2018
STANDARD POSTAGE
STAMP CATALOGUE

ONE HUNDRED AND SEVENTY-FOURTH EDITION IN SIX VOLUMES

VOLUME 2A

C-Cur

EDITOR	Donna Houseman
MANAGING EDITOR	Charles Snee
EDITOR EMERITUS	James E. Kloetzel
SENIOR EDITOR /NEW ISSUES & VALUING	Martin J. Frankevicz
SENIOR VALUING ANALYST	Steven R. Myers
ADMINISTRATIVE ASSISTANT/CATALOGUE LAYOUT	Eric Wiessinger
PRINTING AND IMAGE COORDINATOR	Stacey Mahan
SENIOR GRAPHIC DESIGNER	Cinda McAlexander
ADVERTISING/SALES – EAST	Stephanie Campana
	David Pistello
ADVERTISING/SALES – WEST & FL	Eric Roth

Released May 2017

Includes New Stamp Listings through the March 2017 *Linn's Stamp News Monthly* Catalogue Update

Copyright© 2017 by

AMOS MEDIA

911 Vandemark Road, Sidney, OH 45365-0828

Publishers of *Linn's Stamp News*, *Linn's Stamp News Monthly*, *Coin World* and *Coin World Monthly*.

Vols. 2A-2B Number Additions, Deletions & Changes

Number in 2017 Catalogue	Number in 2018 Catalogue

Cambodia

new 345

Canada

new 104e
new 104f
new 2080b

Ceylon

new MR2c

Cook Islands

new 66a
new 166a

Czech Republic

new 3202a
new 3337a

Egypt

new 4f

Epirus

new 5a
new 6a
new 21a
new 22a

Fernando Po

new 17A

Fiji

new 1154A
new 1193C
new 1194b
new 1254G
new 1254Ga
new 1346a
new 1346b
new 1347a
new 1347b
new 1347c

France

new 37e-37f

Table of Contents

See the following volumes for other country listings:
Volume 1A: United States, United Nations, Abu Dhabi-Australia; Volume 1B: Austria-B
Volume 2B: Cyp-F
Volume 3A: G; Volume 3B: H-I
Volume 4A: J-L; Volume 4B: M
Volume 5A: N-Phil; Volume 5B: Pit-Sam
Volume 6A: San-Tete; Volume 6B: Thai-Z

Scott Catalogue Mission Statement

The Scott Catalogue Team exists to serve the recreational,
educational and commercial hobby needs of stamp collectors and dealers.

We strive to set the industry standard for philatelic information and products by developing and
providing goods that help collectors identify, value, organize and present their collections.

Quality customer service is, and will continue to be, our highest priority.
We aspire toward achieving total customer satisfaction.

Acknowledgments

Our appreciation and gratitude go to the following individuals who have assisted us in preparing information included in this year's Scott Catalogues. Some helpers prefer anonymity. These individuals have generously shared their stamp knowledge with others through the medium of the Scott Catalogue.

Those who follow provided information that is in addition to the hundreds of dealer price lists and advertisements and scores of auction catalogues and realizations that were used in producing the catalogue values. It is from those noted here that we have been able to obtain information on items not normally seen in published lists and advertisements. Support from these people goes beyond data leading to catalogue values, for they also are key to editorial changes.

A special acknowledgment to Liane and Sergio Sismondo of The Classic Collector for their assistance and knowledge sharing that have aided in the preparation of this year's Standard and Classic Specialized Catalogues.

Roland Austin
Robert Ausubel (Great Britain Collectors Club)
John Birkinbine II
Thurston Bland (Bubba Bland Philatelics)
Roger S. Brody
Peter Bylen
Tina & John Carlson (JET Stamps)
Richard A Champagne (Richard A. Champagne, Ltd.)
Henry Chlanda
David & Julia Crawford
Steven D. Crippe (Gradedstamps.com)
Tony L. Crumbley (Carolina Coin & Stamp, Inc.)
Christopher Dahle
Ubaldo Del Toro
Leon Djerahian
Bob & Rita Dumaine (Sam Houston Duck Co.)
Sister Theresa Durand
Mark Eastzer (Markest Stamp Co.)
Paul G. Eckman
George Epstein (Allkor Stamp Co.)
Henry Fisher
Jeffrey M. Forster
Robert S. Freeman
Michael Fuchs
Bob Genisol (Sultan Stamp Center)
Stan Goldfarb
Allen Grant (Rushstamps (Retail) Ltd.)
Daniel E. Grau
Jan E. Gronwall
Bruce Hecht (Bruce L. Hecht Co.)
Peter Hoffman
Armen Hovsepian (Armenstamp)
Philip J. Hughes
Doug Iams
Chris Jackson (Society for Czechoslovak Philately)
John Jamieson (Saskatoon Stamp and Coin)
N. M. Janoowalla
Peter Jeannopoulos
Stephen Joe (International Stamp Service)
William A. Jones
Allan Katz (Ventura Stamp Co.)
Stanford M. Katz
Lewis Kaufman (The Philatelic Foundation)

Jon Kawaguchi (Ryukyu Philatelic Specialist Society)
Roland Kretschmer
William V. Kriebel (Brazil Philatelic Association)
George Krieger
Victor Krievans
Frederick P. Lawrence
Ken Lawrence
John R. Lewis (The William Henry Stamp Co.)
Ulf Lindahl
Ignacio Llach (Filatelia Llach S.L.)
Marilyn R. Mattke
Gary Morris (Pacific Midwest Co.)
Peter Mosiondz, Jr.
Bruce M. Moyer (Moyer Stamps & Collectibles)
Richard H. Muller
Leonard Nadybal
Dr. Tiong Tak Ngo
Nik & Lisa Oquist
Dr. Everett Parker
Don Peterson (International Philippine Philatelic Society)
Stanley M. Piller (Stanley M. Piller & Associates)
Virgil Pirvulescu
Todor Drumev Popov
Peter W. W. Powell
Siddique Mahmudur Rahman
Ghassan D. Riachi
Omar Rodriguez
Mehrdad Sadri (Persiphila)
Theodosios Sampson PhD
Alexander Schauss (Schauss Philatelics)
Jacques C. Schiff, Jr. (Jacques C. Schiff, Jr., Inc.)
Chuck & Joyce Schmidt
Michael Schreiber
Jeff Siddiqui
Sergio & Liane Sismondo (The Classic Collector)
Jay Smith
Frank J. Stanley, III
Alfred E. Staubus
Peter Thy
Scott R. Trepel (Siegel Auction Galleries)
Dan Undersander (United Postal Stationery Society)
Herbert R. Volin
Philip T. Wall

Giana Wayman
Gary B. Weiss
Ralph Yorio
Val Zabijaka (Zabijaka Auctions)
Michal Zika
Steven Zirinsky (Zirinsky Stamps)
Alfonso G. Zulueta, Jr.

SCOTT

What's new for 2018 Scott Standard Volume 2A?

Greetings, Fellow Scott Catalog User:

The 2018 edition of the *Scott Standard Postage Stamp Catalogue* celebrates the 150th anniversary of the Scott catalogs. The title pages of this volume and other volumes in the 2018 Scott Standard catalog state that this is the 174th edition of the catalogs (and it is). In September 1868, John Walter Scott published his first stamp catalog. The catalog, titled *A Descriptive Catalogue of America and Foreign Postage Stamps, Issued from 1840 to Date*, is considered to be the first Scott stamp catalog.

The Scott catalog has come a long way since its humble beginnings as a 24-page bound pamphlet. The Scott Standard catalog lists more than 700,000 stamps from more than 600 stamp-issuing entities. Because the catalog volumes had grown so large that they were literally bursting at the seams, each 2018 Scott Standard catalog has been split into two volumes, A and B.

• More than 150 value changes in Cambodia reflect more increases over decreases. The changes are mostly among key issues. The souvenir sheets of one from the 1951-52 issue (Scott 15a, 16a, and 17a) each increase from $50 mint to $55. The 1974 4th Anniversary of the Republic set (321-323) jumps from $30.50 mint in the 2017 Scott Standard catalog to $36.50 in the 2018 edition. The value for the used set increases from $10 to $13.

Cambodia's 1974 4th Anniversary of the Republic set (Scott 321-323) jumps from $30.50 unused in the 2017 Scott Standard catalog to $36.50 in the 2018 edition.

• Almost 350 value changes were made among the classic issues of China. Value changes for stamps from 1878 through the early 1900s reflect a strong market, with many increases in values, some substantial. The 1897 10-cent-on-12c (Scott 45) soars from $35,000 unused to $50,000, and from $2,750 used to $2,850.

• The early issues of the Republic of China (Taiwan) show a general uptick in values in the 2018 Vol. 2A. The $2 Allegory of Election souvenir sheet of 1951 (No. 1041) rises from $550 unused to $575 and from $350 used to $400. Numerous increases are found among the stamps issued under Japanese occupation.

• The issues of the People's Republic of China continue to show strength, but the stamps no longer are setting record prices. Overall values are slipping, except for values of great rarities. Decreases occur among the Cultural Revolution issues. The very scarce withdrawn 1968 8-fen The Whole Country is Red stamp (Scott 999A) advances from $125,000 mint to $135,000, but falls from $90,000 used to $80,000. The popular 1980 8f Year of the Monkey stamp (1586) sees a slight decrease in the mint value, from $1,800 to $1,750. The value is in italics to denote an item that can be difficult to value accurately.

• Scarcer stamps of Cilicia show increases. Thirty-nine value changes were made. Many of these changes occur among the inverted overprint and double overprint varieties. The 1919 2-para red lilac with inverted overprint (No. 2a) moves from $17.50 both unused and used to $20 both ways, and the double overprint variety of this stamp (2b) increases from $27.50 unused and used to $30 both ways.

• Among the 147 value changes in Costa Rica, all reflect increases, some more substantial than others. The 1889 5-centimo orange in an imperforate pair (Scott 27a) soars from $250 used to $750. The value is in italics to denote that this is an item that can be difficult to value accurately. The same is true of the horizontal pair, imperf between (27b), which increases from $150 unused to $350. A value

of $500 has been added for a used example of the 1889 10c red brown in a vertical or horizontal pair, imperf between (28a).

• Scattered increases were made throughout Cape Verde.

• A sprinkling of increases can be found among the many decreases for Corfu stamps. The 1941 set of postal tax stamps (Scott NRA1-NRA3) increases slightly from $65 for a never-hinged set to $67.50.

• The 60 value changes among the issues of Cuba reflect scattered increases and decreases.

• A mix of increases and decreases occur among the more than 90 values changes in Ceylon.

• A full line-by-line review of Cook Islands results in more than 1,400 value changes. Many decreases in values reflect a weak New Zealand dollar and a slow market. The increases that occur are among the classic stamps. The first-issue 1½-penny violet on toned paper (Scott 2) increases slightly, from $47.50 unused to $50, as does the stamp on white paper (6). A few increases occur among the New Zealand postal fiscal stamps of 1931-32 overprinted in blue or red. The £1 pink of this set (83) moves from $105 unused to $125, and from $190 used to $200. Many decreases occur among issues from 1970 onward. The 1974 50¢ souvenir sheet (377) issued for the 10th British Commonwealth Games drops from $2.60 both mint and used to $1.25 both ways.

Editorial enhancements for Canada

Various notes and footnotes have been clarified or expanded throughout the catalog to further explain complicated listings, and other notes have been screened carefully to ensure accuracy.

The scarce People's Republic of China withdrawn 1968 8-fen The Whole Country is Red stamp (Scott 999A) advances from $125,000 unused to $135,000.

• An ongoing Scott project to include listings for complete booklets among the Canada listings continues this year. The 2016 Vol. 2 included the booklets from 1995 to the present continues this year. In the 2017 catalog, these booklet listings were expanded to include the 1992-1994 booklets, Nos. 1403b to 1536A. The 2018 Vol. 2A expands the listings even further, adding values for complete booklets from 1900-1935 (No. 77b through No. 219a). Detailed notes of explanation also are included. Expect further expansions in future years, first up to Queen Elizabeth II, then filling in up to Scott 1403b, where the modern complete booklet listings start.

• A warning has been added to the listings of Canada's 2006 Flag Over Landscape booklet pane of six (No. 2193b), advising collectors to beware of fake examples that have been found hand cut from printer's waste.

As with the stock market, a softening in the stamp market for some countries can be looked upon as an opportunity to buy stamps to fill spaces in your stamp albums.

As always, we encourage you to pay special attention to the Number Additions, Deletions & Changes found on page 2A in this volume.

While you settle in with your stamp album and Scott catalog, relax and enjoy the world's greatest hobby.

Donna Houseman
Donna Houseman/Catalogue Editor

Addresses, Telephone Numbers, Web Sites, E-Mail Addresses of General & Specialized Philatelic Societies

Collectors can contact the following groups for information about the philately of the areas within the scope of these societies, or inquire about membership in these groups. Aside from the general societies, we limit this list to groups that specialize in particular fields of philately, particular areas covered by the Scott Standard Postage Stamp Catalogue, and topical groups. Many more specialized philatelic society exist than those listed below. These addresses are updated yearly, and they are, to the best of our knowledge, correct and current. Groups should inform the editors of address changes whenever they occur. The editors also want to hear from other such specialized groups not listed. Unless otherwise noted all website addresses begin with http://

American Philatelic Society
100 Match Factory Place
Bellefonte PA 16823-1367
Ph: (814) 933-3803
www.stamps.org
E-mail: apsinfo@stamps.org

American Stamp Dealers Association, Inc.
P.O. Box 692
Leesport PA 19553
Ph: (800) 369-8207
www.americanstampdealer.com
E-mail: asda@americanstampdealer.com

National Stamp Dealers Association
Richard Kostka, President
3643 Private Road 18
Pinckneyville IL 62274-3426
Ph: (800) 875-6633
www.nsdainc.org
E-mail: nsda@nsdainc.org

International Society of Worldwide Stamp Collectors
Joanne Berkowitz, MD
P.O. Box 19006
Sacramento CA 95819
www.iswsc.org
E-mail: executivedirector@iswsc.org

Royal Philatelic Society
41 Devonshire Place
London, W1G 6JY
UNITED KINGDOM
www.rpsl.org.uk
E-mail: secretary@rpsl.org.uk

Royal Philatelic Society of Canada
P.O. Box 929, Station Q
Toronto, ON, M4T 2P1
CANADA
Ph: (888) 285-4143
www.rpsc.org
E-mail: info@rpsc.org

Young Stamp Collectors of America
Janet Houser
100 Match Factory Place
Bellefonte PA 16823-1367
Ph: (814) 933-3820
www.stamps.org/ysca/intro.htm
E-mail: ysca@stamps.org

Philatelic Research Resources
(The Scott editors encourage any additional research organizations to submit data for inclusion in this listing category)

American Philatelic Research Library
Tara Murray
100 Match Factory Place
Bellefonte PA 16823
Ph: (814) 933-3803
www.stamplibrary.org
E-mail: libraryestamps.org

Institute for Analytical Philately, Inc.
P.O. Box 8035
Holland MI 49422-8035
Ph: (616) 399-9299
www.analyticalphilately.org
E-mail: info@analyticalphilately.org

The Western Philatelic Library
P.O. Box 2219
1500 Partridge Ave.
Sunnyvale CA 94087
Ph: (408) 733-0336
www.fwpf.org

Groups focusing on fields or aspects found in worldwide philately (some might cover U.S. area only)

American Air Mail Society
Stephen Reinhard
P.O. Box 110
Mineola NY 11501
www.americanairmailsociety.org
E-mail: sreinhard1@optonline.net

American First Day Cover Society
Douglas Kelsey
P.O. Box 16277
Tucson AZ 85732-6277
Ph: (520) 321-0880
www.afdcs.org
E-mail: afdcs@afdcs.org

American Revenue Association
Eric Jackson
P.O. Box 728
Leesport PA 19533-0728
Ph: (610) 926-6200
www.revenuer.org
E-mail: eric@revenuer.com

American Topical Association
Vera Felts
P.O. Box 8
Carterville IL 62918-0008
Ph: (618) 985-5100
www.americantopicalassn.org
E-mail: americantopical@msn.com

Christmas Seal & Charity Stamp Society
John Denune
234 E. Broadway
Granville OH 43023
Ph: (740) 587-0276
www.seal-society.org
E-mail: john@christmasseals.net

Errors, Freaks and Oddities Collectors Club
Scott Shaulis
P.O. Box 549
Murrysville PA 15668-0549
Ph: (724) 733-4134
www.efocc.org

First Issues Collectors Club
Kurt Streepy, Secretary
3128 E. Mattatha Drive
Bloomington IN 47401
www.firstissues.org
E-mail: secretary@firstissues.org

International Society of Reply Coupon Collectors
Peter Robin
P.O. Box 353
Bala Cynwyd PA 19004
E-mail: peterrobin@verizon.net

The Joint Stamp Issues Society
Richard Zimmermann
29A Rue Des Eviats
Lalaye F-67220
FRANCE
www.philarz.net
E-mail: richard.zimmermann@club-internet.fr

National Duck Stamp Collectors Society
Anthony J. Monico
P.O. Box 43
Harleysville PA 19438-0043
www.ndscs.org
E-mail: ndscs@ndscs.org

No Value Identified Club
Albert Sauvanet
Le Clos Royal B, Boulevard des Pas Enchantes
St. Sebastien-sur Loire, 44230
FRANCE
E-mail: alain.vailly@irin.univ nantes.fr

The Perfins Club
Ken Masters
111 NW 94th Street Apt. 102
Kansas City MO 64155-2993
Ph: (816) 835-5907
www.perfins.org
E-mail: kmasters@aol.com

Postage Due Mail Study Group
John Rawlins
13, Longacre
Chelmsford, CM1 3BJ
UNITED KINGDOM
E-mail: john.rawlins2@ukonline.co.uk.

Post Mark Collectors Club
Bob Milligan
7014 Woodland Oaks
Magnolia TX 77354
Ph: (281) 259-2735
www.postmarks.org
E-mail: bob.milligan@gmail.net

Postal History Society
George McGowan
P.O. Box 482
East Schodack NY 12063-0482
www.postalhistorysociety.org
E-mail: geolotus2003@nycap.rr.com

Precancel Stamp Society
Charles Adrion
P.O. Box 10295
Rochester NY 14610
Ph: (585) 319-0600
www.precancels.com
E-mail: pss.promotion@rochester.rr.com

United Postal Stationery Society
Stuart Leven
1659 Branham Lane Suite F-307
San Jose CA 95118-2291
www.upss.org
E-mail: poststat@gmail.com

United States Possessions Philatelic Society
Daniel F. Ring
P.O. Box 113
Woodstock IL 60098
www.uspps.net
E-mail: danielfring@hotmail.com

Groups focusing on U.S. area philately as covered in the Standard Catalogue

Canal Zone Study Group
Tom Brougham
737 Neilson St.
Berkeley CA 94707
www.CanalZoneStudyGroup.com
E-mail: czsgsecretary@gmail.com

Carriers and Locals Society
Martin Richardson
P.O. Box 74
Grosse Ile MI 48138
www.pennypost.org
E-mail: martinr362@aol.com

Confederate Stamp Alliance
Patricia A. Kaufman
10194 N. Old State Road
Lincoln DE 19960
Ph. (302) 422-2656
www.csalliance.org
E-mail: trishkauf@comcast.net

Hawaiian Philatelic Society
Kay H. Hoke
P.O. Box 10115
Honolulu HI 96816-0115
Ph: (808) 521-5721

Plate Number Coil Collectors Club
Gene Trinks
16415 W. Desert Wren Court
Surprise AZ 85374
Ph: (623) 322-4619
www.pnc3.org
E-mail: gctrinks@cox.net

Ryukyu Philatelic Specialist Society
Laura Edmonds, Secy.
P.O. Box 240177
Charlotte NC 28224-0177
Ph: (336) 509-3739
www.ryukyustamps.org
E-mail: secretary@ryukyustamps.org

United Nations Philatelists
Blanton Clement, Jr.
P.O. Box 146
Morrisville PA 19067-0146
www.unpi.com
E-mail: bclemjr@yahoo.com

United States Stamp Society
Executive Secretary
P.O. Box 6634
Katy TX 77491-6634
www.usstamps.org

U.S. Cancellation Club
Joe Crosby
E-mail: joecrosby@cox.nat

U.S. Philatelic Classics Society
Rob Lund
2913 Fulton St.
Everett WA 98201-3733
www.uspcs.org
E-mail: membershipchairman@uspcs.org

Groups focusing on philately of foreign countries or regions

Aden & Somaliland Study Group
Gary Brown
P.O. Box 106
Briar Hill, Victoria, 3088
AUSTRALIA
E-mail: garyjohn951@optushome.com.au

American Society of Polar Philatelists (Antarctic areas)
Alan Warren
P.O. Box 39
Exton PA 19341-0039
www.polarphilatelists.org

Andorran Philatelic Study Circle
D. Hope
17 Hawthorn Drive
Stalybridge, Cheshire, SK15 1UE
UNITED KINGDOM
E-mail: andorranpsc@btinternet.com

Australian States Study Circle of The Royal Sydney Philatelic Club
Ben Palmer
GPO 1751
Sydney, N.S.W., 2001
AUSTRALIA
www.philas.org.au/states

Austria Philatelic Society
Ralph Schneider
P.O. Box 23049
Belleville IL 62223
Ph: (618) 277-6152
www.austriaphilatelicsociety.com
E-mail: rschneiderstamps@att.net

American Belgian Philatelic Society
Edward de Bary
11 Wakefield Drive Apt. 2105
Asheville NC 28803
E-mail: emdeb@charter.net

Bechuanalands and Botswana Society
Neville Midwood
69 Porlock Lane
Furzton, Milton Keynes, MK4 1JY
UNITED KINGDOM
www.nevsoft.com
E-mail: bbsoc@nevsoft.com

Bermuda Collectors Society
John Pare
405 Perimeter Road
Mount Horeb WI 53572
www.bermudacollectorssociety.com
E-mail: pare16@mhtc.net

Brazil Philatelic Association
William V. Kriebel
1923 Manning St.
Philadelphia PA 19103-5728
www.brazilphilatelic.org
E-mail: info@brazilphilatelic.org

British Caribbean Philatelic Study Group
Duane Larson
2 Forest Blvd.
Park Forest IL 60466
www.bcpsg.com
E-mail: dlarson283@aol.com

The King George VI Collectors Society (British Commonwealth)
Brian Livingstone
21 York Mansions, Prince of Wales Drive
London, SW11 4DL
UNITED KINGDOM
www.kg6.info
E-mail: livingstone484@btinternet.com

British North America Philatelic Society (Canada & Provinces)
Andy Ellwood
10 Doris Avenue
Gloucester, ON, K1T 3W8
CANADA
www.bnaps.org
E-mail: secretary@bnaps.org

British West Indies Study Circle
John Seidl
4324 Granby Way
Marietta GA 30062
Ph: (770) 642-6424
www.bwisc.org
E-mail: john.seidl@gmail.com

Burma Philatelic Study Circle
Michael Whittaker
1, Ecton Leys, Hillside
Rugby, Warwickshire, CV22 5SL
UNITED KINGDOM
www.burmastamps.homecall.co.uk
E-mail: manningham8@mypostoffice.co.uk

Cape and Natal Study Circle
Dr. Guy Dillaway
P.O. Box 181
Weston MA 02493
www.nzsc.demon.co.uk

Ceylon Study Circle
R. W. P. Frost
42 Lonsdale Road, Cannington
Bridgewater, Somerset, TA5 2JS
UNITED KINGDOM
www.ceylonsc.org
E-mail: rodney.frost@tiscali.co.uk

Channel Islands Specialists Society
Richard Flemming
64, Falconers Green, Burbage
Hinckley, Leicestershire, LE10 2SX
UNITED KINGDOM
www.ciss1950.org.uk
E-mail: secretary@ciss1950.org.uk

China Stamp Society
H. James Maxwell
1050 West Blue Ridge Boulevard
Kansas City MO 64145-1216
www.chinastampsociety.org
E-mail: president@chinastampsociety.org

Colombia/Panama Philatelic Study Group (COPAPHIL)
Thomas P. Myers
P.O. Box 522
Gordonsville VA 22942
www.copaphil.org
E-mail: tpmphil@hotmail.com

Association Filatelic de Costa Rica
Giana Wayman
c/o Interlink 102, P.O. Box 52-6770
Miami FL 33152
E-mail: scotland@racsa.co.cr

Society for Costa Rica Collectors
Dr. Hector R. Mena
P.O. Box 14831
Baton Rouge LA 70808
www.socorico.org
E-mail: hrmena@aol.com

International Cuban Philatelic Society
Ernesto Cuesta
P.O. Box 34434
Bethesda MD 20827
www.cubafil.org
E-mail: ecuesta@philat.com

Cuban Philatelic Society of America ®
P.O. Box 141656
Coral Gables FL 33114-1656
www.cubapsa.com
E-mail: cpsa.usa@gmail.com

Cyprus Study Circle
Colin Dear
10 Marne Close, Wem
Shropshire, SY4 5YE
UNITED KINGDOM
www.cyprusstudycircle.org/index.htm
E-mail: colindear@talktalk.net

Society for Czechoslovak Philately
Tom Cossaboom
P.O. Box 4124
Prescott AZ 86302
Ph: (928) 771-9097
www.csphilately.org
E-mail: klfck1@aol.com

Danish West Indies Study Unit of the Scandinavian Collectors Club
Arnold Sorensen
7666 Edgedale Drive
Newburgh IN 47630
Ph: (812) 480-6532
www.scc-online.org
E-mail: valbydwi@hotmail.com

East Africa Study Circle
Michael Vesey-Fitzgerald
Gambles Cottage, 18 Clarence Road
Lyndhurst, SO43 7AL
UNITED KINGDOM
www.easc.org.uk
E-mail: secretary@easc.org.uk

Egypt Study Circle
Mike Murphy
109 Chadwick Road
London, SE15 4PY
UNITED KINGDOM
Trent Ruebush: North American Agent
E-mail: tkruebrush@gmail.com
www.egyptstudycircle.org
E-mail: egyptstudycircle@hotmail.com

Estonian Philatelic Society
Juri Kirsimagi
29 Clifford Ave.
Pelham NY 10803
Ph: (914) 738-3713

Ethiopian Philatelic Society
Ulf Lindahl
21 Westview Place
Riverside CT 06878
Ph: (203) 722-0769
http://ethiopianphilatelicsociety.weebly.com
E-mail: ulindahl@optonline.net

Falkland Islands Philatelic Study Group
Carl J. Faulkner
615 Taconic Trail
Williamstown MA 01267-2745
Ph: (413) 458-4421
www.fipsg.org.uk
E-mail: cfaulkner@taconicwilliamstown.com

Faroe Islands Study Circle
Norman Hudson
40 Queen's Road, Vicar's Cross
Chester, CH3 5HB
UNITED KINGDOM
www.faroeislandssc.org
E-mail: jntropics@hotmail.com

Former French Colonies Specialist Society
COLFRA
BP 628
75367 Paris, Cedex 08
FRANCE
www.colfra.org
E-mail: secretaire@colfra.org

France & Colonies Philatelic Society
Edward Grabowski
111 Prospect St., 4C
Westfield NJ 07090
www.franceandcolps.org
E-mail: edjjg@alum.mit.edu

Germany Philatelic Society
P.O. Box 6547
Chesterfield MO 63006
www.germanyphilatelicusa.org

Plebiscite-Memel-Saar Study Group of the German Philatelic Society
Clayton Wallace
100 Lark Court
Alamo CA 94507
E-mail: claytonwallace@comcast.net

Gibraltar Study Circle
Eric D. Holmes
29 Highgate Road
Woodley, Berkshire RG5 3ND
UNITED KINGDOM
www.gibraltarstudycircle.wordpress.com
E-mail: ericholmes@talktalk.net

Great Britain Collectors Club
Steve McGill
10309 Brookhollow Circle
Highlands Ranch CO 80129
www.gbstamps.com/gbcc
E-mail: steve.mcgill@comcast.net

International Society of Guatemala Collectors
Jaime Marckwordt
449 St. Francis Blvd.
Daly City CA 94015-2136
www.guatemalastamps.com
E-mail: membership@guatamalastamps.com

Haiti Philatelic Society
Ubaldo Del Toro
5709 Marble Archway
Alexandria VA 22315
www.haitiphilately.org
E-mail: u007ubi@aol.com

Federacion Filatelica de la Republica de Honduras (Honduran Philatelic Federation, FFRH)
Mauricio Mejia
Apartado postal 1465
Tegucigalpa
HONDURAS

Hong Kong Stamp Society
Ming W. Tsang
P.O. Box 206
Glenside PA 19038
www.hkss.org
E-mail: hkstamps@yahoo.com

Society for Hungarian Philately
Robert Morgan
2201 Roscomare Road
Los Angeles CA 90077-2222
Ph: (978) 682-0242
www.hungarianphilately.org
E-mail: alan@hungarianstamps.com

India Study Circle
John Warren
P.O. Box 7326
Washington DC 20044
Ph: (202) 564-6876
www.indiastudycircle.org
E-mail: warren.john@epa.gov

Indian Ocean Study Circle
E. S. Hutton
29 Paternoster Close
Waltham Abby, Essex, EN9 3JU
UNITED KINGDOM
www.indianoceanstudycircle.com
E-mail: secretary@indianoceanstudy-circle.com

Society of Indo-China Philatelists
Ron Bentley
2600 N. 24th St.
Arlington VA 22207
www.sicp-online.org
E-mail: ron.bentley@verizon.net

Iran Philatelic Study Circle
Mehdi Esmaili
P.O. Box 750096
Forest Hills NY 11375
www.iranphilatelic.org
E-mail: m.esmaili@earthlink.net

Eire Philatelic Association (Ireland)
David J. Brennan
P.O. Box 704
Bernardsville NJ 07924
www.eirephilatelicassoc.org
E-mail: brennan704@aol.com

Society of Israel Philatelists
Becky Dean
100 Match Factory Place
Bellefonte PA 16823-1367
Ph: (814) 933-3802 ext. 212
www.israelstamps.org
E-mail: israelstamps@gmail.com

Italy and Colonies Study Circle
Richard Harlow
7 Duncombe House, 8 Manor Road
Teddington, TW11 8BE
UNITED KINGDOM
www.icsc.pwp.blueyonder.co.uk
E-mail: harlowr@gmail.com

International Society for Japanese Philately
William Eisenhauer
P.O. Box 230462
Tigard OR 97281
www.isjp.org
E-mail: secretary@isjp.org

Korea Stamp Society
John E. Talmage
P.O. Box 6889
Oak Ridge TN 37831
www.pennfamily.org/KSS-USA
E-mail: jtalmage@usit.net

Latin American Philatelic Society
Jules K. Beck
30½ St. #209
St. Louis Park MN 55426-3551

Liberian Philatelic Society
William Thomas Lockard
P.O. Box 106
Wellston OH 45692
Ph: (740) 384-2020
E-mail: tlockard@zoomnet.net

Liechtenstudy USA (Liechtenstein)
Paul Tremaine
410 SW Ninth St.
Dundee OR 97115
Ph: (503) 538-4500
www.liechtenstudy.org
E-mail: editor@liechtenstudy.org

Lithuania Philatelic Society
John Variakojis
8472 Carlisle Court
Burr Ridge IL 60527
Ph: (630) 974-6525
www.lithuanianphilately.com/lps
E-mail: variakojis@sbcglobal.net

Luxembourg Collectors Club
Gary B. Little
7319 Beau Road
Sechelt, BC, VON 3A8
CANADA
lcc.luxcentral.com
E-mail: gary@luxcentral.com

Malaya Study Group
David Tett
16 Broadway, Gustard Wood
Wheathampstead, Herts, AL4 8LN
UNITED KINGDOM
www.m-s-g.org.uk
E-mail: davidtett@aol.com

Malta Study Circle
Rodger Evans
Ravensbourne, Hook Heath Road
Woking, Surrey, GU22 OLB
UNITED KINGDOM
www.maltastudycircle.org.uk
E-mail: carge@hotmail.co.uk

Mexico-Elmhurst Philatelic Society International
Thurston Bland
50 Regato
Rancho Santa Margarita CA 92688-3003
www.mepsi.org

Asociacion Mexicana de Filatelia
AMEXFIL
Jose Maria Rico, 129, Col. Del Valle
Mexico City DF, 03100
MEXICO
www.amexfil.mx
E-mail: amexfil@gmail.com

Society for Moroccan and Tunisian Philately
S.P.L.M.
206, bld. Pereire
Paris 75017
FRANCE
splm-philatelie.org
E-mail: splm206@aol.com

Nepal & Tibet Philatelic Study Group
Roger D. Skinner
1020 Covington Road
Los Altos CA 94024-5003
Ph: (650) 968-4163
www.fuchs-online.com/ntpsc/
E-mail: colinhepper@hotmail.co.uk

American Society for Netherlands Philately
Hans Kremer
50 Rockport Court
Danville CA 94526
Ph: (925) 820-5841
www.asnp1975.com
E-mail: hkremer@usa.net

New Zealand Society of Great Britain
Michael Wilkinson
121 London Road
Sevenoaks, Kent, TN13 1BH
UNITED KINGDOM
www.nzsgb.org.uk
E-mail: mwilkin799@aol.com

Nicaragua Study Group
Erick Rodriguez
11817 SW 11th St.
Miami FL 33184-2501
clubs.yahoo.com/clubs/
nicaraguastudygroup
E-mail: nsgsec@yahoo.com

Society of Australasian Specialists/Oceania
David McNamee
P.O. Box 37
Alamo CA 94507
www.sasoceania.org
E-mail: treasurer@sasoceania.com

Orange Free State Study Circle
J. R. Stroud
24 Hooper Close
Burnham-on-sea, Somerset, TA8 1JQ
UNITED KINGDOM
orangefreestatephilately.org.uk
E-mail: richardstroudph@gofast.co.uk

Pacific Islands Study Circle
John Ray
24 Woodvale Ave.
London, SE25 4AE
UNITED KINGDOM
www.pisc.org.uk
E-mail: info@pisc.org.uk

Pakistan Philatelic Study Circle
Jeff Siddiqui
P.O. Box 7002
Lynnwood WA 98046
E-mail: jeffsiddiqui@msn.com

Centro de Filatelistas Independientes de Panama
Vladimir Berrio-Lemm
Apartado 0823-02748
Plaza Concordia Panama
PANAMA
E-mail: panahistoria@gmail.com

Papuan Philatelic Society
Steven Zirinsky
P.O. Box 49, Ansonia Station
New York NY 10023
Ph: (718) 706-0616
www.communigate.co.uk/york/pps
E-mail: szirinsky@cs.com

International Philippine Philatelic Society
Donald J. Peterson
P.O. Box 122
Brunswick MD 21716
Ph: (301) 834-6419
www.theipps.info
E-mail: dpeterson4526@gmail.com

Pitcairn Islands Study Group
Dr. Everett L. Parker
117 Cedar Breeze South
Glenburn ME 04401-1734
Ph: (386) 688-1358
www.pisg.net
E-mail: eparker@hughes.net

Polonus Philatelic Society (Poland)
Daniel Lubelski
P.O. Box 60438
Rossford OH 43460
Ph: (419) 410-9115
www.polonus.org
E-mail: info@polonus.org

International Society for Portuguese Philately
Clyde Homen
1491 Bonnie View Road
Hollister CA 95023-5117
www.portugalstamps.com
E-mail: ispp1962@sbcglobal.net

Rhodesian Study Circle
William R. Wallace
P.O. Box 16381
San Francisco CA 94116
www.rhodesianstudycircle.org.uk
E-mail: bwall8rscr@earthlink.net

Rossica Society of Russian Philately
Alexander Kolchinsky
1506 Country Lake Drive
Champaign IL 6821-6428
www.rossica.org
E-mail: alexander.kolchinsky@rossica.org

St. Helena, Ascension & Tristan Da Cunha Philatelic Society
Dr. Everett L. Parker
117 Cedar Breeze South
Glenburn ME 04401-1734
Ph: (386) 688-1358
www.shatps.org
E-mail: eparker@hughes.net

St. Pierre & Miquelon Philatelic Society
James R. (Jim) Taylor
2335 Paliswood Road SW
Calgary, AB, T2V 3P6
CANADA
www.stamps.org/spm

Associated Collectors of El Salvador
Joseph D. Hahn
1015 Old Boalsburg Road Apt G-5
State College PA 16801-6149
www.elsalvadorphilately.org
E-mail: jdhahn2@gmail.com

Fellowship of Samoa Specialists
Donald Mee
23 Leo St.
Christchurch, 8051
NEW ZEALAND
www.samoaexpress.org
E-mail: donanm@xtra.co.nz

Sarawak Specialists' Society
Stephen Schumann
2417 Cabrillo Drive-
Hayward CA 94545
Ph: (510) 785-4794
www.britborneostamps.org.uk
E-mail: sdsch@earthlink.net

Scandinavian Collectors Club
Steve Lund
P.O. Box 16213
St. Paul MN 55116
www.scc-online.org
E-mail: steve88h@aol.com

Slovakia Stamp Society
Jack Benchik
P.O. Box 555
Notre Dame IN 46556

Philatelic Society for Greater Southern Africa
Alan Hanks
34 Seaton Drive
Aurora, ON, L4G 2K1
CANADA
www.psgsa.thestampweb.com

South Sudan Philatelic Society
William Barclay
1370 Spring Hill Road
South Londonderry VT 05155
E-mail: barclayphilatelics@gmail.com

Spanish Philatelic Society
Robert H. Penn
1108 Walnut Drive
Danielsville PA 18038
Ph: (610) 844-8963
E-mail: roberthpenn43@gmail.com

Sudan Study Group
Paul Grigg
19 Howmead
Berkeley, GLOS, GL13 9AR
England
UNITED KINGDOM
www.sudanstamps.org

American Helvetia Philatelic Society (Switzerland, Liechtenstein)
Richard T. Hall
P.O. Box 15053
Asheville NC 28813-0053
www.swiss-stamps.org
E-mail: secretary2@swiss-stamps.org

Tannu Tuva Collectors Society
Ken R. Simon
P.O. Box 385
Lake Worth FL 33460-0385
Ph: (561) 588-5954
www.tuva.tk
E-mail: yurttuva@yahoo.com

Society for Thai Philately
H. R. Blakeney
P.O. Box 25644
Oklahoma City OK 73125
E-mail: HRBlakeney@aol.com

Transvaal Study Circle
Chris Board
36 Wakefield Gardens
London, SE19 2NR
UNITED KINGDOM
www.transvaalstamps.org.uk
E-mail: c.board@macace.net

Ottoman and Near East Philatelic Society (Turkey and related areas)
Bob Stuchell
193 Valley Stream Lane
Wayne PA 19087
www.oneps.org
E-mail: rstuchell@msn.com

Ukrainian Philatelic & Numismatic Society
Martin B. Tatuch
5117 8th Road N.
Arlington VA 22205-1201
www.upns.org
E-mail: treasurer@upns.org

Vatican Philatelic Society
Sal Quinonez
1 Aldersgate, Apt. 1002
Riverhead NY 11901-1830
Ph: (516) 727-6426
www.vaticanphilately.org

British Virgin Islands Philatelic Society
Giorgio Migliavacca
P.O. Box 7007
St. Thomas VI 00801-0007
www.islandsun.com/category/collectables/
E-mail: issun@candwbvi.net

West Africa Study Circle
Martin Bratzel
1233 Virginia Ave.
Windsor, ON, N8S 2Z1
CANADA
www.wasc.org.uk
E-mail: marty_bratzel@yahoo.ca

Western Australia Study Group
Brian Pope
P.O. Box 423
Claremont, Western Australia, 6910
AUSTRALIA
www.wastudygroup.com
E-mail: black5swan@yahoo.com.au

Yugoslavia Study Group of the Croatian Philatelic Society
Michael Lenard
1514 N. Third Ave.
Wausau WI 54401
Ph: (715) 675-2833
E-mail: mjlenard@aol.com

Topical Groups

Americana Unit
Dennis Dengel
17 Peckham Road
Poughkeepsie NY 12603-2018
www.americanaunit.org
E-mail: ddengel@americanaunit.org

Astronomy Study Unit
John Budd
728 Sugar Camp Way
Brooksville FL 34604
Ph: (352) 345-4799
E-mail: jwgbudd@gmail.com

Bicycle Stamp Club
Steve Andreasen
2000 Alaskan Way, Unit 157
Seattle WA 98121
E-mail: steven.w.andreasen@gmail.com

Biology Unit
Alan Hanks
34 Seaton Drive
Aurora, ON, L4G 2K1
CANADA
Ph: (905) 727-6993

Bird Stamp Society
S. A. H. (Tony) Statham
Ashlyns Lodge, Chesham Road,
Berkhamsted, Hertfordshire HP4 2ST
UNITED KINGDOM
www.bird-stamps.org/bss
E-mail: tony.statham@sky.com

Captain Cook Society
Jerry Yucht
8427 Leale Ave.
Stockton CA 95212
www.captaincooksociety.com
E-mail: US@captaincooksociety.com

The CartoPhilatelic Society
Marybeth Sulkowski
2885 Sanford Ave, SW, #32361
Grandville MI 49418-1342
www.mapsonstamps.org
E-mail: secretary@mapsonstamps.org

Casey Jones Railroad Unit
Roy W. Menninger MD
P.O. Box 5511
Topeka KS 66605
Ph: (785) 231-8366
www.uqp.de/cjr/index.htm
E-mail: roymenn85@gmail.com

Cats on Stamps Study Unit
Robert D. Jarvis
2731 Teton Lane
Fairfield CA 94533
www.catstamps.info
E-mail: bobmarci@aol.com

Chemistry & Physics on Stamps Study Unit
Dr. Roland Hirsch
20458 Water Point Lane
Germantown MD 20874
www.cpossu.org
E-mail: rfhirsch@cpossu.org

Chess on Stamps Study Unit
Ray C. Alexis
608 Emery St.
Longmont CO 80501
E-mail: chessstuff911459@aol.com

Christmas Philatelic Club
Jim Balog
P.O. Box 774
Geneva OH 44041
www.christmasphilatelicclub.org
E-mail: jpb4stamps@windstream.net

Cricket Philatelic Society
A.Melville-Brown, President
11 Weppons, Ravens Road
Shoreham-by-Sea
West Sussex, BN43 5AW
UNITED KINGDOM
www.cricketstamp.net
E-mail: mel.cricket.100@googlemail.com

Dogs on Stamps Study Unit
Morris Raskin
202A Newport Road
Monroe Township NJ 08831
Ph: (609) 655-7411
www.dossu.org
E-mail: mraskin@cellurian.com

Earth's Physical Features Study Group
Fred Klein
515 Magdalena Ave.
Los Altos CA 94024
epfsu.jeffhayward.com

Ebony Society of Philatelic Events and Reflections, Inc. (African-American topicals)
Manuel Gilyard
800 Riverside Drive, Suite 4H
New York NY 10032-7412
www.esperstamps.org
E-mail: gilyardmani@aol.com

Europa Study Unit
Tonny E. Van Loij
3002 S. Xanthia St.
Denver CO 80231-4237
Ph: (303) 752-0189
www.europastudyunit.org
E-mail: tvanloij@gmail.com

Fine & Performing Arts
Deborah L. Washington
6922 S. Jeffery Blvd., #7 - North
Chicago IL 60649
E-mail: brasslady@comcast.net

Fire Service in Philately
John Zaranek
81 Hillpine Road
Cheektowaga NY 14227-2259
Ph: (716) 668-3352
E-mail: jczaranek@roadrunner.com

Gay & Lesbian History on Stamps Club
Joe Petronie
P.O. Box 190842
Dallas TX 75219-0842
www.facebook.com/glhsc
E-mail: glhsc@aol.com

Gems, Minerals & Jewelry Study Unit
Mrs. Gilberte Proteau
138 Lafontaine
Beloeil QC J3G 2G7
CANADA
Ph: (978) 851-8283
E-mail: gilberte.ferland@sympatico.ca

Graphics Philately Association
Mark H. Winnegrad
P.O. Box 380
Bronx NY 10462-0380
www.graphics-stamps.org
E-mail: indybruce1@yahoo.com

Journalists, Authors & Poets on Stamps
Ms. Lee Straayer
P.O. Box 6808
Champaign IL 61826
E-mail: lstraayer@dcbnet.com

Lighthouse Stamp Society
Dalene Thomas
1805 S Balsam St., #106
Lakewood CO 80232
Ph: (303) 986-6620
www.lighthousestampsociety.org
E-mail: dalene@lighthousestampsociety.org

Lions International Stamp Club
John Bargus
108-2777 Barry Road RR 2
Mill Bay, BC, V0R 2P2
CANADA
Ph: (250) 743-5782

Mahatma Gandhi On Stamps Study Circle
Pramod Shivagunde
Pratik Clinic, Akluj
Solapur, Maharashtra, 413101
INDIA
E-mail: drnanda@bom6.vsnl.net.in

Masonic Study Unit
Stanley R. Longenecker
930 Wood St.
Mount Joy PA 17552-1926
Ph: (717) 669-9094
E-mail: natsco@usa.net

Mathematical Study Unit
Monty Strauss
4209 88th St.
Lubbock TX 79423-2941
www.mathstamps.org

Medical Subjects Unit
Dr. Frederick C. Skvara
P.O. Box 6228
Bridgewater NJ 08807
E-mail: fcskvara@optonline.net

Military Postal History Society
Ed Dubin
1 S. Wacker Drive, Suite 3500
Chicago IL 60606
www.militaryPHS.org
E-mail: dubine@comcast.net

Mourning Stamps and Covers Club
James Camak, Jr.
3801 Acapulco Ct.
Irving TX 75062
www.mscc.ms
E-mail: jamescamak7@gmail.com

Napoleonic Age Philatelists
Ken Berry
4117 NW 146th St.
Oklahoma City OK 73134-1746
Ph: (405) 748-8646
www.nap-stamps.org
E-mail: krb4117@att.net

Old World Archeological Study Unit
Caroline Scannell
11 Dawn Drive
Smithtown NY 11787-1761
www.owasu.org
E-mail: editor@owasu.org

Petroleum Philatelic Society International
Feitze Papa
922 Meander Dr.
Walnut Creek CA 94598-4239
E-mail: oildad@astound.net

Rotary on Stamps Unit
Gerald L. Fitzsimmons
105 Calla Ricardo
Victoria TX 77904
rotaryonstamps.org
E-mail: glfitz@suddenlink.net

Scouts on Stamps Society International
Lawrence Clay
P.O. Box 6228
Kennewick WA 99336
Ph: (509) 735-3731
www.sossi.org
E-mail: rfrank@sossi.org

Ships on Stamps Unit
Les Smith
302 Conklin Ave.
Penticton, BC, V2A 2T4
CANADA
Ph: (250) 493-7486
www.shipsonstamps.org
E-mail: lessmith440@shaw.ca

Space Unit
David Blog
P.O. Box 174
Bergenfield NJ 07621
www.space-unit.com
E-mail: davidblognj@gmail.com

Sports Philatelists International
Mark Maestrone
2824 Curie Place
San Diego CA 92122-4110
www.sportstamps.org
Email: president@sportstamps.org

Stamps on Stamps Collectors Club
Alf Jordan
156 W. Elm St.
Yarmouth ME 04096
www.stampsonstamps.org
E-mail: ajordan1@maine.rr.com

Windmill Study Unit
Orville Tysseling
9740 Washington Church Rd.
Miamisburg OH 45342-4510
www.wsu.world

Wine On Stamps Study Unit
David Wolfersberger
768 Chain Ridge Road
St. Louis MO 63122-3259
Ph: (314) 961-5032
www.wine-on-stamps.org
E-mail: dewolf2@swbell.net

Women on Stamps Study Unit
Hugh Gottfried
2232 26th St.
Santa Monica CA 90405-1902
E-mail: hgottfried@adelphia.net

Expertizing Services

The following organizations will, for a fee, provide expert opinions about stamps submitted to them. Collectors should contact these organizations to find out about their fees and requirements before submiting philatelic material to them. The listing of these groups here is not intended as an endorsement by Amos Media Co.

General Expertizing Services

American Philatelic Expertizing Service (a service of the American Philatelic Society)
100 Match Factory Place
Bellefonte PA 16823-1367
Ph: (814) 237-3803
Fax: (814) 237-6128
www.stamps.org
E-mail: ambristo@stamps.org
Areas of Expertise: Worldwide

B. P. A. Expertising, Ltd.
P.O. Box 1141
Guildford, Surrey, GU5 0WR
UNITED KINGDOM
E-mail: sec@bpaexpertising.org
Areas of Expertise: British Commonwealth, Great Britain, Classics of Europe, South America and the Far East

Philatelic Foundation
341 W. 38th St., 5th Floor
New York NY 10018
Ph: (212) 221-6555
Fax: (212) 221-6208
www.philatelicfoundation.org
E-mail: philatelicfoundation@verizon.net
Areas of Expertise: U.S. & Worldwide

Philatelic Stamp Authentication and Grading, Inc.
P.O. Box 41-0880
Melbourne FL 32941-0880
Customer Service: (305) 345-9864
www.psaginc.com
E-mail: info@psaginc.com
Areas of Expertise: U.S., Canal Zone, Hawaii, Philippines, Canada & Provinces

Professional Stamp Experts
P.O. Box 6170
Newport Beach CA 92658
Ph: (877) STAMP-88
Fax: (949) 833-7955
www.collectors.com/pse
E-mail: pseinfo@collectors.com
Areas of Expertise: Stamps and covers of U.S., U.S. Possessions, British Commonwealth

Royal Philatelic Society Expert Committee
41 Devonshire Place
London, W1N 1PE
UNITED KINGDOM
www.rpsl.org.uk/experts.html
E-mail: experts@rpsl.org.uk
Areas of Expertise: Worldwide

Expertizing Services Covering Specific Fields Or Countries

China Stamp Society Expertizing Service
1050 W. Blue Ridge Blvd.
Kansas City MO 64145
Ph: (816) 942-6300
E-mail: hjmesq@aol.com
Areas of Expertise: China

Confederate Stamp Alliance Authentication Service
Gen. Frank Crown, Jr.
P.O. Box 278
Capshaw AL 35742-0396
Ph: (302) 422-2656
Fax: (302) 424-1990
www.csalliance.org
E-mail: csaas@knology.net
Areas of Expertise: Confederate stamps and postal history

Errors, Freaks and Oddities Collectors Club Expertizing Service
138 East Lakemont Drive
Kingsland GA 31548
Ph: (912) 729-1573
Areas of Expertise: U.S. errors, freaks and oddities

Estonian Philatelic Society Expertizing Service
39 Clafford Lane
Melville NY 11747
Ph: (516) 421-2078
E-mail: esto4@aol.com
Areas of Expertise: Estonia

Hawaiian Philatelic Society Expertizing Service
P.O. Box 10115
Honolulu HI 96816-0115
Areas of Expertise: Hawaii

Hong Kong Stamp Society Expertizing Service
P.O. Box 206
Glenside PA 19038
Fax: (215) 576-6850
Areas of Expertise: Hong Kong

International Association of Philatelic Experts United States Associate members:

Paul Buchsbayew
119 W. 57th St.
New York NY 10019
Ph: (212) 977-7734
Fax: (212) 977-8653
Areas of Expertise: Russia, Soviet Union

William T. Crowe
P.O. Box 2090
Danbury CT 06813-2090
E-mail: wtcrowe@aol.com
Areas of Expertise: United States

John Lievsay
(see American Philatelic Expertizing Service and Philatelic Foundation)
Areas of Expertise: France

Robert W. Lyman
P.O. Box 348
Irvington on Hudson NY 10533
Ph and Fax: (914) 591-6937
Areas of Expertise: British North America, New Zealand

Robert Odenweller
P.O. Box 401
Bernardsville NJ 07924-0401
Ph and Fax: (908) 766-5460
Areas of Expertise: New Zealand, Samoa to 1900

Sergio Sismondo
The Regency Tower, Suite 1109
770 James Street
Syracuse NY 13203
Ph: (315) 422-2331
Fax: (315) 422-2956
Areas of Expertise: British East Africa, Camerouns, Cape of Good Hope, Canada, British North America

International Society for Japanese Philately Expertizing Committee
132 North Pine Terrace
Staten Island NY 10312-4052
Ph: (718) 227-5229
Areas of Expertise: Japan and related areas, except WWII Japanese Occupation issues

International Society for Portuguese Philately Expertizing Service
P.O. Box 43146
Philadelphia PA 19129-3146
Ph and Fax: (215) 843-2106
E-mail: s.s.washburne@worldnet.att.net
Areas of Expertise: Portugal and Colonies

Mexico-Elmhurst Philatelic Society International Expert Committee
P.O. Box 1133
West Covina CA 91793
Areas of Expertise: Mexico

Ukrainian Philatelic & Numismatic Society Expertizing Service
30552 Dell Lane
Warren MI 48092-1862
Areas of Expertise: Ukraine, Western Ukraine

V. G. Greene Philatelic Research Foundation
P.O. Box 204, Station Q
Toronto, ON, M4T 2M1
CANADA
Ph: (416) 921-2073
Fax: (416) 921-1282
www.greenefoundation.ca
E-mail: vggfoundation@on.aibn.com
Areas of Expertise: British North America

Information on Catalogue Values, Grade and Condition

Catalogue Value

The Scott Catalogue value is a retail value; that is, an amount you could expect to pay for a stamp in the grade of Very Fine with no faults. Any exceptions to the grade valued will be noted in the text. The general introduction on the following pages and the individual section introductions further explain the type of material that is valued. The value listed for any given stamp is a reference that reflects recent actual dealer selling prices for that item.

Dealer retail price lists, public auction results, published prices in advertising and individual solicitation of retail prices from dealers, collectors and specialty organizations have been used in establishing the values found in this catalogue. Amos Media Co. values stamps, but Amos Media is not a company engaged in the business of buying and selling stamps as a dealer.

Use this catalogue as a guide for buying and selling. The actual price you pay for a stamp may be higher or lower than the catalogue value because of many different factors, including the amount of personal service a dealer offers, or increased or decreased interest in the country or topic represented by a stamp or set. An item may occasionally be offered at a lower price as a "loss leader," or as part of a special sale. You also may obtain an item inexpensively at public auction because of little interest at that time or as part of a large lot.

Stamps that are of a lesser grade than Very Fine, or those with condition problems, generally trade at lower prices than those given in this catalogue. Stamps of exceptional quality in both grade and condition often command higher prices than those listed.

Values for pre-1900 unused issues are for stamps with approximately half or more of their original gum. Stamps with most or all of their original gum may be expected to sell for more, and stamps with less than half of their original gum may be expected to sell for somewhat less than the values listed. On rarer stamps, it may be expected that the original gum will be somewhat more disturbed than it will be on more common issues. Post-1900 unused issues are assumed to have full original gum. From breakpoints in most countries' listings, stamps are valued as never hinged, due to the wide availability of stamps in that condition. These notations are prominently placed in the listings and in the country information preceding the listings. Some countries also feature listings with dual values for hinged and never-hinged stamps.

Grade

A stamp's grade and condition are crucial to its value. The accompanying illustrations show examples of Very Fine stamps from different time periods, along with examples of stamps in Fine to Very Fine and Extremely Fine grades as points of reference. When a stamp seller offers a stamp in any grade from fine to superb without further qualifying statements, that stamp should not only have the centering grade as defined, but it also should be free of faults or other condition problems.

FINE stamps (illustrations not shown) have designs that are quite off center, with the perforations on one or two sides very close to the design but not quite touching it. There is white space between the perforations and the design that is minimal but evident to the unaided eye. Imperforate stamps may have small margins, and earlier issues may show the design just touching one edge of the stamp design. Very early perforated issues normally will have the perforations slightly cutting into the design. Used stamps may have heavier than usual cancellations.

FINE-VERY FINE stamps will be somewhat off center on one side, or slightly off center on two sides. Imperforate stamps will have two margins of at least normal size, and the design will not touch any edge. For perforated stamps, the perfs are well clear of the design, but are still noticeably off center. *However, early issues of a country may be printed in such a way that the design naturally is very close to the edges. In these cases, the perforations may cut into the design very slightly.* Used stamps will not have a cancellation that detracts from the design.

VERY FINE stamps will be just slightly off center on one or two sides, but the design will be well clear of the edge. The stamp will present a nice, balanced appearance. Imperforate stamps will be well centered within normal-sized margins. *However, early issues of many countries may be printed in such a way that the perforations may touch the design on one or more sides. Where this is the case, a boxed note will be found defining the centering and margins of the stamps being valued.* Used stamps will have light or otherwise neat cancellations. This is the grade used to establish Scott Catalogue values.

EXTREMELY FINE stamps are close to being perfectly centered. Imperforate stamps will have even margins that are slightly larger than normal. Even the earliest perforated issues will have perforations clear of the design on all sides.

Amos Media Co. recognizes that there is no formally enforced grading scheme for postage stamps, and that the final price you pay or obtain for a stamp will be determined by individual agreement at the time of transaction.

Condition

Grade addresses only centering and (for used stamps) cancellation. *Condition* refers to factors other than grade that affect a stamp's desirability.

Factors that can increase the value of a stamp include exceptionally wide margins, particularly fresh color, the presence of selvage, and plate or die varieties. Unusual cancels on used stamps (particularly those of the 19th century) can greatly enhance their value as well.

Factors other than faults that decrease the value of a stamp include loss of original gum, regumming, a hinge remnant or foreign object adhering to the gum, natural inclusions, straight edges, and markings or notations applied by collectors or dealers.

Faults include missing pieces, tears, pin or other holes, surface scuffs, thin spots, creases, toning, short or pulled perforations, clipped perforations, oxidation or other forms of color changelings, soiling, stains, and such man-made changes as reperforations or the chemical removal or lightening of a cancellation.

Grading Illustrations

On the following two pages are illustrations of various stamps from countries appearing in this volume. These stamps are arranged by country, and they represent early or important issues that are often found in widely different grades in the marketplace. The editors believe the illustrations will prove useful in showing the margin size and centering that will be seen on the various issues.

In addition to the matters of margin size and centering, collectors are reminded that the very fine stamps valued in the Scott catalogues also will possess fresh color and intact perforations, and they will be free from defects.

Examples shown are computer-manipulated images made from single digitized master illustrations.

Stamp Illustrations Used in the Catalogue

It is important to note that the stamp images used for identification purposes in this catlaogue may not be indicative of the grade of stamp being valued. Refer to the written discussion of grades on this page and to the grading illustrations on the following two pages for grading information.

Fine-Very Fine

SCOTT
CATALOGUES
VALUE
STAMPS IN
THIS GRADE

Very Fine

Extremely Fine

Fine-Very Fine

SCOTT
CATALOGUES
VALUE
STAMPS IN
THIS GRADE

Very Fine

Extremely Fine

Fine-Very Fine →

SCOTT
CATALOGUES
VALUE
STAMPS IN
THIS GRADE

Very Fine →

Extremely Fine →

Fine-Very Fine →

SCOTT
CATALOGUES
VALUE
STAMPS IN
THIS GRADE

Very Fine →

Extremely Fine →

For purposes of helping to determine the gum condition and value of an unused stamp, Scott presents the following chart which details different gum conditions and indicates how the conditions correlate with the Scott values for unused stamps. Used together, the Illustrated Grading Chart on the previous pages and this Illustrated Gum Chart should allow catalogue users to better understand the grade and gum condition of stamps valued in the Scott catalogues.

Gum Categories:	MINT N.H.	ORIGINAL GUM (O.G.)				NO GUM
	Mint **Never Hinged** *Free from any disturbance*	**Lightly Hinged** *Faint impression of a removed hinge over a small area*	**Hinge Mark or Remnant** *Prominent hinged spot with part or all of the hinge remaining*	**Large part o.g.** *Approximately half or more of the gum intact*	**Small part o.g.** *Approximately less than half of the gum intact*	**No gum** *Only if issued with gum*
Commonly Used Symbol:	★ ★	★	★	★	★	(★)
Pre-1900 Issues (Pre-1881 for U.S.)	*Very fine pre-1900 stamps in these categories trade at a premium over Scott value*			Scott Value for "Unused"		Scott "No Gum" listings for selected unused classic stamps
From 1900 to break-points for listings of never-hinged stamps	Scott "Never Hinged" listings for selected unused stamps	Scott Value for "Unused" (Actual value will be affected by the degree of hinging of the full o.g.)				
From breakpoints noted for many countries	Scott Value for "Unused"					

Never Hinged (NH; ★★): A never-hinged stamp will have full original gum that will have no hinge mark or disturbance. The presence of an expertizer's mark does not disqualify a stamp from this designation.

Original Gum (OG; ★): Pre-1900 stamps should have approximately half or more of their original gum. On rarer stamps, it may be expected that the original gum will be somewhat more disturbed than it will be on more common issues. Post-1900 stamps should have full original gum. Original gum will show some disturbance caused by a previous hinge(s) which may be present or entirely removed. The actual value of a post-1900 stamp will be affected by the degree of hinging of the full original gum.

Disturbed Original Gum: Gum showing noticeable effects of humidity, climate or hinging over more than half of the gum. The significance of gum disturbance in valuing a stamp in any of the Original Gum categories depends on the degree of disturbance, the rarity and normal gum condition of the issue and other variables affecting quality.

Regummed (RG; (★)): A regummed stamp is a stamp without gum that has had some type of gum privately applied at a time after it was issued. This normally is done to deceive collectors and/or dealers into thinking that the stamp has original gum and therefore has a higher value. A regummed stamp is considered the same as a stamp with none of its original gum for purposes of grading.

Catalogue Listing Policy

It is the intent of Amos Media Co. to list all postage stamps of the world in the *Scott Standard Postage Stamp Catalogue*. The only strict criteria for listing is that stamps be decreed legal for postage by the issuing country and that the issuing country actually have an operating postal system. Whether the primary intent of issuing a given stamp or set was for sale to postal patrons or to stamp collectors is not part of our listing criteria. Scott's role is to provide basic comprehensive postage stamp information. It is up to each stamp collector to choose which items to include in a collection.

It is Scott's objective to seek reasons why a stamp should be listed, rather than why it should not. Nevertheless, there are certain types of items that will not be listed. These include the following:

1. Unissued items that are not officially distributed or released by the issuing postal authority. If such items are officially issued at a later date by the country, they will be listed. Unissued items consist of those that have been printed and then held from sale for reasons such as change in government, errors found on stamps or something deemed objectionable about a stamp subject or design.

2. Stamps "issued" by non-existent postal entities or fantasy countries, such as Nagaland, Occusi-Ambeno, Staffa, Sedang, Torres Straits and others. Also, stamps "issued" in the names of legitimate, stamp-issuing countries that are not authorized by those countries.

3. Semi-official or unofficial items not required for postage. Examples include items issued by private agencies for their own express services. When such items are required for delivery, or are valid as prepayment of postage, they are listed.

4. Local stamps issued for local use only. Postage stamps issued by governments specifically for "domestic" use, such as Haiti Scott 219-228, or the United States non-denominated stamps, are not considered to be locals, since they are valid for postage throughout the country of origin.

5. Items not valid for postal use. For example, a few countries have issued souvenir sheets that are not valid for postage. This area also includes a number of worldwide charity labels (some denominated) that do not pay postage.

6. Egregiously exploitative issues such as stamps sold for far more than face value, stamps purposefully issued in artificially small quantities or only against advance orders, stamps awarded only to a selected audience such as a philatelic bureau's standing order customers, or stamps sold only in conjunction with other products. All of these kinds of items are usually controlled issues and/or are intended for speculation. These items normally will be included in a footnote.

7. Items distributed by the issuing government only to a limited group, club, philatelic exhibition or a single stamp dealer or other private company. These items normally will be included in a footnote.

8. Stamps not available to collectors. These generally are rare items, all of which are held by public institutions such as museums. The existence of such items often will be cited in footnotes.

The fact that a stamp has been used successfully as postage, even on international mail, is not in itself sufficient proof that it was legitimately issued. Numerous examples of so-called stamps from non-existent countries are known to have been used to post letters that have successfully passed through the international mail system.

There are certain items that are subject to interpretation. When a stamp falls outside our specifications, it may be listed along with a cautionary footnote.

A number of factors are considered in our approach to analyzing how a stamp is listed. The following list of factors is presented to share with you, the catalogue user, the complexity of the listing process.

Additional printings — "Additional printings" of a previously issued stamp may range from an item that is totally different to cases where it is impossible to differentiate from the original. At least a minor number (a small-letter suffix) is assigned if there is a distinct change in stamp shade, noticeably redrawn design, or a significantly different perforation measurement. A major number (numeral or numeral and capital-letter combination) is assigned if the editors feel the "additional printing" is sufficiently different from the original that it constitutes a different issue.

Commemoratives — Where practical, commemoratives with the same theme are placed in a set. For example, the U.S. Civil War Centennial set of 1961-65 and the Constitution Bicentennial series of 1989-90 appear as sets. Countries such as Japan and Korea issue such material on a regular basis, with an announced, or at least predictable, number of stamps known in advance. Occasionally, however, stamp sets that were released over a period of years have been separated. Appropriately placed footnotes will guide you to each set's continuation.

Definitive sets — Blocks of numbers generally have been reserved for definitive sets, based on previous experience with any given country. If a few more stamps were issued in a set than originally expected, they often have been inserted into the original set with a capital-letter suffix, such as U.S. Scott 1059A. If it appears that many more stamps

than the originally allotted block will be released before the set is completed, a new block of numbers will be reserved, with the original one being closed off. In some cases, such as the U.S. Transportation and Great Americans series, several blocks of numbers exist. Appropriately placed footnotes will guide you to each set's continuation.

New country — Membership in the Universal Postal Union is not a consideration for listing status or order of placement within the catalogue. The index will tell you in what volume or page number the listings begin.

"No release date" items — The amount of information available for any given stamp issue varies greatly from country to country and even from time to time. Extremely comprehensive information about new stamps is available from some countries well before the stamps are released. By contrast some countries do not provide information about stamps or release dates. Most countries, however, fall between these extremes. A country may provide denominations or subjects of stamps from upcoming issues that are not issued as planned. Sometimes, philatelic agencies, those private firms hired to represent countries, add these later-issued items to sets well after the formal release date. This time period can range from weeks to years. If these items were officially released by the country, they will be added to the appropriate spot in the set. In many cases, the specific release date of a stamp or set of stamps may never be known.

Overprints — The color of an overprint is always noted if it is other than black. Where more than one color of ink has been used on overprints of a single set, the color used is noted. Early overprint and surcharge illustrations were altered to prevent their use by forgers.

Personalized Stamps — Since 1999, the special service of personalizing stamp vignettes, or labels attached to stamps, has been offered to customers by postal administrations of many countries. Sheets of these stamps are sold, singly or in quantity, only through special orders made by mail, in person, or through a sale on a computer website with the postal administrations or their agents for which an extra fee is charged, though some countries offer to collectors at face value personalized stamps having generic images in the vignettes or on the attached labels. It is impossible for any catalogue to know what images have been chosen by customers. Images can be 1) owned or created by the customer, 2) a generic image, or 3) an image pulled from a library of stock images on the stamp creation website. It is also impossible to know the quantity printed for any stamp having a particular image. So from a valuing standpoint, any image is equivalent to any other image for any personalized stamp having the same catalogue number. Illustrations of personalized stamps in the catalogue are not always those of stamps having generic images.

Personalized items are listed with some exceptions. These include:

1. Stamps or sheets that have attached labels that the customer cannot personalize, but which are nonetheless marketed as "personalized," and are sold for far more than the franking value.

2. Stamps or sheets that can be personalized by the customer, but where a portion of the print run must be ceded to the issuing country for sale to other customers.

3. Stamps or sheets that are created exclusively for a particular commercial client, or clients, including stamps that differ from any similar stamp that has been made available to the public.

4. Stamps or sheets that are deliberately conceived by the issuing authority that have been, or are likely to be, created with an excessive number of different face values, sizes, or other features that are changeable.

5. Stamps or sheets that are created by postal administrations using the same system of stamp personalization that has been put in place for use by the public that are printed in limited quantities and sold above face value.

6. Stamps or sheets that are created by licensees not directly affiliated or controlled by a postal administration.

Excluded items may or may not be footnoted.

Se-tenants — Connected stamps of differing features (se-tenants) will be listed in the format most commonly collected. This includes pairs, blocks or larger multiples. Se-tenant units are not always symmetrical. An example is Australia Scott 508, which is a block of seven stamps. If the stamps are primarily collected as a unit, the major number may be assigned to the multiple, with minors going to each component stamp. In cases where continuous-design or other unit se-tenants will receive significant postal use, each stamp is given a major Scott number listing. This includes issues from the United States, Canada, Germany and Great Britain, for example.

Understanding the Listings

On the opposite page is an enlarged "typical" listing from this catalogue. Below are detailed explanations of each of the highlighted parts of the listing.

❶ Scott number — Scott catalogue numbers are used to identify specific items when buying, selling or trading stamps. Each listed postage stamp from every country has a unique Scott catalogue number. Therefore, Germany Scott 99, for example, can only refer to a single stamp. Although the Scott catalogue usually lists stamps in chronological order by date of issue, there are exceptions. When a country has issued a set of stamps over a period of time, those stamps within the set are kept together without regard to date of issue. This follows the normal collecting approach of keeping stamps in their natural sets.

When a country issues a set of stamps over a period of time, a group of consecutive catalogue numbers is reserved for the stamps in that set, as issued. If that group of numbers proves to be too few, capital-letter suffixes, such as "A" or "B," may be added to existing numbers to create enough catalogue numbers to cover all items in the set. A capital-letter suffix indicates a major Scott catalogue number listing. Scott generally uses a suffix letter only once. Therefore, a catalogue number listing with a capital-letter suffix will seldom be found with the same letter (lower case) used as a minor-letter listing. If there is a Scott 16A in a set, for example, there will seldom be a Scott 16a. However, a minor-letter "a" listing may be added to a major number containing an "A" suffix (Scott 16Aa, for example).

Suffix letters are cumulative. A minor "b" variety of Scott 16A would be Scott 16Ab, not Scott 16b.

There are times when a reserved block of Scott catalogue numbers is too large for a set, leaving some numbers unused. Such gaps in the numbering sequence also occur when the catalogue editors move an item's listing elsewhere or have removed it entirely from the catalogue. Scott does not attempt to account for every possible number, but rather attempts to assure that each stamp is assigned its own number.

Scott numbers designating regular postage normally are only numerals. Scott numbers for other types of stamps, such as air post, semi-postal, postal tax, postage due, occupation and others have a prefix consisting of one or more capital letters or a combination of numerals and capital letters.

❷ Illustration number — Illustration or design-type numbers are used to identify each catalogue illustration. For most sets, the lowest face-value stamp is shown. It then serves as an example of the basic design approach for other stamps not illustrated. Where more than one stamp use the same illustration number, but have differences in design, the design paragraph or the description line clearly indicates the design on each stamp not illustrated. Where there are both vertical and horizontal designs in a set, a single illustration may be used, with the exceptions noted in the design paragraph or description line.

When an illustration is followed by a lower-case letter in parentheses, such as "A2(b)," the trailing letter indicates which overprint or surcharge illustration applies.

Illustrations normally are 70 percent of the original size of the stamp. Oversized stamps, blocks and souvenir sheets are reduced even more. Overprints and surcharges are shown at 100 percent of their original size if shown alone, but are 70 percent of original size if shown on stamps. In some cases, the illustration will be placed above the set, between listings or omitted completely. Overprint and surcharge illustrations are not placed in this catalogue for purposes of expertizing stamps.

❸ Paper color — The color of a stamp's paper is noted in italic type when the paper used is not white.

❹ Listing styles — There are two principal types of catalogue listings: major and minor.

Major listings are in a larger type style than minor listings. The catalogue number is a numeral that can be found with or without a capital-letter suffix, and with or without a prefix.

Minor listings are in a smaller type style and have a small-letter suffix or (if the listing immediately follows that of the major number) may show only the letter. These listings identify a variety of the major item. Examples include perforation and shade differences, multiples (some souvenir sheets, booklet panes and se-tenant combinations), and singles of multiples.

Examples of major number listings include 16, 28A, B97, C13A, 10N5, and 10N6A. Examples of minor numbers are 16a and C13Ab.

❺ Basic information about a stamp or set — Introducing each stamp issue is a small section (usually a line listing) of basic information about a stamp or set. This section normally includes the date of issue, method of printing, perforation, watermark and, sometimes, some additional information of note. *Printing method, perforation and watermark apply to the following sets until a change is noted.* Stamps created by overprinting or surcharging previous issues are assumed to have the same perforation, watermark, printing method and other production characteristics as the original. Dates of issue are as precise as Scott is able to confirm and often reflect the dates on first-day covers, rather than the actual date of release.

❻ Denomination — This normally refers to the face value of the stamp; that is, the cost of the unused stamp at the post office at the time of issue. When a denomination is shown in parentheses, it does not appear on the stamp. This includes the non-denominated stamps of the United States, Brazil and Great Britain, for example.

❼ Color or other description — This area provides information to solidify identification of a stamp. In many recent cases, a description of the stamp design appears in this space, rather than a listing of colors.

❽ Year of issue — In stamp sets that have been released in a period that spans more than a year, the number shown in parentheses is the year that stamp first appeared. Stamps without a date appeared during the first year of the issue. Dates are not always given for minor varieties.

❾ Value unused and Value used — The Scott catalogue values are based on stamps that are in a grade of Very Fine unless stated otherwise. Unused values refer to items that have not seen postal, revenue or any other duty for which they were intended. Pre-1900 unused stamps that were issued with gum must have at least most of their original gum. Later issues are assumed to have full original gum. From breakpoints specified in most countries' listings, stamps are valued as never hinged. Stamps issued without gum are noted. Modern issues with PVA or other synthetic adhesives may appear ungummed. Unused self-adhesive stamps are valued as appearing undisturbed on their original backing paper. Values for used self-adhesive stamps are for examples either on piece or off piece. For a more detailed explanation of these values, please see the "Catalogue Value," "Condition" and "Understanding Valuing Notations" sections elsewhere in this introduction.

In some cases, where used stamps are more valuable than unused stamps, the value is for an example with a contemporaneous cancel, rather than a modern cancel or a smudge or other unclear marking. For those stamps that were released for postal and fiscal purposes, the used value represents a postally used stamp. Stamps with revenue cancels generally sell for less.

Stamps separated from a complete se-tenant multiple usually will be worth less than a pro-rated portion of the se-tenant multiple, and stamps lacking the attached labels that are noted in the listings will be worth less than the values shown.

❿ Changes in basic set information — Bold type is used to show any changes in the basic data given for a set of stamps. These basic data categories include perforation gauge measurement, paper type, printing method and watermark.

⓫ Total value of a set — The total value of sets of three or more stamps issued after 1900 are shown. The set line also notes the range of Scott numbers and total number of stamps included in the grouping. The actual value of a set consisting predominantly of stamps having the minimum value of 25 cents may be less than the total value shown. Similarly, the actual value or catalogue value of se-tenant pairs or of blocks consisting of stamps having the minimum value of 25 cents may be less than the catalogue values of the component parts.

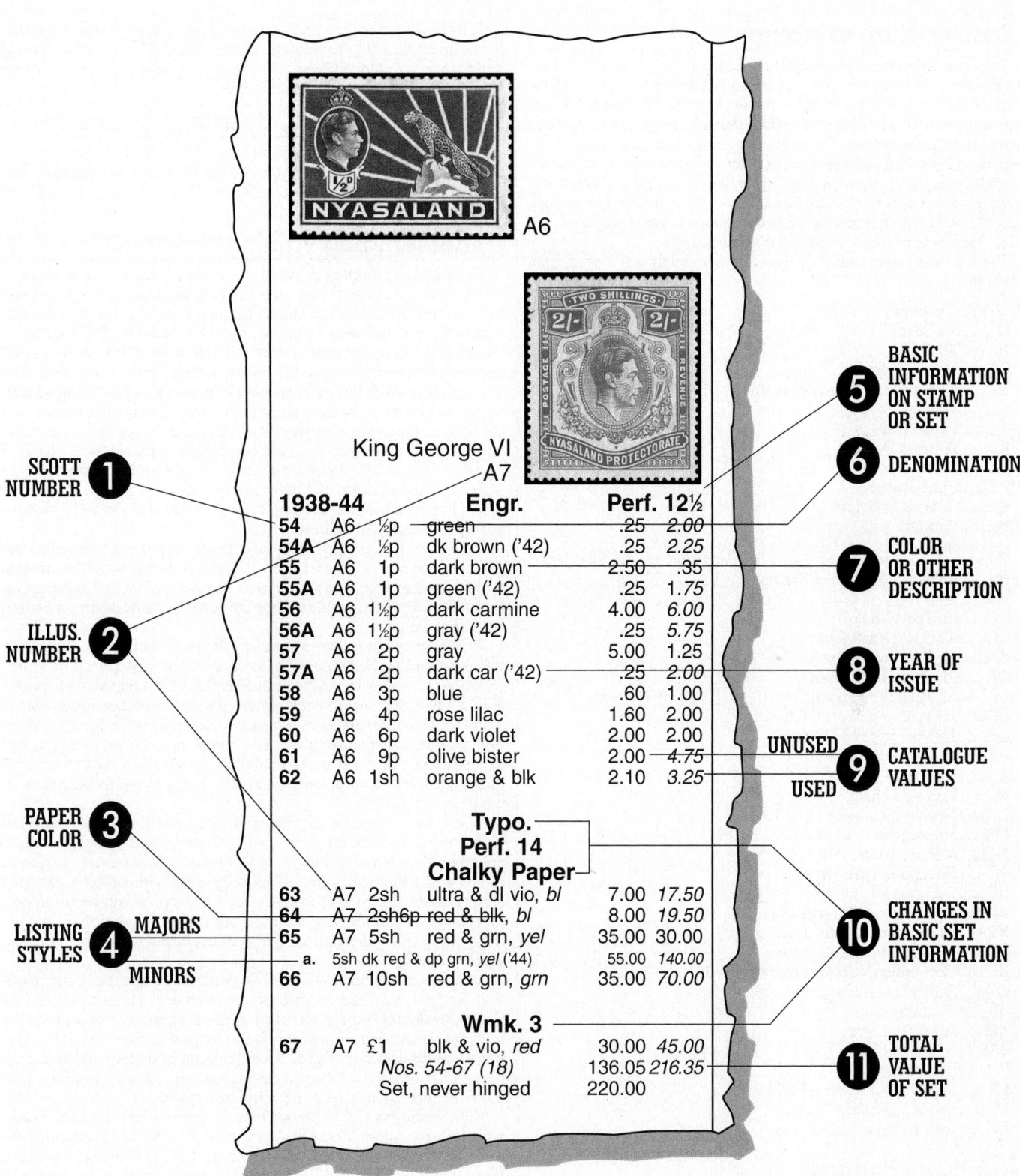

SCOTT NUMBER **1**

ILLUS. NUMBER **2**

PAPER COLOR **3**

LISTING STYLES **4**

MAJORS

MINORS

A6

King George VI
A7

BASIC INFORMATION ON STAMP OR SET **5**

DENOMINATION **6**

COLOR OR OTHER DESCRIPTION **7**

YEAR OF ISSUE **8**

CATALOGUE VALUES **9**

UNUSED

USED

CHANGES IN BASIC SET INFORMATION **10**

TOTAL VALUE OF SET **11**

1938-44			**Engr.**	**Perf. 12½**	
54	A6	½p	green	.25	*2.00*
54A	A6	½p	dk brown ('42)	.25	*2.25*
55	A6	1p	dark brown	2.50	*.35*
55A	A6	1p	green ('42)	.25	*1.75*
56	A6	1½p	dark carmine	4.00	*6.00*
56A	A6	1½p	gray ('42)	.25	*5.75*
57	A6	2p	gray	5.00	*1.25*
57A	A6	2p	dark car ('42)	.25	*2.00*
58	A6	3p	blue	.60	*1.00*
59	A6	4p	rose lilac	1.60	*2.00*
60	A6	6p	dark violet	2.00	*2.00*
61	A6	9p	olive bister	2.00	*4.75*
62	A6	1sh	orange & blk	2.10	*3.25*

Typo.
Perf. 14
Chalky Paper

63	A7	2sh	ultra & dl vio, *bl*	7.00	*17.50*
64	A7	2sh6p	red & blk, *bl*	8.00	*19.50*
65	A7	5sh	red & grn, *yel*	35.00	30.00
a.			5sh dk red & dp grn, *yel* ('44)	55.00	*140.00*
66	A7	10sh	red & grn, *grn*	35.00	*70.00*

Wmk. 3

67	A7	£1	blk & vio, *red*	30.00	*45.00*
		Nos. 54-67 (18)		136.05	*216.35*
		Set, never hinged		220.00	

Special Notices

Classification of stamps

The *Scott Standard Postage Stamp Catalogue* lists stamps by country of issue. The next level of organization is a listing by section on the basis of the function of the stamps. The principal sections cover regular postage, semi-postal, air post, special delivery, registration, postage due and other categories. Except for regular postage, catalogue numbers for all sections include a prefix letter (or number-letter combination) denoting the class to which a given stamp belongs. When some countries issue sets containing stamps from more than one category, the catalogue will at times list all of the stamps in one category (such as air post stamps listed as part of a postage set).

The following is a listing of the most commonly used catalogue prefixes.

Prefix ....Category

C.........Air Post
M........Military
P.........Newspaper
N.........Occupation - Regular Issues
O........Official
Q........Parcel Post
J..........Postage Due
RA......Postal Tax
B.........Semi-Postal
E.........Special Delivery
MR......War Tax

Other prefixes used by more than one country include the following:

H.........Acknowledgment of Receipt
I..........Late Fee
CO......Air Post Official
CQ......Air Post Parcel Post
RAC....Air Post Postal Tax
CF......Air Post Registration
CB......Air Post Semi-Postal
CBO...Air Post Semi-Postal Official
CE......Air Post Special Delivery
EY.......Authorized Delivery
S.........Franchise
G........Insured Letter
GY......Marine Insurance
MC.....Military Air Post
MQ.....Military Parcel Post
NC......Occupation - Air Post
NO......Occupation - Official
NJ........Occupation - Postage Due
NRA....Occupation - Postal Tax
NB......Occupation - Semi-Postal
NE......Occupation - Special Delivery
QY......Parcel Post Authorized Delivery
AR......Postal-fiscal
RAJ.....Postal Tax Due
RAB....Postal Tax Semi-Postal
F.........Registration
EB.......Semi-Postal Special Delivery
EO......Special Delivery Official
QE......Special Handling

New issue listings

Updates to this catalogue appear each month in the *Linn's Stamp News* monthly magazine. Included in this update are additions to the listings of countries found in the *Scott Standard Postage Stamp Catalogue* and the *Specialized Catalogue of United States Stamps and Covers*, as well as corrections and updates to current editions of this catalogue.

From time to time there will be changes in the final listings of stamps from the *Linn's Stamp News* magazine to the next edition of the catalogue. This occurs as more information about certain stamps or sets becomes available.

The catalogue update section of the *Linn's Stamp News* magazine is the most timely presentation of this material available. Annual subscriptions to *Linn's Stamp News* are available from Linn's Stamp News, Box 926, Sidney, OH 45365-0926.

Number additions, deletions & changes

A listing of catalogue number additions, deletions and changes from the previous edition of the catalogue appears in each volume. See Catalogue Number Additions, Deletions & Changes in the table of contents for the location of this list.

Understanding valuing notations

The *minimum catalogue value* of an individual stamp or set is 25 cents. This represents a portion of the cost incurred by a dealer when he prepares an individual stamp for resale. As a point of philatelic-economic fact, the lower the value shown for an item in this catalogue, the greater the percentage of that value is attributed to dealer mark up and profit margin. In many cases, such as the 25-cent minimum value, that price does not cover the labor or other costs involved with stocking it as an individual stamp. The sum of minimum values in a set does not properly represent the value of a complete set primarily composed of a number of minimum-value stamps, nor does the sum represent the actual value of a packet made up of minimum-value stamps. Thus a packet of 1,000 different common stamps — each of which has a catalogue value of 25 cents — normally sells for considerably less than 250 dollars!

The *absence of a retail value* for a stamp does not necessarily suggest that a stamp is scarce or rare. A dash in the value column means that the stamp is known in a stated form or variety, but information is either lacking or insufficient for purposes of establishing a usable catalogue value.

Stamp values in *italics* generally refer to items that are difficult to value accurately. For expensive items, such as those priced at $1,000 or higher, a value in italics indicates that the affected item trades very seldom. For inexpensive items, a value in italics represents a warning. One example is a "blocked" issue where the issuing postal administration may have controlled one stamp in a set in an attempt to make the whole set more valuable. Another example is an item that sold at an extreme multiple of face value in the marketplace at the time of its issue.

One type of warning to collectors that appears in the catalogue is illustrated by a stamp that is valued considerably higher in used condition than it is as unused. In this case, collectors are cautioned to be certain the used version has a genuine and contemporaneous cancellation. The type of cancellation on a stamp can be an important factor in determining its sale price. Catalogue values do not apply to fiscal, telegraph or non-contemporaneous postal cancels, unless otherwise noted.

Some countries have released back issues of stamps in canceled-to-order form, sometimes covering as much as a 10-year period. The Scott Catalogue values for used stamps reflect canceled-to-order material when such stamps are found to predominate in the marketplace for the issue involved. Notes frequently appear in the stamp listings to specify which items are valued as canceled-to-order, or if there is a premium for postally used examples.

Many countries sell canceled-to-order stamps at a marked reduction of face value. Countries that sell or have sold canceled-to-order stamps at *full* face value include United Nations, Australia, Netherlands, France and Switzerland. It may be almost impossible to identify such stamps if the gum has been removed, because official government canceling devices are used. Postally used examples of these items on cover, however, are usually worth more than the canceled-to-order stamps with original gum.

Abbreviations

Scott uses a consistent set of abbreviations throughout this catalogue to conserve space, while still providing necessary information.

COLOR ABBREVIATIONS

amb. amber	crim. crimson	ol ..... olive
anil.. aniline	cr ..... cream	olvn . olivine
ap.... apple	dk .... dark	org... orange
aqua aquamarine	dl ..... dull	pck .. peacock
az .... azure	dp.... deep	pnksh pinkish
bis ... bister	db.... drab	Prus. Prussian
bl..... blue	emer emerald	pur... purple
bld... blood	gldn. golden	redsh reddish
blk... black	gryshgrayish	res ... reseda
bril... brilliant	grn... green	ros ... rosine
brn... brown	grnsh greenish	ryl.... royal
brnsh brownish	hel ... heliotrope	sal ... salmon
brnz. bronze	hn.... henna	saph sapphire
brt.... bright	ind... indigo	scar . scarlet
brnt . burnt	int .... intense	sep .. sepia
car... carmine	lav ... lavender	sien . sienna
cer ... cerise	lem.. lemon	sil..... silver
chlky chalky	lil ..... lilac	sl...... slate
chamchamois	lt ...... light	stl .... steel
chnt . chestnut	mag. magenta	turq.. turquoise
choc chocolate	man. manila	ultra ultramarine
chr... chrome	mar.. maroon	Ven.. Venetian
cit .... citron	mv ... mauve	ver .. vermilion
cl...... claret	multi multicolored	vio ... violet
cob .. cobalt	mlky milky	yel ... yellow
cop .. copper	myr.. myrtle	yelsh yellowish

When no color is given for an overprint or surcharge, black is the color used. Abbreviations for colors used for overprints and surcharges include: "(B)" or "(Blk)," black; "(Bl)," blue; "(R)," red; and "(G)," green.

Additional abbreviations in this catalogue are shown below:

Adm.	Administration
AFL	American Federation of Labor
Anniv.	Anniversary
APS	American Philatelic Society
Assoc.	Association
ASSR.	Autonomous Soviet Socialist Republic
b.	Born
BEP	Bureau of Engraving and Printing
Bicent.	Bicentennial
Bklt.	Booklet
Brit.	British
btwn.	Between
Bur.	Bureau
c. or ca.	Circa
Cat.	Catalogue
Cent.	Centennial, century, centenary
CIO	Congress of Industrial Organizations
Conf.	Conference
Cong.	Congress
Cpl.	Corporal
CTO	Canceled to order
d.	Died
Dbl.	Double
EDU	Earliest documented use
Engr.	Engraved
Exhib.	Exhibition
Expo.	Exposition
Fed.	Federation
GB	Great Britain
Gen.	General
GPO	General post office
Horiz.	Horizontal
Imperf.	Imperforate
Impt.	Imprint

Intl.	International
Invtd.	Inverted
L	Left
Lieut., lt.	Lieutenant
Litho.	Lithographed
LL	Lower left
LR	Lower right
mm	Millimeter
Ms.	Manuscript
Natl.	National
No.	Number
NY	New York
NYC	New York City
Ovpt.	Overprint
Ovptd.	Overprinted
P	Plate number
Perf.	Perforated, perforation
Phil.	Philatelic
Photo.	Photogravure
PO	Post office
Pr.	Pair
P.R.	Puerto Rico
Prec.	Precancel, precanceled
Pres.	President
PTT	Post, Telephone and Telegraph
R	Right
Rio	Rio de Janeiro
Sgt.	Sergeant
Soc.	Society
Souv.	Souvenir
SSR	Soviet Socialist Republic, see ASSR
St.	Saint, street
Surch.	Surcharge
Typo.	Typographed
UL	Upper left
Unwmkd.	Unwatermarked
UPU	Universal Postal Union
UR	Upper Right
US	United States
USPOD	United States Post Office Department
USSR	Union of Soviet Socialist Republics
Vert.	Vertical
VP	Vice president
Wmk.	Watermark
Wmkd.	Watermarked
WWI	World War I
WWII	World War II

Examination

Amos Media Co. will not comment upon the genuineness, grade or condition of stamps, because of the time and responsibility involved. Rather, there are several expertizing groups that undertake this work for both collectors and dealers. Neither will Amos Media Co. appraise or identify philatelic material. The company cannot take responsibility for unsolicited stamps or covers sent by individuals.

All letters, E-mails, etc. are read attentively, but they are not always answered due to time considerations.

How to order from your dealer

When ordering stamps from a dealer, it is not necessary to write the full description of a stamp as listed in this catalogue. All you need is the name of the country, the Scott catalogue number and whether the desired item is unused or used. For example, "Japan Scott 422 unused" is sufficient to identify the unused stamp of Japan listed as "422 A206 5y brown."

Basic Stamp Information

A stamp collector's knowledge of the combined elements that make a given stamp issue unique determines his or her ability to identify stamps. These elements include paper, watermark, method of separation, printing, design and gum. On the following pages each of these important areas is briefly described.

Paper

Paper is an organic material composed of a compacted weave of cellulose fibers and generally formed into sheets. Paper used to print stamps may be manufactured in sheets, or it may have been part of a large roll (called a web) before being cut to size. The fibers most often used to create paper on which stamps are printed include bark, wood, straw and certain grasses. In many cases, linen or cotton rags have been added for greater strength and durability. Grinding, bleaching, cooking and rinsing these raw fibers reduces them to a slushy pulp, referred to by paper makers as "stuff." Sizing and, sometimes, coloring matter is added to the pulp to make different types of finished paper.

After the stuff is prepared, it is poured onto sieve-like frames that allow the water to run off, while retaining the matted pulp. As fibers fall onto the screen and are held by gravity, they form a natural weave that will later hold the paper together. If the screen has metal bits that are formed into letters or images attached, it leaves slightly thinned areas on the paper. These are called watermarks.

When the stuff is almost dry, it is passed under pressure through smooth or engraved rollers - dandy rolls - or placed between cloth in a press to be flattened and dried.

Wove	Laid	Granite
Quadrille	Oblong Quadrille	Laid Batonne

Stamp paper falls broadly into two types: wove and laid. The nature of the surface of the frame onto which the pulp is first deposited causes the differences in appearance between the two. If the surface is smooth and even, the paper will be of fairly uniform texture throughout. This is known as *wove paper*. Early papermaking machines poured the pulp onto a continuously circulating web of felt, but modern machines feed the pulp onto a cloth-like screen made of closely interwoven fine wires. This paper, when held to a light, will show little dots or points very close together. The proper name for this is "wire wove," but the type is still considered wove. Any U.S. or British stamp printed after 1880 will serve as an example of wire wove paper.

Closely spaced parallel wires, with cross wires at wider intervals, make up the frames used for what is known as *laid paper*. A greater thickness of the pulp will settle between the wires. The paper, when held to a light, will show alternate light and dark lines. The spacing and the thickness of the lines may vary, but on any one sheet of paper they are all alike. See Russia Scott 31-38 for examples of laid paper.

Batonne, from the French word meaning "a staff," is a term used if the lines in the paper are spaced quite far apart, like the printed ruling on a writing tablet. Batonne paper may be either wove or laid. If laid, fine laid lines can be seen between the batons.

Quadrille is the term used when the lines in the paper form little squares. *Oblong quadrille* is the term used when rectangles, rather than squares, are formed. Grid patterns vary from distinct to extremely faint. See Mexico-Guadalajara Scott 35-37 for examples of oblong quadrille paper.

Paper also is classified as thick or thin, hard or soft, and by color. Such colors may include yellowish, greenish, bluish and reddish.

Brief explanations of other types of paper used for printing stamps, as well as examples, follow.

Colored — Colored paper is created by the addition of dye in the paper-making process. Such colors may include shades of yellow, green, blue and red. *Surface-colored papers*, most commonly used for British colonial issues in 1913-14, are created when coloring is added only to the surface during the finishing process. Stamps printed on surface-colored paper have white or uncolored backs, while true colored papers are colored through. See Jamaica Scott 71-73.

Pelure — Pelure paper is a very thin, hard and often brittle paper that is sometimes bluish or grayish in appearance. See Serbia Scott 169-170.

Native — This is a term applied to handmade papers used to produce some of the early stamps of the Indian states. Stamps printed on native paper may be expected to display various natural inclusions that are normal and do not negatively affect value. Japanese paper, originally made of mulberry fibers and rice flour, is part of this group. See Japan Scott 1-18.

Manila — This type of paper is often used to make stamped envelopes and wrappers. It is a coarse-textured stock, usually smooth on one side and rough on the other. A variety of colors of manila paper exist, but the most common range is yellowish-brown.

Silk — Introduced by the British in 1847 as a safeguard against counterfeiting, silk paper contains bits of colored silk thread scattered throughout. The density of these fibers varies greatly and can include as few as one fiber per stamp or hundreds. U.S. revenue Scott R152 is a good example of an easy-to-identify silk paper stamp.

Silk-thread paper has uninterrupted threads of colored silk arranged so that one or more threads run through the stamp or postal stationery. See Great Britain Scott 5-6 and Switzerland Scott 14-19.

Granite — Filled with minute cloth or colored paper fibers of various colors and lengths, granite paper should not be confused with either type of silk paper. Austria Scott 172-175 and a number of Swiss stamps are examples of granite paper.

Chalky — A chalk-like substance coats the surface of chalky paper to discourage the cleaning and reuse of canceled stamps, as well as to provide a smoother, more acceptable printing surface. Because the designs of stamps printed on chalky paper are imprinted on what is often a water-soluble coating, any attempt to remove a cancellation will destroy the stamp. *Do not soak these stamps in any fluid.* To remove a stamp printed on chalky paper from an envelope, wet the paper from underneath the stamp until the gum dissolves enough to release the stamp from the paper. See St. Kitts-Nevis Scott 89-90 for examples of stamps printed on this type of chalky paper.

India — Another name for this paper, originally introduced from China about 1750, is "China Paper." It is a thin, opaque paper often used for plate and die proofs by many countries.

Double — In philately, the term double paper has two distinct meanings. The first is a two-ply paper, usually a combination of a thick and a thin sheet, joined during manufacture. This type was used experimentally as a means to discourage the reuse of stamps.

The design is printed on the thin paper. Any attempt to remove a cancellation would destroy the design. U.S. Scott 158 and other Banknote-era stamps exist on this form of double paper.

The second type of double paper occurs on a rotary press, when the end of one paper roll, or web, is affixed to the next roll to save time feeding the paper through the press. Stamp designs are printed over the joined paper and, if overlooked by inspectors, may get into post office stocks.

Goldbeater's Skin — This type of paper was used for the 1866 issue of Prussia, and was a tough, translucent paper. The design was printed in reverse on the back of the stamp, and the gum applied over the printing. It is impossible to remove stamps printed on this type of paper from the paper to which they are affixed without destroying the design.

Ribbed — Ribbed paper has an uneven, corrugated surface made by passing the paper through ridged rollers. This type exists on some copies of U.S. Scott 156-165.

Various other substances, or substrates, have been used for stamp manufacture, including wood, aluminum, copper, silver and gold foil, plastic, and silk and cotton fabrics.

Watermarks

Watermarks are an integral part of some papers. They are formed in the process of paper manufacture. Watermarks consist of small designs, formed of wire or cut from metal and soldered to the surface of the mold or, sometimes, on the dandy roll. The designs may be in the form of crowns, stars, anchors, letters or other characters or symbols. These pieces of metal - known in the paper-making industry as "bits" - impress a design into the paper. The design sometimes may be seen by holding the stamp to the light. Some are more easily seen with a watermark detector. This important tool is a small black tray into which a stamp is placed face down and dampened with a fast-evaporating watermark detection fluid that brings up the watermark image in the form of dark lines against a lighter background. These dark lines are the thinner areas of the paper known as the watermark. Some watermarks are extremely difficult to locate, due to either a faint impression, watermark location or the color of the stamp. There also are electric watermark detectors that come with plastic filter disks of various colors. The disks neutralize the color of the stamp, permitting the watermark to be seen more easily.

Multiple watermarks of Crown Agents and Burma

Watermarks of Uruguay, Vatican City and Jamaica

WARNING: Some inks used in the photogravure process dissolve in watermark fluids (Please see the section on Soluble Printing Inks). Also, see "chalky paper."

Watermarks may be found normal, reversed, inverted, reversed and inverted, sideways or diagonal, as seen from the back of the stamp. The relationship of watermark to stamp design depends on the position of the printing plates or how paper is fed through the press. On machine-made paper, watermarks normally are read from right to left. The design is repeated closely throughout the sheet in a "multiple-watermark design." In a "sheet watermark," the design appears only once on the sheet, but extends over many stamps. Individual stamps may carry only a small fraction or none of the watermark.

"Marginal watermarks" occur in the margins of sheets or panes of stamps. They occur on the outside border of paper (ostensibly outside the area where stamps are to be printed). A large row of letters may spell the name of the country or the manufacturer of the paper, or a border of lines may appear. Careless press feeding may cause parts of these letters and/or lines to show on stamps of the outer row of a pane.

Soluble Printing Inks

WARNING: Most stamp colors are permanent; that is, they are not seriously affected by short-term exposure to light or water. Many colors, especially of modern inks, fade from excessive exposure to light. There are stamps printed with inks that dissolve easily in water or in fluids used to detect watermarks. Use of these inks was intentional to prevent the removal of cancellations. Water affects all aniline inks, those on so-called safety paper and some photogravure printings - all such inks are known as fugitive colors. *Removal from paper of such stamps requires care and alternatives to traditional soaking.*

Separation

"Separation" is the general term used to describe methods used to separate stamps. The three standard forms currently in use are perforating, rouletting and die-cutting. These methods are done during the stamp production process, after printing. Sometimes these methods are done on-press or sometimes as a separate step. The earliest issues, such as the 1840 Penny Black of Great Britain (Scott 1), did not have any means provided for separation. It was expected the stamps would be cut apart with scissors or folded and torn. These are examples of imperforate stamps. Many stamps were first issued in imperforate formats and were later issued with perforations. Therefore, care must be observed in buying single imperforate stamps to be certain they were issued imperforate and are not perforated copies that have been altered by having the perforations trimmed away. Stamps issued imperforate usually are valued as singles. However, imperforate varieties of normally perforated stamps should be collected in pairs or larger pieces as indisputable evidence of their imperforate character.

PERFORATION

The chief style of separation of stamps, and the one that is in almost universal use today, is perforating. By this process, paper between the stamps is cut away in a line of holes, usually round, leaving little bridges of paper between the stamps to hold them together. Some types of perforation, such as hyphen-hole perfs, can be confused with roulettes, but a close visual inspection reveals that paper has been removed. The little perforation bridges, which project from the stamp when it is torn from the pane, are called the teeth of the perforation.

As the size of the perforation is sometimes the only way to differentiate between two otherwise identical stamps, it is necessary to be able to accurately measure and describe them. This is done with a perforation gauge, usually a ruler-like device that has dots or graduated lines to show how many perforations may be counted in the space of two centimeters. Two centimeters is the space universally adopted in which to measure perforations.

Perforation gauge

perce en arc   perce en lignes

perce en points   oblique roulette

perce en scie   perce serpentin

To measure a stamp, run it along the gauge until the dots on it fit exactly into the perforations of the stamp. If you are using a graduated-line perforation gauge, simply slide the stamp along the surface until the lines on the gauge perfectly project from the center of the bridges or holes. The number to the side of the line of dots or lines that fit the stamp's perforation is the measurement. For example, an "11" means that 11 perforations fit between two centimeters. The description of the stamp therefore is "perf. 11." If the gauge of the perforations on the top and bottom of a stamp differs from that on the sides, the result is what is known as *compound perforations*. In measuring compound perforations, the gauge at top and bottom is always given first, then the sides. Thus, a stamp that measures 11 at top and bottom and 10½ at the sides is "perf. 11 x 10½." See U.S. Scott 632-642 for examples of compound perforations.

Stamps also are known with perforations different on three or all four sides. Descriptions of such items are clockwise, beginning with the top of the stamp.

A perforation with small holes and teeth close together is a "fine perforation." One with large holes and teeth far apart is a "coarse perforation." Holes that are jagged, rather than clean-cut, are "rough perforations." *Blind perforations* are the slight impressions left by the perforating pins if they fail to puncture the paper. Multiples of stamps showing blind perforations may command a slight premium over normally perforated stamps.

The term *syncopated perfs* describes intentional irregularities in the perforations. The earliest form was used by the Netherlands from 1925-33, where holes were omitted to create distinctive patterns. Beginning in 1992, Great Britain has used an oval perforation to help prevent counterfeiting. Several other countries have started using the oval perfs or other syncopated perf patterns.

A new type of perforation, still primarily used for postal stationery, is known as microperfs. Microperfs are tiny perforations (in some cases hundreds of holes per two centimeters) that allows items to be intentionally separated very easily, while not accidentally breaking apart as easily as standard perforations. These are not currently measured or differentiated by size, as are standard perforations.

ROULETTING

In rouletting, the stamp paper is cut partly or wholly through, with no paper removed. In perforating, some paper is removed. Rouletting derives its name from the French roulette, a spur-like wheel. As the wheel is rolled over the paper, each point makes a small cut. The number of cuts made in a two-centimeter space determines the gauge of the roulette, just as the number of perforations in two centimeters determines the gauge of the perforation.

The shape and arrangement of the teeth on the wheels varies. Various roulette types generally carry French names:

Perce en lignes - rouletted in lines. The paper receives short, straight cuts in lines. This is the most common type of rouletting. See Mexico Scott 500.

Perce en points - pin-rouletted or pin-perfed. This differs from a small perforation because no paper is removed, although round, equidistant holes are pricked through the paper. See Mexico Scott 242-256.

Perce en arc and *perce en scie* - pierced in an arc or saw-toothed designs, forming half circles or small triangles. See Hanover (German States) Scott 25-29.

Perce en serpentin - serpentine roulettes. The cuts form a serpentine or wavy line. See Brunswick (German States) Scott 13-18.

Once again, no paper is removed by these processes, leaving the stamps easily separated, but closely attached.

DIE-CUTTING

The third major form of stamp separation is die-cutting. This is a method where a die in the pattern of separation is created that later cuts the stamp paper in a stroke motion. Although some standard stamps bear die-cut perforations, this process is primarily used for self-adhesive postage stamps. Die-cutting can appear in straight lines, such as U.S. Scott 2522, shapes, such as U.S. Scott 1551, or imitating the appearance of perforations, such as New Zealand Scott 935A and 935B.

Printing Processes

ENGRAVING (Intaglio, Line-engraving, Etching)

Master die — The initial operation in the process of line engraving is making the master die. The die is a small, flat block of softened steel upon which the stamp design is recess engraved in reverse.

Master die

Photographic reduction of the original art is made to the appropriate size. It then serves as a tracing guide for the initial outline of the design. The engraver lightly traces the design on the steel with his graver, then slowly works the design until it is completed. At various points during the engraving process, the engraver hand-inks the die and makes an impression to check his progress. These are known as progressive die proofs. After completion of the engraving, the die is hardened to withstand the stress and pressures of later transfer operations.

Transfer roll

Transfer roll — Next is production of the transfer roll that, as the name implies, is the medium used to transfer the subject from the master die to the printing plate. A blank roll of soft steel, mounted on a mandrel, is placed under the bearers of the transfer press to allow it to roll freely on its axis. The hardened die is placed on the bed of the press and the face of the transfer roll is applied to the die, under pressure. The bed or the roll is then rocked back and forth under increasing pressure, until the soft steel of the roll is forced into every engraved line of the die. The resulting impression on the roll is known as a "relief" or a "relief transfer." The engraved image is now positive in appearance and stands out from the steel. After the required number of reliefs are "rocked in," the soft steel transfer roll is hardened.

Different flaws may occur during the relief process. A defective relief may occur during the rocking in process because of a minute piece of foreign material lodging on the die, or some other cause. Imperfections in the steel of the transfer roll may result in a breaking away of parts of the design. This is known as a relief break, which will show up on finished stamps as small, unprinted areas. If a damaged relief remains in use, it will transfer a repeating defect to the plate. Deliberate alterations of reliefs sometimes occur. "Altered reliefs" designate these changed conditions.

Plate — The final step in pre-printing production is the making of the printing plate. A flat piece of soft steel replaces the die on the bed of the transfer press. One of the reliefs on the transfer roll is positioned over this soft steel. Position, or layout, dots determine the correct position on the plate. The dots have been lightly marked on the plate in advance. After the correct position of the relief is determined,

the design is rocked in by following the same method used in making the transfer roll. The difference is that this time the image is being transferred from the transfer roll, rather than to it. Once the design is entered on the plate, it appears in reverse and is recessed. There are as many transfers entered on the plate as there are subjects printed on the sheet of stamps. It is during this process that double and shifted transfers occur, as well as re-entries. These are the result of improperly entered images that have not been properly burnished out prior to rocking in a new image.

Modern siderography processes, such as those used by the U.S. Bureau of Engraving and Printing, involve an automated form of rocking designs in on preformed cylindrical printing sleeves. The same process also allows for easier removal and re-entry of worn images right on the sleeve.

Transferring the design to the plate

Following the entering of the required transfers on the plate, the position dots, layout dots and lines, scratches and other markings generally are burnished out. Added at this time by the siderographer are any required *guide lines*, *plate numbers* or other *marginal markings*. The plate is then hand-inked and a proof impression is taken. This is known as a plate proof. If the impression is approved, the plate is machined for fitting onto the press, is hardened and sent to the plate vault ready for use.

On press, the plate is inked and the surface is automatically wiped clean, leaving ink only in the recessed lines. Paper is then forced under pressure into the engraved recessed lines, thereby receiving the ink. Thus, the ink lines on engraved stamps are slightly raised, and slight depressions (debossing) occur on the back of the stamp. Prior to the advent of modern high-speed presses and more advanced ink formulations, paper had to be dampened before receiving the ink. This sometimes led to uneven shrinkage by the time the stamps were perforated, resulting in improperly perforated stamps, or misperfs. Newer presses use drier paper, thus both *wet* and *dry printings* exist on some stamps.

Rotary Press — Until 1914, only flat plates were used to print engraved stamps. Rotary press printing was introduced in 1914, and slowly spread. Some countries still use flat-plate printing.

After approval of the plate proof, older *rotary press plates* require additional machining. They are curved to fit the press cylinder. "Gripper slots" are cut into the back of each plate to receive the "grippers," which hold the plate securely on the press. The plate is then hardened. Stamps printed from these bent rotary press plates are longer or wider than the same stamps printed from flat-plate presses. The stretching of the plate during the curving process is what causes this distortion.

Re-entry — To execute a re-entry on a flat plate, the transfer roll is re-applied to the plate, often at some time after its first use on the press. Worn-out designs can be resharpened by carefully burnishing out the original image and re-entering it from the transfer roll. If the original impression has not been sufficiently removed and the transfer roll is not precisely in line with the remaining impression, the resulting double transfer will make the re-entry obvious. If the registration is true, a re-entry may be difficult or impossible to distinguish. Sometimes a stamp printed from a successful re-entry is identified by having a much sharper and clearer impression than its neighbors. With the advent of rotary presses, post-press re-entries were not possible. After a plate was curved for the rotary press, it was impossible to make a re-entry. This is because the plate had already been bent once (with the design distorted).

However, with the introduction of the previously mentioned modern-style siderography machines, entries are made to the preformed cylindrical printing sleeve. Such sleeves are dechromed and softened. This allows individual images to be burnished out and re-entered on the curved sleeve. The sleeve is then rechromed, resulting in longer press life.

Double Transfer — This is a description of the condition of a transfer on a plate that shows evidence of a duplication of all, or a portion of the design. It usually is the result of the changing of the registration between the transfer roll and the plate during the rocking in of the original entry. Double transfers also occur when only a portion of the design has been rocked in and improper positioning is noted. If the worker elected not to burnish out the partial or completed design, a strong double transfer will occur for part or all of the design.

It sometimes is necessary to remove the original transfer from a plate and repeat the process a second time. If the finished re-worked image shows traces of the original impression, attributable to incomplete burnishing, the result is a partial double transfer.

With the modern automatic machines mentioned previously, double transfers are all but impossible to create. Those partially doubled images on stamps printed from such sleeves are more than likely re-entries, rather than true double transfers.

Re-engraved — Alterations to a stamp design are sometimes necessary after some stamps have been printed. In some cases, either the original die or the actual printing plate may have its "temper" drawn (softened), and the design will be re-cut. The resulting impressions from such a re-engraved die or plate may differ slightly from the original issue, and are known as "re-engraved." If the alteration was made to the master die, all future printings will be consistently different from the original. If alterations were made to the printing plate, each altered stamp on the plate will be slightly different from each other, allowing specialists to reconstruct a complete printing plate.

Dropped Transfers — If an impression from the transfer roll has not been properly placed, a dropped transfer may occur. The final stamp image will appear obviously out of line with its neighbors.

Short Transfer — Sometimes a transfer roll is not rocked its entire length when entering a transfer onto a plate. As a result, the finished transfer on the plate fails to show the complete design, and the finished stamp will have an incomplete design printed. This is known as a "short transfer." U.S. Scott No. 8 is a good example of a short transfer.

TYPOGRAPHY (Letterpress, Surface Printing, Flexography, Dry Offset, High Etch)

Although the word "Typography" is obsolete as a term describing a printing method, it was the accepted term throughout the first century of postage stamps. Therefore, appropriate Scott listings in this catalogue refer to typographed stamps. The current term for this form of printing, however, is "letterpress."

As it relates to the production of postage stamps, letterpress printing is the reverse of engraving. Rather than having recessed areas trap the ink and deposit it on paper, only the raised areas of the design are inked. This is comparable to the type of printing seen by inking and using an ordinary rubber stamp. Letterpress includes all printing where the design is above the surface area, whether it is wood, metal or, in some instances, hardened rubber or polymer plastic.

For most letterpress-printed stamps, the engraved master is made in much the same manner as for engraved stamps. In this instance, however, an additional step is needed. The design is transferred to another surface before being transferred to the transfer roll. In this way, the transfer roll has a recessed stamp design, rather than one done in relief. This makes the printing areas on the final plate raised, or relief areas.

For less-detailed stamps of the 19th century, the area on the die not used as a printing surface was cut away, leaving the surface area raised. The original die was then reproduced by stereotyping or electrotyping. The resulting electrotypes were assembled in the required number and format of the desired sheet of stamps. The plate used in printing the stamps was an electroplate of these assembled electrotypes.

Once the final letterpress plates are created, ink is applied to the raised surface and the pressure of the press transfers the ink impression to the paper. In contrast to engraving, the fine lines of letterpress are impressed on the surface of the stamp, leaving a debossed surface. When viewed from the back (as on a typewritten page), the corresponding line work on the stamp will be raised slightly (embossed) above the surface.

PHOTOGRAVURE (Gravure, Rotogravure, Heliogravure)

In this process, the basic principles of photography are applied to a chemically sensitized metal plate, rather than photographic paper. The design is transferred photographically to the plate through a halftone, or dot-matrix screen, breaking the reproduction into tiny dots. The plate is treated chemically and the dots form depressions, called cells, of varying depths and diameters, depending on the degrees of shade in the design. Then, like engraving, ink is applied to the plate and the surface is wiped clean. This leaves ink in the tiny cells that is lifted out and deposited on the paper when it is pressed against the plate.

Gravure is most often used for multicolored stamps, generally using the three primary colors (red, yellow and blue) and black. By varying the dot matrix pattern and density of these colors, virtually any color can be reproduced. A typical full-color gravure stamp will be created from four printing cylinders (one for each color). The original multicolored image will have been photographically separated into its component colors.

Modern gravure printing may use computer-generated dot-matrix screens, and modern plates may be of various types including metal-coated plastic. The catalogue designation of Photogravure (or "Photo") covers any of these older and more modern gravure methods of printing.

For examples of the first photogravure stamps printed (1914), see Bavaria Scott 94-114.

LITHOGRAPHY (Offset Lithography, Stone Lithography, Dilitho, Planography, Collotype)

The principle that oil and water do not mix is the basis for lithography. The stamp design is drawn by hand or transferred from engraving to the surface of a lithographic stone or metal plate in a greasy (oily) substance. This oily substance holds the ink, which will later be transferred to the paper. The stone (or plate) is wet with an acid fluid, causing it to repel the printing ink in all areas not covered by the greasy substance.

Transfer paper is used to transfer the design from the original stone or plate. A series of duplicate transfers are grouped and, in turn, transferred to the final printing plate.

Photolithography — The application of photographic processes to lithography. This process allows greater flexibility of design, related to use of halftone screens combined with line work. Unlike photogravure or engraving, this process can allow large, solid areas to be printed.

Offset — A refinement of the lithographic process. A rubber-covered blanket cylinder takes the impression from the inked lithographic plate. From the "blanket" the impression is *offset* or transferred to the paper. Greater flexibility and speed are the principal reasons offset printing has largely displaced lithography. The term "lithography" covers both processes, and results are almost identical.

EMBOSSED (Relief) Printing

Embossing, not considered one of the four main printing types, is a method in which the design first is sunk into the metal of the die. Printing is done against a yielding platen, such as leather or linoleum. The platen is forced into the depression of the die, thus forming the design on the paper in relief. This process is often used for metallic inks.

Embossing may be done without color (see Sardinia Scott 4-6); with color printed around the embossed area (see Great Britain Scott 5 and most U.S. envelopes); and with color in exact registration with the embossed subject (see Canada Scott 656-657).

HOLOGRAMS

For objects to appear as holograms on stamps, a model exactly the same size as it is to appear on the hologram must be created. Rather than using photographic film to capture the image, holography records an image on a photoresist material. In processing, chemicals eat away at certain exposed areas, leaving a pattern of constructive and destructive interference. When the photoresist is developed, the result is a pattern of uneven ridges that acts as a mold. This mold is then coated with metal, and the resulting form is used to press copies in much the same way phonograph records are produced.

A typical reflective hologram used for stamps consists of a reproduction of the uneven patterns on a plastic film that is applied to a reflective background, usually a silver or gold foil. Light is reflected off the background through the film, making the pattern present on the film visible. Because of the uneven pattern of the film, the viewer will perceive the objects in their proper three-dimensional relationships with appropriate brightness.

The first hologram on a stamp was produced by Austria in 1988 (Scott 1441).

FOIL APPLICATION

A modern technique of applying color to stamps involves the application of metallic foil to the stamp paper. A pattern of foil is applied to the stamp paper by use of a stamping die. The foil usually is flat, but it may be textured. Canada Scott 1735 has three different foil applications in pearl, bronze and gold. The gold foil was textured using a chemical-etch copper embossing die. The printing of this stamp also involved two-color offset lithography plus embossing.

THERMOGRAPHY

In the 1990s stamps began to be enhanced with thermographic printing. In this process, a powdered polymer is applied over a sheet that has just been printed. The powder adheres to ink that lacks drying or hardening agents and does not adhere to areas where the ink has these agents. The excess powder is removed and the sheet is briefly heated to melt the powder. The melted powder solidifies after cooling, producing a raised, shiny effect on the stamps. See Scott New Caledonia C239-C240.

COMBINATION PRINTINGS

Sometimes two or even three printing methods are combined in producing stamps. In these cases, such as Austria Scott 933 or Canada 1735 (described in the preceding paragraph), the multiple-printing technique can be determined by studying the individual characteristics of each printing type. A few stamps, such as Singapore Scott 684-684A, combine as many as three of the four major printing types (lithography, engraving and typography). When this is done it often indicates the incorporation of security devices against counterfeiting.

INK COLORS

Inks or colored papers used in stamp printing often are of mineral origin, although there are numerous examples of organic-based pigments. As a general rule, organic-based pigments are far more subject to varieties and change than those of mineral-based origin.

The appearance of any given color on a stamp may be affected by many aspects, including printing variations, light, color of paper, aging and chemical alterations.

Numerous printing variations may be observed. Heavier pressure or inking will cause a more intense color, while slight interruptions in the ink feed or lighter impressions will cause a lighter appearance. Stamps printed in the same color by water-based and solvent-based inks can differ significantly in appearance. This affects several stamps in the U.S. Prominent Americans series. Hand-mixed ink formulas (primarily from the 19th century) produced under different conditions (humidity and temperature) account for notable color variations in early printings of the same stamp (see U.S. Scott 248-250, 279B, for example). Different sources of pigment can also result in significant differences in color.

Light exposure and aging are closely related in the way they affect stamp color. Both eventually break down the ink and fade colors, so that a carefully kept stamp may differ significantly in color from an identical copy that has been exposed to light. If stamps are exposed to light either intentionally or accidentally, their colors can be faded or completely changed in some cases.

Papers of different quality and consistency used for the same stamp printing may affect color appearance. Most pelure papers, for example, show a richer color when compared with wove or laid papers. See Russia Scott 181a, for an example of this effect.

The very nature of the printing processes can cause a variety of differences in shades or hues of the same stamp. Some of these shades are scarcer than others, and are of particular interest to the advanced collector.

Luminescence

All forms of tagged stamps fall under the general category of luminescence. Within this broad category is fluorescence, dealing with forms of tagging visible under longwave ultraviolet light, and phosphorescence, which deals with tagging visible only under shortwave light. Phosphorescence leaves an afterglow and fluorescence does not. These treated stamps show up in a range of different colors when exposed to UV light. The differing wavelengths of the light activates the tagging material, making it glow in various colors that usually serve different mail processing purposes.

Intentional tagging is a post-World War II phenomenon, brought about by the increased literacy rate and rapidly growing mail volume. It was one of several answers to the problem of the need for more automated mail processes. Early tagged stamps served the purpose of triggering machines to separate different types of mail. A natural outgrowth was to also use the signal to trigger machines that faced all envelopes the same way and canceled them.

Tagged stamps come in many different forms. Some tagged stamps have luminescent shapes or images imprinted on them as a form of security device. Others have blocks (United States), stripes, frames (South Africa and Canada), overall coatings (United States), bars (Great Britain and Canada) and many other types. Some types of tagging are even mixed in with the pigmented printing ink (Australia Scott 366, Netherlands Scott 478 and U.S. Scott 1359 and 2443).

The means of applying taggant to stamps differs as much as the intended purposes for the stamps. The most common form of tagging is a coating applied to the surface of the printed stamp. Since the taggant ink is frequently invisible except under UV light, it does not interfere with the appearance of the stamp. Another common application is the use of phosphored papers. In this case the paper itself either has a coating of taggant applied before the stamp is printed, has taggant applied during the papermaking process (incorporating it into the fibers), or has the taggant mixed into the coating of the paper. The latter method, among others, is currently in use in the United States.

Many countries now use tagging in various forms to either expedite mail handling or to serve as a printing security device against counterfeiting. Following the introduction of tagged stamps for public use in 1959 by Great Britain, other countries have steadily joined the parade. Among those are Germany (1961); Canada and Denmark (1962); United States, Australia, France and Switzerland (1963); Belgium and Japan (1966); Sweden and Norway (1967); Italy (1968); and Russia (1969). Since then, many other countries have begun using forms of tagging, including Brazil, China, Czechoslovakia, Hong Kong, Guatemala, Indonesia, Israel, Lithuania, Luxembourg, Netherlands, Penrhyn Islands, Portugal, St. Vincent, Singapore, South Africa, Spain and Sweden to name a few.

In some cases, including United States, Canada, Great Britain and Switzerland, stamps were released both with and without tagging. Many of these were released during each country's experimental period. Tagged and untagged versions are listed for the aforementioned countries and are noted in some other countries' listings. For at least a few stamps, the experimentally tagged version is worth far more than its untagged counterpart, such as the 1963 experimental tagged version of France Scott 1024.

In some cases, luminescent varieties of stamps were inadvertently created. Several Russian stamps, for example, sport highly fluorescent ink that was not intended as a form of tagging. Older stamps, such as early U.S. postage dues, can be positively identified by the use of UV light, since the organic ink used has become slightly fluorescent over time. Other stamps, such as Austria Scott 70a-82a (varnish bars) and Obock Scott 46-64 (printed quadrille lines), have become fluorescent over time.

Various fluorescent substances have been added to paper to make it appear brighter. These optical brighteners, as they are known, greatly affect the appearance of the stamp under UV light. The brightest of these is known as Hi-Brite paper. These paper varieties are beyond the scope of the Scott Catalogue.

Shortwave UV light also is used extensively in expertizing, since each form of paper has its own fluorescent characteristics that are impossible to perfectly match. It is therefore a simple matter to detect filled thins, added perforation teeth and other alterations that involve the addition of paper. UV light also is used to examine stamps that have had cancels chemically removed and for other purposes as well.

Gum

The Illustrated Gum Chart in the first part of this introduction shows and defines various types of gum condition. Because gum condition has an important impact on the value of unused stamps, we recommend studying this chart and the accompanying text carefully.

The gum on the back of a stamp may be shiny, dull, smooth, rough, dark, white, colored or tinted. Most stamp gumming adhesives use gum arabic or dextrine as a base. Certain polymers such as polyvinyl alcohol (PVA) have been used extensively since World War II.

The *Scott Standard Postage Stamp Catalogue* does not list items by types of gum. The *Scott Specialized Catalogue of United States Stamps and Covers* does differentiate among some types of gum for certain issues.

Reprints of stamps may have gum differing from the original issues. In addition, some countries have used different gum formulas for different seasons. These adhesives have different properties that may become more apparent over time.

Many stamps have been issued without gum, and the catalogue will note this fact. See, for example, United States Scott 40-47. Sometimes, gum may have been removed to preserve the stamp. Germany Scott B68, for example, has a highly acidic gum that eventually destroys the stamps. This item is valued in the catalogue with gum removed.

Reprints and Reissues

These are impressions of stamps (usually obsolete) made from the original plates or stones. If they are valid for postage and reproduce obsolete issues (such as U.S. Scott 102-111), the stamps are *reissues*. If they are from current issues, they are designated as *second, third,* etc., *printing*. If designated for a particular purpose, they are called *special printings*.

When special printings are not valid for postage, but are made from original dies and plates by authorized persons, they are *official reprints*. *Private reprints* are made from the original plates and dies by private hands. An example of a private reprint is that of the 1871-1932 reprints made from the original die of the 1845 New Haven, Conn., postmaster's provisional. *Official reproductions* or imitations are made from new dies and plates by government authorization. Scott will list those reissues that are valid for postage if they differ significantly from the original printing.

The U.S. government made special printings of its first postage stamps in 1875. Produced were official imitations of the first two stamps (listed as Scott 3-4), reprints of the demonetized pre-1861 issues (Scott 40-47) and reissues of the 1861 stamps, the 1869 stamps and the then-current 1875 denominations. Even though the official imitations and the reprints were not valid for postage, Scott lists all of these U.S. special printings.

Most reprints or reissues differ slightly from the original stamp in some characteristic, such as gum, paper, perforation, color or watermark. Sometimes the details are followed so meticulously that only a student of that specific stamp is able to distinguish the reprint or reissue from the original.

Remainders and Canceled to Order

Some countries sell their stock of old stamps when a new issue replaces them. To avoid postal use, the *remainders* usually are canceled with a punch hole, a heavy line or bar, or a more-or-less regular-looking cancellation. The most famous merchant of remainders was Nicholas F. Seebeck. In the 1880s and 1890s, he arranged printing contracts between the Hamilton Bank Note Co., of which he was a director, and several Central and South American countries. The contracts provided that the plates and all remainders of the yearly issues became the property of Hamilton. Seebeck saw to it that ample stock remained. The "Seebecks," both remainders and reprints, were standard packet fillers for decades.

Some countries also issue stamps *canceled-to-order (CTO)*, either in sheets with original gum or stuck onto pieces of paper or envelopes and canceled. Such CTO items generally are worth less than postally used stamps. In cases where the CTO material is far more prevalent in the marketplace than postally used examples, the catalogue value relates to the CTO examples, with postally used examples noted as premium items. Most CTOs can be detected by the presence of gum. However, as the CTO practice goes back at least to 1885, the gum inevitably has been soaked off some stamps so they could pass as postally used. The normally applied postmarks usually differ slightly from standard postmarks, and specialists are able to tell the difference. When applied individually to envelopes by philatelically minded persons, CTO material is known as *favor canceled* and generally sells at large discounts.

Cinderellas and Facsimiles

Cinderella is a catch-all term used by stamp collectors to describe phantoms, fantasies, bogus items, municipal issues, exhibition seals, local revenues, transportation stamps, labels, poster stamps and many other types of items. Some cinderella collectors include in their collections local postage issues, telegraph stamps, essays and proofs, forgeries and counterfeits.

A *fantasy* is an adhesive created for a nonexistent stamp-issuing authority. Fantasy items range from imaginary countries (Occusi-Ambeno, Kingdom of Sedang, Principality of Trinidad or Torres Straits), to non-existent locals (Winans City Post), or nonexistent transportation lines (McRobish & Co.'s Acapulco-San Francisco Line).

On the other hand, if the entity exists and could have issued stamps (but did not) or was known to have issued other stamps, the items are considered *bogus* stamps. These would include the Mormon postage stamps of Utah, S. Allan Taylor's Guatemala and Paraguay inventions, the propaganda issues for the South Moluccas and the adhesives of the Page & Keyes local post of Boston.

Phantoms is another term for both fantasy and bogus issues.

Facsimiles are copies or imitations made to represent original stamps, but which do not pretend to be originals. A catalogue illustration is such a facsimile. Illustrations from the Moens catalogue of the last century were occasionally colored and passed off as stamps. Since the beginning of stamp collecting, facsimiles have been made for collectors as space fillers or for reference. They often carry the word "facsimile," "falsch" (German), "sanko" or "mozo" (Japanese), or "faux" (French) overprinted on the face or stamped on the back. Unfortunately, over the years a number of these items have had fake cancels applied over the facsimile notation and have been passed off as genuine.

Forgeries and Counterfeits

Forgeries and counterfeits have been with philately virtually from the beginning of stamp production. Over time, the terminology for the two has been used interchangeably. Although both forgeries and counterfeits are reproductions of stamps, the purposes behind their creation differ considerably.

Among specialists there is an increasing movement to more specifically define such items. Although there is no universally accepted terminology, we feel the following definitions most closely mirror the items and their purposes as they are currently defined.

Forgeries (also often referred to as *Counterfeits*) are reproductions of genuine stamps that have been created to defraud collectors. Such spurious items first appeared on the market around 1860, and most old-time collections contain one or more. Many are crude and easily spotted, but some can deceive experts.

An important supplier of these early philatelic forgeries was the Hamburg printer Gebruder Spiro. Many others with reputations in this craft included S. Allan Taylor, George Hussey, James Chute, George Forune, Benjamin & Sarpy, Julius Goldner, E. Oneglia and L.H. Mercier. Among the noted 20th-century forgers were Francois Fournier, Jean Sperati and the prolific Raoul DeThuin.

Forgeries may be complete replications, or they may be genuine stamps altered to resemble a scarcer (and more valuable) type. Most forgeries, particularly those of rare stamps, are worth only a small fraction of the value of a genuine example, but a few types, created by some of the most notable forgers, such as Sperati, can be worth as much as or more than the genuine. Fraudulently produced copies are known of most classic rarities and many medium-priced stamps.

In addition to rare stamps, large numbers of common 19th- and early 20th-century stamps were forged to supply stamps to the early packet trade. Many can still be easily found. Few new philatelic forgeries have appeared in recent decades. Successful imitation of well-engraved work is virtually impossible. It has proven far easier to produce a fake by altering a genuine stamp than to duplicate a stamp completely.

Counterfeit (also often referred to as *Postal Counterfeit* or *Postal Forgery*) is the term generally applied to reproductions of stamps that have been created to defraud the government of revenue. Such items usually are created at the time a stamp is current and, in some cases, are hard to detect. Because most counterfeits are seized when the perpetrator is captured, postal counterfeits, particularly used on cover, are usually worth much more than a genuine example to specialists. The first postal counterfeit was of Spain's 4-cuarto carmine of 1854 (the real one is Scott 25). Apparently, the counterfeiters were not satisfied with their first version, which is now very scarce, and they soon created an engraved counterfeit, which is common. Postal counterfeits quickly followed in Austria, Naples, Sardinia and the Roman States. They have since been created in many other countries as well, including the United States.

An infamous counterfeit to defraud the government is the 1-shilling Great Britain "Stock Exchange" forgery of 1872, used on telegraph forms at the exchange that year. The stamp escaped detection until a stamp dealer noticed it in 1898.

Fakes

Fakes are genuine stamps altered in some way to make them more desirable. One student of this part of stamp collecting has estimated that by the 1950s more than 30,000 varieties of fakes were known. That number has grown greatly since then. The widespread existence of fakes makes it important for stamp collectors to study their philatelic holdings and use relevant literature. Likewise, collectors should buy from reputable dealers who guarantee their stamps and make full and prompt refunds should a purchased item be declared faked or altered by some mutually agreed-upon authority. Because fakes always have some genuine characteristics, it is not always possible to obtain unanimous agreement among experts regarding specific items. These students may change their opinions as philatelic knowledge increases. More than 80 percent of all fakes on the philatelic market today are regummed, reperforated (or perforated for the first time), or bear forged overprints, surcharges or cancellations.

Stamps can be chemically treated to alter or eliminate colors. For example, a pale rose stamp can be re-colored to resemble a blue shade of high market value. In other cases, treated stamps can be made to resemble missing color varieties. Designs may be changed by painting, or a stroke or a dot added or bleached out to turn an ordinary variety into a seemingly scarcer stamp. Part of a stamp can be bleached and reprinted in a different version, achieving an inverted center or frame. Margins can be added or repairs done so deceptively that the stamps move from the "repaired" into the "fake" category.

Fakers have not left the backs of the stamps untouched either. They may create false watermarks, add fake grills or press out genuine grills. A thin India paper proof may be glued onto a thicker backing to create the appearance an issued stamp, or a proof printed on cardboard may be shaved down and perforated to resemble a stamp. Silk threads are impressed into paper and stamps have been split so that a rare paper variety is added to an otherwise inexpensive stamp. The most common treatment to the back of a stamp, however, is regumming.

Some in the business of faking stamps have openly advertised fool-proof application of "original gum" to stamps that lack it, although most publications now ban such ads from their pages. It is believed that very few early stamps have survived without being hinged. The large number of never-hinged examples of such earlier material offered for sale thus suggests the widespread extent of regumming activity. Regumming also may be used to hide repairs or thin spots. Dipping the stamp into watermark fluid, or examining it under longwave ultraviolet light often will reveal these flaws.

Fakers also tamper with separations. Ingenious ways to add margins are known. Perforated wide-margin stamps may be falsely represented as imperforate when trimmed. Reperforating is commonly done to create scarce coil or perforation varieties, and to eliminate the naturally occurring straight-edge stamps found in sheet margin positions of many earlier issues. Custom has made straight-edged stamps less desirable. Fakers have obliged by perforating straight-edged stamps so that many are now uncommon, if not rare.

Another fertile field for the faker is that of overprints, surcharges and cancellations. The forging of rare surcharges or overprints began in the 1880s or 1890s. These forgeries are sometimes difficult to detect, but experts have identified almost all. Occasionally, overprints or cancellations are removed to create non-overprinted stamps or seemingly unused items. This is most commonly done by removing a manuscript cancel to make a stamp resemble an unused example. "SPECIMEN" overprints may be removed by scraping and repainting to create non-overprinted varieties. Fakers use inexpensive revenues or pen-canceled stamps to generate unused stamps for further faking by adding other markings. The quartz lamp or UV lamp and a high-powered magnifying glass help to easily detect removed cancellations.

The bigger problem, however, is the addition of overprints, surcharges or cancellations - many with such precision that they are very difficult to ascertain. Plating of the stamps or the overprint can be an important method of detection.

Fake postmarks may range from many spurious fancy cancellations to a host of markings applied to transatlantic covers, to adding normally appearing postmarks to definitives of some countries with stamps that are valued far higher used than unused. With the increased popularity of cover collecting, and the widespread interest in postal history, a fertile new field for fakers has come about. Some have tried to create entire covers. Others specialize in adding stamps, tied by fake cancellations, to genuine stampless covers, or replacing less expensive or damaged stamps with more valuable ones. Detailed study of postal rates in effect at the time a cover in question was mailed, including the analysis of each handstamp used during the period, ink analysis and similar techniques, usually will unmask the fraud.

Restoration and Repairs

Scott bases its catalogue values on stamps that are free of defects and otherwise meet the standards set forth earlier in this introduction. Most stamp collectors desire to have the finest copy of an item possible. Even within given grading categories there are variances. This leads to a controversial practice that is not defined in any universal manner: stamp *restoration*.

There are broad differences of opinion about what is permissible when it comes to restoration. Carefully applying a soft eraser to a stamp or cover to remove light soiling is one form of restoration, as is washing a stamp in mild soap and water to clean it. These are fairly accepted forms of restoration. More severe forms of restoration include pressing out creases or removing stains caused by tape. To what degree each of these is acceptable is dependent upon the individual situation. Further along the spectrum is the freshening of a stamp's color by removing oxide build-up or the effects of wax paper left next to stamps shipped to the tropics.

At some point in this spectrum the concept of *repair* replaces that of restoration. Repairs include filling thin spots, mending tears by reweaving or adding a missing perforation tooth. Regumming stamps may have been acceptable as a restoration or repair technique many decades ago, but today it is considered a form of fakery.

Restored stamps may or may not sell at a discount, and it is possible that the value of individual restored items may be enhanced over that of their pre-restoration state. Specific situations dictate the resultant value of such an item. Repaired stamps sell at substantial discounts from the value of sound stamps.

Terminology

Booklets — Many countries have issued stamps in small booklets for the convenience of users. This idea continues to become increasingly popular in many countries. Booklets have been issued in many sizes and forms, often with advertising on the covers, the panes of stamps or on the interleaving.

The panes used in booklets may be printed from special plates or made from regular sheets. All panes from booklets issued by the United States and many from those of other countries contain stamps that are straight edged on the sides, but perforated between. Others are distinguished by orientation of watermark or other identifying features. Any stamp-like unit in the pane, either printed or blank, that is not a postage stamp, is considered to be a *label* in the catalogue listings.

Scott lists and values booklet panes. Modern complete booklets also are listed and valued. Individual booklet panes are listed only when they are not fashioned from existing sheet stamps and, therefore, are identifiable from their sheet stamp counterparts.

Panes usually do not have a used value assigned to them because there is little market activity for used booklet panes, even though many exist used and there is some demand for them.

Cancellations — The marks or obliterations put on stamps by postal authorities to show that they have performed service and to prevent their reuse are known as cancellations. If the marking is made with a pen, it is considered a "pen cancel." When the location of the post office appears in the marking, it is a "town cancellation." A "postmark" is technically any postal marking, but in practice the term generally is applied to a town cancellation with a date. When calling attention to a cause or celebration, the marking is known as a "slogan cancellation." Many other types and styles of cancellations exist, such as duplex, numerals, targets, fancy and others. See also "precancels," below.

Coil Stamps — These are stamps that are issued in rolls for use in dispensers, affixing and vending machines. Those coils of the United States, Canada, Sweden and some other countries are perforated horizontally or vertically only, with the outer edges imperforate. Coil stamps of some countries, such as Great Britain and Germany, are perforated on all four sides and may in some cases be distinguished from their sheet stamp counterparts by watermarks, counting numbers on the reverse or other means.

Covers — Entire envelopes, with or without adhesive postage stamps, that have passed through the mail and bear postal or other markings of philatelic interest are known as covers. Before the introduction of envelopes in about 1840, people folded letters and wrote the address on the outside. Some people covered their letters with an extra sheet of paper on the outside for the address, producing the term "cover." Used airletter sheets, stamped envelopes and other items of postal stationery also are considered covers.

Errors — Stamps that have some major, consistent, unintentional deviation from the normal are considered errors. Errors include, but are not limited to, missing or wrong colors, wrong paper, wrong watermarks, inverted centers or frames on multicolor printing, inverted or missing surcharges or overprints, double impressions, missing perforations, unintentionally omitted tagging and others. Factually wrong or misspelled information, if it appears on all examples of a stamp, are not considered errors in the true sense of the word. They are errors of design. Inconsistent or randomly appearing items, such as misperfs or color shifts, are classified as freaks.

Color-Omitted Errors — This term refers to stamps where a missing color is caused by the complete failure of the printing plate to deliver ink to the stamp paper or any other paper. Generally, this is caused by the printing plate not being engaged on the press or the ink station running dry of ink during printing.

Color-Missing Errors — This term refers to stamps where a color or colors were printed somewhere but do not appear on the finished stamp. There are four different classes of color-missing errors, and the catalog indicates with a two-letter code appended to each such listing what caused the color to be missing. These codes are used only for the United States' color-missing error listings.

FO = A *foldover* of the stamp sheet during printing may block ink from appearing on a stamp. Instead, the color will appear on the back of the foldover (where it might fall on the back of the selvage or perhaps on the back of the stamp or another stamp). FO also will be used in the case of foldunders, where the paper may fold underneath the other stamp paper and the color will print on the platen.

EP = A piece of *extraneous paper* falling across the plate or stamp paper will receive the printed ink. When the extraneous paper is removed, an unprinted portion of stamp paper remains and shows partially or totally missing colors.

CM = A misregistration of the printing plates during printing will result in a *color misregistration*, and such a misregistraion may result in a color not appearing on the finished stamp.

PS = A *perforation shift* after printing may remove a color from the finished stamp. Normally, this will occur on a row of stamps at the edge of the stamp pane.

Measurements – When measurements are given in the Scott catalogues for stamp size, grill size or any other reason, the first measurement given is always for the top and bottom dimension, while the second measurement will be for the sides (just as perforation gauges are measured). Thus, a stamp size of 15mm x 21mm will indicate a vertically oriented stamp 15mm wide at top and bottom, and 21mm tall at the sides. The same principle holds for measuring or counting items such as U.S. grills. A grill count of 22x18 points (B grill) indicates that there are 22 grill points across by 18 grill points down.

Overprints and Surcharges — Overprinting involves applying wording or design elements over an already existing stamp. Overprints can be used to alter the place of use (such as "Canal Zone" on U.S. stamps), to adapt them for a special purpose ("Porto" on Denmark's 1913-20 regular issues for use as postage due stamps, Scott J1-J7) or to commemorate a special occasion (United States Scott 647-648).

A *surcharge* is a form of overprint that changes or restates the face value of a stamp or piece of postal stationery.

Surcharges and overprints may be handstamped, typeset or, occasionally, lithographed or engraved. A few hand-written overprints and surcharges are known.

Personalized Stamps — In 1999, Australia issued stamps with se-tenant labels that could be personalized with pictures of the customer's choice. Other countries quickly followed suit, with some offering to print the selected picture on the stamp itself within a frame that was used exclusively for personalized issues. As the picture used on these stamps or labels vary, listings for such stamps are for any picture within the common frame (or any picture on a se-tenant label), be it a "generic" image or one produced especially for a customer, almost invariably at a premium price.

Precancels — Stamps that are canceled before they are placed in the mail are known as precancels. Precanceling usually is done to expedite the handling of large mailings and generally allow the affected mail pieces to skip certain phases of mail handling.

In the United States, precancellations generally identified the point of origin; that is, the city and state. This information appeared across the face of the stamp, usually centered between parallel lines. More recently, bureau precancels retained the parallel lines, but the city and state designations were dropped. Recent coils have a service inscription that is present on the original printing plate. These show the mail service paid for by the stamp. Since these stamps are not intended to receive further cancellations when used as intended, they are considered precancels. Such items often do not have parallel lines as part of the precancellation.

In France, the abbreviation *Affranchts* in a semicircle together with the word *Postes* is the general form of precancel in use. Belgian precancellations usually appear in a box in which the name of the city appears. Netherlands precancels have the name of the city enclosed between concentric circles, sometimes called a "lifesaver." Precancellations of other countries usually follow these patterns, but may be any arrangement of bars, boxes and city names.

Precancels are listed in the Scott catalogues only if the precancel changes the denomination (Belgium Scott 477-478); if the precanceled stamp is different from the non-precanceled version (such as untagged U.S. precancels); or if the stamp exists only precanceled (France Scott 1096-1099, U.S. Scott 2265).

Proofs and Essays — Proofs are impressions taken from an approved die, plate or stone in which the design and color are the same as the stamp issued to the public. Trial color proofs are impressions taken from approved dies, plates or stones in colors that vary from the final version. An essay is the impression of a design that differs in some way from the issued stamp. "Progressive die proofs" generally are considered to be essays.

Provisionals — These are stamps that are issued on short notice and intended for temporary use pending the arrival of regular issues. They usually are issued to meet such contingencies as changes in government or currency, shortage of necessary postage values or military occupation.

During the 1840s, postmasters in certain American cities issued stamps that were valid only at specific post offices. In 1861, postmasters of the Confederate States also issued stamps with limited validity. Both of these examples are known as "postmaster's provisionals."

Se-tenant — This term refers to an unsevered pair, strip or block of stamps that differ in design, denomination or overprint.

Unless the se-tenant item has a continuous design (see U.S. Scott 1451a, 1694a) the stamps do not have to be in the same order as shown in the catalogue (see U.S. Scott 2158a).

Specimens — The Universal Postal Union required member nations to send samples of all stamps they released into service to the International Bureau in Switzerland. Member nations of the UPU received these specimens as samples of what stamps were valid for postage. Many are overprinted, handstamped or initial-perforated "Specimen," "Canceled" or "Muestra." Some are marked with bars across the denominations (China-Taiwan), punched holes (Czechoslovakia) or back inscriptions (Mongolia).

Stamps distributed to government officials or for publicity purposes, and stamps submitted by private security printers for official approval, also may receive such defacements.

The previously described defacement markings prevent postal use, and all such items generally are known as "specimens."

Tete Beche — This term describes a pair of stamps in which one is upside down in relation to the other. Some of these are the result of intentional sheet arrangements, such as Morocco Scott B10-B11. Others occurred when one or more electrotypes accidentally were placed upside down on the plate, such as Colombia Scott 57a. Separation of the tete-beche stamps, of course, destroys the tete beche variety.

Currency Conversion

Country	Dollar	Pound	S Franc	Yen	HK $	Euro	Cdn $	Aus $
Australia	1.3867	1.7008	1.3463	0.0117	0.1788	1.4404	1.0315	—
Canada	1.3443	1.6488	1.3051	0.0114	0.1733	1.3964	—	0.9694
European Union	0.9627	1.1808	0.9347	0.0081	0.1241	—	0.7161	0.6942
Hong Kong	7.7561	9.5130	7.5302	0.0656	—	8.0566	5.7696	5.5932
Japan	118.26	145.05	114.82	—	15.247	122.84	87.971	85.282
Switzerland	1.0300	1.2633	—	0.0087	0.1328	1.0699	0.7662	0.7428
United Kingdom	0.8153	—	0.7916	0.0069	0.1051	0.8469	0.6065	0.5880
United States	—	1.2265	0.9709	0.0085	0.1289	1.0387	0.7439	0.7211

Country	Currency	U.S. $ Equiv.
Cambodia	riel	.0003
Cameroun	Community of French Africa (CFA) franc	.0016
Canada	dollar	.7439
Cape Verde	escudo	.0094
Caribbean Netherlands	US dollar	1.0000
Cayman Islands	dollar	1.2106
Central African Republic	CFA franc	.0016
Chad	CFA franc	.0016
Chile	peso	.0015
China (Taiwan)	dollar	.0309
China (People's Republic)	yuan	.1437
Christmas Island	Australian dollar	.7211
Cocos Island	Australian dollar	.7211
Colombia	peso	.0003
Comoro Islands	franc	.0021
Congo Republic	CFA franc	.0016
Cook Islands	New Zealand dollar	.6909
Costa Rica	colon	.0018
Croatia	kuna	.1374
Curacao	guilder	.5587

*Source: **xe.com** Jan. 3, 2017. Figures reflect values as of Jan. 3, 2017.*

COMMON DESIGN TYPES

Pictured in this section are issues where one illustration has been used for a number of countries in the Catalogue. Not included in this section are overprinted stamps or those issues which are illustrated in each country. Because the location of Never Hinged breakpoints varies from country to country, some of the values in the listings below will be for unused stamps that were previously hinged.

EUROPA
Europa, 1956

The design symbolizing the cooperation among the six countries comprising the Coal and Steel Community is illustrated in each country.

Belgium	496-497
France	805-806
Germany	748-749
Italy	715-716
Luxembourg	318-320
Netherlands	368-369

Nos. 496-497 (2)	9.00	.70
Nos. 805-806 (2)	5.25	1.00
Nos. 748-749 (2)	7.30	1.20
Nos. 715-716 (2)	11.50	1.25
Nos. 318-320 (3)	73.00	50.00
Nos. 368-369 (2)	72.50	1.75
Set total (13) Stamps	178.55	55.90

Europa, 1958

"E" and Dove — CD1

European Postal Union at the service of European integration.

1958, Sept. 13

Belgium	527-528
France	889-890
Germany	790-791
Italy	750-751
Luxembourg	341-343
Netherlands	375-376
Saar	317-318

Nos. 527-528 (2)	4.25	.60
Nos. 889-890 (2)	1.65	.55
Nos. 790-791 (2)	3.65	.65
Nos. 750-751 (2)	1.85	.60
Nos. 341-343 (3)	2.35	1.15
Nos. 375-376 (2)	2.50	.70
Nos. 317-318 (2)	1.05	2.30
Set total (15) Stamps	17.30	6.60

Europa, 1959

6-Link Enless Chain — CD2

1959, Sept. 19

Belgium	536-537
France	929-930
Germany	805-806
Italy	791-792
Luxembourg	354-355
Netherlands	379-380

Nos. 536-537 (2)	1.55	.60
Nos. 929-930 (2)	1.40	.80
Nos. 805-806 (2)	1.55	.65
Nos. 791-792 (2)	.80	.50
Nos. 354-355 (2)	3.50	1.40
Nos. 379-380 (2)	9.90	1.25
Set total (12) Stamps	18.70	5.20

Europa, 1960

19-Spoke Wheel CD3

First anniverary of the establishment of C.E.P.T. (Conference Europeenne des Administrations des Postes et des Telecommunications.) The spokes symbolize the 19 founding members of the Conference.

1960, Sept.

Belgium	553-554
Denmark	379
Finland	376-377
France	970-971
Germany	818-820
Great Britain	377-378
Greece	688
Iceland	327-328
Ireland	175-176
Italy	809-810
Luxembourg	374-375
Netherlands	385-386
Norway	387
Portugal	866-867
Spain	941-942
Sweden	562-563
Switzerland	400-401
Turkey	1493-1494

Nos. 553-554 (2)	1.25	.55
No. 379 (1)	.55	.50
Nos. 376-377 (2)	1.70	1.80
Nos. 970-971 (2)	.50	.50
Nos. 818-820 (3)	2.25	1.50
Nos. 377-378 (2)	9.00	5.00
No. 688 (1)	5.00	2.00
Nos. 327-328 (2)	1.30	1.85
Nos. 175-176 (2)	75.00	14.00
Nos. 809-810 (2)	.70	.50
Nos. 374-375 (2)	1.00	.80
Nos. 385-386 (2)	3.65	1.50
No. 387 (1)	1.25	1.25
Nos. 866-867 (2)	2.25	1.25
Nos. 941-942 (2)	1.50	.75
Nos. 562-563 (2)	1.05	.55
Nos. 400-401 (2)	1.25	.65
Nos. 1493-1494 (2)	2.10	1.35
Set total (34) Stamps	111.30	36.30

Europa, 1961

19 Doves Flying as One — CD4

The 19 doves represent the 19 members of the Conference of European Postal and Telecommunications Administrations C.E.P.T.

1961-62

Belgium	572-573
Cyprus	201-203
France	1005-1006
Germany	844-845
Great Britain	382-384
Greece	718-719
Iceland	340-341
Italy	845-846
Luxembourg	382-383
Netherlands	387-388
Spain	1010-1011
Switzerland	410-411
Turkey	1518-1520

Nos. 572-573 (2)	.75	.50
Nos. 201-203 (3)	2.10	1.20
Nos. 1005-1006 (2)	.50	.50
Nos. 844-845 (2)	.60	.75
Nos. 382-384 (3)	.75	.90
Nos. 718-719 (2)	.80	.50
Nos. 340-341 (2)	1.10	1.60
Nos. 845-846 (2)	.55	.50
Nos. 382-383 (2)	.70	.70
Nos. 387-388 (2)	.55	.50
Nos. 1010-1011 (2)	.70	.55
Nos. 410-411 (2)	1.25	.60
Nos. 1518-1520 (3)	2.45	1.30
Set total (29) Stamps	12.80	10.10

Europa, 1962

Young Tree with 19 Leaves CD5

The 19 leaves represent the 19 original members of C.E.P.T.

1962-63

Belgium	582-583
Cyprus	219-221
France	1045-1046
Germany	852-853
Greece	739-740
Iceland	348-349
Ireland	184-185
Italy	860-861
Luxembourg	386-387
Netherlands	394-395
Norway	414-415
Switzerland	416-417
Turkey	1553-1555

Nos. 582-583 (2)	.65	.65
Nos. 219-221 (3)	76.25	4.40
Nos. 1045-1046 (2)	.60	.50
Nos. 852-853 (2)	.70	.80
Nos. 739-740 (2)	2.25	1.15
Nos. 348-349 (2)	.85	.85
Nos. 184-185 (2)	2.00	1.50
Nos. 860-861 (2)	1.35	.55
Nos. 386-387 (2)	.85	.70
Nos. 394-395 (2)	1.40	.75
Nos. 414-415 (2)	2.25	2.25
Nos. 416-417 (2)	1.65	1.00
Nos. 1553-1555 (3)	3.00	1.55
Set total (28) Stamps	93.80	16.65

Europa, 1963

Stylized Links, Symbolizing Unity — CD6

1963, Sept.

Belgium	598-599
Cyprus	229-231
Finland	419
France	1074-1075
Germany	867-868
Greece	768-769
Iceland	357-358
Ireland	188-189
Italy	880-881
Luxembourg	403-404
Netherlands	416-417
Norway	441-442
Switzerland	429
Turkey	1602-1603

Nos. 598-599 (2)	1.60	.55
Nos. 229-231 (3)	54.75	5.15
No. 419 (1)	1.25	.55
Nos. 1074-1075 (2)	.60	.50
Nos. 867-868 (2)	.50	.55
Nos. 768-769 (2)	5.25	1.90
Nos. 357-358 (2)	1.20	1.20
Nos. 188-189 (2)	4.75	3.25
Nos. 880-881 (2)	.65	.50
Nos. 403-404 (2)	1.00	.80
Nos. 416-417 (2)	2.25	1.00
Nos. 441-442 (2)	4.75	3.00
No. 429 (1)	.90	.60
Nos. 1602-1603 (2)	1.40	.60
Set total (27) Stamps	80.85	20.15

Europa, 1964

Symbolic Daisy — CD7

5th anniversary of the establishment of C.E.P.T. The 22 petals of the flower symbolize the 22 members of the Conference.

1964, Sept.

Austria	738
Belgium	614-615
Cyprus	244-246
France	1109-1110
Germany	897-898
Greece	801-802
Iceland	367-368
Ireland	196-197
Italy	894-895
Luxembourg	411-412
Monaco	590-591
Netherlands	428-429
Norway	458
Portugal	931-933
Spain	1262-1263
Switzerland	438-439
Turkey	1628-1629

No. 738 (1)	1.20	.80
Nos. 614-615 (2)	1.40	.60
Nos. 244-246 (3)	35.75	3.45
Nos. 1109-1110 (2)	.50	.50
Nos. 897-898 (2)	.50	.50
Nos. 801-802 (2)	5.00	1.90
Nos. 367-368 (2)	1.40	1.15
Nos. 196-197 (2)	20.00	4.25
Nos. 894-895 (2)	.55	.50
Nos. 411-412 (2)	.90	.55
Nos. 590-591 (2)	2.50	.70
Nos. 428-429 (2)	1.80	.60
No. 458 (1)	4.50	4.50
Nos. 931-933 (3)	10.00	2.00
Nos. 1262-1263 (2)	1.30	.80
Nos. 438-439 (2)	1.60	.50
Nos. 1628-1629 (2)	2.65	1.35
Set total (34) Stamps	91.55	24.65

Europa, 1965

Leaves and "Fruit" CD8

1965

Belgium	636-637
Cyprus	262-264
Finland	437
France	1131-1132
Germany	934-935
Greece	833-834
Iceland	375-376
Ireland	204-205
Italy	915-916
Luxembourg	432-433
Monaco	616-617
Netherlands	438-439
Norway	475-476
Portugal	958-960
Switzerland	469
Turkey	1665-1666

Nos. 636-637 (2)	.50	.50
Nos. 262-264 (3)	25.35	3.80
No. 437 (1)	1.25	.55
Nos. 1131-1132 (2)	.70	.55
Nos. 934-935 (2)	.50	.50
Nos. 833-834 (2)	2.25	1.15
Nos. 375-376 (2)	2.50	1.75
Nos. 204-205 (2)	20.00	3.35
Nos. 915-916 (2)	.50	.50
Nos. 432-433 (2)	.80	.60
Nos. 616-617 (2)	3.25	1.65
Nos. 438-439 (2)	.75	.55
Nos. 475-476 (2)	4.00	3.10
Nos. 958-960 (3)	10.00	2.75
No. 469 (1)	1.15	.25
Nos. 1665-1666 (2)	3.50	2.10
Set total (32) Stamps	77.00	23.65

Europa, 1966

Symbolic Sailboat — CD9

1966, Sept.

Andorra, French	172
Belgium	675-676
Cyprus	275-277
France	1163-1164
Germany	963-964

Greece		862-863
Iceland		384-385
Ireland		216-217
Italy		942-943
Liechtenstein		415
Luxembourg		440-441
Monaco		639-640
Netherlands		441-442
Norway		496-497
Portugal		980-982
Switzerland		477-478
Turkey		1718-1719

No. 172 (1)	3.00	3.00
Nos. 675-676 (2)	.80	.50
Nos. 275-277 (3)	4.75	1.90
Nos. 1163-1164 (2)	.55	.50
Nos. 963-964 (2)	.50	.55
Nos. 862-863 (2)	2.25	1.05
Nos. 384-385 (2)	4.50	3.50
Nos. 216-217 (2)	7.00	2.00
Nos. 942-943 (2)	.50	.50
No. 415 (1)	.40	.35
Nos. 440-441 (2)	.80	.60
Nos. 639-640 (2)	2.00	.65
Nos. 441-442 (2)	1.50	.65
Nos. 496-497 (2)	5.00	3.00
Nos. 980-982 (3)	9.75	2.25
Nos. 477-478 (2)	1.60	.60
Nos. 1718-1719 (2)	3.35	1.75
Set total (34) Stamps	48.25	23.35

Europa, 1967

Cogwheels
CD10

1967

Andorra, French		174-175
Belgium		688-689
Cyprus		297-299
France		1178-1179
Germany		969-970
Greece		891-892
Iceland		389-390
Ireland		232-233
Italy		951-952
Liechtenstein		420
Luxembourg		449-450
Monaco		669-670
Netherlands		444-447
Norway		504-505
Portugal		994-996
Spain		1465-1466
Switzerland		482
Turkey		B120-B121

Nos. 174-175 (2)	10.75	6.25
Nos. 688-689 (2)	1.05	.55
Nos. 297-299 (3)	4.25	1.75
Nos. 1178-1179 (2)	.55	.50
Nos. 969-970 (2)	.55	.55
Nos. 891-892 (2)	3.75	1.00
Nos. 389-390 (2)	3.00	2.00
Nos. 232-233 (2)	6.15	2.30
Nos. 951-952 (2)	.60	.50
No. 420 (1)	.45	.40
Nos. 449-450 (2)	1.00	.70
Nos. 669-670 (2)	2.75	.70
Nos. 444-447 (4)	.90	1.85
Nos. 504-505 (2)	3.25	2.75
Nos. 994-996 (3)	9.50	1.85
Nos. 1465-1466 (2)	.50	.50
No. 482 (1)	.70	.25
Nos. B120-B121 (2)	3.50	2.75
Set total (38) Stamps	57.30	27.15

Europa, 1968

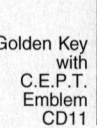

Golden Key
with
C.E.P.T.
Emblem
CD11

1968

Andorra, French		182-183
Belgium		705-706
Cyprus		314-316
France		1209-1210
Germany		983-984
Greece		916-917
Iceland		395-396
Ireland		242-243
Italy		979-980

Liechtenstein		442
Luxembourg		466-467
Monaco		689-691
Netherlands		452-453
Portugal		1019-1021
San Marino		687
Spain		1526
Switzerland		488
Turkey		1775-1776

Nos. 182-183 (2)	16.50	10.00
Nos. 705-706 (2)	1.25	.50
Nos. 314-316 (3)	2.90	1.75
Nos. 1209-1210 (2)	.85	.55
Nos. 983-984 (2)	.50	.55
Nos. 916-917 (2)	3.75	1.65
Nos. 395-396 (2)	3.00	2.20
Nos. 242-243 (2)	3.75	3.00
Nos. 979-980 (2)	.50	.50
No. 442 (1)	.45	.40
Nos. 466-467 (2)	.80	.70
Nos. 689-691 (3)	5.40	.95
Nos. 452-453 (2)	2.10	.70
Nos. 1019-1021 (3)	9.75	2.10
No. 687 (1)	.55	.35
No. 1526 (1)	.25	.25
No. 488 (1)	.45	.25
Nos. 1775-1776 (2)	5.00	2.00
Set total (35) Stamps	57.75	28.40

Europa, 1969

"EUROPA"
and "CEPT"
CD12

Tenth anniversary of C.E.P.T.

1969

Andorra, French		188-189
Austria		837
Belgium		718-719
Cyprus		326-328
Denmark		458
Finland		483
France		1245-1246
Germany		996-997
Great Britain		585
Greece		947-948
Iceland		406-407
Ireland		270-271
Italy		1000-1001
Liechtenstein		453
Luxembourg		475-476
Monaco		722-724
Netherlands		475-476
Norway		533-534
Portugal		1038-1040
San Marino		701-702
Spain		1567
Sweden		814-816
Switzerland		500-501
Turkey		1799-1800
Vatican		470-472
Yugoslavia		1003-1004

Nos. 188-189 (2)	18.50	12.00
No. 837 (1)	.65	.30
Nos. 718-719 (2)	.75	.50
Nos. 326-328 (3)	3.00	1.35
No. 458 (1)	.75	.75
No. 483 (1)	3.50	.75
Nos. 1245-1246 (2)	.55	.50
Nos. 996-997 (2)	.80	.50
No. 585 (1)	.25	.25
Nos. 947-948 (2)	5.00	1.50
Nos. 406-407 (2)	4.20	2.40
Nos. 270-271 (2)	4.00	2.00
Nos. 1000-1001 (2)	.70	.50
No. 453 (1)	.45	.45
Nos. 475-476 (2)	1.00	.70
Nos. 722-724 (3)	10.50	2.00
Nos. 475-476 (2)	2.60	1.15
Nos. 533-534 (2)	3.75	2.35
Nos. 1038-1040 (3)	17.85	2.40
Nos. 701-702 (2)	.90	.90
No. 1567 (1)	.25	.25
Nos. 814-816 (3)	4.00	2.85
Nos. 500-501 (2)	1.85	.60
Nos. 1799-1800 (2)	3.85	2.25
Nos. 470-472 (3)	.75	.75
Nos. 1003-1004 (2)	4.00	4.00
Set total (51) Stamps	94.40	43.95

Europa, 1970

Interwoven
Threads
CD13

1970

Andorra, French		196-197
Belgium		741-742
Cyprus		340-342
France		1271-1272
Germany		1018-1019
Greece		985, 987
Iceland		420-421
Ireland		279-281
Italy		1013-1014
Liechtenstein		470
Luxembourg		489-490
Monaco		768-770
Netherlands		483-484
Portugal		1060-1062
San Marino		729-730
Spain		1607
Switzerland		515-516
Turkey		1848-1849
Yugoslavia		1024-1025

Nos. 196-197 (2)	20.00	8.50
Nos. 741-742 (2)	1.10	.55
Nos. 340-342 (3)	2.70	1.90
Nos. 1271-1272 (2)	.65	.50
Nos. 1018-1019 (2)	.60	.50
Nos. 985,987 (2)	7.75	2.00
Nos. 420-421 (2)	6.00	4.00
Nos. 279-281 (3)	9.50	3.30
Nos. 1013-1014 (2)	.65	.50
No. 470 (1)	.45	.45
Nos. 489-490 (2)	.80	.80
Nos. 768-770 (3)	6.35	2.10
Nos. 483-484 (2)	2.50	1.15
Nos. 1060-1062 (3)	9.85	2.35
Nos. 729-730 (2)	.90	.55
No. 1607 (1)	.25	.25
Nos. 515-516 (2)	1.85	.60
Nos. 1848-1849 (2)	5.00	2.25
Nos. 1024-1025 (2)	.80	.80
Set total (40) Stamps	77.70	33.05

Europa, 1971

"Fraternity,
Cooperation,
Common
Effort"
CD14

1971

Andorra, French		205-206
Belgium		803-804
Cyprus		365-367
Finland		504
France		1304
Germany		1064-1065
Greece		1029-1030
Iceland		429-430
Ireland		305-306
Italy		1038-1039
Liechtenstein		485
Luxembourg		500-501
Malta		425-427
Monaco		797-799
Netherlands		488-489
Portugal		1094-1096
San Marino		749-750
Spain		1675-1676
Switzerland		531-532
Turkey		1876-1877
Yugoslavia		1052-1053

Nos. 205-206 (2)	20.00	7.75
Nos. 803-804 (2)	1.30	.55
Nos. 365-367 (3)	2.60	1.75
No. 504 (1)	5.00	.75
No. 1304 (1)	.45	.40
Nos. 1064-1065 (2)	.60	.50
Nos. 1029-1030 (2)	4.00	1.80
Nos. 429-430 (2)	5.00	3.75
Nos. 305-306 (2)	5.00	1.50
Nos. 1038-1039 (2)	.65	.50
No. 485 (1)	.45	.45
Nos. 500-501 (2)	1.00	.80
Nos. 425-427 (3)	.80	.80
Nos. 797-799 (3)	15.00	2.80
Nos. 488-489 (2)	2.50	1.15
Nos. 1094-1096 (3)	9.75	1.75
Nos. 749-750 (2)	.65	.55
Nos. 1675-1676 (2)	.75	.55
Nos. 531-532 (2)	1.85	.65
Nos. 1876-1877 (2)	5.60	2.50
Nos. 1052-1053 (2)	.50	.50
Set total (43) Stamps	83.45	31.75

Europa, 1972

Sparkles, Symbolic
of Communications
CD15

1972

Andorra, French		210-211
Andorra, Spanish		62
Belgium		825-826
Cyprus		380-382
Finland		512-513
France		1341
Germany		1089-1090
Greece		1049-1050
Iceland		439-440
Ireland		316-317
Italy		1065-1066
Liechtenstein		504
Luxembourg		512-513
Malta		450-453
Monaco		831-832
Netherlands		494-495
Portugal		1141-1143
San Marino		771-772
Spain		1718
Switzerland		544-545
Turkey		1907-1908
Yugoslavia		1100-1101

Nos. 210-211 (2)	21.00	7.00
No. 62 (1)	45.00	45.00
Nos. 825-826 (2)	.95	.55
Nos. 380-382 (3)	5.95	2.45
Nos. 512-513 (2)	7.00	1.40
No. 1341 (1)	.50	.35
Nos. 1089-1090 (2)	1.30	.50
Nos. 1049-1050 (2)	2.00	1.55
Nos. 439-440 (2)	2.90	2.65
Nos. 316-317 (2)	13.00	4.50
Nos. 1065-1066 (2)	.65	.50
No. 504 (1)	.45	.45
Nos. 512-513 (2)	1.00	.80
Nos. 450-453 (4)	1.05	1.40
Nos. 831-832 (2)	5.00	1.40
Nos. 494-495 (2)	3.25	1.15
Nos. 1141-1143 (3)	9.85	1.50
Nos. 771-772 (2)	.70	.50
No. 1718 (1)	.50	.40
Nos. 544-545 (2)	1.65	.60
Nos. 1907-1908 (2)	7.50	3.00
Nos. 1100-1101 (2)	1.20	1.20
Set total (44) Stamps	132.40	78.85

Europa, 1973

Post Horn
and Arrows
CD16

1973

Andorra, French		219-220
Andorra, Spanish		76
Belgium		839-840
Cyprus		396-398
Finland		526
France		1367
Germany		1114-1115
Greece		1090-1092
Iceland		447-448
Ireland		329-330
Italy		1108-1109
Liechtenstein		528-529
Luxembourg		523-524
Malta		469-471
Monaco		866-867
Netherlands		504-505
Norway		604-605
Portugal		1170-1172
San Marino		802-803
Spain		1753
Switzerland		580-581
Turkey		1935-1936
Yugoslavia		1138-1139

Nos. 219-220 (2)	20.00	11.00
No. 76 (1)	.65	.55
Nos. 839-840 (2)	1.00	.65
Nos. 396-398 (3)	4.25	2.10
No. 526 (1)	1.25	.55
No. 1367 (1)	1.25	.75
Nos. 1114-1115 (2)	.90	.50
Nos. 1090-1092 (3)	2.10	1.40
Nos. 447-448 (2)	6.65	3.35

Nos. 329-330 (2)	5.25	2.00
Nos. 1108-1109 (2)	.65	.50
Nos. 528-529 (2)	.60	.60
Nos. 523-524 (2)	.90	1.00
Nos. 469-471 (3)	.90	1.20
Nos. 866-867 (2)	15.00	2.40
Nos. 504-505 (2)	2.85	1.10
Nos. 604-605 (2)	6.25	2.40
Nos. 1170-1172 (3)	13.00	2.15
Nos. 802-803 (2)	1.00	.60
No. 1753 (1)	.35	.25
Nos. 580-581 (2)	1.55	.60
Nos. 1935-1936 (2)	10.00	4.50
Nos. 1138-1139 (2)	1.15	1.10
Set total (46) Stamps	97.50	41.25

Europa, 2000

CD17

2000

Albania	2621-2622
Andorra, French	522
Andorra, Spanish	262
Armenia	610-611
Austria	1814
Azerbaijan	698-699
Belarus	350
Belgium	1818
Bosnia & Herzegovina (Moslem)	358
Bosnia & Herzegovina (Serb)	111-112
Croatia	428-429
Cyprus	959
Czech Republic	3120
Denmark	1189
Estonia	394
Faroe Islands	376
Finland	1129
Aland Islands	166
France	2771
Georgia	228-229
Germany	2086-2087
Gibraltar	837-840
Great Britain (Jersey)	935-936
Great Britain (Isle of Man)	883
Greece	1959
Greenland	363
Hungary	3699-3700
Iceland	910
Ireland	1230-1231
Italy	2349
Latvia	504
Liechtenstein	1178
Lithuania	668
Luxembourg	1035
Macedonia	187
Malta	1011-1012
Moldova	355
Monaco	2161-2162
Poland	3519
Portugal	2358
Portugal (Azores)	455
Portugal (Madeira)	208
Romania	4370
Russia	6589
San Marino	1480
Slovakia	355
Slovenia	424
Spain	3036
Sweden	2394
Switzerland	1074
Turkey	2762
Turkish Rep. of Northern Cyprus	500
Ukraine	379
Vatican City	1152

Nos. 2621-2622 (2)	11.00	11.00
No. 522 (1)	2.00	1.00
No. 262 (1)	1.60	.70
Nos. 610-611 (2)	4.75	4.75
No. 1814 (1)	1.40	1.40
Nos. 698-699 (2)	6.00	6.00
No. 350 (1)	1.75	1.75
No. 1818 (1)	1.40	.60
No. 358 (1)	4.75	4.75
Nos. 111-112 (2)	110.00	110.00
Nos. 428-429 (2)	6.25	6.25
No. 959 (1)	2.10	1.40
No. 3120 (1)	1.00	.40
No. 1189 (1)	3.50	2.25
No. 394 (1)	1.25	1.25
No. 376 (1)	2.40	2.40
No. 1129 (1)	2.00	.60
No. 166 (1)	2.00	1.10
No. 2771 (1)	1.25	.40
Nos. 228-229 (1)	9.00	9.00
Nos. 2086-2087 (2)	4.15	1.90
Nos. 837-840 (4)	5.50	5.30

Nos. 935-936 (2)	2.40	2.40
No. 883 (1)	1.50	1.50
No. 1959 (1)	3.00	3.00
No. 363 (1)	1.90	1.90
Nos. 3699-3700 (2)	6.50	2.50
No. 910 (1)	1.60	1.60
Nos. 1230-1231 (2)	4.75	4.75
No. 2349 (1)	1.50	.40
No. 504 (1)	5.00	2.40
No. 1178 (1)	2.25	1.75
No. 668 (1)	1.50	1.50
No. 1035 (1)	1.40	1.00
No. 187 (1)	3.25	3.25
Nos. 1011-1012 (2)	4.35	4.35
No. 355 (1)	3.50	3.50
Nos. 2161-2162 (2)	2.80	1.40
No. 3519 (1)	1.10	.50
No. 2358 (1)	1.25	.65
No. 455 (1)	1.25	.50
No. 208 (1)	1.25	.50
No. 4370 (1)	2.50	1.25
No. 6589 (1)	2.00	.85
No. 1480 (1)	1.00	1.00
No. 355 (1)	1.25	.55
No. 424 (1)	3.25	1.60
No. 3036 (1)	.75	.40
No. 2394 (1)	3.00	2.25
No. 1074 (1)	2.10	.75
No. 2762 (1)	2.00	2.00
No. 500 (1)	2.50	2.50
No. 379 (1)	4.50	3.00
No. 1152 (1)	1.25	1.25
Set total (68) Stamps	263.20	230.95

The Gibraltar stamps are similar to the stamp illustrated, but none have the design shown above. All other sets listed above include at least one stamp with the design shown, but some include stamps with entirely different designs. Bulgaria Nos. 4131-4132, Guernsey Nos. 802-803 and Yugoslavia Nos. 2485-2486 are Europa stamps with completely different designs.

PORTUGAL & COLONIES
Vasco da Gama

Fleet Departing
CD20

Fleet Arriving at
Calicut — CD21

Embarking at
Rastello
CD22

Muse of
History
CD23

San Gabriel,
da Gama and
Camoens
CD24

Archangel
Gabriel, the
Patron Saint
CD25

Flagship San
Gabriel — CD26

Vasco da
Gama — CD27

Fourth centenary of Vasco da Gama's discovery of the route to India.

1898

Azores	93-100
Macao	67-74
Madeira	37-44
Portugal	147-154
Port. Africa	1-8
Port. Congo	75-98
Port. India	189-196
St. Thomas & Prince Islands	170-193
Timor	45-52

Nos. 93-100 (8)	122.00	76.25
Nos. 67-74 (8)	136.00	96.75
Nos. 37-44 (8)	44.55	34.00
Nos. 147-154 (8)	169.30	43.45
Nos. 1-8 (8)	23.95	21.70
Nos. 75-98 (24)	41.15	34.45
Nos. 189-196 (8)	20.25	12.95
Nos. 170-193 (24)	38.75	34.30
Nos. 45-52 (8)	21.50	10.45
Set total (104) Stamps	617.45	364.30

Pombal
POSTAL TAX
POSTAL TAX DUES

Marquis de
Pombal — CD28

Planning
Reconstruction
of Lisbon,
1755 — CD29

Pombal Monument,
Lisbon — CD30

Sebastiao Jose de Carvalho e Mello, Marquis de Pombal (1699-1782), statesman, rebuilt Lisbon after earthquake of 1755. Tax was for the erection of Pombal monument. Obligatory on all mail on certain days throughout the year. Postal Tax Dues are inscribed "Multa."

1925

Angola	RA1-RA3, RAJ1-RAJ3
Azores	RA9-RA11, RAJ2-RAJ4
Cape Verde	RA1-RA3, RAJ1-RAJ3
Macao	RA1-RA3, RAJ1-RAJ3
Madeira	RA1-RA3, RAJ1-RAJ3
Mozambique	RA1-RA3, RAJ1-RAJ3
Nyassa	RA1-RA3, RAJ1-RAJ3
Portugal	RA11-RA13, RAJ2-RAJ4
Port. Guinea	RA1-RA3, RAJ1-RAJ3
Port. India	RA1-RA3, RAJ1-RAJ3
St. Thomas & Prince Islands	RA1-RA3, RAJ1-RAJ3
Timor	RA1-RA3, RAJ1-RAJ3

Nos. RA1-RA3,RAJ1-RAJ3 (6)	6.60	6.60
Nos. RA9-RA11,RAJ2-RAJ4 (6)	6.60	9.30
Nos. RA1-RA3,RAJ1-RAJ3 (6)	6.00	5.40
Nos. RA1-RA3,RAJ1-RAJ3 (6)	19.50	4.20
Nos. RA1-RA3,RAJ1-RAJ3 (6)	4.35	12.45
Nos. RA1-RA3,RAJ1-RAJ3 (6)	2.55	2.70
Nos. RA1-RA3,RAJ1-RAJ3 (6)	52.50	38.25
Nos. RA11-RA13,RAJ2-RAJ4 (6)	5.80	5.20
Nos. RA1-RA3,RAJ1-RAJ3 (6)	3.30	2.70
Nos. RA1-RA3,RAJ1-RAJ3 (6)	3.45	3.45
Nos. RA1-RA3,RAJ1-RAJ3 (6)	3.60	3.60
Nos. RA1-RA3,RAJ1-RAJ3 (6)	2.10	3.90
Set total (72) Stamps	116.35	97.75

Vasco da Gama
CD34

Mousinho de
Albuquerque
CD35

Dam
CD36

Prince Henry
the Navigator
CD37

Affonso de
Albuquerque
CD38

Plane over
Globe
CD39

1938-39

Angola	274-291, C1-C9
Cape Verde	234-251, C1-C9
Macao	289-305, C7-C15
Mozambique	270-287, C1-C9
Port. Guinea	233-250, C1-C9
Port. India	439-453, C1-C8
St. Thomas & Prince Islands	302-319, 323-340, C1-C18
Timor	223-239, C1-C9

Nos. 274-291,C1-C9 (27)	132.90	22.85
Nos. 234-251,C1-C9 (27)	100.00	31.20
Nos. 289-305,C7-C15 (26)	701.70	135.60
Nos. 270-287,C1-C9 (27)	63.45	11.20
Nos. 233-250,C1-C9 (27)	88.05	30.70
Nos. 439-453,C1-C8 (23)	74.75	25.50
Nos. 302-319,323-340,C1-C18 (54)	319.25	190.35
Nos. 223-239,C1-C9 (26)	149.25	73.15
Set total (237) Stamps	1,629.	520.55

Lady of Fatima

Our Lady of the
Rosary, Fatima,
Portugal — CD40

1948-49

Angola	315-318
Cape Verde	266
Macao	336
Mozambique	325-328
Port. Guinea	271
Port. India	480
St. Thomas & Prince Islands	351
Timor	254

Nos. 315-318 (4)	68.00	17.25
No. 266 (1)	8.50	4.50
No. 336 (1)	40.00	12.00
Nos. 325-328 (4)	20.00	4.50
No. 271 (1)	3.25	3.00
No. 480 (1)	2.50	2.25
No. 351 (1)	7.25	6.50
No. 254 (1)	3.00	3.00
Set total (14) Stamps	152.50	53.00

A souvenir sheet of 9 stamps was issued in 1951 to mark the extension of the 1950 Holy Year. The sheet contains: Angola No. 316, Cape Verde No. 266, Macao No. 336, Mozambique No. 325, Portuguese Guinea No. 271, Portuguese India Nos. 480, 485, St. Thomas & Prince Islands No. 351, Timor No. 254. The sheet also contains a portrait of Pope Pius XII and is inscribed "Encerramento do

Ano Santo, Fatima 1951." It was sold for 11 escudos.

Holy Year

Church Bells and Dove CD41 — Angel Holding Candelabra CD42

Holy Year, 1950.

1950-51

Angola	331-332
Cape Verde	268-269
Macao	339-340
Mozambique	330-331
Port. Guinea	273-274
Port. India	490-491, 496-503
St. Thomas & Prince Islands	353-354
Timor	258-259

Nos. 331-332 (2)	7.60	1.35
Nos. 268-269 (2)	4.75	2.20
Nos. 339-340 (2)	55.00	12.50
Nos. 330-331 (2)	1.75	.85
Nos. 273-274 (2)	3.50	2.60
Nos. 490-491, 496-503 (10)	12.80	5.40
Nos. 353-354 (2)	7.50	4.40
Nos. 258-259 (2)	3.75	3.25
Set total (24) Stamps	96.65	32.55

A souvenir sheet of 8 stamps was issued in 1951 to mark the extension of the Holy Year. The sheet contains: Angola No. 331, Cape Verde No. 269, Macao No. 340, Mozambique No. 331, Portuguese Guinea No. 275, Portuguese India No. 490, St. Thomas & Prince Islands No. 354, Timor No. 258, some with colors changed. The sheet contains doves and is inscribed 'Encerramento do Ano Santo, Fatima 1951.' It was sold for 17 escudos.

Holy Year Conclusion

Our Lady of Fatima — CD43

Conclusion of Holy Year. Sheets contain alternate vertical rows of stamps and labels bearing quotation from Pope Pius XII, different for each colony.

1951

Angola	357
Cape Verde	270
Macao	352
Mozambique	356
Port. Guinea	275
Port. India	506
St. Thomas & Prince Islands	355
Timor	270

No. 357 (1)	5.25	1.50
No. 270 (1)	1.50	1.25
No. 352 (1)	37.50	10.00
No. 356 (1)	2.25	1.00
No. 275 (1)	1.00	.65
No. 506 (1)	1.60	1.00
No. 355 (1)	2.50	2.00
No. 270 (1)	2.00	1.75
Set total (8) Stamps	53.60	19.15

Medical Congress

CD44

First National Congress of Tropical Medicine, Lisbon, 1952. Each stamp has a different design.

1952

Angola	358
Cape Verde	287
Macao	364

Mozambique	359
Port. Guinea	276
Port. India	516
St. Thomas & Prince Islands	356
Timor	271

No. 358 (1)	1.50	.50
No. 287 (1)	.70	.50
No. 364 (1)	9.75	4.25
No. 359 (1)	1.10	.55
No. 276 (1)	.45	.35
No. 516 (1)	4.75	2.00
No. 356 (1)	.30	.30
No. 271 (1)	1.00	1.00
Set total (8) Stamps	19.55	9.45

Postage Due Stamps

CD45

1952

Angola	J37-J42
Cape Verde	J31-J36
Macao	J53-J58
Mozambique	J51-J56
Port. Guinea	J40-J45
Port. India	J47-J52
St. Thomas & Prince Islands	J52-J57
Timor	J31-J36

Nos. J37-J42 (6)	4.05	3.15
Nos. J31-J36 (6)	2.80	2.30
Nos. J53-J58 (6)	17.45	6.85
Nos. J51-J56 (6)	1.80	1.55
Nos. J40-J45 (6)	2.55	2.55
Nos. J47-J52 (6)	6.10	6.10
Nos. J52-J57 (6)	4.15	4.15
Nos. J31-J36 (6)	3.50	3.50
Set total (48) Stamps	42.40	30.15

Sao Paulo

Father Manuel da Nobrega and View of Sao Paulo — CD46

Founding of Sao Paulo, Brazil, 400th anniv.

1954

Angola	385
Cape Verde	297
Macao	382
Mozambique	395
Port. Guinea	291
Port. India	530
St. Thomas & Prince Islands	369
Timor	279

No. 385 (1)	.80	.50
No. 297 (1)	.70	.60
No. 382 (1)	14.00	3.00
No. 395 (1)	.40	.30
No. 291 (1)	.35	.25
No. 530 (1)	.80	.40
No. 369 (1)	.80	.60
No. 279 (1)	.85	.70
Set total (8) Stamps	18.70	6.35

Tropical Medicine Congress

CD47

Sixth International Congress for Tropical Medicine and Malaria, Lisbon, Sept. 1958. Each stamp shows a different plant.

1958

Angola	409
Cape Verde	303
Macao	392
Mozambique	404
Port. Guinea	295
Port. India	569
St. Thomas & Prince Islands	371

Timor	289

No. 409 (1)	3.50	1.10
No. 303 (1)	5.50	2.10
No. 392 (1)	8.00	3.00
No. 404 (1)	4.00	.85
No. 295 (1)	2.75	1.10
No. 569 (1)	1.75	.75
No. 371 (1)	2.75	2.25
No. 289 (1)	3.00	2.75
Set total (8) Stamps	31.25	13.90

Sports

CD48

Each stamp shows a different sport.

1962

Angola	433-438
Cape Verde	320-325
Macao	394-399
Mozambique	424-429
Port. Guinea	299-304
St. Thomas & Prince Islands	374-379
Timor	313-318

Nos. 433-438 (6)	5.50	3.20
Nos. 320-325 (6)	15.25	5.20
Nos. 394-399 (6)	74.00	14.60
Nos. 424-429 (6)	5.70	2.45
Nos. 299-304 (6)	4.95	2.15
Nos. 374-379 (6)	6.75	3.20
Nos. 313-318 (6)	6.40	3.70
Set total (42) Stamps	118.55	34.50

Anti-Malaria

Anopheles Funestus and Malaria Eradication Symbol — CD49

World Health Organization drive to eradicate malaria.

1962

Angola	439
Cape Verde	326
Macao	400
Mozambique	430
Port. Guinea	305
St. Thomas & Prince Islands	380
Timor	319

No. 439 (1)	1.75	.90
No. 326 (1)	1.40	.90
No. 400 (1)	6.50	2.00
No. 430 (1)	1.40	.40
No. 305 (1)	1.25	.45
No. 380 (1)	2.00	1.50
No. 319 (1)	.75	.60
Set total (7) Stamps	15.05	6.75

Airline Anniversary

Map of Africa, Super Constellation and Jet Liner — CD50

Tenth anniversary of Transportes Aereos Portugueses (TAP).

1963

Angola	490
Cape Verde	327
Mozambique	434
Port. Guinea	318
St. Thomas & Prince Islands	381

No. 490 (1)	1.00	.35
No. 327 (1)	1.10	.70
No. 434 (1)	.40	.25

No. 318 (1)	.65	.35
No. 381 (1)	.70	.60
Set total (5) Stamps	3.85	2.25

National Overseas Bank

Antonio Teixeira de Sousa — CD51

Centenary of the National Overseas Bank of Portugal.

1964, May 16

Angola	509
Cape Verde	328
Port. Guinea	319
St. Thomas & Prince Islands	382
Timor	320

No. 509 (1)	.90	.30
No. 328 (1)	1.10	.75
No. 319 (1)	.65	.40
No. 382 (1)	.70	.50
No. 320 (1)	.75	.60
Set total (5) Stamps	4.10	2.55

ITU

ITU Emblem and the Archangel Gabriel — CD52

International Communications Union, Cent.

1965, May 17

Angola	511
Cape Verde	329
Macao	402
Mozambique	464
Port. Guinea	320
St. Thomas & Prince Islands	383
Timor	321

No. 511 (1)	1.25	.65
No. 329 (1)	2.10	1.40
No. 402 (1)	5.00	2.00
No. 464 (1)	.40	.25
No. 320 (1)	1.90	.75
No. 383 (1)	1.50	1.00
No. 321 (1)	1.50	.90
Set total (7) Stamps	13.65	6.95

National Revolution

CD53

40th anniv. of the National Revolution. Different buildings on each stamp.

1966, May 28

Angola	525
Cape Verde	338
Macao	403
Mozambique	465
Port. Guinea	329
St. Thomas & Prince Islands	392
Timor	322

No. 525 (1)	.50	.25
No. 338 (1)	.60	.45
No. 403 (1)	5.00	2.00
No. 465 (1)	.50	.30
No. 329 (1)	.55	.35
No. 392 (1)	.75	.50
No. 322 (1)	1.50	.90
Set total (7) Stamps	9.40	4.75

Navy Club

CD54

Centenary of Portugal's Navy Club. Each stamp has a different design.

1967, Jan. 31

Angola	527-528
Cape Verde	339-340
Macao	412-413
Mozambique	478-479
Port. Guinea	330-331
St. Thomas & Prince Islands	393-394
Timor	323-324

Nos. 527-528 (2)	1.75	.75
Nos. 339-340 (2)	2.00	1.40
Nos. 412-413 (2)	9.50	3.75
Nos. 478-479 (2)	1.20	.65
Nos. 330-331 (2)	1.20	.90
Nos. 393-394 (2)	3.20	1.25
Nos. 323-324 (2)	4.00	2.00
Set total (14) Stamps	22.85	10.70

Admiral Coutinho

CD55

Centenary of the birth of Admiral Carlos Viegas Gago Coutinho (1869-1959), explorer and aviation pioneer. Each stamp has a different design.

1969, Feb. 17

Angola	547
Cape Verde	355
Macao	417
Mozambique	484
Port. Guinea	335
St. Thomas & Prince Islands	397
Timor	335

No. 547 (1)	.85	.35
No. 355 (1)	.35	.25
No. 417 (1)	3.75	1.50
No. 484 (1)	.25	.25
No. 335 (1)	.35	.25
No. 397 (1)	.50	.35
No. 335 (1)	1.10	.85
Set total (7) Stamps	7.15	3.80

Administration Reform

Luiz Augusto Rebello da Silva — CD56

Centenary of the administration reforms of the overseas territories.

1969, Sept. 25

Angola	549
Cape Verde	357
Macao	419
Mozambique	491
Port. Guinea	337
St. Thomas & Prince Islands	399
Timor	338

No. 549 (1)	.35	.25
No. 357 (1)	.35	.25
No. 419 (1)	5.00	1.00
No. 491 (1)	.25	.25
No. 337 (1)	.25	.25
No. 399 (1)	.45	.45
No. 338 (1)	.40	.25
Set total (7) Stamps	7.05	2.70

Marshal Carmona

CD57

Birth centenary of Marshal Antonio Oscar Carmona de Fragoso (1869-1951), President of Portugal. Each stamp has a different design.

1970, Nov. 15

Angola	563
Cape Verde	359
Macao	422
Mozambique	493
Port. Guinea	340
St. Thomas & Prince Islands	403
Timor	341

No. 563 (1)	.45	.25
No. 359 (1)	.55	.35
No. 422 (1)	2.25	1.25
No. 493 (1)	.40	.25
No. 340 (1)	.35	.25
No. 403 (1)	.75	.45
No. 341 (1)	.25	.25
Set total (7) Stamps	5.00	3.05

Olympic Games

CD59

20th Olympic Games, Munich, Aug. 26-Sept. 11. Each stamp shows a different sport.

1972, June 20

Angola	569
Cape Verde	361
Macao	426
Mozambique	504
Port. Guinea	342
St. Thomas & Prince Islands	408
Timor	343

No. 569 (1)	.65	.25
No. 361 (1)	.65	.30
No. 426 (1)	3.25	1.00
No. 504 (1)	.30	.25
No. 342 (1)	.45	.25
No. 408 (1)	.35	.25
No. 343 (1)	.50	.50
Set total (7) Stamps	6.15	2.80

Lisbon-Rio de Janeiro Flight

CD60

50th anniversary of the Lisbon to Rio de Janeiro flight by Arturo de Sacadura and Coutinho, March 30-June 5, 1922. Each stamp shows a different stage of the flight.

1972, Sept. 20

Angola	570
Cape Verde	362
Macao	427
Mozambique	505
Port. Guinea	343
St. Thomas & Prince Islands	409
Timor	344

No. 570 (1)	.35	.25
No. 362 (1)	1.50	.30
No. 427 (1)	22.50	7.50
No. 505 (1)	.25	.25
No. 343 (1)	.25	.25
No. 409 (1)	.35	.25
No. 344 (1)	.25	.40
Set total (7) Stamps	25.45	9.20

WMO Centenary

WMO Emblem — CD61

Centenary of international meterological cooperation.

1973, Dec. 15

Angola	571
Cape Verde	363
Macao	429
Mozambique	509
Port. Guinea	344
St. Thomas & Prince Islands	410

Timor	345

No. 571 (1)	.45	.25
No. 363 (1)	.65	.30
No. 429 (1)	6.25	1.75
No. 509 (1)	.30	.25
No. 344 (1)	.45	.35
No. 410 (1)	.60	.50
No. 345 (1)	1.75	2.00
Set total (7) Stamps	10.45	5.40

FRENCH COMMUNITY
**Upper Volta can be found under
Burkina Faso in Vol. 1
Madagascar can be found under
Malagasy in Vol. 3
Colonial Exposition**

People of French Empire CD70

Women's Heads CD71

France Showing Way to Civilization CD72

"Colonial Commerce" CD73

International Colonial Exposition, Paris.

1931

Cameroun	213-216
Chad	60-63
Dahomey	97-100
Fr. Guiana	152-155
Fr. Guinea	116-119
Fr. India	100-103
Fr. Polynesia	76-79
Fr. Sudan	102-105
Gabon	120-123
Guadeloupe	138-141
Indo-China	140-142
Ivory Coast	92-95
Madagascar	169-172
Martinique	129-132
Mauritania	65-68
Middle Congo	61-64
New Caledonia	176-179
Niger	73-76
Reunion	122-125
St. Pierre & Miquelon	132-135
Senegal	138-141
Somali Coast	135-138
Togo	254-257
Ubangi-Shari	82-85
Upper Volta	66-69
Wallis & Futuna Isls.	85-88

Nos. 213-216 (4)	23.00	18.25
Nos. 60-63 (4)	22.00	22.00
Nos. 97-100 (4)	26.00	26.00
Nos. 152-155 (4)	22.00	22.00
Nos. 116-119 (4)	19.75	19.75
Nos. 100-103 (4)	18.00	18.00
Nos. 76-79 (4)	30.00	30.00
Nos. 102-105 (4)	19.00	19.00
Nos. 120-123 (4)	17.50	17.50
Nos. 138-141 (4)	19.00	19.00
Nos. 140-142 (3)	11.50	11.50
Nos. 92-95 (4)	22.50	22.50
Nos. 169-172 (4)	7.90	5.00
Nos. 129-132 (4)	21.00	21.00
Nos. 65-68 (4)	22.00	22.00
Nos. 61-64 (4)	20.50	20.50
Nos. 176-179 (4)	24.00	24.00
Nos. 73-76 (4)	21.50	21.50
Nos. 122-125 (4)	22.00	22.00
Nos. 132-135 (4)	24.00	24.00
Nos. 138-141 (4)	20.00	20.00
Nos. 135-138 (4)	22.00	22.00
Nos. 254-257 (4)	22.00	22.00

Nos. 82-85 (4)	21.00	21.00
Nos. 66-69 (4)	19.00	19.00
Nos. 85-88 (4)	35.00	35.00
Set total (103) Stamps	552.15	544.50

Paris International Exposition
Colonial Arts Exposition

"Colonial Resources"
CD74   CD77

Overseas Commerce CD75

Exposition Building and Women CD76

"France and the Empire" CD78

Cultural Treasures of the Colonies CD79

Souvenir sheets contain one imperf. stamp.

1937

Cameroun	217-222A
Dahomey	101-107
Fr. Equatorial Africa	27-32, 73
Fr. Guiana	162-168
Fr. Guinea	120-126
Fr. India	104-110
Fr. Polynesia	117-123
Fr. Sudan	106-112
Guadeloupe	148-154
Indo-China	193-199
Inini	41
Ivory Coast	152-158
Kwangchowan	132
Madagascar	191-197
Martinique	179-185
Mauritania	69-75
New Caledonia	208-214
Niger	73-83
Reunion	167-173
St. Pierre & Miquelon	165-171
Senegal	172-178
Somali Coast	139-145
Togo	258-264
Wallis & Futuna Isls.	89

Nos. 217-222A (7)	18.80	20.30
Nos. 101-107 (7)	23.60	27.60
Nos. 27-32, 73 (7)	28.10	32.10
Nos. 162-168 (7)	22.50	24.50
Nos. 120-126 (7)	24.00	28.00
Nos. 104-110 (7)	21.15	36.50
Nos. 117-123 (7)	58.50	75.00
Nos. 106-112 (7)	23.60	27.60
Nos. 148-154 (7)	19.55	21.05
Nos. 193-199 (7)	17.70	19.70
No. 41 (1)	19.00	22.50
Nos. 152-158 (7)	22.20	26.20
No. 132 (1)	9.25	11.00
Nos. 191-197 (7)	19.25	21.75
Nos. 179-185 (7)	19.95	21.70
Nos. 69-75 (7)	20.50	24.50
Nos. 208-214 (7)	39.00	50.50
Nos. 73-83 (11)	42.70	46.70
Nos. 167-173 (7)	21.70	23.20
Nos. 165-171 (7)	49.60	64.00
Nos. 172-178 (7)	21.00	23.80
Nos. 139-145 (7)	25.60	32.60
Nos. 258-264 (7)	20.40	20.40
No. 89 (1)	28.50	37.50
Set total (154) Stamps	616.15	738.70

Curie

Pierre and Marie Curie CD80

40th anniversary of the discovery of radium. The surtax was for the benefit of the Intl. Union for the Control of Cancer.

1938

Cameroun	B1
Cuba	B1-B2
Dahomey	B2
France	B76
Fr. Equatorial Africa	B1
Fr. Guiana	B3
Fr. Guinea	B2
Fr. India	B6
Fr. Polynesia	B5
Fr. Sudan	B1
Guadeloupe	B3
Indo-China	B14
Ivory Coast	B2
Madagascar	B2
Martinique	B2
Mauritania	B3
New Caledonia	B4
Niger	B1
Reunion	B4
St. Pierre & Miquelon	B3
Senegal	B3
Somali Coast	B2
Togo	B1

No. B1 (1)	10.00	10.00
Nos. B1-B2 (2)	8.50	2.40
No. B2 (1)	9.50	9.50
No. B76 (1)	21.00	12.50
No. B1 (1)	24.00	24.00
No. B3 (1)	13.50	13.50
No. B2 (1)	8.75	8.75
No. B6 (1)	10.00	10.00
No. B5 (1)	20.00	20.00
No. B1 (1)	12.50	12.50
No. B3 (1)	11.00	10.50
No. B14 (1)	12.00	12.00
No. B2 (1)	11.00	7.50
No. B2 (1)	11.00	11.00
No. B2 (1)	13.00	13.00
No. B3 (1)	7.75	7.75
No. B4 (1)	16.50	17.50
No. B1 (1)	15.00	15.00
No. B4 (1)	14.00	14.00
No. B3 (1)	21.00	22.50
No. B3 (1)	10.50	10.50
No. B2 (1)	7.75	7.75
No. B1 (1)	20.00	20.00
Set total (24) Stamps	308.25	292.15

Caillie

Rene Caillie and Map of Northwestern Africa — CD81

Death centenary of Rene Caillie (1799-1838), French explorer. All three denominations exist with colony name omitted.

1939

Dahomey	108-110
Fr. Guinea	161-163
Fr. Sudan	113-115
Ivory Coast	160-162
Mauritania	109-111
Niger	84-86
Senegal	188-190
Togo	265-267

Nos. 108-110 (3)	1.20	3.60
Nos. 161-163 (3)	1.20	3.20
Nos. 113-115 (3)	1.20	3.20
Nos. 160-162 (3)	1.05	2.55
Nos. 109-111 (3)	1.05	3.80
Nos. 84-86 (3)	1.05	2.35
Nos. 188-190 (3)	1.05	2.90
Nos. 265-267 (3)	1.05	3.30
Set total (24) Stamps	8.85	24.90

New York World's Fair

Natives and New York Skyline CD82

1939

Cameroun	223-224
Dahomey	111-112
Fr. Equatorial Africa	78-79
Fr. Guiana	169-170
Fr. Guinea	164-165
Fr. India	111-112
Fr. Polynesia	124-125
Fr. Sudan	116-117
Guadeloupe	155-156
Indo-China	203-204
Inini	42-43
Ivory Coast	163-164
Kwangchowan	133-134
Madagascar	209-210
Martinique	186-187
Mauritania	112-113
New Caledonia	215-216
Niger	87-88
Reunion	174-175
St. Pierre & Miquelon	205-206
Senegal	191-192
Somali Coast	179-180
Togo	268-269
Wallis & Futuna Isls.	90-91

Nos. 223-224 (2)	2.80	2.40
Nos. 111-112 (2)	1.60	3.20
Nos. 78-79 (2)	1.60	3.20
Nos. 169-170 (2)	2.60	2.60
Nos. 164-165 (2)	1.60	3.20
Nos. 111-112 (2)	3.00	8.00
Nos. 124-125 (2)	4.80	4.80
Nos. 116-117 (2)	1.60	3.20
Nos. 155-156 (2)	2.50	2.50
Nos. 203-204 (2)	2.05	2.05
Nos. 42-43 (2)	7.50	9.00
Nos. 163-164 (2)	1.50	3.00
Nos. 133-134 (2)	2.50	2.50
Nos. 209-210 (2)	1.50	2.50
Nos. 186-187 (2)	2.35	2.35
Nos. 112-113 (2)	1.40	2.80
Nos. 215-216 (2)	3.35	3.35
Nos. 87-88 (2)	1.40	2.80
Nos. 174-175 (2)	2.80	2.80
Nos. 205-206 (2)	4.80	6.00
Nos. 191-192 (2)	1.40	2.80
Nos. 179-180 (2)	1.40	2.80
Nos. 268-269 (2)	1.40	2.80
Nos. 90-91 (2)	6.00	6.00
Set total (48) Stamps	63.45	86.65

French Revolution

Storming of the Bastille CD83

French Revolution, 150th anniv. The surtax was for the defense of the colonies.

1939

Cameroun	B2-B6
Dahomey	B3-B7
Fr. Equatorial Africa	B4-B8, CB1
Fr. Guiana	B4-B8, CB1
Fr. Guinea	B3-B7
Fr. India	B7-B11
Fr. Polynesia	B6-B10, CB1
Fr. Sudan	B2-B6
Guadeloupe	B4-B8
Indo-China	B15-B19, CB1
Inini	B1-B5
Ivory Coast	B3-B7
Kwangchowan	B1-B5
Madagascar	B3-B7, CB1
Martinique	B3-B7
Mauritania	B4-B8
New Caledonia	B5-B9, CB1
Niger	B2-B6
Reunion	B5-B9, CB1
St. Pierre & Miquelon	B4-B8
Senegal	B4-B8, CB1
Somali Coast	B3-B7
Togo	B2-B6
Wallis & Futuna Isls.	B1-B5

Nos. B2-B6 (5)	60.00	60.00
Nos. B3-B7 (5)	47.50	47.50
Nos. B4-B8, CB1 (6)	120.00	120.00
Nos. B4-B8, CB1 (6)	79.50	79.50
Nos. B3-B7 (5)	47.50	47.50
Nos. B7-B11 (5)	28.75	32.50
Nos. B6-B10, CB1 (6)	122.50	122.50
Nos. B2-B6 (5)	50.00	50.00
Nos. B4-B8 (5)	50.00	50.00
Nos. B15-B19, CB1 (6)	85.00	85.00
Nos. B1-B5 (5)	75.00	87.50
Nos. B3-B7 (5)	43.75	43.75
Nos. B1-B5 (5)	46.25	46.25
Nos. B3-B7, CB1 (6)	65.50	65.50
Nos. B3-B7 (5)	52.50	52.50
Nos. B4-B8 (5)	42.50	42.50
Nos. B5-B9, CB1 (6)	101.50	101.50
Nos. B2-B6 (5)	60.00	60.00
Nos. B5-B9, CB1 (6)	87.50	87.50
Nos. B4-B8 (5)	67.50	72.50
Nos. B4-B8, CB1 (6)	56.50	56.50
Nos. B3-B7 (5)	45.00	45.00
Nos. B2-B6 (5)	42.50	42.50
Nos. B1-B5 (5)	95.00	95.00
Set total (128) Stamps	1,572.	1,593.

Plane over Coastal Area CD85

All five denominations exist with colony name omitted.

1940

Dahomey	C1-C5
Fr. Guinea	C1-C5
Fr. Sudan	C1-C5
Ivory Coast	C1-C5
Mauritania	C1-C5
Niger	C1-C5
Senegal	C12-C16
Togo	C1-C5

Nos. C1-C5 (5)	4.00	4.00
Nos. C1-C5 (5)	4.00	4.00
Nos. C1-C5 (5)	4.00	4.00
Nos. C1-C5 (5)	3.80	3.80
Nos. C1-C5 (5)	3.50	3.50
Nos. C1-C5 (5)	3.50	3.50
Nos. C12-C16 (5)	3.50	3.50
Nos. C1-C5 (5)	3.15	3.15
Set total (40) Stamps	29.45	29.45

Defense of the Empire

Colonial Infantryman — CD86

1941

Cameroun	B13B
Dahomey	B13
Fr. Equatorial Africa	B8B
Fr. Guiana	B10
Fr. Guinea	B13
Fr. India	B13
Fr. Polynesia	B12
Fr. Sudan	B12
Guadeloupe	B10
Indo-China	B19B
Inini	B7
Ivory Coast	B13
Kwangchowan	B7
Madagascar	B9
Martinique	B9
Mauritania	B14
New Caledonia	B11
Niger	B12
Reunion	B11
St. Pierre & Miquelon	B8B
Senegal	B14
Somali Coast	B9
Togo	B10B
Wallis & Futuna Isls.	B7

No. B13B (1)	1.60	
No. B13 (1)	1.20	
No. B8B (1)	3.50	
No. B10 (1)	1.40	
No. B13 (1)	1.40	
No. B13 (1)	1.25	
No. B12 (1)	3.50	
No. B12 (1)	1.40	
No. B10 (1)	1.00	
No. B19B (1)	1.60	
No. B7 (1)	1.75	
No. B13 (1)	1.25	
No. B7 (1)	.85	

No. B9 (1)	1.50	
No. B9 (1)	1.40	
No. B14 (1)	.95	
No. B11 (1)	1.60	
No. B12 (1)	1.40	
No. B11 (1)	1.60	
No. B8B (1)	3.75	
No. B14 (1)	1.25	
No. B9 (1)	1.60	
No. B10B (1)	1.10	
No. B7 (1)	2.40	
Set total (24) Stamps	40.25	

Each of the CD86 stamps listed above is part of a set of three stamps. The designs of the other two stamps in the set vary from country to country. Only the values of the Common Design stamps are listed here.

Colonial Education Fund

CD86a

1942

Cameroun	CB3
Dahomey	CB4
Fr. Equatorial Africa	CB5
Fr. Guiana	CB4
Fr. Guinea	CB4
Fr. India	CB3
Fr. Polynesia	CB4
Fr. Sudan	CB4
Guadeloupe	CB3
Indo-China	CB5
Inini	CB3
Ivory Coast	CB4
Kwangchowan	CB4
Malagasy	CB5
Martinique	CB3
Mauritania	CB4
New Caledonia	CB4
Niger	CB4
Reunion	CB4
St. Pierre & Miquelon	CB3
Senegal	CB5
Somali Coast	CB3
Togo	CB3
Wallis & Futuna	CB3

No. CB3 (1)	1.10	
No. CB4 (1)	.80	5.50
No. CB5 (1)	.80	
No. CB4 (1)	1.10	
No. CB4 (1)	.40	5.50
No. CB3 (1)	.90	
No. CB4 (1)	2.00	
No. CB4 (1)	.40	5.50
No. CB3 (1)	1.10	
No. CB5 (1)	1.10	
No. CB3 (1)	1.25	
No. CB4 (1)	1.00	5.50
No. CB4 (1)	1.00	
No. CB5 (1)	.65	
No. CB3 (1)	1.00	
No. CB4 (1)	.80	
No. CB4 (1)	1.60	
No. CB4 (1)	.35	
No. CB4 (1)	.90	
No. CB3 (1)	5.25	
No. CB5 (1)	.80	6.50
No. CB3 (1)	.70	
No. CB3 (1)	.35	
No. CB3 (1)	2.25	
Set total (24) Stamps	27.60	28.50

Cross of Lorraine & Four-motor Plane CD87

1941-5

Cameroun	C1-C7
Fr. Equatorial Africa	C17-C23
Fr. Guiana	C9-C10
Fr. India	C1-C6
Fr. Polynesia	C3-C9
Fr. West Africa	C1-C3
Guadeloupe	C1-C2

Madagascar.......................... C37-C43
Martinique................................. C1-C2
New Caledonia...................... C7-C13
Reunion............................... C18-C24
St. Pierre & Miquelon.............. C1-C7
Somali Coast.......................... C1-C7

Nos. C1-C7 (7)   6.30   6.30
Nos. C17-C23 (7)   10.40   6.35
Nos. C9-C10 (2)   3.80   3.10
Nos. C1-C6 (6)   9.30   15.00
Nos. C3-C9 (7)   13.75   10.00
Nos. C1-C3 (3)   9.50   3.90
Nos. C1-C2 (2)   3.75   2.50
Nos. C37-C43 (7)   5.60   3.80
Nos. C1-C2 (2)   3.00   1.60
Nos. C7-C13 (7)   8.35   8.35
Nos. C18-C24 (7)   7.05   5.00
Nos. C1-C7 (7)   11.60   9.40
Nos. C1-C7 (7)   13.95   11.10
Set total (71) Stamps   106.35   86.40

Transport
Plane
CD88

Caravan
and Plane
CD89

1942

Dahomey C6-C13
Fr. Guinea C6-C13
Fr. Sudan C6-C13
Ivory Coast.............................. C6-C13
Mauritania................................ C6-C13
Niger.. C6-C13
Senegal C17-C25
Togo.. C6-C13

Nos. C6-C13 (8)   7.15
Nos. C6-C13 (8)   5.75
Nos. C6-C13 (8)   8.00
Nos. C6-C13 (8)   11.15
Nos. C6-C13 (8)   9.75
Nos. C6-C13 (8)   6.90
Nos. C17-C25 (9)   9.45
Nos. C6-C13 (8)   6.75
Set total (65) Stamps   64.90

Red Cross

Marianne
CD90

The surtax was for the French Red Cross
and national relief.

1944

Cameroun...................................... B28
Fr. Equatorial Africa B38
Fr. Guiana B12
Fr. India B14
Fr. Polynesia................................. B13
Fr. West Africa B1
Guadeloupe................................... B12
Madagascar................................... B15
Martinique...................................... B11
New Caledonia............................... B13
Reunion B15
St. Pierre & Miquelon..................... B13
Somali Coast................................. B13
Wallis & Futuna Isls. B9

No. B28 (1)   2.00   1.60
No. B38 (1)   1.60   1.20
No. B12 (1)   1.75   1.25
No. B14 (1)   1.50   1.25
No. B13 (1)   2.00   1.60
No. B1 (1)   6.50   4.75
No. B12 (1)   1.40   1.00
No. B15 (1)   .90   .90
No. B11 (1)   1.20   1.20
No. B13 (1)   1.50   1.50
No. B15 (1)   1.60   1.10
No. B13 (1)   2.75   2.40
No. B13 (1)   1.75   2.00
No. B9 (1)   4.50   3.25
Set total (14) Stamps   30.95   25.00

Eboue

CD91

Felix Eboue, first French colonial administrator to proclaim resistance to Germany after
French surrender in World War II.

1945

Cameroun.................................296-297
Fr. Equatorial Africa 156-157
Fr. Guiana 171-172
Fr. India 210-211
Fr. Polynesia...........................150-151
Fr. West Africa 15-16
Guadeloupe.............................187-188
Madagascar.............................259-260
Martinique................................196-197
New Caledonia 274-275
Reunion 238-239
St. Pierre & Miquelon..............322-323
Somali Coast...........................238-239

Nos. 296-297 (2)   2.40   1.95
Nos. 156-157 (2)   2.55   2.00
Nos. 171-172 (2)   2.45   2.00
Nos. 210-211 (2)   2.20   1.95
Nos. 150-151 (2)   3.60   2.85
Nos. 15-16 (2)   2.40   2.40
Nos. 187-188 (2)   2.05   1.60
Nos. 259-260 (2)   2.00   1.45
Nos. 196-197 (2)   2.05   1.55
Nos. 274-275 (2)   3.40   3.00
Nos. 238-239 (2)   2.40   2.00
Nos. 322-323 (2)   4.40   3.45
Nos. 238-239 (2)   2.45   2.10
Set total (26) Stamps   34.35   28.30

Victory

Victory — CD92

European victory of the Allied Nations in
World War II.

1946, May 8

Cameroun... C8
Fr. Equatorial Africa C24
Fr. Guiana C11
Fr. India C7
Fr. Polynesia................................ C10
Fr. West Africa C4
Guadeloupe.................................... C3
Indo-China.................................... C19
Madagascar.................................. C44
Martinique...................................... C3
New Caledonia.............................. C14
Reunion C25
St. Pierre & Miquelon.................... C8
Somali Coast................................. C8
Wallis & Futuna Isls. C1

No. C8 (1)   1.60   1.20
No. C24 (1)   1.60   1.25
No. C11 (1)   1.75   1.25
No. C7 (1)   1.00   4.00
No. C10 (1)   2.75   2.00
No. C4 (1)   1.60   1.20
No. C3 (1)   1.25   1.00
No. C19 (1)   1.00   .55
No. C44 (1)   1.00   .35
No. C3 (1)   1.30   1.00
No. C14 (1)   2.25   1.25
No. C25 (1)   1.10   .90
No. C8 (1)   2.10   1.75
No. C8 (1)   1.75   1.40
No. C1 (1)   2.50   1.90
Set total (15) Stamps   24.55   21.00

Chad to Rhine

Leclerc's Departure from
Chad — CD93

Battle at Cufra Oasis — CD94

Tanks in Action, Mareth — CD95

Normandy Invasion — CD96

Entering Paris — CD97

Liberation of Strasbourg — CD98

"Chad to the Rhine" march, 1942-44, by
Gen. Jacques Leclerc's column, later French
2nd Armored Division.

1946, June 6

Cameroun.................................. C9-C14
Fr. Equatorial Africa C25-C30
Fr. Guiana C12-C17
Fr. India C8-C13
Fr. Polynesia.......................... C11-C16
Fr. West Africa C5-C10
Guadeloupe............................. C4-C9
Indo-China.............................. C20-C25
Madagascar............................ C45-C50
Martinique............................... C4-C9
New Caledonia....................... C15-C20
Reunion C26-C31
St. Pierre & Miquelon.............. C9-C14
Somali Coast.......................... C9-C14
Wallis & Futuna Isls. C2-C7

Nos. C9-C14 (6)   12.05   9.70
Nos. C25-C30 (6)   14.70   10.80
Nos. C12-C17 (6)   12.65   10.35
Nos. C8-C13 (6)   12.80   15.00
Nos. C11-C16 (6)   17.55   13.40
Nos. C5-C10 (6)   16.05   11.95
Nos. C4-C9 (6)   12.00   9.60
Nos. C20-C25 (6)   6.40   6.40
Nos. C45-C50 (6)   10.30   8.40
Nos. C4-C9 (6)   8.85   7.30
Nos. C15-C20 (6)   13.40   11.90
Nos. C26-C31 (6)   10.25   6.55
Nos. C9-C14 (6)   17.30   14.35

Nos. C9-C14 (6)   18.10   12.65
Nos. C2-C7 (6)   13.75   10.45
Set total (90) Stamps   196.15   158.80

UPU

French Colonials, Globe and
Plane — CD99

Universal Postal Union, 75th anniv.

1949, July 4

Cameroun..................................... C29
Fr. Equatorial Africa C34
Fr. India C17
Fr. Polynesia................................ C20
Fr. West Africa C15
Indo-China................................... C26
Madagascar................................. C55
New Caledonia............................. C24
St. Pierre & Miquelon................... C18
Somali Coast................................ C18
Togo.. C18
Wallis & Futuna Isls. C10

No. C29 (1)   8.00   4.75
No. C34 (1)   16.00   12.00
No. C17 (1)   11.50   8.75
No. C20 (1)   20.00   15.00
No. C15 (1)   12.00   8.75
No. C26 (1)   4.75   4.00
No. C55 (1)   4.00   2.75
No. C24 (1)   8.25   5.25
No. C18 (1)   20.00   12.00
No. C18 (1)   14.00   10.50
No. C18 (1)   8.50   7.00
No. C10 (1)   12.50   8.25
Set total (12) Stamps   139.50   99.00

Tropical Medicine

Doctor
Treating
Infant
CD100

The surtax was for charitable work.

1950

Cameroun...................................... B29
Fr. Equatorial Africa B39
Fr. India B15
Fr. Polynesia................................. B14
Fr. West Africa B3
Madagascar................................... B17
New Caledonia............................... B14
St. Pierre & Miquelon..................... B14
Somali Coast................................. B14
Togo.. B11

No. B29 (1)   7.25   5.50
No. B39 (1)   7.25   5.50
No. B15 (1)   6.00   4.00
No. B14 (1)   10.50   8.00
No. B3 (1)   9.50   7.25
No. B17 (1)   5.50   5.50
No. B14 (1)   6.75   5.25
No. B14 (1)   17.00   13.00
No. B14 (1)   7.75   6.25
No. B11 (1)   5.00   3.50
Set total (10) Stamps   82.50   63.75

Military Medal

Medal, Early Marine
and Colonial
Soldier — CD101

Centenary of the creation of the French Military Medal.

1952

Cameroun.....................................322
Comoro Isls..................................39
Fr. Equatorial Africa 186

Fr. India		233
Fr. Polynesia		179
Fr. West Africa		57
Madagascar		286
New Caledonia		295
St. Pierre & Miquelon		345
Somali Coast		267
Togo		327
Wallis & Futuna Isls.		149

No. 322 (1)	7.25	3.25
No. 39 (1)	50.00	40.00
No. 186 (1)	8.00	5.50
No. 233 (1)	5.50	7.00
No. 179 (1)	13.50	10.00
No. 57 (1)	8.75	6.50
No. 286 (1)	3.75	2.50
No. 295 (1)	7.50	6.00
No. 345 (1)	17.00	13.00
No. 267 (1)	9.00	8.00
No. 327 (1)	5.50	4.75
No. 149 (1)	9.50	7.00
Set total (12) Stamps	145.25	113.50

Liberation

Allied Landing, Victory Sign and Cross of Lorraine — CD102

Liberation of France, 10th anniv.

1954, June 6

Cameroun		C32
Comoro Isls.		C4
Fr. Equatorial Africa		C38
Fr. India		C18
Fr. Polynesia		C22
Fr. West Africa		C17
Madagascar		C57
New Caledonia		C25
St. Pierre & Miquelon		C19
Somali Coast		C19
Togo		C19
Wallis & Futuna Isls.		C11

No. C32 (1)	7.25	4.75
No. C4 (1)	35.00	20.00
No. C38 (1)	12.00	8.00
No. C18 (1)	11.00	8.00
No. C22 (1)	10.00	8.00
No. C17 (1)	12.00	5.50
No. C57 (1)	3.25	2.00
No. C25 (1)	8.25	5.00
No. C19 (1)	18.00	12.00
No. C19 (1)	10.50	8.50
No. C19 (1)	7.00	5.50
No. C11 (1)	12.50	8.25
Set total (12) Stamps	146.75	95.50

FIDES

Plowmen
CD103

Efforts of FIDES, the Economic and Social Development Fund for Overseas Possessions (Fonds d' Investissement pour le Developpement Economique et Social). Each stamp has a different design.

1956

Cameroun		326-329
Comoro Isls.		43
Fr. Equatorial Africa		189-192
Fr. Polynesia		181
Fr. West Africa		65-72
Madagascar		292-295
New Caledonia		303
St. Pierre & Miquelon		350
Somali Coast		268-269
Togo		331

Nos. 326-329 (4)	6.90	3.20
No. 43 (1)	2.25	1.60
Nos. 189-192 (4)	3.20	1.65
No. 181 (1)	4.00	2.00
Nos. 65-72 (8)	16.00	6.35
Nos. 292-295 (4)	2.25	1.20
No. 303 (1)	1.90	1.10
No. 350 (1)	6.50	3.50

Nos. 268-269 (2)	5.35	3.15
No. 331 (1)	4.25	2.10
Set total (27) Stamps	52.60	25.85

Flower

CD104

Each stamp shows a different flower.

1958-9

Cameroun		333
Comoro Isls.		45
Fr. Equatorial Africa		200-201
Fr. Polynesia		192
Fr. So. & Antarctic Terr.		11
Fr. West Africa		79-83
Madagascar		301-302
New Caledonia		304-305
St. Pierre & Miquelon		357
Somali Coast		270
Togo		348-349
Wallis & Futuna Isls.		152

No. 333 (1)	1.60	.80
No. 45 (1)	5.50	4.50
Nos. 200-201 (2)	3.60	1.60
No. 192 (1)	6.50	4.00
No. 11 (1)	10.00	8.00
Nos. 79-83 (5)	10.45	5.60
Nos. 301-302 (2)	1.60	.60
Nos. 304-305 (2)	9.25	3.00
No. 357 (1)	4.50	2.40
No. 270 (1)	4.25	1.40
Nos. 348-349 (2)	1.10	.50
No. 152 (1)	4.50	2.50
Set total (20) Stamps	62.85	34.90

Human Rights

Sun, Dove and U.N. Emblem CD105

10th anniversary of the signing of the Universal Declaration of Human Rights.

1958

Comoro Isls.		44
Fr. Equatorial Africa		202
Fr. Polynesia		191
Fr. West Africa		85
Madagascar		300
New Caledonia		306
St. Pierre & Miquelon		356
Somali Coast		274
Wallis & Futuna Isls.		153

No. 44 (1)	11.00	11.00
No. 202 (1)	2.40	1.25
No. 191 (1)	13.00	8.75
No. 85 (1)	2.40	2.00
No. 300 (1)	.80	.40
No. 306 (1)	3.00	1.50
No. 356 (1)	3.50	2.50
No. 274 (1)	3.50	2.10
No. 153 (1)	5.75	4.00
Set total (9) Stamps	45.35	33.50

C.C.T.A.

CD106

Commission for Technical Cooperation in Africa south of the Sahara, 10th anniv.

1960

Cameroun		339
Cent. Africa		3
Chad		66
Congo, P.R.		90
Dahomey		138
Gabon		150
Ivory Coast		180
Madagascar		317

Mali		9
Mauritania		117
Niger		104
Upper Volta		89

No. 339 (1)	1.60	.75
No. 3 (1)	1.90	.65
No. 66 (1)	1.90	.50
No. 90 (1)	1.00	1.00
No. 138 (1)	.50	.25
No. 150 (1)	1.40	1.10
No. 180 (1)	1.10	.50
No. 317 (1)	.60	.30
No. 9 (1)	1.40	.50
No. 117 (1)	.75	.40
No. 104 (1)	.85	.45
No. 89 (1)	.45	.40
Set total (12) Stamps	13.45	6.80

Air Afrique, 1961

Modern and Ancient Africa, Map and Planes — CD107

Founding of Air Afrique (African Airlines).

1961-62

Cameroun		C37
Cent. Africa		C5
Chad		C7
Congo, P.R.		C5
Dahomey		C17
Gabon		C5
Ivory Coast		C18
Mauritania		C17
Niger		C22
Senegal		C31
Upper Volta		C4

No. C37 (1)	1.00	.50
No. C5 (1)	1.00	.55
No. C7 (1)	1.00	.25
No. C5 (1)	1.75	.90
No. C17 (1)	.80	.40
No. C5 (1)	11.00	6.00
No. C18 (1)	2.00	1.25
No. C17 (1)	2.50	1.25
No. C22 (1)	1.75	.90
No. C31 (1)	.80	.30
No. C4 (1)	.65	.45
Set total (11) Stamps	24.25	12.75

Anti-Malaria

CD108

World Health Organization drive to eradicate malaria.

1962, Apr. 7

Cameroun		B36
Cent. Africa		B1
Chad		B1
Comoro Isls.		B1
Congo, P.R.		B3
Dahomey		B15
Gabon		B4
Ivory Coast		B15
Madagascar		B19
Mali		B1
Mauritania		B16
Niger		B14
Senegal		B16
Somali Coast		B15
Upper Volta		B1

No. B36 (1)	1.00	.45
No. B1 (1)	1.40	1.40
No. B1 (1)	1.25	.50
No. B1 (1)	4.00	4.00
No. B3 (1)	1.40	1.00
No. B15 (1)	.75	.75
No. B4 (1)	1.00	1.00
No. B15 (1)	1.25	1.25
No. B19 (1)	.75	.50
No. B1 (1)	1.25	.60
No. B16 (1)	.80	.80
No. B14 (1)	.60	.60

No. B16 (1)	1.10	.65
No. B15 (1)	7.00	7.00
No. B1 (1)	.95	.95
Set total (15) Stamps	24.50	21.45

Abidjan Games

CD109

Abidjan Games, Ivory Coast, Dec. 24-31, 1961. Each stamp shows a different sport.

1962

Cent. Africa		19-20, C6
Chad		83-84, C8
Congo, P.R.		103-104, C7
Gabon		163-164, C6
Niger		109-111
Upper Volta		103-105

Nos. 19-20,C6 (3)	3.90	2.60
Nos. 83-84,C8 (3)	6.30	1.55
Nos. 103-104,C7 (3)	3.85	1.80
Nos. 163-164,C6 (3)	5.00	3.00
Nos. 109-111 (3)	2.60	1.10
Nos. 103-105 (3)	3.15	1.80
Set total (18) Stamps	24.80	11.85

African and Malagasy Union

Flag of Union CD110

First anniversary of the Union.

1962, Sept. 8

Cameroun		373
Cent. Africa		21
Chad		85
Congo, P.R.		105
Dahomey		155
Gabon		165
Ivory Coast		198
Madagascar		332
Mauritania		170
Niger		112
Senegal		211
Upper Volta		106

No. 373 (1)	2.00	.75
No. 21 (1)	1.25	.60
No. 85 (1)	1.25	.25
No. 105 (1)	1.50	.50
No. 155 (1)	1.25	.90
No. 165 (1)	1.60	1.25
No. 198 (1)	2.10	.75
No. 332 (1)	.80	.80
No. 170 (1)	.75	.50
No. 112 (1)	.80	.40
No. 211 (1)	.80	.50
No. 106 (1)	1.50	.90
Set total (12) Stamps	15.60	8.10

Telstar

Telstar and Globe Showing Andover and Pleumeur-Bodou — CD111

First television connection of the United States and Europe through the Telstar satellite, July 11-12, 1962.

1962-63

Andorra, French		154
Comoro Isls.		C7
Fr. Polynesia		C29
Fr. So. & Antarctic Terr.		C5
New Caledonia		C33
St. Pierre & Miquelon		C26
Somali Coast		C31
Wallis & Futuna Isls.		C17

No. 154 (1)	2.00	1.60
No. C7 (1)	5.00	3.00
No. C29 (1)	11.50	8.00

No. C5 (1)	29.00	21.00
No. C33 (1)	30.00	18.50
No. C26 (1)	7.25	5.50
No. C31 (1)	1.00	1.00
No. C17 (1)	3.50	3.50
Set total (8) Stamps	89.25	62.10

Freedom From Hunger

World Map and Wheat Emblem CD112

U.N. Food and Agriculture Organization's "Freedom from Hunger" campaign.

1963, Mar. 21

Cameroon	B37-B38
Cent. Africa	B2
Chad	B2
Congo, P.R.	B4
Dahomey	B16
Gabon	B5
Ivory Coast	B16
Madagascar	B21
Mauritania	B17
Niger	B15
Senegal	B17
Upper Volta	B2

Nos. B37-B38 (2)	2.25	.75
No. B2 (1)	1.25	1.25
No. B2 (1)	2.00	.50
No. B4 (1)	1.40	1.00
No. B16 (1)	.80	.80
No. B5 (1)	1.00	1.00
No. B16 (1)	1.50	1.50
No. B21 (1)	.60	.45
No. B17 (1)	.80	.80
No. B15 (1)	.60	.60
No. B17 (1)	.80	.50
No. B2 (1)	.95	.95
Set total (13) Stamps	13.95	10.10

Red Cross Centenary

CD113

Centenary of the International Red Cross.

1963, Sept. 2

Comoro Isls.	55
Fr. Polynesia	205
New Caledonia	328
St. Pierre & Miquelon	367
Somali Coast	297
Wallis & Futuna Isls.	165

No. 55 (1)	9.50	7.00
No. 205 (1)	15.00	12.00
No. 328 (1)	9.00	6.75
No. 367 (1)	12.00	6.75
No. 297 (1)	6.25	6.25
No. 165 (1)	4.00	3.50
Set total (6) Stamps	55.75	42.25

African Postal Union, 1963

UAMPT Emblem, Radio Masts, Plane and Mail CD114

Establishment of the African and Malagasy Posts and Telecommunications Union.

1963, Sept. 8

Cameroun	C47
Cent. Africa	C10
Chad	C9
Congo, P.R.	C13

Dahomey	C19
Gabon	C13
Ivory Coast	C25
Madagascar	C75
Mauritania	C22
Niger	C27
Rwanda	36
Senegal	C32
Upper Volta	C9

No. C47 (1)	2.25	1.00
No. C10 (1)	1.90	.85
No. C9 (1)	2.40	.60
No. C13 (1)	1.40	.75
No. C19 (1)	.75	.25
No. C13 (1)	1.90	.80
No. C25 (1)	2.50	1.50
No. C75 (1)	1.25	.80
No. C22 (1)	1.50	.60
No. C27 (1)	1.25	.60
No. 36 (1)	.90	.55
No. C32 (1)	1.75	.50
No. C9 (1)	1.50	.75
Set total (13) Stamps	21.25	9.55

Air Afrique, 1963

Symbols of Flight — CD115

First anniversary of Air Afrique and inauguration of DC-8 service.

1963, Nov. 19

Cameroun	C48
Chad	C10
Congo, P.R.	C14
Gabon	C18
Ivory Coast	C26
Mauritania	C26
Niger	C35
Senegal	C33

No. C48 (1)	1.25	.40
No. C10 (1)	2.40	.60
No. C14 (1)	1.60	.60
No. C18 (1)	1.40	.65
No. C26 (1)	1.00	.50
No. C26 (1)	.70	.25
No. C35 (1)	.90	.50
No. C33 (1)	2.00	.65
Set total (8) Stamps	11.25	4.15

Europafrica

Europe and Africa Linked — CD116

Signing of an economic agreement between the European Economic Community and the African and Malagasy Union, Yaounde, Cameroun, July 20, 1963.

1963-64

Cameroun	402
Cent. Africa	C12
Chad	C11
Congo, P.R.	C16
Gabon	C19
Ivory Coast	217
Niger	C43
Upper Volta	C11

No. 402 (1)	2.25	.60
No. C12 (1)	2.50	1.75
No. C11 (1)	2.00	.50
No. C16 (1)	1.60	1.00
No. C19 (1)	1.40	.75
No. 217 (1)	1.10	.35
No. C43 (1)	.85	.50
No. C11 (1)	1.50	.80
Set total (8) Stamps	13.20	6.25

Human Rights

Scales of Justice and Globe CD117

15th anniversary of the Universal Declaration of Human Rights.

1963, Dec. 10

Comoro Isls.	56
Fr. Polynesia	206
New Caledonia	329
St. Pierre & Miquelon	368
Somali Coast	300
Wallis & Futuna Isls.	166

No. 56 (1)	9.50	7.50
No. 205 (1)	15.00	12.00
No. 329 (1)	8.00	6.00
No. 368 (1)	6.50	3.50
No. 300 (1)	8.50	8.50
No. 166 (1)	8.00	7.50
Set total (6) Stamps	55.50	45.00

PHILATEC

Stamp Album, Champs Elysees Palace and Horses of Marly CD118

Intl. Philatelic and Postal Techniques Exhibition, Paris, June 5-21, 1964.

1963-64

Comoro Isls.	60
France	1078
Fr. Polynesia	207
New Caledonia	341
St. Pierre & Miquelon	369
Somali Coast	301
Wallis & Futuna Isls.	167

No. 60 (1)	4.50	4.00
No. 1078 (1)	.25	.25
No. 206 (1)	15.00	10.00
No. 341 (1)	8.50	6.75
No. 369 (1)	11.00	8.00
No. 301 (1)	7.75	7.75
No. 167 (1)	3.50	3.50
Set total (7) Stamps	50.50	40.25

Cooperation

CD119

Cooperation between France and the French-speaking countries of Africa and Madagascar.

1964

Cameroun	409-410
Cent. Africa	39
Chad	103
Congo, P.R.	121
Dahomey	193
France	1111
Gabon	175
Ivory Coast	221
Madagascar	360
Mauritania	181
Niger	143
Senegal	236
Togo	495

Nos. 409-410 (2)	2.50	.50
No. 39 (1)	1.00	.55
No. 103 (1)	1.00	.25
No. 121 (1)	.80	.35
No. 193 (1)	.80	.35
No. 1111 (1)	.25	.25
No. 175 (1)	.90	.60
No. 221 (1)	1.10	.35

No. 360 (1)	.60	.25
No. 181 (1)	.60	.35
No. 143 (1)	.80	.40
No. 236 (1)	1.60	.85
No. 495 (1)	.70	.25
Set total (14) Stamps	12.65	5.30

ITU

Telegraph, Syncom Satellite and ITU Emblem CD120

Intl. Telecommunication Union, Cent.

1965, May 17

Comoro Isls.	C14
Fr. Polynesia	C33
Fr. So. & Antarctic Terr.	C8
New Caledonia	C40
New Hebrides	124-125
St. Pierre & Miquelon	C29
Somali Coast	C36
Wallis & Futuna Isls.	C20

No. C14 (1)	20.00	10.00
No. C33 (1)	80.00	52.50
No. C8 (1)	200.00	160.00
No. C40 (1)	12.00	9.00
Nos. 124-125 (2)	40.50	34.00
No. C29 (1)	24.00	11.00
No. C36 (1)	15.00	9.00
No. C20 (1)	21.00	15.00
Set total (9) Stamps	412.50	300.50

French Satellite A-1

Diamant Rocket and Launching Installation — CD121

Launching of France's first satellite, Nov. 26, 1965.

1965-66

Comoro Isls.	C16a
France	1138a
Reunion	359a
Fr. Polynesia	C41a
Fr. So. & Antarctic Terr.	C10a
New Caledonia	C45a
St. Pierre & Miquelon	C31a
Somali Coast	C40a
Wallis & Futuna Isls.	C23a

No. C16a (1)	11.00	11.00
No. 1138a (1)	.65	.65
No. 359a (1)	3.50	3.00
No. C41a (1)	14.00	14.00
No. C10a (1)	29.00	24.00
No. C45a (1)	8.25	7.00
No. C31a (1)	15.00	15.00
No. C40a (1)	7.00	7.00
No. C23a (1)	9.25	9.25
Set total (9) Stamps	97.65	90.90

French Satellite D-1

D-1 Satellite in Orbit — CD122

Launching of the D-1 satellite at Hammaguir, Algeria, Feb. 17, 1966.

1966

Comoro Isls.	C17
France	1148

Fr. Polynesia...C42
Fr. So. & Antarctic Terr. C11
New Caledonia.................................C46
St. Pierre & Miquelon......................C32
Somali Coast....................................C49
Wallis & Futuna Isls. C24

No. C17 (1)	4.00	4.00
No. 1148 (1)	.25	.25
No. C42 (1)	7.00	4.75
No. C11 (1)	57.50	40.00
No. C46 (1)	3.00	2.00
No. C32 (1)	10.50	6.50
No. C49 (1)	4.25	2.75
No. C24 (1)	3.50	3.50
Set total (8) Stamps	90.00	63.75

Air Afrique, 1966

Planes and Air Afrique Emblem — CD123

Introduction of DC-8F planes by Air Afrique.

1966

Cameroun...C79
Cent. Africa C35
Chad...C26
Congo, P.R..C42
Dahomey C42
Gabon...C47
Ivory Coast C32
Mauritania...C57
Niger...C63
Senegal C47
Togo..C54
Upper Volta..C31

No. C79 (1)	.80	.25
No. C35 (1)	1.00	.40
No. C26 (1)	1.00	.25
No. C42 (1)	1.00	.25
No. C42 (1)	.75	.25
No. C47 (1)	.90	.35
No. C32 (1)	1.00	.60
No. C57 (1)	.80	.30
No. C63 (1)	.65	.35
No. C47 (1)	.80	.30
No. C54 (1)	.80	.25
No. C31 (1)	.75	.50
Set total (12) Stamps	10.25	4.05

African Postal Union, 1967

Telecommunications Symbols and Map of Africa — CD124

Fifth anniversary of the establishment of the African and Malagasy Union of Posts and Telecommunications, UAMPT.

1967

Cameroun...C90
Cent. Africa C46
Chad...C37
Congo, P.R..C57
Dahomey C61
Gabon...C58
Ivory Coast C34
Madagascar.......................................C85
Mauritania...C65
Niger...C75
Rwanda C1-C3
Senegal C60
Togo..C81
Upper Volta..C50

No. C90 (1)	2.40	.65
No. C46 (1)	2.25	.85
No. C37 (1)	2.00	.60
No. C57 (1)	1.60	.60
No. C61 (1)	1.75	.95
No. C58 (1)	2.25	.95
No. C34 (1)	3.50	1.50
No. C85 (1)	1.25	.60
No. C65 (1)	1.25	.60
No. C75 (1)	1.40	.60

Nos. C1-C3 (3)	2.30	1.25
No. C60 (1)	1.75	.50
No. C81 (1)	1.90	.30
No. C50 (1)	1.80	.70
Set total (16) Stamps	27.40	10.65

Monetary Union

Gold Token of the Ashantis, 17-18th Centuries — CD125

West African Monetary Union, 5th anniv.

1967, Nov. 4

Dahomey 244
Ivory Coast 259
Mauritania...238
Niger...204
Senegal 294
Togo..623
Upper Volta..181

No. 244 (1)	.65	.65
No. 259 (1)	.85	.40
No. 238 (1)	.45	.25
No. 204 (1)	.45	.25
No. 294 (1)	.60	.25
No. 623 (1)	.60	.25
No. 181 (1)	.70	.35
Set total (7) Stamps	4.30	2.40

WHO Anniversary

Sun, Flowers and WHO Emblem CD126

World Health Organization, 20th anniv.

1968, May 4

Afars & Issas.....................................317
Comoro Isls. 73
Fr. Polynesia.............................241-242
Fr. So. & Antarctic Terr. 31
New Caledonia.................................367
St. Pierre & Miquelon......................377
Wallis & Futuna Isls. 169

No. 317 (1)	3.00	3.00
No. 73 (1)	2.75	2.00
Nos. 241-242 (2)	22.00	12.75
No. 31 (1)	65.00	45.00
No. 367 (1)	4.50	2.25
No. 377 (1)	12.00	8.00
No. 169 (1)	6.50	4.50
Set total (8) Stamps	115.75	77.50

Human Rights Year

Human Rights Flame — CD127

1968, Aug. 10

Afars & Issas.............................322-323
Comoro Isls. 76
Fr. Polynesia.............................243-244
Fr. So. & Antarctic Terr. 32
New Caledonia.................................369
St. Pierre & Miquelon......................382
Wallis & Futuna Isls. 170

Nos. 322-323 (2)	6.50	3.70
No. 76 (1)	3.50	3.50
Nos. 243-244 (2)	24.00	14.00
No. 32 (1)	60.00	45.00
No. 369 (1)	3.00	1.50
No. 382 (1)	10.00	5.50
No. 170 (1)	3.75	3.75
Set total (9) Stamps	110.75	76.95

2nd PHILEXAFRIQUE

CD128

Opening of PHILEXAFRIQUE, Abidjan, Feb. 14. Each stamp shows a local scene and stamp.

1969, Feb. 14

Cameroun...C118
Cent. Africa C65
Chad...C48
Congo, P.R..C77
Dahomey C94
Gabon...C82
Ivory Coast C38-C40
Madagascar.......................................C92
Mali...C65
Mauritania...C80
Niger...C104
Senegal C68
Togo..C104
Upper Volta..C62

No. C118 (1)	3.25	1.25
No. C65 (1)	1.90	1.90
No. C48 (1)	2.40	1.00
No. C77 (1)	2.00	1.75
No. C94 (1)	2.25	2.25
No. C82 (1)	2.25	2.25
Nos. C38-C40 (3)	14.50	14.50
No. C92 (1)	1.75	.85
No. C65 (1)	2.00	1.00
No. C80 (1)	1.90	.75
No. C104 (1)	2.75	1.90
No. C68 (1)	2.00	1.40
No. C104 (1)	2.25	.45
No. C62 (1)	4.00	3.75
Set total (16) Stamps	45.20	35.00

Concorde

Concorde in Flight CD129

First flight of the prototype Concorde supersonic plane at Toulouse, Mar. 1, 1969.

1969

Afars & Issas.....................................C56
Comoro Isls. C29
France..C42
Fr. Polynesia....................................C50
Fr. So. & Antarctic Terr. C18
New Caledonia.................................C63
St. Pierre & Miquelon......................C40
Wallis & Futuna Isls. C30

No. C56 (1)	25.00	16.00
No. C29 (1)	24.00	16.00
No. C42 (1)	.75	.35
No. C50 (1)	55.00	35.00
No. C18 (1)	55.00	37.50
No. C63 (1)	35.00	20.00
No. C40 (1)	32.50	12.00
No. C30 (1)	15.00	10.00
Set total (8) Stamps	242.25	146.85

Development Bank

Bank Emblem — CD130

African Development Bank, fifth anniv.

1969

Cameroun...499
Chad...217
Congo, P.R..181-182

Ivory Coast 281
Mali...127-128
Mauritania...267
Niger...220
Senegal 317-318
Upper Volta..201

No. 499 (1)	.80	.25
No. 217 (1)	.70	.25
Nos. 181-182 (2)	.80	.50
No. 281 (1)	.70	.40
Nos. 127-128 (2)	1.25	.50
No. 267 (1)	.60	.25
No. 220 (1)	.60	.30
Nos. 317-318 (2)	1.55	.50
No. 201 (1)	.70	.30
Set total (12) Stamps	7.70	3.25

ILO

ILO Headquarters, Geneva, and Emblem — CD131

Intl. Labor Organization, 50th anniv.

1969-70

Afars & Issas.....................................337
Comoro Isls. 83
Fr. Polynesia.............................251-252
Fr. So. & Antarctic Terr. 35
New Caledonia.................................379
St. Pierre & Miquelon......................396
Wallis & Futuna Isls. 172

No. 337 (1)	2.75	2.00
No. 83 (1)	1.25	.75
Nos. 251-252 (2)	24.00	12.50
No. 35 (1)	18.50	11.00
No. 379 (1)	2.25	1.10
No. 396 (1)	10.00	5.50
No. 172 (1)	3.00	2.90
Set total (8) Stamps	61.75	35.75

ASECNA

Map of Africa, Plane and Airport CD132

10th anniversary of the Agency for the Security of Aerial Navigation in Africa and Madagascar (ASECNA, Agence pour la Securite de la Navigation Aerienne en Afrique et a Madagascar).

1969-70

Cameroun...500
Cent. Africa 119
Chad...222
Congo, P.R..197
Dahomey 269
Gabon...260
Ivory Coast 287
Mali...130
Niger...221
Senegal 321
Upper Volta..204

No. 500 (1)	2.00	.60
No. 119 (1)	2.25	.80
No. 222 (1)	1.00	.25
No. 197 (1)	2.00	.40
No. 269 (1)	.90	.55
No. 260 (1)	1.75	.75
No. 287 (1)	.90	.40
No. 130 (1)	1.00	.40
No. 221 (1)	1.25	.70
No. 321 (1)	1.60	.50
No. 204 (1)	1.75	1.00
Set total (11) Stamps	16.40	6.35

U.P.U. Headquarters

CD133

New Universal Postal Union headquarters, Bern, Switzerland.

1970

Afars & Issas		342
Algeria		443
Cameroun		503-504
Cent. Africa		125
Chad		225
Comoro Isls.		84
Congo, P.R.		216
Fr. Polynesia		261-262
Fr. So. & Antarctic Terr.		36
Gabon		258
Ivory Coast		295
Madagascar		444
Mali		134-135
Mauritania		283
New Caledonia		382
Niger		231-232
St. Pierre & Miquelon		397-398
Senegal		328-329
Tunisia		535
Wallis & Futuna Isls.		173

No. 342 (1)	2.50	1.40
No. 443 (1)	1.10	.40
Nos. 503-504 (2)	2.60	.55
No. 125 (1)	1.90	.70
No. 225 (1)	1.00	.25
No. 84 (1)	5.50	2.00
No. 216 (1)	.80	.25
Nos. 261-262 (2)	20.00	10.00
No. 36 (1)	45.00	29.00
No. 258 (1)	.90	.55
No. 295 (1)	1.10	.50
No. 444 (1)	.55	.25
Nos. 134-135 (2)	1.25	.50
No. 283 (1)	.60	.30
No. 382 (1)	3.00	1.50
Nos. 231-232 (2)	1.20	.60
Nos. 397-398 (2)	34.00	17.50
Nos. 328-329 (2)	1.55	.55
No. 535 (1)	.60	.25
No. 173 (1)	4.00	4.00
Set total (26) Stamps	129.15	71.05

De Gaulle

CD134

First anniversay of the death of Charles de Gaulle, (1890-1970), President of France.

1971-72

Afars & Issas		356-357
Comoro Isls.		104-105
France		1325a
Fr. Polynesia		270-271
Fr. So. & Antarctic Terr.		52-53
New Caledonia		393-394
Reunion		380a
St. Pierre & Miquelon		417-418
Wallis & Futuna Isls.		177-178

Nos. 356-357 (2)	14.50	9.50
Nos. 104-105 (2)	9.00	5.75
No. 1325a (1)	3.00	2.50
Nos. 270-271 (2)	51.50	29.50
Nos. 52-53 (2)	47.00	33.50
Nos. 393-394 (2)	25.00	11.75
No. 380a (1)	9.25	8.00
Nos. 417-418 (2)	57.50	30.00
Nos. 177-178 (2)	24.00	16.25
Set total (16) Stamps	240.75	146.75

African Postal Union, 1971

UAMPT Building, Brazzaville,
Congo — CD135

10th anniversary of the establishment of the African and Malagasy Posts and Telecommunications Union, UAMPT. Each stamp has a different native design.

1971, Nov. 13

Cameroun		C177
Cent. Africa		C89
Chad		C94
Congo, P.R.		C136
Dahomey		C146
Gabon		C120
Ivory Coast		C47
Mauritania		C113
Niger		C164
Rwanda		C8
Senegal		C105
Togo		C166
Upper Volta		C97

No. C177 (1)	2.00	.50
No. C89 (1)	2.25	.85
No. C94 (1)	1.50	.50
No. C136 (1)	1.60	.75
No. C146 (1)	1.75	.80
No. C120 (1)	1.75	.70
No. C47 (1)	2.00	1.00
No. C113 (1)	1.20	.65
No. C164 (1)	1.25	.60
No. C8 (1)	2.75	2.25
No. C105 (1)	1.60	.50
No. C166 (1)	1.25	.40
No. C97 (1)	1.50	.70
Set total (13) Stamps	22.40	10.20

West African Monetary Union

African Couple, City, Village and
Commemorative Coin — CD136

West African Monetary Union, 10th anniv.

1972, Nov. 2

Dahomey		300
Ivory Coast		331
Mauritania		299
Niger		258
Senegal		374
Togo		825
Upper Volta		280

No. 300 (1)	.65	.25
No. 331 (1)	1.00	.50
No. 299 (1)	.75	.25
No. 258 (1)	.55	.30
No. 374 (1)	.50	.30
No. 825 (1)	.60	.25
No. 280 (1)	.60	.25
Set total (7) Stamps	4.65	2.10

African Postal Union, 1973

Telecommunications Symbols and Map
of Africa — CD137

11th anniversary of the African and Malagasy Posts and Telecommunications Union (UAMPT).

1973, Sept. 12

Cameroun		574
Cent. Africa		194
Chad		294
Congo, P.R.		289
Dahomey		311
Gabon		320
Ivory Coast		361
Madagascar		500
Mauritania		304
Niger		287
Rwanda		540
Senegal		393
Togo		849
Upper Volta		297

No. 574 (1)	1.75	.40
No. 194 (1)	1.25	.75
No. 294 (1)	1.75	.40
No. 289 (1)	1.60	.50
No. 311 (1)	1.25	.55
No. 320 (1)	1.40	.75
No. 361 (1)	2.50	1.00
No. 500 (1)	1.10	.35
No. 304 (1)	1.10	.40
No. 287 (1)	.90	.60
No. 540 (1)	3.75	2.00
No. 393 (1)	1.60	.50

No. 849 (1)	1.00	.35
No. 297 (1)	1.25	.70
Set total (14) Stamps	22.20	9.25

Philexafrique II — Essen

CD138

CD139

Designs: Indigenous fauna, local and German stamps. Types CD138-CD139 printed horizontally and vertically se-tenant in sheets of 10 (2x5). Label between horizontal pairs alternately commemorates Philexafrique II, Libreville, Gabon, June 1978, and 2nd International Stamp Fair, Essen, Germany, Nov. 1-5.

1978-1979

Benin		C286a
Central Africa		C201a
Chad		C239a
Congo Republic		C246a
Djibouti		C122a
Gabon		C216a
Ivory Coast		C65a
Mali		C357a
Mauritania		C186a
Niger		C292a
Rwanda		C13a
Senegal		C147a
Togo		C364a

No. C286a (1)	9.00	8.50
No. C201a (1)	7.50	7.50
No. C239a (1)	8.00	4.00
No. C246a (1)	7.00	7.00
No. C122a (1)	8.50	8.50
No. C216a (1)	6.50	4.00
No. C65a (1)	9.00	4.00
No. C357a (1)	7.50	3.00
No. C186a (1)	4.50	4.00
No. C292a (1)	6.00	5.00
No. C13a (1)	4.00	4.00
No. C147a (1)	10.00	4.00
No. C364a (1)	3.00	1.50
Set total (13) Stamps	90.50	70.00

BRITISH COMMONWEALTH OF NATIONS

The listings follow established trade practices when these issues are offered as units by dealers. The Peace issue, for example, includes only one stamp from the Indian state of Hyderabad. The U.P.U. issue includes the Egypt set. Pairs are included for those varieties issued with bilingual designs se-tenant.

Silver Jubilee

Windsor Castle and King George V
CD301

Reign of King George V, 25th anniv.

1935

Antigua		77-80
Ascension		33-36
Bahamas		92-95
Barbados		186-189
Basutoland		11-14

Bechuanaland Protectorate		117-120
Bermuda		100-103
British Guiana		223-226
British Honduras		108-111
Cayman Islands		81-84
Ceylon		260-263
Cyprus		136-139
Dominica		90-93
Falkland Islands		77-80
Fiji		110-113
Gambia		125-128
Gibraltar		100-103
Gilbert & Ellice Islands		33-36
Gold Coast		108-111
Grenada		124-127
Hong Kong		147-150
Jamaica		109-112
Kenya, Uganda, Tanzania		42-45
Leeward Islands		96-99
Malta		184-187
Mauritius		204-207
Montserrat		85-88
Newfoundland		226-229
Nigeria		34-37
Northern Rhodesia		18-21
Nyasaland Protectorate		47-50
St. Helena		111-114
St. Kitts-Nevis		72-75
St. Lucia		91-94
St. Vincent		134-137
Seychelles		118-121
Sierra Leone		166-169
Solomon Islands		60-63
Somaliland Protectorate		77-80
Straits Settlements		213-216
Swaziland		20-23
Trinidad & Tobago		43-46
Turks & Caicos Islands		71-74
Virgin Islands		69-72

The following have different designs but are included in the omnibus set:

Great Britain		226-229
Offices in Morocco (Sp. Curr.)		67-70
Offices in Morocco (Br. Curr.)		226-229
Offices in Morocco (Fr. Curr.)		422-425
Offices in Morocco (Tangier)		508-510
Australia		152-154
Canada		211-216
Cook Islands		98-100
India		142-148
Nauru		31-34
New Guinea		46-47
New Zealand		199-201
Niue		67-69
Papua		114-117
Samoa		163-165
South Africa		68-71
Southern Rhodesia		33-36
South-West Africa		121-124

Nos. 77-80 (4)	20.25	20.50
Nos. 33-36 (4)	58.50	120.00
Nos. 92-95 (4)	25.00	43.00
Nos. 186-189 (4)	30.15	49.30
Nos. 11-14 (4)	12.10	23.00
Nos. 117-120 (4)	17.00	31.25
Nos. 100-103 (4)	18.00	58.25
Nos. 223-226 (4)	18.35	35.50
Nos. 108-111 (4)	15.25	15.35
Nos. 81-84 (4)	19.95	19.50
Nos. 260-263 (4)	10.15	19.10
Nos. 136-139 (4)	39.75	34.40
Nos. 90-93 (4)	18.85	19.85
Nos. 77-80 (4)	51.00	15.75
Nos. 110-113 (4)	15.25	29.00
Nos. 125-128 (4)	12.20	25.25
Nos. 100-103 (4)	28.75	42.75
Nos. 33-36 (4)	31.50	50.00
Nos. 108-111 (4)	26.25	62.85
Nos. 124-127 (4)	16.70	40.60
Nos. 147-150 (4)	59.00	18.75
Nos. 109-112 (4)	19.70	39.00
Nos. 42-45 (4)	8.75	11.00
Nos. 96-99 (4)	35.75	49.60
Nos. 184-187 (4)	22.00	33.70
Nos. 204-207 (4)	47.60	58.25
Nos. 85-88 (4)	10.25	30.25
Nos. 226-229 (4)	17.50	12.05
Nos. 34-37 (4)	13.25	59.75
Nos. 18-21 (4)	16.75	16.25
Nos. 47-50 (4)	39.75	80.25
Nos. 111-114 (4)	31.15	33.25
Nos. 72-75 (4)	11.55	18.50
Nos. 91-94 (4)	16.00	20.80
Nos. 134-137 (4)	9.45	21.25
Nos. 118-121 (4)	17.50	32.50
Nos. 166-169 (4)	24.25	56.00
Nos. 60-63 (4)	27.25	38.00
Nos. 77-80 (4)	18.75	56.75
Nos. 213-216 (4)	15.00	25.10
Nos. 20-23 (4)	6.80	18.25
Nos. 43-46 (4)	14.05	27.75
Nos. 71-74 (4)	9.25	16.25
Nos. 69-72 (4)	24.20	55.25
Nos. 226-229 (4)	7.25	7.45

Nos. 67-70 (4)	14.35	26.10
Nos. 226-229 (4)	8.20	28.90
Nos. 422-425 (4)	3.90	2.00
Nos. 508-510 (3)	18.80	23.85
Nos. 152-154 (3)	45.75	60.35
Nos. 211-216 (6)	26.30	13.35
Nos. 98-100 (3)	9.65	12.00
Nos. 142-148 (7)	23.25	11.80
Nos. 31-34 (4)	12.60	13.85
Nos. 46-47 (2)	4.35	1.70
Nos. 199-201 (3)	21.75	31.75
Nos. 67-69 (3)	10.55	26.50
Nos. 114-117 (4)	9.20	17.00
Nos. 163-165 (3)	4.40	5.50
Nos. 68-71 (4)	57.00	155.00
Nos. 33-36 (4)	27.75	45.25
Nos. 121-124 (4)	14.50	36.10
Set total (245) Stamps	1,320.	2,094.

Coronation

Queen Elizabeth and King George VI
CD302

1937

Aden	13-15
Antigua	81-83
Ascension	37-39
Bahamas	97-99
Barbados	190-192
Basutoland	15-17
Bechuanaland Protectorate	121-123
Bermuda	115-117
British Guiana	227-229
British Honduras	112-114
Cayman Islands	97-99
Ceylon	275-277
Cyprus	140-142
Dominica	94-96
Falkland Islands	81-83
Fiji	114-116
Gambia	129-131
Gibraltar	104-106
Gilbert & Ellice Islands	37-39
Gold Coast	112-114
Grenada	128-130
Hong Kong	151-153
Jamaica	113-115
Kenya, Uganda, Tanzania	60-62
Leeward Islands	100-102
Malta	188-190
Mauritius	208-210
Montserrat	89-91
Newfoundland	230-232
Nigeria	50-52
Northern Rhodesia	22-24
Nyasaland Protectorate	51-53
St. Helena	115-117
St. Kitts-Nevis	76-78
St. Lucia	107-109
St. Vincent	138-140
Seychelles	122-124
Sierra Leone	170-172
Solomon Islands	64-66
Somaliland Protectorate	81-83
Straits Settlements	235-237
Swaziland	24-26
Trinidad & Tobago	47-49
Turks & Caicos Islands	75-77
Virgin Islands	73-75

The following have different designs but are included in the omnibus set:

Great Britain	234
Offices in Morocco (Sp. Curr.)	82
Offices in Morocco (Fr. Curr.)	439
Offices in Morocco (Tangier)	514
Canada	237
Cook Islands	109-111
Nauru	35-38
Newfoundland	233-243
New Guinea	48-51
New Zealand	223-225
Niue	70-72
Papua	118-121
South Africa	74-78
Southern Rhodesia	38-41
South-West Africa	125-132

Nos. 13-15 (3)	3.00	5.75
Nos. 81-83 (3)	1.85	3.75
Nos. 37-39 (3)	2.75	2.75
Nos. 97-99 (3)	1.15	3.05
Nos. 190-192 (3)	1.10	1.95
Nos. 15-17 (3)	1.15	3.00
Nos. 121-123 (3)	.95	3.35
Nos. 115-117 (3)	1.25	5.00
Nos. 227-229 (3)	1.45	3.05
Nos. 112-114 (3)	1.20	2.35
Nos. 97-99 (3)	1.10	2.30
Nos. 275-277 (3)	8.25	10.35

Nos. 140-142 (3)	3.75	6.50
Nos. 94-96 (3)	.85	2.40
Nos. 81-83 (3)	2.90	2.30
Nos. 114-116 (3)	1.35	5.75
Nos. 129-131 (3)	.95	3.95
Nos. 104-106 (3)	2.25	6.45
Nos. 37-39 (3)	.85	2.00
Nos. 112-114 (3)	3.10	10.00
Nos. 128-130 (3)	1.00	.85
Nos. 151-153 (3)	23.00	12.50
Nos. 113-115 (3)	1.35	1.25
Nos. 60-62 (3)	1.00	2.35
Nos. 100-102 (3)	1.55	4.00
Nos. 188-190 (3)	1.25	1.60
Nos. 208-210 (3)	2.05	3.75
Nos. 89-91 (3)	1.00	3.35
Nos. 230-232 (3)	7.00	2.80
Nos. 50-52 (3)	3.25	8.50
Nos. 22-24 (3)	.95	2.25
Nos. 51-53 (3)	1.05	1.30
Nos. 115-117 (3)	1.45	2.05
Nos. 76-78 (3)	.95	2.05
Nos. 107-109 (3)	1.05	2.05
Nos. 138-140 (3)	.80	4.75
Nos. 122-124 (3)	1.20	1.90
Nos. 170-172 (3)	1.95	5.65
Nos. 64-66 (3)	.90	2.00
Nos. 81-83 (3)	1.10	3.40
Nos. 235-237 (3)	3.25	1.60
Nos. 24-26 (3)	1.05	1.75
Nos. 47-49 (3)	1.00	1.00
Nos. 75-77 (3)	1.30	1.55
Nos. 73-75 (3)	2.20	6.90
No. 234 (1)	.25	.25
No. 82 (1)	.80	.80
No. 439 (1)	.35	.25
No. 514 (1)	.55	.55
No. 237 (1)	.35	.25
Nos. 109-111 (3)	.85	.80
Nos. 35-38 (4)	1.15	5.50
Nos. 233-243 (11)	42.20	30.40
Nos. 48-51 (4)	1.40	7.90
Nos. 223-225 (3)	1.40	2.75
Nos. 70-72 (3)	.80	2.05
Nos. 118-121 (4)	1.60	5.25
Nos. 74-78 (5)	9.25	10.80
Nos. 38-41 (4)	3.55	15.50
Nos. 125-132 (8)	5.50	8.45
Set total (189) Stamps	173.85	258.65

Peace

King George VI and Parliament Buildings, London
CD303

Return to peace at the close of World War II.

1945-46

Aden	28-29
Antigua	96-97
Ascension	50-51
Bahamas	130-131
Barbados	207-208
Bermuda	131-132
British Guiana	242-243
British Honduras	127-128
Cayman Islands	112-113
Ceylon	293-294
Cyprus	156-157
Dominica	112-113
Falkland Islands	97-98
Falkland Islands Dep	1L9-1L10
Fiji	137-138
Gambia	144-145
Gibraltar	119-120
Gilbert & Ellice Islands	52-53
Gold Coast	128-129
Grenada	143-144
Jamaica	136-137
Kenya, Uganda, Tanzania	90-91
Leeward Islands	116-117
Malta	206-207
Mauritius	223-224
Montserrat	104-105
Nigeria	71-72
Northern Rhodesia	46-47
Nyasaland Protectorate	82-83
Pitcairn Islands	9-10
St. Helena	128-129
St. Kitts-Nevis	91-92
St. Lucia	127-128
St. Vincent	152-153
Seychelles	149-150
Sierra Leone	186-187
Solomon Islands	80-81
Somaliland Protectorate	108-109
Trinidad & Tobago	62-63
Turks & Caicos Islands	90-91
Virgin Islands	88-89

The following have different designs but are included in the omnibus set:

Great Britain	264-265

Offices in Morocco (Tangier)	523-524
Aden	
Kathiri State of Seiyun	12-13
Qu'aiti State of Shihr and Mukalla	12-13
Australia	200-202
Basutoland	29-31
Bechuanaland Protectorate	137-139
Burma	66-69
Cook Islands	127-130
Hong Kong	174-175
India	195-198
Hyderabad	51-53
New Zealand	247-257
Niue	90-93
Pakistan-Bahawalpur	O16
Samoa	191-194
South Africa	100-102
Southern Rhodesia	67-70
South-West Africa	153-155
Swaziland	38-40
Zanzibar	222-223

Nos. 28-29 (2)	.95	2.50
Nos. 96-97 (2)	.50	.80
Nos. 50-51 (2)	.90	1.80
Nos. 130-131 (2)	.50	1.40
Nos. 207-208 (2)	.50	1.10
Nos. 131-132 (2)	.55	.55
Nos. 242-243 (2)	1.05	1.40
Nos. 127-128 (2)	.50	.50
Nos. 112-113 (2)	.60	.80
Nos. 293-294 (2)	.60	2.10
Nos. 156-157 (2)	1.00	.70
Nos. 112-113 (2)	.50	.50
Nos. 97-98 (2)	.90	1.35
Nos. 1L9-1L10 (2)	1.40	1.00
Nos. 137-138 (2)	.50	1.75
Nos. 144-145 (2)	.50	.95
Nos. 119-120 (2)	.75	1.00
Nos. 52-53 (2)	.50	.50
Nos. 128-129 (2)	1.85	3.75
Nos. 143-144 (2)	.50	.95
Nos. 136-137 (2)	.90	12.50
Nos. 90-91 (2)	.65	.65
Nos. 116-117 (2)	.50	1.50
Nos. 206-207 (2)	.65	2.00
Nos. 223-224 (2)	.50	1.05
Nos. 104-105 (2)	.50	.50
Nos. 71-72 (2)	.70	2.75
Nos. 46-47 (2)	1.25	2.00
Nos. 82-83 (2)	.50	.50
Nos. 9-10 (2)	1.40	1.40
Nos. 128-129 (2)	.65	.70
Nos. 91-92 (2)	.50	.50
Nos. 127-128 (2)	.50	.60
Nos. 152-153 (2)	.50	.50
Nos. 149-150 (2)	.55	.50
Nos. 186-187 (2)	.50	.50
Nos. 80-81 (2)	.50	1.30
Nos. 108-109 (2)	.70	.50
Nos. 62-63 (2)	.50	.50
Nos. 90-91 (2)	.50	.50
Nos. 88-89 (2)	.50	.50
Nos. 264-265 (2)	.50	.70
Nos. 523-524 (2)	1.50	3.00
Nos. 12-13 (2)	.50	.90
Nos. 12-13 (2)	.50	1.25
Nos. 200-202 (3)	1.60	3.00
Nos. 29-31 (3)	2.10	2.60
Nos. 137-139 (3)	2.05	4.75
Nos. 66-69 (4)	1.60	1.30
Nos. 127-130 (4)	2.00	1.85
Nos. 174-175 (2)	6.75	3.15
Nos. 195-198 (4)	4.75	3.60
Nos. 51-53 (3)	1.50	1.70
Nos. 247-257 (11)	3.95	3.90
Nos. 90-93 (4)	1.70	2.20
No. O16 (1)	5.50	7.00
Nos. 191-194 (4)	2.05	1.00
Nos. 100-102 (3)	1.20	4.00
Nos. 67-70 (4)	1.40	1.75
Nos. 153-155 (3)	2.55	3.50
Nos. 38-40 (3)	2.40	5.50
Nos. 222-223 (2)	.65	1.00
Set total (151) Stamps	75.25	114.50

Silver Wedding

King George VI and Queen Elizabeth

CD304   CD305

1948-49

Aden	30-31
Kathiri State of Seiyun	14-15
Qu'aiti State of Shihr and Mukalla	14-15

Antigua	98-99
Ascension	52-53
Bahamas	148-149
Barbados	210-211
Basutoland	39-40
Bechuanaland Protectorate	147-148
Bermuda	133-134
British Guiana	244-245
British Honduras	129-130
Cayman Islands	116-117
Cyprus	158-159
Dominica	114-115
Falkland Islands	99-100
Falkland Islands Dep	1L11-1L12
Fiji	139-140
Gambia	146-147
Gibraltar	121-122
Gilbert & Ellice Islands	54-55
Gold Coast	142-143
Grenada	145-146
Hong Kong	178-179
Jamaica	138-139
Kenya, Uganda, Tanzania	92-93
Leeward Islands	118-119
Malaya	
Johore	128-129
Kedah	55-56
Kelantan	44-45
Malacca	1-2
Negri Sembilan	36-37
Pahang	44-45
Penang	1-2
Perak	99-100
Perlis	1-2
Selangor	74-75
Trengganu	47-48
Malta	223-224
Mauritius	229-230
Montserrat	106-107
Nigeria	73-74
North Borneo	238-239
Northern Rhodesia	48-49
Nyasaland Protectorate	85-86
Pitcairn Islands	11-12
St. Helena	130-131
St. Kitts-Nevis	93-94
St. Lucia	129-130
St. Vincent	154-155
Sarawak	174-175
Seychelles	151-152
Sierra Leone	188-189
Singapore	21-22
Solomon Islands	82-83
Somaliland Protectorate	110-111
Swaziland	48-49
Trinidad & Tobago	64-65
Turks & Caicos Islands	92-93
Virgin Islands	90-91
Zanzibar	224-225

The following have different designs but are included in the omnibus set:

Great Britain	267-268
Offices in Morocco (Sp. Curr.)	93-94
Offices in Morocco (Tangier)	525-526
Bahrain	62-63
Kuwait	82-83
Oman	25-26
South Africa	106
South-West Africa	159

Nos. 30-31 (2)	37.90	45.00
Nos. 14-15 (2)	18.85	17.50
Nos. 14-15 (2)	18.55	14.75
Nos. 98-99 (2)	12.55	12.75
Nos. 52-53 (2)	60.55	57.95
Nos. 148-149 (2)	45.25	40.30
Nos. 210-211 (2)	18.35	13.05
Nos. 39-40 (2)	52.80	55.25
Nos. 147-148 (2)	45.35	50.25
Nos. 133-134 (2)	47.75	55.25
Nos. 244-245 (2)	24.25	28.45
Nos. 129-130 (2)	22.75	53.20
Nos. 116-117 (2)	22.75	28.50
Nos. 158-159 (2)	58.50	78.05
Nos. 114-115 (2)	25.25	32.75
Nos. 99-100 (2)	112.10	83.60
Nos. 1L11-1L12 (2)	4.25	6.00
Nos. 139-140 (2)	18.20	10.75
Nos. 146-147 (2)	21.25	21.25
Nos. 121-122 (2)	61.00	78.00
Nos. 54-55 (2)	14.25	22.75
Nos. 142-143 (2)	35.25	37.75
Nos. 145-146 (2)	21.75	21.75
Nos. 178-179 (2)	303.50	96.50
Nos. 138-139 (2)	30.35	72.75
Nos. 92-93 (2)	52.75	72.75
Nos. 118-119 (2)	7.00	8.25
Nos. 128-129 (2)	29.25	53.25
Nos. 55-56 (2)	35.25	50.25
Nos. 44-45 (2)	35.75	62.75
Nos. 1-2 (2)	35.40	49.75
Nos. 36-37 (2)	28.10	38.20
Nos. 44-45 (2)	28.00	38.05
Nos. 1-2 (2)	40.50	37.80

Nos. 99-100 (2)	27.80	37.75
Nos. 1-2 (2)	33.50	58.00
Nos. 74-75 (2)	30.25	25.30
Nos. 47-48 (2)	35.25	62.75
Nos. 223-224 (2)	40.55	45.25
Nos. 229-230 (2)	17.75	45.25
Nos. 106-107 (2)	9.25	18.25
Nos. 73-74 (2)	17.85	22.80
Nos. 48-49 (2)	92.80	90.25
Nos. 85-86 (2)	19.25	32.75
Nos. 11-12 (2)	49.25	51.00
Nos. 130-131 (2)	32.80	42.80
Nos. 93-94 (2)	11.25	7.25
Nos. 129-130 (2)	22.25	45.25
Nos. 154-155 (2)	27.75	30.25
Nos. 174-175 (2)	55.40	60.40
Nos. 151-152 (2)	16.25	45.75
Nos. 188-189 (2)	24.75	26.25
Nos. 21-22 (2)	116.25	45.40
Nos. 82-83 (2)	13.40	13.40
Nos. 110-111 (2)	8.40	8.75
Nos. 48-49 (2)	40.30	47.75
Nos. 64-65 (2)	32.75	38.25
Nos. 92-93 (2)	15.25	20.30
Nos. 90-91 (2)	15.35	21.35
Nos. 224-225 (2)	29.60	38.00
Nos. 267-268 (2)	40.40	40.25
Nos. 93-94 (2)	20.10	25.35
Nos. 525-526 (2)	23.10	29.25
Nos. 62-63 (2)	38.45	72.50
Nos. 82-83 (2)	45.50	45.50
Nos. 25-26 (2)	46.00	47.50
No. 106 (1)	.90	1.25
No. 159 (1)	1.25	.35
Set total (134) Stamps	2,476.	2,688.

U.P.U.

Mercury and Symbols of Communications — CD306

Plane, Ship and Hemispheres — CD307

Mercury Scattering Letters over Globe CD308

U.P.U. Monument, Bern CD309

Universal Postal Union, 75th anniversary.

1949

Aden	32-35
Kathiri State of Seiyun	16-19
Qu'aiti State of Shihr and Mukalla	16-19
Antigua	100-103
Ascension	57-60
Bahamas	150-153
Barbados	212-215
Basutoland	41-44
Bechuanaland Protectorate	149-152
Bermuda	138-141
British Guiana	246-249
British Honduras	137-140
Brunei	79-82
Cayman Islands	118-121
Cyprus	160-163
Dominica	116-119
Falkland Islands	103-106
Falkland Islands Dep.	1L14-1L17
Fiji	141-144
Gambia	148-151
Gibraltar	123-126
Gilbert & Ellice Islands	56-59

Gold Coast	144-147
Grenada	147-150
Hong Kong	180-183
Jamaica	142-145
Kenya, Uganda, Tanzania	94-97
Leeward Islands	126-129
Malaya	
Johore	151-154
Kedah	57-60
Kelantan	46-49
Malacca	18-21
Negri Sembilan	59-62
Pahang	46-49
Penang	23-26
Perak	101-104
Perlis	3-6
Selangor	76-79
Trengganu	49-52
Malta	225-228
Mauritius	231-234
Montserrat	108-111
New Hebrides, British	62-65
New Hebrides, French	79-82
Nigeria	75-78
North Borneo	240-243
Northern Rhodesia	50-53
Nyasaland Protectorate	87-90
Pitcairn Islands	13-16
St. Helena	132-135
St. Kitts-Nevis	95-98
St. Lucia	131-134
St. Vincent	170-173
Sarawak	176-179
Seychelles	153-156
Sierra Leone	190-193
Singapore	23-26
Solomon Islands	84-87
Somaliland Protectorate	112-115
Southern Rhodesia	71-72
Swaziland	50-53
Tonga	87-90
Trinidad & Tobago	66-69
Turks & Caicos Islands	101-104
Virgin Islands	92-95
Zanzibar	226-229

The following have different designs but are included in the omnibus set:

Great Britain	276-279
Offices in Morocco (Tangier)	546-549
Australia	223
Bahrain	68-71
Burma	116-121
Ceylon	304-306
Egypt	281-283
India	223-226
Kuwait	89-92
Oman	31-34
Pakistan-Bahawalpur	26-29, O25-O28
South Africa	109-111
South-West Africa	160-162

Nos. 32-35 (4)	5.50	7.80
Nos. 16-19 (4)	3.10	3.60
Nos. 16-19 (4)	2.95	3.95
Nos. 100-103 (4)	4.15	6.85
Nos. 57-60 (4)	12.40	10.00
Nos. 150-153 (4)	5.60	9.55
Nos. 212-215 (4)	4.40	14.15
Nos. 41-44 (4)	4.75	10.00
Nos. 149-152 (4)	3.35	7.25
Nos. 138-141 (4)	4.75	5.55
Nos. 246-249 (4)	2.75	4.20
Nos. 137-140 (4)	3.35	4.75
Nos. 79-82 (4)	7.75	6.75
Nos. 118-121 (4)	4.00	6.40
Nos. 160-163 (4)	4.60	8.30
Nos. 116-119 (4)	2.30	5.65
Nos. 103-106 (4)	14.90	17.10
Nos. 1L14-1L17 (4)	15.50	14.00
Nos. 141-144 (4)	3.35	14.00
Nos. 148-151 (4)	3.10	7.10
Nos. 123-126 (4)	5.90	8.75
Nos. 56-59 (4)	4.70	7.85
Nos. 144-147 (4)	3.05	6.95
Nos. 147-150 (4)	2.15	3.55
Nos. 180-183 (4)	57.25	18.25
Nos. 142-145 (4)	2.70	6.00
Nos. 94-97 (4)	2.90	3.40
Nos. 126-129 (4)	3.05	9.60
Nos. 151-154 (4)	4.70	8.90
Nos. 57-60 (4)	4.80	12.00
Nos. 46-49 (4)	4.25	12.65
Nos. 18-21 (4)	4.25	17.30
Nos. 59-62 (4)	3.50	10.75
Nos. 46-49 (4)	3.00	7.25
Nos. 23-26 (4)	5.10	11.75
Nos. 101-104 (4)	3.65	10.75
Nos. 3-6 (4)	3.95	14.25
Nos. 76-79 (4)	4.90	12.30
Nos. 49-52 (4)	4.95	9.75
Nos. 225-228 (4)	4.50	4.85
Nos. 231-234 (4)	4.35	6.70
Nos. 108-111 (4)	3.40	3.85
Nos. 62-65 (4)	1.60	4.10
Nos. 79-82 (4)	24.25	24.25
Nos. 75-78 (4)	2.80	9.25
Nos. 50-53 (4)	5.00	6.50

Nos. 87-90 (4)	4.05	4.05
Nos. 13-16 (4)	18.50	16.50
Nos. 132-135 (4)	4.85	7.10
Nos. 95-98 (4)	3.35	4.70
Nos. 131-134 (4)	2.55	3.85
Nos. 170-173 (4)	2.20	5.05
Nos. 176-179 (4)	9.00	11.10
Nos. 153-156 (4)	3.25	4.10
Nos. 190-193 (4)	3.00	5.10
Nos. 23-26 (4)	20.75	14.20
Nos. 84-87 (4)	4.35	4.90
Nos. 112-115 (4)	3.95	8.70
Nos. 71-72 (2)	1.95	2.25
Nos. 50-53 (4)	2.80	4.65
Nos. 87-90 (4)	3.25	5.25
Nos. 66-69 (4)	3.15	3.15
Nos. 101-104 (4)	3.65	4.00
Nos. 92-95 (4)	2.60	5.90
Nos. 226-229 (4)	5.45	13.50
Nos. 276-279 (4)	1.35	2.10
Nos. 546-549 (4)	3.20	10.15
No. 223 (1)	.60	.55
Nos. 68-71 (4)	5.00	16.75
Nos. 116-121 (6)	7.15	5.30
Nos. 304-306 (3)	3.35	4.25
Nos. 281-283 (3)	5.75	2.70
Nos. 223-226 (4)	35.50	10.50
Nos. 89-92 (4)	6.10	10.25
Nos. 31-34 (4)	5.55	15.75
Nos. 26-29, O25-O28 (8)	2.00	42.00
Nos. 109-111 (3)	2.20	3.00
Nos. 160-162 (3)	3.95	6.00
Set total (309) Stamps	471.55	675.80

University

Arms of University College CD310

Alice, Princess of Athlone CD311

1948 opening of University College of the West Indies at Jamaica.

1951

Antigua	104-105
Barbados	228-229
British Guiana	250-251
British Honduras	141-142
Dominica	120-121
Grenada	164-165
Jamaica	146-147
Leeward Islands	130-131
Montserrat	112-113
St. Kitts-Nevis	105-106
St. Lucia	149-150
St. Vincent	174-175
Trinidad & Tobago	70-71
Virgin Islands	96-97

Nos. 104-105 (2)	1.35	3.25
Nos. 228-229 (2)	1.85	1.55
Nos. 250-251 (2)	1.10	1.25
Nos. 141-142 (2)	1.40	2.15
Nos. 120-121 (2)	1.40	1.75
Nos. 164-165 (2)	1.20	1.60
Nos. 146-147 (2)	.95	.85
Nos. 130-131 (2)	1.35	4.00
Nos. 112-113 (2)	.85	1.50
Nos. 105-106 (2)	.90	1.50
Nos. 149-150 (2)	1.40	1.50
Nos. 174-175 (2)	1.00	2.15
Nos. 70-71 (2)	.75	.75
Nos. 96-97 (2)	1.50	3.40
Set total (28) Stamps	17.00	27.20

Coronation

Queen Elizabeth II — CD312

1953

Aden	47
Kathiri State of Seiyun	28
Qu'aiti State of Shihr and Mukalla	28
Antigua	106
Ascension	61

Bahamas	157
Barbados	234
Basutoland	45
Bechuanaland Protectorate	153
Bermuda	142
British Guiana	252
British Honduras	143
Cayman Islands	150
Cyprus	167
Dominica	141
Falkland Islands	121
Falkland Islands Dependencies	1L18
Fiji	145
Gambia	152
Gibraltar	131
Gilbert & Ellice Islands	60
Gold Coast	160
Grenada	170
Hong Kong	184
Jamaica	153
Kenya, Uganda, Tanzania	101
Leeward Islands	132
Malaya	
Johore	155
Kedah	82
Kelantan	71
Malacca	27
Negri Sembilan	63
Pahang	71
Penang	27
Perak	126
Perlis	28
Selangor	101
Trengganu	74
Malta	241
Mauritius	250
Montserrat	127
New Hebrides, British	77
Nigeria	79
North Borneo	260
Northern Rhodesia	60
Nyasaland Protectorate	96
Pitcairn Islands	19
St. Helena	139
St. Kitts-Nevis	119
St. Lucia	156
St. Vincent	185
Sarawak	196
Seychelles	172
Sierra Leone	194
Singapore	27
Solomon Islands	88
Somaliland Protectorate	127
Swaziland	54
Trinidad & Tobago	84
Tristan da Cunha	13
Turks & Caicos Islands	118
Virgin Islands	114

The following have different designs but are included in the omnibus set:

Great Britain	313-316
Offices in Morocco (Tangier)	579-582
Australia	259-261
Bahrain	92-95
Canada	330
Ceylon	317
Cook Islands	145-146
Kuwait	113-116
New Zealand	280-284
Niue	104-105
Oman	52-55
Samoa	214-215
South Africa	192
Southern Rhodesia	80
South-West Africa	244-248
Tokelau Islands	4

No. 47 (1)	1.25	1.25
No. 28 (1)	.40	1.50
No. 28 (1)	1.10	.60
No. 106 (1)	.50	.75
No. 61 (1)	1.25	2.50
No. 157 (1)	1.25	.75
No. 234 (1)	1.00	.25
No. 45 (1)	.50	.60
No. 153 (1)	.75	.35
No. 142 (1)	.85	.40
No. 252 (1)	.45	.25
No. 143 (1)	.55	.40
No. 150 (1)	.40	1.00
No. 167 (1)	1.50	1.00
No. 141 (1)	.40	.40
No. 121 (1)	.90	1.50
No. 1L18 (1)	1.50	1.50
No. 145 (1)	1.75	.60
No. 152 (1)	.50	.50
No. 131 (1)	.50	.50
No. 60 (1)	.65	2.25
No. 160 (1)	.95	.25
No. 170 (1)	.30	.25
No. 184 (1)	6.00	.35
No. 153 (1)	.95	.25
No. 101 (1)	.40	.25
No. 132 (1)	1.00	2.25

No. 155 (1)	1.40	.30
No. 82 (1)	2.25	.60
No. 71 (1)	1.60	1.60
No. 27 (1)	1.10	1.50
No. 63 (1)	1.40	.65
No. 71 (1)	2.25	.25
No. 27 (1)	1.75	.30
No. 126 (1)	1.60	.25
No. 28 (1)	1.75	4.00
No. 101 (1)	1.75	.25
No. 74 (1)	1.50	1.00
No. 241 (1)	.50	.25
No. 250 (1)	1.00	.25
No. 127 (1)	.65	.50
No. 77 (1)	.75	.60
No. 79 (1)	.45	.25
No. 60 (1)	.70	.25
No. 96 (1)	.75	.75
No. 19 (1)	2.25	2.25
No. 139 (1)	1.25	1.25
No. 119 (1)	.35	.25
No. 156 (1)	.70	.35
No. 185 (1)	.50	.30
No. 196 (1)	2.25	2.25
No. 172 (1)	.80	.80
No. 194 (1)	.40	.40
No. 27 (1)	2.50	.40
No. 88 (1)	1.10	1.10
No. 127 (1)	.40	.25
No. 54 (1)	.30	.25
No. 84 (1)	.25	.25
No. 13 (1)	1.00	1.75
No. 118 (1)	.40	1.10
No. 114 (1)	.40	1.00
Nos. 313-316 (4)	16.35	8.75
Nos. 579-582 (4)	7.40	5.20
Nos. 259-261 (3)	4.60	3.25
Nos. 92-95 (4)	15.25	12.75
No. 330 (1)	.25	.25
No. 317 (1)	1.50	.25
Nos. 145-146 (2)	2.65	2.65
Nos. 113-116 (4)	16.00	8.50
Nos. 280-284 (5)	5.65	6.85
Nos. 104-105 (2)	1.75	1.75
Nos. 52-55 (4)	15.25	6.50
Nos. 214-215 (2)	2.10	1.00
No. 192 (1)	.30	.25
No. 80 (1)	7.25	7.25
Nos. 244-248 (5)	4.90	3.50
No. 4 (1)	2.75	2.75
Set total (105) Stamps	169.50	121.40

Separate designs for each country for the visit of Queen Elizabeth II and the Duke of Edinburgh.

Royal Visit 1953

1953

Aden	62
Australia	267-269
Bermuda	163
Ceylon	318
Fiji	146
Gibraltar	146
Jamaica	154
Kenya, Uganda, Tanzania	102
Malta	242
New Zealand	286-287

No. 62 (1)	.65	2.00
Nos. 267-269 (3)	2.35	1.90
No. 163 (1)	.50	.25
No. 318 (1)	1.25	.25
No. 146 (1)	.65	.35
No. 146 (1)	.50	.30
No. 154 (1)	.50	.25
No. 102 (1)	.50	.25
No. 242 (1)	.35	.25
Nos. 286-287 (2)	.50	.50
Set total (13) Stamps	7.75	6.30

West Indies Federation

Map of the Caribbean
CD313

Federation of the West Indies, April 22, 1958.

1958

Antigua	122-124
Barbados	248-250
Dominica	161-163
Grenada	184-186
Jamaica	175-177
Montserrat	143-145
St. Kitts-Nevis	136-138
St. Lucia	170-172
St. Vincent	198-200
Trinidad & Tobago	86-88

Nos. 122-124 (3)	5.80	3.80
Nos. 248-250 (3)	1.60	2.90
Nos. 161-163 (3)	1.95	1.85

Nos. 184-186 (3)	1.50	1.20
Nos. 175-177 (3)	3.10	4.20
Nos. 143-145 (3)	2.35	1.35
Nos. 136-138 (3)	3.00	1.85
Nos. 170-172 (3)	2.05	2.80
Nos. 198-200 (3)	1.50	1.75
Nos. 86-88 (3)	.75	.90
Set total (30) Stamps	23.60	22.60

Freedom from Hunger

Protein Food
CD314

U.N. Food and Agricultural Organization's "Freedom from Hunger" campaign.

1963

Aden	65
Antigua	133
Ascension	89
Bahamas	180
Basutoland	83
Bechuanaland Protectorate	194
Bermuda	192
British Guiana	271
British Honduras	179
Brunei	100
Cayman Islands	168
Dominica	181
Falkland Islands	146
Fiji	198
Gambia	172
Gibraltar	161
Gilbert & Ellice Islands	76
Grenada	190
Hong Kong	218
Malta	291
Mauritius	270
Montserrat	150
New Hebrides, British	93
North Borneo	296
Pitcairn Islands	35
St. Helena	173
St. Lucia	179
St. Vincent	201
Sarawak	212
Seychelles	213
Solomon Islands	109
Swaziland	108
Tonga	127
Tristan da Cunha	68
Turks & Caicos Islands	138
Virgin Islands	140
Zanzibar	280

No. 65 (1)	1.75	1.75
No. 133 (1)	.35	.35
No. 89 (1)	1.00	1.00
No. 180 (1)	.65	.65
No. 83 (1)	.50	.25
No. 194 (1)	.50	.50
No. 192 (1)	1.00	.50
No. 271 (1)	.45	.25
No. 179 (1)	.65	.25
No. 100 (1)	3.25	2.25
No. 168 (1)	.50	.30
No. 181 (1)	.30	.30
No. 146 (1)	11.50	3.50
No. 198 (1)	5.25	2.75
No. 172 (1)	.50	.25
No. 161 (1)	4.00	2.25
No. 76 (1)	1.40	.40
No. 190 (1)	.30	.25
No. 218 (1)	47.50	7.50
No. 291 (1)	2.00	2.00
No. 270 (1)	.50	.50
No. 150 (1)	.55	.45
No. 93 (1)	.60	.25
No. 35 (1)	10.00	4.50
No. 173 (1)	2.25	1.10
No. 179 (1)	.40	.40
No. 201 (1)	.90	.50
No. 212 (1)	1.60	1.75
No. 213 (1)	.85	.35
No. 109 (1)	2.00	.85
No. 108 (1)	.50	.50
No. 127 (1)	.70	.35
No. 68 (1)	.90	.40
No. 138 (1)	.50	.50
No. 140 (1)	.50	.50
No. 280 (1)	1.50	.80
Set total (36) Stamps	107.60	40.95

Red Cross Centenary

Red Cross and Elizabeth II
CD315

1963

Antigua	134-135
Ascension	90-91
Bahamas	183-184
Basutoland	84-85
Bechuanaland Protectorate	195-196
Bermuda	193-194
British Guiana	272-273
British Honduras	180-181
Cayman Islands	169-170
Dominica	182-183
Falkland Islands	147-148
Fiji	203-204
Gambia	173-174
Gibraltar	162-163
Gilbert & Ellice Islands	77-78
Grenada	191-192
Hong Kong	219-220
Jamaica	203-204
Malta	292-293
Mauritius	271-272
Montserrat	151-152
New Hebrides, British	94-95
Pitcairn Islands	36-37
St. Helena	174-175
St. Kitts-Nevis	143-144
St. Lucia	180-181
St. Vincent	202-203
Seychelles	214-215
Solomon Islands	110-111
South Arabia	1-2
Swaziland	109-110
Tonga	134-135
Tristan da Cunha	69-70
Turks & Caicos Islands	139-140
Virgin Islands	141-142

Nos. 134-135 (2)	1.10	1.50
Nos. 90-91 (2)	8.25	2.70
Nos. 183-184 (2)	2.30	2.55
Nos. 84-85 (2)	1.20	.90
Nos. 195-196 (2)	.95	.85
Nos. 193-194 (2)	2.75	2.55
Nos. 272-273 (2)	1.05	.80
Nos. 180-181 (2)	1.00	2.25
Nos. 169-170 (2)	.95	2.00
Nos. 182-183 (2)	.70	1.05
Nos. 147-148 (2)	19.75	6.00
Nos. 203-204 (2)	4.00	3.55
Nos. 173-174 (2)	.75	1.00
Nos. 162-163 (2)	6.25	5.40
Nos. 77-78 (2)	2.25	3.25
Nos. 191-192 (2)	.80	.50
Nos. 219-220 (2)	35.00	7.35
Nos. 203-204 (2)	.75	1.65
Nos. 292-293 (2)	2.50	4.75
Nos. 271-272 (2)	.90	.90
Nos. 151-152 (2)	1.00	.80
Nos. 94-95 (2)	1.00	.50
Nos. 36-37 (2)	6.50	5.50
Nos. 174-175 (2)	1.70	2.30
Nos. 143-144 (2)	.90	.90
Nos. 180-181 (2)	1.25	1.25
Nos. 202-203 (2)	.90	.90
Nos. 214-215 (2)	1.10	.90
Nos. 110-111 (2)	1.25	1.15
Nos. 1-2 (2)	1.25	1.25
Nos. 109-110 (2)	1.10	1.10
Nos. 134-135 (2)	1.00	1.25
Nos. 69-70 (2)	1.50	1.00
Nos. 139-140 (2)	.95	1.10
Nos. 141-142 (2)	.80	.80
Set total (70) Stamps	115.40	72.20

Shakespeare

Shakespeare Memorial Theatre, Stratford-on-Avon — CD316

400th anniversary of the birth of William Shakespeare.

1964

Antigua	151
Bahamas	201
Bechuanaland Protectorate	197
Cayman Islands	171
Dominica	184
Falkland Islands	149
Gambia	192
Gibraltar	164
Montserrat	153
St. Lucia	196
Turks & Caicos Islands	141
Virgin Islands	143

No. 151 (1)	.40	.25
No. 201 (1)	.60	.35
No. 197 (1)	.35	.35

No. 171 (1)	.35	.30
No. 184 (1)	.35	.35
No. 149 (1)	1.75	.50
No. 192 (1)	.35	.25
No. 164 (1)	.65	.55
No. 153 (1)	.35	.25
No. 196 (1)	.45	.25
No. 141 (1)	.40	.40
No. 143 (1)	.45	.45
Set total (12) Stamps	6.45	4.25

ITU

ITU Emblem
CD317

Intl. Telecommunication Union, cent.

1965

Antigua	153-154
Ascension	92-93
Bahamas	219-220
Barbados	265-266
Basutoland	101-102
Bechuanaland Protectorate	202-203
Bermuda	196-197
British Guiana	293-294
British Honduras	187-188
Brunei	116-117
Cayman Islands	172-173
Dominica	185-186
Falkland Islands	154-155
Fiji	211-212
Gibraltar	167-168
Gilbert & Ellice Islands	87-88
Grenada	205-206
Hong Kong	221-222
Mauritius	291-292
Montserrat	157-158
New Hebrides, British	108-109
Pitcairn Islands	52-53
St. Helena	180-181
St. Kitts-Nevis	163-164
St. Lucia	197-198
St. Vincent	224-225
Seychelles	218-219
Solomon Islands	126-127
Swaziland	115-116
Tristan da Cunha	85-86
Turks & Caicos Islands	142-143
Virgin Islands	159-160

Nos. 153-154 (2)	1.65	1.35
Nos. 92-93 (2)	1.90	1.50
Nos. 219-220 (2)	1.35	1.35
Nos. 265-266 (2)	1.50	1.25
Nos. 101-102 (2)	.85	.65
Nos. 202-203 (2)	1.10	.75
Nos. 196-197 (2)	2.15	2.25
Nos. 293-294 (2)	.60	.55
Nos. 187-188 (2)	.85	.85
Nos. 116-117 (2)	1.75	1.75
Nos. 172-173 (2)	1.00	1.00
Nos. 185-186 (2)	.55	.55
Nos. 154-155 (2)	7.75	3.65
Nos. 211-212 (2)	2.70	2.70
Nos. 167-168 (2)	9.00	5.95
Nos. 87-88 (2)	.95	.75
Nos. 205-206 (2)	.50	.50
Nos. 221-222 (2)	24.50	3.80
Nos. 291-292 (2)	1.20	.65
Nos. 157-158 (2)	1.25	1.15
Nos. 108-109 (2)	.65	.50
Nos. 52-53 (2)	6.25	4.30
Nos. 180-181 (2)	.80	.60
Nos. 163-164 (2)	.80	.60
Nos. 197-198 (2)	1.25	1.25
Nos. 224-225 (2)	.80	.90
Nos. 218-219 (2)	.90	.60
Nos. 126-127 (2)	.70	.55
Nos. 115-116 (2)	.75	.65
Nos. 85-86 (2)	1.15	.65
Nos. 142-143 (2)	.90	.90
Nos. 159-160 (2)	.95	.95
Set total (64) Stamps	78.80	45.50

Intl. Cooperation Year

ICY Emblem
CD318

1965

Antigua	155-156
Ascension	94-95
Bahamas	222-223
Basutoland	103-104

Bechuanaland Protectorate.....204-205
Bermuda............................199-200
British Guiana.....................295-296
British Honduras..................189-190
Brunei.................................118-119
Cayman Islands..................174-175
Dominica............................187-188
Falkland Islands..................156-157
Fiji....................................213-214
Gibraltar............................169-170
Gilbert & Ellice Islands..........104-105
Grenada.............................207-208
Hong Kong.........................223-224
Mauritius............................293-294
Montserrat.........................176-177
New Hebrides, British...........110-111
New Hebrides, French...........126-127
Pitcairn Islands.....................54-55
St. Helena..........................182-183
St. Kitts-Nevis....................165-166
St. Lucia............................199-200
Seychelles..........................220-221
Solomon Islands..................143-144
South Arabia.........................17-18
Swaziland..........................117-118
Tristan da Cunha...................87-88
Turks & Caicos Islands..........144-145
Virgin Islands......................161-162

Nos. 155-156 (2)	.60	.50
Nos. 94-95 (2)	1.30	1.50
Nos. 222-223 (2)	.65	1.40
Nos. 103-104 (2)	.75	.85
Nos. 204-205 (2)	.85	1.00
Nos. 199-200 (2)	2.25	1.25
Nos. 295-296 (2)	.65	.60
Nos. 189-190 (2)	.60	.55
Nos. 118-119 (2)	.85	.85
Nos. 174-175 (2)	1.00	.95
Nos. 187-188 (2)	.55	.55
Nos. 156-157 (2)	7.00	1.90
Nos. 213-214 (2)	2.60	2.35
Nos. 169-170 (2)	1.25	2.75
Nos. 104-105 (2)	.95	.60
Nos. 207-208 (2)	.50	.50
Nos. 223-224 (2)	22.00	3.10
Nos. 293-294 (2)	.70	.70
Nos. 176-177 (2)	.80	.65
Nos. 110-111 (2)	.50	.50
Nos. 126-127 (2)	12.00	12.00
Nos. 54-55 (2)	6.35	4.50
Nos. 182-183 (2)	.95	.50
Nos. 165-166 (2)	.70	.60
Nos. 199-200 (2)	.55	.55
Nos. 220-221 (2)	.90	.65
Nos. 143-144 (2)	.70	.60
Nos. 17-18 (2)	1.20	.50
Nos. 117-118 (2)	.75	.75
Nos. 87-88 (2)	1.35	.75
Nos. 144-145 (2)	.85	.85
Nos. 161-162 (2)	.80	.80
Set total (64) Stamps	73.45	46.10

Churchill Memorial

Winston Churchill and St. Paul's, London, During Air Attack
CD319

1966

Antigua................................157-160
Ascension..............................96-99
Bahamas.............................224-227
Barbados.............................281-284
Basutoland...........................105-108
Bechuanaland Protectorate.....206-209
Bermuda.............................201-204
British Antarctic Territory..........16-19
British Honduras..................191-194
Brunei.................................120-123
Cayman Islands..................176-179
Dominica............................189-192
Falkland Islands..................158-161
Fiji....................................215-218
Gibraltar............................171-174
Gilbert & Ellice Islands..........106-109
Grenada.............................209-212
Hong Kong.........................225-228
Mauritius............................295-298
Montserrat.........................178-181
New Hebrides, British...........112-115
New Hebrides, French...........128-131
Pitcairn Islands.....................56-59
St. Helena..........................184-187
St. Kitts-Nevis....................167-170
St. Lucia............................201-204
St. Vincent.........................241-244
Seychelles..........................222-225
Solomon Islands..................145-148
South Arabia.........................19-22
Swaziland..........................119-122

Tristan da Cunha...................89-92
Turks & Caicos Islands..........146-149
Virgin Islands......................163-166

Nos. 157-160 (4)	3.05	2.55
Nos. 96-99 (4)	10.00	7.15
Nos. 224-227 (4)	2.30	3.20
Nos. 281-284 (4)	3.00	4.45
Nos. 105-108 (4)	2.80	3.25
Nos. 206-209 (4)	2.50	2.50
Nos. 201-204 (4)	4.00	4.00
Nos. 16-19 (4)	41.35	20.00
Nos. 191-194 (4)	2.55	1.80
Nos. 120-123 (4)	8.00	7.25
Nos. 176-179 (4)	3.40	3.55
Nos. 189-192 (4)	1.15	1.15
Nos. 158-161 (4)	12.75	7.80
Nos. 215-218 (4)	5.15	3.45
Nos. 171-174 (4)	3.05	5.30
Nos. 106-109 (4)	1.75	1.30
Nos. 209-212 (4)	1.10	1.10
Nos. 225-228 (4)	52.50	11.40
Nos. 295-298 (4)	4.05	4.05
Nos. 178-181 (4)	1.60	1.55
Nos. 112-115 (4)	2.30	1.00
Nos. 128-131 (4)	10.25	10.25
Nos. 56-59 (4)	11.00	6.75
Nos. 184-187 (4)	1.85	1.95
Nos. 167-170 (4)	1.70	1.70
Nos. 201-204 (4)	1.50	1.50
Nos. 241-244 (4)	1.50	1.75
Nos. 222-225 (4)	3.20	3.60
Nos. 145-148 (4)	1.75	1.75
Nos. 19-22 (4)	2.95	2.20
Nos. 119-122 (4)	1.70	2.55
Nos. 89-92 (4)	5.95	2.70
Nos. 146-149 (4)	1.60	1.75
Nos. 163-166 (4)	1.90	1.90
Set total (136) Stamps	215.20	138.15

Royal Visit, 1966

Queen Elizabeth II and Prince Philip
CD320

Caribbean visit, Feb. 4 - Mar. 6, 1966.

1966

Antigua................................161-162
Bahamas.............................228-229
Barbados.............................285-286
British Guiana......................299-300
Cayman Islands..................180-181
Dominica............................193-194
Grenada.............................213-214
Montserrat.........................182-183
St. Kitts-Nevis....................171-172
St. Lucia............................205-206
St. Vincent.........................245-246
Turks & Caicos Islands..........150-151
Virgin Islands......................167-168

Nos. 161-162 (2)	3.80	2.60
Nos. 228-229 (2)	3.05	3.05
Nos. 285-286 (2)	3.00	2.00
Nos. 299-300 (2)	3.35	1.60
Nos. 180-181 (2)	3.45	1.80
Nos. 193-194 (2)	3.00	.60
Nos. 213-214 (2)	.80	.50
Nos. 182-183 (2)	1.70	1.00
Nos. 171-172 (2)	.80	.75
Nos. 205-206 (2)	1.50	1.35
Nos. 245-246 (2)	2.75	1.35
Nos. 150-151 (2)	1.20	.70
Nos. 167-168 (2)	2.25	2.25
Set total (26) Stamps	30.65	19.55

World Cup Soccer

Soccer Player and Jules Rimet Cup
CD321

World Cup Soccer Championship, Wembley, England, July 11-30.

1966

Antigua................................163-164
Ascension...........................100-101
Bahamas.............................245-246
Bermuda.............................205-206
Brunei.................................124-125
Cayman Islands..................182-183
Dominica............................195-196
Fiji....................................219-220
Gibraltar............................175-176
Gilbert & Ellice Islands..........125-126
Grenada.............................230-231

New Hebrides, British...........116-117
New Hebrides, French...........132-133
Pitcairn Islands.....................60-61
St. Helena..........................188-189
St. Kitts-Nevis....................173-174
St. Lucia............................207-208
Seychelles..........................226-227
Solomon Islands..................167-168
South Arabia.........................23-24
Tristan da Cunha...................93-94

Nos. 163-164 (2)	.85	.50
Nos. 100-101 (2)	2.50	1.80
Nos. 245-246 (2)	.65	.65
Nos. 205-206 (2)	1.75	1.75
Nos. 124-125 (2)	1.40	1.00
Nos. 182-183 (2)	.75	.75
Nos. 195-196 (2)	1.20	.75
Nos. 219-220 (2)	2.00	1.20
Nos. 175-176 (2)	1.85	1.75
Nos. 125-126 (2)	.80	.60
Nos. 230-231 (2)	.65	.95
Nos. 116-117 (2)	1.00	1.00
Nos. 132-133 (2)	7.00	7.00
Nos. 60-61 (2)	5.50	5.00
Nos. 188-189 (2)	1.25	.60
Nos. 173-174 (2)	.85	.80
Nos. 207-208 (2)	1.15	.90
Nos. 226-227 (2)	.85	.85
Nos. 167-168 (2)	.70	.70
Nos. 23-24 (2)	1.90	.55
Nos. 93-94 (2)	1.25	.80
Set total (42) Stamps	35.85	29.90

WHO Headquarters

World Health Organization Headquarters, Geneva — CD322

1966

Antigua................................165-166
Ascension...........................102-103
Bahamas.............................247-248
Brunei.................................126-127
Cayman Islands..................184-185
Dominica............................197-198
Fiji....................................224-225
Gibraltar............................180-181
Gilbert & Ellice Islands..........127-128
Grenada.............................232-233
Hong Kong.........................229-230
Montserrat.........................184-185
New Hebrides, British...........118-119
New Hebrides, French...........134-135
Pitcairn Islands.....................62-63
St. Helena..........................190-191
St. Kitts-Nevis....................177-178
St. Lucia............................209-210
St. Vincent.........................247-248
Seychelles..........................228-229
Solomon Islands..................169-170
South Arabia.........................25-26
Tristan da Cunha...................99-100

Nos. 165-166 (2)	1.05	.55
Nos. 102-103 (2)	6.60	3.50
Nos. 247-248 (2)	.80	.80
Nos. 126-127 (2)	1.35	1.00
Nos. 184-185 (2)	2.25	1.40
Nos. 197-198 (2)	.75	.75
Nos. 224-225 (2)	5.10	3.90
Nos. 180-181 (2)	6.50	4.50
Nos. 127-128 (2)	.80	.70
Nos. 232-233 (2)	.80	.50
Nos. 229-230 (2)	11.25	2.30
Nos. 184-185 (2)	1.00	1.00
Nos. 118-119 (2)	.75	.50
Nos. 134-135 (2)	8.75	8.75
Nos. 62-63 (2)	7.25	6.50
Nos. 190-191 (2)	3.50	1.50
Nos. 177-178 (2)	.65	.65
Nos. 209-210 (2)	.80	.80
Nos. 247-248 (2)	1.15	1.05
Nos. 228-229 (2)	1.25	.75
Nos. 169-170 (2)	.80	.80
Nos. 25-26 (2)	2.10	.70
Nos. 99-100 (2)	1.90	1.25
Set total (46) Stamps	67.15	44.15

UNESCO Anniversary

"Education" — CD323

"Science" (Wheat ears & flask enclosing globe). "Culture" (lyre & columns). 20th anniversary of the UNESCO.

1966-67

Antigua................................183-185
Ascension...........................108-110
Bahamas.............................249-251
Barbados.............................287-289
Bermuda.............................207-209
Brunei.................................128-130
Cayman Islands..................186-188
Dominica............................199-201
Gibraltar............................183-185
Gilbert & Ellice Islands..........129-131
Grenada.............................234-236
Hong Kong.........................231-233
Mauritius............................299-301
Montserrat.........................186-188
New Hebrides, British...........120-122
New Hebrides, French...........136-138
Pitcairn Islands.....................64-66
St. Helena..........................192-194
St. Kitts-Nevis....................179-181
St. Lucia............................211-213
St. Vincent.........................249-251
Seychelles..........................230-232
Solomon Islands..................171-173
South Arabia.........................27-29
Swaziland..........................123-125
Tristan da Cunha.................101-103
Turks & Caicos Islands..........155-157
Virgin Islands......................176-178

Nos. 183-185 (3)	1.90	2.50
Nos. 108-110 (3)	11.00	6.15
Nos. 249-251 (3)	2.35	2.35
Nos. 287-289 (3)	2.50	2.15
Nos. 207-209 (3)	4.30	3.90
Nos. 128-130 (3)	5.00	7.40
Nos. 186-188 (3)	2.50	1.70
Nos. 199-201 (3)	1.60	.75
Nos. 183-185 (3)	6.50	3.25
Nos. 129-131 (3)	2.50	1.65
Nos. 234-236 (3)	1.10	1.20
Nos. 231-233 (3)	69.50	17.50
Nos. 299-301 (3)	2.10	1.50
Nos. 186-188 (3)	2.40	2.40
Nos. 120-122 (3)	1.90	1.90
Nos. 136-138 (3)	7.75	7.75
Nos. 64-66 (3)	7.10	4.75
Nos. 192-194 (3)	5.25	3.65
Nos. 179-181 (3)	.90	.90
Nos. 211-213 (3)	1.15	1.15
Nos. 249-251 (3)	2.30	1.35
Nos. 230-232 (3)	2.40	2.40
Nos. 171-173 (3)	2.00	1.50
Nos. 27-29 (3)	5.50	5.50
Nos. 123-125 (3)	1.45	1.45
Nos. 101-103 (3)	2.00	1.40
Nos. 155-157 (3)	1.05	1.05
Nos. 176-178 (3)	1.30	1.30
Set total (84) Stamps	157.30	90.45

Silver Wedding, 1972

Queen Elizabeth II and Prince Philip — CD324

Designs: borders differ for each country.

1972

Anguilla...............................161-162
Antigua................................295-296
Ascension...........................164-165
Bahamas.............................344-345
Bermuda.............................296-297
British Antarctic Territory...........43-44
British Honduras..................306-307
British Indian Ocean Territory.....48-49
Brunei.................................186-187
Cayman Islands..................304-305
Dominica............................352-353
Falkland Islands..................223-224
Fiji....................................328-329
Gibraltar............................292-293
Gilbert & Ellice Islands..........206-207
Grenada.............................466-467
Hong Kong.........................271-272
Montserrat.........................286-287
New Hebrides, British...........169-170
Pitcairn Islands...................127-128
St. Helena..........................271-272
St. Kitts-Nevis....................257-258
St. Lucia............................328-329
St. Vincent.........................344-345

Seychelles 309-310
Solomon Islands.......................248-249
South Georgia 35-36
Tristan da Cunha.....................178-179
Turks & Caicos Islands 257-258
Virgin Islands.........................241-242

Nos. 161-162 (2)	1.30	1.50
Nos. 295-296 (2)	.50	.50
Nos. 164-165 (2)	.80	.80
Nos. 344-345 (2)	.60	.60
Nos. 296-297 (2)	.50	.50
Nos. 43-44 (2)	7.75	6.10
Nos. 306-307 (2)	.90	.90
Nos. 48-49 (2)	2.30	1.00
Nos. 186-187 (2)	.65	.85
Nos. 304-305 (2)	.75	.75
Nos. 352-353 (2)	.65	.65
Nos. 223-224 (2)	1.10	1.10
Nos. 328-329 (2)	1.00	1.00
Nos. 292-293 (2)	.50	.50
Nos. 206-207 (2)	.50	.50
Nos. 466-467 (2)	.70	.70
Nos. 271-272 (2)	1.70	1.50
Nos. 286-287 (2)	.55	.55
Nos. 169-170 (2)	.50	.50
Nos. 127-128 (2)	.90	.85
Nos. 271-272 (2)	.70	1.20
Nos. 257-258 (2)	.65	.50
Nos. 328-329 (2)	.75	.75
Nos. 344-345 (2)	.55	.55
Nos. 309-310 (2)	.95	.95
Nos. 248-249 (2)	.60	.60
Nos. 35-36 (2)	1.40	1.40
Nos. 178-179 (2)	.70	.70
Nos. 257-258 (2)	.50	.50
Nos. 241-242 (2)	.50	.50
Set total (60) Stamps	31.45	29.00

Princess Anne's Wedding

Princess Anne and Mark Phillips — CD325

Wedding of Princess Anne and Mark Phillips, Nov. 14, 1973.

1973

Anguilla................................179-180
Ascension.................................177-178
Belize.....................................325-326
Bermuda.................................302-303
British Antarctic Territory.............60-61
Cayman Islands.........................320-321
Falkland Islands 225-226
Gibraltar.................................305-306
Gilbert & Ellice Islands............216-217
Hong Kong 289-290
Montserrat 300-301
Pitcairn Islands 135-136
St. Helena 277-278
St. Kitts-Nevis 274-275
St. Lucia 349-350
St. Vincent 358-359
St. Vincent Grenadines 1-2
Seychelles 311-312
Solomon Islands.......................259-260
South Georgia 37-38
Tristan da Cunha.....................189-190
Turks & Caicos Islands 286-287
Virgin Islands.........................260-261

Nos. 179-180 (2)	.55	.55
Nos. 177-178 (2)	.65	.65
Nos. 325-326 (2)	.50	.50
Nos. 302-303 (2)	.50	.50
Nos. 60-61 (2)	1.10	1.10
Nos. 320-321 (2)	.55	.55
Nos. 225-226 (2)	.75	.75
Nos. 305-306 (2)	.55	.55
Nos. 216-217 (2)	.50	.50
Nos. 289-290 (2)	2.65	2.00
Nos. 300-301 (2)	.65	.65
Nos. 135-136 (2)	.70	.60
Nos. 277-278 (2)	.50	.50
Nos. 274-275 (2)	.50	.50
Nos. 349-350 (2)	.50	.50
Nos. 358-359 (2)	.50	.50
Nos. 1-2 (2)	.50	.50
Nos. 311-312 (2)	.70	.70
Nos. 259-260 (2)	.70	.70
Nos. 37-38 (2)	.75	.75
Nos. 189-190 (2)	.50	.50
Nos. 286-287 (2)	.50	.50
Nos. 260-261 (2)	.50	.50
Set total (46) Stamps	15.80	15.05

Elizabeth II Coronation Anniv.

CD326   CD327

CD328

Designs: Royal and local beasts in heraldic form and simulated stonework. Portrait of Elizabeth II by Peter Grugeon. 25th anniversary of coronation of Queen Elizabeth II.

1978

Ascension...................................229
Barbados.....................................474
Belize.......................................397
British Antarctic Territory...............71
Cayman Islands.............................404
Christmas Island 87
Falkland Islands 275
Fiji...384
Gambia......................................380
Gilbert Islands 312
Mauritius...................................464
New Hebrides, British 258
St. Helena 317
St. Kitts-Nevis 354
Samoa.......................................472
Solomon Islands...........................368
South Georgia 51
Swaziland...................................302
Tristan da Cunha..........................238
Virgin Islands.............................337

No. 229 (1)	2.25	2.25
No. 474 (1)	1.35	1.35
No. 397 (1)	1.75	1.75
No. 71 (1)	6.00	6.00
No. 404 (1)	2.00	2.50
No. 87 (1)	3.50	4.00
No. 275 (1)	4.00	4.00
No. 384 (1)	2.75	2.75
No. 380 (1)	1.50	1.50
No. 312 (1)	1.25	1.25
No. 464 (1)	2.75	2.75
No. 258 (1)	1.75	1.75
No. 317 (1)	1.75	1.75
No. 354 (1)	1.00	1.00
No. 472 (1)	2.00	2.00
No. 368 (1)	3.00	3.00
No. 51 (1)	3.00	3.00
No. 302 (1)	1.75	1.75
No. 238 (1)	1.50	1.50
No. 337 (1)	2.25	2.25
Set total (20) Stamps	47.10	48.10

Queen Mother Elizabeth's 80th Birthday

CD330

Designs: Photographs of Queen Mother Elizabeth. Falkland Islands issued in sheets of 50; others in sheets of 9.

1980

Ascension 261
Bermuda.....................................401
Cayman Islands.............................443
Falkland Islands 305
Gambia......................................412
Gibraltar...................................393
Hong Kong 364
Pitcairn Islands 193
St. Helena 341
Samoa.......................................532
Solomon Islands............................426

Tristan da Cunha............................277

No. 261 (1)	.50	.50
No. 401 (1)	.45	.45
No. 443 (1)	.45	.45
No. 305 (1)	.40	.40
No. 412 (1)	.40	.50
No. 393 (1)	.35	.35
No. 364 (1)	1.10	1.00
No. 193 (1)	.60	.60
No. 341 (1)	.50	.50
No. 532 (1)	.55	.55
No. 426 (1)	.50	.50
No. 277 (1)	.45	.45
Set total (12) Stamps	6.25	6.25

Royal Wedding, 1981

Prince Charles and Lady Diana — CD331   CD331a

Wedding of Charles, Prince of Wales, and Lady Diana Spencer, St. Paul's Cathedral, London, July 29, 1981.

1981

Antigua 623-627
Ascension 294-296
Barbados 547-549
Barbuda 497-501
Bermuda 412-414
Brunei 268-270
Cayman Islands.....................471-473
Dominica 701-705
Falkland Islands 324-326
Falkland Islands Dep............1L59-1L61
Fiji 442-444
Gambia 426-428
Ghana 759-764
Grenada 1051-1055
Grenada Grenadines............440-443
Hong Kong 373-375
Jamaica 500-503
Lesotho 335-337
Maldive Islands 906-909
Mauritius 520-522
Norfolk Island 280-282
Pitcairn Islands 206-208
St. Helena 353-355
St. Lucia 543-549
Samoa 558-560
Sierra Leone 509-518
Solomon Islands.......................450-452
Swaziland 382-384
Tristan da Cunha.......................294-296
Turks & Caicos Islands 486-489
Caicos Island................................8-11
Uganda 314-317
Vanuatu 308-310
Virgin Islands...........................406-408

Nos. 623-627 (5)	7.55	2.55
Nos. 294-296 (3)	1.10	1.10
Nos. 547-549 (3)	.90	.90
Nos. 497-501 (5)	10.95	10.95
Nos. 412-414 (3)	2.00	2.00
Nos. 268-270 (3)	2.15	4.50
Nos. 471-473 (3)	1.35	1.35
Nos. 701-705 (5)	8.35	2.35
Nos. 324-326 (3)	1.65	1.70
Nos. 1L59-1L61 (3)	1.45	1.45
Nos. 442-444 (3)	1.70	1.70
Nos. 426-428 (3)	.80	.80
Nos. 759-764 (9)	6.20	6.20
Nos. 1051-1055 (5)	9.85	1.85
Nos. 440-443 (4)	2.35	2.35
Nos. 373-375 (3)	3.30	3.10
Nos. 500-503 (4)	1.50	1.25
Nos. 335-337 (3)	1.10	1.10
Nos. 906-909 (4)	1.70	1.80
Nos. 520-522 (3)	2.75	2.75
Nos. 280-282 (3)	1.35	1.35
Nos. 206-208 (3)	1.10	1.10
Nos. 353-355 (3)	.85	.85
Nos. 543-549 (5)	8.50	8.50
Nos. 558-560 (3)	.85	.85
Nos. 509-518 (10)	15.50	15.50
Nos. 450-452 (3)	1.05	1.05
Nos. 382-384 (3)	1.30	1.25
Nos. 294-296 (3)	.90	.90
Nos. 486-489 (4)	2.20	2.20
Nos. 8-11 (4)	6.25	6.25
Nos. 314-317 (4)	3.30	3.00
Nos. 308-310 (3)	1.15	1.15
Nos. 406-408 (3)	1.30	1.30
Set total (131) Stamps	114.30	97.00

Princess Diana

CD332

CD333

Designs: Photographs and portrait of Princess Diana, wedding or honeymoon photographs, royal residences, arms of issuing country. Portrait photograph by Clive Friend. Souvenir sheet margins show family tree, various people related to the princess. 21st birthday of Princess Diana of Wales, July 1.

1982

Antigua 663-666
Ascension 313-316
Bahamas 510-513
Barbados 585-588
Barbuda 544-547
British Antarctic Territory.............92-95
Cayman Islands.....................486-489
Dominica 773-776
Falkland Islands 348-351
Falkland Islands Dep...........1L72-1L75
Fiji 470-473
Gambia 447-450
Grenada 1101A-1105
Grenada Grenadines............485-491
Lesotho 372-375
Maldive Islands 952-955
Mauritius 548-551
Pitcairn Islands 213-216
St. Helena 372-375
St. Lucia 591-594
Sierra Leone 531-534
Solomon Islands.......................471-474
Swaziland 406-409
Tristan da Cunha.......................310-313
Turks and Caicos Islands 531-534
Virgin Islands...........................430-433

Nos. 663-666 (4)	9.70	9.70
Nos. 313-316 (4)	3.95	3.95
Nos. 510-513 (4)	6.00	3.85
Nos. 585-588 (4)	3.40	3.25
Nos. 544-547 (4)	9.75	7.70
Nos. 92-95 (4)	5.30	3.45
Nos. 486-489 (4)	5.40	2.70
Nos. 773-776 (4)	7.05	7.05
Nos. 348-351 (4)	3.10	3.10
Nos. 1L72-1L75 (4)	2.50	2.60
Nos. 470-473 (4)	4.50	4.50
Nos. 447-450 (4)	2.85	2.85
Nos. 1101A-1105 (7)	16.05	15.55
Nos. 485-491 (7)	17.65	17.65
Nos. 372-375 (4)	4.00	4.00
Nos. 952-955 (4)	7.25	7.25
Nos. 548-551 (4)	5.50	5.50
Nos. 213-216 (4)	2.15	2.15
Nos. 372-375 (4)	2.95	2.95
Nos. 591-594 (4)	9.90	9.90
Nos. 531-534 (4)	7.20	7.20
Nos. 471-474 (4)	2.90	2.90
Nos. 406-409 (4)	3.85	2.25
Nos. 310-313 (4)	3.65	1.45
Nos. 486-489 (4)	2.20	2.20
Nos. 430-433 (4)	3.55	3.55
Set total (110) Stamps	152.30	139.20

250th anniv. of first edition of Lloyd's List (shipping news publication) & of Lloyd's marine insurance.

CD335

Designs: First page of early edition of the list; historical ships, modern transportation or harbor scenes.

1984

Ascension	351-354	
Bahamas	555-558	
Barbados	627-630	
Cayes of Belize	10-13	
Cayman Islands	522-526	
Falkland Islands	404-407	
Fiji	509-512	
Gambia	519-522	
Mauritius	587-590	
Nauru	280-283	
St. Helena	412-415	
Samoa	624-627	
Seychelles	538-541	
Solomon Islands	521-524	
Vanuatu	368-371	
Virgin Islands	466-469	

Nos. 351-354 (4)	3.30	2.55
Nos. 555-558 (4)	4.55	2.95
Nos. 627-630 (4)	6.10	5.15
Nos. 10-13 (4)	3.05	3.05
Nos. 522-526 (5)	9.30	8.45
Nos. 404-407 (4)	3.65	4.00
Nos. 509-512 (4)	6.15	6.15
Nos. 519-522 (4)	4.20	4.30
Nos. 587-590 (4)	8.95	8.95
Nos. 280-283 (4)	2.40	2.35
Nos. 412-415 (4)	2.40	2.40
Nos. 624-627 (4)	2.75	2.45
Nos. 538-541 (4)	5.25	5.25
Nos. 521-524 (4)	4.65	3.95
Nos. 368-371 (4)	2.40	2.40
Nos. 466-469 (4)	5.00	5.00
Set total (65) Stamps	74.10	69.45

Queen Mother 85th Birthday

CD336

Designs: Photographs tracing the life of the Queen Mother, Elizabeth. The high value in each set pictures the same photograph taken of the Queen Mother holding the infant Prince Henry.

1985

Ascension	372-376	
Bahamas	580-584	
Barbados	660-664	
Bermuda	469-473	
Falkland Islands	420-424	
Falkland Islands Dep	1L92-1L96	
Fiji	531-535	
Hong Kong	447-450	
Jamaica	599-603	
Mauritius	604-608	
Norfolk Island	364-368	
Pitcairn Islands	253-257	
St. Helena	428-432	
Samoa	649-653	
Seychelles	567-571	
Zil Elwannyen Sesel	101-105	
Solomon Islands	543-547	
Swaziland	476-480	
Tristan da Cunha	372-376	
Vanuatu	392-396	

Nos. 372-376 (5)	5.35	5.35
Nos. 580-584 (5)	7.95	6.45
Nos. 660-664 (5)	8.00	6.70
Nos. 469-473 (5)	9.90	9.90
Nos. 420-424 (5)	8.25	7.60
Nos. 1L92-1L96 (5)	8.25	8.25
Nos. 531-535 (5)	7.05	7.05
Nos. 447-450 (4)	10.25	8.50
Nos. 599-603 (5)	7.30	8.00
Nos. 604-608 (5)	11.80	11.80
Nos. 364-368 (5)	5.05	5.05
Nos. 253-257 (5)	5.25	5.95
Nos. 428-432 (5)	5.25	5.25
Nos. 649-653 (5)	8.65	7.80
Nos. 567-571 (5)	8.70	8.70
Nos. 101-105 (5)	7.15	7.15
Nos. 543-547 (5)	4.20	4.20
Nos. 476-480 (5)	8.00	7.50
Nos. 372-376 (5)	5.40	5.40
Nos. 392-396 (5)	5.25	5.25
Set total (99) Stamps	147.00	141.85

Queen Elizabeth II, 60th Birthday

CD337

1986, April 21

Ascension	389-393	
Bahamas	592-596	
Barbados	675-679	
Bermuda	499-503	
Cayman Islands	555-559	
Falkland Islands	441-445	
Fiji	544-548	
Hong Kong	465-469	
Jamaica	620-624	
Kiribati	470-474	
Mauritius	629-633	
Papua New Guinea	640-644	
Pitcairn Islands	270-274	
St. Helena	451-455	
Samoa	670-674	
Seychelles	592-596	
Zil Elwannyen Sesel	114-118	
Solomon Islands	562-566	
South Georgia	101-105	
Swaziland	490-494	
Tristan da Cunha	388-392	
Vanuatu	414-418	
Zambia	343-347	

Nos. 389-393 (5)	2.80	2.80
Nos. 592-596 (5)	2.75	3.70
Nos. 675-679 (5)	3.35	3.20
Nos. 499-503 (5)	4.90	4.90
Nos. 555-559 (5)	4.55	4.45
Nos. 441-445 (5)	3.95	4.95
Nos. 544-548 (5)	4.05	4.05
Nos. 465-469 (5)	9.60	6.85
Nos. 620-624 (5)	2.95	3.05
Nos. 470-474 (5)	2.10	2.10
Nos. 629-633 (5)	3.70	3.70
Nos. 640-644 (5)	4.50	4.50
Nos. 270-274 (5)	2.70	2.70
Nos. 451-455 (5)	3.05	3.05
Nos. 670-674 (5)	2.90	2.90
Nos. 592-596 (5)	2.70	2.70
Nos. 114-118 (5)	2.25	2.25
Nos. 562-566 (5)	2.50	2.50
Nos. 101-105 (5)	3.55	3.55
Nos. 490-494 (5)	2.30	2.30
Nos. 388-392 (5)	3.00	3.00
Nos. 414-418 (5)	3.10	3.10
Nos. 343-347 (5)	1.75	1.75
Set total (115) Stamps	79.00	78.05

Royal Wedding

Marriage of Prince Andrew and Sarah Ferguson
CD338

1986, July 23

Ascension	399-400	
Bahamas	602-603	
Barbados	687-688	
Cayman Islands	560-561	
Jamaica	629-630	
Pitcairn Islands	275-276	
St. Helena	460-461	
St. Kitts	181-182	
Seychelles	602-603	
Zil Elwannyen Sesel	119-120	
Solomon Islands	567-568	
Tristan da Cunha	397-398	
Zambia	348-349	

Nos. 399-400 (2)	1.60	1.60
Nos. 602-603 (2)	2.75	2.75
Nos. 687-688 (2)	2.25	1.25
Nos. 560-561 (2)	1.50	2.15
Nos. 629-630 (2)	1.75	1.75
Nos. 275-276 (2)	2.40	2.40
Nos. 460-461 (2)	1.05	1.05
Nos. 181-182 (2)	1.50	1.50
Nos. 602-603 (2)	2.50	2.50
Nos. 119-120 (2)	2.30	2.30
Nos. 567-568 (2)	1.00	1.00
Nos. 397-398 (2)	1.40	1.40
Nos. 348-349 (2)	1.10	1.30
Set total (26) Stamps	23.10	22.95

Queen Elizabeth II, 60th Birthday

Queen Elizabeth II & Prince Philip, 1947 Wedding Portrait — CD339

Designs: Photographs tracing the life of Queen Elizabeth II.

1986

Anguilla	674-677	
Antigua	925-928	
Barbuda	783-786	
Dominica	950-953	
Gambia	611-614	
Grenada	1371-1374	
Grenada Grenadines	749-752	
Lesotho	531-534	
Maldive Islands	1172-1175	
Sierra Leone	760-763	
Uganda	495-498	

Nos. 674-677 (4)	8.00	8.00
Nos. 925-928 (4)	6.75	6.75
Nos. 783-786 (4)	23.15	23.15
Nos. 950-953 (4)	7.25	7.25
Nos. 611-614 (4)	8.25	7.90
Nos. 1371-1374 (4)	6.80	6.80
Nos. 749-752 (4)	6.75	6.75
Nos. 531-534 (4)	5.50	5.50
Nos. 1172-1175 (4)	7.00	7.00
Nos. 760-763 (4)	6.30	6.30
Nos. 495-498 (4)	8.50	8.50
Set total (44) Stamps	94.25	93.90

Royal Wedding, 1986

CD340

Designs: Photographs of Prince Andrew and Sarah Ferguson during courtship, engagement and marriage.

1986

Antigua	939-942	
Barbuda	809-812	
Dominica	970-973	
Gambia	635-638	
Grenada	1385-1388	
Grenada Grenadines	758-761	
Lesotho	545-548	
Maldive Islands	1181-1184	
Sierra Leone	769-772	
Uganda	510-513	

Nos. 939-942 (4)	8.25	8.25
Nos. 809-812 (4)	14.55	14.55
Nos. 970-973 (4)	7.25	7.25
Nos. 635-638 (4)	8.55	8.55
Nos. 1385-1388 (4)	8.30	8.30
Nos. 758-761 (4)	9.00	9.00
Nos. 545-548 (4)	7.95	7.95
Nos. 1181-1184 (4)	10.20	10.20
Nos. 769-772 (4)	5.35	5.35
Nos. 510-513 (4)	9.25	10.00
Set total (40) Stamps	88.65	89.40

Lloyds of London, 300th Anniv.

CD341

Designs: 17th century aspects of Lloyds, representations of each country's individual connections with Lloyds and publicized disasters insured by the organization.

1986

Ascension	454-457	
Bahamas	655-658	
Barbados	731-734	
Bermuda	541-544	
Falkland Islands	481-484	
Liberia	1101-1104	
Malawi	534-537	
Nevis	571-574	
St. Helena	501-504	
St. Lucia	923-926	
Seychelles	649-652	
Zil Elwannyen Sesel	146-149	
Solomon Islands	627-630	
South Georgia	131-134	
Trinidad & Tobago	484-487	
Tristan da Cunha	439-442	
Vanuatu	485-488	

Nos. 454-457 (4)	5.00	5.00
Nos. 655-658 (4)	8.90	4.95
Nos. 731-734 (4)	12.50	8.35
Nos. 541-544 (4)	8.25	5.60
Nos. 481-484 (4)	6.30	4.55
Nos. 1101-1104 (4)	4.25	4.25
Nos. 534-537 (4)	11.00	7.85
Nos. 571-574 (4)	8.35	8.35
Nos. 501-504 (4)	8.70	7.15
Nos. 923-926 (4)	9.40	9.40
Nos. 649-652 (4)	13.10	13.10
Nos. 146-149 (4)	11.25	11.25
Nos. 627-630 (4)	7.90	4.45
Nos. 131-134 (4)	6.30	3.70
Nos. 484-487 (4)	10.25	6.35
Nos. 439-442 (4)	7.60	7.60
Nos. 485-488 (4)	5.90	5.90
Set total (68) Stamps	144.95	117.80

Moon Landing, 20th Anniv.

CD342

Designs: Equipment, crew photographs, spacecraft, official emblems and report profiles created for the Apollo Missions. Two stamps in each set are square in format rather than like the stamp shown; see individual country listings for more information.

1989

Ascension	468-472	
Bahamas	674-678	
Belize	916-920	
Kiribati	517-521	
Liberia	1125-1129	
Nevis	586-590	
St. Kitts	248-252	
Samoa	760-764	
Seychelles	676-680	
Zil Elwannyen Sesel	154-158	
Solomon Islands	643-647	
Vanuatu	507-511	

Nos. 468-472 (5)	9.40	8.60
Nos. 674-678 (5)	23.00	19.70
Nos. 916-920 (5)	27.40	23.50
Nos. 517-521 (5)	12.50	12.50
Nos. 1125-1129 (5)	8.50	8.50
Nos. 586-590 (5)	7.50	7.50
Nos. 248-252 (5)	8.00	8.00
Nos. 760-764 (5)	9.60	9.05
Nos. 676-680 (5)	16.05	16.05
Nos. 154-158 (5)	26.85	26.85
Nos. 643-647 (5)	12.75	11.60
Nos. 507-511 (5)	9.90	9.90
Set total (60) Stamps	171.45	161.75

Queen Mother, 90th Birthday

CD343   CD344

Designs: Portraits of Queen Elizabeth, the Queen Mother. See individual country listings for more information.

1990

Ascension	491-492
Bahamas	698-699
Barbados	782-783
British Antarctic Territory	170-171
British Indian Ocean Territory	106-107
Cayman Islands	622-623
Falkland Islands	524-525
Kenya	527-528
Kiribati	555-556
Liberia	1145-1146
Pitcairn Islands	336-337
St. Helena	532-533
St. Lucia	969-970
Seychelles	710-711
Zil Elwannyen Sesel	171-172
Solomon Islands	671-672
South Georgia	143-144
Swaziland	565-566
Tristan da Cunha	480-481

Nos. 491-492 (2)	4.75	5.65
Nos. 698-699 (2)	5.65	5.65
Nos. 782-783 (2)	4.00	3.70
Nos. 170-171 (2)	6.75	6.75
Nos. 106-107 (2)	20.75	21.25
Nos. 622-623 (2)	5.10	6.75
Nos. 524-525 (2)	5.25	5.25
Nos. 527-528 (2)	7.00	7.00
Nos. 555-556 (2)	5.60	5.60
Nos. 1145-1146 (2)	3.25	3.25
Nos. 336-337 (2)	4.25	4.25
Nos. 532-533 (2)	5.25	5.25
Nos. 969-970 (2)	5.25	5.25
Nos. 710-711 (2)	6.60	6.60
Nos. 171-172 (2)	8.25	8.25
Nos. 671-672 (2)	6.50	6.40
Nos. 143-144 (2)	5.75	5.75
Nos. 565-566 (2)	4.35	4.35
Nos. 480-481 (2)	5.60	5.60
Set total (38) Stamps	119.90	122.55

Queen Elizabeth II, 65th Birthday, and Prince Philip, 70th Birthday

CD345

CD346

Designs: Portraits of Queen Elizabeth II and Prince Philip differ for each country. Printed in sheets of 10 + 5 labels (3 different) between. Stamps alternate, producing 5 different triptychs.

1991

Ascension	506a
Bahamas	731a
Belize	970a
Bermuda	618a
Kiribati	572a
Mauritius	734a
Pitcairn Islands	349a
St. Helena	555a
St. Kitts	319a
Samoa	791a
Seychelles	724a
Zil Elwannyen Sesel	178a
Solomon Islands	689a
South Georgia	150a
Swaziland	587a
Vanuatu	541a

No. 506a (1)	3.50	3.75
No. 731a (1)	4.00	4.00
No. 970a (1)	3.75	3.75
No. 618a (1)	4.00	4.00
No. 572a (1)	4.00	4.00
No. 734a (1)	3.75	3.75
No. 349a (1)	3.25	3.25
No. 555a (1)	2.75	2.75
No. 319a (1)	3.00	3.00

No. 791a (1)	4.25	4.25
No. 724a (1)	5.00	5.00
No. 178a (1)	6.50	6.50
No. 689a (1)	4.50	4.50
No. 150a (1)	7.00	7.00
No. 587a (1)	4.25	4.25
No. 541a (1)	2.50	2.50
Set total (16) Stamps	66.00	66.25

Royal Family Birthday, Anniversary

CD347

Queen Elizabeth II, 65th birthday, Charles and Diana, 10th wedding anniversary: Various photographs of Queen Elizabeth II, Prince Philip, Prince Charles, Princess Diana and their sons William and Henry.

1991

Antigua	1446-1455
Barbuda	1229-1238
Dominica	1328-1337
Gambia	1080-1089
Grenada	2006-2015
Grenada Grenadines	1331-1340
Guyana	2440-2451
Lesotho	871-875
Maldive Islands	1533-1542
Nevis	666-675
St. Vincent	1485-1494
St. Vincent Grenadines	769-778
Sierra Leone	1387-1396
Turks & Caicos Islands	913-922
Uganda	918-927

Nos. 1446-1455 (10)	21.95	20.30
Nos. 1229-1238 (10)	125.00	119.50
Nos. 1328-1337 (10)	30.20	30.20
Nos. 1080-1089 (10)	24.65	24.40
Nos. 2006-2015 (10)	25.45	22.10
Nos. 1331-1340 (10)	23.85	23.35
Nos. 2440-2451 (12)	21.40	21.15
Nos. 871-875 (5)	13.55	13.55
Nos. 1533-1542 (10)	29.60	29.60
Nos. 666-675 (10)	25.65	25.65
Nos. 1485-1494 (10)	26.75	25.90
Nos. 769-778 (10)	25.40	25.40
Nos. 1387-1396 (10)	26.55	26.55
Nos. 913-922 (10)	31.65	30.00
Nos. 918-927 (10)	26.60	26.60
Set total (147) Stamps	478.25	464.25

Queen Elizabeth II's Accession to the Throne, 40th Anniv.

CD348

Various photographs of Queen Elizabeth II with local Scenes.

1992

Antigua	1513-1518
Barbuda	1306-1311
Dominica	1414-1419
Gambia	1172-1177
Grenada	2047-2052
Grenada Grenadines	1368-1373
Lesotho	881-885
Maldive Islands	1637-1642
Nevis	702-707
St. Vincent	1582-1587
St. Vincent Grenadines	829-834
Sierra Leone	1482-1487
Turks and Caicos Islands	978-987
Uganda	990-995
Virgin Islands	742-746

Nos. 1513-1518 (6)	16.00	14.10
Nos. 1306-1311 (6)	125.25	83.65
Nos. 1414-1419 (6)	12.50	12.50
Nos. 1172-1177 (6)	16.60	16.35
Nos. 2047-2052 (6)	15.95	15.95
Nos. 1368-1373 (6)	17.00	15.35
Nos. 881-885 (5)	11.90	11.90
Nos. 1637-1642 (6)	17.55	17.55
Nos. 702-707 (6)	13.80	13.80
Nos. 1582-1587 (6)	14.40	14.40
Nos. 829-834 (6)	19.65	19.65
Nos. 1482-1487 (6)	22.50	22.50
Nos. 913-922 (10)	31.65	30.00
Nos. 990-995 (6)	19.50	19.50
Nos. 742-746 (5)	15.50	15.50
Set total (92) Stamps	369.75	322.70

CD349

1992

Ascension	531-535
Bahamas	744-748
Bermuda	623-627
British Indian Ocean Territory	119-123
Cayman Islands	648-652
Falkland Islands	549-553
Gibraltar	605-609
Hong Kong	619-623
Kenya	563-567
Kiribati	582-586
Pitcairn Islands	362-366
St. Helena	570-574
St. Kitts	332-336
Samoa	805-809
Seychelles	734-738
Zil Elwannyen Sesel	183-187
Solomon Islands	708-712
South Georgia	157-161
Tristan da Cunha	508-512
Vanuatu	555-559
Zambia	561-565

Nos. 531-535 (5)	6.35	6.35
Nos. 744-748 (5)	6.90	4.70
Nos. 623-627 (5)	8.20	7.30
Nos. 119-123 (5)	24.75	21.00
Nos. 648-652 (5)	7.60	7.10
Nos. 549-553 (5)	6.80	8.20
Nos. 605-609 (5)	5.15	5.50
Nos. 619-623 (5)	5.65	2.65
Nos. 563-567 (5)	9.10	9.10
Nos. 582-586 (5)	3.85	3.85
Nos. 362-366 (5)	5.35	5.35
Nos. 570-574 (5)	5.70	5.70
Nos. 332-336 (5)	6.60	5.50
Nos. 805-809 (5)	8.10	6.15
Nos. 734-738 (5)	10.80	10.80
Nos. 183-187 (5)	9.40	9.40
Nos. 708-712 (5)	7.95	7.30
Nos. 157-161 (5)	5.85	5.75
Nos. 508-512 (5)	8.75	8.30
Nos. 555-559 (5)	3.65	3.65
Nos. 561-565 (5)	5.60	5.60
Set total (105) Stamps	162.10	149.25

Royal Air Force, 75th Anniversary

CD350

1993

Ascension	557-561
Bahamas	771-775
Barbados	842-846
Belize	1003-1008
Bermuda	648-651
British Indian Ocean Territory	136-140
Falkland Is.	573-577
Fiji	687-691
Montserrat	830-834
St. Kitts	351-355

Nos. 557-561 (5)	16.70	14.85
Nos. 771-775 (5)	26.00	22.20
Nos. 842-846 (5)	13.65	12.35
Nos. 1003-1008 (6)	19.40	18.70
Nos. 648-651 (4)	10.50	9.95
Nos. 136-140 (5)	17.50	17.50
Nos. 573-577 (5)	11.25	11.25
Nos. 687-691 (5)	18.95	18.95
Nos. 830-834 (5)	14.35	14.35
Nos. 351-355 (5)	24.45	23.95
Set total (50) Stamps	172.75	164.05

Royal Air Force, 80th Anniv.

Design CD350 Re-inscribed

1998

Ascension	697-701
Bahamas	907-911
British Indian Ocean Terr	198-202
Cayman Islands	754-758
Fiji	814-818
Gibraltar	755-759
Samoa	957-961
Turks & Caicos Islands	1258-1265
Tuvalu	763-767
Virgin Islands	879-883

Nos. 697-701 (5)	17.35	17.35
Nos. 907-911 (5)	14.25	13.55
Nos. 136-140 (5)	17.50	17.50
Nos. 754-758 (5)	15.75	15.75
Nos. 814-818 (5)	15.50	15.50
Nos. 755-759 (5)	9.70	9.70
Nos. 957-961 (5)	16.70	15.90
Nos. 1258-1265 (2)	32.00	32.00
Nos. 763-767 (5)	9.75	9.75
Nos. 879-883 (5)	17.00	17.00
Set total (47) Stamps	165.50	164.00

End of World War II, 50th Anniv.

CD351

CD352

1995

Ascension	613-617
Bahamas	824-828
Barbados	891-895
Belize	1047-1050
British Indian Ocean Territory	163-167
Cayman Islands	704-708
Falkland Islands	634-638
Fiji	720-724
Kiribati	662-668
Liberia	1175-1179
Mauritius	803-805
St. Helena	646-654
St. Kitts	389-393
St. Lucia	1018-1022
Samoa	890-894
Solomon Islands	799-803
South Georgia	198-200
Tristan da Cunha	562-566

Nos. 613-617 (5)	21.50	21.50
Nos. 824-828 (5)	22.00	18.70
Nos. 891-895 (5)	14.20	11.90
Nos. 1047-1050 (4)	7.45	6.75
Nos. 163-167 (5)	16.25	16.25
Nos. 704-708 (5)	18.15	14.45
Nos. 634-638 (5)	17.90	17.40
Nos. 720-724 (5)	21.35	21.35
Nos. 662-668 (7)	16.30	16.30
Nos. 1175-1179 (5)	15.25	11.15
Nos. 803-805 (3)	7.50	7.50
Nos. 646-654 (9)	26.10	26.10
Nos. 389-393 (5)	13.60	13.60
Nos. 1018-1022 (5)	14.25	11.15
Nos. 890-894 (5)	14.25	13.50
Nos. 799-803 (5)	17.50	17.50
Nos. 198-200 (3)	14.00	14.00
Nos. 562-566 (5)	20.10	20.10
Set total (91) Stamps	297.65	279.20

UN, 50th Anniv.

CD353

1995

Bahamas		839-842
Barbados		901-904
Belize		1055-1058
Jamaica		847-851
Liberia		1187-1190
Mauritius		813-816
Pitcairn Islands		436-439
St. Kitts		398-401
St. Lucia		1023-1026
Samoa		900-903
Tristan da Cunha		568-571
Virgin Islands		807-810

Nos. 839-842 (4)	8.00	7.05
Nos. 901-904 (4)	7.00	5.75
Nos. 1055-1058 (4)	5.70	5.60
Nos. 847-851 (5)	6.50	5.95
Nos. 1187-1190 (4)	9.65	9.65
Nos. 813-816 (4)	3.90	3.90
Nos. 436-439 (4)	8.15	8.15
Nos. 398-401 (4)	6.15	6.15
Nos. 1023-1026 (4)	7.50	7.25
Nos. 900-903 (4)	9.35	8.20
Nos. 568-571 (4)	13.50	13.50
Nos. 807-810 (4)	9.45	9.45
Set total (49) Stamps	94.85	90.60

Queen Elizabeth, 70th Birthday

CD354

1996

Ascension		632-635
British Antarctic Territory		240-243
British Indian Ocean Territory		176-180
Falkland Islands		653-657
Pitcairn Islands		446-449
St. Helena		672-676
Samoa		912-916
Tokelau		223-227
Tristan da Cunha		576-579
Virgin Islands		824-828

Nos. 632-635 (4)	5.90	5.90
Nos. 240-243 (4)	10.50	8.90
Nos. 176-180 (5)	11.50	11.50
Nos. 653-657 (5)	14.35	11.90
Nos. 446-449 (4)	8.60	8.60
Nos. 672-676 (5)	12.70	12.70
Nos. 912-916 (5)	11.50	11.50
Nos. 223-227 (5)	11.35	11.35
Nos. 576-579 (4)	8.35	8.35
Nos. 824-828 (5)	12.30	12.30
Set total (46) Stamps	107.05	103.00

Diana, Princess of Wales (1961-97)

CD355

1998

Ascension		696
Bahamas		901A-902
Barbados		950
Belize		1091
Bermuda		753
Botswana		659-663
British Antarctic Territory		258
British Indian Ocean Terr.		197
Cayman Islands		752A-753

Falkland Islands		694
Fiji		819-820
Gibraltar		754
Kiribati		719A-720
Namibia		909
Niue		706
Norfolk Island		644-645
Papua New Guinea		937
Pitcairn Islands		487
St. Helena		711
St. Kitts		437A-438
Samoa		955A-956
Seycelles		802
Solomon Islands		866-867
South Georgia		220
Tokelau		252B-253
Tonga		980
Niuafo'ou		201
Tristan da Cunha		618
Tuvalu		762
Vanuatu		718A-719
Virgin Islands		878

No. 696 (1)	5.50	5.50
Nos. 901A-902 (2)	5.30	5.30
No. 950 (1)	5.00	5.00
No. 1091 (1)	5.50	5.50
No. 753 (1)	5.50	5.50
Nos. 659-663 (5)	10.25	10.10
No. 258 (1)	6.25	6.25
No. 197 (1)	6.50	6.50
Nos. 752A-753 (3)	7.75	7.75
No. 694 (1)	4.75	4.75
Nos. 819-820 (2)	6.00	6.00
No. 754 (1)	4.75	4.75
Nos. 719A-720 (2)	4.85	4.85
No. 909 (1)	1.90	1.90
No. 706 (1)	5.50	5.50
Nos. 644-645 (2)	5.25	5.25
No. 937 (1)	6.50	6.50
No. 487 (1)	4.75	4.75
No. 711 (1)	4.25	4.25
Nos. 437A-438 (2)	5.15	5.15
Nos. 955A-956 (2)	7.00	7.00
No. 802 (1)	6.25	6.25
Nos. 866-867 (2)	6.90	6.90
No. 220 (1)	5.25	5.25
Nos. 252B-253 (2)	6.75	6.75
No. 980 (1)	5.75	5.75
No. 201 (1)	7.75	7.75
No. 618 (1)	5.00	5.00
No. 762 (1)	4.00	4.00
Nos. 718A-719 (2)	8.00	8.00
No. 878 (1)	5.50	5.50
Set total (46) Stamps	179.35	179.20

Wedding of Prince Edward and Sophie Rhys-Jones

CD356

1999

Ascension		729-730
Cayman Islands		775-776
Falkland Islands		729-730
Pitcairn Islands		505-506
St. Helena		733-734
Samoa		971-972
Tristan da Cunha		636-637
Virgin Islands		908-909

Nos. 729-730 (2)	5.90	5.90
Nos. 775-776 (2)	5.50	5.50
Nos. 729-730 (2)	15.00	15.00
Nos. 505-506 (2)	7.00	7.00
Nos. 733-734 (2)	5.00	5.00
Nos. 971-972 (2)	5.00	5.00
Nos. 636-637 (2)	7.50	7.50
Nos. 908-909 (2)	8.30	8.30
Set total (16) Stamps	59.20	59.20

1st Manned Moon Landing, 30th Anniv.

CD357

1999

Ascension		731-735
Bahamas		942-946
Barbados		967-971
Bermuda		778
Cayman Islands		777-781
Fiji		853-857
Jamaica		889-893
Kirbati		746-750
Nauru		465-469
St. Kitts		460-464
Samoa		973-977
Solomon Islands		875-879
Tuvalu		800-804
Virgin Islands		910-914

Nos. 731-735 (5)	13.90	13.90
Nos. 942-946 (5)	14.10	14.10
Nos. 967-971 (5)	8.65	7.75
No. 778 (1)	8.00	8.00
Nos. 777-781 (5)	10.30	10.30
Nos. 853-857 (5)	10.40	10.40
Nos. 889-893 (5)	10.20	10.00
Nos. 746-750 (5)	8.85	8.85
Nos. 465-469 (5)	8.90	10.15
Nos. 460-464 (5)	12.00	12.00
Nos. 973-977 (5)	13.45	13.30
Nos. 875-879 (5)	10.00	9.85
Nos. 800-804 (5)	7.45	7.45
Nos. 910-914 (5)	15.00	15.00
Set total (66) Stamps	151.20	151.05

Queen Mother's Century

CD358

1999

Ascension		736-740
Bahamas		951-955
Cayman Islands		782-786
Falkland Islands		734-738
Fiji		858-862
Norfolk Island		688-692
St. Helena		740-744
Samoa		978-982
Solomon Islands		880-884
South Georgia		231-235
Tristan da Cunha		638-642
Tuvalu		805-809

Nos. 736-740 (5)	17.00	17.00
Nos. 951-955 (5)	14.00	12.90
Nos. 782-786 (5)	9.15	9.15
Nos. 734-738 (5)	30.75	27.75
Nos. 858-862 (5)	15.00	15.00
Nos. 688-692 (5)	10.30	10.30
Nos. 740-744 (5)	16.15	16.15
Nos. 978-982 (5)	12.50	12.10
Nos. 880-884 (5)	10.00	9.45
Nos. 231-235 (5)	30.25	29.75
Nos. 638-642 (5)	18.00	18.00
Nos. 805-809 (5)	8.65	8.65
Set total (60) Stamps	191.75	186.20

Prince William, 18th Birthday

CD359

2000

Ascension		755-759
Cayman Islands		797-801
Falkland Islands		762-766
Fiji		889-893
South Georgia		257-261
Tristan da Cunha		664-668
Virgin Islands		925-929

Nos. 755-759 (5)	17.75	17.75
Nos. 797-801 (5)	13.05	12.75
Nos. 762-766 (5)	27.15	23.75
Nos. 889-893 (5)	14.00	14.00
Nos. 257-261 (5)	29.00	29.00
Nos. 664-668 (5)	21.50	21.50
Nos. 925-929 (5)	14.75	14.75
Set total (35) Stamps	137.20	133.50

Reign of Queen Elizabeth II, 50th Anniv.

CD360

2002

Ascension		790-794
Bahamas		1033-1037
Barbados		1019-1023
Belize		1152-1156
Bermuda		822-826
British Antarctic Territory		307-311
British Indian Ocean Territory		239-243
Cayman Islands		844-848
Falkland Islands		804-808
Gibraltar		896-900
Jamaica		952-956
Nauru		491-495
Norfolk Island		758-762
Papua New Guinea		1019-1023
Pitcairn Islands		552
St. Helena		788-792
St. Lucia		1146-1150
Solomon Islands		931-935
South Georgia		274-278
Swaziland		706-710
Tokelau		302-306
Tonga		1059
Niuafo'ou		239
Tristan da Cunha		706-710
Virgin Islands		967-971

Nos. 790-794 (5)	16.25	16.25
Nos. 1033-1037 (5)	15.75	15.75
Nos. 1019-1023 (5)	13.15	13.15
Nos. 1152-1156 (5)	15.50	15.15
Nos. 822-826 (5)	18.50	18.50
Nos. 307-311 (5)	25.00	25.00
Nos. 239-243 (5)	22.00	22.00
Nos. 844-848 (5)	14.25	14.25
Nos. 804-808 (5)	23.50	22.50
Nos. 896-900 (5)	6.65	6.65
Nos. 952-956 (5)	18.25	18.25
Nos. 491-495 (5)	18.75	18.75
Nos. 758-762 (5)	19.50	19.50
Nos. 1019-1023 (5)	14.50	14.50
No. 552 (1)	9.25	9.25
Nos. 788-792 (5)	19.75	19.75
Nos. 1146-1150 (5)	12.25	12.25
Nos. 931-935 (5)	16.00	16.00
Nos. 274-278 (5)	28.50	28.50
Nos. 706-710 (5)	12.75	12.75
Nos. 302-306 (5)	17.00	17.00
No. 1059 (1)	8.00	8.00
No. 239 (1)	7.00	7.00
Nos. 706-710 (5)	18.50	18.50
Nos. 967-971 (5)	19.00	19.00
Set total (113) Stamps	409.55	408.20

Queen Mother Elizabeth (1900-2002)

CD361

2002

Ascension		799-801
Bahamas		1044-1046
Bermuda		834-836
British Antarctic Territory		312-314

British Indian Ocean Territory 245-
247
Cayman Islands........................857-861
Falkland Islands 812-816
Nauru...................................499-501
Pitcairn Islands.......................561-565
St. Helena 808-812
St. Lucia 1155-1159
Seychelles 830
Solomon Islands.......................945-947
South Georgia 281-285
Tokelau 312-314
Tristan da Cunha.....................715-717
Virgin Islands.........................979-983

Nos. 799-801 (3)	9.75	9.75
Nos. 1044-1046 (3)	9.35	9.35
Nos. 834-836 (3)	12.50	12.50
Nos. 312-314 (3)	19.25	19.25
Nos. 245-247 (3)	19.50	19.50
Nos. 857-861 (5)	15.00	15.00
Nos. 812-816 (5)	31.50	31.50
Nos. 499-501 (3)	16.00	16.00
Nos. 561-565 (5)	15.25	15.25
Nos. 808-812 (5)	12.00	12.00
Nos. 1155-1159 (5)	13.00	13.00
No. 830 (1)	6.50	6.50
Nos. 945-947 (3)	11.00	11.00
Nos. 281-285 (5)	20.00	20.00
Nos. 312-314 (3)	14.25	13.75
Nos. 715-717 (3)	16.25	16.25
Nos. 979-983 (5)	26.50	26.50
Set total (63) Stamps	267.60	267.10

Head of Queen Elizabeth II

CD362

2003

Ascension...............................822
Bermuda..................................865
British Antarctic Territory.................322
British Indian Ocean Territory 261
Cayman Islands...........................878
Falkland Islands 828
St. Helena 820
South Georgia 294
Tristan da Cunha............................731
Virgin Islands.............................1003

No. 822 (1)	13.50	13.50
No. 865 (1)	55.00	55.00
No. 322 (1)	10.00	10.00
No. 261 (1)	12.50	12.50
No. 878 (1)	17.00	17.00
No. 828 (1)	10.00	10.00
No. 820 (1)	9.00	9.00
No. 294 (1)	9.00	9.00
No. 731 (1)	10.00	10.00
No. 1003 (1)	10.00	10.00
Set total (10) Stamps	156.00	156.00

Coronation of Queen Elizabeth II, 50th Anniv.

CD363

2003

Ascension................................823-825
Bahamas 1073-1075
Bermuda...............................866-868
British Antarctic Territory..........323-325
British Indian Ocean Territory 262-
264
Cayman Islands........................879-881
Jamaica 970-972
Kiribati 825-827
Pitcairn Islands.........................577-581
St. Helena 821-823
St. Lucia 1171-1173
Tokelau 320-322
Tristan da Cunha.....................732-734
Virgin Islands........................1004-1006

Nos. 823-825 (3)	13.50	13.50
Nos. 1073-1075 (3)	13.00	13.00
Nos. 866-868 (3)	14.25	14.25
Nos. 323-325 (3)	26.00	26.00
Nos. 262-264 (3)	31.00	31.00
Nos. 879-881 (3)	20.25	20.25

Nos. 970-972 (3)	11.75	11.75
Nos. 825-827 (3)	13.50	13.50
Nos. 577-581 (5)	14.40	14.40
Nos. 821-823 (3)	7.25	7.25
Nos. 1171-1173 (3)	8.75	8.75
Nos. 320-322 (3)	20.00	20.00
Nos. 732-734 (3)	16.75	16.75
Nos. 1004-1006 (3)	25.00	25.00
Set total (44) Stamps	235.40	235.40

Prince William, 21st Birthday

CD364

2003

Ascension......................................826
British Indian Ocean Territory 265
Cayman Islands.......................882-884
Falkland Islands 829
South Georgia 295
Tokelau 323
Tristan da Cunha............................735
Virgin Islands........................1007-1009

No. 826 (1)	7.50	7.50
No. 265 (1)	9.00	9.00
Nos. 882-884 (3)	7.65	7.65
No. 829 (1)	14.50	14.50
No. 295 (1)	9.00	9.00
No. 323 (1)	7.25	7.25
No. 735 (1)	6.00	6.00
Nos. 1007-1009 (3)	10.00	10.00
Set total (12) Stamps	70.90	70.90

2016 Scott Supplements

Whether you're updating your album or decided to start collecting a new country, Scott supplements are the way to go. Heavy acid-free paper and the use of Scott numbers for easy identification makes collecting easy.

Country	Item No.	Retail	AA	Release Date
NATIONAL SERIES				
U.S. National	100S016	22.99	19.99	February
U.S. Minuteman	180S016	22.99	19.99	February
U.S. Pony Express	178S016	22.99	19.99	March
U.S. Platinum Hingeless	199S016	78.99	67.99	April
American (U.S. & U.N.)	170S016	34.99	29.99	March
U.S. Commemorative Singles	130S016	16.99	13.99	February
U.S. Commemorative & Air Plate Blocks	120S016	19.99	16.99	April
U.S. Regular & Air Plate Blocks	125S016	11.99	9.99	April
U.S. Small Panes	118S016	34.99	29.99	April
U.S. Booklet Panes	101S016	16.99	13.99	April
U.S. Plate Number Coils–Simplified	113S016	11.99	9.99	January
U.S. Plate Number Coils–Comprehensive	114S016	19.99	16.99	January
U.S. Plate Number Coil Singles	117S016	19.99	16.99	January
U.S. Federal & State Duck Stamps	115S016	22.99	19.99	October
U.S. Computer Vended Postage	103S016	11.99	9.99	March
U.N. Singles & Postal Stationery	551S016	25.99	21.99	March
U.N. Minuteman	181S016	25.99	21.99	March
U.N. Imprint Blocks	552S016	19.99	16.99	March
Republic of the Marshall Islands	111MA16	22.99	19.99	April
Republic of Palau	111PA16	34.99	29.99	April
Federated States of Micronesia	111MI16	34.99	29.99	April
SPECIALTY SERIES				
Argentina	642S016	19.99	16.99	September
Australia	210S016	22.99	19.99	September
Austria	300S016	19.99	16.99	May
Baltic States	361S016	19.99	16.99	August
Belgium	303S016	22.99	19.99	August
Brazil	644S016	19.99	16.99	September
Canada	240S016	25.99	21.99	May
Canada Master	245S016	28.99	24.99	May
Cyprus	203CY16	11.99	9.99	May
Czech Republic & Slovakia	307S016	22.99	19.99	August
Denmark	345DM16	16.99	13.99	June
Dependencies of Australia	211S016	22.99	19.99	September
Dependencies of New Zealand	221S016	34.99	29.99	September
Dominican Republic	648S016	16.99	13.99	September
Faroe Islands	345FI16	11.99	9.99	June
Finland & Aland	345FN16	22.99	19.99	June
France	310S016	34.99	29.99	May
French Polynesia	625S016	11.99	9.99	August
French Southern & Antarctic Territory	626S016	16.99	13.99	August

Country	Item No.	Retail	AA	Release Date
SPECIALTY SERIES				
Germany	315S316	16.99	13.99	May
Gibraltar	203GB16	16.99	13.99	May
Great Britain	200S016	22.99	19.99	May
Greece	320S016	22.99	19.99	June
Greenland	345GR16	16.99	13.99	June
Guernsey & Alderney	202GN16	22.99	19.99	May
Hong Kong	275HK16	22.99	19.99	May
Hungary	323S016	22.99	19.99	August
Iceland	345IC16	11.99	9.99	June
India	618S016	22.99	19.99	July
Ireland	201S016	16.99	13.99	May
Isle of Man	202IM16	22.99	19.99	May
Israel Singles	500S016	16.99	13.99	August
Israel Tab Singles	501S016	19.99	16.99	August
Italy	325S016	22.99	19.99	July
Japan	510S016	45.99	39.99	July
Jersey	202JR16	22.99	19.99	May
Liechtenstein	367S016	11.99	9.99	June
Luxembourg	330S016	11.99	9.99	August
Malta	203ML16	16.99	13.99	May
Mexico	430S016	19.99	16.99	September
Monaco & French Andorra	333S016	19.99	16.99	May
Netherlands	335S016	40.99	34.99	August
New Zealand	220S016	22.99	19.99	September
Norway	345NR16	11.99	9.99	June
People's Republic of China	520S016	22.99	19.99	July
Poland	338S016	19.99	16.99	August
Portugal/Azores/Maderia	340S016	22.99	19.99	July
Republic of China Taiwan	530S016	22.99	19.99	July
Russia	360S016	34.99	29.99	September
San Marino	328S016	11.99	9.99	July
Singapore	275SG16	22.99	19.99	May
South Africa	669S016	22.99	19.99	October
Spain & Spanish Andorra	355S016	22.99	19.99	July
Sri Lanka	622S016	19.99	16.99	July
Sweden	345SW16	16.99	13.99	September
Switzerland	365S016	16.99	13.99	June
Thailand	540S016	22.99	19.99	July
Turkey	505S016	22.99	19.99	July
Ukraine	362UK16	19.99	16.99	August
Vatican City	375S016	11.99	9.99	July
International Part A	852P116	160.99	140.00	December
International Part B	852P216	160.99	140.00	December

Visit AmosAdvantage.com
or Call 1-800-572-6885
Outside U.S. & Canada 937-498-0800 • Mail to: P.O. Box 4129, Sidney OH 45365

SHIPPING & HANDLING: United States: Order total $0-$10.00 charged $3.99 shipping. United States - Order total $10.01-$79.99 charged $7.99 shipping. United States - Order total $80.00 or more charged 10% of order total for shipping. Maximum Freight Charge $45.00. Canada: 20% of order total. Minimum charge $19.99 Maximum charge $200.00. Foreign orders are shipped via FedExl Intl. or USPS and billed actual freight.

ORDERING INFORMATION: *AA prices apply to paid subscribers of Amos Media titles, or orders placed online. Prices, terms and product availability subject to change. Shipping and handling rates will apply.

British Commonwealth of Nations

Dominions, Colonies, Territories, Offices and Independent Members

Comprising stamps of the British Commonwealth and associated nations.

A strict observance of technicalities would bar some or all of the stamps listed under Burma, Ireland, Kuwait, Nepal, New Republic, Orange Free State, Samoa, South Africa, South-West Africa, Stellaland, Sudan, Swaziland, the two Transvaal Republics and others but these are included for the convenience of collectors.

1. Great Britain

Great Britain: Including England, Scotland, Wales and Northern Ireland.

2. The Dominions, Present and Past

AUSTRALIA

The Commonwealth of Australia was proclaimed on January 1, 1901. It consists of six former colonies as follows:

New South Wales	Victoria
Queensland	Tasmania
South Australia	Western Australia

The following islands and territories are, or have been, administered by Australia: Australian Antarctic Territory, Christmas Island, Cocos (Keeling) Islands, Nauru, New Guinea, Norfolk Island, Papua.

CANADA

The Dominion of Canada was created by the British North America Act in 1867. The following provinces were former sepa- rate colonies and issued postage stamps:

British Columbia and	Newfoundland
Vancouver Island	Nova Scotia
New Brunswick	Prince Edward Island

FIJI

The colony of Fiji became an independent nation with dominion status on Oct. 10, 1970.

GHANA

This state came into existence Mar. 6, 1957, with dominion status. It consists of the former colony of the Gold Coast and the Trusteeship Territory of Togoland. Ghana became a republic July 1, 1960.

INDIA

The Republic of India was inaugurated on January 26, 1950. It succeeded the Dominion of India which was proclaimed August 15, 1947, when the former Empire of India was divided into Pakistan and the Union of India. The Republic is composed of about 40 predominantly Hindu states of three classes: governor's provinces, chief commissioner's provinces and princely states. India also has various territories, such as the Andaman and Nicobar Islands.

The old Empire of India was a federation of British India and the native states. The more important princely states were autonomous. Of the more than 700 Indian states, these 43 are familiar names to philatelists because of their postage stamps.

CONVENTION STATES

Chamba	Jhind
Faridkot	Nabha
Gwalior	Patiala

FEUDATORY STATES

Alwar	Jammu and Kashmir
Bahawalpur	Jasdan
Bamra	Jhalawar
Barwani	Jhind (1875-76)
Bhopal	Kashmir
Bhor	Kishangarh
Bijawar	Kotah
Bundi	Las Bela
Bussahir	Morvi
Charkhari	Nandgaon
Cochin	Nowanuggur
Dhar	Orchha
Dungarpur	Poonch
Duttia	Rajasthan
Faridkot (1879-85)	Rajpeepla
Hyderabad	Sirmur
Idar	Soruth
Indore	Tonk
Jaipur	Travancore
Jammu	Wadhwan

NEW ZEALAND

Became a dominion on September 26, 1907. The following islands and territories are, or have been, administered by New Zealand:

Aitutaki	Ross Dependency
Cook Islands (Rarotonga)	Samoa (Western Samoa)
Niue	Tokelau Islands
Penrhyn	

PAKISTAN

The Republic of Pakistan was proclaimed March 23, 1956. It succeeded the Dominion which was proclaimed August 15, 1947. It is made up of all or part of several Moslem provinces and various districts of the former Empire of India, including Bahawalpur and Las Bela. Pakistan withdrew from the Commonwealth in 1972.

SOUTH AFRICA

Under the terms of the South African Act (1909) the self-governing colonies of Cape of Good Hope, Natal, Orange River Colony and Transvaal united on May 31, 1910, to form the Union of South Africa. It became an independent republic May 3, 1961.

Under the terms of the Treaty of Versailles, South-West Africa, formerly German South-West Africa, was mandated to the Union of South Africa.

SRI LANKA (CEYLON)

The Dominion of Ceylon was proclaimed February 4, 1948. The island had been a Crown Colony from 1802 until then. On May 22, 1972, Ceylon became the Republic of Sri Lanka.

3. Colonies, Past and Present; Controlled Territory and Independent Members of the Commonwealth

Aden	Bechuanaland
Aitutaki	Bechuanaland Prot.
Anguilla	Belize
Antigua	Bermuda
Ascension	Botswana
Bahamas	British Antarctic Territory
Bahrain	British Central Africa
Bangladesh	British Columbia and
Barbados	Vancouver Island
Barbuda	British East Africa
Basutoland	British Guiana
Batum	

British Honduras
British Indian Ocean Territory
British New Guinea
British Solomon Islands
British Somaliland
Brunei
Burma
Bushire
Cameroons
Cape of Good Hope
Cayman Islands
Christmas Island
Cocos (Keeling) Islands
Cook Islands
Crete,
  British Administration
Cyprus
Dominica
East Africa & Uganda
  Protectorates
Egypt
Falkland Islands
Fiji
Gambia
German East Africa
Gibraltar
Gilbert Islands
Gilbert & Ellice Islands
Gold Coast
Grenada
Griqualand West
Guernsey
Guyana
Heligoland
Hong Kong
Indian Native States
  (see India)
Ionian Islands
Jamaica
Jersey

Kenya
Kenya, Uganda & Tanzania
Kuwait
Labuan
Lagos
Leeward Islands
Lesotho
Madagascar
Malawi
Malaya
  Federated Malay States
  Johore
  Kedah
  Kelantan
  Malacca
  Negri Sembilan
  Pahang
  Penang
  Perak
  Perlis
  Selangor
  Singapore
  Sungei Ujong
  Trengganu
Malaysia
Maldive Islands
Malta
Man, Isle of
Mauritius
Mesopotamia
Montserrat
Muscat
Namibia
Natal
Nauru
Nevis
New Britain
New Brunswick
Newfoundland
New Guinea

New Hebrides
New Republic
New South Wales
Niger Coast Protectorate
Nigeria
Niue
Norfolk Island
North Borneo
Northern Nigeria
Northern Rhodesia
North West Pacific Islands
Nova Scotia
Nyasaland Protectorate
Oman
Orange River Colony
Palestine
Papua New Guinea
Penrhyn Island
Pitcairn Islands
Prince Edward Island
Queensland
Rhodesia
Rhodesia & Nyasaland
Ross Dependency
Sabah
St. Christopher
St. Helena
St. Kitts
St. Kitts-Nevis-Anguilla
St. Lucia
St. Vincent
Samoa
Sarawak
Seychelles
Sierra Leone
Solomon Islands
Somaliland Protectorate
South Arabia
South Australia
South Georgia

Southern Nigeria
Southern Rhodesia
South-West Africa
Stellaland
Straits Settlements
Sudan
Swaziland
Tanganyika
Tanzania
Tasmania
Tobago
Togo
Tokelau Islands
Tonga
Transvaal
Trinidad
Trinidad and Tobago
Tristan da Cunha
Trucial States
Turks and Caicos
Turks Islands
Tuvalu
Uganda
United Arab Emirates
Victoria
Virgin Islands
Western Australia
Zambia
Zanzibar
Zululand

POST OFFICES IN FOREIGN COUNTRIES
Africa
  East Africa Forces
  Middle East Forces
Bangkok
China
Morocco
Turkish Empire

Colonies, Former Colonies, Offices, Territories Controlled by Parent States

Belgium
Belgian Congo
Ruanda-Urundi

Denmark
Danish West Indies
Faroe Islands
Greenland
Iceland

Finland
Aland Islands

France
COLONIES PAST AND PRESENT, CONTROLLED TERRITORIES
Afars & Issas, Territory of
Alaouites
Alexandretta
Algeria
Alsace & Lorraine
Anjouan
Annam & Tonkin
Benin
Cambodia (Khmer)
Cameroun
Castellorizo
Chad
Cilicia
Cochin China
Comoro Islands
Dahomey
Diego Suarez
Djibouti (Somali Coast)
Fezzan
French Congo
French Equatorial Africa
French Guiana
French Guinea
French India
French Morocco
French Polynesia (Oceania)
French Southern & Antarctic Territories
French Sudan
French West Africa
Gabon
Germany
Ghadames
Grand Comoro
Guadeloupe
Indo-China
Inini
Ivory Coast
Laos
Latakia
Lebanon
Madagascar
Martinique
Mauritania
Mayotte
Memel
Middle Congo
Moheli
New Caledonia
New Hebrides
Niger Territory

Nossi-Be
Obock
Reunion
Rouad, Ile
Ste.-Marie de Madagascar
St. Pierre & Miquelon
Senegal
Senegambia & Niger
Somali Coast
Syria
Tahiti
Togo
Tunisia
Ubangi-Shari
Upper Senegal & Niger
Upper Volta
Viet Nam
Wallis & Futuna Islands

POST OFFICES IN FOREIGN COUNTRIES
China
Crete
Egypt
Turkish Empire
Zanzibar

Germany
EARLY STATES
Baden
Bavaria
Bergedorf
Bremen
Brunswick
Hamburg
Hanover
Lubeck
Mecklenburg-Schwerin
Mecklenburg-Strelitz
Oldenburg
Prussia
Saxony
Schleswig-Holstein
Wurttemberg

FORMER COLONIES
Cameroun (Kamerun)
Caroline Islands
German East Africa
German New Guinea
German South-West Africa
Kiauchau
Mariana Islands
Marshall Islands
Samoa
Togo

Italy
EARLY STATES
Modena
Parma
Romagna
Roman States
Sardinia
Tuscany
Two Sicilies
  Naples
  Neapolitan Provinces
  Sicily

FORMER COLONIES, CONTROLLED TERRITORIES, OCCUPATION AREAS
Aegean Islands
  Calimno (Calino)
  Caso
  Cos (Coo)
  Karki (Carchi)
  Leros (Lero)
  Lipso
  Nisiros (Nisiro)
  Patmos (Patmo)
  Piscopi
  Rodi (Rhodes)
  Scarpanto
  Simi
  Stampalia
Castellorizo
Corfu
Cyrenaica
Eritrea
Ethiopia (Abyssinia)
Fiume
Ionian Islands
  Cephalonia
  Ithaca
  Paxos
Italian East Africa
Libya
Oltre Giuba
Saseno
Somalia (Italian Somaliland)
Tripolitania

POST OFFICES IN FOREIGN COUNTRIES
"ESTERO"*
Austria
China
  Peking
  Tientsin
Crete
Tripoli
Turkish Empire
  Constantinople
  Durazzo
  Janina
Jerusalem
Salonika
Scutari
Smyrna
Valona
*Stamps overprinted "ESTERO" were used in various parts of the world.

Netherlands
Aruba
Caribbean Netherlands
Curacao
Netherlands Antilles (Curacao)
Netherlands Indies
Netherlands New Guinea
St. Martin
Surinam (Dutch Guiana)

Portugal
COLONIES PAST AND PRESENT, CONTROLLED TERRITORIES
Angola
Angra
Azores

Cape Verde
Funchal
Horta
Inhambane
Kionga
Lourenco Marques
Macao
Madeira
Mozambique
Mozambique Co.
Nyassa
Ponta Delgada
Portuguese Africa
Portuguese Congo
Portuguese Guinea
Portuguese India
Quelimane
St. Thomas & Prince Islands
Tete
Timor
Zambezia

Russia
ALLIED TERRITORIES AND REPUBLICS, OCCUPATION AREAS
Armenia
Aunus (Olonets)
Azerbaijan
Batum
Estonia
Far Eastern Republic
Georgia
Karelia
Latvia
Lithuania
North Ingermanland
Ostland
Russian Turkestan
Siberia
South Russia
Tannu Tuva
Transcaucasian Fed. Republics
Ukraine
Wenden (Livonia)
Western Ukraine

Spain
COLONIES PAST AND PRESENT, CONTROLLED TERRITORIES
Aguera, La
Cape Juby
Cuba
Elobey, Annobon & Corisco
Fernando Po
Ifni
Mariana Islands
Philippines
Puerto Rico
Rio de Oro
Rio Muni
Spanish Guinea
Spanish Morocco
Spanish Sahara
Spanish West Africa

POST OFFICES IN FOREIGN COUNTRIES
Morocco
Tangier
Tetuan

Dies of British Colonial Stamps

DIE A:

1. The lines in the groundwork vary in thickness and are not uniformly straight.

2. The seventh and eighth lines from the top, in the groundwork, converge where they meet the head.

3. There is a small dash in the upper part of the second jewel in the band of the crown.

4. The vertical color line in front of the throat stops at the sixth line of shading on the neck.

DIE B:

1. The lines in the groundwork are all thin and straight.

2. All the lines of the background are parallel.

3. There is no dash in the upper part of the second jewel in the band of the crown.

4. The vertical color line in front of the throat stops at the eighth line of shading on the neck.

DIE I:

1. The base of the crown is well below the level of the inner white line around the vignette.

2. The labels inscribed "POSTAGE" and "REVENUE" are cut square at the top.

3. There is a white "bud" on the outer side of the main stem of the curved ornaments in each lower corner.

4. The second (thick) line below the country name has the ends next to the crown cut diagonally.

DIE Iа.	DIE Ib.
1 as die II.	1 and 3 as die II.
2 and 3 as die I.	2 as die I.

DIE II:

1. The base of the crown is aligned with the underside of the white line around the vignette.

2. The labels curve inward at the top inner corners.

3. The "bud" has been removed from the outer curve of the ornaments in each corner.

4. The second line below the country name has the ends next to the crown cut vertically.

Wmk. 1
Crown and C C

Wmk. 2
Crown and C A

Wmk. 3
Multiple Crown
and C A

Wmk. 4
Multiple Crown
and Script C A

Wmk. 4a

Wmk. 314
St. Edward's Crown
and C A Multiple

Wmk. 373

Wmk. 384

Wmk. 406

British Colonial and Crown Agents Watermarks

Watermarks 1 to 4, 314, 373, 384 and 406, common to many British territories, are illustrated here to avoid duplication.

The letters "CC" of Wmk. 1 identify the paper as having been made for the use of the Crown Colonies, while the letters "CA" of the others stand for "Crown Agents." Both Wmks. 1 and 2 were used on stamps printed by De La Rue & Co.

Wmk. 3 was adopted in 1904; Wmk. 4 in 1921; Wmk. 314 in 1957; Wmk. 373 in 1974; Wmk. 384 in 1985; Wmk 406 in 2008.

In Wmk. 4a, a non-matching crown of the general St. Edwards type (bulging on both sides at top) was substituted for one of the Wmk. 4 crowns which fell off the dandy roll. The non-matching crown occurs in 1950-52 printings in a horizontal row of crowns on certain regular stamps of Johore and Seychelles, and on various postage due stamps of Barbados, Basutoland, British Guiana, Gold Coast, Grenada, Northern Rhodesia, St. Lucia, Swaziland and Trinidad and Tobago. A variation of Wmk. 4a, with the non-matching crown in a horizontal row of crown-CA-crown, occurs on regular stamps of Bahamas, St. Kitts-Nevis and Singapore.

Wmk. 314 was intentionally used sideways, starting in 1966. When a stamp was issued with Wmk. 314 both upright and sideways, the sideways varieties usually are listed also – with minor numbers. In many of the later issues, Wmk. 314 is slightly visible.

Wmk. 373 is usually only faintly visible.

CAMBODIA

kam-'bō-dē-ə

(Kampuchea)

(Khmer Republic)

LOCATION — Southern Indo-China
GOVT. — Republic
AREA — 69,898 sq. mi.
POP. — 11,626,520 (1999 est.)
CAPITAL — Phnom Penh

Before 1951, Cambodia used stamps of Indo-China. In October, 1970, the Kingdom of Cambodia became the Khmer Republic.
From 1978 to 1980 money was abolished.

100 Cents = 1 Piaster
100 Cents = 1 Riel (1955)

Imperforates
Most Cambodia stamps exist imperforate in issued and trial colors, and also in small presentation sheets in issued colors.

Catalogue values for all unused stamps in this country are for Never Hinged items.

Apsaras — A1   King Norodom Sihanouk — A3

Enthronement Hall — A2

1951-52   Unwmk.   Engr.   Perf. 13

1	A1	10c dk blue green	.90	3.00
2	A1	20c cl & org brn	.60	1.25
3	A1	30c pur & indigo	.60	.50
4	A1	40c ultra & brt bl grn	.80	.80
5	A2	50c dk grn & dk ol grn	.70	.70
6	A3	80c bl blk & dk bl grn	1.50	2.50
7	A2	1pi indigo & purple	1.40	1.00
8	A3	1.10pi dp car & brt red	1.75	2.50
9	A3	1.50pi blk brn & red brn ('51)	1.75	1.25
10	A1	1.50pi dp car & cerise	1.75	1.75
11	A2	1.50pi indigo & dp ultra	1.75	1.25
12	A3	1.90pi indigo & dp ultra	3.50	5.75
13	A2	2pi dp car & org brn	2.50	1.00
14	A3	3pi dp car & org brn	3.75	2.00
15	A1	5pi indigo & purple	12.00	6.50
a.		Souvenir sheet of 1	55.00	
16	A1	10pi purple & indigo	14.00	11.00
a.		Souvenir sheet of 1	55.00	
17	A3	15pi dk pur & pur	32.50	22.50
a.		Souvenir sheet of 1	55.00	
		Nos. 1-17 (17)	81.75	65.25

Nos. 15a, 16a, 17a sold in a booklet. Value, $300.
Stamps with completely white gum and no toning sell for a premium.
For surcharges see Nos. B1-B4.

Phnom Daun Penh — A4

East Gate, Angkor Thom — A5

Arms of Cambodia — A6   Methods of Mail Transport — A7

1954-55   Unwmk.   Perf. 13

18	A4	10c rose carmine	1.25	1.75
a.		Souvenir sheet of 5 ('55)	42.50	42.50
19	A4	20c dark green	1.50	.45
20	A4	30c indigo	1.40	2.10
21	A4	40c dark purple	1.60	.70
22	A4	50c dk violet brn	1.50	.30
23	A5	70c chocolate	2.00	3.00
a.		Souvenir sheet of 5 ('55)	42.50	42.50
24	A5	1pi red violet	2.00	1.60
25	A5	1.50pi red	2.00	.50
26	A6	2pi rose red	2.00	.40
a.		Souvenir sheet of 5 ('55)	42.50	42.50
27	A6	2.50pi green	2.00	.55
28	A7	2.50pi blue green	2.00	.50
a.		Souvenir sheet of 5 ('55)	42.50	42.50
29	A6	3pi ultra	2.10	1.50
30	A7	4pi black brown	3.00	2.75
31	A6	4.50pi purple	2.75	2.75
32	A7	5pi rose red	3.50	1.60
33	A6	6pi chocolate	3.00	2.25
34	A7	10pi purple	3.75	2.50
35	A7	15pi deep blue	4.50	4.50
36	A5	20pi ultra	10.00	4.75
37	A5	30pi blue green	16.00	7.50
		Nos. 18-37 (20)	67.85	41.95
		Nos. 18a//28a, Set of 4	160.00	

The 4 souvenir sheets each contain 5 stamps: No. 18a (10c, 20c, 30c, 40c, 50c); #23a (70c, 1pi, 1.50pi, 20pi, 30pi); No. 26a (2pi, 2.50pi green, 3pi, 4.50pi, 6pi); No. 28a (2.50pi blue green, 4pi, 5pi, 10pi, 15pi). Size of No. 18a, 26a and 28a: 120x120mm. Size of No. 23a: 160x92mm. Values are for very fine, unblemished sheets. Examples with toning and/or gum bends sell for less.
For overprints see Nos. 99-100.

King Norodom Suramarit — A8

King Norodom Suramarit and Queen Kossamak Nearirat Serey Vathana A9

Portraits: 50c (No. 39), 2.50r, 4r, 6r, 15r, Queen Kossamak Nearirat Serey Vathana.

Perf. 14x13(A8), 13(A9)
1955, Nov. 24   Engr.   Unwmk.

38	A8	50c violet	.40	.40
39	A8	50c indigo	.40	.40
40	A8	1r car lake	.50	.45
41	A9	1.50r dk brown	.80	.50
42	A9	2r black & indigo	.70	.45
43	A8	2r dp ultra	.80	.60
44	A9	2.50r dk vio brn	1.10	.60
45	A9	3r brn org & car	1.00	.60
46	A8	4r dark green	1.40	.90
47	A9	5r blk & dk grn	1.50	1.10
48	A8	6r deep plum	1.75	1.10
49	A8	7r dark brown	2.00	1.10
50	A9	10r brn car & vio	2.50	1.25
51	A8	15r purple	3.00	2.00
52	A8	20r deep green	4.75	2.75
		Nos. 38-52 (15)	22.60	14.20

Coronation of King Norodom Suramarit and Queen Kossamak Nearirat Serey Vathana.
See Nos. 74-75. For surcharge see No. 122.

King Norodom Suramarit — A10

Portrait: 3r, 5r, 50r, Queen Kossamak Nearirat Serey Vathana.

1956, Mar. 8   Perf. 13

53	A10	2r dark red	2.25	2.00
54	A10	3r dark blue	3.25	2.75
55	A10	5r yellow green	4.50	3.75
56	A10	10r dark green	9.00	7.50
57	A10	30r dark violet	21.00	18.00
58	A10	50r rose lilac	40.00	37.50
		Nos. 53-58 (6)	80.00	71.50

Coronation of King Norodom Suramarit and Queen Kossamak Nearirat Serey Vathana.

Prince Sihanouk, Globe and Flags — A11

1957, Mar. 1

59	A11	2r grn, ultra & car	1.50	1.10
60	A11	4.50r ultra	1.50	1.10
61	A11	8.50r carmine	1.50	1.10
		Nos. 59-61 (3)	4.50	3.30

Admission to the UN, 1st anniv. (in 1956).

Type of Semi-Postal Stamps, 1957
1957, May 12   Unwmk.   Perf. 13

62	SP1	1.50r vermilion	1.00	1.00
63	SP1	6.50r bluish violet	1.25	1.25
64	SP1	8r dark green	1.50	1.50
		Nos. 62-64 (3)	3.75	3.75

2500th anniv. of the birth of Buddha.

King Ang Duong A12

1958, Mar. 4

65	A12	1.50r purple & brown	.60	.60
66	A12	5r olive gray & olive	.80	.80
67	A12	10r claret & dull brn	1.50	1.50
a.		Souvenir sheet of 3, #65-67	7.00	6.00
		Nos. 65-67 (3)	2.90	2.90

King Ang Duong (1795-1860).
No. 67a sold for 25r.

King Norodom I — A13

1958-59   Engr.   Perf. 12½x13

68	A13	2r ultra & olive	.70	.50
69	A13	6r orange & sl grn	1.00	.70
70	A13	15r green & ol gray	2.00	1.40
a.		Souv. sheet of 3, #68-70 ('59)	7.00	6.00
		Nos. 68-70 (3)	3.70	2.60

King Norodom I (1835-1904).
No. 70a sold for 32r.
Issued: Nos. 68-70, 11/3/58; No. 70a, 1/31/59.
For surcharge see No. 184.

Children of the World — A14

1959, Dec. 9   Unwmk.   Perf. 13

71	A14	20c rose violet	.30	.30
72	A14	50c blue	.55	.55
73	A14	80c rose carmine	1.10	1.10
		Nos. 71-73 (3)	1.95	1.95

Issued to promote friendship among the children of the world.
For surcharges see Nos. 115, B8-B10.

Nos. 49 and 52 with Black Border

1960   Perf. 14x13

74	A8	7r dk brown & blk	4.50	4.50
75	A8	20r dp green & blk	4.50	4.50

Death of King Norodom Suramarit.

Port of Sihanoukville, Prince Sihanouk and Serpent Naga — A15

20r (double size)

1960, Apr.   Perf. 13x12½

76	A15	2r carmine & sepia	.65	.65
a.		Cambodian 20r	3.50	3.50
77	A15	5r ultra & dp brown	.65	.65
a.		Cambodian 20r	4.00	4.00
78	A15	20r lilac & dk blue	2.40	2.40
		Nos. 76-78 (3)	3.70	3.70

Opening of the port of Sihanoukville. By error the denomination in Cambodian on the 2r and 5r was engraved as 20r; it was corrected later.

Ceremonial Plow — A16

1960   Perf. 12

79	A16	1r magenta	.65	.65
80	A16	2r brown	.90	.90
81	A16	3r bluish green	1.25	1.25
		Nos. 79-81 (3)	2.80	2.80

Feast of the Sacred Furrow.

Fight Against Illiteracy A17

Water Conservation, Dam at Chhouksar — A18

Dove, Factory and Books A19

Buddhist Ceremony A20

Works of Sangkum: 6r, Workman and house. 10r, Woman in rice field.

1960, Sept. 1   **Engr.**   **Perf. 13**
82	A17	2r dk grn, brn & dk bl	.65	.40
a.		Souvenir sheet of 3	8.00	8.00
83	A18	3r brown & green	.80	.40
a.		Souvenir sheet of 3	8.00	8.00
84	A19	4r rose car, vio & grn	.80	.55
85	A17	6r brown, org & grn	.90	.70
86	A17	10r ultra, grn & bis	2.25	1.40
87	A20	25r dk car, red & mag	4.50	2.75
		Nos. 82-87 (6)	9.90	6.20

No. 82a contains one each of Nos. 82, 85 and 87, and sold for 42r. No. 83a contains one each of Nos. 83, 84 and 86, and sold for 23r. Nos. 82a-83a were issued Dec. 5, 1960.

Cambodian Flag and Dove — A21

1960, Dec. 24   **Engr.**   **Perf. 13**
Flag in Ultramarine and Red
88	A21	1.50r brown & green	.40	.25
89	A21	5r orange red	.60	.35
90	A21	7r green & ultra	1.25	1.00
a.		Souvenir sheet of 3, #88-90	17.00	17.00
b.		Souv. sheet of 3 (colors changed)	12.00	12.00
		Nos. 88-90 (3)	2.25	1.60

Peace propaganda. No. 90a sold for 16r. No. 90b contains one of each denomination with colors changed to: 1.50r orange red, 5r green & ultramarine, 7r brown & green and sold for 20r.

Frangipani — A22

1961, July 1   **Unwmk.**   **Perf. 13**
91	A22	2r shown	.65	.65
92	A22	5r Oleander	1.10	1.10
93	A22	10r Amaryllis	2.75	2.75
a.		Souvenir sheet of 3, #91-93	9.00	9.00
		Nos. 91-93 (3)	4.50	4.50

No. 93a sold for 20r.

Krishna in Chariot, Khmer Frieze — A23

1961-63   **Typo.**   **Perf. 14x13½**
94	A23	1r lilac	.40	.25
94A	A23	2r blue ('63)	3.25	1.60
95	A23	3r emerald	.90	.40
96	A23	6r orange	.90	.40
a.		Souvenir sheet of 3	7.50	7.50
		Nos. 94-96 (4)	5.45	2.65

Issued to honor Cambodian armed forces. No. 94A issued in coils. No. 96a contains one each of Nos. 94, 95, 96. Sold for 12r.

Independence Monument — A24

1961, Nov. 9   **Engr.**   **Perf. 13x12½**
97	A24	2r green	.50	.50
98	A24	4r gray brown	.50	.50
a.		Souvenir sheet of 2, #97-98	5.00	5.00
		Nos. 97-98,C15-C17 (5)	9.40	7.05

10th anniv. of Independence. For surcharge see No. 116.

Nos. 27 and 31 Overprinted in Red

1961, Nov. 11   **Perf. 13**
99	A6	2.50pi green	1.10	.65
100	A6	4.50pi purple	1.75	1.00

Sixth World Conference of Buddhism.

Highway (American Aid) — A25

Foreign Aid: 2r, Power station (Czech aid). 4r, Textile factory (Chinese aid). 5r, Hospital (Russian aid). 6r, Airport (French aid).

1961, Dec.   **Engr.**   **Perf. 13**
101	A25	2r org & rose car	.45	.30
102	A25	3r bl, grn & org brn	.45	.30
103	A25	4r dl bl, org brn & mag	.45	.40
104	A25	5r dl grn & lil rose	.65	.40
105	A25	6r dk bl & org brn	1.25	.55
a.		Souvenir sheet of 5, #101-105	8.00	8.00
		Nos. 101-105 (5)	3.25	1.95

Malaria Eradication Emblem — A26

1962, Apr. 7   **Unwmk.**   **Perf. 13**
106	A26	2r magenta & brown	.50	.40
107	A26	4r green & dk brown	.50	.40
108	A26	6r violet & olive bister	.75	.45
		Nos. 106-108 (3)	1.75	1.25

WHO drive to eradicate malaria. For surcharges see Nos. B11-B12.

Fruits A27

1962, June 4   **Engr.**
109	A27	2r Cardamom	.60	.45
110	A27	4r Sugar apple	1.10	.75
111	A27	6r Mangosteens	1.10	.75
a.		Souvenir sheet of 3, #109-111	6.00	6.00
		Nos. 109-111 (3)	2.80	1.95

Nos. 111a sold for 15r.

Pineapples — A28

1962   **Unwmk.**   **Perf. 13**
112	A28	2r shown	.90	.50
113	A28	5r Sugar cane	1.40	.75
114	A28	9r Sugar palms	1.75	.70
		Nos. 112-114 (3)	4.05	1.95

No. 73 Surcharged

1962, Nov. 9   **Perf. 13**
115	A14	50c on 80c rose car	.70	.40

No. 97 Srchd. in Red and Ovptd. in Black

1962
116	A24	3r on 2r green	1.00	.40

Dedication of Independence Monument. See No. C18.

Corn, Rice and FAO Emblem A29

1963, Mar. 21   **Engr.**   **Perf. 13**
117	A29	3r multicolored	.70	.55
118	A29	6r org red, vio bl & ocher	.70	.55

FAO "Freedom from Hunger" campaign.

Preah Vihear, Ancient Temple — A30

1963, June 15   **Perf. 12½x13**
119	A30	3r clar, brn & sl grn	.50	.40
120	A30	6r org, sl grn & grnsh blk	.90	.65
121	A30	15r blue, choc & green	1.40	1.10
		Nos. 119-121 (3)	2.80	2.15

Return by Thailand of Preah Vihear on the Mekong River. For overprint see No. 176.

No. 44 Surcharged

1963   **Engr.**   **Perf. 14x13**
122	A8	3r on 2½r dk violet brn	.90	.55

Tonsay Lake — A31

7r, Popokvil Falls. 20r, Beach, horiz.

Perf. 12x12½, 12½x12

1963, Aug. 1   **Photo.**
123	A31	3r multicolored	.50	.50
124	A31	7r multicolored	.80	.70
125	A31	20r multicolored	2.50	1.10
		Nos. 123-125 (3)	3.80	2.30

UNESCO Emblem, Scales and Globe A32

1963, Dec. 10   **Engr.**   **Perf. 13**
126	A32	1r vio bl, rose cl & grn	.50	.50
127	A32	3r yel grn, vio bl & rose cl	.90	.90
128	A32	12r rose cl, yel grn & vio bl	1.60	1.60
		Nos. 126-128 (3)	3.00	3.00

15th anniversary of the Universal Declaration of Human Rights. For surcharge see No. 183.

Kouprey A33

1964, Mar. 3   **Unwmk.**   **Perf. 13**
129	A33	50c grn, dk brn & org brn	.95	.55
130	A33	3r org, brn, dk brn & grn	1.40	.95
131	A33	6r blue, dk brn & grn	2.10	1.40
		Nos. 129-131 (3)	4.45	2.65

Black-billed Magpie — A34

1964, May 2   **Engr.**   **Perf. 13**
132	A34	3r shown	1.40	.65
133	A34	6r Kingfisher	2.10	1.00
134	A34	12r Gray heron	3.75	2.00
		Nos. 132-134 (3)	7.25	3.65

For overprint & surcharge see Nos. 303, B16.

Emblem of Royal Cambodian Airline A35

1964 Unwmk. Perf. 13x12½
135 A35 1.50r rose car & purple .40 .25
136 A35 3r ver & dk blue .55 .40
137 A35 7.50r ultra & car 1.25 .60
Nos. 135-137 (3) 2.20 1.25

8th anniv. of the Royal Cambodian Airline.

Prince Norodom Sihanouk — A36

1964 Engr. Perf. 12½x13
138 A36 2r purple .55 .40
139 A36 3r red brown .80 .50
140 A36 10r dark blue 1.60 .90
Nos. 138-140 (3) 2.95 1.80

10th anniv. of the Sangkum (political party). For overprints see Nos. 144-145.

A set of three stamps, imperf, showing clasped hands, was prepared for International Cooperation Year but were never issued. Value, $200.

Woman Weaver A37

Khmer Handicrafts: 3r, Metal worker. 5r, Basket maker.

1965, Feb. 1 Perf. 13x12½
141 A37 1r multicolored .40 .40
142 A37 3r red lil, red brn & gray ol .65 .40
143 A37 5r green, dk brn & car 1.10 .85
Nos. 141-143 (3) 2.15 1.65

Nos. 139-140 Overprinted in Black or Red

1965, Mar. 1 Perf. 12½x13
144 A36 3r red brown .70 .40
145 A36 10r dark blue (R) 1.00 .55

Conference of the people of Indo-China.

ITU Emblem, Old and New Communication Equipment — A38

1965, May 17 Engr. Perf. 13
146 A38 3r green & olive bister .40 .30
147 A38 4r red & blue .70 .40
148 A38 10r violet & rose lilac 1.00 .70
Nos. 146-148 (3) 2.10 1.40

Centenary of the ITU.

Cotton Plant — A39

3r, Peanut plant. 7.50r, Coconut palm.

1965, Aug. 2 Perf. 12½x13
149 A39 1.50r org, sl grn & pur .55 .40
150 A39 3r blue, yel, grn & brn .90 .60
151 A39 7.50r org brn & sl grn 1.50 1.00
Nos. 149-151 (3) 2.95 2.00

Preah Ko Temple, Rolouoh — A40

Temples at Angkor: 5r, Baksei Chamkrong, Rolouoh. 7r, Banteay Srei (Citadel of Women). 9r, Angkor Wat. 12r, Bayon, Angkor Thom.

1966, Feb. 1 Engr. Perf. 13
152 A40 3r gray ol, sal & dl grn 1.25 .80
153 A40 5r lil, dk grn & redsh brn 1.50 .85
154 A40 7r dk grn, redsh brn & bis 2.00 1.60
155 A40 9r vio bl, pur & dk grn 2.75 2.10
156 A40 12r dk grn, rose car & ver 3.25 2.75
Nos. 152-156 (5) 10.75 8.10

For overprints see Nos. 172-175, 177.

WHO Headquarters, Geneva — A41

1966, July 1 Photo. Perf. 12½x13
WHO Emblem in Blue and Yellow
157 A41 2r black & pale rose .40 .25
158 A41 3r black & yel grn .50 .40
159 A41 5r black & lt bl .80 .55
Nos. 157-159 (3) 1.70 1.20

Inauguration of WHO Headquarters, Geneva.

Tree Planting — A42

1966, July 22 Engr. Perf. 12½x13
160 A42 1r brn, dull brn & brt grn .30 .25
161 A42 3r org, dull brn & brt grn .55 .30
162 A42 7r gray, dull brn & brt grn .85 .40
Nos. 160-162 (3) 1.70 .95

Issued for Arbor Day.

UNESCO Emblem — A43

1966 Photo. Perf. 13
163 A43 3r multicolored .50 .40
164 A43 7r multicolored .75 .55

20th anniv. of UNESCO.

Wrestlers and Games' Emblem A44

GANEFO Games (Games Emblem and): 3r, Stadium, Phnom Penh. 7r, Swordsmen. 10r, Indian club swingers. Bas-reliefs from Angkor Wat.

1966, Nov. 25 Engr. Perf. 13
165 A44 3r violet blue .40 .25
166 A44 4r green .45 .30
167 A44 7r dk car rose .70 .50
168 A44 10r dark brown 1.10 .65
Nos. 165-168 (4) 2.65 1.70

Indian Wild Boar A45

Perf. 13x12½, 12½x13
1967, Feb. 20 Engr.
169 A45 3r shown 1.25 .40
170 A45 5r Muntjac, vert. 1.60 .65
171 A45 7r Elephant 2.25 .95
Nos. 169-171 (3) 5.10 2.00

Nos. 152-153, 155-156 and 121 Overprinted in Red

1967, Apr. 27 Engr. Perf. 13
172 A40 3r multicolored .85 .75
173 A40 5r multicolored .90 .75
174 A40 9r multicolored 1.40 1.25
175 A40 12r multicolored 1.75 1.50
176 A30 15r multicolored 2.10 1.75
Nos. 172-176 (5) 7.00 6.00

International Tourist Year, 1967.

No. 154 Overprinted in Red

1967, Apr. 27
177 A40 7r multicolored 1.50 .60

Banteay Srei Temple at Angkor, millennium.

Royal Ballet Dancer — A46

Various Dancers

1967, June Engr. Perf. 13
178 A46 1r orange .50 .40
179 A46 3r Prus blue .90 .60
180 A46 5r ultra 1.40 .55
181 A46 7r carmine rose 2.00 .80
182 A46 10r multicolored 2.50 1.00
Nos. 178-182 (5) 7.30 3.35

Cambodian Royal Ballet.

Nos. 128 and 70 Srchd. in Red

1967, Sept. 8 Engr.
183 A32 6r on 12r multi 1.10 .50
184 A13 7r on 15r grn & olive gray 1.40 .70

Intl. Literacy Day, Sept. 8. The surcharge on No. 184 is adapted to fit the shape of the stamp.

Symbolic Water Cycle — A47

1967, Nov. 1 Typo. Perf. 13x14
185 A47 1r black, bl & org .30 .25
186 A47 6r lilac, lt bl & org .60 .30
187 A47 10r dk blue, emer & org .90 .50
Nos. 185-187 (3) 1.80 1.05

Hydrological Decade (UNESCO), 1965-74.

Royal University, Kompong Cham A48

6r, Engineering School, Phnom Penh. 9r, University Center, Sangkum Reastr Niyum.

1968, Mar. 1 Engr. Perf. 13
188 A48 4r violet bl & multi .50 .40
189 A48 6r slate & multi .65 .40
190 A48 9r Prus blue & multi .90 .55
Nos. 188-190 (3) 2.05 1.35

Vaccination and WHO Emblem A49

WHO, 20th Anniv.: 7r, Malaria control and WHO emblem (man spraying DDT).

1968, July 8 Engr. Perf. 13
191 A49 3r ultramarine .60 .40
192 A49 7r deep blue .90 .55

Stadium, Mexico City — A50

1968, Oct. 12 Engr. Perf. 13
193 A50 1r shown .65 .55
194 A50 2r Wrestling .80 .55
195 A50 3r Bicycling .90 .55
196 A50 5r Boxing, vert. 1.10 .55
197 A50 7.50r Torch bearer, vert. 1.50 .75
Nos. 193-197 (5) 4.95 2.95

19th Olympic Games, Mexico City, 12/12-27.

Red Cross Team
A51

1968, Nov. 1　　Engr.　　Perf. 13
198　A51　3r Prus bl, grn & red　　1.50　.50

Issued to honor the Cambodian Red Cross.

Prince Norodom Sihanouk
A52

8r, Soldiers wading through swamp.

1968, Nov. 9
199　A52　7r emer, ultra & pur　　.50　.40
200　A52　8r bl, grn & dp brn　　.75　.55

15th anniversary of independence.

Human Rights Flame and Prince Sihanouk
A53

1968, Dec. 10　　Engr.　　Perf. 13
201　A53　3r blue　　　　　　.45　.25
202　A53　5r bright plum　　.80　.35
203　A53　7r multicolored　　1.10　.55
　　Nos. 201-203 (3)　　2.35　1.15

International Human Rights Year.

ILO Emblem
A54

1969, May 1　　Engr.　　Perf. 13
204　A54　3r ultra　　　　　.50　.25
205　A54　6r dp carmine　　.70　.40
206　A54　9r blue green　　1.00　.55
　　Nos. 204-206 (3)　　2.20　1.20

ILO, 50th anniversary.

Globe, Red Cross, Crescent, Lion and Sun Emblems
A55

1969, May 8
207　A55　1r blue, red & yel　　.40　.25
208　A55　3r sl grn, red & vio brn　　.65　.40
209　A55　10r brt lil, red & brn　　1.40　.60
　　Nos. 207-209 (3)　　2.45　1.25

50th anniv. of the League of Red Cross Societies.

Papilio Oeacus
A56

Butterflies: 4r, Papilio agamenon. 8r, Danaus plexippus.

1969, Oct. 10　　Engr.　　Perf. 13
210　A56　3r lilac, blk & yel　　3.25　1.00
211　A56　4r ver, blk & grn　　4.25　2.00
212　A56　8r yel grn, dk brn & org　6.00　3.00
　　Nos. 210-212 (3)　　13.50　6.00

Map of Cambodia and Diesel Engine
A57

Various railroad stations and trains.

1969, Nov. 27　　Engr.　　Perf. 13
213　A57　3r multicolored　　1.00　.75
214　A57　6r slate grn & lt brn　　2.00　1.50
215　A57　8r black　　　　　3.25　2.25
216　A57　9r dk green & blue　　3.75　2.40
　　Nos. 213-216 (4)　　10.00　6.90

Issued to publicize the new rail link between Phnom Penh and Sihanoukville.

Fish — A58

1970, Jan. 29　　Photo.　　Perf. 13
217　A58　3r Tripletail　　1.75　.90
218　A58　7r Sleeper goby　　4.00　1.50
219　A58　9r Snakehead　　5.75　2.00
　　Nos. 217-219 (3)　　11.50　4.40

Wat Maniratanaram — A59

Monasteries: 2r, Wat Tepthidaram, vert. 6r, Wat Patumavati. 8r, Wat Unnalom.

1970, Apr. 29　　Photo.　　Perf. 13
220　A59　2r multicolored　　.35　.40
221　A59　3r multicolored　　.40　.40
222　A59　6r multicolored　　.85　.40
223　A59　8r multicolored　　1.60　.55
　　Nos. 220-223 (4)　　3.20　1.75

UPU Headquarters and Monument, Bern — A60

1970, May 20
224　A60　1r green & multi　　.35　.25
225　A60　3r scarlet & multi　　.50　.30
226　A60　4r dp blue & multi　　.65　.30
227　A60　10r brown & multi　　1.00　.60
　　Nos. 224-227 (4)　　2.50　1.45

New UPU Headquarters in Bern.

Open Book and Satellite Earth Receiving Station — A61

1970, May 17　　Photo.　　Perf. 13
228　A61　3r dk vio bl & multi　　.30　.25
229　A61　4r sl grn & multi　　.40　.25
230　A61　9r brn ol & multi　　.85　.35
　　Nos. 228-230 (3)　　1.55　.85

World Telecommunications Day.

Nelumbium Speciosum
A62

Flowers: 4r, Eichhornia crassipes. 13r, Nymphea lotus.

1970, Aug. 17　　Photo.　　Perf. 13
231　A62　3r multicolored　　.70　.30
　　a.　Cambodian and Arabic 3's transposed　　37.50　37.50
232　A62　4r multicolored　　1.40　.45
233　A62　13r multicolored　　3.00　.70
　　Nos. 231-233 (3)　　5.10　1.45

Elephant God, Bas relief at Banteay Srei — A63

1970, Sept. 21　　Engr.　　Perf. 13
234　A63　3r lil rose & dp grn　　.35　.25
235　A63　4r bl grn, grn & lil rose　　.55　.25
236　A63　7r bl grn, dk brn & grn　　.85　.40
　　Nos. 234-236 (3)　　1.75　.90

Issued for World Meteorological Day.

Khmer Republic

Globe, Rocket, Dove and UN Emblem
A64

1970, Nov. 9　　Photo.　　Perf. 12½x12
237　A64　3r black & multi　　.30　.25
238　A64　5r brown red & multi　　.45　.25
239　A64　10r dp violet & multi　　.90　.50
　　Nos. 237-239 (3)　　1.65　1.00

25th anniversary of the United Nations.

Education Year Emblem
A65

1970, Nov. 9　　Engr.　　Perf. 13x12½
240　A65　1r blue　　　　　.25　.25
241　A65　3r brt rose lilac　　.35　.25
242　A65　8r blue green　　.75　.45
　　Nos. 240-242 (3)　　1.35　.95

Issued for International Education Year.

Chuon-Nath — A66

1971, Jan. 27　　Photo.　　Perf. 13
243　A66　3r ol grn & multi　　.35　.25
244　A66　8r purple & multi　　.75　.35
245　A66　9r violet & multi　　1.00　.55
　　Nos. 243-245 (3)　　2.10　1.15

In memory of Chuon-Nath (1883-1969), Cambodian language expert.
For surcharge see No. 322.

Soldiers in Battle
A67

1971, Mar. 18　　Photo.　　Perf. 13
246　A67　1r gray & multi　　.45　.25
247　A67　3r bister & multi　　.70　.40
248　A67　10r blue & multi　　1.75　.75
　　Nos. 246-248 (3)　　2.90　1.40

National territorial defense.
For overprint see No. 321.

UN Emblem, Men of Four Races
A68

1971, Mar. 21
249　A68　3r blue & multi　　.65　.25
250　A68　7r green & multi　　1.25　.40
251　A68　8r brt rose & multi　　2.00　.55
　　Nos. 249-251 (3)　　3.90　1.20

Intl. year against racial discrimination.

General Post Office, Phnom Penh — A69

1971, Apr. 19
252　A69　3r blue & multi　　.35　.25
253　A69　9r lilac rose & multi　　.65　.35
254　A69　10r black & multi　　1.05　.40
　　Nos. 252-254 (3)　　2.05　1.00

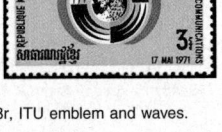

Symbolic Globe and Waves
A70

Design: 7r, 8r, ITU emblem and waves.

1971, May 17　　Photo.　　Perf. 13
255　A70　3r green, blk & bl　　.25　.25
256　A70　4r yellow & multi　　.40　.25
257　A70　7r lilac, blk & red　　.50　.25
258　A70　8r sal pink, blk & red　　.60　.30
　　Nos. 255-258 (4)　　1.75　1.05

3rd World Telecommunications Day.

Erythrina Indica
A71

Wild Flowers: 3r, Bauhinia variegata. 6r, Butea frondosa. 10r, Lagerstroemia floribunda, vert.

1971, July 5　　Perf. 13x12½, 12½x13
259　A71　2r lt ultra & multi　　.55　.45
260　A71　3r yel grn & multi　　.65　.55
261　A71　6r blue & multi　　1.40　1.10
262　A71　10r brown & multi　　1.75　1.40
　　Nos. 259-262 (4)　　4.35　3.50

Khmer Coat of Arms — A72

Flag and Square of the Republic — A73

1971, Oct. 9   Engr.   Perf. 13
263 A72 3r brt grn & bis   .25 .25
264 A73 3r purple & multi   .30 .25
265 A73 4r dp claret & multi   .40 .25
266 A72 6r orange & bis   .50 .25
267 A72 10r lt brn & bis   .80 .30
 a. Souv. sheet of 3, #263, 266-267 3.00 3.00
268 A73 10r slate grn & multi   .80 .35
 a. Souv. sheet of 3, #264-265, 268 3.00 3.00
      Nos. 263-268 (6)   3.05 1.65

Republic, 1st anniv.
No. 267a sold for 25r, No. 268a for 20r.
For overprints and surcharges see Nos. 301-302, B13-B14.

UNICEF Emblem — A74

1971, Dec. 11
269 A74 3r black brown   .35 .25
270 A74 5r ultra   .50 .25
271 A74 9r dk pur & brn red   1.00 .45
      Nos. 269-271 (3)   1.85 .95

25th anniv. of UNICEF.
This set and others exist with overprint "RPK," both with and without frame. Status has not been determined.

Book Year Emblem A75

1972, Feb. 7
272 A75 3r blue, grn & vio   .40 .25
273 A75 8r violet, grn & bl   .60 .30
274 A75 9r emerald & multi   1.00 .50
 a. Souvenir sheet of 3, #272-274 3.00 3.00
      Nos. 272-274 (3)   2.00 1.05

Intl. Book Year. No. 274a sold for 23r.

Lion of St. Mark A76

Designs: 5r, Waves engulfing St. Mark's Basilica. 10r, Bridge of Sighs, vert.

1972, Feb. 7   Engr.   Perf. 13
275 A76 3r lil rose & org brn   .50 .25
276 A76 5r yel grn & org brn   1.00 .40
277 A76 10r org brn, bl & yel grn 1.25 .50
 a. Souvenir sheet of 3, #275-277 3.00 3.00
      Nos. 275-277 (3)   2.75 1.15

UNESCO campaign to save Venice. No. 277a sold for 23r.

UN Emblem A77

1972, Mar. 28
278 A77 3r deep carmine   .50 .25
279 A77 6r deep blue   .75 .35
280 A77 9r deep orange   .90 .50
 a. Souvenir sheet of 3, #278-280 3.00 3.00
      Nos. 278-280 (3)   2.15 1.10

25th anniv. UN Economic Commission for Asia and the Far East (ECAFE). No. 280a sold for 23r.

Dancing Apsarases — A78

1972, May 5   Engr.   Perf. 13
281 A78 1r golden brn   .25 .25
282 A78 3r violet   .35 .25
283 A78 7r rose claret   .45 .30
284 A78 8r olive brn   .60 .30
285 A78 9r blue grn   .70 .30
286 A78 10r ultra   1.10 .30
287 A78 12r purple   1.40 .30
288 A78 14r Prus blue   1.75 .45
      Nos. 281-288 (8)   6.60 2.45

"UIT" A79

1972, May 17   Litho.
289 A79 3r blk, yel & grnsh bl   .40 .25
290 A79 9r blk, dp lil rose & bl grn .75 .30
291 A79 14r blk, brn & bl grn   1.10 .45
      Nos. 289-291 (3)   2.25 1.00

4th World Telecommunications Day.

"Human Environment" — A80

1972, June 5   Engr.
292 A80 3r org, plum & grn   .50 .25
293 A80 12r brt grn & plum   .75 .30
294 A80 15r plum & brt grn   1.25 .50
 a. Souvenir sheet of 3, #292-294 3.00 3.00
      Nos. 292-294 (3)   2.50 1.05

UN Conf. on Human Environment, Stockholm, June 5-16. No. 294a sold for 35r.
For overprints and surcharges see Nos. 304-305, B15, B17.

Javan Rhinoceros A81

1972, Aug. 1   Engr.   Perf. 13
295 A81 3r shown   .60 .25
296 A81 4r Serow   .70 .25
297 A81 6r Malayan sambar   1.40 .30
298 A81 7r Banteng   2.00 .30
299 A81 8r Water buffalo   2.50 .50
300 A81 10r Gaur   3.25 .60
      Nos. 295-300 (6)   10.45 2.20

Nos. 263, 267, 134, 293, 294 Overprinted in Red

1972, Sept. 9   Engr.   Perf. 13
301 A72 3r brt grn & bister   .75 .30
302 A72 10r orange & bister   1.50 .65
303 A34 12r multicolored   1.50 .80
304 A80 12r brt grn & plum   1.60 .80
305 A80 15r plum & brt grn   2.10 1.00
      Nos. 301-305 (5)   7.45 3.55

20th Olympic Games, Munich, 8/26-9/11.

Raising Khmer Flag — A82

1972, Oct. 9   Photo.   Perf. 12½x13
306 A82 3r multicolored   .25 .25
307 A82 5r brt rose & multi   .40 .30
308 A82 9r yel grn & multi   .90 .50
      Nos. 306-308 (3)   1.55 1.05

2nd anniversary of the establishment of the Khmer Republic.
For surcharge see No. 323.

Stupa and Crest — A83

1973, May 12   Engr.   Perf. 13
309 A83 3r ocher & multi   .45 .25
310 A83 12r yel grn & multi   .45 .25
311 A83 14r blue & multi   .75 .50
 a. Souvenir sheet of 3, #309-311 3.25 3.25
      Nos. 309-311 (3)   1.65 1.00

New Constitution. No. 311a sold for 34r.

Apsaras — A84

Sculptures from Angkor Wat: 8r, 10r, Devata, diff.

1973, July 23   Engr.   Perf. 13
312 A84 3r brown black   .50 .25
313 A84 8r Prus green   .65 .30
314 A84 10r olive bister   1.60 .50
 a. Souvenir sheet of 3, #312-314 3.00 3.00
      Nos. 312-314 (3)   2.75 1.05

No. 314a sold for 25r.

INTERPOL Emblem — A85

1973, Oct. 2   Engr.   Perf. 13
315 A85 3r green & multi   .45 .25
316 A85 7r red brn & multi   .55 .30
317 A85 10r olive & multi   .75 .45
 a. Souvenir sheet of 3, #315-317 4.50 4.50
      Nos. 315-317 (3)   1.75 1.00

50th anniv. of the Intl. Criminal Police Org. No. 317a sold for 30r.

Marshal Lon Nol — A86

1973, Oct. 9
318 A86 3r lt grn, blk & brn   .40 .25
319 A86 8r brown, ol & blk   .60 .30
320 A86 14r black & brn   1.00 .40
 a. Souvenir sheet of 3   5.00 5.00
      Nos. 318-320 (3)   2.00 .95

Marshal Lon Nol, 1st pres. of the Republic. No. 320a contains stamps similar to Nos. 318-320 in changed colors. Sold for 50r.

Nos. 248, 243 and 307 Srchd. & Ovptd. in Red or Silver

1974   Photo.   Perf. 13, 12½x13
321 A67 10r multi (R)   4.50 2.50
322 A66 50r on 3r multi   9.50 4.00
323 A82 100r on 5r multi   22.50 6.50
      Nos. 321-323 (3)   36.50 13.00

4th anniversary of the Republic.

Copernicus and "Nerva" — A87

Copernicus, various spacecraft and events: 5r, Mariner II. 10r, Apollo. 25r, Telstar. 50r, Space walk. 100r, Moon landing. 150r, Separation of spaceship and module.

1974, Sept. 10   Litho.   Perf. 13
324 A87 1r shown   .35 .30
325 A87 5r multicolored   .45 .30
326 A87 10r multicolored   .75 .40
327 A87 25r multicolored   1.75 .75
328 A87 50r multicolored   3.25 1.50
329 A87 100r multicolored   7.00 3.75
330 A87 150r multicolored   10.00 5.00
      Nos. 324-330 (7)   23.55 12.50
      Nos. 324-330,C46-C47 (9) 48.55 28.00

500th anniversary of the birth of Nicolaus Copernicus (1473-1543), Polish astronomer.

Carrier Pigeon and UPU Emblem — A88

Design: 60r, Sailing ship and UPU emblem.

1974, Nov. 2
331 A88 10r multicolored   1.50 1.50
332 A88 60r multicolored   4.50 4.50
      Nos. 331-332,C50 (3)   17.50 17.50

Cent. of UPU. Souvenir sheets of one exist, both imperf. and simulated perfs for Nos. 331 and 332. Value, set of 3, $30 each. Also, set of 2 souvenirs sheets of one each No. 332 and

No. C50 with silver borders, perf. and imperf. (simulated perfs.) Value, set $9 perf., $40 imperf.

A set of 8 stamps picturing musical instruments, overprinted and surcharged for use by the Khmer Republic just before the fall of the government in Apr. 1975, exists. Value, $1,100. Value for same set without surcharge, $500.

A89

1976 Summer Olympic Games, Montreal — A90

1r, 18th cent. swordsmen. 5r, Modern fencers. 10r, Ancient Olympic runner. 25r, Modern runner. 50r, Ancient rowers. 100r, Modern kayakers. 150r, Ancient horseman. 200r, Modern equestrian competitor. 250r, Buildings, Olympic flame.

1975, Jan. 2   Litho.   Perf. 13½
333-341 A89 Set of 9   11.50
Litho. & Embossed
342 A90 1200r gold & multi   25.00
Souvenir Sheets
343 A89 200r silver & multi   9.00
344 A89 250r silver & multi   9.00
345 A89 1,200r gold & multi   25.00

Nos. 337-344 are airmail.
Nos. 342-345 exist imperf.

A91

1974 World Cup Soccer
Championships — A92

Soccer players and arms of: 1r, Hamburg. 5r, Gelsenkirchen. 10r, Dortmund. 25r, Stuttgart. 50r, Dusseldorf. 100r, Hannover. 150r, Frankfurt. 200r, Munich. 250r, Berlin.

Litho. (#346-354, 356-357)
Litho. & Embossed (#355, 358)
1975, Feb. 13
346-354 A91 Set of 9   12.00
355 A92 1200r gold & multi   20.00
Souvenir Sheets
356 A91 200r gold & multi   6.50
357 A91 250r gold & multi   6.50
358 A92 1200r gold & multi   17.50

Nos. 350-358 are airmail. Nos. 346-354 exist in imperforate souvenir sheets.

UPU, Cent. — A93

Designs: 15r, Letter carrier, pack mule. 20r, Biplane. 70r, Post coach. 160r, Biplane, Concorde. 180r, Steam-powered wagon. 235r, Postrider, tail of mailplane. 500r, Railway mail car. 1000r, Airship. 2000r, Caravel.

1975, Apr. 12
359-367 A93 Set of 9   9.00
366a   Souvenir sheet of 1   4.75
367a   Souvenir sheet of 1   4.75

Nos. 365-367 are airmail. Nos. 366a and 367a exist imperf. Values, each $25.

People's Republic of Kampuchea

Soldiers — A94

Designs, horiz.: 20c, People, flag. 50c, Fishermen. 1r, Soldiers passing flag.

1980, Apr. 10   Litho.   Perf. 11
368-371 A94 Set of 4   70.00 70.00

Soviet Union,
60th
Anniv. — A95

Designs: 50c, Globe, Kremlin. 1r, Buildings, map of USSR.

1982, Dec. 30   Perf. 12x12½
372-373 A95 Set of 2   1.60 .55

People's Republic of Kampuchea, 4th
Anniv. — A96

Designs: 50c, Natl. arms, vert. 1r, shown. 3r, Map, stylized figures, vert. 6r, Temple, vert.

1983, Jan. 7   Litho.   Perf. 13
374-376 A96 Set of 3   4.75 1.25
Souvenir Sheet
377 A96 6r multicolored   6.00 2.25

1984
Summer
Olympic
Games,
Los
Angeles
A97

Designs: 20c, Runner with torch. 50c, Javelin. 80c, Pole vault. 1r, Discus. 1.50r, Relay race. 2r, Swimming. 3r, Basketball.
20c-1r, 3r are vert.

1983, Jan. 20   Litho.   Perf. 13
378-384 A97 Set of 7   7.00 1.50
Souvenir Sheet
385 A97 6r Soccer   5.25 3.00

No. 385 contains one 32x40mm stamp.

Butterflies — A98

20c, Salatura genutia. 50c, Euploea althaea. 80c, Byasa polyeuctes. 1r, Stichophthalma howqua. 1.50r, Kallima inachus. 2r, Precis orithya. 3r, Catopsilia pomona.
20c, 50c, 1.50r, 2r, 3r are vert.

1983, Feb. 18   Litho.   Perf. 13
386-392 A98 Set of 7   10.00 2.00

Khmer
Culture
A99

Designs: 20c, Ruins, Srah Srang. 50c, Temple, Bakong. 80c, Ta Son. 1r, North Gate, Angkor Thom. 1.50r, Two winged figures. 2r, Apsara, Angkor. 3r, Statue of Banteai Srei.
80c-3r are vert.

1983, Mar. 15
393-399 A99 Set of 7   7.00 1.75

Folk Dances
A100

Various dances. Denominations 50c, 1r, 3r.

1983, Apr. 17   Litho.   Perf. 13
400-402 A100 Set of 3   4.00 1.25
Souvenir Sheet
403 A100 6r Native, "buffalo"   6.50 1.40

No. 403 contains one 32x40mm stamp.

Raphael (1483-1520) — A101

Parnassus (details): No. 404, 20c, Dante, Ennius, Homer. No. 406, 80c, Horace, Ovid, others. No. 409, 2r, The Muses. No. 410, 3r, Alcaeus, Petrarch, others.
School at Athens (details): No. 407, 1r, Euclid, disciples. No. 408, 1.50r, Telange, Pythagoras.
Details from: No. 405, 50c, Mass of Bolsena. 6r, Angels from Dispute of the Holy Sacrament, horiz.

1983, May 10 Litho.   Perf. 12½x13
404-410 A101 Set of 7   6.50 2.25
Souvenir Sheet
Perf. 13
411 A101 6r multicolored   7.25 2.50

No. 411 contains one 40x32mm stamp.

1st Hot Air
Balloon
Ascension,
Bicent.
A102

Designs: 20c, Montgolfier. 30c, Ville d'Orleans. 50c, Hydrogen balloon. 1r, Blanchard & Jeffries, 1785. 1.50r, Ascension in Arctic. 2r, Stratosphere balloon. 3r, Balloon race. 6r, Balloons over town.

1983, June 3   Perf. 12½
412-418 A102 Set of 7   6.50 2.00
Souvenir Sheet
Perf. 13
419 A102 6r multicolored   7.25 1.50

Reptiles — A103

Designs: 20c, Iguana. 30c, Cobra. 80c, Trionyx turtle. 1r, Chameleon. 1.50r, Boa constrictor. 2r, Crocodile. 3r, Turtle.
30c, 1r, 1.50r are vert.

1983, June 28
420-426 A103 Set of 7   8.00 2.50

Birds
A104

Designs: 20c, Lorikeet. 50c, Swallow. 80c, Eagle. 1r, Vulture. 1.50r, Turtle dove. 2r, Magpie. 3r, Hornbill.
20c-50c, 2r-3r are vert.

1983, Sept. 20
427-433 A104 Set of 7   10.50 2.50

Flowers — A105

20c, Sunflower. 50c, Caprifoliacae. 80c, Bougainvillea. 1r, Renonculacae. 1.50r, Nyctaginaceae. 2r, Cockscomb. 3r, Roses.

1983, Oct. 18 **Perf. 13**
434-440 A105 Set of 7   7.50 1.75

1984 Winter Olympic Games, Sarajevo — A106

Designs: 1r, Luge. 2r, Biathlon. 4r, Ski jumping. 5r, Two-man bobsled. 7r, Hockey. 6r, Cross-country skiing.

1983, Nov. 10 **Perf. 12½**
441-445 A106 Set of 5   15.00 2.75
Souvenir Sheet
446 A106 6r multicolored   6.50 1.75
No. 446 contains one 40x32mm stamp.

Fish A107

20c, 1.50r, 2r, 3r, Various Cyprinidae. 50c, Trout. 80c, Catfish. 1r, Moray eel.

1983, Nov. 16 **Perf. 13**
447-453 A107 Set of 7   8.00 2.00

Festival of Rebirth — A108

50c, Factory. 1r, Bull, tractor. 3r, Bridge, ship, train. 6r, Radio antenna. 50c, 3r, 6r vert.

Perf. 12½x13, 13x12½
1983, Dec. 2 **Litho.**
454-456 A108 Set of 3   3.50 1.00
Souvenir Sheet
457 A108 6r multicolored   6.50 1.50
No. 457 contains one 32x40mm stamp.

People's Republic of Kampuchea, 5th Anniv. — A109

Designs: 50c, Red Cross. 1r, Soldiers. 3r, People celebrating. 6r, Man carrying water.

1984, Jan. 7 **Litho.** **Perf. 13**
458-460 A109 Set of 3   3.75 1.25
Souvenir Sheet
461 A109 6r multicolored   6.50 1.50
No. 461 contains one 32x40mm stamp.
For surcharges see Nos. 775-776.

1984 Winter Olympics, Sarajevo A110

Designs: 20c, Speed skating. 50c, Hockey. 80c, Slalom skiing. 1r, Ski jumping. 1.50r, Biathlon. 2r, Cross-country skiing. 3r, Pairs figure skating. 6r, Women's figure skating.

1984, Jan. 6 **Litho.** **Perf. 13**
462-468 A110 Set of 7   7.25 2.00
Souvenir Sheet
469 A110 6r multicolored   5.50 1.40
No. 469 contains one 32x40mm stamp.

Birds — A111

Designs: 10c, Bubulcus ibis. 40c, Lanius schach. 80c, Psittacula himalayana. 1r, Chloropsis aurifrons. 1.20r, Clamator coromandus. 2r, Motacilla cinerea. 2.50r, Dendronanthus indicus.

1984, Feb. 2
470-476 A111 Set of 7   15.00 3.00

Intl. Peace in Southeast Asia Forum — A112

Background color: 50c, Green. 1r, Blue. 3r, Violet.

1984, Feb. 25 **Perf. 13x12½**
477-479 A112 Set of 3   3.75 1.00

Space Exploration — A113

Designs: 10c, Luna 1. 40c, Luna 2. 80c, Luna 3. 1r, Soyuz 6. 1.20r, Soyuz 7. 2r, Soyuz 8. 2.50r, Book, rocket, S.P. Koralev. 6r, Salyut space station.
1r-2.50r are vert.

1984, Mar. 8 **Perf. 12½**
480-486 A113 Set of 7   6.50 2.00
Souvenir Sheet
487 A113 6r multicolored   6.50 1.75
No. 487 contains one 40x32mm stamp.

1984 Summer Olympic Games, Los Angeles A114

Designs: 20c, Discus. 50c, Long jump. 80c, Hurdles. 1r, Relay race. 1.50r, Pole vault. 2r, Javelin. 3r, High jump. 6r, Sprint race.

1984, Apr. 20 **Perf. 13**
488-494 A114 Set of 7   8.00 2.50
Souvenir Sheet
495 A114 6r multicolored   6.75 2.25
No. 495 contains one 32x40mm stamp.

Souvenir Sheet

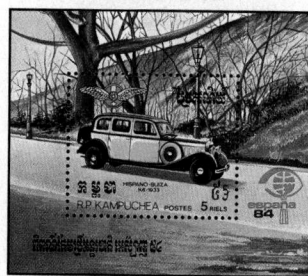

ESPAÑA '84, Madrid — A115

5r, 1933 Hispano-Suiza K6.

1984, Apr. 24 **Perf. 12½**
496 A115 5r multicolored   6.50 2.25

Wild Animals A116

Designs: 10c, Canis latrans. 40c, Canis dingo. 80c, Lycaon pictus. 1r, Canis aureus. 1.20r, Vulpes vulpes. 2r, Chrysocyon brachyurus, vert. 2.50r, Canis lupus.

1984, May 5 **Perf. 13**
497-503 A116 Set of 7   9.50 1.60

Locomotives — A117

Designs: 10c, BB-1002, France, 1966. 40c, BB-1052, France, 1966. 80c, Franco-Belgian, 1945. 1r, #231-505, Franco-Belgian, 1929. 1.20r, #803, Germany, 1968. 2r, BDE-405, France, 1957. 2.50r, DS-01, France, 1979.

1984, June 15 **Litho.** **Perf. 12½**
504-510 A117 Set of 7   8.75 1.75

Flowers A118

Designs: 10c, Magnolia. 40c, Plumeria. 80c, Himenoballis. 1r, Peltophorum roxburghii.

1.20r, Couroupita guianensis. 2r, Lagerstroemia. 2.50r, Thevetia perubiana.

1984, July 10 **Litho.** **Perf. 13**
511-517 A118 Set of 7   11.00 2.00

Classic Automobiles — A119

Designs: 20c, Mercedes-Benz. 50c, Bugatti. 80c, Alfa Romeo. 1r, Franklin. 1.50r, Hispano-Suiza. 2r, Rolls Royce. 3r, Tatra. 6r, Mercedes Benz, diff.

1984, Sept. 15 **Perf. 13x12½**
518-524 A119 Set of 7   9.50 2.00
Souvenir Sheet
Perf. 12½
525 A119 6r multicolored   7.25 1.50
No. 525 contains one 40x32mm stamp.

Musical Instruments — A120

Designs: 10c, Sra Lai. 40c, Skor drum. 80c, Skor thom. 1r, Thro khmer. 1.20r, Raneat ek. 2r, Raneat kong. 2.50r, Thro khe.
10c, 80c are vert.

1984, Oct. 10 **Perf. 13**
526-532 A120 Set of 7   7.50 1.75

Wild Animals A121

Designs: 10c, Gazelle. 40c, Capreolus capreolus. 80c, Lepus. 1r, Cervus elaphus. 1.20r, Elephas maximus. 2r, Genet. 2.50r, Bibos sauveli.
10c-40c, 1r-1.20r are vert.

1984, Nov. 11 **Perf. 13**
533-539 A121 Set of 7   7.50 1.75

Correggio (1489-1534) — A122

Details from paintings: 20c, Rest on Flight into Egypt. 50c, Martyrdom of the Four Saints. 80c, Mystic Marriage of St. Catherine with Saints Francis and Dominic. 1r, Madonna & Child with Saints John the Baptist, Geminian, Peter Martyr and George. 1.50r, Mystic Marriage of St. Catherine. 2r, The Deposition. 2.50r, The Deposition, diff. 6r, Virgin Crowned by Christ.

1984, Dec. 10   *Perf. 12½x13*
540-546 A122 Set of 7   5.00 1.00
Souvenir Sheet
Perf. 12½
547 A122 6r multicolored   6.00 1.00
No. 547 contains one 40x32mm stamp.

Natl. Festival — A123

50c, Oxcart. 1r, Horse-drawn cart. 3r, Elephants. 6r, Oxcart with passengers, vert.

1985, Jan. 5   *Perf. 12½x12*
548-550 A123 Set of 3   4.50 1.00
Souvenir Sheet
Perf. 12½
551 A123 6r multicolored   6.50 1.00
No. 551 contains one 32x40mm stamp.

1986 World Cup Soccer
Championships, Mexico — A124

Various soccer players; 20c, vert. 50c, vert. 80c, vert. 1r. 1.50r. 2r, vert. 3r, vert.

1985, Feb. 4   *Perf. 13*
552-558 A124 Set of 7   5.25 1.25
Souvenir Sheet
559 A124 6r multicolored   6.00 1.00
No. 559 contains one 40x32mm stamp.

Motorcycles — A125

20c, 1939 Eska-Mofa. 50c, 1939 Wanderer. 80c, 1929 Premier. 1r, 1939 Ardie. 1.50r, 1932 Jawa. 2r, 1983 Simson. 3r, 1984 CZ-125.

1985, Mar. 8   *Litho.*   *Perf. 13*
560-566 A125 Set of 7   5.50 1.75
Souvenir Sheet
567 A125 6r 1984 MBA   6.50 1.50
No. 567 contains one 40x32mm stamp.

Mushrooms — A126

Designs: 20c, Gymnopilus spectabilis. 50c, Coprinus micaceus. 80c, Amanita panterina. 1r, Hebelona crustuliniforme. 1.50r, Amanita muscaria. 2r, Coprinus comatus. 3r, Amanita caesarea.
Nos. 569-574 are vert.

1985, Apr. 4   *Perf. 13*
568-574 A126 Set of 7   8.50 1.40

Soviet Space Achievements — A127

Designs: 20c, Sputnik. 50c, Yuri Gagarin, rocket. 80c, Valentina Tereshkova, Vostok 6. 1r, Cosmonaut walking in space. 1.50r, Soyuz 4 docked with Soyuz 5. 2r, Lunar rover. 3r, Apollo-Soyuz mission. 6r, Soyuz capsule.

1985, Apr. 12   *Perf. 13*
575-581 A127 Set of 7   5.25 1.25
Souvenir Sheet
582 A127 6r multicolored   6.00 1.00
No. 582 contains one 40x32mm stamp.

Traditional Dances — A128

Designs: 50c, Four dancers. 1r, Three dancers. 3r, One dancer, vert.

1985, Apr. 13   *Litho.*   *Perf. 12½*
583-585 A128 Set of 3   3.50 1.25

End of World
War II, 40th
Anniv.
A129

Designs: 50c, Soldiers celebrating. 1r, Victory parade, Moscow. 3r, Tank battle.

1985, May 9   *Litho.*   *Perf. 12x12½*
586-588 A129 Set of 3   4.25 1.50

Cats — A130

Various cats: 20c, 50c, 80c, 1r, 1.50r, 2r, 3r.

1985, May 16   *Litho.*   *Perf. 12x12½*
589-595 A130 Set of 7   6.25 1.50

Flowers — A131

20c, Lilium Black Dragon. 50c, Iris delavayi. 80c, Crocus aureus. 1r, Cyclamen persicum, wild form. 1.50r, Primula malacoides. 2r, Viola tricolor. 3r, Crocus purpureus.

1985, June 5   *Litho.*   *Perf. 13*
596-602 A131 Set of 7   6.00 1.25

Intl. Music
Year — A132

Paintings: 20c, Mezzetin, by Watteau. 50c, St. Cecilia and the Angel, by Saraceni. 80c, Still Life with Violin, Flute and Guitar, by Oudry, horiz. 1r, Three Musicians, by F. Leger. 1.50r, Opera Orchestra, by Degas. 2r, St. Cecilia, by Schedoni. 3r, Young Harlequin with Violin, by Caillard. 6r, The Fifer, by Manet.

1985, June 13   *Perf. 13*
603-609 A132 Set of 7   4.75 1.25
Souvenir Sheet
610 A132 6r multicolored   4.75 1.25
No. 610 contains one 32x40mm stamp.

Lenin (1870-
1924)
A133

1r, Portrait. 3r, Lenin standing, map of Soviet Union.

1985, June 20   *Litho.*   *Perf. 13*
611-612 A133 Set of 2   3.50 1.00

ARGENTINA '85 — A134

Birds: 20c, Xanthopsar flavus. 50c, Sicalis flaveola. 80c, Thraupis bonariensis. 1r, Amblyramphus holosericeus. 1.50r, Chiloroceryle amazona. 2r, Ramphastos toco. 3r, Turdus rufiventris.
20c-80c, 1.50r-2r are vert.

1985, July 5   *Litho.*   *Perf. 12½*
613-619 A134 Set of 7   8.75 2.00

Ships
A135

Designs: 10c, River boat, 1942. 40c, River boat, 1948. 80c, Tugboat, Japan, 1913. 1r, Dredge. 1.20r, Tugboat, US. 2r, Freighter. 2.50r, Tanker, Panama.

1985, Aug. 8
620-626 A135 Set of 7   4.75 1.40

ITALIA
85 — A136

Paintings: 20c, The Flood, by Michelangelo. 50c, Virgin & St. Margaret, by Il Parmigianino (Filippo Mazzola). 80c, Martyrdom of St. Peter Martyr, by Domenichino. 1r, Spring, by Botticelli. 1.50r, Sacrifice of Abraham, by Veronese. 2r, Meeting of St. Joachim and St. Anne, by Giotto. 3r, Bacchus, by Caravaggio.
6r, Early train.

1985, Oct. 25
627-633 A136 Set of 7   6.00 1.10
Souvenir Sheet
634 A136 6r multicolored   4.50 1.25
No. 634 contains one 32x40mm stamp.

Son Ngoc
Minh — A137

1985, Dec. 2   *Litho.*   *Perf. 12x12½*
635-637 A137 Set of 3, 50c, 1r, 3r   2.50 1.25

Fish
A138

20c, Barbus tetrazona. 50c, Ophiocephalus micropeltes. 80c, Carassius auratus. 1r, Trichogaster leeri. 1.50r, Puntius hexazona. 2r, Betta splendens. 3r, Datnioides microlepis.

1985, Dec. 28   *Litho.*   *Perf. 13*
638-644 A138 Set of 7   6.50 1.50

1986 World Cup
Soccer
Championships,
Mexico — A139

Various soccer players: 20c, 50c, 80c, 1r, 1.50r, 2r, 3r.

1986, Jan. 29
645-651 A139 Set of 7   4.75 1.25
Souvenir Sheet
652 A139 6r multicolored   6.00 1.00
No. 652 contains one 32x40mm stamp.

Horses
A140

Designs: 20c, Cob. 50c, Arabian. 80c, Australian pony. 1r, Appaloosa. 1.50r, Quarter horse. 2r, Vladimir heavy draft. 3r, Andalusian.

1986, Feb. 15
653-659 A140 Set of 7   5.50 1.50

27th Soviet Communist Party Congress A141

Designs: 50c, Space capsules. 1r, Lenin. 5r, Statue, rocket lift-off.

1986, Feb. 25   *Perf. 12x12½*
660-662 A141 Set of 3   4.25 1.25

Prehistoric Animals — A142

Designs: 20c, Edaphosaurus, horiz. 50c, Sauroctonus, horiz. 80c, Mastodonsaurus, horiz. 1r, Rhamphorhynchus. 1.50r, Brachiosaurus. 2r, Tarbosaurus. 3r, Indricotherium.

1986, Mar. 20   *Perf. 12½*
663-669 A142 Set of 7   11.00 3.00

Manned Space Flight, 25th Anniv. — A143

10c, Luna 16. 40c, Luna 3. 80c, Vostok. 1r, Alexei Leonov walking in space. 1.20r, Apollo-Soyuz mission. 2r, Soyuz capsule docking with Salyut station. 2.50r, Yuri Gagarin.

1986, Apr. 12   *Perf. 12½*
670-676 A143 Set of 7   5.25 1.50

Khmer Culture — A144

20c, Temple. 50c, Head of Buddha. 80c, Temple entrance. 1r, 1.50r, 2r, 3r, Various fans.

1986, Apr. 12   *Perf. 13*
677-683 A144 Set of 7   4.00 1.60

Mercedes-Benz Automobiles — A145

20c, 1885 3-wheel. 50c, 1935 sedan. 80c, 1907 open touring car. 1r, 1920 convertible. 1.50r, 1932 cabriolet. 2r, 1938 2-door. 3r, 1985 sedan.

1986, May 14   *Perf. 13x12½*
684-690 A145 Set of 7   5.25 1.50

Butterflies A146

Designs: 20c, Danaus genutia. 50c, Graphium amtiphates. 80c, Papilio demoleus. 1r, Danaus sita. 1.50r, Idea blanchardi. 2r, Papilio polytes. 3r, Dabasa payeni.

1986, June 19   *Perf. 13*
691-697 A146 Set of 7   5.50 1.75

Ships A147

20c, English cog. 50c, Cog. 80c, Nile barge. 1r, Galley. 1.50r, Viking long ship. 2r, Two-masted lateen-rigged ship. 3r, Cog, diff.

1986, July 7   *Perf. 13*
698-704 A147 Set of 7   4.75 1.50

Halley's Comet — A148

Designs: 10c, Solar system, Copernicus, Galileo, Brahe. 20c, Comet above Adoration of the Magi in painting by Giotto. 50c, Comet, observatory. 80c, Edmond Halley. 1.20r, Giotto probe. 1.50r, Vega probe. 2r, Computer-enhanced images of comet. 6r, Vega probe, diff.

1986, July 21   *Litho.*   *Perf. 12x12½*
705-711 A148 Set of 7   3.75 1.40
Souvenir Sheet
Perf. 13
712 A148 6r multicolored   4.75 1.25
No. 712 contains one 32x40mm stamp.

STOCKHOLMIA 86 — A149

Chess masters: 20c, Ruy Lopez. 50c, Francois Philador. 80c, Adolph Anderssen. 1r, Wilhelm Steinetz. 1.50r, Emanuel Lasker. 2r, José Capablanca. 3r, Alexander Alekhine. 6r, Chess pieces.

1986, Aug. 28   *Litho.*   *Perf. 12½*
713-719 A149 Set of 7   6.00 1.40
Souvenir Sheet
Perf. 13
720 A149 6r multicolored   7.25 1.40
No. 720 contains one 40x32mm stamp.

Cactus — A150

20c, Parodia maasii. 50c, Rebutia marsoneri. 80c, Melocactus evae. 1r, Gymnocalycium valnicekianum. 1.50r, Discocactus silichromus. 2r, Neochilenia simulans. 3r, Weingartia chiqichuquensis.

1986, Sept. 25   *Perf. 13*
721-727 A150 Set of 7   5.50 1.40

Fruit — A151

Designs: 10c, Bananas. 40c, Papayas. 80c, Mangos. 1r, Breadfruit. 1.20r, Litchi. 2r, Pineapple. 2.50r, Grapefruit, horiz.

1986, Oct. 4   *Perf. 12½*
728-734 A151 Set of 7   4.00 1.50

Aircraft — A152

20c, Concorde. 50c, DC-10. 80c, 747. 1r, IL-62. 1.50r, IL-86. 2r, AN-124. 3r, A-300.

1986, Nov. 21
735-741 A152 Set of 7   4.75 1.60

Silverware — A153

Designs: 50c, Elephant, containers. 1r, Covered bowl. 3r, Serving dish.

1986, Dec. 2   *Perf. 13*
742-744 A153 Set of 3   3.75 1.40

World Wildlife Fund A154

Designs: No. 745, 20c, Kouprey. No. 746, 20c, Gaur. 80c, Banteng. 1.50r, Buffalo.

1986, Dec. 30   *Litho.*   *Perf. 13*
745-748 A154 Set of 4   14.00 4.00

Tou Samouth A155

Denominations and background colors: 50c, green. 1r, blue, 3r, yellow.

1987, Jan. 7   *Litho.*   *Perf. 13*
749-751 A155 Set of 3   2.75 1.00

1988 Winter Olympic Games, Calgary — A156

Designs: 20c, Biathlon. 50c, Women's figure skating. 80c, Speed skating. 1r, Hockey. 1.50r, Luge. 2r, Two-man bobsled. 3r, Cross-country skiing. 6r, Slalom skiing.

1987, Jan. 14   *Perf. 13x12½*
752-758 A156 Set of 7   4.75 1.25
Souvenir Sheet
Perf. 12½
759 A156 6r multicolored   4.75 1.10
No. 759 contains one 40x32mm stamp.

1988 Summer Olympic Games, Seoul — A157

Designs: 20c, Weight lifting, vert. 50c, Archery. 80c, Fencing. 1r, Gymnastics, vert. 1.50r, Discus. 2r, Javelin, vert. 3r, Hurdles. 6r, Wrestling.

1987, Feb. 2   *Perf. 12½x13, 13x12½*
760-766 A157 Set of 7   4.75 1.25
Souvenir Sheet
Perf. 13
767 A157 6r multicolored   4.75 1.25
No. 767 contains one 40x32mm stamp.

Dogs A158

Designs: 20c, shown. 50c, Greyhound. 80c, Great Dane. 1r, Doberman pinscher. 1.50r, Samoyed. 2r, Borzoi. 3r, Collie.

1987, Mar. 3 *Perf. 13*
768-774 A158 Set of 7   8.00 1.50

Nos. 458, 463 Surcharged

1987, Mar.   **Litho.**   *Perf. 13*
775 A110 35r on 50c #463   5.00
776 A109 50r on 50c #458   5.00

Soviet
Spacecraft
A159

Designs: 20c, Sputnik. 50c, Weather satellite. 80c, Proton. 1r, Vostok 1. 1.50r, Electron-2. 2r, Kosmos. 3r, Luna 2. 6r, Electron-4.

1987, Apr. 12   **Litho.**   *Perf. 13*
777-783 A159 Set of 7   4.75 1.60
Souvenir Sheet
784 A159 6r multicolored   4.75 1.25
No. 784 contains one 40x32mm stamp.

Silverware — A159a

Designs: 50c, Long-necked pot, vert. 1r, Box. 1.50r, Tea set. 3r, Sword.

1987, Apr. 13 *Perf. 13*
785-788 A159a Set of 4   3.50 1.00

CAPEX 87 — A160

Birds: 20c, Merops nubicus. 50c, Upupa epops. 80c, Balearica pavonina. 1r, Tyto alba. 1.50r, Halcyon leucocephala. 2r, Pycnonotus jocosus. 3r, Ardea purpurea. 6r, Terpsiphone paradisi.
50c-1.50r, 3r are vert.

1987, May 5 *Perf. 13*
789-795 A160 Set of 7   5.25 1.25
Souvenir Sheet
796 A160 6r multicolored   5.25 1.25
No. 796 contains one 32x40mm stamp.

Early
Aircraft
Designs
A161

Designs by: 20c, Horatio F. Phillips, 1893. 50c, John Stringfellow, 1848. 80c, Thomas Moy, 1875. 1r, Leonardo da Vinci, 1490. 1.50r, Sir George Cayley, 1840. 2r, Sir Hiram Maxim, 1894. 3r, William S. Henson, 1842. 6r, Da Vinci, diff.

1987, Aug. 7 *Perf. 13*
797-803 A161 Set of 7   5.25 1.40
Souvenir Sheet
Perf. 12½
804 A161 6r multicolored   4.75 1.00
No. 804 contains one 32x40mm stamp.

Reptiles
A162

Designs: 20c, Testudo gigantea. 50c, Uromastix acanthinuros. 80c, Cyclura macleayi. 1r, Phrynosoma coronatum. 1.50r, Sauromalus obesus. 2r, Ophisaurus apodus. 3r, Thamnophis sirtalis.

1987, Sept. 9 *Perf. 13*
805-811 A162 Set of 7   4.75 1.75

HAFNIA 87 — A163

Helicopters: 20c, Kamov KA-15. 50c, Kamov KA-18. 80c, Westland Lynx WG-13. 1r, Sud Aviation Gazelle. 1.50r, Sud Aviation Puma. 2r, Boeing CH-47 Chinook. 3r, Boeing UTTAS. 6r, Fairey Rotodyne.

1987, Oct. 16 *Perf. 12½x12*
812-818 A163 Set of 7   4.75 1.40
Souvenir Sheet
Perf. 13
819 A163 6r multicolored   4.75 1.25
No. 819 contains one 40x32mm stamp.

Russian October Revolution, 70th
Anniv. — A164

1987   **Litho.**   *Perf. 12x12¼*
820 A164 2r Soldiers, horse   1.25 .30
821 A164 3r Soldiers   1.75 .50
822 A164 5r Lenin, aides   3.50 .80
Two additional stamps were issued in this set. The editors would like to examine them.

Fire
Trucks
A165

1987, Nov. 24   **Litho.**   *Perf. 13*
823-829 A165   20c, 50c, 80c, 1r, 1.50r, 2r, 3r, set of 7   5.50 2.00

Telecommunications — A166

50c, Dish antenna, vert. 1r, Broadcast center, vert. 3r, Dish antenna, broadcast center.

Perf. 13x12½, 12x12½, 12½x12
1987, Dec. 2
830-832 A166 Set of 3   3.00 1.10
No. 830 is 29x40mm. No. 831 is 28x44mm. No. 832 printed with se-tenant label.

1988
Winter
Olympic
Games,
Calgary
A167

Designs: 20c, Speed skating. 50c, Hockey. 80c, Downhill skiing. 1r, Ski jumping. 1.50r, Biathlon. 2r, Pairs figure skating. 3r, Cross-country skiing. 6r, Four-man bobsled.

1988, Jan. 7 *Perf. 12½*
833-839 A167 Set of 7   4.75 1.00
Souvenir Sheet
Perf. 13
840 A167 6r multicolored   3.25 1.10
No. 840 contains one 32x40mm stamp.

Water
Projects
A168

Designs: 50c, Canal. 1r, Dam under construction. 3r, Dam, bridge.

1988, Jan. 7   **Litho.**   *Perf. 13*
841-843 A168 Set of 3   3.00 1.25

1988 Summer Olympic Games,
Seoul — A169

Designs: 20c, Balance beam, vert. 50c, Uneven bars. 80c, Rhythmic gymnastics ribbon, vert. 1r, Rhythmic gymnastics hoop, vert. 1.50r, Rhythmic gymnastics clubs, vert. 2r, Rhythmic gymnastics ball. 3r, Floor exercise. 6r, Rhythmic gymnastics, diff.

Perf. 12½x13, 13x12½
1988, Feb. 2   **Litho.**
844-850 A169 Set of 7   4.50 1.50
Souvenir Sheet
Perf. 12½
851 A169 6r multicolored   4.75 1.50
No. 851 contains one 32x40mm stamp.

JUVALUX
88
A170

Various cats. Denominations: 20c, 50c, 80c, 1r, 1.50r, 2r, 3r. Nos. 853-854, 856-858 are vert.

1988, Mar. 15 *Perf. 12½*
852-858 A170 Set of 7   5.25 1.25
Souvenir Sheet
Perf. 13
859 A170 6r multicolored   6.00 1.25
No. 859 contains one 40x32mm stamp.

ESSEN 88 — A171

Ships: 20c, Passenger liner. 50c, Passenger liner, diff. 80c, Research ship. 1r, Communications ship. 1.50r, Tanker. 2r, Hydrofoil. 3r, Hovercraft.

1988, Apr. 14   **Litho.**   *Perf. 12½*
860-866 A171 Set of 7   6.50 1.50
Souvenir Sheet
Perf. 13
867 A171 6r Hydrofoil   5.25 1.10

Satellites — A172

Various satellites. Denominations: 20c, 80c, 1r, 1.50r, 2r, 3r. Nos. 868-870 are vert.

1988, Apr. 24   *Perf. 12½x13, 13x12½*
868-874 A172 Set of 7   4.25 1.50
Souvenir Sheet
Perf. 13
875 A172 6r multicolored   4.75 1.25
No. 875 contains one 40x32mm stamp.

FINLANDIA 88 — A173

Fish: 20c, Xiphophorus helleri. 50c, Hemigrammus ocellifer. 80c, Macropodus opercularis. 1r, Carassius auratus. 1.50r, Hyphessobrycon inesi. 2r, Corynopoma riisei. 3r, Mollienisia latipinna.
6r, Pterophyllum scalare.

1988, Jun 10   **Litho.**   *Perf. 13x12½*
876-882 A173 Set of 7   6.50 1.50
Souvenir Sheet
Perf. 12½
883 A173 6r multicolored   5.50 1.25
No. 883 contains one 32x40mm stamp.

Shells — A174

Designs: 20c, Helicostyla florida. 50c, Helicostyla marinduquensis. 80c, Helicostyla fulgens. 1r, Helicostyla woodiana. 1.50r, Chloraea sirena. 2r, Helicostyla mirabilis. 3r, Helicostyla limansauensis.

1988, Aug. 5   **Litho.**   *Perf. 13x12½*
884-890 A174 Set of 7   5.25 1.50

Insects — A175

Designs: 20c, Coccinellidae. 50c, Zonabride geminata. 80c, Carabus auronitens. 1r, Apis mellifera. 1.50r, Praying mantis. 2r, Odonata. 3r, Malachius aeneus.

1988, Sept. 6   *Perf. 13x12½*
891-897 A175 Set of 7   6.50 1.40

Orchids
A176

Designs: 20c, Cattleya aclandiae. 50c, Odontoglossum Royal Sovereign. 80c, Cattleya labiata. 1r, Ophrys apifera. 1.50r, Laelia anceps. 2r, Laelia pumila. 3r, Stanhopea tigrina, horiz.

1988, Oct. 10   *Perf. 12½x13, 13x12½*
898-904 A176 Set of 7   4.75 1.25

Reptiles — A177

Designs: 20c, Naja haje, vert. 50c, Iguana iguana, vert. 80c, Dryophis nasuta. 1r, Terrapene carolina. 1.50r, Cyclura macleayi. 2r, Bothrops bicolor. 3r, Naja naja, with hood spread, vert.

1988, Nov. 7   *Perf. 12x12½, 12½x12*
905-911 A177 Set of 7   6.50 1.75

Dance of the Peacock A178

50c, 3 dancers, vert. 1r, shown. 3r, 2 dancers.

1988, Dec. 2   *Perf. 13*
912-914 A178 Set of 3   3.50 1.25
  For surcharges see Nos. 1195-1196.

Bridges — A179

1989   *Perf. 13x12½*
915-917 A179 50c, 1r, 3r, set of 3   3.25 1.40

Decade of Progress — A180

3r, Telecommunications station. 12r, Central Electrical Plant No. 4. 30r, Cement plant, vert.

1989
918-920 A180 Set of 3   2.75 1.50

1990 World Cup Soccer Championships, Italy — A181

Various soccer players. Denominations: 2r, 3r, 5r, 10r, 15r, 20r, 35r.

1989   *Perf. 12½x13*
921-927 A181 Set of 7   6.50 1.50
Souvenir Sheet
Perf. 13
928 A181 45r multicolored   4.75 1.00
  No. 928 contains one 32x40mm stamp.

Trains
A182

Various locomotives. Denominations: 2r, 3r, 5r, 10r, 15r, 20r, 35r.

1989   *Perf. 13*
929-935 A182 Set of 7   6.75 1.50
Souvenir Sheet
Perf. 12½
936 A182 45r multicolored   6.00 1.00
  No. 936 contains one 40x32mm stamp.

A183

1989   *Perf. 13*
937 A183 12r red & black   1.25 .55
  Cuban Revolution, 30th anniv.

Birds — A184

20c, Ara macao. 80c, Kakatoe galerita. 3r, Psittacula krameri. 6r, Ara ararauna. 10r, Poicephalus robustus. 15r, Amazona aestiva. 25r, Pionus senilis, horiz. 45r, Cyanoramphus novaezelandiae.

1989
938-944 A184 Set of 7   6.75 1.25
Souvenir Sheet
Perf. 12½
945 A184 45r multicolored   5.50 1.00
  No. 945 contains one 40x32mm stamp.

1992 Winter Olympic Games, Albertville A185

2r, Slalom skiing. 3r, Biathlon. 5r, Crosscountry skiing. 10r, Ski jumping. 15r, Speed skating. 20r, Hockey. 35r, Bobsled. 45r, Pairs figure skating.

1989, Mar. 30   *Perf. 13*
946-952 A185 Set of 7   6.50 1.50
Souvenir Sheet
Perf. 12½
953 A185 45r multicolored   4.75 1.50
  No. 953 contains one 32x40mm stamp.

Water Lilies A186

20c, Nymphaea capensis (pink). 80c, Nymphaea capensis (purple). 3r, Nymphaea lotus. 6r, Nymphaea Dir. Geo. T. Moore. 10r, Nymphaea Sunrise. 15r, Nymphaea Escarboncle. 25r, Nymphaea Cladstoniana. 45r, Nymphaea Paul Hariot.

1989   *Perf. 12½x13*
954-960 A186 Set of 7   4.50 1.25
Souvenir Sheet
Perf. 12½
961 A186 45r multicolored   4.75 1.00
  No. 961 contains one 32x40mm stamp.

1992 Summer Olympic Games, Barcelona — A187

Designs: 2r, Wrestling. 3r, Pommel horse, vert. 5r, Shot put. 10r, Running, vert. 15r, Fencing. 20r, Canoeing, vert. 35r, Steeplechase, vert. 45r, Weight lifting, vert.

1989   *Perf. 13*
962-968 A187 Set of 7   6.50 1.50
Souvenir Sheet
Perf. 12½
969 A187 45r multicolored   5.25 1.50
  No. 969 contains one 32x40mm stamp.

Mushrooms
A188

Designs: 20c, Xerocomus subtomentosus. 80c, Inocybe patouillardii. 3r, Armillaria mellea. 6r, Agaricus campestris. 10r, Paxillus involutus. 15r, Coprinus comatus. 25r, Lepiota procera.

1989   *Perf. 12½x13*
970-976 A188 Set of 7   5.25 1.10

Horses — A189

Designs: 2r, Shire. 3r, Brabant. 5r, Bolounais. 10r, Breton. 15r, Vladimir heavy draft. 20r, Italian heavy draft. 35r, Freiberger. 45r, Horse-drawn cart.

1989   *Perf. 12½*
977-983 A189 Set of 7   5.50 1.50
Souvenir Sheet
984 A189 45r multicolored   4.75 1.10
  Nos. 977-983 printed with se-tenant label.
  No. 984 contains one 40x32mm stamp.

Angkor Wat — A190

Denominations: 35r, 50r, 80r, 100r.

1989, May 15   Litho.   *Perf. 13¼*
985-988 A190 Set of 4   *175.00 175.00*

Cambodia

PHILEXFRANCE 89 — A191

Mail coaches: 2r, 17th cent. 3r, Paris-Lyon, 1720. 5r, 1793. 10r, 1805. 15r, Royal Mail. 20r, Paris-Lille, 1837, vert. 45r, 1815, vert.

1989   Litho.   *Perf. 13*
989-995 A191 Set of 7   5.75 1.50
Souvenir Sheet
Perf. 12½
996 A191 45r multicolored   3.25 1.50
  No. 996 contains one 23x40mm stamp.

BRASILIANA
89 — A192

Butterflies: 2r, Papilio zagreus. 3r, Morpho catenarius. 5r, Morpho aega. 10r, Callithea sapphira. 15r, Catagramma sorana. 20r, Pierella nereis. 35r, Papilio brasiliensis. 45r, Thacia marsyas, horiz.

1989   *Perf. 13*
997-1003 A192   Set of 7   7.00 1.50
Souvenir Sheet
1004 A192 45r multicolored   6.00 1.50
   No. 1004 contains one 40x32mm stamp.

Khmer Boats
A193

Various pirogues. Denominations: 3r, 12r, 30r.

1989, Dec. 2   **Litho.**   *Perf. 12½*
1005-1007 A193   Set of 3   3.00 1.25

Natl. Organizations — A194

3r, Youth, vert. 12r, Labor. 30r, Natl. Front.

1990, Jan. 7   **Litho.**   *Perf. 13*
1008-1010 A194   Set of 3   3.50 1.25

1990 World Cup Soccer Championships, Italy — A195

Various soccer players. Denominations: 2r, 3r, 5r, 10r, 15r, 20r, 35r.

1990, Jan. 5   **Litho.**   *Perf. 13*
1011-1017 A195   Set of 7   5.50 1.50
Souvenir Sheet
1018 A195 45r multicolored   4.00 1.00
   No. 1018 contains one 32x40mm stamp.
   For surcharges see Nos. 1072-1076A.

STAMPWORLD LONDON 90 — A196

Various mail coaches. Denominations: 2r, 3r, 5r, 10r, 15r, 20r, 35r.
   45r, Single horse van for rural deliveries.

1990   *Perf. 12½x12*
1019-1025 A196   Set of 7   5.50 1.25
Souvenir Sheet
Perf. 13
1026 A196 45r multicolored   4.75 1.00
   Nos. 1019-1025 are printed with se-tenant label. No. 1026 contains one 40x32mm stamp.

Rice — A197

Designs: 3r, Woman, rice. 12r, People hauling rice, horiz. 30r, Women threshing rice.

1990, June 19   **Litho.**   *Perf. 13*
1027-1029 A197   Set of 3   3.50 1.25

1992 Winter Olympic Games, Albertville A198

2r, 4-man bobsled. 3r, Speed skating. 5r, Pairs figure skating. 10r, Hockey. 15r, Biathlon. 20r, Luge. 35r, Ski jumping. 45r, Hockey goalie.

1990   **Litho.**   *Perf. 13*
1030-1036 A198   Set of 7   5.50 1.50
Souvenir Sheet
1037 A198 45r multicolored   4.50 1.00
   No. 1037 contains one 32x40mm stamp.

1992 Summer Olympic Games, Barcelona A199

Designs: 2r, Shooting. 3r, Shot put. 5r, Weight lifting. 10r, Boxing. 15r, Pole vault. 20r, Basketball. 35r, Fencing. 45r, Rhythmic gymnastics.

1990
1038-1044 A199   Set of 7   5.50 1.50
Souvenir Sheet
1045 A199 45r multicolored   4.00 1.00
   No. 1045 contains one 32x40mm stamp.

Khmer Culture A200

Designs: 3r, Facade, Bantey Srei. 12r, Relief. 30r, Ruins, Banon.

Perf. 12½, 12½x13 (#1048)
1990, Dec. 2   **Litho.**
1046-1048 A200   Set of 3   3.75 1.25
   No. 1048 is 36x21mm.

Dogs
A201

20c, Poodle. 80c, Shetland. 3r, Samoyed. 6r, Springer spaniel. 10r, Fox terrier. 15r, Afghan. 25r, Dalmatian. 45r, Bernese.

1990   **Litho.**   *Perf. 13*
1049-1055 A201   Set of 7   5.50 1.25
Souvenir Sheet
1056 A201 45r multicolored   4.25 1.00
   No. 1056 contains one 40x32mm stamp.

Cacti — A202

Designs: 20c, Cereus hexagonus. 80c, Arthrocereus rondonianus. 3r, Matucana multicolor. 6r, Hildewintera aureispina. 10r, Opuntia retrosa. 15r, Erdisia tenuicula. 25r, Mamillaria yaquensis.

1990
1057-1063 A202   Set of 7   5.00 1.50

NEW ZEALAND 90 — A203

Butterflies: 2r, Zizina oxleyi. 3r, Cupha prosope. 5r, Heteronympha merope. 10r, Dodonidia helmsi. 15r, Argirophenga antipodum. 20r, Tysonotis danis. 35r, Pyrameis gonnarilla. 45r, Pyrameis itea.

1990   *Perf. 13*
1064-1070 A203   Set of 7   8.00 1.50
Souvenir Sheet
Perf. 12½
1071 A203 45r multicolored   5.50 1.25
   No. 1071 contains one 40x32mm stamp.

Nos. 1012-1017 Surcharged in Red
1990   **Litho.**   *Perf. 13*
1072   A195   200r on 3r #1012
1073   A195   300r on 5r #1013
1074   A195   500r on 10r #1014
1075   A195   800r on 15r #1015
1076   A195   1000r on 20r #1016
1076A   A195   2000r on 35r #1017

Intl. Literacy Year — A204

Denominations: 3r, 12r, 30r.

1990   **Litho.**   *Perf. 13*
1077-1079 A204   Set of 3   5.25 1.50

Ships
A205

Designs: 20c, English, 1200. 80c, Spanish galleon, 16th cent. 3r, Dutch ship, 1627. 6r, La Couronne, 1638. 10r, L'Astrolabe, 1826. 15r, French packet, Louisiana, 1864. 25r, Clipper ship, 1900, vert. 45r, Merchant ship, 1800.

1990   **Litho.**   *Perf. 13*
1080-1086 A205   Set of 7   6.50 1.50
Souvenir Sheet
Perf. 12½
1087 A205 45r multicolored   4.50 1.00
   No. 1087 contains one 32x40mm stamp.

Natl. Building Campaign — A206

3r, Railroad. 12r, Cargo ship, Kampong Som. 30r, Fishing boats, Kampong Som.

1990   **Litho.**   *Perf. 13*
1088-1090 A206   Set of 3   5.50 1.25

PARIS
90 — A207

Chess pieces and: 2r, Sacré Coeur. 3r, Equestrian statue. 5r, Winged Victory of Samothrace. 10r, Chateau, Azay le Riddeau. 15r, Sculpture, "The Dance." 20r, Eiffel Tower. 35r, Arc de Triomphe.
   45r, Chess pieces, horiz.

1990, Nov. 15   **Litho.**   *Perf. 13*
1091-1097 A207   Set of 7   6.50 2.00
Souvenir Sheet
1098 A207 45r multicolored   5.50 1.50
   No. 1098 contains one 40x32mm stamp.

Space
Day — A208

Designs: 2r, Vostok. 3r, Soyuz. 5r, Artificial satellite. 10r, Luna 10. 15r, Mars 1. 20r, Venera 3. 35r, Energia, Buran. 45r, Mir.

1990   **Litho.**   *Perf. 13*
1099-1105 A208   Set of 7   5.50 1.50
Souvenir Sheet
1106 A208 45r multicolored   4.00 1.00
   No. 1106 contains one 32x40mm stamp.
   For surcharges see Nos. 1145-1151.

Discovery of America, 500th Anniv. (in 1992) — A209

Designs: 2r, Columbus. 3r, Queen Isabella's jewelry chest. 5r, Queen Isabella. 10r, Santa Maria. 15r, Juan de la Cosa. 20r, Columbus Monument. 35r, Pyramid, Yucatan.
45r, Columbus, diff.

1990, Oct. 12   Litho.   *Perf. 13*
1107-1113 A209 Set of 7   7.50 2.00
Souvenir Sheet
1114 A209 45r multicolored   4.75 1.25
No. 1114 contains one 32x40mm stamp.

Natl. Festival A210

Designs: 100r, Tire production. 300r, Rural infirmary. 500r, Fisherman, vert.

Perf. 12½, 13 (#1117)
1991, Jan. 7   Litho.
1115-1117 A210 Set of 3   5.00 1.75
No. 1117 is 28x40mm.

1994 World Cup Soccer Championships, US — A211

Various soccer players. Denominations: 5r, 25r, 70r, 100r, 200r, 400r, 1000r.

1991, Feb. 15   Litho.   *Perf. 13*
1118-1124 A211 Set of 7   6.25 1.75
Souvenir Sheet
1125 A211 900r multicolored   3.50 1.10
No. 1125 contains one 32x40mm stamp.

1992 Winter Olympic Games, Albertville A212

Designs: 5r, Speed skating. 25r, Slalom skiing. 70r, Hockey. 100r, Bobsled. 200r, Freestyle skiing. 400r, Pairs figure skating. 1000r, Downhill skiing.
900r, Ski jumping.

1991, Mar. 30   Litho.   *Perf. 12½*
1126-1132 A212 Set of 7   7.00 2.00
Souvenir Sheet
Perf. 13
1133 A212 900r multicolored   4.75 1.25
No. 1133 contains one 32x40mm stamp.

Khmer Culture A213

Statues: 100r, Garuda, 10th cent. 300r, Torso of Vishnu reclining, 11th cent. 500r, Reclining Nandin, 7th cent.

1991, Apr. 13   Litho.   *Perf. 12½*
1134-1136 A213 Set of 3   3.50 2.00

1992 Summer Olympic Games, Barcelona A214

Designs: 5r, Pole vault. 25r, Table tennis. 70r, Women's running. 100r, Wrestling. 200r, Women's gymnastics. 400r, Tennis. 1000r, Boxing.
900r, Balance beam.

1991, Apr. 25   Litho.   *Perf. 12½x13*
1137-1143 A214 Set of 7   5.75 1.50
Souvenir Sheet
Perf. 13
1144 A214 900r multicolored   4.00 1.00
No. 1144 contains one 32x40mm stamp.

Nos. 1099-1105 Surcharged in Red
1991		Litho.	*Perf. 13*
1145	A208	100r on 2r #1099	—
1146	A208	150r on 3r #1100	75.00
1147	A208	200r on 5r #1101	75.00
1148	A208	300r on 10r #1102	75.00
1149	A208	500r on 15r #1103	75.00
1150	A208	1500r on 20r #1104	—
1151	A208	2000r on 35r #1105	75.00

Aircraft — A215

Designs: 5r, DC-10-30. 25r, MD-11. 70r, IL-96-300. 100r, A-310. 200r, YAK-42. 400r, TU-154. 1000r, DC-9

1991, June 15   Litho.   *Perf. 13x12½*
1152-1158 A215 Set of 7   6.00 1.75

ESPAMER 91 — A216

Pre-Columbian pottery: 5r, Catamarca. 25r, Catamarca, vert. 70r, Tucuman, vert. 100r, Santiago del Estero. 200r, Santiago del Estero, diff. 400r, Tucuman, diff., vert. 1000r, Catamarca, diff.
900r, Catamarca, diff.

1991, July 10   *Perf. 13*
1159-1165 A216 Set of 7   6.50 2.00
Souvenir Sheet
Perf. 12½
1166 A216 900r multicolored   4.50 1.25
No. 1166 contains one 40x32mm stamp.

Discovery of America, 500th Anniv. (in 1992) — A217

Designs: 5r, Pinta, vert. 25r, Niña, vert. 70r, Santa Maria, vert. 100r, Landing of Columbus. 200r, Encountering new cultures. 400r, First European settlement in Americas. 1000r, Native village.
900r, Columbus.

1991, Oct. 12   *Perf. 12½x13, 13x12½*
1167-1173 A217 Set of 7   7.00 2.00
Souvenir Sheet
Perf. 12½
1174 A217 900r multicolored   4.00 1.10
No. 1174 contains one 40x32mm stamp.

PHILANIPPON 91 — A218

Butterflies: 5r, Neptis pryeri. 25r, Papilio xuthus. 70r, Cyrestis thyodamas. 100r, Argynnis anadiomene. 200r, Lethe marginalis. 400r, Artopoetes pryeri. 1000r, Danaus chrysippus.
900r, Ochlodes subhyalina.

1991, Nov. 16   *Perf. 13*
1175-1181 A218 Set of 7   8.50 2.00
Souvenir Sheet
Perf. 12½
1182 A218 900r multicolored   7.00 1.25
No. 1182 contains one 40x32mm stamp.

Natl. Building Campaign A219

Designs: 100r, Fishing port. 300r, Preparing palm sugar, vert. 500r, Harvesting peppers.

1991, Dec. 2   Litho.   *Perf. 12½*
1183-1185 A219 Set of 3   4.75 2.40

Natl. Festival — A220

Traditional costumes: 150r, Chakdomuk. 350r, Longvek. 1000r, Angkor.

1992, Jan. 7   *Perf. 13*
1186-1188 A220 Set of 3   4.50 1.25

1992 Summer Olympic Games, Barcelona A221

5r, Wrestling. 15r, Soccer. 80r, Weight lifting. 400r, Archery. 1500r, Balance beam. 1000r, Equestrian.

1992, Jan.   Litho.   *Perf. 13*
1189-1193 A221 Set of 5   4.50 1.25
Souvenir Sheet
Perf. 12½
1194 A221 1000r multicolored   4.25 1.00
No. 1194 contains one 32x40mm stamp.

Nos. 913-914 Surcharged in Red
1992, Jan.   Litho.   *Perf. 13*
1195 A178 200r on 3r #914
1196 A178 300r on 1r #913

Fish A222

Designs: 5r, Hyphessobrycon innesi. 15r, Betta splendens. 80r, Nematobrycon palmen. 400r, Colisa lalia. 1500r, Hoplosternum thoracatum.
1000r, Pterophyllum scalare.

1992, Feb. 8   Litho.   *Perf. 12½*
1197-1201 A222 Set of 5   5.25 1.50
Souvenir Sheet
1202 A222 1000r multicolored   4.00 1.00
No. 1202 contains one 40x32mm stamp.

1994 World Cup Soccer Championships, US — A223

Various soccer plays. Denominations: 5r, 15r, 80r, 400r, 1500r. Nos. 1203, 1205-1207 are vert.

1992, Mar. 6   Litho.   *Perf. 12½*
1203-1207 A223 Set of 5   4.50 1.50
Souvenir Sheet
1208 A223 1000r multicolored   3.25 1.00
No. 1208 contains one 40x32mm stamp.

Khmer Culture — A224

19th cent. structures: 150r, Monument. 350r, Stupa. 1000r, Library of Mandapa.

1992, Apr. 13   Litho.   *Perf. 12½*
1209-1211 A224 Set of 3   5.50 3.25

Leonardo da Vinci (1452-1519) — A225

Designs: 5r, Automobile. 15r, Container ship. 80r, Helicopter. 400r, Scuba gear. 1500r, Parachute, vert. 1000r, Portrait.

1992, Apr. 15   Litho.   Perf. 12x12½
1212-1216 A225 Set of 5   7.00 1.50
Souvenir Sheet
Perf. 13
1217 A225 1000r multicolored   4.75 1.00

Nos. 1212-1216 each printed with se-tenant labels showing Da Vinci's conceptions of the items shown on the stamps. No. 1217 contains one 32x40mm stamp.

EXPO 92, Seville A226

Inventors, builders: 5r, De la Cierva, autogyro. 15r, Edison, electric light bulb. 80r, Morse, telegraph. 400r, Monturiol, submarine. No. 1222, 1500r, Bell, telephone.
No. 1223, 1500r, Fulton, steamship.

1992, Apr. 23   Perf. 12½
1218-1222 A226 Set of 5   4.75 1.25
Souvenir Sheet
Perf. 13
1223 A226 1000r pink & black   3.50 1.00

No. 1223 contains one 32x40mm stamp.

1992 Summer Olympic Games, Barcelona — A227

Designs: 5r, Weight lifting. 15r, Boxing. 80r, Basketball. 400r, Sprints. 1500r, Water polo. 1000r, Women's gymnastics.

1992, May 15   Perf. 13
1224-1228 A227 Set of 5   8.00 1.50
Souvenir Sheet
Perf. 12½
1229 A227 1000r multicolored   5.50 1.25

No. 1229 contains one 40x32mm stamp.

Environmental Protection — A228

Designs: 5r, Women filling water jars. 15r, Pagoda. 80r, Palm trees. 400r, Boy riding water buffalo. 1500r, Lake, swimmers. 1000r, Angkor Wat.

1992, June 16   Litho.   Perf. 12½
1230-1234 A228 Set of 5   6.75 1.75
Souvenir Sheet
Perf. 13
1235 A228 1000r multicolored   5.00 1.25

No. 1235 contains one 42x32mm stamp.

GENOA 92 — A229

Explorers, ship: 5r, Bougainville, Boudeuse. 15r, Cook, Endeavour. 80r, Darwin, Beagle. 400r, Cousteau, Calypso. 1500r, Heyerdahl, Kon Tiki.
1000r, Columbus.

1992, Aug. 1   Litho.   Perf. 12x12½
1236-1240 A229 Set of 5   5.50 1.50
Souvenir Sheet
Perf. 12½
1241 A229 1000r multicolored   4.75 1.00

No. 1241 contains one 32x40mm stamp.

Mushrooms A230

Designs: 5r, Albatrellus confluens. 15r, Boletus calopus. 80r, Stropharia aeruginosa. 400r, Telamonia armillata. 1500r, Cortinarius traganus.

1992, Sept. 25   Perf. 13
1242-1246 A230 Set of 5   5.50 1.50

Seaplanes — A231

Designs: 5r, Bellanca Pacemaker, 1930. 15r, Canadair CL-215, 1965. 80r, G-21A Goose, 1937. 400r, Sealand SA-6, 1947. 1500r, Short S-23, 1936.
1000r, G-44 Widgeon, 1940.

1992, Oct. 16   Perf. 12½x12
1247-1251 A231 Set of 5   4.50 1.25
Souvenir Sheet
Perf. 13
1252 A231 1000r multicolored   3.50 1.00

No. 1252 contains one 32x40mm stamp.

Natl. Development A232

Designs: 150r, Dish antenna. 350r, Dish antenna, flags. 1000r, Hotel Cambodiana.

1992, Dec. 2   Litho.   Perf. 12½
1253-1255 A232 Set of 3   5.50 1.25

Natl. Festival A233

Designs: 50r, Sociological Institute. 450r, Motel Cambodiana. 1000r, Theater.

1993, Jan. 7   Litho.   Perf. 12½
1256-1258 A233 Set of 3   5.50 1.25

Dolphin, Bathyscaph — A234

Fauna, machine: 150r, shown. 200r, Falcon, jet fighter. 250r, Beaver, dam. 500r, Bat, satellite. 900r, Hummingbird, helicopter.

1993, Feb. 5   Litho.   Perf. 13
Without Gum
1259-1263 A234 Set of 5   4.75 1.25

Flowers — A235

Designs: 150r, Datura suaveolens. 200r, Convolvulus tricolor. 250r, Hippeastrum hybrid. 500r, Camellia hybrid. 900r, Lilium speciosum.
1000r, Datura suaveolens, camellia, lilium speciosum.

1993, Mar. 15   Perf. 13
Without Gum
1264-1268 A235 Set of 5   6.25 1.25
Souvenir Sheet
Perf. 12½
1269 A235 1000r multicolored   3.75 1.00

No. 1269 contains one 40x32mm stamp.

Khmer Culture A236

Designs: 50r, Statue of a Nandin. 450r, Temple Vihear. 1000r, Man with offerings.

1993, Apr. 13   Litho.   Perf. 12½
1270-1272 A236 Set of 3   5.50 2.75

Wildlife — A237

150r, Cynocephalus volans. 200r, Petuarista petuarista. 250r, Ptychozoon homalocephalum. 500r, Rhacophorus nigropalmatus. 900r, Draco volans.

1993, May 4   Litho.   Perf. 12½x12
Without Gum
1273-1277 A237 Set of 5   5.00 1.50

BRASILIANA 93 — A238

Butterflies: 250r, Symbrenthia hypselis. 350r, Sithon nedymond. 600r, Geitoneura minyas. 800r, Argyreus hyperbius. 1000r, Argyrophenga antipodum.
1500r, Pararge schakra.

1993, June 15   Perf. 12½x12
Without Gum
1278-1282 A238 Set of 5   8.50 1.50
Souvenir Sheet
Perf. 12½
1283 A238 1500r multicolored   5.75 1.25

No. 1283 contains one 40x32mm stamp.

UN Transitional Authority in Cambodia (UNTAC) Pacification Program A239

150r, Cambodian soldiers approaching UN base. 200r, Cambodians entering camp. 250r, Cambodians surrendering weapons to UN. 500r, Vocational training. 900r, Cambodians re-entering society.
1000r, Returning to homes and family.

1993, Aug. 4   Litho.   Perf. 12½
1284-1288 A239 Set of 5   5.75 1.50
Souvenir Sheet
Perf. 13
1289 A239 1000r blue & black   4.50 1.25

No. 1289 contains one 32x40mm stamp.

Ships A240

150r, Venetian caravel. 200r, Phoenician galley. 250r, Egyptian merchantman. 500r, Genoese merchantman. 900r, English merchantman.

1993, Aug. 27   Litho.   Perf. 13
Without Gum
1290-1294 A240 Set of 5   4.75 1.25

Alberto Santos-Dumont (1873-1932) — A241

Designs: 150r, Portrait, Balloon, Eiffel Tower, vert. 200r, 14-bis, 1906. 250r, Demoiselle. 500r, EMB-201A. 900r, EMB-111.

1993, Sept. 10   Perf. 13
Without Gum
1295-1299 A241 Set of 5   4.75 1.25

1994 World Cup Soccer Championships, US — A242

Various soccer plays. Denominations: 250r, 350r, 600r, 800r, 1000r, vert.

1993, Sept. 23   Litho.   Perf. 12½
1300-1304 A242 Set of 5   6.00 1.75
Souvenir Sheet
1305 A242 1500r multicolored   5.00 1.50
No. 1305 contains one 40x32mm stamp.

BANGKOK 93 — A243

Ducks: 250r, Anas penelope. 350r, Anas formosa. 600r, Aix galericulata. 800r, Aix sponsa. 1000r, Histrionicus histrionicus. 1500r, Head of Air galericulata.

1993, Oct. 1   Litho.   Perf. 13
Without Gum
1306-1310 A243 Set of 5   6.00 1.75
Souvenir Sheet
1311 A243 1500r multicolored   4.00 1.10
No. 1311 contains one 40x32mm stamp.

Vertical Take-Off Aircraft — A244

Designs: 150r, First helicopter model, France, 1784, vert. 200r, Steam helicopter model, 1863, vert. 250r, New York-Atlanta-Miami autogyro flight, 1927. 500r, Sikorsky helicopter, 1943. 900r, French VTOL jet. 1000r, Juan de la Cierva's autogyro C-4, 1923.

Perf. 12x12½, 12½x12
1993, Nov. 6   Without Gum
1312-1316 A244 Set of 5   4.75 1.25
Souvenir Sheet
Perf. 12½
1317 A244 1000r multicolored   3.50 1.00
No. 1317 contains one 40x32mm stamp.

Insects — A245

Designs: 50r, Cnaphalocrosis medinalis. 450r, Cicadelle brune. 500r, Scirpophaga incertulas. No. 1321, 1000r, Diopsis macrophthlalma. No. 1322, Leptocorisa oratorius.

1993, Dec. 2   Perf. 13
1318-1321 A245 Set of 4   5.00 1.25
Souvenir Sheet
Perf. 12½
1322 A245 1000r multicolored   4.00 1.00
Issued without gum.
No. 1322 contains one 32x40mm stamp.

Independence, 40th Anniv. — A246

Designs: 300r, Ministry of Posts and Tele-communications. 500r, Independence Monument, 1953, vert. 700r, Natl. flag.

1993   Litho.   Perf. 12½
1323-1325 A246 Set of 3   5.25 2.00

Hummel Figurines A247

Designs: 50r, Boy riding pony. 100r, Girl with baby carriage. 150r, Girl bathing doll. 200r, Girl holding doll. 250r, Boys playing. 300r, Girls pulling boy in cart. 350r, Girls playing ring-around-the-rosie. 600r, Boys with stick and drum.

1993   Litho.   Perf. 12½
1326-1333 A247 Set of 8   6.25 1.75

1994 Winter Olympic Games, Lillehammer — A248

150r, Women's figure skating, vert. 250r, Two-man luge. 400r, Downhill skiing. 700r, Biathlon. 1000r, Speed skating, vert. 1500r, Curling, vert.

1994, Jan. 23   Perf. 13
1334-1338 A248 Set of 5   6.00 1.50
Souvenir Sheet
1339 A248 1500r multicolored   4.00 1.25
No. 1339 contains one 32x40mm stamp.

Classic Automobiles — A249

Designs: 150r, 1924 Opel. 200r, 1901 Mercedes. 250r, 1927 Model T Ford. 500r, 1907 Rolls Royce. 900r, 1908 Hutton. 1000r, 1931 Duesenberg.

1994, Feb. 20   Perf. 13
1340-1344 A249 Set of 5   6.50 1.25
Souvenir Sheet
1345 A249 1000r multicolored   5.75 1.25
No. 1345 contains one 32x40mm stamp.

1996 Summer Olympic Games, Atlanta — A250

Designs: 150r, Women's gymnastics. 200r, Soccer. 250r, Javelin. 300r, Canoeing. 600r, Running. 1000r, Diving, horiz. 1500r, Equestrian.

1994, Mar. 20   Perf. 13
1346-1351 A250 Set of 6   5.50 1.50
Souvenir Sheet
1352 A250 1500r multicolored   4.75 1.25
No. 1352 contains one 32x40mm stamp.

Khmer Statues — A251

Designs: 300r, Siva and Uma. 500r, Vishnu. 700r, King Jayavarman VII.

1994, Apr. 13
1353-1355 A251 Set of 3   5.50 2.75

Intl. Olympic Committee, Cent. — A252

Designs: 100r, Olympic Flag. 300r, Flag, Torch. 600r, Flag, Baron de Coubertin.

1994, Apr. 23   Perf. 12½
1356-1358 A252 Set of 3   3.25 1.40

Prehistoric Animals — A253

150r, Mesonyx. 250r, Doedicurus. 400r, Mylodon. 700r, Uintatherium. 1000r, Hyrachyus.

1994, May 10   Perf. 12½
1359-1363 A253 Set of 5   6.50 2.00

1994 World Cup Soccer Championships, U.S. — A254

Various soccer plays. Denominations: 150r, 250r, 400r, 700r, 1000r.

1994, June 17   Perf. 12½
1364-1368 A254 Set of 5   6.25 1.50
Souvenir Sheet
1369 A254 1500r multicolored   4.50 1.25
No. 1369 contains one 32x40mm stamp.

Statues A255

Designs: 300r, shown. 500r, Soldiers in combat, vert. 700r, Lions, vert.

1994   Perf. 13
1370-1372 A255 Set of 3   4.50 2.75

Beetles A256

Designs: 150r, Chlorophanus viridis. 200r, Chrysochroa fulgidissima. 250r, Lytta vesicatoria. 500r, Purpuricenus kaehleri. 900r, Dynastes hercules. 1000r, Timarcha tenebricosa.

1994, July 7   Perf. 12½
1373-1377 A256 Set of 5   6.50 1.50
Souvenir Sheet
1378 A256 1000r multicolored   4.00 1.00
No. 1378 contains one 40x32mm stamp.

Submarines — A257

Designs: 150r, Halley's diving bell, 1690, vert. 200r, Gimnote, 1886. 250r, Peral, 1888. 500r, Nuclear-powered Nautilus, 1954. 900r, Bathyscaphe Trieste, 1953. 1000r, Ictineo, 1885.

1994, Aug. 12   Perf. 13
1379-1383 A257 Set of 5   5.75 1.50
Souvenir Sheet
Perf. 12½
1384 A257 1000r multicolored   3.75 1.00
No. 1384 contains one 40x32mm stamp.

Chess Champions — A258

Designs: 150r, Francois-André Philador, 1795. 200r, Louis de la Bourdonnais, 1821. 250r, Adolph Anderssen, 1851. 500r, Paul Morphy, 1858. 900r, Wilhelm Steinitz, 1866. 1000r, Emanuel Lasker, 1894.

1994, Sept. 20   Perf. 13
1385-1389 A258 Set of 5   5.50 1.50
Souvenir Sheet
1390 A258 1000r multicolored   3.50 1.00
No. 1390 contains one 32x40mm stamp.

Aircraft
A259

Designs: 150r, Sikorsky S-42 flying boat. 200r, Vought-Sikorsky VS-300A helicopter. 250r, Sikorsky S-37 biplane. 500r, Sikorsky S-35 biplane. 900r, Sikorsky S-43 amphibian. 1000r, 1st 4-engine bomber, Ilya Mourometz.

1994, Oct. 6   *Perf. 13*
1391-1395 A259   Set of 5   5.25 1.50
Souvenir Sheet
Perf. 12½
1396 A259 1000r multicolored   3.75 1.00
No. 1396 contains one 40x32mm stamp.

Birds
A260

Designs: 150r, Remiz pendulinus, vert. 250r, Panurus biarmicus. 400r, Emberiza rustica. 700r, Emberiza schoeniclus. 1000r, Regulus regulus. 1500r, Pitta angolensis.

1994, Nov. 20   *Perf. 12½*
1397-1401 A260   Set of 5   6.50 1.50
Souvenir Sheet
Perf. 13
1402 A260 1500r multicolored   4.25 1.40
No. 1402 contains one 32x40mm stamp.

Independence Festival — A261

Designs: 300r, Postal Service float. 500r, Soldiers marching. 700r, Army unit marching.

1994, Dec. 9   *Perf. 13*
1403-1405 A261   Set of 3   5.00 1.75

Natl. Development — A262

Designs: 300r, Chruoi Changwar Bridge. 500r, Olympic Commercial Center. 700r, Sakamony Chedei Temple.

1994, Dec. 10
1406-1408 A262   Set of 3   5.00 1.50

Prehistoric Animals — A263

100r, Psittacosaurus. 200r, Protoceratops. 300r, Montanoceraptors. 400r, Centrosaurus. 700r, Styracosaurus. 800r, Triceratops.

1995, Jan. 10
1409-1414 A263   Set of 6   7.00 1.50

Butterflies
A264

100r, Anthocharis cardamines. 200r, Iphiclides podalirius. 300r, Mesoacidalia aglaja. 600r, Vanessa atalanta. 800r, Inachis io.

1995, Feb. 12
1415-1419 A264   Set of 5   7.50 1.50

1996 Summer Olympic Games, Atlanta
A265

Designs: 100r, Swimming. 200r, Rhythmic gymnastics. 400r, Basketball. 800r, Soccer. 1000r, Cycling. 1500r, Running.
200r-1500r are vert.

1995, Mar. 9
1420-1424 A265   Set of 5   6.25 1.50
Souvenir Sheet
1425 A265 1500r multicolored   4.00 1.00
No. 1425 contains one 32x40mm stamp.

Mushrooms
A266

Designs: 100r, Amanita phalloides. 200r, Cantharellus cibarius. 300r, Armillaria mellea. 600r, Agaricus campestris. 800r, Amanita muscaria.

1995, Mar. 23
1426-1430 A266   Set of 5   5.75 1.50

Statues — A267

Designs: 300r, Kneeling ascetic. 500r, Parasurama. 700r, Siva.

1995, Apr. 13   *Perf. 12½*
1431-1433 A267   Set of 3   4.50 1.40

Protected Wildlife — A268

Designs: 300r, Bos gaurus. 500r, Bos sauveli, vert. 700r, Grus antigone, vert.

1995, May 5   *Perf. 13*
1434-1436 A268   Set of 3   4.50 1.25

Parrots — A269

Designs: 100r, Lorus lory. 200r, Polytelis alexandrae. 400r, Eclectus voratus. 800r, Ara macao. 1000r, Melopsittacus undulatus. 1500r, Amazona ochrocephala.

1995, May 23   *Perf. 13*
1437-1441 A269   Set of 5   7.00 1.50
Souvenir Sheet
Perf. 12½
1442 A269 1500r multicolored   5.50 1.50
No. 1442 contains one 32x40mm stamp.

Tourism
A270

Public gardens: 300r, Sculpture of Garuda. 500r, Fountain. 700r, Sculpture of mythological figures.

1995, July 15   *Perf. 12½*
1443-1445 A270   Set of 3   4.00 1.50

Locomotives — A271

100r, Richard Trevithick's steam locomotive, 1804. 200r, George Stephenson's Rocket, 1830. 300r, Stephenson's Locomotion, 1825. 600r, Lafayette, 1837. 800r, Best Friend of Charleston, 1830.
1000r, Stephenson, vert.

1995, Aug. 17
1446-1450 A271   Set of 5   5.25 1.50
Souvenir Sheet
1451 A271 1000r multicolored   3.50 1.25
No. 1451 contains one 32x40mm stamp.

World War II Aircraft
A272

100r, Bristol Blenheim II, vert. 200r, North American B-25. 300r, Avro Anson. 600r, Avro Manchester. 800r, Consolidated B-24. 1000r, Boeing B-17E.

Perf. 12x12½, 12½x12
1995, Sept. 15
1452-1456 A272   Set of 5   5.50 1.50
Souvenir Sheet
Perf. 12½
1457 A272 1000r multicolored   3.75 1.00
No. 1457 contains one 32x40mm stamp.

FAO, 50th Anniv.
A273

Designs: 300r, Separating rice plants. 500r, Transplanting rice. 700r, Model rice farm.

1995, Oct. 24   *Perf. 13*
1458-1460 A273   Set of 3   3.50 1.00

UN, 50th Anniv.
A274

Designs: 300r, Bridge. 500r, People on bridge. 700r, Central spans of bridge.

1995, Oct. 24   *Perf. 12½*
1461-1463 A274   Set of 3   4.00 1.50

Queen Monineath
A275

700r, shown. 800r, King Norodom Sihanouk.

1995, Nov. 9   *Perf. 12½x13*
1464-1465 A275   Set of 2   4.75 1.50

Fish
A276

100r, Heniochus acuminatus. 200r, Chelmon rostratus. 400r, Amphirion percula. 800r, Paracanthurus hepatus. 1000r, Holocanthus ciliaris. 1500r, Coris angulata, vert.

1995, Nov. 19   *Perf. 12½*
1466-1470 A276   Set of 5   6.25 1.50
Souvenir Sheet
1471 A276 1500r multicolored   5.00 1.00

Main Post Office, Cent.
A277

Denominations: 300r, 500r, 700r.

1995, Dec. 2   *Perf. 12½*
1472-1474 A277   Set of 3   6.00 1.40

Admission to UN, 40th Anniv. — A278

300r, Independence Monument. 400r, Angkor Wat. 800r, Natl. flag, vert.

Perf. 12½x13, 13x12½

1995, Dec. 14 **Litho.**
1475-1477 A278 Set of 3   5.50 1.25

1996 Summer Olympic Games, Atlanta — A279

Designs: 100r, Tennis. 200r, Volleyball. 300r, Soccer. No. 1480A, 500r, Running. 900r, Baseball. 1000r, Basketball. 1500r, Windsurfing.

1996, Jan. 10 **Litho.** **Perf. 12½x13**
1478-1482 A279 Set of 6   6.00 1.50
Souvenir Sheet
Perf. 12½
1483 A279 1500r multicolored   3.50 1.00
No. 1483 contains one 32x40mm stamp.

A280

50r, Kep State Chalet. 100r, Power station. 200r, Wheelchair. 500r, Wheelchair basketball. 800r, Making crutches, vert. 1000r, Kep beach. 1500r, Serpent Island.

1996, Jan. 30 **Perf. 12½**
1484 A280   50r multi   .25 .25
1485 A280   100r multi   .25 .25
1486 A280   200r multi   .30 .25
1487 A280   500r multi   .60 .25
1488 A280   800r multi   1.00 .25
1489 A280   1000r multi   1.40 .35
1490 A280   1500r multi   2.00 .45
    Nos. 1484-1490 (7)   5.80 2.05

Wild Cats A281

100r, Felis libyca, vert. 200r, Felis silvestris. 300r, Felis caracal. 500r, Felis geoffroyi. 900r, Felis nigripes. 1000r, Felis planiceps.

1996, Feb. 8 **Perf. 13**
1491-1496 A281 Set of 6   6.25 2.00

1998 World Cup Soccer Championships, France — A282

Various soccer players. Denominations: 100r, 200r, 300r, 500r, 900r, 1000r. No. 1502 is horiz.

1996, Mar. 15 **Perf. 13**
1497-1502 A282 Set of 6   6.00 1.50
Souvenir Sheet
1503 A282 1500r multicolored   4.25 1.00
No. 1503 contains one 32x40mm stamp.

Khmer Culture — A283

100r, Tusmukh. 500r, Ream Iso. 900r, Isei.

1996, Apr. 13 **Litho.** **Perf. 12½x13**
1504-1506 A283 Set of 3   3.75 1.50

Locomotives — A284

100r, Pacific Type. 200r, Unidentified, 1902. 300r, Unidentified, 1930. 500r, Unidentified, 1914. 900r, LMS #6202, 1930. 1000r, Snake, 1864. 1500r, Canadian Pacific.

1996, Apr. 20
1507-1512 A284 Set of 6   5.00 1.50
Souvenir Sheet
1513 A284 1500r multicolored   3.50 1.00
No. 1513 contains one 40x32mm stamp. CAPEX 96 (No. 1513).

Birds A285

Designs: 100r, Kittacinela malabarica, vert. 200r, Leiothrix lutea. 300r, Parus varius, vert. 500r, Oriolus chinensis. 900r, Cettia diphone. 1000r, Cyanoptila cyanomelana, vert.

1996, May 7
1514-1519 A285 Set of 6   5.25 1.50

Olymphilex '96 — A286

Designs: 100r, Rhythmic gymnastics. 200r, Judo. 300r, High jump. 500r, Wrestling. 900r, Weight lifting. 1000r, Soccer. 1500r, Diving.

1996, June 14 **Litho.** **Perf. 13x12½**
1520-1525 A286 Set of 6   6.50 1.25
Souvenir Sheet
Perf. 12½
1526 A286 1500r multicolored   5.00 1.25
No. 1526 contains one 32x40mm stamp.

Early Aircraft — A287

100r, Douglas M-2, 1926. 200r, Pitcairn PA-5 Mailwing, 1928. 300r, Boeing 40 B, 1928. 500r, Potez 25, 1925. 900r, Stearman C-3MB, 1927. 1000r, De Havilland DH4, 1918. 1500r, Standard JR-1B, 1918.

1996, July 5 **Perf. 12½x12**
1527-1532 A287 Set of 6   4.75 1.50
Souvenir Sheet
Perf. 13
1533 A287 1500r multicolored   3.25 1.00
No. 1533 contains one 40x32mm stamp.

Historic Sites — A288

50r, 100r, 200r, Diff. Apsaras, Tonle Bati. No. 1537, Statue, Angkor Wat. No. 1538, Statue of a Goddess. 500r, Carved wall, Tonle Bati. No. 1540, 1000r, No. 1543, Various structures, Tonle Bati. No. 1541, No. 1544, 1700r, 2500r, 3000r, Various views of Angkor Wat.
Nos. 1539, 1543, 1545-1547 are horiz.

1996-97 **Litho.** **Perf. 12½**
1534 A288   50r black & yel org   .25 .25
1535 A288   100r black & blue   .25 .25
1536 A288   200r black & tan   .40 .25
1537 A288   300r blk & light bl   .30 .25
1538 A288   300r black & red   .30 .25
1539 A288   500r blk & bright bl   .80 .25
1540 A288   800r blk & yel grn   1.00 .25
1541 A288   800r blk & yel grn   .60 .25
1542 A288   1000r black & green   1.10 .40
1543 A288   1500r black & bister   1.40 .50
1544 A288   1500r black & brown   1.40 .50
1545 A288   1700r black & org brn   1.50 .30
1546 A288   2500r black & blue   2.00 .40
1547 A288   3000r black & dk grn   3.50 .50
    Nos. 1534-1547 (14)   14.80 4.35

Issued: 50r, 100r, 200r, 500r, No. 1540, 1000r, No. 1543, 7/30/96; others, 3/26/97. See Nos. 1686-1692, 1846-1852.

Dinosaurs — A289

No. 1548: a, 50r, Coelophysis. b, 100r, Euparkeria. c, 150r, Plateosaurus. d, 200r, Herrerasaurus.
No. 1549: a, 250r, Dilophosaurus. b, 300r, Tuojiangosaurus. c, 350r, Camarasaurus. d, 400r, Ceratosaurus.
No. 1550: a, 500r, Spinosaurus. b, 700r, Ouranosaurus. c, 800r, Avimimus. d, 1200r, Deinonychus.

1996, Aug. 8 **Litho.** **Perf. 13**
1548 A289   Sheet of 4, #a.-d.   1.00 .25
1549 A289   Sheet of 4, #a.-d.   2.75 .60
1550 A289   Sheet of 4, #a.-d.   6.75 1.50

Chess Champions A290

100r, José Raul Capablanca. 200r, Alexander Alekhine. 300r, Vassily Smyslov. 500r, Mikhail Tal. 900r, Bobby Fischer. 1000r, Anatoly Karpov. 1500r, Garry Kasparov.

1996, Sept. 10 **Perf. 13**
1551-1556 A290 Set of 6   5.50 1.50
Souvenir Sheet
Perf. 12½
1557 A290 1500r multicolored   3.50 1.00
No. 1557 contains one 32x40mm stamp.

Wild Animals A291

Designs: 100r, Ursus arctos. 200r, Panthera leo. 300r, Tapirus indicus. 500r, Camelus ferus. 900r, Capra ibex. 1000r, Zalophus californianus.

1996, Oct. 3 **Perf. 13x12½**
1558-1563 A291 Set of 6   4.75 1.25

Dogs — A292

Designs: 200r, Collie. 300r, Labrador retriever. 500r, Doberman pinscher. 900r, German shepherd. 1000r, Boxer.

1996, Nov. 8 **Perf. 12½x13**
1564-1568 A292 Set of 5   4.75 1.25

Independence — A293

100, 500, 900r, Various water treatment plants.

1996, Nov. 9 **Perf. 13**
1569-1571 A293 Set of 3   3.75 1.50

Ships A294

Designs: 200r, Chinese junk. 300r, Galley. 500r, Roman galley. 900r, Clipper ship, 19th cent. 1000r, Paddle steamer Sirius, 1838. 1500r, Great Eastern, 1858.

1996, Dec. 15 **Perf. 12½x13**
1572-1576 A294 Set of 5   4.75 1.25
Souvenir Sheet
Perf. 12½
1577 A294 1500r multicolored   3.25 1.00
No. 1577 contains one 40x32mm stamp.

Cambodia's Admission to UPU, 45th
Anniv. — A295

Denominations: 200r, 400r, 900r.

1996, Dec. 21   *Perf. 12½*
1578-1580 A295 Set of 3   3.75 1.50

New Year 1997 (Year of the
Ox) — A296

Paintings of oxen, attributed to Han Huang
723-87): a, Facing left. b, Looking right. c,
Brown & white spotted. d, Facing left, head
down.

1996, Dec. 28   *Perf. 13x12½*
1581 A296 500r Strip of 4, #a.-d.
            + label   3.00 .90

UN Intl. Day of Volunteers — A297

Designs: 100r, Phnom Kaun Sat Dam. 900r,
Chrey Krem Dam. 1500r, Angkrung Canal.

1996, Dec. 30
1582-1584 A297 Set of 3   4.00 1.50

Greenpeace,
25th
Anniv. — A298

Helicopter: 200r, Hovering over cargo. 300r,
Hovering over ship. 500r, On helipad. 900r,
Lifting cargo.
1000r, Close-up of helicopter.

1996, Dec. 30   *Perf. 12½x13*
1585-1588 A298 Set of 4   6.00 1.75
Souvenir Sheet
Perf. 12½
1589 A298 1000r multicolored   5.50 1.00
No. 1589 contains one 32x40mm stamp.

1998 World Cup
Soccer
Championships,
France — A299

Various soccer plays. Denominations: 100r,
200r, 300r, 500r, 900r, 1000r.

1997, Jan. 6   Litho.   Perf. 12½x13
1590-1595 A299 Set of 6   5.25 1.50
Souvenir Sheet
Perf. 13
1596 A299 2000r multicolored   3.25 1.00
No. 1596 contains one 40x32mm stamp.

Elephas Maximus — A300

World Wildlife Fund: a, 300r, Two walking. b,
500r, Three standing. c, 900r, Two fighting. d,
1000r, Adult, calf.

1997, Feb. 12   *Perf. 12½x12*
1597 A300 Strip of 4, #a.-d.   8.00 3.00

Birds — A301

600r, Bombycilla garrulus. 900r, Lanius
excubitor. 1000r, Passer montanus. 2000r,
Phoenicurus phoenicurus. 2500r, Emberiza
schoeniclus. 3000r, Emberiza hortulana.

1997, Feb. 20   *Perf. 13x12½*
1598-1603 A301 Set of 6   15.00 4.50
Express mail service.

Fire
Fighting
Vehicles
A302

Designs: 200r, English, 1731. 500r, Putnam,
1863. 900r, Merryweather, 1894. 1000r,
Shand Mason Co., 1901. 1500r, Maxim Motor
Co., Ford, 1949. 4000r, Merryweather, 1950.
5400r, Mack Truck Co., 1953.

1997, Mar. 11   *Perf. 12½x13*
1604-1609 A302 Set of 6   7.00 1.50
Souvenir Sheet
Perf. 13
1610 A302 5400r multicolored   4.75 1.10
No. 1610 contains one 40x32mm stamp.

Ducks
A303

Designs: 200r, Polysticta stelleri. 500r, Alopochen aegyptiacus. 900r, Anas americana.
1000r, Anas falcata. 1500r, Melanitta perspicillata. 4000r, Anas discors.
5400r, Anas formosa, vert.

1997, Apr. 7   *Perf. 12½x13*
1611-1616 A303 Set of 6   5.00 1.50
Souvenir Sheet
Perf. 12½
1617 A303 5400r multicolored   3.75 1.10
No. 1617 contains one 32x40mm stamp.

Heinrich Von
Stephan (1831-
1897), Founder
of UPU — A304

Denominations: 500r, 1500r, 2000r.

1997, Apr. 8   *Perf. 12½x13*
1618-1620 A304 Set of 3   3.50 1.00

Khmer
Culture — A305

Various views of Bantea Srei Temple.
Denominations: 500r, 1500r, 2000r.

1997, Apr. 13   *Perf. 13x12½*
1621-1623 A305 Set of 3   3.75 1.00

Cats — A306

Designs: 200r, Birman. 500r, Exotic shorthair. 900r, Persian. 1000r, Turkish. 1500r,
American short-hair. 4000r, Scottish fold.
5400r, Sphinx.

1997, May 8   *Perf. 13x12½*
1624-1629 A306 Set of 6   9.00 1.75
Souvenir Sheet
Perf. 13
1630 A306 5400r multicolored   4.00 1.10
No. 1630 contains one 32x40mm stamp.

Trains
A307

200r, 4-4-2T, #488. 500r, Frederick Smith 4-
6-0. 900r, 0-8-0, #3131. 1000r, Transport #1,
London #L44, 0-4-4. 1500r, 0-6-2, #1711.
4000r, 4-6-2, #60523.
5400r, North Yorkshire Moor (K1), 2-6-0,
#2005.

1997, Jun 9   *Perf. 12½x12*
1631-1636 A307 Set of 6   5.50 1.50
Souvenir Sheet
Perf. 13
1637 A307 5400r multicolored   3.75 1.00
No. 1637 contains one 40x32mm stamp.

Dogs
A308

Designs: 200r, Shar-pei. 500r, Tchin-tchin.
900r, Pekinese. 1000r, Chow-chow, vert.
1500r, Pug, vert. 4000r, Akita, vert.
5400r, Tufted Chinese, vert.

1997, July 4   Perf. 12½x13, 13x12½
1638-1643 A308 Set of 6   4.75 1.50
Souvenir Sheet
Perf. 12½
1644 A308 5400r multicolored   3.50 1.25
No. 1644 contains one 32x40mm stamp.

ASEAN,
30th
Anniv.
A309

Designs: 500r, Dunalom Wat. 1500r, Royal
Palace. 2000r, Natl. Museum.

1997, Aug. 5   *Perf. 12½x13*
1645-1647 A309 Set of 3   4.00 1.00

Ships
A310

Designs: 200r, Caravelle, 15th cent. 500r,
Spanish galleon, 16th cent. 900r, Galleon
"Great Harry," 16th cent. 1000r, Galleon "Le
Couronne," 17th cent. 1500r, Cargo ship, 18th
cent. 4000r, Clipper ship, 19th cent.
5400r, HMS Victory.

1997, Sept. 10   *Perf. 12½x12*
1648-1653 A310 Set of 6   5.50 1.50
Souvenir Sheet
Perf. 13
1654 A310 5400r multicolored   4.25 1.10
No. 1654 contains one 40x32mm stamp.

A311

Nos. 1655-1658, Various public gardens.
Nos. 1659-1661, Various dams. No. 1657 is
vert.

1997, Sept. 30   *Perf. 12½*
1655 A311 300r black & yel grn   .30 .25
1656 A311 300r black & red   .30 .25
1657 A311 800r black & citron   .65 .25
1658 A311 1500r black & org brn 1.25 .30
1659 A311 1700r blk & red brn   1.40 .35
1660 A311 2500r blk & grn bl   1.60 .50
1661 A311 3000r black & blue   2.00 .65
      Nos. 1655-1661 (7)   7.50 2.55

Mushrooms
A312

Designs: 200r, Boletus satanas. 500r, Amanita regalis. 900r, Morchella semilibera. 1000r,
Gomphus clavatus. 1500r, Hygrophorus
hypothejus. 4000r, Albatrellus confluens.
5400r, Boletus chrysenteron.

1997, Oct. 5   *Perf. 12½x13*
1662-1667 A312 Set of 6   6.00 1.50
Souvenir Sheet
Perf. 12½
1668 A312 5400r multicolored   4.00 1.10
No. 1668 contains one 32x40mm stamp.

Fish
A313

200r, Betta imbellis. 500r, Colisa fasciata. 900r, Puntius conchonius. 1000r, Macropodus concolor. 1500r, Epalzeorhynchos frenatus. 4000r, Capoeta tetrazona.
5400r, Rasbora heteromorpha.

1997, Nov. 8　　　**Perf. 12½x13**
1669-1674 A313　Set of 6　　5.25　1.50
Souvenir Sheet
Perf. 13

1675 A313 5400r multicolored　　3.50　1.00
No. 1675 contains one 40x32mm stamp.

Independence, 44th Anniv. — A314

Post Offices: 1000r, Kampot. 3000r, Prey Veng.

1997, Nov. 9　　　**Perf. 13**
1676-1677 A314　Set of 2　　3.25　1.00

Orchids — A315

200r, Orchis milicaris. 500r, Orchiaceras bivonae. 900r, Orchiaceras spuria. 1000r, Gymnadenia conopsea. 1500r, Serapias neglecta. 4000r, Pseudorhiza bruniana.
5400r, Dactylodenia wintonii.

1997, Dec. 12　　　**Perf. 13**
1678-1683 A315　Set of 6　　9.00　1.75
Souvenir Sheet

1684 A315 5400r multicolored　　6.75　1.10
No. 1684 contains one 32x40mm stamp.

Princess Diana (1961-97) A316

Designs: a, 100r, In dark blue jacket. b, 200r, In black dress. c, 300r, Holding hand to throat. d, 500r, Wearing face shield. e, 1000r, Watching mine clearing operation. f, 1500r, With Elizabeth Dole. g, 2000r, Holding land mine. h, 2500r, With members of Mother Teresa's Order.

1997, Dec. 30　　　**Perf. 12x12½**
1685 A316　Sheet of 8, #a.-h. + label　　7.00　1.75

Historic Sites Type of 1996-97

Temples: 300r, Prasat Suorprat. 500r, Preah Kumlung, horiz. 1200r, Prasat Bapuon, horiz. 1500r, Palilai. 1700r, Prasat Prerup, horiz. 2000r, Prasat Preah Khan, horiz. 3000r, Prasat Bayon.

1998　　**Litho.**　　**Perf. 12½**
1686 A288　300r black & orange　.25　.25
1687 A288　500r black & pink　　.30　.25
1688 A288　1200r black & buff　　.70　.25
1689 A288　1500r black & buff　　.90　.30
1690 A288　1700r black & blue　1.00　.35
1691 A288　2000r black & green　1.25　.45
1692 A288　3000r black & violet　1.75　.65
Nos. 1686-1692 (7)　　　　　6.15　2.50

New Year 1998 (Year of the Tiger) A317

Various pictures of panthera tigris: 200r, vert., 500r, vert., 900r, vert., 1000r, 1500r, 4000r.
5400r, Tiger, vert.

1998　　　　**Perf. 13**
1693-1698 A317　Set of 6　　5.00　1.50
Souvenir Sheet
Perf. 12½

1699 A317 5400r multicolored　　4.25　1.00
No. 1699 contains one 32x40mm stamp.

1998 World Cup Soccer Championships, France — A318

Designs showing portion of soccer player at left, various plays at right, stadium: 200r, 500r, 900r, 1000r, 1500r, 4000r.
5400r, Two players kicking ball.

1998　　　　**Perf. 13**
1700-1705 A318　Set of 6　　4.50　1.50
Souvenir Sheet

1706 A318 5400r multicolored　　3.25　1.00
No. 1706 contains one 40x32mm stamp.

Domestic Cats A319

Designs: 200r, Scottish fold. 500r, Ragdoll. 900r, Welsh. 1000r, Devon rex. 1500r, American curl. 4000r, Sphinx.
5400r, Japanese bobtail.

1998
1707-1712 A319　Set of 6　　4.50　1.50
Souvenir Sheet

1713　A319 5400r multi　　3.50　1.00
No. 1713 contains one 40x32mm stamp.

Italia '98, Intl. Philatelic Exhibition A320

Paintings: 200r, Baptism of Christ from triptych, Jean de Trompes, by Gerard David. 500r, The Virgin of Martin van Niuwenhoven, by Hans Memling. 900r, Baptism of Christ, by Hendrich Goltzius. 1000r, Christ Carrying the Cross, by Luis de Morales. 1500r, Angel in the Desert, by Dirk Bouts. 4000r, The Virgin, by Petrus Christus.
5400r, The Immaculate Conception, by Bartolomé Esteban Murillo.

1998　　**Litho.**　**Perf. 12½x13**
1714-1719 A320　Set of 6　　5.50　1.50

Souvenir Sheet
Perf. 12½
1720 A320 5400r multicolored　　4.00　1.00
No. 1720 contains one 40x32mm stamp.

Butterflies — A321

200r, Phyciodes tharos. 500r, Pararge mergera. 900r, Danaus plexippus. 1000r, Parnassius apollo. 1500r, Papilio machaon. 4000r, Eumenis semele.
5400r, Morpho rhetenor.

1998　　　　**Perf. 12½**
1721-1726 A321　Set of 6　　5.50　1.50
Souvenir Sheet

1727 A321 5400r multicolored　　5.00　1.00
No. 1727 contains one 40x32mm stamp.

Mail Boxes — A322

Designs: 1000r, 1997. 3000r, 1951.

1998　　**Litho.**　　**Perf. 13**
1728-1729 A322　Set of 2　　2.75　1.00

Trains — A323

No. 1730a, 200r, Oakland, Antioch & Eastern. No. 1730b, 500r, New York, Westchester & Boston. No. 1731a, 900r, Spokane & Inland. No. 1731b, 1000r, International Railway. No. 1732a, 1500r, British columbia Electric Railway. No. 1732b, 4000r, Southern Pacific.
5400r, Storage battery locomotive.

1998, Mar. 2　　**Litho.**　**Perf. 12½**
Pairs, #a.-b.
1730-1732 A323　Set of 3　　6.50　1.50
Souvenir Sheet

1733 A323 5400r multicolored　　5.50　1.25

Dogs — A324

200r, Rottweiler. 500r, Beauceron. 900r, Boxer. 1000r, Siberian husky. 1500r, Welsh corgi (Pembroke). 4000r, Basset hound.
5400r, Schnauzer.

1998, Mar. 30　　**Litho.**　**Perf. 12¼**
1734-1739 A324　Set of 6　　4.75　1.50
Souvenir Sheet
Perf. 12½
1740 A324 5400r multicolored　　3.25　1.00

Insects A325

200r, Lucanus cervus. 500r, Carabus auronitens. 900r, Rosalia alpina. 1000r, Geotrupes. 1500r, Megasoma elephas. 4000r, Chalcosoma.
5400r, Leptura rubra.

1998, Apr. 10　**Litho.**　**Perf. 12½**
1741-1746 A325　Set of 6　　5.00　1.50
Souvenir Sheet

1747 A325 5400r multicolored　　4.25　1.25

Khmer Culture A326

Designs: 500r, Prasat Prerup. 1500r, Prasat Bayon. 2000r, Angkor Wat.

1998, Apr. 13　**Litho.**　**Perf. 12¾**
1748-1750 A326　Set of 3　　3.75　1.10

Historic Ships A327

200r, Cutter. 500r, Steamship "Britannia." 900r, Viking ship. 1000r, Steamship "Great Britain." 1500r, Coaster. 4000r, Frigate.
5400r, Tartan.

1998, May 7　**Litho.**　**Perf. 12¾**
1751-1756 A327　Set of 6　　5.75　1.50
Souvenir Sheet
Perf. 13
1757 A327 5400r multicolored　　3.50　1.00
No. 1757 contains one 40x32mm stamp.

Flowers — A328

200r, Petasites japonica. 500r, Gentiana triflora. 900r, Doronicum cordatum. 1000r, Scabiosa japonica. 1500r, Magnolia sieboldii. 4000r, Erythronium japonica.
5400r, Callistephus chinensis.

1998　　**Litho.**　　**Perf. 12¾**
1758-1763 A328　Set of 6　　4.75　1.50
Souvenir Sheet
Perf. 13

1764 A328 5400r multicolored　　3.25　1.00
No. 1764 contains one 32x40mm stamp.

Turtles A329

200r, Platysternon megacephalum. 500r, Chelonia mydas. 900r, Trionyx spiniferus. 1000r, Eretmochelys imbricata. 1500r, Megalochelys gigantea. 4000r, Dermochelys coriacea.
5400r, Chelus fimbriatus.

1998, Nov. 8 **Litho.** *Perf. 12¾*
1765-1770 A329 Set of 6   5.00 1.50
Souvenir Sheet
Perf. 13x13¼

1771 A329 5400r multi   4.75 1.00
No. 1771 contains one 40x32mm stamp.

Independence, 45th Anniv. — A330

Various dancers: 500r, 1500r, 2000r.

1998, Nov. 9 Litho. *Perf. 12½x12¼*
1772-1774 A330 Set of 3   2.75 1.00

Gemstones
A331

Designs: 200r, Aquamarine. 500r, Cat's eye. 900r, Malachite. 1000r, Emerald. 1500r, Turquoise. 4000r, Ruby.
5400r, Diamond, horiz.

1998, Dec. 28 **Litho.** *Perf. 12¾*
1775-1780 A331 Set of 6   4.75 1.50
Souvenir Sheet
Perf. 13

1781 A331 5400r multi   3.75 1.00
No. 1781 contains one 40x32mm stamp.

Wild
Cats
A332

Designs: 200r, Acinonyx juabatus. 500r, Panthera uncia. 900r, Felis pardalis. 1000r, Panthera pardus. 1500r, Felis serval. 4000r, Panthera onca.
5400r, Panthera tigris.

1998 **Litho.** *Perf. 12½x12¼*
1782-1787 A332 Set of 6   5.00 1.50
Souvenir Sheet
Perf. 13

1788 A332 5400r multi   4.00 1.00
No. 1788 contains one 32x40mm stamp.

New Year
1999
(Year of
the
Rabbit)
A333

Various rabbits: 200r, 500r, 900r, 1000r, 1500r, 4000r. 4000r is vert.

1999, Jan. 5 **Litho.** *Perf. 12¾*
1790-1795 A333 Set of 6   6.75 1.50
Souvenir Sheet
Perf. 13

1796 A333 5400r Rabbit, diff.   5.00 1.00
No. 1796 contains one 40x32mm stamp.

Trains — A334

Designs: 200r, Stourbridge Lion. 500r, Atlantic. 900r, 035. 100r, Iron Duke. 1500r, 4-6-0. 4000r, 4-4-2.

Perf. 12½x12¼
1999, Nov. 20 **Litho.**
1797-1802 A334 Set of 6   5.75 1.50
Souvenir Sheet
Perf. 12½

1803 A334 5400r Firefly   3.75 1.00
No. 1803 contains one 40x32mm stamp.

Dogs
A335

Designs: 200r, Shiba inu, vert. 500r, Shih tzu. 900r, Tibetan spaniel. 1000r, Ainu, vert. 1500r, Lhasa apso. 4000r, Tibetan terrier.

Perf. 12¼x12½ (200, 1000r), 12¾
1999, Feb. 3 **Litho.**
1804-1809 A335 Set of 6   5.75 1.50
Souvenir Sheet
Perf. 12½

1810 A335 5400r Tosa inu, vert.   3.50 1.00
Size of Nos. 1804, 1807: 48x30mm. No. 1810 contains one 32x40mm stamp.

Antique Automobiles — A336

Designs: 200r, 1881 La Rapide. 500r, 1895 Duryea. 900r, 1898 Barbarou. 1000r, 1898 Panhard. 1500r, 1901 Mercedes-Benz. 4000r, 1915 Ford.
5400r, 1875 Siegfried Marcus.

1999, Mar. 5 **Litho.** *Perf. 13x12¾*
1811-1816 A336 Set of 6   4.75 1.50
Souvenir Sheet
Perf. 13

1817 A336 5400r multi   3.75 1.00
No. 1817 contains one 40x32mm stamp.

Cats — A337

Designs: 200r, Ragdoll. 500r, Russian blue. 900r, Bombay. 1000r, Snowshoe. 1500r, Oriental. 4000r, Somali.

1999, Mar. 30 **Litho.** *Perf. 13*
1818-1823 A337 Set of 6   5.75 1.50
Souvenir Sheet

1824 A337 5400r Egyptian mau   3.50 1.00
No. 1824 contains one 32x40mm stamp.

Butterflies
A338

Designs: 200r, Araschnia levana. 500r, Vanessa cardui, horiz. 900r, Clossiana euphrosyne. 1000r, Coenonympha hero. 1500r, Parnassius apollo, horiz. 4000r, Plebejus argus.
5400r, Palaeochrysophanus hippothoe.

1999, Apr. 25 *Perf. 12¾*
1825-1830 A338 Set of 6   6.75 1.50
Souvenir Sheet
Perf. 12½

1831 A338 5400r multi   4.75 1.00
No. 1831 contains one 32x40mm stamp.

Dinosaurs — A339

Designs: 200r, Saurornitholestes. 500r, Prenocephalus. 900r, Wuerhosaurus. 1000r, Muttaburrasaurus. 1500r, Shantungosaurus. 4000r, Microceratops.
5400r, Daspletosaurus.

1999, May 10 **Litho.** *Perf. 12¾*
1832-1837 A339 Set of 6   4.75 1.50
Souvenir Sheet
Perf. 13

1838 A339 5400r multi   3.25 1.00
No. 1838 contains one 40x32mm stamp.

Molluscs
A340

Designs: 200r, Flabellina affinis. 500r, Octopus macropus. 900r, Helix hortensis. 1000r, Lima hians. 1500r, Arion empiricorum. 4000r, Anodonta cygnaea.
5400r, Eledone aldrovandii.

1999, May 31 **Litho.** *Perf. 12¾*
1839-1844 A340 Set of 6   4.75 1.50
Souvenir Sheet
Perf. 12½

1845 A340 5400r multi   3.50 1.00
No. 1845 contains one 32x40mm stamp.

Historic Sites Type of 1996-97

Designs: 100r, Prasat Neak Poan, horiz. 300r, Statue, Prasat Neak Poan, horiz. 500r, Prasat Banteay Srey. 1400r, Prasat Banteay Samré, horiz. 1600r, Prasat Banteay Srey, horiz. 1800r, Bas-relief, Angkor Wat. 1900r, Prasat Takeo, horiz.

1999 **Litho.** *Perf. 12½*
Vignette Colors

1846	A288	100r blue	.30 .25
1847	A288	300r red	.30 .25
1848	A288	500r olive green	.40 .25
1849	A288	1400r bright green	1.00 .30
1850	A288	1600r pink	1.10 .30
1851	A288	1800r violet	1.25 .35
1852	A288	1900r brown	1.50 .45
		Nos. 1846-1852 (7)	5.85 2.15

Khmer
Culture
A341

Designs: 500r, Dragon Bridge. 1500r, Temple with 100 columns, Kratie. 2000r, Krapum Chhouk stupa, Kratie.

1999, Apr. 13 *Perf. 13*
1853-1855 A341 Set of 3   3.00 .85

UPU,
125th
Anniv.
A342

1999 **Litho.** *Perf. 12½x12¼*
1856 A342 1600r multi   1.50 .85

Independence — A343

People and: 500r, Map. 1500r, Ship, airplane, dove, public works. 2000r, Buildings.

1999, Nov. 9 *Perf. 12½*
1857-1859 A343 Set of 3   2.75 1.00

Snakes
A344

Designs: 200r, Aspidelaps lubricus. 500r, Epicrates cenchria. 900r, Eunectes notaeus. 1000r, Diadophis punctatus. 1500r, Micrurus fulvius. 4000r, Telescopus semiannulatus.
5400r, Chondropython viridis.

1999, Dec. 6 *Perf. 12¾*
1860-1865 A344 Set of 6   5.75 1.50
Souvenir Sheet
Perf. 13

1866 A344 5400r multi   3.25 1.00
No. 1866 contains one 39x31mm stamp.

Birds of
Prey
A345

Designs: 200r, Harpia harpyja. 500r, Terthopius ecaudatus, vert. 900r, Neophron pernopterus, vert. 1000r, Falco peregrinus, vert. 1500r, Buteo jamaicensis, vert. 4000r, Haliaetus leucocephalus.
5400r, Milvus milvus.

1999, Oct. 5 **Litho.** *Perf. 12¾*
1867-1872 A345 Set of 6   5.75 1.50
Souvenir Sheet
Perf. 12½

1873 A345 5400r multi   3.50 1.00
No. 1873 contains one 31x39mm stamp.

Philex
France
99 — A346

Still life paintings by: 200r, Henri Fantin-
Latour. 500r, Paul Cézanne. 900r, André Der-
ain. 1000r, Henri Matisse. 1500r, Othon
Friesz. 4000r, Matisse, diff.
5400r, Cézanne, diff.

1999, June 10   Litho.   Perf. 12½
1874-1879 A346   Set of 6   7.50 1.50
Souvenir Sheet
Perf. 13
1880 A346 5400r multi   5.25 1.00

Souvenir Sheet

China 1999 World Philatleic
Exhibition — A347

Pagodas: a, 200r, Tongzhou. b, 500r, Tian-
ing Temple. c, 900r, Summer Palace. d, 900r,
Temple of the Clouds. e, 1000r, Bei Hai. f,
1000r, Perfumed Hill. g, 1500r, Yunju. h,
4000r, Miaoying Temple.

Perf. 12¼x12½
1999, Aug. 12   Litho.
1881 A347   Sheet of 8, #a-h, +
                     label   6.75 2.00

Orchids
A348

Designs: 200r, Cymbidium insigne. 500r,
Papillonanthe teres. 900r, Panisea uniflora.
1000r, Euanthe sanderiana. 1500r, Dendrobium trigonopus. 4000r, Vanda coerulea.
5400r, Paphiopedilum callosum.

1999, Aug. 5   Litho.   Perf. 12¾
1889-1894 A348   Set of 6   5.75 1.50
Souvenir Sheet
Perf. 12½
1895 A348 5400r multi   5.00 1.25
No. 1895 contains one 32x40mm stamp.

Birds
A349

Designs: 200r, Pyrrhula pyrrhula. 500r, Coccothraustes coccothraustes. 900r, Carduelis
chloris. 1000r, Dendroica petechia. 1500r,
Lanius excubitor. 4000r, Parus caeruleus.
5400r, Erithacus rubecula.

1999, Sept. 5   Litho.   Perf. 12¾
1896-1901 A349   Set of 6   6.50 1.50
Souvenir Sheet
Perf. 13
1902 A349 5400r multi   5.75 1.25
No. 1902 contains one 40x32mm stamp.

Fish
A350

Designs: 200r, Capoeta tetrazona. 500r,
Epalzeorhynchus frenatus. 900r, Rasbora
kalochroma. 1000r, Etroplus maculatus.
1500r, Betta imbellis. 4000r, Colisa sota.
5400r, Tetraodon biocellatus.

Perf. 12½x12¼
1999, Sept. 20   Litho.
1903-1908 A350   Set of 6   6.00 1.50
Souvenir Sheet
Perf. 13
1909 A350 5400r multi   4.50 1.00
No. 1909 contains one 40x32mm stamp.

Wildlife — A351

Designs: 200r, Ailuropada melanoleuca.
500r, Bos mutus. 900r, Hydropotes inermis.
1000r, Neomys fodiens, horiz. 1500r, Lutra
lutra, horiz. 4000r, Panthera tigris, horiz.
5400r, Elaphurus davidianus, vert.

1999, Nov. 20   Litho.   Perf. 12¾
1910-1915 A351   Set of 6   6.50 1.50
Souvenir Sheet
Perf. 12½
1916 A351 5400r multi   5.75 1.00
No. 1916 contains one 32x40mm stamp.

Bangkok 2000 Stamp
Exhibition — A352

Turtle-shaped objects and turtles: 200r,
Cuora amboinensis, vert. 500r, Cuora
flavomarginata, vert. 900r, Geoemyda spen-
gleri. 1000r, Manouria impressa. 1500r,
Chinemys reevesi. 4000r, Heosemys spinosa.
4500r, Hieremys annandalei.

2000, Feb. 27   Perf. 12¾
1917-1922 A352   Set of 6   7.00 1.50
Souvenir Sheet
Perf. 13
1923 A352 4500r multi   5.00 1.00
No. 1923 contains one 40x32mm stamp.

Dinosaurs — A353

Designs: 200r, Iguanodon. 500r,
Euoplocephalus. 900r, Dilophosaurus. 1000r,
Diplodocus. 1500r, Stegoceras. 4000r,
Stegosaurus.
4500r, Brachiosaurus, vert.

2000, Jan. 30   Litho.   Perf. 12½x12¼
1924-1929 A353   Set of 6   4.50 1.50
Souvenir Sheet
Perf. 12½
1930 A353 4500r multi   3.00 1.00
No. 1930 contains one 32x40mm stamp.

Beetles
A354

Designs: 200r, Calosoma sycophanta. 500r,
Oryctes nasicornis. 900r, Diochrysa fastuosa.
1000r, Blaps gigas. 1500r, Cincindela
campestris. 4000r, Cissistes cephalotes.
4500r, Scarabeus aegyptiorum.

2000, Feb. 5   Litho.   Perf. 12¾
1931-1936 A354   Set of 6   6.00 1.50
Souvenir Sheet
Perf. 13
1937 A354 4500r multi   2.75 1.00
No. 1937 contains one 40x32mm stamp.

New Year 2000
(Year of the
Dragon) — A355

Various dragons. Denominations: 200r,
500r, 900r, 1000r, 1500r, 4000r.

2000, Jan. 20   Litho.   Perf. 12¼x12½
1938-1943 A355   Set of 6   7.00 1.50
Souvenir Sheet
Perf. 13
1944 A355 4500r multi   3.25 1.00
No. 1944 contains one 32x40mm stamp.

Bettas — A356

Designs: 200r, Unimaculata, Pugnax. 500r,
Macrostoma, Taeniata. 900r, Foerschi, Imbellis. 1000r, Tessyae, Picta. 1500r, Edithae, Bel-
lica. 4000r, Smaragdina.
4500r, Splendens.

2000, Apr. 10   Litho.   Perf. 12½x12¼
1945-1950 A356   Set of 6   5.00 1.50
Souvenir Sheet
Perf. 13
1951 A356 4500r multi   3.75 1.00
No. 1951 contains one 40x32mm stamp.

Mushrooms
A357

Designs: 200r, Amanita muscaria. 500r,
Amanita pantherina. 900r, Clitocybe oleana.
1000r, Lactarius scrobiculatus. 1500r, Scleroderma vulgare. 4000r, Amanita verna.
4500r, Amanita phalloides.

2000, Mar. 20   Litho.   Perf. 12¾
1952-1957 A357   Set of 6   5.00 1.50
Souvenir Sheet
Perf. 13
1958 A357 4500r multi   3.00 1.00
No. 1958 contains one 32x40mm stamp.

Khmer
Culture — A358

Designs: 500r, Srei Snam. 1500r, Srei
Snam, diff. 2000r, Srei Krub Lakhna,

2000, Apr. 13   Litho.   Perf. 13
1959-1961 A358   Set of 3   3.00 1.10

Growing
Rice — A359

Designs: 100r, Transporting seedlings. 300r,
Harrowing. 500r, Threshing. 1400r, Winnowing. 1600r, Transplanting. 1900r, Plowing.
2200r, Harvesting.

2000, Mar. 1   Perf. 12¼x12½
Vignette Color
1962 A359   100r brt yel grn   .25   .25
1963 A359   300r brt blue   .30   .25
1964 A359   500r brt pink   .40   .25
1965 A359   1400r brn orange   1.10   .25
1966 A359   1600r dull blue   1.25   .30
1967 A359   1900r bister brn   1.50   .35
1968 A359   2200r red   1.75   .40
     Nos. 1962-1968 (7)   6.55 2.05

Locomotives — A360

Designs: 200r, Jules Petiet. 500r, Longue
Chaudiere. 900r, Les Grand Chocolats. 1000r,
Glehn du Bousquet. 1500r, Le Pendule Fran-
çais. 4000r, TGV 001.
4500r, Le Shuttle.

2000, Mar. 5   Litho.   Perf. 12½x12¼
1969-1974 A360   Set of 6   6.75 1.50
Souvenir Sheet
Perf. 13
1975 A360 4500r multi   3.25 1.00
WIPA 2000 Philatelic Exhibition, Vienna
(No. 1975). No. 1975 contains one 80x32mm
stamp.

Birds
A361

Designs: 200r, Diomedea irrorata. 500r, Charadrius alexandrinus, vert. 900r, Sula nebouxii. 1000r, Sterna hirundo. 1500r, Larus argentatus, vert. 4000r, Chlidonia hybrida. 4500r, Sula bassana.

2000, May 8		Perf. 12¾
1976-1981 A361	Set of 6	5.00 1.50

Souvenir Sheet
Perf. 13

1982 A361 4500r multi	3.25 1.00

No. 1982 contains one 40x32mm stamp.

Orchids — A362

Designs: 200r, Cypripedium macranthum. 500r, Vandopsis gigantea. 900r, Calypso bulbosa. 1000r, Vanda luzonica. 1500r, Paphiopedilum villosum. 4000r, Vanda merrillii. 4500r, Paphiopedilum victoria.

2000, May 30		Perf. 12¾
1983-1988 A362	Set of 6	6.00 1.50

Souvenir Sheet
Perf. 13

1989 A362 4500r multi	4.00 1.00

No. 1989 contains one 32x40mm stamp.

Children's
Stories — A363

Designs: 200r, The Courageous Little Tailor, vert. 500r, Tom Thumb, vert. 900r, Thumbelina, vert. 1000r, Pinocchio. 1500r, The Crayfish. 4000r, Peter Pan. 4500r, The Pied Piper, vert.

2000, Nov. 20	Litho.	Perf. 12¾
1990-1995 A363	Set of 6	5.25 5.25

Souvenir Sheet
Perf. 12½

1996 A363 4500r multi	2.75 3.00

No. 1996 contains one 32x40mm stamp.

Water
Festival
and
Tourism
A364

Designs: 500r, Men rowing canoe. 1500r, Men at canoe prow. 2000r, Temples, elephant, woman.

2000, June 1	Litho.	Perf. 13
1997-1999 A364	Set of 3	4.25 2.75

Fire
Trucks
A365

Designs: 200r, Metz DLK 23-6. 500r, Iveco-Magirus SLF24/100. 900r, Metz SLF 7000 WS. 1000r, Iveco-Magirus TLF 24/50. 1500r, Saval-Kronenburg RFF 11000. 4000r, Metz TLF 24/50. 4500r, Metz TLF 16/25.

2000, July 30		Perf. 12¾
2000-2005 A365	Set of 6	5.25 5.25

Souvenir Sheet
Perf. 13

2006 A365 4500r multi	3.50 3.50

No. 2006 contains one 40x32mm stamp.

Independence, 47th Anniv. — A366

Flag, temple and: 500r, Flowers. 1500r, Dove. 2000r, People carrying torch.

2000, Oct. 9		Perf. 12¾
2007-2009 A366	Set of 3	4.25 2.75

Antique Automobiles — A367

Designs: 200r, 1912 Rover 12C. 500r, 1907, Austin 30CV. 900r, 1909 Rolls-Royce Silver Ghost. 1000r, 1929 Graham Paige Phaeton DC. 1500r, 1937 Austin 12. 4000r, 1957 Mercedes-Benz 300SL. 4500r, 1936 MG.

2000, Sept. 30		Perf. 12¾
2010-2015 A367	Set of 6	5.00 2.50

Souvenir Sheet
Perf. 13

2016 A367 4500r multi	3.50 2.00

España 2000 Intl. Philatelic Exhibition (No. 2016). No. 2016 contains one 40x32mm stamp.

Dachshunds — A368

Designs: 200r, Smooth-haired dachshund. 500r, Wire-haired dachshund. 900r, Long-haired dachshund. 1000r, Two dachshunds. 1500r, Dachshund with pups. 4000r, Dachshunds resting. 4500r, Wire-haired dachshund, vert.

2000, Aug. 30		Perf. 13
2017-2022 A368	Set of 6	5.75 2.50

Souvenir Sheet
Perf. 12½

2023 A368 4500r multi	2.75 2.00

No. 2023 contains one 32x40mm stamp.

Cats
and Art
A369

Cat or cats and: 200r, Korean silk painting, 18th cent. 500r, Portuguese tile, 18th cent. 900r, Japanese ceramic cat. 1000r, Egyptian metallic cat. 1500r, Scandinavian engraving. 4000r, Japanese painting. 4500r, Cat on hind legs.

2000, Oct. 5		Perf. 12½x12¼
2024-2029 A369	Set of 6	5.75 2.50

Souvenir Sheet
Perf. 13x13¼

2030 A369 4500r multi	3.00 1.50

No. 2030 contains one 40x32mm stamp.

Birds
A370

Designs: 200r, Creatophora cinerea. 500r, Sturnus vulgaris. 900r, Leiothrix lutea. 1000r, Rupicola rupicola. 1500r, Prunella collaris. 4000r, Panurus biarnicus. 4500r, Muscicapula pallipes, vert.

2000, Dec. 10		Perf. 13
2031-2036 A370	Set of 6	6.00 3.50

Souvenir Sheet
Perf. 13

2037 A370 4500r multi	3.75 2.00

No. 2037 contains one 32x40mm stamp.

Sports — A371

Designs: 200r, Weight lifting. 500r, Rhythmic gymnastics. 900r, Baseball. 1000r, Women's tennis. 1500r, Basketball. 4000r, Women's high jump.

Perf. 12¾, 12½ (#2044)

2000, June 30		Litho.
2038-2043 A371	Set of 6	5.75 2.75

Souvenir Sheet

2044 A371 4500r Runners	2.75 1.75

No. 2044 contains one 32x40mm stamp.

New Year 2001
(Year of the
Snake) — A372

Various stylized snakes with background colors of: 200r, Beige. 500r, Dull bister. 900r, Light blue. 1000r, Greenish blue. 1500r, Dull green. 4000r, Blue. 5400r, Blue, horiz.

2001, Jan. 15	Litho.	Perf. 12¼x12½
2045-2050 A372	Set of 6	6.00 3.50

Souvenir Sheet
Perf. 13x13¼

2051 A372 5400r multi	4.50 2.75

No. 2051 contains one 40x32mm stamp.

Millennium — A373

Designs: 200r, Johannes Gutenberg, printers. 500r, Michael Faraday, electric motor. 900r, Samuel F. B. Morse, telegraph. 1000r, Alexander Graham Bell, telephone. 1500r, Enrico Fermi, nuclear energy. 4000r, Edward Roberts, computer.
No. 2058: a, Christopher Columbus, ships. b, Neil Armstrong, lunar module.

2001, Jan. 5	Litho.	Perf. 12¾
2052-2057 A373	Set of 6	7.00 4.00

Souvenir Sheet
Perf. 12½

2058 A373 5400r Sheet of 2, #a-b + label	8.00 8.00

No. 2058 contains two 40x32mm stamps.

Fire and
Rescue
Equipment
A374

Designs: 200r, 1910 Sandou ladder wagon. 500r, 1899 Gallo cart. 900r, Merryweather pumper, 1950s. 1000r, 1940 Merryweather ambulance. 1500r, 1972 Man-Metz pumper. 4000r, Roman Diesel pumper, 1970s. 5400r, 1898 Metropolitan steam pumper.

2001, Feb. 5		Perf. 12¾
2059-2064 A374	Set of 6	7.00 4.00

Souvenir Sheet
Perf. 13x13¼

2065 A374 5400r multi	4.00 4.00

No. 2065 contains one 40x32mm stamp.

Mushrooms — A375

Designs: 200r, Lycoperdon perlatum. 500r, Trametes versicolor. 900r, Hipholoma sublateritium. 1000r, Amanita muscaria. 1500r, Lycoperdon umbrinum. 4000r, Cortinarius orellanus. 5400r Amanita phalloides, vert.

2001, Feb. 25		Perf. 12¾
2066-2071 A375	Set of 6	7.00 4.00

Souvenir Sheet
Perf. 12½

2072 A375 5400r multi	4.00 4.00

No. 2072 contains one 32x40mm stamp.

Belgica 2001 Intl. Stamp Exhibition,
Brussels — A376

Butterflies: 200r, Nymphalis polychloros. 500r, Cethosia hypsea. 900r, Papilio palinurus. 1000r, Apatura ilia. 1500r, Parthenos sylvia. 4000r, Morpho grandensis. 5400r, Heliconius melpomene.

2001, Apr. 5   *Perf. 12¾*
2073-2078 A376   Set of 6   7.00 4.00
Souvenir Sheet
Perf. 13x13¼
2079 A376 5400r multi   4.00 2.50

Film Personalities A377

Designs: 200r, Gary Cooper. 500r, Marlene Dietrich. 900r, Walt Disney. 1000r, Clark Gable. 1500r, Jeanette MacDonald. 4000r, Melvyn Douglas.
No. 2086: a, Rudolph Valentino. b, Marilyn Monroe.

2001, Apr. 25   Litho.   *Perf. 12¾*
2080 A377   200r multi   .25 .25
2081 A377   500r multi   .50 .30
2082 A377   900r multi   .70 .40
2083 A377   1000r multi   .90 .50
2084 A377   1500r multi   1.25 .75
2085 A377   4000r multi   3.25 1.75
    Nos. 2080-2085 (6)   6.85 3.95
Souvenir Sheet
Perf. 13
2086 A377 5400r Sheet of 2, #a-b   9.00 6.00

Natl. Culture Day A378

Sculptures: 500r, Angkor. 1500r, Bayon. 2000r, Bayon, diff.

2001, Apr. 3   Litho.   *Perf. 12¾*
2087-2089 A378   Set of 3   3.50 2.00

Temples — A379

Designs: 200r, Preah Vihear. 300r, Thonmanom. 600r, Tasom. 1000r, Kravan. 1500r, Takeo. 1700r, Mebon. 2200r, Banteay Kdei.

2001, Mar. 15   *Perf. 12¼x12½*
2090-2096 A379   Set of 7   6.00 3.50

Automobiles — A380

Designs: 200r, 1972 TVR Series M. 500r, 1958 Ferrari 410. 900r, 1995 Peugeot 405. 1000r, 1953 Fiat 8VZ. 1500r, 1997 Citroen Xsara. 4000r, 1997 Renault Espace.
5400r, 1963 Ferrari 250 GT SWB.

2001, June 5   Litho.   *Perf. 12¾*
2097-2102 A380   Set of 6   7.00 4.00
Souvenir Sheet
Perf. 13x13¼
2103 A380 5400r multi   3.50 2.50
No. 2103 contains one 40x32mm stamp.

Tourism A381

Designs: 500r, Sourire de Bayon. 1500r, Bayon. 2000r, Bayon, diff.

2001, June 5   *Perf. 12¾*
2104-2106 A381   Set of 3   3.25 2.50

Philanippon '01 — A382

Locomotives: 200r, 4-6-0. 500r, 4-6-4. 900r, 4-4-0. 1000r, 4-6-4, diff. 1500r, 4-6-2. 4000r, 4-8-2.
5400r, Undescribed locomotive.

2001, July 5   *Perf. 12½x12¼*
2107-2112 A382   Set of 6   7.50 6.00
Souvenir Sheet
Perf. 13x13¼
2113 A382 5400r multi   5.50 4.50
No. 2113 contains one 40x32mm stamp.

Penguins A383

Designs: 200r, Aptenodytes forsteri. 500r, Spheniscus demersus. 900r, Spheniscus humboldti. 1000r, Eudypes cristatus. 1500r, Aptenodytes patagonica. 4000r, Pygoscelis antarctica.
5400r, Pygoscelis papua.

2001, Aug. 5   *Perf. 12¾*
2114-2119 A383   Set of 6   8.25 5.50
Souvenir Sheet
Perf. 13x13¼
2120 A383 5400r multi   6.00 5.00
No. 2120 contains one 40x32mm stamp.

Cats A384

Designs: 200r, Singapura. 500r, Cymric. 900r, Exotic shorthair. 1000r, Ragdoll. 1500r, Manx. 4000r, Somali.
5400r, Egyptian Mau.

2001, Aug. 25   *Perf. 12½x12¼*
2121-2126 A384   Set of 6   8.25 6.00
Souvenir Sheet
Perf. 13x13¼
2127 A384 5400r multi   5.75 4.75
No. 2127 contains one 40x32mm stamp.

Kites A385

Designs: 300r, Khleng Chak. 500r, Khleng Kanton. 1000r, Khleng Phnong. 1500r, Khleng Kaun Morn. 3000r, Khleng Me Ambao.

2001, Sept. 7   *Perf. 12¾*
2128-2132 A385   Set of 5   6.50 5.50

Cacti — A386

Designs: 200r, Parodia cintiensis. 500r, Astrophytum astenas. 900r, Parodia faustiana. 1000r, Coryphantha sulcolanata. 1500r, Neochilenia hankena. 4000r, Mammilaria boolii.
5400r, Mammilaria swinglei.

2001, Sept. 15   *Perf. 12¾*
2133-2138 A386   Set of 6   8.25 6.00
Souvenir Sheet
Perf. 12½
2139 A386 5400r multi   6.25 5.00
No. 2139 contains one 32x40mm stamp.

Khmer Culture A387

Designs: 500r, Fish Dance. 1500r, Red Fish Ballet. 2000r, Apsara Ballet.

2001, Oct. 9   *Perf. 12¾*
2140-2142 A387   Set of 3   4.25 3.50

Wolves and Foxes A388

Designs: 200r, Canis lupus occidentalis. 500r, Canis lupus tundrorum, vert. 900r, Vulpes fulvas. 1000r, Canis latrans. 1500r, Vulpes zerda, vert. 4000r, Alopex lagopus.
5400r, Canis lupus signatus, vert.

2001, Oct. 15   *Perf. 12¾*
2143-2148 A388   Set of 6   8.25 6.00
Souvenir Sheet
Perf. 12½
2149 A388 5400r multi   3.50 3.00
No. 2103 contains one 32x40mm stamp.

Human Evolution — A389

Designs: 100r, Australopithecus anamensis. 200r, Australopithecus afarensis. 300r, Australopithecus africanus. No. 2153, 500r, Australopithecus rudolfensis. No. 2154, 500r, Australopithecus boisei. 1000r, Homo habilis. 1500r, Homo erectus. 4000r, Homo sapiens neanderthalensis.
5400r, Homo sapiens sapiens.

2001, Oct. 25   *Perf. 13*
2150-2157 A389   Set of 8   9.50 6.00
Souvenir Sheet
2158 A389 5400r multi   6.50 5.00
No. 2158 contains one 40x32mm stamp.

King Norodom Sihanouk, 80th Birthday (in 2002) A389a

Various photos: 100r, 200r, 300r, 400r, 500r, 600r, 700r, 800r, 900r, 1000r, 1500r, 2000r, 3000r.

2001, Oct. 31   Litho.   *Perf. 13*
2158A-2158M A389a   Set of 13   17.00 10.00

Chess A390

Designs: 200r, Rook. 500r, Pawn. 900r, King. 1000r, Bishop. 1500r, Queen. 4000r, Knight.
5400r, Pieces of Oriental chess-like game.

2001, Dec. 25   *Perf. 12¾*
2159-2164 A390   Set of 6   7.00 6.00
Souvenir Sheet
Perf. 13
2165 A390 5400r multi   5.50 4.00
No. 2165 contains one 40x32mm stamp.

Italian Soccer A391

Designs: 200r, 1934 World Cup championship team. 500r, 1938 World Cup championship team. 900r, 1968 European Cup championship team. 1000r, 1982 World Cup championship team. 1500r, 2002 World Cup team. 4000r, Italian soccer federation emblem.

2001   *Perf. 12¾*
2166-2171 A391   Set of 6   7.00 7.00

ASEAN Post, 10th Anniv A392

Temples: 500r, Prasat Preah Vihear. 1000r, Prasat Preah Ko. 1500r, Prasat Banteay Srei. 2500r, Prasat Bayon. 3500r, Prasat Angkor Wat.

2002, July 9   *Perf. 13*
2172-2176 A392   Set of 5   11.00 10.00

Sugar Palm — A393

Designs: 300r, Tree. 500r, Female flower. 700r, Male flower. 1500r, Fruit.

2003, June 20   **Litho.**
2177-2180 A393   Set of 4   7.50 7.00

Japanese Grant Aid — A394

Designs: 100r, Drawing of Bridge No. 26, Highway 6A. 200r, Bridge No. 26, Highway 6A. 400r, Chroy Changvar Bridge. 800r, Kizuna Bridge. 3500r, Monument, vert.

2003, Apr. 25
2181-2185 A394   Set of 5   7.50 6.00

Cambodian Red Cross — A395

Designs: 100r, Ox cart. 200r, Woman carrying rice bag, vert. 300r, Queen with Red Cross volunteers. 400r, Queen and women. 500r, Queen and elderly people. 700r, Queen and women, diff. 800r, Queen and Prime Minister's wife giving items to people. 1000r, Like 800r, diff. 1900r, Like 800r, diff., vert. 2100r, Like 800r, diff., vert. 4000r, Queen and Prime Minister's wife with baby.

2003, May 8
2186-2196 A395   Set of 11   12.00 12.00

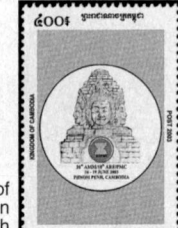

Cambodia/People's Republic of China Diplomatic Relations, 50th Anniv. — A396

No. 2197: a, Angkor Wat. b, Great Wall of China.

2003, July 19   **Perf. 12¼x12**
2197 A396 2000r Horiz. pair,
     #a-b   5.00 4.00

Association of South East Asian Nations, 36th Anniv. — A397

Designs: 400r, Conference emblem. 500r, Apsara dancer. 600r, Apsara dancer, diff. 1600r, Apsara dancers. 1900r, Temonorom dancers.

2003, Aug. 8   **Perf. 13**
2198-2202 A397   Set of 5   8.00 6.50

King Norodom Sihanouk — A398

Designs: 200r, Pointing at map. 400r, Meeting rural Cambodians, vert. 500r, Sitting in forest, vert. 800r, Pointing in forest, vert. 1000r, Saluting, vert. 2000r, Saluting, with flag and Independence Monument, vert. 5000r, With handicapped people.

2003, Nov. 9
2203-2209 A398   Set of 7   10.00 7.00

Khmer Culture A399

Sculptures: 100r, Bayon. 200r, Banteay Srei. 400r, Banteay Srei, diff. 800r, Bayon, vert. 3500r, Banteay Srei, vert. 2000r, Unattributed sculpture, vert.

2004, Apr. 3
2210-2214 A399   Set of 5   5.00 4.00
Souvenir Sheet
2215 A399 2000r multi   3.25 2.00

Rural Areas A400

Designs: 600r, Mill. 900r, House, field and cattle. 2000r, House and trees. 2000r, Ox cart and driver.

2004, Apr. 13
2216-2218 A400   Set of 3   6.00 4.00
Souvenir Sheet
2219 A400 2000r multi   3.00 2.25

Tepmonorum Dancers — A401

Dancers with: 400r, Yellow costumes. 1000r, Blue costumes. 2100r, Blue and yellow costumes.
2100r, Blue and yellow costumes, diff.

2004, May 5
2220-2222 A401   Set of 3   5.00 4.00
Souvenir Sheet
2223 A401 2000r multi   3.00 2.50

Flowers — A402

Designs: 600r, Cassia fistula. 700r, Butea monosperma. 900r, Couroupita quianensis.

1000r, Delonix regia, horiz. 1800r, Lagerstroemia floribunda.
2000r, Lagerstroemia floribunda, horiz.

2004, Aug. 25   **Litho.**   **Perf. 13**
2224-2228 A402   Set of 5   5.50 4.00
Souvenir Sheet
2229 A402 2000r multi   3.25 1.75

Tourism — A403

Designs: 200r, Prasat Preah Khan. 500r, Prasat Preup. 600r, PrasatBanteay Samre. 1600r, Prasat Bayon. 1900r, Angkor Wat. 2000r, Prasat Bayon, vert.

2004, Sept. 27   **Litho.**   **Perf. 13**
2230-2234 A403   Set of 5   5.00 3.50
Souvenir Sheet
2235 A403 2000r multi   3.25 2.00

Coronation of King Norodom Shiamoni A404

Various photos: 100r, 400r, 500r, 600r, 700r, 900r, 2100r, 2200r, 4000r. 700r-4000r are horiz.

2004, Oct. 29
2236-2244 A404   Set of 9   8.00 8.00

Ancient Fishing Tools A405

Various scoops and baskets: 100r, 200r, 800r, 1700r, 2200r. 1700r and 2200r are vert. 2000r, Child with basket, vert.

2004, Dec. 5
2245-2249 A405   Set of 5   5.50 4.00
Souvenir Sheet
2250 A405 2000r multi   4.25 2.50

Cambodian Red Cross, 50th Anniv. — A406

Designs: 400r, Emblem. 700r, Volunteers, horiz. 800r, Volunteers, diff., horiz. 1900r, Volunteers, diff., horiz. 2100r, Volunteers, diff. horiz. 2200r, Royalty on dais, horiz.

2005, Feb. 18
2251-2256 A406   Set of 6   7.25 7.25

Apsaras Dance — A407

Dancer with background color of: 800r, Pink. 900r, Light blue. 1400r, Green. 1600r, Rose. 2000r, Blue.
4000r, Brown.

2005, Apr. 12
2257-2261 A407   Set of 5   6.50 5.00
Souvenir Sheet
2262 A407 4000r multi   4.25 3.00

Khmer Culture A408

Designs: 500r, Banteay Kdei. 700r, Elephant Terrace. 1000r, Thommanon. 2000r, Ta Prohm. 2500r, Angkor Wat.
4000r, Ta Reach, vert.

2005, May 16
2263-2267 A408   Set of 5   6.25 5.00
Souvenir Sheet
2268 A408 4000r multi   4.25 3.00

Flowers — A409

Nymphaea lotus in: 100r, Purple. 500r, White. 1200r, Blue. 2000r, Yellow. 2500r, Red. 4000r, Red flowers in canoe, horiz.

2005, July 25   **Litho.**   **Perf. 13**
2269-2273 A409   Set of 5   6.00 4.50
Souvenir Sheet
2274 A409 4000r multi   4.25 3.00

Fish A410

Designs: 700r, Pangasionodon gigas. 800r, Catlocarpio siamensis. 1000r, Mekongina erythrospila. 1900r, Probarbus labeaminor, vert. 2200r, Wallago leeri, vert.
4000r, Scleropages formosus.

2005, Sept. 5   **Perf. 13**
2275-2279 A410   Set of 5   6.25 5.50
Souvenir Sheet
2280 A410 4000r multi   4.25 3.75

Coronation of King Norodom Sihamoni, 1st Anniv. — A411

Frame colors: 500r, Green. 1500r, Blue. 2200r, Red.

2005, Oct. 29   **Litho.**   **Perf. 13**
2281-2283   A411   Set of 3   3.25 3.25

Miniature Sheet

Birds — A412

No. 2284: a, 200r, Great egret. b, 400r, Great-billed heron. c, 1000r, Painted stork. d, 1200r, Spot-billed pelican. e, 1800r, Sarus crane, horiz. f, 3500r, Greater adjutant, horiz.

2005, Dec. 5
2284   A412   Sheet of 6, #a-f   8.00 8.00

Khmer Culture A413

Women at work: 100r, Scooping dyes. 800r, Washing clothes. 1500r, Weaving. 2200r, Spinning thread. 3500r, Weaving, diff.
5400r, Weaving, diff.

2006, Jan. 26
2285-2289   A413   Set of 5   6.75 6.00
       Souvenir Sheet
2290   A413   5400r multi   4.00 3.00

Marine Mammals — A414

Designs: 500r, Sousa chinensis. 900r, Neophocaena phocaenoides. 1400r, Dolphinus capensis tropicalis. 2100r, Stenella longirostris roseinventris. 3500r, Tursiops aduncus.
5400r, Neophocaena phocaenoides and boat.

2006, Mar. 9
2291-2295   A414   Set of 5   7.50 6.50
       Souvenir Sheet
2296   A414   5400r multi   4.00 3.00

Reamker Legend — A415

Designs: 1000r, Jup Leak and Ream Leak. 1400r, Preah Ream, vert. 1600r, Neang Seda,

vert. 1900r, Krong Reap, vert. 2100r, Hanuman, vert.
5400r, Two characters in water.

2006, Apr. 13
2297-2301   A415   Set of 5   6.50 5.50
       Souvenir Sheet
2302   A415   5400r multi   4.25 3.25

Elephants — A416

Designs: 400r, Adult and juvenile elephant. 700r, Elephants in water. 1600r, Elephant, vert. 2200r, Elephant facing right. 3500r, Elephant facing left.
5400r, Elephants in water, diff.

2006, June 15   **Litho.**   **Perf. 13**
2303-2307   A416   Set of 5   7.00 5.50
       Souvenir Sheet
2308   A416   5400r multi   4.25 3.50

Dances — A417

Designs: 600r, Chhai Yaim dance. 1900r, Sacrifice of Buffalo dance. 2200r, Mouth Organ dance. 3500r, Rice Harvest dance.

2006, Aug. 17
2309-2312   A417   Set of 4   6.50 5.50

Birds A418

Designs: 600r, Threskionis melanocephalus. 800r, Plegadis facinellus. 1500r, Houbaropsis bengalensis. 2100r, Pseudibis gigantea. 3500r, Pseudibis davisoni.
5400r, Pseudibis gigantea, vert.

2006, Nov. 8   **Litho.**   **Perf. 13**
2313-2317   A418   Set of 5   7.50 6.00
       Souvenir Sheet
2318   A418   5400r multi   7.00 5.50

Condom Use Program — A419

Designs: 300r, Man, woman, program emblem. 500r, Man, motorcycle, program emblem. 2200r, Men on boat, flag with program emblem.

2006, Dec. 1   **Litho.**   **Perf. 13**
2319-2321   A419   Set of 3   2.25 2.25
       World AIDS Day.

Cambodian Red Cross HIV/AIDS Campaign — A420

Campaign leader Bun Rany, wife of Prime Minister Hun Sen and captions: 1500r, Caring. 1900r, Stop discrimination, vert. 2000r, Give hope to families. 2100r, National and Asia-Pacific Leadership Forum Champion. 2200r, National and Asia-Pacific Leadership Forum Champion, diff.

2007   **Litho.**   **Perf. 13**
2322-2326   A420   Set of 5   6.50 6.50

Sculpture A421

Flags of Viet Nam and Cambodia A422

2007, June 24
2327   A421   500r shown   .45 .45
2328   A421   800r Sculpture, diff.   .65 .65
2329   A421   1000r Sculpture, diff.   .75 .75
2330   A421   1500r Sculpture, diff.   1.25 1.25
2331   A422   1900r shown   1.50 1.50
    Nos. 2327-2331 (5)   4.60 4.60
Diplomatic relations between Cambodia and Viet Nam, 40th anniv.

Handicap International, 25th Anniv. — A423

Denominations: 1000r, 1500r.

2007, July 25
2332-2333   A423   Set of 2   2.00 2.00

Dancers — A424

Architecture — A425

Various dancers with denominations of: 800r, 900r, 1400r, 1600r, 2000r.
No. 2339: a, Secretariat Building, Bandar Seri Begawan, Brunei. b, National Museum of Cambodia. c, Fatahillah Museum, Jakarta, Indonesia. d, Typical house, Laos. e, Malayan Railway Headquarters Building, Kuala Lumpur, Malaysia. f, Yangon Post Office, Myanmar (Burma). g, Malacañang Palace, Philippines. h, National Museum of Singapore. i, Vimanmek Mansion, Bangkok, Thailand. j, Presidential Palace, Hanoi, Viet Nam.

2007, Aug. 8
2334-2338   A424   Set of 5   5.00 5.00
2339   A425   1000r Sheet of 10,
       #a-j   10.00 10.00
    Association of South East Asian Nations (ASEAN), 40th anniv. See Brunei No. 607, Burma No. 370, Indonesia Nos. 2120-2121, Laos Nos. 1717-1718, Malaysia No. 1170, Philippines Nos. 3103-3105, Singapore No. 1265, Thailand No. 2315, and Viet Nam Nos. 3302-3311.

Friendship Between Cambodia and People's Republic of China, 50th Anniv. — A427

No. 2346: a, Tian An Men Rostrum, flag of People's Republic of China. b, Royal Palace, flag of Cambodia.

2008, July 25   **Litho.**   **Perf. 12**
2346   A427   2000r Horiz. pair, #a-
       b   2.00 2.00

A430

Pottery Making — A431

Various women making pottery: 100r, 700r, 1900r, 2000r, 2200r.
6000r, Oxcart with pottery.

2008, Dec. 5   **Litho.**   ***Perf. 13***
2359-2363   A430   Set of 5   3.50   3.50

Souvenir Sheet
Perf. 13¾x13½

2364   A431   6000r multi   3.00   3.00

Ancient Agricultural Tools — A434

Designs: 300r, Plow. 1200r, Harrow. 1700r, Spiked roller. 1800r, Water wheel. 2800r, Cart. 6000r, Farmer operating water wheel, vert.

2010, Mar. 30   **Litho.**   ***Perf. 13***
2377-2381   A434   Set of 5   3.75   3.75

Souvenir Sheet
Perf. 13¾x13½

2382   A434   6000r multi   3.00   3.00

Environmental Protection
A435

Designs: 200r, Filled trash can, face on Earth. 800r, Watering can pouring water on Earth, cars in flood. 1400r, Tree inside split Earth. 1700r, Buildings in hourglass. 3000r, Tree in hands.
6000r, Cars in flood, palm trees.

2010, May 25   **Litho.**   ***Perf. 13***
2383-2387   A435   Set of 5   3.50   3.50

Souvenir Sheet
Perf. 13¾x13½

2388   A435   6000r multi   3.00   3.00

Diplomatic Relations Between Cambodia and the United States, 60th Anniv. — A436

2010, July 11   **Litho.**   ***Perf. 13***
2389   A436   2800r multi   1.40   1.40

Campaign Against AIDS — A437

Red AIDS ribbon and: 1000r, Wrapped and unwrapped condoms, condom with face. 1500r, Man, woman and child. 2800r, Men and woman at night club. 4000r, Two birds.

2011, June 29   **Litho.**   ***Perf. 13***
2390-2393   A437   Set of 4   4.75   4.75

First day cancels show a June 5 date, but the stamps were not sold until June 29.

Fish
A438

Designs: 500r, Barbonymus schwanenfeldii. 1500r, Hypsibarbus lagleri. 2800r, Puntioplites falcifer. 3000r, Osteochilus melanopleurus. 3500r, Hampala macrolepidota.
6000r, Fish, fishermen and nets.

2011, Aug. 8   **Litho.**   ***Perf. 13***
2394-2398   A438   Set of 5   5.75   5.75

Souvenir Sheet
Perf. 13½x13¾

2399   A438   6000r multi   3.00   3.00

SEMI-POSTAL STAMPS

Nos. 8, 12, 14 and 15 Surcharged in Black

1952, Oct. 20   **Unwmk.**   ***Perf. 13***
B1   A3   1.10pi + 40c   4.75   8.50
B2   A3   1.90pi + 60c   4.75   8.50
B3   A3   3pi + 1pi   4.75   8.50
B4   A1   5pi + 2pi   4.75   8.50
   Nos. B1-B4 (4)   19.00   34.00

For students assistance.

Preah Stupa — SP1

1957, Mar. 15   **Engr.**   ***Perf. 13***
B5   SP1   1.50r + 50c ind, ol & red   2.00   2.00
B6   SP1   6.50r + 1.50r red lil, ol & red   3.00   3.00
B7   SP1   8r + 2r bl, ol & red   5.00   5.00
   Nos. B5-B7 (3)   10.00   10.00

Birth of Buddha, 2,500th anniv. See #62-64.

Regular Issue, 1959, with Red Typographed Surcharge

1959, Dec. 9
B8   A14   20c + 20c rose vio   .50   .50
B9   A14   50c + 30c blue   .80   .80
B10   A14   80c + 50c rose car   1.75   1.75
   Nos. B8-B10 (3)   3.05   3.05

The surtax was for the Red Cross.

Nos. 107-108 Surcharged and Overprinted in Red

1963, Oct. 1   **Unwmk.**   ***Perf. 13***
B11   A26   4r + 40c grn & dk brn   1.00   1.00
B12   A26   6r + 60c vio & ol bis   1.50   1.50

Centenary of International Red Cross.

Nos. 263, 267, 293-294, 134 Surcharged in Red

1972, Nov. 15   **Engr.**   ***Perf. 13***
B13   A72   3r + 2r multi   .60   .40
B14   A72   10r + 6r multi   .90   .80
B15   A80   12r + 7r multi   1.00   .90
B16   A34   12r + 7r multi   1.00   .90
B17   A80   15r + 8r multi   1.50   1.50
   Nos. B13-B17 (5)   5.00   4.50

Surtax was for war victims. Surcharge arranged differently on Nos. B15-B17.

AIR POST STAMPS

Kinnari — AP1

Unwmk.
1953, Apr. 16   **Engr.**   ***Perf. 13***
C1   AP1   50c deep green   2.00   1.00
  a.   Souv. sheet of 4, #C1, C3, C5, C9   85.00   85.00
C2   AP1   3pi red brown   2.00   1.25
  a.   Souv. sheet of 3, #C2, C4, C8   85.00   85.00
C3   AP1   3.30pi rose violet   3.00   2.00
C4   AP1   4pi dk brn & dp bl   2.00   2.00
C5   AP1   5.10pi brn, red & org   3.75   3.00
C6   AP1   6.50pi dk brn & lil rose   3.75   3.25
  a.   Souv. sheet of 2, #C6-C7   85.00   85.00
C7   AP1   9pi lil rose & dp grn   4.50   5.00
C8   AP1   11.50pi multi   9.00   7.00
C9   AP1   30c dk brn, bl grn & org   17.50   12.00
   Nos. C1-C9 (9)   47.50   36.50

No. C1a sold for 50pi, No. C2a for 25pi, No. C6a for 20pi.
Souvenir sheets with completely white gum, no toning and no gum bends sell for a premium.

AP2

1957, Dec. 11
C10   AP2   50c maroon   .40   .25
C11   AP2   1r emerald   .70   .25
C12   AP2   4r ultra   2.25   .75
C13   AP2   50r carmine rose   8.75   4.00
C14   AP2   100r grn, bl & car   16.00   6.00
  a.   Souv. sheet of 5, #C10-C14   35.00   35.00
   Nos. C10-C14 (5)   28.10   11.25

No. C14a sold for 160r.
See note after No. C9.

Independence Type of 1961
1961, Nov. 9   ***Perf. 13x12½***
C15   A24   7r multicolored   .90   .80
C16   A24   30r grn, car & ultra   3.00   2.25
C17   A24   50r ind, grn & ol   4.50   3.00
  a.   Souv. sheet of 3, #C15-C17   10.00   10.00
   Nos. C15-C17 (3)   7.55   7.55

No. C15 Srchd. in Red and Ovptd. in Black

1962, Nov. 9
C18   A24   12r on 7r multi   2.25   1.25

Dedication of Independence Monument.

Hanuman, Monkey God — AP3

1964, Sept. 1   **Engr.**   ***Perf. 13***
C19   AP3   5r multicolored   1.10   .55
C20   AP3   10r ol bis, lil rose & grn   1.60   .65
C21   AP3   20r vio, bl & ol bis   2.50   1.40
C22   AP3   40r bl, ol bis & dk bl   6.00   2.25
C23   AP3   80r multicolored   10.00   6.00
   Nos. C19-C23 (5)   21.20   10.85

Nos. C19-C22 Surcharged in Red

1964, Oct.
C24   AP3   3r on 5r multi   .90   .55
C25   AP3   6r on 10r multi   1.40   .85
C26   AP3   9r on 20r multi   1.75   1.10
C27   AP3   12r on 40r multi   3.50   2.00
   Nos. C24-C27 (4)   7.55   4.50

18th Olympic Games, Tokyo, Oct. 10-25.

1972 Summer Olympic Games, Munich — AP4

Designs: No. C28, shown. No. C29, Munich churches, Olympic emblem, vert.

Litho. & Embossed

1972, Sept. 28   *Perf. 13½*
C28 AP4 900r gold & multi	42.50	42.50
C29 AP4 900r gold & multi	42.50	42.50
a. Souvenir sheet of 2, #C28-C29		90.00

No. C29a exists imperf. Value, $110.

Apollo 16 AP5

Designs: No. C30, Astronauts in Lunar Rover. No. C31, Astronaut walking on moon.

1972, Sept. 28
C30 AP5 900r gold & multi	45.00	45.00
C31 AP5 900r gold & multi	45.00	45.00
a. Souvenir sheet of 2, #C30-C31		85.00

No. C31a exists imperf. Value, $130.

Pres. Nixon's Visit to the People's Republic of China — AP6

Nixon, Mao Zedong: No. C32, Large portraits (shown). No. C33, Small portraits.

1972, Sept. 28   *Perf. 12½*
C32 AP6 900r gold & multi	80.00	80.00
C33 AP6 900r gold & multi	80.00	80.00

Garuda, 12th Century, Angkor Thom — AP7

1973, Jan. 18   Engr.   *Perf. 13*
C34 AP7 3r carmine	.35	.25
C35 AP7 30r violet blue	2.00	1.00
C36 AP7 50r dull purple	3.75	2.00
C37 AP7 100r dull green	5.25	3.00
Nos. C34-C37 (4)	11.35	6.25

1972 Summer Olympic Games, Munich AP8

Gold medalists: No. C38, Heide Rosendahl. No. C39, Mark Spitz.

Litho. & Embossed

1973, May 18   *Perf. 13½*
C38 AP8 900r gold & multi	35.00	35.00
C39 AP8 900r gold & multi	35.00	35.00
a. Souvenir sheet, #C38-C39		72.50

No. C39a exists imperf. Value $100.

Nos. C38-C39 Overprinted

1973, Nov. 19
C40 AP8 900r on C38	40.00	40.00
C41 AP8 900r on C39	40.00	40.00
a. Souvenir sheet, #C40-C41		80.00

No. C41a exists imperf. Value, $160.

1974 World Cup Soccer Championships, Munich — AP9

Designs: No. C42, Trophy, players. No. C43, Trophy, players, vert.

1973, Nov. 19   Litho. & Embossed
C42 AP9 900r gold & multi	35.00	35.00
C43 AP9 900r gold & multi	35.00	35.00
a. Souvenir sheet, #C42-C43		70.00

No. C43a exists imperf. Value, $100.

John F. Kennedy, Apollo 11 — AP10

No. C44, shown. No. C45, Kennedy, Apollo 17.

1974, Feb. 18
C44 AP10 1100r gold & multi	95.00	95.00
C45 AP10 1100r gold & multi	95.00	95.00
a. Souv. sheet of 2, #C44-C45		200.00

Nos. C44-C45a exist imperf. Values slightly higher.

Copernicus Type of 1974 and

Copernicus, Sun — AP11

200r, Copernicus and Skylab III. 250r, Copernicus, Concorde and solar eclipse. No. C48, shown. No. C49, Moon, Skylab, hand holding symbol of sun.

1974, Sept. 10   Litho.   *Perf. 13*
C46 A87 200r multi	10.00	5.50
C47 A87 250r multi	15.00	10.00

Litho. & Engraved
Perf. 13½
C48 AP11 1200r gold & multi	30.00	30.00

Souvenir Sheet of 1
C49 AP11 1200r gold & multi	30.00	30.00

Nos. C46-C47 exist in perf or imperf souvenir sheets of 1. Values, $25 perf., $50 imperf. Nos. C48-C49 exist imperf. Values, each $55.

UPU Type of 1974 and

AP12

700r, Rocket, globe and UPU emblem. No. C51, UPU Headquarters. No. C52, US #1434-1435.

1974, Nov. 2   Litho.   *Perf. 13*
C50 A88 700r gold & multi	11.50	11.50

Litho. & Embossed
Perf. 13½
C51 AP12 1200r gold & multi	20.00	20.00

Souvenir Sheet
C52 AP12 1200r gold & multi		30.00

Nos. C50-C51 exist in souvenir sheets of one. Nos. C51-C52 exist imperf.

UPU, Cent. (in 1974) AP13

UPU emblem and: No. C53, Biplane, train. No. C54, Satellite, sailboat.

Litho. & Embossed

1975, Apr. 12   *Perf. 13¼*
C53 AP13 2000r gold & multi	13.50	—

Souvenir Sheet
C54 AP13 2000r gold & multi	40.00	—

No. C53 exists in a souvenir sheet of 1.

Post Aerienne at Right — AP14

Denominations: 5r, 10r, 15r, 25r.

1984, Feb. 1   Litho.   *Perf. 12x12½*
C55-C58 AP14 Set of 4	45.00	8.50

Post Aerienne at Left — AP15

Denominations: 5r, 10r, 15r, 25r.

1986, Mar. 4   Litho.   *Perf. 12x12½*
C59-C62 AP15 Set of 4	40.00	8.00

POSTAGE DUE STAMPS

D1

1957   Unwmk.   Typo.   *Perf. 13½*
Denomination in Black
J1 D1 10c ver & pale blue	.30	.30
J2 D1 50c ver & pale blue	.55	.55
J3 D1 1r ver & pale blue	.85	.85
J4 D1 3r ver & pale blue	1.25	1.25
J5 D1 5r ver & pale blue	2.00	2.00
Nos. J1-J5 (5)	4.95	4.95

Frieze, Angkor Wat — D2

1974, Feb. 18   Engr.   *Perf. 12½x13*
J6 D2 2r ocher	.30	.30
J7 D2 6r green	.45	.45
J8 D2 8r deep carmine	.70	.70
J9 D2 10r violet blue	1.00	1.00
Nos. J6-J9 (4)	2.45	2.45

CAMEROONS

ˌka-mə-'rüns

LOCATION — West coast of Africa, north of equator
GOVT. — British Trust Territory
AREA — 34,081 sq. mi.
POP. — 868,637 (estimated)
CAPITAL — Buea

Prior to World War I, Cameroons (Kamerun) was a German Protectorate. It was occupied during the War by Great Britain and France and in 1922 was mandated to these countries by the League of Nations. Stamps of Nigeria were used in the British part until 1960. The northern section of the British Cameroons became part of the independent state of Nigeria in 1960, and the southern section became a United Kingdom Trust Territory. After a referendum, this U.K.T.T. joined the independent State of Cameroun to form the Federal Republic of Cameroun, Oct. 1, 1961.

Stamps of the German Protectorate, the French Mandate, the independent state and the Cameroun Federal Republic are listed under Cameroun.

> Catalogue values for unused stamps in this country are for Never Hinged items.

United Kingdom Trust Territory

Stamps and Type of Nigeria, 1953, Ovptd. in Red

		Perf. 13½, 14		
1960, Oct. 1		**Wmk. 4**		**Engr.**
		Size: 35½x22½mm		
66	A17	½p red org & black	.25	1.75
67	A17	1p ol gray & black	.25	.60
68	A17	1½p blue green	.25	.25
69	A17	2p gray (II)	.65	2.00
70	A17	3p purple & black	.25	.25
71	A17	4p ultra & black	.25	2.25
72	A18	6p blk & org brn, perf. 14	.40	.25
a.		Perf. 13x13½ ('61)	.35	2.25
73	A17	1sh brown vio & blk	.35	.25
		Size: 40½x24½mm		
74	A17	2sh6p green & black	2.00	.80
75	A17	5sh ver & black	2.75	3.00
76	A17	10sh red brn & blk	3.75	6.50
		Size: 42x31½mm		
77	A17	£1 violet & black	18.50	27.50
		Nos. 66-77 (12)	29.65	45.40

Nos. 66-77 were withdrawn in Northern Cameroons on May 31, 1961, when that territory joined Nigeria and in Southern Cameroons Sept. 30, 1961, when that territory joined the Cameroun Federal Republic.

CAMEROUN

ˌka-mə-'rün

(Kamerun)

LOCATION — On the west coast of Africa, north of the equator
GOVT. — Republic
AREA — 183,520 sq. mi.
POP. — 15,456,092 (1999 est.)
CAPITAL — Yaounde

Before World War I, Cameroun (Kamerun) was a German Protectorate. It was occupied during the war by Great Britain and France and in 1922 was mandated to these countries by the League of Nations. The French-mandated part became the independent State of Cameroun on January 1, 1960.

The Southern Cameroons, a United Kingdom Trust Territory, joined this state to form the Federal Republic of Cameroon on October 1, 1961. The name was changed to United Republic of Cameroon on May 20, 1972.

Stamps of Southern Cameroons are listed under Cameroons.

100 Pfennig = 1 Mark
12 Pence = 1 Shilling
100 Centimes = 1 Franc

> Catalogue values for unused stamps in this country are for Never Hinged items, beginning with Scott 296 in the regular postage section, Scott B29 in the semipostal section, Scott C8 in the airpost section, Scott J24 in the postage due section, and Scott M1 in the military stamp section.

Watermark

Wmk. 125 — Lozenges

TOR C
CART
TOR C
CART

Wmk. 385

Issued under German Dominion

Stamps of Germany Overprinted in Black

1897		**Unwmk.**	**Perf. 13½x14½**	
1	A9	3pf yel brn	11.00	16.00
a.		3pf red brown	45.00	130.00
b.		3pf dark brown	16.00	37.50
c.		3pf olive brown	8.75	37.50
2	A9	5pf green	5.25	8.00
3	A10	10pf carmine	3.75	4.50
4	A10	20pf ultra	4.00	8.00
a.		Diagonal half used as 10pf on cover		18,750.
5	A10	25pf orange	20.00	37.50
6	A10	50pf red brn	16.00	29.00
		Nos. 1-6 (6)	60.00	103.00

A3

Kaiser's Yacht "Hohenzollern" — A4

1900		**Unwmk.**	**Typo.**	**Perf. 14**
7	A3	3pf brown	1.25	1.60
8	A3	5pf green	13.50	1.20
9	A3	10pf carmine	40.00	1.25
10	A3	20pf ultra	25.00	2.25
a.		Vertical half used as 10pf on cover (Longji, '11)		6,750.
11	A3	25pf org & blk, yel	1.50	5.00
12	A3	30pf org & blk, sal	2.00	4.00
13	A3	40pf lake & blk	2.00	4.00
14	A3	50pf pur & blk, sal	2.00	6.00
15	A3	80pf lake & blk, rose	2.75	11.00
		Engr.		**Perf. 14½x14**
16	A4	1m carmine	67.50	67.50
17	A4	2m blue	5.25	65.00
18	A4	3m blk vio	5.25	105.00
19	A4	5m slate & car	140.00	450.00
		Nos. 7-19 (13)	308.00	723.80

1905-18		**Wmk. 125**		**Typo.**
20	A3	3pf brown ('18)	.70	
21	A3	5pf green	.70	1.60
a.		Bklt. pane of 6	15.00	
b.		Bklt. pane of 6, 2 #21 + 4 #22	62.50	
c.		Bklt. pane of 5 + label	375.00	
22	A3	10pf carmine ('06)	2.25	1.50
a.		Bklt. pane of 6	17.50	
b.		Booklet pane of 5 + label	500.00	
23	A3	20pf ultra ('14)	3.00	125.00
24	A4	1m carmine ('15)	12.00	
25	A4	5m slate & car ('13)	40.00	4,250.
		Nos. 20-25 (6)	68.35	

The 3pf and 1m were not placed in use. Nos. 21a, 22a were made from sheet stamps.

Issued under British Occupation

Stamps of German Cameroun Surcharged

No. 53

No. 62

Wmk. Lozenges (125) (#54-56, 65); Unwmk. (Other Values)

1915			**Perf. 14, 14½**	
		Blue Surcharge		
53	A3	½p on 3pf brn	15.00	60.00
54	A3	½p on 5pf grn	7.75	11.00
a.		Double surcharge		1,100.
b.		Black surcharge		
55	A3	1p on 10pf car	1.45	11.00
a.		"1" with thin serifs	15.00	75.00
b.		Double surcharge	475.00	
c.		Black surcharge	18.00	65.00
d.		As "c," "1" with thin serifs	300.00	
		Black Surcharge		
56	A3	2p on 20pf ultra	4.00	24.00
57	A3	2½p on 25pf org & blk, yel	18.50	60.00
a.		Double surcharge	15,000.	
58	A3	3p on 30pf org & blk, sal	15.00	65.00
59	A3	4p on 40pf lake & blk	15.00	65.00
60	A3	6p on 50pf pur & blk, sal	15.00	65.00
61	A3	8p on 80pf lake & blk, rose	15.00	65.00
62	A4	1sh on 1m car	220.00	1,000.
a.		"S" inverted	1,100.	4,000.
63	A4	2sh on 2m bl	250.00	1,050.
a.		"S" inverted	1,100.	4,000.
64	A4	3sh on 3m blk vio	250.00	1,050.
a.		"S" inverted	1,100.	4,400.
b.		Double surcharge	16,500.	
65	A4	5sh on 5m sl & car	300.00	1,100.
a.		"S" inverted	1,425.	4,750.
		Nos. 53-65 (13)	1,127.	4,626.

The letters "C. E. F." are the initials of "Cameroons Expeditionary Force."
Numerous overprint varieties exist for Nos. 53-65.

Counterfeits exist of Nos. 54a, 54b.

See Cameroons for Nos. 66-77.

Issued under French Occupation

Gabon Nos. 37, 49-52, 54, 57-58, 60, 62-64, 66, 69-70 Overprinted

1915		**Unwmk.**	**Perf. 13½x14**	
		Inscribed "Congo Français"		
101	A10	10c red & car	32.50	24.00
		Inscribed "Afrique Equatoriale"		
102	A10	1c choc & org	110.00	47.50
103	A10	2c blk & choc	200.00	150.00
104	A10	4c vio & dp bl	200.00	150.00
105	A10	5c ol gray & grn	40.00	24.00
105A	A10	10c red & car	21,500.	24,000.
106	A10	20c ol brn & dk vio	210.00	210.00
107	A11	25c dp bl & choc	60.00	47.50
108	A11	30c gray blk & red	200.00	200.00
109	A11	35c dk vio & grn	67.50	45.00
a.		Double overprint	1,900.	
110	A11	40c choc & ultra	200.00	200.00
111	A11	45c car & vio	225.00	225.00
112	A11	50c bl grn & gray	225.00	225.00
113	A11	75c org & choc	275.00	225.00
114	A12	1fr dk brn & bis	260.00	225.00
115	A12	2fr car & brn	300.00	260.00
		Nos. 101-105,106-115 (15)	2,605.	2,258.

The overprint is vertical, reading up, on Nos. 101-106, 114-115, and horizontal on Nos. 107-113.

Stamps of Middle Congo, Issue of 1907, Overprinted

1916			**Unwmk.**	
116	A1	1c ol gray & brn	110.00	110.00
117	A1	2c violet & brn	110.00	110.00
118	A1	4c blue & brown	120.00	120.00
119	A1	5c dk green & blue	32.50	32.50
120	A2	35c violet brn & bl	110.00	75.00
121	A2	45c violet & red	87.50	75.00

The overprint is vert., reading down, on Nos. 120-121.

Same Overprint On Stamps of French Congo, 1900

Wmk. Branch of Thistle (122)

122	A4	15c dull vio & ol grn	120.00	120.00
a.		Inverted overprint	200.00	180.00

Wmk. Branch of Rose Tree (123)

123	A5	20c yellow grn & grn	140.00	92.50
124	A5	30c car rose & org	110.00	87.50
125	A5	40c org brn & brt grn	105.00	80.00
126	A5	50c gray vio & lil	110.00	87.50
127	A5	75c red vio & org	110.00	85.00

Wmk. Branch of Olive (124)

128	A6	1fr gray lilac & ol	125.00	120.00
129	A6	2fr carmine & brn	160.00	120.00
		Nos. 116-129 (14)	1,550.	1,315.

The overprint is horiz. on No. 122. The overprint is vert., reading down or up, on Nos. 123-129. Values are for the cheaper variety. See the Scott Classic Specialized Catalogue of Stamps & Covers for detailed listings.

Values are for stamps centered in the grade of fine.
Counterfeits exist of Nos. 101-129.

Stamps of Middle Congo, Issue of 1907 Overprinted

1916-17			**Unwmk.**	
130	A1	1c ol gray & brn	.40	.40
131	A1	2c violet & brn	.50	.50
132	A1	4c blue & brn	.75	.75

133	A1	5c dk green & bl	.50	.40
134	A1	10c carmine & bl	1.10	.80
135	A1	15c brn vio & rose ('17)	2.00	.80
136	A1	20c brown & bl	.80	.80
137	A2	25c blue & grn	.80	.80
a.		Triple overprint	550.00	700.00
138	A2	30c scarlet & grn	1.25	.80
a.		Double overprint	400.00	575.00
139	A2	35c vio brn & bl	.80	.80
140	A2	40c dull grn & brn	2.40	1.60
141	A2	45c violet & red	2.40	1.60
142	A2	50c blue grn & red	2.40	1.60
143	A2	75c brown & blue	2.40	1.60
144	A3	1fr dp grn & vio	2.00	1.60
145	A3	2fr vio & gray grn	8.00	6.75
146	A3	5fr blue & rose	13.50	11.00
		Nos. 130-146 (17)	42.00	32.60

Nos. 130-146 exist on ordinary paper and, with the exception of No. 135, on chalk surfaced paper. Nos. 137-146 are known with inverted 'S' in 'Francaise' and without period after 'Francaise.' See the *Scott Classic Specialized Catalogue of Stamps & Covers* for detailed listings.

On Nos. 137-146 there is 7mm between "Cameroun" and "Occupation."

Provisional French Mandate

Types of Middle Congo, 1907, Overprinted **CAMEROUN**

1921

147	A1	1c ol grn & org	.35	.30
148	A1	2c brown & rose	.35	.30
149	A1	4c gray & lt grn	.55	.55
150	A1	5c dl red & org	.55	.55
a.		Double overprint	1,200.	
151	A1	10c bl grn & lt grn	1.25	.90
152	A1	15c blue & org	.55	.55
153	A1	20c red brn & ol	.80	.80
154	A2	25c slate & org	1.20	.80
155	A2	30c rose & ver	1.25	.80
156	A2	35c gray & ultra	.80	.80
157	A2	40c brown & rose	.80	.80
158	A2	45c brown & rose	.80	.80
159	A2	50c blue & ultra	1.25	.80
160	A2	75c red brn & lt grn	1.25	.80
161	A3	1fr slate & org	2.40	2.40
162	A3	2fr ol grn & rose	6.50	5.50
163	A3	5fr dull red & gray	9.50	8.00
		Nos. 147-163 (17)	30.60	25.45

The 1c, 2c, 4c, 15c, 20c, 25c and 50c exist with overprint omitted. For listings, see the *Scott Specialized Catalogue of Stamps & Covers.*

Nos. 152, 162, 163, 158, 160 Surcharged with New Value and Bars

1924-25

164	A1	25c on 15c bl & org ('25)	1.25	1.25
165	A3	25c on 2fr ol grn & rose	1.25	1.60
166	A3	25c on 5fr red & gray	1.25	1.60
a.		Pair, one without new value and bars	2.00	2.00
167	A2	65c on 45c brn & rose ('25)	2.00	2.00
168	A2	85c on 75c red brn & lt grn ('25)	2.40	2.40
		Nos. 164-168 (5)	8.15	8.85

French Mandate

Herder and Cattle Crossing Sanaga River — A5

Tapping Rubber Tree — A6

Rope Suspension Bridge — A7

1925-38   Typo.   Perf. 14x13½

170	A5	1c ol grn & brn vio, *lav*	.25	.25
171	A5	2c rose & grn, *grnsh*	.25	.25
172	A5	4c blue & blk	.25	.25
173	A5	5c org & red vio, *lav*	.25	.25
174	A5	10c red brn & org, *yel*	.45	.40
175	A5	15c sl grn & grn	.45	.40
176	A5	15c lilac & red ('27)	1.00	.80

Perf. 13½x14

177	A6	20c ol brn & red brn	.70	.40
178	A6	20c green ('26)	.65	.50
179	A6	20c brn red & ol brn ('27)	.65	.65
180	A6	25c lt green & blk	.95	.50
181	A6	30c bluish grn & ver	.50	.30
182	A6	30c dk grn & grn ('27)	.90	.65
183	A6	35c brown & black	1.10	.50
184	A6	35c dl grn & grn ('38)	1.90	1.20
185	A6	40c orange & vio	2.00	1.20
186	A6	45c dp rose & cer	.80	.50
187	A6	45c vio & org brn ('27)	2.25	1.60
188	A6	50c lt green & cer	.80	.30
189	A6	55c ultra & car ('38)	1.60	1.60
190	A6	60c red vio & blk	.80	.55
191	A6	60c brown red ('26)	.95	.55
192	A6	65c indigo & brn	1.20	1.20
193	A6	75c indigo & dp bl	.80	.80
194	A6	75c grn brn & red vio ('27)	1.40	1.10
195	A6	80c carmine & brn ('38)	1.40	1.20
196	A6	85c dp rose & bl	1.60	1.20
197	A6	90c brn red & cer ('27)	2.75	1.20

Perf. 14x13½

198	A7	1fr indigo & brn	1.20	1.20
199	A7	1fr dull bl	.80	.55
200	A7	1fr ol brn & red vio ('27)	1.10	.80
201	A7	1fr grn & dk brn ('29)	2.40	1.20
202	A7	1.10fr rose red & dk brn ('28)	4.75	*6.50*
203	A7	1.25fr gray & dp bl ('33)	4.75	3.50
204	A7	1.50fr dull bl ('27)	1.20	.80
205	A7	1.75fr brn & org ('33)	1.60	1.20
206	A7	1.75fr dk bl & lt bl ('38)	2.40	1.60
207	A7	2fr dl grn & brn org	2.00	1.20
208	A7	3fr ol brn & red vio ('27)	8.00	2.75
209	A7	5fr brn & blk, *bluish*	3.50	2.00
a.		Cliché of 2fr in plate of 5fr	1,450.	
b.		As "a," in pair with #209	1,700.	
210	A7	10fr org & vio ('27)	14.50	7.25
211	A7	20fr rose & ol grn ('27)	21.00	15.00
		Nos. 170-211 (42)	97.80	65.85

Shades exist for several values.
For overprints and surcharge see Nos. 212, 264, 276, 278, 279, B7-B9, B21.

No. 199 Surcharged with New Value and Bars in Red

1926

212	A7	1.25fr on 1fr dull blue	1.20	.80

Common Design Types pictured following the introduction.

Colonial Exposition Issue
Common Design Types
Name of Country in Black

1931   Engr.   Perf. 12½

213	CD70	40c deep green	5.50	4.00
214	CD71	50c violet	5.50	4.75
215	CD72	90c red orange	5.50	4.75
216	CD73	1.50fr dull blue	6.50	4.75
		Nos. 213-216 (4)	23.00	18.25

Paris International Exposition Issue
Common Design Types

1937   Perf. 13

217	CD74	20c deep violet	1.75	1.75
218	CD75	30c dark green	1.75	1.75
219	CD76	40c car rose	1.75	1.75
220	CD77	50c dark brown	1.75	1.75
221	CD78	90c red	1.90	1.90
222	CD79	1.50fr ultramarine	1.90	1.90
		Nos. 217-222 (6)	10.80	10.80

French Colonial Art Exhibition
Common Design Type
Souvenir Sheet

1937   Imperf.

222A	CD77	3fr org red & blk	8.00	*9.50*

New York World's Fair Issue
Common Design Type

1939   Perf. 12½x12

223	CD82	1.25fr carmine lake	1.40	1.20
224	CD82	2.25fr ultra	1.40	1.20

For overprints and surcharges see Nos. 280-281, B14-B17, B23, B25.

Mandara Woman — A19   Falls on M'bam River near Banyo — A20

Elephants A21

Man in Yaré — A22

1939-40   Engr.   Perf. 13

225	A19	2c black brn	.25	.25
226	A19	3c magenta ('40)	.25	.25
227	A19	4c deep ultra	.25	.25
228	A19	5c red brown	.25	.25
229	A19	10c dp bl grn	.25	.25
230	A19	15c rose red	.30	.30
231	A19	20c plum	.30	.30
232	A20	25c black brn	.65	.65
233	A20	30c dk red	.80	.70
234	A20	40c ultra ('40)	.80	.80
235	A20	45c sl grn ('40)	2.60	2.25
236	A20	50c brown car	.90	.70
237	A20	60c pck blue ('40)	.75	.65
238	A20	70c plum ('40)	3.25	2.90
239	A21	80c Prus blue	2.60	2.10
240	A21	90c Prus blue	.95	.75
241	A21	1fr car rose	1.90	.95
242	A21	1fr choc ('40)	1.40	.80
243	A21	1.25fr car rose	4.00	3.25
244	A21	1.40fr red rose ('40)	1.25	.95
245	A21	1.50fr chocolate	1.20	.95
246	A21	1.60fr black brn ('40)	2.50	2.25
247	A21	1.75fr dk blue	1.40	.95
248	A21	2fr dk green	.90	.90
249	A21	2.25fr dk blue	1.40	.90
250	A21	2.50fr brt red vio ('40)	1.20	1.00
251	A21	3fr dk violet	1.40	.80
252	A22	5fr black brn	1.40	.95
253	A22	10fr brt red vio	2.00	1.60
254	A22	20fr dk green	4.00	3.25
		Nos. 225-254 (30)	41.10	32.85

For overprints and surcharges see Nos. 255-263, 265-275, 277, 278A, 279A, B10-B13, B22, B24.

Stamps of 1925-40 Overprinted in Black or Orange

1940   Perf. 14x13½, 13½x14, 13

255	A19	2c blk brn (O)	1.60	1.60
256	A19	3c magenta	2.40	2.40
257	A19	4c dp ultra (O)	1.60	1.60
258	A19	5c red brn	5.50	5.50
259	A19	10c dp bl grn (O)	1.60	1.60
260	A19	15c rose red	2.40	2.40
260A	A19	20c plum (O)	13.50	13.50

261	A20	25c blk brn	1.60	1.60
261A	A20	30c dk red	14.50	14.50
262	A20	40c ultra	5.50	5.50
263	A20	45c slate green	4.00	4.00
264	A6	50c lt grn & cer	2.40	1.60
a.		Inverted overprint	225.00	
265	A20	60c pck bl	6.50	6.50
266	A20	70c plum	3.25	3.25
267	A21	80c Prus bl (O)	5.50	5.50
268	A21	90c Prus bl (O)	1.60	1.60
269	A21	1.25fr car rose	1.60	1.60
270	A21	1.40fr org red	4.75	4.75
271	A21	1.50fr chocolate	1.60	1.60
272	A21	1.60fr blk brn (O)	3.25	3.25
273	A21	1.75fr dk bl (O)	2.40	2.40
274	A21	2.25fr dk bl (O)	1.60	1.60
275	A21	2.50fr brt red vio	1.60	1.60
276	A7	5fr brn & blk, *bluish*	24.00	24.00
277	A22	5fr black brn	24.00	16.00
278	A7	10fr org & vio	32.50	32.50
278A	A22	10fr brt red vio	65.00	45.00
279	A7	20fr rose & ol grn	55.00	55.00
279A	A22	20fr dk green	190.00	190.00

Same Overprint on Stamps of 1939
Perf. 12½x12

280	CD82	1.25fr car lake	12.00	12.00
281	CD82	2.25fr ultra	12.00	12.00
		Nos. 255-281 (31)	504.75	475.95

Issued to note Cameroun's affiliation with General de Gaulle's "Free France" movement. Numerous overprint varieties exist.

Cattle Fording Sanaga River and Marshal Petain A22a

1941   Engr.   Perf. 12½x12

281A	A22a	1fr green		.40
281B	A22a	2.50fr dark blue		.40
		Set, never hinged		1.60

Nos. 281A-281B were issued by the Vichy government in France, but were not placed on sale in Cameroun.
For surcharges, see Nos. B25A-B25B.

Lorraine Cross and Joan of Arc Shield — A23

1941   Photo.   Perf. 14x14½

282	A23	5c brown	.25	.25
283	A23	10c dk blue	.25	.25
284	A23	25c emerald	.25	.25
285	A23	30c dp orange	.25	.25
286	A23	40c dk slate green	.25	.25
287	A23	50c red brown	.50	.25
288	A23	1fr dp red lilac	.50	.50
289	A23	1.50fr brt red	.50	.50
290	A23	2fr gray black	.75	.50
291	A23	2.50fr brt ultra	.80	.50
292	A23	4fr dull violet	.90	.75
293	A23	5fr bister	.95	.90
294	A23	10fr dp brown	.95	.90
295	A23	20fr dp green	1.90	1.40
		Nos. 282-295 (14)	9.00	7.45

For surcharges see Nos. 297A-303.

> **Catalogue values for unused stamps in this section, from this point to the end of the section, are for Never Hinged items.**

Eboue Issue
Common Design Type

1945   Unwmk.   Engr.   Perf. 13

296	CD91	2fr black	.80	.55
297	CD91	25fr Prus green	1.60	1.40

Nos. 282, 284, 291 Surcharged with New Values and Bars in Red, Carmine or Black

1946   Perf. 14x14½

297A	A23	50c on 5c (R)	.65	.50
298	A23	60c on 5c (R)	.75	.55
a.		Inverted surcharge	200.00	
299	A23	70c on 5c (R)	1.00	.75
300	A23	1.20fr on 5c (C)	1.00	.75
301	A23	2.40fr on 25c	.95	.75

302	A23	3fr on 25c	1.40	1.00
302A	A23	4.50fr on 25c	1.90	1.40
303	A23	15fr on 2.50fr (C)	2.00	1.50
		Nos. 297A-303 (8)	9.65	7.20

Zebu and Herder A25

Tikar Women — A26

Porters Carrying Bananas — A27

Bowman A28

Lamido Horsemen A29

Farmer — A30

1946		Engr.	Perf. 12½x12, 12x12½	
304	A25	10c blue grn	.50	.30
305	A25	30c brown org	.50	.30
306	A25	40c brt ultra	.50	.30
307	A26	50c olive brn	.50	.30
308	A26	60c dp plum	.65	.30
309	A26	80c chnt brn	.80	.50
310	A27	1fr org red	.50	.25
311	A27	1.20fr dp green	.90	.50
312	A27	1.50fr dk car	2.25	1.40
313	A28	2fr black	.50	.25
314	A28	3fr dk carmine	.65	.30
314A	A28	3.60fr red brn	1.60	1.10
315	A28	4fr dp blue	.90	.40
316	A29	5fr brown car	1.00	.65
317	A29	6fr ultra	1.00	.55
318	A29	10fr slate green	1.75	.50
319	A30	15fr grnsh blue	2.40	.90
320	A30	20fr dk green	3.25	.90
321	A30	25fr black	3.25	1.40
		Nos. 304-321 (19)	23.40	11.10

Shades exist for most values.
For surcharges see Nos. 343-344, 346.

Imperforates
Most Cameroun stamps from 1952 onward exist imperforate in issued and trial colors, and also in small presentation sheets in issued colors.

Military Medal Issue
Common Design Type
Engraved and Typographed

1952		Unwmk.	Perf. 13	
322	CD101	15fr multicolored	7.25	3.25

Porters Carrying Bananas — A32

Picking Coffee Beans — A33

1954			Engr.	
323	A32	8fr red vio, org brn & vio bl	1.20	.80
324	A32	15fr brn red, yel & blk brn	1.60	.80
325	A33	40fr blk brn, org brn & lil rose	2.00	.80
		Nos. 323-325 (3)	4.80	2.40

FIDES Issue
Common Design Type

Designs: 5fr, Plowmen. 15fr, Wouri bridge. 20fr, Technical instruction. 25fr, Mobile medical station.

1956		Unwmk.	Perf. 13	
326	CD103	5fr org brn & dk brn	1.20	.50
327	CD103	15fr aqua, slate & blk	1.60	.80
328	CD103	20fr grnsh bl & dp ultra	1.60	.80
329	CD103	25fr dp ultra	2.50	1.10
		Nos. 326-329 (4)	6.90	3.20

For surcharges see Nos. 345, 347.

Coffee Issue

Coffee A35

1956		Engr.	Perf. 13	
330	A35	15fr car & brt red	1.60	.80

For surcharge see No. 348.

Autonomous Government

Flag and Woman Holding Child A36

1958				
331	A36	20fr multicolored	1.60	.80

Anniv. of the installation of the 1st autonomous government of Cameroun.

Men Looking to the Sun — A37

1958				
332	A37	20fr sepia & brn red	1.60	.80

10th anniv. of the signing of the Universal Declaration of Human Rights.

Flower Issue
Common Design Type

Design: 20fr, Randia malleifera.

1959		Photo.	Perf. 12½x12	
333	CD104	20fr dp grn, yel & rose	1.60	.80

Loading Bananas A38

Harvesting Bananas — A39

1959		Engr.	Perf. 13	
334	A38	20fr dk grn & org	1.20	.40
335	A39	25fr maroon & slate grn	1.60	.80

For surcharge see No. 349.

Independent State

Map and Flag of Cameroun — A40

Prime Minister Ahmadou Ahidjo — A41

1960		Unwmk.	Engr.	Perf. 13
336	A40	20fr multicolored		.80 .25
337	A41	25fr blk, grn & pale lem		.85 .25

Declaration of independence, Jan. 1, 1960.
For surcharge see No. 350.

Uprooted Oak Emblem A42

1960				
338	A42	30fr red brn, ultra & yel grn	1.10	.45

World Refugee Year, 7/1/59-6/30/60.
For surcharge see No. 351.

C.C.T.A. Issue
Common Design Type

1960				
339	CD106	50fr dull claret & slate	1.60	.75

UN Headquarters, NYC, and Flag — A43

1961, May 20			Perf. 13	

Flag in Green, Red and Yellow

340	A43	15fr grn, dk bl & brn	.60	.30
341	A43	25fr dk blue & grn	.75	.30
342	A43	85fr red, dk bl & vio brn	2.40	1.20
		Nos. 340-342 (3)	3.75	1.80

Cameroun's admission to the UN, Sept. 20, 1960.

Federal Republic

Stamps of 1946-60 Surcharged in Red or Black

Type I

Type II

Two types of 2sh6p:
I — Large figures. "2/6" measures 8x3¾mm.
II — Small figures. "2/6" measures 6x2½mm.

	Perf. 12x12½, 13			
1961, Oct. 1			Engr.	
343	A27	½p on 1fr (#310)	.35	.25
344	A28	1p on 2fr (#313)	.45	.30
345	CD103	1½p on 5fr (#326)	.55	.35
346	A29	2p on 10fr (#318)	1.00	.45
347	CD103	3p on 15fr (#327)	1.40	.60
348	A35	4p on 15fr (Bk) (#330)	1.10	.70
349	A38	6p on 20fr (#334)	2.40	1.00
350	A41	1sh on 25fr (#337)	2.75	1.50
351	A42	2sh6p on 30fr (#338) (I)	5.00	5.00
a.		Type II	21.00	21.00
		Nos. 343-351 (9)	15.00	10.15

Issued for use in the former United Kingdom Trust Territory of Southern Cameroons.
The "Republique Federale" overprint is in one line on Nos. 345, 347-349, in two vertical lines on No. 350. See Nos. C38-C40.

President Ahidjo and Prime Minister Foncha A45

1962, Jan. 1		Unwmk.		
		Engr.	Perf. 13	
352	A45	20fr vio & choc	8.00	7.00
353	A45	25fr dk grn & brn	14.00	11.00
354	A45	60fr car & dl grn	40.00	32.50
		Nos. 352-354 (3)	62.00	50.50

Surcharged for Use in Southern Cameroons

355	A45	3p on 20fr	175.00	160.00
356	A45	6p on 25fr	175.00	160.00
357	A45	2sh6p on 60fr	175.00	160.00
		Nos. 355-357 (3)	525.00	480.00

Reunification of the former French and British Sections of Cameroun. It is reported that Nos. 352-357 were withdrawn after a few days and destroyed.

Mustache
Monkey
A46

Designs: 1fr, 4fr, Elephant, Ntem Falls.
1.50fr, 3fr, Buffon's kob, Dschang. 2fr, 5fr, Hippopotamus. 6fr, 15fr, Mustache monkey. 8fr,
30fr, Manatee, Lake Ossa. 10fr, 25fr, Buffalo,
Batouri. 20fr, 40fr, Giraffes, Waza Reservation, vert.

1962	Unwmk.	Engr.	Perf. 12	
358 A46	50c brn, brt grn & bl		.25	.25
359 A46	1fr gray brn, bl grn & org		.25	.25
360 A46	1.50fr brn, lt grn & sl grn		.25	.25
361 A46	2fr dk gray, grnsh bl & grn		.25	.25
362 A46	3fr brn, org & lil rose		.25	.25
363 A46	4fr brn, yel grn & bl grn		.25	.25
364 A46	5fr gray brn, grn & sal		.25	.25
365 A46	6fr brn, yel & bl		.45	.25
366 A46	8fr dk bl, red & grn		.90	.50
367 A46	10fr ol blk, org & brt bl		.75	.25
368 A46	15fr brn, Prus bl & bl		1.00	.40
369 A46	20fr brn & gray		1.25	.40
370 A46	25fr red brn, grn & yel		3.25	1.00
371 A46	30fr blk, org & bl		4.50	1.10
372 A46	40fr dp cl, yel grn & blk		7.50	1.50
Nos. 358-372 (15)			21.35	7.15

See Nos. 396-397.

African and Malagasy Union Issue
Common Design Type

1962, Sept. 8   Perf. 12½x12
373 CD110 30fr multicolored   2.00 .75

Village and
Map of
Cameroun
A48

Designs: 20fr, 25fr, Sun rising over city.
50fr, Hands holding scroll.

1962, Oct. 1   Engr.   Perf. 13
374 A48	9fr pur, olive & dk brn	.40	.25
375 A48	18fr grn, org brn & dk bl	.50	.25
376 A48	20fr lil rose, ol bis & ind	.50	.25
377 A48	25fr bl, red org & sep	.60	.25
378 A48	50fr dk red, sepia & bl	1.75	.50
Nos. 374-378 (5)		3.75	1.50

1st anniv. of the reunification of Cameroun.

"School under the
Trees" — A49

1962, Nov. 5   Photo.   Perf. 12½x12½
379 A49 20fr ver, emerald & yel   1.00 .35
Literacy and popular education campaign.

Telstar and
Globe
A50

High Frequency
Transmission
Station, Mt.
Bankolo — A51

1963, Feb. 9   Engr.   Perf. 13
Size: 36x22mm
380 A50	1fr dk bl, olive & pur	.25	.25
381 A50	2fr dk bl, claret & grn	.25	.25
382 A50	3fr dk grn, ol & dp cl	.25	.25
383 A50	25fr grn, dp cl & brt bl	.75	.40
Nos. 380-383,C45 (5)		4.00	1.80

1st TV connection of the US and Europe
through the Telstar satellite, July 11-12, 1962.

1963, May 18   Photo.   Perf. 12x12½
384 A51	15fr multicolored	.45	.25
385 A51	20fr multicolored	.60	.25
Nos. 384-385,C46 (3)		3.55	1.15

Issued to publicize the high frequency telegraph connection Douala-Yaounde.

"Yaoundé-Regional Center of Textbook
Production" — A52

1963, Aug. 10   Unwmk.   Perf. 12½
386 A52	20fr emer, blk & red	.45	.25
387 A52	25fr org, blk & red	.60	.25
388 A52	100fr gold, blk & red	2.10	.60
Nos. 386-388 (3)		3.10	1.10

UNESCO regional center for the production
of school books at Yaounde.

Pres. Ahmadou
Ahidjo and
Flag — A53

Design: 18fr, Flag and map of Cameroun.

1963, Oct. 1   Perf. 12x12½
Flag in Green, Red and Yellow
389 A53	9fr grn, bl & dk brn	.45	.25
390 A53	18fr grn, bl & lil	.65	.25
391 A53	20fr grn, blk & yel grn	.70	.25
Nos. 389-391 (3)		1.80	.75

Second anniversary of reunification.

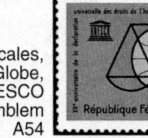

Scales,
Globe,
UNESCO
Emblem
A54

1963, Dec. 10   Photo.   Perf. 12½x12
392 A54	9fr ultra, blk & sal	.40	.25
393 A54	18fr brt yel grn, blk & rose red	.50	.25
394 A54	25fr rose red, blk & brt yel grn	.70	.25
395 A54	75fr yel, blk & ultra	2.00	.50
Nos. 392-395 (4)		3.60	1.25

Universal Declaration of Human Rights,
15th anniv.

Animal Type of 1962
Design: 10fr, 25fr, Lion, Waza National
Park, North Cameroun.

1964, June 20   Engr.   Perf. 13
396 A46	10fr red brn, bis & grn	1.25	.40
397 A46	25fr green & bister	3.00	1.25

Soccer
Game in
Stadium
A55

18fr, Pile of sports equipment. 30fr, Stadium
(outside), flags and map of Africa.

1964, July 11   Engr.   Perf. 13
398 A55	10fr grn, bl & red brn	.50	.25
399 A55	18fr car, grn & vio	.60	.35
400 A55	30fr blk, dk bl & org brn	1.00	.50
Nos. 398-400 (3)		2.10	1.10

Tropics Cup Games, Yaounde, July 11-19.

Europafrica Issue
Common Design Type and

Palace of Justice, Yaounde — A56

40fr, Emblems of Science, Agriculture,
Industry and Education and two sunbursts.

1964, July 20   Photo.   Perf. 12x13
401 A56	15fr multicolored	1.25	.25
402 CD116	40fr multicolored	2.25	.60

1st anniv. of the economic agreement
between the European Economic Community
and the African and Malgache Union.

Hurdling and Olympic Flame — A57

Design: 10fr, Runners, vert.

1964, Oct. 10   Engr.   Perf. 13
403 A57	9fr red, yel grn & blk	1.50	.40
404 A57	10fr red, vio & ol gray	2.25	.40
Nos. 403-404,C49 (3)		11.25	2.80

18th Olympic Games, Tokyo, Oct. 10-25.

Bamileke Dance
Dress — A58

Ntem Falls,
Ebolowa
Region — A59

Designs: 18fr, Dance mask, Bamenda
region. 25fr, Fulani horseman, North Cameroun, horiz.

1964   Unwmk.   Perf. 13
405 A58	9fr red, yel grn & bl	.55	.25
406 A58	18fr bl, red & brn	.70	.25
407 A59	20fr dk car, grn & ol	.90	.25
408 A58	25fr dk brn, org & car	1.40	.25
Nos. 405-408,C50 (5)		4.55	1.35

Cooperation Issue
Common Design Type

1964, Nov. 7   Engr.
409 CD119	18fr dk bl, yel grn & dk brn	1.00	.25
410 CD119	30fr red brn, bl grn & dk brn	1.50	.25

Memorial
Stone — A60

1965, Jan. 1   Engr.   Perf. 13
411 A60 12fr bl, indigo & grn   1.00 .25

Diesel Train
A61

Typo.   Perf. 14x13
412 A61 20fr rose car, yel & grn   2.50 .25

Laying of the 1st rail of the Mbanga-Kumba
Railroad, Mar. 28, 1964.

Red Cross
Station and
Ambulance
A62

50fr, Red Cross nurse and infant, vert.

1965, May 8   Engr.   Perf. 13
413 A62	25fr car, slate grn & ocher	.95	.25
414 A62	50fr gray, red & red brn	2.25	.30

Issued for the Cameroun Red Cross.

Coins Inserted in
Map of Cameroun,
and
Bankbook — A63

Savings Bank Building — A64

Design: 20fr, Bankbook and coins inserted
in cacao pod-shaped bank, vert.

1965, June 10   Size: 22x37mm
415 A63 9fr grn, red & org   .45 .25

Size: 48x27mm, 27x48mm
416 A64	15fr choc, ultra & grn	.55	.25
417 A63	20fr ocher, brt grn & brn	.65	.25
Nos. 415-417 (3)		1.65	.75

Federal Postal Savings Banks.

Soccer Players and Africa Cup — A65

Unwmk.

1965, June 26   Engr.   Perf. 13
418 A65   9fr car, brn & yel   .55   .25
419 A65   20fr car, slate bl & yel   1.40   .25

Cameroun Oryx Club, winner of the club champions' Africa Cup, February 1965.

Symbolic Map of Europe and Africa — A66

40fr, Delegates around conference table.

1965, July 20   Photo.   Perf. 12x12½
420 A66   5fr car, blk & lilac   .30   .25
421 A66   40fr brn, buff, grn & ul-
          tra   1.50   .35

2nd, anniv. of the economic agreement between the European Economic Community and the African and Malgache Union.

UPU Monument, Bern A67

1965, July 26   Engr.   Perf. 13
422 A67   30fr black & red   .80   .25

Cameroun's admission to the UPU, 5th anniv.

ICY Emblem — A68

1965, Sept. 11   Unwmk.   Perf. 13
423 A68   10fr dk bl & car rose   .45   .25

Issued for the International Cooperation Year, 1964-65. See No. C57.

Pres. Ahidjo and Government House — A69

Design: 9fr, 20fr, Pres. Ahidjo and Government House, vert.

Perf. 12x12½, 12½x12
1965, Oct. 1   Photo.   Unwmk.
424 A69   9fr multicolored   .25   .25
425 A69   18fr multicolored   .55   .25
426 A69   20fr multicolored   .65   .25
427 A69   25fr multicolored   .80   .25
          Nos. 424-427 (4)   2.25 1.00

Reelection of Pres. Ahmadou Ahidjo.

National Tourist Office, Yaoundé A70

Designs: 9fr, Pouss Musgum houses. 18fr, Great Calao's dance (North Cameroon). 20fr, Gate of Sultan's Palace, Foumban, vert.

1965   Engr.   Perf. 13
428 A70   9fr brn, rose red & grn   .45   .25
429 A70   18fr brt bl, brn & grn   .65   .25
430 A70   20fr bl, brn & choc   1.00   .25
431 A70   25fr mar, emer & gray   .90   .25
          Nos. 428-431 (4)   3.00 1.00

See No. C58.

Mountain Hotel, Buea — A71

Designs: 20fr, Hotel of the Deputies, Yaoundé. 35fr, Dschang Health Center.

1966
432 A71   9fr sl grn, rose cl &
          brn   .35   .25
433 A71   20fr brt bl, sl grn & blk .45   .25
434 A71   35fr brn, sl grn & car   .80   .30
          Nos. 432-434,C63-C69 (10) 15.10 4.90

Bas-relief, Foumban A72

Designs: 18fr, Ekoi mask, vert. 20fr, Mother and child, carving, Bamiléké, vert. 25fr, Ceremonial stool, Bamoun.

1966, Apr. 15   Unwmk.
435 A72   9fr red & blk   .60   .25
436 A72   18fr brt grn, org brn &
          choc   .75   .25
437 A72   20fr brt bl, red brn & pur 1.15 .25
438 A72   25fr pur & dk brn   1.25   .25
          Nos. 435-438 (4)   3.75 1.00

Intl. Negro Arts Festival, Dakar, Senegal, 4/1-24.

New WHO Headquarters, Geneva — A73

1966, May 3   Photo.   Perf. 12½x13
439 A73   50fr ultra, red brn & yel .75   .50

ITU Headquarters, Geneva — A74

1966, May 3   Photo.   Perf. 12½x13
440 A74   50fr ultra & yellow   1.25   .50

Phaeomeria Magnifica — A75

Flowers: 18fr, Hibiscus (rose of China). 20fr, Mountain rose.

1966, May 20   Perf. 12x12½
Flowers in Natural Colors
Size: 22x36mm
441 A75   9fr red brown   .55   .25
442 A75   18fr green   .70   .25
443 A75   20fr dark green   .70   .25
          Nos. 441-443,C70-C72 (6) 7.55 1.50

See No. 469.

"6" and Men Dancing around UN Emblem — A76

Design: 50fr, UN General Assembly, horiz.

1966, Sept. 20   Engr.   Perf. 13
444 A76   50fr ultra, grn & vio brn .90   .25
445 A76   100fr red brn, grn & ul-
          tra   2.00   .50

6th anniv. of Cameroun's admission to the UN.

Prime Minister's Residence, Buea — A77

Designs (Prime Minister's Residences): 18fr, at Yaoundé, front view. 20fr, at Yaoundé, side view. 25fr, at Buea, front view.

1966, Oct. 1   Photo.
446 A77   9fr multicolored   .45   .25
447 A77   18fr multicolored   .65   .25
448 A77   20fr multicolored   .60   .35
449 A77   25fr multicolored   .80   .35
          Nos. 446-449 (4)   2.50 1.20

5th anniversary of re-unification.

Learning to Write and UNESCO Emblem A78

No. 451, Children's heads & UNICEF emblem.

1966, Nov. 24   Engr.   Perf. 13
450 A78   50fr red lil, bl & brn   1.40   .30
451 A78   50fr red lil, blk & brt bl 1.40 .30

20th anniv. of UNESCO, 20th anniv. of UNICEF.

Independence Proclamation — A79

1967, Jan. 1   Engr.   Perf. 13
452 A79   20fr grn, red & yel   2.25   .60

7th anniversary of independence.

Map of Africa and Madagascar, Railroad Tracks and Symbols — A80

25fr, Map of Africa and Madagascar and train.

1967, Feb. 21   Photo.   Perf. 13
453 A80   20fr multicolored   3.50 1.50
454 A80   25fr multicolored   5.00 2.00

5th Conf. of African and Madagascan Railroad Technicians.

Lions Emblem and Forest — A81

Design: 100fr, Lions emblem and palms.

1967, Mar. 3
455 A81   50fr multicolored   .90   .35
456 A81   100fr multicolored   2.10   .65

Lions International, 50th anniversary.

Jet and I.C.A.O. Emblem — A82

Dove and I.A.E.A. Emblem A83

Perf. 13x12½, 12½x13
1967, Mar. 15   Photo.
457 A82   50fr ultra, lt bl, brn & gold 1.40 .35
458 A83   50fr ultra & emer   1.40   .35

UN agencies: No. 457, the ICAO; No. 458, the Intl. Atomic Energy Agency.

Rotary International Emblem — A84

1967, Apr. 17   Photo.   Perf. 12½
459 A84 25fr crim, vio bl & gold   1.25 .25

10th anniversary of the Douala, Cameroun, branch of Rotary International.

Grapefruit — A85

1967, May 10   Photo.   Perf. 12x12½
460 A85 1fr shown   .25 .25
461 A85 2fr Papaya   .25 .25
462 A85 3fr Custard apple .25 .25
463 A85 4fr Breadfruit   .25 .25
464 A85 5fr Coconut   .35 .25
465 A85 6fr Mango   .45 .25
466 A85 8fr Avacado   .90 .25
467 A85 10fr Pineapple   1.40 .25
468 A85 30fr Bananas   3.50 .25
        Nos. 460-468 (9)   7.60 2.25

For surcharges see Nos. 550, 593.

Bird of Paradise Flower — A86

1967, June 22 Photo. Perf. 12x12½
Size: 22x36mm
469 A86 15fr lt blue & multi   .90 .25

Sanaga Falls and ITY Emblem — A87

1967, Aug. 14 Photo. Perf. 13x12½
470 A87 30fr multicolored   .85 .25

Issued for International Tourist Year 1967.

Art of Cameroun: Coconut Harvest A88

Carved Bas-relief: 20fr, Lion hunt. 30fr, Women carrying baskets. 100fr, Carved chest.

1967, Sept. 22   Perf. 12½x13
471 A88 10fr brn, bl & car   .35 .25
472 A88 20fr brn, yel & grn   .55 .25
473 A88 30fr emer, brn & car .90 .25

474 A88 100fr red org, brn & emer   2.25 .40
        Nos. 471-474 (4)   4.05 1.15

Coat of Arms A89

1968, Jan. 1   Litho.   Perf. 12½x13
475 A89 30fr gold & multi   1.00 .25

Spiny Lobster A90

Designs (Fish and Crustaceans): 10fr, River crayfish. 15fr, Nile mouth-breeder. 20fr, Sole. 25fr, Common pike. 30fr, Crab. 40fr, Spadefish, vert. 50fr, Shrimp, vert. 55fr, African snakehead. 60fr, Threadfin.

1968, July 25   Engr.   Perf. 13
476 A90 5fr brn, vio bl & dl grn   .30 .25
477 A90 10fr ultra, brn ol & slate   .30 .25
478 A90 15fr sal, red lil & sepia   .85 .25
479 A90 20fr red brn, dp bl & sep   1.00 .25
480 A90 25fr lt brn, emer & slate   1.10 .25
481 A90 30fr mag, dk bl & dk brn   1.50 .25
482 A90 40fr slate bl & org   2.25 .25
483 A90 50fr emer, gray & rose car   3.00 .25
484 A90 55fr lt brn, Prus bl & dk brn   4.50 .25
485 A90 60fr brn, bl grn & indigo   6.75 .35
        Nos. 476-485 (10)   21.55 2.60

Tanker, Refinery and Map of Area Served — A91

1968, July 30   Photo.   Perf. 12½
486 A91 30fr multicolored   1.60 .25

Port Gentil (Gabon) Refinery opening, 6/12/68.

Human Rights Flame A92

1968, Sept. 14   Photo.   Perf. 12½x13
487 A92 15fr blue & salmon   .65 .25

Intl. Human Rights Year. See No. C110.

Pres. Ahmadou Ahidjo A93

1969, Apr. 10   Photo.   Perf. 12½x12
488 A93 30fr carmine & multi   .80 .25

Chocolate Vat — A94

Designs: 30fr, Chocolate factory. 50fr, Candy making, vert.

1969, Apr. 24   Engr.   Perf. 13
489 A94 15fr red brn, ind & choc   .50 .25
490 A94 30fr grn, blk & red brn   .80 .25
491 A94 50fr brown & multi   1.10 .25
        Nos. 489-491 (3)   2.40 .75

Cameroun chocolate industry.

Fertility Symbol, Abbia — A95

Art and Folklore from Abbia: 10fr, Two toucans, horiz. 15fr, Forest symbol. 30fr, Vulture attacking monkey, horiz. 70fr, Oliphant player.

1969, May 30   Engr.   Perf. 13
492 A95 5fr ultra, Prus bl & brt rose lil   .25 .25
493 A95 10fr bl, ol gray & org   .35 .25
494 A95 15fr ultra, dk red & blk   .50 .25
495 A95 30fr brt bl, lem & grn   .90 .25
496 A95 70fr brt bl, dk grn & ver   1.90 .50
        Nos. 492-496 (5)   3.90 1.50

Diesel Train on Bridge — A96

Design: 30fr, Kumba Railroad station, horiz.

Perf. 12½x13, 13x12½
1969, July 11   Photo.
497 A96 30fr blue & multi   1.25 .30
498 A96 50fr black & multi   3.25 .60

Opening of Mbanga-Kumba Railroad.

Development Bank Issue
Common Design Type

1969, Sept. 10   Engr.   Perf. 13
499 CD130 30fr vio bl, grn & ocher   .80 .25

African Development Bank, 5th anniv.

ASECNA Issue
Common Design Type

1969, Dec. 12   Engr.   Perf. 13
500 CD132 100fr slate green   2.00 .60

Red Sage — A99

Design: 30fr, Passionflower.

1970, Mar. 24 Photo. Perf. 12x12½
Size: 22x36½mm
501 A99 15fr yel grn & multi   .45 .25
502 A99 30fr multicolored   1.00 .25
        Nos. 501-502,C140-C141 (4) 5.60 1.75

UPU Headquarters Issue
Common Design Type

1970, May 20   Engr.   Perf. 13
503 CD133 30fr blue, pur & grn   1.00 .25
504 CD133 50fr gray, red & bl   1.60 .30

Brewery A100

Design: 30fr, Cellar with barrels.

1970, July 9   Engr.   Perf. 13
505 A100 15fr brn, gray & dk grn   .50 .25
506 A100 30fr bl grn, dk brn & brn red   1.00 .30

Cameroun brewing industry.

Ozila Dancers — A101

Design: 50fr, Ozila dancer and drummer.

1970, Oct. 19   Engr.   Perf. 13
507 A101 30fr multicolored   1.00 .35
508 A101 50fr red & multi   1.25 .75

Cameroun Doll — A102

Designs: 15fr, Doll in short skirt. 30fr, Doll with basket on back.

1970, Nov. 2
509 A102 10fr car & multi   .60 .25
510 A102 15fr dk grn & multi   .70 .25
511 A102 30fr brn red & multi 1.90 .30
        Nos. 509-511 (3)   3.20 .80

Cogwheels and Grain A103

1970, Feb. 9   Photo.   Perf. 13
512 A103 30fr multicolored   .85 .25

Europafrica Economic Conference.

Federal
University,
Yaoundé
A104

1971, Jan. 19   **Engr.**
513 A104 50fr multicolored   1.00   .25
Inauguration of Federal University at
Yaoundé.

Presidents Ahidjo and Pompidou,
Flags of Cameroun and
France — A105

1971, Feb. 9   Photo.   Perf. 13
514 A105 30fr multicolored   1.50   .35
Visit of Georges Pompidou, Pres. of France.

Young
People,
Globe, Map
of
Cameroun
A106

1971, Feb. 11
515 A106 30fr blue & multi   .90   .30
Fifth National Youth Festival, Feb. 11.

Gerbera
Hybrida — A107

Designs: 40fr, Opuntia polyantha (cactus).
50fr, Hemerocallis hybrida (lily).

1971, Mar. 14   **Photo.**
516 A107 20fr multicolored   .60   .25
517 A107 40fr green & multi   1.50   .25
518 A107 50fr blue & multi   2.10   .25
    Nos. 516-518 (3)   4.20   .75

Men of Four
Races — A108

Design: 30fr, Hands and globe.

1971, Mar. 21   Perf. 13x12½
519 A108 20fr green & multi   .55   .25
520 A108 30fr ultra & multi   .75   .25
Intl. year against racial discrimination.

Crowned
Cranes at
Waza
Camp
A109

20fr, Canoe on Sanaga River. 30fr, Sanaga
River.

1971, Apr. 9.   Engr.   Perf. 13
521 A109 10fr red, grn & blk   1.50   .25
522 A109 20fr dk grn, brn & red   1.00   .25
523 A109 30fr red, dk grn & brt
         bl   1.50   .25
    Nos. 521-523 (3)   4.00   .75

International Court, The
Hague — A110

1971, June 14   Engr.   Perf. 13
524 A110 50fr ultra, org brn & sl
         grn   1.25 .35
25th anniversary of the International Court
in The Hague, Netherlands.

Liana
Bridge — A111

Local
Market
A112

1971, Aug. 16   Photo.   Perf. 13
525 A111 40fr multicolored   1.60   .25
526 A112 45fr multicolored   1.60   .25

Bamoun
Horseman
A113

African Art: 15fr, Animal fetish statuette.

1971, Sept. 18
527 A113 10fr brown & yellow   .50   .50
528 A113 15fr dp brn & org yel   .50   .50

Communications Satellite and
Globe — A114

1971, Oct. 14   Perf. 13x12½
529 A114 40fr Prus bl, sl grn &
         org   .80   .25
Pan-African telecommunications system.

UNICEF
Emblem
A115

50fr, UNICEF emblem and grain, vert.

1971, Dec. 11   Engr.   Perf. 13
530 A115 40fr sl grn, bl grn &
         plum   .95   .25
531 A115 50fr dp bl, dk red & lt
         grn   1.25 .25
    25th anniv. of UNICEF.

Houses from South-Central
Region — A116

Design: 15fr, Adamaua round houses.

1972, Jan. 15   Photo.   Perf. 13
532 A116 10fr dk blue & multi   .25   .25
533 A116 15fr black & multi   .55   .25

Giraffe — A117

Designs: 5fr, Home industries. 10fr, Smith,
horiz. 15fr, Women carrying burdens.

Perf. 13x13½, 13½x13
1972, Feb. 18   **Litho.**
534 A117 2fr multicolored   .30   .25
535 A117 5fr black, org & red   .30   .25
536 A117 10fr multicolored   .30   .25
537 A117 15fr multicolored   .30   .25
    Nos. 534-537 (4)   1.20 1.00
    Youth Day 1972.

Soccer Players and Field — A118

Designs: 20fr, African Soccer Cup, vert.
45fr, Team captains shaking hands, vert.

1972, Feb. 22   **Perf. 13½**
538 A118 20fr gray & multi   .55   .25
539 A118 40fr gray & multi   .95   .25
540 A118 45fr yellow & multi   1.50 .25
    Nos. 538-540 (3)   3.00 .75
African Soccer Cup, Yaoundé, 2/23-3/5.

Government Building, Yaoundé, and
Laurel — A119

1972, Apr. 6   Photo.   Perf. 12½x12
541 A119 40fr multicolored   .80   .25
110th session of Inter-Parliamentary Council, Yaoundé, Apr. 1972.

"Fantasia,"
North
Cameroun
A120

Bororo
Woman — A121

40fr, Boat on Wouri River & Mt. Cameroun.

1972, Apr. 24   Perf. 13x12½, 12½x13
542 A120 15fr dk vio & multi   .35   .25
543 A121 20fr multicolored   .45   .25
544 A120 40fr multicolored   1.50 .25
    Nos. 542-544 (3)   2.30 .75

Chemical
Apparatus
A122

1972, May 15   Engr.   Perf. 13
545 A122 40fr lilac, red & green   .80   .25
President Ahmadou Ahidjo Prize.

United Republic

Solanum
Macranthum
A123

Design: 45fr, Wax plant.

1972, July 20   Photo.   Perf. 13
546 A123 40fr multicolored   .95   .25
547 A123 45fr yellow & multi   1.25 .25

Charaxes
Ameliae
A124

Design: 45fr, Papilio tynderaeus.

1972, Aug. 20   Photo.   Perf. 13
548 A124 40fr bl, dk bl & gold   4.00   .40
549 A124 45fr lt grn, blk & gold   5.50   .60

No. 468 Surcharged

1972, Aug. 30   Photo.   Perf. 12x12½
550 A85 40fr on 30fr multicolored   1.00 .25

Resurrection Lily — A125

Flowers: 45fr, Candlestick cassia. 50fr, Amaryllis.

1972, Sept. 16 **Perf. 13**
551 A125 40fr lt green & multi 1.00 .25
552 A125 45fr multicolored 1.25 .25
553 A125 50fr lt blue & multi 1.50 .35
Nos. 551-553 (3) 3.75 .85

Great Blue Touraco — A126

Design: 45fr, Red-faced lovebirds, horiz.

Perf. 12½x13, 13x12½
1972, Nov. 20 **Litho.**
554 A126 10fr yellow & multi 1.75 .25
555 A126 45fr yellow & multi 3.75 .25

Cotton (North) — A127

10fr, Cacao (south central). 15fr, Logging (southeast & southern coast). 20fr, Coffee (west). 45fr, Tea (northwest & southwest).

1973, Mar. 26 **Photo.** **Perf. 12½x13**
556 A127 5fr black & multi .25 .25
557 A127 10fr black & multi .25 .25
558 A127 15fr black & multi .75 .25
559 A127 20fr black & multi 1.50 .25
560 A127 45fr black & multi 2.50 .40
Nos. 556-560 (5) 5.25 1.40

Third 5-Year Plan.
For surcharge see No. 568.

Flag and Map of Cameroon, Pres. Ahidjo and No. 331 — A128

Design: 20fr, Proclamation of independence, Pres. Ahidjo and No. 336.

1973, May 20 **Engr.** **Perf. 13**
561 A128 10fr ultra & multi .65 .25
562 A128 20fr multicolored 1.00 .25
Nos. 561-562,C200-C201 (4) 3.45 1.15

United Republic of Cameroun, 1st anniv.

Bamoun Mask — A129

Designs: Various Bamoun masks.

1973, July 10 **Engr.** **Perf. 13**
563 A129 5fr green, brn & blk .25 .25
564 A129 10fr lilac, brn & blk .25 .25
565 A129 45fr red, brn & blk .75 .25
566 A129 100fr ultra, brn & blk 2.00 .40
Nos. 563-566 (4) 3.25 1.15

Dr. Hansen — A130

1973, July 25 **Engr.** **Perf. 13**
567 A130 45fr multicolored 2.00 .25

Centenary of the discovery by Dr. Armauer G. Hansen of the Hansen bacillus, the cause of leprosy.

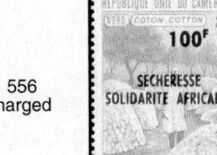

No. 556 Surcharged

1973, Aug. 16 **Photo.** **Perf. 12½x13**
568 A127 100fr on 5fr 1.75 .40

African solidarity in drought emergency.

Dancers, South West Africa — A131

Designs: Southwest African dances.

1973, Aug. 17 **Perf. 13**
569 A131 10fr multicolored .25 .25
570 A131 25fr multicolored .55 .25
571 A131 45fr multicolored 1.10 .25
Nos. 569-571 (3) 1.90 .75

WMO Emblem — A132

1973, Sept. 1 **Engr.** **Perf. 13**
572 A132 45fr green & ultra 1.60 .25

Cent. of intl. meteorological cooperation.

Garoua Party Headquarters — A133

1973, Sept. 1 **Photo.**
573 A133 40fr multicolored .80 .25

7th anniv. of Cameroun National Union.

African Postal Union Issue, 1973
Common Design Type
1973, Sept. 12 **Engr.**
574 CD137 100fr brt bl, bl & sl grn 1.75 .40

Avocados — A135

1973, Sept. 20
575 A135 10fr shown .70 .25
576 A135 20fr Mangos .80 .25
577 A135 45fr Plums 2.00 .25
578 A135 50fr Custard apple 2.50 .25
Nos. 575-578 (4) 6.00 1.00

Kirdi Village A136

45fr, Mabas village. 50fr, Fishing village.

1973, Oct. 25 **Engr.** **Perf. 13**
579 A136 15fr black, bis & grn .25 .25
580 A136 45fr magenta, brn & org .90 .25
581 A136 50fr green, blk & org 1.25 .25
Nos. 579-581 (3) 2.40 .75

Handshake on Map of Africa — A137

1974, May 15 **Engr.** **Perf. 12½x13**
582 A137 40fr carmine & multi .55 .25
583 A137 45fr indigo & multi .70 .25

Organization for African Unity, 10th anniv.

Spinning Mill — A138

1974, May 25 **Engr.** **Perf. 13x12½**
584 A138 45fr multicolored .80 .25

CICAM Industrial Complex.

Carved Panel from Bilinga A139

Cameroun Art (Carvings): 40fr, Detail from Bubinga chair. 45fr, Detail Acajou Ngollon panel.

1974, May 30
585 A139 10fr brt grn & ocher .25 .25
586 A139 40fr red & brown .80 .25
587 A139 45fr blue & rose brn 1.10 .25
Nos. 585-587 (3) 2.15 .75

Zebu — A140

1974, June 1 **Perf. 13½**
588 A140 40fr multicolored 1.40 .25

North Cameroun cattle raising. See No. C210.

Laying Rail Section A141

Designs: 5fr, Map showing line Yaoundé to Ngaoundéré, vert. 40fr, Welding rail joint, vert. 100fr, Train on Djerem River Bridge.

Perf. 12½x13, 13x12½
1974, June 10 **Engr.**
589 A141 5fr multicolored .65 .25
590 A141 20fr multicolored 1.25 .30
591 A141 40fr multicolored 2.00 .60
592 A141 100fr multicolored 3.25 .90
Nos. 589-592 (4) 7.15 2.05

Opening of Yaoundé-Ngaoundéré railroad line.
For surcharge see No. 596.

No. 466 Surcharged

1974, June 1 **Photo.** **Perf. 12x12½**
593 A85 40fr on 8fr multi .80 .25

UPU Emblem, Hands Holding Letters A142

1974, Oct. 8 **Engr.** **Perf. 13**
594 A142 40fr multicolored .90 .25
Nos. 594,C218-C219 (3) 5.90 1.75

Cent. of the UPU.

Presidents and Flags of Cameroun, CAR, Congo, Gabon and Meeting Center — A143

1974, Dec. 8   **Photo.**   *Perf. 13*
595 A143 40fr gold & multi   1.50   .25

10th anniversary of Central African Customs and Economic Union (Union Douanière et Economique de l'Afrique Centrale, UDEAC). See No. C223.

No. 589 Surcharged in Violet Blue

1974, Dec. 10   **Engr.**   *Perf. 12½x13*
596 A141 100fr on 5fr multi   2.50   .85

Virgin of Autun, 15th Century Sculpture A144

Christmas: 45fr, Virgin and Child, by Luis de Morales (c. 1509-1586).

1974, Dec. 20   **Photo.**   *Perf. 13*
597 A144 40fr gold & multi   .95   .25
598 A144 45fr gold & multi   1.25   .25

Tropical Plants — A145

5fr, Cockscomb. 40fr, Costus spectabilis. 45fr, Mussaenda erythrophylla.

1975, Mar. 10   **Photo.**   *Perf. 13*
599 A145 5fr multicolored   .30   .25
600 A145 40fr multicolored   1.50   .25
601 A145 45fr multicolored   1.90   .35
   Nos. 599-601 (3)   3.70   .85

Fishing by Night — A146

1975, Apr. 1   **Engr.**   *Perf. 13*
602 A146 40fr shown   1.75   .40
603 A146 45fr Fishing by day   1.75   .40

Afo Akom Statue and Chief's Stool — A147

1975, Apr. 1   **Photo.**
604 A147 40fr multicolored   .65   .25
605 A147 45fr multicolored   .85   .25
606 A147 200fr multicolored   2.50   .75
   Nos. 604-606 (3)   4.00   1.25

Tree Fungus — A148

1975, Apr. 14
607 A148 15fr shown   125.00   2.00
608 A148 40fr Chrysalis   85.00   1.00

Ministry of Posts and Telecommunications — A149

1975, July 21   **Engr.**   *Perf. 13*
609 A149 40fr brn, grn & Prus bl   .65   .25
610 A149 45fr Prus bl, brn & grn   .90   .25

Presbyterian Church, Elat — A150

Designs: No. 612, Foumban Mosque. 45fr, Catholic Church, Ngaoundere.

1975, Aug. 20   **Engr.**   *Perf. 13*
611 A150 40fr multicolored   .45   .25
612 A150 40fr multicolored   .45   .25
613 A150 45fr multicolored   .65   .25
   Nos. 611-613 (3)   1.55   .75

Plowing A151

Design: No. 615, Corn harvest, vert.

Perf. 13x12½, 12½x13
1975, Dec. 15   **Photo.**
614 A151 40fr deep grn & multi   .70   .25
615 A151 40fr deep grn & multi   .70   .25
   Green revolution.

Zamengoe Satellite Monitoring Station — A152

1976, May 20   **Litho.**   *Perf. 13*
616 A152 40fr shown   .50   .25
617 A152 100fr Radar, vert.   1.25   .40

Porcelain Rose — A153

Design: 50fr, Flower of North Cameroun.

1976, July 20   **Litho.**   *Perf. 12½*
618 A153 40fr multicolored   1.00   .25
619 A153 50fr multicolored   1.40   .35

Leopard Dance — A154

1976, Sept. 15   **Litho.**   *Perf. 12*
620 A154 40fr gray & multi   .80   .25
   Nos. 620,C233-C234 (3)   2.55   .85

Telephone Exchange A155

1976, Oct. 5   *Perf. 13*
621 A155 50fr multicolored   .80   .25

Centenary of first telephone call by Alexander Graham Bell, Mar. 10, 1876.

Young Men Building House — A156

Design: 45fr, Young women working in field.

1976, Oct. 10   **Litho.**   *Perf. 12*
622 A156 40fr multicolored   .35   .25
623 A156 45fr multicolored   .60   .25
   10th National Youth Day.

Konrad Adenauer (1876-1967), German Chancellor, Cologne Cathedral A157

1976, Oct. 20
624 A157 100fr multicolored   .95   .40

Party Headquarters, Douala — A158

No. 626, Party Headquarters, Yaoundé.

1976, Dec. 28   **Litho.**   *Perf. 12*
625 A158 50fr orange & multi   .45   .25
626 A158 50fr blue & multi   .45   .25

10th anniv. of the Cameroun National Union.

Bamoun Copper Pipe — A159

1977, Feb. 4   **Litho.**   *Perf. 12½*
627 A159 50fr multicolored   .70   .25

2nd World Black and African Festival, Lagos, Nigeria, 1/15-2/12. See No. C239.

Ostrich — A160

1977, Mar. 20   **Litho.**   *Perf. 12*
628 A160 30fr shown   2.50   .40
629 A160 50fr Crowned cranes   3.00   .75

Cameroun No. 609 and Switzerland No. 3L1 — A161

1977, June 5   **Litho.**   *Perf. 12*
630 A161 50fr multicolored   1.00   .30
   Nos. 630,C252-C253 (3)   4.35   1.25

Jufilex Philatelic Exhibition, Bern, Switzerland. See Nos. C252-C253.

Winter Olympics 1976, set of five, 40, 50fr, airmail 140, 200, 350fr, and airmail souv. sheet, 500fr, issued Aug. 10, 1977. Nos. 7701-7706. Value, set $7.50, souvenir sheet $5.

Apollo-Soyuz — A163

Designs: 40fr, Astronaut Thomas P. Stafford, Apollo lifting off. 60fr, Cosmonaut Alexei Leonov, Soyuz lifting off.

1977, Aug. 10   Litho.   Perf. 14x13½
633 A163 40fr multicolored   .45   .25
634 A163 60fr multicolored   .70   .50
    Nos. 633-634,C256-C258 (5)   7.55   2.60

No. 617 Overprinted in French and English

1977, Aug. 22   Litho.   Perf. 13
635 A152 100fr multicolored   .90   .40
Palestinian fighters and their families.

Chairman Mao and Great Wall A164

1977, Sept. 9   Engr.   Perf. 13
636 A164 100fr olive & brown   4.25   .55
Mao Tse-tung (1893-1976), Chinese communist leader, first death anniversary.

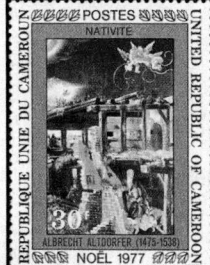

Nativity, by Albrecht Altdorfer A165

50fr, Madonna of the Grand Duke, by Raphael.

1977, Dec. 15   Litho.   Perf. 12½x12
637 A165 30fr multicolored   .55   .25
638 A165 50fr multicolored   1.10   .25
    Nos. 637-638,C264-C265 (4)   7.65   2.50
Christmas 1977.

Gazelle and Rotary Emblem — A166

1978, Feb. 11   Litho.   Perf. 12
639 A166 50fr orange & multi   .70   .25
Rotary Club of Yaounde, 20th anniversary.

Pres. Ahidjo, Flag and Map of Cameroun A167

1978, Apr. 3   Litho.   Perf. 12½
640 A167 50fr multicolored   .90   .25
New flag of Cameroun. See No. C266.

Cardioglossa Escalerae — A168

Design: 60fr, Cardioglossa elegans.

1978, Apr. 5
641 A168 50fr multicolored   1.75   .25
642 A168 60fr multicolored   3.00   .25
    Nos. 641-642,C267 (3)   8.50   1.25

Jules Verne and "From Earth to Moon" — A169

1978, Oct. 10   Litho.   Perf. 12
643 A169 250fr multicolored   2.25   1.40
Jules Verne (1828-1905), science fiction writer, birth sesquicentennial. See No. C276.

Hypolimnas Salmacis Drury — A170

Butterflies: 25fr, Euxanthe trajanus ward. 30fr, Euphaedra cyparissa cramer.

1978, Oct. 15
644 A170 20fr multicolored   2.00   .60
645 A170 25fr multicolored   2.25   .60
646 A170 30fr multicolored   3.75   .60
    Nos. 644-646 (3)   8.00   1.80

Men Planting Seedlings — A171

1978, Oct. 30   Perf. 12½
647 A171 10fr multicolored   .25   .25
648 A171 15fr multicolored   .35   .25
Green barrier against the desert.

Carved Bamun Drum — A172

60fr, String instrument (Gueguerou), horiz.

1978, Nov. 20   Litho.   Perf. 12½
649 A172 50fr multicolored   .45   .25
650 A172 60fr multicolored   .90   .25
    Nos. 649-650,C277 (3)   2.60   .90

Pres. Ahidjo, Giscard D'Estaing, Flags of Cameroun and France — A173

1979, Feb. 8   Photo.   Perf. 13
651 A173 60fr multicolored   1.50   .60
Visit of Pres. Valery Giscard D'Estaing of France to Cameroun.

Human Rights Emblem, Globe, Scroll and African — A174

1979, Feb. 11   Litho.   Perf. 12x12½
652 A174 5fr multicolored   .25   .25
Universal Declaration of Human Rights, 30th anniversary (in 1978). See No. C278. See No. 803.

Boy and Girl Greeting Sun — A175

1979, Aug. 15   Litho.   Perf. 12
653 A175 50fr multicolored   .80   .25
International Year of the Child.

Protected Animals A176

Nos. 655, 658 vert.

1979, Sept. 20   Perf. 12½
654 A176 50fr Rhinoceros   1.40   .30
655 A176 60fr Giraffe   1.90   .40
656 A176 60fr Gorilla   1.90   .40
657 A176 100fr Leopard   2.90   .60
658 A176 100fr Elephant   2.90   .60
    Nos. 654-658 (5)   11.00   2.30

Eugene Jamot, Map of Cameroun, Tsetse Fly — A177

1979, Nov. 5   Engr.   Perf. 13
659 A177 50fr multicolored   3.00   .40
Eugene Jamot (1879-1937), discoverer of sleeping sickness cure.

Annunciation, by Fra Filippo Lippi — A178

Paintings; 50fr, Rest During the Flight to Egypt, c. 1620. No. 622, Flight into Egypt, by Jan Joest, No. 663, Nativity, by Joest. 100fr, Nativity, by Botticelli.

1979, Dec. 6   Litho.   Perf. 12½x12
660 A178 10fr multicolored   .25   .25
661 A178 50fr multicolored   .60   .25
662 A178 60fr multicolored   .75   .30
663 A178 60fr multicolored   .75   .30
a.   Pair, #662-663   1.50   1.50
664 A178 100fr multicolored   1.50   .40
    Nos. 660-664 (5)   3.85   1.50
Christmas 1979.

Piper Capense A179

Medicinal Plants: 60fr, Bracken fern.

1979, Dec. 15   Litho.   Perf. 12½
665 A179 50fr multicolored   1.25   .30
666 A179 60fr multicolored   1.50   .40

Pres. Ahidjo, Cameroun Map, Arms and No. 331 A180

1980, Feb. 12   Litho.   Perf. 12½
667 A180 50fr multicolored   .65   .25
Independence, 20th anniversary.

Congress Building, Bafoussam A181

1980, Feb. 12
668 A181 50fr multicolored .65 .25
Cameroun National Union, 3rd Ordinary Congress, Bafoussam, Feb. 12-17.

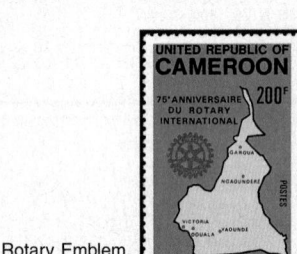

Rotary Emblem, Map of Cameroun A182

Rotary Intl., 75th Anniv.: No. 670, Anniv. emblem.

1980, Mar. 15   Litho.   Perf. 12½
669 A182 200fr multicolored 2.00 .80
670 A182 200fr multicolored 2.00 .80
a.   Souvenir sheet of 2, #669-670 5.25 4.00

Voacanga Medicinal Beans A183

60fr, Voacanga tree, vert. 100fr, Voacanga flower, vert.

1980, Dec. 3   Litho.   Perf. 12½
671 A183 50fr shown 1.00 .25
672 A183 60fr multicolored 1.25 .25
673 A183 100fr multicolored 1.75 .40
    Nos. 671-673 (3) 4.00 .90

Violet Mellowstone A184

60fr, Patula. 100fr, Cashmere bouquet.

1980, Dec. 5
674 A184 50fr shown .70 .25
675 A184 60fr multicolored 1.00 .25
676 A184 100fr multicolored 1.60 .40
    Nos. 674-676 (3) 3.30 .90

Occupation of Mecca by Mohammed, 1350th Anniversary — A185

1980, Dec. 9
677 A185 50fr multicolored 1.00 .30

African Slender-snouted Crocodile (Endangered Species) — A186

300fr, Buffon's antelope, vert.

1980, Dec. 24
678 A186 200fr shown 3.25 .80
679 A186 300fr multicolored 4.00 1.20
    See Nos. 888-889.

Bororo Girls and Roumsiki Peaks — A187

60fr, Dschang tourist center.

1980, Dec. 29
680 A187 50fr shown .55 .25
681 A187 60fr multicolored .55 .25

Banana Tree A188

1981, Feb. 5
682 A188 50fr shown .65 .30
683 A188 60fr Cattle, vert. .80 .40

Girl on Crutches — A189

150fr, Boy in motorized wheelchair.

1981, Feb. 20   Litho.   Perf. 12½
684 A189 60fr shown .55 .25
685 A189 150fr multicolored 1.25 .65
    International Year of the Disabled.

Air Terminal, Douala Airport — A190

200fr, Boeing 747. 300fr, Douala Intl. Airport.

1981, Apr. 4   Litho.   Perf. 12½
686 A190 100fr shown 1.00 .55
687 A190 200fr multi 2.00 1.10
688 A190 300fr multi 3.00 1.60
    Nos. 686-688 (3) 6.00 3.25
    Cameroun Airlines, 10th anniv.

Pres. Ahidjo Presenting Trophy to Canon Soccer Team — A191

No. 690, Union team captain.

1981, Apr. 20
689 A191 60fr shown .90 .40
690 A191 60fr multicolored .90 .40
    1979 African Soccer Cup champions.

Scaly Anteater A192

Designs: Endangered species.

1981, July 20   Litho.   Perf. 12½
691 A192 50fr Moutourou 1.50 .25
692 A192 50fr Tortoise 1.50 .25
693 A192 100fr shown 3.25 .40
    Nos. 691-693 (3) 6.25 .90

Prince Charles and Lady Diana, St. Paul's Cathedral A193

No. 695, Couple, royal coach.

1981, July 29   Litho.   Perf. 12½
694 A193 500fr shown 4.50 2.00
695 A193 500fr multicolored 4.50 2.00
a.   Souvenir sheet of 2, #694-695 10.00 4.00
    Royal wedding.

Bafoussam-Bamenda Highway — A194

1981, Sept. 10   Litho.   Perf. 12½
696 A194 50fr multicolored .55 .25

Freighter Cam Iroko (Cameroun Shipping Line) A195

1981, Sept. 25
697 A195 60fr multicolored 1.00 .40

20th Anniv. of Reunification — A196

1981, Oct. 10   Perf. 12½x13
698 A196 50fr multicolored .70 .25

Medicinal Plants — A197

60fr, Voacanga thouarsii. 70fr, Cassia alata.

1981, Dec. 31   Litho.   Perf. 12½
699 A197 60fr multicolored 1.10 .30
700 A197 70fr multicolored 1.40 .40

Easter 1982 — A198

Paintings: 100fr, Christ in the Garden of Olives, by Delacroix. 200fr, Descent from the Cross, by Giotto. 250fr, Pieta in the Countryside, by Bellini.

1982, Apr. 10   Litho.   Perf. 13
701 A198 100fr multicolored .90 .35
702 A198 200fr multicolored 1.75 .65
703 A198 250fr multicolored 2.25 .90
    Nos. 701-703 (3) 4.90 1.90

PHILEXFRANCE '82 Stamp Exhibition, Paris, June 11-21 — A199

1982, Apr. 25   Perf. 12
704 A199 90fr multicolored 1.90 .40

Snakeskin Handbag — A200

1982, Apr. 30   Perf. 12½
705 A200 60fr shown .70 .25
706 A200 70fr Clay water jug .80 .35

10th Anniv. of Republic — A201

1982, May 20 **Perf. 13**
707 A201 500fr multicolored 4.50 2.00

Town Hall, Douala — A202

1982, June 15 **Litho.** **Perf. 12½**
708 A202 40fr shown .45 .25
709 A202 60fr Yaounde .65 .25

See Nos. 730-731, 757-758, 790-791, 867.

1982 World Cup — A203

100fr, National team. 200fr, Semi-finalists.
300fr, Players, vert. 400fr, National team 2nd
lineup.

1982, July 10 **Perf. 13**
710 A203 100fr multi 1.40 .40
711 A203 200fr multi 2.75 .75
712 A203 300fr multi 4.50 1.25
713 A203 400fr multi 5.75 1.60
  a. Souvenir sheet of 2, #713 14.50 3.50
  Nos. 710-713 (4) 14.40 4.00

Partridge — A204

Bongo Antelope
— A204a

15fr, Turtle dove. 20fr, Swallow. 300fr, Black
colobus.

1982 **Perf. 12½x13**
714 A204 10fr shown 2.50 .40
715 A204 15fr multi 3.00 .85
716 A204 20fr multi 5.50 1.10
717 A204a 200fr shown 3.00 .80
718 A204a 300fr multi 4.00 1.25
  Nos. 714-718 (5) 18.00 4.40

Issued: 200fr, 300fr, July 20; others Aug. 10.
See No. 804.

Scouting
Year
A205

1982, Sept. 30 **Litho.** **Perf. 13x12½**
719 A205 200fr Campfire 2.50 .80
720 A205 400fr Baden-Powell 4.50 1.60

25th Anniv. of the Presbyterian Church
in Cameroun — A206

45fr, Buea Chapel. 60fr, Nyasoso Chapel,
vert.

1982, Oct. 30 **Perf. 13x12½, 12½x13**
721 A206 45fr multi .55 .25
722 A206 60fr multi .65 .25

ITU
Plenipotentiaries
Conference,
Nairobi,
Sept. — A207

1982, Oct. 5 **Litho.** **Perf. 12½x13**
723 A207 70fr multicolored .70 .25

Italy's Victory in 1982 World
Cup — A208

1982, Nov. **Perf. 13**
724 A208 500fr multicolored 5.50 2.00
725 A208 1000fr multicolored 10.50 4.00

30th Anniv. of
Customs
Cooperation
Council — A209

No. 726, Emblem. No. 727, Headquarters,
Brussels.

1983, Jan. 10 **Perf. 12½x13**
726 A209 250fr multicolored 2.25 .80
727 A209 250fr multicolored 2.25 .80

2nd Yaoundé Medical
Conference — A210

1983, Jan. 23 **Litho.** **Perf. 13**
728 A210 60fr grn & multi .70 .25
729 A210 70fr brn & multi .90 .25

City Hall Type of 1982

1983, Feb. 25 **Litho.** **Perf. 12½**
730 A202 60fr Bafoussam .60 .25
731 A202 70fr Garoua .70 .30

Homage to
Women — A211

1983, Apr. 25 **Litho.** **Perf. 12½**
733 A211 60fr Nurse .75 .25
734 A211 70fr Lawyer .75 .25

11th Anniv. of Independence — A212

Flag and Pres. Paul Biya.

1983, May 18 **Litho.** **Perf. 13**
735 A212 60fr dk grn & multi .55 .25
736 A212 70fr dk bl & multi .70 .30

25th Anniv.
of Intl.
Maritime
Org.
A213

1983, May 23 **Perf. 13x12½**
737 A213 500fr multicolored 5.50 1.50

Eagle — A214

1983, June 15 **Litho.** **Perf. 12½x13**
738 A214 25fr shown 1.50 .40
739 A214 30fr Sparrowhawk 2.50 .75
740 A214 50fr Purple heron 4.50 1.00
  Nos. 738-740 (3) 8.50 2.15

See Nos. 798-800, 873, 882, 886.

A215

60fr, Pearl mask, by Wery-Nwen-Nto, 1899.
70fr, Basket with lid.

1983, July 25 **Litho.** **Perf. 12**
741 A215 60fr multicolored .70 .25
742 A215 70fr multicolored .90 .30

A216

90fr, Mobile Post Office, horiz. 150fr, Telegraph Operator. 250fr, Tom-tom.

1983, Aug. 20 **Litho.** **Perf. 12**
743 A216 90fr multicolored .90 .25
744 A216 150fr multicolored 1.40 .35
745 A216 250fr multicolored 2.75 .55
  Nos. 743-745 (3) 5.05 1.15

World Communications Year.

Endangered Species — A217

1983, Sept. 22 **Perf. 12**
746 A217 200fr Civet Cat 2.75 .50
747 A217 200fr Gorilla, vert 2.75 .50
748 A217 350fr Cobaya, vert 4.50 1.25
  Nos. 746-748 (3) 10.00 2.25

See No. 887.

Lake Tizon — A218

1983, Nov. 25 **Litho.** **Perf. 13**
749 A218 60fr shown .55 .25
750 A218 70fr Mt. Cameroon .70 .25

Human Rights
Declaration, 35th
Anniv — A219

1983, Dec. 20   Litho.   *Perf. 12½x13*
751 A219 60fr multicolored   .55   .25
752 A219 70fr multicolored   .70   .25

Christmas 1983 — A220

60fr, Christmas tree. 200fr, Stained glass window, Yaoundé Cathedral. No. 755, Rest during Flight into Egypt, by Philipp Otto Runge. No. 756, Angel of the Annunciation. 60fr, 200fr, No. 756 vert.

1983, Dec. 20   Litho.   *Perf. 12½*
753 A220   60fr   multicolored   .45   .25
754 A220 200fr multicolored   1.75   .50
755 A220 500fr multicolored   4.50   1.25
756 A220 500fr multicolored   4.50   1.25
   a.   Souvenir sheet of 3, #754-756   12.50   12.50
    Nos. 753-756 (4)   11.20   3.25

City Hall Type of 1982
1984, Apr. 20   Litho.   *Perf. 12½*
757 A202 60fr Bamenda   .55   .25
758 A202 70fr Mbalmayo   .70   .25

Catholic Church, Zoetele — A221

70fr, Protestant Church, Yaounde.

1984, July 25   Litho.   *Perf. 13*
759 A221 60fr shown   .55   .25
760 A221 70fr multicolored   .70   .25

Endangered Species — A222

1984, Aug. 15
761 A222 250fr Wild pig   3.50   .75
762 A222 250fr Deer   3.50   .75

1984, Oct. 10   Litho.   *Perf. 13½*
763 A222 60fr Nightingale   4.50   1.00
764 A222 60fr Vultures   4.50   1.00
    See No. 883.

Bamenda Farming Fair — A223

1984, Dec. 10   Litho.   *Perf. 13*
765 A223   60fr Corn   .60   .25
766 A223   70fr Cattle   .90   .25
767 A223 300fr Potatoes   3.50   .90
    Nos. 765-767 (3)   5.00   1.40

International Civil Aviation Organization, 40th Anniv. — A224

No. 768, Icarus. No. 769, ICAO emblem, vert. No. 770, Boeing 747. No. 771, Solar Princess painting.

1984, Dec. 20   Litho.   *Perf. 12½*
768 A224 200fr multi   1.75   .60
769 A224 200fr multi   1.75   .60
770 A224 300fr multi   2.75   .90
771 A224 300fr multi   3.25   .90
    Nos. 768-771 (4)   9.50   3.00

Olymphilex '85, Lausanne — A225

150fr, Wrestlers, exhibition emblem.

Wmk. 385
1985, Apr. 5   Photo.   *Perf. 13*
772 A225 150fr multicolored   1.50   .40

Domestic Musical Instruments A226

60fr, Balafons (xylophone). 70fr, Guitar. 100fr, Flute.

1985, Apr. 23   *Perf. 13½*
773 A226   60fr multicolored   .65   .25
774 A226   70fr multicolored   .80   .25
775 A226 100fr multicolored   1.10   .30
    Nos. 773-775 (3)   2.55   .80

INTELSAT Org., 20th Anniv. — A227

125fr, Intelsat V. 200fr, Intelcam, Yaounde.

1985, May 8   *Perf. 13*
776 A227 125fr multicolored   1.60   .35
777 A227 200fr multicolored   2.10   .60

New York Headquarters — A228

1985, May 30
778 A228 250fr multicolored   2.40   1.10
779 A228 500fr multicolored   4.50   2.25
    UN, 40th anniv.

Pres. Mitterand, Biya — A229

1985, June 20
780 A229 60fr multicolored   2.25   .25
781 A229 70fr multicolored   2.50   .25
    Visit of Pres. Mitterand of France.

UNICEF A230

UN Infant Survival Campaign A231

1985, July 15
782 A230   60fr multicolored   .55   .25
783 A231 300fr multicolored   2.75   1.00

Visit of Pope John Paul II, Aug. 10-14 — A232

60fr, Pope, papal arms. 70fr, Pope, crosier. 200fr, Pres. Biya, John Paul II.

1985, Aug. 9   *Perf. 13x12½*
784 A232 60fr multi   1.10   .40
785 A232 70fr multi   1.25   .55

Size: 55x38mm
786 A232 200fr multi   4.00   2.25
   a.   Souv. sheet of 3, #784-786   8.00   8.00
    Nos. 784-786 (3)   6.35   3.20

Landscapes — A233

60fr, Lake Barumbi, Kumba. 70fr, Bonando Pygmy Village, Doume. 150fr, Cameroun River.

1985, July 25   Litho.   *Perf. 12½*
787 A233   60fr multicolored   .70   .25
788 A233   70fr multicolored   .70   .25
789 A233 150fr multicolored   1.40   .40
    Nos. 787-789 (3)   2.80   .90

City Hall Type of 1982
1985, July 30
790 A202 60fr Ngaoundere   .55   .25
791 A202 60fr D'Ebolowa   .55   .25

Wildlife — A234

1985, Aug. 20   *Perf. 13½*
792 A234 125fr Porcupine   1.50   .40
793 A234 200fr Squirrel   2.50   .60
794 A234 350fr Hedgehog   4.00   1.10
    Nos. 792-794 (3)   8.00   2.10

Wood Sculptures A235

60fr, Mask. 70fr, Mask, diff. 100fr, Wood bas-relief, horiz.

1985, Sept. 15
795 A235   60fr multicolored   .65   .25
796 A235   70fr multicolored   .90   .25
797 A235 100fr multicolored   1.25   .30
    Nos. 795-797 (3)   2.80   .80

Bird Type of 1983 Redrawn
140fr, Toucans. 150fr, Rooster. 200fr, Red-throated bee-eater.

1985, Nov. 10
798 A214 140fr multicolored   2.25   .50
799 A214 150fr multicolored   2.25   .55
800 A214 200fr multicolored   3.25   .70
    Nos. 798-800 (3)   7.75   1.75

    Nos. 798-800 inscribed "Republic of Cameroon".
    See No. 873. For surcharge see No. 871.

American Peace Corps in Cameroun, 25th Anniv. — A237

1986, Jan. 1   Litho.   *Perf. 12½*
801 A237 70fr multicolored   .70   .25
802 A237 100fr multicolored   1.00   .30

Stamps of 1979-1982 Redrawn
1986, Mar.   *Perf. 13, 13½*
803 A174   5fr multicolored   .35   .35
804 A204 10fr multicolored   .35   .35

    Nos. 803-804 inscribed "Republic of Cameroon" instead of "United Republic of Cameroon."

Easter — A238

Paintings: 210fr, Head of the Virgin, by Pierre-Paul Prud'Hon (1758-1823). 350fr, The Stoning of St. Steven, by Van Scorel (1495-1562).

1986, Apr. 15   **Perf. 13½**
805 A238 210fr multicolored   1.75   .60
806 A238 350fr multicolored   3.00   1.00

Insects — A239

1986, Apr. 20
807 A239 70fr Honeybee   1.75   .40
808 A239 70fr Dragonfly   1.75   .40
809 A239 100fr Grasshopper   2.50   .65
    Nos. 807-809 (3)   6.00   1.45
    Nos. 808-809 horiz.

Flags, Conference Center — A240

1986, Apr. 25   **Litho.**   **Perf. 13**
810 A240 100fr Map, vert.   1.00   .30
811 A240 175fr shown   1.20   .60

Conference of Ministers of the Economic Commission for Africa, Apr. 9-29.

Statues — A241

70fr, Bronze earth mother. 100fr, Wood funerary figure. 130fr, Wood equestrian figure.

1986, July 5   **Litho.**   **Perf. 13½**
812 A241 70fr multicolored   .85   .25
813 A241 100fr multicolored   .95   .30
814 A241 130fr multicolored   1.60   .40
    Nos. 812-814 (3)   3.40   .95

Queen Elizabeth II, 60th Birthday — A242

100fr, Elizabeth. 175fr, Elizabeth, Pres. Biya. 210fr, Elizabeth, diff.

1986, July 15   **Litho.**   **Perf. 13**
815 A242 100fr multicolored   1.00   .40
816 A242 175fr multicolored   1.40   .60
817 A242 210fr multicolored   2.00   .75
    Nos. 815-817 (3)   4.40   1.75

Natl. Democratic Party, 1st Anniv. — A243

No. 818, Party headquarters, Bamenda. No. 819, Pres. Biya, vert. No. 820, Presidential address, vert.

1986, July 25   **Perf. 12½**
818 A243 70fr multicolored   .70   .25
819 A243 70fr multicolored   .70   .25
820 A243 100fr multicolored   1.00   .35
    Nos. 818-820 (3)   2.40   .85

Kwem Mask Dancers of the Northeast — A244

1986, Aug. 1   **Perf. 13½**
821 A244 100fr multicolored   1.00   .35
822 A244 130fr multicolored   1.25   .45

Endangered Species — A245

1986, Aug. 20
823   300fr Varanus niloticus   3.50   1.00
824   300fr Panthera pardus   3.50   1.00
    For surcharge see No. 872.

A246

Intl. Peace Year: 175fr, 200fr, Desmond Tutu, South Africa, Nobel Peace Prize winner. 250fr, UN and IPY emblems.

1986, Sept. 7   **Litho.**   **Perf. 13½**
825 A246 175fr multicolored   1.75   1.10
826 A246 200fr multicolored   2.00   1.25
827 A246 250fr multicolored   2.50   1.50
    Nos. 825-827 (3)   6.25   3.85

A247

1986, Oct. 30   **Litho.**   **Perf. 13½**
828 A247 70fr multicolored   .65   .25

Natl. Fed. of Associations for the Handicapped.

African Vaccination Year — A248

70fr, Family under umbrella. 100fr, Child immunization.

1986, Nov. 9
829 A248 70fr multicolored   .90   .25
830 A248 100fr multicolored   1.10   .35

Arbor Day — A249

70fr, Afforestation map. 100fr, Hands, seedling.

1986, Dec. 20   **Litho.**   **Perf. 13½**
831 A249 70fr multicolored   .90   .25
832 A249 100fr multicolored   1.10   .35

Agricultural Development — A250

No. 833, ONCPB seminar. No. 834, Coconut farming, Dibombari. No. 835, Pineapple farm.

1986, Dec. 24
833 A250 70fr multicolored   .75   .40
834 A250 70fr multicolored   .75   .40
835 A250 200fr multicolored   2.00   1.10
    Nos. 833-835 (3)   3.50   1.90

Insects Destructive to Agriculture A251

70fr, Antestiopsis lineaticollis intricata. 100fr, Distantiella theobroma.

1987, Sept. 25   **Litho.**   **Perf. 13½**
836 A251 70fr multicolored   1.50   .50
837 A251 100fr multicolored   2.00   .70

4th African Games, Nairobi — A252

1987, Oct. 1   **Perf. 12½**
838 A252 100fr Shot put   .90   .70
839 A252 140fr Pole vault   1.25   1.00

Maroua Agricultural Show — A253

1988, Jan. 6
840 A253 70fr Millet field   .90   .50
841 A253 100fr Cotton   1.10   .70
842 A253 150fr Cattle   1.60   1.10
    Nos. 840-842 (3)   3.60   2.30

World Wildlife Fund — A254

Baboons, Papio leucophaeus: 30fr, Adult. 40fr, Adult grooming young. 70fr, Baboon on branch. 100fr, Adult carrying young.

1988, Apr. 25   **Litho.**   **Perf. 13**
843 A254 30fr multicolored   1.75   .75
844 A254 40fr multicolored   2.25   .75
845 A254 70fr multicolored   3.50   1.25
846 A254 100fr multicolored   6.00   1.75
    Nos. 843-846 (4)   13.50   4.50

Interparliamentary Union, Cent. — A255

1989   **Litho.**   **Perf. 13½**
847 A255 50fr Natl. Assembly   .60   .30

World Cup Soccer Championships, Italy — A256

No. 849, Players, diff. No. 850, Goalkeeper, flags. No. 851, Team.

1990, Oct. 27   **Litho.**   **Perf. 11½**
       Granite Paper
848 A256 200fr shown   1.75   1.00
849 A256 250fr multicolored   2.25   1.25
850 A256 250fr multicolored   2.25   1.25
851 A256 300fr multicolored   3.00   1.50
a.   Souv. sheet of 4, #848-851   9.00   6.50
    Nos. 848-851 (4)   9.25   5.00

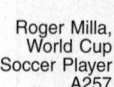

Roger Milla,
World Cup
Soccer Player
A257

1990, July 4　Litho.　Perf. 11½
Granite Paper
852　A257　500fr multicolored　　6.50　3.50
　a.　Souv. sheet of 1　　　　　　9.00　6.00

Agriculture
A258

70fr, Treating cacao plants. 100fr, Sheep.

1990, Dec. 1　Litho.　Perf. 13½
853　A258　70fr multicolored　　1.25　.55
854　A258　100fr multicolored　　1.75　.80
　a.　Sheet of 2, #853-854, perf. 12½　8.00　8.00

For surcharges see Nos. 894-895.

UN Development Program, 40th
Anniv. — A259

1990, Dec. 31　Litho.　Perf. 13½
855　A259　50fr multicolored　　.60　.40

Intl.
Literacy
Year
A260

1990, Dec. 31
856　A260　200fr bl, blk, & lt bl　　2.00　.75

Independence, 30th Anniv. — A261

1000fr, Flag, Palace, #336.

1991, Jan. 1　　　　　　Perf. 13
857　A261　150fr shown　　1.75　1.25
858　A261　1000fr multi　　9.00　8.00
　a.　Souv. sheet of 2, #857-858　12.50　12.50

A262

Fight
Against
AIDS —
A262a

1991, Jan. 15
859　A262　15fr Hearts, map, vert.　.25　.25
860　A262a 25fr shown　　　　　　.35　.25

See Nos. 884-885.

Birds
A263

Designs: Nos. 861, 864, Pie grieche, vert.
Nos. 862, 863, Picathartes chauve.

1991, May 3　Litho.　Perf. 13½
861　A263　70fr grn & multi　　.75　.35
862　A263　70fr bl & multi　　.75　.40
863　A263　300fr blk & multi　　3.25　2.00
864　A263　350fr blk & multi　　3.50　2.25
　a.　Souv. sheet of 2, #863-864　9.00　5.50
　　　Nos. 861-864 (4)　　　　8.25　5.00

Wild
Animals
A264

1991, May 8　　　　　　Perf. 13½
865　A264　125fr Elephant　　1.60　1.00
866　A264　250fr Water buffalo　3.00　2.00
　a.　Souvenir sheet of 2, #865-866,
　　　perf. 12½　　　　　　　　9.00　3.50

City Hall Type of 1982 Redrawn
1991　　　　　　　　　　　Perf. 13
867　A202　40fr multicolored　　.60　.25

No. 867 inscribed "Republic of Cameroon"
instead of "United Republic of Cameroon."

Cameroun
Catholic
Church,
Cent. (in
1990)
A265

125fr, Mvolye church. 250fr, Akono church.

1991, Dec. 8　Litho.　Perf. 13½
868　A265　125fr multicolored　　1.25　.75
　a.　Booklet pane of 4
　　　Complete booklet, #868a
869　A265　250fr multicolored　　2.25　1.75
　a.　Souvenir sheet of 2, #868-869
　　　perf. 12½x13　　　　　　4.00　3.00
　b.　Booklet pane of 4
　　　Complete booklet, #869a

Issued: Nos. 868a, 869b, 1993.

Intl.
Savings
Banks
Institute,
7th
Meeting
of the
African
Group
A266

1991, Dec. 9
870　A266　250fr multicolored　　2.40　1.60
　a.　Souv. sheet of 1, perf. 12½x13　3.00　2.00

No. 799
Surcharged

No. 824
Surcharged

1992　　　　　　　　　　Perf. 13½
871　A214　20fr on 150fr #799　1.75　.25
872　A245　70fr on 300fr #824　5.75　.55

Bird Type of 1983
1992　Litho.　　Perf. 13½
873　A214　125fr like #800　　1.50　.95

Dated 1985.

Cameroun
Soccer
League
A267

125fr, Mbappe Mbappe Samuel (1936-85),
soccer player, vert. 250fr, Linafoote League
emblem, vert. 400fr, Linafoote emblem, diff.
500fr, Stadium.

1992, Aug.　　　　　　Perf. 11½
874　A267　125fr multicolored　1.25　.75
875　A267　250fr multicolored　2.40　1.75
876　A267　400fr multicolored　3.50　2.75
877　A267　500fr multicolored　5.50　3.50
　　　Nos. 874-877 (4)　　　12.65　8.75

See Nos. 896-896B.

Discovery
of
America,
500th
Anniv.
A268

Columbus and: 125fr, Fleet of ships. 250fr,
Landing in New World. 400fr, Meeting with
natives. 500fr, Map, ships.

1992, Aug.
878　A268　125fr multicolored　1.40　.75
879　A268　250fr multicolored　2.10　1.75
880　A268　400fr multicolored　3.50　2.75
881　A268　500fr multicolored　5.00　3.50
　　　Nos. 878-881 (4)　　　12.00　8.75

Types of 1983-84 Redrawn
1992　Litho.　　Perf. 13½
882　A214　200fr like #739　2.25　1.40
　a.　Booklet pane of 5
　　　Complete booklet, #882a
883　A222　350fr like #763　3.75　2.50

Nos. 882-883 inscribed "Republic of
Cameroon".

AIDS Type of 1991
1993　Litho.　　Perf. 13½
884　A262　100fr like #859　1.10　.70
885　A262　175fr like #860　1.90　1.25

Types of 1983 Redrawn
886　A214　370fr like #738　3.50　2.50

Perf. 13
887　A217　410fr like #746　4.50　2.90

Nos. 886-887 inscribed "Republic of
Cameroon".

Wild Animal Type of 1980 Redrawn
125fr, Crocodile. 250fr, Buffon's antelope,
vert.

1993　Litho.　Serpentine Die Cut 9½
Booklet Stamps
Self-Adhesive
888　A186　125fr multicolored　　1.40　.65
　a.　Booklet pane of 4　　　5.75
889　A186　250fr multicolored　　2.75　1.25
　a.　Booklet pane of 4　　　11.50

Nos. 888-889 inscribed "Republic of
Cameroon".
By their nature, Nos. 888a, 889a are complete booklets. The peelable backing serves
as a booklet cover.

1994 World Cup Soccer
Championships, US — A270

Designs: 125fr, Pres. Paul Biya holding soccer ball, lion. 250fr, Logo, lion, player, map.
450fr, Players, globe, World Cup, flag. 500fr,
US eagle, Cameroun lion, soccer ball.

1994, Mar. 28　　　　Perf. 13
890　A270　125fr multicolored　　.75　.40
891　A270　250fr multicolored　1.50　.75
892　A270　450fr multicolored　2.75　1.75
893　A270　500fr multicolored　3.00　1.75
　a.　Min. sheet of 4, #890-893　80.00　60.00
　　　Nos. 890-893 (4)　　　8.00　4.40

Nos. 853-
854 Srchd.
in Gold
and Black

1993　Litho.　　Perf. 13½
894　A258　125fr on 70fr #853　　—　—
895　A258　125fr on 100fr #854　　—　—
　a.　With gold obliterator, new de-
　　　nomination in black omitted　—　—

**Cameroun Soccer League Type of
1992**
1992-93　Litho.　　Perf. 11½
896　A267　10fr like #876　　—　—
896A　A267　25fr like #875　　—　—
896B　A267　50fr like #874　　—　—

Nos. 896-896A dated 1993.
Issued: 50fr, 8/1/92; others, 1993.

Psittacus
Erithacus — A271

1995　Litho.　Perf. 11½
Granite Paper
897　A271　125fr multicolored　3.00　1.00

Visit of
Pope John
Paul II
A272

125fr, Pope, open text, cross.

1995, Sept. 14　　　　Perf. 12½
898　A272　55fr shown　　　.35　.25
　a.　Souvenir sheet of 1
899　A272　125fr multicolored　.95　.50
　a.　Souvenir sheet of 1

UN, 50th
Anniv.
A273

1995, Oct. 24   *Perf. 11½*
900 A273 200fr shown   1.25 .60
901 A273 250fr "50," people   1.50 .80

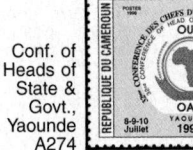

Conf. of
Heads of
State &
Govt.,
Yaounde
A274

Perf. 12½, 14¾x14 (200fr, 250fr)
1996-97   **Litho.**
902   A274 125fr blue & multi   1.00 .50
c.   A274 125fr Perf. 14¾x14
902A   A274 200fr lt grn & multi
         ('97)   1.50 .75
902B   A274 250fr yel & multi ('97)   2.00 1.00
903   A274 410fr pink & multi,
         vert.   3.00 2.00
   No. 902c is dated "1997."

World
Records Set
at 1996
Summer
Olympic
Games,
Atlanta
A275

125fr, Baily, M. Johnson. 250fr, Harrison,
Galfione, Perec, vert.

1996   *Perf. 11½*
904 A275 125fr multi   — 1.00
905 A275 250fr multi   — 1.50

Universal
Declaration of
Human Rights,
50th
Anniv. — A279

1998   **Litho.**   *Perf. 14x14¾*
918 A279 370fr multicolored   — 2.00

1998 World Cup Soccer
Championships, France — A280

Design: 125fr, Flag of Cameroun, World
Cup trophy, vert.

1998   **Litho.**   *Perf. 13*
922 A280 125fr multicolored   — 2.00
923 A280 250fr multicolored   — 2.50

Shrike
A281

1998   **Litho.**   *Perf. 13x13½*
926 A281 125fr multicolored   — 3.00

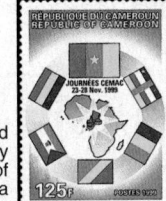

Economic and
Monetary
Community of
Central Africa
Week — A281a

Design: 125fr, Flags surrounding map of
Africa. 225fr, Flags above map of Africa.

1999   **Litho.**   *Perf. 14½*
927 A281a 125fr multi   — —
928 A281a 225fr multi   — —

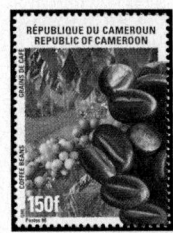

Flora &
Fauna — A282

2000   **Litho.**   *Perf. 14x14½*
929   A282 100fr Pineapple   — 2.00
930   A282 125fr Pineapple   — 2.00
930A A282 150fr Coffee beans   — —
930B A282 175fr Crowned crane   — —
931   A282 200fr Baboon   — 2.00
932   A282 250fr Coffee beans   — 2.00
934   A282 410fr Crowned crane   — 2.00
       Dated 1998.

Peace, Work,
Country
A283

Map and
Scenes — A284

Airplane and
Wildlife — A285

2000   **Litho.**   *Perf. 11¾*
935 A283 125fr multi   — 2.00
936 A284 200fr multi   — 2.00
937 A285 250fr multi   — 2.00

Palais des
Congrés,
Yaounde
A286

Perf. 11¾x11½
2001, Mar. 26   **Litho.**
938 A286 125fr multi
   Cooperation between Cameroun and People's Republic of China, 30th anniv.

Campaign
Against
AIDS — A287

Design: 125fr, Woman vaccinating child,
Chantal Biya Foundation emblem. 250fr,

Chantal Biya Foundation emblem, globe, ribbon, woman with fetus.

2001   **Litho.**   *Perf. 13¼x13*
939 A287 125fr multi   — —
941 A287 250fr multi   — —
a.   Souvenir sheet, #939, 941   150.00 —
    Nos. 939-941 (2)   40.00 —

2002 World Cup Soccer
Championships, Japan and Korea —
A287a

Indomitable
Lions
Soccer
Team, 20th
Anniv. of
Success
A288

2002, June 20   **Litho.**   *Perf. 13¾*
943 A287a 125fr multi
       Perf. 13x13¼
944 A288 250fr multi
    Nos. 943-944 (2)   100.00
     Souvenir Sheet
945   Sheet of 2, #943, 945a   100.00
a.   As #944, 40x44mm, perf. 13½

71st Interpol
General
Assembly,
Yaounde — A289

2002   **Litho.**   *Perf. 13¼x13*
946 A289   125fr multi   4.00 —
a.   Souvenir sheet of 1   8.00 8.00

Cooperation Between Cameroun and
Japan — A290

2005   **Litho.**   *Perf. 13*
948 A290 100fr multi   2.00 1.00
949 A290 125fr multi   2.00 —
950 A290 200fr multi   — —
951 A290 250fr multi   — —
952 A290 370fr multi   2.75 1.50
953 A290 410fr multi   3.00 2.00
954 A290 500fr multi   3.50 —
955 A290 1000fr multi   6.50 —
   Nos. 948-951, 954-955 exist with "2005"
year date.

   Cameroun postal officials have
declared as illegal a stamp inscribed
"Republic of Cameroon" dated "2005"
marking the 70th birthday of Elvis
Presley.

Postal Savings
Bank — A291

2006   **Litho.**   *Perf. 15x14*
956 A291 500fr multi

   No. 956 was issued in 1997 as a stamp to
pay fees for opening an account with the Postal Savings Bank. It was made available for
postal use in 2006.

Visit of
Pope
Benedict
XVI to
Cameroun
A292

Flags of Vatican City and Cameroun, Pope
Benedict XVI, Pres. Paul Biya and background
color of: 200fr, Yellow. 250fr, Bright pink.

2009   **Litho.**   *Perf. 13x13¼*
957-958 A292   Set of 2   6.00

New Challenges for Africa Conference,
Yaounde — A293

Colors: 125fr, Black & gray. 250fr,
Multicolored.

2010   **Litho.**   *Perf. 13½*
959-960 A293   Set of 2   5.00

Reunification and
Independence,
50th
Anniv. — A294

Designs: 125fr, Cameroun flag shown
rotated 90 degrees clockwise. 200fr, 50th
anniversary emblem. 250fr, Arms of Cameroun. 500fr, Pres. Paul Biya in black.
1000fr, Pres. Biya in color.

2010
961-964 A294   Set of 4   40.00 —
964a   Horiz. strip of 4, #961-964   — —
964b   Booklet pane of 8, 2 each
      #961-964   — —
     Complete booklet, #964b   — —
     Souvenir Sheet
965 A294 1000fr multi   20.00 —
   No. 965 sold for 1500fr.

Diplomatic Relations Between
Cameroun and People's Republic of
China, 25th Anniv.
A295

Designs: 125fr, Workers digging trenches
for optical fibers. 200fr, Gynecological, Obstetrics and Pediatric Hospital, Yaounde. 250fr,
Multi-purpose Sports Complex, Yaounde.
500fr, Cameroun Pres. Paul Biya and Chinese
Pres. Hu Jintao shaking hands.

2011, Mar. 26   *Perf. 12*
966-969 A295   Set of 4   20.00 —
968a   Souvenir sheet of 3, #966-968   15.00 —
   See Nos. 975-976.

First Douala-Paris Camair-Co
Flight — A296

Litho. & Embossed
2011, Mar. 28   Perf. 13x13¼

		Denomination	Color
970	A296 250fr green	—	—
971	A296 500fr white	—	—
a.	Souvenir sheet of 2, #970-971	—	—

Discovery
of AIDS
and HIV,
30th Anniv.
A297

Designs: 100fr, Emblem of Cameroun
National Committee for the Campaign Against
AIDS. 250fr, AIDS ribbon, map of Africa.
500fr, Chantal Biya, First Lady of Cameroun
and founder of Synergies Africaines charity.

2011, June 3   Litho.
972-974 A297   Set of 3   —   —

Diplomatic Relations Type of 2011
Souvenir Sheets

Design as before.

2011, Sept. 14   Litho.   Perf. 12
975 A295 500fr multi   —   —

Litho. With Three-Dimensional Plastic Affixed
Without Gum

976 A295 500fr multi   —   —

No. 975 contains one 60x40mm stamp. No.
976 contains one 76x50mm stamp.

SEMI-POSTAL STAMPS

Curie Issue
Common Design Type
1938   Unwmk.   Perf. 13
B1 CD80 1.75fr + 50c brt ultra   10.00   10.00

French Revolution Issue
Common Design Type
Photogravure; Name and Value Typographed in Black
1939
B2	CD83	45c + 25c green	11.50	11.50
B3	CD83	70c + 30c brown	11.50	11.50
B4	CD83	90c + 35c red org	11.50	11.50
B5	CD83	1.25fr +1fr rose pink	11.50	11.50
B6	CD83	2.25fr + 2fr blue	14.00	14.00
		Nos. B2-B6 (5)	60.00	60.00

Stamps of
1925-33
Srchd. in
Black

1940   Perf. 14x13½
B7	A7	1.25fr + 2fr gray & dp bl	32.50	24.00
B8	A7	1.75fr + 3fr brn & org	32.50	24.00
B9	A7	2fr + 5fr dl grn & brn org	32.50	24.00
		Nos. B7-B9 (3)	97.50	72.00

The surtax was used for war relief work.

Regular Stamps of
1939 Surcharged in
Black

1940   Perf. 13
B10	A20	25c + 5fr blk brn	130.00	110.00
B11	A20	45c + 5fr slate grn	130.00	110.00
B12	A20	60c + 5fr peacock bl	130.00	120.00
B13	A20	70c + 5fr plum	130.00	120.00
		Nos. B10-B13 (4)	520.00	460.00

The surtax was used to purchase Spitfire
planes for the Free French army.

Common Design Type and

Military
Doctor
SP2

Cameroun
Militiaman — SP4

1941   Photo.   Perf. 13½
B13A	SP2	1fr + 1fr red		1.60
B13B	CD86	1.50fr + 3fr maroon		1.60
B13C	SP4	2.50fr + 1fr dk bl		1.60
		Nos. B13A-B13C (3)		4.80

Nos. B13A-B13C were issued by the Vichy
government in France, but were not placed on
sale in Cameroun.

Nos. 223-
224
Surcharged
in Black or
Blue

1941   Perf. 12½x12
B14	CD82	1.25fr + 10fr car lake	120.00	120.00
B15	CD82	2.25fr + 10fr ultra	120.00	120.00

Nos. 223-
224
Surcharged
in Black or
Blue

1941
B16	CD82	1.25fr + 10fr car lake (Bl)	40.00	40.00
B17	CD82	2.25fr + 10fr ultra (Bk)	40.00	40.00

The surtax was used to purchase ambulances for the Free French army.

Regular
Stamps of
1933-39
Surcharged
in Black

1943   Perf. 14x13½, 13, 12½x12
B21	A7	1.25fr + 100 gray & dp bl	27.50	27.50
B22	A21	1.25fr + 100fr car rose	27.50	27.50
B23	CD82	1.25fr + 100fr car lake	27.50	27.50
B24	A21	1.50fr + 100fr choc	27.50	27.50

B25	CD82	2.25fr + 100fr ul-tra	27.50	27.50
		Nos. B21-B25 (5)	137.50	137.50

Nos. 281A-
281B
Surcharged
in Black or
Red

1944   Engr.   Perf. 12½x12
B25A	50c + 1.50fr on 2.50fr deep blue (R)		.40
B25B	+ 2.50fr on 1fr green		.40

Colonial Development Fund.
Nos. B25A-B25B were issued by the Vichy
government in France, but were not placed on
sale in Cameroun.

Red Cross Issue
Common Design Type
1944   Photo.   Perf. 14½x14
B28 CD90 5fr + 20fr rose   2.00   1.60

The surtax was for the French Red Cross
and national relief.

> Catalogue values for unused
> stamps in this section, from this
> point to the end of the section, are
> for **Never Hinged** items.

Tropical Medicine Issue
Common Design Type
1950   Engr.   Perf. 13
B29 CD100 10fr + 2fr dk bl grn
& dk grn   7.25   5.50

The surtax was for charitable work.

Independent State

Map and
Flag — SP7

Unwmk.
1961, Mar. 25   Engr.   Perf. 13
B30	SP7	20fr + 5fr grn, car & yel	1.10	1.00
B31	SP7	25fr + 10fr multi	1.40	1.25
B32	SP7	30fr + 15fr car, yel & grn	2.00	1.75
		Nos. B30-B32 (3)	4.50	4.00

The surtax was for the Red Cross.

Federal Republic

Map of Cameroun, Lions Emblem and
Physician Helping Leper
SP8

1962, Jan. 28
B33	SP8	20fr + 5fr multi	.70	.40
B34	SP8	25fr + 10fr multi	.90	.50
B35	SP8	50fr + 15fr multi	1.75	.85
		Nos. B33-B35 (3)	3.35	1.75

Issued for leprosy relief work.

Anti-Malaria Issue
Common Design Type
1962, Apr. 7   Perf. 12½x12
B36 CD108 25fr + 5fr rose lilac   1.00   .45

WHO drive to eradicate malaria.

Freedom from Hunger Issue
Common Design Type
1963, Mar. 21   Engr.   Perf. 13
B37	CD112 18fr + 5fr multi	1.00	.35
B38	CD112 25fr + 5fr multi	1.25	.40

Antelopes — SP9

Designs: 125fr+10fr, Ourebia ourebi.
250fr+20fr, Kobus defassa.

1991, Apr. 30   Litho.   Perf. 13½x13
B39	SP9	125fr + 10fr multi	2.00	1.10
B40	SP9	250fr + 20fr multi	3.00	2.25
a.	Souvenir sheet of 2, #B39-B40, perf. 12½		8.00	8.00

AIR POST STAMPS

Common Design Type
1942 Unwmk. Photo. Perf. 14½x14
C1	CD87	1fr dk orange	.30	.30
C2	CD87	1.50fr brt red	.30	.30
C3	CD87	5fr brown red	.65	.65
C4	CD87	10fr black	.80	.80
C5	CD87	25fr ultra	1.10	1.10
C6	CD87	50fr dk green	1.40	1.40
C7	CD87	100fr plum	1.75	1.75
		Nos. C1-C7 (7)	6.30	6.30

Types AP9 and AP10 without "RF" and

Plane Over
Coast
AP3

1943-44   Photo.   Perf. 13, 13½
C7A	AP9	25c brown red		.25
C7B	AP9	50c green		.25
C7C	AP9	1fr brt violet		.30
C7D	AP10	5fr red brown		.55
C7E	AP10	10fr black		.65
C7F	AP10	12fr orange		.70
C7G	AP10	20fr crimson		.95
C7H	AP10	50fr blue		1.10
C7I	AP3	100fr lilac brown		1.25
		Nos. C7A-C7I (9)		6.00

Nos. C7A to C7I were issued by the Vichy
Government in France, but were not placed on
sale in Cameroun.
For Types AP9 and AP10 inscribed RF, see
Nos. C15-C24.

> Catalogue values for unused
> stamps in this section, from this
> point to the end of the section, are
> for **Never Hinged** items.

Victory Issue
Common Design Type
1946, May 8   Engr.   Perf. 12½
C8 CD92 8fr dk violet brn   1.60   1.20

European victory of the Allied Nations in
WWII.

Chad to Rhine Issue
Common Design Types
1946, June 6
C9	CD93	5fr dk blue grn	1.60	1.25
C10	CD94	10fr dk rose vio	1.60	1.25
C11	CD95	15fr red	2.00	1.60
C12	CD96	20fr brt blue	2.00	1.60
C13	CD97	25fr orange red	2.10	1.75
C14	CD98	50fr gray	2.75	2.25
		Nos. C9-C14 (6)	12.05	9.70

Plane and Map — AP9

Seaplane
Alighting
AP10

Plane and Freighters AP11

1946 Photo. Perf. 13, 13½

C15	AP9	25c brown red	.40 .25
C16	AP9	50c green	.40 .25
C17	AP9	1fr brt violet	.50 .30
C18	AP10	2fr olive grn	.65 .50
C19	AP10	3fr chocolate	.65 .50
C20	AP10	4fr deep ultra	.65 .50
C21	AP10	6fr blue grn	.65 .50
C22	AP10	7fr brt violet	1.10 .80
C23	AP10	12fr orange	5.50 3.50
C24	AP10	20fr crimson	1.90 1.40
C25	AP11	50fr dk ultra	2.75 1.90
	Nos. C15-C25 (11)		15.15 10.40

Nos. C15 to C25 were issued in 1941 in France by the Vichy Government, but were not sold in Cameroun until 1946.
See Nos. C7A-C7H for stamps without "RF."

Birds over Mountains — AP12

Cavalry and Plane — AP13

Warrior, Dance Mask and Nose of Plane — AP14

Perf. 12½

1947, Feb. 10 Unwmk. Engr.

C26	AP12	50fr dk green	3.25 1.20
C27	AP13	100fr brn red	4.75 1.20
C28	AP14	200fr black	7.25 2.40
	Nos. C26-C28 (3)		15.25 4.80

UPU Issue
Common Design Type

1949, July Perf. 13

C29	CD99	25fr multicolored	8.00 4.75

Rhumsiki Peak — AP16

1953, Feb. 16

C30	AP16	500fr grnsh blk, dk vio & vio bl	26.00 4.00

For surcharge see No. C40.

Edéa Dam and Sacred Ibis — AP17

1953, Nov. 18

C31	AP17	15fr choc, brn lake & ultra	5.50 1.60

Dedication of Edea Dam on the Sanaga River.

Liberation Issue
Common Design Type

1954, June 6

C32	CD102	15fr dk grnsh bl & bl grn	7.25 4.75

Dr. Eugene Jamot, Research Laboratory and Tsetse Flies — AP19

1954, Nov. 29

C33	AP19	15fr dk grn, ind & dk brn	4.75 2.75

75th anniv. of the birth of Dr. Eugene Jamot.

Logging — AP20

100fr, Giraffes. 200fr, Port of Douala.

1955, Jan. 24

C34	AP20	50fr ol grn, brn & vio brn	4.00 .80
C35	AP20	100fr grnsh bl, brn & dk brn	8.00 1.60
C36	AP20	200fr dk grn, choc & dp ultra	10.50 2.40
	Nos. C34-C36 (3)		22.50 4.80

For surcharges see Nos. C38-C39.

Federal Republic
Air Afrique Issue
Common Design Type
Unwmk.

1962, Feb. 17 Engr. Perf. 13

C37	CD107	25fr mar, pur & lt grn	1.00 .50

Nos. C35-C36 and C30 Surcharged in Red

Type I

Two types of 5sh:
I — "5/-" measures 6½x4mm.
II — "5/" measures 3¾x3mm, No dash after diagonal line.

Three types of 10sh:
I — "10/-" measures 9x3¾mm.
II — "10/-" measures 7x2½-3mm.
III — "1" of "10/" vertically in line with last "E" of "FEDERALE".

Two types of £1:
I — "REPUBLIQUE / FEDERALE" 17¼mm wide.
II — "REPUBLIQUE / FEDERALE" 22mm wide.

1961, Oct. 1 Engr. Perf. 13

C38	AP20	5sh on 100fr (I)	10.00 6.00
a.		Type II	32.50 18.00
C39	AP20	10sh on 200fr (I)	22.00 13.00
a.		Type II	77.50 42.50
b.		Type III	32.50 30.00
C40	AP16	£1 on 500fr (I)	35.00 22.00
a.		Type II	60.00 35.00
	Nos. C38-C40 (3)		67.00 41.00

Issued for use in the former United Kingdom Trust Territory of Southern Cameroons.

Kapsikis Mokolo — AP21

Designs: 50fr, Cocotieres Hotel, Douala. 100fr, Cymothoe sangaris butterflies. 200fr, Ostriches, Waza Reservation.

1962, June 15

C41	AP21	50fr sl grn, bl & dl red	.90 .25
C42	AP21	100fr multicolored	5.75 .60
C43	AP21	200fr dk grn, blk & bis	8.00 1.40
C44	AP21	500fr vio brn, bl & ocher	9.00 2.25
	Nos. C41-C44 (4)		23.65 4.50

Telstar Type of Regular Issue

1963, Feb. 9 Size: 48x27mm

C45	A50	100fr dk grn & red brn	2.50 .65

Edéa Relay Station — AP22

1963, May 18 Photo. Perf. 12x12½

C46	AP22	100fr multicolored	2.50 .65

Issued to publicize the high frequency telegraph connection Douala-Yaoundé.

African Postal Union Issue
Common Design Type

1963, Sept. 8 Unwmk. Perf. 12½

C47	CD114	85fr ultra, ocher & red	2.25 1.00

Air Afrique Issue, 1963
Common Design Type

1963, Nov. 19 Perf. 13x12

C48	CD115	50fr pink, gray, blk & grn	1.25 .40

Olympic Games Type of 1964

300fr, Greco-Roman wrestlers (ancient).

1964, Oct. 10 Engr. Perf. 13

C49	A57	300fr red, dk brn & dl grn	7.50 2.00
a.		Sheet of 3, #403-404, C49	13.50 4.25

Kribi Port — AP25

1964, Oct. 26 Unwmk. Perf. 13

C50	AP25	50fr red brn, ultra & grn	1.00 .35

Black Rhinoceros — AP26

1964, Dec. 15 Engr. Perf. 13

C51	AP26	250fr brn red, grn & dk brn	10.00 3.00

Pres. John F. Kennedy — AP27

1964, Dec. 8 Photo. Perf. 12½

C52	AP27	100fr grn, yel grn & brn	2.50 1.10
a.		Souvenir sheet of 4	10.00 4.50

Pres. John F. Kennedy (1917-63).

Abraham Lincoln — AP28

1965, Apr. 20 Unwmk. Perf. 13

C53	AP28	100fr multicolored	2.50 .80

Abraham Lincoln, death centenary.

Syncom Satellite and ITU Emblem — AP29

1965, May 17 Engr.

C54	AP29	70fr red, dk bl, & blk	1.60 .60

Cent. of the ITU.

Sir Winston Spencer Churchill, Statesman and World War II Leader — AP30

Designs: 12fr, Churchill giving V sign. 18fr, Churchill, battleship and oak leaves with acorns.

Perf. 13x12½

1965, May 28 Photo. Unwmk.

C55	12fr multicolored		1.00 .50
C56	18fr multicolored		1.00 .50
a.	AP40 Strip of 2, #C55-C56 + label		2.75 1.40

ICY Type of Regular Issue

1965, Sept. 11 Engr. Perf. 13

C57	A68	100fr dk red & dk bl	2.25 .70

Racing Boat, Sanaga River, Edéa — AP31

1965, Oct. 27   **Unwmk.**   **Perf. 13**
C58 AP31 50fr brn, dk grn & sl   2.25 .35

Edward H. White Floating in Space and Gemini IV — AP32

Designs: 50fr, Vostok 6. 200fr, Gemini V and REP (rendezvous evaluation pod). 500fr, Gemini VI & VII rendezvous.

1966, Mar. 30   **Engr.**   **Perf. 13**
C59 AP32 50fr car rose & dk sl grn	.90	.35
C60 AP32 100fr red lil & vio bl	2.10	.65
C61 AP32 200fr ultra & dk pur	3.75	1.40
C62 AP32 500fr brt bl & indigo	9.00	3.00
Nos. C59-C62 (4)	15.75	5.40

Man's conquest of space.

Hotel Type of Regular Issue

18fr, Mountain Hotel, Buea. 25fr, Hotel Akwa Palace, Douala. 50fr, Terminus Hotel, Yaoundé. 60fr, Imperial Hotel, Yaoundé. 85fr, Independence Hotel, Yaoundé. 100fr, Hunting Lodge, Mora, vert. 150fr, Boukarous (round huts), Waza Camp.

1966
C63 A71 18fr sl grn, brt bl & blk	.45	.25
C64 A71 25fr car, ultra & sl	.65	.25
C65 A71 50fr choc, grn & ocher	2.50	.90
C66 A71 60fr choc, grn & brt bl	1.50	.50
C67 A71 85fr dk car rose, dl bl & grn	1.90	.60
C68 A71 100fr brn, grn & sl	2.75	.70
C69 A71 150fr brn, dl bl & ocher	3.75	.90
Nos. C63-C69 (7)	13.50	4.05

Issued: Nos. C63-C64, 4/6; Nos. C65-C69, 6/4.

Flower Type of Regular Issue

Flowers: 25fr, Hibiscus mutabilis. 50fr, Delonix regia. 100fr, Bougainvillea.

1966, May 20   **Photo.**   **Perf. 12½**
Flowers in Natural Colors
Size: 26x45mm
C70 A75 25fr slate green	.75	.25
C71 A75 50fr brt grnsh bl	1.60	.25
C72 A75 100fr gold	3.25	.25
Nos. C70-C72 (3)	5.60	.65

Military Police — AP33

25fr, "Army," soldier, tanks & parachutes. 60fr, "Navy," & "Vigilante." 100fr, "Air Force," plane.

1966, June 21   **Engr.**   **Perf. 13**
C73 AP33 20fr vio bl, org brn & dl pur	.55	.25
C74 AP33 25fr dk grn, dl pur & brn	.55	.25
C75 AP33 60fr bl grn, bl & ind	1.60	.30
C76 AP33 100fr brn, Prus bl & car rose	2.75	.65
Nos. C73-C76 (4)	5.45	1.45

Issued to honor Cameroun's armed forces.

Wembley Stadium, London — AP34

1966, July 20
C77 AP34 50fr shown	1.40	.25
C78 AP34 200fr Soccer	4.75	1.10

8th World Cup Soccer Championship, Wembley, England, July 11-30.

Air Afrique Issue, 1966
Common Design Type

1966, Aug. 31   **Photo.**   **Perf. 13**
C79 CD123 25fr red lil, blk & gray   .80 .25

Yaoundé Cathedral — AP35

18fr, Buea Cathedral. 30fr, Orthodox Church, Yaoundé. 60fr, Mosque, Garoua.

1966, Dec. 19   **Engr.**   **Perf. 13**
C80 AP35 18fr choc, bl & grn	.45	.25
C81 AP35 25fr brn, grn & brt vio	.55	.25
C82 AP35 30fr lil, grn & dl red	.70	.25
C83 AP35 60fr mar, brt grn & grn	1.40	.35
Nos. C80-C83 (4)	3.10	1.10

Pioneer A and Moon — AP36

1967, Apr. 30   **Engr.**   **Perf. 13**
C84 AP36 25fr shown	.50	.25
C85 AP36 50fr Ranger 6	.90	.35
C86 AP36 100fr Luna 9	2.25	.65
C87 AP36 250fr Luna 10	4.75	2.00
Nos. C84-C87 (4)	8.40	3.25

"Conquest of the Moon."

Flower Type of Regular Issue

200fr, Thevetia Peruviana. 250fr, Amaryllis.

1967, June 22   **Photo.**   **Perf. 12½**
Size: 26x46mm
C88 A86 200fr multi	4.50	.90
C89 A86 250fr multi	5.50	1.10

African Postal Union Issue, 1967
Common Design Type

1967, Sept. 9   **Engr.**   **Perf. 13**
C90 CD124 100fr red brn, Prus bl & brt lil   2.40 .65

Skis, Ice Skates, Olympic Flame and Emblem — AP38

1967, Oct. 11   **Engr.**   **Perf. 13**
C91 AP38 30fr ultra & sepia   1.60 .25

Issued to publicize the 10th Winter Olympic Games, Grenoble, Feb. 6-8, 1968.

Cameroun Exhibit, EXPO '67 — AP39

100fr, Bangwa house poles carved with ancestor figures. 200fr, Canadian Pavilions.

1967, Oct. 18
C92 AP39 50fr mag, ol & mar	1.00	.25
C93 AP39 100fr dk grn, mar & dk brn	3.25	.70
C94 AP39 200fr brn, lil rose & sl grn	4.25	1.25
Nos. C92-C94 (3)	8.50	2.20

EXPO '67, International Exhibition, Montreal, Apr. 28-Oct. 27, 1967.
See note after No. C116 regarding 1969 moon overprint.

Konrad Adenauer (1876-1967), Chancellor of West Germany (1949-63) and Cologne Cathedral AP40

70fr, Adenauer and Chancellery, Bonn.

1967, Dec. 1   **Photo.**   **Perf. 12½**
C95 AP40 30fr multi	.90	.25
C96 AP40 70fr multi	1.50	.40
a. Pair, #C95-C96 + label	3.50	2.50

Pres. Ahidjo, King Faisal and View of Mecca — AP41

60fr, Pres. Ahidjo, Pope Paul VI & view of Rome.

1968, Feb. 18   **Photo.**   **Perf. 12½**
C97 AP41 30fr multi	.90	.25
C98 AP41 60fr multi	2.10	.30

Issued to commemorate President Ahidjo's Pilgrimage to Mecca and visit to Rome.

Earth on Television Transmitted by Explorer VI — AP42

30fr, Molniya spacecraft. 40fr, Earth on television screen transmitted by Molniya.

1968, Apr. 20   **Engr.**   **Perf. 13**
C99 AP42 20fr multi	.55	.25
C100 AP42 30fr multi	.80	.25
C101 AP42 40fr multi	1.10	.25
Nos. C99-C101 (3)	2.45	.75

Telecommunication by satellite.

Forge — AP43

No. C103, Tea harvest. No. C104, Trans-Cameroun railroad (diesel train emerging from tunnel). 40fr, Rubber harvest. 60fr, Douala Harbor, horiz.

1968, June 5   **Engr.**   **Perf. 13**
C102 AP43 20fr red brn, dk grn & ind	.60	.25
C103 AP43 30fr dk brn, grn & ultra	1.10	.35
C104 AP43 30fr ind, sl grn & bis brn	7.50	2.50
C105 AP43 40fr ol bis, dk grn & bl grn	1.10	.35
C106 AP43 60fr ultra, dk brn & sl	3.00	1.00
Nos. C102-C106 (5)	13.30	4.45

Second Economic Development Five-Year Plan.

Boxing — AP44

50fr, Long jump. 60fr, Athlete on rings.

1968, Aug. 19   **Engr.**   **Perf. 13**
C107 AP44 30fr brt grn, dk grn & choc	.65	.25
C108 AP44 50fr brt grn, brn red & choc	1.25	.30
C109 AP44 60fr brt grn, ultra & choc	1.50	.35
a. Min. sheet of 3, #C107-C109	4.00	4.00
Nos. C107-C109 (3)	3.40	.90

19th Olympic Games, Mexico City, 10/12-27.

Human Rights Type of Regular Issue

1968, Sept. 14   **Photo.**   **Perf. 12½x13**
C110 A92 30fr grn & brt pink   .80 .25

Martin Luther King, Jr. — AP45

Portraits: No. C112, Mahatma Gandhi and map of India. 40fr, John F. Kennedy. 60fr, Robert F. Kennedy. No. C115, Rev. Martin Luther King, Jr. No. C116, Mahatma Gandhi.

1968, Dec. 5   Photo.   Perf. 12½
C111 AP45 30fr bl & blk   .60   .25
C112 AP45 30fr multi   .60   .25
C113 AP45 40fr pink & blk   1.00   .50
C114 AP45 60fr bluish lil & blk 1.25 .50
C115 AP45 70fr yel grn & blk   1.40   .60
a.   Souvenir sheet of 4,
      #C112-C115   8.00   8.00
C116 AP45 70fr multi   1.40   .60
   Nos. C111-C116 (6)   6.25   2.70

Issued to honor exponents of non-violence. The 2 King stamps (Nos. C111 and C115), the 2 Gandhi stamps (Nos. C112 and C116) and the 2 Kennedy stamps (Nos. C113-C114) are each printed as triptychs with a descriptive label between.

In 1969 Nos. C111-C116 and C94 were overprinted in carmine capitals: "Premier Homme / sur la Lune / 20 Juillet 1969" and "First Man / Landing on Moon / 20 July 1969". Two types of overprints were used: Type I - English and French text 25mm apart; Type II - English and French text close together. Values: on No. C94, $50; on Nos. C111-C116, $325; on No. C115a (2 different souvenir sheets, with both overprint types on different stamps), each $300.

PHILEXAFRIQUE Issue

The Letter, by Armand Cambon AP46

1968, Dec. 10
C117 AP46 100fr multi   3.25   1.25

PHILEXAFRIQUE, Philatelic Exhibition in Abidjan, Feb. 14-23, 1969. Printed with alternating light green label.

2nd PHILEXAFRIQUE Issue
Common Design Type

Design: Cameroun #199 and Wouri Bridge.

1969, Feb. 14   Engr.   Perf. 13
C118 CD128 50fr multi   3.25   1.25

Caladium Bicolor — AP47

Flowers: 50fr, Aristolochia elegans. 100fr, Gloriosa simplex.

1969, May 14   Photo.   Perf. 12½
C119 AP47 30fr lil & multi   .75   .25
C120 AP47 50fr grn & multi   1.50   .40
C121 AP47 100fr brn & multi   3.50   1.00
   Nos. C119-C121 (3)   5.75   1.65

3rd Intl. Flower Show, Paris, Apr. 23-Oct. 5.

Douala Post Office — AP48

50fr, Buèa P.O. 100fr, Bafoussam P.O.

1969, June 19   Engr.   Perf. 13
C122 AP48 30fr grn, vio bl &
           brn   .55   .25
C123 AP48 50fr sl, emer & red
           brn   .90   .25
C124 AP48 100fr dk brn, brt grn
           & brn   1.75   .50
   Nos. C122-C124 (3)   3.20   1.00

Coronation of Napoleon I, by Jacques Louis David — AP49

Napoleon Crossing Saint Bernard, after J. L. David — AP50

1969, July 4   Photo.   Perf. 12x12½
C125 AP49   30fr vio bl & multi 1.00 .40

Die-cut Perf. 10
Embossed on Gold Foil
C126 AP50 1000fr gold   45.00 45.00

Bicentenary of birth of Napoleon I.

William E. B. Du Bois (1868-1963), American Writer — AP51

15fr, Dr. Price Mars, Haiti (1876-1969). No. C128, Aimé Cesaire, Martinique (1913-). No. C130, Langston Hughes, US (1902-67). No. C131, Marcus Garvey, Jamaica (1887-1940). 100fr, René Maran, Martinique (1887-1960).

1969, Sept. 25   Photo.   Perf. 12½
C127 AP51 15fr lt bl & blk   .45   .25
C128 AP51 30fr lem & blk   .55   .25
C129 AP51 30fr rose brn & blk .55   .25
C130 AP51 50fr gray & blk   .80   .25
C131 AP51 50fr emer & blk   .80   .25
C132 AP51 100fr yel & blk   2.00   .60
a.   Min. sheet of 6, #C127-C132 6.75 4.50
   Nos. C127-C132 (6)   5.15   1.85

Issued to honor Negro writers.

ILO Emblem — AP52

1969, Oct. 29   Photo.   Perf. 13
C133 AP52 30fr blk, bl grn & gray .80 .25
C134 AP52 50fr blk, dp lil rose &
           gray   1.40   .35

50th anniv. of the ILO.

Armstrong, Collins and Aldrin Splashdown in the Pacific — AP53

Design: 500fr, Landing module and Nell A. Armstrong's first step on moon.

1969, Nov. 29   Photo.   Perf. 12½
C135 AP53 200fr multi   5.00   1.25
C136 AP53 500fr multi   12.00 3.00

See note after Algeria No. 427.

Pres. Ahidjo, Arms and Map of Cameroun — AP54

Embossed on Gold Foil
1970, Jan. 1   Die-cut Perf. 10
C137 AP54 1000fr gold & multi 26.00 25.00

10th anniversary of independence.

Hotel Mont Fébé, Yaoundé — AP55

1970, Jan. 15   Engr.   Perf. 13
C138 AP55 30fr lt brn, sl grn &
           gray   .80   .25

Lenin — AP56

1970, Jan. 25   Photo.   Perf. 12½
C139 AP56 50fr org & blk   2.00   .55

Plant Type of Regular Issue

Designs: 50fr, Cleome speciosa (caper). 100fr, Mussaenda erythrophylla (madder).

1970, Mar. 24   Photo.   Perf. 12½
            Size: 26x46mm
C140 A99 50fr blk & multi   1.40   .35
C141 A99 100fr multi   2.75   .90

Map of Africa and Lions Emblem Pinpointing Yaoundé — AP57

1970, May 2   Photo.   Perf. 12½
C142 AP57 100fr multi   2.25   .75

13th Lions International Congress of District 13, Yaoundé, May 2, 1970.

UN Emblem and Doves — AP58

Design: 50fr, UN emblem and dove, vert.

1970, June 26   Engr.   Perf. 13
C143 AP58 30fr brn & org   1.00   .25
C144 AP58 50fr Prus bl & sl bl 1.25   .40

25th anniversary of the United Nations.

Japanese Pavilion and EXPO Emblem — AP59

Designs (EXPO Emblem and): 100fr, Map of Japan, vert. 150fr, Australian pavilion.

1970, Aug. 1   Engr.   Perf. 13
C145 AP59 50fr ind, lt grn & ver .90 .30
C146 AP59 100fr bl, lt grn & red 2.00 .55
C147 AP59 150fr choc, bl & gray 3.25 .65
   Nos. C145-C147 (3)   6.15   1.50

EXPO '70 International Exhibition, Osaka, Japan, Mar. 15-Sept. 13.

Charles de Gaulle — AP60

Design: 200fr, de Gaulle in unifrom.

1970, Aug. 27
C148 100fr grn, vio bl & ol brn 2.25 .80
C149 200fr ol brn, vio bl & grn 4.50 1.40
a.   AP60 Pair, #C148-C149 +
       label   8.00   8.00

Rallying of the Free French, 30th anniv. For overprints see Nos. C159-C160.

Pelé and Team — AP61

Designs: 50fr, Aztec Stadium, Mexico City, horiz. 100fr, Mexican soccer team, horiz.

1970, Oct. 14   Photo.   Perf. 12½
C150	AP61	50fr multi	.90	.30
C151	AP61	100fr multi	2.00	.65
C152	AP61	200fr multi	3.50	1.00
		Nos. C150-C152 (3)	6.40	1.95

9th World Soccer Championships for the Jules Rimet Cup, Mexico City, May 30-June 21, and the final victory of Brazil over Italy.

Ludwig van Beethoven (1770-1827), Composer AP62

1970, Nov. 23   Engr.   Perf. 13
| C153 | AP62 | 250fr multi | 5.75 | 1.75 |

Christ at Emmaus, by Rembrandt — AP63

150fr, The Anatomy Lesson, by Rembrandt.

1970, Dec. 5   Photo.   Perf. 12x12½
| C154 | AP63 | 70fr grn & multi | 1.40 | .35 |
| C155 | AP63 | 150fr multi | 2.75 | .75 |

Charles Dickens — AP64

Designs: 50fr, Scenes from David Copperfield. 100fr, Dickens holding quill.

1970, Dec. 22   Perf. 13
C156	AP64	40fr blk & rose	.95	.25
C157	AP64	50fr bis & multi	1.00	.30
C158	AP64	100fr rose & multi	2.00	.65
a.		Strip of 3, #C156-C158	5.00	2.00

Charles Dickens (1812-1870), English novelist.

De Gaulle Type of 1970 Overprinted

1971, Jan. 15   Engr.   Perf. 13
C159	100fr vio bl, emer & brn red	2.75	.75
C160	200fr brn red, emer & vio bl	5.00	1.25
a.	AP60 Pair, #C159-C160 + label	8.00	8.00

In memory of Gen. Charles de Gaulle (1890-1970), President of France.

Timber Storage, Douala — AP65

Industrialization: 70fr, ALUCAM aluminum plant, Edea, vert. 100fr, Mbakaou Dam.

1971, Feb. 14   Engr.   Perf. 13
C161	AP65	40fr dk red, bl grn & ol brn	.55	.25
C162	AP65	70fr ol brn, sl grn & brt bl	1.10	.30
C163	AP65	100fr Prus bl, yel grn & red brn	1.75	.40
		Nos. C161-C163 (3)	3.40	.95

Relay Race — AP66

50fr, Torch bearer, vert. 100fr, Discus.

1971, Apr. 24   Engr.   Perf. 13
C164	AP66	30fr dk brn, ver & ind	.65	.25
C165	AP66	50fr blk, bl & choc	.80	.25
C166	AP66	100fr multi	1.75	.40
		Nos. C164-C166 (3)	3.20	.90

75th anniv. of revival of Olympic Games.

Fishing Trawler — AP67

Designs: 40fr, Local fishermen, Northern Cameroun. 70fr, Fishing harbor, Douala. 150fr, Shrimp boats, Douala.

1971, May 14   Engr.   Perf. 13
C167	AP67	30fr lt brn, bl & grn	.70	.30
C168	AP67	40fr sl grn, bl & dk brn	.90	.30
C169	AP67	70fr dk brn, bl & red org	2.00	.40
C170	AP67	150fr multi	4.25	1.00
		Nos. C167-C170 (4)	7.85	2.00

Cameroun fishing industry.

Cameroun No. 123 and War Memorial, Yaoundé — AP68

Designs (Cameroun Stamps): 25fr, No. C33 and Jamot memorial. 40fr, No. 431 and government buildings, Yaoundé. 50fr, No. 19 and Imperial German postal emblem. 100fr, No. 101 and World War II memorial.

1971, Aug. 1   Engr.   Perf. 13
C171	AP68	20fr grn, ocher & dk brn	.45	.25
C172	AP68	25fr dk brn, vio bl & sl grn	.65	.25
C173	AP68	40fr grn, mar & sl	.80	.25
C174	AP68	50fr dk brn, blk & ver	1.25	.25
C175	AP68	100fr mar, sl grn & org	1.75	.50
		Nos. C171-C175 (5)	4.90	1.50

PHILATECAM 1971 Philatelic Exhibition.

Cameroun Flag, Pres. Ahidjo and Reunification Highway — AP69

Typographed, Silk Screen, Embossed

1971, Oct. 1   Perf. 12½
| C176 | AP69 | 250fr gold & multi | 6.00 | 4.50 |

PHILATECAM Philatelic Exhibition, Yaoundé-Douala.

African Postal Union Issue, 1971
Common Design Type

1971, Nov. 13   Photo.   Perf. 13x13½
| C177 | CD135 | 100fr bl & multi | 2.00 | .50 |

Annunciation, by Fra Angelico — AP71

Christmas (Paintings): 45fr, Virgin and Child, by Andrea del Sarto. 150fr, Christ Child with Lamb, detail from Holy Family, by Raphael, vert.

1971, Dec. 19   Perf. 13x13½, 13½x13
C178	AP71	40fr multi	.55	.25
C179	AP71	45fr multi	.70	.25
C180	AP71	150fr multi	3.25	.75
		Nos. C178-C180 (3)	4.50	1.25

Cameroun Airlines Emblem AP72

1972, Feb. 2   Photo.   Perf. 12½x12
| C181 | AP72 | 50fr lt bl & multi | .80 | .25 |

Inauguration of Cameroun Airlines.

Doge's Palace, by Ippolito Caffi AP73

100fr, 200fr, Details from "Regatta on the Grand Canal," by School of Canaletto.

1972, Mar. 19   Photo.   Perf. 13
C182	AP73	40fr gold & multi	.70	.25
C183	AP73	100fr gold & multi	1.75	.40
C184	AP73	200fr gold & multi	4.00	.80
		Nos. C182-C184 (3)	6.45	1.45

UNESCO campaign to save Venice.

Cosmonauts Patsayev, Dobrovolsky and Volkov — AP74

1972, May 1   Photo.   Perf. 13x13½
| C185 | AP74 | 50fr multi | 1.00 | .30 |

Salute-Soyuz 11 space mission, and in memory of the Russian cosmonauts Victor I. Patsayev, Georgi T. Dobrovolsky and Vladislav N. Volkov, who died during Soyuz 11 space mission, June 6-30, 1971.

UN Headquarters, Chinese Flag and Gate of Heavenly Peace — AP75

1972, May 19   Perf. 13
| C186 | AP75 | 50fr blk, scar & gold | 3.25 | .35 |

Admission of People's Republic of China to UN.

United Republic

Olympic Rings, Swimming AP76

Designs (Olympic Rings and): No. C188, Boxing, vert. 200fr, Equestrian.

1972, Aug. 1   Engr.   Perf. 13
C187	AP76	50fr lake & slate grn	.90	.25
C188	AP76	50fr choc & slate	.90	.25
C189	AP76	200fr cl, gray & dk brn	3.50	1.00
a.		Min. sheet of 3	5.75	5.75
		Nos. C187-C189 (3)	5.30	1.50

20th Olympic Games, Munich, Aug. 26-Sept. 11. No. C189a contains stamps similar to Nos. C187-C189, but in changed colors. The 50fr (swimming) is Prussian blue, violet & brown; the 50c (boxing) lilac, Prussian blue & brown; the 200fr, Prussian blue & brown.

Nos. C187-C189 Overprinted in Red or Black

a

b

c

1972, Oct. 23   Engr.   Perf. 13
C190 AP76(a) 50fr (R)   .90 .25
C191 AP76(b) 50fr   .90 .25
C192 AP76(c) 200fr   3.50 1.00
    Nos. C190-C192 (3)   5.30 1.50

Gold Medal Winners in 20th Olympic Games: Mark Spitz, US, swimming (No. C190); Dieter Kottysch, West Germany, light middleweight boxing (No. C191); Richard Meade, Great Britain, 3-day equestrian (No. C192).

Madonna with Angels, by Cimabue AP77

Christmas: 140fr, Madonna of the Rose Arbor, by Stefan Lochner.

1972, Dec. 21   Photo.   Perf. 13
C193 AP77 45fr gold & multi   1.00 .25
C194 AP77 140fr gold & multi 2.75 1.00

St. Teresa, the Little Flower — AP78

100fr, Lisieux Cathedral and St. Teresa.

1973, Jan. 2   Engr.
C195 AP78 45fr vio bl, pur & mar .70 .25
C196 AP78 100fr mag, ultra & brn 1.75 .40

Centenary of the birth of St. Teresa of Lisieux (1873-1897), Carmelite nun.

African Unity Hall, Addis Ababa and Emperor Haile Selassie — AP79

1973, Mar. 14   Photo.   Perf. 13
C197 AP79 45fr yellow & multi 1.00 .25

80th birthday of Emperor Haile Selassie of Ethiopia.

Corn, Grain, Healthy and Starving People — AP80

1973, Apr. 10   Typo.   Perf. 13
C198 AP80 45fr multi   .80 .25

World Food Program, 10th anniversary.

Hearts and Blood Vessels — AP81

1973, May 5   Engr.
C199 AP81 50fr dk car rose & dk
    vio bl   1.00 .25

"Your Heart is Your Health" and for the 25th anniv. of the WHO.

Type of Regular Issue

Designs: 45fr, Map of Cameroun, Pres. Ahidjo and No. C176. 70fr, National colors and commemorative inscriptions.

1973, May 20   Engr.   Perf. 13
C200 A128 45fr grn & multi   .80 .25
C201 A128 70fr red & multi   1.00 .40

Scout Emblem and Flags — AP82

1973, July 31   Typo.   Perf. 13
C202 AP82 40fr multi   1.00 .25
C203 AP82 45fr multi   1.25 .35
C204 AP82 100fr multi   3.25 .60
    Nos. C202-C204 (3)   5.50 1.20

Cameroun's admission to the World Scout Conference, Mar. 26, 1971.

African Weeks Issue

Head and City Hall, Brussels — AP83

1973, Sept. 17   Engr.   Perf. 13
C205 AP83 40fr dp brn & rose
    claret   .80 .25

African Weeks, Brussels, Sept. 15-30.

Map of Africa with Cameroun — AP84

1973, Sept. 29   Engr.   Perf. 13
C206 AP84 40fr blk, red & grn .80 .25

Help for handicapped children.

Zamengoe Radar Station AP85

1973, Dec. 8   Engr.   Perf. 13
C207 AP85 100fr bl, lt brn & grn 1.50 .45

Chancellor Rolin Madonna, by Van Eyck AP86

Christmas: 140fr, Nativity, by Federigo Barocei.

1973, Dec. 11   Photo.   Perf. 13
C208 AP86 45fr gold & multi 1.00 .30
C209 AP86 140fr gold & multi 2.75 1.00

Zebu Type of 1974

1974, June 1   Litho.   Perf. 13
C210 A140 45fr Zebu herd   1.40 .35

Churchill and Union Jack AP87

1974, July 10   Engr.   Perf. 13
C211 AP87 100fr blk, bl & red 1.60 .45

Winston Churchill (1874-1965).

Soccer, Arms of Frankfurt, Dortmund, Gelsenkirchen and Stuttgart — AP88

100fr, Soccer & arms of Berlin, Hamburg, Hanover & Düsseldorf. 200fr, Soccer cup & game.

1974, Aug. 5   Photo.   Perf. 13
C212 AP88 45fr gray, sl & org .70 .25
C213 AP88 100fr gray, sl & org 1.25 .40
C214 AP88 200fr org, slate & bl 2.75 1.00
  a.   Strip of 3, Nos. C212-C214 5.00 5.00

World Cup Soccer Championship, Munich, June 13-July 7.

Nos. C212-C214 Overprinted in Dark Blue

1974, Sept. 16   Photo.   Perf. 13
C215 AP88 45fr multi   .65 .25
C216 AP88 100fr multi   1.25 .40
C217 AP88 200fr multi   2.40 1.00
  a.   Strip of 3, Nos. C215-C217 5.00 5.00

World Cup Soccer Championship, 1974, victory of German Federal Republic.

UPU Type of 1974

100fr, Cameroun #503. 200fr, Cameroun #C29.

1974, Oct. 8   Engr.   Perf. 13
C218 A142 100fr blue & multi 1.75 .50
C219 A142 200fr red & multi 3.25 1.00

Copernicus and Planets Circling Sun — AP89

1974, Oct. 15   Engr.   Perf. 13
C220 AP89 250fr multi   3.50 1.25

500th anniversary of the birth of Nicolaus Copernicus (1473-1543), Polish astronomer.

21st Chess Olympiad, Nice, France, June 6-30 — AP90

1974, Nov. 3   Photo.   Perf. 13x12½
C221 AP90 100fr Chess pieces 5.25 1.00

Mask and ARPHILA Emblem — AP91

1974, Nov. 30   Engr.   Perf. 13
C222 AP91 50fr choc & magenta .80 .25

ARPHILA 75, Paris, June 6-16, 1975.

Presidents and Flags of Cameroun, CAR, Gabon and Congo — AP92

1974, Dec. 8   **Photo.**
C223 AP92 100fr gold & multi   2.25   .45
See note after No. 595.

Man Landing on Moon — AP93

1974, Dec. 15   **Engr.**
C224 AP93 200fr brn, bl & car   3.25   1.00
5th anniv. of man's 1st landing on the moon.

Charles de Gaulle and Félix
Eboué — AP94

1975, Feb. 24   **Typo.**   **Perf. 13**
C225 AP94 45fr multi   1.50   .35
C226 AP94 200fr multi   5.00   1.50

Felix A. Eboué (1884-1944), Governor of Chad, first colonial governor to join Free French in WWII, 30th death anniversary.

Marquis de
Lafayette
AP95

American Bicentennial: 140fr, Washington and soldiers. 500fr, Franklin and Independence Hall.

1975, Oct. 20   **Engr.**   **Perf. 13**
C227 AP95 100fr vio bl & multi   2.25   .60
C228 AP95 140fr brn & multi   2.40   .65
C229 AP95 500fr grn & multi   7.25   2.00
    Nos. C227-C229 (3)   11.90   3.25

The
Burning
Bush, by
Nicolas
Froment
AP96

Painting: 500fr, Adoration of the Kings, by Gentile da Fabriano, horiz.

1975, Dec. 25   **Photo.**   **Perf. 13**
C230 AP96 50fr gold & multi   .90   .30
C231 AP96 500fr gold & multi   7.25   3.00
    Christmas 1975.

Concorde and Route: Paris-Dakar-Rio
de Janeiro — AP97

1976, July 20   **Litho.**   **Perf. 13**
C232 AP97 500fr lt bl & multi   6.50   1.60
   a.   Souvenir sheet of 1   9.00   9.00
1st commercial flight of supersonic jet Concorde from Paris to Rio de Janeiro, Jan. 21. No. C232a sold for 600fr.
For overprint see No. C263.

Dance Type of 1976

50fr, Dancers & drummer. 100fr, Woman dancer.

1976, Sept. 15   **Litho.**   **Perf. 12**
C233 A154 50fr gray & multi   .65   .25
C234 A154 100fr gray & multi   1.10   .35

Virgin and Child, by Giovanni
Bellini — AP98

Paintings: 30fr, Adoration of the Shepherds, by Le Brun. 60fr, Adoration of the Kings, by Rubens. 500fr, The Newborn, by Georges de la Tour.

1976, Dec. 15   **Litho.**   **Perf. 12½**
C235 AP98 30fr gold & multi   .70   .25
C236 AP98 60fr gold & multi   .90   .25
C237 AP98 70fr gold & multi   1.25   .35
C238 AP98 500fr gold & multi   9.00   3.00
   a.   Souv. sheet of 4, #C235-
      C238   12.50   12.00
    Nos. C235-C238 (4)   11.85   3.85
    Christmas 1976.

Festival Type of 1977

Traditional Chief on his throne, sculpture.

1977, Feb. 4   **Litho.**   **Perf. 12½**
C239 A159 60fr multi   1.10   .25

Easter — AP99

75fr, Crucifixion, by Matthias Grunewald. 125fr, Christ on the Cross, by Velazquez, vert. 150fr, The Deposition, by Titian.

1977, Apr. 2   **Litho.**   **Perf. 12½**
C240   50fr gold & multi   .90   .25
C241   125fr gold & multi   1.75   .45
C242   150fr gold & multi   2.50   .65
   a.   AP99 Souv. sheet of 3, #C240-
      C242, perf. 12   6.75   1.75
    Nos. C240-C242 (3)   5.15   1.35
    No. C242a sold for 350fr.

Lions Emblem,
Map of
Africa — AP100

1977, Apr. 29   **Litho.**   **Perf. 12½**
C243 AP100 250fr multi   3.00   1.00
Lions Club of Douala, 19th Cong., 4/29-30.

Rotary Emblem
AP101

1977, May 18
C244 AP101 60fr multi   .70   .25
Rotary Club of Douala, 20th anniversary.

Antoine de Saint-
Exupéry
AP102

Charles Lindbergh and Spirit of St.
Louis — AP103

Designs: 50fr, Jean Mermoz and his plane. 80fr, Maryse Bastié and her plane. 100fr, Sikorsky S-43. 300fr, Concorde.

1977, May 20   **Engr.**   **Perf. 13**
C245 AP103 50fr org & bl   .90   .25
C246 AP102 60fr mag & org   .95   .25
C247 AP103 80fr mag & bl   1.25   .30
   a.   Souv. sheet, #C245-C247   3.25   3.25
C248 AP103 100fr grn & yel   1.50   .40
C249 AP103 300fr multi   5.50   1.25
C250 AP103 500fr multi   8.00   2.50
   a.   Souv. sheet, #C248-C250   14.50   14.50
    Nos. C245-C250 (6)   18.10   4.95

Aviation pioneers and events. No. C247a sold for 200fr. No. C250a sold for 1000fr.
For overprint see No. C262.

Sassenage Castle, Grenoble — AP104

1977, May 21   **Litho.**   **Perf. 12½**
C251 AP104 70fr multi   1.60   1.00
10th anniv. of Intl. French Language Council.

Jufilex Type of 1977

Designs: 70fr, Switzerland (Zurich) No. 1L1 and Cameroun No. 16. 100fr, Switzerland (Geneva) No. 2L1 and Cameroun No. 254.

1977, June 5   **Litho.**   **Perf. 12**
C252 A161 70fr multi   1.25   .35
C253 A161 100fr multi   2.10   .60

Apollo-Soyuz Type

100fr, Astronaut Vance Brand, Apollo in orbit. 250fr, Apollo and Soyuz docking. 350fr, Cosmonaut Valery Kubasov, Soyuz in orbit. 500fr, Astronaut Donald Slayton, handshake.

1977, Aug. 10   **Litho.**   **Perf. 14x13½**
C256 A163 100fr multicolored   .90   .25
C257 A163 250fr multicolored   2.25   .60
C258 A163 350fr multicolored   3.25   1.00
    Nos. C256-C258 (3)   6.40   5.85

Souvenir Sheet

C259 A163 500fr multicolored   5.00   5.00

Diseased
Knee, WHO
Emblem
AP105

1977, Oct. 15   **Engr.**   **Perf. 13**
C260 AP105 70fr multi   .70   .25
    World Rheumatism Year.

**Nos. C249 and C232 Overprinted in
Red**

Engraved, Lithographed
1977, Nov. 22   **Perf. 13**
C262 AP103 300fr multi   3.25   1.25
C263 AP97 500fr multi   5.00   2.00

Concorde, 1st commercial flight Paris to NY.

Christmas Type of 1977

Paintings: 60fr, Virgin and Child with 4 Saints, by Bellini, horiz. 400fr, Adoration of the Shepherds, by George de la Tour, horiz.

1977, Dec. 15   **Litho.**   **Perf. 12x12½**
C264 A165 60fr multi   1.00   .25
C265 A165 400fr multi   5.00   1.75

Flag Type of 1978

60fr, New flag, Pres. Ahidjo and spear.

1978, Apr. 3   **Litho.**   **Perf. 12½**
C266 A167 60fr multi   .55   .25

Frog Type of 1978

Design: 100fr, Cardioglossa trifasciata.

1978, Apr. 5
C267 A168 100fr multi   3.75   .75

L'Arlesienne, by Van Gogh — AP106

No. C269, Burial of Christ, by Albrecht Dürer.

1978, May 15   Litho.   Perf. 12½
C268 AP106 200fr multi   4.25 1.10
C269 AP106 200fr multi   5.75 1.10

Leprosy Distribution on World Map, Raoul Follereau — AP107

1978, June 6   Litho.   Perf. 12
C270 AP107 100fr multi   1.10 .55
25th World Leprosy Day.

Capt. Cook and Siege of Quebec — AP108

Design: 250fr, Capt. Cook, Adventure and Resolution, map of voyages.

1978, July 26   Engr.   Perf. 13
C271 AP108 100fr multi   2.10 .55
C272 AP108 250fr multi   5.00 1.40
Capt. James Cook (1728-1779), explorer.

Argentine Soccer Team, Coat of Arms and Rimet Cup — AP109

200fr, Two soccer players, vert. 1000fr, Soccer ball illuminating world map, vert.

1978, Sept. 1   Litho.   Perf. 13
C273 AP109 100fr multi   1.00 .55
C274 AP109 200fr multi   1.75 1.10
C275 AP109 1000fr multi   10.00 5.50
     Nos. C273-C275 (3)   12.75 7.15
11th World Cup Soccer Championship, Argentina, June 1-25.

Jules Verne Type of 1978

Design: 400fr, Jules Verne and "20,000 Leagues Under the Sea," horiz.

1978, Oct. 10   Litho.   Perf. 12
C276 A169 400fr multi   4.00 2.00

Musical Instrument Type of 1978

Design: 100fr, Man playing Mvet zither.

1978, Nov. 20   Litho.   Perf. 12½
C277 A172 100fr multi   1.25 .40

Human Rights Type of 1979
1979, Feb. 11   Litho.   Perf. 12x12½
C278 A174 500fr multi   5.50 2.50

Lions Emblem, Map of District 403 — AP110

1979, Apr. 26   Litho.   Perf. 12½
C279 AP110 60fr multi   .70 .25
21st Congress of Lions Club of Yaoundé.

Penny Black, Hill, Cameroun No. 9 — AP111

1979, Oct. 10   Engr.   Perf. 13
C280 AP111 100fr multi   1.00 .40
Sir Rowland Hill (1795-1879), originator of penny postage.

"TELECOM 79" — AP112

1979, Sept. 26   Litho.   Perf. 13x12½
C281 AP112 100fr multi   1.10 .40
3rd World Telecommunications Exhibition, Geneva, Sept. 20-26.

Pope Paul VI — AP113

1979, Oct. 23   Engr.   Perf. 12½x13
C282 AP113 100fr shown   2.25 .50
C283 AP113 100fr John Paul I   2.25 .50
C284 AP113 100fr John Paul II   2.25 .50
     Nos. C282-C284 (3)   6.75 1.50

"Double Eagle" over French Coastline AP114

Design: No. C286, Balloonists and balloon.

1979, Dec. 15   Litho.   Perf. 12½
C285 AP114 500fr multi   5.00 2.25
C286 AP114 500fr multi   5.00 2.25
First Transatlantic balloon crossing.

100-Meter Race — AP115

Designs: 150fr, Figure skating pairs. 200fr, Javelin. 300fr, Wrestling.

1980, Dec. 18   Litho.   Perf. 12½
C287 AP115 100fr yel brn & brn .90 .50
C288 AP115 150fr bl & brn   1.25 .70
C289 AP115 200fr grn & brn   1.75 1.00
C290 AP115 300fr red & brn   2.50 1.40
     Nos. C287-C290 (4)   6.40 3.60
22nd Summer Olympic Games, Moscow, July 19-Aug. 3; 13th Winter Olympic Games, Lake Placid, Feb. 12-24 (150fr).

Alan Shepard and Freedom 7 — AP116

No. C292, Yuri Gagarin, Vostok I.

1981, Sept. 15   Litho.   Perf. 12½
C291 AP116 500fr shown   5.00 2.25
C292 AP116 500fr multi   5.00 2.25
Manned space flight, 20th anniv.

4th African Scouting Conference, Abidjan, June — AP117

100fr, Emblem, salute, badge. 500fr, Scout saluting.

1981, Oct. 5
C293 AP117 100fr multi   .70 .40
C294 AP117 500fr multi   4.50 2.00

Guernica (detail), by Pablo Picasso (1881-1973) — AP118

No. C296, Landscape, by Paul Cezanne (1839-1906).

1981, Nov. 10   Litho.   Perf. 12½
C295 AP118 500fr multi   6.00 2.00
C296 AP118 500fr multi   6.00 2.00

Christmas 1981 — AP119

Designs: 50fr, Virgin and Child, by Froment, vert. 60f, San Zeno Altarpiece, by Mantegna, vert. 400fr, Flight into Egypt, by Giotto.

1981, Dec. 1   Litho.   Perf. 12½
C297 AP119 50fr multi   .45 .25
C298 AP119 60fr multi   .65 .30
C299 AP119 400fr multi   3.50 2.00
   a.   Souv. sheet of 3, #C297-
         C299, perf. 13x13½   9.00 9.00
     Nos. C297-C299 (3)   4.60 2.55

Still Life, by Georges Braque (1882-1963) — AP120

Paintings: No. C301, Olympia, by Edouard Manet (1832-1883).

1982, Dec. 5   Litho.   Perf. 13
C300 AP120 500fr multi   5.00 2.00
C301 AP120 500fr multi   5.00 2.00

Pres. John F. Kennedy (1917-63) AP121

1983, Mar. 15   Litho.   Perf. 13
C302 AP121 500fr multi   4.50 2.00

Lions District 403 (Douala), 2nd Convention, May — AP122

1983, May 5   Litho.   Perf. 12½
C303 AP122 70fr multi   .55 .30
C304 AP122 150fr multi   1.25 .65

Jeanne of Aragon by Raphael AP123

No. C306, Massacre of Scio by Delacroix.

1983, Oct. 15   Litho.   Perf. 13
C305 AP123 500fr multi   5.00   1.00
C306 AP123 500fr multi   5.00   1.00

Easter 1984 — AP124

200fr, Pieta, by G. Hernandez. 500fr, Martyrdom of St. John the Evangelist, by C. Le Brun.

1984, Mar. 30   Litho.   Perf. 13
C307 AP124 200fr multi   1.75   .50
C308 AP124 500fr multi   4.50   1.40
a.   Souv. sheet of 2, #C307-
          C308   7.25   7.25

1984 Summer
Olympics
AP125

1984, Apr. 30   Perf. 12½
C309 AP125 100fr High jump   .90   .25
C310 AP125 150fr Volleyball   1.25   .35
C311 AP125 250fr Handball   2.25   .55
C312 AP125 500fr Bicycling   4.50   1.10
      Nos. C309-C312 (4)   8.90   2.25

See Nos. C321-C324.

European Soccer
Championship,
June 12-
27 — AP126

No. C313, Player in red shorts. No. C314, Yellow shorts. No. C315, Players.

1984, June 5   Litho.   Perf. 12½
C313 AP126 250fr multicolored   2.25   .65
C314 AP126 250fr multicolored   2.25   .65
C315 AP126 500fr multicolored   4.50   1.25
a.   Souvenir sheet of 3   10.00 10.00
      Nos. C313-C315 (3)   9.00   2.55

No. C315a contains Nos. C313-C315 in changed panel colors.

Presidential Oath — AP127

1984   Litho.   Perf. 13
C316 AP127 60fr French in-
                    scription   .55   .25
a.   English inscription   .55   .25
C317 AP127 70fr French in-
                    scription   .55   .25
a.   English inscription   .55   .25

C318 AP127 200fr French in-
                     scription   1.75   .40
a.   English inscription   1.75   .40
      Nos. C316-C318 (3)   2.85   .90

Issue dates: French, Sept. 15; English, Nov.

Paintings — AP128

No. C319, Diana in the Bath, by Watteau (1684-1721). No. C320, Portrait of Diderot (1713-1784).

1984, Sept. 20   Litho.   Perf. 13
C319 AP128 500fr Watteau   5.00   1.00
C320 AP128 500fr Diderot, vert. 5.00   1.00

Nos. C309-C312 in Changed Colors with Added Inscriptions

MOEGENBURG
(R.F.A.) 11-08-
84

U.S.A. 11-08-84

YOUGOSLAVIE
9-08-84

GORSKI
(U.S.A.) 3-08-84

1984, Sept. 25   Litho.   Perf. 12½
C321 AP125 100fr multi   .90   .25
C322 AP125 150fr multi   1.25   .30
C323 AP125 250fr multi   2.25   .60
C324 AP125 500fr multi   4.50   1.00
      Nos. C321-C324 (4)   8.90   2.05

Moon Landing,
15th
Anniv. — AP129

No. C325, Neil Armstrong. No. C326, Apollo 12 launching.

1984, Nov. 15   Litho.   Perf. 12½
C325 AP129 500fr multi   4.50   1.50
C326 AP129 500fr multi   4.50   1.50

Louis Pasteur (1822-1895), Chemist,
Microbiologist — AP130

No. C328, Mourning Woman (detail), Mausoleum of Henri Claude d'Harcourt, by sculptor Jean Baptiste Pigalle (1714-1785).

1985, Oct. 10   Litho.   Perf. 13
C327 AP130 500fr multi   6.00   1.75
C328 AP130 500fr multi   6.00   1.75

Christmas
AP131

250fr, Children's gifts. 300fr, Akono Church. 400fr, Holy Family & drummer boy. 500fr, The Virgin with the Blue Diadem, by Raphael.

1985, Dec. 20   Litho.   Perf. 13
C329 AP131 250fr multi   2.25   .90
C330 AP131 300fr multi   2.50   1.10
C331 AP131 400fr multi   3.25   1.50
C332 AP131 500fr multi   5.00   2.00
      Nos. C329-C332 (4)   13.00   5.50

1986 World Cup Soccer
Championships, Mexico — AP132

250fr, Argentina, winner. 300fr, Stadium. 400fr, Mexican team.

1986   Perf. 13½
C333 AP132 250fr multi   2.75   1.40
C334 AP132 300fr multi   2.75   1.60
C335 AP132 400fr multi   3.50   2.25
      Nos. C333-C335 (3)   9.00   5.25

Issued: 300fr, 400fr, 5/15; 250fr, 7/26.

Famous Men — AP133

No. C336, Pierre Curie (1859-1906), chemist, atom, and elements. No. C337, Jean Mermoz (1901-1936), aviator, and aircraft.

1986, Sept. 10   Litho.   Perf. 12½
C336 AP133 500fr multi   6.25   2.00
C337 AP133 500fr multi   6.25   2.00

AIR POST SEMI-POSTAL STAMPS

Doctor Examining
Child — SPAP1

Unwmk.
1942, June 22   Engr.   Perf. 13
CB1 SPAP1 1.50fr + 50c green   1.00
CB2 SPAP1 2fr + 6fr brn &
                 red brn   1.00

Native children's welfare fund.
Nos. CB1-CB2 were issued by the Vichy government in France, but were not placed on sale in Cameroun.

Colonial Education Fund
Common Design Type
1942, June 22
CB3 CD86a 1.20fr + 1.80fr blue
                 & red   1.10

No. CB3 was issued by the Vichy government in France, but was not placed on sale in Cameroun.

POSTAGE DUE STAMPS

Man Felling
Tree — D1

Perf. 14x13½
1925-27   Unwmk.   Typo.
J1   D1 2c lt bl & blk   .30   .50
J2   D1 4c ol bis & red vio   .30   .50
J3   D1 5c vio & blk   .65   .80
J4   D1 10c red & blk   .65   .80
J5   D1 15c gray & blk   .75   .95
J6   D1 20c olive grn & blk   .75   .95
J7   D1 25c yel & blk   1.40   1.60
J8   D1 30c blue & org   1.60   1.90
J9   D1 50c brn & blk   2.00   2.40
J10 D1 60c bl grn & rose red   2.00   2.40
J11 D1 1fr dl red & grn,
                  grnsh   2.40   3.25
J12 D1 2fr red & vio ('27)   4.75   5.50
J13 D1 3fr org brn & ultra
                  ('27)   7.25   8.00
      Nos. J1-J13 (13)   24.80 29.55

Shades occur for several values.

Carved Figures — D2

1939   Engr.   Perf. 14x13

J14	D2	5c brt red vio	.25	.80
J15	D2	10c Prus blue	.75	.90
J16	D2	15c car rose	.25	.40
J17	D2	20c blk brn	.25	.40
J18	D2	30c ultra	.50	.65
J19	D2	50c dk grn	.50	.65
J20	D2	60c brn vio	.85	1.00
J21	D2	1fr dk vio	1.10	1.20
J22	D2	2fr org red	1.60	1.60
J23	D2	3fr dark blue	2.25	2.40
		Nos. J14-J23 (10)	8.30	10.00

1944   Type D2 without "RF"

J23A	D2	10c Prussian blue	.80

No. J23A was issued by the Vichy government in France, but was not placed on sale in Cameroun.

> Catalogue values for unused stamps in this section, from this point to the end of the section, are for Never Hinged items.

D3

1947   Unwmk.   Perf. 13

J24	D3	10c dark red	.40	.30
J25	D3	30c dp org	.40	.30
J26	D3	50c grnsh blk	.40	.30
J27	D3	1fr dark car	.50	.40
J28	D3	2fr dp yel grn	.65	.55
J29	D3	3fr dp red lil	.65	.55
J30	D3	4fr dp ultra	.90	.70
J31	D3	5fr red brn	1.00	.90
J32	D3	10fr peacock bl	1.90	1.60
J33	D3	20fr sepia	2.75	2.25
		Nos. J24-J33 (10)	9.55	7.85

Federal Republic

Hibiscus
D4

Flowers: No. J35, Erythrina. No. J36, Plumeria lutea. No. J37, Ipomoea. No. J38, Hoodia gordonii. No. J39, Crinum. No. J40, Ochna. No. J41, Gloriosa. No. J42, Costus spectabilis. No. J43, Bougainvillea spectabilis. No. J44, Delonix regia. No. J45, Haemanthus. No. J46, Ophthalmophyllum. No. J47, Titanopsis. No. J48, Amorphophallus. No. J49, Zingiberacee.

Unwmk.
1963, Apr. 10   Engr.   Perf. 11

J34	D4	50c car, bl, grn & yel	.25	.25
J35	D4	50c car, bl, grn & yel	.25	.25
a.		Pair, #J34-J35	.55	.45
J36	D4	1fr mag, grn & yel	.25	.25
J37	D4	1fr mag, grn & yel	.25	.25
a.		Pair, #J36-J37	.55	.45
J38	D4	1.50fr dk grn, lil & yel	.25	.25
J39	D4	1.50fr dk grn, lil & yel	.25	.25
a.		Pair, #J38-J39	.55	.45
J40	D4	2fr org ver, yel & grn	.25	.25
J41	D4	2fr org ver, yel & grn	.25	.25
a.		Pair, #J40-J41	.55	.45
J42	D4	5fr mag, grn & yel	.25	.25
J43	D4	5fr mag, grn & yel	.25	.25
a.		Pair, #J42-J43	.55	.45
J44	D4	10fr crim, grn & yel	.50	.25
J45	D4	10fr crim, grn & yel	.50	.25
a.		Pair, #J44-J45	1.20	.45
J46	D4	20fr grn, yel & lil	1.10	.45
J47	D4	20fr grn, yel & lil	1.10	.45
a.		Pair, #J46-J47	2.40	1.00
J48	D4	40fr lilac & yel	2.00	.80
J49	D4	40fr lilac & yel	2.00	.80
a.		Pair, #J48-J49	4.25	1.75
		Nos. J34-J49 (16)	9.70	5.50

The pairs are se-tenant at the base.

MILITARY STAMPS

> Catalogue values for unused stamps in this section are for Never Hinged items.

M1

Unwmk.
1963, July 1   Typo.   Perf. 13

M1	M1	rose claret	3.00 3.00

Type of 1963 Inscribed
"REPUBLIC UNIE DU CAMEROUN / UNITED REPUBLIC OF CAMEROUN"

1976?   Litho.   Perf. 13x13½

M2	M1	rose claret	

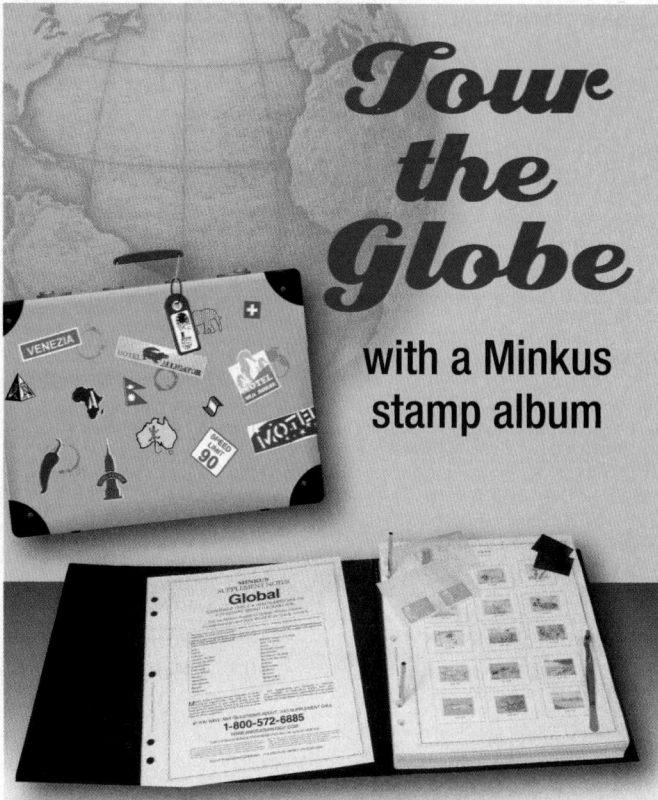

CANADIAN PROVINCES

BRITISH COLUMBIA & VAN-COUVER IS.

'bri-tish kə-'ləm-bē-ə

and van-'kü-vər 'i-lənd

LOCATION — On the northwest coast of North America
GOVT. — British Colony
AREA — 355,900 sq. mi.
POP. — 694,300

In 1871 the colony became a part of the Canadian Confederation and the postage stamps of Canada have since been used.

12 Pence = 1 Shilling
20 Shillings = 1 Pound
100 Cents = 1 Dollar (1865)

Values for unused stamps are for examples with original gum as defined in the catalogue introduction. Very fine examples of Nos. 2 and 5-18 will have perforations touching the design on at least one side due to the narrow spacing of the stamps on the plates. Stamps with perfs clear of the design on all four sides are extremely scarce and will command much higher prices.

Queen Victoria — A1

1860   Unwmk.   Typo.   Imperf.
1   A1   2½p dull rose   25,000.

No. 1 was not placed in use and may be a proof or reprint. Most examples are without gum. Value without gum, $18,000.

Perf. 14
2   A1   2½p dull rose   1,000.   240.

VANCOUVER ISLAND

A2   A3

1865   Wmk. 1   Imperf.
3   A2   5c rose   75,000.   10,000.
   No gum   37,500.
4   A3   10c blue   5,000.   1,100.

Perf. 14
5   A2   5c rose   500.   300.
6   A3   10c blue   475.   300.

BRITISH COLUMBIA

Seal of British Columbia — A4

1865, Nov. 1
7   A4   3p blue   160.00   110.00

Type A4 of 1865 Surcharged in Various Colors

1867-69   Perf. 14
8   2c on 3p brown
       (Bk)   160.00   150.00
9   5c on 3p brt red
       (Bk) ('69)   300.00   250.00
10   10c on 3p lilac rose
       (Bl)   1,900.
11   25c on 3p orange
       (V) ('69)   400.00   325.00
12   50c on 3p violet (R)   900.00   1,050.
13   $1 on 3p green (G)   2,000.

Nos. 10 and 13 were not placed in use.

1869   Perf. 12½
14   5c on 3p brt red
       (Bk)   2,250.   1,300.
15   10c on 3p lilac rose
       (Bl)   1,300.   1,000.
16   25c on 3p orange
       (V)   1,100.   800.00
17   50c on 3p violet (R)   1,600.   1,000.
18   $1 on 3p green (G)   2,500.   1,750.

NEW BRUNSWICK

'nü 'brənz-ˌwik

LOCATION — Eastern Canada, bordering on the Bay of Fundy and the Gulf of St. Lawrence.
GOVT. — British Province
AREA — 27,985 sq. mi.
POP. — 285,594 (1871)
CAPITAL — Fredericton

At one time a part of Nova Scotia, New Brunswick became a separate province in 1784. Upon joining the Canadian Confederation in 1867 its postage stamps were superseded by those of Canada.

12 Pence = 1 Shilling
100 Cents = 1 Dollar (1860)

Crown of Great Britain and Heraldic Flowers of the United Kingdom A1

1851   Unwmk.   Engr.   Imperf.
Blue Paper
1   A1   3p red   5,500.   550.
   a.   3p dark red   5,750.   600.
   b.   Half used as 1½p on
      cover   4,750.
2   A1   6p olive yellow   7,000.   1,200.
   a.   6p orange yellow   7,000.   1,200.
   b.   Half used as 3p on cover   3,500.
   c.   Quarter used as 1½p on
      cover   30,000.
   d.   6p mustard yellow   10,000.   1,400.
3   A1   1sh brt red violet   32,500.   6,500.
   a.   Half used as 6p on cover   22,500.
   b.   Quarter used as 3p on
      cover   22,500.
4   A1   1sh dull violet   40,000.   7,500.
   a.   Half used as 6p on cover   22,500.
   b.   Quarter used as 3p on
      cover   22,500.

The reprints are on stout white paper. The 3p is printed in orange and the 6p and 1sh in violet black. Value about $275 per set of 3.

Charles Connell — A2

1860   Perf. 12
5   A2   5c brown   14,000.

No. 5 was prepared for use but not issued. Most examples of No. 5 have creases or other faults. Value of an average example is about half that shown here.

Locomotive   Victoria
A3   A4

A5   A6

Steam and   Edward VII
Sailing   as Prince of
Ship — A7   Wales — A8

1860-63   White Paper   Perf. 12
6   A3   1c red lilac   42.50   37.50
   a.   1c brown violet   100.00   70.00
   b.   Horiz. pair, imperf. vert.   700.00
7   A4   2c orange ('63)   20.00   15.00
   a.   Vertical pair, imperf. horiz.   750.00
8   A5   5c yellow green   30.00   22.50
   a.   5c blue green   35.00   22.50
   b.   5c olive green   175.00   37.50
9   A6   10c vermilion   55.00   47.50
   a.   Half used as 5c on cover   750.00
   b.   Double impression   350.00   175.00
10   A7   12½c blue   100.00   75.00
11   A8   17c black   55.00   65.00
      Nos. 6-11 (6)   302.50   262.50
      Set, never hinged   647.50

NEWFOUNDLAND

'nü-fən̩dˌ-lənd

LOCATION — Island in the Atlantic Ocean off the coast of Canada, and Labrador, a part of the mainland
GOVT. — British Dominion
AREA — 42,734 sq. mi.
POP. — 321,177 (1945)
CAPITAL — St. John's

Newfoundland was a self-governing Dominion of the British Empire from 1855 to 1933, when it became a Crown Colony. In 1949 it united with Canada.

12 Pence = 1 Shilling
100 Cents = 1 Dollar (1866)

Values for unused stamps are for examples with original gum as defined in the catalogue introduction. However, very fine examples of Nos. 2-7, 9, 11, 12, 13 and 15 without gum are often traded at values very close to those for examples with original gum.

Watermark

Wmk. 224
Coat of Arms

As the watermark 224 does not show on every stamp in the sheet, pairs are found one with and one without watermark. This applies to all stamps with watermark 224.

Crown of Great Britain and Heraldic Flowers of the United Kingdom — A1

Rose, Thistle and Shamrock — A3

A2   A4

A5   A6

A7   A8

1857   Unwmk.   Engr.   Imperf.
Thick Porous Wove Paper with Mesh
1   A1   1p brn vio   125.00   200.00
   a.   Half used as ½p on
      cover   20,000.
2   A2   2p scar ver   17,500.   7,000.
   a.   Vert. half used as 1p
      on cover   27,500.
3   A3   3p green   575.00   500.00
4   A4   4p scar ver   12,000.   4,250.
   a.   Half used as 2p on
      cover   27,500.
5   A1   5p brn vio   325.00   425.00
6   A5   6p scar ver   25,000.   5,000.
7   A6   6½p scar ver   5,000.   4,000.
8   A7   8p scar ver   400.00   475.00
   a.   Half used as 4p on
      cover   4,500.
9   A8   1sh scar ver   45,000.   10,000.
   a.   Half used as 6p on
      cover   20,000.

1860
Thin to Thick Wove Paper, No Mesh
11   A2   2p orange   475.00   475.00
11A   A3   3p green   85.00   110.00
12   A4   4p orange   3,750.   1,350.
   b.   Half used as 2p on
      cover   27,500.
12A   A1   5p vio brown   85.00   150.00
13   A5   6p orange   5,250.   1,100.
15   A8   1sh orange   37,500.   12,000.
   b.   Half used as 6p on
      cover   20,000.

A 6½p orange exists as a souvenir item.
A 1sh exists in orange on horizontally or vertically laid paper. Most authorities consider these to be proofs. Value, $10,500.

1861-62

15A	A1	1p vio brown	175.00	250.00
16	A1	1p reddish brown	12,500.	
17	A2	2p rose	175.00	175.00
18	A4	4p rose	37.50	70.00
a.		Half used as 2p on cover		—
19	A1	5p reddish brown	75.00	77.50
20	A5	6p rose	22.50	62.50
a.		Half used as 3p on cover		18,000.
21	A6	6½p rose	85.00	275.00
22	A7	8p rose	85.00	300.00
23	A8	1sh rose	42.50	250.00
a.		Half used as 6p on cover		18,000.

Some sheets of Nos. 11-23 are known with the papermaker's watermark "STACEY WISE 1858" in large capitals. Values unused and used about 25% more than values shown, except about 50% more for unused Nos. 12 and 13, and 75% more for unused No. 16.

No. 16 was prepared but not issued.

False cancellations are found on Nos. 1, 3, 5, 8, 11, 11A, 12A and 17-23.

Forgeries exist of most or all of Nos. 1-23.

Codfish — A9

Harp Seal — A10

Prince Albert — A11

Victoria — A12

Fishing Ship — A13

Victoria — A14

1865-94   *Perf. 12*

White Paper (#24, 27, 28)
Thin Yellowish Paper (#25-26, 29-31)

24	A9	2c green	110.00	35.00
a.		Thin yellowish paper	140.00	70.00
b.		Half used as 1c on cover		8,000.
25	A10	5c brown	600.00	375.00
a.		Half used as 2c on cover		10,000.
26	A10	5c black ('68)	350.00	200.00
27	A11	10c black	375.00	60.00
a.		Thin yellowish paper	425.00	115.00
b.		Half used as 5c on cover		9,000.
28	A12	12c pale red brn	85.00	47.50
a.		Thin yellowish paper	600.00	190.00
b.		Half used as 6c on cover		4,000.
29	A12	12c brn, *white* ('94)	70.00	55.00
30	A13	13c orange	250.00	115.00
31	A14	24c blue, thin transluscent paper	75.00	35.00
a.		Thicker white paper ('70)	375.00	300.00

See Nos. 38, 40.

Edward VII as Prince of Wales — A15

Queen Victoria — A16

1868-94

32	A15	1c violet	75.00	60.00
32A	A15	1c brn lil (re-engr. '71)	115.00	75.00
33	A16	3c ver ('70)	400.00	190.00
34	A16	3c blue ('73)	375.00	75.00
35	A16	6c dull rose ('70)	35.00	17.50
36	A16	6c car lake ('94)	50.00	22.50
		Nos. 32-36 (6)	1,050.	440.00

In the re-engraved 1c the top of the letters "N" and "F" are about ½mm from the ribbon with "ONE CENT." In No. 32 they are fully 1mm away. There are many small differences in the engraving.

1876-79   *Rouletted*

37	A15	1c brn lilac ('77)	160.00	52.50
38	A9	2c green ('79)	200.00	52.50
39	A16	3c blue ('77)	425.00	15.00
40	A10	5c blue	275.00	15.00
		Nos. 37-40 (4)	1,060.	135.00

A17   A19

A18

A20

1880-96   *Perf. 12*

41	A17	1c violet brown	60.00	11.50
42	A17	1c gray brown	60.00	11.50
43	A17	1c brown ('96)	140.00	70.00
44	A17	1c deep green ('87)	27.50	4.25
45	A17	1c green ('97)	27.50	4.25
46	A19	2c yellow green	75.00	14.00
47	A19	2c green ('96)	120.00	27.50
48	A19	2c red org ('87)	40.00	9.50
a.		Imperf., pair	325.00	
49	A18	3c blue ('96)	70.00	7.00
51	A18	3c umber brn ('87)	65.00	4.75
52	A18	3c vio brown ('96)	130.00	90.00
53	A20	5c pale blue	375.00	14.00
54	A20	5c dark blue ('87)	200.00	10.00
55	A20	5c bright bl ('94)	70.00	6.50
		Nos. 41-55 (14)	1,460.	284.75

Newfoundland Dog — A21

Schooner — A22

1887-96

56	A21	½c rose red	12.50	7.50
57	A21	½c org red ('96)	85.00	45.00
58	A21	½c black ('94)	15.00	7.25
59	A22	10c black	140.00	67.50
		Nos. 56-59 (4)	252.50	127.25
		Set, never hinged	462.50	

Queen Victoria — A23

1890

60	A23	3c slate	35.00	1.60
a.		3c gray lilac	35.00	1.60
b.		3c brown lilac	55.00	1.60
c.		3c lilac	40.00	1.60
d.		3c slate violet	75.00	3.00
e.		Vert. pair, imperf. horiz.	750.00	

For surcharges see Nos. 75-77.

Victoria — A24

Cabot (John?) — A25

Cape Bonavista A26

Caribou Hunting A27

Mining — A28

Logging — A29

Fishing — A30

Cabot's Ship "Matthew" A31   Willow Ptarmigan A32

Seals — A33

Salmon Fishing — A34

Colony Seal — A35   Iceberg off St. John's — A36

Henry VII — A37

1897, June 24

61	A24	1c deep green	1.75	1.75
62	A25	2c carmine lake	2.25	1.40
63	A26	3c ultramarine	4.25	1.40
64	A27	4c olive green	5.75	2.75
65	A28	5c violet	12.00	2.75
66	A29	6c red brown	6.00	3.25
67	A30	8c red orange	25.00	15.00
68	A31	10c black brown	25.00	7.50
69	A32	12c dark blue	30.00	15.00
70	A33	15c scarlet	22.50	13.00
71	A34	24c gray violet	30.00	12.00
72	A35	30c slate	65.00	55.00
73	A36	35c red	120.00	60.00
74	A37	60c black	18.00	11.50
		Nos. 61-74 (14)	367.50	202.30
		Set, never hinged	736.50	

400th anniv. of John Cabot's discovery of Newfoundland; 60th year of Victoria's reign. The ship on the 10c was previously used by the American Bank Note Co. as the "Flagship of Columbus" on US No. 232. The portrait on the 2c, intended to be of John Cabot, is said to be a Holbein painting of his son, Sebastian.

For surcharges and overprints see Nos. 127-130, C2-C4.

No. 60a Surcharged

No. 75   No. 76

No. 77   ONE CENT

Available Oct. 19 through Dec. 3, 1897

75	A23	1c on 3c gray lil	90.00	50.00
a.		Dbl. surch., one diagonal	2,000.	
b.		Vert. pair, "ONE CENT" and lower bar omitted on bottom stamp	4,250.	
76	A23	1c on 3c gray lil	300.00	225.00
77	A23	1c on 3c gray lil	875.00	700.00
		Nos. 75-77 (3)	1,265.	975.00
		Set, never hinged	2,680.	

Most examples of Nos. 75-77 are poorly centered. Fine examples sell for about 60% of the values given. No. 75b is valued in the grade of fine.

Trial surcharges of Nos. 75-77 exist with red surcharge and with double surcharge, one in red and one in black, but these were not issued.

Edward VIII as a Child — A38

Victoria — A39

Edward VII as Prince of Wales — A40

Queen Alexandra as Princess of Wales — A41

Queen Mary as Duchess of York — A42   George V as Duke of York — A43

1897-1901				Engr.
78	A38	½c olive green ('98)	4.50	2.75
79	A39	1c carmine rose ('97)	5.50	5.00
80	A39	1c yel grn ('98)	5.50	.35
b.		Vert. pair, imperf. horiz.	450.00	
81	A40	2c orange ('97)	7.00	4.25
82	A40	2c ver ('98)	12.50	.75
b.		Pair, imperf. between	575.00	
83	A41	3c orange ('98)	32.50	.75
a.		Vert. pair, imperf. horiz.	500.00	
84	A42	4c violet ('01)	42.50	4.50
85	A43	5c blue ('99)	42.50	3.00
		Nos. 78-85 (8)	152.50	21.35
		Set, never hinged	305.00	

No. 80b is valued in the grade of fine.

Imperf., Pairs

78a	A38	½c		600.00	800.00
81a	A40	2c			425.00
82a	A40	2c		350.00	950.00
83b	A41	3c		425.00	
84a	A42	4c		700.00	

No. 82a used is valued on cover. Three such covers are recorded.

Imperf., Pairs

Newfoundland imperforates virtually always are proofs on stamp paper or "postmaster's perquisites." Most part-perforate varieties also are "postmaster's perquisites." These items were not regularly issued, but rather were sold or given to favored persons.

Map of Newfoundland — A44

1908, Sept.

86	A44	2c rose carmine	55.00	3.50
		Never hinged	110.00	

Guy Issue

James I — A45

Arms of the London and Bristol Co. — A46

John Guy A47

Guy's Ship, the "Endeavour" A48

View of Cupids — A49

Lord Bacon — A50

View of Mosquito — A51

Logging Camp — A52

Paper Mills — A53

Edward VII — A54

George V — A55

Type I

Type II

SIX CENT TYPES
I — "Z" of "COLONIZATION" reversed.
II — "Z" of normal.

1910, Aug. 15			Litho.	*Perf.* 12
87	A45	1c deep green, perf. 12x11	2.25	1.10
a.		Perf. 12	4.75	1.90
b.		Perf. 12x14	7.50	2.25
c.		Horiz. pair, imperf. btwn.	400.00	
d.		Vert. pair, imperf. btwn.	475.00	
h.		Perf. 12x12x12x11		—
88	A46	2c carmine	11.00	1.15
a.		Perf. 12x14	8.50	.85
b.		As "a," horiz. pair, imperf. between	900.00	
c.		Perf. 12x11½	750.00	350.00
89	A47	3c brown olive	25.00	14.00
90	A48	4c dull violet	25.00	14.00
91	A49	5c ultramarine, perf. 14x12	27.50	4.50
a.		Perf. 12	32.50	7.50
92	A50	6c claret, type I	100.00	70.00
92A	A50	6c claret, type II	50.00	37.50
b.		Imperf., pair	450.00	
93	A51	8c pale brown	75.00	55.00
94	A52	9c olive green	75.00	55.00
95	A53	10c vio black	75.00	55.00
96	A54	12c lilac brown	75.00	55.00
a.		Imperf., pair	375.00	
97	A55	15c gray black	80.00	65.00
		Nos. 87-97 (12)	620.75	427.25
		Set, never hinged	1,242.	

Tercentenary of the Colonization of Newfoundland.

On No. 87 printing flaws such as "NFW" and "JANES" exist.

1911			Engr.	*Perf.* 14
98	A50	6c brown vio	35.00	22.50
b.		Horiz. pair, imperf. btwn.	1,100.	
99	A51	8c bister brn	75.00	67.50
b.		Horiz. pair, imperf. btwn.	1,200.	
100	A52	9c olive grn	75.00	60.00
b.		Horiz. pair, imperf. btwn.	1,200.	
101	A53	10c violet blk	100.00	95.00
b.		Horiz. pair, imperf. btwn.	1,200.	
102	A54	12c red brown	75.00	75.00
b.		Horiz. pair, imperf. btwn.	1,200.	
103	A55	15c slate grn	75.00	75.00
b.		Horiz. pair, imperf. btwn.	1,200.	
		Nos. 98-103 (6)	435.00	395.00
		Set, never hinged	810.00	

Nos. 100 and 103 are known with papermaker's watermark "E. TOWGOOD FINE." Values, unused or used: No. 100, $800; No. 103, $1,000.

Imperf., Pairs

98a	A50	6c	325.00
99a	A51	8c	325.00
100a	A52	9c	325.00
101a	A53	10c	325.00
102a	A54	12c	325.00
103a	A55	15c	325.00

Nos. 98a-103a were made with and without gum. Values the same.

Royal Family Issue

Queen Mary — A56

George V — A57

Prince of Wales (Edward VIII) — A58

Prince Albert (George VI) — A59

Princess Mary — A60

Prince Henry — A61

Prince George A62

Prince John A63

Queen Alexandra A64

Duke of Connaught A65

Seal of Colony — A66

1911, June 19   Perf. 13½x14, 14

104	A56	1c yellow grn	3.00	.25
105	A57	2c carmine	2.75	1.00
106	A58	3c red brown	35.00	19.00
107	A59	4c violet	35.00	13.50
108	A60	5c ultra	22.50	1.90
109	A61	6c black	32.50	22.50
110	A62	8c blue (paper colored through)	85.00	65.00
a.		8c peacock blue	95.00	70.00
111	A63	9c bl violet	35.00	20.00
112	A64	10c dark green	55.00	37.50
113	A65	12c plum	42.50	37.50
114	A66	15c magenta	35.00	37.50
	Nos. 104-114 (11)		383.25	255.65
	Set, never hinged		764.00	

Coronation of King George V.

Imperf., Pairs Without Gum

104a	A56	1c	325.00
105a	A57	2c	325.00
108a	A60	5c	325.00
113a	A65	12c	425.00
114a	A66	15c	140.00

Trail of the Caribou Issue

Caribou
A67   A68

1919, Jan. 2   Perf. 14

115	A67	1c green	2.75	.35
116	A68	2c scarlet	3.00	.50
117	A67	3c red brown	3.50	.30
118	A67	4c violet	5.00	1.40
119	A68	5c ultramarine	9.00	1.40
120	A67	6c gray	22.50	22.50
121	A68	8c magenta	25.00	19.00
122	A67	10c dark green	20.00	5.50
123	A68	12c orange	75.00	45.00
124	A67	15c dark blue	42.50	42.50
125	A67	24c bister	45.00	42.50
126	A67	36c olive green	37.50	35.00
	Nos. 115-126 (12)		290.75	215.95
	Set, never hinged		581.50	

Services of the Newfoundland contingent in WWI.

Each denomination of type A67 is inscribed with the name of a different action in which Newfoundland troops took part.

For overprint and surcharge see Nos. C1, C5.

A shipment delay of the Trail of the Caribou issue led to trial surcharges of No. 74 reading "TWO / 2 / CENTS" in red. Fifty stamps were so surcharged, including examples with double surcharge. Value, $1,500.

Imperf., Pairs Without Gum

115a	A67	1c	275.00
116a	A68	2c	275.00
117a	A67	3c red brown	275.00
118a	A67	4c	275.00
119a	A68	5c	275.00
120a	A67	6c	275.00
121a	A68	8c	275.00
122a	A67	10c	275.00
123a	A68	12c	275.00
124a	A67	15c	275.00
125a	A67	24c	275.00
126a	A67	36c	275.00

No. 72 Surcharged in Black

TWO CENTS

Available Sept. 24 through Sept. 27, 1920

127	A35	2c on 30c slate	5.75	5.50
		Never hinged	8.75	
a.		Inverted surcharge	1,100.	

No. 127 with red surcharge is an unissued color trial. 25 examples are known. Value, $1,000.

Nos. 70 and 73 Surcharged in Black

THREE CENTS

THREE CENTS

Type I — Bars 10½mm apart.
Type II — Bars 13½mm apart.

Available Sept. 13 through Oct. 3, 1920

128	A33	3c on 15c scar (I)	230.00	250.00
		Never hinged	350.00	
a.		Inverted surcharge	*3,000.*	
129	A33	3c on 15c scar (II)	19.00	11.00
		Never hinged	35.00	
130	A36	3c on 35c red	11.50	9.50
		Never hinged	20.00	
		Lower bar omitted	150.00	135.00

Trial surcharges of "THREE CENTS" between bars on No. 66 in red or brown are known. Twenty-five of each were produced, Value, $1,000.

Twin Hills, Tor's Cove — A70

South West Arm, Trinity — A71

131b	A70	1c	200.00
132b	A71	2c	200.00
133a	A72	3c	300.00
134a	A73	4c	250.00
135a	A74	5c	250.00
136a	A75	6c	250.00
137a	A76	8c	250.00
138a	A77	9c	250.00
139a	A78	10c	250.00
140a	A79	11c	250.00
141a	A80	12c	250.00
142a	A81	15c	160.00

Nos. 133a-139a, 141a-142a are without gum. Others are either with or without gum; values about the same.

War Memorial, St. John's A72

Humber River A73

Coast of Trinity — A74

Upper Steadies, Humber River — A75

Quidi Vidi, near St. John's — A76

Caribou Crossing Lake — A77

Humber River Canyon A78

Shell Bird Island A79

Mt. Moriah, Bay of Islands A80

Humber River near Little Rapids A81

Placentia, from Mt. Pleasant A82

Topsail Falls near St. John's A83

1923-24   Engr.   Perf. 14, 13½x14

131	A70	1c gray green	1.90	.30
a.		Booklet pane of 8	500.00	
132	A71	2c carmine	1.90	.30
a.		Booklet pane of 8	300.00	
133	A72	3c brown	2.50	.30
134	A73	4c brn violet	2.75	1.80
135	A74	5c ultramarine	7.00	2.25
136	A75	6c gray black	6.50	6.00
137	A76	8c dull violet	5.00	4.50
138	A77	9c slate green	42.50	27.50
139	A78	10c dark violet	4.50	2.50
140	A79	11c olive green	7.50	7.00
141	A80	12c lake	7.50	7.50
142	A81	15c deep blue	9.50	8.00
143	A82	20c red brn ('24)	13.00	7.50
144	A83	24c blk brn ('24)	85.00	50.00
	Nos. 131-144 (14)		197.05	125.45
	Set, never hinged		317.50	

For surcharge see No. 160.

Imperf., Pairs

Map of Newfoundland A84

Steamship "Caribou" A85

Queen Mary, George V — A86

Prince of Wales — A87

Express Train — A88

Newfoundland Hotel, St. John's — A89

Heart's Content — A90

Cabot Tower, St. John's — A91

War Memorial, St. John's — A92

GPO, St. John's — A93

First Nonstop Transatlantic Flight, 1919 — A94

Colonial Building, St. John's — A95

Grand Falls, Labrador — A96

Perf. 14, 13½x13, 13x13½
1928, Jan. 3

145	A84	1c deep green	1.85	.75
146	A85	2c deep carmine	2.50	.70
a.		Imperf., pair	300.00	
147	A86	3c brown	2.75	.50
148	A87	4c lilac rose	3.50	1.80
149	A88	5c slate green	10.00	4.25
150	A89	6c ultramarine	5.75	5.00
151	A90	8c lt red brown	7.25	4.50
152	A91	9c myrtle green	7.00	7.00
153	A92	10c dark violet	9.00	4.25
154	A93	12c brn carmine	5.00	5.00
155	A91	14c red brown	10.50	7.00
156	A94	15c dark blue	9.25	7.00
157	A95	20c gray black	12.50	6.50
158	A93	28c gray green	35.00	27.50
159	A96	30c olive brown	17.50	7.50
	Nos. 145-159 (15)		139.85	89.25
	Set, never hinged		280.25	

See Nos. 163-182.

No. 136 Surcharged
in Red or Black

Type I — 5mm between "CENTS" and bar.
Type II — 3mm between "CENTS" and bar.

Available Aug. 23-Aug. 30, 1929

160 A75 3c on 6c gray black
　　(II) (R) 　　　4.25　4.25
　　Never hinged 　　6.75
　a.　Inverted surcharge (II)　1,000.

The stamps with black surcharge, type I and II, were trial surcharges, and were not issued. There were 50 examples of each. Value, each $1,750.

Types of 1928 Issue Re-engraved

1c — On No. 145 the lines of the engraving are thinner and the impression is clearer than on No. 163. On the former "C. BAULD" is above "C. NORMAN." On the latter these words are transposed.

2c — On the 1928 stamp the "D" of "NEW-FOUNDLAND" is 1mm from the scroll at the right; the flag at the stern is lower than the top of the boat davit. On the 1929 stamp the "D" is ½mm from the scroll and the flag rises above the davits.

3c — On the 1928 stamp the pearls at the top of the crown, the jewels of the tiara and the pillars flanking the portraits are all unshaded. On the reengraved stamp there are small curved lines inside the pearls, the jewels of the tiara are in solid color, and the pillars have vertical shading lines. On the 1928 stamps the tablets with "THREE" and "CENTS" have a background of crossed lines (vertical and horizontal). On the 1929 stamp the background is of horizontal lines only.

4c — On the 1928 stamp the figures "4" have shading of horizontal and diagonal crossed lines. There are six circles at each side of the portrait.
On the 1929 stamp the "4s" have shading of horizontal lines only. There are five roses at each side of the portrait.

5c — The crossbars of the telegraph pole touch the frame at the left on the 1929 stamp but just clear it on the 1928 stamp. In the 1928 issue the foliate ornaments beside and below the figures "5" end in small scrolls and a small spur. These spurs are omitted on the 1929 stamp.

6c — On the re-engraved stamp the columns at right and left of the picture have heavy wavy outlines on the inner sides. There is no period after "JOHNS." The numerals in the lower corners are 1½mm wide instead of 1¼mm.

8c — The impression of the 1928 stamp is clear, that of 1931 is slightly blurred. The 1928 stamp has three horizontal lines above "EIGHT CENTS" and four berries on the laurel branch at the right side. On the 1931 stamp there are two horizontal lines and three berries.

10c — On the re-engraved stamp there is no period after "ST. JOHN'S." The letters of "TEN CENTS" are slightly larger and the numerals "10" slightly smaller than in 1928. Inside the "0" of "10" at the right there are two vertical lines instead of three. The clouds are fainter in 1929 and the cross upheld by the figure on the monument is more distinct. On the 1928 stamp the torch at the left side terminates in a single tongue of flame. On the 1929-30 stamp it terminates in two tongues.

15c — On the 1928 stamp the "N" of "NEW-FOUNDLAND" is 1½mm from the left frame, the "L" of "LEAVING" is under the first "A" of "AIRPLANE" and the apostrophe in "JOHN'S" breaks the first line above it.
On the 1929 stamp the "N" of "NEW-FOUNDLAND" is 1mm from the left frame, the "L" of "LEAVING" is below the "T" of "FIRST" and the apostrophe in "JOHN'S" does not touch the line above it.

20c — On the 1928 stamp the points of the "W" of "NEWFOUNDLAND" are truncated. The "O" is wide and nearly round. The columns that form the sides of the frame have a shading of evenly spaced horizontal lines at their inner sides.
On the 1929-31 stamp the points of the "W" form sharp angles. The "O" is narrow and has a small opening. Many lines have been added to the shading on the inner sides of the columns, making it almost solid.

30c — 1928 stamp. Size: 19¼x24½mm. At the outer side of the right column there are three strong and two faint vertical lines. Faint period after "FALLS."
1931 stamp. Size: 19x25mm. At the outer side of the right column there are two strong vertical lines and a fragment of the lower end of a faint one. Clear period after "FALLS." A great many of the small lines of the design have been deepened making the whole stamp appear darker.

1929-31　Unwmk.　Perf. 13½ to 14

163 A84 1c green 　　　2.25　.65
　a.　Double impression
166a A87　4c 　　　145.00
164a A85 2c pale carmine, cream 　145.00
　b.　2c dark carmine 　145.00
165a A86 3c 　　　145.00
166a A87 4c 　　　145.00

No. 164b is without gum, others with gum.

163	A84	1c green	2.25	.65
a.		Double impression		
b.		Vert. pair, imperf. btwn.	210.00	
164	A85	2c deep carmine	2.25	.70
165	A86	3c dp red brown	2.50	.70
166	A87	4c magenta	3.75	1.25
167	A88	5c slate green	7.50	2.50
168	A89	6c ultramarine	10.00	9.00
169	A92	10c dark violet	8.75	2.25
170	A94	15c deep blue ('30)	50.00	37.50
171	A95	20c gray blk ('31)	75.00	27.50
		Nos. 163-171 (9)	162.00	82.05
		Set, never hinged	324.50	

Imperf., Pairs

163c	A84	1c	120.00
164a	A85	2c pale carmine, cream	145.00
b.		2c dark carmine	145.00
165a	A86	3c	145.00
166a	A87	4c	145.00

No. 164b is without gum, others with gum.

Types of 1928 Issue　Re-engraved

1931　Wmk. 224　Perf. 13½x14

172	A84	1c green, perf. 13½	2.25	1.30
a.		Horiz. pair, imperf. btwn.	425.00	
173	A85	2c red	7.00	1.30
174	A86	3c red brown	3.50	1.30
175	A87	4c rose	4.25	2.75
176	A88	5c grnsh gray	12.50	7.00
177	A89	6c ultramarine	17.50	17.50
178	A90	8c lt red brn	22.50	17.50
179	A92	10c dk violet	15.00	9.00
180	A94	15c deep blue	45.00	27.50
181	A95	20c gray black	55.00	17.50
182	A96	30c olive brown	45.00	25.00
		Nos. 172-182 (11)	229.50	127.65
		Set, never hinged	459.00	

Codfish — A97

George V — A98

Queen Mary — A99

Prince of Wales — A100

Caribou A101

Princess Elizabeth A102

Salmon Leaping Falls — A103

Newfoundland Dog — A104

Harp Seal Pup — A105

Cape Race — A106

Sealing Fleet — A107

Fishing Fleet Leaving for "The Banks" — A108

Type I

Type II

FIVE CENT
Die I — Antlers even, or equal in height.
Die II — Antler under "T" higher.

1932-37　Engr.　Perf. 13½, 14

183	A97	1c green	2.75	.50
a.		Booklet pane of 4, perf. 13	75.00	
c.		Vert. pair, imperf. btwn.	200.00	
184	A97	1c gray black	.60	.25
a.		Bklt. pane of 4, perf. 13½	57.50	
b.		Booklet pane of 4, perf. 14	72.50	
185	A98	2c rose	2.25	.35
a.		Booklet pane of 4, perf. 13½	35.00	
b.		Booklet pane of 4, perf. 13	47.50	
186	A98	2c green	1.10	.25
a.		Bklt. pane of 4, perf. 13½	55.00	
b.		Booklet pane of 4, perf. 14	35.00	
d.		Horiz. pair, imperf. btwn.	160.00	
187	A99	3c orange brn	1.10	.35
a.		Bklt. pane of 4, perf. 13½	55.00	
b.		Booklet pane of 4, perf. 14	67.50	
c.		Booklet pane of 4, perf. 13	75.00	
e.		Vert. pair, imperf. btwn.	300.00	
188	A100	4c deep violet	7.00	2.00
189	A100	4c rose lake	.75	.50
b.		Vert. pair, imperf. btwn.	120.00	
c.		Horiz. pair, imperf. btwn.	120.00	
190	A101	5c vio brn, perf. 13½ (Die I)	9.50	2.00
191	A101	5c dp vio, perf. 13½ (Die II)	1.10	.40
c.		5c dp vio, perf. 13½ (Die I)	14.00	1.25
e.		Horiz. pair, imperf. btwn. (I)	240.00	
g.		Horiz. pair, imperf. btwn. (II)	240.00	
192	A102	6c dull blue	11.00	11.00
193	A103	10c olive black	1.40	.85
194	A104	14c int black	3.25	2.75
195	A105	15c magenta	2.50	2.25
196	A106	20c gray green	2.50	1.00
197	A107	25c gray	2.75	2.00
b.		Horiz. pair, imperf. btwn.	450.00	
c.		Vert. pair, imperf. btwn.	450.00	
198	A108	30c ultra	32.50	24.00
b.		Vert. pair, imperf. btwn.	1,000.	
199	A108	48c red brn ('37)	11.00	5.25
		Nos. 183-199 (17)	93.05	55.70
		Set, never hinged	134.55	

Two dies were used for 2c green, one for 2c rose.

See Nos. 253-266.

Imperf., Pairs

183b	A97	1c	240.00
184c	A97	1c	47.50
185c	A98	2c	250.00
186c	A98	2c	47.50
187d	A99	3c	95.00
189a	A100	4c	60.00
190a	A101	5c	200.00
191b	A101	5c (II)	75.00
191d	A101	5c (I)	100.00
192a	A102	6c	175.00
193a	A103	10c	110.00
194a	A103	14c	130.00
195a	A103	15c	130.00
196a	A106	20c	225.00
197a	A107	25c	225.00
198a	A108	30c	750.00
199a	A108	48c	120.00

All with gum. Nos. 186c, 187d, 192a, 193a and 196a also made without gum; values about 10% less.

Queen Elizabeth when Duchess of York — A109

Corner Brook Paper Mills — A110

Loading Iron Ore at Bell Island — A111

1932

208	A109	7c red brown	1.40	1.25
a.		Imperf., pair	160.00	
b.		Horiz. pair, imperf. between	600.00	
209	A110	8c orange red	1.40	1.10
a.		Imperf., pair	140.00	
210	A111	24c light blue	2.75	2.75
a.		Imperf., pair	200.00	
b.		Double impression	1,500.	
		Nos. 208-210 (3)	5.55	5.10
		Set, never hinged	7.75	

No. 208a was made both with and without gum. Values about the same.
See Nos. 259, 264.

No. C9 Overprinted Bars and

1933, Feb. 9　Wmk. 224　Perf. 14

211	AP6	15c brown	11.00	9.50
		Never hinged	17.00	
a.		Vert. pair, one without overprint	7,500.	
b.		Overprint reading up	4,750.	

The end of the period of use and availability of No. 211 is unknown.
"L. & S." stands for "Land and Sea."

Sir Humphrey Gilbert Issue

Sir Humphrey Gilbert — A112

Compton Castle, Home of the Gilbert Family — A113

Gilbert Coat of Arms — A114

Eton College — A115

Token from Queen Elizabeth I — A116

Sir Humphrey Receiving Royal Patents for Colonization A117

Sir Humphrey's Ships Leaving Plymouth, 1583 — A118

The Ships Arriving at St. John's — A119

Annexation of Newfoundland, Aug. 5, 1583 — A120

Coat of Arms of England A121

Sir Humphrey on the Deck of the "Squirrel" A122

Capt. John Mason's Map of Newfoundland, 1626 — A123

Queen Elizabeth I A124

Gilbert Statue at Truro A125

Wmk. 224

1933, Aug. 3		**Engr.**	**Perf. 13½**	
212	A112	1c gray black	1.40	.75
213	A113	2c green	1.40	.75
b.		Double impression	600.00	
214	A114	3c yellow brn	3.00	.75
215	A115	4c carmine	2.25	.75
216	A116	5c dull violet	3.50	1.10
217	A117	7c blue	19.00	12.50
218	A118	8c orange red	8.50	7.00
219	A119	9c ultramarine	10.00	7.50
220	A120	10c red brown	8.50	6.25
221	A121	14c black	17.50	15.00
222	A122	15c claret	17.50	15.00
223	A123	20c deep green	15.00	10.00
224	A124	24c vio brown	27.50	22.50
225	A125	32c gray	27.50	22.50
		Nos. 212-225 (14)	162.55	122.35
		Set, never hinged	233.05	

350th anniv. of annexation of Newfoundland to England, Aug. 5, 1583, by authority of Letters Patent issued by Queen Elizabeth I to Sir Humphrey Gilbert.

Imperf., Pairs

212a	A112	1c	45.00
213a	A113	2c	45.00
214a	A114	3c	375.00
215a	A115	4c	50.00
216a	A116	5c	375.00
219a	A119	9c	500.00
220a	A120	10c	500.00
221a	A120	14c	400.00
222a	A120	15c	240.00
224a	A124	24c	225.00

No. 212a was made both with and without gum. Value of pair without gum about 10% less.

Common Design Types pictured following the introduction.

Silver Jubilee Issue
Common Design Type

1935, May 6		**Wmk. 4**	**Perf. 11x12**	
226	CD301	4c bright rose	2.25	.70
227	CD301	5c violet	2.25	.85
228	CD301	7c dark blue	4.00	3.50
229	CD301	24c olive green	9.00	7.00
		Nos. 226-229 (4)	17.50	12.05
		Set, never hinged	25.35	

Coronation Issue
Common Design Type

1937, May 12		**Perf. 11x11½**		
230	CD302	2c deep green	1.75	.70
231	CD302	4c carmine rose	1.75	.70
232	CD302	5c dark violet	3.50	1.40
		Nos. 230-232 (3)	7.00	2.80
		Set, never hinged	9.80	

Codfish A126

Map of Newfoundland — A127

Caribou A128

Corner Brook Paper Mills A129

Salmon A130

Newfoundland Dog — A131

Harp Seal Pup A132

Cape Race A133

Loading Iron Ore at Bell Island A134

Sealing Fleet A135

Fishing Fleet Leaving for "The Banks" A136

Type I	Type II

Two types of the 3c
Type I — Fine impression; no lines on bridge of nose.
Type II — Coarse impression; lines on bridge of nose.

Perf. 13½, 14 (#234-235)

1937, May 12			**Wmk. 224**	
233	A126	1c gray black	.70	.30
234	A127	3c org brn, die I	3.00	1.10
a.		Die II	2.25	1.10
b.		Vert. pair, imperf. btwn. (I)	850.00	
c.		Vert. pair, imperf. btwn. (II)	850.00	
d.		Horiz. pair, imperf. btwn. (I)	575.00	
e.		Horiz. pair, imperf. btwn. (II)	575.00	
f.		Imperf., pair	240.00	
I.		Horiz. pair, imperf. vert., never hinged	1,600.	
235	A128	7c blue	3.00	2.50
236	A129	8c orange red	3.00	2.50
a.		Vert. pair, imperf. between	350.00	
b.		Horiz. pair, imperf. vert.	2,000.	
237	A130	10c olive gray	4.25	4.25
a.		Double impression	280.00	
238	A131	14c black	4.25	3.50
a.		Imperf., pair	400.00	
239	A132	15c rose lake	4.25	3.50
a.		Vert. pair, imperf. between	1,400.	
240	A133	20c green	4.25	2.25
a.		Vert. pair, imperf. between	1,500.	
241	A134	24c turq blue	4.25	3.25
a.		Vert. pair, imperf. between	2,500.	
242	A135	25c gray	4.25	3.25
a.		Imperf., pair	275.00	
243	A136	48c dark violet	7.00	4.00
a.		Vert. pair, imperf. between	2,500.	
b.		Imperf., pair	275.00	
		Nos. 233-243 (11)	42.20	30.40
		Set, never hinged	60.85	

Imperfs are with gum. No. 243b also made without gum; value the same.

Princess Elizabeth — A139

Designs: 2c, King George VI. 3c, Queen Elizabeth. 7c, Queen Mother Mary.

1938, May 12			**Perf. 13½**	
245	A139	2c green	1.75	.25
246	A139	3c dark carmine	1.75	.25
247	A139	4c light blue	2.40	.25
248	A139	7c dark ultra	1.60	1.10
		Nos. 245-248 (4)	7.50	1.85
		Set, never hinged	9.50	

See Nos. 254-256, 258, 269.

Imperf., Pairs

245a	A139	2c	120.00
246a	A139	3c	120.00
247a	A139	4c	120.00
248a	A139	7c	120.00
		Set, never hinged	700.00

George VI and Queen Elizabeth A141

1939, June 17			**Unwmk.**	
249	A141	5c violet blue	1.25	1.10
		Never hinged	1.75	

Visit of King George and Queen Elizabeth.

No. 249 Surcharged in Brown or Red

Available Nov. 21 and exhausted by Dec. 16, 1939

250	A141	2c on 5c vio blue (Br)	1.40	1.00
251	A141	4c on 5c vio blue (R)	1.10	1.00
		Set, never hinged	3.30	

There are many varieties of broken letters and figures in the settings of the surcharges.

Sir Wilfred Grenfell and "Strathcona II" — A142

1941, Dec. 1			**Perf. 12**	
252	A142	5c dull blue	.40	.30
		Never hinged	.50	

Grenfell Mission, 50th anniv.

Types of 1931-38

1941-44			**Wmk. 224**	**Perf. 12½**
253	A97	1c dark gray	.35	.25
a.		Imperf., pair	150.00	
254	A139	2c deep green	.35	.25
255	A139	3c rose carmine	.50	.25
a.		Imperf., pair	275.00	
256	A139	4c blue	.70	.30
257	A101	5c violet (Die I)	1.00	.25
a.		Imperf., pair	200.00	
b.		Horiz. pair, imperf. vert.	650.00	
c.		Double impression	650.00	
258	A139	7c vio blue ('42)	1.20	1.00
259	A110	8c red	1.40	.65
260	A103	10c brownish blk	1.40	.60
261	A104	14c black	2.10	1.75
a.		Imperf., pair	240.00	
c.		Vert. pair, imperf. horiz.	500.00	
262	A105	15c pale rose vio	2.00	1.40
263	A106	20c green	2.00	1.10
264	A111	24c deep blue	2.25	2.00
265	A107	25c slate	2.25	2.00
266	A108	48c red brown ('44)	3.25	1.75
		Nos. 253-266 (14)	20.75	13.55
		Set, never hinged	26.60	

Nos. 254 and 255 are re-engraved.

Memorial University College A143

1943, Jan. 2		**Unwmk.**	**Perf. 12**	
267	A143	30c carmine	1.40	1.00
		Never hinged	1.85	

No. 267 Surcharged in Black

Available Mar. 21 through April 1, 1946

268	A143	2c on 30c carmine	.30	.30
		Never hinged	.40	

Princess Elizabeth — A144

		Wmk. 224		
1947, Apr. 21		**Engr.**	**Perf. 12½**	
269	A144	4c light blue	.30	.25
		Never hinged	.40	
a.		Imperf., pair	240.00	
b.		Horiz. pair, imperf. vert.	400.00	

Princess Elizabeth's 21st birthday.

Deck of the Matthew A145

1947, June 24

270	A145	5c rose violet	.30	.25
		Never hinged	.40	
a.		Horiz. pair, imperf. between	1,350.	
b.		Imperf., pair	240.00	

Cabot's arrival off Cape Bonavista, 450th anniv.

AIR POST STAMPS

No. 117 Overprinted in Black

Manuscript "Aerial Atlantic Mail JAR"

1919, Apr. 12   Unwmk.   *Perf. 14*

C1	A67	3c red brown	25,000.	15,000.
		Never hinged	35,000.	
a.		Manuscript "Aerial Atlantic Mail JAR"	75,000.	25,000.

No. 70 Surcharged in Black on Block of 25 with Selvage Removed

Trans-Atlantic AIR POST, 1919. ONE DOLLAR.

1919, June 9   *Perf. 12*

C2	A33	$1 on 15c scarlet	225.00	225.00
		Never hinged	375.00	
a.		Without comma after "Post"	240.00	275.00
b.		As "a," without period after "1919"	450.00	450.00

No. 73 Overprinted in Black on Block of 25 with Selvage Removed

AIR MAIL to Halifax, N.S. 1921

1921, Nov. 7

C3	A36	35c red, 2½mm between "AIR" and "MAIL"	140.00	190.00
a.		Inverted overprint	6,000.	
b.		With period after "1921"	150.00	200.00
c.		As "b," inverted overprint	6,500.	

No. 74 Overprinted in Red on Block of 50 with Selvage

Air Mail DE PINEDO 1927

1927, May 21

C4	A37	60c black	45,000.	20,000.
		Never hinged	60,000.	

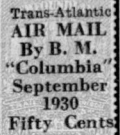

No. 126 Surcharged in Black on Block of 4

Trans-Atlantic AIR MAIL By B. M. "Columbia" September 1930 Fifty Cents

1930, Sept. 25   *Perf. 14*

C5	A67	50c on 36c ol grn	9,500.	9,500.
		Never hinged	14,000.	

Dog Sled and Airplane — AP6

First Transatlantic Mail Airplane and Packet Ship — AP7

Routes of Historic Transatlantic Flights — AP8

1931, Jan. 2   Engr.   Unwmk.

C6	AP6	15c brown	11.00	7.50
a.		Horiz. pair, imperf. between	950.00	
b.		Vert. pair, imperf. between	950.00	
c.		Imperf., pair	625.00	
C7	AP7	50c green	35.00	25.00
a.		Horiz. pair, imperf. between	1,350.	825.00
b.		Vert. pair, imperf. between	1,350.	
c.		Imperf., pair	725.00	
C8	AP8	$1 blue	70.00	55.00
a.		Horiz. pair, imperf. between	1,000.	
b.		Vert. pair, imperf. between	1,000.	
c.		Imperf., pair	725.00	
		Nos. C6-C8 (3)	116.00	87.50
		Set, never hinged	195.00	

1931   Wmk. 224 Sideways

C9	AP6	15c brown	11.00	7.50
a.		Horiz. pair, imperf. between	950.00	
b.		Vert. pair, imperf. between	1,100.	
c.		Imperf., pair	600.00	
C10	AP7	50c green	40.00	35.00
a.		Horiz. pair, imperf. between	950.00	
b.		Vert. pair, imperf. between	950.00	
c.		Horiz. pair, imperf. vert.	950.00	
C11	AP8	$1 blue	100.00	90.00
a.		Vert. pair, imperf. between	1,000.	
c.		Horiz. pair, imperf. between	1,000.	
d.		Vert. pair, imperf. horiz.	1,000.	
e.		Imperf., pair	600.00	
		Nos. C9-C11 (3)	151.00	132.50
		Set, never hinged	263.50	

As the watermark 224 does not show on every stamp in the sheet, pairs are found one with and one without watermark.

For overprint and surcharge see Nos. 211, C12.

No. C11 Surcharged in Red on Block of 4

TRANS-ATLANTIC WEST TO EAST Per Dornier DO-X May, 1932. One Dollar and Fifty Cents

1932, May 19

C12	AP8	$1.50 on $1 blue	275.00	275.00
		Never hinged	425.00	
a.		Inverted surcharge	20,000.	
		Never hinged	25,000.	

NEWFOUNDLAND 1932 FIRST TRANSATLANTIC AIR MAIL AND PASSENGER FLIGHT 1932 AIR MAIL POSTAGE ONE DOLLAR

A stamp of this design was produced in the US in 1932 by a private company under contract with Newfoundland authorities. The government canceled the contract and the stamp was not valid for prepayment of postage. Value, $35.

"Put to Flight" — AP9

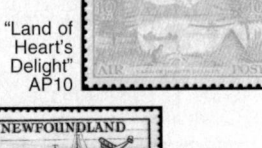

"Land of Heart's Delight" AP10

"Spotting the Herd" AP11

"News from Home" AP12

"Labrador, The Land of Gold" AP13

Perf. 11½ (10, 60c), 14 (5, 30, 75c)

1933, June 9   Engr.

C13	AP9	5c lt brown	11.00	11.00
b.		Horiz. pair, imperf. between	1,150.	
c.		Vert. pair, imperf. between	1,150.	
C14	AP10	10c yellow	19.00	17.50
C15	AP11	30c blue	30.00	30.00
C16	AP12	60c green	65.00	57.50
C17	AP13	75c bister, perf. 14.3	60.00	57.50
b.		Horiz. pair, imperf. between	2,500.	
c.		Vert. pair, imperf. between	2,500.	
		Nos. C13-C17 (5)	185.00	173.50
		Set, never hinged	262.50	

Beware of clever forgeries of Nos. C13b, C13c, C17b and C17c. Certificates of authenticity are highly recommended.

Imperf., Pairs

C13a	AP9	5c	275.00
C14a	AP10	10c	200.00
C15a	AP11	30c	725.00
C16a	AP12	60c	725.00
C17a	AP13	75c	725.00
		Set, never hinged	3,150.

No. C17 Surcharged in Black

1933 GEN. BALBO FLIGHT. $4.50

1933, July 24   *Perf. 14.3*

C18	AP13	$4.50 on 75c bister	325.00	350.00
		Never hinged	500.00	
a.		Inverted surcharge	120,000.	
		Never hinged	150,000.	

On return from the Chicago World Fair "Century of Progress" with his "armada" of 24 seaplanes, Gen. Italo Balbo made a stopover in Shoal Harbour and accepted mail to Italy of about 1,150 covers.

No. C18a was not regularly issued.

The $4.50 on No. C14, 10c yellow, is a proof. Value, $62,500.

View of St. John's AP14

1943, June 1   Unwmk.   *Perf. 12*

C19	AP14	7c bright ultra	.35	.30
		Never hinged	.45	

POSTAGE DUE STAMPS

D1

Perf. 10-10½, Compound

1939-49   Litho.   Unwmk.

J1	D1	1c yellow green, perf. 11 ('49)	4.25	5.50
a.		Perf. 10-10½	7.00	5.50
J2	D1	2c vermilion	7.00	5.50
a.		Perf. 11x9 ('46)	7.00	5.50
J3	D1	3c ultramarine	7.00	5.50
a.		Perf. 11x9 ('49)	7.50	7.50
b.		Perf. 9	3,750.	
J4	D1	4c yel org, perf. 11x9 ('49)	9.50	9.50
a.		Perf 10-10½	15.00	15.00
J5	D1	5c pale brown	15.00	4.25
J6	D1	10c dark violet	7.00	6.50
		Nos. J1-J6 (6)	49.75	36.75
		Set, never hinged	80.50	

1949   Wmk. 224   *Perf. 11*

J7	D1	10c dark violet	11.00	*15.00*
		Never hinged	19.00	
a.		Vert. pair, imperf. between	850.00	

For used examples of Nos. J1-J7 with dated cancels from 1939-49, triple the values shown.

NOVA SCOTIA

ˌnō-və-'skō-shə

LOCATION — Eastern coast of Canada between the Gulf of St. Lawrence and the Atlantic Ocean
GOVT. — British Crown Colony
AREA — 21,428 sq. mi.
POP. — 386,500 (1871)
CAPITAL — Halifax

Nova Scotia joined the Canadian Confederation in 1867 and is now a province of the Dominion. Postage stamps of Canada are used.

12 Pence = 1 Shilling
100 Cents = 1 Dollar (1860)

Values for unused stamps are for examples with original gum as defined in the catalogue introduction except for Nos. 4-7, which are rarely found with any remaining original gum.

Queen Victoria — A1

Crown of Great Britain and Heraldic Flowers of the Empire — A2

Blue Paper

1851-57	**Unwmk.**	**Engr.**	**Imperf.**	
1	A1	1p red brown ('53)	2,500.	525.
a.	Half used as ½p on cover			
2	A2	3p bright blue	1,750.	250.
a.	Half used as 1 ½p on cover			3,750.
b.	3p pale blue ('57)	1,750.	275.
c.	As "b," half used as 1 ½p on cover			3,750.
3	A2	3p dark blue	2,250.	300.
a.	Half used as 1 ½p on cover			4,500.
4	A2	6p yellow green	5,500.	850.
a.	Half used as 3p on cover			4,500.
5	A2	6p dark green ('57)	11,000.	2,250.
a.	Half used as 3p on cover			5,000.
b.	Quarter used as 1 ½p on cover			47,500.
6	A2	1sh reddish pur ('57)	25,000.	5,250.
a.	Half used as 6p on cover			30,000.
b.	1sh deep purple	27,500.	6,000.
7	A2	1sh dull violet	25,000.	6,000.
a.	Half used as 6p on cover			47,500.
b.	Quarter used as 3p on cover			55,000.

Reprints are on thin hard white paper. 1p in brown, 3p in blue, 6p dark green. 1sh violet black. Value about $300 per set.

No. 6 was reproduced by the collotype process in a souvenir sheet distributed at the London International Stamp Exhibition 1950.

Queen Victoria — A3

A5

A6

White or Yellowish Paper

1860-63				**Perf. 12**
8	A3	1c black	15.00	7.50
a.	White paper	15.00	7.50
b.	Half used as ½c on cover		5,750.
c.	Horiz. pair, imperf. vert.	325.00	
9	A3	2c lilac	15.00	12.50
a.	Yellowish paper	15.00	12.50
b.	Half used as 1c on cover		3,250.
10	A3	5c blue	425.00	12.00
a.	Yellowish paper	425.00	12.00
b.	Half used as 2 ½c on cover		5,000.
11	A5	8 ½c green	15.00	22.00
a.	White paper	15.00	22.00
12	A5	10c vermilion	15.00	12.00
a.	Yellowish paper	15.00	12.00
b.	Half used as 5c on cover		1,200.
13	A6	12 ½c black	42.50	37.50
a.	White paper	42.50	37.50
		Nos. 8-13 (6)	527.50	103.50
		Set, never hinged	1,460.	

The stamps of Nova Scotia were replaced by those of Canada.

PRINCE EDWARD ISLAND

ˈprinˌt̩s 'ed-wərd 'ī-lənd

LOCATION — In the Gulf of St. Lawrence, opposite the provinces of New Brunswick and Nova Scotia
GOVT. — British Crown Colony
AREA — 2,184 sq. mi.
POP. — 92,000 (estimated)
CAPITAL — Charlottetown

Originally annexed to Nova Scotia, Prince Edward Island was a separate colony from 1769 to 1873, when it became a part of the Canadian Confederation. Postage stamps of Canada are now used.

12 Pence = 1 Shilling
100 Cents = 1 Dollar (1872)

A1

A2

Queen Victoria — A3

1861, Jan. 1	**Unwmk.**	**Typo.**	**Perf. 9**	
1	A1	2p dull rose	1,100.	325.
a.	2p deep rose	1,350.	350.
b.	Rouletted		22,500.
c.	Horiz. pair, imperf. between	6,500.	
d.	Diagonal half used as 1p on cover		1,900.
2	A2	3p blue	2,250.	750.
a.	Diagonal half used as 1 ½p on cover		2,250.
b.	Double impression	4,750.	

No. 2b is valued with very small faults.

3	A3	6p yellow green	2,750.	1,200.

A4

A5

White or Yellowish Paper

1862-65			**Perf. 11½-12**	
4	A4	1p yellow orange	42.50	35.00
a.	1p brown orange. perf. 11	50.00	35.00
b.	Imperf., pair	200.00	
c.	Half used as ½p on cover		2,000.
5	A1	2p rose	8.50	7.50
a.	Yellowish paper	15.00	7.50
b.	Imperf., pair	100.00	
c.	Horiz. pair, imperf. vert.	275.00	
d.	Vert. pair, imperf. horiz.	375.00	
e.	Diagonal half used as 1p on cover		1,900.
f.	"TWC" for "TWO"	75.00	60.00

6	A2	3p blue	16.00	15.00
a.	Yellowish paper	32.50	15.00
b.	Imperf., pair	150.00	
c.	Vert. pair, imperf. horiz.	400.00	
d.	Horiz. pair, imperf. vert.	400.00	
e.	Diagonal half used as 1 ½p on cover		250.00
f.	Imperf. pair with gutter btwn.	950.00	
g.	Imperf. tete-beche pair with gutter btwn.		2,250.
7	A3	6p yellow green	125.00	95.00
a.	6p blue green	125.00	95.00
c.	Diagonal half used as 3p on cover		3,000.
8	A5	9p violet	95.00	80.00
a.	Imperf., pair	375.00	
b.	Horiz. pair, imperf. vert.	450.00	
c.	Diagonal half used as 4 ½p on cover		2,250.
		Nos. 4-8 (5)	287.00	232.50
		Set, never hinged	465.00	

Queen Victoria — A6

1868				
9	A6	4p black	9.00	19.00
a.	Yellowish paper	15.00	20.00
b.	Horiz. pair, imperf. vert.	190.00	
c.	Diagonal half used as 2p on cover		2,250.
d.	Imperf., pair	140.00	
e.	Horiz. pair, imperf. between	160.00	
g.	Horiz. strip of 3, imperf. btwn.	1,100.	

Queen Victoria — A7

1870, June 1		**Engr.**	**Perf. 12**	
10	A7	4 ½p brown	90.00	75.00

A8

A9

A10

A11

A12

A13

1872, Jan. 1		**Typo.**	**Perf. 12, 12½**	
11	A8	1c brown orange	7.00	7.50
a.	Imperf., pair	240.00	
12	A9	2c ultra	35.00	42.50
a.	Imperf., pair	450.00	
b.	Diagonal half used as 1c on cover		—
13	A10	3c rose	30.00	22.50
a.	Imperf., pair	400.00	
b.	Diagonal half used as 1 ½c on cover		—
c.	Horiz. or vert. pair, imperf. between	275.00	
14	A11	4c green	11.50	16.00
a.	Imperf., pair	400.00	
b.	Diagonal half used as 2c on cover		2,000.
15	A12	6c black	7.50	13.00
a.	Horiz. pair, imperf. btwn.	250.00	
b.	Half used as 3c on cover		900.00
16	A13	12c violet	7.50	30.00
a.	Imperf., pair	425.00	
b.	Half used as 6c on cover		—
		Nos. 11-16 (6)	98.50	131.50
		Set, never hinged	138.50	

CANADA

'ka-nə-də

LOCATION — Northern part of North American continent, except for Alaska
GOVT. — Self-governing dominion in the British Commonwealth of Nations
AREA — 3,851,809 sq. mi.
POP. — 28,846,761 (1996)
CAPITAL — Ottawa

Included in the dominion are British Columbia, Vancouver Island, Prince Edward Island, Nova Scotia, New Brunswick and Newfoundland, all of which formerly issued stamps.

12 Pence = 1 Shilling
100 Cents = 1 Dollar (1859)

> Catalogue values for unused stamps in this country are for Never Hinged items, beginning with Scott 268 in the regular postage section, Scott B1 in the semipostal section, Scott C9 in the air post section, Scott CE3 in the air post special delivery section, Scott CO1 in the air post official section, Scott E11 in the special delivery section, Scott EO1 in the special delivery official section, Scott J15 in the postage due section, and Scott O1 in the official section.

Values for unused stamps of Nos. 1-33 are for examples with partial original gum. Stamps without gum often trade at prices very close to those of stamps with partial gum. Examples with full original gum and lightly hinged are extremely scarce and generally sell for substantially more than the values listed.

Very fine examples of the perforated issues between Nos. 11-20 will have perforations touching the design or frameline on at least one side due to the narrow spacing of the stamps on the plates. Stamps with perfs clear of the designs on all four sides are extremely scarce and will command much higher prices.

Province of Canada

Beaver — A1

Prince Albert — A2

Queen Victoria — A3

1851	**Unwmk.**	**Engr.**	**Imperf.**	
		Laid Paper		
1	A1	3p red	40,000.	1,000.
2	A2	6p slate violet	40,000.	1,650.
a.	Diagonal half used as 3p on cover		32,500.
3	A3	12p black	175,000.	135,000.

On some stamps the laid lines of Nos. 1-3 are practically invisible.

1852-57			**Wove Paper**	
4	A1	3p red	1,500.	225.
a.	3p brown red ('53)	1,700.	250.
b.	Diagonal half used as 1 ½p on cover		32,500.
c.	Ribbed paper	4,500.	575.
d.	Thin paper	1,600.	225.
5	A2	6p slate gray ('55)	30,000.	1,200.
a.	6p brownish gray	40,000.	1,750.
b.	6p greenish gray	30,000.	1,200.

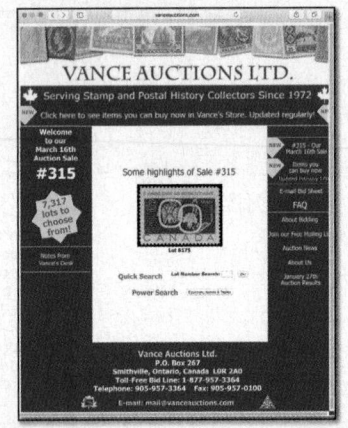
c.	Diagonal half used as 3p on cover			17,500.
d.	Thick hard paper (gray vio) ('57)		30,000.	3,000.

Re-entries of the 3p are numerous. The main re-entry is distinguishable most easily by the line through "EE" and "PEN".

Most authorities believe the 12p black does not exist on wove paper.

Jacques Cartier — A4

1855
7	A4	10p blue	12,000.	1,650.
a.	Thick paper		13,000.	2,250.

Queen Victoria
A5   A6

1857
8	A5	½p rose	1,100.	700.
a.	Horizontally ribbed paper		10,000.	2,500.
b.	Vertically ribbed paper		10,000.	3,750.
9	A6	7½p green	10,000.	3,500.

Very Thick Soft Wove Paper
10	A2	6p reddish pur	32,500.	7,500.
a.	Half used as 3p on cover			25,000.

1858-59   Wove Paper   Perf. 12
11	A5	½p rose	4,250.	1,900.
12	A1	3p red	17,500.	1,350.
13	A2	6p brown vio ('59)	22,500.	7,500.
a.	6p gray violet		22,500.	7,500.
b.	Diagonal half used as 3p on cover			17,500.

Nos. 11-13 values are for examples with perfs touching the design.

A7   A8

A9   A10

A11

1859
14	A7	1c rose	425.00	90.00
a.	Imperf., pair		5,500.	
b.	1c deep rose		575.00	150.00
15	A8	5c ver	575.00	37.50
		On cover		47.50
a.	Imperf., pair		15,000.	
b.	Diagonal half used as 2½c on cover			6,000.
c.	5c brick red		625.00	42.50

16	A9	10c black brn, perf. 11¾	20,000.	6,500.
a.	Half used as 5c on cover			9,000.
17	A9	10c red lilac	1,400.	175.00
a.	10c violet		2,000.	160.00
b.	10c brown		1,400.	140.00
c.	Imperf., pair		11,000.	
d.	Diagonal half used as 5c on cover			5,500.
e.	10c deep red purple		3,250.	1,100.
18	A10	12½c yel green	900.00	130.00
a.	12½c blue green		1,100.	125.00
b.	Imperf., pair		5,750.	
19	A11	17c blue	1,250.	200.00
a.	17c slate blue		1,300.	225.00
b.	Imperf., pair		5,250.	

Values for Nos. 14-19 are for examples with perfs touching the design.

No. 15b was used with a 10c for a 12½c rate.

No. 16 was to be accompanied by a certificate of authenticity issued by a recognized expertizing authority. Less expensive dark brown shades of the 10c often are offered as the rare black brown.

Imperfs. are without gum.

Re-entries of the 5c are numerous. Many of them are slight and have only small premium value. The major re-entry has many lines of the design double, especially the outlines of the ovals and frame at left. Value, used, about $800.

A12

1864
20	A12	2c rose	650.00	300.00
a.	2c deep claret rose		750.00	350.00
b.	Imperf., pair		3,500.	

Imperfs. are without gum.
Values are for examples with perfs touching the design.

Dominion of Canada

Queen Victoria
A13   A14

A15   A16

A17   A18

A19   A20

1868-76   Perf. 12, 11½x12 (5c)
21	A13	½c black	110.00	80.00
a.	Perf. 11½x12 ('73)		150.00	90.00
b.	Watermarked		22,500.	11,000.
c.	Thin paper		150.00	80.00
22	A14	1c brn red	800.00	160.00
a.	Watermarked		3,250.	500.00
b.	Thin paper		950.00	140.00
23	A14	1c yell org	1,750.	225.00
a.	1c deep orange		2,500.	260.00
24	A15	2c green	900.00	100.00
a.	Watermarked		3,250.	425.00
b.	Thin paper		950.00	110.00

---

c.	Diagonal half used as 1c on cover			4,000.
25	A16	3c red	2,250.	40.00
a.	Watermarked		5,250.	475.00
b.	Thin paper		2,500.	55.00
26	A17	5c ol grn ('75)	2,000.	225.00
a.	Perf. 12		8,000.	1,000.
b.	Imperf., pair		32,500.	
27	A18	6c dk brn	2,250.	140.00
a.	6c yellow brown		2,000.	125.00
b.	Watermarked		24,000.	2,500.
c.	Thin paper		2,100.	160.00
d.	Diagonal half used as 3c on cover			3,000.
e.	Vert. half used as 3c on cover			—
f.	6c black brown, thin paper (Mar. '68, 1st printing)		3,250.	250.00
28	A19	12½c blue	1,250.	125.00
a.	Watermarked		7,000.	425.00
b.	Thin paper		1,200.	150.00
c.	Horiz. pair, imperf. vert.			—
d.	Vert. pair, imperf. horiz.			16,000.
29	A20	15c gray vio	90.00	65.00
a.	Perf. 11½x12 ('74)		1,750.	425.00
b.	15c red lilac		1,000.	125.00
c.	Watermarked		12,500.	1,250.
d.	Imperf., pair		1,200.	
e.	Thin paper		800.00	150.00
30	A20	15c gray	90.00	65.00
a.	Perf. 11½x12 ('73)		1,600.	400.00
b.	15c blue gray ('75)		135.00	75.00
c.	Very thick paper (dp vio)		5,250.	1,600.
d.	Script wmk., Perf. 11½x12, ('76)		25,000.	9,000.
e.	15c deep blue		1,850.	425.00

The watermark on Nos. 21a, 22a, 24a, 25a, 27b, 28a and 29c consists of double-lined letters reading: "E. & G. BOTHWELL CLUTHA MILLS." The script watermark on No. 30d reads in full: "Alexr. Pirie & Sons." Values for all these watermarked stamps are for fine examples. Very fine examples are rare, seldom traded, and generally command premiums of about 100% over the values listed.

No. 21b unused and used, and Nos. 26a and 26b unused are valued in the grade of fine. No. 26b is a unique pair.

The existence of No. 28c has been questioned.

1868   Laid Paper
31	A14	1c brown red	40,000.	9,000.
32	A15	2c green		250,000.
33	A16	3c bright red	25,000.	2,250.

Only three examples of No. 32 are recorded, none being very fine.

Montreal and Ottawa Printings

A21   A22

A23

A24   A25

A26   A27

1870-89   Wove Paper   Perf. 12
34	A21	½c black ('82)	22.50	10.00
a.	Imperf., pair		650.00	
b.	Horiz. pair, imperf. between		1,000.	
35	A22	1c yellow	50.00	1.25
a.	1c orange ('70)		300.00	11.00
b.	Imperf., pair		475.00	
c.	Diagonal half used as ½c on circular			4,500.
36	A23	2c green ('72)	85.00	2.50
a.	Imperf., pair		725.00	
b.	Diagonal half used as 1c on cover			2,100.

c.	Vertical half used as 1c on cover			2,100.
d.	2c blue green ('89)		110.00	5.00
f.	Double impression		*6,000.*	—
37	A24	3c org red ('73)	175.00	1.50
a.		3c rose ('71)	625.00	17.50
b.		3c copper red ('70)	1,750.	65.00
c.		3c dull red ('72)	175.00	3.25
38	A25	5c sl green ('76)	800.00	27.50
39	A26	6c yel brn ('72)	600.00	27.50
a.		Diagonal half used as 3c on cover		4,500.
c.		Imperf., pair	3,500.	
40	A27	10c dull rose lil ('77)	1,600.	90.00
a.		10c magenta ('80)	1,600.	90.00
b.		10c deep lilac rose	1,600.	90.00

No. 34a was made with and without gum; values the same.

Examples of Nos. 36b and 36c postmarked "Halifax" are a private speculation.

No. 39c is unique and in the form of a strip of three.

1870   **Perf. 12½**

37d	A24	3c copper red (Ottawa)	11,000.	1,500.

1873-79   **Perf. 11½x12**

35d	A22	1c orange	500.00	20.00
36e	A23	2c green	750.00	25.00
37e	A24	3c red	450.00	12.50
38a	A25	5c slate green	1,250.	52.50
39b	A26	6c yellow brown	1,000.	65.00
40c	A27	10c dull rose lilac	1,700.	260.00

The gum on Nos. 35d-40c is always dull and usually blotchy or streaky. It is distinct from the earlier clear, smooth gum and from the bright shiny gums of the later periods.

Nos. 38 and 40 were printed at Montreal. Printings of Nos. 34 to 37, and 39 were made at Ottawa or Montreal and can be separated only by differences in paper and gum.

Ottawa Printing

    A28   A29

1888-97   **Perf. 12**

41	A24	3c brt vermilion	65.00	.80
a.		3c rose carmine	525.00	15.00
42	A25	5c gray	230.00	5.00
43	A26	6c red brown	240.00	12.50
a.		6c chocolate ('90)	400.00	32.50
44	A28	8c viol blk ('93)	260.00	7.00
a.		8c blue gray	425.00	8.50
b.		8c slate	300.00	7.00
c.		8c gray	300.00	7.00
45	A27	10c brn red ('97)	725.00	65.00
a.		10c dull rose	625.00	55.00
b.		10c pink	725.00	65.00
46	A29	20c ver ('93)	425.00	125.00
47	A29	50c dp blue ('93)	425.00	85.00

Stamps of the 1870-93 issues are found on paper varying from very thin to thick, also occasionally on paper showing a distinctly ribbed surface.

The gum on Nos. 41-47 appears bright and shiny, often with a yellowish tint.

Imperf., Pairs

41b	A24	3c	500.
42a	A25	5c	750.
43b	A26	6c	625.
44d	A28	8c	850.
45c	A27	10c	625.
46a	A29	20c	1,500.
47a	A29	50c	1,500.

Nos. 41b-45c made with and without gum. Without gum sell for the same as the unused hinged price.

Imperforates and Part-Perforates

From 1859 through 1943 (Nos. 14a/262a), imperforate stamps were printed. The earliest imperforates through perhaps 1917 most likely were from imprimatur sheets (i.e. the first sheets from the approved plates, normally kept in government files) or proof sheets on stamp paper that once were in the post office archives. The imperforates from approximately 1927 to 1943 (often made both with and without gum) were specially created and traded for classic stamps needed for the post office museum, given as gifts to governmental or other dignitaries, or sold or given to favored persons.

The only imperforates from this entire period that were issued to the public were Nos. 90A and 136-138.

Similarly, almost all stamps that are known part-perforate (i.e. horizontal pairs imperforate vertically and vertical pairs imperforate horizontally) were specially made for trading purposes or as presentation items to be given to favored persons. These part-perforates are not listed here, but they are listed in *Scott Classic Specialized Catalogue of Stamps & Covers.* Part-perforate error stamps that are believed to have been actually issued to the public are listed in this catalogue.

See the similar imperforates in the air post, Nos. CE1a and CE2a, special delivery, No. F2c (but not No. F1c which was an issued error), postage dues, and Nos. MR4b and MR4c.

Jubilee Issue

Queen Victoria, "1837" and "1897" — A30

1897, June 19   **Unwmk.**   **Perf. 12**

50	A30	½c black	110.00	110.00
		Never hinged	275.00	
51	A30	1c orange	30.00	8.00
		Never hinged	75.00	
52	A30	2c green	37.50	15.00
		Never hinged	92.50	
53	A30	3c bright rose	30.00	2.50
		Never hinged	75.00	
54	A30	5c deep blue	70.00	45.00
		Never hinged	180.00	
55	A30	6c yell brn	230.00	175.00
		Never hinged	575.00	
56	A30	8c dark violet	130.00	70.00
		Never hinged	325.00	
57	A30	10c brown violet	175.00	120.00
		Never hinged	425.00	
58	A30	15c steel blue	275.00	190.00
		Never hinged	675.00	
59	A30	20c vermilion	275.00	190.00
		Never hinged	650.00	
60	A30	50c ultra	375.00	190.00
		Never hinged	775.00	
61	A30	$1 lake	1,000.	700.00
		Never hinged	2,900.	
62	A30	$2 dk purple	1,400.	600.00
		Never hinged	4,000.	
63	A30	$3 yel bister	1,400.	1,100.
		Never hinged	4,000.	
64	A30	$4 purple	1,400.	1,100.
		Never hinged	4,000.	
65	A30	$5 olive green	1,500.	1,100.
		Never hinged	4,250.	
		Nos. 50-60 (11)	1,738.	1,116.
		Set, never hinged	4,097.	

60th year of Queen Victoria's reign.
Roller and smudged cancels on Nos. 61-65 sell for less.

    A31

1897-98

66	A31	½c black	15.00	8.50
		Never hinged	37.50	
67	A31	1c blue green	45.00	2.00
		Never hinged	115.00	
68	A31	2c purple	50.00	2.25
		Never hinged	125.00	
69	A31	3c carmine ('98)	80.00	2.00
		Never hinged	200.00	
70	A31	5c dk bl, *bluish*	150.00	10.00
		Never hinged	375.00	

71	A31	6c brown	140.00	45.00
		Never hinged	350.00	
72	A31	8c orange	325.00	21.00
		Never hinged	800.00	
73	A31	10c brn vio ('98)	600.00	100.00
		Never hinged	1,500.	
		Nos. 66-73 (8)	1,405.	190.75
		Set, never hinged	3,503.	

For surcharge see No. 87.

Imperf., Pairs

66a	A31	½c	500.
		Never hinged	950.
67a	A31	1c	400.
		Never hinged	750.
68a	A31	2c	500.
		Never hinged	950.
69a	A31	3c	800.
		Never hinged	1,450.
70a	A31	5c	500.
		Never hinged	750.
71a	A31	6c	800.
		Never hinged	1,450.
72a	A31	8c	700.
		Never hinged	1,250.
73a	A31	10c	700.
		Never hinged	1,250.

Nos. 66a, 67a, 68a and 70a made with and without gum. Specialists can distinguish printings made with and without gum by shade and paper quality. Without gum sell for about 80% of the unused hinged price.

A32

Type I   Type II

TWO CENTS:
Type I — Frame of four very thin lines.
Type II — Frame of a thick line between two thin ones.

1898-1902

74	A32	½c black	12.50	2.75
		Never hinged	25.00	
75	A32	1c gray green	50.00	.75
		Never hinged	100.00	
76	A32	2c purple (I)	40.00	.75
		Never hinged	80.00	
a.		Thick paper ('99)	175.00	12.00
		Never hinged	350.00	
77	A32	2c car (I) ('99)	55.00	.75
		Never hinged	110.00	
a.		2c carmine (II) ('99)	70.00	.60
		Never hinged	140.00	
b.		Booklet pane of 6 (II) ('00)	1,600.	—
		Never hinged	3,000.	
		Complete booklet, 2 #77b	3,250.	
78	A32	3c carmine	90.00	1.10
		Never hinged	180.00	
79	A32	5c blue, *bluish* ('99)	220.00	3.00
		Never hinged	440.00	
80	A32	6c brown	200.00	57.50
		Never hinged	400.00	
81	A32	7c ol yel ('02)	150.00	22.50
		Never hinged	300.00	
82	A32	8c orange	375.00	27.50
		Never hinged	750.00	
83	A32	10c brown vio	425.00	30.00
		Never hinged	850.00	
84	A32	20c ol grn ('00)	650.00	110.00
		Never hinged	1,300.	
		Nos. 74-84 (11)	2,268.	256.60
		Set, never hinged	4,515.	

For surcharges see Nos. 88-88C.

Imperf., Pairs

74a	A32	½c	500.
		Never hinged	800.
75a	A32	1c	1,250.
		Never hinged	2,250.
77c	A32	2c (I)	475.
		Never hinged	775.
77d	A32	2c (II)	*1,250.*
e.		As No. 77b, imperf., 2 panes tete beche ('00)	15,000.
79a	A32	5c	1,200.
		Never hinged	1,900.
80a	A32	6c	1,200.
		Never hinged	1,900.
81a	A32	7c	600.
82a	A32	8c	1,200.
		Never hinged	1,900.
83a	A32	10c	1,200.
		Never hinged	1,900.
84a	A32	20c	5,500.

Nos. 77d, 77e, 81a and 84a were made only without gum. No. 80a was made only with gum. Others either with or without gum and of these those without gum sell for about ⅔ of the values shown for unused hinged. Specialists can distinguish printings made with and without gum by shade and paper quality.

Values for complete booklets from No. 77b to No. 219a are for booklets with uncreases and very fine covers containing never-hinged panes with normal centering, which is fine. Booklets with very fine panes will sell for more. Values are for the most common booklet covers; other cover types exist for some booklets from No. 104a to 167a, and these may sell for more.

Imperial Penny Postage Issue

Map of British Empire on Mercator Projection A33

No. 86

1898, Dec. 7   Engr. & Typo.

85	A33	2c black, lav & car	45.00	9.00
		Never hinged	100.00	
a.		Imperf., pair	550.00	
86	A33	2c black, bl & car	45.00	9.00
		Never hinged	100.00	
a.		Imperf., pair	550.00	

Imperfs. are without gum.

Nos. 69 and 78 Surcharged in

2 CENTS

1899, July

87	A31	2c on 3c carmine	17.50	7.50
		Never hinged	45.00	
88	A32	2c on 3c carmine	32.50	6.00
		Never hinged	82.50	

No. 78 Surcharged in Blue or Violet

A32a   A32b

1899, Jan. 5

88B	A32a	1(c) on ⅓ of 3c, on cover (Bl)	7,750.
88C	A32b	2(c) on ⅔ of 3c, on cover (V)	7,250.

Nos. 88B-88C were prepared and used on Jan. 5 only at Port Hood, Nova Scotia, without official authorization.

Nos. 88B-88C must be accompanied by certificates from recognized expertizing organizations. Covers reported to date were backdated and never saw postal use.

King Edward VII — A34

Type I   Type II

Two types of 2c carmine.
Type I — Has breaks in the upper left shading lines above "DA" in Canada.
Type II — Has solid lines, no breaks.

1903-08   Engr.

89	A34	1c green	45.00	.40
		Never hinged	115.00	
90	A34	2c carmine, type II	55.00	.40
		Never hinged	135.00	
b.		Booklet pane of 6	1,600.	1,250.
		Never hinged	2,750.	
		Complete booklet, 2 #90b	3,500.	
e.		2c carmine, type I	160.00	2.00
		Never hinged	400.00	
f.		Vert. pair, imperf. btwn at either top or bottom	5,000.	
91	A34	5c blue, *blue*	250.00	5.75
		Never hinged	625.00	
92	A34	7c olive bister	260.00	6.25
		Never hinged	650.00	
93	A34	10c brown lilac	425.00	15.00
		Never hinged	1,050.	
94	A34	20c ol grn ('04)	800.00	50.00
		Never hinged	2,000.	
95	A34	50c purple ('08)	950.00	175.00
		Never hinged	2,350.	
		Nos. 89-95 (7)	2,785.	252.80
		Set, never hinged	6,925.	

Values for Nos. 94 and 95 used are for examples with contemporaneous circular datestamps. Stamps with heavy cancellations or parcel cancellations sell for much less.
Issued: 1c-10c, 7/1/03; 20c, 9/27/04; 50c, 11/19/08.

Imperf., Type II

90A	A34	2c carmine	40.00	40.00
		Never hinged	80.00	

No. 90A is the only imperforate Canada stamp besides Nos. 136-138 regularly issued to the public. 100,000 were issued.

Imperf., Pairs, Without Gum

89a	A34	1c	725.00
90c	A34	2c Type I	850.00
d.		As No. 90c, imperf, 2 panes tete beche	20,000.
91a	A34	5c	1,200.
92a	A34	7c	800.
93a	A34	10c	1,200.

Quebec Tercentenary Issue

Prince and Princess of Wales, 1908 — A35

Jacques Cartier and Samuel de Champlain A36

Queen Alexandra and King Edward A37

Champlain's Home in Quebec A38

Generals Montcalm and Wolfe — A39

View of Quebec in 1700 — A40

Champlain's Departure for the West — A41

Arrival of Cartier at Quebec A42

1908, July 16   *Perf. 12*

96	A35	½c black brown	8.00	5.00
		Never hinged	19.00	
97	A36	1c blue green	30.00	6.00
		Never hinged	75.00	
98	A37	2c carmine	40.00	3.00
		Never hinged	100.00	
99	A38	5c dark blue	85.00	70.00
		Never hinged	210.00	
100	A39	7c olive green	160.00	100.00
		Never hinged	400.00	
101	A40	10c dark violet	200.00	125.00
		Never hinged	500.00	
102	A41	15c red orange	225.00	160.00
		Never hinged	625.00	
103	A42	20c yellow brown	250.00	225.00
		Never hinged	625.00	
		Nos. 96-103 (8)	998.00	694.00
		Set, never hinged	2,479.	

Imperf., Pairs

96a	A35	½c	750.
		Never hinged	1,300.
97a	A36	1c	750.
		Never hinged	1,300.
98a	A37	2c	750.
		Never hinged	1,300.
99a	A38	5c	750.
		Never hinged	1,300.
100a	A39	7c	750.
		Never hinged	1,300.
101a	A40	10c	750.
		Never hinged	1,300.
102a	A41	15c	750.
		Never hinged	1,300.
103a	A42	20c	750.
		Never hinged	1,300.

100 pairs of imperfs made, 50 with gum and 50 without. Due to demand, pairs without gum generally sell for 90-95% of the unused hinged price.

King George V — A43

Type I

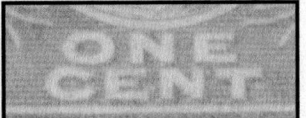

Type II

Two types of 1c.
Type I — The "N" of "ONE" is separated from the oval above it.
Type II — The "N" of "ONE" almost touches the oval above it.

Type I   Type II

Two types of 3c carmine.
Type I — The "R" of "THREE" is separated from the oval above it. The bottom line of the vignette does not touch the heavy diagonal stroke at right.

Type II — The "R" of "THREE" almost touches the oval above it. The bottom horizontal line of the vignette touches the heavy diagonal stroke at right.

Note that the values for Nos. 104-122 are for sheet stamps with perforations on four sides. Single stamps from booklet panes Nos. 104a, 105a, 105b, 106a, 106d, 107b, 107c, 108a and 109a all have natural straight edges on one or two sides, and (except for No. 107d singles) they are worth much less than the listed sheet stamps.

See note on booklet panes and complete booklets after Nos. 74-84. Values for listed booklet panes throughout this catalog are for very fine panes.

1911-25

104	A43	1c dark green	25.00	.25
		Never hinged	60.00	
a.		As "b," booklet pane of 6	150.00	150.00
		Never hinged	300.00	
		Complete booklet, 4 #104a	750.00	
d.		As "c," booklet pane of 6	180.00	180.00
		Never hinged	325.00	
		Complete booklet, 4 #104d	875.00	
e.		1c yellow green	25.00	.25
		Never hinged	60.00	
f.		As "e," booklet pane of 6	35.00	35.00
		Never hinged	70.00	
		Complete booklet, 4 #104f	180.00	
105	A43	1c org yell (I) ('22)	25.00	.25
		Never hinged	60.00	
a.		Booklet pane of 4 + 2 labels	55.00	55.00
		Never hinged	110.00	
b.		Booklet pane of 6	62.50	62.50
		Never hinged	125.00	
		Complete booklet, 4 #105b	375.00	
d.		1c org yellow (II)	20.00	.25
		Never hinged	50.00	
106	A43	2c carmine	25.00	.25
		Never hinged	60.00	
a.		Booklet pane of 6	40.00	40.00
		Never hinged	80.00	
		Complete booklet, 2 #106a	140.00	
b.		2c pink	150.00	18.00
		Never hinged	350.00	
c.		2c rose carmine	25.00	.25
		Never hinged	60.00	
d.		As "c," booklet pane of 6	160.00	160.00
		Never hinged	320.00	
107	A43	2c yel grn ('22)	27.50	.25
		Never hinged	65.00	
a.		Thin paper ('24)	20.00	2.50
		Never hinged	50.00	
b.		Booklet pane of 4 + 2 labels ('22)	70.00	80.00
		Never hinged	140.00	
c.		Booklet pane of 6 ('22)	350.00	325.00
		Never hinged	625.00	
		Complete booklet, 2 #107c	800.00	
108	A43	3c brown ('18)	25.00	.40
		Never hinged	60.00	
a.		Booklet pane of 4 + 2 labels	90.00	95.00
		Never hinged	180.00	
		Complete booklet, 2 #108a	550.00	
		Complete booklet, #105a, 107b, 108a	475.00	
109	A43	3c car (I) ('23)	17.50	.25
		Never hinged	42.50	
a.		Booklet pane of 4 + 2 labels	70.00	75.00
		Never hinged	140.00	
		Complete booklet, 2 #109a	325.00	
		Complete booklet, #105a, 107b, 109a	350.00	
c.		Die II ('24)	50.00	.25
		Never hinged	125.00	
110	A43	4c ol bis ('22)	47.50	4.50
		Never hinged	120.00	
111	A43	5c dark blue ('12)	175.00	1.75
		Never hinged	450.00	
112	A43	5c violet ('22)	40.00	1.00
		Never hinged	100.00	
a.		Thin paper ('24)	35.00	7.50
		Never hinged	87.50	
113	A43	7c yel ocher ('12)	75.00	3.50
		Never hinged	180.00	
114	A43	7c red brn ('24)	22.50	10.00
		Never hinged	55.00	
115	A43	8c blue ('25)	37.50	10.00
		Never hinged	92.50	
116	A43	10c plum ('12)	275.00	4.00
		Never hinged	675.00	
117	A43	10c blue ('22)	47.50	2.00
		Never hinged	115.00	
118	A43	10c bis brn ('25)	40.00	2.00
		Never hinged	95.00	
119	A43	20c ol grn ('25)	110.00	1.75
		Never hinged	275.00	
120	A43	50c blk brn ('25)	90.00	3.75
		Never hinged	225.00	
a.		50c black ('12)	300.00	12.00
		Never hinged	725.00	
122	A43	$1 orange ('23)	95.00	10.00
		Never hinged	240.00	
		Nos. 104-122 (18)	1,200.	55.90
		Set, never hinged	2,920.	

For type A43 perforated 12x8 see No. 184.
For surcharges see Nos. 139-140.
Issued: Nos. 104, 106, 12/22/11; No. 105, 6/7/22; No. 108, 8/6/18; No. 109, 12/18/23; 4c, 7/7/22; No. 111, 1/17/12; No. 112, 2/2/22; No. 113, 116, 11/12/12; No. 114, 12/12/24; 8c, 9/1/25; No. 117, 2/20/22; No. 118, 8/1/25; 20c, 1/23/12; 50c, 1/26/12; $1, 7/22/23.

Imperf., Panes

105c		As No. 105b, imperf, 2 panes tete beche	15,000.
107d		As No. 107c, imperf, 2 panes tete beche	15,000.
109b		As No. 109a, imperf, 2 panes tete beche	15,000.

Imperf., Pairs

110a	A43	4c	2,250.	
		Never hinged	4,000.	
112b	A43	5c	2,250.	
		Never hinged	4,000.	
114a	A43	7c	2,250.	
		Never hinged	4,000.	
115a	A43	8c	2,250.	
		Never hinged	4,000.	
118a	A43	10c	2,250.	
		Never hinged	4,000.	
119a	A43	20c	2,250.	
		Never hinged	4,000.	
120b	A43	50c	3,000.	
		Never hinged	6,000.	
122a	A43	$1	2,250.	
		Never hinged	4,000.	

Nos. 105c and 109b made without gum, others with gum. About half of the No. 120b pairs have creases; value thus $500.

Coil Stamps

1913   Perf. 8 Horizontally

123	A43	1c dark green	110.00	65.00
		Never hinged	275.00	
124	A43	2c carmine	120.00	65.00
		Never hinged	300.00	

1912-24   Perf. 8 Vertically

125	A43	1c green	25.00	2.00
		Never hinged	50.00	
126	A43	1c org yell (II) ('23)	12.00	7.50
		Never hinged	24.00	
a.		As #126, block of 4 (II)	65.00	50.00
		Never hinged	100.00	
b.		1c org yellow (I)	30.00	11.00
		Never hinged	60.00	
c.		As "b," block of 4 (I)	700.00	
		Never hinged	1,200.	
127	A43	2c carmine	40.00	2.00
		Never hinged	80.00	
128	A43	2c green ('22)	25.00	1.10
		Never hinged	50.00	
a.		Block of 4	65.00	60.00
		Never hinged	100.00	
129	A43	3c brown ('18)	30.00	1.30
		Never hinged	60.00	
130	A43	3c carmine (I) ('24)	75.00	9.00
		Never hinged	150.00	
a.		Block of 4 (I)	1,050.	750.00
		Never hinged	1,650.	
b.		Die II	100.00	10.00
		Never hinged	200.00	
		Nos. 125-130 (6)	207.00	22.90
		Set, never hinged	386.50	

Nos. 126a and 128a were issued to the public. Nos. 126c and 130a were issued "by favor" as were the various other imperf and part-perfs of this era.
Beware of fakes of No. 130a made from No. 138.

1915-24   Perf. 12 Horizontally

131	A43	1c dark green	7.50	6.50
		Never hinged	15.00	
132	A43	2c carmine	40.00	10.00
		Never hinged	80.00	
133	A43	2c yell grn ('24)	85.00	75.00
		Never hinged	170.00	
134	A43	3c brown ('21)	12.50	6.50
		Never hinged	25.00	
		Nos. 131-134 (4)	145.00	98.00
		Set, never hinged	290.00	

"The Fathers of Confederation" — A44

1917, Sept. 15   Perf. 12

135	A44	3c brown	47.50	2.25
		Never hinged	120.00	
a.		Imperf., pair	600.00	

50th anniv. of the Canadian Confederation. Imperfs. are without gum.

1924   Imperf.

136	A43	1c orange yellow (I)	35.00	35.00
		Never hinged	65.00	
		Pair	87.50	87.50
		Never hinged	160.00	
137	A43	2c green	35.00	35.00
		Never hinged	65.00	
		Pair	87.50	87.50
		Never hinged	160.00	
138	A43	3c carmine (I)	17.50	17.50
		Never hinged	32.50	
		Pair	42.50	42.50
		Never hinged	77.50	
		Nos. 136-138 (3)	87.50	87.50
		Set, never hinged	162.50	

No. 109 Surcharged

a   b

1926   Perf. 12

139	A43(a)	2c on 3c carmine (I)	55.00	55.00
		Never hinged	90.00	
a.		Pair, one without surcharge	725.00	
		Never hinged	1,150.	
b.		Double surcharge	275.00	
		Never hinged	425.00	
c.		Die II	850.00	
		Never hinged	1,500.	
140	A43(b)	2c on 3c carmine	27.50	30.00
		Never hinged	47.50	
a.		Double surcharge	250.00	225.00
		Never hinged	390.00	
b.		Triple surcharge	250.00	250.00
		Never hinged	390.00	
c.		Double surch., one invtd.	400.00	
		Never hinged	600.00	

Sir John A.   Sir Wilfrid
Macdonald   Laurier
A45   A48

"The Fathers of Confederation" — A46

Parliament Building at Ottawa
A47

Map of Canada
A49

1927, June 29

141	A45	1c orange	3.00	1.30
		Never hinged	5.50	
142	A46	2c green	2.00	.25
		Never hinged	3.75	
143	A47	3c brown carmine	8.75	6.50
		Never hinged	16.00	
144	A48	5c violet	4.25	3.50
		Never hinged	8.00	
145	A49	12c dark blue	25.00	6.50
		Never hinged	45.00	
		Nos. 141-145 (5)	43.00	18.05
		Set, never hinged	78.25	

60th year of the Canadian Confederation. Nos. 141-145 exist partly perforated.

Imperf., Pairs

141a	A45	1c	125.00	
		Never hinged	180.00	
142a	A46	2c	125.00	
		Never hinged	180.00	
143a	A47	3c	125.00	
		Never hinged	180.00	
144a	A48	5c	125.00	
		Never hinged	180.00	
145a	A49	12c	125.00	
		Never hinged	180.00	

Thomas d'Arcy
McGee — A50

Laurier and
Macdonald
A51

Robert
Baldwin and
Sir Louis
Hypolyte
Lafontaine
A52

1927, June 29

146	A50	5c violet	4.00	3.00
		Never hinged	7.25	
147	A51	12c green	10.00	5.50
		Never hinged	18.00	
148	A52	20c brown carmine	27.50	6.50
		Never hinged	50.00	
		Nos. 146-148 (3)	41.50	15.00
		Set, never hinged	75.25	

Nos. 146-148 were to have been issued in July, 1926, as a commemorative series, but were withheld and issued June 29, 1927.

Imperf., Pairs

146a	A50	5c	125.00	
		Never hinged	180.00	
147a	A51	12c	125.00	
		Never hinged	180.00	
148a	A52	20c	125.00	
		Never hinged	180.00	

King George V — A53

Mt. Hurd from Bell-Smith's Painting
"The Ice-crowned Monarch of the
Rockies"
A54

Quebec
Bridge
A55

Harvesting
Wheat
A56

Schooner
"Bluenose"
A57

Parliament
Building
A58

1928-29

149	A53	1c orange	3.50	.40
		Never hinged	6.50	
a.		Booklet pane of 6	27.50	25.00
		Never hinged	40.00	
		Complete booklet, 4 #149a	150.00	
150	A53	2c green	1.90	.25
		Never hinged	3.50	
a.		Booklet pane of 6	27.50	25.00
		Never hinged	40.00	
		Complete booklet, 2 #150a	95.00	
151	A53	3c dk carmine	27.50	12.50
		Never hinged	50.00	
152	A53	4c bister ('29)	25.00	6.00
		Never hinged	45.00	
153	A53	5c dp violet	16.00	3.00
		Never hinged	30.00	
a.		Booklet pane of 6	200.00	140.00
		Never hinged	280.00	
		Complete booklet, 3 #149a, 2 #150a, 1 #153a	600.00	
154	A53	8c blue	18.00	9.00
		Never hinged	32.50	
155	A54	10c green	22.50	2.50
		Never hinged	42.50	
156	A55	12c gray ('29)	45.00	9.00
		Never hinged	85.00	
157	A56	20c dk car ('29)	65.00	12.00
		Never hinged	120.00	
158	A57	50c dk blue ('29)	225.00	65.00
		Never hinged	450.00	
159	A58	$1 ol grn ('29)	300.00	80.00
		Never hinged	600.00	
		Nos. 149-159 (11)	749.40	199.65
		Set, never hinged	1,465.	

Imperf., Panes

149c		As No. 149a, imperf, 2 panes tete beche	1,000.
		Never hinged	1,450.
150c		As No. 150a, imperf, 2 panes tete beche	1,000.
		Never hinged	1,450.
153c		As No. 153a, imperf, 2 panes tete beche	1,000.
		Never hinged	1,450.

Imperf., Pairs

149b	A53	1c	100.00
		Never hinged	140.00
150b	A53	2c	100.00
		Never hinged	140.00
151a	A53	3c	120.00
		Never hinged	170.00
152a	A53	4c	120.00
		Never hinged	170.00
153b	A53	5c	100.00
		Never hinged	140.00
154a	A53	8c	120.00
		Never hinged	170.00
155a	A54	10c	200.00
		Never hinged	280.00
156a	A55	12c	200.00
		Never hinged	280.00
157a	A56	20c	200.00
		Never hinged	280.00
158a	A57	50c	800.00
		Never hinged	1,150.
159a	A58	$1	725.00
		Never hinged	1,050.

Coil Stamps

1929 *Perf. 8 Vertically*

160	A53	1c orange	40.00	22.50
		Never hinged	75.00	
		Precanceled		22.50
161	A53	2c green	40.00	3.50
		Never hinged	75.00	

King George
V
A59

Library of
Parliament
A60

The Citadel
at Quebec
A61

Harvesting
Wheat
A62

Museum at
Grand Pré
and
Monument to
Evangeline
A63

Mt. Edith
Cavell
A64

Type I   Type II

Two types of 1c.
Type I — Three thick and one thin colored lines between "P" at right and ornament above it.
Type II — Four thick colored lines. Curved line in ball of ornament at right is longer than in die I.

Type I   Type II

Two types of 2c.
Type I — The top of the letter "P" encloses a tiny dot of color.
Type II — The top of the "P" encloses a larger spot of color than in die I. The "P" appears almost like a "D."

1930-31 *Perf. 11*

162	A59	1c orange	1.25	.70
		Never hinged	2.50	
163	A59	1c dp grn (II)	2.00	.25
		Never hinged	4.00	
a.		Booklet pane of 4 + 2 labels (II)	120.00	100.00
		Never hinged	180.00	
b.		Die I	2.00	.25
		Never hinged	4.00	
c.		Booklet pane of 6 (I)	22.50	20.00
		Never hinged	35.00	
		Complete booklet, 4 #163c	180.00	
164	A59	2c dull green (I)	1.75	.25
		Never hinged	3.50	
a.		Booklet pane of 6	32.50	32.50
		Never hinged	47.50	
		Complete booklet, 2 #164a	180.00	
165	A59	2c deep red (I)	1.75	.30
		Never hinged	3.50	
a.		Die II	1.90	.25
		Never hinged	3.75	
b.		Booklet pane of 6 (I)	25.00	22.50
		Never hinged	37.50	
		Complete booklet, 2 #165b	90.00	

166	A59	2c dk brn (II) ('31)	1.75	.25
		Never hinged	3.50	
a.		Booklet pane of 4 + 2 labels (II)	130.00	130.00
		Never hinged	200.00	
b.		Die I	5.00	4.00
		Never hinged	10.00	
c.		Booklet pane of 6 (I)	57.50	57.50
		Never hinged	87.50	
		Complete booklet, 2 #166c	225.00	
167	A59	3c deep red ('31)	3.00	.25
		Never hinged	6.00	
a.		Booklet pane of 4 + 2 labels	40.00	40.00
		Never hinged	60.00	
		Complete booklet, 2 #167a	110.00	
		Complete booklet, #163a, 166a, 167a	450.00	
168	A59	4c yel bister	15.00	7.50
		Never hinged	30.00	
169	A59	5c dull violet	7.25	5.00
		Never hinged	14.50	
170	A59	5c dull blue	8.50	1.25
		Never hinged	17.00	
171	A59	8c dark blue	27.50	13.50
		Never hinged	55.00	
172	A59	8c red orange	8.50	5.50
		Never hinged	17.00	
173	A60	10c olive green	11.00	1.30
		Never hinged	22.00	
174	A61	12c gray black	30.00	6.50
		Never hinged	60.00	
175	A62	20c brown red	50.00	1.40
		Never hinged	100.00	
176	A63	50c dull blue	175.00	14.00
		Never hinged	350.00	
177	A64	$1 dk ol green	175.00	27.50
		Never hinged	350.00	
		Nos. 162-177 (16)	519.25	85.45
		Set, never hinged	1,037.	

No. 169 rotary printing is distinguished unused from No. 169a flat plate printing by the former having gum ridges about 5mm apart. See No. 201. For surcharge see No. 191. For overprint see No. 203.

Imperf., Pairs

163d	A59	1c (II)	1,600.
		Never hinged	2,500.
173a	A60	10c	1,600.
		Never hinged	2,500.
174a	A61	12c	900.
		Never hinged	1,350.
175a	A62	2c	900.
		Never hinged	1,350.
176a	A63	50c	1,000.
		Never hinged	1,550.
177a	A64	$1	1,000.
		Never hinged	1,550.

Coil Stamps

1930-31   *Perf. 8½ Vertically*

178	A59	1c orange	15.00	10.00
		Never hinged	30.00	
179	A59	1c deep green	9.00	5.75
		Never hinged	18.00	
180	A59	2c dull green	6.00	3.00
		Never hinged	12.00	
181	A59	2c deep red	25.00	2.50
		Never hinged	50.00	
182	A59	2c dark brown ('31)	14.00	.75
		Never hinged	28.00	
183	A59	3c deep red ('31)	18.00	.75
		Never hinged	36.00	
		Nos. 178-183 (6)	87.00	22.75
		Set, never hinged	174.00	

George V Type of 1912-25

1931, June 24   *Perf. 12x8*

184	A43	3c carmine	8.00	4.50
		Never hinged	20.00	

Sir Georges Etienne Cartier — A65

1931, Sept. 30   *Perf. 11*

190	A65	10c dark green	14.00	.25
		Never hinged	30.00	
a.		Imperf., pair	500.00	
		Never hinged	750.00	

Nos. 165, 165a Surcharged

1932, June 21

191	A59	3c on 2c dp red (II)	1.40	.25
		Never hinged	2.25	
a.		Die I	3.00	1.90
		Never hinged	5.00	

King George V — A66

Edward, Prince of Wales — A67

Allegory of British Empire A68

1932, July 12

192	A66	3c deep red	1.25	.25
		Never hinged	2.50	
193	A67	5c dull blue	7.00	3.00
		Never hinged	14.00	
194	A68	13c deep green	10.00	7.00
		Never hinged	20.00	
		Nos. 192-194 (3)	18.25	10.25
		Set, never hinged	36.50	

Imperial Economic Conference, Ottawa.

Type of 1930 and

King George V — A69

Type I   Type II

Two types of 3c.
Type I — Upper left tip of "3" level with horizontal line to its left.
Type II — Raised "3"; upper left tip of "3" is above horizontal line.

1932, Dec. 1

195	A69	1c dk green	1.25	.25
		Never hinged	2.50	
a.		Booklet pane of 4 + 2 labels ('33)	90.00	85.00
		Never hinged	135.00	
b.		Booklet pane of 6 ('33)	47.50	47.50
		Never hinged	72.50	
		Complete booklet, 4 #195b	250.00	
196	A69	2c black brown	1.40	.25
		Never hinged	2.80	
a.		Booklet pane of 4 + 2 labels ('33)	120.00	110.00
		Never hinged	180.00	
b.		Booklet pane of 6 ('33)	90.00	70.00
		Never hinged	135.00	
		Complete booklet, 2 #196b	375.00	
197	A69	3c deep red (I)	1.40	.25
		Never hinged	2.80	
c.		Die II	1.50	.25
		Never hinged	3.00	
d.		Booklet pane of 4 + 2 labels, die II ('33)	42.50	37.50
		Never hinged	85.00	
		Complete booklet, 2 #197d	125.00	
		Complete booklet, #195a, 196a, 197d	250.00	
198	A69	4c ocher	50.00	7.00
		Never hinged	100.00	
199	A69	5c dark blue	11.50	.50
		Never hinged	23.00	
a.		Horiz. pair, imperf. vert.	1,600.	
		Never hinged	2,250.	
200	A69	8c red orange	42.50	3.50
		Never hinged	85.00	
201	A61	13c dull violet	42.50	3.50
		Never hinged	85.00	
		Nos. 195-201 (7)	150.55	15.25
		Set, never hinged	306.10	

Type A66 has at the foot of the stamp "OTTAWA-CONFERENCE 1932". This inscription does not appear on the stamps of type A69.

Imperf., Pairs

195c	A69	1c	240.00
		Never hinged	360.00
196c	A69	2c	240.00
		Never hinged	360.00
197b	A69	3c (I)	240.00
		Never hinged	360.00
197e	A69	3c (II)	2,000.
198a	A69	4c	240.00
		Never hinged	360.00
199b	A69	5c	240.00
		Never hinged	360.00

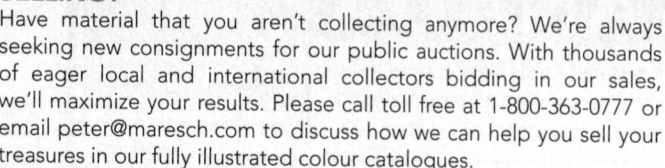

200a	A69	8c	240.00
		Never hinged	360.00
201a	A69	13c	800.00
		Never hinged	1,200.

No. 197e exists as one unused block of 4.

Government Buildings, Ottawa — A70

1933, May 18   *Perf. 11*

202	A70 5c dark blue	10.00	3.75
	Never hinged	18.50	
a.	Imperf., pair	625.00	
	Never hinged	950.00	

Meeting of the Executive Committee of the UPU at Ottawa, May and June, 1933.

No. 175 Overprinted in Blue

1933, July 24

203	A62 20c brown red	45.00	14.00
	Never hinged	80.00	
a.	Imperf., pair	625.00	
	Never hinged	950.00	

World's Grain Exhibition and Conference at Regina.

Steamship Royal William — A71

1933, Aug. 17

204	A71 5c dark blue	11.00	3.75
	Never hinged	20.00	
a.	Imperf., pair	700.00	
	Never hinged	1,100.	

Centenary of the linking by steam of the Dominion, then a colony, with Great Britain, the mother country. The Royal William's 1833 voyage was the first Trans-Atlantic passage under steam all the way.

George V Type of 1932
Coil Stamps

1933		*Perf. 8½ Vertically*	
205	A69 1c dark green	15.00	3.00
	Never hinged	26.00	
206	A69 2c black brown	20.00	1.10
	Never hinged	35.00	
207	A69 3c deep red	20.00	.40
	Never hinged	35.00	
	Nos. 205-207 (3)	55.00	4.50
	Set, never hinged	96.00	

Cartier's Arrival at Quebec — A72

1934, July 1   *Perf. 11*

208	A72 3c blue	4.50	1.40
	Never hinged	9.00	
a.	Imperf., pair	625.00	
	Never hinged	950.00	

Landing of Jacques Cartier, 400th anniv.

Group from Loyalists Monument, Hamilton, Ontario A73

1934, July 1

209	A73 10c olive green	28.00	7.50
	Never hinged	52.50	
a.	Imperf., pair	1,400.	
	Never hinged	2,100.	

Emigration of the United Empire Loyalists from the US to Canada, 150th anniv.

Seal of New Brunswick — A74

1934, Aug. 16

210	A74 2c red brown	2.75	2.25
	Never hinged	5.00	
a.	Imperf., pair	650.00	
	Never hinged	1,000.	

150th anniv. of the founding of the Province of New Brunswick.

Princess Elizabeth A75

Duke of York A76

King George V and Queen Mary — A77

Prince of Wales — A78

Windsor Castle A79

Royal Yacht Britannia A80

1935, May 4   *Perf. 12*

211	A75 1c green	.75	.35
	Never hinged	1.10	
212	A76 2c brown	.80	.25
	Never hinged	1.15	
213	A77 3c carmine	2.00	.25
	Never hinged	3.25	
214	A78 5c blue	4.25	3.00
	Never hinged	7.00	
215	A79 10c green	8.50	3.00
	Never hinged	13.50	
216	A80 13c dark blue	10.00	6.50
	Never hinged	16.00	
	Nos. 211-216 (6)	26.30	13.35
	Set, never hinged	42.00	

25th anniv. of the accession to the throne of George V.

Imperf., Pairs

211a	A75	1c	275.00
		Never hinged	425.00
212a	A76	2c	275.00
		Never hinged	425.00
213a	A77	3c	275.00
		Never hinged	425.00
214a	A78	5c	275.00
		Never hinged	425.00
215a	A79	10c	275.00
		Never hinged	425.00
216b	A80	13c	275.00
		Never hinged	425.00

King George V — A81

Royal Canadian Mounted Police — A82

Confederation Conference at Charlottetown, 1864 — A83

Niagara Falls — A84

Parliament Buildings, Victoria, B.C. — A85

Champlain Monument, Quebec A86

1935, June 1   *Perf. 12*

217	A81 1c green	.35	.25
	Never hinged	.50	
a.	Bklt. pane of 4 + 2 labels	70.00	70.00
	Never hinged	105.00	
b.	Booklet pane of 6	50.00	50.00
	Never hinged	80.00	
	Complete booklet, 4 #217b	200.00	
218	A81 2c brown	.35	.25
	Never hinged	.50	
a.	Bklt. pane of 4 + 2 labels	70.00	70.00
	Never hinged	105.00	
b.	Booklet pane of 6	55.00	55.00
	Never hinged	82.50	
	Complete booklet, 2 #218b	130.00	
219	A81 3c dk carmine	.75	.25
	Never hinged	1.10	
a.	Bklt. pane of 4 + 2 labels	40.00	40.00
	Never hinged	60.00	
	Complete booklet, 2 #219a	100.00	
	Complete booklet, 2 #217a, 218a, 219a	225.00	
c.	Printed on gummed side	600.00	
220	A81 4c yellowish org	2.50	.55
	Never hinged	3.75	
221	A81 5c blue	3.25	.35
	Never hinged	5.00	
a.	Horiz. pair, imperf. vert.	225.00	
	Never hinged	340.00	
222	A81 8c dp orange	2.75	2.25
	Never hinged	4.25	
223	A82 10c car rose	9.00	.25
	Never hinged	14.00	
224	A83 13c violet	9.00	.75
	Never hinged	14.00	
225	A84 20c olive green	18.00	.75
	Never hinged	27.50	
226	A85 50c dull violet	27.50	6.00
	Never hinged	40.00	
227	A86 $1 deep blue	60.00	11.00
	Never hinged	90.00	
	Nos. 217-227 (11)	133.45	22.65
	Set, never hinged	200.60	

No. 219c is valued in the grade of fine. Very fine examples are rare and sell for much more.

Imperf., Pairs

217c	A81	1c	200.00
		Never hinged	290.00
218c	A81	2c	200.00
		Never hinged	290.00
219b	A81	3c	200.00
		Never hinged	290.00
220a	A81	4c	200.00
		Never hinged	290.00
221b	A81	5c	200.00
		Never hinged	290.00
222a	A81	8c	200.00
		Never hinged	290.00
223a	A82	10c	300.00
		Never hinged	450.00
224a	A83	13c	300.00
		Never hinged	450.00
225a	A84	20c	300.00
		Never hinged	450.00
226a	A85	50c	300.00
		Never hinged	450.00
227a	A86	$1	350.00
		Never hinged	525.00

Coil Stamps

1935		*Perf. 8 Vertically*	
228	A81 1c green	15.00	3.25
	Never hinged	22.50	
229	A81 2c brown	19.00	1.00
	Never hinged	28.50	
230	A81 3c dark carmine	16.00	.60
	Never hinged	24.00	
	Nos. 228-230 (3)	50.00	4.85
	Set, never hinged	75.00	

George VI — A87

1937   *Perf. 12*

231	A87 1c green	.30	.25
	Never hinged	.45	
a.	Booklet pane of 4 + 2 labels	20.00	25.00
	Never hinged	30.00	
b.	Booklet pane of 6	7.50	20.00
	Never hinged	11.50	
232	A87 2c brown	.70	.25
	Never hinged	1.05	
a.	Booklet pane of 4 + 2 labels	20.00	22.50
	Never hinged	30.00	
b.	Booklet pane of 6	12.00	15.00
	Never hinged	18.00	
233	A87 3c carmine	.70	.25
	Never hinged	1.05	
a.	Booklet pane of 4 + 2 labels	9.00	14.00
	Never hinged	10.50	
234	A87 4c yellow	2.75	.25
	Never hinged	4.00	
235	A87 5c blue	3.50	.25
	Never hinged	5.00	
236	A87 8c orange	2.75	.45
	Never hinged	4.00	
	Nos. 231-236 (6)	10.70	1.70

Set, never hinged		15.55	

Imperf., Pairs

231c	A87	1c	300.00
	Never hinged		450.00
232c	A87	2c	300.00
	Never hinged		450.00
233b	A87	3c	300.00
	Never hinged		450.00
234a	A87	4c	300.00
	Never hinged		450.00
235a	A87	5c.	300.00
	Never hinged		450.00
236a	A87	8c	300.00
	Never hinged		450.00

George VI and Queen Elizabeth A88

1937, May 10

237	A88	3c carmine	.35	.25
	Never hinged		.40	
a.	Imperf., pair		625.00	
	Never hinged		950.00	

Coronation of King George VI and Queen Elizabeth.

George VI Types of 1937
Coil Stamps

1937   **Perf. 8 Vertically**

238	A87	1c green	3.00	1.10
	Never hinged		4.50	
239	A87	2c brown	5.50	.40
	Never hinged		8.25	
240	A87	3c carmine	9.00	.25
	Never hinged		13.50	
	Nos. 238-240 (3)		17.50	1.75
	Set, never hinged		26.25	

Memorial Chamber, Parliament Building, Ottawa — A89

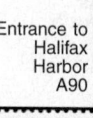

Entrance to Halifax Harbor A90

Fort Garry Gate, Winnipeg A91

Vancouver Harbor A92

Chateau de Ramezay, Montreal A93

1938   **Perf. 12**

241	A89	10c dk carmine	8.50	.25
	Never hinged		13.00	
a.	10c carmine rose		8.00	.25
	Never hinged		12.00	
242	A90	13c deep blue	12.00	.60
	Never hinged		18.00	
243	A91	20c red brown	16.00	.45
	Never hinged		24.00	
244	A92	50c green	37.50	6.00
	Never hinged		55.00	
245	A93	$1 dull violet	75.00	7.75
	Never hinged		115.00	
a.	Vert. pair, imperf., horiz.		4,750.	
	Never hinged		6,750.	
	Nos. 241-245 (5)		149.00	15.05

Set, never hinged		225.00	

Imperf., Pairs

241b	A89	10c dark carmine	500.00
	Never hinged		750.00
241c	A89	10c carmine rose	500.00
	Never hinged		750.00
242a	A90	13c	500.00
	Never hinged		750.00
243a	A91	20c	500.00
	Never hinged		750.00
244a	A92	50c	500.00
	Never hinged		750.00
245b	A93	$1	700.00
	Never hinged		1,050.

Princess Elizabeth and Princess Margaret Rose — A94

War Memorial, Ottawa — A95

King George VI and Queen Elizabeth A96

Unwmk.

1939, May 15   **Engr.**   **Perf. 12**

246	A94	1c green & black	.35	.25
	Never hinged		.40	
247	A95	2c brown & black	.35	.25
	Never hinged		.40	
248	A96	3c dk car & black	.35	.25
	Never hinged		.40	
	Nos. 246-248 (3)		1.05	.75
	Set, never hinged		1.20	

Visit of George VI and Queen Elizabeth to Canada and the US.

Imperf., Pairs

246a	A94	1c	550.00
	Never hinged		800.00
247a	A95	2c	550.00
	Never hinged		800.00
248a	A96	3c	550.00
	Never hinged		800.00

A97   A98

King George VI — A99

Grain Elevators A100   Farm Scene A101

Parliament Buildings — A102

"Ram" Tank — A103

Corvette A104

Munitions Factory A105

Destroyer A106

1942-43   **Engr.**   **Perf. 12**

249	A97	1c green	.35	.25
	Never hinged		.45	
a.	Booklet pane of 4 + 2 labels		3.50	3.75
	Never hinged		5.25	
b.	Booklet pane of 6		5.00	5.50
	Never hinged		7.50	
c.	Booklet pane of 3 ('43)		2.50	5.00
	Never hinged		3.75	
250	A98	2c brown	.40	.25
	Never hinged		.60	
a.	Booklet pane of 4 + 2 labels ('43)		7.00	8.00
	Never hinged		10.50	
b.	Booklet pane of 6		10.50	11.50

	Never hinged		16.00	
d.	Vert. strip of 3, imperf. horiz.		5,500.	
251	A99	3c dk carmine	.60	.25
	Never hinged		.90	
a.	Booklet pane of 4 + 2 labels		4.25	5.25
	Never hinged		6.50	
252	A99	3c rose violet ('43)	.50	.25
	Never hinged		.70	
a.	Booklet pane of 4 + 2 labels		3.25	4.50
	Never hinged		5.00	
b.	Booklet pane of 3		3.25	4.50
	Never hinged		4.75	
c.	Booklet pane of 6 ('47)		3.75	4.00
	Never hinged		5.50	
253	A100	4c greenish black	1.25	.60
	Never hinged		1.90	
254	A98	4c dk car ('43)	.70	.25
	Never hinged		1.00	
a.	Booklet pane of 6		5.25	10.00
	Never hinged		8.00	
b.	Booklet pane of 3		3.25	4.50
	Never hinged		4.75	
255	A97	5c deep blue	1.20	.25
	Never hinged		1.80	
256	A101	8c red brown	1.60	.50
	Never hinged		2.40	
257	A102	10c brown	4.75	.25
	Never hinged		7.00	
258	A103	13c dull green	5.00	3.60
	Never hinged		7.50	
259	A103	14c dull grn ('43)	7.50	.35
	Never hinged		11.25	
260	A104	20c chocolate	9.00	.25
	Never hinged		13.50	
261	A105	50c violet	30.00	1.75
	Never hinged		45.00	
262	A106	$1 deep blue	65.00	7.50
	Never hinged		100.00	
	Nos. 249-262 (14)		127.85	16.30
	Set, never hinged		194.00	

Canada's contribution to the war effort of the Allied Nations.

No. 250d totally imperf horiz. is unique and is valued in the grade of fine. Beware of strips with blind perfs; these sell for much less.

For overprints see Nos. O1-O4.

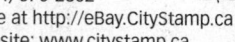

Imperf., Pairs

249d	A97	1c		300.00
		Never hinged		450.00
250c	A98	2c		300.00
		Never hinged		450.00
251b	A99	3c		300.00
		Never hinged		450.00
252d	A99	3c		300.00
		Never hinged		450.00
253a	A100	4c		300.00
		Never hinged		450.00
254c	A98	4c		300.00
		Never hinged		450.00
255a	A97	5c		300.00
		Never hinged		450.00
256a	A100	8c		300.00
		Never hinged		450.00
257a	A102	10c		450.00
		Never hinged		675.00
258a	A103	13c		450.00
		Never hinged		675.00
259a	A103	14c		450.00
		Never hinged		675.00
260a	A104	20c		450.00
		Never hinged		675.00
261a	A105	50c		450.00
		Never hinged		675.00
262a	A106	$1		600.00
		Never hinged		900.00

Types of 1942
Coil Stamps

1942-43　　　　Perf. 8 Vertically

263	A97	1c green ('43)	1.50	.55
		Never hinged	2.25	
264	A98	2c brown	2.25	1.10
		Never hinged	3.40	
265	A99	3c dark carmine	2.25	1.10
		Never hinged	3.40	
266	A99	3c rose violet ('43)	4.00	.40
		Never hinged	6.00	
267	A98	4c dk carmine ('43)	6.00	.30
		Never hinged	9.00	
		Nos. 263-267 (5)	16.00	3.45
		Set, never hinged	24.05	

See Nos. 278-281.

> Catalogue values for unused stamps in this section, from this point to the end of the section, are for Never Hinged items.

Farm Scene, Ontario
A107

Great Bear Lake, Mackenzie
A108

Hydroelectric Station, Saint Maurice River
A109

Combine
A110

Logging, British Columbia
A111

Train Ferry, Prince Edward Island
A112

1946, Sept. 16　　Engr.　　Perf. 12

268	A107	8c red brown	2.00	.25
269	A108	10c olive	2.75	.25
270	A109	14c black brown	4.25	.25
271	A110	20c slate black	5.00	.25

272	A111	50c dk blue green	20.00	1.75
273	A112	$1 red violet	45.00	3.00
		Nos. 268-273 (6)	79.00	6.20

For overprints see Nos. O6-O10, O21-O23, O25.

Alexander Graham Bell — A113

1947, Mar. 3

274　A113　4c deep blue　　　.25　.25

Birth centenary of Alexander Graham Bell.

Citizen of Canada — A114

1947, July 1

275　A114　4c deep blue　　　.25　.25

Issued on the 80th anniv. of the Canadian Confederation, to mark the advent of Canadian Citizenship.

Princess Elizabeth — A115

1948, Feb. 16

276　A115　4c deep blue　　　.25　.25

Marriage of Princess Elizabeth to Lieut. Philip Mountbatten, R. N., on Nov. 20, 1947.

Parliament Buildings Ottawa
A116

1948, Oct. 1

277　A116　4c gray　　　.25　.25

Centenary of Responsible Government.

George VI Types of 1942
Coil Stamps

1948　　　　Perf. 9½ Vertically

278	A97	1c green	7.00	2.00
279	A98	2c brown	22.50	8.50
280	A99	3c rose violet	15.00	2.00
281	A98	4c dark carmine	22.50	2.25
		Nos. 278-281 (4)	67.00	14.75

John Cabot's Ship "Matthew" A117

1949, Apr. 1　　Engr.　　Perf. 12

282　A117　4c deep green　　　.25　.25

Entry of Newfoundland into confederation with Canada.

"Founding of Halifax, 1749"
A118

1949, June 21　　　　Unwmk.

283　A118　4c purple　　　.25　.25

200th anniv. of the founding of Halifax, Nova Scotia.

A119　　　　　A120

A121

A122　　　　　A123

1949, Nov. 15

284	A119	1c green	.25	.25
a.		Booklet pane of 3 ('50)	.75	2.00
285	A120	2c sepia	.30	.25
286	A121	3c rose violet	.35	.25
a.		Booklet pane of 3 ('50)	2.50	6.50
b.		Booklet pane of 4 + 2 labels ('50)	3.25	3.75
287	A122	4c dk carmine	.60	.25
a.		Booklet pane of 3 ('50)	12.50	12.50
b.		Booklet pane of 6 ('50)	18.00	18.00
288	A123	5c deep blue	1.25	.65
		Nos. 284-288 (5)	2.75	1.65

Stamps from booklet panes of 3 are imperf. on 2 or 3 sides.

"POSTES POSTAGE" Omitted

1950, Jan. 19

289	A119	1c green	.25	.25
290	A120	2c sepia	.35	.25
291	A121	3c rose violet	.35	.25
292	A122	4c dark carmine	.40	.25
293	A123	5c deep blue	1.50	1.00
		Nos. 289-293 (5)	2.85	2.00

See Nos. 295-300, 305-306, 309-310. For overprints see Nos. O12-O20.

Oil Wells, Alberta
A124

1950, Mar. 1　　Engr.　　Perf. 12

294　A124　50c dull green　　8.50　1.30

Development of oil wells in Canada. For overprints see Nos. O11, O24.

Types of 1949
"POSTES POSTAGE" Omitted
Coil Stamps

1950　　　　Perf. 9½ Vertically

295	A119	1c green	.75	.30
296	A121	3c rose violet	1.10	.55

With "POSTES POSTAGE"
Perf. 9½ Vertically

297	A119	1c green	.45	.25
298	A120	2c sepia	3.50	1.30
299	A121	3c rose violet	2.25	.25
300	A122	4c dark carmine	19.00	.75
		Nos. 297-300 (4)	25.20	2.55

See note after No. 288.

Indians Drying Skins on Stretchers
A125

1950, Oct. 2　　　　Perf. 12

301　A125　10c black brown　　.90　.25

Canada's fur resources. For overprint see No. O26.

Fishing
A126

1951, Feb. 1　　　　Unwmk.

302　A126　$1 bright ultra　42.50　10.00

Canada's fish resources. For overprint see No. O27.

Sir Robert Laird Borden
A127

William L. Mackenzie King
A128

1951, June 25　　　　Perf. 12

303	A127	3c turquoise green	.25	.25
304	A128	4c rose pink	.30	.25

George VI Types of 1949

1951　　　　Perf. 12

305	A120	2c olive green	.25	.25
306	A122	4c orange vermilion	.35	.25
a.		Booklet pane of 3	5.25	2.75
b.		Booklet pane of 6	5.00	5.00

For overprints see Nos. O28-O29.

Coil Stamps
Perf. 9½ Vertically

309	A120	2c olive green	1.40	.60
310	A122	4c orange vermilion	3.00	.70

Trains of 1851 and 1951 — A129

"Threepenny Beaver" of 1851 — A130

Designs: 5c, Steamships City of Toronto and Prince George. 7c, Stagecoach and Plane.

1951, Sept. 24　　Unwmk.　　Perf. 12

311	A129	4c dark gray	.60	.25
312	A129	5c purple	1.80	1.25
313	A129	7c deep blue	1.10	.30
314	A130	15c bright red	1.20	.30
		Nos. 311-314 (4)	4.70	2.10

Centenary of British North American postal administration.

Princess Elizabeth and Duke of Edinburgh
A131

1951, Oct. 26　　　　Engr.

315　A131　4c violet　　　.25　.25

Visit of Princess Elizabeth, Duchess of Edinburgh and the Duke of Edinburgh to Canada and the US.

Symbols of
Newsprint
Paper
Production
A132

1952, Apr. 1   Unwmk.   Perf. 12
316 A132 20c gray   1.60 .25
    Canada's paper production. For overprint
see No. O30.

Red Cross
on
Sun — A133

1952, July 26   Engr. and Litho.
317 A133 4c blue & red   .25 .25
    18th Intl. Red Cross Conf., Toronto, July
1952.

Sir John J. C.   Alexander
Abbott   Mackenzie
A134   A135

1952, Nov. 3   Engr.
318 A134 3c rose lilac   .25 .25
319 A135 4c orange vermilion   .25 .25

Canada
Goose
A136

1952, Nov. 3
320 A136 7c blue   .40 .25
    For overprint see No. O31.

Pacific Coast Indian
House and Totem
Pole — A137

1953, Feb. 2
321 A137 $1 gray   5.75 .90
    For overprint see No. O32.

Natl. Wildlife
Week — A138

1953, Apr. 1
322 A138 2c Polar bear   .25 .25
323 A138 3c Moose   .25 .25
324 A138 4c Bighorn sheep   .25 .25
        Nos. 322-324 (3)   .75 .75

Elizabeth II — A139

1953, May 1
325 A139 1c violet brown   .25 .25
  a.   Booklet pane of 3   1.40 1.40
326 A139 2c green   .25 .25
327 A139 3c carmine rose   .25 .25
  a.   Booklet pane of 3   1.90 1.40
  b.   Booklet pane of 4 + 2 labels   1.30 1.75
328 A139 4c violet   .25 .25
  a.   Booklet pane of 3   1.90 1.75
  b.   Booklet pane of 6   1.40 1.40
329 A139 5c ultramarine   .35 .25
        Nos. 325-329 (5)   1.35 1.25
    Stamps from booklet panes of 3 are imperf.
on 2 or 3 sides.
    See Nos. 331-333. For overprints see Nos.
O33-O37.

Coronation Issue

Queen
Elizabeth II — A140

1953, June 1
330 A140 4c violet   .25 .25

Coil Stamps
1953   Perf. 9½ Vertically
331 A139 2c green   1.40 .90
332 A139 3c carmine rose   1.40 .90
333 A139 4c violet   3.25 1.40
        Nos. 331-333 (3)   6.05 3.20
    See note after No. 329.
    Issued: 2c, 7/30; 3c, 7/27; 4c, 9/3.

Bobbin, Cloth
and Spinning
Wheel
A141

1953, Nov. 2   Perf. 12
334 A141 50c light green   2.75 .25
    For overprint see No. O38.

Walrus   Beaver
A142   A143

1954, Apr. 1
335 A142 4c gray   .30 .25
336 A143 5c ultramarine   .35 .25
  a.   Booklet pane of 5 + label   1.75 1.40
    National Wildlife Week, 1954.

Elizabeth II   Gannet
A144   A145

1954-61
337 A144 1c violet brn   .25 .25
  a.   Booklet pane of 5 + label
            ('56)   1.10 1.10
338 A144 2c green   .25 .25
  a.   Pane of 25 ('61)   3.75 3.75
339 A144 3c carmine rose   .25 .25
  a.   Horiz. pair, imperf. vert.   1,400.
340 A144 4c violet   .25 .25
  a.   Booklet pane of 5 + label
            ('56)   1.40 1.40
  b.   Booklet pane of 6 ('55)   3.00 3.00
341 A144 5c bright blue   .25 .25
  a.   Booklet pane of 5 + label   1.10 1.10
  b.   Pane of 20 (5 x 4) ('61)   6.50 6.50
  c.   Horiz. pair, imperf. vert.   6,000.
342 A144 6c orange   .50 .25
343 A145 15c gray   1.50 .25
        Nos. 337-343 (7)   3.25 1.75
    Panes of 20 and 25 are imperf. on 4 sides.
    Issued: 5c, 15c, 4/1; others, 6/10.
    For overprints see Nos. O40-O44.

Luminescence
    The overprinting of regular stamps
with vertical luminescent bands began
experimentally in 1962 when Nos.
337p-341p were released at Winnipeg.
The bands are of varying number, position and chemical content.
    Tagged varieties of stamps which
were issued both untagged and with
luminescent overprint are listed with
suffix letter "p".

1962, Jan. 13   Tagged
337p A144 1c violet brown   1.30 .95
338p A144 2c green   1.30 .95
339p A144 3c carmine rose   1.30 .95
340p A144 4c violet   3.75 3.25
341p A144 5c bright blue   4.00 2.25
        Nos. 337p-341p (5)   11.65 8.35

Coil Stamps
1954   Perf. 9½ Vertically
345 A144 2c green   .55 .25
347 A144 4c violet   1.50 .25
348 A144 5c bright blue   2.25 .25
        Nos. 345-348 (3)   4.30 .75
    Issued: 2c, 9/9; 3c, 8/23; 4c, 7/6.

Sir John   Sir Mackenzie
Sparrow   Bowell
David   A147
Thompson
A146

1954, Nov. 1
349 A146 4c violet   .35 .25
350 A147 5c bright blue   .35 .25

Eskimo and
Kayak
A148

1955, Feb. 21
351 A148 10c violet brown   .40 .25
    For overprint see No. O39.

Musk Ox — A149

Whooping
Cranes
A150

1955, Apr. 4
352 A149 4c purple   .35 .25
353 A150 5c blue   .40 .25
    National Wildlife Week, April 10-16.

Torch, Dove and
Maple
Leaves — A151

1955, June 1   Unwmk.
354 A151 5c light blue   .40 .25
    ICAO, 10th anniversary.

Pioneer
Settlers
A152

1955, June 30   Perf. 12
355 A152 5c ultramarine   .40 .25
    50th anniv. of the founding of the provinces
of Alberta and Saskatchewan.

Globe and
Scout
Emblem
A153

1955, Aug. 20   Engr.
356 A153 5c green & org brown   .40 .25
    8th Boy Scout World Jamboree, Niagara-on-
the-Lake, Ont.

Richard
Bedford
Bennett
A154

Sir Charles
Tupper
A155

1955, Nov. 8
357 A154 4c violet .35 .25
358 A155 5c ultramarine .35 .25

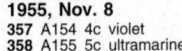

Ice Hockey
Players
A156

1956, Jan. 23
359 A156 5c ultramarine .35 .25

Issued to publicize Canada's most popular winter sport.

Caribou
A157

Mountain
Goat
A158

1956, Apr. 12
360 A157 4c deep violet .40 .25
361 A158 5c ultramarine .40 .25

National Wildlife Week, 1956.

"Paper
Industry"
A159

"Chemical
Industry" — A160

1956, June 7 **Engr.**
362 A159 20c green 1.40 .25
363 A160 25c red 1.50 .25

For overprint see No. O45.

House on Fire — A161

1956, Oct. 9 **Unwmk.** **Perf. 12**
364 A161 5c gray & red .35 .25

Issued to emphasize the needless waste caused by preventable fires.

Canada's
Outdoor
Recreation
Facilities
A162

1957, Mar. 7
365 A162 5c Fishing .40 .25
366 A162 5c Swimming .40 .25
367 A162 5c Hunter and dog .40 .25
368 A162 5c Skiing .40 .25
  a. Block of 4, #365-368 1.60 1.10

All four designs are printed alternating in sheet of 50, with various combinations possible.

Loon — A163

1957, Apr. 10 **Perf. 12**
369 A163 5c black .35 .25

David
Thompson
and Map of
Western
Canada
A164

1957, June 5 **Unwmk.**
370 A164 5c ultramarine .35 .25

David Thompson (1770-1857), explorer and geographer.

Parliament Building,
Ottawa — A165

Post Horn
and Globe
A166

1957, Aug. 14 **Perf. 12**
371 A165 5c dark blue .35 .25
372 A166 15c dark blue 2.25 2.00

UPU, 14th Congress, Ottawa, Aug. 1957.

Miner With Pneumatic
Drill — A167

1957, Sept. 5
373 A167 5c black .30 .25

Canada's mining industry; 6th Commonwealth Mining and Metallurgical Congress, Vancouver, Sept. 8-Oct. 8.

Elizabeth II and
Prince
Philip — A168

1957, Oct. 10 **Unwmk.**
374 A168 5c black .30 .25

Visit of Queen Elizabeth II and Prince Philip to Canada, Oct. 12-16.

Newspapers
and Symbols
of Industry
A169

1958, Jan. 22 **Engr.**
375 A169 5c black .35 .25

Canadian press; the importance of a free press.

Microscope and
Globe — A170

1958, Mar. 5 **Perf. 12**
376 A170 5c blue .35 .25

Intl. Geophysical Year, 1957-1958.

Miner
Panning
Gold — A171

1958, May 8
377 A171 5c bluish green .35 .25

Province of British Columbia, cent.

La Verendrye
A172

1958, June 4
378 A172 5c bright ultra .35 .25

Pierre Gaultier de Varenne, Sieur de la Verendrye, 18th century French explorer of Western Canada.

Champlain
and View of
Quebec
A173

1958, June 26
379 A173 5c dk green & bis brn .35 .25

Founding of Quebec, 350th anniv.

Nurse — A174

1958, July 30 **Engr.**
380 A174 5c rose lilac .35 .25

Importance of health, both to the individual and to the nation.

Kerosene Lamp
and
Refinery — A175

1958, Sept. 10 **Perf. 12**
381 A175 5c olive & red .35 .25

Centennial of Canada's oil industry.

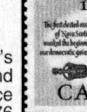

Speaker's
Chair and
Mace
A176

1958, Oct. 2
382 A176 5c slate blue .35 .25

Bicentennial of the meeting of the first House of Representatives in Canada, Halifax, Oct. 2, 1758.

"Silver Dart"
and Delta
Wing Planes
A177

1959, Feb. 23
383 A177 5c blue & black .35 .25

50th anniv. of the 1st airplane flight in Canada near Baddeck, N. S., with J. A. D. McCurdy as pilot.

Globe and
Dove — A178

1959, Apr. 2
384 A178 5c violet blue .35 .25

NATO, 10th anniversary.

Woman Tending
Tree — A179

1959, May 13
385 A179 5c apple green & blk .35 .25

Associated Country Women of the World.

Elizabeth II — A180

1959, June 18
386 A180 5c dark carmine .35 .25

Visit of Queen Elizabeth and Prince Philip to Canada, June 18-Aug. 1.

Great Lakes,
Maple Leaf
and Eagle
Emblems
A181

1959, June 26 **Engr.**
387 A181 5c red & blue .35 .25
  a. Center inverted 9,500. 8,000.

Opening of the St. Lawrence Seaway, June 26, 1959.
See United States No. 1131.

British Lion, Fleur-de-Lis and Maple Leaves A182

1959, Sept. 10   *Perf. 12*
388 A182 5c crim rose & dk green   .35 .25
  Bicentenary of the Battle of the Plains of Abraham.

Girl Guide Emblem — A183

1960, Apr. 20   **Unwmk.**
389 A183 5c brown org & ultra   .35 .25
  Canadian Girl Guides Assoc., 50th anniv.

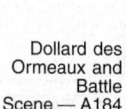

Dollard des Ormeaux and Battle Scene — A184

1960, May 19
390 A184 5c ultra & bis brown   .35 .25
  Battle of the Long Sault, 300th anniv.

Compass Rose, Earth Mover and Surveyor — A185

1961, Feb. 8   **Engr.**
391 A185 5c green & vermilion   .35 .25
  Development of Canada's Northland.

Emily Pauline Johnson — A186

1961, Mar. 10
392 A186 5c green & red   .35 .25
  Emily Pauline Johnson (1861-1913), Mohawk princess and poet.

Arthur Meighen — A187

1961, Apr. 19
393 A187 5c ultramarine   .35 .25
  Arthur Meighen, Prime Minister of Canada, (1920-21, 1926).

Power Plant and Men Holding Blueprint A188

1961, June 28   **Unwmk.**
394 A188 5c lt red brn & blue   .35 .25
  10th anniv. of the Colombo Plan, initiated to assist underdeveloped countries by providing trained manpower and resources.

Natural Resources and Hands Holding Cogwheel — A189

1961, Oct. 12   **Engr.**
395 A189 5c brown & blue grn   .35 .25
  Canada's "Resources for Tomorrow Program" and to publicize the close link between industry and the country's renewable natural resources.

Young Adults and Education Symbols — A190

1962, Feb. 28
396 A190 5c black & lt red brn   .35 .25
  Issued to stimulate public awareness of the importance of education.

Scottish Settler and Lord Selkirk A191

1962, May 3
397 A191 5c lt green & vio brn   .35 .25
  150th anniv. of the Red River Settlement in Western Canada (Prairie Provinces).

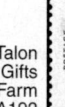

Jean Talon Presenting Gifts to Young Farm Couple — A192

1962, June 13   **Unwmk.**
398 A192 5c dark blue   .35 .25
  Jean Talon, administrator of New France (Canada), 1665-1668.

British Columbia Legislative Building and Stamp of 1860 — A193

1962, Aug. 22   **Engr.**
399 A193 5c black & reddish org   .35 .25
  Centenary of Victoria as incorporated city.

In middle to late 1962, Canadian Bank Note Co. changed their perforation equipment from a gauge of 11.95 to gauge 11.85. The gauge 11.85 perforation holes are slightly larger than those of the 11.95 gauge.

This change affected some of the reprintings of then-current low- and medium-value Wilding definitives (including Nos. 320, 321, 334, 338, 340, 343, 351, 362, 363, 411), at least one commemorative (No. 399), low-value Cameo definitives (Nos. 401a, 402a, 404a, 405b, 405p), a low-value Centennial booklet (No. 458a) and several postage dues (Nos. J15-J20). Other issues may be affected and the editors would like to hear of any new discoveries.

Arms of the Provinces A194

1962, Aug. 31
400 A194 5c brown orange & black   .35 .25
  Official opening of the Trans-Canada Highway, Rogers Pass, Glacier National Park, Sept. 4.

Queen Elizabeth II and Wheat — A195

  Designs (Symbol in upper left corner): 1c, Mineral crystals. 2c, Tree. 3c, Fish. 4c, Electric high tension tower.

1962-63   **Engr.**   *Perf. 12*
401 A195 1c dp brn ('63)   .25 .25
  a.   Booklet pane of 5 + label ('63)   3.00 3.00
402 A195 2c green ('63)   .25 .25
  a.   Pane of 25 ('63)   7.50 7.50
403 A195 3c purple ('63)   .25 .25
404 A195 4c carmine ('63)   .25 .25
  a.   Booklet pane of 5 + label ('63)   3.00 3.00
  b.   Pane of 25 ('63)   11.00 11.00
405 A195 5c violet blue   .25 .25
  a.   Booklet pane of 5 + label ('63)   3.00 3.00
  b.   Pane of 20 ('63)   13.00 13.00
  c.   Imperf., pair (#405b)   3,750.
  d.   Vert. pair, imperf. horiz.   4,000. 575.00
    Nos. 401-405 (5)   1.25 1.25

  Nos. 402a, 404b, and 405b are imperf. on four sides.
  Used examples of No. 405d are canceled "Gonor, MB." Beware of examples with traces of blind perfs; a certificate of authenticity is recommended.
  Issued: 5c, 10/3; 1c, 4c, 2/4/63; 2c, 3c, 5/2/63.
  For overprints see Nos. O46-O49.

1963   **Tagged**
401p A195 1c deep brown   .25 .25
402p A195 2c green   .25 .25
403p A195 3c purple   .25 .25
404p A195 4c carmine   .75 .50
405p A195 5c violet blue   .45 .25
  q.   Pane of 20   42.50 42.50
    Nos. 401p-405p (5)   1.95 1.50
    See note after No. 343.

Coil Stamps

1962-63   *Perf. 9½ Horiz.*
406 A195 2c green   4.75 2.25
407 A195 3c purple   3.50 1.75
408 A195 4c carmine   4.75 2.25
  a.   Pair, imperf between   3,000.
409 A195 5c violet blue   4.75 1.00
    Nos. 406-409 (4)   17.75 7.25

  No. 408a is valued in the grade of fine. Beware of dangerous fakes; a certificate of authenticity is necessary.
  Issued: 5c, 10/3; 4c, 2/4/63; 2c, 3c, 5/2/63.

Sir Casimir Stanislaus Gzowski (1813-98), Engineer, Soldier and Educator — A196

1963, Mar. 5   **Unwmk.**   *Perf. 12*
410 A196 5c rose lilac   .30 .25

Export Crate and Mercator Map — A197

1963, June 14
411 A197 $1 rose carmine   9.00 2.25

Sir Martin Frobisher (1535-1594), Explorer and Discoverer of Frobisher Bay — A198

1963, Aug. 21
412 A198 5c ultramarine   .30 .25

Postrider and First Land Mail Routes A199

1963, Sept. 25
413 A199 5c green & red brn .30 .25
Bicentennial of the 1st regular postal service between Quebec, Three Rivers & Montreal.

Jet at Ottawa Airport — A200   Canada Geese — A201

1963-64
414 A200 7c blue ('64) .50 .40
415 A201 15c deep ultra 1.80 .25
See No. 436. For surcharge see No. 430.

"Peace on Earth" — A202

1964, Apr. 8   Engr. & Litho.
416 A202 5c grnsh blue, Prus bl & ocher .30 .25
Issued to promote world peace.

Three-Maple-Leaf Emblem (Canadian Unity) — A203

White Trillium and Arms of Ontario A204

No. 419, White garden lily and arms of Quebec. No. 420, Mayflower (trailing arbutus) and arms of Nova Scotia. No. 421, Purple violet and arms of New Brunswick. No. 422, Prairie crocus and arms of Manitoba. No. 423, Dogwood and arms of British Columbia. No. 424, Lady's slipper and arms of Prince Edward Island. No. 425, Prairie lily and arms of Saskatchewan. No. 426, Wild rose and arms of Alberta. No. 427, Pitcher plant and arms of Newfoundland. No. 428, Fireweed and arms of Yukon. No. 429, Mountain avens and arms of Northwest Territories. No. 429A, Maple leaf and arms of Canada.

1964-66	Engr. & Litho.	Perf. 12	
417	A203 5c lt blue & dk car	.25	.25
418	A204 5c red brn, buff & green	.25	.25
419	A204 5c grn, yel & org	.25	.25
420	A204 5c blue, pink & grn	.25	.25
421	A204 5c car, green & vio	.25	.25
422	A204 5c red brn, lil & dl grn	.25	.25
423	A204 5c lilac, grn & bis	.25	.25
424	A204 5c vio, grn & dp rose	.25	.25
425	A204 5c sepia, org & grn	.25	.25
426	A204 5c dl grn, yel & car	.25	.25
427	A204 5c black, grn & car	.25	.25
428	A204 5c dk bl, rose & grn	.25	.25
429	A204 5c ol, yel & green	.25	.25
429A	A204 5c dk blue & dp red	.25	.25
	Nos. 417-429A (14)	3.50	3.50

Issued: No. 417, 5/14/64; Nos. 418-419, 6/30/64; Nos. 420-421, 2/3/65; Nos. 422-423, 4/28/65; No. 424, 7/21/65; Nos. 425-426, 1/19/66; No. 427, 2/23/66; Nos. 428-429, 3/23/66; No. 429A, 6/30/66.

No. 414 Surcharged

1964, July 15   Engr.
430 A200 8c on 7c blue .45 .25
a. Pair, one without surcharge 11,500.
b. Surcharge on reverse, inverted 3,750.
Nos. 430a and 430b are each unique.

Fathers of Confederation Memorial, Charlottetown — A205

1964, July 29
431 A205 5c black .30 .25
Centenary of the Charlottetown, P.E.I., Conference, Sept. 1-9, 1864, which led to the creation of the Canadian nation in 1867.

Maple Leaf and Hand Holding Quill Pen — A206

1964, Sept. 9
432 A206 5c dark brown & rose .25 .25
Centenary of the Quebec Conference, Oct. 10-27, 1864, which led to the creation of the Canadian nation.

Elizabeth II — A207

1964, Oct. 5
433 A207 5c claret .25 .25
Queen Elizabeth's visit, Oct. 6-13.

Family and Star of Bethlehem — A208

1964, Oct. 14   Perf. 12
434 A208 3c red .25 .25
a. Pane of 25 7.50 7.50
p. Tagged .65 .35
q. As "a," tagged 11.00 11.00
435 A208 5c blue .25 .25
p. Tagged 1.10 .35
Panes of 25 are imperf. on four sides.

Jet Type of 1964
1964, Nov. 18   Unwmk.
436 A200 8c blue .40 .25

Maple Leaf and ICY Emblem A209

1965, Mar. 3
437 A209 5c slate green .25 .25
International Cooperation Year.

Sir Wilfred Grenfell at Wheel of Hospital Ship Strathcona II A210

1965, June 9
438 A210 5c Prussian blue .25 .25
Sir Wilfred Grenfell, author, medical missionary and founder of the Grenfell Mission, birth cent.

Canada's Maple Leaf Flag, 1965 A211

1965, June 30
439 A211 5c blue & red .25 .25

Winston Churchill — A212

1965, Aug. 12   Litho.   Perf. 12
440 A212 5c brown .25 .25
Sir Winston Spencer Churchill (1874-1965).

Peace Tower, Ottawa — A213

1965, Sept. 8   Engr.
441 A213 5c slate green .25 .25
Meeting of the Inter-Parliamentary Union, Ottawa, Sept. 8-17.

Parliament and Ottawa River A214

1965, Sept. 8
442 A214 5c brown .25 .25
Centenary of the final selection of Ottawa as national capital.

Gifts of the Wise Men — A215

1965, Oct. 13
443 A215 3c olive .25 .25
a. Pane of 25 6.25 6.25
p. Tagged .25 .25
q. As "a," tagged 8.50 8.50
444 A215 5c violet blue .25 .25
p. Tagged .35 .25
Christmas. Panes of 25 are imperf. on four sides.

Alouette II Orbiting Globe — A216

1966, Jan. 5
445 A216 5c dark violet blue .25 .25
Launching (in California) of the Canadian satellite Alouette II, Nov. 28, 1965, as part of the Canadian-American program of space research.

La Salle, Map of 17th Century Canada, Ship, Canoe, Spyglass and Compass — A217

1966, Apr. 13
446 A217 5c blue green .25 .25
Tercentenary of the arrival in Canada of Rene Robert Cavelier, Sieur de La Salle (1643-1687).

Traffic Signs — A218

1966, May 2
447 A218 5c black, blue & yel .25 .25
Issued to publicize traffic safety.

House of Commons, Thames River and Canadian Delegates A219

1966, May 26
448 A219 5c brown .25 .25
Centenary of the London Conf., Dec. 4, 1866, which resulted in the British North America Act.

Atomic Reactor, Heavy Water Atom Symbol and Microscope A220

1966, July 27
449 A220 5c deep ultra .25 .25
Peaceful uses of atomic power. The design shows a stylized view of the Douglas Point Nuclear Power Station, Lake Huron, Ontario.

Parliamentary Library, Ottawa — A221

1966, Sept. 8
450 A221 5c plum .25 .25
12th General Conf. of the Commonwealth Parliamentary Assoc., Ottawa, Sept. 8-Oct. 5.

Praying Hands, by
Albrecht Dürer — A222

1966, Oct. 12

451	A222	3c carmine rose	.25	.25
a.		Pane of 25	3.75	3.75
p.		Tagged	.25	.25
q.		As "a," tagged	5.00	5.00
452	A222	5c orange	.25	.25
p.		Tagged	.45	.25

Christmas. Panes of 25 are imperf. on four sides.

Canadian Flag over Globe and Centennial Emblem — A223

1967, Jan. 11

453	A223	5c blue & red	.25	.25
p.		Tagged	.40	.30

Canada's centenary as a nation.

Northern Lights and Dog Team — A224

"Alaska Highway" by A. Y. Jackson A225

Two Types of 6c Black

Type I   Type II

Designs: 2c, Totem pole (Pacific Area). 3c, Combine and oil rig (Prairie Region). 4c, Ship in lock (Central Canada). 5c, Lobster traps and boat (Atlantic Provinces). 6c, Transportation means. 10c, "The Jack Pine" by Tom Thomson. 15c, "Bylot Island" by Lawren Harris. 20c, "The Ferry, Quebec" by James Wilson Morrice. 25c, "The Solemn Land" by J. E. H. MacDonald. 50c, "Summer's Stores" by John Ensor (grain elevators). $1, Oilfield near Edmonton, by H. G. Glyde.

1967-72   **Engr.**   **Perf. 12**

454	A224	1c brown	.25	.25
a.		Booklet pane of 5 + label	.45	.35
b.		Bklt. pane, 1 #454d, 4 #459 + label, perf. 10 ('68)	3.00	2.50
c.		Bklt. pane, 5 #454d + 5 #457d, perf. 10 ('68)	1.40	1.40
d.		Perf. 10 ('68)	.25	.25
e.		Perf. 12½x12 ('71)	.25	.25
f.		Printed on gummed side	1,000.	
455	A224	2c green	.25	.25
a.		Bklt. pane, 4 #455, 4 #456 with gutter btwn. ('70)	1.45	1.45
456	A224	3c dull purple	.25	.25
a.		Perf. 12½x12 ('71)	.75	.30
457	A224	4c car rose	.25	.25
a.		Booklet pane of 5 + label	1.25	1.25
b.		Pane of 25 (5x5)	25.00	20.00
c.		Booklet pane of 25 + 2 labels, perf. 10 ('68)	7.50	7.00
d.		Perf. 10	.50	.25
458	A224	5c blue	.25	.25
a.		Booklet pane of 5 + label	5.25	5.25
b.		Pane of 20	30.00	27.50
c.		Bklt. pane of 20, perf. 10 ('68)	7.50	7.50
d.		Perf. 10	.60	.25
459	A224	6c org., perf. 10	.25	.25
a.		Bklt. pane of 25 + 2 labels, perf. 10 ('68)	7.50	7.50
b.		Perf. 12½x12 ('69)	.25	.25
460	A224	6c black (I), perf. 12½x12	.25	.25
a.		Bklt. pane of 25 + 2 labels (I), perf. 10 ('70)	11.00	7.50
b.		As "a," perf. 12½x12	15.00	13.00

c.		Type II, perf. 12½x12	.25	.25
d.		As "c," booklet pane of 4	3.50	3.25
e.		As "d," perf. 10 ('70)	10.00	6.00
f.		Type II, perf. 12 ('72)	.35	.25
g.		Type I, perf. 10	1.50	.30
h.		Type II, perf. 10	2.00	.65
i.		As "f," printed on gummed side		18.00
461	A225	8c violet brown	.25	.25
462	A225	10c olive green	.25	.25
463	A225	15c dull purple	.45	.25
464	A225	20c dark blue	.55	.25
465	A225	25c slate green	1.50	.25
465A	A225	50c brown org	3.75	.25
465B	A225	$1 carmine rose	6.00	.75
		Nos. 454-465B (14)	14.50	4.00

Nos. 454d, 454e, 456a, 457d, 458d, 460c, 460g and 460h are from booklet panes. Issued: No. 459, 11/1/68; No. 460, 1/7/70; others, 2/8/67.
See Nos. 543-544, 549-550.

Tagged

454p	A224	1c brown	.25	.25
ep.		Perf. 12½x12 ('71)	.25	.25
455p	A224	2c green	.25	.25
456p	A224	3c dull purple	.25	.25
457p	A224	4c car rose	.60	.25
458p	A224	5c blue	.60	.25
bp.		Pane of 20	55.00	47.50
459p	A224	6c org., perf. 10	.70	.25
bp.		Perf. 12½x12 ('69)	.75	.30
460p	A224	6c black (I), perf. 12½x12	.35	.25
cp.		Type II ('70)	.45	.50
fp.		As "cp," perf. 12 ('72)	.25	.25
462p	A225	10c olive green	.90	.35
463p	A225	15c dull purple	.90	.35
464p	A225	20c dark blue	1.50	.55
465p	A225	25c slate green	7.00	2.25
		Nos. 454p-465p (11)	13.30	5.25

Nos. 454ep and 460cp are from booklet panes Nos. 544p-544s. Issued: 1c-5c, 2/8/67; No. 459p, 11/1/68; No. 460p, 1/7/70; others, 12/9/69.
See note after No. 343.

Coil Stamps

1967-70   **Perf. 9½ Horiz.**

466	A224	3c dull purple	3.75	.85
467	A224	4c carmine rose	1.10	.50
468	A224	5c blue	2.25	.65

Perf. 10 Horiz.

468A	A224	6c orange	.45	.25
c.		Imperf., pair	275.00	
468B	A224	6c black, die II	.35	.25
d.		Imperf., pair	2,500.	
		Nos. 466-468B (5)	7.90	2.50

Horizontal pairs or blocks of Nos. 468A and 468B may be found with a fine vertical score line between the stamps. These sell for little more than vertical pairs or strips.
Issued: No. 468A, 1/69; No. 468B, 8/70; others, 2/8/67.

EXPO '67 Emblem and Canadian Pavilion A226

1967, Apr. 28   **Engr.**   **Perf. 12**

469	A226	5c blue & red	.25	.25

EXPO '67, Intl. Exhib., Montreal, Apr. 28-Oct. 27.

Symbolic Woman and Ballot — A227

1967, May 24   **Litho.**

470	A227	5c black & rose lilac	.25	.25

50th anniversary of woman suffrage.

Elizabeth II — A228

1967, June 30   **Engr.**

471	A228	5c deep org & purple	.25	.25

Centennial Year visit of Queen Elizabeth II and the Duke of Edinburgh.

Runner A229

1967, July 19

472	A229	5c red	.25	.25

Pan-American Games, Winnipeg, Manitoba, July 22-Aug. 7.

Globe and Flash A230

1967, Aug. 31

473	A230	5c deep ultra	.25	.25

50th anniv. of the Canadian Press, news gathering and distributing service.

Georges Philias Vanier A231

1967, Sept. 15   **Engr. & Litho.**

474	A231	5c black	.25	.25

Georges Philias Vanier (1888-1967), Governor General of Canada, 1959-1967.

Toronto in 1967 and Citizens of 1867 — A232

1967, Sept. 28

475	A232	5c sl grn & sal pink	.25	.25

Centenary of Toronto as capital of Ontario.

Singing Children and Peace Tower, Ottawa — A233

1967, Oct. 11

476	A233	3c carmine	.25	.25
a.		Pane of 25	3.25	3.25
p.		Tagged	.25	.25
q.		As "a" tagged	4.50	4.50
477	A233	5c green	.25	.25
p.		Tagged	.30	.25

Christmas. Panes of 25 are imperf. on four sides.

Gray Jays — A234

1968, Feb. 15   **Litho.**

478	A234	5c green, blk & red	.45	.25

Weather Map and Composite of Instruments A235

1968, Mar. 13   **Perf. 11**

479	A235	5c dk & lt blue, yel & red	.25	.25

200th anniv. of Canada's first long-term fixed point weather observations at Fort Prince of Wales, Churchill, by William Wales and Joseph Dymond.

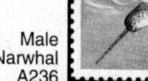

Male Narwhal A236

1968, Apr. 10

480	A236	5c multicolored	.25	.25

Weighing Rain Gauge, World Map and Maple Leaf A237

1968, May 8

481	A237	5c multicolored	.25	.25

Intl. Hydrological Decade, 1965-74.

The Nonsuch A238

Photo. & Engr.

1968, June 5   **Perf. 10**

482	A238	5c dk blue & multi	.25	.25

300th anniv. of the voyage of the Nonsuch which opened the way to Canada's West through the fur trade.

Contemporary and Indian Lacrosse Players — A239

1968, July 3

483	A239	5c yel, black & red	.25	.25

George Brown, "Globe" Front Page and Legislature, Prince Edward Island A240

1968, Aug. 21

484	A240	5c multicolored	.25	.25

George Brown (1818-1880), founder of Toronto "Globe" and political leader.

Henri Bourassa and Newspaper Page — A241

Litho. & Engr.

1968, Sept. 4   **Perf. 12**
485 A241 5c ver, buff & black   .25 .25
Henri Bourassa (1868-1952), jounalist and statesman.

Canadian Memorial, Near Vimy, France — A242

1968, Oct. 15   **Engr.**
486 A242 15c slate   2.00 1.25
50th anniv. of the Armistice which ended WWI. The stamp shows "The Defenders and the Breaking of the Sword," a detail from the memorial designed by W. S. Allward.

John McCrae and "Flanders Fields" A243

1968, Oct. 15   **Litho. & Engr.**
487 A243 5c multicolored   .25 .25
50th death anniv. of Lt. Col. John McCrae (1872-1918), author of "In Flanders Fields."

Eskimo Family, Carving — A244

Eskimo soapstone carving: 6c, Mother and infant, by Munamee of Cape Dorset.

1968, Nov.   **Photo.**
488 A244 5c brt blue & black   .25 .25
 a.   Booklet pane of 10   3.00 3.00
 p.   Tagged   .25 .25
 q.   As "a," tagged   3.75 3.75
489 A244 6c dp bister & black   .25 .25
 p.   Tagged   .25 .25
Christmas. Issued: 5c, Nov. 1; 6c, Nov. 15.

Curling A245

Photo. & Engr.

1969, Jan. 15   **Perf. 10**
490 A245 6c black, brt blue & car .25 .25

Vincent Massey — A246

Litho. & Engr.

1969, Feb. 20   **Perf. 12**
491 A246 6c yel olive & dk brn   .25 .25
Vincent Massey (1887-1967), 1st Canadian-born Gov. General of Canada, 1952-59.

Return from the Harvest Field, by Aurele de Foy Suzor-Cote A247

1969, Mar. 14   **Photo.**
492 A247 50c multicolored   3.50 2.50
Aurele de Foy Suzor-Cote (1869-1937), painter.

Globe and Tools of Various Trades A248

1969, May 21   **Engr.**   **Perf. 12x12½**
493 A248 6c dk olive green   .25 .25
50th anniv. of the ILO.

Vickers Vimy, 1919, and Map of the Atlantic A249

1969, June 13   **Photo. and Engr.**
494 A249 15c red brn, yel grn & lt ultra   1.75 1.50
50th anniv. of the first non-stop Atlantic flight from Newfoundland to Ireland of Capt. John Alcock and Lt. Arthur Whitten Brown.

Sir William Osler — A250

1969, June 23   **Perf. 12½x12**
495 A250 6c dk blue & lt red brn   .25 .25
Osler (1849-1919), physician, professor of physiology and pathology in Canada, US and England.

Ipswich Sparrow A251

Birds: 6c, White-throated sparrows, vert. 25c, Hermit thrush.

1969, July 23   **Litho.**   **Perf. 12**
496 A251 6c multicolored   .35 .25
497 A251 10c ultra & multi   .70 .40
498 A251 25c black & multi   1.75 1.50
        Nos. 496-498 (3)   2.80 2.15

Map of Prince Edward Island A252

Photo. & Engr.

1969, Aug. 15   **Perf. 12x12½**
499 A252 6c ultra, org brn & black .25 .25
Bicentenary of Charlottetown as capital of Prince Edward Island.

Flags of Summer and Winter Canada Games — A253

Litho. & Engr.

1969, Aug. 15   **Perf. 12**
500 A253 6c ultra, brt green & red .25 .25
1st Canada Summer Games, Halifax and Dartmouth, N.S., Aug. 16-24.

Sir Isaac Brock and Memorial Queenston Heights — A254

1969, Sept. 12
501 A254 6c yel brn, brn & pale sal .25 .25
Major General Sir Isaac Brock (1769-1812), administrator of Upper Canada and leader in the war of 1812.

Children of Various Races — A255

1969, Oct. 8   **Litho.**
502 A255 5c blue & multi   .25   .25
 a.   Booklet pane of 10   3.00 3.00
 p.   Tagged   .25   .25
 q.   As "a" tagged   3.75 3.75
503 A255 6c red & multi   .25   .25
 a.   Black (inscriptions & frame line) omitted 1,750. 1,500.
 p.   Tagged   .25   .25
                 Christmas.

Stephen Leacock, Comedy Mask and Mariposa View A256

Photo. & Engr.

1969, Nov. 12   **Perf. 12x12½**
504 A256 6c multicolored   .25 .25
Stephen Butler Leacock (1869-1944), humorist, historian and economist.

Manitoba, Crossroads of Canada A257

1970, Jan. 27   **Litho.**   **Perf. 12**
505 A257 6c violet blue & multi   .25 .25
 p.   Tagged   .30 .25
Centenary of the province of Manitoba.

Enchanted Owl, by Kenojuak — A258

1970, Jan. 27   **Engr.**
506 A258 6c dark red & black   .25 .25
Centenary of Nortwest Territories.

Microscopic View of Inside of Leaf A259

1970, Feb. 18   **Photo. & Engr.**
507 A259 6c green, lt org & blue   .25 .25
Canada's participation in the Intl. Biological Program, 1967-1972.

Emblems of EXPO '67 and '70 — A260

EXPO '70 Emblem and Dogwood, British Columbia A261

Designs: No. 510, EXPO '70 emblem and white garden lily, Quebec. No. 511, EXPO '70 emblem and white trillium, Ontario.

1970, Mar. 18   **Litho.**
508 A260 25c red emblem   2.00 2.00
 p.   Tagged   2.50 2.50
509 A260 25c violet emblem   2.00 2.00
 p.   Tagged   2.50 2.50
510 A261 25c green emblem   2.00 2.00
 p.   Tagged   2.50 2.50
511 A261 25c blue emblem   2.00 2.00
 p.   Tagged   2.50 2.50
 a.   Block of 4, #508-511   8.00 8.00
 b.   As "a," tagged   10.00 10.00
        Nos. 508-511 (4)   8.00 8.00
EXPO '70 Intl. Exhibition, Osaka, Japan, Mar. 15-Sept. 13. Nos. 508-511 printed se-tenant in panes of 50 (5x10), with various combinations possible.

Henry Kelsey A262

Photo. & Engr.

1970, Apr. 15   **Perf. 12½x12½**
512 A262 6c multicolored   .25 .25
300th birth anniv. of Henry Kelsey, explorer of Canada's western plains.

"A Divided World, with Energy Focused on Unification..." — A263

1970, May 13   **Litho.**   **Perf. 11**
513 A263 10c blue   .70   .55
 p.   Tagged   .85   .85
514 A263 15c lilac & dk red   1.10 .70
 p.   Tagged   1.50 1.50
25th anniversary of the United Nations.

Louis Riel — A264

1970, June 19   **Photo.**   **Perf. 12½x12**
515 A264 6c red & brt blue   .25 .25
Louis Riel (1844-1885), Metis leader who became president of the Council of Assiniboin in 1870.

Mackenzie Rock,
Dean
Channel — A265

1970, June 25   Engr.   Perf. 12
516 A265 6c brown   .25   .25
Sir Alexander Mackenzie (1764-1820), Scottish explorer who in 1793 completed the first crossing of the North American continent north of Mexico.

Sir Oliver
Mowat and
Parliament,
Ottawa
A266

Photo. & Engr.
1970, Aug. 12   Perf. 12x12½
517 A266 6c red & black   .25   .25
Sir Oliver Mowat (1820-1903), government leader and a Father of Confederation.

Isle of
Spruce, by
Arthur Lismer
A267

1970, Sept. 18   Litho.   Perf. 11
518 A267 6c multicolored   .25   .25
50th anniv. of "The Group of Seven," Canadian landscape artists.

Santa
Claus — A268

Christ
Child — A269

Child in the Manger and Star-studded
Sky — A270

Christmas, Designs by Canadian School Children: No. 519, 527 Santa Claus. No. 520, Horse-drawn Sleigh. No. 521, Nativity. No. 522, Children Skiing. No. 523, Snowmen and Christmas Tree. No. 524, 529 Christ Child. No. 525, Christmas Tree and Children. No. 526, Toy Store. . No. 528, Church. No. 530, Snowmobile and Trees.

1970, Oct. 7   Litho.   Perf. 12
519 A268 5c multicolored   .30   .25
520 A268 5c multicolored   .30   .25
521 A268 5c multicolored   .30   .25
522 A268 5c multicolored   .30   .25
523 A268 5c multicolored   .30   .25
 a.   Strip of 5, #519-523   2.75   2.25
 b.   As "a," triple impression of
      black   550.00
524 A269 6c multicolored   .35   .25
525 A269 6c multicolored   .35   .25
526 A269 6c multicolored   .35   .25
527 A269 6c multicolored   .35   .25
528 A269 6c multicolored   .35   .25
 a.   Strip of 5, #524-528   3.00   2.50
529 A270 10c multicolored   .40   .35
530 A270 15c multicolored   .90   .90
      Nos. 519-530 (12)   4.55   3.75

Tagged
519p A268 5c multicolored   .35   .25
520p A268 5c multicolored   .35   .25
521p A268 5c multicolored   .35   .25
522p A268 5c multicolored   .35   .25
523p A268 5c multicolored   .35   .25
 ap.   Strip of 5, #519p-523p   3.25   2.75
524p A269 6c multicolored   .40   .25
525p A269 6c multicolored   .40   .25
526p A269 6c multicolored   .40   .25
527p A269 6c multicolored   .40   .25
528p A269 6c multicolored   .40   .25
 ap.   Strip of 5, #524p-528p   4.50   3.00
529p A270 10c multicolored   .50   .50
530p A270 15c multicolored   1.10   1.10
      Nos. 519p-530p (12)   5.35   4.10

Christmas.
The sheets of 100 of both 5c and 6c contain all 5 designs, generally alternating, and arranged to permit vertical and horizontal pairs of each design in the two center vertical and horizontal rows. The center block of 4 is entirely of No. 522 (5c) and 525 (6c). The sheet may also be broken to provide 20 strips of 5, each stamp of different design.

Sir Donald Alexander
Smith — A271

1970, Nov. 4
531 A271 6c dk grn, yel & black   .25   .25
Smith (1820-1914), railroad builder and Canadian High Commissioner, 1896-1914.

Big Raven, by
Emily
Carr — A272

1971, Feb. 12
532 A272 6c multicolored   .25   .25
Emily Carr (1871-1945), painter and writer.

Laboratory
Equipment Used for
Insulin
Discovery — A273

1971, Mar. 3   Perf. 11
533 A273 6c multicolored   .25   .25
Discovery of insulin by Dr. Frederick G. Banting and Dr. Charles H. Best, 50th anniversary.

A274

1971, Mar. 24
534 A274 6c red, org & black   .25   .25
Sir Ernest Rutherford (1871-1937), physicist, developer of theory of spontaneous disintegration of the atom.

Spring, Winged
Maple Seed — A275

1971
535 A275 6c shown   .30   .25
 a.   Imperf., pair   850.00 750.00
536 A275 6c Summer   .30   .25
537 A275 7c Autumn   .30   .25
538 A275 7c Winter   .30   .25
      Nos. 535-538 (4)   1.20   1.00

Issue dates: No. 535, Apr. 14; No. 536, June 16; No. 537, Sept. 3; No. 538, Nov. 19.

Louis Joseph
Papineau — A276

Litho. & Engr.
1971, May 7   Perf. 12½x12
539 A276 6c multicolored   .25   .25
Louis Joseph Papineau (1786-1871), member of Legislative Assembly and leader of French Canadian Patriote party.

Map of
Copper
Mine River
Basin
A277

1971, May 7   Perf. 12x12½
540 A277 6c buff, red & brown   .25   .25
Bicentenary of Samuel Hearne's expedition to the Copper Mine River.

Maple
Leaves
A278

1971, June 1
541 A278 15c blk, red org & yel   1.70   1.10
 p.   Tagged   2.40   2.25
Inauguration of new transmitters for Radio Canada International.

Computer Tape
and
Reels — A279

1971, June 1
542 A279 6c black, ultra & red   .25   .25
Centenary of measured progress through census.

Migrating Phosphor
Canada's "Ottawa/General" tagging of engraved stamps printed March-October, 1972, used a phosphor which migrates onto or through other stamps, booklet covers and album pages. It fluoresces yellow under ultraviolet light.
This bleeding, contaminating "OP4" phosphor can be somewhat contained in mounts or envelopes of acetate, glassine or polyethylene, but it may leak or penetrate.
The migrating phosphor is found on all examples of Nos. 560p-561p, and on some of Nos. 544p, 544q, 544r, 544s, 562p-565p and 594-598.

Transportation
Means — A280

Design: 8c, Library of Parliament.

1971-72   Engr.   Perf. 12½x12
543 A280 7c slate green   .35   .25
 a.   Booklet pane of 5 + label
      (#454e, #456a + 3#543)   7.50   4.50
 b.   Booklet pane of 20 (4 #454e, 4
      #456a, 12 #543)   8.00   6.50
 p.   Tagged   .60   .25
544 A280 8c slate   .25   .25
 a.   Booklet pane of 6 (3 #454e, 1
      #460c, 2 #544)   3.50   1.75
 b.   Booklet pane of 18 (6 #454e, 1
      #460c, 11 #544)   5.25   3.00
 c.   Booklet pane of 10 (4 #454e, 1
      #460c, 5 #544 ('72)   2.25   2.25
 p.   Tagged   .30   .25
 q.   As "a," tagged   1.75   1.75
 r.   As "b," tagged   3.25   3.25
 s.   As "c," tagged   2.00   2.00

Coil Stamps
1971   Perf. 10 Horiz.
549 A280 7c slate green   .40   .25
 a.   Imperf, pair   1,050.
550 A280 8c slate   .30   .25
 a.   Imperf, pair   600.00
 p.   Tagged   .25   .25
 q.   As "p," imperf, pair   1,000.

See note below No. 468B.
Issued: 7c, 6/30/71; 8c, 12/30/71.

Abstract
"BC"
A282

1971, July 20   Litho.   Perf. 12
552 A282 7c multicolored   .25   .25
Centenary of British Columbia's entry into Canadian Confederation.

Indian Encampment on Lake Huron,
by Kane — A283

1971, Aug. 11   Perf. 12½
553 A283 7c multicolored   .40   .25
Paul Kane (1810-1871), painter.

Snowflake — A284

1971, Oct. 6   Engr.   Perf. 12
Size: 24x30mm
554 A284 6c dark blue   .25   .25
 p.   Tagged   .25   .25
 a.   All color omitted (from
      foldover)   2,000.
 b.   Printed on gummed side
      (from foldover)   1,200.
555 A284 7c bright green   .25   .25
 p.   Tagged   .30   .25

Litho. and Engr.
Size: 30x30mm
556 A284 10c dp car & silver   .35   .30
 p.   Tagged   .45   .30
557 A284 15c lt ultra, dp car
      & silver   .70   .65
 p.   Tagged   .90   .75
      Nos. 554-557 (4)   1.55   1.45
Christmas.

Pierre Laporte — A285

1971, Oct. 20   **Perf. 12½x12**
558 A285 7c black   .25 .25

Pierre Laporte (1921-1970), Minister of Labor, kidnapped and killed.

Figure Skating — A286

1972, Mar. 1   **Litho.**   **Perf. 12**
559 A286 8c deep red lilac   .25 .25

World Figure Skating Championships, Calgary, Alberta, Mar. 6-12.

"Your Heart is your Health" A287

1972, Apr. 7   **Engr.**   **Perf. 12x12½**
560 A287 8c red   .30 .25
p.   Tagged   .55 .35

World Health Day, Apr. 7.

Frontenac, by Philippe Hébert and Fort Saint Louis, Quebec A288

1972, May 17   **Photo. and Engr.**
561 A288 8c red brown & multi   .25 .25
p.   Tagged   .75 .75

Tercentenary of the appointment of Louis de Buade, Count of Frontenac and Palluau (1622-1698), as Governor of New France.

Indians of Canada

Buffalo Chase, by George Catlin A289

Thunderbird, Assiniboin Pattern — A290

No. 563, Plains Indian artifacts. No. 565, Ceremonial sun dance costume.
In Nos. 562-581, the first two and last two stamps of each annual set are printed checkerwise in same sheet of 50.

1972   **Litho.**   **Perf. 12x12½**
562 A289 8c shown   .40 .25
p.   Tagged   .55 .30
563 A289 8c multicolored   .40 .25
p.   Tagged   .55 .30
a.   Pair, #562-563   .80 .50
b.   As "a," tagged   1.10 .75

Perf. 12½x12
Photo. & Engr.
564 A290 8c shown   .35 .25
p.   Tagged   .55 .30
565 A290 8c multicolored   .35 .25
p.   Tagged   .55 .30
a.   Pair, #564-565   .70 .50
b.   As "a," tagged   1.10 .75

Plains Indians of Canada.
Issued: Nos. 562-563, 7/6; Nos. 564-565, 10/4.

Tagged (Nos. 566-581)

No. 566, Algonkian artifacts. No. 567, "Micmac Indians." No. 568, Thunderbird and belt. No. 569, Algonkian man and woman.

1973   **Litho.**   **Perf. 12x12½**
566 A289 8c multicolored   .35 .25
567 A289 8c multicolored   .35 .25
a.   Pair, #566-567   .70 .50

Perf. 12½x12
Photo. & Engr.
568 A290 8c multicolored   .30 .25
569 A290 8c multicolored   .30 .25
a.   Pair, #568-569   .60 .50

Algonkian-speaking Indians of Canada (Malecite, Micmac, Montagnais, Algonquin and Ojibwa).
Issued: Nos. 566-567, 2/21; Nos. 568-569, 11/28.

1974   **Litho.**   **Perf. 12x12½**

No. 570, Nootka Sound, house, inside. No. 571, Artifacts. No. 572, Chief wearing Chilkat blanket. No. 573, Thunderbird from Kwakiutl house.

570 A289 8c multicolored   .30 .25
571 A289 8c multicolored   .30 .25
a.   Pair, #570-571   .60 .50

Perf. 12½x12
Photo. & Engr.
572 A290 8c multicolored   .30 .25
573 A290 8c multicolored   .30 .25
a.   Pair, #572-573   .60 .50

Pacific Coast Indians of Canada (Haida, Salish, Tsimshian, Chilkat and Kwakiutl).
Issued: Nos. 570-571, 1/16; Nos. 572-573, 2/22.

1975, Apr. 4   **Litho.**   **Perf. 13½**

No. 574, Montagnais-Naskapi artifacts. No. 575, Dance of the Kutcha-Kutchin. No. 576, Kutchin ceremonial costume. No. 577, Ojibwa thunderbird and Naskapi pattern.

574 A289 8c multicolored   .25 .25
575 A289 8c multicolored   .25 .25
a.   Pair, #574-575   .50 .50

Perf. 12½
576 A290 8c multicolored   .25 .25

Litho. and Embossed
577 A290 8c multicolored   .25 .25
a.   Pair, #576-577   .50 .50

Subarctic Indians.

1976, Sept. 17   **Litho.**   **Perf. 13½**

No. 578, Cornhusk mask, artifacts. No. 579, Iroquoian Encampment, by George Heriot. No. 580, Iroquoian thunderbird. No. 581, Iroquoian man, woman.

578 A289 10c multicolored   .25 .25
579 A289 10c multicolored   .25 .25
a.   Pair, #578-579   .50 .50

Perf. 12½
Litho. & Embossed
580 A290 10c multicolored   .25 .25

Litho.
581 A290 10c multicolored   .25 .25
a.   Pair, #580-581   .50 .50
Nos. 562-581 (20)   6.00 5.00

Iroquois (Mohawk, Cayuga, Seneca, Oneida, Onondaga and Tuscarora).

Geological Fault — A291

No. 583, Bird's eye view of town. No. 584, Aerial map photography. No. 585, Contour lines.

1972, Aug. 2   **Perf. 12**
582 A291 15c shown   1.50 1.10
p.   Tagged   2.00 1.50

---

583 A291 15c multicolored   1.50 1.10
p.   Tagged   2.00 1.50
584 A291 15c multicolored   1.50 1.10
p.   Tagged   2.00 1.50
585 A291 15c multicolored   1.50 1.10
p.   Tagged   2.00 1.50
a.   Block of 4, #582-585   6.00 5.50
b.   As "a," tagged   8.00 11.00
Nos. 582-585 (4)   6.00 4.40

Earth sciences: 24th Intl. Geological Cong. (No. 582); 22nd Intl. Geographical Cong. (No. 583); 12th Cong. of Intl. Soc. of Photogrammetry (No. 584); 6th Cong. of Intl. Cartographic Assoc. (No. 585).

Sir John A. Macdonald A292

Elizabeth II A292a

Forest, Central Canada — A293

Vancouver, B.C. — A294

Designs: 2c, Sir Wilfrid Laurier. 3c, Sir Robert L. Borden. 4c, William Lyon Mackenzie King. 5c, Richard Bedford Bennett. 6c, Lester B. Pearson. 7c, Louis St. Laurent. 15c, Mountain sheep, Western Canada. 20c, Grain fields, Prairie. 25c, Polar bears, North. 50c, Seashore. $2, Quebec.

1972-76   **Engr.**   **Perf. 12x12½**
Tagged
586 A292 1c orange ('73)   .25 .25
a.   Booklet pane, 3 #586, 1
   #591, 2 #593 ('74)   1.25 1.10
b.   Bklt. pane, 6 #586, 1
   #591, 11 #593 ('75)   1.50 1.50
c.   Bklt. pane, 2 #586, 4
   #587, 4 #593Ac ('76)   1.25 1.10
d.   Printed on gummed side   900.00
587 A292 2c green ('73)   .25 .25
588 A292 3c brown ('73)   .25 .25
589 A292 4c black ('73)   .25 .25
590 A292 5c lilac ('73)   .25 .25
591 A292 6c dk red ('73)   .25 .25
a.   Printed on gummed side   180.00
592 A292 7c dk brn ('74)   .25 .25
593 A292a 8c ultra ('73)   .25 .25
b.   Perf. 13x13½ ('76)   .75 .25

Perf. 13x13½
593A A292a 10c dk car ('76)   .25 .25
c.   Perf. 12x12½   .35 .25

Perf. 12½x12
Photo. & Engr.
594 A293 10c multicolored   .30 .25
595 A293 15c multicolored   .50 .25
596 A293 20c multicolored   .50 .25
597 A293 25c multicolored   .55 .25
598 A293 50c multicolored   1.20 .25
599 A294 $1 multi ('73)   2.50 .50

Perf. 11
Litho. & Engraved
600 A294 $1 multicolored   6.00 1.60
601 A294 $2 multicolored   4.50 2.25
Nos. 586-601 (17)   18.30 7.85

No. 599 has engraved shading added in some areas.
Plates 1 and 2 of the scenic 10c differ in impression and colors. Plate 1 has distinct crosshatching of "Canada" background. On plate 2, released in 1974, this area appears solidly inked.
A 1976 printing of the 15c shows the blue trees on the hillside as solid color, while the 1972 printing shows clear detail on the trees.
A 1974 printing of the 50c has darker shading and a deeper tone for the dark blue areas of the photogravure impression.
Nos. 600 and 601 are untagged.

1976-77   **Photo. & Engr.**   **Perf. 13½**
594a A293 10c multicolored   .30 .25
595a A293 15c multicolored   .45 .25
596a A293 20c multicolored   .60 .25

597a A293 25c multicolored   .65 .25
598a A293 50c multicolored   1.75 .25
599a A294 $1 multi ('77)   2.50 .30
Nos. 594a-599a (6)   6.25 1.55

Coil Stamps

1974-76   **Engr.**   **Perf. 10 Vert.**
604 A292a 8c ultramarine   .25 .25
a.   Imperf., horiz. pair   150.00
605 A292a 10c dk carmine
  ('76)   .30 .25
a.   Imperf., horiz. pair   160.00

See note below No. 468B. No. 604 also exists in vertical multiples without score line.

Candles — A295

Candles and Fruit A296

Christmas: 8c, Like 6c. 15c, Candles, 15th century prayer book, boxes and brass vase.

1972, Nov. 1   **Litho.**   **Perf. 12½x12**
606 A295 6c red & multi   .25 .25
p.   Tagged   .30 .25
607 A295 8c vio blue & multi   .25 .25
p.   Tagged   .35 .25

Perf. 11
608 A296 10c green & multi   .45 .35
p.   Tagged   .65 .55
609 A296 15c yel bister & multi   .70 .70
p.   Tagged   1.25 1.20
Nos. 606-609 (4)   1.65 1.55

"The Blacksmith's Shop," by Krieghoff — A297

1972, Nov. 29   **Perf. 12½**
610 A297 8c multicolored   .30 .25
p.   Tagged   .35 .25

Cornelius Krieghoff (1815-1872), painter.

Tagged
From No. 611 onward, all stamps are tagged unless otherwise noted.

Monsignor de Laval — A298

1973, Jan. 31   **Perf. 11**
611 A298 8c silver, ultra & gold   .25 .25

Francois-Xavier de Montmorency-Laval de Montigny (1623-1708), 1st Bishop of Quebec and founder of many educational institutions; one of the builders of New France.

Commissioner G. A. French and Map of 1874 Trek — A299

10c, Spectrograph. 15c, R.C.M.P. Musical Ride.

1973, Mar. 9
612 A299 8c dk brn, org & red .25 .25
613 A299 10c dk blue & multi .35 .30
614 A299 15c yel grn & multi .75 .50
a. Imperf., pair 375.00
Nos. 612-614 (3) 1.35 1.05

Royal Canadian Mounted Police, cent.
Imperfs of No. 614 with a double impression and examples with 15c printed on 10c are from printer's waste.

Jeanne Mance A300

1973, Apr. 18
615 A300 8c multicolored .25 .25
a. Printed on gummed side 750.00

Jeanne Mance (1606-1673), first secular nurse in North America and founder of first hospital, the Hôtel-Dieu in Montreal settlement.

Joseph Howe — A301

1973, May 16
616 A301 8c gold & black .25 .25

Joseph Howe (1804-1873), journalist, poet and Lieutenant-Governor of Nova Scotia.

Mist Fantasy, by James MacDonald A302

1973, June 8 **Perf. 12½**
617 A302 15c multicolored .60 .50

Centenary of the birth of James E. H. MacDonald (1873-1932), painter.

Oaks on Shore A303

Photo. & Engr.
1973, June 22 **Perf. 12x12½**
618 A303 8c orange & red brn .25 .25

Centenary of Prince Edward Island's entry into Confederation.

Scottish Settlers and "Hector" A304

1973, July 20
619 A304 8c multicolored .25 .25

Bicentenary of arrival of Scottish settlers at Pictou, N.S.

Queen Elizabeth II — A305

1973, Aug. 2 **Photo. and Engr.**
620 A305 8c silver & multi .25 .25
621 A305 15c gold & multi .70 .60

Visit to Ottawa of Elizabeth II and the Duke of Edinburgh, July 31-Aug. 4, and meeting of Commonwealth Heads of Government, Ottawa, Aug. 2-10.

Nellie McClung — A306

1973, Aug. 29 **Litho.** **Perf. 10½x11**
622 A306 8c multicolored .25 .25

Nellie McClung (1873-1951), leader of women's suffrage movement, social reformer and writer.

Montreal Olympic Games — A307

1973, Sept. 20 **Perf. 12x12½**
Size: 26x44mm
623 A307 8c silver & multi .25 .25
624 A307 15c gold & multi .60 .50

21st Olympic Games, Montreal, 1976.
See Nos. B1-B3.

Ice Skate — A308

Santa Claus — A309

8c, Dove. 15c, Shepherd and star.

1973, Nov. 7 **Perf. 12½x12**
625 A308 6c multicolored .25 .25
a. Double impression of black 110.00
626 A308 8c multicolored .25 .25
Perf. 10½
627 A309 10c multicolored .30 .30
628 A309 15c multicolored .60 .60
Nos. 625-628 (4) 1.40 1.40

Christmas.

Children Diving from Dock — A310

1974, Mar. 22 **Engr.** **Perf. 12**
629 A310 8c shown .35 .25
630 A310 8c Joggers .35 .25
631 A310 8c Bicycling family .35 .25
632 A310 8c Hikers .35 .25
a. Block of 4, #629-632 1.40 1.00

"Keep Fit." 21st Summer Olympic Games, Montreal, 1976. When stamps are observed at an angle the Montreal Olympic Games' emblem can be seen.

Main St. and Portage Ave., Winnipeg, 1872 — A311

Litho. & Engr.
1974, May 3 **Perf. 12x12½**
633 A311 8c multicolored .25 .25

Winnipeg's incorporation as a city, cent.

Postmaster A312

No. 635, Mail collector and truck. No. 636, Mail handler. No. 637, Mail sorters. No. 638, Mailman. No. 639, Rural mail delivery.

1974, June 11 **Litho.** **Perf. 13½x13**
634 A312 8c shown .35 .30
635 A312 8c multicolored .35 .30
636 A312 8c multicolored .35 .30
637 A312 8c multicolored .35 .30
638 A312 8c multicolored .35 .30
639 A312 8c multicolored .35 .30
a. Block of 6, #634-639 2.25 2.25

Centenary of letter carrier delivery service. Printed in sheets of 50 (5x10).

Agricultural Education A313

1974, July 12 **Perf. 12½x12**
640 A313 8c multicolored .25 .25

Ontario Agricultural College centenary.

Pedestal, Gallows Frame and Contempra Telephones A314

1974, July 26 **Perf. 12½**
641 A314 8c multicolored .25 .25
a. Imperf., pair 1,500.

Centenary of the idea for the telephone by Alexander Graham Bell while visiting Brantford, Canada.

Bicycle Wheel and Cycling Emblem A315

Photo. & Engr.
1974, Aug. 7 **Perf. 12x12½**
642 A315 8c black, red & silver .25 .25

World Cycling Championships, Montreal, Aug. 14-25.

Mennonite Settlers A316

1974, Aug. 28 **Litho.** **Perf. 12x12½**
643 A316 8c multicolored .25 .25

Centenary of arrival of Mennonite settlers in Manitoba.

Snowshoeing A317

1974, Sept. 23 **Engr.** **Perf. 13½**
644 A317 8c shown .35 .25
645 A317 8c Skiing .35 .25
646 A317 8c Skating .35 .25
647 A317 8c Curling .35 .25
a. Block of 4, #644-647 1.40 1.40
b. Block or strip of 4, printed on gummed side 3,000.

"Keep Fit." 1976 Winter Olympic Games. When the stamps are observed at an angle the Montreal Olympic Games' emblem can be seen.
Warning: No. 647b must show each design; blocks exist that contain 2 No. 645 but no example of No. 647. Value thus, $1,500.

Mercury with Winged Horses, UPU Emblem A318

Photo. & Engr.
1974, Oct. 9 **Perf. 12x12½**
648 A318 8c violet, red & blue .25 .25
649 A318 15c violet, red & blue .90 .75

Centenary of Universal Postal Union.

Nativity, by Jean Paul Lemieux A319

Skaters at Hull, by Henri Masson — A320

Christmas (Paintings): 10c, The Ice Cone, Montmorency Falls, by Robert C. Todd. 15c, Village in the Laurentian Mountains, by Clarence A. Gagnon.

1974, Nov. 1 **Litho.** **Perf. 13½**
650 A319 6c multicolored .25 .25
651 A320 8c multicolored .25 .25
652 A319 10c multicolored .35 .30
653 A319 15c multicolored .60 .55
Nos. 650-653 (4) 1.45 1.35

Marconi and St. John's, Newfoundland, from Signal Hill — A321

1974, Nov. 15　　　　　　*Perf. 13*
654 A321 8c multicolored　　　.25　.25

Guglielmo Marconi (1874-1937), Italian electrical engineer and inventor.

Merritt and Welland Canal A322

Litho. & Engr.
1974, Nov. 29　　　　*Perf. 13x13½*
655 A322 8c multicolored　　　.25　.25

Sesquicentennial of the start of construction of the Welland Canal between Lakes Ontario and Erie, a project conceived and supervised by William Hamilton Merritt (1793-1862). Portrait by Robert Whale.

The Sprinter — A323

The Plunger — A324

Designs: Sculptures by Robert Tait McKenzie, M.D. (1867-1938), and Montreal Olympic Games' emblem.

Perf. 12½x12, 12x12½
1975, Mar. 14　　**Litho.; Embossed**
656 A323 $1 multicolored　　2.25　2.25
657 A324 $2 multicolored　　4.50　4.50

21st Olympic Games, Montreal, July 17-Aug. 1, 1976.

A325

No. 658, Anne of Green Gables. No. 659, Maria Chapdelaine.

1975, May 15　　　**Litho.**　　*Perf. 13*
658　　8c blue & multi　　　.25　.25
659　　8c brown & multi　　.25　.25
　a.　A325 Pair, #658-659　　　.50　.50

Birth centenary of Lucy Maud Montgomery (1874-1942), writer and author of "Anne of Green Gables"; Louis Hémon (1880-1913), writer and author of "Maria Chapdelaine." Nos. 658-659 printed checkerwise.

Marguerite Bourgeoys A327

Alphonse Desjardins A328

1975, May 30　Litho.　*Perf. 12½x12*
660 A327 8c red & multi　　.25　.25
661 A328 8c red & multi　　.25　.25

Marguerite Bourgeoys (1620-1700), founder of the Congrégation de Notre-Dame, Montreal, first girls' school in New France; Alphonse Desjardins (1854-1920), journalist, founder of first credit union in North America.

A329

No. 662, Samuel Dwight Chown (1853-1933), Methodist minister, leader of temperance movement, founder of United Church. No. 663, Dr. John Cook (1805-92), 1st Moderator of the United Presbyterian Church in Canada.
Nos. 662-663 printed checkerwise.

Photo. & Engr.
1975, May 30　　　　*Perf. 12x12½*
662　　8c dk brown, yel & buff　　.25　.25
663　　8c dk brown, yel & buff　　.25　.25
　a.　A329 Pair, #662-663　　　　　.50　.50

Pole Vaulting — A331

Hurdling — A332

Design: 25c, Marathon running and Montreal Olympic Games' emblem.

1975, June 11　Litho.　*Perf. 12x12½*
664 A331 20c dk blue & multi　　.60　.45
665 A331 25c maroon & multi　　.75　.50
666 A332 50c green & multi　　1.50　1.00
　　Nos. 664-666 (3)　　　　2.85　1.95

21st Olympic Games, Montreal, July 17-Aug. 1, 1976.

"Untamed" (Wild Horse Race) A333

1975, July 3
667 A333 8c gray & multi　　　.25　.25

Centenary of the founding of Calgary.

Female Symbol — A334

Photo. & Engr.
1975, July 14　　　　*Perf. 13*
668 A334 8c dp yel, gray & black　.25　.25

International Women's Year.

"Justice," by Walter S. Allward — A335

1975, Sept. 2　Litho.　*Perf. 12½*
669 A335 8c multicolored　　.25　.25

Supreme Court of Canada, centenary.

"Wm. D. Lawrence" A336

Photo. & Engr.
1975, Sept. 24　　　　*Perf. 13*
670 A336 8c shown　　　.35　.30
671 A336 8c "Beaver"　　.35　.30
672 A336 8c "Neptune"　　.35　.30
673 A336 8c "Quadra"　　.35　.30
　a.　Block of 4, #670-673　　1.40　1.40

Coastal ships.

Santa Claus — A337

Child — A338

Trees — A339

Designs by Canadian School Children: "What Christmas Means to Me" — No. 675, Skater. No. 677, Family and Christmas tree. No. 678, Gift box.

1975, Oct. 22　　Litho.　　*Perf. 13½*
674 A337　6c shown　　　　.25　.25
675 A337　6c multicolored　　.25　.25
　a.　Pair, #674-675　　　　.50　.50
676 A338　8c shown　　　　.25　.25
677 A338　8c multicolored　　.25　.25
　a.　Pair, #676-677　　　　.50　.50
　b.　Double impression of black　90.00
　c.　As "a," triple impression of black　　　　　　　300.00
678 A338　10c multicolored　.25　.25
679 A339　15c shown　　　.45　.45
　　Nos. 674-679 (6)　　1.70　1.70

Christmas. Stamps of same denomination printed checkerwise.

Legion Emblem and Bugle A340

Photo. & Engr.
1975, Nov. 10　　　　*Perf. 13*
680 A340 8c gray & multi　　.25　.25

Royal Canadian Legion, 50th anniversary.

Olympic Torch Ignited by Satellite in Canada A341

Montreal Olympic Games' Emblem and: 20c, Canadian athletes carrying Olympic flag. 25c, Women athletes receiving Olympic medals.

1976, June 18　　Litho.　　*Perf. 13*
681 A341　8c black & multi　　.25　.25
682 A341　20c black & multi　.70　.55
683 A341　25c black & multi　.90　.60
　　Nos. 681-683 (3)　　1.85　1.40

1976 Olympic Games ceremonies.

Communication Arts — A342

25c, Handicraft tools. 50c, Performing arts.

1976, Feb. 6　Photo.　*Perf. 12x12½*
684 A342 20c gray & multi　　1.25　.60
685 A342 25c ocher & multi　1.50　.75
686 A342 50c blue & multi　2.50　1.25
　　Nos. 684-686 (3)　　5.25　2.60

Olympic Fine Arts and Cultural Program.

High-rise Tower, Notre Dame Church, Montreal, and Games' Emblem — A343

Design: $2, Olympic Stadium, Velodrome, flags and emblem.

Photo. & Engr.
1976, Mar. 12　　　　*Perf. 13*
687 A343 $1 silver & multi　　3.25　2.25
688 A343 $2 gold & multi　　5.25　4.50

Nos. 681-688 were issued in commemoration of, or in connection with the 21st Olympic Games, Montreal, July 17-Aug. 1. Nos. 687-688 were issued in panes of 8.

Snowflake, Winter Olympics' Emblem — A344

Photo. and Embossed

1976, Feb. 6 **Perf. 12½**
689 A344 20c multicolored .90 .65

12th Winter Olympic Games, Innsbruck, Austria, Feb. 4-15.

Flower Growing from City — A345

1976, May 12 Litho. Perf. 12x12½
690 A345 20c multicolored .60 .45

Habitat, UN Conference on Human Settlements, Vancouver, May 31-June 11.

Franklin and Map of North America, 1776 A346

Litho. & Engr.

1976, June 1 Perf. 13
691 A346 10c multicolored .35 .25

American Bicentennial; Benjamin Franklin (1706-1790), deputy postmaster general for the colonies (1753-1774).
See US No. 1690.

Royal Military College, Kingston, Ont., Cent. — A347

No. 692, Color Parade, Memorial Arch. No. 693, Wing Parade, Mackenzie Building.

1976, June 1 Litho. Perf. 12
692 8c red & multi .25 .25
693 8c red & multi .25 .25
  a. A347 Pair, #692-693 .50 .50
  b. As "a," imperf. 2,000.
  c. Block of 4, imperf. horiz. 650.00
  d. As "a," double impression 3,500.

A few used singles exist of Nos. 692-693 with double impression. Very rare.

Archer in Wheelchair A349

1976, Aug. 3 Perf. 12x12½
694 A349 20c green & multi .60 .50

Olympiad for the Physically Disabled (25th Stoke Mandeville Games), Toronto, Aug. 3-11.

A350

No. 695, The Cremation of Sam McGee. No. 696, The Outlander.

1976, Aug. 17 Perf. 13½
695 8c multicolored .25 .25
696 8c multicolored .25 .25
  a. A350 Pair, #695-696 .50 .50

Robert W. Service (1874-1958), author of poem "The Cremation of Sam McGee"; Germaine Guevremont, author of "Le Survenant" (The Outlander).

Nativity, St. Michael's, Toronto — A352

Stained-glass windows: 10c, Nativity, St. Jude, London, Ontario. 20c, Nativity, by Yvonne Williams.

1976, Nov. 3 Perf. 13½
697 A352 8c multicolored .25 .25
698 A352 10c multicolored .25 .25
699 A352 20c multicolored .40 .40
  Nos. 697-699 (3) .90 .90

Christmas.

Inland Vessels A353

Litho. & Engr.

1976, Nov. 19 Perf. 12
700 A353 10c Northcote .35 .30
701 A353 10c Passport .35 .30
  a. Double impression of purple 275.00
702 A353 10c Chicora .35 .30
  a. Double impression of blue 275.00
703 A353 10c Athabasca .35 .30
  a. Block of 4, #700-703 1.40 1.25

Elizabeth II A354

Litho. and Typo.

1977, Feb. 4 Perf. 12½x12
704 A354 25c silver & multi .70 .50
  a. Silver omitted 1,100.

25th anniv. of the reign of Elizabeth II. Authentication strongly recommended for No. 704a. Fakes exist.

Bottle Gentian A355 Elizabeth II A356

Parliament, Ottawa A357

Trembling Aspen A358

Main Street, Prairie Town — A359

Fundy National Park — A359a

Designs: 2c, Western columbine. 3c, Canada lily. 4c, Hepatica. 5c, Shooting star. 10c, Franklin's lady's-slipper. No. 712, Jewelweed. No. 715, Parliament, Ottawa. No. 716, Queen Elizabeth II. 20c, Douglas fir. 25c, Maple. 30c, Red oak. 35c, White pine. 60c, Street scene, Ontario City. 75c, Old houses, eastern City Street. 80c, Street leading to the sea, Eastern Maritime Provinces. $2 Kluane National Park.

Litho. & Engr.

1977-82 Perf. 12x12½
705 A355 1c multicolored .25 .25
  a. Printed on gummed side, precanceled 1,100.
707 A355 2c multicolored .25 .25
  a. Printed on gummed side 950.00
708 A355 3c multicolored .25 .25
709 A355 4c multicolored .25 .25
  a. Printed on gummed side 300.00
710 A355 5c multicolored .25 .25
711 A355 10c multicolored .25 .25
  a. Perf. 13x13½ ('78) .25 .25

Photo. & Engr.

Perf. 13x13½
712 A355 12c multi ('78) .30 .25
713 A356 12c blue & multi .25 .25
  a. Perf. 12x12½ .30 .25

Engraved

Perf. 13x13½
714 A357 12c blue .25 .25
  a. Printed on gummed side 300.00
715 A357 14c red ('78) .25 .25
  a. Printed on gummed side 37.50
  b. All color omitted 400.00

Photo. & Engr.

Perf. 13x13½
716 A356 14c red & blk ('78) .25 .25
  a. Perf. 12x12½ .25 .25
  b. As "a," booklet pane of 25 + 2 labels ('78) 5.50 6.00
  c. Red omitted 1,150.

Perf. 13½
717 A358 15c multi .45 .25
718 A358 20c multi .35 .25
  a. Black (denomination) omitted 750.00
719 A358 25c multi .50 .25
720 A358 30c multi ('78) .60 .25
721 A358 35c multi ('79) .60 .25
723 A359 50c multi ('78) 1.10 .25
723A A359 50c multi, litho. & engr. ('78) .90 .25
  b. Dark brown (engr., all inscriptions, etc.) omitted 2,000.
  c. Magenta (litho.) and dark brown (engr.) missing (from foldover) 15,000.
723C A359 60c multi, litho. ('82) 1.25 .25
724 A359 75c multi ('78) 1.30 .30
725 A359 80c multi ('78) 1.50 .25

Lithographed and Engraved
726 A359a $1 multi ('79) 1.50 .55
  a. Untagged 2.50 .70
  b. As "a," blk inscriptions omitted 500.00 500.00

---

727 A359a $2 multi ('79) 3.60 1.40
  a. Silver inscriptions omitted 300.00
  b. Double impression of silver inscriptions 750.00
  Nos. 705-727 (23) 16.45 7.35

On No. 715b, a strong embossed impression from the plate, without color, is evident.
On No. 723A license plate on yellow car reads "1978."
No. 723Ac is unique.
Certificate of authenticity recommended for No. 727b. "Kiss prints" also exist that are not true double impressions.
See Nos. 781-806, 934-937, 1084.

Coil Stamps

1977-78 Engr. Perf. 10 Vert.
729 A357 12c blue .25 .25
  a. Imperf., pair 150.00
730 A357 14c red ('78) .30 .25
  a. Imperf., pair 170.00

See note below No. 468B.

Eastern Cougar A360

1977, Mar. 30 Litho. Perf. 12½
732 A360 12c multicolored .25 .25

Wildlife protection.

April in Algonquin Park, by Thomson — A361

No. 734, Autumn Birches, by Tom Thomson.

1977, May 26 Perf. 12
733 A361 12c black & multi .25 .25
734 A361 12c ocher & multi .25 .25
  a. Pair, #733-734 .50 .50

Tom Thomson (1877-1917), landscape painter, birth centenary. Nos. 733-734 printed checkerwise.

Names of Governors General and Standard A362

1977, June 30 Perf. 12½
735 A362 12c vio blue & multi .25 .25

Honoring Canadian-born Governors General: Vincent Massey, Georges Philias Vanier, Daniel Roland Michener and Jules Léger.

Order of Canada A363

Litho. & Embossed

1977, June 30
736 A363 12c multicolored .25 .25

Order of Canada, 10th anniversary.

Peace Bridge, Canadian, US and UN Flags A364

1977, Aug. 4 Litho.
737 A364 12c blue & multi .25 .25

50th anniversary of the Peace Bridge, connecting Fort Erie, Ontario, with Buffalo, N.Y.

Joseph E. Bernier, CGS Arctic A365

Sandford Fleming, Railroad Bridge A366

1977, Sept. 16   Engr.   Perf. 13
738	A365	12c dark blue	.25	.25
739	A366	12c brown	.25	.25
a.		Pair, #738-739	.50	.50

Joseph-Elzéar Bernier (1852-1934), explorer; Sandford Fleming (1827-1915), mapped route for Intercolonial Railway and designed Canada's first stamp.
Nos. 738-739 printed checkerwise.

Peace Tower, Parliament, Ottawa A367

1977, Sept. 19   Litho.   Perf. 12½
| 740 | A367 | 25c multicolored | .75 | .65 |

23rd Commonwealth Parliamentary Conference, Ottawa, Sept. 19-25.

Hunters Following Star — A368

Christmas: 12c, Angelic choir in northern light. 25c, Christ Child in Ring of Glory blessing chiefs from afar. Illustrations for Canada's first Christmas carol, written by Father Brébeuf, 1649.

1977, Oct. 26   Perf. 13½
741	A368	10c multicolored	.25	.25
a.		Horiz. pair, imperf between	1,050.	
b.		Printed on gummed side	650.00	
c.		Imperf., pair	1,150.	
742	A368	12c multicolored	.25	.25
a.		Left margin block of 4, left vert. pair imperf, right pair part perf	1,900.	
b.		Double impression of purple, blue, green; quadruple impression of black (inscriptions)	650.00	
743	A368	25c multicolored	.45	.35
		Nos. 741-743 (3)	.95	.85

Pinky A369

Canadian sailing ships — No. 745, Tern schooner. No. 746, 5-masted schooner. No. 747, Mackinaw boat.

Litho. and Engr.

1977, Nov. 18   Perf. 12x12½
744	A369	12c shown	.25	.25
745	A369	12c multicolored	.25	.25
746	A369	12c multicolored	.25	.25
747	A369	12c multicolored	.25	.25
a.		Block of 4, #744-747	1.00	1.00
b.		As "a," #745, 747 imperf; #744, 746 part perf	3,500.	

See Nos. 776-779.

Seal Hunter, Soapstone Sculpture A370

Disguised Caribou Hunter, Print — A371

Inuit Art: No. 749, Spear fishing. No. 751, Walrus hunt. Nos. 749-751 are after stonecut prints.

1977, Nov. 18   Litho.
748	A370	12c multicolored	.25	.25
749	A371	12c multicolored	.25	.25
a.		Pair, #748-749	.50	.50
b.		As "a," gray (inscriptions) omitted on No. 749	2,250.	
750	A371	12c multicolored	.25	.25
751	A371	12c multicolored	.25	.25
a.		Pair, #750-751	.50	.50
		Nos. 748-751 (4)	1.00	1.00

Inuit hunting. Nos. 748-749 and Nos. 750-751 printed se-tenant checkerwise.

Peregrine Falcon A372

1978, Jan. 18
| 752 | A372 | 12c multicolored | .25 | .25 |

Endangered wildlife.

Canada No. 3, 1851 — A373

1978   Photo. & Engr.   Perf. 13½
753	A373	12c shown	.25	.25
754	A373	14c No. 7	.25	.25
755	A373	30c No. 8	.55	.30
756	A373	$1.25 No. 2	2.00	1.00
a.		Souvenir sheet of 3	3.25	3.25
		Nos. 753-756 (4)	3.05	1.80

CAPEX '78, Canadian Intl. Phil. Exhib., Toronto, June 9-18 (cent. of Canada's admission to UPU).
No. 756a contains one each of Nos. 754-756 ($1.25 untagged). Value of No. 756 untagged, $2.75.
Issue dates: 12c, Jan. 18; others, June 10.

Games' Emblem A374

Design: 30c, Badminton.

1978, Mar. 31   Litho.   Perf. 12½
| 757 | A374 | 14c silver & multi | .25 | .25 |
| 758 | A374 | 30c silver & multi | .55 | .45 |

Stadium A375

No. 760, Running. No. 761, Alberta Legislature building, Edmonton. No. 762, Lawn bowling.

1978, Aug. 3
759	A375	14c silver & multi	.30	.25
760	A375	14c silver & multi	.30	.25
a.		Pair, #759-760	.60	.50
761	A375	30c silver & multi	.55	.50
762	A375	30c silver & multi	.55	.50
a.		Pair, #761-762	1.10	1.00
		Nos. 759-762 (4)	1.70	1.50

Nos. 757-762 commemorate 11th Commonwealth Games, Edmonton, Aug. 3-12.
Nos. 760a, 762a printed checkerwise.

A376

No. 763, Capt. Cook, by Nathaniel Dance. No. 764, Nootka Sound, by John Webber.

1978, Apr. 26   Perf. 13
763		14c multicolored	.25	.25
764		14c multicolored	.25	.25
a.		A376 Pair, #763-764	.60	.50

Capt. James Cook (1728-1779), explorer of Canada's East and West Coasts and bicentenary of his anchorage near Anchorage, June 1, 1778. Nos. 763-764 printed checkerwise.

Silver Mine, Cobalt Lake A378

Stripmining, Athabasca Tar Sands A379

1978, May 19   Perf. 12½
765	A378	14c multicolored	.25	.25
766	A379	14c multicolored	.25	.25
a.		Pair, #765-766	.50	.50
b.		As "a," No. 766 with double impression of brown (inscriptions)	600.00	

Development of national resources. Nos. 765-766 printed checkerwise.

Prince's Gate A380

1978, Aug. 16
| 767 | A380 | 14c multicolored | .25 | .25 |

Canadian National Exhibition, centenary.

Mère d'Youville and Miracle of Food — A381

1978, Sept. 21   Perf. 13x13½
| 768 | A381 | 14c multicolored | .25 | .25 |

Marguerite d'Youville (1701-1771), founder of the Gray Nuns, beatified 1959.

Woman Walking, by Pitseolak A382

Migration, Soapstone by Joe Talurinili A383

Works by Eskimo Artists: No. 771, Plane over village, stonecut and stencil print by Pudlo. No. 772, Dogteam and sled, ivory sculpture by Abraham Kingmeatook.

1978, Sept. 27   Perf. 13½
769	A382	14c multicolored	.25	.25
770	A383	14c multicolored	.25	.25
a.		Pair, #769-770	.50	.50
771	A382	14c multicolored	.25	.25
772	A383	14c multicolored	.25	.25
a.		Pair, #771-772	.50	.50
		Nos. 769-772 (4)	1.00	1.00

Travels of the Inuit. Printed checkerwise.

Madonna of the Flowering Pea, Cologne School — A384

Renaissance Paintings in National Gallery of Canada: 14c, Virgin and Child, by Hans Memling. 30c, Virgin and Child, by Jacopo Di Cione.

1978, Oct. 20   Perf. 12½
773	A384	12c multicolored	.25	.25
774	A384	14c multicolored	.25	.25
a.		Black omitted	1,000.	
775	A384	30c multicolored	.55	.25
		Nos. 773-775 (3)	1.05	.75

Christmas.

Sailing Ships Type of 1977

No. 776, "Chief Justice Robinson," 1842. No. 777, "St. Roch," 1928. No. 778, "Northern Light," 1928. No. 779, "Labrador," 1954.

1978, Nov. 15   Litho. & Engr.   Perf. 13
776	A369	14c multicolored	.30	.25
777	A369	14c multicolored	.30	.25
778	A369	14c multicolored	.30	.25
779	A369	14c multicolored	.30	.25
a.		Block of 4, #776-779	1.25	1.10

Ice vessels.

Quebec Carnival — A386

1979, Feb. 1   Litho.   Perf. 13½
| 780 | A386 | 14c multicolored | .25 | .25 |

Flower, Queen & Parliament Types

1c, Bottle gentian. 2c, Western columbine. 3c, Canada lily. 4c, Hepatica. 5c, Shooting star. 10c, Franklin's lady's-slipper. 15c, Canada violet. No. 789, Elizabeth II. No. 790, Parliament, Ottawa.

Photo. & Engr., Engr. (#790)

1977-83   Perf. 13x13½
781	A355	1c multi ('79)	.25	.25
a.		Perf. 12x12½ ('77)	.25	.25
b.		Bklt. pane, 2 #781a, 4 #713a	1.00	1.00
782	A355	2c multi ('79)	.25	.25
a.		Bklt. pane, 4 #782b, 3 #716a + label	1.00	1.00
b.		Perf. 12x12½ ('78)	.25	.25
783	A355	3c multi ('79)	.25	.25
784	A355	4c multi ('79)	.25	.25
785	A355	5c multi ('79)	.25	.25
786	A355	10c multi ('79)	.25	.25
787	A355	15c multi ('79)	.30	.25
789	A356	17c green & blk ('79)	.30	.25
a.		Perf. 12x12½	.35	.25
b.		Bklt. pane of 25 #789a + 2 labels	6.50	7.50
c.		Horiz. pair, imperf. btwn. and at left and bottom	1,800.	
d.		Black inscriptions omitted	950.00	
790	A357	17c slate green ('79)	.25	.25
a.		Printed on gummed side	37.50	
791	A356	30c multi ('82)	.45	.25
a.		Black (engr.) omitted	2,250.	
792	A356	32c multi ('83)	.50	.25
		Nos. 781-792 (11)	3.30	2.75

Nos. 781a, 782b, 789a are from booklet panes. No. 782b has one straight edge, others one or two.

Beware of examples purported to be No. 791a that actually have tiny amounts of black present. Only two examples have been confirmed with 100% omission. Certification strongly recommended.

No. 789d also shows the horiz. perfs. shifted.

Parliament Type of 1977
Booklet Stamps

1979, Mar. 28		**Engr.**	**Perf. 12x12½**
797	A357 1c slate blue	.40	.25
a.	Bklt. pane, 1 #797, 3 #800, 2 #789a	1.40	
800	A357 5c violet brown	.30	.25

No. 797 has one straight edge, No. 800 has one or two.

Coil Stamps

1979, Mar. 8		**Perf. 10 Vert.**	
806	A357 17c slate green	.25	.25
a.	Imperf., pair	150.00	

Endangered Wildlife A392

1979, Apr. 10	**Litho.**	**Perf. 12½**	
813	A392 17c Soft-shelled turtle	.30	.25
814	A392 35c Bowhead whale	.75	.40

Ribbon Around Woman's Finger — A393

No. 816, String around man's finger.

1979, Apr. 10			
815	A393 17c multicolored	.25	.25
816	A393 17c multicolored	.25	.25
a.	Pair, #815-816	.50	.50
b.	As "a," double impression of black	110.00	
c.	As "a," triple impression of black	225.00	
d.	As "a," double impression of red	110.00	

Use postal code. Printed checkerwise.

Fruits of the Earth, by F. P. Grove A394

The Golden Vessel, by Emile Nelligan A395

1979, May 3		**Perf. 13x13½**	
817	A394 17c multicolored	.25	.25
a.	Double impression of brown	375.00	
818	A395 17c multicolored	.25	.25
a.	Double impression of blue	375.00	
b.	Pair, #817-818	.50	.55
c.	As "b," left margin block of 4, left vert. pair imperf, right pair part perf	2,000.	2,000.

Frederick Philip Grove (1879-1948), teacher and writer; Emile Nelligan (1879-1941), French-Canadian poet. Nos. 817-818 printed checkerwise.

Warning: horizontal pairs exist of No. 818a that appear to be imperforate. These actually are pairs made from No. 818c with normal perforations trimmed off the right edge.

A396

1979, May 11		**Perf. 13½**	
819	17c De Salaberry	.25	.25
820	17c John By	.25	.25
a.	A396 Pair, #819-820	.50	.50

Charles-Michel d'Irumberry de Salaberry (1778-1829), and John By (1779-1836), Canadian colonels. Printed checkerwise.

Flag of Ontario A398

Provincial and Territorial flags: No. 822, Quebec. No. 823, Nova Scotia. No. 824, New Brunswick. No. 825, Manitoba. No. 826, British Columbia. No. 827, Prince Edward Island. No. 828, Saskatchewan. No. 829, Alberta. No. 830, Newfoundland. No. 831, Northwest Territories. No. 832, Yukon Territory.

1979, June 15		**Perf. 13½**	
821	A398 17c shown	.30	.25
822	A398 17c multicolored	.30	.25
823	A398 17c multicolored	.30	.25
824	A398 17c multicolored	.30	.25
825	A398 17c multicolored	.30	.25
826	A398 17c multicolored	.30	.25
827	A398 17c multicolored	.30	.25
828	A398 17c multicolored	.30	.25
829	A398 17c multicolored	.30	.25
830	A398 17c multicolored	.30	.25
831	A398 17c multicolored	.30	.25
832	A398 17c multicolored	.30	.25
a.	Pane of 12, #821-832	4.00	3.75

White Water Kayak Race A399

1979, July 3		**Perf. 12½**	
833	A399 17c multicolored	.30	.25

Canoe-Kayak (Slalom and Wild Water) World Championships, Jonquière and Desbiens, Quebec, June 30-July 8.

Women's Field Hockey A400

1979, Aug. 16			
834	A400 17c multicolored	.30	.25

Women's Field Hockey Championship, Vancouver, B.C., Aug. 16-30.

Summer Tent, Print by Kiakshuk A401

Eskimos Building Igloo, by Abraham of Povungnituk A402

Works by Eskimo Artists: No. 837, The Dance, print by Kalvak of Holman Island. No. 838, Two soapstone figures from Repulse Bay, by Madeleine Isserkut and Jean Mapsalak.

1979, Sept. 13		**Perf. 13½**	
835	A401 17c multicolored	.25	.25
836	A402 17c multicolored	.25	.25
a.	Pair, #835-836	.50	.50
837	A401 17c multicolored	.25	.25
838	A402 17c multicolored	.25	.25
a.	Pair, #837-838	.50	.50
	Nos. 835-838 (4)	1.00	1.00

Inuit shelters and community. Printed checkerwise.

Painted Wooden Train A403

Antique Toys: 17c, Horse, pull toy. 35c, Knitted doll, vert.

1979, Oct. 17		**Perf. 13**	
839	A403 15c multicolored	.25	.25
840	A403 17c multicolored	.30	.25
841	A403 35c multicolored	.60	.30
a.	Gold (and tagging) omitted	1,100.	700.00
	Nos. 839-841 (3)	1.15	.80

Christmas.

Girl Watering Tree of Life — A404

1979, Oct. 24			
842	A404 17c multicolored	.25	.25

International Year of the Child.

Curtiss HS-2L A405

No. 844, Canadair CL-215. No. 845, Vickers Vedette. No. 846, Consolidated Canso.

1979, Nov. 15		**Perf. 12½**	
843	A405 17c shown	.30	.25
844	A405 17c multicolored	.30	.25
a.	Pair, #843-844	.65	.55
845	A405 35c multicolored	.65	.50
846	A405 35c multicolored	.65	.50
a.	Pair, #845-846	1.30	1.25
	Nos. 843-846 (4)	1.90	1.50

Map of Canada Showing Arctic Islands A406

1980, Jan. 23		**Perf. 13½**	
847	A406 17c multicolored	.25	.25

Acquisition of the Arctic Islands, centenary.

Downhill Skiing A407

1980, Jan. 23			
848	A407 35c multicolored	.65	.45

13th Winter Olympic Games, Lake Placid, NY, Feb. 12-24.

Meeting of the School Trustees, by Robert Harris A408

Royal Canadian Academy of Arts Centenary: No. 850, Inspiration, bronze sculpture, by Louis-Philippe Hebert (1850-1917). No. 851, Parliament Buildings, by Thomas Fuller (1822-1919). No. 852, Sunrise on the Saguenay, by Lucius O'Brien (1832-99).

1980, Mar. 6			
849	A408 17c multicolored	.30	.25
850	A408 17c multicolored	.30	.25
a.	Pair, #849-850	.60	.55
851	A408 35c multicolored	.65	.50
852	A408 35c multicolored	.65	.50
a.	Pair, #851-852	1.30	1.25
	Nos. 849-852 (4)	1.90	1.50

Printed checkerwise.

Atlantic Whitefish A409

Endangered wildlife. No. 854, Greater prairie chicken.

1980, May 6		**Perf. 12½**	
853	A409 17c multicolored	.35	.25
854	A409 17c multicolored	.35	.25

Garden — A410

1980, May 29		**Perf. 13½**	
855	A410 17c multicolored	.25	.25

Intl. Flower Show, Montreal, May 17-Sept. 1.

Helping Hands — A411

Litho. & Embossed

1980, May 29		**Perf. 12½**	
856	A411 17c ultra & gold	.25	.25

14th World Congress of Rehabilitation International, Winnipeg, June 22-27.

"O Canada" Opening Bars A412

Composers Lavallee, Routhier, Weir A413

1980, June 6		**Litho.**	
857	A412 17c multicolored	.25	.25
858	A413 17c multicolored	.25	.25
a.	Pair, #857-858	.50	.50

"O Canada" centenary. Printed checkerwise in sheets of 16.

John George Diefenbaker (1895-1979), Prime Minister, 1956-63 — A414

1980, June 20   **Engr.**   *Perf. 13½*
859 A414 17c dark blue   .25 .25

Emma Albani (1847-1930), Soprano — A415

No. 861, Healey Willan (1880-1968), organist, composer. Printed checkerwise.

1980, July 4   **Litho.**
860 A415 17c multicolored   .25 .25
861 A415 17c multicolored   .25 .25
    a.   Pair, #860-861   .50 .50

Ned Hanlan (1855-1908), Oarsman A416

1980, July 4
862 A416 17c multicolored   .25 .25

Wheat Fields, Saskatchewan A417

No. 864, Strip farming and town, Alberta.

1980, Aug. 27
863 A417 17c multicolored   .25 .25
864 A417 17c multicolored   .25 .25

75th anniversary of Saskatchewan's and Alberta's creation as Provinces.

Uraninite Molecular Structure A418

1980, Sept. 3
865 A418 35c multicolored   .65 .50
    a.   Printed on gummed side   850.00

Discovery of uranium in Canada, 80th anniversary.

Sedna, by Ashoona Kiawak A419

Return of the Sun, Print by Kenojouak A420

Works by Eskimo Artists: No. 868, Bird Spirit, by Doris Hagiolok. No. 869, Shaman, print by Simon Tookoome.

1980, Sept. 25
866 A419 17c multicolored   .25 .25
867 A420 17c multicolored   .25 .25
    a.   Pair, #866-867   .50 .50
868 A419 35c multicolored   .55 .55
869 A420 35c multicolored   .55 .55
    a.   Pair, #868-869   1.10 1.10
    b.   As No. 869, double impression of gray   675.00
    Nos. 866-869 (4)   1.60 1.60

Inuit spirits. Printed checkerwise.

Christmas Morning, by Frank Charles Hennessey — A421

Christmas (Greeting Cards, 1931): 17c, Sleigh Ride, by Joseph Sydney Hallam. 35c, McGill Cab Stand, by Kathleen Morris.

1980, Oct. 22   *Perf. 12½x12*
870 A421 15c multicolored   .25 .25
871 A421 17c multicolored   .25 .25
872 A421 35c multicolored   .55 .45
    Nos. 870-872 (3)   1.05 .95

Avro Canada CF-100, 1950 A422

Military Aircraft: No. 874, Avro Lancaster, 1941. No. 875, Curtiss JN-4 Canuck. No. 876, Hawker Hurricane, 1935.

1980, Nov. 10   *Perf. 13x13½*
873 A422 17c multicolored   .30 .25
874 A422 17c multicolored   .30 .25
    a.   Pair, #873-874   .60 .55
875 A422 35c multicolored   .65 .55
876 A422 35c multicolored   .65 .55
    a.   Pair, #875-876   1.30 1.25
    Nos. 873-876 (4)   1.90 1.60

Printed checkerwise.

Emmanuel-Persillier Lachapelle, Caduceus — A423

1980, Dec. 5   *Perf. 13½*
877 A423 17c multicolored   .25 .25

Lachapelle (1845-1918), physician, founded Notre Dame Hospital, Montreal, 1880.

Mandora, 18th Century A424

1981, Jan. 19   *Perf. 12½*
878 A424 17c multicolored   .25 .25

"The Look of Music" rare musical instrument exhibition, Vancouver, Nov. 2, 1980-Apr. 5, 1981.
No. 878 exists printed on gummed side with gold color and tagging omitted, from printer's waste.

Emily Stowe (1831-1903) and Toronto General Hospital — A425

Designs: No. 880, Louise McKinney, (1868-1931) Alberta legislative building. No. 881, Idola Saint-Jean, (1875-1945) Quebec legislative building. No. 882, Henrietta Edwards, (1849-1931) clubwomen.

1981, Mar. 4   *Perf. 13x13½*
879 A425 17c multicolored   .35 .25
880 A425 17c multicolored   .35 .25
881 A425 17c multicolored   .35 .25
882 A425 17c multicolored   .35 .25
    a.   Block of 4, #879-882   1.40 1.25

Vancouver Island Marmot, by Michael Dumas A426

Endangered Wildlife: 35c, Wood bison, by Robert Bateman.

1981, Apr. 6
883 A426 17c multicolored   .30 .25
884 A426 35c multicolored   .70 .60

Kateri Tekakwitha ("Lily of the Mohawks"), by Emile Brunet — A427

Brunet Sculpture: No. 886, Marie de L'Incarnation.

1981, Apr. 24   *Perf. 12½*
885 A427 17c brown & pale grn   .25 .25
886 A427 17c lt blue & ultra   .25 .25
    a.   Pair, #885-886   .50 .50

Beatification of Kateri Tekakwitha (1656-1680), first North American Indian saint, and Marie De L'Incarnation (1599-1672), founder of Ursuline Order.

At Baie Saint-Paul, by Marc-Aurele Fortin (1888-1970) — A428

Paintings: No. 888, Self-portrait, by Frederick H. Varley (1881-1969). 35c, Untitled No. 6, by Paul-Emile Borduas (1905-60).

1981, May 22
887 A428 17c multi   .25 .25
888 A428 17c multi, vert.   .25 .25
    a.   Imperf, pair   *1,500.*

Photo.
Perf. 13
889 A428 35c multi, vert.   .60 .60
    Nos. 887-889 (3)   1.10 1.10

Map of Canada Showing Provincial Boundaries, 1867 — A429

1981, June 30   **Litho.**   *Perf. 13½*
890 A429 17c shown   .30 .25
891 A429 17c 1873   .30 .25
892 A429 17c 1905   .30 .25
893 A429 17c 1949   .30 .25
    a.   Strip of 4, #890-893   1.20 1.20

Canada Day.

Frere Marie-Victorin (1885-1944) Botanist — A430

Botanists: No. 895, John Macoun (1831-1920).

1981, July 22   *Perf. 12½*
894 A430 17c multicolored   .25 .25
895 A430 17c multicolored   .25 .25
    a.   Pair, #894-895   .50 .50

Montreal Rose — A431

1981, July 22   *Perf. 13½*
896 A431 17c multicolored   .25 .25

A432

1981, July 31   **Photo. & Engr.**
897 A432 17c multicolored   .25 .25

Niagara-on-the-Lake (1st capital of Upper Canada).

A433

1981, Aug. 14   **Litho.**
898 A433 17c multicolored   .25 .25

Acadian Congress centenary.

A434

1981, Sept. 8
899 A434 17c multicolored   .25 .25

Aaron Mosher (1881-1959), Labor Congress founder.

A435

1981, Nov. 16   **Litho.**
900 A435 15c 1781   .25 .25
901 A435 15c 1881   .25 .25
902 A435 15c 1981   .25 .25
    Nos. 900-902 (3)   .75 .75

Christmas; bicentenary of 1st illuminated Christmas tree in Canada.

Canadair
CL-41 Tutor
A436

No. 904, de Havilland Tiger Moth. No. 905, Avro Canada C-102. No. 906, de Havilland Canada Dash-7.

1981, Nov. 24   **Perf. 12½**
903 A436 17c shown   .30 .25
904 A436 17c multicolored   .30 .25
   a.   Pair, #903-904   .60 .55
905 A436 35c multicolored   .60 .55
906 A436 35c multicolored   .60 .55
   a.   Pair, #905-906   1.20 1.10
    Nos. 903-906 (4)   1.80 1.60

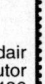

A437

1981, Dec. 29   **Engr.**   **Perf. 13x13½**
907 A437 (30c) red   .90 .25
   a.   Printed on gummed side   750.00

Coil Stamp
Perf. 10 Vert.
908 A437 (30c) red   .75 .25
   a.   Imperf., pair   375.00 225.00

See Nos. 923-924, 940, 943-946, 950-951.

CANADA '82 Intl. Philatelic Youth Exhibition, Toronto, May 20-24 — A438

1982   **Litho.**   **Perf. 13½**
909 A438 30c No. 1   .50 .25
910 A438 30c No. 102   .50 .25
911 A438 35c No. 223   .60 .50
912 A438 35c No. 155   .60 .50
913 A438 60c No. 158   1.20 .75
   a.   Souvenir sheet of 5, #909-913   3.75 3.75
   b.   As No. 913, triple impression of reddish brown   1,400.
    Nos. 909-913 (5)   3.40 2.25

Issued: Nos. 909, 911, 3/11; others, 5/20.

Jules Leger
(1913-1980), 26th
Governor
General — A439

1982, Apr. 2
914 A439 30c multicolored   .45 .25

Terry Fox (1958-1981), Marathon of Hope — A440

1982, Apr. 13   **Perf. 12½**
915 A440 30c multicolored   .45 .25

1982 Constitution — A441

1982, Apr. 16   **Perf. 12x12½**
916 A441 30c multicolored   .45 .25

Types of 1979-81 and

18th-19th
Cent.
Artifacts
A442

Parliament
(Library)
A443

Parliament
(West
Block) — A444

Parliament
(East
Block) — A445

Elizabeth II — A446

Designs: 1c, Duck decoy. 2c, Fishing spear. 3c, Stable lantern. 5c, Bucket. 10c, Weathercock. 20c, Ice skates. 37c, Wooden plow. 39c, Settle-bed. 48c, Cradle. 50c, Sleigh. 64c, Wood stove. 68c, Spinning wheel. $1, Glacier National Park. $1.50, Waterton Lakes National Park. $2, Moraine Lake, Banff National Park. $5, Point Pelee National Park.

1982-87   **Litho.**   **Perf. 14x13½**
917 A442 1c multicolored   .25 .25
   a.   Perf. 13x13½ ('85)   .25
918 A442 2c multicolored   .25 .25
   a.   Perf. 13x13½ ('84)   .25
   b.   Bottom margin block of 4, bottom pair imperf, top pair part perf   2,100.
   c.   As "a," printed on gummed side   60.00
919 A442 3c multicolored   .25 .25
   a.   Perf. 13x13½ ('85)   .25
920 A442 5c multicolored   .25 .25
   a.   Perf. 13x13½ ('84)   .25
921 A442 10c multicolored   .25 .25
   a.   Perf. 13x13½ ('85)   .25
922 A442 20c multicolored   .30 .25

The previously listed No. 922 variety with "brown omitted" has been determined to be a normal No. 922 with a color shade or a color changeling.

Photo. & Engr.
Perf. 13x13½
923 A437 30c lt blue, bl, & red   .50 .25
   a.   Bklt. pane of 20, perf. 12x12½   10.00
   b.   Perf. 12x12½   1.40 .45
924 A437 32c beige, red & brn   .50 .25
   a.   Bklt. pane of 25, perf. 12x12½   12.50 13.50
   b.   Perf. 12x12½   1.00 .70
   c.   As #924, beige (and tagging) omitted   900.00

Litho.
Perf. 13½x13
925 A443 34c multicolored   .55 .25
   a.   Booklet pane of 25   13.75
   b.   Perf. 13½x14 ('86)   .75 .25
   c.   Bklt. pane of 25, perf. 13½x14   14.00 16.50

Photo. & Engr.
Perf. 13x13½
926 A446 34c lt bl & int bl   .55 .25
926A A446 36c plum   3.00 2.25

Perf. 13½x13
926B A443 36c multicolored   .55 .25
   c.   Booklet pane of 10 #926Be   5.50
   d.   Booklet pane of 25 #926Be   17.50
   e.   Perf. 13½x14 ('87)   .70 .25
   f.   Left margin block of 4, left vert. pair imperf, right pair part perf   1,500.
   g.   Imperf., horiz. pair   600.00
   h.   All color missing   1,500.

No. 926Bh was caused by an extraneous piece of paper overlaying the pane during printing. Two such panes are recorded, one with two color-missing stamps and the other with 16 color-missing stamps. All adjoining stamps have some to most color missing, and if the panes are broken, the color-missing variety must be left se-tenant with a partially printed stamp.

Litho.   **Perf. 12x12½**
Size A442: 26x20mm
927 A442 37c multi   .55 .25
928 A442 39c multi   .60 .25
929 A442 48c multi   .75 .30
930 A442 50c multi   .75 .25
932 A442 64c multi   .95 .35
933 A442 68c multi   1.10 .35

Litho. & Engr.
Perf. 13½
934 A359a $1 multi   1.50 .50
   a.   Blue inscriptions omitted   900.00
   b.   Imperf., pair   3,000.
935 A359a $1.50 multi   3.25 .55
   a.   Black omitted   2,250.
936 A359a $2 multi   3.25 1.10
   a.   Bluish green inscriptions omitted   1,100.
937 A359a $5 multi   9.00 2.00
    Nos. 917-937 (22)   28.90 10.90

Issued:1c-20c, 10/19; 30c, 5/11; $1.50, 6/18; $5, 1/10/83; 32c, 2/10/83; 37c, 48c, 64c, 4/8/83; $1, 8/15/84; No. 925, $2, 6/21/85; No. 926, 7/12/85; 39c, 50c, 68c, 8/1/85; No. 926B, 3/30/87; No. 926A, 10/1/87.
For former No. 931, see new No. 723C.

Booklet Stamps
Perf. 12x12½ (A437), 12½x12
Engr.
938 A445 1c sage green ('87)   .25 .25
939 A444 2c myrtle grn ('85)   .25 .25
   a.   2c slate green ('89)   .25 .25
940 A437 5c deep claret   .25 .25
941 A445 5c dp brown ('85)   .25 .25
942 A444 6c henna brn ('87)   .25 .25
943 A437 8c dk blue ('83)   .50 .25
944 A437 10c dark green   .45 .25
945 A437 30c red   .75 .30
   a.   Bklt. pane of 4 + 2 labels (2 #940, 944, 945)   1.20 1.40
946 A437 32c brown ('83)   .60 .25
   b.   Bklt. pane of 4 + 2 labels (2 #940, 943, 946)   1.10 1.30
947 A434 34c dp slate bl ('85)   1.15 .70
   a.   Bklt. pane of 6 (3 #939, 2 #941, #947)   1.70 1.25
948 A443 36c dark lil rose ('87)   1.35 .70
   b.   Bklt. pane of 5 + label (2 #938, 2 #942, #948)   2.25 1.40

Issued: No. 940, 10c, 30c, 3/1; 8c, 32c, 2/15/83; No. 941, 30c, 6/21/85; 1c, 6c, 36c, 3/30/87.

Coil Stamps
Engr.   **Perf. 10 Vert.**
950 A437 30c red   .90 .25
   a.   Imperf., pair   325.00
951 A437 32c brown ('83)   .75 .25
   a.   Imperf., pair   160.00

Perf. 10 Horiz.
952 A443 34c dull red brn ('85)   .75 .25
   a.   Imperf., pair   150.00
953 A443 36c dark red ('87)   .75 .25
   a.   Imperf., pair   275.00

Issued: 30c, 5/11; 32c, 2/10/83; 34c, 8/1/85; 36c, 5/19/87.
See Nos. 1080-1083, 1186-1188, 1194-1194A.

Centenary of Salvation Army in Canada
A457

1982, June 25   **Litho.**   **Perf. 13**
954 A457 30c multicolored   .50 .25

Canada Day
A458

Paintings: No. 955, The Highway near Kluana Lake, by A.Y. Jackson. No. 956, Montreal Street Scene, by Adrien Hebert. No. 957, Breakwater, by Christopher Pratt. No. 958, Along Great Slave Lake, by Rene Richard. No. 959, Tea Hill, by Molly Lamb. No. 960, Family and Rainstorm, by Alex Colville. No. 961, Brown Shadows, by Dorothy Knowles. No. 962, The Red Brick House, by David Milne. No. 963, Campus Gates, by Bruno Bobak. No. 964, Prairie Town—Early Morning, by Illingworth Kerr. No. 965, Totems at Ninstints, by Joe Plaskett. No. 966, Doc Snider's House, by Lionel LeMoine FitzGerald.

1982, June 30   **Perf. 12½x12**
955 A458 30c multicolored   .65 .65
956 A458 30c multicolored   .65 .65
957 A458 30c multicolored   .65 .65
958 A458 30c multicolored   .65 .65
959 A458 30c multicolored   .65 .65
960 A458 30c multicolored   .65 .65
961 A458 30c multicolored   .65 .65
962 A458 30c multicolored   .65 .65
963 A458 30c multicolored   .65 .65
964 A458 30c multicolored   .65 .65
965 A458 30c multicolored   .65 .65
966 A458 30c multicolored   .65 .65
   a.   Min. pane of 12, #955-966   8.00 8.00

Regina
Centenary
A459

1982, Aug. 3   **Perf. 13½x13**
967 A459 30c multicolored   .50 .25

Centenary of Royal Canadian Henley Regatta, St. Catharines, Aug. 4-8 — A460

1982, Aug. 4
968 A460 30c multicolored   .50 .25

Fairchild
FC-2W1
A461

No. 970, De Havilland Canada Beaver. No. 971, Noorduyn Norseman. No. 972, Fokker Super Universal.

1982, Oct. 5   **Litho.**   **Perf. 12½**
969 A461 30c shown   .75 .25
970 A461 30c multicolored   .75 .25
   a.   Pair, #969-970   1.50 1.10
971 A461 60c multicolored   1.10 .75
972 A461 60c multicolored   1.10 .75
   a.   Pair, #971-972   2.20 1.75
    Nos. 969-972 (4)   3.70 2.00

Christmas
A462

Designs: Creche figures.

1982, Nov. 3 **Perf. 13½**
973 A462 30c Holy Family .45 .25
a.   All colors except black
    omitted *11,000.*
b.   Printed on gummed side,
    black omitted *11,000.*
974 A462 35c Shepherds .55 .45
975 A462 60c Three Kings .90 .75
    Nos. 973-975 (3) 1.90 1.45

Nos. 973a and 973b are each unique and were caused by a paper foldover.

World
Communications
Year — A463

1983, Mar. 10 Litho. **Perf. 12x12½**
976 A463 32c multicolored .50 .25
a.   Double impression of central
    multicolored globe 750.00

Commonwealth Day — A464

1983, Mar. 14
977 A464 $2 multicolored 9.00 3.75

Scene from
Angeline de
Montbrun, by
Laure Conan
(1845-1924),
Painted by
Rene
Milot — A465

Design: No. 979, Sea Gulls, by Edwin John Pratt (1882-1966), woodcut by Claire Pratt.

1983, Apr. 22 Litho. **Perf. 13½**
978 A465 32c multicolored .50 .25
979 A465 32c multicolored .50 .25
a.   Pair, #978-979 1.00 .90
b.   As "a," all color missing 4,000.

No. 979b resulted from an extraneous piece of paper receiving the colors. After removal, the issued pane shows two horizontal pairs without color plus six other stamps with only partial color.

St. John
Ambulance
Centenary
A466

1983, June 3 **Perf. 13½**
980 A466 32c Emblem .50 .25

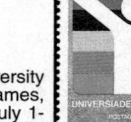

World University
Games,
Edmonton, July 1-
11 — A467

1983, June 28 **Perf. 13½**
981 A467 32c multicolored .50 .25
a.   Printed on gummed side 900.00
982 A467 64c multicolored 1.10 .75

Canada Day — A468

No. 983, Fort Henry, Ontario. No. 984, Fort William, Ontario. No. 985, Fort Rodd Hill, British Columbia. No. 986, Fort Wellington, Ontario. No. 987, Fort Prince of Wales, Manitoba. No. 988, Halifax Citadel, Nova Scotia. No. 989, Fort Chambly, Quebec. No. 990, Fort No. 1, Point Levis, Quebec. No. 991, Fort at Coteau-du-Lac, Quebec. No. 992, Fort Beausejour, New Brunswick. Sizes: Nos. 983, 988: 44x22mm; Nos. 984-985, 989-990, 36x22mm; Nos. 986-987, 991-992, 28x22mm.

Booklet Stamps

1983, June 30 **Perf. 12½x13**
983 A468 32c multicolored .75 .75
984 A468 32c multicolored .75 .75
985 A468 32c multicolored .75 .75
986 A468 32c multicolored .75 .75
987 A468 32c multicolored .75 .75
988 A468 32c multicolored .75 .75
989 A468 32c multicolored .75 .75
990 A468 32c multicolored .75 .75
991 A468 32c multicolored .75 .75
992 A468 32c multicolored .75 .75
a.   Booklet pane of 10, #983-992 7.50 7.50

Scouting
Year — A469

1983, July 6 **Perf. 13½**
993 A469 32c multicolored .50 .25

Church Council
Emblem — A470

1983, July 22 **Litho.**
994 A470 32c tan & green .50 .25

6th World Council of Churches Assembly, Vancouver, July 24-Aug. 10.

Humphrey
Gilbert — A471

1983, Aug. 3 **Litho.**
995 A471 32c multicolored .50 .25

400th anniv. of discovery of Newfoundland by Sir Humphrey Gilbert (1537-1583).

Centenary
of
Discovery
of Nickel,
Sudbury,
Ontario
A472

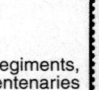

Litho. & Typo.
1983, Aug. 12 **Perf. 13**
996 A472 32c multicolored .55 .25
a.   Silver (and tagging) omitted 675.00

Beware of forgeries of No. 996a. A certificate of authenticity is mandatory.

Josiah Henson (1789-1883),
Preacher — A473

1983, Sept. 16 Litho. **Perf. 13x13½**
997 A473 32c multicolored .50 .25

Antoine
Labelle (1833-
1891), Deputy
Minister for
Settlement
A474

1983, Sept. 16 **Perf. 13½**
998 A474 32c multicolored .50 .25

Locomotives — A475

No. 999, Toronto 4-4-0, 1853. No. 1000, Dorchester 0-4-0, 1836. No. 1001, Samson 0-6-0, 1838. No. 1002, Adam Brown 4-4-0, 1860.

1983, Oct. 3 **Perf. 12½x13**
999 A475 32c multicolored .50 .25
1000 A475 32c multicolored .50 .25
a.   Pair, #999-1000 1.00 .90
1001 A475 37c multicolored .60 .60
1002 A475 64c multicolored 1.10 .90
    Nos. 999-1002 (4) 2.70 2.00

Dalhousie
Law School
Centenary
A476

1983, Oct. 28 **Perf. 13**
1003 A476 32c Arms .50 .25

Christmas
A477

32c, Urban church. 37c, Family going to church. 64c, Rural church.

1983, Nov. 3 **Perf. 13½**
1004 A477 32c multicolored .50 .25
1005 A477 37c multicolored .55 .45
1006 A477 64c multicolored .95 .75
    Nos. 1004-1006 (3) 2.00 1.45

Army Regiments,
Centenaries
A478

19th Cent. Uniforms: No. 1007, Royal Canadian Regiment, British Columbia Regiment. No. 1008, Royal Winnipeg Rifles, Royal Canadian Dragoons.

1983, Nov. 10 **Perf. 13½x13**
1007 A478 32c shown .50 .25
1008 A478 32c multicolored .50 .25
a.   Pair, #1007-1008 1.00 .90

Yellowknife, 50th
Anniv. — A479

1984, Mar. 15 **Perf. 13½**
1009 A479 32c Gold mine .50 .25

50th Anniv.
of Montreal
Symphony
Orchestra
A480

1984, Mar. 24 **Perf. 12½**
1010 A480 32c multicolored .50 .25

450th
Anniv. of
Cartier's
Landing in
Quebec
A481

1984, Apr. 20 **Photo. & Engr.**
1011 A481 32c multicolored .50 .25

See France No. 1923.

Voyage of Tall
Ships, Saint-Malo,
France, to
Quebec
City — A482

1984, May 18 Litho. **Perf. 12x12½**
1012 A482 32c multicolored .50 .25

450th anniv. of Cartier's landing in Quebec.

Canadian Red
Cross Society,
75th
Anniv. — A483

32c, Meritorious Service Medal.

1984, May 28 **Perf. 13**
1013 A483 32c multicolored .50 .25

New Brunswick, Bicentenary A484

1984, June 18 **Photo. & Engr.**
1014 A484 32c Galleys .50 .25

St. Lawrence Seaway, 25th Anniv. — A485

32c, Seaway, Lake Superior.

1984, June 26 **Litho.**
1015 A485 32c multicolored .50 .25

Canada Day A486

Provincial Landscapes by Jean Paul Lemieux (b. 1904): No. 1016, New Brunswick. No. 1017, British Columbia. No. 1018, Yukon Territory. No. 1019, Quebec. No. 1020, Manitoba. No. 1021, Alberta. No. 1022, Prince Edward Island. No. 1023, Saskatchewan. No. 1024, Nova Scotia, vert. No. 1025, Northwest Territories. No. 1026, Newfoundland. No. 1027, Ontario, vert.

1984, June 29
1016 A486 32c multicolored .55 .40
1017 A486 32c multicolored .55 .40
1018 A486 32c multicolored .55 .40
1019 A486 32c multicolored .55 .40
1020 A486 32c multicolored .55 .40
1021 A486 32c multicolored .55 .40
1022 A486 32c multicolored .55 .40
1023 A486 32c multicolored .55 .40
1024 A486 32c multicolored .55 .40
1025 A486 32c multicolored .55 .40
1026 A486 32c multicolored .55 .40
1027 A486 32c multicolored .55 .40
 a. Min. pane of 12, #1016-1027 6.75 6.25

Nos. 1018 and 1025 incorrectly inscribed. No. 1018 shows Northwest Territories landscape; No. 1025, Yukon Territory church.

Loyalists, British Flag (1606-1801) — A487

1984, July 3
1028 A487 32c multicolored .50 .25

United Empire Loyalists, American colonists who remained loyal to British throne and emigrated to Canada during American Revolution.

Roman Catholic Church in Newfoundland A488

32c, St. John's Basilica.

1984, Aug. 17 **Perf. 13½**
1029 A488 32c multicolored .50 .25

Papal Visit A489

1984, Aug. 31 **Perf. 12½**
1030 A489 32c multicolored .50 .25
1031 A489 64c multicolored 1.10 .65

Lighthouses — A490

No. 1032, Louisbourg, 1734. No. 1033, Fisgard, 1860. No. 1034, Ile Verte, 1809. No. 1035, Gibraltar Point, 1808.

1984, Sept. 21
1032 A490 32c multicolored .55 .25
1033 A490 32c multicolored .55 .25
1034 A490 32c multicolored .55 .25
1035 A490 32c multicolored .55 .25
 a. Block of 4, #1032-1035 2.20 1.20

Steam Locomotives — A491

No. 1036, Scotia. No. 1037, Countess of Dufferin. No. 1038, Grand Trunk Class E3. No. 1039, Canadian Pacific D10a.

1984, Oct. 25 **Perf. 12½x13**
1036 A491 32c multicolored .50 .25
1037 A491 32c multicolored .50 .25
 a. Pair, #1036-1037 1.00 .90
1038 A491 37c multicolored .75 .65
1039 A491 64c multicolored 1.30 .90
 a. Souvenir sheet 3.00 3.00
 Nos. 1036-1039 (4) 3.05 2.05

No. 1039a contains Nos. 1036-1039 in changed colors.
See Nos. 1071-1074, 1118-1121.

Christmas A492

Paintings: 32c, The Annunciation, by Jean Dallaire. 37c, The Three Kings, by Simone Mary Bouchard. 64c, Snow in Bethlehem, by David Milne.

1984, Nov. 2 **Perf. 13**
1040 A492 32c multicolored .50 .25
1041 A492 37c multicolored .55 .55
1042 A492 64c multicolored .95 .75
 Nos. 1040-1042 (3) 2.00 1.55

Royal Canadian Air Force — A493

1984, Nov. 9 **Perf. 12x12½**
1043 A493 32c Pilots .50 .25

Cent. of La Presse — A494

32c, Treffle Berthiaume.

1984, Nov. 16 **Perf. 13x13½**
1044 A494 32c multicolored .50 .25

Heart, Arrow, Jeans A495

1985, Feb. 8 **Perf. 12½**
1045 A495 32c multicolored .50 .25

International Youth Year.

Canadians in Space — A496

1985, Mar. 15 **Perf. 13½**
1046 A496 32c Astronaut .55 .25

Therese Casgrain (1896-1981), Suffragist A497

Emily Murphy (1868-1933), Writer A498

1985, Apr. 17
1047 A497 32c multicolored .50 .25
1048 A498 32c multicolored .50 .25
 a. Pair, #1047-1048 1.00 .90

Gabriel Dumont (1837-1906), Metis Leader — A499

1985, May 6 **Perf. 13**
1049 A499 32c multicolored .50 .25

Centenary of the Northwest Rebellion.

Canada Day — A500

No. 1050, Lower Ft. Garry, Manitoba. No. 1051, Ft. Anne, Nova Scotia. No. 1052, Ft. York, Ontario. No. 1053, Castle Hill, Newfoundland. No. 1054, Ft. Whoop Up, Alberta. No. 1055, Ft. Erie, Ontario. No. 1056, Ft. Walsh, Saskatchewan. No. 1057, Ft. Lennox,

Quebec. No. 1058, York Redoubt, Nova Scotia. No. 1059, Ft. Frederick, Ontario.
Sizes: Nos. 1050, 1055: 48x26mm. Nos. 1051-1052, 1056-1057: 40x26mm. Nos. 1053-1054, 1058-1059, 32x26mm.

Booklet Stamps

1985, June 28 **Perf. 12½x13**
1050 A500 34c multicolored .95 .65
1051 A500 34c multicolored .95 .65
1052 A500 34c multicolored .95 .65
1053 A500 34c multicolored .95 .65
1054 A500 34c multicolored .95 .65
1055 A500 34c multicolored .95 .65
1056 A500 34c multicolored .95 .65
1057 A500 34c multicolored .95 .65
1058 A500 34c multicolored .95 .65
1059 A500 34c multicolored .95 .65
 a. Bkt. pane of 10, #1050-1059 9.50 12.50

Intl. Pharmaceutical Federation Congress — A501

Design: Louis Hebert (1575-1627), 1st French Apothecary in North America.

1985, Aug. 30 **Perf. 12½**
1060 A501 34c multicolored .50 .25

Interparliamentary Union '85, Ottawa — A502

1985, Sept. 3 **Perf. 13½**
1061 A502 34c multicolored .50 .25

Guide, Brownie Saluting — A503

1985, Sept. 12 **Photo.** **Perf. 13½x13**
1062 A503 34c multicolored .50 .25

Natl. Girl Guides movement, cent.

Lighthouses A504

1985, Oct. 3 **Litho.** **Perf. 13½**
1063 A504 34c Sisters Islets .70 .25
1064 A504 34c Pelee Passage .70 .25
1065 A504 34c Haut-fond Prince .70 .25
1066 A504 34c Rose Blanche .70 .25
 a. Block of 4, #1063-1066 2.80 2.50
 b. Souv. sheet of 4, #1063-1066 4.50 4.50

Santa Claus Parade A505

Paintings by Barbara Carroll: 34c, Santa Claus. 39c, Horse-drawn coach. 68c, Christmas tree. No. 1070, 32c, Polar float.

1985, Oct. 23
1067	A505	34c multicolored	.50	.25
1068	A505	39c multicolored	.60	.55
1069	A505	68c multicolored	1.25	.90

Perf. 13½ on 3 Sides
1070	A505	32c multicolored	1.10	.50
a.		Booklet pane of 10	11.00	10.00
		Nos. 1067-1070 (4)	3.45	2.20

No. 1070 printed in booklets only.

Locomotives Type of 1984

No. 1071, Grand Trunk K2. No. 1072, Canadian Pacific P2a. No. 1073, Canadian Northern O10a. No. 1074, Canadian Govt. Railways H4D.

1985, Nov. 7 *Perf. 12½x13*
1071	A491	34c multicolored	.75	.25
1072	A491	34c multicolored	.75	.25
a.		Pair, #1071-1072	1.50	1.10
1073	A491	39c multicolored	.75	.70
1074	A491	68c multicolored	1.30	1.00
		Nos. 1071-1074 (4)	3.55	2.20

1910 Gunner's Mate, World War II Officer, 1985 Woman Recruit — A507

1985, Nov. 8 *Perf. 13½x13*
1075	A507	34c multicolored	.50	.25

Royal Canadian Navy, 75th anniv.

Old Holton House, Sherbrooke Street, Montreal, by James Wilson Morrice (1865-1924) A508

1985, Nov. 15 *Perf. 13½*
1076	A508	34c multicolored	.50	.25

Montreal Museum of Fine Arts, 120th anniv.

Southwestern Alberta, Computer Design Map — A509

1986, Feb. 13 Litho. *Perf. 12½x13*
1077	A509	34c multicolored	.50	.25

1988 Winter Olympics, Calgary, Alberta, Feb. 13-28.

EXPO '86, Vancouver, May 2-Oct. 13 — A510

1986, Mar. 7 Photo. & Engr.
1078	A510	34c Canada Pavilion	.50	.25
1079	A510	39c Communications	.65	.55

Artifacts Type of 1982

Designs: 25c Butter stamp. 42c, Linen chest. 55c, Iron kettle. 72c, Hand-drawn cart.

1987, May 6 Litho. *Perf. 14x13½*
1080	A442	25c multicolored	.55	.30

Size: 20x26mm
Perf. 12x12½
1081	A442	42c multicolored	1.10	.25
1082	A442	55c multicolored	1.40	.30
1083	A442	72c multicolored	1.70	.35
a.		Imperf., pair	900.00	
		Nos. 1080-1083 (4)	4.75	1.20

Park Type of 1979

Design: La Mauricie National Park.

Litho. & Engr.
1986, Mar. 14 *Perf. 13½*
1084	A359a	$5 multi	9.00	2.00
a.		Dark blue inscriptions omitted	2,500.	1,500.

No. 1084a is valued in the grade of fine as all known examples are centered thus.

Philippe Aubert de Gaspe (1786-1871), Novelist A511

Molly Brant (1736-1796), Iroquois Leader and Loyalist A512

1986, Apr. 14 Litho. *Perf. 12½*
1090	A511	34c multicolored	.50	.25

Perf. 13½
1091	A512	34c multicolored	.50	.25

EXPO '86 — A513

34c, Expo Center, Vancouver. 68c, Transportation, horiz.

Photo. & Engr.
1986, Apr. 28 *Perf. 13x13½*
1092	A513	34c multicolored	.50	.25
1093	A513	68c multicolored	1.10	.70

Canadian Forces Postal Service, 75th Anniv. A514

1986, May 9 Litho. *Perf. 13½*
1094	A514	34c multicolored	.50	.25

Indigenous Birds — A515

1986, May 22
1095	A515	34c Great blue heron	.70	.30
1096	A515	34c Snow goose	.70	.30
1097	A515	34c Great horned owl	.70	.30
1098	A515	34c Spruce grouse	.70	.30
a.		Block of 4, #1095-1098	2.80	2.50

19th Intl. Ornithological Congress, Ottawa, June 22-29.

Canada Day — A516

Invention blueprints: No. 1099, Rotary snowplow, 1869. No. 1100, Canadarm, 1986. No. 1101, Anti-gravity flight suit, 1938. No. 1102, Variable pitch propeller, 1923.

1986, June 27
1099	A516	34c multicolored	.75	.25
1100	A516	34c multicolored	.75	.25
1101	A516	34c multicolored	.75	.25
1102	A516	34c multicolored	.75	.25
a.		Block of 4, #1099-1102	3.00	2.50

Canadian Broadcasting Corp., 50th Anniv. — A517

1986, July 23 *Perf. 12½*
1103	A517	34c Emblem, map	.50	.25

Exploration of Canada A518

No. 1104, Siberian Indians discover and inhabit America, 10,000 B.C. No. 1105, Viking settlement, A.D. 1000. No. 1106, John Cabot lands, 1498. No. 1107, Henry Hudson pioneers Hudson Strait and Bay, 1610.

1986, Aug. 29 *Perf. 12½x13*
1104	A518	34c multicolored	.55	.30
1105	A518	34c multicolored	.55	.30
1106	A518	34c multicolored	.55	.30
1107	A518	34c multicolored	.55	.30
a.		Block of 4, #1104-1107	2.20	2.00
b.		Souv. sheet of 4, #1104-1107	3.00	3.00

No. 1107b issued Oct. 1 for CAPEX '87.
See Nos. 1126-1129, 1199-1202, 1233-1236.

Peacemakers of the Frontier, 1870s — A519

Designs: No. 1108, Crowfoot (1830-1890), Blackfoot Indian chief. No. 1109, James F. Macleod (1836-1894), asst. commissioner of Northwest Mounted Police.

1986, Sept. 5 *Perf. 13x13½*
1108	A519	34c scar, gray & ind	.50	.25
1109	A519	34c ind, gray & scar	.50	.25
a.		Pair, #1108-1109	1.00	.90

Intl. Peace Year — A520

Litho. & Embossed
1986, Sept. 16 *Perf. 13½*
1110	A520	34c multicolored	.50	.25

1988 Calgary Winter Olympics — A521

1986, Oct. 15 *Perf. 13½x13*
1111	A521	34c Ice hockey	.50	.25
1112	A521	34c Biathlon	.50	.25
a.		Pair, #1111-1112	1.00	.90

See Nos. 1130-1131, 1152-1153, 1195-1198.

Christmas Angels — A522

1986, Oct. 29 *Perf. 12½*
1113	A522	34c multicolored	.50	.25
1114	A522	39c multicolored	.65	.55
1115	A522	68c multicolored	1.10	.80

Booklet Stamps
Size: 72x26mm
Perf. 13½ Horiz.
1116	A522	29c multicolored	1.40	1.10
a.		Booklet pane of 10	14.00	13.00
b.		Perf. 12½ horiz.	6.00	2.25
c.		Bklt. pane of 10, #1116b	60.00	52.50
		Nos. 1113-1116 (4)	3.65	2.70

No. 1116 has bar code at left, for use on covers with printed postal code matrix.

John Molson (1763-1836), Entrepreneur — A523

1986, Nov. 4
1117	A523	34c multicolored	.50	.25

Locomotives Type of 1984

Locomotives, 1925-1945.

1986, Nov. 21 *Perf. 12½x13*
1118	A491	34c CN V1a	.75	.30
1119	A491	34c CP T1a	.75	.30
a.		Pair, #1118-1119	1.50	1.10
1120	A491	39c CN U2a	.90	.75
1121	A491	68c CP H1c	1.30	1.10
		Nos. 1118-1121 (4)	3.70	2.45

CAPEX '87 — A524

34c, 1st Toronto P.O. 36c, Nelson-Miramichi P.O. 42c, Saint Ours P.O. 72c, Battleford P.O.

1987 Litho. & Engr. *Perf. 13x13½*
1122	A524	34c multicolored	.50	.25
1123	A524	36c multicolored	.55	.25
1124	A524	42c multicolored	.75	.65
1125	A524	72c multicolored	1.30	1.10
		Nos. 1122-1125 (4)	3.10	2.25

Souvenir Sheet
Yellow Green Inscription
1125A		Sheet of 4	3.00	3.00
b.	A524	36c like #1122	.60	.60
c.	A524	36c like #1123	.60	.60
d.	A524	42c like #1124	.70	.70
e.	A524	72c like #1125	1.10	1.10

Issue dates: 34c, Feb. 16; others, June 12.

Exploration Type of 1986

Pioneers of New France: No. 1126, Etienne Brule (c. 1592-1633), 1st European to see the Great Lakes. No. 1127, Pierre Esprit Radisson (c. 1636-1710) & Medard Chouart des Groseilliers 1625-98), British expedition to Hudson Bay, 1668. No. 1128, Louis Jolliet (1645-1700)

& Fr. Jacques Marquette (1637-75) discovering the Mississippi River, 1673. No. 1129, Recollet wilderness mission, 1615.

1987, Mar. 13   Litho.   Perf. 12½x13

1126	A518	34c multicolored	.55	.30
1127	A518	34c multicolored	.55	.30
1128	A518	34c multicolored	.55	.30
1129	A518	34c multicolored	.55	.30
a.		Block of 4, #1126-1129	2.20	2.00

Olympics Type of 1986

1987, Apr. 3   Perf. 13½x13

1130	A521	36c Speed skating	.55	.25
1131	A521	42c Bobsledding	.75	.65

Volunteers Week — A525

1987, Apr. 13   Perf. 12½x13

1132	A525	36c multicolored	.55	.25

Law Day — A526

1987, Apr. 15   Perf. 14x13½

1133	A526	36c Coat of arms	.55	.25
a.		Imperf, pair	1,500.	

Canadian Charter of Rights and Freedoms, 5th anniv.

Engineering Institute of Canada, Cent. — A527

1987, May 19   Perf. 12½x13

1134	A527	36c multicolored	.55	.25

Canada Day — A528

Inventors & communications innovations: No. 1135, Reginald Aubrey Fessenden (1866-1932), AM radio, 1900. No. 1136, Charles Fenerty, newsprint, 1838. No. 1137, Georges-Edouard Desbarats and William Leggo, halftone engraving, 1869. No. 1138, Frederick Newton Gisborne, No. America's 1st undersea cable, 1852, New Brunswick-Prince Edward Island.

1987, June 25   Perf. 13½

1135	A528	36c multicolored	.60	.30
1136	A528	36c multicolored	.60	.30
1137	A528	36c multicolored	.60	.30
1138	A528	36c multicolored	.60	.30
a.		Block of 4, #1135-1138	2.40	2.20

Steamships A529

No. 1139, Segwun, 1887. No. 1140, Princess Marguerite, 1948.

1987, July 20   Perf. 13½x13

1139	A529	36c multicolored	.55	.30

51x22mm

1140	A529	36c multicolored	.55	.30
a.		Pair, #1139-1140	1.10	1.00

Shipwrecks A530

No. 1141, Hamilton & Scourge, 1813. No. 1142, San Juan, 1565. No. 1143, Breadalbane, 1853. No. 1144, Ericsson, 1892.

1987, Aug. 7

1141	A530	36c multicolored	.55	.30
1142	A530	36c multicolored	.55	.30
1143	A530	36c multicolored	.55	.30
1144	A530	36c multicolored	.55	.30
a.		Block of 4, #1141-1144	2.20	2.00

Air Canada, 50th Anniv. — A531

1987, Sept. 1   Perf. 13½

1145	A531	36c multicolored	.55	.25

2nd Intl. Francophone Summit, Quebec, 9/2-4 — A532

1987, Sept. 2   Perf. 13x12½

1146	A532	36c multicolored	.55	.25

9th Commonwealth Meeting, Vancouver, Oct. 13-17 — A533

1987, Oct. 13

1147	A533	36c multicolored	.55	.25

Christmas A534

36c, Poinsettia. 42c, Holly wreath. 72c, Mistletoe, Christmas tree. 31c, Gifts, Christmas tree.

1987, Nov. 2   Litho.   Perf. 13½

1148	A534	36c multicolored	.55	.25
1149	A534	42c multicolored	.75	.65
1150	A534	72c multicolored	1.20	.90

Size: 39x25mm

1151	A534	31c multicolored	.75	.75
a.		Booklet pane of 10	7.50	10.00
b.		Imperf. btwn., pair, from miscut bklt. pane	2,600.	
		Nos. 1148-1151 (4)	3.25	2.55

No. 1151 has bar code at left, for use on covers with printed postal code matrix. Issued in booklets only.

Olympics Type of 1986

No. 1152, Cross-country skiing. No. 1153, Ski jumping.

1987, Nov. 13   Perf. 13½x13

1152	A521	36c multicolored	.55	.25
1153	A521	36c multicolored	.55	.25
a.		Pair, #1152-1153	1.10	.90

75th Grey Cup, Vancouver, Nov. 29 — A535

1987, Nov. 20   Perf. 12½

1154	A535	36c multicolored	.55	.25

Types of 1982 and

Queen Elizabeth II A536

Mammals A538

Parliament (Center Block)
A537   A539

Architecture — A540

Flag and Clouds A541

Flag A542

Natl. Flag, Deciduous Forest A543

Flag and Mountains A544

Designs: No. 1155, Flying squirrel. 2c, Prickly porcupine. 3c, Muskrat. No. 1158, Varying hare. No. 1159, Red fox. 10c, Skunk. 25c, Beaver. 43c, Lynx. 44c, Walrus. 45c, Pronghorn. 46c, Wolverine. 57c, Killer whale. 59c, Musk-ox. 61c, Timber wolf. 63c, Harbor porpoise. 74c, Wapiti. 76c, Grizzly bear. 78c, Beluga whale. 80c, Peary caribou. $1, Runnymede Library, Toronto. $2, McAdam Railway Station, New Brunswick. $5, Bonsecours Market, Montreal. No. 1192, Flag and field. No. 1193, Flag and seacoast.

Sizes Vary on A536, A538

1987-91   Litho.   Perf. 13½x13½

1155	A538	1c multicolored	.25	.25
a.		Perf. 13x12½	4.00	.85
b.		Imperf, pair	750.00	
1156	A538	2c multicolored	.25	.25
a.		Imperf, pair	750.00	
1157	A538	3c multicolored	.25	.25
a.		Imperf, pair	900.00	
1158	A538	5c multicolored	.25	.25
a.		Imperf, pair	1,500.	
1159	A538	6c multicolored	.25	.25
a.		Horiz. pair, imperf	2,250.	
1160	A538	10c multicolored	.25	.25
a.		Perf. 13x12½	6.00	.40
b.		Imperf., pair	750.00	
1161	A538	25c multicolored	.40	.25

Perf. 13½x13

1162	A536	37c multicolored	.75	.25
1163	A537	37c multicolored	.75	.25
a.		Bklt. pane of 10, #1163c	7.50	7.50
b.		Bklt. pane of 25, #1163c	19.00	17.50
c.		Perf. 13½x14	1.40	.40

Perf. 13x12½

1164	A536	38c multicolored	.75	.25
a.		Perf. 13x13½	.75	.35
b.		As "a," bklt. pane of 10 + 2 labels	7.50	7.00
c.		Vert. block of 10, middle pair imperf, 2nd and 4th pairs part perf	1,050.	
d.		As "a," horiz. pair, imperf btwn.	900.00	
e.		Bottom margin horiz. pair, imperf	—	

Perf. 13x13½ on 3 or 4 Sides

1165	A539	38c multicolored	.75	.25
a.		Bklt. pane of 10 + 2 labels	7.50	7.50
b.		Bklt. pane of 25 + 2 labels	19.00	19.00
c.		Printed on gummed side	90.00	
d.		Double impression of all litho colors except black	225.00	

Perf. 13½x13

1166	A541	39c multicolored	.75	.25
a.		Bklt. pane of 10 + 2 labels	7.50	
b.		Bklt. pane of 25 + 2 labels	19.00	
c.		Perf. 12½x13	18.00	.75
d.		Imperf, pair	575.00	

Perf. 13x13½

1167	A536	39c multicolored	.75	.25
a.		Bklt. pane of 10 + 2 labels	7.50	7.50
b.		Perf. 13	15.00	.85
c.		Imperf, pair	500.00	
d.		Horiz. pair, imperf btwn.	325.00	
1168	A536	40c multicolored	.75	.25
a.		Bklt. pane of 10 + 2 labels	7.50	7.00

Perf. 13½x13

1169	A544	40c multicolored	.75	.25
a.		Bklt. pane of 25 + 2 labels	25.00	
b.		Bklt. pane of 10 + 2 labels	7.50	

Perf. 12x12½

1170	A538	43c multicolored	1.10	.40

Perf. 14½x14

1171	A538	44c multicolored	1.40	.25
a.		Perf. 12½x13	2.75	1.75
b.		As "a," bklt. pane of 5 + label	12.50	11.50
c.		Perf. 13½x13	425.00	425.00
1172	A538	45c multicolored	.90	.25
b.		As "f," bklt. pane of 5 + label	13.00	14.00
d.		Perf. 13	20.00	1.20
f.		Perf. 12½x13	2.60	.50
h.		Imperf., pair	800.00	

Perf. 13

1172A	A538	46c multicolored	.90	.25
c.		Perf. 12½x13	1.25	.50
e.		As "c," bklt. pane of 5 + label	6.25	5.50
g.		Perf. 14½x14	5.25	.40

Perf. 12x12½

1173	A538	57c multicolored	1.10	.35

Perf. 14½x14

1174	A538	59c multicolored	1.20	.30
a.		Perf. 13	10.00	2.50
1175	A538	61c multicolored	1.20	.35
a.		Perf. 13	80.00	6.50
1176	A538	63c multicolored	3.00	.40
a.		Perf. 13	6.50	3.00

Perf. 12x12½

1177	A538	74c multicolored	1.90	.75

Perf. 14½x14

1178	A538	76c multicolored	1.90	.75
a.		Perf. 12½x13	3.00	2.50
b.		As "a," bklt. pane of 5 + label	15.00	15.00
c.		Perf. 13	37.50	14.00
1179	A538	78c multicolored	2.20	.75
a.		As "c," bklt. pane of 5	15.00	15.00
b.		Perf. 13	35.00	6.00
c.		Perf. 12½x13	3.50	2.00
d.		Imperf, pair	900.00	

Perf. 13

1180	A538	80c multicolored	1.80	.75
a.		Perf. 12½x13	3.00	1.10
b.		As "a," bklt. pane of 5 + label	15.00	15.00
c.		Perf. 14½x14	5.50	2.25
d.		Imperf, pair	1,100.	

Perf. 13½
Litho. & Engr.

1181	A540	$1 multicolored	1.50	.55
a.		Engr. inscriptions inverted	13,000.	
b.		Imperf., pair	1,250.	
1182	A540	$2 multicolored	3.75	1.00
		Imperf., pair	850.00	
b.		Vert. strip of 5, stamps 3 and 4 imperf vert., horiz. imperf btwn. stamps 2 and 3, and btwn. stamps 3 and 4	1,500.	
1183	A540	$5 multicolored	7.50	2.25
		Vert. strip of 5, top stamp imperf on 3 sides, stamp 4 imperf at top and sides	2,600.	
		Nos. 1155-1183 (30)	39.25	13.10

A later printing of No. 1182 has more intense and clearly defined green shading on the roofline and the deep orange background extends closer to the roofline.

Imperfs exist of Nos. 1155-1157 and 1160, from printer's waste.

Issued: 1c, 2c, 3c, 5c, 6c, 10c, 25c, 10/3/88; 37c, 12/30/87; 38c, 12/29/88; 43c, 57c, 74c, 1/18/88; 44c, 59c, 76c, 1/18/89; $1, $2, 5/5/89; No. 1166, 12/28/89; 45c, 61c, 78c, No. 1167, 1/12/90; $5, 5/28/90; 40c, 46c, 63c, 80c, 12/28/90.

Booklet Stamps
Perf. 13½x14 on 3 Sides
Litho.

1184	A542	1c multicolored	.25	.25
a.		Perf. 12½x13	11.00	11.00
1185	A542	5c multicolored	.25	.25
a.		Perf. 12½x13	7.50	7.50

Perf. 12½x12 on 2 or 3 sides
Engr.

1186	A445	6c dark purple	.70	.30
1187	A443	37c dark blue	.90	.70
a.		Bklt. pane of 4 + 2 labels (#938, 2 #942, #1187)	1.40	1.40
1188	A443	38c dark blue	.90	.40
a.		Bklt. pane of 5 (3 #939a, #1186, #1188)	1.40	1.40

Perf. 13½x14 on 3 Sides
Litho.

1189	A542	39c multicolored	.90	.40
a.		Bklt. pane of 4 (#1184, 2 #1185, #1189)	1.65	.65
b.		Perf. 12½x13	12.00	12.00
c.		Bklt. pane of 4 (#1184a, 2 #1185a, 1189b)	37.50	37.50
1190	A542	40c multicolored	1.50	.55
a.		Bklt. pane of 4 (#1184, #1185, #1190)	2.40	1.20
b.		As "a," imperf	1,400.	

Nos. 1190a, 1190c sold for 50c.

Issued: No. 1187, 2/3/88; No. 1188, 1/18/89; No. 1186, 1989; Nos. 1184-1185, 1189, 1/12/90; No. 1190, 12/28/90.

Self-Adhesives
Die Cut
Booklet Stamps

1191	A543	38c multicolored	1.50	.75
a.		Booklet of 12	18.00	
b.		Blue omitted	1,900.	
c.		Yellow omitted	900.00	
1192	A543	39c multicolored	1.40	.75
a.		Booklet of 12	17.00	
1193	A543	40c multicolored	1.40	.75
a.		Booklet of 12	17.00	

Issued: 38c, 6/30/89; 39c, 2/8/90; 40c, 1/11/91.

Issued on peelable paper backing serving as booklet cover. Nos. 1191a, 1192a sold for $5, No. 1193a for $5.25.

Coil Stamps
Perf. 10 Horiz.
Engr.

1194	A443	37c dark blue	.75	.25
d.		Imperf., pair	170.00	
1194A	A443	38c dark green	1.10	.25
e.		Imperf., pair	375.00	
1194B	A542	39c violet	.75	.25
f.		Imperf., pair	150.00	
1194C	A542	40c blue gray	.75	.25
g.		Imperf., pair	275.00	
h.		All color omitted (tagged)	400.00	

Issued: 37c, 2/22/88; 38c, 2/1/89; 39c, 2/8/90; 40c, 12/28/90.

No. 1194Ch must be collected in a pair with normal or misperfed stamp or (more often) in a strip of four with a pair of normal (or misperfed) stamps and a pair of the color-omitted stamps.

See Nos. 1356-1362, 1375-1376, 1388, 1394-1396, 1682-1683, 1687, 1695, 1698.

Olympics Type of 1986

1988, Feb. 12   Litho.   Perf. 12x12½

1195	A521	37c Alpine skiing	.60	.25
1196	A521	37c Curling	.60	.25
a.		Pair, #1195-1196	1.20	.90
1197	A521	43c Figure skating	.65	.65
1198	A521	74c Luge	1.20	.90
		Nos. 1195-1198 (4)	3.05	2.05

Exploration Type of 1986

18th Cent. explorers of the western territories: No. 1199, Anthony Henday, who traveled the Prairies in 1754 from the Hayes River to Red Deer, Alberta. No. 1200, George Vancouver (1757-1798), who circumnavigated Vancouver Is. and explored the Pacific Coast, 1792-94. No. 1201, Simon Fraser (1776-1862), fur trader who discovered and navigated the Fraser River. No. 1202, John Palliser (1807-1887), geographer who determined the topographical boundary between Canada and the US from Lake Superior to the Pacific Coast.

1988, Mar. 17   Litho.   Perf. 12½x13

1199	A518	37c multicolored	.55	.35
1200	A518	37c multicolored	.55	.35
1201	A518	37c multicolored	.55	.35
1202	A518	37c multicolored	.55	.35
a.		Block of 4, #1199-1202	2.20	2.00

The Young Reader, by Ozias Leduc A546

Photo. & Engr. with Foil Application
1988, May 20   Perf. 13x13½

1203	A546	50c multicolored	1.10	.90

Masterpieces of Canadian art. Printed in sheets of 16.

See Nos. 1241, 1271, 1310, 1419, 1466, 1516, 1545, 1602, 1635, 1754, 1800, 1863, 1916, 1945.

Wildlife and Habitat Conservation A547

1988, June 1   Litho.   Perf. 13x13½

1204	A547	37c Duck landing	.55	.35
1205	A547	37c Moose at water hole	.55	.35
a.		Pair, #1204-1205	1.10	.90

Grey Owl, born Archibald Belaney, (b. 1888), conservationist; Ducks Unlimited Canada, 50th anniv.

Science and Technology — A548

Inventions: No. 1206, Kerosene, invented by Abraham Gesner (1797-1864), patented in 1854. No. 1207, Marquis wheat, developed in 1908 by Charles Saunders. No. 1208, Electron microscope, developed in 1938 at the University of Toronto by James Hillier and Albert Prebus under the supervision of Eli Burton. No. 1209, Cobalt cancer therapy, introduced by Dr. Harold Johns and Atomic Energy of Canada, Ltd., in 1951.

1988, June 17   Perf. 12½x13

1206	A548	37c multicolored	.55	.30
1207	A548	37c multicolored	.55	.30
1208	A548	37c multicolored	.55	.30
1209	A548	37c multicolored	.55	.30
a.		Block of 4, #1206-1209	2.20	2.00

Intl. Entomology Congress, Vancouver A549

No. 1210, Short-tailed swallowtail. No. 1211, Northern blue. No. 1212, Macoun's Arctic. No. 1213, Canadian tiger swallowtail.

1988, July 4   Perf. 12

1210	A549	37c multicolored	.55	.35
1211	A549	37c multicolored	.55	.35
1212	A549	37c multicolored	.55	.35
1213	A549	37c multicolored	.55	.35
a.		Block of 4, #1210-1213	2.20	1.80

St. John's, Newfoundland, Cent. of Incorporation — A550

37c, Harbor entrance, skyline.

1988, July 22   Perf. 13½x13

1214	A550	37c multicolored	.55	.25

Canadian 4-H Council, 75th Anniv. A551

37c, Motto, farm, young scientists.

1988, Aug. 5

1215	A551	37c multicolored	.55	.25

Les Forges Du St. Maurice (1738-1883), Canada's 1st Industrial Complex — A552

Litho. & Engr.
1988, Aug. 19   Perf. 13½

1216	A552	37c multicolored	.55	.25

Canadian Kennel Club, Cent. A553

No. 1217, Tahltan bear dog. No. 1218, Nova Scotia duck-tolling retriever. No. 1219, Canadian Eskimo dog. No. 1220, Newfoundland.

1988, Aug. 26   Perf. 12½x12

1217	A553	37c multicolored	.90	.40
1218	A553	37c multicolored	.90	.40
1219	A553	37c multicolored	.90	.40
1220	A553	37c multicolored	.90	.40
a.		Block of 4, #1217-1220	3.60	2.75

A554

1988, Sept. 14   Litho.   Perf. 13½x13

1221	A554	37c multicolored	.55	.25

Sesquicentennial of the 1st baseball game played in Canada, June 4, 1838 at Beachville, Upper Canada.

A555

Christmas (Icons of the Eastern Church): 32c, Nativity. 37c, Conception. 43c, Virgin and Child. 74c, Virgin and Child, diff.

1988, Oct. 27   Perf. 13½

1222	A555	37c multicolored	.60	.25
1223	A555	43c multicolored	.75	.65
1224	A555	74c multicolored	1.50	.45

Booklet Stamp
Size: 35½x21mm
Perf. 12½x13½

1225	A555	32c multicolored	.90	.75
a.		Booklet pane of 10	9.00	9.00
		Nos. 1222-1225 (4)	3.75	2.55

Millennium of Christianity in the Ukraine. No. 1225 has bar code at left; for use on covers with printed postal code matrix.

Inglis and Anglican Church A556

1988, Nov. 1   Perf. 12½x12

1226	A556	37c multicolored	.55	.25

Charles Inglis (1734-1816), Canada's 1st Anglican bishop and founder of the Kings-Edgehill School, Nova Scotia, and the University of King's College at Halifax, bicent.

Hopkins and *Canoe Manned by Voyageurs* A557

1988, Nov. 18   Perf. 13½x13

1227	A557	37c multicolored	.55	.25

Frances Ann Hopkins (1838-1918), painter.

The Bluenose and Capt. Walters — A558

1988, Nov. 18   Perf. 13½

1228	A558	37c multicolored	.60	.25

Angus Walters (1882-1968), mariner.

Small Craft
A559

1989, Feb. 1   Perf. 13½x13
1229 A559 38c Chipewyan canoe   .55   .35
1230 A559 38c Haida canoe   .55   .35
1231 A559 38c Inuit kayak   .55   .35
1232 A559 38c Micmac canoe   .55   .35
a.   Block of 4, #1229-1232   2.20 2.00

See Nos. 1266-1269, 1317-1320.

Exploration Type of 1986

Explorers of the North: No. 1233, Matonab-bee (c. 1737-1782), Indian guide who led 1st overland European expedition to the Arctic Ocean. No. 1234, Relics of expedition led by Sir John Franklin (1786-1847) that proved the existence of the Northwest Passage. No. 1235, Relics of the discovery of the Alberta fossil bed by geologist Joseph Burr Tyrrell (1858-1957). No. 1236, Vilhjalmur Stefansson (1879-1962), American ethnologist who discovered the last uncharted islands in the Arctic Archipelago.

1989, Mar. 22   Perf. 12½x13
1233 A518 38c multicolored   .55   .35
1234 A518 38c multicolored   .55   .35
1235 A518 38c multicolored   .55   .35
1236 A518 38c multicolored   .55   .35
a.   Block of 4, #1233-1236   2.20 2.00

Photography in Canada,
Sesquicentennial — A560

Photographers and their work: No. 1237, William Notman (1826-1891). No. 1238, W. Hanson Boorne (1859-1945). No. 1239, Alexander Henderson (1831-1913). No. 1240, Jules-Ernest Livernois (1851-1933).

1989, June 23   Perf. 12½x12
1237 A560 38c multicolored   .55   .35
1238 A560 38c multicolored   .55   .35
1239 A560 38c multicolored   .55   .35
1240 A560 38c multicolored   .55   .35
a.   Block of 4, #1237-1240   2.20 2.00

Art Type of 1988

Ceremonial Frontlet (headpiece) Worn by Tsimshian Indian Chiefs, Early 20th Cent.

Litho. with Foil Application
1989, June 29   Perf. 12½x13
1241 A546 50c multicolored   1.10   .90

Masterpieces of Canadian Art and opening of the Museum of Civilization.

Poets — A562

No. 1243, Louis Frechette (1839-1908). No. 1244, Archibald Lampman (1861-1899).

1989, July 7   Litho.   Perf. 13½
1243 A562 38c multicolored   .55   .35
1244 A562 38c multicolored   .55   .35
a.   Pair, #1243-1244   1.10   .90

Mushrooms
A563

No. 1245, Clavulinopsis fusiformis. No. 1246, Boletus mirabilis. No. 1247, Cantharellus cinnabarinus. No. 1248, Morchella esculenta.

1989, Aug. 4
1245 A563 38c multicolored   .55   .35
1246 A563 38c multicolored   .55   .35
1247 A563 38c multicolored   .55   .35
1248 A563 38c multicolored   .55   .35
a.   Block of 4, #1245-1248   2.20 2.00

Infantry
Regiments,
75th
Anniv.
A564

No. 1249, Princess Patricia's Canadian Light Infantry. No. 1250, Royal 22nd Regiment.

Litho. & Engr.
1989, Sept. 8   Perf. 13
1249 A564 38c multicolored   .75   .40
1250 A564 38c multicolored   .75   .40
a.   Pair, #1249-1250   1.50 1.25

Intl. Trade
A565

1989, Oct. 2   Litho.   Perf. 13½x13
1251 A565 38c multicolored   .55   .25

Performing
Arts — A566

No. 1252, Dancers. No. 1253, Musicians. No. 1254, Camera, director. No. 1255, Youth and adult entertainers.

1989, Oct. 4   Perf. 13x13½
1252 A566 38c multicolored   .55   .35
1253 A566 38c multicolored   .55   .35
1254 A566 38c multicolored   .55   .35
1255 A566 38c multicolored   .55   .35
a.   Block of 4, #1252-1255   2.20 1.80

Royal Winnipeg Ballet 50th anniv. (No. 1252), Vancouver Opera 30th anniv. (No. 1253), Natl. Film Board 50th anniv. (No. 1254), and Confederation Center of the Arts, Charlottetown, P.E.I., 25th anniv. (No. 1255).

A566a

A567

Winter landscapes: 33c, *Champ-de-Mars, Winter*, 1892, by William Brymner (1855-1925). 38c, *Bend in the Gosselin River, Arthabaska*, c. 1906, by Marc-Aurele de Foy Suzor-Cote (1869-1937). 44c, *Snow II*, 1915, by Lawren S. Harris (1885-1970). 76c, *Ste. Agnes*, c. 1925-30, by Albert H. Robinson (1881-1956). Nos. 1256-1258 vert.

1989, Oct. 26
Size of 44c, 76c: 25x31mm
1256 A566a 38c multi   .55   .25
a.   Bkt. pane of 10, #1256b 45.00 45.00
b.   Perf. 13x12½   4.50 4.50
           Perf. 13½
1257 A566a 44c multi   .75   .60
a.   Booklet pane of 5 + label 15.00 15.00
1258 A566a 76c multi   1.30   .90
a.   Booklet pane of 5 + label 27.50 27.50

Booklet Stamp
Size: 35x21mm
Perf. 12½x13½
1259 A567 33c shown   1.50 1.50
a.   Booklet pane of 10   15.00
b.   Horiz. pair, imperf btwn. 2,250.
c.   As "a," imperf. vert. between 11,000.
     Nos. 1256-1259 (4)   4.10 3.25

Christmas. No. 1259 has bar code at left; for use on covers with printed postal code matrix. Booklet panes separate easily.

Declaration of War, 1939 — A568

Political and military actions taken by Canada at the outbreak of World War II: No. 1261, Army mobilization. No. 1262, Navy convoy system. No. 1263, Commonwealth Air Training Plan.

1989, Nov. 10   Perf. 13½
1260 A568 38c shown   .75   .55
1261 A568 38c multicolored   .75   .55
1262 A568 38c multicolored   .75   .55
1263 A568 38c multicolored   .75   .55
a.   Block of 4, #1260-1263 3.00 2.50

See Nos. 1298-1301, 1345-1348, 1448-1451, 1503-1506, 1537-1544.

Norman Bethune (1890-1939),
Surgeon — A569

Litho. & Engr.
1990, Mar. 2   Perf. 13x13½
1264 A569 39c In Canada   .90   .40
1265 A569 39c In China   .90   .40
a.   Pair, #1264-1265   1.80 1.10

See People's Republic of China Nos. 2263-2264.

Small Craft Type of 1989
1990, Mar. 15   Litho.   Perf. 13½x13
1266 A559 39c Dory   .70   .35
1267 A559 39c Pointer   .70   .35
1268 A559 39c York boat   .70   .35
1269 A559 39c North canoe   .70   .35
a.   Block of 4, #1266-1269 2.80 2.40

Mail Trucks
A571   A572

1990, May 3   Litho.   Perf. 13½
Booklet Stamps
1272 A571 39c multicolored   .75   .55
1273 A572 39c multicolored   .75   .55
a.   Bkt. pane of 8+printed margin (4 each #1272-1273) 6.00 6.00
b.   Bkt. pane of 9+3 labels, printed margin (5 #1272, 4 #1273) 11.50 11.50

Dolls
A573

1990, June 8   Perf. 12½x12
1274 A573 39c Native   .65   .35
1275 A573 39c Settlers   .65   .35
1276 A573 39c 4 Commercial   .65   .35
1277 A573 39c 5 Commercial   .65   .35
a.   Block of 4, #1274-1277 2.60 2.40

Natl. Flag, 25th
Anniv. — A574

39c, Flag, fireworks.

1990, June 29   Perf. 13x12½
1278 A574 39c multicolored   .60   .25
a.   Silver (inscriptions) omitted 2,000.

Printed in sheets of 16.

Prehistoric
Life
A575

Litho. & Engr.
1990, July 12   Perf. 13x13½
1279 A575 39c Trilobite   .65   .35
1280 A575 39c Sea scorpion   .65   .35
1281 A575 39c Fossil algae   .65   .35
1282 A575 39c Soft invertebrate .65   .35
a.   Block of 4, #1279-1282 2.60 2.20

See Nos. 1306-1309.

Canadian
Forests
A576

No. 1283, Acadian. No. 1284, Great Lakes-St. Lawrence. No. 1285, Coast. No. 1286, Boreal.

1990, Aug. 7   Litho.   Perf. 12½x13
1283 A576 39c multicolored   .65   .30
     Pane of 4   9.00 7.50
1284 A576 39c multicolored   .65   .30
     Pane of 4   9.00 7.50
1285 A576 39c multicolored   .65   .30
     Pane of 4   9.00 7.50
1286 A576 39c multicolored   .65   .30
a.   Block of 4, #1283-1286 2.60 2.20
b.   Pane of 4   9.00 7.50

Panes of four sold for $1 each through Petro-Canada gas stations, and for full face value through the philatelic bureau. Issue date: Sept. 7.

Multicultural Heritage of Canada
A570

Litho. & Engr.
1990, Apr. 5   Perf. 13
1270 A570 39c multicolored   .60   .25
a.   Black (inscriptions) omitted 1,200.

Art Type of 1988
Painting: *The West Wind*, by Tom Thomson.

Litho. with Foil Application
1990, May 3   Perf. 12½x13
1271 A546 50c multicolored   1.10   .90

Masterpieces of Canadian Art.

Weather Observations in Canada,
150th Anniv. — A577

1990, Sept. 5   **Perf. 12½x13½**
1287 A577 39c multicolored   .60 .25

The left and right margin singles of No. 1287 differ slightly in design from stamps from columns 2-4, due to the nature of the continuous cloud design across the pane.

Intl. Literacy
Year — A578

1990, Sept. 7   **Perf. 13½x13**
1288 A578 39c multicolored   .60 .25

Legendary
Creatures
A579

1990, Oct. 1   **Perf. 12½x13½**
1289	A579	39c	Sasquatch	.75	.75
1290	A579	39c	Kraken	.75	.75
1291	A579	39c	Werewolf	.75	.75
1292	A579	39c	Ogopogo	.75	.75
a.			Block of 4, #1289-1292	3.00	3.00
b.			As "a," imperf.	1,500.	

Perf. 12½x12
1289a	A579	39c		11.00	3.75
1290a	A579	39c		11.00	3.75
1291a	A579	39c		11.00	3.75
1292c	A579	39c		11.00	3.75
d.			Block of 4, #1289a-1292c	45.00	32.50

Agnes Campbell
Macphail (1890-
1954), First Woman
Member of
Parliament — A580

1990, Oct. 9   **Perf. 13x13½**
1293 A580 39c multicolored   .60 .25

Virgin Mary with
Christ Child and
St. John the
Baptist by Norval
Morrisseau
A581

Rebirth by
Jackson
Beardy
A582

Indian Art: 45c, Sculpture of Mother and Child by an Inuit artist. 78c, Children of the Raven by Bill Reid.

1990, Oct. 25   **Perf. 13½**
| 1294 | A581 | 39c multicolored | .75 | .25 |
| a. | | Booklet pane of 10 | 7.50 | 9.00 |

1295	A581	45c multicolored	.75	.65
a.		Bklt. pane of 5 + label	3.75	4.00
1296	A581	78c multicolored	1.50	1.10
a.		Bklt. pane of 5 + label	7.50	6.50

Booklet Stamp
Perf. 12½x13 on 2 or 3 Sides
1297	A582	34c multicolored	.85	.30
a.		Booklet pane of 10	8.50	10.00
		Nos. 1294-1297 (4)	3.85	2.30

Christmas. No. 1297 has bar code at left; for use on covers with printed postal code matrix.

World War II Type of 1989

No. 1298, Home front. No. 1299, Communal war efforts. No. 1300, Food production. No. 1301, Science and war.

1990, Nov. 9   **Perf. 12½x12**
1298	A568	39c multicolored	.75	.60
1299	A568	39c multicolored	.75	.60
1300	A568	39c multicolored	.75	.60
1301	A568	39c multicolored	.75	.60
a.		Block of 4, #1298-1301	3.00	3.00

A583

Physicians: No. 1302, Jennie Trout (1841-1921), first licensed Canadian woman physician. No. 1303, Wilder Penfield (1891-1976), neurosurgeon. No. 1304, Sir Frederick Banting (1891-1941), discoverer of insulin. No. 1305, Harold Griffith (1894-1985), anesthesiologist.

1991, Mar. 15   **Perf. 13½**
1302	A583	40c multicolored	.65	.35
1303	A583	40c multicolored	.65	.35
1304	A583	40c multicolored	.65	.35
1305	A583	40c multicolored	.65	.35
a.		Block of 4, #1302-1305	2.60	2.20

Prehistoric Life Type of 1990

1991, Apr. 5   **Perf. 12½x13½**
1306	A575	40c	Microfossils	.65	.35
1307	A575	40c	Early tree	.65	.35
1308	A575	40c	Early fish	.65	.35
1309	A575	40c	Land reptile	.65	.35
a.			Block of 4, #1306-1309	2.60	2.20

Art Type of 1988

Forest, British Columbia by Emily Carr.

Litho. with Foil Application
1991, May 7   **Perf. 12½x13**
1310 A546 50c multicolored   1.10 .90

Masterpieces of Canadian Art.

A584

Public Gardens: No. 1311, Butchart Gardens, Victoria, B.C. No. 1312, Intl. Peace Garden, Boissevain, Manitoba. No. 1313, Royal Botanical Gardens, Hamilton, Ontario. No. 1314, Montreal Botanical Gardens. No. 1315, Halifax Public Gardens, Nova Scotia.

Booklet Stamps
1991, May 22   **Litho.**   **Perf. 13x12½**
1311	A584	40c multicolored	.75	.40
1312	A584	40c multicolored	.75	.40
1313	A584	40c multicolored	.75	.40
1314	A584	40c multicolored	.75	.40
1315	A584	40c multicolored	.75	.40
a.		Strip of 5, #1311-1315	3.75	2.75
b.		Bklt. pane, 2 each #1311-1315	7.50	7.00

Canada
Day — A585

1991, June 28   **Perf. 13½x13**
1316 A585 40c multicolored   .75 .25

Small Craft Type of 1989

1991, July 18
1317	A559	40c	Verchere rowboat	.65	.35
1318	A559	40c	Touring kayak	.65	.35
1319	A559	40c	Sailing dinghy	.65	.35
1320	A559	40c	Cedar strip canoe	.65	.35
a.			Block of 4, #1317-1320	2.60	2.25

Canadian
Rivers — A586

No. 1321, South Nahanni. No. 1322, Athabasca. No. 1323, Boundary Waters-Voyageur Waterway. No. 1324, Jacques Cartier. No. 1325, Main.

Booklet Stamps
1991, Aug. 20   **Perf. 13x12½**
1321	A586	40c multicolored	.75	.40
1322	A586	40c multicolored	.75	.40
1323	A586	40c multicolored	.75	.40
1324	A586	40c multicolored	.75	.40
1325	A586	40c multicolored	.75	.40
a.		Strip of 5, #1321-1325	3.75	3.25
b.		Bklt. pane, 2 each #1321-1325	7.50	6.75

See Nos. 1408-1412, 1485-1489, 1511-1515.

Arrival of
Ukrainians,
Cent. — A587

Paintings by William Kurelek: No. 1326, Leaving homeland. No. 1327, Winter in Canada. No. 1328, Clearing land. No. 1329, Growing wheat.

1991, Aug. 29   **Perf. 13½x13**
1326	A587	40c multicolored	.65	.35
1327	A587	40c multicolored	.65	.35
1328	A587	40c multicolored	.65	.35
1329	A587	40c multicolored	.65	.35
a.		Block of 4, #1326-1329	2.60	2.20

Dangerous Public
Service
Occupations
A588

1991, Sept. 23   **Perf. 13½**
1330	A588	40c	Ski Patrol	1.10	.35
1331	A588	40c	Police	1.10	.35
1332	A588	40c	Fire fighters	1.10	.35
1333	A588	40c	Search & Rescue	1.10	.35
a.			Block of 4, #1330-1333	4.40	2.60

Folktales
A589

1991, Oct. 1   **Litho.**   **Perf. 13½x12½**
1334	A589	40c	Witched Canoe	.75	.30
1335	A589	40c	Orphan Boy	.75	.30
1336	A589	40c	Chinook Wind	.75	.30
1337	A589	40c	Buried Treasure	.75	.30
a.			Block of 4, #1334-1337	3.00	2.50

Queen's
University,
Kingston, Ont.,
Sesqui. — A590

1991, Oct. 16
| 1338 | A590 | 40c multicolored | .75 | .55 |
| a. | | Bklt. pane of 10 + 2 labels | 7.50 | 6.00 |

A591

Santa
Claus
A592

1991, Oct. 23   **Perf. 13½**
1339	A591	40c	At fireplace	.75	.25
a.			Booklet pane of 10	7.50	6.00
1340	A591	46c	With white horse, tree	.75	.50
a.			Bklt. pane of 5 + label	3.75	3.00
1341	A591	80c	Sinterklaas, girl	1.30	.90
a.			Bklt. pane of 5 + label	6.50	6.00

Booklet Stamp
Perf. 12½x13 on 2 or 3 Sides
1342	A592	35c	With punchbowl	.75	.25
a.			Booklet pane of 10	7.50	4.50
			Nos. 1339-1342 (4)	3.55	1.90

Christmas. No. 1342 has bar code at left; for use on covers with printed postal code matrix.

Basketball,
Cent. — A593

1991, Oct. 25   **Perf. 13x13½**
1343 A593 40c multicolored   .75 .25

Souvenir Sheet
1344		Pane of 3	5.00	5.00
a.	A593	40c like #1343	1.10	1.10
b.	A593	46c Player shooting, diff.	1.50	1.50
c.	A593	80c Player dribbling	2.20	2.20

No. 1344a has 3-line inscription.

World War II Type of 1989

No. 1345, Women's Armed Forces. No. 1346, War industry. No. 1347, Cadets and veterans. No. 1348, Defense of Hong Kong.

1991, Nov. 8   **Perf. 13½**
1345	A568	40c multicolored	.75	.55
1346	A568	40c multicolored	.75	.55
1347	A568	40c multicolored	.75	.55
1348	A568	40c multicolored	.75	.55
a.		Block or strip of 4, #1345-1348	3.00	2.50

Types of 1987-91 and

Edible
Berries — A594

Flag and
Hills — A595

Flag and
Prairie
A596

Flag and
Building
A597

Trees — A598

Designs: 1c, Blueberry. 2c, Wild strawberry. 3c, Black crowberry. 5c, Rose hip. 6c, Black raspberry. 10c, Kinnikinnick. 25c, Saskatoon berry. 49c, McIntosh apple. 49c, Delicious apple. 50c, Snow apple. 52c, Gravenstein apple. 65c, Black walnut. 67c, Beaked hazelnut. 69c, Shagbark hickory. 71c, American chestnut. 84c, Stanley plum. 86c, Bartlett pear. 88c, Westcot apricot. 90c, Elberta peach. $1, Court House, Yorkton, Saskatchewan. $2, Provincial Normal School, Truro, Nova Scotia. $5, Carnegie Public Library, Victoria, British Columbia. No. 1388, Flag and mountains. No. 1389, Flag and estuary shore.

1991-98   Litho.   Perf. 13x13½

1349	A594	1c multicolored	.25	.25
a.		Imperf., pair	650.00	
1350	A594	2c multicolored	.25	.25
a.		Imperf., pair	650.00	
1351	A594	3c multicolored	.25	.25
a.		Imperf., pair	650.00	
1352	A594	5c multicolored	.25	.25
a.		Imperf., pair	650.00	
1353	A594	6c multicolored	.25	.25
a.		Imperf., pair	650.00	
1354	A594	10c multicolored	.25	.25
a.		Horiz. pair, imperf at sides and bottom	1,100.	
b.		Imperf., pair	650.00	
1355	A594	25c multicolored	.75	.25
a.		Imperf., pair	650.00	

Perf. 13½x13

1356	A595	42c multicolored	.80	.25
a.		Booklet pane of 10	7.50	5.75
b.		Bklt. pane of 50 + 2 labels	90.00	75.00
c.		Bklt. pane of 25 + 2 labels	17.50	12.50
d.		Vert. pair, imperf between	900.00	

Perf. 13x13½

1357	A536	42c multicolored	.75	.25
a.		Booklet pane of 10	7.50	6.00
1358	A536	43c multicolored	.90	.25
a.		Booklet pane of 10	9.00	8.50
b.		Imperf., pair	900.00	

Perf. 13½x13

1359	A596	43c multicolored	.90	.25
a.		Booklet pane of 10	9.00	7.00
b.		Bklt. pane of 25 + 2 labels	22.50	17.50
c.		Perf. 14½	1.10	.25
d.		As "c," bklt. pane of 10	9.00	7.50
e.		As "c," bklt. pane of 25 + 2 labels	25.00	25.00
f.		Vert. pair, imperf between (from #1359e)	750.00	
g.		Imperf., pair	700.00	

Perf. 13x13½

1360	A536	45c multicolored	.75	.25
a.		Booklet pane of 10	7.50	6.00
		Complete booklet, #1360a	7.50	

Perf. 14½

1361	A597	45c multicolored	.75	.25
a.		Booklet pane of 10	7.50	7.00
		Complete booklet, #1361a	7.50	
b.		Bklt. pane of 25 + 2 labels	27.50	22.50
		Complete booklet, #1361b	27.50	
c.		Perf. 13½x13	.75	.25
d.		As "c," bklt. pane of 10	7.50	6.75
		Complete booklet, #1361d	7.50	
e.		As "b," bklt. pane of 25 + 2 labels	19.00	
		Complete booklet, #1361e	19.00	

Perf. 13x13½

Size: 16x20mm

1362	A597	45c multicolored	.65	.25
a.		Booklet pane of 10	6.50	8.25
		Complete booklet, #1362a	6.50	
b.		Booklet pane of 30	22.50	22.50
		Complete booklet, #1362b	22.50	
c.		Imperf, pair	500.00	

No. 1361 is 17x21mm.

Perf. 13

1363	A598	48c multicolored	1.00	.25
a.		Perf. 14½x14 on 3 sides	1.50	.40
b.		As "a," bklt. pane of 5 + label	7.50	5.75
c.		Imperf., pair	850.00	
1364	A598	49c multicolored	.90	.25
a.		Perf. 14½x14	2.60	.35
b.		As "a," bklt. pane of 5 + 1 label	13.00	6.00
c.		Booklet pane of 5 + label	12.00	9.50
1365	A598	50c multicolored	.90	.30
a.		Booklet pane of 5 + label	6.50	5.00
b.		Perf. 14½x14	2.25	.45
c.		As "b," bklt. pane of 5 + label	13.00	11.50
1366	A598	52c multicolored	1.50	.40
a.		Booklet pane of 5 + label	7.50	6.00
		Complete booklet, #1366a	8.00	
b.		Perf. 14½x14	2.25	.55
c.		As "b," bklt. pane of 5 + label	11.50	10.00
		Complete booklet, #1366c	12.00	
1367	A598	65c multicolored	1.10	.40
a.		Imperf., pair	1,000.	
1368	A598	67c multicolored	1.10	.40
a.		Imperf., pair	1,500.	
1369	A598	69c multicolored	1.10	.35
1370	A598	71c multicolored	1.10	.35
a.		Perf. 14½x14	70.00	7.50
1371	A598	84c multicolored	1.50	.40
a.		Perf. 14½x14 on 3 sides	2.25	.60
b.		As "a," bklt. pane of 5 + label	11.50	9.00
c.		Imperf., pair	1,350.	
1372	A598	86c multicolored	1.80	.55
a.		Perf. 14½x14	3.00	1.50
b.		As "a," bklt. pane of 5 + 1 label	15.00	12.50
c.		Booklet pane of 5 + label	17.00	15.00
1373	A598	88c multicolored	1.50	.50
a.		Booklet pane of 5 + label	11.00	7.50
b.		Perf. 14½x14	4.00	1.25
c.		As "b," bklt. pane of 5 + label	20.00	15.00
1374	A598	90c multicolored	1.80	.45
a.		Booklet pane of 5 + label	10.00	8.00
		Complete booklet, #1374a	10.50	
b.		Perf. 14½x14	3.75	1.50
c.		As "b," bklt. pane of 5+label	9.00	13.00
		Complete booklet, #1374c	20.00	

Size: 48x40mm
Litho. & Engr.
Perf. 14½x14

1375	A540	$1 multicolored	1.80	.55
a.		Dk bl (inscriptions) omitted	1,250.	
b.		Perf 13½x13	1.80	.55
c.		As "b," dk bl (inscriptions) omitted	1,350.	
1376	A540	$2 multicolored	3.75	1.00
a.		Dk grn (inscriptions) omitted	900.00	
c.		Engr. inscriptions inverted	8,500.	
c.		Perf. 13½x13	3.75	1.10
d.		As "c," dk grn (inscriptions) omitted	1,500.	

Perf. 13½x13

1378	A540	$5 multicolored	7.50	2.20
		Nos. 1349-1378 (29)	36.10	11.85

Self-Adhesive
Die Cut
Imperf
Booklet Stamps

1388	A543	42c multicolored	1.10	.75
a.		Booklet of 12	13.50	
1389	A543	43c multicolored	1.10	.75
a.		Booklet of 12	13.50	

Nos. 1388a, 1389a issued on peelable paper backing serving as booklet cover and sold for $5.25.

Coil Stamps
Perf. 10 Horiz.
Engr.

1394	A542	42c red	.75	.25
a.		Imperf., pair	170.00	
1395	A542	43c olive green	.75	.25
a.		Imperf., pair	150.00	
1396	A542	45c blue green	.75	.25
a.		Imperf., pair	150.00	
		Nos. 1394-1396 (3)	2.25	.75

Nos. 1349-1363 are known imperf from printer's waste. Items exist imperf in wrong colors and with wrong denominations. These may be essays or printer's waste.

Issued: 1c-25c, 8/5/92; Nos. 1356-1357, 1394, 48c, 65c, 84c, 12/27/91; No. 1388, 1/28/92; Nos. 1358-1359, 1364, 1368, 1372, 1395, 12/30/92; No. 1389, 2/15/93; Nos. 1359c-1359e, 1/18/94; Nos. 1364c, 1372c, 1/7/94; 50c, 69c, 88c, 2/25/94; $1, $2, 2/21/94; NOs. 1375b, 1376c, 2/20/95; Nos. 1365c,

1373c, 3/27/95; Nos. 1360-1361, 1396, 52c, 71c, 90c, 7/31/95; $5, 2/29/96; No. 1362, 2/2/98.

1992
Winter
Olympics,
Albertville
A601

No. 1399, Ski jumping. No. 1400, Pairs figure skating. No. 1401, Hockey. No. 1402, Bobsledding. No. 1403, Alpine skiing.

Booklet Stamps

1992, Feb. 7   Litho.   Perf. 12½x13

1399	A601	42c multicolored	.75	.40
1400	A601	42c multicolored	.75	.40
1401	A601	42c multicolored	.75	.40
1402	A601	42c multicolored	.75	.40
1403	A601	42c multicolored	.75	.40
a.		Strip of 5, #1399-1403	3.75	3.00
b.		Bklt. pane, 2 each #1399-1403	7.50	7.50
		Complete booklet, #1403b	8.50	

See Nos. 1414-1418.

City of Montreal, 350th Anniv. — A602

Designs: No. 1404, City of Montreal, modern times. No. 1405, Early settlement of Montreal (Ville-Marie). 48c, Jacques Cartier's chart of Canada, snowshoe, ship's mast. 84c, World map, nocturnal and Aztec calendar stone.

1992, Mar. 25   Perf. 13½

1404	A602	42c multicolored	.60	.30
1405	A602	42c multicolored	.60	.30
a.		Pair, #1404-1405	1.20	.75
1406	A602	48c multicolored	.75	.70
1407	A602	84c multicolored	1.30	.90
a.		Souvenir sheet of 4, #1404-1407	4.00	4.00
		Nos. 1404-1407 (4)	3.25	2.20

Discovery of America, 500th anniv. (No. 1407).
Nos. 1404-1405 printed checkerwise. No. 1407a with engraved signatures in margin was produced in limited quantities for World Philatelic Youth Exhibition catalogue which sold for $12.

Canadian Rivers Type of 1991

No. 1408, Margaree. No. 1409, West (Eliot). No. 1410, Ottawa. No. 1411, Niagara. No. 1412, South Saskatchewan.

Booklet Stamps

1992, Apr. 22   Perf. 12½

1408	A586	42c multicolored	.75	.40
1409	A586	42c multicolored	.75	.40
1410	A586	42c multicolored	.75	.40
1411	A586	42c multicolored	.75	.40
1412	A586	42c multicolored	.75	.40
a.		Strip of 5, #1408-1412	3.75	3.25
b.		Bklt. pane, 2 each #1408-1412	7.50	
		Complete booklet, #1412b	8.50	

Nos. 1408-1412 are horiz.

Alaska Highway,
50th
Anniv. — A603

1992, May 15   Perf. 13½

1413	A603	42c multicolored	.65	.25

1992 Olympic Games Type

1992, June 15   Perf. 12½x13

1414	A601	42c Gymnastics	.75	.40
1415	A601	42c Running	.75	.40
1416	A601	42c Diving	.75	.40
1417	A601	42c Cycling	.75	.40
1418	A601	42c Swimming	.75	.40
a.		Strip of 5, #1414-1418	3.75	3.75
b.		Bklt. pane, 2 each #1414-1418	7.50	7.50
		Complete booklet, #1418b	8.50	

1992 Summer Olympics, Barcelona. Stamps in bottom row of No. 1418b are in different sequence than those in No. 1418a.

Art Type of 1988

Painting: Red Nasturtiums, by David Milne.

Litho. with Foil Application
1992, June 29

1419	A546	50c multicolored	.90	.75

Masterpieces in Canadian Art.

Miniature Sheet

Canada
Day
A604

No. 1420, Nova Scotia. No. 1421, Ontario. No. 1422, Prince Edward Island. No. 1423, New Brunswick. No. 1424, Quebec. No. 1425, Saskatchewan. No. 1426, Manitoba. No. 1427, Northwest Territories. No. 1428, Alberta. No. 1429, British Columbia. No. 1430, Yukon. No. 1431, Newfoundland.

1992, June 29

1420	A604	42c multicolored	1.50	1.50
1421	A604	42c multicolored	1.50	1.50
1422	A604	42c multicolored	1.50	1.50
1423	A604	42c multicolored	1.50	1.50
1424	A604	42c multicolored	1.50	1.50
1425	A604	42c multicolored	1.50	1.50
1426	A604	42c multicolored	1.50	1.50
1427	A604	42c multicolored	1.50	1.50
1428	A604	42c multicolored	1.50	1.50
1429	A604	42c multicolored	1.50	1.50
1430	A604	42c multicolored	1.50	1.50
1431	A604	42c multicolored	1.50	1.50
a.		Pane of 12, #1420-1431 + 13 labels	18.00	18.00

Canadian
Folklore — A605

Legendary heroes: No. 1432, Jerry Potts, guide, interpreter. No. 1433, Captain William Jackman, rescuer. No. 1434, Laura Secord, patriot. No. 1435, Jos Monferrand, lumberjack.

1992, Sept. 8   Perf. 12½

1432	A605	42c multicolored	.75	.35
1433	A605	42c multicolored	.75	.35
1434	A605	42c multicolored	.75	.35
1435	A605	42c multicolored	.75	.35
a.		Block of 4, #1432-1435	3.00	2.50

Minerals
A606

1992, Sept. 21

1436	A606	42c Copper	.90	.40
1437	A606	42c Sodalite	.90	.40
1438	A606	42c Gold	.90	.40
1439	A606	42c Galena	.90	.40
1440	A606	42c Grossular	.90	.40
a.		Strip of 5, #1436-1440	4.50	4.50
b.		Bklt. pane, 2 each #1436-1440	9.00	9.00
		Complete booklet, #1440b	8.50	

Canada in
Space
A607

No. 1441, Anik E2 satellite. No. 1442, Earth,
space shuttle.

1992, Oct. 1   **Perf. 13**
1441 A607 42c multicolored   .75   .80
   a.   Silver omitted   2,750.   2,000.

Size: 32x26mm
1442 A607 42c multicolored   1.10   1.10
   a.   Pair, #1441-1442   1.80   *1.80*
   b.   As "a," hologram omitted
     on #1442   1,500.   1,400.

No. 1442 has a holographic image. Soaking
in water may affect the hologram.

Natl.
Hockey
League,
75th Anniv.
A608

Designs: No. 1443, Skates, stick, puck, photograph from the early years (1917-1942). No.
1444, Photograph, team emblems from the
six-team years (1942-1967). No. 1445,
Goalie's mask, gloves, photograph from the
expansion years (1967-1992).

Booklet Stamps
1992, Oct. 9   **Perf. 13x12½**
1443 A608 42c multicolored   .75   .25
   a.   Bklt. pane of 8 + 4 labels   6.00   5.00
1444 A608 42c multicolored   .75   .25
   a.   Bklt. pane of 8 + 4 labels   6.00   5.00
1445 A608 42c multicolored   .75   .25
   a.   Bklt. pane of 9 + 3 labels   6.75   5.25
     Complete booklet, #1443a,
     1444a, 1445a   21.00
     Nos. 1443-1445 (3)   2.25   .75

A609

No. 1446, Order of Canada, 25th anniv. No.
1447, Daniel Roland Michener (1900-1991),
Governor General.

1992, Oct. 21   **Perf. 12½**
1446   42c multicolored   .65   .25
1447   42c multicolored   .65   .30
   a.   A609 Pair, #1446-1447   1.30   1.10

Nos. 1446-1447 printed in panes of 25 containing 16 No. 1446 and 9 No. 1447.

World War II Type of 1989
No. 1448, War reporting. No. 1449, New-
foundland air bases. No. 1450, Raid on
Dieppe. No. 1451, U-boats offshore.

1992, Nov. 10   **Perf. 13½**
1448 A568 42c multicolored   .75   .45
1449 A568 42c multicolored   .75   .45
1450 A568 42c multicolored   .75   .45
1451 A568 42c multicolored   .75   .45
   a.   Block or strip of 4, #1448-1451   3.00   2.50

A611

Santa
Claus
A612

1992, Nov. 13   **Perf. 12½**
1452 A611 42c Jouluvana   .65   .25
   a.   Perf. 13½   .90   .25
   b.   As "a," booklet pane of 10   9.00   5.00
     Complete booklet, #1452b   10.00

           Perf. 13½
1453 A611 48c La Befana   1.10   .75
   a.   Booklet pane of 5 + label   5.50   4.75
     Complete booklet, #1453a   6.00
1454 A611 84c Weihnachtsmann   1.50   .75
   a.   Booklet pane of 5 + label   7.50   6.00
     Complete booklet, #1454a   8.50

Booklet Stamp
     Perf. 12½x13
1455 A612 37c Santa Claus   .75   .75
   a.   Booklet pane of 10   7.50
     Complete booklet, #1455a   8.50
     Nos. 1452-1455 (4)   4.00   2.50

Christmas. No. 1455 has bar code at left; for
use on covers with printed postal code matrix.

A613

Canadian Women: No. 1456, Adelaide
Sophia Hoodless (1857-1910), founder of Victorian Order of Nurses. No. 1457, Marie-
Josephine Gerin-Lajoie (1890-1971), founder
of Notre-Dame du Bon Conseil Institute. No.
1458, Pitseolak Ashoona (c. 1904-83), Inuit
graphic artist. No. 1459, Helen Alice Kinnear
(1894-1970), first woman appointed King's
Counsel and first federally appointed woman
judge.

1993, Mar. 8   **Perf. 12½**
1456 A613 43c multicolored   .65   .30
1457 A613 43c multicolored   .65   .30
1458 A613 43c multicolored   .65   .30
1459 A613 43c multicolored   .65   .30
   a.   Block or strip of 4, #1456-1459   2.60   2.25

Natl. Council of Women of Canada
(NCWC), and Natl. office of YWCA, cent.

Stanley Cup,
Cent. — A614

1993, Apr. 16   **Perf. 13½**
1460 A614 43c multicolored   .75   .25

Handcrafted Textiles — A615

No. 1461, Coverlet, New Brunswick. No.
1462, Pieced quilt, Ontario. No. 1463,
Doukhobor bedcover, Saskatchewan. No.
1464, Kwakwaka'wakw ceremonial robe, British Columbia. No. 1465, Boutonne coverlet,
Quebec.

Booklet Stamps
   Perf. 13x12½ on 3 Sides
1993, Apr. 30
1461 A615 43c multicolored   .75   .40
1462 A615 43c multicolored   .75   .40
1463 A615 43c multicolored   .75   .40

1464 A615 43c multicolored   .75   .40
1465 A615 43c multicolored   .75   .40
   a.   Strip of 5, #1461-1465   3.75   3.00
   b.   Bklt. pane, 2 ea #1461-1465   7.50
     Complete booklet, #1465b   8.50

Stamps in bottom row of No. 1465b are in
different sequence than those in No. 1465a.

Art Type of 1988

Painting: Drawing for The Owl, by Kenojuak
Ashevak.

Litho. with Foil Application
1993, May 17   **Perf. 12½x13½**
1466 A546 86c multicolored   1.50   1.10

Intl. Year of Indigenous People.

Historic
Canadian
Pacific
Railway
Hotels
A616

No. 1467, Empress, Victoria, B.C. No. 1468,
Banff Springs, Banff, Alberta. No. 1469, Royal
York, Toronto, Ont. No. 1470, Chateau Fron-
tenac, Quebec. No. 1471, Algonquin, St.
Andrews, N.B.

Booklet Stamps
1993, June 14   **Perf. 13½ on 3 Sides**
1467 A616 43c multicolored   .90   .60
1468 A616 43c multicolored   .90   .65
1469 A616 43c multicolored   .90   .60
1470 A616 43c multicolored   .90   .60
1471 A616 43c multicolored   .90   .60
   a.   Strip of 5, #1467-1471   4.50   3.50
   b.   Booklet pane, 2 #1471a   9.00
     Complete booklet, #1471b   10.00

Opening of Chateau Frontenac, cent.

Miniature Sheet

Canada
Day
A617

Provincial and Territorial Parks: No. 1472,
Algonquin, Ontario. No. 1473, De la Gaspesie,
Quebec. No. 1474, Cedar Dunes, Prince
Edward Island. No. 1475, Cape St. Mary's
Seabird Ecological Reserve, Newfoundland.
No. 1476, Mount Robson, British Columbia.
No. 1477, Writing-On-Stone, Alberta. No.
1478, Spruce Woods, Manitoba. No. 1479,
Herschel Island, Yukon. No. 1480, Cypress
Hills, Saskatchewan. No. 1481, The Rocks,
New Brunswick. No. 1482, Blomidon, Nova
Scotia. No. 1483, Katannilik, Northwest
Territories.

1993, June 30   **Perf. 13**
1472 A617 43c multicolored   1.00   1.00
1473 A617 43c multicolored   1.00   1.00
1474 A617 43c multicolored   1.00   1.00
1475 A617 43c multicolored   1.00   1.00
1476 A617 43c multicolored   1.00   1.00
1477 A617 43c multicolored   1.00   1.00
1478 A617 43c multicolored   1.00   1.00
1479 A617 43c multicolored   1.00   1.00
1480 A617 43c multicolored   1.00   1.00
1481 A617 43c multicolored   1.00   1.00
1482 A617 43c multicolored   1.00   1.00
1483 A617 43c multicolored   1.00   1.00
   a.   Pane of 12, #1472-1483   12.00   12.00

Algonquin Park, centennial.

City of Toronto,
Bicent. — A618

1993, Aug. 6   **Perf. 13½x13**
1484 A618 43c multicolored   .75   .25

Canadian Rivers Type of 1991
Booklet Stamps

1993, Aug. 10   **Perf. 13x12½**
1485 A586 43c Fraser   .75   .40
1486 A586 43c Yukon   .75   .40
1487 A586 43c Red   .75   .40
1488 A586 43c St. Lawrence   .75   .40
1489 A586 43c St. John   .75   .40
   a.   Strip of 5, #1485-1489   3.75   3.50
   b.   Bklt. pane, 2 each #1485-
     1489   7.50
     Complete booklet, #1489b   8.50
   c.   As "a," imperf   3,000.

Miniature Sheet

Historic Automobiles — A619

a, 1867 H.S. Taylor Steam Buggy. b, 1908
Russell Model L Touring Car. c, 1914 Ford
Model T Open Touring Car. d, 1950 Stude-
baker Champion Deluxe Starlight Coupe. e,
1928 McLaughlin-Buick Model 28-496 Special
Car. f, 1923-24 Gray-Dort 25-SM Luxury
Sedan.

1993, Aug. 23   **Perf. 12½x13**
1490 A619   Pane of 6   7.50   7.50
   a.-b.   43c any single, 35x22mm   .75   .75
   c.-d.   49c any single, 43x22mm   .90   .90
   e.-f.   86c any single, 51x22mm   1.50   1.40

See Nos. 1527, 1552, 1604-1605.

Folk Songs
A620

Designs: No. 1491, The Alberta Home-
steader, Alberta. No. 1492, Les Raftmans,
Quebec. No. 1493, I'se the B'y That Builds the
Boat, Newfoundland. No. 1494, Onkwa:ri
tenhanonniahkwe, Kanien'kehaka (Mohawk).

1993, Sept. 7   **Perf. 12½**
1491 A620 43c multicolored   .65   .30
1492 A620 43c multicolored   .65   .30
1493 A620 43c multicolored   .65   .30
1494 A620 43c multicolored   .65   .30
   a.   Block of 4, #1491-1494   2.60   2.20

Dinosaurs — A621

No. 1495, Massospondylus. No. 1496,
Styracosaurus. No. 1497, Albertosaurus. No.
1498, Platecarpus.

1993, Oct. 1   **Perf. 13½**
1495 A621 43c multicolored   .65   .30
1496 A621 43c multicolored   .65   .30
1497 A621 43c multicolored   .65   .30
1498 A621 43c multicolored   .65   .30
   a.   Block or strip of 4, #1495-
     1498   2.60   2.20
   b.   As "a," imperf.   2,750.

See Nos. 1529-1532.

A622

Santa Claus A623

43c, Swiety Mikolaj. 49c, Ded Moroz. 86c, Father Christmas, Australia. No. 1502, 38c, Santa Claus.

1993, Nov. 4
1499	A622	43c multicolored	.65	.25
a.		Booklet pane of 10	6.50	5.00
		Complete booklet, #1499a	7.50	
b.		Horiz. pair, imperf between	*1,200.*	
1500	A622	49c multicolored	.75	.45
a.		Booklet pane of 5 + label	3.75	3.25
		Complete booklet, #1500a	4.75	
1501	A622	86c multicolored	1.50	.55
a.		Booklet pane of 5 + label	7.50	6.50
		Complete booklet, #1501a	8.50	

Booklet Stamp
Perf. 13
1502	A623	38c multicolored	.75	.60
a.		Booklet pane of 10	7.50	7.00
		Complete booklet, #1502a	8.50	
		Nos. 1499-1502 (4)	3.65	1.85

Christmas. No. 1502 has bar code at left; for use on covers with printed postal code matrix.

World War II Type of 1989
No. 1503, Aid to Allies. No. 1504, Bomber forces. No. 1505, Battle of the Atlantic. No. 1506, Italian campaign.

1993, Nov. 8   **Perf. 13½**
1503	A568	43c ol grn & blk	.75	.45
1504	A568	43c dp turq grn & blk	.75	.45
1505	A568	43c blue & black	.75	.45
1506	A568	43c org brn & blk	.75	.45
a.		Block or strip of 4, #1503-1506	3.00	2.50

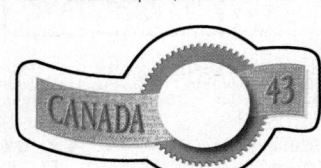

Greetings — A624

Design: No. 1508, "Canada" at right.

1994, Jan. 28   **Die Cut**
Self-Adhesive
1507	A624	43c multicolored	.90	.70
1508	A624	43c multicolored	.90	.70
a.		Bklt. pane of 10, 5 each #1507-1508	9.00	

No. 1508a also contains 35 self-adhesive greetings labels in seven designs that complete the design when placed in the central circle of Nos. 1507-1508.
See Nos. 1568-1569, 1600-1601.

Jeanne Sauve (1922-93), Governor General — A625

1994, Mar. 8   **Perf. 12½x13**
1509	A625	43c + label, multi	.75	.30
a.		Block or horiz. strip of 4 + 4 labels	3.00	2.25

No. 1509 issued se-tenant with label in sheets of 20 + 20 labels in four designs. In alternating rows, labels appear on left or right side of stamp.

T. Eaton Company, 125th Anniv. — A626

1994, Mar. 17   **Perf. 13½x13**
1510	A626	43c multicolored	.75	.30
a.		Booklet pane of 10 + 2 labels	7.50	6.25
		Complete booklet, #1510a	8.50	

Canadian Rivers Type of 1991
Booklet Stamps
1994, Apr. 22   **Perf. 13½**
1511	A586	43c Saguenay	.90	.45
1512	A586	43c French	.90	.45
1513	A586	43c Mackenzie	.90	.45
1514	A586	43c Churchill	.90	.45
1515	A586	43c Columbia	.90	.45
a.		Strip of 5, #1511-1515	4.50	3.50
b.		Bklt. pane, 2 ea #1511-1515	9.00	9.00
		Complete booklet, #1515b	10.00	

Art Type of 1988
Vera, by Frederick H. Varley (1881-1969).
Litho. with Foil Application
1994, May 6   **Perf. 14x14½**
1516	A546	88c multicolored	1.50	1.10

XV Commonwealth Games, Victoria, BC — A627

No. 1517, Lawn bowls. No. 1518, Lacrosse. No. 1519, Wheelchair marathon. No. 1520, High jump. No. 1521, Diving. No. 1522, Cycling.

1994   **Litho.**   **Perf. 14**
1517	A627	43c multicolored	.75	.25
1518	A627	43c multicolored	.75	.25
a.		Pair, #1517-1518	1.50	1.10
1519	A627	43c multicolored	.75	.25
1520	A627	43c multicolored	.75	.25
a.		Pair, #1519-1520	1.50	1.10
1521	A627	50c multicolored	.90	.75
a.		Gold ("CANADA 50") omitted	1,400.	
1522	A627	88c multicolored	1.50	.90
a.		Gold ("CANADA 88") omitted	1,800.	
		Nos. 1517-1522 (6)	5.40	2.65

Certificates of authenticity recommended for Nos. 1521a and 1522a.
Issued: Nos. 1517-1518, 5/20; Nos. 1519-1522, 8/5.

Souvenir Sheet

Intl. Year of the Family — A628

Designs: a, Mother and infant. b, Adults, children playing. c, Elderly woman, child. d, Adults, children in class. e, Judge, health care worker, child.

1994, June 2
1523	A628	Pane of 5	3.75	3.75
a.-e.		43c any single	.75	.75

Canada Day — A629

Maple trees: a, Big leaf. b, Sugar. c, Silver. d, Striped. e, Norway. f, Manitoba. g, Black. h, Douglas. i, Mountain. j, Vine. k, Hedge. l, Red.

1994, June 30   **Perf. 13x13½**
1524	A629	Pane of 12	9.00	9.00
a.-l.		43c any single	.75	.75

A630

No. 1525, Billy Bishop (1894-1956), Fighter Ace. No. 1526, Mary Travers, "La Bolduc" (1894-1941), folk singer.

1994, Aug. 12   **Perf. 13**
1525		43c multicolored	.65	.30
1526		43c multicolored	.65	.30
a.	A630	Pair, #1525-1526	1.30	.90

Historic Vehicles Type of 1993
Miniature Sheet
Designs: a, 1942 Ford F60L-AMB military ambulance. b, 1925 REO Speed Wagon Police Wagon. c, 1927 Sicard Snow Remover/Snowblower. d, 1936 Bickle Chieftain Fire Engine. e, 1894 Ottawa Car Company Streetcar. f, 1950 Motor Coach Industries Courier 50 Skyview bus.

1994, Aug. 19   **Perf. 12½x13**
1527		Pane of 6	6.75	6.75
a.-b.	A619	43c any single	.75	.75
c.-d.	A619	50c any single	.90	.90
e.-f.	A619	88c any single	1.70	1.60

ICAO, 50th Anniv. A632

1994, Sept. 16   **Perf. 13**
1528	A632	43c multicolored	1.10	.25

Dinosaur Type of 1993
Prehistoric animals: No. 1529, Coryphodon. No. 1530, Megacerops. No. 1531, Short-faced bear. No. 1532, Woolly mammoth.

1994, Sept. 26
1529	A621	43c multicolored	.65	.30
1530	A621	43c multicolored	.65	.30
1531	A621	43c multicolored	.65	.30
1532	A621	43c multicolored	.65	.30
a.		Block or strip of 4, #1529-1532	2.60	2.20

Family Singing Carols A633

Soloist A634

1994, Nov. 3   **Perf. 13½**
1533	A633	43c multicolored	.65	.25
a.		Booklet pane of 10	6.50	6.50
		Complete booklet, #1533a	7.00	
1534	A633	50c Choir, vert.	.75	.55
a.		Booklet pane of 5 + label	5.00	4.00
		Complete booklet, #1534a	5.50	
1535	A633	88c Caroling, vert.	1.50	.90
a.		Booklet pane of 5 + label	7.50	7.00
		Complete booklet, #1535a	8.00	

Booklet Stamp
Perf. 13
1536	A634	38c multicolored	.75	.55
a.		Booklet pane of 10	7.50	6.00
		Complete booklet, #1536a	8.00	
		Nos. 1533-1536 (4)	3.65	2.25

Christmas. No. 1536 has bar code at left; for use on covers with printed postal code matrix.
Examples exist of 52c and 90c denominations with the same designs as Nos. 1534 (52c) and 1535 (90c). These were prepared in advance in anticipation of a rate increase that was not approved. Virtually all were destroyed, but a small quantity are known in private hands. None were regularly issued or sold at post offices. Values: 52c, $150; 90c, $475.

World War II Type of 1989
No. 1537, D-Day beachhead. No. 1538, Artillery-Normandy. No. 1539, Tactical Air Forces. No. 1540, Walcheren and the Scheldt.

1994, Nov. 7   **Perf. 13½**
1537	A568	43c multicolored	.90	.35
1538	A568	43c multicolored	.90	.35
1539	A568	43c multicolored	.90	.35
1540	A568	43c multicolored	.90	.35
a.		Block or strip of 4, #1537-1540	3.60	2.20

World War II Type of 1989
No. 1541, Veterans return home. No. 1542, Freeing the POW. No. 1543, Liberation of civilians. No. 1544, Crossing the Rhine.

1995, Mar. 20
1541	A568	43c multicolored	.90	.35
1542	A568	43c multicolored	.90	.35
1543	A568	43c multicolored	.90	.35
1544	A568	43c multicolored	.90	.35
a.		Block or strip of 4, #1541-1544	3.60	3.00

Art Type of 1988
Painting: Floraison, by Alfred Pellan (1906-88).

Litho. with Foil Application
1995, Apr. 21   **Perf. 13**
1545	A546	88c multicolored	1.70	1.10
a.		Gold foil omitted	1,400.	

Flag Over Lake — A635

1995, May 1   **Litho.**   **Perf. 13½x13**
1546	A635	(43c) multicolored	.90	.25

No. 1546 was valued at the first class domestic letter rate on day of issue.

Fortress of Louisbourg, 275th Anniv. — A636

No. 1547, Louisbourg Harbor, ships near Dauphin Gate. No. 1548, Walls, streets, buildings of Louisbourg. No. 1549, Museum behind King's Bastion. No. 1550, Drawing of King's Garden, Convent, Hospital and barracks. No. 1551, Partially eroded fortifications.

1995, May 5   **Perf. 12½x13**
1547	A636	(43c) 48x32mm	.75	.40
1548	A636	(43c) 32x32mm	.75	.40
1549	A636	(43c) 40x32mm	.75	.40
1550	A636	(43c) 56x32mm	.75	.40
1551	A636	(43c) 48x32mm	.75	.40
a.		Strip of 5, #1547-1551	3.75	3.25
b.		Booklet pane, 2 #1551a	7.50	6.75
		Complete booklet, #1551b	7.75	

Nos. 1547-1551 were valued at the first class domestic letter rate on day of issue. No. 1551a is a continuous design.

Historic Vehicles Type of 1993
Miniature Sheet
Farm, frontier vehicles: a, 1950 Cockshutt "30" farm tractor. b, 1970 Bombardier Ski-Doo Olympique 335 snowmobile. c, 1948 Bombardier B-12 CS multi-passenger snowmobile. d, 1924 Gotfredson model 20 farm truck. e, 1962 Robin-Nodwell RN 110 tracked carrier. f, 1942 Massey-Harris No. 21 self-propelled combine.

1995, May 26
1552		Pane of 6	7.00	7.00
a.-b.	A619	43c any single, 35x22mm	.75	.75
c.-d.	A619	50c any single, 43x22mm	.95	.95
e.-f.	A619	88c any single, 43x22mm	1.80	1.80

Golf in Canada A637

Designs: No. 1553, Banff Springs Golf Club. No. 1554, Riverside Country Club. No. 1555, Glen Abbey Golf Club. No. 1556, Victoria Golf Club. No. 1557, Royal Montreal Golf Club.

Booklet Stamps
Perf. 13½x13 on 3 Sides

1995, June 6

1553	A637	43c multicolored	.90	.40
1554	A637	43c multicolored	.90	.40
1555	A637	43c multicolored	.90	.40
1556	A637	43c multicolored	.90	.40
1557	A637	43c multicolored	.90	.40
a.	Strip of 5, #1553-1557		4.50	3.75
b.	Booklet pane, 2 #1557a		9.00	8.00
	Complete booklet, #1557b		9.50	

Nat. Golf Week. Canadian Amateur Golf Championship, cent. Royal Canadian Golf Assoc., cent.

Lunenburg Academy, Cent. — A638

1995, June 29 *Perf. 13*

1558	A638	43c multicolored	.65	.25

Souvenir Sheets

Group of Seven — A639

Painting, original members: No. 1559a, October Gold, by Franklin Carmichael. b, From the North Shore, Lake Superior, by Lawren Harris. c, Evening, Les Eboulements, Quebec, by A.Y. Jackson.

No. 1560a, Serenity, Lake of the Woods, by Frank H. Johnston. b, A September Gale, Georgian Bay, by Arthur Lismer. c, Falls, Montreal River, by J.E.H. MacDonald. d, Open Window, by Frederick Horsman Varley.

Painting, new members: No. 1561a, Mill Houses, by Alfred J. Casson. b, Pembina Valley, by Lionel LeMoine FitzGerald. c, The Lumberjack, by Edwin Headley Holgate.

1995, June 29

1559	A639	Pane of 3	2.75	2.75
a.-c.	43c any single		.90	.90
1560	A639	Pane of 4	3.60	3.60
a.-d.	43c any single		.90	.90
1561	A639	Pane of 3	2.75	2.75
a.-c.	43c any single		.90	.90

Manitoba's Entry Into Confederation, 125th Anniv. — A640

1995, July 14 *Perf. 13½x13*

1562	A640	43c multicolored	.65	.30

Migratory Wildlife — A641

No. 1563, Monarch butterfly. No. 1564, Belted kingfisher. No. 1565, Northern pintail. No. 1566, Hoary bat.

1995, Aug. 15 *Perf. 13x12½*

1563	A641	45c multicolored	.75	.25
1564	A641	45c multicolored	.75	.40
1565	A641	45c multicolored	.75	.25
1566	A641	45c multicolored	.75	.25
a.	Block or strip of 4, #1563-1566		3.00	2.50

No. 1564 with Revised Inscription

1995, Sept. 26

1567	A641	45c like #1564	.90	.75
a.	Block or strip of 4, #1563, 1565-1567		3.60	3.60

No. 1564 inscribed "aune," No. 1567 "Faune." See Mexico No. 1924.

Greetings Type of 1994
Designs: No. 1568, "Canada" at left. No. 1569, "Canada" at right.

Self-Adhesive
Size: 46x22mm

1995, Sept. 1 *Die Cut*

1568	A624	45c green & multi	.90	.75
1569	A624	45c green & multi	.90	.75
a.	Bklt. pane, 5 ea #1568-1569		9.00	

By its nature, No. 1569a is a complete booklet. The peelable backing serves as a booklet cover.

No. 1569a also contains 15 self-adhesive greetings labels in four designs that complete the design when placed in the central circle of Nos. 1568-1569.

No. 1569a exists with special cover and labels commemorating the Canadian Memorial Chiropractic College, Toronto, 50th anniv.

Bridges A642

No. 1570, Quebec Bridge, Quebec. No. 1571, Highway 403-401-410 interchange, Ontario. No. 1572, Hartland Covered Wooden Bridge, New Brunswick. No. 1573, Alex Fraser Bridge, British Columbia.

1995, Sept. 1 *Perf. 12½x13*

1570	A642	45c multicolored	.75	.30
1571	A642	45c multicolored	.75	.30
1572	A642	45c multicolored	.75	.30
1573	A642	45c multicolored	.75	.30
a.	Block or strip of 4, #1570-1573		3.00	2.50

Canadian Arctic A643

No. 1574, Polar bear, caribou. No. 1575, Arctic poppy, cargo canoe. No. 1576, Inuk man, igloo, sled dogs. No. 1577, Dog-sled team, ski plane. No. 1578, Children.

Booklet Stamps

1995, Sept. 15 *Perf. 13x12½*

1574	A643	45c multicolored	.75	.30
1575	A643	45c multicolored	.75	.30
1576	A643	45c multicolored	.75	.30
1577	A643	45c multicolored	.75	.30
1578	A643	45c multicolored	.75	.30
a.	Strip of 5, #1574-1578		3.75	3.25
b.	Bklt. pane, 2 #1578a		7.50	7.50
	Complete booklet, #1578b		8.00	

Stamps in bottom row of No. 1578b are in different sequence.

Comic Book Characters A644

No. 1579, Superman. No. 1580, Johnny Canuck. No. 1581, Nelvana. No. 1582, Captain Canuck. No. 1583, Fleur de Lys.

Booklet Stamps

1995, Oct. 2 *Perf. 13x12½*

1579	A644	45c multi	1.10	.40
1580	A644	45c multi	1.10	.40
1581	A644	45c multi	1.10	.40
1582	A644	45c multi	1.10	.40
1583	A644	45c multi	1.10	.40
a.	Strip of 5, #1579-1583		5.50	5.00
b.	Booklet pane, 2 #1583a		11.00	11.00
	Complete booklet, #1583b		11.50	

Stamps in the bottom row of No. 1583b are in different sequence.

UN, 50th Anniv. A645

1995, Oct. 24 *Perf. 13½*

1584	A645	45c blue & multi	1.20	.25

No. 1584 printed in panes of 10 with top label equal to 10 stamps. Label shows details of Canadian participation in UN activities. UN emblem on No. 1584 is stamped in blue foil.

Capital Sculptures, by Emile Brunet (1893-1977), Sainte-Anne-de-Deaupre Basilica — A646

Holly A647

45c, The Nativity. 52c, The Annunciation. 90c, Flight to Egypt.

1995, Nov. 2

1585	A646	45c multicolored	.65	.25
a.	Booklet pane of 10		6.50	5.50
	Complete booklet, #1585a		7.00	
1586	A646	52c multicolored	.75	.50
a.	Booklet pane of 5 + label		3.75	3.75
	Complete booklet, #1586a		4.00	
1587	A646	90c multicolored	1.30	.60
a.	Booklet pane of 5 + label		6.50	6.00
	Complete booklet, #1587a		7.00	

Booklet Stamp
Perf. 12½x13

1588	A647	40c multicolored	.75	.75
a.	Booklet pane of 10		7.50	10.00
	Complete booklet, #1588a		7.75	
	Nos. 1585-1588 (4)		3.45	2.10

Christmas. No. 1588 has bar code at left; for use on covers with printed postal code matrix.

La Francophonie's Agency for Cultural and Technical Cooperation, 25th Anniv. — A648

1995, Nov. 6 *Perf. 13x13½*

1589	A648	45c multicolored	.65	.25

End of the Holocaust, 50th Anniv. — A649

1995, Nov. 9 *Perf. 12½x13*

1590	A649	45c multicolored	.65	.25

Birds A650

No. 1591, American kestrel. No. 1592, Atlantic puffin. No. 1593, Pileated woodpecker. No. 1594, Ruby-throated hummingbird.

1996, Jan. 9 *Perf. 13½*

1591	A650	45c multicolored	.75	.30
1592	A650	45c multicolored	.75	.30
1593	A650	45c multicolored	.75	.30
1594	A650	45c multicolored	.75	.30
a.	Strip of 4, Nos. 1591-1594		3.00	2.75

Issued in panes of 12 stamps, printed checkerwise, and in uncut sheets of 5 panes. See Nos. 1631-1634, 1710-1713, 1770-1777, 1839-1846, 1886-1893.

High Technology Industries — A651

Designs: No. 1595, Ocean technology. No. 1596, Aerospace technology. No. 1597, Information technology. No. 1598, Biotechnology.

Booklet Stamps

1996, Feb. 15 *Perf. 13½ on 3 Sides*

1595	A651	45c multicolored	.90	.35
1596	A651	45c multicolored	.90	.35
1597	A651	45c multicolored	.90	.35
1598	A651	45c multicolored	.90	.35
a.	Booklet pane of 12, 3 each Nos. 1595-1598		11.00	7.50
	Complete booklet, No. 1598a		11.50	
	Nos. 1595-1598 (4)		3.60	1.40

Greetings Type of 1994
"Canada": No. 1600, at L. No. 1601, at R.

Self-Adhesive
Size: 51x25mm

1996, Jan. 15 *Die Cut*

1600	A624	45c green & multi	1.50	1.20
1601	A624	45c green & multi	1.50	1.20
a.	Booklet pane, 5 ea #1600-1601		15.00	
b.	As "a," die cutting omitted		3,500.	

By its nature No. 1601a is a complete booklet. The peelable backing serves as a booklet cover.

No. 1601a also contains 35 self-adhesive greetings labels in seven designs that complete the design when placed in the central circle of Nos. 1600-1601.

Art Type of 1988

Sculpture: The Spirit of Haida Gwaii, by Bill Reid.

Litho. with Foil Application

1996, Apr. 30		Perf. 12½x13
1602 A546 90c multicolored		1.50 1.00

AIDS Awareness — A652

1996, May 8	Litho.	Perf. 13½
1603 A652 45c multicolored		.65 .25

Historic Vehicles Type of 1993

No. 1604: a, 1899 Still Motor Co. Ltd. Electric Van. b, 1914 Waterous Engine Works Road Roller. c, 1938 International D-35 Delivery Truck. d, 1936 Champion Road Grader. e, 1947 White Model WA 122 Tractor Trailer. f, 1975 Hayes HDX 45-115 Logging Truck.

No. 1605: a, like #1490a. b, like #1490b. c, like 1527a. d, like #1527b. e, like #1552b. f, like #1604a. g, like #1604b. h, like #1552a. i, like #1604c. j, like 1604d. k, like #1527e. l, like #1527f. m, like #1604e. n, like #1604f. o, like #1490a. p, like #1490d. q, like #1527d. r, like #1490e. s, like #1490f. t, like #1527c. u, like #1552c. v, like #1552d. w, like #1552e. x, like #1552f. y, 1975 Bricklin SV-1 Sports car.

1996		Perf. 12½x13
1604 A619 Pane of 6		6.50 6.50
a.-b.	45c any single	.80 .80
c.-d.	52c any single	.90 .90
e.-f.	90c any single	1.50 1.50
1605 A619 Pane of 25		9.00 9.00
a.-j.	5c any single	.25 .25
k.-n.	10c any single	.30 .30
o.-x.	20c any single	.45 .45
y.	45c multicolored	1.00 1.00

Nos. 1604e-1604f, 1605k-1605n, 1605y are 51x22mm. Nos. 1605o-1605x are 43x21mm.

Yukon Gold Rush, Cent. — A653

Designs: a, "Skookum" Jim Mason's discovery on Rabbit (Bonanza) Creek, 1896. b, Miners trekking to gold fields, boats on Lake Laberge. c, Supr. Sam Steele, North West Mounted Police, Alaska-Yukon border. d, Dawson, boom town, city of entertainment. e, Klondike gold fields.

1996, June 13		Perf. 13½
1606 A653 Strip of 5		5.50 4.75
a.-e.	45c any single	1.10 .60

CAPEX '96. No. 1606 was issued in panes of 10 stamps.

Canada Day — A654

Self-Adhesive

1996, June 28		Die Cut
1607 A654 45c multicolored		.75 .25
a.	Pane of 12	9.00 4.00

Canadian Olympic Gold Medalists A655

No. 1608, Ethel Catherwood, high jump, 1928. No. 1609, Etienne Desmarteau, 56 lb.

---

weight throw, 1904. No. 1610, Fanny Rosenfeld, 100m, 400m relay, 1928. No. 1611, Gerald Ouellette, smallbore rifle, prone, 1956. No. 1612, Percy Williams, 100m, 200m, 1928.

Booklet Stamps
Litho. & Typo.

1996, July 8		Perf. 13x12½
1608 A655 45c multicolored		1.00 .60
1609 A655 45c multicolored		1.00 .60
1610 A655 45c multicolored		1.00 .60
1611 A655 45c multicolored		1.00 .60
1612 A655 45c multicolored		1.00 .60
a.	Strip of 5, #1608-1612	5.00 4.00
b.	Booklet pane, 2 #1612a	10.00
	Complete booklet, #1612b	10.50

British Columbia's Entry Into Confederation, 125th Anniv. — A656

1996, July 19		
1613 A656 45c multicolored		.65 .25

Canadian Heraldry — A657

1996, Aug. 19	Litho.	Perf. 12½x12
1614 A657 45c multicolored		.65 .25

Motion Pictures, Cent. — A658

Film strips from motion pictures: No. 1615a, L'arrivée d'un train en gare, Lumière cinematography, 1896. b, Back to God's Country, Nell & Ernest Shipman, 1919. c, Hen Hop, Norman McLaren, 1942. d, Pour la suite du monde, Pierre Perrault, Michel Brault, 1963. e, Goin' Down the Road, Don Shebib, 1970.

No. 1616a, Mon oncle Antoine, Claude Jutra, 1971. b, The Apprenticeship of Duddy Kravitz, Ted Kotcheff, 1974. c, Les Ordres, Michel Brault, 1974. d, Les Bons Débarras, Francis Mankiewiez, 1980. e, The Grey Fox, Philip Borsos, 1982.

Self-Adhesive

1996, Aug. 22		Die Cut
1615	Pane of 5	3.25 3.25
a.-e.	A658 45c Any single	.65 .65
1616	Pane of 5	3.25 3.25
a.-e.	A658 45c Any single	.65 .65

Edouard Montpetit (1881-1954), Educator A659

1996, Sept. 26		Perf. 12½
1617 A659 45c multicolored		.65 .25

Winnie the Pooh A660

Designs: No. 1618, Winnie, Lt. Colebourne, 1914. No. 1619, Winnie, Christopher Robin, 1925. No. 1620, Milne and Shepard's Winnie the Pooh, 1926. No. 1621, Winnie the Pooh at Walt Disney World, 1996.

1996, Oct. 1		Perf. 12½x13
1618 A660 45c multicolored		.75 .40
1619 A660 45c multicolored		.75 .40
1620 A660 45c multicolored		.75 .40
1621 A660 45c multicolored		.75 .40
a.	Block of 4, #1618-1621	3.00 2.50
b.	Souv. sheet of 4, #1618-1621	7.50 7.50
c.	Booklet pane of 16, 4 each #1618-1621	12.00 12.00
	Complete booklet, #1621c	12.50

No. 1621c was issued with the halves of the booklet pane printed tete-beche. The booklet pane of 16 was used as a cover for a souvenir story booklet.

Walt Disney World, 25th anniv.

Authors — A661

No. 1622, Margaret Laurence (1926-87). No. 1623, Donald G. Creighton (1902-79). No. 1624, Gabrielle Roy (1909-83). No. 1625, Felix-Antoine Savard (1896-1982). No. 1626, Thomas C. Haliburton (1796-1865).

Booklet Stamps
Perf. 13½x13 on 3 Sides

1996, Oct. 10		Litho. & Engr.
1622 A661 45c multicolored		1.10 .40
1623 A661 45c multicolored		1.10 .40
1624 A661 45c multicolored		1.10 .40
1625 A661 45c multicolored		1.10 .40
1626 A661 45c multicolored		1.10 .40
a.	Strip of 5, #1622-1626	5.50 5.00
b.	Booklet pane, 2 #1626a	11.00 12.00
	Complete booklet, #1626b	11.50

A662

Christmas: 45c, Children on snowshoes, sled. 52c, Santa Claus skiing. 90c, Children skating.

Perf. 13½ (#1627, 1629a), 12¾x12¼ (#1628, 1629), 13½x13 (#1627a, 1628a)

1996, Nov. 1		Litho.
1627 A662 45c multicolored		.65 .25
a.	Booklet pane of 10	6.50 6.50
	Complete booklet, #1627a	7.00
1628 A662 52c multicolored		.80 .25
a.	Booklet pane of 5 + label	4.00 4.50
	Complete booklet, #1628a	4.25
1629 A662 90c multicolored		1.30 .50
a.	Booklet pane of 5 + label	6.50 7.00
	Complete booklet, #1629a	7.00

UNICEF, 50th anniv.

New Year 1997 (Year of the Ox) — A663

1997, Jan. 7		Perf. 13x12½
1630 A663 45c multicolored		.90 .25
a.	Souvenir sheet of 2	2.60 2.60
b.	As No. 1630, gold omitted	4,000.
c.	As "a," gold omitted	9,000.

No. 1630a is fan shaped.

No. 1630a with Hong Kong 97 overprint was sold as a limited edition only at the show. Value $7.50.

Bird Type of 1996

No. 1631, Mountain bluebird. No. 1632, Western grebe. No. 1633, Northern gannet. No. 1634, Scarlet tanager.

1997, Jan. 10		Perf. 12½x13
1631 A650 45c multicolored		.75 .25
1632 A650 45c multicolored		.75 .25
1633 A650 45c multicolored		.75 .25
1634 A650 45c multicolored		.75 .25
a.	Block or strip of 4, #1631-1634	3.00 2.50

Nos. 1631-1634 were issued in panes of 20, 5 each, printed checkerwise to contain 4 complete blocks or 5 strips.

Art Type of 1988

Painting: York Boat on Lake Winnipeg, by Walter J. Phillips.

Litho. with Foil Application

1997, Feb. 17		
1635 A546 90c gold & multi		1.80 1.10

Canadian Tire, 75th Anniv. A664

1997, Mar. 3	Litho.	Perf. 13x13½
1636 A664 45c multicolored		.75 .25

Father Charles-Emile Gadbois (1906-81), Musicologist A665

1997, Mar. 20		Perf. 13½x13
1637 A665 45c multicolored		.75 .25

Québec en Fleurs 97, Intl. Horticultural Exhibition A666

Booklet Stamps
Perf. 13x12½ on 3 Sides

1997, Apr. 4		
1638 A666 45c Blue poppy		.75 .25
a.	Booklet pane of 12	9.00 10.00
	Complete booklet, #1638a	9.50

Victorian Order of Nurses for Canada, Cent. A667

1997, May 12		Perf. 12½x13
1639 A667 45c multicolored		.75 .25

Law Society of Upper Canada, Bicent. — A668

1997, May 23		Perf. 13½x13
1640 A668 45c multicolored		.75 .25

Salt Water Fish A669

No. 1641, Great white shark. No. 1642, Pacific halibut. No. 1643, Atlantic sturgeon. No. 1644, Bluefin tuna.

1997, May 30   *Perf. 12½x13*
1641	A669	45c multicolored	.65	.25
1642	A669	45c multicolored	.65	.25
1643	A669	45c multicolored	.65	.25
1644	A669	45c multicolored	.65	.25
a.		Block or strip of 4, #1641-1644	2.60	2.20

Opening of the Confederation Bridge — A670

No. 1645, Lighthouse, bridge. No. 1646, Bridge, bird.

1997, May 31
1645	A670	45c multicolored	.65	.25
1646	A670	45c multicolored	.65	.25
a.		Pair, #1645-1646 + label	1.30	1.10

Gilles Villeneuve (1950-82), Formula One Race Car Driver — A671

45c, Villeneuve winning race in Ferrari T-4. 90c, Close-up, racing in Number 12 Ferrari T-3.

1997, June 12
1647	A671	45c multicolored	.75	.25
1648	A671	90c multicolored	1.50	.90
a.		Pair, #1647-1648	2.25	2.25
b.		Pane of 4 #1648a	9.00	9.00

John Cabot's Voyage to Canada, 500th Anniv. A672

1997, June 24
1649	A672	45c multicolored	.75	.25

See Italy No. 2162.

Scenic Canadian Highways — A673

Designs: No. 1650, Sea to Sky Highway, British Columbia. No. 1651, The Cabot Trail, Nova Scotia. No. 1652, The Wine Route, starting in Ontario. No. 1653, The Big Muddy, Saskatchewan.

1997, June 30
1650	A673	45c multicolored	.65	.40
1651	A673	45c multicolored	.65	.40
1652	A673	45c multicolored	.65	.40
1653	A673	45c multicolored	.65	.40
a.		Block or strip of 4, #1650-1653	2.60	2.20

See Nos. 1739-1742, 1780-1783.

Canadian Industrial Design — A674

1997, July 23
1654	A674	45c multicolored	.65	.25

No. 1654 was issued with se-tenant label in panes of 24 + 24 labels. The 12 different labels each appear twice in different colors. In alternating rows, labels appear on left or right side of stamp.

Association of Canadian Industrial Designers, 50th anniv. and 20th Intl. Congress of Intl. Council of Societies of Industrial Design.

Highland Games, Maxville, Ontario — A675

1997, Aug. 1
1655	A675	45c multicolored	.65	.25

Knights of Columbus in Canada, Cent. — A676

1997, Aug. 5   *Perf. 13*
1656	A676	45c multicolored	.65	.25

28th World Congress of Postal, Telegraph and Telephone Intl. Labor Union, Montreal A677

1997, Aug. 18
1657	A677	45c multicolored	.65	.25

Asia Pacific Year A678

1997, Aug. 25   *Perf. 13½*
1658	A678	45c multicolored	.65	.25

Canada-USSR Ice Hockey "Series of the Century," 25th Anniv. — A679

Designs: No. 1659, Canadian players, Paul Henderson, Yvan Cournoyer (No. 12), after scoring winning goal in final game. No. 1660, Canadian team members celebrating victory.

Booklet Stamps

1997, Sept. 20   *Perf. 14x13*
1659	A679	45c multicolored	.75	.30
1660	A679	45c multicolored	.75	.30
a.		Bklt. pane, 5 ea #1659-1660	7.50	8.00
		Complete booklet, #1660a	8.00	

Famous Politicians A680

No. 1661, Martha Black (1866-1957). No. 1662, Lionel Chevrier (1903-87). No. 1663, Judy LaMarsh (1924-80). No. 1664, Réal Caouette (1917-76).

1997, Sept. 26   *Perf. 13½x13*
1661	A680	45c multicolored	.65	.35
1662	A680	45c multicolored	.65	.35
1663	A680	45c multicolored	.65	.35
a.		Double impression of "Canada 45"		55.00
b.		Quadruple impression of "Canada 45"		300.00
1664	A680	45c multicolored	.65	.35
a.		Quintuple impression of "Canada 45"		375.00
b.		Block or strip of 4, #1661-1664	2.60	2.00

Supernatural — A681

1997, Oct. 1   *Perf. 13x12½*
1665	A681	45c Vampire	.65	.35
1666	A681	45c Werewolf	.65	.35
1667	A681	45c Ghost	.65	.35
1668	A681	45c Goblin	.65	.35
a.		Block of 4, #1665-1668	2.60	2.20

Christmas — A682

Stained glass windows: 45c, "Our Lady of the Rosary," Holy Rosary Cathedral, Vancouver. 52c, "Nativity Scene," United Church, Leith, Ontario. 90c, Madonna and Child, St. Stephen's Ukrainian Byzantine Rite Roman Catholic Church, Calgary.

1997, Nov. 3   *Perf. 12½x13*
1669	A682	45c multicolored	.70	.25
a.		Booklet pane of 10	7.00	7.00
		Complete booklet, #1669a	7.50	
1670	A682	52c multicolored	.80	.35
a.		Booklet pane of 5	4.00	4.00
		Complete booklet, #1670a	4.25	
1671	A682	90c multicolored	1.40	.55
a.		Booklet pane of 5	7.00	7.00
		Complete booklet, #1671a	7.50	
		Nos. 1669-1671 (3)	2.90	1.15

75th Royal Agriculture Winter Fair, Toronto A683

1997, Nov. 6
1672	A683	45c multicolored	.65	.25

Types of 1987-98 and

Traditional Handiwork A684

Maple Leaf A685

Loon A686

Moose — A687

Flag and Inukshuk — A688

Designs: 1c, Bookbinding. 2c, Ironwork. 3c, Glass blowing. 4c, Oyster farmer. 5c, Weaving. 9c, Quilting. 10c, Artistic woodworking. 25c, Leatherwork. Nos. 1682, 1698, Flag over icebergs. No. 1688, White-tailed deer. No. 1689, Atlantic walrus. No. 1690, Polar bear. No. 1691, Peregrine falcon. No. 1692, Sable Island horses. $8, Grizzly bear.

1997-2005   **Litho.**   *Perf. 13¼*
1673	A684	1c multicolored	.25	.25
a.		Gray (in numeral "1") omitted	300.00	
1674	A684	2c multicolored	.25	.25
1675	A684	3c multicolored	.25	.25
1676	A684	4c multicolored	.25	.25
a.		Imperf., pair	950.00	
1677	A684	5c multicolored	.25	.25
1678	A684	9c multicolored	.25	.25
1679	A684	10c multicolored	.25	.25
a.		Imperf, single	—	
b.		Block of 4, top two stamps imperf (cut between)	750.00	
1680	A684	25c multicolored	.40	.25

     Perf. 13¼x13
1681	A536	46c multicolored	.70	.25

     Perf. 13x13¼
1682	A541	46c multicolored	.75	.25
a.		Booklet pane of 10	7.50	11.00
		Complete booklet, #1682a	8.00	

     Perf. 13¼x13
1683	A536	47c multicolored	.70	.25
a.		Imperf, pair	650.00	

     Perf. 13x13¼
1684	A685	55c multicolored	.90	.25
a.		Booklet pane of 5 + label	4.50	3.75
		Complete booklet, #1684a	4.75	
1685	A685	73c multicolored	1.10	.40
1686	A685	95c multicolored	1.70	.50
a.		Booklet pane of 5 + label	8.50	8.00
		Complete booklet, #1686a	9.00	

Litho. & Engr.

     Perf. 13¼x13
1687	A686	$1 multicolored	1.50	.55

     Perf. 12½x13
1688	A686	$1 multicolored	1.50	.55
1689	A686	$1 multicolored	1.50	.55
a.		Pair, #1688-1689	3.00	2.50
b.		Souvenir sheet, 2 each #1688-1689	7.50	7.50

     Perf. 13¼x13
1690	A686	$2 multicolored	3.00	1.00

     Perf. 12½x13
1691	A686	$2 multicolored	3.00	1.00
1692	A686	$2 multicolored	3.00	1.00
a.		Pair, #1691-1692	6.00	4.75

b. Souvenir sheet, 2 each #1691-1692   14.00   14.00

Size 63x48mm
1693 A687 $5 multicolored   7.50   2.00
a. Engraved colors (Moose, etc.) omitted   5,250.
1694 A687 $8 multicolored   12.00   4.50
Nos. 1673-1694 (22)   41.00   15.05

Coil Stamp
Engr.
Perf. 10 Horiz.
1695 A542 46c red   .75   .25
a. Imperf, pair   170.00

Photo.
Booklet Stamp
Self-Adhesive
Die Cut
1696 A685 45c multicolored   1.30   2.00
a. Booklet pane of 18   25.00

Typo. & Embossed
Die Cut Perf. 13
Coil Stamp
1697 A685 45c multicolored   1.10   .75

Litho.
Booklet Stamps
Die Cut
1698 A541 46c multicolored   .90   .25
a. Booklet pane of 30   27.00
b. Imperf, pair   300.00

Photo.
1699 A685 46c multicolored   2.75   2.75
a. Booklet pane of 18   50.00

Litho.
1700 A688 47c multicolored   .75   .25
a. Booklet of 10   7.50
b. Booklet of 30   22.50
c. All colors omitted   225.00
d. As "a," all colors omitted   2,250.
e. As "a," die cutting omitted   1,900.

Nos. 1696a, 1698a-1699a are complete booklets. The peelable backing serves as a booklet cover.
Issued: Nos. 1681, 1682, 1684-1686, 1695, 1698-1700, 12/28/98; No. 1693, 12/19/03; No. 1694, 10/15; No. 1696, 4/14/98. No. 1697, 9/30/98; No. 1687, 1690, 10/27/98; Nos. 1673-1680, 4/29/99; No. 1683, 12/28/00; Nos. 1688-1689, 10/20/05; Nos. 1691-1692, 12/19/05.
No. 1697 does not have the "POSTAGE / POSTES" and copyright inscriptions found in No. 1696. The gold on No. 1697 is embossed and brighter than that on No. 1696.
On Nos. 1700c and 1700d, the booklet cover on the reverse side is properly printed.
See Nos. 1928-1930.

New Year 1998 (Year of the Tiger) A690

1998, Jan. 8   Litho.   *Perf. 13x12½*
1708 A690 45c multicolored   .75   .25
a. Souvenir sheet of 2   1.60   1.40

No. 1708a overprinted exists. Value $3.

Provincial Leaders — A691

Designs: a, John P. Robarts (1917-82), Ontario. b, Jean Lesage (1912-80), Quebec. c, John B. McNair (1889-1968), New Brunswick. d, Tommy Douglas (1904-86), Saskatchewan. e, Joseph R. Smallwood (1900-91), Newfoundland. f, Angus L. MacDonald (1890-1954), Nova Scotia. g, W.A.C. Bennett (1900-79), British Columbia. h, Ernest C. Manning (1908-95), Alberta. i, John Bracken (1883-1969), Manitoba. j, J. Walter Jones (1878-1954), Prince Edward Island.

1998, Feb. 18   *Perf. 13½*
1709 A691 Sheet of 10   11.00   9.00
a.-j. 45c any single   1.10   .75

Bird Type of 1996
No. 1710, Hairy woodpecker. No. 1711, Great crested flycatcher. No. 1712, Eastern

screech owl. No. 1713, Gray-crowned rosy-finch.

1998, Mar. 13   *Perf. 13x13½*
1710 A650 45c multicolored   .75   .30
1711 A650 45c multicolored   .75   .30
1712 A650 45c multicolored   .75   .30
1713 A650 45c multicolored   .75   .30
a. Block or strip of 4, #1710-1713   3.00   2.25

Nos. 1710-1713 were issued in panes of 20, 5 each, printed checkerwise to contain 4 complete blocks or 5 strips.

Fly Fishing in Canada — A693

Lure, type of fish: No. 1715, Coquihalla orange, steelhead trout. No. 1716, Steelhead bee, steelhead trout. No. 1717, Dark Montreal, brook trout. No. 1718, Lady Amherst, Atlantic salmon. No. 1719, Coho blue, coho salmon. No. 1720, Cosseboom special, Atlantic salmon.

1998, Apr. 16   *Perf. 12½x13*
1715 A693 45c multicolored   .90   .45
1716 A693 45c multicolored   .90   .45
1717 A693 45c multicolored   .90   .45
1718 A693 45c multicolored   .90   .45
1719 A693 45c multicolored   .90   .45
1720 A693 45c multicolored   .90   .45
a. Vertical strip of 6, #1715-1720   5.50   4.50
b. Bklt. pane, 2 ea #1715-1720   11.00
Complete booklet, #1720a   11.50

Canadian Institute of Mining, Metallurgy and Petroleum, Cent. — A694

1998, May 4   *Perf. 12½*
1721 A694 45c multicolored   .75   .25

Imperial Penny Post, Cent. A695

St. Edward's Crown, #86, Sir William Mulock.

1998, May 29   *Perf. 12½x13*
1722 A695 45c multicolored   .75   .25
No. 1722 was issued in panes of 14 + 1 label.

Sumo Wrestling Tournament, Vancouver — A696

Rising sun, mapleleaf and: No. 1723, Two wrestlers. No. 1724, Sumo champion performing bow twirling ceremony.

1998, June 5   Litho. & Embossed
1723 A696 45c multicolored   .75   .25
1724 A696 45c multicolored   .75   .25
a. Horiz. or Vert. Pair, #1723-1724 + 4 labels   1.50   1.50
b. Souvenir sheet, #1723-1724   3.75   3.75

Nos. 1723-1724 were printed checkerwise in panes of 20, 10 each + 40 labels.

Canals of Canada — A697

No. 1725, St. Peters Canal, Nova Scotia. No. 1726, St. Ours Canal, Quebec. No. 1727, Port Carling Lock, Ontario. No. 1728, Locks, Rideau Canal, Ontario. No. 1729, Peterborough lift lock, Trent-Severn Waterway, Ontario. No. 1730, Chambly Canal, Quebec. No. 1731, Lachine Canal, Quebec. No. 1732, Ice skating on Rideau Canal, Ottawa. No. 1733, Boat on Big Chute Marine Railway, Trent-Severn Waterway, Ontario. No. 1734, Sault Ste. Marie Canal, Ontario.

Booklet Stamps
1998, June 17   Litho.   *Perf. 12½*
1725 A697 45c multicolored   1.10   .75
1726 A697 45c multicolored   1.10   .75
1727 A697 45c multicolored   1.10   .75
1728 A697 45c multicolored   1.10   .75
1729 A697 45c multicolored   1.10   .75
1730 A697 45c multicolored   1.10   .75
1731 A697 45c multicolored   1.10   .75
1732 A697 45c multicolored   1.10   .75
1733 A697 45c multicolored   1.10   .75
1734 A697 45c multicolored   1.10   .75
a. Bklt. pane, #1725-1734 + 10 labels   14.00
Complete booklet, #1734a   15.00

Health Professionals A698

Litho. & Embossed with Foil Application
1998, June 25
1735 A698 45c multicolored   .65   .25

Royal Canadian Mounted Police, 125th Anniv. — A699

No. 1736, Male mountie, native, horse. No. 1737, Female mountie, helicopter, cityscape.

1998, July 3   *Perf. 12½x13*
1736 A699 45c multicolored   .65   .25
1737 A699 45c multicolored   .65   .25
a. Pair, #1736-1737 + 2 labels   1.30   1.10
b. Souvenir sheet, #1736-1737 + 1 label   1.50   1.50
c. As "b," with signature   3.00   3.00
d. As "b," with Portugal 98 emblem   4.50   4.50
e. As "b," with Italia 98 emblem   4.50   4.50
f. As "d," gold embossed emblem omitted   750.00

Nos. 1737c-1737e have added inscriptions in gold. Issued: No. 1737c, 7/3; No. 1737d, 9/4; No. 1737e, 10/23.

William James Roué (1879-1970), Naval Architect — A700

Litho. & Engr.
1998, July 24   *Perf. 13*
1738 A700 45c multicolored   .75   .25

Scenic Highway Type of 1997
Designs: No. 1739, Dempster Highway, Yukon. No. 1740, Dinosaur Trail, Alberta. No. 1741, River Valley Scenic Drive, New Brunswick. No. 1742, Blue Heron Route, Prince Edward Island.

1998, July 28   Litho.   *Perf. 12½x13*
1739 A673 45c multicolored   .65   .35
1740 A673 45c multicolored   .65   .35
1741 A673 45c multicolored   .65   .35
1742 A673 45c multicolored   .65   .35
a. Block or strip of 4, #1739-1742   2.60   2.30

Publication of "Refus Global" by The Automatistes, 50th Anniv. — A701

Painting, artist: No. 1743, "Peinture," Jean-Paul Riopelle. No. 1744, "La dernière campagne de Napoléon," Fernand Leduc. No. 1745, "Jet fuligineux sur noir torturé," Jean-Paul Mousseau. No. 1746, "Le fond du garde-robe," Pierre Gauvreau. No. 1747, "Joie lacustre," Paul-Emile Borduas. No. 1748, "Syndicat des gens de mer," Marcelle Ferron. No. 1749, "Le tumulte á la machoire crispée," Marcel Barbeau.

Self-Adhesive
Booklet Stamps
1998, Aug. 7   *Die Cut*
1743 A701 45c multicolored   1.10   1.10
1744 A701 45c multicolored   1.10   1.10
1745 A701 45c multicolored   1.10   1.10
1746 A701 45c multicolored   1.10   1.10
1747 A701 45c multicolored   1.10   1.10
1748 A701 45c multicolored   1.10   1.10
1749 A701 45c multicolored   1.10   1.10
a. Booklet pane, #1743-1749   7.75

No. 1746 is 34x48mm. No. 1749a is a complete booklet. The peelable paper backing serves as a booklet cover.

Legendary Canadians A702

No. 1750, Napoléon-Alexandre Comeau (1848-1923), outdoorsman, "King of the North Shore." No. 1751, Phyllis Munday (1894-1990), mountaineer, community service worker. No. 1752, Bill Mason (1929-88), film maker, canoe enthusiast. No. 1753, Harry "Red" Foster (1905-1985), founder of Canadian Special Olympics, sports enthusiast.

1998, Aug. 15   *Perf. 13½*
1750 A702 45c multicolored   .65   .25
1751 A702 45c multicolored   .65   .25
1752 A702 45c multicolored   .65   .25
1753 A702 45c multicolored   .65   .25
a. Block or strip of 4, #1750-1753   2.60   2.20

Art Type of 1988
Painting: The Farmer's Family (detail), by Bruno Bobak.

Litho. with Foil Application
1998, Sept. 8   *Perf. 12½x13*
1754 A546 90c gold & multi   1.50   .90

Housing in Canada A703

a, Native peoples. b, Settler. c, Regional. d, Heritage preservation. e, Multiple unit. f, Prefabricated. g, Veterans. h, Planned community. i, Innovative.

1998, Sept. 23   **Litho.**

1755	Pane of 9	10.00	10.00
a.-i.	A703 45c Any single	1.10	1.10

University of Ottawa, 150th Anniv. — A704

1998, Sept. 25   **Perf. 13**

1756	A704 45c multicolored	.65	.25

The Circus — A705

Various circus clowns and: No. 1757, Elephant, bear performing tricks. No. 1758, Woman standing on horse, aerial act. No. 1759, Lion tamer. No. 1760, Contortionists, acrobats.

Booklet Stamps

1998, Oct. 1   **Perf. 13 on 3 Sides**

1757	A705	45c multicolored	.65	.30
1758	A705	45c multicolored	.65	.30
1759	A705	45c multicolored	.65	.30
1760	A705	45c multicolored	.65	.30
a.	Bklt. pane, 3 ea #1757-1760		6.50	6.50
	Complete booklet, #1760a		7.00	
b.	Souvenir sheet, #1757-1760		4.50	3.75

Stamps in No. 1760b are perforated on all four sides.

John Peters Humphrey (1905-95), Author of Universal Declaration of Human Rights A706

1998, Oct. 7   **Perf. 13**

1761	A706 45c multicolored	.65	.25

Canadian Naval Reserve, 75th Anniv. — A707

No. 1762, HMCS Sackville. No. 1763, HMCS Shawinigan.

1998, Nov. 4   **Perf. 12½x13**

1762	A707 45c multicolored	.75	.25
1763	A707 45c multicolored	.75	.25
a.	Pair, #1762-1763	1.50	1.40

Christmas — A708

Sculpted wooden angels: 45c, "Angel of Last Judgment" blowing trumpet. 52c, "Adoring Angel" raising hand. 90c, "Adoring Angel, Kneeling," by Thomas Baillairgé.

1998, Nov. 6   **Perf. 13**

1764	A708 45c multicolored	.75	.25
a.	Booklet pane of 10	32.50	32.50
	Complete booklet, #1764a	35.00	
b.	Perf 13x13½	350.00	16.00
c.	As "b," booklet pane of 10	15.00	13.50
	Complete booklet, #1764c	16.00	

The values for No. 1764b are for singles perfed on all four sides from sheet format. These are extremely scarce. Single stamps from booklet pane No. 1764c have a straight edge on one side. Value, booklet single, unused $1.50, used $.30.

Perf. 13x13½

1765	A708 52c multicolored	.80	.40
a.	Booklet pane of 5 + label	22.50	22.50
	Complete booklet, #1765a	23.50	
b.	Perf 13	1.10	.60
c.	As "b," booklet pane of 5 + label	5.50	5.00
	Complete booklet, #1765c	6.00	
1766	A708 90c multicolored	1.50	.75
a.	Booklet pane of 5 + label	37.50	37.50
	Complete booklet, #1766a	40.00	
b.	Perf 13	1.50	.75
c.	As "b," booklet pane of 5 + label	7.50	6.75
	Complete booklet, #1766c	8.00	
	Nos. 1764-1766 (3)	3.05	1.40

New Year 1999 (Year of the Rabbit) A709

1999, Jan. 8   **Perf. 13½**

1767	A709 46c multicolored	.75	.25
a.	Red and tagging omitted	800.00	

Souvenir Sheet
Perf. 12½x13

1768	A709 95c Pane of 1	2.25	2.00
a.	Single stamp	1.50	1.25
b.	Red and tagging omitted	950.00	

No. 1768 with China 99 overprint was sold only at the show. Value same as unoverprinted pane. Also known with red and tagging omitted. Value $1,750.

Le Theatre du Rideau Vert, 50th Anniv. — A710

1999, Feb. 17   **Perf. 13x12½**

1769	A710 46c multicolored	.70	.25

Bird Type of 1996

Designs: No. 1770, Northern goshawk. No. 1771, Red-winged blackbird. No. 1772, American goldfinch. No. 1773, Sandhill crane.

1999, Feb. 24   **Perf. 12½x13**

1770	A650	46c multicolored	.70	.30
1771	A650	46c multicolored	.70	.30
1772	A650	46c multicolored	.70	.30
1773	A650	46c multicolored	.70	.30
a.	Block or strip of 4, #1770-1773		2.80	1.50

Booklet Stamps
Self-Adhesive
Die Cut Perf. 11½

1774	A650	46c like #1770	.90	.35
1775	A650	46c like #1771	.90	.35
1776	A650	46c like #1772	.90	.35
1777	A650	46c like #1773	.90	.35
a.	Booklet pane, 2 each #1774-1775, 1 each #1776-1777		5.50	
b.	Booklet pane, 1 each #1776-1777, 1 each #1774-1775		5.50	
	Complete booklet, #1777a, #1777b		11.00	

Nos. 1770-1773 were issued in panes of 20, 5 each, printed checkerwise to contain 4 complete blocks or strips.

The peelable paper backing of Nos. 1777a, 1777b serves as the booklet cover.

Univ. of British Columbia's Museum of Anthropology, 50th Anniv. — A711

1999, Mar. 9   **Perf. 13½**

1778	A711 46c multicolored	.70	.25

Sailing Ship Marco Polo — A712

1999, Mar. 19   **Perf. 13x12½**

1779	A712 46c multicolored	.70	.25
a.	Pane of 2, #1779b, Australia #1631 perf. 13½	2.75	2.75
b.	Perf 13 (from No. 1779a)	1.80	1.80

Australia '99 World Stamp Expo. See Australia No. 1631a.

Scenic Highway Type of 1997

No. 1780, Gaspé Peninsula, Highway 132, Quebec. No. 1781, Yellowhead Highway (PTH 16), Manitoba. No. 1782, Dempster Highway 8, Northwest Territories. No. 1783, Discovery Trail, Route 230N, Newfoundland.

1999, Mar. 31   **Perf. 12½x13**

1780	A673	46c multicolored	.70	.35
1781	A673	46c multicolored	.70	.35
1782	A673	46c multicolored	.70	.35
1783	A673	46c multicolored	.70	.35
a.	Block or strip of 4, #1780-1783		2.80	2.50

Creation of the Nunavut Territory — A713

1999, Apr. 1

1784	A713 46c multicolored	.70	.25

Intl. Year of Older Persons — A714

1999, Apr. 12   **Perf. 13½**

1785	A714 46c multicolored	.70	.25

A715

1999, Apr. 19   **Perf. 13**

1786	A715 46c multicolored	1.80	.40

Baisakhi, Religious Holiday of Sikh Canadians, 300th Anniv.

A716

Paintings (Canadian Orchids): No. 1787, Arethusa bulbosa, by Poon-Kuen Chow. No. 1788, Amerorchis rotundifolia, by Yakman Lai. No. 1789, Platanthera psycodes, by Lai. No. 1790, Cypripedium pubescens, by Chow.

Booklet Stamps

1999, Apr. 27   **Perf. 13x12½**

1787	A716	46c multicolored	.90	.30
1788	A716	46c multicolored	.90	.30
1789	A716	46c multicolored	.90	.30
1790	A716	46c multicolored	.90	.30
a.	Bklt. pane, 3 ea #1787-1790		11.00	
	Complete booklet, #1790a		11.50	
b.	Souvenir sheet, #1787-1790		3.75	3.75

China '99 World Philatelic Exhibition, Beijing. Designs of some stamps contained in No. 1790a extend into selvage of booklet pane. Issued: No. 1790b, 8/21/99.

Horses A717

No. 1791, Northern Dancer, thoroughbred race horse. No. 1792, Kingsway Skoal, bucking horse. No. 1793, Big Ben, show horse. No. 1794, Armbro Flight, harness race horse.

1999, June 2   **Perf. 13x13½**

1791	A717	46c multicolored	.90	.40
1792	A717	46c multicolored	.90	.40
1793	A717	46c multicolored	.90	.40
1794	A717	46c multicolored	.90	.40
a.	Block or strip of 4, #1791-1794		3.60	3.00

Booklet Stamps
Self-Adhesive
Serpentine Die Cut 11½

1795	A717	46c like #1791	1.10	.30
1796	A717	46c like #1792	1.10	.30
1797	A717	46c like #1793	1.10	.30
1798	A717	46c like #1794	1.10	.30
a.	Block of 4, #1795-1798		4.40	
b.	Complete booklet, 3 each #1795-1798		13.25	

Nos. 1791-1794 were issued in panes of 16, 4 each, printed checkerwise to contain 4 complete blocks or strips.

Quebec Bar Assoc., 150th Anniv. — A718

1999, June 3   **Perf. 13½**

1799	A718 46c multicolored	.70	.25

Art Type of 1988

Coq Licorne, by Jean Dallaire (1916-65).

Litho. with Foil Application

1999, July 3   **Perf. 12½x13¼**

1800	A546 95c Rose gold & multi	1.50	1.10
a.	Silver omitted	1,250.	

1999 Pan
American
Games,
Winnipeg
A719

Designs: No. 1801, Track & field. No. 1802,
Cycling, weight lifting, gymnastics. No. 1803,
Swimming, sailboarding, kayaking. No. 1804,
Soccer, tennis, medal winners.

1999, July 12	Litho.	Perf. 13¼	
1801	A719 46c multicolored	.70	.35
1802	A719 46c multicolored	.70	.35
1803	A719 46c multicolored	.70	.35
1804	A719 46c multicolored	.70	.35
a.	Block of 4, #1801-1804	2.80	2.50

Issued in panes of 16 stamps.

23rd World Rowing Championships,
St. Catharines, Ont. — A720

1999, Aug. 22		Perf. 12½x13	
1805	A720 46c multicolored	.70	.25

UPU, 125th Anniv. — A721

1999, Aug. 26			
1806	A721 46c multicolored	.70	.25

Airplanes — A722

No. 1807: a, Fokker DR-1, CT-114 Tutors. b,
Tutors, H101 Salto sailplane. c, De Havilland
DH100 Vampire MKIII. d, Stearman A-75.

No. 1808: a, De Havilland Mosquito FBVI. b,
Sopwith F1 Camel. c, De Havilland Canada
DHC-3 Otter. d, De Havilland Canada CC-108
Caribou. e, Canadair CL-28 Argus MK 2. f,
North American F-86 Sabre 6. g, McDonnell
Douglas CF-18 Hornet. h, Sopwith SF-1
Dolphin. i, Armstrong Whitworth Siskin IIIA. j,
Canadian Vickers (Northrop) Delta II. k, Sikor-
sky CH-124A Sea King helicopter. l, Vickers-
Armstrong Wellington MKII. m, Avro Anson
MKI. n, Canadair (Lockheed) CF-104G
Starfighter. o, Burgess-Dunne seaplane. p,
Avro 504K.

1999, Sept. 4

1807	A722 Pane of 4	4.40	4.40
a.-d.	46c any single	1.10	.90
1808	A722 Pane of 16	18.00	18.00
a.-p.	46c any single	1.00	1.00

Canadian Intl. Air Show, 50th anniv. (No.
1807). Royal Canadian Air Force, 75th anniv.
(No. 1808). Nos. 1808a-1808p are each
56x28mm.

NATO, 50th Anniv. — A723

1999, Sept. 21

1809	A723 46c multicolored	.75	.25

Frontier
College,
100th
Anniv.
A724

1999, Sept. 24   Perf. 13x13½

1810	A724 46c multicolored	.70	.25

Kites
A725

Designs: a, Master Control, sport kite by
Lam Hoac (triagular). b, Indian Garden Flying
Carpet, edo kite by Skye Morrison (trapezoi-
dal). c, Gibson Girl, manufactured box kite
(rectangular). d, Dragon centipede kite by
Zhang tian Wei (oval).

Die cut in various patterns

1999, Oct. 1		Self-Adhesive	
1811	Complete booklet, 2 each #a.-d.	8.00	
a.-d.	A725 46c any single	1.00	.35

A726

A727

Millennium
A728

Self-Adhesive (46c)

1999, Oct. 12	Holography		Die Cut
1812	A726 46c silver	1.00	.40
	Pane of 4	4.75	4.75

Litho.
Perf. 13¼

1813	A727 55c multicolored	1.00	.80
	Pane of 4	4.75	4.75

Engr.
Perf. 12¾

1814	A728 95c brown	1.70	1.50
	Pane of 4	7.00	7.00
	Nos. 1812-1814 (3)	3.70	2.70

Nos. 1812-1814 each exist in souvenir
sheets of 1 with decorative border.

Christmas — A729

1999, Nov. 4	Litho.	Perf. 13¼	
1815	A729 46c Angel, drum	.70	.25
a.	Booklet pane of 10	7.00	8.00
	Complete booklet	7.50	
b.	Horiz. pair, imperf. btwn.	1,750.	
1816	A729 55c Angel, toys	.80	.35
a.	Booklet pane of 5 + label	4.00	6.00
	Complete booklet	4.50	
1817	A729 95c Angel, candle	1.50	.75
a.	Booklet pane of 5 + label	8.00	10.00
	Complete booklet	8.50	
b.	Horiz. pair, imperf. btwn.	1,200.	
	Nos. 1815-1817 (3)	3.00	1.35

Souvenir Sheets

Millennium — A730

No. 1818 — Media Technologies: a, IMAX
movies. b, Softimage animation software. c,
Ted Rogers, Sr. (1900-39) and radio tube. d,
Invention of radio facsimile device for trans-
mission of photographs for publishing by Sir
William Stephenson (1896-1989).

No. 1819 — Canadian Entertainment: a,
Calgary Stampede. b, Performers from Cirque
du Soleil. c, Hockey Night in Canada. d, La
Soiree du Hockey.

No. 1820 — Entertainers: a, Portia White
(1911-68), singer. b, Glenn Gould (1932-82),
pianist. c, Guy Lombardo (1902-77), band
leader. d, Félix Leclerc (1914-88), singer,
guitarist.

No. 1821 — Fostering Canadian Talent: a,
Royal Canadian Academy of Arts (men viewing painting). b, Canada Council (sky, musical
staff, "A"). c, National Film Board of Canada.
d, Canadian Broadcasting Corporation.

No. 1822 — Medical Innovators: a, Sir Frederick Banting (1891-1941), co-discoverer of
insulin, syringe and dog. b, Dr. Armand Frap-
pier (1904-91), microbiologist, holding flask. c,
Dr. Hans Selye (1907-82), endocrinologist,
and molecular diagram. d, Maude Abbott
(1869-1940), pathologist, and roses.

No. 1823 — Social Progress: a, Nun, doctor, hospital. b, Statue of woman holding
decree. c, Alphonse Desjardins (1854-1920)
and wife Dorimène (1858-1932), credit union
founders, and credit union emblem. d, Father
Moses Coady (1882-1959), educator of adults.

No. 1824 — Charity: a, Canadian International Development Agency (hands and tools).
b, Dr. Lucille Teasdale (1929-96), hospital
administrator in Uganda. c, Marathon of Hope
inspired by Terry Fox (1958-81). d, Meals on
Wheels program.

No. 1825 — Humanitarians and
Peacekeepers: a, Raoul Dandurand (1861-
1942). b, Pauline Vanier (1898-1991), Red
Cross volunteer, and Elizabeth Smellie (1884-
1968), head of various nursing services. c,
Lester B. Pearson (1897-1972), prime minister, and Nobel Peace Prize winner, and dove.
d, Amputee and shadow (Ottawa Convention
on Land Mines).

No. 1826 — Canada's First People: a, Chief
Pontiac (c. 1720-69). b, Tom Longboat (1887-
1949), marathon runner. c, Inuit sculpture of
shaman. d, Medicine man.

No. 1827 — Canada's Cultural Fabric: a,
Norse boat, L'Anse aux Meadows. b, Immigrants on Halifax's Pier 21. c, Neptune Theater, Halifax (head of Neptune). d, Stratford
Festival (actor and theater).

No. 1828 — Literary Legends: a, W. O.
Mitchell (1914-98), novelist, and prairie scene.
b, Gratien Gélinas (1909-99), actor and playwright, and stars. c, Le Cercle du Livre de
France book club. d, Harlequin paperback
books.

No. 1829 — Great Thinkers: a, Marshall
McLuhan (1911-80), philosopher, and television set. b, Northrop Frye (1912-91), literary
critic, and word "code." c, Roger Lemelin
(1919-92), novelist, and cast of "The Plouffe
Family" TV series. d, Hilda Marion Neatby
(1904-75), historian, and farm scene.

No. 1830 — A Tradition of Generosity: a,
Hart Massey (1823-96), Hart House, University of Toronto. b, Dorothy (1899-1965) and
Izaak Killam (1885-1955), philanthropists, and
molecular model. c, Eric Lafferty Harvie
(1892-1975), philanthropist, and mountain
scene. d, Macdonald Stewart Foundation.

No. 1831 — Engineering and Technological
Marvels: a, Map of Rogers Pass, locomotive,
tunnel diggers. b, Manic Dams. c, Canadian
satellites, Remote Manipulator Arm. d, CN
Tower.

No. 1832 — Fathers of Invention: a, George
Klein (1904-92), gearwheels. b, Abraham
Gesner (1797-1864), beaker of kerosene and
lamp. c, Alexander Graham Bell (1847-1922),
passenger-carrying kite, hydrofoil. d, Joseph-
Armand Bombardier (1907-64), snowmobile.

No. 1833 — Food: a, Sir Charles Saunders
(1867-1937), Marquis wheat. b, Pablum. c, Dr.
Archibald Gowanlock Huntsman (1883-1973),
marketer of frozen fish. d, Products of McCain
Foods, Ltd., tractor.

No. 1834 — Enterprising Giants: a, Hudson's Bay Company (Colonist, Indian, canoe).
b, Bell Canada Enterprises (earth, satellite,
string of binary digits). c, Vachon Co. snack
cakes. d, George Weston Limited (Baked
goods, eggs).

1999-2000	Litho.	Perf. 13¼	
1818	A730 Pane of 4	6.50	6.50
a.-d.	46c any single	1.60	1.25
1819	A730 Pane of 4	6.50	6.50
a.-d.	46c any single	1.60	1.25
1820	A730 Pane of 4	6.50	6.50
a.-d.	46c any single	1.60	1.25
1821	A730 Pane of 4	6.50	6.50
a.-d.	46c any single	1.60	1.25
1822	A730 Pane of 4	6.50	6.50
a.-d.	46c any single	1.60	1.25
1823	A730 Pane of 4	6.50	6.50
a.-d.	46c any single	1.60	1.25
1824	A730 Pane of 4	6.50	6.50
a.-d.	46c any single	1.60	1.25
1825	A730 Pane of 4	6.50	6.50
a.-d.	46c any single	1.60	1.25
1826	A730 Pane of 4	6.50	6.50
a.-d.	46c any single	1.60	1.25
1827	A730 Pane of 4	6.50	6.50
a.-d.	46c any single	1.60	1.25
1828	A730 Pane of 4	6.50	6.50
a.-d.	46c any single	1.60	1.25
1829	A730 Pane of 4	6.50	6.50
a.-d.	46c any single	1.60	1.25
1830	A730 Pane of 4	6.50	6.50
a.-d.	46c any single	1.60	1.25
1831	A730 Pane of 4	6.50	6.50
a.-d.	46c any single	1.60	1.25
1832	A730 Pane of 4	6.50	6.50
a.-d.	46c any single	1.60	1.25
1833	A730 Pane of 4	6.50	6.50
a.-d.	46c any single	1.60	1.25
1834	A730 Pane of 4	6.50	6.50
a.-d.	46c any single	1.60	1.25
	Nos. 1818-1834 (17)	110.50	110.50

Issued: Nos. 1818-1821, 12/17; Nos. 1822-
1825, 1/17/00; Nos. 1826-1830, 2/17/00; Nos.
1831-1834, 3/17/00.

Stamps similar to these were printed in a
hardcover book produced by Canada Post
Sept. 15, 1999 that sold for $59.99. Stamps
from souvenir panes show a distinct upward
turn of the tails of the nines in the small 1999
date at upper left. The tails of the nines on
stamps from the book are flat.

Millennium — A731

2000, Jan. 1		Perf. 13x12½	
1835	A731 46c multicolored	.75	.25

New Year 2000 (Year of the Dragon) — A732

Litho. & Embossed

2000, Jan. 5 **Perf. 12½x12¾**
1836 A732 46c multicolored .75 .25
　　a.　Red and tagging omitted 1,100.

Souvenir Sheet
Perf. 13¾x13¼
1837 A732 95c multicolored 1.70 1.70
　　a.　Orange and tagging omit-
　　　　ted 1,500.

No. 1837 has rounded corners and contains one 56x29mm stamp.

50th National Hockey League All-Star Game A733

Famous NHL players: a, Wayne Gretzky (Oilers jersey No. 99). b, Gordie Howe (Red Wings jersey No. 9). c, Maurice Richard (red, white and blue Canadiens jersey No. 9). d, Doug Harvey (Canadiens jersey No. 2). e, Bobby Orr (Bruins jersey No. 4). f, Jacques Plante (Canadiens jersey No. 1).

2000, Feb. 5 **Litho.** **Perf. 12¾**
1838　　Pane of 6 4.50 4.50
　　a.-f.　A733 46c any single .75 .60

Bird Type of 1996

Designs: Nos. 1839, 1843, Canada warbler. Nos. 1840, 1844, Osprey. Nos. 1841, 1845, Pacific loon. Nos. 1842, 1846, Blue jay.

2000, Mar. 1 **Litho.** **Perf. 12½x13¼**
1839 A650 46c multi .90 .30
1840 A650 46c multi .90 .30
1841 A650 46c multi .90 .30
1842 A650 46c multi .90 .30
　　a.　Block or strip of 4 3.60 2.50

Booklet Stamps
Self-Adhesive
Die Cut 11½x11¼
1843 A650 46c multi .90 .30
1844 A650 46c multi .90 .30
1845 A650 46c multi .90 .30
1846 A650 95c multi .90 .30
　　a.　Booklet pane, 2 each #1843-
　　　　1844, 1 each #1845-1846 5.50
　　b.　Booklet pane, 2 each #1845-
　　　　1846, 1 each #1843-1844 5.50
　　　　Complete bklt., #1846a,
　　　　1846b 11.00

Nos. 1839-1842 were issued in panes of 20, 5 each printed checkerwise to contain 4 complete blocks or strips.

Supreme Court, 125th Anniv. A734

2000, Apr. 10 **Perf. 12½x13¼**
1847 A734 46c multi .75 .25

Ritual of the Calling of an Engineer, 75th Anniv. — A735

2000, Apr. 25
1848 A735 46c multi .75 .25
　　a.　Tete-beche pair 1.50 1.10
　　b.　Silver ("CANADA 46")
　　　　omitted 2,250.

Decorated Rural Mailboxes — A736

Mailboxes with: No. 1849, Ship, fish, house designs. No. 1850, Flower, cow and church designs. No. 1851, Tractor design. No. 1852, Goose head, house designs.

Booklet Stamps
Perf. 12½x13¼ on 3 sides
2000, Apr. 28
1849 A736 46c multi .90 .40
1850 A736 46c multi .90 .40
1851 A736 46c multi .90 .40
1852 A736 46c multi .90 .40
　　a.　Block of 4, #1849-1852 3.60 2.75
　　b.　Bklt. pane, 3 ea #1849-1852 11.00
　　　　Complete booklet, #1852a 11.50

Picture Frame A737

Self-Adhesive
Serpentine Die Cut 11½
2000, Apr. 28
1853 A737 46c multi .90 .60
　　a.　Booklet pane of 5 + 5 differ-
　　　　ent labels 4.50
　　　　Complete booklet, #1853a 5.00
　　b.　Pane of 25 + stickers 75.00

No. 1853b sold for $24.95 each for one or two panes, and $22.95 for three to ten panes. Twenty-five self-adhesive, die cut address labels and reproductions of a photo sent in by the customer are on the reverse of No. 1853b. These panes were not available at post offices or through the philatelic bureau, but special orders from the printer, Ashton-Potter. The front cover of the booklet containing No. 1853a served as the order blank for No. 1853b.

See Nos. 1872, 1882.

A738

A739

A740

A741

A742

A743

A744

A745

A746

Fresh Waters — A747

Self-Adhesive
Serpentine Die Cut 2½ Horiz.
2000, Feb. 23
1854　　Complete booklet, #a.-e. 7.50
　　a.　A738 55c multi 1.50 .90
　　b.　A739 55c multi 1.50 .90
　　c.　A740 55c multi 1.50 .90
　　d.　A741 55c multi 1.50 .90
　　e.　A742 55c multi 1.50 .90
1855　　Complete booklet, #a.-e. 9.50
　　a.　A743 95c multi 1.90 1.50
　　b.　A744 95c multi 1.90 1.50
　　c.　A745 95c multi 1.90 1.50
　　d.　A746 95c multi 1.90 1.50
　　e.　A747 95c multi 1.90 1.50

Queen Mother (b. 1900) A748

2000, May 23 **Perf. 13x13¼**
1856 A748 95c multi 1.50 .90
　　a.　Imperf., pair 750.00

Boys and Girls Clubs of Canada, Cent. — A749

2000, June 1 **Perf. 13**
1857 A749 46c multi .70 .25

World Session of Seventh Day Adventist Church, Toronto A750

2000, June 29 **Perf. 13½x13¼**
1858 A750 46c multi .90 .25

Stampin' the Future Children's Stamp Design Contest Winners A751

Designs: No. 1859, Rainbow, space vehicle, astronauts, flag, by Rosalie Anne Nardelli. No. 1860, Three children in space vehicle, three children on ground, by Sarah Lutgen. No. 1861, Children and map of Canada, by Christine Weera. No. 1862, Two astronauts in space vehicle, planets, by Andrew Wright.

2000, July 1 **Perf. 13¼**
1859 A751 46c multi .70 .35
1860 A751 46c multi .70 .35
1861 A751 46c multi .70 .35
1862 A751 46c multi .70 .35
　　a.　Block or strip, #1859-1862 2.80 2.25
　　b.　Souvenir sheet, #1859-1862 4.50 3.00

Art Type of 1988

The Artist at Niagara, by Cornelius Krieghoff.

Litho. with Foil Application
2000, July 7 **Perf. 12½x13¼**
1863 A546 95c multi 1.40 .90

Tall Ships in Halifax Harbor — A752

Various ships: No. 1864, Denomination at L. No. 1865, Denomination at R.

Self-Adhesive
Booklet Stamps
Serpentine Die Cut 4¾x5
2000, July 19 **Litho.**
1864 A752 46c multicolored .90 .40
1865 A752 46c multicolored .90 .40
　　a.　Pair, #1864-1865 1.80
　　b.　Booklet, 5 #1864a 9.00

Dept. of Labor, Cent. — A753

2000, Sept. 1 **Perf. 12½x13¼**
1866 A753 46c multi .70 .25

Petro-Canada, 25th Anniv. — A754

Self-Adhesive Booklet Stamp

2000, Sept. 13 — *Die Cut*

1867	A754	46c multi	.90	.40
a.		Booklet pane of 12	11.00	
		Booklet, #1867a	11.50	
b.		Die cutting inverted (2 points jut at T, L)	7.50	7.50

No. 1867a is the cover of an informational booklet about Petro-Canada. No. 1867b was issued in collector packs.

Cetaceans — A755

No. 1868, Monodon monoceros. No. 1869, Balaenoptera musculus. No. 1870, Balaena mysticetus. No. 1871, Delphinapterus leucas.

2000, Oct. 2 — *Perf. 12½x13*

1868	A755	46c multi	.75	.30
1869	A755	46c multi	.75	.30
1870	A755	46c multi	.75	.30
1871	A755	46c multi	.75	.30
a.		Block of 4, #1868-1871	3.00	2.25

Christmas A756

Self-Adhesive Booklet Stamp

Serpentine Die Cut 11¾

2000, Oct. 5

1872	A756	46c multi	.90	.80
a.		Booklet pane of 5 + 5 labels	4.50	
		Booklet, #1872a	5.00	
b.		Pane of 25 + stickers	75.00	

See No. 1882f.

Christmas A757

Designs: 46c, Adoration of the shepherds. 55c, Creche. 95c, Flight into Egypt.

2000, Nov. 3 — *Perf. 13¼*

1873	A757	46c multi	.70	.25
a.		Booklet pane of 10	7.00	8.50
		Booklet, #1873a	7.50	
1874	A757	55c multi	.80	.35
a.		Booklet pane of 6	5.00	6.00
		Booklet, #1874a	5.50	
1875	A757	95c multi	1.40	.65
a.		Booklet pane of 6	8.50	9.50
		Booklet, #1875a	9.00	
		Nos. 1873-1875 (3)	2.90	1.25

Regiments A758

No. 1876, Lord Strathcona's Horse Regiment. No. 1877, Les Voltigeurs de Quebec.

2000, Nov. 11 — *Perf. 13¼x13*

1876	A758	46c multi	.70	.30
1877	A758	46c multi	.70	.30
a.		Pair, #1876-1877	1.40	.90

Maple Leaves A759

Animals A760

Designs: 60c, Red fox. 75c, Gray wolf. $1.05, White-tailed deer.

Coil Stamps

Serpentine Die Cut 8½ Horiz.

2000, Dec. 28 — *Self-Adhesive*

1878	A759	47c multi	.70	.25
a.		Blue inscriptions omitted	600.00	
1879	A760	60c multi	1.00	.35
a.		Booklet pane of 6	10.00	
1880	A760	75c multi	1.10	.45
1881	A760	$1.05 multi	1.60	.75
a.		Booklet pane of 6	11.00	
		Nos. 1878-1881 (4)	4.40	1.80

Nos. 1879a and 1881a are complete booklets. See No. 1927.

Frame Type of 2000

No. 1882: a, Silver. b, Like #1853. c, Mahogany. d, Love (roses). e, Christmas.

Booklet Stamps

Serpentine Die Cut 11¾

2000, Dec. 28 — *Self-Adhesive*

1882		Bklt. pane of 5 + 5 labels	4.50	
a.-e.		A737 47c any single	.90	.90
		Booklet, #1882	5.00	
f.		Pane of 25 + stickers	75.00	

No. 1882f was available only by special order.

New Year 2001 (Year of the Snake) A761

Litho. & Embossed

2001, Jan. 5 — *Perf. 13¼*

1883	A761	47c green & multi	.75	.25
a.		Gold omitted	1,300.	

Souvenir Sheet

1884	A761	$1.05 brown & multi	2.25	2.25

National Hockey League Stars A762

No. 1885: a, Jean Beliveau (Montreal Canadiens jersey No. 4). b, Terry Sawchuk (goalie in Detroit Red Wings uniform). c, Eddie Shore (Boston Bruins jersey No. 2). d, Denis Potvin (Islanders jersey No. 5). e, Bobby Hull (Chicago Black Hawks jersey No. 9). f, Syl Apps, Sr. (Toronto Maple Leafs jersey).

Perf. 12½x13 on 3 sides

2001, Jan. 18 — *Litho.*

1885		Sheet of 6 + 3 labels	4.50	4.50
a.-f.		A762 47c any single	.75	.45
g.		Strip of 3 (#1885a, 1885c, 1885e), blue circle and text omitted	8,000.	

Bird Type of 1996

Designs: Nos. 1886, 1890, Golden eagle. Nos. 1887, 1891, Arctic tern. Nos. 1888, 1892, Rock ptarmigan. Nos. 1889, 1893, Lapland longspur.

2001, Feb. 1 — *Perf. 12½x13*

1886	A650	47c multi	.75	.30
1887	A650	47c multi	.75	.30
1888	A650	47c multi	.75	.30
1889	A650	47c multi	.75	.30
a.		Block or strip of 4, #1886-1889	3.00	2.25

Booklet Stamps Self-Adhesive

Die Cut Perf 11½x11¼

1890	A650	47c multi	.90	.35
1891	A650	47c multi	.90	.35
1892	A650	47c multi	.90	.35
1893	A650	47c multi	.90	.35
a.		Booklet pane, 2 each #1890-1891, 1 each #1892-1893	5.50	
b.		Booklet pane, 2 each #1892-1893, 1 each #1890-1891	5.50	
		Booklet, #1893a, 1893b	11.00	

Nos. 1886-1889 were issued in panes of 20, 5 each printed checkerwise to contain 4 complete blocks or strips.

Games of La Francophonie, Ottawa and Hull — A763

2001, Feb. 28 — *Perf. 13¼*

1894		47c High jumper	.70	.25
1895		47c Dancer	.70	.25
a.		A763 Horiz. pair, #1894-1895	1.40	.90

World Figure Skating Championships, Vancouver — A764

Designs: No. 1896, Pairs. No. 1897, Ice dancing. No. 1898, Men's singles. No. 1899, Women's singles.

2001, Mar. 19 — *Perf. 13x12½*

1896	A764	47c shown	.70	.30
1897	A764	47c multi	.70	.30
1898	A764	47c multi	.70	.30
1899	A764	47c multi	.70	.30
a.		Block of 4, #1896-1899	2.80	2.25

First Canadian Postage Stamps, 150th Anniv. — A765

Litho. & Engr.

2001, Apr. 6 — *Perf. 13*

1900	A765	47c multi	.75	.25

Toronto Blue Jays Baseball Team, 25th Anniv. A766

Self-Adhesive

2001, Apr. 9 — *Litho.* — *Die Cut*

1901	A766	47c multi	.90	.25
a.		Booklet pane of 8	7.25	

No. 1901a is a complete booklet.

Summit of the Americas, Quebec — A767

2001, Apr. 20 — *Perf. 13¼x13*

1902	A767	47c multi	.75	.25

Tourist Attractions — A768

No. 1903: a, Butchart Gardens, British Columbia. b, Apple Blossom Festival, Nova Scotia. c, White Pass and Yukon Route. d, Sugar bushes, Quebec. e, Niagara-on-the-Lake, Ontario.

No. 1904: a, The Forks, Manitoba. b, Barkerville, British Columbia. c, Canadian Tulip Festival, Ontario. d, Auyuittuq National Park, Nunavut. e, Signal Hill National Historic Site, Newfoundland.

Self-Adhesive

2001, May 11 — *Die Cut Perf. 11x11¼*

1903		Booklet of 5	4.50	
a.-e.		A768 60c any single	.90	.75
1904		Booklet of 5	8.50	
a.-e.		A768 $1.05 any single	1.70	1.10

See Nos. 1952-1953, 1989-1990, 2019-2023.

Armenian Church, 1,700th Anniv. — A769

2001, May 16 — *Perf. 13x12½*

1905	A769	47c multi	.70	.25

Royal Military College of Canada, 125th Anniv. — A770

2001, June 1 — *Perf. 12½x13*

1906	A770	47c multi	.70	.25

Eighth Intl. Amateur Athletic Federation World Championships, Edmonton — A771

2001, June 25 — *Perf. 12¾x12½*

1907		47c Pole vault	.70	.25
1908		47c Runner	.70	.25
a.		A771 Pair, #1907-1908	1.40	.90

Pierre Elliott Trudeau (1919-2000), Prime Minister — A772

2001, July 1   **Perf. 13x12½**
1909 A772 47c multi   .70   .25
  a.   Souvenir sheet of 4   3.00 3.00

Roses — A773

Designs: Nos. 1910a, 1911, Morden Centennial. Nos. 1910b, 1912, Agnes. Nos. 1910c, 1913, Champlain. Nos. 1910d, 1914, Canadian White Star.

Souvenir Sheet
2001, Aug. 1   **Perf. 12½x13**
1910 Pane of 4   4.40 4.40
  a.-d. A773 47c Any single   1.10 1.10

Booklet Stamps
Die Cut
1911 A773 47c multi   .75   .30
1912 A773 47c multi   .75   .30
1913 A773 47c multi   .75   .30
1914 A773 47c multi   .75   .30
  a.   Booklet pane, #1911-1914 3.00
  b.   Booklet, 3 #1914a   9.00

Phila Nippon '01, Japan (No. 1910). Die cutting on Nos. 1911-1914 has "thorn" at the center of each side, pointing outward at top and left and toward the design at bottom and right.

Great Peace of Montreal, 300th Anniv. — A774

2001, Aug. 3   **Perf. 12½x13**
1915 A774 47c multi   .70   .25

Art Type of 1988

Design: The Space Between Columns #21 (Italian), by Jack Shadbolt.

Litho. with Foil Application
2001, Aug. 24   **Perf. 13x13¼**
1916 A546 $1.05 multi   1.70   .90

Shriners — A775

2001, Sept. 19 Litho.   Perf. 13¼x13
1917 A775 47c multi   .70   .25

Frame Type of 2000 Inscribed "Domestic Lettermail / Poste-lettres du régime intérieur"

No. 1918: a, Like #1882a. b, Like #1882b. c, Baby toys and flowers. d, Like #1882d. e, Like #1882e.

Serpentine Die Cut 11¾
2001, Sept. 21   **Self-Adhesive**
1918   Bklt. pane of 5 + 5 labels   5.00
  a.-e. A737 (47c) Any single   1.00 1.00
          Booklet, #1918   5.50
  f.   Pane of 25 + stickers   75.00
  g.   Pane of 10 + stickers   60.00

Nos. 1918f and 1918g were available only by special order.

Theater Anniversaries — A776

Designs: No. 1919, Théatre du Nouveau Monde, Montreal, 50th anniv. No. 1920, Grand Theater, London, Ont., cent.

2001, Sept. 28   **Perf. 12½x12¾**
1919 A776 47c multi   .75   .25
1920 A776 47c multi   .75   .25
  a.   Horiz. pair, #1919-1920   1.50   .90

Hot Air Balloons A777

Background colors: a, Green. b, Blue violet. c, Red violet. d, Olive.

Self-Adhesive
2001, Oct. 1   **Die Cut**
1921   Booklet, 2 each #a-d   7.25
  a.-d. A777 47c Any single   .90   .40

Christmas A778

Illuminated trees and: 47c, Horse-drawn sleigh. 60c, Skaters. $1.05, Children making snowman.

2001, Nov. 1   **Perf. 12½x13¼**
1922 A778   47c multi   .75   .25
  a.   Booklet pane of 10   7.50 7.50
          Booklet, #1922a   8.00
1923 A778   60c multi   .90   .40
  a.   Booklet pane of 6   5.50 5.50
          Booklet, #1923a   6.00
1924 A778 $1.05 multi   1.65   .60
  a.   Booklet pane of 6   10.00 10.00
          Booklet, #1924a   10.50

YMCA in Canada, 150th Anniv. — A779

2001, Nov. 8   **Perf. 13¼**
1925 A779 47c multi   .75   .25

Royal Canadian Legion, 75th Anniv. — A780

2001, Nov. 11   **Perf. 12½x13**
1926 A780 47c multi   .75   .25

Maple Leaves Type of 2000, Traditional Handiwork Type of 1999 and

Flag and Canada Post Headquarters, Ottawa — A781

Designs: 65c, Jewelry making, horiz. 77c, Basket weaving, horiz. $1.25, Sculpture, horiz.

Self-Adhesive
Coil Stamps
Serpentine Die Cut 8½ Horiz.
2002, Jan. 2
1927 A759   48c multi   .75   .25
1928 A684   65c multi   1.00   .30
  a.   Booklet of 6   6.00
1929 A684   77c multi   1.10   .40
1930 A684 $1.25 multi   1.80   .65
  a.   Booklet of 6   11.00

Booklet Stamp
Serpentine Die Cut 8½
1931 A781   48c multi   .75   .25
  a.   Booklet of 10   7.50
  b.   Booklet of 30   22.50
  c.   Blue omitted   375.00
       Nos. 1927-1931 (5)   5.40 1.85

By separating the booklet along the columns of rouletting, No. 1931b could be broken up into three separately obtainable examples of No. 1931a. See No. 1991.

Reign of Queen Elizabeth II, 50th Anniv. A782

2002, Jan. 2   **Perf. 13¼x12½**
1932 A782 48c multi   .70   .25
  a.   Imperf, pair   1,200.
  b.   Gold omitted   1,300.

New Year 2002 (Year of the Horse) — A783

Horse and: 48c, Bamboo leaves. $1.25, Peach blossoms.

Litho. & Embossed With Foil Application
2002, Jan. 3   **Perf. 13¼**
1933 A783   48c multi   .75   .25
  a.   Foil (horse) omitted   1,150.

Souvenir Sheet
1934 A783 $1.25 multi   2.25 2.25

National Hockey League Stars A784

No. 1935: a, Tim Horton (Toronto Maple Leafs jersey No. 7). b, Guy Lafleur (Montreal Canadiens jersey No. 10). c, Howie Morenz (Canadiens jersey, with brown gloves). d, Glenn Hall (Chicago Black Hawks jersey No. 1). e, Red Kelly (Maple Leafs jersey No. 4). f, Phil Esposito (Boston Bruins jersey no. 7).

Perf. 12½x13 on 3 Sides
2002, Jan. 12
1935   Pane of 6 + 3 labels   5.00 5.00
  a.-f. A784 48c Any single   .80   .60

2002 Winter Olympics, Salt Lake City — A785

Designs: No. 1936, Short track speed skating. No. 1937, Curling. No. 1938, Freestyle aerial skiing. No. 1939, Women's hockey.

2002, Jan. 25   **Perf. 13¼x13**
1936 A785 48c multi   .75   .35
1937 A785 48c multi   .75   .35
1938 A785 48c multi   .75   .35
1939 A785 48c multi   .75   .35
  a.   Block or strip of 4, #1936-1939 3.00 2.50

Appointment of First Canadian Governor General, 50th Anniv. — A786

2002, Feb. 1   **Perf. 13¼x12½**
1940 A786 48c multi   .75   .25

Universities — A787

Design: No. 1941, University of Manitoba, 125th anniv. No. 1942, Laval University, 150th anniv. No. 1943, University of Trinity College, 150th anniv. No. 1944, Saint Mary's University, Halifax, 200th anniv.

2002   Booklet Stamp   Perf. 13½
1941 A787 48c multi   .75   .25
  a.   Booklet pane of 8   6.00 6.00
          Booklet, #1941a   6.50
1942 A787 48c multi   .75   .25
  a.   Booklet pane of 8   6.00 6.00
          Booklet, #1942a   6.50
1943 A787 48c multi   .75   .25
  a.   Booklet pane of 8   6.00 6.00
          Booklet, #1943a   6.50
1944 A787 48c multi   .75   .25
  a.   Booklet pane of 8   6.00 6.00
          Booklet, #1944a   6.50
       Nos. 1941-1944 (4)   3.00 1.00

Issued: No. 1941, 2/28. No. 1942, 4/4. No. 1943, 4/30. No. 1944, 5/27.

Art Type of 1988

Design: Church and Horse, by Alex Colville.

Litho. with Foil Application
2002, Mar. 22   **Perf. 12½x13**
1945 A546 $1.25 multi   1.80 1.10
  a.   Foil only (all other colors and tagging omitted)   1,500.
  b.   Imperf, pair   1,350.

Tulips — A788

Tulip varieties: a, City of Vancouver. b, Monte Carlo. c, Ottawa. d, The Bishop.

No. 1947: a, Like #1946a. b, Like #1946b. c, Like #1946c. d, Like #1946d.

Self-Adhesive
2002, May 3   Litho.   Die Cut
1946   Booklet pane of 4   3.00
a.-d.   A788 48c Any single   .75   .30
    Booklet, 2 #1946   6.00

Souvenir Sheet
Perf. 13x12½
1947   Pane of 4   3.25   3.25
a.-d.   A788 48c Any single   .80   .80

Issued: No. 1946, 5/3; No. 1947, 8/30.

Dendronepthea Giagantea and Dendronepthea Corals — A789

Tubastrea and Echinogorgia Corals — A790

North Atlantic Pink Tree, Pacific Orange Cup and North Pacific Horn Corals — A791

North Atlantic Giant Orange Tree and Black Corals — A792

2002, May 19   Perf. 12½x13
1948   A789 48c multi   .70   .30
1949   A790 48c multi   .70   .30
1950   A791 48c multi   .70   .30
1951   A792 48c multi   .70   .30
a.   Block of 4, #1948-1951   2.80   2.00
b.   Souvenir sheet #1948-1951, perf. 13¼x13   3.75   3.75

See Hong Kong Nos. 979-982.

Tourist Attractions Type of 2001
No. 1952: a, Yukon Quest, Yukon Territory. b, Icefields Parkway, Alberta. c, Agawa Canyon, Ontario. d, Old Port of Montreal, Quebec. e, Kings Landing, New Brunswick.

No. 1953: a, Northern Lights, Northwest Territories. b, Stanley Park, Vancouver, British Columbia. c, Head-Smashed-In Buffalo Jump, Alberta. d, Saguenay Fjord, Quebec. e, Peggy's Cove, Nova Scotia.

Self-Adhesive
2002, June 1   Die Cut Perf. 11x11¼
1952   Booklet of 5   5.50
a.-e.   A768 65c Any single   1.10   .75
1953   Booklet of 5   10.00
a.-e.   A768 $1.25 Any single   2.00   1.10

Sculpture — A793

Designs: No. 1954, Embacle, by Charles Daudelin. No. 1955, Lumberjacks, by Leo Mol.

2002, June 10   Perf. 13¼
1954   A793 48c multi   .75   .25
1955   A793 48c multi   .75   .25
a.   Horiz. or vert. pair, #1954-1955   1.50   .90

Canadian Postmasters and Assistants Association, Cent. — A794

2002, July 5   Perf. 13¼x12½
1956   A794 48c multi   .75   .25

Printed in panes of 16 stamps + 12 labels.

17th World Youth Day, Toronto — A795

Self-Adhesive Booklet Stamp
2002, July 23   Die Cut
1957   A795 48c multi   .75   .30
a.   Booklet of 8   6.00

Public Services International World Congress, Ottawa — A796

2002, Sept. 4   Perf. 12½x13
1958   A796 48c multi   .75   .25

Public Pensions, 75th Anniv. — A797

2002, Sept. 10   Perf. 13¼
1959   A797 48c multi   .75   .25

Souvenir Sheet

Intl. Year of Mountains — A798

No. 1960: a, Mt. Logan, Canada. b, Mt. Elbrus, Russia. c, Puncak Jaya, Indonesia. d, Mt. Everest, Nepal and China. e, Mt. Kilimanjaro, Tanzania. f, Vinson Massif, Antarctica. g, Mt. Aconcagua, Argentina. h, Mt. McKinley, Alaska.

Self-Adhesive
2002, Oct. 1   Die Cut
1960   A798   Pane of 8 + 8 labels   7.25
a.-h.   48c Any single   .90   1.10

World Teachers' Day — A799

2002, Oct. 4   Perf. 12½x13
1961   A799 48c multi   .75   .25

Toronto Stock Exchange, 150th Anniv. — A800

2002, Oct. 24
1962   A800 48c multi   .75   .25

Communication Technology Centenaries — A801

Part of map of North America and: No. 1963, Sir Sandford Fleming (1827-1915), cable-laying ship. No. 1964, Guglielmo Marconi (1874-1937), radio and transmission towers.

2002, Oct. 31   Perf. 13x12½
1963   48c multi   .75   .25
1964   48c multi   .75   .25
a.   A801 Horiz. pair, #1963-1964   1.50   1.10

Cent. of first telegraph message sent over transpacific cable (No. 1963); first transatlantic radio message (No. 1964).

Christmas A802

Art by aboriginals: 48c, Genesis, by Daphne Odjig. 65c, Winter Travel, by Cecil Youngfox. $1.25, Mary and Child, sculpture by Irene Katak Angutitaq.

2002, Nov. 4   Perf. 12½x13
1965   A802   48c multi   .75   .25
a.   Booklet pane of 10   7.50   7.50
    Booklet, #1965a   8.00
1966   A802   65c multi   1.00   .40
a.   Booklet pane of 6   6.00   6.00
    Booklet, #1966a   6.50
1967   A802 $1.25 multi   2.00   .75
a.   Booklet pane of 6   12.00   12.00
    Booklet, #1967a   12.50
    Nos. 1965-1967 (3)   3.75   1.40

Quebec Symphony Orchestra, Cent. A803

2002, Nov. 7
1968   A803 48c multi   .80   .30

New Year 2003 (Year of the Ram) — A804

Litho. & Embossed with Foil Application
2003, Jan. 3   Perf. 13
1969   A804   48c shown   .75   .25
a.   Gold omitted   400.00
b.   Imperf, pair   2,000.

Souvenir Sheet
Perf. 13¼
1970   A804 $1.25 Ram, diff.   2.50   2.50

No. 1970 contains one 33x58mm stamp. Slits replace perforations on the vertical sides of the stamps between the point of the acute angle made with the curving perforations and the point perpendicular to where the perforations on the opposite side form the obtuse angle with the curving perforations.

National Hockey League Stars A805

Designs: Nos. 1971a, 1972a, Frank Mahovlich (orange panel). Nos. 1971b, 1972b, Raymond Bourque (lilac panel). Nos. 1971c, 1972c, Serge Savard (blue panel). Nos. 1971d, 1972d, Stan Mikita (red violet panel). Nos. 1971e, 1972e, Mike Bossy (bright pink panel). Nos. 1971f, 1972f, Bill Durnan (green panel).

Perf. 12½x13¼ on 3 Sides
2003, Jan. 18
1971   Pane of 6 + 3 labels   14.00   —
a.-f.   A805 48c Any single   2.25   1.50

Self-Adhseive
Die Cut
1972   Pane of 6   65.00   —
a.-f.   A805 48c Any single   7.00   1.50

Universities A806

Design: No. 1973, Bishop's University, Lennoxville, Quebec, 150th anniv. No. 1974, University of Western Ontario, London, Ont., 125th anniv. No. 1975, St. Francis Xavier University, Antigonish, N. S., 150th Anniv. No. 1976, Macdonald Institute, Guelph, Ont., cent. No. 1977, University of Montreal, 125th anniv.

Booklet Stamps
2003   Perf. 13¼x13½
1973   A806 48c multi   .75   .25
a.   Booklet pane of 8   6.00   6.00
    Booklet, #1973a   6.50
1974   A806 48c multi   .75   .25
a.   Booklet pane of 8   6.00   6.00
    Booklet, #1974a   6.50
1975   A806 48c multi   .75   .25
a.   Booklet pane of 8   6.00   6.00
    Complete booklet, #1975a   6.50
1976   A806 48c multi   .75   .25
a.   Booklet pane of 8   6.00   6.00
    Complete booklet, #1976a   6.50
1977   A806 48c multi   .75   .25
a.   Booklet pane of 8   6.00   6.00
    Complete booklet, #1977a   6.50

Issued: No. 1973, 1/28. No. 1975, 4/4. No. 1976, 6/20. No. 1977, 9/4. No. 1974, 3/19. See Nos. 2033-2034, 2089, 2172, 2209-2210.

Bird Paintings by John James
Audubon — A807

Designs: No. 1979, Leach's storm petrel.
No. 1980, Brant. No. 1981, Great cormorant.
No. 1982, Common murre. 65c, Gyrfalcon,
vert.

2003, Feb. 21　　　　**Perf. 13¼x12½**
1979	A807	48c multi	.75	.35
1980	A807	48c multi	.75	.35
1981	A807	48c multi	.75	.35
1982	A807	48c multi	.75	.35
a.		Block of 4, #1979-1982	3.00	2.25

Booklet Stamp
Self-Adhesive
Die Cut

1983	A807	65c multi	1.10	.75
a.		Booklet pane of 6	6.75	
		Nos. 1979-1983 (5)	4.10	2.15

Canadian Rangers — A808

2003, Mar. 3　　　　**Perf. 12½x13¼**
| 1984 | A808 | 48c multi | .75 | .25 |

American
Hellenic
Educational
Progressive
Association In
Canada, 75th
Anniv. — A809

2003, Mar. 25
| 1985 | A809 | 48c multi | .75 | .25 |

Volunteer Firefighters — A810

2003, May 30　　　　**Perf. 13¼**
| 1986 | A810 | 48c multi | .75 | .25 |

Coronation
of Queen
Elizabeth II,
50th Anniv.
A811

2003, June 2　　　　**Perf. 13x12½**
| 1987 | A811 | 48c multi | .75 | .25 |

Quebec City, Seal of Sovereign
Council of New France, Signature of
Pedro da Silva — A812

2003, June 6　　　　**Perf. 13**
| 1988 | A812 | 48c multi | .75 | .25 |

Pedro da Silva, first courier in New France,
50th anniv. of Portuguese immigration to
Canada.

Tourist Attractions Type of 2001

No. 1989: a, Wilberforce Falls, Nunavut. b,
Inside Passage, B. C. c, Royal Canadian
Mounted Police Depot Division, Regina, Sask.
d, Casa Loma, Toronto, Ont. e, Gatineau Park,
Que.
No. 1990: a, Dragon boat races, Vancouver,
B. C. b, Polar bear watching, Man. c, Niagara
Falls, Ont. d, Magdalen Islands, Que. e,
Charlottestown, P. E. I.

Self-Adhesive

2003, June 12　　　**Die Cut Perf. 11¼**
1989		Booklet of 5	5.50	
a.-e.	A768	65c Any single	1.10	.75
1990		Booklet of 5	10.00	
a.-e.	A768	$1.25 Any single	2.00	1.10

"Vancouver 2010"
Added in Red

Self-Adhesive
Booklet Stamp
Serpentine Die Cut 8½

2003, July 11　　　　**Litho.**
1991	A781	48c multi	1.50	1.20
a.		Booklet of 10	15.00	
b.		Booklet of 30	45.00	
e.		Die cutting omitted, pair	800.00	

Selection of Vancouver as site of 2010 Winter Olympics. By separating the booklet along
the columns of rouletting, No. 1991b could be
broken up into three separately obtainable
examples of No. 1991a.

Canada-Alaska Cruise
Scenes — A813

Mountains and: No. 1991C, Totem pole. No.
1991D, Whale's tail.

Self-Adhesive

2003, July 19　　　　**Die Cut**
1991C	A813	($1.25) multi	7.50	7.50
1991D	A813	($1.25) multi	7.50	7.50
e.		Horiz. pair, #19901C-1991D	15.00	

Nos. 1991C-1991D were printed in panes of
10 containing five of each stamp. The blank
spaces in each stamp and the three stamp-like
vignettes at the left of the pane that lack die
cutting and "Postage Paid / Port Payé" inscription could be personalized on cruise ships.
Personalized panes sold for $19.95 in US cur-
rency, while unpersonalized panes sold for
$12.50. Value, unpersonalized complete pane
$85.

Lutheran World
Federation, 10th
Assembly,
Winnipeg
A814

2003, July 21　　　　**Perf. 12½x13**
| 1992 | A814 | 48c multi | .75 | .25 |

Korean War Armistice Agreement,
50th Anniv. — A815

2003, July 25　　　　**Perf. 12¾**
| 1993 | A815 | 48c multi | .75 | .25 |

Authors
A816

Designs: No. 1994, Anne Hébert (1916-
2000). No. 1995, Hector de Saint-Denys Garneau (1912-43). No. 1996, Morley Callaghan
(1903-90). No. 1997, Susanna Moodie (1803-
85), and Catharine Parr Traill (1802-99).

Booklet Stamps

2003, Sept. 8　　　　**Perf. 13¼x12½**
1994	A816	48c multi	.75	.35
1995	A816	48c multi	.75	.35
1996	A816	48c multi	.75	.35
1997	A816	48c multi	.75	.35
a.		Block of 4, #1994-1997	3.00	2.25
b.		Booklet pane, 2 #1997a	6.00	
		Complete booklet, #1997b	6.50	

2003 Road Cycling World
Championships, Hamilton,
Ont. — A817

Booklet Stamp

2003, Sept. 10　　　　**Perf. 12½x13**
1998	A817	48c multi	.75	.55
a.		Booklet pane of 8	6.00	—
		Complete booklet, #1998a	6.50	

Canadian
Astronauts
A818

No. 1999: a, Marc Garneau. b, Roberta
Bondar. c, Steve MacLean. d, Chris Hadfield.
e, Robert Thirsk. f, Bjarni Tryggvason. g, Dave
Williams. h, Julie Payette.

Self-Adhesive
Litho. With Foil Application

2003, Oct. 1　　　　**Die Cut**
| 1999 | | Pane of 8 | 8.00 | |
| a.-h. | A818 | 48c Any single | .90 | .90 |

Trees of Canada
and
Thailand — A819

Designs: No. 2000, Acer saccharum leaves
(Canada). No. 2001, Cassia fistula (Thailand).

2003, Oct. 4　**Litho.**　**Perf. 12¾x12½**
2000	A819	48c multi	.75	.25
2001	A819	48c multi	.75	.25
a.		Pair, #2000-2001	1.50	1.10
b.		Souvenir sheet, #2000-2001	7.50	4.00
c.		As "a," imperf	900.00	
d.		As "b," imperf	1,250.	

Bangkok 2003 Intl. Philatelic Exhibition (No.
2001b).
See Thailand No. 2090.

L'Hommage à Rosa Luxemburg, by
Jean-Paul Riopelle — A820

Painting details — No. 2002; a, Red and
blue dots between birds at LR. b, Bird with
yellow beak at center. c, Three birds in circle
at R. d, Sun at UR. e, Birds with purple outlines at L. f, Bird with red outline in circle at R.
$1.25, Pink bird in red circle at R.

2003, Oct. 7　　　　**Perf. 12½x13**
| 2002 | A820 | Pane of 6 | 7.50 | 7.50 |
| a.-f. | | 48c Any single | 1.25 | 1.25 |

Souvenir Sheet
Perf. 12¾
| 2003 | A820 | $1.25 multi | 3.00 | 3.00 |

Christmas
A821

Gift boxes and: 48c, Ice skates. 65c, Teddy
bear. $1.25, Toy duck.

Self-Adhesive
Booklet Stamps

2003, Nov. 4　　　　**Die Cut**
2004	A821	48c multi	.75	.25
a.		Booklet pane of 6	4.50	
		Complete booklet, 2 #2004a	9.00	
b.		Pair, die cutting omitted	375.00	
2005	A821	65c multi	1.00	.60
a.		Booklet pane of 6	6.00	
b.		As "a," die cutting omitted	1,500.	
c.		Die cutting omitted, pair	450.00	
2006	A821	$1.25 multi	2.00	1.00
a.		Booklet pane of 6	12.00	
b.		Die cutting omitted, pair	450.00	
		Nos. 2004-2006 (3)	3.75	1.85

Maple Leaf and Samara
A822

Maple Leaf on Twig
A823

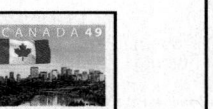

Flag Over Edmonton, Alberta
A824

Queen Elizabeth II
A825

Coil Stamps
Serpentine Die Cut 8½ Horiz.
2003, Dec. 19   **Self-Adhesive**
2008 A822 49c multi   .75   .25
   a. Die cutting omitted, pair   150.00

Serpentine Die Cut 8½ Vert.
2009 A823 80c red & multi   1.20   .40
2010 A823 $1.40 grn & multi   3.00   .55

Booklet Stamps
Die Cut
2011 A824 49c multi   .75   .25
   a. Booklet pane of 10   7.50
   b. Die cutting omitted, pair   150.00
   c. As "a," die cutting omitted   750.00
2012 A825 49c multi   .75   .25
   a. Booklet pane of 10   7.50
2013 A823 80c red & multi   1.50   .40
   a. Booklet pane of 6   9.00
2014 A823 $1.40 grn & multi   2.25   .50
   a. Booklet pane of 6   13.50
   Nos. 2008-2014 (7)   10.20   2.85

See Nos. 2053-2055, 2075.

New Year 2004 (Year of the Monkey) — A826

Scenes from Chinese story *Journey to the West.* 49c, Monkey King. $1.40, Monkey King, Xuan Zang, Sandy, Pigsy and horse.

Litho. & Embossed with Foil Application
2004, Jan. 8   *Perf. 13x12½*
2015 A826 49c multi   .75   .25

Souvenir Sheet
2016 A826 $1.40 multi   3.00   3.00
   a. As No. 2016, with 2004 Hong Kong Stamp Expo ovpt. in margin   3.75   3.75

No. 2016 has rouletted tab at right showing bar code.

National Hockey League Stars
A827

Designs: Nos. 2017a, 2018a, Larry Robinson (blue background). Nos. 2017b, 2018b, Marcel Dionne (orange background). Nos. 2017c, 2018c, Ted Lindsay (red background). Nos. 2017d, 2018d, Johnny Bower (green background). Nos. 2017e, 2018e, Brad Park (brown background). Nos. 2017f, 2018f, Milt Schmidt (purple background).

Perf. 12½x13¼ on 3 Sides
2004, Jan. 24   **Litho.**
2017   Pane of 6 + 3 labels   6.50   6.50
   a.-f. A827 49c Any single   .75   .60

Self-Adhesive
Die Cut
2018   Pane of 6   6.50
   a.-f. A827 49c Any single   .75   .55

Tourist Attractions Type of 2001
Design: No. 2019, Quebec Winter Carnival; No. 2020, St. Joseph's Oratory, Montreal, Quebec; No. 2021, International Jazz Festival, Montreal. No. 2022, Traversée Internationale du Lac St. Jean Swimming Marathon, Quebec; No. 2023, Canadian National Exhibition, Toronto.

Self-Adhesive
Booklet Stamp
2004, Jan. 29   *Die Cut*
2019 A768 49c multi   .75   .35
   a. Booklet of 6   5.00
2020 A768 49c multi   .75   .35
   a. Booklet of 6   5.00
2021 A768 49c multi   .75   .35
   a. Booklet of 6   5.00
2022 A768 49c multi   .75   .35
   a. Booklet of 6   5.00
2023 A768 49c multi   .75   .35
   a. Booklet of 6   5.00

Issued: No. 2019, 1/29; No. 2020, 4/2; No. 2021, 6/1; No. 2022, 6/18; No. 2023, 7/19.

Governor General Ramon John Hnatyshyn (1934-2002) — A828

2004, Mar. 16   *Perf. 12½x13*
2024 A828 49c multi   .75   .25

Royal Canadian Army Cadets, 125th Anniv.
A829

Self-Adhesive
Booklet Stamp
2004, Mar. 26   *Die Cut*
2025 A829 49c multi   .75   .30
   a. Booklet pane of 4   3.00
    Complete booklet, 2 #2025a   6.00

The Fram, Ship of Otto Sverdrup (1854-1930), Arctic Explorer — A830

Litho. & Engr.
2004, Mar. 26   *Perf. 13¼*
2026 A830 49c multi   .75   .25

Souvenir Sheet
2027 A830 $1.40 multi + 2 labels   3.00   3.00
See Greenland No. 426, Norway Nos. 1398-1399.

Urban Transit and Light Rail Systems — A831

Train cars, station names and system emblems of: No. 2028, Toronto Transit Commission. No. 2029, TransLink SkyTrain, Vancouver. No. 2030, Société de Transport de Montreal. No. 2031, Calgary Transit Light Rail.

2004, Mar. 30   **Litho.**   *Perf. 12½x13*
2028 A831 49c multi   .75   .30
2029 A831 49c multi   .75   .30
2030 A831 49c multi   .75   .30
2031 A831 49c multi   .75   .30
   a. Vert. strip of 4, #2028-2031   3.00   2.50

Home Hardware, 40th Anniv. — A832

Self-Adhesive
Booklet Stamp
2004, Apr. 19   *Die Cut Perf. 11*
2032 A832 49c multi   .75   .30
   a. Booklet pane of 10 + label   7.50
    Complete booklet, #2032a   8.00

No. 2032a is the inside front cover of the complete booklet. Fifteen self-adhesive seals are on the inside back cover of the complete booklet.

Universities Type of 2003
Designs: No. 2033, Sherbrooke University, Sherbrooke, Quebec, 50th anniv. No. 2034, University of Prince Edward Island, Charlottetown, bicent.

Booklet Stamps
2004   *Perf. 13¼x13½*
2033 A806 49c multi   .75   .30
   a. Booklet pane of 8   6.00   6.00
    Complete booklet, #2033a   6.50
2034 A806 49c multi   .75   .30
   a. Booklet pane of 8   6.00   6.00
    Complete booklet, #2034a   6.50

Issued: No. 2033, 5/4; No. 2034, 5/8.

Montreal Children's Hospital, Cent. — A833

Self-Adhesive
Booklet Stamp
2004, May 6   *Die Cut Perf. 9½x10¾*
2035 A833 49c multi   .75   .30
   a. Booklet pane of 4   3.00
    Complete booklet, 2 #2035a   6.00

Bird Paintings by John James Audubon
A834

Designs: No. 2036, Ruby-crowned kinglet. No. 2037, White-winged crossbill. No. 2038, Bohemian waxwing. No. 2039, Boreal chickadee. 80c, Lincoln's sparrow.

2004, May 14   *Perf. 12½x13*
2036 A834 49c multi   .75   .35
2037 A834 49c multi   .75   .35
2038 A834 49c multi   .75   .35
2039 A834 49c multi   .75   .35
   a. Block of 4, #2036-2039   3.00   2.50

Self-Adhesive
Booklet Stamp
Die Cut
2040 A834 80c multi   1.20   .75
   a. Booklet pane of 6   7.25
    Nos. 2036-2040 (5)   4.20   2.15

Pioneers of Transatlantic Mail Service — A835

Designs: No. 2041, Sir Samuel Cunard (1787-1865). No. 2042, Sir Hugh Allan (1810-82).

Self-Adhesive
2004, May 28   *Perf. 13¼x12½*
2041 49c multi   .75   .30
2042 49c multi   .75   .30
   a. A835 Horiz. pair #2041-2042   1.50   1.10

D-Day, 60th Anniv.
A836

2004, June 6   *Perf. 13x12½*
2043 A836 49c multi   .75   .30

Pierre Dugua de Mons, Leader of First French Settlement in Acadia, and Ship
A837

2004, June 26   *Litho. & Engr.*
2044 A837 49c multi   .75   .30
See France No. 3032.

Butterfly and Flower
A838

Children on Beach
A839

Rose
A840

Dog
A841

Self-Adhesive
Booklet Stamps
Serpentine Die Cut 11¾
2004, June   **Litho.**
2045 A838 (49c) multi   22.50   13.00
   a. Booklet pane of 2   45.00
    Complete booklet, #2045a + phonecard in greeting card   50.00

2046	A839	(49c) multi	9.00	*13.00*
a.		Booklet pane of 2	18.00	
		Complete booklet, #2046a + phonecard in greeting card	22.00	
2047	A840	(49c) multi	9.00	*13.00*
a.		Booklet pane of 2	18.00	
		Complete booklet, #2047a + phonecard in greeting card	22.00	
2048	A841	(49c) multi	9.00	*13.00*
a.		Booklet pane of 2	18.00	
		Complete booklet, #2048a + phonecard in greeting card	22.00	
	Nos. 2045-2048 (4)		49.50	52.00

Nos. 2045-2048, have a frame like No. 1918a, and are similarly inscribed "Domestic Lettermail" and "Poste-lettres du régime intérieur," but Nos. 2045-2048 have the vignettes printed on the stamps, while any vignettes found on No. 1918a are affixed stickers. Nos. 2045a-2048a are affixed to the insides of greeting cards that contain detachable phonecards valid for 15 minutes calling time on any touchtone phone in Canada or the United States. The stamps were available only in the greeting card, which sold for $5.99 along with a blank envelope for sending the greeting card.

2004 Summer Olympics, Athens — A842

Olympic rings and: No. 2049, Spyros Louis, 1896 Marathon gold medalist, diagram of track, "Athens" in Greek, and stylized runner. No. 2050, Soccer net inscribed "Canada," girls playing soccer.

2004, July 28			**Perf. 12½x13¼**	
2049	A842	49c multi	.75	.30
2050	A842	49c multi	.75	.30
a.		Horiz. pair, #2049-2050	1.50	1.10

Canadian Open Golf Championship, Cent. — A843

Crowd, trophy and golfer: No. 2051, Finishing swing. No. 2052, Ready to putt.

Self-Adhesive

Litho. & Embossed With Foil Application

2004, Aug. 12		*Serpentine Die Cut*		
2051	A843	49c multi	.75	.30
2052	A843	49c multi	.75	.30

Nos. 2051-2052 were issued in a sheet containing four of each stamp.

Maple Leaf Types of 2003
Self-Adhesive Coil Stamps

2004, Aug. 18		**Litho.**	**Die Cut**	
2053	A822	49c multi	.75	.25
a.		Die cutting omitted, pair	180.00	
	Serpentine Die Cut 8¼ Horiz.			
2054	A823	80c red & multi	2.00	.50
2055	A823	$1.40 grn & multi	3.75	.90
a.		Die cutting omitted, pair		
	Nos. 2053-2055 (3)		6.50	1.65

Die cut gauges on Nos. 2054-2055 vary widely within the roll, from 8¼-8¾. Gauge 8¼ is the most common.

Montreal Heart Institute, 50th Anniv. — A844

Self-Adhesive Booklet Stamp

2004, Sept. 15		*Die Cut Perf. 13½*		
2056	A844	49c multi	.75	.30
a.		Booklet pane of 4	3.00	
		Complete booklet, 2 #2056	6.00	

Pets
A845

Self-Adhesive Booklet Stamps

2004, Oct. 1			**Die Cut**	
2057	A845	49c Fish	.80	.35
2058	A845	49c Cats	.80	.35
2059	A845	49c Rabbit	.80	.35
2060	A845	49c Dog	.80	.35
a.		Booklet pane, #2057-2060	3.25	
		Complete booklet, 2 #2060a	6.50	

Nobel Laureates in Chemistry — A846

Designs: No. 2061, Gerhard Herzberg, 1971 laureate, and molecular structures. No. 2062, Michael Smith, 1993 laureate, and DNA double helix.

2004, Oct. 4			**Perf. 12½x13**	
2061	A846	49c multi	.75	.30
2062	A846	49c multi	.75	.30
a.		Pair, #2061-2062	1.50	1.10

Ribbon Frame
A847

Picture Album Frame
A848

Serpentine Die Cut 12¾x13				
2004, Oct. 8			**Self-Adhesive**	
2063	A847	(49c) multi	1.50	1.25
2064	A848	(49c) multi	1.50	1.25

Nos. 2063 and 2064 were each printed in panes of 21 that sold for $9.80. These panes were split by a row of rouletting in the center, with 20 stamps on one side and one on the other side. Panes of 21 with vignettes that could be personalized by the customer were available for $24.95. Panes of 40 stamps with personalized vignettes were also available for $39.95.

Victoria Cross, 150th Anniv. — A849

Designs: No. 2065, Victoria Cross. No. 2066, Design for Canadian Victoria Cross, approved with Queen Elizabeth II's signature.

Litho. & Embossed

2004, Oct. 21			**Perf. 13x12½**	
2065	A849	49c multi	.75	.30
		Litho.		
2066	A849	49c multi	.75	.30
a.		Pair, #2065-2066	1.50	1.20

Paintings by Jean Paul Lemieux — A850

Designs: 49c, Self-portrait. 80c, A June Wedding, horiz. (53x35mm). $1.40, Summer, horiz. (64x31mm).

2004, Oct. 22			**Perf. 13x13¼**	
2067	A850	49c multi	.75	.30
a.		Perf. 13	1.50	1.50
		Souvenir Sheet		
		Perf. 13		
2068		Sheet, #2067a, 2068a, 2068b	4.00	4.00
a.		A850 80c multi	1.50	1.50
b.		A850 $1.40 multi	2.20	2.20

Christmas — A851

Santa Claus and: 49c, Sleigh. 80c, Automobile. $1.40, Train.

Booklet Stamps

Serpentine Die Cut 7¼ Horiz.				
2004, Nov. 2			**Self-Adhesive**	
2069	A851	49c multi	.75	.25
a.		Booklet pane of 6	4.50	
		Complete booklet, 2 #2069a	9.00	
b.		Printed on gummed side	11.00	
c.		As "a," printed on gummed side	150.00	
2070	A851	80c multi	1.20	.45
a.		Booklet pane of 6	7.25	
b.		Printed on gummed side	—	
2071	A851	$1.40 multi	2.10	.75
a.		Booklet pane of 6	12.50	
b.		Printed on gummed side	45.00	
c.		As "a," printed on gummed side	750.00	

Queen Type of 2003 and

Red Calla Lilies
A852

Flag and Saskatoon, Saskatchewan
A853

Flag and Durrell, Newfoundland
A854

Flag and Shannon Falls, British Columbia
A855

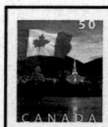

Flag and Mont-Saint-Hilaire, Quebec — A856

Flag and Toronto — A857

Designs: 85c, Yellow calla lily. $1.45, Dutch iris.

Coil Stamps

Serpentine Die Cut 6½-8¾ Horiz.				
2004-05			**Self-Adhesive**	
2072	A852	50c multi	.75	.25
a.		Serpentine die cut 6¾ horiz. ('05)	.75	.25
b.		Die cutting omitted, pair	75.00	
2073	A852	85c multi	1.25	.25
a.		Serpentine die cut 6¾ horiz. ('05)	1.50	.25
2074	A852	$1.45 multi	2.25	.60
a.		Serpentine die cut 6¾ horiz. ('05)	5.50	2.25

The die cutting gauge on Nos. 2072-2074a will vary between stamps on a roll and between stamps on one roll and other rolls.
Issued: Nos. 2072, 2073, 2074, 12/20/04. Nos. 2072a, 2073a, 2074a, 2/2005. Die cuttings on these issues are variable.

Booklet Stamps

Die Cut				
2075	A825	50c multi	.75	.25
a.		Booklet pane of 10	7.50	
2076	A853	50c multi	.75	.25
2077	A854	50c multi	.75	.25
2078	A855	50c multi	.75	.25
2079	A856	50c multi	.75	.25
2080	A857	50c multi	.75	.25
a.		Booklet pane, 2 each #2076-2080	7.50	
b.		As "a," printed on gummed side	70.00	
2081	A852	85c multi	1.65	.40
a.		Booklet pane of 6	10.00	
b.		As "a," black inscriptions omitted	5,000.	
2082	A852	$1.45 multi	2.20	.60
a.		Booklet pane of 6	13.25	
	Nos. 2072-2082 (11)		12.60	3.60

New Year 2005 (Year of the Cock) — A858

Rooster with: 50c, Red tail feathers. $1.45, Gold tail feathers.

Litho. & Embossed with Foil Application

2005, Jan. 7			**Perf. 13¼**	
2083	A858	50c multi	.75	.30
a.		Red omitted	1,400.	
		Souvenir Sheet		
		Perf. 12½x13		
2084	A858	$1.45 multi	2.25	2.25
a.		With dates, Canadian and Chinese flags added in sheet margin	3.00	3.00

Canada — People's Republic of China diplomatic relations, 35th anniv. (No. 2084a). No. 2084 contains one 40x40mm stamp.

National Hockey League Stars
A859

Designs: Nos. 2085a, 2086a, Henri Richard (blue background). Nos. 2085b, 2086b, Grant Fuhr (orange background). Nos. 2085c, 2086c, Allan Stanley (red background). Nos. 2085d, 2086d, Pierre Pilote (green background). Nos. 2085e, 2086e, Bryan Trottier (purple background). Nos. 2085f, 2086f, John Bucyk (yellow background).

Perf. 12½x13¼ on 3 Sides

2005, Jan. 29   **Litho.**
2085   Pane of 6 + 3 labels   4.75   4.75
  a.-f.   A859 50c Any single   .80   .55

Self-Adhesive
Die Cut

2086   A859   Pane of 6   4.75
  a.-f.   A859 50c Any single   .80   .55

Fishing Flies — A860

Designs: Nos. 2087a, 2088a, Alevin. Nos. 2087b, 2088b, Jock Scott. Nos. 2087c, 2088d, P. E. I. Fly. Nos. 2087d, 2088c, Mickey Finn.

2005, Feb. 4   **Perf. 12½x13¼**
2087   A860   Pane of 4   7.25   5.50
  a.-d.   50c Any single   1.80   1.10

Self-Adhesive
Serpentine Die Cut 10 Syncopated

2088   A860   Booklet pane of 4   3.60
  a.-d.   50c Any single   .90   .35
     Complete booklet, 2 #2088   7.25

Universities Type of 2003

Design: Nova Scotia Agricultural College, cent.

Booklet Stamp

Die Cut Perf. 12¾x13¼

2005, Feb. 14   **Self-Adhesive**
2089   A806 50c multi   .75   .30
  a.   Booklet pane of 4   3.00
     Complete booklet, 2 #2089a   6.00

Expo 2005, Aichi, Japan — A861

2005, Mar. 4   **Perf. 13½**
2090   A861 50c multi   .75   .30

Daffodils
A862

Designs: Nos. 2091a, 2092, Yellow daffodils, green and yellow background. Nos. 2091b, 2093, White daffodils, red orange and yellow background.

Souvenir Sheet

2005, Mar. 10   **Perf. 13x13¼**
2091   Pane of 2   2.20   2.20
  a.-b.   A862 50c Either single   1.10   .75

Booklet Stamps
Self-Adhesive
Die Cut Perf. 10

2092   A862 50c multi   .80   .30
2093   A862 50c multi   .80   .30
  a.   Booklet pane, 5 each #2092-2093 + 10 stickers   8.00

Pacific Explore 2005 World Stamp Expo, Sydney, Australia (No. 2091).

TD Bank Financial Group, 150th Anniv. — A863

Self-Adhesive
Booklet Stamp

2005, Mar. 18   **Die Cut Perf. 11¼**
2094   A863 50c multi   .75   .35
  a.   Booklet pane of 10   7.50
     Complete booklet, #2094a   10.00

The booklet pane of 10 is the inside front cover of the booklet. Fifteen stickers are on inside back cover.

Bird Paintings by John James Audubon — A864

Designs: No. 2095, Horned lark. No. 2096, Piping plover. No. 2097, Stilt sandpiper. No. 2098, Willow ptarmigan. 85c, Double-crested cormorant.

2005, Mar. 23   **Perf. 12½x13¼**
2095   A864 50c multi   .75   .40
2096   A864 50c multi   .75   .40
2097   A864 50c multi   .75   .40
2098   A864 50c multi   .75   .40
  a.   Block of 4, #2095-2098   3.00   2.50

Booklet Stamp
Self-Adhesive
Size: 48x39mm
Die Cut

2099   A864 85c multi   1.10   .45
  a.   Booklet pane of 6   6.50

Bridges — A865

Designs: No. 2100, Jacques Cartier Bridge, Quebec. No. 2101, Souris Swinging Bridge, Manitoba. No. 2102, Angus L. Macdonald Bridge, Nova Scotia. No. 2103, Canso Causeway, Nova Scotia.

Self-Adhesive

2005, Apr. 2   **Perf. 12½x13**
2100   A865 50c multi   .75   .45
2101   A865 50c multi   .75   .45
2102   A865 50c multi   .75   .45
2103   A865 50c multi   .75   .45
  a.   Block or strip of 4, #2100-2103   3.00   2.75
  b.   As "a," imperf.   1,500.

Maclean's Magazine, Cent. A866

2005, Apr. 12
2104   A866 50c multi   .75   .30

Biosphere Reserves in Canada and Ireland — A867

Designs: No. 2105, Saskatoon berries, Waterton Lakes National Park, Canada. No. 2106, Deer, Killarney National Park, Ireland.

2005, Apr. 22
2105   A867 50c multi   .75   .30
2106   A867 50c multi   .75   .30
  a.   Pair, #2105-2106   1.50   1.10
  b.   Souvenir sheet, #2105-2106   2.25   2.25

See Ireland Nos. 1611-1612.

Battle of the Atlantic, World War II — A868

2005, Apr. 29
2107   A868 50c multi   .75   .30

Opening of Canadian War Museum, Ottawa — A869

Booklet Stamp
Serpentine Die Cut 8x8½ Syncopated

2005, May 6   **Self-Adhesive**
2108   A869 50c multi   .75   .30
  a.   Booklet pane of 4   3.00
     Complete booklet, 2 #2108a   6.00

Paintings by Homer Watson (1855-1936) — A870

Designs: 50c, Down in the Laurentides. 85c, The Flood Gate (54x40mm)

2005, May 27   **Perf. 13¼x13**
2109   A870 50c multi   .75   .30
  a.   Perf. 13½x13   1.50   1.50

Souvenir Sheet
Perf. 13½x13

2110   Pane of 2, Nos. 2109a, 2110a   4.50   4.50
  a.   A870 85c multi   3.00   3.00

Miniature Sheet

Search and Rescue — A871

No. 2111: a, Rescuer and dog at plane crash. b, Rescuers at shipwreck. c, Helicopter, airplane and rescuers. d, Mountainside rescuers.

2005, June 13   **Perf. 13x13¼**
2111   A871   Pane of 8, 2 each #a-d   6.00   6.00
  a.-d.   50c Any single   .75   .55

No. 2111 contains two horizontal strips, one of which is inverted, so that a tete-beche pair of No. 2111c and two tete-beche pairs containing Nos. 2111b and 2111d can be created.

Ellen Fairclough (1905-2004), First Female Cabinet Minister — A872

2005, June 21   **Perf. 13x12½**
2112   A872 50c multi   .75   .30

Diver   Swimmer
A873   A874

2005, July 5   **Perf. 13¼**
2113   A873 50c multi   .75   .45
2114   A874 50c multi   .75   .45
  a.   Horiz. pair, #2113-2114   1.50   .90

9th FINA World Championships, Montreal. In No. 2114a, the denomination for one stamp is on the opposite side of the pair from that of the other stamp.

Founding of Port-Royal, Nova Scotia, 400th Anniv. A875

Litho. & Engr.
2005, July 16   **Perf. 13x12½**
2115   A875 50c multi   .75   .30

Province of Alberta, Cent. — A876

Self-Adhesive

2005, July 21   **Litho.**   **Perf. 12½x13**
2116   A876 50c multi   .75   .30

Printed in panes of 8 with each stamp having a different design on the backing.

Province of Saskatchewan, Cent. — A877

2005, Aug. 2   **Perf. 13x12½**
2117   A877 50c multi   .75   .30

Oscar Peterson, Pianist, 80th Birthday — A878

2005, Aug. 15
2118 A878 50c multi   .75   .30
  a.   Souvenir sheet of 4   3.00   3.00

No. 176 and Acadian Flag A879

2005, Aug. 15
2119 A879 50c multi   .75   .30
Acadian Deportation, 250th anniv.

Children Playing and Leg Braces — A880

2005, Sept. 2   **Perf. 12½x13**
2120 A880 50c multi   .75   .30
Mass polio vaccinations in Canada, 50th anniv.

Youth Sports — A881

No. 2121: a, Wall climbing. b, Skateboarding. c, Mountain biking. d, Snowboarding.

Self-Adhesive
2005, Oct. 1   **Die Cut**
2121   Complete booket, 2
     each #a-d   6.00
  a.-d. A881 50c Any single   .75   .40

Wild Cats — A882

Designs: No. 2122, Puma concolor. No. 2123, Panthera pardus orientalis.

Perf. 13½x13¼ Syncopated
2005, Oct. 13
2122   50c multi   .75   .40
2123   50c multi   .75   .40
  a.   A882 Horiz. pair, #2122-2123   1.50   .90
  b.   Souvenir sheet, #2123a   1.80   1.80

Diplomatic relations with People's Republic of China, 35th anniv. (No. 2123b). The perforation column between the two stamps, which gauges perf. 13½, has a maple leaf shaped syncopation.

See People's Republic of China Nos. 3458-3459.

Snowman — A883

Self-Adhesive
Litho. with Hologram Applied
Serpentine Die Cut 8¼ Horiz.
2005, Nov. 2   **Booklet Stamp**
2124 A883 50c multi   .75   .30
  a.   Booklet pane of 6   4.50
     Complete booklet, 2 #2124a   9.00

A884   A885

Creche Figures, St. Joseph's Oratory, Montreal — A886

Self-Adhesive
Serpentine Die Cut 6¾ Horiz.
2005, Nov. 2   **Booklet Stamps**
2125 A884 50c multi   .75   .30
  a.   Booklet pane of 6   4.50
     Complete booklet, 2 #2125a   9.00
Serpentine Die Cut 6½ Horiz.
2126 A885 85c multi   1.25   .60
  a.   Booklet pane of 6   7.50
Serpentine Die Cut 6¾ Horiz.
2127 A886 $1.45 multi   2.20   1.10
  a.   Booklet pane of 6   13.00

Flowers — A887

Designs: 51c, Red bergamot. 89c, Yellow lady's slipper. $1.05, Pink fairy slipper. $1.49, Himalayan blue poppy.

Coil Stamps
Serpentine Die Cut 7 to 9¼ Horiz.
2005, Dec. 19   **Self-Adhesive**
2128 A887 51c multi   .75   .25
2129 A887 89c multi   1.30   .45
2130 A887 $1.05 multi   1.50   .60
2131 A887 $1.49 multi   2.20   .90

Booklet Stamps
             Die Cut
2132 A887 89c multi   1.50   .40
  a.   Booklet pane of 6   9.00
2133 A887 $1.05 multi   1.80   .65
  a.   Booklet pane of 6   11.00
2134 A887 $1.49 multi   2.20   1.00
  a.   Booklet pane of 6   13.00
     Nos. 2128-2134 (7)   11.25   4.25

Flag and Houses, New Glasgow, Prince Edward Island A888

Flag and Bridge, Bouctouche, New Brunswick A889

Flag and Windmills, Pincher Creek, Alberta A890

Flag and Lower Fort Garry, Manitoba A891

Flag and Dogsled, Yukon Territory — A892

Self-Adhesive
Booklet Stamps
2005, Dec. 19   **Die Cut**
2135 A888 51c multi   .75   .25
2136 A889 51c multi   .75   .25
2137 A890 51c multi   .75   .25
2138 A891 51c multi   .75   .25
2139 A892 51c multi   .75   .25
  a.   Booklet pane, 2 each
     #2135-2139   7.50
  b.   As "a," die cutting omitted   1,500.
     Nos. 2135-2139 (5)   3.75   1.25

New Year 2006 (Year of the Dog) — A893

Litho. & Embossed With Foil Application
2006, Jan. 6   **Perf. 13¼**
2140 A893 51c shown   .75   .30

Souvenir Sheet
2141 A893 $1.49 Dog and pup   2.20   2.20

Queen Elizabeth II, 80th Birthday A894

Self-Adhesive
Booklet Stamp
Serpentine Die Cut 10
2006, Jan. 12   **Litho.**
2142 A894 51c multi   .75   .30
  a.   Booklet pane of 10   7.50
  b.   Die cutting omitted, pair   250.00
     See No. 2150.

2006 Winter Olympics, Turin, Italy A895

Designs: No. 2143, Team pursuit speed skating. No. 2144, Skeleton.

2006, Feb. 3   **Perf. 12½x13**
2143 A895 51c multi   .75   .30
2144 A895 51c multi   .75   .30
  a.   Horiz. pair, #2143-2144   1.50   .90

Gardens — A896

No. 2145: a, Shade garden and black-throated blue warbler. b, Flower garden and American painted lady butterfly. c, Water garden and green darner dragonfly. d, Rock garden and blue-spotted salamander.

Self-Adhesive
2006, Mar. 8   *Serpentine Die Cut 10*
2145   Complete booklet, 2
     each #a-d   6.00
  a.-d. A896 51c Any single   .75   .45

Party Balloons A897

Booklet Stamp
Serpentine Die Cut 6¾ Horiz.
2006, Apr. 3   **Self-Adhesive**
2146 A897 51c multi   .75   .30
  a.   Booklet pane of 6   6.00

Paintings by Dorothy Knowles — A898

Designs: 51c, The Field of Rapeseed. 89c, North Saskatchewan River, vert. (42x51mm).

2006, Apr. 7   **Perf. 13¼x12½**
2147 A898 51c multi   .75   .30
  a.   Perf. 12¾x12½   1.50   1.50
Souvenir Sheet
        Perf. 13
2148   Pane, Nos. 2147a,
     2148a   3.75   3.75
  a.   A898 89c multi   2.20   2.20

Canadian Labor Congress, 50th Anniv. — A899

2006, Apr. 20   **Perf. 13½x13¼**
2149 A899 51c multi   .75   .30

Queen Elizabeth II, 80th Birthday
Type of 2006
Souvenir Sheet
2006, Apr. 21   **Perf. 12½x13**
2150   Pane of 2, No. 2150a   4.50   4.50
  a.   A894 149c multi, 36x28mm   2.25   2.25

McClelland & Stewart Publishing House, Cent. — A900

Self-Adhesive
Booklet Stamp

2006, Apr. 26   *Die Cut Perf. 11¼x11*
2151	A900	51c slate grn & sil	.75	.30
a.		Booklet pane of 4 + 4 stickers	3.00	
		Complete booklet, 2 #2151a	6.00	

Northwest Coast Transformation Mask and Northwest Coast Exhibit — A901

Booklet Stamp

Serpentine Die Cut 8 Horiz. Syncopated

2006, May 11   **Self-Adhesive**
2152	A901	89c multi	1.30	.80
a.		Booklet pane of 4	3.25	
		Complete booklet, 2 #2152a	7.00	
b.		Die cutting omitted, pair	750.00	

Canadian Museum of Civilization, 150th anniv.

Canadians in Hollywood A903

Actors and actresses: Nos. 2153a, 2154a, John Candy (1950-94). Nos. 2153b, 2154c, Fay Wray (1907-2004). Nos. 2153c, 2154d, Lorne Greene (1915-87). Nos. 2153d, 2154b, Mary Pickford (1893-1979).

2006, May 26   *Perf. 13x12½*
2153		Souvenir sheet of 4	4.50	4.50
a.-d.		A903 51c Any single	1.10	1.10

Self-Adhesive
Serpentine Die Cut 9¾x10
2154		Booklet pane of 4 + 4 stickers	3.00	
a.-d.		A903 51c Any single	.75	.45
		Complete booklet, 2 #2154	6.00	

Complete booklets were issued with four different covers depicting the featured actors or actresses.
See Nos. 2279-2280.

A904

Exploration of Eastern Coast by Samuel de Champlain, 400th Anniv. — A905

Litho. & Engr.
2006, May 28   *Perf. 13x12½*
2155	A904	51c multi	.75	.30

Souvenir Sheet
Perf. 11
2156	A905	Pane of 2 #2156a, 2 US #4074a	7.50	7.00
a.		A904 51c multi	1.45	1.10

Washington 2006 World Philatelic Exhibition (No. 2156). No. 2156, sold only by Canada Post for $2, has bar code in pane margin at lower left. United States No. 4074, sold only by the United States Postal Service, lacks this bar code.

Vancouver Aquarium, 50th Anniv. — A906

Self-Adhesive
Booklet Stamp
Serpentine Die Cut 9½
2006, June 15   **Litho.**
2157	A906	51c multi	.75	.30
a.		Booklet pane of 5	3.75	
		Complete booklet, 2 #2157a	7.50	

Canadian Forces Snowbirds Aerobatics Team — A907

Designs: No. 2158, Pilot in cockpit, two airplanes. No. 2159, Three airplanes, Snowbirds emblem.

2006, June 28   *Perf. 12½x13¼*
2158	A907	51c multi	.75	.30
2159	A907	51c multi	.75	.30
a.		Horiz. pair, #2158-2159	1.50	1.10
b.		Souvenir sheet, #2159a	2.20	2.20

James White, Dividers and Map of Canada A908

2006, June 30   *Perf. 13¼x12½*
2160	A908	51c multi	.75	.30

Atlas of Canada, cent. Printed in panes of 16 + 4 labels.

World Lacrosse Championships, London, Ontario — A909

Booklet Stamp
Serpentine Die Cut 11¾ Horiz.
2006, July 6   **Self-Adhesive**
2161	A909	51c multi	.75	.30
a.		Booklet pane of 8	6.00	

Alpine Club of Canada, Cent. — A910

Self-Adhesive
Booklet Stamp
2006, July 19   *Die Cut Perf. 12½x13*
2162	A910	51c multi	.75	.30
a.		Booklet pane of 8	6.00	

Ducks and Duck Decoys A911

Designs: No. 2163, Barrow's goldeneyes. No. 2164, Mallards. No. 2165, American black ducks. No. 2166, Redbreasted mergansers.

2006, Aug. 3   *Perf. 13¼x12½*
2163	A911	51c blue & multi	.75	.45
2164	A911	51c yel & multi	.75	.45
2165	A911	51c red & multi	.75	.45
2166	A911	51c grn & multi	.75	.45
a.		Block of 4, #2163-2166	3.00	2.20
b.		Souvenir sheet, #2163-2166	3.75	3.75

Society of Graphic Designers of Canada, 50th Anniv. — A912

2006, Aug. 16   *Perf. 12½x13*
2167	A912	51c multi	.75	.30

Canadian Wines A913

Canadian Cheeses A914

Designs: No. 2168, Three glasses of wine. No. 2169, Wine taster, barrels. No. 2170, Various cheeses. No. 2171, Woman with tray of cheeses and fruit.

Self-Adhesive
Booklet Stamps
2006, Aug. 23   **Die Cut**
2168	A913	51c multi	.75	.45
2169	A913	51c multi	.75	.45
2170	A914	51c multi	.75	.45
2171	A914	51c multi	.75	.45
a.		Booklet pane, 2 each #2168-2171	6.00	
		Nos. 2168-2171 (4)	3.00	1.80

Universities Type of 2003
Design: Macdonald College, Sainte-Anne-de-Bellevue, Quebec, cent.

Booklet Stamp
Die Cut Perf. 12¾x13¼
2006, Sept. 26   **Self-Adhesive**
2172	A806	51c multi	.75	.30
a.		Booklet pane of 4	3.00	
		Complete booklet, 2 #2172a	6.00	

Endangered Animals — A915

Designs: Nos. 2173a, 2174, Newfoundland marten. Nos. 2173b, 2175, Blotched tiger salamander. Nos. 2173c, 2176, Blue racer snake. Nos. 2173d, 2177, Swift fox.

2006, Sept. 29   *Perf. 13¼*
2173		Pane of 4 + 4 labels	4.50	4.00
a.-d.		A915 51c Any single	1.10	.90

Booklet Stamps
Self-Adhesive
Size: 47x24mm
Die Cut
2174	A915	51c multi	.75	.45
2175	A915	51c multi	.75	.45
2176	A915	51c multi	.75	.45
2177	A915	51c multi	.75	.45
a.		Block of 4, #2174-2177	3.00	
b.		Booklet pane, 2 #2177a	6.00	

See Nos. 2229-2233, 2285-2289.

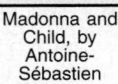

Opera Singers — A916

Designs: No. 2178, Maureen Forrester. No. 2179, Raoul Jobin (1906-74). No. 2180, Léopold Simoneau (1916-2006) and Pierrette Alarie. No. 2181, Jon Vickers. No. 2182, Edward Johnson (1878-1959).

2006, Oct. 17   *Perf. 13½x13*
2178	A916	51c multi	.75	.45
2179	A916	51c multi	.75	.45
2180	A916	51c multi	.75	.45
2181	A916	51c multi	.75	.45
2182	A916	51c multi	.75	.45
a.		Vert. strip of 5, #2178-2182	3.75	3.75

Madonna and Child, by Antoine-Sébastien Falardeau A917

Christmas Card Art A918

Designs: No. 2184, Snowman, by Yvonne McKague Housser. 89c, Winter Joys, by J. E. Sampson. $1.49, Contemplation, by Edwin Holgate.

Self-Adhesive
Booklet Stamp
2006, Nov. 1   *Die Cut*
2183	A917	51c multi	.75	.25
a.		Booklet pane of 12	9.00	

Serpentine Die Cut 13¼ Horiz.
2184	A918	51c multi	.75	.25
a.		Booklet pane of 12	9.00	
2185	A918	89c multi	1.30	.55
a.		Booklet pane of 6	8.00	
2186	A918	$1.49 multi	2.20	.90
a.		Booklet pane of 6	13.25	
		Nos. 2183-2186 (4)	5.00	1.95

Spotted
Coralroot
A919

Queen
Elizabeth II
A920

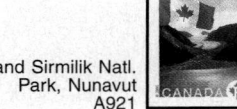

Flag and Sirmilik Natl.
Park, Nunavut
A921

Flag and Cliff Near
Chemainus, British
Columbia
A922

Flag and Polar Bears
Near Churchill, Manitoba
A923

Flag and Bras d'Or
Lake, Nova Scotia
A924

Flag and Tuktut Nogait
Natl. Park, Northwest
Territories — A925

**Self-Adhesive
Coil Stamp**

Serpentine Die Cut 7½-9 Horiz.

2006, Nov. 16			Litho.	
2187	A919	P multi	1.25	.25

Booklet Stamps
Die Cut

2188	A920	P multi	1.25	.25
a.		Booklet pane of 10	12.50	
2189	A921	P multi	1.25	.25
2190	A922	P multi	1.25	.25
2191	A923	P multi	1.25	.25
2192	A924	P multi	1.25	.25
2193	A925	P multi	1.25	.25
a.		Booklet pane, 2 each #2189-2193	12.50	
b.		Booklet pane, 6 each #2189-2193	37.50	
		Nos. 2187-2193 (7)	8.75	1.75

Nos. 2187-2193 each sold for 51c on day of issue. On Nos. 2188a, 2193a and 2193b, adjacent stamps that are on both sides of the booklet fold have rouletting rather than die cutting between them. No. 2193b is sold folded into thirds. Each of the thirds has selvage surrounding the ten stamps on it, unlike No. 2193a. Beware of fake examples of No. 2139b that have been found hand cut from printer's waste.

See No. 2194a.

Spotted Coralroot Type of 2006 and

Flat-leaved
Bladderwort — A926

Designs: $1.10, Marsh skullcap. $1.55, Little larkspur.

2006, Dec. 19			Perf. 13¼x13	
2194		Souvenir sheet of 4	7.50	7.50
a.	A919	P multi	1.25	.75
b.	A926	93c multi	1.50	1.10
c.	A926	$1.10 multi	1.65	1.25
d.	A926	$1.55 multi	2.20	2.20

**Self-Adhesive
Coil Stamps**

Serpentine Die Cut 7½-9 Horiz.

2195	A926	93c multi	1.35	.40
2196	A926	$1.10 multi	1.65	.60

2197	A926	$1.55 multi	2.25	.60

Booklet Stamps
Die Cut

2198	A926	93c multi	1.50	.60
a.		Booklet pane of 6	9.00	
2199	A926	$1.10 multi	1.75	.75
a.		Booklet pane of 6	10.50	
2200	A926	$1.55 multi	2.50	1.10
a.		Booklet pane of 6	15.00	
		Nos. 2195-2200 (6)	11.00	4.05

No. 2194a sold for 51c on day of issue. See Nos. 2243, 2245-2247, 2254-2256.

New
Year
2007
(Year
of the
Pig)
A927

Pig facing: 52c, Left. $1.55, Right.

**Litho. & Embossed with Foil
Application**

2007, Jan. 5			Perf. 13½x13	
2201	A927	52c red & multi	.75	.30
a.		Gold foil omitted	75.00	

Souvenir Sheet

2202	A927	$1.55 grn & multi	2.50	2.50

Confetti and
Streamers
A928

**Self-Adhesive
Booklet Stamp**

Serpentine Die Cut 6¾ Horiz.

2007, Jan. 15			Litho.	
2203	A928	52c multi	.75	.30
a.		Booklet pane of 6	4.50	

International Polar Year — A929

Designs: No. 2204, Somateria spectabilis. No. 2205, Crossota millsaeare.

Perf. 13½ Syncopated

2007, Feb. 12				
2204		52c multi	.75	.30
2205		52c multi	.75	.30
a.		A929 Horiz. pair, #2204-2205	1.50	.90
b.		Souvenir sheet, #2205a	2.20	2.20

Lilacs — A930

Color of lilacs: Nos. 2206a, 2207, White. Nos. 2206b, 2208, Purple.

Souvenir Sheet

2007, Mar. 1			Perf. 12¾	
2206	A930	Pane of 2	2.20	2.20
a.-b.		52c Either single	1.10	.75

Booklet Stamps
Self-Adhesive
Die Cut

2207	A930	52c multi	.75	.30
2208	A930	52c multi	.75	.30
a.		Booklet pane of 10, 5 each #2207-2208	7.50	

Universities Type of 2003

Design: No. 2209, HEC Montreal, cent. No. 2210, University of Saskatchewan, cent.

**Self-Adhesive
Booklet Stamp**

2007		*Die Cut Perf. 12¾x13¼*		
2209	A806	52c multi	.75	.30
a.		Booklet pane of 4	2.00	
		Complete booklet, 2 #2209a	6.00	
2210	A806	52c multi	.75	.30
a.		Booklet pane of 4	3.00	
		Complete booklet, 2 #2210a	6.00	

Issued: No. 2209, 3/12. No. 2210, 4/3.

Art
by
Mary
Pratt
A931

Designs: 52c, Jelly Shelf. $1.55 Iceberg in the North Atlantic (58x36mm).

2007, Mar. 15			Perf. 13x12½	
2211	A931	52c multi	.75	.30

Souvenir Sheet

2212		Pane, #2211, 2212a	3.50	3.50
a.	A931	$1.55 multi	2.20	2.20

Selection of Ottawa as National
Capital, 150th Anniv. — A932

**Litho., Litho & Embossed with Foil
Application (#2213b)**

2007, May 3			Perf. 13¼	
2213		Pane of 2, #2213a, 2213b	3.50	3.50
a.	A932	52c multi	1.10	1.10
b.	A932	$1.55 multi	2.20	2.20

**Booklet Stamp
Self-Adhesive**

Serpentine Die Cut 7¼ Horiz.

2214	A932	52c multi	.85	.30
a.		Booklet pane of 4	3.50	
		Complete booklet, 2 #2214a	7.00	

Royal Architectural Institute of Canada,
Cent. — A933

Buildings: No. 2215, University of Lethbridge, by Arthur Erickson. No. 2216, St. Mary's Church, by Douglas Cardinal. No. 2217, Ontario Science Centre, by Raymond Moriyama. No. 2218, National Gallery of Canada, by Moshe Safdie.

2007, May 9			Litho.	Perf. 13	
2215	A933	52c multi + label	.75	.45
2216	A933	52c multi + label	.75	.45
2217	A933	52c multi + label	.75	.45
2218	A933	52c multi + label	.75	.45
a.		Vert. strip of 4, #2215-2218, + 4 labels	3.00	2.20

Nos. 2215-2218 were printed in panes containing two of each stamp. Labels flank the stamps, with labels on the left showing drawings of the buildings and the labels on the right showing the architect.

Capt. George
Vancouver (1757-98),
Explorer — A934

Litho. & Embossed

2007, June 22			Perf. 13x12½	
2219	A934	$1.55 multi	2.20	1.00
a.		Souvenir sheet of 1, perf. 13	2.20	2.20

FIFA Under-20 World Soccer
Championships, Canada — A935

2007, June 26		Litho.	Perf. 12½x13	
2220	A935	52c multi	.75	.30
a.		Imperf., pair	950.00	

Popular Singers — A936

Designs: Nos. 2221a, 2222a, Gordon Lightfoot. Nos. 2221b, 2222b, Joni Mitchell. Nos. 2221c, 2222c, Anne Murray. Nos. 2221d, 2222d, Paul Anka.

2007, June 29			Perf. 12½x13	
2221	A936	Pane of 4	3.00	3.00
a.-d.		52c Any single	.75	.75

Self-Adhesive
Serpentine Die Cut 13½

2222	A936	Booklet pane of 4	3.00	
a.-d.		52c Any single	.75	.40
		Complete booklet, 2 #2222	6.00	

Complete booklets were issued with four different covers depicting the featured singers.

National Parks — A937

Designs: No. 2223, Terra Nova National Park, Newfoundland, 50th anniv. No. 2224, Jasper National Park, Alberta, cent.

**Self-Adhesive
Booklet Stamps**

2007		*Serpentine Die Cut 13½*		
2223	A937	52c multi	.75	.30
a.		Booklet pane of 5	3.75	
		Complete booklet, 2 #2223a	7.50	
2224	A937	52c multi	.75	.30
a.		Booklet pane of 5	3.75	
		Complete booklet, 2 #2224a	7.50	
b.		Gutter pane, 5 each #2223-2224	11.00	

Issued: No. 2223, 7/6; No. 2224, 7/20.

Scouting,
Cent.
A938

**Self-Adhesive
Booklet Stamp**

2007, July 25
2225	A938 52c multi	.75	.30
a.	Booklet pane of 4 + 4 labels	3.00	
	Complete booklet, 2 #2225a	6.00	

Henri Membertou, Grand Chief of Mi'kmaq Tribe — A939

2007, June 26   Engr.   Perf. 13x12½
2226	A939 52c multi	.75	.30

Law Society of Saskatchewan, Cent. — A940

2007, Sept. 13   Litho.   Perf. 13
2227	A940 52c multi	1.50	.75

Printed in panes of 8 + 8 labels.

Law Society of Alberta, Cent. A941

2007, Sept. 13   Perf. 12½x13
2228	A941 52c multi	.75	.30

Endangered Animals Type of 2006

Designs: Nos. 2229a, 2230, North Atlantic right whale. Nos. 2229b, 2231, Northern cricket frog. Nos. 2229c, 2232, White sturgeon. Nos. 2229d, 2233, Leatherback turtle.

2007, Oct. 1   Perf. 13¼
2229	Pane of 4 + 4 labels	3.00	3.00
a.-d.	A915 52c Any single	.75	.75

Booklet Stamps
Self-Adhesive
Size: 47x24mm
Die Cut
2230	A915 52c multi	.80	.30
2231	A915 52c multi	.80	.30
2232	A915 52c multi	.80	.30
2233	A915 52c multi	.80	.30
a.	Block of 4, #2230-2233	3.20	
b.	Booklet pane, 2 #2233a	6.50	

Beneficial Insects — A942

Designs: 1c, Convergent lady beetle (Hippodamia convergens). 3c, Golden-eyed lacewing (Chrysopa oculata). 5c, Northern bumblebee (Bombus polaris). 10c, Canada darner (Aeshna canadensis). 25c, Cecropia moth (Hyalophora cecropia).

No. 2235

No. 2235a

2007, Oct. 12   Perf. 13¼x13
2234	A942 1c multi	.25	.25
2235	A942 3c multi	.25	.25
a.	"Canada" shifted to right, touching "Oculata" (pos. 11-14)	.40	.25
b.	Dated "2012," with added microprinting and small design features (#2409b)	.25	.25
2236	A942 5c multi	.25	.25
2237	A942 10c multi	.25	.25
2238	A942 25c multi	.40	.25
a.	Souvenir sheet, #2234-2238	1.10	1.00
	Nos. 2234-2238 (5)	1.40	1.25

No. 2235a occurs four times on each pane of 50. Panes printed in 2010 correct the errors. See Nos. 2328, 2406-2410, 2708.
Issued: No. 2235b, 10/16/12.

Christmas
A943   A944

Designs: No. 2239, Reindeer and snowflakes. No. 2240, Holy Family. 93c, Angel over town. $1.55, Dove.

Booklet Stamps
Litho. With Hologram Affixed
Serpentine Die Cut 8¼ Horiz.
2007, Nov. 1   Self-Adhesive
2239	A943 (52c) multi	1.25	.25
a.	Booklet pane of 6	7.50	
	Complete booklet, 2 #2239a	15.00	
b.	Die cutting omitted, pair	500.00	

Litho.
Serpentine Die Cut 13½
2240	A944 (52c) multi	1.25	.25
a.	Booklet pane of 6	7.50	
	Complete booklet, 2 #2240a	15.00	
2241	A944 93c multi	1.30	.40
a.	Booklet pane of 6	8.00	
2242	A944 $1.55 multi	2.20	.60
a.	Booklet pane of 6	13.25	
b.	Die cutting omitted, pair	575.00	
	Nos. 2239-2242 (4)	6.00	1.50

Flowers Type of 2006 and

Odontioda Island Red Orchid A945

Queen Elizabeth II A946

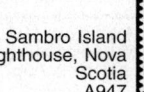

Flag and Sambro Island Lighthouse, Nova Scotia A947

Flag and Point Clark Lighthouse, Ontario A948

Flag and Cap-des-Rosiers Lighthouse, Quebec — A949

Flag and Warren Landing Lighthouse, Manitoba A950

Flag and Pachena Point Lighthouse, British Columbia A951

Flag and Pachena Point Lighthouse, British Columbia — A951a

Designs: 96c, Potinara Janet Elizabeth "Fire Dancer" orchid. $1.15, Laeliocattleya Memoria Evelyn Light orchid. $1.60, Masdevallia Kaleidoscope "Conni" orchid.

2007, Dec. 27   Litho.   Perf. 13¼x13
2243	Pane of 4	6.75	6.75
a.	A945 P multi	1.25	.85
b.	A926 96c multi	1.50	1.20
c.	A926 $1.15 multi	1.65	1.30
d.	A926 $1.60 multi	2.20	1.80

Self-Adhesive
Coil Stamps
Serpentine Die Cut 8-9½ Horiz.
2244	A945 P multi	1.25	.25

Serpentine Die Cut 9.2 Horiz.
2244A	A945 P multi	1.45	1.45

Serpentine Die Cut 8-9½
2245	A926 96c multi	1.25	.30
2246	A926 $1.15 multi	1.80	.45
2247	A926 $1.60 multi	2.50	.60
	Nos. 2244-2247 (5)	8.25	3.05

Die cutting is irregular across the stamp (saw tooth tips) on Nos. 2244 and 2245-2247 compared to being consistent across the stamp (rounded tips) on No. 2244A. On No. 2244, stamps are vertically contiguous on the backing paper, while on No. 2244A the stamps are separated on horizontal backing paper that is taller than the stamp.

Booklet Stamps
Serpentine Die Cut 13¼
2248	A946 P multi	1.25	.25
a.	Booklet pane of 10	12.50	
2249	A947 P multi	1.25	.25
2250	A948 P multi	1.25	.25
2251	A949 P multi	1.25	.25
2252	A950 P multi	1.25	.25
2253	A951 P multi	1.25	.25
a.	Booklet pane of 10, 2 each #2249-2253	12.50	

Serpentine Die Cut 13¼
2253B	A951a P multi	1.25	.25
c.	Booklet pane of 10, 2 each #2249-2252, 2253B	12.50	
d.	Booklet pane of 30, 6 each #2249-2252, 2253B	37.50	

Die Cut
2254	A926 96c multi	1.50	.25
a.	Booklet pane of 6	9.00	
2255	A926 $1.15 multi	1.80	.40
a.	Booklet pane of 6	11.00	
2256	A926 $1.60 multi	2.40	.60
a.	Booklet pane of 6	14.50	
	Nos. 2248-2256 (10)	14.45	3.00

Nos. 2243a, 2244, 2248-2253 each sold for 52c on day of issue.
No. 2244A issued 2/21/08.
No. 2253B issued 5/1/08. No. 2253Bd was separated into thirds by two rows of rouletting. The separated thirds of this booklet have the same contents as No. 2253Bc, but have different selvage markings.

New Year 2008 (Year of the Rat) — A952

Designs: 52c, Rat with umbrella. $1.60, Rat with fan.

Litho. & Embossed With Foil Application
2008, Jan. 8   Perf. 13
2257	A952 52c multi	.75	.30

Souvenir Sheet
2258	A952 $1.60 multi	3.00	3.00

No. 2257 printed in panes of 25 + 20 labels.

Fireworks A953

Self-Adhesive
Booklet Stamp
Serpentine Die Cut 13½ Horiz.
2008, Jan. 15   Litho.
2259	A953 P multi	1.25	.30
a.	Booklet pane of 6	7.50	

No. 2259 sold for 52c on day of issue.

Peonies — A954

Peony color: Nos. 2260a, 2261, Pink. Nos. 2260b, 2262, Red.

2008, Mar. 3   Litho.   Perf. 13¼
2260	Pane of 2	2.20	2.20
a.-b.	A954 52c Either single	1.10	.75

Booklet Stamps
Self-Adhesive
Serpentine Die Cut 13¼
2261	A954 52c multi	.75	.30
2262	A954 52c multi	.75	.30
a.	Pair, #2261-2262	1.50	
b.	Booklet pane, 5 each #2261-2262, + 10 stickers	7.50	
c.	Die cutting omitted, pair	375.00	

The country name and denomination are closer to the flowers on Nos. 2261-2262 than on Nos. 2260a-2260b.

Universities A955

Designs: No. 2263, University of Alberta, cent. No. 2264, University of British Columbia, cent.

Self-Adhesive
Serpentine Die Cut 13¼
2008, Mar. 7   Booklet Stamps
2263	A955 52c multi	.75	.25
a.	Booklet pane of 8	6.00	
b.	Die cutting omitted, pair	325.00	
2264	A955 52c multi	.75	.25
a.	Booklet pane of 8	6.00	
b.	Gutter pane, 4 each #2263-2264	11.00	

2008 Intl. Ice Hockey Federation Championships, Halifax and Quebec — A956

Self-Adhesive
Serpentine Die Cut 13½
2008, Apr. 3   Booklet Stamp
2265	A956 52c multi	.75	.25
a.	Booklet pane of 10	7.50	
b.	Die cutting omitted, pair	300.00	

No. 2265a was printed with two different booklet covers.

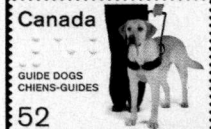

Guide Dog — A957

Self-Adhesive
Booklet Stamp

Serpentine Die Cut 13½x13
2008, Apr. 21   Litho. & Embossed
2266 A957 52c multi   .75   .25
  a.   Booklet pane of 10   7.50
Montreal Association for the Blind, cent.

Oil and Gas Anniversaries — A958

Designs: No. 2267, Welder welding Trans-Canada Pipeline. No. 2268, James M. Williams, Charles Tripp, Oil Springs, Ontario oil field.

Self-Adhesive
Booklet Stamps
Serpentine Die Cut 13¼
2008, May 2   Litho.
2267 A958 52c multi   .75   .25
  a.   Die cutting omitted, pair   750.00
2268 A958 52c multi   .75   .25
  a.   Die cutting omitted, pair   750.00
  b.   Booklet pane of 10, 5 each
         #2267-2268   7.50
Trans-Canada Pipeline, 50th anniv., First commercial oil well in Canada, 150th anniv.

Quebec City, 400th Anniv. — A959

Litho. & Engr.
2008, May 16   Perf. 13x12½
2269 A959 52c multi   .75   .30
  See France No. 3437. A souvenir sheet containing No. 2269 and France No. 3437 sold for $4.99.

Photographic Portraits by Yousuf Karsh (1908-2008) A960

Designs: 52c, Self-portrait, 1952. 96c, Audrey Hepburn, 1956. $1.60, Sir Winston Churchill, 1941.

2008, May 21   Litho.   Perf. 13x12½
2270 A960   52c multi   .75   .30
Souvenir Sheet
2271   Pane of 3, #2270,
          2271a, 2271b   4.00 4.00
  a.   A960 96c multi   1.50 1.10
  b.   A960 $1.60 multi   2.40 2.20
Booklet Stamps
Self-Adhesive
2272 A960   96c multi   1.50 .60
  a.   Booklet pane of 4   6.00
         Complete booklet, 2 #2272a 12.00
2273 A960 $1.60 multi   2.40 .90
  a.   Booklet pane of 4   9.50
         Complete booklet, 2 #2273a 19.00
  b.   Gutter pane, #2272a, 2273a 15.00
No. 2270 printed in panes of 16 + 4 labels.

1908 Fifty-cent Coin — A961

Litho. & Embossed
2008, June 4   Perf. 13x13¼
2274 A961 52c multi   .75   .30
  Royal Canadian Mint, cent. Printed in panes of 16 + 4 labels.

Canadian Nurses Association, Cent. — A962

Self-Adhesive
Booklet Stamp
Serpentine Die Cut 13¼
2008, June 16   Litho.
2275 A962 52c multi   .75   .25
  a.   Booklet pane of 10   7.50

Publication of *Anne of Green Gables,* by Lucy Maud Montgomery, Cent. — A963

Designs: Nos. 2276a, 2277, Anne holding buttercups. Nos. 2276b, 2278, Green Gables House.

Perf. 13½ Syncopated
2008, June 20
Souvenir Sheet
2276   A963   Pane of 2   2.40 2.40
  a.-b. 52c Either single   1.20   .75
Booklet Stamps
Self-Adhesive
Serpentine Die Cut 13¼x13
2277 A963 52c multi   .75   .30
2278 A963 52c multi   .75   .30
  a.   Booklet pane of 10, 5 each
         #2277-2278 + 10 stickers   7.50
  b.   Die cutting omitted, pair
         (#2277-2278)   375.00
  See Japan No. 3028.

Canadians in Hollywood Type of 2006
  Actors and actresses: Nos. 2279a, 2280c, Norma Shearer (1902?-83). Nos. 2279b, 2280b, Chief Dan George (1899-1981). Nos. 2279c, 2280a, Marie Dressler (1868-1934). Nos. 2279d, 2280d, Raymond Burr (1917-93).

2008, June 30   Perf. 13x12½
2279   Souvenir sheet of 4   4.40 4.40
  a.-d. A903 52c Any single   1.10   .90
Self-Adhesive
Serpentine Die Cut 13½x13¼
2280   Booklet pane of 4 + 4
          stickers   3.00
  a.-d. A903 52c Any single   .75   .30
          Complete booklet, 2 #2280 6.00
  Complete booklets were issued with four different covers depicting the featured actors or actresses. The order of the stamps and labels in the booklet pane differed in the four booklets.

2008 Summer Olympics, Beijing — A964

Self-Adhesive
Serpentine Die Cut 13½
2008, July 18   Booklet Stamp
2281 A964 52c multi   .75   .30
  a.   Booklet pane of 10   7.50
  b.   Die cutting omitted, strip of
         3   900.00

Lifesaving Society, Cent. A965

Self-Adhesive
Serpentine Die Cut 13¼x12¾
2008, July 25   Booklet Stamp
2282 A965 52c multi   .75   .25
  a.   Booklet pane of 10   7.50

British Columbia, 150th Anniv. — A966

Self-Adhesive
2008, Aug. 1   Perf. 12½x13
2283 A966 52c multi   .75   .30

R. Samuel McLaughlin (1871-1972), Automobile Manufacturer, and Buick Automobile — A967

2008, Sept. 8   Perf. 12½x13
2284 A967 52c multi   .75   .30

Endangered Animals Type of 2006
  Designs: Nos. 2285a, 2286, Prothonotary warbler. Nos. 2285b, 2287, Taylor's checkerspot butterfly. Nos. 2285c, 2288, Roseate tern. Nos. 2285d, 2289, Burrowing owl.

2008, Oct. 1   Perf. 13¼
2285   Pane of 4 + 4 labels   3.00 3.00
  a.-d. A915 52c Any single   .75   .75
Booklet Stamps
Self-Adhesive
Size: 48x24mm
Die Cut
2286 A915 52c multi   .75   .30
2287 A915 52c multi   .75   .30
2288 A915 52c multi   .75   .30
2289 A915 52c multi   .75   .30
  a.   Block of 4, #2286-2289   3.00
  b.   Booklet pane, 2 #2289a   6.00

12th Francophone Summit, Quebec — A968

2008, Oct. 15   Perf. 12½x13¼
2290 A968 52c multi   .75   .30

A969

Christmas — A970

Child: Nos. 2291a, 2293, Making snow angel. Nos. 2291b, 2294, Skiing. Nos. 2291c, 2295, Tobogganing.

Souvenir Sheet
2008, Nov. 3   Perf. 13½
2291   Pane of 3   5.25 5.25
  a.   A969 P multi   1.25   .90
  b.   A969 96c multi   1.50 1.50
  c.   A969 $1.60 multi   2.40 2.40
Booklet Stamps
Self-Adhesive
Serpentine Die Cut 13¼
2292 A970   P multi   1.25 .25
  a.   Booklet pane of 6   7.50
         Complete booklet, 2 #2292a 15.00
  b.   Die cutting omitted, pair   600.00
Serpentine Die Cut 13¾
2293 A969   P multi   1.25 .25
  a.   Booklet pane of 6   7.50
         Complete booklet, 2 #2293a 15.00
2294 A969   96c multi   1.50 .60
  a.   Booklet pane of 6   9.00
2295 A969 $1.60 multi   2.40 .90
  a.   Booklet pane of 6   14.50
  b.   Gutter pane, #2294a, 2295a 24.00
  Nos. 2292-2295 (4)   6.40 2.00
Nos. 2291a, 2292 and 2293 each sold for 52c on day of issue.
See No. 2343a.

A971

New Year 2009 (Year of the Ox) A972

Litho. & Embossed With Foil Application

2009, Jan. 8   *Perf. 12½*
2296   A971   P multi   1.25   .25

Souvenir Sheet
2297   A972 $1.65 multi   2.40   2.40
   a.   With China 2009 emblem overprinted in gold in pane margin   3.25   3.25

No. 2296 sold for 54c on day of issue.

Queen Elizabeth II — A973

Self-Adhesive
Booklet Stamp

Serpentine Die Cut 13½x13¼

2009, Jan. 12   *Litho.*
2298   A973   P multi   1.25   .25
   a.   Booklet pane of 10   12.50

No. 2298 sold for 54c on day of issue.

Sports of the Winter Olympics and Paralympics
A974   A975

Designs: Nos. 2299a, 2303, Curling. Nos. 2299b, 2302, Bobsledding. Nos. 2299c, 2304, Snowboarding. Nos. 2299d, 2300, Freestyle skiing. Nos. 2299e, 2301, Ice-sled hockey.

2009, Jan. 12   *Perf. 13¼x13*
2299   Pane of 5   6.25   3.75
   a.-d.   A974 P Any single   1.25   .90
   e.   A975 P multi   1.25   .90
   f.   As No. 2299, with "Vancouver / 2010" overprinted in sheet margin in silver   17.50   17.50

Booklet Stamps
Self-Adhesive

Serpentine Die Cut 13¼x13½

2300   A974   P multi   1.25   .25
2301   A975   P multi   1.25   .25
2302   A974   P multi   1.25   .25
2303   A974   P multi   1.25   .25
2304   A974   P multi   1.25   .25
   a.   Booklet pane of 10, 2 each #2300-2304   12.50
   b.   Booklet pane of 30, 6 each #2300-2304   37.50

On day of issue, Nos. 2299a-2299e, 2300-2304 each sold for 54c.

No. 2299f was originally sold with a set of coins in 2009. It was made available in 2010 in a set of 3 sheets, Nos. 2299f, 2305f, and 2366c that sold for $8.73.

2010 Vancouver Winter Olympics Emblem
A976

2010 Vancouver Winter Paralympics Emblem
A977

Miga, Winter Olympics Mascot — A978

Sumi, Paralympics Mascot — A979

Quatchi, Winter Olympics Mascot — A980

2009   *Perf. 13¼x13*
2305   Pane of 5   9.00   9.00
   a.   A976 P multi   1.25   .90
   b.   A977 P multi   1.25   .90
   c.   A978 98c multi   1.50   1.50
   d.   A979 $1.18 multi   1.75   1.75
   e.   A980 $1.65 multi   2.40   2.40
   f.   As No. 2305, with "Vancouver / 2010" overprinted in sheet margin in bronze   18.00   18.00

Self-Adhesive
Coil Stamps

Serpentine Die Cut 9¼ (Rounded Tips)

2306   A976   P multi   1.40   1.40
2307   A977   P multi   1.40   1.40

Serpentine Die Cut 7¾-9½ (Sawtooth Tips)

2307A   A976   P multi   1.25   .25
2307B   A977   P multi   1.25   .25
   c.   Vert. pair, #2307A-2307B   2.50
2308   A978   98c multi   1.50   .30
2309   A979 $1.18 multi   1.80   .45
2310   A980 $1.65 multi   2.40   .60

Booklet Stamps

Serpentine Die Cut 9¼ (Rounded Tips)

2311   A978   98c multi   1.40   .25
   a.   Booklet pane of 6   8.50
2312   A979 $1.18 multi   1.80   .40
   a.   Booklet pane of 6   11.00
2313   A980 $1.65 multi   2.40   .55
   a.   Booklet pane of 6   14.50
     Nos. 2306-2313 (10)   16.60   5.85

Issued: Nos. 2305, 2309, 2312, 2/12; Nos. 2306-2308, 2310-2311, 2313, 1/12. On day of issue, Nos. 2305a, 2305b, 2306-2307B each sold for 54c. Rolls of Nos. 2306 and 2307 have horizontal pairs of the same stamp that do not abut each other. Stamps from rolls containing Nos. 2307A and 2307B have pairs of different stamps that abut each other vertically.

No. 2305f was originally sold with a set of coins in 2009. It was made available in 2010 in a set of 3 sheets, Nos. 2299f, 2305f, and 2366c that sold for $8.73.

Celebration A981

Self-Adhesive

Serpentine Die Cut 13½ Horiz.

2009, Feb. 2   Booklet Stamp
2314   A981   P multi   1.25   .30
   a.   Booklet pane of 6   7.50

No. 2314 sold for 54c on day of issue.

Rosemary Brown (1930-2003)
A982

Abraham Doras Shadd (1801-82)
A983

2009, Feb. 2   *Perf. 13x12½*
2315   A982   54c multi   .75   .30
2316   A983   54c multi   .75   .30
   a.   Pair, #2315-2316   1.50   .40

Black History Month. Brown and Shadd were the first black woman and man elected to public office in Canada.

First Airplane Flight in Canada, Cent. — A984

Self-Adhesive

2009, Feb. 23   *Perf. 12½x13*
2317   A984   P multi   1.25   .30

No. 2317 sold for 54c on day of issue.

Rhododendrons — A985

Color of rhododendrons: Nos. 2318a, 2319, White and pink. Nos. 2318b, 2320, Pink.

2009, Mar. 13   *Perf. 13¼*
2318   A985   Pane of 2   2.20   2.20
   a.-b.   54c Either single   1.10   .75

Booklet Stamps
Self-Adhesive

Serpentine Die Cut 13½x12¾

2319   A985   54c multi   .75   .30
2320   A985   54c multi   .75   .30
   a.   Booklet pane of 10, 5 each #2319-2320   7.50
   b.   Die cutting omitted, pair   550.00

Paintings by Jack Bush (1909-77) A986

Designs: 54c, Striped Column. $1.65, Chopsticks, horiz. (57x23mm).

2009, Mar. 20   *Perf. 13x13¼*
2321   A986   54c multi   .75   .30
   a.   Perf. 12½x13¼   1.10   1.10

Souvenir Sheet
Perf. 12½x13¼

2322   Pane, #2321a, 2322a   3.75   3.75
   a.   A986 $1.65 multi   2.20   2.20

Souvenir Sheet

Intl. Year of Astronomy — A987

Designs: Nos. 2323a, 2324, Dominion Astrophysical Observatory, Saanich, British Columbia, and Horsehead Nebula. Nos. 2323b, 2325, Canada-France-Hawaii Telescope, Hawaii, and Eagle Nebula.

2009, Apr. 2   *Perf. 13¼x13*
2323   A987   Pane of 2   2.20   2.20
   a.-b.   54c Either single   1.10   .75
   c.   As #2323, with buff background behind product code   3.75   3.75

Booklet Stamps
Size: 24x34mm
Self-Adhesive

Serpentine Die Cut 13½

2324   A987   54c multi   .75   .30
2325   A987   54c multi   .75   .30
   a.   Booklet pane, 5 each #2324-2325   7.50

The product code on No. 2323 is "063491072031," and on No. 2323c, "063491072024." The background behind the product code on No. 2323 is white. No. 2323c also has a fluorescent overprint in the margin, not found on No. 2323. Nos. 2323a and 2323b are 27x36mm.

Preservation of Polar Regions and Glaciers — A988

2009, Apr. 9   *Perf. 13x12¾*
2326   A988   54c Polar bear   .75   .30
2327   A988   54c Arctic tern   .75   .30
   a.   Pair, #2326-2327   1.50   .90
   b.   Souvenir sheet, #2326-2327   1.80   1.80

Beneficial Insects Type of 2007

Design: Danaus plexippus caterpillar.

2009, Apr. 22   *Perf. 13¼x13*
2328   A942   2c multi   .25   .25

Horses A989

Designs: No. 2329, Canadian horse. No. 2330, Newfoundland pony.

Self-Adhesive

Serpentine Die Cut 13¼

2009, May 15   Booklet Stamps
2329   A989   54c multi   .90   .30
2330   A989   54c multi   .90   .30
   a.   Booklet pane of 10, 5 each #2329-2330   9.00

Department of Foreign Affairs and International Trade, Cent.
A990

2009, June 1   *Perf. 13¼x13*
2331   A990   54c multi   .80   .30

Boundary Waters Treaty, Cent.
A991

2009, June 12   *Perf. 13¼*
2332   A991   54c multi   .80   .30

Popular Singers — A992

Designs: Nos. 2333a, 2334d, Robert Charlebois. Nos. 2333b, 2334c, Edith Butler. Nos. 2333c, 2334b, Stompin' Tom Connors. Nos. 2333d, 2334a, Bryan Adams.

2009, July 2		**Perf. 12½x13**	
2333	A992 Pane of 4	3.20	3.20
a.-d.	54c Any single	.80	.80

Self-Adhesive
Serpentine Die Cut 13½

2334	A992 Booklet pane of 4	3.20	
a.-d.	54c Any single	.80	.40
	Complete booklet, 2 #2334	6.50	

Complete booklets were issued with four different covers depicting the featured singers. The order of the stamps is different in each booklet.

Roadside Attractions — A993

Designs: Nos. 2335a, 2336a, Mr. PG, Prince George, British Columbia. Nos. 2335b, 2336b, Sign Post Forest, Watson Lake, Yukon Territory. Nos. 2335c, 2336c, Inukshuk, Hay River, Northwest Territories. Nos. 2335d, 2336d, Pysanka, Vegreville, Alberta.

2009, July 6		**Perf. 13**	
2335	A993 Pane of 4	3.20	3.20
a.-d.	54c Any single	.80	.80

Self-Adhesive
Serpentine Die Cut 13½

2336	A993 Booklet pane of 4	3.20	
a.-d.	54c Any single	.80	.40
	Complete booklet, 2 #2336	6.50	

Captain Robert Abram Bartlett (1875-1946), Arctic Explorer — A994

2009, July 10		**Perf. 13**	
2337	A994 54c multi	.80	.30

Sports Invented By Canadians — A995

No. 2338: a, Five-pin bowling. b, Ringette. c, Lacrosse. d, Basketball.

Serpentine Die Cut 13¼
2009, Aug. 10

2338	Booklet pane of 4	3.20	
a.-d.	A995 54c Any single	.80	.40
	Complete booklet, 2 #2338	6.50	

Montreal Canadiens Hockey Jersey — A996

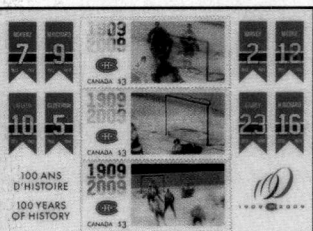

500-Goal Scorers of the Montreal Canadiens — A997

No. 2340 — 500th goal of: a, Maurice Richard. b, Jean Béliveau. c, Guy Lafleur.

Self-Adhesive
Serpentine Die Cut 13½x13¼

2009, Oct. 17		**Booklet Stamp**	
2339	A996 P multi	1.25	.30
a.	Booklet pane of 10	12.50	

Souvenir Sheet
Litho. With Three-Dimensional Plastic Affixed
Serpentine Die Cut 13x13¼
Self-Adhesive

2340	A997 Pane of 3	14.00	14.00
a.-c.	$3 Any single	4.50	4.50
d.	Die cutting omitted, pane of 3	1,800.	

Montreal Canadiens hockey team, cent. No. 2339 sold for 54c on day of issue.

Soaking of No. 2340 may cause the stamps to separate into layers. Soaking of used examples also may cause the cancellations to dissolve.

National War Memorial, Ottawa, and Poppy — A998

2009, Oct. 19	**Litho.**	**Perf. 12½**	
2341	A998 P multi	1.25	.55
a.	Souvenir sheet of 2	2.50	1.10

Booklet Stamp
Self-Adhesive
Serpentine Die Cut 13¼

2342	A998 P multi	1.25	.25
a.	Booklet pane of 10	12.50	

End of World War I, 91st anniv. On day of issue, Nos. 2341-2342 each sold for 54c. No. 2341 was issued only in the souvenir sheet of 2.

Christmas Type of 2008 and

Christmas
A999   A1000

Designs: Nos. 2343b, 2345, Madonna and child. 98c, Magus. $1.65, Shepherd and lamb.

2009, Nov. 2		**Perf. 13x12½**	
2343	Pane of 4 + 6 labels	7.25	7.25
a.	A970 P multi	1.25	.90
b.	A999 P multi	1.25	.90
c.	A999 98c multi	1.50	1.50
d.	A999 $1.65 multi	2.40	2.40

Booklet Stamps
Self-Adhesive
Litho. With Hologram Affixed
Serpentine Die Cut 8¼ Horiz.

2344	A1000 P multi	1.25	.25
a.	Booklet pane of 6	7.50	
	Complete booklet, 2 #2344a	15.00	

Litho.
Serpentine Die Cut 13½

2345	A999 P multi	1.25	.25
a.	Booklet pane of 6	7.50	
	Complete booklet, 2 #2345	15.00	
2346	A999 98c multi	1.40	.60
a.	Booklet pane of 6	8.50	
2347	A999 $1.65 multi	2.30	.90
a.	Booklet pane of 6	14.00	
b.	Booklet pane of 12, 6 each #2346-2347	28.00	
	Nos. 2344-2347 (4)	6.20	2.00

On day of issue, Nos. 2343a, 2343b, 2344, and 2345 each sold for 54c. No. 2347b is Nos. 2346a and 2347a unseparated but with horizontal slits cut in margin between the panes.

New Year 2010 (Year of the Tiger) — A1001

Designs: P, Seal impression of tiger in circle. $1.70, Sculpted tiger seal.

Litho. & Embossed With Foil Application

2010, Jan. 8		**Perf. 12½**	
2348	A1001 P multi	1.25	.25

Souvenir Sheet

2349	A1001 $1.70 multi	2.40	2.40

No. 2348 sold for 57c on day of issue.

Flag Over Watson's Mill, Manotick, Ont. A1002

Flag Over Keremeos Grist Mill, Keremeos, B.C. A1003

Flag Over Old Stone Mill Natl. Historic Site, Delta, Ont. — A1004

Flag Over Riordon Grist Mill, Caraquet, N. B. — A1005

Flag Over Cornell Mill, Stanbridge East, Que. — A1006

2010, Jan. 11	**Litho.**	**Perf. 13x13¼**	
2350	Souvenir sheet of 5	6.50	5.00
a.	A1002 P multi	1.25	.80
b.	A1003 P multi	1.25	.80
c.	A1004 P multi	1.25	.80
d.	A1005 P multi	1.25	.80
e.	A1006 P multi	1.25	.80

Booklet Stamps
Self-Adhesive
Serpentine Die Cut 13¼

2351	A1002 P multi	1.25	.25
2352	A1003 P multi	1.25	.25
2353	A1004 P multi	1.25	.25
2354	A1005 P multi	1.25	.25
2355	A1006 P multi	1.25	.25
a.	Booklet pane of 10, 2 each #2351-2355	12.50	
b.	Booklet pane of 30, 6 each #2351-2355	37.50	
	Nos. 2351-2355 (5)	6.25	1.25

On day of issue, Nos. 2350a-2350e and 2351-2355 each sold for 57c.

Striped Coralroot Orchid — A1007   **Giant Helleborine Orchid — A1008**

Rose Pogonia Orchid — A1009   **Grass Pink Orchid — A1010**

2010, Jan. 11		**Perf. 13¼x13**	
2356	Souvenir sheet of 4	6.75	6.75
a.	A1007 P multi	1.25	.90
b.	A1008 $1 multi	1.50	1.10
c.	A1009 $1.22 multi	1.65	1.30
d.	A1010 $1.70 multi	2.20	1.80

Coil Stamps
Self-Adhesive
Serpentine Die Cut 8 to 9½ (Sawtooth Tips)

2357	A1007 P multi	1.20	.25
2358	A1008 $1 multi	1.35	.30
2359	A1009 $1.22 multi	1.80	.40
2360	A1010 $1.70 multi	2.50	.60

Horiz. pairs, imperf. between, of No. 2357 are from uncut press panels of 100. Value unused, $4.

Serpentine Die Cut 9¼ (Rounded Tips)

2361	A1007 P multi	1.40	1.40
	Nos. 2357-2361 (5)	8.25	2.95

Booklet Stamps

2362	A1008 $1 multi	1.50	.30
a.	Booklet pane of 6	9.00	
2363	A1009 $1.22 multi	1.80	.45
a.	Booklet pane of 6	11.00	
2364	A1010 $1.70 multi	2.40	.60
a.	Booklet pane of 6	14.50	
	Nos. 2362-2364 (3)	5.70	1.35

On day of issue, Nos. 2356a and 2357 each sold for 57c. No. 2357 was printed in vertical rolls with stamps that are adjacent. No. 2361 was printed in horizontal rolls with stamps that are separated.

Queen Elizabeth II — A1011

Self-Adhesive
Serpentine Die Cut 13¼

2010, Jan. 11		**Booklet Stamp**	
2365	A1011 P multi	1.25	.25
a.	Booklet pane of 10	12.50	

No. 2365 sold for 57c on day of issue.

Venues of the 2010 Winter Olympics — A1012

Designs: Nos. 2366a, 2367, Whistler, B.C. Nos. 2366b, 2368, Vancouver.

2010, Jan. 12   *Perf. 13½x13¼*
2366	A1012	Souvenir sheet of 2	2.20	2.20
a.-b.		57c Either single	1.00	.75
c.		As No. 2366, with "Vancouver / 2010" overprinted in sheet margin in gold	12.00	12.00

Booklet Stamps
Self-Adhesive
Serpentine Die Cut 13¼
2367	A1012	57c multi	.85	.30
2368	A1012	57c multi	.85	.30
a.		Booklet pane of 10, 5 each #2367-2368, + 10 stickers	8.50	

No. 2366c was sold in a package of 3 sheets that also contained Nos. 2299f and 2305f.

William Hall (1827-1904), First Black Recipient of Victoria Cross — A1013

2010, Feb. 1   *Perf. 12¾x12½*
2369	A1013	57c multi	.85	.30

Roméo LeBlanc (1927-2009), Governor-General — A1014

2010, Feb. 8   *Perf. 12½*
2370	A1014	57c multi	.85	.30

Gold Medal From Vancouver Winter Olympics A1015

2010, Feb. 15   *Perf. 12½*
2371		Sheet of 2 #2371a	2.20	2.20
a.		A1015 57c Single stamp	1.10	.75

First day cancels have a Feb. 14 date, which was the date on which the first gold medal was awarded to a Canadian on home soil, but which also was a Sunday. Post offices in Vancouver had the stamp available for sale on Feb. 15.

Booklet Stamp
Self-Adhesive
Serpentine Die Cut 13½
2372	A1015	57c multi	.85	.30
a.		Booklet pane of 10	8.50	

Awarding of first gold medal to a Canadian on home soil.

Spirit of the Winter Olympics — A1016

Winter Olympic athletes and: Nos. 2373a, 2374, Woman with painted face at left. Nos. 2373b, 2375, Woman with painted face at right.

2010, Feb. 22   *Perf. 13*
2373	A1016	Souvenir sheet of 2	2.20	2.20
a.-b.		57c Either single	1.10	.75

Booklet Stamps
Self-Adhesive
Serpentine Die Cut 13¼
2374	A1016	57c multi	.85	.30
2375	A1016	57c multi	.85	.30
a.		Booklet pane of 10, 5 each #2374-2375	8.50	

African Violet Hybrids — A1017

Flower colors: Nos. 2376a, 2377, Red (Descelles' Avalanche). Nos. 2376b, 2378, Purple (Picasso).

2010, Mar. 3   *Litho.*   *Perf. 13*
2376	A1017	Souvenir sheet of 2	2.50	2.25
a.-b.		P Either single	1.25	.75

Booklet Stamps
Self-Adhesive
Serpentine Die Cut 13½
2377	A1017	P multi	1.25	.30
2378	A1017	P multi	1.25	.30
a.		Booklet pane of 10, 5 each #2377-2378	12.50	

On day of issue, Nos. 2376a, 2376b, 2377 and 2378 each sold for 57c.

Friendship Between Canada and Israel, 60th Anniv. A1018

Booklet Stamp
Self-Adhesive
Serpentine Die Cut 13¼
2010, Apr. 14   *Litho.*
2379	A1018	$1.70 multi	2.50	.90
a.		Booklet pane of 3 + label	7.50	
		Complete booklet, 2 #2379a	15.00	

See Israel No. 1812.

Indian Kings — A1019

Portraits by John Verelst of: No. 2380, Tee Yee Neen Ho Ga Row. No. 2381, Sa Ga Yeath Qua Pieth Tow. No. 2382, Ho Nee Yeath Taw No Row. No. 2383, Etow Oh Koam.

2010, Apr. 19   *Litho.*   *Perf. 12½*
2380	A1019	57c multi	.85	.40
2381	A1019	57c multi	.85	.40
2382	A1019	57c multi	.85	.40
2383	A1019	57c multi	.85	.40
a.		Block or strip of 4, #2380-2383	3.20	2.20
b.		Souvenir sheet of 4, #2380-2383	3.75	3.75
c.		As "b," with London 2010 emblem on sheet margin	5.50	5.50
		Nos. 2380-2383 (4)	3.40	1.60

Meeting of the four Indian Kings and Queen Anne in London, 300th anniv.

Canadian Navy, Cent. — A1020

Designs: Nos. 2384a, 2385, Male sailor, HMCS Niobe. Nos. 2384b, 2386, Female sailor, HMCS Halifax.

2010, May 4   *Litho.*   *Perf. 12½*
2384	A1020	Sheet of 2	2.20	2.20
a.-b.		57c Either single	1.10	.75

Booklet Stamps
Self-Adhesive
Serpentine Die Cut 13¼x13½
2385	A1020	57c multi	.85	.30
2386	A1020	57c multi	.85	
a.		Booklet pane of 10, 5 each #2385-2386	8.50	

Sea Mammals — A1021

Designs: No. 2387a, Harbor porpoise. No. 2387b, Sea otter.

Perf. 13x12¼x13x13 Syncopated (#2387a), 13x13x13x12¼ Syncopated (#2387b)
2010, May 13   *Litho. & Engr.*
2387	A1021	Sheet of 2	2.20	2.20
a.-b.		57c Either single	1.10	.75
c.		As "a," perf. 13x12¾ syncopated	1.10	.35
d.		As "b," perf. 13x12¾ syncopated	1.10	.35
e.		Booklet pane of 8, 4 each #2387c-2387d	8.75	8.75
		Complete booklet, #2387e	9.00	

Nos. 2387a and 2387b have syncopation on left and right side, with the syncopation between the stamps in the shape of a maple leaf. Nos. 2387c and 2387d have syncopation on one side only, with the syncopation between pairs of stamps in the shape of conjoined ovals.

See Sweden No. 2638.

Canadian Geographic's Wildlife Photography of the Year — A1022

Designs: Nos. 2388a, 2393, Ardia herodias, by Martin Cooper. Nos. 2388b, 2392, Vulpes vulpes, by Ben Boulter. Nos. 2388c, 2391, Tettigoniidae, by Julie Bazinet. Nos. 2388d, 2390, Tachycineta bicolor, by Mark Bradley. Nos. 2388e, 2389, Selasphorus rufus, by Wing Yan Tam.

2010, May 22   *Litho.*   *Perf. 12½x13*
2388	A1022	Sheet of 5	4.25	4.25
a.-e.		57c Any single	.85	.75

Booklet Stamps
Self-Adhesive
Serpentine Die Cut 13¼
2389	A1022	57c multi	.85	.30
2390	A1022	57c multi	.85	.30
2391	A1022	57c multi	.85	.30
2392	A1022	57c multi	.85	.30
2393	A1022	57c multi	.85	.30
a.		Booklet pane of 10, 2 each #2389-2393	8.50	
		Nos. 2389-2393 (5)	4.25	1.50

Rotary International in Canada, Cent. A1023

Self-Adhesive
Booklet Stamp
Serpentine Die Cut 13½x12¾
2010, June 18   *Litho.*
2394	A1023	57c multi	.85	.30
a.		Booklet pane of 8	6.75	

Paintings by Prudence Heward (1896-1947) A1024

Designs: 57c, Rollande. $1.70, At the Theatre, horiz. (42x40mm).

2010, July 2   *Perf. 13¼x13*
2395	A1024	57c multi	.85	.30

Souvenir Sheet
2396		Sheet of 2, #2395, 2396a	3.00	3.00
a.		A1024 $1.70 multi	2.20	2.20

Roadside Attractions — A1025

Designs: Nos. 2397a, 2398, Coffee Pot, Davidson, Saskatchewan. Nos. 2397b, 2399, Happy Rock, Gladstone, Manitoba. Nos. 2397c, 2400, Wawa Goose, Wawa, Ontario. Nos. 2397d, 2401, Puffin, Longue-Pointe-de-Mingan, Quebec.

2010, July 5   *Perf. 13*
2397	A1025	Sheet of 4	5.00	3.50
a.-d.		P Any single	1.25	.90

Booklet Stamps
Self-Adhesive
Serpentine Die Cut 13½
2398	A1025	P multi	1.25	.35
2399	A1025	P multi	1.25	.35
2400	A1025	P multi	1.25	.35
2401	A1025	P multi	1.25	.35
a.		Booklet pane of 4, #2398-2401	5.00	
		Complete booklet, 2 #2401a	10.00	

On day of issue, Nos. 2397a-2397d, 2398-2401 each sold for 57c.

Girl Guides, Cent. — A1026

Self-Adhesive
Serpentine Die Cut 13¾
2010, July 8   **Booklet Stamp**
2402	A1026	P multi	1.25	.25
a.		Booklet pane of 10	12.50	

No. 2402 sold for 57c on day of issue.

Founding of Cupids, Newfoundland
Settlement, 400th Anniv. — A1027

2010, Aug. 17   *Perf. 12½*
2403 A1027 57c multi   .85   .30

Year of
British
Home
Children
A1028

2010, Sept. 1
2404 A1028 57c multi   .85   .30

Blue Whale — A1029

Litho., Engr. & Silk-screened
2010, Oct. 4   *Perf. 12½x13*
2405 A1029 $10 multi   15.00   5.50
    Printed in sheets of 2.

Beneficial Insects Type of 2007

Designs: 4c, Paper wasp (Polistes fuscatus). 6c, Assassin bug (Zelus luridus). 7c, Large milkweed bug (Oncopeltus fasciatus). 8c, Margined leatherwing (Chauliognathus marginatus). 9c, Dogbane beetle (Chrysochus auratus).

2010, Oct. 19 Litho. *Perf. 13¼x13*
2406 A942 4c multi   .25   .25
  a.   With added microprinting and
       small design features
       (#2409b)   .25   .25
2407 A942 6c multi   .25   .25
2408 A942 7c multi   .25   .25
2409 A942 8c multi   .25   .25
  a.   With added microprinting and
       small design features
       (#2409b)   .25   .25
  b.   Souvenir sheet of 3, #2235b,
       2406a, 2409a   .25   .25
2410 A942 9c multi   .25   .25
  a.   Souvenir sheet, #2406-2410 2.20   .40
       Nos. 2406-2410 (5)   1.25   1.25
Issued: Nos. 2406a, 2409a, 2409b, 10/16/12.

Christmas   Madonna and
Ornaments   Child, Sculpture
A1030   by Antonio
                  Caruso
                  A1031

Designs: Nos. 2411a, 2413, Three red ornaments, greenish blue background. $1, Two blue ornaments, purple background. $1.70, Three red ornaments, dull blue background.

2010, Nov. 1   Litho.   *Perf. 12½*
2411   Souvenir sheet of 3   5.25   4.75
  a.   A1030 P multi   1.25   .90
  b.   A1030 $1 multi   1.50   1.50
  c.   A1030 $1.70 multi   2.50   2.50

Booklet Stamps
Self-Adhesive
Serpentine Die Cut 13¼
2412 A1031   P multi   1.25   .25
  a.   Booklet pane of 6   7.50

Complete booklet, 2 #2412a   15.00
Serpentine Die Cut 13½
2413 A1030   P multi   1.25   .25
  a.   Booklet pane of 6   7.50
       Complete booklet, 2 #2413a 15.00
2414 A1030 $1 multi   1.50   .60
  a.   Booklet pane of 6   9.00
2415 A1030 $1.70 multi   2.50   .90
  a.   Booklet pane of 6   15.00
  b.   Gutter pane, #2414a, 2415a 26.00
       Nos. 2412-2415 (4)   6.50   2.00
Nos. 2411a, 2412 and 2413 each sold for 57c on day of issue.

New Year 2011
(Year of
the Rabbit)
A1032

Design: $1.75, Two rabbits in circle.

Litho. & Embossed With Foil
Application
2011, Jan. 7   *Perf. 12½*
2416 A1032   P shown   1.25   .25
Souvenir Sheet
2417 A1032 $1.75 multi   2.50   2.50
No. 2416 sold for 59c on day of issue.

Canadian Flag on
Soldier's Uniform
A1033

Canadian Flag on Hot-
air Balloon
A1034

Canadian Flag on
Search and Rescue
Team's Uniform
A1035

Canadian Flag on
Canadarm
A1036

Canadian Flag on
Backpack — A1037

2011, Jan. 17   Litho.   *Perf. 13x13¼*
2418   Sheet of 5   6.25   4.75
  a.   A1033 P multi   1.25   .90
  b.   A1034 P multi   1.25   .90
  c.   A1035 P multi   1.25   .90
  d.   A1036 P multi   1.25   .90
  e.   A1037 P multi   1.25   .90
Booklet Stamps
Self-Adhesive
Serpentine Die Cut 13¼
2419 A1033 P multi   1.25   .25
2420 A1034 P multi   1.25   .25
2421 A1035 P multi   1.25   .25
2422 A1036 P multi   1.25   .25
2423 A1037 P multi   1.25   .25
  a.   Booklet pane of 10, 2 each
       #2419-2423   12.50
  b.   Booklet pane of 30, 6 each
       #2419-2423   37.50
       Nos. 2419-2423 (5)   6.25   3.00
On day of issue, Nos. 2418a-2418e, 2419-2423 each sold for 59c.

Juvenile
Wildlife — A1038

Designs: P, Arctic hare leverets. $1.03, Red fox kit in hollow log. $1.25, Canada goslings. $1.75, Polar bear cub.

2011, Jan. 17   *Perf. 13¼x13*
2424   Sheet of 4   8.00   8.00
  a.   A1038 P multi   1.25   .90
  b.   A1038 $1.03 multi   1.50   1.10
  c.   A1038 $1.25 multi   1.75   1.30
  d.   A1038 $1.75 multi   2.50   1.80
Coil Stamps
Self-Adhesive
Serpentine Die Cut 9¼ Horiz.
2425 A1038   P multi   1.40   1.40
Serpentine Die Cut 8¼ Horiz.
2426 A1038   P multi   1.25   .25
2427 A1038 $1.03 multi   1.35   .30
Horiz. pairs, imperf. between, of No. 2426 are from uncut press panels of 100. Value unused, $3.25.
Serpentine Die Cut 8½ Horiz.
2428 A1038 $1.25 multi   1.80   .45
Serpentine Die Cut 8¼ Horiz.
2429 A1038 $1.75 multi   2.50   .60
Booklet Stamps
Serpentine Die Cut 9¼ Horiz.
2430 A1038 $1.03 multi   1.50   .30
  a.   Booklet pane of 6   9.00
2431 A1038 $1.25 multi   1.80   .45
  a.   Booklet pane of 6   11.00
2432 A1038 $1.75 multi   2.40   .60
  a.   Booklet pane of 6   14.50
       Nos. 2425-2432 (8)   18.70   9.40
On day of issue, Nos. 2424a, 2425 and 2426 each sold for 59c. On rolls of No. 2425, stamps do not touch each other and pairs are horizontal. On rolls of No. 2426, stamps touch each other and pairs are vertical.
See Nos. 2504-2512, 2602-2610, 2692, 2692A, 2709-2717.

Black History
Month — A1039

Order of Canada recipients: No. 2433, Carrie Best (1903-2001), journalist. No. 2434, Ferguson Jenkins, baseball player.

Self-Adhesive
Serpentine Die Cut 13½x13¾
2011, Feb. 1   **Booklet Stamps**
2433 A1039 59c multi   .85   .30
  a.   Booklet pane of 10   8.50
2434 A1039 59c multi   .85   .30
  a.   Booklet pane of 10   8.50

Gift
Box — A1040

Self-Adhesive
Serpentine Die Cut 13½ Horiz.
2011, Feb. 7   **Booklet Stamp**
2435 A1040 P multi   1.25   .25
  a.   Booklet pane of 6   7.50
No. 2435 sold for 59c on day of issue.

Paintings of
Daphne
Odjig
A1041

Paintings: 59c, Pow-wow Dancer. $1.03, Pow-wow (32x39mm). $1.75, Spiritual Renewal (56x39mm).

2011, Feb. 21   *Perf. 12½*
2436 A1041 59c multi   .85   .30
Souvenir Sheet
2437   Sheet of 3, #2436,
        2437a-2437b   4.00   4.00
  a.   A1041 $1.03 multi   1.50   1.50
  b.   A1041 $1.75 multi   2.50   2.50
Booklet Stamps
Self-Adhesive
Serpentine Die Cut 13½x13¼
2438 A1041 $1.03 multi   1.50   .60
  a.   Booklet pane of 6   9.00
2439 A1041 $1.75 multi   2.50   .90
  a.   Booklet pane of 6   15.00

Sunflower
A1042   A1043

Sunflower varieties: Nos. 2440a, 2441, 2443, Prado Red. Nos. 2440b, 2442, 2444, Sunbright (yellow flower).

2011, Mar. 3   Litho.   *Perf. 13¼*
Souvenir Sheet
2440   Sheet of 2   2.50   2.00
  a.-b. A1042 P Either single 1.25   .90
Coil Stamps
Self-Adhesive
Serpentine Die Cut 8¼ Horiz.
2441 A1043 P multi   1.25   .35
2442 A1043 P multi   1.25   .35
  a.   Vert. pair, #2441-2442 2.50
Booklet Stamps
Serpentine Die Cut 13½
2443 A1042 P multi   1.25   .30
2444 A1042 P multi   1.25   .30
  a.   Booklet pane of 10, 5 each
       #2443-2444   12.50
On day of issue, Nos. 2440a-2440b, 2441-2444 each sold for 59c.

Signs of the
Zodiac — A1044

No. 2445: a, Aries. b, Taurus. c, Gemini. d, Cancer. No. 2446: a, Leo. b, Virgo. c, Libra. d, Scorpio. No. 2447: a, Sagittarius. b, Capricorn. c, Aquarius. d, Pisces.
No. 2448: a, Aries. b, Taurus. c, Gemini. d, Cancer. e, Leo. f, Virgo. g, Libra. h, Scorpio. i, Sagittarius. j, Capricorn. k, Aquarius. l, Pisces. No. 2449, Aries. No. 2450, Taurus. No. 2451, Gemini. No. 2452, Cancer. No. 2453, Leo. No. 2454, Virgo. No. 2455, Libra. No. 2456, Scorpio. No. 2457, Sagittarius. No. 2458, Capricorn. No. 2459, Aquarius. No. 2460, Pisces.

2011-13   Litho.   *Perf. 12½*
2445   Sheet of 4   5.00   3.75
  a.-d. A1044 P Any single   1.25   .90
2446   Sheet of 4   5.00   3.75
  a.-d. A1044 P Any single   1.25   .90
2447   Sheet of 4   5.00   3.75
  a.-d. A1044 P Any single   1.25   .90
          Perf. 12½x13
2448   Sheet of 12   15.00 11.00
  a.-l. A1044 P Any single   1.25   .90
Booklet Stamps
Self-Adhesive
Serpentine Die Cut 13½
2449 A1044 P multi   1.25   .30
  a.   Booklet pane of 10   12.50
2450 A1044 P multi   1.25   .30
  a.   Booklet pane of 10   12.50
  b.   Gutter pane of 12, 6 each
       #2449-2450   15.00
2451 A1044 P multi   1.25   .30
  a.   Booklet pane of 10   12.50
2452 A1044 P multi   1.25   .30
  a.   Booklet pane of 10   12.50
  b.   Gutter pane of 12, 6 each
       #2451-2452   15.00
2453 A1044 P multi   1.25   .30
  a.   Booklet pane of 10   12.50
2454 A1044 P multi   1.25   .30
  a.   Booklet pane of 10   12.50
2455 A1044 P multi   1.25   .30
  a.   Booklet pane of 10   12.50

2456	A1044	P multi		1.25	.30
a.		Booklet pane of 10		12.50	
b.		Gutter pane of 24, 6 each			
		#2453-2456		30.00	
2457	A1044	P multi		1.25	.30
a.		Booklet pane of 10		12.50	
2458	A1044	P multi		1.25	.30
a.		Booklet pane of 10		12.50	
2459	A1044	P multi		1.25	.30
a.		Booklet pane of 10		12.50	
2460	A1044	P multi		1.25	.30
a.		Booklet pane of 10		12.50	
b.		Gutter pane of 24, 6 each			
		#2457-2460		30.00	
		Nos. 2449-2460 (12)		15.00	3.60

Issued: No. 2449, 3/21; Nos. 2450, 2450b, 4/21; No. 2451, 5/20; Nos. 2445, 2452, 2452b, 6/22, Nos. 2446, 2453-2456, 2456b, 7/23/12. Nos. 2447-2448, 2457-2460, 2460b, 2/20/13. Nos. 2445a-2445d, 2449-2452 each sold for 59c on day of issue. Nos. 2446a-2446d, 2453-2456 each sold for 61c on day of issue. Nos. 2447a-2447d, 2448a-2448l, 2457-2460 each sold for 63c on day of issue.

Intl. Year of Forests — A1045

Designs: Nos. 2461a, 2462, Tree. Nos. 2461b, 2463, Mushrooms and plants on forest floor.

2011, Apr. 21	Litho.	Perf. 13½x13		
2461	A1045	Sheet of 2	2.50	2.25
a.-b.		P Either single	1.25	.90

Booklet Stamps
Self-Adhesive

Serpentine Die Cut 13x13¼

2462	A1045	P multi		1.25	.30
2463	A1045	P multi		1.25	.30
a.		Booklet pane of 8, 4 each			
		#2462-2463		10.00	

On day of issue, Nos. 2461a-2461b, 2462-2463 each sold for 59c.

Wedding of Prince William and Catherine Middleton — A1046

Couple with Prince William at: P, Right. $1.75, Left.

2011, Apr. 29			Perf. 12¾x13¼		
2464	A1046	P multi		1.25	.30
2465	A1046	$1.75 multi		2.50	1.10
a.		Horiz. pair, #2464-2465		3.75	1.50
b.		Souvenir sheet, #2464-2465		4.00	4.00
c.		As "b," with arms of Prince William overprinted in sheet margin in gold		4.50	4.50

Booklet Stamps
Self-Adhesive

Serpentine Die Cut 13¼

2466	A1046	P multi		1.25	.30
a.		Booklet pane of 10		12.50	

2467	A1046	$1.75 multi		2.50	1.10
a.		Booklet pane of 10		25.00	
b.		Gutter pane, 6 #2466, 4 #2467		55.00	

On day of issue, Nos. 2464 and 2468 each sold for 59c.

Methods of Mail Delivery — A1047

Designs: No. 2468, Ponchon. No. 2469, Dog sled.

2011, May 13		Perf. 12½		
2468		59c multi	.85	.30
2469		59c multi	.85	.30
a.	A1047	Horiz. pair, #2468-2469	1.70	.75

Parks Canada, Cent. — A1048

Self-Adhesive

Serpentine Die Cut 13½

2011, May 19		Booklet Stamp		
2470	A1048	59c multi	.85	.30
a.		Booklet pane of 10	8.50	

Details of Art Deco Structures — A1049

Designs: Nos. 2471a, 2472, Burrard Bridge, Vancouver. Nos. 2471b, 2473, Cormier House, Montreal. Nos. 2471c, 2474, R. C. Harris Water Treatment Plant, Toronto. Nos. 2471d, 2475, Supreme Court of Canada, Ottawa. Nos. 2471e, 2476, Dominion Building, Regina, Saskatchewan.

2011, June 9		Litho.	Perf. 13x12½		
2471	A1049	Sheet of 5 + 5 labels		6.25	4.25
a.-e.		P Any single		1.25	.90

Booklet Stamps
Self-Adhesive

Serpentine Die Cut 13¼x13½

2472	A1049	P multi		1.25	.30
2473	A1049	P multi		1.25	.30
2474	A1049	P multi		1.25	.30
2475	A1049	P multi		1.25	.30
2476	A1049	P multi		1.25	.30
a.		Booklet pane of 10, 2 each #2472-2476		12.50	
		Nos. 2472-2476 (5)		6.25	1.50

On day of issue, Nos. 2471a-2471e, 2472-2476 each sold for 59c.

Duke and Duchess of Cambridge on Their Wedding Day — A1050

2011, June 22		Perf. 12¾x13¼		
2477		Sheet of 2 #2477a	2.50	1.90
a.	A1050	P multi	1.25	.90
b.		Sheet similar to #2477, with Royal Tour emblem overprinted in gold in sheet margin	2.50	1.90

Popular Singers
A1051

Booklet Stamp
Self-Adhesive

Serpentine Die Cut 13¼

2478	A1050	P multi		1.25	.30

On day of issue, Nos. 2477a and 2478 each sold for 59c. Margin of No. 2477 depicts Westminster Abbey, and that of No. 2477b depicts the Canadian Parliament.

Designs: Nos. 2479, 2483c, Ginette Reno. Nos. 2480, 2483a, Bruce Cockburn. Nos. 2481, 2483d, Robbie Robertson. Nos. 2482, 2483b, Kate and Anna McGarrigle.

2011			Perf. 12½		
2479	A1051	P multi		1.50	1.50
a.		Perf. 12½x13		1.30	.90
2480	A1051	P multi		1.50	1.50
a.		Perf. 12½x13		1.30	.90
2481	A1051	P multi		1.50	1.50
a.		Perf. 12½x13		1.30	.90
2482	A1051	P multi		1.50	1.50
a.		Perf. 12½x13		1.30	.90
b.		Souvenir sheet of 4, #2479a-2482a		5.25	3.50
		Nos. 2479-2482 (4)		6.00	6.00

Self-Adhesive
Serpentine Die Cut 13½

2483		Booklet pane of 4	5.00	
a.-d.	A1051	P Any single	1.25	.40
		Complete booklet, 2 #2483	10.00	

Issued: Nos. 2479-2482, 7/30; Nos. 2479a-2482a, 2482b, 2483, 6/30. On day of issue, Nos. 2479a2482, 2479a-2482a and 2483a-2483d each sold for 59c.

Complete booklets were issued with four different covers depicting the featured singers. The order of the stamps is different in each booklet.

Roadside Attractions — A1052

Designs: Nos. 2484a, 2485a, World's Largest Lobster, Shediac, New Brunswick. Nos. 2484b, 2485b, Wild Blueberry, Oxford, Nova Scotia. Nos. 2484c, 2485c, Big Potato, O'Leary, Prince Edward Island. Nos. 2484d, 2485d, Giant Squid, Glover's Harbour, Newfoundland.

2011, July 7			Perf. 12¾		
2484	A1052	Sheet of 4		5.00	3.50
a.-d.		P Any single		1.25	.90

Self-Adhesive
Serpentine Die Cut13½

2485	A1052	Booklet pane of 4	5.00	
a.-d.		P Any single	1.25	.35
		Complete booklet, 2 #2485	10.00	

Third Consecutive Victory of Intl. Harmsworth Trophy by Miss Supertest III Hydroplane — A1053

Designs: P, Miss Supertest III. $1.75, Miss Supertest III, diff.

2011, Aug. 8		Litho.	Perf. 13¼		
2486	A1053	Sheet of 2		4.25	4.00
a.		P multi		1.25	.90
b.		$1.75 multi		2.85	2.60

Booklet Stamp
Self-Adhesive

Serpentine Die Cut 13¼ Horiz.

2487	A1053	P multi		1.25	.30
a.		Booklet pane of 10		12.50	

Nos. 2486a and 2487 each sold for 59c on day of issue.

Canadian Inventions — A1054

No. 2488: a, Pacemaker, developed by Dr. John Hopps. b, BlackBerry, developed by Research in Motion. c, Electric oven, developed by Thomas Ahearn. d, Electric wheelchair, developed by George J. Klein.

Serpentine Die Cut 13¼

2011, Aug. 17		Self-Adhesive		
2488		Booklet pane of 4	3.50	
a.-d.	A1054	59c Any single	.85	.40
		Complete booklet, 2 #2488	7.00	

Dr. John Charles Polanyi, Winner of 1986 Nobel Prize for Chemistry A1055

Self-Adhesive
Booklet Stamp

Serpentine Die Cut 13½

2011, Oct. 3			Litho.		
2489	A1055	P multi		1.25	.30
a.		Booklet pane of 10		12.50	

Intl. Year of Chemistry. No. 2489 sold for 59c on day of issue.

Christmas
A1056   A1057

Stained-glass windows, Cathedral of Saint Mary of the Immaculate Conception, Kingston, Ontario: Nos. 2490a, 2492, Angel. $1.03, Nativity. $1.75, Epiphany.

2011, Nov. 1		Litho.	Perf. 13x12½		
2490		Sheet of 3		5.25	4.75
a.	A1056	P multi		1.25	.90
b.	A1056	$1.03 multi		1.50	1.50
c.	A1056	$1.75 multi		2.50	2.50

Booklet Stamps
Self-Adhesive
Litho. With Hologram Affixed

Serpentine Die Cut 8¼ Horiz.

2491	A1057	P multi		1.25	.25
a.		Booklet pane of 6		7.50	
		Complete booklet, 2 #2491a		15.00	

Litho.

Serpentine Die Cut 13¼

2492	A1056	P multi		1.25	.25
a.		Booklet pane of 6		7.50	
		Complete booklet, 2 #2492a		15.00	
2493	A1056	$1.03 multi		1.50	.60
a.		Booklet pane of 6		9.00	
2494	A1056	$1.75 multi		2.50	.90
a.		Booklet pane of 6		15.00	
b.		Gutter pane of 2493a, 2494a		25.00	
		Nos. 2491-2494 (4)		6.50	2.00

On day of issue, Nos. 2490a, 2491 and 2492 each sold for 59c.

New Year 2012
(Year of the
Dragon)
A1058

Design: $1.80, Dragon's head.

Litho. & Embossed With Foil Application

2012, Jan. 10			Perf. 12½
2495 A1058	P shown	1.25	.25

Souvenir Sheet

| 2496 A1058 | $1.80 multi | 2.50 | 2.50 |
| a. | Souvenir sheet of 2, #2417, 2496 | 5.00 | 5.00 |

Booklet Stamp Self-Adhesive Litho.

Serpentine Die Cut 13½

| 2497 A1058 | $1.80 multi | 2.50 | .90 |
| a. | Booklet pane of 6 | 15.00 | |

No. 2495 sold for 61c on day of issue.

Flag on Coast Guard Ship A1059

Flag in Van Window A1060

Olympic Athlete Carrying Flag A1061

Flag on Bobsled A1062

Inuit Child Waving Flag — A1063

2012, Jan. 16	Litho.	Perf. 13x13¼
2498	Souvenir sheet of 5	6.25 4.75
a.	A1059 P multi	1.25 .90
b.	A1060 P multi	1.25 .90
c.	A1061 P multi	1.25 .90
d.	A1062 P multi	1.25 .90
e.	A1063 P multi	1.25 .90

Booklet Stamps Self-Adhesive

Serpentine Die Cut 13¼

2499 A1059	P multi	1.25	.25
a.	With "Canada" visible on reverse of stamp	7.25	.35
2500 A1060	P multi	1.25	.25
a.	With "Canada" visible on reverse of stamp	2.25	.35
2501 A1061	P multi	1.25	.25
a.	With "Canada" visible on reverse of stamp	2.25	.35
2502 A1062	P multi	1.25	.25
a.	Microprinting with corrected spelling "Lueders"	1.50	.25
b.	As "a," with "Canada" visible on reverse of stamp	2.25	.35
2503 A1063	P multi	1.25	.25
a.	Booklet pane of 10, 2 each #2499-2503	12.50	
b.	Booklet pane of 30, 6 each #2499-2503	37.50	
c.	Booklet pane of 10, 2 each #2499-2502, 2502a, 2503	18.00	
d.	With "Canada" visible on reverse of stamp	2.25	.35
e.	Booklet pane of 10, 2 each #2499a, 2500a, 2501a, 2502b, 2503d	22.50	
	Nos. 2499-2503 (5)	6.25	1.25

On day of issue, Nos. 2498a-2498e, 2499-2503 each sold for 61c. The printing on the backing paper on No. 2503a differs from that on the backing paper of any of the component thirds of No. 2503b.
Issued: Nos. 2502a, 2503c, 9/28/12; Nos. 2499a, 2500a, 2501a, 2502b, 2503d, 2013. Nos. 2498d and 2502 have incorrect spelling in microprinting of "Leuders."

Juvenile Wildlife Type of 2011

Designs: P, Three raccoon kits. $1.05, Two caribou calves. $1.29, Adult loon and two chicks. $1.80, Moose calves.

2012, Jan. 16		Perf. 13¼x13
2504	Souvenir sheet of 4	7.00 5.75
a.	A1038 P multi	1.25 .90
b.	A1038 $1.05 multi	1.50 1.10
c.	A1038 $1.29 multi	1.80 1.30
d.	A1038 $1.80 multi	2.50 1.80

Self-Adhesive Coil Stamps

Serpentine Die Cut 9¼ Horiz.

| 2505 A1038 | P multi | 1.40 1.40 |

Serpentine Die Cut 8¼ Horiz.

2506 A1038	P multi	1.25 .25
2507 A1038	$1.05 multi	1.50 .30
2508 A1038	$1.29 multi	1.80 .45
2509 A1038	$1.80 multi	2.50 .55
	Nos. 2505-2509 (5)	8.45 2.95

Booklet Stamps

Serpentine Die Cut 9¼ Horiz.

2510 A1038	$1.05 multi	1.50	.30
a.	Booklet pane of 6	9.00	
2511 A1038	$1.29 multi	1.80	.45
a.	Booklet pane of 6	11.00	
2512 A1038	$1.80 multi	2.50	.60
a.	Booklet pane of 6	15.00	
	Nos. 2510-2512 (3)	5.80	1.35

On day of issue, Nos. 2504a, 2505 and 2506 each sold for 61c. On rolls of No. 2505, stamps do not touch each other and pairs are horizontal. On rolls of No. 2506, stamps touch each other and pairs are vertical.

A1064

Reign of Queen Elizabeth II, 60th Anniv. — A1065

Designs: No. 2513, Crown, Canada #330. No. 2514, Map of Canada, Canada #471. No. 2515, Document, pen, Canada #704. No. 2516, Jubilee bouquet, Canada #1168. No. 2517, Tiara details, Canada #1932. Nos. 2518, 2519, Queen Elizabeth II wearing robe and tiara.

2012	Litho.	Perf. 13¼
2513 A1064	P multi	1.25 .75
2514 A1064	P multi	1.25 .75
2515 A1064	P multi	1.25 .75
2516 A1064	P multi	1.25 .75
2517 A1064	P multi	1.25 .75

Perf. 13¼x12½

| 2518 A1065 | P multi | 1.25 .75 |

Booklet Stamp Self-Adhesive

| 2519 A1065 | P multi | 1.25 | .30 |
| a. | Booklet pane of 10 | 12.50 | |

Issued: Nos. 2513, 2519, 1/16; No. 2514, 2/6; No. 2515, 3/6; No. 2516, 4/10; No. 2517, 5/7; No. 2518, 6/1. On day of issue, Nos. 2513-2519 each sold for 61c. Nos. 2513-2518 each were printed in sheets of 4.

Black History Month — A1066

Designs: No. 2520, John Ware (c. 1845-1905), cattle driver and rancher. No. 2521, Viola Desmond (1914-65), civil rights activist.

Self-Adhesive Booklet Stamps

Serpentine Die Cut 13½

2012, Feb. 1		Litho.
2520 A1066	P multi	1.25 .30
a.	Booklet pane of 10	12.50
2521 A1066	P multi	1.25 .30
a.	Booklet pane of 10	12.50
b.	Gutter pane of 12, 6 each #2520-2521	15.00

On day of issue, Nos. 2520-2521 each sold for 61c.

Sculptures by Joe Fafard — A1067

Designs: P, Smoothly She Shifted. $1.05, Dear Vincent, vert. (32x40mm). $1.80, Capillery, horiz. (64x32mm).

2012, Feb. 23		Perf. 12½
2522 A1067	P multi	1.25 .30

Souvenir Sheet

2523	Sheet of 3, #2522, 2523a, 2523b	5.25 4.50
a.	A1067 $1.05 multi	1.50 1.70
b.	A1067 $1.80 multi	2.50 2.90

Booklet Stamps Self-Adhesive

Serpentine Die Cut 13½

| 2524 A1067 | $1.05 multi | 1.50 | .60 |
| a. | Booklet pane of 6 | 9.00 | |

Serpentine Die Cut 13¼

2525 A1067	$1.80 multi	2.50	.90
a.	Booklet pane of 6	15.00	
b.	Gutter pane of 6, 3 each #2524-2525	15.00	

No. 2522 sold for 61c on day of issue.

A1068

Daylilies — A1069

Color of daylily: Nos. 2526a, 2527, 2529, Orange. Nos. 2526b, 2528, 2530, Purple.

2012, Mar. 1		Perf. 13¼
2526	Souvenir Sheet Sheet of 2	2.50 1.80
a.-b.	A1068 P Either single	1.25 .90

Coil Stamps Self-Adhesive

Serpentine Die Cut 8¼ Horiz.

2527 A1069	P multi	1.25 .30
2528 A1069	P multi	1.25 .30
a.	Vert. pair, #2527-2528	2.50

Booklet Stamps

Serpentine Die Cut 13½

2529 A1068	P multi	1.25	.30
2530 A1068	P multi	1.25	.30
a.	Booklet pane of 10, 5 each #2529-2530	12.50	

On day of issue, Nos. 2526a, 2526b, 2527-2530 each sold for 61c.

A1070

Sinking of the Titanic, Cent. — A1071

Flag of the White Star Line and: Nos. 2531, 2536, Bow of Titanic, map showing Halifax, Nova Scotia. Nos. 2532, 2537, Bow of Titanic, map showing Southampton, England. No. 2533, Propellers of Titanic, three men. No. 2534, Propellers of Titanic, six men. $1.80, Titanic, map of North Atlantic, flag of the White Star Line.

2012, Apr. 5	Litho.	Perf. 12½
2531 A1070	P multi	1.25 .45
2532 A1070	P multi	1.25 .45
2533 A1070	P multi	1.25 .45
2534 A1070	P multi	1.25 .45
a.	Block of 4, #2531-2534	5.00 2.25
	Nos. 2531-2534 (4)	5.00 1.80

Souvenir Sheet

Perf. 13

| 2535 A1071 | $1.80 multi | 2.50 2.50 |

Booklet Stamps Self-Adhesive

Serpentine Die Cut 13½

2536 A1070	P multi	1.25	.30
2537 A1070	P multi	1.25	.30
a.	Booklet pane of 10, 5 each #2536-2537	12.50	
2538 A1071	$1.80 multi	2.50	1.50
a.	Booklet pane of 6	15.00	
	Nos. 2536-2538 (3)	5.00	2.10

On day of issue, Nos. 2531-2534, 2536-2537 each sold for 61c.

Thomas Douglas, 5th Earl of Selkirk (1771-1820), Founder of Red River Settlement, and Settlers — A1072

2012, May 3	Litho.	Perf. 13¼
2539 A1072 P multi		1.25 .30

Red River Settlement, bicent. No. 2539 sold for 61c on day of issue.

Reign Of Queen Elizabeth II, 60th Anniv. A1073

2012, May 7	Engr.	Perf. 11½
2540 A1073	$2 purple	3.00 1.50
a.	Souvenir sheet of 1	3.75 3.75

Franklin the Turtle, Children's Book Character by Paulette Bourgeois — A1074

Designs: Nos. 2541a, 2542, Franklin, beaver and teddy bear. Nos. 2541b, 2543, Franklin helping young turtle to read book. Nos. 2541c, 2544, Franklin and snail. Nos. 2541d, 2545, Franklin watching bear feed fish in bowl.

2012, May 11		Perf. 13x12½
2541	Miniature sheet of 4	5.00 4.50
a.-d.	A1074 P Any single	1.25 .90

Booklet Stamps Self-Adhesive

Serpentine Die Cut 13¼

2542 A1074	P multi	1.25 .35
2543 A1074	P multi	1.25 .35
2544 A1074	P multi	1.25 .35

2545	A1074	P multi	1.25	.35
a.		Booklet pane of 12, 3 each #2542-2545	15.00	
		Nos. 2542-2545 (4)	5.00	1.40

Nos. 2541a-2541d, 2542-2545 each sold for 61c on day of issue.

Calgary Stampede, Cent. — A1075

Designs: P, Saddle on rodeo horse. $1.05, Commemorative belt buckle.

2012, May 17   **Perf. 13x13¼**

2546		Souvenir sheet of 2	3.00	2.50
a.	A1075	P multi	1.25	.90
b.	A1075	$1.05 multi	1.80	1.60

Booklet Stamps
Self-Adhesive

Serpentine Die Cut 13¼x13

2547	A1075	P multi	1.25	.30
a.		Booklet pane of 10	12.50	
2548	A1075	$1.05 multi	1.50	.60
a.		Booklet pane of 10	15.00	
b.		Gutter pane of 10, 6 #2547, 4 #2548	15.00	

Nos. 2546a and 2547 each sold for 61c on day of issue.

Order of Canada Recipients A1076

Designs: Nos. 2549a, 2550, Louise Arbour, president of International Crisis Group. Nos. 2549b, 2551, Rick Hansen, founder of Rick Hansen Foundation (spinal cord injury research). Nos. 2549c, 2552, Sheila Watt-Cloutier, Inuit rights activist. Nos. 2549d, 2553, Michael J. Fox, actor, founder of Michael J. Fox Foundation for Parkinson's Research.

2012, May 22   **Litho.**   **Perf. 12½**

2549		Miniature sheet of 4	5.00	4.50
a.-d.	A1076	P Any single	1.25	.90

Booklet Stamps
Self-Adhesive

Serpentine Die Cut 13½

2550	A1076	P multi	1.25	.30
a.		Booklet pane of 10	12.50	
2551	A1076	P multi	1.25	.30
a.		Booklet pane of 10	12.50	
2552	A1076	P multi	1.25	.30
a.		Booklet pane of 10	12.50	
2553	A1076	P multi	1.25	.30
a.		Booklet pane of 10	12.50	
		Nos. 2550-2553 (4)	5.00	1.20

On day of issue Nos. 2549a-2549d, 2550-2553 each sold for 61c.

War of 1812, Bicent. — A1077

Designs: No. 2554, Sir Isaac Brock (1769-1812), British Major General. No. 2555, Tecumseh (1768-1813), leader of Indian confederacy.

2012, June 15   **Perf. 13¼x12½**

2554		P multi	1.25	.30
2555		P multi	1.25	.30
a.		A1077 Horiz. pair, #2554-2555	2.50	1.25

On day of issue, Nos. 2554-2555 each sold for 61c. See Guernsey No. 1172.

2012 Summer Olympics, London A1078

Self-Adhesive
Booklet Stamp

2012, June 27   *Serpentine Die Cut 8*

2556	A1078	P multi	1.25	.35
a.		Booklet pane of 10	12.50	

No. 2556 sold for 61c on day of issue.

Tommy Douglas (1904-86), Politician A1079

2012, June 29   **Perf. 12½**

2557	A1079	P multi	1.25	.30

Passage of Saskatchewan's Medical Care Insurance Act, 50th anniv. (start of socialized medicine in Canada). No. 2557 sold for 61c on day of issue.

Canadian Football League Team Emblems — A1080

Designs: Nos. 2558a, 2559, British Columbia Lions. Nos. 2558b, 2560, Edmonton Eskimos. Nos. 2558c, 2561, Calgary Stampeders. Nos. 2558d, 2562, Saskatchewan Roughriders. Nos. 2558e, 2563, Winnipeg Blue Bombers. Nos. 2558f, 2564, Hamilton Tiger-Cats. Nos. 2558g, 2565, Toronto Argonauts. Nos. 2558h, 2566, Montreal Alouettes.

2012, June 29   **Perf. 13¼x13**

2558	A1080	Sheet of 8	10.00	8.00
a.-h.		P Any single	1.25	.90

Coil Stamps
Self-Adhesive

Serpentine Die Cut 8¼ Horiz.

2559	A1080	P multi	1.25	.30
2560	A1080	P multi	1.25	.30
2561	A1080	P multi	1.25	.30
2562	A1080	P multi	1.25	.30
2563	A1080	P multi	1.25	.30
2564	A1080	P multi	1.25	.30
2565	A1080	P multi	1.25	.30
2566	A1080	P multi	1.25	.30
		Nos. 2559-2566 (8)	10.00	2.40

On day of issue, Nos. 2558a-2558h, 2559-2566 each sold for 61c. See No. 2754.

Grey Cup, Cent. — A1081

Grey Cup and: Nos. 2567a, 2568, Two football players, "100." Nos. 2567b, 2569, British Columbia Lions player Geroy Simon, kicker and holder in 1994 game. Nos. 2567c, 2570, Edmonton Eskimos player Tom Wilkinson, quarterback ready to throw pass. Nos. 2567d,

---

2571, Calgary Stampeders player "Thumper" Wayne Harris, running back and tacklers from 1948 game. Nos. 2567e, 2572, Saskatchewan Roughriders player George Reed, players celebrating in 1989 game. Nos. 2567f, 2573, Winnipeg Blue Bombers player Ken Pipen, players in fog in 1962 game. Nos. 2567g, 2574, Hamilton Tiger-Cats player Danny Mcmanus, player catching ball in 1972 game. Nos. 2567h, 2575, Toronto Argonauts player Michael "Pinball" Clemons, players on muddy field in 1950 game. Nos. 2567i, 2576, Montreal Alouettes player Anthony Calvillo, players at line of scrimmage in 1977 game.

Litho. & Embossed

2012, Aug. 16   **Perf. 12½**

2567	A1081	Sheet of 9	11.25	8.00
a.-i.		P Any single	1.25	.85

Litho.
Booklet Stamps
Self-Adhesive

Serpentine Die Cut 13¼

2568	A1081	P multi	1.25	.30
a.		Booklet pane of 10	12.50	
2569	A1081	P multi	1.25	.30
a.		Booklet pane of 10	12.50	
2570	A1081	P multi	1.25	.30
a.		Booklet pane of 10	12.50	
2571	A1081	P multi	1.25	.30
a.		Booklet pane of 10	12.50	
2572	A1081	P multi	1.25	.30
a.		Booklet pane of 10	12.50	
2573	A1081	P multi	1.25	.30
a.		Booklet pane of 10	12.50	
2574	A1081	P multi	1.25	.30
a.		Booklet pane of 10	12.50	
2575	A1081	P multi	1.25	.30
a.		Booklet pane of 10	12.50	
2576	A1081	P multi	1.25	.30
a.		Booklet pane of 10	12.50	
		Nos. 2568-2576 (9)	11.25	2.70

Nos. 2567a-2567i, 2568-2576 each sold for 61c on day of issue. For overprint, see No. 2598.

Military Regiments, 150th Anniv. A1082

Uniforms of: Nos. 2577a, 2578, Black Watch (Royal Highland) Regiment of Canada. Nos. 2577b, 2579, Royal Hamilton Light Infantry (Wentworth Regiment). Nos. 2577c, 2580, Royal Regiment of Canada

2012, Oct. 11   **Litho.**   **Perf. 13x13½**

2577		Souvenir sheet of 3	3.75	3.00
a.-c.	A1082	P Any single	1.25	.90

Booklet Stamps
Self-Adhesive

Serpentine Die Cut 13¼x13

2578	A1082	P multi	1.25	.35
a.		Booklet pane of 10	12.50	
2579	A1082	P multi	1.25	.35
a.		Booklet pane of 10	12.50	
2580	A1082	P multi	1.25	.35
a.		Booklet pane of 10	12.50	
		Nos. 2578-2580 (3)	3.75	1.05

On day of issue, Nos. 2577a-2577c, 2578-2580 each sold for 61c.

Gingerbread Cookies A1083

Stained Glass Window From St. Mary's of the Immaculate Conception Cathedral, Kingsoton, Ontario A1084

Ribbons on Christmas cookies shaped as: P, Man and woman. $1.05, Five-pointed star. $1.80, Snowflake.

Souvenir Sheet

2012, Oct. 15   **Perf. 13¾x13¼**

2581		Sheet of 3	5.50	4.50
a.	A1083	P multi	1.25	.90
b.	A1083	$1.05 multi	1.50	1.50
c.	A1083	$1.80 multi	2.60	2.60

Booklet Stamps
Self-Adhesive

Serpentine Die Cut 13¼

2582	A1084	P multi	1.25	.25
a.		Booklet pane of 12	15.00	

Serpentine Die Cut 13¼x13

2583	A1083	P multi	1.25	.25
a.		Booklet pane of 12	12.50	
2584	A1083	$1.05 multi	1.50	.60
a.		Booklet pane of 6	9.00	
2585	A1083	$1.80 multi	2.90	1.00
a.		Booklet pane of 6	17.50	
		Nos. 2582-2585 (4)	6.90	2.10

Christmas. On day of issue, Nos. 2581a, 2582 and 2583 each sold for 61c.

Dots — A1085

Frame — A1086

Creatures A1088

Hearts A1087

Butterflies A1089

Maple Leaves A1090

Flowers A1091

Snowflakes A1092

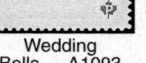

Wedding Bells — A1093

Doves and Flowers — A1094

Balloons, Stars, Party Hat — A1095

Holly — A1096

Serpentine Die Cut 13¼

2012, Nov. Self-Adhesive Litho.

2586	A1085 P gray	2.25	2.25
a.	Personalized version, any denomination or orientation	—	—
2587	A1086 P gray	2.25	2.25
a.	Personalized version, any denomination or orientation	—	—
2588	A1087 P gray & red	2.25	2.25
a.	Personalized version, any denomination or orientation	—	—
2589	A1088 P multi	2.25	2.25
a.	Personalized version, any denomination or orientation	—	—
2590	A1089 P multi	2.25	2.25
a.	Personalized version, any denomination or orientation	—	—
2591	A1090 P multi	2.25	2.25
a.	Personalized version, any denomination or orientation	—	—
2592	A1091 P multi	2.25	2.25
a.	Personalized version, any denomination or orientation	—	—
2593	A1092 P multi	2.25	2.25
a.	Personalized version, any denomination or orientation	—	—
2594	A1093 P gray & black	2.25	2.25
a.	Personalized version, any denomination or orientation	—	—
2595	A1094 P gray	2.25	2.25
a.	Personalized version, any denomination or orientation	—	—
2596	A1095 P multi	2.25	2.25
a.	Personalized version, any denomination or orientation	—	—
2597	A1096 P multi	2.25	2.25
a.	Personalized version, any denomination or orientation	—	—
	Nos. 2586-2597 (12)	27.00	27.00

Nos. 2586-2597 had a franking value on the day of issue of 61c, and were sold together in a package of single stamps that sold for $7.32. Each vertically-oriented stamp in the package had a gray image area. Horizontally-oriented stamps were not made available in these packages. First day covers of Nos. 2586-2597 are dated 11/5.

Nos. 2586a-2597a have personalized photographs in the image area, and were available with vertical or horizontal orientations and in various denominations. On Nov. 16-24 personalized stamps were offered for sale on iPad and iPhone apps at the P rate (with a franking value of 61c), $1.05, $1.29 and $1.80. It is not known if any personalized stamps of the $1.05, $1.29 and $1.80 denominations were created for customers through these apps during this brief period. On Nov. 24 stamps at the P rate (with a franking value of 61c), $1.10, $1.34 and $1.85 were offered to customers through the Picture Postage page of the Canada Post website, as well as through the apps. Additional stamps with different denominations may be offered for sale later. A $1.29 stamp featuring the image of a Turtle was made available on Nov. 1. It was only available affixed to packages containing a box of Nestle's Turtles candy. A box of candy and affixed stamp sold at post offices for $4.99, and the package could only be sent to Canadian addresses.

Except for the stamp with the turtle's image, the stamps of the various denominations were each made available in sheets of 26, sheets of 50 and booklet panes of 12 (a minimum of three booklet panes needed to be ordered). The selling prices of the personalized sheets and booklets were substantially higher than the face value of the stamps within them.

Vertically oriented stamps have the denomination in the lower right corner of the stamp, with the "C" of "Canada" at the upper left of the stamp, as shown in the illustrations. Horizontally oriented stamps have the denomination in the lower right corner of the stamp, with the "C" of "Canada" at the lower left corner. The dots, frame, hearts, creatures and butterflies images on horizontally-oriented stamps differ from those shown on the vertically-oriented stamps.

No. 2568 Overprinted in Dark Blue, Light Blue, Black and Silver

Booklet Stamp

Serpentine Die Cut 13¼

2012, Nov. 28 Litho.

Self-Adhesive

2598	A1081 P multi	1.25	.30
a.	Booklet pane of 10	12.50	

Grey Cup victory of Toronto Argonauts. No. 2598 sold for 61c on day of issue.

New Year 2013 (Year of the Snake) — A1097

Design: $1.85, Snake's head.

Litho. & Embossed

2013, Jan. 8 Perf. 12½

2599	A1097 P shown	1.25	.30

Souvenir Sheet

Litho. & Embossed With Foil Application

2600	A1097 $1.85 multi	2.75	2.75
a.	Souvenir sheet of 2, #2496, 2600	5.25	4.75

Booklet Stamp

Self-Adhesive

Litho.

Serpentine Die Cut 13½

2601	A1097 $1.85 multi	2.90	1.20
a.	Booklet pane of 6	17.50	

No. 2599 sold for 63c on day of issue. See No. 2700a.

Juvenile Wildlife Type of 2011

Designs: P, Four woodchuck pups. $1.10, Porcupette. $1.34, Fawn. $1.85, Bear cub.

2013, Jan. 14 Perf. 13¼x13

2602	Souvenir sheet of 4	7.25	6.25
a.	A1038 P multi	1.25	.90
b.	A1038 $1.10 multi	1.50	1.10
c.	A1038 $1.34 multi	1.80	1.30
d.	A1038 $1.85 multi	2.50	1.80

Self-Adhesive

Coil Stamps

Serpentine Die Cut 9¼ Horiz.

2603	A1038 P multi	1.50	1.50

Serpentine Die Cut 8¼ Horiz.

2604	A1038 P multi	1.25	.25
2605	A1038 $1.10 multi	1.50	.30
2606	A1038 $1.34 multi	1.80	.40
2607	A1038 $1.85 multi	2.50	.55

Booklet Stamps

Serpentine Die Cut 9¼ Horiz.

2608	A1038 $1.10 multi	1.60	.30
a.	Booklet pane of 6	9.50	
2609	A1038 $1.34 multi	2.00	.45
a.	Booklet pane of 6	12.00	
2610	A1038 $1.85 multi	2.75	.60
a.	Booklet pane of 6	16.50	
	Nos. 2603-2610 (8)	14.90	4.35

On day of issue, Nos. 2602a, 2603 and 2604 each sold for 63c. On rolls of No. 2603, stamps do not touch each other and pairs are horizontal. On rolls of No. 2604, stamps touch each other and pairs are vertical.

See No. 2692.

Flag Design on Chairs A1098

Flag on Hay Roll A1099

Flag Design on Spinnaker A1100

Flag in Flower Bed A1101

Flag Design on Hut — A1102

2013, Jan. 14 Litho. Perf. 13x13¼

2611	Souvenir sheet of 5	6.25	4.50
a.	A1098 P multi	1.25	.90
b.	A1099 P multi	1.25	.90
c.	A1100 P multi	1.25	.90
d.	A1101 P multi	1.25	.90
e.	A1102 P multi	1.25	.90

Booklet Stamps

Self-Adhesive

Serpentine Die Cut 13¼

2612	A1098 P multi	1.25	.25
a.	With "Canada" visible on reverse of stamp	1.25	.25
2613	A1099 P multi	1.25	.25
a.	With "Canada" visible on reverse of stamp	1.25	.25
2614	A1100 P multi	1.25	.25
a.	With "Canada" visible on reverse of stamp	1.25	.25
2615	A1101 P multi	1.25	.25
a.	With "Canada" visible on reverse of stamp	1.25	.25
2616	A1102 P multi	1.25	.25
a.	With "Canada" visible on reverse of stamp	1.25	.25
b.	Booklet pane of 10, 2 each #2612-2616	12.50	
c.	Booklet pane of 10, 2 each #2612a-2616a	12.50	
d.	Booklet pane of 30, 6 each #2612-2616	37.50	
e.	Booklet pane of 30, 6 each #2612a-2616a	37.50	
	Nos. 2612-2616 (5)	6.25	1.25

On day of issue, Nos. 2611a-2611e, 2612-2616, 2612a-2616a each sold for 63c. The printing on the backing paper on Nos. 2616b and 2616c differs from that on the backing paper of any of the component thirds of Nos. 2616d and 2616e.

See Nos. 2693-2697.

Queen Elizabeth II — A1103

Booklet Stamp

Serpentine Die Cut 13¼

2013, Jan. 14 Self-Adhesive

2617	A1103 P multi	1.25	.25
a.	Booklet pane of 10	12.50	
b.	As #2617,with "Canada" visible on reverse of stamp	1.25	.25
c.	Booklet pane of 10 #2617b	12.50	

No. 2617 sold for 63c on day of issue. Issued: Nos. 2617b, 2617c, 6/1. See No. 2698.

Raoul Wallenberg (1912-47), Swedish Diplomat Who Rescued Jews During World War II — A1104

Booklet Stamp

Serpentine Die Cut 13¼

2013, Jan. 17 Self-Adhesive

2618	A1104 185c multi	2.75	1.10
a.	Booklet pane of 6	16.50	

Oliver Jones, Jazz Musician — A1105

Joe Fortes (1863-1922), First Official Lifeguard of Vancouver — A1106

Booklet Stamps

Serpentine Die Cut 13¼

2013, Feb. 1 Self-Adhesive

2619	A1105 P multi	1.25	.30
a.	Booklet pane of 10	12.50	
2620	A1106 P multi	1.25	.30
a.	Booklet pane of 10	12.50	

On day of issue, Nos. 2619-2620 each sold for 63c.

Magnolias A1107   A1108

Magnolia varieties: Nos. 2621a, 2622, 2624, Yellow Bird (yellow flower). Nos. 2621b, 2623, 2625, Eskimo (lilac and white flower).

2013, Mar. 4 Litho. Perf. 13¼

Souvenir Sheet

2621	Sheet of 2	2.50	2.00
a.-b.	A1107 P Either single	1.25	.90

Coil Stamps

Self-Adhesive

Serpentine Die Cut 8¼ Horiz.

2622	A1108 P multi	1.25	.30
2623	A1108 P multi	1.25	.30
a.	Vert. pair, #2622-2623	2.50	

Booklet Stamps

Serpentine Die Cut 13½

2624	A1107 P multi	1.25	.30
2625	A1107 P multi	1.25	.30
a.	Booklet pane of 10, 5 each #2624-2625	12.50	

On day of issue, Nos. 2621a-2621b, 2622-2625 each sold for 63c.

Photography — A1109

Designs: Nos. 2626a, 2629, Louis-Joseph Papineau, by Thomas Coffin Doane, 1852. Nos. 2626b, 2630, The Kitchen Sink, by Margaret Watkins, 1919. Nos. 2626c, 2632, Kootuck-tuck, by Geraldine Moodie, 1903-05. Nos. 2627a, 2628, Hot Properties #1, by Jim Breukelman, 1987, horiz. Nos. 2627b, 2631, Andor Pasztor, by Gabor Szilasi, 1978, horiz. $1.10, Basement Camera Shop circa 1937, by Rodney Graham, 2011, horiz. $1.85, Yousuf Karsh, by Arnaud Maggs, 1981, horiz.

2013, Mar. 22 Perf. 13¼

2626	A1109 Sheet of 3	3.75	3.25
a.-c.	P Any single	1.25	.90
2627	A1109 Sheet of 4	7.00	6.25
a.-b.	P Any single	1.25	.90
c.	$1.10 multi	1.60	1.50
d.	$1.85 multi	2.75	2.50

Booklet Stamps

Self-Adhesive

Serpentine Die Cut 13½

2628	A1109 P multi	1.25	.30
2629	A1109 P multi	1.25	.30
2630	A1109 P multi	1.25	.30
2631	A1109 P multi	1.25	.30

2632	A1109	P multi	1.25	.30
a.		Booklet pane of 10, 2 each		
		#2628-2632	12.50	
2633	A1109	$1.10 multi	1.60	.75
a.		Booklet pane of 6	9.50	
2634	A1109	$1.85 multi	2.75	1.10
a.		Booklet pane of 6	16.50	
		Nos. 2628-2634 (7)	10.60	3.35

On day of issue, Nos. 2626a-2626c, 2627a, 2627b, 2628-2632 each sold for 63c.
See Nos. 2756-2764, 2814-2822, 2902-2910.

The Prince of Wales' Own Regiment, 150th Anniv. A1110

Serpentine Die Cut 13¼x13
2013, Apr. 9   Self-Adhesive
Booklet Stamp

2635	A1110	P multi	1.25	.35
a.		Booklet pane of 10	12.50	

No. 2635 sold for 63c on day of issue.

Pet Adoption — A1111

Designs: Nos. 2636a, 2637, Cat with bird on branch in background (24x32mm). Nos. 2636b, 2638, Parrot on perch (24x24mm). Nos. 2636c, 2639, Dog with squirrel, butterfly, flower and ball in background (24x40mm). Nos. 2636d, 2640, Dog with fireplace, dog bed and bone in background (40x40mm). Nos. 2636e, 2641, Cat with cat toys in background (24x32mm).

Perf. 12½ (#2636a, 2636e), 13¼ (#2636b), 12½x13¼
2013, Apr. 22

2636	A1111	Sheet of 5	6.25	5.00
a.-e.		P Any single	1.25	.90

Booklet Stamps
Self-Adhesive
Serpentine Die Cut 13x13¼

2637	A1111	P multi	1.25	.30

Serpentine Die Cut 13

2638	A1111	P multi	1.25	.30

Serpentine Die Cut 13½

2639	A1111	P multi	1.25	.30
2640	A1111	P multi	1.25	.30

Serpentine Die Cut 13x13¼

2641	A1111	P multi	1.25	.30
a.		Booklet pane of 10, 2 each		
		#2637-2641	12.50	
		Nos. 2637-2641 (5)	6.25	1.50

On day of issue, Nos. 2636a-2636e, 2637-2641 each sold for 63c.

Chinatown Gates — A1112

Gates in: Nos. 2642a, 2643a, Toronto. Nos. 2642b, 2643b, Montreal. Nos. 2642c, 2643c, Winnipeg. Nos. 2642d, 2643d, Edmonton. Nos. 2642e, 2643d, Vancouver. Nos. 2642f, 2643f, Ottawa. Nos. 2642g, 2643g, Mississauga, Ontario. Nos. 2642h, 2643h, Victoria.

Litho. With Foil Application
2013, May 1   Perf. 12½

2642	A1112	Miniature sheet of 8 + central label	10.00	7.50
a.-h.		P Any single	1.25	.90

An imperf. pane of 8 exists of No. 2642. Sold only in a "Gates of Chinatown Collection," along with a normal No. 2642 and two coins, for $88.88. Value of imperf. pane, $140.

Litho.
Booklet Stamps
Self-Adhesive
Serpentine Die Cut 13½

2643	A1112	Booklet pane of 8	10.00	
a.-h.		P Any single	1.25	.30

On day of issue Nos. 2642a-2642h, 2643a-2643h each sold for 63c. Label on No. 2642 has a die cut square opening in center.

Coronation of Queen Elizabeth II, 60th Anniv. — A1113

Serpentine Die Cut 13¼   Litho.
2013, May 8
Booklet Stamp
Self-Adhesive

2644	A1113	P multi	1.25	.30
a.		Booklet pane of 10	12.50	

No. 2644 sold for 63c on day of issue.

Big Brothers Big Sisters of Canada, Cent. — A1114

Serpentine Die Cut 13x13½   Litho.
2013, May 14
Booklet Stamp
Self-Adhesive

2645	A1114	P multi	1.25	.30
a.		Booklet pane of 10	12.50	

No. 2645 sold for 63c on day of issue.

Motorcycles — A1115

Designs: Nos. 2646a, 2647, 1908 CCM. Nos. 2646b, 2648, 1914 Indian.

2013, June 5   Perf. 12½x13
Souvenir Sheet

2646	A1115	Sheet of 2	2.50	1.80
a.-b.		P Either single	1.25	.90

Booklet Stamps
Self-Adhesive
Serpentine Die Cut 13¼

2647	A1115	P multi	1.25	.30
2648	A1115	P multi	1.25	.30
a.		Booklet pane of 10, 5 each		
		#2647-2648	12.50	

On day of issue, Nos. 2646a-2646b, 2647-2648 each sold for 63c.

Quebec Harbor Scene and Benjamin Franklin (1706-90), British North America Deputy Postmaster A1116

Booklet Stamp
Serpentine Die Cut 13½
2013, June 10   Self-Adhesive

2649	A1116	P multi	1.25	.30
a.		Booklet pane of 10	12.50	

Mail packet service from Montreal to New York, 250th anniv. No. 2649 sold for 63c on day of issue.

War of 1812 — A1117

Heroic figures of War of 1812: No. 2650, Lieutenant Colonel Charles de Salaberry (1778-1829). No. 2651, Laura Secord (1775-1868).

2013, June 20   Perf. 13x12½

2650		P multi	1.25	.30
2651		P multi	1.25	.30
a.	A1117	Horiz. pair, #2650-2651	2.50	.90

On day of issue, Nos. 2650-2651 each sold for 63c.

Children's Literature — A1118

Characters from series of *Stella* books, by Marie-Louise Gay: Nos. 2652a, 2653, Stella hanging by legs from tree. Nos. 2652b, 2654, Stella, brother Sam, and dog, Fred.

2013, July 5   Perf. 12½
Souvenir Sheet

2652	A1118	Sheet of 2	2.50	2.25
a.-b.		P Either single	1.25	.90

Booklet Stamps
Self-Adhesive
Serpentine Die Cut 13¼

2653	A1118	P multi	1.25	.30
2654	A1118	P multi	1.25	.30
a.		Booklet pane of 10, 5 each		
		#2653-2654	12.50	

On day of issue, Nos. 2652a-2652b, 2653-2654 each sold for 63c.

Canadian Bands — A1119

Designs: Nos. 2655a, 2656, The Tragically Hip (36x28mm). Nos. 2655b, 2657, Rush (28x28mm). Nos. 2655c, 2658, Beau Dommage (36x28mm). Nos. 2655d, 2659, The Guess Who (28x28mm).

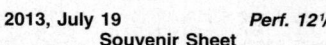

2013, July 19   Perf. 12½
Souvenir Sheet

2655	A1119	Sheet of 4	5.00	4.25
a.-d.		P Any single	1.25	.90

Booklet Stamps
Self-Adhesive
Serpentine Die Cut 13½

2656	A1119	P multi	1.25	.30
a.		Booklet pane of 10	12.50	
2657	A1119	P multi	1.25	.30
a.		Booklet pane of 10	12.50	
2658	A1119	P multi	1.25	.30
a.		Booklet pane of 10	12.50	
2659	A1119	P multi	1.25	.30
a.		Booklet pane of 10	12.50	
		Nos. 2656-2659 (4)	5.00	1.20

On day of issue, Nos. 2655a-2655d, 2656-2659 each sold for 63c.

Robertson Davies (1913-95), Writer — A1120

Booklet Stamp
Serpentine Die Cut 13¼
2013, Aug. 28   Self-Adhesive

2660	A1120	63c multi	.90	.35
a.		Booklet pane of 10	9.00	

Pucks With Emblems of Canadian National Hockey League Teams — A1121

Pucks with emblem of: Nos. 2661a, 2662, Vancouver Canucks. Nos. 2661b, 2663, Edmonton Oilers. Nos. 2661c, 2664, Toronto Maple Leafs. Nos. 2661d, 2665, Montreal Canadiens. Nos. 2661e, 2666, Calgary Flames. Nos. 2661f, 2667, Winnipeg Jets. Nos. 2661g, 2668, Ottawa Senators.

2013, Sept. 3   Litho.   Perf. 13¼x13

2661	A1121	Sheet of 7	7.00	6.50
a.-g.		63c Any single	1.00	.80

Coil Stamps
Self-Adhesive
Serpentine Die Cut 8¼ Horiz.

2662	A1121	63c multi	.90	.30
2663	A1121	63c multi	.90	.30
2664	A1121	63c multi	.90	.30
2665	A1121	63c multi	.90	.30
2666	A1121	63c multi	.90	.30
2667	A1121	63c multi	.90	.30
2668	A1121	63c multi	.90	.30
		Nos. 2662-2668 (7)	6.30	2.10

Player and Fans Wearing Home and Away Uniforms of Canadian National Hockey League Teams A1122

Uniforms of: Nos. 2669a, 2670, Vancouver Canucks. Nos. 2669b, 2671, Montreal Canadiens. Nos. 2669c, 2672, Edmonton Oilers. Nos. 2669d, 2673, Ottawa Senators. Nos. 2669e, 2674, Calgary Flames. Nos. 2669f, 2675, Winnipeg Jets. Nos. 2669g, 2676, Toronto Maple Leafs.

Serpentine Die Cut 13¼x13½
2013, Sept. 3   Litho. & Embossed

2669	A1122	Sheet of 7 + 2 labels	7.00	6.50
a.-g.		63c Any single	1.00	.80

Litho.
Booklet Stamps
Self-Adhesive

2670	A1122	63c multi	.90	.30
a.		Booklet pane of 10	9.00	
2671	A1122	63c multi	.90	.30
a.		Booklet pane of 10	9.00	

2672 A1122 63c multi	.90	.30
a. Booklet pane of 10	9.00	
2673 A1122 63c multi	.90	
a. Booklet pane of 10	9.00	
2674 A1122 63c multi	.90	.30
a. Booklet pane of 10	9.00	
2675 A1122 63c multi	.90	.30
a. Booklet pane of 10	9.00	
2676 A1122 63c multi	.90	.30
a. Booklet pane of 10	9.00	
Nos. 2670-2676 (7)	6.30	2.10

A1123

A1124

A1125

A1126

A1127

Superman Comics, 75th Anniv. — A1128

2013, Sept. 10   **Perf. 12½**

2677 Sheet of 5	6.25	5.50
a. A1123 P multi	1.25	.90
b. A1124 P multi	1.25	.90
c. A1125 P multi	1.25	.90
d. A1126 P multi	1.25	.90
e. A1127 P multi	1.25	.90

Coil Stamp
Self-Adhesive
Die Cut Perf. 13½

2678 A1128 P multi	1.25	.40

Booklet Stamps
Serpentine Die Cut 13½x13¼

2679 A1123 P multi	1.25	.30
2680 A1124 P multi	1.25	.30
2681 A1125 P multi	1.25	.30
2682 A1126 P multi	1.25	.30

2683 A1127 P multi	1.25	.30
a. Booklet pane of 10, 2 each #2679-2683	12.50	
Nos. 2678-2683 (6)	7.50	1.90

Nos. 2677a-2677e, 2678-2683 each sold for 63c on day of issue.

Hastings and Prince Edward Regiment, 150th Anniv.
A1129

Serpentine Die Cut 13¼x13

2013, Oct. 18   **Litho.**
Booklet Stamp
Self-Adhesive

2684 A1129 P multi	1.25	.30
a. Booklet pane of 10	12.50	

No. 2684 sold for 63c on day of issue.

Birth of Prince George of Cambridge
A1130

2013, Oct. 22   Litho.   Perf. 12½

2685 Sheet of 2 #2685a	2.50	1.80
a. A1130 P Single stamp	1.25	.90

Booklet Stamp
Self-Adhesive
Serpentine Die Cut 13½

2686 A1130 P multi	1.25	.30
a. Booklet pane of 10	12.50	

On day of issue, Nos. 2685a and 2686 each sold for 63c.

Christmas
A1131   A1132

Designs: Nos. 2687a, 2689, Cross-stitched horn. $1.10, Cross-stitched reindeer. $1.85, Cross-stitched Christmas tree. No. 2688, St. Anne with the Christ Child, by Georges de La Tour.

2013, Oct. 22   Litho.   Perf. 13½x13¼

2687 Sheet of 3	5.25	5.25
a. A1131 63c multi	.90	.90
b. A1131 $1.10 multi	1.60	1.50
c. A1131 $1.85 multi	2.75	2.60

Booklet Stamps
Self-Adhesive
Serpentine Die Cut 13½

2688 A1132 63c multi	.90	.25
a. Booklet pane of 12	11.00	

Serpentine Die Cut 13¼x13

2689 A1131 63c multi	.90	.25
a. Booklet pane of 12	11.00	
2690 A1131 $1.10 multi	1.50	.60
a. Booklet pane of 6	9.00	
2691 A1131 $1.85 multi	2.75	.90
a. Booklet pane of 6	16.50	
Nos. 2688-2691 (4)	6.05	2.00

Juvenile Wildlife Type of 2011

Design: 63c, Four woodchuck pups.

Serpentine Die Cut 9¼ Horiz.

2013, Dec. 11   **Litho.**
Coil Stamps
Self-Adhesive

2692 A1038 63c multi	.90	.25
b. Without repeating "Canada" underprint on reverse	75.00	8.00

Serpentine Die Cut 8¼ Horiz.

2692A A1038 63c multi	1.10	1.10

Coils containing No. 2692A are adjacent in vertical strips. Coils containing No. 2692 are in horizontal strips with stamps separated.

Flag Types of 2013
Serpentine Die Cut 13¼

2013, Dec. 11   **Litho.**
Booklet Stamps
Self-Adhesive

2693 A1098 63c multi	.90	.25
2694 A1099 63c multi	.90	.25
2695 A1100 63c multi	.90	.25
2696 A1101 63c multi	.90	.25
2697 A1102 63c multi	.90	.25
a. Booklet pane of 10, 2 each #2693-2697	9.00	
Nos. 2693-2697 (5)	4.50	1.25

Queen Elizabeth II Type of 2013
Serpentine Die Cut 13¼

2013, Dec. 11   **Litho.**
Booklet Stamp
Self-Adhesive

2698 A1103 63c multi	.90	.25
a. Booklet pane of 10	9.00	

New Year 2014 (Year of the Horse) — A1133

Design: $1.85, Horse, diff.

Litho. & Embossed

2014, Jan. 13   **Perf. 12½**

2699 A1133 63c multi	.90	.30

Litho. & Embossed With Foil Application
Souvenir Sheet

2700 A1133 $1.85 multi	2.75	2.75
a. Souvenir sheet of 2, #2600, 2700	5.50	5.50

Litho. With Foil Application
Booklet Stamp
Self-Adhesive
Serpentine Die Cut 13½

2701 A1133 $1.85 multi	2.75	2.40
a. Booklet pane of 6	16.50	

African-Canadian Neighborhoods — A1134

Residents and buildings of: No. 2702, Africville, neighborhood of Halifax, Nova Scotia. No. 2703, Hogan's Alley, neighborhood of Vancouver, British Columbia.

Serpentine Die Cut 13¼

2014, Jan. 30   **Litho.**
Booklet Stamps
Self-Adhesive

2702 A1134 63c multi	.90	.35
a. Booklet pane of 10	9.00	
2703 A1134 63c multi	.90	.35
a. Booklet pane of 10	9.00	

Female Athletes — A1135

Designs: Nos. 2704a, 2705, Barbara Ann Scott (1928-2012), figure skater. Nos. 2704b, 2706, Sandra Schmirler (1963-2000), curler. Nos. 2704c, 2707, Sarah Burke (1982-2012), freestyle skier.

2014, Feb. 3   **Litho.**   **Perf. 13**
Souvenir Sheet

2704 Sheet of 3	2.75	2.75
a.-c. A1135 63c Any single	.90	.90

Booklet Stamps
Self-Adhesive
Serpentine Die Cut 13¼

2705 A1135 63c multi	.90	.30
a. Booklet pane of 10	9.00	
2706 A1135 63c multi	.90	.30
a. Booklet pane of 10	9.00	
2707 A1135 63c multi	.90	.30
a. Booklet pane of 10	9.00	
Nos. 2705-2707 (3)	2.70	.90

Beneficial Insects Type of 2007

Design: 22c, Monarch butterfly.

2014, Mar. 31   Litho.   Perf. 13¼x13

2708 A942 22c multi	.30	.25

Juvenile Wildlife Type of 2011

Designs: P, Beaver kits. $1, Burrowing owl chicks. $1.20, Mountain goat kid. $1.80, Puffin chicks. $2.50, Newborn wapiti.

2014, Mar. 31   Litho.   Perf. 13¼x13

2709 Souvenir sheet of 5	11.00	10.00
a. A1038 P multi	1.25	.90
b. A1038 $1 multi	1.50	1.50
c. A1038 $1.20 multi	1.75	1.60
d. A1038 $1.80 multi	2.60	2.50
e. A1038 $2.50 multi	3.75	3.75

Coil Stamps
Self-Adhesive
Die Cut Perf. 13½

2710 A1038 $1 multi	1.50	.25

Serpentine Die Cut 9¼ Horiz.

2710A A1038 P multi	1.40	1.40

Serpentine Die Cut 8¼ Horiz.

2711 A1038 P multi	1.25	.25
2712 A1038 $1.20 multi	1.75	.30
2713 A1038 $1.80 multi	2.60	.60
2714 A1038 $2.50 multi	3.75	.90
Nos. 2710-2714 (5)	10.85	2.30

Booklet Stamps
Serpentine Die Cut 9¼ Horiz.

2715 A1038 $1.20 multi	1.75	.30
a. Booklet pane of 6	10.50	
2716 A1038 $1.80 multi	2.60	.60
a. Booklet pane of 6	15.50	
2717 A1038 $2.50 multi	3.75	.90
a. Booklet pane of 6	22.50	
Nos. 2715-2717 (3)	8.10	1.80

On day of issue, Nos. 2709a, 2710A, 2711 each sold for 85c. On rolls of No. 2710A, stamps do not touch each other and pairs are horizontal. On rolls of No. 2711, stamps touch each other and pairs are vertical.

Gros Morne National Park, Newfoundland and Labrador
A1136

Joggins Fossil Cliffs, Nova Scotia
A1137

Canadian Rocky Mountain Parks, Alberta and British Columbia
A1138

Nahinni National Park, Northwest Territories
A1139

Miguasha National Park, Quebec — A1140

2014, Mar. 31   Litho.   Perf. 13¼x13

2718 Souvenir sheet of 5	6.25	5.75
a. A1136 P multi	1.25	.90
b. A1137 P multi	1.25	.90
c. A1138 P multi	1.25	.90
d. A1139 P multi	1.25	.90
e. A1140 P multi	1.25	.90

Booklet Stamps
Self-Adhesive
Serpentine Die Cut 13¼

2719	A1136	P multi	1.25	.25
2720	A1139	P multi	1.25	.25
2721	A1137	P multi	1.25	.25
2722	A1140	P multi	1.25	.25
2723	A1138	P multi	1.25	.25
a.	Booklet pane of 10, 2 each #2719-2723		12.50	
b.	Booklet pane of 30, 6 each #2719-2723		37.50	
Nos. 2719-2723 (5)			6.25	1.25

UNESCO World Heritage Sites. On day of issue, Nos. 2718a-2718f, 2719-2723 each sold for 85c.

Shiva Natajara Sculpture, Mummified Cat and Bison — A1141

Hadrasaur Skeleton and Luohan Chinese Sculpture A1142

2014, Apr. 14   Litho.   *Perf. 12½*

2724		Souvenir sheet of 2	2.50	2.50
a.	A1141	P multi	1.25	.90
b.	A1142	P multi	1.25	.90

Booklet Stamps
Self-Adhesive
Serpentine Die Cut 13½x13¼

2725	A1141	P multi	1.25	.30
2726	A1142	P multi	1.25	.30
a.	Booklet pane of 10, 5 each #2725-2726		12.50	

Royal Ontario Museum, cent. On day of issue, Nos. 2724a-2724b, 2725-2726 each sold for 85c.

Roses

A1143   A1144

Rose varieties: Nos. 2727a, 2729, 2730, Konrad Henkel (red) rose. Nos. 2727b, 2728, 2731, Maid of Honor (white) rose.

2014, Apr. 23   Litho.   *Perf. 13*
Souvenir Sheet

2727		Sheet of 2	2.50	2.50
a.-b.	A1143	P Either single	1.25	.90

Coil Stamps
Self-Adhesive
Serpentine Die Cut 8¼ Horiz.

2728	A1144	P multi	1.25	.30
2729	A1144	P multi	1.25	.30
a.	Vert. pair, #2728-2729		2.50	

Booklet Stamps
Serpentine Die Cut 13¼

2730	A1143	P multi	1.25	.30
2731	A1143	P multi	1.25	.30
a.	Booklet pane of 10, 5 each #2730-2731		12.50	
Nos. 2728-2731 (4)			5.00	1.20

On day of issue, Nos. 2727a-2727b, 2728-2731 each sold for 85c.

Komagata Maru Incident, Cent. — A1145

Serpentine Die Cut 13x12¾
2014, May 1   Litho.
Booklet Stamp
Self-Adhesive

2732	A1145	$2.50 multi	3.75	1.50
a.	Booklet pane of 6		22.50	

National Film Board, 75th Anniv. — A1146

Scenes from Canadian films: Nos. 2733a, 2734, *Flamenco at 5:15,* 1983. Nos. 2733b, 2735, *The Railrodder,* 1965. Nos. 2733c, 2736, *Mon Oncle Antoine,* 1971. Nos. 2733d, 2737, *Log Driver's Waltz,* 1979. Nos. 2733e, 2738, *Neighbours,* 1952.

2014, May 2   Litho.   *Perf. 13¼x12½*

2733	A1146	Sheet of 5 + label	6.25	6.00
a.-e.		P Any single	1.25	.90

Booklet Stamps
Self-Adhesive
Serpentine Die Cut 13¼

2734	A1146	P multi	1.25	.30
2735	A1146	P multi	1.25	.30
2736	A1146	P multi	1.25	.30
2737	A1146	P multi	1.25	.30
2738	A1146	P multi	1.25	.30
a.	Booklet pane of 10, 2 each #2734-2738		12.50	
Nos. 2734-2738 (5)			6.25	1.50

On day of issue, Nos. 2733a-2733e and 2734-2738 each sold for 85c.

UNESCO World Heritage Sites — A1147

Designs: Nos. 2739a, 2741, Head-Smashed-In Buffalo Jump, Alberta. Nos. 2739b, 2740, Old Town Lunenburg, Nova Scotia. Nos. 2739c, 2742, Landscape of Grand Pré, Nova Scotia. Nos. 2739d, 2743, SGang Gwaay, British Columbia. Nos. 2739e, 2744, Rideau Canal, Ontario.

2014, May 16   Litho.   *Perf. 12½*
Miniature Sheet

2739	A1147	Sheet of 5	12.75	11.00
a.-c.		$1.20 Any single	1.75	1.50
d.-e.		$2.50 Either single	3.75	2.20

Booklet Stamps
Self-Adhesive
Serpentine Die Cut 13¼x13½

2740	A1147	$1.20 multi	1.75	1.10
2741	A1147	$1.20 multi	1.75	1.10
2742	A1147	$1.20 multi	1.75	1.10
a.	Booklet pane of 6, 2 each #2740-2742		10.50	

2743	A1147	$2.50 multi	3.75	2.20
2744	A1147	$2.50 multi	3.75	2.20
a.	Booklet pane of 6, 3 each #2743-2744		22.50	
Nos. 2740-2744 (5)			12.75	7.70

Sinking of the RMS Empress of Ireland, Cent. — A1148

Designs: P, Empress of Ireland facing right. $2.50, Empress of Ireland facing left, horiz.

2014, May 29   Litho.   *Perf. 12½*

2745	A1148	P multi	1.25	.45

Souvenir Sheet
Perf. 12¾

2746	A1148	$2.50 multi	3.75	3.25

Booklet Stamp
Self-Adhesive
Serpentine Die Cut 13½

2747	A1148	P multi	1.25	.30
a.	Booklet pane of 10		12.50	

On day of issue, Nos. 2745 and 2747 each sold for 85c. No. 2745 was printed in sheets of 16 + 4 labels. No. 2746 contains one 80x32mm stamp.

Haunted Canada A1149

Designs: Nos. 2748a, 2749, Ghost bride, Banff Springs, Alberta. Nos. 2748b, 2751, Ghost train, St. Louis, Saskatchewan. Nos. 2748c, 2753, Apparitions of Fort George, Ontario. Nos. 2748d, 2752, Count of Frontenac Apparition, Château Frontenac Hotel, Quebec. Nos. 2748e, 2750, Phantom ship off Nova Scotia and Prince Edward Island.

2014, June 13   Litho.   *Perf. 12½*

2748		Sheet of 5	6.25	5.75
a.-e.	A1149	P Any single	1.25	.90

Booklet Stamps
Self-Adhesive
Serpentine Die Cut 13¼

2749	A1149	P multi	1.25	.30
2750	A1149	P multi	1.25	.30
2751	A1149	P multi	1.25	.30
2752	A1149	P multi	1.25	.30
2753	A1149	P multi	1.25	.30
a.	Booklet pane of 10, 2 each #2749-2753		12.50	
Nos. 2749-2753 (5)			6.25	1.50

On day of issue, Nos. 2748a-2748e, 2749-2753 each sold for 85c.

Canadian Football League Team Emblems Type of 2012 and

Russ Jackson in Ottawa Rough Riders Uniform, TD Place Stadium, Ottawa Redblacks Emblem A1150

Design: No. 2754, Ottawa Redblacks emblem.

Serpentine Die Cut 8¼ Horiz.
2014, June 19   Litho.
Coil Stamp
Self-Adhesive

2754	A1080	P multi	1.25	.30

Booklet Stamp

2755	A1150	P multi	1.25	.30
a.	Booklet pane of 10		12.50	

On day of issue, Nos. 2754 and 2755 each sold for 85c.

Photography Type of 2013

Designs: Nos. 2756a, 2762, Unidentified Chinese Man, by C. D. Hoy, c. 1912. Nos. 2756b, 2759, St. Joseph's Convent School, by Michel Lambeth, 1960. Nos. 2756c, 2763, Sitting Bull and Buffalo Bill, Montreal, by William Notman, 1885. Nos. 2757a, 2761, Untitled, by Lynne Cohen, 1970, horiz. Nos. 2757b, 2760, La Ville de Québec en Hiver (Quebec City in Winter), by Louis-Prudent Vallée, 1894, horiz. Nos. 2757c, 2758, Bogner's Grocery, by Fred Herzog, 1960, horiz. Nos. 2757d, 2764, Railcuts: #1, by Edward Burtynsky, 1985, horiz.

2014, July 7   Litho.   *Perf. 13¼*

2756		Sheet of 3	4.25	3.50
a.-b.		A1109 P Either single	1.25	.90
c.		A1109 $1.20 multi	1.75	1.50
2757		Sheet of 4	7.50	7.50
a.-c.		A1109 P Any single	1.25	.90
d.		A1109 $2.50 multi	3.75	3.75

Booklet Stamps
Self-Adhesive
Serpentine Die Cut 13¼

2758	A1109	P multi	1.25	.30
2759	A1109	P multi	1.25	.30
2760	A1109	P multi	1.25	.30
2761	A1109	P multi	1.25	.30
2762	A1109	P multi	1.25	.30
a.	Booklet pane of 10, 2 each #2758-2762		12.50	
2763	A1109	$1.20 multi	1.75	.65
a.	Booklet pane of 6		10.50	
2764	A1109	$2.50 multi	3.75	1.10
a.	Booklet pane of 6		22.50	
Nos. 2758-2764 (7)			11.75	3.25

On day of issue, Nos. 2756a-2756b, 2757a-2757c, 2758-2762 each sold for 85c.

Hank Snow (1914-99), Country Music Recording Artist A1151

Renée Martel, Country Music Recording Artist A1152

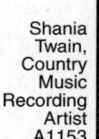

Shania Twain, Country Music Recording Artist A1153

Tommy Hunter, Country Music Recording Artist A1154

K. D. Lang, Country Music Recording Artist A1155

2014, July 31   Litho.   *Perf. 12½*

2765		Sheet of 5	6.25	5.75
a.	A1151	P multi	1.25	.90
b.	A1152	P multi	1.25	.90
c.	A1153	P multi	1.25	.90
d.	A1154	P multi	1.25	.90
e.	A1155	P multi	1.25	.90

Booklet Stamps
Self-Adhesive
Serpentine Die Cut 13¼

2766	A1151	P multi	1.25	.30
a.	Booklet pane of 10		12.50	
2767	A1152	P multi	1.25	.30
a.	Booklet pane of 10		12.50	
2768	A1153	P multi	1.25	.30
a.	Booklet pane of 10		12.50	

2769	A1154 P multi	1.25	.30
a.	Booklet pane of 10	12.50	
2770	A1155 P multi	1.25	.30
a.	Booklet pane of 10	12.50	
	Nos. 2766-2770 (5)	6.25	1.50

On day of issue, Nos. 2765a-2765e, 2766-2770 each sold for 85c.

Canadian Museum for Human Rights, Winnipeg — A1156

Serpentine Die Cut 13¼
2014, Aug. 20   Litho.
Booklet Stamp
Self-Adhesive

2771	A1156 P multi	1.25	.30
a.	Booklet pane of 10	12.50	

No. 2771 sold for 85c on day of issue.

Comedians — A1157

Designs: Nos. 2772a, 2773, Mike Myers. Nos. 2772b, 2774, Martin Short. Nos. 2772c, 2775, Catherine O'Hara. Nos. 2772d, 2776, Olivier Guimond (1914-71). Nos. 2772e, 2777, Jim Carrey.

2014, Aug. 29   Litho.   **Perf. 12½x13**

2772	Sheet of 5 + label	6.25	5.75
a.-e.	A1157 P Any single	1.25	.90

Booklet Stamps
Self-Adhesive
Serpentine Die Cut 13¼

2773	A1157 P multi	1.25	.30
a.	Booklet pane of 10, #2774-2777, 6#2773	12.50	
2774	A1157 P multi	1.25	.30
a.	Booklet pane of 10, #2773, 2775-2777, 6#2774	12.50	
2775	A1157 P multi	1.25	.30
a.	Booklet pane of 10, #2773-2774, 2776-2777, 6#2775	12.50	
2776	A1157 P multi	1.25	.30
a.	Booklet pane of 10, #2773-2775, 2777, 6#2776	12.50	
2777	A1157 P multi	1.25	.30
a.	Booklet pane of 10, #2773-2776, 6#2777	12.50	
	Nos. 2773-2777 (5)	6.25	1.50

On day of issue, Nos. 2772a-2772e, 2773-2777 each sold for 85c.

Zamboni With Canadian National Hockey League Team Emblems — A1158

Zamboni with emblem of: Nos. 2778a, 2779, Winnipeg Jets. Nos. 2778b, 2780, Ottawa Senators. Nos. 2778c, 2781, Toronto Maple Leafs. Nos. 2778d, 2782, Montreal Canadiens. Nos. 2778e, 2783, Vancouver Canucks. Nos. 2778f, 2784, Calgary Flames. Nos. 2778g, 2785, Edmonton Oilers.

2014, Oct. 3   Litho.   **Perf. 13¼x13**
Miniature Sheet

2778	Sheet of 7	8.75	8.25
a.-g.	A1158 P Any single	1.25	.90

Coil Stamps
Self-Adhesive
Serpentine Die Cut 8¼ Horiz.

2779	A1158 P multi	1.25	.30
2780	A1158 P multi	1.25	.30
2781	A1158 P multi	1.25	.30
2782	A1158 P multi	1.25	.30
2783	A1158 P multi	1.25	.30
2784	A1158 P multi	1.25	.30
2785	A1158 P multi	1.25	.30
	Nos. 2779-2785 (7)	8.75	2.10

On day of issue, Nos. 2778a-2778g, 2779-2785 each sold for 85c.

Defensemen in National Hockey League Hall of Fame — A1159

Designs: Nos. 2786a, 2787a, 2788, Tim Horton (1930-74). Nos. 2786b, 2787b, 2789, Doug Harvey. Nos. 2786c, 2787c, 2790, Bobby Orr. Nos. 2786d, 2787d, 2791, Harry Howell. Nos. 2786e, 2787e, 2792, Pierre Pilote. Nos. 2786f, 2787f, 2793, Red Kelly.

Litho., Sheet Margin Litho. & Embossed With Foil Application
2014, Oct. 3   **Perf. 12½x13**
Miniature Sheet

2786	Sheet of 6	7.50	6.50
a.-f.	A1159 P Any single	1.25	.90

Litho.
Booklet Stamps
Self-Adhesive
Serpentine Die Cut 13¼x13½

2787	Booklet pane of 6	7.50	
a.-f.	A1159 P Any single	1.25	.30

Souvenir Sheets
Serpentine Die Cut 13½x13¼

2788	A1159 $2.50 multi	3.75	1.80
2789	A1159 $2.50 multi	3.75	1.80
2790	A1159 $2.50 multi	3.75	1.80
2791	A1159 $2.50 multi	3.75	1.80
2792	A1159 $2.50 multi	3.75	1.80
2793	A1159 $2.50 multi	3.75	1.80
	Nos. 2788-2793 (6)	22.50	10.80

Nos. 2786a-2786f, 2787a-2787f each sold for 85c on day of issue. Nos. 2788-2793 each contain one 52x78mm stamp. Nos. 2788-2793 were sold together in a sealed opaque plastic package. One of every 50 packages contained a souvenir sheet that was autographed by one of the 5 living players depicted.

"Wait for Me Daddy," Photograph by Claude P. Dettloff — A1160

2014, Oct. 4   Litho.   **Perf. 13½x13¼**

2794	A1160 P multi	1.25	.45

Booklet Stamp
Self-Adhesive
Serpentine Die Cut 13¼x13½

2795	A1160 P multi	1.25	.30
a.	Booklet pane of 10	12.50	

Dedication of statue depicting photograph in New Westminster, British Columbia. Nos. 2794 and 2795 each sold for 85c on day of issue. No. 2794 was printed in sheets of 5.

Santa Claus A1161

The Virgin and Child with St. John the Baptist, by Abraham Janssens van Nuyssen A1162

Santa Claus: P, Writing letter. $1.20, Carrying sack. $2.50, With dove.

2014, Oct. 23   Litho.   **Perf. 13½x13¼**
Souvenir Sheet

2796	Sheet of 3	6.75	5.25
a.	A1161 P multi	1.25	.90
b.	A1161 $1.20 multi	1.75	1.50
c.	A1161 $2.50 multi	3.75	2.60

Booklet Stamps
Self-Adhesive
Serpentine Die Cut 13½

2797	A1162 P multi	1.25	.25
a.	Booklet pane of 12	15.00	

Serpentine Die Cut 13¼x13

2798	A1161 P multi	1.25	.25
a.	Booklet pane of 12	15.00	
2799	A1161 $1.20 multi	1.75	.60
a.	Booklet pane of 6	10.50	
2800	A1161 $2.50 multi	3.75	.90
a.	Booklet pane of 6	27.00	
	Nos. 2797-2800 (4)	8.00	2.00

Christmas. Nos. 2796a, 2797 and 2798 each sold for 85c on day of issue.

New Year 2015 (Year of the Ram) — A1163

Design: $2.50, Ram facing left.

Litho. & Embossed With Foil Application
2015, Jan. 8   **Perf. 12½**

2801	A1163 P multi	1.25	.35

Souvenir Sheet

2802	A1163 $2.50 multi	3.75	3.50
a.	Souvenir sheet of 2, #2700, 2802	6.50	5.75
b.	Perf. 13¼ (#2885a)	3.75	3.75

Litho. With Foil Application
Booklet Stamp
Self-Adhesive
Serpentine Die Cut 13½

2803	A1163 $2.50 multi	3.75	1.65
a.	Booklet pane of 6	22.50	

No. 2801 sold for 85c on day of issue.
Issued: No. 2802b, 2/1/16.

Sir John A. Macdonald (1815-91), First Prime Minister of Canada A1164

Serpentine Die Cut 13¼
2015, Jan. 11   Litho.
Self-Adhesive
Booklet Stamp

2804	A1164 P multi	1.25	.30
a.	Booklet pane of 10	12.50	

No. 2804 sold for 85c on day of issue.

Nelson Mandela (1918-2013), President of South Africa — A1165

2015, Jan. 30   Litho.   **Perf. 12½x13**
Souvenir Sheet

2805	A1165 $2.50 multi	3.75	3.25

Booklet Stamp
Self-Adhesive
Size: 33x33mm
Serpentine Die Cut 13¼

2806	A1165 P multi	1.25	.30
a.	Booklet pane of 10	12.50	

No. 2806 sold for 85c on day of issue.

A1166

Canadian Flag, 50th Anniv. — A1167

Serpentine Die Cut 13¼x13½
2015, Feb. 15   Litho.
Booklet Stamp
Self-Adhesive

2807	A1166 P multi	1.25	.30
a.	Booklet pane of 10	12.50	

Souvenir Sheet
On Rayon Fabric
Serpentine Die Cut 9½

2808	A1167 $5 multi	7.50	3.50

No. 2807 sold for 85c on day of issue.

Pansies
A1168   A1169

Designs: Nos. 2809a, 2810, 2812, Delta Premium Pure Light Blue pansy (blue and yellow flower). No. 2809b, 2811, 2813, Midnight Glow pansy (purple and yellow flower).

2015, Mar. 2   Litho.   **Perf. 13x13¼**
Souvenir Sheet

2809	Sheet of 2	2.50	2.50
a.-b.	A1168 P Either single	1.25	.90

Coil Stamps
Self-Adhesive
Serpentine Die Cut 8¼ Horiz.

2810	A1169 P multi	1.25	.30
2811	A1169 P multi	1.25	.30
a.	Vert. pair, #2810-2811	2.50	

Booklet Stamps
Serpentine Die Cut 13½

2812	A1168 P multi	1.25	.30
2813	A1168 P multi	1.25	.30
a.	Booklet pane of 10, 5 each #2812-2813	12.50	

On day of issue Nos. 2809a-2809b, 2810-2813 each sold for 85c.

Photography Type of 2013

Designs: Nos. 2814a, 2820, Shoeshine Stand, by Nina Raginsky, 1974. Nos. 2814b, 2817, Southan Sisters, Montreal, by Harold Mortimer-Lamb, c. 1915-19, horiz. Nos. 2814c, 2822, La Voie Lactée, by Geneviève Cadieux, 1992, horiz. Nos. 2815a, 2816, Angels, Saint-Jean-Baptiste Day, by Sam Tata, 1962, horiz. Nos. 2815b, 2819, Isaac's First Swim, Lambton County, Ontario, Canada, by Larry Towell, 1996, horiz. Nos. 2815c, 2818, Friends and Family and Trips. In Front of Simpsons, by Conrad Poirer, 1936, horiz. Nos. 2815d, 2821, Alex Colville on the Tantramar Marshes, by Geoffrey James, c. 1970, horiz.

2015, Apr. 8   Litho.   **Perf. 12¾**

2814	A1109 Sheet of 3	6.25	6.00
a.-b.	P Either single	1.25	.90
c.	$2.50 multi	3.75	3.75
2815	A1109 Sheet of 4	5.50	5.00
a.-c.	P Any single	1.25	.90
d.	$1.20 multi	1.75	1.50

Booklet Stamps
Self-Adhesive
Serpentine Die Cut 13¼

2816	A1109 P multi	1.25	.30
2817	A1109 P multi	1.25	.30
2818	A1109 P multi	1.25	.30
2819	A1109 P multi	1.25	.30

2820	A1109	P multi	1.25 .30
a.		Booklet pane of 10, 2 each	
		#2816-2820	12.50
2821	A1109	$1.20 multi	1.75 .65
a.		Booklet pane of 6	10.50
2822	A1109	$2.50 multi	3.75 1.50
a.		Booklet pane of 6	22.50
		Nos. 2816-2822 (7)	11.75 3.65

On day of issue, Nos. 2814a-2814b, 2815a-2815c, 2816-2820 each sold for 85c.

Dinosaurs
A1170

Designs: Nos. 2823a, 2827, Euplocephalus tutus (33x28mm). Nos. 2823b, 2826, Chasmosaurus belli (28x28mm). Nos. 2823c, 2824, Tyrannosaurus rex. Nos. 2823d, 2828, Ornithomimus edmontonicus. Nos. 2823e, 2825, Tylosaurus pembinensis.

Litho. & Embossed With Foil Application
Serpentine Die Cut 13¼
2015, Apr. 3   **Self-Adhesive**

2823		Sheet of 5	6.25 5.75
a.-e.	A1170	P Any single	1.25 .90

Booklet Stamps
Litho. With Foil Application

2824	A1170	P multi	1.25 .30
2825	A1170	P multi	1.25 .30
2826	A1170	P multi	1.25 .30
2827	A1170	P multi	1.25 .30
2828	A1170	P multi	1.25 .30
a.		Booklet pane of 10, 2 each	
		#2824-2828	12.50

On day of issue, Nos. 2823a-2823e, 2824-2828 each sold for 85c.

Love Your Pet
A1171

Designs: Nos. 2829a, 2830, Cat in head cone sniffing flowers. Nos. 2829b, 2831, Dog chasing snowball. Nos. 2829c, 2832, Veterinarian examining cat. Nos. 2829d, 2834, Dog drinking water from bowl. Nos. 2829e, 2833, Cat on leash wearing identification tags.

2015, May 2   **Litho.**   *Perf. 13*

2829		Sheet of 5	6.25 5.75
a.-e.	A1171	P Any single	1.25 .90

Booklet Stamps
Self-Adhesive
Serpentine Die Cut 13¼

2830	A1171	P multi	1.25 .30
2831	A1171	P multi	1.25 .30
2832	A1171	P multi	1.25 .30
2833	A1171	P multi	1.25 .30
2834	A1171	P multi	1.25 .30
a.		Booklet pane of 10, 2 each	
		#2830-2834	12.50
		Nos. 2830-2834 (5)	6.25 1.50

On day of issue, Nos. 2829a-2829e, 2830-2834 each sold for 85c.

In Flanders Fields, Poem by John McCrae, Cent. A1172

2015, May 3   **Litho.**   *Perf. 12½*

2835	A1172	P multi	1.25 .45

Booklet Stamp
Self-Adhesive
Serpentine Die Cut 13¼x13½

2836	A1172	P multi	1.25 .30
a.		Booklet pane of 10	12.50

On day of issue, Nos. 2835-2836 each sold for 85c. No. 2835 was printed in sheets of 5.

2015 Women's World Cup Soccer Championships, Canada — A1173

Serpentine Die Cut 13¼x13½
2015, May 6   **Booklet Stamp**   **Litho.**
Self-Adhesive

2837	A1173	P multi	1.25 .30
a.		Booklet pane of 10	12.50

No. 2837 sold for 85c on day of issue.

Weather Phenomena — A1174

Designs: Nos. 2838a, 2839, Lightning. Nos. 2838b, 2842, Double rainbow. Nos. 2838c, 2843, Sun dog over Iqaluit, Nunavut. Nos. 2838d, 2841, Fog near Cape Spear Lighthouse. Nos. 2838e, 2840, Hoar frost on tree.

Perf. 12½x13¼
2015, June 18   **Litho.**

2838	A1174	Sheet of 5 + label	6.25 5.75
a.-e.		P any single	1.25 .90

Booklet Stamps
Self-Adhesive
Serpentine Die Cut 13¼

2839	A1174	P multi	1.25 .30
2840	A1174	P multi	1.25 .30
2841	A1174	P multi	1.25 .30
2842	A1174	P multi	1.25 .30
2843	A1174	P multi	1.25 .30
a.		Booklet pane of 10, 2 each	
		#2839-2843	12.50

Nos. 2838a-2838e, 2839-2843 each sold for 85c on day of issue.

Hoodoos, Alberta A1175

Wood Buffalo National Park, Alberta and Northwest Territories A1176

Red Bay Basque Whaling Station, Newfoundland and Labrador — A1177

Waterton Glacier International Peace Park, Alberta and Montana — A1178

Kluane National Park, Yukon, Wrangell-St. Elias and Glacier Bay National Parks, Alaska, Tatshenshini-Alsek Park, British Columbia — A1179

2015, July 3   **Litho.**   *Perf. 12½*

2844		Sheet of 5	42.50 42.50
a.	A1175	$1.20 multi	30.00 15.00
b.	A1176	$1.20 multi	1.80 .90
c.	A1177	$1.20 multi	1.80 .90
d.	A1178	$2.50 multi	3.75 1.90
e.	A1179	$2.50 multi	3.75 1.90

Booklet Stamps
Self-Adhesive
Serpentine Die Cut 13¼

2845	A1175	$1.20 multi	15.00 7.50
2846	A1177	$1.20 multi	1.80 .90
2847	A1176	$1.20 multi	1.80 .90
a.		Booklet pane of 6, 2 each	
		#2845-2847	37.50
2848	A1178	$2.50 multi	3.75 1.90
2849	A1179	$2.50 multi	3.75 1.90
a.		Booklet pane of 6, 3 each	
		#2848-2849	22.50

UNESCO World Heritage Sites. Nos. 2844 and 2847a were withdrawn from sale on July 6 after it was discovered that illustration A1175 shows hoodoos not located in Dinosaur Provincial Park in Alberta. See Nos. 2857-2858.

Alice Munro, 2013 Nobel Literature Laureate — A1180

Serpentine Die Cut 13¾
2015, July 10   **Litho.**
Booklet Stamp
Self-Adhesive

2850	A1180	P multi	1.25 .30
a.		Booklet pane of 10	12.50

No. 2850 sold for 85c on day of issue.

HMS Erebus Trapped in Ice — A1181

Map of Northern Canadian Islands — A1182

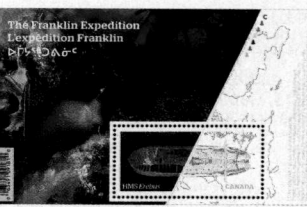

Wreckage and Diagram of HMS Erebus — A1183

Litho & Embossed, Litho (A1183)
2015, Aug. 6   *Perf. 12½*

2851	A1181	P multi	1.25 .70
2852	A1182	P multi	1.25 .70
a.		Horiz. pair, #2851-2852	2.50 1.40

Souvenir Sheet
Perf. 13¼

2853	A1183	$2.50 multi	3.75 1.90

Booklet Stamps
Serpentine Die Cut 13½x13¼

2854	A1181	P multi	1.25 .70
2855	A1182	P multi	1.25 .70
a.		Booklet pane of 10, 5 each	
		#2854-2855	12.50

Serpentine Die Cut 13¼x13¾

2856	A1183	$2.50 multi	3.75 1.90
a.		Booklet pane of 6	22.50
		Nos. 2854-2856 (3)	6.25 3.30

Discovery of wreckage of HMS Erebus, 1st anniv. Nos. 2851-2852, 2854-2855 each sold for 85c on day of issue.

Dinosaur Provincial Park, Alberta A1184

2015, Aug. 21   **Litho.**   *Perf. 12½*

2857		Sheet of 5, #2844b-2844e, 2857a	14.00 14.00
a.	A1184	$1.20 multi	1.90 .95

Booklet Stamp
Self-Adhesive

2858	A1184	$1.20 multi	1.80 .95
a.		Booklet pane of 6, 2 each	
		#2846, 2847, 2858	11.00

UNESCO World Heritage Sites. Nos. 2857a and 2858 show correct images of landscapes in Dinosaur Provincial Park.

Queen Elizabeth II, Longest-Reigning British Monarch — A1185

Serpentine Die Cut 13¼
2015, Sept. 9   **Litho.**
Booklet Stamp
Self-Adhesive

2859	A1185	P multi	1.25 .70
a.		Booklet pane of 10	12.50

No. 2859 sold for 85c on day of issue.

Haunted Canada — A1186

Designs: Nos. 2860a, 2861, Brakeman ghost, Vancouver, British Columbia. Nos. 2860b, 2864, Red River Trail Oxcart, Winnipeg, Manitoba. Nos. 2860c, 2863, Gray Lady of the Citadel, Halifax, Nova Scotia. Nos.

2860d, 2862, Ghost of Marie-Josephte Corriveau, Lévis, Quebec. Nos. 2860e, 2865, Ghost of Caribou Hotel, Carcross, Yukon.

Litho. With Holographic Foil

2015, Sept. 14		Perf. 12½x13	
2860	A1186	Sheet of 5	6.25	6.25
a.-e.		P Any single	1.25	.70

Booklet Stamps
Self-Adhesive

Serpentine Die Cut 13¼

2861	A1186	P multi	1.25	.70
2862	A1186	P multi	1.25	.70
2863	A1186	P multi	1.25	.70
2864	A1186	P multi	1.25	.70
2865	A1186	P multi	1.25	.70
a.		Booklet pane of 10, 2 each #2861-2865	12.50	
		Nos. 2861-2865 (5)	6.25	3.50

On day of issue, Nos. 2860a-2860e, 2861-2865 each sold for 85c.

A1187

Hockey Goaltenders — A1188

Designs: Nos. 2866a, 2867, 2873, Ken Dryden. Nos. 2866b, 2868, 2874, Tony Esposito. Nos. 2866c, 2869, 2875, Johnny Bower. Nos. 2866d, 2870, 2876, Gump Worsley (1929-2007). Nos. 2866e, 2871, 2877, Bernie Parent. Nos. 2866f, 2872, 2878, Martin Brodeur.

Litho., Sheet Margin Litho. & Embossed With Foil Application

2015, Oct. 2		Perf. 12½	
2866		Sheet of 6 + 3 labels	8.50	8.50
a.-f.	A1187	P Any single	1.40	.70

Booklet Stamps
Self-Adhesive
Litho.

Serpentine Die Cut 13¼x13½

2867	A1187	P multi	1.25	.70
2868	A1187	P multi	1.25	.70
2869	A1187	P multi	1.25	.70
2870	A1187	P multi	1.25	.70
2871	A1187	P multi	1.25	.70
2872	A1187	P multi	1.25	.70
a.		Booklet pane of 6, #2867-2872	7.50	
		Nos. 2867-2872 (6)	7.50	4.20

Souvenir Sheets

Serpentine Die Cut 13½x13¼

2873	A1188	$1.80 multi	2.75	1.40
2874	A1188	$1.80 multi	2.75	1.40
2875	A1188	$1.80 multi	2.75	1.40
2876	A1188	$1.80 multi	2.75	1.40
2877	A1188	$1.80 multi	2.75	1.40
2878	A1188	$1.80 multi	2.75	1.40
		Nos. 2873-2878 (6)	16.50	8.40

Nos. 2866a-2866f, 2867-2872 each sold for 85c on day of issue. Nos. 2873-2878 each contain one 52x78mm stamp. Nos. 2873-2878 were sold together in a sealed opaque plastic package. One of every 40 packages contained a souvenir sheet signed by Esposito, Bower, Parent or Brodeur.

A1189

Christmas — A1190

Designs: Nos. 2879a, 2881, Moose. Nos. 2879b, 2882, Beaver. Nos. 2879c, 2883, Polar bear. No. 2880, Adoration of the Magi, by Adriaen Isenbrandt.

2015, Nov. 2		Litho.	Perf. 13¾x13¼	
2879		Sheet of 3	6.50	6.50
a.	A1189	P multi	1.25	.70
b.	A1189	$1.20 multi	1.50	.95
c.	A1189	$2.50 multi	3.75	2.00

Booklet Stamps
Self-Adhesive

Serpentine Die Cut 13¼x13½

2880	A1190	P multi	1.25	.70
a.		Booklet pane of 12	15.00	

Serpentine Die Cut 13¼x13

2881	A1189	P multi	1.25	.70
a.		Booklet pane of 12	15.00	
2882	A1189	$1.20 multi	1.80	.95
a.		Booklet pane of 6	11.00	
2883	A1189	$2.50 multi	3.75	2.00
a.		Booklet pane of 6	22.50	
		Nos. 2880-2883 (4)	8.05	4.35

Nos. 2879a, 2880 and 2881 each sold for 85c on day of issue.

New Year 2016 (Year of the Monkey) A1191

Design: $2.50, Monkey's head.

Litho. & Embossed With Foil Application

2016			Perf. 13¼	
2884	A1191	P multi	1.25	.60

Souvenir Sheet

2885	A1191	$2.50 multi	3.75	3.75
a.		Souvenir sheet of 2, #2802b, 2885	7.50	7.50
b.		Perf. 12½ (#2960a)	3.75	1.90

Litho.

Booklet Stamps
Self-Adhesive

Serpentine Die Cut 13½

2886	A1191	P multi	1.25	.60
a.		Booklet pane of 10	12.50	
2887	A1191	$2.50 multi	3.75	1.90
a.		Booklet pane of 6	22.50	

Issued: Nos. 2884, 2886, 1/11; Nos. 2885, 2887, 2/1. No. 2885a, 1/9/17. No. 2885b, 1/9/17. Nos. 2884 and 2886 each sold for 85c on day of issue.

Queen Elizabeth II — A1192

Serpentine Die Cut 13½x13¾

2016, Jan. 11			Litho.

Booklet Stamp
Self-Adhesive

2888	A1192	P multi	1.25	.60
a.		Booklet pane of 10	12.50	

No. 2888 sold for 85c on day of issue.

Landscape of Grand Pré, Nova Scotia A1193

Rideau Canal, Ontario A1194

SGang Gwaay, British Columbia — A1195

Head-Smashed-In Buffalo Jump, Alberta — A1196

Old Town Lunenburg, Nova Scotia — A1197

2016, Jan. 11		Litho.	Perf. 13¼x13	

Souvenir Sheet

2889		Sheet of 5	6.25	6.25
a.	A1193	P multi	1.25	.60
b.	A1194	P multi	1.25	.60
c.	A1195	P multi	1.25	.60
d.	A1196	P multi	1.25	.60
e.	A1197	P multi	1.25	.60

Booklet Stamps
Self-Adhesive

Serpentine Die Cut 13¾x13½

2890	A1193	P multi	1.25	.60
2891	A1195	P multi	1.25	.60
2892	A1197	P multi	1.25	.60
2893	A1194	P multi	1.25	.60
2894	A1196	P multi	1.25	.60
a.		Booklet pane of 10, 2 each #2890-2894	12.50	
b.		Booklet pane of 30, 6 each #2890-2894	37.50	

UNESCO World Heritage Sites. On day of issue, Nos. 2889a-2889e, 2890-2894 each sold for 85c.

Organization of No. 2 Construction Battalion (First Black Battalion), Cent. — A1198

Serpentine Die Cut 13½

2016, Feb. 1			Litho.

Booklet Stamp
Self-Adhesive

2895	A1198	P multi	1.25	.60
a.		Booklet pane of 10	12.50	

No. 2895 sold for 85c on day of issue.

Hydrangeas
A1199   A1200

Designs: Nos. 2896a, 2897, 2899, Hydrangea macrophylla. Nos. 2896b, 2898, 2900, Hydrangea arborescens.

2016, Mar. 1		Litho.	Perf. 13	

Souvenir Sheet

2896		Sheet of 2	2.50	2.50
a.-b.	A1199	P Either single	1.25	.65

Coil Stamps
Self-Adhesive

Serpentine Die Cut 8¼ Vert.

2897	A1200	P multi	1.25	.65
2898	A1200	P multi	1.25	.65
a.		Horiz. pair, #2897-2898	2.50	

Booklet Stamps

Serpentine Die Cut 13¼

2899	A1199	P multi	1.25	.65
2900	A1199	P multi	1.25	.65
a.		Booklet pane of 10, 5 each #2899-2900	12.50	
		Nos. 2897-2900 (4)	5.00	2.60

On day of issue, Nos. 2896a-2896b, 2897-2900 each sold for 85c.

Woman Suffrage, Cent. — A1201

Serpentine Die Cut 13½x13¾

2016, Mar. 8	Self-Adhesive	Litho.

Booklet Stamp

2901	A1201	P black & gold	1.25	.70
a.		Booklet pane of 10	12.50	

No. 2901 sold for 85c on day of issue.

Photography Type of 2013

Designs: Nos. 2902a, 2904, Toronto, by Lutz Dille, 1960, horiz. Nos. 2902b, 2905, Window, by Angela Grauerholz, 1988, horiz. Nos. 2902c, 2907, Victoria Bridge, Grand Trunk Railway, by Alexander Henderson, c. 1878, horiz. Nos. 2902d, 2906, Freighter's Boat on the Banks of the Red River, Manitoba, by Humphrey Lloyd Hime, 1858, horiz. Nos. 2903a, 2908, Sans Titre 0310/La Chambre Noire, by Michel Campeau, 2005-10, vert. Nos. 2903b, 2909, Climbing Mt. Habel, by Byron Harmon, c. 1909, horiz. Nos. 2903c, 2910, Grey Owl, by Yousuf Karsh, 1936, vert.

2016, Apr. 13		Litho.	Perf. 12¾	
2902	A1109	Sheet of 4	5.00	5.00
a.-d.		P Any single	1.25	.70
2903	A1109	Sheet of 3	6.80	6.80
a.		P multi	1.25	.70
b.		$1.20 multi	1.80	.95
c.		$2.50 multi	3.75	2.00

Booklet Stamps
Self-Adhesive

Serpentine Die Cut 13¼

2904	A1109	P multi	1.25	.70
2905	A1109	P multi	1.25	.70
2906	A1109	P multi	1.25	.70
2907	A1109	P multi	1.25	.70
2908	A1109	P multi	1.25	.70
a.		Booklet pane of 10, 2 each #2904-2908	12.50	
2909	A1109	$1.20 multi	1.80	.95
a.		Booklet pane of 6	11.00	
2910	A1109	$2.50 multi	3.75	2.00
a.		Booklet pane of 6	22.50	
		Nos. 2904-2910 (7)	11.80	6.45

On day of issue, Nos. 2902a-2902d, 2903a, 2904-2908 each sold for 85c.

U.S.S. Enterprise NCC-1701 A1202

Klingon Battle Cruiser A1203

Captain James T. Kirk A1204

Klingon Commander Kor — A1205

Dr. Leonard "Bones" McCoy A1206

Lieutenant Commander Montgomery "Scotty" Scott — A1207

Commander Spock — A1208

Characters From *Star Trek* Television Series — A1209

No. 2922: a, McCoy, Kirk, Spock and Scott in transporter room. b, Spock, Kirk and planet.

2016, May 5   Litho.   Perf. 13¼x13
2911	Sheet of 2	2.50	2.50
a.	A1202 P multi	1.25	.70
b.	A1203 P multi	1.25	.70

Perf. 13¼
2912	Sheet of 5	12.00	12.00
a.	A1204 P multi	1.25	.70
b.	A1205 $1 multi	1.50	.80
c.	A1206 $1.20 multi	1.80	.95
d.	A1207 $1.80 multi	2.70	1.40
e.	A1208 $2.50 multi	3.75	2.00
f.	Booklet pane of 4 #2912a	5.00	—
g.	Booklet pane of 3, #2912c, 2912e, 2912e	7.25	—
h.	Booklet pane of 1 #2912b	1.50	—
i.	Booklet pane of 5, #2912a-2912e	11.00	—

Coil Stamps
Self-Adhesive
Serpentine Die Cut 8¼ Horiz.
2913	A1202 P multi	1.25	.70
2914	A1203 P multi	1.25	.70
a.	Vert. pair, #2913-2914	2.50	

Booklet Stamps
Serpentine Die Cut 13¾
2915	A1202 P multi	1.25	1.40
2916	A1203 P multi	1.25	1.40
a.	Booklet pane of 2, #2915-2916	2.80	
	Complete booklet, #2912f, 2912g, 2912h, 2912i, 2916a	31.00	

Serpentine Die Cut 13¼x13¼
2917	A1204 P multi	1.25	.70
2918	A1207 P multi	1.25	.70
2919	A1205 P multi	1.25	.70
2920	A1208 P multi	1.25	.70
2921	A1206 P multi	1.25	.70
a.	Booklet pane of 10, 2 each #2917-2921	12.50	
	Nos. 2915-2921 (7)	8.75	6.30

Souvenir Sheet
Litho. With Three-Dimensional Plastic Affixed
Perf. 14¾
2922	A1209 Sheet of 2	15.00	15.00
a.-b.	$5 Either single	7.50	7.50

Star Trek television series, 50th anniv. Nos. 2911a, 2911b, 2912a, 2913, 2914, 2917-2921 each sold for 85c on day of issue. Complete booklet sold for $19.95. Nos. 2915-2916 each had a franking value of 85c on day of issue.

Dinosaurs A1210

Designs: Nos. 2923a, 2924, Troodon inequalis. Nos. 2923b, 2926, Dimetrodon borealis. Nos. 2923c, 2928, Comox Valley elasmosaur. Nos. 2923d, 2925, Cypretherium coarctatum. Nos. 2923e, 2927, Acrotholus audeti.

2016, May 26   Litho.   Perf. 13
2923	Sheet of 5	6.25	6.25
a.-e.	A1210 P Any single	1.25	.70

Booklet Stamps
Self-Adhesive
Serpentine Die Cut 13¼
2924	A1210 P multi	1.25	.70
2925	A1210 P multi	1.25	.70
2926	A1210 P multi	1.25	.70
2927	A1210 P multi	1.25	.70
2928	A1210 P multi	1.25	.70
a.	Booklet pane of 10, 2 each #2924-2928	12.50	
	Nos. 2924-2928 (5)	6.25	3.50

On day of issue, Nos. 2923a-2923e, 2924-2928 each sold for 85c.

Birds — A1211

Designs: Nos. 2929a, 2934, Lagopus muta. Nos. 2929b, 2931, Bubo virginianus. Nos. 2929c, 2933, Corvus corax. Nos. 2929d, 2932, Fratercula arctica. Nos. 2929e, 2930, Tympanuchus phasianellus.

2016, July 12   Litho.   Perf. 13x13¼
2929	A1211 Sheet of 5 + label	6.25	6.25
a.-e.	P Any single	1.25	.70

Booklet Stamps
Self-Adhesive
Serpentine Die Cut 13½x13¾
2930	A1211 P multi	1.25	.70
2931	A1211 P multi	1.25	.70
2932	A1211 P multi	1.25	.70
2933	A1211 P multi	1.25	.70
2934	A1211 P multi	1.25	.70
a.	Booklet pane of 10, 2 each #2930-2934	12.50	
	Nos. 2930-2934 (5)	6.25	3.50

On day of issue, Nos. 2929a-2929e, 2930-2934 each sold for 85c.

Haunted Canada — A1212

Designs: Nos. 2935a, 2936, Bell Island Hag, Newfoundland and Labrador. Nos. 2935b, 2937, Dungarvon Whooper, New Brunswick. Nos. 2935c, 2939, Ghost of the Winter Garden Theater, Toronto, Ontario. Nos. 2935d, 2938, Lady in White of Montmorency Falls, Quebec. Nos. 2935e, 2940, Phantom Bell Ringers of the Kirk of St. James, Charlottetown, Prince Edward Island.

Litho. With Holographic Foil
2016, Sept. 8   Perf. 13
2935	A1212 Sheet of 5	7.00	7.00
a.-e.	P Any single	1.40	.70

Booklet Stamps
Self-Adhesive
Serpentine Die Cut 13½
2936	A1212 P multi	1.40	.70
2937	A1212 P multi	1.40	.70
2938	A1212 P multi	1.40	.70
2939	A1212 P multi	1.40	.70
2940	A1212 P multi	1.40	.70
a.	Booklet pane of 10, 2 each #2936-2940	14.00	
	Nos. 2936-2940 (5)	7.00	3.50

On day of issue, Nos. 2935a-2935e, 2936-2940 each sold for 85c.

A1213

Hockey Forwards — A1214

Designs: Nos. 2941a, 2942, 2948, Sidney Crosby. Nos. 2941b, 2943, 2949, Phil Esposito. Nos. 2941c, 2944, 2950, Guy Lafleur. Nos. 2941d, 2945, 2951, Steve Yzerman. Nos. 2941e, 2946, 2952, Mark Messier. Nos. 2941f, 2947, 2953, Darryl Sittler.

Litho., Sheet Margin Litho. &
Embossed With Foil Application
2016, Sept. 23   Perf. 12½x13
2941	Sheet of 6 + 3 labels	8.50	8.50
a.-f.	A1213 P Any single	1.40	.70

Booklet Stamps
Self-Adhesive
Litho.
Serpentine Die Cut 13¼x13½
2942	A1213 P multi	1.40	.70
2943	A1213 P multi	1.40	.70
2944	A1213 P multi	1.40	.70
2945	A1213 P multi	1.40	.70
2946	A1213 P multi	1.40	.70
2947	A1213 P multi	1.40	.70
a.	Booklet pane of 6, #2942-2947	8.50	
	Nos. 2942-2947 (6)	8.40	4.20

Souvenir Sheets
Serpentine Die Cut 13½x13¼
2948	A1214 $1.80 multi	2.75	1.40
2949	A1214 $1.80 multi	2.75	1.40
2950	A1214 $1.80 multi	2.75	1.40
2951	A1214 $1.80 multi	2.75	1.40
2952	A1214 $1.80 multi	2.75	1.40
2953	A1214 $1.80 multi	2.75	1.40
	Nos. 2948-2953 (6)	16.50	8.40

Nos. 2941a-2941f, 2942-2947 each sold for 85c on day of issue. Nos. 2948-2953 each contain one 52x78mm stamp. Nos. 2873-2878 were sold together in a sealed opaque plastic package. One of every 40 packages contained a souvenir sheet signed by Crosby, Esposito, Lafleur, Yzerman, Messier or Sittler.

A1215

Christmas — A1216

Designs: Nos. 2954a, 2956, Santa Claus and Christmas tree. Nos. 2954b, 2957, Stocking cap on Christmas tree. Nos. 2954c, 2958, Dove and Christmas tree. No. 2955, Virgin and Child, by Master of the Castello Nativity.

2016, Nov. 1 Litho.   Perf. 12¾x12½
2954	Sheet of 3	7.25	7.25
a.	A1215 P multi	1.40	.70
b.	A1215 $1.20 multi	1.90	.95
c.	A1215 $2.50 multi	3.75	1.90

Booklet Stamps
Self-Adhesive
Serpentine Die Cut 13¼x13½
2955	A1216 P multi	1.40	.70
a.	Booklet pane of 12	17.00	

Serpentine Die Cut 13
2956	A1215 P multi	1.40	.70
a.	Booklet pane of 12	17.00	
2957	A1215 $1.20 multi	1.90	.95
a.	Booklet pane of 6	11.50	
2958	A1215 $2.50 multi	3.75	1.90
a.	Booklet pane of 6	22.50	
	Nos. 2955-2958 (4)	8.45	4.25

Nos. 2954a, 2955 and 2956 each sold for 85c on day of issue.

New Year 2017 (Year of the Rooster) A1217

Designs: P, Rooster. $2.50, Head of rooster.

Litho. With Foil Application, Litho.
(#2961)
2017, Jan. 9   Perf. 12½x13¼
2959	A1217 P gold & multi	1.25	.60
a.	Perf. 13¼x12½	1.25	.60
b.	Pair, #2959, 2959a	2.50	1.25

Souvenir Sheet
Perf. 12½
2960	A1217 $2.50 gold & multi	3.75	3.75
a.	Souvenir sheet of 2, #2885b, 2960	7.50	7.50

Booklet Stamps
Serpentine Die Cut 13½
2961	A1217 P multi	1.25	.60
a.	Booklet pane of 10	12.50	
2962	A1217 $2.50 gold & multi	3.75	1.90
a.	Booklet pane of 6	22.50	

Nos. 2959 and 2961 each sold for 85c on day of issue. On No. 2959b, one stamp of the pair is rotated 90 degrees in relation to the other stamp. Blocks of four contain stamps with four different orientations.

The tagging for all Canada stamps issued in 2017 will include the text "Canada 150."

Dinosaur Provincial Park, Alberta A1218

Mistaken Point, Newfoundland and Labrador A1219

Historic District
of Old Quebec
A1220

L'Anse aux
Meadows
National
Historic Site,
Newfoundland
and Labrador
A1221

Red Bay Basque
Whaling Station,
Newfoundland and
Labrador — A1222

2017, Jan. 16   Litho.   Perf. 13¼x13
2963   Sheet of 5   6.25 6.25
a.   A1218 P multi   1.25   .60
b.   A1219 P multi   1.25   .60
c.   A1220 P multi   1.25   .60
d.   A1221 P multi   1.25   .60
e.   A1222 P multi   1.25   .60

Booklet Stamps
Self-Adhesive
Serpentine Die Cut 13
2964   A1218 P multi   1.25   .60
2965   A1220 P multi   1.25   .60
2966   A1222 P multi   1.25   .60
2967   A1219 P multi   1.25   .60
2968   A1221 P multi   1.25   .60
a.   Booklet pane of 10, 2 each
           #2964-2968   12.50
b.   Booklet pane of 30, 6 each
           #2964-2968   37.50
        Nos. 2964-2968 (5)   6.25 3.00

UNESCO World Heritage Sites. Nos.
2963a-2963e, 2964-2968 each sold for 85c on
day of issue.

SEMI-POSTAL STAMPS

> Catalogue values for unused
> stamps in this section are for
> Never Hinged items.

Olympic Type of 1973
Size: 20x36mm
1974, Apr. 17   Litho.   Perf. 12½
B1   A307   8c + 2c multi   .35   .35
B2   A307   10c + 5c multi   .55   .55
B3   A307   15c + 5c multi   .75   .75
        Nos. B1-B3 (3)   1.65 1.65

SP1

1975, Feb. 5   Perf. 13
B4   SP1   8c + 2c Swimming   .35   .35
B5   SP1   10c + 5c Rowing   .60   .60
B6   SP1   15c + 5c Sailing   .75   .75
        Nos. B4-B6 (3)   1.70 1.70

SP2

1975, Aug. 6
B7   SP2   8c + 2c Fencing   .35   .35
B8   SP2   10c + 5c Boxing   .60   .60
B9   SP2   15c + 5c Judo   .75   .75
        Nos. B7-B9 (3)   1.70 1.70

1976, Jan. 7
B10   SP2   8c + 2c Basketball   .35   .35
B11   SP2   10c + 5c Vaulting   .60   .60
B12   SP2   20c + 5c Soccer   .90   .90
        Nos. B10-B12 (3)   1.85 1.85

21st Olympic Games, Montreal, July 17-
Aug. 1. The surtax was for the Canadian
Olympic Committee.

Literacy — SP3

1996, Sept. 9   Litho.   Perf. 13x12½
B13   SP3 45c +5c multi   1.00   .60
a.   Booklet pane of 10   10.00
        Complete booklet   11.50

No. B13 has die cut opening in center to
represent missing puzzle piece.
Surcharge donated to ABC CANADA literacy organization.

Mental
Health — SP4

Self-Adhesive
Booklet Stamp
Serpentine Die Cut 13¼
2008, Oct. 6   Litho.
B14   SP4 P +10c multi   1.40   .45
a.   Booklet pane of 10   14.00

No. B14 had a franking value of 52c on day
of issue. Surtax for Canada Post Foundation
for Mental Health.

Mental
Health — SP5

Self-Adhesive
Booklet Stamp
Serpentine Die Cut 13¼
2009, Sept. 14   Litho.
B15   SP5 P +10c multi   1.40   .45
a.   Booklet pane of 10   14.00

No. B15 had a franking value of 54c on day
of issue. Surtax for Canada Post Foundation
for Mental Health.

Mental
Health — SP6

Self-Adhesive
Booklet Stamp
Serpentine Die Cut 13¼
2010, Sept. 7   Litho.
B16   SP6 P + 10c multi   1.10   .45
a.   Booklet pane of 10   11.00

No. B16 had a franking value of 57c on day
of issue. Surtax for Canada Post Foundation
for Mental Health.

Mental
Health — SP7

2011, Sept. 6   Litho.   Perf. 12¾x13¼
B17   Souvenir sheet of 2
        #B17a   2.75 1.80
a.   SP7 P+10c multi   1.35   .75

Booklet Stamp
Self-Adhesive
Serpentine Die Cut 13¼
B18   SP7 P+10c multi   1.35   .45
a.   Booklet pane of 10   13.50

Nos. B17a and B18 each had a franking
value of 59c on day of issue. Surtax was for
Canada Post Foundation for Mental Health.

Hands and
Heart — SP8

Self-Adhesive
Serpentine Die Cut 13x13¼
2012, Sept. 17   Litho.
Booklet Stamp
B19   SP8 P +10c multi   1.35   .45
a.   Booklet pane of 10   13.50

No. B19 had a franking value of 61c on day
of issue. Surtax for Canada Post Community
Foundation.

Floating Abroad,
Children's Art by
Ezra Peters — SP9

Serpentine Die Cut 13x12½
2013, Sept. 30   Booklet Stamp
Self-Adhesive
B20   SP9 63c+10c multi   .95   .45
a.   Booklet pane of 10   9.50

Surtax for Canada Post Community
Foundation.

Children in
Paper Sailboat
SP10

Serpentine Die Cut 13½
2014, Sept. 29   Litho.
Booklet Stamp
Self-Adhesive
B21   SP10 P+10c multi   1.35   .45
a.   Booklet pane of 10   13.50

No. B21 had a franking value of 85c. Surtax
for Canada Post Community Foundation.

Children Reading
Story Under Tented
Bedsheet — SP11

Serpentine Die Cut 13x12½
2015, Sept. 28   Litho.
Booklet Stamp
Self-Adhesive
B22   SP11 P+10c multi   1.40 1.40
a.   Booklet pane of 10   14.00

No. B22 had a franking value of 85c on day
of issue. Surtax for Canada Post Community
Foundation.

Stylized
Bird — SP12

Serpentine Die Cut 13½
2016, Sept. 26   Litho.
Booklet Stamp
Self-Adhesive
B23   SP12 P+10c blue & multi 1.50 1.50
B24   SP12 P+10c apple grn &
           multi   1.50 1.50
a.   Booklet pane of 10, 5 each
           #B23-B24   15.00

Nos. B23-B24 each had a franking value of
85c on day of issue. Surtax for Canada Post
Community Foundation.

AIR POST STAMPS

Allegory of
Flight — AP1

Unwmk.
1928, Sept. 21   Engr.   Perf. 12
C1   AP1 5c brown olive   15.00 5.50
        Never hinged   27.50
a.   Imperf., pair   275.00
        Never hinged   375.00

No. C1 is known imperforate horizontally
and imperforate vertically.
For surcharge see No. C3.

For information on imperforate and
part-perforate varieties, see note following No. 47a.

Allegory-Air
Mail Circles
Globe
AP2

1930, Dec. 4   Perf. 11
C2   AP2 5c olive brown   70.00 24.00
        Never hinged   120.00

For surcharge see No. C4.

No. C1
Surcharged

1932, Feb. 22   Perf. 12
C3   AP1 6c on 5c brown olive 11.00 4.00
        Never hinged   20.00
a.   Inverted surcharge   225.00
        Never hinged   325.00
b.   Double surcharge   650.00
        Never hinged   925.00
c.   Triple surcharge   400.00
        Never hinged   550.00
d.   Pair, one without surcharge 950.00
        Never hinged   1,350.

Counterfeit surcharges exist.
No. C3b is valued in the grade of fine.

No. C2 Surcharged in Dark Blue

1932, July 12   *Perf. 11*
C4   AP2 6c on 5c olive brown   40.00 14.00
    Never hinged   70.00

Daedalus
AP3

1935, June 1   *Perf. 12*
C5   AP3 6c red brown   4.25 1.25
    Never hinged   6.00
a.   Horiz. pair, imperf. vert.   7,500.
b.   Imperf., pair   600.00
    Never hinged   900.00

No. C5a is unique and is the result of a pre-perforating paper foldover.

Mackenzie River Steamer and Seaplane AP4

1938, June 15
C6   AP4 6c blue   3.75 .40
    Never hinged   5.25
a.   Imperf., pair   650.00
    Never hinged   1,000.

Planes and Student Flyers AP5

1942-43
C7   AP5 6c deep blue   6.50 1.30
    Never hinged   7.50
a.   Imperf., pair   650.00
    Never hinged   1,000.
C8   AP5 7c deep blue ('43)   1.10 .25
    Never hinged   1.60
a.   Imperf., pair   650.00
    Never hinged   1,000.

Canada's contribution to the war effort of the Allied Nations.

Catalogue values for unused stamps in this section, from this point to the end of the section, are for Never Hinged items.

Canada Geese in Flight — AP6

1946, Sept. 16
C9   AP6 7c deep blue   1.10 .25
a.   Booklet pane of 4   4.00 3.50

For overprints see Nos. CO1, CO2.

AIR POST SPECIAL DELIVERY STAMPS

Trans-Canada Airplane and Aerial View of a City — APSD1

1942-43   **Unwmk.**   **Engr.**   *Perf. 12*
CE1   APSD1 16c bright ultra   2.50 2.00
    Never hinged   3.50
a.   Imperf., pair   650.00
    Never hinged   1,025.
CE2   APSD1 17c brt ultra ('43)   3.25 3.00
    Never hinged   4.75
a.   Imperf., pair   650.00
    Never hinged   1,025.

Canada's contribution to the war effort of the Allied Nations.

Catalogue values for unused stamps in this section, from this point to the end of the section, are for Never Hinged items.

DC-4 Transatlantic Mail Plane Over Quebec — APSD2

1946, Sept. 16
CE3   APSD2 17c bright ultra   7.50 4.75

Circumflex accent on second "E" of "EXPRES."

1946, Dec. 3   **Corrected Die**
CE4   APSD2 17c bright ultra   7.50 6.00

Grave accent on the 2nd "E" of "EXPRES."

AIR POST OFFICIAL STAMPS

Catalogue values for unused stamps in this section are for Never Hinged items.

No. C9 Overprinted in Black

1949   **Unwmk.**   *Perf. 12*
CO1   AP6 7c deep blue   12.00 4.75
a.   No period after "S"   110.00 60.00

Same Overprinted

1950
CO2   AP6 7c deep blue   17.50 13.50

SPECIAL DELIVERY STAMPS

SD1

1898, June 28   **Unwmk.**   **Engr.**   *Perf. 12*
E1   SD1 10c blue green   125.00 11.00
    Never hinged   350.00

SD2

1922, Aug. 21
E2   SD2 20c carmine   100.00 9.00
    Never hinged   220.00

Five Stages of Mail Transportation SD3

1927, June 29
E3   SD3 20c orange   35.00 22.50
    Never hinged   70.00
a.   Imperf., pair   225.00
    Never hinged   400.00

No. E3 forms part of the Confederation Commemorative issue. It is known imperforate vertically and imperforate horizontally.

SD4

1930, Sept. 2   *Perf. 11*
E4   SD4 20c henna brown   65.00 17.50
    Never hinged   125.00

SD5

1932, Dec. 24
E5   SD5 20c henna brown   60.00 17.50
    Never hinged   115.00
a.   Imperf., pair   650.00
    Never hinged   950.00

Allegory of Progress — SD6

1935, June 1   *Perf. 12*
E6   SD6 20c dark carmine   12.00 7.50
    Never hinged   20.00
a.   Imperf., pair   650.00
    Never hinged   950.00

Arms of Canada — SD7

1938-39
E7   SD7 10c dk green (4/1/39)   9.50 3.50
    Never hinged   15.50
a.   Imperf., pair   600.00
    Never hinged   1,000.
E8   SD7 20c dark carmine (6/15/38)   30.00 25.00
    Never hinged   50.00
a.   Imperf., pair   600.00
    Never hinged   1,000.

No. E8 Surcharged in Black

1939, Mar. 1
E9   SD7 10c on 20c dk car   8.00 6.50
    Never hinged   12.00

Coat of Arms and Flags SD8

1942, July 1
E10   SD8 10c green   3.50 2.00
    Never hinged   5.00
a.   Imperf., pair   600.00
    Never hinged   950.00

Canada's contribution to the war effort of the Allied Nations.

Catalogue values for unused stamps in this section, from this point to the end of the section, are for Never Hinged items.

Arms of Canada — SD9

1946, Sept. 16
E11   SD9 10c green   4.50 1.25

The laurel and olive branches symbolize Victory and Peace.
For overprints see Nos. EO1, EO2.

SPECIAL DELIVERY OFFICIAL STAMPS

Catalogue values for unused stamps in this section are for Never Hinged items.

No. E11 Overprinted in Black

1950   Unwmk.   Perf. 12
EO1   SD9   10c green   17.50   12.50

Same Overprinted

EO2   SD9   10c green   25.00   17.50

REGISTRATION STAMPS

R1

1875-88   Unwmk.   Engr.   Perf. 12
F1	R1	2c orange	115.00	6.00

F1   R1   2c orange   115.00   6.00
  Never hinged   250.00
  a. 2c vermilion   170.00   15.00
   Never hinged   375.00
  b. 2c rose carmine   340.00   110.00
   Never hinged   725.00
  c. As "a," imperf., pair   3,000.
  d. Perf. 12x11½   575.00   110.00
   Never hinged   1,200.
F2   R1   5c dark green   150.00   6.00
  Never hinged   300.00
  a. 5c blue green ('88) 160.00   6.00
   Never hinged   325.00
  b. 5c yellow green   240.00   7.50
   Never hinged   475.00
  c. Imperf., pair   1,200.
   Never hinged   2,250.
  d. Perf. 12x11½   2,250.   280.00
   Never hinged   4,500.
F3   R1   8c dull blue ('76) 600.00   350.00
  Never hinged   1,500.
  Nos. F1-F3 (3)   865.00   362.00

The used No. F1c is unique (fine centering).

POSTAGE DUE STAMPS

D1

1906-28   Unwmk.   Engr.   Perf. 12
J1   D1   1c violet   25.00   4.75
  Never hinged   40.00
  a. Thin paper ('24)   45.00   7.50
   Never hinged   80.00
  b. Imperf., pair   400.00
J2   D1   2c violet   25.00   1.00
  Never hinged   40.00
  a. Thin paper ('24)   45.00   11.00
   Never hinged   80.00
  b. Imperf., pair   400.00
J3   D1   4c violet ('28)   65.00   22.50
  Never hinged   110.00
J4   D1   5c violet   25.00   2.00
  Never hinged   40.00
  a. As "c," thin paper 35.00   7.50
   Never hinged   60.00
  b. Imperf., pair   400.00
  c. 5c reddish violet ('28) 25.00   2.00
   Never hinged   40.00
J5   D1   10c violet ('28)   100.00   14.00
  Never hinged   190.00
  Nos. J1-J5 (5)   240.00   44.25
Set, never hinged   390.00

In 1924 there was a printing of Nos. J1, J2 and J4 on thin semi-transparent paper. Imperf pairs are without gum.

D2

1930-32   Perf. 11
J6   D2   1c dark violet   12.50   4.25
  Never hinged   22.50
J7   D2   2c dark violet   7.00   1.10
  Never hinged   12.50
J8   D2   4c dark violet   15.00   5.50
  Never hinged   25.00
J9   D2   5c dark violet   25.00   6.50
  Never hinged   42.50
J10 D2   10c dark violet ('32) 110.00   10.00
  Never hinged   200.00
  a. Vert. pair, imperf. horiz. 1,750.   —
   Never hinged   2,750.
  Nos. J6-J10 (5)   169.50   27.35
Set, never hinged   312.50

No. J10a is valued in the grade of fine.

D3

1933-34
J11 D3   1c dark violet ('34) 15.00   6.50
  Never hinged   27.50
  a. Imperf., pair   400.00
   Never hinged   575.00
J12 D3   2c dark violet   9.00   1.25
  Never hinged   16.50
J13 D3   4c dark violet   15.00   8.00
  Never hinged   27.50
J14 D3   10c dark violet   35.00   7.25
  Never hinged   57.50
  Nos. J11-J14 (4)   74.00   23.00
Set, never hinged   115.50

> **Catalogue values for unused stamps in this section, from this point to the end of the section, are for Never Hinged items.**

D4

1935-65   Perf. 12
J15 D4   1c dark violet   .30   .25
  a. Imperf., pair   200.00
J16 D4   2c dark violet   .30   .25
  a. Imperf., pair   200.00
J16B D4   3c dark vio ('65)   2.00   1.50
J17 D4   4c dark violet   .35   .25
  a. Imperf., pair   200.00
J18 D4   5c dark vio ('48)   .40   .35
J19 D4   6c dark vio ('57)   2.25   1.75
J20 D4   10c dark violet   .40   .25
  a. Imperf., pair   200.00
  Nos. J15-J20 (7)   6.00   4.60

D5

Size: 20x17mm

1967, Feb. 8   Litho.   Perf. 12
J21 D5   1c carmine rose   .25   .25
J22 D5   2c carmine rose   .25   .25
J23 D5   3c carmine rose   .25   .25
J24 D5   4c carmine rose   .30   .25
J25 D5   5c carmine rose   1.50   1.50
J26 D5   6c carmine rose   .30   .25
J27 D5   10c carmine rose   .40   .30
  Nos. J21-J27 (7)   3.25   3.05

Size: 20x15¾mm

1969-78   Perf. 12
J28 D5   1c car rose ('70)   .45   .30
  a. Perf. 12½x12 ('77) .25   .25
J29 D5   2c car rose ('72)   .25   .25
J30 D5   3c car rose ('74)   .25   .25
J31 D5   4c carmine rose   .40   .30
  a. Perf. 12½x12 ('77) .25   .25
J32 D5   5c car rose, perf. 12½x12 ('77) .25   .25
  a. Perf. 12   16.00   12.50
J33 D5   6c car rose ('72)   .25   .25
J34 D5   8c car rose ('74)   .25   .25
  a. Perf. 12½x12 ('78) .40   .30
J35 D5   10c carmine rose   .55   .25
  a. Perf. 12½x12 ('77) .25   .25

J36 D5   12c carmine rose   .75   .60
  a. Perf. 12½x12 ('77) 1.50   .70
J37 D5   16c carmine rose ('74) .40   .25

Perf. 12½x12
J38 D5   20c carmine rose ('77) .55   .40
J39 D5   24c carmine rose ('77) .65   .40
J40 D5   50c carmine rose ('77) 1.00   .75
  Nos. J28-J40 (13)   6.00   4.50

WAR TAX STAMPS

WT1

Unwmk.

1915, Mar. 25   Engr.   Perf. 12
MR1 WT1   1c green   25.00   .40
  Never hinged   60.00
MR2 WT1   2c carmine   25.00   .40
  Never hinged   60.00

In 1915 postage stamps of 5, 20 and 50 cents were overprinted "WAR TAX" in two lines. These stamps were intended for fiscal use, the war tax on postal matter being 1 cent. A few of these stamps were used to pay postage.

WT2

Type I   Type II

TWO TYPES:
Type I — There is a colored line between two white lines below the large letter "T."
Type II — The right half of the colored line is replaced by two short diagonal lines and five small dots.

1916
MR3 WT2   2c + 1c car (I)   40.00   .25
  Never hinged   100.00
  a. 2c + 1c carmine (II) 275.00   4.50
   Never hinged   625.00
  b. 2c + 1c rose red (I) 50.00   .40
   Never hinged   120.00
MR4 WT2   2c + 1c brn (II)   25.00   .25
  Never hinged   62.50
  a. 2c + 1c brown (I) 800.00   10.00
   Never hinged   1,500.
  b. Imperf., pair (I) 175.00
  c. Imperf., pair (II) 2,250.

Nos. MR4b and MR4c were made without gum.

Perf. 12x8
MR5 WT2   2c + 1c car (I)   65.00   30.00
  Never hinged   140.00

Coil Stamps
Perf. 8 Vertically
MR6 WT2   2c + 1c car (I)   150.00   10.00
  Never hinged   350.00
MR7 WT2   2c + 1c brn (II)   50.00   2.25
  Never hinged   110.00
  a. 2c + 1c brown (I) 200.00   7.50
   Never hinged   500.00

OVERPRINTED OFFICIAL STAMPS

> **Catalogue values for unused stamps in this section are for Never Hinged items.**

With Perforated Initials O H M S
On March 28, 1939 the Treasury Board ruled that on and after June 30, 1939 all stamps used by government departments throughout the country should be perforated O H M S (On His Majesty's Service) and that "the Post Office Department is to make arrangements required to provide that all stamps sold to Government Departments are perforated with the letters O H M S." The sale of such perforated stamps was discontinued in 1948.

For listings see the *Scott Classic Specialized Catalogue.*

Nos. 249, 250, 252 and 254 Overprinted in Black

1949-50   Unwmk.   Perf. 12
O1   A97   1c green   2.25   1.75
  a. No period after "S" 150.00   75.00
O2   A98   2c brown   10.00   7.50
  a. No period after "S" 150.00   75.00
O3   A99   3c rose violet   2.25   1.25
O4   A98   4c dark carmine   3.00   .75

Nos. 269 to 273 Overprinted in Black

O6   A108 10c olive   3.50   .60
  a. No period after "S" 85.00   60.00
O7   A109 14c black brown   6.50   2.25
  a. No period after "S" 125.00   80.00
O8   A110 20c slate black   17.50   3.25
  a. No period after "S" 150.00   80.00
O9   A111 50c dk blue grn   200.00   110.00
  a. No period after "S" 1,000.   600.00
O10 A112 $1 red violet   70.00   35.00
  a. No period after "S" 6,000.   3,000.
  Nos. O1-O4, O6-O10 (9) 315.00   162.35

It is recommended that a certificate of authenticity be acquired for No. O10a.

Same Overprint on No. 294

1950
O11 A124 50c dull green   40.00   15.00

Nos. 284 to 288 Overprinted in Black

1950
O12 A119 1c green   .40   .35
O13 A120 2c sepia   1.10   .80
O14 A121 3c rose violet   1.10   .50
O15 A122 4c dark carmine   1.10   .25
  b. No period after "S" 400.00   275.00
O15A A123 5c deep blue   2.25   1.50
  c. No period after "S" 80.00   60.00
  Nos. O12-O15A (5)   5.95   3.40

It is recommended that a certificate of authenticity be acquired for No. O15b.

Stamps of 1946-50 Overprinted in Black

a

b

c

1950

O16	A119(a)	1c grn (#284)	.50	.25
O17	A120(a)	2c sep (#285)	1.30	.90
O18	A121(a)	3c rose vio (#286)	1.30	.25
O19	A122(a)	4c dk car (#287)	1.30	.25
O20	A123(a)	5c dp bl (#288)	1.60	.90
O21	A108(b)	10c olive	4.25	.50
O22	A109(b)	14c black brn	8.50	2.00
O23	A110(b)	20c slate blk	14.00	1.00
O24	A124(b)	50c dull green	10.00	5.50
O25	A112(b)	$1 red violet	100.00	85.00
		Nos. O16-O25 (10)	142.75	96.55

Nos. 301-302 Overprinted Type "b"
1950-51

O26	A125	10c black brown	1.30	.25
a.		Pair, one without "G"	850.00	600.00
O27	A126	$1 brt ultra ('51)	100.00	60.00

It is recommended that a certificate of authenticity be acquired for No. O26a.

Nos. 305-306 Overprinted Type "a"
1951-52   Unwmk.   Perf. 12

O28	A120	2c olive green	.60	.25
O29	A122	4c orange ver ('52)	.95	.25

No. 316 Overprinted Type "b"
1952

O30	A132	20c gray	2.25	.25

Nos. 320-321 Overprinted Type "b"
1952-53

O31	A136	7c blue	4.00	1.25
O32	A137	$1 gray ('53)	12.00	7.50

Same Overprints on #325-329, 334
1953-61

O33	A139(a)	1c violet brown	.35	.25
O34	A139(a)	2c green	.35	.25
O35	A139(a)	3c carmine rose	.35	.25
O36	A139(a)	4c violet	.45	.25
O37	A139(a)	5c ultramarine	.45	.25
O38	A141(b)	50c light green	5.00	2.00
a.		Overprinted type "c" ('61)	5.00	2.00
		Nos. O33-O38 (6)	6.95	2.45

No. 351 Overprinted Type "b"
1955-62

O39	A148	10c violet brown	.90	.25
a.		Overprinted type "c" ('62)	1.90	1.25

#337-338, 340-341 Ovptd. Type "a"
1955-56

O40	A144	1c vio brown ('56)	.35	.30
O41	A144	2c green ('56)	.35	.25
O43	A144	4c violet ('56)	1.00	.25
O44	A144	5c bright blue	.60	.25
		Nos. O40-O44 (4)	2.30	1.05

No. 362 Overprinted Type "b"
1956-62

O45	A159	20c green	1.75	.25
a.		Overprinted type "c" ('62)	7.00	.50

#401-402, 404-405 Ovptd. Type "a"
1963, May 15   Engr.   Perf. 12

O46	A195	1c deep brown	.75	.70
a.		Double overprint	750.00	
O47	A195	2c green	.75	.70
a.		Pair, one without "G"	1,000.	
O48	A195	4c carmine	.80	.70
O49	A195	5c violet blue	.70	.50
		Nos. O46-O49 (4)	3.00	2.60

CAPE JUBY

'kāp 'jü-bē

LOCATION — Northwest coast of Africa in Spanish Sahara
GOVT. — Spanish administration
AREA — 12,700 sq. mi.
POP. — 9,836
CAPITAL — Villa Bens (Cape Juby)

By agreement with France, Spain's Sahara possessions were extended to include Cape Juby and in 1916 Spanish troops occupied the territory. It was attached for administrative purposes to Spanish Sahara.

100 Centimos = 1 Peseta

Stamps of Rio de Oro, 1914 Surcharged in Violet, Red, Green or Blue

1916   Unwmk.   Perf. 13

1	A6	5c on 4p rose (V)	240.00	19.00
a.		Inverted surcharge	250.00	30.00
d.		Double surcharge	325.00	30.00
2	A6	10c on 10p dl vio (R)	50.00	19.00
a.		Inverted surcharge	55.00	30.00
d.		Double surcharge	75.00	50.00
2E	A6	10c on 10p dl vio (V)	125.00	72.50
f.		Double surcharge (R, V)	150.00	90.00
2G	A6	10c on 10p dl vio (R)	125.00	72.50
3	A6	15c on 50c dk brn (G)	52.50	30.00
a.		Inverted surcharge	57.50	30.00
4	A6	15c on 50c dk brn (R)	50.00	19.00
a.		Inverted surcharge	55.00	30.00
5	A6	40c on 1p red vio (G)	87.50	35.00
a.		Inverted surcharge	75.00	37.50
6	A6	40c on 1p red vio (R)	85.00	26.00
a.		Inverted surcharge	75.00	42.50
		Nos. 1-6 (8)	815.00	293.00
		Set, never hinged		

Very fine examples of Nos. 1-6 will be somewhat off center. Well centered examples are uncommon and will sell for more.

Stamps of Spain, 1876-1917, Overprinted in Red or Black

1919   Imperf.

7	A21	¼c bl grn (R)	.30	.30

Perf. 13x12½, 14

8	A46	2c dk brn (Bk)	.30	.30
a.		Double overprint	50.00	60.00
b.		Double overprint (Bk + R)	100.00	52.50
9	A46	5c grn (R)	.85	.75
a.		Double overprint	40.00	50.00
b.		Inverted overprint	30.00	47.50
10	A46	10c car (Bk)	1.00	.70
a.		Double overprint (Bk + R)	100.00	52.50
b.		Double overprint	40.00	50.00
11	A46	15c ocher (Bk)	4.00	3.50
b.		Double overprint	40.00	50.00
c.		Red control #	6.50	3.75
d.		As "c," inverted overprint	13.00	
12	A46	20c ol grn (R)	27.50	16.00
13	A46	25c dp bl (R)	3.75	3.00
a.		Double overprint	40.00	50.00
14	A46	30c bl grn (R)	3.75	3.75
15	A46	40c rose (Bk)	4.00	3.75
16	A46	50c sl bl (R)	4.50	4.50
17	A46	1p lake (Bk)	13.00	11.00
18	A46	4p dp vio (R)	57.50	55.00
19	A46	10p org (Bk)	80.00	75.00
		Nos. 7-19 (13)	200.45	177.55
		Set, never hinged	400.00	

Nos. 8-19 have blue control number on back. For imperfs, see the *Scott Classic Catalogue.*

Same on Stamps of Spain, 1920-21
1922   Imperf.

20	A47	1c blue green (R)	25.00	14.00
		Never hinged	45.00	

Engr.   Perf. 13x12½
Blue Control Number on Back

23	A46	20c violet	145.00	42.50

A 2c and a 15c exist, values $400 and $10, respectively, for unused, hinged examples, $600 and $15 for never hinged. Overprint on 2c privately applied.

Same on Stamps of Spain, 1922-23
1925   Perf. 13½x13

25	A49	5c red vio	5.25	3.50
26	A49	10c bl grn	13.00	3.50
28	A49	20c violet	27.50	10.00
		Nos. 25-28 (3)	45.75	17.00
		Set, never hinged	72.50	

Exists on Spain No. 331, 2c olive green. Value $425 unused hinged and $650 never hinged. Overprint was privately applied.

Seville-Barcelona Exposition Issue

Stamps of Spain, 1929, Overprinted in Red or Blue

1929   Perf. 11

29	A52	5c rose lake (Bl)	.40	.40
30	A53	10c green (R)	.40	.40
31	A53	15c Prus bl (R)	.40	.40
32	A51	20c pur (R)	.40	.40
33	A50	25c brt rose (Bl)	.40	.40
34	A52	30c blk brn (R)	.40	.40
35	A53	40c dk bl (R)	.40	.40
36	A51	50c dp org (Bl)	.55	.55
37	A52	1p bl blk (R)	15.00	15.00
38	A53	4p dp brn (R)	18.50	19.50
39	A53	10p brn (Bl)	18.50	19.50
		Nos. 29-39 (11)	55.35	57.35
		Set, never hinged	120.00	

Stamps of Spanish Morocco, 1928-33, Overprinted in Black or Red

1934   Perf. 14

40	A7	1c brt rose (Bk)	.55	.55
41	A2	2c dk vio (R)	5.00	5.00
42	A2	5c dp bl (R)	5.75	5.75
43	A2	10c dk grn (R)	14.00	11.50
43A	A10	10c dk grn (R)	3.50	3.50
44	A2	15c org brn (Bk)	32.50	29.00
45	A7	20c sl grn (R)	13.00	10.00
46	A2	25c cop red (Bk)	6.00	5.50
47	A10	30c red brn (Bk)	11.00	10.00
48	A13	40c dp bl (R)	40.00	37.50
49	A13	50c red org (Bk)	80.00	70.00
50	A4	1p yel grn (Bk)	57.50	57.50
51	A5	2.50p red vio (Bk)	120.00	115.00
52	A6	4p ultra (R)	160.00	145.00

No. 43A and 1c, 20c, 30c, 40c, 50c, with control numbers.

Same Overprint in Black on Stamp of Spanish Morocco, 1932

53	A2	1c car rose ("Ct")	2.40	2.40
		Nos. 40-53 (15)	551.20	508.20
		Set, never hinged	900.00	

Stamps of Spanish Morocco, 1933-35, Overprinted in Black, Blue or Red

1935-36

54	A8	2c grn (R)	1.25	1.00
55	A9	5c mag (Bk)	3.50	3.50
55A	A10	10c dk grn (R) ('36)	21.00	21.00
56	A11	15c yel (Bl)	8.00	8.00
57	A12	25c crim (Bk)	100.00	85.00
58	A8	1p sl blk (R)	13.50	12.50
59	A9	2.50p brn (Bl)	60.00	47.50
60	A11	4p yel grn (R)	100.00	90.00
61	A12	5p blk (R)	85.00	65.00
		Nos. 54-61 (9)	392.25	328.50
		Set, never hinged	750.00	

Same Overprint in Black or Red on Stamps of Spanish Morocco, 1935
1935   Perf. 13½

62	A14	25c vio (R)	4.00	4.00
63	A15	30c crim (Bk)	4.00	4.00
64	A14	40c org (Bk)	5.75	5.25
65	A15	50c brt bl (R)	15.00	11.00

66	A14	60c dk bl grn (R)	17.50	14.00
67	A15	2p brn lake (Bk)	95.00	75.00

Same Overprint on Stamps of Spanish Morocco, 1933
Perf. 13½, 14

68	A7	1c brt rose (Bk)	.30	.30

Perf. 14

69	A7	20c slate grn (R)	6.75	6.75
		Nos. 62-69 (8)	148.30	120.30
		Set, never hinged	200.00	

Same Overprint on Stamps of Spanish Morocco, 1937
1937   Perf. 13½

70	A21	1c dk bl (Bk)	.50	.50
71	A21	2c org brn (Bk)	.50	.50
72	A21	5c cer (R)	.50	.50
73	A21	10c emer (Bk)	.50	.50
74	A21	15c brt bl (Bk)	.50	.50
75	A21	20c red brn (Bk)	.50	.50
76	A21	25c mag (R)	.50	.50
77	A21	30c red org (Bk)	.50	.50
78	A21	40c org (Bk)	1.60	1.60
79	A21	50c ultra (R)	1.60	1.60
80	A21	60c yel grn (Bk)	1.60	1.60
81	A21	1p bl vio (Bk)	1.60	1.60
82	A21	2p Prus bl (Bk)	87.50	87.50
83	A21	2.50p gray blk (R)	87.50	87.50
84	A21	4p dk brn (Bk)	87.50	87.50
85	A22	10p vio blk (R)	87.50	87.50
		Nos. 70-85 (16)	360.40	360.40
		Set, never hinged	600.00	

1st Year of the Revolution.

Same Overprint in Black on Types of Spanish Morocco, 1939

Designs: 5c, Spanish quarter. 10c, Moroccan quarter. 15c, Street scene, Larache. 20c, Tetuan.

1939   Photo.   Perf. 13½

86	A25	5c vermilion	.50	.50
87	A25	10c deep green	.50	.50
88	A25	15c brown lake	.50	.50
89	A25	20c bright blue	.50	.50
		Nos. 86-89 (4)	2.00	2.00
		Set, never hinged	4.00	

Same Overprint in Black or Red on Stamps of Spanish Morocco, 1940
1940   Perf. 11½x11

90	A26	1c dk brn (Bk)	.25	.25
91	A27	2c ol grn (R)	.25	.25
92	A28	5c dk bl (R)	.25	.25
93	A29	10c dk red lil (Bk)	.25	.25
94	A30	15c dk grn (R)	.25	.25
95	A31	20c pur (R)	.30	.30
96	A32	25c blk brn (R)	.30	.30
97	A33	30c brt grn (Bk)	.35	.35
98	A34	40c slate grn (R)	.85	.75
99	A35	45c org ver (Bk)	.85	.75
100	A36	50c brn org (Bk)	.90	.90
101	A37	70c saph (R)	2.40	2.25
102	A39	1p ind & brn (Bk)	5.00	5.00
103	A39	2.50p choc & dk grn (Bk)	14.00	12.50
104	A40	5p dk cer & sep (Bk)	14.00	13.00
105	A41	10p dk ol grn & brn org (Bk)	40.00	35.00
		Nos. 90-105 (16)	80.20	72.35
		Set, never hinged	150.00	

Imperfs exist. Value, set $300.

Stamps of Spanish Morocco, 1944, Overprinted in Black or Red

1944, Oct. 2   Unwmk.   Perf. 12½

106	A47	1c choc & lt bl	.25	.25
107	A48	2c slate grn & lt grn	.25	.25
108	A49	5c choc & grnsh blk (R)	.25	.25
109	A50	10c brt ultra & red org	.25	.25
110	A51	15c sl grn & lt grn	.25	.25
111	A52	20c dp cl & blk (R)	.25	.25
112	A53	25c lt bl & choc	.25	.25
113	A47	30c yel grn & brt ultra (R)	.25	.25
114	A48	40c choc & red vio	.25	.25
115	A49	50c brt ultra, & red brn	.25	.25
116	A50	75c yel grn & brt ultra (R)	1.25	1.25
117	A51	1p brt ultra & choc	1.40	1.40
118	A52	2.50p blk & brt ultra (R)	3.25	3.25
119	A53	10p sal & gray blk (R)	25.00	25.00
		Nos. 106-119 (14)	33.40	33.40
		Set, never hinged	70.00	

Same Overprint on Stamps of Spanish Morocco, 1946

1946, Mar.   **Perf. 10½x10**

120	A54	1c pur & brn	.25	.25
121	A55	2c dk Prus grn & vio blk (R)	.25	.25
122	A54	10c dp org vio bl	.25	.25
123	A55	15c dk bl & bl grn	.25	.25
124	A54	25c yel grn & ultra	.25	.25
125	A56	40c dk bl & brn (R)	.30	.30
126	A55	45c blk & rose	.45	.45
127	A57	1p dk Prus grn & dp bl	1.60	1.60
128	A58	2.50p dp org & grnsh gray (R)	4.75	4.75
129	A59	10p dk bl & gray (R)	13.50	13.50
		Nos. 120-129 (10)	21.85	21.85
		Set, never hinged	40.00	

Same Overprint in Carmine, Black or Brown on Stamps of Spanish Morocco, 1948

1948, Jan. 1   **Perf. 10, 10x10½**

130	A64	2c pur & brn	.40	1.00
131	A65	5c dp claret & vio	.25	.25
132	A66	15c brt ultra & bl grn (Bk)	.25	.25
133	A67	25c blk & Prus grn	.25	.25
134	A65	35c brt ultra & gray blk	.25	.25
135	A68	50c red & vio (Br)	.25	.25
136	A66	70c dk gray grn & ultra (Bk)	.25	.25
137	A67	90c cer & dk gray grn (Bk)	.30	.30
138	A68	1p brt ultra & vio (Br)	.45	.45
139	A64	2.50p vio brn & sl grn	1.60	1.60
140	A69	10p blk & dp ultra	3.00	3.00
		Nos. 130-140 (11)	7.25	7.85
		Set, never hinged	12.00	

SEMI-POSTAL STAMPS

Types of Semi-Postal Stamps of Spain, 1926, Overprinted

1926   **Unwmk.**   **Perf. 12½, 13**

B1	SP1	1c orange	11.50	11.50
B2	SP2	2c rose	11.50	11.50
B3	SP3	5c blk brn	3.00	3.00
B4	SP4	10c dk grn	1.60	1.60
B5	SP1	15c dk vio	1.10	1.10
B6	SP4	20c vio brn	1.10	1.10
B7	SP5	25c dp car	1.10	1.10
B8	SP1	30c ol grn	1.10	1.10
B9	SP3	40c ultra	.45	.45
B10	SP2	50c red brn	.45	.45
B11	SP4	1p vermilion	.45	.45
B12	SP3	4p bister	2.00	2.00
B13	SP5	10p lt vio	3.00	3.00
		Nos. B1-B13 (13)	38.35	38.35
		Set, never hinged	65.00	

Nos. B12-B13 surcharged "Alfonso XIII" and new value are listed as Spain Nos. B68-B69. See Spain No. B6a.

AIR POST STAMPS

Spanish Morocco, Nos. C1 to C10 Overprinted "CABO JUBY" as on #54-61

1938, June 1   **Unwmk.**   **Perf. 13½**

C1	AP1	5c brown	.25	.25
C2	AP1	10c brt grn	.25	.25
C3	AP1	25c crimson	.25	.25
C4	AP1	40c light blue	2.10	2.10
C5	AP2	50c brt mag	.25	.25
C6	AP2	75c dk bl	.25	.25
C7	AP1	1p sepia	.25	.25
C8	AP1	1.50p dp vio	1.90	1.90
C9	AP1	2p dp red brn	2.75	2.75
C10	AP1	3p brn blk	7.25	7.25
		Nos. C1-C10 (10)	15.50	15.50
		Set, never hinged	45.00	

Moroccan Views — AP3

Designs: 5c, Ketama landscape. 10c, Mosque, Tangier. 15c, Velez. 90c, Sanjurjo. 5p, Strait of Gibraltar.

1942, Apr. 1   **Photo.**   **Perf. 12½**

C11	AP3	5c deep blue	.25	.25
C12	AP3	10c org brn	.25	.25
C13	AP3	15c grnsh blk	.25	.25
C14	AP3	90c dk rose	.50	.50
C15	AP3	5p black	1.75	1.75
		Nos. C11-C15 (5)	3.00	3.00
		Set, never hinged	4.00	

SPECIAL DELIVERY STAMPS

Special Delivery Stamp of Spain Ovptd. "CABO JUBY" as on #7-28

1919   **Unwmk.**   **Perf. 14**

E1	SD1	20c red (Bk)	3.25	3.25
b.		Double overprint	27.50	13.00

Spanish Morocco #E4 Overprinted "CABO JUBY" as on #40-52 in Red

1934

E2	SD2	20c black	10.00	10.00

Spanish Morocco No. E5 Overprinted "CABO JUBY" as on Nos. 54-61

1935

E3	SD3	20c vermilion	3.50	3.50

Same Ovpt. on Spanish Morocco #E6

1937   **Perf. 13½**

E4	SD4	20c bright carmine	1.10	1.10

1st Year of the Revolution.

Same Ovpt. on Spanish Morocco #E8

1940   **Perf. 11½x11**

E5	SD5	25c scarlet	.65	.65

SEMI-POSTAL SPECIAL DELIVERY STAMP

Type of Semi-Postal Special Delivery Stamp of Spain, 1926, Overprinted "CABO-JUBY" as on Nos. B1-B13

1926   **Unwmk.**   **Perf. 12½, 13**

EB1	SPSD1	20c ultra & black	3.50	3.50

CAPE OF GOOD HOPE

ˈkāp əv ˈgu̇d ˈhōp

LOCATION — In the extreme southern part of South Africa
GOVT. — Former British Colony
AREA — 276,995 sq mi. (1911)
POP. — 2,564,965 (1911)
CAPITAL — Cape Town

Cape of Good Hope joined with Natal, the Transvaal and the Orange River Colony in 1910, forming the Union of South Africa.

12 Pence = 1 Shilling

Watermarks

Wmk. 15 — Anchor   Wmk. 16 — Anchor

"Hope" Seated A1

Printed by Perkins, Bacon & Co.

Wmk. 15

1853, Sept. 1   **Engr.**   **Imperf.**

1	A1	1p brick red, bluish paper		
			3,500.	400.00
a.		1p pale brick red, deeply blued paper	4,500.	450.00
b.		1p deep brick red, deeply blued paper	10,500.	475.00
2	A1	4p deep blue, lightly blued paper	1,750.	170.00
a.		4p deep blue, deeply blued paper	3,500.	375.00
b.		4p blue, bluish paper	3,250.	200.00

Counterfeits exist.

			White Paper	
1855-58				
3	A1	1p rose ('57)	850.00	325.00
a.		1p dull red	1,100.	425.00
b.		1p brick red	6,000.	1,050.
4	A1	4p blue	700.00	85.00
a.		Half used as 2p on cover		42,000.
d.		4p deep blue	900.00	90.00
e.		4p bright blue	900.00	90.00
5	A1	6p pale lilac ('58)	1,200.	300.00
a.		6p rose lilac	2,500.	400.00
b.		6p grayish lilac on bluish paper	5,000.	540.00
c.		6p slate purple on bluish paper	4,150.	1,200.
d.		Half used as 3p on cover		—
6	A1	1sh yellow grn ('58)	4,000.	300.00
a.		1sh dark green	450.00	600.00
b.		Half used as 6p on cover		—

Nos. 3-6 are known rouletted unofficially. Counterfeits exist.
No. 4 was reproduced by the collotype process in an unwatermarked souvenir sheet distributed at the London Intl. Stamp Exhib. 1950.

A2

Printed by Saul Solomon & Co.

			Unwmk.	Typo.
1861		**Laid Paper**		
7	A2	1p vermilion	17,000.	2,750.
a.		1p carmine	42,500.	4,000.
b.		1p red	50,000.	5,000.
c.		1p milky blue (error)	200,000.	32,500.
d.		1p pale blue (error)		36,000.
9	A2	4p milky blue	40,000.	2,500.
a.		4p pale blue	42,000.	3,250.
b.		4p blue	45,000.	3,500.
c.		4p dark blue	120,000.	5,750.
d.		As #9, right corner retouched		7,750.
e.		As #9a, right corner retouched		7,750.
f.		4p vermilion (error)	200,000.	65,000.
g.		4p carmine (error)		112,500.

Nos. 7 and 9 are usually called Wood Blocks. The plates were made locally and composed of clichés mounted on wood. The errors were caused by a cliché of each value being mounted in the plate of the other value.
In 1883 plate proofs of both values on white paper, usually called "reprints," were made. The 1p is in dull orange red; the 4p in dark blue. These are known canceled, as a few were misused as stamps. The proofs do not include the errors.
Counterfeits exist.

Printed by De La Rue & Co.

			Wmk. 15	Engr.
1863-64				
12	A1	1p dark carmine	325.00	325.00
a.		1p reddish brown	650.00	350.00
b.		1p brownish red	650.00	350.00
13	A1	4p dark blue	325.00	135.00
a.		4p slate blue	2,500.	600.00
14	A1	6p purple	450.00	500.00
15	A1	1sh emerald	675.00	725.00
a.		1sh pale emerald	1,400.	

Nos. 12-15 can be distinguished from Nos. 3-6 not only by colors but because Nos. 12-15 often appear in a granular ink or with the background lightly printed in whole or part.
No. 12a, Wmk. 1, is believed to be a proof. Value, $29,000.
Counterfeits exist.

"Hope" and Symbols of Colony — A3

Frame Line Around Stamp

		Typo.	Wmk. 1	Perf. 14
1864-77				
16	A3	1p rose ('65)	130.00	42.50
17	A3	4p blue ('65)	210.00	4.50
a.		4p pale blue		4.50
b.		4p dull ultramarine	350.00	65.00
c.		4p deep blue ('72)	275.00	4.50
18	A3	6p bright vio ('77)	235.00	1.75
a.		6p dull violet	375.00	8.25
b.		6p pale lilac	225.00	28.00
19	A3	1sh yellow green	225.00	4.75
a.		1sh blue green	250.00	6.00
		Nos. 16-19 (4)	800.00	53.50

Imperf. stamps are believed to be proofs.
For surcharges see Nos. 20-21, N3.
For types A3 and A6 with manuscript surcharge of 1d or overprints "G. W." or "G," see Griqualand West listings.

Stamps of 1864 Surcharged in Red or Black

 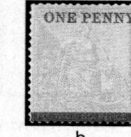

a   b

1868-74   **Red Surcharge**
20	A3(a)	4p on 6p	625.00	19.00
a.	"Peuce" for "Pence"		2,500.	900.00
b.	"Fonr" for "Four"			850.00
21	A3(b)	1p on 6p ('74)	800.00	140.00
a.	"E" of "PENNY" omitted			1,800.

Space between words and bars varies from 12½-16mm on No. 20, and 16½-18mm on No. 21.

1876   **Black Surcharge**
22	A3 (b)	1p on 1sh green	160.00	80.00

"Hope" and Symbols of Colony — A6

Without Frame Line Around Stamp
1871-81   **Perf. 14**
23	A6	½p gray black ('75)	37.50	17.50
24	A6	1p rose ('72)	55.00	1.25
25	A6	3p lilac rose ('80)	375.00	42.50
26	A6	3p claret ('81)	190.00	4.50
27	A6	4p blue ('76)	190.00	.90
a.	4p ultramarine		350.00	60.00
28	A6	5sh orange	650.00	25.00
	Nos. 23-28 (6)		1,498.	91.65

For surcharges see Nos. 29-32, 39, 55.

No. 27 Surcharged in Red

1879
29	A6	3p on 4p blue	200.00	3.00
a.	"THE.EE"		3,500.	350.00
b.	"PENCB"		4,000.	275.00
c.	Double surcharge		13,000.	4,500.
d.	As "a," double surcharge		—	—

Type of 1871 Surcharged in Black

1880
30	A6	3p on 4p lilac rose	145.00	3.25

No. 25 Surcharged in Black

e   f

31	A6(e)	3p on 3p lilac rose	400.00	12.00
a.	Inverted surcharge		13,000.	1,600.
32	A6(f)	3p on 3p lilac rose	130.00	2.25
a.	Inverted surcharge		1,600.	47.50

1882-83   **Wmk. 2**
33	A6	½p gray black	47.50	3.25
34	A6	1p rose	90.00	2.50
35	A6	2p bister	150.00	1.75
36	A6	3p claret	13.00	1.75
37	A3	6p bright violet	160.00	1.00
38	A6	5sh orange ('83)	950.00	300.00

For overprint see Rhodesia No. 49.

Nos. 26 and 36 Surcharged in Black

1882   **Wmk. 1**
39	A6	½p on 3p claret	7,000.	180.00
a.	Hyphen omitted			4,000.

Wmk. 2
40	A6	½p on 3p claret	60.00	8.00
a.	"ENNY"		2,500.	825.00
b.	"PENN"		2,000.	800.00
c.	Hyphen omitted		900.00	425.00

1884-98   **Wmk. 16**
41	A6	½p gray black ('86)	12.00	.25
42	A6	½p yel green ('96)	1.80	.60
43	A6	1p rose ('85)	15.00	.25
44	A6	2p bister	15.00	.25
45	A6	2p choc brown ('97)	4.00	3.50
46	A6	3p red violet ('98)	25.00	1.20
47	A6	4p blue ('90)	26.00	1.50
48	A6	4p pale ol grn ('97)	12.00	4.25
49	A3	6p violet	16.00	.50
50	A3	1sh dull bluish grn ('89)	180.00	1.25
51	A6	1sh blue grn ('94)	110.00	8.50
52	A6	1sh yel buff ('96)	19.00	3.25
53	A6	5sh orange ('87)	190.00	9.50
54	A6	5sh brown org ('96)	140.00	5.00
	Nos. 41-54 (14)		765.80	39.80

For surcharges see Nos. 58, 162, 165-166.
For overprints see Rhodesia Nos. 43, 45-48.

Type of 1871 Surcharged in Black

1891, Mar.
55	A6	2½p on 3p deep magenta	8.00	.25
a.	"1" of "½" has straight serif		95.00	37.50

Hope Seated — A13

1892-96
56	A13	2½p sage green	26.00	.25
57	A13	2½p ultra ('96)	13.00	.25

For surcharge see No. N4. For overprint see Orange River Colony No. 55.

No. 44 Surcharged in Black

1893, Mar.
58	A6	1p on 2p bister	6.00	.60
a.	Double surcharge			600.00
b.	No period after "PENNY"		100.00	25.00

Hope Standing — A15

1893-1902
59	A15	½p green ('98)	11.00	.25
60	A15	1p carmine	4.00	.25
61	A15	3p red violet ('02)	8.00	3.50
	Nos. 59-61 (3)		23.00	4.00

For surcharges see Nos. 163-164, N2. For overprints see Orange River Colony Nos. 54, 56, Rhodesia No. 44, Transvaal Nos. 236-236A.

Table Mountain and Bay; Coat of Arms — A16

1900, Jan.
62	A16	1p carmine rose	8.50	.25

King Edward VII — A17

Various frames.

1902-04   **Wmk. 16**
63	A17	½p emerald	4.00	.25
64	A17	1p car rose	3.50	.25
65	A17	2p brown ('04)	24.00	.95
66	A17	2½p ultra ('04)	5.75	13.00
67	A17	3p red violet ('03)	18.50	1.40
68	A17	4p ol green ('03)	20.00	.80
69	A17	6p violet ('03)	30.00	.60
70	A17	1sh bister	20.00	1.25
71	A17	5sh brown org ('03)	175.00	27.50
	Nos. 63-71 (9)		300.75	46.00

Imperf. stamps are proofs.

Cape of Good Hope stamps were replaced by those of Union of South Africa.

ISSUED IN MAFEKING

Excellent forgeries of Nos. 162-179 are known.

Stamps of Cape of Good Hope Surcharged

1900, Mar. 24
162	A6	1p on ½p grn	325.00	85.00
163	A15	1p on ½p grn	375.00	125.00
164	A15	3p on 1p rose	325.00	65.00
165	A6	6p on 3p red vio	45,000.	350.00
166	A6	1sh on 4p pale ol grn	8,000.	425.00

Stamps of Bechuanaland Protectorate Surcharged

1900   **Wmk. 30**
167	A54	1p on ½p ver	325.00	85.00
a.	Inverted surcharge		—	8,000.
b.	Vert. pair, surcharge tête bêche			40,000.
168	A40	3p on 1p lilac	1,000.	155.00
a.	Double surcharge			37,500.
169	A56	6p on 2p grn & car	3,000.	125.00
170	A58	6p on 3p vio, yel	7,500.	425.00
a.	Inverted surcharge			42,500.
b.	Double surcharge			

The lettering of "Mafeking Besieged" shows varying breaks in various letters, and may have either a period or no punctuation after "Mafeking."

On Stamps of Bechuanaland
Wmk. 29
171	A1	6p on 3p vio & blk	550.00	95.00

Wmk. 30
172	A59	1sh on 4p brn & grn	1,650.	110.00
a.	Double surch., one inverted		—	30,000.
b.	Triple surcharge		—	30,000.
c.	Inverted surcharge		—	
d.	Double surcharge		—	30,000.

Stamps of Bechuanaland Protectorate Surcharged

173	A40	3p on 1p lil	1,100.	100.00
a.	Double surcharge		—	11,000.
174	A56	6p on 2p grn & car	1,600.	100.00
175	A62	1sh on 6p vio, rose	7,500.	130.00

On Stamps of Bechuanaland
176	A62	1sh on 6p vio, rose	45,000.	900.00
177	A65	2sh on 1sh green	15,000.	650.00

Sgt. Major Goodyear M1   Gen. Robert S. S. Baden-Powell M2

Wmk. OCEANA FINE Photographic Print
1900, Apr.   **Perf. 12**
Laid Paper
178	M1	1p blue, *blue*	1,300.	475.00
	On cover			12,000.
a.	Imperf. pair		27,000.	
179	M2	3p blue, *blue*, 18½mm wide	1,900.	525.00
	On cover			9,000.
a.	Horiz. pair, imperf. between		—	120,000.
b.	Double impression		—	30,000.
c.	Reversed design		120,000.	80,000.
180	M2	3p blue, *blue*, 21mm wide	13,000.	1,650.
	On cover			16,500.
a.	3p deep blue		15,000.	1,500.
	On cover			18,000.

The color of the paper varies from pale to deep blue.

OCEANA FINE is a sheet watermark and does not appear on every stamp.

Imperfs of No. 178 are proofs.

There is one used pair of No. 179a privately owned. A single used, partially imperf. example of No. 179 exists. Value, $45,000. There are four used examples of No. 179b reported. There are 2 unused and 6 used examples of No. 179c privately owned.

Issued: No. 179, Apr. 6; Nos. 178 and 180, Apr. 10.

ISSUED IN VRYBURG

Under Boer Occupation

Cape of Good Hope Stamps of 1884-96 Surcharged

"Z.A.R." stands for Zuid Afrikaansche Republiek (South African Republic).

Two Types of Surcharge:
Type I — Surcharge 10mm high. Space between lines 5½mm.
Type II — Surcharge 12mm high. Space between lines 7½mm.

1899, Nov.   **Wmk. 16**   **Perf. 14**
N1	A6	½p on ½p emer (I)	240.	95.
a.	Type II		2,000.	825.
N2	A15	1p on 1p rose (I)	275.	120.
a.	Double surcharge			
b.	Type II		2,250.	950.
N3	A3	2p on 6p vio (II)	2,500.	600.
N4	A13	2½p on 2½p ultra (I)	2,000.	500.
a.	Type II		12,000.	5,000.

"Z.A.R." stands for Zuid Afrikaansche Republiek (South African Republic).
The italic "Z" variety (Nos. N1b-N4b) occurs in one position in the setting of 60.

Under British Occupation

Transvaal Stamps of
1895-96 Handstamped

1900		Unwmk.	*Perf. 12½*
N5	A13	½p green	— 3,500.
N6	A13	1p rose & grn	14,000. 6,000.
N7	A13	2p brown & grn	— 47,500.
N8	A13	2½p ultra & grn	— 47,500.

No. N5 exists used with double handstamp.
Nos. N5 and N6 exist inverted (overprint reading down).

CAPE VERDE

ˈkāp ˈvərd

LOCATION — A group of 10 islands and five islets in the Atlantic Ocean, about 500 miles due west of Senegal.
GOVT. — Republic
AREA — 1,557 sq. mi.
POP. — 405,748 (1999 est.)
CAPITAL — Praia

The Portuguese territory of Cape Verde became independent on July 5, 1975.

1000 Reis = 1 Milreis
100 Centavos = 1 Escudo (1913)

Catalogue values for unused stamps in this country are for Never Hinged items, beginning with Scott 268 in the regular postage section, Scott J31 in the postage due section, and Scott RA6 in the postal tax section.

Crown of Portugal — A1

1877		Unwmk. Typo.	*Perf. 12½*
1	A1	5r black	6.00 2.00
2	A1	10r yellow	70.00 11.00
3	A1	20r bister	3.00 1.40
4	A1	25r rose	2.50 1.40
5	A1	40r blue	85.00 50.00
b.		Cliche of Mozambique in Cape Verde plate, in pair with #5	2,200. 1,400.
6	A1	50r green	165.00 72.50
7	A1	100r lilac	8.25 3.50
8	A1	200r orange	6.00 3.75
9	A1	300r brown	7.00 3.75
		Nos. 1-9 (9)	352.75 150.80

For expanded treatment of Nos. 1-9, see the *Scott Classic Catalogue.*

1881-85			*Perf. 12½*
10	A1	10r green	2.75 2.10
11	A1	20r carmine ('85)	5.50 3.75
12	A1	25r violet ('85)	4.00 3.00
13	A1	40r yellow buff	2.40 1.75
a.		Imperf.	40.00
b.		Cliche of Mozambique in Cape Verde plate, in pair with #13	110.00 110.00
c.		As "b," imperf.	
14	A1	50r blue	7.00 4.25
		Nos. 10-14 (5)	21.65 14.85

Reprints of the 1877-85 issues are on smooth white chalky paper, ungummed, and on thin white paper with shiny white gum. They are perf 13½.
For expanded treatment of nos. 10-14, see the *Scott Classic Catalogue.*

King Luiz — A2

1886		Embossed	*Perf. 12½, 13½*
		Chalk-Surfaced Paper	
15	A2	5r black	4.50 3.00
16	A2	10r green	6.75 3.00
17	A2	20r carmine	9.00 5.25
18	A2	25r violet	10.00 5.50
19	A2	40r chocolate	10.00 3.50
20	A2	50r blue	10.00 3.50
21	A2	100r yel brown	10.00 4.00
22	A2	200r gray lilac	20.00 10.50
23	A2	300r orange	24.00 4.25
		Nos. 15-23 (9)	104.25 43.00

The 25r, 50r and 100r have been reprinted in aniline colors with clean-cut Perf. 13½.
For expanded treatment of nos. 15-19, see the *Scott Classic Catalogue.*
For surcharges see Nos. 59-67, 184-187.

King Carlos — A3

1894-95		Typo.	*Perf. 11½, 12½, 13½*
24	A3	5r orange	3.00 1.25
25	A3	10r redsh violet	3.00 1.25
26	A3	15r chocolate	5.00 2.60
a.		Perf. 12½	150.00 120.00
27	A3	20r lavender	4.00 2.60
28	A3	25r dp green	4.00 2.25
a.		Perf. 12½	4.00 3.25
29	A3	50r lt blue	4.00 2.25
a.		Perf. 13 1/2	14.00 4.50
30	A3	75r carmine ('95)	11.50 5.75
a.		Perf. 13½	55.00 42.00
31	A3	80r yel grn ('95)	12.00 6.50
a.		Perf. 13½	45.00 35.00
32	A3	100r brn, *buff* ('95)	12.00 5.25
a.		Perf. 12½	100.00 55.00
33	A3	150r car, *rose* ('95)	50.00 27.00
a.		Perf. 12½	400.00 300.00
b.		Perf. 11½	70.00 45.00
34	A3	200r dk blue, *lt blue* ('95)	50.00 27.00
a.		Perf. 12½	150.00 120.00
35	A3	300r dk blue, *sal* ('95)	60.00 17.00
		Nos. 24-35 (12)	218.50 100.70

For surcharges see Nos. 68-78, 137, 189-193, 201-205.

King Carlos — A4

1898-1903			*Perf. 11½*
		Name and Value in Black except 500r	
36	A4	2½r gray	.40 .30
37	A4	5r orange	.50 .30
38	A4	10r lt green	.55 .30
39	A4	15r brown	5.50 2.00
40	A4	15r gray grn ('03)	1.90 1.25
41	A4	20r gray violet	1.60 1.00
42	A4	25r sea green	3.50 1.25
a.		Perf 12½	300.00 180.00
43	A4	25r carmine ('03)	1.00 .40
44	A4	50r dark blue	3.50 1.50
45	A4	50r brown ('03)	3.75 2.40
46	A4	65r slate blue ('03)	60.00 30.00
47	A4	75r rose	10.00 3.50
48	A4	75r lilac ('03)	3.50 2.25
49	A4	80r violet	8.50 3.50
50	A4	100r dk blue, *blue*	3.50 2.00
51	A4	115r org brn, *pink* ('03)	15.00 13.50
52	A4	130r brown, *straw* ('03)	15.00 13.50
53	A4	150r brown, *straw* ('03)	10.00 6.75
54	A4	200r red vio, *pnksh*	4.00 3.00
55	A4	300r dk blue, *rose*	10.00 5.00
56	A4	400r dull blue, *straw* ('03)	16.00 10.50
57	A4	500r blk & red, *blue* ('01)	15.00 5.00
58	A4	700r violet, *yelsh* ('01)	30.00 17.50
		Nos. 36-58 (23)	222.70 126.70

For overprints and suecharges see Nos. 80-99, 139, 200.

Regular Issues Surcharged in Red or Black

Two spacing types of surcharge. See note above Angola No. 61.

On Issue of 1886

1902, Dec. 1			*Perf. 12½, 13½*
59	A2	65r on 5r black (R)	7.00 3.75
60	A2	65r on 200r gray lil	7.00 3.75
61	A2	65r on 300r orange	7.00 3.75
62	A2	115r on 10r green	7.00 3.75
63	A2	115r on 20r rose	7.00 3.75
a.		Perf 13½	60.00 35.00
64	A2	130r on 50r blue	7.00 3.75
65	A2	130r on 100r brown	7.00 3.75
66	A2	400r on 25r violet	6.00 2.60
67	A2	400r on 40r choc	12.00 3.75
a.		Perf 13½	50.00 35.00

On Issue of 1894

			Perf. 11½, 12½, 13½
68	A3	65r on 10r red vio	7.00 3.75
69	A3	65r on 20r lavender	7.00 3.75
70	A3	65r on 100r brn, *buff*	8.50 5.25
a.		Perf 12½	26.00 24.00
71	A3	115r on 5r orange	5.00 3.00
a.		Inverted surcharge	60.00 60.00
72	A3	115r on 25r blue grn	4.00 2.10
a.		Perf 11½	55.00 55.00
73	A3	115r on 150r car, *rose*	9.00 6.50
a.		Perf 13½	55.00 25.00
74	A3	130r on 75r car	5.00 3.00
a.		Perf 13½	250.00 200.00
75	A3	130r on 80r yel grn	4.00 2.00
76	A3	130r on 200r dk blue, *blue*	4.00 2.60
77	A3	400r on 50r lt blue	9.00 3.00
a.		Inverted surcharge	65.00 55.00
b.		Perf 13½	300.00 300.00
78	A3	400r on 300r dk blue, *sal*	4.00 1.75

On Newspaper Stamp of 1893

79	N1	400r on 2½r brown	1.60 1.50
a.		Inverted surcharge	30.00
b.		Perf 12½	225.00 200.00
		Nos. 59-79 (21)	135.10 70.80

Reprints of Nos. 59, 66, 67, and 77 have shiny white gum and clean-cut perforation 13½.
For overprint and surcharge see Nos. 137, 205-206.

Overprinted in Black On Nos. 39, 42, 44, 47

1902-03			*Perf. 11½*
80	A4	15r brown	2.00 1.25
81	A4	25r sea green	2.00 1.25
82	A4	50r blue ('03)	2.00 1.25
83	A4	75r rose ('03)	3.75 2.75
a.		Inverted overprint	42.50 42.50
		Nos. 80-83 (4)	9.75 6.50

For overprint see No. 139.

No. 46 Surcharged in Black

1905, July 1			
84	A4	50r on 65r slate blue	6.00 3.00

Stamps of 1898-1903 Overprinted in Carmine or Green

1911, Aug. 20			
85	A4	2½r gray	.25 .25
86	A4	5r orange	.25 .25
87	A4	10r lt green	1.00 .80
88	A4	15r gray green	.90 .45
89	A4	20r gray violet	1.50 .80
90	A4	25r carmine (G)	.90 .45
91	A4	50r brown	8.50 6.00
92	A4	75r red lilac	1.40 .80
93	A4	100r dk blue, *blue*	1.40 .80
94	A4	115r org brn, *pink*	1.40 .80
95	A4	130r brown, *straw*	1.40 .80
96	A4	200r red vio, *pnksh*	6.50 4.00
97	A4	400r dull bl, *straw*	3.50 1.25
98	A4	500r blk & red, *bl*	3.50 1.25
99	A4	700r violet, *straw*	3.50 1.40
		Nos. 85-99 (15)	35.90 20.10

King Manuel II — A5

Overprinted in Carmine or Green

1912			*Perf. 11½x12*
100	A5	2½r violet	.25 .25
101	A5	5r black	.25 .25
102	A5	10r gray grn	.45 .40
103	A5	20r carmine (G)	2.40 1.40
104	A5	50r vio brown	.45 .25
105	A5	50r dk blue	5.00 3.50
106	A5	75r bister brn	1.10 1.00
107	A5	100r brown, *lt grn*	1.10 1.00
108	A5	200r dk green, *sal*	1.75 1.10
109	A5	300r black, *azure*	1.75 1.10
		Perf. 14½x15	
110	A5	400r black & blue	3.75 3.00
111	A5	500r ol grn & vio brn	3.75 3.00
		Nos. 100-111 (12)	22.00 16.25

Common Design Types pictured following the introduction.

Vasco da Gama Issue of Various Portuguese Colonies

Common Design Types CD20-CD27 Surcharged

On Stamps of Macao

1913, Feb. 13			*Perf. 12½ to 16*
112		¼c on ½a blue grn	3.00 .85
113		½c on 1a red	3.00 .85
114		1c on 2a red violet	3.00 .85
115		2½c on 4a yel grn	3.00 .85
116		5c on 8a dk blue	7.00 6.00
117		7½c on 12a vio brn	5.75 2.40
118		10c on 16a bister brn	2.25 1.60
119		15c on 24a bister	5.75 3.50
		Nos. 112-119 (8)	32.75 16.90

On Stamps of Portuguese Africa

			Perf. 14 to 15
120		¼c on 2½r bl grn	2.00 .60
121		½c on 5r red	2.00 .60
122		1c on 10r red vio	2.00 .60
123		2½c on 25r yel grn	2.00 .60
124		5c on 50r dk blue	2.00 1.50
125		7½c on 75r vio brn	3.75 3.00
126		10c on 100r bis brn	2.00 1.90
127		15c on 150r bister	2.50 2.50
		Nos. 120-127 (8)	18.25 11.30

On Stamps of Timor

128		¼c on ½a bl grn	2.00 .85
129		½c on 1a red	2.00 .85
130		1c on 2a red vio	2.00 .85
131		2½c on 4a yel grn	2.00 .85
132		5c on 8a dk blue	7.00 5.50
133		7½c on 12a vio brn	5.50 3.00
134		10c on 16a bis brn	2.25 1.90
135		15c on 24a bister	4.50 2.40
		Nos. 128-135 (8)	27.25 16.20
		Nos. 112-135 (24)	78.25 44.40

For surcharges see Nos. 197-198.

No. 75 Overprinted in Red

1913			*Perf. 11½, 12½, 13½*
137	A3	130r on 80r yel grn	6.00 3.75

Nos. 73 and 76 overprinted but not issued. Values, $20, $25.

Same Overprint on No. 83 in Green

1914			*Perf. 12*
139	A4	75r rose	6.00 3.75
a.		"PROVISORIO" double (G and R)	80.00 57.50

Ceres — A6

1914 Typo. Perf. 15x14
Name and Value in Black
Chalky Paper

144	A6	¼c olive brn	.75	.55
145	A6	½c black	.45	.30
146	A6	1c blue grn	5.25	4.75
147	A6	1½c lilac brown	.75	.55
148	A6	2c carmine	1.25	.70
149	A6	2½c lt violet	.60	.50
150	A6	5c deep blue	1.00	.80
151	A6	7½c yel brn	1.25	.70
152	A6	8c slate	1.25	.75
153	A6	10c orange brn	2.00	.90
154	A6	15c brn rose ('22)	8.50	5.00
155	A6	20c yel grn	2.00	.90
156	A6	30c brown, *grn*	5.00	3.00
157	A6	40c brown, *pink*	5.00	3.00
158	A6	50c orange, *sal*	5.00	3.00
159	A6	1e green, *blue*	3.00	3.00
		Nos. 144-159 (16)	43.05	28.40

1916
Enamel-Surfaced Paper

160	A6	¼c olive brn	.45	.30
161	A6	5c deep blue	.75	.45

Ordinary Paper

162	A6	¼c olive brn	.25	.25
163	A6	½c black	.25	.25
164	A6	1c blue grn	.85	.75
165	A6	1c yel grn ('22)	.25	.25
166	A6	1½c lilac brown	.25	.25
167	A6	2c carmine	.25	.25
168	A6	2½c lt violet	.25	.25
169	A6	3c org ('22)	.30	.25
170	A6	4c rose ('22)	.25	.25
171	A6	12c blue grn ('22)	.35	.25
172	A6	15c plum	.90	.75
		Nos. 162-172 (11)	4.15	3.75

1920-26 Perf. 12x11½

173	A6	¼c olive brn	.25	.25
174	A6	½c black	.25	.25
175	A6	1c yel grn ('22)	.25	.25
176	A6	1½c lilac brown	.25	.25
177	A6	2c carmine	.25	.25
178	A6	2c gray ('26)	.25	.25
179	A6	2½c lt violet	.25	.25
180	A6	3c org ('22)	2.40	2.25
181	A6	4c rose ('22)	.35	.50
182	A6	4½c gray ('22)	.25	.25
183	A6	5c brt blue ('22)	.25	.25
183A	A6	6c lilac ('22)	.25	.50
183B	A6	7c ultra ('22)	.25	.50
183C	A6	7½c yel brn	.25	.50
183D	A6	8c slate	.40	.30
183E	A6	10c orange brn	.25	.25
183F	A6	12c blue grn ('22)	.35	.25
183G	A6	15c plum	.30	.30
183H	A6	20c yel grn	.25	.25
183I	A6	24c ultra ('26)	1.50	1.40
183J	A6	25c choc ('26)	1.50	1.40
183K	A6	30c gray grn ('26)	.75	.25
183L	A6	40c turq blue ('22)	2.00	.25
183M	A6	50c violet ('26)	2.00	.30
183N	A6	60c dk blue ('22)	2.00	.45
183O	A6	60c rose ('26)	2.00	.45
183P	A6	80c brt rose ('22)	2.00	1.10
		Nos. 173-183P (27)	21.05	13.70

For surcharge see No. 214.

Glazed Paper

183Q	A6	1e rose ('22)	7.00	2.25
183R	A6	1e dp blue ('26)	9.00	1.50
183S	A6	2e dk violet ('22)	10.00	4.00
183T	A6	5e buff ('26)	45.00	12.00
183U	A6	10e pink ('26)	150.00	60.00
183V	A6	20e pale turq ('26)	200.00	80.00
		Nos. 183Q-183V (6)	421.00	159.75

Provisional Issue of 1902 Overprinted in Carmine

1915 Perf. 11½, 12½, 13½
184 A2 115r on 10r green
　(11½)　　　2.50　2.00
　a. Perf. 13½　　100.00　100.00
185 A2 115r on 20r rose
　(12½)　　　2.75　1.75
　a. Perf. 13½　　30.00　30.00
186 A2 130r on 50r blue
　(12½)　　　2.50　1.25
187 A2 130r on 100r brown
　(12½)　　　1.60　1.00

188 A3 115r on 5r org (11½)　1.40　.75
　a. Inverted overprint　　45.00
189 A3 115r on 25r blue grn
　(12½)　　　2.50　1.75
　a. Perf. 11½　　70.00　70.00
190 A3 115r on 150r car,
　rose (11½)　　1.00　.75
191 A3 130r on 75r car
　(12½)　　　2.50　1.00
192 A3 130r on 80r yel grn
　(11½)　　　2.50　1.00
　a. Inverted overprint　　50.00
193 A3 130r on 200r bl, *bl*
　(13½)　　　2.00　1.00
　a. Perf. 12½　　90.00　80.00
　Nos. 184-193 (10)　21.25　12.25

War Tax Stamps of Portuguese Africa Srchd.

1921, Feb. 3 Perf. 15x14
194 WT1 ¼c on 1c green　　.60　.40
195 WT1 ½c on 1c green　　.70　.50
　a. "1/2" instead of "½" as
　shown　　17.50　15.00
196 WT1 1c green　　　.65　.50
　　　Perf. 12x11½
194B WT1 ¼c on 1c green　1.20　1.00
195B WT1 ½c on 1c green　1.20　1.00
　a. "1/2" instead of "½" as
　shown　　25.00　19.00
196B WT1 1c green　　　1.10　.95
Nos. 194B-196B also exist on enameled paper. The values are the same.

Nos. 127 and 126 Surcharged

Perf. 14 to 15
197 CD27 2c on 15c on
　150r　　　2.25　1.50
198 CD26 4c on 10c on
　100r　　　2.75　2.60
　a. On No. 118 (error)　300.00　175.00
The 4c surcharge also exists on No. 134. Value, $500.

No. 50 Surcharged

Perf. 12
200 A4 6c on 100r dk bl, *bl*　2.75　2.10
　a. No accent on "U" of surcharge　17.50　15.00
　Nos. 194-200 (6)　9.70　7.60
No. 200 has an accent on the "U" of the surcharge.

Stamps of 1913-15 Surcharged

1922, Apr. Perf. 11½, 12½, 13½
On No. 137
201 A3 4c on 130r on 80r　1.25　1.25
On Nos. 191-193
202 A3 4c on 130r on 75r　1.60　1.60
203 A3 4c on 130r on 80r　1.25　1.25
204 A3 4c on 130r on 200r　1.00　.80
　a. Perf. 12½　　15.00　15.00
　Nos. 201-204 (4)　5.10　4.90
Surcharge of Nos. 201-204 with smaller $ occurs once in sheet of 28. Value eight times normal.

Nos. 78-79 Surcharged

1925 Perf. 13½, 11½
205 A3 40c on 400r on 300r　1.50　.80
206 N1 40c on 400r on 2½r　1.50　.75

No. 176 Surcharged

1931, Nov. Perf. 12x11½
214 A6 70c on 80c brt rose　3.75　2.50

Ceres — A7

1934, May 1 Wmk. 232

215	A7	1c bister	.25	.25
216	A7	5c olive brown	.25	.25
217	A7	10c violet	.25	.25
218	A7	15c black	.25	.25
219	A7	20c gray	.25	.25
220	A7	30c dk green	.25	.25
221	A7	40c red org	.25	.25
222	A7	45c brt blue	2.00	.85
223	A7	50c brown	.90	.55
224	A7	60c olive grn	.90	.55
225	A7	70c brown org	.90	.55
226	A7	80c emerald	.90	.55
227	A7	85c deep rose	4.00	2.60
228	A7	1e maroon	2.75	.50
229	A7	1.40e dk blue	3.75	3.00
230	A7	2e dk violet	4.50	2.60
231	A7	5e apple green	21.00	5.00
232	A7	10e olive bister	32.50	18.00
233	A7	20e orange	60.00	24.00
		Nos. 215-233 (19)	135.85	60.50

For surcharge see No. 256.

Vasco da Gama Issue
Common Design Types
1938 Unwmk. Perf. 13½x13
Name and Value in Black

234	CD34	1c gray green	.25	.25
235	CD34	5c orange brn	.25	.25
236	CD34	10c dk carmine	.25	.25
237	CD34	15c dk vio brn	1.00	.85
238	CD34	20c slate	.50	.25
239	CD35	30c rose vio	.50	.25
240	CD35	35c brt green	.50	.25
241	CD35	40c brown	.50	.25
242	CD35	50c brt red vio	.50	.25
243	CD36	60c gray blk	.50	.25
244	CD36	70c brown vio	.50	.25
245	CD36	80c orange	.45	.25
246	CD36	1e red	.60	.25
247	CD37	1.75e blue	1.90	.70
248	CD37	2e dk blue grn	3.50	2.00
249	CD37	5e ol grn	8.00	2.00
250	CD38	10e blue vio	13.00	2.60
251	CD38	20e red brown	37.50	5.00
		Nos. 234-251 (18)	70.20	16.15

For surcharges see Nos. 255, 271-276, 288-292.

Outline Map of Africa — A8

1939, June 23 Litho. Perf. 11½x12
252 A8 80c vio, *pale rose*　5.00　3.50
253 A8 1.75e blue, *pale bl*　40.00　30.00
254 A8 20e brown, *buff*　85.00　26.00
　Nos. 252-254 (3)　130.00　59.50
Visit of the President of Portugal in 1939.

Nos. 239 and 221 Surcharged with New Value and Bars in Black
1948 Unwmk. Perf. 13½x13
255 CD35 10c on 30c rose violet　2.00　1.25
　　　Perf. 12x11½
　　　Wmk. 232
256 A7 25c on 40c red orange　2.00　1.25

Machado Pt., Sao Vicente — A9

Brava Creek, Sao Nicoláo — A10

Designs: 10c, Ribeira Grande. 1e, Harbor, Sao Vicente. 1.75e, Mindelo, distant view. 2e, Joao de Evora Beach. 5e, Mindelo. 10e, Volcano, Fire Island. 20e, Mt. Paul.

Perf. 14½
1948, Oct. 1 Litho. Unwmk.

257	A9	5c vio brn & bis	.35	.30
258	A9	10c ol grn & pale grn	.35	.30
259	A10	50c mag & lil rose	.65	.30
260	A10	1e brn vio & rose lil	2.00	1.25
261	A10	1.75e ultra & grnsh bl	3.00	2.25
262	A10	2e dk brn & buff	6.00	2.00
263	A10	5e ol grn & yel	12.00	5.00
264	A10	10e red & cream	22.50	16.00
265	A10	20e dk vio & bis	50.00	32.00
		Nos. 257-265 (9)	96.85	59.40

Lady of Fatima Issue
Common Design Type
1948, Dec.
266 CD40 50c dark blue　8.50　4.50

UPU Symbols — A10a

1949, Oct. Perf. 14
267 A10a 1e red vio & pink　7.00　3.00
UPU, 75th anniversary.

Catalogue values for unused stamps in this section, from this point to the end of the section, are for **Never Hinged** items.

Holy Year Issue
Common Design Types
1950, May Perf. 13x13½
268 CD41 1e orange brown　1.00　.45
269 CD42 2e slate　　3.75　1.75

Holy Year Conclusion Issue
Common Design Type
1951, Oct. Unwmk. Perf. 14
270 CD43 2e pur & lil + label　1.50　1.25
Stamps without labels sell for less.

Nos. 240, 244-245, 247, 250 Surcharged with New Value and Bars
Perf. 13½x13
1951, May 21 Unwmk.

271	CD35	10c on 35c	.70	.55
272	CD36	20c on 70c	.90	.65
273	CD36	40c on 70c	1.10	.65
274	CD36	50c on 80c	1.10	.65
275	CD37	1e on 1.75e	1.25	.65
276	CD38	2e on 10e	5.75	2.00
	a.	1e on 10e	250.00	125.00
		Nos. 271-276 (6)	10.80	5.15

Map of Cape Verde Islands, 1502 — A11

Vicente Dias and Gonçalo de Cintra A12

Portraits: 30c, Diogo Alfonso and Alvaro Fernandes. 50c, Lançarote and Soeiro da Costa. 1e, Diogo Gomes and Antonio da Nola. 2e, Prince Fernando and Prince Henry the Navigator. 3e, Antao Gonçalves and Dinis Dias. 5e, Alfonso Goncalves Baldaia and Joao Fernandes. 10e, Dinis Eanes da Gra and Alvaro de Freitas. 20e, Map of Cape Verde Islands, 1502.

1952, Feb. 24			Perf. 14	
277	A11	5c multicolored	.25	.25
278	A12	10c multicolored	.25	.25
279	A12	30c multicolored	.25	.25
280	A12	50c multicolored	.25	.25
281	A12	1e multicolored	.25	.25
282	A12	2e multicolored	1.50	.25
283	A12	3e multicolored	11.50	1.50
284	A12	5e multicolored	4.00	.70
285	A12	10e multicolored	8.00	1.75
286	A11	20e multicolored	14.00	2.40
		Nos. 277-286 (10)	40.25	7.85

Medical Congress Issue
Common Design Type

Design: Hypodermic Injection.

1952, June		Perf. 13½	
287	CD44 20c ol grn & dk brn	.70	.50

No. 247 Surcharged with New Values and "X" in Black

1952, Jan. 25			Perf. 13½x13	
288	CD37	10c on 1.75e	2.00	1.10
289	CD37	20c on 1.75e	2.00	1.10
290	CD37	50c on 1.75e	8.00	5.00
291	CD37	1e on 1.75e	1.50	.25
292	CD37	1.50e on 1.75e	1.50	.25
		Nos. 288-292 (5)	15.00	7.70

Facade of Jeronymos Convent A13

		Perf. 13½	
1953, Jan.		**Unwmk.**	**Litho.**
293	A13 10c brown & pale olive	.25	.25
294	A13 50c purple & fawn	.90	.40
295	A13 1e dark green & fawn	2.10	1.10
	Nos. 293-295 (3)	3.25	1.75

Exhibition of Sacred Missionary Art held at Lisbon in 1951.

Stamp of Portugal and Arms of Colonies — A13a

1953		Photo.	
296	A13a 50c multicolored	1.75	1.10

Centenary of Portuguese stamps.

Sao Paulo Issue
Common Design Type

1954		Litho.	Perf. 13½	
297	CD46 1e green, cream & gray	.70	.60

Belem Tower, Lisbon, and Colonial Arms — A14

1955, May 15		Litho.	Perf. 13½	
298	A14	1e multicolored	.50	.25
299	A14	1.60e buff & multi	.75	.60

Visit of Pres. Francisco H. C. Lopes.

Arms of Praia — A15

1958, June 14		Perf. 12x11½	
300	A15 1e multicolored	.65	.45
301	A15 2.50e pink & multi	1.10	.90

Centenary of city of Praia.

Fair Emblem, Globe and Arms — A15a

1958		Perf. 12x11½	
302	A15a 2e multicolored	.90	.40

World's Fair, Brussels, Apr. 17-Oct. 19.

Tropical Medicine Congress Issue
Common Design Type

1958, Sept. 5		Perf. 13½	
303	CD47 3e Aloe vera	5.50	2.10

Prince Henry — A16

1960, June 25		Litho.	Perf. 13½	
304	A16 2e multicolored	.50	.25

500th anniv. of the death of Prince Henry the Navigator.

Antonio da Nola — A17

Design: 2.50e, Diogo Gomes.

1960, Oct.		Unwmk.	Perf. 14½	
305	A17 1e multicolored	.75	.45
306	A17 2.50e multicolored	2.50	1.00

Discovery of Cape Verde, 500th anniv.

School Children A18

1960			
307	A18 2.50e multicolored	1.25	.65

10th anniv. of the Commission for Technical Cooperation in Africa South of the Sahara (C.C.T.A.).

Arms of Praia — A19

Arms of various cities & towns of Cape Verde.

1961, July		Litho.	Perf. 13½	
308	A19	5c shown	.25	.25
309	A19	15c Nova Sintra	.25	.25
310	A19	20c Ribeira Brava	.25	.25
311	A19	30c Assomada	.25	.25
312	A19	1e Maio	.65	.25
313	A19	2e Mindelo	.65	
314	A19	2.50e Santa Maria	1.00	.25
315	A19	3e Pombas	2.00	.50
316	A19	5e Sal-Rei	2.00	.50
317	A19	7.50e Tarrafal	3.00	.90
318	A19	15e Maria Pia	5.00	.90
319	A19	30e San Felipe	9.00	2.50
		Nos. 308-319 (12)	24.30	7.05

Sports Issue
Common Design Type

Sports: 50c, Javelin. 1e, Discus. 1.50e, Cricket. 2.50e, Boxing. 4.50e, Hurdling. 12.50e, Golf.

1962, Jan. 18			Perf. 13½	
320	CD48	50c lt brown	.25	.25
321	CD48	1e lt green	.75	.25
322	CD48	1.50e lt blue grn	10.00	2.00
323	CD48	2.50e pale vio bl	.75	.35
324	CD48	4.50e orange	1.10	.75
325	CD48	12.50e beige	2.40	1.60
		Nos. 320-325 (6)	15.25	5.20

Anti-Malaria Issue
Common Design Type

Design: Anopheles pretoriensis.

1962		Litho.	Perf. 13½	
326	CD49 2.50e multicolored	1.40	.90

Airline Anniversary Issue
Common Design Type

1963, Oct.		Unwmk.	Perf. 14½	
327	CD50 2.50e gray & multi	1.10	.70

National Overseas Bank Issue
Common Design Type

Design: 1.50e, Jose da Silva Mendes Leal.

1964, May 16		Perf. 13½	
328	CD51 1.50e multicolored	1.10	.75

ITU Issue
Common Design Type

1965, May 17		Litho.	Perf. 14½	
329	CD52 2.50e buff & multi	2.10	1.40

Militia Drummer, 1806 — A20

Designs: 1e, Soldier, Militia, 1806. 1.50e, Grenadier officer, 1833. 2.50e, Grenadier, 1833. 3e, Cavalry officer, 1834. 4e, Grenadier, 1835. 5e, Artillery officer, 1848. 10e, Drum major, infantry, 1856.

1965, Dec. 1			Litho.	Perf. 14½	
330	A20	50c multicolored	.25	.25
331	A20	1e multicolored	.45	.25
332	A20	1.50e multicolored	.45	.40
333	A20	2.50e multicolored	1.25	.35
334	A20	3e multicolored	2.50	.55
335	A20	4e multicolored	1.10	.55
336	A20	5e multicolored	1.25	.55
337	A20	10e multicolored	2.75	1.75
		Nos. 330-337 (8)	10.00	4.65

National Revolution Issue
Common Design Type

1e, Dr. Adriano Moreira School & Health Center.

1966, May 28		Litho.	Perf. 12	
338	CD53 1e multicolored	.60	.45

Navy Club Issue
Common Design Type

Designs: 1e, Capt. Fontoura da Costa and gunboat Mandovy. 1.50e, Capt. Carvalho Araujo and minesweeper Augusto Castilho.

1967, Jan. 31		Litho.	Perf. 13	
339	CD54	1e multicolored	.75	.50
340	CD54	1.50e multicolored	1.25	.90

Virgin Mary Statue — A21

1967, May 13		Litho.	Perf. 12½x13	
341	A21 1e multicolored	.35	.25

50th anniv. of the apparition of the Virgin Mary to 3 shepherd children at Fatima.

Pres. Rodrigues Thomaz — A22

1968, Feb. 9		Litho.	Perf. 13½	
342	A22 1e multicolored	.35	.25

Issued to commemorate the 1968 visit of Pres. Americo de Deus Rodrigues Thomaz.

Cabral Issue

Pedro Alvares Cabral — A23

1e, Cantino's world map, 1502, horiz.

1968, Apr. 22		Litho.	Perf. 14	
343	A23	1e multicolored	.85	.70
344	A23	1.50e multicolored	1.40	.75

See note after Angola No. 545.
For overprint see No. 365.

Sao Vicente Harbor — A24

Physic Nut — A25

Designs: 1.50e, Peanut plant. 2.50e, Castor-oil plant. 3.50e, Yams. 4e, Date palm. 4.50e, Guavas. 5e, Tamarind. 10e, Bitter cassava. 30e, Woman carrying fruit baskets.

1968, Oct. 15			Litho.	Perf. 14	
345	A24	50c multicolored	.25	.25
346	A25	1e multicolored	.50	.25
347	A25	1.50e multicolored	.50	.25
348	A25	2.50e multicolored	.50	.25
349	A25	3.50e multicolored	.50	.25
350	A25	4e multicolored	.50	.25
351	A25	4.50e multicolored	1.00	.25
352	A25	5e multicolored	2.00	.30
353	A25	10e multicolored	2.00	.60
354	A25	30e multicolored	4.00	2.50
		Nos. 345-354 (10)	11.75	5.15

For overprint see No. 372.

Admiral Coutinho Issue
Common Design Type

Adm. Coutinho & map showing route of 1st flight from Lisbon to Rio de Janeiro.

1969, Feb. 17   Litho.   Perf. 14
355 CD55 30c multi, vert.   .35   .25
For surcharge see No. 388.

Vasco da Gama Issue

Vasco da Gama — A26

1969, Aug. 29   Litho.   Perf. 14
356 A26 1.50e multicolored   .35   .25
Vasco da Gama (1469-1524), navigator.

Administration Reform Issue
Common Design Type

1969, Sept. 25   Litho.   Perf. 14
357 CD56 2e multicolored   .35   .25

King Manuel I Issue

King Manuel I — A27

1969, Dec. 1   Litho.   Perf. 14
358 A27 3e multicolored   .55   .35
500th anniv. of the birth of King Manuel I.

Marshal Carmona Issue
Common Design Type

Design: 2.50e, Antonio Oscar Carmona in marshal's uniform.

1970, Nov. 15   Litho.   Perf. 14
359 CD57 2.50e multi   .55   .35
    Nos. 359 (1)   .55   .35

Galleons on Sanaga River — A28

1972, May 25   Litho.   Perf. 13
360 A28 5e lilac rose & multi   1.00   .30
4th centenary of the publication of The Lusiads by Luiz Camoens.

Olympic Games Issue
Common Design Type

4e, Basketball & boxing, Olympic emblem.

1972, June 20   Perf. 14x13½
361 CD59 4e multicolored   .65   .30
For surcharge see No. 371.

Lisbon-Rio de Janeiro Flight Issue
Common Design Type

Design: "Lusitania" landing at San Vicente.

1972, Sept. 20   Litho.   Perf. 13½
362 CD60 3.50e multi   1.50   .30

WMO Centenary Issue
Common Design Type

1973, Dec. 15   Litho.   Perf. 14
363 CD61 2.50e ultra & multi   .65   .30
For overprint see No. 387.

Mindelo Desalination Plant — A29

1974   Litho.   Perf. 13½
364 A29 4e multicolored   1.25   .85
Opening of the Mindelo desalination plant. For surcharge see No. 371A.

Republic

No. 343 Overprinted

1975, Dec. 19   Litho.   Perf. 14
365 A23 1e multicolored   .35   .25
Proclamation of Independence.

Amilcar Cabral, Flag and Crowd — A30

1976, Jan. 20
366 A30 5e multicolored   .55   .25
3rd anniv. of the assassination of Amilcar Cabral (1924-73), revolutionary leader.

Rising Sun, Coat of Arms, Liberated People — A31

1976, July 5   Litho.   Perf. 14
367 A31 50c multicolored   .25   .25
368 A31 3e multicolored   .90   .25
369 A31 15e multicolored   2.00   .35
370 A31 50e multicolored   6.25   1.25
 a. Miniature sheet, #367-370   12.00   12.00
    Nos. 367-370 (4)   9.40   2.10
First anniversary of independence.

Nos. 351, 361, 364 Overprinted

1976   Litho.   Perf. 14
371   CD59 4e multi   1,150.   —
371A A29 4e multi   50.00   27.50
372   A25 4.50e multi   4.25   2.25

Amilcar Cabral, Map and Flag of Cape Verde A32

1976, Sept. 19   Perf. 14
373 A32 1e multicolored   .45   .25
Party of Intl. Action (PAICC), 20th anniv.

Electronic Tree and ITU Emblem — A33

1977, May 17   Litho.   Perf. 13½x13
374 A33 5.50e multi   .45   .25
World Telecommunications Day.

Ashtray — A34

Carved Coconut Shells: 30c, Bell on stand. 50c, Lamp with Adam and Eve. 1e, Hollow shell with Nativity. 1.50e, Desk lamp. 5e, Jar. 10e, Jar with hinged cover. 20e, Tobacco jar with palms. 30e, Stringed instrument.

1977, July 5   Litho.   Perf. 14
375 A34 20c lilac & multi   .25   .25
376 A34 30c rose & multi   .25   .25
377 A34 50c salmon & multi   .25   .25
378 A34 1e lt green & multi   .35   .25
379 A34 1.50e orange yel & multi   .35   .25
380 A34 5e gray & multi   .75   .35
381 A34 10e lt blue & multi   1.25   .55
382 A34 20e yellow & multi   2.00   1.25
383 A34 30e rose lilac & multi   3.25   1.40
    Nos. 375-383 (9)   8.70   4.80

Cape Verde No. 1 and Coat of Arms — A35

1977, Sept. 12   Litho.   Perf. 13½
384 A35 4e blue & multi   .40   .25
385 A35 8e lilac & multi   .80   .35
Centenary of Cape Verde stamps.

Congress Emblem — A36

1977, Nov. 15   Perf. 14
386 A36 3.50e multi   .60   .25
African Party of Independence of Guinea-Bissau and Cape Verde (PAIGC), 3rd cong., Nov. 15-20.

No. 363 Overprinted

1978, May 1   Perf. 12
387 CD61 2.50e ultra & multi   .60   .25

No. 355 Surcharged

1978, May 1   Perf. 14
388 CD55 3e on 30c multi   2.25   .35

Antenna and ITU Emblem — A37

1978, May 17   Litho.   Perf. 14
389 A37 3.50e silver & multi   .55   .25
10th World Telecommunications Day.

Freighter Cabo Verde — A38

1978, June 25   Litho.   Perf. 14
391 A38 1e multicolored   .70   .25
First ship of Cape Verde merchant marine.

Map of Africa and Equality Emblem — A39

1978, June 21
392 A39 4.50e multicolored   .55   .25
Anti-Apartheid Year.

Human Rights Emblem — A40

1978, Dec. 10   Litho.   Perf. 14
393 A40 1.50e multicolored   .35   .25
394 A40 2e multicolored   .55   .35
Universal Declaration of Human Rights, 30th anniversary.

Children and Balloons, IYC Emblem — A41

IYC Emblem and Child's Drawing: 3.50e,
Children and flowers.

1979, June 1   Litho.   Perf. 14
395 A41 1.50e multi   .65 .25
396 A41 3.50e multi   1.10 .35
International Year of the Child.

Pindjiguiti
Massacre
Monument — A42

1979, Aug. 3   Perf. 13
397 A42 4.50e multi   3.00 .25
Massacre of Pindjiguiti, 20th anniversary.

Natl. Youth Week
— A42a

1979, Sept. 1   Litho.   Perf. 14
397A A42a 3.50e Poster   1.10 .25

Centenary of Mindelo — A43

1980, Apr. 23   Litho.   Perf. 12½
398 A43 4e multicolored   .70 .25

Flag of Cape
Verde — A44

Stylized Bird,
"V" — A45

1980   Litho.   Perf. 12½
399 A44 4e multicolored   1.25 .25
400 A45 4e multicolored   .45 .25
401 A45 7e multicolored   .80 .35
402 A45 11e multicolored   1.10 .45
Nos. 399-402 (4)   3.60 1.30
5th anniversary of independence.
Issued: No. 399, June 1; others July 5.

A45a

1980, May 13
402A A45a 3.50e multi   .55 .25
402B A45a 4.50e multi   .70 .25
1980 Natl. census.

A46

1980, June 6
403 A46   1e Running   .25 .25
404 A46   2.50e Boxing   .25 .25
405 A46   3e Basketball   .35 .25
406 A46   4e Volleyball   .50 .30
407 A46   20e Swimming   1.40 .90
408 A46   50e Tennis   4.00 1.75
Nos. 403-408 (6)   6.75 3.70

Souvenir Sheet
Perf. 13
409 A46 30e Soccer, horiz.   18.00 18.00
22nd Summer Olympic Games, Moscow,
July 19-Aug. 3.

Thunnus
Alalunga
A47

4.50e, Trachurus trachurus. 8e, Muraena
helena. 10e, Corvina nigra. 12e, Katsuwonus
pelamis. 50e, Prionace glauca.

1980, Nov. 11   Litho.   Perf. 13
410 A47 50c shown   .25 .25
411 A47 4.50e multicolored   .50 .25
412 A47 8e multicolored   .90 .25
413 A47 10e multicolored   1.50 .35
414 A47 12e multicolored   2.00 .60
415 A47 50e multicolored   5.00 1.90
Nos. 410-415 (6)   10.15 3.60

Lochnera
Rosea — A48

4.50e, Poinciana regia-bojer. 8e, Mirabilis
jalapa. 10e, Nerium oleander. 12e, Bougainvil-
lia litoralis. 30e, Hibiscus.

1980, Dec. 29
416 A48 50c shown   .25 .25
417 A48 4.50e multicolored   .30 .25
418 A48 8e multicolored   .75 .35
419 A48 10e multicolored   .95 .45
420 A48 12e multicolored   1.10 .55
421 A48 30e multicolored   2.60 1.50
Nos. 416-421 (6)   5.95 3.35

WHO Anti-smoking Campaign — A48a

1980, Sept. 19   Perf. 12½
421A A48a 4e multicolored   .50 .25
421B A48a 7e multicolored   1.10 .35

Arca
Verde
A49

1980, Nov. 30 Litho.   Perf. 12½x12
422 A49 3e shown   .30 .25
423 A49 5.50e Ilha do Maio   .50 .25
424 A49 7.50e Ilha de Komo   .95 .55
425 A49 9e Boa Vista   1.25 .75
426 A49 12e Santo Antao   1.40 .55
427 A49 30e Santiago   3.25 1.40
Nos. 422-427 (6)   7.65 3.75

Hand-woven Bag, Map — A49a

Various hand-woven articles. 10e, vert.

1978, May 21   Litho.   Perf. 14
427A A49a 50c multi   .25 .25
427B A49a 1.50e multi   .25 .25
427C A49a 2e multi   .55 .25
427D A49a 3e multi   .55 .30
427E A49a 10e multi   1.40 .70
Nos. 427A-427E (5)   3.00 1.75

Desert Erosion Prevention
Campaign — A50

1981, Mar. 30   Litho.   Perf. 13
428 A50 4.50e multi   .60 .25
429 A50 10.50e multi   1.25 .50

6th Anniv. of
Constitution
A51

1981, Apr. 15
430 A51 4.50e multicolored   .60 .25

Souvenir Sheet

Austria No. B336 — A52

1981, May 18
431 A52 50e multicolored   6.50 6.50
WIPA '81 Philatelic Exhibition, Vienna, Austria, May 22-31.

Antenna — A53

1981, Aug. 25   Litho.   Perf. 12½
432 A53 4.50e shown   .65 .25
433 A53 8e Dish antenna   .95 .40
434 A53 20e Dish antenna, diff. 2.00 .95
Nos. 432-434 (3)   3.60 1.60

Intl. Year
of the
Disabled
A54

1981, Dec. 25   Litho.   Perf. 12½
435 A54 4.50e multicolored   .65 .35

Purple
Gallinule
A55

1981, Dec. 30
436 A55 1e Egret, vert.   .60 .25
437 A55 4.50e Barn owl, vert. 1.25 .40
438 A55 8e Passerine, vert.   2.75 .55
439 A55 10e shown   3.00 .65
440 A55 12e Guinea fowl   3.75 .75
Nos. 436-440 (5)   11.35 2.60

Souvenir Sheet
Perf. 13
441 A55 50e Razo Isld. lark   9.50 9.50
No. 441 contains 31x39mm one stamp.

CILSS Congress, Praia, Jan.
17 — A56

1982, Jan. 17   Perf. 13x12½
442 A56 11.50e multicolored   1.40 .65

Amilcar Cabral Soccer
Championship — A57

Designs: Soccer players and flags.

1982, Feb. 10   Litho.   Perf. 12½
443 A57 4.50e multicolored   .55 .25
444 A57 7.50e multicolored   .85 .40
445 A57 11.50e multicolored   1.40 .70
Nos. 443-445 (3)   2.80 1.35

1982 World
Cup — A58

Designs: Soccer players and ball.

1982, Apr. 25
446	A58	1.50e multi	.25	.25
447	A58	4.50e multi	.50	.25
448	A58	8e multi	.85	.35
449	A58	10.50e multi	1.00	.45
450	A58	12e multi	1.25	.55
451	A58	20e multi	2.25	.90
		Nos. 446-451 (6)	6.10	2.75

Souvenir Sheet
452	A58	50e multi	6.25	6.25

First Anniv. of Women's
Organization — A59

1982, Apr. 15   Litho.   Perf. 12½x12
453	A59	4.50e Marching	.55	.25
454	A59	8e Farming	1.10	.40
455	A59	12e Child care	1.60	.70
		Nos. 453-455 (3)	3.25	1.35

Estaleiros Navais Port, St. Vincent
A59a

1982, July 5   Litho.   Perf. 13x12½
455A	A59a	10.50e multi	1.75	.60

Natl. independence, 7th anniv.

Return of Barque Morrissey-
Ernestina — A60

1982, July 5   Litho.   Perf. 13
456	A60	12e multi	2.00	.80

Butterflies — A61

2e, Hypolimnas misippus. 4.50e, Melanitis
lede. 8e, Catopsilia florella. 10.50e, Colias
electo. 11.50e, Danaus chrysippus. 12e,
Papilio demodecus.

1982, July 27   Litho.
457	A61	2e multicolored	.35	.25
458	A61	4.50e multicolored	.70	.25
459	A61	8e multicolored	1.10	.35
460	A61	10.50e multicolored	1.50	.40

461	A61	11.50e multicolored	1.60	.60
462	A61	12e multicolored	2.75	.70
		Nos. 457-462 (6)	8.00	2.45

Francisco Xavier da Cruz (1905-1958),
Composer — A62

14e, Eugenio Tavares (1867-1930), poet.

1983, Feb. 20   Litho.   Perf. 13
463	A62	7e multicolored	.45	.30
464	A62	14e multicolored	1.90	.80

World Communications Year — A63

1983, Oct. 10   Litho.
465	A63	13e multicolored	1.60	.80

Local
Seashells — A64

1983, Nov. 30   Perf. 13½
466	A64	50c Conus ateralbus	.25	.25
467	A64	1e Conus decoratus	.25	.25
468	A64	3e Conus salreiensis	.35	.25
469	A64	10e Conus verdensis	1.50	.55
470	A64	50e Conus cuneolus	5.00	2.75
		Nos. 466-470 (5)	7.35	4.05

40th Anniv.
of Intl. Civil
Aviation
Org.
A65

Airplanes: 50c, Ogma-Auster D5/160, 1966.
2e, De Havilland DH-104 Dove, 1945. 10e,
Hawker Siddeley 748-200, 1972. 13e, De Hav-
illand Dragon Rapide, 1945. 20e, De Havilland
Twin Otter, 1977. 50e, Britten-Norman
Islander, 1971.

1984, Feb. 15   Litho.
471	A65	50c multicolored	.25	.25
472	A65	2e multicolored	.30	.25
473	A65	10e multicolored	1.10	.50
474	A65	13e multicolored	1.25	.85
475	A65	20e multicolored	1.90	1.25
476	A65	50e multicolored	4.50	2.50
		Nos. 471-476 (6)	9.30	5.60

Amilcar
Cabral — A66

1983, Jan. 17   Litho.   Perf. 14½
477	A66	7e multi	1.00	.50
478	A66	10.50e multi	1.50	.90
a.		Souvenir sheet of 2, #477-478	30.00	30.00

Amilcar Cabral Symposium, Jan. 17-20.
No. 478a sold for 30e.

Cross Over
Islands — A67

1983, Dec. 10   Photo.   Perf. 14½
479	A67	7e multicolored	1.10	.50

Christianity in Cape Verde, 450th anniv.

Natl. Solidarity
Campaign
A68

1984, Sept. 12   Perf. 13½
480	A68	6.50e multicolored	1.10	.25
481	A68	13.50e multicolored	2.10	.85

2nd Conference
of Natl. Women's
Orgs., Mar. 23-
27 — A69

1985, Mar. 27   Litho.   Perf. 13½
482	A69	8e multicolored	3.00	1.50

Miniature Sheet
483	A69	30e multicolored	100.00	100.00

Natl.
Independence,
10th
Anniv. — A70

1985, July 5   Litho.   Perf. 14
484	A70	8c multicolored	1.25	.55
485	A70	12e multicolored	1.90	.80

Intl. Youth
Year — A71

1985, Sept. 12   Litho.   Perf. 14
486	A71	12e multicolored	2.50	.90

Vapor, by
Hundertwasser
A72

Photogravure and Engraved
1986, Apr. 25   Perf. 14
Black Surcharge
487	A72	30e on 10e multi	22.50	4.00

Souvenir Sheets
Background Color
488		Sheet of 4	150.00	
a.	A72	50e yellow & multi	17.50	17.50
489		Sheet of 4	150.00	
a.	A72	50e red & multi	17.50	17.50
490		Sheet of 4	150.00	
a.	A72	50e green & multi	17.50	17.50

No. 487 exists without surcharge. Value $40.

World
Wildlife
Fund — A73

8e, Mabuya vaillanti. 10e, Tarentola gigas
brancoensis. 15e, Tarentola gigas gigas. 30e,
Hemidactylus bouvieri.
No. 495a, Mabuya vaillanti. No. 495b,
Hemidactylus bouvieri.

Perf. 13½x14½
1986, June 15   Litho.
491	A73	8e multicolored	6.50	2.50
492	A73	10e multicolored	8.00	3.25
493	A73	15e multicolored	12.00	4.00
494	A73	30e multicolored	24.00	5.00
		Nos. 491-494 (4)	50.50	14.75

Souvenir Sheet
495		Sheet of 2	30.00	22.50
a.	A73	50e multi	14.00	10.00
b.	A73	50e multi	14.00	10.00

No. 495 printed with center label picturing
progress union emblem. Nos. 495a-495b
printed without WWF emblem.

World Food
Day — A74

1986, June 20   Perf. 14
496	A74	8e Cauldron	.50	.25
497	A74	12e Mortar & pestle	.80	.35
498	A74	15e Quern stone	1.40	.50
		Nos. 496-498 (3)	2.70	1.10

Intl. Peace
Year — A75

1986, Dec. 24   Litho.   Perf. 14
499	A75	12e multicolored	.60	.25
500	A75	30e multicolored	2.10	1.40

Natl. Child
Survival
Campaign
A76

1987, Mar. 27   Litho.   Perf. 14
501	A76	8e multicolored	.45	.25
502	A76	10e multicolored	.55	.25
503	A76	12e multicolored	.65	.35
504	A76	16e multicolored	.95	.50
505	A76	100e multicolored	4.50	2.75
		Nos. 501-505 (5)	7.10	4.10

Tourism
A77

1987, May 17
506	A77	1e Bay, Mindelo	.25	.25
507	A77	2.50e Hill country	.25	.25
508	A77	5e Mountain peak	.25	.25
509	A77	8e Monument	.45	.25
510	A77	10e Mountain peaks	1.00	.30
511	A77	12e Beached boats	1.00	.40
512	A77	100e Harbor	5.25	3.00
		Nos. 506-512 (7)	8.45	4.70

For surcharge see No. 710.

Ships — A78

1987, Aug. 3 Perf. 13½x14½
513	A78	12e Carvalho, 1937	.75	.25
514	A78	16e Nauta, 1943	1.25	.25
515	A78	50e Maria Sony, 1911	3.75	1.25
		Nos. 513-515 (3)	5.75	1.75

Souvenir Sheet
516		Sheet of 2	9.00	9.00
a.		A78 60e Madalan, 1928	4.00	4.00

Crop
Protection
A80

50c, Identification of insect plague. 2e, Use of insecticides. 9e, Import of parasites. 13e, Import of predators. 16e, Locust. 19e, Estimation of crop loss.
50e, Agricultural Research Institute.

1988, May 9 Litho. Perf. 13½
518	A80	50c multicolored	.25	.25
519	A80	2e multicolored	.25	.25
520	A80	9e multicolored	.50	.25
521	A80	13e multicolored	.60	.25
522	A80	16e multicolored	1.00	.40
523	A80	19e multicolored	1.25	.60
		Nos. 518-523 (6)	3.85	2.00

Souvenir Sheet
524	A80	50e multicolored	5.00	5.00

Maps — A81

1e, Dutch, 17th cent. 2.50e, Belgian, 18th cent. 4.50e, French, 18th cent. 9.50e, English, 18th cent. 19.50e, English, 19th cent. 20e, French, 18th cent., vert.

1988, July 5 Litho. Perf. 14
525	A81	1e multicolored	.25	.25
526	A81	2.50e multicolored	.25	.25
527	A81	4.50e multicolored	.30	.25
528	A81	9.50e multicolored	.60	.25
529	A81	19.50e multicolored	1.25	.55
530	A81	20e multicolored	1.40	.65
		Nos. 525-530 (6)	4.05	2.20

Churches
A82

5e, St. Amaro Abade, Tarrafal, Santiago Is. 8e, Our Lady of the Light, Maio Is. 10e, Nazarene, Praia, Santiago Is. 12e, Our Lady of Rosa'rio, Sao Nicolau Is. 15e, Nazarene, Mindelo, Sao Vicente Is. 20e, Our Lady of Grace, Praia, Santiago Is.

1988, Aug. 15 Perf. 13½x14½
531	A82	5e multicolored	.25	.25
532	A82	8e multicolored	.45	.25
533	A82	10e multicolored	.55	.25
534	A82	12e multicolored	.60	.25
535	A82	15e multicolored	.85	.35
536	A82	20e multicolored	1.25	.45
		Nos. 531-536 (6)	3.95	1.80

Water Conservation — A83

1988, Sept. 26 Litho. Perf. 14
537	A83	12e multicolored	.75	.35

Intl. Red Cross, 125th Anniv. — A84

1988, Oct. 20
538	A84	7e multi	.60	.25

3rd Communist Party (PAICV)
Congress — A85

Portrait of Pres. Pereira, PAICV secretary-general, and: 7e, S. Jorginho Vocational Training Center. 10.50e, UN Secretary-General Perez de Cuellar. 30e, 100e, Star and text.

Perf. 14½x13½
			Litho.	
539	A85	7e multi	.40	.25
540	A85	10.50e multi	.60	.25
541	A85	30e multi	1.75	.75
		Nos. 539-541 (3)	2.75	1.25

Souvenir Sheet
542	A85	100e multi	6.25	6.25

1988 Summer
Olympics,
Seoul — A86

1988, Dec. 26
543	A86	12e shown	.60	.25
544	A86	15e Tennis	.90	.35
545	A86	20e Soccer	1.25	.50
546	A86	30e Boxing	1.75	.90
		Nos. 543-546 (4)	4.50	2.00

Souvenir Sheet
547	A86	50e Long jump	4.00	4.00

Roberto
Duarte
Silva
(1837-89),
Chemist —
A86a

1989, May 2 Litho. Perf. 14¼x14
547A	A86a	12.50e multi	.45	.25

2nd JAAC-
CV
Congress,
Sept. 7-
12 — A87

1989, Apr. 7 Litho. Perf. 14
548	A87	30e Hot air balloon	1.10	.75

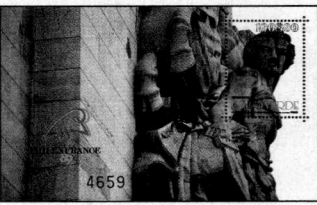

Liberty Guiding the People — A88

Relief, Arc de Triomphe — A89

1989, July 7 Litho. Perf. 14
549	A88	20e multicolored	.85	.45
550	A88	24e multicolored	1.10	.55
551	A88	25e multicolored	1.25	.65
		Nos. 549-551 (3)	3.20	1.65

Souvenir Sheet
Perf. 14½x13½
552	A89	100e multicolored	5.50	5.50

French revolution, bicent.

Interparliamentary Union, Cent. — A90

1989, Sept. 18 Litho. Perf. 14
553	A90	2e shown	.25	.25
554	A90	4e Dove	.25	.25
555	A90	13e Natl. Assembly Bldg.	.45	.25
		Nos. 553-555 (3)	.95	.75

Traditional
Ceramics
A91

1989, Nov. 13 Litho. Perf. 13½
Panel Colors
556	A91	13e lilac	.50	.25
557	A91	20e red, vert.	.70	.40
558	A91	24e brown	.90	.50
559	A91	25e orange, vert.	1.00	.55
		Nos. 556-559 (4)	3.10	1.70

Outdoor
Toys — A92

1989, Dec. 23
560	A92	1e Yellow truck	.25	.25
561	A92	6e Car	.25	.25
562	A92	8e White truck	.35	.25
563	A92	11.50e Trucks	.45	.25
564	A92	18e Scooter	.75	.45
565	A92	100e Boat	4.00	2.25
		Nos. 560-565 (6)	6.05	3.70

Visit of Pope John
Paul II — A93

1990, Jan. 25
566	A93	13e blue & multi	.40	.25
567	A93	20e purple & multi	.75	.40

Souvenir Sheet
568	A93	200e multi, diff.	8.00	8.00

Turtles
A94

50c, Chelonia mydas. 1e, Dermochelys coriacea. 5e, Lepidochelys olivacea. 10e, Caretta caretta. 42e, Eretmochelys imbricata.

1990, May 17 Litho. Perf. 13½
569	A94	50c multicolored	.30	.25
570	A94	1e multicolored	.30	.25
571	A94	5e multicolored	.50	.25
572	A94	10e multicolored	.70	.25
573	A94	42e multicolored	3.00	.90
		Nos. 569-573 (5)	4.80	1.90

Women's
Congress
A95

1990, Aug. 13
574	A95	9e multicolored	.50	.25

A96

Various drawings of soccer players in action.

1990, Aug. 7
575	A96	4e multicolored	.25	.25
576	A96	7.50e multicolored	.25	.25
577	A96	8e multicolored	.25	.25
578	A96	100e multicolored	3.50	2.10
		Nos. 575-578 (4)	4.25	2.85

Souvenir Sheet
579	A96	100e multi, diff.	4.50	4.50

World Cup Soccer Championships, Italy.
For surcharges see Nos. 711-712.

A97

Vaccinations: 5e, Emile Roux (1853-1933), diphtheria. 13e, Robert Koch (1843-1910), tuberculosis. 20e, Gaston Ramon (1886-1963), tetanus. 24e, Jonas Salk (1914-95), polio.

Granite Paper

1990, Oct. 15   **Perf. 11½**
580 A97 5e multicolored   .35   .25
581 A97 13e multicolored   1.00   .25
582 A97 20e multicolored   1.40   .40
583 A97 24e multicolored   1.75   .50
     Nos. 580-583 (4)   4.50 1.40

Intl. Literacy Year — A98

Designs: 3e, Adult literacy class. 15e, Teacher holding flash card, children. 19e, Teacher, student at blackboard.

1990, Sept. 28   **Granite Paper**
584 A98 2e shown   .50   .25
585 A98 3e multicolored   .50   .25
586 A98 15e multicolored   .75   .25
587 A98 19e multicolored   1.00   .30
     Nos. 584-587 (4)   2.75 1.05

Traditional Fairy Tales A99

2.50e, Man catching mermaid. 12e, Woman, snake. 25e, Man, eggs, woman.

1990, Dec. 20   **Litho.**   **Perf. 12½**
588 A99 50c shown   .25   .25
589 A99 2.50e multicolored   .25   .25
590 A99 12e multicolored   .50   .45
591 A99 25e multicolored   1.00   .40
     Nos. 588-591 (4)   2.00 1.35

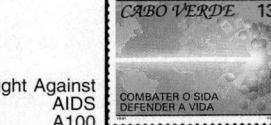

Fight Against AIDS A100

1991, Feb. 20   **Litho.**   **Perf. 14**
     Granite Paper
592 A100 13e multicolored   .75   .30
593 A100 24e multi, diff.   1.25   .75

Fishing — A101

24e, Man removing hook from fish. 25e, Fishing boats. 50e, Two men long-line fishing.

1991, Apr. 23   **Litho.**   **Perf. 11½**
594 A101 10e multicolored   .35   .25
595 A101 24e multicolored   1.10   .60
596 A101 25e multicolored   1.25   .65
597 A101 50e multicolored   2.40 1.50
     Nos. 594-597 (4)   5.10 3.00

Medicinal Plants — A102

10e, Lavandula rotundifolia. 15e, Micromeria forbesii. 21e, Sarcostemma daltonii. 24e, Periploca chevalieri. 30e, Echium hypertropicum. 35e, Erysimum caboverdeanum.

1991, July 5   **Litho.**   **Perf. 11½**
598 A102 10e multicolored   .30   .25
599 A102 15e multicolored   .55   .25
600 A102 21e multicolored   1.00   .30
601 A102 24e multicolored   1.25   .35
602 A102 30e multicolored   2.00   .45
603 A102 35e multicolored   3.00   .55
     Nos. 598-603 (6)   8.10 2.15

Landmarks in Old Ribeira Grande on Santiago Island A103

12.50e, Church of Our Lady of the Rosary, 1495. 15e, Ruins of the Cathedral, 1556. 20e, Fortress of San Felipe, 1587. 30e, Ruins of the Convent of St. Francis, 1642. 100e, Pillory, 1520, vert.

1991, June 25   **Litho.**   **Perf. 11½**
604 A103 12.50e multicolored   .45   .25
605 A103 15e multicolored   .55   .25
606 A103 20e multicolored   .75   .45
607 A103 30e multicolored   1.10   .75
     Nos. 604-607 (4)   2.85 1.70

     Souvenir Sheet
608 A103 100e multicolored   4.00 4.00

Musical Instruments — A104

1991, Oct. 9   **Litho.**   **Perf. 11½**
609 A104 10e 6-string guitar   .35   .25
610 A104 20e Violin   .85   .55
611 A104 29e 5-string guitar   1.40   .65
612 A104 47e Cimba   2.00 1.25
     Nos. 609-612 (4)   4.60 2.70

     Souvenir Sheet
613 A104 60e Accordion, horiz.   3.00 3.00

Christmas A105

1991, Dec. 20   **Litho.**   **Perf. 11½**
614 A105 31e Nativity scene   1.10   .50
615 A105 50e Nativity scene, diff.   1.75   .90

Discovery of America, 500th Anniv. A106

1992, Mar. 31   **Litho.**   **Perf. 11½**
616 A106 40e shown   2.00 1.10
617 A106 40e Columbus on ship   2.00 1.10
  a.   Pair, #616-617   4.50 4.50
     Souvenir Sheet
618 A106   Sheet of 2   8.00 8.00

Stamps in No. 618 are smaller, without white border and "Luis Duran" and "Courvoisier" inscriptions. No. 618 was printed in continuous design and sold for 150e.

     Souvenir Sheet

Granada '92 — A107

1992, Apr. 24   **Perf. 11½**
619 A107 50e multicolored   8.00 8.00
     No. 619 sold for 150e.

Tropical Fruits A108

16e, Syzygium jambos. 25e, Mangifera indica. 31e, Anacardium occidentale. 32e, Persea americana.

1992, Feb. 29   **Perf. 12x11½**
620 A108 16e multicolored   .65   .30
621 A108 25e multicolored   1.10   .50
622 A108 31e multicolored   1.40   .65
623 A108 32e multicolored   1.60   .75
     Nos. 620-623 (4)   4.75 2.20

1992 Summer Olympics, Barcelona A109

16e, Women's javelin. 20e, Weight lifting. 32e, Women's pole vault. 40e, Women's shot put.
100e, Women's gymnastics.

1992, June 30   **Litho.**   **Perf. 13½**
624 A109 16e multicolored   .60   .25
625 A109 20e multicolored   .75   .30
626 A109 32e multicolored   1.40   .65
627 A109 40e multicolored   1.60   .85
     Nos. 624-627 (4)   4.35 2.05

     Souvenir Sheet
628 A109 100e multicolored   4.25 4.25

Sugar Cane Production — A110

Designs: 19e, Oxen, sugar cane. 20e, Oxen yoked to press. 37e, Man placing cane inside press. 38e, Refining process.

1992, Nov.   **Litho.**   **Perf. 11**
629 A110 19e multicolored   .65   .30
630 A110 20e multicolored   .65   .30
631 A110 37e multicolored   1.25   .60
632 A110 38e multicolored   1.40   .60
     Nos. 629-632 (4)   3.95 1.80

Domestic Animals A111

1992, Nov.   **Perf. 13½**
633 A111 16e Cat   .65   .40
634 A111 31e Chickens   1.10   .80
635 A111 32e Dog, vert.   1.25   .90
636 A111 50e Horse   2.00 1.25
     Nos. 633-636 (4)   5.00 3.35

Corals A112

5e, Tubastrea aurea. 31e, Corallium rubrum. 37e, Porites porites. 50e, Millepora alcicornis.

1993, Apr. 29   **Litho.**   **Perf. 11½**
637 A112 5e multicolored   .25   .25
638 A112 31e multicolored   1.25   .80
639 A112 37e multicolored   1.50 1.00
640 A112 50e multicolored   2.00 1.25
     Nos. 637-640 (4)   5.00 3.30

Treaty of Tordesillas, 500th Anniv. (in 1994) — A113

Designs: No. 641, King Ferdinand, Queen Isabella of Spain, Pope Alexander VI. No. 642, Pope Julius II, King John II of Portugal. No. 643, Astrolabe, treaty signing. No. 644, Compass rose, map.

1993, Aug. 1   **Litho.**   **Perf. 12x11½**
641   37e multicolored   1.50   .65
642   37e multicolored   1.50   .65
  a.   A113 Pair, #641-642   3.50 3.25
643   38e multicolored   1.50   .65
644   38e multicolored   1.50   .65
  a.   A113 Pair, #643-644   3.50 3.25
     Nos. 641-644 (4)   6.00 2.60

     Souvenir Sheet

Santiago Island, 1806 — A114

1993, July 30   **Perf. 13½**
645 A114 100e multicolored   5.00 5.00
     Brasiliana '93.

Lobsters — A115

2e, Palinurus charlestoni. 10e, Panulirus echinatus. 17e, Panulirus regius. 38e, Scyllarides latus.
100e, Panulirus regius, diff.

1993, Sept. 29   Litho.   Perf. 11½
646 A115 2e multicolored .35 .25
647 A115 10e multicolored .70 .25
648 A115 17e multicolored 1.25 .50
649 A115 38e multicolored 2.75 1.00
Nos. 646-649 (4) 5.05 2.00

Souvenir Sheet
650 A115 100e multicolored 6.50 6.50
No. 650 contains one 51x36mm stamp.

Birds
A116

10e, Calonectris edwardsii. 30e, Sula leucogaster. 40e, Fregata magnificens. 41e, Phaeton aethereus.

1993, Oct. 29   Litho.   Perf. 12x11½
651 A116 10e multicolored .75 .25
652 A116 30e multicolored 3.00 .85
653 A116 40e multicolored 4.00 1.10
a. Souvenir sheet of 1 12.00 11.00
654 A116 41e multicolored 4.00 1.10
Nos. 651-654 (4) 11.75 3.30

Hong Kong '94 (No. 653a).
No. 653a sold for 150e.

Flowers
A117

1993, Dec. 16   Litho.   Perf. 12x11½
655 A117 5e Rosa alexandra .25 .25
656 A117 30e Strelitzia reginae 1.10 .80
657 A117 37e Dianthus barbatus 1.50 1.00
a. Souvenir sheet of 1 7.50 7.50
658 A117 50e Dahlia 1.90 1.25
Nos. 655-658 (4) 4.75 3.30

Singapore '95 (No. 657a). Issued 9/1/95.
No. 657a sold for 150e.

1994 World Cup Soccer
Championships, US — A118

Players, US flag, and: 1e, Giant's Stadium, New Jersey. 20e, Rose Bowl Stadium, Pasadena. 37e, Foxboro Stadium, Boston. 38e, Silverdome, Pontiac. 100e, RFK Stadium, Washington DC.

1994, May 31   Litho.   Perf. 11½
659 A118 1e multicolored .25 .25
660 A118 20e multicolored .85 .50
661 A118 37e multicolored 1.50 1.00
662 A118 38e multicolored 1.60 1.10
Nos. 659-662 (4) 4.20 2.85

Souvenir Sheet
663 A118 100e multicolored 5.50 5.50

Prince Henry the Navigator (1394-1460) — A119

1994, Mar. 4   Litho.   Perf. 12
664 A119 37e multicolored 3.00 1.00
See Brazil No. 2463, Macao No. 719, Portugal No. 1987.

Sharks
A120

21e, Eugomphodus taurus. 27e, Carcharhinus limbatus. 37e, Rhiniodon typus. 38e, Etmopterus spinax.

1994, June 27   Litho.   Perf. 12x11½
665 A120 21e multicolored 1.00 .60
666 A120 27e multicolored 1.25 .75
667 A120 37e multicolored 1.75 1.25
668 A120 38e multicolored 2.00 1.40
Nos. 665-668 (4) 6.00 4.00

Bananas
A121

1994, Aug. 16   Litho.   Perf. 11½
669 A121 12e Prata, vert. .50 .25
670 A121 16e Pao .75 .40
671 A121 30e Ana roberta, vert. 1.50 .85
672 A121 40e Roxa, vert. 2.00 1.10
Nos. 669-672 (4) 4.75 2.60

Souvenir Sheet
673 A121 100e Prata, diff., vert. 9.00 9.00
PHILAKOREA '94, SINGPEX '94 (No. 673).
No. 673 sold for 150e.

Lighthouses — A122

2e, Fontes Pereira de Melo. 37e, Morro Negro. 38e, Amelia, vert. 50e, Maria Pia, vert.

1994, Oct. 17   Litho.   Perf. 12
674 A122 2e multicolored .25 .25
675 A122 37e multicolored 1.75 1.00
676 A122 38e multicolored 1.75 1.10
677 A122 50e multicolored 2.25 1.40
Nos. 674-677 (4) 6.00 3.75

Wilhelm Roentgen (1845-1923),
Discovery of the X-Ray, Cent. — A123

1995, Mar. 31   Litho.   Perf. 12
678 A123 20e yellow & multi .80 .50
679 A123 37e blue & multi 1.50 1.00
a. Souvenir sheet of 2, #678-679 4.50 4.50
No. 679a sold for 100e.

A124

FAO, 50th
Anniv. — A125

1995, May 17   Litho.   Perf. 12
680 A124 37e multicolored 1.50 .90
681 A125 38e multicolored 1.50 .90

Dogs
A126

Dog, scene depicting story of dogs: 1e, Fox terrier, Two foxhounds and fox terrier, by John Emms. 10e, Cavalier King Charles, Shooting over Dogs, by Richard Ansdell. 40e, Rough collie, German shepherd. 50e, Braco, Hounds at Full Cry, by Thomas Blinks.

1995, June 16   Litho.   Perf. 12x11½
682 A126 1e multicolored .25 .25
683 A126 10e multicolored .55 .25
684 A126 40e multicolored 2.25 1.25
685 A126 50e multicolored 2.75 1.10
Nos. 682-685 (4) 5.80 2.85

Independence,
20th
Anniv. — A127

1995, July 20   Litho.   Perf. 12
686 A127 37e multicolored 1.90 1.25

Traditional
Festival
A128

Designs: 2e, Horse race. 10e, Horseman leading parade. 37e, People singing, playing drums. 40e, Playing game on horseback.

1995, Oct. 9   Litho.   Perf. 12x11½
687 A128 2e multicolored .25 .25
688 A128 10e multicolored .45 .25
689 A128 37e multicolored 1.50 .85
690 A128 40e multicolored 1.75 1.00
Nos. 687-690 (4) 3.95 2.35

Children's
Stories
A130

Designs: 10e, The cicadas making music, ants. 25e, Cicada being exposed to light. 38e, Cicada with guitar, ants working. 45e, Ants at table making fun of cicada.

1995, Dec. 15   Litho.   Perf. 11½
692 A130 10e multicolored .40 .55
693 A130 25e multicolored .85 .85
694 A130 38e multicolored 1.40 1.10
695 A130 45e multicolored 1.60 1.00
Nos. 692-695 (4) 4.25 3.50

Endangered
Plants — A131

20e, Sonchus daltonii. 37e, Echium vulcanorum. 38e, Nauplius smithii. 50e, Campanula jacobaea.

1996, Apr. 24   Litho.   Perf. 11½
696 A131 20e multicolored .65 .40
697 A131 37e multicolored 1.20 .75
698 A131 38e multicolored 1.20 .75
699 A131 50e multicolored 1.60 1.10
Nos. 696-699 (4) 4.65 3.00

1996
Summer
Olympic
Games,
Atlanta
A132

1996, June 30   Litho.   Perf. 11½
700 A132 1e Tennis .25 .25
701 A132 37e Gymnastics 1.10 .75
702 A132 100e Athletics 3.25 2.10
Nos. 700-702 (3) 4.60 3.10

UNICEF, 50th
Anniv. — A133

1996, Aug. 1   Litho.   Perf. 12
703 A133 20e Young girl .90 .40
704 A133 40e Mother, child 1.75 .85

Water
Sports — A134

Designs: 2.50e, Fishing. 10e, Windsurfing. 22e, Jet skiing. No. 708, Surfing, horiz. No. 709, Diver's hand, pufferfish, horiz.

1996, Oct. 9   Litho.   Perf. 12
705 A134 2.50e multicolored .25 .25
706 A134 10e multicolored .35 .25
707 A134 22e multicolored .70 .45
708 A134 100e multicolored 3.25 2.10
Nos. 705-708 (4) 4.55 3.05

Souvenir Sheet
709 A134 100e multicolored 4.50 4.50
No. 709 contains one 80x61mm stamp.

Nos. 507, 575-576 Surcharged

a

b

1997 Litho. Perf. 14
710 A77(a) 3e on 2.50e #507 .25 .25
Perf. 13½
711 A96(b) 37e on 4e #575 3.00 .75
712 A96(a) 38e on 7.50e #576 3.00 .75
Nos. 710-712 (3) 6.25 1.75

Natl. Symbols A135

1997 Perf. 12
713 A135 25e Arms .80 .50
714 A135 37e Anthem 1.10 .75
715 A135 50e Flag 1.60 1.00
Nos. 713-715 (3) 3.50 2.25

World Wildlife Fund — A136

Pristis pectinata: a, On seabed. b, Swimming, school of small fish. c, Swimming along seabed, small fish. d, Two near seabed.

1997 Litho. Perf. 11½
716 A136 15e Strip of 4, #a.-d. 10.00 10.00

Legends of the Sea — A137

a, Fish, dolphins. b, Merman, mermaid. c, Fish swimming through portal, moray eel.

1997 Litho. Perf. 11½
717 A137 45e Strip of 3, #a.-c. 5.00 5.00

Fish A138

Designs: 13e, Thunnus albacares. 21e, Thunnus obesus. 41e, Euthynnus alletteratus. 45e, Katsuwonus pelamis.

1997 Litho. Perf. 12
718 A138 13e multicolored .50 .30
719 A138 21e multicolored 1.00 .60
720 A138 41e multicolored 1.75 1.25
721 A138 45e multicolored 2.00 1.50
Nos. 718-721 (4) 5.25 3.65

1998 World Cup Soccer Championships, France — A139

Designs: 30e, Soccer ball in net, vert. 45e, Soccer player, ball, vert. 50e, Globe, ball, World Cup trophy, fans in stadium.

1998 Litho. Perf. 12x11½, 11½x12
722 A139 10e shown .30 .25
723 A139 30e multicolored .80 .80
724 A139 45e multicolored 1.25 1.25
725 A139 50e multicolored 1.50 1.40
Nos. 722-725 (4) 3.85 3.70

Traditional Cuisine A140

5e, Boiled fish. 25e, Xerém com friginato. 35e, Cachupa. 40e, Molho de Saint-Nicholas.

1998 Litho. Perf. 12x11½
726 A140 5e multicolored .25 .25
727 A140 25e multicolored .65 .65
728 A140 35e multicolored 1.00 1.00
729 A140 40e multicolored 1.10 1.10
Nos. 726-729 (4) 3.00 3.00

Early Exploration — A141

a, Quotation from Lusiadas, two men looking at maps. b, Man with sword, man & woman. c, Compass, map, sailing ship, buildings on cliff.

1998 Perf. 11½
730 A141 50e Strip of 3, #a.-c. 6.00 6.00

Women's Traditional Costumes — A142

1998 Litho. Perf. 12
731 A142 10e Brava .25 .25
732 A142 18e Fogo .50 .50
733 A142 30e Boa Vista .80 .80
734 A142 50e Santiago 1.40 1.40
Nos. 731-734 (4) 2.95 2.95

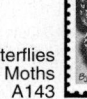

Butterflies and Moths A143

Designs: 5e, Byblia ilithyia. 10e, Aganais speciosa. 20e, Utetheisia pulchella. 30e, Vanessa cardui. 50e, Trichoplusia ni. 100e, Grammodes congenita.

1999, Mar. 16 Litho. Perf. 11¾
735 A143 5e multi .25 .25
736 A143 10e multi .25 .25
737 A143 20e multi .50 .50
738 A143 30e multi .80 .80
a. Souvenir sheet #737-738 4.00 4.00
739 A143 50e multi 1.25 1.25
740 A143 100e multi 2.60 2.60
Nos. 735-740 (6) 5.65 5.65
No. 738a sold for 100e.

First Concorde Flight, 30th Anniv. A144

Concorde: 30e, In flight. 50e, On ground.

1999, June 14 Litho. Perf. 12
741-742 A144 Set of 2 2.75 2.75

Famous People — A145

Design: 30e, Alain Gerbault (1893-1941), sailor, boats at dock. 50e, Roberto Duarte Silva (1837-89), chemist, Eiffel Tower.

1999, July 2 Litho. Perf. 14½
743 A145 30e multi 2.00 2.00
744 A145 50e multi 3.25 3.25
a. Souvenir sheet, #743-744 6.50 6.50
Philex France 99 (No. 744a).

A146

UPU, 125th Anniv. A147

1999, Sept. 15 Perf. 12x11¾
745 A146 30e shown 20.00 20.00
746 A147 50e shown 20.00 20.00

With Country Name Added

No. 747

No. 748

747 A146 30e multi .65 .65
748 A147 50e multi 1.10 1.10
Nos. 745-748 (4) 41.75 41.75

Dance A148

Designs: 10e, Colá Sanjon, vert. 30e, Contradança, vert. 50e, Desfile de tabanca. 100e, Batuque.

Perf. 11¾x12, 12x11¾
1999, Nov. 5 Litho.
749-752 A148 Set of 4 5.00 5.00

Millennium — A149

Designs: 40e, Globe, hourglass and open antique book inscribed "2000," vert. 50e, "2000 Milenio."

2000, Jan. 31 Litho. Perf. 11¾x11½
753-754 A149 Set of 2 2.50 2.50

SOS Children's Villages A150

Emblem and child: 50e, Seated, vert. 100e, With arms outstretched.

Perf. 11¾x12, 12x11¾
2000, Apr. 28 Litho.
755-756 A150 Set of 2 4.00 4.00

Independence, 25th Anniv. — A151

2000, July 5 Perf. 11¾
757 A151 50e multi 2.00 1.25

2000 Summer Olympics, Sydney A152

Designs: 10e, Women's gymnastics. 40e, Taekwondo. 50e, Women's hurdles.

2000, Sept. 15 Litho. Perf. 11¾
758-760 A152 Set of 3 2.60 2.60
760a Souvenir sheet of 3, #758-760 2.75 2.75

Dragoeiro Tree — A153

2000, Oct. 9 Litho. Perf. 11¾x11½
761 A153 5e green .25 .25
762 A153 40e red 1.00 1.00
763 A153 60e brown 1.60 1.60

Sao Nicolau Seminary and School — A154

No. 764: a, Seminarians and students (denomination at LR, 27x26mm). b, Seminarians and students (denomination at LL, 29x26mm). c, José Alves Feijo, Dr. Julio Dias and Canon António Bouças (56x26mm).

2000, Dec. 15 Perf. 14½
764 A154 60e Horiz. strip of 3, #a-c 5.00 5.00

Fish A155

Designs: 10e, Diplodus sargus lineatus. 22e, Diplodus prayensis. 28e, Lithognathus mormyrus. 48e, Diplodus fasciatus. 60e, Diplodus puntazzo.

2001, Apr. 24 Perf. 12x11¾
765-769 A155 Set of 5 5.00 5.00

Spiders
A156

Designs: 13e, Thomisus onustus. 16e, Scytodes velutina. 40e, Hersiliola simoni. 100e, Loxosceles rufescens.

2001, May 28
770-773   A156   Set of 4   5.00 5.00

Trees — A156a

Designs: 50e, Acacia albida. 60e, Ficus sycomorus.

2001, June 9   Litho.   Perf. 11¾x11½
773A-773B   A156a   Set of 2   2.75 2.75

Souvenir Sheet

Belgica 2001 Intl. Stamp Exhibition, Brussels — A157

Perf. 11¾x11½
2001, June 9   Photo.
774   A157   100e multi   2.75 2.75

Medicinal Plants — A157a

Designs: 20e, Artimisia gorgonum. 27e, Globularia amygdalifolia. 47.50e, Sidereoxylon marginata, horiz. 50e, Umbilicus schmidtii, horiz. 60e, Verbascum cystolithicum. 100e, Limonium lobinii.

Perf. 11¾x12, 12x11¾
2001, Sept. 27   Litho.
774A-774F   A157a   Set of 6   8.00 8.00

Year of Dialogue Among Civilizations — A158

2001, Oct. 9   Litho.   Perf. 11¾x12
775   A158   60e multi   1.60 1.60

António Aurélio Gonçalves (1901-84), Writer — A159

2001, Dec. 20   Perf. 12¼
776   A159   100e multi   2.75 2.75

Medicinal Plants A160

Designs: 10e, Euphorbia tuckeyna. 50e, Limonium sunding, vert. 60e, Aeonium gorgoneum, vert. 100e, Polycarpaea gayi, vert.

Perf. 12x11¾, 11¾x12
2002, Apr. 26   Litho.
777-780   A160   Set of 4   5.75 5.75

2002 World Cup Soccer Championships, Japan and Korea — A161

Designs: 60e, Player heading ball towards goal. 100e, Player kicking ball towards goal.

2002, July 22   Perf. 12x11¾
781-782   A161   Set of 2   4.00 4.00

Caretta Caretta A162

Designs: 10e, Pair mating. 20e, Female laying eggs, vert. 30e, Eggs hatching. 60e, Hatchlings heading for sea, vert. No. 787, 100e, Turtle swimming underwater. No. 788, 100e, Turtle on beach.

2002, Sept. 9   Perf. 12x11¾, 11¾x12
783-787   A162   Set of 5   6.50 6.50
Souvenir Sheet
788   A162   100e multi   3.00 3.00
No. 788 contains one 80x60mm stamp.

Basketry A163

Baskets and basket weavers from: 20e, Sao Nicolau Island. 33e, Santo Antao Island. 60e, Santiago Island. 100e, Boa Vista Island.

2002, Oct. 29   Perf. 12x11¾
789-792   A163   Set of 4   6.50 6.50

Composers and Poets A164

Designs: 12e, Katcháss (1951-88), composer. 20e, Jorge Monteiro (1913-98), composer. 32e, Luis Rendall (1898-1986), composer. 47.50e, Jorge Barbosa (1902-71), poet.

60e, Januário Leite (1865-1930), poet. 100e, José Lopes (1872-1962), poet.

2003, Feb. 24
793-798   A164   Set of 6   7.50 7.50

Birds — A165

Designs: 10e, Ardea bournei. 27e, Ardea cinerea. 42e, Bubulcus ibis. 60e, Egretta garzeta.

2003, July 9   Perf. 14x13¾
799-802   A165   Set of 4   4.00 4.00

Cesaria Evora, Singer A166

Designs: 60e, Evora at left. 100e, Evora at right. 200e, Feet of Evora.

2003, May 26   Perf. 13¾x14
803-804   A166   Set of 2   4.50 4.50
Souvenir Sheet
Perf. 12¼x12
805   A166   200e multi + label   6.00 6.00
No. 805 contains one 50x38mm stamp.

Scouting in Cape Verde A167

Emblem and scout of: 60e, Scouts Association of Cape Verde. 100e, Cape Verde Scouts Corps.

2003, Oct. 24   Litho.   Perf. 13¾x14
806-807   A167   Set of 2   4.50 4.50

Whales A168

Designs: 10e, Balaenoptera musculus. 20e, Physeter macrocephalus. 50e, Megaptera novaeangliae. 60e, Globicephala macrorhynchus.

2003, Nov. 25   Perf. 12
808-811   A168   Set of 4   12.00 12.00

First Dakar — Praia Seaplane Flight of Europe — Africa — South America Airmail Service, 75th Anniv. — A169

Seaplane and: 10e, Crew. 42e, Pilot Paulin Paris, map of South America — Africa route. 60e, Map of entire route. 100e, Like 10e.

2003, Dec. 11   Perf. 14
812-814   A169   Set of 3   3.25 3.25
Souvenir Sheet
815   A169   100e multi   3.00 3.00

Election of Pope John Paul II, 25th Anniv. — A170

Pope John Paul II and: 30e, Girl. 60e, Boats, horiz. 100e, Censer and crucifix.

2003, Dec. 29   Perf. 14x13¾, 13¾x14
816-817   A170   Set of 2   2.40 2.40
Souvenir Sheet
818   A170   100e multi   3.00 3.00

Trees — A171

Designs: 20e, Khaya senegalensis. 27e, Acacia nilotica. 60e, Ceiba pentandra. 100e, Phoenix atlantica.

2004, Jan. 25   Perf. 14x13¾
819-822   A171   Set of 4   5.50 5.50

Windmill — A172

Colors: 20e, Blue. 60e, Red. 100e, Green.

2004, June 3   Perf. 13¼x13
823-825   A172   Set of 3   4.75 4.75

2004 Summer Olympics, Athens — A173

Designs: 10e, Taekwondo. 60e, Rhythmic gymnastics. 100e, Boxing, horiz.

Perf. 13¼x13, 13x13¼
2004, Aug. 13   Litho.
826-828   A173   Set of 3   4.75 4.75

Lighthouses A174

Designs: 10e, Ponta do Barril Lighthouse, Sao Nicolau Island. 30e, Ponta Jalunga Lighthouse, Brava Island. 40e, D. Luis Lighthouse,

Passaros Islands, horiz. 50e, Ponta Preta Lighthouse, Santiago Island, horiz.

2004, Sept. 7
829-832 A174 Set of 4 4.00 4.00

Houses on Fogo Island A175

Various houses: 20e, 40e, 50e, 60e.

2004, Oct. 9 *Perf. 13x13¼*
833-836 A175 Set of 4 4.75 4.75

Telephones — A176

Old telephones and: 10e, Switchboard. 40e, Operator. 60e, Telephone directory. 100e, Truck and telephone poles.

2004, Nov. 12
837-840 A176 Set of 4 5.50 5.50

Oral Stories and Legends A177

Designs: 10e, Stória Stória. 20e, Era um Vez! 30e, Sapatinha Ribera Baxu. 60e, Quem ki Sabi Mas, Conta Midjor!, vert.

Perf. 13x13¼, 13¼x13
2005, Feb. 21 *Litho.*
841-844 A177 Set of 4 3.50 3.50

Amilcar Cabral (1924-73), Revolutionary Leader — A178

2005, June 30 Litho. *Perf. 13¼x13*
845 A178 60e multicolored 1.60 1.60
Independence, 30th anniv.

Shells A179

Designs: 30e, Conus evorai. 40e, Harpa doris. 50e, Strombus lotus. 60e, Phyllonotus duplex.

2005, July 18 *Perf. 13x13¼*
846-849 A179 Set of 4 6.00 6.00

Birds — A180

Designs: 19e, Passer iagoensis. 42e, Estrilda astrild. 44e, Passer domesticus. 55e, Acrocephalus brevipennis.

2005, Aug. 8 *Perf. 13¼x13*
850-853 A180 Set of 4 4.25 4.25

World Summit on the Information Society, Tunis A181

2005, Nov. 16 Litho. *Perf. 13x13¼*
854 A181 60e multi 2.00 2.00

Artifacts of the Slave Trade A182

Designs: 5e, Pipe. 10e, Telescope. 30e, Cannon. 60e, Nautical instrument. 100e, Shackles.

2006, Jan. 31
855-858 A182 Set of 4 3.00 3.00
Souvenir Sheet
859 A182 100e multi 3.00 3.00
No. 859 contains one 80x60mm stamp.

Whaling A183

Designs: 10e, Ship and map. 20e, Whalers in ship and longboat chasing whales off shore. 40e, Ship, longboat and whale. 60e, Crew on whaling ship.

2006, May 18 Litho. *Perf. 13¼x13½*
Granite Paper
860-863 A183 Set of 4 7.00 7.00

2006 World Cup Soccer Championships, Germany — A184

Designs: 30e, Emblem and soccer players. 40e, Emblem, vert. 60e, World Cup trophy and soccer players.

Perf. 13x13¼, 13¼x13
2006, Oct. 18 *Litho.*
Granite Paper
864-866 A184 Set of 3 4.00 4.00

Ribeira Grande and the International Slave Route — A185

Designs: 24e, Ship and buildings. 36e, Ship, slaves, map of Africa, North America and South America. 50e, Ship, slaves, map of Europe, North America, South America and Africa. 60e, Ship, small boat and buildings.

2006, Oct. 30 Litho. *Perf. 13x13¼*
Granite Paper
867-870 A185 Set of 4 5.00 5.00
An additional stamp was issued in this set. The editors would like to examine any example of it.

Community of Portuguese-Speaking Nations, 10th Anniv. — A186

2006, Nov. 2
872 A186 60e multi 2.40 2.40

Sir Francis Drake (c. 1540-96), Explorer — A187

Drake and: 5e, Sextant. 16e, Ship, map of Cape Verde, compass wheel, horiz. 44e, Ships, horiz. 60e, Old map of Atlantic Ocean, horiz.

2006, Nov. 27 *Perf. 13¼x13*
Granite Paper (5e, 16e, 60e)
873 A187 5e multi — —
874 A187 16e multi — —
875 A187 44e multi — —
876 A187 60e multi — —

Aeronautics — A188

Designs: 10e, Map of Rome-Rio de Janeiro flight via Ilha do Sal, airplane and hangar on Ilha do Sal. 20e, Seaplane, map of Portugal-Brazil flight, monument. 40e, Zeppelin in flight over town. 50e, Ferdinand von Zeppelin, Zeppelins in flight. 60e, Graf Zeppelin in flight, Cape Verde newspaper article.

2006, Dec. 15 *Perf. 13x13¼*
Granite Paper
877-881 A188 Set of 5 7.50 7.50

Writers — A189

Designs: No. 882, 60e, Manuel Lopes (1907-2005). No. 883, 60e, Baltasar Lopes da Silva (Osvaldo Alcantara) (1907-89).

2007 *Perf. 13¼*
882-883 A189 Set of 2 4.75 4.75

Pico do Fogo Volcano A190

Various depictions of erupting volcano: 10e, 50e, 55e, 60e. 50e and 55e are vert.

2007 *Perf. 13x13¼, 13¼x13*
884-887 A190 Set of 4 7.00 7.00

Luis de Cadamosto (1432-88), Discoverer of Cape Verde Islands — A191

Designs: 16e, Cadamosto and ship. 44e, Ship and compass rose. 60e, Cadamosto. 100e, Cadamosto, ship and astrolabe.

2007 *Perf. 13¼x13*
888 A191 16e multi — —
889 A191 44e multi — —
890 A191 60e multi — —
891 A191 100e multi — —

Whaling A192

Designs: 20e, Whale, map of Cape Verde and world showing whale reproduction sites. 30e, Crew on whaling ship stripping whale. 40e, Whale and ship near shore. 60e, Whale breaching near ship.

2007, June 14 Litho. *Perf. 13x13¼*
Granite Paper
892-895 A192 Set of 4 8.00 8.00

Aviation A193

Designs: 10e, Airplane, map of South America, Cape Verde, and Africa. 50e, Concorde. 60e, Airplane, map of Africa and Asia. 100e, Airplane over airport.

2007 *Perf. 13x13¼*
896-899 A193 Set of 4 6.00 6.00

Local Cuisine A194

Designs: 10e, Cozido (stew). 20e, Cuscus com mel (couscous with honey), vert. 60e, Trotxida. 100e, Xerem (cornmeal puree).

2008 *Perf. 13x13¼, 13¼x13*
900-903 A194 Set of 4 9.75 9.75

Occupations
A195

Designs: 30e, Engraxador (shoe polisher).
40e, Vendedeira de pao (bread seller). 50e,
Vendedeira de leite (milk seller), horiz. 100e,
Vendedeira de peixe (fish seller).

2008   **Perf. 13¼x13, 13x13¼**
904-907 A195   Set of 4   10.50 10.50

Souvenir Sheet

Praia, 150th Anniv. — A196

2008   **Perf. 13¼x13**
908 A196 200e multi   9.75 9.75

Peace Corps in
Cape Verde, 20th
Anniv. — A197

2008
909 A197 60e multi   3.00 3.00

Birds of
Prey — A198

Designs: 5e, Buteo bannermani. 20e, Falco
tinnunculus. 40e, Pandion haliaetus. 60e,
Falco peregrinus madeus.

2008
910-913 A198   Set of 4   4.75 4.75

Louis
Braille
(1809-52),
Educator
of the
Blind
A199

Designs: No. 914, 60e, Hands reading
Braille text. No. 915, 60e, Blind man with cane.
No. 916, 60e, Blind children. No. 917, 60e,
Blind man with seeing-eye dog, vert.

2009   **Perf. 13x13¼, 13¼x13**
Granite Paper
914-917 A199   Set of 4   7.50 7.50

Charles Darwin (1809-82),
Naturalist — A200

No. 918 — Map of Darwin's voyages and: a,
Darwin, skulls. b, Skull, ship, Darwin's legs. c,
Darwin and octopus.

2009   **Perf. 13½x13¼**
918   A200 Horiz. strip of 3   8.25 8.25
 a.-c.   60e Any single   2.75 2.75

Red Cross,
150th
Anniv.
A201

2009   **Litho.**   **Perf. 13x13¼**
Granite Paper
919 A201 100e multi   2.75 2.75

Flora and
Fauna
A202

Designs: 5e, Chioninia delalandii. 10e,
Tornabenea annua. 20e, Tarentola darwini.
30e, Satureja forbesii, vert. 40e, Campylnatus
glaber glaber, vert. 60e, Chioninia vailanti.

2009   **Perf. 13x13¼, 13¼x13**
Granite Paper
920-925 A202   Set of 6   4.50 4.50

Souvenir Sheet

Serra Malagueta Protected
Areas — A203

No. 926 — Various views of Serra
Malagueta: a, 50e. b, 100e.

2009   **Granite Paper**   **Perf. 13¼**
926 A203   Sheet of 2, #a-b   4.25 4.25

Discovery of Cape Verde Islands,
550th Anniv. — A204

No. 927: a, Two ships. b, Map of Cape
Verde and Africa, compass rose, birds, "14." c,
Ship, rowboat, map of Africa and Asia, com-
pass rose, "60."

2010 **Granite Paper** **Perf. 13½x13¼**
927   A204   Horiz. strip of 3   4.50 4.50
 a.-c.   60e Any single   1.50 1.50

Monte Gordo
Protected
Areas — A205

Flora and birds of Monte Gordo Protected
Areas: 5e, Diplotaxis gracilis. 20e, Theresia.
30e, Verbascum capitis-viridis. 40e, Coturnix
coturnix, horiz. 50e, Corvus ruficollis, horiz.
60e, Columba livia, horiz.
100e, Monte Gordo, horiz.

2010   **Perf. 13¼x13, 13x13¼**
928-933 A205   Set of 6   5.25 5.25

Souvenir Sheet
934 A205 100e multi   2.50 2.50

2010 World Cup Soccer
Championships, South Africa — A206

Designs: 40e, Mascot, silhouettes of players. 50e, Emblem, players, vert. 60e, Mascot,
players. 100e, World Cup, silhouettes of
players.

2010   **Perf. 13x13¼, 13¼x13**
935-938 A206   Set of 4   6.25 6.25

Independence, 35th Anniv. — A207

2010, July 5   **Litho.**   **Perf. 13¼**
939 A207 100e multi   4.75 4.75

Campaigns
Against
Chronic
Diseases
A208

Campaign against: 10e, Alcoholism. 20e,
Alcoholism, diff. 30e, Diabetes. 40e, Diabetes,
diff. 50e, Tuberculosis. 60e, Tuberculosis, diff.

2010, Aug. 12   **Perf. 13x13¼**
940-945 A208   Set of 6   10.00 10.00

Assoc. of Postal and
Telecommunications Operators of
Portuguese-Speaking Countries and
Territories, 20th Anniv. — A209

2010
946 A209 100e multi   4.75 4.75

Rebellions — A210

Rebellions at: 40e, Mindelo, 1934. 50e,
Paul, 1894. 60e, Rubon Manel, 1910.

2010   **Perf. 13½**
947-949 A210   Set of 3   7.25 7.25

Heart
Health
A211

Designs: 20e, Hearts, electrocardiogram
waves, mother lifting child. 40e, Heart and
stethoscope. 60e, Family, hearts, electrocardiogram waves. 100e, Heart and arteries.

2011   **Perf. 13x13¼**
950-953 A211   Set of 4   6.25 6.25

Nudibranchs — A212

Designs: 5e, Flabelina arveleoi. 10e, Flabelina bulbosa. 20e, Aplysia dactylomela. 40e,
Pleurobranchus garciagomezis. 60e, Hyp-
selodoris sp., vert.

2011   **Perf. 13x13¼, 13¼x13**
954-958 A212   Set of 5   3.75 3.75

Flora and Fauna
of Cha das
Caldeiras
Protected
Area — A213

Designs: 5e, Halcion leucocephala. 10e,
Verbascum cystolithicum. 20e, Acrocephalus
brevipennis. 40e, Echium vulcanorum. 60e,
Pterodroma feae. 100e, Erisimum
caboverdeanum.
150e, Halcion leucocephala, Acrocephalus
brevipennis, horiz.

2011   **Perf. 13¼x13**
959-964 A213   Set of 6   6.75 6.75
Souvenir Sheet
Perf. 13x13¼
965 A213 150e multi   4.25 4.25

Baltazar
Lopes da
Silva
(1907-89),
Writer
A214

2012   **Perf. 13x13¼**
966 A214 100e multi   2.75 2.75

Old Household
Objects — A215

Designs: No. 967, 60e, Oil burner (Fogao a
petróleo). No. 968, 60e, Oil lamp (Conddeeiro
a petróleo). No. 969, 60e, Washbasin
(Lavatório). No. 970, 60e, Iron (Ferro de
engomar a carvao), horiz.

2012   **Perf. 13¼x13, 13x13¼**
967-970 A215   Set of 4   6.75 6.75

Emigration
A216

Designs: 30e, Compass rose, man on boat waving to family on dock. 50e, Man writing on envelope. 60e, Agricultural worker, hand picking cacao pod. 100e, Man wheeling suitcase, world map, horiz.

2012		**Perf. 13¼x13, 13x13¼**	
971-974	A216	Set of 4	6.75 6.75

Composers and Musicians — A217

Designs: 10e, Ano Nobu (1933-2004), composer. 20e, Ildo Lobo (1953-2004), singer. 30e, Renato Cardoso (1951-89), composer. 40e, Manuel d'Novas (1938-2009), composer. 50e, Codé di Dona (1940-2010), composer. 60e, Orlando Pantera (1967-2001), composer.

2012	**Litho.**	**Perf. 13¼**	
975-980	A217	Set of 6	6.00 6.00

Cape Verde National Soccer Team
A218

Designs: 40e, Team emblem. 60e, Team jersey, vert. 100e, Like 40e.

2012		**Perf. 13x13¼, 13¼x13**	
981-982	A218	Set of 2	2.75 2.75
		Souvenir Sheet	
983	A218	100e multi	2.75 2.75

Flora and Fauna of Santo Antao Proctected Area — A219

Designs: 10e, Buteo bannermani. 20e, Pterodroma feae. 30e, Sideroxylon marginata. 40e, Carex antolensis, horiz. 50e, Tarentola caboverdiana caboverdiana, horiz. 60e, Papaver gorgoneum, horiz.
100e, Birds in flight over Coza Natural Park, horiz.

2012		**Perf. 13¼x13, 13x13¼**	
984-989	A219	Set of 6	6.00 6.00
		Souvenir Sheet	
990	A219	100e multi	2.75 2.75

Brasiliana 2013 Intl. Philatelic Exhibition, Rio de Janeiro
A220

Brasiliana 2013 emblem, Brazil Nos. 1, 2 and 3, and: 60e, Map of Brazil and circle indicating location of Cape Verde. 150e, Cape Verde #1, map of Cape Verde, label without denomination similar to 60e.

2013	**Litho.**	**Perf. 13½**	
991	A220	60e multi	1.50 1.50
		Size: 145x81mm	
		Imperf	
992	A220	150e multi + label	4.00 4.00

African Union, 50th Anniv. — A221

2013	**Litho.**	**Perf. 13½**	
993	A221	60e multi	1.50 1.50

Father Custódio Ferreira de Campos and Church
A222

2013, Oct. 9	**Litho.**	**Perf. 13x13¼**	
994	A222	60e multi	1.50 1.50

Carnaval — A223

Carnaval participants and animators: No. 995, 60e, Capote (1916-85). No. 996, 60e, Artur Boxe (1910-2004). No. 997, 60e, Negro Sarafe (1924-92).

2014, Feb. 28	**Litho.**	**Perf. 13½**	
995-997	A223	Set of 3	4.50 4.50

Portuguese Language, 800th Anniv.
A224

2014, May 5	**Litho.**	**Perf. 12x12½**	
998	A224	60e multi	1.50 1.50

Intl. Children's Day
A226

2014, June 1	**Litho.**	**Perf. 13x13½**	
999	A225	60e multi	1.50 1.50
1000	A226	60e multi	1.50 1.50

A227

A228

Corn Processing
A229

2014, Oct. 9	**Litho.**	**Perf. 13x13½**	
1001	A227	60e multi	2.00 2.00
1002	A228	60e multi	2.00 2.00
1003	A229	60e multi	2.00 2.00
		Nos. 1001-1003 (3)	6.00 6.00

Intl. Association of Portuguese-Speaking Countries, 25th Anniv. — A230

2015, Apr. 27	**Litho.**	**Perf. 13¼x13**	
1004	A230	60e multi	1.25 1.25

See Angola No. , Brazil No. 3300, Guinea-Bissau No. , Macao No. 1440, Mozambique No. , Portugal Nos. 3694-3695, St. Thomas & Prince Islands No. 2954, and Timor No.

Independence, 40th Anniv. — A231

		Perf. 14½x14¼	
2015, June 23		**Litho.**	
1005	A231	60e multi	1.25 1.25

Economic Community of West African States, 40th Anniv.
A232

2015, July	**Litho.**	**Perf. 13x13¼**	
1006	A232	60e multi	1.25 1.25

Admission to United Nations, 40th Anniv.
A233

2015, Oct. 6	**Litho.**	**Perf. 13x13¼**	
1007	A233	60e multi	1.25 1.25

United Nations Food and Agriculture Organization, 70th Anniv. — A234

Designs: No. 1008, 60e, Seeds and peas. No. 1009, 60e, Terraced farmland. No. 1010, 60e, Plate of food.

2015, Oct. 16	**Litho.**	**Perf. 13¼**	
		Stamp + Label	
1008-1010	A234	Set of 3	3.75 3.75

Kriol Jazz Festival, Praia
A235

2016, Apr. 8	**Litho.**	**Perf. 13¼**	
1011	A235	60e multi	1.25 1.25

Emblem of Atlantic Music Expo — A236

2016, Apr. 12	**Litho.**	**Perf. 13½**	
1012	A236	60e multi	1.25 1.25

Values are for stamps with surrounding selvage.

Kavala Fresk Festival — A237

2016, July 9	**Litho.**	**Perf. 14¼x14½**	
1013	A237	60e multi	1.25 1.25

AIR POST STAMPS

Common Design Type
Name and Value in Black
Perf. 13½x13

1938, July 26			**Unwmk.**	
C1	CD39	10c red orange	.60	.50
C2	CD39	20c purple	.60	.50
C3	CD39	50c orange	.60	.50
C4	CD39	1e ultra	.60	.50
C5	CD39	2e lilac brown	1.40	.80
C6	CD39	3e dk green	1.75	1.40
C7	CD39	5e red brown	5.50	2.10
C8	CD39	9e rose carmine	9.00	3.75
C9	CD39	10e magenta	9.75	5.00
		Nos. C1-C9 (9)	29.80	15.05
		Set, never hinged	50.00	

No. C7 exists with overprint "Exposicao Internacional de Nova York, 1939-1940" and Trylon and Perisphere.

POSTAGE DUE STAMPS

D1

1904		Unwmk.	Typo.	Perf. 12	
J1	D1	5r yellow grn		.40	.25
J2	D1	10r slate		.40	.25
J3	D1	20r yellow brn		.50	.40
J4	D1	30r red orange		1.25	.40
J5	D1	50r gray brown		.50	.35
J6	D1	60r red brown		9.25	4.25
J7	D1	100r lilac		1.75	1.25
J8	D1	130r dull blue		1.90	1.25
J9	D1	200r carmine		1.60	1.60
J10	D1	500r dull violet		5.00	3.00
		Nos. J1-J10 (10)		22.55	13.00

Overprinted in Carmine or Green

1911					
J11	D1	5r yellow grn		.30	.25
J12	D1	10r slate		.30	.25
J13	D1	20r yellow brn		.35	.25
J14	D1	30r orange		.35	.25
J15	D1	50r gray brown		.65	.40
J16	D1	60r red brown		.65	.40
J17	D1	100r lilac		.65	.40
J18	D1	130r dull blue		.75	.65
J19	D1	200r carmine (G)		2.00	1.50
J20	D1	500r dull violet		2.50	1.75
		Nos. J11-J20 (10)		8.50	6.10

D2

1921			Perf. 11½	
J21	D2	½c yellow grn	.30	.25
J22	D2	1c slate	.30	.25
J23	D2	2c red brown	.30	.25
J24	D2	3c orange	.30	.25
J25	D2	5c gray brown	.30	.25
J26	D2	6c lt brown	.30	.25
J27	D2	10c red violet	.30	.25
J28	D2	13c dull blue	.55	.40
J29	D2	20c carmine	.60	.50
J30	D2	50c gray	1.75	1.10
		Nos. J21-J30 (10)	5.00	3.75

Catalogue values for unused stamps in this section, from this point to the end of the section, are for Never Hinged items.

Common Design Type
Photogravure and Typographed

1952		Unwmk.	Perf. 14	

Numeral in Red, Frame Multicolored

J31	CD45	10c chocolate	.30	.25
J32	CD45	30c black brown	.30	.25
J33	CD45	50c dark blue	.30	.25
J34	CD45	1e dark blue	.40	.30
J35	CD45	2e red brown	.40	.30
J36	CD45	5e olive green	1.10	1.00
		Nos. J31-J36 (6)	2.80	2.30

NEWSPAPER STAMP

N1

1893	Typo.	Unwmk.	Perf. 11½	
P1	N1 2½r brown		1.50	.60
a.	Perf. 12½		3.00	1.50
b.	Perf. 13½		6.50	3.00

For surcharges see Nos. 79, 206.

POSTAL TAX STAMPS

Pombal Issue
Common Design Types

1925		Unwmk.	Engr.	Perf. 12½	
RA1	CD28	15c dull vio & blk		1.25	1.10
RA2	CD29	15c dull vio & blk		1.25	1.10
RA3	CD30	15c dull vio & blk		1.25	1.10
		Nos. RA1-RA3 (3)		3.75	3.30

St. Isabel — PT1

1948		Litho.	Perf. 11	
RA4	PT1	50c dark green	3.75	2.40
RA5	PT1	1e henna brown	7.50	3.00

Catalogue values for unused stamps in this section, from this point to the end of the section, are for Never Hinged items.

No. RA5 Surcharged with New Value and Bars

1959				
RA6	PT1	50c on 1e henna brown	1.40	1.10

		Perf. 14		
RA7	PT1	50c carmine rose	2.10	1.00
RA8	PT1	1e blue	2.10	1.00

St. Isabel Type Redrawn

1967-73		Litho.	Perf. 14	
RA9	PT1	30c (blue panel)	.50	.50
RA9A	PT1	30c (orange panel)	.50	.50
RA10	PT1	50c (lilac rose panel)	.85	.85
RA11	PT1	50c (red panel) ('72)	.50	.50
RA12	PT1	1e (brn panel)	1.00	1.00
RA13	PT1	1e (red lilac panel) ('72)	1.00	1.00
		Nos. RA9-RA13 (6)	4.35	4.35

Nos. RA9-RA13 are inscribed "ASSISTENCIA" in large letters in bottom panel and "PORTUGAL" and "CABO VERDE" in small letters in upper left corner.

Revenue Stamps Surcharged in Green, Blue or Black — PT2

Black "CABO VERDE" & Value Pale Green Burelage

1967-72		Typo.	Perf. 12	
RA14	PT2	50c on 1c org (Bl) ('71)	1.40	.90
a.	Black surcharge ('68?)		20.00	14.50
RA15	PT2	50c on 2c org (Bk) ('69)	25.00	14.50
c.	Inverted surcharge		50.00	35.00
RA16	PT2	50c on 3c org (G) ('72)	1.10	.60
RA17	PT2	50c on 5c org (G) ('72)	1.10	.60
RA18	PT2	50c on 10c org (G) ('71)	1.25	1.00
RA19	PT2	1e on 1c org (Bk)	2.75	2.10
RA20	PT2	1e on 2c org (G) ('71)	2.00	1.75
a.	Blue surcharge ('71)		3.00	1.10
b.	Black surcharge		4.00	2.10
		Nos. RA14-RA20 (7)	34.60	21.45

POSTAL TAX DUE STAMPS

Pombal Issue
Common Design Types

1925		Unwmk.	Perf. 12½	
RAJ1	CD28	30c dull vio & blk	.75	.70
RAJ2	CD29	30c dull vio & blk	.75	.70
RAJ3	CD30	30c dull vio & blk	.75	.70
		Nos. RAJ1-RAJ3 (3)	2.25	2.10

CARIBBEAN NETHERLANDS

ˈkar-ē-bbe-ə-n ˈne-thər-lənˌdz

LOCATION — The islands of Bonaire (north of Venezuela), Saint Eustatius and Saba (south of Anguilla)
AREA — 125 sq. mi.
POP. — 18,012 (2010)
CAPITAL — Kralendijk, Bonaire; Oranjestad, Saint Eustatius; The Bottom, Saba

On Oct. 10, 2010, Caribbean Netherlands, formerly part of Netherlands Antilles, became special municipalities within the Kingdom of the Netherlands.

100 Cents = 1 Gulden
100 Cents = 1 Dollar (2011)

Catalogue values for all unused stamps in this country are for Never Hinged items.

Map of Islands and West Indies, Arms, Queen Beatrix A1

	Perf. 13¾		
2010, Oct. 10	**Litho.**	**Unwmk.**	
1	A1 111c multicolored	1.50	1.50

New Constitutional Status — A2

Designs: 63c, Triangle with flags of Bonaire, Saint Eustatius and Saba, Acropora palmata. 81c, Three Glassy sweepers with elements of flags of Bonaire, Saint Eustatius and Saba. 93c, Two Yellowcheek wrasses with elements of Bonaire flag. 96c, Parrotfish with elements of Saint Eustatius flag. 159c, Blue tang surgeonfish with elements of Saba flag.

2011, June 1		**Perf. 13¼x13**	
2-6	A2 Set of 5	10.00	10.00

Greetings — A3

Inscriptions: 33c, Thinking of you. 63c, Always in my prayers. 93c, Celebrate another year. 159c, Love U so much. 226c, For you my cup of tea.

2011, July 11		**Perf. 13x13¼**	
7-11	A3 Set of 5	8.50	8.50

Corals — A4

Designs: 45c, Scolymia wellsi. 63c, Diodogorgia nodulifera, vert. 159c, Eusmilia fastigiata. 226c, Acropora palmata, vert.

	Perf. 13¼x13, 13x13¼	
2011, Sept. 11		
12-15	A4 Set of 4	8.00	7.00

Visit of Queen Beatrix — A5

Queen Beatrix: 81c, Without hat. 159c, Wearing hat.
250c, Queen Beatrix in coach, horiz.

2011, Nov. 4		**Perf. 14**	
16-17	A5 Set of 2	5.00	5.00
		Souvenir Sheet	
18	A5 250c multi	5.00	5.00

Holiday Light Decorations A6

Designs: 63c, Snowflakes. 81c, Reindeer. 93c, Flowers. 159c, Bells.

2011, Nov. 11		**Perf. 13½x12¾**	
19-22	A6 Set of 4	8.00	8.00

Sailboats A7

Designs: 66c, Catamaran. 99c, Optimist. 101c, Sunfish. 168c, Laser, vert.

	Perf. 13½x12¾, 12¾x13½	
2012, Feb. 1		
23-26	A7 Set of 4	8.75	8.75

Parrots — A8

Designs: 100c, Ara chloropterus. 150c, Aratinga pertinax. 200c, Amazona ochrocephala ochrocephala. 250c, Anodorhynchus hyacinthinus.

2012, June 1		**Perf. 12¾x13½**	
27-30	A8 Set of 4	14.00	14.00

Rafflesia Flower — A9

Mandala — A10

2012, June 18   **Perf. 13½x12¾**
31 A9   10c multicolored   .25 .25

Souvenir Sheet
Perf.
32 A10   200c multicolored   4.00 4.00

Indoensia 2012 World Stamp Exhibition, Jakarta.

Miniature Sheet

Dutch Queens and Heraldry — A11

No. 33: a, Queen Emma. b, Queen Wilhelmina. c, Queen Juliana. d, Queen Beatrix. e, Royal arms.

Litho. & Embossed
2012, Sept. 3   **Perf. 12¾x13½**
33 A11   300c Sheet of 5, #a-e   30.00 30.00

Arms and Christmas Ornaments A12

Designs: 66c, Arms of Saba, ornament in shape of Saba, ornament with Saba flag elements. 99c, Arms of St. Eustatius, ornament in shape of St. Eustatius, ornament with St. Eustatius flag elements. 101c, Arms of Bonaire, ornament in shape of Bonaire, ornament with Bonaire flag elements. 168c, Arms of Netherlands, ornaments with flag elements of Saba, St. Eustatius and Bonaire.

2012, Nov. 1   **Litho.**   **Perf. 13¼x13**
34-37 A12   Set of 4   8.75 8.75

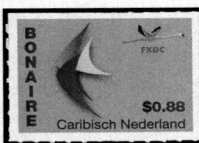

Emblem and Flamingo A13

No. 38 — Inscribed: a, Bonaire. b, Saba. c, St, Eustatius. d, Bonaire. e, Saba. f, St. Eustatius.

2014, Oct. 10   **Litho.**   **Rouletted 6½**
38   Horiz. strip of 6   11.50 11.50
   a.-c.   A13 88c Any single   1.75 1.75
   d.-f.   A13 99c Any single   2.00 2.00

Miniature Sheets

Flamingos — A14

Pelicans — A15

Hummingbirds — A16

Various birds, as shown.

Perf. 13¼x13½
2014, Nov. 10   **Litho.**
Inscribed "Bonaire"
39 A14   99c Sheet of 5, #a-e   10.00 10.00
Inscribed "Saba"
40 A15   99c Sheet of 5, #a-e   10.00 10.00
Inscribed "St. Eustatius"
41 A16   99c Sheet of 5, #a-e   10.00 10.00
    Nos. 39-41 (3)   30.00 30.00

Personalized Stamp — A17

Serpentine Die Cut 14¼
2014, Nov. 10   **Litho.**
Self-Adhesive
42 A17   99c multi + label   2.00 2.00

No. 42 was printed in sheets of 10 + 10 labels. The label shown is a generic label. Two other generic labels, depicting scenes of Saba and St. Eustatius were created. Labels could also be personalized. Sheets containing personalized labels sold for $15.

Miniature Sheet

Flag and King Willem-Alexander — A18

Flag of Bonaire (No. 43), Saba (No. 44) or St. Eustatius (No. 45) with King Willem-Alexander in: a, 99c, Sepia. b, 99c, Full color. c, $1.36, Sepia. d, $1.36, Full color. e, $1.98, Sepia, f, $1.98, Full color. g, $2.82, Sepia, h, $2.82, Full color. i, $4.40, Sepia. j, $4.40, Full color.

2015, Apr. 30   **Litho.**   **Perf. 14x13½**
Inscribed "Bonaire"
43 A18   Sheet of 10, #a-j   46.50 46.50

Inscribed "Saba"
44 A18   Sheet of 10, #a-j   46.50 46.50
Inscribed "St. Eustatius"
45 A18   Sheet of 10, #a-j   46.50 46.50
    Nos. 43-45 (3)   139.50 139.50

SEMI-POSTAL STAMPS

Intl. Year of Cooperatives SP1

2012, Oct. 9   **Litho.**   **Perf. 13½x12¾**
B1 SP1   99c+45c multi   3.00 3.00

CAROLINE ISLANDS

ˈkar-ə-ˌlin ˈī-lənds

LOCATION — A group of about 549 small islands in the West Pacific Ocean, north of the Equator.
GOVT. — German colony
AREA — 550 sq. mi.
POP. — 40,000 (approx. 1915)

100 Pfennig = 1 Mark

Watermark

Wmk. 125 — Lozenges

Stamps of Germany 1889-90 Overprinted in Black

Overprinted at 56 degree Angle

1900   **Unwmk.**   **Perf. 13½x14½**
1   A9   3pf dk brown   13.00   14.00
2   A9   5pf green   18.00   18.00
3   A10   10pf carmine   19.00   19.00
4   A10   20pf ultra   24.00   30.00
5   A10   25pf orange   55.00   65.00
6   A10   50pf red brown   55.00   65.00
    Nos. 1-6 (6)   184.00   211.00

Overprinted at 48 degree Angle

1899
1a   A9   3pf light brown   625.00   750.00
2a   A9   5pf green   650.00   650.00
3a   A10   10pf carmine   65.00   150.00
4a   A10   20pf ultra   65.00   150.00
5a   A10   25pf orange   1,650.   3,100.
6a   A10   50pf red brown   900.00   1,600.

A3

Kaiser's Yacht "Hohenzollern" — A4

1901, Jan.   **Typo.**   **Perf. 14**
7   A3   3pf brown   1.10   1.75
8   A3   5pf green   1.10   2.10
9   A3   10pf carmine   1.10   5.00
   a.   Half used as 5pf on cover, back-stamped in Jaluit ('05)   120.00
10   A3   20pf ultra   1.25   9.00
   a.   Half used as 10pf on cover ('10)   8,500.
11   A3   25pf org & blk, yel   1.60   14.50
12   A3   30pf org & blk, sal   1.60   14.50
13   A3   40pf lake & blk   1.60   16.50
14   A3   50pf pur & blk, sal   2.00   22.50
15   A3   80pf lake & blk, rose   3.00   25.00
    Engr.   **Perf. 14½x14**
16   A4   1m carmine   4.50   62.50
17   A4   2m blue   7.25   87.50
18   A4   3m black violet   10.00   150.00
19   A4   5m slate & car   160.00   550.00
    Nos. 7-19 (13)   196.10   960.85

No. 9a is known as the "typhoon provisional" the stock of 5pf stamps having been destroyed during a typhoon. Covers (cards) without backstamp, value about $72.50.
Forged cancellations are found on #7-19.

No. 7 Handstamp Surcharged

1910, July 12
20   A3   5pf on 3pf brown   5,500.
   a.   Inverted surcharge   7,750.
   b.   Double surcharge   11,000.

Values are for stamps tied to cover. Stamps on piece sell for about 40% less.

1915-19   **Wmk. 125**   **Typo.**
21   A3   3pf brown ('19)   .90
22   A3   5pf green   12.50
    Engr.
23   A4   5m slate & carmine   35.00
    Nos. 21-23 (3)   48.40

Nos. 21-23 were not placed in use.

CASTELLORIZO

ˌkäs-tə-'lor-ə-ˌzō

(Castelrosso)

LOCATION — A Mediterranean island in the Dodecanese group lying close to the coast of Asia Minor and about 60 miles east of Rhodes.
GOVT. — Former Italian Colony
AREA — 4 sq. mi.
POP. — 2,238 (1936)

Formerly a Turkish possession, Castellorizo was occupied by the French in 1915 and ceded to Italy after World War I. In 1945 it became part of Greece.

25 Centimes = 1 Piaster
100 Centimes = 1 Franc

> Used values in italics are for postally used copies. Stamps with CTO cancels sell for about the same as hinged, unused stamps.

Issued under French Occupation

Stamps of French Offices in Turkey Overprinted

B. N. F. CASTELLORIZO

1920   Unwmk.   Perf. 14x13½

1	A2	1c gray	45.00	65.00
a.		Inverted overprint	175.00	250.00
b.		Double overprint	175.00	350.00
2	A2	2c vio brn	50.00	70.00
a.		Double overprint	225.00	300.00
3	A2	3c red org	45.00	65.00
a.		Inverted overprint	175.00	250.00
4	A2	5c green	75.00	90.00
a.		Inverted overprint	225.00	300.00
5	A3	10c rose	90.00	125.00
6	A3	15c pale red	115.00	150.00
a.		Inverted overprint	450.00	625.00
7	A3	20c brn vio	125.00	150.00
8	A5	1pi on 25c blue	115.00	125.00
a.		Pair, one without overprint	750.00	800.00
9	A3	30c lilac	125.00	150.00
10	A4	40c red & pale bl (down)	200.00	250.00
a.		Inverted ovpt (reading up)	850.00	900.00
11	A6	2pi on 50c bis brn & lav (down)	225.00	275.00
a.		Inverted ovpt (reading up)	900.00	1,000.
b.		Double overprint	1,250.	1,300.
12	A6	4pi on 1fr cl & ol grn (down)	275.00	350.00
a.		Double overprint	1,300.	1,350.
b.		Inverted overprint (reading up)	1,050.	1,100.
13	A6	20pi on 5fr dk bl & buff	625.00	800.00
a.		Double overprint	1,850.	2,000.
		Nos. 1-13 (13)	2,110.	2,665.
		Set, never hinged	4,500.	

No. 1-9 were overprinted in blocks of 25. Position 4 had "CASTELLORIZO" inverted and Positions 8 and 18 had "CASTELLORISO." The later variety also occurred in the setting of the form for Nos. 10-13.
"B. N. F." are the initials of "Base Navale Francaise".

Overprinted in Black or Red

O. N. F. Castellorizo

1920

On Stamps of French Offices in Turkey

14	A2	1c gray	34.00	40.00
15	A2	2c vio brn	37.50	50.00
16	A2	3c red org	67.50	80.00
17	A2	5c green (R)	32.50	37.50
19	A3	10c rose	40.00	47.50
20	A3	15c pale red	70.00	80.00
21	A3	20c brn vio	105.00	110.00
22	A5	1pi on 25c bl (R)	67.50	70.00
23	A3	30c lilac (R)	77.50	85.00
24	A4	40c red & pale bl	72.50	75.00
25	A6	2pi on 50c bis brn & lav	72.50	80.00

26	A6	4pi on 1fr claret & ol grn	115.00	140.00
28	A6	20pi on 5fr dk bl & buff	400.00	450.00
		Nos. 14-28 (13)	1,192.	1,345.

On Nos. 25, 26 and 28 the two lines of the overprint are set wider apart than on the lower values.
"O.N.F." are the initials of "Occupation Navale Francaise."
"Casetlorizo" and "astellorizo" varieties are known on Nos. 14-23.
Overprint on 5c in black and on 8pi on 2fr (#37) were prepared but not issued. Values: 5c, $1,300; 8pi on 2fr, $1,450.

On Stamps of France

30	A22	10c red	50.00	60.00
a.		Inverted overprint	200.00	250.00
31	A22	25c blue (R)	50.00	60.00
a.		Inverted overprint	200.00	250.00

This overprint exists on 8 other 1900-1907 denominations of France (5c, 15c, 20c, 30c, 40c, 50c, 1fr, 5fr). These are believed not to have been issued or postally used. Values: 5c, $750; 15c, $750; 20c, $800; 30c, $1,300; 40c, $1,300; 50c, $1,300; 1fr, $1,400; 5fr, $12,500.

Stamps of France, 1900-1907, Handstamped in Black or Violet

O F CASTELLORISO

1920

33	A22	5c green	175.00	200.00
a.		Overprint inverted (reading up)		1,300.
b.		Double overprint		1,000.
34	A22	10c red	175.00	200.00
35	A22	20c vio brn	175.00	200.00
a.		Overprint inverted (reading up)		1,500.
36	A22	25c blue	175.00	200.00
b.		Double overprint		1,000.
37	A18	50c bis brn & lav	1,000.	1,200.
a.		Double overprint		1,700.
38	A18	1fr cl & ol grn (V)	1,000.	1,200.
		Nos. 33-38 (6)	2,700.	3,200.
		Set, never hinged	5,400.	

French Offices in Turkey Nos. 25//38 are handstamped as Nos. 33-38 locally by the officers in charge of the French Navy postal facilities but were not issued. Values: 5c, 10c, 15c, 20c, 1pi on 25c, each $1,000; 40c, 2pi on 50c, each $2,000; 4pi on 1fr, $2,350; 20pi on 5fr, $10,000.

Covers: Values for covers are for commercial items. Philatelic covers sell for less.
Forgeries of overprints on Nos. 1-38 exist. They abound of Nos. 33-38.

Issued under Italian Dominion

100 Centesimi = 1 Lira

Italian Stamps of 1906-20 Overprinted

CASTELROSSO

1922, July 22   Wmk. 140   Perf. 14

51	A48	5c green	5.00	30.00
52	A48	10c claret	3.50	30.00
53	A48	15c slate	3.50	30.00
54	A50	20c brn org	3.50	30.00
a.		Double overprint	500.00	
b.		Vertical pair, one without overprint		2,250.
55	A49	25c blue	3.50	30.00
56	A49	40c brown	48.00	35.00
57	A49	50c violet	50.00	37.50
58	A49	60c carmine	50.00	57.50
a.		Diagonal overprint		800.00
59	A49	85c chocolate	5.50	65.00
		Nos. 51-59 (9)	172.50	345.00
		Set, never hinged	450.00	

Map of Castellorizo; Flag of Italy — A1

1923, Jan.

60	A1	5c gray green	6.00	40.00
61	A1	10c dull rose	6.00	40.00
62	A1	25c dull blue	6.00	40.00
63	A1	50c gray lilac	6.00	40.00
64	A1	1 l brown	6.00	40.00
		Nos. 60-64 (5)	30.00	200.00
		Set, never hinged	65.00	

Italian Stamps of 1901-20 Overprinted

1924, March

65	A48	5c green	2.50	30.00
66	A48	10c claret	2.50	30.00
67	A48	15c slate	2.50	40.00
68	A50	20c brn orange	2.50	40.00
a.		Double overprint	145.00	
69	A49	25c blue	2.50	30.00
70	A49	40c brown	2.50	30.00
71	A49	50c violet	2.50	40.00
72	A49	60c carmine	2.50	50.00
a.		Double overprint	450.00	
73	A49	85c red brown	2.50	60.00
74	A46	1 l brn & green	2.50	60.00
		Nos. 65-74 (10)	25.00	410.00
		Set, never hinged	55.00	

Ferrucci Issue

Italian Stamps of 1930, Ovptd. in Red or Blue

CASTELROSSO

1930, Oct. 20   Wmk. Crowns (140)

75	A102	20c violet	10.00	6.00
76	A103	25c dark green	10.00	25.00
77	A103	50c black	10.00	6.00
78	A103	1.25 l deep blue	10.00	25.00
79	A104	5 l + 2 l dp car (Bl)	10.00	77.50
		Nos. 75-79 (5)	50.00	139.50
		Set, never hinged	150.00	

Garibaldi Issue

Types of Italian Stamps of 1932, Overprinted like Nos. 75-79 in Red or Blue

1932, Aug. 28

80	A138	10c brown	20.00	25.00
81	A138	20c red brn (Bl)	20.00	25.00
82	A138	25c dp grn	20.00	25.00
83	A138	30c bluish slate	20.00	25.00
84	A138	50c red vio (Bl)	20.00	25.00
85	A141	75c cop red (Bl)	20.00	25.00
86	A141	1.25 l dull blue	20.00	25.00
87	A141	1.75 l + 25c brn	20.00	25.00
88	A144	2.55 l + 50c org (Bl)	20.00	25.00
89	A145	5 l + 1 l dl vio	20.00	25.00
		Nos. 80-89 (10)	200.00	250.00
		Set, never hinged	400.00	

CAYMAN ISLANDS

ˌkā-'man 'ī-lənds

LOCATION — Three islands in the Caribbean Sea, about 200 miles northwest of Jamaica
GOVT. — British Crown Colony, formerly a dependency of Jamaica
AREA — 100 sq. mi.
POP. — 39,335 (1999 est.)
CAPITAL — George Town, located on Grand Cayman

12 Pence = 1 Shilling
20 Shilling = 1 Pound
100 Cents = 1 Dollar (1969)

> Catalogue values for unused stamps in this country are for Never Hinged items, beginning with Scott 112.

Victoria — A1

1900   Typo.   Wmk. 2   Perf. 14

1	A1	½p pale green	15.00	22.50
2	A1	1p carmine rose	16.00	4.25

Edward VII — A2

1901-03

3	A2	½p green ('02)	5.50	30.00
4	A2	1p car rose ('03)	12.00	12.00
5	A2	2½p ultramarine	12.00	21.00
6	A2	6p chocolate	35.00	70.00
7	A2	1sh brown orange	72.50	125.00
		Nos. 3-7 (5)	137.00	258.00

1905   Wmk. 3

8	A2	½p green	12.00	17.50
9	A2	1p carmine rose	24.00	20.00
10	A2	2½p ultramarine	12.00	5.50
11	A2	6p chocolate	19.00	45.00
12	A2	1sh brown orange	37.50	55.00
		Nos. 8-12 (5)	104.50	143.00

For surcharge see No. 17.

1907, Mar. 13

13	A2	4p brown & blue	40.00	67.50
14	A2	6p gr red & rose	45.00	80.00
15	A2	1sh violet & green	65.00	95.00
16	A2	5sh ver & green	225.00	350.00
		Nos. 13-16 (4)	375.00	592.50

Numerals of 4p, 1sh and 5sh of type A2 are in color on colorless tablet.
For surcharges see Nos. 18-20.

Nos. 9, 16, 13 Handstamped

One Halfpenny.
No. 17

D / 2
No. 18

1D
No. 19

2½D
No. 20

1907-08

17	A2	½p on 1p	60.00	92.50
18	A2	½p on 5sh	325.00	525.00
a.		Inverted surcharge	100,000.	
b.		Double surcharge	12,750.	12,750.
c.		Double surcharge, one inverted		
d.		Pair, one without surcharge	100,000.	
19	A2	1p on 5sh	350.00	525.00
a.		Double surcharge	22,500.	20,000.
b.		Inverted surcharge	150,000.	
20	A2	2½p on 4p ('08)	2,000.	3,750.
a.		Double surcharge	60,000.	30,000.

No. 19b is unique. It exists on the upper left stamp in an upper left corner margin plate no. 1 block of four that is lightly hinged in the top margin only.
The 1p on 4p is a revenue stamp not authorized for postal use, although postally used examples exist. Value for unused is about $300.

A3

1907-09   Perf. 14

21	A3	½p green	5.25	5.50
22	A3	1p carmine rose	2.10	1.10
23	A3	2½p ultramarine	7.50	3.00

Chalky Paper

24	A3	3p violet, yellow	4.50	3.75
25	A3	4p blk & red, yel	67.50	100.00
26	A3	6p purple & br pur	72.50	52.50
27	A3	1sh black, grn	11.00	32.50
28	A3	5sh grn & red, yel	60.00	90.00
		Nos. 21-28 (8)	185.35	288.35

Issued: ½p, 1p, 12/27/07; 2½p, 3p, 4p, 5sh, 3/30/08; 6d, 10/2/08; 1sh, 4/5/09.
Forged cancellations are found on No. 28.

1908, Mar. 30   Wmk. 2
29	A3	1sh black, *green*	85.00	125.00
30	A3	10sh grn & red, *grn*	225.00	400.00

Numerals of 3p, 4p, 1sh and 5sh of type A3 are in color on plain tablet.
Forged cancellations are found on No. 30.

A4

1908   Wmk. 3   Ordinary Paper
31	A4	¼p brown	6.00	1.00

King George V — A5

1912-20
32	A5	¼p brown ('13)	1.25	.50
33	A5	½p green	3.25	6.00
34	A5	1p carmine ('13)	4.00	3.00
35	A5	2p gray	1.25	12.50
36	A5	2½p ultra ('14)	8.50	13.50

Chalky Paper
37	A5	3p vio, *yel* ('13)	3.00	22.50
38	A5	4p blk & red, *yel* ('13)	1.25	12.50
39	A5	6p vio & red vio ('13)	4.50	9.00
40	A5	1sh blk, *grn* ('13)	4.25	32.50
41	A5	2sh vio & ultra, *bl*	14.50	65.00
42	A5	3sh green & vio	22.50	77.50
43	A5	5sh grn & red, *yel* ('14)	90.00	190.00
44	A5	10sh grn & red, *bl grn, olive back* ('18)	125.00	250.00
a.		10sh green & red, *grn* ('14)	150.00	250.00
		Nos. 32-44 (13)	283.25	694.50

The first printings of the 3p, 1sh and 10sh have a white back.
For surcharges, see Nos. MR1-MR7.

1913, Nov. 19   Surface-colored Paper
45	A5	3p violet, *yel*	4.25	9.50
46	A5	1sh black, *green*	4.25	4.25
47	A5	10sh grn & red, *grn*	130.00	190.00
		Nos. 45-47 (3)	138.50	203.75

Numeral of ¼p, 2p, 3p, 4p, 1sh, 2sh, 3sh and 5sh of type A5 are in color on plain tablet.

King George V — A6

1921-26   Wmk. 4   Perf. 14
50	A6	¼p yel brown	.60	1.75
51	A6	½p gray green	.60	.35
52	A6	1p rose red	1.75	1.00
53	A6	1½p orange brn	2.10	.35
54	A6	2p gray	2.10	4.75
55	A6	2½p ultramarine ('22)	.60	.60
56	A6	3p violet, *yel*	3.25	5.25
57	A6	4½p olive grn	4.00	3.75
58	A6	6p claret	6.50	37.50
59	A6	1sh black, *grn* ('25)	11.50	37.50
60	A6	2sh violet, *blue*	17.00	30.00
61	A6	3sh violet	27.50	19.00
62	A6	5sh green, *yel*	30.00	55.00
63	A6	10sh car, *green*	72.50	100.00
		Nos. 50-63 (14)	180.00	296.80

Issued: 1½p, 4/4/21; ¼p, ½p, 1p, 2p, 2½p, 6p, 2sh, 3sh, 4/1/22; 3p, 4½p, 6/29/23; 5sh, 2/15/25; 1sh, 5/15/25; 10sh, 9/5/26.

1921-22   Wmk. 3
64	A6	3p violet, *org*	1.75	9.50
65	A6	4p red, *yel*	1.25	6.50
66	A6	1sh black, *green*	2.25	11.50
67	A6	5sh green, *yel*	19.00	85.00
a.		5sh deep green, *pale yellow*	110.00	170.00
		Nos. 64-68 (4)	24.25	112.50

Issued: 4p, 4/1/22; others, 4/4/21.

King William IV, King George V
A7

1932, Dec. 5   Wmk. 4   Engr.
69	A7	¼p brown	1.90	1.40
70	A7	½p green	3.25	11.00
71	A7	1p carmine	3.25	15.00
72	A7	1½p orange	3.25	3.75
73	A7	2p gray	3.25	4.75
74	A7	2½p ultramarine	3.25	2.00
75	A7	3p olive green	8.00	6.75
76	A7	6p red violet	13.00	30.00
77	A7	1sh brn & black	20.00	42.50
78	A7	2sh ultra & blk	55.00	100.00
79	A7	5sh green & blk	100.00	160.00
80	A7	10sh car & black	350.00	475.00
		Nos. 69-80 (12)	564.15	852.15
		Set, never hinged	1,250.	

Centenary of the formation of the Cayman Islands Assembly.

Common Design Types
pictured following the introduction.

Silver Jubilee Issue
Common Design Type

1935, May 6   Perf. 13½x14
81	CD301	½p green & black	.35	1.50
82	CD301	2½p blue & brown	5.50	1.75
83	CD301	6p ol grn & lt bl	1.60	4.75
84	CD301	1sh brt vio & ind	12.50	11.50
		Nos. 81-84 (4)	19.95	19.50
		Set, never hinged	24.00	

King George V
A8

Catboat
A9

Red-footed Boobies
A10

Conches and Coconut Palms — A11

Hawksbill Turtles
A12

1935-36   Perf. 12½
85	A8	¼p brown & blk	.60	1.25
86	A9	½p yel grn & ultra	1.25	1.25
87	A10	1p car & ultra	5.00	3.00
88	A11	1½p org & black	1.75	2.40
89	A9	2p brown vio & ultra	4.50	1.50
90	A12	2½p dp blue & blk	4.00	1.60
91	A8	3p ol grn & blk	3.00	3.75
92	A12	6p red vio & blk	8.00	6.00
93	A9	1sh org & ultra	7.00	8.50
94	A10	2sh black & ultra	55.00	50.00

95	A12	5sh green & blk	60.00	65.00
96	A11	10sh car & black	100.00	110.00
		Nos. 85-96 (12)	250.10	254.25
		Set, never hinged	525.00	

Issued: No. 86, 2½p, 6p, 1sh, 1/1/36; others, 5/1/35.

Coronation Issue
Common Design Type

1937, May 13   Perf. 11x11½
97	CD302	½p deep green	.25	1.50
98	CD302	1p dark carmine	.30	.25
99	CD302	2½p deep ultra	.55	.55
		Nos. 97-99 (3)	1.10	2.30
		Set, never hinged	2.25	

Beach View, Grand Cayman
A13

Dolphin — A14

Map of the Islands
A15

Hawksbill Turtles — A16

Cayman Schooner
A17

Perf. 12½; 11½x13 or 13x11½ (A14, #111); 14 (#104, 107)
1938-43   Engr.
100	A13	¼p red orange	.55	.75
a.		Perf. 13½x12½ ('43)	.25	.85
101	A14	½p yel green	.85	.75
a.		Perf. 14 ('43)	1.50	1.75
102	A15	1p carmine	.25	1.00
103	A13	1½p black	.25	.25
104	A16	2p dp violet ('43)	.50	.35
a.		Perf. 11½x13	3.00	.40
105	A17	2½p ultra	.40	.25
106	A15	3p orange	.40	.25
107	A16	6p dk ol grn ('43)	2.50	2.50
a.		Perf. 11½x13	7.25	5.25
108	A14	1sh reddish brown	5.00	2.00
a.		Perf. 14 ('43)	4.00	2.50
109	A13	2sh green	22.50	18.00
110	A17	5sh deep rose	24.50	19.00
111	A16	10sh dark brown	22.50	12.00
a.		Perf. 14 ('43)	20.00	12.00
		Nos. 100-111 (12)	80.20	57.10
		Set, never hinged	125.00	

See Nos. 114-115.

> Catalogue values for unused stamps in this section, from this point to the end of the section, are for Never Hinged items.

Peace Issue
Common Design Type

1946, Aug. 26   Wmk. 4   Perf. 13½
112	CD303	1½p black	.30	.40
113	CD303	3p orange	.30	.40

Types of 1938   Perf. 12½
114	A17	2½p orange	3.50	.65
115	A15	3p ultramarine	3.50	.45

Silver Wedding Issue
Common Design Types

1948, Nov. 29 Photo.   Perf. 14x14½
116	CD304	½p dark green	.25	1.00

Perf. 11½x11
Engr.; Name Typo.
117	CD305	10sh blue violet	22.50	27.50

UPU Issue
Common Design Types
Engr.; Name Typo. on #119, 120

1949, Oct. 10   Perf. 13½, 11x11½
118	CD306	2½p orange	.40	1.00
119	CD307	3p indigo	1.90	2.50
120	CD308	6p olive	.85	2.50
121	CD309	1sh red brown	.85	.40
		Nos. 118-121 (4)	4.00	6.40

Catboat
A18

Designs: ½p, Coconut grove. 1p, Green turtle. 1½p, Thatch rope industry. 2p, Caymanian seamen. 2½p, Map. 3p, Parrot fish. 6p, Bluff, Cayman Brac. 9p, George Town harbor. 1sh, Turtle "crawl". 2sh, Cayman schooner. 5sh, Boat-building. 10sh, Government offices.

Perf. 11½x11
1950, Oct. 2   Wmk. 4   Engr.
122	A18	¼p rose red & blue	.25	.80
123	A18	½p bl grn & red vio	.25	1.75
124	A18	1p dp blue & olive	.75	1.00
125	A18	1½p choc & bl grn	.45	1.00
126	A18	2p rose car & vio	1.75	2.00
127	A18	2½p sepia & aqua	1.75	.85
128	A18	3p bl & blue grn	2.10	2.00
129	A18	6p db bl & org brn	2.50	1.75
130	A18	9p dk grn & rose red	12.00	2.50
131	A18	1sh red org & brn	4.50	3.75
132	A18	2sh red vio & vio	13.00	14.50
133	A18	5sh vio & olive	22.50	9.50
134	A18	10sh rose red & blk	27.50	20.00
		Nos. 122-134 (13)	89.30	61.40

Types of 1950 with Portrait of Queen Elizabeth II and

Lighthouse, South Sound — A20

Elizabeth II and Turtles — A21

Perf. 11½x11, 11x11½
1953-59   Engr.
135	A18	¼p rose red & bl	1.40	.80
136	A18	½p bl grn & red vio	1.10	.75
137	A18	1p dp bl & olive	1.00	.70
138	A18	1½p choc & bl grn	.75	.35
139	A18	2p rose car & vio	3.50	1.40
140	A18	2½p black & aqua	4.25	1.25
141	A18	3p blue & bl grn	5.25	1.00
142	A20	4p dp blue & blk	2.50	.70
143	A18	6p db bl & red brn	2.10	.30
144	A18	9p dk grn & rose red	8.50	.40
145	A18	1sh red org & brn	4.75	.40
146	A18	2sh red vio & vio	16.00	11.50
147	A18	5sh vio & olive	17.50	10.00
148	A18	10sh rose red & blk	19.00	11.50
149	A21	£1 bright blue	37.50	16.00
		Nos. 135-149 (15)	125.10	57.05

Issued: 4p, 3/2; 2p, 2½p, 9p, 6/2/54; ½p, 1p, 1½p, 6p, 7/7/54; ¼p, 3p, 1sh-10sh, 2/21/55; £1, 1/6/59.

Coronation Issue
Common Design Type

1953, June 2   Perf. 13½x13
150	CD312	1p brt green & black	.40	1.00

Arms of Cayman Islands A22

Perf. 12

1959, July 4   Wmk. 4   Photo.
151 A22 2½p dull blue & blk   .65 1.25
152 A22 1sh red orange & blk   .70   .50

Granting of a new constitution.

Cayman Parrot — A23

Catboat A24

1 ½p, Orchid. 2p, Map of Islands. 2 ½p, Fisherman casting net. 3p, West Bay Beach. 4p, Green turtle. 6p, Cayman schooner. 9p, Angler with kingfish. 1sh, Iguana. 1sh3p, Swimming pool, Cayman Brac. 1sh9p, Girl and sailboat. 5sh, Fort George. 10sh, Coat of Arms. £1, Queen Elizabeth II.

Perf. 11x11½, 11½x11

1962, Nov. 28   Wmk. 314   Engr.
153 A23 ¼p rose red & emer   1.10   1.50
154 A24 1p olive & black   .95   .40
155 A24 1 ½p purple & yel   4.75   1.25
156 A24 2p sepia & blue   1.20   .50
157 A24 2 ½p green & vio   .95   1.50
158 A24 3p car & blue   .45   .40
159 A24 4p pur & green   1.50   .95
160 A24 6p sepia & green   3.50   .55
161 A23 9p pur & vio bl   2.50   .85
162 A24 1sh rose & sepia   .95   .25
163 A24 1sh3p brn org & lt grn   4.00   3.50
164 A24 1sh9p vio & bl grn   16.50   2.25
165 A24 5sh grn & dl pur   13.00   9.50
166 A23 10sh blue & olive   22.50 13.00
167 A23 £1 blk & car rose   22.50 24.00
         Revenue cancel   .80
     Nos. 153-167 (15)   96.35 60.40

Freedom from Hunger Issue
Common Design Type
1963, June 4   Photo.   Perf. 14x14½
168 CD314 1sh9p car rose   .50   .30

Red Cross Centenary Issue
Common Design Type
Wmk. 314
1963, Sept. 2   Litho.   Perf. 13
169 CD315 1p black & red   .25   .25
170 CD315 1sh9p ultra & red   .70   1.75

Shakespeare Issue
Common Design Type
1964, Apr. 23   Photo.   Perf. 14x14½
171 CD316 6p deep lilac rose   .35   .30

ITU Issue
Common Design Type
1965, May 17   Litho.   Wmk. 314
172 CD317 1p ultra & red lil   .25   .25
173 CD317 1sh3p rose lil & grn   .75   .75

Intl. Cooperation Year Issue
Common Design Type
1965, Oct. 25   Wmk. 314   Perf. 14½
174 CD318 1p blue grn & claret   .30   .25
175 CD318 1sh lt vio & green   .70   .70

Churchill Memorial Issue
Common Design Type
1966, Jan. 24   Photo.   Perf. 14
Design in Black, Gold and Carmine Rose
176 CD319 ¼p bright blue   .25   1.50
177 CD319 1p green   .50   .50
178 CD319 1sh brown   .90   .65
179 CD319 1sh9p violet   1.75   .90
     Nos. 176-179 (4)   3.40   3.55

Royal Visit Issue
Common Design Type
1966, Feb. 4   Litho.   Perf. 11x12
180 CD320 1p violet blue   .70   .30
181 CD320 1sh9p dk car rose   2.75   1.50

World Cup Soccer Issue
Common Design Type
1966, July 1   Litho.   Perf. 14
182 CD321 1 ½p multicolored   .25   .25
183 CD321 1sh9p multicolored   .50   .50

WHO Headquarters Issue
Common Design Type
1966, Sept. 20   Litho.   Perf. 14
184 CD322 1p multicolored   .65   .30
185 CD322 1sh3p multicolored 1.60   1.10

UNESCO Anniversary Issue
Common Design Type
1966, Dec. 1   Litho.   Perf. 14
186 CD323 1p "Education"   .25   .25
187 CD323 1sh9p "Science"   .75   .35
188 CD323 5sh "Culture"   1.50   1.10
     Nos. 186-188 (3)   2.50   1.70

Telephone and Map of Caymans — A25

Perf. 14½x14

1966, Dec. 5   Litho.   Wmk. 314
189 A25 4p multicolored   .25   .25
190 A25 9p multicolored   .30   .30

Linking of the Cayman telephone system with the intl. system.

BAC 1-11 Jet Liner over Schooner — A26

1966, Dec. 17
191 A26 1sh blue, ol & black   .35   .35
192 A26 1sh9p ultra, grn & sepia   .60   .60

Opening of the Grand Cayman Airport jet service.

Water Skiing and ITY Emblem A27

ITY Emblem and: 6p, Skin diving. 1sh, Sport fishing. 1sh9p, Sailing.

Perf. 14½x14

1967, Dec. 1   Photo.   Wmk. 314
193 A27 4p multi & gold   .35   .25
 a.   Gold omitted   250.00 225.00
194 A27 6p multi & gold   .35   .25
195 A27 1sh multi & gold   .35   .35
196 A27 1sh9p multi & gold   .50   .75
     Nos. 193-196 (4)   1.55   1.60

International Tourist Year.

Human Rights Flame and Freed Slaves A28

1968, June 3   Photo.   Wmk. 314
197 A28 3p slate bl, grn & gold   .25   .25
198 A28 9p lt brn, grn & gold   .25   .25
199 A28 5sh ultra, grn & gold   .70   .70
     Nos. 197-199 (3)   1.20   1.20

International Human Rights Year.

Long Jump A29

1sh3p, High jump. 2sh, Pole vault, vert.

1968, Oct. 1   Litho.   Perf. 13½
200 A29 1sh multicolored   .25   .25
201 A29 1sh3p multicolored   .25   .25
202 A29 2sh yellow & multi   .30   .30
     Nos. 200-202 (3)   .80   .80

19th Olympic Games, Mexico City, 10/12-27.

Adoration of Shepherds, by Carel Fabritius — A30

Christmas: 1p, 8p, 2sh, Adoration of the Shepherds, by Rembrandt.

Perf. 14x14½

1968, Nov. 18   Photo.   Wmk. 314
203 A30 ¼p brown & multi   .25   .25
 a.   Gold omitted   250.00
204 A30 1p violet & multi   .25   .25
205 A30 6p multicolored   .25   .25
206 A30 8p car & multi   .25   .25
207 A30 1sh3p multicolored   .30   .30
208 A30 2sh gray & multi   .30   .30
     Nos. 203-208 (6)   1.60   1.60

1969, Jan. 8   Unwmk.
209 A30 ¼p red lilac & multi   .75   .35

Grand Cayman Thrush A31

1p, Brahman cattle. 2p, Blowholes on coast. 2 ½p, Map of Grand Cayman. 3p, Town scene in George Town. 4p, Royal poinciana. 6p, Map of Cayman Brac and Little Cayman. 8p, Motor vessels at berth. 1sh, Basket making. 1sh3p, Beach scene. 1sh6p, Rope making. 2sh, Barracudas. 4sh, Government House. 10sh, Coat of arms. £1, Queen Elizabeth II.

Unwmk.

1969, June 5   Litho.   Perf. 14
210 A31 ¼p multi   .25   .90
211 A31 1p multi   .25   .25
212 A31 2p multi   .25   .25
213 A31 2 ½p multi   .25   .25
214 A31 3p multi   .25   .25
215 A31 4p multi   .25   .25
216 A31 6p multi   .25   .25
217 A31 8p multi   .25   .25
218 A31 1sh multi   .25   .25
219 A31 1sh3p multi   .30   1.90
220 A31 1sh6p multi   .35   1.90
221 A31 2sh multi   1.25   1.40
222 A31 4sh multi   .60   1.40

223 A31 10sh multi, vert.   1.25   2.50
224 A31 £1 multi, vert.   3.00   3.50
     Nos. 210-224 (15)   9.00 15.50

See Nos. 262-276. For surcharges see Nos. 227-241.

1969, Aug. 11   Wmk. 314 Sideways
225 A31 ¼p multicolored   .70   .70

Type of 1969 Surcharged

1969, Sept. 8   Wmk. 314   Perf. 14
227 A31 ¼c on ¼p multi   .25   .85
228 A31 1c on 1p multi   .25   .25
229 A31 2c on 2p multi   .25   .25
230 A31 3c on 4p multi   .25   .25
231 A31 4c on 2 ½p multi   .25   .25
232 A31 5c on 6p multi   .25   .25
233 A31 7c on 8p multi   .25   .25
234 A31 8c on 3p multi   .25   .25
235 A31 10c on 1s multi   .35   .25
236 A31 12c on 1sh3p multi   .45   1.90
237 A31 15c on 1sh6p multi   .25   1.25
238 A31 20c on 2sh multi   2.00   2.10
239 A31 40c on 4sh multi   .55   1.25
240 A31 $1 on 10sh multi   1.45   3.75
241 A31 $2 on £1 multi   2.25   4.50
     Nos. 227-241 (15)   9.60 17.60

The surcharge is arranged differently on various denominations.

Madonna and Child, by Alvise Vivarini — A32

Christmas: 1c, 7c, 20c, The Adoration of the Kings, by Jan Gossaert.

1969, Nov. 4   Photo.   Perf. 14
242 A32 ¼c blue & multi   .25   .25
243 A32 ¼c emer & multi   .25   .25
244 A32 ¼c red org & multi   .25   .25
245 A32 ¼c brt pink & multi   .25   .25
246 A32 1c vio blue & multi   .25   .25
247 A32 5c red org & multi   .25   .25
248 A32 7c dk green & multi   .25   .25
249 A32 12c emer & multi   .25   .25
250 A32 20c multicolored   .25   .25
     Nos. 242-250 (9)   2.25   2.25

"Noli me Tangere," by Titian — A33

1970, Mar. 23   Litho.   Unwmk.
251 A33 ¼c dull grn & multi   .25   .25
252 A33 ¼c dk car & multi   .25   .25
253 A33 ¼c violet & multi   .25   .25
254 A33 ¼c bister & multi   .25   .25
255 A33 10c vio blue & multi   .25   .25
256 A33 12c red brn & multi   .25   .25
257 A33 40c brn vio & multi   .60   .60
     Nos. 251-257 (7)   2.10   2.10

Easter.

Barnaby from "Barnaby Rudge" by Dickens (1812-70), English Novelist — A34

Characters from Charles Dickens: 12c, Sairey Gamp, from "Martin Chuzzlewit." 20c, Mr. Micawber and David, from "David Copperfield." 40c, The Marchioness from "The Old Curiosity Shop."

1970, June 17 Photo. Perf. 14½x14

258	A34	1c ol green, yel & blk	.25	.25
259	A34	12c red brn, brick red & black	.25	.25
260	A34	20c dk ol bis, gold & black	.35	.35
261	A34	40c dp ultra, lt bl & blk	.60	.60
		Nos. 258-261 (4)	1.45	1.45

Type of Regular Issue 1969 Values in Cents and Dollars

Designs: ¼c, Grand Cayman thrush. 1c, Brahman cattle. 2c, Blowholes on coast. 3c, Royal poinciana. 4c, Map of Grand Cayman. 5c, Map of Cayman Brac and Little Cayman. 7c, Motor vessels at berth. 8c, Town scene in George Town. 10c, Basket making. 12c, Beach scene. 15c, Rope making. 20c, Barracudas. 40c, Government House. $1, Coat of arms, vert. $2, Queen Elizabeth II, vert.

Wmk. 314

1970, Sept. 8 Litho. Perf. 14

262	A31	¼c multicolored	.60	.30
263	A31	1c multicolored	.25	.25
264	A31	2c multicolored	.25	.25
265	A31	3c multicolored	.25	.25
266	A31	4c multicolored	.25	.25
267	A31	5c multicolored	.45	.25
268	A31	7c multicolored	.40	.25
269	A31	8c multicolored	.40	.25
270	A31	10c multicolored	.40	.25
271	A31	12c multicolored	1.00	1.10
272	A31	15c multicolored	1.10	3.50
273	A31	20c multicolored	2.50	1.75
274	A31	40c multicolored	.85	.85
275	A31	$1 multicolored	1.10	5.75
276	A31	$2 multicolored	1.75	5.75
		Nos. 262-276 (15)	11.55	21.00

The Three Wise Men A35

Christmas: 1c, 10c, 20c, Nativity and globe.

1970, Oct. 8 Litho. Perf. 14

277	A35	¼c brt grn & yel grn	.25	.25
278	A35	1c bl grn, yel grn & blk	.25	.25
279	A35	5c dp claret & org	.25	.25
280	A35	10c red org, yel & blk	.25	.25
281	A35	12c ultra & lt grnsh bl	.25	.25
282	A35	20c grn, yel grn & blk	.25	.25
		Nos. 277-282 (6)	1.50	1.50

Grand Cayman Terrapin A36

Cayman Islands Turtles: 7c, Green turtle. 12c, Hawksbill turtle. 20c, Turtle farm.

1971, Jan. 28 Perf. 14x14½

283	A36	5c multicolored	.70	.40
284	A36	7c multicolored	.85	.40
285	A36	12c multicolored	1.75	.50
286	A36	20c multicolored	3.00	2.00
		Nos. 283-286 (4)	6.30	3.30

Dendrophylax Fawcetii — A37

Wild Orchids of West Indies: 2c, Schomburgkia thomsoniana. 10c, Vanilla claviculata. 40c, Oncidium variegatum.

1971, Apr. 7 Wmk. 314 Perf. 14

287	A37	¼c brown & multi	.35	1.60
288	A37	2c ol green & multi	1.00	1.25
289	A37	10c gray bl & multi	3.50	3.50
290	A37	40c lt violet & multi	5.00	4.00
		Nos. 287-290 (4)	9.85	7.60

Adoration of the Kings, 15th Century — A38

Christmas: 1c, 15c, Nativity (detail), Paris, 14th cent. 5c, 20c, Adoration of the Kings (detail), Burgundian, 15th cent.

1971, Sept. 27 Perf. 14

291	A38	¼c gold & multi	.25	.25
292	A38	1c gold & multi	.25	.25
293	A38	5c gold & multi	.25	.25
294	A38	12c gold & multi	.25	.25
295	A38	15c gold & multi	.30	.30
296	A38	20c gold & multi	.40	.40
a.		Souvenir sheet of 6, #291-296	4.75	4.75
		Nos. 291-296 (6)	1.70	1.70

Underwater Cable, Turtle and Telephone — A39

1972, Jan. 10

297	A39	2c multicolored	.25	.25
298	A39	10c multicolored	.25	.25
299	A39	40c multicolored	.75	.75
		Nos. 297-299 (3)	1.25	1.25

Coaxial cable for world communications.

Courthouse — A40

Designs: 15c, 40c, Legislative Assembly Building, George Town.

1972, Aug. 15 Perf. 13½x14

300	A40	5c dp car & multi	.25	.25
301	A40	15c lilac rose & multi	.25	.25
302	A40	25c dull grn & multi	.25	.25
303	A40	40c dk blue & multi	.40	.40
a.		Souvenir sheet of 4, #300-303	1.10	1.10
		Nos. 300-303 (4)	1.15	1.15

New Cayman Islands government buildings.

Silver Wedding Issue, 1972
Common Design Type

Design: Queen Elizabeth II, Prince Philip, hawksbill turtle and conch.

1972, Nov. 20 Photo. Perf. 14x14½

304	CD324	12c vio black & multi	.25	.25
305	CD324	30c olive & multi	.50	.50

$1 Note and 1c Coin A41

6c, $5 note and 5c coin. 15c, $10 note and 10c coin. 25c, $25 note and 25c coin.

1973, Jan. 15

306	A41	3c emerald & multi	.25	.25
307	A41	6c yellow & multi	.30	.60
308	A41	15c lilac & multi	.65	.50
309	A41	25c orange & multi	1.25	.90
a.		Souvenir sheet of 4, #306-309	4.00	4.00
		Nos. 306-309 (4)	2.45	2.25

First Cayman Islands coinage and bank notes, May 1, 1972.

Last Supper A42

Stained Glass Windows: 10c, Christ Carrying Cross, vert. 12c, Resurrection, vert. 30c, Crucifixion.

Perf. 14½x14, 14x14½

1973, Apr. 11 Litho.

310	A42	10c pink & multi	.25	.25
311	A42	12c yel green & multi	.25	.25
312	A42	20c lt blue & multi	.30	.30
313	A42	30c yellow & multi	.40	.40
a.		Souvenir sheet of 4	1.45	1.45
		Nos. 310-313 (4)	1.20	1.20

Easter. No. 313a contains 4 stamps similar to Nos. 310-313 with simulated perforations.

Nativity — A43

Christmas: 5c, 12c, 25c, Adoration of the Magi, from Breviary of Queen Isabella. 9c, 15c, Like 3c, Nativity from Sforza Book of Hours.

1973, Oct. 2 Perf. 14½

314	A43	3c dull green & multi	.25	.25
315	A43	5c dull pur & multi	.25	.25
316	A43	9c sepia & multi	.25	.25
317	A43	12c dk blue & multi	.25	.25
318	A43	15c dp rose & multi	.25	.25
319	A43	25c black & multi	.40	.40
		Nos. 314-319 (6)	1.65	1.65

Princess Anne's Wedding Issue
Common Design Type

1973, Nov. 14 Wmk. 314 Perf. 14

320	CD325	10c brt green & multi	.25	.25
321	CD325	30c lilac & multi	.30	.30

White-winged Dove — A44

10c, Vitelline warblers. 12c, Greater Antillean grackles. 20c, West Indian red-bellied woodpecker. 30c, Stripe-headed tanagers. 50c, Yucatan vireos.

1974, Jan. 2 Litho. Perf. 14x14½

322	A44	3c shown	2.75	.40
323	A44	10c multicolored	3.50	.40
324	A44	12c multicolored	3.50	.40
325	A44	20c multicolored	5.75	1.00
326	A44	30c multicolored	7.25	2.25
327	A44	50c multicolored	9.75	6.25
		Nos. 322-327 (6)	32.50	10.70

See Nos. 354-359.

One-room Schoolhouse — A45

Designs: 20c, New comprehensive school. 30c, Creative Arts Center, Mona, Jamaica.

1974, May 1 Perf. 14

328	A45	12c multicolored	.25	.25
329	A45	20c multicolored	.25	.25
330	A45	30c multicolored	.30	.30
		Nos. 328-330 (3)	.80	.80

25th anniv. of the University College of the West Indies.

Hermit Crab and Pirate Gold (#346) A46

Coat of Arms (#344) — A47

Elizabeth II (#348) — A48

Designs: 3c, Pirate, treasure chest and lion's paw. 4c, Spotted scorpionfish and crown. 6c, Flint-lock pistol and brain coral. 6c, Blackbeard on Grand Cayman and green turtle. 8c, 9c, Jeweled pomander and porkfish. 10c, Spiny lobster and gold coins. 12c, Jeweled sword, dagger and sea fan. 15c, Cabrit's murex and jeweled necklace. 20c, Queen conch, pistol and gold cup. 25c, Hogfish and pirate chest. 40c, Gold chalice and sea whip.

Wmk. 314 Upright, Sideways (#331-332, 336, 344-345)

1974-75 Litho. Perf. 14

Size: 41x26.5mm

331	A46	1c multi ('75)	4.25	1.75
a.		Wmk. upright	3.75	1.25
332	A46	3c multicolored	4.25	1.75
a.		Wmk. upright	3.75	.70
333	A46	4c multicolored	.70	.95
334	A46	5c multicolored	3.50	1.00
335	A46	6c multicolored	.50	2.75
336	A46	8c multicolored	3.00	9.50
337	A46	9c multicolored	5.00	12.50
338	A46	10c multicolored	5.50	1.10
339	A46	12c multicolored	.50	2.25
340	A46	15c multicolored	.55	1.75
341	A46	20c multicolored	5.00	4.00
342	A46	25c multicolored	.60	.85
343	A46	40c multicolored	5.00	1.50
344	A47	$1 multicolored	3.25	3.50
345	A48	$2 multicolored	9.50	10.00
		Nos. 331-345 (15)	51.10	55.15

Issued: No. 332, 11/12; 8c, 12/16; No. 331, 9/29; others, 8/1.

1976-77 Wmk. 373

332b	A46	3c multicolored	1.00	4.50
333a	A46	4c multicolored ('77)	1.50	5.00
334a	A46	5c multi ('77)	7.50	7.50
336b	A46	8c multicolored	8.50	6.25
338b	A46	10c multicolored	3.75	5.00
341b	A46	20c multicolored	4.25	3.50
344a	A47	$1 multi ('77)	7.50	11.00
345b	A48	$2 multicolored	8.50	9.25
		Nos. 332b-345b (8)	42.50	52.00

Issued: 3c, 8c, 10c, 20c, $2, 9/3; 4c, 5c, $1, 10/19.

Design Smaller
Size: 39.5x25mm
Wmk. 373 (Sideways on 1c-40c)

1978-80

346	A46	1c multicolored		1.25	1.75
346A	A46	3c multicolored		1.00	.75
346B	A46	5c multi ('79)		2.75	3.00
347	A46	10c multicolored		2.00	1.00
347A	A46	20c multicolored		4.00	1.75
347B	A46	40c multi ('79)		15.00	22.50
347C	A47	$1 multi ('80)		22.50	7.00
348	A48	$2 multi ('80)		6.50	25.00
		Nos. 346-348 (8)		55.00	62.75

Issued: 1c, 3c, 3/16; 10c, 20c, 5/25; 5c, 12/11; $2, 4/3; $1, 7/30.

Sea Captain and Ship — A49

1974, Oct. 7   Wmk. 314   *Perf. 14*

349	A49	8c shown		.25	.25
350	A49	12c Thatch weaver		.25	.25
351	A49	20c Farmer		.55	.50
	a.	Miniature sheet of 3, #349-351		2.00	2.50
		Nos. 349-351 (3)		1.05	1.00

Arms of Cinque   Churchill Coat of
Ports and Lord   Arms — A51
Warden's
Flag — A50

1974, Nov. 30

352	A50	12c multicolored		.25	.25
353	A51	50c multicolored		.70	.70
	a.	Souvenir sheet of 2, #352-353		1.10	1.25

Sir Winston Churchill (1874-1965).

Bird Type of 1974

3c, Yellow-shafted flicker. 10c, West Indian tree duck. 12c, Yellow warblers. 20c, White-bellied dove. 30c, Magnificent frigate bird. 50c, Cayman amazon.

Wmk. 314

1975, Jan. 1   Litho.   *Perf. 14*

354	A44	3c multicolored		.70	.45
355	A44	10c multicolored		1.25	.45
356	A44	12c multicolored		1.60	.70
357	A44	20c multicolored		2.50	2.50
358	A44	30c multicolored		3.75	4.25
359	A44	50c multicolored		4.50	11.50
	a.	Wmk. 362 (Lesotho)		650.00	
		Nos. 354-359 (6)		14.30	19.85

Ivory Crosier with
Crucifixion — A52

Design: 35c, Crucifixion, ivory and gilt. Designs show heads of 14th century French pastoral staffs.

Wmk. 314

1975, Mar. 24   Litho.   *Perf. 14*

360	A52	15c plum & multi		.25	.25
361	A52	35c gray & multi		.65	.65
	a.	Souvenir sheet of 2, #360-361		1.10	1.10

Easter. No. 361a exists imperf.
See Nos. 366-367.

Israel
Hands
A53

Designs: Pirates and various scenes.

1975, July 25   Wmk. 314

362	A53	10c shown		.50	.25
363	A53	12c John Fenn		.50	.25
364	A53	20c Thomas Anstis		.85	.50
365	A53	30c Edward Low		1.10	1.50
		Nos. 362-365 (4)		2.95	2.50

Easter Type of 1975

Designs after ivory carved pastoral staffs showing Virgin and Child with angels, French, 14th century.

Wmk. 373

1975, Oct. 31   Litho.   *Perf. 14*

366	A52	12c dk green & multi		.25	.25
367	A52	50c multicolored		.70	.70
	a.	Souvenir sheet of 2, #366-367		1.50	1.90

Christmas.

Registered Letter with Nos. 1-2;
Cayman Brac Government House and
Sub Post Office — A54

Cayman Islands 1st postage stamps, 75th anniv.: 20c, Cayman Islands #1 and cancelation used 1890-94; 30c, #2, 20; 50c, #1-2.

1976, Mar. 12   Litho.   *Perf. 13½x14*

368	A54	10c lt blue & multi		.25	.25
369	A54	20c pink & multi		.25	.25
370	A54	30c multicolored		.40	.40
371	A54	50c yellow & multi		.60	.60
	a.	Souvenir sheet of 4, #368-371		4.00	4.00
		Nos. 368-371 (4)		1.50	1.50

Seals of Georgia, Delaware and New
Hampshire — A55

15c, Seals of SC, NJ, MD. 20c, Seals of VA, RI, MA. 25c, Seals of NY, CT, NC. 30c, Seal of PA, Liberty Bell and Great Seal of the US.

Wmk. 373

1976, May 29   Litho.   *Perf. 14*

372	A55	10c olive & multi		.35	.25
373	A55	15c blue & multi		.45	.25
374	A55	20c multicolored		.60	.50
375	A55	25c blue grn & multi		.90	.60
376	A55	30c red brn & multi		1.10	.85
	a.	Souvenir sheet of 5 + label		6.25	6.25
		Nos. 372-376 (5)		3.40	2.25

American Bicentennial. Nos. 372-376 printed in sheets of 5. No. 376a contains one each of Nos. 372-376 and corner label inscribed "USA 200."

French Class 470
Racing
Dinghies — A56

Design: 50c, One racing dinghy.

1976, Aug. 16   Litho.   *Perf. 14*

377	A56	20c multicolored		.60	.45
378	A56	50c multicolored		1.10	1.10

21st Olympic Games, Montreal, Canada, July 17-Aug. 1.

Queen Elizabeth
II — A57

8c, Prince Charles, 1973 visit. 50c, Preparation for anointing ceremony, horiz.

Perf. 14x13½, 13½x14

1977, Feb. 7   Litho.   Wmk. 373

379	A57	8c multicolored		.25	.25
380	A57	30c multicolored		.25	.25
381	A57	50c multicolored		.25	.25
		Nos. 379-381 (3)		.75	.75

25th anniv. of the reign of Elizabeth II.

Scuba
Diving
A58

10c, Divers examining underwater wreck. 20c, Fairy basslets (fish). 25c, Sergeant majors (fish).

1977, July 25   *Perf. 13½*

382	A58	5c multicolored		.25	.25
383	A58	10c multicolored		.25	.25
384	A58	20c multicolored		.45	.45
385	A58	25c multicolored		.60	.60
	a.	Souvenir sheet of 4		3.00	3.00
		Nos. 382-385 (4)		1.55	1.55

Tourist publicity. No. 385a contains one each of Nos. 382-385, perf. 14½.

Composia Fidelissima — A59

Butterflies: 8c, Heliconius charitonius. 10c, Danaus gilippus. 15c, Agraulis vanillae. 20c, Junonia evarete. 30c, Anartia jatrophae.

1977, Dec. 2   Wmk. 373   *Perf. 14x13*

386	A59	5c multicolored		1.10	.25
387	A59	8c multicolored		1.25	.30
388	A59	10c multicolored		1.35	.35
389	A59	15c multicolored		1.60	.55
390	A59	20c multicolored		1.75	.60
391	A59	30c multicolored		2.00	1.10
		Nos. 386-391 (6)		9.05	3.15

Cruise Ship
"Southward"
A60

Designs: 5c, "Renaissance." 30c, New harbor, vert. 50c, "Daphne," vert.

1978, Jan. 23   Litho.   *Perf. 14*

392	A60	3c multicolored		.45	.25
393	A60	5c multicolored		.45	.25
394	A60	30c multicolored		1.25	.50
395	A60	50c multicolored		1.50	.75
		Nos. 392-395 (4)		3.65	1.75

New harbor and cruise ships.

Crucifixion, by
Dürer — A61

Etchings by Dürer: 15c, Christ at Emmaus. 20c, Entry into Jerusalem. 30c, Christ washing Peter's feet.

1978, Mar. 20   Litho.   *Perf. 12*

396	A61	10c multicolored		.30	.25
397	A61	15c multicolored		.45	.30
398	A61	20c multicolored		.55	.40
399	A61	30c multicolored		.65	.55
	a.	Souvenir sheet of 4, #396-399		6.50	6.50
		Nos. 396-399 (4)		1.95	1.50

Easter; Albrecht Dürer (1471-1528). Nos. 396-399 issued in sheets of 6.

Explorers, Singing
Game — A62

10c, Girls' Brigade presenting flag. 20c, Guides studying Bible, playing guitar, tennis and volleyball. 50c, Guides setting table.

1978, Apr. 25   Litho.   *Perf. 14*

400	A62	3c multicolored		.25	.25
401	A62	10c multicolored		.35	.35
402	A62	20c multicolored		.60	.60
403	A62	50c multicolored		1.25	1.25
		Nos. 400-403 (4)		2.45	2.45

3rd Intl. Council Meeting of Girls' Brigade.

Elizabeth II Coronation Anniversary
Issue
Common Design Types
Souvenir Sheet

1978, June 2   Unwmk.   *Perf. 15*

404	Sheet of 6		2.00	2.50
a.	CD326 30c Yale of Beaufort		.30	.30
b.	CD327 30c Elizabeth II		.30	.30
c.	CD328 30c Screech owl		.30	.30

No. 404 contains 2 se-tenant strips of Nos. 404a-404c, separated by horizontal gutter with commemorative and descriptive inscriptions.

A63

A63a

A63: 1c, Trumpetfish. 3c, Nassau grouper. 5c, French angelfish. 10c, Schoolmaster snappers. 20c, Banded butterflyfish. 50c, Black-bar soldierfish.

A63a: 3c, Four-eyed butterflyfish. 5c, Grey angel fish. 10c, Squirrelfish. 15c, Parrotfish. 20c, Spanish hogfish. 30c, Queen angelfish.

1978-79   Wmk. 373   Litho.   *Perf. 14*

405	A63	1c multicolored		.25	.25
406	A63	3c multicolored		.35	.25
407	A63a	3c multicolored		.30	.25
408	A63a	5c multicolored		.35	.25
409	A63	5c multicolored		.30	.25
412	A63a	10c multicolored		.55	.25
413	A63	10c multicolored		.55	.25
414	A63a	15c multicolored		.65	.35
415	A63a	20c multicolored		.85	.45

416	A63	20c multicolored		1.05	.45
417	A63a	30c multicolored		1.75	.70
418	A63	50c multicolored		2.75	1.10
		Nos. 405-418 (12)		9.70	4.80

Issued: design A63, 4/20/79; design A63a, 8/28/78.

Lockheed Lodestar — A64

Aircraft: 5c, Consolidated PBY. 10c, Vickers Viking. 15c, BAC1-11. 20c, Piper Cheyenne, HS 125 and Bell 47. 30c, BAC1-11.

1979, Feb. 5   **Perf. 14½**

420	A64	3c multicolored		.40	.25
421	A64	5c multicolored		.40	.25
422	A64	10c multicolored		.45	.25
423	A64	15c multicolored		.75	.40
424	A64	20c multicolored		.95	.45
425	A64	30c multicolored		1.10	.55
		Nos. 420-425 (6)		4.05	2.15

Opening of Owen Roberts Airport, 25th anniv.

Rowland Hill and No. 2 — A65

Sir Rowland Hill (1795-1879), originator of penny postage, and: 10c, Great Britain #132. 20c, Cayman Islands #149. 50c, Cayman Islands #20.

Perf. 13½x14½

1979, Aug. 15   **Litho.**

426	A65	5c multicolored		.25	.25
427	A65	10c multicolored		.25	.25
428	A65	20c multicolored		.60	.60
		Nos. 426-428 (3)		1.10	1.10

Souvenir Sheet

429	A65	50c multicolored		1.50	1.50

Flight into Egypt A66

Christmas: 20c, Shepherds, Star of Bethlehem. 30c, Nativity. 40c, Three Kings, Star of Bethlehem.

1979, Nov. 20   **Litho.**   **Perf. 13½**

430	A66	10c multicolored		.25	.25
431	A66	20c multicolored		.25	.25
432	A66	30c multicolored		.40	.25
433	A66	40c multicolored		.70	.30
		Nos. 430-433 (4)		1.60	1.05

Bonaventure House, Rotary Emblem — A67

30c, Paul P. Harris, vert. 50c, Anniversary emblem, vert.

Perf. 14x13½, 13½x14

1980, Feb. 14   **Litho.**   **Wmk. 373**

434	A67	20c shown		.30	.25
435	A67	30c multicolored		.50	.25
436	A67	50c multicolored		.80	.50
		Nos. 434-436 (3)		1.60	1.00

Rotary International, 75th anniversary.

Mailman, London 1980 Emblem A68

1980, May 6   **Litho.**   **Perf. 14**

437	A68	5c shown		.25	.25
438	A68	10c Cat boat		.25	.25
439	A68	15c Mounted mailman		.25	.25
440	A68	30c Mail wagon		.40	.35
441	A68	40c Mailman on bicycle		.50	.45
442	A68	$1 Mail truck		1.00	.90
		Nos. 437-442 (6)		2.65	2.45

London '80 Intl. Stamp Exhib., May 6-14.

Queen Mother Elizabeth Birthday Issue
Common Design Type

1980, Aug. 4   **Litho.**   **Perf. 14**

443	CD330	20c multicolored		.45	.45

Spondylus Americanus A69

10c, Murex brevifrons. 30c, Cymatium femorale. 50c, Vasum muricatum.

1980, Aug. 12   **Perf. 14½x14**

444	A69	5c shown		.80	.25
445	A69	10c multicolored		.80	.30
446	A69	30c multicolored		1.60	.65
447	A69	50c multicolored		1.75	1.25
		Nos. 444-447 (4)		4.95	2.45

See Nos. 502-505, 518-521.

Lantana — A70

1980, Oct. 21   **Litho.**   **Perf. 14**

448	A70	5c shown		.25	.25
449	A70	15c Bauhinia		.30	.25
450	A70	30c Hibiscus		.55	.30
451	A70	$1 Milk and wine lily		1.45	1.40
		Nos. 448-451 (4)		2.55	2.20

See Nos. 478-481.

Juvenile Tarpon and Fire Sponges — A71

5c, Mangrove root oysters. 10c, Mangrove crab. 15c, Lizard, crescent spot butterfly. 20c, Tricolored heron. 30c, Red mangrove flower. 40c, Red mangrove seeds. 50c, Waterhouse's leaf-nosed bat. $1, Black-crowned night heron. $2, Cayman Islands arms. $4, Queen Elizabeth II.

1980, Dec. 9   **Litho.**   **Perf. 13½x13**
Without Imprint

452	A71	3c shown		1.10	2.25
453	A71	5c multicolored		1.25	1.10
d.		Wmk. 384		8.00	8.00
e.		Wmk. 384, perf. 14		6.75	7.00
454	A71	10c multicolored		.65	1.10
d.		Wmk. 384, perf. 14		10.00	9.75
455	A71	15c multicolored		1.10	2.25
456	A71	20c multicolored		1.50	2.75
457	A71	30c multicolored		.90	1.40
458	A71	40c multicolored		.95	1.25
459	A71	50c multicolored		1.50	1.75
460	A71	$1 multicolored		6.00	5.50

461	A71	$2 multicolored		2.25	3.75
462	A71	$4 multicolored		4.25	4.25
		Nos. 452-462 (11)		21.45	27.35

Nos. 453d, 453e and 454d inscribed "1986" below design. Issued: No. 453d, 4/86; Nos. 453e, 454fa, 6/86.

1982, June 14   Inscribed "1982"

452a	A71	3c shown		5.00	4.00
453a	A71	5c multicolored		1.25	.90
454a	A71	10c multicolored		1.25	.90
455a	A71	15c multicolored		4.50	2.00
456a	A71	20c multicolored		2.50	2.25
457a	A71	30c multicolored		1.50	1.50
458a	A71	40c multicolored		1.50	1.50
459a	A71	50c multicolored		2.00	2.00
460a	A71	$1 multicolored		6.00	5.00
461a	A71	$2 multicolored		4.00	4.00
462a	A71	$4 multicolored		9.00	9.00
		Nos. 452a-462a (11)		38.50	33.05

Issued: No. 453a, 4/86; No. 454a, 6/86.

1984   Inscribed "1984"

453b	A71	5c multicolored		2.50	2.50

Issued: No. 453b, 6/86.

1985   Inscribed "1985"

453c	A71	5c multicolored		1.25	1.25
454c	A71	10c multicolored		1.25	1.25
455c	A71	15c multicolored		4.50	4.50
456c	A71	20c multicolored		2.50	2.50
457c	A71	30c multicolored		1.50	1.50
458c	A71	40c multicolored		1.50	1.50
459c	A71	50c multicolored		2.00	2.00
460c	A71	$1 multicolored		6.00	5.00
461c	A71	$2 multicolored		5.00	5.00
		Nos. 453c-461c (9)		25.50	24.50

Bread and Wine — A72

1981, Mar. 17   **Wmk. 373**   **Perf. 14**

463	A72	3c shown		.25	.25
464	A72	10c Crown of thorns		.25	.25
465	A72	20c Crucifix		.25	.25
466	A72	$1 Christ		.60	1.10
		Nos. 463-466 (4)		1.35	1.85

Easter.

Wood Slave A73

1981, June 16   **Litho.**   **Perf. 13½**

467	A73	20c shown		.40	.40
468	A73	30c Cayman iguana		.60	.60
469	A73	40c Lion lizard		.80	.80
470	A73	50c Freshwater turtle		.95	.95
		Nos. 467-470 (4)		2.75	2.75

Royal Wedding Issue
Common Design Type

1981, July 22   **Litho.**   **Perf. 14**

471	CD331	20c Bouquet		.25	.25
472	CD331	30c Charles		.30	.30
473	CD331	$1 Couple		.80	.80
		Nos. 471-473 (3)		1.35	1.35

Intl. Year of the Disabled A74

5c, Scuba divers. 15c, Old School for Handicapped. 20c, New School for Handicapped. $1, Beach scene.

1981, Sept. 29   **Litho.**   **Perf. 14**

474	A74	5c multicolored		.25	.25
475	A74	15c multicolored		.25	.25
476	A74	20c multicolored		.35	.35
477	A74	$1 multicolored		1.40	1.40
		Nos. 474-477 (4)		2.25	2.25

Flower Type of 1980

1981, Oct. 20   **Litho.**   **Perf. 14**

478	A70	3c Bougainvillea		.25	.25
479	A70	10c Morning glory		.25	.25
480	A70	20c Wild amaryllis		.55	.55
481	A70	$1 Cordia		2.25	2.25
		Nos. 478-481 (4)		3.30	3.30

TB Bacillus Centenary — A75

15c, Koch, horizontal microscope. 30c, Koch, vert. microscope. 40c, Microscope, vert. 50c, Koch, diff., vert.

1982, Mar. 24   **Litho.**   **Perf. 14½**

482	A75	15c multicolored		.30	.30
483	A75	30c multicolored		.65	.65
484	A75	40c multicolored		.80	.80
485	A75	50c multicolored		1.10	1.10
		Nos. 482-485 (4)		2.85	2.85

Princess Diana Issue
Common Design Type

1982, July 1   **Litho.**   **Perf. 13**

486	CD333	20c Arms		.50	.40
487	CD333	30c Diana		.90	.55
488	CD333	40c Wedding		1.00	.75
489	CD333	50c Portrait		3.00	1.00
		Nos. 486-489 (4)		5.40	2.70

Scouting Year A76

1982, Aug. 24   **Wmk. 373**   **Perf. 14**

490	A76	3c Pitching tent		.30	.25
491	A76	20c Cooking		.65	.65
492	A76	30c Troop		1.10	1.10
493	A76	50c Boating skills		1.50	1.50
		Nos. 490-493 (4)		3.55	3.50

Christmas 1982 — A77

Virgin and Child Paintings by Raphael.

1982, Oct. 26   **Perf. 14½**

494	A77	3c multicolored		.25	.25
495	A77	10c multicolored		.30	.30
496	A77	20c multicolored		.60	.60
497	A77	30c multicolored		.85	.85
		Nos. 494-497 (4)		2.00	2.00

Representative Govt. Sesquicentennial — A78

3c, Mace. 10c, Old Courthouse. 20c, Commonwealth Parliamentary Assoc. arms. 30c, Legislative Assembly building.

1982, Nov. 9   **Litho.**   **Wmk. 373**

498	A78	3c multicolored		.25	.25
499	A78	10c multicolored		.25	.25
500	A78	20c multicolored		.40	.40
501	A78	30c multicolored		.60	.60
		Nos. 498-501 (4)		1.50	1.50

Shell Type of 1980

5c, Natica canrena. 10c, Cassis tuberosa. 20c, Strombus gallus. $1, Cypraecassis testiculus.

1983, Jan. 11   **Litho.**   **Perf. 13½**
502	A69	5c multicolored	.25	.25
503	A69	10c multicolored	.40	.40
504	A69	20c multicolored	.85	.85
505	A69	$1 multicolored	3.50	3.50
		Nos. 502-505 (4)	5.00	5.00

Visit of Queen Elizabeth II and Prince Philip A79

20c, Legislative Building, Cayman Brac. 30c, Leg. Bldg., Grand Cayman. 50c, Prince Philip. $1, Queen Elizabeth II.

1983, Feb. 15   **Litho.**   **Perf. 14**
506	A79	20c multicolored	.50	.50
507	A79	30c multicolored	.85	.75
508	A79	50c multicolored	1.50	1.25
509	A79	$1 multicolored	2.50	2.50
a.		Souvenir sheet of 4, #506-509	6.50	6.50
		Nos. 506-509 (4)	5.35	5.00

A80

1983, Mar. 14
510	A80	3c Globe	.30	.25
511	A80	15c Flags	.65	.60
512	A80	20c Fisherman	.70	.70
513	A80	40c Elizabeth II	1.10	.95
		Nos. 510-513 (4)	2.75	2.50

Commonwealth Day.

Manned Flight Bicentenary and Mosquito Research and Control Unit — A81

Airplanes: 3c, MRCU Cessna. 10c, Consolidated Catalina PBY. 20c, Boeing 727. 40c, Hawker Siddeley HS-748.

1983, Oct. 10   **Litho.**   **Perf. 14½**
514	A81	3c multicolored	.95	.70
515	A81	10c multicolored	1.10	.70
516	A81	20c multicolored	1.90	1.90
517	A81	40c multicolored	2.50	3.75
		Nos. 514-517 (4)	6.45	7.05

Shell Type of 1980

3c, Natica floridana. 10c, Conus austini. 30c, Colubrania obscura. 50c, Turbo cailletii.

1984, Jan. 18   **Perf. 14x14½**
518	A69	3c multicolored	1.25	.40
519	A69	10c multicolored	1.60	.40
520	A69	30c multicolored	4.50	4.50
521	A69	50c multicolored	4.75	4.75
		Nos. 518-521 (4)	12.10	10.05

Lloyd's List Issue
Common Design Type

1984, May 16   **Litho.**   **Perf. 14**
522	CD335	5c Cruise ship	.65	.65
523	CD335	10c The Old Harbor	.75	.30
524	CD335	25c Ridgefield	1.40	1.40
525	CD335	50c Goldfield	3.00	3.00
		Nos. 522-525 (4)	5.80	4.95

Souvenir Sheet

526	CD335	$1 Goldfield, diff.	3.50	3.50

No. 525 Overprinted

1984, June 18
527	CD335	50c multicolored	2.00	2.00

Local Birds — A82

Perf. 14x14½
1984, Aug. 15   **Litho.**   **Wmk. 373**
528	A82	5c Snowy egret	1.25	.65
529	A82	10c Bananaquit	1.25	.65
530	A82	35c Kingfisher	4.00	2.50
531	A82	$1 Brown booby	7.50	9.50
		Nos. 528-531 (4)	14.00	13.30

Christmas — A83

Nos. 532a-532d, evening beach scenes. Nos. 533a-533d, daytime boating and beach scenes.

1984, Oct. 17   **Litho.**   **Perf. 14**
532	A83	Strip of 4	5.00	5.00
a.-d.		5c Any single	1.25	1.25
533	A83	Strip of 4	6.00	5.00
a.-d.		25c Any single	1.50	1.25

Souvenir Sheet

534	A83	$1 Bonfire, diff.	6.75	6.75

No. 534 contains one stamp 29x48mm.

Orchids — A84

5c, Schomburgkia thomsoniana var. 10c, Schomburgkia thomsoniana. 25c, Encyclia plicata. 50c, Dendrophylax fawcetti.

1985, Mar. 13   **Litho.**   **Perf. 14x13½**
535	A84	5c multicolored	1.50	.55
536	A84	10c multicolored	1.50	.55
537	A84	25c multicolored	3.75	1.25
538	A84	50c multicolored	4.75	3.50
		Nos. 535-538 (4)	11.50	5.85

Shipwrecks A85

Unspecified shipwrecks found in Cayman waters.

1985, May 22   **Perf. 14**
539	A85	5c multicolored	1.25	.55
540	A85	25c multicolored	4.00	1.50
541	A85	35c multicolored	4.25	2.75
542	A85	40c multicolored	4.50	3.75
		Nos. 539-542 (4)	14.00	8.55

Intl. Youth Year — A86

5c, Natl. Athletic Assoc. track competition. 15c, High school students studying in Grand Cayman Campus Library. 25c, Amateur League Competition Football. 50c, Natl. Netball Assoc. competition.

1985, Aug. 14   **Perf. 14½**
543	A86	5c multicolored	.25	.25
544	A86	15c multicolored	.45	.40
545	A86	25c multicolored	.95	.85
546	A86	50c multicolored	1.90	1.90
		Nos. 543-546 (4)	3.55	3.40

Telecommunications, 50th Anniv. — A87

Designs: 5c, Morse Code transmitter, 1935. 10c, Hand-cranked telephone, 1935. 25c, Tropospheric scatter dish, 1966. 50c, Earth dish receiver, 1979.

1985, Oct. 25   **Perf. 14**
547	A87	5c multicolored	.55	.55
548	A87	10c multicolored	.60	.60
549	A87	25c multicolored	1.75	1.10
550	A87	50c multicolored	2.75	3.50
		Nos. 547-550 (4)	5.65	5.75

Birds A88

10c, Magnificent frigatebird. 25c, West Indian whistling duck. 35c, La Sagra's flycatcher. 40c, Yellow-faced grassquit.

1986, Mar. 20   **Litho.**   **Wmk. 384**
551	A88	10c multicolored	2.25	1.00
552	A88	25c multicolored	3.00	1.60
553	A88	35c multicolored	3.50	3.50
554	A88	40c multicolored	4.00	4.00
		Nos. 551-554 (4)	12.75	10.10

Nos. 552-553 vert.

Queen Elizabeth II 60th Birthday
Common Design Type

Designs: 5c, As bridesmaid at wedding of Lady Mary Cambridge, 1931. 10c, Royal visit to Norway, 1955. 25c, Inspecting West Indian troop, royal tour, 1985. 50c, Gulf tour, 1979. $1, Visiting Crown Agents' offices, 1983.

1986, Apr. 21   **Perf. 14x14½**
555	CD337	5c scar, blk & sil	.25	.25
556	CD337	10c ultra, blk & sil	.25	.25
557	CD337	25c grn & multi	1.75	.95
558	CD337	50c vio & multi	.90	1.10
559	CD337	$1 rose vio & multi	1.40	1.90
		Nos. 555-559 (5)	4.55	4.45

Royal Wedding Issue, 1986
Common Design Type

Designs: 5c, Informal portrait. 50c, Andrew in uniform, helicopter.

Perf. 14½x14
1986, July 23   **Litho.**   **Wmk. 384**
560	CD338	5c multicolored	.30	.25
561	CD338	50c multicolored	1.20	1.90

Marine Life — A89

5c, Rhynchocinetes rigeus. 10c, Nemaster rubiginosa. 15c, Calcinus tibicen. 20c, Rhodactis sanctithomae. 25c, Spirobranchus gigantea. 35c, Diodon holacanthus. 50c, Pseudocorynactis aribbeorum. 60c, Astrophyton muricatum. 75c, Cyphoma gibbosum. $1, Conolylactis gigantea. $2, Malacoctenus boehlkei. $4, Lima scabra.

Perf. 13½x13
1986, Sept. 15   **Wmk. 373**
Inscribed "1986"
562	A89	5c multicolored	.80	.65
563	A89	10c multicolored	.80	.65
c.		Wmk. 384, inscribed "1990"	2.75	3.00
564	A89	15c multicolored	.70	.75
565	A89	20c multicolored	.70	.95
566	A89	25c multicolored	.45	3.00
567	A89	35c multicolored	.70	3.25
568	A89	50c multicolored	.80	5.00
569	A89	60c multicolored	3.50	9.50
570	A89	75c multicolored	9.50	12.00
571	A89	$1 multicolored	2.25	3.25
572	A89	$2 multicolored	5.00	5.25
573	A89	$4 multicolored	10.00	8.25
		Nos. 562-573 (12)	35.20	52.50

1987   Inscribed "1987"
562a	A89	5c multicolored	.80	1.60
563a	A89	10c multicolored	.80	1.25
564a	A89	15c multicolored	.70	1.50
565a	A89	20c multicolored	.70	2.00
571a	A89	$1 multicolored	2.25	6.50
572a	A89	$2 multicolored	5.00	10.50
573a	A89	$4 multicolored	10.00	17.50
		Nos. 562a-573a (7)	20.25	40.85

1990   Inscribed "1990"
562b	A89	5c multicolored	2.75	5.00
563b	A89	10c multicolored	2.75	4.00
564b	A89	15c multicolored	2.50	5.00
565b	A89	20c multicolored	2.50	7.00
566b	A89	25c multicolored	1.50	10.00
567b	A89	35c multicolored		—
568b	A89	50c multicolored		—
571b	A89	$1 multicolored	8.00	10.00
572b	A89	$2 multicolored	17.50	17.50
		Nos. 562b-572b (7)	37.50	58.50

Tourism A90

Perf. 13x13½
1987, Jan. 26   **Wmk. 384**
574	A90	10c Golfing	2.50	1.00
575	A90	15c Sailing	2.60	1.00
576	A90	25c Snorkeling	2.60	1.50
577	A90	35c Parasailing	2.60	2.00
578	A90	$1 Fishing	5.75	9.75
		Nos. 574-578 (5)	16.05	15.25

Fruit — A91

1987, May 20   **Perf. 14½**
579	A91	5c Akee	1.00	1.00
580	A91	25c Breadfruit	2.25	.75
581	A91	35c Papaya	2.25	1.00
582	A91	$1 Soursop	6.00	7.50
		Nos. 579-582 (4)	11.50	10.25

Lizards — A92

1987, Aug. 26   Litho.   Perf. 14
583	A92	10c Lion lizard	2.00	1.00
584	A92	50c Iguana	5.25	4.50
585	A92	$1 Anole	6.25	8.75
		Nos. 583-585 (3)	13.50	14.25

Flowers — A93

1987, Nov. 18   Perf. 14½x14
586	A93	5c Poinsettia	1.25	.55
587	A93	25c Periwinkle	3.00	.90
588	A93	35c Yellow allamanda	3.00	1.25
589	A93	75c Blood lily	5.25	6.00
		Nos. 586-589 (4)	12.50	8.70

Butterflies
A94

Designs: 5c, Hemiargus ammon erembis and Strymon martialis. 25c, Phocides pigmalion batabano. 50c, Anaea troglodyta cubana. $1, Papilio andraemon andraemon.

1988, Mar. 29   Wmk. 384   Perf. 14
590	A94	5c multicolored	1.60	.65
591	A94	25c multicolored	3.50	1.40
592	A94	50c multicolored	5.25	5.25
593	A94	$1 multicolored	6.75	6.75
		Nos. 590-593 (4)	17.10	14.05

Herons — A95

5c, Butorides striatus. 25c, Egretta tricolor. 50c, Nycticorax violaceus. $1, Egretta caerulea.

1988, Jan. 26   Litho.   Perf. 14
594	A95	5c multicolored	2.40	.65
595	A95	25c multicolored	4.50	.90
596	A95	50c multicolored	5.50	5.25
597	A95	$1 multicolored	6.00	5.50
		Nos. 594-597 (4)	18.40	12.30

1988
Summer
Olympics,
Seoul — A96

10c, Cycling. 50c, Natl. team, passenger jet. $1, Yachting.
No. 601, Tennis.

1988, Sept. 21   Perf. 14½
598	A96	10c multicolored	2.25	.65
599	A96	50c multicolored	3.75	2.75
600	A96	$1 multicolored	4.00	4.00
		Nos. 598-600 (3)	10.00	7.40

Souvenir Sheet
Wmk. 373
601	A96	$1 multicolored	6.25	6.25

No. 601 commemorates the 75th anniv. of the Intl. Tennis Federation.

Visit of Princess
Alexandra
A97

1988, Nov. 1   Wmk. 373   Perf. 15
602	A97	5c Portrait	2.75	1.25
603	A97	$1 Seated in garden	9.75	7.50

Cayman
Islands P.O.,
Cent. — A98

Designs: 5c, P.O., Georgetown, 1889, and Jamaica #24, canceled. 25c, S.S. Orinoco and Cayman Isls. #1. 35c, Grand Cayman G.P.O. and #442. $1, Cayman Airways mail plane and #191.

1989, Apr. 12   Wmk. 384   Perf. 14½
604	A98	5c multicolored	1.25	1.25
605	A98	25c multicolored	2.75	1.50
606	A98	35c multicolored	3.00	1.75
607	A98	$1 multicolored	11.00	11.00
		Nos. 604-607 (4)	18.00	15.50

A99

Mutiny on the Bounty: a, Capt. Bligh. b, HMS Providence, two crewmen. c, HMS Assistant, transplanted breadfruit. d, Moving breadfruit on land, in longboat. e, Midshipman among casks and crates.

1989, May 24   Perf. 14
608		Strip of 5	32.50	32.50
a.-e.	A99	50c any single	6.50	6.50

A100

5c, Panton House. 10c, Town Hall. 25c, Old Courts House. 35c, Elmslie Memorial Church. $1, Post office.

Perf. 14½x14
1989, Oct. 18   Litho.   Wmk. 373
609	A100	5c multicolored	1.00	1.00
610	A100	10c multicolored	1.00	1.00
611	A100	25c multicolored	2.25	.90
612	A100	35c multicolored	2.25	1.25
613	A100	$1 multicolored	5.50	5.75
		Nos. 609-613 (5)	12.00	9.90

Natl. Trust emblem & architecture, George Town.

Island
Surveys
A101

Maps or survey ships: 5c, Navigational instruments and George Gauld's map of 1773.

25c, Instruments and map created by surveyors aboard HMS Vidal, 1956. 50c, Mutine, 1914. $1, HMS Vidal.

1989, Nov. 15
614	A101	5c multicolored	1.75	1.40
615	A101	25c multicolored	4.50	1.75
616	A101	50c multicolored	7.00	5.25
617	A101	$1 multicolored	11.00	11.00
		Nos. 614-617 (4)	24.25	19.40

Angelfish
A102

1990, Apr. 25   Wmk. 384   Perf. 14
618	A102	10c French	2.10	.65
619	A102	25c Gray	3.75	1.40
620	A102	50c Queen	5.50	5.50
621	A102	$1 Rock beauty	9.00	9.00
		Nos. 618-621 (4)	20.35	16.55

Queen Mother, 90th Birthday
Common Design Types

50c, King, Queen Elizabeth, 1948. $1, King, Queen with Churchill, 1940.

1990, Aug. 4   Wmk. 384   Perf. 14x15
622	CD343	50c multicolored	1.60	2.50

Perf. 14½
623	CD344	$1 multicolored	3.50	4.25

Butterflies
A103

5c, Soldier. 25c, Pygmy blue. 35c, Cayman crescent spot. $1, Gulf fritillary.

1990, Oct. 24   Perf. 14½x14
624	A103	5c multicolored	1.35	1.25
625	A103	25c multicolored	3.00	2.40
626	A103	35c multicolored	3.75	2.75
627	A103	$1 multicolored	8.75	10.50
		Nos. 624-627 (4)	16.85	16.90

Expo '90, International Garden and Greenery Exposition, Osaka, Japan.

Hurricane Awareness — A104

Designs: 5c, Goes weather satellite. 30c, Meteorologist tracks storm. 40c, Hurricane damage. $1, Lockheed WP-3D Orion flying in hurricane's eye.

1991, Aug. 8   Perf. 14
628	A104	5c multicolored	1.40	1.40
629	A104	30c multicolored	3.25	1.75
630	A104	40c multicolored	3.50	2.10
631	A104	$1 multicolored	8.50	8.50
		Nos. 628-631 (4)	16.65	13.75

Christmas
A105

Local flowers and Christmas scenes: 5c, Angel's trumpet, angels with trumpets. 30c, Golden trumpet, Mary on donkey led by Joseph. 40c, Christmas flower, Adoration of the Magi. 60c, Tree of life, nativity scene.

1991, Nov. 6   Wmk. 373
632	A105	5c multicolored	1.00	1.00
633	A105	30c multicolored	3.00	.85
634	A105	40c multicolored	3.25	1.40
635	A105	60c multicolored	3.75	5.00
		Nos. 632-635 (4)	11.00	8.25

Island
Scenes
A106

5c, Coconut tree, vert. 15c, Beach scene. 20c, Poincianas in bloom. 30c, Blowholes. 40c, Police band. 50c, Downtown scene, vert. 80c, The Bluff, Cayman Brac. 80c, Coat of arms, vert. 90c, View of Hell. $1, Sportfishing. $2, Harbor scene, vert. $8, Queen Elizabeth II, vert.

Perf. 12½x13, 13x12½
1991, Dec. 11   Litho.   Wmk. 373
636	A106	5c multicolored	.75	.55
a.		Inscribed "1994"	1.00	.75
637	A106	15c multicolored	1.60	.55
638	A106	20c multicolored	.85	.70
639	A106	30c multicolored	2.25	.90
640	A106	40c multicolored	3.75	2.25
641	A106	50c multicolored	3.00	2.25
642	A106	60c multicolored	2.50	3.50
643	A106	80c multicolored	2.25	3.75
644	A106	90c multicolored	2.25	3.75
645	A106	$1 multicolored	4.50	3.75
646	A106	$2 multicolored	9.50	9.00
647	A106	$8 multicolored	22.50	25.00
		Nos. 636-647 (12)	55.70	55.95

Queen Elizabeth II's Accession to the Throne, 40th Anniv.
Common Design Type
Wmk. 373, 384 (40c)
1992, Feb. 6   Litho.   Perf. 14
648	CD349	5c multicolored	.45	.45
649	CD349	20c multicolored	1.40	.50
650	CD349	30c multicolored	1.50	.75
651	CD349	40c multicolored	1.50	1.40
652	CD349	$1 multicolored	2.75	4.00
		Nos. 648-652 (5)	7.60	7.10

1992
Summer
Olympics,
Barcelona
A107

15c, Cyclist. 40c, Two cyclists. 60c, Feet, pedals. $1, Two cyclists, diff.

1992, Aug. 5   Wmk. 373
653	A107	15c multicolored	2.00	.55
654	A107	40c multicolored	3.50	1.50
655	A107	60c multicolored	4.00	4.00
656	A107	$1 multicolored	5.00	5.00
		Nos. 653-656 (4)	14.50	11.05

Island
Heritage — A108

5c, Lady with donkey. 30c, Making fish nets. 40c, Maypole dancing. 60c, Basket making. $1, Cooking on caboose.

1992, Oct. 21
657	A108	5c multicolored	.70	.70
658	A108	30c multicolored	1.75	1.00
659	A108	40c multicolored	3.00	1.60
660	A108	60c multicolored	3.50	3.50
661	A108	$1 multicolored	4.25	4.25
		Nos. 657-661 (5)	13.20	11.05

Rays
A109

5c, Yellow stingray. 30c, Southern stingray. 40c, Spotted eagle ray. $1, Manta ray.

Perf. 13½x14
1993, June 16 Litho. Wmk. 373
662	A109	5c multicolored	.95	.85
663	A109	30c multicolored	2.40	1.60
664	A109	40c multicolored	2.75	1.90
665	A109	$1 multicolored	6.25	6.25
		Nos. 662-665 (4)	12.35	10.60

A110

Tourism: No. 666a, Turtle, sailboats. b, Diver, coral, boats. c, Golf. d, Beach, tennis. e, Pirates, sailing ship.
No. 667: a, Cruise ship, boat, sailboat. b, City street scene. c, Submarines. d, Cyclist, scooters. e, Jet planes.

Perf. 14x13½
1993, Sept. 30 Litho. Wmk. 373
666	A110	15c Strip of 5, #a.-e.	11.50	11.50
667	A110	30c Strip of 5, #a.-e.	12.50	12.50
f.		Booklet pane of 10, #666-667	32.50	

A111

Various views of Grand Cayman Parrot.

1993, Oct. 29 Perf. 14
668	A111	5c green & multi	1.25	1.25
669	A111	5c red & multi	1.25	1.25
670	A111	30c yellow & multi	3.00	3.00
671	A111	30c blue & multi	3.00	3.00
		Nos. 668-671 (4)	8.50	8.50

Christmas A112

Christmas scenes, orchids: 5c, Manger, Ionopsis utricularioides. 40c, Shepherd, lamb, Encyclia cochleata. 60c, Magi, Vanilla pompona. $1, Virgin in prayer, Oncidium caymanense.

Perf. 13½x14
1993, Dec. 6 Litho. Wmk. 384
672	A112	5c multicolored	1.40	.75
673	A112	40c multicolored	3.75	1.00
674	A112	60c multicolored	4.75	4.75
675	A112	$1 multicolored	6.25	6.25
		Nos. 672-675 (4)	16.15	12.75

Souvenir Sheet

Reef Life — A113

Designs: a, Holocanthus ciliaris. b, Bodianus pulchellus, anisotremus virginicus. c, Holocanthus tricolor, gramma loreto. d, Pomacanthus paru, chaeton striatus.

Perf. 14½x13
1994, Feb. 18 Litho. Wmk. 373
676	A113	60c Sheet of 4, #a.-d.	13.50	13.50

Hong Kong '94.

Royal Visit — A114

Designs: 5c, Cayman Islands, United Kingdom flags. 15c, Royal yacht Britannia. 30c, Queen Elizabeth II. $2, Queen, Prince Philip.

1994, Feb. 22 Perf. 14½
677	A114	5c multicolored	2.00	.95
678	A114	15c multicolored	3.75	1.60
679	A114	30c multicolored	3.75	1.75
680	A114	$2 multicolored	10.50	10.50
		Nos. 677-680 (4)	20.00	14.80

West Indian Whistling Duck A115

5c, One standing. 15c, Landing in water. 20c, Four ducks, various activities. 80c, One raising wings. $1, Adult, chick.

Wmk. 373
1994, Apr. 21 Litho. Perf. 14
681	A115	5c multi, vert.	1.75	.90
682	A115	15c multi	2.50	.95
683	A115	20c multi	2.50	1.00
684	A115	80c multi, vert.	5.50	6.00
685	A115	$1 multi	6.25	6.50
a.		Souvenir sheet of 1	13.00	13.00
		Nos. 681-685 (5)	18.50	15.35

No. 685a has a continuous design and contains Cayman Islands Natl. Trust emblem.

Butterflies A116

No. 686: a, Fulvous hairstreak. b, Atala butterfly.
No. 687: a, Barred sulphur. b, Dorantes skipper.

Wmk. 373
1994, Aug. 16 Litho. Perf. 13½
686	A116	10c Pair, #a.-b.	2.75	3.00
687	A116	$1 Pair, #a.-b.	13.00	13.00

Wreck of the Ten Sail, Bicent. — A117

Perf. 13½x14
1994, Oct. 12 Litho. Wmk. 373
688	A117	10c shown	.75	.75
689	A117	10c multicolored	.75	.75
690	A117	15c multicolored	1.25	.60
691	A117	20c multicolored	1.50	.70
692	A117	$2 multicolored	7.75	7.75
		Nos. 688-692 (5)	12.00	10.55

Sea Turtles A118

Animals of the Nativity.

1995, Nov. 1 Perf. 14
710	A121	10c Ox	.90	.30
711	A121	20c Sheep, lamb	1.40	.50
712	A121	30c Donkey	2.25	.60

Wmk. 384
1995, Feb. 28 Litho. Perf. 14
693	A118	10c Green	.75	.45
694	A118	20c Kemp's ridley	1.10	.55
695	A118	25c Hawksbill	1.25	.65
696	A118	30c Leatherback	1.45	.75
697	A118	$1.30 Loggerhead	5.25	5.25
698	A118	$2 Pacific ridley	6.50	6.50
a.		Souvenir sheet, #693-698	16.50	16.50
		Nos. 693-698 (6)	16.30	14.15

1995 CARIFTA & IAAF Games A119

1995, Apr. 15 Litho. Perf. 14
699	A119	10c Running	1.00	.55
700	A119	20c Pole vault	1.50	1.10
701	A119	30c Javelin	2.10	1.25
702	A119	$1.30 Sailing	7.25	7.25
		Nos. 699-702 (4)	11.85	10.15

Souvenir Sheet
703	A119	$2 Medal winners	11.00	11.00

End of World War II, 50th Anniv.
Common Design Type

10c, Two soldiers, Cayman Home Guard. 25c, Freighter Comayagua torpedoed off Caymans, 5/14/42. 40c, Type IXc U-Boat U-125. $1, Navy airship L-3 used for U-boat patrol. $1.30, Reverse of War Medal 1939-45.

Wmk. 373
1995, May 8 Litho. Perf. 13½
704	CD351	10c multicolored	1.40	.55
705	CD351	25c multicolored	2.75	.90
706	CD351	40c multicolored	3.25	2.25
707	CD351	$1 multicolored	5.75	5.75
		Nos. 704-707 (4)	13.15	9.45

Souvenir Sheet
Perf. 14
708	CD352	$1.30 multicolored	5.00	5.00

Souvenir Sheet

Queen Mother, 95th Birthday — A120

1995, Aug. 25 Perf. 14½
709	A120	$4 multicolored	12.00	12.00

Singapore '95.

A121

713	A121	$2 Camels	8.50	10.50
a.		Souvenir sheet of 4, #710-713	14.00	14.00
		Nos. 710-713 (4)	13.05	11.90

Wild Fruit — A122

10c, Sea grape. 25c, Guava. 40c, West Indian cherry. $1, Tamarind.

Wmk. 384
1996, Mar. 21 Litho. Perf. 14
714	A122	10c multicolored	.60	.50
715	A122	25c multicolored	1.25	.70
716	A122	40c multicolored	2.00	1.25
717	A122	$1 multicolored	4.00	5.25
		Nos. 714-717 (4)	7.85	7.70

Modern Olympic Games, Cent. — A123

Perf. 14x13½
1996, June 19 Litho. Wmk. 384
718	A123	10c Sailing	.65	.45
719	A123	20c Sailboarding	1.25	.55
720	A123	30c Sailing, diff.	1.60	.80
721	A123	$2 Running	6.50	6.50
		Nos. 718-721 (4)	10.00	8.30

Symbols of National Identity — A124

Designs: 10c, Guitar, music, natl. song. 20c, Boeing 737. 25c, Queen Elizabeth II opening Legislative Assembly. 30c, Seven Mile Beach. 40c, Scuba diver, stingrays. 60c, School children, Cayman Turtle Farm. 80c, Cayman parrot, natl. bird. 90c, Silver thatch palm, natl. tree. $1, Natl. flag. $2, Wild banana orchid, natl. flower. $4, Natl. arms. $6, Natl. currency.

Wmk. 373
1996, Sept. 26 Litho. Perf. 14
Inscribed "1996"
722	A124	10c multicolored	.50	.45
		Complete booklet, 10 #722	5.25	
a.		Inscribed "1997"	.50	.45
723	A124	20c multicolored	1.10	.85
724	A124	25c multicolored	1.25	.80
725	A124	30c multicolored	1.25	.80
		Complete booklet, 10 #725	13.00	
726	A124	40c multicolored	1.60	1.25
		Complete booklet, 10 #726	17.00	
727	A124	60c multicolored	2.25	1.60
728	A124	80c multicolored	3.75	3.00
a.		Souvenir sheet of 1	4.25	4.25
729	A124	90c multicolored	2.50	3.00
730	A124	$1 multicolored	4.00	3.25
731	A124	$2 multicolored	7.25	7.00
732	A124	$4 multicolored	13.00	16.00
733	A124	$6 multicolored	17.00	20.00
		Nos. 722-733 (12)	55.45	58.00

No. 728a for Hong Kong '97. Issued 2/3/97.

1999, Feb. 5 Wmk. 373 Sideways
723a	A124	20c multicolored	1.10	.85
725a	A124	30c multicolored	1.25	.80
727a	A124	60c multicolored	2.25	1.60
		Nos. 723a-727a (3)	4.60	3.25

Christmas
A125

Designs: 10c, Christmas time on North Church Street. 25c, Santa "Gone Fishing." 30c, "Claus Encounters." $2, "Caymanian Christmas."

Wmk. 373

1996, Nov. 12	Litho.		Perf. 14	
734	A125	10c multicolored	.65	.35
735	A125	25c multicolored	1.60	.90
736	A125	30c multicolored	2.00	1.25
737	A125	$2 multicolored	4.50	4.50
		Nos. 734-737 (4)	8.75	7.00

Queen Elizabeth II and Prince Philip, 50th Wedding Anniv. — A126

No. 738, Queen. No. 739, Royal Guard. No. 740, Young Prince riding horse. No. 741, Queen in blue, Prince in military attire in open carriage. No. 742 Prince holding horse's reins. No. 743, Queen looking at horses.
$1, Queen, Prince in open carriage.

Perf. 14x13½

1997, July 10	Litho.		Wmk. 373	
738	A126	10c multicolored	1.25	1.25
739	A126	10c multicolored	1.25	1.25
a.		Pair, #738-739	2.50	2.50
740	A126	30c multicolored	2.00	2.00
741	A126	30c multicolored	2.00	2.00
a.		Pair, #740-741	4.00	4.00
742	A126	40c multicolored	2.40	2.40
743	A126	40c multicolored	2.40	2.40
a.		Pair, #742-743	5.00	5.00
		Nos. 738-743 (6)	11.30	11.30

Souvenir Sheet

744	A126	$1 multicolored	7.25	7.25

Telecommunications — A127

Designs: 10c, Children using the Internet. 25c, Cable and wireless ship. 30c, Children wearing numbers of new area code, "345." 60c, Cable and wireless satellite communications.

Perf. 14x14½

1997, Oct. 10	Litho.		Wmk. 384	
745	A127	10c multicolored	.45	.30
746	A127	25c multicolored	1.25	.80
747	A127	30c multicolored	1.40	.95
748	A127	60c multicolored	2.25	2.25
		Nos. 745-748 (4)	5.35	4.30

Christmas
A128

Santa Claus: 10c, Relaxing in hammock, Little Cayman. 30c, With children on bluff, Cayman Brac. 40c, Playing golf. $1, Diving with stingrays.

Wmk. 373

1997, Dec. 3	Litho.		Perf. 13	
749	A128	10c multicolored	.35	.25
750	A128	30c multicolored	.80	.45
751	A128	40c multicolored	1.75	.80
752	A128	$1 multicolored	3.00	3.50
		Nos. 749-752 (4)	5.90	5.00

Diana, Princess of Wales (1961-97)
Common Design Type

Portraits: a, 10c. b, 20c. c, 40c. d, $1.

Perf. 14½x14

1998	Litho.		Wmk. 373	
752A	CD355	10c Like #753a	.75	.75
752B	CD355	20c Like #753b	1.50	1.50

Sheet of 4

753	CD355	#a.-d.	5.50	5.50

No. 753 sold for $1.70 + 30c, with surtax from international sales being donated to the Princess Diana Memorial Fund and surtax from national sales being donated to designated local charity.

Royal Air Force, 80th Anniv.
Common Design Type of 1993 Re-Inscribed

Designs: 10c, Hawker Horsley. 20c, Fairey Hendon. 25c, Hawker Siddeley Gnat. 30c, Hawker Siddeley Dominie.
No. 758: a, 40c, Airco DH-9. b, 60c, Spad 13 Scout. c, 80c, Airspeed Oxford. d, $1, Martin Baltimore.

Wmk. 373

1998, Apr. 1	Litho.		Perf. 14	
754	CD350	10c multicolored	1.00	1.00
755	CD350	20c multicolored	1.25	1.25
756	CD350	25c multicolored	1.60	1.60
757	CD350	30c multicolored	1.90	1.90
		Nos. 754-757 (4)	5.75	5.75

Souvenir Sheet

758	CD350	Sheet of 4, #a.-d.	10.00	10.00

Birds — A129

Designs: 10c, West Indian whistling duck. 20c, Magnificent frigatebird. 60c, Red footed booby. $1, Grand Cayman parrot.

1998	Litho.	Wmk. 373		Perf. 13½
759	A129	10c multicolored	1.10	.60
760	A129	20c multicolored	2.00	.60
761	A129	60c multicolored	3.50	3.50
762	A129	$1 multicolored	4.25	4.25
		Nos. 759-762 (4)	10.85	8.95

Christmas
A130

Santa at various island locations: 10c, At Blowholes. 30c, Diving on wreck of MV Capt. Keith Tibbetts. 40c, Visiting Pedro Castle. 60c, Arriving at Little Cayman.

1998			Perf. 14x14½	
763	A130	10c multicolored	.40	.40
764	A130	30c multicolored	1.10	.85
765	A130	40c multicolored	1.50	1.10
766	A130	60c multicolored	3.00	3.00
		Nos. 763-766 (4)	6.00	5.35

Easter
A131

Artworks by Miss Lassie (Gladwyn Bush): 10c, "They Rolled the Stone Away." 20c, "Ascension," vert. 30c, "The World Praying for Peace." 40c, "Calvary," vert.

Wmk. 373

1999, Mar. 26	Litho.		Perf. 13	
767	A131	10c multicolored	.50	.50
768	A131	20c multicolored	.90	.90
769	A131	30c multicolored	1.40	1.40
770	A131	40c multicolored	1.50	1.50
		Nos. 767-770 (4)	4.30	4.30

Vision 2008
A132

Children's drawings: 10c, "Cayman House." 30c, "Coral Reef." 40c, "Fisherman on North Sound." $2, "Three Fish and A Turtle."

1999, June			Perf. 13½	
771	A132	10c multicolored	.30	.30
772	A132	30c multicolored	1.10	1.10
773	A132	40c multicolored	1.25	1.25
774	A132	$2 multicolored	6.50	6.50
		Nos. 771-774 (4)	9.15	9.15

Wedding of Prince Edward and Sophie Rhys-Jones
Common Design Type

Perf. 13¾x14

1999, June 16	Litho.	Wmk. 384		
775	CD356	10c Separate portraits	.50	.50
776	CD356	$2 Couple	5.00	5.00

1st Manned Moon Landing, 30th Anniv.
Common Design Type

Designs: 10c, Coast Guard during launch. 25c, 3rd stage fires and puts rocket in orbit. 30c, Aldrin descends to lunar surface. 60c, Lander module sent back to moon.
$1.50, Looking at earth from moon.

1999, July 20			Perf. 14x13¾	
777	CD357	10c multicolored	.45	.45
778	CD357	25c multicolored	1.10	1.10
779	CD357	30c multicolored	1.25	1.25
780	CD357	60c multicolored	2.50	2.50
		Nos. 777-780 (4)	5.30	5.30

Souvenir Sheet
Perf. 14

781	CD357	$1.50 multicolored	5.00	5.00

No. 781 contains one circular stamp 40mm in diameter.

Queen Mother's Century
Common Design Type

Queen Mother: 10c, Looking at London's defenses, 1940. 20c, At Clarence House, 94th birthday. 30c, With Princes Charles and William. 40c, Reviewing the Chelsea Pensioners, 1986.
$1.50, At her wedding.

Wmk. 384

1999, Aug. 18	Litho.		Perf. 13¼	
782	CD358	10c multicolored	.45	.45
783	CD358	20c multicolored	.80	.80
784	CD358	30c multicolored	1.40	1.40
785	CD358	40c multicolored	1.75	1.75
		Nos. 782-785 (4)	4.40	4.40

Souvenir Sheet

786	CD358	$1.50 multicolored	4.75	4.75

Christmas — A133

Wmk. 373

1999, Nov. 17	Litho.		Perf. 13¼	
787	A133	10c #242, vert.	.40	.35
788	A133	30c #532d, vert.	1.10	.90
789	A133	40c #749, vert.	1.50	1.25
790	A133	$1 #431	3.00	3.00
a.		Souv. sheet, #787-790, perf. 12	6.00	6.00
		Nos. 787-790 (4)	6.00	5.50

British Monarchs — A134

No. 792: a, Henry VIII. b, Mary I. c, Charles II. d, Anne. e, George IV. f, George V.

Wmk. 373

2000, Feb. 29	Litho.		Perf. 14	
791	A134	10c Henry VII	.70	.70

Sheet of 6

792	A134	40c #a.-f.	10.00	10.00

The Stamp Show 2000, London.

Sesame Street — A135

Designs: 10c, Ernie. 30c, Big Bird.
No. 795: a, Grover. b, Zoe. c, Oscar the Grouch. d, The Count. e, Like 30c. f, Cookie Monster. g, Like 10c. h, Bert. i, Elmo in pond.
No. 796, Elmo collecting stamps.

Perf. 14½x14¾

2000, Mar. 15	Litho.		Wmk. 373	
793	A135	10c multi	.40	.40
794	A135	30c multi	1.10	1.10
795	A135	20c Sheet of 9, #a-i	6.25	6.25

Souvenir Sheet

796	A135	20c multi	1.90	1.90

Prince William, 18th Birthday
Common Design Type

10c, In checked shirt and in sweater and checked shirt. 20c, In white shirt and black bow tie. 30c, In blue casual shirt, vert. 40c, As child, with beret, vert. $1, As infant.

Perf. 14¼x13¾, 13¾x14¼

2000, June 21	Litho.		Wmk. 373	
Stamps With White Border				
797	CD359	10c multi	.50	.40
798	CD359	20c multi	1.00	.95
799	CD359	30c multi	1.40	1.25
800	CD359	40c multi	1.90	1.90
		Nos. 797-800 (4)	4.80	4.50

Souvenir Sheet
Stamps Without White Border
Perf. 14¼

801		Sheet of 5	8.25	8.25
a.	CD359	10c multi	.35	.35
b.	CD359	20c multi	.75	.75
c.	CD359	30c multi	1.00	1.00
d.	CD359	40c multi	1.40	1.40
e.	CD359	$1 multi	4.00	4.00

Marine Life
A136

10c, Green turtle. 20c, Queen angelfish. 30c, Parrotfish. $1, Green moray eel.

Wmk. 384

2000, Aug. 25	Litho.		Perf. 14	
802-805	A136	Set of 4	7.25	7.25

National
Drug
Council
A137

Various children's drawings. Denominations, 10c, 15c, 30c, $2.

2000, Aug. 25
806-809 A137 Set of 4　　　11.00 11.00

Christmas
A138

10c, Backing sand. 30c, Christmas dinner. 40c, Yard dance. 60c, Conch shell border.

Perf. 14½x14¼
2000, Nov. 14　　　　　　**Wmk. 373**
810-813 A138 Set of 4　　　8.50 8.50

UN Women's
Human Rights
Campaign — A139

Wmk. 373
2001, Mar. 8　Litho.　　*Perf. 14*
814 A139 10c multi　　　　　.90　.90

Cayman
Brac
A140

Designs: 15c, Red mangrove. 20c, Peter's Cave, vert. 25c, Bight Road stairway, vert. 30c, Westerly Pond. 40c, Aerial view. 60c, Marshes.

2001, Apr. 21
815-820 A140 Set of 6　　　9.50　9.50

Non-profit Organizations — A141

Designs: Nos. 821, 826a, 15c, National Council of Voluntary Organizations. Nos. 822, 826b, 20c, Cayman Humane Society. Nos. 823, 826c, 25c, Red Cross/Red Crescent. Nos. 824, 826d, 30c, Cayman Islands Cancer Society, vert. Nos. 825, 826e, 40c, Lions Club of Tropical Gardens, vert.

Wmk. 373
2001, Aug. 15　Litho.　*Perf. 14*
Stamps With White Margins
821-825 A141 Set of 5　　　11.00 11.00
Souvenir Sheet
Stamps With Pink Margins
826 A141 Sheet of 5, #a-e　11.00 11.00
No. 826 sold for $1.80, 50c of which went to the various organizations honored.

Transportation — A142

Designs: No. 827, Walking home. No. 828, Boy on donkey. 20c, Bananas by canoe. 25c, Horse and buggy. 30c, Catboats. 40c, Schooner. 60c, Police bicycle, vert. 80c, Lady drivers. 90c, Launching Cimboco, vert. $1, Seaplane. $4, Freighter. $10, Boeing 767.

Perf. 14¼x14½, 14½x14¼
2001, Sept. 29　Litho.　**Wmk. 373**
827 A142 15c multi　　　.40　.40
828 A142 15c multi　　　.40　.40
829 A142 20c multi　　　.55　.55
830 A142 25c multi　　　.70　.70
831 A142 30c multi　　　.80　.80
832 A142 40c multi　　1.10　1.10
833 A142 60c multi　　1.60　1.60
834 A142 80c multi　　2.25　2.25
835 A142 90c multi　　2.50　2.50
836 A142 $1 multi　　　2.75　2.75
837 A142 $4 multi　　 11.00 11.00
838 A142 $10 multi　　26.00 26.00
　　Nos. 827-838 (12)　　50.05 50.05

Christmas
A143

Santa Claus: 15c, With children on dock. 30c, On eagle ray. 40c, In catboat. 60c, Parasailing.

Perf. 14¼x14½
2001, Nov. 21　Litho.　**Wmk. 373**
839-842 A143 Set of 4　　　7.50 7.50

In Remembrance of Sept. 11, 2001
Terrorist Attacks — A144

Perf. 14x14¾
2002, Jan. 22　Litho.　**Wmk. 373**
843 A144 $1 multi　　　　4.25 4.25

Reign Of Queen Elizabeth II, 50th Anniv. Issue
Common Design Type

Designs: Nos. 844, 848a, 15c, Princess Elizabeth as child. Nos. 845, 848b, 20c, In 1976. Nos. 846, 848c, 30c, With Princess Margaret, 1942. Nos. 847, 848d, 80c, In 1996. No. 848e, $1, 1955 portrait by Annigoni (38x50mm).

Perf. 14¼x14½, 13¾ (#848e)
2002, Feb. 6　Litho.　**Wmk. 373**
With Gold Frames
844 CD360 15c multicolored　　.45　.45
845 CD360 20c multicolored　　.65　.65
846 CD360 30c multicolored　　.90　.90
847 CD360 80c multicolored　2.25 2.25
　　Nos. 844-847 (4)　　　　　4.25 4.25
Souvenir Sheet
Without Gold Frames
848 CD360 Sheet of 5, #a-e 10.00 10.00

Peanuts
Comic
Strip
Characters
A145

Designs: 15c, Snoopy painting Woodstock at Cayman Brac Bluff. 20c, Charlie Brown and Sally at Hell Post Office. 25c, Peppermint Patty and Marcie at Little Cayman beach. 30c, Snoopy and Boeing 737-200. 40c, Linus and

Snoopy at Point of Sand. 60c, Charlie Brown at Links Golf Course.

Wmk. 373
2002, Mar. 9　Litho.　　*Perf. 14*
849-854 A145 Set of 6　　8.50 8.50
854a　　　Souvenir sheet, #849-854　8.50 8.50

2002 World Cup
Soccer
Championships,
Japan and
Korea — A146

Denominations: 30c, 40c.

2002, Apr. 30　　　　*Perf. 13¾*
855-856 A146 Set of 2　　4.25 4.25

Queen Mother Elizabeth (1900-2002)
Common Design Type

Designs: 15c, Wearing hat (sepia photograph). 30c, Wearing dark blue hat. Nos. 859, 861a, 40c, Wearing hat (black and white photograph). Nos. 860, 861b, $1, Wearing tiara.

Perf. 13¾x14¼, 14¼ (#859-860)
2002, Aug. 5　Litho.　**Wmk. 373**
With Purple Frames
857 CD361 15c multicolored　　.65　.65
858 CD361 30c multicolored　1.25 1.25
859 CD361 40c multicolored　1.60 1.60
860 CD361 $1 multicolored　4.00 4.00
　　Nos. 857-860 (4)　　　　7.50 7.50
Souvenir Sheet
Without Purple Frames
Perf. 14½x14¼
861 CD361　Sheet of 2, #a-b　7.50 7.50

Christmas
A147

Designs: 15c, Hail Mary. 20c, Journey to Bethlehem. 30c, Her firstborn Son. 40c, I bring good tidings. 60c Star in the east.

Wmk. 373
2002, Oct. 18　Litho.　*Perf. 14*
Stamps + labels
862-866 A147 Set of 5　　5.50 5.50
866a　　Souvenir sheet of 5, #862-
　　　　866 + 5 labels　　　6.50 6.50

Aviation in
the
Cayman
Islands,
50th Anniv.
A148

Designs: 15c, PBY Catalina Flying Boat. 20c, First landing at Grand Cayman Airport, 1952. 25c, Cayman Brac Airways AC 50. 30c, Cayman Airways B-737. 40c, Concorde at original airport, 1984. $1.30, Island Air DHC6.

2002, Nov. 8
867-872 A148 Set of 6　　12.50 12.50

Children's
Games
A149

Designs: 15c, Rope skipping. 20c, Maypole dancing. 25c, Gig. 30c, Hopscotch. $1, Marbles.

Wmk. 373
2003, May 27　Litho.　*Perf. 13¾*
873-877 A149 Set of 5　　8.00 8.00

Head of Queen Elizabeth II
Common Design Type

Wmk. 373
2003, June 2　Litho.　*Perf. 13¾*
878 CD362 $4 multi　　　17.00 17.00

Coronation of Queen Elizabeth II, 50th Anniv.
Common Design Type

Designs: Nos. 879, 15c, 881a, 20c, Queen wearing crown. Nos. 880, $2, 881b, $4, Queen holding symbols of office.

Perf. 14¼x14½
2003, June 2　Litho.　**Wmk. 373**
Vignettes Framed, Red Background
879 CD363 15c multicolored　　.50　.50
880 CD363 $2 multicolored　6.75 6.75
Souvenir Sheet
Vignettes Without Frame, Purple Panel
881 CD363　Sheet of 2, #a-b 13.00 13.00

Prince William, 21st Birthday
Common Design Type

Color photographs: 15c, William with backpack at right. 40c, William in suit and tie at left
No. 884: a, William with hand on chin at right. b, William with white bow tie at left.

Wmk. 373
2003, June 21　Litho.　*Perf. 14¼*
882 CD364 15c multi　　　.50　.50
883 CD364 40c multi　　1.40 1.40
884　　　Horiz. pair　　　5.75 5.75
a.　CD364 80c multi　　2.50 2.50
b.　CD364 $1 multi　　　3.25 3.25
　　Nos. 882-884 (3)　　7.65 7.65

Discovery of
the Cayman
Islands,
500th Anniv.
A150

Designs: 15c, Turtle hatchlings. No. 886, 20c, Old waterfront. No. 887, 20c, Turtle and ship of Christopher Columbus. 25c, Nassau grouper. 30c, Cayman Brac schooner "Kirk-B." 40c, George Town harbor. 60c, Musical instruments. 80c, Smokewood tree. 90c, Little Cayman Baptist Church. $1, Thatch rope. $1.30, Children's dance troupe. $2, Parliament in session.

Wmk. 373
2003, July 24　Litho.　*Perf. 13¾*
885-896 A150 Set of 12　29.00 29.00
896a　　Souvenir sheet, #885-896　29.00 29.00

Holiday
Greetings
A151

Various Christmas decorations and inscriptions of: 15c, Merry Christmas. 20c, Celebrate With Family. 30c, Happy New Year. 40c, Happy Holidays. 60c, Seasons Greetings.

Wmk. 373
2003, Nov. 4　Litho.　*Perf. 13¼*
897-901 A151 Set of 5　　8.00 8.00

Worldwide
Fund for
Nature
(WWF)
A152

Short-finned pilot whale: 15c, Adult and calf. 20c, Pod of four whales. 30c, Two whales at surface. 40c, One adult.

2003, Nov. 26 — Perf. 14

902-905 A152 Set of 4 7.00 7.00
905a Sheet, 4 each #902-905 30.00 30.00

Shipping Registry, Cent. — A153

Ships: 15c, Lady Slater. 20c, Seanostrum. 30c, Kirk Pride. $1, Boadicea.

Perf. 14x14¾

2004, Jan. 29 Litho. Wmk. 373
906-909 A153 Set of 4 9.50 9.50

Easter — A154

Designs: 15c, Jesus Carrying His Cross. 30c, The Ascension.

2004, Mar. 16 — Perf. 14¾x14
910-911 A154 Set of 2 3.25 3.25

2004 Summer Olympics, Athens — A155

Designs: 15c, Swimmer. 40c, Runner. 60c, Long jumper. 80c, Swimmers.

Perf. 13½x13¼

2004, Aug. 23 Litho. Wmk. 373
912-915 A155 Set of 4 6.50 6.50

Blue Iguana A156

Designs: 15c, Adult on rocks. 20c, Eggs. 25c, Four juveniles. 30c, Juvenile on finger. 40c, Adult with open mouth. 90c, Eye.
No. 922: a, 60c, On rock facing right. b, 80c, On rock facing left.

2004, Oct. 26 Litho. Perf. 13¾
916-921 A156 Set of 6 8.50 8.50
Souvenir Sheet
922 A156 Sheet of 2, #a-b 7.00 7.00
No. 922 sold for $1.90.

Battle of Trafalgar, Bicent. — A157

Designs: 15c, HMS Victory. 20c, HMS Tonnant tangles into the bow of the Algesiras. 25c, Flint cannon lock and linstock. No. 926, 60c,

Royal Navy boatswain's mate. $1, Adm. Horatio Nelson, vert. No. 928, $2, HMS Orion in action against the Intrepide.
No. 929, vert.: a, 60c, French gunship Pluton. b, $2, HMS Tonnant.

Wmk. 373, Unwmkd. (15c)

2005, June 8 Litho. Perf. 13¼
923-928 A157 Set of 6 12.00 12.00
Souvenir Sheet
929 A157 Sheet of 2, #a-b 7.00 7.00
No. 923 has particles of wood from the HMS Victory embedded in the areas covered by a thermographic process that produces a raised, shiny effect.

Rotary International, Cent. — A158

Designs: 15c, Centennial emblem. 30c, PolioPlus emblem.

2005, June 30 Wmk. 373 Perf. 13¾
930-931 A158 Set of 2 2.50 2.50

Orchids A159

Designs: 15c, Myrmecophila albopurpurea. 20c, Prosthechea boothiana. 30c, Tolumnia calochila, vert. 40c, Encyclia phoenicia. 80c, Prosthechea cochleata, vert. $1.50, Encyclia kingsii.

2005, July 28 — Perf. 14
932-936 A159 Set of 5 7.25 7.25
Souvenir Sheet
937 A159 $1.50 multi 6.00 6.00

Pope John Paul II (1920-2005) A160

2005, Aug. 18
938 A160 30c multi 1.75 1.75

A161

Butterflies A162

Designs: 15c, Queen. 20c, Mexican fritillary. 25c, Malachite. 30c, Cayman crescent spot. 40c, Cloudless sulphur. 90c, Swallowtail.

Wmk. 373

2005, Sept. 21 Litho. Perf. 14
939 A161 15c multi .60 .60
940 A161 20c multi .75 .75
941 A161 25c multi .85 .85
942 A161 30c multi 1.10 1.10
943 A161 40c multi 1.60 1.60
944 A161 90c multi 3.25 3.25
Nos. 939-944 (6) 8.15 8.15

Booklet Stamps
Self-Adhesive
Unwmk.
Serpentine Die Cut 9½x9

945 A162 15c multi .60 .60
a. Booklet pane of 10 6.00
946 A162 20c multi .70 .70
a. Booklet pane of 6 4.20
947 A162 30c multi 1.00 1.00
a. Booklet pane of 10 10.00
Nos. 945-947 (3) 2.30 2.30

Christmas A163

Designs: 15c, Angels. 30c, Magi, horiz. 40c, Holy Family. 60c, Shepherds, horiz.

Perf. 14x14¾, 14¾x14

2005, Oct. 26 Wmk. 373
948-951 A163 Set of 4 5.50 5.50
951a Souvenir sheet, #948-951, perf. 14¾ 5.50 5.50

Trees and Blossorns — A164

Designs: 15c, Wash wood. 20c, Red mangrove. 30c, Ironwood. 60c, West Indian cedar. $2, Spanish elm.

Wmk. 373

2006, Feb. 23 Litho. Perf. 13¼
Stamp + Label
952-956 A164 Set of 5 12.00 12.00

Queen Elizabeth II, 80th Birthday A165

Designs: 15c, As child. 40c, Wearing uniform and cap. $1, Wearing tiara. $2, Wearing sunglasses.
No. 961: a, 40c, Like #958. b, $1, Like #959.

2006, Apr. 21 — Perf. 14
With White Frames
957-960 A165 Set of 4 12.00 12.00
Souvenir Sheet
Without White Frames
961 A165 Sheet of 2, #a-b 12.00 12.00

A166

Marine Life — A167

Designs: Nos. 962, 967a, 968, Hawksbill turtle. Nos. 963, 967b, 969, Gray angelfish. Nos. 964, 967c, 970, Queen angelfish. Nos. 965, 967c, 971, Diamond blenny. Nos. 966, 967e, Juvenile spotted drum, vert. Nos. 964 and 967c are vert.

Wmk. 373

2006, July 18 Litho. Perf. 14
With White Margins
962 A166 25c multi 1.00 1.00
963 A166 25c multi 1.00 1.00
964 A166 60c multi 2.50 2.50
965 A166 75c multi 3.25 3.25
966 A166 $1 multi 4.25 4.25
Nos. 962-966 (5) 12.00 12.00

Souvenir Sheet
Without White Margin
967 A166 Sheet of 5, #a-e 12.00 12.00

Booklet Stamps
Self-Adhesive
Serpentine Die Cut 9½x9
Unwmk.

968 A167 25c multi .70 .70
a. Booklet pane of 10 7.00
969 A167 25c multi .70 .70
a. Booklet pane of 10 7.00
970 A167 60c multi 1.75 1.75
a. Booklet pane of 10 17.50
971 A167 75c multi 2.00 2.00
a. Booklet pane of 10 20.00
Nos. 968-971 (4) 5.15 5.15

Birds A168

Designs: 25c, Bananaquit. 50c, Vitelline warbler. 75c, Grand Cayman parrot. 80c, Caribbean dove. $1, Caribbean elaenia. $1.50, West Indian woodpecker. $1.60, Thick-billed vireo. $2, Northern flicker. $4, Cuban bullfinch. $5, Western spindalis. $10, Loggerhead kingbird. $20, Red-legged thrush.

Perf. 13½x13¾

2006, Oct. 9 Litho. Wmk. 373
972 A168 25c multi .60 .60
973 A168 50c multi 1.25 1.25
974 A168 75c multi 1.90 1.90
975 A168 80c multi 2.00 2.00
976 A168 $1 multi 2.50 2.50
977 A168 $1.50 multi 3.75 3.75
978 A168 $1.60 multi 4.00 4.00
979 A168 $2 multi 5.00 5.00
980 A168 $4 multi 9.75 9.75
981 A168 $5 multi 12.00 12.00
982 A168 $10 multi 24.00 24.00
983 A168 $20 multi 50.00 50.00
Nos. 972-983 (12) 116.75 116.75

Booklet Stamps
Self-Adhesive
Unwmk.
Serpentine Die Cut 10x9½
Size:29x24mm

983A A168 25c multi .60 .60
d. Booklet pane of 10 6.00
983B A168 75c multi 1.90 1.90
e. Booklet pane of 10 19.00
983C A168 80c multi 2.00 2.00
f. Booklet pane of 10 20.00
Nos. 983A-983C (3) 4.50 4.50

Christmas A169

Designs: 25c, "Faith," Magi. 75c, "Hope," Prophet with scroll. 80c, "Joy," angel. $1, "Love," Madonna and Child.

Perf. 12½x13¼

2006, Oct. 26 Litho. Wmk. 373
984-987 A169 Set of 4 12.50 12.50

Island Scenes
A170

Designs: 20c, Brac Reed dock. 25c, Water-front buildings, Hog Sty Bay. 30c, East End blowholes, vert. 40c, Man in hammock, vert. 75c, Poinciana blooms. $1, Driftwood on Little Cayman.

Wmk. 373

2007, June 26	**Litho.**	**Perf. 13¾**	
988-993	A170	Set of 6	10.50 10.50

Scouting, Cent.
A171

Designs: 25c, Wolf Cubs and leaders, hands lashing rope. 75c, Cub Scouts and leaders, hands with trumpet. 80c, Scouts camping, hand with compass. $1, Scout Drill Team, poppies.
No. 998, vert.: a, 50c, Scouts marching. b, $1.50, Lord Robert Baden-Powell and dog.

2007, July 9			
994-997	A171	Set of 4	9.00 9.00
Souvenir Sheet			
998	A171	Sheet of 2, #a-b	5.50 5.50

Wedding of Queen Elizabeth II and Prince Philip, 60th Anniv. — A172

Designs: 50c, Couple and wedding coach. 75c, Elizabeth wearing bridal veil. 80c, Princess Elizabeth, Philip, Queen Mother Elizabeth, King George VI, Princess Margaret. $1, Wedding procession, Westminster Abbey. $2, Couple.

Wmk. 373

2007, Sept. 12	**Litho.**	**Perf. 13¾**	
999-1002	A172	Set of 4	10.50 10.50
Souvenir Sheet			
Perf. 14			
1003	A172	$2 multi	6.50 6.50

No. 1003 contains one 42x57mm stamp.

Christmas
A173

Stained-glass windows from local churches: 25c, Nativity, Wesleyan Holiness Church. 50c, Jesus Praying, Elmslie Memorial Church. 75c, Jesus Calling First Disciples, St. George's Anglican Church. 80c, Dove, East End Adventist Church. $1, Orb, First Baptist Church of Grand Cayman. $1.50, Shepherd, Frank Sound Church of God.

2007, Oct. 22		**Perf. 15x14**	
1004-1009	A173	Set of 6	15.00 15.00

A174

Greetings
A175

Nos. 1010-1015: a, Hello. b, Good Luck. c, Congratulations. d, You're Invited. e, Best Wishes. f, Love.
No. 1016, Hello. No. 1017, Congratulations. No. 1018, You're Invited. No. 1019, Love.

Wmk. 373

2008, Feb. 5		**Litho.**	**Perf. 14¼**	
1010	A174	20c Sheet of 6, #a-f	3.00	3.00
1011	A174	25c Sheet of 6, #a-f	3.75	3.75
1012	A174	50c Sheet of 6, #a-f	7.50	7.50
1013	A174	75c Sheet of 6, #a-f	11.00	11.00
1014	A174	80c Sheet of 6, #a-f	12.00	12.00
1015	A174	$1 Sheet of 6, #a-f	15.00	15.00
Nos. 1010-1015 (6)			52.25	52.25

Booklet Stamps

Self-Adhesive

Serpentine Die Cut 9½x9

Unwmk.

1016	A175	20c multi	.60	.60
a.		Booklet pane of 10	6.00	
1017	A175	25c multi	.70	.70
a.		Booklet pane of 10	7.00	
1018	A175	25c multi	.60	.60
a.		Booklet pane of 10	7.00	
1019	A175	25c multi	.70	.70
a.		Booklet pane of 10	7.00	
Nos. 1016-1019 (4)			2.60	2.60

Darwin Initiative
A176

Fauna: 20c, Land crab. 25c, Needlecase. 75c, Little Cayman green anole, vert. 80c, Cayman Brac ground boa. $1, White-shouldered bat.
$2, Caribbean reef squid, vert.

Wmk. 373

2008, July 9	**Litho.**	**Perf. 14**	
1020-1024	A176	Set of 5	11.00 11.00
Souvenir Sheet			
1025	A176	$2 multi	6.50 6.50

2008 Olympic Games, Beijing
A177

Designs: 20c, Lanterns, swimming. 25c, Fish, swimming. 50c, Bamboo, running. 75c, Dragon, hurdles.

Wmk. 373

2008, Aug. 8	**Litho.**	**Perf. 13¼**	
1026-1029	A177	Set of 4	6.75 6.75

Water Authority, 25th Anniv.
A178

Children's art: 25c, Stop Water Pollution. 75c, Water droplets. $2, Splash of Life.

Wmk. 373

2008, Oct. 16	**Litho.**	**Perf. 13¼**	
1030-1032	A178	Set of 3	11.50 11.50

Christmas
A179

Santa Claus and: 25c, Ship. 75c, Horse-drawn carriage. 80c, Helicopter. $1, Race car.

2008, Nov. 12		**Perf. 13¾**	
1033-1036	A179	Set of 4	11.00 11.00

A180

No. 1037: a, Silver thatch plant. b, People making rope strands. c, Man cobbing rope. d, Thatch products. e, Traditional home.

Wmk. 406

2009, Jan. 28		**Litho.**	**Perf. 13¾**	
1037	A180	Horiz. strip of 5	5.00	5.00
a.-e.		25c Any single	1.00	1.00
		Complete booklet, 2 #1037	10.00	

Island Scenes
A181

Designs: 20c, Hammock, palm trees, boat. 25c, House. 75c, Hammock under shelter at beach, palm trees, vert. 80c, Three cruise liners. $1, Direction signs near bus depot, vert. $1.50, Limestone pinnacles, Hell.
$2, Iguana.

2009, Apr. 9			**Perf. 12½**	
1038-1043	A181	Set of 6	12.50	12.50
Souvenir Sheet				
Perf. 13				
1044	A181	$2 multi	5.75	5.75

Space Exploration
A182

Designs: 20c, Mars Rover, 2004. 25c, Space Shuttle STS-71 launch, 1995. 75c, Hubble Space Telescope. $1, Apollo 11 launch, 1969. $1.50, International Space Station.
$2, Lunar Rover on Moon, painting by Capt. Alan Bean, vert.

Wmk. 406

2009, July 20		**Litho.**	**Perf. 13¼**	
1045-1049	A182	Set of 5	9.00	9.00
Souvenir Sheet				
Perf. 13x13¼				
1050	A182	$2 multi	5.00	5.00

No. 1050 contains one 40x60mm stamp. Nos. 1045-1049 each were printed in sheets of 6.

Equality Through Democracy
A183

Designs: No. 1051, 25c, Hands holding pens signing voting rolls. No. 1052, 25c, George Town Town Hall. 50c, Woman casting ballot.

Wmk. 406

2009, Sept. 23		**Litho.**	**Perf. 13¾**	
1051-1053	A183	Set of 3	2.75	2.75
1053a		Sheet of 3, #1051-1053	2.75	2.75

Woman suffrage and Cayman Islands constitution, 50th anniv.

Christmas — A184

Images of Christmas stamps of 1997: 25c, Cayman Islands #749. 75c, Cayman Islands #750. 80c, Cayman Islands #751. $1, Cayman Islands #752.

Wmk. 406

2009, Oct. 22	**Litho.**	**Perf. 14**	
1054-1057	A184	Set of 4	7.00 7.00

Shells
A185

Designs: 20c, Hawk-wing conch. 25c, Ornate scallop. 60c, Chestnut turban. 75c, Beautiful mitre. 80c, Four-toothed nerite. $1.60, White-spotted marginella.
$3, Queen conch.

Wmk. 406

2010, June 30	**Litho.**	**Perf. 13¼**	
1058-1063	A185	Set of 6	12.00 12.00
Souvenir Sheet			
1064	A185	$3 multi	8.50 8.75

Shells — A186

Designs: 25c, Ornate scallop. 75c, Beautiful mitre.

Serpentine Die Cut 9½x9

2010, June 30			**Unwmk.**	
Booklet Stamps				
Self-Adhesive				
1065	A186	25c multi	.90	.90
a.		Booklet pane of 10	9.00	
1066	A186	75c multi	2.10	2.10
a.		Booklet pane of 10	21.00	

Girld Guides, Cent.
A187

Girl Guides: 20c Uniforms. 25c, Camping. 50c, Parade. 80c, Badges.

Wmk. 406

2010, Dec. 17   **Litho.**   **Perf. 12½**
1067-1070 A187   Set of 4   4.75 4.75

Wedding of Prince
William and
Catherine
Middleton — A188

Designs: 25c, Couple kissing. 75c, Couple in carriage waving, horiz. 80c, Couple holding hands. $2, Couple and father of the bride, horiz.

2011, Aug. 4   **Perf. 14**
1071-1074 A188   Set of 4   9.50 9.50

Catboats
A189

Designs: No. 1075, 20c, Men in catboats catching turtles. Nos. 1076, 1081, 25c, Men building catboat. No. 1077, 25c, Catboat sailing around Cayman Brac's Bluff. No. 1078, 50c, Catboats racing regatta style. No. 1079, $1.60, Catboats unloading cargo. No. 1080, $2, Women sewing catboat sail.

2011, Aug. 31   **Wmk. 406**   **Perf. 14**
1075-1080 A189   Set of 6   11.50 11.50
Booklet Stamp
Self-Adhesive
Size:30x25mm
Serpentine Die Cut 9½x9
Unwmk.
1081 A189 25c multi   .60   .60
  a.   Booklet pane of 10   6.00

Christmas
A190

Designs: 25c, Frontispiece for 1611 edition of the King James Bible. 75c, King James I. 80c, William Tyndale, Bible tanslator. $1, Printers printing the King James Bible. $1.60, Translators in the Jerusalem Chamber.

2011, Nov. 8   **Wmk. 406**   **Perf. 12½**
1082-1086 A190   Set of 5   10.50 10.50

King James Bible, 400th anniv.

Famous
Cayman
Islanders
A191

Designs: 20c, Almerian Labertha McLaughlin Tomlinson (1882-1974), midwife. 25c, Captain Rayal Brazley Bodden (1885-1976), shipwright and builder. 75c, Irskie Leila Yates (1899-1996), maternity nurse. $1.50, Major Joseph Rodriguez Watler (1890-1965), police inspector.

Perf. 13¼x13¾
2011, Nov. 11   **Wmk. 406**
1087 A191 20c multi   .50   .50
  a.   Booklet pane of 6   3.00
       Complete booklet, #1087a   3.00
1088 A191 25c multi   .60   .60
  a.   Booklet pane of 6   3.75
       Complete booklet, #1088a   3.75

1089 A191 75c multi   1.75   1.75
  a.   Booklet pane of 6   10.50
       Complete booklet   10.50
1090 A191 $1.50 multi   3.50   3.50
  a.   Booklet pane of 6   21.00
       Complete booklet, #1090a   21.00
     Nos. 1087-1090 (4)   6.35   6.35

A192

Reign of Queen
Elizabeth II, 60th
Anniv. — A193

Various photographs of Queen Elizabeth II: 25c, 80c, $1, $1.50.

2012, June 12   **Wmk. 406**   **Perf. 14**
1091-1094 A192   Set of 4   8.25 8.25
Booklet Stamp
Self-Adhesive
Serpentine Die Cut 9½x9
Unwmk.
1095 A193 25c multi   .60   .60
  a.   Booklet pane of 10   6.00

2012
Summer
Olympics,
London
A194

Designs: 25c, Runner. 50c, Hurdler. 75c, Swimmer. 80c, Two runners. $1.60, Swimmer, diff.

Wmk. 406
2012, Aug. 2   **Litho.**   **Perf. 13¼**
1096-1100 A194   Set of 5   9.50 9.50

A195

A195a

Emergency Services: 20c, Patrol boats. 25c, Ambulance service. 75c, Fire department. $1.50, 911 public safety communications. $2, Police helicopter.

2012, Aug. 30   **Wmk. 406**   **Perf. 14**
1101-1105 A195   Set of 5   12.00 12.00
1101a   Dated "2013"   .50   .50
Booklet Stamps
Self-Adhesive
Unwmk.
Serpentine Die Cut 9½x9
1105A A195a 25c multi   .65   .65
  c.   Booklet pane of 10   6.50
1105B A195a 75c multi   1.90   1.90
  d.   Booklet pane of 10   19.00

A196

A197

Marine Life: 25c, Stoplight parrotfish. 50c, Green sea turtle. 75c, Common sea fan, Yellow tube sponge. 80c, Upside-down jellyfish. $1, Juvenile yellowtail damselfish. $1.50, Spotted trunkfish. $1.60, Caribbean spiny lobster. $2, Giant barrel sponge. $4, Caribbean reef shark. $5, Great barracuda. $10, Southern stingray.$20, West Indian spider crab.

2012, Oct. 9   **Wmk. 406**   **Perf. 14**
1106 A196 25c multi   .60   .60
1107 A196 50c multi   1.25   1.25
1108 A196 75c multi   1.90   1.90
1109 A196 80c multi   2.00   2.00
1110 A196 $1 multi   2.50   2.50
  a.   Souvenir sheet of 4   10.00   10.00
1111 A196 $1.50 multi   3.75   3.75
1112 A196 $1.60 multi   4.00   4.00
1113 A196 $2 multi   5.00   5.00
1114 A196 $4 multi   9.75   9.75
1115 A196 $5 multi   12.50   12.50
1116 A196 $10 multi   25.00   25.00
1117 A196 $20 multi   50.00   50.00
     Nos. 1106-1117 (12)   118.25   118.25
Booklet Stamps
Self-Adhesive
Die Cut Perf. 14x15¼
Unwmk.
1118 A197 25c multi   .60   .60
  a.   Booklet pane of 10   6.00
1119 A197 75c multi   1.90   1.90
  a.   Booklet pane of 10   19.00
1120 A197 80c multi   2.00   2.00
  a.   Booklet pane of 10   20.00
     Nos. 1118-1120 (3)   4.50   4.50

Christmas
A198

Paintings by Gladwyn K. Bush: 25c, Mary and Jesus. 75c, His Name is Jesus. 80c, Every Knee Shall Bow. $1, Nativity.

2012, Dec. 6   **Wmk. 406**   **Perf. 14**
Stamps + Label
1121-1124 A198   Set of 4   7.00 7.00

A199

Shipwrecks and
Anchors — A200

Shipwreck: 20c, Mathusalem. Nos. 1126, 1130, 25c, Inga. No. 1127, 25c, Topsy. $1.50, Tofa. $2, Glamis.

Wmk. 406
2013, Aug. 2   **Litho.**   **Perf. 14**
1125-1129 A199   Set of 5   10.50 10.50
Booklet Stamp
Self-Adhesive
Die Cut Perf. 14x15¼
Unwmk.
1130 A200 25c multi   .60   .60
  a.   Booklet pane of 10   6.00

Birth of Prince
George of
Cambridge
A201

Designs: 20c, Prince George. 25c, Duchess of Cambridge holding Prince George. 80c, Duke of Cambridge holding Prince George. $2, Duke and Duchess of Cambridge, Prince George.

Wmk. 406
2013, Oct. 31   **Litho.**   **Perf. 12½**
1131-1134 A201   Set of 4   7.75 7.75

Christmas
A202

Santa Claus and: 25c, Old Government House. 75c, Old Homestead. 80c, Bodden Town Mission House. $1, Old District Administration Building.

Wmk. 406
2013, Nov. 5   **Litho.**   **Perf. 13**
1135-1138 A202   Set of 4   6.75 6.75

Houses
on Little
Cayman
and
Cayman
Brac
A203

Designs: 20c, Captain Theo's Villa, Little Cayman. 25c, Carter's House, Cayman Brac. 75c, Captain Charlie's House, Cayman Brac. $1, Foster's House, Cayman Brac.

Wmk. 406
2014, June 10   **Litho.**   **Perf. 13**
1139-1142 A203   Set of 4   5.50 5.50

A204

20th
Commonwealth
Games,
Glasgow,
Scotland — A205

Scottish flag and: 20c, Cycling. 25c, Swimming. 55c, Boxing. 80c, Squash. $1, Shooting. $1.60, Gymnastics. $2, Javelin.

Perf. 13¼x13
2014, Oct. 3   **Litho.**   **Wmk. 406**
1143-1149 A204   Set of 7   16.00 16.00
Booklet Stamp
Self-Adhesive
Serpentine Die Cut 13¾x14
Unwmk.
1150 A205 25c multi   .60   .60
  a.   Booklet pane of 10   6.00

A206

Christmas
A207

Christmas ornaments, poinsettia and: Nos. 1151, 1154, 25c, Little Cayman Baptist Church. Nos. 1152, 1155, 25c, South Sound United Church. Nos. 1153, 1156, 25c, Stake Bay Baptist Church.

Wmk. 406

2014, Nov. 15		Litho.		Perf. 13¾
1151-1153	A206	Set of 3	1.90	1.90

Booklet Stamps
Self-Adhesive
Die Cut Perf. 14x15¼
Unwmk.

| 1154-1156 | A207 | Set of 3 | 1.90 | 1.90 |
| 1156a | | Booklet pane of 12, 4 each #1154-1156 | 7.75 | |

Famous Cayman Islanders Type of 2011

Designs: 25c, Timothy E. McField (1928-95), educator. 50c, Annie Huldah Bodden (1908-89), politician. 80c, Ormond L. Panton (1920-92), politician. $1, Captain Keith P. Tibbetts, Sr. (1916-96), politician.

Perf. 13¼x13¾

2015, May 20		Litho.		Wmk. 406
1157	A191	25c multi	.60	.60
a.		Booklet pane of 6	3.75	—
		Complete booklet, #1157a	3.75	
1158	A191	50c multi	1.25	1.25
a.		Booklet pane of 6	7.50	—
		Complete booklet, #1158a	7.50	
1159	A191	80c multi	2.00	2.00
a.		Booklet pane of 6	12.00	—
		Complete booklet, #1159a	12.00	
1160	A191	$1 multi	2.50	2.50
a.		Booklet pane of 6	15.00	—
		Complete booklet, #1160a	15.00	
		Nos. 1157-1160 (4)	6.35	6.35

A208

Christmas
A209

Winning designs in children's Christmas stamp design contest depicting: 20c, Christmas tree, presents and crab, by Arianna Anglin. Nos. 1162, 1165, 25c, Parrot, by Clementine Bonnie Lumsden. 75c, Turtle, by Zara Garofolo. 80c, Sun, sailboat, Christmas stockings, by Cerys Martin.

Wmk. 406

2015, Dec. 2		Litho.		Perf. 13
1161-1164	A208	Set of 4	5.00	5.00

Booklet Stamp
Self-Adhesive
Serpentine Die Cut 13¾x14
Unwmk.

| 1165 | A209 | 25c multi | .60 | .60 |
| a. | | Booklet pane of 10 | 6.00 | |

Cayman Islands
National Museum,
25th
Anniv. — A210

Designs: No. 1166, 25c, Ship's sextant, 1960s. No. 1167, 25c, Caymanian Woman, wood carving by Clarice Carter, 1960s. 75c, Coffee grinder, early 1900s. $1.60, Monkey jar, early 1900s.

Wmk. 406

2015, Dec. 3		Litho.		Perf. 14
1166-1169	A210	Set of 4	7.00	7.00

Ships
A211

Designs: 25c, Kirk B. 80c, Nunoca. $1, Rembro. $2, Clara C. Scott. $4, HMS Dragon.

Wmk. 406

2016, May 16		Litho.		Perf. 13
1170-1173	A211	Set of 4	10.00	10.00

Souvenir Sheet

| 1174 | A211 | $4 multi | 9.75 | 9.75 |

WAR TAX STAMPS

No. 36 Surcharged

a

b

1917, Feb. 26		Wmk. 3		Perf. 14
MR1	A5(a)	1 ½p on 2 ½p	20.00	25.00
a.		Fraction bar omitted	275.00	300.00
b.		Period missing after "STAMP"	900.00	
MR2	A5(b)	1 ½p on 2 ½p	2.10	7.25
a.		Fraction bar omitted	85.00	150.00

On No. 1 the distance between "WAR STAMP" and "1 ½" varies.

Surcharged

1917, Sept. 4				
MR3	A5	1 ½p on 2 ½p ultra	850.00	2,500.

Surcharged

1917, Sept. 4				
MR4	A5	1 ½p on 2 ½p ultra	.30	.65

No. 33 Overprinted

1919, Feb. 4				
MR5	A5	½p green	.70	3.00

The "brownish paper" variety comes from the interleaving used for shipment from England.

Type of 1912-16
Surcharged

1919, Feb. 4				
MR6	A5	1 ½p on 2 ½p orange	1.25	2.50

No. 35 Surcharged

1920, Mar. 10				
MR7	A5	1 ½p on 2p gray	5.50	9.50

The "rose-tinted paper" variety comes from the interleaving used for shipment from England.
A surcharge in red was not issued.

CENTRAL AFRICAN REPUBLIC

'sen-trəl 'a-fri-kən ri-'pə-blik

LOCATION — Western Africa, north of equator
GOVT. — Republic
AREA — 241,243 sq. mi.
POP. — 3,444,951 (1999 est.)
CAPITAL — Bangui

The former French colony of Ubangi-Shari, a unit in French Equatorial Africa, proclaimed itself the Central African Republic Dec. 1, 1958. It became the Central African Empire Dec. 4, 1976. It became the Central African Republic again in 1979.

100 Centimes = 1 Franc

> **Catalogue values for all unused stamps in this country are for Never Hinged items.**

Watermark

Wmk. 385

Premier Barthélemy
Boganda and
Flag — A1

Design: 25fr, Boganda and flag, horiz.

Unwmk.

1959, Dec. 1		Engr.		Perf. 13
1	A1	15fr multi	.40	.25
2	A1	25fr multi	.60	.25

1st anniv. of the Republic and honoring Premier Barthélemy Boganda (1910-59).
For overprints & surcharge see Nos. 12, 59, M1-M2.

Imperforates

Many stamps of Central African Republic exist imperforate in issued and trial colors, and also in small presentation sheets in issued colors.

Common Design Types
pictured following the introduction.

C.C.T.A. Issue
Common Design Type

1960, May 21		Unwmk.		Perf. 13
3	CD106	50fr lt grn & dk bl	1.90	.65

Dactyloceras Widenmanni — A2

Designs: Various butterflies.

1960-61

4	A2	50c bl grn & dk red	.25	.25
5	A2	1fr multi	.25	.25
6	A2	2fr dk grn & brn	.25	.25
7	A2	3fr yel grn & dk red	.30	.25
8	A2	5fr multi	.35	.25
9	A2	10fr multi	.85	.35
10	A2	20fr multi	2.00	.50
11	A2	85fr multi	8.00	1.60
		Nos. 4-11 (8)	12.25	3.70

Issued: 50c-3fr, 6/10/61; others, 9/3/60.

No. 2
Overprinted

1960, Dec. 1

12	A1	25fr multi	1.60	1.60

National Holiday, Dec. 1, 1960.

Louis
Pasteur
and
Pasteur
Institute,
Bangui
A3

1961, Feb. 25   Unwmk.   Perf. 13

13	A3	20fr multi	1.25	.80

Opening of Pasteur Institute at Bangui.

Flag, Map,
and UN
Emblem
A4

1961, Mar. 4   Engr.

14	A4	15fr multi	.50	.30
15	A4	25fr multi	.50	.30
16	A4	85fr multi	1.75	1.00
		Nos. 14-16 (3)	2.75	1.60

Admission to the UN.

No. 15
Overprinted
in Green

1961, Dec. 1

17	A4	25fr multi	2.25	2.25

National Holiday, Dec. 1.

No. 16
Srchd. in
Red Brown

1962, Mar. 25

18	A4	50fr on 85fr multi	1.90	1.90

Conf. of the African and Malgache Union at Bangui, Mar. 25-27.

Abidjan Games Issue
Common Design Type
1962, July 21 Photo. Perf. 12½x12
19	CD109	20fr Hurdling	.45	.30
20	CD109	50fr Bicycling	1.20	.80
		Nos. 19-20,C6 (3)	3.90	2.60

African-Malgache Union Issue
Common Design Type
1962, Sept. 8 Unwmk.
| 21 | CD110 | 30fr multi | 1.25 | .60 |

African and Malgache Union, 1st anniv.

Pres. David
Dacko — A5

1962 Perf. 12
| 22 | A5 | 20fr multi | .40 | .25 |
| 23 | A5 | 25fr multi | .60 | .25 |

For surcharge see No. 60.

Soldiers with
Flag — A6

1963, Aug. 13 Photo.
| 24 | A6 | 20fr blk & multi | .75 | .35 |

National Army, third anniversary.

Waves
Around
Globe
A6a

Design: 100fr, Orbit patterns around globe.

1963, Sept. 19 Unwmk. Perf. 12½
| 25 | A6a | 25fr plum & grn | .75 | .55 |
| 26 | A6a | 100fr org, bl & grn | 1.90 | 1.50 |

Issued to publicize space communications.

Young
Pioneers
A7

1963, Oct. 14 Engr. Perf. 12½
| 27 | A7 | 50fr grnsh bl, vio bl & brn | .90 | .50 |

Issued to honor Young Pioneers.

Boali Falls — A8

1963, Oct. 28 Perf. 13
| 28 | A8 | 30fr bl, grn & red brn | .90 | .45 |

Colotis
Evippe
A9

Designs: Various butterflies.

1963, Nov. 18 Photo. Perf. 12½x13
29	A9	1fr multi	.25	.25
30	A9	3fr multi	.75	.25
31	A9	4fr multi	.85	.30
32	A9	60fr multi	6.00	3.00
		Nos. 29-32 (4)	7.85	3.80

For surcharge see No. 58.

UNESCO
Emblem,
Scales and
Tree — A9a

1963, Dec. 10 Perf. 13
| 33 | A9a | 25fr grn, ol & red brn | 1.00 | .55 |

15th anniversary of the Universal Declaration of Human Rights.

Leaves and
IQSY
Emblem
A10

1964, Apr. 20 Engr. Perf. 13
| 34 | A10 | 25fr org, Prus grn & bis | 1.25 | .75 |

International Quiet Sun Year, 1964-65.

Child — A11

Designs: Heads of Children.

1964, Aug. 13 Unwmk. Perf. 13
35	A11	20fr multi	.35	.25
36	A11	25fr multi	.40	.30
37	A11	40fr multi	.55	.45
38	A11	50fr multi	.70	.45
a.		Miniature sheet of 4, #35-38	3.00	3.00
		Nos. 35-38 (4)	2.00	1.45

Cooperation Issue
Common Design Type
1964, Nov. 7 Engr.
| 39 | CD119 | 25fr grn, mag & dk brn | 1.00 | .55 |

"All Men Are
Men" — A12

1964, Dec. 1 Litho. Perf. 13x12½
| 40 | A12 | 25fr multi | 1.00 | .45 |

Issued to publicize National Unity.

Putting
Yoke on
Oxen
A13

Designs: 50fr, Ox pulling harrow. 85fr, Team of oxen in field. 100fr, Hay wagon.

1965, Apr. 28 Engr. Perf. 13
41	A13	25fr sl grn, sep & rose	.60	.30
42	A13	50fr sl grn, lt bl & brn	1.00	.45
43	A13	85fr bl, grn & red brn	1.40	.70
44	A13	100fr multi	1.90	.90
		Nos. 41-44 (4)	4.90	2.35

For surcharges see Nos. 63-64.

Telegraph Receiver by Pouget-
Maisonneuve — A14

ITU cent.: 30fr, Chappe telegraph, vert. 50fr, Doignon regulator, vert. 85fr, Pouillet telegraph transcriber.

1965, May 17 Unwmk.
45	A14	25fr red, grn & ultra	.60	.40
46	A14	30fr lake & grn	.65	.40
47	A14	50fr car & vio	1.00	.60
48	A14	85fr red lil & slate	1.90	1.00
		Nos. 45-48 (4)	4.15	2.40

"Health"
A15

25fr, "Clothes;" shuttle, cloth & women. 60fr, "Teaching;" student & school. 85fr, "Food;" mother feeding child, tractor in wheat field.

1965, June 10 Engr. Perf. 13
49	A15	25fr ultra, brt grn & brn	.50	.30
50	A15	50fr ultra, brn & grn	.90	.45
51	A15	60fr grn, ultra & brn	1.00	.60
52	A15	85fr multi	1.40	.70
		Nos. 49-52 (4)	3.80	2.05

Issued to publicize the slogans and aims of "M.E.S.A.N." (Mouvement d'Évolution Sociale de l'Afrique Noire). See No. C30.

Caterpillars and
Moth on Coffee
Branch — A16

Designs: 3fr, Hawk moth and caterpillar on coffee leaves, horiz. 30fr, Platyedra moth and larvae on cotton plant.

1965, Aug. 25 Engr. Perf. 13
53	A16	2fr dk pur, dp org & sl grn	.40	.25
54	A16	3fr blk, sl grn & red	1.00	.25
55	A16	30fr red lil, red & sl grn	6.50	.90
		Nos. 53-55 (3)	7.90	1.40

Issued to publicize plant protection.

Boy Scout,
Tents and
Animals
A17

Design: 25fr, Campfire and Scout emblem.

1965, Sept. 27 Unwmk. Perf. 13
| 56 | A17 | 25fr red org, bl & red lil | 1.00 | .25 |
| 57 | A17 | 50fr brn & Prus bl | 1.25 | .60 |

Issued to honor the Boy Scouts.

Nos. 30, 1 and 22
Surcharged in Black
or Brown

Engraved; Photogravure
Perf. 13, 12, 12½x13
1965, Aug. 26 Unwmk.
58	A9	2fr on 3fr multi	5.75	5.75
59	A1	5fr on 15fr multi	4.50	4.50
60	A5	10fr on 20fr multi (Br)	6.25	6.25
		Nos. 58-60 (3)	16.50	16.50

The surcharges are adjusted to shape of stamps.

UN
Emblem
and Wheat
A18

1965, Oct. 16 Engr. Perf. 13
| 61 | A18 | 50fr ocher, sl grn & brt bl | 1.25 | .70 |

FAO "Freedom from Hunger Campaign."

Diamond
Cutter
A19

1966, Mar. 14 Engr. Perf. 13
| 62 | A19 | 25fr car rose, dk pur & brn | 1.40 | .45 |

Nos. 43-44
Surcharged

1966, Feb.
| 63 | A13 | 5fr on 85fr multi | .40 | .40 |
| 64 | A13 | 10fr on 100fr multi | .65 | .65 |

Issue dates: 5fr, Feb. 17; 10fr, Feb. 15.

Statue of Mbaka
Woman
Porter — A20

1966, Apr. 9 Photo. Perf. 13x12½
| 65 | A20 | 25fr multi | 1.00 | .45 |

Intl. Negro Arts Festival, Dakar, Senegal, Apr. 1-24.

WHO Headquarters,
Geneva — A21

1966, May 3 Photo. Unwmk.
| 66 | A21 | 25fr pur, bl & yel | 1.00 | .45 |

Inauguration of the WHO Headquarters, Geneva.

Eulophia Cucullata — A22

Orchids: 5fr, Lissochilus horsfalii. 10fr, Tridactyle bicaudata. 15fr, Polystachya. 20fr, Eulophia alta. 25fr, Microcelia macrorrhynchium.

1966, May 16 Photo. Perf. 12x12½
Orchids in Natural Colors
67	A22	2fr dk red	.30	.25
68	A22	5fr brn org & vio	.75	.25
69	A22	10fr bl grn & blk	.90	.40
70	A22	15fr lt grn & dk brn	1.40	.65
71	A22	20fr dk grn	2.00	.70
72	A22	25fr lt ultra & brn	3.00	.80
	Nos. 67-72 (6)		8.35	3.05

For surcharge see No. 78.

Congo Forest Mouse A23

Rodents: 10fr, One-stripe mouse. 20fr, Dollman's tree mouse, vert.

1966, Sept. 15 Photo. Perf. 12½x12
73	A23	5fr yel & multi	.65	.30
74	A23	10fr tan & multi	1.25	.45
75	A23	20fr lt grn & multi	2.10	.80
	Nos. 73-75 (3)		4.00	1.55

UNESCO Emblem — A24

1966, Dec. 5 Photo. Perf. 13
76	A24	30fr multi	.80 .40

20th anniv. of UNESCO.

Pres. Jean Bedel Bokassa — A25

1967, Jan. 1 Perf. 12x12½
77	A25	30fr yel grn, blk & bis brn	.75 .35

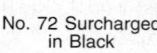

No. 72 Surcharged in Black

1967, May 8 Photo. Perf. 12x12½
78	A22	10fr on 25fr multi	.80 .30

See No. C43.

Central Market, Bangui A26

1967, Aug. 8 Photo. Perf. 12½x13
79	A26	30fr multi	1.00 .40

Safari Hotel, Bangui A27

1967, Sept. 26 Photo. Perf. 12½x13
80	A27	30fr multi	1.00 .40

Leucocoprinus Africanus — A28

Various Mushrooms

1967, Oct. 3 Photo. Perf. 13
81	A28	5fr dk brn, ol & ocher	10.00	.80
82	A28	10fr dk brn, ultra & yel	15.00	1.25
83	A28	15fr dk brn, sl grn & yel	17.50	1.40
84	A28	30fr multi	50.00	4.00
85	A28	50fr multi	75.00	6.00
	Nos. 81-85 (5)		167.50	13.45

Map, Radio Tower, Projector and People A29

1967, Oct. 31 Engr.
86	A29	30fr emer, ocher & indigo	1.00 .45

Radiovision service.

African Hair Style — A30

Various African Hair Styles.

1967, Nov. 7 Engr. Perf. 13
87	A30	5fr ultra, dk brn & bis brn	.30	.25
88	A30	10fr car, dk brn & bis brn	.50	.25
89	A30	15fr dp grn, dk brn & bis brn	.75	.40
90	A30	20fr org, dk brn & bis brn	.75	.50
91	A30	30fr red lil, dk brn & bis brn	1.40	.65
	Nos. 87-91 (5)		3.70	2.05

Nurse Vaccinating Children A31

1967, Nov. 14
92	A31	30fr dk red brn & brt grn	.90 .50

Vaccination campaign, 1967-70.

Douglas DC-3 A32

1967, Nov. 24
93	A32	1fr shown	.35	.25
94	A32	2fr Beechcraft Baron	.35	.25
95	A32	5fr Douglas DC-4	.35	.25
	Nos. 93-95,C47-C49 (6)		23.05	7.55

Pierced Stone, Kwe Tribe — A33

Designs: 30fr, Primitive dwelling at Toulou, horiz. 100fr, Megaliths, Bouar. 130fr, Rock painting (people), Toulou, horiz.

1967, Dec. 26 Engr. Perf. 13
96	A33	30fr crim, ind & mar	.85	.45
97	A33	50fr ol brn, ocher & dk grn	1.60	.90
98	A33	100fr dk brn, brt bl & brn	3.00	1.20
99	A33	130fr dk red, brn & dk grn	3.25	1.20
	Nos. 96-99 (4)		8.70	3.75

6th Pan-African Prehistoric Cong., Dakar.

Tanker, Refinery and Map of Area Served — A33a

1968, July 30 Photo. Perf. 12½
100	A33a	30fr multi	1.00 .30

Issued to commemorate the opening of the Port Gentil (Gabon) Refinery, June 12, 1968.

Bulldozer Clearing Land — A34

Designs: 10fr, Baoule cattle. 20fr, 15,000-spindle spinning machine. No. 104, Automatic Diederichs looms. No. 105, Bulldozer.

1968, Oct. 1 Engr. Perf. 13
101	A34	5fr blk, grn & dk brn	.40	.25
102	A34	10fr blk, pale grn & bis brn	.55	.30
103	A34	20fr grn, red brn & yel	.90	.30
104	A34	30fr brn, ol & ultra	1.40	.55
105	A34	30fr ind, red brn & sl grn	1.40	.55
	Nos. 101-105 (5)		4.65	1.95

Issued to publicize "Operation Bokassa."

Bangui Mosque A35

1968, Oct. 14
106	A35	30fr grn, bl & ocher	.85 .40

Hunting Knife of Baya and Boufi Tribes A36

20fr, Hunting knife of Nzakara tribe. 30fr, Crossbow of Babinga & Babenzele (pygmy) tribes.

1968, Nov. 19 Engr. Perf. 13
107	A36	10fr lem, Prus bl & ultra	.50	.25
108	A36	20fr ultra, dk ol & sl grn	.70	.30
109	A36	30fr sl grn, ultra & brn org	1.25	.40
	Nos. 107-109 (3)		2.45	.95

"Ville de Bangui," 1958 — A37

River Boats: 30fr, "J. B. Gouandjia," 1968. 50fr, "Lamblin," 1944.

1968, Dec. 10 Engr. Perf. 13
Size: 36x22mm
110	A37	10fr mag, brt grn & vio bl	.65	.40
111	A37	30fr bl, grn & brn	1.25	.45
112	A37	50fr brn, sl & ol grn	2.00	.55
	Nos. 110-112,C62-C63 (5)		9.40	3.65

Woman Javelin Thrower — A38

1969, Mar. 18 Photo. Perf. 13x12½
113	A38	5fr shown	.30	.25
114	A38	10fr Women runners	.30	.25
115	A38	15fr Soccer	.50	.25
	Nos. 113-115,C71-C72 (5)		4.45	1.65

BIT and ILO Emblems and Worker A39

1969, May 20 Photo. Perf. 12½x13
116	A39	30fr dp bl, grn & ol brn	1.00 .40
117	A39	50fr dp car, grn & ol brn	1.50 .55

50th anniv. of the ILO.

Pres. Bokassa — A40

1969, Dec. 1 Litho. Perf. 13x13½
118	A40	30fr vermilion & multi	.65 .30

ASECNA Issue
Common Design Type
1969, Dec. 12 Engr. Perf. 13
119	CD132	100fr dp bl	2.25 .80

Garayah — A41

Musical Instuments: 15fr, Ngombi (harp) horiz. 30fr, Xylophone, horiz. 50fr, Ndala (lute) horiz. 130fr, Gatta and babyon (drums).

1970, Jan. 6   Engr.   Perf. 13
120 A41 10fr yel grn, dk grn & ocher   .60   .25
121 A41 15fr bl grn, ocher & dk brn   .60   .25
122 A41 30fr mar, ocher & dk brn   1.00   .45
123 A41 50fr rose car & ind   1.50   .55
124 A41 130fr brt bl, brn & ol   4.75   .95
    Nos. 120-124 (5)   8.45 2.45

UPU Headquarters Issue
Common Design Type
1970, May 20   Engr.   Perf. 13
125 CD133 100fr ultra, ver & red brn   1.90   .70

Loading Platform and Flour Storage Bins A42

50fr, Flour milling machinery. 100fr, View of mill.

1970, Feb. 24   Litho.   Perf. 14
126 A42 25fr sl & multi   11.00   .70
127 A42 50fr lil & multi   26.50   1.50
128 A42 100fr red & multi   37.50   2.50
    Nos. 126-128 (3)   75.00   4.70

Inauguration of SICPAD (Société Industrielle Centrafricaine des Produits Alimentaires et Dérivés), a part of Operation Bokassa, 2/22/68.

Pres. Bokassa — A43

1970, Aug. 13   Litho.   Perf. 14
129 A43 30fr multi   9.00   5.00
130 A43 40fr multi   10.00   5.00

Cheese Factory, Sarki — A44

Silk Worm — A45

10fr, M'Bali Ranch. 20fr, Zebu, vert.

Perf. 13x13½, 13½x13
1970, Sept. 15
131 A44 5fr red & multi   .55   .30
132 A44 10fr red & multi   6.50 4.25
133 A44 20fr red & multi   1.40   .55
134 A44 40fr red & multi   3.00   .95
    Nos. 131-134,C83 (5)   15.95 7.15

Issued to publicize Operation Bokassa, a national development plan.
Nos. 131-134 exist perf 10. See No. C83.

Gnathonemus Monteiri — A46

River Fish: 20fr, Mormyrus proboscirostris. 30fr, Marcusenius wilverthi. 40fr, Gnathonemus elephas. 50fr, Gnathonemus curvirostris.

1971, Apr. 6   Photo.   Perf. 12½
135 A46 10fr multi   .40   .25
136 A46 20fr multi   .75   .30
137 A46 30fr multi   1.10   .60
138 A46 40fr multi   2.50   .70
139 A46 50fr multi   2.75 1.10
    Nos. 135-139 (5)   7.50 2.95

Berberati Cathedral A47

1971, July 20   Litho.   Perf. 13½
140 A47 5fr grn & multi   .65   .25
New Roman Catholic Cathedral at Berberati.

Charles de Gaulle — A48

1971, Aug. 20   Perf. 13½x13
141 A48 100fr brt bl & multi   3.50 2.00
In memory of Gen. Charles de Gaulle (1890-1970), president of France.

Gray Galago — A49

Designs: 40fr, Elegant galago. 100fr, Calabar potto, horiz. 150fr, Bosman's potto, horiz. 200fr, Oustalet's colobo, horiz.

1971, Oct. 25   Photo.   Perf. 13
142 A49 30fr pink & multi   .70   .45
143 A49 40fr lt bl & multi   .90   .55
144 A49 100fr multi   2.75 1.10
145 A49 150fr multi   4.75 1.75
146 A49 200fr multi   5.75 2.25
    Nos. 142-146 (5)   14.85 6.10

Alan B. Shepard — A50

No. 148, Yuri Gagarin. No. 149, Edwin E. Aldrin, Jr. No. 150, Alexei Leonov. No. 151, Neil A. Armstrong on moon. No. 152, Lunokhod I on moon.

1971, Nov. 19   Litho.   Perf. 14
147 A50 40fr vio & multi   .50   .30
148 A50 40fr vio & multi   .50   .30
149 A50 100fr multi   1.25   .45
150 A50 100fr multi   1.25   .45
151 A50 200fr red & multi   2.50 1.10
152 A50 200fr red & multi   2.50 1.10
    Nos. 147-152 (6)   8.50 3.70

Space achievements of US and Russia.

"Operation Bokassa" and Pres. Bokassa A51

1971, Dec. 1   Photo.   Perf. 13
153 A51 40fr red & multi   .80   .40
12th anniversary of independence.

Racial Equality Emblem A52

1971, Dec. 6   Litho.
154 A52 50fr multi   .90   .45
Intl. Year Against Racial Discrimination.

Bokassa School Emblem and Cadets — A53

1972, Jan. 1   Photo.
155 A53 30fr gold & multi   .90   .45
J. B. Bokassa Military School.

Book Year Emblem — A54

1972, Mar. 11   Photo.   Perf. 12½x13
156 A54 100fr red brn, gold & org   3.00 1.00
International Book Year 1972.

"Your Heart is your Health" A55

1972, Apr. 7   Photo.   Perf. 13x12½
157 A55 100fr yel, blk & car   1.75   .85
World Health Day.

Red Cross Workers in Village — A56

1972, May 8   Perf. 13
158 A56 150fr multi   3.00 1.40
25th World Red Cross Day.

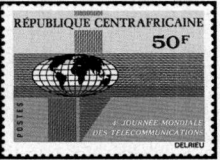

Globe A57

1972, May 17   Litho.
159 A57 50fr yel, blk & dp org   .90   .55
4th World Telecommunications Day.

Pres. and Mrs. Bokassa and Family — A58

1972, May 28   Perf. 14
160 A58 30fr yel & multi   .65   .35
Mother's Day. Mothers' gold medal awarded to Catherine Bokassa.

Pres. Bokassa Planting Cotton, Map of Africa — A59

1972, June 5   Photo.   Perf. 13
161 A59 40fr yel & multi   .90   .45
Operation Bokassa, a natl. development plan.

Postal Checking and Savings Center A60

1972, June 21
162 A60 30fr yel org & multi .65 .40

Irrigated Rice Fields — A61

"Le Pacifique" Apartment House A62

25fr, Plowing rice field. No. 166, Swimming pool, Hotel St. Sylvestre. No. 167, Entrance, Hotel St. Sylvestre. No. 168, J. B. Bokassa University.

1972	Litho.	Perf. 13x13½
163 A61 5fr multi	1.25	.25
164 A61 25fr multi	2.10	.30

	Engr.	Perf. 13
165 A62 30fr multi	.40	.25
166 A62 30fr multi	.50	.25
167 A62 40fr multi	.60	.40
168 A62 40fr multi	.65	.40
Nos. 163-168 (6)	5.50	1.90

Operation Bokassa. Issued: 5fr, 25fr, 11/10; No. 165, 6/27; Nos. 166-167, 12/9; No. 168, 8/26.

Bull Chasing Woman on Clock Face — A63

Scenes Painted on Clock Faces: 10fr, Men & open cooking fire. 20fr, Fishermen. 30fr, Palms, monkeys & giraffe. 40fr, Warriors.

1972, July 31	Photo.	Perf. 12½
169 A63 5fr dk red & multi	.30	.30
170 A63 10fr brt bl & multi	.30	.30
171 A63 20fr grn & multi	.60	.30
172 A63 30fr yel & multi	.85	.45
173 A63 40fr vio & multi	1.25	.60
Nos. 169-173 (5)	3.30	1.95

HORCEN Central African clock and watch factory.

Protestant Youth Center — A64

10fr, Postal runner carrying mail in cleft stick.

1972, Aug. 12		Perf. 13
174 A64 10fr multi, vert.	.30	.30
175 A64 20fr multi	.50	.30
Nos. 174-175,C95-C98 (6)	8.35	5.10

Centraphilex 1972, Central African Philatelic Exhibition, Bangui.

Mail Truck A65

1972, Oct. 23	Photo.	Perf. 13
176 A65 100fr ocher & multi	1.90	.70

Universal Postal Union Day.

Mother Teaching Child to Write — A66

Central African Mothers: 10fr, Caring for infant. 15fr, Combing child's hair. 20fr, Teaching to read. 180fr, Nursing. 190fr, Teaching to walk.

1972, Dec. 27		Perf. 13½x13
177 A66 5fr multi	.25	.25
178 A66 10fr lil & multi	.30	.25
179 A66 15fr dl org & multi	.30	.25
180 A66 20fr yel grn & multi	.50	.25
181 A66 180fr multi	2.75	1.25
182 A66 190fr pink & multi	2.75	1.25
Nos. 177-182 (6)	6.85	3.50

Farmer Carrying Sheaf — A67

1973, May 30	Photo.	Perf. 13
183 A67 50fr vio bl & multi	.90	.45

10th anniv. of the World Food Program.

Garcinia Punctata A68

African Flora: 20fr, Bertiera racemosa. 30fr, Corynanthe pachyceras. 40fr, Combretodendron africanum. 50fr, Xylopia Villosa, vert.

1973, June 8		
184 A68 10fr pale bl & multi	.50	.25
185 A68 20fr multi	.85	.30
186 A68 30fr lt gray & multi	1.00	.45
187 A68 40fr multi	1.60	.60
188 A68 50fr multi	2.00	.80
Nos. 184-188 (5)	5.95	2.40

For surcharge see No. 193.

Pygmy Chameleon A69

1973, June 26	Photo.	Perf. 13
189 A69 15fr multi	1.50	.40

Caterpillar — A70

Designs: Various caterpillars.

1973, Aug. 6	Photo.	Perf. 13
190 A70 3fr multi	1.25	.30
191 A70 5fr multi	2.00	.40
192 A70 25fr multi	4.00	.60
Nos. 190-192 (3)	7.25	1.30

For surcharge see No. 259.

No. 184 Srchd. and Ovptd. in Red

1973, Aug. 16
193 A68 100fr on 10fr multi 1.75 1.00

African solidarity in drought emergency.

African Postal Union Issue
Common Design Type

1973, Sept. 12	Engr.	Perf. 13
194 CD137 100fr dk brn, red org & ol	1.25	.75

Pres. Bokassa and CAR Flag — A71

1973, Nov. 30	Photo.	Perf. 12½
195 A71 1fr brn & multi	.25	.25
196 A71 2fr pur & multi	.25	.25
197 A71 3fr vio bl & multi	.25	.25
198 A71 5fr ocher & multi	.25	.25
199 A71 10fr multi	.40	.25
200 A71 15fr org & multi	.40	.25
201 A71 20fr multi	.50	.25
202 A71 30fr dk grn & multi	.50	.30
203 A71 40fr dk brn & multi	.65	.40
Nos. 195-203,C117-C118 (11)	5.60	3.55

INTERPOL Emblem A72

1973, Dec. 20		Perf. 13x12½
204 A72 50fr yellow & multi	1.40	.60

Intl. Criminal Police Organization, 50th anniv.

Catherine Bokassa Center A73

40fr, Ambulance in front of Catherine Bokassa Center.

1974, Jan. 24	Engr.	Perf. 13
205 A73 30fr multi	.40	.25
206 A73 40fr multi	.55	.30

Catherine Bokassa Center for Mothers and Children.

Cigarette-making Machine — A74

10fr, Cigarette in ashtray, & factory. 30fr, Hand lighting cigarette, & Administration Building.

1974, Jan. 29		
207 A74 5fr slate grn & multi	.25	.25
208 A74 10fr slate grn & multi	.40	.25
209 A74 30fr slate grn & multi	.50	.25
Nos. 207-209 (3)	1.15	.75

Publicity for Centra cigarettes.

"Communications" A75

1974, June 8	Photo.	Perf. 12½x13
210 A75 100fr multi	1.75	.85

World Telecommunications Day.
For surcharge see No. 280.

People and WPY Emblem A76

1974, June 20	Engr.	Perf. 13
211 A76 100fr red, slate grn & brn	1.25	.65

World Population Year.
For surcharge see No. 281.

Mother, Child, WHO Emblem — A77

1974, July 10		
212 A77 100fr multi	1.75	.70

26th anniv. of WHO.
For surcharge see No. 282.

Hoeing — A78

Veterans' activities: 10fr, Battle scene ("yesterday"). 15fr, Pastoral scene ("today"). 20fr, Rice planting. 25fr, Storehouse. 40fr, Veterans Headquarters. Borders show tanks and tractors.

1974, Nov. 15	Litho.	Perf. 13
213 A78 10fr multi	.25	.25
214 A78 15fr multi	.30	.25
215 A78 20fr multi	.30	.25
216 A78 25fr multi	.40	.25
217 A78 30fr multi	.40	.25
218 A78 40fr multi	.60	.25
Nos. 213-218 (6)	2.25	1.50

For surcharges see Nos. 260, 265, 267.

Presidents and Flags of Cameroun,
CAR, Congo, Gabon and Meeting
Center — A79

1974, Dec. 8   Photo.   Perf. 13
219 A79 40fr gold & multi   .65   .40
See No. C126 and note after Cameroun No.
595.
For surcharge see No. 272.

House in
OCAM
City — A80

Scenes in housing development, OCAM
City.

1975, Feb. 1   Photo.   Perf. 13
220 A80 30fr multi   .40   .25
221 A80 40fr multi   .50   .30
222 A80 50fr multi   .60   .30
223 A80 100fr multi   1.00   .55
        Nos. 220-223 (4)   2.50 1.40
For surcharges see Nos. 269, 273.

1975, Feb. 22
Cottage scenes in J. B. Bokassa "pilot
village."
224 A80 25fr multi   .30   .25
225 A80 30fr multi   .40   .25
226 A80 40fr multi   .50   .30
        Nos. 224-226 (3)   1.20   .80
For surcharges see Nos. 268, 270, 274.

Foreign
Ministry
A81

Television
Station
A82

1975, Feb. 28   Perf. 13x12½
227 A81 40fr multi   .65   .40
                Perf. 13
228 A82 40fr multi   .65   .40
Public buildings, Bangui.
For surcharges see Nos. 275-276.

Bokassa's Saber — A83

Design: 40fr, Bokassa's baton.

1975, Feb. 22   Photo.   Perf. 13
229 A83 30fr dp bl & multi   .55   .30
230 A83 40fr vio bl & multi   .55   .30
Jean Bedel Bokassa, President for Life and
Marshal of the Republic. See Nos. C127-
C128. For surcharge see No. 286.

Traffic Signs
A84

1975, Mar. 20
231 A84 5fr Do Not Enter   .25   .25
232 A84 10fr Stop   .25   .25
233 A84 20fr No parking   .30   .25
234 A84 30fr School   .50   .25
235 A84 40fr Intersection   .75   .30
        Nos. 231-235 (5)   2.05 1.30
For surcharges see Nos. 261, 277.

Buffon's
Kob — A85

1975, June 24   Photo.   Perf. 13
236 A85 10fr shown   .45   .25
237 A85 15fr Wart hog   1.10   .35
238 A85 20fr Waterbuck   1.50   .25
239 A85 30fr Lion   1.50   .40
        Nos. 236-239 (4)   4.55 1.25
For surcharges see Nos. 262-263, 266, 271.

Crane
Lifting Log
onto Truck
A86

Designs: 10fr, Forest, vert. 15fr, Tree felling, vert. 100fr, Log pile. 150fr, Logs trans-
ported by raft. 200fr, Lumberyard.

1975, Nov. 28   Engr.   Perf. 13
240 A86 10fr multi   .25   .25
241 A86 15fr multi   .30   .25
242 A86 20fr multi   .55   .25
243 A86 100fr multi   1.50   .55
244 A86 150fr multi   1.75 1.00
245 A86 200fr multi   2.25 1.10
        Nos. 240-245 (6)   6.60 3.40
Promotion of Central African wood.
For surcharges see Nos. 264, 279.

Alexander
Graham
Bell — A88

1976, Mar. 25   Litho.   Perf. 12½x13
248 A88 100fr yel & blk   2.25 1.00
Centenary of first telephone call by Alexander Graham Bell, Mar. 10, 1876.
For surcharge see No. 283.

Satellite and ITU Emblem — A89

No. 250, UPU emblem, various forms of
mail transport.

1976   Engr.   Perf. 13
249 A89 100fr vio bl, claret & grn   1.90 1.00
250 A89 100fr car, grn & ocher   1.60   .80
World Telecommunications Day (No. 249);
Universal Postal Union Day (No. 250).
For surcharges see Nos. 284-285.

Soyuz on Launching Pad — A90

Design: 50fr, Apollo rocket.

1976, June 14   Litho.   Perf. 14x13½
251 A90 40fr multi   .55   .25
252 A90 50fr multi   .80   .25
        Nos. 251-252,C135-C137 (5)   6.45 2.25
Apollo Soyuz space test project, Russo-
American cooperation, launched July 15, link-
up July 17, 1975.
For surcharges see Nos. 287, 290, C161,
C168, C173, C177.

Drurya Antimachus — A91

Butterfly: 40fr, Argema mittrei, vert.

1976, Sept. 20   Litho.   Perf. 12½
253 A91 30fr ocher & multi   7.00 1.00
254 A91 40fr ultra & multi   9.00 1.00
        Nos. 253-254,C145-C146 (4) 43.00 5.50
For surcharge see No. 278.

Slalom, Piero Gros — A92

60fr, Karl Schnabel and Toni Innauer.

1976, Sept. 23   Perf. 13½
255 A92 40fr multi   .65   .25
256 A92 60fr multi   1.00   .30
        Nos. 255-256,C147-C149 (5)   8.05 2.45
12th Winter Olympic Games winners,
Innsbruck.
For surcharges see Nos. 288, 291, C164,
C170, C174, C178.

Viking
Components
A93

Design: 60fr, Viking take-off.

1976, Dec.
257 A93 40fr multi   .65   .25
258 A93 60fr multi   1.00   .30
        Nos. 257-258,C151-C153 (5)   8.05 2.40
Viking Mars project.
For surcharges and overprints see Nos.
289, 292, 391-392, C165, C171, C175, C179.

Central African Empire
Stamps of 1973-76 Overprinted in
Black, Green, Violet Blue, Silver,
Carmine, Brown or Red

Nos. 259, 278, 283

Nos. 260, 265, 267, 269, 273, 276,
279

Nos. 261,
277

Nos. 262-
263, 266,
271

Nos. 264, 282

Nos. 268,
270, 274,
280, 284-
285

Nos. 272, 275

No. 281

Printing and Perforations as Before
1977, Mar.

259	A70	3fr	(#190; B)	.50	.45
260	A78	10fr	(#213;B)	.35	.35
261	A84	10fr	(#232;VB)	.35	.35
262	A85	10fr	(#236;C)	.50	.50
263	A85	15fr	(#237;C)	.85	.85
264	A86	15fr	(#241;B)	.35	.35
265	A78	20fr	(#215;B)	.50	.50
266	A85	20fr	(#238;C)	.50	.50
267	A78	25fr	(#216;B)	.40	.40
268	A80	25fr	(#224;B)	.40	.40
269	A80	30fr	(#220;VB)	.50	.50
270	A80	30fr	(#225;B)	.50	.50
271	A85	30fr	(#239;C)	.60	.60
272	A79	40fr	(#219;B)	.50	.50
273	A80	40fr	(#221;VB)	.50	.50
274	A80	40fr	(#226;B)	.50	.50
275	A81	40fr	(#227;B & S)	.70	.70
276	A82	40fr	(#228;B)	.75	.75
277	A84	40fr	(#235;VB)	.75	.75
278	A91	40fr	(#254;B)	1.00	1.00
279	A86	50fr	(#242;Br)	1.00	1.00
280	A75	100fr	(#210;B)	1.90	1.90
281	A76	100fr	(#211;B)	1.90	1.90
282	A77	100fr	(#212;G)	2.25	2.25
283	A88	100fr	(#248;B)	1.90	1.90
284	A89	100fr	(#249;B)	2.25	2.25
285	A89	100fr	(#250;B)	2.50	2.50
	Nos. 259-285 (27)			24.70	24.65

Stamps of 1975-76 Overprinted in
Black on Silver Panel

1977, Apr. 1

286	A83	40fr multi	(#230)	.90	.90
287	A90	40fr multi	(#251)	.70	.70
288	A92	40fr multi	(#255)	.70	.70
289	A93	40fr multi	(#257)	.70	.70
290	A90	50fr multi	(#252)	1.00	1.00
291	A92	60fr multi	(#256)	.90	.90
292	A93	60fr multi	(#258)	.90	.90
	Nos. 286-292 (7)			5.80	5.80

Pierre and Marie Curie — A94

Design: 60fr, Wilhelm C. Roentgen.

1977, Apr. 1   Litho.   Perf. 13½

293	A94	40fr multi	1.00	.30
294	A94	60fr multi	1.00	.40
	Nos. 293-294,C180-C182 (5)		14.25	2.75

Nobel Prize winners.

Italy No. C42 and Faustine Temple,
Rome — A95

60fr, Russia #C12 & St. Basil's Cathedral,
Moscow.

1977, Apr. 11   Litho.   Perf. 11

295	A95	40fr multi	1.00	.25
296	A95	60fr multi	1.10	.40
	Nos. 295-296,C184-C186 (5)		9.75	2.55

75th anniversary of the Zeppelin.

Lindbergh over Paris — A96

Designs: 60fr, Santos Dumont and "14 bis."
100fr, Bleriot and monoplane. 200fr, Roald
Amundsen and "N24." 300fr, Concorde. 500fr,
Lindbergh and Spirit of St. Louis.

1977, Sept. 30   Litho.   Perf. 13½

297	A96	50fr multi	.65	.25
298	A96	60fr multi	1.00	.25
299	A96	100fr multi	1.75	.40
300	A96	200fr multi	2.50	.55
301	A96	300fr multi	5.00	1.25
	Nos. 297-301 (5)		10.90	2.70

Souvenir Sheet

302	A96	500fr multi	6.00	2.00

History of aviation, famous fliers.

Shot
on
Goal
A97

Designs: 60fr, Heading ball in net. 100fr,
Backfield defense. 200fr, Argentina '78
poster. 300fr, Mario Zagalo and stadium.
500fr, Ferenc Puskas.

1977, Nov. 18   Litho.   Perf. 13½

303	A97	50fr multi	.50	.25
304	A97	60fr multi	.65	.25
305	A97	100fr multi	1.25	.30
306	A97	200fr multi	2.10	.55
307	A97	300fr multi	3.50	.90
	Nos. 303-307 (5)		8.00	2.25

Souvenir Sheet

308	A97	500fr multi	5.50	1.75

World Soccer Championships, Argentina,
June 1-25, 1978.
For overprints see Nos. 370-375.

Emperor
Bokassa I,
Central
African
Flag — A98

1977, Dec. 4   Litho.   Perf. 13½

309	A98	40fr multi	.40	.25
310	A98	60fr multi	.55	.25
311	A98	100fr multi	1.00	.45
312	A98	150fr multi	1.40	.60
	Nos. 309-312,C188-C189 (6)		8.00	3.60

Coronation of Emperor Bokassa I, Dec. 4.

Lilium — A99

1977   Litho.   Perf. 13½x14

313	A99	5fr shown	.55	.30
314	A99	10fr Hibiscus	1.10	.55

For overprints see Nos. 408-409.

Electronic Tree, ITU
Emblem — A100

1977

315	A100	100fr blk, org & brn	3.00	2.00

World Telecommunications Day.

Bible and
People
A101

1977   Litho.   Perf. 14x13½

316	A101	40fr multi	8.00	1.25

Bible Week.

People and
Rotary
Emblem
A102

1977

317	A102	60fr multi	4.50	2.00

Rotary Club of Bangui, 20th anniversary.

Holy Family,
by Rubens
A103

Rubens Paintings: 150fr, Marie de Medicis.
200fr, Son of artist. 300fr, Neptune. 500fr,
Marie de Medicis, diff.

1978, Jan. 26

318	A103	60fr multi	.60	.25
319	A103	150fr multi	1.50	.40
320	A103	200fr multi	2.40	.60
321	A103	300fr multi	3.50	.80
	Nos. 318-321 (4)		8.00	2.05

Souvenir Sheet

322	A103	500fr gold & multi	6.00	2.00

Peter Paul Rubens (1577-1640).

Rhinoceros — A104

Endangered Animals and Wildlife Fund
Emblem: 50fr, Slender-nosed crocodile. 60fr,
Leopard, vert. 100fr, Giraffe, vert. 200fr, Ele-
phant. 300fr, Gorilla, vert.

1978, Feb. 21   Litho.   Perf. 13½

323	A104	40fr multi	1.75	.30
324	A104	50fr multi	2.50	.35
325	A104	60fr multi	2.75	.55
326	A104	100fr multi	4.75	.90
327	A104	200fr multi	12.00	1.25
328	A104	300fr multi	14.00	2.00
	Nos. 323-328 (6)		37.75	5.35

Bokassa
Sports
Palace
A105

Design: 60fr, Sports Palace, side view.

1978   Perf. 14

329	A105	40fr multi	.50	.25
330	A105	60fr multi	.65	.40

Automatic
Telephone
Exchange,
Bangui
A106

1978

331	A106	40fr multi	.50	.25
332	A106	60fr multi	.65	.40

Diligence and Satellite — A107

Designs (UPU Emblem and): 50fr, Steam
locomotive and communications via satellite.
60fr, Paddle-wheel steamer and ship-to-shore
communication via satellite. 80fr, Old mail
truck and satellite.

1978, May 17   Perf. 13½

333	A107	40fr multi	.25	.25
334	A107	50fr multi	3.00	1.25
335	A107	60fr multi	.30	.25
336	A107	80fr multi	.40	.25
	Nos. 333-336,C191-C192 (6)		6.15	2.55

Posts and telecommunications, cent. of
progress.

Mask — A108

Designs: 30fr, Mask. 60fr, Women dancers, horiz. 100fr, Men dancers, horiz.

Perf. 13½x14, 14x13½

1978, July 11			**Litho.**	
337	A108	20fr blk & yel	.75	.30
338	A108	30fr blk & brt bl	.75	.30
339	A108	60fr blk & multi	1.90	.60
340	A108	100fr blk & multi	3.25	.95
	Nos. 337-340 (4)		6.65	2.15

Black-African World Arts Festival, Lagos. For overprints see Nos. 411-412.

Capt. Cook on "Endeavour" A109

60fr, Resolution off Hawaii. 200fr, Hawaiians welcoming Capt. Cook. 350fr, Masked rowers in Hawaiian boat.

1978, Aug. 30			**Perf. 14½**	
341	A109	60fr multi, horiz.	.75	.25
342	A109	80fr multi	1.25	.25
343	A109	200fr multi, horiz.	2.50	.70
344	A109	350fr multi, horiz.	4.50	1.25
	Nos. 341-344 (4)		9.00	2.45

Capt. James Cook (1728-1779), explorer.

Dürer, Self-portrait A110

Dürer Paintings: 80fr, The Four Apostles. 200fr, Virgin and Child. 350fr, Emperor Maximilian I.

1978, Oct. 24		**Litho.**	**Perf. 13½**	
345	A110	60fr multi	.65	.25
346	A110	80fr multi	1.10	.25
347	A110	200fr multi	2.50	.85
348	A110	350fr multi	4.75	1.40
	Nos. 345-348 (4)		9.00	2.75

Albrecht Dürer (1471-1528), German painter.

Tutankhamen's Gold Mask — A111

Treasures of Tutankhamen: 60fr, King and Queen, gold back panel of throne. 80fr, Gilt folding chair. 100fr, King wearing crowns of Upper and Lower Egypt, painted wood sculpture. 120fr, Lion's head. 150fr, Tutankhamen,

wood stature. 180fr, Gold throne. 250fr, Gold miniature coffin.

1978, Nov. 22				
349	A111	40fr multi	.60	.30
350	A111	60fr multi	.70	.40
351	A111	80fr multi	1.10	.55
352	A111	100fr multi	1.25	.55
353	A111	120fr multi	1.75	.60
354	A111	150fr multi	2.00	.70
355	A111	180fr multi	2.50	.85
356	A111	250fr multi	3.00	1.10
	Nos. 349-356 (8)		12.90	5.05

Tutankhamen, c. 1358 B.C., King of Egypt.

Lenin at Smolny Institute — A112

Soviet Union, 60th anniv.: 60fr, 200fr, 300fr, Various Lenin portraits. 100fr, Ulyanov family, horiz. 150fr, Lenin, Cruiser "Aurora" and flag, horiz. 500fr, "Aurora" and star.

1978, Nov.			**Perf. 14**	
357	A112	40fr multi	.50	.30
358	A112	60fr multi	.60	.30
359	A112	100fr blk & gold	1.00	.45
360	A112	150fr blk, gold & red	1.90	.70
361	A112	200fr multi	3.00	1.00
362	A112	300fr multi	4.00	1.40
	Nos. 357-362 (6)		11.00	4.25

Souvenir Sheet

363	A112	500fr multi	6.00	4.00

Catherine Bokassa A113

Design: 60fr, Emperor Bokassa.

1978, Dec. 4		**Litho.**	**Perf. 13**	
364	A113	40fr multi	.65	.25
365	A113	60fr multi	.90	.30

1st anniv. of coronation. See No. C202.

Rowland Hill, Letter Scale and G.B. No. 1 — A114

Rowland Hill and: 50fr, US #1, mailman on bicycle. 60fr, Austria #P4, 19th cent. mailman. 80fr, Switzerland #2L1, postilion and mailcoach.

1978, Dec. 9		**Litho.**	**Perf. 13½**	
366	A114	40fr multi	.65	.30
367	A114	50fr multi	.65	.30
368	A114	60fr multi	.90	.40
369	A114	80fr multi	1.00	.50
	Nos. 366-369,C203-C204 (6)		8.95	3.55

Sir Rowland Hill (1795-1879), originator of penny postage.

Nos. 303-307 Overprinted in Silver

1978, Dec. 27				
370	A97	50fr multi	.55	.25
371	A97	60fr multi	.65	.30
372	A97	100fr multi	1.00	.55
373	A97	200fr multi	2.25	1.00
374	A97	300fr multi	3.25	1.40
	Nos. 370-374 (5)		7.70	3.50

Souvenir Sheet
No. 308 Overprinted in Silver

375	A97	500fr multi	5.00	5.00

Argentina's victory in World Cup Soccer Championship 1978.

Children Painting and Dutch Portrait — A115

UNICEF, Eagle Emblems and: 50fr, Eskimo children skiing, ski jump. 60fr, Children with toy racing car, Carl Benz with early car model. 80fr, Children launching rocket, Mariner 5.

1979, Mar. 6		**Litho.**	**Perf. 13½**	
376	A115	40fr multi	.65	.25
377	A115	50fr multi	.75	.25
378	A115	60fr multi	.90	.25
379	A115	80fr multi	1.25	.30
	Nos. 376-379,C206-C207 (6)		7.70	2.10

International Year of the Child.

High Jump, Moscow '80 Emblem and "M" — A116

Designs (Moscow '80 Emblem, Various Sports and): 50fr, Bicycling and "O." 60fr, Weight lifting and "C." 80fr, Judo and "K."

1979, Mar. 16		**Litho.**	**Perf. 13**	
380	A116	40fr multi	.55	.25
381	A116	50fr multi	.65	.25
382	A116	60fr multi	.75	.25
383	A116	80fr multi	1.10	.30
	Nos. 380-383,C209-C210 (6)		6.25	2.05

22nd Olympic Games, Moscow, July 19-Aug. 3, 1980. Background letters on Nos. 380-383, C209-C210 spell "Mockba." A 1500fr gold embossed stamp showing emblems and Discobolus exists.

Memorial, Bangui, Butterfly, Hibiscus — A117

Design: 150fr, Canoe, truck and letters.

1979, June 8	**Litho.**	**Perf. 12x12½**		
384	A117	60fr multi	3.00	1.25
385	A117	150fr multi	5.50	2.50

Philexafrique II, Libreville, Gabon, June 8-17. Nos. 384, 385 each printed in sheets of 10 with 5 labels showing exhibition emblem.

Schoolgirl A118

1979, July 25	**Litho.**	**Perf. 12½x12**		
386	A118	70fr multi	.95	.40

Intl. Bureau of Education, Geneva, 50th anniv.

Chicken A119

1979, Aug.			**Perf. 13**	
387	A119	10fr shown	1.90	1.10
388	A119	20fr Bull	1.90	1.10
389	A119	40fr Sheep	4.00	2.10
	Nos. 387-389,C211 (4)		13.55	6.30

National Husbandry Assoc.

Souvenir Sheet

Virgin and Child, by Dürer — A120

1979, Aug.			**Perf. 13½**	
390	A120	500fr lt grn & dl red	5.50	1.60

Albrecht Dürer (1471-1528), German engraver and printer.

Central African Republic

Nos. 257-258 Overprinted

1979, Nov. 11 Litho. Perf. 13½
391 A93 40fr multi .65 .30
392 A93 60fr multi .75 .40
Nos. 391-392,C212-C214 (5) 7.05 3.35

Apollo 11 moon landing, 10th anniversary.

Girl and Rose A121

30fr, Butterfly and girl, vert. 60fr, Hansel and Gretel, vert. 200fr, The Little Match Girl. 250fr, Mermaid, vert.

1979, Dec. 15
393 A121 30fr multicolored .30 .25
394 A121 40fr shown .50 .25
395 A121 60fr multicolored .55 .25
396 A121 200fr multicolored 2.25 .70
397 A121 250fr multicolored 2.75 .80
Nos. 393-397 (5) 6.35 2.25

International Year of the Child.

Locomotive, U.S. Type A27, Hill — A122

Locomotives, Hill and Stamps: 100fr, France #1. 150fr, Germany type A11. 250fr, Great Britain #32. 500fr, CAR #2.

1979, Dec. 20
398 A122 60fr multi .55 .25
399 A122 100fr multi 1.10 .30
400 A122 150fr multi 1.75 .45
401 A122 250fr multi 3.00 .95
Nos. 398-401 (4) 6.40 1.95

Souvenir Sheet
402 A122 500fr multi 5.75 2.00

Sir Rowland Hill (1795-1879), originator of penny postage.

Basketball, Moscow '80 Emblem — A123

Pre-Olympic Year: Men's or women's basketball.

1979, Dec. 28 Litho. Perf. 14½
403 A123 50fr multi .50 .25
404 A123 125fr multi 1.10 .35
405 A123 200fr multi 1.90 .55
406 A123 300fr multi 3.25 .80
407 A123 500fr multi 5.00 1.40
Nos. 403-407 (5) 11.75 3.35

For overprints see Nos. 425-429.

Nos. 313-314 Overprinted in Black on Silver Panel

and

Balambo Chair A124

and

Nos. 337-338 Overprinted in Black on Silver Panel

Perf. 13½x14, 14x13½
1980, Mar. 20 Litho.
408 A99 5fr multi .35 .30
409 A99 10fr multi .35 .30
410 A124 20fr multi .25 .25
411 A108 20fr multi .25 .25
412 A108 30fr multi .40 .25
Nos. 408-412 (5) 1.60 1.35

Apollo-Soyuz — A125

40fr, Viking Satellite. 50fr, Apollo-Soyuz. 60fr, Voyager. 100fr, European Space Agency emblem, flags.

1980, Apr. 8 Perf. 13½
413 A125 40fr multicolored .55 .25
414 A125 50fr multicolored .65 .25
415 A125 60fr multicolored .75 .25
416 A125 100fr multicolored 1.25 .30
Nos. 413-416,C221-C222 (6) 6.70 2.00

Walking, Olympic Medal, Moscow '80 Emblem — A126

1980, July 25 Litho. Perf. 13½
417 A126 30fr shown .50 .25
418 A126 40fr Relay race .55 .25
419 A126 70fr Running .75 .25
420 A126 80fr High jump .90 .25
Nos. 417-420,C231-C232 (6) 5.30 1.65

For overprints see Nos. 462-465, C248-C250.

Fruit — A126a

1980, Aug. 1 Litho. Perf. 13½
420A A126a 40fr multicolored — —
420B A126a 70fr green & multi — —

Agricultural Development A127

40fr, Telecommunications. 70fr, Engineering. 100fr, Civil engineering.

1980, Nov. 4 Litho. Perf. 13½
421 A127 30fr shown .30 .25
422 A127 40fr multicolored .50 .25
423 A127 70fr multicolored .90 .25
424 A127 100fr multicolored 1.10 .40
Nos. 421-424,C234-C235 (6) 6.20 2.25

Europe-Africa cooperation.

Nos. 403-407 Overprinted in Black

1980, Nov. 12 Perf. 14½
425 A123 50fr multi .55 .25
426 A123 125fr multi 1.10 .40
427 A123 190fr multi 1.90 .55
428 A123 300fr multi 3.60 .90
429 A123 500fr multi 5.00 1.60
Nos. 425-429 (5) 12.15 3.70

Virgin and Child, by Raphael — A128

Christmas: Paintings by Raphael.

1980, Dec. 20 Perf. 12½
430 A128 60fr multi .65 .25
431 A128 150fr multi 1.60 .60
432 A128 250fr multi 3.00 1.10
Nos. 430-432 (3) 5.25 1.95

African Postal Union, 5th Anniversary A129

1980, Dec. 24 Photo. Perf. 13½
433 A129 70fr multi .85 .45

Peruvian Soccer Team, Soccer Cup — A130

1981, Jan. 13 Litho. Perf. 13½
434 A130 10fr shown .25 .25
435 A130 15fr Scotland .25 .25
436 A130 20fr Mexico .30 .25
437 A130 25fr Sweden .30 .25
438 A130 30fr Austria .40 .25
439 A130 40fr Poland .50 .25
440 A130 50fr France .55 .25
441 A130 60fr Italy .65 .25
442 A130 70fr Germany .75 .25
443 A130 80fr Brazil .90 .25
Nos. 434-443,C237-C238 (12) 7.60 3.30

ESPANA '82 World Cup Soccer Championship.

13th World Telecommunications Day — A131

1981, May 17 Litho. Perf. 12½
444 A131 150fr multi 1.40 .70

Apollo 15 Crew on Moon — A132

Space Exploration: Columbia space shuttle.

1981, June 10 Litho. Perf. 14
445 A132 100fr multi .90 .30
446 A132 150fr multi 1.50 .40
447 A132 200fr multi 2.10 .60
448 A132 300fr multi 3.50 1.00
Nos. 445-448 (4) 8.00 2.30

Souvenir Sheet
449 A132 500fr multi 5.00 1.60

Family of Acrobats with Monkey, by Picasso A133

Picasso Birth Cent.: 50fr, The Balcony. 80fr, The Artist's Son as Pierrot. 100fr, The Three Dancers.

1981, June 30 Perf. 13½
450 A133 40fr multi .50 .25
451 A133 50fr multi .65 .25
452 A133 80fr multi 1.10 .25
453 A133 100fr multi 1.40 .40
Nos. 450-453,C245-C246 (6) 8.40 2.20

First Anniv. of Zimbabwe's Independence — A134

1981, July 9   Litho.   Perf. 12½
454 A134 100fr multi   1.10   .45
455 A134 150fr multi   1.50   .55
456 A134 200fr multi   2.25   .70
        Nos. 454-456 (3)   4.85   1.70

Royal Wedding
A135

75fr, Charles. 100fr, Diana. 150fr, St. Paul's Cathedral. 175fr, Prince Charles and Lady Diana.
    500fr, Couple.

1981, July, 24   Perf. 14
457 A135 75fr multicolored   .50   .25
458 A135 100fr multicolored   .70   .25
459 A135 150fr multicolored   1.20   .40
460 A135 175fr multicolored   1.50   .40
        Nos. 457-460 (4)   3.90   1.30
Souvenir Sheet
461 A135 500fr multicolored   5.00   1.40
        For overprints see Nos. 529-533.

Nos. 417-420 Overprinted in Gold

1981   Litho.   Perf. 13½
462 A126 30fr multi   .35   .25
463 A126 40fr multi   .50   .25
464 A126 70fr multi   .85   .30
465 A126 80fr multi   .85   .40
        Nos. 462-465,C248-C249 (6)   4.95   1.85

Prince Charles and Lady
Diana — A136

50fr, Crowned Prince of Wales. 80fr, Diana. 100fr, Naval training.

1981, Aug. 20   Litho.   Perf. 13½
466 A136 40fr shown   .50   .25
467 A136 50fr multicolored   .50   .25
468 A136 80fr multicolored   .85   .30
469 A136 100fr multicolored   1.10   .40
        Nos. 466-469,C251-C252 (6)   6.65   2.15
        Royal wedding.

1906 Renault — A137

40fr, Mercedes-Benz, 1937. 50fr, Matra-Ford, 1969. 110fr, Tazio Nuvolari, 1927. 150fr, Jackie Stewart, 1965.
    450fr, Finish line, 1914.

1981, Sept. 22   Litho.   Perf. 12½
470 A137 20fr shown   .30   .25
471 A137 40fr multicolored   .65   .25
472 A137 50fr multicolored   .75   .25
473 A137 110fr multicolored   1.50   .40
474 A137 150fr multicolored   2.25   .55
        Nos. 470-474 (5)   5.45   1.70
Souvenir Sheet
Perf. 10
475 A137 450fr multicolored   6.00   6.00
    Grand Prix of France, 75th anniv.

World Food
Day
A138

1981, Oct. 16
476 A138 90fr multi   .95   .30
477 A138 110fr multi   1.10   .40

Navigators and their Ships — A139

1981, Sept. 4   Litho.   Perf. 13½
478 A139 40fr C.V. Rietschoten   .50   .30
479 A139 50fr M. Pajot   .55   .45
480 A139 60fr K. Jaworski   .75   .55
481 A139 80fr M. Birch   1.00   .60
        Nos. 478-481,C254-C255 (6)   6.30   4.00

Downfall
of Empire
A140

5fr, Bayonet through crown. 25fr, Victory holding map. 90fr, Toppled Bokassa statue.

1981, Oct. 6
482 A140 5fr multicolored   .25   .25
483 A140 10fr like #482   .25   .25
484 A140 25fr multicolored   .30   .25
485 A140 60fr like #484   .75   .25
486 A140 90fr multicolored   1.10   .40
487 A140 500fr like #486   4.75   2.00
        Nos. 482-487 (6)   7.40   3.40

Komba — A141

1981, Nov. 17
488 A141 50fr shown   .65   .25
489 A141 90fr Dodoro, horiz.   1.25   .30
490 A141 140fr Kaya, horiz.   2.10   .40
        Nos. 488-490 (3)   4.00   .95

Central
African
States
Bank
A142

1981, Dec. 12   Litho.   Perf. 12½x13
491 A142 90fr multi   1.00   .30
492 A142 110fr multi   1.10   .40

Christmas
1981 — A143

Virgin and Child Paintings: 50fr, Fra Angelico, 1430. 60fr, Cosimo Tura, 1484. 90fr, Bramantino. 110fr, Memling.

1981, Dec. 24
493 A143 50fr multicolored   1.00   .30
494 A143 60fr multicolored   1.10   .40
495 A143 90fr multicolored   1.75   .45
496 A143 110fr multicolored   2.25   .70
        Nos. 493-496,C260-C261 (6)   13.10   3.00

Scouting Year — A144

100fr, Hiking. 150fr, Scouts, horiz. 200fr, Leaning against railing. 300fr, Salute, flag, vert.
    500fr, Scout, Baden-Powell, vert.

1982, Jan. 13   Perf. 12½
497 A144 100fr multicolored   1.25   .40
498 A144 150fr multicolored   1.90   .55
499 A144 200fr multicolored   2.75   .80
500 A144 300fr multicolored   3.75   1.25
        Nos. 497-500 (4)   9.65   3.00
Souvenir Sheet
Perf. 13
501 A144 500fr multicolored   6.25   1.60

Elephant
A145

1982, Jan. 22   Perf. 13½
502 A145 60fr shown   .90   .25
503 A145 90fr Giraffes   1.10   .30
504 A145 100fr Addaxes   1.25   .30
505 A145 110fr Okapi   1.50   .45
        Nos. 502-505,C263-C264 (6)   13.50   3.35

Norman
Rockwell
Illustrations
A146

30fr, Grandfather snowman. 60fr, Croquet players. 110fr, Women talking. 150fr, Searching.

1982, Feb. 17   Perf. 13½x14
506 A146 30fr multicolored   .30   .25
507 A146 60fr multicolored   .75   .30
508 A146 110fr multicolored   1.25   .40
509 A146 150fr multicolored   1.75   .55
        Nos. 506-509 (4)   4.05   1.50

AT 16
Dirigible
A147

10fr, Beyer-Garrat locomotive. 20fr, Bugatti 24 "Royale," 1924. 110fr, Vickers "Valentia," 1928.

1982, Feb. 27   Litho.   Perf. 13½
510 A147 5fr shown   .25   .25
511 A147 10fr multicolored   .25   .25
512 A147 20fr multicolored   .30   .25
513 A147 110fr multicolored   1.40   .40
        Nos. 510-513,C266-C267 (6)   11.45   3.20

Bellvue Garden, by Edouard
Manet — A148

Anniversaries: 400fr, Goethe, vert. Nos. 519-520, Princess Diana, 21st birthday, July 1, vert. 300fr, George Washington, vert.

1982, Apr. 6   Litho.   Perf. 13
517   A148 200fr multi   3.25   1.00
517A A148 300fr multi   3.00   1.00
518   A148 400fr multi   4.00   1.25
519   A148 500fr multi   5.00   2.00
        Nos. 517-519 (4)   15.25   5.25
Souvenir Sheet
520   A148 500fr multi   5.50   1.40

23rd Olympic Games, Los Angeles,
1984 — A149

1982, July 24   Litho.   Perf. 13½
521 A149 5fr Soccer   .25   .25
522 A149 10fr Boxing   .25   .25
523 A149 20fr Running   .30   .25
524 A149 110fr Long jump   1.00   .30
        Nos. 521-524,C269-C270 (6)   9.80   3.25

21st Birthday of Princess
Diana — A150

Portraits.

1982, July 20　　Litho.　　Perf. 13½
525	A150	5fr multi	.25	.25
526	A150	10fr multi	.25	.25
527	A150	20fr multi	.30	.25
528	A150	110fr multi	1.00	.30
	Nos. 525-528,C272-C273 (6)		10.55	3.25

Nos. 457-461
Overprinted in
Blue

1982, Aug. 20　　Perf. 14
529	A135	75fr multi	.55	.25
530	A135	110fr multi	.75	.40
531	A135	150fr multi	1.40	.55
532	A135	175fr multi	2.25	.80
	Nos. 529-532 (4)		4.95	2.00

Souvenir Sheet
533	A135	500fr multi	5.50	3.75

Birth of Prince William of Wales, June 21.

2nd UN
Conference
on Peaceful
Uses of Outer
Space,
Vienna, Aug.
9-21 — A151

Various satellites and space scenes.

1982, Aug. 15　　Litho.　　Perf. 13½
534	A151	5fr multi	.25	.25
535	A151	10fr multi	.25	.25
536	A151	20fr multi	.30	.25
537	A151	110fr multi	1.00	.30
	Nos. 534-537,C277-C278 (6)		9.80	3.25

Sakpa
Basket
A152

Baskets and bowls: 25fr, Ngbenda gourd,
vert. 120fr, Ta ti ngou jugs. 175fr, Kangu
bowls. 300fr, Kolongo bowls, vert.

1982, Sept. 2　　Perf. 13
538	A152	5fr shown	.25	.25
539	A152	10fr like 5fr	.25	.25
540	A152	25fr multicolored	.30	.25
541	A152	60fr like 25fr	.75	.25
542	A152	120fr multicolored	1.60	.40
543	A152	175fr multicolored	1.75	.60
544	A152	300fr multicolored	3.50	1.25
	Nos. 538-544 (7)		8.40	3.25

For surcharges see Nos. 792A-792B.

1982 World Cup Soccer
Championships, Spain — A152a

Various soccer plays.

1982, Sept.　　Litho.　　Perf. 13½x13
Overprinted in Silver or Gold
545	A152a	60fr Italy, 1st, 2nd	.90	.25
546	A152a	150fr Poland, 3rd	1.75	.55
547	A152a	300fr France, 4th	3.50	1.25
	Nos. 545-547 (3)		6.15	2.05

Souvenir Sheet
548	A152a	500fr Italy, 1st (G)	5.75	1.40

Not issued without overprint.

13th World UPU
Day — A153

1982, Oct. 9
549	A153	60fr multi	.60	.25
550	A153	120fr multi	1.40	.45

Comb and
Hairpins
A154

1982, Oct. 20　　Perf. 13x12½
551	A154	20fr multi	.25	.25
552	A154	30fr multi	.40	.25
553	A154	60fr multi	.75	.30
554	A154	80fr multi	1.10	.40
555	A154	120fr multi	1.50	.45
	Nos. 551-555 (5)		4.00	1.65

Artist Pierre
Ndarata and
No.69
A155

1982, Oct.　　Perf. 13
556	A155	40fr Jean Tubind at		
		easel, vert.	.25	.25
557	A155	70fr shown	.45	.25
558	A155	90fr like 70fr	.55	.25
559	A155	140fr like 40fr	1.00	.35
	Nos. 556-559 (4)		2.25	1.10

TB Bacillus
Centenary
A156

1982, Nov. 30　　Perf. 13½x13
560	A156	100fr vio & blk	1.40	.30
561	A156	120fr red org & blk	1.60	.45
562	A156	175fr bl & blk	2.25	.80
	Nos. 560-562 (3)		5.25	1.55

10th Anniv.
of UN
Conference
on Human
Environment
A157

1982, Dec. 8
563	A157	120fr multi	1.40	.40
564	A157	150fr multi	1.50	.55
565	A157	300fr multi	3.00	1.00
	Nos. 563-565 (3)		5.90	1.95

Granary
A158

1982, Dec. 15　　Perf. 13
566	A158	60fr multi	.65	.25
567	A158	80fr multi	1.00	.40
568	A158	120fr multi	1.40	.60
569	A158	200fr multi	2.40	1.20
	Nos. 566-569 (4)		5.45	2.45

A159

1982, Dec.
570	A159	100fr multi	1.00	.40
571	A159	120fr multi	1.40	.45

ITU Plenipotentiaries Conf., Nairobi, Sept.

A160

5fr, Modes of communication. 120fr, Map,
jet.

1983, Jan. 31　　Litho.　　Perf. 13½x13
572	A160	5fr multicolored	.25	.25
573	A160	60fr like 5fr	.75	.30
574	A160	120fr multicolored	1.40	.40
575	A160	175fr like 120fr	1.75	.55
	Nos. 572-575 (4)		4.15	1.50

UN Decade for African Transportation and
Communication, 1978-88.

Chess Champions — A161

Men and Chess Pieces: 5fr, Steinitz, first
world champion, 1886. 10fr, Aaron
Niemzovitch, castle. 20fr, Alexander Alekhine,
knights. 110fr, Botvinnik. 300fr, Boris
Spassky, glass pieces. 500fr, Bobby Fischer,
king, knight. 600fr, Korchnoi, Karpov, pawn.
No. 582A, Bobby Fischer. No. 582B, Reti, Larsen, Petrossian, and Mecking, horiz.

1983, Jan. 15
576	A161	5fr multi	.25	.25
577	A161	10fr multi	.25	.25
578	A161	20fr multi	.35	.25
579	A161	110fr multi	1.40	.25

580	A161	300fr multi	3.75	.75
581	A161	500fr multi	5.50	1.40
	Nos. 576-581 (6)		11.50	3.15

Souvenir Sheet
582	A161	600fr multi	7.00	2.00

Litho. & Embossed
Perf. 13½
Size: 35x60mm
582A	A161	1500fr gold & multi	42.50	3.50

Souvenir Sheet
582B	A161	1500fr gold & multi	10.00	10.00

No. 582 contains one 56x33mm stamp, No.
582B one 35x60mm stamp. 300fr, 500fr,
600fr, Nos. 582A and 582B are airmail.

Marshal Tito
(1892-1980)
A162

20fr, George Washington.

1983, Jan. 22
583	A162	20fr multicolored	.25	.25
a.		Souvenir sheet	5.50	—
584	A162	110fr shown	1.25	.30
a.		Souvenir sheet	5.50	—

1982 World Cup Soccer
Championships, Spain — A162a

Trophy, flags, scores, players: 5fr, Hamilton,
Pezzey. 10fr, Borovski, Boniek. 20fr, Littbarski,
Zamora. 110fr, Zico, Passarella. 300fr, Rossi,
Smolarek. 500fr, Rummenigge, Giresse.
600fr, Rossi, Rummenigge. No. 584I, Platini.
No. 584J, Rossi.

1983, Feb. 8　　Litho.　　Perf. 13½
584B	A162a	5fr multi	.25	.25
584C	A162a	10fr multi	.25	.25
584D	A162a	20fr multi	.40	.25
584E	A162a	110fr multi	1.50	.30
584F	A162a	300fr multi	3.25	.70
584G	A162a	500fr multi	5.50	1.40
	Nos. 584B-584G (6)		11.15	3.15

Souvenir Sheet
584H	A162a	600fr multi	5.50	4.25

Litho. & Embossed
584I	A162a	1500fr gold & multi	35.00	6.50

Souvenir Sheet
584J	A162a	1500fr gold & multi	10.00	10.00

Nos. 584F-584J are airmail.

Easter
1983
A163

Rembrandt Paintings: 100fr, Entombment. 300fr, Crucifixion. 400fr, Descent from the Cross.

1983, Apr. 16
585	A163	100fr multicolored	1.00	.40
586	A163	300fr multicolored	3.00	1.25
587	A163	400fr multicolored	4.00	1.75
		Nos. 585-587 (3)	8.00	3.40

Vintage Cars and their Makers A164

A164a

Designs: 10fr, Emile Levassor, Rene Panhard, 1895 car. 20fr, Henry Ford, 1896 car. 30fr, Louis Renault, 1899 car. 80fr, Ettore Bugatti, type 37, 1925. 400fr, Enzo Ferrari, 815 sport, 1940. 500fr, Ferdinand Porsche, 356 coupe, 1951. 600fr, Karl Benz, velocipede, 1886. No. 594A, F.H. Royce and C.S. Rolls, 1911 Rolls-Royce Silver Ghost. No. 594B, G. Daimler, 1900 Mercedes 35CV.

1983, June 3   Litho.   Perf. 13½
588	A164	10fr multi	.25	.25
589	A164	20fr multi	.25	.25
590	A164	30fr multi	.30	.25
591	A164	80fr multi	1.00	.30
592	A164	400fr multi	4.50	1.10
593	A164	500fr multi	5.50	1.40
		Nos. 588-593 (6)	11.80	3.55

Souvenir Sheet
594	A164	600fr multi	5.75	1.60

Litho. & Embossed
594A	A164a	1500fr gold & multi	25.00	4.00

Souvenir Sheet
594B	A164a	1500fr gold & multi	10.00	6.00

Nos. 592-594B are airmail.

25th Anniv. of Intl. Maritime Org. — A165

1983, July 8   Litho.   Perf. 12½x13
595	A165	40fr multi	.50	.25
596	A165	100fr multi	1.00	.40

World Communications Year — A166

1983, July 22
597	A166	50fr multi	.50	.25
598	A166	130fr multi	1.40	.45

Pre-Olympics, Los Angeles A167

1984 Summer Olympics, Los Angeles A167a

5fr, Gymnast. 40fr, Javelin throwing. 60fr, Pole vault. 120fr, Fencing. 200fr, Cycling. 300fr, Sailing.

600fr, Handball. No. 605A, 1500fr, Shot put. No. 605B, 1500fr, Dressage, horiz.

1983, Aug. 3   Litho.   Perf. 13
599	A167	5fr multi	.25	.25
600	A167	40fr multi	.40	.25
601	A167	60fr multi	.65	.25
602	A167	120fr multi	1.40	.30
603	A167	200fr multi	2.25	.40
604	A167	300fr multi	3.25	.80
		Nos. 599-604 (6)	8.20	2.25

Souvenir Sheet
605	A167	600fr multi	5.00	1.60

Litho. & Embossed
Perf. 13½
605A	A167a	1500fr multi	35.00	3.50

Souvenir Sheet
605B	A167a	1500fr multi	10.00	10.00

Nos. 603-605B are airmail.

Namibia Day — A168

1983, Sept. 16   Litho.   Perf. 13
606	A168	100fr multi	1.10	.40
607	A168	200fr multi	1.90	.80

Manned Flight Bicentenary — A169

A169a

Designs: 50fr, J. Montgolfier and his balloon, 1783. 100fr, J.P. Blanchard, English Channel crossing, 1785. 200fr, L.-J. Gay-Lussac, 4000-meter balloon ascent, 1804. 300fr, Giffard and his dirigible, 1852. 400fr, Santos Dumont, dirigible, Eiffel Tower. 500fr, A. Laquot, captive observation balloon, 1914. 600fr, J.A. Charles, first gas balloon; G. Tissandier, dirigible, 1883. No. 614, Marquis d'Arlandes and Jean Francois Pilatre de Rozier, Montgolfier balloon. No. 614B, Ferdinand von Zeppelin, Graf Zeppelin, horiz.

1983, Sept. 30   Litho.   Perf. 13½
608	A169	50fr multi	.50	.25
609	A169	100fr multi	1.10	.40
610	A169	200fr multi	2.50	.80
611	A169	300fr multi	3.25	1.10
612	A169	400fr multi	4.25	1.50
613	A169	500fr multi	5.75	1.90
		Nos. 608-613 (6)	17.35	5.95

Souvenir Sheet
614	A169	600fr multi	5.50	1.40

Litho. & Embossed
614A	A169a	1500fr gold & multi	37.50	4.00

Souvenir Sheet
614B	A169a	1500fr gold & multi	10.00	10.00

Nos. 612-614B are airmail.

Black Rhinoceros and World Wildlife Emblem — A170

Various black rhinoceroses.

1983, Nov. 14
615	A170	10fr multi	1.25	.50
616	A170	40fr multi	1.50	.75
617	A170	70fr multi	2.25	1.00
618	A170	180fr multi	6.75	2.00
		Nos. 615-618 (4)	11.75	4.25

Nos. 615-618 were issued in support of the World Wildlife Fund.
See Nos. C291A-C293.

UPU Day, World Communications Year — A171

1983, Nov. 2   Litho.   Perf. 13
619	A171	205fr multi	2.00	.90

2nd Anniv. of the Natl. Military Committee A172

Gen. Andre Kolingba, head of state.

1983, Sept. 1   Perf. 12½
620	A172	65fr sil & multi	.55	.25
621	A172	130fr gold & multi	1.40	.45

Earth Satellite Receiving Station, Bangui M'Poko — A173

1983   Perf. 13
622	A173	130fr multi	1.40	.55

Natl. Day of the Handicapped and the Elderly — A174

1983, Dec. 20   Engr.   Perf. 13x12½
623	A174	65fr vio & org	.55	.30
624	A174	130fr ultra & org	1.10	.45
625	A174	205fr dk grn & org	1.75	.80
		Nos. 623-625 (3)	3.40	1.55

Fishing Resources A175

1983, Dec. 31   Litho.   Perf. 12½
626	A175	25fr Breeding tank	.25	.25
627	A175	65fr Net fishing	1.10	.25
628	A175	100fr Dam fishing	1.25	.40
629	A175	130fr Still life with fish	2.50	.70
630	A175	205fr Basket trap	2.75	.70
		Nos. 626-630 (5)	7.85	2.30

Wildlife Protection — A176

1984, Jan. 25   Perf. 13
631	A176	30fr Forest fire	3.50	.40
632	A176	130fr Hunters	5.00	1.10

CC-1500 Locomotive — A177

110fr, CC-1500 locomotive. 240fr, PLM series 210, 1868. 350fr, 231-726 locomotive, 1937. 440fr, Pacific S3/6, 1908. 500fr, Henschel 151 series 45, 1937.

1984, July 16   Litho.   Perf. 12½
633	A177	110fr multicolored	1.40	.30
634	A177	240fr multicolored	3.00	.85
635	A177	350fr multicolored	4.25	1.10
636	A177	440fr multicolored	5.75	1.25
637	A177	500fr multicolored	6.75	1.60
		Nos. 633-637 (5)	21.15	5.10

For overprints see Nos. 702, 704.

Packet Ship Pericles — A177a

120fr, Three-master Pereire. 250fr, Admella. 400fr, Royal William. 500fr, Great Britain.

1984, July 23		Litho.	Perf. 12½	
638	A177a	65fr shown	.90	.30
639	A177a	120fr multicolored	1.40	.55
640	A177a	250fr multicolored	3.00	1.10
641	A177a	400fr multicolored	5.50	1.90
642	A177a	500fr multicolored	6.25	2.40
		Nos. 638-642 (5)	17.05	6.25

For overprints see Nos. 701, 703.

J. W. Goethe, Scene from Faust A178

Designs: 100fr, Henri Dunant, Red Cross Founder, Battle of Solferino, 125th anniv. 200fr, Alfred Nobel, Nobel Foundation headquarters. 300fr, Lord Baden-Powell, World Scouting Jamboree, Alberta, 1983. 400fr, John F. Kennedy, first man on the Moon, 1969. 500fr, 600fr, wedding of Prince and Princess of Wales.

1984, Feb. 25		Litho.	Perf. 13½	
643	A178	50fr multi	.55	.25
644	A178	100fr multi	1.10	.40
645	A178	200fr multi	2.50	.55
646	A178	300fr multi	3.25	1.10
647	A178	400fr multi	4.50	1.10
648	A178	500fr multi	5.50	1.10
		Nos. 643-648 (6)	17.40	4.50

Souvenir Sheet

649	A178	600fr multi	5.00	1.40

Nos. 647-649 are airmail.

Old Masters A179

Paintings: 50fr, Madonna and Child, by Raphael. 100fr, Madonna with Pear, by Durer. 200fr, Aldobrandini Madonna, by Raphael. 300fr, Madonna with Carnation, by Durer. 400fr, Virgin and Child, by Correggio. 500fr, La Bohemienne, by Modigliani. 600fr, Madonna and Child on the Throne, by Raphael.

1984, Mar. 30		Litho.	Perf. 13½	
650	A179	50fr multi	.60	.25
651	A179	100fr multi	1.10	.25
652	A179	200fr multi	2.50	.45
653	A179	300fr multi	3.50	.85
654	A179	400fr multi	4.75	1.90
655	A179	500fr multi	5.75	2.50
		Nos. 650-655 (6)	18.20	6.20

Miniature Sheet

656	A179	600fr multi	5.50	1.40

No. 656 contains 1 stamp, size 30x59mm. Nos. 654-656 are airmail.

Space — A180

20fr, Galileo, Ariane rocket. 70fr, Piccard, X-15, balloon. 150fr, Oberth, satellite. 205fr, Einstein, satellites. 300fr, Curie, Viking vehicle. 500fr, Merbold, Spacelab. 600fr, Armstrong, Apollo 11, horiz.

1984, Aug. 6		Litho.	Perf. 13½	
657	A180	20fr multicolored	.30	.25
658	A180	70fr multicolored	.75	.25
659	A180	150fr multicolored	1.50	.45
660	A180	205fr multicolored	2.25	.55
661	A180	300fr multicolored	3.50	.80
662	A180	500fr multicolored	5.00	1.00
		Nos. 657-662 (6)	13.30	3.30

Miniature Sheet

663	A180	600fr multicolored	5.00	1.50

No. 663 contains 1 stamp, size: 42x36mm. 300fr, 500fr and 600fr are airmail.

Forestry Resources A181

1984, Oct. 9		Litho.	Perf. 13x12½	
664	A181	70fr Forest	1.00	.30
665	A181	130fr Logging	2.00	.55

UNICEF — A182

1984, Oct. 27		Litho.	Perf. 13x12½	
666	A182	10fr Weighing child	.25	.25
667	A182	30fr Vaccinating child	.50	.30
668	A182	65fr Giving liquids	.60	.40
669	A182	100fr Balancing diet	1.25	.55
		Nos. 666-669 (4)	2.60	1.50

Fishing Traps A183

1984, Nov. 6		Litho.	Perf. 13	
670	A183	50fr Bangui-Kette	.85	.30
671	A183	80fr Mbres	1.10	.55
672	A183	150fr Bangui-Kette	2.50	.90
		Nos. 670-672 (3)	4.45	1.75

Mushrooms A184

5fr, Leptoporus lignosus. 10fr, Phlebopus sudanicus. 40fr, Termitomyces letestui. 130fr, Lepiota esculenta. 300fr, Termitomyces auraniacus. 500fr, Termitomyces robustus. 600fr, Tricholoma- lobayensis.

1984, Nov. 15		Litho.	Perf. 13½	
673	A184	5fr multicolored	.25	.25
674	A184	10fr multicolored	.25	.25
675	A184	40fr multicolored	.75	.30
676	A184	130fr multicolored	2.25	.30
677	A184	300fr multicolored	3.50	.80
678	A184	500fr multicolored	6.25	1.25
		Nos. 673-678 (6)	13.25	3.15

Souvenir Sheet

679	A184	600fr multicolored	6.50	2.00

Nos. 677-679 are airmail.

1984 Winter Olympics, Sarajevo A184a

Gold medalists, communications satellite and events: 30fr, Gaetan Boucher, Canada, 1000 and 1500-meter speed skating. 90fr, W. Hoppe, R. Wetzig, D. Schauerhammer and A. Kirchner, German Democratic Republic, 4-man bobsled. 140fr, Paoletta Magoni, Italy, women's slalom. 200fr, Jayne Torvill and Christopher Dean, Great Britain, ice dancing. 400fr, Matti Nykaenen, Finland, 90-meter ski jumping. 500fr, USSR, ice hockey. 600fr, Bill Johnson, US, men's downhill.

1984, Nov. 30		Litho.	Perf. 13½	
679A	A184a	30fr multi	.30	.25
679B	A184a	90fr multi	1.00	.30
679C	A184a	140fr multi	1.50	.40
679D	A184a	200fr multi	2.25	.55
679E	A184a	400fr multi	4.00	1.00
679F	A184a	500fr multi	5.25	1.25
		Nos. 679A-679F (6)	14.30	3.75

Souvenir Sheet

679G	A184a	600fr multi	5.50	1.60

Nos. 679E-679G are airmail.

Flowers — A185

65fr, Hibiscus. 130fr, Canna Indica. 205fr, Eichlornia Crassipes.

1984, Nov. 22		Litho.	Perf. 13½	
680	A185	65fr multicolored	1.10	.40
681	A185	130fr multicolored	1.90	.50
682	A185	205fr multicolored	3.00	1.00
		Nos. 680-682 (3)	6.00	1.90

Economic Campaign — A186

25fr, Cotton planting. 40fr, Selling cotton crop. 130fr, Cotton market.

1984, Dec. 3		Litho.	Perf. 13½	
683	A186	25fr multicolored	.40	.25
684	A186	40fr multicolored	.65	.40
685	A186	130fr multicolored	1.70	.55
		Nos. 683-685 (3)	2.75	1.20

World Food Day A187

1984, Dec. 10		Litho.	Perf. 13½	
686	A187	205fr Picking corn	2.50	.90

OLYMPHILEX '85 — A188

Publicity posters from previous Games and host city landmarks: 5fr, Stockholm, 1912. 10fr, Paris, 1924. 20fr, London, 1948. 100fr, Tokyo, 1964. 400fr, Mexico. 500fr, Munich, 1972.

600fr, Athens, 1896, Baron Pierre de Coubertin.

1985, Mar 18		Litho.	Perf. 13½	
687	A188	5fr multicolored	.25	.25
688	A188	10fr multicolored	.25	.25
689	A188	20fr multicolored	.30	.25
690	A188	100fr multicolored	5.25	1.00
691	A188	400fr multicolored	2.25	.45
692	A188	500fr multicolored	2.75	.55
		Nos. 687-692 (6)	11.05	2.75

Souvenir Sheet

693	A188	600fr multicolored	5.50	1.50

Nos. 691-693 are airmail. No. 693 contains one 60x30mm stamp.

Anniversaries and Events — A189

Famous men: 50fr, Abraham Lincoln, American Civil War soldiers. 90fr, Auguste Piccard (1884-1962), inventor, bathyscaphe Trieste. 120fr, Gottlieb Daimler (1834-1900), 1938 Mercedes Type 540. 200fr, Louis Bleriot (1872-1936), inventor, plane. 350fr, Anatoly Karpov, world chess champion. 400fr, Jean Henri Dunant (1828-1910), Red Cross founder, worker caring for wounded soldier.

1984, Dec. 22		Litho.	Perf. 13½	
694	A189	50fr multi	.55	.25
695	A189	90fr multi	1.00	.30
696	A189	120fr multi	1.60	.40
697	A189	200fr multi	2.50	.55
698	A189	350fr multi	3.75	.80
698A	A189	400fr multi	3.75	.90
		Nos. 694-698A (6)	13.15	3.20

Nos. 698-698A are airmail.

Souvenir Sheet

Queen Mother, 85th Birthday — A189a

1984		Litho.	Perf. 13½	
698B	A189a	600fr multi	5.50	1.60

Bangui Rotary Club and Water — A190

1984, Dec. 29
699	A190	130fr multi	1.90	.45
700	A190	205fr multi	2.75	.80

Nos. 635//641, C302A Overprinted with Exhibitions in Red

1985, Mar. 13   Litho.   Perf. 12½
701	A177	250fr Argentina '85, Buenos Aires (#640)	2.75	1.25
702	A177a	350fr Tsukuba Expo '85 (#635)	3.50	1.60
703	A177	400fr Italia '85, Rome (#641)	5.00	2.25
704	A177a	440fr Mophila '85, Hamburg (#636)	5.50	2.40
		Nos. 701-704 (4)	16.75	7.50

Souvenir Sheet
Perf. 13½x13
705	AP89	500fr Olymphilex '85, Lausanne	5.50	5.50

500fr airmail.

Beetles — A191

15fr, Chelorrhina polyphemus. 20fr, Fornasinius russus. 25fr, Goliathus giganteus. 65fr, Goliathus meleagris.

1985, Mar.   Litho.   Perf. 13½
706	A191	15fr multicolored	.25	.25
707	A191	20fr multicolored	.45	.25
708	A191	25fr multicolored	.65	.25
709	A191	65fr multicolored	1.50	.30
		Nos. 706-709 (4)	2.85	1.05

Audubon Birth Bicentenary — A192

Illustrations of North American bird species by John Audubon: 40fr, Cyanocitta cristata. 80fr, Caprimulgus carolinensis. 130fr, Campephilus principales. 250fr, Calocitta formosa. 300fr, Coccizus minor, horiz. 500fr, Hirundo rustica, horiz.
600fr, Dryocopus pileatus, horiz.

1985, Mar. 25   Litho.   Perf. 13½
710	A192	40fr multicolored	.90	.25
711	A192	80fr multicolored	1.25	.25
712	A192	130fr multicolored	2.40	.25
713	A192	250fr multicolored	3.25	.55
714	A192	300fr multicolored	3.50	.60
715	A192	500fr multicolored	5.75	1.10
		Nos. 710-715 (6)	17.05	3.00

Souvenir Sheet
716	A192	600fr multicolored	7.75	2.50

Nos. 714-716 are airmail.

Intl. Youth Year A193

Famous children's book authors and scenes from their best-known novels: 100fr, The Jungle Book, 1894, by Kipling, vert. 200fr, Les

Cavaliers, 1967, by Joseph Kessel (1898-1979). 300fr, Twenty-Thousand Leagues Under the Sea, 1873, by Verne. 400fr, The Adventures of Tom Sawyer, 1876, by Twain.

1985, Apr.   Litho.   Perf. 13
718	A193	100fr multi	1.40	.45
719	A193	200fr multi	2.50	.85
720	A193	300fr multi	3.00	1.25
721	A193	400fr multi	4.50	2.10
		Nos. 718-721 (4)	11.40	4.65

Philexafrica '85, Lome — A194

No. 722, UPU emblem, Postmen unloading parcel post van. No. 723, Exhibition emblem, scout troop.

1985, May 15   Perf. 13x12½
722	A194	200fr multi	2.50	.90
723	A194	200fr multi	2.50	.90
a.		Pair, #722-723 + label	5.25	4.50

Rabies Vaccine Cent., Louis Pasteur (1822-95), Chemist, Microbiologist — A195

Anniversaries and events: 200fr, Battle of Solferino, founding of the Red Cross, 125th Anniv., founder Jean-Henri Dunant (1828-1910), horiz. 300fr, Girl Guides, 75th anniv. 450fr, Elizabeth, the Queen Mother, 85th birthday. 500fr, Statue of Liberty, cent.

1985, June   Perf. 13
724	A195	150fr multi	2.50	.50
725	A195	200fr multi	3.00	.60
726	A195	300fr multi	2.50	.90
727	A195	450fr multi	4.50	1.50
728	A195	500fr multi	5.50	1.75
		Nos. 724-728 (5)	18.00	5.25

1986 World Cup Soccer Championships, Mexico — A196

Famous soccer players and match scenes: 5fr, Pele. 10fr, Tony Schumacher. 20fr, Paolo Rossi. 350fr, Kevin Keegan. 400fr, Michel Platini. 500fr, Karl Heinz Rummenigge. 600fr, Diego Armando Maradona.

1985, July 24   Litho.   Perf. 13½
730	A196	5fr multicolored	.25	.25
731	A196	10fr multicolored	.25	.25
732	A196	20fr multicolored	.25	.25
733	A196	350fr multicolored	3.50	.90
734	A196	400fr multicolored	4.00	.90
735	A196	500fr multicolored	5.00	1.10
		Nos. 730-735 (6)	13.25	3.65

Souvenir Sheet
736	A196	600fr multicolored	5.00	1.40

Nos. 734-736 are airmail.

Kotto Waterfalls A197

1985, July 27   Litho.   Perf. 13½
737	A197	65fr multi	1.00	.30
738	A197	90fr multi	1.10	.40
739	A197	130fr multi	1.75	.60
		Nos. 737-739 (3)	3.85	1.30

State Visit of Pope John Paul II — A198

Portraits.

1985, Aug. 14
740	A198	65fr multi	1.25	.40
741	A198	130fr multi	2.50	.80

Natl. Economic Development Campaign — A199

Designs: 5fr, Troops plowing. 60fr, Soldier preparing field for planting, vert. 130fr, Planting cotton seeds, vert.

1985, Sept. 1   Perf. 13
742	A199	5fr multi	.25	.25
743	A199	60fr multi	.75	.30
744	A199	130fr multi	1.50	.45
		Nos. 742-744 (3)	2.50	1.00

Queen Mother, 85th Birthday — A200

100fr, Age 4, with brother. 200fr, Duchess of York, 1923. 300fr, Reviewing Irish Guards, 1928. 350fr, Family portrait, 1936. 400fr, George VI coronation, 1937. 500fr, Wedding anniv., 1948. 600fr, Christening Prince Charles, 1948.

1985, Sept. 16   Litho.   Perf. 13½
745	A200	100fr multicolored	.90	.25
746	A200	200fr multicolored	2.10	.35
747	A200	300fr multicolored	3.25	.70
748	A200	350fr multicolored	3.50	.75
749	A200	400fr multicolored	4.25	.90
750	A200	500fr multicolored	5.50	1.00
		Nos. 745-750 (6)	19.50	3.95

Souvenir Sheet
751	A200	600fr multicolored	4.50	1.40

Nos. 749-751 are airmail.

Dr. Rene Labusquiere (1919-1977), Promoter of Preventive Medicine — A201

1985, Sept. 22   Litho.   Perf. 13½
752	A201	10fr multi	.25	.25
753	A201	45fr multi	.50	.25
754	A201	110fr multi	.75	.45
		Nos. 752-754 (3)	1.50	.95

Natl. Postal Service — A202

15fr, Loading mail van. 60fr, Bangui P.O., van. 150fr, Hdqtrs, Bangui, and vans.

1985, Oct. 9   Perf. 12½
755	A202	15fr multicolored	.25	.25
756	A202	60fr multicolored	.65	.25
757	A202	150fr multicolored	1.60	.80
		Nos. 755-757 (3)	2.50	1.30

Space Research — A203

Designs: 40fr, Yuri Gagarin, Soviet cosmonaut, and Sergei Korolev, rocket engineer. 110fr, Nicolaus Copernicus, Cassini probe. 240fr, Galileo, Viking orbiter. 300fr, Theodor von Karman (1881-1963), American aeronautical engineer, and space shuttle recovering Palapa B satellite. 450fr, Percival Lowell (1855-1916), American astronomer, and Viking probe. 500fr, Dr. U. Merbold and orbiting space station project Colombo. 600fr, Apollo 11 Project, first step on Moon by Neil Armstrong.

1985, Oct. 31   Litho.   Perf. 13½
758	A203	40fr multi	.25	.25
759	A203	110fr multi	1.00	.30
760	A203	240fr multi	2.75	.55
761	A203	300fr multi	3.50	.80
762	A203	450fr multi	5.50	1.00
763	A203	500fr multi	6.00	1.10
		Nos. 758-763 (6)	19.00	4.00

Souvenir Sheet
Imperf
764	A203	600fr multi	5.00	1.40

Nos. 762-764 are airmail.

Solar Energy Apparatus, Damara A204

1985, Nov. 4   Litho.   Perf. 13½
765	A204	65fr multi	.65	.30
766	A204	130fr multi	1.40	.55

Girl Guides Nature Study — A205

No. 768, Quaka Sugar Refinery.

1985, Nov. 16   Perf. 13
767	A205	250fr shown	4.50	1.75
768	A205	250fr multicolored	4.50	1.75
a.		Pair, #767-768 + label	13.00	6.50

PHILEXAFRICA '85, Lome, Togo, 11/16-24.

State Visit of Pres. Mitterand of France, Dec. 12-13 — A206

1985-86   **Litho.**   *Perf. 13x12½*
769	A206	65fr multi	.75	.25
770	A206	130fr multi	1.50	.55
770A	A206	160fr multi ('86)	2.10	.80
		Nos. 769-770A (3)	4.35	1.60

Issued: Nos. 769-770, Dec. 12.

UN 40th Anniv., Central Africa Admission, 25th Anniv. — A207

1985, Dec. 18   *Perf. 13½*
771	A207	140fr multi	1.40	.55

Intl. Youth Year A208

Designs: 40fr, David, by Andrea del Verrocchio; Madonna with the Carnation, 1470, by Leonardo da Vinci. 80fr, Johann Sebastian Bach. 100fr, St. John at Patmos, 1619, by Velazquez. 250fr, The Erl King score, by Franz Schubert. 400fr, Portrait of Vicente Osorio de Moscoso, by Goya. 500fr, The Young Mozart Playing in Paris, 1764. 600fr, Woman in a Plumed Hat, 1901, by Picasso.

1985, Dec. 28
772	A208	40fr multi	.40	.25
773	A208	80fr multi	.90	.25
774	A208	100fr multi	1.25	.25
775	A208	250fr multi	2.50	.55
776	A208	400fr multi	4.50	.90
777	A208	500fr multi	5.00	1.10
		Nos. 772-777 (6)	14.55	3.30

Souvenir Sheet
778	A208	600fr multi	5.25	1.40

Nos. 776-778 are airmail.

Halley's Comet A209

100fr, Edmond Halley, British astronomer. 200fr, Sir Isaac Newton's telescope & comet sighting. 300fr, Halley & Newton observing comet. 350fr, US probe. 400fr, Soviet probe plotting comet's perihelion. 500fr, Isodensity photograph of comet. 600fr, Comet, Earth, Sun & probe.

1985, Dec. 31
779	A209	100fr multi	.90	.30
780	A209	200fr multi	2.00	.45
781	A209	300fr multi	3.00	.90
782	A209	350fr multi	3.50	1.10
783	A209	400fr multi	4.25	1.00
784	A209	500fr multi	5.25	1.25
		Nos. 779-784 (6)	18.90	5.00

Souvenir Sheet
785	A209	600fr multi	6.00	1.75

Nos. 783-785 are airmail.

Christopher Columbus — A210

Various events leading to the discovery of America and beyond: 90fr, Plotting course. 110fr, Receiving blessing. 240fr, Fleet in port. 300fr, Trade with natives. 400fr, Storm at sea. 500fr, Fleet at sea.
600fr, Portrait.

1986
786	A210	90fr multicolored	1.00	.30
787	A210	110fr multicolored	1.40	.45
788	A210	240fr multicolored	2.75	.60
789	A210	300fr multicolored	3.50	.90
790	A210	400fr multicolored	4.75	1.00
791	A210	500fr multicolored	5.50	2.40
		Nos. 786-791 (6)	18.90	5.65

Souvenir Sheet
792	A210	600fr multicolored	6.50	1.75

Nos. 790-792 are airmail.

Nos. 543-544 Surcharged

No. 792A, Kangu bowls. No. 792B, Kolongo bowls.

1986, Apr. 1   **Litho.**   *Perf. 13*
792A	A152	30fr on 175fr	
792B	A152	65fr on 300fr	

Hairstyles A211

1986, May 21   **Litho.**   *Perf. 12½*
793	A211	20fr multi	.45	.25
794	A211	30fr multi	.55	.25
795	A211	65fr multi	.80	.40
796	A211	160fr multi	2.75	.70
		Nos. 793-796 (4)	4.55	1.60

France - Central Africa Week — A212

1986, May 26
797	A212	40fr	Communications, horiz.	.50	.25
798	A212	65fr	Youth, horiz.	.65	.30
799	A212	100fr	Basket maker	1.40	.45
800	A212	130fr	Bicycling	2.00	.60
			Nos. 797-800 (4)	4.55	1.60

Centrapalm Palm Oil — A213

25fr, 65fr, Refinery, Bossongo, and palm tree. 120fr, 160fr, Refinery and palm tree.

1986, Aug. 12   **Litho.**   *Perf. 13½*
801	A213	25fr multi	.30	.25
802	A213	65fr multi	.75	.40
803	A213	120fr multi, vert.	1.40	.80
804	A213	160fr multi, vert.	1.90	.60
		Nos. 801-804 (4)	4.35	2.05

Dogs and Cats A214

10fr, Pointer. 20fr, Egyptian mau. 200fr, Newfoundland. 300fr, Borzoi. 400fr, Persian red.
500fr, Spaniel, Burmese-Malayan.

1986, Sept. 9
805	A214	10fr multicolored	.25	.25
806	A214	20fr multicolored	.50	.25
807	A214	200fr multicolored	3.00	.55
808	A214	300fr multicolored	3.75	.60
809	A214	400fr multicolored	5.50	.85
		Nos. 805-809 (5)	13.00	2.50

Souvenir Sheet
810	A214	500fr multicolored	7.00	1.75

Nos. 808-810 are airmail.

African Coffee Producers Organization, 25th Anniv. — A215

1986, Sept. 25   **Litho.**   *Perf. 13*
811	A215	160fr multi	1.60	.55

1986 World Cup Soccer Championships, Mexico — A216

Satellites, final scores, World Cup and athletes: 30fr, Muller, Socrates. 110fr, Scifo, Ceulemans. 160fr, Stopyra, Platini. 350fr, Brehme, Schumacher. 450fr, Maradona. 500fr, Schumacher, Burruchaga.

1986, Nov. 12   *Perf. 13½*
812	A216	30fr multi	.30	.25
813	A216	110fr multi	1.00	.25
814	A216	160fr multi	1.40	.30
815	A216	350fr multi	3.25	.80
816	A216	450fr multi	4.50	1.10
		Nos. 812-816 (5)	10.45	2.70

Souvenir Sheet
817	A216	500fr multi	5.50	1.40

Nos. 816-817 are airmail.

US Anniversaries and Events A217

15fr, Judith Resnik. 25fr, Frederic Auguste Bartholdi. 70fr, Elvis Presley. 300fr, Ronald McNair. 450fr, Christa McAuliffe. 500fr, Challenger Astronauts: McAuliffe, Scobee, Smith, Resnik, Onizuka, McNair, Jarvis.

1986, Nov. 19
818	A217	15fr multi	.25	.25
819	A217	25fr multi	.40	.25
820	A217	70fr multi	1.90	.25
821	A217	300fr multi	3.00	.60
822	A217	450fr multi	4.50	1.10
		Nos. 818-822 (5)	10.05	2.45

Souvenir Sheet
823	A217	500fr multi	6.25	1.50

US space shuttle Challenger explosion; Statue of Liberty, cent. Nos. 822-823 are airmail.
For surcharges & overprint see Nos. 851-851B.

Flora and Fauna A218

25fr, Allamanda neriifolia. 65fr, Taurotragus eurycerus. 160fr, Plumieria acuminata. 300fr, Acinonyx jubatus. 400fr, Eulophia erthoplata. 500fr, Leopard.
600fr, Derby's eland, eulophia cucullata.

1986, May 30   **Litho.**   *Perf. 13½*
824	A218	25fr multicolored	.25	.25
825	A218	65fr multicolored	.90	.25
826	A218	160fr multicolored	2.10	.30
827	A218	300fr multicolored	4.50	.80
828	A218	400fr multicolored	4.75	.90
829	A218	500fr multicolored	6.50	1.10
		Nos. 824-829 (6)	19.00	3.60

Souvenir Sheet
830	A218	600fr multi	5.75	1.75

Nos. 824, 826, 828 vert. Nos. 828-830 are airmail. No. 830 contains one 51x30mm stamp.

Intl. Peace Year — A219

1986, Nov. 29
831	A219	160fr multi	2.00	.75

Air Africa, 25th Anniv. — A220

1986, Dec. 15
832	A220	200fr multi	1.90	.80

UNICEF, 40th
Anniv. — A221

130fr, Child immunization. 160fr, Youth,
food, map.

1986, Dec. 24

833	A221	15fr shown	.25	.25
834	A221	130fr multicolored	1.50	.55
835	A221	160fr multicolored	1.75	.70
	Nos. 833-835 (3)		3.50	1.50

German Railways
Sesquicentenary — A222

Inventors and locomotives: 40fr, Alfred de
Glehn, Prussian Railways DH2 Green Elephant. 70fr, Rudolf Diesel, S3/6 No. 1829 Rheingold. 160fr, Carl Golsdorf, Trans-Europe
Express train Type 103. 300fr, Wilhelm
Schmidt, Beyer Garratt locomotive. 400fr,
Monsieur Du Bousquet, Series 3500 compound locomotive. 500fr, Werner von Siemens, 1980s electric locomotive.

1986, Dec. 31

836	A222	40fr multi	.55	.25
837	A222	70fr multi	1.00	.25
838	A222	160fr multi	2.25	.40
839	A222	300fr multi	3.75	.60
840	A222	400fr multi	4.50	1.10
	Nos. 836-840 (5)		12.05	2.60

Souvenir Sheet

841	A222	500fr multi	5.00	1.40

Nos. 840-841 are airmail. No. 841 contains
one 42x36mm stamp.

Agriculture
Radio Project
A223

265fr, Satellite communication.

1986, Dec. 27   Litho.   Perf. 13½

842	A223	170fr shown	2.25	.90
843	A223	265fr multicolored	3.25	1.40

Pan-African Telecommunications Union
congress, Dec. 7, 1986.
No. 842 exists in souvenir sheet of one.

Space
A224

Scientists and inventions: 5fr, Sir William
Herschel (1738-1822), British astronomer, and
Mariner Mark II. 65fr, Wernher von Braun
(1912-1977), American engineer, and Mars
rover. 160fr, Rudolf Hanel, Mariner Mark II and
Titan. 300fr, Patrick Baudry, Hermes shuttle
and Eureka platform. 400fr, U. Keller, Halley's

Comet and Giotto probe. 500fr, Wubbo Ock-
els, Ulf Merbold and Columbus European
Space Station. 600fr, Wilhelm Obers (1758-
1840) and Mariner Mark II surveying aster-
oids. No. 850 horiz.

1987, Jan. 27

844	A224	25fr multi	.35	.25
845	A224	65fr multi	.75	.25
846	A224	160fr multi	1.75	.30
847	A224	300fr multi	3.00	.75
848	A224	400fr multi	3.25	.90
849	A224	500fr multi	4.00	1.25
	Nos. 844-849 (6)		13.10	3.70

Souvenir Sheet

850	A224	600fr multi	6.25	1.75

Nos. 848-850 are airmail.

No. 820
Surcharged

1987, Feb. 20   Litho.   Perf. 13½

851	A217	485fr on 70fr Elvis Presley	7.75	2.00

Nos. 820 and
851
Overprinted
in Black

1987, Feb. 20   Litho.   Perf. 13½

851A	A217	70fr multi	1.40	.40
851B	A217	485fr on 70fr multi	6.50	2.00

Overprint in red exists.

1992
Barcelona
Olympics
A225

Athletes and landmarks or sights: 30fr, Soc-
cer player, Lady with Umbrella fountain. 150fr,
Judo, Barcelona Cathedral. 265fr, Cyclist,
Church of the Holy Family, by Gaudi. 350fr,
Gymnast, Tomb of Columbus. 495fr, Runner,
human tower. 500fr, Swimmer, Statue of
Columbus.

1987, June 4

852	A225	30fr multi	.40	.25
853	A225	150fr multi	1.40	.45
854	A225	265fr multi	2.50	.80
855	A225	350fr multi	3.50	1.00
856	A225	495fr multi	5.50	1.40
	Nos. 852-856 (5)		13.30	3.90

Souvenir Sheet

857	A225	500fr multi	4.50	1.40

Nos. 855-857 are airmail.

A226

1988 Winter Olympics,
Calgary — A227

20fr, Two-man luge. 140fr, Cross-country
skiing. 250fr, Women's figure skating. 300fr,
Hockey. 400fr, Men's slalom.
500fr, Downhill skiing.

1987, June 26

858	A226	20fr multicolored	.30	.25
859	A226	140fr multicolored	1.40	.45
860	A226	250fr multicolored	2.25	.80
861	A226	300fr multicolored	3.00	.90
862	A226	400fr multicolored	3.75	1.10
	Nos. 858-862 (5)		10.70	3.50

Souvenir Sheet

863	A227	500fr multicolored	4.50	1.40

Nos. 861-863 are airmail.

Intl. Peace
Year — A228

1987, July 20

864	A228	50fr dull ultra, sepia & blk	.50	.25
865	A228	160fr lt ol grn, sep & blk	1.40	.60

Intl. Decade
of Drinkable
Water —
A228a

Designs: 5fr, Woman at village pump; 10fr,
Two women at village pump; 200fr, Three
women at village pump.

1987, Sept. 22   Litho.   Perf. 13½

865A	A228a	5fr multi	32.50	—
865B	A228a	10fr multi	32.50	—
865C	A228a	200fr multi	37.50	—
	Nos. 865A-865C (3)		102.50	

Butterflies
A229

100fr, Charaxes candiope. 120fr, Graphium
leonidas. 130fr, Charaxes brutus. 160fr, Salamis aetiops.

1987, Oct. 5   Litho.   Perf. 13½

866	A229	100fr multicolored	2.00	.85
867	A229	120fr multicolored	2.75	.90
868	A229	130fr multicolored	3.00	.90
869	A229	160fr multicolored	3.25	1.10
	Nos. 866-869 (4)		11.00	3.75

Pygmy Soccer Team from
Nola — A230

1987, Nov. 30   Litho.   Perf. 13

870	A230	90fr multi	1.50	.75
871	A230	160fr multi	2.25	1.25

Integration of the pygmy people into Central
African society.

Dinosaurs — A231

50fr, Brontosaurus. 65fr, Triceratops. 100fr,
Ankylosaurus. 160fr, Stegosaurus. 200fr,
Tyrannosaurus rex. 240fr, Corythosaurus.
300fr, Allosaurus. 350fr, Brachiosaurus.

Perf. 14x13½, 13½x14

1988, Mar. 19   Litho.

872	A231	50fr multicolored	.45	.25
873	A231	65fr multicolored	.80	.25
874	A231	100fr multicolored	1.10	.40
875	A231	160fr multicolored	1.90	.60
876	A231	200fr multicolored	2.00	.80
877	A231	240fr multicolored	3.00	.90
878	A231	300fr multicolored	3.50	1.25
879	A231	350fr multicolored	4.25	1.50
	Nos. 872-879 (8)		17.00	5.95

Nos. 876-879 vert.

Anniversaries
and Events
A232

Designs: 40fr, Pres. James Madison and
"We the People..." from the US Constitution.
160fr, Elizabeth II and Duke of Edinburgh.
200fr, Steffi Graf, tennis champion. 300fr,
Garri Kasparov of Russia, 1985 world chess
champion. 400fr, Boris Becker, 1985-86 Wimbledon champion. 500fr, Christoph Willibald
Gluck (1714-87), composer. Nos. 880-884
vert.

1988, Feb. 15   Perf. 13½

880	A232	40fr multi	.40	.25
881	A232	160fr multi	1.50	.25
882	A232	200fr multi	1.90	.45
883	A232	300fr multi	3.00	.80
884	A232	400fr multi	3.50	1.25
	Nos. 880-884 (5)		10.30	3.00

Souvenir Sheet

885	A232	500fr multi	6.25	1.75

US Constitution bicentennial (40fr); 40th
wedding anniv. of Elizabeth II and Prince
Philip (160fr). Nos. 883-885 are airmail.

World Health
Organization,
40th
Anniv. — A233

1988, Apr. 7   Litho.   Perf. 13½
886 A233 70fr multi   .65   .40
887 A233 120fr multi   1.00   .55

Scout
Ornithological
Activities
A234

Scouts and: 25fr, *Merops nubicus.* 170fr,
Euplectes hordeacea. 300fr, *Ceryle rudis.*
400fr, *Estrilda bengala.* 450fr, *Kaupifalco
monogrammicus.* 500fr, *Lamprotornis
splendidus.*

1988, July 1   Litho.   Perf. 13½
888 A234 25fr multi   .25   .25
889 A234 170fr multi   1.50   .70
890 A234 300fr multi   3.00   2.00
891 A234 400fr multi   4.25   2.00
892 A234 450fr multi   5.00   2.40
       Nos. 888-892 (5)   14.00   7.35
Souvenir Sheet
893 A234 500fr multi   6.25   1.75
Nos. 891-893 are airmail.
For surcharges see Nos. 921-924.

1988
Summer
Olympics,
Seoul
A235

1988, Sept. 30
894 A235 150fr Running, vert.   1.25   .25
895 A235 300fr Judo, vert.   2.75   .70
896 A235 400fr Soccer, vert.   3.00   1.00
897 A235 450fr Tennis, vert.   3.50   1.10
       Nos. 894-897 (4)   10.50   3.05
Souvenir Sheet
898 A235 500fr Boxing   5.00   1.50
Nos. 896-898 are airmail.

1988 Winter Olympics,
Calgary — A236

170fr, Cross-country skiing. 350fr, Ice
hockey. 400fr, Downhill skiing. 450fr,
Freestyle.

1988, Sept. 30   Litho.   Perf. 13½
899 A236 170fr multicolored   1.40   .30
900 A236 350fr multicolored   2.25   .60
901 A236 400fr multicolored   3.00   .90
902 A236 450fr multicolored   3.25   1.00
       Nos. 899-902 (4)   9.90   2.80
Souvenir Sheet
903 A236 500fr shown   5.50   1.50
Nos. 899-902 vert. Nos. 901-903 are airmail.

Natl. Arbor
Day — A237

50fr, Students planting trees. 130fr, Forest
(before and after).

1988, July 16   Litho.   Perf. 13½
904 A237 50fr multicolored   .50   .25
905 A237 100fr like 50fr   1.00   .55
906 A237 130fr multicolored   1.40   .60
       Nos. 904-906 (3)   2.90   1.40

L'Amitie
Hospital, 1st
Anniv.
A238

1988, Nov. 30
907 A238 5fr shown   .25   .25
908 A238 60fr Aerial view   .65   .40
909 A238 160fr Front gate   1.40   .80
       Nos. 907-909 (3)   2.30   1.45

Proclamation of
Central African
Republic, 30th
Anniv. A238a

Design: 65fr, 160fr, Dove, map, flag, people.
240fr, Government buildings, horiz.

1988 (?)   Litho.   Perf. 13½
909A A238a 65fr multi   52.50   —
909B A238b 160fr multi   52.50   —
909C A238a 240fr multi   52.50   —

A239

Olympic Medalists, Seoul, 1988: 150fr, Kris-
tine Otto, DDR, swimming. 240fr, Matt Biondi,
US, swimming. 300fr, Florence Griffith-Joyner,
US, running. 450fr, Pierre Durand, France,
equestrian. 600fr, Carl Lewis, US, running.

1989, Apr. 1
910 A239 150fr multi   2.25   .55
911 A239 240fr multi   3.50   .80
912 A239 300fr multi   4.50   1.10
913 A239 450fr multi   7.50   1.75
  a.   Souv. sheet of 4, #910-913   17.50
       Nos. 910-913 (4)   17.75   4.20
Souvenir Sheet
914 A239 600fr multi   5.75   2.00
Nos. 913-914 airmail. No. 914 contains one
37x43mm stamp.

A240

Transportation Innovations, Inventors: 20fr,
Hebmuller and 1953 Volkswagen Beetle.
205fr, Werner von Siemens (1816-1892) and
1879 Locomotive B. 300fr, Dennis Conner,

skipper of *Stars and Stripes,* winner of the
1988 America's Cup. 400fr, Andre Citroen
(1878-1935) and 1955 Citroen-15 SIX. 450fr,
Marc Seguin (1786-1875) and 1895
Decauville-Mallet 020-020. 750fr, Frederick S.
Duesenberg (1876-1932), brother August, US
flag and 1929 J Phaeton.

1989, Apr. 10   Litho.   Perf. 13½
915 A240 20fr multi   .25   .25
916 A240 205fr multi   1.90   .55
917 A240 300fr multi   2.50   .60
918 A240 400fr multi   3.50   1.10
919 A240 450fr multi   4.50   1.25
       Nos. 915-919 (5)   12.65   3.75
Souvenir Sheet
920 A240 750fr multi   6.25   1.50
Nos. 919-920 airmail. No. 920 contains one
43x37mm stamp.
Nos. 915-919 exist in souvenir sheets of 1.

**Nos. 889-892 Surcharged in Black
or Silver**
1988, Oct. 7   Litho.   Perf. 13½
921 A234 30fr on 170fr (B)   .40   .25
922 A234 70fr on 300fr   1.10   .55
923 A234 160fr on 400fr   1.90   .85
924 A234 200fr on 450fr   2.50   1.10
       Nos. 921-924 (4)   5.90   2.75
Nos. 923-924 are airmail.

PHILEXFRANCE '89, French
Revolution Bicent. — A241

Designs: 200fr, Allegory in Honor of Liberty.
300fr, Declaration of Human Rights and Citizenship. 500fr, The Bastille, horiz.

1989, July 7   Litho.   Perf. 13
925 A241 200fr multi   1.90   .80
926 A241 300fr multi   4.00   1.25
  a.   Pair, #925-926 + label   6.50   6.50
Souvenir Sheet
927 A241 500fr multi   6.25   3.75

Souvenir Sheet

Statue of Liberty — A242

Designs: a, Crown and torch observatories
lit at night. b, Working on statue's coiffure. c,
Face and scaffolding. d, Workman sanding
copper sheeting around the crown observatory. e, Re-opening ceremony, 1986. f, Crown
observatory at night.

Wmk. 385
1989, July   Litho.   Perf. 13
928 A242 Sheet of 6   11.00 11.00
  a.-c.   150fr any single   1.60   .60
  d.-f.   200fr any single   1.75   .70
Statue of Liberty cent. (in 1986). Photograph of the statue is reversed.

M. Champagnat (1789-1840), Founder
of the Marist Order — A243

15fr, Madonna and child, map. 50fr, Cross,
Earth.

1989   Litho.   Unwmk.   Perf. 13½
929 A243 15fr multicolored   .25   .25
930 A243 50fr multicolored   .45   .25
931 A243 160fr shown   1.75   1.25
       Nos. 929-931 (3)   2.45   1.75
Nos. 929-930 vert.

Harvest
Feast,
Bambari
A244

1989, Oct. 15
932 A244 100fr Produce   1.25   .60
933 A244 160fr Ox plow   1.75   .80

World Food
Day
A245

60fr, Domestic animals. 240fr, Arresting
ivory poachers.

1989, Oct. 16
934 A245 60fr multicolored   .55   .30
935 A245 240fr multicolored 2.25   1.00

French Revolution, Bicent. — A246

Battle scenes and leaders: 160fr, Brig.-Gen.
Francois-Christophe Kellermann (1735-1820),
Battle of Valmy, Sept. 22, 1792. 200fr, Minister
of War Charles-Francois du Perier Dumouriez
(1739-1823), Battle of Jemappes, Nov. 7,
1792. 500fr, Gen. Jean-Charles Pichegru
(1761-1804), capture of the Dutch fleet, Jan.
22, 1795. 600fr, Gen. Louis-Lazare Hoche
(1768-97), Battle of Quiberon Bay, July 21,
1795. 1000fr, Napoleon at the Battle of Rivoli
Veronese, Jan. 15, 1797. 1500fr, General
Jean-Baptiste Jourdan.

1989, Dec. 5   Litho.   Perf. 13½
936 A246 160fr multicolored   1.40   .40
937 A246 200fr multicolored   1.75   .55
938 A246 500fr multicolored   5.50   1.10
939 A246 600fr multicolored   5.00   1.00
  a.   Souvenir sheet of 4, #936-
       939   15.00 15.00
       Nos. 936-939 (4)   13.65   3.05
Souvenir Sheet
940 A246 1000fr multicolored 10.00   3.00
Litho. & Embossed
940A A246 1500fr gold & multi   —   —
PHILEXFRANCE '89. Nos. 938-940A are
airmail.
No. 936 is incorrectly inscribed "Francois-
Etienne." Jemappes is incorrectly spelled on
No. 937. No. 940 is incorrectly inscribed "January 14."

1990 World Cup Soccer Championships, Italy — A247

Various athletes and Italian landmarks: 20fr, Bell tower, Palermo Cathedral. 120fr, Trinity of the Mount, Rome. 160fr, St. Francis Church apse, Bologna. 200fr, Palace, Florence. 1000fr, Milan Cathedral.

1989, Dec. 23

941	A247	20fr multicolored	.25	.25
942	A247	120fr multicolored	1.25	.40
943	A247	160fr multicolored	1.40	.40
944	A247	200fr multicolored	1.60	.55
		Nos. 941-944 (4)	4.50	1.60

Souvenir Sheet

945	A247	1000fr multicolored	9.25	2.00

Nos. 942 and 945 are airmail.

Save the Forests A247a

1989   **Litho.**   **Perf. 13½**

945A	A247a	160fr multicolored	2.00	.75

Town of Bangui, Cent. A247b

Designs: 100fr, Governor's Palace, 1906. 160fr, Outpost. 200fr, A. Dolisie, founder of Bangui, vert. 1000fr, Signing of peace treaty between Michel Dolisie and Chief Gbembo, 1889, vert.

1989   **Litho.**   **Perf. 13½**

945B	A247b	100fr multi	1.25	.40
945C	A247b	160fr multi	1.75	1.00
945D	A247b	200fr multi	2.50	.95
945E	A247b	1000fr multi	10.50	4.25
		Nos. 945B-945E (4)	16.00	6.60

Championship Team from Central Africa, 1987 — A248

1990, Feb. 23   **Litho.**   **Perf. 13½**

946	A248	160fr Flag, players, trophy	1.60	.75
947	A248	240fr shown	2.25	1.00
948	A248	500fr like 160fr	5.50	2.25
		Nos. 946-948 (3)	9.35	4.00

African Basketball Championships. Dated 1988. Nos. 946 and 948 vert.

A249

1990, Feb. 23   **Litho.**   **Perf. 13½**

949	A249	100fr multicolored	1.00	.40
950	A249	130fr multicolored	1.10	.55

Central Africa, winner of the 1987 African Basketball Cup Championships, Tunis. Dated 1989.

A250

1992 Winter Olympics, Albertville: 10fr, Speed skating. 60fr, Cross-country skiing. 500fr, Slalom. 750fr, Figure skating. 1000fr, Downhill skiing. No. 955A, Slalom skier. No. 955B, Pairs figure skating.

1990, Mar. 12   **Litho.**   **Perf. 13½**

951	A250	10fr multi	.25	.25
952	A250	60fr multi	.55	.25
953	A250	500fr multi	4.50	1.00
954	A250	750fr multi	6.25	1.40
		Nos. 951-954 (4)	11.55	2.90

Souvenir Sheet

955	A250	1000fr multi	8.75	2.00

Litho. & Embossed

955A	A250	1500fr gold & multi	12.00	3.50

Souvenir Sheet

955B	A250	1500fr gold & multi	30.00	30.00

Nos. 953-955B are airmail. No. 955 contains one 36x42mm stamp. Nos. 951-954 exist in souvenir sheets of one.

Scout, *Euphaera eusemoides* — A251

Boy scouts and butterflies: 65fr, *Cymothoe beckeri.* 160fr, *Pseudacraea clarki.* 250fr, *Charaxes castor.* 300fr, *Euphaedra gausape.* 500fr, *Graphium ridleyanus.* 1000fr, *Euphaedra edwardsi.* No. 962A, Antanartia delius. No. 962B, Spotted flycatcher. No. 962C, Cymothoe sangaris.

1990, Mar. 26

956	A251	25fr multicolored	.30	.25
957	A251	65fr multicolored	.65	.35
958	A251	160fr multicolored	1.60	.45
959	A251	250fr multicolored	2.75	.75
960	A251	300fr multicolored	3.00	.90
961	A251	500fr multicolored	5.25	1.25
		Nos. 956-961 (6)	13.55	3.95

Souvenir Sheet

962	A251	1000fr multicolored	11.00	2.25

Litho. & Embossed
Perf. 12½

962A	A251	1500fr gold & multi	15.00	5.00

Perf. 13½

962B	A251	1500fr gold & multi	45.00	4.00

Souvenir Sheet

962C	A251	1500fr gold & multi	12.00	12.00

Nos. 962A-962C are airmail. No. 962A exists in a souvenir sheet of 1.

1992 Summer Olympics, Barcelona A252

1990, Apr. 1   **Litho.**   **Perf. 13½**

963	A252	10fr Javelin	.25	.25
964	A252	40fr Runner	.40	.25
965	A252	130fr Tennis	1.25	.45
966	A252	240fr Hurdles	2.50	.55
967	A252	400fr Yachting	4.00	1.00
968	A252	500fr Soccer	5.25	1.25
		Nos. 963-968 (6)	13.65	3.75

Souvenir Sheet

969	A252	1000fr Boxing	10.00	2.25

Nos. 963-965 vert. Nos. 967-969 are airmail.

Pres. Gorbachev, Pres. Bush — A253

Pres. Gorbachev, Pope John Paul II — A254

1990, July 27   **Litho.**   **Perf. 13½**

970	A253	120fr multicolored	1.00	.30
971	A254	200fr multicolored	2.00	.45

Pope John Paul II-Gorbachev meeting Dec. 2, 1989. Bush-Gorbachev Summit Meeting Dec. 3, 1989. Nos. 970-971 exist in souvenir sheets of 1. Value, each $20.

Great Britain No. 1, Sir Rowland Hill (1795-1879) — A255

1990, July 27

972	A255	130fr multicolored	1.40	.30

No. 972 exists in a souvenir sheet of 1.

Events and Anniversaries — A256

Designs: 160fr, Galileo Probe to Jupiter. 240fr, Neil Armstrong, 1st man on moon. 250fr, Concorde, rapid-transit train, Rotary Intl. emblem.

A258

1990, July 27   **Litho.**   **Perf. 13½**

973	A256	160fr multicolored	1.50	.40
974	A256	240fr multicolored	2.40	.50
975	A256	250fr multicolored	2.75	.75
		Nos. 973-975 (3)	6.65	1.65

Wildlife Protection — A258a

100fr, Declining elephant population.

1991, Jan. 25   **Litho.**   **Perf. 13½**

976	A258	15fr gold & multi	.75	.25
977	A258	60fr multicolored	2.40	.40
978	A258a	100fr multicolored	3.25	.55
		Nos. 976-978 (3)	6.40	1.20

Eutropius A259

Design: 240fr, Distichodus.

1991, Jan. 26

979	A259	50fr multicolored	1.25	.25
980	A259	160fr gold & multi	2.75	.75
981	A259	240fr multicolored	3.50	.50
		Nos. 979-981 (3)	7.50	1.50

Fight Against AIDS A260

Design: 120fr, Class speaker, vert.

1991, Jan. 24

982	A260	5fr gold & multi	.90	.25
983	A260	70fr multicolored	2.75	.55
984	A260	120fr multicolored	3.50	.80
		Nos. 982-984 (3)	7.15	1.60

Central African Diamonds A260a

Designs: 65fr, Woman polishing diamond, 160fr, Map, diamond.

1991, Feb. 14   **Litho.**   **Perf. 11½**
Granite Paper

984A	A260a	65fr multicolored	—	
984B	A260a	160fr multicolored	—	

Assumption of
Power by Pres.
Andre Kolingba,
10th Anniv. (in
1991) — A261

1992, Sept. 1   **Litho.**   **Perf. 13x13½**
985   A261   160fr multicolored   3.00   .60

Anniversaries and Events — A262

Designs: 80fr, Maybach Zeppelin, zeppelin
airship, Count Ferdinand Zeppelin. 140fr,
Child being comforted, Jean-Henri Dunant.
160fr, Benetton-Ford B 192, Michael Schumacher. 350fr, Konrad Adenauer signing Constitution of German Republic. 500fr, Pope
John Paul II, mother and child, map. 600fr,
Wolfgang Amadeus Mozart. 1000fr, Columbus
at La Rabida, sailing ship, and building in
Seville, Spain.

1992, Sept. 22   **Litho.**   **Perf. 13½**
986   A262   80fr multicolored   1.00   .25
987   A262   140fr multicolored   1.60   .50
988   A262   160fr multicolored   2.00   .75
989   A262   350fr multicolored   4.50   1.10
990   A262   500fr multicolored   6.25   1.40
991   A262   600fr multicolored   8.25   1.50
   Nos. 986-991 (6)   23.60   5.50

Souvenir Sheet
992   A262   1000fr multicolored   10.00   2.00

Count Zeppelin, 75th anniv. of death (No.
986). Jean-Henri Dunant, first recipient of
Nobel Peace Prize, 90th anniv. (in 1991) (No.
987). Grand Prix of Monaco (No. 988). Bran-
denburg Gate, bicent (No. 989). Visit of Pope
John Paul II to Africa (No. 990). Wolfgang
Amadeus Mozart, bicent. of death (in 1991)
(No. 991). Discovery of America, 500th anniv.
and Expo '92, Seville (No. 992).
Nos. 990-992 are airmail. Nos. 986-991
exist in souvenir sheets of 1.
For overprint see No. 1073.

A264

Elvis Presley
(1935-1977)
— A264a

Portrait of Presley, song or movie: 200fr,
Heartbreak Hotel, 1956. 300fr, Love Me
Tender, 1957. 400fr, Jailhouse Rock, 1957.
600fr, Harem Scarum, 1965.
1000fr, With guitar, at microphone.
No. 1001A, Holding microphone. No.
1001B, Playing guitar.

1993, July 12   **Litho.**   **Perf. 13½**
997   A264   200fr multi   2.40   .25
998   A264   300fr multi   3.50   .50
999   A264   400fr multi   4.25   .60
1000   A264   600fr multi   6.00   1.00
   Nos. 997-1000 (4)   16.15   2.35

Souvenir Sheet
1001   A264   1000fr multi   9.50   2.40

Litho. & Embossed
1001A   A264a   1500fr gold &
      multi   20.00   7.50

Souvenir Sheet
1001B   A264a   1500fr gold &
      multi   13.00   8.00

Nos. 1000-1001B are airmail. Nos. 997-
1000, 1001A exist imperf. and in souvenir
sheets of one. Nos. 1001, 1001B exist imperf.

A265

Wedding
of Japan's
Crown
Prince
Naruhito
and
Masako
Owada —
A265a

Designs: 50fr, Princess Masako, parents.
65fr, Crown Prince Naruhito, parents. 160fr,
Princess Masako, Harvard University 450fr,
Crown Prince Naruhito, Oxford University.
750fr, Crown Prince, Princess.

1993, July 12   **Litho.**   **Perf. 13½**
1002   A265   50fr multi   .40   .25
1003   A265   65fr multi   .65   .25
1004   A265   160fr multi   1.75   .25
1005   A265   450fr multi   4.50   1.00
   Nos. 1002-1005 (4)   7.30   1.75

Souvenir Sheet
1006   A265   750fr multi   7.75   3.00

Litho. & Embossed
1006A   A265a   1500fr gold &
      multi   26.00   4.00

Nos. 1005-1006A are airmail. Nos. 1002-
1005, 1006A exist imperf. and in souvenir
sheets of one. No. 1006 exists imperf.

A266

1994 World Cup Soccer
Championships, US — A266a

Designs show winning team, scenes from:
40fr, Amsterdam, 1928; Montevideo, 1930.
50fr, Rome, 1934; Paris, 1938. 60fr, Rio,
1950; Berne, 1954. 80fr, Stockholm, 1958;
Santiago, 1962. 160fr, London, 1966; Mexico
City, 1970. 200fr, Munich, 1974; Buenos
Aires, 1978. 400fr, Madrid, 1982; Mexico City,
1986. 500fr, Rome, 1990; emblem for US
competition, 1994.
1000fr, 1990 German team; 1994 US team.
No. 1015A, Pele, Brazil. No. 1015B, Gerd
Muller, Germany.

1993, Oct. 9   **Litho.**   **Perf. 13½**
1007   A266   40fr multi   .40   .25
1008   A266   50fr multi   .40   .25
1009   A266   60fr multi   .50   .25
1010   A266   80fr multi   .65   .25
1011   A266   160fr multi   1.40   .40
1012   A266   200fr multi   1.90   .70
1013   A266   400fr multi   3.50   .70
1014   A266   500fr multi   5.00   1.00
   Nos. 1007-1014 (8)   13.75   3.80

Souvenir Sheet
1015   A266   1000fr multi   10.00   2.75

Litho. & Embossed
1015A   A266a   1500fr gold &
      multi   26.00

Souvenir Sheet
1015B   A266a   1500fr gold &
      multi   13.50

No. 1015 contains one 60x30mm stamp.
No. 1007-1014 exist in souvenir sheets of one.
Nos. 1015A-1015B are airmail.

Miniature Sheets

Modern Olympic Games, Cent. (in
1996) — A267

No. 1016: a, Ancient olympian. b, Baron de
Coubertin, 1896. c, Charles Bennett, 1900. d,
Etienne Desmarteau, 1904. e, Harry Porter,
1908. f, Patrick MacDonald, 1912. g, No
games, 1916. h, Frank Loomis, 1920. i, Albert
White, 1924.
No. 1017: a, El Ouafi, 1928. b, Eddie Tolan,
1932. c, Jesse Owens, 1936. d, No games,
1940. e, No games, 1944. f, Tapio Rautavaara,
1948. g, Jean Boiteux, 1952. h, Petrus Kas-
terman, 1956. i, Sante Gaiardoni, 1960.
No. 1018: a, Anton Geesink, 1964. b, Bob
Beamon, 1968. c, Mark Spitz, 1972. d, Nadia
Comaneci, 1976. e, Aleksandre Dityatin, 1980.
f, J.F. Lamour, 1984. g, Pierre Durand, 1988.
h, Michael Jordan, 1992. i, Soccer player,
1996.

1993   **Litho.**   **Perf. 13½**
1016   A267   90fr Sheet of 9,
      #a.-i.   7.50   3.25
1017   A267   100fr Sheet of 9,
      #a.-i.   9.00   3.75
1018   A267   160fr Sheet of 9,
      #a.-i.   15.00   5.75

Miniature Sheet

Dinosaurs — A268

Designs: No. 1019a, 25fr, Saltoposuchus. b,
25fr, Rhamphorhynchus. c, 25fr,
Dimorphodon. d, 25fr, Archaeopteryx. e, 30fr,
Compsognathus longipes. f, 30fr, Cryptocle-
idus oxoniensis. g, 30fr, Stegosaurus. h, 30fr,
Cetiosaurus. i, 50fr, Brontosaurus. j, 50fr,
Corythosaurus casuarius. k, 50fr,
Styracosaurus. l, 50fr, Gorgosaurus. m, 500fr,
Scolosaurus. n, 500fr, Trachodon. o, 500fr,
Struthiomimus. p, 500fr, Tarbosaurus.
No. 1020, Tylosaur.

1993, Dec. 3
1019   A268   Sheet of 16, #a.-p.   26.00   26.00

Souvenir Sheet
1020   A268   1000fr multicolored   10.50   2.75

No. 1020 is airmail and contains one
51x60mm stamp.

Biodiversity
A269

Various fauna surrounding: 100fr, Man
planting tree. 130fr, Man with local fauna, vert.

1993, Oct. 20   **Litho.**   **Perf. 13½**
1021   A269   100fr multicolored   3.50   .75
1022   A269   130fr multicolored   5.00   1.00

M'Bali
Dam — A270

200fr, Women, men with fish.

1993, Jan. 14   **Litho.**   **Perf. 13**
1023   A270   160fr shown   1.60   .30
1024   A270   200fr multi   2.25   .40

Cooperation Council, 40th
Anniv. — A271

1993, Jan. 26
1025   A271   240fr multicolored   2.50   .50

Intl. Conference on Nutrition, Rome — A272

1993, Apr. 1
1026 A272 90fr shown .75 .45
1027 A272 140fr Fresh foods 1.40 .75

University of Bangui A273

1993, Apr. 8
1028 A273 100fr multicolored 1.00 .45
Dated 1992.

Environmental Development A274

Designs: 160fr, Woman with vegetables, fruit. 240fr, Woman cooking food.

1993, Oct. 27 Litho. Perf. 13½
1029 A274 160fr multicolored 1.75 .80
1030 A274 240fr multicolored 2.50 .95

Miniature Sheets

1994 Winter Olympics, Lillehammer — A275

Past Winter Olympic champions: 1031a, Th. Haug, Nordic combined skiing, Chamonix, 1924. b, J. Heaton, 1-man sled, St. Moritz, 1928. c, B. Ruud, ski jumping, Lake Placid, 1932. d, I. Ballangrud, speed skating, Garmisch-Partenkirchen, 1936. e, G. Fraser, women's slalom skiing, St. Moritz, 1948. f, German 4-man bobsled, Oslo, 1952. g, USSR hockey team, Cortina D'Ampezzo, 1956. h, J. Vuarnet, downhill skiing, Squaw Valley, 1960.
No. 1032a, M. Goitschel, giant slalom, Innsbruck, 1964. b, Jean-Claude Killy, slalom skiing, Grenoble, 1968. c, U. Wehling, Nordic combined, Sapporo, 1972. d, Rodnina & Zaitsev, pairs figure skating, Innsbruck, 1976. e, E. Heiden, speed skating, Lake Placid, 1980. f, K. Witt, figure skating, Sarajevo, 1984. g, J. Mueller, luge, Calgary, 1988. h, E. Grospiron, freestyle skiing, Albertville, 1992. i, Speed skiing, Lillehammer, 1994.

1994, Jan. 14 Litho. Perf. 13½
1031 A275 100fr Sheet of 8, #a.-h. + label 9.00 9.00
1032 A275 200fr Sheet of 9, #a.-i. 15.00 15.00

1994 Winter Olympics, Lillehammer — A276

Design: 1500fr, Women figure skaters.

1994 Litho. & Embossed Perf. 13½
1033 A276 1500fr gold & multi 15.00
No. 1033 is airmail & exists in a souvenir sheet of 1. Value $24.

Flowers, Vegetables, Fruit, & Mushrooms A277

Flowers: No. 1034a, 25fr, Ansellia africana. b, 60fr, Polystachia bella. c, 90fr, Aerangis rhodosticta. d, 500fr, Angraecum eburneum.
Vegetables: No. 1035a, 30r, Yams. b, 65fr, Manioc. c, 100fr, Corn. d, 400fr, Sweet potato.
Fruits: No. 1036a, 40fr, Orange. b, 70fr, Banana. c, 160fr, Mango. d, 300fr, Coffee.
Mushrooms: No. 1037a, 50fr, Termitomyces schimperi. b, 80fr, Sympodia arborescens. c, 200fr, Phlebopus sudanicus. d, 600fr, Leucocoprinus africanus.

1994, Jan. 21 Litho. Perf. 13½
1034 A277 Strip of 4, #a.-d. 5.50 2.50
1035 A277 Strip of 4, #a.-d. 5.00 2.25
1036 A277 Strip of 4, #a.-d. 4.50 2.00
1037 A277 Strip of 4, #a.-d. 8.75 3.75
e. Sheet of 16, #1034-1037 26.00 12.00

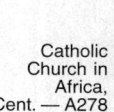

Catholic Church in Africa, Cent. — A278

Designs: 130fr, Monsignor Augouard, founder of mission, St. Paul of the Rapids. 160fr, Monsignor Grandin, Abbe Boganda, first sacred ordainment, 1938. 240fr, Father Louis Godart, House of Charity, Bangui.

1994, June 2 Litho. Perf. 13½
1038 A278 130fr multicolored .65 .45
1039 A278 160fr multicolored .80 .45
1040 A278 240fr multicolored 1.40 .60
Nos. 1038-1040 (3) 2.85 1.50

Relics from Early Civilizations, Landmarks — A279

Designs: 10fr, Cabin-shaped cinerary urn, Rome. 25fr, Face of the secret denunciation, Venice, vert. 30fr, Statue of the Tetrarchs, Venice, vert. 50fr, Little cube-shaped building, Palermo, vert. 65fr, Frieze, The Alhambra, Granada, vert. 90fr, Grand Chateau, Bellinzona. 100fr, Museum D'Orsay, Paris, vert. 130fr, Granary, Galicia. 140fr, Mural, by Diego Rivera, Mexico, vert. 160fr, Guacamaya mask, Mexico, vert. 200fr, Ivory mask, Western

Africa, vert. 240fr, La Sagrada Familia, Barcelona, vert. 260fr, Casbah of Amerhidil. 300fr, Gold aureus of Sulla, Rome, 82 BC. 400fr, Chimborazo volcano.

1994, June 2 Perf. 13
1041-1055 A279 Set of 15 12.00 4.50

D-Day, 50th Anniv. — A280

Pegasus Bridge, June 6: No. 1056a, British troops crossing bridge, piper. b, Glider, British and German soldiers. c, German soldiers.
Operation COBRA, July 24: a, Tank, monument, soldiers. b, Bombers, soldiers, gun barrel. c, Tank, soldiers up close.

1994, Oct. 25 Litho. Perf. 13½
1056 A280 600fr Strip of 3, #a.- c. 10.00 3.75
1057 A280 600fr Strip of 3, #a.- c. 10.00 3.75

Nos. 1056b, 1057b are 30x46mm. Nos. 1056-1057 are continuous designs. See No. C359.

Anniversaries & Events — A281

No. 1058, 600fr — Characters from "Star Wars:" a, Han Solo, Chewbaca. b, Darth Vader, Princess Leia, Luke Skywalker, R2D2, C3PO. c, Obi Wan Kenobi.
No. 1059 — First manned moon landing, 25th anniv.: a, 400fr, Buzz Aldrin. b, 500fr, Neil Armstrong, Apollo 11 liftoff. c, 600fr, Michael Collins.
No. 1060: a, 400fr, Theodor von Karman. b, 500fr, Apollo 11 command module, Wernher von Braun. c, 600fr, Hermes Rocket, Hermann Oberth.

1994, Oct. 25 Litho. Perf. 13½
1058 A281 Strip of 3, #a.-c. 8.00 3.50
1059 A281 Strip of 3, #a.-c. 7.50 3.00
1060 A281 Strip of 3, #a.-c. 7.50 3.00

Motion Pictures, cent. (No. 1058).
Nos. 1058b, 1059b, 1060b are 60x51mm. Nos. 1058-1060 are continuous design and exist in a souvenir sheet of 1.

Natl. Assembly A282

1994, Dec. 8
1061 A282 65fr blue & multi .35 .25
1062 A282 430fr yel brn & multi 1.90 .90

Antoine de Saint-Exupery (1900-44), Aviator, Author — A283

1994, Dec 16
1063 A283 80fr Airplane .50 .30
1064 A283 235fr Portrait, vert. 1.00 .50

Inauguration of Pres. Ange-Felix Patasse, 1st Anniv. — A284

1994, Oct. 22
1065 A284 65fr blue & multi .40 .25
1066 A284 300fr yellow & multi 1.60 .60
1067 A284 385fr green & multi 2.00 .75
Nos. 1065-1067 (3) 4.00 1.60

A285

Intl. Olympic Committee, Cent. — A286

1994, Oct. 25
1068 A285 60fr bl grn & multi .35 .25
1069 A285 405fr yel grn & multi 1.75 .80
Souvenir Sheet
1070 A286 675fr Pierre de Coubertin 3.00 1.40
No. 1070 is airmail.

Nos. 1031-1032 Ovptd. with Medalist & Country Name in Gold

Overprints on No. 1031: No. 1071a, "F.B. LUNDBERG / NORVEGE." b, "G. HACKL / ALLEMAGNE." c, "B. DAEHLIE / NORVEGE." d, "J.O. KOSS / NORVEGE." e, "V. SCHNEIDER / SUISSE." f, "MEDAILLE D'OR / ALLEMAGNE." g, "MEDAILLE D'OR / SUEDE." h, "T. MOE / U.S.A."
Overprints on No. 1032: No. 1072a, "M. WASMEIER / ALLEMAGNE." b, "T. STANGASSINGER / AUTRICHE." c, "MEDAILLE D'OR / PAR EQUIPES / JAPON." d, "Y. GORDEYEVA / S. GRINKOV / RUSSIE." e, "D. JANSEN / U.S.A." f, "O. BAYUL / UKRAINE." g, "G. HACKL / ALLEMAGNE." h, "J.-L. BRASSARO / CANADA." i, "K. SEIZINGER / ALLEMAGNE."

1994
1071 A275 100fr Sheet of 8, #a.-h. + label 6.50 3.00
1072 A275 200fr Sheet of 9, #a.-i. 15.00 7.00

No. 988 Overprinted in Silver

1994, Dec. 28 Litho. Perf. 13½
1073 A262 160fr multicolored 10.00 4.50
No. 1073 also exists in a souvenir sheet of 1.

1995 Boy Scout
Jamboree,
Holland — A287

Scout with mushrooms or butterflies: 300fr, Armillariela mellea. 385fr, Charaxes pleione. 405fr, Charaxes candiope. 430fr, Charaxes pollux. 500fr, Volvaria esculenta. 1000fr, Cortinarius.
2000fr, Euphaedra medon.

1995, May 24
1074-1079 A287 Set of 6   15.00 7.00
1077a   Sheet, #1075-1077   10.00 2.75
1079a   Sheet, #1074, #1078-1079 14.50 4.00
Souvenir Sheet
1080 A287 2000fr multicolored   18.00 4.25
Nos. 1074-1079 exist in souvenir sheets of 1. No. 1080 is airmail and contains one 39x57mm stamp.

1994 World Cup Soccer
Championships, US — A288

Stadium: 300fr, Citrus Bowl, Orlando. 385fr, RFK Stadium, Washington, DC. 405fr, Soldier Field, Chicago. 430fr, Cotton Bowl, Dallas. 500fr, Giants Stadium, East Rutherford, NJ. 1000fr, Foxboro Stadium, Foxboro, MA.
2000fr, Rose Bowl, vert.

1995, July 14   Litho.   Perf. 13½
1081-1086 A288 Set of 6   14.00 6.50
Souvenir Sheet
1087 A288 2000fr multicolored   12.50 5.75
No. 1087 is airmail.

African
Development
Bank, 30th
Anniv. — A289

1995, June 29
1088 A289 70fr multicolored   .35   .25
1089 A289 200fr multicolored   1.00   .45
Nos. 1088-1089 also exist in souvenir sheet of 1.

Fish
A290

Designs, 25fr, 300fr, Auchenoglanis. 30fr, 50fr, Chrisicntys.

1995, June 22
1090-1093 A290 Set of 4   2.75   .90

Entertainers
A291

Designs: 300fr, Freddie Mercury (Queen). 385fr, Jimi Hendrix. 430fr, Marilyn Monroe. 500fr, Michael Jackson. 600fr, Jerry Garcia (Grateful Dead). 800fr, Elvis Presley.
1500fr, Charlton Heston in "Planet of the Apes." 2000fr, Marilyn Monroe, diff.

1995, July 21
1094-1099 A291 Set of 6   15.00 6.50
Souvenir Sheets
1099B A291 1500fr multicolored   8.25 3.25
1100   A291 2000fr multicolored 10.50 4.25
Nos. 1094-1099 exist in souvenir sheets of 1. No. 1100 is airmail. No. 1099B contains one 51x60mm airmail stamp.

Volleyball,
Cent. — A292

1995, Oct. 3   Litho.   Perf. 13½
1101 A292 300fr multicolored   1.50   .65
No. 1101 exists in a souvenir sheet of 1. Value $10.

Sports
Figures
A293

400fr, Andre Agassi, tennis. 500fr, Boris Becker, tennis. 700fr, Ayrton Senna (1960-94) race car driver. 800fr, Michael Schumacher, F-1 world driving champion.
2000fr, Michael Schumacher, diff.

1996, June 20   Litho.   Perf. 13½
1102-1105 A293 Set of 4   12.00 5.50
Souvenir Sheet
1106 A293 2000fr multicolored   10.00 4.50
No. 1102-1105 exist in souvenir sheets of 1. Value $30.

1996 Summer
Olympic
Games,
Atlanta
A294

Olympic athletes, sites in Atlanta: 170fr, Atlanta-Fulton County Stadium. 300fr, Martin Luther King Memorial. 350fr, Alexander H.

Stephens Monument. 600fr, High Museum of Art.
2000fr, Pierre de Coubertin, runner.

1996, June 20
1107-1110 A294 Set of 4   7.50 3.25
Souvenir Sheet
1110A A294 2000fr multicolored   9.50 4.00
No. 1110A contains one 42x51mm stamp.

UN, 50th
Anniv. (in
1995)
A295

1996, July 15   Perf. 14
1111 A295 5fr "50," emblem,
           vert.   .25   .25
1112 A295 430fr shown   2.25   .90
Nos. 1111-1112 each exist in souvenir sheets of 1. Value, set of two sheets $2.75.

1996
Summer
Olympic
Games,
Atlanta
A296

1900 Summer Olympics, Paris: 235fr, Alvin Kraenzlein, vert. 300fr, Paris Stadium. 385fr, Irving Baxter. 430fr, British soccer team.
Past Olympic medalists: No. 1117a, Miruts Yifter, 5,000-meters, 1980. b, Germany, team dressage, 1976. c, Bruce Jenner, decathlon, 1976. d, Mark Gorski, 1000-meter match sprint, 1984. e, Randy Williams, long jump, 1972. f, Shinodu Sekine, judo, 1972. g, Kiyomi Kato, wrestling, 1972. h, Mitsuo Tsukahama, gymnastics, 1976. i, Hartwig Steenken, Germany, 1972.
Each 1000fr: No. 1118, Betty Cuthbert, 100-meters, 1956. No. 1119, Gerhard Stock, javelin, 1936.

1996, July 19
1113-1116 A296 Set of 4   6.00 2.75
1117 A296 200fr Sheet of 9, #a.-
           i.   8.00 3.50
Souvenir Sheets
1118-1119 A296 Set of 2   8.75 4.00
Olymphilex '96 (Nos. 1113-1116, 1118-1119).

Francophonie, 25th Anniv. (in
1995) — A297

300fr, "25 ANS" surrounded by "1970-1995."

1996, July 22
1120 A297 235fr multicolored   1.00   .50
1121 A297 300fr multicolored   1.50   .60
Nos. 1120-1121 each exist in souvenir sheets of 1. Value, set of two sheets $7.50.

FAO, 50th
Anniv. (in
1995)
A298

Designs: 10fr, Fish being lifted in net, vert. 385fr, Boy drinking water.

1996
1122 A298 10fr multicolored   .25   .25
1123 A298 385fr multicolored   2.00   .75
Nos. 1122-1123 each exist in souvenir sheets of 1. Value, set of two sheets $2.75.

Queen Elizabeth II, 70th
Birthday — A299

a, Formal portrait. b, In blue suit. c, In red hat.
1000fr, Balmoral Castle.

1996, July 24   Perf. 13½x14
1124 A299 300fr Strip of 3, #a.-
           c.   3.75 1.75
Souvenir Sheet
1125 A299 1000fr multicolored   4.50 2.00
Nos. 1124 was issued in sheets of 9 stamps.

Pets — A300

1996   Litho.   Perf. 13½
1126 A300 250fr Dog   1.25   .60
1127 A300 600fr Cat   3.00 1.40
Nos. 1126-1127 exist in souvenir sheets of 1.

1998 World Cup Soccer
Championships, France — A301

Winning country, year, player: No. 1128a, Uruguay 1930, Pedro Cea (Argentina), Italy 1934. b, Italy 1938, Piola (Italy), Uruguay 1950. c, Germany 1954, Brazil 1958, Walter, (Germany). d, Amarildo, (Brazil), Brazil 1962, England 1966.
No. 1129: a, Brazil 1970, Pele (Brazil), Germany 1974. b, Kempes (Argentina), Argentina 1978, Italy 1982. c, Argentina 1986, Mattaus (Germany), Germany 1990. d, Platini (France), Brazil 1994.

1996   Litho.   Perf. 13½
1128 A301 375fr Sheet of 4, #a.-
           d.   7.25 3.25
1129 A301 425fr Sheet of 4, #a.-
           d.   8.25 3.75

Dinosaur Eggs — A302

Denomination at: a, LR. b, LL.

1996, Apr. 28
1130 A302 140fr Pair, #a.-b.   2.10   .65
c.   Souv. Sheet, #1130a-1130b   3.00   .65
CHINA '96 (No. 1130c).

Scouting
A303

Raptors, butterflies, mushrooms: 175fr, Buzzard. 200fr, H. misippus. 300fr, Lepiota aspera. 350fr, Raptor with feathers ruffled. 450fr, Amanita caesarea. 500fr, Morpho portis-nymphalidae.

1996 Litho. Perf. 13½
1131-1136 A303 Set of 6   10.00 4.50
Nos. 1132-1133, 1135-1136 exist in souvenir sheets of 1.

Horses — A304

No. 1137, 235fr: a, Appaloosa. b, Arabian. c, Quarter horse. d, Belgian. e, Pure blood English. f, Mustang. g, Haflinger. h, Welsh pony.
No. 1138, 235fr: a, Pinto. b, Palomino. c, Welara. d, Morgan. e, Standard American. f, Norwegian fjord. g, Shetland. h, Shire.
1000fr, Saddlebred.

1996, Nov. 20 Perf. 14
Sheets of 8, #a-h
1137-1138 A304 235fr Set of 2   16.00 7.50
Souvenir Sheet
1139 A304 1000fr multicolored   4.50 2.25

Great Nebula, Andromeda — A305

Designs: b, Halley's Comet. c, Jupiter. d, Saturn. e, Moon. f, Mars.

1996, Nov. 22
1140 A305 300fr Sheet of 6, #a.-f.   8.00 3.50

Wildlife — A306

Flowers: a, Bomax costatum. b, Clappertonia flcifolia. c, Canarina abyssinica. d,

---

Kigelia africana. e, Adenium obesum. f, Oncoba spinosa. g, Orinum ornatum. h, Gloriosa simplex. i, Strophanthus gratus.
Bird: 1500fr, Sagittarius serpentarius.

1997, Feb. 6 Litho. Perf. 14
1141 A306 205fr Sheet of 9, #a.-i.   8.25 3.75
Souvenir Sheet
1142 A306 1500fr multicolored   8.25 3.00

Intl. Express Mail Service A307

300fr, Globe, international express mail routes. 405fr, Emblem of hand holding letter.

1996 Litho. Perf. 13½
1143 A307 300fr multicolored   1.40 .65
1144 A307 405fr multicolored   1.90 .90
No. 1144 exists in a souvenir sheet of 1.

Human Rights Advocates — A308

Designs: a, Dalai Lama. b, Martin Luther King. c, John F. Kennedy. d, Nelson Mandela. e, Mother Teresa. f, Mahatma Gandhi.

1996
1145 A308 175fr Sheet of 6, #a.-f. + 2 labels   5.00 2.25

Red Cross and Red Crescent Societies — A309

Designs: a, Doctor with patient. b, Man sifting grain. c, Using stethoscope on patient. d, Wounded man. e, Bandaging patient. f, Aiding infant.

1996
1146 A309 250fr Sheet of 6, #a.-f. + 2 labels   7.25 3.25

Boy Scouts — A310

Boy scout: a, With dog. b, Riding horse. c, Holding cat. d, Holding butterfly. e, On bicycle. f, Playing game.
Butterfly: 2000fr, Saturnidae, horiz.

1996 Litho. Perf. 13½
1147 A310 300fr Sheet of 6, #a.-f. + 2 labels   9.00 4.00
Souvenir Sheet
1148 A310 2000fr multicolored   10.00 4.50
No. 1148 contains one 42x36mm stamp.

Lions Intl., Rotary Intl. — A311

Designs: a, Child drinking from cup. b, Child carrying sack. c, Girl holding sheaves of grain. d, Man breaking bread. e, Woman cooking over fire. f, Boy, corn stalk.

1996
1149 A311 500fr Sheet of 6, #a.-f. + 2 labels   14.00 6.50

Flora and Fauna A312

15fr, Cucumis sativus, vert. 20fr, Phyllochistis citrella. 40fr, Cetonia aurata. 65fr, Nomadacris septemfasciata. 100fr, Crocodilus vulgaris. 140fr, Athyrium filix, vert. 405fr, Rhopalo ceres.

1996
1150-1156 A312 Set of 7   5.00 1.75
Nos. 1151, 1156 exist in sourvenir sheets of 1.

UN, UNICEF, 50th Anniv. — A313

Designs: a, Futuristic space vehicle. b, MIR space station. c, US space shuttle, space station. d, Woman carrying food. e, Child receiving vaccination. f, Baby being weighed.

1996
1157 A313 350fr Sheet of 6, #a.-f. + 2 labels   10.00 4.50

Elizabeth Taylor, Actress — A314   Princess Diana — A315

Various portraits.

1997, Apr. 10 Litho. Perf. 14
1158 A314 300fr Sheet of 6, #a.-f.   8.00 3.50
1159 A315 300fr Sheet of 6, #a.-f.   8.00 3.50
Souvenir Sheets
1160 A314 1500fr multicolored   6.50 3.00
1161 A315 1500fr multicolored   6.50 3.00
For overprints see Nos. 1181-1182.

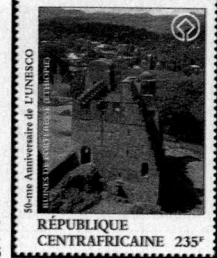

UNESCO, 50th Anniv. A316

No. 1162, 235fr: a, Fortress ruins, Ethiopia. b, Victoria Falls, Zambia. c, River during dry season, Zimbabwe. d, Nature Reserve, Niger. e, Pelican, Natl. Park, Mauritania. f, Native huts in village, Niokolo-Kobo Natl. Park, Senegal. g, M'Zab Valley, Algeria. h, Mosque, Morocco.
No. 1163, 235fr: a, c, Ruins of Roman Amphitheater, France. b, Split, Croatia. d, e, Quedlinberg, Germany. f, h, Tower of London, England. g, Olympic Natl. Park, US.
No. 1164, 235fr: a, Horyu-Ji, Japan. b, Waterfalls, Amazon River, Los Katios Natl. Park, Colombia. c, Abu Mena Church, Egypt. d, Boat on river, Fortress of Suomenlinna, Finland. e, Venice, Italy. f, Mural, Potala Palace, Lhasa, Tibet, China. g, Cathedral, town of Olinda, Brazil. h, Monastery, Mystras, Greece.
No. 1165, 1000fr, Jiuzhaigou Valley, China. No. 1166, 1000fr, Interior, Pilgrimage Church of Wies, Germany. No. 1167, 1000fr Ruins of Fountains Abbey, Studley Park, England.

1997, Apr. 30 Perf. 13½x14
Sheets of 8, #a-h + Label
1162-1164 A316 Set of 3   25.00 12.00
Souvenir Sheets
1165-1167 A316 Set of 3   13.00 6.00

UNICEF, 50th Anniv. — A317

No. 1168: a, 200fr, UN headquarters building. b, 250fr, Baby. c, 500fr, Danny Kaye seated inside vehicle. 1500fr, Child.

1997, Apr. 30 Perf. 14
1168 A317 Sheet of 3, #a.-c.   4.00 1.90
Souvenir Sheet
1169 A317 1500fr multicolored   6.50 3.00

US Pres. Bill Clinton and His Cat, "Socks" — A318

Designs: a, b, c, e, g, h, i, Socks in various poses. d, f, Clinton, Socks.

1996
1170 A318 200fr Sheet of 9, #a.-i.   9.00 3.75

Conquest of Space — A319

Events in 1977: No. 1171: a, Voyager 1, US. b, Space Shuttle Enterprise, US. c, Meteosat 1, US. d, Salyut 6 Space Station, USSR.

Events in 1982: No. 1172: a, Salyut 7 Space Station, USSR. b, Landsat 4 Satellite, US. c, Venera 13, USSR. d, IRAS Infrared Telescope, US.

Events of 1967: No. 1173: a, Cosmos 186 & 188. b, Molniya satellite. c, Surveyor 3. d, Mariner 5.

Events in 1972: No. 1174: a, Copernicus probe, US. b, Pioneer 10, US. c, Apollo 16, US. d, Apollo 17, John F. Kennedy.

Events of 1962: No. 1175: a, Mariner 2, US. b, OSO 1, US. c, John Glenn. d, Mars 1, USSR.

Events of 1957: No. 1176: a, Vostok 1, Yuri Gagarin, USSR. b, Sputnik 2, USSR. c, Sputnik 1, USSR. d, Bell X15, US.

2000fr, Voyager, Pioneer 10, Apollo 11, US.

1997			**Perf. 13½**	
1171	A319	250fr Sheet of 4, #a.-d.	5.00	2.00
1172	A319	350fr Sheet of 4, #a.-d.	6.50	3.00
1173	A319	450fr Sheet of 4, #a.-d.	9.00	3.75
1174	A319	500fr Sheet of 4, #a.-d.	10.00	4.00
1175	A319	600fr Sheet of 4, #a.-d.	11.00	5.00
1176	A319	800fr Sheet of 4, #a.-d.	14.50	6.50

Souvenir Sheet

1177	A319	2000fr multicolored	10.00	4.00

No. 1177 contains one 60x30mm stamp.
No. 1173 exists imperf.

Marilyn Monroe (1926-62) — A320

Various portraits.

1997				
1178	A320	375fr Sheet of 9, #a.-i.	16.00	6.50

John F. Kennedy (1917-63) — A321

Various portraits.

1997				
1179	A321	300fr Sheet of 9, #a.-i.	13.00	5.00

Bruce Lee (1940-73), Actor — A322

Various portraits.

1997		**Litho.**	**Perf. 13½**	
1180	A322	200fr Sheet of 9, #a.-i.	9.00	3.25

Nos. 1159, 1161 Ovptd. "In Memoriam"

1997			**Perf. 14**	
1181	A315	300fr Sheet of 6, #a.-f.	9.00	3.50

Souvenir Sheet

1182	A315	1500fr multicolored	7.50	3.00

Nos. 1181-1182 each contain "Diana, Princess of Wales (1961-1997) IN MEMORIAM" in sheet margin and on each stamp in No. 1181.

Dogs & Cats — A323

Dogs: No. 1183: a, Chinese crested. b, King Charles spaniel. c, Dachshund. d, Borzoi. e, Chow chow. f, Welsh springer. g, Rottweiler. h, Keeshond.

Cats: No. 1184: a, Birman. b, Black and white Persian. c, Siamese kitten. d, Red and black. e, American curl. f, Cornish rex. g, Silver shaded. h, White-footed cat.

1500fr, Pekingese. 2000fr, Somali.

1997		**Litho.**	**Perf. 13½**	
1183	A323	175fr Sheet of 8, #a.-h.	6.50	2.50
1184	A323	250fr Sheet of 8, #a.-h.	9.00	3.75

Souvenir Sheets

1185	A323	1500fr multicolored	7.50	2.75
1186	A323	2000fr multicolored	10.00	3.75

Nos. 1185-1186 each contain one 42x51mm stamp.

Return of Hong Kong to China — A324

No. 1187: a, Tung Chee-Hwa, taking down British flag. b, Raising Chinese flag, Chris Patten, British flag. c, Jiang Zemin, skyline at night. d, City lights, Queen Elizabeth II.

600fr, Tung Chee-Hwa.

1997				
1187	A324	175fr Sheet of 4, #a.-d.	3.25	1.50

Souvenir Sheet

1188	A324	600fr multicolored	3.25	1.25

No. 1188 contains one 38x42mm stamp.

Paintings by Hiroshige (1797-1858) A325

No. 1189: a, Minami-Shinagawa and Samezu Coast. b, Plum Garden, Kamata. c, The Kawaguchi Ferry and Zenkoji Temple. d, Armor-Hanging Pine, Hakkeizaka. e, Robe-Hanging Pine, Senzoku Pond. f, Benten Shrine, Inokashira Pond.

No. 1190: a, A Little Brown Owl on a Pine Branch with a Crescent Moon Behind. b, Sparrows and Camellia in snow. c, Three Wild Geese Flying Downward across the Moon. d, A Blue Bird on a Yellow-flowered Hibiscus. e, Five Swallows in flight.

No. 1191: a, Sparrows and Wild Rose. b, Peonies. c, Morning Glory and Cricket. d, Blossoming Plum Tree. e, Kingfisher above a Yellow-flowered Water Plant.

No. 1192, 1500fr, Haneda Ferry and Benten Shrine. No. 1193, 1500fr, A Bird Clinging to a Tendril of Wisteria. No. 1194, 1500fr, Butterfly and Peony.

1998, Feb. 20		**Litho.**	**Perf. 14**	
1189	A325	300fr Sheet of 6, #a.-f.	9.00	3.00
1190	A325	430fr Sheet of 5, #a.-e.	11.00	3.75
1191	A325	500fr Sheet of 5, #a.-e.	9.25	4.25

Souvenir Sheets

1192-1194	A325	Set of 3	18.00	7.50

Nos. 1190-1191 each contain five 26x72mm stamps. Nos. 1192-1194 each contain one 26x72mm stamp.

Chinese Lunar New Year A326

Animals representing lunar year: a, Rat. b, Ox. c, Tiger. d, Hare. e, Dragon. f, Snake. g, Horse. h, Sheep. i, Monkey. j, Rooster. k, Dog. l, Boar.

1000fr, Tiger, diff.

Intl. Scouting, 90th Anniv. — A327

1998		**Litho. & Typo.**	**Perf. 14**	
1195	A326	150fr Sheet of 12, #a.-l.	8.00	3.75

Souvenir Sheet

1196	A326	1000fr gold & multi	3.75	1.75

Insects: No. 1196A: b, Apis mellifica. c, Lucanus cervus. d, Oryctes nasicornis. e, Pseudacraea boisduvalii. f, Helictopleurus quadripunctatus, euchroea spininasuta. g, Bombus terrestris. h, Charaxes smaragdalis. i, Euchroea coelestis, mantis religiosa.

Wildlife — No. 1197: a, Coracias caudata, Otocyon megalotis. b, Gnu. c, Milvus aegyptus, pelecanus onocrotalus. d, Panthera leo. e, Loxondonta africana. f, Buffalo. g, Hippopotamus amphibius. h, Acinonyx jubatus.

Raptors — No. 1198: a, Buteo rufinus. b, Circus aeruginosus. c, Aquila verreauxii. d, Circaetus gallicus. e, Terathopius ecaudatus. f, Haliaeetus vocifer. g, Milvus milvus. h, Accipiter badius.

1997(?)		**Litho.**	**Perf. 13**	
1196A	A327	200fr Sheet of 8, #b.-i.	7.00	3.00
1197	A327	300fr Sheet of 8, #a.-h.	10.00	4.50
1198	A327	350fr Sheet of 8, #a.-h.	13.00	5.25

1998 World Cup Soccer Championships, France — A328

Player, country, vert: No. 1199, 300fr, Moore, England. No. 1200, 300fr, Rahn, Germany. No. 1201, 300fr, Paulao, Angola. No. 1202, 300fr, Shearer, England.

No. 1203: a, Seaman, England. b, Schillaci, Italy. c, Romario, Brazil. d, McCoist, Scotland. e, Makanaky, Angola. f, Moore, England. g, Muller, Germany. h, Schmeichel, Denmark.

No. 1204, 1500fr, Moore, England, diff. No. 1205, 1500fr, Pele, Brazil.

1998, June 2		**Perf. 13½x14, 14x13½**		
1199-1202	A328	Set of 4	4.50	2.00
1203	A328	205fr Sheet of 8, #a-h, + label	7.00	7.00

Souvenir Sheets

1204-1205	A328	Set of 2	12.00	12.00

Diana, Princess of Wales (1961-97) — A329

Various portraits.

1998 — Perf. 13½

1206	A329	200fr Sheet of 9, #a.-i.	8.00	3.50
1207	A329	250fr Sheet of 9, #a.-i.	10.00	4.50

Diana, Princess of Wales (1961-97) — A330

Diana wearing gowns in one of four seasons: No. 1208, White gown, spring. No. 1209, Blue gown, summer. No. 1210, Bridal gown, fall. No. 1211, High-collared white gown, winter.

1998 — Litho. — Perf. 13½
Souvenir Sheets

1208	A330	1500fr multicolored	7.50	2.50
1209	A330	1500fr multicolored	7.50	2.50
1210	A330	2000fr multicolored	9.00	3.50
1211	A330	2000fr multicolored	9.00	3.50

Nos. 1208-1211 each contain one 50x60mm stamp.

Jacqueline Kennedy Onassis (1929-94) A331

Various portraits.

1997 — Litho. — Perf. 13½

1212	A331	250fr Sheet of 9, #a.-i.	10.50	4.25

1998 Winter Olympic Games, Nagano — A332

Mirror images of vignette with different backgrounds, denomination at — No. 1213: a, Bobsled, LR. b, Slalom skier, CL. c, Ski jumper, CL. d, Bobsled, LL. e, Slalom skier, CR. f, Ski jumper, CR.
No. 1214: a, Ice hockey, LR. b, Cross-country skier, CR. c, Speed skater, LR. d, Ice hockey, LL. e, Cross-country skier, CL. f, Speed skater, LL.
No. 1215: a, Snow boarding, UR. b, Downhill skier, CR. c, Pairs figure skating, CR. d, Snow boarding, UL. e, Downhill skier, CL. f, Pairs figure skating, CL.
No. 1216, Cross-country, freestyle skiers.

1998

1213	A332	180fr Sheet of 6, #a.-f.	4.00	1.75
1214	A332	300fr Sheet of 6, #a.-f.	7.00	3.00
1215	A332	350fr Sheet of 6, #a.-f.	8.25	3.75

Souvenir Sheet

1216	A332	2000fr multicolored	9.25	3.50

Sports — A333

No. 1217 — Cyclists: a, Woman wearing helmet. b, Woman in pink, white & black outfit. c, Man in black & white outfit. d, Man in yellow & black outfit.
No. 1218 — Female tennis players: a, Holding racket above head. b, Wearing black head band. c, Wearing white head band. d, Wearing dreadlocks.
No. 1219 — Male tennis players: a, Holding racket with his right hand. b, In blue shirt, shorts. c, Holding racket behind head. d, Wearing cap backwards.
No. 1220 — Golfers: a, Completing swing. b, Hitting ball in sand trap. c, In orange knickers, argyle socks. d, Lining up putt.

1998 — Litho. — Perf. 13½

1217	A333	350fr Sheet of 4, #a.-d.	6.50	3.00
1218	A333	375fr Sheet of 4, #a.-d.	7.50	3.50
1219	A333	450fr Sheet of 4, #a.-d.	8.50	3.50
1220	A333	500fr Sheet of 4, #a.-d.	9.00	3.50

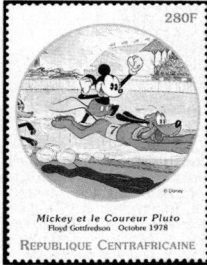

Mickey Mouse, 70th Birthday A334

Scenes from various Disney films drawn by Floyd Gottfredson.
No. 1221: a, 10/78. b, 11/78. c, 3/79. d, 7/79. e, 9/79.
No. 1222: a, 10/79. b, 2/80. c, 4/80. d, 6/80. e, 7/80.
No. 1223: a, 11/80. b, 3/81. c, 6/81. d, 9/81. e, 3/82.
No. 1224: a, 5/82. b, 7/82. c, 10/82. d, 3/83. e, 5/83.
No. 1225, 1500fr, Mickey with camera, flashlight. No. 1226, 1500fr, Mickey with pearl in box. No. 1227, 2000fr, Mickey and magic lamp. No. 1228, 2000fr, Floyd Gottfredson.

Perf. 13½x14, 14x13½
1999, Feb. 10 — Litho.

1221	A334	280fr Sheet of 5, #a.-e., + label	7.00	3.00
1222	A334	365fr Sheet of 5, #a.-e., + label	9.00	3.50
1223	A334	390fr Sheet of 5, #a.-e., + label	10.00	4.00
1224	A334	440fr Sheet of 5, #a.-e., + label	11.00	4.00

Souvenir Sheets

1225-1226	A334	1500fr Set of 2	15.00	5.00
1227-1228	A334	2000fr Set of 2	20.00	6.50

Birds of Africa — A335

Designs: No. 1229, 500fr, Pandion haliaetus. No. 1230, 500fr, Chaetops frenatus. No. 1231, 500fr, Tachymarptis melba. No. 1232, 500fr, Ceratogymna bucinator. No. 1233, 500fr, Laniarius atrococcineus. No. 1234, 500fr, Coturnix coturnix.
No. 1235: a, Lamprotornis superbus. b, Agapornis personatus. c, Coracias spatulata. d, Euplectes jacksoni. e, Nectarinia violacea. f, Emberiza schoeniclus. g, Pica pica. h, Tauraco erythrolophus. i, Sitta europaea.
No. 1236: a, Merops apiaster. b, Coracias garrulus. c, Cuculus canorus. d, Hirundo rustica. e, Motacilla flava. f, Ardea cinerea. g, Falco tinnunculus. h, Tyto alba. i, Charadrius hiaticula.
1500fr, Eremophila alpestris. 2000fr, Delichon urbica.

1999, Mar. 10 — Litho. — Perf. 14

1229-1234	A335	Set of 6	11.00	5.00
1235	A335	280fr Sheet of 9, #a.-i.	9.25	4.25
1236	A335	490fr Sheet of 9, #a.-i.	16.00	7.50

Souvenir Sheets

1237	A335	1500fr multicolored	5.50	2.50
1238	A335	2000fr multicolored	7.50	3.50

World Wildlife Fund — A336

Balaeniceps rex: a, Eating fish. b, Up close. c, Standing. d, One in flight, one up close.

1999

1239	A336	200fr Strip of 4, #a.-d.	5.00	4.00

No. 1239 was issued in sheets of 16 stamps.

Trains A337

No. 1240: a, 40fr, 2-4-0 Steam locomotive. b, 50fr, German Mallat. c, 60fr, Shunting locomotive. d, 260fr, Rhodesian 14A 2-6-2+2-6-2 Garrat. e, 280fr, Steam train. f, 390fr, Engine No. 7, 0-6-0 Baldwin, 1920. g, 440fr, Amtrak passenger train. h, 460fr, German TEE diesel. i, 490fr, "Sir Nigel Gresley."
No. 1241: a, 40fr, Steam train. b, 50fr, 4-4-0, LNWR, 1897. c, 60fr, 2-4-0 locomotive, Midland. d, 260fr, Class XC. e, 280fr, 2-6-0T Sernada and Aveiro, 1910. f, 390fr, East Daggafontein Mines train, Great Britain. g, 440fr, Union Pacific. h, 460fr, Engine No. 6, Baldwin. i, 490fr, 4-4-2 aerodynamic train, Belgium, 1939.
No. 1242, 2000fr, Fairlie, Snake and Auckland, New Zealand, 1874. No. 1243, 2000fr, Steam train arriving at the London-Brighton Depot.

1999, Mar. 11 — Sheets of 9

1240-1241	A337	Set of 2	25.00	10.00

Souvenir Sheets

1242-1243	A337	Set of 2	18.00	6.50

Prehistoric Animals — A338

No. 1244: a, Archaeopteryx. b, Stegosaurus. c, Placerias. d, Rutiodon. e, Tyrannosaurus rex. f, Lystrosaurus.
No. 1245: a, Spinosaurus. b, Cynognathus. c, Kuehneosaurus. d, Compsognathus. e, Triceratops. f, Euoplocephalus. 2000fr, Desmatosuchus.

1998 — Litho. — Perf. 13½

1244	A338	250fr Sheet of 6, #a.-f.	7.50	2.75
1245	A338	300fr Sheet of 6, #a.-f.	8.50	3.25

Souvenir Sheet

1246	A338	2000fr multicolored	9.00	3.75

No. 1246 contains one 51x36mm stamp.

Transportation — A339

No. 1247 — Antique automobiles: a, 1899 Fiat. b, First Chevrolet. c, Serpolet steam carriage. d, 130HP Fiat.
No. 1248 — Cyclists: a, Swiss rider. b, US rider. c, Miguel Indurain (riding to right). d, Jan Ullrich (riding to left).
No. 1249 — Sports cars: a, Porsche Boxster. b, Corvette. c, Jaguar S-type. d, Maserati 3200 GT.
No. 1250 — High-speed trains: a, TGV Atlantique. b, Shin Kansen. c, ETR X-500. d, Advanced passenger train.
No. 1251 — Trains: a, Cornish Riviera Express. b, Lancashire and Yorkshire Railway. c, Type 230. d, Pacific Mallard.
No. 1252 — Fire trucks: a, 1916 Seagrave. b, 1927 Ahrens-Fox Model JS-2. c, 1992 Diesel. d, 1958 Mack Bulldog, Type B-95.
No. 1253 — Space flight of John Glenn: a, Portrait in business suit. b, In Project Mercury spacesuit. c, In shuttle launch suit, 1998. d, Orbiting earth, Space Shuttle.
No. 1254 — Supersonic airplanes: a, Boeing 2707. b, Transatmospheric prototype. c, Tupolev 144. d, Project of European Supersonic ESRP.

1998

1247	A339	300fr Sheet of 4, #a.-d.	6.00	3.00
1248	A339	350fr Sheet of 4, #a.-d.	6.50	2.50
1249	A339	400fr Sheet of 4, #a.-d.	8.00	3.00
1250	A339	450fr Sheet of 4, #a.-d.	9.00	3.50
1251	A339	500fr Sheet of 4, #a.-d.	9.00	3.75
1252	A339	600fr Sheet of 4, #a.-d.	11.00	4.50
1253	A339	800fr Sheet of 4, #a.-d.	15.00	6.00
1254	A339	1000fr Sheet of 4, #a.-d.	20.00	7.50

Scouting — A340

No. 1255 — Scouts with flowers: a, Vanilla planifolia. b, Flamboyant. c, Angraecum sesquipedale.
No. 1256 — Scouts with butterflies or bird: a, Hesperie a bande. b, Philepitte souimanga. c, Dryope.
No. 1257 — Scouts with dogs, cats, and their young: a, Basenji. b, Egyptian mau cat. c, White dog.
No. 1258 — Scouts with minerals: a, Tourmaline. b, Jasper. c, Madgascar corundum.
No. 1259 — Scouts administering Red Cross aid: a, Girl Scout wiping child's tears. b, Scout bandaging child. c, Scout kneeling to help child.
No. 1260 — Scouts in leisure activities: a, Playing table tennis. b, Playing chess. c, Riding horse.

1998 — Litho. — Perf. 13½

1255	A340	400fr Sheet of 3, #a.-c.	6.00	2.25
1256	A340	475fr Sheet of 3, #a.-c.	7.00	2.50
1257	A340	500fr Sheet of 3, #a.-c.	8.00	2.75
1258	A340	600fr Sheet of 3, #a.-c.	9.00	3.25

1259 A340 700fr Sheet of 3, 10.00 3.75
  #a.-c.
1260 A340 800fr Sheet of 3, 10.00 4.50
  #a.-c.

Minerals — A341

No. 1261: a, Hematite (red). b. Challophyllite. c, Fer natif. d, Sylvanite. e. Hematite (specularite). f, Spodumene.
No. 1262: a, Amber. b, Opal. c, Struvite. d, Rhodochrosite. e, Polybasite. f, Silver.

1998 Litho. Perf. 13½
1261 A341 400fr Sheet of 6, 12.00 4.50
  #a.-f.
1262 A341 600fr Sheet of 6, 17.00 6.75
  #a.-f.

A number has been reserved for a souvenir sheet to go with this set.

Mushrooms A342

40fr, Jelly babies. 50fr, Herald of winter. 65fr, Dentate elf cup. 280fr, Pink wax cap. 345fr, Tripe fungus. 485fr, Funnel tooth. Common white saddle. 600fr, False morel.
No. 1272: a, Parrot wax cap. b, Orange naval cap. c, Amethyst deceiver. d, Plums and custard. e, Blue legs. f, Tawny funnel cap. g, Goblet. h, Spindle-shank. i, Buttery tough shank.
No. 1273: a, Fetid mummy cap. b, Stainer. c, Lilac bonnet. d, Firm-fleshed brittle gill. e, Fly agaric. f, Arched bonnet. g, King bolete. h, Orange birch bolete. i, Dog stinkhorn.
1500fr, Hedgehog puffball. 2000fr, Striated earth star.

1999, June 11 Litho. Perf. 14
1264-1271 A342 Set of 8 9.50 4.25
1272 A342 390fr Sheet of 9, 15.00 6.50
  #a.-i.
1273 A342 440fr Sheet of 9, 20.00 6.75
  #a.-i.
Souvenir Sheets
1274 A342 1500fr multicolored 9.00 4.00
1275 A342 2000fr multicolored 11.00 5.00

Birds — A343

No. 1276: a, Psittacula himalayama. b, Anodorhynchus hyacinthinus. c, Trichoglossus haematodus. d, Xipholena punicea. e, Chloebia gouldiae. f, Ramphastos tucanus.
No. 1277: a, Falco sparverius. b, Polyborus plancus. c, Terathopius ecaudatus. d, Tyto alba. e, Glaucidium passerinum. f, Speotyto cunicularia.

1999 Litho. Perf. 13½
1276 A343 350fr Sheet of 6, 12.00 4.00
  #a.-f.
1277 A343 500fr Sheet of 6, 17.50 5.25
  #a.-f.

Dogs, Cats, & Horses A344

Designs: 60fr, Doberman, vert. 280fr, Domestic cat, vert. No. 1280, 390fr, Korat, vert. No. 1281, 390fr, Hanoverian, vert. 440fr, Ardennais. 490fr, Lhasa apso.
Dogs — No. 1284: a, Alaskan malamute. b, Musterlander. c, German shepherd. d, Borzoi. e, Afghan hound. f, Irish terrier. g, Komondor. h, Finnish spitz.
Cats — No. 1285: a, American bobtail. b, American curl. c, Singapura. d, Burmese. e, Tortoise shell. f, Scottish fold. g, British shorthair blue. h, Turkish van.
Horses — No. 1286: a, Shire. b, Clydesdale. c, Arabian. d, Soviet work horse. e, Finnish work horse. f, Percheron. g, Draco. h, North Swedish.
No. 1287, 2000fr, Beagle. No. 1288, 2000fr, Havana. No. 1289, 2000fr, Hanoverian.

1999, July 9 Litho. Perf. 14
1278-1283 A344 Set of 6 12.00 5.00
1284 A344 465fr Sheet of 8, 20.00 9.00
  #a.-h.
1285 A344 485fr Sheet of 8, 20.00 8.00
  #a.-h.
1286 A344 515fr Sheet of 8, 20.00 9.00
  #a.-h.
Souvenir Sheets
1287-1289 A344 Set of 3 30.00 10.50
Nos. 1287-1289 each contain one 44x56mm stamp.

Butterflies A345

Designs: 40fr, Heliconius melpomene. 65fr, Large oak blue. 280fr, Danaus chrysippus. 345fr, Aricia agestis. 485fr, Danis danis. 600fr, Plebejus argus.
No. 1296: a, Delias mysis. b, Ornithoptera priamus. c, Phoebis philea. d, Heliconius doris. e, Thecla coronata f, Lycaena dispar. g, Bematistes aganise. h, Pereute leucodrosime.
No. 1297: a, Colotis danae. b, Eueides isabella. c, Papilio cresphontes. d, Mimacraea marshalli. e, Parathyma nefte. f, Appias nero. g, Uraneis ucubis. h, Eurema brigitta.
No. 1298: a, Heliconius melpomene, diff. b, Mylothris chloris. c, Catopsilia florella. d, Hebomoia glaucippe. e, Palla ussheri. f, Papilio glaucus. g, Colias erytheme. h, Euploea corus.
No. 1299, 1500fr, Unnamed. No. 1300, 1500fr, Papilio, glaucus, vert.

1999, Dec. Litho. Perf. 14
1290-1295 A345 Set of 6 9.00 3.25
1296 A345 280fr Sheet of 8, 12.50 5.00
  #a.-h.
1297 A345 390fr Sheet of 8, 16.00 6.00
  #a.-h.
1298 A345 465fr Sheet of 8, 19.00 6.50
  #a.-h.
Souvenir Sheets
1299-1300 A345 Set of 2 15.00 6.00

Trains A346

Designs: No. 1301, 280fr, Le Capitole, France. No. 1302, 390fr, Montreaux-Bern Line, Switzerland. No. 1303, 485fr, Zugspitzbahn, Switzerland. No. 1304, 485fr, Rhatische Bahn, Swizerland.
No. 1305: a, Schwebebahn, Germany. b, Reichsbahn Class 44, Germany. c, Rembrandt, Germany. d, Trans-Europe Express, Germany. e, Inter-city, Germany. f, Steam locomotive, Germany.
No. 1306: a, ETR300, Italy. b, Mistral, France. c, ER200, Russia. d, Pendoline, Italy. e, Class 1100, Netherlands. f, Rheingold Express, Germany.
No. 1307, 1500fr, TGV, France. No. 1308, 1500fr, Austrian train.

2000, Jan. 25
1301-1304 A346 Set of 4 8.50 3.00
1305 A346 280fr Sheet of 6, 9.00 3.00
  #a.-f.
1306 A346 390fr Sheet of 6, 12.00 4.25
  #a.-f.
Souvenir Sheets
1307-1308 A346 Set of 2 17.50 5.00

Flowers — A347

No. 1309: a, Orchid. b, Water crinum. c, Flame lily. d, Narcissus poeticus. e, Belladonna lily. f, Table Mountain orchid. g, Upland cotton. h, Narcissus jonquilla.
No. 1310: a, Moore's crinum. b, Cyrtanthus brachyscyphus. c, Namaqualand daisy. d, "Narcissus poeticus," diff. e, Painted homeria. f, Helen O'Connor. g, Pink oxalis. h, Pink oxalis and pink arum.
No. 1311: a, Yellow wild iris. b, White arum lily (mountains in background). c, Blue tulip. d, Osteospermum. e, Table Mountain orchid, diff. f, White arum lily (with stems and leaves). g, Daisy. h, Meadow saffron.
No. 1312, 1500fr, Amaryllis belladonna, horiz. No. 1313, 1500fr, African tulip tree, horiz. No. 1314, 1500fr, Bird of paradise, horiz.

2000, Feb. 24
1309 A347 280fr Sheet of 8, 12.00 3.50
  #a.-h.
1310 A347 390fr Sheet of 8, 16.00 4.75
  #a.-h.
1311 A347 515fr Sheet of 8, 20.00 6.00
  #a.-h.
Souvenir Sheets
1312-1314 A347 Set of 3 22.50 8.00
Inscription on No. 1310d is incorrect.

Birds A348

Designs: 100fr, Dendrocygna bicolor, vert. 150fr, Tockis flavirostris, vert. 200fr, Treron calva. 300fr, Ardeola ralloides. 450fr, Passer melanus, vert. 750fr, Sturnus vulgaris, vert.
No. 1321, vert.: a, Trachyphonus vaillantii. b, Polyhierax semitorquatus. c, Tockus nasutus. d, Estrilda astrild. e, Merops persicus. f, Amandava subflava. g, Guttera pucherani. h, Oriolus oriolus. i, Bycanistes brevis.
No. 1322: a, Butoides striatus. b, Limnocorax flavirostra. c, Terathopius ecaudatus. d, Mycteria ibis. e, Actophilornis africanus. f, Poicephalus rueppellii. g, Alopochen aegyptiacus. h, Morus capensis. i, Sagittarius serpentarius.
No. 1323: a, Gyps africanus. b, Tyto alba. c, Pelecanus onocrotalus. d, Ephippiorhynchus senegalensis. e, Ardea goliath. f, Sylvia communis. g, Buteo rufofuscus. h, Parus caeruleus. i, Dromas ardeola.
No. 1324, 2000fr, Buphagus africanus. No. 1325, 2000fr, Haliaeetus vocifer. No. 1326, 2000fr, Erythropgia coryphaeus, vert.

2000, Feb. 25
1315-1320 A348 Set of 6 8.50 3.00
1321 A348 390fr Sheet of 9, 16.00 5.25
  #a.-i.
1322 A348 440fr Sheet of 9, 18.00 6.00
  #a.-i.
1323 A348 485fr Sheet of 9, 18.00 6.50
  #a.-i.
Souvenir Sheets
1324-1326 A348 Set of 3 27.50 10.00

Aviation A349

Designs: 280fr, Spirit of St. Louis. 345fr, Hindenburg. 465fr, Flight at Kitty Hawk. 485fr, AH-1 Cobra.
No. 1331: a, Fokker triplane. b, Spad XIII. c, Blériot XI. d, Nieuport 12. e, Sopwith Camel. f, 1920s US Mail plane. g, Otto Lilienthal's hang glider. h, Hydrogen-filled balloon of J. A. C. Charles.

No. 1332: a, Mitchell-B25. b, P-38E Lightning. c, Vought F-4U Corsair. d, Mitsubishi Zero. e, B-17 Flying Fortress. f, P-51 Mustang. g, Flying Tiger plane. h, Messerschmitt Bf-109.
No. 1333: a, X-1. b, B-52C. c, Boeing 707. d, F-16C. e, Sabre jet. f, MiG-15. g, F-4 Phantom. h, F-117A Stealth.
No. 1334, 1500fr, Concorde. No. 1335, 1500fr, Space shuttle "Enterprise."

2000, Feb. 28
1327-1330 A349 Set of 4 7.50 2.40
1331 A349 345fr Sheet of 8, 13.00 4.25
  #a.-h.
1332 A349 390fr Sheet of 8, 14.50 4.75
  #a.-h.
1333 A349 515fr Sheet of 8, 19.00 6.25
  #a.-h.
Souvenir Sheets
1334-1335 A349 1500fr Set of 2 13.00 5.00

Chess Players — A350

No. 1336, 280fr: a, Otto IV of Brandenburg. b, Mme. de Verzu and Chevalier de Bourgogne. c, Chess Players by Estienne Porcher. d, Fresco by F. Pella.
No. 1337, 300fr: a, Two Nobles. b, Depiction from book of Jean Wauquelin. c, Girolamo de Cremona. d, Ashtapada.
No. 1338, 390fr: a, Ulysses and Palamedes. b, Christian cavalier and Muslim. c, Two Moorish women. d, Burzurgmikhr and Kannuja.
No. 1339, 465fr: a, Two men, 18th Cent. b, Napoleon and Cornwallis. c, Adolf Anderssen and Wilhelm Steinitz. d, Queen Victoria.
No. 1340, 485fr: a, Two women. b, Chess on an enlarged board. c, Xerxes. d, King Evil-Merodach.
No. 1341, 515fr: a, King Henry VIII of England. b, Queen Elizabeth I of England. c, King Charles I of England. d, Russian czarevitch.

1999 Litho. Perf. 13½
Sheets of 4, #a-d
1336-1341 A350 Set of 6 45.00 18.00

Cosmonauts and Astronauts — A351

No. 1342, 485fr: a, Vladimir Soloviev. b, Georgi Beregovoy. c, Alexei Leonov. d, Pavel Popovich. e, Yuri Gagarin. f, Valentina Tereshkova. g, Helena Kondakova. h, Gherman Titov. i, Alexander Volkov.
No. 1343, 515fr: a, Neil Armstrong. b, Edwin Aldrin. c, Michael Collins. d, Alan Bean. e, James Lovell. f, Alan Shepard. g, David Scott. h, John Young. i, Eugene Cernan.
2000fr, Armstrong and Gagarin, horiz.

1999 Sheets of 9, #a-i
1342-1343 A351 Set of 2 35.00 14.00
Souvenir Sheet
1344 A351 2000fr multi 9.00 3.25
No. 1344 contains one 60x51mm stamp.

Millennium — A352

2000, Mar. 31   **Perf. 14**
1345 A352 515fr multicolored   2.50 1.00
Issued in sheets of six.

2000 Summer Olympics,
Sydney — A353

No. 1346, 300fr: a, Individual dressage. b, Rhythmic gymnastics. c, Women's 100-meter hurdles. d, Cycling.
No. 1347, 485fr: a, Tennis. b, Diving. c, Soccer. d, Pole vault.
No. 1348, 750fr: a, Long jump. b, Judo. c, Basketball. d, Show jumping.
No. 1349, 800fr: a, Boxing. b, Table tennis. c, Women's 200-meter sprint. d, Individual three-day equestrian event.

2000   **Perf. 13½**
     Sheets of 4, #a-d
1346-1349 A353 Set of 4   40.00 15.00

2002 Winter Olympics, Salt Lake
City — A354

No. 1350, 280fr: a, Freestyle skiing. b, Cross-country skiing. c, Bobsled. d, Men's slalom.
No. 1351, 390fr: a, Luge. b, Women's ski relay. c, Downhill skiing. d, Short track skating.
No. 1352, 465fr: a, Women's figure skating. b, Hockey. c, Ski jumping. d, Biathlon.
No. 1353, 515fr, a, Pairs figure skating. b, Women's giant slalom. c, Speed skating. d, Nordic combined.

2000   **Sheets of 4, #a-d**
1350-1353 A354 Set of 4   30.00 12.00

UPU, 125th Anniv. — A355

UPU emblem and various men: 280fr, 300fr, 390fr, 465fr, 485fr, 515fr, 750fr, 800fr.

2000, Sept. 8   **Litho.**   **Perf. 13¼**
1354-1361 A355 Set of 8   18.00 6.50

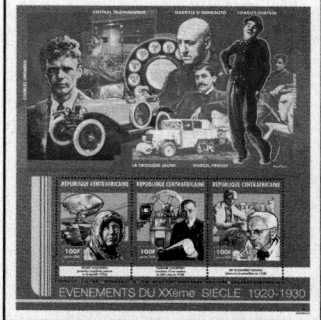

Millennium — A356

No. 1362: a, Roald Amundsen, first polar exploration by dirigible, 1926. b, Vladimir Zworykin, inventor of television camera, 1928. c, Sir Alexander Fleming, discoverer of penicillin, 1928.
No. 1363: a, Henri Dunant, 1901 Nobel Peace prize winner. b, Wilbur and Orville Wright, first airplane, 1903. c, Enrico Caruso, opera singer.
No. 1364: a, Theodore Roosevelt, opening of Panama Canal, 1914. b, Albert Einstein, theory of general relativity, 1916. c, Battle of Verdun, 1916.
No. 1365: a, Auguste Piccard, flight to stratosphere in balloon, 1931. b, Robert Goddard, rocketry pioneer, 1935. c, Ferdinand von Zeppelin and Graf Zeppelin, 1928-37.
No. 1366: a, Felix Eboue, governor of Chad, 1940. b, Mahatma Gandhi, independence of India, 1947. c, Marilyn Monroe (1926-62), actress.
No. 1367: a, Juan Manuel Fangio, race car driver. b, James Dean (1931-55), actor. c, Sputnik 1, 1957.
No. 1368: a, Charles De Gaulle (1890-1970), French general and political leader. b, Yuri Gagarin (1934-68), Soviet Cosmonaut. c, Neil Armstrong (1930-), American Astronaut.
No. 1369: a, Apollo-Soyuz. b, Elvis Presley (1935-77), American entertainer. c, Muhammad Ali (1942-), American boxer.
No. 1370: a, John Young, Space Shuttle, 1981. b, Mikhail Gorbachev, fall of the Berlin Wall, 1989. c, Dalai Lama, 1989 Nobel Peace prize winner.
No. 1371: a, Nelson Mandela, 1993 Nobel Peace prize winner. b, Galileo probe reaches Jupiter, 1995. c, Mars Pathfinder, 1998.

2000, Sept. 28   **Perf. 13¼**
1362 A356 100fr Sheet of 3,
       #a-c   1.50 .75
1363 A356 280fr Sheet of 3,
       #a-c   4.00 1.50
1364 A356 300fr Sheet of 3,
       #a-c   4.50 2.25
1365 A356 390fr Sheet of 3,
       #a-c   6.00 2.25
1366 A356 465fr Sheet of 3,
       #a-c   7.50 3.00
1367 A356 485fr Sheet of 3,
       #a-c   7.50 3.00
1368 A356 515fr Sheet of 3,
       #a-c   7.50 3.00
1369 A356 750fr Sheet of 3,
       #a-c   9.00 4.50
1370 A356 800fr Sheet of 3,
       #a-c   12.00 4.50
1371 A356 1000fr Sheet of 3,
       #a-c   15.00 6.50
   Nos. 1362-1371 (10)   74.50 31.25

Flora, Dinosaurs and
Mushrooms — A357

No. 1372 — Butterflies: a, Cymothoe lurida. b, Charaxes lasti. c, Charaxes lactetinctus. d, Charaxes opinatus. e, Charaxes subornatus. f, Coelides hanno.

No. 1373 — Butterflies: a, Charaxes cithaeron. b, Charaxes anticlea. c, Bebearia plistonax. d, Charaxes jahlusa. e, Charaxes acraeoides. f, Bebearia oxione.
No. 1374 — Dinosaurs: a, Compsognathus. b, Kritosaurus. c, Nodosaurus. d, Tuojiangosaurus. e, Homalocephalus. f, Tsintaosaurus.
No. 1375 — Birds: a, Veuve royale. b, Travailleur cardinal. c, Gonolek a ventre rouge. d, Touraco de Schalow. e, Touraco Pauline. f, Souimanga orange.
No. 1376 — Dinosaurs: a, Monoclonius. b, Dryosaurus. c, Anatosaurus. d, Styracosaurus. e, Pinacosaurus. f, Kentrosaurus.
No. 1377 — Birds: a, Bateleur de savanes. b, Corbeau a nuque blanche. c, Corvinelle pie. d, Cordon-bleu violace. e, Fauvette passerinette. f, Crombec a face rousse.
No. 1378 — Mushrooms: a, Lentinus sajorcaju. b, Lentinus velutinus. c, Pleurotus luteoalbus. d, Pluteus congolensis. e, Lentinus crinitus. f, Leucoagaricus ferruginosus.
No. 1379 — Mushrooms: a, Lentinus squarrosulus. b, Phlebopus colossus. c, Lentinus tuberregium. d, Phlebopus sudanicus. e, Phlebopus silvaticus. f, Volvariella congolensis.
No. 1380 — Dogs: a, Briard. b, Pyrenees shepherd. c, Chow chow. d, Cocker spaniel. e, Puli. f, Yorkshire terrier.
No. 1381 — Cats: a, American wirehair. b, California spangled cat. c, Chinchilla. d, Exotic shorthair. e, Selkirk Rex. f, Oriental.
No. 1382 — Dogs: a, Greenland dog. b, Alaskan malamute. c, Samoyed. d, Siberian husky.

2001, May 28   **Litho.**   **Perf. 13¼**
1372 A357 280fr Sheet of 6,
       #a-f   7.25 3.00
1373 A357 300fr Sheet of 6,
       #a-f   7.75 3.00
1374 A357 300fr Sheet of 6,
       #a-f   7.75 3.00
1375 A357 350fr Sheet of 6,
       #a-f   9.50 3.50
1376 A357 390fr Sheet of 6,
       #a-f   9.50 4.00
1377 A357 390fr Sheet of 6,
       #a-f   9.50 4.00
1378 A357 390fr Sheet of 6,
       #a-f   9.50 4.00
1379 A357 465fr Sheet of 6,
       #a-f   11.50 4.50
1380 A357 465fr Sheet of 6,
       #a-f   11.00 4.50
1381 A357 485fr Sheet of 6,
       #a-f   12.00 4.50
1382 A357 600fr Sheet of 4,
       #a-d   10.00 4.00
   Nos. 1372-1382 (11)   105.25 42.00

Fauna and Fish
A358

Designs: 280fr, Salamandra salamandra. No. 1384, 300fr, Epiplatys annualatus. No. 1385, 350fr, Pseudotropheus zebra. 400fr, Trichechus senegalensis. 450fr, Pelomedusa subrufa. 500fr, Xenomystus nigri.
No. 1389, vert.: a, Damaliscus dorcas. b, Manis temmincki. c, Hyaena brunnea. d, Lycaon pictus. e, Diceros bicornis. f, Osteolaemis tetraspis. g, Cercocebus torquatus. h, Bunologus monticularis. i, Myosciurus pumilia.
No. 1390, vert.: a, Plotosus lineatus. b, Protopterus dolloi. c, Calamoichthys calabaricus. d, Malapterurus electricus. e, Discoglossus pictus. f, Dugong dugon.
No. 1391, 1500fr, Julidochromis ornatus, vert. No. 1392, 1500fr, Hippopotamus amphibius, vert. No. 1393, 1500fr, Afropavo congensis, vert.

   Perf. 13¼x13½, 13½x13¼
2001, July 12
1383-1388 A358   Set of 6   10.00 3.00
1389 A358 300fr Sheet of 9, #a-
       i   12.50 3.50
1390 A358 350fr Sheet of 6, #a-
       f   9.50 2.75
     Souvenir Sheets
1391-1393 A358   Set of 3   21.00 7.50

Reptiles and Amphibians — A359

No. 1394, 350fr: a, Boa arc-en-ciel. b, Crapaud marine. c, Basilic vert. d, Grenouille taureau. e, Tortue happante. f, Pseudoeurycea leprosa.
No. 1395, 350fr: a, Trionix epinelix. b, Iguane rhinoceros. c, Boa constrictor. d, Boa canin. e, Tortue d'etang. f, Dermophis mexicanus.
No. 1396, 1500fr, Serpent des arbres. No. 1397, 1500fr, Grenouille poison.

2001, July 12   **Perf. 13¼x13½**
     Sheets of 6, #a-f
1394-1395 A359   Set of 2   20.00 5.50
     Souvenir Sheets
1396-1397 A359   Set of 2   14.00 6.00

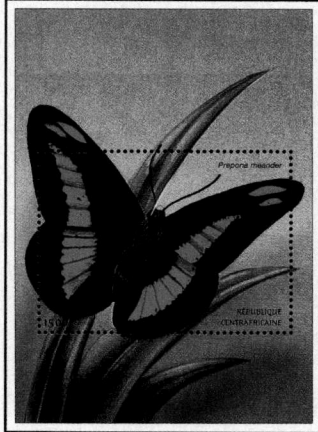

Butterflies — A360

No. 1398, 350fr, vert.: a, Papilio garamus. b, Eunica orphise. c, Parides lysander. d, Julia dryas iulia. e, Adelpha mythra. f, Thecla coronata.
No. 1399, 350fr, vert.: a, Battus polydamas. b, Mesene phareus. c, Anartia jatrophae. d, Siproeta epaphus. e, Uraneis ucubis. f, Pereute leucodrosine.
No. 1400, 1500fr, Prepona meander. No. 1401, 1500fr, Morpho peleides. No. 1402, 1500fr, Pieris rapae. No. 1403, 1500fr, Helconius melpomene.

2001, July 12   **Perf. 13½x13¼**
     Sheets of 6, #a-f
1398-1399 A360   Set of 2   20.00 6.00
     Souvenir Sheets
1400-1403 A360   Set of 4   27.50 10.00

Nos. 1398-1399 each contain six 28x42mm stamps.

A361

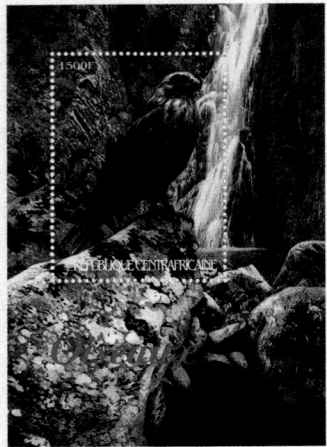

Birds — A362

Designs: 50fr, Macareux moine. 75fr, Harfang des neiges, vert. 100fr, Manchots, vert. 150fr, Fou à pieds bleus, vert.

No. 1408, 325fr: a, Perruche soleil. b, Toucan de cuviée. c, Colibri. d, Ara hyacinthe. e, Pione a tete bleue. f, Perruche flavéolée. g, Pelican. h, Flamant rose. i, Toucan toco.

No. 1409, 325fr: a, Touraco à gros bec. b, Martin-chaseur à poitrine bleue. c, Faucon lanier. d, Inséparable masqué. e, Loriquet à tete bleue. f, Perroquet jaco. g, Perenoptere d'Egypte. h, Grue grise couronnée. i, Marabou.

No. 1410, 350fr, vert.: a, Colibri caraibe. b, Jaseur des cèdres. c, Colibri d'abeille. d, Bruant indigo. e, Tourterelle pleureuse. f, Talève pourprée.

No. 1411, 350fr: a, Gros-bec bleu. b, Fauvette à gorge orangée. c, Pic flamboyant. d, Passerin nonpareil. e, Fauvette à capuchon. f, Bananaquit.

No. 1412, 1500fr, Cygne, vert. No. 1413, 1500fr, Pygargue à tete blanche, vert. No. 1414, 1500fr, shown. No. 1415, 1500fr, Balbuzard, vert.

Perf. 13¼x13½, 13½x13¼
2001, July 19
1404-1407 A361 Set of 4   3.75 1.50
Sheets of 9, #a-i
1408-1409 A361 Set of 2   26.50 8.25
Sheets of 6, #a-f
Perf. 13¼x13, 13x13¼
1410-1411 A362 Set of 2   20.00 6.00
Souvenir Sheets
Perf. 13½x13¼
1412-1413 A361 Set of 2   14.00 5.00
Perf. 13¼
1414-1415 A362 Set of 2   14.00 5.00

No. 1410 contains six 30x40mm stamps; No. 1411 contains six 40x30mm stamps.

Mushrooms A363

Designs: 550fr, Coltricia montagnei. 600fr, Inocybe fuscodisca. 650fr, Hydnum imbricatum. 700fr, Hygrophorus miniatus.

No. 1420: a, Coprinus picaceus. b, Crinipellis zonata. c, Naematoloma fasciculare. d, Cortinarius caerulescens. e, Amanita muscaria. f, Cortinarius obtusus. g, Entoloma serrulatum. h, Strobilomyces floccopus.

1500fr, Sarcosphaera crassa, horiz.

Perf. 13½x13¼, 13¼x13½
2001, July 26
1416-1419 A363 Set of 4   12.00 3.50
1420 A363 350fr Sheet of 8,
               #a-h   13.00 4.00
Souvenir Sheet
1421 A363 1500fr multi   7.00 2.50

Prehistoric Animals — A364

Designs: 50fr, Anatasaurus. 100fr, Apatosaurus. 150fr, Allosaurus. 200fr, Velociraptor.

No. 1426, 240fr: a, Rhamphorhynchus. b, Pteranodon. c, Tyrannosaurus rex. d, Deinonychus antirrhopus. e, Parasaurolophus. f, Corythosaurus. g, Patagosaurus. h, Triceratops. i, Brachylophosaurus. j, Europlocephalus. k, Dimetrodon. l, Leptoceratops.

No. 1427, 240fr: a, Perosaur. b, Albertosaurus. c, Dryptosaurus. d, Archaeopteryx. e, Ouranosaurus. f, Myahuera. g, Camptosaurus. h, Ichthyosaurus. i, Geosaurus. j, Trilobita. k, Plesiosaurus. l, Lewisiceras.

No. 1428, 1500fr, Herrerasaurus. No. 1429, 1500fr, Stegosaurus.

2001, July 31   Perf. 12½
1422-1425 A364 Set of 4   2.50 .70
Sheets of 12, #a-l, + 8 labels
1426-1427 A364 Set of 2   27.50 8.25
Souvenir Sheets
1428-1429 A364 Set of 2   14.00 4.25

Dinosaurs A365

Designs: 250fr, Apatosaurus. 300fr, Baryonyx. 325fr, Albertosaurus. 375fr, Dimetrodon.

No. 1434, 350fr: a, Triceratops. b, Ornithocherius. c, Brachiosaurus. d, Utahraptor. e, Tyrannosaurus rex. f, Stegosaurus.

No. 1435, 350fr: a, Diplodicus. b, Pachycephalosaurus. c, Archaeopteryx. d, Pteranodon. e, Herrerasaurus. f, Struthiomimus.

No. 1436, 1500fr, Rhamphorhynchus. No. 1437, 1500fr, Proleratops and Deinonychus.

2001, July 31   Perf. 13¼x13½
1430-1433 A365 Set of 4   6.00 1.75
Sheets of 6, #a-f
1434-1435 A365 Set of 2   20.00 6.00
Souvenir Sheets
1436-1437 A365 Set of 2   12.00 5.00

Belgica 2001 Intl. Stamp Exhibition, Brussels (Nos. 1434-1437).

2001 Catastrophes — A366

No. 1438: a, Jan. 26 earthquake, India. b, Sept. 11 terrorist attacks, US. c, Dec. 26 fires, Australia. d, Hurricane Michelle, Cuba, Oct. 27. e, July 4 tornado, Canada. f, July 24 eruption of Mt. Etna, Italy.

2002, July 23   Perf. 13¼
1438 A366 390fr Sheet of 6, #a-f 9.00 4.00

Each stamp in sheet exists in a souvenir sheet of 1.

Painters and Paintings — A367

No. 1439, 390fr: a, Claude Monet. b, Woman with an Umbrella, by Monet. c, Argenteuil, by Edouard Manet. d, Manet. e, Joseph Mallord William Turner. f, Mornings Amongst the Conniston Falls, Cumberland, by Turner.

No. 1440, 390fr: a, Girl with a Mandolin, by Pablo Picasso. b, Picasso. c, Georges Braque. d, The Musician, by Braque. e, Woman in Blue, by Fernand Leger. f, Leger.

2002, July 23   Sheets of 6, #a-f
1439-1440 A367 Set of 2   17.00 7.00

Chess — A368

No. 1441: a, Board from match between Garry Kasparov and Viswantathan Anand. b, Kasparov. c, Anand. d, Board from match between Anand and Shirov. e, Board from match between Ruslan Ponomariov and Vassily Ivanchuk. f, Ponomariov.

2002, July 23
1441 A368 605fr Sheet of 6, #a-
             f   13.00 5.50

Each horizontal pair in the sheet exists in a souvenir sheet of 2 stamps.

Cosmonauts — A369

No. 1442: a, Yuri Gagarin, Vostok 1. b, Pavel Vinogradov, Mir 24. c, Valentina Tereshkova, Vostok 6. d, Valeri Kubasov, Apollo-Soyuz. e, Alexei Leonov, Voskhod 2. f, Sergei Treschev, Intl. Space Station.

2002, July 23
1442 A369 605fr Sheet of 6, #a-
             f   13.00 5.50

Zeppelin NT and Concorde — A370

No. 1443: a, Zeppelin NT over Friedrichshafen, Germany. b, Concorde over Rio de Janeiro. c, Concorde over Alaska. d, Zeppelin NT over Lake Constance. e, Zeppelin NT over Orly Airport, Paris. f, Concorde over New York.

2002, July 23
1443 A370 665fr Sheet of 6, #a-
             f   15.00 6.00

Each stamp in sheet exists in a souvenir sheet of 1.

Famous People — A371

No. 1444: a, Paul Harris, founder of Rotary International. b, Princess Diana, Intl. Red Cross Ambassador against land mines. c, Pope John Paul II. d, Sir Alexander Fleming. e, Mother Teresa. f, Melvin Jones, founder of Lions Club International.

2002, July 23
1444 A371 665fr Sheet of 6, #a-
f   15.00 6.00

Each stamp in sheet exists in a souvenir sheet of 1.

Rotary and Lions Emblems and Animals — A372

No. 1445, 390fr — Turtles: a, Eretmochelys imbricata. b, Lepidochelys olivacea. c, Natator depressa.
No. 1446, 600fr — Dinosaurs: a, Sauropelta. b, Chasmosaurus. c, Herrerasaurus.

2002, Dec. 23   Sheets of 3, #a-c
1445-1446 A372 Set of 2   11.00 4.75

Scouts — A373

No. 1447, 605fr — Orchids: a, Dactylorhiza markusii. b, Cephalanthera rubra. c, Neotinea maculata.
No. 1448, 665fr — Mushrooms: a, Agaricus ostreatus. b, Russula virescens. c, Lactarius deliciosus.
No. 1449, 815fr — Dinosaurs: a, Brachiosaurus. b, Sarcosuchus. c, Gigantosaurus carolinii.
No. 1450, 840fr — Minerals: a, Guilleminite. b, Torbernite. c, Bornite.
Nos. 1451-1452A (each 3000fr), Scout playing: Nos. 1451, 1451A, Chess. Nos. 1452, 1452A, Table tennis.

2002, Dec. 23   Sheets of 3, #a-c
1447-1450 A373 Set of 4   32.50 14.00

A373a

Litho. & Embossed
Perf. 13½
1451	A373a	gold & multi	9.50	9.50
1451A	A373a	sil & multi	9.50	9.50
1452	A373a	gold & multi	9.50	9.50
1452A	A373a	sil & multi	9.50	9.50
	Nos. 1451-1452A (4)		38.00	38.00

Each stamp in each sheet and Nos. 4151-4152A exists in a souvenir sheet of 1.

Famous People A374

Designs: No. 1453, 485fr, Christopher Columbus (1450-1506), explorer. No. 1454, 485fr, Admiral Horatio Nelson (1758-1805). No. 1455, 605fr, Jacques Cartier (1491-1557), explorer. No. 1456, 605fr, Vladimir Yourkevitch (1885-1964), naval designer. No. 1457, 665fr, Columbus, diff. No. 1458, 665fr, Sir Francis Drake (1540-96), explorer. No. 1459, 815fr, Jean-François Champollion (1790-1832), Egyptologist. No. 1460, 815fr, Queen Mother Elizabeth of England (1900-2002). No. 1461, 840fr, Marilyn Monroe (1926-62), actress. No. 1462, 840fr, Elvis Presley (1935-77), singer. No. 1463, 1000fr, Pres. John F. Kennedy (1917-63). No. 1464, 1000fr, French President Charles de Gaulle (1890-1970).

2003, May 15   Litho.   Perf. 13½
1453-1464 A374   Set of 12   40.00 16.00

Dated 2002. Each stamp also exists in souvenir sheet of 1.

2004 Summer Olympics, Athens A375

Designs: 390fr, Boxing. 485fr, Basketball. 605fr, Equestrian. 655fr, Tennis. 815fr, Table tennis.

2004, Mar. 3   Litho.   Perf. 13½
1465-1469 A375   Set of 5   14.00 5.75

Dated 2003. Each stamp also exists in souvenir sheet of 1.

2006 World Cup Soccer Championships, Germany — A376

Various soccer players and stadia: 160fr, 390fr, 485fr, 605fr, 815fr.

2004, Mar. 3   Litho.   Perf. 13½
1470-1474	A376	Set of 5	9.25	9.25
1474a		Horiz. strip of 5, #1470-1474	9.25	9.25

Each stamp also exists in a souvenir sheet of 1.

2004 Summer Olympics, Athens — A376a

Designs: Nos. 1475, 1476, Table tennis. Nos. 1477, 1478, Tennis.

Litho. & Embossed
2004, Mar. 3   Perf. 13½
1475	A376a	3000fr gold & multi	11.00	11.00
1476	A376a	3000fr sil & multi	11.00	11.00
1477	A376a	3000fr gold & multi	11.00	11.00
1478	A376a	3000fr sil & multi	11.00	11.00
	Nos. 1475-1478 (4)		44.00	44.00

Europa Stamps, 50th Anniv. (in 2006) — A377

Top stamp: 5fr, Netherlands #387. 20fr, Italy #810. 100fr, San Marino #1065. 150fr, Greece #718. 300fr, Italy #1039. 390fr, Italy #916. 465fr, Liechtenstein #368. 485fr, Germany #996. 515fr, Spain #941. 750fr, Finland #419. 800fr, Italy #979. 1500fr, Belgium #840.

2005, Apr. 10   Litho.   Perf. 13½
1479-1490 A377   Set of 12   22.00 22.00

Gen. François Bozizé, President of Central Africa — A378

2005 ?   Litho.   Perf. 13¼
Frame Color
1493	A378	15fr purple	—
1498	A378	100fr blue	—
1501	A378	300fr red	—
1504	A378	515fr bister	—

Nos. 1498, 1501 and 1504 are dated 2004. No. 1493 is dated 2006. Ten additional stamps were issued in this set. The editors would like to examine any examples.

Pope John Paul II (1920-2005) — A379

Various portraits of Pope John Paul II: 280fr, 1000fr.

2007, Aug. 24   Litho.   Perf. 13¼
1505-1506 A379   Set of 2   5.50 2.75

Each stamp also exists in a souvenir sheet of 1.

2008 Summer Olympics, Beijing — A380

Designs: 300fr, Chinese female athlete, swimmer. 390fr, Chinese soccer players, stadium. 1000fr, Chinese table tennis players, building.

2007, Apr. 24
1507-1509 A380   Set of 3   7.00 3.50

Each stamp also exists in a souvenir sheet of 1.

Princess Diana (1961-97) — A381

Princess Diana with: No. 1510, 390fr, Mother Teresa. No. 1511, 390fr, Pope John Paul II.

2007, Aug. 24   Litho.   Perf. 13¼
1510-1511 A381   Set of 2   3.25 3.25

Nos. 1510 and 1511 each exist in souvenir sheets of 1.

Worldwide Fund For Nature (WWF) — A382

Civettictis civetta: 390fr, Standing in grass. 485fr, Adult and juvenile at den. 515fr, Head. 750fr, On branch.

2007, Aug. 24
1512-1515 A382   Set of 4   9.00 9.00

Nos. 1512-1515 exist with printer's inscription at lower left in a souvenir sheet of 4.

A386

No. 1522, 650fr — Rhinoceroses: a, Two rhinocersoses facing left. b, Head of rhinoceros facing right, rhinoceros walking left. c, Two rhinoceroses, one facing right, one facing forward. d, Three rhinoceroses.
No. 1523, 650fr — Gorillas: a, Gorilla beringei, adult and juvenile at left, large gorilla at right. b, Gorilla beringei, gorilla in foliage at left, large gorilla at right. c, Gorilla gorilla, large gorilla at left. d, Gorilla beringei, adult and juvenile at left, large gorilla showing teeth at right.
No. 1524, 650fr — Bats: a, Two Rousettus lanosus. b, Three Rousettus lanosus. c, Two Megaloglossus woermanni. d, Two Hipposideros abae.
No. 1525, 650fr — Lions: a, Male and female. b, Two females in tree. c, Three cubs, two playing, one front paws on rock. d, Head of male, cub chewing on stick.
No. 1526, 650fr — Wild cats: a, Felis margarita. b, Pardofelis temminckii. c, Felis silvestris lybica. d, Caracal aurata.
No. 1527, 650fr — Dogs: a, Dogues de Bordeaux. b, Irish terriers. c, Basenjis. d, Boerboels.
No. 1528, 650fr — Elephants: a, Two Loxondonta africana, grass in foreground. b, Two Loxodonta cyclotis, grass in foreground. c, Two Loxodonta africana, elephant with raised trunk at left. d, Loxodonta cyclotis, elephant eating at right..
No. 1529, 650fr — Horses: a, Horse leaping in background. b, Horse running left in background. c, Light brown horses. d, White horse at left, brown horse in background.
No. 1530, 650fr — Dolphins: a, Sousa teuszii, Tursiops truncatus. b, Two Tursiops truncatus, Latin name at LR. c, Two Sousa teuszii. d, Two Tursiops truncatus, Latin name at LL.
No. 1531, 650fr — Whales: a, Balaenoptera acutorostrata, Latin name at LL. b, Eubalaena australis. c, Balaenoptera acutorostrata, Latin name at center left. d, Megaptera novaeangliae.
No. 1532, 650fr — Birds of prey: a, Aquila rapax rapax. b, Terathopius ecaudatus. c, Buteo augur. d, Haliaeetus vocifer.
No. 1533, 650fr — Parrots: a, Poicephalus senegalus, Latin name in white. b, Poicephalus rueppellii. c, Psittacus erithacus. d, Poicephalus senegalus, Latin name in black.

No. 1534, 650fr — Peacocks (Afropavo congensis) with Latin name at: a, UR, denomination at LL. b, LL, denomination at top center. c, UR, denomination at right center. d, LR, denomination at UL.

No. 1535, 650fr — Kingfishers: a, Ceryle rudis, Latin name at top. b, Merops apiaster. c, Megaceryle maxima. d, Ceryle rudis, Latin name at right.

No. 1536, 650fr — Owls: a, Asio madagascariensis. b, Asio capensis. c, Bubo africanus. d, Asio flammeus.

No. 1537, 650fr — Owls: a, Scotopelia peli. b, Strix aluco yamadae. c, Scotopelia peli, Strix aluco aluco. d, Strix aluco aluco, denomination at LL.

No. 1538, 650fr — Bees: a, Apis mellifera scutellata and Jean-Henri Fabre (1823-1915), entomologist. b, Apis mellifera monticola and Charles Valentine Riley (1843-95), entomologist. c, Apis mellifera scutellata and Pierre André Latreille (1762-1833), zoologist. d, Apis mellifera scutellata and Léon Provancher (1820-92), naturalist.

No. 1539, 650fr — Beetles: a, Chrysocarabus auronitens, Cleridae. b, Cortodera humeralis, Goliathus goliathus. c, Cleridae. d, Ips typographus, Stictoleptura tripartita.

No. 1540, 650fr — Butterflies: a, Papilio demodocus. b, Phalanta phalantha, Latin name at top center. c, Tarucus thespis. d, Phalanta phalantha, Latin name at left center.

No. 1541, 650fr — Butterflies: a, Tarucus theophrastus, Melanitis leda. b, Catopsilia florella. c, Colotis danae. d, Junonia hierta.

No. 1542, 650fr — Fish: a, Sphyraena barracuda. b, Balistes vetula. c, Pomacanthus imperator. d, Naso elegans.

No. 1543, 650fr — Marine life (Homarus gammarus) and: a, Ostreidae. b, Pecten maximus. c, Tripneustes ventricosus. d, Sepia officinalis.

No. 1544, 650fr — Cacti: a, Opuntia ficus-indica, denomination at UR. b, Opuntia ficus-indica, denomination at LR. c, Brachycereus nesioticus, Rhipsalis baccifera. d, Euphorbia lactea.

No. 1545, 650fr — Orchids: a, Spathoglottis kimballiana and Pierre Marie Auguste Broussonet (1761-1807), naturalist. b, Spathoglottis plicata and Jean-Baptiste de Lamarck (1744-1829), naturalist. c, Eurychone galeandrae and Antoine Gouan (1733-1821), naturalist. d, Eulophia alta and Joseph Pitton de Tournefort (1656-1708), botanist.

No. 1546, 650fr — Minerals: a, Hématite and rutile. b, Limonite, denomination at LL. c, Limonite, denomination at LR. d, Gold.

No. 1547, 650fr — Worldwide Fund for Nature stamps of other countries: a, Botswana #915. b, Niue #730. c, Sierra Leone #588. d, British Antarctic Territory #192.

No. 1548, 2400fr, Two rhinoceroses, diff. No. 1549, 2400fr, Gorilla gorilla and Dian Fossey (1932-85), primatologist. No. 1550, 2400fr, Epomops franqueti. No. 1551, 2400fr, Two male lions. No. 1552, 2400fr, Profelis aurata. No. 1553, 2400fr, Azawakhs. No. 1554, 2400fr, Two elephants, diff. No. 1555, 2400fr, Horse and man. No. 1556, 2400fr, Cephalorhynchus heavisidii. No. 1557, 2400fr, Caperea marginata, Balaenoptera acutorostrata. No. 1558, 2400fr, Aquila nipalensis, Aquila rapax. No. 1559, 2400fr, Poicephalus senegalus, Poicephalus gulielmi. No. 1560, 2400fr, Two Afropavo congensis, diff. No. 1561, 2400fr, Megaceryle maxima, diff. No. 1562, 2400fr, Asio capensis, diff. No. 1563, 2400fr, Strix butleri, Scotopelia peli. No. 1564, 2400fr, Apis mellifera scutellata and Fabre, diff. No. 1565, 2400fr, Phchynoteus, Goliathus goliathus. No. 1566, 2400fr, Belenois aurota and boy with butterfly net. No. 1567, 2400fr, Leptotes pirithous, Eurema hecabe. No. 1568, 2400fr, Ctenochaetus hawaiiensis. No. 1569, 2400fr, Homarus, Venerupis decussata. No. 1570, 2400fr, Opuntia ficus-indica and bat. No. 1571, 2400fr, Eulophia alta and Jean Jules Linden (1817-98), botanist. No. 1572, 2400fr, Quartz and boy. No. 1573, 2400fr, Slovenia #247c.

2011, Dec. 20   Litho.   Perf. 13¼
Sheets of 4, #a-d

| 1522-1547 | A386 | Set of 26 | 275.00 | 275.00 |

Souvenir Sheets

| 1548-1573 | A386 | Set of 26 | 250.00 | 250.00 |

A387

No. 1574, 1000fr — Wedding of Prince William and Catherine Middleton: a, Couple. b, Couple and archbishop. c, Couple, vert.

No. 1575, 1000fr — Princess Diana (1961-97): a, Visiting child in Japanese hospital, 1995. b, Visiting child at Mother Teresa Hospice, 1995. c, Holding Camila Fiocco at Northwick Park Hospital, 1997, vert.

No. 1576, 1000fr — Mohandas K. Gandhi (1869-1948), Indian nationalist: a, Leading march, 1931. b, Addressing crowd in Calcutta, 1919. c, With Sarojini Naidu in Salt March, 1930, vert.

No. 1577, 1000fr — Pope John Paul II (1920-2005), papal arms and: a, African animals. b, Map of Africa. c, Tree, vert.

No. 1578, 1000fr — Yuri Gagarin (1934-68), first man in space, and: a, MiG-15. b, His children, monument to Gagarin in Moscow. c, Vostok 1 lifting off, vert.

No. 1579, 1000fr — Marilyn Monroe (1926-62), actress: a, With camera and flag in background. b, With flag stripes in background. c, With mouth open, vert.

No. 1580, 1000fr — Brigitte Bardot, actress, and scene from: a, Viva Maria!, 1965. b, Don Juan, 1973. c, Shalako, 1968, vert.

No. 1581, 1000fr — Romy Schneider (1938-82), actress, and scene from: a, Max and the Junkmen, 1971. b, 10:30 P.M. Summer, 1966. c, Otley, 1968, vert.

No. 1582, 1000fr — Elvis Presley (1935-77), playing guitar, and: a, Denomination at UL. b, Wife, Priscilla, and daughter, Lisa Marie. c, White star in background, vert.

No. 1583, 1000fr — Composers: a, Felix Mendelssohn (1809-47). b, Johann Sebastian Bach (1685-1750). c, Johannes Brahms (1833-97), vert.

No. 1584, 1000fr — Presidents of France: a, Charles de Gaulle (1890-1970). b, Jacques Chirac and Nicolas Sarkozy. c, Georges Pompidou (1911-74), vert.

No. 1585, 1000fr — Nobel Prize winners: a, Ada Yonath, 2009 Chemistry laureate, and ribosome. b, Andre Geim, 2010 Physics laureate, and graphene lattice. c, Elizabeth Blackburn, 2009 Physiology or Medicine laureate, and telomerase, vert.

No. 1586, 1000fr — Impressionist painters and their paintings: a, View of Pontoise: Quai du Pothuis, by Camille Pissarro (1830-1903). b, Flood at Port Marly, by Alfred Sisley (1839-99). c, The Absinthe Drinker, by Edgar Degas (1834-1917), vert.

No. 1587, 1000fr — Entomologists: a, Andrey Avinoff (1884-1949), and Daphnis nerii. b, Eleanor Anne Ormerod (1828-1901), and Junonia orithya. c, Jean-Henri Fabre (1823-1915), and Graphium agamemnon, vert.

No. 1588, 1000fr — Mycologists: a, William Murrill (1869-1957), and Cantharellus aurantiacus. b, Fred Jay Seaver (1877-1970), and Stropharia viridula. c, Arthur Henry Reginald Buller (1874-1944), and Amanita mappa, vert.

No. 1589, 1000fr — Mineralogists: a, Florence Bascom (1862-1945), and kyanite. b, Otto Wilhelm Herrmann von Abich (1806-86), and abichite. c, Auguste Michel-Lévy (1844-1911), and calcaires, vert.

No. 1590, 1000fr — Sports of 2012 Summer Olympics, London: a, Taekwondo. b, Boxing. c, Archery, vert.

No. 1591, 1000fr — Table tennis players: a, Timo Boll. b, Wang Liqin. c, Liu Shiwen, vert.

No. 1592, 1000fr — World chess champions: a, Paul Morphy (1837-84). b, Mikhail Botvinnik (1911-95). c, Alexander Alekhine (1892-1946), vert.

No. 1593, 1000fr — Scouts: a, Five Boy Scouts. b, Boy Scout bugler, Boy Scout with pigeons. c, Boy Scouts adjusting tent, Olave Baden-Powell (1889-1977), vert.

No. 1594, 1000fr — Survivors of the sinking of the Titanic: a, Eva Hart (1905-96). b, Dorothy Gibson (1889-1946). c, Ruth Elizabeth Becker (1899-1990), vert.

No. 1595, 1000fr — New Year 2012 (Year of the Dragon): a, Dragon, denomination at UL. b, Dragon, denomination at UR. c, Dragon, vert.

No. 1596, 1000fr — Indonesia 2012 Intl. Philatelic Exhibition emblem and: a, Rinjani Volcano, Panthera tigris sumatrae. b, Ijen volcanic crater, Pongo abelii, vert. c, Krakatoa Volcano, Elephas maximus borneensis, vert.

No. 1597, 2700fr, Prince William and Catherine Middleton, diff. No. 1598, 2700fr, Princess Diana with child at Hindu temple, London. No. 1599, 2700fr, Gandhi and young girl. No. 1600, 2700fr, Pope John Paul II kissing ground at Bangui Airport. No. 1601, 2700fr, Gagarin and Vostok 1 lifting off, diff. No. 1602, 2700fr, Monroe, diff. No. 1603, 2700fr, Bardot, diff. No. 1604, 2700fr, Schneider, scene from Adorable Sinner, 1959. No. 1605, 2700fr, Presley, diff. No. 1606, 2700fr, Wolfgang Amadeus Mozart (1756-91), composer. No. 1607, 2700fr, French President Nicolas Sarkozy, U.S. President Barack Obama. No. 1608, 2700fr, Robert G. Edwards, 2010 Physiology and Medicine Nobel laureate and in-vitro fertilization. No. 1609, 2700fr, Impression, Soleil Levant, by Clause Monet (1840-1926). No. 1610, 2700fr, Evelyn Cheesman (1881-1969), entomologist and Phalacrognathus muelleri. No. 1611, 2700fr, Elsie Maud Wakefield (1886-1972), mycologist, and Lactaria vellerea. No. 1612, 2700fr, Ignacy Domeyko (1802-89), mineralogist, and domeykite. No. 1613, 2700fr, Dressage. No. 1614, 2700fr, Table tennis player Ding Ning. No. 1615, 2700fr, World chess champion Anatoly Karpov. No. 1616, 2700fr, Boy Scouts and Lord Robert Baden-Powell (1857-1941). No. 1617, 2700fr, Lolo and Edmond Navratil, survivors of sinking of the Titanic. No. 1618, 2700fr, Dragon, diff. No. 1619, 2700fr, Indonesia 2012 Intl. Philatelic Exhibition emblem and Varanus komodoensis, vert.

2011, Dec. 27   Litho.   Perf. 13¼
Sheets of 3, #a-c

| 1574-1596 | A387 | Set of 23 | 275.00 | 275.00 |

Souvenir Sheets

| 1597-1619 | A387 | Set of 23 | 250.00 | 250.00 |

A388

A389

Art — A390

No. 1620, 400fr — Inscriptions: a, Adam et Eve. b, Marie-Madeleine Pénitente. c, La Vierge à L'Enfant.

No. 1621, 400fr — Inscriptions: a, Venus en Devant le Miroir. b, La Flore. c, Le Suicide de Lucrèce.

No. 1622, 400fr — Inscriptions: a, Noli Me Tangere. b, Mater Dolorosa. c, Marei avec L'Enfant et des Saintes.

No. 1623, 400fr, horiz. — Inscriptions: a, La Venus d'Urbino (woman in background). b, La Venus d'Urbino (no woman in background). c, Danaé avec Nourrice.

No. 1624, 3200fr, Like #1620a. No. 1625, 3200fr, Like #1620b. No. 1626, 3200fr, Like #1620c. No. 1627, 3200fr, Like #1621a. No. 1628, 3200fr, Like #1621b. No. 1629, 3200fr, Like #1621c. No. 1630, 3200fr, Like #1622a. No. 1631, 3200fr, Like #1622b. No. 1632, 3200fr, Like #1622c, horiz. No. 1633, 3200fr, Like #1623a (image flipped). No. 1634, 3200fr, Like #1623b. No. 1635, 3200fr, Like #1623c.

No. 1636, 4000fr, Venus et Adonis.

No. 1637, 400fr — Inscriptions: a, La Toilette de Venus. b, Hercuse et Omfala. c, Marquise de Pompadour.

No. 1638, 400fr — Inscriptions: a, Venus Consoler Amour. b, Jeune Femme avec un Bouquet de Roses. c, Venus Fin Cupidon.

No. 1639, 400fr — Inscriptions: a, Portrait d'une Femme. b, Putti avec des Oiseaux. c, Diana au Bain.

No. 1640, 400fr, horiz. — Inscriptions: a, Portrait de Marie-Louise O'Murphy. b, L'Odalisque. c, Léda et la Cygne.

No. 1641, 3200fr, Like #1637a. No. 1642, 3200fr, Like #1637b. No. 1643, 3200fr, Like #1637c. No. 1644, 3200fr, Like #1638a. No. 1645, 3200fr, Like #1638b. No. 1646, 3200fr, Like #1638c. No. 1647, 3200fr, Like #1639a. No. 1648, 3200fr, Like #1639b. No. 1649, 3200fr, Like #1639c, horiz. No. 1650, 3200fr, Like #1640a. No. 1651, 3200fr, Like #1640b. No. 1652, 3200fr, Like #1640c.

No. 1653, 4000fr, Renaud et Armide.

No. 1654, 400fr — Inscriptions: a, Portrait de Victor Jaquemont. b, Déjeuner sur l'Herbe de l'Etude. c, Peupliers le Long du Fleuve Epte.

No. 1655, 400fr — Inscriptions: a, Camille avec un Petit Chien. b, Camille Monet en Costume Japonais. c, Femme à l'Ombrelle.

No. 1656, 400fr — Inscriptions: a, Femme à l'Ombrelle Tournée vers la Droite. b, Poly, Pêcheur de Belle-Ile. c, Le Déjeuner.

No. 1657, 400fr, horiz. — Inscriptions: a, Le Pont sur la Seine. b, Le Pont, D'Amsterdam. c, Chambres du Parlement, Coucher de Soleil.

No. 1658, 3200fr, Like #1654a. No. 1659, 3200fr, Like #1654b. No. 1660, 3200fr, Like #1654c. No. 1661, 3200fr, Like #1655a. No. 1662, 3200fr, Like #1655b. No. 1663, 3200fr, Like #1655c. No. 1664, 3200fr, Like #1656a. No. 1665, 3200fr, Like #1656b. No. 1666, 3200fr, Like #1656c. No. 1667, 3200fr, Like #1657a. No. 1668, 3200fr, Like #1657b. No. 1669, 3200fr, Like #1657c.

No. 1670, 4000fr, Camille Monet et un Enfant dans le Jardin de l'Artiste à Argenteuil.

No. 1671, 400fr — Inscriptions: a, Sainte-Anne avec la Vierge et l'Enfant. b, Portrait d'une Jeune Femme Vénitienne. c, Christ comme l'Homme des Douleurs. d, Portrait de Maximilien I. e, Portrait d'Elsbeth Tucher. f, Portrait de Oswolt Krel.

No. 1672, 400fr — Inscriptions: a, Madone et l'Enfant. b, Adam et Eve. c, Lamentations sur le Christ Mort. d, Vierge et l'Enfant avant d'une Arcade. e, Le Vol à Destination de l'Egypte Résineux. f, Jérôme Pénitent.

No. 1673, 3200fr, Like #1671a. No. 1674, 3200fr, Like #1671b. No. 1675, 3200fr, Like #1671c. No. 1676, 3200fr, Like #1671d. No. 1677, 3200fr, Like #1671e. No. 1678, 3200fr, Like #1671f. No. 1679, 3200fr, Like #1672a. No. 1680, 3200fr, Like #1672b. No. 1681, 3200fr, Like #1672c. No. 1682, 3200fr, Like #1672e. No. 1683, 3200fr, Like #1672e. No. 1684, 3200fr, Like #1672f.

No. 1685, 4000fr, Bacchanales avec Silene.

No. 1686, 400fr — Inscriptions: a, David (statue). b, La Pietà (statue). c, Jugement Dernier Christ Juge. d, Le Prophète Zacharie. e, Le Prophète Jérémie. f, La Sibylle de Cumes.

No. 1687, 400fr — Inscriptions: a, Le Prophète Joel. b, Le Prophète Jessaja. c, Le Prophète Ezéchiel. d, La Sibylle d'Erythrée. e, La Sibylle de Delphes. f, La Sibylle de Libye.

No. 1688, 3200fr, Like #1686a. No. 1689, 3200fr, Like #1686b. No. 1690, 3200fr, Like #1686c. No. 1691, 3200fr, Like #1686d. No. 1692, 3200fr, Like #1686e. No. 1693, 3200fr, Like #1686f. No. 1694, 3200fr, Like #1687a. No. 1695, 3200fr, Like #1687b. No. 1696,

3200fr, Like #1687c. No. 1697, 3200fr, Like #1687d. No. 1698, 3200fr, Like #1687e. No. 1699, 3200fr, Like #1687f.

No. 1700, 400fr, La Chapelle Sixtine.

No. 1701, 400fr — Inscriptions: a, Le Christ Bénissant. b, La Vierge Colonna. c, Saint-George aux Prises avec les Dragons. d, Madone du Chardonneret. e, La Vierge Garvagh. f, La Madone Sixtine.

No. 1702, 400fr — Inscriptions: a, Saint-Michel. b, Le Portrait d'une Jeune Femme. c, Sainte-Catherine d'Alexandrie. d, Madonna del Baldacchio. e, La Sainte Famille avec les Saints Elizabeth et John. f, La Vierge de la Maison d'Orléans.

No. 1703, 3200fr, Like #1701a. No. 1704, 3200fr, Like #1701b. No. 1705, 3200fr, Like #1701c. No. 1706, 3200fr, Like #1701d. No. 1707, 3200fr, Like #1701e. No. 1708, 3200fr, Like #1701f. No. 1709, 3200fr, Like #1702a. No. 1710, 3200fr, Like #1702b. No. 1711, 3200fr, Like #1702c. No. 1712, 3200fr, Like #1702d. No. 1713, 3200fr, Like #1702e. No. 1714, 3200fr, Like #1702f.

No. 1715, 4000fr, La Dispute du Saint Sacrement.

No. 1716, 400fr — Inscriptions: a, Alexandre et de Roxane. b, Viol des Filles de Leucippe. c, Le Débarquement de Marie de Médicis à Marseille. d, Bethsabée à la Fontaine. e, Persée Libératrice Andromède. f, Diane et ses Nymphes Surpris par les Faunes.

No. 1717, 400fr — Inscriptions: a, L'Union de la Terre et de l'Eau. b, Bacchus. c,Vénus à un Miroir. d, Les Trois Grâces. e, Isabelle, Gouverneur des Pays Bas. f, Erection de la Croix.

No. 1718, 3200fr, Like #1716a. No. 1719, 3200fr, Like #1716b. No. 1720, 3200fr, Like #1716c. No. 1721, 3200fr, Like #1716d. No. 1722, 3200fr, Like #1716e. No. 1723, 3200fr, Like #1716f. No. 1724, 3200fr, Like #1717a. No. 1725, 3200fr, Like #1717b. No. 1726, 3200fr, Like #1717c. No. 1727, 3200fr, Like #1717d. No. 1728, 3200fr, Like #1717e. No. 1729, 3200fr, Like #1717f.

No. 1730, 4000fr, Ixion.

No. 1731, 400fr — Inscriptions: a, Philadelphie et Elisabeth Cary. b, Marchesa Durazzo. c, Saint-Pierre. d, Susanna & Aînés. e, Saint Jean le Baptiste dans le Desert. f, St. Rosalie Intercédant pour les Pestiférés de Palerme.

No. 1732, 400fr — Inscriptions: a, Charles Ier de Chasse. b, Golgotha. c, Silène Ivre. d, L'Homme en Armure avec Foulard Rouge. e, Portrait de Famille. f, Tête d'une Jeune Femme.

No. 1733, 3200fr, Like #1731a. No. 1734, 3200fr, Like #1731b. No. 1735, 3200fr, Like #1731c. No. 1736, 3200fr, Like #1731d. No. 1737, 3200fr, Like #1731e. No. 1738, 3200fr, Like #1731f. No. 1739, 3200fr, Like #1732a. No. 1740, 3200fr, Like #1732b. No. 1741, 3200fr, Like #1732c. No. 1742, 3200fr, Like #1732d. No. 1743, 3200fr, Like #1732e. No. 1744, 3200fr, Like #1732f.

No. 1745, 4000fr, Déploration du Christ.

No. 1746, 400fr — Inscriptions: a, Saskia en Flore. b, Artemis. c, Une Jeune Femme qui Tente sur Boucles d'Oreilles. d, David et Jonathan. e, La Sainte Famille (Jesus in cradle). f, La Sainte Famille (Mary holding Jesus).

No. 1747, 400fr — Inscriptions: a, Abraham le Sacrifice. b, Balaam Ass. c, Tobie Accusant Anna de Voler le Kid. d, La Fête de la Musique. e, Christ dans la Tempête sur le Lac de Galilée. f, Enlèvement de Ganymède.

No. 1748, 3200fr, Like #1746a. No. 1749, 3200fr, Like #1746b. No. 1750, 3200fr, Like #1746c. No. 1751, 3200fr, Like #1746d. No. 1752, 3200fr, Like #1746e. No. 1753, 3200fr, Like #1746f. No. 1754, 3200fr, Like #1747a. No. 1755, 3200fr, Like #1747b. No. 1756, 3200fr, Like #1747c. No. 1757, 3200fr, Like #1747d. No. 1758, 3200fr, Like #1747e. No. 1759, 3200fr, Like #1747f.

No. 1760, 4000fr, La Scène de l'Enfant Prodigue dans la Taverne.

No. 1761, 400fr — Inscriptions: a, Baigneuse Arrangeant ses Cheveux. b, Femme Endormie. c, Baigneuse aux Cheveux Longs. d, La Promenade. e, Une Femme Jouant de la Guitare. f, Femme Arranger ses Cheveux.

No. 1762, 400fr — Inscriptions: a, Femme de Baignade. b, Jeanne Samary. c, Junge Badende. d, La Loge. e, Gabrielle à la Rose. f, Deux Soeurs sur la Terrasse.

No. 1763, 3200fr, Like #1761a. No. 1764, 3200fr, Like #1761b. No. 1765, 3200fr, Like #1761c. No. 1766, 3200fr, Like #1761d. No. 1767, 3200fr, Like #1761e. No. 1768, 3200fr, Like #1761f. No. 1769, 3200fr, Like #1762a. No. 1770, 3200fr, Like #1762b. No. 1771, 3200fr, Like #1762c. No. 1772, 3200fr, Like #1762d. No. 1773, 3200fr, Like #1762e. No. 1774, 3200fr, Like #1762f.

No. 1775, 4000fr, Oarsmen at Chatou.

No. 1776, 400fr — Inscriptions: a, Après le Bain (woman kneeling, striped floral wallpaper in background). b, Les Buveurs d'Absinthe. c, Après le Bain (woman standing with leg lifted). d, La Ballerine. e, Après le Bain (woman kneeling, plain background). f, Petit-Déjeuner Après un Bain.

No. 1777, 400fr — Inscriptions: a, Danseuse Assise. b, Inclinaison Dancer. c, Mademoiselle Malo. d, Femme se Coiffant Devant un Miroir. e, Musiciens de l'Orchestre. f, Six Amis de l'Artiste.

No. 1778, 3200fr, Like #1776a. No. 1779, 3200fr, Like #1776b. No. 1780, 3200fr, Like #1776c. No. 1781, 3200fr, Like #1776d. No. 1782, 3200fr, Like #1776e. No. 1783, 3200fr, Like #1776f. No. 1784, 3200fr, Like #1777a. No. 1785, 3200fr, Like #1777b. No. 1786, 3200fr, Like #1777c. No. 1787, 3200fr, Like #1777d. No. 1788, 3200fr, Like #1777e. No. 1789, 3200fr, Like #1777f.

No. 1790, 4000fr, Filles Spartiates Difficile Garçons.

Illustrations on Nos. 1776a-1776f, 1777a-1777f are flipped in comparison to Nos. 1778-1789.

No. 1791, 400fr — Inscriptions: a, Ange. b, Chef de une Vielle Femme dans un Bonnet Blanc. c, Portrait de Camille Roulin. d, Joseph Etienne Roulin. e, Chef de une Vielle Femme dans un Bonnet Blanc (woman with hand touching her face). f, Le Zouave Assis.

No. 1792, 400fr — Inscriptions: a, Vase avec Douze Tournesols. b, Irisews (Irises). c, Portrait du Père Tanguy. d, Chef de une Paysanne avec un Bonnet de Dentelles Verdatre. e, Van Gogh Chair. f, Berceuse.

No. 1793, 3200fr, Like #1791a. No. 1794, 3200fr, Like #1791b. No. 1795, 3200fr, Like #1791c. No. 1796, 3200fr, Like #1791d. No. 1797, 3200fr, Like #1791e. No. 1798, 3200fr, Like #1791f. No. 1799, 3200fr, Like #1792a. No. 1800, 3200fr, Like #1792b. No. 1801, 3200fr, Like #1792c. No. 1802, 3200fr, Like #1792d. No. 1803, 3200fr, Like #1792e. No. 1804, 3200fr, Like #1792f.

No. 1805, 4000fr, Village de Rue et Escalier avec Chiffres.

No. 1806, 400fr — Inscriptions: a, Nu Assis (blue area at LL). b, Jeanne Hebuterne (head). c, Portrait de Madame Kisling. d, Nu Assis sur un Canapé. e, Portrait de Chaim Soutner. f, Portrait de Celso Lagar.

No. 1807, 400fr — Inscriptions: a, Femme nue. b, Jeanne Hebuterne (seated). c, Nu Assis (seated, dark blue background). d, Nu Assis (seated, blue green background). e, Madame Pompadour. f, Jeune Fille Assise.

No. 1808, 3200fr, Like #1806a. No. 1809, 3200fr, Like #1806b. No. 1810, 3200fr, Like #1806c. No. 1811, 3200fr, Like #1806d. No. 1812, 3200fr, Like #1806e. No. 1813, 3200fr, Like #1806f. No. 1814, 3200fr, Like #1807a. No. 1815, 3200fr, Like #1807b. No. 1816, 3200fr, Like #1807c. No. 1817, 3200fr, Like #1807d. No. 1818, 3200fr, Like #1807e. No. 1819, 3200fr, Like #1807f.

No. 1820, 4000fr, Nu Couché.

No. 1821, 400fr — Inscriptions: a, A. S. Pouchkine. b, Bateau à Voile. c, Mer (Etude). d, Tapez Leandrovoy Tour à Constantinople. e, Navire dans la Mer Orageuse. f, Acropole d'Athènes. g, Portrait de l'Épouse de l'Artiste.

No. 1822, 400fr, horiz. — Inscriptions: a, Brigue "Mercury" Attaque par Deux Navires Turcs. b, L'Arrivée de Flotille Colomb. c, La Bataille dans la Manche Chios. d, Examen de la Flotte de la Mer Noire en 1849. e, Bataille Navale Russo-Turque de Sinop. f, La Bataille de Navarin. g, Bataille près de Sinop.

No. 1823, 400fr, horiz. — Inscriptions: a, Paysage Italien. b, Napoléon. c, La Flotte de la Mer Noire à Feodosiya. d, Vue de Saint-Pétersbourg. e, Vue de Kertch. f, Pêcheurs sur Littoral. g, Pouchkine.

No. 1824, 400fr, horiz — Inscriptions: a, Un Naufrage près du Mont Athos. b, La Tempête. c, Tempête sur la Mer. d, Sur l'Ile de Crète. e, La Neuvième Vague. f, Signal de la Tempête. g, Le Bulow

No. 1825, 4000fr, Tempête.

2011, Dec. 29   Litho.   Perf. 13¾
Works of Titian (Tiziano Vecelli)
Sheets of 3, #a-c, + label
1620-1623 A388   Set of 4   19.50   19.50
Souvenir Sheets
Perf. 13x13¼, 13¼x13
1624-1635 A389   Set of 12   155.00   155.00
1636 A390 4000fr multi   16.00   16.00
Works of François Boucher
Sheets of 3, #a-c, + label
1637-1640 A388   Set of 4   19.50   19.50
Souvenir Sheets
Perf. 13x13¼, 13¼x13
1641-1652 A389   Set of 12   155.00   155.00
1653 A390 4000fr multi   16.00   16.00
Works of Claude Monet
Sheets of 3, #a-c, + label
1654-1657 A388   Set of 4   19.50   19.50
Souvenir Sheets
Perf. 13x13¼, 13¼x13
1658-1669 A389   Set of 12   155.00   155.00
1670 A390 4000fr multi   16.00   16.00
Works of Albrecht Dürer
Sheets of 6, #a-f, + 2 labels
Perf. 13¾
1671-1672 A388   Set of 2   19.50   19.50

Souvenir Sheets
Perf. 13x13¼
1673-1684 A389   Set of 12   155.00   155.00
1685 A390 4000fr multi   16.00   16.00
Works of Michelangelo
Sheets of 6, #a-f, + 2 labels
Perf. 13¾
1686-1687 A388   Set of 2   19.50   19.50
Souvenir Sheets
Perf. 13x13¼
1688-1699 A389   Set of 12   155.00   155.00
1700 A390 4000fr multi   16.00   16.00
Works of Raphael (Raffaello Sanzio)
Sheets of 6, #a-f, + 2 labels
Perf. 13¾
1701-1702 A388   Set of 2   19.50   19.50
Souvenir Sheets
Perf. 13x13¼
1703-1714 A389   Set of 12   155.00   155.00
1715 A390 4000fr multi   16.00   16.00
Works of Peter Paul Rubens
Sheets of 6, #a-f, + 2 labels
Perf. 13¾
1716-1717 A388   Set of 2   19.50   19.50
Souvenir Sheets
Perf. 13x13¼
1718-1729 A389   Set of 12   155.00   155.00
1730 A390 4000fr multi   16.00   16.00
Works of Anthony van Dyck
Sheets of 6, #a-f, + 2 labels
Perf. 13¾
1731-1732 A388   Set of 2   19.50   19.50
Souvenir Sheets
Perf. 13x13¼
1733-1744 A389   Set of 12   155.00   155.00
1745 A390 4000fr multi   16.00   16.00
Works of Rembrandt van Rijn
Sheets of 6, #a-f, + 2 labels
Perf. 13¾
1746-1747 A388   Set of 2   19.50   19.50
Souvenir Sheets
Perf. 13x13¼
1748-1759 A389   Set of 12   155.00   155.00
1760 A390 4000fr multi   16.00   16.00
Works of Pierre-Auguste Renoir
Sheets of 6, #a-f, + 2 labels
Perf. 13¾
1761-1762 A388   Set of 2   19.50   19.50
Souvenir Sheets
Perf. 13x13¼
1763-1774 A389   Set of 12   155.00   155.00
1775 A390 4000fr multi   16.00   16.00
Works of Edgar Degas
Sheets of 6, #a-f, + 2 labels
Perf. 13¾
1776-1777 A388   Set of 2   19.50   19.50
Souvenir Sheets
Perf. 13x13¼
1778-1789 A389   Set of 12   155.00   155.00
1790 A390 4000fr multi   16.00   16.00
Works of Vincent van Gogh
Sheets of 6, #a-f, + 2 labels
Perf. 13¾
1791-1792 A388   Set of 2   19.50   19.50
Souvenir Sheets
Perf. 13x13¼
1793-1804 A389   Set of 12   155.00   155.00
1805 A390 4000fr multi   16.00   16.00
Works of Amedeo Modigliani
Sheets of 6, #a-f, + 2 labels
Perf. 13¾
1806-1807 A388   Set of 2   19.50   19.50
Souvenir Sheets
Perf. 13x13¼
1808-1819 A389   Set of 12   155.00   155.00
1820 A390 4000fr multi   16.00   16.00
Works of Ivan Aivazovsky
Sheets of 7, #a-g, + label
Perf. 13¾
1821-1824 A388   Set of 4   45.00   45.00
Souvenir Sheets
Perf. 13x13¼
1825 A390 4000fr multi   16.00   16.00

SEMI-POSTAL STAMPS

Anti-Malaria Issue
Common Design Type
Perf. 12½x12
1962, Apr. 7   Engr.   Unwmk.
B1 CD108 25fr + 5fr slate   1.40   1.40
WHO drive to eradicate malaria.

Freedom from Hunger Issue
Common Design Type
1963, Mar. 21   Perf. 13
B2 CD112 25fr + 5fr multi   1.25   1.25

Guinea Fowl and Partridge SP1

Designs: 10fr+5fr, Yellow-backed duiker and snail. 20fr+5fr, Elephant, tortoise and hippopotamus playing tug-of-war. 30fr+10fr, Cuckoo and tortoise. 50fr+20fr, Patas monkey and leopard.

1971, Feb. 9   Photo.   Perf. 12½x12
B3 SP1 5fr + 5fr multi   4.50   2.00
B4 SP1 10fr + 5fr multi   5.75   2.50
B5 SP1 20fr + 5fr multi   7.50   2.75
B6 SP1 30fr + 10fr multi   10.00   7.00
B7 SP1 50fr + 20fr multi   16.00   12.00
   Nos. B3-B7 (5)   43.75   26.25

Lengué Dancer — SP2

Dancers: 40fr+10fr, Le Lengué. 100fr+40fr, Teke. 140fr+40fr, Englabolo.

1971   Litho.   Perf. 13
B8 SP2 20fr + 5fr multi   .65   .25
B9 SP2 40fr + 10fr multi   1.10   .40
B10 SP2 100fr + 40fr multi   2.50   1.25
B11 SP2 140fr + 40fr multi   3.25   1.50
   Nos. B8-B11 (4)   7.50   3.40

AIR POST STAMPS

Abyssinian Roller — AP1

Birds: 200fr, Gold Coast touraco. 500fr, African fish eagle.

Unwmk.
1960, Sept. 3   Engr.   Perf. 13
C1 AP1 100fr vio bl, org brn & emer   2.50   .70
C2 AP1 200fr multi   4.75   2.00
C3 AP1 500fr Prus bl, emer & red brn   14.75   4.75
   Nos. C1-C3 (3)   22.00   7.45

**French Equatorial Africa No. C37
Surcharged in Red**

1960, Dec. 15   *Perf. 13*
C4 AP8 250fr on 500fr grnsh
        blk, blk & slate   9.00 8.25
17th Olympic Games, Rome, 8/25-9/11.

Air Afrique Issue
Common Design Type
1962, Feb. 17 Unwmk. Perf. 13
C5 CD107 50fr vio, lt grn & red
        brn   1.00 .55
Founding of Air Afrique airline.

Pole
Vault — AP1a

1962, July 21 Photo. Perf. 12x12½
C6 AP1a 100fr grn, yel, brn &
        blk   2.25 1.50
Abidjan games.

Red-faced Lovebirds — AP2

1962-63 Engr. Perf. 13
C7 AP2 50fr Great blue touraco 2.25 .55
C8 AP2 250fr shown ('63)   7.00 2.50
Issued: 50fr, Nov. 15; 250fr, Mar. 11, 1963.

Runner with
Torch and Palm
Branch — AP3

1962, Dec. 24
C9 AP3 100fr gray grn, brn &
        car   2.25 1.25
Tropics Cup Games, Bangui, Dec. 24-31.

African Postal Union Issue
Common Design Type
1963, Sept. 8 Photo. Perf. 12½
C10 CD114 85fr emer, ocher &
        red   1.90 .85

Sun Shining on Africa — AP4

1963, Nov. 9   *Perf. 13x12*
C11 AP4 25fr bl, yel & vio bl   .75 .40
Issued for African unity.

Europafrica Issue
Common Design Type
1963, Nov. 30   *Perf. 12x13*
C12 CD116 50fr ultra, yel & dk
        brn   2.50 1.75

Diesel Engine — AP5

Various Locomotives; 25fr, 50fr, vertical.

1963, Dec. 1 Engr. Perf. 13
C13 AP5 20fr brn, cl & dk grn   .70 .70
C14 AP5 25fr brn, bl & choc   .80 .80
C15 AP5 50r brn, red lil &
        vio   2.75 2.75
C16 AP5 100fr brn, grn & dl
        red brn   3.75 3.75
a. Min. sheet of 4, #C13-C16 12.00 12.00
    Nos. C13-C16 (4)   8.00 8.00
Bangui-Douala railroad project.

Bangui Cathedral — AP6

1964, Jan. 21 Unwmk. Perf. 13
C17 AP6 100fr yel grn, org brn &
        bl   1.90 1.00

Radar Tracking Station and WMO
Emblem — AP7

1964, Mar. 23 Engr. Perf. 13
C18 AP7 50fr org brn, bl & pur   1.25 1.25
World Meteorological Day.

Map and
Presidents
of Chad,
Congo,
Gabon and
Central
African
Republic
AP8

1964, June 23 Photo. Perf. 12½
C19 AP8 100fr multi   2.00 .80
5th anniversary of the Conference of Chiefs
of State of Equatorial Africa.

Javelin Throwers — AP9

Designs: 50fr, Basketball game. 100fr,
Four runners. 250fr, Swimmers, one in water.

1964, June 23 Engr. Perf. 13
C20 AP9 25fr grn, dk brn & lt
        vio bl   .55 .30
C21 AP9 50fr blk, car & grn   1.10 .45
C22 AP9 100fr grn, vio bl & dk
        brn   2.50 .95
C23 AP9 250fr grn, blk & car   6.75 2.50
a. Min. sheet of 4, #C20-C23 18.00 18.00
    Nos. C20-C23 (4)   10.90 4.20
18th Olympic Games, Tokyo, 10/10-25/64.

John F.
Kennedy — AP10

1964, July 4 Photo. Perf. 12½
C24 AP10 100fr lil, brn & blk   2.50 1.50
a. Min. sheet of 4   10.00 10.00

Industrial Symbols, Maps of Africa and
Europe — AP11

1964, Dec. 19 Unwmk. Perf. 13x12
C25 AP11 50fr yel, org & grn   1.50 .85
See note after Cameroun No. 402.

International Cooperation Year
Emblem — AP12

1965, Jan. 2   *Perf. 13*
C26 AP12 100fr red brn, yel & bl 1.75 .75
International Cooperation Year.

Nimbus Weather Satellite — AP13

1965, Mar. 23 Engr. Perf. 13
C27 AP13 100fr org brn, ultra &
        blk   1.90 .80
Fifth World Meteorological Day.

Lincoln and Statue of Liberty — AP14

1965, Apr. 15 Photo. Perf. 13
C28 AP14 100fr bluish grn, ind &
        bis   1.75 .75
Centenary of death of Abraham Lincoln.

ITU Emblem and Relay
Satellite — AP15

1965, May 17 Engr. Perf. 13
C29 AP15 100fr dk grn vio bl &
        brn   1.90 1.10
Centenary of the ITU.

"Housing," New Home in
Village — AP16

1965, June 10   *Unwmk.*
C30 AP16 100fr ultra, brn & sl grn 1.10 .65
See note after No. 52.

Europafrica Issue

Tractor, Cotton
Picker, Cotton,
Sun and
Emblem — AP17

1965, Nov. 7 Photo. Perf. 12x13
C31 AP17 50fr multi   .90 .65
See note after Chad No. C11.

Mercury by
Antoine
Coysevox
AP18

1965, Dec. 5 Engr. Perf. 13
C32 AP18 100fr red brn, bl & blk 2.75 1.10
5th anniv. of Central African Republic's
admission to the UPU.

Father Holding Sick Child — AP19

Design: 100fr, Mother and child.

1965, Dec. 12
C33 AP19 50fr dk bl, car & blk 1.25 .45
C34 AP19 100fr red brn, red & brt grn 2.75 1.10

Issued to honor the Red Cross.

Air Afrique Issue
Common Design Type
1966, Aug. 31   Photo.   Perf. 13
C35 CD123 25fr bl, blk & lem 1.00 .40

For surcharge see No. C43.

Surveyor Spacecraft on Moon — AP20

Designs: No. C37, Luna 9 on Moon and Earth. 200fr, Rocket take-off, Jules Verne's "From the Earth to the Moon."

1966, Oct. 24   Photo.   Perf. 12x12½
C36 AP20 130fr multi 1.60 .95
C37 AP20 130fr multi 1.60 .95
C38 AP20 200fr multi 3.00 1.75
a.   Souv. sheet of 3, #C36-C38 9.00 9.00
    Nos. C36-C38 (3) 6.20 3.65

Conquest of the Moon.
For surcharges see Nos. C58, C61.

Eugene A. Cernan, Gemini 9 and Agena Rocket — AP21

No. C40, Pavel R. Popovich and rocket.

1966, Nov. 14   Photo.   Perf. 13
C39 AP21 50fr multi 1.10 .50
C40 AP21 50fr multi 1.10 .50

American and Russian astronauts.

Diamant Rocket, D-1 Satellite and Globe with Map of Africa — AP22

1966, Nov. 14   Engr.
C41 AP22 100fr brt rose lil & brn 1.75 .85

Issued to commemorate the launching of France's first satellite, Nov. 26, 1965, and the launching of the D-1 satellite, Feb. 17, 1966.

Exchange of Agricultural and Industrial Products between Africa and Europe — AP23

1966, Dec. 5   Photo.   Perf. 12x13
C42 AP23 50fr multi 1.25 .85

See note after Gabon No. C46.

No. C35 Surcharged

1967, May 8   Perf. 13
C43 CD123 5fr on 25fr multi .55 .30

The surcharge obliterates the "2" of the original 25fr denomination.

DC-8F Over M'Poko Airport, Bangui — AP24

1967, July 3   Engr.   Perf. 13
C44 AP24 100fr sl, dk grn & brn 2.50 1.00

View of EXPO '67, Montreal — AP25

1967, July 17
C45 AP25 100fr vio bl, dk red brn & dk grn 2.25 .80

International Exposition. EXPO '67, Montreal, Apr. 28-Oct. 27.

African Postal Union Issue, 1967
Common Design Type
1967, Sept. 9   Engr.   Perf. 13
C46 CD124 100fr brt grn, dk car rose & plum 2.25 .85
    Nos. C46 (1) 2.25 .85

Potez 25 TOE — AP26

1967, Nov. 24   Engr.   Perf. 13
C47 AP26 100fr shown 2.50 .80
C48 AP26 200fr Junkers 52 5.50 1.75
C49 AP26 500fr Caravelle 11R 14.00 4.25
    Nos. C47-C49 (3) 22.00 6.80

For surcharges see Nos. C59-C60.

Presidents Boganda and Bokassa — AP27

1967, Dec. 1   Photo.   Perf. 12½
C50 AP27 130fr org, red, lt bl & blk 2.00 1.00

9th anniversary of the republic.

Pres. Jean Bedel Bokassa AP28

1968, Jan. 1   Perf. 12½x12
C51 AP28 30fr multi .80 .40

Human Rights Flame, Men and Globe — AP29

1968, Mar. 26   Photo.   Perf. 13
C52 AP29 200fr brt grn, vio & ver 3.50 1.40

International Human Rights Year.

Man, WHO Emblem and Tsetse Fly — AP30

1968, Apr. 8   Engr.
C53 AP30 200fr multi 4.00 2.00

20th anniv. of WHO.

Javelin Thrower — AP31

1968, Apr. 16   Engr.   Perf. 13
C54 AP31 200fr shown 4.50 3.00
C55 AP31 200fr Downhill skier 4.50 3.00

The 1968 Olympic Games.

Space Probe Landing on Venus — AP32

1968, Apr. 23
C56 AP32 100fr ultra, dk & brt grn 1.75 .95

Venus exploration by Venera 4, 10/18/67.

Marie Curie and "Cancer Destroyed" — AP33

1968, Apr. 30
C57 AP33 100fr vio, brt bl & brn 2.75 1.10

Marie Curie (1867-1934), scientist.

Nos. C36-C37 and C47-C48 Surcharged with New Value
Photogravure; Engraved
1968, Sept. 16   Perf. 12x12½, 13
C58 AP20 5fr on 130fr multi .25 .25
C59 AP26 10fr on 100fr multi .30 .25
C60 AP26 20fr on 200fr multi .50 .30
C61 AP20 50fr on 130fr multi 1.10 .55
    Nos. C58-C61 (4) 2.15 1.35

On No. C58 the old denomination has been obliterated with "XIX," on No. C61 the obliteration is a rectangular bar. On Nos. C59-C60 the last zero of the old denomination has been obliterated with a black square.

River Boat Type of Regular Issue
Craft: 100fr, "Pie X," Bangui, 1894. 130fr, "Ballay," Bangui, 1891.

1968, Dec. 10   Engr.   Perf. 13
Size: 48x27mm
C62 A37 100fr bl, dk brn & ol 2.50 1.00
C63 A37 130fr brt pink, sl grn & slate 3.00 1.25

PHILEXAFRIQUE Issue

Mme. de Sévigné, French School, 17th Century AP34

1968, Dec. 17   Photo.   Perf. 12½
C64 AP34 100fr brn & multi 3.00 2.25

Issued to publicize PHILEXAFRIQUE, Philatelic Exhibition in Abidjan, Feb. 14-23. Printed with alternating brown label.

2nd PHILEXAFRIQUE Issue
Common Design Type
Design: 50fr, Ubangi-Shari No. J16, cotton field and Pres. Bokassa.

1969, Feb. 14   Engr.   Perf. 13
C65 CD128 50fr bis brn, blk & dk grn 1.90 1.90

Holocerina Angulata Aur. — AP35

Butterflies and Moths: 20fr, Nudaurelia dione fabr. 30fr, Eustera troglophylla hamp., vert. 50fr, Aurivillius aratus west. 100fr, Epiphora albida druce.

1969, Feb. 25   **Photo.**
C66 AP35 10fr yel & multi   1.10 .35
C67 AP35 20fr vio & multi   1.60 .55
C68 AP35 30fr multi   3.75 1.00
C69 AP35 50fr multi   5.25 2.25
C70 AP35 100fr multi   9.00 3.25
   Nos. C66-C70 (5)   20.70 7.40

Boxing — AP36

1969, Mar. 18   **Photo.**   **Perf. 13**
C71 AP36 50fr shown   1.10 .30
C72 AP36 100fr Basketball   2.25 .60

Apollo 8 over Moonscape — AP37

1969, May 27   **Photo.**   **Perf. 13**
C73 AP37 200fr dp bl, gray & yel   3.50 1.75
   US Apollo 8 mission, the 1st men in orbit around the moon, Dec. 21-27, 1968.
   For overprint see No. C81.

Market Cross, Nuremberg, and Toys — AP38

1969, June 3
C74 AP38 100fr blk, brt rose lil & emer   2.25 .95
   Intl. Toy Fair in Nuremberg, Germany.

Napoleon as First Consul, by Anne-Louis Girodet-Trioson — AP39

Designs: 130fr, Napoleon meeting Emperor Francis II, by Antoine Jean Gros, horiz. 200fr, The Wedding of Napoleon and Marie-Louise, by Georges Rouget, horiz.

1969, Nov. 4   **Photo.**   **Perf. 12½**
C75 AP39 100fr multi   2.25 1.25
C76 AP39 130fr brn & multi   3.25 1.50
C77 AP39 200fr multi   5.50 2.75
   Nos. C75-C77 (3)   11.00 5.50
   Napoleon Bonaparte (1769-1821).

Pres. Bokassa, Map of Africa and Flag — AP40

1970, Jan. 1   **Die-cut; Perf. 10½**
Embossed on Gold Foil
C78 AP40 2000fr gold   40.00 40.00

Franklin Delano Roosevelt — AP41

1970   **Litho.**   **Perf. 13½x14**
C79 AP41 100fr shown   2.00 1.00
C80 AP41 100fr Lenin   3.00 1.25
   Roosevelt, 25th death anniv., Lenin, birth cent.
   Issue dates: No. C79, Apr. 29; No. C80. Apr. 22.

No. C73 Overprinted in Red

1970, June 1   **Photo.**   **Perf. 13**
C81 AP37 200fr multi   15.00 9.00
   Moon landing mission of Apollo 12, 11/14-24/69.

AP42

1970, Sept. 15   **Litho.**   **Perf. 10**
C82 AP42   Pair + label   4.50 3.00
   a.   100fr Dancer   1.90 .55
   b.   100fr Still life   1.90 .55
   Knokphila 70, 6th Intl. Phil. Exhib. at Knokke, Belgium, July 4-10. Imperf. between stamps and label.

Sericulture Type of Regular Issue
1970, Sept. 15   **Perf. 10**
C83 A45 140fr multi   4.50 1.10

C.A.R. Flag, EXPO Emblem and Pavilion AP43

1970, Dec. 18   **Litho.**   **Perf. 13½x13**
C84 AP43 200fr red & multi   3.50 1.50
   Intl. Exposition EXPO '70, Osaka, Japan.

Soccer — AP44

1970, Dec. 8   **Perf. 13x13½**
C85 AP44 200fr multi   3.50 1.50
   World Soccer Championships, Mexico, May 30-June 21, 1970.

Dove — AP45

1970, Dec. 31
C86 AP45 200fr bl, yel & blk   3.50 1.50
   25th anniversary of the United Nations.

Presidents Mobutu, Bokassa, and Tombalbaye — AP46

1971, Jan. 10
C87 AP46 140fr multi   3.00 1.00
   Return of Central African Republic to the United States of Central Africa which also includes Congo Democratic Republic and Chad.

Satellite over Globe — AP47

1971, May 17   **Photo.**   **Perf. 12½**
C88 AP47 100fr multi   2.25 .85
   3rd World Telecommunications Day.

African Postal Union Issue, 1971
Common Design Type
   Design: 100fr, Carved head and UAMPT building, Brazzaville, Congo.

1971, Nov. 13   **Photo.**   **Perf. 13x13½**
C89 CD135 100fr bl & multi   2.25 .85

Child and Education Year Emblem — AP48

1971, Nov. 11   **Litho.**   **Perf. 13x13½**
C90 AP48 140fr multi   2.25 .80
   25th anniv. of UNESCO.

Fight Against Cancer — AP49

1971, Nov. 20   **Photo.**   **Perf. 12½**
C91 AP49 100fr grn & multi   2.75 1.10

Gamal Abdel Nasser — AP50

1972, Jan. 15
C92 AP50 100fr dk red, blk & bister   2.50 .85
   In memory of Gamal Abdel Nasser (1918-1970), president of Egypt.

Olympic Rings and Boxing — AP51

No. C94, Track and Olympic rings, vert.

1972, May 26   **Engr.**   **Perf. 13**
C93 AP51 100fr brn org & sepia   1.75 .80
C94 AP51 100fr green & violet   1.75 1.10
   a.   Miniature sheet of 2   5.00 5.00
   20th Olympic Games, Munich, Aug. 26-Sept. 10. No. C94a contains 2 stamps similar to Nos. C93-C94, but in changed colors. The boxing stamp is red lilac and green, the track stamp ocher and red lilac.
   For overprints see Nos. C100-C101.

Tiling's Mail Rocket, 1931, and
Mailman — AP52

Designs: 50fr, DC-3 and mailman riding
camel, vert. 150fr, Sirio satellite and rocket,
vert. 200fr, Intelsat 4 and rocket.

1972, Aug. 12
C95 AP52 40fr bl, org & indigo .65 .45
C96 AP52 50fr bl, brn & org .90 .55
C97 AP52 150fr brn, org & gray 2.50 1.25
C98 AP52 200fr brn, bl & org 3.50 2.25
a. Souv. sheet of 4, #C95-C98 9.25 9.25
Nos. C95-C98 (4) 7.55 4.50
Centraphilex 1972, Central African Philatelic
Exhibition, Bangui.

Europafrica Issue

Arrows with
Symbols of
Agriculture and
Industry — AP53

1972, Nov. 17 Litho. Perf. 13
C99 AP53 100fr multi 1.75 .80

Nos. C93-C94, C94a Overprinted

(a)

(b)

1972, Nov. 24 Engr.
C100 AP51 (a) 100fr 1.75 .95
C101 AP51 (b) 100fr 1.75 .95
a. Miniature sheet of 2 3.75 3.75
Gold Medal Winners in 20th Olympic
Games: Viatscheslav Lemechev, USSR, mid-
dleweight boxing; Randy Williams, US, broad
jump.

Lunar Rover and Module — AP54

1972, Dec. 18 Engr. Perf. 13
C102 AP54 100fr slate grn, bl &
gray 1.75 .80
Apollo 16 US moon mission, 4/15-27/72.

Virgin and
Child, by
Francesco
Pesellino
AP55

Christmas: 150fr, Adoration of the Child
with St. John the Baptist and St. Romuald, by
Fra Filippo Lippi.

1972, Dec. 25 Photo.
C103 AP55 100fr gold & multi 1.60 .85
C104 AP55 150fr gold & multi 2.75 1.25

Parthenon, Athens, Spyridon Louis,
Marathon, 1896 — AP56

Olympic Rings and: 40fr, Arc de Triomphe,
Paris, H. Barrelet, single scull, 1900. 50fr, Old
Courthouse and Western Arch, St. Louis,
Myer Prinstein, triple jump, 1904. 100fr, Tower,
London, Henry Taylor, swimming, 1908. 150fr,
City Hall, Stockholm, Greco-Roman wrestling,
1912.

1972, Dec. 28 Engr.
C105 AP56 30fr brt grn, mag &
brn .40 .25
C106 AP56 40fr vio bl, emer &
brn .50 .25
C107 AP56 50fr car rose, vio bl
& Prus bl .55 .40
C108 AP56 100fr sl, red lil & brn 1.10 .45
C109 AP56 150fr red lil, blk &
Prus bl 1.75 1.10
Nos. C105-C109 (5) 4.30 2.45
Olympic Games 1896-1912.

WHO Emblem, Surgeon and
Nurse — AP57

1973, Apr. 7 Photo. Perf. 13
C110 AP57 100fr multi 1.50 .75
WHO, 25th anniv.

World Map,
Arrows,
Waves — AP58

1973, May 17 Litho. Perf. 12½
C111 AP58 200fr multicolored 2.50 1.00
5th International Telecommunications Day.

AP58a

Head and City Hall, Brussels.

1973, Sept. 17 Engr. Perf. 13
C112 AP58a 100fr pur, ocher &
brn 1.40 .70
African Weeks, Brussels, Sept. 15-30, 1973.

Europafrica Issue

Map of Central African Republic with
Industry and Agriculture, Young
Man — AP59

1973, Sept. 28 Engr. Perf. 13
C113 AP59 100fr sepia, grn & org 1.75 .80

Carrier Pigeon with Letter and UPU
Emblem — AP60

1973, Oct. 9 Photo.
C114 AP60 200fr multi 2.50 1.10
Universal Postal Union Day.

WMO Emblem, Weather Map — AP61

1973, Oct. 20 Engr. Perf. 13
C115 AP61 150fr brt ultra & sl
grn 2.75 1.00
Cent. of intl. meteorological cooperation.

Copernicus, Heliocentric
System — AP62

1973, Nov. 2 Photo.
C116 AP62 100fr gold & multi 3.00 1.75
Copernicus (1473-1543), Polish astronomer.

Pres.
Bokassa
AP63

Pres.
Bokassa — AP64

1973, Nov. 30 Photo. Perf. 12½
C117 AP63 50fr multi .75 .40
C118 AP64 100fr multi 1.40 .70

Rocket Launch
and Apollo 17
Badge — AP65

65fr, Capsule over moonscape, horiz.
100fr, Moon landing, horiz. 150fr, Astronauts
on moon. 200fr, Splashdown with parachutes
and badge.

1973, Dec. 15 Engr. Perf. 13
C119 AP65 50fr ver, gray grn &
brn .55 .30
C120 AP65 65fr dk brn, brn red
& sl grn .75 .40
C121 AP65 100fr ver, slate &
choc 1.25 .60
C122 AP65 150fr brn, ol & sl grn 1.90 .80
C123 AP65 200fr red, bl & sl grn 2.25 1.10
Nos. C119-C123 (5) 6.70 3.20
Apollo 17 US moon mission, 12/7-19/72.

St.
Teresa — AP66

1973, Dec. 25
C124 AP66 500fr vio bl & grnsh
bl 6.75 3.50
St. Teresa of the Infant Jesus, the Little
Flower (1873-1897), Carmelite nun.

UPU Emblem,
Letter — AP67

1974, Oct. 9   Engr.   Perf. 13
C125 AP67 500fr multi   7.50 4.00
  Centenary of Universal Postal Union.
For surcharge see No. C159.

Presidents and Flags of Cameroun,
CAR, Gabon and Congo — AP68

1974, Dec. 8   Photo.   Perf. 13
C126 AP68 100fr gold & multi   1.40 .80
  See note after Cameroun No. 595.
For surcharge see No. C155.

Marshal
Bokassa
AP69

100fr, Bokassa in Marshal's uniform with
cape.

1975, Feb. 22   Photo.   Perf. 13
C127 AP69 50fr & multi   .65 .40
C128 AP69 100fr tan & multi   1.40 .45
  Jean Bedel Bokassa, President for Life and
Marshal of the Republic.

Mask, Map of
Africa, Arphila
Emblem — AP70

1975, Aug. 25   Engr.   Perf. 13
C129 AP70 100fr brt bl, red brn &
        red   1.40 .60
  ARPHILA 75 International Philatelic Exhibi-
tion, Paris, June 6-16.
For surcharge see No. C156.

Albert Schweitzer
and Dugout,
Lambarene
AP71

1975, Sept. 30   Engr.   Perf. 13
C130 AP71 200fr blk, ultra & ol   5.00 2.00
  Dr. Albert Schweitzer (1875-1965), medical
missionary and musician.
For surcharge see No. C158.

Pres. Bokassa's Houseboat,
Bow — AP72

40fr, Pres. Bokassa's houseboat, stern.

1976, Feb. 22   Litho.   Perf. 13
C131 AP72 30fr multi   .65 .30
C132 AP72 40fr multi   .85 .45

Monument
to Franco-
CAR
Cooperation
AP73

Presidents
and Flags
of France
and CAR
AP74

1976, Mar. 5
C133 AP73 100fr multi   1.40 .80
C134 AP74 200fr multi   2.50 1.25
  Official visit of Pres. Valery Giscard
d'Estaing to Central African Republic, 3/5-8.
For surcharge see No. C157.

Apollo Soyuz Type, 1976

Designs: 100fr, Soyuz space ship. 200fr,
Apollo space ship. 300fr, Astronauts and cosmonauts in cabin. 500fr, Apollo and Soyuz
after link-up.

1976, June 14   Litho.   Perf. 14x13½
C135 A90 100fr multi   .90 .25
C136 A90 200fr multi   1.60 .55
C137 A90 300fr multi   2.60 .95
    Nos. C135-C137 (3)   6.45 1.75
Souvenir Sheet
C138 A90 500fr multi   5.00 1.75
  For surcharges see Nos. C161, C168,
C173, C177.

French
Hussar
AP75

Uniforms: 125fr, Scottish "Black Watch."
150fr, German dragoon. 200fr, British grenadier. 250fr, American ranger. 450fr, American
dragoon.

1976, July 4   Perf. 13½
C139 AP75 100fr multi   .90 .30
C140 AP75 125fr multi   1.00 .45
C141 AP75 150fr multi   1.25 .45
C142 AP75 200fr multi   1.90 .55
C143 AP75 250fr multi   2.50 .95
    Nos. C139-C143 (5)   7.55 2.70
Souvenir Sheet
C144 AP75 450fr multi   7.50 2.00
  American Bicentennial.
For surcharges see Nos. C162, C166-C167,
C169, C172, C176.

Acherontia Atropos — AP76

100fr, Papilio nireus & niocha marnois.

1976, Sept. 20   Litho.   Perf. 12½
C145 AP76 50fr multi   9.00 1.50
C146 AP76 100fr multi   18.00 2.00
  For surcharges see Nos. C160, C163.

Olympic Winners Type, 1976

Designs: 100fr, Women's figure skating,
Dorothy Hamill, vert. 200fr, Ice skating, Alexander Gorshkov and Ludmilla Pakhomova.
300fr, Men's figure skating, John Curry, vert.
500fr, Downhill skiing, Rosi Mittermaier, vert.

1976, Sept. 23   Litho.   Perf. 13½
C147 A92 100fr multi   .75 .30
C148 A92 200fr multi   2.40 .60
C149 A92 300fr multi   3.25 1.00
    Nos. C147-C149 (3)   6.40 1.90
Souvenir Sheet
C150 A92 500fr multi   6.00 1.75
  For surcharges see Nos. C164, C170,
C174, C178.

Viking Mars Type, 1976

Designs: 100fr, Phases of Mars landing.
200fr, Viking descending on Mars, horiz.
300fr, Viking probe. 500fr, Viking flight to
Mars, horiz.

1976, Dec.
C151 A93 100fr multi   1.00 .30
C152 A93 200fr multi   2.40 .60
C153 A93 300fr multi   3.00 .95
    Nos. C151-C153 (3)   6.40 1.85
Souvenir Sheet
C154 A93 500fr multi   5.50 1.75
  For surcharges and overprints see Nos.
C165, C171, C175, C179, C212-C215.

Central African Empire
Stamps of 1973-76 Overprinted in
Black, Violet Blue or Gold

**Printing and Perforations as Before
1977, Mar.**
C155 AP68 100fr (#C126;B)   1.10 1.10
C156 AP70 100fr (#C129;VB)   1.10 1.10
C157 AP73 100fr (#C133;G)   1.10 1.10
C158 AP71 200fr (#C130;B)   3.25 1.50
C159 AP67 500fr (#C125;B)   10.00 10.00
    Nos. C155-C159 (5)   16.55 14.80
  No bar on No. C159.

Stamps of 1976 Overprinted in
Black on Silver Panel

1977, Apr. 1
C160 AP76 50fr (#C145)   .55 .55
C161 A90 100fr (#C135)   1.10 1.10
C162 AP75 100fr (#C139)   1.10 1.10
C163 AP76 100fr (#C146)   1.10 1.10
C164 A92 100fr (#C147)   1.10 1.10
C165 A93 100fr (#C151)   1.10 1.10
C166 AP75 125fr (#C140)   1.40 1.40
C167 AP75 150fr (#C141)   1.60 1.60
C168 A90 200fr (#C136)   2.75 2.75
C169 AP75 200fr (#C142)   2.50 2.50
C170 A92 200fr (#C148)   2.25 2.25
C171 A93 200fr (#C152)   2.25 2.25
C172 AP75 250fr (#C143)   2.75 2.75
C173 A90 300fr (#C137)   3.50 3.50
C174 A92 300fr (#C149)   3.50 3.50
C175 A93 300fr (#C153)   3.50 3.50
    Nos. C160-C175 (16)   32.05 32.05
Souvenir Sheets
C176 AP75 450fr (#C144)   5.50 5.50
C177 A90 500fr (#C138)   8.00 8.00
C178 A92 500fr (#C150)   5.50 5.50
C179 A93 500fr (#C154)   5.50 5.50
  Overprint on type AP75 is in upper and
lower case letters.

Nobel Prize Type, 1977

Designs: 100fr, Rudyard Kipling. 200fr,
Ernest Hemingway. 300fr, Luigi Pirandello.
500fr, Rabindranath Tagore.

1977, Apr. 1   Litho.   Perf. 13½
C180 A94 100fr multi   2.00 .40
C181 A94 200fr multi   4.00 .70
C182 A94 300fr multi   6.25 .95
    Nos. C180-C182 (3)   12.25 2.05
Souvenir Sheet
C183 A94 500fr multi   6.00 1.75

Zeppelin Type of 1977

100fr, Germany #C42 and North Pole.
200fr, Germany #C44 and Science and Industry Building, Chicago. 300fr, Germany #C35
and Brandenburg Gate, Berlin. 500fr, US
#C14 and US Capitol.

1977, Apr. 11   Litho.   Perf. 11
C184 A95 100fr multi   1.40 .30
C185 A95 200fr multi   2.75 .60
C186 A95 300fr multi   3.50 1.00
    Nos. C184-C186 (3)   7.65 1.90
Souvenir Sheet
C187 A95 500fr multi   5.50 2.00
  75th anniversary of Zeppelin.

Bokassa Type of 1977

1977, Dec. 4   Litho.   Perf. 13½
C188 A98 200fr multi   1.90 .80
C189 A98 300fr multi   2.75 1.25
  a. Souvenir sheet, 500fr   6.00 2.50
  Coronation of Emperor Bokassa I, Dec. 4.
No. C189a contains a horizontal stamp in simi-
lar design. A 2500fr gold embossed horizontal
stamp in similar design exists. Value $25.

Vaccination
AP77

1977   Litho.   Perf. 14x13½
C190 AP77 150fr multi   4.00 1.25
  World Health Day.

Communications Type of 1978

Designs: 100fr, Balloon and spaceships docking in space. 200fr, Hydrofoil and Concorde. 500fr, Tom-tom and Zeppelin. No. C193A, Early postman and rider, UPU emblem, Concorde. No. C193B, Mail coach, dove, satellites.

1978, May 17	Litho.	Perf. 13½		
C191	A107	100fr multi	1.10	.25
C192	A107	200fr multi	1.10	.30

Souvenir Sheet

C193	A107	500fr multi	5.75	2.25

Cent. of progress of posts and telecommunications. No. C193 contains one 53x35mm stamp.

1978, Mar. 21   Litho. & Embossed
Size: 57x39mm

C193A	A107	1500fr gold & multi	55.00	4.00

Souvenir Sheet

C193B	A107	1500fr gold & multi	15.00	4.75

Nos. C193A-C193B exist imperf. No. C193A exists in a souvenir sheet of one. No. C193B contains one 57x39mm stamp.

Clement Ader and his Plane — AP78

Designs: 50fr, Wilbur and Orville Wright and plane. 60fr, John W. Alcock, Arthur W. Brown and plane. 100fr, Alan Cobham and plane. 150fr, Claude Dornier and hydroplane. 500fr, Wilbur and Orville Wright and plane.

1978, Sept. 19		Perf. 14		
C194	AP78	40fr multi	.55	.25
C195	AP78	50fr multi	.55	.25
C196	AP78	60fr multi	.65	.25
C197	AP78	100fr multi	1.25	.40
C198	AP78	150fr multi	1.90	.60
	Nos. C194-C198 (5)		4.90	1.75

Souvenir Sheet

C199	AP78	500fr multi	6.00	1.75

History of aviation.

Philexafrique II-Essen Issue
Common Design Types

No. C200, Crocodile, #C3. No. C201, Birds, Mecklenburg-Schwerin #1.

1978, Nov. 1		Litho.	Perf. 12½	
C200	CD138	100fr multi	1.90	1.10
C201	CD139	100fr multi	1.90	1.10
a.	Pair, #C200-C201 + label		7.50	7.50

Bokassa Type of 1978

150fr, Catherine & Jean Bedel Bokassa.

1978, Dec. 4		Litho.	Perf. 13	
C202	A113	150fr multi, horiz.	1.90	.70

First anniv. of coronation. A 1000fr gold embossed souvenir sheet showing Emperor Bokassa exists. Value $9.

Rowland Hill Type of 1978

Designs (Rowland Hill and): 100fr, Mailman and Tuscany No. 23. 200fr, Balloon and France No. 1. 500fr, Central Africa Nos. 1-2.

1978, Dec. 27				
C203	A114	100fr multi	4.00	1.40
C204	A114	200fr multi	1.75	.65

Souvenir Sheet

C205	A114	500fr multi	5.50	1.75

Sir Rowland Hill (1795-1879), originator of penny postage. No. C205 contains one 37½x39mm stamp. 1500fr gold embossed stamp and souvenir sheet exist.

IYC Type of 1979

Designs (UNICEF, Eagle Emblems and): 100fr, Chinese girl flying kites and German Do-X flying boat, 1929. 200fr, Boys playing leapfrog, hurdler and Olympic emblem. 500fr, Child with abacus and Albert Einstein with his equation.

1979, Mar. 6			Perf. 13½	
C206	A115	100fr multi	1.40	.40
C207	A115	200fr multi	2.75	.65

Souvenir Sheet

C208	A115	500fr multi	5.50	1.75

International Year of the Child. No. C208 contains one 56x33mm stamp. 1500fr gold embossed stamp and souvenir sheet exist.

Olympic Type of 1979

Moscow '80 Emblem, various sports and: 100fr, Hurdles & "B." 200fr, Broad jump & "A." 500fr, Pole vault, horiz.

1979, Mar. 16		Litho.	Perf. 13	
C209	A116	100fr multi	1.10	.35
C210	A116	200fr multi	2.10	.65

Souvenir Sheet

C210A	A116	500fr multi	—	—

22nd Olympic Games, Moscow, July 19-Aug. 3, 1980. No. C210A contains one 57x39mm stamp. A 1500fr gold embossed souvenir sheet exists showing diver, runner and javelin.

National Husbandry Association Type

1979, Aug.		Litho.	Perf. 13	
C211	A119	60fr Horse	5.75	2.00

Central African Republic

Nos. C151-C154 Overprinted in Black or Silver

1979, Oct.		Litho.	Perf. 14x13½	
C212	A93	100fr multi	1.00	.55
C213	A93	200fr multi	1.90	.85
C214	A93	300fr multi	2.75	1.25
	Nos. C212-C214 (3)		5.65	2.65

Souvenir Sheet

C215	A93	500fr multi (S)	5.50	5.50

Apollo 11 moon landing, 10th anniversary.

Ski Jump, Lake Placid '80 Emblem — AP79

1979, Nov. 11		Litho.	Perf. 13½	
C216	AP79	60fr shown	.65	.25
C217	AP79	100fr Downhill skiing	1.10	.40
C218	AP79	200fr Hockey	2.25	.85
C219	AP79	300fr Slalom	3.25	1.25
	Nos. C216-C219 (4)		7.25	2.75

Souvenir Sheet

C220	AP79	500fr Bobsledding	5.50	1.75

13th Winter Olympics Games, Lake Placid, NY, Feb. 12-24, 1980.
For overprints see Nos. C224-C228.

Space Type of 1980

150fr, Early satellites. 200fr, Space shuttle. 500fr, Apollo 11, Armstrong. No. C223A, Armstrong, Apollo 11. No. C223B, Space shuttle, horiz.

1980, Apr. 8		Litho.	Perf. 13½	
C221	A125	150fr multi	1.60	.40
C222	A125	200fr multi	1.90	.55

Souvenir Sheet

C223	A125	500fr multi	5.50	1.40

Litho. & Embossed
Size: 51x57mm

C223A	A125	1500fr multi	50.00	3.00

Souvenir Sheet

C223B	A125	1500fr multi	10.00	

C223A-C223B exist imperf. No. C223A exists in a souvenir sheet of one. Value $40. No. C223B contains one 57x51mm stamp.

Nos. C216-C220 Overprinted

a

b

c

d

e

1980, May 12		Litho.	Perf. 13½	
C224	AP79 (a)	60fr multi	.50	.25
C225	AP79 (b)	100fr multi	.75	.40
C226	AP79 (c)	200fr multi	1.90	.85
C227	AP79 (d)	300fr multi	2.75	1.25
	Nos. C224-C227 (4)		5.90	2.75

Souvenir Sheet

C228	AP79 (e)	500fr multi	5.00	5.00

World Telecommunications Day — AP80

1980, June 26		Litho.	Perf. 12½	
C229	AP80	100fr multi	1.10	.55
C230	AP80	150fr multi, vert.	1.40	.80

Olympic Type of 1980

100fr, Boxing. 150fr, Hurdles. 250fr, Long jump. No. C233A, Relay race, diff. No. C233B, Basketball, vert.

1980, July 25		Litho.	Perf. 13½	
C231	A126	100fr multi	1.00	.25
C232	A126	150fr multi	1.60	.40

Souvenir Sheet

C233	A126	250fr multi	3.00	.65

Litho. & Embossed

C233A	A126	1500fr multi	35.00	4.00

Souvenir Sheet

C233B	A126	1500fr multi	11.00	4.75

22nd Summer Olympic Games, Moscow, July 19-Aug. 3. No. C233 contains one 39x36mm stamp.
For overprints see Nos. C248-C250B.

Europe-Africa Type of 1980

150fr, Meteorology. 200fr, Aviation. 500fr, Concorde jet. No. C236A, Boy Scouts. No. C236B, Concorde.

1980, Nov. 4		Litho.	Perf. 13½	
C234	A127	150fr multi	1.50	.50
C235	A127	200fr multi	1.90	.60

Souvenir Sheet

C236	A127	500fr multi	5.50	1.60

No. C236 contains one 41½x29mm stamp.

Litho. & Embossed
Size: 42x39mm

C236A	A127	1500fr multi	15.00	4.00

Souvenir Sheet

C236B	A127	1500fr multi	12.00	4.75

Nos. C236A-C236B exist imperf. No. C236B contains one 42x39mm stamp.
No. C236A exists in a souvenir sheet of one. Value $30.

Soccer Type of 1981

100fr, Netherlands. 200fr, Spain. 500fr, Argentina. No. C239A, Players, trophy. No. C239B, Players, trophy, diff.

1981, Jan. 13		Litho.	Perf. 13½	
C237	A130	100fr multi	1.00	.25
C238	A130	200fr multi	1.75	.55

Souvenir Sheet

C239	A130	500fr multi	6.25	1.75

Litho. & Embossed
Size: 57x39mm

C239A	A130	1500fr multi	24.00	5.50

Souvenir Sheet

C239B	A130	1500fr multi	10.00	4.00

No. C239A exists with tabs for either Philexafrique II or Essen 78.
Nos. C239A-C239B exist imperf. No. C239A exists in a souvenir sheet of one. Value $38. No. C239B contains one 36x60mm stamp.

Jacob Wrestling with the Angel, by Rembrandt AP81

Rembrandt Paintings: 90fr, Christ during the Storm. 150fr, Jeremiah Mourning the Destruction of Jerusalem. 250fr, Tobit Accusing Anne of Theft of a Goat. 500fr, Belshazzar's Feast, horiz.

1981, Feb. 20			Perf. 12½	
C240	AP81	60fr multi	.55	.25
C241	AP81	90fr multi	1.00	.25
C242	AP81	150fr multi	1.75	.65
C243	AP81	250fr multi	3.00	.75
	Nos. C240-C243 (4)		6.30	1.90

Souvenir Sheet

C244	AP81	500fr multi	6.00	1.75

Picasso Type of 1981

Paintings: 150fr, Woman in Mirror with Self-portrait. 200fr, Woman Sleeping, The Dream. 500fr, Portrait of Maia (the Artist's Daughter). No. C247A, Two Women and Glasses, Picasso. No. C247B, Woman with Handbag, statue of standing woman, vert.

1981, June 30	Litho.	Perf. 13½		
C245	A133	150fr multi	2.25	.45
C246	A133	200fr multi	2.50	.60
		Souvenir Sheet		
C247	A133	500fr multi	5.75	1.40

No. C247 contains one 42x46mm stamp.

	Litho. & Embossed			
	Size: 57x39mm			
C247A	A133	1500fr gold & multi	17.50	6.00
		Souvenir Sheet		
C247B	A133	1500fr gold & multi	12.00	

Nos. C247A-C247B exist imperf. No. C247A exists in a souvenir sheet of one. Value $30. No. C247B contains one 39x58mm stamp.

Nos. C231-C233B Overprinted in Gold

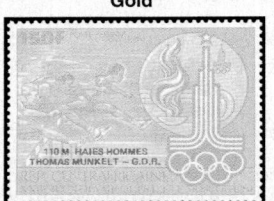

1981		Litho.	Perf. 13½		
C248	A126	100fr multi		1.00	.25
C249	A126	150fr multi		1.40	.40
		Souvenir Sheet			
C250	A126	250fr multi		3.00	.65
		Litho. & Embossed			
C250A	A126	1500fr on #C233A		14.00	
		Souvenir Sheet			
C250B	A126	1500fr on #C233B		15.00	

No. C250A exists in a souvenir sheet of 1. Value $35.

Royal Wedding Type of 1981

150fr, Prince of Wales arms. 200fr, Palace. 500fr, St. Paul's Cathedral. No. C253A, Diana, Charles. No. C253B, Charles, Diana, ship.

1981, Aug. 20	Litho.	Perf. 13½		
C251	A136	150fr multi	1.60	.40
C252	A136	200fr multi	2.10	.55
		Souvenir Sheet		
C253	A136	500fr multi	4.75	1.40

No. C253 contains one 60x32mm stamp.

	Litho. & Embossed			
	Size: 51x42mm			
C253A	A136	1500fr multi	15.00	4.00
		Souvenir Sheet		
C253B	A136	1500fr multi	12.00	

Nos. C253A-C253B exist imperf. No. C253A exists in a souvenir sheet of one. Value $21. No. C253B contains one 51x42mm stamp.

Navigator Type of 1981

100fr, O. Kersauson. 200fr, Chichester. 500fr, A. Colas. No. C256A, Riguidel. No. C256B, Tabarly.

1981, Sept. 4	Litho.	Perf. 13½		
C254	A139	100fr multi	1.10	.70
C255	A139	200fr multi	2.40	1.40
		Souvenir Sheet		
C256	A139	500fr multi	6.50	1.40
		Litho. & Embossed		
		Size: 51x42mm		
C256A	A139	1500fr multi	16.00	4.50
		Souvenir Sheet		
C256B	A139	1500fr multi	13.00	

Nos. C256A-C256B exist imperf. No. C256A exists in a souvenir sheet of one. Value $40. No. C256B contains one 51x42mm stamp.

Lizard
AP82

1981, Oct. 30		Perf. 12½x13		
C257	AP82	30fr shown	1.00	.25
C258	AP82	60fr Snake	1.25	.30
C259	AP82	110fr Crocodile	2.50	.45
	Nos. C257-C259 (3)		4.75	1.00

Christmas Type of 1981

140fr, Correggio. 200fr, Gentileschi, 1610. 500fr, Holy Family, by Cranach. No. C262A, Hans Memling, c. 1470. No. C262B, Fra Angelico, 1438.

1981, Dec. 24		Perf. 13½		
C260	A143	140fr multi	2.50	.45
C261	A143	200fr multi	4.50	.70
		Souvenir Sheet		
C262	A143	500fr multi	6.75	1.75

No. C262 contains one 41x50mm stamp.

	Litho. & Embossed			
	Size: 30x60mm			
C262A	A143	1500fr multi	15.00	4.50
		Souvenir Sheet		
C262B	A143	1500fr multi	11.00	

Nos. C262A-C262B exist imperf. No. C262A exists in a souvenir sheet of one. Value $25. No. C262B contains one 30x60mm stamp.

Animal Type of 1982

300fr, Mandrill. 500fr, Lion. 600fr, Nile crocodiles. No. C265A, Leopard, Rotary emblem. No. C265B, Emblem, eagle, horiz.

1982, Jan. 22	Litho.	Perf. 13½		
C263	A145	300fr multi	3.25	.65
C264	A145	500fr multi	5.50	1.40
		Souvenir Sheet		
C265	A145	600fr multi	6.75	1.60

No. C265 contains one 47x38mm stamp.

	Litho. & Embossed			
	Size: 51x57mm			
C265A	A145	1500fr multi	15.00	4.00
		Souvenir Sheet		
C265B	A145	1500fr multi	13.00	

Nos. C265A-C265B exist imperf. No. C265A exists in a souvenir sheet of one. Value $42.50. No. C265B contains one 57x51mm stamp.

Transportation Type of 1982 and

AP82a

Designs: 300fr, Savannah cargo ship. 500fr, Columbia space shuttle. 600fr, Spirit of Locomotion emblem. No. C268A, Space shuttle launch, horiz. No. C268B, Shuttle, space telescope.

1982, Feb. 27	Litho.	Perf. 13½		
C266	A147	300fr multi	3.75	.65
C267	A147	500fr multi	5.50	1.40
		Souvenir Sheet		
C268	A147	600fr multi	5.50	1.60

	Litho. & Embossed			
C268A	AP82a	1500fr gold & multi	15.00	4.50
		Souvenir Sheet		
C268B	AP82a	1500fr gold & multi	11.50	

No. C268 contains one 39x43mm stamp. No. C268B contains one 51x42mm stamp. No. C268A exists in a souvenir sheet of 1. Value $50.

Olympic Type of 1982

1982, July 24	Litho.	Perf. 13½		
C269	A149	300fr Diving	3.00	.80
C270	A149	500fr Equestrian	5.00	1.40
		Souvenir Sheet		
C271	A149	600fr Basketball	5.50	1.60

No. C271 contains one 38x56mm stamp.

Diana Type of 1982

1982, July 20	Litho.	Perf. 13½		
C272	A150	300fr multi	3.25	.80
C273	A150	500fr multi	5.50	1.40
		Souvenir Sheet		
C274	A150	600fr multi	5.75	1.60

No. C274 contains one 56x32mm stamp.

Christmas
1982
AP83

Raphael Paintings: 150fr, Beautiful Gardener. 500fr, Holy Family.

1982, Dec.		Perf. 13		
C275	AP83	150fr multi	2.00	.50
C276	AP83	500fr multi	5.50	1.40

Space Type of 1982

Designs: Various satellites and space scenes. No. C279A, European communications satellite, controller. No. C279B, Viking on Mars, vert.

1982, Aug. 15	Litho.	Perf. 13½		
C277	A151	300fr multi	3.00	.80
C278	A151	500fr multi	5.00	1.40
		Souvenir Sheet		
C279	A151	600fr multi	5.00	1.60

	Litho. & Embossed			
	Size: 60x36mm			
C279A	A151	1500fr gold & multi	15.00	4.50
		Souvenir Sheet		
C279B	A151	1500fr gold & multi	12.00	

Nos. C279A-C279B exist imperf. No. C279A exists in a souvenir sheet of one. Value $55. No. C279B contains one 36x60mm stamp.

Birth of Prince
William of Wales,
June 21,
1982 — AP84

500fr, Diana, William. 600fr, Family. No. C281A, Diana, William, Charles. No. 281B, Diana, William, vert.

1983, Jan. 22				
C280	AP84	500fr multi	5.50	1.40
		Souvenir Sheet		
C281	AP84	600fr multi	5.50	4.00
		Litho. & Embossed		
C281A	AP84	1500fr gold & multi	15.00	3.50
		Souvenir Sheet		
C281B	AP84	1500fr gold & multi	10.00	

No. C281A exists in a souvenir sheet of 1. Value $40.

Manned
Flight
Bicentenary
AP85

65fr, Robert's & Hullin's balloon. 130fr, John Wise's, 1859. 350fr, Mail balloon, 1870. 400fr, Dirigible Underberg. 500fr, Montgolfiere, 1783.

1983, Apr.				
C282	AP85	65fr multicolored	1.00	.25
C283	AP85	130fr multicolored	1.50	.35
C284	AP85	350fr multicolored	3.25	.90
C285	AP85	400fr multicolored	4.25	1.10
	Nos. C282-C285 (4)		10.00	2.60
		Souvenir Sheet		
C286	AP85	500fr multicolored	5.75	1.40

Pre-Olympics — AP86

Various equestrian events.

1983, July	Litho.	Perf. 13		
C287	AP86	100fr multi	1.00	.40
C288	AP86	200fr multi	2.10	.60
C289	AP86	300fr multi	2.75	.80
C290	AP86	400fr multi	3.50	1.10
	Nos. C287-C290 (4)		9.35	2.90
		Souvenir Sheet		
C291	AP86	500fr multi	5.75	1.40

Animal Type of 1983

Endangered Animals, Rotary Emblem: 400fr, Black rhinoceros, parrot, zebra, scouts. 500fr, Lions, parrot, antelope, elephant, flag, Rotary Int'l emblem. 600fr, Leopard.

1983, Nov. 14	Litho.	Perf. 13½		
C291A	A170	400fr multicolored	10.00	3.00
C292	A170	500fr multicolored	12.00	3.50
		Souvenir Sheet		
C293	A170	600fr multicolored	16.00	4.00

15th World Scout Jamboree, Alberta (400fr). No. C293 contains one 47x32mm stamp.

Christmas
1983
AP88

Paintings: 130fr, Annunciation, by da Vinci. 205fr, Virgin of the Rocks, by da Vinci. 350fr, Adoration of the Shepherds, by Rubens. 500fr, Virgin and Child with Donor, by Rubens.

1984, Jan. 3	Litho.	Perf. 13		
C294	AP88	130fr multi	1.25	.35
C295	AP88	205fr multi	2.00	.50
C296	AP88	350fr multi	3.50	1.00
C297	AP88	500fr multi	5.00	1.25
	Nos. C294-C297 (4)		11.75	3.10

1984 Summer Olympics — AP89

Various gymnastic and rhythmic gymnastic events. 65fr, 100fr, 205fr, 350fr vert. 500fr, Rhythmic formation.

		1984, Mar. 13	Litho.	Perf. 13	
C298	AP89	65fr	multi	.55	.25
C299	AP89	100fr	multi	1.10	.25
C300	AP89	130fr	multi	1.40	.30
C301	AP89	205fr	multi	2.25	.60
C302	AP89	350fr	multi	4.00	1.00
		Nos. C298-C302 (5)		9.30	2.40

Souvenir Sheet
Perf. 13½x13

C302A	AP89	500fr	multi	5.00	1.25

For overprint see No. 705.

Summer Olympics Winners AP90

60fr, 400 meter relay. 140fr, 400 meter hurdles. 300fr, 5000 meter race. 440fr, Decathlon. 550fr, 800 meter race, horiz.

		1985, Jan. 7	Litho.	Perf. 14	
C303	AP90	60fr	multicolored	.55	.25
C304	AP90	140fr	multicolored	1.75	.40
C305	AP90	300fr	multicolored	3.50	.80
C306	AP90	440fr	multicolored	4.50	1.00
		Nos. C303-C306 (4)		10.30	2.45

Souvenir Sheet

C307	AP90	500fr	multicolored	5.00	4.50

Christmas 1984 — AP91

Paintings by Titian: 130fr, Virgin and Infant Jesus. 350fr, Virgin with Rabbit. 400fr, Virgin and Child.

		1985, Jan. 17	Litho.	Perf. 13	
C308	AP91	130fr	multi	1.25	.55
C309	AP91	350fr	multi	2.75	1.10
C310	AP91	400fr	multi	3.75	1.25
		Nos. C308-C310 (3)		7.75	2.90

Audubon Bicentenary — AP92

60fr, Otus asio. 110fr, Coccizus minor, vert. 200fr, Zenaidura macroura, vert. 500fr, Aix sponsa.

		1985, Jan. 25	Litho.	Perf. 13	
C311	AP92	60fr	multicolored	.80	.25
C312	AP92	110fr	multicolored	1.25	.45
C313	AP92	200fr	multicolored	2.10	1.00
C314	AP92	500fr	multicolored	5.25	2.50
		Nos. C311-C314 (4)		9.40	4.20

Christmas 1985 AP93

Religious paintings: 100fr, Virgin with Angels, by the Master of Burgo de Osma. 200fr, Nativity, by Louis Le Nain (1593-1648). 400fr, Virgin and Child with Dove, by Piero de Cosimo (1462-1521).

		1985, Dec. 24	Litho.	Perf. 13	
C315	AP93	100fr	multi	1.10	.40
C316	AP93	200fr	multi	2.50	.85
C317	AP93	400fr	multi	4.75	1.90
		Nos. C315-C317 (3)		8.35	3.15

Halley's Comet — AP94

110fr, Edmond Halley. 130fr, Giotto probe. 200fr, Comet, planet. 300fr, Vega probe. 400fr, Space shuttle.

1986, Mar. 8

C318	AP94	110fr	multicolored	1.00	.25
C319	AP94	130fr	multicolored	1.40	.25
C320	AP94	200fr	multicolored	2.25	.50
C321	AP94	300fr	multicolored	3.00	.75
C322	AP94	400fr	multicolored	4.50	1.00
		Nos. C318-C322 (5)		12.15	2.75

Christmas AP95

Painting details: 250fr, Nativity, by Giotto. 440fr, Adoration of the Magi, by Botticelli, vert. 500fr, Nativity, by Giotto, diff.

		1986, Dec. 24	Litho.	Perf. 13½	
C323	AP95	250fr	multi	2.50	1.10
C324	AP95	440fr	multi	4.25	1.75
C325	AP95	500fr	multi	5.25	2.10
		Nos. C323-C325 (3)		12.00	4.95

Tennis at the 1988 Olympics — AP96

Various plays.

		1986, Dec. 31		Perf. 12½	
C326	AP96	150fr	multi	1.60	.60
C327	AP96	250fr	multi, vert.	3.00	.70
C328	AP96	440fr	multi, vert.	3.75	1.25
C329	AP96	600fr	multi	6.25	1.40
		Nos. C326-C329 (4)		14.60	3.95

1988 Summer Olympics, Seoul — AP97

100fr, Triple jump, vert. 200fr, High jump. 300fr, Long jump. 400fr, Pole vault, vert. 500fr, High jump, diff.

		1987, June 15	Litho.	Perf. 13	
C330	AP97	100fr	multicolored	.90	.40
C331	AP97	200fr	multicolored	1.75	.80
C332	AP97	300fr	multicolored	2.60	1.10
C333	AP97	400fr	multicolored	3.50	1.60
		Nos. C330-C333 (4)		8.75	3.90

Souvenir Sheet

C334	AP97	500fr	multicolored	4.50	3.25

1988 Summer Olympics, Seoul — AP98

Stamps on stamps and gymnasts: 90fr, No. C94, balance beam, vert. 200fr, No. C21, balance beam, diff. 300fr, No. C22, pommel horse. 400fr, No. C23, parallel bars. 500fr, No. C93, rings.

		1988, July 26	Litho.	Perf. 13	
C335	AP98	90fr	multi	.90	.30
C336	AP98	200fr	multi	2.00	.50
C337	AP98	300fr	multi	3.00	.90
C338	AP98	400fr	multi	4.00	1.40
		Nos. C335-C338 (4)		9.90	3.10

Souvenir Sheet

C339	AP98	500fr	multi	5.00	2.75

1st Moon Landing, 20th Anniv. AP99

		1989, Aug. 4	Litho.	Perf. 13	
C340	AP99	40fr	Apollo 11	.35	.25
C341	AP99	80fr	Apollo 15	.75	.30
C342	AP99	130fr	Apollo 16	1.50	.55
C343	AP99	1000fr	Apollo 17	10.00	2.75
		Nos. C340-C343 (4)		12.60	3.85

World Cup Soccer Championships, Italy — AP100

		1990, July 7	Litho.	Perf. 13	
C344	AP100	5fr	multicolored	.25	.25
C345	AP100	30fr	multi, diff.	.30	.25
C346	AP100	500fr	multi, diff.	5.00	1.00
C347	AP100	1000fr	multi, diff.	9.25	1.60
		Nos. C344-C347 (4)		14.80	3.10

Charles de Gaulle (1890-1979) — AP101

		1990, July 27		Perf. 13½	
C348	AP101	500fr	multicolored	3.75	.90

No. C348 exists in a souvenir sheet of 1. For overprint see No. C360.

Don Mattingly, Baseball Player — AP102

Saturn V Rocket, Apollo 11 Astronauts — AP103

Charles de Gaulle, Birth Cent. AP104

No. C352, De Gaulle and Cross of Lorraine.

		1990, July 27	Litho.	Perf. 13½	
C349	AP102	300fr	multicolored	2.50	.80

Souvenir Sheet

C350	AP103	1000fr	multicolored	8.25	1.75

Litho. & Embossed

C351	AP104	1500fr	gold & multi	15.00	5.00

Souvenir Sheet

C352	AP104	1500fr	gold & multi	11.00	

No. C351 exists in souvenir sheet of 1. Value $14. This souvenir sheet also exists imperf. and with an overprint in the sheet margin.
For overprints see Nos. C355-C356.

Visit of Pope
John Paul II
to Africa
AP105

Pope John Paul II and: No. C353, Mother Theresa, portrait. No. C354, Papal arms, globe.

1993 Litho. & Embossed *Perf. 13½*
C353 AP105 1500fr gold & multi   15.00 5.00

Souvenir Sheet
C354 AP105 1500fr gold & multi   20.00

No. C353 exists in a souvenir sheet of 1. Value $20.

No. C351
Overprinted

Litho. & Embossed
1994, June 6   ***Perf. 13½***
C355 AP104 1500fr gold & multi   12.00 9.00

No. C352 Ovptd. in Silver in Sheet Margin
Souvenir Sheet
C356 AP104 1500fr gold & multi   12.00 9.00

Overprint on No. C356 contains map, soldiers and "50 eme ANNIVERSAIRE DU /DEBARQUEMENT."
No. C355 exists in souvenir sheet of 1. Value $12.

Souvenir Sheets

Japanese Exploration of
Antarctica — AP106

No. C357, Nobu Shirase. No. C358, Schooner Kainman Maru, horiz.

1994, Oct. 25
C357 AP106 1200fr multi   5.00 4.75
C358 AP106 1200fr multi   5.00 4.75

D-Day, 50th Anniv. (in 1994) — AP107

Designs: a, Gliders over Pegasus Bridge, Sword beach. b, Fighter planes over Juno, Gold and Omaha beaches. c, Planes over Utah beach, St. Mere Eglise.

Litho. & Embossed
1995, Oct. 25   ***Perf. 13½***
C359 AP107 1000fr Strip of 3,
     #a.-c.   13.00 13.00
No. C359b is 60x45mm.

Souvenir Sheet
No. C348 Overprinted

IN MEMORIAM
1970 - 1995

1995, Oct. 10   **Litho.**   ***Perf. 13½***
C360 AP101 500fr multicolored   11.50 11.50

AIR POST SEMI-POSTAL STAMPS

Isis of Kalabsha
SPAP1

Unwmk.
1964, Mar. 7   **Engr.**   ***Perf. 13***
CB1 SPAP1 25fr + 10fr multi   1.40 1.40
CB2 SPAP1 50fr + 10fr multi   2.25 2.25
CB3 SPAP1 100fr + 10fr multi   3.50 3.50
    Nos. CB1-CB3 (3)   7.15 7.15

UNESCO world campaign to save historic monuments in Nubia.

African Infants and Globe — SPAP2

1971, Dec. 11   **Litho.**   ***Perf. 13x13½***
CB4 SPAP2 140fr + 50fr multi   3.25 1.75
25th anniv. of UNICEF, and Children's Day.

POSTAGE DUE STAMPS

Sternotomis Virescens — D1

Beetles: No. J2, Sternotomis gama. No. J3, Augosoma centaurus. No. J4, Phosphorus virescens, ceroplesis carabarica. No. J5, Cetoine scaraboidae. No. J6, Ceroplesis S.P. No. J7, Macrorhina S.P. No. J8, Cetoine scaraboidae. No. J9, Phryneta leprosa. No. J10, Taurina longiceps. No. J11, Monohamus griseoplagiatus. No. J12, Jambonus trifasciatus.

Unwmk.
1962, Oct. 15   **Engr.**   ***Perf. 11***
J1   D1 50c grn & dp org   .25 .25
J2   D1 50c grn & dp org   .25 .25
  a.   Pair, #J1-J2   .45
J3   D1 1fr blk, brn & lt grn   .30 .30
J4   D1 1fr blk, brn & lt grn   .30 .30
  a.   Pair, #J3-J4   .75
J5   D1 2fr blk, org & yel grn   .40 .40
J6   D1 2fr blk & red org   .40 .40
  a.   Pair, #J5-J6   .85
J7   D1 5fr brn, org & grn   .55 .55
J8   D1 5fr brn, org, grn & red   .55 .55
  a.   Pair, #J7-J8   1.25
J9   D1 10fr blk, grn & brn   1.00 1.00
J10 D1 10fr blk, brn & grn   1.00 1.00
  a.   Pair, #J9-J10   2.25
J11 D1 25fr blk, bl grn & brn   3.00 2.40
J12 D1 25fr blk, brn & bl grn   3.00 2.40
  a.   Pair, #J11-J12   6.50
    Nos. J1-J12 (12)   11.00 9.80

Pairs se-tenant at the base.

Giant Anteater — D2

1985, Jan. 25   **Litho.**   ***Perf. 12½***
J13 D2 5fr multi   .50 .50
J14 D2 20fr multi   .90 .90
J15 D2 30fr multi   1.10 1.10
    Nos. J13-J15 (3)   2.50 2.50

MILITARY STAMPS

No. 1 Overprinted

Unwmk.
1962, Jan. 1   **Engr.**   ***Perf. 13***
M1 A1   bl, car, grn & yel   15.00 —

No. 1 Overprinted

1963
M2 A1   bl, car, grn & yel   16.00 —

OFFICIAL STAMPS

Coat of Arms — O1

Imprint: "d'après G. RICHER
SO.GE.IM."

Perf. 13x12½
1965-69   **Litho.**   **Unwmk.**
Arms in Original Colors
O1 O1 1fr blk & brn org   .25 .25
O2 O1 2fr blk & violet   .25 .25
O3 O1 5fr blk & gray   .25 .25
O4 O1 10fr blk & green   .25 .25

O5   O1 20fr blk & red brn   .55 .25
O6   O1 30fr blk & emer ('69)   1.10 .55
O7   O1 50fr blk & dk bl   1.25 .70
O8   O1 100fr blk & bister   2.75 1.10
O9   O1 130fr blk & ver ('69)   4.25 2.25
O10 O1 200fr blk & claret   6.25 2.75
    Nos. O1-O10 (10)   17.15 8.60

Redrawn
Imprint: "d'après G. RICHER
DELRIEU"

1971   **Photo.**   ***Perf. 12x12½***
Arms in Original Colors
O11 O1 5fr blk & gray   .25 .25
O12 O1 30fr blk & emer   .50 .25
O13 O1 40fr blk & dp claret   .65 .30
O14 O1 100fr blk & bister   1.50 .55
O15 O1 140fr blk & lt bl   2.75 .85
O16 O1 200fr blk & claret   3.25 1.40
    Nos. O11-O16 (6)   8.90 3.60

Empire

Nos. O11, O13-O16
Overprinted in Black

1977   **Litho.**   ***Perf. 12x12½***
O17 O1 5fr multi   .35 .25
O18 O1 40fr multi   .50 .30
O19 O1 100fr multi   1.40 .45
O20 O1 140fr multi   1.75 .70
O21 O1 200fr multi   2.75 1.00
    Nos. O17-O21 (5)   6.75 2.70

**Type of 1965 Inscribed: "EMPIRE
CENTRAFRICAIN"**
1978, July   **Litho.**   ***Perf. 12½***
O22 O1 1fr multi   .25 .25
O23 O1 2fr multi   .25 .25
O24 O1 5fr multi   .25 .25
O25 O1 10fr multi   .25 .25
O26 O1 15fr multi   .25 .25
O27 O1 20fr multi   .25 .25
O28 O1 30fr multi   .30 .25
O29 O1 40fr multi   .40 .25
O30 O1 50fr multi   .55 .30
O31 O1 60fr multi   .75 .40
O32 O1 100fr multi   1.00 .55
O33 O1 130fr multi   1.60 .95
O34 O1 140fr multi   1.75 .95
O35 O1 200fr multi   3.50 1.25
    Nos. O22-O35 (14)   11.35 6.40

CENTRAL LITHUANIA

'sen-trəl ˌli-thə-'wā-nē-ə

LOCATION — North of Poland and east of Lithuania
CAPITAL — Vilnius

At one time Central Lithuania was a grand duchy of Lithuania but at the end of the 18th Century it fell under Russian rule. After World War I, Lithuania regained her sovereignty but certain areas were occupied by Poland. During the Russo-Polish war this territory was seized by Lithuania whose claim was promptly recognized by the Soviet Government. Under the leadership of the Polish General Zeligowski the territory was recaptured and it was during this occupation the stamps of Central Lithuania came into being. Subsequently the territory became a part of Poland.

100 Fennigi = 1 Markka

Coat of Arms — A1

Perf. 11½, Imperf.

1920-21		Typo.	Unwmk.	
1	A1	25f red	.40	.55
2	A1	25f dark grn ('21)	.40	.55
3	A1	1m blue	.40	.55
4	A1	1m dark brn ('21)	.40	.55
5	A1	2m violet	.40	.55
6	A1	2m orange ('21)	.40	.55
		Nos. 1-6 (6)	2.40	3.30

For surcharges see Nos. B1-B5.

Lithuanian Stamps of 1919 Surcharged in Blue or Black

Perf. 11½x12, 12½x11½, 14

1920, Nov. 23			Wmk. 145	
13	A5	2m on 15sk lil	47.50	55.00
a.		Inverted surcharge	200.00	900.00
14	A5	4m on 10sk red	47.50	52.50
a.		Inverted surcharge	150.00	
15	A5	4m on 20sk dl bl (Bk)	47.50	52.50
a.		Inverted surcharge	150.00	
16	A5	4m on 30sk buff	47.50	52.50
a.		Inverted surcharge	150.00	
17	A6	6m on 50sk lt grn	47.50	52.50
a.		4m on 50sk (error)	200.00	
b.		10m on 50sk (error)	200.00	
c.		Surcharge inverted		—
18	A6	6m on 60sk vio & red	47.50	52.50
a.		4m on 60sk (error)	200.00	
b.		10m on 60sk (error)	200.00	
19	A6	6m on 75sk bis & red	47.50	52.50
a.		4m on 75sk (error)	200.00	
b.		10m on 75sk (error)	200.00	
20	A8	10m on 1auk gray & red	95.00	110.00
a.		Inverted surcharge	210.00	
21	A8	10m on 3auk lt brn & red	1,400.	1,800.
22	A8	10m on 5auk bl grn & red	1,400.	1,800.
		Nos. 13-20 (8)	427.50	480.00
		Nos. 13-22 (10)	3,228.	4,080.

The overprint on Nos. 17-19 is down-reading, i.e., the top of the overprint is at the right of the original design, the bottom at the left. The inverted overprint on No. 17c is up-reading.
Reprints of Nos. 17a, 17b, 18a, 18b, 19a, 19b. Value, each $45.
Counterfeits of Nos. 21-22 exist.

Lithuanian Girl — A2

Warrior — A3

Holy Gate of Vilnius — A4

Rector's Insignia — A6

Gen. Lucien Zeligowski — A7

Tower and Cathedral, Vilnius — A5

Perf. 11½, Imperf.

1920		Litho.	Unwmk.	
23	A2	25f gray	.25	.75
24	A3	1m orange	.25	.75
25	A4	2m claret	.45	1.00
26	A5	4m gray grn & buff	.60	1.25
27	A6	6m rose & gray	2.00	2.75
28	A7	10m brown & yellow	3.00	4.00
		Nos. 23-28 (6)	6.55	10.50

For surcharges see Nos. B13-B14, B17-B19.

St. Anne's Church, Vilnius — A8

St. Stanislas Cathedral, Vilnius — A9

White Eagle, White Knight Vytis — A10

Queen Hedwig and King Ladislas II Jagello — A11

Coat of Arms of Vilnius — A12

Poczobut Astronomical Observatory A13

Union of Lithuania and Poland — A14

Tadeusz Kosciuszko and Adam Mickiewicz A15

Perf. 14, Imperf.

1921				
35	A8	1m dk gray & yel	.65	1.10
36	A9	2m rose & green	.65	1.10
37	A10	3m dark green	.65	1.10
38	A11	4m brown & buff	.65	1.10
39	A12	5m red brown	.65	1.10
40	A13	6m slate & buff	.65	1.40
41	A14	10m red vio & buff	.90	2.25
42	A15	20m blk brn & buff	.90	2.25
		Nos. 35-42 (8)	5.70	11.40

Set, perf. 13½, $150.

Peasant Girl Sowing — A16

White Eagle and Vytis — A17

Great Theater at Vilnius — A18

Allegory: Peace and Industry — A19

Gen. Zeligowski Entering Vilnius — A20

Gen. Zeligowski — A21

Perf. 11½, Imperf.

1921-22				
53	A16	10m brown ('22)	3.25	6.25
54	A17	25m red & yel ('22)	3.50	8.00
55	A18	50m dk blue ('22)	5.00	12.00
56	A19	75m violet ('22)	6.00	22.50
57	A20	100m bl & bister	2.50	5.25
58	A21	150m ol grn & brn	3.50	6.75
		Nos. 53-58 (6)	23.75	60.75

Opening of the Natl. Parliament, Nos. 53-56; anniv. of the entry of General Zeligowski into Vilnius, Nos. 57-58.

SEMI-POSTAL STAMPS

Nos. 1-6 Surcharged in Black or Red

Perf. 11½, Imperf.

1921		Unwmk.		
B1	A1	25f + 2m red (Bk)	1.00	1.75
B2	A1	25f + 2m dk green	1.00	1.75
B3	A1	1m + 2m blue	1.10	1.75
B4	A1	1m + 2m dk brown	1.10	1.75
B5	A1	2m + 2m violet	1.10	1.75
B6	A1	2m + 2m orange	1.10	1.75
		Nos. B1-B6 (6)	6.40	10.50

The surcharge means "For Silesia 2 marks." The stamps were intended to provide a fund to assist the plebiscite in Upper Silesia.

Nos. 25, 26 Surcharged

a

b

Perf. 11½, Imperf.

B13	A4	(a) 2m + 1(m) claret	1.00	2.00
B14	A5	(b) 4m + 1m gray green & buff	1.00	2.00

Nos. 25-26, 28 with inset

Perf. 11½, Imperf.

B17	A4	2m + 1m claret	.65	1.25
B18	A5	4m + 1m gray green & buff	.65	1.25
B19	A7	10m + 2m brn & yel	.90	1.25
		Nos. B13-B19 (5)	4.20	7.75

POSTAGE DUE STAMPS

University, Vilnius — D1

Castle Hill, Vilnius — D2

Castle Ruins, Troki D3

Holy Gate, Vilnius D4

St. Stanislas Cathedral D5

St. Anne's Church, Vilnius D6

1920-21		Unwmk.	Perf. 11½, Imperf.	
J1	D1	50f red violet	.40	1.25
J2	D2	1m green	.40	1.25
J3	D3	2m red violet	.50	1.25
J4	D4	3m red violet	.85	1.60
J5	D5	5m red violet	1.00	2.50
J6	D6	20m scarlet	2.00	3.25
		Nos. J1-J6 (6)	5.15	11.10

CEYLON

si-'län

LOCATION — An island in the Indian Ocean separated from India by the Gulf of Manaar

GOVT. — Independent republic within the British Commonwealth

AREA — 25,332 sq. mi.

POP. — 12,670,000 (est. 1971)

CAPITAL — Colombo

Ceylon changed its name to Republic of Sri Lanka on May 22, 1972.

12 Pence = 1 Shilling
100 Cents = 1 Rupee (1872)

Values for unused stamps are for examples with original gum as defined in the catalogue introduction except for Nos. 2, 5, 8-9 which seldom have any remaining trace of their original gum. Many unused stamps of Ceylon, especially between Nos. 59 and 274, have toned gum or tropical stains. Values quoted are for stamps with fresh gum. Toned stamps have lower values, and common stamps with toned gum are worth very little.

Very fine examples of Nos. 1-15 will be cut square, will have small margins, but will show an intact design. Inferior examples with the design partly cut away will sell for much less, and examples with large margins will command higher prices. Very fine examples of Nos. 17-58b will have perforations just cutting into the design on one or more sides due to the narrow spacing of the stamps on the plates and to imperfect perforating methods. Stamps with perfs clear on all four sides are extremely scarce and will command substantially higher prices.

Catalogue values for unused stamps in this country are for Never Hinged items, beginning with Scott 290 in the regular postage section and Scott B1 in the semi-postal section.

Watermarks

Wmk. 1a —
22½mm high,
Oval Letters

Wmk. 1b —
21mm high,
Round Letters

Wmk. 6 — Large Star

Wmk. 290 —
Lotus and "Sri"
Multiple

Queen Victoria
A1   A2

1857		Engr.	Wmk. 6	Imperf.

Blued Paper

| 1 | A1 | 1p blue | — | 240. |
| 2 | A1 | 6p plum | 12,500. | 525. |

1857-59				**White Paper**
3	A1	1p dp turq	1,150.	47.50
4	A1	2p deep grn	210.00	75.00
a.		2p yellow green	575.00	105.00
5	A2	4p dl rose ('59)	75,000.	5,250.
6	A1	5p org brown	1,750.	175.00
6A	A1	6p plum	2,850.	170.00
7	A1	6p brown	10,500.	575.00
8	A2	8p brown ('59)	30,000.	1,750.
9	A2	9p lil brn ('59)	62,500.	1,050.
10	A1	10p vermilion	950.00	350.00
11	A1	1sh violet	5,750.	225.00
12	A2	1sh9p green ('59)	950.00	925.00
a.		1sh9p yellow green	5,500.	3,500.
13	A2	2sh blue ('59)	6,750.	1,400.

Stamps of type A2 frequently have repaired corners.

Nos. 3-4 exist unofficially rouletted. See the *Scott Classic Specialized Catalogue of Stamps & Covers* for listings.

Beware of Nos. 17-57 trimmed to resemble Nos. 3-13. Values are for stamps with clear margins on all sides.

No. 5 was reproduced by the collotype process in a souvenir sheet distributed at the London International Stamp Exhibition 1950. The paper is unwatermarked.

A3

1857-58		Typo.		Unwmk.
14	A3	½p lilac ('58)	200.	250.
15	A3	½p lilac, *bluish*	4,250.	650.

Values are for stamps without cracking of the surface, and examples showing cracking should be discounted.

		Clean-Cut Perf. 14 to 15½		
1861		**Wmk. 6**		**Engr.**
17	A1	1p blue	210.00	18.00
18	A1	2p yel grn	275.00	27.50
b.		Vert. pair, imperf between		
19	A2	4p dull rose	2,300.	350.00
20	A1	5p org brown	125.00	10.00
20A	A1	6p brown	3,200.	190.00
b.		6p bister brown	2,250.	290.00
21	A2	8p brown	2,600.	575.00
22	A2	9p lilac brown	16,000.	275.00
23	A1	1sh violet	145.00	17.50
24	A2	2sh blue	4,750.	875.00
		Rough Perf. 14 to 15½		
25	A1	1p blue	170.00	12.50
b.		Blued paper	850.00	27.50
26	A1	2p yel green	475.00	92.50
27	A2	4p rose red	600.00	130.00
28	A1	6p olive brown	1,250.	120.00
a.		6p deep brown	1,350.	130.00
b.		6p bister brown	2,300.	200.00
29	A2	8p brown	1,775.	675.00
30	A2	8p yel brown	1,800.	425.00
31	A2	9p olive brown	875.00	85.00
32	A2	9p deep brown	160.00	120.00
33	A1	10p vermilion	325.00	30.00
a.		Imperf. vert., pair		

34	A1	1sh violet	300.00	17.50
35	A2	1sh9p green	825.00	
36	A2	2sh blue	800.00	160.00

The 1sh9p green was never placed in use.

1863			**Perf. 12½**	
37	A1	10p vermilion	340.00	22.50

1864		**Typo.**	**Unwmk.**	
38	A3	½p lilac	260.00	210.00

See note following No. 15.

1862		**Engr.**	**Perf. 13**	
39	A1	1p blue	180.00	7.00
40	A1	5p car brown	1,850.	175.00
41	A1	6p deep brown	210.00	30.00
42	A2	9p brown	1,400.	120.00
43	A1	1sh grayish violet	2,100.	95.00

Parts of the papermaker's sheet watermark, "T. H. SAUNDERS 1862," may be found on some examples of Nos. 39-43.

			Perf. 12	
44	A1	1p blue	1,900.	150.00
a.		Horiz. pair, imperf. btwn.	18,000.	

Two Types of Watermark Crown and CC (1)

1863-67		**Typo.**	**Wmk. 1a**	**Perf. 12½**
45	A3	½p lilac	80.00	50.00
a.		½p reddish lilac	90.00	65.00
			Engr.	
46	A1	1p blue	180.00	9.00
a.		1p dark blue	180.00	9.00
c.		Perf. 11½	3,650.	350.00
47	A1	2p gray green	100.00	15.00
48	A1	2p emerald	190.00	120.00
48A	A1	2p yel green	10,000.	475.00
48B	A1	2p bottle green		4,250.
49	A1	2p olive	325.00	275.00
50	A2	4p rose	550.00	130.00
a.		4p carmine rose	900.00	275.00
51	A1	5p car brown	325.00	110.00
52	A1	5p olive green	1,700.	350.00
e.		5p deep sage green	2,100.	425.00
53	A1	6p choc brown	250.00	7.50
a.		Perf. 13	2,850.	260.00
b.		6p black brown	300.00	11.50
c.		As "b," double impression		4,500.
d.		6p reddish brown	350.00	14.00
54	A2	8p red brown	150.00	80.00
55	A2	9p brown	360.00	52.50
c.		Perf. 13	6,750.	1,100.
56	A1	10p vermilion	5,000.	70.00
		10p orange	7,500.	500.00
58	A2	2sh blue	375.00	45.00

The ½p, 1p blue, 2p olive, 4p and 5p green exist imperf.

			Wmk. 1b	
46d	A1	1p blue	325.00	17.50
		1p dark blue	275.00	16.00
49d	A1	2p orange yellow	135.00	8.00
e.		2p olive yellow	175.00	14.00
f.		2p olive green	175.00	30.00
50b	A2	4p rose	325.00	65.00
c.		4p carmine rose	125.00	40.00
52b	A1	5p myrtle green	160.00	25.00
c.		5p olive green	150.00	27.50
d.		5p bronze green	60.00	60.00
53e	A1	6p chocolate brown	140.00	11.00
f.		6p brown	190.00	9.00
54a	A2	8p red brown	140.00	80.00
55a	A2	9p dark brown	70.00	74.00
b.		9p bister brown	975.00	40.00
56b	A1	10p orange	150.00	17.00
		10p orange red	90.00	18.00
d.		10p vermilion	5,500.	170.00
57	A1	1sh purple	150.00	12.00
		1sh reddish lilac	325.00	32.50
58a	A2	2sh deep blue	160.00	17.50
		2sh indigo	300.00	22.50

The 1p blue and 6p brown exist imperf.
For overprints see Nos. O2, O4-O7.

A4   A5

1866		**Typo.**	**Wmk. 1**	**Perf. 12½**
59	A5	3p rose	300.00	105.00
a.		Imperf., pair	1,000.	

For overprint see No. O3.

1868			**Perf. 14**	
61	A4	1p blue	30.00	12.00
62	A5	3p rose	95.00	52.50

For overprint see No. O1.

A6   A7

A8   A9

A10   A11

A12   A13

A14   A15

1872-80			**Perf. 14**	
63	A6	2c brown	32.50	4.50
64	A7	4c gray	50.00	1.75
65	A7	4c lil rose ('80)	75.00	1.60
66	A8	8c orange	55.00	7.25
a.		8c orange yellow	45.00	8.00
67	A9	16c violet	150.00	3.00
68	A10	24c green	90.00	2.25
69	A11	32c slate bl ('77)	190.00	16.00
70	A12	36c blue	210.00	30.00
71	A13	48c rose	110.00	9.50
72	A14	64c red brn ('77)	325.00	77.50
73	A15	96c olive gray	300.00	30.00
		Nos. 63-73 (11)	1,588.	183.35

For surcharges see Nos. 83-84, 94A-110, 112-114. For types surcharged see Nos. 124-129.

1872			**Perf. 12½**	
74	A6	2c brown	4,750.	275.00
75	A7	4c gray	3,250.	350.00

A16

1879			**Perf. 14x12½**	
77	A6	2c brown	450.00	75.00
78	A7	4c gray	2,600.	40.00
79	A8	8c orange	500.00	57.50
			Perf. 12½x14	
82	A16	2r50c claret	825.00	440.00

The 32c and 64c are known perf. 14x12½, but were not regularly issued.

No. 82, perf. 12½, was not regularly issued. See Nos. 142, 158. For surcharges see Nos. 111, 115, 130. For types surcharged see Nos. 160-161.

Nos. 68, 72 Surcharged

SIXTEEN
16
CENTS

1882   *Perf. 14*

83	A10	16c on 24c green	42.50	10.00
a.	Inverted surcharge		—	
84	A14	20c on 64c red brn	14.50	10.00
a.	Double surcharge		1,850.	

1883-99   *Wmk. 2*

85	A6	2c pale brown	75.00	3.50
86	A6	2c green ('84)	3.25	.25
a.	Perf. 12		7,000.	
87	A6	2c org brn ('99)	5.00	.40
88	A7	4c lilac rose	6.50	.50
89	A7	4c rose ('84)	7.75	13.50
a.	Perf. 12		7,250.	
90	A7	4c brt rose ('98)	13.00	15.00
91	A7	4c yellow ('99)	4.25	4.00
92	A8	8c orange	8.00	14.00
93	A9	16c violet	2,100.	180.00
94	A10	24c purple brown	1,750.	
b.	Perf. 12		7,750.	

Nos. 86a, 89a, 94 and 94b were never placed in use. A 48c brown, perf. 12, was prepared but not issued.

For surcharges and overprints see Nos.116-123, 143-151D, 155-156. O8-O9.

Issues of 1872-82 Surcharged

a   b

c   d

1885   *Wmk. 1*   *Perf. 14*

94A	A9 (a)	5c on 16c		3,250.
95	A10 (a)	5c on 24c	6,750.	115.00
96	A11 (a)	5c on 32c	72.50	20.00
a.	Inverted surcharge			3,000.
97	A12 (a)	5c on 36c	325.00	13.50
a.	Inverted surcharge			2,850.
98	A13 (a)	5c on 48c	2,550.	75.00
99	A14 (a)	5c on 64c	145.00	14.00
a.	Double surcharge			3,750.
100	A15 (a)	5c on 96c	575.00	75.00
101	A9 (b)	10c on 16c	12,500.	3,250.
102	A10 (b)	10c on 24c	525.00	145.00
103	A12 (b)	10c on 36c	500.00	290.00
104	A14 (b)	10c on 64c	475.00	275.00
105	A10 (b)	20c on 24c	80.00	30.00
106	A11 (c)	20c on 32c	95.00	80.00
107	A11 (c)	25c on 32c	27.50	8.25
108	A13 (c)	28c on 48c	45.00	11.50
a.	Double surcharge			3,250.
109	A12 (b)	30c on 36c	16.00	12.50
a.	Inverted surcharge		350.00	160.00
110	A15 (b)	50c on 96c	37.50	27.50

Perf. 12½

111	A16 (d)	1r12c on 2r50c	750.00	115.00

Perf. 14x12½

112	A11 (a)	5c on 32c	900.00	57.50
113	A14 (a)	5c on 64c	975.00	57.50
114	A14 (b)	10c on 64c	100.00	175.00
a.	Vert. pair, imperf. btwn.			6,750.

Perf. 12½x14

115	A16 (d)	1r12c on 2r50c	115.00	55.00

Perf. 14   *Wmk. 2*

117	A7 (a)	5c on 4c rose	27.50	6.00
a.	Inverted surcharge			350.00
118	A8 (a)	5c on 8c org	100.00	12.00
a.	Inverted surcharge			4,400.
b.	Double surcharge			4,000.
119	A9 (a)	5c on 16c vio	190.00	18.00
a.	Inverted surcharge			260.00
120	A10 (a)	5c on 24c pur brn	—	600.00
121	A9 (b)	10c on 16c vio	13,500.	1,800.
122	A10 (b)	10c on 24c pur brn	18.50	11.50
123	A9 (b)	15c on 16c vio	15.50	11.50

A 5c on 4c lilac rose and a 5c on 24c green are known to exist and are considered to be a forgeries.

Types of 1872-80 Surcharged

e   f

g

1885-87

124	A 8 (e)	5c on 8c lilac	27.50	1.60
125	A10 (f)	10c on 24c pur brn	14.50	9.00
126	A 9 (f)	15c on 16c org	62.50	15.50
127	A11 (f)	28c on 32c sl bl	30.00	2.75
128	A12 (f)	30c on 36c ol grn	30.00	16.00
129	A15 (f)	56c on 96c ol gray	55.00	18.00

Wmk. 1 Sideways

130	A16 (g)	1r12c on 2r50c cl	62.50	145.00
	Nos. 124-130 (7)		282.00	207.85

A23

Type I   Type II

FIVE CENTS
Type I — Thin lines in background. Hair and curl clear.
Type II — Thicker lines in background. Heavier shading under chin.

1886   *Wmk. 2*

131	A23	5c lilac, type I	4.00	.25
a.	Type II		4.00	.25

For overprint see No. O12.

A24

1886-1900

132	A24	3c org brn & green ('93)	7.00	.50
133	A24	3c green ('00)	5.00	.60
134	A24	6c rose & blk ('99)	3.25	.50
135	A24	12c ol grn & car ('00)	5.50	9.00
136	A24	15c olive green	9.00	2.40
137	A24	15c ultra ('00)	8.00	1.50
138	A24	25c brown	5.75	2.00
a.	25c brown, value in ol yel		155.00	90.00
139	A24	28c slate	25.00	1.50
140	A24	30c vio & org brown ('93)	4.75	3.50
141	A24	75c blk & org brown ('00)	9.50	9.50
	Nos. 132-141 (10)		82.75	31.00

Numeral tablet of 3c, 12c and 75c has lined background with colorless value and "c."

For surcharges & overprints see Nos. 152-154, 157, 159, O10-O11, O13-O17.

1887   *Wmk. 1*

142	A16	1r12c claret	32.50	30.00

For overprint see No. O18.

Issue of 1883-84 Surcharged

1888-90   *Wmk. 2*

143	A7	2c on 4c lilac rose	1.60	.95
a.	Inverted surcharge		25.00	24.00
b.	Double surcharge, one invtd.		400.00	
144	A7	2c on 4c rose	2.75	.35
a.	Inverted surcharge		20.00	21.00
b.	Double surcharge		400.00	

Surcharged

145	A7	2c on 4c lilac rose	1.10	.30
a.	Inverted surcharge		42.50	42.50
b.	Double surcharge		100.00	110.00
c.	Double surcharge, one invtd.		85.00	85.00
146	A7	2c on 4c rose	8.00	.25
a.	Double surcharge, one invtd.		105.00	125.00
b.	Double surcharge		110.00	125.00
c.	Inverted surcharge		425.00	

Surcharged

147	A7	2c on 4c lilac rose	82.50	35.00
a.	Inverted surcharge		175.00	47.50
b.	Double surcharge, one inverted		210.00	
148	A7	2c on 4c rose	4.00	1.00
a.	Inverted surcharge		19.00	10.00
b.	Double surcharge, one inverted		9.50	15.00
c.	Double surcharge		210.00	175.00

Surcharged

149	A7	2c on 4c lilac rose	67.50	30.00
a.	Inverted surcharge		200.00	32.50
150	A7	2c on 4c rose	3.00	1.25
a.	Inverted surcharge		19.00	8.50
b.	Double surcharge		160.00	150.00
c.	Double surcharge, one inverted		19.00	11.00

Surcharged

151	A7	2c on 4c rose	13.50	1.20
a.	Inverted surcharge		24.00	7.50
b.	Double surcharge		135.00	135.00
c.	Double surch., one invtd.		27.50	13.50
i.	"S" of "Cents" inverted		525.00	350.00
151D	A7	2c on 4c lilac rose	67.50	37.50
e.	Inverted surcharge		95.00	42.50
f.	Double surcharge		450.00	
g.	Double surch., one invtd.		150.00	150.00
h.	"S" of "Cents" inverted		750.00	

Counterfeit errors of surcharges of Nos. 143 to 151D are prevalent.

No. 136 Surcharged

1890

152	A24	5c on 15c ol green	4.00	2.75
a.	"Five" instead of "Five"		140.00	100.00
b.	"REVENUE" omitted		225.00	200.00
c.	Inverted surcharge		65.00	75.00
d.	Double surcharge		125.00	145.00
e.	As "a," inverted surcharge		—	1,800.
f.	Inverted "s" in "Cents"		130.00	120.00
g.	As "f," inverted surcharge		2,200.	
h.	As "b," invtd. "s" in "Cents"		1,800.	

Nos. 138-139 Surcharged

1891

153	A24	15c on 25c brown	20.00	20.00
154	A24	15c on 28c slate	21.00	10.00

Nos. 88, 89 and 139 Surcharged

1892

155	A7	3c on 4c lilac rose	1.10	3.50
156	A7	3c on 4c rose	7.25	11.00
a.	Double surcharge, one invtd.			
157	A24	3c on 28c slate	6.25	5.75
a.	Double surcharge		180.00	
	Nos. 155-157 (3)		14.60	20.25

Type of 1879

1898

158	A16	2r50c violet, *red*	42.50	65.00

No. 136 Surcharged in Black

1899

159	A24	6c on 15c olive green	1.35	.85

Surcharged Type "g" in Black

1899   *Wmk. 1*

160	A16	1r50c on 2r50c gray	24.00	55.00
161	A16	2r25c on 2r50c yel	50.00	95.00

A35

1900   *Wmk. 1*

162	A35	1r50c car rose	35.00	55.00
163	A35	2r25c dull blue	37.50	55.00

Nos. 166-292 exist in many different shades, representing different printings for each stamp.

King Edward VII
A36   A37

A38   A39

A40

1903-05   *Wmk. 2*

166	A36	2c org brown	2.40	.25
167	A37	3c green	2.40	1.20
168	A37	4c yel & blue	2.40	6.00
169	A38	5c dull lilac	2.75	.70

170	A39	6c car rose	11.00	1.75
171	A37	12c ol grn & car	5.50	11.50
172	A40	15c ultra	6.75	3.50
173	A40	25c bister	5.00	4.25
174	A40	30c vio & green	3.50	4.25
175	A37	75c bl & org ('05)	3.50	24.00
176	A40	1r50c gray ('04)	67.50	67.50
177	A40	2r25c brn & grn ('04)	95.00	60.00
		Nos. 166-177 (12)	207.70	192.65
		Set, never hinged	400.00	

For overprints see Nos. O19-O24.

1904-10 — **Wmk. 3**

178	A36	2c orange brown	2.75	.25
a.		2c orange	1.60	.60
179	A37	3c green	1.75	.25
180	A37	4c yel & blue	3.00	1.75
181	A38	5c dull lilac	3.50	1.50
a.		Booklet pane of 12	7.50	.75
b.		5c dull lilac, "chalky paper"		
182	A39	6c car rose	5.25	.25
183	A40	10c ol grn & vio ('10)	2.50	3.50
184	A37	12c ol grn & car	1.75	2.00
185	A40	15c ultra	3.75	.70
186	A40	25c bister ('05)	6.25	4.00
187	A40	25c slate ('10)	2.75	3.00
188	A40	30c vio & grn ('05)	2.75	3.25
189	A40	50c brown ('10)	4.25	7.75
190	A37	75c bl & org ('05)	5.50	8.25
191	A40	1r vio, yel ('10)	8.50	13.00
192	A40	1r50c gray ('05)	32.50	14.00
193	A40	2r scar, yel ('10)	16.00	30.00
194	A40	2r25c brn & grn	26.00	32.50
195	A40	5r blk, grn ('10)	50.00	125.00
196	A40	10r blk, red ('10)	150.00	325.00
		Nos. 178-196 (19)	328.75	575.95
		Set, never hinged	600.00	

A41

A42

1908

197	A41	5c deep red violet	7.75	.25
a.		Booklet pane of 12		
198	A42	6c carmine rose	3.50	.25

1911, July 5

199	A40	3c green	1.10	.85

A44

King George V — A45

Type I

Type II

3 AND 6 CENTS

Type I — Small "c" after value, 2¼mm wide and 2mm high.

Type II — Large "c" after value, 2½mm wide and 2¼mm high.

1, 5 AND 9 CENTS are Type II, other denominations Type I.

For description of dies I and II see "Dies of British Colonial Stamps" in the Table of Contents.

1912-25 — **Die I** — **Wmk. 3**

200	A44	1c dp brn (Die Ib) ('20)	1.20	.25
201	A44	2c brown org	.45	.25
202	A44	3c dp grn (Die Ia, type II)	5.75	.50
a.		3c deep green, die I, type I	6.75	2.40
203	A44	5c red viol	1.20	.70
a.		5c purple	12.00	3.00
204	A44	6c car (Die Ib, type II)	1.75	1.60
a.		6c carmine, die I, type I	20.00	1.25
b.		As "a", bklt. pane of 6		
205	A44	10c olive green	3.50	2.00
206	A44	15c ultra	3.75	1.50

Chalky Paper

207	A44	25c yel & ultra	2.10	2.10
208	A44	30c green & vio	4.75	3.75
209	A44	50c black & scar	1.75	2.10
210	A44	1r violet, yel	5.25	4.25
211	A44	2r blk & red, yel	3.75	15.00
212	A44	5r blk, green	20.00	42.50
a.		5r black, bl grn, olive back	25.00	45.00
b.		5r blk, emer (Die II) ('20)	52.50	120.00
213	A44	10r vio & blk, red	85.00	105.00
a.		Die II ('20)	95.00	165.00
214	A44	20r blk & red, bl	165.00	175.00
215	A45	50r dull violet	675.00	1,300.
216	A45	100r gray black	3,000.	
217	A45	500r gray green	8,000.	
218	A45	1000r vio, red ('25)	35,000.	
		Nos. 200-214 (15)	305.20	356.50
		Set, never hinged	600.00	

Although Nos. 217 and 218 were theoretically available for postage it is not probable that they were ever used for other than fiscal purposes.

The 1r through 100r with revenue cancellations sell for minimal prices.

For surcharge & overprints see Nos. 223, MR1-MR3.

Die I

1913-14 — **Surface-colored Paper**

220	A44	1r violet, yellow	5.00	5.75
221	A44	2r black & red, yel	3.25	15.00
222	A44	5r black, green	26.00	42.50
		Nos. 220-222 (3)	34.25	63.25

No. 203 Surcharged

ONE CENT

1918

223	A44	1c on 5c red violet	3.50	3.50
a.		1c on 5c purple	.25	.30

For overprint see No. MR4.

Die I

1921-33 — **Wmk. 4** — **Ordinary Paper**

225	A44	1c dp brn (Die Ib) ('27)	1.20	.40
226	A44	2c brn org (Die II)	.85	.30
227	A44	3c green (Die Ia, type II)	5.75	.90
228	A44	3c slate (Die Ia, type II) ('22)	.90	.25
229	A44	5c red vio (Die I)	.70	.25
230	A44	6c carmine (Die Ib, type II)	3.50	.90
231	A44	6c vio (Die Ib, type II) ('22)	3.00	.25
232	A44	9c red, yel (Die II) ('26)	3.25	.45
233	A44	10c olive green	1.60	.45
a.		Die II	2.10	.70
234	A44	12c scarlet, Die II	1.20	6.00
a.		Die I ('25)	10.00	12.50
235	A44	15c ultramarine	4.00	22.50
236	A44	15c green, yel, Die II	5.00	1.20
a.		Die I ('22)	5.75	6.00
237	A44	20c ultra, Die II ('24)	4.25	.50
a.		Die I ('22)	6.00	7.25
238	A44	25c yel & blue	3.25	2.25
a.		Die II	3.75	1.50

For surcharges see Nos. 248-249.

Chalky Paper

239	A44	30c green & violet	1.90	6.75
a.		Die I	6.25	1.50
240	A44	50c blk & scar (Die II)	2.25	.95
a.		Die I	65.00	100.00
241	A44	1r vio, yel, Die II	26.00	42.50
a.		Die I	16.00	52.50
242	A44	2r blk & red, yel (Die II)	8.50	15.00
243	A44	5r blk, emer, (Die II)	52.50	97.50
244	A44	20r blk & red, bl, (Die II)	260.00	425.00
245	A45	50r dull vio	825.00	1,500.
246	A45	100r gray black	3,250.	
247	A45	100r ultra & dl vio ('27)	2,500.	
		Nos. 225-244 (20)	389.60	624.30
		Set, never hinged	675.00	

Nos. 228, 231
Surcharged

2 Cents.

1926

248	A44	2c on 3c slate	3.50	1.20
a.		Double surcharge	85.00	
b.		Bar omitted	90.00	100.00
249	A44	5c on 6c violet	1.25	.45
a.		Double surcharge		

A46

1927-29 — **Chalky Paper** — **Wmk. 4**

254	A46	1r red vio & dl vio ('28)	3.00	1.50
255	A46	2r car & green ('29)	4.50	3.25
256	A46	5r brn vio & grn ('28)	17.50	24.00
257	A46	10r org & green	52.50	115.00
258	A46	20r ultra & dl vio	190.00	340.00
		Nos. 254-258 (5)	267.50	483.75
		Set, never hinged	450.00	

Common Design Types pictured following the introduction.

Silver Jubilee Issue
Common Design Type

1935, May 6 — **Engr.** — **Perf. 13½x14**

260	CD301	6c gray blk & ultra	.70	.35
261	CD301	9c indigo & green	.70	2.50
262	CD301	20c blue & brown	4.00	2.75
263	CD301	50c brt vio & ind	7.45	13.50
		Nos. 260-263 (4)	10.15	19.10
		Set, never hinged	20.00	

Tapping Rubber Tree — A47

Colombo Harbor — A49

Adam's Peak — A48

Picking Tea — A50

Coconut Palms — A53

Rice Terraces A51

River Scene A52

Temple of the Tooth, Kandy A54

Ancient Reservoir A55

Wild Elephants A56

View of Trincomalee A57

Perf. 11x11½, 11½x11; 11½x13, 13x11½ (A47, A48, A53); 14 (A56)

1935-36 — **Wmk. 4**

264	A47	2c car rose & blk	.45	.55
a.		Perf. 14	12.00	.55
265	A48	3c olive & black	.50	.55
a.		Perf. 14	35.00	.40
266	A49	6c blue & black	.45	.40
267	A50	9c org red & ol grn	1.50	.90
268	A51	10c dk vio & blk	1.75	3.25
269	A52	15c grn & org brn	1.50	.70
270	A53	20c ultra & black	2.50	3.50
271	A54	25c choc & dk ultra	2.00	1.75
272	A55	30c green & lake	3.00	3.25
273	A56	50c dk vio & blk	15.00	2.50
274	A57	1r brown & vio	35.00	24.00
		Nos. 264-274 (11)	63.65	41.85
		Set, never hinged	200.00	

Issued: 2c, 15c, 25c, 5/1/35; 10c, 6/1/35; 1r, 7/1/35; 30c, 8/1/35; 3c, 10/1/35; 6c, 9c, 20c, 50c, 1/1/36.

Coronation Issue
Common Design Type

1937, May 12 — **Perf. 11x11½**

275	CD302	6c dark carmine	.75	1.10
a.		Booklet pane of 10	20.00	
276	CD302	9c deep green	3.00	4.75
a.		Booklet pane of 10	300.00	
277	CD302	20c deep ultra	4.50	4.50
		Nos. 275-277 (3)	8.25	10.35
		Set, never hinged	16.00	

Types of 1935 with "Postage & Revenue Removed" and Picturing George VI and

Sigiriya (Lion Rock) — A61

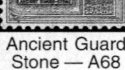

Ancient Guard Stone — A68

George VI — A69

Perf. 11x11½, 11½x11; 12 (#286)

1938-52 — **Engr.** — **Wmk. 4**

278	A47	2c car rose & blk ('44)	.45	1.25
a.		Perf. 13½x13 ('38)	100.00	2.00
b.		Perf. 13½ ('38)	2.00	.25
c.		Perf. 12 ('49)	1.25	4.50
d.		Perf. 11½x13 ('38)	10.00	2.75
279	A48	3c dk grn & blk ('42)	.50	.25
a.		Perf. 13x13½ ('38)	225.00	12.50
b.		Perf. 14 ('41)	100.00	1.10
c.		Perf. 13½ ('38)	3.50	.25
d.		Perf. 12 ('46)	.70	.25
e.		Perf. 13x11½	8.00	2.50
280	A49	6c blue & black	.25	.25
281	A61	10c blue & black	1.75	.25
282	A52	15c red brn & grn	1.25	.25
283	A50	20c dull bl & blk	2.25	.25
284	A54	25c choc & dk ultra	3.25	.30
285	A55	30c dk grn & rose car	8.00	3.75

286	A56	50c dk vio & blk ('46)	2.75 .25
a.		Perf. 14 ('42)	90.00 29.00
b.		Perf. 13x11½ ('38)	140.00 52.50
c.		Perf. 13x13½ ('38)	300.00 3.00
d.		Perf. 13½ ('38)	15.00 .55
e.		Perf. 11½x11 ('42)	4.00 4.25
287	A57	1r dk brn & bl vio	10.50 1.60
288	A68	2r dark car & blk	9.25 4.00

Perf. 14
Typo.

289	A69	5r brn vio & grn	27.50 13.50
289A	A69	10r yel org & dl grn ('52)	50.00 50.00

Nos. 278-289A (13) 117.70 75.90
Set, never hinged 360.00

No. 289A differs from type A69 in having "REVENUE" inscribed vertically at either side of the frame. This revenue 10r was valid for postage Dec. 1, 1952-Mar. 14, 1954.
See Nos. 292, 295. For surcharges see Nos. 290-291.

> Catalogue values for unused stamps in this section, from this point to the end of the section, are for Never Hinged items.

No. 283 Surcharged
in Black

3 CENTS

1940, Nov. 5   **Perf. 11x11½**
290 A50 3c on 20c dull bl & blk 4.50 4.50

No. 280 Surcharged

3 CENTS

1941, May 10
291 A49 3c on 6c blue & black .65 *1.00*

Coconut
Palms — A70

1943-47   **Wmk. 4**   **Engr.**   **Perf. 12**
292 A70 5c red org & ol grn ('47) 1.75 .35
a.   Perf. 13½ ('43) .35 .25

Peace Issue
Common Design Type
1946, Dec. 10   **Perf. 13½x14**
293 CD303 6c deep blue .30 *.35*
294 CD303 15c brown .30 *1.75*

Guard Stone Type of 1938
1947, Mar. 15   **Perf. 11x11½**
295 A68 2r violet & black . 2.40 *2.75*

Parliament Building, Colombo — A71

Adam's Peak   Dagoba at
A72   Anuradhapura
    A74

Temple
of the
Tooth,
Kandy
A73

1947, Nov. 25   **Perf. 11x12, 12x11**
296 A71 6c deep ultra & black .25 .25
297 A72 10c car, orange & black .25 .40
298 A73 15c red vio & grnsh blk .25 .80
299 A74 25c brt green & bister .25 *1.75*
Nos. 296-299 (4) 1.00 3.20
New constitution of 1947.

National Flag   D. S.
A75   Senanayake
    A76

Engr., Flag Typo. (A75); Engr. (A76)
Perf. 12½x12, 12x12½, 13x12½
1949   **Wmk. 4**
300 A75 4c org brn, car & yel .25 .25
301 A76 5c dark green & brn .25 .25

Wmk. 290
302 A75 15c red org, car & yel 1.00 .40
303 A76 25c dp blue & brown .25 1.00
Nos. 300-303 (4) 1.75 1.90

Size of No. 302: 28x22¼mm.
1st anniv. of Ceylon's independence.
Issued: Nos. 300-301, Feb. 4; Nos. 302-303, Apr. 5.

A77

A78

Design: 15c, Lion Rock and UPU symbols.

Wmk. 290
1949, Oct. 10   **Engr.**   **Perf. 12**
304 A77 5c dk green & brown .85 .25
305 A77 15c dark car & black 1.25 2.75
306 A78 25c ultra & black 1.25 1.25
Nos. 304-306 (3) 3.35 4.25
75th anniv. of the UPU.

Kandyan   Kiri Vehera,
Dancer   Polonnaruwa
A79   A80

Vesak   Sigiriya — A82
Orchid — A81

Vatadage
Ruins at
Madirigiriya
A84

1950, Feb. 4   **Perf. 12x12½**
307 A79 4c bright red & choc .25 .25
308 A80 5c green .25 .25
309 A81 15c pur & blue green 2.75 .50
310 A82 30c carmine & yel .40 .70

Perf. 11x11½, 11½x11
311 A83 75c red org & blue 8.50 .25
312 A84 1r red brn & dp blue 2.50 .45
Nos. 307-312 (6) 14.65 2.40
See Nos. 340-345.

Coconut   Star
Palms — A85   Orchid — A86

1951-52 Unwmk. Photo.   **Perf. 11½**
313 A85 10c gray & dark green 1.25 .75
314 A86 35c dk grn & rose brn ('52) 1.50 1.50
a.   Corrected inscription ('54) 6.00 .70

On No. 314a a dot has been added above the third character in the second line of the Tamil inscription.
Issue dates: 10c, Aug. 1; 35c, Feb. 1.
See No. 351.

Mace and
Symbols of
Industry
A87

Perf. 12½x14
1952, Feb. 23   **Wmk. 290**
315 A87 5c green .25 .30
316 A87 15c brt ultramarine .40 .60
Colombo Plan Exhibition, February 1952.

Coronation Issue

Queen
Elizabeth II — A88

1953, June 2   **Engr.**   **Perf. 12x12½**
317 A88 5c green 1.50 .25

Royal
Procession
A89

1954, Apr. 10   **Perf. 13x12½**
318 A89 10c deep blue 1.25 .25
Visit of Queen Elizabeth II and the Duke of Edinburgh, 1954.

Sambar in   Rubber
Ruhuna   Trees — A91
National
Park — A90

Designs: 3c, Ancient guard stone. 6c and 10r, Harvesting rice. 25c, Sigiriya fresco. 50c, Outrigger fishing canoe. 85c, Tea Picker. 2r, Gal Oya dam. 5r, Bas-relief, "The Lovers."

1954   **Unwmk.**   **Photo.**   **Perf. 11½**
Size: 21x25½mm
319 A90 2c green & brown .25 *1.25*
320 A90 3c violet & black .25 *1.00*
321 A90 6c yel grn & blk brn .25 *.30*
322 A90 25c vio bl, bl & brn orange .25 .25

Size: 25½x21mm
323 A91 40c black brown 5.50 1.25
324 A91 50c indigo .45 .25

Size: 23x32½mm, 32½x23mm
325 A90 85c dk grn & gray 1.50 .40
326 A91 2r blue & blk brn 9.25 1.40
327 A90 5r dp org & blk brn 8.00 1.50
328 A90 10r brown 60.00 20.00
Nos. 319-328 (10) 85.70 27.60

See Nos. 346-356.
Issued: 25c, 50c, 5r, 10r, 3/15; others, 5/15. Nos. 327-328 with revenue cancellations sell for minimal prices.

King
Coconuts — A92

1954, Dec. 1
329 A92 10c brown & orange .30 .25
See No. 349.

Symbols of
Agriculture
A93

Perf. 14x14½
1955, Dec. 10   **Wmk. 290**
330 A93 10c orange & brown .30 .25
Royal Agricultural and Food Exhibition.

House of Representatives — A94

1956, Mar. 26   Unwmk.   Perf. 11½
Granite Paper
331 A94 10c deep green   .25 .25
   25th anniv. of Prime Minister Sir John Kote-lawala's entry into the Ceylon Legislature.

Arrival of Vijaya in Ceylon — A95

Dharmachakra Encircling Globe — A96

1956, May 23   Granite Paper
332 A95 3c dull vio gray & saph   .25 .25
333 A96 15c ultramarine   .25 .25
   Birth of Buddha, 2500th anniv. See Nos. B1-B2.

Methods of Transportation — A97

   35c, 85c, Ceylon's 1st stamp & coat of arms.

1957, Apr. 1   Photo.   Perf. 12½x13
334 A97 4c blue green & ver   .80 .50
335 A97 10c blue & vermilion   .80 .25
Perf. 11½
336 A97 35c blue, yel & brown   .40 .55
337 A97 85c dull grn, yel & brn   .85 1.60
   Nos. 334-337 (4)   2.85 2.90
   Ceylon's 1st postage stamps, cent.

Nos. B1-B2 Overprinted with Black Bars and Squares

1958, Jan. 15   Unwmk.
Granite Paper
338 SP1 4c dp blue & lt yel   .25 .25
 a. Inverted overprint   15.00 20.00
 b. Double overprint   22.50 29.00
339 SP1 10c dk gray, yel & brt pink .25 .25
 a. Inverted overprint   15.00 17.00
   The overprint obliterates the surtax and inscription at right.

Types of 1950-54 Redrawn
Perf. 12x12½
1958-59   Engr.   Wmk. 290
340 A79 4c brt red & choco-late   .25 .25
341 A80 5c green   .25 1.60
342 A81 15c purple & blue grn   3.50 1.10
343 A82 30c car & yel ('59)   .25 1.50
Perf. 11½x11
344 A83 75c red org & bl ('59)   9.50 3.25
Perf. 11x11½
345 A84 1r red brn & dp blue   .65 .25
   Nos. 340-345 (6)   14.40 7.95
   Issued: 4c, 5/14; 5c, 15c, 1r, 10/1; 30c, 75c, 5/1.
   For surcharge see No. 368.

No. 328

No. 356

1958-59 Unwmk. Photo. Perf. 11½
Granite Paper
346 A90 2c green & brown   .25 .50
347 A90 3c violet & black   .25 .70
348 A90 6c yel grn & blk brn   .25 .65
349 A92 10c brown & orange   .25 .25
350 A90 25c vio bl, bl & brn orange .25 .25
351 A86 35c dk grn & rose brn   7.75 .40
352 A91 50c indigo   .25 .25
353 A90 85c dark green & gray   4.50 8.50
354 A91 2r blue & blk brn   2.00 .30
355 A90 5r dp org & blk brn   10.00 .40
356 A90 10r brown   12.00 1.40
   Nos. 346-356 (11)   37.75 13.60

   Designs and sizes of Nos. 340-356 remain as before, but wording has been changed to be predominantly Singhalese. "Ceylon" appears in small letters only in English and Tamil.
   Nos. 355-356 with revenue cancellations sell for minimal prices.
   Issue dates: 35c, 50c, July 15; 10c, Oct. 1; 85c, May 1, 1959; others, May 14, 1958.
   For surcharges, see Sri Lanka Nos. 1572, 1577.

Hands Reaching for UN Symbol A98

Perf. 13x12½
1958, Dec. 10   Photo.   Unwmk.
357 A98 10c red brown & red   .25 .25
358 A98 85c Prus green & red   .30 .30
   10th anniv. of the signing of the Universal Declaration of Human Rights.

Pirivena Universities and Founders A99

1959, Dec. 31
359 A99 10c brt ultra & dp org   .30 .30
   Institution of Pirivena Universities; founders Hikkaduwe Sri Sumangala Nayaka Thero and Ratmalane Sri Dharmaloka Nayake Thero.

Uprooted Oak Emblem — A100

1960, Apr. 7   Photo.   Perf. 11½
Granite Paper
360 A100 4c chocolate & gold   .25 .85
361 A100 25c vio blue & gold   .25 .25
   World Refugee Year, 7/1/59-6/30/60.

Prime Minister Bandaranaike A101

Type I

Type II

   Two types:
   I — Gray hair at temple.
   II — Dark hair at temple (redrawn).

1961, Jan. 8   Granite Paper
362 A101 10c vio bl & gray bl (I)   .40 .60
 a. Type II   .90 .25
   Solomon West Ridgeway Dias Bandaranaike, assassinated Sept. 26, 1959.

Badge of Singhalese Scouts — A102

1962, Feb. 26   Unwmk.   Perf. 11½
Granite Paper
363 A102 35c dark blue & ocher   .35 .25
   Boy Scouts of Ceylon, 50th anniv.

Malaria Eradication Emblem — A103

Perf. 14½x14
1962, Apr. 7   Photo.   Wmk. 290
364 A103 25c lt sep, red org & brn .40 .40
   WHO drive to eradicate malaria.

Monoplane 1938, and De Havilland Comet IV — A104

1963, Feb. 28   Unwmk.   Perf. 11½
Granite Paper
365 A104 50c lt grnsh blue & blk   .60 .60
   25th anniv. of Ceylonese airmail service.

Stylized Vase and Wheat Emblem A105

1963, Mar. 21   Granite Paper
366 A105 5c blue & orange ver   .75 2.50
367 A105 25c olive & brown   3.00 3.25
   FAO "Freedom from Hunger" campaign.

No. 340 Surcharged

Perf. 12x12½
1963, June 1   Engr.   Wmk. 290
368 A79 2c on 4c brt red & choc   .40 .40
 a. Inverted surcharge   20.00
 b. Double surcharge   40.00

Rural Life — A106

1963, July 5   Photo.   Perf. 14x14½
369 A106 60c dull red & black   2.00 .75
   50th anniv. of the Cooperative Movement.

Landscape and Elephant A107

1963, Dec. 2   Wmk. 290
370 A107 5c blue & black   .65 .45
   National Conservation Week.

S.W.R.D. Bandaranaike A108

Perf. 11½
1963, Sept. 26   Unwmk.   Engr.
Granite Paper
371 A108 10c blue   .30 .30

Redrawn
Granite Paper
1964, July 1   Photo.
372 A108 10c grnsh gray & bl vio   .30 .30
   Frame redrawn on No. 372; inscription in bottom panel replaced by ornament.
   For surcharge see No. 389.

Anagarika Dharmapala — A109

1964, Sept. 16   Unwmk.   Perf. 11½
Granite Paper
373 A109 25c gray brn & dull yel   .30 .30
Anagarika Dharmapala, Buddhist missionary, birth cent.

Ceylon Jungle Fowl — A110

Tea Picker — A112

Vatadage Ruins at Madirigiriya A111

Designs: 5c, Hill myna. 15c, Blue peafowl. 75c, Asiatic black-headed oriole. 5r, Girls, working in rice field. 10r, Map of Ceylon on scroll, showing agricultural development stations.

Wmk. 290, Unwmkd. (20c)
1964-69   Photo.   Perf. 14, 11½ (20c)
374 A110 5c brt bl, blk, yel
          & grn   2.00 1.40
375 A110 15c yel, grn, blk,
          brt bl & rose   3.75   .30
376 A111 20c dk red brn,
          buff   .25   .25
377 A110 60c yel & multi   4.50 1.10
  a.   Blue omitted   50.00
  b.   Red omitted   50.00
378 A110 75c ol, blk, org &
          brn   3.00   .75
  a.   Souvenir sheet of 4   10.00 14.00
  b.   As "a," overprinted   10.00
379 A112 1r brown & grn   1.00   .25
  c.   Brown omitted   750.00
379A A111 5r multicolored   9.50   9.50
379B A112 10r brown & multi   22.50   3.50
    Nos. 374-379B (8)   46.50 17.05

No. 378a contains four imperf. stamps with simulated perforations similar to Nos. 374-375 and 377-378.
No. 378b is overprinted "First National Stamp Exhibition 1967" in two lines of black capitals.
No. 376 is on granite paper.
Issued: 20c, 1r, 10/1; 5c, 15c, 60c, 75c, 2/5/66; 5r, 8/15/69; 10r, 10/1/69.
See No. 325.

Exhibition Buildings, Cogwheels — A113

"Industrial Exhibition" in Singhalese and English
1964, Dec. 1   Unwmk.   Perf. 11
380 A113 5c multicolored   .25   .75
"Industrial Exhibition" in Singhalese and Tamil
381 A113 5c multicolored   .25   .75
  a.   Pair, #380-381   .35 2.50
    1965 Industrial Exhibition.

Railroad Trains, 1864-1964 A114

"Railway Centenary" in Singhalese and English

Wmk. 290
1964, Dec. 21   Photo.   Perf. 14
382 A114 60c lil rose, bl & yel
          grn   3.25   .55
"Railway Centenary" in Singhalese and Tamil
383 A114 60c lil rose, bl & yel
          grn   3.25   .55
  a.   Vertical pair, #382-383 7.75 7.75
    Centenary of Ceylonese railroads.

ITU Emblem, Old and New Communication Equipment — A115

1965, May 17   Perf. 14
384 A115 2c ultra & red   1.60 1.40
385 A115 30c brown & red   4.50   .55
    ITU, centenary.

ICY Emblem A116

1965, June 26   Unwmk.   Perf. 11½
Granite Paper
386 A116 3c rose car & dk bl   1.50 1.25
387 A116 50c gold, rose car &
          blk   4.00   .60
    International Cooperation Year.

Municipal Council Building A117

1965, Oct. 29   Photo.   Perf. 11½
Granite Paper
388 A117 25c gray & green   .30   .30
    Centenary of Colombo Municipal Council.

No. 372 Surcharged

1965, Dec. 18   Photo.   Perf. 11½
389 A108 5c on 10c   .30 1.25

D. S. Senanayake — A118

1966, Mar. 22   Unwmk.   Perf. 11½
Granite Paper
390 A118 10c bright green   .85   .25
    D. S. Senanayake, first prime minister of Ceylon, 14th death anniv. See No. 418.

View and Arms of Kandy — A119

Perf. 14x13½
1966, June 15   Photo.   Wmk. 290
391 A119 25c multicolored   .30   .30
    Centenary of Kandy Municipal Council.

Opening of WHO Headquarters, Geneva A120

Unwmk.
1966, Oct. 8   Litho.   Perf. 14
392 A120 4c multicolored   2.50 3.00
393 A120 1r multicolored   8.00 1.60

Rice, Map of Ceylon, FAO Emblem — A121

Design: 30c, Rice and globe.

1966, Oct. 25   Photo.   Perf. 11½
Granite Paper
394 A121 6c dk green, org &
          brn   .25   .75
395 A121 30c brt blue, org & brn .50   .25
    Intl. Rice Year under sponsorship of the FAO.

UNESCO Emblem A122

1966, Nov. 3   Litho.   Perf. 12
396 A122 3c tan & multi   4.00 4.00
397 A122 50c brt green & multi 7.75 1.00
    20th anniv. of UNESCO.
    For surcharge, see Sri Lanka No. 1578.

Map of Ceylon and UNESCO Emblem — A123

1966, Dec. 1   Unwmk.   Perf. 14
398 A123 2c yel brn, yel & blue .35 1.00
399 A123 2r multicolored   1.50 2.25
    Intl. Hydrological Decade (UNESCO), 1965-74.

Worshippers at Buddhist Shrine A124

Designs: 20c, Muhintale Rock. 35c, Sacred Bo Tree. 60c, Adam's Peak.

1967, Jan. 2   Photo.   Perf. 12
400 A124 5c multicolored   .25   .60
401 A124 20c multicolored   .25   .25
402 A124 35c multicolored   .25   .25
403 A124 60c multicolored   .25   .25
    Nos. 400-403 (4)   1.00 1.35
    1st anniv. of the Poya Holiday System, Buddhist holiday replacing Sunday.
    For surcharge, see Sri Lanka No. 1573.

Dutch Ramparts, Clock Tower and Arms of Galle A125

1967, Jan. 5   Litho.   Perf. 14x13½
404 A125 25c dk green & multi   .80   .25
    Centenary of Galle Municipal Council.

Tea Research A126

40c, Tea tasting (cup & loose tea). 50c, Tea picking. 1r, Tea export (crate & freighter).

1967, Aug. 1   Unwmk.   Perf. 13½
405 A126 4c multicolored   .60   .60
406 A126 40c multicolored   1.75 1.60
407 A126 50c multicolored   1.75   .40
408 A126 1r multicolored   1.75   .25
    Nos. 405-408 (4)   5.85 2.85
    Centenary of the Ceylonese tea industry.

Elephant and ITY Emblem A127

1967, Aug. 15   Litho.
409 A127 45c multicolored   3.00   .85
    Intl. Tourist Year.

Girl Guide, Jubilee Emblem and Flag — A128

1967, Sept. 19   Perf. 12x12½
410 A128 3c green & multi   .60   .25
411 A128 25c org yel & multi   .90   .25
    Ceylon Girl Guide Assoc., 50th anniv.

Henry S. Olcott and Buddhist Flag A129

Perf. 13½
1967, Dec. 12   Unwmk.   Litho.
412 A129 15c multicolored   .40   .25
    Colonel Henry S. Olcott (1832-1907), an American who reorganized the Buddhist hierarchy and school system in Ceylon and was the first president of the Theosophical Society.

Independence Memorial, Colombo A130

Design: 1r, Flag of Ceylon and mace.

1968, Feb. 4   Wmk. 290   Perf. 14
413 A130 5c multicolored   .25   .55
414 A130 1r multicolored   .60   .25
    20th anniversary of independence.

D. B.
Jayatilaka — A131

1968, Feb. 14   **Photo.**
415   A131   25c brown   .30   .30
Sir Don Baron Jayatilaka (1868-1944), Buddhist leader and scholar.

Hygiene
Institute,
Kalutara
A132

Perf. 11½x12
1968, Apr. 4   **Litho.**   **Wmk. 290**
416   A132   50c multicolored   .30   .30
WHO, 20th anniversary.

Jet over
Colombo
Terminal
A133

1968, Aug. 5   **Perf. 13½**
417   A133   60c org brn, dk bl &
            org   .75   .25
Opening of Colombo Airport.

D. S.
Senanayake — A134

1968, Sept. 23   **Photo.**   **Perf. 14**
418   A134   10c deep green   .25   .25
See No. 390.

Open Koran
A135

1968, Oct. 14   **Photo.**   **Perf. 14**
419   A135   25c org brn, blk, blue &
            emerald   .30   .30
1,400th anniversary of the Koran.

Human Rights
Flame
A136

Perf. 12½x13½
1968, Dec. 10   **Unwmk.**
420   A136   2c multicolored   .25   .30
421   A136   20c multicolored   .25   .25
422   A136   40c multicolored   .25   .25
423   A136   2r multicolored   .90   4.00
      Nos. 420-423 (4)   1.65   4.80
International Human Rights Year.

Ceylon Buddhist Headquarters,
Colombo — A137

1968, Dec. 19   **Litho.**   **Perf. 13½**
424   A137   5c multicolored   .40   .60
All-Ceylon Buddhist Cong., 50th anniv.
A multicolored 50c showing the Sri Padmaya (Sacred Footprint) on Adam's Peak was prepared but the issuance order was countermanded on Dec. 18. Some were sold in ignorance of the withdrawal order. Value $65.

E. W. Perera — A138

Wmk. 290
1969, Feb. 17   **Photo.**   **Perf. 14**
425   A138   60c brown   .30   .50
E. W. Perera, member of Legislative Council.

"Strength in
Saving" — A139

1969, Mar. 20
426   A139   3c blue, yel & black   .30   .40
National Savings Movement, 25th anniv.

A140

4c, Seat of Enlightenment under Bodhi Tree. 6c, Buduresmala (disk symbolic of six-fold Buddha rays).

Wmk. 290
1969, Apr. 10   **Litho.**   **Perf. 15**
427   A140   4c orange & multi   .25   .50
428   A140   6c gold & multi   .25   .50
429   A140   35c scarlet & multi   .25   .25
      Nos. 427-429 (3)   .75   1.25
Vesak Day, which commemorates the birth, enlightenment and death of Buddha.
For surcharges see Nos. 463, 466.

A141

1969, Apr. 29   **Photo.**   **Perf. 14x14½**
430   A141   15c org yel & multi   .30   .30
Alexander Ekanayake Goonesingha (1891-1967), trade unionist, political leader and diplomat.

ILO, 50th
Anniv.
A142

1969, May 4   **Perf. 14½x14**
431   A142   5c grnsh bl & black   .25   .25
432   A142   25c car rose & black   .25   .25

Convocation
Hall,
University of
Ceylon
A143

Elephant Lamp (Ath
Pana) — A144

35c, "Lamp of Education," globe & flags. 50c, Uranium atom diagram. 60c, Symbols of science education. 1r, Aerial view of Sigiriya rock fortress.

Inscribed: "SIYAWASA"

Unwmk.
1969, Aug. 1   **Litho.**   **Perf. 14**
433   A143   4c yellow & multi   .25   .80
434   A144   6c multicolored   .40   1.50
435   A143   35c multicolored   .25   .25
436   A144   50c red & multi   .25   .25
437   A143   60c blue & multi   .30   .25
438   A144   1r yel & multi   .40   .25
      Nos. 433-438 (6)   1.85   3.30
Centenary of public education and archaeological research.
For surcharges see Nos. 464-467.

Wild Water
Buffalo
A145

15c, Slender loris. 50c, Axis deer. 1r, Leopard.

Perf. 14x13½
1970, May 11   **Litho.**   **Unwmk.**
439   A145   5c lt blue & multi   1.25   1.40
440   A145   15c buff & multi   2.00   1.00
441   A145   50c salmon & multi   1.50   1.40
442   A145   1r gray & multi   1.50   1.90
      Nos. 439-442 (4)   6.25   5.70

Symbols of
Agriculture
and Industry
A146

1970, June 17
443   A146   60c multicolored   .30   .30
Asian Productivity Year.

Inauguration
of UPU
Headquarters,
Bern — A147

1970, Aug. 14   **Litho.**   **Unwmk.**
444   A147   50c org, black & blue   .50   .25
445   A147   1.10r red, black & blue   4.50   .60

Caduceus and
Oil
Lamp — A148

1970, Sept. 1   **Perf. 13½x14**
446   A148   5c multicolored   1.00   1.40
447   A148   45c gray & multi   1.00   1.10
Centenary of the Ceylon Medical School.

Victory March
and S.W.R.D.
Bandaranaike
A149

1970, Sept. 25   **Perf. 14**
448   A149   10c red & multi   .25   .25
For surcharge see No. 465.

UN Emblem
and
Dove — A150

1970, Oct. 24   **Photo.**   **Perf. 12½x14**
449   A150   2r dp orange & multi   3.00   3.50
25th anniversary of the United Nations.

Keppetipola
Dissawe — A151

1970, Nov. 26   **Litho.**   **Perf. 14x14½**
450   A151   25c multicolored   .30   .25
The 152nd anniversary of the execution of Keppetipola Dissawe, leader of the Great Rebellion of 1817-18.

Ola Leaf Manuscript and Education
Year Emblem — A152

1970, Dec. 21   **Photo.**   **Perf. 13**
451   A152   15c brown & multi   2.75   1.75
International Education Year.

Charles Henry de
Soysa — A153

1971, Mar. 3   **Litho.**   **Perf. 14x13½**
452   A153   20c orange & multi   .40   .50
de Soysa (1836-90), philanthropist who founded hospitals and schools.

Edward Henry
Pedris — A154

1971, July 8   Litho.   Perf. 14x14½
453 A154 25c blue & multi   .40 .40
Edward Henry Pedris (1888-1925), patriot.

A 5c stamp for the 10th Conf. of World Fellowship of Buddhists, Ceylon, May 9-13, was supposedly not issued without "1972" overprint. See Sri Lanka No. 471.

Lenin (1870-1924) — A156

1971, Aug. 31   Perf. 14½
455 A156 40c dp car & multi   .55 .55

Cumaratunga
Munidasa — A157

Poets and Philosophers: No. 457, Ananda Coomaraswamy (1887-1947). No. 458, Rev. S. Mahinda Thero (1905-51). No. 459, Ananda Rajakaruna (1885-1957). No. 460, Arumuga Navalar (1822-78).

1971, Oct. 29   Perf. 14
456 A157 5c brown   .25 .25
457 A157 5c slate   .25 .25
458 A157 5c deep orange   .25 .25
459 A157 5c dp vio blue   .25 .25
460 A157 5c brown red   .25 .25
     Nos. 456-460 (5)   1.25 1.25

CARE
Package
A158

1971, Dec. 28   Perf. 14x13
461 A158 50c purple, blue & pink   .55 .35
25th anniv. of CARE, a US-Canadian Co-operative for American Relief Everywhere.

Map of
Ceylon,
Colombo
Plan
Emblem
A159

1971, Dec. 28   Litho.   Perf. 14x14½
462 A159 20c multicolored   .40 .40
20th anniversary of the Colombo Plan.

Issues of 1969-70 Surcharged

a

b

c

d

e

Wmk. 290, Unwmkd.
1971, Dec. 5   Perf. 15, 14
463 A140 (a) 5c on 4c (#427)   6.00 2.50
464 A143 (b) 5c on 4c (#433)   .25 1.90
465 A149 (c) 15c on 10c (#448) .25   .50
466 A140 (d) 25c on 6c (#428)   .65   .95
467 A144 (e) 25c on 6c (#434)   .65 3.25
     Nos. 463-467 (5)   7.80 9.10
Nos. 463-466 exist with surcharge inverted.

WHO Emblem
and
Heart — A160

1972, May 2   Unwmk.   Perf. 13x13½
468 A160 25c multicolored   3.00 .90
"Your heart is your health," World Health Day.

UN
Emblem,
Map
Showing
Asian
Highway
A161

1972, May 2   Perf. 13x12½
469 A161 85c lt blue & multi   5.25 3.25
Economic Commission for Asia and the Far East (ECAFE), 25th anniversary.

SEMI-POSTAL STAMPS

Catalogue values for unused stamps in this section are for Never Hinged items.

Lamp and
Dharmachakra
SP1

Design: 10c+5c, Hand of Peace.

Perf. 11½
1956, May 10   Unwmk.   Photo.
Granite Paper
B1 SP1 4c + 2c dp bl & lt yel   .35   .75
B2 SP1 10c + 5c dk gray, yel &
              brt pink   .50 1.00
2500th anniv. of the birth of Buddha. The surtax went to the Buddha Jayanti Fund. For overprints, see Nos. 338-339.

WAR TAX STAMPS

Nos. 201, 202, 202a
and 203 Overprinted

Die I
1918   Wmk. 3   Perf. 14
MR1 A44 2c brown orange   .25   .45
  a.   Double overprint   35.00 47.50
  b.   Inverted overprint   75.00 85.00
MR2 A44 3c dp grn (Die Ia,
            type II)   4.00   .45
  a.   3c dp green (Die I, type I) .25 .60
  b.   Double overprint (Die I) 110.00 130.00
  c.   5c Double overprint (Die
       Ia, type II)   150.00
MR3 A44 5c red violet   4.75 3.50
  a.   Double overprint   75.00 85.00
  b.   Inverted overprint   120.00
  c.   5c purple   .60   .35

No. 223 Overprinted in
Black

MR4 A44 1c on 5c red violet   3.50 4.50
  a.   Double overprint   210.00
  b.   1c on No. 223a   .60   .45
     Nos. MR1-MR4 (4)   12.50 8.90

OFFICIAL STAMPS

Regular Issues
Overprinted

Black Overprint
1869   Wmk. 1   Perf. 12½, 14
O1 A4 1p blue   77.50
O2 A1 2p yellow   77.50
O3 A5 3p rose   155.00
O4 A2 8p red brown   77.50
O5 A1 1sh gray lilac   175.00

Red Overprint
O6 A1 6p brown   77.50
O7 A2 2sh blue   125.00
  a.   Imperf.   1,150.
     Nos. O1-O7 (7)   765.00
Nos. O1-O7 were never placed in use. The overprint measures 15mm on Nos. O1, O3.

Regular Issues
Overprinted in Black or
Red

1895-1900   Wmk. 2   Perf. 14
O8   A6   2c green   21.00   .75
O9   A6   2c org brn ('00)   13.00   .65
O10 A24 3c org brn & grn   13.00 3.00
O11 A24 3c green ('00)   14.00 5.00
O12 A23 5c lilac   5.75   .35
O13 A24 15c olive green   25.00   .75
O14 A24 15c ultra ('00)   28.00   .75
O15 A24 25c brown   13.50 3.50
O16 A24 30c vio & org brn   13.50   .65
O17 A24 75c blk & org brn
              (R) ('99)   11.00 11.00

O18 A16 1r12c claret   100.00 67.50
     Nos. O8-O18 (11)   257.75 93.90

1903-04   Wmk. 2
O19 A36 2c orange brown   24.00 1.75
O20 A37 3c green   17.50 2.40
O21 A38 5c dull lilac   34.00 1.60
O22 A40 15c ultramarine   45.00 3.25
O23 A40 25c bister   40.00 22.50
O24 A40 30c violet & green   22.50 2.25
     Nos. O19-O24 (6)   183.00 33.75

CHAD

'chad

(Tchad)

LOCATION — Central Africa, south of Libya
GOVT. — Republic
AREA — 495,572 sq. mi.
POP. — 7,557,436 (1999 est.)
CAPITAL — N'Djamena

A former dependency of Ubangi-Shari, Chad became a separate French colony in 1920. In 1934, the colonies of Chad, Gabon, Middle Congo and Ubangi-Shari were grouped in a single administrative unit known as French Equatorial Africa, with the capital at Brazzaville. The Republic of Chad was proclaimed November 28, 1958.

100 Centimes = 1 Franc

Catalogue values for unused stamps in this country are for Never Hinged items, beginning with Scott 64 in the regular postage section, Scott B1 in the semi-postal section, Scott C1 in the air post section, Scott CB1 in the air post semi-postal section, Scott J23 in the postage due section, Scott M1 in the military stamp section, and Scott O1 in the officials section.

See French Equatorial Africa No. 190 for stamp inscribed "Tchad."

Types of Middle Congo, 1907-17, Overprinted

Perf. 14x13½, 13½x14

1922 Unwmk.

1	A1	1c red & violet	.40	.55
a.		Overprint omitted	225.00	
2	A1	2c ol brn & salmon	.40	.80
a.		Overprint omitted	260.00	
3	A1	4c ind & vio	1.20	1.60
4	A1	5c choc & grn	1.25	1.60
5	A1	10c dp grn & gray grn	2.40	2.75
6	A1	15c vio & red	2.50	2.75
7	A1	20c grn & vio	4.00	4.75
8	A2	25c ol brn & brn	12.00	12.00
9	A2	30c rose & pale rose	2.40	2.00
10	A2	35c dl bl & dl rose	3.25	3.25
11	A2	40c choc & grn	4.00	4.00
12	A2	45c vio & grn	3.25	3.25
13	A2	50c dk bl & pale bl	3.25	4.00
14	A2	60c on 75c vio, pnksh	4.00	4.75
a.		"TCHAD" omitted	300.00	
b.		"60" omitted	300.00	
15	A1	75c red & violet	4.00	4.00
16	A3	1fr indigo & salmon	12.00	16.00
17	A3	2fr indigo & violet	24.00	24.00
18	A3	5fr ind & olive brn	24.00	24.00
		Nos. 1-18 (18)	108.30	116.05

See Nos. 26a, 32a, 38a, 55a.

Stamps of 1922 Overprinted in Various Colors

Nos. 19-28

Nos. 29-50

1924-33

19	A1	1c red & vio	.40	.80
a.		"TCHAD" omitted	225.00	250.00
b.		Double overprint	300.00	
c.		Violet omitted	300.00	
20	A1	2c ol brn & sal	.40	.50
a.		"TCHAD" omitted	225.00	
b.		Double overprint	240.00	
21	A1	4c ind & vio	.40	.50
a.		"TCHAD" omitted	950.00	
22	A1	5c choc & grn (Bl)	1.60	2.00
a.		"TCHAD" omitted	200.00	225.00
23	A1	5c choc & grn	.80	.70
a.		"TCHAD" omitted	225.00	
24	A1	10c dp grn & gray grn (Bl)	1.60	1.40
25	A1	10c dp grn & gray grn	1.60	1.40
26	A1	10c red org & blk	.60	.25
a.		"Afrique Equatoriale Francaise" omitted	225.00	250.00
b.		"TCHAD" omitted	240.00	260.00
27	A1	15c vio & red	.80	.85
28	A1	20c grn & vio	.80	.80
a.		"TCHAD" omitted	225.00	
b.		"Afrique Equatoriale Francaise" doubled	340.00	
29	A2	25c ol brn & brn	.80	.85
a.		"Afrique Equatoriale Francaise" doubled	160.00	
30	A2	30c rose & pale rose	.80	1.10
31	A2	30c gray & bl (R) ('25)	.40	.80
32	A2	30c dk grn & grn ('27)	1.20	1.60
a.		"Afrique Equatoriale Francaise" omitted	340.00	
33	A2	35c indigo & dl rose	.80	.85
34	A2	40c choc & grn	1.25	1.60
a.		Double overprint (R + Bk)	275.00	
35	A2	45c vio & grn	1.20	1.40
a.		Double overprint (R + Bk)	275.00	
36	A2	50c dk bl & pale bl (R)	2.40	1.90
a.		Inverted overprint	160.00	
37	A2	50c grn & vio ('25)	2.40	2.40
38	A2	65c org brn & bl ('28)	2.40	2.40
a.		"Afrique Equatoriale Francaise" omitted	260.00	
39	A2	75c red & vio (Bl)	2.00	1.90
40	A2	75c dp bl & lt bl (R) ('25)	.80	1.20
a.		"TCHAD" omitted	260.00	
41	A2	75c rose & dk brn ('28)	3.25	3.25
42	A2	90c brn red & pink ('30)	8.00	12.00
43	A3	1fr ind & salmon	2.40	2.50
44	A3	1.10fr dl grn & bl ('28)	4.00	4.00
45	A3	1.25fr org brn & lt bl ('33)	8.00	9.50
46	A3	1.50fr ultra & bl ('30)	8.00	12.00
47	A3	1.75fr ol brn & vio ('33)	40.00	45.00
48	A3	2fr ind & blk	3.25	3.50
a.		Double impression of frame	550.00	
49	A3	3fr red vio ('30)	12.00	16.00
50	A3	5fr ind & ol brn	4.00	4.75
		Nos. 19-50 (32)	118.35	139.85

See No. 58a.

Types of 1922 Overprinted like Nos. 29-50 and Surcharged with New Values

1924-27

51	A2	60c on 75c dk vio, pnksh	.80	1.20
a.		"60" omitted	200.00	
52	A3	65c on 1fr brn & ol grn ('25)	2.50	2.00
53	A3	85c on 1fr brn & ol grn ('25)	2.50	2.00
54	A2	90c on 75c brn red & rose red ('27)	2.50	2.00
55	A3	1.25fr on 1fr dk bl & ultra (R) ('26)	1.25	.80
a.		"Afrique Equatoriale Francaise" omitted	175.00	
56	A3	1.50fr on 1fr ultra & bl ('27)	2.50	2.00
57	A3	3fr on 5fr org brn & dl red ('27)	6.50	6.00
58	A3	10fr on 5fr ol grn & cer ('27)	16.00	14.50
a.		"10fr" omitted	400.00	400.00
59	A3	20fr on 5fr vio & ver ('27)	20.00	21.00
		Nos. 51-59 (9)	54.55	51.50

Common Design Types pictured following the introduction.

Colonial Exposition Issue
Common Design Types

1931 Engr. Perf. 12½
Name of Country in Black

60	CD70	40c deep green	5.50	5.50
61	CD71	50c violet	5.50	5.50
62	CD72	90c red orange	5.50	5.50
63	CD73	1.50fr dull blue	5.50	5.50
		Nos. 60-63 (4)	22.00	22.00

Catalogue values for unused stamps in this section, from this point to the end of the section, are for Never Hinged items.

Republic

"Birth of the Republic" A1

"Solidarity of the Community" A2

1959 Unwmk. Engr. Perf. 13

64	A1	15fr ultra, grn & maroon	.80	.25
65	A2	25fr dk grn & dp claret	1.00	.25

1st anniv. of the proclamation of the Republic.

Imperforates

Most Chad stamps from 1959 onward exist imperforate in issued and trial colors, and also in small presentation sheets in issued colors.

C.C.T.A. Issue
Common Design Type

1960

66	CD106	50fr rose lil & dk pur	1.90	.50

Flag and Map of Chad and UN Emblem — A3

Unwmk.
1961, Jan. 11 Engr. Perf. 13
Flag in blue, yellow and carmine

67	A3	15fr brn & dk bl	.60	.25
68	A3	25fr org brn & dk bl	.90	.25
69	A3	85fr slate grn & dk bl	2.50	.40
		Nos. 67-69 (3)	4.00	.90

Admission of Chad to United Nations.

Chari Bridge and Hippopotamus — A4

Abtouyoua Mountain and Ox — A5

Designs: 50c, Biltine and dorcas gazelle. 1fr, Logone and elephant. 2fr, Batha and lion. 3fr, Salamat and buffalo. 4fr, Ouaddai and Kudu. 15fr, Bessada and giant eland. 20fr, Tibesti mountains and mouflon. 25fr, Rocherg and antelope. 30fr, Kanem and cheetah. 60fr, Borkou and oryx. 85fr, Gorge of Archet and addax.

Perf. 13½x14, 14x13½

1961-62 Typo.

70	A5	50c yel grn & dk grn ('62)	.25	.25
71	A5	1fr bl grn & dk bl grn ('62)	.25	.25
72	A5	2fr dk red brn & blk ('62)	.25	.25
73	A5	3fr ocher & dl grn ('62)	.25	.25
74	A5	4fr dk crim & blk ('62)	.25	.25
75	A4	5fr yellow & blk	.25	.25
76	A5	10fr pink & blk	.35	.25
77	A5	15fr lilac & blk ('62)	.70	.25
78	A5	20fr red & blk	.85	.25
79	A5	25fr blue & blk ('62)	.90	.25
80	A5	30fr ultra & blk ('62)	1.00	.25
81	A5	60fr yel & ol grn ('62)	2.25	.25
82	A5	85fr org & blk	2.75	.25
		Nos. 70-82 (13)	10.30	3.25

First anniversary of Independence.
For overprint see No. M1.

Abidjan Games Issue
Common Design Type

1962, July 21 Photo. Perf. 12½x12

83	CD109	20fr Relay race	.80	.25
84	CD109	50fr High jump	2.00	.30
		Nos. 83-84,C8 (3)	6.30	1.55

African-Malgache Union Issue
Common Design Type

1962, Sept. 8 Unwmk.

85	CD110	30fr dk bl, bluish grn, red & gold	1.25	.25

Pres. Ngarta Tombalbaye — A7

1963, Apr. 22 Perf. 12x12½

86	A7	20fr multi	.65	.25
87	A7	85fr multi	1.75	.30

For surcharge, see No. 125.

Space Communications Issue

Waves Around Globe — A8

Design: 100fr, Orbit patterns around globe.

Perf. 12½

1963, Sept. 19 Unwmk. Photo.

88	A8	25fr grn & pur	1.00	.25
89	A8	100fr pink & ultra	3.00	.60

Ancestral Mask — A9

Excavated Sao Art: 5fr, Clay weight. 25fr, Ancestral clay statuette. 60fr, Gazelle, bronze. 80fr, Bronze pectoral.

1963, Dec. 2 Engr. Perf. 13

90	A9	5fr brt grn & red brn	.25	.25
91	A9	15fr gray, dl cl & red	.45	.25
92	A9	25fr dk bl & org brn	1.10	.25

93	A9	60fr org brn & slate grn	2.75	.35
94	A9	80fr org red & olive	3.00	.40
		Nos. 90-94 (5)	7.55	1.50

UNESCO Emblem, Scales and Tree — A10

1963, Dec. 10
95 A10 25fr green & maroon 1.00 .25

15th anniv. of the Universal Declaration of Human Rights.

Potter A11

Perf. 12½
1964, Feb. 5   Unwmk.   Engr.
96	A11	10fr shown	.35	.25
97	A11	30fr Boatmaker	.90	.25
98	A11	50fr Weaver	1.50	.25
99	A11	85fr Smiths	2.25	.35
		Nos. 96-99 (4)	5.00	1.10

Barograph and WMO Emblem A12

1964, Mar. 23   Perf. 13
100 A12 50fr red lil, pur & ultra 1.40 .25

Fourth World Meteorological Day.

Cotton A13

1964, Apr. 6   Photo.   Perf. 12½x13
101 A13 20fr shown 1.75 .35
102 A13 25fr Royal poinciana 2.00 .40

Co-operation Issue
Common Design Type
1964, Nov. 7   Engr.   Perf. 13
103 CD119 25fr ver, dk bl & dk
       brn 1.00 .25

National Guard and Map of Chad A14

Design: 25fr, Infantry, flag and map, vert.

Perf. 12½x13, 13x12½
1964, Dec. 11   Photo.
104 A14 20fr multi .85 .25
105 A14 25fr lt bl & multi 1.00 .25

Issued to honor the army of Chad.

Aoudad or Barbary Sheep A15

10fr, Addax. 20fr, Oryx. 25fr, Derby's eland, vert. 30fr, Giraffe, buffalo & lion, Zakouma Park, vert. 85fr, Great kudu at water hole, vert.

Perf. 12½x12, 12x12½
1965, Jan. 11   Unwmk.
106	A15	5fr dk brn, ultra & yel	.50	.25
107	A15	10fr ultra, org & blk	.75	.25
108	A15	20fr multi	1.50	.25
109	A15	25fr multi	1.75	.25
110	A15	30fr multi	2.50	.40
111	A15	85fr multi	5.00	.75
		Nos. 106-111 (6)	12.00	2.15

Olsen Perforator A16

Designs: 60fr, Mildé telephone, vert. 100fr, Distributor of Baudot telegraph.

1965, May 17   Engr.   Perf. 13
112	A16	30fr multi	.75	.25
113	A16	60fr multi	1.25	.45
114	A16	100fr multi	2.00	.60
		Nos. 112-114 (3)	4.00	1.30

Cent. of the ITU.

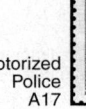

Motorized Police A17

Perf. 12½x12
1965, June 22   Photo.   Unwmk.
115 A17 25fr ol, dk grn, gold &
       brn 1.00 .25

Issued to honor the national police.

Drum and stool — A18

Musical Instruments from National Museum: 2fr, Guitar. 3fr, Shoulder drums, vert. 15fr, Viol. 60fr, Harp, vert.

1965, Oct. 26   Engr.   Perf. 13
Size: 22x36mm, 36x22mm
116	A18	1fr car, emer & brn	.25	.25
117	A18	2fr red, brt lil & brn	.25	.25
118	A18	3fr red & sepia	.25	.25
119	A18	15fr red, ocher & sl grn	.75	.25
120	A18	60fr maroon & slate grn	1.75	.60
		Nos. 116-120,C23 (6)	6.00	2.60

See No. C23.

Head and Bowl — A19

Sao Art: 20fr, Head. 60fr, Head with crown. 80fr, Circlet with human head. From excavations at Bouta Kebira and Gawi.

1966, Apr. 1   Engr.   Perf. 13
121	A19	15fr ol, choc & ultra	.40	.25
122	A19	20fr dk red, brn & bl grn	.75	.25
123	A19	60fr brt bl, choc & ver	1.75	.50
124	A19	80fr brn org, grn & pur	2.50	1.60
		Nos. 121-124 (4)	5.40	1.60

Issued to publicize the International Negro Arts Festival, Dakar, Senegal, Apr. 1-24.

No. 86 Surcharged in Orange

1966, Apr. 15   Photo.   Perf. 12x12½
125 A7 25fr on 20fr multi 1.00 .30

WHO Headquarters, Geneva — A20

1966, May 3
126 A20 25fr car, lt ultra & yel .90 .25
127 A20 32fr emer, ultra & yel 1.00 .25

New WHO Headquarters, Geneva.

Staff of Mercury and Map of Africa A21

1966, May 24   Perf. 12½x12
128 A21 30fr multi 1.00 .25

Central African Customs and Economic Union (Union Douaniere et Economique de l'Afrique Centrale, UDEAC).

Soccer Player — A22

Design: 60fr, Soccer player facing left.

1966, July 12   Engr.   Perf. 13
129 A22 30fr grn, bl grn & mar 1.00 .25
130 A22 60fr dk bl, gray & car 2.00 .40

8th World Cup Soccer Championship, Wembley, England, July 11-30.

Young Men, Flag and Emblem A23

1966, Aug. 11   Photo.   Perf. 12½x13
131 A23 25fr dk bl & multi 1.00 .25

Chad Youth Movement.

Greek Columns and UNESCO Emblem — A24

1966, Aug. 23   Engr.   Perf. 13
132 A24 32fr sl bl, vio & car rose 1.00 .25

20th anniv. of UNESCO.

Reconstructed Skull of Chadanthropus — A25

1966, Sept. 20   Engr.   Perf. 13
133 A25 30fr gray, red & ocher 2.00 .50

Yves Coppens' discovery of Lake Chad man.

Stone Axe — A26

Prehistoric Tools: 30fr, Flint arrow head. 85fr, Bone harpoon. 100fr, Sandstone millstone with grinder.

1966, Dec. 11   Engr.   Perf. 13
134	A26	25fr dp bl, red & dk brn	.70	.25
135	A26	30fr brn, dp bl & blk	.80	.25
136	A26	85fr dk red, brt bl & brn	2.50	.50
137	A26	100fr Prus grn, dk brn & bis brn	2.75	.65
a.		Miniature sheet of 4, #134-137	15.00	8.00
		Nos. 134-137 (4)	6.75	1.65

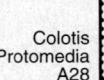

Map of Chad and Various Sports — A27

1967, Apr. 10   Photo.   Perf. 12x12½
138 A27 25fr multi 1.00 .30

Issued for Sports Day, Apr. 10, 1967.

Colotis Protomedia A28

Various Butterflies.

1967, May 23   Photo.   Perf. 12½x12
139	A28	5fr blue & multi	2.00	.30
140	A28	10fr emerald & multi	4.25	.75
141	A28	20fr orange & multi	8.50	1.50
142	A28	130fr red & multi	17.50	2.50
		Nos. 139-142 (4)	32.25	5.05

WHO Headquarters,
Brazzaville — A29

1967, Sept. 23 Photo. *Perf. 12½x13*
143 A29 30fr vio bl & multi   1.00   .25
   Opening of the Regional Office of the WHO,
Brazzaville.

Jamboree
Emblem
and Boy
Scouts
A30

32fr, Jamboree emblem and Boy Scout.

1967, Oct. 17 Photo. *Perf. 12½x13*
144 A30 25fr multi   .90   .25
145 A30 32fr multi   1.00   .25
   12th Boy Scout World Jamboree, Farragut
State Park, Idaho, Aug. 1-9.

Great Mills
of Chad
A31

30fr, Lake reclamation project, grain fields.

1967, Nov. 14 Engr. *Perf. 13*
146 A31 25fr brt bl, ind & sep   .90   .25
147 A31 30fr ultra, emer & ol brn   1.00   .25
   Economic development of Chad.

Woman and
Harp Player
A32

Rock Paintings: 30fr, Giraffes. 50fr, Camel
rider hunting ostrich.

1967, Dec. 19 Engr. *Perf. 13*
Size: 36x22mm
148 A32 15fr bl, sal & mar   2.00   .25
149 A32 30fr grnsh bl, sal &
            mar   4.00   .40
150 A32 50fr emer, sal & mar   5.50   .55
   Nos. 148-150,C38-C39 (5)   28.50   3.65
   Balloud expedition in the Ennedi Mountains.
See Nos. 163-166.

Rotary
Emblem — A33

1968, Jan. 9 Photo. *Perf. 13x12½*
151 A33 50fr multi   2.00   .50
   Rotary Club of Chad, 10th anniversary.

Map of Chad, WHO
Emblem, Well,
Physicians, Mother
and Child — A34

1968, Apr. 6 *Perf. 13x12½*
152 A34 25fr multi   .90   .25
153 A34 32fr multi   1.10   .25
   20th anniv. of WHO.

"Water"
Aiding
Agriculture
and
Industry
A35

1968, Apr. 23 Engr. *Perf. 13*
154 A35 50fr grnsh bl, brn & brt
            grn   1.10   .25
   Hydrological Decade (UNESCO), 1965-74.

National Administration School — A36

1968, Aug. 20 Engr. *Perf. 13*
155 A36 25fr slate, brn red &
            rose vio   1.00   .25

Boy
Learning to
Write
A37

1968, Sept. 10
156 A37 60fr dk bl, dk brn & blk   2.00   .50
   Issued for National Literacy Day.

Cotton
Harvest
A38

Loom, Fort
Archambault
Factory — A39

1968, Sept. 24 Engr. *Perf. 13*
157 A38 25fr Prus bl, choc & dk
            grn   .90   .25
158 A39 30fr brt grn, ol & ultra   1.00   .25
   Issued to publicize the cotton industry.

Tiger Moth — A40

Moths: 30fr, Owlet. 50fr, Saturnid (Gynanisa
maja). 100fr, Saturnid (Epiphora bauhiniae).

1968, Oct. 1   Photo.
159 A40 25fr multi   5.25   .60
160 A40 30fr multi   6.25   .75
161 A40 50fr multi   9.50   .85
162 A40 100fr multi   11.00   1.50
   Nos. 159-162 (4)   32.00   3.70

Rock Paintings Type of 1967
   Rock Paintings: 2fr, Archers. 10fr, Costumes (4 women, 1 man). 20fr, Funeral vigil.
25fr, Dispute.

1968, Nov. 19 Engr. *Perf. 13*
Size: 36x22mm
163 A32 2fr scar, salmon & brn   .65   .25
164 A32 10fr pur, salmon & dk
            red   1.60   .25
165 A32 20fr grn, salmon & mar   3.25   .50
166 A32 25fr bl, salmon & ma-
            roon   3.50   .60
   Nos. 163-166 (4)   9.00   1.60

Man and Human
Rights Flame — A41

1968, Dec. 10 Engr. *Perf. 13*
167 A41 32fr grn, brt bl & red   1.00   .25
   International Human Rights Year.

St. Paul — A42

   Apostles: 1fr, St. Peter. 2fr, St. Thomas. 5fr,
St. John the Evangelist. 10fr, St. Bartholomew.
20fr, St. Matthew. 25fr, St. James the Less.
30fr, St. Andrew. 40fr, St. Jude. 50fr, St.
James the Greater. 85fr, St. Philip. 100fr, St.
Simon.

1969, May 6 Litho. *Perf. 12½x13*
168 A42 50c multi   .25   .25
169 A42 1fr multi   .25   .25
170 A42 2fr multi   .25   .25
171 A42 5fr multi   .25   .25
172 A42 10fr multi   .25   .25
173 A42 20fr multi   .30   .25
174 A42 25fr multi   .40   .25
175 A42 30fr multi   .50   .25
176 A42 40fr multi   .60   .25
177 A42 50fr multi   .70   .25
178 A42 85fr multi   1.10   .40
179 A42 100fr multi   1.25   .40
   a.   Sheet of 12, #168-179   6.00   1.75
Jubilee Year of the Catholic Church in Chad.

Tractors and
Trucks — A43

1969, June 19 Engr. *Perf. 13*
180 A43 32fr grn, red brn & ind   .75   .25
   50th anniv. of the ILO.

Deborah
Meyer, US, 200
Meter Freestyle
A44

Woman with
Flowers, by
Veneto — A45

Portrait of an
African
Woman, by
Bezombes —
A45a

   Winners of 1968 Olympic Games: No. 182,
Roland Matthes, East Germany, 100m back-
stroke. No. 183, Klaus DiBiasi, Italy, spring-
board diving. No. 184, Bruno Cipolla, Primo
Baran and Renzo Sambo, Italy, pair with cox-
swain. No. 185, Annemarie Zimmermann and
Rosewitha Esser, West Germany, women's
kayak tandem. No. 186, Sailing, G.B. No. 187,
Pierre Trentin, France, 1000 meter bicycling.
No. 188, Pier Franco Vianelli, Italy, 196k bicy-
cle road race. No. 189, Daniel Morelon and
Pierre Trentin, France, tandem.
   No. 190, Daniel R. Rebillard, France, 4000m
pursuit (bicycle). No. 191, Ingrid Becker, West
Germany, pentathlon. No. 192, Jean J. Guyon,
France, equestrian. No. 193, Olympic
dressage team, West Germany. No. 194,
Bernd Klinger, West Germany, small bore rifle.
No. 195, Manfred Wolke, East Germany, wel-
terweight. No. 196, Randy Matson, US, shot
put. No. 197, Colette Besson, France, 400m
run. No. 198, Mohammed Gammoudi, Tunisia,
5,000m run. No. 199, Tommie Smith, US,
200m run.
   No. 200, David Hemery, G.B., 200m hurdles. No. 201, Willie Davenport, US, 110m
hurdles. No. 202, Bob Beamon, US, long
jump. No. 203, Sawao Kato, Japan, all around
gymnastics. No. 204, Dick Fosbury, US, high
jump.
   Paintings: No. 206, Holy Family, by Murillo,
horiz. No. 207, Adoration of the Magi, by
Rubens. No. 209, Three Black Men, by
Rubens. No. 210, Mother and Child, by
Gauguin.

1969, June 30 Litho. *Perf. 12½x13*
181-204 A44 1fr set of 24   8.00   8.00
       Perf. 12½x13, 13x12½
205 A45 1fr shown   .35   .35
206 A45 1fr multi   .35   .35
207 A45 1fr multi   .35   .35
208 A45a 1fr shown   .35   .35
209 A45 1fr multi   .35   .35
210 A45 1fr multi   .35   .35
Issued to stress the brotherhood of mankind.
   For overprints see Nos. 244A-244F, 245A-
245X.

Cochlospermum Tinctorium — A46

   Flowers: 4fr, Parkia biglobosa. 10fr, Pancratium trianthum. 15fr, Morning glory.

1969, July 8 Photo. *Perf. 12½x13*
211 A46 1fr pink, yel & blk   .60   .25
212 A46 4fr dk grn, yel & red   .90   .25
213 A46 10fr dk grn, yel & gray   1.10   .25
214 A46 15fr vio bl & multi   1.90   .25
   Nos. 211-214 (4)   4.50   1.00

Meat Freezer, Farcha A47

30fr, Cattle at Farcha slaughterhouse.

1969, Aug. 19　　Engr.　　Perf. 13
215　A47　25fr sl grn, ocher & red
　　　　　brn　　　　　　　　.60　.25
216　A47　30fr red brn, sl grn &
　　　　　gray　　　　　　　.75　.25
　Economic development in Chad.

Development Bank Issue
Common Design Type
1969, Sept. 10
217　CD130　30fr dl red, grn &
　　　　　　ocher　　　　　　.70　.25

Tilapia Nilotica A48

Fish: 3fr, Citharinus latus. 5fr, Tetraodon fahaka strigosus. 20fr, Hydrocyon forskali.

1969, Nov. 25　　Engr.　　Perf. 13
218　A48　2fr choc, grn & gray　.55　.25
219　A48　3fr gray, red & bl　1.10　.25
220　A48　5fr ocher, blk & yel　1.75　.25
221　A48　20fr blk, red & grn　4.75　.60
　　　　　Nos. 218-221 (4)　　8.15　1.35

ASECNA Issue
Common Design Type
1969, Dec. 12　　Engr.　　Perf. 13
222　CD132　30fr orange　　1.00　.25

Pres. François Tombalbaye A49

1970, Jan. 11　　Litho.　　Perf. 14
223　A49　25fr multi　　　1.00　.25

Lenin — A50

1970, Apr. 22　　Photo.　　Perf. 11½
224　A50　150fr gold, blk & buff　3.25　1.10
　Lenin (1870-1924), Russian communist leader.

UPU Headquarters Issue
Common Design Type
1970, May 20　　Engr.　　Perf. 13
225　CD133　30fr dk red, pur & brn　1.00　.25

During the 1970-73 period three different agents had entered into contracts to produce stamps with various officials of the Chad government, apparently including Pres. Tombalbaye.

In June 1973, Tombalbaye declared that some of the stamps produced by these agents were not recognized by the Chad government but might be put on sale at a later date, and that other stamps produced and shipped to Chad were refused by the government.

In July 1973, the Chad government announced that the stamps that were not recognized would be put on sale by the end of the year. We have no evidence that this actually happened.

Apollo Program A50a

Designs: 15fr, Apollo 11 in Lunar orbit. 25fr, Apollo 12 astronaut deploying lunar research equipment. 40fr, Astronaut, lunar module on moon. 50fr, Astronauts Conrad and Bean in life raft after splashdown, horiz.

1970, June 12　Litho.　Perf. 12x12½
225A　A50a　Strip of 3, #b-d　　6.00　—
　　　　　Souvenir Sheet
　　　　　Perf. 13½x13
225E　A50a　50fr multicolored　10.00　—
　No. 225E contains one 66x44mm stamp.
15fr, 25fr are airmail.

Expo '70, Japan — A50b

Japanese prints of women: 50c, by Kiyonaga. 1fr, by Utamaro. 2fr, from Heian period.

1970, June 12　Litho.　Perf. 12x12½
225F　A50b　Strip of 3, #a-c　　13.50　—
　For overprint see No. 239C.

Adult Education Class and UN Emblem — A52

1970, June 16　　Litho.　　Perf. 14
226　A52　100fr blue & multi　2.00　.60
　International Education Year.

Bull's Head, Symbols of Weather and Agriculture — A53

1970, July 22　　Engr.　　Perf. 13
227　A53　50fr org, gray & grn　1.00　.25
　Issued for World Meteorological Day.

1970 World Cup Soccer Championships, Mexico City — A53a

Designs: 1fr, Three players, Italian flag. 4fr, Franz Beckenbauer, German flag. Nos. 227C, 227E, English players receiving World Cup trophy, 1966. No. 227D, Three players, Brazilian flag. No. 227F, Four players, "1970."

1970-71　　Litho.　　Perf. 12
227A　A53a　1fr multicolored
227B　A53a　4fr multicolored
227C　A53a　15fr multicolored
227D　A53a　40fr multicolored
　　　　Nos. 227A-227D (4)　　3.75　—
　　　　　Embossed
　　　　　Die Cut Perf 13
227E　A53a　5fr gold　　　17.50　—
　　　　　Souvenir Sheet
　　　　　Litho.
　　　　　Perf. 13½x13
227F　A53a　15fr multicolored　6.25　—
　No. 227F contains one 66x44mm stamp. Nos. 227D, 227F are airmail.
　Issued: Nos. 227A-227D, 227F, 7/2; No. 227E, 11/1/71.
　For overprints see Nos. 267A-267E.

Christmas A53b

Virgin and Child by: 3fr, Solario. 25fr, Durer. 32fr, Fouquet.

1970, Aug. 19　Litho.　Perf. 12x12½
227G　A53b　3fr multicolored
227H　A53b　25fr multicolored
227I　A53b　32fr multicolored
　　　　Nos. 227G-227I (3)　　13.50　—
　No. 227I is airmail.

Ahmed Mangue, Minister of Education — A54

1970, Sept. 15　　　Litho. & Engr.
228　A54　100fr gold, car & blk　2.00　.50

1972 Summer Olympics, Munich — A54a

Designs: No. 228A, 3fr, Horses pulling chariot. 8fr, Men running. 10fr, No. 228C, Woman hurdling. No. 228B, 20fr, Equestrian. 35fr, Woman diving. No. 228D, Woman diver in tuck position.

1970　　　Litho.　　Perf. 12½x12
228A　A54a　Strip of 3, #a-c　4.00　—
　　　　　Perf. 12x12½
228B　A54a　Pair, #a-b + la-
　　　　　bel　　　　　　4.00　—
　　　　　Embossed
　　　　　Die Cut Perf 13
228C　A54a　10fr gold　　　17.50　—
　　　　　Souvenir Sheet
　　　　　Litho.
　　　　　Perf. 13½x13
228D　A54a　40fr multicolored　10.00　—
　10fr, 35fr, Nos. 228C-228D are airmail. No. 228D contains one 66x43mm stamp.
　Issued: Nos. 228A-228B, 228D, Sept; No. 228C, 10/14.
　For overprints see Nos. 239D-239F.

Tanner A55

Designs: 2fr, Cloth dyer, vert. 3fr, Camel turning oil press. 4fr, Water carrier, vert.. 5fr, Copper worker.

1970, Oct. 10　　Engr.　　Perf. 13
229　A55　1fr ol brn, bl & brn　.25　.25
229A　A55　2fr dk brn, ol & ind　.25　.25
229B　A55　3fr pur, ol brn & rose
　　　　　car　　　　　　.40　.25
229C　A55　4fr choc, lem & bl grn　.50　.25
229D　A55　5fr red, choc & sl grn　.50　.25
　　　　　Nos. 229-229D (5)　1.90　1.25

UN Emblem, Grain and Dove — A56

1970, Oct. 24　　Photo.　　Perf. 12x12½
230　A56　32fr dk bl & multi　1.00　.25
　25th anniversary of United Nations.

OCAM Headquarters, Map of Africa, Stars — A57

1971, Jan. 23 Photo. Perf. 12½x12
231 A57 30fr dk grn & multi 1.00 .25
OCAM (Organisation Commune Africaine, Malgache et Mauricienne) Summit Conference, N'djamena, Jan. 22-30.

Space Exploration — A57a

10fr, Apollo 11. 35fr, Soviet space station.
40fr, John F. Kennedy, Apollo spacecraft, vert.

1971, Feb. 16 Litho. Perf. 13x13½
231A A57a 8fr shown .60 —
231B A57a 10fr multi .90 —
231C A57a 35fr multi 6.25 —
  Nos. 231A-231C (3) 7.75

Embossed
Die Cut Perf 13
231D A57a 8fr gold, like #231A 8.25 —
  f. Sheet of 1, Imperf.

Souvenir Sheet
Perf. 13½x13
231E A57a 40fr multi 10.00 —
Nos. 231C, 231E are airmail. No. 231Df contains one 73x45mm stamp with same size design as No. 231D. No. 231E contains one 33x50mm stamp.

Nos. 231D, 231Df probably were not available in Chad.

1972 Winter Olympics, Sapporo A57b

Paintings by Kiyonaga: 50c, Cherry Trees in Bloom, Tokyo. 1fr, Snowy Morning. 2fr, Sake Party.

1971 Litho. Perf. 12x12½
231G A57b 50c multicolored .80 —
231H A57b 1fr multicolored 1.40 —
231I A57b 2fr multicolored 2.25 —
  Nos. 231G-231I (3) 4.45

Embossed
Die Cut Perf 13
231J A57b 2fr gold, like #231I 17.50 —
  k. Sheet of 1, Imperf. 35.00 —
Issued: Nos. 231G-231I, 2/16; Nos. 231J-231Jk, 11/1. No. 231Jk contains one 43x54mm stamp with same size design as No. 231I.

For overprints see Nos. 246A-246C.

Nos. 231J-231Jk probably were not available in Chad.

Portraits of French Royalty — A57c

Designs: No. 232A, 25fr, The Dauphin (Louis XVII), by J.M. Vien the Younger. 32fr, Marie Antoinette, by E. Vigee-Lebrun. 60fr, Louis XVI, by J.S. Duplessis.
No. 232B, 25fr, Comtesse du Barry, by E. Vigee-Lebrun. 40fr, Louis XV, by M.Q. Delatour.
No. 232C, 40fr, Marie Antoinette, by Charpentier. 50fr, Louis XVI (Dauphin), by Michel Van Loo.
No. 232D, 35fr, Madame de Pompadour (detail), by Delatour. 70fr, Louis XV by Delatour.
No. 232E, 30fr, Madame de Pompadour (entire), by Delatour. 60fr, Marie Leszczynska, by Jean Marc Nattier. 80fr, Louis XV, by Van Loo.
No. 232F, 40fr, Duc D'Orleans as Regent, by 19th cent. French school. 200fr, Louis XIV, by H. Rigaud.
No. 232G, 100fr, Madame de Montespan, by Henry Gascard. 100fr, Madame de Maintenon, by Pierre Mignard.
No. 232H, 50fr, Colbert, by Claude Lefebvre. 200fr, Louis XIV, by J. Garnier.
No. 232J, 50fr, Marie Therese, by Mignard. 200fr, Louis XIV, by Marot.
No. 232K, 50fr, Marie de la Valliere, by English school. 200fr, Louis XIV, by French school.
No. 232L, 100fr, Giulio Cardinal Mazarin, by Mignard. 100fr, Anne of Austria, by Rubens.
No. 232M, 50fr, Vicomte de Turenne, by Champaigne. 200fr, Louis XIV as a Boy, by Mignard.
No. 232N, 100fr, Marquis de Cinq-Mars, by M. le Nain. 150fr, Cardinal Richelieu, by Champaigne.
No. 232P, 150fr, Anne of Austria, by Rubens. 250fr, Louis XIII (detail), by Simon Vouet.
No. 232Q, 150fr, Marriage of Marie de Medicis (looking right), by Rubens. 150fr, Mirror image.
No. 232R, 150fr, Duke of Sully, by Quesnel. 150fr, Mirror image.
No. 232S, 150fr, Henry IV, by Rubens. 150fr, Marie de Medicis, by Rubens.
No. 232T, 200fr, Gabrielle d'Estrees, by unknown artist. 250fr, Henry IV, by French school, c. 1595.
No. 232U, 150fr, Jeanne d'Albret, by Francois Clouet. 200fr, Marie de Medicis as a Girl, by Angelo Bronzino.
No. 232V, 200fr, Henry III, by Clouet. 250fr, Ambroise Pare, by 16th century French school.
No. 232W, 150fr, Catherine de Medicis, by Clouet. 250fr, Henry II, by Clouet.
No. 233A, 200fr, Elizabeth of Austria, by Clouet. 250fr, Charles IX, by Clouet.
No. 233B, 200fr, Mary Stuart, by 16th cent. Scottish school. 300fr, Diane of Poitiers, by Fontainbleu school.
No. 233C, 200fr, Elizabeth of Valois, by Alonso S. Coello. 250fr, Francis, Duke of Alencon, by Clouet.
No. 233D, 150fr, Marguerite d'Angouleme, by Clouet. 300fr, Francis I, by Clouet.
No. 233E, 200fr, Francis I, by Titian. 300fr, Francis I as Dauphin, by Corneille of Lyon.
No. 233F, 100fr, Anne of Austria, by Coello. 250fr, Louis XIII, by Champaigne.
No. 233G, 200fr, Marie de Medicis, by Rubens. 200fr, Marie de Medicis, Louis XIII, by Rubens.
No. 233H, 150fr, The Exchange of Princess Elizabeth of France and Princess Anne of Austria on the Andaye River, by Rubens. 250fr, Louis XIII of France and Navarre, by Vouet.
No. 233J, 250fr, Marie de Medicis, by Rubens. 250fr, Henry IV, by Rubens.
No. 233K, Louis XV and the Dauphin at Battle of Fontenoy, by Mignard. No. 233L, The Grand Dauphin and his Family, by Mignard. No. 233M, Madame de Montespan, horiz. No. 233N, Madame de la Valliere and her Children. No. 233P, The Birth of Louis XIII at Fontainebleau, by Rubens. No. 233Q, Reconciliation of the Queen and Louis XIII, by Rubens. No. 233R, Henry IV Entrusting Regency to Marie de Medici, by Rubens. No. 233S, The Majority of Louis XIII, by Rubens. No. 233T, The Apotheosis of Henry IV and the Proclamation of Regency, by Rubens. No. 233U, Felicity of the Regency, by Rubens.

Small numbers appear at the lower right on Nos. 232A-233J. To ease identication, these numbers are shown in parentheses after each listing.

1971-73 Litho. Perf. 12½x13
232A A57c Strip of 3, #aa-ac (58-60) 3.00
232B A57c Pair, #aa-ab (53-54) 2.00
232C A57c Pair, #aa-ab (56-57) 2.00
232D A57c Pair, #aa-ab (51-52) 2.00
232E A57c Strip of 3, #aa-ac (48-50) 4.00
232F A57c Pair, #aa-ab (45, 47) 4.00
232G A57c Pair, #aa-ab (44, 45B) 3.00
232H A57c Pair, #aa-ab (42-43) 4.00
232J A57c Pair, #aa-ab (40-41) 4.00
232K A57c Pair, #aa-ab (38-39) 4.00
232L A57c Pair, #aa-ab (36-37) 2.50
232M A57c Pair, #aa-ab (34-35) 4.00
232N A57c Pair, #aa-ab (32-33) 4.00
232P A57c Pair, #aa-ab (30-31) 6.00
232Q A57c Pair, #aa-ab (22-23) 4.00
232R A57c Pair, #aa-ab (22A-22B) 4.50
232S A57c Pair, #aa-ab (26, 27A) 4.50
232T A57c Pair, #aa-ab (18-19) 7.50
232U A57c Pair, #aa-ab (16-17) 5.50
232V A57c Pair, #aa-ab (16-16A) 7.50
232W A57c Pair, #aa-ab (14-15) 6.50
233A A57c Pair, #aa-ab (13-13A) 7.50
233B A57c Pair, #aa-ab (11-12) 8.00
233C A57c Pair, #aa-ab (10, 11A) 6.50
233D A57c Pair, #aa-ab (8-9) 7.50
233E A57c Pair, #aa-ab (7, 8A) 8.00
233F A57c Pair, #aa-ab (29, 32B) 6.00
233G A57c Pair, #aa-ab (24-25) 6.00
233H A57c Pair, #aa-ab (27-28) 6.00
233J A57c Pair, #aa-ab (20-21) 7.50
  Nos. 232A-233J (30) 151.50

Souvenir Sheets
Perf. 13x13½, 13½x13, 13½
233K A57c 75fr multi 6.50
233L A57c 100fr multi 6.00
233M A57c 200fr multi 6.00
233N A57c 300fr multi 6.00
233P A57c 350fr multi 12.00
233Q A57c 400fr multi 16.00
233R A57c 400fr multi 10.00
233S A57c 400fr multi 10.00
233T A57c 400fr multi 6.00
233U A57c 500fr multi 13.50
  Nos. 233K-233U (10) 92.00

Nos. 232A 60fr, 232B 40fr, 232C 50fr, 232D 70fr, 232E 80fr, 232F 200fr, 232G, 232H 200fr, 232J 200fr, 232K, 232L, 232M 200fr, 232N-233U are airmail.
Issued: 1971 — No. 232A, 2/24; No. 232B, 3/30; No. 232C, 3/4; Nos. 232D, 233K, 3/15; No. 232E, 4/12; Nos. 232F, 233L, 4/26; No. 232G, 8/10; No. 232H, 9/6; No. 232J, 9/23; No. 232K, 10/6; No. 232L, 10/26; No. 232M, 11/16; No. 232N, 11/20.
1972 — Nos. 232P, 233P, Jan.; Nos. 232Q, 233M-233N, Feb.; Nos. 233Q-233R, May; Nos. 232R, 233S, 6/15; Nos. 232S, 233T, 6/26; No. 232T, 8/8; No. 232U, 8/17; No. 232V, 8/30; Nos. 232W, 233U, 12/11; No. 233A, 12/18; No. 233B, 12/28.
1973 — Nos. 233C-233J.
Nos. 233K-233L, 233T-233U each contain one 37x62mm stamp. No. 233N, 233P each contain one 32x50mm stamp. No. 233M contains one 45x65mm stamp. Nos. 233Q-233R, 233U each contain one 65x45mm stamp.
Nos. 232Q-232V, 233G, 233J, 233R-233U and possibly 232P, 232W-233F, 233H probably were not available in Chad.

Symbolic Tree — A58

1971, Mar. 21 Engr. Perf. 13
236 A58 40fr bl grn, dk red & grn 1.00 .25
Intl. year against racial discrimination.

Paintings of Flowers A58a

Designs: 1fr, The Three Graces (detail), by Rubens. 4fr, Imperial Bouquet, by Van Os. 5fr, Bouquet, by Jan Brueghel.

1971, Apr. 28 Litho. Perf. 12x12½
236A A58a Strip of 3, #a-c 5.50 —
For overprint see No. 278A.

Summer Olympic Games — A58b

15fr, Swimming. 20fr, Women's relay races. 25fr, Swimming, medals. 50fr, Running.

Perf. 12x12½, 12½x12
1971, Apr. 28 Litho.
236B A58b 5fr multi, vert. 1.75 —
236C A58b 20fr multi, vert. 2.75 —
236D A58b 25fr multi 3.50 —
  Nos. 236B-236D (3) 8.00

Embossed
Perf. 13
236E A58b 25fr gold, like No. 236D 17.50 —

Souvenir Sheet
Litho.
Die Cut Perf 13
236F A58b 50fr multicolored 10.00 —
Nos. 236D-236F are airmail. No. 236F contains one 62x36mm stamp.
Issued: Nos. 236B-236D, 236F, 4/28; No. 236E, 11/1.
For overprints see Nos. 251A-251D.
No. 236E probably was not available in Chad.

Map of Africa, Radar Antenna A59

Map of Africa and: 40fr, Communications tower. 50fr, Communications satellite.

1971, May 17 Engr. Perf. 13
237 A59 5fr ultra, org & dk red .25 .25
238 A59 40fr pur, emer & brn .75 .25
239 A59 50fr dk red, blk & brn 1.00 .25
  Nos. 237-239 (3) 2.00 .75
3rd World Telecommunications Day.

Apollo 11 — A59a

1971, July 5   Embossed   *Perf. 13*
239A A59a 10fr gold   22.50
  b.   Sheet of 1, Imperf.   40.00
  No. 239Ab contains one 73x45mm stamp
with same size design as No. 239A.
  Nos. 239A-239Ab probably were not available in Chad.

No. 225F
Overprinted
in Gold

1971, July 17   Litho.   *Perf. 12x12½*
239C A50b Strip of 3, #a-c   6.00
  1972 Winter Olympics, Sapporo.

**Nos. 228A-228B, 228D Ovptd. with
"MUNICH 72" and Olympic Rings in
Gold**
Perf. 12½x12, 12x12½
1971, Nov. 1   Litho.
239D A54a Strip of 3, #a-c   10.00
239E A54a Pair, #a-b + label   6.00
Souvenir Sheet
Perf. 13½x13
239F A54a 40fr on #228D   20.00

UNICEF Emblem
and
Children — A60

1971, Dec. 11   Engr.   *Perf. 13*
240 A60 50fr Prus bl, emer & brt
            pink   2.00   .25
  25th anniv. of UNICEF.

Gorane
Nangara
Dancers
A61

  Dancers: 15fr, Girls' initiation dance, Yondo.
30fr, Women of M'Boum, vert. 40fr, Men of
Sara Kaba, vert.

1971, Dec. 18   Litho.   *Perf. 13*
241 A61 10fr blk & multi   .75   .25
242 A61 15fr brn org & multi   1.10   .25
243 A61 30fr bl & multi   1.50   .25
244 A61 40fr yel grn & multi   1.90   .25
    Nos. 241-244 (4)   5.25 1.00

Nos. 205-210
Ovptd. in Gold

1971   Litho.   *Perf. 12½x13, 13x12½*
244A-244F A45 1fr on #205-210   4.50
  Nos. 244A-244F probably were not available in Chad.

Presidents Pompidou and Tombalbaye,
Map with Paris and Fort Lamy — A62

1972, Jan. 25   Photo.   *Perf. 13*
245 A62 40fr blue & multi   1.75   .25
  Visit of Pres. Georges Pompidou of France,
Jan. 1972.

Nos. 181-204
Ovptd. in Gold

1972, Feb. 7   Litho.   *Perf. 12½x13*
245A-245X A44 1fr on #181-
                  204   20.00
  Nos. 245A-245X probably were not available in Chad.

Nos. 231G-231I Ovptd. in Gold

a

b

1972, Feb.   Litho.   *Perf. 12x12½*
246A A57b 50c Pair, #d.-e.   1.50
246B A57b 1fr Pair, #f.-g.   2.25
246C A57b 2fr Pair, #h.-i.   2.75
  Nos. 246A-246C probably were not available in Chad.

President Tombalbaye — A63

1972, Apr. 13   Litho.   *Perf. 13*
247   A63 30fr multi   .40   .25
247A A63 40fr multi   .60   .25
  Nos. 247-247A,C112-C113 (4)   3.00 1.15

Downhill Skiing — A64

  75fr, Women's figure skating. 150fr, Luge.

1972, Apr. 13   *Perf. 13½*
248 A64 25fr multi   .30   .25
249 A64 75fr multi   .75   .25
250 A64 150fr multi   1.50   .45
  Nos. 248-250,C114-C115 (5)   6.45 2.00
  11th Winter Olympic Games, Sapporo,
Japan.

Heart — A65

1972, Apr. 25   Engr.   *Perf. 13*
251 A65 100fr purple, bl & car 1.75   .25
  "Your heart is your health," World Health
Month.

Nos. 236B-
236D, 236F
Ovptd. in
Gold

1972   Litho.   *Perf. 12x12½, 12½x12*
251A A58b 15fr multicolored   3.25
251B A58b 20fr multicolored   5.00
251C A58b 25fr multicolored   7.75
  Nos. 251A-251C (3)   16.00
Souvenir Sheet
Die Cut Perf 13
251D A58b 50fr multicolored   47.50
  Nos. 251C-251D are airmail.

Gorrizia
Dubiosa — A66

  Insects and Spiders: 2fr, Spider (argiope
sector). 3fr, Silk spider (nephila senegalense).
4fr, Beetle (oryctes boas). 5fr, Dragonfly
(hemistigma albipunctata).

1972, May 6   Photo.
252 A66 1fr green & multi   1.40   .25
253 A66 2fr blue & multi   2.25   .25
254 A66 3fr car rose & multi   2.50   .30
255 A66 4fr yellow grn & multi 4.50   .40
256 A66 5fr dp green & multi   5.00   .60
  Nos. 252-256 (5)   15.65 1.80

Trains — A66a

  10fr, Orient Express. 40fr, Osaka Express.
50fr, St. Germain. 150fr, Blue train. 200fr,
Trans-Europe Express.
  300fr, Rogers "Madison," 1855.

1972   Litho.   *Perf. 12*
256A A66a 10fr multi   1.00
256B A66a 40fr multi   2.25
256C A66a 50fr multi   2.50
256D A66a 150fr multi   5.00
256E A66a 200fr multi   9.25
  Nos. 256A-256E (5)   20.00
Souvenir Sheet
256F A66a 300fr multi   14.00
  No. 256F contains one 60x40mm stamp.
See note before No. 225A.

Scout Greeting — A67

  70fr, Mountain climbing. 80fr, Canoeing.

1972, May 15   Photo.
257 A67 30fr multi   .75   .25
258 A67 70fr multi   1.40   .25
259 A67 80fr multi   1.75   .25
  Nos. 257-259,C118-C119 (5)   8.55 1.65
  Scout Jamboree.

Hurdles,
Motion and
Olympic
Emblems
A68

  Motion and Olympic Emblems and: 130fr,
Gymnast on rings. 150fr, Swimming. 300fr,
Bicycling.

1972, June 9   Litho.   Perf. 13½
260 A68 50fr blk & multi   .75 .25
261 A68 130fr blk & multi   1.90 .25
262 A68 150fr blk & multi   2.25 .30
  Nos. 260-262 (3)   4.90 .80
Souvenir Sheet
263 A68 300fr blk & multi   5.00 2.00
20th Olympic Games, Munich, Aug. 26-Sept. 10.

Ski Jump, Kasaya, Japan — A69

Designs: 75fr, Cross-country skiing, P. Tyldum, Sweden. 100fr, Figure-skating, pairs, L. Rodnina and A. Ulanov, USSR. 130fr, Men's speed skating, A. Schenk, Netherlands.

1972, June 15   Perf. 14½
264 A69 25fr gold & multi   .40 .25
265 A69 75fr gold & multi   1.00 .25
266 A69 100fr gold & multi   1.50 .40
267 A69 130fr gold & multi   1.90 .50
  Nos. 264-267,C130-C131 (6)   11.55 3.15
11th Winter Olympic Games, gold-medal winners. Nos. 264-267 exist se-tenant with label showing earth satellite.

Nos. 227A-227D, 227F Ovptd. in Gold

1972   Litho.   Perf. 12
267A A53a 1fr multicolored   .95
267B A53a 4fr multicolored   1.20
267C A53a 5fr multicolored   1.90
267D A53a 5fr multicolored   1.90
  Nos. 267A-267D (4)   5.95
Souvenir Sheet
Perf. 13½x13
267E A53a 15fr multicolored   9.00
Nos. 267D-267E are airmail.
Nos. 267A-267E probably were not available in Chad.

TV Tower and Weight-lifting — A70

Designs (TV Tower, Munich and): 40fr, Woman sprinter. 60fr, Soccer goalkeeper.

1972, Aug. 15   Litho.   Perf. 14½
268 A70 20fr gold & multi   .65 .25
269 A70 40fr gold & multi   .80 .25
270 A70 60fr gold & multi   1.40 .25
  Nos. 268-270,C135-C137 (6)   10.70 2.65
20th Summer Olympic Games, Munich. Nos. 268-270 exist se-tenant with label showing arms of Munich.

Domestic Animals A71

1972, Aug. 29   Engr.   Perf. 13
271 A71 25fr Dromedary   1.75 .25
272 A71 30fr Horse   2.25 .25
273 A71 40fr Dog   3.25 .30
274 A71 45fr Goat   3.75 .40
  Nos. 271-274 (4)   11.00 1.20
For surcharge see No. 293.

Tobacco Cultivation A72

1972, Oct. 24   Engr.   Perf. 13
275 A72 40fr shown   .75 .25
276 A72 50fr Plowing   1.25 .25

Massa Warrior — A73

Design: 20fr, Moundang warrior.

1972, Nov. 15   Photo.   Perf. 14x13
277 A73 15fr orange & multi   .75 .25
278 A73 20fr yellow & multi   1.00 .25

No. 236A Overprinted in Gold

1972   Litho.   Perf. 12x12½
278A A58a Strip of 3, #a-c   5.50
No. 278A probably was not available in Chad.

King Faisal and Pres. Tombalbaye — A74

1972, Nov. 17   Litho.   Perf. 13
279 A74 100fr gold & multi   2.50 .75
Visit of King Faisal of Saudi Arabia. See No. C143.

Gen. Gowon and Pres. Tombalbaye — A75

1972, Dec. 7
280 A75 70fr multi   1.00 .25
Visit of Gen. Yakubu Gowon of Nigeria.

Olympic Emblem and 100-meter Sprint, Valeri Borzov, USSR — A76

Designs (Olympic Emblem and): 20fr, Shotput, Komar, Poland. 40fr, Hammer throw, Bondartchuk, USSR. 60fr, Discus, Danek, Czechoslovakia.

1972, Dec. 22   Perf. 11
281 A76 10fr multi   .55 .25
282 A76 20fr multi   .55 .25
283 A76 40fr multi   .70 .25
284 A76 60fr multi   1.10 .30
  Nos. 281-284,C148-C149 (6)   10.15 2.40
20th Summer Olympic Games, winners.

Olympic Emblem and Fencing, Woyda, Poland — A77

Olympic Emblem and: 30fr, 3-day equestrian event, Richard Meade, Gt. Britain. 50fr, Two-man sculls, Brietzke-Mager, East Germany.

1972, Dec. 22
285 A77 20fr gold & multi   .65 .25
286 A77 30fr gold & multi   .65 .25
287 A77 50fr gold & multi   1.00 .30
  Nos. 285-287,C151-C152 (5)   10.55 2.50
20th Summer Olympic Games, winners.

1972 Summer Olympics Gold Medalists — A77a

20fr, Teofilo Stevenson, boxing, Cuba. 25fr, Yugoslavia, team handball. 30fr, M. Peters, pentathlon, Great Britain. 40fr, basketball, USSR. No. 287E, W. Ruska, judo, Netherlands. No. 287F, Women's gymnastics, Ludmila Tourischeva, USSR. 75fr, Men's volleyball, Japan. No. 287H, A. Scalzone, shooting, Italy. No. 287I, Soccer, Poland. 130fr, J. Williams, archery, US. No. 287K, A.

Nakayama, men's rings, Japan. No. 287L, Field hockey, West Germany. 200fr, Vassily Alexeiev, weight lifting, USSR. 250fr, D. Morelon, cycling, France.

1972, Dec. 22   Litho.   Perf. 11½
287A A77a 20fr multicolored
287B A77a 25fr multicolored
287C A77a 30fr multicolored
287D A77a 40fr multicolored
287E A77a 50fr multicolored
287F A77a 50fr multicolored
287G A77a 75fr multicolored
287H A77a 100fr multicolored
287I A77a 100fr multicolored
287J A77a 130fr multicolored
287K A77a 150fr multicolored
287L A77a 150fr multicolored
  Nos. 287A-287L (12)   19.00
Souvenir Sheets
Perf. 15
287M A77a 200fr multicolored   13.50
287N A77a 250fr multicolored   13.50
Nos. 287G-287N are airmail.

Soviet Flag and Shield — A78

1972, Dec. 30   Litho.   Perf. 12
288 A78 150fr red & multi   1.90 .40
50th anniversary of the Soviet Union.

High Jump — A79

Designs (Games Emblem and): 125fr, Running. 200fr, Shot put. 250fr, Discus.

1973, Jan. 17   Litho.   Perf. 13½x13
289 A79 50fr vio bl & multi   .75 .25
290 A79 125fr olive & multi   1.60 .40
291 A79 200fr lilac & multi   3.00 .65
  Nos. 289-291 (3)   5.35 1.30
Souvenir Sheet
292 A79 250fr brn & multi   3.75 2.25
2nd African Games, Lagos, Nigeria, 1/7-18.

Paintings with Musical Instruments — A79a

Details from Paintings: 30fr, Madeleine Playing her Lute, by unknown artist. 70fr, A Concert, by Lorenzo Costa. 100fr, Bass and Sheet Music, by Jean-Baptiste Oudry, horiz. 15fr, St. Cecilia and Angel, by Carlo Saraceni. 150fr, Woman Listening to Violinist, by Gabriel Metsu. 300fr, Still Life with Musical Instruments, by Pieter Claesz, horiz.

1973, Apr.   Litho.   Perf. 11½
292A A79a 30fr multicolored
292B A79a 70fr multicolored
292C A79a 100fr multicolored
292D A79a 125fr multicolored
292E A79a 150fr multicolored

Nos. 292A-292E (5) 13.50

Souvenir Sheet
Perf. 15

292F A79a 300fr multicolored 13.50

Nos. 292D-292F are airmail.

No. 271 Srchd. and Ovptd. in Red

1973, Aug. 16 Engr. Perf. 13
293 A71 100fr on 25fr multi 2.25 .50

African solidarity in drought emergency.

African Postal Union Issue
Common Design Type

1973, Sept. 17 Engr. Perf. 13
294 CD137 100fr multicolored 1.75 .40

Easter A79b

Details from paintings: 40fr, Christ on the Cross, by Lucas Cranach. 60fr, Supper in Emmaus, by Titian, horiz. 120fr, The Crucifixion, by Durer. 150fr, The Tribute, by Titian. 250fr, The Pieta, by Botticelli. 400fr, Entombment of Christ, by Gaspard Isenmann, horiz.

1973 Litho. Perf. 11½
294A A79b 40fr multicolored
294B A79b 60fr multicolored
294C A79b 120fr multicolored
294D A79b 150fr multicolored
294E A79b 250fr multicolored
Nos. 294A-294E (5) 13.50

Souvenir Sheet
Perf. 15
294F A79b 400fr multicolored 13.50

Nos. 294A, 294D-294F are airmail.

Animals A79c

1973 Litho. Perf. 13½
294G A79c 20fr Sheep
294H A79c 30fr Camels
294J A79c 100fr Cats
294K A79c 130fr Dogs
294L A79c 150fr Horses
Nos. 294G-294L (5) 13.50

Nos. 294J-294L are airmail.
See note before No. 225A.

Christmas — A79d

30fr, The Virgin & Infant Surrounded by Saints, by Lorenzo Lotto. 40fr, Madonna and Child with St. Peter and a Martyred Saint, by Paolo Veronese (not Tintoretto), vert. 55fr, Nativity Scene, by Martin Schongauer, vert. 60fr, Nativity Scene, by Federico Barocci, vert. 250fr, Adoration of the Magi, by Stephan Lochner, vert. 400fr, Epiphany, by Hans Memling.

1973 Litho. Perf. 11½
294M A79d 30fr multicolored
294N A79d 40fr multicolored
294P A79d 55fr multicolored
294Q A79d 60fr multicolored
294R A79d 250fr multicolored
Nos. 294M-294R (5) 13.50

Souvenir Sheet
Perf. 15
294S A79d 400fr multicolored 13.50

Nos. 294Q-294S are airmail.
See note before No. 225A.

Insects — A80

No. 295, Dinothrombium Tinctorium. No. 296, Bupreste sternocera. No. 297, Diptere hyperechia. No. 298, Chrysis. No. 299, Longicorn beetle. No. 300, Spider.

1974, Sept. 3 Photo. Perf. 13
295 A80 25fr multicolored 1.50 .25
296 A80 30fr multicolored 2.25 .25
297 A80 40fr multicolored 2.75 .25
298 A80 50fr multicolored 3.25 .35
299 A80 100fr multicolored 4.75 .65
300 A80 150fr multicolored 7.50 .95
Nos. 295-300 (6) 22.00 2.70

Rotary Emblem — A81

1975, Apr. 11 Typo. Perf. 13
301 A81 50fr multi 1.00 .25

Rotary International, 70th anniversary.

Craterostigma Plantagineum — A82

Flowers: 10fr, Tapinanthus globiferus. 15fr, Commelina forskalaei, vert. 20fr, Adenium obesum. 25fr, Yellow hibiscus. 30fr, Red hibiscus. 40fr, Kigelia africana.

1975, Sept. 25 Photo. Perf. 13
302 A82 5fr org & multi .40 .25
303 A82 10fr gray bl & multi .60 .25
304 A82 15fr yel grn & multi .75 .25
305 A82 20fr lt brn & multi 1.00 .25
306 A82 25fr lil & multi 1.75 .25
307 A82 30fr bis & multi 1.90 .35
308 A82 40fr ultra & multi 3.00 .50
Nos. 302-308 (7) 9.40 2.10

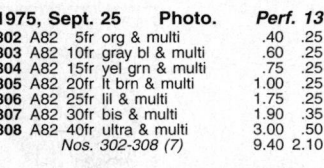

A. G. Bell, Satellite and Waves — A83

1976, June 10 Litho. Perf. 12½
309 A83 100fr bl, brn & ocher 1.40 .40
310 A83 125fr brn, brn & ocher 1.90 .60

Centenary of first telephone call by Alexander Graham Bell, Mar. 10, 1876.

Ice Hockey, USSR — A84

90fr, Ski jump, Karl Schnabl, Austria.

1976, June 21 Perf. 14
311 A84 60fr multi .75 .25
312 A84 90fr multi 1.25 .25
Nos. 311-312,C178-C179 (4) 8.25 2.10

12th Winter Olympic Games, winners. See No. C180.

High Hurdles A85

1976, July 12 Litho. Perf. 13½
313 A85 45fr multi .70 .25
Nos. 313,C187-C189 (4) 8.70 1.70

21st Summer Olympic Games, Montreal, Canada. See No. C190.

Mars Landing and Viking Rocket A86

1976, July 23 Perf. 14
314 A86 45fr multi .50 .25
315 A86 90fr multi 1.00 .25
Nos. 314-315,C191-C193 (5) 7.35 2.10

Mars Landing and: 90fr, Viking trajectory, Earth to Mars.

Viking Mars project.

For overprints see Nos. 379-380.

Robert Koch, Medicine — A87

Design: 90fr, Anatole France, literature.

1976, Dec. 15
316 A87 45fr multi .75 .25
317 A87 90fr multi 1.50 .25
Nos. 316-317,C196-C198 (5) 9.75 2.05

Nobel Prize winners.

Map and Flag of Chad, Clasped Hands A88

120fr, Map of Chad, people & occupations.

1976, Sept. 15 Litho. Perf. 12½x13
318 A88 30fr multi .60 .25
319 A88 60fr orange & multi 1.10 .30
320 A88 120fr brown & multi 2.25 .50
Nos. 318-320 (3) 3.95 1.05

National reconciliation.

Freed Political Prisoners — A89

Designs: 60fr, Parade of cadets.

1976, Sept. 25 Litho. Perf. 12½
321 A89 30fr blue & multi .30 .25
322 A89 60fr black & multi .75 .25
323 A89 120fr red & multi 1.40 .25
Nos. 321-323 (3) 2.45 .75

Revolution of Apr. 13, 1975, 1st anniv.

Decorated Calabashes — A90

Designs: Various pyrographed calabashes.

1976, Nov. Litho. Perf. 12½x13
324 A90 30fr multi .40 .25
325 A90 60fr multi .90 .25
326 A90 120fr multi 1.75 .25
Nos. 324-326 (3) 3.05 .75

Germany No. C57 and
Friedrichshafen, Germany — A91

1977, Mar. 30   *Perf. 14*
327 A91 100fr multi   1.40   .25
    Nos. 327,C206-C209 (5)   11.55 2.10
    75th anniversary of the Zeppelin.

Elizabeth II in Coronation Regalia and
Clergy — A92

Design: 450fr, Elizabeth II and Prince Philip.

1977, June 15 Litho.   Perf. 14x13½
328 A92 250fr multi   3.25   .75
              Souvenir Sheet
329 A92 450fr multi   5.75 2.50
    25th anniv. of the reign of Elizabeth II.
    Nos. 328-329 exist imperf. For overprints
see Nos. 347-348.

Simon
Bolivar
A93

Famous Personalities: 175fr, Joseph J. Roberts. No. 332, Queen Wilhelmina of Netherlands. No. 333, Charles de Gaulle. 325fr, King
Baudouin and Queen Fabiola of Belgium.

1977, June 15   *Perf. 13½x14*
330 A93 150fr multi   1.50   .30
331 A93 175fr multi   2.25   .45
332 A93 200fr multi   3.00   .65
333 A93 200fr multi   3.00   .75
334 A93 325fr multi   4.00 1.00
    Nos. 330-334 (5)   13.75 3.15

Post and Telecommunications
Emblem — A94

Map of Chad and
Waves — A95

Society
Emblem — A96

1977, Aug. 15   Litho.   Perf. 13
335 A94 30fr yel & blk   .50   .25
              Perf. 12½
336 A95 60fr multi   .75   .25
              Perf. 13½x13
337 A96 120fr multi   1.60   .50
    Nos. 335-337 (3)   2.85 1.00
    Telecommunications (30fr); Natl. Telecom-
munications School, 10th anniv. (60fr); Intl.
Telecommunication Soc. of Chad (120fr).

WHO Emblem
and Man (Back
Pain) — A97

World Rheumatism Year (WHO Emblem
and): 60fr, Woman's head (neck pain), horiz.
120fr, Leg (knee pain).

         Perf. 12½x13, 13x12½
1977, Nov. 10   **Engr.**
338 A97 30fr multi   .50   .25
339 A97 60fr multi   1.00   .25
340 A97 120fr multi   1.40   .40
    Nos. 338-340 (3)   2.90   .90

World Cup Emblems and Saving a
Goal — A98

Designs (Argentina '78, World Cup
Emblems and): 60fr, Heading the ball. 100fr,
Referee whistling a goal. 200fr, World Cup
poster. 300fr, Pelé. 500fr, Helmut Schoen and
Munich stadium.

1977, Nov. 25   Litho.   Perf. 13½
341 A98 40fr multi   .50   .25
342 A98 60fr multi   .75   .25
343 A98 100fr multi   1.10   .25
344 A98 200fr multi   2.50   .50
345 A98 300fr multi   3.75   .75
    Nos. 341-345 (5)   8.60 2.00
              Souvenir Sheet
346 A98 500fr multi   5.75 3.00
    World Cup Soccer Championship, Argentina
'78.
    For overprints see Nos. 359-364.

Nos. 328-329 Overprinted in Silver

1978, Sept. 13   *Perf. 14x13½*
347 A92 250fr multi   3.00 1.00
              Souvenir Sheet
348 A92 450fr multi   5.50 4.50
    25th anniv. of coronation of Elizabeth II.

Abraham and Melchisedek, by
Rubens — A99

Rubens Paintings: 120fr, Helene Fourment,
vert. 200fr, David and the Elders of Israel.
300fr, Anne of Austria, vert. 500fr, Marie de
Medicis, vert.

1978, Nov. 23   Litho.   Perf. 13½
349 A99 60fr multi   .75   .25
350 A99 120fr multi   1.75   .35
351 A99 200fr multi   3.00 1.00
352 A99 300fr multi   4.50 1.25
    Nos. 349-352 (4)   10.00 2.60
              Souvenir Sheet
353 A99 500fr multi   6.75 3.00
    Peter Paul Rubens (1577-1640).

Dürer
Portrait
A100

Dürer Paintings: 150fr, Jacob Muffel. 250fr,
Young Woman. 350fr, Oswolt Krel.

1978, Nov. 23
354 A100 60fr multi   .60   .25
355 A100 150fr multi   1.75   .50
356 A100 250fr multi   3.00   .80
357 A100 350fr multi   4.50 1.25
    Nos. 354-357 (4)   9.85 2.80

Head, Village and
Fly — A101

1978, Nov. 28   *Perf. 13*
358 A101 60f multi   .75   .25
    National Health Day.

Nos. 341-346 Overprinted in Silver

a

b

c

d

e

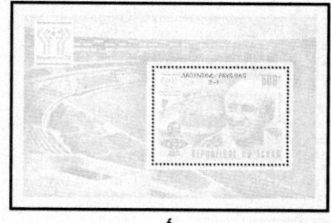

f

1978, Dec. 30   Litho.   Perf. 13½
359 A98(a) 40fr multi   .50   .25
360 A98(b) 60fr multi   .75   .25
361 A98(c) 100fr multi   1.40   .40
362 A98(d) 200fr multi   2.50   .75
363 A98(e) 300fr multi   3.50 1.25
    Nos. 359-363 (5)   8.65 2.90
              Souvenir Sheet
364 A98(f) 500fr multi   5.75 5.00
    World Soccer Championship winners.

UPU Emblems, Camel Caravan,
Satellites — A102

Design: 150fr, Obus woman and houses,
Massa Territory, hibiscus.

1979, June 8   Litho.   Perf. 12x12½
365 A102 60fr multi   3.00   .25
366 A102 150fr multi   5.00   .40

    Philexafrique II, Libreville, Gabon, June 8-
17. Nos. 365, 366 each printed in sheets of 10
with 5 labels showing exhibition emblem.

Wildlife Fund Emblem and
Gazelle — A103

Protected Animals.

1979, Sept. 15	Litho.	Perf. 14½	
367	A103	40fr shown	2.00	.30
368	A103	50fr Addax	2.25	.50
369	A103	60fr Oryx antelope	2.75	.75
370	A103	100fr Cheetah	4.25	1.40
371	A103	150fr Zebra	5.75	1.90
372	A103	300fr Rhinoceros	11.50	3.00
	Nos. 367-372 (6)		28.50	7.85

Souvenir Sheet

Holy Family, by Dürer — A104

1979, Sept. 1		Perf. 13½	
373	A104	500fr brown & dull red	6.75	2.50

Boy and Handpainted Doors — A105

IYC Emblem and: 75fr, Oriental girl. 100fr,
Caucasian girl, doves. 150fr, African boys.
250fr, Pencil and outlines of child's hands.

1979, Sept. 19	Litho.	Perf. 13½	
374	A105	65fr multi	.60	.25
375	A105	75fr multi	.75	.25
376	A105	100fr multi	1.00	.25
377	A105	150fr multi	1.50	.40
	Nos. 374-377 (4)		3.85	1.15

Souvenir Sheet

378	A105	250fr multi	3.00	1.50

Nos. 314-
315
Overprinted

1979, Nov. 26	Litho.	Perf. 13½x14	
379	A86	45fr multi	.60	.25
380	A86	90fr multi	1.00	.30
	Nos. 379-380,C240-C242 (5)		7.45	2.55

Apollo 11 moon landing, 10th anniversary.

Ski Jump, Lake Placid '80
Emblem — A106

Lake Placid '80 Emblem and: 20fr, Slalom,
vert. 40fr, Biathlon, vert. 150fr, Women's slalom, vert. 350fr, Cross-country skiing. 500fr,
Downhill skiing.

1979, Dec. 18		Perf. 14½	
381	A106	20fr multi	.30	.25
382	A106	40fr multi	.65	.25
383	A106	60fr multi	.80	.25
384	A106	150fr multi	1.75	.50
385	A106	350fr multi	3.00	1.40
386	A106	500fr multi	4.50	1.90
	Nos. 381-386 (6)		11.00	4.55

13th Winter Olympic Games, Lake Placid,
NY, Feb. 12-24, 1980.

Jet over
Map of
Africa
A107

1980, Feb. 20	Litho.	Perf. 12½	
387	A107	15fr yellow & multi	.25	.25
388	A107	30fr blue & multi	.40	.25
389	A107	60fr red & multi	.60	.25
	Nos. 387-389 (3)		1.25	.75

ASECNA (Air Safety Board), 20th anniv.

A set of four stamps (50fr, 80fr, 100fr
air post, 200fr air post) commemorating
cooperation between Chad and Libya
were prepared for use in 1981 but not
issued. Value, $300.

1982 World Cup Soccer
Championships, Spain — A108

1982	Litho.	Perf. 13½	
390	A108	30fr Hungary	.30	.25
391	A108	40fr Italy	.40	.25
392	A108	50fr Algeria	.50	.25
393	A108	60fr Argentina	.60	.25
	Nos. 390-393,C258-C259 (6)		5.80	1.75

21st
Birthday
of
Princess
Diana
A109

1982, July 2	Litho.	Perf. 13½	
395	A109	30fr 1961	.30	.25
396	A109	40fr 1965	.40	.25
397	A109	50fr 1967	.50	.25
398	A109	60fr 1975	.60	.25
	Nos. 395-398,C260-C261 (6)		5.80	2.20

For overprints see Nos. 413-419B.

A110

1984 Summer Olympics, Los
Angeles — A110a

No. 405A, Runner. No. 405B, Long jumper,
vert.

1982, Aug. 2	Litho.	Perf. 13½	
399	A110	30fr Gymnast	.30	.25
400	A110	40fr Equestrian	.40	.25
401	A110	50fr Judo	.50	.25
402	A110	60fr High jump	.60	.25
403	A110	80fr Hurdles	1.00	.25
404	A110	300fr Woman gymnast	3.00	.95
	Nos. 399-404 (6)		5.80	2.20

Souvenir Sheet

405	A110	500fr Relay race	5.50	1.50

For surcharge see No. C302.

1982, July 31	Litho. & Embossed	
405A	A110a	1500fr gold & multi	16.00

Souvenir Sheet

405B	A110a	1500fr gold & multi	12.00

No. 405 contains one 56x39mm stamp.
Nos. 403-405B airmail.
No. 405A exists in a souvenir sheet of 1.
Value $47.50.

Scouting Year — A111

Boy Scouts,
75th Anniv.
A111a

Scouts from various countries. No. 412A,
Lord Robert Baden-Powell. No. 412B, Scouts
at campsite, Baden-Powell, horiz.

1982, July 15		
406	A111	30fr West Germany	.30	.25
407	A111	40fr Upper Volta	.40	.25
408	A111	50fr Mali	.50	.25
409	A111	60fr Scotland	.60	.25
410	A111	80fr Kuwait	1.00	.25
411	A111	300fr Chad	3.00	.95
	Nos. 406-411 (6)		5.80	2.20

Souvenir Sheet

412	A111	500fr Chad, diff.	5.50	2.00

Litho. & Embossed

412A	A111a	1500fr gold & multi	17.00

Souvenir Sheet

412B	A111a	1500fr gold & multi	17.00

No. 412 contains one 53x35mm stamp.
Nos. 410-412B airmail.
No. 412A exists in a souvenir sheet of 1.
Value $40.
For overprints see Nos. 466-472B.

Nos. 395-398, C260-C262B
Overprinted "21 JUIN 1982 /
WILLIAM ARTHUR PHILIP LOUIS/
PRINCE DE GALLES"

1982, Oct. 4	Litho.	Perf. 13½	
413	A109	30fr multi	.30	.25
414	A109	40fr multi	.40	.25
415	A109	50fr multi	.50	.25
416	A109	60fr multi	.60	.25
417	A109	80fr multi	1.00	.25
418	A109	300fr multi	3.00	.95
	Nos. 413-418 (6)		5.80	2.20

Souvenir Sheet

419	A109	500fr multi	5.50	1.60

Litho. & Embossed

419A	AP71b	1500fr on #C262A	16.00

Souvenir Sheet

419B	AP71b	1500fr on #C262B	13.50

Birth of Prince William of Wales, June 21.
Nos. 417-419B airmail.
No. 419A exists in a souvenir sheet of 1.
Value $42.50.

A112

1982 World Cup Soccer
Championships, Spain — A112a

Various players and flags. No. 426A, Dino
Zoff, Italy, holding World Cup trophy. No.
426B, Paolo Rossi, Italy, two players, trophy,
horiz.

1982, Nov. 30		
420	A112	30fr multi	.30	.25
421	A112	40fr multi	.40	.25
422	A112	50fr multi	.50	.25
423	A112	60fr multi	.60	.25
424	A112	80fr multi	1.00	.25
425	A112	300fr multi	3.00	.95
	Nos. 420-425 (6)		5.80	2.20

Souvenir Sheet

426	A112	500fr multi	5.50	2.00

Litho. & Embossed

426A	A112a	1500fr gold & multi	16.00

Souvenir Sheet

426B	A112a	1500fr gold & multi	16.00

No. 426 contains one 56x32mm stamp.
Nos. 424-426B airmail.
No. 426A exists in a souvenir sheet of 1.
Value $42.50.
For surcharge see No. C306.

A113

Chess Champions — A113a

30fr, Philidor. 40fr, Paul Morphy. 50fr, Howard Staunton. 60fr, Capablanca. 80fr, Boris Spassky. 300fr, Anatoly Karpov.
500fr, Victor Korchnoi. No. 433A, Bobby Fischer. No. 433B, William Steinitz.

1982, Dec. 24
427	A113	30fr multi	1.00	.25
428	A113	40fr multi	1.10	.25
429	A113	50fr multi	1.25	.25
430	A113	60fr multi	1.40	.25
431	A113	80fr multi	2.10	.25
432	A113	300fr multi	3.75	.75
	Nos. 427-432 (6)		10.60	2.00

Souvenir Sheet
433	A113	500fr multi	9.00	3.00

Litho. & Embossed
433A	A113a	1500fr gold & multi	17.50

Souvenir Sheet
433B	A113a	1500fr gold & multi	12.00

No. 433 contains one 53x35mm stamp. Nos. 431-433B airmail.
No. 433A exists in a souvenir sheet of 1. Value $50.
For overprints see Nos. 459-465.

2nd UN Conference on Peaceful Uses of Outer Space, Vienna, Aug. 9-21 — A114

A114a

Inventors and Satellites: 30fr, K.E. Tsiolkovsky, Soyuz. 40fr, R.H. Goddard, space telescope design. 50fr, Korolev, ultraviolet telescope. 60fr, von Braun, Columbia space shuttle. 80fr, Esnault Pelterie, Ariana rocket. 300fr, H. Oberth, orbital space station. 500fr, Pres. Kennedy, Apollo 11 badge, lunar rover. No. 440A, Sir Bernard Lovell, Viking I & II. No. 440B, Sir Isaac Newton, satellite TDF 1.

1983, Feb. 1   Litho.   Perf. 13½
434	A114	30fr multi	.30	.25
435	A114	40fr multi	.40	.25
436	A114	50fr multi	.50	.25
437	A114	60fr multi	.60	.25
438	A114	80fr multi	1.00	.25
439	A114	300fr multi	3.00	.95
	Nos. 434-439 (6)		5.80	2.20

Souvenir Sheet
440	A114	500fr multi	5.50	2.50

Litho. & Embossed
440A	A114a	1500fr gold & multi	16.00

Souvenir Sheet
440B	A114a	1500fr gold & multi	12.00

No. 440 contains one 42x50mm stamp. Nos. 438-440B airmail.
No. 440A exists in a souvenir sheet of 1. Value $50.

Bobsledding — A115

Woman Figure Skater A115a

40fr, Speed skating. 50fr, Cross-country skiing. 60fr, Hockey. 80fr, Ski jumping. 300fr, Downhill skiing.
500fr, Figure skating. No. 447B, Slalom skier, horiz.

1983, Apr. 25   Litho.   Perf. 13½
441	A115	30fr shown	.30	.25
442	A115	40fr multi	.40	.25
443	A115	50fr multi	.50	.25
444	A115	60fr multi	.60	.25
445	A115	80fr multi	1.00	.30
446	A115	300fr multi	3.00	1.10
	Nos. 441-446 (6)		5.80	2.40

Souvenir Sheet
447	A115	500fr multi	5.50	1.60

Litho. & Embossed
447A	A115a	1500fr gold & multi	16.00

Souvenir Sheet
447B	A115a	1500fr gold & multi	12.00

14th Winter Olympic Games, Sarajevo, Yugoslavia, Feb. 8-19, 1984.
Nos. 445-447B airmail.
No. 447A exists in a souvenir sheet of 1. Value $45.
For surcharge see No. C298.

First Manned Balloon Flight, 200th Anniv. A116

Designs: 25fr, Hot air balloon, Montgolfier Brothers. 45fr, Captive balloon, Pilatre De Rozier. 50fr, First parachute descent, Jacques Garnerin. 60fr, Chelsea balloon, J.P. Blanchard.

1983, May 30   Litho.   Perf. 13½
448	A116	25fr multi	.30	.25
449	A116	45fr multi	.40	.25
450	A116	50fr multi	.50	.25
451	A116	60fr multi	.60	.25
	Nos. 448-451,C268-C269 (6)		5.80	1.65

Automobiles — A116a

Automobiles and their builders: 25fr, 1927 Mercedes Type S, Gottlieb Daimler and Karl Benz. 45fr, 1913 Torpedo Martini Type GC 32-2, 6L, Friedrich Martini. 50fr, 1926 Chrysler "70," Walter P. Chrysler. 60fr, 1929 Alfa Romeo 6C 1750 Grand Sport, Nicola Romeo. 80fr, 1934 Phantom II Continental, Stewart Rolls and Henry Royce. 250fr, 1948 Talbot Lago, Lord Shrewsbury and Talbot.

1983, July 15   Litho.   Perf. 13½
451A	A116a	25fr multicolored	
451B	A116a	45fr multicolored	
451C	A116a	50fr multicolored	
451D	A116a	60fr multicolored	
451E	A116a	80fr multicolored	
451F	A116a	250fr multicolored	
	Nos. 451A-451F (6)		6.75 1.60

Nos. 451E-451F are airmail.

1984 Summer Olympics, Los Angeles A117

A117a

1983, Nov. 15   Litho.   Perf. 13½
452	A117	25fr Kayak	.30	.25
453	A117	45fr Long jump	.60	.25
454	A117	50fr Boxing	.70	.25
455	A117	60fr Discus	.75	.25
456	A117	80fr Running	1.00	.25
457	A117	350fr Equestrian	3.50	.75
	Nos. 452-457 (6)		6.85	2.00

Souvenir Sheet
458	A117	500fr Gymnastics	5.50	2.50

Litho. & Embossed
458A	A117a	1500fr Hurdles	16.00

Souvenir Sheet
458B	A117a	1500fr Equestrian, vert.	12.00

Nos. 456-458B are airmail.
No. 458A exists in a souvenir sheet of 1. Value $47.50.

Pres. Hissein Habre — A117b

Designs: Nos. 458D, 458H, Sources of food. Nos. 458E, 458I, Dove of peace, different tribal groups, country map.

1983, Dec. 26   Litho.   Perf. 13½
458C	A117b	50fr multicolored	.60	.25
458D	A117b	50fr multicolored	.60	.25
458E	A117b	50fr multicolored	.60	.25
458F	A117b	80fr multicolored	.70	.25
458G	A117b	80fr multicolored	.90	.25
458H	A117b	80fr multicolored	.90	.25
458I	A117b	80fr multicolored	.90	.25
458J	A117b	100fr multicolored	1.10	.35
	See Nos. C276-C279.			

Nos. 427-433 Overprinted: "60e ANNIVERSAIRE FEDERATION / MONDIALE D'ECHECS 1924-1984"

1983, Dec. 27   Litho.   Perf. 13½
459	A113	30fr multi	.90	.25
460	A113	40fr multi	1.10	.25
461	A113	50fr multi	1.40	.25
462	A113	60fr multi	1.75	.25
463	A113	80fr multi	2.25	.30
464	A113	300fr multi	4.50	.75
	Nos. 459-464 (6)		11.90	2.05

Souvenir Sheet
465	A113	500fr multi	4.50	2.50

World Chess Fedn., 60th anniv.

Nos. 406-412B Ovptd. with Emblem for the 15th World Scout Jamboree, Alberta, Canada, 1983

1983, Dec. 27   Litho.   Perf. 13½
466	A111	30fr multi	.30	.25
467	A111	40fr multi	.40	.25
468	A111	50fr multi	.50	.25
469	A111	60fr multi	.60	.25
470	A111	80fr multi	.70	.25
471	A111	300fr multi	3.00	.50
	Nos. 466-471 (6)		5.50	1.75

Souvenir Sheet
472	A111	500fr multi	6.00	2.50

Litho. & Embossed
472A	A111a	1500fr on #412A	16.00

Souvenir Sheet
472B	A111a	1500fr on #412B	12.00

Locomotive "Lady," 1879 — A118

200fr, Sailboat, Lake Chad. 300fr, Graf Zeppelin, 1930. 350fr, Renault desert transport. 400fr, Bloch 120 monoplane. 500fr, Air Africa DC-8.
600fr, Intelsat V satellite.

1984, Mar. 15
473	A118	50fr shown	.60	.25
474	A118	200fr multicolored	2.40	.60
475	A118	300fr multicolored	3.25	.90
476	A118	350fr multicolored	4.00	1.10
477	A118	400fr multicolored	4.25	1.25
478	A118	500fr multicolored	5.50	1.50
	Nos. 473-478 (6)		20.00	5.60

Souvenir Sheet
479	A118	600fr multicolored	5.75	5.00

Nos. 477-479 airmail. For surcharge see No. 579.

Liberation, 2nd Anniv. — A119

1984, June 6   Perf. 12½
480	A119	50fr multi	.60	.25

Pres. Hissein
Habre — A120

1984, June 18   **Perf. 12½x13**
481 A120 125fr multi   1.50   .40

Anniversaries and Events — A121

Designs: 50fr, Pres. Habre, civil war martyrs. 200fr, Paul Harris, Rotary Intl. headquarters, Illinois. 300fr, Alfred Nobel, will establishing fund for Prizes. 350fr, Raphael, detail from Virgin with Child and St. John the Baptist. 400fr, Rembrandt, detail from The Holy Family. 500fr, J.W. Goethe, scene from Faust. 600fr, Rubens, detail from Helene Fourment and Her Two Children.

1984, Jan. 16   Litho.   Perf. 13½
482 A121 50fr multi   .50   .25
483 A121 200fr multi   1.90   .30
484 A121 300fr multi   3.00   .45
485 A121 350fr multi   3.75   .55
486 A121 400fr multi   4.50   .60
487 A121 500fr multi   5.75   .70
   Nos. 482-487 (6)   19.40 2.85

Souvenir Sheet
488 A121 600fr multi   6.75 2.50

Nos. 486-488 are airmail.

Homage to Our
Martyred
Dead — A122

1984, Feb. 22   Litho.   Perf. 13½
500 A122 50fr multi   .50   .25
501 A122 80fr multi   .75   .25
502 A122 120fr multi   1.10   .25
503 A122 200fr multi   1.90   .40
504 A122 250fr multi   2.50   .50
   Nos. 500-504 (5)   6.75 1.65

Nos. 503-504 airmail. For surcharge see Nos. 228A-228B, 228D Ovptd. with "MUNICH 72" and Olympic Rings in GoldC303.

World Communications Year — A123

1984, Feb. 29   Litho.   Perf. 13½
505 A123 50fr sil & multi   .50   .25
506 A123 60fr sil & multi   .60   .25
507 A123 70fr sil & multi   .75   .25
508 A123 125fr sil & multi   1.10   .25
509 A123 250fr sil & multi   2.50   .50
   Nos. 505-509 (5)   5.45 1.50

Nos. 508-509 airmail. For surcharge see Nos. 228A-228B, 228D Ovptd. with "MUNICH 72" and Olympic Rings in GoldC304.

Anniversaries and Events — A123a

50fr, Durer, detail from Madonna of the Rosary. 200fr, Henri Dunant, Red Cross founder, Battle of Solferino. 300fr, Early telephone, Goonhilly Downs Satellite Station, Britain. 350fr, J.F. Kennedy, Neil Armstrong's 1st step on Moon, 1969. 400fr, Europe-Africa Satellite infrared photograph. 500fr, Prince Charles & Lady Diana. 600fr, Wedding photograph of Prince Charles & Lady Diana.

1984
510 A123a 50fr multi   .50   .25
511 A123a 200fr multi   2.10   .30
512 A123a 300fr multi   3.00   .45
513 A123a 350fr multi   3.50   .50
514 A123a 400fr multi   3.75   .55
515 A123a 500fr multi   5.00   .80
   Nos. 510-515 (6)   17.85 2.85

Souvenir Sheet
516 A121 600fr multicolored   5.25

A souvenir sheet of 6 containing Nos. 510-515 exists. Nos. 514-516 are airmail.
For surcharge see No. 578.

Development of
Communications — A123b

Ships and locomotives: 90fr, Indiaman, East India Co. 100fr, Nord 701, 1885. 125fr, Vera Cruz. 150fr, Columbia, 1888. 200fr, Carlisle Castle. 250fr, Rete Mediterranea, 1900. 300fr, Britannia. 350fr, Mav 114.

1984, Aug. 1   Litho.   Perf. 12½
517 A123b 90fr multi   1.10   .25
518 A123b 100fr multi   1.10   .25
519 A123b 125fr multi   1.75   .25
520 A123b 150fr multi   1.75   .25
521 A123b 200fr multi   2.50   .25
522 A123b 250fr multi   3.00   .30
523 A123b 300fr multi   3.25   .35
524 A123b 350fr multi   3.75   .50
   Nos. 517-524 (8)   18.20 2.40

Christmas — A124

1984, Dec. 28   Litho.   Perf. 13
525 A124 50fr lt bl & org brn   .50   .25
526 A124 60fr ver & org brn   .60   .25
527 A124 80fr emer & org brn   .75   .25
528 A124 85fr rose lil & org brn .75 .25
529 A124 100fr org yel & org brn 1.00 .30
530 A124 135fr dp bl vio & org
               brn   1.25   .40
   Nos. 525-530 (6)   4.85 1.70

European Music
Year — A125

Instruments.

1985, Apr. 30   Litho.   Perf. 12x12½
531 A125 20fr Guitar   .25   .25
532 A125 25fr Harp   .30   .25
533 A125 30fr Xylophone   .40   .25
534 A125 50fr Shoulder drum   .50   .25
535 A125 70fr like #534   .70   .25
536 A125 80fr like #532   .75   .30
537 A125 100fr like #531   1.00   .40
538 A125 250fr like #533   2.50   .80
   Nos. 531-538 (8)   6.40 2.75

Mushrooms
A126

25fr, Chlorophyllum molybdites. 30fr, Tulostoma volvulatum. 50fr, Lentinus tuber-regium. 80fr, Podaxis pistillarus.

1985, May 15   Litho.   Perf. 12½
539 A126 25fr multi   .60   .25
540 A126 30fr multi   .70   .25
541 A126 50fr multi   1.00   .25
542 A126 70fr like #541   1.40   .25
543 A126 80fr multi   1.60   .25
544 A126 100fr like #539   2.50   .35
   Nos. 539-544 (6)   7.80 1.60

Anniversaries and Events — A127

25fr, Abraham Lincoln. 45fr, Henri Dunant, Geneva birthplace and red cross. 50fr, Gottlieb Daimler, 1887 Motor Carriage. 60fr, Louis Bleriot, Bleriot XI monoplane, 1909. 80fr, Paul Harris, Chicago site of Rotary Intl. founding. 350fr, Auguste Piccard, bathyscaphe Trieste, 1953.
600fr, Anatoly Karpov, 1981 world chess champion. 1500fr, Paul Harris on Medal.

1985, May 25   Litho.   Perf. 13½
545 A127 25fr multi   .30   .25
546 A127 45fr multi   .60   .25
547 A127 50fr multi   .75   .25
548 A127 60fr multi   1.00   .25
549 A127 80fr multi   1.10   .35
550 A127 350fr multi   4.00 1.25
   Nos. 545-550 (6)   7.75 2.60

Souvenir Sheets
551 A127 600fr multi   6.75 5.00

Litho. & Embossed
551A A127 1500fr multi   14.50

No. 551A contains one 130x90mm stamp. Nos. 548-551A are airmail.
Souvenir sheets of 1 exist for Nos. 545-551.

Intl. Youth
Year — A128

70fr, Development levels. 200fr, Globe, horiz.

1985, May 30   Litho.   Perf. 13
552 A128 70fr multi   .70   .25
553 A128 200fr multi   1.75   .50

A129

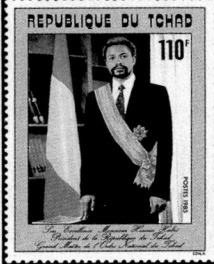

3rd Anniv.
of the
Republic
A130

Perf. 13, 12½x13
1985, June 7   Litho.
554 A129 70fr Hand, claw   .70   .25
555 A129 70fr Hands, map   .70   .25
556 A130 70fr Pres. Hissein
               Habre   .70   .25
557 A129 110fr like #554   1.10   .40
558 A129 110fr like #555   1.25   .40
559 A130 110fr like #556   1.25   .40
   Nos. 554-559 (6)   5.70 1.95

Audubon Birth
Bicent. — A131

1985, July 20   Engr.   Perf. 13
560 A131 70fr Stork   1.10   .30
561 A131 110fr Ostrich   1.60   .40
562 A131 150fr Marabou   2.25   .65
563 A131 200fr Snake eagle   3.00   .90
   Nos. 560-563 (4)   7.95 2.25

Souvenir Sheet
564 A131 500fr like 200fr   6.75 5.00

Mammals
A132

1985, Aug. 25
565 A132 50fr Waterbuck   .75   .25
566 A132 70fr Kudus, horiz.   1.00   .40
567 A132 250fr Shaggy mouflon 3.25 1.25
   Nos. 565-567 (3)   5.00 1.90

Souvenir Sheet
568 A132 500fr White rhinoceros 5.75 5.00

UN, 40th Anniv. — A133

1985, Nov. 24
569 A133 200fr brt bl, red & brn   2.25 .75

Chad Admission
to UN, 25th
Anniv. — A134

1985, Nov. 24
570 A134 300fr red, brt bl & yel   3.25 1.00

President's
Visit to the
Nation's
Interior
A135

1986, June 7   Litho.   Perf. 12½x13
571 A135 100fr multi   1.10 .25
572 A135 170fr multi   2.25 .35
573 A135 200fr multi   2.50 .45
    Nos. 571-573 (3)   5.85 1.05

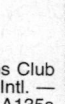

Lions Club
Intl. —
A135a

100fr, Sick child. 170fr, Three children,
horiz. 200fr, Eye exam, horiz.

1987   Litho.   Perf. 14
573A A135a 30fr Like #573C   50.00 —
573C A135a 100fr multi
573E A135a 170fr multi
573F A135a 200fr multi

There are two additional stamps in this set.
The editors would like to examine them.

World Wildlife Fund — A136

Various mouflons, *Ammotragus lervia.*

1988, Nov. 10   Litho.   Perf. 13
574 A136 25fr shown   2.50 .50
575 A136 45fr Adult, young   3.25 .75
576 A136 70fr Two adults, diff.   4.25 1.25
577 A136 100fr Adults, young   6.00 1.75
    Nos. 574-577 (4)   16.00 4.25

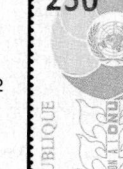

Nos. 475, 512
and 570
Surcharged

Methods and Perfs. As Before
1989
578 A123a 170fr on 300fr #512
578A A134 230fr on 300fr #570
579 A118 240fr on 300fr #475

Liberation — A137

1989   Perf. 11½x12
580 A137 20fr multi   .50 .30
581 A137 25fr multi   .60 .30
582 A137 40fr multi   1.00 .50
583 A137 100fr multi   1.50 .75
584 A137 170fr multi   2.50 1.25
    Nos. 580-584 (5)   6.10 3.10

World Post Day —
A137a

1989, Oct. 9   Photo.   Perf. 12
Granite Paper
584A A137a 100fr grn bl & multi
584B A137a 120fr red & multi
584C A137a 170fr pur & multi
584D A137a 250fr ol & multi
    Nos. 584A-584D (4)   160.00

Visit of Pope John Paul II — A138

Cathedral in Chad and: 20fr, 100fr, Pope
holding crosier. 80fr, 170fr, Pope, diff.

1989, Dec. 20   Litho.   Perf. 13
585 A138 20fr multicolored   .35 .25
586 A138 80fr multicolored   1.10 .40
587 A138 100fr multicolored   1.40 .50
588 A138 170fr multicolored   2.25 1.10
    Nos. 585-588 (4)   5.10 2.25

Traditional Hair
Styles — A139

1989, Oct. 9   Photo.   Perf. 12
Granite Paper
589 A139 100fr apple grn &
            multi
590 A139 120fr purple & multi

---

591 A139 170fr pink & multi
592 A139 250fr org yel & multi
    Nos. 589-592 (4)   160.00

Vaccinations
A140

1991, Dec. 1   Photo.   Perf. 11½
Granite Paper
593 A140 30fr brown & multi   .30 .25
594 A140 100fr green & multi   1.00 .45
595 A140 170fr vio & multi   1.60 .75
596 A140 180fr blue & multi   1.75 .80
597 A140 200fr red & multi   1.90 .90
    Nos. 593-597 (5)   6.55 3.15

Liberty and
Democracy Day —
A141

1991, Dec. 1   Litho.
598 A141 10fr green & multi   .25 .25
599 A141 20fr lilac & multi   .25 .25
600 A141 40fr yellow & multi   .40 .25
601 A141 70fr blue & multi   .65 .30
602 A141 130fr tan & multi   1.25 .75
603 A141 200fr pink & multi   1.90 1.00
    Nos. 598-603 (6)   4.70 2.80

Fight Against
Insect Pests —
A141a

1992, Sept. 1   Photo.   Perf. 12
603A A141a 25fr multi   30.00 15.00
603B A141a 45fr multi   30.00 15.00
603C A141a 100fr multi   30.00 15.00
603D A141a 150fr multi   30.00 15.00
603E A141a 170fr multi   30.00 15.00
    Nos. 603A-603E (5)   150.00 75.00

A142

1992, Nov. 15   Litho.   Perf. 11½
604 A142 20fr bright yel & multi   .25 .25
605 A142 45fr golden yel & mul-
            ti   .40 .25
606 A142 85fr pink & multi   .75 .35
607 A142 170fr blue & multi   1.50 .70
608 A142 300fr gray & multi   3.00 1.40
    Nos. 604-608 (5)   5.90 2.95

Doctors Without Borders, 20th anniv.

Campaign
Against
Illiteracy
A143

1992, Nov. 30
609 A143 25fr yel grn & multi   .25 .25
610 A143 40fr golden yel & mul-
            ti   .40 .25
611 A143 70fr pink & multi   .60 .30
612 A143 100fr lilac & multi   .75 .40
613 A143 180fr blue & multi   1.60 .60
614 A143 200fr gray & multi   1.75 .70
    Nos. 609-614 (6)   5.35 2.50

Intl. Conference on
Nutrition,
Rome — A144

1992, Dec. 15
615 A144 10fr yellow & multi   .25 .25
616 A144 60fr pink & multi   1.00 .25
617 A144 120fr yel grn & multi   1.75 .40
618 A144 500fr blue & multi   4.50 1.60
    Nos. 615-618 (4)   7.50 2.50

Palace of
the People
A145

1993, Apr. 15   Litho.   Perf. 11½
619 A145 80fr multi   40.00 5.00
620 A145 100fr multi   40.00 5.00
621 A145 130fr multi   40.00 5.00
622 A145 400fr multi   40.00 5.00
    Nos. 619-622 (4)   160.00 20.00

Natl.
Conference — A146

1993, Dec. 1   Litho.   Perf. 11¾
Granite paper
623 A146 55fr multi   .80 .35
624 A146 70fr multi   1.00 .45
625 A146 110fr multi   1.40 .80
626 A146 125fr multi   1.75 .90
    Nos. 623-626 (4)   4.95 2.50

OAU, 30th
Anniv. — A147

1993, Dec. 4   Litho.   Perf. 11½x11¾
627 A147 15fr multi   .25 .25
628 A147 30fr multi   .30 .25
629 A147 110fr multi   1.10 .80
630 A147 190fr multi   2.00 1.50
    Nos. 627-630 (4)   3.65 2.80

Victor
Schoelcher
(1804-93),
Abolitionist
A148

Perf. 11¾x11½
1993, Dec. 26   Litho.
631 A148 55fr multi   .40 .40
632 A148 105fr multi   1.10 .75
633 A148 125fr multi   1.40 1.10
634 A148 300fr multi   2.75 2.00

Tourism
A149

Perf. 11¾x11½

1993, Dec. 27   **Litho.**
635 A149 15fr multi   40.00 20.00
636 A149 95fr multi   40.00 20.00
637 A149 100fr multi   40.00 20.00
638 A149 190fr multi   — 20.00

Bank of Central African States A150

1994   **Litho.**   **Perf. 11½**
639 A150 20fr multicolored   .25 .25
640 A150 30fr pink & multi   .40 .25
641 A150 105fr blue & multi   .90 .30
642 A150 190fr lilac & multi   1.60 .90
   Nos. 639-642 (4)   3.15 1.70

Huts for Storing Grain A151

Designs: 75fr, Arabe, kim. 150fr, Sara, moundang. 300fr, Boulala, kotoko. 450fr, Ouaddai, kenga.

1995, Oct. 15   **Litho.**   **Perf. 14**
643 A151 75fr multicolored   .50 .25
644 A151 150fr multicolored   .90 .30
645 A151 300fr multicolored   1.50 .75
646 A151 450fr multicolored   2.50 1.00
   Nos. 643-646 (4)   5.40 2.30

Souvenir Sheet

Chinese Post, Cent. — A151a

1996   **Litho.**   **Perf. 13¼**
646A A151a 270fr multi   2.25 2.00

1996 Olympic Games, Atlanta A151b

No. 646B: e, Tennis. f, Equestrian. g, Soccer. h, Boxing.
No. 646C: i, Judo. j, Running. k, Cycling. l, Table tennis. 1500fr, Hurdler.

1996   **Litho.**   **Perf. 13¼**
646B A151b 250fr Sheet of 4, #e-h   4.00 4.00

646C A151b 300fr Sheet of 4, #i-l   5.00 5.00

Souvenir Sheet
646D A151b 1500fr multi   6.25 6.25
No. 646D contains one 39x57mm stamp.

1995 Boy Scout Jamboree, Holland — A152

Mushrooms: 150fr, Amanita phalloides. 170fr, Phallus impudicus. 200fr, Lyloperdon perlatum. 350fr, Hydne commun. 450fr, Agaricus bisporus. 800fr, Cortinarius orellanus.
1500fr, Pleurotus ostreatus.

1996, Apr. 15   **Litho.**   **Perf. 13½**
647-652 A152 Set of 6   9.25 4.75
   a.   Souvenir sheet, #647-652   9.25 4.75

Souvenir Sheet
653 A152 1500fr multicolored   6.50 5.00
Nos. 647-652 exist in souvenir sheets of 1.

Butterflies, Mushrooms and Minerals A152a

No. 653A: g, Papilio zalmoxis. h, Anacridium melanorhodon. i, Otidea leporina. j, Haliaetus vocifer.
No. 653B: k, Amanita phalloides, Papilio dardanus. l, Papilio antimachus, Cortinarius praestans. m, Phallus impudicus, Chrysidia croesus. n, Papilio dardanus, Lycoperon perlatum.
No. 653C: o, Charaxes brutus. p, Epiphora albida. q, Euchloron megaera. r, Salamis duprei.
No. 653D: s, Disthene. t, Olivine. u, Sphene. v, Hemimorphite.
No. 653E, Argema mittrei. No. 653F, Zoisite.

1996   **Litho.**   **Perf. 13¼**
653A A152a 350fr Sheet of 4, #g-j   7.00 6.00
653B A152a 400fr Sheet of 4, #k-n   8.00 7.00
653C A152a 650fr Sheet of 4, #o-r   12.00 10.00
653D A152a 800fr Sheet of 4, #s-v   15.00 12.00
   Nos. 653A-653D (4)   42.00 35.00

Souvenir Sheets
653E A152a 2000fr multi   8.50 8.50
653F A152a 2000fr multi   8.50 8.50
A number has been reserved for an additional sheet in this set. Nos. 653E-653F each contain one 42x36mm stamp.

Greenpeace, 25th Anniv. — A153

No. 654: a, 170fr, Green coral, school of small fish. b, 200fr, Yellow & orange coral. c, 300fr, Red orange coral. d, 350fr, White coral. 1500fr, Diver, coral, vert.

1996, July 16
654 A153 Block of 4, #a.-d.   5.00 5.00
Souvenir Sheet
655 A153 1500fr multicolored   9.50 9.50

Entertainers A154

Designs: No. 656, 170fr, Bob Marley. No. 657, 170fr, Marilyn Monroe. No. 658, 200fr, Elvis Presley. No. 659, 200fr, Monroe. No. 660, 300fr, Monroe. No. 661, 350fr, Stevie Wonder. No. 662, 350fr, Presley. No. 663, 400fr, John Lennon. No. 664, 500fr, Presley. No. 665, 600fr, Lennon. No. 666, 700fr, Madonna. No. 667, 800fr, Presley. No. 668, 1000fr, Monroe.
No. 669, 1500fr, Tina Turner. No. 670, 1500fr, Clint Eastwood. No. 670A, 1500fr, Presley.

1996, May 15
656-668 A154 Set of 13   29.00 22.50
   665a   Sheet of 2, #663, 665   4.50 2.25
   667a   Sheet of 4, #658, 662, 664, 667   8.00 3.75
   668a   Sheet of 4, #657, 659-660, 668   7.00 3.50

Souvenir Sheets
669-670A A154 Set of 3   20.00 10.00
Nos. 656-668 exist in souvenir sheets of 1. No. 670A contains one 51x90mm stamp. See No. 674.

A155

No. 671: a, Pres. Bill Clinton. b, Elvis Presley in white jumpsuit.
No. 672: a, Pres. Richard Nixon. b, Presley in white shirt, black jacket.

1996, Dec. 17   **Litho.**   **Perf. 13½**
671 A155 1500fr Sheet of 2, #a.-b.   16.00 16.00
672 A155 1500fr Sheet of 2, #a.-b.   16.00 16.00

Giant Panda — A156

No. 673: a, Holding branch, left claw out. b, Holding branch. c, Lying on back. d, Holding branch in mouth.

1996, Oct. 15
673 A156 100fr Sheet of 4, #a.-d.   2.00 2.00

Entertainers Type of 1996
1996   **Litho.**   **Perf. 13½**
674 A154 500fr Jerry Garcia   2.50 1.75
No. 674 exists in a souvenir sheet of 1.

1998 World Cup Soccer Championships, France — A157

1998 World Cup Soccer Championships, France — A157a

Unidentified players, stadium: No. 675, 150fr, The Beaujoire, Nantes. No. 676, 200fr, Lescure Park, Bordeaux. No. 676A, 300fr, Municipal Stadium, Toulouse. No. 676B, 600fr, Felix Bollaert, Lens.
No. 677A: b, Player in white shirt. c, Player in red shirt.

1996, Dec. 17
675-676B A157 Set of 4   6.00 4.50
Souvenir Sheet
677 A157a 1500fr George Weah   7.50 5.00
677A A157a 3000fr Sheet of 2, #b-c   13.00 11.00

Dinosaurs, Dog & Cats, Butterflies & Insects — A158

No. 678 — Dinosaurs: a, Heterodontosaurus. b, Ornitholestes. c, Dromaeosaurus. d, Pinacosaurus.
No. 679 — Dinosaurs: a, Corythosaurus. b, Ankylosaurides. c, Ornithomimus. d, Styracosaurus.
No. 680 — Dogs & cats: a, Artois. b, Bengal. c, Persian. d, Vendeen.
No. 681 — Butterflies & insects: a, Euphaedra zaddachi. b, Pseudacraea dolomena. c, Cicindela barbara. d, Goliath.

1996, Oct. 15
678 A158 150fr Sheet of 4, #a.-d.   3.00 3.00
679 A158 200fr Sheet of 4, #a.-d.   3.75 3.75
680 A158 250fr Sheet of 4, #a.-d.   5.00 5.00
681 A158 300fr Sheet of 4, #a.-d.   6.00 4.00

Ovptd. in Gold in Sheet Margin
1997   **Litho.**   **Perf. 13½**
678e   Sheet of 4   3.00 3.00
679e   Sheet of 4   3.75 3.75
680e   Sheet of 4   5.00 5.00

Gold overprints on Nos. 678e-680e contain two-line inscription in Chinese and Hong Kong '97 exhibition emblem.

UNICEF, UN, 50th Anniv., Lions Intl. — A159

No. 682 — UNICEF, 50th anniv: a, 150fr, Girl, boy turtles. b, 400fr, Feeding small child.
No. 683 — UN, 50th anniv: a, 170fr, Huygens probe, starving child. b, 500fr, Man with plant, Marsnet probe.

No. 684 — Lions Intl.: a, 200fr, Man carrying sack of grain. b, 800fr, Men examining plants, native man stirring kettle over fire.

1996, Oct. 15   **Litho.**   **Perf. 13½**
682	A159	Pair, #a.-b. + label	3.00	2.00
683	A159	Pair, #a.-b. + label	3.50	2.50
684	A159	Pair, #a.-b. + label	5.50	3.50

Nos. 682-684 exist as souvenir sheets with colored margins. Value, each $13.

1996 European Soccer Championships — A160

No. 685: a, Oliver Bierhoff holding trophy. b, Two players. c, Two players, referee. d, Queen Elizabeth II, player holding trophy.

1996, Dec. 17
685	A160	350fr Sheet of 4, #a.-d.	6.75	5.00

Michael Schumacher, 1995 World Driving Champion — A161

No. 686: a, Ferrari Formula-1 race car. b, Schumacher close-up. c, Schumacher in Benetton uniform. d, Benetton Formula-1 race car.
No. 687, Schumacher with arms raised. No. 687A, Winner of 1996 Italian Grand Prix.

1997, June 16
686	A161	700fr Sheet of 4, #a.-d.	13.50	10.00

Souvenir Sheets
687	A161	2000fr multicolored	10.00	7.50
687A	A161	2000fr multicolored	10.00	7.50

No. 687 contains one 36x51mm stamp.

1998 Winter Olympic Games, Nagano, Japan A162

Designs: 100fr, Women's figure skating. 170fr, Hockey. 350fr, Downhill skiing. 750fr, Speed skating. 1500fr, Slalom skiing.

1996, Dec. 17
688-691	A162	Set of 4	6.75	5.00

Souvenir Sheet
692	A162	1500fr multicolored	7.50	5.00

World Wildlife Fund — A163

No. 693 — Struthio camelus rothschildi: a, Female. b, Male. c, Chicks. d, Male, female up close.

1996, Dec. 17   **Litho.**   **Perf. 13½**
693	A163	200fr Block of 4, #a.-d.	17.00	17.00

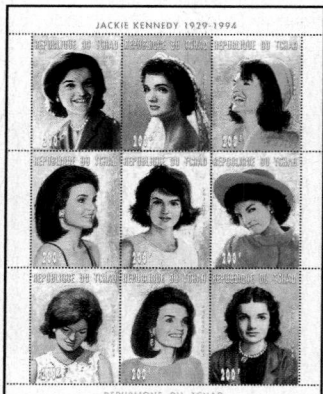

Jacqueline Kennedy Onassis (1929-94) — A164

Various portraits.

1996, Dec. 17
694	A164	200fr Sheet of 9, #a.-i.	9.50	7.00

Intl. Red Cross, Rotary Intl., Scouts — A165

No. 695 — Intl. Red Cross: a, 100fr, Woman, airplane. b, 350fr, Man, train.
No. 696 — Rotary Intl.: a, 300fr, Boy, water coming through pipes. b, 700fr, Native boy and man, volunteers.
No. 697 — Scouts: a, 250fr, Boy scout holding book, hyena. b, 1000fr, Garry Kasparov, chess player, scout.

1996, Oct. 15   **Litho.**   **Perf. 13¼**
695	A165	Pair, #a.-b. + label	2.50	1.75
696	A165	Pair, #a.-b. + label	5.50	3.50
697	A165	Pair, #a.-b. + label	6.50	4.50

Nos. 695-697 exist in souvenir sheets with colored margins. Value, each $13.

Japanese Sumo Wrestling — A166

Various wrestlers in ring.

1996, Dec. 17   **Litho.**   **Perf. 13½**
698	A166	400fr Sheet of 4, #a.-d.	8.00	6.00

China '96 — A168

Various paintings showing mountains and trees.

1996
704	A168	100fr Sheet of 9, #a.-i.	4.50	3.50

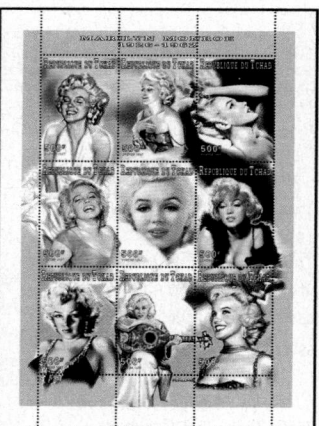

Marilyn Monroe — A168a

Various portraits.

1997   **Litho.**   **Perf. 13¼**
704J	A168a	500fr Sheet of 9, #k-s	16.00	16.00

History of Space Travel — A169

No. 705: a, Lunar N1 rocket, USSR, Saturn 1, US, Apollo 1 crew, Grissom, White, Chaffee. b, Launch of Soyuz, USSR, V.M.

Komarov. c, US Lunar Orbiter 4. d, Neil Armstrong, US, Molniya 1, USSR. e, Venera 4, USSR, Mariner, US. f, Surveyor 3, US.
No. 706: a, Ariane 1, Landsat 4, US. b, Spacelab & space shuttle, NASA, ESA, Thomas Mattingly, US. c, L-Sat Telecom Satelite, ESA. d, J.L. Chretien, Soviet Salyut 7, US Space Shuttle. e, Venera 13, USSR. f, Intelsat 6, US.
No. 707: a, John Glenn, Atlas rocket, Mercury capsule. b, Mariner 2, US. c, Scott Carpenter, US. d, Telstar, Tiros 6, US. e, Vostok capsule, USSR, Bell X15 airplane, US. f, Mars 1, USSR.
No. 708: a, "Sounds of Earth" record, Voyager 1 & 2, US. b, Himawari 1, MU-3H, Japan, Atlas Centaur, US. c, Soviet Salyut 6, Proton rocket, Galileo (1564-1642). d, Meteosat, SMS Geos, Atlas EF, US. e, Boeing 747, space shuttle, US. f, ISEE, US.
No. 709: a, Saturn 5, US, OAO 3 Copernicus. b, Pioneer 10, US. c, Luna 20, USSR, John F. Kennedy. d, Landsat 1, US. e, Apollo 16, US astronauts Mattingly, Duke, Young. f, Lunar Rover, US Apollo 17 astronauts Schmitt, Evans, Cernan.
No. 710: a, RD 107 rocket, USSR, Vanguard rocket, US, Vanguard 1, US. b, Aerobee, Goddard rockets, Robert H. Goddard. c, Laika, 1st dog in space, USSR. d, Theodor von Karman, V2A, Gird 09 rockets, USSR. e, Sputnik 1, USSR, Korolev airplane. f, Sanger, Bell X1 airplanes, US, Eugene Sanger.
No. 711, US Astronauts, Neil Armstrong, Michael Collins, Edwin E. Aldrin, Jr., USSR animals in space, Laika, Felix the cat.
Illustration reduced.

1997   **Litho.**   **Perf. 13½**
705	A169	150fr Sheet of 6, #a.-f.	4.00	4.00
706	A169	250fr Sheet of 6, #a.-f.	6.00	6.00
707	A169	300fr Sheet of 6, #a.-f.	7.50	7.50
708	A169	450fr Sheet of 6, #a.-f.	9.00	9.00
709	A169	475fr Sheet of 6, #a.-f.	11.50	11.00
710	A169	800fr Sheet of 6, #a.-f.	18.00	18.00

Souvenir Sheet
711	A169	2000fr multicolored	8.25	8.25

No. 711 contains one 80x85mm stamp.

Elvis Presley — A169a

Various portraits.

1997   **Litho.**   **Perf. 13¼**
711A	A169a	300fr Sheet of 9, #b-j	12.00	12.00

Jacqueline Kennedy Onassis (1929-94) — A170

Various portraits.

1997, July 15   Litho.   Perf. 13½
712 A170 150fr Sheet of 9, #a.-i.   5.75 2.75

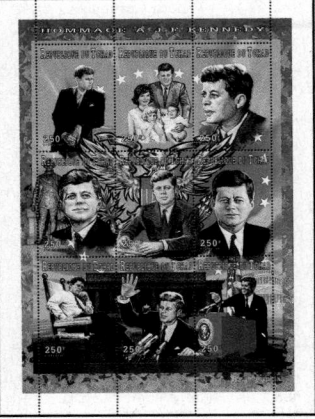

Pres. John F. Kennedy — A170a

No. 712J: k, Standing, looking right. l, With family. m, Looking left. n, With statue of George Washington. o, Seated, with Great Seal of the United States. p, Facing forward, with stars and arrows. q, In chair. r, With statue of Lincoln. s, Behind podium, with flag and Capitol.

1997   Litho.   Perf. 13¼
712J A170a 250fr Sheet of 9, #k-s   9.00 9.00

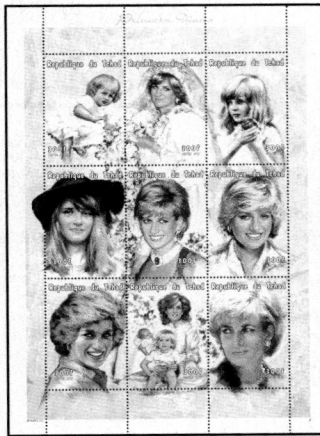

Diana, Princess of Wales (1961-97) — A171

Various portraits.

1997
713 A171 300fr Sheet of 9, #a.-i.   11.00 11.00

714 A171 450fr Sheet of 9, #a.-i.   16.00 16.00
Souvenir Sheet
715 A171 2000fr multicolored   8.25 7.50
No. 715 contains one 42x60mm stamp.

Deng Xiaoping and Bruce Lee — A171a

No. 715A — Deng and: c, Child. d, Chinese flag. e, Dancer. f, Boats in water. g, Farmers. h, Cityscape.
No. 715B — Lee and movie titles: i, Operation Dragon. j, La Fureur du Dragon. k, La Fureur de Vaincre. l, La Flute Silencieuse. m, Le Jeu de la Mort. n, Le Retour du Dragon. 1000fr, Deng and stars.

1997   Litho.   Perf. 13¼
715A A171a 75fr Sheet of 6, #c-h   1.75 1.75
715B A171a 125fr Sheet of 6, #i-n   3.00 3.00
Souvenir Sheet
715O A171a 1000fr multi   —   —
No. 715O contains one 36x41mm stamp.

Mahatma Gandhi (1869-1948), Mother Teresa (1910-97) — A172

No. 716: a, Gandhi seated, dendrobium speciosum. b, Mother Teresa with Indian people. c, Bulbophyllum umbellatum, Gandhi with 2 women.

1998, Feb. 5   Litho.   Perf. 13½
716 A172 150fr Sheet of 3, #a.-c. 1.90 1.90

Famous Men — A173

Designs: 300fr, Nelson Mandela, Pres. of South Africa, diamond. 450fr, Albert Einstein (1879-1955), physicist, satellite. 800fr, Robert Barany (1876-1936), physician, Felix the space cat.
2000fr, Alfred Nobel (1833-96).

1998, Feb. 5
717-719 A173 Set of 3   7.00 5.50
Souvenir Sheet
720 A173 2000fr multicolored   8.25 7.50
Nos. 717-719 exist in souvenir sheets of 1.
No. 720 contains one 41x60mm stamp.
See Nos. 729-734.

The Beatles — A174

No. 721: a-i, Various portraits of John Lennon.
No. 722 — The Beatles: a, Paul McCartney. b, Silhouettes. c, John Lennon. d, George Harrison, Lennon. e, Four faces. f, McCartney, Ringo Starr. g, Starr. h, Four in Sgt. Pepper's costumes. i, Harrison.
No. 723 — Life of John Lennon: a, Yoko Ono. b, With McCartney. c, In profile. d, Wearing suit. e, Wearing white shirt, tie. f, With mother. g, Wearing dark glasses. h, With guru. i, In white suit.
No. 724: Various portraits of Lennon, McCartney, Harrison, Starr.
No. 724J, Beatles in suits and ties. No. 724K, Beatles in Sgt. Pepper uniforms.

1996   Litho.   Perf. 13½
721 A174 100fr Sheet of 9, #a-f   3.50 3.50
722 A174 170fr Sheet of 9, #a.-i.   7.00 7.00
723 A174 200fr Sheet of 9, #a.-i.   6.75 6.75
724 A174 300fr Sheet of 9, #a.-i.   14.00 14.00
Souvenir Sheets
724J A174 1500fr multi   7.50 6.00
724K A174 1500fr multi   7.50 6.00

Antelopes — A175

Designs: a, 170fr, Damaliscus dorcas. b, 350fr, Oryx gazella. c, 500fr, Addax nasomaculatus. d, 600fr, Aepyceros melampus.

1996, Dec. 17
725 A175 Block of 4, #a.-d.   7.00 7.00
Nos. 725a-725d exist in souvenir sheets of 1.

No. 725 Overprinted in Gold

1996
726 A175 Block of 4, #a.-d.   7.00 7.00
Nos. 726a-726d exist in souvenir sheets of 1.

Marilyn Monroe (1926-1962) — A176

Various portraits.

1996
727 A176 250fr Sheet of 9, #a.-i.   10.50 9.00
Souvenir Sheet
728 A176 1500fr multicolored   6.00 6.00
No. 728 contains one 51x90mm stamp.

Famous People Type of 1997

Nobel Prize winners: 100fr, Mother Teresa (1910-97), humanitarian. 150fr, Martin Luther King, Jr. (1929-68), civil rights leader. 475fr, Otto Hahn (1879-1968), chemist, nuclear powered ship. 500fr, Ivan Pavlov (1849-1936), physiologist, Russian space dog, Laika. 600fr, Johannes van der Waals (1837-1923), physicist. 1000fr, Sir Edward Appleton (1892-1965), physicist, Concorde jet.

1998, Feb. 5
729-734 A173 Set of 6   14.50 10.00
Nos. 729-734 exist in souvenir sheets of 1.

Scouting A177

Wild animals: No. 735: a, Hyena. b, Mongoose.
No. 736: a, Wildcat. b, Addax nasomaculatus.
No. 737: a, Fennec. b, Hyena, diff.

1998, Feb. 6
735 A177 150fr Pair, #a.-b.   2.00 2.00
736 A177 550fr Pair, #a.-b.   5.75 5.75
737 A177 600fr Pair, #a.-b.   7.00 7.00

Cats and Dogs — A178

No. 738: a, Maine coon. b, Singapore.
No. 739: a, Siberian husky. b, Malamute.
No. 740: a, Spitz. b, Eskimo.
No. 741: a, Siamese. b, Common cat.
No. 742, 1500fr, Abyssinian. No. 743, 1500fr, Samoyed.

1998, Feb. 6

738	A178	300fr Pair, #a.-b.	2.75	2.75
739	A178	450fr Pair, #a.-b.	3.00	3.00
740	A178	475fr Pair, #a.-b.	3.75	3.75
741	A178	500fr Pair, #a.-b.	4.00	4.00

Souvenir Sheets

742-743	A178	Set of 2	12.50	12.50

Nos. 742-743 each contain one 42x60mm stamp.

Airplanes, Ships, & Trains — A179

No. 743A — Early aircraft: b, Latecoere 28, France. c, D'Equeuilly, France. d, Liore et Olivier Leo-213, France. e, Louis Bleriot monoplane. f, Graf Zeppelin LZ 127. g, Caproni CA 133, Italy.

No. 744 — Airplanes: a, Sikorsky VS-44A. b, Short S25/V Sandringham 4. c, Bristol 167 Brabazon 1. d, Savoia S13 Bis. e, Curtiss CR-3. f, Curtiss R3C-2.

No. 745 — Ships: a, Normandy, 1935. b, Persia, 1856. c, Queen Elizabeth II, 1968. d, Christian Radich, 1937. e, Amerigo Vespucci, 1933. f, Tovarich, 1933.

No. 745G — Classic sports cars: h, 1963-65 Porsche 356 SC. i, 1961-66 AC Cobra. j, 1960-61 Maserati Tipo 63 Birdcage. k, 1962-63 Austin Healey 3000 MK11. l, 1959-62 Ferrari 250 GT Berlinetta SWB. m, 1958 Aston Martin DB4.

No. 746 — Trains: a, BRB cog steam train. b, AE 4/7 10969. c, Crocodile of Saint-Gothard BE 6/8 111. d, RAE 2/4 1001. e, Steam train, Spain. f, RE 6/6 11612 express.

No. 746G — High speed trains: h, ETR 470, Italy. i, TGV Metro, France. j, Hikari, Japan. k, TGV 001 turbotrain, France. l, Eurostar 3203/3204 Metro train, France, Germany, Great Britain. m, 990 ICE train, Germany.

1500fr, Steam locomotive, C5/6 2978. 2000fr, TGV, France.

1998, Feb. 4

743A	A179	150fr Sheet of 6, #b.-g.	4.00	4.00
744	A179	200fr Sheet of 6, #a.-f.	5.00	5.00
745	A179	250fr Sheet of 6, #a.-f.	6.25	6.25
745G	A179	300fr Sheet of 6, #h.-m.	7.50	7.50
746	A179	350fr Sheet of 6, #a.-f.	9.00	9.00
746G	A179	400fr Sheet of 6, #h.-m.	10.00	11.00

Souvenir Sheets

747	A179	1500fr multicolored	6.25	6.25
748	A179	2000fr multicolored	8.25	8.25

Nos. 747-748 contain one 36x42mm stamp. Swiss rail service, 150th anniv. (Nos. 746-747).

Issued: No. 745G, 2/6.

See No. 758.

Diana, Princess of Wales (1961-97) A180

Various portraits. 2000fr, Portrait wearing high lace collar.

1997   **Litho.**   **Perf. 13½**

749	A180	250fr Sheet of 9, #a.-i.	9.00	9.00

Souvenir Sheet

749J	A180	2000fr multicolored	8.50	7.50

Literacy Campaign A181

1997, June 16

750	A181	150fr olive & multi	.80	.80
751	A181	300fr buff & multi	1.75	1.60
752	A181	475fr salmon & multi	2.50	2.50
		Nos. 750-752 (3)	5.05	4.90

Kellou Dahalob — A182

1998, Apr. 8

753	A182	50fr pink & multi	.30	.30
754	A182	100fr blue & multi	.40	.40
755	A182	150fr green & multi	.65	.65
756	A182	300fr lilac & multi	1.10	1.10
757	A182	400fr yellow & multi	1.50	1.50
		Nos. 753-757 (5)	3.95	3.95

Transportation Type of 1997

No. 758 — Modern aircraft: a, SAT, France, Germany. b, BAC/Aerospatiale Concorde. c, X001, Japan. d, Bell X-2, US. e, Douglas X-3, US. f, Aerospatiale STS 2000, France.

1998, Feb. 4   **Litho.**   **Perf. 13½**

758	A179	475fr Sheet of 6, #a.-f.	12.00	12.00

Women — A183

Women: 50fr, 100fr, 150fr, Using grindstone. 300fr, 450fr, 500fr, Kneeling.

1997, June 16

759	A183	50fr vio & multi, vert.	.30	.30
760	A183	100fr grn & multi, vert.	.40	.40
761	A183	150fr yel & multi, vert.	.55	.55
762	A183	300fr vio & multi	1.10	1.10
763	A183	450fr grn & multi	1.75	1.75
764	A183	500fr yel & multi	1.90	1.90
		Nos. 759-764 (6)	6.00	6.00

Protect the Ozone Layer — A184

1998   **Litho.**   **Perf. 13½**

765	A184	150fr blue & multi	.60	.60
766	A184	300fr green & multi	1.25	1.25
767	A184	475fr pink & multi	1.90	1.60
768	A184	500fr blue green & multi	1.90	1.90
		Nos. 765-768 (4)	5.65	5.35

Fauna — A185

No. 769 — Bats: a, Holding mouse, tree branch. b, Drinking. c, One in flight, bottom of mouse. d, One flying left. e, One flying right. f, Mouse on rock, bat landing.

No. 769G — Horses: h, Gray Arabian. i, Brown Arabian. j, Przewalski's. k, Australian brumbies. l, Camargue. m, Zebras.

No. 769N — Sea mammals: o-t, Various portraits of Trichechus senegalensis.

No. 770 — Gorillas & chimpanzees: a, Chimpanzee scratching head. b, Gorilla walking on all fours. c, Gorilla seated. d, Chimpanzee swinging from branch. e, Chimpanzee using stick. f, Two gorillas.

No. 771 — Raptors: a, Terathopius ecaudatus. b, Buteo buteo. c, Sagittarius serpentarius. d, Polemaetus belligosus. e, Circaetus allicus. f, Aquila chrysaetos.

No. 771G — Reptiles: h, Crocodylus niloticus. i, Drendroaspis angusticeps. j, Bitis nasicornis. k, Chamaeleo johnstoni. l, Naja nigricolis. m, Meroles cuneirostris.

No. 771N — Mushrooms: o, Coprinus atramentarius. p, Romaria botrytis. q, Aleuria aurantia. r, Amanita muscaria. s, Macrolepiota rhacodes. t, Helvella crispa.

No. 771U — Mushrooms: v, Morchella vulgaris. w, Tuber aestiuum. x, Tuber melanosporum. y, Mitrophora hybrida. z, Morchella conica. aa, Choeromyces meandriformis.

No. 772 — Butterflies: a, Charaxes jasius. b, Hamanumidia daedalus. c, Charaxes bohemani. d, Hallimoides rumia, denomination LL. e, Hallimoides rumia, denomination LR. f, Pseudacraea boisduuali.

1500fr, Coelogyne ovalis, palla ussheri. 2000fr, Baleniceps, Neurophyllum clauatum.

1998, June 20

769	A185	150fr Sheet of 6, #a.-f.	5.00	5.00
769G	A185	250fr Sheet of 6, #h.-m.	5.50	5.50
769N	A185	300fr Sheet of 6, #o.-t.	6.50	6.50
770	A185	300fr Sheet of 6, #a.-f.	8.00	8.00
771	A185	350fr Sheet of 6, #a.-f.	10.00	10.00
771G	A185	450fr Sheet of 6, #h.-m.	12.00	12.00
771N	A185	475fr Sheet of 6, #o.-t.	10.50	10.50
771U	A185	500fr Sheet of 6, #v.-aa.	12.00	12.00
772	A185	600fr Sheet of 6, #a.-f.	16.00	8.00

Souvenir Sheets

773	A185	1500fr multicolored	6.50	6.50
773A	A185	2000fr multicolored	7.50	7.50

Nos. 773-773A contain one 51x42mm stamp.

Bela Lugosi as Dracula — A185a

Lugosi in various poses.

1998, Dec. 11   **Litho.**   **Perf. 13½**

773B	A185a	250fr Sheet of 9, #d.-l.	8.50	8.50

Souvenir Sheet

773C	A185a	1500fr multi, horiz.	5.75	5.75

Diana, Princess of Wales — A186

No. 774 — Various portraits: a, 200fr. b, 250fr. c, 300fr. d, 400fr. e, 475fr. f, 500fr. g, 800fr. h, 900fr. i, 1000fr.

1999, Jan. 10   **Litho.**   **Perf. 12½**

774	A186	Sheet of 9, #a.-i.	18.00	18.00

Birds — A187

Designs: 75fr, Ibis ibis. 150fr, Ephippiorhynchus senegalensis. 200fr, Phoenicopterus ruber. 300fr, Leptoptilus crumeniferus. 400fr, Scopus umbretta. 475fr, Platalea alba. 1000fr, Balaeniceps rex.

1999, Jan. 15   **Litho.**   **Perf. 12¾**

775-780	A187	Set of 6	5.75	5.75

Souvenir Sheet

781	A187	1000fr multicolored	3.50	3.50

No. 781 contains one 32x40mm stamp.

Fire Trucks A188

Designs: 50fr, 1840 model. 150fr, 1920 Fiat. 200fr, 1915 Mack. 300fr, 1930 Renault. 400fr, Pegaso M 1090. 500fr, 1960 Jet Fire Power. 700fr, 1720 King George III Fire Company.

1998, Dec. 30

782-787	A188	Set of 6	5.75	5.75

Souvenir Sheet

788	A188	700fr multicolored	2.50	2.50

No. 788 contains one 35x28mm stamp.

Minerals — A188a

No. 788A: a, Opal. b, Cyanite. c, Chalcopyrite. d, Apatite. e, Celestite. f, Scorodite.
No. 788B: a, Agate. b, Wulfenite. c, Barytine. d, Tanzanite. e, Amazonite. f, Malachite.

1998   Litho.   Perf. 13½
788A A188a 475fr Sheet of 6,
        #a.-f.   11.00 11.00
788B A188a 500f Sheet of 6,
        #a.-f.   11.50 11.50

Dinosaurs — A188b

No. 788C: a, Dilophosaurus. b, Argentinosaurus. c, Kritosaurus. d, Scutellosaurus. e, Ornithomimosaurus. f, Bactrosaurus.
No. 788D: a, Coelophysis. b, Kannemeyeria. c, Apatosaurus. d, Scipionyx. e, Lystrosaurus. f, Kentrosaurus.
No. 788E, Giganotosaurus, vert.

1998, Nov. 12   Litho.   Perf. 13¼
            Sheets of 6
788C A188b 400fr #a.-f.   9.25   9.25
788D A188b 450fr #a.-f.   10.50 10.50
            Souvenir Sheet
788E A188b 2000fr multi   7.50   7.50

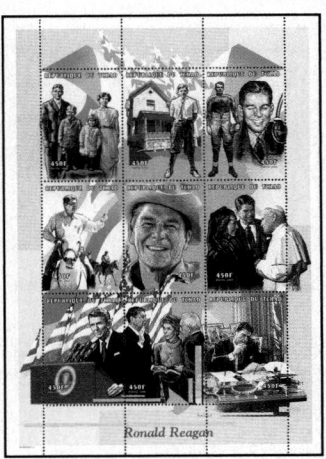

US Pres. Ronald Reagan — A189

No. 789: a, Family portrait as young boy. b, In front of family home. c, In football uniform, as radio announcer. d, Riding horse. e, Up close portrait. f, With Nancy, greeting Pope John Paul II. g, Making speech at podium. h, Being sworn in as president. i, At desk in Oval Office.
2000fr, At desk, White House.

1999, Feb. 2   Litho.   Perf. 13½
789 A189 450fr Sheet of 9,
        #a.-i.   16.00 18.00
            Souvenir Sheet
790 A189 2000fr multicolored   8.00   8.00

American Railroads — A190

No. 791 — Train, railroad pioneer: a, "Alco" Santa Fe, 1945, Cyrus Holliday. b, Rio Grande, 1961, J.F. Stevens. c, Amtrak, 1976, Thomas Dehone Judah. d, 250 Gobernador, 1884, Mark Hopkins. e, Meeting of Central Pacific and Union Pacific at Promontory Point, 1869, Leland Stanford, Thomas Durant. f, Great Northern W1, 1947, Jim Hill. g, Union Pacific Railroad, 1951, G.M. Dodge. h, Pennsylvania GG1, 1934, S.M. Vauclain. i, 151 Santa Fe U.P., 1917, S. Barstow Strong.

1998, Dec. 11
791 A190 200fr Sheet of 9, #a.-i. 7.00 7.00

Fossils and Cave Paintings — A191

No. 792: a, Harlania enigmatica. b, Spirophyton. c, Fossils, dunes of Djourab. d, Chain of people, oxen, Bardai. e, Man of Gonoa. f, Oxen, Kozen, Borkou.

1998, Dec. 11
792 A191 150fr Sheet of 6, #a.-f. 4.00 4.00

Frank Sinatra — A191a

No. 792G — Sinatra with: h, Blonde actress. i, Green jacket. j, Ava Gardner. k, Striped suit. l, Actor. m, Gun. n, Dark green hat. o, Oscar statuette. p, Military cap.

1998, Dec. 30   Litho.   Perf. 13½
792G A191a 300fr Sheet of 9,
        #h.-p.   11.00 11.00

James Dean (1931-55), Actor — A192

Various portraits.

1999, Feb. 2
793 A192 200fr Sheet of 9, #a.-i. 7.00 7.00

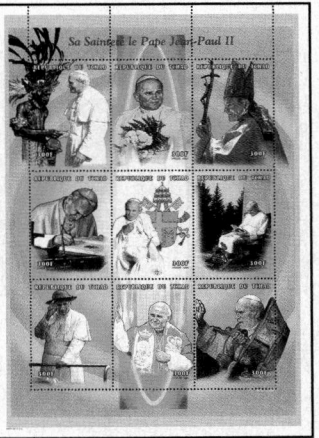

Pope John Paul II — A193

Various portraits.

1999, Feb. 2
794 A193 300fr Sheet of 9,
        #a.-i.   10.50 10.50
            Souvenir Sheet
795 A193 1500fr multicolored   6.00   5.50
No. 795 contains one 58x51mm stamp.

John Glenn's Return to Space — A194

Various portraits.

1999, Feb. 11   Litho.   Perf. 13½
796 A194 500fr Sheet of 9,
        #a.-i.   17.50 17.50
            Souvenir Sheet
797 A194 2000fr multicolored   8.00   8.00
No. 797 contains one 57x51mm stamp.

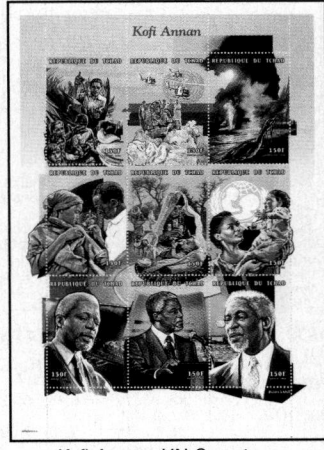

Kofi Annan, UN Secretary-
General — A195

Various portraits.

1998, Dec. 11
798 A195 150fr Sheet of 9, #a.-i. 5.25 5.25

Chess — A196

No. 798J: k, Paul Morphy. l, Chess board, Morphy-Anderssen, 1858. m, Adolf Anderssen. n, Emanuel Lasker. o, Chess board, Lasker-Capablanca, 1914. p, José Raul Capablanca. q, David Bronstein. r, Chess board, Bronstein-Botvinnik, 1951. s, Mikhail Botvinnik.
a, Bobby Fischer. b, Chess board, Fischer-Tal, 1961. c, Mikhail Tal. d, Boris Spassky. e, Chess board, Spassky-Petrosian, 1969. f, Tigran Petrosian. g, Garry Kasparov. h, Chess board, Kasparov-Karpov, 1960. i, Anatoly Karpov.
No. 800, Margrave Othon IV of Brandenburg.
No. 800A, King Louis XVI playing chess, horiz.

1999, Feb. 20
798J A196 375fr Sheet of 9,
        #k.-s.   13.00 13.00
799 A196 500fr Sheet of 9,
        #a.-i.   17.50 17.50
            Souvenir Sheets
800   A196 2000fr multi   7.75   7.75
800A A196 2000fr multi   7.75   7.75
Dated 1998. No. 800 contains one 58x51mm stamp. No. 800A contains one 58x51mm stamp. Sheets of 3 stamps, containing Nos. 798Jk-798Jm, 798Jn-798Jp, 798Jq-798Js, 799a-799c, 799d-799f, or 799g-799i exist.

Souvenir Sheets

France, 1998 World Cup
Champions — A197

No. 801: a, Bikente Lizarazu. b, Christian Karembeu. c, Frank Leboeuf. d, Emmanuel Petit.
No. 802: a, Fabien Barthez. b, Marcel Desailly. c, Didier Deschamps. d, Christophe Dugarry.
No. 803: Youri Djorkaeff. b, Aime Jacquet. c, Lilian Thuram. d, Zinedine Zidane.
2000fr, Deschamps holding World Cup.

1999, Feb. 20   **Litho.**   **Perf. 13½**
801 A197   300fr Sheet of 4,
     #a.-d.   4.50   4.50
802 A197   400fr Sheet of 4,
     #a.-d.   6.25   6.25
803 A197   500fr Sheet of 4,
     #a.-d.   8.00   8.00
     Perf. 13¼
804 A197   2000fr multicolored   8.00   8.00
No. 804 contains one 57x51mm stamp.

Hokusai
Paintings
A198

Designs: a, Voyagers Crossing the Oi River. b, Bird. c, On Totomi Mountain. d, Evening at Ueno. e, Higashimachi-matsuri-yatai-tenjou. f, Evening shower at Yoshiwara. g. Woman with Umbrella. h, Cascade. i, Courtesan.

1999, Sept. 10   **Litho.**   **Perf. 13½**
805 A198   475fr Sheet of 9,
     #a.-i.   17.50   17.50
     Japex '99.

Millennium — A199

No. 806 — Highlights of 1000-1899: a, Commercial routes in West Africa. b, Crusades. c, Notre Dame Cathedral. d, Ming dynasty tombs. e, Discovery of America. f, Albrecht Dürer. g, Sir Isaac Newton. h, American Independence. i, Napoleon.
No. 807 — 1900-24: a, Return of Halley's Comet. b, Lord Baden-Powell founds Scouting movement. c, Sinking of the Titanic. d, 1st film in Technicolor. e, Marconi sends 1st message across Atlantic, birth of radio. f, Harry Houdini. g, Capablanca-Lasker chess matches. h,

Pierre & Marie Curie win Nobel Prize. i, Theft of the Mona Lisa.
No. 808 — 1925-49: a, Birth of Marilyn Monroe. b, Discovery of Pluto. c, Laurel and Hardy. d, Independence of India. e, Alexander Fleming discovers penicillin. f, Introduction of Volkswagen Beetle & Vespa motor scooter. g, Opening of film "Dracula." h, World War II. i, Discovery of Lascaux cave drawings.
No. 809 — 1950-74: a, 1st flight of the Concorde, 7 original astronauts. b, Death of Buddy Holly. c, 1st Super Bowl. d, Death of Eva Peron. e, Art by Andy Warhol. f, The Beatles. g, Cultural Revolution in China. h, Assassination of Pres. John F. Kennedy. i, Cuban Revolution.
No. 810 — 1975-99: a, Death of Princess Diana. b, Death of Enzo Ferrari. c, Akira. d, Argentina, 1986 World Cup Soccer champions. e, B. Lara breaks cricket records. f, France, 1998 World Cup Soccer champions. g, Explosion of the Space Shuttle Challenger. h, Pope John Paul II meets Lech Walesa. i, Deaths of Frank Sinatra, Freddie Mercury.

1999, Sept. 10
806 A199   150fr Sheet of 9,
     #a.-i.
807 A199   300fr Sheet of 9,   5.25   5.25
     #a.-i.
808 A199   450fr Sheet of 9,   10.00   10.00
     #a.-i.
809 A199   475fr Sheet of 9,   15.00   15.00
     #a.-i.
810 A199   500fr Sheet of 9,   16.00   16.00
     #a.-i.   16.00   16.00
     Nos. 806-810 (5)   62.25   62.25

Souvenir Sheet

PhilexFrance '99 — A200

1999, Sept. 10
811 A200   1500fr multi   6.00   6.00

I Love Lucy — A201

No. 812: a, Lucy leaning against tree, Ricky. b, Lucy, Ricky kissing. c, Lucy pointing gun. d, Ricky falling to ground. e, Lucy in apartment. f, Ricky holding animal. g, Ricky drinking from canteen. h, Lucy, Ricky talking. i, Lucy behind bush.
No. 813, Lucy in grape vat. No. 814, Lucy, Ricky in bed.

1999, Feb. 20   **Litho.**   **Perf. 13¼**
812 A201   450fr Sheet of 9,
     #a.-i.   18.00   18.00
     Souvenir Sheets
813 A201   1500fr multi   7.00   7.00
814 A201   2000fr multi   9.00   9.00
     Dated 1998.
     See Nos. 865-867.

Betty Boop — A202

No. 815: a, With cat and dog. b, In flowered dress. c, Looking back over shoulder. d, With hammer, dresser. e, As majorette. f, In red dress with fur collar. g, Holding paper. h, Holding blue dress. i, Holding telephone.
No. 816, With feathered hat. No. 817, In leopard-spotted blouse.

1999, Feb. 20   **Litho.**   **Perf. 13¼**
815 A202   450fr Sheet of 9,
     #a.-i.   18.00   18.00
     Souvenir Sheets
816 A202   1500fr multi   7.00   7.00
817 A202   2000fr multi   9.00   9.00
     Dated 1998.
     See Nos. 856-858.

Antique Automobiles — A203

150fr, 1900 F.N. 300fr, 1906 Bianchi. 400fr, 1906 Renault. 500fr, 1919 Pierce-Arrow. 700fr, 1919 Citroen 5CV. 900fr, 1928 Ford. 1000fr, 1898 Renault.

1999   **Litho.**   **Perf. 13x12¾**
818-823 A203   Set of 6   14.00   14.00
     Souvenir Sheet
     Perf. 13x13¼
824 A203   1000fr multi   5.00   5.00
No. 824 contains one 40x31mm stamp.

Locomotives — A204

Designs: 150fr, 0-4-0. 300fr, Red 0-4-0. 400fr, Green 0-6-0. 500fr, Brown 0-4-0. 700fr, Blue 0-4-0. 900fr, Blue 0-6-0. 1000fr, Electric locomotive.

1999   **Perf. 12¾**
825-830 A204   Set of 6   14.00   14.00
     Souvenir Sheet
     Perf. 13x13¼
831 A204   1000fr multi   5.00   5.00
No. 831 contains one 36x28mm stamp.

Wonders of Forgotten
Cultures — A205

Designs: 50fr, Easter Island. 150fr, Stonehenge. 300fr, Jericho. 400fr, Machu Picchu. 500fr, Valley of Statues. 700fr, Chichén Itzá. 900fr, Persepolis.

1999   **Perf. 12¾**
832-838 A205   Set of 7   15.00   15.00

Chad postal officials have declared the following items to be "not authorized:"
Set of six stamps of various denominations: New Year 2000 (Year of the Dragon)
Sheet of nine stamps of various denominations: Orchids
Sheet of nine 150fr stamps: Spanish Impressionist paintings
Sheet of nine 300fr stamps: Millennium (Composers), Van Gogh paintings
Sheet of nine 450fr stamps: Millennium (Marilyn Monroe), French Impressionist paintings
Sheet of nine 475fr stamps: Impressionist paintings
Sheet of nine 500fr stamps: Renoir nudes, Elvis Presley, Olympics
Souvenir sheets of one: Millennium (three 300fr, two 450fr, one 475fr, three 500fr, one 1500fr), New Year 2000 (1000fr), Palace of Versailles (1500fr, 2000fr), Hiroshige paintings (1500fr, 2000fr).

Minerals
A206

Designs: 150fr, Wulfenite. 200fr, Argentite. 400fr, Siderite. 500fr, Dolomite and quartz. 700fr, Azurite. 900fr, Spinel and calcite. 1000fr, Cassiterite.

2000, Jan. 15   **Litho.**   **Perf. 12¾**
839-844 A206   Set of 6   14.00   14.00
     Souvenir Sheet
845 A206   1000fr multi   5.00   5.00
     Dated 1999.

Dogs — A206a

Designs: 150fr, Caucasian Mountain dog (Berger caucasique). 300fr, Belgian shepherd (Berger Belgue). 400fr, Spanish mastiff (Mâtin Espagne). 500fr, Kuvasz. 700fr, Beauceron. 900fr, Rough collie.

2000, Jan. 15   **Litho.**   **Perf. 13**
845A A206a   150fr multi   —
845B A206a   300fr multi   —
845C A206a   400fr multi   —
845D A206a   500fr multi   —
845E A206a   700fr multi   —
845F A206a   900fr multi   —
     Dated 1999.

Elvis Presley — A207

No. 846: a, Playing guitar, wearing red jacket. b, Holding microphone and guitar, wearing red jacket. c, Holding guitar, wearing gold jacket. d, Playing guitar wearing black leather jacket. e, Playing guitar, wearing black jacket. f, Playing guitar, wearing blue jacket. g, Holding microphone, wearing blue shirt. h, Singing, wearing brown jacket. i, Holding microphone, wearing striped yellow jacket.

2000, Mar. 10   *Perf. 13¼*
846 A207 300fr Sheet of 9, #a-i   12.00 12.00
   Dated 1999.

Carl Benz and Mercedes-Benz Automobiles — A208

No. 847: a, 1934 W-25. b, 1934 500 K. c, 1964 230 SL. d, 1935 150. e, 1954 300 SL. f, 1971 280 SE.
   2000fr, 1934 500 K, diff.

2000, Mar. 10
847 A208 250fr Sheet of 6, #a-f   7.00 7.00
Souvenir Sheet
848 A208 2000fr multi   9.00 9.00
   No. 847 contains six 30x30mm stamps. Dated 1999.

Trains — A209

No. 849: a, FES 3228, European Union flag. b, TGV Duplex, French flag. c, 500 Series Unit W1, Japanese flag. d, AVE Class 100, Spanish flag. e, ICE3, German flag. f, ETR 500, Italian flag.
   2000fr, TGC 001 V56, TGV Duplex, Etienne Chambron.

2000, Mar. 10
849 A209 600fr Sheet of 6, #a-f   11.50 11.50
Souvenir Sheet
850 A209 2000fr multi   6.50 6.50
   No. 849 contains six 30x30mm stamps. Dated 1999.

French Rulers — A210

No. 851, 150fr: a, Charlemagne. b, King Charles VIII. c, King Francis I. d, King Henry II. e, Catherine de Medici. f, King Henry III.
   No. 852, 200fr: a, King Louis XII. b, King Louis XIII. c, King Louis XIV. d, King Louis XV. e, King Louis XVI. f, King Louis XVIII.
   No. 853, 300fr — Napoleon Bonaparte: a, Standing, wearing red cape. b, On horseback, wearing red cape. c, On horseback, with soldier at right. d, On horseback, with crowd at right. e, Standing with other people. f, On white horse, leading battle.

2000, Mar. 10   **Sheets of 6, #a-f**
851-853 A210   Set of 3   17.50 17.50
   Dated 1999.

Pope John Paul II — A211

No. 854 — Pope John Paul II and: a, Dalai Lama. b, Fidel Castro. c, King Hassan II of Morocco. d, Grand Rabbi Elio Toaff. e, Patriarch Bartholomew I. f, Mother Teresa.

2000, Mar. 10
854 A211 475fr Sheet of 6, #a-f   13.00 13.00
   Dated 1999.

Space — A212

No. 855: a, Sputnik, dog Laika. b, Yuri Gagarin, Vostok 1. c, Konstantin Feoktistov, Vladimir Komarov, Boris Yegorov, Voskhod 1. d, Luna 1, chimpanzee Ham. e, Neil Armstrong, Michael Collins, Edwin Aldrin, Apollo 11. f, Aldrin, splashdown of capsule.

2000, Mar. 10
855 A212 500fr Sheet of 6, #a-f   13.00 13.00
   Dated 1999.

Betty Boop Type of 1999

No. 856: a, Wearing red and violet striped leotard, kicking leg up. b, As cheerleader. c, At football field, holding pennant. d, At ice cream shop. e, Wearing yellow and green striped leotard. f, Wearing baseball cap and orange shorts. g, Wearing baseball cap and checked shirt. h, Seated, drinking beverage. i, Wearing cut-off shorts.
   No. 857, 1500fr, Riding bicycle. No. 858, 2000fr, Wearing glasses, elbow and knee pads.

2000, Mar. 30
856 A202 250fr Sheet of 9, #a-i   10.00 10.00
Souvenir Sheets
857-858 A202   Set of 2   16.00 16.00

The Three Stooges — A213

No. 859, 250fr, horiz.: a, Larry, in surgeon's gown, and Curly. b, Curly, Moe, Larry around barrel. c, Moe, Larry and Curly on horse. d, Larry attacking man. e, Moe getting hair pulled. f, Moe with mallet. g, Curly, Moe and Larry in western outfits, outdoors. h, Larry, Curly and Moe in white doctor's jackets. i, Man looking at Moe.
   No. 860, 300fr, horiz.: a, Larry grabbing Moe's chin. b, Moe and Larry holding scrolls. c, Moe, yellow background. d, Larry, blue background. e, Moe, Shemp and Larry. f, Shemp, blue background. g, Shemp, yellow background. h, Shemp pointing bellows at Larry. i, Moe and Larry in white.
   No. 861, 1500fr, Moe in surgeon's gown. No. 862, 1500fr, Moe wearing hat. No. 863, 2000fr, Curly, Moe and Larry in western outfits, outdoors. No. 864, 2000fr, Larry with violin.

2000   **Sheets of 9, #a-i**
859-860 A213   Set of 2   22.50 22.50
Souvenir Sheets
861-864 A213   Set of 4   32.50 32.50
   Issued: Nos. 859, 861, 863, 3/30; Nos. 860, 862, 864, 5/29.

I Love Lucy Type of 1999

No. 865: a, Lucy dancing, man in background. b, Lucy dancing, with knees bent and arms extended. c, Lucy in doorway. d, Lucy dancing behind sofa. e, Lucy kicking out leg. f, Lucy being caught by two men. g, Lucy with one arm extended. h, Lucy being sprayed with seltzer water. i, Lucy with leg on dance rail.
   No. 866, 1500fr, Lucy looking at clock, horiz. No. 867, 2000fr, Lucy with clown costume and arms extended.

2000, May 29
865 A201 225fr Sheet of 9, #a-i   9.00 9.00
Souvenir Sheets
866-867 A201   Set of 2   16.00 16.00

N'Djamena, Cent. — A213a

Background colors: 150fr, Blue. 300fr, Red. 475fr, Green.

2000, May 29   **Litho.**   *Perf. 13¼*
867A-867C A213a   Set of 3   — —

Chadian Political History — A214

No. 868, 150fr: a, Louis Léon César Faidherbe. b, François Joseph Lamy. c, Henri Eugène Gouraud. d, Gustav Nachtigal. e, Head of Rabah on spike. f, Fernand Foureau.
   No. 869, 300fr: a, Pierre Savorgnan de Brazza. b, Philippe Marie de Hautecloque Leclerc. c, Emile Gentil. d, Gabriel Lisette. e, Charles de Gaulle. f, Felix Eboué.

2000, May 29   *Perf. 13½*
Sheets of 6, #a-f
868-869 A214   Set of 2   18.00 18.00

Wildlife, Map of Chad, Scouting Emblem — A215

No. 870, 150fr — Giraffa camelopardalis: a, Pair, one with head lowered. b, Pair, both with heads extended. c, Pair near forest. d, Trio.
   No. 871, 200fr: a, Pair of Gazella granti in field. b, Gazella cuiveri. c, Gazella dorcas. d, Pair of Gazella granti at waterhole.
   No. 872, 250fr — Addax nasomaculatus: a, View of head. b, Lying in grass. c, Standing. d, Grazing.
   No. 873, 300fr — Ammotragus lervia: a, Pair. b, View of head. c, Standing on mountain ledge. d, Standing, with purple mountain in background.
   No. 874, 375fr — Diceros bicornis: a, View of head. b, Facing right, line of dark green foliage in background. c, Facing left. d, Facing right, with trees in background.
   No. 875, 400fr — Panthera pardus: a, On tree branch. b, Lying in grass. c, Standing. d, View of head.
   No. 876, 450fr: a, Head of Theropithecus gelada. b, Cercopithecus aethiops. c, Papio anubis. d, Adult and juvenile Thereopithecus gelada.
   No. 877, 450fr — Hippopotamus amphibius: a, Pair laying in mud. b, With open mouth. c, Standing. d, Herd.
   No. 878, 475fr — Oryx dammah: a, Facing right, green foliage in background. b, View of head. c, Pair. d, Grazing, mountain in background.
   No. 879, 500fr — Panthera leo: a, Male on female. b, Females at waterhole. c, Female and cub. d, Female and male.
   No. 880, 600fr — Loxodonta africana: a, With tree at right. b, Facing right. c, View of head. d, With tree and mountain in background.
   No. 881, 750fr — Syncerus caffer: a, Juvenile, adult grazing. b, Adult in field. c, Pair lying on ground. d, With grass in mouth.
   No. 882, 1000fr, Pair of Diceros bicornis. No. 883, 1000fr, Pair of Hippopotamus amphibius fighting. No. 884, 1500fr, Panthera leo with kill.
   Illustration reduced.

2000, Aug. 1   *Perf. 13¼*
Horiz. Strips of 4, #a-d
870-881 A215   Set of 12   90.00 90.00
Souvenir Sheets
882-884 A215   Set of 3   16.00 16.00
   Nos. 882-884 each contain one 36x51mm stamp.

Miniature Sheet

Baseball Player — A216

2000, Oct. 11   Litho. & Embossed
885 A216 3000fr gold & multi   10.00 10.00
Exists with silver background.

High-five of Teenagers — A217

No. 886: a, Moon Hee-jun and Lee Jae-won. b, Jang Woo-hyuk and ear of Tony An. c, Tony an and Kang Ta. d, Jang Woo-hyuk. e, Entire group. f, Kang Ta. g, Moon Hee-jun. h, Lee Jae-won. i, Tony An.

2000   Litho.
886 A217 150fr Sheet of 9, #a-i   4.50 4.50

Sports and Chess — A218

No. 887, 30fr — Dogs involved in sport activities: a, Sled dogs. b, Dog racing. c, Hunting dogs. d, Dogs and skier.
No. 888, 70fr — Various sports: a, Petanque. b, Rugby. c, Archery. d, Jai alai.
No. 889, 250fr — 2000 Summer Olympics, Sydney: a, Fencing. b, Judo. c, Tennis. d, Boxing.
No. 890, 300fr — 2000 Summer Olympics, Sydney: a, Cycling. b, Basketball. c, Beach volleyball. d, Baseball.
No. 891, 400fr — Soccer players: a, Zinedine Zidane. b, Lilian Thuram. c, Yuri Djorkaeff. d, Nicolas Anelka
No. 892, 475fr — 2000 Summer Olympics, Sydney: a, Table tennis. b, Equestrian. c, Swimming. d, Kayaking.
No. 893, 500fr — Golf: a, Man with white pants swinging club. b, Golfer analyzing putt. c, Man with black pants swinging club. d, Woman golfer.
No. 894, 750fr — Formula I race drivers: a, Michael Schumacher. b, Mikka Hakkinen. c, Ralf Schumacher. d, David Coulthard.

No. 895, 1000fr — Chess: a, Knight with shield. b, Knight on donkey. c, Knight with attendant. d, Horses and wheeled castle. 2000fr, Venus Williams.

2001, Jan. 31   Perf. 13¼
Sheets of 4, #a-d
887-895 A218   Set of 9   85.00 85.00
Souvenir Sheet
896 A218 2000fr multi   9.00 9.00
2000 Summer Olympics, Sydney (No. 896). No. 896 contains one 36x51mm stamp.

Trains — A219

No. 897, 200fr: a, Mallard, 1935. b, P8 Prussian, 1908. c, F2A, 1936. b, 240 P, 1940.
No. 898, 300fr: a, NSB No. 3641. b, New Zealand Railways Sereis EW. c, Series 277, Renfe. d, Series DF4 Vent d'Est IV Co-Co.
No. 899, 400fr: a, SNCF Series 9100 2-D-2, 1950. b, SNCF Series 72000 C-C, 1967. c, CC 21000, 1969. d, VL-80, 1963.
No. 900, 475fr: a, GNER Eurostar. b, Electric EMU ETR 500. c, DER OBB 1016 001. d, GNER train.
No. 901, 500fr: a, OL-49, 1951. b, Pacific Series 16E, 1935. c, Andaluces 030, 1877. d, Franco-Crosti Gr. 743, 1937.
No. 902, 500fr: a, JR West 8-car unit E4. b, TGV KTX. c, 300 Series unit J3. d, E3 Series unit R6.
No. 903, 500fr: a, 2D2 PO, 1926. b, Metropolitan BB Vickers, 1920. c, DB ET 491, 1935. d, Series D, 1925.
No. 904, 600fr: a, Electric EMU 490. b, Acela, 2001. c, CFF-FFS Electric EMU RABe 500. d, ICE-T Bavereihe 41.
No. 905, 750fr: a, Single Driver, 1870. b, Great Western Railway Castle, 1923. c, Schools Class, 1930. d, 230 Besa, 1905.
No. 906, 750fr: a, TGV Thalys. b, TGV Duplex. c, TGV La Poste. d, TGV Atlantique. 1500fr, SAR Series 26 2-D-2. 2000fr, TGV Sud-est.

2001, June 22   Litho.
Sheets of 4, #a-d
897-906 A219   Set of 10   90.00 90.00
Souvenir Sheets
907-908 A219   Set of 2   16.00 16.00
Nos. 907-908 each contain one 51x36mm stamp.

British Royalty — A220

No. 909, 300fr — Queen Mother: a, With King George VI. b, With young daughter. c, With Prince Charles. d, Waving. e, Wearing tiara and yellow dress. f, Wearing pink dress and hat. g, Wearing green dress and hat. h, Holding flowers. i, With dogs.
No. 910, 300fr — Prince William wearing: a, Black suit with lapel handkerchief. b, Suit with red and blue vest. c, Suit with gold vest. d, Sweater, looking right. e, Black suit and dark blue tie. f, Sweater, facing forward. g, Blue shirt with button. h, Dark blue shirt without button. i, Light blue suit.

2001, July 22   Perf. 13¼
Sheets of 9, #a-i
909-910 A220   Set of 2   24.00 24.00
No. 910 contains nine 36x51mm stamps.

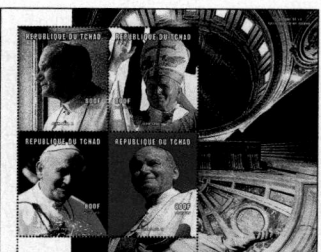

French Rulers — A221

No. 911, 300fr: a, King Francis I. b, King Louis XIII. c, Elizabeth of Austria, consort of King Charles IX. d, King John II the Good.
No. 912, 375fr: a, King Louis XIV. b, King Francis I, diff. c, King Louis XVI. d, King Louis XVIII.
No. 913, 475fr: a, King Louis XV as child. b, King Louis XV as adult. c, Queen Marie Antoinette. d, King Charles VII.
No. 914, 500fr — Napoleon Bonaparte wearing: a, White tunic. b, Black jacket. c, Emperor's robes. d, Red tunic.

2001, July 22   Sheets of 4, #a-d
911-914 A221   Set of 4   30.00 30.00
Stamps of Nos. 911-913 exist in souvenir sheets of 1. Value, set $70.

Pope John Paul II — A222

No. 915, 800fr: a, Standing in room, looking left. b, Waving. c, Holding flowers. d, With blue sky background.
No. 916, 1000fr: a, Wearing red hat. b, Wearing miter, waving. c, Bending to kiss ground. d, Wearing miter, holding crucifix. 4000fr, Wearing zucchetto.

2001   Litho.   Perf. 13¼
Sheets of 4, #a-d
915-916 A222   Set of 2   32.50 32.50
Miniature Sheet
Litho. & Embossed
917 A222 4000fr gold & multi   22.50 22.50
Issued: Nos. 915-916, 7/22; No. 917, 7/23. No. 917 contains one 60x90mm stamp and exists with a silver background. Stamps of Nos. 915-916 exist in souvenir sheets of 1. Value, set $60.

Famous Men — A223

Designs: 200fr, Charles Darwin (1809-82), naturalist. 250fr, Christopher Columbus (1451-1506), explorer. 300fr, Jacques-Yves Cousteau (1910-97), marine scientist. 350fr, Albert Schweitzer (1875-1965), missionary. 400fr, Juan Manuel Fangio (1911-95), race car driver. 450fr, Nicolaus Copernicus (1473-1543), astronomer. 500fr, Robert Stephenson (1803-59), engineer. 550fr, Etienne Chambron, high speed rail pioneer. 600fr, Garry Kasparov, chess player. 750fr, Lord Robert

Baden-Powell (1857-1941), founder of scouting. 800fr, Neil Armstrong, astronaut. 1000fr, Sir Alexander Fleming (1881-1955), bacteriologist.

2001, Oct. 30   Litho.
918-929 A223   Set of 12   29.00 29.00
Nos. 918-929 exist in souvenir sheets of 1. Value, set $115.

Fossils, Dinosaurs, Meteorites and Minerals — A224

No. 930, 300fr — Fossils: a, Stenosaurus bollensis. b, Rhamphorhynchus. c, Archaeopteryx lithographica. d, Keichousaurus hui.
No. 931, 375fr — Dinosaurs: a, Mesadactylus. b, Pteranodon. c, Tropeognathus. d, Quetzalcoatlus.
No. 932, 400fr — Meteorites found in: a, India. b, Nigeria. c, US. d, Australia.
No. 933, 500fr — Dinosaurs: a, Deinonychus. b, Seismosaurus. c, Pleurocoelus, Acrocanthosaur. d, Styracosaurus.
No. 934, 500fr — Minerals: a, Fluorite. b, Pyrite. c, Wulfenite. d, Merovingian scoria.
No. 935, 550fr — Meteorites found in: a, Antarctica. b, Libya. c, USSR. d, China.
No. 936, 600fr — Minerals: a, Magnetite. b, Kunzite. c, Apophyllite, Stilbite. d, Fluorite, diff.
No. 937, 750fr — Minerals: a, Quartz. b, Merovingian scoria, diff. c, Epidote. d, Amethyst, agate.
3000fr, Tyrannosaurus rex, vert.

2001, Dec. 27   Litho.
Sheets of 4, #a-d
930-937 A224   Set of 8   77.50 77.50
Miniature Sheet
Litho. & Embossed
938 A224 3000fr gold & multi   17.00 17.00
No. 938 contains one 60x90mm stamp and exists with silver background.

French Kings — A225

Designs: No. 939, 3000fr, Louis IX. No. 940, 3000fr, Francis I. No. 941, 3000fr, Henry IV. No. 942, 3000fr, Louis XIII. No. 943, 3000fr, Louis XV.

2002, Apr. 10   Litho. & Embossed
Gold & Multicolored
939-943 A225   Set of 5   50.00 50.00
Nos. 939-943 exist with silver background.

Egyptian Treasures A225a

Designs: No. 943A, 3000fr, Painted wooden box. No. 943B, 3000fr, Nekhbet vulture. No. 943C, 3000fr, Oushebti of Tutankhamen, vert. No. 943D, 3000fr, Pair of royal scepters, vert. No. 943E, 3000fr, Diadem, vert. No. 943F, 3000fr, Gold-plated throne, vert. No. 943G, 3000fr, Cynocephalic pectoral, vert. No. 943H, 3000fr, Coffin of Tutankhamen, vert. No. 943I, 3000fr, Statue of Ka, vert. No. 943J, 3000fr, Duck earring, vert. No. 943K, 3000fr, Lion-shaped vase, vert. No. 943L, 3000fr, Canopic dais and chapel, vert.

Embossed on Gold Paper
2002, Apr. 10   **Perf. 13¼**
943A-943L A225a Set of
12   140.00 140.00

Artists and Their Paintings — A226

On Nos. 944-957, painting titles (in French) and artist's birth and death dates are in margins adjacent to each stamp. On Nos. 958-962 painting titles are not shown, but artist's name is in sheet margin
No. 944, 150fr: a, Berthe Morisot (1841-95). b, Cache-cache. c, Le Berceau. d, Au bal. e, Jeune femme se poudrant. f, Paule Gobillard peignant.
No. 945, 200fr: a, Marc Chagall (1887-1985). b, Nature morte. c, Le violoniste vert. d, La maison bleue. e, Mariage. f, Le soldat ivre.
No. 946, 250fr: a, Camille Pissarro (1830-1903). b, Les chataigniers a Osny. c, Le verger. d, Le repos des glaneuses. e, Jeune paysanne prenant son cafe. f, Le bergére.
No. 947, 300fr: a, Alfred Sisley (1839-99). b, Le pont de Villeneuve la Garenne, c, Allee de jardin a Louveciennes. d, Meule de foin bord du Loing. e, Moret sur Loing. f, Moulin a Moret.
No. 948, 325fr: a, Paul Delvaux (1897-1994). b, La voix publique. c, Nocturnes. d, Balgnade des Nymphes. e, Pygmalion. f, Jeunes femmes revant.
No. 949, 350fr: a, Edouard Manet (1832-83). b, Le Déjeuner sur l'herbe. c, Olympia. d, Le fifre. e, La serveuse de bocks. f, Le balcon.
No. 950, 375fr: a, Vincent van Gogh (1853-90). b, Champ de blé avec cypres. c, Rue a Auvers. d, La sieste. e, Chambre jaune a Arles. f, Rue de village.
No. 951, 400fr: a, Salvador Dali (1904-89). b, Cannibalisme en automne. c, Corpus Hypercubicus. d, Le sommeil. e, Le tentation de St. Antoine. f, Meditation sur harpe.
No. 952, 425fr: a, Paul Cézanne (1839-1906). b, Les baigneurs. c, Les grandes baigneuses (light blue background). d, Les grandes baigneuses, diff. (dark blue background). e, Les baigneueses. f, Les baigneurs au repos.
No. 953, 450fr: a, Pablo Picasso (1881-1973). b, Les demoiselles d'Avignon. c, Femme a l'eventail. d, La danse. e, La vie. f, La mere et son fils.
No. 954, 475fr: a, Amadeo Modigliani (1884-1920). b, Nu souche sur un divan. c, Nu debout. d, Cariatide debout. e, Nu allongé. f, Nu assis de dos.
No. 955, 500fr: a, Auguste Renoir (1841-1919). b, Diane chasseresse. c, Nu allongé. d, Baigneuses. e, Baigneuse assise. f, Nymphe au printemps.
No. 956, 550fr: a, Edgar Degas (1834-1917). b, Femme se coiffant. c, Aprés le bain (view of front of seated woman). d, Femme se peignant. e, Aprés le bain (view of back of woman). f, Aprés le bain (woman dressing).
No. 957, 600fr: a, Henri Matisse (1869-1954). b, Le nu bleu. c, Le genou levé. d, Nu assis sur un fauteuil. e, Odalisques. f, Nu allongé.
No. 958, 1500fr, Gustave Caillebotte. No. 959, 1500fr, Picasso, diff. No. 960, 1500fr, Auguste Renoir, diff. No. 961, 2000fr, Pablo Picasso, diff. No. 962, 2000fr, Van Gogh, diff.

2002, Apr. 10   **Perf. 12¾x13¼**
Sheets of 6, #a-f
944-957 A226 Set of 14 140.00 140.00
Souvenir Sheets
Perf. 13¼x12¾
958-962 A226 Set of 5 27.50 27.50
Nos. 944a-955a and 957a exist in souvenir sheets of 1 that are perf. 13¼x12¾. Value, set $92.50.

Miniature Sheet

Zeppelin NT — A227

No. 963: a, 475fr, Over Lake Constance. b, 500fr, Over Frankfurt. c, 600fr, Over Nürburgring, Germany. d, 750fr, At 2001 Salon du Bourget.

2002, Oct. 30   **Perf. 13¼**
963 A227 Sheet of 4, #a-d 11.00 11.00
Nos. 963a-963d exist in souvenir sheets of 1. Value, set $45.

Fauna and Mushrooms — A228

No. 964, 150fr: a, Hemichromis lifalili. b, Trichechus senegalensis. c, Synodontis nigriventris. d, Gnathonemus petersii. e, Ctenopoma ansorgii. f, Pseudocrenilabrus multicolor.
No. 965, 300fr, vert.: a, Nectarina venusta. b, Lamprotornis splendidus. c, Poicephalus meyeri. d, Halcyon leucocephala. e, Quelea quelea. f, Merops pusillus.
No. 966, 300fr, vert.: a, Terathopius ecaudatus. b, Gymnogyps californianus. c, Buteo jamaicensis. d, Lophaetus occipitalis. e, Aquila rapax. f, Melierax metabates.
No. 967, 375fr, vert.: a, Elanus caeruleus. b, Harpia harpyja. c, Gyps rueppellii. d, Milvus migrans. e, Torgos tracheliotus. f, Aquila chrysaetos.
No. 968, 550fr: a, Kallimoides rumia. b, Zophopetes dysmephila. c, Megalopalpus zymna. d, Coeliades forestan. e, Catopsilia florella. f, Anaphaesis aurota.
No. 969, 600fr: a, Amanita muscaria. b, Amanita rubescens. c, Cortinarius orellanus. d, Hygrophorus hypothejus. e, Leccinum piceinum. f, Strobilomyces strobilaceus.

2003, June 2   **Litho.**
Sheets of 6, #a-f
964-969 A228 Set of 6 55.00 55.00
Stamps of Nos. 965-969 exist in a set of twelve souvenir sheets of two, with each souvenir sheet of two containing adjacent stamps found in the sheet of six. Value, set $160.

Chad - Taiwan Cooperation — A229

Flags and: 50fr, Grain. 100fr, Surgeon's hands, Red Cross. 150fr, Bridge. 300fr, Handshake, maps.

2003, Dec. 1
970-973 A229 Set of 4 2.50 2.50
973a Booklet pane, 2 each #970-973 5.00 —
Complete booklet, #973a 5.00
973b Souvenir sheet, #970-973 2.50 2.50

AIDS Prevention
A230

Red ribbon and: 50fr, People under umbrella. 100fr, Man and woman. 150fr, Doctor. 300fr, "Prudence, Abstinence, Fidelité."

2004, July 7 **Litho.** **Perf. 13x12¾**
974-977 A230 Set of 4 2.50 2.50

Opening of Petroleum Refinery, 1st Anniv.
A231

Pres. Idriss Deby opening pipeline and: 150fr, Storage tank. 350fr, Storage tanks. 400fr, Refinery. 500fr, Tower, vert.

2004, Oct. 10 **Perf. 12¾x13, 13x12¾**
978-981 A231 Set of 4 6.50 6.50

Women's Hairstyles
A232

Designs: 150fr, Figuerier. 350fr, Sakkindjala. 550fr, Kileskou. 575fr, Dabbou.

2005, Mar. 8   **Perf. 13**
982-985 A232 Set of 4 8.00 8.00

Toumaï Skull
A233

Color of skull: 25fr, Purple. 50fr, Green. 100fr, Gray. 150fr, Red. 1500fr, Gray.

2005, July 19 **Litho.** **Perf. 12¾x13**
986-989 A233 Set of 4 1.40 1.40
Souvenir Sheet
990 A233 1500fr multi 5.75 5.75

Campaign Against Trypanosomiasis, 10th Anniv. — A234

Tsetse fly and: 150fr, Trypanosomiasis protozoa, eradication campaign emblem. 300fr, Eradication campaign emblem, map of Africa. 350fr, Pan-African Postal Union emblem, eradication campaign emblem, map of Africa.

550fr, Trypanosomiasis protozoa, maps of Chad and Africa.

2010   **Perf. 12¾**
991-994 A234 Set of 4 5.50 5.50

Independence, 50th Anniv. — A235

Emblem with denomination color of: 150fr, Red. 300fr, White. 350fr, Yellow. 550fr, Blue.

2010
995-998 A235 Set of 4 5.50 5.50

A236

Designs: No. 999, 150fr, Cyphotilapia frontosa, Lysmata amboinensis. No. 1000, 150fr, Cyrtocara moorii, Potamonautes maculata. No. 1001, 150fr, Placidochromis milomo, Sesarma mederi. No. 1002, 150fr, Tropheus brichardi, Atyopsis gabonensis. No. 1003, 200fr, Phocidae, Swakopmund Lighthouse, Namibia. No. 1004, 200fr, Odobenus rosmarus, Nosy Iranja Lighthouse, Madagascar. No. 1005, 200fr, Lobodon carcinophaga, Pelican Point Lighthouse, Namibia. No. 1006, 200fr, Odobenus rosmarus, Katsepy Lighthouse, Madagascar. No. 1007, 300fr, Morus capensis, Pointe-Noire Lighthouse, Congo. No. 1008, 300fr, Phalacrocorax capensis, Slangkop Point Lighthouse, South Africa. No. 1009, 300fr, Fregata magnificens, Cap Agulhas Lighthouse, South Africa. No. 1010, 300fr, Phalacrocorax melanoleucos, Ngombe Lighthouse, Gabon. No. 1011, 300fr, Strombus gibberulus albus, Grand Bassam Lighthouse, Ivory Coast. No. 1012, 300fr, Argonauta cornuta, Cap Blanc Lighthouse, Mauritania. No. 1013, 300fr, Calpurnus verrucosus, Conakry Lighthouse, Guinea. No. 1014, 300fr, Haliotis queketti, Cap Miné Lighthouse, Madagascar. No. 1015, 350fr, Galeocerdo cuvier, Cherchell Lighthouse, Algeria. No. 1016, 350fr, Isurus paucus, l'ilot d'Arzew Lighthouse, Algeria. No. 1017, 350fr, Sphyrna mokarran, Amirauté Lighthouse, Algeria. No. 1018, 350fr, Carcharodon carcharias, Cap Ivi Lighthouse, Algeria. No. 1019, 500fr, Amanita jacksonii, Eugaster spinulosa. No. 1020, 500fr, Amanita caesarea, Zographus regalis. No. 1021, 500fr, Armillaria gallica, Megaponera foetens. No. 1022, 500fr, Sarcoscypha coccinea, Mylabris sp. No. 1023, 600fr, Cystodermella cinnabarina, Schistocerca gregaria. No. 1024, 600fr, Marasmius rotula, Palpopleura lucia. No. 1025, 600fr, Periphragmoides lysurus, Myrmeleontidae. No. 1026, 600fr, Boletus edulis, Trithemis kirbyi. No. 1027, 750fr, Fluorine. No. 1028, 750fr, Malachite. No. 1029, 750fr, Pyrite. No. 1030, 750fr, Vanadinite.

2012, Sept. 4 **Litho.** **Perf. 13¼**
999-1030 A236 Set of 32 50.00 50.00
Nos. 999-1030 each exist in souvenir sheets of 1.

SEMI-POSTAL STAMPS

Catalogue values for unused stamps in this section are for Never Hinged items.

Anti-Malaria Issue
Common Design Type
Perf. 12½x12
1962, Apr. 7 **Engr.** **Unwmk.**
B1 CD108 25fr + 5fr orange 1.25 .50

Freedom from Hunger Issue
Common Design Type
1963, Mar. 21   **Perf. 13**
B2 CD112 25fr + 5fr dk grn, dk
bl & brn 2.00 .50

Red Cross, Mother and Children — SP1

1974, Oct. 2   Photo.   Perf. 12½x13
B3   SP1 30fr + 10fr multi   1.00   .40
Red Cross of Chad, first anniversary.

AIR POST STAMPS

Catalogue values for unused stamps in this section are for Never Hinged items.

Olympic Games Issue
French Equatorial Africa No. C37 Surcharged in Red

Unwmk.
1960, Dec. 15   Engr.   Perf. 13
C1   AP8 250fr on 500fr grnsh
        blk, blk & slate   12.00 7.50
17th Olympic Games, Rome, Aug. 25-Sept. 11. Surcharge 46mm wide.

Red Bishops — AP1

Birds in pairs: 100fr, Scarlet-chested sunbird. 200fr, African paradise flycatcher. 250fr, Malachite kingfisher. 500fr, Nubian carmine bee-eater.

1961-63   Unwmk.   Engr.   Perf. 13
C2   AP1 50fr dk grn, mag &
        blk   1.25   .35
C3   AP1 100fr multi   3.75 1.25
C4   AP1 200fr multi   6.50 1.90
C5   AP1 250fr dk bl, grn & dp
        org ('63)   10.00 3.00
C6   AP1 500fr multi   22.50 9.50
     Nos. C2-C6 (5)   44.00 16.00

Air Afrique Issue
Common Design Type
1962, Feb. 17   Unwmk.   Perf. 13
C7   CD107 25fr lt bl, org brn &
        blk   1.00   .25

Abidjan Games Issue

Discus Thrower — AP2

1962, July 21   Photo.   Perf. 12x12½
C8   AP2 100fr brn, lt grn & blk   3.50 1.00

African Postal Union Issue
Common Design Type
1963, Sept. 8   Photo.   Perf. 12½
C9   CD114 85fr dk bl, ocher &
        red   2.40   .60

Air Afrique Issue, 1963
Common Design Type
1963, Nov. 19   Perf. 13x12
C10 CD115 50fr multi   2.40   .60

Europafrica Issue
Common Design Type
1963, Nov. 30   Photo.   Perf. 12x13
C11 CD116 50fr dp grn, yel & dk
        brn   2.00   .50

Mail Truck and Broussard Plane — AP4

Unwmk.
1963, Dec. 16   Engr.   Perf. 13
C12 AP4 100fr sl grn, ultra & red
        brn   4.00   .90

Chiefs of State Issue

Map and Presidents of Chad, Congo, Gabon and Central African Republic — AP4a

1964, June 23   Photo.   Perf. 12½
C13 AP4a 100fr multi   2.40   .60
See note after Central African Republic No. C19.

Europafrica Issue

Globe and Emblems of Industry and Agriculture — AP5

1964, July 20   Perf. 13x12
C14 AP5 50fr brn, pur & dp org   2.00   .40
See note after Cameroun No. 402.

Soccer — AP6

Designs: 50fr, Javelin throw, vert. 100fr, High jump, vert. 200fr, Runners.

1964, Aug. 12   Engr.   Perf. 13
C15 AP6 25fr yel grn, sl grn &
        org brn   1.00   .30
C16 AP6 50fr org brn, ind &
        brt bl   2.00   .60
C17 AP6 100fr blk, red & brt grn   3.50 1.00
C18 AP6 200fr bis, blk & car   6.00 2.00
  a. Min. sheet of 4, #C15-C18 18.00 6.50
     Nos. C15-C18 (4)   12.50 3.90
18th Olympic Games, Tokyo, 10/10-25/64.

Communications Symbols — AP7

1964, Nov. 2   Litho.   Perf. 12½x13
C19 AP7 25fr lil, dk brn & lt red
        brn   1.00   .25
Pan-African and Malagasy Posts and Tele-communications Cong., Cairo, Oct. 24-Nov. 6.

President John F. Kennedy (1917-63) — AP8

1964, Nov. 3   Photo.   Perf. 12½
C20 AP8 100fr multi   3.00 1.00
  a. Souvenir sheet of 4   12.00 6.00

ICY Emblem — AP9

1965, July 5   Photo.   Perf. 13
C21 AP9 100fr multi   2.00   .60
International Cooperation Year, 1965.

Abraham Lincoln — AP10

1965, Sept. 7   Unwmk.   Perf. 13
C22 AP10 100fr multi   3.00   .75
Centenary of death of Abraham Lincoln.

Musical Instrument Type
Design: 100fr, Xylophone (marimba).

1965, Oct. 26   Engr.   Perf. 13
Size: 48x27mm
C23 A18 100fr ocher, brt bl & vio
        bl   2.75 1.00

Sir Winston Spencer Churchill (1874-1965) AP11

1965, Nov. 23   Engr.   Perf. 13
C24 AP11 50fr dk grn & blk   2.00   .50

Dr. Albert Schweitzer and Outstretched Hands — AP12

1966, Feb. 15   Photo.   Perf. 12½
C25 AP12 100fr multi   2.75   .80
Dr. Albert Schweitzer (1875-1965), medical missionary, theologian and musician.

Air Afrique Issue, 1966
Common Design Type
1966, Aug. 31   Photo.   Perf. 13
C26 CD123 30fr yel grn, blk &
        gray   1.00   .25

White-throated Bee-eater — AP13

Birds: 50fr, Blue-eared glossy starling. 200fr, African pygmy kingfisher. 250fr, Red-throated bee-eater. 500fr, Little green bee-eater.

1966-67   Photo.   Perf. 13x12½
C27 AP13 50fr gold & multi   1.50   .40
C28 AP13 100fr bluish gray &
        multi   3.50 1.00
C29 AP13 200fr grnsh gray &
        multi   6.75 1.75
C30 AP13 250fr pale bl & multi   7.50 1.75
C31 AP13 500fr pale sal & multi 14.00 3.25
     Nos. C27-C31 (5)   33.25 8.15
Issued: 100fr, 200fr, 500fr, 8/18/66; others, 3/21/67.
For surcharges see Nos. C67-C69.

Congress Hall — AP14

1967, Jan. 5   Photo.   Perf. 12½
C32 AP14 25fr multi   1.00   .25
Opening of the new Congress Hall.

Breguet 19 Biplane — AP15

Planes: 30fr, Latécoère 631 hydroplane. 50fr, Douglas DC-3. 100fr, Piper Cherokee 6.

1967, Aug. 1   Engr.   Perf. 13
C33 AP15 25fr sky bl, sl grn & lt
            brn   .75   .25
C34 AP15 30fr sky bl, indigo &
            grn   1.00   .30
C35 AP15 50fr sky bl, ol bis &
            sl grn   1.75   .60
C36 AP15 100fr dk bl, sl grn &
            dk red   3.50   .90
    Nos. C33-C36 (4)   7.00 2.05
  First anniversary of Air Chad.

African Postal Union Issue, 1967
Common Design Type
1967, Sept. 9   Engr.   Perf. 13
C37 CD124 100fr ol, brt pink &
             red brn   2.00   .60

Rock Painting Type of Regular Issue
1967, Dec. 19   Engr.   Perf. 13
Size: 48x27mm
C38 A32 100fr Masked dancers   8.00   .95
C39 A32 125fr Rabbit hunt   9.00 1.50

Downhill Skiing — AP16

1968, Feb. 5   Engr.   Perf. 13
C40 AP16 30fr shown   1.25   .30
C41 AP16 100fr Ski jump, vert.   3.25   .90
  10th Winter Olympic Games, Grenoble, France, Feb. 6-18.

Konrad Adenauer (1876-1967), Chancellor of West Germany (1949-63) AP17

1968, Mar. 19   Photo.   Perf. 12½
C42 AP17 52fr grn, dk brn & lt lil 1.50   .50
  a.   Souvenir sheet of 4   6.00 4.50

The Snake Charmer, by Henri Rousseau — AP18

Design: 130fr, "War" by Henri Rousseau.

1968, May 14   Photo.   Perf. 13½
Size: 41x41mm
C43 AP18 100fr ultra & multi   3.50 1.00

Size: 48x35mm
Perf. 12½
C44 AP18 130fr brn & multi   5.50 1.50

Hurdlers — AP19

1968, Oct. 16   Engr.   Perf. 13
C45 AP19 32fr shown   1.20   .40
C46 AP19 80fr Relay race   2.75   .80
  19th Olympic Games, Mexico City, 10/12-27.

PHILEXAFRIQUE Issue

The Actor Wolf (Bernard), by Jacques L. David AP20

1969, Jan. 15   Photo.   Perf. 12½
C47 AP20 100fr multi   3.75 1.75
  PHILEXAFRIQUE, Philatelic Exhib. in Abidjan, Feb. 14-23. Printed with alternating label. Value is for stamp with label attached.

2nd PHILEXAFRIQUE Issue
Common Design Type
50fr, Chad #J12 and Moundang Dancers.
1969, Feb. 14   Engr.   Perf. 13
C48 CD128 50fr red, brt bl, brn &
             grn   2.40 1.00

Gustav Nachtigal and Tibesti Gorge, 1869 — AP21

No. C50, Heinrich Barth & Lake Chad, 1851.

1969, Feb. 17
C49 AP21 100fr vio bl, dk brn &
            brn   2.40   .60
C50 AP21 100fr grn, pur & bl   2.40   .60
  German explorers Gustav Nachtigal (1834-85) and Heinrich Barth (1821-65), and state visit of the Pres. of West Germany Heinrich Lubke.

Apollo 8, Earth and Moon — AP22

1969, Apr. 10   Photo.   Perf. 13
C51 AP22 100fr multi   3.00   .75
  US Apollo 8 mission, the 1st men in orbit around the moon, Dec. 21-27, 1968.

Mahatma Gandhi — AP23

No. C53, John F. Kennedy. No. C54, Dr. Martin Luther King, Jr. No. C55, Robert F. Kennedy.

1969, May 20   Photo.   Perf. 12½
C52 AP23 50fr blk & lt grn   1.25   .40
C53 AP23 50fr blk & tan   1.25   .40
C54 AP23 50fr blk & pink   1.25   .40
C55 AP23 50fr blk & lt vio bl   1.25   .40
  a.   Souvenir sheet of 4, #C52-C55 6.00 6.00
    Nos. C52-C55 (4)   5.00 1.60
  Issued to honor exponents of non-violence.

Presidents Tombalbaye and Mobutu, Map and Flags of Chad and Congo — AP24

Embossed on Gold Foil
1969   Die-cut Perf. 13½
C56 AP24 1000fr gold, dk bl &
            red   27.50 27.50
  1st anniv. of the establishment of the Union of Central African States, comprising Chad, Congo Democratic Republic and Central African Republic.

Napoleon Visiting Hospital, by Alexandre Veron-Bellecourt — AP25

Paintings: 85fr, Battle of Wagram, by Horace Vernet. 130fr, Battle of Austerlitz, by Francois Pascal Gerard.

1969, July 23   Photo.   Perf. 12x12½
C57 AP25 30fr multi   1.20   .40
C58 AP25 85fr multi   2.50   .75
C59 AP25 130fr multi   4.50 1.25
    Nos. C57-C59 (3)   8.20 2.40
  Bicentenary of birth of Napoleon I.

Apollo 11 Issue

Astronaut on Moon — AP26

Embossed on Gold Foil
1969, Oct. 17   Die-cut Perf. 13½
C60 AP26 1000fr gold   27.50 27.50
  See note after Algeria No. 427.

Village Life, by Goto Narcisse — AP27

No. 62, Women at the Market, by Iba N'Diaye. No. 63, Woman with Flowers, by Iba N'Diaye, vert.

1970 Photo. Perf. 12x12½, 12½x12
C61 AP27 100fr multi   3.25   .75
C62 AP27 250fr grn & multi   5.00 1.00
C63 AP27 250fr brn & multi   5.00 1.00
    Nos. C61-C63 (3)   13.25 2.75
  Issued: 100fr, Mar. 17; Nos. C62-C63, Aug. 28.

Napoleon — AP27a

Designs: Nos. C63A, C63E, Napoleon II, Duke of Reichstadt, vert.
No. C63B: g, 10fr, Crossing the Grand St. Bernard, by David. h, 25fr, Emperor Napoleon, by Gerard. i, 32fr, Marriage of Napoleon and Marie Louise, by Rouget.
40fr, Napoleon after return from Elba, vert.

Perf. 12x12½, 12½x12
1970-71   Litho.
C63A AP27a 10fr multicolored   4.00   —
C63B AP27a Strip of 3,
              #g.-i.   14.00   —

Embossed
Perf. 13
C63C AP27a 10fr gold   20.00   —
  f.   Sheet of 1, Imperf.   37.50   —

Souvenir Sheets
Litho.
Perf. 13x13½
C63D AP27a 40fr multicolored   10.00   —

Embossed
Imperf
C63E AP27a 10fr gold, like
              #C63A   37.50   —

No. C63A is printed se-tenant with label. No. C63D contains one 43x67mm stamp. No. C63Cf contains one 53x42mm stamp with same size design as No. C63Bg. No. C63E contains one 43x104mm stamp with same size design as No. C63A.
No. C63E probably was not available in Chad.
Issued: No. C63B, 6/12; Nos. C63A, C63D-C63E, 4/1971; No. C63C, 11/1/71.

EXPO Emblem and Osaka Print — AP28

EXPO Emblem and: 100fr, Tower of the Sun. 125fr, Osaka print, diff.

1970, June 30   Engr.   Perf. 13

C64	AP28	50fr bl, red brn & sl grn	.70	.25
C65	AP28	100fr red, yel grn & Prus bl	1.40	.40
C66	AP28	125fr blk, dk red & bis	1.90	.60
		Nos. C64-C66 (3)	4.00	1.25

Issued to publicize EXPO '70 International Exhibition, Osaka, Japan, Mar. 15-Sept. 13.

1968 Summer Olympics, 1970 World Cup Soccer Championships, Mexico
AP28a

5fr, Flags, soccer players. 15fr, Olympic torch, soccer player.

1970, July 1   Litho.   Perf. 12½x12

C66A	AP28a	5fr multicolored	1.50

Souvenir Sheet
Perf. 13½x13

C66C	AP28a	15fr multicolored	6.50

No. C66A printed in sheets of 2 + 2 labels. No. C66C contains one 66x43mm stamp. For overprints see Nos. C88A-C88B.

Nos. C28-C30 Surcharged and Overprinted in Carmine

a

b

c

1970, July 9   Photo.   Perf. 13x12½

C67	AP13 (a)	50fr on 100fr	1.90	.25
C68	AP13 (b)	100fr on 200fr	3.25	.45
C69	AP13 (c)	125fr on 250fr	4.75	.55
		Nos. C67-C69 (3)	9.90	1.25

Space missions of Apollo 11, 12 and 13.

DC-8 "Fort Lamy" over Airport — AP29

1970, Aug. 5   Perf. 12½

C70	AP29	30fr dk sl grn & multi	1.20	.30

Souvenir Sheet

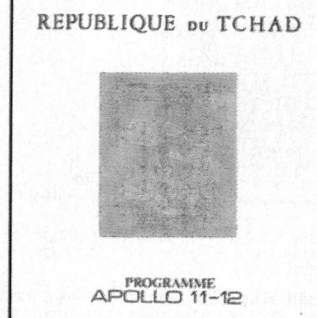

Apollo 12 — AP29a

1970, Sept.   Embossed   Perf. 12¾

C70A	AP29a	25fr gold	18.00

No. C70A exists imperf. Value, $35. No. C70A probably was not available in Chad.

The Visitation, Venetian School, 15th Century
AP30

Paintings, Venetian School: 25fr, Nativity, 15th century. 30fr, Virgin and Child, c. 1350.

1970, Dec. 15   Photo.   Perf. 12½x12

C71	AP30	20fr gold & multi	.75	.25
C72	AP30	25fr gold & multi	1.10	.25
C73	AP30	30fr gold & multi	1.25	.25
		Nos. C71-C73 (3)	3.10	.75

Christmas 1970. See Nos. C144-C147.

Post Office Mauritius and Emblem
AP31

1971, Jan. 23   Engr.   Perf. 13

C74	AP31	10fr shown	.25	.25
C75	AP31	20fr Tuscany #23	.40	.25
C76	AP31	30fr France #8	.60	.25
C77	AP31	60fr US #2	1.10	.30
C78	AP31	80fr Japan #8	1.50	.60
C79	AP31	100fr Saxony #1	1.90	.75
a.		Souvenir sheet of 6, #C74-C79	8.00	5.00
		Nos. C74-C79 (6)	5.75	2.40

Publicity for PHILEXOCAM, philatelic exhibition, Fort Lamy, Jan. 23-30.

Gamal Abdel Nasser — AP32

1971, Feb. 16   Photo.   Perf. 12½

C80	AP32	75fr multi	2.00	.50

In memory of Gamal Abdel Nasser (1918-1970), President of Egypt.

Presidents Mobutu, Bokassa and Tombalbaye — AP33

1971, Apr. 28   Photo.   Perf. 13

C81	AP33	100fr multi	2.00	.60

Return of Central African Republic to the United States of Central Africa which also includes Congo Democratic Republic and Chad.

Map of Africa, Communications Network and Symbols — AP34

1971, May 17   Engr.   Perf. 13

C82	AP34	125fr ultra, sl grn & brn red	3.00	.75

Pan-African telecommunications system.

Boys Around Campfire, Torii
AP35

1971, Aug. 24   Photo.   Perf. 12½

C83	AP35	250fr multi	1.50	.40

13th Boy Scout World Jamboree, Asagiri Plain, Japan, Aug. 2-10.

White Egret — AP36

1971, Sept. 28   Photo.   Perf. 13x12½

C84	AP36	1000fr blk, dk bl & ocher	75.00	12.50

Greek Marathon Runners — AP37

45fr, Ancient Olympic Stadium. 75fr, Greek wrestlers. 130fr, Olympic Stadium, Athens, 1896.

1971, Oct. 5   Perf. 12½

C85	AP37	40fr multi	.75	.25
C86	AP37	45fr multi	1.00	.25
C87	AP37	75fr multi	1.75	.40
C88	AP37	130fr multi	2.00	.75
		Nos. C85-C88 (4)	5.50	1.65

75th anniv. of modern Olympic Games.

Nos. C66A, C66C Ovptd. in Gold

1971   Litho.   Perf. 12½x12

C88A	AP28a	5fr multi	2.50

Souvenir Sheet
Perf. 13½x13

C88B	AP28a	15fr multi	5.50

Overprint on No. C88B is 36mm long.

Duke Ellington — AP38

50fr, Sidney Bechet. 100fr, Louis Armstrong.

1971, Oct. 20   Litho.   Perf. 13

C89	AP38	50fr multi	2.00	.50
C90	AP38	75fr lt bl & multi	3.00	.70
C91	AP38	100fr multi	5.00	.85
		Nos. C89-C91 (3)	10.00	2.05

Famous American jazz musicians.

Charles de Gaulle — AP39

Design: No. C93, Félix Eboué.

Lithographed and Embossed
1971, Nov. 9   Perf. 12½

C92	AP39	200fr grn, yel grn & gold	8.00	4.00
C93	AP39	200fr bl, lt bl & gold	8.00	4.00
a.		Souv. sheet, #C92-C93 + label	20.00	20.00

Charles de Gaulle (1890-1970), pres. of France.

African Postal Union Issue, 1971
Common Design Type

Design: 100fr, Sao antelope head and UAMPT building, Brazzaville, Congo.

1971, Nov. 13   Photo.   Perf. 13x13½

C94	CD135	100fr bl & multi	1.50	.50

Apollo 15 Rocket
AP40

80fr, Apollo 15 capsule, horiz. 150fr, Lunar module on Moon, horiz. 250fr, Astronaut making tests. 300fr, Moon-buggy. No. C100, Successful splashdown, horiz. No. C101, Apollo 15 insignia.

1972, Jan. 5   **Litho.**   **Perf. 13½**
C95   AP40   40fr multi   .50   .25
C96   AP40   80fr multi   .90   .25
C97   AP40   150fr multi   1.50   .30
C98   AP40   250fr multi   2.50   .45
C99   AP40   300fr multi   3.00   .60
C100   AP40   500fr multi   5.50   1.40
    Nos. C95-C100 (6)   13.90   3.25

Souvenir Sheet
C101   AP40   500fr multi   8.00   2.50

Apollo 15 moon landing.

Soyuz 11 Link-up — AP41

Designs: 30fr, Soyuz 11 on launching pad, vert. 50fr, No. C108, Cosmonauts in uniform. 200fr, V. I. Patsayev. No. C106, V. N. Volkov. 400fr, G. L. Dobrovolsky. No. C109, Three cosmonauts.

1972, Jan. 5   **Perf. 13½x13**
C102   AP41   30fr multi   .25   .25
C103   AP41   50fr multi   .45   .25
C104   AP41   100fr multi   .80   .25
C105   AP41   200fr multi   2.00   .50
C106   AP41   300fr multi   3.25   .75
C107   AP41   400fr multi   4.25   1.10
    Nos. C102-C107 (6)   11.00   3.10

Souvenir Sheets
C108   AP41   300fr multi   3.50   1.25
C109   AP41   400fr multi   4.00   1.50

Soyuz 11 link-up project.

Bobsledding — AP42

Design: 100fr, Slalom.

1972, Feb. 24   **Engr.**   **Perf. 13**
C110   AP42   50fr Prus bl & rose red   1.00   .30
C111   AP42   100fr red lil & slate grn   1.90   .50

11th Winter Olympic Games, Sapporo, Japan, Feb. 3-13.

Pres. Tombalbaye Type, 1972

1972, Apr. 13   **Litho.**   **Perf. 13**
C112   A63   70fr multi   .90   .30
C113   A63   80fr multi   1.10   .35

11th Winter Olympic Type, 1972

130fr, Speed skating. No. C115, Ice hockey. No. C116, Ski jumping. 250fr, 4-man bobsled.

1972, Apr. 13   **Perf. 13½**
C114   A64   130fr multi   1.40   .45
C115   A64   200fr multi   2.50   .60

Souvenir Sheets
C116   A64   200fr multi   3.50   1.25
C117   A64   250fr multi   4.50   1.50

Scout Jamboree Type, 1972

Designs: 100fr, Cooking preparation. 120fr, Lord Baden Powell. 250fr, Hiking.

1972, May 15
C118   A67   100fr multi   2.25   .40
C119   A67   120fr multi   2.40   .50

Souvenir Sheet
C120   A67   250fr multi   8.50   1.75

Zebras — AP43

African wild animals: 30fr, Mandrills. 100fr, African elephants. 130fr, Gazelles. 150fr, Hippopotamuses. 200fr, Lion cub.

1972, May 15   **Litho.**   **Perf. 13**
C121   AP43   20fr multi   .35   .25
C122   AP43   30fr multi   .50   .25
C123   AP43   100fr multi   1.40   .35
C124   AP43   130fr multi   2.25   .50
C125   AP43   150fr multi   3.50   .75
    Nos. C121-C125 (5)   8.00   2.10

Souvenir Sheet
C126   AP43   200fr multi   35.00   25.00

View of Venice, by Caffi — AP44

Paintings by Ippolito Caffi: 40fr, Sailing ship and Doge's Palace, vert. 140fr, Grand Canal, vert.

1972, May 23   **Photo.**
C127   AP44   40fr gold & multi   1.10   .25
C128   AP44   45fr gold & multi   1.90   .25
C129   AP44   140fr gold & multi   3.50   .60
    Nos. C127-C129 (3)   6.50   1.10

UNESCO campaign to save Venice.

11th Winter Olympic Winners Type, 1972

Designs: 150fr, Slalom, B. Cochran, US. 200fr, Women's figure skating, B. Schuba, Austria. 250fr, Ice hockey, USSR. 300fr, 2-man bobsled. W. Zimmerer and P. Utzschneider, West Germany.

1972, June 15   **Perf. 14½**
C130   A69   150fr gold & multi   3.00   .75
C131   A69   300fr gold & multi   3.75   1.00

Souvenir Sheets
C132   A69   250fr gold & multi   3.25   2.75
C133   A69   300fr gold & multi   3.75   3.00

Nos. C130-C131 exist se-tenant with label showing earth satellite.

Daudet, "Tartarin de Tarascon," Book Year Emblem — AP45

1972, July 22   **Engr.**   **Perf. 13**
C134   AP45   100fr dk red, lil & dk brn   2.00   .60

Intl. Book Year, 1972, and to honor Alphonse Daudet (1840-1897), French writer.

20th Summer Olympics Type, 1972

Designs (TV Tower, Munich and): 100fr, Gymnast. 120fr, Pole vault. 150fr, Fencing. 250fr, Hammer throw. 300fr, Boxing.

1972, Aug. 15   **Perf. 14½**
C135   AP70   100fr gold & multi   2.10   .50
C136   AP70   120fr gold & multi   2.50   .60
C137   AP70   150fr gold & multi   3.25   .80
    Nos. C135-C137 (3)   7.85   1.90

Souvenir Sheets
C138   A70   250fr gold & multi   3.50   2.75
C139   A70   300fr gold & multi   4.00   3.00

Nos. C135-C137 exist se-tenant with label showing arms of Munich.

Lunokhod on Moon — AP46

Russian moon missions: 100fr, Luna 16 on moon and rocket in flight, vert.

1972, Sept. 19   **Perf. 13**
C140   AP46   100fr dk bl, pur & bis   1.90   .50
C141   AP46   150fr slate, brn & lil   2.50   .75

Farcha Laboratory, Cattle, Scientist — AP47

1972, Nov. 11   **Photo.**   **Perf. 13**
C142   AP47   75fr yellow & multi   1.40   .30

20th anniversary of the Farcha Laboratory for veterinary research.

King Faisal and Holy Kaaba, Mecca — AP48

1972, Nov. 17
C143   AP48   75fr multi   1.40   .40

Visit of King Faisal of Saudi Arabia.

Christmas Type of 1970

Christmas: 40fr, Virgin and Child, by Giovanni Bellini. 75fr, Virgin and Child, by Dall'Occhio. 80fr, Nativity, by Fra Angelico, horiz. 95fr, Adoration of the Kings, by Il Perugino.

1972, Dec. 15   **Photo.**   **Perf. 13**
C144   AP30   40fr gold & multi   .25   .25
C145   AP30   75fr gold & multi   1.75   .30
C146   AP30   80fr gold & multi   2.00   .40
C147   AP30   95fr gold & multi   2.00   .50
    Nos. C144-C147 (4)   6.00   1.45

Summer Olympic Winners Type, 1972

Olympic Emblems and: 150fr, Pole vault, Nordwig, East Germany. 250fr, Hurdles, Milburn, US. 300fr, Javelin, Wolfermann, West Germany.

1972, Dec. 22   **Perf. 11**
C148   A76   150fr multi   3.00   .60
C149   A76   250fr multi   4.25   .75

Souvenir Sheet
C150   A76   300fr multi   15.00   3.00

Summer Olympic Winners Type, 1972

Olympic Emblem and: 150fr, Dressage, Mancinelli, Italy. No. C152, Finn class sailing, Serge Maury, France. No. C153, Swimming, Mark Spitz.

1972, Dec. 22   **Litho.**   **Perf. 11**
C151   A77   150fr gold & multi   3.25   .75
C152   A77   250fr gold & multi   5.00   1.00

Souvenir Sheet
C153   A77   250fr multi   15.00   3.00

Copernicus and Solar System — AP49

1973, Mar. 31   **Engr.**   **Perf. 13**
C154   AP49   250fr gray, mag & brn   5.25   1.25

500th anniversary of the birth of Nicolaus Copernicus (1473-1543), Polish astronomer.

Horses — AP49a

Details from paintings: 20fr, A Horse Frightened by Lightning, by Theodore Gericault. 60fr, The White Horse, by Paul Potter. 100fr, Mares and Foals, by George Stubbs. 150fr, Horse Head, by Theodore Gericault, vert. 500fr, The Carriage, by Vernet.

1973   **Litho.**   **Perf. 11½**
C154A   AP49a   20fr multi
C154B   AP49a   60fr multi
C154C   AP49a   100fr multi
C154D   AP49a   150fr multi
    Nos. C154A-C154D (4)   14.00

Souvenir Sheet
Perf. 15
C154E   AP49a   500fr multi   15.00

See note before No. 225A.

Airplanes — AP49b

5fr, Fokker F VII/3M. 25fr, DH 89A Rapide. 70fr, Viscount. 150fr, Boeing 747. 200fr, Concorde.
350fr, Concorde, diff.

1973   **Litho.**   **Perf. 12**
C154F   AP49b   5fr multi
C154G   AP49b   25fr multi
C154H   AP49b   70fr multi
C154J   AP49b   150fr multi
C154K   AP49b   200fr multi
    Nos. C154F-C154K (5)   14.00

Souvenir Sheet
Perf. 12
C154L   AP49b   350fr multi   14.00

Nos. C154L contains one 60x40mm stamp. See note before No. 225A.

Skylab over Africa — AP50

1974, Aug. 6   **Engr.**   **Perf. 13**
C155   AP50   100fr shown   1.50   .25
C156   AP50   150fr Skylab   2.50   .60

Exploits of Skylab, US manned space station.

Soccer — AP51

125fr, 150fr, Soccer players; 125fr, vert.

1974, Oct. 22   Engr.   Perf. 13
C157 AP51 50fr dl red & choc   .75   .25
C158 AP51 125fr red & dp grn   1.75   .50
C159 AP51 150fr grn & rose red   2.50   .75
    Nos. C157-C159 (3)   5.00 1.50

World Cup Soccer Championship, Munich, June 13-July 7.

Family and WPY Emblem — AP52

1974, Nov. 11
C160 AP52 250fr multi   4.00 1.25
World Population Year.

Mail Delivery by Canoe — AP53

UPU Cent.: 40fr, Diesel train. 100fr, Jet. 150fr, Spacecraft.

1974, Dec. 20   Engr.   Perf. 13
C161 AP53 30fr car & multi   .60   .25
C162 AP53 40fr ultra & blk   1.00   .25
C163 AP53 100fr brn, ultra & blk 1.90   .40
C164 AP53 150fr grn, lil & ol   2.40   .55
    Nos. C161-C164 (4)   5.90 1.45

Women of Different Races, IWY Emblem — AP54

1975, June 25   Photo.   Perf. 13
C165 AP54 250fr bl & multi   4.50 1.25
International Women's Year 1975.

Apollo and Soyuz Before Link-up — AP55

130fr, Apollo and Soyuz after link-up.

1975, July 15   Engr.   Perf. 13
C166 AP55 100fr ultra, choc & grn   1.50   .40
C167 AP55 130fr vio bl, brn & grn   2.00   .50

Apollo Soyuz space test project (Russo-American space cooperation), launching 7/15; link-up 7/17.
    For overprints see Nos. C171-C172.

Soccer Player, View of Montreal — AP56

Olympic Rings, Montreal Skyline: 100fr, Discus thrower. 125fr, Runner.

1975, Oct. 14   Engr.   Perf. 13
C168 AP56 75fr car & slate grn 1.00   .25
C169 AP56 100fr car, choc & bl grn 1.40   .40
C170 AP56 125fr brn, bl & car   1.90   .75
    Nos. C168-C170 (3)   4.30 1.40
    Pre-Olympic Year 1975.

**Nos. C166-C167 Overprinted:
"JONCTION / 17 JUILLET 1975"**

1975, Nov. 4   Engr.   Perf. 13
C171 AP55 100fr multi   1.75   .25
C172 AP55 130fr multi   2.10   .35

Apollo-Soyuz link-up in space, July 17.

Stylized British and American Flags, "200" — AP57

1975, Dec. 5   Engr.   Perf. 13
C173 AP57 150fr vio bl, car & ol bis   2.25   .75

American Bicentennial.

Adoration of the Shepherds, by Murillo — AP58

Christmas (Paintings): 75fr, Adoration of the Shepherds, by Georges de La Tour. 80fr, Virgin and Child with Bible, by Rogier van der Weyden, vert. 100fr, Holy Family, by Raphael, vert.

1975, Dec. 15   Litho.   Perf. 13x12½
C174 AP58 40fr yel & multi   .75   .25
C175 AP58 75fr yel & multi   1.25   .35
C176 AP58 80fr yel & multi   1.75   .40
C177 AP58 100fr yel & multi   2.75   .75
    Nos. C174-C177 (4)   6.50 1.75

12th Winter Olympic Winners Type, 1976

250fr, 4-man bobsled, West Germany. 300fr, Speed skating, J. E. Storholt, Norway. 500fr, Downhill skiing, F. Klammer, Austria.

1976, June 21   Perf. 14
C178 A84 250fr multi   2.75   .60
C179 A84 300fr multi   3.50 1.00

Souvenir Sheet

C180 A84 500fr multi   6.00 3.00

Paul Revere's Ride and Portrait by Copley — AP59

American Bicentennial: 125fr, Washington crossing Delaware. 150fr, Lafayette offering his services to America. 200fr, Rochambeau at Yorktown with Washington. 250fr, Franklin presenting Declaration of Independence. 400fr, Count de Grasse's victory at Cape Charles.

1976, July 4   Litho.   Perf. 14
C181 AP59 100fr multi   1.10   .30
C182 AP59 125fr multi   1.25   .35
C183 AP59 150fr multi   1.90   .40
C184 AP59 200fr multi   2.25   .50
C185 AP59 250fr multi   3.00   .55
    Nos. C181-C185 (5) 9.50 2.10

Souvenir Sheet

C186 AP59 400fr multi   6.00 3.00

Summer Olympics Type, 1976

1976, July 12   Perf. 13½
C187 A85 100fr Boxing   1.50   .30
C188 A85 200fr Pole vault 2.50   .50
C189 A85 300fr Shot put   4.00   .65
    Nos. C187-C189 (3)   8.00 1.45

Souvenir Sheet

C190 A85 500fr Sprint   6.00 3.00

Viking Mars Project Type, 1976

Mars Lander and: 100fr, Viking landing on Mars. 200fr, Capsule over Mars. 250fr, Lander over Mars. 450fr, Lander and probe.

1976, July 23   Litho.   Perf. 14
C191 A86 100fr multi   1.10   .30
C192 A86 200fr multi   2.25   .55
C193 A86 250fr multi   2.50   .75
    Nos. C191-C193 (3) 5.85 1.60

Souvenir Sheet

C194 A86 450fr multi   7.50 3.00
For overprints see Nos. C240-C243.

Concorde — AP60

1976, Oct. 15   Litho.   Perf. 12½
C195 AP60 250fr bl, blk & ver   6.00 1.75

First commercial flight of supersonic jet Concorde, Jan. 21.

Nobel Prize Type, 1976

100fr, Albert Einstein, physics. 200fr, Dag Hammarskjold, peace. 300fr, Shinichiro Tomanaga, physics. 500fr, Alexander Fleming, medicine.

1976, Dec. 15   Perf. 14
C196 A87 100fr multi   1.50   .30
C197 A87 200fr multi   2.50   .55
C198 A87 300fr multi   3.50   .70
    Nos. C196-C198 (3) 7.50 1.55

Souvenir Sheet

C199 A87 500fr multi   8.00 3.50

Adoration of the Shepherds, by Gerard van Honthorst — AP61

Christmas (Paintings): 30fr, Nativity, by Albrecht Altdorfer, vert. 60fr, Nativity, by Hans Holbein, vert. 150fr, Adoration of the Kings, by Gerard David.

1976, Dec. 22   Litho.   Perf. 12½
C200 AP61 30fr gold & multi   .50   .25
C201 AP61 60fr gold & multi   .75   .25
C202 AP61 120fr gold & blk   1.50   .50
C203 AP61 150fr gold & blk   2.25   .75
    Nos. C200-C203 (4)   5.00 1.75

Lesdiguières Bridge, by Jongkind — AP62

Design: 120fr, Sailing Ship and Boats, by Johan Barthold Jongkind (1819-1891).

1976, Dec. 27   Photo.   Perf. 13
C204 AP62 100fr multi   1.75   .55
C205 AP62 120fr multi   2.25   .60

Centenary of impressionism.

Zeppelin Type of 1977

125fr, Germany #C40, North Pole. 150fr, Germany #C45, Chicago department store. 175fr, Germany #C38 and scenes of NYC and London. 200fr, 500fr, US #C15, NYC.

1977, Mar. 30   Perf. 11
C206 A91 125fr multi   1.90   .35
C207 A91 150fr multi   2.25   .40
C208 A91 175fr multi   2.75   .50
C209 A91 200fr multi   3.25   .60
    Nos. C206-C209 (4) 10.15 1.85

Souvenir Sheet

C210 A91 500fr multi   8.00 3.00

Sassenage Castle, Grenoble — AP63

1977, May 21   Litho.   Perf. 12½
C211 AP63 100fr multi   1.00   .30

Intl. French Language Council, 10th Anniv.

Lafayette and Ships — AP64

American Bicentennial: 120fr, Abraham Lincoln, eagle and flags, vert. 150fr, James Madison and family.

1977, July 30   Engr.   Perf. 13
C212 AP64 100fr multi   1.40   .35
C213 AP64 120fr multi   1.75   .40
C214 AP64 150fr multi   2.25   .50
    Nos. C212-C214 (3) 5.40 1.25

Lindbergh and Spirit of St. Louis — AP65

100fr, Concorde. 150fr, 200fr, 300fr, Various Lindbergh portraits & Spirit of St. Louis.

1977, Sept. 27

C215	AP65	100fr multi	1.25	.30
C216	AP65	120fr multi	1.25	.40
C217	AP65	150fr multi	1.40	.55
C218	AP65	200fr multi	2.25	.65
C219	AP65	300fr multi	3.00	.90
	Nos. C215-C219 (5)		9.15	2.80

Charles A. Lindbergh's solo transatlantic flight from NY to Paris, 50th anniv., and 1st supersonic transatlantic flight of Concorde.
For overprint see No. C227.

Mariner 10 — AP66

Spacecraft: 200fr, Lunokhod on moon, Luna 21. 300fr, Viking on Mars.

1977, Oct. 10   Engr.   Perf. 13

C220	AP66	100fr multi	1.25	.40
C221	AP66	200fr multi	2.00	.70
C222	AP66	300fr multi	2.75	.90
	Nos. C220-C222 (3)		6.00	2.00

Running — AP67

1977, Oct. 24   Engr.   Perf. 13

C223	AP67	30fr shown	.40	.25
C224	AP67	60fr Volleyball	.85	.25
C225	AP67	120fr Soccer	1.50	.45
C226	AP67	125fr Basketball	1.25	.50
	Nos. C223-C226 (4)		4.00	1.45

No. C215 Overprinted: "PARIS NEW-YORK / 22.11.77"

1977, Nov. 22

C227	AP65	100fr multi	3.25	.25

Concorde, 1st commercial flight Paris-NYC.

Virgin and Child, by Rubens AP68

Rubens Paintings: 60fr, Virgin and Child and Two Donors. 100fr, Adoration of the Shepherds. 125fr, Adoration of the Kings.

1977, Dec. 20   Litho.   Perf. 12½x12

C228	AP68	30fr multi	.75	.25
C229	AP68	60fr multi	1.10	.40
C230	AP68	100fr multi	1.50	.40
C231	AP68	125fr multi	1.90	.60
	Nos. C228-C231 (4)		5.25	1.55

Christmas 1977.

Antoine de Saint-Exupéry — AP69

50fr, Wilbur & Orville Wright & Flyer. 80fr, Hugo Junkers & his plane. 100fr, Gen. Italo Balbo & his plane. 120fr, Concorde. 500fr, Wilbur & Orville Wright & Flyer.

1978, Oct. 25   Litho.   Perf. 13½

C232	AP69	40fr multi	.60	.25
C233	AP69	60fr multi	.75	.25
C234	AP69	80fr multi	1.10	.30
C235	AP69	100fr multi	1.50	.40
C236	AP69	120fr multi	1.75	.50
	Nos. C232-C236 (5)		5.70	1.70

Souvenir Sheet

C237	AP69	500fr multi	6.75	2.00

History of aviation and 75th anniversary of 1st powered flight.

Philexafrique II-Essen Issue
Common Design Types

No. C238, Rhinoceros & Chad #C6. No. C239, Kingfisher & Mecklenburg-Strelitz #1.

1978, Nov. 1   Perf. 12½

C238	CD138	100fr multi	3.00	1.00
C239	CD139	100fr multi	3.00	1.00
a.	Pair, #C238-C239 + label		8.00	4.00

Nos. C191-C194 Overprinted "ALUNISSAGE/APOLLO XI/ JUILLET 1969"

1979, Nov. 26   Litho.   Perf. 13½x14

C240	A86	100fr multi	1.10	.35
C241	A86	200fr multi	2.25	.65
C242	A86	250fr multi	2.50	1.00
	Nos. C240-C242 (3)		5.85	2.00

Souvenir Sheet

C243	A86	450fr multi	5.50	4.50

Apollo 11 moon landing, 10th anniversary.

Hurdles, Moscow '80 Emblem — AP70

Emblem and: 30fr, Field hockey. 250fr, Swimming. 350fr, Running. 500fr, Yachting.

1979, Nov. 30   Perf. 13½

C244	AP70	15fr multi	.25	.25
C245	AP70	30fr multi	.30	.25
C246	AP70	250fr multi	1.90	.60
C247	AP70	350fr multi	3.00	1.10
	Nos. C244-C247 (4)		5.45	2.20

Souvenir Sheet

C248	AP70	500fr multi	5.75	3.00

Pre-Olympic Year.
For overprints see Nos. C254-C255.

Austria Jubilee Issue of 1910, Canoe, Hill — AP71

Hill, Stamps & Vessels: 100fr, US design A97, dhow. 200fr, France #21, Sidewheeler. 300fr, Holstein #16, ocean liner. 500fr, Chad #J13, ocean liner.

1979, Dec. 3   Perf. 14x13½

C249	AP71	65fr multi	.60	.25
C250	AP71	100fr multi	1.40	.25
C251	AP71	200fr multi	2.25	.45
C252	AP71	300fr multi	2.75	.70
	Nos. C249-C252 (4)		7.00	1.65

Souvenir Sheet

C253	AP71	500fr multi	5.75	3.00

Sir Rowland Hill (1795-1879), originator of penny postage.
For overprints see Nos. C256-C257.

Nos. C244-C245, C249-C250 Overprinted: "POSTES 1981" in Red or Overprinted and Surcharged Silver on Red
Perf. 13½, 14x13½

1981, Nov. 15   Litho.

C254	AP70	30fr on 15fr multi	1.25	.40
C255	AP70	30fr multi	1.25	.40
C256	AP71	60fr on 65fr multi	2.25	.70
C257	AP71	60fr on 100fr multi	2.25	.70
	Nos. C254-C257 (4)		7.00	2.20

Soccer Type of 1982 and

1982 World Cup Soccer Championships, Spain — AP71a

80fr, Brazil. 300fr, W. Germany.
No. C259C, Soccer players, ball, & trophy, vert.

1982   Litho.   Perf. 13½

C258	A108	80fr multi	1.00	.25
C259	A108	300fr multi	3.00	.50

Souvenir Sheet

C259A	A108	500fr like 300fr	6.00	2.00

Litho. & Embossed

C259B	AP71a	1500fr shown	16.00	

Souvenir Sheet

C259C	AP71a	1500fr gold & multi	14.00	

No. C259A contains one 42x51mm stamp.
No. C259B exists in a souvenir sheet of 1. Value $42.50.
For surcharge see No. C305.

Diana Type of 1982 and

Princess Diana, 21st Birthday — AP71b

Design: No. C262A, Portrait, horiz.

1982, July 2   Litho.   Perf. 13½

C260	A109	80fr 1977	1.00	.25
C261	A109	300fr 1980	3.00	.95

Souvenir Sheet

C262	A109	500fr 1981	5.50	2.00

Litho. & Embossed

C262A	AP71b	1500fr gold & multi	16.00	

Souvenir Sheet

C262B	AP71b	1500fr gold & multi	16.00	

No. C262A exists in a souvenir sheet of 1. Value $42.50.
For overprints see Nos. 419A-419B.

Manned Flight Bicentenary AP72

Balloons: 100fr, Charles' & Roberts', 1783. 200fr, J.P. Blanchard, Berlin, 1788. 300fr, Charles Green, London, 1837. 400fr, Modern blimp. 500fr, Montgolfiere, 1783.

1983, Apr.   Litho.   Perf. 13

C263	AP72	100fr multi, vert.	1.25	.25
C264	AP72	200fr multi, vert.	2.50	.40
C265	AP72	300fr multi, vert.	3.50	.60
C266	AP72	400fr multi, vert.	4.75	.75
	Nos. C263-C266 (4)		12.00	2.00

Souvenir Sheet

C267	AP72	500fr multi, vert.	5.75	2.50

Balloon Type and

First Balloon Ascension, Bicent. — AP72a

80fr, Steam Powered Airship, H. Giffard. 250fr, Graf Zeppelin; Airship L-1, 1st flight. 300fr, 1st Balloon Flight, Montgolfier & Rozier. No. C270A, Airship Hindenburg, Count Ferdinand von Zeppelin. No. C270B, Jean-Francois Pilatre de Rozier & Marquis d'Arlandes, 1st balloon ascension.

1983, May 30   Litho.   Perf. 13½

C268	A116	80fr multi	1.00	.25
C269	A116	250fr multi	3.00	.40

Souvenir Sheet

C270	A116	300fr multi	3.75	2.50

Litho. & Embossed
Perf. 13½

C270A	AP72a	1500fr gold & multi	16.00	

Souvenir Sheet

C270B	AP72a	1500fr gold & multi	12.00	

No. C270A exists in a souvenir sheet of 1. Value $25.
For surcharge see No. C299.

1984 Summer Olympics — AP73

Various kayak scenes.

1984, Mar. 1 Litho. *Perf.* 13
C271 AP73 100fr multi 1.00 .25
C272 AP73 200fr multi 2.00 .25
C273 AP73 300fr multi 3.00 .50
C274 AP73 400fr multi 4.00 .60
  Nos. C271-C274 (4) 10.00 1.60

Souvenir Sheet

C275 AP73 500fr multi 5.00 3.50

Natl. Goals
AP73a

Nos. C276, C278, Peace & reconciliation. Nos. C277, C279, Self-sufficiency in food production.

1983, Dec. 26 Litho. *Perf.* 13½
C276 AP73a 150fr multi 1.50 .40
C277 AP73a 150fr multi 1.50 .40
C278 AP73a 200fr multi 2.25 .55
C279 AP73a 200fr multi 2.25 .55
  Nos. C276-C279 (4) 7.50 1.90

For surcharges see Nos. C300-C301.

Souvenir Sheet

Paul P. Harris (1868-1947), Founder of Rotary Intl. — AP73b

Litho. & Embossed

1984, Jan. 16 *Perf.* 13½
C279B AP73b 1500fr gold & multi 12.00

IYY, PHILEXAFRICA '85 — AP74

No. C280, Boy scout, tree. No. C281, Air Chad Fokker 27.

1985, May 2 Litho. *Perf.* 13
C280 AP74 200fr multicolored 3.00 1.50
C281 AP74 200fr multicolored 3.00 1.50
  a. Pair, #C280-C281 + label 6.75 5.00

IYY, PHILEXAFRICA Type of 1985

No. C283, Girl, Scout ceremony. No. C284, Communications and transportation.

1985, Nov. 1 Litho. *Perf.* 13x12½
C283 AP74 250fr multicolored 3.00 1.50
C284 AP74 250fr multicolored 3.00 1.50
  a. Pair, #C283-C284 + label 6.75 5.00

ASCENA Airlines, 25th Anniv. — AP75

1985, Aug. 25 *Perf.* 12½
C285 AP75 70fr bl & multi .60 .25
C286 AP75 110fr org & multi 1.00 .25
C287 AP75 250fr yel & multi 2.25 .80
  Nos. C285-C287 (3) 3.85 1.30

Victor Hugo (1802-1885), French Novelist — AP76

Scene from Les Miserables.

1985, Nov. 24 Engr. *Perf.* 13
C288 AP76 70fr org brn, chlky bl & dp brn .75 .25
C289 AP76 110fr lake, dk brn & dk grn 1.00 .30
C290 AP76 250fr brt org, blk & dk red 2.50 .80
C291 AP76 300fr dk red, cl & sl bl 2.75 .90
  Nos. C288-C291 (4) 7.00 2.25

Adoration of the Magi — AP77

1985, Dec. 22 Litho. *Perf.* 13½
C292 250fr multicolored 2.25 .60

Christmas 1985.

1988 Summer Olympics, Seoul — AP78

100fr, 400-Meter hurdles, vert. 170fr, 5000-Meter race. 200fr, Long jump. 600fr, Triple jump, vert.
750fr, 10,000-Meter race, vert.

1988, June 1 Litho. *Perf.* 13
C293 AP78 100fr multi 1.10 .30
C294 AP78 170fr multi 1.75 .55
C295 AP78 200fr multi 2.25 .65
C296 AP78 600fr multi 5.75 2.00
  Nos. C293-C296 (4) 10.85 3.50

Souvenir Sheet

C297 AP78 750fr multi 8.00 6.00

Stamps of 1982-84 Surcharged

1989 *Perfs. as Before*
C298 A115 100 on 300fr #446
C299 A116 100 on 250fr #C269
C300 AP73a 100 on 200fr #C278
C301 AP73a 100 on 200fr #C279
C302 A110 170 on 300fr #404
C303 A122 170 on 200fr #503
C304 A123 170 on 250fr #509
C305 A108 170 on 300fr #C259
C306 A112 240 on 300fr #425

AIR POST SEMI-POSTAL STAMPS

Catalogue values for unused stamps in this section are for Never Hinged items.

Ramses II Battling the Hittites (from Abu Simbel) — SPAP1

Unwmk.

1964, Mar. 9 Engr. *Perf.* 13
CB1 SPAP1 10fr + 5fr multi .75 .25
CB2 SPAP1 25fr + 5fr multi 1.40 .40
CB3 SPAP1 50fr + 5fr multi 2.75 .75
  Nos. CB1-CB3 (3) 4.90 1.40

UNESCO world campaign to save historic monuments in Nubia.

Lions Emblem
SPAP2

1967, July 5 Photo. *Perf.* 13
CB4 SPAP2 50fr + 10fr multi 2.00 .25

50th anniv. of Lions Intl. and to publicize the Lions work for the blind.

POSTAGE DUE STAMPS

Postage Due Stamps of France Overprinted

1928 Unwmk. *Perf.* 14x13½
J1 D2 5c light blue .80 1.20
J2 D2 10c gray brown .80 1.20
J3 D2 20c olive green .80 1.20
J4 D2 25c bright rose 1.20 1.60
J5 D2 30c light red 1.20 1.60
J6 D2 45c blue green 1.60 2.00
J7 D2 50c brown violet 2.40 2.40
J8 D2 60c yellow brown 2.40 2.40
J9 D2 1fr red brown 2.40 2.75
J10 D2 2fr orange red 5.50 6.00
J11 D2 3fr bright violet 4.75 5.50
  Nos. J1-J11 (11) 23.85 27.85

Huts — D3

Canoe — D4

1930 Typo. *Perf.* 14x13½, 13½x14
J12 D3 5c dp bl & olive .40 .80
J13 D3 10c dk red & brn .40 .80
J14 D3 20c grn & brn 1.20 1.60
J15 D3 25c lt bl & brn 1.20 2.40
J16 D3 30c bis brn & Prus bl 1.60 2.00
J17 D3 45c Prus bl & olive 2.40 2.75
J18 D3 50c red vio & brn 2.40 4.00
J19 D3 60c gray lil & bl blk 3.25 4.75
J20 D4 1fr bis brn & bl blk 3.25 4.75

J21 D4 2fr vio & brn 8.00 8.00
J22 D4 3fr dp red & brn 35.00 40.00
  Nos. J12-J22 (11) 59.10 71.85

In 1934 stamps of Chad were superseded by those of French Equatorial Africa.

Catalogue values for unused stamps in this section, from this point to the end of the section, are for Never Hinged items.

Republic

Rhinoceros — D5

Tibesti Pictographs: #J24, Kudu. #J25, 2 antelopes. #J26, 3 antelopes. #J27, Ostrich. #J28, Horned bull. #J29, Bull. #J30, Wild swine. #J31, Elephant. #J32, Rhinoceros. #J33, Warrior with spear and shield. #J34, Masked archer.

Unwmk.

1962, Apr. 20 Engr. *Perf.* 13
J23 D5 50c olive bister .30 .25
J24 D5 50c brown red .30 .25
  a. Pair, #J23-J24 .55
J25 D5 1fr blue .40 .25
J26 D5 1fr green .40 .25
  a. Pair, #J25-J26 .75
J27 D5 2fr vermilion .50 .25
J28 D5 2fr maroon .50 .25
  a. Pair, #J27-J28 1.00
J29 D5 5fr slate green .75 .40
J30 D5 5fr violet blue .75 .40
  a. Pair, #J29-J30 1.50
J31 D5 10fr brown 1.40 .75
J32 D5 10fr orange brown 1.40 .75
  a. Pair, #J31-J32 2.75
J33 D5 25fr carmine rose 3.25 1.75
J34 D5 25fr violet 3.25 1.75
  a. Pair, #J33-J34 6.50
  Nos. J23-J34 (12) 13.20 7.30

Dolls — D6

1969, Sept. 19 Engr. *Perf.* 14x13
J35 D6 1fr Kanem .25 .25
J36 D6 2fr Kotoko .25 .25
J37 D6 5fr Leather .40 .25
J38 D6 10fr Kotoko .50 .25
J39 D6 25fr Guera .60 .25
  Nos. J35-J39 (5) 2.00 1.25

MILITARY STAMPS

Catalogue values for unused stamps in this section are for Never Hinged items.

No. 78 Overprinted "F.M."
1965 Typo. *Perf.* 14x13½
M1 A5 20fr red & black 300.00 300.00

Flag Bearer and Map of Chad — M1

1968 Unwmk. Litho. *Perf.* 13x12½
M2 M1 tan & multi 2.00 5.00

1st Regiment
Emblem — M2

1972, Jan. 21   Photo.   Perf. 13
M3   M2   blue & multi   1.00 2.00

OFFICIAL STAMPS

Catalogue values for unused stamps in this section are for Never Hinged items.

Flag and Map of Chad — O1

Perf. 13½x14
1966-71   Typo.   Unwmk.
Flag in blue, yellow and carmine

O1	O1	1fr light blue	.25	.25
O2	O1	2fr gray	.25	.25
O3	O1	5fr black	.25	.25
O4	O1	10fr violet blue	.25	.25
O5	O1	25fr orange	.30	.25
O6	O1	30fr bright green	.50	.25
O7	O1	40fr carmine ('71)	.75	.25
O8	O1	50fr red lilac	.75	.25
O9	O1	85fr green	1.10	.30
O10	O1	100fr brown	1.75	.35
O11	O1	200fr red	3.00	.50
		Nos. O1-O11 (11)	9.15	3.15

**Flag and Map Type of 1966-71
Redrawn with "N'Djamena" as
Capital on Map**
Perf. 13½x13¼, 11¾ (100fr)
1993-2000 ?   Litho.
**Center Flag Stripe in Yellow
Frame Color**

O13	O1	100fr brown	—	—
O14	O1	200fr red	—	—

Nos. O13 and O14 have a large "F" in denomination, "POSTES" without serifs, and has printer's inscription of "COURVOISIER."

**Center Flag Stripe in Orange
Frame Color**

O17	O1	50fr green	—	—
O18	O1	85fr orange	—	—
O19	O1	100fr red orange	—	—
O20	O1	150fr blue green	—	—
O21	O1	200fr green	—	—
O22	O1	250fr lilac	—	—
O23	O1	300fr blue	—	—
O24	O1	500fr red	—	—
O25	O1	1000fr dark green	—	—

Additional stamps may have been issued in this set. The editors would like to examine any examples. Numbers may change.

CHILE

'chi-lē

LOCATION — Southwest corner of South America
GOVT. — Republic
AREA — 284,520 sq. mi.
POP. — 14,973,843 (1999 est.)
CAPITAL — Santiago

100 Centavos = 1 Peso
1000 Milésimos = 100 Centésimos = 1 Escudo (1960)
100 Centavos = 1 Peso (1975)

Catalogue values for unused stamps in this country are for Never Hinged items, beginning with Scott 257 in the regular postage section, Scott B3 in the semipostal section, Scott C125 in the airpost section, and Scott CB1 in the airpost semi-postal section.

Issues of the Republic

Unused values for Nos. 1-14 are for stamps without gum. Examples with original gum are very scarce and are worth considerably more.

Pen cancellations are common on the 1862-67 issues. Such stamps sell for much less than the quoted values which are for those with handstamped postal cancellations.

Watermarks

| a | b | c | d |
| e | f | g |

Wmk. 215 — Small Star in Shield, Multiple

Christopher Columbus — A1

London Prints

1853   Wmk. b   Engr.   Imperf.
Blued Paper

1	A1	5c brown red	650.00	150.00
a.		White paper		250.00

Wmk. e
White Paper

2	A1	10c dp brt bl	1,000.	175.00
a.		Blued paper		225.00
b.		Diag. half used as 5c on cover		800.00
c.		Horiz. half used as 5c on cover		800.00
d.		Vert. half used as 5c on cover		800.00

1867   Unwmk.   Perf. 12

15	A2	1c orange	70.00	15.00
		Pen cancellation		1.25
16	A2	2c black	80.00	30.00
		Pen cancellation		2.00
17	A2	5c red	60.00	4.00
		Pen cancellation		.40
18	A2	10c blue	80.00	6.00
		Pen cancellation		1.25

Santiago Prints
Impressions Fine and Clear

1854   Wmk. b and e
White Paper

3	A1	5c pale red brn	600.00	67.50
a.		5c deep red brown	650.00	67.50
b.		5c chestnut	1,000.	200.00
e.		Double impression		275.00
4	A1	5c burnt sienna	1,800.	300.00
a.		5c dull chocolate	3,500.	2,000.
5	A1	10c deep blue	1,200.	275.00
a.		10c slate blue		275.00
b.		10c greenish blue		475.00
d.		Diag. half used as 5c on cover		450.00
e.		Horiz. half used as 5c on cover		450.00
f.		Vert. half used as 5c on cover		450.00
6	A1	10c lt dl bl	800.00	150.00
a.		10c pale blue		190.00
b.		Diag. half used as 5c on cover		425.00
c.		Horiz. half used as 5c on cover		425.00
d.		Vert. half used as 5c on cover		425.00

Litho.

7	A1	5c pale brown	1,200.	300.00

London Print

1855   Blued Paper   Wmk. c   Engr.

8	A1	5c brown red	220.00	16.00
		Fiscal cancellation		2.75

Santiago Prints
Impressions Worn and Blurred

1856-62   Wmk. b and e
White Paper

9	A1	5c rose red ('58)	60.00	8.00
		Fiscal cancellation		1.40
a.		5c carmine ('62)	90.00	20.00
b.		5c orange red ('61)	225.00	100.00
c.		5c dull redsh brn ('57)	250.00	27.50
f.		Printed on both sides	450.00	250.00
g.		Double impression	450.00	140.00
10	A1	10c sky blue ('57)	160.00	40.00
		Fiscal cancellation		1.40
a.		10c deep blue	160.00	40.00
b.		10c light blue ('59)	160.00	40.00
c.		10c indigo blue ('60)	175.00	50.00
k.		Printed on both sides		350.00
n.		As "j," half used as 5c on cover		165.00
o.		Any shade, horiz. half used as 5c on cover		200.00
p.		Any shade, vert. half used as 5c on cover		200.00

London Prints

1862   Wmk. a, f and g

11	A1	1c lemon yellow	67.50	40.00
		Fiscal cancellation		1.50
a.		Double impression, one inverted		200.00
12	A1	10c bright blue	40.00	15.00
		Fiscally used		1.50
a.		10c deep blue	32.50	21.00
b.		Blued paper	—	17.50
c.		Wmkd. "20" (error)	5,000.	5,200.
d.		Diag. half used as 5c on cover		110.00
e.		Horiz. half used as 5c on cover		125.00
f.		Vert. half used as 5c on cover		125.00
13	A1	20c green	160.00	67.50
		Fiscally used		6.75
		Nos. 11-13 (3)	267.50	122.50

No. 11a is only known fiscally used.

Santiago Print

1865   Wmk. d

14	A1	5c rose red	80.00	20.00
		Fiscally used		1.50
a.		5c carmine red	80.00	20.00
b.		Printed on both sides	375.00	200.00
c.		Laid paper		90.00
d.		Double impression, entire stamp	825.00	160.00

The 5c rose red (shades) on unwatermaked paper, either wove or ribbed, and on paper watermarked Chilean arms in the sheet are reprints made about 1870.

No. 13 has been reprinted in the color of issue and in fancy colors, both from the original engraved plate and from lithographic transfers. The reprints are on paper without watermark or with watermark CHILE and Star.

A2

A3

1877   Rouletted

20	A3	1c gray	10.00	3.00
		Pen cancellation		.60
21	A3	2c orange	30.00	3.00
		Pen cancellation		.60
22	A3	5c dull lake	24.00	2.00
		Pen cancellation		.40
23	A3	10c blue	18.00	2.75
a.		Diagonal half used as 5c on cover		—
24	A3	20c green	20.00	4.50
		Nos. 20-24 (5)	102.00	15.25

The panel inscribed "CENTAVO" is straight on No. 22.

A4

A5

Columbus — A6

1878-99   Rouletted

25	A4	1c green ('81)	1.00	.25
26	A4	2c rose ('81)	1.00	.25
27	A5	5c dull lake ('78)	7.25	.90
28	A5	5c ultra ('83)	1.90	.50
29	A5	10c orange ('85)	2.75	.35
a.		10c yellow	9.00	1.90
30	A5	15c dk grn ('92)	3.00	.55
31	A5	20c gray ('86)	3.00	.55
32	A5	25c org brn ('92)	3.00	.55
33	A5	30c rose car ('99)	7.25	3.75
34	A5	50c lilac ('78)	45.00	27.50
35	A5	50c violet ('85)	3.00	2.00
36	A6	1p dk brn & blk ('92)	19.00	2.75
a.		Imperf. horiz. or vert., pair	75.00	
		Nos. 25-36 (12)	97.15	39.90

For surcharge and overprint see Nos. 50, O16.

Columbus — A7

1894   Re-engraved

37	A7	1c blue green	.90	.25
38	A7	2c carmine lake	.90	.25

In type A4 there is a small colorless ornament at each side of the base of the numeral, above the "E" and "V" of "CENTAVO." In type A7 these ornaments are missing, the figure "1" is broader than in type A4 and the head of the figure "2" is formed by a curved line instead of a ball.

Columbus — A8

Type I   Type II

Type I — There is a heavy shading of short horizontal lines below "Chile" and the adjacent ornaments.
Type II — There is practically no shading below "Chile" and the ornaments.

Type I

1900-01

39	A8	1c yel grn	.80	.25
40	A8	2c brn rose	1.25	.25
41	A8	5c dp bl	6.50	.35
42	A8	10c violet	6.50	.70
43	A8	20c gray	6.50	2.50
44	A8	30c dp org ('01)	6.50	2.50
45	A8	50c red brn	7.50	2.50
		Nos. 39-45 (7)	35.55	9.05

Type II

46	A8	1c yel grn ('01)	.85	.25
47	A8	2c rose ('01)	.85	.30
48	A8	5c dull blue ('01)	5.00	.25
a.		Printed on both sides		
49	A8	10c vio ('01)	6.00	.85
		Nos. 46-49 (4)	12.70	1.65

For surcharge see No. 57.

No. 33 Surcharged in Black

1900   Black Surcharge

50	A5	5c on 30c rose car	1.25	.35
a.		Inverted surcharge	32.50	24.00
b.		Double surcharge	90.00	60.00
c.		Double surcharge, both invtd.	90.00	60.00
d.		Double surcharge, one invtd.	90.00	60.00

Columbus — A10

1901-02   Perf. 12

51	A10	1c green	.50	.30
52	A10	2c carmine	.65	.25
53	A10	5c ultra	1.50	.25
54	A10	10c red & blk	2.25	.35
55	A10	30c vio & blk	6.75	2.25
56	A10	50c red org & blk	7.25	2.25
		Nos. 51-56 (6)	18.90	4.25

No. 44 Surcharged in Dark Blue

1903   Rouletted

57	A8	10c on 30c orange	1.90	.75
a.		Inverted surcharge	18.00	12.00
b.		Double surcharge	25.00	15.00
c.		Double surch., one inverted	25.00	15.00
d.		Double surch., both invtd.	25.00	15.00
e.		Stamp design printed on both sides		

Telegraph Stamps Surcharged or Overprinted in Black

Pedro de Valdivia — A11   Coat of Arms — A12

1854 (column, Unused values for Nos. 15-19)

19	A2	20c green	80.00	8.00
		Pen cancellation		1.60
		Nos. 15-19 (5)	370.00	61.00

Unused values for Nos. 15-19 are for stamps with original gum.

Type I   **Type II**

Type I — Animal at left has neither mane nor tail.
Type II — Animal at left has mane and tail.

1904   **Perf. 12**
58	A11	1c on 20c ultra	.40	.30
a.		Imperf. horiz., pair	40.00	40.00
b.		Inverted surcharge	50.00	50.00
59	A13	2c yel brn, I	.35	.25
a.		Inverted overprint	20.00	20.00
b.		Pair, one without overprint	50.00	50.00
60	A13	5c red, I	.55	.25
a.		Inverted overprint	20.00	20.00
c.		Pair, one without overprint	50.00	50.00
61	A13	10c ol grn, I	1.50	.50
a.		Inverted overprint	50.00	50.00
		Nos. 58-61 (4)	2.80	1.30

Perf. 12½ to 16
62	A13	2c yel, brn, II	5.25	4.50
63	A11	3c on 5c brn red	37.50	32.50
a.		Inverted surcharge		
64	A12	3c on 1p brn, II	.45	.30
a.		Double surcharge	50.00	50.00
65	A13	5c red, II	6.25	5.50
a.		Inverted overprint		
66	A13	10c ol grn, II	14.50	10.00
67	A11	12c on 5c brn red	1.00	.45
a.		No star at left of "Centavos"	3.00	2.50
b.		Inverted surcharge	40.00	40.00
c.		Double surcharge	50.00	50.00
		Nos. 62-67 (6)	64.95	53.25

Counterfeits exist of the overprint and surcharge varieties of Nos. 57-67.
For overprint see No. O12.

A14   **A15**

Columbus — A16

1905-09   **Perf. 12**
68	A14	1c green	.25	.25
69	A14	2c carmine	.30	.25
70	A14	3c yel brn	.65	.30
71	A14	5c ultra	.70	.25
72	A15	10c gray & blk	1.10	.25
73	A15	12c lake & blk	5.50	2.25
74	A15	15c vio & blk	1.25	.25
75	A15	20c org brn & blk	2.25	.25
76	A15	30c bl grn & blk	3.50	.35
77	A15	50c ultra & blk	3.50	.40
78	A16	1p gold, grn & gray	16.00	11.00
		Nos. 68-78 (11)	35.00	15.80

A 20c dull red and black, type A15, was prepared but not issued. Value $125. "Specimen" examples of Nos. 74, 76-78 exist, punched to prevent postal use.
For surcharges and overprints see Nos. 79-82, O9, O11-O15.

Nos. 73, 78 Surcharged in Blue or Red

a   **b**

1910
79	A15 (a)	5c on 12c (Bl)	.50	.25
80	A16 (b)	10c on 1p (R)	1.10	.30
81	A16 (b)	20c on 1p (R)	1.60	.60
82	A16 (b)	1p (R)	3.00	1.10
		Nos. 79-82 (4)	6.20	2.25

The 1p is overprinted "ISLAS DE JUAN FERNANDEZ" only. The use of these stamps throughout Chile was authorized.

Independence Centenary Issue

Oath of Independence — A17

Monument to O'Higgins — A26   **Adm. Lord Thomas Cochrane — A29**

Designs: 2c, Battle of Chacabuco. 3c, Battle of Roble. 5c, Battle of Maipu. 10c, Naval Engagement of "Lautaro" and "Esmeralda." 12c, Capturing the "Maria Isabel." 15c, First Sortie of Liberating Forces. 20c, Abdication of O'Higgins. 25c, Chile's First Congress. 50c, Monument to José M. Carrera. 1p, Monument to San Martin. 2p, Gen. Manuel Blanco Encalada. 5p, Gen. José Ignacio Zenteno.

1910   **Center in Black**
83	A17	1c dk green	.25	.25
a.		Center inverted	7,000.	
84	A17	2c lake	1.10	.75
85	A17	3c red brown	.80	.45
86	A17	5c dp blue	.45	.25
87	A17	10c gray brn	1.20	.30
88	A17	12c vermilion	2.50	1.00
89	A17	15c slate	1.90	.55
90	A17	20c red orange	2.50	.85
91	A17	25c ultra	3.25	2.00
92	A26	30c violet	3.25	1.40
93	A26	50c olive grn	6.75	2.25
94	A26	1p yel org	14.00	5.25
95	A29	2p red	14.00	5.25
96	A29	5p yel grn	37.50	17.50
97	A29	10p dk violet	35.00	16.00
		Nos. 83-97 (15)	124.45	54.05

Columbus A32   **De Valdivia A33**

Mateo de Toro Zambrano A34   **Bernardo O'Higgins A35**

1912-13   **Engr.**   **Perf. 12**
113	A47	2c scarlet	.25	.25
114	A48	4c black brn	.30	.25
115	A49	8c gray	1.00	.25

Ramón Freire — A36   **F. A. Pinto — A37**

Joaquín Prieto — A38   **Manuel Bulnes — A39**

Manuel Montt — A40   **José Joaquín Pérez — A41**

Federico Errázuriz Zanartu — A42   **José de Balmaceda — A43**

Designs: 1p, Anibal Pinto, 2p, Domingo Santa María. 10p, Federico Errázuriz Echaurren.

Outer backgrounds consist of horizontal and diagonal lines

1911   **Engr.**   **Perf. 12**
98	A32	1c dp green	.25	.25
99	A33	2c scarlet	.25	.25
100	A34	3c sepia	.75	.25
101	A35	5c dk blue	.25	.25
102	A36	10c gray & blk	.75	.25
a.		Center inverted	800.00	600.00
103	A37	12c carmine & blk	1.00	.25
104	A38	15c violet & blk	.90	.25
a.		Center inverted	1,000.	
105	A39	20c org red & blk	1.75	.25
a.		Center inverted	50.00	50.00
106	A40	25c lt blue & blk	2.75	.60
107	A41	30c bis brn & blk	4.00	.30
108	A42	50c myr grn & blk	5.00	.30
109	A43	1p green & blk	9.00	.40
110	A43	2p ver & blk	17.50	1.75
111	A43	5p ol grn & blk	50.00	9.50
112	A43	10p org yel & blk	45.00	8.50
		Nos. 98-112 (15)	139.15	23.35

See Nos. 117, 121, 123, 127-128, 133-141, 143, 155A, 157-161, 165-169,171-172 and designs A47-A55, A57. For overprints see Nos. C6, C6B-C6D, C7-C8, C10-C11, C13-C21, O19-O22, O24-O27, O30-O34, O40.

Columbus A47   **Toro Zambrano A48**

Freire A49   **O'Higgins A50**

116	A50	10c blue & blk	1.00	.25
a.		Center inverted	500.00	400.00
b.		Imperf. horiz. or vert., pair	50.00	
117	A37	14c car & blk	1.50	.25
121	A38	40c violet & blk	5.75	.60
123	A40	60c lt blue & blk	14.00	1.75
		Nos. 113-123 (7)	23.80	3.60

See Nos. 125-126, 131, 164, 170, 173. For overprints see Nos. C6E, O18, O23, O28, O29.

Cochrane — A52

1915   **Engr.**   **Perf. 13½x14**
124	A52	5c slate blue	.60	.35
a.		Imperf., pair	11.50	

See Nos. 155, 162-163. For overprints see Nos. O17, O37.

1918
125	A49	8c slate	17.50	.80

No. 125 is from a plate made in Chile to resemble No. 115. The top of the head is further from the oval, the spots of color enclosed in the figures "8" are oval instead of round, and there are many small differences in the design.

1921   **Worn Plate**
126	A49	8c gray	20.00	5.00

No. 126 differs from No. 125 in not having diagonal lines in the frame and only a few diagonal lines above the shoulders (due to wear), while No. 125 has diagonal lines in the oval up to the level of the forehead.

Columbus — A53

1915-25   **Typo.**   **Perf. 13½ to 14½**
127	A32	1c gray green	.25	.25
128	A33	2c red	.25	.25
129	A53	4c brown ('18)	.25	.25

Frame Litho.; Head Engr.
131	A50	10c bl & blk	1.25	.25
a.		10c dark blue & black	1.25	.25
b.		Imperf., pair	110.00	
c.		Center inverted	325.00	
133	A38	15c vio & blk	.90	.25
134	A39	20c org red & blk	1.40	.25
a.		20c brown orange & blk	1.75	
135	A40	25c dl bl & blk	.55	.25
136	A41	30c bis brn & blk	1.75	.25
137	A42	50c dp grn & blk	1.75	.25

Perf. 14
138	A43	1p grn & blk	8.00	.25
139	A43	2p red & blk	9.75	.25
a.		2p vermilion & black	32.50	.60
140	A43	5p ol grn & blk ('20)	24.00	.60
141	A43	10p org & blk ('25)	25.00	1.75
		Nos. 127-141 (13)	75.10	5.10

The frames have crosshatching on the 15c, 20c, 30c, 2p, 5p and 10p. They have no crosshatching on the 10c, 25c, 50c and 1p.

Nos. 131a and 134a are printed from new head plates which give blacker and heavier impressions. No. 131a exists with; (a) frame litho., head engr.; (b) frame typo., head engr.; (c) frame typo., head litho. No. 134a is with frame typo., head engr.

A 4c stamp with portrait of Balmaceda and a 14c with portrait of Manuel de Salas were prepared but not placed in use. Both stamps were sent to the paper mill at Puente Alto for destruction. They were not all destroyed as some were privately preserved and sold.

Columbus — A54

Types of 1915-20 Redrawn

1918-20   *Perf. 13½x14½*
143 A32 1c gray grn ('20)   .30   .25
144 A54 4c brown   .50   .25
No. 143 has all the lines much finer and clearer than No. 127. The white shirt front is also much less shaded.

Manuel Rengifo — A55

1921
145 A55 40c dk vio & blk   2.00   .40
For overprints see Nos. C6A, C9.

Pan-American Congress Building — A56

1923, Apr. 25   **Typo.**   *Perf. 14½x14*
146 A56 2c red   .25   .25
147 A56 4c brown   .25   .25
Typo.; Center Engr.
148 A56 10c blue & blk   .25   .25
149 A56 20c orange & blk   .75   .25
150 A56 40c dl vio & blk   1.00   .30
151 A56 1p green & blk   1.25   .50
152 A56 2p red & blk   5.00   .60
153 A56 5p dk grn & blk   17.00   4.50
   Nos. 146-153 (8)   25.75   6.90
Fifth Pan-American Congress.

Adm. Juan José Latorre — A57

Typographed; Head Engraved
1927   *Perf. 13½x14½*
154 A57 80c dk brn & blk   2.00   .60

Types of 1915-25 Issues
Inscribed: "Chile Correos"
Perf. 13½x14½
1928-31   **Engr.**   **Wmk. 215**
155 A52 5c slate blue   1.40   .25
Frame Typo.; Center Engr.
155A A38 15c violet & blk   2,200.
156 A55 40c dk vio & blk   .60   .25
157 A42 50c dp grn & blk   2.50   .25
Perf. 14
158 A43 1p green & blk   1.00   .25
159 A43 2p red & blk   5.00   .25
160 A43 5p ol grn & blk   9.75   .45
161 A43 10p orange & blk   9.75   1.90
   Nos. 155,156-161 (7)   30.00   3.60
Paper of Nos. 155-161 varies from thin to thick.

Types of 1915-25 Issues
Inscribed: "Correos de Chile"
1928   **Engr.**   *Perf. 13½x14½*
162 A52 5c deep blue   .35   .25
1929   **Litho.**
163 A52 5c light green   .50   .25
Frame Litho.; Center Engr.
164 A50 10c blue & blk   2.00   .25
165 A38 15c violet & blk   2.40   .25
166 A39 20c org red & blk   5.75   .25
167 A40 25c blue & blk   .95   .25
168 A41 30c brown & blk   .75   .25
169 A42 50c dp grn & blk   .65   .25
   Nos. 163-169 (7)   13.00   1.75

Redrawn
1929   **Frame Typo.; Center Litho.**
170 A50 10c blue & blk   3.00   .25
171 A38 15c violet & blk   2.75   .25
172 A39 20c org red & blk   4.25   .25
   Nos. 170-172 (3)   10.00   .75
1931   **Unwmk.**
173 A50 10c blue & blk   .70   .25
In the redrawn stamps the lines behind the portraits are heavier and completely fill the ovals. There are strong diagonal lines above the shoulders. On No. 170 the head is larger than on Nos. 164, 173.

A58

Prosperity of Saltpeter Trade
A59   A60

Perf. 13½x14
1930, July 21   **Litho.**   **Wmk. 215**
Size: 20x25mm
175 A58 5c yellow grn   .60   .40
176 A58 10c red brown   .60   .30
177 A58 15c violet   .60   .30
178 A59 25c deep gray   1.90   .60
179 A60 70c dark blue   4.50   1.50
Perf. 14
Size: 24½x30mm
180 A60 1p dk gray grn   3.75   .75
   Nos. 175-180 (6)   11.95   3.85
Cent. of the 1st shipment of saltpeter from Chile, July 21, 1830.

Manuel Bulnes — A61

1931   *Perf. 13½, 14*
181 A61 20c dark brown   1.00   .30
For overprints see Nos. O35, O39.

Bernardo O'Higgins — A62

1932
182 A62 10c deep blue   1.50   .45
For overprints see Nos. O36, O38.

Mariano Egana — A63   Joaquin Tocornal — A64

1934   *Perf. 13½x14*
183 A63 30c magenta   .60   .25
Perf. 14
184 A64 1.20p bright blue   1.00   .25
Centenary of the constitution.

José Joaquín Pérez — A65

1934   *Perf. 13½x14*
185 A65 30c bright pink   1.60   .35

Atacama Desert — A66

Designs: 10c, Fishing boats. 20c, Coquito palms. 25c, Sheep. 30c, Mining. 40c, Lonquimay forest. 50c, Colliery at Port Lota. 1p, Shipping at Valparaiso. 1.20p, Puntiagudo volcano. 2p, Diego de Almagro. 5p, Cattle. 10p, Mining saltpeter.

Wmk. 215
1936, Mar. 1   **Litho.**   *Perf. 14*
186 A66 5c vermilion   .60   .30
187 A66 10c violet   .30   .25
188 A66 20c magenta   .40   .25
189 A66 25c grnsh blue   3.00   .80
190 A66 30c lt green   .40   .25
191 A66 40c blk, *cream*   3.25   .85
192 A66 50c bl, *bluish*   1.75   .30
Engr.
193 A66 1p dk green   1.75   .50
194 A66 1.20p dp blue   2.00   .70
195 A66 2p dk brown   2.50   .80
196 A66 5p copper red   5.75   2.25
197 A66 10p dk violet   14.00   8.00
   Nos. 186-197 (12)   35.70   15.25
400th anniv. of the discovery of Chile by Diego de Almagro.

Laja Waterfall — A78   Fishing in Chiloé — A84

Designs: 10c, Agriculture. 15c, Boldo tree. 20c, Nitrate Industry. 30c, Mineral spas. 40c, Copper mine. 50c, Mining. 1.80p, Osorno Volcano. 2p, Mercantile marine. 5p, Lake Villarrica. 10p, State railways.

Perf. 13½x14
1938-40   **Litho.**   **Wmk. 215**
198 A78 5c brn car ('39)   .25   .25
199 A78 10c sal pink ('39)   .25   .25
200 A78 15c brn org ('40)   .25   .25
201 A78 20c light blue   .25   .25
202 A78 30c brt pink   .25   .25
203 A78 40c lt grn ('39)   .25   .25
204 A78 50c violet   .25   .25
Engr.   *Perf. 14*
205 A84 1p orange brn   .25   .25
206 A84 1.80p deep blue   .45   .40
207 A84 2p car lake   .25   .25
208 A84 5p dk slate grn   .35   .25
209 A84 10p rose vio ('40)   .90   .25
   Nos. 198-209 (12)   3.95   3.15
See Nos. 217-227. For surcharge and overprints see Nos. 253, O41-O66, O70-O71.

Map of the Americas — A89

Unwmk.
1940, Sept. 11   **Litho.**   *Perf. 14*
210 A89 40c dl grn & yel grn   .35   .25
Pan American Union, 50th anniversary.

Camilo Henríquez — A90

Founding of Santiago A93

Designs: 40c, Pedro de Valdivia. 1.10p, Benjamin Vicuna Mackenna. 3.60p, Diego Barros Arana.

Perf. 14½x14, 14½
1941, Jan. 23   **Engr.**   **Wmk. 215**
211 A90 10c carmine lake   .25   .25
212 A90 40c green   .35   .25
213 A90 1.10p red   1.25   .70
214 A93 1.80p blue   1.25   .70
215 A90 3.60p indigo   3.75   2.75
   Nos. 211-215 (5)   6.85   4.65
400th anniversary of Santiago.

Types of 1938
Perf. 13½x14
1942-46   **Unwmk.**   **Litho.**
217 A78 10c sal pink ('43)   .25   .25
218 A78 15c brown org ('43)   .25   .25
219 A78 20c lt blue ('43)   .25   .25
220 A78 30c brt pink ('43)   .25   .25
221 A78 40c yellow grn   .80   .25
222 A78 50c violet ('43)   .25   .25
Engr.   *Perf. 14*
223 A84 1p brown orange   1.50   .25
225 A84 2p car lake ('43)   .25   .25
226 A84 5p dk sl grn ('43)   .50   .25
227 A84 10p rose violet ('46)   .90   .25
   Nos. 217-227 (10)   5.20   2.50

Valentin Letelier — A95   University of Chile — A98

Designs: 40c, Andrés Bello. 90c, Manuel Bulnes. 1.80p, Manuel Montt.

1942, Nov. 1   *Perf. 14x14½, 14 (1p)*
228 A95 30c rose red   .25   .25
229 A95 40c deep green   .25   .25
230 A95 90c rose violet   1.90   1.50
231 A98 1p deep brown   1.10   .90
232 A95 1.80p dark blue   3.50   3.00
   Nos. 228-232 (5)   7.00   5.90
University of Chile cent. See No. C89.

Manuel Bulnes — A100

Map Showing Strait of Magellan — A104

Designs: 30c, Juan Williams Wilson. 40c, Diego Duble Almeida. 1p, José Mardones.

1944, Mar. 2　Litho.　Perf. 14
233	A100	15c black	.25	.25
234	A100	30c deep rose	.25	.25
235	A100	40c yellow green	.25	.25
236	A100	1p brown carmine	.95	.25
237	A104	1.80p ultra	1.40	.95
		Nos. 233-237 (5)	3.10	1.95

100th anniversary of the occupation of the Strait of Magellan.

Red Cross and Lamp of Life — A105

Serpent and Cup — A106

1944, Oct. 18　Unwmk.
| 238 | A105 | 40c green, red & blk | .30 | .25 |
| 239 | A106 | 1.80p ultra & red | .90 | .45 |

80th anniv. of the Intl. Red Cross Soc.

Bernardo O'Higgins — A107

"Embrace of Maipú" (O'Higgins Joining San Martin) — A108

Designs: 40c, Abdication of O'Higgins. 1.80p, Battle of Rancagua.

1945　Engr.　Perf. 14 (15c), 14½
Center in Black
240	A107	15c carmine	.30	.25
241	A108	30c brown	.30	.25
242	A108	40c deep green	.30	.25
243	A108	1.80p dark blue	1.40	.90
		Nos. 240-243 (4)	2.30	1.65

Death of Bernardo O'Higgins in 1842, cent.

A111

Proposed Columbus lighthouse.

Wmk. 215
1945, Sept. 10　Litho.　Perf. 14
| 244 | A111 | 40c light green | .50 | .25 |

. Issued in honor of the discovery of America by Columbus and the Memorial Lighthouse to be erected in his memory.

A112

1946　　Engr.
| 245 | A112 | 40c dark green | .25 | .25 |
| 246 | A112 | 1.80p dark blue | .25 | .25 |

80th anniv. of the death of Andrés Bello, poet and educator.

Map Showing Chile's Claims of Antarctic Territory A113

1947, May 12　Litho.　Perf. 14½
| 247 | A113 | 40c carmine | .60 | .30 |
| 248 | A113 | 2.50p deep blue | 1.60 | .50 |

Eusebio Lillo and Ramon Carnicer A114

1947, Sept. 18　　Engr.
| 249 | A114 | 40c dark green | .25 | .25 |

Centenary of national anthem.

Miguel de Cervantes Saavedra A115

1947, Oct. 11　　Wmk. 215
| 250 | A115 | 40c dk carmine | .25 | .25 |

400th anniv. of the birth of Cervantes, novelist, playwright and poet.

Arturo Prat Chacón and Iquique Naval Battle A116

1948, Dec. 24　　Perf. 14½
| 251 | A116 | 40c deep blue | .25 | .25 |

Centenary of the birth of Arturo Prat Chacon, Chilean naval hero.

Bernardo O'Higgins — A117

Perf. 13½x14
1948　Wmk. 215　　Litho.
| 252 | A117 | 60c black | .25 | .25 |

See No. 262. For surcharges see Nos. 266-267.

No. 203 Surcharged in Black

1948
| 253 | A78 | 20c on 40c lt grn | .25 | .25 |

Chilean Pigeons — A118

FAUNA: a, Chilean Otter. b, tree. d, American skunk. f, Southern sea lions. g, Sugarcane borer moth. h, Emperor penguins. i, Bat. j, Chinchilla. k, Grant's stag beetle. l, Trevally (fish). m, Chilean slender lizard. o, Crested caracara. q, Red-gartered coot. r, Chilean guemal (deer). s, Spiny rock lobster. u, Tilefish. v, Praying mantis. x, Torrent duck. y, Red conger.

FLORA: b, Araucarian pine (monkey puzzle tree). e, Evening primrose. n, Chilean red bell flower. p, Loxodon (flower). t, Boldo tree. w, Coquito palm trees.

Wmk. 215
1948, Dec. 6　Litho.　Perf. 14
254		60c Block of 25	60.00	60.00
a.-y.	A118	any single	1.00	.80
255		2.60p Block of 25	90.00	90.00
a.-y.	A118	any single	1.75	1.25

Issued in panes of 100.
Cent. (in 1944) of the publication of the 1st volume of Claudio Gay's Natural History of Chile. See No. C124.

> Catalogue values for unused stamps in this section, from this point to the end of the section, are for Never Hinged items.

Benjamin Vicuna Mackenna — A121

1949, Mar. 22　Engr.　Perf. 13½x14
| 257 | A121 | 60c deep blue | .30 | .25 |

See No. C126.

Symbols of Arts and Crafts Education — A122

Design: 2.60p, Badge and book.

Unwmk.
1949, Nov. 11　Litho.　Perf. 14
258	A122	60c lilac rose	.25	.25
259	A122	2.60p violet blue	.40	.30
		Nos. 258-259,C127-C128 (4)	2.90	1.55

Cent. of the foundation of Chile's School of Arts and Crafts.

Heinrich von Stephan — A123

1950, Jan. 6　　Engr.
260	A123	60c deep carmine	.25	.25
261	A123	2.50p deep blue	.70	.50
		Nos. 260-261,C129-C130 (4)	2.55	1.60

UPU, 75th anniv.

O'Higgins Type of 1948
1950　Litho.　Perf. 13x14
| 262 | A117 | 60c black | .25 | .25 |

For surcharge see No. 266.

San Martín — A124

Wmk. 215
1951, Mar. 16　Engr.　Perf. 14
| 263 | A124 | 60c deep blue | .40 | .25 |

Cent. of the death of Gen. José de San Martin. See No. C165.

Isabella I — A125

1952, Mar. 20
| 264 | A125 | 60c brt blue | .35 | .25 |

500th anniv. of the birth of Queen Isabella I of Spain. See No. C166.

Bernardo O'Higgins — A126

1952 Unwmk. Litho. Perf. 13½x14
| 265 | A126 | 1p dk blue grn | .30 | .25 |

See No. 275. For overprints see Nos. O67-O69.

No. 262 Surcharged in Red, Numbers & Letters Thicker

No. 252 Surcharged in Red, Numbers & Letters Thinner

1952, Sept.
| 266 | A117 | 40c on 60c black | .35 | .25 |

Wmk. 215
| 267 | A117 | 40c on 60c black | .35 | .25 |

Mateo de Toro Zambrano — A127

1953, Mar. 13   Wmk. 215
268 A127 80c green   .25 .25
See No. 285.

Valdivia Arms — A128

Old Fort — A129

3p, Modern Valdivia. 5p, Street in ancient Valdivia.

1953, May   Perf. 14
269 A128 1p brt ultra   .40 .25
270 A129 2p dull rose vio   .40 .25
271 A129 3p blue green   .50 .25
272 A129 5p deep brown   .50 .25
   Nos. 269-272,C167 (5)   4.05 1.45
4th centenary of the founding of Valdivia, capital of Valdivia province.

José Toribio Medina (1852-1930), Historian and Bibliographer A130

1953, June   Engr.   Perf. 14½
273 A130 1p brown   .35 .25
274 A130 2.50p deep blue   .45 .25

O'Higgins Type of 1952
Perf. 13½x14
1953, Oct.   Wmk. 215   Litho.
275 A126 1p dk blue green   .35 .25
For overprint see No. O69.

Stamp of 1853 — A131

1953, Oct. 15   Engr.   Perf. 14½
276 A131 1p brown   .50 .25
Centenary of Chile's first postage stamps.
   Souvenir sheet including No. 276 is noted below No. C168.

A132

Census chart and map.

1953, Nov. 5   Litho.   Perf. 13½x14
277 A132 1p blue green   .30 .25
278 A132 2.50p violet blue   .30 .25
279 A132 3p chocolate   .50 .25
280 A132 4p carmine   .50 .25
   Nos. 277-280 (4)   1.60 1.00
12th general census of population and housing.

Arms of Angol — A133

1954, May 28   Unwmk.   Perf. 14
281 A133 2p deep carmine   .35 .25
400th anniversary of the founding of Angol, capital of Malleco province.

Ignacio Domeyko — A134

1954, Aug. 16   Engr.   Perf. 13½x14
282 A134 1p greenish blue   .35 .25
150th anniversary of the birth of Ignacio Domeyko (1802-89), mineralogist and educator. See No. C171.

Early Steam Locomotive — A135

1954, Sept. 10   Wmk. 215   Perf. 14½
283 A135 1p red   .60 .30
Centenary (in 1951) of the first South American railroad. See No. C172.

Adm. Arturo Prat Chacón — A136

1954   Unwmk.   Litho.   Perf. 14
284 A136 2p dk violet blue   .35 .25
75th anniv. of the naval Battle of Iquique.

Toro Zambrano Type of 1953
1954, Nov. 6   Perf. 13½x14
285 A127 80c green   .30 .25

Arms of Viña del Mar — A137

Design: 2p, Arms of Valparaiso.

1955, Mar. 5   Wmk. 215   Perf. 14
286 A137 1p violet blue   .35 .25
287 A137 2p carmine   .35 .25
1st Intl. Phil. Exhib., Valparaiso, Mar. 1955.

Dr. Alejandro del Rio — A138

1955, May 24   Perf. 13½x14
288 A138 2p violet blue   .40 .25
14th Pan-American Sanitary Conference.

Christ of the Andes, Emblems of Chile, Argentina A139

1955, Aug. 31   Unwmk.   Perf. 14½
289 A139 1p violet blue   .35 .25
Reciprocal visits of Presidents Juan D. Peron and Carlos Ibanez del Campo. See No. C173.

Manuel Rengifo — A140

5p, Mariano Egana. 50p, Diego Portales.

1955-56   Unwmk.   Perf. 14x14½
290 A140 3p violet blue   .35 .25
291 A140 5p dk car rose   .35 .25
292 A140 50p rose lilac ('56) 1.90 .45
   Nos. 290-292 (3)   2.60 .95
Joaquin Prieto (1786-1854), soldier and political leader; president, 1831-41. See No. QRA1.

Jose M. Carrera A141

Ramón Freire A142

Portraits: 5p, Manuel Bulnes. 10p, Pres. Francisco A. Pinto. 50p, Manuel Montt.

Perf. 14x14½
1956-58   Unwmk.   Litho.
293 A141 2p purple   .30 .25
293A A142 3p lt violet blue .25 .25
294 A141 5p redsh brn
            (19½x23mm)   .30 .25
   a. Size 19x22mm   .30 .25
295 A142 10p vio (19x22¼mm) .30 .25
   a. Perf. 13½x14 (19¼x22½mm)
            ('58)   .55 .25
296 A141 50p rose red   .50 .25
   Nos. 293-296 (5)   1.65 1.25

Wmk. 215
297 A141 2p dull purple   .30 .25
298 A142 3p violet blue   .30 .25
No. 294 has yellow gum; No. 294a, white gum.
For overprints see Nos. O72-O76.

Federico Santa Maria — A143

Unwmk.
1957, Jan. 31   Engr.   Perf. 14
299 A143 5p dk red brown   .30 .25
25th anniv. of the Federico Santa Maria Technical University. See Nos. C190-C191.
   Souvenir sheet including No. 299 is noted below No. C191.

Gabriela Mistral — A144

1958, Jan. 10
300 A144 10p red brown   .45 .25
Issued in honor of Gabriela Mistral, poet and educator. See No. C192.

Arms of Osorno — A145

Design: 50p, Garcia Hdo. de Mendoza.

1958, Mar. 23   Litho.   Perf. 14
301 A145 10p carmine   .25 .25
Engr.
302 A145 50p green   .40 .25
400th anniversary of the founding of the city of Osorno, capital of Osorno province.
   Souvenir sheet including No. 302 in red brown is noted below No. C193.

Arms of Santiago — A146

1958, Oct. 18   Unwmk.   Perf. 14
303 A146 10p dark violet   .30 .25
Natl. Philatelic Exposition, Santiago, Oct. 18-26.
   Souvenir sheet including No. 303 in deep red is noted below No. C194.

Symbolical Savings Bank — A147

1958, Dec. 18
304 A147 10p dark blue   .40 .25
Savings Bank for Public Employees, cent.
   Souvenir sheet including No. 304 in violet is noted below No. C195.

Modern Map of Antarctica — A148

1958, Aug. 28   Unwmk.   Perf. 14
305 A148 40p rose carmine   .60 .60
IGY, 1957-1958. See No. C214.

Antarctic Map and "La Araucana" A149

Map of Strait of Magellan, 1588 — A150

1958 **Litho.** **Perf. 14**
310 A149 10p violet blue .75 .25

Engr.
311 A150 200p dull purple 2.75 1.75
Nos. 310-311,C199-C200 (4) 7.75 4.00
For overprint see No. O77.

Valdivia River Bridge — A153

1959, Feb. 9 **Engr.** **Perf. 14**
319 A153 40p green .45 .25
Cent. of the German School in Valdivia and to publicize the Valdivia Phil. Exhib., 2/9-18. Souvenir sheet including No. 319 is noted below No. C213.

Strait of Magellan, Map by Pedro Sarmiento de Gamboa, c. 1582 — A154

1959, Aug. 27 **Litho.**
320 A154 10p dull purple .45 .25
Juan Ladrillero expedition to explore the Strait of Magellan, 1557-58, 400th anniv. See No. C215.

Diego Barros Arana — A155

1959, Aug. 27
321 A155 40p ultra .45 .25
50th anniv. of the death of Diego Barros Arana (1830-1907), historian. See No. C216.

Henri Dunant — A156

1959, Oct. 6 **Unwmk.** **Perf. 14**
322 A156 20p red & red brn .45 .25
Cent. of the Red Cross idea. See No. C217.

Manuel Bulnes — A157

Francisco A. Pinto — A158

Choshuenco Volcano A159

No. 326, Choshuenco volcano, redrawn. 5c, Manuel Montt. 10c, Maule River Valley. 20c, 1e, Inca Lake.

1960-67 **Litho.** **Perf. 13x14**
323 A157 5m bluish grn .25 .25
324 A158 1c carmine .25 .25
Perf. 14
Size: 29x25mm
325 A159 2c ultra ('61) .25 .25
Perf. 14x13
Size: 23½x18mm
326 A159 2c ultra ('62) .25 .25
Perf. 13x14
327 A157 5c blue .25 .25
Perf. 14
Size: 29x25mm
328 A159 10c green ('62) .25 .25
329 A159 20c Prus blue ('62) .35 .25
329A A159 1e bluish grn ('67) .65 .25
Nos. 323-329A (8) 2.50 2.00
On No. 325 "Volcan Choshuenco" is at upper left, below "Correos." On No. 326, it is at bottom, above "Centesimos."
For overprint and surcharge see Nos. B7, O79, RA1.

Refugee Family A160

1960, Apr. 7 **Perf. 14½**
330 A160 1c green .30 .25
WRY, July 1, 1959-June 30, 1960. A souvenir sheet is noted below No. C218.

Type of Air Post Issue, 1962, and

Arms of Chile A161

José M. Carrera A162

No. 332, Palace of Justice. 5c, Natl. Memorial. 10c, Manuel de Toro y Zambrano and Martinez de Rozas. 20c, Manuel de Salas and Juan Egana. 50c, Manuel Rodriguez and Juan Mackenna.

Wmk. 215 (#331, 1e); Unwmk.
1960-65 **Engr.** **Perf. 14½**
331 A161 1c maroon & sepia .25 .25
332 A161 1c brn & claret ('62) .25 .25
333 A162 5c grn & Prus grn ('61) .25 .25
334 AP54 10c brn & vio brn ('64) .40 .25
334A AP54 20c ind & bl grn ('65) .40 .25
335 AP54 50c red brn & mar ('65) .70 .25
336 A162 1e gray ol & brn 1.25 .40
Nos. 331-336,C218A-C220D (14) 6.90 3.80
150th anniv. of the formation of the 1st Natl. Government. A souvenir sheet is noted below No. C220B. See No. C285.

Family — A163

Design: 10c, Various buildings.

Unwmk.
1960, Jan. 18 **Litho.** **Perf. 14**
337 A163 5c green .25 .25
338 A163 10c brt violet .25 .25
13th population census (No. 337) and 2nd housing census (No. 338).

Chamber of Deputies A164

1961, Aug. 14 **Unwmk.** **Perf. 14½**
339 A164 2c red brown .65 .25
150th anniv. of the 1st National Congress. See No. C245.

Soccer Players and Globe A165

Design: 5c, Goalkeeper and stadium, vert.

1962, May 30 **Engr.** **Perf. 14½**
340 A165 2c blue .40 .25
341 A165 5c green .55 .25
World Soccer Championship, Chile, May 30-June 17. Note on souvenir sheet follows No. C247.

Mother and Child — A166

1963, Mar. 21 **Litho.** **Perf. 14**
342 A166 3c maroon .35 .25
FAO "Freedom from Hunger" campaign. See No. C248.

Centenary Emblem — A167

1963, Aug. 23 **Unwmk.** **Perf. 14**
343 A167 3c red & gray .35 .25
Cent. of the Intl. Red Cross. See No. C249.

Fireman Carrying Woman — A168

1963, Dec. 20 **Unwmk.** **Perf. 14**
344 A168 3c violet .45 .25
Centenary of the Santiago Fire Brigade. See No. C250.

Enrique Molina — A169

Design: No. 346, Magr. Carlos Casanueva.

1964, Nov. 14 **Litho.** **Perf. 14**
345 A169 4c bister brown .35 .25
346 A169 4c rose claret .35 .25
Nos. 345-346,C257-C258 (4) 1.30 1.00
Enrique Molina, founder of the University of Concepcion, and Msgr. Carlos Casanueva, rector of the Catholic University, 1920-53.

Easter Island Statue — A170

Copihue, National Flower — A171

Design: 30c, Robinson Crusoe.

1965-69 **Litho.** **Perf. 14x14½**
347 A170 6c rose lilac .95 .25
347A A170 10c rose pink ('68) .30 .25
Perf. 14
348 A171 15c yel grn & rose red .75 .25
348A A171 20c yel grn & rose red ('69) .35 .25
Perf. 14x14½
349 A170 30c rose claret .55 .25
Nos. 347-349 (5) 2.90 1.25
For surcharge see No. RA2.

Skier — A172

1965, Aug. 30 **Perf. 14**
350 A172 4c blue green .40 .25
World Skiing Championships, Chile, 1966.

Lorenzo Sazie — A173

1966, Feb. 9   Litho.   Perf. 14x14½
351 A173 1e green   .95 .25
Cent. of the death of Dr. Lorenzo Sazie, dean of the Faculty of Medicine, University of Santiago.

German Riesco, President in 1901-1906 — A174

Portrait: 30c, Jorge Montt (1847-1922), president in 1891-1896.

1966   Unwmk.   Perf. 13x14
354 A174 30c violet   .30 .25
355 A174 50c dull brown   .35 .25
For surcharge see No. 450.

William Wheelwright and S.S. Chile — A175

1966, Aug. 2   Perf. 14½
358 A175 10c ultra & lt bl   .35 .25
125th anniv. (in 1965) of the arrival of the paddle steamers "Chile" and "Peru." See No. C268.

Learning to Read — A176

1966, Aug. 13   Litho.   Perf. 14
359 A176 10c red brown   .35 .25
Literacy campaign.

UN and ICY Emblems A177

1966, Oct. 28   Unwmk.   Perf. 14½
360 A177 1e green & brown   1.40 .25
Intl. Cooperation Year, 1965. See No. C269.

Capt. Luis Pardo and Ship in Antarctica — A178

1967, Jan.   Litho.   Perf. 14½
361 A178 20c turquoise blue   .45 .25
Rescue of the Shackleton South Pole expedition by Capt. Luis Pardo of Chile, 50th anniv. See No. C271.

Family — A179

1967, Apr. 13   Unwmk.   Perf. 14
362 A179 10c magenta & blk   .35 .25
8th Intl. Conf. for Family Planning, Santiago, Apr. 1967. See No. C272.

Trees and Mountains A180

1967, June 9   Litho.   Perf. 14½
363 A180 10c blue grn & lt bl   .35 .25
Reforestation Campaign. See No. C274.

Lions Emblem — A181

1967, July 12   Litho.   Perf. 14
364 A181 20c Prus blue & yel   .35 .25
Nos. 364,C275-C276 (3)   1.85 .80
50th anniv. of Lions Intl.

Chilean Flag A182

1967, Oct. 20   Unwmk.   Perf. 14½
365 A182 80c crimson & ultra   .60 .25
Natl, flag, 150th anniv. See No. C277.

José Maria Cardinal Caro — A183

1967, Dec. 4   Engr.   Perf. 14½
366 A183 20c deep carmine   .75 .35
Cent. of the birth of José Maria Cardinal Caro, the first Chilean cardinal. See No. C279.

San Martin and O'Higgins — A184

1968, Apr. 23   Litho.   Unwmk.
367 A184 3e blue   .65 .25
Sesquicentennial of the Battles of Chacabuco and Maipu. See No. C280.

Farm Couple — A185

1968, June 18   Perf. 14½
368 A185 20c black, org & grn   .40 .25
Agrarian reforms. See No. C281.

Juan I. Molina A186

1968, Aug. 27   Litho.   Perf. 14½
369 A186 2e red lilac   .60 .25
Issued to honor Juan I. Molina, educator and scientist. See No. C282.

Hand Holding Cogwheel — A187

1968, Sept.   Perf. 14x14½
370 A187 30c deep carmine   .30 .25
Fourth census of manufacturers.

Map of Chiloé Province, Sailing Ship and Coastal Vessel A188

1968, Oct. 7   Perf. 14½
371 A188 30c ultra   .40 .25
Anniversaries of the founding of five towns in Chiloé Province. See No. C283.

Automobile Club Emblem A189

1968, Nov. 10   Engr.   Perf. 14½x14
372 A189 1e carmine rose   .35 .25
40th anniversary of the Automobile Club of Chile. See No. C284.

Francisco Garcia Huidobro A190

Design: 5e, King Philip V of Spain.

1968, Dec. 31   Litho.   Perf. 14½
373 A190 2e pale rose & ultra   .40 .25
374 A190 5e brown & yel grn   .40 .25
Nos. 373-374,C288-C289 (4)   1.40 1.00
225th anniv. of the founding of the State Mint (Casa de Moneda de Chile).

Satellite and Radar Station A191

1969, May 20   Litho.   Perf. 14½
375 A191 30c blue   .30 .25
Inauguration of ENTEL-Chile, the 1st commercial satellite communications ground station, Longovilo.
See No. C290. For surcharges see Nos. 397, C308.

Red Cross, Crescent and Lion and Sun Emblems A192

1969, Sept.   Litho.   Perf. 14½
376 A192 2e violet blue & red   .40 .25
50th anniversary of the League of Red Cross Societies. See No. C291.

Rapel Hydroelectric Plant — A193

1969, Nov. 18   Litho.   Perf. 14½
377 A193 40c green   .30 .25
See No. C292. For surcharge see No. B8.

Col. Rodriguez Monument — A194

1969, Nov. 24
378 A194 2e rose claret .40 .25
150th anniversary of the death of Col. Manuel Rodriguez. See No. C293.

EXPO '70 Emblem — A195

1969, Dec. 2   Litho.   Perf. 14
379 A195 3e blue .55 .25
EXPO '70 Intl. Exhibition, Osaka, Japan, Mar. 15-Sept. 13, 1970. See No. C294.

Open Book A196

1969, Dec. 3   Perf. 14½
380 A196 40c red brown .40 .25
Translation of the Bible into Spanish by Casiodoro de Reina, 400th anniv. See No. C295. For surcharge see No. B10.

Globes and ILO Emblem A197

1969, Dec. 17   Perf. 14½
381 A197 1e green & blk .35 .25
ILO, 50th anniv. See No. C296.

Human Rights Flame A198

1969, Dec. 18
382 A198 4e blue & red .60 .25
Human Rights Year, 1968. See No. C297.

Policarpo Toro and Easter Island A199

1970, Jan. 26   Perf. 14½
383 A199 5e lilac .90 .25
80th anniversary of the acquisition of Easter Island. See No. C298.

Sailing Ship and Arms of Valdivia A200

1970, Feb. 4   Litho.   Perf. 14½
384 A200 40c dk carmine .60 .25
150th anniv. of the capture of Valdivia during Chile's war of independence by Thomas Cochrane (1775-1860), naval commander. See No. C299.

Paul Harris and Rotary Emblem — A201

1970, Mar. 18   Litho.   Perf. 14
385 A201 10e violet blue 1.10 .25
Cent. of the birth of Paul Harris (1868-1947), founder of Rotary Intl. See No. C300.

Mahatma Gandhi — A202

1970, Apr. 1   Litho.   Perf. 14½
386 A202 40c blue green 3.50 .30
Mohandas K. Gandhi (1869-1948), leader in India's fight for independence, birth cent. See No. C301. For surcharge see No. 449.

Santo Domingo Church, Santiago, Chile — A203

Designs: 2e, Casa de Moneda de Chile, horiz. 3e, Pedro de Valdivia. 5e, Bridge, horiz. 10e, Ambrosio O'Higgins.

1970, Apr. 30   Engr.
387 A203 2e violet brown .40 .25
388 A203 3e dark red .40 .25
389 A203 4e dark blue .30 .25
390 A203 5e brown .30 .25
391 A203 10e green .30 .25
     Nos. 387-391 (5) 1.70 1.25
Exploration and development of Chile by Spanish explorers.
A sheet containing imperf examples of Nos. 388, 390 and 391 exists. It was not valid for postage.

Education Year Emblem — A204

1970, July 17   Litho.   Perf. 14½
392 A204 2e claret .35 .25
International Education Year. See No. C302.

Virgin and Child — A205

1970, July 28
393 A205 40c green .30 .25
O'Higgins National Shrine at Maipu. See No. C303. For surcharge see No. 454.

Torch and Snake — A206

1970, Aug. 11
394 A206 40c claret & light blue .50 .25
International Cancer Congress, Houston, Texas, May 22-29. See No. C304.

Copper Symbol, Chile Arms — A207

1970, Oct. 21   Litho.   Perf. 14½
395 A207 40c car & lt red brn .35 .25
Nationalization of the copper industry. See No. C305. For surcharges see Nos. 459, B9.

Dove and World Map A208

1970, Oct. 22
396 A208 3e rose magenta & pur .40 .25
25th anniv. of the UN. See No. C306.

1970, Dec. 24   Litho.   Perf. 14½
397 A191 52c on 30c blue .45 .25

Freighter and Ship's Wheel — A209

1971, Jan. 18   Litho.   Perf. 14
398 A209 52c deep carmine .35 .25
Natl. Maritime Commission. See No. C307.

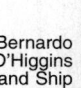

Bernardo O'Higgins and Ship A210

1971, Feb. 3   Perf. 14½
399 A210 5e grnsh bl & grn .55 .25
150th anniv. of the expedition to liberate Peru from Spanish rule. See No. C309.

Youth, Girl and UN Emblem A211

1971, Feb. 11   Litho.   Perf. 14½
400 A211 52c dk blue & brn .35 .25
1st meeting in Latin America of the Executive Council of UNICEF, Santiago, May 20-31, 1969. See No. C310.

Chilean Boy Scout Emblem — A212

1971, Feb. 10   Perf. 14
401 A212 1e green & brn .45 .25
Founding of Chilean Boy Scouts, 60th anniversary. See No. C311.

Satellite and Radar Station A213

1971, May 25   Litho.   Perf. 14½
402 A213 40c dull green .50 .25
First commercial Chilean satellite communications ground station, Longovilo. See No. C312.

Diver with Harpoon Gun A214

1971, Sept. 1
403 A214 1.15e lt & dk green ..... 1.10 .25
404 A214 2.35e vio bl & dp vio bl ..... .40 .25

10th World Championship of Underwater Fishing.

Ferdinand Magellan and Sailing Ship — A215

1971, Nov. 3
405 A215 35c lt vio & brn vio ..... .35 .25

450th anniv. of 1st trip through and discovery of the Strait of Magellan, Oct. 21-Nov. 28, 1520.

Dagoberto Godoy and Plane over Andes — A216

1971, Nov. 4
406 A216 1.15e blue & grn ..... .40 .25

First trans-Andean flight, Dec. 12, 1918.

Virgin of San Cristobal — A217

Chilean Flag and Congress Emblem A218

Congress Emblem and: 4.35e, Church of San Francisco. 9.35e, Central post office, horiz. 18.35e, La Posada (Inn) del Corregidor, horiz.

1971
407 A217 1.15e dk blue ..... .60 .30
408 A218 2.35e ultra & car ..... .60 .30
409 A217 4.35e brown red ..... .60 .30
410 A217 9.35e violet ..... .60 .30
411 A217 18.35e lilac rose ..... 1.25 .30
    Nos. 407-411 (5) 3.65 1.50

10th Cong. of the Postal Union of the Americas and Spain, Santiago.
An imperf souvenir sheet containing Nos. 407-411 was not valid for postage. Value $11. Issued: 2.35e, 4.35e, Nov. 5; 1.15e, Nov. 11; 9.35e, Nov. 18; 18.35e, Nov. 19.

Observation Dome, Cerro el Tololo Observatory — A219

1971, Dec. 18
412 A219 1.95e lt & dk blue ..... .35 .25

Boeing 707 over Easter Island A220

1971, Dec. 18
413 A220 2.35e dk brn & yel ..... .45 .25

Inauguration of regular flights: Santiago, Easter Island, Tahiti.

Alonso de Ercilla y Zuniga — A221

1972, Mar. 20 Engr. Perf. 14
414 A221 1e dark red ..... .40 .25

4th centenary (in 1969) of "La Araucana," by Alonso de Ercilla y Zuniga (1533-1596), Spanish author. See No. C313.

Map of Antarctica and Dog Sled — A222

1972, Mar. 20 Litho. Perf. 14½x15
415 A222 1.15e vio bl & blk ..... .65 .30
416 A222 3.50e blue grn & grn ..... 1.10 .30

10th anniversary (in 1971) of the Antarctic Treaty pledging peaceful uses of and scientific cooperation in Antarctica.
For surcharge see No. 630.

"Your Heart is your Health" — A223

1972, Apr. 2 Litho. Perf. 14½
417 A223 1.15e black & car ..... .40 .25

World Health Month.
For surcharge see No. 631.

People and Statement by Pres. Allende — A224

Conference Hall and UN Emblem — A225

1972, Apr. 13 Litho. Perf. 14½
418 A224 35c dl grn & buff ..... .35 .25
419 A225 1.15e ultra & pur ..... .40 .25
420 A224 4e dk pur & pale rose ..... .60 .35
421 A225 6e orange & vio bl ..... .50 .25
    Nos. 418-421 (4) 1.85 1.10

3rd UN Conf. on Trade and Development (UNCTAD III), Santiago, Apr.-May 1972. Design A224 is perf. horiz. in the middle.

Soldier, 1822, Andes, Military College Emblem A226

1972, June 9
422 A226 1.15e blue & yel ..... .35 .25

Sesquicentennial of Bernardo O'Higgins Military College.

Miner Holding Copper Ingot, Chilean Flag — A227

1972, July 11 Litho. Perf. 15x14½
423 A227 1.15e blue & rose red ..... .35 .25
424 A227 5e blue, blk & rose red ..... .45 .25

Nationalization of copper industry.

Sailing Ship — A228

1972, Aug. 4
425 A228 1.15e violet brown ..... .55 .25

Arturo Pratt Naval Training School, sesqui.

Mt. Calan Observatory — A229

1972, Aug. 31 Litho. Perf. 14½
426 A229 50c ultra ..... .40 .25

University of Chile Mt. Calan Observatory.

Carrier Pigeon — A230

1972, Oct. 9 Litho. Perf. 14½
427 A230 1.15e red lilac & vio ..... .40 .25

Intl. Letter Writing Week, Oct. 9-15.

René Schneider and Army Flag — A231

1972, Oct. 25 Perf. 14
428 A231 2.30e multi ..... .40 .30

2nd anniv. of the death of Gen. René Schneider. No. 428 is perforated vertically in the middle.

Book and Young People A232

1972, Oct. 31 Perf. 14½
429 A232 50c black & dp org ..... .40 .25

International Book Year 1972.

Guitar and Earthen Jar A233

Designs: 2.65e, Fish and produce. 3.50e, Stove, pots and rug, vert.

1972, Nov. 20 Litho. Perf. 14½
430 A233 1.15e red & blk ..... .30 .25
431 A233 2.65e ultra & rose lake ..... .40 .25
432 A233 3.50e red & red brn ..... .40 .25
    Nos. 430-432 (3) ..... 1.10 .75

Tourism Year of the Americas.

José M. Carrera
Before Execution
A234

1973, Feb. 1   Litho.   Perf. 14½
433 A234 2.30e lt ultra   .40   .25
   Sesquicentennial of the death of José
Miguel Carrera (1785-1821), Chilean revolutionist and dictator.

Map of
Antarctica, Flag
at Base — A235

1973, Feb. 8
434 A235 10e ultra & red   .90   .25
   Bernardo O'Higgins Antarctic Base, 25th
anniv.

Naval Air Service
Emblem,
Destroyer
A236

1973, Mar. 16   Litho.   Perf. 14½
435 A236 20e brt bl & ocher   .45   .25
   Chilean Naval Aviation, 50th anniversary.

La Silla
Observatory
A237

1973, Apr. 25   Litho.   Perf. 14½
436 A237 2.30e ultra & blk   .40   .25

INTERPOL
Emblem
A238

   Designs: 50e, Fingerprint over globe.

1973, Sept. 23   Litho.   Perf. 14½
437 A238 30e bister & ultra   .65   .30
438 A238 50e black & red   .85   .30
   50th anniversary of International Criminal
Police Organization.

Grapes — A239

   Chilean wine export: 100e, Globe inscribed
"Chile Exporta Vino."

1973, Dec. 10   Litho.   Perf. 14½
439 A239 20e buff & lilac   .45   .25
440 A239 100e blue & claret   1.00 .25

UPU Headquarters, Bern — A240

1974, Apr. 4
441 A240 500e on 45c green   .75   .25
   UPU cent. No. 441 was not issued without
dark green surcharge and overprint.

Bernardo O'Higgins, Armed Forces
Emblems — A241

   No. 443, Soldiers with mortar. No. 444,
Navy anti-aircraft gunners. No. 445, Pilot in
cockpit. No. 446, Mounted policeman.

1974, Apr. 11   Litho.   Perf. 14½
442 A241 30e shown   .30   .25
443 A241 30e multicolored   .30   .25
444 A241 30e multicolored   .30   .25
445 A241 30e multicolored   .30   .25
446 A241 30e multicolored   .30   .25
      Nos. 442-446 (5)   1.50 1.25
   Honoring the Armed Forces.

Soccer Ball and
Globe — A242

   1000e, Soccer ball and stadium, horiz.

1974   Litho.   Perf. 14
447 A242 500e dk red & org   .60   .25
448 A242 1000e bl & indigo   1.25 .30
   World Cup Soccer Championship, Munich,
June 13-July 7.
   A souvenir sheet contains 2 imperf. stamps
similar to Nos. 447-448, with blue marginal
inscription. Printed on thin card. Size:
90x119mm. Value, $15.

Nos. 386, 355
Surcharged

1974, June   Litho.   Perf. 14½
449 A202 100e on 40c bl grn   .35   .25
      Perf. 13x14
450 A174 300e on 50c dl brn   .40   .25

Traffic
Police — A243

1974, June 20   Perf. 14½
451 A243 30e red brn & grn   .40   .25
   Traffic safety.

Santiago-Australia Air Service — A244

1974, Sept. 5   Litho.   Perf. 14½x14
452 A244 Block of 4   4.75 3.00
   a. 200e Easter Island turtle .70   .30
   b. 200e Polynesian dancer   .70   .30
   c. 200e Map of Fiji Islands   .70   .30
   d. 200e Kangaroo   .70   .30
   Inauguration of air service by LAN (Chile's
national airline) from Santiago to Easter
Island, Tahiti, Fiji, Australia.

Globe Cut to Show
Mantle and
Core — A245

1974, Sept. 9   Perf. 14x14½
453 A245 500e red brn & org   1.00 .25
   International Volcanology Congress, Santiago, Sept. 9-14.

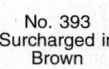

No. 393
Surcharged in
Brown

1974, Oct. 24   Litho.   Perf. 14½
454 A205 100e on 40c green   .40   .25
   Inauguration of the O'Higgins National
Shrine at Maipu, Oct. 24, 1974.

Juan Fernandez Archipelago — A246

1974, Nov. 22   Litho.   Perf. 14½x14
455 A246 Block of 4   5.00 2.50
   a. 200e Robinson Crusoe Island .75 .35
   b. 200e Chonta palms   .75   .35
   c. 200e Mountain goat   .75   .35
   d. 200e Spiny rock lobster   .75   .35
   400th anniversary of discovery of Juan Fernandez Archipelago.

O'Higgins
and
Bolivar
A247

1974, Dec. 9   Perf. 14½
456 A247 100e red brn & buff   .30   .25
   Sesquicentennial of the Battles of Junin and
Ayacucho.

F. Vidal Gormaz
and Institute
Seal — A248

1975, Jan. 22   Litho.   Perf. 14½
457 A248 100e rose claret & bl .35   .25
   Centenary of the Naval Hydrographic Institute; F. Vidal Gormaz was first commandant.

Albert
Schweitzer — A249

1975, Apr. 7   Litho.   Perf. 14x14½
458 A249 500e yel & red brn   .70   .25
   Dr. Albert Schweitzer (1875-1965), medical
missionary, birth centenary.

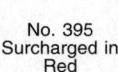

No. 395
Surcharged in
Red

1975, Apr. 7   Perf. 14½
459 A207 70e on 40c car & lt red
             brn   .35   .25

Volunteer Lifeboat Service — A250

1975, Apr. 15   Litho.   Perf. 14½x14
460 A250 Block of 4   6.00 3.75
   a. 150e Lighthouse   .85   .30
   b. 150e Shipwreck   .85   .30

| c. | 150e Lifeboat | .85 | .30 |
| d. | 150e Sailor reaching for life preserver | .85 | .30 |

Valparaiso Volunteer Lifeboat service, 50th anniversary.

Note: souvenir cards were issued by Chile starting in 1975 for various issues. They were printed on thin card. These are not souvenir sheets.

Frigate Lautaro A251

No. 462, Corvette Baquedano. No. 463, Cruiser Chacabuco. No. 464, Brigantine Goleta Esmeralda.

1975, May 21   **Photo. & Engr.**

461	A251	500e shown	.75	.30
462	A251	500e multi	.75	.30
463	A251	500e multi	.75	.30
464	A251	500e multi	.75	.30
a.		Block of 4, #461-464	7.50	7.50
465	A251	800e like #461	1.00	.35
466	A251	800e like #462	1.00	.35
467	A251	800e like #463	1.00	.35
468	A251	800e like #464	1.00	.35
a.		Block of 4, #465-468	10.00	10.00
469	A251	1000e like #461	1.50	.50
470	A251	1000e like #462	1.50	.50
471	A251	1000e like #463	1.50	.50
472	A251	1000e like #464	1.50	.50
a.		Block of 4, #469-472	12.50	12.50
		Nos. 461-472 (12)	13.00	4.60

Shipwreck of training frigate Lautaro, 30th anniversary. Se-tenant in sheets of 25 (5x5) with 7 Lautaro stamps and 6 each of the others.

Happy Mother, by Alfredo Valenzuela P. — A252

Paintings: No. 474, Young Girl, by Francisco Javier Mandiola. No. 475, Lucía Guzman, by Pedro Lira Rencoret. No. 476, Woman, by Magdalena Mira Mena.

1975, Oct. 13   **Litho.**   **Perf. 14½**

473	A252	50c multicolored	.90	.25
474	A252	50c multicolored	.90	.25
475	A252	50c multicolored	.90	.25
476	A252	50c multicolored	.90	.25
		Nos. 473-476 (4)	3.60	1.00

International Women's Year 1975. Gray inscription on back, printed beneath gum, gives details about painting shown.

Diego Portales, Finance Minister — A253

Inscribed: D. Portales

1975-78   **Litho.**   **Perf. 13½x14½**

477	A253	10c gray grn	.30	.25
478	A253	20c violet ('76)	.30	.25
479	A253	30c orange ('76)	.30	.25
480	A253	50c lt brown	.30	.25
481	A253	1p blue	.30	.25
482	A253	1.50p ocher ('76)	.30	.25
483	A253	2p gray ('77)	.30	.25
483A	A253	2.50p citron ('78)	.30	.25
483B	A253	3.50p pnksh rose ('78)	.35	.25
484	A253	5p rose claret	.35	.25
		Nos. 477-484 (10)	3.10	2.50

See Nos. 635-639. For surcharge see No. 533.

Cochrane and Liberating Squadron, 1820 — A254

No. 486, Capture of Valdivia, 1820. No. 487, Capture of Three-master Esmeralda, 1820. No. 488, Cruiser Cochrane, 1874. No. 489, Destroyer Cochrane, 1962.

1976, Jan. 6   **Perf. 14½**

485	A254	1p multicolored	.70	.25
486	A254	1p multicolored	.70	.25
487	A254	1p multicolored	.70	.25
488	A254	1p multicolored	.70	.25
489	A254	1p multicolored	.70	.25
a.		Strip of 5, #485-489	4.00	4.00

Lord Thomas Cochrane, first commander of Chilean Navy, birth bicentenary.

Flags of Chile and Bolivia A255

1976, May 25   **Litho.**   **Perf. 14½**

| 490 | A255 | 1.50p multicolored | 1.50 | .25 |

Sesquicentennial of Bolivia's independence.

Lake of the Inca, OAS Emblem A256

1976, June 11

| 491 | A256 | 1.50p multicolored | 1.40 | .25 |

6th General Assembly of the Organization of American States.

George Washington A257

1976, July 3

| 492 | A257 | 5p multicolored | .80 | .25 |

American Bicentennial.

Minerva and Academy Emblem A258

1976, July

| 493 | A258 | 2.50p multicolored | 1.50 | .25 |

Polytechnic Military Academy, 50th anniv.

Araucan Indian — A259

Designs: 2p, Condor with broken chain. 3p, Winged woman, symbolizing rebirth.

1976, Sept. 20   **Litho.**   **Perf. 14½**

494	A259	1p blue & multi	.30	.25
495	A259	2p blue & multi	1.50	.75
496	A259	3p yellow & multi	.60	.25
a.		Strip of 3, #494-496	2.75	2.00

3rd anniversary of the Military Junta.

View, Antarctica — A260

1977, Feb. 10   **Litho.**   **Perf. 14½**

| 497 | A260 | 2p multicolored | 9.00 | .50 |

Visit of President Augusto Pinochet to Antarctica.

School Emblem, Planted Field — A261

1977, Mar. 10   **Perf. 14½**

| 498 | A261 | 2p multicolored | 1.50 | .30 |

Cent. of advanced agricultural education.

Justice — A262

1977, Mar. 30   **Litho.**   **Perf. 14½**

| 499 | A262 | 2p brown & slate | 1.60 | .35 |

Supreme Court of Justice, sesquicentennial.

Eye with Globe, Caduceus — A263

1977, Mar. 30   **Litho.**   **Perf. 14½**

| 500 | A263 | 2p multicolored | 2.00 | .55 |

11th Pan-American Ophthalmological Cong.

Mounted Policeman A264

Designs: No. 502, Policewoman with children. No. 503, Paine Peaks and Osorno Volcano, crossed rifle emblem. No. 504, Crossed rifle emblem, mounted and motorcycle policemen, helicopter and automobile, horiz.

1977, Apr. 27

501	A264	2p multicolored	.45	.25
502	A264	2p multicolored	.45	.25
503	A264	2p multicolored	.45	.25
504	A264	2p multicolored	.45	.25
		Nos. 501-504 (4)	1.80	1.00

Chilean police organization, 50th anniv.

Intelsat Satellite over Globe — A265

1977, May 17   **Litho.**   **Perf. 14½**

| 505 | A265 | 2p multi | .90 | .35 |

World Telecommunications Day.

El Mercurio's First Front Page, Press and Ship — A266

1977, July 5   **Litho.**   **Perf. 14½**

| 506 | A266 | 2p multi | .40 | .25 |

El Mercurio de Valparaiso, first Chilean newspaper, 150th anniversary.

St. Francis, Birds and Cross — A267

1977, July 26   **Litho.**   **Perf. 14½**

| 507 | A267 | 5p multi | 1.75 | .30 |

St. Francis of Assisi, 750th death anniv.

Science and Technology A268

1977, Aug. 26   **Litho.**   **Perf. 14½**

| 508 | A268 | 4p multi | .55 | .25 |

Young Mother
Weaving — A269

No. 510, Handicapped boy in wheelchair &
nurse. No. 511, Children dancing in circle. No.
512, Old man & home.

1977, Sept. 13   Litho.   Perf. 14½
509 A269 5p multi   .60   .25
510 A269 5p multi   .60   .25
511 A269 10p multi, horiz.   1.25   .25
512 A269 10p multi, horiz.   1.25   .25
     Nos. 509-512 (4)   3.70 1.00

4th anniversary of Government Junta and
social services of armed forces.

Diego de
Almagro — A270

1977, Oct. 31   Engr.   Perf. 14½
513 A270 5p rose & carmine   .40   .25

Diego de Almagro (1475-1538), leader of
Spanish expedition to Chile.

Bell,
Letters,
Dove and
Child
A271

1977, Dec. 12   Litho.   Perf. 14½
514 A271 2.50p multi   .40   .25

Christmas 1977.

Loading
Timber
A272

1978   Litho.   Perf. 15
515 A272 10p multi   1.25   .25
516 A272 20p multi   1.75   .35

No. 516 inscribed "CORREOS," ship is flying Chilean flag.

Papal Arms
and Globe
A273

University — A274

1978   Litho.   Perf. 14½
521 A273 10p multi   1.00   .30
522 A274 25p multi   2.25   .75

World Peace Day (10p); Catholic University
of Valparaiso, 50th anniversary. Issue
dates: 10p, July 28; 25p, July 31.

O'Higgins, by
Gil de
Castro — A275

1978, Aug. 20   Litho.   Perf. 15
523 A275 10p multi   .90   .30

Bernardo O'Higgins (1778-1842), soldier
and statesman.

Chacabuco
Victory
Monument
A276

1978, Sept. 11
524 A276 10p multi   .90   .30

160th anniv. of O'Higgins victory at Chacabuco, and 5th anniv. of military government.

Teacher Writing on
Blackboard — A277

1978, Sept. 21
525 A277 15p multi   1.00   .25

10th anniversary and 9th Reunion of Inter-
american Council for Education, Science and
Culture (C.I.E.C.C.), Sept. 21-29.

First National Fleet, by Thomas
Somerscales — A278

Design: 30p, Last Moments of Rancagua
Battle, by Pedro Subercaseaux.

1978   Litho.   Perf. 15
526 A278 20p multi   2.25   .55
527 A278 30p multi   2.75   .90

Bernardo O'Higgins (1778-1842), soldier
and statesman.
     Issue dates: 20p, Oct. 9; 30p, Oct. 2.

San Martin-O'Higgins Medal, by Rene
Thenot, 1942 — A279

1978, Oct. 20
528 A279 7p multi   .50   .25

José de San Martin and Bernardo
O'Higgins, 200th birth anniversaries.

Council
Emblem — A280

1978, Nov. 27   Litho.   Perf. 14½
529 A280 50p multi   5.25 2.10

Intl. Council of Military Sports, 30th anniv.

Three
Kings — A281

Virgin and
Child — A282

1978, Dec. 14   Litho.   Perf. 14½
530 A281 3p multi   .75   .25
531 A282 11p multi   1.40   .40

Christmas 1978.

Philippi
Brothers
A283

1978, Dec. 29   Litho.   Perf. 14½x15
532 A283 3.50p multi   .70   .25

Bernardo E. Philippi (1811-1852) and
Rodulfo A. Philippi (1808-1904), scientists and
travelers.

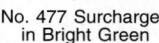

No. 477 Surcharged
in Bright Green

1979   Litho.   Perf. 13x14
533 A253 3.50p on 10c gray grn   .30   .25

Flags of Chile
and Salvation
Army — A284

1979, Mar. 17   Litho.   Perf. 14½
534 A284 10p multi   1.25   .65

Salvation Army in Chile, 70th anniversary.

Pope Paul VI (1897-1978) — A285

1979, Mar. 30
535 A285 11p multi   1.50   .90

Battle of Maipu Monument — A286

1979, Apr. 17   Litho.   Perf. 14½
536 A286 8.50p multi   1.40   .50

Bernardo O'Higgins (1778-1842), Liberator
of Chile.

Naval
Battles
A287

1979, May 21   Litho.   Perf. 14½
537 A287 3.50p Angamos   .80   .30
538 A287 3.50p Iquique   .80   .30
539 A287 3.50p Punta Gruesa   .80   .30
     Nos. 537-539 (3)   2.40   .90

Centenary of victorious naval battles against
Peru.

1903 Ambulance and Red
Cross — A288

1979, June 29   Litho.   Perf. 14½
540 A288 25p multi   4.00 1.10

75th anniversary of Chilean Red Cross.

Diego
Portales — A289

1979-86   Litho.   Perf. 13½
542 A289 1.50p ocher   .25   .25
543 A289 2p gray ('81)   .25   .25
544 A289 3.50p red   .30   .25

545	A289	4.50p bl grn ('81)	.40	.25
546	A289	5p rose claret	.50	.25
547	A289	6p emerald	.60	.30
548	A289	7p yellow ('82)	.55	.30
549	A289	10p blue ('82)	.80	.30
550	A289	12p orange ('86)	.35	.25
		Nos. 542-550 (9)	4.00	2.40

1.50p, 3.50p, 5p and 6p inscribed "D. Portales."

People and Flag — A290

1979, Aug. 28   Litho.   Perf. 14½
551 A290 10p multi   1.00   .60

Yugoslavian immigration, centenary.

Coat of Arms and Mt. Castillo A290a

1979, Oct. 12   Litho.   Perf. 14½
552 A290a 20p multi   2.25   1.00

Coyhaique 50th anniv.

IYC Emblem, Playground — A291

IYC Emblem, Children's Drawings: 11p, Girl and shadow, vert. 12p, Dancing.

1979, Oct. 9   Perf. 14½
553 A291 9.50p multi   .95   .60
554 A291 11p multi   1.10   .75
555 A291 12p multi   1.60   .85
Nos. 553-555 (3)   3.65   2.20

International Year of the Child.

Telecom 79 A292

1979, Oct. 26   Litho.   Perf. 14½
556 A292 15p multi   1.50   .75

3rd World Telecommunications Exhibition, Geneva, Sept. 20-26.

Puerto Williams, 25th Anniversary — A293

1979, Nov. 21
557 A293 3.50p multi   .60   .25

Adoration of the Kings A294

1979, Dec. 4   Litho.   Perf. 15
558 A294 3.50p multi   .60   .25

Christmas 1979.

Rafael Sotomayor, Minister of War — A295

Military heroes: No. 560, Erasmo Escala. No. 561, Emilio Sotomayor. No. 562, Eleuterio Ramirez.

1979, Dec. 29   Perf. 13½
559 A295 3.50p ocher & brn   .50   .25
560 A295 3.50p multi   .50   .25
561 A295 3.50p multi   .50   .25
562 A295 3.50p multi   .50   .25
a.   Block of 4, #559-562   2.00   2.00

Bell UH-1 Rescue Helicopter at Tinguiririca Volcano, by S.O. Mococain — A296

Air Force, 50th Anniversary: No. 564, Flying boat Catalina Skua over Antarctic, by E.F. Alvarez. No. 565, F5-E Tiger II over Andes, by M.M. Barria.

1980, Mar. 21   Litho.   Perf. 13½
563 A296 3.50p shown   .50   .25
564 A296 3.50p Jet   .50   .25
565 A296 3.50p Sea plane   .50   .25
Nos. 563-565 (3)   1.50   .75

The Death of Bueras, by Pedro Leon Carmona — A297

1980, Apr. 14   Litho.   Perf. 13½
566 A297 12p multi   1.50   .50

Charge of Bueras, Battle of Maipo, 1818.

Rotary International, 75th Anniversary — A298

1980, Apr. 15
567 A298 10p multi   1.25   .45

Gen. Manuel Baquedano, by Pedro Subercaseaux A299

Gen. Pedro Lagos, Battle Scene, by Subercaseaux — A300

Battle of Morro de Arica Centenary (Subercaseaux Paintings): No. 570, Commander Juan J. San Martin, battle scene.

1980, June 7   Litho.   Perf. 13½
568 A299 3.50p multi   .40   .25
569 A300 3.50p multi   .40   .25
570 A300 3.50p multi   .40   .25
Nos. 568-570 (3)   1.20   .75

Score and Perez's Silhouette — A301

1980, June 27   Litho.   Perf. 13½
571 A301 6p multi   .60   .30

Osman Perez Freire (1880-1930), composer, and fragment from his song "Ay, Ay, Ay."

Mt. Gasherbrum II, Chilean Flag, Ice Pick — A302

1980, July 9
572 A302 15p multi   1.40   .60

Chilean Himalayan expedition, June 1979.

"Charity," Stained-glass Window A303

1980, July 18
573 A303 10p multi   1.50   .35

Daughters of Charity, 125th anniv. in Chile.

Condor, Colors of Chile — A304

1980, Sept. 11   Litho.   Perf. 13½
574 A304 3.50p multi   .40   .25

Plebiscite to vote on new constitution.

Inca Child Mummy — A305

1980, Sept. 14
575 A305 5p shown   .60   .25
576 A305 5p Claudio Gay   .60   .25
a.   Pair, #575-576 + label   1.40   1.25

Natl. Museum of Natural History (founded by Claudio Gay, 1800-73) sesqui.

Pablo Burchard, by Pedro Lira — A306

1980, Sept. 27   Litho.   Perf. 13½
577 A306 3.50p multi   .45   .25

Museum of Fine Art centenary (directed by Burchard, 1932).

Santiago International Fair — A307

1980, Oct. 30
578 A307 3.50p multi   .50   .25

Nativity — A308

Christmas 1980: 3.50p, Family, vert.

1980, Nov. 25   Litho.   Perf. 13½
579 A308 3.50p multi   .80   .30
580 A308 10.50p multi   2.00   .55

Infantryman
1879 — A309

Pacific War period uniforms, 1879.

1980, Nov. 27
581	A309	3.50p shown	.75	.25
582	A309	3.50p Cavalry officer	.75	.25
583	A309	3.50p Artillery officer	.75	.25
584	A309	3.50p Engineer colonel	.75	.25
a.		Block of 4, #581-584	4.00	4.00

See Nos. 606-609.

Congress
Emblem — A310

1980, Dec. 1
585	A310	11.50p multi	2.00	.60

23rd Intl. Cong. of Military Medicine & Pharmacy.

Eradication of
Hoof and
Mouth
Disease
A311

1981, Jan. 16   Litho.   Perf. 13½
586	A311	9.50p multi	.90	.25

Moai Statues, Easter Island — A312

No. 588, Robinson Crusoe Island. No. 589, Penguins, Antarctic Territory.

1981, Jan. 28   Litho.   Perf. 13½
587	A312	3.50p shown	.45	.35
588	A312	3.50p multi	.80	.35
589	A312	10.50p multi	3.50	1.00
		Nos. 587-589 (3)	4.75	1.70

National Heroine Javiera Carrera, by
O.M. Pizarro, Birth
Bicentenary — A313

1981, Mar. 20
590	A313	3.50p multi	.40	.25

UPU
Membership
Centenary
A314

1981, Apr. 1
591	A314	3.50p multi	.40	.25

C130 Hercules Air Force Transport
Plane Unloading Cargo — A315

1981, Apr. 21
592	A315	3.50p multi	1.25	.40

Lieutenant Marsh Air Force Base, 1st anniv.

13th World Telecommunications
Day — A316

1981, May 17   Litho.   Perf. 13½
593	A316	3.50p multi	.45	.25

Arturo
Prat
Naval
Base
A317

1981, June 23   Litho.   Perf. 13½
594	A317	3.50p multi	1.50	.25

Capt. Jose
Luis Araneda
A318

1981, June 26
595	A318	3.50p multi	.45	.25

Battle of Sangrar centenary.

Philatelic
Society of
Chile, 90th
Anniv.
A319

1981, July 29   Litho.   Perf. 13½
596	A319	4.50p multi	.40	.25

Minister Recabarren and Chief
Conuepan Giving Speeches, by Hector
Robles Acuna — A320

1981, Aug. 7
597	A320	4.50p multi	1.00	.25

Temuco city centenary.

Exports
A321

1981, Aug. 31   Litho.   Perf. 13½
598	A321	14p multi	.90	.35

Presidential Palace — A322

1981, Sept. 11
599	A322	4.50p multi	.80	.25

Natl. liberation, 8th anniv.

St. Vincent de
Paul, 400th
Birth Anniv.
A323

1981, Sept. 27   Litho.   Perf. 13½
600	A323	4.50p multi	.50	.25

Andres Bello,
Poet and
Sholar, Birth
Bicentenary
A324

1981, Sept. 29
601	A324	4.50p Coin	.45	.25
602	A324	9.50p Bust, books	.75	.25
603	A324	11.50p Statue, arms	1.10	.40
		Nos. 601-603 (3)	2.30	.95

2nd Congress
of South
American
Uniformed
Police
A325

1981, Oct. 15
604	A325	4.50p multi	.55	.25

World
Food
Day
A326

1981, Oct. 16
605	A326	5.50p multi	.55	.25

Uniform Type of 1980

1879 Parade Uniforms.

1981, Nov. 6   Perf. 13½
606	A309	5.50p Infantry private	.80	.25
607	A309	5.50p Cadet	.80	.25
608	A309	5.50p Cavalryman	.80	.25
609	A309	5.50p Artilleryman	.80	.25
a.		Block of 4, #606-609	4.00	3.00

Intl. Year of
the Disabled
A327

1981, Nov. 11
610	A327	5.50p multi	1.10	.30

Christmas 1981 — A328

1981, Nov. 25
611 A328 5.50p Nativity .50 .25
612 A328 11.50p Three Kings 1.00 .40

50th Anniv. of Federico Santa Maria
Technical University — A329

1981, Dec 1 Litho. Perf. 13½
613 A329 5.50p multi .50 .25

Dario Salas
(1881-1941),
Educator — A330

1981, Dec. 4
614 A330 5.50p multi .50 .25

FIDA '82, 2nd Natl. Air Force
Fair — A331

1982, Mar. 6 Litho. Perf. 13½
615 A331 4.50p multi .50 .25

1980 Constitution — A332

4.50p, Cardinal Caro, family. 11p, Diego
Portales. 30p, Bernardo O'Higgins.

1982, Mar. 11
616 A332 4.50p multi .50 .25
617 A332 11p multi 1.25 .40
618 A332 30p multi 3.00 .90
 Nos. 616-618 (3) 4.75 1.55

Panamerican
Institute of
Geography
and History,
12th General
Assembly
A333

1982, Mar. 22 Litho. Perf. 13½
619 A333 4.50p multi .50 .25

American Air Forces Cooperation
System — A334

1982, Apr. 12
620 A334 4.50p multi .45 .25

Pedro Montt — A335

1982, Mar. 27
621 A335 4.50p light vio .50 .25

Fish
Exports — A336

1982, May 3 Litho. Perf. 13½
622 A336 20p multi 2.25 .75

Scouting Year — A337

No. 623b, Robert Baden-Powell.

1982, May 21 Litho. Perf. 13
623 A337 Pair 42.50 32.50
a.-b. 4.50p, either single 15.00 8.00

Battle of
Concepcion
Centenary
A338

Chacabuco Regiment officers killed in
battle.

1982, June 18 Litho. Perf. 13½
624 Block of 4 2.50 2.50
a. A338 4.50p I. Carrera Pinto .50 .25
b. A338 4.50p A. Perez Canto .50 .25
c. A338 4.50p J. Montt Salamanca .50 .25
d. A338 4.50p L. Cruz Martinez .50 .25

UN World Assembly on Aging, July
26-Aug. 6 — A339

1982, Aug. 5
625 A339 4.50p multi .40 .25

TB Bacillus
Centenary
A340

1982, Aug. 31
626 A340 4.50p multi .40 .25

9th Anniv. of National
Liberation — A341

1982, Sept. 11 Litho. Perf. 13½
627 A341 4.50p multi .40 .25

Christmas 1982 — A342

Children's drawings.

1982, Nov. 2
628 A342 10p multi 1.00 .25
629 A342 25p multi, vert. 1.50 .60

Nos. 416 Surcharged in Green

Nos. 417
Surcharged in
Black

1982, Nov. Perf. 14½x15, 14½
630 A222 1p on 3.50p bl grn &
 grn (G) .25 .25
631 A223 2p on 1.15p blk & car .25 .25

Marist Alumni, 9th
World Congress
A342a

Virgin Mary & Marcellus Champagnat
(founder of Marist Brotherhood), stained glass
window, Church of the Sacred Heart of Jesus,
Barcelona.

1982, Nov. 11 Litho. Perf. 13½
631A A342a 7p multi 1.50 .40

El Sur
Newspaper
Centenary
A342b

7p, Wooden handpress, masthead.

1982, Nov. 15
631B A342b 7p multi .50 .25

110th Anniv. of South American
Steamship Co. — A342c

1982, Dec. 20
631C A342c 7p Steamer Copiapo 1.00 .35

60th Anniv. of
Radio Club of
Chile — A342d

1982, Dec. 29
631D A342d 7p multi .50 .25

First Anniv. of Postal Agreement with
Order of Malta — A343

1983, Mar. 30 Litho. Perf. 13½
632 25p Arms of Order of Malta 2.00 .40
633 50p Chile 4.00 .80
a. Pair, #632-633 8.00 6.50

D.D. No. 20
This and similar inscriptions indicate
that the stamps would be sold at a discount if purchased in large quantities.

D. Portales Type of 1975 Inscribed Diego Portales and

Ramon Barros Luco
A344

Juan Luis Sanfuentes
A344a

1983-88		Litho.	Perf. 13½	
634	A344	1p grnsh bl	.25	.25
635	A253	1p chalky bl	.25	.25
636	A253	1.50p ocher	.25	.25
637	A344	2p dl vio ('84)	.25	.25
638	A253	2p ol gray	.25	.25
639	A253	2.50p lemon	.25	.25
640	A253	5p red lilac	.35	.25
641	A344	5p crim rose	.25	.25
642	A344a	5p red ('84)	.25	.25
643	A344	7p ultra	.30	.25
644	A344a	9p brn ('84)	.25	.25
645	A344a	9p grn ('84)	.25	.25
646	A344	10p black	.25	.25
646A	A344a	10p gray ('84)	.25	.25
647	A344a	15p ultra ('87)	.25	.25
a.		Booklet pane of 10	1.50	
648	A344a	20p yel ('88)	.25	.25
b.		Booklet pane of 10	2.00	

Nos. 644, 647, 648 inscribed "D.S. No. 20."
Issued: No. 640, 8/85.
For surcharge see No. 779.

50th Anniv. of Bureau of Investigation
A345

1983, June 19	Litho.	Perf. 13½	
649 A345 20p multi		1.25	.50

Antonio Cardinal Samore (1905-1983) — A346

1983, June 26
650 A346 30p multi   2.00   .60

Centenary of Cliff Elevators in Valparaiso
A347

1983, Aug. 19	Litho.	Perf. 13½	
651 A347 40p multi		4.00	.45

Pucara de Quitor Settlement Ruins, San Pedro de Atacama — A348

No. 653, Llamas, rock painting, Rio Ibanez, Aisen. No. 654, Duck-shaped jug with human head, Diaguita cultures. No. 655, Puoko Tangata carved stone head, Easter Isld.

1983, Aug. 26
652 A348 7p multi	1.00	.40
653 A348 7p multi	1.00	.40
654 A348 7p multi	1.00	.40
655 A348 7p multi, vert.	.25	.25
Nos. 652-655 (4)	3.25	1.45

10th Anniv. of National Liberation — A349

1983, Sept. 11	Litho.	Perf. 13½	
656 A349	7p Angel with broken chains	.60	.25
657 A349	7p Couple, flag	.60	.25
658 A349	10p Family, torch	.60	.25
659 A349	40p Coat of arms, "10"	2.00	.75
a.	Strip of 4, #656-659	5.00	3.50

For surcharges see Nos. 669-670.

Famous Hondurans
A350

No. 660, Francisco Morazan (1792-1842), Advocate of United Central America. No. 661, Jose Cecilio Del Valle (1777-1834), Scholar and Leader of Pan Americanism.

1983, Oct. 3	Litho.	Perf. 13½	
660 A350 7p multi		.40	.25
661 A350 7p multi		.40	.25
a. Pair, #660-661		.80	.80

World Communications Year — A351

1983, Oct. 13	Litho.	Perf. 13½	
662	7p Central P.O.	.85	.25
663	7p Challenger spaceship	.85	.25
a.	A351 Pair, #662-663	1.75	1.75

Christmas 1983 — A353

Childrens' Drawings: 10p Chilean Peasant, Hanny Chacon. 30p, Holy Family. Lucrecia Cardenas, vert.

1983, Nov. 14	Litho.	Perf. 13	
664 A353 10p multi		.50	.25
665 A353 30p multi		1.50	.40

Design descriptions printed on back on top of gum.

State Railways Centenary — A354

Train Cars: a, Presidential coach, 1911. b, Service coach, 1910; tender, 1929. c, Locomotive Type 80, 1929.

1984, Jan. 4	Litho.	Perf. 13½	
666 A354 Strip of 3		10.00	8.75
a.-c.	9p, any single	2.40	.45

3rd Intl. Air Fair, Santiago, Mar. 3-11 — A355

1984, Jan. 31	Litho.	Perf. 13½	
667 A355 9p Flags, plane		1.00	.25

20th Anniv. of Nuclear Energy Commission — A356

1984, Apr. 16	Litho.	Perf. 13	
668 A356 9p multi		.50	.25

Nos. 656-657 Surcharged in Purple

1984, June 11	Litho.	Perf. 13½	
669 A349 9p on 7p #656		.45	.25
670 A349 9p on 7p #657		.45	.25
a. Pair, #669-670		1.25	.95

Antarctic Colonization — A357

No. 671, Women's expedition. No. 672, Villa las Estrellas Station. No. 673, Scouts, flag, Air Force base.

1984, June 18
671 A357 15p multicolored	.75	.35
672 A357 15p multicolored	.75	.35
673 A357 15p multicolored	.75	.35
a. Strip of 3, #671-673	5.75	5.50

10th Anniv. of Regionalization — A358

Designs: a, Parinacota Church, Tarapaca. b, El Tatio geyser, Antofagasta. c, Copper mining, Atacama. d, Tololo Observatory, Coquimbo. e, Valparaiso Harbor, Valparaiso. f, Ahu Akivi head sculptures, Easter Isld. g, St.

Francis Church, Santiago. h, El Hunique House, O'Higgins. i, Colburn Machicura Dam and Hydroelectric Power Station, Maule. j, Sta. Juana de Guadalcazar Fort, Bio-Bio. k, Indian woman, Araucania. l, Guar Isld. Church, Los Lagos. m, Main road, Gen. del Campo. n, Shepherds' Monument, Magellanes and Antarctic. o, Family, Villa las Estrellas Station, Antarctic.

1984, July 11
674	Sheet of 15	15.00	15.00
a.-o. A358 9p multi, any single		.75	.40

Capt. Pedro Sarmiento de Gamboa, Map, 1584 — A359

1984, July 31	Litho.	Perf. 13	
675 A359 100p multi		5.25	1.10

400th anniv. of Spanish presence in Straits of Magellan.

State Bank of Chile Centenary — A360

35p, Founder Antonio Varas de la Barra, coin.

1984, Sept. 6	Litho.	Perf. 13½	
676 A360 35p multi		1.25	.55

11th Anniv. of Liberation — A361

20p, Monument to O'Higgins.

1984, Sept. 11
677 A361 20p multi	1.10	.30

Circus Centenary — A362

1984, Sept. 28	Litho.	Perf. 13½	
678 A362 45p Clown		1.50	.70

Endangered Species, World Wildlife Emblem — A363

1985, July   Litho.   Perf. 13½
679	A363	9p Chinchilla	9.00	2.50
680	A363	9p Blue whale	9.00	2.50
681	A363	9p Sea lions	9.00	2.50
682	A363	9p Chilean huemuls	9.00	2.50
a.		Block of 4, #679-682	48.00	25.00

Christmas 1984 — A364

Children's drawings.

1984, Nov. 20   Litho.   Perf. 13½
683	A364	9p Shepherds	.40	.25
684	A364	40p Bethlehem	1.50	.40

Santiago University Planetarium Opening — A365

1984, Dec. 29
685	A365	10p multi	.70	.25

Flora and Fauna — A366

Wildlife: a, Conepatus chinga. b, Leucocoryne purpurea. c, Himantopus himantopus. d, Lutra felina. e, Balbisia peduncularis. f, Psittacus cyanalysias. g, Pudu pudu. h, Fuschia magellanica. i, Diuca diuca. j, Dusicyon griseus. k, Alstroemeria sierrae. l, Glaucidium nanum.

1985, Feb.
686		Block of 12	15.00	10.00
a.-l.	A366	10p, Any single	.75	.40

American Airforces Cooperation System, 25th Anniv. A367

1985, Mar. 26
687	A367	45p Emblem, flags	2.00	1.10

Chile-Argentina Peace Treaty — A368

1985, May 2   Litho.   Perf. 13½
688	A368	20p Papal arms, flags	3.00	.60

Fr. Joseph Kentenich (1885-1968), Founder, Intl. Schonstatt Movement of Catholic Laymen A369

40p, Portrait, La Florida Sanctuary, Santiago.

1985, May 19   Litho.   Perf. 13½
689	A369	40p multi	.70	.40

Antarctic Treaty, 25th Anniv. — A370

Resources, research: 15p, Krill, pack ice, map. 20p, Seismological Station, O'Higgins' Base. 35p, Georeception Station, dish receiver.

1985, June 21
690	A370	15p multi	.65	.35
691	A370	20p multi	.85	.50
692	A370	35p multi	1.50	.75
		Nos. 690-692 (3)	3.00	1.60

Canis Fulvipes — A371

Endangered wildlife: b, Phoenicoparrus jamesi. c, Fulica gigantea. d, Lutra provocax.

1985, Aug. 9   Litho.   Perf. 13½
693	A371	Block of 4	13.00	4.50
a.-d.		20p, any single	1.75	.35

Intl. Youth Year A372

UN, 40th Anniv. A373

1985, Aug. 31
694	A372	15p multi	.50	.25
695	A373	15p multi	.50	.25
a.		Pair, #694-695	1.50	1.50

Gen. Jose Miguel Carrera Verdugo (1785-1821) — A374

1985, Oct. 8   Litho.   Perf. 13½
696	A374	40p multi	2.25	.55

Farmer and Ox-drawn Hay Cart — A375

Folklore: b, Street photographer, wet plate camera. c, One-man band. d, Basket maker.

1985, Oct.
697	A375	Block of 4	1.25	.90
a.-d.		10p, any single	.25	.25

For surcharges see Nos. 770-771.

Christmas 1985 — A376

Winning children's drawings, 7th natl. design contest.

1985, Nov. 4
698	A376	15p Nativity	.55	.25
699	A376	100p Father Christmas, vert.	3.75	1.00

Nos. 698-699 inscribed in black on gummed side with child's name, age, school and region.

Holy Family — A376a

1985   Litho.   Perf. 13½
699A	A376a	10p buff & brn	.60	.25

For surcharge see No. 768.

16th Armed Forces Conference — A377

20p, Cavalryman, Directorial Escort, 1818. 35p, Officer, Grand Guard, 1813.

1985, Nov. 15   Litho.   Perf. 13½
700	A377	20p multicolored	.75	.25
701	A377	35p multicolored	1.25	.35

Halley's Comet — A378

1985, Nov. 29   Litho.   Perf. 13½
702	A378	45p multicolored	1.00	.25
a.		Souvenir sheet	20.00	20.00

No. 702a exists imperf. Value $30.

Natl. Solidarity Campaign — A379

1985
703	A379	5p red & blue	.50	.50

Campaign for Prevention of Forest Fires — A380

1985, Dec. 27
704		40p Forest	.75	.40
705		40p Fire destruction	.75	.40
a.	A380	Pair, #704-705	2.75	1.50

No. 705a has continuous design.

Dungeness Point Lighthouse, Straits of Magellan — A381

1986, Jan. 26
706	A381	45p shown	1.40	.45
707	A381	45p Evangelistas Lighthouse	1.40	.45
a.		Pair, #706-707	4.00	2.50

No. 707a continuous design.

View of Santiago, Mackenna — A382

1986, Jan. 28
708	A382	30p multi	.45	.25

Benjamin Vicuna Mackenna (d. 1886), municipal superintendent of Santiago, 1872-1875.

Diego Portales, Natl. Crest, Text — A382a

1986, Feb.   Litho.   Perf. 13½
708A	A382a	12p on 3.50p multi	.45	.25

No. 708A not issued without surcharge.

1986 World Cup Soccer
Championships, Mexico — A383

Host stadiums: 15p, Natl. Stadium, Chile, 1962. 20p, Aztec Stadium, Mexico, 1970. 35p, Maracana Stadium, Brazil, 1950. 50p, Wembley Stadium, Great Britain, 1966.

1986, Feb. 18
709	A383	15p multi	.40	.25
710	A383	20p multi	.55	.25
711	A383	35p multi	.80	.35
712	A383	50p multi	1.25	.50
	Nos. 709-712 (4)		3.00	1.35

Environmental Conservation — A384

1986, Feb. 28
713	A384	20p Water	.75	.25
714	A384	20p Air	.75	.25
715	A384	20p Soil	.75	.25
	Nos. 713-715 (3)		2.25	.75

Sailing Ship Santiaguillo, Flags — A385

1986, Mar. 20
716	A385	40p multi	1.00	.55

Discovery of Valparaiso Bay, 450th anniv.

A386

1986, Apr. 9
717	A386	45p multi	1.00	.45

Interamerican Development Bank, 25th anniv.

A387

1986, Apr. 30   Litho.   Perf. 13½
718	A387	15p multi	.65	.25

St. Rosa de Lima (1586-1617), sanctuary at Pelequen.

Moai Statues, Easter Is. — A388

60p, Raraku Volcano. 100p, Tongariki Ruins.

1986, May 15
719	A388	60p multi	2.50	.60
a.		Souvenir sheet	12.50	12.50
720	A388	100p multi	5.00	1.00
a.		Souvenir sheet	19.00	19.00

AMERIPEX '86 — A389

1986, May 23
721	A389	100p multi	2.50	1.10

Historic Naval Ships — A390

No. 722, Schooner Ancud, 1843. No. 723, Armed merchantman Aguilar, 1830. No. 724, Corvette Esmeralda, 1856. No. 725, Frigate O'Higgins, 1834.

1986, May 30
722	A390	35p multi	1.25	.60
723	A390	35p multi	1.25	.60
724	A390	35p multi	1.25	.60
725	A390	35p multi	1.25	.60
a.		Block of 4, #722-725	7.00	6.50

See Nos. 752-753.

Paintings by Juan Francisco Gonzalez (1853-1933) A391

No. 726, Rush and Chrysanthemums. No. 727, Gate of La Serena.

1986, June 24
726	A391	30p multi	1.00	.35
727	A391	30p multi	1.00	.35
a.		Pair, #726-727	2.50	1.75

Exports — A392

Designs: a, Saltpeter. b, Iron. c, Copper. d, Molybdenum.

1986   Litho.   Perf. 13½
728	A392	Block of 4	1.60	1.25
a.-d.		12p, any single	.25	.25

Antarctic Fauna — A393

a, Sterna vittata. b, Phalacrocorax atriceps. c, Aptenodytes forsteri. d, Catharacta lonnberg.

1986, July 16   Litho.   Perf. 13½
729		Block of 4	9.00	5.50
a.-d.	A393	40p, any single	1.75	.70

Writers — A394

No. 730, Pedro de Ona (1570-1643). No. 731, Vicente Huidobro (1893-1948).

1986, Aug. 19
730	A394	20p multi	.65	.40
731	A394	20p multi	.65	.40
a.		Pair, #730-731	1.75	1.00

Has continuous design.

Military Academy, Cent. — A395

No. 732, Major-General, 1878. No. 733, Major, 1950.

1986, Sept. 8   Litho.   Perf. 13½
732	A395	45p multi	.75	.40
733	A395	45p multi	.75	.40
a.		Pair, #732-733	1.75	1.10

Art A396

No. 734, Diaguita urn, duck jug. No. 735, Mapuche silver ornament, embroidery.

1986, Oct. 17   Perf. 13½
734	A396	30p multi	.65	.40
735	A396	30p multi	.65	.40
a.		Pair, #734-735	2.50	1.60

Christmas — A397

8th Natl. design contest-winning children's drawings.

1986, Nov. 19   Litho.   Perf. 13½
736	A397	15p multi	.65	.25
737	A397	105p multi	2.75	.70

Nos. 736-737 inscribed in black on gummed side with child's name, age, school and region.

Christmas A397a

Design: Shepherds see star, Bethlehem.

1986, Nov.   Litho.   Perf. 13½
737A	A397a	12p multi	.35	.25

Intl. Peace Year — A398

1986, Nov. 26
738	A398	85p multi	1.50	.60

Natl. Women Volunteers — A399

1986, Dec. 15   Litho.   Perf. 13½
739	A399	15p multi	.70	.25

Crowning of Our Lady of Mt. Carmel, Patron of Chile, by Pius XI, 60th Anniv. — A400

1986, Dec. 19
740	A400	25p multi	.70	.25

Andean Railways Kitson-Meyer No. 59, 1907, Designed by Robert Sterling — A401

1987, Jan. 27   Litho.   Perf. 13½
741 A401 95p multi   3.00 1.25

Arturo Prat Naval Base, Greenwich Island, the Antarctic, 40th Anniv. — A402

No. 742, Storage and power supplies. No. 743, Working and living quarters.

1987, Feb. 6
742 100p multi   4.50 2.00
743 100p multi   4.50 2.00
a. A402 Pair, #742-743   10.00 7.75

State Visit of Pope John Paul II, Apr. 1-6, 1987 — A403

Pope John Paul II and: 20p, Christ the Redeemer statue. 25p, Votive Church, Maipu. 90p, Cross of the Seas, Straits of Magellan. 115p, Virgin of the Hill.

1987   Litho.   Perf. 13½
744 A403 20p multi   .30   .25
745 A403 25p multi   .40   .25
746 A403 90p multi   1.40   .60
747 A403 115p multi   1.90   .95
a.   Souv. sheet of one   5.25 5.25
747B A403 115p multi   2.00 1.00
    Nos. 744-747B (5)   6.00 3.05

No. 747a sold for 250p.
No. 747B differs from No. 747 in that the Statue of the Virgin has a halo and Pope John Paul II is smiling.
Issue date: Nos. 744-747a, Apr. 6.

Los Carabineros (Natl. Guard), 60th Anniv. — A404

No. 748, Cavalry showmanship. No. 749, Air-sea rescue.

1987, Apr. 21
748 A404 50p multi   .80   .35
749 A404 50p multi   .80   .35
a.   Pair, #748-749   2.40 2.00

World Youth Soccer Championships A405

b, Concepcion Stadium, kick play. c, Antofagasta Stadium, dribbling the ball. d, Valparaiso Stadium, heading the ball.

1987, May 28
750   Block of 4   4.50 4.50
a.-d.   A405 45p any single   1.10   .60
        Souvenir Sheet
751 A405 45p Four players   5.00 5.00
        No. 751 sold for 150p.

Naval Ships Type of 1986
No. 752, Battleship Almirante Latorre, 1913. No. 753, Cruiser O'Higgins, 1936.

1987, May 29
752 A390 60p multi   1.00   .60
753 A390 60p multi   1.00   .60
a.   Pair, #752-753   3.75 2.25

Diego Portales (1793-1837), Finance Minister — A406

1987, June 16
754 A406 30p multi   .50   .25

Public Works Ministry, Cent. — A407

1987, June 26
755 A407 25p multi   .55   .30

Infantry School, Cent. — A408

1987, July 9
756 A408 50p Entrance   .50   .25
757 A408 100p Soldiers, natl.
                flag   1.00   .50

        Miniature Sheet

Flora and Fauna — A409

Designs: a, Chiasognathus granti. b, Calidris alba. c, Hippocamelus antisensis. d, Jubaea chilensis. e, Colias vauthieri. f, Pandion haliaetus. g, Cephalorhynchus commersonii. h, Austrocedrus chilensis. i, Jasus frontalis. j, Stephanoides fernandensis. k, Vicugna vicugna. l, Thyrsopteris elegans. m, Lithodes antarctica. n, Pterocnemia pennata. o, Lagidium viscacia. p, Cereus atacamensis.

1987, July 30
758   Sheet of 16   15.00 15.00
a.-p.   A409 25p any single   .55   .30

Intl. Year of Shelter for the Homeless A410

1987, Aug. 6
759 A410 40p multi   .60   .30

Legends and Folk Tales — A411

a, The Guitarist of Quinchamali. b, El Caleuche. c, El Pihuychen. d, La Lola.

1987, July   Litho.   Perf. 13½
760 A411 Block of 4   1.60 1.00
a.-d.   15p any single   .25   .25
    Nos. 760a-760d exist ovptd. "D.S. No 20." in golden brown on back. Value $2.50.
    For surcharges see Nos. 812, 1104.

FISA '87, Santiago — A412

1987, Oct. 16   Litho.   Perf. 13½
761 A412 20p multi   .40   .25
    25th Intl. agriculture and exports exhibition.

Rear Admiral Carlos Condell de la Haza (1843-1887), Naval Hero at the Battle of the Pacific — A413

1987, Nov. 7
762 A413 50p multi   1.50   .90

Christmas 1987 — A414

Children's drawings: 30p, Holy Family. 100p, Star Over Bethlehem, horiz.

1987, Nov. 13
763 A414 30p multi   .75   .30
764 A414 100p multi   3.00   .95

COBRE '87, Intl. Conf. on Copper — A415

1987, Nov. 23
765 A415 40p Foundry   2.10   .60
a.   Souv. sheet of one   2.50 2.50
        No. 765 sold for 150p.

Natl. Antarctic Exploration Commission, 25th Anniv. — A415a

1987, Dec. 11   Litho.   Perf. 13½
765B A415a 45p multi   1.25   .55

Ramon Freire Serrano (1787-1851), Chief of State — A416

1987, Dec. 29   Perf. 13x13½
766 A416 20p pale lil & rose clar-
                et   .40   .30

To Smoke Is To Contaminate — A417

1987, Dec.   Litho.   Perf. 13½
767 A417 15p blue & ver   .40   .25
Natl. Commission for the Control of Smoking.

No. 699A Surcharged in Green

1987   Litho.   Perf. 13½
768 A376a 12p on 10p buff & brn   .30   .25

Christmas 1987 — A418

1987, Dec.
769 A418 15p ultra, org yel & blk   .30   .25
a.   Bklt. pane of 10   4.50
    No. 769a exists ovptd. "D.S. No 20." on back.

No. 697 Surcharged in Black and Rose Red

1987, Dec.

770	A375	Block of 4	1.10	.80
a.-d.		12p on 10p, #697a-697d	.25	.25
771	A375	Block of 4	1.10	.80
a.-d.		15p on 10p, #697a-697d	.25	.25

St. John Bosco (1815-1888), Educator Canonized in 1934 — A419

1988, Jan. 29

772	A419	40p multi	.75	.30

20th Music Week, Frutillar — A420

1988, Jan. 27

773	A420	30p multi	.75	.25

FIDA '88, 5th Intl. Aviation Fair — A421

1988, Mar. 4   Litho.   Perf. 13½

774	A421	60p dark blue & blue	.90	.60

1988 Summer Olympics, Seoul — A422

Flags of Chile and Korea, events: 50p, Shot put, pole vault, javelin. 100p, Swimming, cycling, running.

1988, Mar. 18   Perf. 13½

775	A422	50p multi	1.25	.60
776	A422	100p multi	2.50	1.00
a.		Souv. sheet of 2, #775-776	3.75	3.75

No. 776a sold for 250p.

Natl. Agricultural Soc., 150th Anniv. — A423

1988, Apr. 8

777	A423	45p multi	1.40	.35

Intl. Red Cross and Red Crescent Organizations, 125th Annivs. — A424

1988, May 10

778	A424	150p multi	2.10	.65

No. 645 Surcharged

1988   Litho.   Perf. 13½

779	A344a	20p on 9p green	.25	.25

Easter Island Folk Art — A425

Designs: Nos. 780, 782, Carved wooden head from Kava Kava. Nos. 781, 783, Bird man stone carving from Tangata Manu.

1988, Apr. 1   Litho.   Perf. 13½

780	A425	20p brick red & blk	.30	.25
781	A425	20p brick red & blk	.30	.25
a.		Bklt. pane, 6 #780, 4 #781	4.00	
b.		Pair, #780-781	2.40	2.40
782	A425	20p yel & blk	.30	.25
783	A425	20p yel & blk	.30	.25
a.		Bklt. pane, 6 #782, 4 #783	4.00	
b.		Pair, #782-783	2.40	2.40
		Nos. 780-783 (4)	1.20	1.00

Nos. 782-783 inscribed "D.S. No 20."
For surcharges see Nos. 813-816, 955-956.

Merino, Biplane, Jet Passenger Plane and Supersonic Fighter Plane — A426

1988, May 17   Litho.   Perf. 13½

784	A426	35p multi	.90	.25

Commodore Arturo Merino Benitez (b. 1888), aviation pioneer.

Naval Tradition — A427

Designs: No. 785, Training ship *Esmeralda*. No. 786, Capt. Arturo Pratt, a stained-glass window in the Naval Museum, Valparaiso.

1988, May 23

785		50p multi	.90	.50
786		50p multi	.90	.50
a.	A427	Pair, #785-786	2.25	1.75

Pontifical Catholic University of Chile, Santiago, Cent. — A429

1988, June 21

787	A429	40p Papal & university arms	.90	.25

Locomotives — A430

No. 788, Esslingen No. 3331. No. 789, North British No. 45.

1988, July 22   Litho.   Perf. 13½

788		60p multi	1.00	.70
789		60p multi	1.00	.70
a.		Souv. sheet, #788-789, imperf	7.00	7.00
b.	A430	Pair, #788-789	2.40	2.40

Arica-La Paz Railway, 75th anniv. (No. 788); Antofagasta Bolivia Railway, cent. (No. 789).

Jose Miguel Carrera Natl. Institute, 175th Anniv. — A431

1988, Aug. 10   Litho.   Perf. 13½

790	A431	45p multi	.70	.35

Annexation of Easter Is., Cent. — A432

1988, Sept. 9

791		50p Ship, officer	1.00	.40
792		50p Map, globe	1.00	.40
a.	A432	Pair, #791-792	2.50	1.50
793		100p Easter Is. folk dancers	1.50	.75
794		100p Stone ruins	1.50	.75
a.		Souv. sheet of 4, #791-794, imperf.	7.00	6.50
b.	A432	Pair, #793-794	5.00	3.00
		Nos. 791-794 (4)	5.00	2.30

Miniature Sheet

Flowers — A433

Designs: a, Chloraea chrysantha. b, Lapageria rosea. c, Nolana paradoxa. d, Rhodophiala advena. e, Schizanthus hookeri. f, Acacia caven. g, Cordia decandra. h, Leontochir ovallei. i, Alstroemeria pelegrina. j, Copiapoa cinerea. k, Salpiglossis sinuata. l, Leucocoryne coquimbensis. m, Eucryphia glutinosa. n, Calandrinia longiscapa. o, Desfontainia spinosa. p, Sophora macrocarpa.

1988, Aug. 23   Litho.   Perf. 13½

795		Sheet of 16	20.00	20.00
a.-p.	A433	30p any single	.85	.40

First Domestic Airmail Route, 1919 — A434

150p, Clodomiro Figueroa Ponce's aircraft.

1988, Oct. 11

796	A434	150p multi	2.25	1.10

Christmas 1988
A435   A436

Children's drawings: 35p, Nativity, by Paulette Thiers, age 8. 100p, Going to church, by Jose M. Lamas, age 9, horiz.

1988, Nov. 17

797	A435	20p rose lake & org yel	.45	.25
a.		Bklt. pane of 10	6.50	
798	A435	20p rose lake & org yel	.45	.25
a.		Bklt. pane of 10	6.50	
799	A436	35p multi	.65	.25
800	A436	100p multi	1.10	.40
		Nos. 797-800 (4)	2.65	1.15

No. 798 inscribed "D.S. No 20."

Artisans — A437

1988, Oct. 25   Litho.   Perf. 13½

801		25p Potter	.70	.25
802		25p Weaver	.70	.25
a.	A437	Pair, #801-802	1.60	1.25

No. 802a has continuous design.

Natl. Philatelic Soc., Cent. — A438

1988, Nov. 24
803 A438 40p No. 38, cancellation .60 .25

School Crossing Guards — A439

1988, Oct. 26
804 A439 45p multi .60 .25

A440

Battle scenes and: No. 805, Manuel Bulnes (1799-1866) Commander. No. 806, Cavalryman, Servicemen. No. 807, Roberto Simpson, Commander. No. 808, Seaman, Servicemen.

1989, Jan. 12   Litho.   Perf. 13½
805	50p multi	.85	.40
806	50p multi	.85	.40
a.	A440 Pair, #805-806	3.00	1.00
807	100p multi	1.60	.85
808	100p multi	1.60	.85
a.	A440 Pair, #807-808	3.50	2.10
	Nos. 805-808 (4)	4.90	2.50

Battles of 1839: Yungay (50p) and Casma (100p). Nos. 806a, 808a have continuous designs.

Municipal Annivs. A442

Municipal coats of arms and: 30p, San Ambrosio Church. 35p, Craftsman sculpting marble. 45p, Laja Spring and falls.

1989, Jan. 20
809	A442 30p multi	.30	.25
810	A442 35p multi	.45	.25
811	A442 45p multi	.50	.25
	Nos. 809-811 (3)	1.25	.75

Founding of Vallenar, 200th anniv. (30p); founding of Combarbala, 200th anniv. (35p); founding of Los Angeles, 250th anniv. (45p).

Nos. 760a-760d and 780-783 Surcharged

a   b

1989, Mar. 20   Litho.   Perf. 13½
812	Block of 4	1.25	.75
a.-d.	A411(a) 25p on 15p #760a-760d, any single	.25	.25
813	A425(b) 25p on 20p #780	.25	.25
814	A425(b) 25p on 20p #781	.25	.25
	Complete booklet, 6 #813, 4 #814	2.50	

815	A425(b) 25p on 20p #782	.25	.25
816	A425(b) 25p on 20p #783	.25	.25
	Complete booklet, 6 #815, 4 #816	2.50	
	Nos. 812-816 (5)	2.25	1.75

Surcharge differs on Nos. 814, 816.
Issued: Nos. 812-814, 3/20. Nos. 815-816, 11/30.

Women Beatified — A443

No. 818, Sr. Teresa de Los Andes. No. 819, Laura Vicuna.

1989, Mar. 21   Litho.   Perf. 13½
818	A443 40p multicolored	.75	.35
819	A443 40p multicolored	.75	.35
a.	Pair, #818-819	1.75	1.10

No. 819a has continuous design.

EXFINA '89, Santiago — A444

No. 820, Christopher Columbus. No. 821, Galleons.

1989, Mar. 31
820	100p multi	1.75	.80
821	100p multi	1.75	.80
a.	A444 Pair, #820-821	4.00	3.25
b.	Souvenir sheet of 2, #820-821	7.00	5.25
c.	Souvenir sheet of 2, #820-821	10.50	6.25

No. 821a has continuous design. No. 821b margin pictures Columbus's coat of arms and the Order of the Great Admiralty. No. 821c margin Nos. 55, 69, 18, 76, 37, 1, 20 and 98.

CORFO Development Corp., 50th Anniv. — A445

1989, Apr. 4
822	A445 60p Shipping	.60	.30
823	A445 60p Lumber	.60	.30
824	A445 60p Communication	.60	.30
825	A445 60p Coal	.60	.30
a.	Block of 4, #822-825	3.00	2.50

Gabriela Mistral (1889-1957), Poet — A446

1989, Apr. 7   Litho.   Perf. 13½
826	A446 30p Poet, steeple	.50	.25
827	A446 30p Poet, children	.50	.25
828	A446 30p Poet working	.50	.25
829	A446 30p Receiving Nobel Prize, 1945	.50	.25
a.	Block of 4, #826-829	3.25	2.00

Exports — A447

Nos. 830, 832, Grapes. Nos. 831, 833, Apple.

1989, Apr. 19
830	A447 25p indigo & brt yel grn	.45	.25
831	A447 25p ver & brt yel grn	.45	.25
a.	Bklt. pane, 5 each #830-831	3.50	
b.	Pair, #830-831	2.00	1.00
832	A447 25p indigo & pale yel org	.45	.25
833	A447 25p ver & pale yel org	.45	.25
a.	Bklt. pane, 5 each #832-833	3.50	
b.	Pair, #832-833	2.00	1.00
	Nos. 830-833 (4)	1.80	1.00

Nos. 832-833 inscribed "D.S. No 20."
See Nos. 861-864, 943-946. For surcharges see Nos. 956B-956C, 1085-1088.

Military Justice Department, 150th Anniv. — A448

1989, Apr. 24   Litho.   Perf. 13½
834	A448 50p multicolored	.60	.25

Monument to the Martyrs of Carabineros de Chile — A449

1989, Apr. 26
835	A449 35p multicolored	.50	.25

Surveyor and Penguins — A450

1989, May 29
836	A450 150p multicolored	2.75	1.00

Antarctic Research Institute expeditions, 25th anniv.

Naval Engineers, Cent. — A451

No. 837, Naval school. No. 838, Seamen in boiler room. No. 839, Ship, helicopter, submarine. No. 840, *Aquiles* launch, Asmar-Talcahuano.

1989, May 31
837	A451 45p multicolored	.75	.25
838	A451 45p multicolored	.75	.25
839	A451 45p multicolored	.75	.25
840	A451 45p multicolored	.75	.25
a.	Block of 4, #837-840	3.50	3.50

Horse-drawn Carriage (Victoria), Vina del Mar — A452

Early transportation: 35p, Launch off Chiloe Is., vert. 40p, Cart, Cautin. 45p, Ferry, Rio Palena. 50p, Car transport, Lake Gral, Carretta. 60p, Incline railroad, Valparaiso. 100p, Cable car (funicular), Santiago.

1989-92   Litho.   Perf. 13½
841	A452 30p black & orange	.55	.25
842	A452 60p black & lemon	1.00	.45
843	A452 60p like No. 842	.85	.25
844	A452 100p black & brt yel grn	1.75	.85

1989-91
845	A452 35p black & brt blue	.55	.25
846	A452 40p black & olive	.65	.25
847	A452 45p blk & pale blue grn	.65	.25
a.	Inscribed "1991"	.65	.25
848	A452 45p black & lt ol grn	.35	.25
849	A452 50p black & scarlet	.45	.25
a.	Inscribed "1992"	.45	.25
	Nos. 841-849 (9)	6.80	3.05

Nos. 843, 848 inscribed DS No. 20.
Issued: Nos. 841-842, 844, 4/22/89; No. 848, 2/1/91; No. 843, 1992; others, 8/1989. For surcharge see No. 1002.

Export Type of 1989

Nos. 861, 863, Grapes. Nos. 862, 864, Apple.

1989, May 22
861	A447 5p dark blue & gray	.40	.40
862	A447 5p brt red, dark blue & gray	.40	.40
a.	Pair, #861-862	.90	.90
863	A447 10p dark blue & gray	.40	.40
864	A447 10p brt red, dark blue & gray	.40	.40
a.	Pair, #863-864	.90	.90

World Stamp Expo '89 — A453

1989, Aug. 25   Litho.   Perf. 13½
865	A453 250p multicolored	3.50	1.40
a.	Souvenir sheet of 1	8.00	8.00

A454

UPAE emblem and pre-Columbian peoples: 30p, Atacamena potter. 150p, Selk'nam-onas bow hunter.

1989, Oct. 12
866	A454 30p multicolored	.75	.25
867	A454 150p multicolored	3.00	.95

Drawing by Christina Lopez — A455

1989, Nov. 20   Litho.   Perf. 13½
868 A455 100p multicolored   1.40   .45
Christmas.

Christmas Ornaments — A456

Nos. 869, 871, Balls. Nos. 870, 872, Bells.

1989
869 A456 25p dull green & org   .45   .25
870 A456 25p dull green & org   .45   .25
  a.   Bklt. pane, 5 each Nos. 869-870   4.50
  b.   Pair, #869-870   1.00   .70
871 A456 25p dull green & ver   .45   .25
872 A456 25p dull green & ver   .45   .25
  a.   Bklt. pane, 5 each Nos. 871-872   4.50
  b.   Pair, #871-872   1.00   .70
       Nos. 869-872 (4)   1.80 1.00

Nos. 871-872 inscribed "D.S. No 20."

Miniature Sheet

Wildlife, Natl. Parks — A457

Designs: a, Vicuna, Lauca Park. b, Chilean flamingos, Salar de Surire. c, Cactus, La Chimba Reserve. d, Guanaco, Pan de Azucar Park. e, Song bird, Father Jorge Park. f, Terns, Rapa Nui Park. g, Ferret, La Campana Park. h, Duck, Rio Clarillo Park. i, Cypress tree, Rio de Los Cipreses Reserve. j, Black-headed swan, Laguna de Torca Reserve. k, Puma, Laguna del Laja Park. l, Araucaria tree, Villarrica Park. m, Flower, Vicente Perez Rosales Park. n, Lenga tree, Dos Lagunas. o, Sea lion, Laguna San Rafael Park. p, Rhea, Torres del Paine Park.

1990, Jan. 25
873   Sheet of 16   18.00 13.00
  a.-p. A457 35p any single   .65   .25

1990 World Cup Soccer Championships, Italy — A458

1990, Feb. 23
874 A458 50p Cleated shoe   .60   .25
875 A458 50p Hand   .60   .25
876 A458 50p Soccer ball   .60   .25
877 A458 50p Athlete   .60   .25
  a.   Block of 4, #874-877   3.00   2.40

Natl. Air Force A459

Various aircraft: No. 878, Vickers Wibault. No. 879, Curtiss O1E Falcon. No. 880, Pitts S2A. No. 881, Extra 300.

1990, Mar. 16   Litho.   Perf. 13½
878 A459 40p multicolored   .70   .25
879 A459 40p multicolored   .70   .25
880 A459 40p multicolored   .70   .25
881 A459 40p multicolored   .70   .25
  a.   Souvenir sheet of 4, #878-881   3.50 2.00
       Nos. 878-881 (4)   2.80   1.00
              FIDAE '90.

Discovery of America 500th Anniv. (in 1992) — A460

Maps and 16th cent. men: No. 882, Incan. No. 883, Spanish infantryman.

1990, Apr. 20   Perf. 13½
882   60p multicolored   1.00   .25
883   60p multicolored   1.00   .25
  a.   A460 Pair, #882-883   4.00   3.00

Port Cities A462

1990, Apr. 27
884 A462 40p Valparaiso   .60   .25
885 A462 40p San Vicente   .60   .25
  a.   Pair, #884-885   1.60   1.25

Democracy — A463

1990, June 8   Litho.   Perf. 13½
886 A463 20p Sunrise   .25   .25
887 A463 30p Peace dove   .55   .25
888 A463 60p Pleasure   .90   .40
889 A463 100p Star   1.60   .75
  a.   Souvenir sheet of 4, #886-889   6.25 6.25
       Nos. 886-889 (4)   3.30   1.65

Equality — A464

1990, June 8
890 A464 45p multicolored   .75   .30
  a.   Souvenir sheet   2.50   2.50

No. 890a margin continues the design.

Naval Tradition — A465

No. 891, Transport ship Piloto Pardo. No. 892, Oceanographic research ship Yelcho.

1990, May 30   Litho.   Perf. 13½
891 A465 50p multicolored   .60   .25
892 A465 50p multicolored   .60   .25
  a.   Pair, #891-892   1.50   1.00

A466

1990, June 12
893 A466 250p Sir Rowland Hill   3.50   1.25
  a.   Souvenir sheet of 1   6.00   4.50
       Penny Black, 150th anniv.
No. 893a margin continues the design.

A467

1990, June 21
894 A467 150p multicolored   1.75   .75
Organization of American States, cent.

Marine Resources — A468

Designs: a, Scallop. b, Clam. c, Swordfish. d, Crab. e, Fish. f, Baiting, processing.

1990, July 27   Litho.   Perf. 13½
895   Block of 6   4.00   3.00
  a.-f. A468 40p any single   .40   .25

Curimon Convent A469

1990, Aug. 1
896 A469 50p multicolored   .60   .25
250th anniversary of San Felipe.

Environmental Protection — A470

1990, Sept. 1   Litho.   Perf. 13½
897 A470 35p Aerosol propel-
                lants   .35   .25
898 A470 35p Deforestation   .35   .25
899 A470 35p Smokestacks   .35   .25
900 A470 35p Oil slick, shore   .35   .25
901 A470 35p Forest fire   .35   .25
  a.   Strip of 5, #897-901   2.75   2.00
  b.   Bklt. pane, 2 each #897-901   7.25
            Inscribed "D.S. No 20"
902 A470 35p Aerosol propel-
                lants   .35   .25
903 A470 35p Deforestation   .35   .25
904 A470 35p Smokestacks   .35   .25
905 A470 35p Oil slick, shore   .35   .25
906 A470 35p Forest fire   .35   .25
  a.   Strip of 5, #902-906   2.75   2.00
  b.   Bklt. pane, 2 each #902-906   7.25
       Nos. 897-906 (10)   3.50   2.50
              See Nos. 988-997.

Presidents of Chile — A471

No. 912, Salvador Allende. No. 913, Eduardo Frei. No. 914, Jorge Alessandri. No. 915, Gabriel Gonzalez V. No. 916, Juan Antonio Rios. No. 917, Pedro Aguirre Cerda. No. 918, Juan E. Montero. No. 919, Carlos Ibanez. No. 920, Emiliano Figueroa. No. 921, Arturo Alessandri.

1990, Sept. 4
912 A471 35p multicolored   .35   .25
913 A471 35p multicolored   .35   .25
914 A471 40p multicolored   .50   .25
  a.   Inscribed "1992"   .50   .25
915 A471 45p multicolored   .55   .25
916 A471 50p multicolored   .65   .35
917 A471 60p multicolored   .70   .40
918 A471 70p multicolored   .85   .40
  a.   Inscribed "1992"   .85   .40
919 A471 80p multicolored   1.00   .50
920 A471 90p multicolored   1.10   .55
  a.   Inscribed "1992"   1.10   .55
921 A471 100p multicolored   1.25   .65
  a.   Inscribed "1992"   1.75   .90
       Nos. 912-921 (10)   7.30   3.85

Rodeos — A472

Designs: a, Rodeo ring. b, Men on horses. c, Man stopping horse. d, Men, horses, bull.

1990, Sept. 24
926   Block of 4   2.75   2.00
  a.-d. A472 45p any single   .45   .25

Discovery of America, 500th Anniv. (in 1992) — A473

30p, Phoenicopterus chilensis. 150p, Arctocephalus australis.

1990, Oct. 12   Litho.   Perf. 13½
927 A473 30p multicolored   1.00   .25
928 A473 150p multicolored   4.00   .85

King and Queen of Spain's Visit — A474

No. 930, Arms of King Juan Carlos I, Chilean Arms.

1990, Oct. 18
929 A474 100p shown   1.25   .60
930 A474 100p Denomination at
                LR   1.25   .60
  a.   Pair, #929-930   3.25   2.25

Malleco Bridge, Cent. — A475

Design: No. 932, Boy waving at train on bridge.

1990, Oct. 26　Litho.　Perf. 13½

931	A475	60p multicolored	1.25	.55
932	A475	60p multicolored	1.25	.55
a.		Pair, #931-932	3.00	2.10

Chilean Antarctic Territorial Claims, 50th Anniv. — A476

Design: No. 934, Penguins, helicopter, camp.

1990, Nov. 6　　　　　　Perf. 13½

933	A476	250p multicolored	2.75	1.40
934	A476	250p multicolored	2.75	1.40
a.		Pair, #933-934	8.00	8.00
b.		Souvenir sheet of 2, #933-934	12.00	12.00

A477

Christmas — A478

150p, Underwater dwelling.

1990, Nov. 20　Litho.　Perf. 13½

935	A477	35p lt green & bl grn	.45	.25
a.		Booklet pane of 10	4.00	
936	A477	35p dull org & bl grn	.30	.25
a.		Booklet pane of 10	4.00	
937	A478	35p shown	.65	.25
938	A478	150p multi	2.75	1.50
		Nos. 935-938 (4)	4.15	2.25

No. 936 inscribed "D.S. No.20."

National Congress — A479

No. 939, Congress chamber. No. 940, Early congressional session.

1990, Dec. 21　Litho.　Perf. 13½

939	A479	100p multicolored	1.25	.55
940	A479	100p multicolored	1.25	.55
a.		Pair, #939-940	2.75	1.75

City of Santiago, 450th Anniv. — A480

1991, Feb. 7

941	A480	100p Colorado House	1.25	.55
942	A480	100p Skyline	1.25	.55
a.		Pair, #941-942	4.00	2.50
b.		Souvenir sheet of 2, #941-942	5.00	5.00

Exports Type of 1989

Nos. 943, 945, Grapes. Nos. 944, 946, Apple.

1991, Feb. 8　Perf. 13½ on 3 Sides

943	A447	45p indigo & brt pink	.50	.25
944	A447	45p ver & brt pink	.50	.25
a.		Bklt. pane, 5 each #943-944	8.25	

945	A447	45p indigo & yel	.50	.25
946	A447	45p ver & yel	.50	.25
a.		Bklt. pane, 5 each #945-946	8.25	
		Nos. 943-946 (4)	2.00	1.00

Nos. 945-946 inscribed "D.S. No.20." For surcharges see Nos. 1085-1088.

Historical Aircraft — A481

Designs: a, Voisin. b, S.E. 5a. c, Morane Saulnier MS 35. d, Consolidated PBY-5A/OA-10 Catalina.

1991, Mar. 21　Litho.　Perf. 13½

947	A481	150p Block of 4, #a.-d.	7.25	4.50

American Soccer Cup, Chile — A482

1991, Apr. 12　Litho.　Perf. 13½

948		100p Player, map	1.10	.40
949		100p Ball, goalie	1.10	.40
a.		A482 Pair, #948-949	2.25	1.00

Coal Mining A483

Design: No. 951, Miners dumping cart of coal.

1991, Apr. 18

950	A483	200p shown	2.00	.95
951	A483	200p multicolored	2.00	.95
a.		Pair, #950-951	4.50	3.00

Cultural Art — A484

1991, Apr. 29

952		90p multicolored	1.00	.50
953		90p multicolored	1.00	.50
a.		A484 Pair, #952-953	2.25	1.40

Chilean Scientific Society, Cent. — A485

1991, Apr. 29

954	A485	45p blue grn & blk	.50	.25

Nos. 782-783 Surcharged

a

b

1991, Apr. 30

955	A425(a)	45p on 20p, #782	.30	.25
956	A425(b)	45p on 20p, #783	.30	.25
a.		Pair, #955-956	1.00	.75

Nos. 832-833 Surcharged

1991, May 6　Litho.　Perf. 13½

956B	A447	45p on 25p, #832	.70	.25
956C	A447	45p on 25p, #833	.70	.25
d.		Pair, #956B-956C	1.60	1.10

Santiago Cathedral A486

1991, May 9　　　　Litho. & Engr.

957	A486	300p red brn, sal & blk	3.75	1.75

World Telecommunications Day — A487

1991, May 17　　　　　　　　Litho.

958	A487	90p multicolored	1.25	.30

A488

1991, May 23

959	A488	100p Pope Leo XIII	1.00	.40

Rerum Novarum Encyclical, cent.

A489

Rescue of Shackleton Expedition, 75th anniv.: a, Lt. Luis Pardo, Sir Ernest Shackleton. b, Rescue ship, Yelcho. c, Sailor pointing to survivors. d, Shackleton's ship, Endurance.

21st General Assembly of Organization of American States, Santiago — A490

1991, June 5

961	A490	70p multicolored	.70	.25

New Carabinero School — A491

1991, June 12

962	A491	50p multicolored	.60	.25

Natl. Merchant Marine Day — A492

1991, June 26

963	A492	45p black & red	.60	.25

11th Pan American Games, Havana — A493

1991, July 23

964	A493	100p Runners, torch, flags	.90	.35
965	A493	100p Cycling, running, basketball	.90	.35
a.		Pair, #964-965	2.25	1.60

Founding of the City of Los Andes, Bicent. — A494

1991, July 29

966	A494	100p multicolored	1.25	.40

Miniature Sheet

Marine Life — A495

1991, May 28　Litho.　Perf. 13½

960	A489	50p Block of 4, #a.-d.	2.50	1.50
e.		Miniature sheet, #960	2.50	2.50

Designs: No. 967a, Octopus vulgaris. b, Durvillaea antarctica. c, Paralichthys adpersus. d, Austromegabalanus psittacus. e, Concholepas concholepas. f, Cancer setosus. g, Lessonia nigrescens. h, Loxechinus albus. i, Homalaspis plana. j, Porphyra columbina. k, Oplegnathus insignis. l, Chorus giganteus. m, Rhynchocinetes typus. n, Engraulis ringens. o, Gracilaria spp. p, Pyura chilensis.

1991, Aug. 20   **Litho.**   **Perf. 13½**
967   Sheet of 16   16.00   7.50
a.-p.   A495 50p any single   .90   .25

1891 Revolution, Cent. — A496

Jose M. Balmaceda (1840-1891) and: No. 968, Machinery. No. 969, Teacher, students at Valentin Letelier School of Medicine.

1991, Aug. 29
968   A496 100p multicolored   1.00   .45
969   A496 100p multicolored   1.00   .45
a.   Pair, #968-969   2.25   1.25

Chilean Art — A497

Paintings: 50p, Woman in Red, by Pedro Reszka. 70p, The Traveler, by Camilo Mori. 200p, Head of Child, by Benito Rebolledo. 300p, Boy Wearing a Fez, by A. Valenzuela Puelma.

1991, Sept. 26
970   A497 50p multicolored   .60   .25
971   A497 70p multicolored   .60   .30
972   A497 200p multicolored   2.40   .85
973   A497 300p multicolored   3.50   1.25
   Nos. 970-973 (4)   7.10   2.65

Antarctic Treaty, 30th Anniv. — A498

1991, Oct. 7   **Litho.**   **Perf. 13½**
974   A498 80p shown   1.75   .70
975   A498 80p Birds, sea life   1.75   .70
a.   Pair, #974-975   4.50   1.60

Intl. Letter Writing Week A499

1991, Oct. 9
976   A499 45p shown   .45   .25
977   A499 70p Envelope filled with people   .70   .30

America Issue — A500

UPAEP emblem, sailing ships and: 150p, Navigator.

1991, Oct. 14
978   A500 50p multicolored   .75   .25
979   A500 150p multicolored   2.10   .75

A501

1991, Oct. 21
980   A501 45p blue hat   .45   .25
981   A501 45p red hat   .45   .25
a.   Pair, #980-981   1.50   .75
b.   Souvenir sheet of 2, #980-981   2.75   2.75

Pablo Neruda, (1904-1973), Nobel Prize winner for literature, 1971. Nos. 981a has a continuous design.

A502

1991, Nov. 4
982   A502 45p Boy with stars   .50   .25
983   A502 100p Girl with stars   1.00   .50
   Christmas.

A503   A504
Christmas

1991, Nov. 18   **Litho.**   **Perf. 13½**
984   A503 45p violet & brt pink   .45   .25
985   A504 45p violet & brt pink   .45   .25
a.   Pair, #984-985   1.10   .25
b.   Bklt. pane of 5 #985a   7.00
986   A503 45p violet & brt pink   .45   .25
987   A504 45p violet & brt pink   .45   .25
a.   Pair, #986-987   1.10   .25
b.   Bklt. pane of 5 #987a   7.00
   Nos. 984-987 (4)   1.80   1.00

Nos. 986-987 inscribed "D.S. No. 20."
For surcharges see Nos. 1016-1019.

Environmental Protection Type of 1990

1992, Jan. 28   **Litho.**   **Perf. 13½**
Lemon & Black

988   A470 60p like #897   .55   .25
989   A470 60p like #898   .55   .25
990   A470 60p like #899   .55   .25
991   A470 60p like #900   .55   .25
992   A470 60p like #901   .55   .25
a.   Strip of 5, #988-992   4.00   2.50
b.   Bklt. pane, 2 each #988-992   8.00

Inscribed "D.S. No. 20"
Orange & Dark Green

993   A470 60p like #902   .55   .25
994   A470 60p like #903   .55   .25
995   A470 60p like #904   .55   .25
996   A470 60p like #905   .55   .25
997   A470 60p like #906   .55   .25
a.   Strip of 5, #993-997   4.00   2.50
b.   Bklt. pane, 2 each #993-997   8.00
   Nos. 988-997 (10)   5.50   2.50

Wolfgang Amadeus Mozart, Death Bicent. (in 1991) — A505

1992, Jan. 31
998   A505 60p shown   .60   .25
999   A505 200p Hands at piano   1.90   .90
a.   Sheet of 2, #998-999   4.00   4.00

FIDAE '92, Intl. Air and Space Fair — A506

1992, Mar. 5   **Litho.**   **Perf. 13½**
1000   A506 60p multicolored   .60   .25

16th Population and Housing Census A507

1992, Mar.
1001   A507 60p multicolored   .60   .25

No. 847 Surcharged in Red Brown

1992, Mar.
1002   A452 60p on 45p   .60   .25

Chilean Cities — A508

Cities' coat of arms and: 80p, Church of San Jose de Maipo. 90p, People making pottery. 100p, Lircunlauta House. 150p, Wine and lumber industries. 250p, Huilquilemu cultural center.

1992, Apr. 10   **Litho.**   **Perf. 13½**
1003   A508 80p multicolored   .65   .25
1004   A508 90p multicolored   .75   .25
1005   A508 100p multicolored   .95   .35
1006   A508 150p multicolored   1.50   .50
1007   A508 250p multicolored   2.40   .80
   Nos. 1003-1007 (5)   6.25   2.15

80p, San Jose de Maipo, 200th anniv. 90p, Melipilla, 250th anniv. 100p, San Fernando, 250th anniv. 150p, Cauquenes, 250th anniv. 250p, Talca, 250th anniv.

Expo '92, Seville A509

1992, Apr. 23
1008   A509 150p Pavilion   1.40   .50
1009   A509 200p Iceberg   2.00   .65
a.   Sheet of 2, #1008-1009   *4.50   4.50*

A510

Easter Island — A511

Marine life: No. 1010a, Morula praecipua, Strombus maculatus, Cypraea caputdraconis. b, Codium pocockiae. c, Myripristis tiki. d, Sargassum skottsbergii. e, Pseudolabrus fuentesi. f, Pocillopora danae. g, Panulirus pascuensis. h, Tripneustes gratilla.
No. 1011b, Natives, airplane, petroglyph.

1992, June 9   **Litho.**   **Perf. 13½**
1010   A510 60p Sheet of 8, #a.-h.   5.00   2.75
1011   A511 200p Pair, #a.-b.   4.00   1.50

Natl. Council of the Disabled — A512

1992, June 23
1012   A512 60p multicolored   .60   .25

Military Chiefs of Staff, 50th Anniv. — A513

1992, July 3
1013   A513 60p multicolored   .60   .25

Submarine Forces, 75th Anniv. — A514

Coat of arms and: 250p, Officer using periscope, control room.

1992, July 4
1014   A514 150p multicolored   1.60   .50
1015   A514 250p multicolored   2.40   .90

Nos. 984-987 Surcharged

1992, Aug. 11　　Litho.　　Perf. 13½
1016	A503	60p on 45p No. 984	.45　.25
1017	A504	60p on 45p No. 985	.45　.25
a.		Pair, #1016-1017	1.90　.90
1018	A503	60p on 45p No. 986	.45　.25
1019	A504	60p on 45p No. 987	.45　.25
a.		Pair, #1018-1019	1.90　.90
		Nos. 1016-1019 (4)	1.80　1.00

Nos. 1018-1019 inscribed "D.S. No. 20."

Emperor
Penguins — A515

1992, Sept. 28　　Litho.　　Perf. 13½
1020	A515	200p shown	1.00　.75
1021	A515	250p Adults with young	2.40　1.00
a.		Souv. sheet of 2, #1020-1021	6.25　6.25

Central Post Office, Santiago,
1772 — A516

1992, Oct. 9
1022	A516	200p multicolored	1.75　.70

Discovery of America, 500th
Anniv. — A517

UPAEP emblem and: 200p, Calendar stone, astrolabe, Columbus. 250p, Church, map of Central and South America, sailing ship.

1992, Oct. 20
1023	A517	200p multicolored	1.75　.65
1024	A517	250p multicolored	2.25　.75

Radio Chile, 75th
Anniv. — A518

1992, Oct. 22
1025	A518	250p multicolored	2.00　.80

Bernardo
O'Higgins (1778-1842)
A519

1992, Oct. 23
1026	A519	60p multicolored	.60　.25

Claudio Arrau, Pianist — A520

1992, Nov. 12　　Litho.　　Perf. 13½
1027	A520	150p As child	1.25　.55
1028	A520	200p As adult	1.60　.75
a.		Souv. sheet of 2, #1027-1028	3.50　3.50

Natl. Human Rights Day — A521

1992, Dec. 10
1029	A521	100p multicolored	.80　.40
a.		Souvenir sheet of 1	1.50　1.50

Christmas — A522

Designs: Nos. 1030, 1032, Denomination at LR. Nos. 1031, 1033, Denomination at LL.

1992, Dec. 12　　Litho.　　Perf. 13½
1030	A522	60p buff & brown	.45　.25
1031	A522	60p buff & brown	.45　.25
a.		Pair, #1030-1031	1.00　.45
b.		Booklet pane of 5 #1031a	4.50　4.50
1032	A522	60p buff & red	.45　.25
1033	A522	60p buff & red	.45　.25
a.		Pair, #1032-1033	1.00　.45
b.		Booklet pane of 5 #1033a	4.50
		Nos. 1030-1033 (4)	1.80　1.00

Nos. 1032-1033 inscribed "DS/20."

A523

University of Chile, 150th Anniv.: a, Statue. b, Coat of arms, facade of building.

1992, Nov. 19　　Litho.　　Perf. 13½
1034	A523	200p Pair, #a.-b.	3.00　1.25
c.		Souvenir sheet of 1, #1034	4.00　4.00

Nos. 1034a-1034b have a continuous design.

A524

1992, Dec. 12
1035	A524	70p black & yellow	.60　.25

23rd meeting of Latin American Energy Ministers.

Churches of
Chiloe — A525

Nos. 1036, 1038, Achao. Nos. 1037, 1039, Castro.

1993, Mar. 1　　Litho.　　Perf. 13½
1036	A525	70p black & pink	.70　.55
1037	A525	70p black & pink	.70　.55
a.		Pair #1036-1037	1.50　1.50
b.		Booklet pane of 5 #1037a	7.50

Inscribed "DS/20"
1038	A525	70p black & yellow	.70　.55
1039	A525	70p black & yellow	.70　.55
a.		Pair, #1038-1039	1.50　1.50
b.		Booklet pane of 5 #1039a	7.50
		Nos. 1036-1039 (4)	2.80　2.20

See Nos. 1053-1060, 1093-1098.
For surcharges see Nos. 1129-1130.

Arrival of the
Jesuits, 400th
Anniv. — A526

Canonization of
St. Teresa of the
Andes,
1993 — A527

200p, St. Ignatius of Loyola. 300p, St. Teresa of the Andes.

1993　　　　Litho.　　Perf. 13½
1040	A526	200p multicolored	1.50　.60
a.		Souvenir sheet of 1	2.50　2.50
1041	A527	300p multicolored	2.50　1.00

Issue dates: 200p, Mar. 15; 300p, Mar. 31. No. 1040a sold for 250p.

World Festival of
Theatre of the
Nations — A528

1993, Apr. 22
1042	A528	250p multicolored	2.00　.75

Second Space Conference of the
Americas — A529

1993, Apr. 26
1043	A529	150p multicolored	1.50　.75
a.		Souvenir sheet of 1	3.25　3.25

No. 1043a sold for 350p.

Clotario Blest
(1899-1990),
Syndicalist
A530

1993, Apr. 30
1044	A530	70p multicolored	.60　.25

Intl. Labor Day.

Vicente Huidobro,
Poet (1893-1948)
A531

1993, May 19　　Litho.　　Perf. 13½
1045	A531	100p shown	.80　.40
1046	A531	100p Portrait, seated	.80　.40
a.		Pair, #1045-1046	1.75　1.10

Antique Fire Engines — A532

Nos. 1047, 1902 Watterous Engineering Co. Ltd., Canada. Nos. 1048, 1872 Merryweather, England.

1993, June 30　　Litho.　　Perf. 13½
1047	A532	100p multicolored	1.10　.40
1048	A532	100p multicolored	1.10　.40
a.		Souv. sheet of 2, #1047-1048	2.50　2.50

No. 1048a sold for 400p.

Aircraft — A533

Designs: No. 1049, Douglas B-26 Invader. No. 1050, Mirage M50 Panther. No. 1051, Sanchez Besa. No. 1052, Bell 47D1 helicopter.

1993, July 13
1049	A533	100p multicolored	.65	.35
1050	A533	100p multicolored	.65	.35
1051	A533	100p multicolored	.65	.35
1052	A533	100p multicolored	.65	.35
a.		Block of 4, #1049-1052	3.50	3.00

Church Type of 1993

Designs: 10p, Chonchi. 20p, Vilupulli. 30p, Llau-llao. 40p, Dalcahue. 50p, Tenaun. 80p, Quinchao. 90p, Quehui. 100p, Nercon.

1993, July   Litho.   Perf. 13½
1053	A525	10p green & black	.25	.25
1054	A525	20p black & brown	.25	.25
1055	A525	30p black & ver	.25	.25
1056	A525	40p black & blue	.30	.30
1057	A525	50p blk & grn blue	.35	.35
1058	A525	80p black & buff	.55	.55
a.		Booklet pane of 10	8.25	
b.		Inscribed "1994"	.60	.60
1059	A525	90p olive & black	.60	.60
a.		Booklet pane of 10	8.25	
		Complete booklet, #1059a	8.25	
1060	A525	100p gray vio & blk	.65	.65
a.		Booklet pane of 10	8.25	
		Nos. 1053-1060 (8)	3.20	3.20

Issued: No. 1058a, 1/1/94; No. 1059a, 1995; No. 1060a, 2/1/96.
See No. 1093 for 80p black and violet.

Natl. Dance, "La Cueca" — A534

1993, Sept. 15   Litho.   Perf. 13½
1061	A534	70p Cueca chilota	.60	.25
1062	A534	70p Cueca central	.60	.25
1063	A534	70p Cueca nortina	.60	.25
		Nos. 1061-1063 (3)	1.80	.75

Paintings — A535

Designs: 80p, Tarde Amanecer, by Mario Carreno, horiz. 90p, Summer, by Gracia Barrios, horiz. 150p, Figura Protegida, by Roser Bru. 200p, Tangueria-Valparaiso, by Nemesio Antunez, horiz.

1993, Sept. 28
1064	A535	80p multicolored	.55	.25
1065	A535	90p multicolored	.60	.25
1066	A535	150p multicolored	1.00	.40
1067	A535	200p multicolored	1.40	.55
		Nos. 1064-1067 (4)	3.55	1.45

Chilean Mint, 250th Anniv. A536

1993, Oct. 7   Litho. & Engr.
1068	A536	250p multicolored	2.40	.95
a.		Souvenir sheet of 1	3.50	3.50

A537

1993, Oct. 19   Litho.
1069	A537	80p multicolored	.70	.25

Urban transportation system, 25th anniv.

A538

150p, Cyanoliseus patagonus. 200p, Hippocamelus bisulcus.

1993, Oct. 12   Litho.   Perf. 13½
1070	A538	150p multicolored	1.50	.55
1071	A538	200p multicolored	2.50	.75

America issue.

Chilean Possession of Straits of Magellan, 150th Anniv. — A539

1993, Oct. 21
1072	A539	100p multicolored	3.50	.35

Naval Anniversaries — A540

1993, Oct. 27
1073	A540	80p Sailing ships	.75	.30
1074	A540	80p Schooner	.75	.30
1075	A540	80p Assault ship	.75	.30
1076	A540	80p Patrol boat	.75	.30
		Nos. 1073-1076 (4)	3.00	1.20

Sailing of first naval squadron (No. 1073), Arturo Prat Naval Academy (No. 1074), Marine Corps (No. 1075), 175th anniversaries. Alejandro Navarette School for Cadets (No. 1076), 125th anniv.

Intl. Year of Indigenous Peoples — A541

1993, Nov. 24
1077	A541	100p multicolored	.90	.40

Christmas — A542

1993, Dec. 1   Litho.   Perf. 13½
1078	A542	70p tan & violet	.55	.25
a.		Booklet pane of 10	6.00	
1079	A542	70p green & blue	.65	.25
a.		Booklet pane of 10	7.00	

No. 1079 inscribed "DS/20."
For surcharge see No. 1131.

Pygoscelis Adelie — A543

1993, Dec. 3
1080	A543	200p Nesting	1.60	.60
1081	A543	250p Adult, chicks	2.00	.80
a.		Souv. sheet of 2, #1080-1081, imperf.	4.75	4.75

Chilean Antarctica.
No. 1081a has simulated perfs.

Chilean Cities — A544

1993, Dec. 15
1082	A544	80p Rancagua	.70	.25
1083	A544	80p Curico	.70	.25
1084	A544	80p Ancud	.70	.25
		Nos. 1082-1084 (3)	2.10	.75

Rancagua and Curico, 250th anniv. Ancud, 225th anniv.

Nos. 943-946 Surcharged

1993   Litho.   Perf. 13½ on 3 Sides
1085	A447	60p on 45p, #943	.35	.25
1086	A447	60p on 45p, #944	.35	.25
a.		Bklt. pane, 5 each #1085-1086	3.50	
1087	A447	60p on 45p, #945	.35	.25
1088	A447	60p on 45p, #946	.35	.25
a.		Bklt. pane, 5 each #1087-1088	3.50	
		Nos. 1085-1088 (4)	1.40	1.00

Nos. 1087-1088 inscribed "D.S. No. 20."

Intl. Year of the Family — A545

1994, Jan. 17   Litho.   Perf. 13½
1089	A545	100p multicolored	.70	.25

Musical Instruments — A546

Designs: a, Violin. b, Cello.

1994, Jan. 27   Litho.   Perf. 13½
1091	A546	150p Pair, #a.-b.	3.25	3.25

No. 1091 has a continuous design.

Church Type of 1993

Designs: 80p, Quinchao. 90p, Quehui. Nos. 1097, 1098, Nercon.

1994-96   Litho.   Perf. 13½
1093	A525	80p black & violet	.50	.25
1095	A525	90p red & black	.50	.25
a.		Booklet pane of 10	4.75	
		Complete booklet, #1095a	4.75	
1097	A525	100p yellow & black	.55	.30
a.		Booklet pane of 10	6.00	
		Complete booklet, #1097a	6.00	
1098	A525	100p gray vio & blk	.60	.30
a.		Booklet pane of 10	6.50	
		Complete booklet, #1098a	6.50	
		Nos. 1093-1098 (4)	2.15	1.10

Issued: 80p, 1/1/94; 90p, 1995; Nos. 1097-1098, 2/1/96.
Nos. 1093, 1095, 1097 inscribed "DS/20."

Souvenir Sheet

Natl. Aviation Museum, 50th Anniv. — A547

Aircraft: a, Sukhoi SU-30 Flanker. b, Vought-Sikorsky OS-2U3 Kingfisher. c, Lockheed F-117A Nighthawk. d, Northrop F-5E Tiger III.

1994, Mar. 17   Litho.   Perf. 13
1102	A547	300p Sheet of 4, #a.-d. + 2 labels	9.00	5.50

Intl. Air and Space Fair, FIDAE '94.
See No. 1159.

College of Agronomy, 50th Anniv. — A548

1994, Apr. 28   Litho.   Perf. 13
1103	A548	220p multicolored	1.50	.75

No. 760 Surcharged

1994, May 1   Litho.   Perf. 13½
1104   Block of 4   2.75 1.50
a.-d. A411 80p on 15p any single   .60 .25

Concepcion University, 75th
Anniv. — A549

Sections of mural, by Jorge Gonzalez
Camarena: No. 1105, Cactus plant, skeletons.
No. 1106, Flags, pillars, nude woman, faces.
No. 1107, Flags, bodies, woman, soldier in
armor. No. 1108, Women's faces, pipelines.

1994, May 14   Litho.   Perf. 13
1105 A549 250p multicolored   1.75 .75
1106 A549 250p multicolored   1.75 .75
1107 A549 250p multicolored   1.75 .75
1108 A549 250p multicolored   1.75 .75
a.   Strip of 4, #1105-1108 + label 7.50 5.00

No. 1108a is a continuous design.

Chilean Antarctic Institute, 30th
Anniv. — A550

Designs: No. 1109, Penguins, buildings. No.
1110, Buildings, coastal waters.

1994, May 31   Perf. 13
1109   300p multicolored   2.00 1.10
1110   300p multicolored   2.00 1.10
a.   A550 Pair, #1109-1110   4.50 2.50

No. 1110a is a continuous design.

Antique Fire Engines — A551

No. 1111, Merryweather steam pumper,
England, 1869. No. 1112, Western lever
pumper, US, 1863. No. 1113, Mieusset steam
pumper, France, 1905. No. 1114, Merryweather pumper, England, 1903.

1994, July 19   Litho.   Perf. 13
1111 A551 150p multicolored   .90 .50
1112 A551 150p multicolored   .90 .50
1113 A551 150p multicolored   .90 .50
1114 A551 150p multicolored   .90 .50
a.   Block of 4, #1111-1114   4.50 3.50

Javiera Carrera Girls' School,
Cent. — A552

1994, Aug. 10
1115 A552 200p multicolored   1.25 .60

Arms, Sights from Chilean
Cities — A553

Designs: 90p, Porvenir, cent. 100p, Villa
Alemana, cent. 150p, Constitucion, bicent.
200p, Linares, bicent. 250p, Copiapo, 250th
anniv. 300p, La Serena, 450th anniv.

1994, Aug. 26
1116 A553   90p multicolored   .50 .25
1117 A553 100p multicolored   .60 .30
1118 A553 150p multicolored   .95 .40
1119 A553 200p multicolored   1.40 .55
1120 A553 250p multicolored   1.75 .65
1121 A553 300p multicolored   2.00 .85
       Nos. 1116-1121 (6)   7.20 3.00

Butterflies — A554

Designs: a, Vanessa terpsichore. b, Hyp-
sochila wagenknechti. c, Battus polydamas. d,
Polythysana apollina. e, Satyridae. f,
Tetraphloebia stellygera. g, Eroessa chilensis.
h, Phoebis sennae.

1994, June 24   Litho.   Perf. 13
1122 A554 100p Sheet of 8, #a.-
                       h.   9.00 9.00

20th Intl.
Conference on
Data
Bases — A555

1994, Sept. 21   Litho.   Perf. 13½
1123 A555 100p multicolored   .60 .30

America Issue — A556

Early postal transport vehicles: 80p, Van.
220p, DH-60-G, Gypsy Moth.

1994, Oct. 12
1124 A556   80p multicolored   1.00 .30
1125 A556 220p multicolored   2.00 .70

A557

1994, Oct. 31   Litho. & Engr.
1126 A557 300p multicolored   2.00 1.00

Beatification of Father Alberto Hurtado.

A558

1994   Litho.   Perf. 13½
1127 A558 80p multicolored   .60 .25
a.   Booklet pane of 10   6.00
          Complete booklet, #1127a   6.00

Inscribed "DS/20"

1128 A558 80p multicolored   .60 .25
a.   Booklet pane of 10   7.00
          Complete booklet, #1128a   7.00

Christmas.

Nos. 1036-1037,
1079 Surcharged

Perf. 13½ on 3 Sides
1994, Nov. 4   Litho.
1129 A525 80p on 70p #1036   .45 .25
1130 A525 80p on 70p #1037   .45 .25
a.   Pair, #1129-1130   .90 .50
b.   Booklet pane, 5 #1130b   7.00
          Complete booklet, #1130b 7.00
1131 A542 80p on 70p #1079   .45 .25
a.   Booklet pane, 10 #1131   7.00
          Complete booklet, #1131a 7.00

Size and location of surcharge varies.

Miniature Sheet

Intl. Women's Day — A559

Designs: a, Star, "Women enriching the
future." b, Moon, sun, "Women bringing harmony." c, Bird, "Women bringing peace." d,
Earth, "Women changing the world."

1995, Mar. 8   Litho.   Perf. 13½
1132 A559 90p Sheet of 4, #a.-d. 5.00 2.50

Ancud Seminary
of Conciliation,
150th
Anniv. — A560

1995, Apr. 27
1133 A560 200p multicolored   1.25 .60

Destroyer
Admiral
Williams
A561

1995, Apr. 21
1134 A561 100p multicolored   .70 .30

World Conference
on Social
Development
A562

1995, Apr. 25
1135 A562 150p multicolored   1.00 .45

Order of St. Augustine in Chile, 400th
Anniv. — A563

Stained glass, Cathedral of Santiago.

1995, Apr. 28
1136 A563 250p multicolored   1.60 .75

Petroglyphs — A564

Designs: a, Ceremonial mask, Buitre, Limari
Province. b, Lamas, Taira Sector, El Loa Prov-
ince. c, Harpooned whale, El Medano, Taltal
Province. d, Two masks, Encanto, Ovalle.

1995, June 16   Litho.   Perf. 13½
1137 A564 150p Block of 4, #a.-
                       d.   7.00 4.00

Miniature Sheet

Motion Pictures,
Cent. — A565

Posters: a, Director's chair, camera. b,
Charlie Chaplin in "The Kid." c, Lumiere broth-
ers' 1895 Cinematographe. d, "Valparaiso, My
Love", with Aldo Francia.

1995, June 21
1138 A565 100p Sheet of 4, #a.-
                       d.   7.00 3.00

City of
Parral,
Bicent.
A566

1995, June 30   Litho.   Perf. 13½
1139 A566 200p multicolored   1.60 .85

Miniature Sheet

FLORA Y FAUNA DE CHILE

Chile $100

Insects and Cacti — A567

a, Cheloderus childreni. b, Eulychnia acida. c, Chiasognathus grantii. d, Browningia candelaris. e, Copiapoa dealbata. f, Acanthinodera cummingi. g, Neoporteria subgibbosa. h, Semiotus luteipennis.

1995, Aug. 10   Litho.   Perf. 13½
1140 A567 100p Sheet of 8,
  #a.-h.   10.00 7.50

2nd World Congress of Police, Santiago — A568

1995, Oct. 2
1141 A568 200p multicolored   1.60 .80

Ministry of Housing and Urban Development, 30th Anniv. — A569

Design: Tower of Babel V, by Mario Toral.

1995, Oct. 5   Litho.   Perf. 13½
1142 A569 200p multicolored   1.60 .85

Andres Bello (1781-1865), Scholar, Author A570

1995, Oct. 9   Litho. & Engr.
1143 A570 250p dk brn & blk   1.75 .85
Andres Bello Covenant, 25th anniv.

UNESCO, UN, FAO, 50th Anniv. — A571

Designs: a, Hands holding book, UNESCO emblem. b, Hands clasped between two

globes, UN emblem. c, Hand holding seedling, FAO emblem.

1995, Oct. 10   Litho.   Perf. 13½
1144 A571 100p Strip of 3, #a.-c. 2.75 1.40
  No. 1144 is a continuous design.

America Issue — A572

Children's drawings of environmental protection: 100p, Family in garden, trees, vert. 250p, Three people working with trees.

1995, Oct. 12   Litho.   Perf. 13½
1145 A572 100p multicolored   1.00 .45
1146 A572 250p multicolored   2.50 1.10

A573

Chilean Soccer, Cent.: a, Carlos Dittborn. b, Hugo Lepe. c, Eladio Rojas. d, Honorino Landa.

1995, Nov. 13   Litho.   Perf. 13½
1147 A573 100p Sheet of 4, #a.-
  d.   3.00 1.40

A574

1995, Oct. 24   Litho.   Perf. 13½
1148 A574 250p multicolored   1.60 .95
51st World Congress of Cape Horn captains.

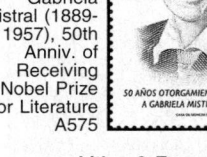

Gabriela Mistral (1889-1957), 50th Anniv. of Receiving Nobel Prize for Literature A575

Litho. & Engr.
1995, Nov. 15   Perf. 13½
1149 A575 300p blue black & blk 2.00 1.00

Eudyptes Chrysolophus A576

1995, Nov. 22   Litho.   Perf. 13½
1150 A576 100p shown   1.25 .45
1151 A576 250p Penguins, diff. 2.25 1.10
 a.   Souv. sheet, #1150-1151 5.00 5.00
  No. 1151a sold for 600p.

Chilean Export Assoc., 60th Anniv. — A577

Cargo ship and: a, Kiwi fruit. b, Grapes. c, Peaches. d, Apples.
Jet plane and: e, Various berries.

1995, Dec. 1
1152 A577 100p Strip of 5, #a.-e. 3.50 3.50

Christmas
A578   A579

1995, Nov. 13   Booklet Stamps
1153 A578 90p brt blue & blue .60 .30
1154 A579 90p brt blue & blue .60 .30
 a.   Bklt. pane, 5 ea #1153-1154 6.50
     Complete booklet, #1154a   6.75
1155 A578 90p brt grn & brown .60 .30
1156 A579 90p brt grn & brown .60 .30
 a.   Bklt. pane, 5 ea #1155-1156 6.50
     Complete booklet, #1156a   6.75
  Nos. 1155-1156 inscribed "DS/20."

End of World War II, 50th Anniv. A580

1995, Dec. 20   Litho.   Perf. 13½
1157 A580 200p multicolored   1.50 .75

Petroleum Production in Chile, 50th Anniv. — A581

Designs: a, Off-shore oil derrick, one main tower. b, Refinery, road trees, building. c, Refinery, up close. d, Off-shore oil derrick, four towers.

1995, Dec. 29
1158 A581 100p Block of 4, #a.-
  d.   3.00 3.00

Aviation Type of 1994

Designs: a, Embraer EMB-145. b, Mirage M5M Elkan. c, DHC-6 Twin Otter Series 300. d, SAAB JAS 39, Gripen.

1996, Mar. 9   Litho.   Perf. 13½
1159 A547 400p Sheet of 4,
  #a.-d.   13.00 8.50
  Intl. Air and Space Fair, FIDAE '96.

Men's High School, La Serena, 175th Anniv. — A582

1996, Apr. 12
1160 A582 100p multicolored   .70 .35

Espamer '96, World Philatelic Exhibition — A583

Designs: No. 1161, Old Train Station, Cordoba. No. 1162, Lope de Vega Theater.

1996, Apr. 25
1161 A583 200p multicolored   1.25 .70
1162 A583 200p multicolored   1.25 .70
 a.   Pair, #1161-1162   3.00 3.00

Accident Prevention A584

Traffic safety: No. 1163a, Cross street at crosswalk. b, Respect traffic police. c, Obey traffic signals. d, Wait for ride on sidewalk. e, Don't cross street between parked cars. f, Never ride on side of bus. g, Walk beside road facing oncoming traffic. h, Pay attention to where you are walking. i, Don't play on streets. j, Obey traffic rules while riding a bicycle.
Safety in the home: No. 1164a, Extinguish matches after using. b, Be careful with boiling water. c, Curb sharp objects. d, Protect electrical outlets. e, Don't improvise electrical connections. f, Don't play radio or TV too loudly. g, Check all gas connections. h, Don't overload electrical outlets. i, Keep flammable materials away from furnace. j, Keep toys off floor.
Recreational safety: No. 1165a, Swim only in designated areas. b, Keep hands, head inside the car. c, Don't get a sunburn. d, Don't contaminate water with detergents. e, Don't litter. f, Extinguish camp fires. g, Don't bother others when swimming. h, Check car safety features. i, Keep kites away from electrical wires. j, Don't run in swimming pool area.
Safety in the workplace: No. 1166a, Use protective gear. b, Use only safe tools. c, Keep you mind on your work. d, Use proper tools. e, Avoid work accidents. f, Keep stairs free of objects. g, Don't carry objects that obstruct your view. h, Check ladder before using. i, Keep area clean, organized. j, Be aware of protruding nails.
Proper use of drugs and alcohol: No. 1167a, Don't drink and drive. b, Don't drink if you are pregnant. c, Don't encourage friends to drink. d, Alcohol and work don't mix. e, Drinking could destroy your family. f, Drugs can't make you happy. g, Drugs don't make you successful. h, Be happy without drugs. i, For your family say "no" to drugs. j, Drug free, happy and confident.

Safety in schools: No. 1168a, Keep calm in case of fire. b, Don't run along sides of buildings. c, Don't play dangerous jokes. d, Don't sit or stand in high dangerous places. e, Don't run on stairs. f, Don't walk and drink at the same time. g, Don't rock on chairs. h, Don't play with sharp objects. i, Don't open doors abruptly. j, Don't talk to strangers outside the school.

1996, May 2
1163	A584	50p	Block of 10, #a.-j.	4.75	2.25
1164	A584	50p	Block of 10, #a.-j.	4.75	2.25
1165	A584	50p	Block of 10, #a.-j.	4.75	2.25
1166	A584	50p	Block of 10, #a.-j.	4.75	2.25
1167	A584	50p	Block of 10, #a.-j.	4.75	2.25
1168	A584	50p	Block of 10, #a.-j.	4.75	2.25

No. 1 Dry Dock, Talcahuano, Cent. — A585

1996, May 20
1169	A585	200p multicolored	1.40	.70

Sculptures — A586

No. 1170, Mariner's Compass, by Ricardo Mesa, vert. No. 1171, Friendship, by Francisca Cerda, vert. No. 1172, Andes Winds, by Benito Rojo. No. 1173, Memory, by Fernando Undurraga.

1996, June 20   Litho.   Perf. 13½
1170	A586	150p multicolored	1.75	.90
1171	A586	150p multicolored	1.75	.90
a.		Pair, #1170-1171	4.75	4.75
1172	A586	200p multicolored	2.25	.90
1173	A586	200p multicolored	2.25	.90
a.		Pair, #1172-1173	6.00	6.00
		Nos. 1170-1173 (4)	8.00	3.60

Intl. Day Against Use of Illegal Drugs and Drug Trafficking — A587

1996, June 26
1174	A587	250p multicolored	2.00	1.25

1996 Summer Olympic Games, Atlanta — A588

Designs: a, Boxer's glove. b, Runner's shoe. c, Roller blade. d, Ball.

1996, July 3
1175	A588	450p	Block of 4, #a.-d.	13.50 11.00

Order of Mother of God, 50th Anniv. of Presence in Chile — A589

1996, Aug.   Litho.   Perf. 13½
1176	A589	200p multicolored	1.50	.75

Lyceum of San Fernando, 150th Anniv. — A590

1996, Aug. 2
1177	A590	200p multicolored	1.50	.75

4th Intl. Congress of Earth Sciences — A591

Globe showing portions of continents, and: a, Forest fire. b, Smoke stacks creating air pollution. c, Cutting down trees. d, Surveying equipment, desert.

1996, Aug. 5   Litho.   Perf. 13½
1178	A591	200p	Block of 4, #a.-d.	6.75 6.75

Minerals — A592

a, Kroehnkita. b, Lapis lazuli. c, Bornite. d, Azurite.

1996, Aug. 9
1179	A592	150p	Block of 4, #a.-d.	5.00 4.25

German Immigration, 150th Anniv. — A593

Designs: 250p, House, lake, mountain. 300p, Monument showing arrival on boat.

1996, Aug. 22
1180	A593	250p multicolored	1.90	.90
1181	A593	300p multicolored	2.10 1.00

Aptenodytes Patagonica A594

1996, Sept. 9   Litho.   Perf. 13½
1182	A594	250p shown	2.00 1.00
1183	A594	300p Molting	2.10 1.10
a.		Souvenir sheet, #1182-1183	5.75 5.75

Castro Fire Dept., Cent. A595

Designs: a, 1937 Italian pumper. b, 1940 Ford fire truck. c, Gorlitz G.A. Fischer manual 4-speed pumper. d, 1907 pumper.

1996, Sept. 14
1184	A595	200p	Block of 4, #a.-d.	6.00 6.00

Ecotourism in National Parks — A596

Designs: a, River rafting. b, Horseback riding. c, Snow skiing. d, Hiking around cacti.

1996, Sept. 27
1185	A596	100p	Sheet of 4, #a.-d.	3.25 3.25

Juan José Latorre Benavente (1846-1912), Admiral — A597

1996, Oct. 8
1186	A597	200p multicolored	1.50	.75

Historical Costumes — A598

America issue: No. 1187, Two women, child, dog, vert. No. 1188, Two men with horse, vert. 250p, Two men on horseback.

1996, Oct. 23
1187	A598	100p multicolored	.95	.50
1188	A598	100p multicolored	.95	.50
a.		Pair, #1187-1188	2.00 2.00
1189	A598	250p multicolored	1.75 1.10

Church, City of Arica — A599

150p, Fauna, mountains, Parinacota Park.

1996, Nov. 18   Litho.   Perf. 13½
1190	A599	100p multicolored	.65	.35
1191	A599	150p multicolored	.85	.45

Christmas — A600

1996, Nov. 25
1192	A600	100p black & multi	.70	.30
a.		Booklet pane of 10	7.50	
		Complete booklet, #1192a	8.00	
1193	A600	100p orange & multi	.70	.30
a.		Booklet pane of 10	7.50	
		Complete booklet, #1193a	8.00	

No. 1193 is inscribed DS/20.

Mythology
A601   A602

1997, Feb. 12   Litho.   Perf. 13½
1194	A601	40p black & blue	.25	.25
1195	A602	110p black & green	.80	.40
a		Booklet pane of 10	8.00	
		Complete booklet, #1195a	8.50	
1196	A602	110p black & orange	.80	.40
a.		Booklet pane of 10	8.00	
		Complete booklet, #1196a	8.50	

No. 1195 inscribed DS/20.

Sixth Summit of Spanish-Americana Heads of State and Government — A603

Mural, Visual Memory of the Nation, by Mario Toral: No. 1198, Left half. No. 1199, Right half.

1996, Nov. 6
1198	A603	110p multicolored	.90	.45
1199	A603	110p multicolored	.90	.45
a.		Pair, #1198-1199	2.00	.95

No. 1199a is a continuous design.

State Visit of King Carl XVI Gustaf, Queen Silvia of Sweden — A604

Design: Nobel Laureates Pablo Neruda, Gabriela Mistral, Nobel medal.

1996, Dec. 3
1200 A604 300p multicolored 2.25 1.10

UNICEF, 50th
Anniv. — A605

1996, Dec. 11
1201 A605 200p multicolored 1.50 .75

Frontier Region, Cent. — A606

No. 1202, Christian Alliance & Missionary Church, cent. No. 1203, Lonquimay municipality, cent.

1997
1202 A606 110p multicolored .80 .40
1203 A606 110p multicolored .90 .45

Issued: No. 1202, 1/19; No. 1203, 1/25.

Arturo Prat Antarctic Naval Base, 50th
Anniv. — A607

1997, Feb. 6 Litho. Perf. 13½
1204 A607 250p Aerial view, vert. 1.90 .95
1205 A607 300p shown 2.40 1.10

Controller General of the Republic,
70th Anniv. — A608

1997, Mar. 26
1206 A608 110p multicolored 2.00 .40

Opening of Metro Line 5 — A609

1997, Apr. 2
1207 A609 200p multicolored 1.50 .75

Interamerican Masonic Confederation,
50th Anniv. — A610

1200p, Emblems, compass, square, book.

1997, Apr. 8
1208 A610 250p shown 2.00 1.00
Souvenir Sheet
1209 A610 1200p multicolored 9.00 9.00
No. 1209 contains one 48x60mm stamp.

Heinrich von
Stephan
(1831-97)
A611

1997, Apr. 15
1210 A611 250p multicolored 2.00 1.00

World Book and Copyright
Day — A612

1997, Apr. 23
1211 A612 110p multicolored .80 .45

Details from "Death to the Invader," by David Alfaro Siqueiros (1896-1974), Muralist — A613

1997, June 26 Litho. Perf. 13½
1212 A613 150p shown 1.50 .40
1213 A613 200p Detail, diff. 1.75 .60
Souvenir Sheets
1214 A613 1000p like #1212 6.25 6.25
1215 A613 1000p like #1213 6.25 6.25
Nos. 1214-1215 each contain one 48x36mm stamp.

Providencia, Cent. — A614

1997, July 17
1216 A614 250p multicolored 1.60 .90

A615

1997, Sept. 1
1217 A615 300p multicolored 2.00 1.10
Diplomatic relations between Chile and Japan, cent. See Japan No. 2578.

A616

1997, Oct. 1 Litho. Perf. 13½
1218 A616 110p Quality .80 .40

1st Radio Broadcast in Chile, 75th
Anniv. — A617

1997 Litho. Perf. 13½
1219 A617 110p multicolored .80 .50

Chilean
Opera
Singers
A618

Singer, opera: 120p, Carlo Morelli, "Rigoletto." 200p, Pedro Navia, "La Bohéme." 250p, Renato Zanelli, "Faust." 300p, Rayèn Quitral, "The Magic Flute." 500p, Ramón Vinay, "Othello."

1997, Oct. 15
1220 A618 120p multicolored 1.00 .55
1221 A618 200p multicolored 1.75 .85
1222 A618 250p multicolored 2.25 1.10
1223 A618 300p multicolored 2.50 1.25
1224 A618 500p multicolored 4.25 2.25
Nos. 1220-1224 (5) 11.75 6.00

America Issue — A619

Life of a postman: 110p, Delivering mail on bicycle. 250p, Delivering mail on horseback.

1997, Oct. 12 Litho. Perf. 13½
1225 A619 110p multicolored 1.00 .45
1226 A619 250p multicolored 2.50 1.00

Christmas — A620

1997 Litho. Perf. 13½
1227 A620 110p multicolored .80 .40
  a. Booklet pane of 10 8.00
     Complete booklet, #1227a 8.50
1228 A620 110p multicolored .80 .40
  a. Booklet pane of 10 8.00
     Complete booklet, #1228a 8.50
No. 1228 is inscribed D/S20 and was only issued in booklets.

Chilean Post,
250th Anniv.
A621

Designs: 120p, Postman canceling letters. 300p, Man depositing letter into postbox.

1997, Dec. 22
1229 A621 120p multicolored .75 .40
1230 A621 300p multicolored 1.90 .95

Dogs
A622   A623

1998 Litho. Perf. 13½
1231 A622 120p Great Dane .60 .25
1232 A623 120p Dalmatian .60 .25
  a. Pair, #1231-1232 1.25 1.00
  b. Booklet pane, 5 #1232a 7.00
     Complete booklet, #1232b 7.00
1233 A622 120p Great Dane .60 .25
1234 A623 120p Dalmatian .60 .25
  a. Pair, #1233-1234 1.25 1.00
  b. Booklet pane, 5 #1234a 7.00
     Complete booklet, #1234b 7.00
Nos. 1233-1234 are inscribed DS/20.

2nd Summit of the
Americas,
Santiago — A624

1998, Apr. 17   Litho.   Perf. 13½
1235 A624 150p multicolored   .85   .40

Souvenir Sheet
1236 A624 1000p Logo, diff.   10.00 10.00

No. 1236 contains one 26x42mm stamp.

Paintings — A625

350p, "Los Zambos de Calama," by Mauricio Moran. 400p, "Sandia Calada," by Roser Bru.

1998, May 14   Litho.   Perf. 13½
1237 A625 350p multicolored   2.10 1.25
1238 A625 400p multicolored   2.40 1.50

Capuchin Order in Chile, 150th Anniv. — A626

Designs: 150p, Native village, friar writing in book. 250p, Friar aiding injured man.

1998, May 18
1239 A626 150p multicolored   .90   .50
1240 A626 250p multicolored   1.40   .70

1998 World Cup Soccer Championships, France — A627

Players and: 250p, Crowd. 350p, World Cup Trophy. 500p, Map of France. 700p, Chilean flag.
1500p, Player, vert.

1998, May 23
1241 A627 250p multicolored   1.50   .70
1242 A627 350p multicolored   2.00 1.00
1243 A627 500p multicolored   3.00 1.50
1244 A627 700p multicolored   4.25 2.00
    Nos. 1241-1244 (4)   10.75 5.20

Souvenir Sheet
1245 A627 1500p multicolored   9.00 9.00

A628

Antarctic Research: 250p, Logo, penguin. 350p, Penguins, map, logo.

1998, July 22
1246 A628 250p multicolored   1.50   .75
1247 A628 350p multicolored   2.25 1.10

No. 1246, Scientific Committee on Antarctic Research, 25th meeting. No. 1247, Natl. Administrators of Antarctic Programs, 10th meeting.

A629

1998, Apr. 3
1248 A629 120p multicolored   .80   .40
Captain Arturo Prat Chacon, 150th birth anniv.

Army Veterinarian Service, Cent. — A630

350p, Veterinarian listening to horse's heartbeat.

1998, Apr. 20
1249 A630 250p multicolored   1.50   .75
1250 A630 350p multicolored   2.25 1.10

Merchant Marine's Director General of Maritime Territory, 150th Anniv. — A631

1998, Aug. 31   Litho.   Perf. 13½
1251 A631 500p multicolored   3.25 1.40
Intl. Year of the Ocean.

Intl. Year of the Ocean A632

No. 1252, Nautical cartography. No. 1253, Iceberg. 500p, Silhouette of stone head, Easter Island.

1998, Sept. 10
1252 A632 400p multicolored   2.50 1.25
1253 A632 400p multicolored   2.50 1.25
1254 A632 500p multicolored   3.25 1.50
    Nos. 1252-1254 (3)   8.25 4.00

Folk Singers and Composers — A633

Designs: 200p, Clara Solovera Cortes (1909-92). 250p, Francisco Flores del Campo (1908-93). 300p, Victor Jara Martinez (1932-73). 350p, Violeta Parra Sandoval (1917-67).

1998, Sept. 14
1255 A633 200p multicolored   1.00   .50
1256 A633 250p multicolored   1.40   .60
1257 A633 300p multicolored   1.50   .70
1258 A633 350p multicolored   1.90   .80
    Nos. 1255-1258 (4)   5.80 2.60

World Stamp Day A634

1998, Oct. 9   Litho.   Perf. 13½
1259 A634 250p multicolored   1.25   .60

Francisco Bilbao (1823-65), Writer A635

Litho. & Engr.
1998, Oct. 29   Perf. 13½
1260 A635 250p multicolored   1.75   .85

Chilean Painters — A636

Designs: 300p, Self-portrait, by Augusto Eguiluz (1894-1969), vert. 450p, Landscape, by Agustin Abarca (1882-1953). 1500p, "Two Nudes," by Henriette Petit (1894-1983).

1998, Nov. 3   Litho.
1261   A636   300p multi   1.50   .80
1262   A636   450p multi   2.25 1.10

Souvenir Sheet
1262A A636 1500p multi   8.00 8.00

No. 1262A contains one 36x47mm stamp.

Catholic University of Valparaiso, 70th Anniv. — A637

1998, Nov. 18   Litho.   Perf. 13½
1263 A637 130p multicolored   .70   .35

Prominent Women from the University of Chile — A638

America Issue: 120p, Amanda Labarca, educator. 250p, Marta Brunet, writer.

1998, Nov. 19   Litho.   Perf. 13½
1264 A638 120p multicolored   .80   .45
1265 A638 250p multicolored   1.60   .85

1999 World Scout Jamboree, Chile — A639

Scouting emblems and: 120p, Children of two races, stylized tents. 200p, Robert Baden-Powell. 250p, Stylized doves. 300p, Scout, stylized tents. 1000p, Scouts, leaders seated in semi-circle, vert.
3000p, Jamboree emblem over drawing of Jamboree site at Picarquin, emblems of past jamborees, Intl. Scouting Emblem.

1998, Dec. 27
1266 A639 120p multicolored   .75   .35
1267 A639 200p multicolored   1.10   .55
1268 A639 250p multicolored   1.40   .70
1269 A639 300p multicolored   1.50   .80
1270 A639 1000p multicolored   5.25 2.75
    Nos. 1266-1270 (5)   10.00 5.15

Imperf
Size: 126x104mm
1270A A639 3000p multi   17.00 17.00

Birds — A640

Designs: 10p, Zonotrichia capensis. 20p, Curaeus curaeus.

1998, Nov. 29
1271 A640 10p multicolored   .80   .25
    a.   Inscribed "2000"   .80   .25
1272 A640 20p multicolored   .80   .25
    a.   Inscribed "2000"   .80   .25

See Nos. 1313-1314, 1356, 1385-1386, 1418-1419.

World Equestrian High Jump Record, 50th Anniv. — A641

Captain Alberto Larraguibel and Huaso.

1999, Feb. 5   Litho.   Perf. 13½
1273 A641 200p multicolored   1.10   .65

Temuco Fire Dept., Cent. — A642

Designs: 140p, 1900 pumper. 200p, 1929 Ford. 300p, 1955 Ford K tanker. 350p, 1967 Mercedes Benz hook and ladder truck.
1500p, Firefighter rescuing victim, vert.

1999, Feb. 18   Litho.   Perf. 13½
1274 A642 140p multicolored   .65   .30
1275 A642 200p multicolored   .95   .40
1276 A642 300p multicolored   1.50   .60
1277 A642 350p multicolored   1.75   .70
    Nos. 1274-1277 (4)   4.85 2.00

Souvenir Sheet
1278 A642 1500p multicolored   8.50 8.50

Chilean Chamber of Deputies, 1000th Session — A643

1999, Mar. 3   **Perf. 13½**
1279 A643 140p multicolored   .70   .50

Sacred Heart College, 150th Anniv. — A644

1999, Mar. 15
1280 A644 250p multicolored   1.25   .85

Economic Development Corporation (CORFO), 60th Anniv. — A645

Pedro Aguirre Cerda, former president of Chile.

1999, Apr. 29   **Perf. 13½**
1281 A645 140p multicolored   .80   .50

Chilean Insurance Assoc., Cent. — A646

1999, May 18   Litho.   Perf. 13½
1282 A646 140p multicolored   .65   .50

Chilean Antarctica A647

Designs: 360p, Leptonychotes weddellii. 450p, Pygoscelis antarctica. 1500p, Arctocephalus gazella, penguins.

1999, June 15
1283 A647 360p multicolored   1.75   .90
1284 A647 450p multicolored   3.25 1.25
Souvenir Sheet
1285 A647 1500p multicolored   8.50 8.50
No. 1285 contains one 35x48mm stamp.

Easter Island A648

1999, June 25
1286 A648 360p multicolored   2.00 2.00

Souvenir Sheet

Barcelona Soccer Club, Cent. — A649

1999
1287 A649 1000p multicolored   5.00 5.00

University of Santiago, 150th Anniv. — A650

Designs: 140p, Monument, students in training room, School of Arts and Sciences, 1849. 250p, Technical equipment, building on campus, State Technical University, 1947. 300p, Student looking into microscope, computer, modern building, 1999.

1999, July 6   Litho.   Perf. 13½
1288 A650 140p multicolored   .75   .35
1289 A650 250p multicolored   1.25   .60
1290 A650 300p multicolored   1.60   .75
     Nos. 1288-1290 (3)   3.60 1.70

Alexander von Humboldt (1769-1859), 200th Anniv. of Scientific Research in Latin America — A651

Face from monument and: 300p, Bust of Humboldt, wildlife, mountains. 360p, Portrait of Humboldt, penguins, sea.

1999, July 16
1291 A651 300p multicolored   1.75   .75
1292 A651 360p multicolored   1.90   .95

China '99, World Philatelic Exhibition, Beijing — A652

Chinese, Chilean flags and: 140p, Pagoda. 450p, Chinese junk. 1500p, Great Wall of China, Gate of Heavenly Peace.

1999, Aug. 10
1293 A652 140p multicolored   .75   .35

1294 A652 450p multicolored   2.10 1.10
Souvenir Sheet
1295 A652 1500p multicolored   8.00 5.00
No. 1295 contains one 60x48mm stamp.

City of Quilpue, Cent. — A653

1999, Aug. 20
1296 A653 250p multicolored   1.60   .80

Holy Year 2000 — A654

140p, Raúl Cardinal Silva Henriquez (1907-99). 200p, Walking in street clothes, administering sacrament, face of Christ.

1999, Aug. 9
1297 A654 140p shown   .80   .40
1298 A654 200p multicolored   1.00   .50

A655

1999, Sept. 23   Litho.   Perf. 13½
1299 A655 140p multicolored   .70   .35
Red Cross blood donation campaign.

2000 World Congress of Authors & Composers, Santiago — A656

1999, Oct. 5
1300 A656 170p multicolored   .90   .45

Intl. Year of Older Persons — A657

1999, Oct. 6
1301 A657 250p multicolored   1.25   .60

UPU, 125th Anniv. A658

1999, Oct. 9
1302 A658 300p Red mailbox   2.75   .90
1303 A658 360p Gold mailbox   2.75 1.10
a.   Pair, #1302-1303 + label   6.75 5.25
Nos. 1302-1303 printed in sheets of 16 pairs, with label in central column.

America Issue, A New Millennium Without Arms — A659

1999, Oct. 12
1304 A659 140p shown   1.25   .30
1305 A659 320p Broken bomb   1.75   .65

Labor Management, 75th Anniv. — A660

1999, Aug. 23
1306 A660 320p multicolored   1.50   .75

Interamerican Development Bank, 40th Anniv. — A661

1999, Oct. 29   Litho.   Perf. 13½
1307 A661 360p multicolored   1.75   .85

Holy Year 2000 — A662

1999, Dec. 1
1308 A662 450p multicolored   2.10 1.10

A663

1999, Dec. 1
1309 A663 170p multicolored   .90   .45

Inscribed "D.S. 20"

1310	A663 170p multicolored	.90	.45
a.	Booklet pane of 10	10.00	
	Complete booklet, #1310a	11.00	
b.	Booklet pane of 5	5.50	
	Complete booklet, #1310b	6.00	

Nos. 1309-1310 each were issued se-tenant with two labels that served as a lottery ticket and stub.

Union Leaders — A664

No. 1311, Luis Emilio Recabarren Serrano (1876-1924), Clotario Leopoldo Blest Riffo (1899-1990). No. 1312, Tucapel Jiménez Alfaro (1921-82), Manuel Bustos Huerta (1943-99).

1999, Dec. 29   Litho.   Perf. 13½

1311	A664 200p multi	.90	.50
1312	A664 200p multi	.90	.50
a.	Pair, #1311-1312 + label	4.00	3.00

Bird Type of 1998

Designs: 50p, Campephilus magellanicus, vert. 100p, Falco peregrinus cassini, vert.

2000, Feb.   Perf. 13½

1313	A640 50p multi	.25	.25
1314	A640 100p multi	.90	.25

Discovery of Juan Fernández, Archipelago, 425th Anniv. — A665

a, Más Afuera (Alejandro Selkirk) Island, Santa Clara Island, tip of Más a Tierra (Robinson Crusoe) Island. b, Más a Tierra Island. c, Dendroseris litoralis. d, Rhaphythamnus venustus. e, Lobster. f, Lobster's antenna, boat. g, Boat, Gavilea insularis. h, Gavilea insularis.

2000, Feb. 29   Perf. 13¼

1315	A665 360p Sheet of 8,	16.00	16.00
	#a.-h.		

Condorito, Cartoon Character by Rene Rios Boettiger Pepo — A666

Condorito: 150p, Celebrating millennium. 260p, As soccer player. 480p, As fire fighter. 980p, On horse. 2000p, With people.

2000, Mar. 20   Perf. 13½

1316	A666 150p multi	.75	.30
1317	A666 260p multi	1.50	.50
1318	A666 480p multi	2.50	.95
1319	A666 980p multi	5.25	2.00
	Nos. 1316-1319 (4)	10.00	3.75

Souvenir Sheet

1320	A666 2000p multi	11.00	11.00

Easter Island — A667

Designs: 200p, Dancer, stone weapon. 260p, Stone statue and carvings. 340p, Island native, stone statue. 480p, Female dancer, inscribed tablet, map of island.

2000, Apr. 27   Litho.   Perf. 13¼

1321	A667 200p multi	1.10	.60
1322	A667 260p multi	1.50	.70
1323	A667 340p multi	2.00	1.00
1324	A667 480p multi	2.75	1.40
	Nos. 1321-1324 (4)	7.35	3.70

Town of Carahue, Cent. (in 1998) — A668

Bridge and: No. 1325, Locomotive, pottery. No. 1326, Potatoes.

2000, May 5

1325	220p multi	1.10	.55
1326	220p multi	1.10	.55
a.	A668 Pair, #1325-1326	2.50	2.00

El Mercurio Newspaper, Cent. — A669

2000, June 1

1327	A669 370p multi	2.00	1.00

4th Natl. Masonic Convention — A670

2000, June 23

1328	A670 460p multi	2.50	1.25

Medicinal Plants — A671

Designs: 200p, Quillaja saponaria. 360p, Fabiana imbricata.

2000, July 3

1329	A671 200p multi	1.25	.60
1330	A671 360p multi	3.00	1.50

Discovery of Brazil, 500th Anniv. — A672

Designs: 260p, Map of Brazil, butterfly, girl. 1500p, Monkey, parrots, boy.

2000, July 10

1331	A672 260p multi	1.50	.75

Souvenir Sheet

1332	A672 1500p multi	8.50	8.50

No. 1332 contains one 48x36mm stamp.

Folklore A673

Religious festivals: 150p, Dancer in devil costume, La Tirana. 200p, Festival of San Pedro de Atacama. 370p, Candlemas Festival, Copiapo. 460p, Chinese dancers, Andacollo.

2000, July 13

1333	A673 150p multi	.80	.40
1334	A673 200p multi	1.10	.55
1335	A673 370p multi	2.00	1.00
1336	A673 460p multi	2.50	1.25
	Nos. 1333-1336 (4)	6.40	3.20

Prehistoric Animals — A674

No. 1337: a, Milodon. b, Titanosaurus. c, Plesiosaurus. d, Iguanodon.

2000

1337	A674 150p Block of 4, #a-d	2.75	1.40

José de San Martín (1778-1850) — A675

2000, Aug. 25   Litho.   Perf. 13½

1338	A675 320p multi	1.60	.80

World Meteorological Organization, 50th Anniv. — A676

2000, Aug. 28

1339	A676 320p multi	1.60	.80

Antarctic Fauna — A677

450p, Sphenis magellanicus, vert. 650p, Megaptera novaeangliae. 940p, Orcinus orca. 2000p, Mirounga leonina, vert.

2000, Sept. 15

1340-1342	A677 Set of 3	25.00	19.00

Souvenir Sheet

1343	A677 2000p multi	25.00	15.00

No. 1343 contains one 36x48mm stamp.

2000 Summer Olympics, Sydney — A678

Sydney Opera House, Olympic flag and: a, 290p, Chilean flag, tennis player, soccer player, sprinter. b, 290p, Australian flag, archer, high jumper, cyclist.

2000, Sept. 20

1344	A678 Pair, #a-b	4.50	2.25

City of Concepcion, 450th Anniv. — A679

Mural by Gregorio De la Fuente: a, Indian holding stick. b, Soldier on white horse. c, Finger pointing upward. d, Seated figure, arms, horse-drawn carriage. e, Horse, statue, train. f, People and rainbow.

2000, Oct. 2

1345	Horiz. strip of 6	10.00	10.00
a.-f.	A679 250p Any single	1.50	.75

America Issue, World AIDS Day — A680

Designs: 150p, Heart, clasped hands of adult and child. 220p, Clasped hands.

2000, Oct. 12

1346-1347	A680 Set of 2	3.00	1.50

Penal Reform — A681

Designs: 150p, Flag, court proceedings. 2000p, People, doors of Justice Ministry.

2000, Nov. 16
1348 A681 150p multi   .80   .40
Souvenir Sheet
1349 A681 2000p multi   11.50 11.50

Christmas — A682

Designs: a, Star of Bethlehem. b, Santa Claus flying over town. c, Three Magi on camels. d, Star on top of Christmas tree. e, Boy at mailbox. f, Sleeping child. g, Two Magi, cow. h, Baby Jesus, cow. i, Mary, Joseph. j, Girl putting ornaments on tree.

2000, Nov. 20   *Perf. 13½*
1350   Block of 10   10.00 10.00
a.-j. A682 150p Any single   .75   .40
Inscribed "DS/20"
Perf. 13½ on 3 sides
1351   Booklet pane of 10   10.00
a.-j. A682 150p Any single   .90   .45
     Booklet, #1351   10.00

National Zoo, 75th Anniv. — A683

Various animals and birds, denomination in: a, LL. b, LR. c, UL. d, UR.

2001, Jan. 13   **Litho.**   *Perf. 13½*
1352 A683 160p Block of 4, #a-d   5.50   5.50

San Sebastian Festival, Yumbel — A684

2001, Jan. 18
1353 A684 210p multi   1.50   .75

Father Alberto Hurtado (1901-52) A685

Hurtado and: 160p, Truck. 340p, Children.

2001, Jan. 20
1354-1355 A685   Set of 2   2.50   1.25

Bird Type of 1998

No. 1356, vert.: a, Sephanoides fernandensis. b, Mimus thenca. c, Pteroptochos megapodius. d, Enicognathus leptorhynchus. Size of Nos. 1356a-1356d: 24x29mm.

2001, Jan. 29
1356 A640 160p Block of 4, #a-d   4.50   4.50

Assembly of Governors of Inter-American Development Bank and Investment Corporation — A686

2001, Mar. 16
1357 A686 230p multi   1.10   .55

Souvenir Sheet

Air Force Anniversaries — A687

No. 1358: a, Lockheed C-130 Hercules, map of Antarctica. b, Flugzeugbau Extra-300, acrobatic squadron. c, North American AT-6 Texan. d, Consolidated PBY-5A/OA-10 Catalina, map of Easter Island.

2001, Mar. 29
1358 A687 260p Sheet of 4, #a-d   5.50   5.50

Air Force presence in Antarctica, 50th anniv. (No. 1358a); Halcones acrobatic squadron, 20th anniv. (No. 1358b); Aviation Group No. 1, 75th anniv. (No. 1358c); First flight ot Easter Island, 50th anniv. (No. 1358d).

Nationalization of Copper Industry, 30th Anniv. — A688

Design: 2000p, Miner and equipment.

2001, Apr. 26   **Litho.**   *Perf. 13¼*
1359 A688 400p multi   2.25   1.10
Souvenir Sheet
1359A A688 2000p multi   12.50 12.50

Organ Donation — A689

2001, May 3
1360 A689 160p multi   1.10   .45

Easter Island — A690

Designs: No. 1361, Stone carvings, map of island and: a, Compass rose. b, Bird and native. No. 1361C, Artifact and map of island.

2001, June 25
1361 A690 260p Horiz. pair,
     #a-b   3.25   3.25
Souvenir Sheet
1361C A690 2000p multi   11.50 11.50

Lynchailurus Colocolo — A691

2001
1362 A691 100p multi   .60   .30
Endangered species. See Nos. 1394-1395.

Valparaiso Firefighting Corps, 150th Anniv. — A692

Firefighters and: 160p, Manuel Blanco Encalada. 260p, Old pumper, building on fire, modern fire truck. 350p, Flags, building. 490p, Helicopter, rail tank car.
    2000p, Helicopter, modern fire truck.

2001, June 28   **Litho.**   *Perf. 13¼*
1363-1366 A692   Set of 4   6.75   3.25
Souvenir Sheet
1367 A692 2000p multi   11.50 11.50

Mushrooms A693

Designs: 300p, Macrolepiota rhacodes. 400p, Laccata ohiensis.

2001, July 25   **Litho.**   *Perf. 13¼*
1368-1369 A693   Set of 2   4.50   2.75

24th Conference of American Armies, Santiago — A694

2001, Aug. 13
1370 A694 350p multi   2.00   .95

Bernardo O'Higgins (1778-1842), Soldier and Statesman — A695

2001, Aug. 17
1371 A695 260p multi   1.50   .70

Chilean Antarctic Research — A696

Designs: 350p, Researcher, Leptonychotes weddellii. 700p, Researchers, Macronectes giganteus. 2000p, Chionis alba.

2001, Aug. 29
1372-1373 A696   Set of 2   5.75   2.75
Souvenir Sheet
1374 A696 2000p multicolored   11.50 11.50

America Issue — UNESCO World Heritage — A697

World Heritage Sites and stamps: 160p, Quinchao Church, #1058. 230p, Tenaun Church, #1057.

2001, Oct. 9   **Litho.**   *Perf. 13¼*
1375-1376 A697   Set of 2   9.00   2.50

Cape Horn A698

2001, Nov. 22
1377 A698 220p multi   1.25   .60

El Indice del Indice, by Roberto Matta (1911-2002) — A699

2001, Nov. 5   **Litho.**   *Perf. 13¼*
1378 A699 300p multi   1.75   .85

Railroads in Chile, 150th Anniv. — A700

No. 1379 (50x29mm): a, Caldera Station, train cars. b, Locomotive and Copiapó Station. 220p, Train on bridge.

2001, Nov. 20
1379 A700 200p Horiz. pair, #a-b   3.00   1.50
1380 A700 220p multi   1.50   .85

Christmas — A701

Designs: a, Heads of three shepherds. b, Shepherd and cow. c, Joseph and Mary. d, Donkey and Magus. e, Cow and two Magi. f, Head of shepherd. g, Two sheep. h, Infant Jesus. i, Shepherd with staff. j, One sheep.

2001, Nov.
1381 A701 160p Block of 10,
     #a-j   8.00   8.00
Inscribed "DS/20"
1382 A701 160p Block of 10,
     #a-j   9.00   9.00
k.   Booklet pane, #1382 with
     straight edge at right   10.00   —
     Complete booklet, #1382k   10.00

Rotary Intl. Emblem, Map of Chile, Globe, Tropic of Capricorn Monument — A702

2001, Dec. 21
1383 A702 240p multi   1.40 .70

Antofagasta Rotary Club, 75th anniv.

Taxation Department, Cent. — A703

2002, Jan. 14
1384 A703 180p multi   .80 .40

Bird Type of 1998

Designs: 10p, Turdus falcklandii. 20p, Sturnella loyca.

2002, Jan. 25
1385 A640 10p multi   .55 .25
1386 A640 20p multi   .55 .25

City of Valdivia, 450th Anniv. — A704

2002, Feb. 9
1387 A704 260p multi   1.25 .65

Carabinero Force, 75th Anniv. — A705

2002, Apr. 8
1388 A705 250p multi   1.25 .65

Ignacy Domeyko (1802-89), Mineralogist — A706

2002, Apr. 11
1389 A706 290p multi   *5.00* .85

See Poland No. 3645.

City of Villarrica, 450th Anniv. — A707

2002, Apr. 26
1390 A707 290p multi   1.50 .75

Town of Calbuco, 400th Anniv. — A708

2002, May 2
1391 A708 230p multi   1.25 .60

Barros Arana Natl. Boarding School — A709

2002, May 20
1392 A709 250p multi   1.25 .65

Abolition of Death Penalty, 1st Anniv. — A710

2002, May 29
1393 A710 240p multi   1.25 .65

Endangered Species Type of 2001

Designs: 10p, Oreailurus jacobita. 20p, Oncifelis geoffroyi.

2002, June 5
1394 A691 10p multi   .55 .25
1395 A691 20p multi   .55 .25

Easter Island A711

Map of Easter Island and: 250p, Toromiro sophora, moai. 450p, Bird, row of moai statues, native in traditional costume. 2000p, Toromiro sophora and bird.

2002, July 1
1396-1397 A711 Set of 2   3.50 1.75
Souvenir Sheet
1398 A711 2000p multi   10.50 10.50

No. 1398 contains one 47x47mm stamp.

World Heritage Sites — A712

Churches and stamps: 230p, Achao, #1036. 290p, Dalcahue, #1056.

2002, July 27
1399-1400 A712 Set of 2   2.25 1.10

America Issue — Youth, Education, and Literacy — A713

Designs: 230p, Adult students. 450p, Woman reading to child, teacher, boy at computer.

2002, Sept. 9
1401-1402 A713 Set of 2   3.25 1.60

Children's Toys — A714

Designs: 290p, Pinwheel. 380p, Kite, vert.

2002, Sept. 16
1403-1404 A714 Set of 2   3.00 1.50

Observatories — A715

Designs: 450p, Cerro-Tololo. 550p, Paranal. 2000p, Cerro-Tololo, diff.

2002, Sept. 27
1405-1406 A715 Set of 2   4.00 2.00
Souvenir Sheet
1407 A715 2000p multi   8.50 8.50

No. 1407 contains one 47x47mm stamp.

University of Chile Clinical Hospital, 50th Anniv. — A716

2002, Oct. 17
1408 A716 250p multi   1.10 .55

Forestry Education, 50th Anniv. — A717

2002, Oct. 22
1409 A717 250p multi   1.10 .55

12th Convention on International Trade in Endangered Species Conference — A718

Designs: 300p, Phoenicoparrus andinus. 450p, Vicugna vicugna. 2000p, Chinchilla lanigera.

2002, Oct. 29
1410-1411 A718 Set of 2   4.00 2.00
Souvenir Sheet
1412 A718 2000p multi   10.00 10.00

No. 1412 contains one 47x47mm stamp.

Protected Whales — A719

Designs: 250p, Eubalaena australis. 500p, Balaenoptera acutorostrata. 2000p, Physeter macrocephalus.

2002, Nov. 2
1413-1414 A719 Set of 2   3.50 1.50
Souvenir Sheet
1415 A719 2000p multi   10.00 10.00

Violence Against Women Prevention Day — A720

2002, Nov. 22
1416 A720 230p multi   1.00 .50

Town of Puerto Varas, 150th Anniv. A721

2002, Nov. 29
1417 A721 190p multi   1.00 .50

Bird Type of 1998

Designs: 500p, Campephilus magellanicus, vert. 1000p, Falco peregrinus cassini, vert.

2003, Jan. 15   Litho.   Perf. 13¼
1418 A640 500p multi   2.10 .75
1419 A640 1000p multi   4.00 1.75

Puerto Montt, 150th Anniv. A722

2003, Feb. 13
1420 A722 240p multi   1.00 .45

Claudio Arrau (1903-91), Pianist — A723

2003, June 9   Litho.   Perf. 13¼
1421 A723 200p multi   .85 .30

First Chilean Postage Stamps, 150th Anniv. — A724

No. 1422 — Mailbox, building and: a, #1. b, #2.
2000p, Building, #1 and various other stamps.

2003, July 1
1422 A724   300p Horiz. pair,
           #a-b   2.50 1.25
Souvenir Sheet
1423 A724 2000p multi   8.00 3.00

America Issue — Flora and Fauna — A725

Designs: 240p, Trees, flowers, cactus. 300p, Frog, fox, butterfly, pudu, parrot.

2003, Oct. 12   Litho.   Perf. 13¼
1424-1425 A725   Set of 2   2.00 1.00

Supreme Court, 180th Anniv. — A726

2003, Nov. 5
1426 A726 200p multi   .85 .35

Chilean Red Cross, Cent. A727

2003, Nov. 18
1427 A727 200p black & red   .85 .35

Christmas — A728

2003, Nov. 28
1428 A728 190p multi   .80 .30
Inscribed "DS-20"
1429 A728 190p multi   .80 ,30

Powered Flight, Cent. — A729

2003, Dec. 11
1430 A729 200p multi   .85 .35

Cristo Redentor Statue, Cent. A730

2004, Apr. 22   Litho.
1431 A730 200p multi   .85 .30

Seventh World Conference of Grand Masonic Lodges — A731

2004, May 5   Perf. 13¼
1432 A731 190p multi   1.25 .30

Pablo Neruda (1904-73), Poet — A732

2004, June 11
1433 A732 300p multi   1.25 .45

Social Security, 80th Anniv. — A733

2004, Aug. 18
1434 A733 190p multi   .80 .30

America Issue — Environmental Protection — A734

Designs: 100p, Burnt forest, logs, field of flowers, puma, flower. 600p, Flower, wildlife, tanker truck, smokestacks.

2004, Sept. 27
1435-1436 A734   Set of 2   2.60 1.50

German Institute, Osorno, 150th Anniv. — A735

2004, Oct. 6
1437 A735 250p multi   18.00 18.00

Tematica 2004 National Philatelic Exhibition A736

2004, Oct. 19
1438 A736 310p multi   1.40 .55

Naval Telecommunications, Cent. — A737

2004, Nov. 5
1439 A737 400p multi   1.75 .80

Electricity and Fuel Superintendency, Cent. — A738

2004, Dec. 7
1440 A738 240p multi   1.00 .40

Chilean Air Force, 75th Anniv. — A739

2005, Mar. 15   Litho.   Perf. 13¼
1441 A739 230p multi   1.00 .40

Law No. 20,000 — A740

2005, May 4
1442 A740 220p multi   1.00 .40

Pope John Paul II (1920-2005) — A741

Pope John Paul II and: a, Child, condor, mountain. b, Crucifix, Chilean flag, mountain. c, Church, Chilean flag.

2005, May 13
1443 A741   Horiz. strip of 3   3.25 1.75
a.-c.   230p Any single   1.00 .50

Rotary International, Cent. — A742

2005, June 30   Litho.   Perf. 13¼
1444 A742 230p multi   1.00 .40

Treasury Building, Bicent. — A743

2005, June 30
1445 A743 230p multi   1.00 .40

Publication of
Don Quixote,
400th Anniv.
A744

No. 1446: a, Don Quixote on horseback. b,
Windmill. c, Windmills. d, Miguel de
Cervantes, author.

2005, July 14
1446   Horiz. strip of 4   .50   .50
a.-b. A744 10p Either single   .25   .25
c.-d. A744 20p Either single   .25   .25
          See No. 1462.

El Teniente Copper Mine,
Cent. — A745

2005, Aug. 3
1447 A745 390p multi   1.90 .75

Undersecretariat of Aviation, 75th
Anniv. — A746

2005, Aug. 19
1448 A746 400p multi   1.75 1.00

Valparaiso Customs House, 150th
Anniv. — A747

2005, Sept. 1
1449 A747 390p multi   1.75 .75

Bicentennial Fountain,
Santiago — A748

2005, Sept. 5
1450 A748 230p multi   1.00 .45

America Issue — Fight Against
Poverty — A749

No. 1451: a, Denomination at right. b,
Denomination at left.

2005, Oct. 3   Litho.   Perf. 13¼
1451 A749 250p Horiz. pair, #a-b 2.25 .95

Canonization of Father Alberto
Hurtado (1901-52) — A750

2005, Oct. 13   Litho.   Perf. 13¼
1452 A750 390p multi   1.75 .75

Expo Austral 2005 Philatelic
Exhibition, Punta Arenas — A751

2005, Oct. 22
1453 A751 390p multi   1.75 .75

New Civil
Matrimony
Law — A752

2005, Nov. 18   Litho.   Perf. 13¼
1454 A752 260p multi   1.40 .60

German Clinic, Cent. — A753

2005, Nov. 23
1455 A753 230p multi   1.25 .55

Restoration
of Central
Post Office,
Santiago
A754

2005, Nov. 30
1456 A754 230p multi   1.25 .55

Political
Constitution
A755

2005, Dec. 1
1457 A755 230p multi   1.25 .55

Department of Physical Education,
Sports and Recreation, Cent. — A756

2006, Mar. 6   Litho.   Perf. 13¼
1458 A756 230p multi   1.25 .55

Intl. Women's Day — A757

2006, Mar. 7
1459 A757 390p multi   1.75 .75

Wulff Castle, Cent. — A758

No. 1460 — Castle, arms of Vina del Mar
and: a, Birds. b, Windmill.

2006, Mar. 21
1460   Horiz. pair   3.00 1.50
a. A758 230p multi   1.00 .55
b. A758 390p multi   1.75 .85

Tourism — A759

No. 1461: a, Morro de Arica. b, Moais,
Easter Island. c, Palafittes, Castro. d, Torres
del Paine. e, Penguins, Chilean Antarctic
Territory.

2006, May 19
1461   Horiz. strip of 5   6.25 3.00
a.-e. A759 230p Any single   1.10 .55

Don Quixote Type of 2005

No. 1462: a, Building. b, Windmills. c, Windmill, country name at LR. d, Don Quixote and
Sancho Panza.

2006, May 31
1462   Horiz. strip of 4   .25   .25
a.-d. A744 10p Any single   .25   .25

Catholic University of the North, 50th
Anniv. — A760

No. 1463: a, Students using computers,
denomination at UR. b, Students, denomination at LL.

2006, June 9
1463   Horiz. pair   2.50 1.25
a.-b. A760 230p Either single   1.10 .55

Citizenship Plaza, Santiago — A761

2006, July 7
1464 A761 390p multi   1.75 .85

World Quality Forum — A762

No. 1465: a, Building. b, Building and flags.

2006, Aug. 29   Litho.   Perf. 13¼
1465 A762 230p Horiz. pair, #a-b 2.50 1.25

America Issue, Energy
Conservation — A763

No. 1466: a, River and mountains. b,
Clouds. c, Oil rigs in water. d, Windmill.

2006, Sept. 29
1466 A763 390p Block of 4, #a-d 7.25 3.50

Adventist University of Chile, Cent. — A764

No. 1467 — University emblem and: a, Building, 1906. b, Family and building, 1922. c, Building, 1960-70. d, Building, 2006.

2006, Oct. 20
1467   Horiz. strip of 4 + central label   4.50 2.25
a.-d. A764 250p Any single   1.10 .55

Antarctic Wildlife — A765

No. 1468 — Chilean and Estonian flags and: a, Balaenoptera acutorostrata. b, Aptenodytes forsteri.

2006, Oct. 25   **Perf. 13½**
1468 A765 500p Horiz. pair, #a-b 4.50 2.25
See Estonia No. 555.

Anniversaries — A766

No. 1469: a, Colonization of the Straits of Magellan area, 160th anniv. b, Fort Bulnes, 160th anniv.

2006, Dec. 7   **Perf. 13¼**
1469 A766 250p Horiz. pair, #a-b 2.25 2.10

Gasco, 150th Anniv. — A767

No. 1470: a, San Borja facility. b, Gasco headquarters.

2006, Dec. 14
1470 A767 250p Horiz. pair, #a-b 2.25 1.10

Federico Santa Maria Technical University, 75th Anniv. — A768

2006, Dec. 20
1471 A768 250p multi   1.10 .50

Carabineros, 80th Anniv. — A769

No. 1472: a, Carabineros and mountains. b, Carabineros on horseback.

2007, Apr. 10   **Litho.**   **Perf. 13¼**
1472 A769 250p Pair, #a-b   2.25 1.10

Tourism — A770

No. 1473: a, Valley of the Moon, Antofagasta Region. b, Easter Island, Valparaiso Region. c, Tourism emblem. d, Villarrica-Pucón Volcano, Araucania Region. e, Penguin in Chilean Antarctic.

2007, May 9
1473   Horiz. strip of 5   9.00 4.50
a.-e. A770 390p Any single   1.75 .90

Church Centenaries — A771

No. 1474: a, Parinacota Church. b, San Pedro de Atacama Church.

Litho. With Foil Application
2007, June 29
1474 A771 250p Pair, #a-b   2.25 1.10

Raul Cardinal Silva Henríquez (1907-99) — A772

No. 1475 — Color of portrait and panel: a, Blue violet. b, Red violet. c, Red orange. d, Green.

2007, Aug. 21   **Litho.**
1475   Horiz. strip of 4 + central label   4.50 2.25
a.-d. A772 250p Any single   1.10 .55

A773

A774

A775

Sculptures by Marta Colvin (1907-95) — A776

2007, Aug. 24   **Perf. 13¼**
1476   Horiz. strip of 4 + central label   4.50 2.25
a. A773 250p multi   1.10 .55
b. A774 250p multi   1.10 .55
c. A775 250p multi   1.10 .55
d. A776 250p multi   1.10 .55

Las Condes, 106th Anniv. — A777

2007, Aug. 28
1477 A777 330p multi   1.50 .75

Museums in Santiago A778

Designs: 10p, Artequin Museum. 20p, National Museum of Fine Arts. 30p, National Museum of Natural History. 50p, Museum of Santiago.

2007, Aug. 31   **Engr.**
1478 A778 10p green   .25 .25
1479 A778 20p black   .25 .25
1480 A778 30p purple   .25 .25
1481 A778 50p red   .25 .25
Nos. 1478-1481 (4)   1.00 1.00

Los Rios Region — A779

No. 1482: a, Lake Ranco. b, Huilo Huilo Waterfall. c, Bridge, Valdivia. d, Choshuenco Volcano.

2007, Oct. 2   **Litho.**
1482   Horiz strip of 4 + central label   7.25 3.75
a.-d. A779 390p Any single   1.75 .90

Arica and Parinacota Region — A780

No. 1483: a, Morro de Arica. b, Parinacota Volcano. c, Anzota Caves. d, Vicunas.

2007, Oct. 8
1483   Horiz strip of 4 + central label   4.50 2.25
a.-d. A780 250p Any single   1.10 .55

Chilean Postal Service, 260th Anniv. — A781

No. 1484: a, Half of original General Post Office, Santiago (denomination at UR). b, Half of modern General Post Office, Santiago

(denomination at UL). c, Original and modern General Post Offices.
3000p, Statue of postal carrier on bicycle.

Litho. With Foil Application
2007, Oct. 9
1484 A781 390p Horiz. strip of 3, #a-c   5.50 2.75
Souvenir Sheet
1485 A781 3000p multi   13.50 6.75

Comptroller of the Navy, 80th Anniv. — A782

Arms of Chilean Navy and: a, Chilean Navy Building, denomination at UL. b, Naval and Maritime Museum, denomination at UR.

2007, Oct. 11   **Litho.**   **Perf. 13¼**
1486 A782 390p Horiz. pair, #a-b 3.50 1.75

America Issue, Education For All — A783

No. 1487: a, Children at computer. b, Boy watching chemistry experiment. c, Children running. d, Children playing musical instruments. e, Boy pointing to globe.

2007, Nov. 5
1487   Horiz. strip of 5   5.75 2.75
a.-e. A783 250p Any single   1.10 .55

Christmas — A784

No. 1488 — Santa Claus: a, In chimney. b, In automobile. c, Near sleigh. d, In front of fan.

Litho. With Foil Application
2007, Nov. 16
1488 A784 250p Block of 4, #a-d 4.50 2.25

Malleco National Reserve, Cent. — A785

No. 1489: a, Tree, flower. b, Tree, puma. c, Waterfall, flowers. d, Forest, fox.

2007, Nov. 20   **Litho.**
1489   Horiz. strip of 4 + central label   4.50 2.25
a.-d. A785 250p Any single   1.00 .50

La Nación Newspaper, 90th Anniv. — A786

No. 1490 — Newspaper's office building, Chilean flag and: a, Newspapers at end of production line. b, Newspaper pages.

2007, Dec. 7
1490　A786　250p Horiz. pair, #a-b　2.25　1.10

Santa María de Iquique Massacre, Cent. — A787

No. 1491: a, People, ships. b, Man raising shovel. c, School, dead on ground. d, Wagon, people weeping. e, People hugging, woman weeping.
3000p, Family, vert.

2007, Dec. 19
1491　　　　Horiz. strip of 5　5.75　2.75
　a.-e.　A787 250p Any single　　1.10　.55

Souvenir Sheet
1492　A787　3000p multi　　　15.00　7.00

Miniature Sheet

Easter Island — A788

No. 1493 — Natives in traditional garb and: a, Ahu Koteriku moais overlooking water. b, Motu Nui, Motu Iti and Motu Kaokao Islets. c, Rock painting. d, Petroglyphs. e, Orongo stone houses. f, Ahu Tahai moai. g, Anakena Beach. h, Rano Kau Volcanic Lake.
No. 1494, vert.: a, Native male. b, Native female.

2008, Jan. 18
1493　A788　390p Sheet of 8,
　　　　　　　#a-h　　　　15.00　7.50

Souvenir Sheet
1494　A788　1500p Sheet of 2,
　　　　　　　#a-b　　　　15.00　7.50

Miniature Sheet

Intl. Polar Year — A789

No. 1495: a, Antarctic base, penguins. b, Ship and icebergs. c, Helicopter and direction signs. d, Cargo airplane and snow vehicle. e, Man directing small airplane. f, People on snowmobiles.

2008, Jan. 29　　　　　　**Perf. 13¼**
1495　A789　250p Sheet of 6, #a-f　7.50　3.75

Occupations — A790

No. 1496, 20p: a, Knife grinder. b, Street sweeper.
No. 1497, 30p: a, Photographer. b, Peanut vendor.
No. 1498, 50p: a, Ice cream vendor. b, Shoeshine man.
No. 1499, 100p: a, Laundry worker. b, Organ grinder.
No. 1500, 500p: a, Street musician. b, Newspaper vendor.

2008, Feb. 25　　**Pairs, #a-b**　　**Litho.**
1496-1500　A790　　Set of 5　　7.50　3.75

Visit to Chile of Italian Pres. Giorgio Napolitano — A791

No. 1501 — Chilean poet Pablo Neruda and: a, His house on Isla Negra, Chile, Chilean flag. b, His house on Isle of Capri, Italy, Italian flag. c, His house on Isla Negra, flags of Chile and Italy. d, Rocks off Capri, flags of Chile and Italy.

2008, Mar. 17
1501　A791　280p Block of 4, #a-d　5.25　2.10

Miniature Sheets

Ensenar la Eternidad, by Roberto Matta — A792

Foyer du Moi, by Matta — A793

Espejo de Cronos, by Matta — A794

Nos. 1502-1504 — Portion of painting: a, Upper left. b, Top center. c, Upper right. d, Left center. e, Center. f, Right center. g, Lower left. h, Bottom center. i, Lower right.

2008, Mar. 25　　　　　**Perf. 13¼**
1502　A792　280p Sheet of 9,
　　　　　　　#a-i　　　12.00　6.00
1503　A793　410p Sheet of 9,
　　　　　　　#a-i　　　17.00　8.50
1504　A794　410p Sheet of 9,
　　　　　　　#a-i　　　17.00　8.50
　Nos. 1502-1504 (3)　　46.00　23.00

Pres. Salvador Allende (1908-73) — A795

2008, June 26　**Litho.**　**Perf. 13¼**
1505　A795　410p multi　　　2.00　1.00

Taltal, 150th Anniv. A796

2008, July 18
1506　A796　280p multi　　　1.40　.70

Women's Under-20 Soccer World Championships, Chillán — A797

No. 1507 — Quarter of soccer ball and stadium and: a, Cross. b, Group of people. c, Fruits and vegetables. d, Pottery.

2008, July 31
1507　A797　280p Block of 4, #a-d　5.50　2.75

Chilean Accountancy Association, 50th Anniv. — A798

No. 1508 — Emblem and: a, Accountants, building. b, Map of Western hemisphere.

2008, Aug. 14
1508　A798　280p Horiz. pair, #a-b　2.75　1.25

Bishop Francisco Valdés Subercaseaux (1908-82) — A799

No. 1509 — Bishop Valdés Subercaseaux and: a, Christ of Tromen. b, Osorno Cathedral.

2008, Sept. 5　　**Litho.**　　**Perf. 13¼**
1509　A799　280p Horiz. pair, #a-b　2.25　1.10

Miniature Sheet

La Vida Allende la Muerte, by Roberto Matta — A800

No. 1510 — Section of painting: a, Upper left. b, Top center. c, Upper right. d, Left center. e, Center. f, Right center. g, Lower left. h, Bottom center. i, Lower right.

2008, Sept. 15
1510　A800　410p Sheet of 9,
　　　　　　　#a-i　　　13.00　6.50

America Issue, National Festivals — A801

Designs; 10p, Cuasimodo. 200p, La Vendimia. 1000p, La Tirana. 2000p, Fiestas Patrias. 5000p, El Rodeo.

2008, Oct. 30
1511　A801　10p multi　　　.25　.25
1512　A801　200p multi　　1.90　.90
1513　A801　1000p multi　　4.50　4.50
1514　A801　2000p multi　　9.00　9.00
1515　A801　5000p multi　22.50　22.50
　Nos. 1511-1515 (5)　38.15　37.15

Miniature Sheet

Torres del Paine National Park, 50th Anniv. — A802

No. 1516: a, Fox, Torres del Paine. b, Puma, Grey Glacier. c, Condor (at right), Paine Grande. d, Condor (at left), Cuernos del Paine. e, Guanaco, Cuernos del Paine. f, Guemal, Macizo Paine and Cordillera Paine.

2008, Nov. 21
1516　A802　500p Sheet of 6, #a-f　9.00　4.50

Telethon, 30th Anniv. — A803

2008, Nov. 25
1517　A803　280p multi　　　1.00　.40

Christmas — A804

No. 1518 — Children's art: a, Drawing by Antonia Retamal Figueroa. b, Drawing by Lucas Bastidas Escobar. c, Drawing by Oscar Maya Lazo. d, Drawing of girl, Christmas tree, mountains, Santa Claus. e, Drawing of Christmas tree, cross and handprints.

2008, Nov. 26
1518   Horiz. strip of 5   5.00   2.10
a.-e.   A804 280p Any single   .85   .40

Osorno, 450th Anniv. — A805

2008, Nov. 28
1519   A805 280p multi   1.25   .40

General Carlos Ibáñez del Campo Carabineros School, Cent. — A806

No. 1520: a, Carabineros, old school building (sepia photograph). b, Carabineros, new school building (color photograph).

2008, Dec. 10
1520   A806 310p Horiz. pair, #a-b   2.90   2.00

Expo Antarctica Chile 2009 Philatelic Exhibition, Pres. Eduardo Frei Montalva Antarctic Base — A807

Designs: 470p, Map of Antarctica, Pres. Eduardo Frei Montalva Antarctic Base. 3000p, Villa Las Estrellas, horiz.

2009, Mar. 12
1521   A807 470p multi   2.00   .85
Souvenir Sheet
1522   A807 3000p multi   19.00   19.00

Antarctic Treaty, 50th anniv. No. 1522 contains one 48x30mm stamp.

Preservation of Polar Regions and Glaciers — A808

Nos. 1523, 1524 — Emblem and map of: a, Arctic area. b, Antarctic area. No. 1524 has vert. stamps.

Litho. with Foil Application
2009, Mar. 18   **Perf. 13¼**
1523   A808   470p Vert. pair,
     #a-b   4.00   2.00
Souvenir Sheet
1524   A808 1500p Sheet of 2,
     #a-b   19.00   19.00

Miniature Sheets

Independence, Bicent. — A809

No. 1525: a, Chile #92. b, Chile #93. c, Chile #94. d, Chile #95. e, Chile #96. f, Chile #97.
No. 1526, horiz.: a, Chile #83. b, Chile #84. c, Chile #85. d, Chile #86. e, Chile #87. f, Chile #88. g, Chile #89. h, Chile #90. i, Chile #91. j, Bicentennial emblem.

2009, Apr. 20   **Litho.**
1525   A809 310p Sheet of 6,
     #a-f   6.50   3.25
1526   A809 310p Sheet of
     10, #a-j   10.50   5.25

University of Concepción, 90th Anniv. — A810

No. 1527: a, Homage to the Founders, sculpture by Samuel Román. b, Campanile.

2009, May 14
1527   A810 310p Horiz. pair, #a-b   2.25   1.10

Santa María de Los Angeles Diocese, 50th Anniv. — A811

No. 1528: a, Virgin Mary, Jesus and angels. b, Los Angeles Cathedral.

2009, June 10
1528   A811 470p Horiz. pair, #a-b   3.50   1.75

Protected Birds — A812

Designs: 10p, Condor. 20p Tricahue parrot. 50p, Chilean flamingo. 100p, Humboldt penguin. 500p, Black-necked swan.

2009, July 15   **Litho.**   **Perf. 13¼**
1529   A812   10p black   .25   .25
1530   A812   20p black   .25   .25
1531   A812   50p black   .25   .25
1532   A812 100p black   .55   .25
1533   A812 500p black   2.25   .95
     Nos. 1529-1533 (5)   3.55   1.95

21st UPAEP Congress, Santiago — A813

2009, Aug. 17   **Litho.**   **Perf. 13¼**
1534   A813 500p multi   2.60   .95

Mutual de Seguros Insurance Company, 90th Anniv. — A814

No. 1535: a, Old building, emblem with black gear. b, Modern building, emblem with blue gray gear.

Litho. With Foil Application
2009, Oct. 14   **Perf. 13¼**
1535   A814 310p Horiz. pair, #a-b   2.75   1.40

A815

Winning Art in Bicentennial Stamp Design Contest — A816

No. 1536: a, Flag with mountains and city, by Andrea Barreda, elementary school competition. b, City, by Javiera Monreal Arcil, middle school competition.
No. 1537: a, People in various costumes, by Patricio Díaz Donay, visual arts competition. b, Pepper, by Joshua Arévalo Carreño, university and technical school competition.

2009, Oct. 15   **Litho.**   **Perf. 13¼**
1536   A815 310p Pair, #a-b   2.40   1.25
1537   A816 310p Horiz. pair, #a-b   2.40   1.25

America Issue, Traditional Games — A817

Designs: 310p, Spinning top. 470p, Girl flying kite.

2009, Oct. 30
1538-1539 A817   Set of 2   3.50   1.75

Christmas — A818

No. 1540 — Children: a, Painting nativity scene. b, Drawing pictures of Santa Claus. c, Opening presents under Christmas tree. d, Looking out of window.

2009, Nov. 26
1540   A818 310p Block of 4, #a-d   5.00   2.50

Gabriela Mistral (1889-1957), 1945 Nobel Laureate in Literature — A819

No. 1451: a, Mistral at left, mountain at right. b, Church at left, Mistral at right. c, Mistral at left, church at right. d, Mountain at left, Mistral at right.

2009, Dec. 18
1541 A819 500p Block of 4, #a-d 8.00 4.00

Chile Philatelic Society, 120th Anniv. — A820

2009, Dec. 30
1542 A820 500p multi 2.00 1.00

Bicentennial Art by National Art Prize Winners — A821

No. 1543 — Works of art by: a, José Balmes. b, Eugenio Dittborn. c, Guillermo Núñez.

2010, Mar. 3
1543 Horiz. strip of 3 6.75 3.50
a.-c. A821 290p Any single 2.25 1.10

Bicentenary Regatta — A822

No. 1544 — Flags and: a, Ships. b, Map of South America, ship.

2010, Apr. 15 Litho. Perf. 13¼
1544 A822 430p Horiz. pair, #a-b 3.75 1.75

Pres. Eduardo Frei Montalva Antarctic Air Base, 40th Anniv. — A823

No. 1545: a, People near cargo airplane. b, Hangar. c, Airplane over base. d, Helicopter. e, Small airplane. f, Penguin, people, base.

2010, May 4
1545 A823 500p Sheet of 6, #a-
f 11.50 5.75

Bauer Tower, Vicuña, 105th Anniv. — A824

Designs: 500p, Tower. 3000p, Tower, diff.

2010, May 7
1546 A824 500p multi 1.90 .95
Souvenir Sheet
1547 A824 3000p multi 11.50 5.75

2010 World Cup Soccer Championships, South Africa — A825

No. 1548 — Flags of Chile and South Africa, emblem of Chile Soccer Federation and: a, Soccer ball and players. b, Map of Africa, leopard skin.

2010, June 25
1548 A825 500p Vert. pair, #a-b 5.00 2.00

Inauguration of Mini University of Tokyo Atacama Observatory Telescope, Mt. Chajnantor — A826

2010, July 7 Litho. Perf. 13¼
1549 A826 430p multi 1.60 .80
Souvenir Sheet
1550 A826 3000p multi 11.00 5.50

Valparaiso, UNESCO World Heritage Site — A827

No. 1551: a, British Arch. b, Heroes of Iquique Monument.
No. 1552, horiz.: a, Palacio Polanco. b, Palacio Lyon.
No. 1553: a, Polanco Funicular. b, Artillería Funicular.
No. 1554, horiz.: a, Trolley bus with doors closed. b, Trolley bus with front doors open.

2010, July 12 Litho. Perf. 13¼
1551 A827 10p Horiz. pair, #a-b .25 .25
1552 A827 20p Horiz. pair, #a-b .25 .25
1553 A827 50p Horiz. pair, #a-b .40 .25
1554 A827 100p Horiz. pair, #a-b .75 .40
Nos. 1551-1554 (4) 1.65 1.15

Independence of Latin America, Bicent. — A828

2010, Sept. 10
1555 A828 430p multi 1.75 .85

La Serena — A829

No. 1556: a, Monumental Lighthouse. b, Plaza de Armas Fountain.

2010, Sept. 15
1556 A829 420p Pair, #a-b 3.50 1.75

Bicentennial Naval Review — A830

No. 1557: a, Steamship from 1910 naval review. b, Ships and sailing vessel with flags hoisted from 1910 naval review. c, Ships from 2010, denomination at UR. d, Ships from 2010, denomination at UL.

2010, Sept. 20
1557 A830 430p Block of 4, #a-d 7.75 4.00

Antofagasta — A831

No. 1558: a, La Portada. b, Fishing terminal. c, Costanera Avenue. d, Historic District. e, Huanchaca Ruins. f, Antofagasta at night.

2010, Sept. 24
1558 A831 500p Sheet of 6, #a-
f 12.50 6.25

Arica — A832

No. 1559: a, Fountain, Morro de Arica. b, Fuerza del Sol Carnival.

2010, Sept. 30 Litho. Perf. 13¼
1559 A832 420p Horiz. pair, #a-b 3.50 1.75

America Issue, National Symbols — A833

2010, Oct. 12 Litho. Perf. 13¼
1560 A833 290p multi 2.60 .60

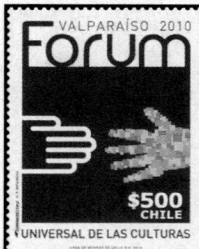

Third International Culture Forum, Valparaíso A834

2010, Oct. 19
1561 A834 500p multi 2.10 1.10

Irishmen Involved With Chilean Independence — A835

No. 1562: a, Commander General John Mackenna (1771-1814). b, Supreme Director Bernardo O'Higgins (1778-1842).

2010, Oct. 28
1562 A835 500p Horiz. pair, #a-b 4.25 2.10
See Ireland Nos. 1902-1903.

Bicentennial Clock, La Serena University — A836

2010, Oct. 29 **Litho.** **Perf. 13¼**
1563 A836 420p multi 1.75 .90
Souvenir Sheet
1564 A836 3000p Clock, vert. 12.50 6.25

Chile 2010 Bicentennial Philatelic Exhibition — A837

2010, Nov. 12 **Litho.** **Perf. 13¼**
1565 A837 290p multi 1.25 .60

Christmas A838

2010, Nov. 26
1566 A838 290p multi 1.25 .60

Miniature Sheet

Chilean Army, Bicent. — A839

No. 1567: a, Cavalry, back of army vehicle. b, Army vehicle, helicopter, tank, rocket launcher. c, Soldiers, flag, truck. d, Soldiers, people awaiting humanitarian aid. e, Soldiers at fort. f, Bulldozer and road grader. g, Soldiers working on railroad track and building. h, Soldiers on pontoon bridge beside damaged bridge.

2010, Dec. 2
1567 A839 500p Sheet of 8, #a-h 21.00 21.00

Purranque, Cent. — A840

2011, Apr. 8
1568 A840 290p multi 1.25 .60

Pres. Eduardo Frei Montalva (1911-82) A841

2011, May 6
1569 A841 290p multi 1.25 .60

Postal Union of the Americas, Spain and Portugal (UPAEP), Cent. — A842

2011, May 20
1570 A842 290p multi 1.25 .60

National Congress, Bicent. — A843

2011, July 3
1571 A843 290p multi 1.25 .60

First Competition of Urban Intervention Ideas — A844

2011, July 29 **Litho.** **Perf. 13¼**
1572 A844 500p multi 2.25 1.10

Rapa Nui Face Decorations — A845

Various face decorations.

2011, Aug. 5
1573 A845 10p brown .25 .25
1574 A845 20p lt brown .25 .25
1575 A845 50p lt brown .25 .25
1576 A845 100p brown .45 .25
Nos. 1573-1576 (4) 1.20 1.00

FAMAE (Weapons Manufacturer for Chilean Armed Forces), Bicent. — A846

2011, Sept. 30
1577 A846 290p multi 1.25 .60

El Tabo, Cent. — A847

No. 1578 — Arms of El Tabo and: a, Nuestra Senora del Rosario Church, El Tabo. b, La Asuncion Church, Las Cruces.

2011, Oct. 7
1578 A847 290p Horiz. pair, #a-b 4.25 2.25

Talca University, 30th Anniv. — A848

No. 1579 — Sculpture and: a, Legal and Social Sciences Building. b, Kinetic Frieze, by Matilde Perez. c, Botanical Garden. d, Curicó Campus Engineering Building.

2011, Oct. 12
1579 A848 290p Block of 4, #a-d 4.75 2.40

Mailbox A849

2011, Oct. 21
1580 A849 290p multi 1.60 .60
America issue.

Christmas — A850

2011, Nov. 28
1581 A850 310p multi 1.50 .60

Carabineros, 85th Anniv. — A851

No. 1582 — Anniversary emblem and: a, Male and female carabineros. b, Flag and silhouettes of carabineros.

2012, Apr. 24
1582 A851 310p Horiz. pair, #a-b 2.60 1.40

Diplomatic Relations Between Chile and South Korea, 50th Anniv. — A852

2012, July 23 **Perf. 13¼**
1583 A852 310p multi 1.40 .70

University of Chile, 170th Anniv. — A853

No. 1584: a, University building. b, Statue of first University rector. c, Valentín Letelier, (1852-1919) rector. d, Amanda Labarca (1886-1975), educator.

2012, Sept. 7
1584 A853 500p Block of 4, #a-d 8.50 4.25

Trauco (Mythological Forest Dweller) A854

2012, Oct. 22
1585 A854 310p multi 1.40 .70
America issue.

Puente Alto, 120th Anniv. — A855

2012, Nov. 12
1586 A855 310p multi   1.40 .70

Christmas — A856

No. 1587: a, Boy and open mail box. b, Children opening Christmas gifts.

2012, Nov. 30
1587 A856 310p Horiz. pair, #a-b 2.75 1.40

Diplomatic Relations Between Thailand and Chile, 50th Anniv. — A857

2012, Dec. 5
1588 A857 500p multi   2.25 1.10

Pontifical Catholic University of Chile, 125th Anniv. — A858

2013, May 15
1589 A858 500p multi   2.10 1.00

Arica-La Paz Railway, Cent. — A859

No. 1590: a, Steam locomotive. b, Diesel locomotive.

2013, May 29
1590 A859 310p Horiz. pair, #a-b 2.50 1.25

Salvador Allende School of Public Health at University of Chile, 70th Anniv. — A860

No. 1591: a, Dr. Benjamin Viel (1913-98), Dr. Abraham Horwitz (1910-2000), Dr. Hugo Behm (1913-2011). b, Building.

2013, June 7
1591 A860 500p Pair, #a-b   4.50 2.00

Historic Aircraft — A861

No. 1592: a, Voisin biplane, 1910 (airplane used in first flight in Chile). b, Batuco biplane, 1913 (first airplane made in Chile).
No. 1593: a, De Havilland DH-60G "Gipsy Moth," 1929 (airplane used on first airmail route in Chile). b, Junkers R42, 1930 (seaplane flown from Puerto Montt to Straits of Magellan).
No. 1594: a, Blériot XI, 1916 (airplane used in first military flight and first airmail flight in Chile). b, Bristol M1C, 1918 (first airplane to cross the Andes at highest point).
No. 1595: a, Let L-13 "Blanik," 1964 (first glider to cross Andes). b, Bell 47 D-1 "Sioux" helicopter, 1960 (helicopter used in airlift after Valdivia earthquake).
No. 1596: a, PBY-5A Catalina, 1951 (seaplane used in first flight to Easter Island). b, Vought Sikorsky OS2U-3 "Kingfisher," 1947 (seaplane used in first flight from Chile to Antarctica).

2013, Aug. 9   **Litho.**   **Perf. 13¼**
1592   Horiz. pair   .25 .25
a.-b.   A861 10p Either single   .25 .25
1593   Horiz. pair   .25 .25
a.-b.   A861 20p Either single   .25 .25
1594   Horiz. pair   .40 .25
a.-b.   A861 50p Either single   .25 .25
1595   Horiz. pair   .60 .30
a.-b.   A861 70p Either single   .30 .25
1596   Horiz. pair   .80 .40
a.-b.   A861 100p Either single   .40 .25
     Nos. 1592-1596 (5)   2.30 1.45

Annexation of Easter Island, 125th Anniv. — A862

2013, Sept. 27   **Litho.**   **Perf. 13¼**
1597 A862 500p multi   2.00 1.00

National Library, 200th Anniv. — A863

2013, Sept. 30   **Litho.**   **Perf. 13¼**
1598 A863 310p multi   1.25 .60

General José Miguel Carrera National Institute (School for Boys), 200th Anniv. — A864

2013, Sept. 30   **Litho.**   **Perf. 13¼**
1599 A864 430p multi   1.75 .85

Federation of Catholic University Students, 75th Anniv. — A865

2013, Oct. 8   **Litho.**   **Perf. 13¼**
1600 A865 310p multi   1.25 .60

Campaign Against Discrimination A866

2013, Oct. 25   **Litho.**   **Perf. 13¼**
1601 A866 310p multi   1.25 .60

America Issue.

Miniature Sheet

San José Mine Rescue, 3rd Anniv. — A867

No. 1602: a, Fénix 2 rescue capsule. b, Names of 33 rescued miners. c, Note indicating condition and number of miners sent to surface on probe. d, Monument to the rescue of the miners. e, Drilling equipment at surface. f, 33 Chilean flags.

2013, Oct. 30   **Litho.**   **Perf. 13¼**
1602 A867 500p Sheet of 6, #a-f   11.50 5.75

Christmas A868

2013, Nov. 27   **Litho.**   **Perf. 13¼**
1603 A868 310p multi   1.25 .60

Public Education in Chile, Cent. — A869

2013, Dec. 30   **Litho.**   **Perf. 13¼**
1604 A869 310p multi   1.25 .60

Philatelic Society of Chile, 125th Anniv. — A870

2014, Mar. 18   **Litho.**   **Perf. 13¼**
1605 A870 310p multi   5.25 2.50

Los Angeles, 275th Anniv. — A871

No. 1606: a, Statue of Bernardo O'Higgins. b, Liceo de Hombres. c, Laguna Esmeralda. d, Laja Waterfalls.

2014, May 26   **Litho.**   **Perf. 13¼**
1606 A871 310p Block of 4, #a-d 5.50 3.00

Printed in sheets containing four blocks of 4 + 4 labels.

2014 World Cup Soccer Championships, Brazil — A872

2014, June 16   **Litho.**   **Perf. 13¼**
1607 A872 500p multi   1.90 .95

Battle of Rancagua, 200th Anniv. — A873

No. 1608 — Soldiers and: a, Angel holding shield. b, Swordsmen on horseback.

2014, Sept. 30   **Litho.**   **Perf. 13¼**
1608 A873   Horiz pair   2.50 1.25
a.-b.   310p Either single   1.10 .55

Printed in sheets containing 12 pairs and 6 labels.

Exfina 2014 Philatelic Exhibition, Santiago — A874

Designs: 470p, Chile #1. 500p, Chile #2. 1500p, Emblem of Philatelic Society of Chile.

2014, Oct. 14   Litho.   Perf. 13¼
1609-1610 A874   Set of 2   3.50 1.75
Souvenir Sheet
1611 A874 1500p multi   5.75 4.50
Philatelic Society of Chile, 125th anniv.

America Issue — A875

No. 1612: a, Lautaro (c. 1534-1557), Mapuche leader of resistance to Spanish rule. b. Caupolicán (d. 1558), Mapuche military leader.

2014, Oct. 30   Litho.   Perf. 13¼
1612 A875 310p Vert. pair, #a-b   2.10 1.10

Christmas
A876

2014, Nov. 10   Litho.   Perf. 13¼
1613 A876 310p multi   1.00 .50

Chinchorro Mummies — A877

No. 1614: a, Mummy of a child with stake point at top of head. b, Mummy with outer coating missing under eye.

2014, Nov. 28   Litho.   Perf. 13¼
1614 A877 500p Horiz. pair, #a-b 3.25 1.60

Chilean Nuclear Energy Commission, 50th Anniv. — A878

No. 1615 — Stylized atom with inscription: a, Salud (health). b, Alimentos (food). c, Industria (industry). d, Minería (mining).

2014, Dec. 10   Litho.   Perf. 13¼
1615 A878 310p Block of 4, #a-d 4.25 2.10

Miniature Sheet

Talcahuano, 250th Anniv. — A879

No. 1616: a, Cacique Talcahueñu, painting by Héctor Robles Acuña. b, R.H. Huáscar. c, David Fuentes Sosa and his Blériot airplane "Talcahuano." d, Alcalde Luis Macera Dellarossa Coliseum. e, Boats in water near Caleta Tumbes. f, Sailboats off Talcahuano.

2014, Dec. 12   Litho.   Perf. 13¼
1616 A879 500p Sheet of 6, #a-
    f   10.00 5.00

Hippocamelus Bisulcus — A880

No. 1617 — Huemul: a, Head, with foliage in background. b, Entire animal on hill, head at right. c, Entire animal with head at left. d, Head, Moon in clouds.

2015, Apr. 7   Litho.   Perf. 13¼
1617 A880 600p Block of 4, #a-d 8.00 4.00
Protection of the huemul.

Miniature Sheet

Chuquicamata, Cent. — A881

No. 1618: a, Pres. Ramón Barros Luco. b, Steam shovel. c, Chuquicamata Mine. d, Chuquicamata Arch. e, Chile Theater. f, El Salvador Church.

2015, June 3   Litho.   Perf. 13¼
1618 A881 500p Sheet of 6, #a-f 9.50 4.75

2015 Copa América Soccer Championships, Chile — A882

No. 1619 — Map of chile and; a, Soccer ball. b, Mascot and soccer ball.

2015, June 8   Litho.   Perf. 13¼
1619 A882 500p Horiz. pair, #a-b 3.25 1.60

Josefina Martínez Children's Hospital, 75th Anniv. — A883

2015, July 28   Litho.   Perf. 13¼
1620 A883 310p multi   .95 .45

Campaign Against Human Trafficking A884

Designs: 310p, Man. 500p, Woman.

2015, Oct. 26   Litho.   Perf. 13¼
1621-1622 A884   Set of 2   2.40 1.25
America Issue.

State Defence Council, 120th Anniv. — A885

2015, Oct. 29   Litho.   Perf. 13¼
1623 A885 310p multi   .90 .45

Maps — A886

Map of: 10p, Santiago, 1541. 50p, Antarctica, 1739. 60p, Antarctica, present day. 80p, Robinson Crusoe Island, 1753. 100p, Robinson Crusoe Island, 1744.

No. 1629 — Map of Easter Island from: a, 1770. b, 1777.

2015, Nov. 4   Litho.   Perf. 13¼
1624 A886 10p multi   .25 .25
1625 A886 50p multi   .25 .25
1626 A886 60p multi   .25 .25
1627 A886 80p multi   .25 .25
1628 A886 100p multi   .30 .25
1629   Horiz. pair   5.50 2.80
a.-b. A886 1000p Either single 2.75 1.40
    Nos. 1624-1629 (6)   6.80 4.05

Christmas — A887

2015, Nov. 25   Litho.   Perf. 13¼
1630 A887 310p multi   .90 .45

Nacimiento — A888

No. 1631 — Arms of Nacimiento and: a, Nacimiento Fort. b, Potter and pottery.

2015, Dec. 21   Litho.   Perf. 13¼
1631   Horiz. pair + flanking
    label   3.50 1.75
a.-b. A888 600p Either single 1.75 .85

Pelluhue — A889

No. 1632 — Arms of Pelluhue and: a, Caleta Curanipe. b, Municipal Stadium. c, Pueño-La Sirena. d, Arcos de Calan, Tregualemu.

2015, Dec. 28   Litho.   Perf. 13¼
1632 A889 310p Block of 4, #a-d 3.50 1.75

Miniature Sheet

Symbols of Chilean Justice — A890

No. 1633: a, Supreme Court Building. b, Statues at Supreme Court Building. c, Stained-glass window. d, Statue of Blind Justice. e, Court building and eagle sculpture. f, Court building and sculpture of Justice.

2015, Dec. 29   Litho.   Perf. 13¼
1633 A890 500p Sheet of 6, #a-f 8.50 4.25

Naval Aviation — A891

No. 1634: a, Dornier Wal No. 16, 1928. b, Fairey III-F Mk 1, 1927.

2016, Mar. 16 Litho. Perf. 13¼
1634 A891 600p Horiz. pair, #a-b 3.75 1.90

Lieutenant Hernan Merino Correa (1936-65), Soldier Killed in Laguna del Desierto Incident — A892

2016, Apr. 25 Litho. Perf. 13¼
1635 A892 500p multi 1.50 .75

POSTAL FISCAL STAMPS

Revenue stamps and telegraph stamp authorized for postal use until the end of 1914.

Arms — PF1

1880-91	**Engr.**	**Unwmk.**	**Perf. 12**	
AR1	PF1	1c red	1.75	1.50
		Revenue cancel		.25
AR2	PF1	2c brown	3.50	2.75
		Revenue cancel		.25
AR3	PF1	5c blue	3.50	1.50
		Revenue cancel		.25
AR4	PF1	10c green ('91)	5.25	3.50
		Revenue cancel		.25
AR5	PF1	20c orange ('91)	7.50	6.25
		Revenue cancel		.25

Printed by the American Banknote Co. Issued: 1c, 2c, 11/27/80; 5c, 7/3/80; 10c, 20c, 4/1/91.

Arms — PF2

1891, Apr. 21				
AR6	PF2	2c yellow brown	3.25	2.00
		Telegraph cancel		.35
AR7	PF2	10c olive green	1.00	2.50
		Telegraph cancel		.35
AR8	PF2	20c blue	8.50	3.25
		Telegraph cancel		.35
AR9	PF2	1p brown	1.50	—
		Revenue cancel		1.00

Printed by Bradbury, Wilkinson & Co. Nos. AR6-AR9 are telegraph stamps, authorized for postal use.

PF3

1900-13			**Perf. 14**	
AR10	PF3	1c vermilion	1.00	.25
		Revenue cancel		.25

AR11	PF3	2c brown ('13)	1.00	.35
		Revenue cancel		.25
AR12	PF3	5c blue	2.00	.35
		Revenue cancel		.25

Printed by Waterlow & Sons, London. Issued: 1c, 10/25/00; 2c, 1/21/13; 5c, 12/6/00.

SEMI-POSTAL STAMPS

S. S. Abtao and Captain Policarpo Toro SP1

S. S. Abtao and Brother Eugenio Eyraud SP2

Perf. 14½x15

1940, Mar. 1	**Engr.**	**Unwmk.**		
B1	SP1	80c + 2.20p dk grn & lake	2.50	2.00
B2	SP2	3.60p + 6.40p lake & dk grn	2.50	2.00
a.		Pair, #B1-B2	10.00	8.00
		Set, never hinged	8.00	

50th anniv. of Chilean ownership of Easter Is. Surtax used for charitable institutions. Sheets containing 15 of each value, with 9 se-tenant pairs.

> **Catalogue values for unused stamps in this section, from this point to the end of the section, are for Never Hinged items.**

Pedro de Valdivia — SP3

Portraits: 10c+10c, Jose Toribio Medina.

1961, Apr. 29 Photo.		**Perf. 13x12½**		
B3	SP3	5c + 5c pale brn & sl grn	1.40	.45
B4	SP3	10c + 10c buff & vio blk	1.00	.35

Printed without charge by the Spanish Mint as a gift to Chile. The surtax was to aid the 1960 earthquake victims and to increase teachers' salaries. See Nos. CB1-CB2.

No. 402 Surcharged in Dark Green

1974, Mar. 25 Litho.		**Perf. 14½**		
B5	A213	27e + 3e on 40c dl grn	.50	.25

Cent. of intl. meteorological cooperation. The 3e surtax of Nos. B5-B10 was for modernization of the postal system.

No. 412 Surcharged in Dark Blue

1974, Apr. 25 Litho.		**Perf. 14½**		
B6	A219	27e + 3e on 1.95e	1.00	.30

500th anniversary of the birth of Nicolaus Copernicus (1473-1534), Polish astronomer.

No. 329A Surcharged

1974, May 2 Litho.		**Perf. 14**		
B7	A159	27e + 3e on 1e bluish grn	.40	.30

Centenary of the city of Vina del Mar.

No. 377 Surcharged in Blk, Nos. 395, 380 in Red

1974 Litho.		**Perf. 14½**		
B8	A193	47e + 3e on 40c grn	.40	.30
B9	A207	67e + 3e on 40c multi	.60	.40
B10	A196	97e + 3e on 40c red brn	.40	.30
		Nos. B8-B10 (3)	1.40	1.00

Issued: No. B8, 6/7; No. B9, 7/9; No. B10, 6/20.

AIR POST STAMPS

Surcharged in Black

Lithographed; Center Engraved

1927	**Unwmk.**		**Perf. 13½x14**	
	Black Brown & Blue			
C1	40c on 10c		400.00	50.00
C2	80c on 10c		400.00	65.00
C3	1.20p on 10c		400.00	75.00
C4	1.60p on 10c		400.00	75.00
C5	2p on 10c		400.00	75.00
	Nos. C1-C5 (5)		2,000.	340.00

Issued for air post service between Santiago and Valparaiso. The stamps picture Bernardo O'Higgins and are not known without surcharge.

Regular Issues of 1915-28 Overprinted or Surcharged in Black, Red or Blue

Inscribed: "Chile Correos"

1928-29		**Perf. 13½x14, 14**		
C6	A39	20c brn org & blk (Bk)	.50	.30
C6A	A55	40c dk vio & blk (R)	.50	.30
C6B	A43	1p grn & blk (Bl)	1.60	.70
C6C	A43	2p red & blk (Bl)	2.60	.40
f.		2p ver & blk (Bl)	120.00	30.00
C6D	A43	5p ol grn & blk (Bl)	4.00	1.10
C6E	A50	6p on 10c dp bl & blk (R)	65.00	22.50

C7	A43	10p org & blk (Bk) ('29)	16.00	4.50
C8	A43	10p org & blk (Bl)	60.00	35.00
		Nos. C6-C8 (8)	150.20	64.80

On Nos. C6B to C6D, C7 and C8 the overprint is larger than on the other stamps of the issue.

Same Overprint or Surcharge on Nos. 155, 156, 158-161
Inscribed: "Chile Correos"

1928-32		**Wmk. 215**		
C9	A55	40c vio & blk (R)	.70	.40
C10	A43	1p grn & blk (Bl)	1.90	.60
C11	A43	2p red & blk (Bl)	11.00	2.25
C12	A52	3p on 5c sl bl (R)	65.00	40.00
C13	A43	5p ol grn & blk (Bl)	8.50	2.00
C14	A43	10p org & blk (Bk)	45.00	11.00
		Nos. C9-C14 (6)	132.10	56.50

Same Overprint on Nos. 166-169, 172 and 158 in Black or Red
Inscribed: "Correos de Chile"

1928-30				
C15	A39	20c (#166) ('29)	1.20	.70
C16	A39	20c (#172) ('30)	.50	.25
C17	A40	25c bl & blk (R)	.60	.25
C18	A41	30c brn & blk	.40	.25
a.		Double ovpt., one inverted	250.00	250.00
C19	A42	50c dp grn & blk (R)	.50	.25
		Nos. C15-C19 (5)	3.20	1.70

Inscribed: "Chile Correos"

1932		**Perf. 13½x14, 14**		
C21	A43	1p yel grn & blk (Bk)	2.75	1.50

Condor on Andes — AP1a

Airplane Crossing Andes — AP3

Los Cerrillos Airport — AP2

1931 Litho.		**Perf. 13½x14, 14½x14**		
C22	AP1a	5c yellow grn	.25	.25
C23	AP1a	10c yellow brn	.25	.25
C24	AP1a	20c rose	.25	.25
C25	AP2	50c dark blue	1.50	.50
C26	AP3	50c black brn	.75	.25
C27	AP3	1p purple	.60	.25
C28	AP3	2p blue blk	.90	.30
a.		2p bluish slate	1.00	.45
C29	AP2	5p lt red	3.00	.30
		Nos. C22-C29 (8)	7.50	2.35

For surcharges see Nos. C51-C53.

Airplane over City — AP4

Two Airplanes over Globe — AP9

Designs: 30c, 40c, 50c, Wings over Chile. 60c, Condor. 70c, Airplane and Star of Chile. 80c, Condor and Statue of Canpolican. 3p, 4p, 5p, Seaplane. 6p, 8p, 10p, Airplane. 20p, 30p, Airplane and Southern Cross. 40p, 50p, Airplane and symbols of space.

		Perf. 13½x14		
1934-39	**Engr.**		**Wmk. 215**	
C30	AP4	10c yel grn ('35)	.30	.25
C31	AP4	15c dk grn ('35)	.45	.25
C32	AP4	20c dp bl ('36)	.25	.25
C33	AP4	30c blk brn ('35)	.25	.25
C34	AP4	40c indigo ('38)	.25	.25
C35	AP4	50c dk brn ('36)	.25	.25
C36	AP4	60c vio blk ('35)	.25	.25
C37	AP4	70c blue ('35)	.45	.25
C38	AP4	80c ol blk ('35)	.25	.25

Perf. 14

C39	AP9	1p slate blk	.25	.25
C40	AP9	2p grnsh bl	.25	.25
C41	AP9	3p org brn ('35)	.30	.25
C42	AP9	4p brn ('35)	.30	.25
C43	AP9	5p org red	.30	.25
C44	AP9	6p yel brn ('35)	.45	.25
a.		6p brown ('39)	2.75	1.90
C45	AP9	8p grn ('35)	.40	.25
C46	AP9	10p brn lake	.45	.25
C47	AP9	20p olive	.45	.25
C48	AP9	30p gray blk	.50	.25
C49	AP9	40p gray vio	1.40	.70
C50	AP9	50p brn vio	1.60	.70
		Nos. C30-C50 (21)	9.35	6.15

Nos. C30-C50 have been re-issued in slightly different colors, with white gum. The first printings are considerably scarcer.
See Nos. C90-C107B, C148-C154.

Types of 1931 Surcharged in Black or Red

Perf. 13½x14, 14½x14

1940   **Wmk. 215**

C51	AP1a	80c on 20c lt rose	.70	.25
C52	AP2	1.60p on 5p lt red	4.25	1.50
C53	AP3	5.10p on 2p sl bl (R)	3.50	1.75
		Nos. C51-C53 (3)	8.45	3.50

The surcharge on No. C52 measures 21½mm.

Plane and Weather Vane — AP14

Plane and Caravel — AP23

Designs (Plane and): 20c, Globe. 30c, Chilean flag. 40c, Star of Chile and Southern Cross. 50c, Mountains. 60c, Tree. 70c, Lakes. 80c, Shore. 90c, Sunrise. 2p, Compass. 3p, Telegraph lines. 4p, Rainbow. 5p, Factory. 10p, Snow-capped mountain.

1941-42   **Wmk. 215**   **Litho.**   **Perf. 14**

C54	AP14	10c ol gray	.25	.25
C55	AP14	20c dp rose	.25	.25
C56	AP14	30c blue vio	.25	.25
C57	AP14	40c dl red brn	.25	.25
C58	AP14	50c red org ('42)	.35	.25
C59	AP14	60c dp green	.25	.25
C60	AP14	70c rose	.30	.25
C61	AP14	80c ultra ('42)	1.50	.45
C62	AP14	90c dk brown	.45	.25
C63	AP23	1p brt blue	.30	.25
C64	AP23	2p rose lake	.80	.30
C65	AP23	3p dk bl grn & yel grn	1.20	.60
C66	AP23	4p bl vio & buff	1.75	1.00
C67	AP23	5p dk org red ('42)	17.00	6.00
C68	AP23	10p gray grn & bl grn	9.50	6.00
		Nos. C54-C68 (15)	34.40	16.60

The 1p, dated "1541-1941," commemorates the 400th anniversary of Santiago.

1942-46   **Unwmk.**

C69	AP14	10c ultra ('43)	.25	.25
C70	AP14	10c rose lil ('45)	.25	.25
C71	AP14	20c dull grn ('43)	.25	.25
C72	AP14	20c cop brn ('45)	.25	.25
C73	AP14	30c dull vio ('44)	.25	.25
C74	AP14	30c ol blk ('45)	.25	.25
C75	AP14	40c red brn ('44)	.30	.25
C76	AP14	40c ultra ('45)	.25	.25
C77	AP14	50c rose ('43)	.25	.25
C78	AP14	50c org red ('45)	.25	.25
C79	AP14	60c orange	.25	.25
C79B	AP14	60c dp grn ('46)	.25	.25
C80	AP14	70c rose ('45)	.45	.35
C81	AP14	80c slate grn	.45	.35
C82	AP14	90c brown ('45)	.45	.35
C83	AP23	1p gray grn & lt bl ('43)	.25	.25
C84	AP23	2p org red ('43)	.45	.25
C85	AP23	3p dk pur & pale org ('43)	.45	.25

C86	AP23	4p bl grn & yel grn	.45	.35
C87	AP23	5p dk rose car ('43)	.35	.25
a.		5p dk car rose ('44)	.45	.25
C88	AP23	10p sapphire ('43)	.45	.35
		Nos. C69-C88 (21)	6.60	5.65

No. C83 is without dates "1541-1941."
See Nos. C109-C123. For surcharges see Nos. C145-C147

Coat of Arms and Plane AP29

1942, Nov. 5   **Engr.**   **Perf. 14½**

C89	AP29	100p car lake	25.00	20.00

University of Chile centenary.

Types of 1934-39
Perf. 13½x14

1944-55   **Unwmk.**   **Engr.**

C90	AP4	10c yel grn ('55)	.25	.25
C92	AP4	20c deep blue	.25	.25
C93	AP4	30c black brn	.25	.25
C94	AP4	40c indigo	.25	.25
C95	AP4	50c dk brn ('47)	.25	.25
C96	AP4	60c slate vio	.25	.25
C97	AP4	70c blue ('48)	.25	.25
C98	AP4	80c olive blk	.25	.25

Perf. 14

C99	AP9	1p slate blk	.25	.25
C100	AP9	2p grnsh bl	.25	.25
C101	AP9	3p org brn ('45)	.25	.25
C102	AP9	4p brown	.25	.25
C103	AP9	5p org red	.35	.25
C104	AP9	6p yel brn ('46)	.40	.25
C105	AP9	8p green	.40	.25
C106	AP9	10p brn lake	1.10	.25
C107	AP9	20p ol gray ('45)	.75	.25
a.		Imperf., pair	70.00	
C107B	AP9	50p rose vio ('50)	17.50	2.50
		Nos. C90-C107B (18)	23.50	6.75

Plane and Radio Tower — AP30

1945   **Unwmk.**   **Litho.**   **Perf. 14**

C108	AP30	1.60p brt violet	.55	.25

See Nos. C118-C119.

Types of 1941-45

1946-48   **Wmk. 215**

C109	AP14	10c rose lil ('47)	.25	.25
C110	AP14	20c dk red brn ('48)	.25	.25
C111	AP14	20c dull grn ('48)	1.50	.30
C112	AP14	30c black ('48)	.25	.25
C113	AP14	40c ultra ('48)	.25	.25
C114	AP14	60c ol grn ('48)	.25	.25
C115	AP14	80c ol blk ('48)	.25	.25
C116	AP14	90c choc ('48)	.25	.25
C117	AP23	1p gray grn & lt bl ('48)	.25	.25
C118	AP30	1.60p brt violet	.25	.25
C119	AP30	1.80p brt vio ('48)	.25	.25
C119A	AP23	2p org red	.40	.25
C120	AP23	3p dk pur & pale org ('47)	1.50	.30
C121	AP23	4p bl grn & yel grn ('48)	1.10	.45
C122	AP23	5p rose car ('47)	.80	.25
C123	AP23	10p sapphire ('47)	1.00	.25
		Nos. C109-C123 (16)	8.80	4.30

No. C117 is without dates "1541-1941." For surcharges see Nos. C145, C147.

Flora and Fauna Type of 1948

1948

C124	A118	3p Block of 25	80.00	80.00
		Never hinged	110.00	
a.-y.		any single	2.00	1.50

Air Line Emblem and Planes — AP32

1949   **Wmk. 215**   **Litho.**   **Perf. 14**

C125	AP32	2p ultra	.45	.25

20th anniversary of the establishment of Chile's National Air Line.

Benjamin Vicuna Mackenna — AP33

1949, Mar. 22   **Engr.**   **Perf. 13½x14**

C126	AP33	3p dk car rose	.30	.25

Factory, Badge and Book — AP34

Design: 10p, Column and cogwheel.

Unwmk.

1949, Nov. 11   **Litho.**   **Perf. 14**

C127	AP34	5p green	.85	.45
C128	AP34	10p red brown	1.40	.55

Centenary of the founding of Chile's School of Arts and Crafts.

Plane and Globe — AP35

1950, Jan.   **Engr.**

C129	AP35	5p green	.60	.25
C130	AP35	10p red brown	1.00	.60

75th anniv. of the UPU.

Plane over Snow-capped Mountain AP36

Araucarian Pine and Plane — AP38

Plane and: 40c, Coast and Sunrise. 60c, Over fishing boat. 2p, Chilean flag. 3p, Dock crane. 4p, Above river. 5p, Blast furnace. 10p, Mountain lake. 20p, Cable cars.

Imprint: "Especies Valoradas-Chile"

1950-54   **Wmk. 215**   **Litho.**   **Perf. 14**

C135	AP36	20c yel brn ('54)	.35	.25
C136	AP36	40c purple ('52)	.35	.25
C137	AP36	60c lt bl ('53)	1.60	.90
C138	AP38	1p dull green	.35	.25
C139	AP38	2p brown red	.35	.25
C140	AP38	3p violet bl	.35	.25
C141	AP38	4p red org ('54)	.35	.25
C142	AP38	5p violet	.35	.25

C143	AP38	10p yel grn ('53)	.35	.25
C144	AP38	20p red brn ('54)	.60	.25
		Nos. C135-C144 (10)	5.00	3.15

See Nos. C155-C164, C207-C212.

Nos. C115, C81 and C116 Surcharged with New Value in Carmine or Black

1951-52   **Wmk. 215**

C145	AP14	40c on 80c ol blk (C) ('52)	.25	.25

Unwmk.

C146	AP14	40c on 80c sl grn (C) ('52)	5.50	3.50

Wmk. 215

C147	AP14	1p on 90c choc	.25	.25
		Nos. C145-C147 (3)	6.00	4.00

Types of 1934-39

1951-53   **Unwmk.**   **Engr.**   **Perf. 14**

C148	AP9	1p deep blue	.25	.25
C149	AP9	2p blue	.35	.25
C150	AP9	6p bis brn ('52)	.45	.25
C151	AP9	30p dk gray ('53)	.60	.90
C152	AP9	40p dk pur brn	18.00	2.40
C153	AP9	50p dark purple	25.00	5.00
		Nos. C148-C153 (6)	44.65	9.05

Wmk. 215

C154	AP9	50p dk pur ('52)	.80	.40

Types of 1950-54
Designs as Before
Imprint: "Especies Valoradas-Chile"

1951-55   **Unwmk.**   **Litho.**   **Perf. 14**

C155	AP36	20c yel brn ('54)	.25	.25
C156	AP36	40c purple	.25	.25
C157	AP36	60c lt blue ('53)	.25	.25
C158	AP38	1p dk bl grn ('55)	.25	.25
C159	AP38	2p brown red	.25	.25
C160	AP38	3p violet bl	.25	.25
C161	AP38	4p red org ('52)	.30	.25
C162	AP38	5p violet	.30	.25
C163	AP38	10p emerald	.30	.25
C164	AP38	20p brown	.40	.25
		Nos. C155-C164 (10)	2.80	2.50

San Martin Crossing Andes AP40

Wmk. 215

1951, Mar. 16   **Engr.**   **Perf. 14½**

C165	AP40	5p red violet	.90	.50

Gen. José de San Martín, death cent.

Isabella Type of Regular Issue, 1952

1952, Mar. 21   **Perf. 14**

C166	A125	10p carmine	.70	.40

A souvenir card without franking value was issued for the Hispano-Chilean Philatelic Exhibition at Santiago, Oct. 12, 1969. It contains 2 imperf. stamps similar to Nos. 264 and C166-60c green and 10p rose red. Size: 115x137½mm.

Ancient Fortress AP42

1953, Apr. 28

C167	AP42	10p brown car	2.25	.45

4th centenary of the founding of Valdivia.

Stamp Centenary Type of 1953

1953, Oct. 15   **Engr.**   **Perf. 14½**

C168	A131	100p dp grnsh bl	2.75	1.00

An imperf. souvenir sheet contains one each of Nos. 276 and C168, with inscriptions in black at top and bottom center. Sheet measures 178x229mm. It is stated that this sheet was not valid for postage.

Early Plane and
Stylized Modern
Version — AP44

Unwmk.

1954, May 26   Engr.   Perf. 14
C170 AP44 3p deep blue   .30   .25
25th anniversary of the founding of Chile's
National Air Line.

**Domeyko Type of Regular Issue,
1954**

1954, Aug. 16   Perf. 13½x14
C171 A134 5p orange brown   .30   .25

**Railroad Type of Regular Issue,
1954**

1954, Sept. 10   Wmk. 215   Perf. 14½
C172 A135 10p dk purple   1.50   .25
An imperforate souvenir sheet contains one
each of Nos. 283 and C172.
Size: 174x232mm. Value, $200.

Presidential Visits Type of 1955

1955, May 24
C173 A139 100p red   1.50 1.25

Jet Plane in
Clouds — AP48

Comet Air
Liner — AP49

Designs: 2p, Helicopter over bridge. 10p, Oil
derricks and plane. 50p, Control tower and
plane. 200p, Beechcraft monoplane. 500p,
Douglas DC-6.

Perf. 14½x14, 14x13½ (AP49)
1955-56   Engr.   Wmk. 215
C174 AP48 1p dk red lil ('56)   .25   .25
C175 AP48 2p pale brn ('56)   .25   .25
C176 AP48 10p bluish grn
                        ('56)   .25   .25
C177 AP48 50p rose ('56)   .60   .25
C178 AP49 100p green   1.00   .25
C179 AP49 200p dp ultra   6.50   .90
C180 AP49 500p dk carmine   7.50   .90
   Nos. C174-C180 (7)   16.35 3.05
Stamps similar to type AP49, but inscribed
in escudo currency, are listed as type AP58.

1956-58   Unwmk.

Designs: 5p, Train and plane. 20p, Jet
plane and Easter Island statue.

C183 AP48 5p violet   .25   .25
C184 AP48 10p grn ('57)   .25   .25
C185 AP48 20p ultra   .25   .25
C186 AP48 50p rose ('57)   .25   .25
C187 AP49 100p bl grn ('57)   .55   .25
  a.   Lithographed ('60)   .55   .25
C188 AP49 200p dp ultra ('57)   .65   .25
C189 AP49 500p car ('58)   .85   .25
   Nos. C183-C189 (7)   3.05 1.75

Symbols of University
Departments — AP50

Design: 100p, View of the University.

1956, Dec. 15   Unwmk.   Perf. 14½
C190 AP50 20p green   .35   .25
C191 AP50 100p dk vio bl   1.40   .80
25th anniversary of the Federico Santa
Maria Technical University, Valparaiso.
   A souvenir sheet contains one each of Nos.
299, C190-C191, imperf. It was not issued for
postal use, though some served postally. Size:
127x160mm. Value, $125.

Mistral Type of Regular Issue, 1958
1958, Jan. 10   Engr.   Perf. 14
C192 A144 100p green   .25   .25

Ambrosio
O'Higgins — AP51

1958, Mar. 23
C193 AP51 100p lt blue   .40   .25
Founding of the city of Osorno, 500th anniv.
   A souvenir sheet contains one each of Nos.
302 and C193, imperf. and printed in red
brown. It was not issued for postal use, though
some served postally. Size: 155x138mm.
Value, $70.

Exhibition Type of Regular Issue
1958, Oct. 18   Unwmk.
C194 A146 50p dull green   .45   .45
   A souvenir sheet contains one each of Nos.
303 and C194, imperf. and printed in deep
red. It was not issued for postal use, though
some served postally. Size: 188x220mm.
Value, $55.

Bank Type of Regular Issue, 1958
1958, Dec. 18   Engr.   Perf. 14
C195 A147 50p redsh brown   .25   .25
   A souvenir sheet contains one each of Nos.
304 and C195, printed in dull violet, imperf. It
was not issued for postal use, though some
served postally. Value, $190.

Antarctic Types of Regular Issue
1958   Litho.   Perf. 14
C199 A149 20p violet   .50   .25
               Engr.
C200 A150 500p dark blue   3.75 1.75

Symbols of
Various
Religions
AP52

Perf. 14½
1959, Jan. 23   Unwmk.   Engr.
C206 AP52 50p dk car rose   .30   .25
10th anniversary of the Universal Declaration of Human Rights.

Types of 1950-54

Designs: 50p, Plane silhouette over shore.
100p, Plane over map of Antarctica. 200p,
Plane over natural arch rock.

**Imprint: "Casa de Moneda de
Chile"**

1959   Litho.   Perf. 14
C207 AP38 1p dk blue grn   .85   .50
  a.   Wmk. 215   30.00
C208 AP38 10p emerald   .55   .25
C209 AP38 20p red brown   .35   .25
C210 AP38 50p yellow grn   .35   .25
C211 AP38 100p car rose   .35   .25
C212 AP38 200p brt blue   .55   .25
   Nos. C207-C212 (6)   3.00 1.75

Carlos Anwandter
AP53

1959, June 18   Engr.   Perf. 14
C213 AP53 20p rose carmine   .25   .25
Centenary of the German School in
Valdivia, founded by Carlos Anwandter.
   A souvenir sheet contains one each of Nos.
319 and C213, imperf. It was not issued for
postal use, though some served postally.
Value, $75.

IGY Type of Regular Issue, 1958
1959, Aug. 28   Unwmk.   Perf. 14
C214 A148 50p green   .70   .25

Ladrillero Type of Regular Issue
1959, Aug. 28   Litho.
C215 A154 50p green   .50   .25

Barros Arana Type of Regular Issue
1959, Aug. 28
C216 A155 100p purple   .50   .25

Red Cross Type of Regular Issue
1959, Oct. 6
C217 A156 50p red & blk   .60   .25

WRY Type of Regular Issue, 1960
1960, Apr. 7   Unwmk.   Perf. 14½
C218 A160 10c violet   .35   .25
   A souvenir sheet contains two stamps similar to Nos. 330 and C218, the 1c printed in
blue, the 10c airmail in maroon. The sheet is
imperf., printed on thin cardboard. Size:
160x204mm. Value, $125.

Type of Regular Issue, 1960-62, and

José Agustin Eyzaguirre and José
Miguel Infante — AP54

Designs: 2c, Palace of Justice. 5c, National
memorial. No. C220, Arms of Chile. No.
C220A, José Gaspar Marin and J. Gregorio
Argomedo. 50c, Archbishop J. I. Cienfuegos
and Brother Camilo Henriquez. 1e, Bernardo
O'Higgins.

1960-65   Unwmk.   Engr.   Perf. 14½
C218A AP54 2c mar & gray vio
                     ('62)   .25   .25
C219 A162 5c vio bl & dl pur
                     ('61)   .25   .25
               Wmk. 215
C220 A161 10c dk brn & red
                     brn   .25   .25
               Unwmk.
C220A AP54 10c vio brn & brn
                     ('64)   .40   .25
C220B AP54 20c dk bl & dl pur
                     ('64)   .25   .25
C220C AP54 50c bl grn & ind
                     ('65)   1.00   .25
C220D A162 1e dk red & red
                     brn ('63)   1.00   .40
   Nos. C218A-C220D (7)   3.40 1.90
   150th anniv. of the formation of the 1st Natl.
Government.
   A souvenir sheet contains two airmail
stamps: a 5c brown similar to No. C219
(National Memorial) and a 10c green, type
A161. The sheet is imperf., printed on heavy
paper with papermaker's watermark. Size:
120x168mm. Value, $85.

Map and Rotary
Emblem — AP55

Unwmk.

1960, Dec. 1   Litho.   Perf. 14
C221 AP55 10c blue   .50   .25
South American Rotary Regional Confer-
ence, Santiago, 1960.
   A souvenir sheet contains one 10c maroon,
type AP55, with brown marginal inscription.
Size: 118x158mm. Value, $65.
   The souvenir sheet was overprinted in green
"El Mundo Unida Contra la Malaria" and the
outline of a mosquito, and released in Octo-
ber, 1962. Value, $110.

Araucan Pine
and
Plane — AP56

Designs: 2m, Chilean flag and plane. 3m,
Plane and dock crane. 4m, Plane above river
(vignette AP39). 5m, Blast furnace. 1c,
Plane over mountain lake. 2c, Plane over
cable cars. 5c, Plane silhouette over shore.
10c, Plane over map of Antarctica. 20c, Plane
over natural arch rock.

**Imprint: "Casa de Moneda de
Chile"**

1960-62   Litho.   Perf. 14
C222 AP56 1m orange   .25   .25
C223 AP56 2m yellow grn   .25   .25
C224 AP56 3m violet   .25   .25
C225 AP56 4m gray olive   .25   .25
C226 AP56 5m brt bl grn   .25   .25
C227 AP56 1c ultra   .25   .25
C228 AP56 2c red brn ('61)   .35   .25
C229 AP56 5c yel grn ('61)   1.75   .25
C230 AP56 10c car rose ('62)   .45   .25
C231 AP56 20c brt bl ('62)   .50   .25
   Nos. C222-C231 (10)   4.55 2.50

Oil Derricks and
Douglas DC-
6 — AP57

Beechcraft
Monoplane
AP58

5m, Train and plane. 2c, Jet plane & Easter
Island statue. 5c, Control tower & plane. 10c,
Comet airliner. 50c, Douglas DC-6.

Perf. 14x13½
1960-67   Unwmk.   Litho.
C234 AP57 5m red brown   .35   .35
C235 AP57 1c dull blue   .35   .35
C236 AP57 2c ultra ('62)   .35   .35
C237 AP57 5c rose red ('64)   .35   .35
C238 AP58 10c ultra ('67)   .35   .35
C239 AP58 20c car ('62)   .35   .35
C240 AP58 50c green ('63)   .35   .35
   Nos. C234-C240 (7)   2.45 2.45

Stamps similar to type AP58, but inscribed
in peso ($) currency, are listed as type AP49.

Congress Type of Regular Issue
1961, Oct. 5   Perf. 14½
C245 A164 10c gray green   .95   .60

Soccer Type of Regular Issue, 1962
Designs: 5c, Goalkeeper and stadium, vert.
10c, Soccer players and globe.

1962, May 30   Unwmk.   Engr.
C246 A165 5c rose lilac   .25   .25
C247 A165 10c dk carmine   .25   .25

A souvenir sheet of four contains one each
of Nos. 340-341, C246-C247, imperf., with

light brown marginal inscriptions. Size: 123x194mm. Sold for 7.50 escudos (face value, 22 centavos). Value $12.

Hunger Type of Regular Issue

20c, Mother with empty bowl, horiz.

1963, Mar. 21   Litho.   Perf. 14
C248 A166 20c green   .25 .25

Red Cross Type of Regular Issue

Design: 20c, Centenary emblem and plane silhouette, horiz.

1963, Sept. 6   Unwmk.   Perf. 14
C249 A167 20c gray & red   .25 .25

Fire Engine of 1860's AP59

1963, Dec. 20   Litho.   Perf. 14½
C250 AP59 30c red   .50 .25
Centenary of the Santiago Fire Brigade.

Western Hemisphere AP60

1964, Apr. 9   Unwmk.   Perf. 14½
C254 AP60 4c ultra   .40 .25
Issued in memory of President John F. Kennedy and to honor the Alliance for Progress.

Battle of Rancagua — AP61

1965, May 7   Engr.   Perf. 14½
C255 AP61 5c dull grn & sepia   .40 .25
Battle of Rancagua, 10/7/14, 150th anniv.

ITU Emblem, Old and New Communication Equipment AP62

1965, May 7   Litho.   Perf. 14½x14
C256 AP62 40c red & maroon   .40 .25
ITU centenary.

Portrait Type of 1964

Portraits: No. C257, Enrique Molina. No. C258, Msgr. Carlos Casanueva.

1965, June   Litho.   Perf. 14
C257 A169 60c brt violet   .30 .25
C258 A169 60c green   .30 .25
See note after No. 346.

Skier Type of Regular Issue 1965

Design: 20c, Skier, horiz.

1965, Aug. 30   Unwmk.   Perf. 14
C259 A172 20c ultra   .30 .25

Fishing Boats, Angelmo Harbor AP63

Aviators' Monument AP64

1965
C260 AP63 40c brown   .30 .25
Perf. 14x14½
C262 AP64 1e car rose   .30 .25

Andrés Bello (1780?-1865), Venezuela-born Writer and Educator — AP65

1965, Nov. 29   Engr.   Unwmk.
C263 AP65 10c dk car rose   .35 .35

Skiers — AP66

1966, Apr. 6   Litho.   Perf. 14
C264 AP66 4e dk bl & red brn   1.25 .25
World Skiing Championships, Partillo, Aug. 1966.

Basketball AP67

1966, Apr. 28
C265 AP67 13c rose carmine   .40 .25
International Basketball Championships.

Slalom AP68

Perf. 14½x15
1966, July 20   Litho.   Unwmk.
C266 AP68 75c rose car & lil   .40 .25
C267 AP68 3e ultra & lt bl   .40 .25
Intl. Skiing Championships, Partillo, August 1966. A souvenir sheet of 2 contains imperf. stamps similar to Nos. C266-C267. No gum. Size: 109x140mm. Value $36.

Ship Type of Regular Issue

1966   Litho.   Perf. 14½
C268 A175 70c Prus grn & yel grn .35 .25
See note below No. 358.

ICY Type of Regular Issue

1966, Oct. 28   Unwmk.   Perf. 14½
C269 A177 3e blue & carmine   .50 .25
A souvenir sheet of 2 contains imperf. stamps similar to Nos. 360 and C269. No gum. Size: 111x140mm. Value $7.50.

Chilean Flag and Ships — AP69

1966, Nov. 21   Litho.   Perf. 14
C270 AP69 13c dull red brn   .40 .25
Centenary of the city of Antofagasta.

Pardo Type of Regular Issue

40c, Pardo & map of Chile's claim to Antarctica.

1967, Jan. 6   Unwmk.   Perf. 14½
C271 A178 40c ultra   .50 .25
See note below No. 361.

Family Type of Regular Issue

1967, Apr. 13   Litho.   Perf. 14
C272 A179 80c brt bl & blk   .35 .25

Ruben Dario and Title Page of "Azul" AP70

1967, May 15   Engr.   Perf. 14½
C273 AP70 10c dark blue   .30 .25
Ruben Dario (pen name of Felix Ruben Garcia Sarmiento, 1867-1916), Nicaraguan poet, newspaper correspondent and diplomat.

Tree Type of Regular Issue

1967, June 9   Litho.
C274 A180 75c grn & pale rose   .35 .25

Lions Type of Regular Issue

1967   Litho.   Perf. 14
C275 A181 1e purple & yel   .40 .25
C276 A181 5e blue & yel   1.10 .30
A souvenir sheet without franking value contains 3 imperf. stamps, 20c, 1e and 5e, in violet blue and yellow. Size: 110x140mm. Value, $13.50.
Issue dates: 1e, July 12; 5e, Aug. 11.

Flag Type of Regular Issue

1967, Oct. 20   Unwmk.   Perf. 14½
C277 A182 50c ultra & crimson   .35 .25

ITY Emblem AP71

1967, Nov. 22   Litho.   Perf. 14½
C278 AP71 30c lt vio bl & blk   .35 .25
Issued for International Tourist Year, 1967.

Caro Type of Regular Issue, 1967

1967, Dec. 4   Engr.   Perf. 14½
C279 A183 40c violet   .70 .35

Type of Regular Issue, 1968

1968, Apr. 23   Litho.   Perf. 14½
C280 A184 2e brt violet   .60 .25
Sesquicentennial of the Battles of Chacabuco and Maipu. A souvenir sheet of 2 contains imperf. stamps similar to Nos. 367 and C280. Value, $12. A second sheet exists with the 2e in green and the 3e in brown. Size: 139½x100mm. Value, $12.

Farm Type of Regular Issue

1968, June 18   Unwmk.
C281 A185 50c blk, org & grn   .35 .25

Juan I. Molina, Educator and Scientist AP72

1968, Aug. 27   Litho.   Perf. 14½
C282 AP72 1e bright green   .30 .25

Map of Chiloé Province — AP73

Perf. 14½
1968, Oct. 7   Unwmk.   Litho.
C283 AP73 1e rose claret   .35 .35
Anniversaries of the founding of five towns in Chiloé Province.

Auto Club Type of Regular Issue

1968, Nov. 10   Engr.   Perf. 14½x14
C284 A189 5e ultra   .35 .25

British Crown and Map of Chile — AP74

50c, Chilean coat of arms (horiz.; similar to type A161). 3e, British coat of arms, horiz.

1968, Nov. 12   Litho.   Perf. 14½
C285 AP74 50c green & brn   .25 .25
C286 AP74 3e lt bl & org brn   .40 .25
Engr.
C287 AP74 5e purple & mag   .60 .25
   Nos. C285-C287 (3)   1.25 .75
Visit of Queen Elizabeth II of Great Britain, Nov. 11-18. A souvenir sheet of 3 contains imperf., lithographed stamps similar to Nos. C285-C287. Size: 124½x190mm. The souvenir sheet also publicizes the British-Chilean Philatelic Exhibition. Value, $20.

First Coin Minted in Chile and Coin Press AP75

Design: 1e, Chile No. 128.

1968, Dec. 31   Litho.   Perf. 14½
C288 AP75 50c ocher & vio brn   .30 .25
C289 AP75 1e lt bl & dp org   .30 .25
225th anniversary of the founding of the State Mint (Casa de Moneda de Chile).
A souvenir sheet of 4 contains imperf. stamps similar to Nos. 373-374, C288-C289. Size: 150x119mm. Value, $10.

Satellite Type of Regular Issue

1969, May 20   Litho.   Perf. 14½
C290 A191 2e rose lilac   .30 .25

Red Cross Type of Regular Issue

1969, Sept.   Litho.   Perf. 14½
C291 A192 5e black & red   .50 .25
A souvenir card contains 2 imperf. stamps similar to Nos. 376 and C291, with red marginal inscription. Size: 109x140mm. Value $5.

Dam Type of Regular Issue
1969, Nov. 18   Litho.   *Perf. 14½*
C292 A193 3e blue   .50 .25

Rodriguez Type of Regular Issue
1969, Nov. 24
C293 A194 30c brown   .35 .25

EXPO '70 Type of Regular Issue
1969, Dec. 1   Litho.   *Perf. 14*
C294 A195 5e red   .35 .25

Bible Type of 1969
1969, Dec. 2   *Perf. 14½*
C295 A196 1e green   .30 .25

ILO Type of Regular Issue
1969, Dec. 17   *Perf. 14½*
C296 A197 2e rose lil & blk   .35 .25

Human Rights Year Type of 1969
1969, Dec. 18
C297 A198 4e brown & red   .35 .35

A souvenir sheet of 2 contains imperf. stamps similar to Nos. 382 and C297. Size: 110x140mm. Value, $9.

Easter Island Type of 1970
1970, Jan. 26
C298 A199 50c dull grnsh bl   .70 .25

Ship Type of Regular Issue
1970, Feb. 4   Litho.   *Perf. 14½*
C299 A200 2e deep ultra   .40 .25

Rotary Type of Regular Issue
1970, Mar. 18   Litho.   *Perf. 14*
C300 A201 1e rose claret   .35 .25

Gandhi Type of Regular Issue
1970, Apr. 1   Litho.   *Perf. 14½*
C301 A202 1e red brown   .40 .25

Education Year Type of 1970
1970, July 17   Litho.   *Perf. 14½*
C302 A204 4e red brown   .30 .25

National Shrine Type of 1970
1970, July 28   Litho.   *Perf. 14½*
C303 A205 1e ultra   .35 .25

Cancer Type of Regular Issue
1970, Aug. 11
C304 A206 2e brn & lt olive   .40 .25

A few stampss are known inscribed "Correos de Chile." instead of "Correos Aereo Chile." Value $350.

Copper Type of Regular Issue
1970, Oct. 21   Litho.   *Perf. 14½*
C305 A207 3e grn & lt red brn   .50 .25

United Nations Type of 1970
1970, Oct. 22
C306 A208 5e dk car & grn   .50 .25

Freighter Type of Regular Issue
1971, Jan. 18   Litho.   *Perf. 14*
C307 A209 5e lt red brown   .50 .25

No. C290 Surcharged in Red

1971, Jan. 21   Litho.   *Perf. 14½*
C308 A191 52c on 2e rose lil   .40 .25

Liberation Type of Regular Issue
1971, Feb. 3   *Perf. 14½*
C309 A210 1e gray bl & brn   .40 .25

UNICEF Type of Regular Issue
1971, Feb. 11   Litho.   *Perf. 14½*
C310 A211 2e blue & grn   .30 .25

Boy Scout Type of Regular Issue
1971, Feb. 10   *Perf. 14*
C311 A212 5c dk car & ol   .40 .25

Satellite Type of Regular Issue
1971, May 25   Litho.   *Perf. 14½*
C312 A213 2e brown   .40 .25

De Ercilla Type of Regular Issue
1972, Mar. 20   Engr.   *Perf. 14*
C313 A221 2e Prussian blue   .30 .25

A souvenir card contains impressions of Nos. 414 and C313 with black marginal inscription commemorating España 75 Philatelic Exhibition. Size: 165x220mm. Value $19.

AIR POST SEMI-POSTAL STAMPS

> **Catalogue values for unused stamps in this section are for Never Hinged items.**

Type of Semi-Postal Stamps, 1961
Portraits: 10c+10c, Alonso de Ercilla. 20c+20c, Gabriela Mistral.

Perf. 13x12½
1961, Apr. 29   Photo.   Unwmk.
CB1 SP3 10c + 10c salmon & choc   1.00 .30
CB2 SP3 20c + 20c gray & dp cl   1.00 .30

Printed without charge by the Spanish Mint as a gift to Chile. The surtax was to aid the 1960 earthquake victims and to increase teachers' salaries.

ACKNOWLEDGMENT OF RECEIPT STAMPS

AR1

1894   Unwmk.   *Perf. 11½*
H1 AR1 5c brown   .75 .50
a.   Imperf., pair   3.00

The black stamp of design similar to AR1 inscribed "Avis de Paiement" was prepared for use on notices of payment of funds but was not regularly issued.

POSTAGE DUE STAMPS

D1   D2

Handstamped
1894   Unwmk.   *Perf. 13*
J1 D1 2c black, *straw*   15.00 8.00
J2 D1 4c black, *straw*   15.00 8.00
J3 D1 6c black, *straw*   15.00 8.00
J4 D1 8c black, *straw*   14.00 8.00
J5 D2 10c black, *straw*   15.00 8.00
J6 D1 16c black, *straw*   15.00 8.00
J7 D1 20c black, *straw*   15.00 8.00
J8 D1 30c black, *straw*   15.00 8.00
J9 D1 40c black, *straw*   15.00 8.00
Nos. J1-J9 (9)   134.00 72.00

J1a D1 2c black, *yellow*   85.00 80.00
J2a D1 4c black, *yellow*   55.00 40.00
J3a D1 6c black, *yellow*   80.00 35.00
J4a D1 8c black, *yellow*   16.00 16.00
J5a D2 10c black, *yellow*   16.00 16.00
J6a D1 16c black, *yellow*   16.00 16.00
J7a D1 20c black, *yellow*   16.00 16.00
J8a D1 30c black, *yellow*   16.00 16.00
J9a D1 40c black, *yellow*   16.00 16.00
Nos. J1a-J9a (9)   316.00 251.00

Counterfeits exist.

D3

1895   Litho.   *Perf. 11*
J19 D3 1c red, *yellow*   7.50 3.00
J20 D3 2c red, *yellow*   7.50 3.00
J21 D3 4c red, *yellow*   6.00 3.00
J22 D3 6c red, *yellow*   7.50 3.00
J23 D3 8c red, *yellow*   4.50 3.00
J24 D3 10c red, *yellow*   4.50 4.50
J25 D3 20c red, *yellow*   4.50 2.25
J26 D3 40c red, *yellow*   4.50 3.00
J27 D3 50c red, *yellow*   4.50 3.00
J28 D3 60c red, *yellow*   9.00 4.50
J29 D3 80c red, *yellow*   9.00 6.00
J30 D3 1p red, *yellow*   9.50 9.50
Nos. J19-J30 (12)   78.50 44.75

Nos. J19-J30 were printed in sheets of 100 (10x10) containing all 12 denominations. Counterfeits of Nos. J19-J42 exist.

1896   *Perf. 13½*
J31 D3 1c red, *straw*   .90 .50
J32 D3 2c red, *straw*   .90 .50
J33 D3 4c red, *straw*   1.10 .50
J34 D3 6c red, *straw*   2.50 1.00
J35 D3 8c red, *straw*   1.10 .60
J36 D3 10c red, *straw*   .90 .60
J37 D3 20c red, *straw*   .90 .60
J38 D3 40c red, *straw*   18.00 15.00
J39 D3 50c red, *straw*   18.00 15.00
J40 D3 60c red, *straw*   18.00 15.00
J41 D3 80c red, *straw*   25.00 17.50
J42 D3 100c red, *straw*   36.00 30.00
Nos. J31-J42 (12)   123.30 96.80

D4

1898   *Perf. 13*
J43 D4 1c scarlet   .50 .30
J44 D4 2c scarlet   1.25 .60
J45 D4 4c scarlet   .50 .30
J46 D4 10c scarlet   .50 .30
J47 D4 20c scarlet   .50 .30
Nos. J43-J47 (5)   3.25 1.80

D5

1924   *Perf. 11½, 12½*
J48 D5 2c blue & red   1.10 .90
J49 D5 4c blue & red   1.10 .90
J50 D5 8c blue & red   1.10 .90
J51 D5 10c blue & red   1.10 .90
J52 D5 20c blue & red   1.10 .60
J53 D5 40c blue & red   1.10 .90
J54 D5 60c blue & red   1.10 .90
J55 D5 80c blue & red   1.10 .90
J56 D5 1p blue & red   1.50 1.10
J57 D5 2p blue & red   2.60 1.90
J58 D5 5p blue & red   2.60 1.90
Nos. J48-J58 (11)   15.50 11.80

Nos. J48-J58 were printed in sheets of 150 containing all 11 denominations, and a second printing was printed in sheets of 50 containing the five lower denominations, providing various se-tenants. Stamps from the second printing are of a slightly different shade of red.

All values of this issue exist imperforate, also with center inverted, but are not believed to have been regularly issued. Those with inverted centers sell for about 10 times normal value.

OFFICIAL STAMPS

For Domestic Postage

O1

Single-lined frame
Control number in violet
1907   Unwmk.   *Imperf.*
O1 O1 dl bl, "CARTA" org   125.00 80.00
O2 O1 red, "OFICIO" bl   125.00 80.00
O3 O1 vio, "PAQUETE" red   125.00 80.00
O4 O1 org, bl, "EP" vio   125.00 80.00
Nos. O1-O4 (4)   500.00 320.00

The diagonal inscription in differing color indicates type of usage: CARTA for letters of ordinary weight; OFICIO, heavy letters to 100 grams; PAQUETE, parcels to 100 grams; E P (Encomienda Postal), heavier parcels; C (Certificado), as on No. O8, registration including postage.

Varieties include CARTA, PAQUETE and E P inverted, OFICIO omitted, etc.

Double-lined frame
Large control number in black
Perf. 11
O5 O1 bl, "CARTA" yel   32.50 25.00
O6 O1 red, "OFICIO" bl   50.00 40.00
O7 O1 brn, "PAQUETE" grn   50.00 40.00
O8 O1 grn, "C" red   600.00 600.00
Nos. O5-O8 (4)   732.50 705.00

Nos. O5-O8 exist in tête bêche pairs; with CARTA, OFICIO or PAQUETE double or inverted, and other varieties.
Counterfeits of Nos. O1-O8 exist.

For Foreign Postage

Regular Issues of 1892-1909 Overprinted in Red — a

On Stamps of 1904-09
1907   *Perf. 12*
O9 A14 1c green   25.00 40.00
a.   Inverted overprint   75.00
O10 A12 3c on lp brn   50.00 60.00
a.   Inverted overprint   150.00
O11 A14 5c ultra   40.00 50.00
a.   Inverted overprint   120.00
O12 A15 10c gray & blk   40.00 65.00
O13 A15 15c vio & blk   40.00 65.00
O14 A15 20c org brn & blk   40.00 65.00
O15 A15 50c ultra & blk   75.00 100.00

On Stamp of 1892
Rouletted
O16 A6 1p dk brn & blk   350.00 500.00
Nos. O9-O16 (8)   660.00 945.00

Counterfeits of Nos. O9-O16 exist.

Regular Issues of 1915-25 Overprinted in Red or Blue — b

1926   *Perf. 13½x14, 14*
O17 A52 5c slate bl (R)   2.50 .50
O18 A50 10c bl & blk (R)   4.00 .75
O19 A39 20c org red & blk (Bl)   2.00 .40
O20 A42 50c dp grn & blk (Bl)   2.00 .40
O21 A43 1p grn & blk (R)   2.75 .70
O22 A43 2p ver & blk (Bl)   4.00 1.00
Nos. O17-O22 (6)   17.25 3.75

Nos. O21 and O22 are overprinted vertically at each side.
Nos. O17 to O22 were for the use of the Biblioteca Nacional.

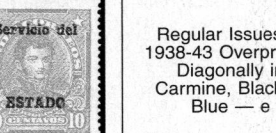

Regular Issue of
1915-25 Overprinted
in Red — c

1928   *Perf. 13½x14, 14*
O23	A50	10c bl & blk	6.50	2.00
O24	A39	20c brn org & blk	3.00	1.00
O25	A40	25c dl bl & blk	7.50	1.00
O26	A42	50c dp grn & blk	4.00	1.00
O27	A43	1p grn & blk	5.00	1.50
	Nos. O23-O27 (5)		26.00	6.50

The overprint on Nos. O23 to O26 is
16½mm high; on No. O27 it is 20mm.

Regular Issues of
1928-30 Overprinted
in Red — d

**On Stamp Inscribed: "Correos de
Chile"**

1930-31
O28	A50	10c bl & blk	3.00	1.50

Wmk. 215
**On Stamps Inscribed: "Correos de
Chile"**
O29	A50	10c bl & blk	6.00	3.00
O30	A39	20c org red & blk	.75	.50
O31	A40	25c bl & blk	.75	.50
O32	A42	50c dp grn & blk	1.50	.75

**On Stamps Inscribed: "Chile
Correos"**
O33	A42	50c dp grn & blk	1.50	.75
O34	A43	1p grn & blk	1.50	.75
	Nos. O28-O34 (7)		15.00	7.75

Same Overprint on No. 181
1933   *Perf. 13½x14*
O35	A61	20c dk brn	.75	.25

Same Overprint in Red on No. 182
1935   **Wmk. 215**
O36	A62	10c deep blue	.75	.50

**No. 163 Ovptd. Type "b" in Red
Inscribed: "Correos de Chile"**
1934
O37	A52	5c lt grn	.60	.50

Overprint "b" on No. 182
1935
O38	A62	10c dp bl	.50	.50

Same Overprint in Black on No. 181
1936   **Wmk. 215**   *Perf. 13½x14*
O39	A61	20c dk brn	10.00	.50

Overprint "b" in Red on No. 158
1938   *Perf. 14*
O40	A43	1p grn & blk	2.50	1.00

**Nos. 204 and 205 Overprinted Type
"d" in Black**
1939   *Perf. 13½x14, 14*
O41	A78	50c violet	4.00	2.50
O42	A84	1p org brn	5.00	4.00

**Stamps of 1938-40 Overprinted Type
"b" in Black, Red or Blue**
1940-46   *Perf. 13½x14, 14*
O43	A78	10c sal pink ('45)	2.00	1.75
O44	A78	15c brn org	1.00	.40
O45	A78	20c lt bl (R) ('42)	1.50	.60
O46	A78	30c brn pink (Bl)	.75	.40
O47	A78	40c lt grn	.75	.40
O48	A78	50c vio ('45)	4.00	.75
O49	A84	1p org brn ('42)	2.50	.75
O50	A84	1.80p dp bl (R) ('45)	10.00	6.00
O51	A84	2p car lake ('42)	2.00	1.25
	Nos. O43-O51 (9)		24.50	12.30

**Overprint "b" in Black on Nos. 223,
225**
Unwmk.
O58	A84	1p brn org	2.50	1.50
O59	A84	2p car lake ('46)	5.00	2.00

Regular Issues of
1938-43 Overprinted
Diagonally in
Carmine, Black or
Blue — e

Wmk. 215, Unwmkd.
1948-54   *Perf. 13½x14, 14*
O60	A78	20c lt bl, #219 (C)	.75	.35
O61	A78	30c brt pink, #202 (Bl)		
		('54)	1.50	.50
O62	A78	40c brt grn, #203 ('54)	2.50	1.25
O63	A78	50c vio #222 ('49)	.75	.40
O64	A84	1p org brn, #205	2.50	1.00
O65	A84	2p car lake, #207		
		('54)	1.00	.50
O66	A84	5p dk sl grn, #208		
		(C) ('51)	1.75	1.00
	Nos. O60-O66 (7)		10.75	5.00

**Overprint "e" Diagonally on Nos.
265 and 275 in Red or Black**
Wmk. 215, Unwmkd.
1953-55   *Perf. 13½x14, 13x14*
O67	A126	1p dk bl grn, #265 (R)	1.00	.50
O68	A126	1p dk bl grn, #265		
		(Bk) ('55)	.75	.50
O69	A126	1p dk bl grn, #275 (R)		
		('55)	.75	.50
	Nos. O67-O69 (3)		2.50	1.50

**Overprint "e" Horizontally on Nos.
207, 209 in Black or Blue**
1955-56   **Wmk. 215**   *Perf. 14*
O70	A84	2p car lake ('56)	1.75	.75
O71	A84	10p rose vio (Bl)	2.75	1.75

**Overprint "e" Horizontally on Nos.
293-295 and Types of 1956 Regular
Issue in Black or Red**
1956   **Unwmk.**   *Perf. 14x14½*
O72	A141	2p purple	1.00	.60
O73	A142	3p lt vio bl (R)	3.00	2.00
O74	A141	5p redsh brn	.75	.35
O75	A142	10p vio (19x22¼mm)		
		(R)	3.00	1.75
a.		Perf. 13½x14 (19½x22½mm)		
		('58)	.50	.40
O76	A141	50p rose red	2.50	1.00

**No. 310 Overprinted in Red
Vertically, Reading Down, Similar to
Type "e"**
Size of Overprint: 21x2½mm
1958   **Litho.**   *Perf. 14*
O77	A149	10p vio blue	200.00	30.00

**Overprint "e" Horizontally on No.
327 in Red**
1960   **Unwmk.**   *Perf. 13x14*
O79	A157	5c blue	1.75	.70

POSTAL TAX STAMPS

Talca Issue.
A 10c blue postal tax stamp,
inscribed "Bicentenario de Talca" and
picturing a coat of arms, was issued in
1942. It was sold only in Talca and was
required for a time on all domestic letters sent from that city. The tax helped
pay for Talca's bicentenary celebration.
Value 20 cents.

Nos. 326 and 347
Surcharged

1970   **Unwmk.**   **Litho.**   *Perf. 14x13*
RA1	A159	10c on 2c ultra	.25	.25

Perf. 14x14½
RA2	A170	10c on 6c rose lil	.25	.25

Chilean Arms — PT1

Perf. 14½x14
1970, Apr. 23   **Litho.**   **Unwmk.**
RA3	PT1	10c blue	.30	.25

See No. RA6.

No. RA3 Surcharged in Red

        a   b

1971-72
RA4	PT1	(a) 15c on 10c bl	.30	.25
RA5	PT1	(b) 15c on 10c bl ('72)	.30	.25

Type of 1970
1972, July   **Litho.**   *Perf. 14½x14*
RA6	PT1	15c rose red	.30	.25

**No. RA6 Surcharged in
Ultramarine**

1972-73
RA7	PT1	20c on 15c rose red	.30	.25
RA8	PT1	50c on 15c rose red		
		('73)	.30	.25

No. RA8 has 9 bars instead of 8.
The surtax on Nos. RA1-RA8 was for modernization of postal system. Compulsory on
all inland mail.

PARCEL POST POSTAL TAX STAMP

Pres. J. J. Prieto
V. — PPT1

Unwmk.
1957, Apr. 8   **Litho.**   *Perf. 14*
QRA1	PPT1	15p green	.35	.30

The surtax aided the Prieto Foundation. No.
QRA1 was required on parcel post entering or
leaving Chile.

CHINA

'chī-nə

LOCATION — Eastern Asia
GOVT. — Republic
AREA — 2,903,475 sq. mi.
POP. — 462,798,093 (1948)

10 Candareen = 1 Mace
10 Mace = 1 Tael
100 Cents = 1 Dollar (Yuan) (1897)

Watermarks

Wmk. 103 —
Yin-Yang Symbol

Wmk. 261 —
Character Yu
(Post) Multiple

Issues of the Imperial Maritime Customs Post

Imperial
Dragon — A1

1878   Unwmk. Typo.   Perf. 12½
Thin Paper
Stamps printed 2½-3¼mm apart

1	A1	1c green	650.00	550.00
a.		1c dark green	775.00	600.00
2	A1	3c brown red	750.00	450.00
a.		3c vermilion	925.00	500.00
3	A1	5c orange	875.00	400.00
a.		5c bister orange	1,200.	500.00

Imperforate essays of Nos. 1-3 have an extra circle near the dragon's lower left foot. Examples with the circle completely or mostly removed are proofs or unfinished stamps.

1882
Thin or Pelure Paper
Stamps printed 4½mm apart

4	A1	1c green	700.00	400.00
a.		1c dark green	800.00	425.00
5	A1	3c brown red	1,350.	375.00
6	A1	5c orange yellow	25,000.	1,500.

1883   Rough to smooth Perf. 12½
Medium to Thick Opaque Paper
Stamps printed 2½ to 3¼mm apart

7	A1	1c green	775.00	475.00
a.		1c dark green	875.00	525.00
b.		1c light green	925.00	575.00
c.		Vert. pair, imperf. between	160,000.	
8	A1	3c brown red	1,350.	500.00
a.		3c vermilion	1,600.	400.00
b.		Vert. pair, imperf. between		230,000.
9	A1	5c yellow	2,350.	650.00
a.		5c chrome yellow	2,650.	875.00
b.		Horiz. pair, imperf. btwn.		60,000.

Nos. 1-9 were printed from plates of 25, 20 or 15 individual copper dies, but only No. 5 exists in the 15-die setting. Many different printings and plate settings exist. All values occur in a wide variety of shades and papers. The effect of climate on certain papers has produced the varieties on so-called toned papers in Nos. 1-15.

Value for No. 8b is for a damaged example.

Counterfeits, frequently with forged cancellations, occur in all early Chinese issues.

Imperial Dragon — A2

1885   Wmk. 103   Perf. 12½

10	A2	1c green	190.00	100.00
a.		Vert. pair, imperf. btwn.	20,000.	17,500.
b.		Horiz. pair, imperf. btwn.		—
11	A2	3c lilac	450.00	130.00
a.		Horiz. pair, imperf. btwn.	22,000.	17,500.
b.		Vert. pair, imperf. btwn.		24,000.
12	A2	5c grnsh yellow	400.00	130.00
a.		5c bister brown	700.00	160.00
b.		Vert. pair, imperf. btwn.	24,000.	24,000.
c.		Horiz. pair, imperf. btwn.		52,500.
		Nos. 10-12 (3)	1,040.	360.00

1888   Perf. 11½-12

13	A2	1c green	100.00	60.00
14	A2	3c lilac	275.00	100.00
b.		Double impression		1,100.
15	A2	5c grnsh yellow	500.00	150.00
b.		Horiz. pair, imperf. vert.		50,000.
c.		Double impression	1,100.	1,100.
		Nos. 13-15 (3)	875.00	310.00

Nos. 10-15 were printed from plates made of 40 individual copper dies, arranged in two panes of 20 each. Several different settings exist of all values.

Imperforates of Nos. 13-15 are considered proofs by most authorities.

Stamps overprinted "Formosa" in English or Chinese are proofs.

For surcharges see Nos. 25-27, 75-77.

"Shou" and "Wu Fu" — A3

Dragon and Hydrangea Leaves — A4

"Pa Kua" Signs in Corners — A5

Dragon and Peony — A6

Carp, the Messenger Fish — A7

Dragon, "Pa Kua" and Immortelle A8

Dragons and "Shou" A9

Dragons and Giant Peony — A10

Junk on the Yangtse A11

1894   Lithographed in Shanghai

16	A3	1c orange red	60.00	50.00
a.		Vert. pair, imperf. btwn.	2,250.	2,100.
b.		Horiz. pair, imperf. btwn.	17,500.	12,000.
c.		Vert. pair, imperf. horiz.	3,250.	3,250.
17	A4	2c green	65.00	55.00
a.		Horiz. pair, imperf. btwn.	3,750.	3,500.
18	A5	3c orange	57.50	30.00
a.		Horiz. pair, imperf. btwn.	3,350.	3,500.
b.		Vert. pair, imperf. btwn.	5,000.	3,800.
19	A6	4c rose pink	200.00	250.00
a.		Horiz. pair, imperf. btwn.	14,000.	
20	A7	5c dull orange	350.00	400.00
a.		Horiz. pair, imperf. btwn.	18,000.	18,000.
21	A8	6c dark brown	150.00	60.00
a.		Vert. pair, imperf. btwn.	24,000.	
b.		Horiz. pair, imperf. btwn.	12,500.	
22	A9	9c dark green	175.00	120.00
a.		Imperf., pair	2,250.	
b.		Horiz. pair, imperf. vert.	4,250.	3,750.
c.		Vert. pair, imperf. horiz.	4,250.	
d.		Vert. pair, imperf. btwn.	4,750.	4,250.
e.		Tete beche pair, vert.	2,000.	1,800.
f.		Tete beche pair, imperf. horiz.	5,500.	
g.		Tete beche pair, imperf. vert.	5,500.	4,750.
h.		Vert. strip of 3, imperf. btwn.	5,500.	
i.		Tete beche pair, horiz.	1,500.	1,300.
23	A10	12c orange	650.00	250.00
24	A11	24c carmine	800.00	300.00
a.		Vert. pair, imperf. btwn.	30,000.	
		Nos. 16-24 (9)	2,508.	1,515.

60th birthday of Tsz'e Hsi, the Empress Dowager. All values exist in several distinct shades.

On Mar. 20, 1896, the Customs Post was changed, by Imperial Edict, effective Jan. 1, 1897, to a National Post and the dollar was adopted as the unit of currency.

Time was required to work out details of the Imperial Post and design new stamps. As a provisional measure, stocks of Nos. 16-24 were ordered surcharged with new values in dollars and cents. It is believed that only the Shanghai office stock of Nos. 16-24 (plus any reserve stock at the printers) was surcharged with small figures of value. Other post offices throughout China were instructed to return all unoverprinted stocks on receipt of the new surcharges.

Early in the year it was apparent that all stamps would be exhausted before the new issues were ready (Nos. 86-97), and since the stones from which Nos. 16-24 had been printed were no longer existed, new stones were made from the original transfers. A printing from the new stones was made early in 1897 and surcharged with large figures of value spaced 2½mm below the Chinese characters. During the surcharging, sheets from the 1894 (original) printing were received from outlying post offices and surcharged as they arrived. A small quantity of the 1897 printing reached the public without surcharge (Nos. 16n-24n).

Additional stamps were still required and another printing was made from the new stones and surcharged with large figures, but in a new setting with 1½mm between the Chinese characters and the value. Additional sheets of the 1894 printing were received from the most distant post offices and were also surcharged with the 1½mm setting. Thus there are four different sets of the large-figure surcharges. All these stamps were regularly issued but no attempt was made by the post office to separate printings. Some values are difficult to distinguish as to printing, particularly in used condition.

See No. 73. For surcharges see Nos. 28-72, 74.

1897   Lithographed in Shanghai

16n	A3	1c pink		1,300.
17n	A4	2c olive green		1,300.
18n	A5	3c chrome yellow	850.00	
p.		3c yellow buff	1,100.	
19n	A6	4c pale rose	925.00	
20n	A7	5c yellow	1,000.	
21n	A8	6c red brown	1,100.	
22n	A9	9c yellowish green	3,900.	
p.		9c emerald green		—
23n	A10	12c yellowish orange	6,000.	
24n	A11	24c purplish red	3,900.	

The colors of the 1897 printings are pale or dull; the gum is thin and white. The 1894 printing has a thicker, yellowish gum.

The set of 9 values on thick unwatermarked paper is a special printing of 5,000 sets ordered by P. G. von Mollendorf, a Customs official, for presentation purposes. Value, set $2,400.

For surcharges see Nos. 47-55, 65-72.

Issues of the Chinese Government Post

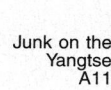

Preceding Issues Surcharged in Black

Small Numerals 2½mm Below Chinese Characters
Surcharged on Nos. 13-15

1897, Jan. 2   Perf. 11½-12

25	A2	1c on 1c	72.50	85.00
26	A2	2c on 3c	300.00	120.00
27	A2	5c on 5c	100.00	57.50
a.		Double surcharge		
		Nos. 25-27 (3)	472.50	262.50

Surcharged on Nos. 16-24
On No. 28 the ½ is 3mm high.

28	A5	½c on 3c	45.00	35.00
a.		"1" instead of "½"	450.00	450.00
b.		Horiz. pair, imperf. btwn.	9,750.	
c.		Vert. pair, imperf. horiz.	9,000.	3,000.
d.		Double surcharge	12,000.	11,000.
e.		Vert. pair, imperf. btwn.	9,000.	
29	A3	1c on 1c	45.00	30.00
a.		Inverted surcharge	50,000.	10,000.
30	A4	2c on 3c	40.00	22.50
a.		Horiz. pair, imperf. vert.	6,000.	
b.		Vert. pair, imperf. btwn.	6,000.	
c.		Double surcharge	14,000.	
d.		Inverted surcharge		15,000.
e.		Horiz. pair, imperf. btwn.	2,000.	
31	A6	4c on 4c	45.00	27.50
a.		Double surcharge	30,000.	20,000.
b.		Vert. pair, imperf. btwn.	10,000.	10,000.
c.		Horiz. pair, imperf. btwn.	10,000.	10,000.
32	A7	5c on 5c	50.00	22.50
a.		Vert. pair, imperf. btwn.	15,000.	10,000.
33	A8	8c on 6c	60.00	35.00
a.		Vert. pair, imperf. btwn.	2,750.	2,250.
b.		Vert. strip of 3, imperf. btwn.	4,200.	2,100.
c.		Horiz. pair, imperf. btwn.	2,500.	2,500.
34	A8	10c on 6c	140.00	90.00
a.		Horiz. pair, imperf. btwn.	7,500.	2,500.
b.		Vert. pair, imperf. btwn.	2,400.	2,400.
35	A9	10c on 9c	475.00	200.00
a.		Double surcharge	40,000.	40,000.
b.		Inverted surcharge	450,000.	
36	A10	10c on 12c	500.00	225.00
a.		Horiz. pair, imperf. horiz.	4,000.	
b.		Vert. pair, imperf. btwn.	4,500.	4,500.
37	A11	30c on 24c	600.00	240.00
a.		Vert. pair, imperf. btwn.	20,000.	
		Nos. 28-37 (10)	2,000.	927.50

Small Numerals 4mm Below Chinese Characters

25a	A2	1c on 1c green	75.00	85.00
28f	A4	½c on 3c orange	60.00	60.00
29b	A3	1c on 1c vermilion	75.00	75.00
30f	A4	2c on 2c dark green	55.00	55.00
31d	A6	4c on 4c dark pink	70.00	55.00
32b	A7	5c on 5c dull orange	70.00	55.00
33d	A8	8c on 6c brown	100.00	100.00
35c	A9	10c on 9c dark green	450.00	375.00
37b	A11	30c on 24c dark red	500.00	500.00

Preceding Issues Surcharged in Black

No. 38 the ½ is 4mm high.

Large Numerals Numerals 2½mm below Chinese characters
Surcharged on Nos. 16-24

1897, Mar.

38	A5	½c on 3c	2,500.	875.00
b.		Inverted surcharge		10,000.
39	A3	1c on 3c	700.00	200.00
40	A4	2c on 2c	375.00	350.00
41	A6	4c on 4c	475.00	375.00
b.		Horiz. pair, imperf. btwn.	11,000.	
42	A7	5c on 5c	225.00	200.00
43	A8	8c on 6c	2,250.	1,750.
44	A9	10c on 9c	800.00	375.00
45	A10	10c on 12c	50,000.	2,850.
46	A11	30c on 24c	1,200.	1,300.
b.		2mm spacing between "30" and "cents."		
			15,000.	

Same Surcharge on Nos. 16n-24n

47	A5	½c on 3c	37.50	40.00
a.		"cen" for "cent"	850.00	850.00
b.		Vert. pair, imperf. btwn.	3,000.	3,000.
c.		Vert. pair, imperf. horiz.	2,700.	2,700.
d.		As "a" and "c"	9,500.	9,500.
e.		As "a" and "b"	7,500.	7,500.
f.		Horiz. pair, imperf. btwn.	3,000.	3,000.
48	A3	1c on 1c	40.00	25.00
a.		Horiz. pair, imperf. btwn.		4,000.
49	A4	2c on 2c	32.50	19.00
50	A6	4c on 4c	40.00	19.00
a.		Horiz. pair, imperf. btwn.	6,000.	6,000.
b.		Vert. pair, imperf. btwn.		5,000.
51	A7	5c on 5c	50.00	30.00
52	A8	8c on 6c	600.00	300.00
53	A9	10c on 9c	300.00	125.00
a.		10c on 9c emerald	400.00	150.00
b.		Pair, one without surcharge	3,000.	2,500.

54	A10	10c on 12c	375.00	90.00
55	A11	30c on 24c	1,200.	400.00
a.		2mm spacing btwn "30" and "cents"	1,500.	750.00
b.		Vert. pair, imperf. btwn.	15,000.	

All recorded unused examples of No. 45 are flawed.

Numerals 1½mm below Chinese characters

1897, May
Surcharged on Nos. 16-24

56	A5	½c on 3c org yel	550.00	375.00
57	A3	1c on 1c	375.00	300.00
58	A4	2c on 2c	175,000.	5,000.
59	A6	4c on 4c	300.00	250.00
60	A7	5c on 5c	400.00	300.00
61	A8	8c on 6c	1,600.	1,350.
62	A9	10c on 9c	375.00	250.00
63	A10	10c on 12c	1,750.	1,100.
64	A11	30c on 24c	75,000.	—

Same Surcharge on Nos. 16n-24n

65	A5	½c on 3c	25.00	30.00
a.		Inverted surcharge	4,500.	4,500.
b.		½mm spacing	3,500.	3,500.
66	A3	1c on 1c	40.00	25.00
67	A4	2c on 2c	35.00	17.50
a.		Inverted surcharge	25,500.	8,750.
b.		Vert. pair, imperf. btwn.		20,000.
68	A6	4c on 4c	300.00	200.00
a.		Inverted surcharge	3,500.	3,500.
69	A7	5c on 5c	300.00	225.00
70	A9	10c on 9c	225.00	110.00
a.		Inverted surcharge	4,000.	3,000.
71	A10	10c on 12c	400.00	190.00
72	A11	30c on 24c	13,000.	2,600.

Same Surcharge (1½mm Spacing) on Type A12, and

A12   A12a

Redrawn Designs
Printed from New Stones

1897

73	A12	½c on 3c yel	275.00	200.00
a.		½mm spacing	7,000.	5,000.
74	A12a	2c on 2c yel grn	75.00	35.00
a.		Horiz. pair, imperf. btwn.	10,000.	5,000.

Nos. 73 and 74 were surcharged on stamps printed from new stones, which differ slightly from the originals. On No. 73 the numeral "3" and symbols in the four corner panels have been enlarged and strengthened. On No. 74, the numeral "2" has a thick, flat base.

Surcharged on Nos. 13-15

75	A2	1c on 1c green	500.00	625.00
76	A2	2c on 3c lilac	1,000.	1,000.
77	A2	5c on 5c grnsh yel	350.00	500.00

Revenue Stamps Surcharged in Black

A13

a   one cent.

b   c

d   e

f   1 dollar.   g   1 dollar.

1897   Unwmk.   Perf. 12 to 15

78	A13 (a)	1c on 3c red	525.00	350.00
a.		No period after "cent"	600.00	400.00
b.		Central character with large "box"	625.00	550.00
79	A13 (b)	2c on 3c red	850.00	450.00
a.		Inverted surcharge	40,000.	30,000.
b.		Inverted "S" in "CENTS"	1,000.	600.00
c.		No period after "CENTS"	1,000.	600.00
d.		Comma after "CENTS"	950.00	550.00
e.		Double surcharge	80,000.	40,000.
f.		Dbl. surch., both inverted	100,000.	
g.		Double surch. (blk & grn)	220,000.	
80	A13 (c)	2c on 3c red	600.00	400.00
81	A13 (d)	4c on 3c red	100,000.	75,000.
a.		Double surcharge (blk & vio)	250,000.	250,000.
82	A13 (e)	4c on 3c red	1,650.	600.00
83	A13 (f)	$1 on 3c red	900,000.	—
a.		No period after "r"	—	
84	A13 (g)	$1 on 3c red	9,000.	3,500.
85	A13 (g)	$5 on 3c red	90,000.	60,000.
a.		Inverted surcharge	140,000.	100,000.

A few examples of the 3c red exist without surcharge; one canceled. Value, unused

$60,000. No. 79 with green surcharge is a trial printing. Value for faulty upper left corner block, $190,000.

No. 79g is unique. The only canceled example of No. 83 is in a museum.

Dragon — A14   Carp — A15

Wild Goose — A16

"Imperial Chinese Post"
Lithographed in Japan
Perf. 11, 11½, 12

1897, Aug. 16   Wmk. 103

86	A14	½c purple brn	5.50	4.50
a.		Horiz. pair, imperf. btwn.	800.00	
87	A14	1c yellow	7.00	4.00
88	A14	2c orange	6.50	3.75
a.		Vert. pair, imperf. horiz.	2,000.	
89	A14	4c brown	11.00	3.75
a.		Horiz. pair, imperf. btwn.	2,000.	
90	A14	5c rose red	14.00	5.00
91	A14	10c dk green	40.00	3.75
92	A15	20c maroon	85.00	19.00
93	A15	30c red	140.00	32.50
94	A15	50c yellow grn	100.00	45.00
a.		50c black green	1,750.	
b.		50c blue green	3,600.	
95	A16	$1 car & rose	325.00	200.00
a.		Horiz. pair, imperf. vert.	4,000.	
96	A16	$2 orange & yel	3,000.	1,400.
a.		Horiz. pair, imperf. vert.	15,000.	
97	A16	$5 yel grn & pink	1,800.	1,000.

The inner circular frames and outer frames of Nos. 86-91 differ for each denomination.

No. 97 imperforate was not regularly issued. **Examples have been privately perforated and offered as No. 97.** Shades occur in most values of this issue.

A17   A18

A19

"Chinese Imperial Post"
Engraved in London

1898   Wmk. 103   Perf. 12 to 16

98	A17	½c chocolate	6.00	2.75
a.		Vert. pair, imperf. btwn.	850.00	475.00
b.		Vert. pair, imperf. horiz.	850.00	475.00
99	A17	1c ocher	6.50	2.75
a.		Vert. pair, imperf. btwn.	300.00	250.00
b.		Horiz. pair, imperf. btwn.	400.00	350.00
100	A17	2c scarlet	8.00	2.75
a.		Vert. pair, imperf. btwn.	400.00	200.00
b.		Horiz. pair, imperf. vert.	400.00	200.00
101	A17	4c orange brn	7.50	2.75
a.		Vert. pair, imperf. btwn.	575.00	
b.		Horiz. pair, imperf. btwn.	500.00	300.00
c.		Horiz. pair, imperf. btwn.	700.00	600.00
d.		Horiz. strip of 3, imperf. btwn.	2,250.	1,500.
102	A17	5c salmon	11.00	4.00
a.		Vert. pair, imperf. btwn.	400.00	300.00
b.		Horiz. pair, imperf. btwn.	775.00	500.00
c.		Vert. pair, imperf. horiz.	600.00	500.00
d.		5c pale reddish orange	16.00	5.50
e.		As "d," vert pair, imperf.		
103	A17	10c dk blue grn	17.50	3.00
a.		Vert. or horiz, pair, imperf. btwn	600.00	500.00
104	A18	20c claret	70.00	9.00
a.		Horiz. pair, imperf. btwn.	850.00	750.00
b.		Vert. pair, imperf. horiz.	850.00	750.00
c.		Vert. pair, imperf. btwn.	900.00	800.00

105	A18	30c dull rose	60.00	15.00
a.		Horiz. pair, imperf. btwn.	2,000.	
b.		Vert. pair, imperf. horiz.	1,750.	
c.		Vert. pair, imperf. btwn.	1,750.	
106	A18	50c lt green	85.00	20.00
a.		Vert. pair, imperf. btwn.	2,250.	
107	A19	$1 red & pale rose	375.00	50.00
108	A19	$2 brn, red & yel	625.00	100.00
109	A19	$5 dp grn & sal	950.00	350.00
a.		Horiz. pair, imperf. btwn.	77,500.	
b.		Vert. pair, imperf. btwn.	20,000.	
		Nos. 98-109 (12)	2,222.	563.00

No. 98 surcharged "B. R. A.-5-Five Cents" in three lines in black or green, was surcharged by British military authorities shortly after the Boxer riots for use from military posts in an occupied area along the Peking-Mukden railway. Usually canceled in violet.
See note following No. 122.

1900(?)-06   Unwmk.   Perf. 12 to 16

110	A17	½c brown	4.00	2.75
a.		Horiz. pair, imperf. btwn.	400.00	400.00
b.		Vert. pair, imperf. btwn.	400.00	400.00
111	A17	1c ocher	4.25	2.75
a.		Horiz. pair, imperf. btwn.	350.00	350.00
b.		Vert. pair, imperf. btwn.	350.00	350.00
c.		Vert. pair, imperf. horiz.	350.00	350.00
112	A17	2c scarlet	6.25	2.75
a.		Horiz. pair, imperf. btwn.	300.00	325.00
b.		Vert. pair, imperf. btwn.	300.00	300.00
c.		Vert. pair, imperf. horiz.	300.00	300.00
d.		Horiz. pair, imperf. vert.	300.00	300.00
e.		Vert. strip of 3, imperf. btwn.	1,250.	750.00
113	A17	4c orange brn	6.00	3.25
a.		Horiz. pair, imperf. btwn.	300.00	300.00
b.		Vert. pair, imperf. btwn.	300.00	300.00
114	A17	5c rose red	30.00	5.00
a.		Horiz. pair, imperf. btwn.	300.00	300.00
b.		Vert. pair, imperf. horiz.	275.00	275.00
115	A17	5c orange	35.00	6.00
a.		5c yellow	200.00	27.50
b.		Vert. pair, imperf. btwn.	475.00	475.00
c.		Horiz. pair, imperf. btwn.	475.00	475.00
116	A17	10c green	20.00	2.75
a.		Vert. pair, imperf. btwn.	425.00	
b.		Horiz. pair, imperf. btwn.	725.00	
c.		Vert. pair, imperf. horiz.	425.00	
d.		Vert. strip of 3, imperf. btwn.	700.00	
117	A18	20c red brown	30.00	2.75
a.		Horiz. pair, imperf. btwn.	600.00	
b.		Vert. pair, imperf. btwn.	500.00	
c.		Vert. pair, imperf. horiz.	500.00	
118	A18	30c dull red	30.00	2.75
a.		Horiz. pair, imperf. btwn.	850.00	
119	A18	50c yellow grn	55.00	2.75
a.		Horiz. pair, imperf. btwn.	1,000.	
120	A19	$1 red & pale rose ('06)	175.00	27.50
121	A19	$2 brn red & yel ('06)	375.00	60.00
122	A19	$5 dp grn & sal ('06)	240.00	
		Nos. 110-122 (13)	1,371.	361.00

See No. 124-130. For surcharges and overprints see Nos. 123, 134-177, J1-J6, Offices in Tibet 1-11.

Diagonal Half of No. 112 Surcharged on Stamp and Envelope

1903

123	A17	1c on half of 2c scarlet, on cover		1,600.

Used Oct. 22 to Oct. 24. Value is for cover mailed to post office other than sending office (Foochow) and bearing backstamp showing arrival date. Locally addressed or unaddressed covers without backstamps properly used are worth approximately $1,000. Others are worth less.

Forgeries are plentiful, particularly on pieces of cover. Certificates of authenticity are mandatory.

1905-10

124	A17	2c green ('08)	3.25	3.25
a.		Horiz. pair, imperf. btwn.	325.00	325.00
b.		Vert. pair, imperf. btwn.	325.00	325.00
c.		Vert. pair, imperf. vert.	325.00	325.00
d.		Horiz. strip of 4, imperf. btwn.	800.00	800.00
125	A17	3c slate grn ('10)	5.00	2.50
a.		Horiz. pair, imperf. btwn.	250.00	
b.		Vert. pair, imperf. btwn.	250.00	
126	A17	4c vermilion ('09)	6.75	2.75
127	A17	5c violet	8.50	2.50
a.		5c lilac	10.00	2.75
b.		Horiz. pair, imperf. btwn.	.55000	
c.		Vert. pair, imperf. btwn.	1,000.	
d.		Vert. pair, imperf. horiz.	600.00	
128	A17	7c maroon ('10)	20.00	10.00
129	A17	10c ultra ('08)	25.00	2.75
a.		Horiz. pair, imperf. btwn.	400.00	
b.		Vert. pair, imperf. btwn.	400.00	
c.		Vert. pair, imperf. horiz.		400.00
130	A18	16c olive grn ('07)	60.00	17.50
		Nos. 124-130 (7)	128.50	41.25

Temple of
Heaven,
Peking — A20

1909 — Perf. 14

131	A20	2c orange & green	8.50	9.00
132	A20	3c orange & blue	10.00	17.50
133	A20	7c orange & brn vio	11.00	12.00
		Nos. 131-133 (3)	29.50	38.50

1st year of the reign of Hsuan T'ung, who later became Henry Pu-yi and then Emperor Kang Teh of Manchukuo.

Stamps of 1902-10 Overprinted with Chinese Characters
Foochow Issue

Overprinted in Red or Black

1912 — Perf. 12 to 16

134	A17	3c slate grn (R)	300.	160.
135	A19	$1 red & pale rose	3,000.	2,500.
136	A19	$2 brn red & yel	5,000.	3,500.
137	A19	$5 dp grn & sal	4,000.	4,000.

The overprint "Ling Shih Chung Li" or "Provisional Neutrality," signified that the P.O. was conducted neutrally by agreement between the Manchu and opposing forces.

Nanking Issue

Overprinted in Red or Black

138	A17	1c ocher (R)	275.	175.
139	A17	3c slate grn (R)	300.	175.
140	A17	7c maroon	550.	375.
141	A18	16c olive grn (R)	2,750.	2,500.
142	A18	50c yellow grn (R)	3,500.	2,250.
143	A19	$1 red & pale rose	3,750.	1,800.
144	A19	$2 brn red & yel	6,000.	4,400.
145	A19	$5 dp green & sal	12,750.	10,000.

Vertical overprint reads: "Chung Hwa Min Kuo" (Republic of China).
Stamps of this issue were also used in Shanghai and Hankow.
Additional values were overprinted but not issued. Excellent forgeries of the overprints of Nos. 134-145 exist.

Issues of the Republic

Overprinted in Black or Red

Overprinted by the Maritime Customs Statistical Department, Shanghai

146	A17	½c brown	1.50	1.25
a.		Inverted overprint	50.00	50.00
b.		Double overprint	100.00	
147	A17	1c ocher (R)	2.25	1.25
a.		Vert. pair, imperf. horiz.	200.00	200.00
b.		Inverted overprint	175.00	125.00
c.		Double overprint	200.00	175.00
d.		Horiz. pair, imperf. btwn.	300.00	250.00
e.		Horiz. pair, imperf. vert.	175.00	
f.		Pair, one without overprint	175.00	
148	A17	2c green (R)	2.50	1.75
a.		Vert. pair, imperf. btwn.	350.00	300.00
149	A17	3c slate grn (R)	3.00	1.50
a.		Inverted overprint	125.00	75.00
b.		Horiz.. pair, imperf. btwn.	300.00	300.00
c.		Vert. pair, imperf btwn.	300.00	300.00
d.		Horiz. pair, imperf. vert.	125.00	
e.		Horiz. strip of 3, imperf btwn.	450.00	
f.		Horiz. strip of 5, imperf btwn.	975.00	

150	A17	4c vermilion	4.75	1.75
a.		Vert. pair, imperf. btwn.	800.00	
151	A17	5c violet (R)	6.25	1.75
a.		Horiz. pair, imperf. btwn.		
152	A17	7c maroon	8.25	3.50
153	A17	10c ultra (R)	8.50	1.75
a.		Double overprint	250.00	
b.		Pair, one without overprint	900.00	
c.		Brownish red overprint	22.50	9.00
d.		Inverted overprint	275.00	275.00
154	A18	16c olive grn (R)	22.50	8.50
155	A18	20c red brown	19.00	5.00
156	A18	30c rose red	24.00	6.00
157	A18	50c yel grn (R)	40.00	6.00
158	A19	$1 red & pale rose	400.00	35.00
a.		Inverted overprint		27,500.
159	A19	$2 brn red & yel	350.00	75.00
a.		Inverted overprint	600.00	600.00
160	A19	$5 dp grn & sal	750.00	500.00
		Nos. 146-160 (15)	1,643.	650.00

Stamps with blue overprint similar to the preceding were not an official issue but were privately made by a printer in Tientsin.

Overprinted in Red

Overprinted by the Commercial Press, Shanghai.
This type differs in that the top character is shifted slightly to right and the bottom character is larger and has small "legs".

161	A17	1c ocher	7.00	2.00
a.		Inverted overprint	375.00	375.00
b.		Vert. pair, imperf. btwn.	450.00	
c.		Double overprint	450.00	
162	A17	2c green	37.50	3.50
a.		Inverted overprint	1,100.	900.00
b.		Vert. pair, imperf. btwn.	800.00	
c.		Horiz. pair, imperf. btwn.	700.00	
d.		Horiz. strip of 3, imperf. btwn.	850.00	

Overprinted in Blue, Carmine or Black

Overprinted by Waterlow & Sons, London

163	A17	½c brown (Bl)	2.50	2.00
a.		Vert. pair, imperf. btwn.	1,400.	1,275.
164	A17	1c ocher (Bl)	2.50	2.00
a.		Horiz. pair, imperf. btwn.	825.00	
165	A17	2c green (C)	3.25	2.00
166	A17	3c slate grn (C)	4.00	1.75
a.		Inverted overprint		1,750.
167	A17	4c vermilion (Bk)	5.00	2.25
168	A17	5c violet (C)	11.00	2.25
169	A17	7c maroon (Bk)	35.00	37.50
170	A17	10c ultra (C)	17.50	2.75
a.		Vert. pair, imperf. btwn.	1,500.	2,600.
171	A18	16c olive grn (R)	50.00	19.00
172	A18	20c red brn (Bk)	32.50	3.50
173	A18	30c dull red (Bk)	100.00	6.75
174	A18	50c yellow grn (R)	150.00	17.50
175	A19	$1 red & pale rose (Bk)	225.00	27.50
176	A19	$2 brn red & yel (Bk)	475.00	225.00
177	A19	$5 dp grn & sal (Bk)	750.00	525.00
		Nos. 163-177 (15)	1,863.	876.75

Due to instructions issued to postmasters throughout China at the time of the Revolution, a number of them prepared unauthorized overprints using the same characters as the overprints prepared by the government. While many were made in good faith, some, like the blue overprints from Tientsin, were bogus, and the status of certain others is extremely dubious.

Dr. Sun Yatsen — A21

1912, Dec. 14 — Perf. 14½

President Yuan Shih-kai — A22

178	A21	1c orange	4.75	3.25
179	A21	2c yellow grn	4.75	3.25
180	A21	3c slate grn	4.75	3.25
181	A21	5c rose lilac	9.50	3.25
182	A21	8c dp brown	9.50	5.00
183	A21	10c dull blue	9.50	5.00
184	A21	16c olive grn	27.50	17.50
185	A21	20c maroon	37.50	10.00
186	A21	50c dk green	100.00	40.00
187	A21	$1 brown red	260.00	60.00
188	A21	$2 yellow brn	750.00	300.00
189	A21	$5 gray	275.00	225.00
		Nos. 178-189 (12)	1,493.	675.50

Honoring the leader of the Revolution.

1912, Dec. 14

190	A22	1c orange	3.00	1.75
191	A22	2c yellow green	3.00	1.75
192	A22	3c slate green	3.00	1.75
193	A22	5c rose lilac	3.75	2.00
194	A22	8c deep brown	11.50	4.00
195	A22	10c dull blue	9.50	2.50
196	A22	16c olive green	10.00	12.00
197	A22	20c maroon	9.00	10.00
198	A22	50c dark green	55.00	35.00
199	A22	$1 brown red	175.00	60.00
200	A22	$2 yellow brown	225.00	75.00
201	A22	$5 gray	675.00	325.00
		Nos. 190-201 (12)	1,183.	530.75

Honoring the 1st pres. of the Republic.

Junk — A24

Reaping Rice — A25

Gateway, Hall of Classics, Peking — A26

DESIGN A24
London Printing: Vertical shading lines under top panel fine, junk with clear diagonal shading lines on sails, right pennant of junk usually long, lines in water weak except directly under junk.
Peking Printing: Vertical shading lines under top panel and inner vertical frame line much heavier, water and sails of junk more evenly and strongly colored, white wave over "H" of "CHINA" pointed upward, touching the junk.

DESIGN A25
London: Front hat brim thick and nearly straight, left foot touches shadow.

Peking: Front hat brim thin and strongly upturned, left foot and sickle clearly outlined in white, shadow of middle tree lighter than those of the right and left trees.

DESIGN A26
London: Light colored walk clearly defined almost to the doorway, figure in right doorway "T" shaped with strong horizontal cross-bar, white panel in base of central tower rectangular, vertical stroke in top left character uniformly thick at its base, tree to right of doorway ends in minute dots.
Peking: Walk more heavily shaded near doorway, especially at right; figure in right doorway more like a "Y", white panel at base of central tower is a long oval, right vertical stroke in top left character incurved near its base, tree at right has five prominent dots at top.

London Printing: By Waterlow & Sons, London, perf. 14 to 15.
Peking Printing: By the Chinese Bureau of Engraving and Printing, Peking, perf. 14.

London Printing

1913, May 5 — Perf. 14-15

202	A24	½c black brn	.75	.40
a.		Horiz. or vert. pair, imperf. btwn.	200.00	
203	A24	1c orange	.75	.40
a.		Horiz. pair, imperf. btwn.	250.00	
b.		Vert. pair, imperf. btwn.	175.00	
c.		Horiz. strip of 5, imperf. btwn	650.00	
204	A24	2c yellow grn	2.75	.40
a.		Horiz. pair, imperf. btwn.	400.00	
205	A24	3c blue grn	6.75	.45
a.		Horiz. pair, imperf. btwn.	200.00	
b.		Vert. pair, imperf. btwn.		400.00
206	A24	4c scarlet	9.50	.70
207	A24	5c rose lilac	30.00	.60
208	A24	6c gray	5.00	.90
209	A24	7c violet	22.50	8.75
210	A24	8c brown org	42.50	2.50
211	A24	10c dk blue	37.50	1.10
a.		Horiz. pair, imperf. btwn.	375.00	375.00
b.		Vert. pair, imperf. btwn.	400.00	300.00
212	A25	15c brown	32.50	5.75
213	A25	16c olive grn	17.50	2.25
214	A25	20c brown red	30.00	2.75
215	A25	30c brown vio	32.50	2.00
a.		Horiz. pair, imperf. btwn.	400.00	400.00
216	A25	50c green	60.00	3.50
217	A26	$1 ocher & blk	175.00	3.00
218	A26	$2 blue & blk	275.00	19.00
219	A26	$5 scarlet & blk	550.00	125.00
220	A26	$10 yel grn & blk	1,500.	950.00
		Nos. 202-220 (19)	2,831.	1,129.

First Peking Printing

1915 — Perf. 14

221	A24	½c black brn	.80	.35
222	A24	1c orange	.80	.35
223	A24	2c yellow grn	1.60	.35
224	A24	3c blue grn	1.75	.35
225	A24	4c scarlet	20.00	.35
226	A24	5c rose lilac	8.50	.35
a.		Booklet pane of 4	140.00	
227	A24	6c gray	16.00	.35
228	A24	7c violet	25.00	4.50
229	A24	8c brown org	14.00	.40
230	A24	10c dk blue	15.00	.70
a.		Booklet pane of 4	140.00	

231	A25	15c brown	42.50	4.50
232	A25	16c olive grn	17.50	.70
233	A25	20c brown red	18.50	.70
234	A25	30c brown vio	17.50	.70
235	A25	50c green	42.50	.80
236	A26	$1 ocher & blk	140.00	.85
237	A26	$2 blue & blk	350.00	5.00
a.		Center inverted	200,000.	—
238	A26	$5 scarlet & blk	800.00	40.00
239	A26	$10 yel grn & blk	1,100.	275.00
		Nos. 221-239 (19)	2,632.	336.30

1919

240	A24	1½c violet	3.75	.60
241	A24	13c brown	9.50	.70
242	A26	$20 yellow & blk	4,900.	3,250.

Nos. 226 and 230 overprinted in red with five characters in vertical column were for postal savings use.

The higher values of the 1913-19 issues are often overprinted with Chinese characters, which are the names of various postal districts. Stamps were frequently stolen while in transit to post offices. The overprints served to protect them, since the stamps could only be used in the districts for which they were overprinted.

Compare designs A24-A26 with designs A29-A31. For surcharges and overprints see Nos. 247, 288, B1-B3, Sinkiang 1-38.

Yeh Kung-cho, Hsu Shi-chang and Chin Yun-peng A27

1921, Oct. 10

243	A27	1c orange	6.00	1.75
244	A27	3c blue green	6.50	1.50
245	A27	6c gray	7.50	5.00
246	A27	10c blue	8.50	4.00
		Nos. 243-246 (4)	28.50	12.25

National Post Office, 25th anniversary.
For overprints see Sinkiang Nos. 39-42.

No. 224 Surcharged in Red

1922

247	A24	2c on 3c blue green	3.50	.70
a.		Inverted surcharge	175,000.	—

Second Peking Printing

A29   A30

A31

Types of 1913-19 Issues Re-engraved

Type A29: Most of the whitecaps in front of the junk have been removed and the water made darker. The shading lines have been removed from the arabesques and pearls above the top inscription. The inner shadings at the top and sides of the picture have been cut away.

Type A30: The heads of rice in the side panels have a background of crossed lines instead of horizontal lines. The Temple of Heaven is strongly shaded and has a door. There are rows of pearls below the Chinese characters in the upper corners. The arabesques above the top inscription have been altered and are without shading lines.

Type A31: The curved line under the inscription at top is single instead of double. There are four vertical lines, instead of eight, at each side of the picture. The trees at the sides of the temple had foliage in the 1913-19 issues, but now the branches are bare. There are numerous other alterations in the design.

1923   *Perf. 14*

248	A29	½c black brown	1.75	.30
a.		Horiz. pair, imperf. btwn.	175.00	175.00
b.		Horiz. pair, imperf. vert.	150.00	150.00
249	A29	1c orange	1.00	.30
a.		Imperf., pair	125.00	
b.		Horiz. pair, imperf. vert.	125.00	
c.		Booklet pane of 6	90.00	
d.		Booklet pane of 4	45.00	
250	A29	1½c violet	3.50	.90
251	A29	2c yellow grn	2.00	.30
252	A29	3c blue green	6.00	.30
a.		Booklet pane of 6	80.00	
253	A29	4c gray	27.50	.80
254	A29	5c claret	4.00	.50
a.		Booklet pane of 4	100.00	
255	A29	6c scarlet	8.50	.50
256	A29	7c violet	8.50	.50
257	A29	8c orange	17.50	.50
258	A29	10c blue	14.50	.30
a.		Booklet pane of 6	120.00	
b.		Booklet pane of 2	150.00	
259	A30	13c brown	32.50	.60
260	A30	15c dp blue	10.00	.60
261	A30	16c olive grn	11.00	.60
262	A30	20c brown red	8.50	.40
263	A30	30c purple	32.50	.40
264	A30	50c dp green	60.00	.55
265	A31	$1 org brn & sep	65.00	.65
266	A31	$2 blue & red brn	85.00	1.00
267	A31	$5 red & slate	140.00	4.25
268	A31	$10 green & claret	700.00	70.00
269	A31	$20 plum & blue	1,450.	200.00
		Nos. 248-269 (22)	2,689.	284.25

Nos. 249 and 275 exist with webbing watermark from experimental printing.

To prevent speculation and theft, the dollar denominations were overprinted with single characters in red for use in Kwangsi ($1-$20) and Kweichow ($1-$5).

See Nos. 275, 324. For surcharges and overprints see Nos. 274, 289, 311, 325, 330, 339-340, Szechwan 1-3, Yunnan 1-20, Manchuria 1-20, Sinkiang 47-69, 114, C1-C4.

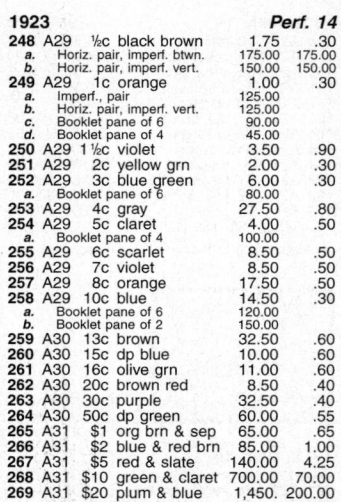

Temple of Heaven, Peking — A32

1923, Oct. 17   *Perf. 14*

270	A32	1c orange	5.00	1.00
271	A32	3c blue green	5.50	2.25
272	A32	4c red	10.50	2.50
273	A32	10c blue	16.50	3.50
		Nos. 270-273 (4)	37.50	9.25

Adoption of Constitution, October, 1923.
For overprints see Sinkiang Nos. 43-46.

No. 253 Surcharged in Red

1925

274	A29	3c on 4c gray	3.50	.35
a.		Inverted surcharge	300,000.	275,000.
b.		Vert. pair, imperf. btwn.		

Junk Type of 1923

1926

275	A29	4c olive green	1.60	.25
a.		Horiz. pair, imperf. vert.	200.00	
b.		Horiz. pair, imperf. btwn.	200.00	
c.		Horiz. strip of 3, imperf. btwn.	250.00	

Marshal Chang Tso-lin — A34

1928, Mar. 1   *Perf. 14*

276	A34	1c brown orange	1.50	1.50
277	A34	4c olive green	3.00	3.00
278	A34	10c dull blue	7.50	5.00
279	A34	$1 red	60.00	65.00
		Nos. 276-279 (4)	72.00	75.00

Assumption of office by Marshal Chang Tso-lin. The stamps of this issue were only available for postage in the Provinces of Chihli and Shantung and at the Offices in Manchuria and Sinkiang.

For overprints see Manchuria Nos. 21-24, Sinkiang 70-73.

President Chiang Kai-shek — A35

1929, May

280	A35	1c brown orange	1.00	.40
281	A35	4c olive green	1.50	.75
282	A35	10c dark blue	12.50	1.50
283	A35	$1 dark red	75.00	55.00
		Nos. 280-283 (4)	90.00	57.65

Unification of China.
For overprints see Yunnan Nos. 21-24, Manchuria 25-28, Sinkiang 74-77.

Sun Yat-sen Mausoleum, Nanking — A36

1929, May 30   *Perf. 14*

284	A36	1c brown orange	1.25	.75
285	A36	4c olive green	1.00	1.25
286	A36	10c dark blue	9.00	2.50
287	A36	$1 dark red	75.00	35.00
		Nos. 284-287 (4)	86.25	39.50

The transfer of Dr. Sun Yat-sen's remains from Peiping to the mausoleum at Nanking.
For overprints see Yunnan Nos. 25-28, Manchuria 29-32, Sinkiang 78-81.

Nos. 224 and 252 Surcharged in Red

1930

288	A24	1c on 3c blue green	1.25	2.25
289	A29	1c on 3c blue green	1.00	.40
a.		No period after "Ct"	18.00	18.00
		See Nos. 311, 325, 330.		

Dr. Sun Yat-sen — A37

Type I   Type II

Type I — Double-lined circle in the sun.
Type II — Heavy, single-lined circle in the sun.

Printed by De la Rue & Co., Ltd., London

Perf. 11½x12½, 12½x13, 12½, 13½

1931, Nov. 12   Type I   Engr.

290	A37	1c orange	.55	.30
291	A37	2c olive green	.65	.40
292	A37	4c green	1.10	.30
293	A37	20c ultra	1.40	.30
294	A37	$1 org brn & dk brn	12.00	.50
295	A37	$2 blue & org brn	35.00	3.00
296	A37	$5 dull red & blk	50.00	5.00
		Nos. 290-296 (7)	100.70	9.80

1931-37   **Type II**

297	A37	2c olive grn	.45	.25
298	A37	4c green	.65	.25
299	A37	5c green ('33)	.40	.25
300	A37	15c dk green	4.25	1.25
301	A37	15c scarlet ('34)	.45	.25
302	A37	20c ultra ('37)	.85	.25
303	A37	25c ultra	.45	.65
304	A37	$1 org brn & dk brn	14.00	.50
305	A37	$2 blue & org brn	25.00	1.25
306	A37	$5 dull red & blk	47.50	5.00
		Nos. 297-306 (10)	94.00	9.90

Stamps issued prior to 1933 were printed by a wet-paper process, and owing to shrinkage such stamps are 1-1½mm narrower than the later dry-printed stamps.

Early printings are perf. 12½x13. Nos. 304, 305 and 306 were later perf. 11½x12½.

See Nos. 631-635. For surcharges and overprints see Nos. 341, 343, 678, 682, 684-685, 689-691, 768, 843, 1N1, 2N1-2N5, 2N57-2N59, 2N83-2N84, 2N101-2N103, 2N116, 2N124-2N126, 3N1-3N5, 4N1-4N5, 5N1-5N4, 6N1-6N5, 7N1-7N4, 7N54, 8N2-8N3, 8N43-8N44, 8N54, 8N57, 8N69-8N71, 8N85, 9N1-9N5, Taiwan 19, 21-22, Northeastern Provinces 44, Szechwan 4-11, Yunnan 29-44, Sinkiang 82-97.

"Nomads in the Desert" — A38

1932   **Unwmk.**   *Perf. 14*

307	A38	1c deep orange	29.00	29.00
308	A38	4c olive green	29.00	29.00
309	A38	5c claret	29.00	29.00
310	A38	10c deep blue	29.00	29.00
		Nos. 307-310 (4)	116.00	116.00

Northwest Scientific Expedition of Sven Hedin. A small quantity of this issue was sold at face at Peking and several other cities. The bulk of the issue was furnished to Hedin and sold at $5 (Chinese) a set for funds to finance the expedition.

No. 252 Surcharged in Black Like 288

1932

311	A29	1c on 3c blue green	2.50	1.10

Martyrs Issue

Teng Keng   Ch'en Ying-shih
A39   A40

Chu Chih-hsin   Sung Chiao-jen
A45   A46

Huang Hsing   Liao Chung-kai
A47   A48

1932-34   *Perf. 14*

312	A39	½c black brown	.25	.25
313	A40	1c orange ('34)	.25	.25
314	A39	2½c rose lilac ('33)	.25	.25
315	A48	3c dp brown ('33)	.25	.25
316	A45	8c brown orange	.50	.30
317	A46	10c dull violet	.60	.30
318	A45	13c blue green	.65	.30
319	A40	17c brown olive	.55	.30
320	A47	20c brown red	1.10	.30
321	A48	30c brown violet	1.50	.30
322	A47	40c orange	1.40	.35
323	A40	50c green ('34)	3.00	.60
		Nos. 312-323 (12)	12.30	3.65

Perfs. 12 to 13 and compound and with secret marks are listed as Nos. 402-439. No. 316 re-drawn is No. 485.

For overprints and surcharge see Nos. 342, 472, 474, 478-479, 486-487, 490, 531-536, 539-541, 544-549, 616, 619, 622-624, 647-659, 662-663, 665, 669, 672, 698, 704, 711, 713-715, 720-721, 831, 846-847, 867, 870,

Marshal Chang Tso-lin — A34

872, 881-882, J120-J121, 1N14-1N15, 1N59, 2N6-2N9, 2N32-2N56, 2N60, 2N76-2N82, 2N85, 2N87-2N90, 2N107-2N115, 2N118, 2N121-2N123, 3N6-3N10, 3N34-3N55, 3N59, 4N6-4N9, 4N39-4N64, 4N69, 5N5-5N8, 5N34-5N60, 5N65, 6N6-6N8, 6N35-6N61, 6N66, 7N5-7N7, 7N30-7N53, 7N55, 7N59, 8N1, 8N4, 8N28-8N42, 8N45, 8N47-8N50, 8N60-8N61, 8N68, 8N73, 8N76-8N79, 8N89, 8N97, 8N99-8N100, 8N103-8N104, 9N72-9N77, Taiwan 14-17, 20, 28A, 74, Northeastern Provinces 6-8, 11, Szechwan 12-23, Yunnan 49-60, Sinkiang 102-113, 140-161, 197.

Junk Type of 1923

1933			Perf. 14	
324	A29	6c brown	20.00	1.25

No. 275 Surcharged in Red Like 288

1933				
325	A29	1c on 4c olive green	1.75	.35
a.		No period after "Ct"	21.00	21.00

Tan Yuan-chang — A49

1933, Jan. 9				
326	A49	2c olive green	2.50	1.25
327	A49	5c green	4.00	.40
328	A49	25c ultra	10.00	1.75
329	A49	$1 red	72.50	35.00
		Nos. 326-329 (4)	89.00	38.40

Tan Yuan-chang, more commonly known as Tan Yen-kai, a prominent statesman in China since the revolution of 1912 and Pres. of the Executive Dept. of the Natl. Government. Placed on sale Jan. 9, 1933, the date of the ceremony in celebration of the completion of the Tan Yuan-chang Memorial Hall and Tomb at Mukden.

For overprints see Yunnan Nos. 45-48, Sinkiang 98-101.

No. 251 Surcharged in Red Like 288

1935			Perf. 14	
330	A29	1c on 2c yellow grn	2.50	.25

Emblem of New Life Movement A50   Four Virtues of New Life A51

Lighthouse — A52

1936, Jan. 1				
331	A50	2c olive green	1.75	.75
332	A50	5c green	2.00	.25
333	A51	20c dark blue	6.00	.70
334	A52	$1 rose red	40.00	11.00
		Nos. 331-334 (4)	49.75	12.70

"New Life" movement.

Methods of Mail Transportation A53

Maritime Scene — A54

Shanghai General Post Office — A55

Ministry of Communications, Nanking — A56

1936, Oct. 10				
335	A53	2c orange	3.00	.70
336	A54	5c green	1.50	.25
337	A55	25c blue	5.00	.80
338	A56	$1 dk carmine	30.00	9.00
		Nos. 335-338 (4)	39.50	10.45

Founding of the Chinese PO, 40th anniv.

Nos. 260 and 261 Surcharged in Red

1936, Oct. 11				
339	A30	5c on 15c dp blue	1.75	.50
340	A30	5c on 16c olive grn	3.00	1.00

No. 298 Surcharged in Red

1937				
341	A37	1c on 4c green, type II	1.25	.50
a.		Upper left character missing		

Nos. 322 and 303 Surcharged in Black or Red

1938			Perf. 12½, 14	
342	A47	8c on 40c orange (Bk)	2.00	.75
343	A37	10c on 25c ultra (R)	1.75	.30

Dr. Sun Yat-sen — A57

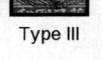

Type I   Type II   Type III

Type I — Coat button half circle. Six lines of shading above head. Top frame partially shaded with vertical lines.

Type II — Coat button complete circle. Nine lines of shading above head. Top frame partially shaded with vertical lines.

Type III — Coat button complete circle. Nine lines of shading above head. Top frame line fully shaded with vertical lines.

Printed by the Chung Hwa Book Co.

Type I

1938	Unwmk.	Engr.	Perf. 12½	
344	A57	$1 henna & dk brn	85.00	12.00
345	A57	$2 dp blue & org brn	17.50	4.25
346	A57	$5 red & grnsh blk	150.00	19.00
		Nos. 344-346 (3)	252.50	35.25

1939			Type II	
347	A57	$1 henna & dk brn	16.00	1.00
348	A57	$2 dp blue & org brn	18.00	4.00

1939-43			Type III	
349	A57	2c olive green	.25	.25
350	A57	3c dull claret	.25	.25
351	A57	5c green	.25	.25
352	A57	5c olive green	.25	.25
353	A57	8c olive green	.25	.25
354	A57	10c green	.25	.25
355	A57	15c scarlet	1.25	2.25
356	A57	15c dk vio brn ('43)	17.50	32.50
357	A57	16c olive gray	1.75	.45
358	A57	25c dk blue	.35	.75
359	A57	$1 henna & dk brn	2.00	.75
360	A57	$2 dp blue & org brn	4.50	.55
a.		Imperf., pair	300.00	
361	A57	$5 red & grnsh blk	2.75	.50
362	A57	$10 dk green & dull pur	17.50	2.25
363	A57	$20 rose lake & dk blue	60.00	50.00
		Nos. 349-363 (15)	109.10	91.50

Several values exist imperforate, but these were not regularly issued. No. 361 imperforate is printer's waste.

See Nos. 368-401, 506-524. For surcharges and overprints see Nos. 440-448, 473, 475-477, 480-481, 482-484, 489, 537-538, 615, 618, 620, 660-661, 664, 666-668, 673-676, 680-681, 686, 688, 699-703, 707-709, 717, 719, 830, J67-J68, M2, M11-M12, 1N2-1N13, 1N23-1N42, 1N57-1N58, 2N2-2N31, 2N61-2N75, 2N86, 2N91-2N93, 2N117, 2N119-2N120, 3N11-3N33, 3N56-3N58, 3N60-3N61, 4N10-4N38, 4N65-4N68, 4N70-4N71, 5N9-5N33, 5N61-5N64, 5N66-5N68, 6N9-6N34, 6N62-6N65, 6N67-6N69, 7N8-7N29, 7N56-7N58, 7N60-7N61, 8N5-8N27, 8N46, 8N51-8N53, 8N55-8N56, 8N58-8N59, 8N62-8N67, 8N72, 8N74-8N75, 8N80-8N84, 8N86-8N88, 8N90, 8N95-8N96, 8N98, 8N101-8N102, 8N105-8N106, 9N6-9N71, 9N97, 9N99, Taiwan 78, 84, Northeastern Provinces 9-10, Sinkiang 115-139, 174-188, 196, 198.

Chinese and American Flags and Map of China — A58

Printed by American Bank Note Co.
Frame Engr., Center Litho.

1939, July 4	Unwmk.		Perf. 12	
Flag in Deep Rose and Ultramarine				
364	A58	5c dark green	1.75	.50
365	A58	25c deep blue	1.75	.90
366	A58	50c brown	4.00	1.10
367	A58	$1 rose carmine	6.50	2.25
		Nos. 364-367 (4)	14.00	4.75

150th anniv. of the US Constitution.

Type of 1939-41 Re-engraved

2c, 1939-41   Re-engraved

8c, 1939-41   Re-engraved

1940			Perf. 12½	
368	A57	2c olive green	.25	.25
369	A57	8c olive green	.25	.25

Type of 1938-41
Type III

1940	Unwmk.		Perf. 14	
370	A57	2c olive green	2.50	1.00
371	A57	5c green	5.00	2.10
372	A57	$1 henna & dk brn	110.00	22.50
373	A57	$2 dp blue & org brn	21.00	5.00
374	A57	$5 red & grnsh blk	26.00	16.50
375	A57	$10 dk green & dull pur	72.50	12.50
		Nos. 370-375 (6)	237.00	59.60

See surcharge note following No. 363.

Type of 1939-41

1940	Wmk. 261		Perf. 12½	
			Type III	
376	A57	$1 henna & dk brn	7.00	9.00
377	A57	$2 dp blue & org brn	9.00	9.00
378	A57	$5 red & grnsh blk	10.00	18.00
379	A57	$10 dk green & dull pur	15.00	30.00
380	A57	$20 rose lake & dp blue	19.00	30.00
		Nos. 376-380 (5)	60.00	96.00

See surcharge note following No. 363.

Printed by the Dah Tung Book Co.
Five Cent

Type III - Characters joined

Secret Mark - Characters not joined

Eight Cent

Type III - Characters not joined

Secret Mark - Characters joined

Ten Cent

Type III - Characters sharp and well shaped

Secret Mark - Characters coarse and varying in thickness

Dollar Values

Type III

Secret Mark

1940   Unwmk.   Perf. 14
Type III with Secret Marks

381	A57	5c green	.25	.25
382	A57	5c olive green	.25	.25
383	A57	8c olive green	.40	.25
a.		Without "star" in uniform button	1.50	2.50
384	A57	10c green	.25	.25
385	A57	30c scarlet	.35	.25
386	A57	50c dk blue	.45	.25
387	A57	$1 org brn & sepia	2.50	.25
388	A57	$2 dp blue & yel brn	1.00	.35
389	A57	$5 red & slate grn	1.00	.45
390	A57	$10 dk grn & dull pur	4.00	2.25
391	A57	$20 rose lake & dk blue	12.00	3.50
		Nos. 381-391 (11)	22.45	8.30

Type III with Secret Marks

1940   Wmk. 261   Perf. 14

392	A57	5c green	.25	.25
393	A57	5c olive green	.25	.25
394	A57	10c green	.35	.25
395	A57	30c scarlet	.25	.25
396	A57	50c dk blue	.55	.25
397	A57	$1 org brn & sepia	4.50	2.75
398	A57	$2 dp blue & yel brn	12.50	13.00
399	A57	$5 red & slate grn	11.50	12.00
400	A57	$10 dk grn & dull pur	16.00	17.00
401	A57	$20 rose lake & dk blue	25.00	20.00
		Nos. 392-401 (10)	71.15	66.00

Nos. 383, 384, 385, 397, 400 and 401 exist perf. 12½, but were not issued with this perforation.

See surcharge note following No. 363.

Types of 1932-34 Martyrs Issue with Secret Mark

1932-34 Issue. In the left Chinese character in bottom row, the two parts are not joined.

Secret Mark, 1940-41 Issue. The two parts are joined

Perf. 12½, 13 and Compound
1940-41   Wmk. 261

402	A39	½c olive blk	.25	.25
403	A40	1c orange	.25	.25
404	A46	2c dp blue ('41)	.25	.25
405	A39	2½c rose lilac	.25	.25
406	A48	3c dp yellow brn	.30	.25
407	A39	4c pale vio ('41)	.30	.25
408	A48	5c dull red org ('41)	.30	.25
409	A45	8c dp orange	.25	.25
410	A45	10c dull violet	.25	.25
411	A45	13c dp yellow grn	.35	.25
412	A46	15c brown car	.25	.25
413	A46	17c brown olive	.25	.25
414	A47	20c lt blue	.25	.25
415	A45	21c olive brn ('41)	1.10	1.25
416	A40	25c red vio ('41)	.25	.25
417	A40	28c olive ('41)	.30	.25
418	A48	30c brown car	.45	.25
a.		Vert. pair, imperf. btwn.	140.00	
419	A47	40c orange	.25	.25
420	A40	50c green	.30	.25

Unwmk.

421	A39	½c olive black	.25	.25
422	A40	1c orange	.25	.25
a.		Without secret mark	2.75	2.75
b.		Horiz. pair, imperf. vert.	110.00	
423	A46	2c dp blue	.25	.25
a.		Vert. pair, imperf. horiz.	100.00	
b.		Horiz. pair, imperf. between	160.00	
424	A39	2½c rose lilac	.25	.25
425	A48	3c dp yellow brn	.25	.25
426	A39	4c pale violet	.25	.25
427	A48	5c dull red org	.25	.25
428	A45	8c dp orange	.25	.25
429	A46	10c dull violet	3.25	.40
430	A45	13c dp yel grn	.25	.65
431	A48	15c brown car	.35	.60
432	A46	17c brn olive	.40	.25
433	A47	20c lt blue	.30	.25
a.		Vert. pair, imperf. horiz.	125.00	
b.		Horiz. pair, imperf. vert.	125.00	
434	A45	21c olive brn	.50	.35
435	A40	25c rose vio	.50	.50
436	A46	28c olive	.70	.50
437	A48	30c brown car	2.50	2.50
438	A47	40c orange	.35	.35
439	A40	50c green	3.50	.40
		Nos. 402-439 (38)	20.65	14.50

Several values exist imperforate, but they were not regularly issued.
Used values are for favor cancels. Postally used examples sell for more.
See surcharge note following No. 323.

Regional Surcharges.

The regional surcharges, Nos. 440-448, 482-484, 486-491, 525-549, have been listed according to the basic stamps, with black or red surcharges. The surcharges of the individual provinces, plus Hong Kong and Shanghai, are noted in small type. The numeral following each letter is the surcharge denomination. These surcharges are identified by the following letters:

a — Hong Kong	i — Kwangsi
b — Shanghai	j — Kwangtung
bx — Anhwei	k — Western Szechwan
c — Hunan	l — Yunnan
d — Kansu	m — Honan
e — Kiangsi	n — Shensi
f — Eastern Szechwan	o — Kweichow
g — Chekiang	p — Hupeh
h — Fukien	

Regional Surcharges on Stamps of 1939-40

Hong Kong — a4

Shanghai — b3

Hunan — c3

Kansu — d3

Kiangsi — e3

Eastern Szechwan — f3

Chekiang — g3

1940-41   Unwmk.   Perf. 12½, 14
Carmine Surcharge

440	A57	4c on 5c ol grn (#382)	.60	.60
r.		Lower right character duplicated at left	30.00	32.50

Black Surcharge

441	A57	3c on 5c grn (#351) (b3)	1.25	1.40
442	A57	3c on 5c ol grn (#352) (c3, d3)	.65	2.00
443	A57	3c on 5c grn (#381) (b3)	.60	1.25
444	A57	3c on 5c ol grn (#382) (e3)	.70	1.00
r.		Lower left character duplicated at right (Kiangsi)	42.50	42.50
		(b3) Shanghai	.65	1.40
		(f3) Eastern Szechwan	.65	1.60

The Kansu surcharges of No. 442 are of 6 types. Differences include formation of top part of fen character (at left of "3"), fen with low right hook, height of "3" (5-4mm), space between upper and lower characters (6-9mm), etc.

1940-41   Wmk. 261   Perf. 14

445	A57	3c on 5c grn (#392) (e3)	.60	1.40
r.		Lower left character duplicated at left (Kiangsi)	35.00	35.00
		(b3, c3) Shanghai, Hunan	.60	1.60
446	A57	3c on 5c grn (#393) (f3)	.70	1.75
		(b3) Shanghai	.95	1.75
r.		Lower right character duplicated at right (f3)	60.00	65.00

Red Surcharge

447	A57	3c on 5c grn (#392) (g3)	1.25	3.25
448	A57	3c on 5c ol grn (#393) (g3)	6.00	6.00

Dr. Sun Yat-sen — A59

Printed by American Bank Note Co.

1941   Unwmk.   Engr.   Perf. 12

449	A59	½c sepia	.25	.30
450	A59	1c orange	.25	.25
451	A59	2c brt ultra	.25	.25
452	A59	5c green	.25	.25
453	A59	8c red orange	.60	.70
454	A59	8c turq green	.30	.25
455	A59	10c brt green	.25	.25
456	A59	17c olive	4.50	12.00
457	A59	25c rose violet	.30	1.00
458	A59	30c scarlet	.35	.25

459	A59	50c dk blue	.50	.25
460	A59	$1 brown & blk	.60	.25
461	A59	$2 blue & blk	.75	.25
a.		Center inverted	180,000.	
462	A59	$5 scarlet & blk	1.75	.65
463	A59	$10 green & blk	5.00	2.75
464	A59	$20 rose vio & blk	4.00	6.00
		Nos. 449-464 (16)	19.90	25.65

For surcharges see Nos. 488, 491, 542-543, 617, 621, 670, 677, 687, 705-706, 712, 716, 718, M1, M3-M4, 1N16-1N22, 1N43-1N56, 9N78-9N96, 9N98, 9N100.

Industry and Agriculture — A60

1941, June 21   Perf. 12½

465	A60	8c green	.50	.50
466	A60	21c red brown	.65	.65
467	A60	28c dk olive grn	.85	.85
468	A60	33c vermilion	1.10	1.50
469	A60	50c dp ultra	1.25	1.25
470	A60	$1 dk violet	1.75	1.75
		Nos. 465-470 (6)	6.10	6.50

Souvenir Sheet
Imperf
Typo.

471		Sheet of 6	70.00	70.00
a.	A60	8c dull green	6.50	6.50
b.	A60	21c dark orange brown	6.50	6.50
c.	A60	28c dull yellow green	6.50	6.50
d.	A60	33c red	6.50	6.50
e.	A60	50c dull blue	6.50	6.50
f.	A60	$1 dark violet	6.50	6.50

The Thrift Movement and its aim to "Save for Reconstruction."
Issued in sheets measuring 155x171mm, without gum.
This sheet exists with additional blue marginal overprints in Russian, French and Chinese reading "Souvenir of the Exhibition of the Russian Philatelic Society in China, Shanghai, China, Feb. 28, 1943." Value, $800.
The overprinting was applied by the society, and when so overprinted this sheet had no franking power.

Stamps of 1939-41 Overprinted in Carmine or Blue

1941, Oct. 10   Perf. 12½, 14, 13

472	A40	1c dull orange	.25	.60
473	A57	2c olive grn (C)	.25	.60
474	A39	4c pale violet (C)	.25	.60
475	A57	8c ol grn (#369) (C)	.25	.60
476	A57	10c green (#354) (C)	.25	.60
477	A57	16c ol gray (#357) (C)	.25	.60
478	A45	21c olive brn (C)	.25	.60
479	A46	28c olive (C)	.60	1.65
480	A57	30c scarlet	1.00	3.25
481	A57	$1 hn & dk brn (#359) (C)	4.00	4.00
		Nos. 472-481 (10)	7.35	13.10

Chinese Republic, 30th anniversary.

Kiangsi — e7

Eastern Szechwan — f7

Chekiang — g7

Fukien — h7

1941   Unwmk.   Perf. 12½, 14

482	A57	7c on 8c (#353) (g7, h7)	1.00	1.10
483	A57	7c on 8c (#369) (f7)	1.00	.55

484	A57	7c on 8c (#383) (h7)	1.00	.90

(e7)	Kiangsi	1.00	1.00
(g7)	Chekiang	1.00	1.10
r.	Without "star" in uniform button	70.00	

Type of 1932-34 Re-engraved

1941   Unwmk.   Perf. 14

485	A45	8c deep orange	13.00	57.50

The original stamps are 19½mm wide, the re-engraved 21mm.

Eleven other values of the Martyrs Issue and types A37 and A57 exist re-engraved, but were not issued.

Hunan — c1

Kiangsi — e1

Fukien — h1

Kwangsi — i1

Kwangtung — j1

1942   Red Surcharge

486	A39	1c on ½c blk brn (#312) (i1)	1.00	1.75
(c1)	Hunan		2.00	2.75
487	A39	1c on ½c ol blk (#421) (e1)	.75	1.60
(c1)	Hunan		.85	2.00
(i1)	Kwangsi		1.65	2.50
(h1)	Fukien		6.00	9.50
488	A59	1c on ½c sepia (#449) (j1)	1.00	1.60
(c1)	Hunan		1.25	2.50

Hunan — c40

Eastern Szechwan — f40

Western Szechwan — k40

Yunnan — l40

Red Surcharge

489	A57	40c on 50c dk bl (#386) (f40)	.75	1.25
(k40)	Western Szechwan		4.25	6.00
(l40)	Yunnan		3.75	5.50
r.	Inverted surcharge (Yunnan)	110.00	

Wmk. 261

490	A40	40c on 50c grn (#420) (c40)	1.75	6.50

Unwmk.

491	A59	40c on 50c dk bl (#459) (c40)	3.25	8.25

Dr. Sun Yat-sen — A62

Central Trust Printing
Perf. 10½-11, 11½-12½, 13 and Compounds

1942-43   Without Gum   Typo.

492	A62	10c dp green ('43)	.25	1.50
493	A62	16c dull ol brn	13.50	47.50
a.	Perf 10½		550.00	550.00
494	A62	20c dk ol grn ('43)	.25	1.50
a.	Perf. 11		13.50	11.00
495	A62	25c brown vio	.25	1.00
496	A62	30c dull ver	.25	1.00
a.	Perf. 11		3.00	5.00
497	A62	40c dk red brn ('43)	.25	1.00
a.	Perf. 11x13		85.00	
b.	Perf. 11		14.00	14.00
498	A62	50c sage green	.25	.25
a.	Perf. 11		7.00	13.50
499	A62	$1 rose lake	.35	.25
a.	Perf. 11		40.00	40.00
500	A62	$1 dull grn ('43)	.35	.35
501	A62	$1.50 dp blue ('43)	.35	.45
a.	Perf. 11		290.00	290.00
502	A62	$2 dk blue grn	.35	.35
503	A62	$3 dk yel ('43)	.35	.35
504	A62	$4 red brown	.40	.45
505	A62	$5 cerise ('43)	.35	.35
		Nos. 492-505 (14)	17.50	56.30

Many shades and part-perforate varieties exist.

See Nos. 550 to 563 for other stamps of type A62 with secret mark and new values and colors. For surcharges and overprints see Nos. 525-530, 671, 683, 692-694, 696, 771, 773, 807-809, 811-820, 824-827, 832, 834-834A, 836, 848-850, 852-854, 857, 860-863, 876, 879, M5-M10, Taiwan 55, 86, 99, Kwangsi 6-7, Sinkiang 162-173, 194-195.

Type of 1938
Thin Paper Without Gum

1942-44   Unwmk.   Engr.   Imperf.

506	A57	$10 red brown	1.75	1.25
507	A57	$20 blue grn	1.75	1.00
508	A57	$20 rose red ('44)	17.00	11.00
509	A57	$30 dull vio ('43)	1.25	1.00
510	A57	$40 rose red ('43)	1.40	1.00
511	A57	$50 blue	2.00	1.25
512	A57	$100 org brn ('43)	8.00	5.00

Rouletted

513	A57	$5 lilac gray ('44)	14.00	14.00
a.	Rouletted x perf. 12½		25.00	30.00
514	A57	$10 red brown	6.75	5.00
515	A57	$50 blue	7.25	6.00
a.	Rouletted x imperf.		125.00	125.00
		Nos. 506-515 (10)	61.15	46.50

1942-45   Perf. 12½ to 15

516	A57	$4 dp blue ('43)	.80	1.25
517	A57	$5 lil gray ('43)	1.75	1.25
518	A57	$10 red brown	1.75	1.25
519	A57	$20 blue grn ('43)	1.75	1.00
520	A57	$20 rose red ('45)	100.00	125.00
521	A57	$30 dull vio ('43)	1.25	1.00
522	A57	$40 rose ('43)	1.25	1.00
523	A57	$50 blue	5.50	2.50
524	A57	$100 org brn ('45)	110.00	125.00
		Nos. 516-524 (9)	224.05	259.25

Beware of Nos. 508 and 512 with faked perforations that are offered as Nos. 520 and 524. See surcharge note following No. 363.

No. 493 Overprinted in Black or Red

1942

525	A62 (i)	16c (Bk)	85.00	100.00
(c)	Hunan		500.00	
(k)	Western Szechwan		190.00	190.00
(m)	Honan		850.00	850.00
(n)	Shensi		250.00	260.00
r.	Perf. 10½ (Kwangsi)		550.00	
s.	Inverted ovpt. (Shensi)		300.00	
526	A62 (d)	16c (R)	60.00	50.00
(bx)	Anhwei		550.00	550.00
(e)	Kiangsi		77.50	60.00
(f)	Eastern Szechwan		120.00	75.00
(h)	Fukien		300.00	225.00
(j)	Kwangtung		675.00	675.00
(l)	Yunnan		60.00	50.00
(o)	Kweichow		275.00	200.00
(p)	Hupeh, perf. 10½		925.00	850.00
r.	Perf. 10½ (E. Szechwan)		550.00	
s.	Horiz. pair, imperf. btwn (Yunnan)		650.00	—
t.	Perf. 13 (Hupeh)		—	—

This overprint means "Domestic Ordinary Letter Surcharge Paid." It was applied in various sizes and types by 14 districts, 9 using red ink, 5 using black. (The Anhwei overprint comes in two types.) These overprinted stamps were briefly sold for $1.16 before the government ordered their sale suspended. The vertical bars and 50c surcharge of Nos. 527-528 were then applied.

Nos. 525-526 Surcharged "50 cents" and 2 Vertical Bars in Black or Red

Anhwei — bx

Hunan — c

Kansu — d

Kiangsi — e

Eastern Szechwan — f

Fukien — h

Kwangsi — i

Kwangtung — j

Western Szechwan — k

Yunnan — l

Honan — m

Kweichow — o

Shensi — n

Hupeh — p

1942   Unwmk.

527	A62	50c on 16c (Bk) (c,f)	3.25	3.00
(i)	Kwangsi		6.00	6.00
(k)	Western Szechwan		11.00	8.50
(m)	Honan		11.50	10.00
(n)	Shensi		4.25	5.00
r.	Inverted surch. (W. Szech.)		250.00	
s.	"k" surcharge on #493		350.00	
528	A62	50c on 16c (R) (p)	5.00	5.00
(bx)	Anhwei		95.00	300.00
(d)	Kansu		3.25	3.00
(e)	Kiangsi		5.50	10.00
(h)	Fukien		6.50	8.50
(j)	Kwangtung		6.50	6.00
(l)	Yunnan		6.50	8.00
(o)	Kweichow		4.00	7.00
r.	"o" surcharge inverted		300.00	
s.	"p" surch. on #526(f)		100.00	47.50

Many varieties of Nos. 527-528 exist, including narrow or wide spacing between the two top characters, or between the vertical bars, or both.

Surcharges on stamps perf. 10½ (basic No. 493a) usually sell at much higher prices.

No. 493 Surcharged in Black, Red or Carmine

General Issue

Hunan — c50

Eastern Szechwan — f50

Chekiang — g50

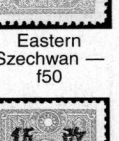

Kwangsi — i50

Kwangtung — j50

Western Szechwan — k50

Honan — m50

Shensi — n50

Kweichow — o50

1943   Unwmk.

529	A62	50c on 16c (Bk) (m50)	11.00	11.00
(n50)	Shensi		11.00	11.00
r.	Perf. 11x13 (Shensi)		95.00	
530	A62	50c on 16c (C) (c50)	1.00	2.00
(c50)	Hunan		3.00	6.00
(f50)	Eastern Szechwan		3.75	2.75
(g50)	Chekiang		42.50	50.00
(i50)	Kwangsi		6.50	7.50
(j50)	Kwangtung		5.00	7.00
(k50)	Western Szechwan		5.00	6.50
(m50)	Honan		6.50	9.50
(o50)	Kweichow		11.00	13.00
r.	Inverted surch. (Hunan)		65.00	
s.	"05" instead of "50" (Kweichow)		450.00	

Many varieties of Nos. 529-530 exist, such as narrow or wide spacing horizontally or vertically between the overprinted Chinese characters.

Surcharges on No. 493a (perf. 10½) usually sell at much higher prices.

The General Issue type, No. 530, was distributed to all head offices, which in turn supplied the post offices under their direction. It is surcharged in carmine; the other stamps listed under No. 530 are surcharged in red or carmine.

Hunan — c20

Kansu — d20

Kiangsi — e20

Eastern Szechwan — f20

Fukien — h20

Kwangsi — i20

Kwangtung — j20

Western Szechwan — k20

Yunnan — l20

Honan — m20

Shensi — n20

Kweichow — o20

Hupeh — p20

On No. 318

**1943				Wmk. 261, Unwmkd.**
531	A45	20c on 13c (k20)	2.25	5.00
	(d20) Kansu		2.25	6.00
	(n20) Shensi		3.50	5.50
532	A45	20c on 13c (i20;R)	1.00	2.75
	(c20) Hunan		1,100.
	(e20) Kiangsi		275.00
	(j20) Kwangtung		85.00	95.00
	(p20) Hupeh		2.00	4.00

On No. 411
533	A45	20c on 13c (n20)	2.25	4.25
	(d20) Kansu		2.75	7.50
	(k20) Western Szechwan	2.00	7.50
	(l20) Yunnan		21.00	35.00
	(m20) Honan		350.00
534	A45	20c on 13c (p20;R)	1.75	5.25
	(c20) Hunan		2.50	1.75
	(e20) Kiangsi		9.00	2.10
	(f20) Eastern Szechwan	2.50	2.75
	(h20) Fukien		9.50	11.00
	(i20) Kwangsi		2.00	2.75
	(j20) Kwangtung		22.00	22.00
	(o20) Kweichow		3.75	3.25

On No. 430
535	A45	20c on 13c (l20)	2.25	4.75
	(d20) Kansu		2.25	2.75
	(k20) Western Szechwan	35.00	42.50
	(m20) Honan		9.50	9.25
	(n20) Shensi		3.50	5.50
536	A45	20c on 13c	2.25	3.50
	(f20;i20;R)
	(c20) Hunan		11.00	9.75
	(e20) Kiangsi		4.50	4.00
	(j20) Kwangtung		2.25	2.75
	(o20) Kweichow		2.25	10.00
	(p20) Hupeh		2.25	4.00

On No. 357
537	A57	20c on 16c (k20)	2.25	2.75
	(c20) Hunan		3.50	13.50
	(d20) Kansu		3.50	13.50
	(m20) Honan		11.00	17.50
	(n20) Shensi		3.50	13.50
538	A57	20c on 16c (e20,	2.25	13.50
	o20; R)
	(c20) Hunan		11.00	17.50
	(i20) Kwangsi		11.00	13.50

		(j20) Kwangtung	52.50	55.00

On No. 413
539	A46	20c on 17c (c20;R)	2.75	4.25
	(i20) Kwangsi		2.25	2.75
	(j20) Kwangtung		30.00	42.50

On No. 432
540	A46	20c on 17c (k20)	3.50	5.50
	(d20) Kansu		3.50	6.50
	(m20) Honan		40.00	47.50
541	A46	20c on 17c (e20;R)	2.25	5.50
	(j20) Kwangtung		3.75	15.00
	(o20) Kweichow		2.50	6.75

On No. 456
542	A59	20c on 17c (m20)	210.00	275.00
543	A59	20c on 17c (c20)	18.00	30.00

On No. 415
544	A45	20c on 21c (e20;R)	11.00	12.00

On No. 434
545	A45	20c on 21c (c20,	2.25	4.00
	k20)
	(d20) Kansu		2.50	6.75
	(l20) Yunnan		2.50	4.00
	(m20) Honan		2.50	9.25
546	A45	20c on 21c (f20;R)	1.75	4.25
	(e20) Kiangsi		1.75	5.50
	(h20) Fukien		2.50	4.75
	(i20) Kwangsi		2.75	4.00
	(j20) Kwangtung		3.75	5.00
	(o20) Kweichow		2.50	2.75
	(p20) Hupeh		2.50	5.50

On No. 417
547	A46	20c on 28c (e20;R)	775.00	725.00

On No. 436
548	A46	20c on 28c (l20)	3.50	6.25
	(d20) Kansu		17.50	24.00
	(k20) Western Szechwan	25.00	65.00
	(m20) Honan		40.00	47.50
549	A46	20c on 28c (e20;R)	1.75	3.25
	(c20) Hunan		1.90	4.75
	(h20) Fukien		3.50	4.75
	(i20) Kwangsi		4.25	6.25
	(j20) Kwangtung		4.25	5.00
	(o20) Kweichow		4.75	4.75

Many varieties of Nos. 531-549 exist, such as narrow or wide spacing between the overprinted Chinese characters, and "20" higher or lower than illustrated.

Type of 1942-43 Pacheng Printing
**1944-46		Unwmk.		Perf. 12**
Without Gum
550	A62	30c chocolate	.40	13.00
551	A62	$1 green	4.00	5.00
552	A62	$2 dk vio brn	.25	.25
	a.	Imperf., pair	30.00	25.00
553	A62	$2 dk bl grn	.25	.25
	a.	Perf. 10½	47.50	35.00
554	A62	$2 deep blue	1.75	6.00
555	A62	$3 lt yellow	1.60	.80
556	A62	$4 violet brn	.25	.25
	a.	Imperf., pair	60.00
557	A62	$5 car ('46)	.25	.25
	a.	Perf. 10½	75.00	75.00
558	A62	$6 gray vio ('45)	.25	.40
559	A62	$10 red brn ('45)	.25	.25
	a.	Imperf., pair	60.00
560	A62	$20 dp ultra ('46)	.25	.25
561	A62	$50 dk green ('46)	4.00	.25
562	A62	$70 lilac ('46)	5.00	.25
563	A62	$100 lt brown ('46)	.30	.25
	Nos. 550-563 (14)		18.80	27.45

In the Pacheng printing of the Central Trust type stamps, the secret mark "C" has been added below the lower left foliate ornament beneath the sun emblem. On the $3, it is below the right ornament. New values also include a "P" at right of sun emblem on the $6 and $10, and at right of necktie on the $20.

Seven different varieties of paper were used in the printing of Nos. 550-563. Some values exist on laid paper with elephant watermark in sheet.

See surcharge note following No. 505.

Dr. Sun Yat-sen — A63

**1944-46	Unwmk.	Typo.	Perf. 12½**
Without Gum
565	A63	40c brown red	.35	.35
566	A63	$2 gray brown	.35	.35
567	A63	$3 red	.35	.35
	a.	$3 orange red	4.00	4.00
568	A63	$3 lt red brn ('45)	.95	.75
569	A63	$6 pale lilac gray	.35	.45
	('45)
570	A63	$10 dull lake ('45)	.35	.35
571	A63	$20 rose ('45)	.35	.45
	a.	Perf. 16	400.00	400.00
572	A63	$50 lt brown ('46)	.45	.55
573	A63	$70 rose vio ('46)	.55	.55
	Nos. 565-573 (9)		4.05	4.05

For surcharges see Nos. 772, 774, 828, 833, 835, 836A, 839, 842, 851, 864, 868, 873-

875, 877, 880. Taiwan 81, 98, Sinkiang 200-201.

Allegory of Savings — A64

**1944-45		Engr.		Perf. 13**
Without Gum
574	A64	$40 indigo ('45)	.35	.90
575	A64	$50 yellow grn ('45)	.35	.35
576	A64	$100 yellow brn	.35	.35
577	A64	$200 dk green ('45)	.35	.35
	Nos. 574-577 (4)		1.40	1.95

All four values were printed on thick paper; the first three were also printed on thin paper. For surcharges see Szechwan Nos. F1, F3.

A65

**1944, Dec. 25		Litho.**
Without Gum
578	A65	$2 deep green	.70	2.00
579	A65	$5 fawn	.70	2.00
580	A65	$6 dull rose vio	1.40	3.50
581	A65	$10 violet blue	2.75	7.00
582	A65	$20 carmine	5.25	9.00
	Nos. 578-582 (5)		10.80	23.50

50th anniversary of the Kuomintang.

Dr. Sun Yat-sen — A66

**1945, Mar. 12		Without Gum**
583	A66	$2 gray green	.45	1.75
584	A66	$5 red brown	.55	1.75
585	A66	$6 dk vio blue	.65	2.25
586	A66	$10 lt blue	1.00	1.75
587	A66	$20 rose	1.25	4.00
588	A66	$30 buff	2.00	6.00
	Nos. 583-588 (6)		5.90	17.50

Death of Dr. Sun Yat-sen, 20th anniv.

Dr. Sun Yat-sen — A67

**1945-46	Without Gum	Perf. 12½**
589	A67	$2 green	.25	.35
590	A67	$5 dull green	.25	.35
591	A67	$10 dk blue	.25	.35
	a.	Imperf., pair	120.00
592	A67	$20 carmine ('46)	.25	.35
	a.	Imperf., pair	120.00
	Nos. 589-592 (4)		1.00	1.40

For surcharges see Nos. 695, 697, 837, 855, Taiwan 58, 82, 87-88.

Statue of Liberty, Map of China, Flags of Great Britain, China and United States, and Chiang Kai-shek — A68

Unwmk.
**1945, July 7	Engr.	Perf. 12**
Flags in Dark Blue and Red
593	A68	$1 deep blue	.50	.50
594	A68	$2 dull green	.50	1.00
595	A68	$5 olive gray	.50	1.00
596	A68	$6 brown	1.00	1.25
597	A68	$10 rose lilac	5.00	7.00
598	A68	$20 carmine rose	5.00	9.50
	Nos. 593-598 (6)		12.50	20.25

Signing of a Treaty in 1943 between Great Britain, the US and China.

Pres. Lin Sen (1864-1943) — A69

**1945, Aug.		Unwmk.		Perf. 12**
599	A69	$1 dp ultra & blk	.65	2.00
600	A69	$2 myrtle grn & blk	.65	2.00
601	A69	$5 red & blk	.65	2.00
602	A69	$6 purple & blk	.90	2.00
603	A69	$10 choc & blk	4.00	4.00
604	A69	$20 olive grn & blk	4.25	6.00
	Nos. 599-604 (6)		11.10	18.00

Pres. Chiang Kai-shek — A70

1945, Oct. 10
Flag in Rose Red and Violet Blue
605	A70	$2 green	.45	1.00
606	A70	$4 dark blue	.50	1.00
607	A70	$5 olive gray	.50	1.50
608	A70	$6 bister brown	1.50	2.25
609	A70	$10 gray	4.00	7.00
610	A70	$20 red violet	5.00	7.00
	Nos. 605-610 (6)		11.95	19.75

Inauguration of Chiang Kai-shek as president, Oct. 10, 1943.

President Chiang Kai-shek — A71

**1945, Oct. 10	Typo.	Perf. 13**
Without Gum
Flag in Carmine and Blue
611	A71	$20 green & blue	.25	.25
612	A71	$50 bister brn & bl	.50	.50
613	A71	$100 blue	.50	.40
614	A71	$300 rose red & blue	.50	.40
	Nos. 611-614 (4)		1.75	1.55

Victory of the Allied Nations over Japan.

C. N. C. Surcharges
The green surcharges on Nos. 615 to 621, and the surcharges on Nos. 647 to 721, and 768 to 774 represent Chinese National Currency and were applied at Shanghai.

Stamps of 1938-41 Srchd. in Black with Chinese Characters and New Value in Checkered Rectangle at Bottom, Resrchd. in Green

**1945		Perf. 12, 12½**
615	A57	10c on $20 on 3c	.25	1.00
	(#350)
616	A46	15c on $30 on 2c	.25	1.00
	(#423)
	a.	Horiz. pair, imperf. between	90.00
	b.	Vert. pair, imperf. between	85.00
617	A59	25c on $50 on 1c	.25	.90
	(#450)

618 A57 50c on $100 on 3c
(#350) .25 .50
619 A40 $1 on $200 on 1c
(#422) .25 .25
a. Horiz. pair, imperf. between 90.00
620 A57 $2 on $400 on 3c
(#350) .25 .30
621 A59 $5 on $1000 on 1c
(#450) .25 .25
Nos. 615-621 (7) 1.75 4.20

The black (first) surcharges on Nos. 615 to 621 represent Nanking puppet government currency.

In the green surcharge, the characters at the left express the new value and are either two or four in number.

Types of 1932-34,
Re-engraved, and
Srchd. in Green with
Horiz. Bar and Four
or Five Chinese
Characters and
Ovptd. in Black

Perf. 14

622 A47 $10 on 20c brown red 8.00 12.00
623 A47 $20 on 40c orange 25.00 29.00
a. Green surcharge inverted 60.00
624 A48 $50 on 30c violet brn 18.50 22.00
Nos. 622-624 (3) 51.50 63.00

These provisional surcharges were applied in Honan in National currency to stamps of the Hwa Pei (North China) government. The black overprint reads: "Hwa Pei."

The two-character "Hwa Pei" overprint was applied to various stamps in 1941-43 by the North China puppet government. See Nos. 8N1-8N53, 8N60-8N84.

Dr. Sun Yat-
sen — A72

1945, Dec.   Typo.   Perf. 12
Without Gum

625 A72 $20 dp carmine .25 .25
626 A72 $30 dp blue .25 .25
627 A72 $40 orange .60 1.25
628 A72 $50 green 1.00 .35
629 A72 $100 dk brown .25 .25
630 A72 $200 brown violet .25 .25
Nos. 625-630 (6) 2.60 2.60

For surcharges see Nos. 810, 829, 838, 865, J110-J119, Taiwan 75, Kwangsi F2, Szechwan F2, F4, Yunnan 66-71.

Type of 1931-37
Perf. 12½, 13x12½, 13½

1946   Unwmk.

631 A37 $1 dk violet .30 1.50
632 A37 $2 olive green .30 3.00
633 A37 $20 brt yellow grn .30 .55
634 A37 $30 chocolate .30 .50
635 A37 $50 red orange .30 .50
Nos. 631-635 (5) 1.50 6.05

$4 blue and $5 red values were prepared but not issued. Value $400.

For surcharges see Nos. 678, 684, 689-690, 768, 843.

Dr. Sun Yat-
sen — A73

1946-47   Engr.   Perf. 14
Without Gum

636 A73 $20 carmine 6.25 .25
637 A73 $30 dk blue ('47) .35 .25
638 A73 $50 purple .25 .25
639 A73 $70 red org ('47) 18.50 3.00
640 A73 $100 dk carmine .25 .25
641 A73 $200 olive grn ('47) .25 .25
642 A73 $500 brt bl grn ('47) .35 .25
643 A73 $700 red brown ('47) .25 .25
644 A73 $1000 rose lake .35 .35
645 A73 $3000 blue 1.00 .40
646 A73 $5000 dp green & ver 1.00 .40
Nos. 636-646 (11) 28.80 5.40

For surcharges see Nos. 679, 769, 775, 823, 837A, 844-845, 856, 866, 875A, 878, Taiwan 18, 23-28, 54, 76-77, 100, Northeastern Provinces 41-43, Fukien 5-6, Hunan 1, E1, Kwangsi 11, F2, Szechwan F5-F8, Sinkiang

202-204, People's Republic of China 3L53, 3L67-3L68, 6L28.

Stamps of 1932-41
Surcharged in Black

Perf. 12½, 13, 13x12, 14
Wmk. 261

647 A45 $20 on 8c
(#409) .25 .65
648 A39 $30 on ½c
(#402) 2,000.
649 A45 $50 on 21c
(#415) .25 .25
650 A45 $70 on 13c
(#411) .25 .25
651 A46 $100 on 28c
(#417) .25 .65

Unwmk.

652 A39 $3 on 2½c
(#424) 7.50 6.25
653 A48 $10 on 15c
(#431) .25 .25
654 A45 $20 on 8c
(#428) .25 .25
655 A47 $20 on 20c
(#433) .35 .35
656 A39 $30 on ½c
(#421) .25 .25
657 A45 $50 on 21c
(#434) .40 .55
657A A45 $70 on 13c
(#318) 210.00 210.00
658 A45 $70 on 13c
(#430) .40 .55
659 A46 $100 on 28c
(#436) .40 .40

Forgeries of No. 648 exist.

Stamps and Types of
1931-1946 Surcharged
in Black or Carmine

Perf. 12½, 13, 14

1946-47   Wmk. 261

660 A57 $50 on 5c green
(#392) .35 .85
661 A57 $50 on 5c ol grn
(#393) 21.00 20.00
662 A48 $50 on 5c dl red org
(#408) .25 1.25
663 A40 $100 on 1c org
(#403) .25 1.10

Perf. 12, 12½, 12½x13, 13, 14

1946-47   Unwmk.

664 A57 $20 on 3c (#350) .25 .35
665 A45 $20 on 8c (#428) .25 .25
666 A57 $50 on 3c (#350) .25 .25
667 A57 $50 on 3c (#352) .25 .25
668 A57 $50 on 5c (#382) .95 1.75
669 A48 $50 on 5c (#427) .25 .25
670 A59 $50 on 5c (#452) .25 .25
671 A62 $50 on $1 (#500) .25 .25
672 A40 $100 on 1c (#422) .25 .25
a. Without secret mark
(#422a) 67.50 67.50
673 A57 $100 on 3c (#350) .25 .25
674 A57 $100 on 8c (#353) 14.00 14.00
675 A57 $100 on 8c (#369) 2.00 .35
676 A57 $100 on 8c (#383) .35 .35
a. Without "star" in uniform
button (No. 383a) 25.00 16.00
677 A59 $100 on 8c (#454) .25 .25
678 A37 $100 on $1 (#631) .25 .25
679 A73 $100 on $20
(#636) .35 .35
680 A57 $200 on 10c
(#354) .75 .25
681 A57 $200 on 10c
(#384) .40 1.10
682 A37 $200 on $4 dl bl .50 .25
a. Double surcharge 16.00
683 A62 $250 on $1.50
(#501) .30 2.50
a. Perf. 11 250.00 250.00
684 A37 $250 on $2 (#632) .50 .25
685 A37 $250 on $5 car .50 .25
686 A57 $300 on 10c
(#354) .25 .25
687 A59 $300 on 10c
(#455) .25 .25
688 A57 $500 on 3c (#350) .50 .25
689 A37 $500 on $20
(#633) .25 .25
690 A37 $800 on $30
(#634) .30 .25
691 A37 $1000 on 2c (#297) .65 .25
692 A62 $1000 on $2 (#552) .30 .25
a. Imperf., pair 30.00 20.00

693 A62 $1000 on $2 (#553) .25 .25
694 A62 $1000 on $2 (#554) .25 .55
695 A67 $1000 on $5 (#589) .25 .25
696 A62 $2000 on $5 (#557) .30 .25
697 A67 $2000 on $5 dl grn
(C) (#590) .25 .25
Nos. 664-697 (34) 27.15 27.65

Nos. 660-697 have a double row of dots in the surcharge box frame.

Nos. 682 and 685 were not issued without surcharge. No. 682 is perf. 13x13½; No. 685, perf. 12x12½.

The characters at the left express the new value and vary in number.

Stamps of 1938-41
Surcharged in Black

Perf. 12, 12½, 13, 14

1946   Wmk. 261

698 A45 $20 on 8c (#409) 200.00 175.00
699 A57 $50 on 5c (#392) .25 .65
700 A57 $50 on 5c (#393) .50 1.25

1946-48   Unwmk.

700A A57 $20 on 5c (#381) 1,050.
701 A57 $20 on 8c (#353) .25 .35
702 A57 $20 on 8c (#369) .35 .35
703 A57 $20 on 8c (#383) .25 .50
a. Without "star" in uniform
button (No. 383a) 4.50 4.50
b. Inverted surcharge 20.00
c. Dbl. surch., one on back 32.50 32.50
d. Double surcharge 32.50
704 A45 $20 on 8c (#428) .25 .25
a. Double surcharge 22.50
705 A59 $20 on 8c (#453) .25 .25
706 A59 $20 on 8c (#454) .25 .25
a. Inverted surcharge 13.00
b. Double surcharge 13.00
707 A57 $50 on 5c (#351) 7.25 6.75
708 A57 $50 on 5c (#352) .25 .25
a. Inverted surcharge 27.50
709 A57 $50 on 5c (#381) .70 .70
710 A57 $50 on 5c (#382) .50 .35
711 A48 $50 on 5c (#427) .25 .25
a. Inverted surcharge 27.50
712 A59 $50 on 5c (#452) .50 .25
a. Double surcharge 16.00

Stamps of 1939-41
Surcharged in Blue or
Red

1946   Wmk. 261   Perf. 12½

713 A40 $10 on 1c org
(#403) .25 .25
a. Inverted surcharge 40.00
714 A48 $20 on 3c dp yel
brn (#406) 800.00 800.00

Forgeries of No. 714 exist.

1946   Unwmk.   Perf. 12, 12½, 13

715 A40 $10 on 1c org (#422) .25 .25
a. Without secret mark (#422a) 10.00 12.00
b. Inverted surcharge 8.00 10.00
716 A59 $10 on 1c org (#450) .25 .25
a. Double surcharge 27.50
717 A57 $20 on 2c ol grn (R)
(#368) .25 .25
718 A59 $20 on 2c brt ultra
(R) (#451) .25 .25
a. Inverted surcharge 20.00
b. Double surcharge 16.00
719 A57 $20 on 3c dl cl (#350) .25 .25
a. Double surcharge 22.50
720 A48 $20 on 3c dp yel brn
(#425) .25 .35
721 A39 $30 on 4c pale vio
(R) (#426) .25 .25
a. Inverted surcharge 9.00
Nos. 715-721 (7) 1.75 1.85

President Chiang
Kai-shek — A74

Perf. 10½-11½

1946, Oct. 31   Engr.   Unwmk.

722 A74 $20 carmine .50 .55
723 A74 $30 green .50 .75
724 A74 $50 vermilion .50 .65
725 A74 $100 yellow grn .60 1.10

726 A74 $200 yellow org .95 1.00
727 A74 $300 magenta .95 .65
Nos. 722-727 (6) 4.00 4.70

60th birthday of Chiang Kai-shek.
Printed by Dah Yeh Printing Co.; the earlier ones are gumless, the later ones gummed.

For stamps of Type A74 with additional characters on either side of the portrait see Taiwan Nos. 29-34, Northeastern Provinces 30-35.

Printed by Dah Tung Book Co.
Without Gum
Perf. 14

722a A74 $20 carmine 1.10 1.50
723a A74 $30 green 1.10 1.50
724a A74 $50 vermilion 1.10 1.50
725a A74 $100 yellow green 3.00 3.00
726a A74 $200 yellow orange 2.00 2.00
727a A74 $300 magenta 2.50 2.50
Nos. 722a-727a (6) 10.80 12.00

Assembly
House,
Nanking
A75

1946, Nov. 15   Litho.   Perf. 14
Without Gum

728 A75 $20 green .75 .40
729 A75 $30 blue .75 .40
730 A75 $50 dk brown .75 .40
a. Horiz. pair, imperf. between 95.00 95.00
731 A75 $100 carmine .75 .40
Nos. 728-731 (4) 3.00 1.60

Convening of National Assembly.
For surcharges see Taiwan Nos. 10-13, Northeastern Provinces 26-29.

Entrance to
Dr. Sun Yat-
sen
Mausoleum
A76

1947, May 5   Engr.

732 A76 $100 dp green .35 .35
733 A76 $200 deep blue .35 .35
734 A76 $250 carmine .35 .35
735 A76 $350 lt brown .35 .35
736 A76 $400 dp claret .35 .35
Nos. 732-736 (5) 1.75 1.75

First anniversary of return of Chinese National Government to Nanking.

See Taiwan Nos. 35-39, Northeastern Provinces 36-40.

Dr. Sun Yat-
sen — A77

1947   Perf. 12½, 11½x12½

737 A77 $500 olive green .25 .25
738 A77 $1000 green & car .25 .25
739 A77 $2000 dp blue & red brn .30 .25
740 A77 $5000 org red & blk .30 .25
Nos. 737-740 (4) 1.10 1.00

For surcharge see Szechwan No. 50.

Confucius
A78

Confucius'
Lecturing School
A79

Tomb of
Confucius
A80

Temple of Confucius A81

1947, Aug. 27   Litho.   Perf. 14
Without Gum
741 A78 $500 carmine rose .60 .65
Engr.
742 A79 $800 yellow brown .50 .80
743 A80 $1250 blue green .50 1.25
744 A81 $1800 blue .50 1.90
    Nos. 741-744 (4) 2.10 4.60

Sun Yat-sen and Plum Blossoms — A82

1947-48   Engr.   Perf. 14
Without Gum
745 A82 $150 dk blue .25 .25
746 A82 $250 dp lilac .35 .25
747 A82 $500 blue grn .25 .25
748 A82 $1000 red .25 .25
749 A82 $2000 vermilion .25 .25
750 A82 $3000 blue .25 .25
751 A82 $4000 gray ('48) .25 .25
752 A82 $5000 dk brown .25 .25
753 A82 $6000 rose lil ('48) .25 .25
754 A82 $7000 lt red brn
            ('48) .25 .25
755 A82 $10,000 dp blue & car 1.10 .25
756 A82 $20,000 car & yel grn .35 .25
757 A82 $50,000 grn & dk bl 1.25 .25
758 A82 $100,000 dl yel & ol
            grn ('48) 1.80 .25
759 A82 $200,000 vio brn & dp
            bl ('48) 2.25 .45
760 A82 $300,000 sep & org
            brn ('48) 2.25 .55
761 A82 $500,000 lt Prus grn
            & sep ('48) 3.00 .55
    Nos. 745-761 (17) 14.60 5.05

See Nos. 788-799. For similar type see Formosa A1. For surcharges see Nos. 770, 804-806, 821-822, 840-841, 858-859, 869, 871, 880A-880B, 885A-885E, 1025-1036, Taiwan 56-57, 59, 89, Fukien 1-4, 7-12, 19-23, Hunan 2-5, C1, F1, Kiangsi 1-3, C1, E1, F1-F2, Kwangsi 8-10, 12-17, Shensi 1-2, C1, E1, Szechwan 24-49, Yunnan 61-62, 69, 205-207, People's Republic of China 3L69-3L70, 3L76, 4L63-4L64, 6L22, 6L27, 6L29, 6L32.

Chinese Flag and Map of Taiwan — A83

1947, Oct. 25   With Gum
762 A83 $500 carmine .35 1.00
763 A83 $1250 deep green .35 1.00
Restoration of Taiwan to China, 2nd anniv.

Mobile Post Office — A84

Street-Corner Branch Post Office — A85

1947, Nov. 5
764 A84 $500 carmine .25 .50
765 A85 $1000 lilac .25 .50
766 A85 $1250 green .25 .85
767 A84 $1800 deep blue .25 1.10
    Nos. 764-767 (4) 1.00 2.95

Stamps and Type of 1943-47 Surcharged in Black or Green

1947-48   Unwmk.   Perf. 12½, 13, 14
768 A37 $500 on $20 brt yel
            grn (#633) .25 .25
769 A73 $1250 on $70 red org
            (#639) .25 .25
770 A82 $1800 on $350 yel org .25 .25
771 A62 $2000 on $3 dk yel ('48)
            (#503) .50 .25
772 A63 $2000 on $3 red (#567) .25 .25
    a. On #567a 6.50 2.25
773 A62 $3000 on $3 lt yel ('48)
            (#555) .25 .25
774 A63 $3000 on $3 lt red brn
            (G) ('48) (#568) .25 .25
    Nos. 768-774 (7) 2.00 1.75

Nos. 768-774 have a single row of dots in the surcharge box frame.
The characters at the left express the new value and vary in number.

No. 640 Surcharged

1948, Aug.   Perf. 14
775 A73 $5000 on $100 dk car 7.00 70.00
No. 775 received its surcharge in Kwangsi for use in that province.

Map of China and Mail-carrying Vehicles A86

Rural Mail Delivery — A87

Early and Modern Mail Transportation A88

1947, Dec. 16   Engr.   Perf. 12
776 A86 $100 violet .25 1.00
777 A87 $200 brt green .25 1.00
778 A87 $300 red brown .25 1.00
779 A88 $400 scarlet .25 1.00
780 A88 $500 brt vio blue .25 1.00
    Nos. 776-780 (5) 1.25 5.00
Chinese Postal Administration, 50th anniv.

National Assembly Building and New Constitution A89

1947, Dec. 25   Perf. 14
Without Gum
781 A89 $2000 brt red .50 .60
782 A89 $3000 blue .50 .60
783 A89 $5000 deep green .50 .60
    Nos. 781-783 (3) 1.50 1.80
1st anniv. of the adoption of China's new constitution, Dec. 25, 1946.

Chinese Stamps of 1947 and 1912 — A90

Perf. 14, Imperf.
1948, Mar. 20   Litho.
Without Gum
784 A90 $5000 dk car rose 1.00 4.00
    a. Vert. pair, imperf. btwn 40.00
785 A90 $5000 dk green 1.00 4.00
    a. Vert. pair, imperf. btwn 40.00
Stamp exhibitions at Nanking, Mar. 20 (No. 784), and at Shanghai, May 19 (No. 785).

Sun Yat-sen Memorial Hall, Taipei — A91

1948, Apr. 28   Engr.   Perf. 14
786 A91 $5000 violet .30 1.25
787 A91 $10000 red .30 1.25
Restoration of Formosa to China, 3rd anniv.

Sun Yat-sen Type of 1947-48
1948   Without Gum
788 A82 $20000 rose pink .50 .35
789 A82 $30000 chocolate .25 .25
790 A82 $40000 green .25 .25
791 A82 $50000 dp blue .25 .25
792 A82 $100000 dull grn .25 .25
793 A82 $200000 brn vio .75 .25
794 A82 $300000 yel grn 2.75 1.00
795 A82 $500000 lil rose 1.25 .25
796 A82 $1000000 claret .75 .25
797 A82 $2000000 vermilion 1.50 .25
798 A82 $3000000 ol bis 3.00 .55
799 A82 $5000000 ultra 6.00 .90
    Nos. 788-799 (12) 17.50 4.80
Zeros for "cents" omitted.
For surcharges see Nos. 841, 871, 880A-880B, 885A-885E, 1025-1028, 1031-1036.

Early Ship and Modern Hai Tien — A92

Passenger Ship Kiang Ya — A93

1948, Aug. 16   Without Gum
800 A92 $20000 blue .60 1.75
801 A92 $30000 rose lilac .60 1.75
802 A93 $40000 yel brown .60 2.75
803 A93 $60000 vermilion .60 2.75
    Nos. 800-803 (4) 2.40 9.00
75th anniversary of the China Merchants' Steam Navigation Company.

Type of 1947-48 Surcharged in Black

1948   Unwmk.   Perf. 14
804 A82 $4000 on $100 car .25 25.00
805 A82 $5000 on $100 car .25 .25
806 A82 $8000 on $700 red brn .35 .90
    Nos. 804-806 (3) .85 26.15

Stamps of 1942-46 Surcharged in Black or Red

1948   Perf. 12½, 13
807 A62 $5000 on $1 (#500) .25 .25
808 A62 $5000 on $1 (#551) 20.00 20.00
809 A62 $5000 on $2 (#502) .25 .25
810 A72 $10000 on $20 (#625) .25 .25
811 A62 $20000 on 10c (#492) .25 .25
812 A62 $20000 on 50c
            (#498;R) .25 .50
813 A62 $30000 on 30c (#496) .25 .50
    a. Perf. 10½ 22.00 22.00
    Nos. 807-813 (7) 21.50 22.00

Nos. 492, 556 and 558 Surcharged in Black or Carmine

1948
814 A62 $15,000 on 10c dp grn .25 .25
815 A62 $15,000 on $4 vio brn .25 .25
816 A62 $15,000 on $6 gray vio
            (C) .25 .25
    Nos. 814-816 (3) .75 .75

No. 498, 494 and 504 Surcharged in Black

1948   Unwmk.   Perf. 11½, 13
817 A62 $15,000 on 50c, perf.
            13 .25 .50
    a. Perf. 11½ 10.00 10.00
818 A62 $40,000 on 20c dk ol
            grn .25 .90
    a. Perf. 11 10.00 7.50
819 A62 $60,000 on $4 red
            brn .45 .50
    Nos. 817-819 (3) .95 1.90

Gold Yuan Surcharges
(Nos. 820-885E)

Stamps of 1942-47 Surcharged in Black, Carmine or Red

1948   Perf. 14, 13, 11
820 A62 ½c on 30c (#496) .25 5.00
821 A82 ½c on $500 (Bk)
            (#747) .25 .25
822 A82 ½c on $500 (C)
            (#747) .25 .90
823 A73 1c on $20 (#636) .25 2.25
824 A62 2c on $1.50 (R)
            (#501) .25 3.25
825 A62 3c on $5 (#505) .25 3.25
826 A62 4c on $1 (#499) .25 3.25
827 A62 5c on 50c (#498) .25 .45
    a. Perf. 11 6.50 6.50
    Nos. 820-827 (8) 2.00 18.60

On No. 820-827, the position of the surcharged denomination and "Gold Yuan" characters varies, the aim being to obliterate the original denomination.

Stamps of 1940-48 Surcharged in Black, Violet, Carmine, Blue or Green

Perf. 12, 12½, 13, 14, 12½x13
1948-49
828 A63 5c on $20
            (#571) .25 1.10
829 A72 5c on $30 (C)
            (#626) .25 1.40
    a. Double surcharge 17.50
830 A57 10c on 2c
            (#368) .25 1.75
831 A39 10c on 2½c
            (#424) .25 1.10

832	A62	10c on 25c (V) (#495)	.25	1.25
833	A63	10c on 40c (#565)	.25	1.40
834	A62	10c on $1 (#500)	.25	.35
834A	A62	10c on $1 (#551)	275.00	250.00
835	A63	10c on $2 (#566)	.25	.25
836	A62	10c on $20 (C) (#560)	.25	.25
836A	A63	10c on $20 (#571)	300.00	300.00
837	A67	10c on $20 (#592)	.25	.25
837A	A73	10c on $20 (#636)	1.00	3.50
838	A72	10c on $30 (C) (#626)	.25	1.50
839	A63	10c on $70 (#573)	.25	.50
a.		Double surcharge	15.00	
840	A82	10c on $7000 (#754)	1.00	1.00
841	A82	10c on $20,000 (#788)	.25	4.75
842	A63	20c on $6 (#569)	.25	.35
843	A37	20c on $30 (#634)	.45	4.75
844	A73	20c on $30 (C) (#637)	.65	3.75
845	A73	20c on $100 (#640)	.25	3.00
a.		Inverted surcharge	22.00	
b.		Double surcharge	16.00	
846	A39	50c on ½c (#312)	75.00	75.00
847	A39	50c on ½c (#421)	.25	.65
a.		Inverted surcharge	30.00	
848	A62	50c on 20c (#494)	.25	.50
849	A62	50c on 30c (Bl) (#496)	.25	1.40
850	A62	50c on 40c (V) (#497)	.25	.90
a.		Perf. 11	9.00	10.00
851	A63	50c on 40c (V) (#565)	.25	1.00
852	A62	50c on $4 (#556)	1.00	3.50
853	A62	50c on $4 (Bl) (#556)	.25	2.00
854	A62	50c on $20 (C) (#560)	.25	.25
855	A67	50c on $20 (V) (#592)	.50	1.50
856	A73	50c on $20 (#636)	.25	1.25
857	A62	50c on $70 (C) (#562)	.30	.30
858	A82	50c on $6000 (#753)	2.00	3.50
859	A82	50c on $6000 (Bl) (#753)	.25	1.50
860	A62	$1 on 30c (#550)	.25	.25
a.		Perf. 11	22.00	22.00
861	A62	$1 on 40c (#497)	.25	.25
a.		Perf. 11	4.00	4.00
862	A62	$1 on $1 (#499)	.55	2.00
863	A62	$1 on $5 (#557)	.70	.40
864	A63	$2 on $2 (R) (#566)	.25	.25
865	A72	$2 on $20 (#625)	.25	.25
866	A73	$2 on $100 (#640)	.25	.25
867	A46	$5 on 17c (#432)	.90	.90
868	A63	$5 on $2 (#566)	.25	.25
869	A82	$5 on $3000 (C) (#750)	.25	1.50
870	A47	$8 on 20c (#433)	.50	.50
871	A82	$8 on $30,000 (C) (#789)	.25	2.50
872	A47	$10 on 40c (#438)	1.25	1.00
873	A63	$10 on $2 (G) (#566)	.25	.35
874	A63	$10 on $2 (C) (#566)	.25	.25
875	A62	$20 on $2 (C) (#566)	.25	.25
875A	A73	$20 on $20 (#636)	4.75	3.00
876	A62	$50 on 30c (#496)	.25	.30
877	A63	$50 on $2 (Bl) (#566)	.30	.30
878	A73	$80 on $20 (#636)	1.00	1.00
879	A62	$100 on $1 (#551)	.25	1.00
a.		Perf. 11	65.00	65.00
880	A63	$100 on $2 (C) (#566)	.35	.35
880A	A82	$50,000 on $20,000 (#788)	1.40	.40

880B	A82	$100,000 on $30,000 (V) (#789)	2.75	.90

Wmk. 261

881	A39	10c on 2½c (#405)	.40	4.00
882	A39	50c on ½c (#402)	.25	.85
		Nos. 828-882 (61)	680.50	698.65

Characters at left express the new value. Style of characters and numerals varies.

Nos. Q7 to Q9 Surcharged in Black or Carmine

1948 Unwmk. Perf. 12½

883	PP2	$200 on $3000 red org	.70	.50
884	PP2	$500 on $5000 dk bl (C)	.70	.50
885	PP2	$1000 on $10,000 vio	.70	.50
		Nos. 883-885 (3)	2.10	1.45

Nos. 788-791 Surcharged in Gold Yuan in Red (Nos. 885A, 885D-885E) or Black (Nos. 885B-885C) at Foochow

1949, Apr. 30 Unwmk. Perf. 14

885A	$20,000 on $40,000	15.00	21.00
885B	$50,000 on $30,000	15.00	21.00
885C	$100,000 on $20,000	15.00	21.00
885D	$200,000 on $40,000	15.00	21.00
885E	$200,000 on $30,000	15.00	21.00
	Nos. 885A-885E (5)	75.00	105.00

Issued in Fukien Postal District.

Dr. Sun Yat-sen — A94

1949 Unwmk. Engr. Perf. 14
Without Gum

886	A94	$1 orange	.45	.65
887	A94	$10 green	.50	.65
888	A94	$20 vio brown	.45	.65
889	A94	$50 dk Prus grn	.45	.65
890	A94	$100 org brn	.45	.65
891	A94	$200 red org	.45	.65
892	A94	$500 rose lilac	.45	.65
893	A94	$800 car rose	.45	2.50
894	A94	$1000 blue	.45	.65

Redrawn
Engr.
Perf. 12½

895	A94	$10 green	.45	5.00
a.		Perf. 14	4.00	8.00
b.		Perf. 13	.45	5.50
896	A94	$20 violet brn	.45	.55
a.		Perf. 14	1.10	4.50
b.		Perf. 13	.45	.90
		Nos. 886-896 (11)	5.00	13.25

Small "T" at left of necktie on Nos. 895-896a.

Redrawn
1949 Litho.
Without Gum Perf. 12½

897	A94	$50 grnsh gray	.30	2.75
898	A94	$100 dk org brn	.30	.50
899	A94	$200 orange red	.60	3.00
900	A94	$500 rose lilac	.30	.50
901	A94	$1000 deep blue	.30	.50
902	A94	$2000 violet	.30	1.50
903	A94	$5000 light blue	.30	.45
904	A94	$10,000 sepia	.30	.45
905	A94	$20,000 apple grn	.30	1.50
906	A94	$50,000 rose pink	.30	.45
907	A94	$80,000 brn red	.70	4.50
908	A94	$100,000 bl grn	.45	.45
		Nos. 897-908 (12)	4.45	16.55

Diagonal lines have been added to the background of the redrawn design.
Zeros for "cents" omitted on No. 908.
See Nos. 973-981. For surcharges see Nos. 991-1006, 1057-1060, Fukien 13-17, Szechwan 51, Tsingtau 1-4, Yunnan 63-65, 68, 70, People's Republic of China 4L34-4L44, 4L48-4L60, 5L43-5L50, 5L54-5L59, 5L91-5L95, 6L1-6L16, 6L23-6L26, 6L30-6L31, 7L6-7L8, 7L13-7L16, 8L12-8L13, 8L48-8L51.

Plane, Train and Ship — A95

Gold Yuan Surcharge in Black or Other Colors on Revenue Stamps

Two types, 50c on $20:
I — Thick numerals in "20." Vertical stroke in lower right corner of vignette. (Dah Tung Book Co.)
II — Thin "20." No vertical stroke in corner. (Central Trust.)

Two types, $2 on $50, $10 on $30, $100 on $50 and $300 on $50:
III — "Y" in lower right corner of vignette. (Dah Yeh Printing Co.)
IV — No "Y" in corner. (Dah Tung, Central Trust or Chung Ming.)

Two types, $50 on $300 and $1000 on $100:
V — Projection on left frame column below foliate ornament. (Dah Yeh Printing Co.)
VI — No projection. (Dah Tung Book Co.)

Litho.; Nos. 923, 933, 935-936 Engr.
1949 Perf. 12½, 13, 14
Without Gum

913	A95	50c on $20 red brn, I	.25	.50
a.		50c on $20 brown, II	.25	.50
914	A95	$1 on $15 red org	.25	9.00
915	A95	$2 on $50 dk bl, IV (C)	.25	1.00
a.		Type III	.40	1.25
916	A95	$3 on $50 dk bl (Bl)	.25	1.00
917	A95	$3 on $50 dk bl	.25	1.00
918	A95	$5 on $50 brn	.25	.90
919	A95	$10 on $30 dk vio, III (Bl)	.25	.45
a.		Type IV	.70	1.75
b.		Double surcharge, IV		
920	A95	$15 on $20 org brn (Bl)	.25	.45
921	A95	$25 on $20 org brn (G)	.25	.45
922	A95	$50 on $50 dk bl (R O)	.25	.45
923	A95	$50 on $300 grn, VI (C)	.25	.60
a.		$50 on $300 yel grn, V (C)	.25	.50
924	A95	$80 on $50 dk bl (Dk Br)	.25	1.25
925	A95	$100 on $50 dk bl, IV	1.00	.60
a.		Type III	5.00	17.50
926	A95	$200 on $50 dk bl	.90	.90
927	A95	$200 on $500 brn (Bl)	.60	.70
928	A95	$300 on $50 dk bl, III (C)	1.25	1.25
a.		Type IV	1.75	2.00
929	A95	$300 on $50 dk bl (Br)	2.00	2.00
930	A95	$500 on $15 red org (Bl)	1.50	4.25
931	A95	$500 on $30 dk vio	.75	3.00
932	A95	$1000 on $50 dk bl (C)	9.00	9.00
933	A95	$1000 on $100 ol grn, V	3.00	4.50
a.		Type VI	14.00	15.00
934	A95	$1500 on $50 dk bl (Bl)	2.50	3.00
935	A95	$2000 on $300 grn	.45	.65
a.		Horiz. pair, imperf. between		
936	A95	$5000 on $100 ol grn (C)	350.00	
		Nos. 913-936 (24)	375.95	
		Nos. 913-935 (23)	25.95	46.90

No. 936 was officially authorized, but never issued.

Key pattern of overprinted border inverted and in 2 or 3 detached sections at top and bottom in Blue, Black or Green
Without Gum
Type A95

1949		**Hankow Prints**		**Litho.**
937	A95	$50 on $10 (Bk)	9.50	11.00
938	A95	$100 on $10 (Bk)	11.00	14.00
939	A95	$500 on $10 (Bk)	9.00	6.50

940	A95	$1000 on $10	7.00	7.00
941	A95	$5000 on $20	29.00	25.00
942	A95	$10,000 on $20 (Bk)	17.50	14.00
943	A95	$50,000 on $20	20.00	25.00
944	A95	$100,000 on $20 (Bk)	25.00	25.00
945	A95	$500,000 on $20	350.00	300.00
946	A95	$2,000,000 on $20 (G)	900.00	375.00
947	A95	$5,000,000 on $20	1,600.	750.00
		Nos. 937-944 (8)	128.00	127.50

The $10 stamp is slate green, the $20 red brown.
The basic revenue stamps of Nos. 915-947 were the work of several printers. There are three main types, differing in the bottom label. Nos. 922 and 925 are in a second type: Nos. 923 and 930 in a third. Varieties of paper, color and overprint exist.
Counterfeits exist of Nos. 945-947.
For surcharges and overprints see Nos. 960-970, C63, E13, F3, J122-J126, Hupeh 1-2, People's Republic of China 5L51-5L53, 6L17-6L21.

Redrawn Coarse Impression
1949 Litho. Without Gum
Size: 18¼x20¾mm

951	A94	$50 green	.40	40.00
952	A94	$1000 dp blue	.50	2.00
953	A94	$5000 carmine	.65	2.00
954	A94	$10,000 brown	4.00	7.50
955	A94	$20,000 orange	1.25	2.00
956	A94	$50,000 blue	3.00	3.50
957	A94	$200,000 violet	5.00	3.75
958	A94	$500,000 brn	6.00	3.00
		Nos. 951-958 (8)	20.80	63.75

Zeros for "cents" omitted on Nos. 957-958.
See surcharge note following No. 900.

Locomotive and Ship — A96

1949, May 1 Litho. Perf. 12½
Without Gum

959	A96	orange	5.00	2.50
a.		Rouletted	13.50	10.00

Nos. 959, C62, E12 and F2 were printed without denomination and sold at the daily rate of the yuan. This was necessitated by the gold yuan inflation.
For surcharges and overprints see Nos. 1130, 1213, Taiwan 97, Fukien 18, Kansu 1, People's Republic of China 24-29, 101-104, 4L31-4L33, 4L45-4L47, 4L61-4L62, 7L9-7L12, 8L52-8L54.

Revenue Stamps Overprinted in Black

1949, May Perf. 12½, 13, 14
Without Gum

960	A95	$30 dark violet	125.00	120.00

Engr.

961	A95	$200 violet brown	15.00	12.00
962	A95	$500 dark green	20.00	20.00
		Nos. 960-962 (3)	160.00	152.00

A similar overprint appears on Nos. C63, E13, F3, differing in 2nd and 3rd characters of bottom row.

Silver Yuan Surcharge in Black or Other Colors

1949 Litho.

963	A95	1c on $5000 brn (G)	8.50	5.50
964	A95	4c on $100 ol grn (Bl)	6.00	3.75
965	A95	4c on $3000 org)	6.00	4.50

966	A95	10c on $50 dk bl (RV)	8.50	2.75
967	A95	10c on $1000 car	8.50	3.25
a.		Inverted surcharge	60.00	
968	A95	20c on $1000 red (V)	8.50	5.00
b.		Inverted surcharge		
968A	A95	50c on $30 dk vio (C)	47.50	6.00
969	A95	50c on $50 dk bl (C)	21.00	2.75
970	A95	$1 on $50 dk bl	25.00	35.00
		Nos. 963-970 (9)	139.50	66.00

Nos. 963-965 and 967 are engraved.

Sun Type of 1949 Redrawn Coarse Impression

1949   *Perf. 12½, 13 or Compound*

973	A94	1c apple green	29.00	11.00
974	A94	2c orange	9.00	17.50
975	A94	4c blue green	.35	2.00
976	A94	10c deep lilac	.35	2.00
977	A94	16c orange red	.75	17.50
978	A94	20c blue	.45	5.50
979	A94	50c dk brown	2.40	48.00
980	A94	100c deep blue	475.00	475.00
981	A94	500c scarlet	525.00	525.00
		Nos. 973-981 (9)	1,042.	1,104.

For surcharges see Nos. 1057-1060.

Flying Geese Over Globe — A97

1949, May   **Litho.**   *Perf. 12½*
Without Gum

984	A97	$1 brown org	15.00	17.50
985	A97	$2 blue	75.00	30.00
986	A97	$5 car rose	75.00	32.50
987	A97	$10 blue grn	75.00	65.00
		Nos. 984-987 (4)	240.00	145.00

Five other denominations — 10c, 16c, 50c, $20 and $50 — were also printed at Shanghai, but were not issued.

For surcharges see Nos. 1007-1011, 1042-1045, 1061-1063, People's Republic of China 49-56, 5LQ17-5LQ26, 7L17-7L18, 8L14-8L16.

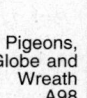

Pigeons, Globe and Wreath A98

Engraved and Typographed
1949, Aug. 1   Without Gum   *Imperf.*

988	A98	$1 org red & blk	12.00	17.50

75th anniv. of the UPU.
Exists with black denomination omitted.

Summer Palace, Peiping — A99

Bronze Bull and Kunming Lake — A100

Engraved and Typographed
1949, Aug.   Rouletted
Without Gum

989	A99	15c org brn & grn	8.00	9.50
990	A100	40c dl grn & car	9.25	9.50
a.		2nd and 3rd characters at top transposed	160.00	200.00

Silver Yuan Surcharge in Black on 1949 Sun Yat-sen Issues

1949   *Perf. 12½, 14*

991	A94	1c on $100 org brn (890)	15.00	10.00
992	A94	1c on $100 dk org brn (898)	15.00	10.00
993	A94	2½c on $500 rose lil (892)	19.00	11.00
a.		Inverted surcharge	60.00	
994	A94	2½c on $500 rose lil (900)	21.00	12.00
995	A94	15c on $10 grn (887)	30.00	40.00
a.		Inverted surcharge	67.50	
996	A94	15c on $20 vio brn (896)	42.50	65.00
		Nos. 991-996 (6)	142.50	148.00

Silver Yuan Surcharge in Black or Carmine

997	A94	2½c on $50 grn (951)	2.75	3.75
998	A94	2½c on $50,000 bl (956)	7.50	3.75
999	A94	5c on $1000 dp bl (952) (C)	6.00	3.75
1000	A94	5c on $20,000 org (955)	4.00	3.25
1001	A94	5c on $200,000 vio (957) (C)	5.50	3.25
1002	A94	5c on $500,000 vio brn (958)	5.50	3.25
1003	A94	10c on $5000 car (953)	11.00	8.00
1004	A94	10c on $10,000 brn (954)	11.00	8.00
1005	A94	15c on $200 red org (891)	13.50	16.00
1006	A94	25c on $100 dk org brn (896)	27.50	30.00
		Nos. 997-1006 (10)	94.25	83.00

REPUBLIC OF CHINA

ri-'pə-blik of 'chī-nə

(Taiwan)

LOCATION — Taiwan (since 1949) (Formosa)
GOVT. — Republic
AREA — 13,970 sq. mi.
POP. — 22,113,250 (1999 est.)
CAPITAL — Taipei

Stamps issued and used in Taiwan after Communist forces occupied the Chinese mainland include Taiwan Nos. 91-96, 101-103, J10-J17.

> Catalogue values for unused stamps in this country are for Never Hinged items, beginning with Scott 1124 in the regular postage section, Scott B17 in the semi-postal section, Scott C69 in the airpost section, and Scott J142 in the postage due section.

Watermarks

Wmk. 281 — Wavy Lines

Wmk. 323 — Seal Character (found with "Yu" in various arrangements)

Wmk. 368 — JEZ Multiple

Wmk. 370 — Geometrical Design

Type of 1949 with Value Omitted Surcharged in Various Colors

1950, Jan. 1   Unwmk.   Perf. 12½

1007	A97	$1 green (Bk)	225.00	14.00
1008	A97	$2 green (C)	260.00	25.00
1009	A97	$5 green (V)	2,750.	140.00
1010	A97	$10 green (Br)	3,750.	325.00
1011	A97	$20 green (Dk Bl)	6,500.	1,100.
		Nos. 1007-1011 (5)	13,485.	1,604.

Two printings of the $1 and $2 show minor differences.

Cheng Ch'eng-kung (Koxinga) — A101

1950, June 26   Typo.   Rouletted
Without Gum

1012	A101	3c dk gray grn	4.00	1.10
1013	A101	10c orange brn	3.00	.30
1014	A101	15c orange yel	14.25	3.25
1015	A101	20c emerald	4.00	.25
1016	A101	30c claret	60.00	17.50
1017	A101	40c red orange	4.50	.30
1018	A101	50c chocolate	7.50	1.10

1019	A101	80c carmine	22.00	3.75
1020	A101	$1 ultra	18.50	1.10
1021	A101	$1.50 green	70.00	14.00
1022	A101	$1.60 blue	60.00	1.75
1023	A101	$2 red violet	25.00	1.40
1024	A101	$5 aqua	175.00	27.50
		Nos. 1012-1024 (13)	467.75	73.30

Part perf pairs exist of the 10c, 20c, 80c. The 10c and 20c were reprinted from new plates. There are slight differences.

For surcharges see Nos. 1070-1072, 1105-1108, 1118-1119.

Nos. 751, 753, 788-791, 793, 795-799 Surcharged in Carmine or Black

1950   **Engr.**   *Perf. 14*

1025	A82	3c on $30,000	3.75	2.25
1026	A82	3c on $40,000 (C)	3.25	2.25
1027	A82	3c on $50,000 (C)	3.25	3.00
1028	A82	5c on $200,000	3.75	2.50
1029	A82	10c on $4000	32.50	4.00
1030	A82	10c on $6000	24.00	4.00
1031	A82	10c on $20,000	24.00	4.00
1032	A82	10c on $2,000,000	24.00	4.00
1033	A82	20c on $500,000	35.00	4.00
1034	A82	20c on $1,000,000	60.00	8.00
1035	A82	30c on $3,000,000	90.00	10.00
1036	A82	50c on $5,000,000 (C)	150.00	10.00
		Nos. 1025-1036 (12)	453.50	58.00

Issued: Nos. 1025-1027, 3/6; No. 1028, 3/25; No. 1031, 6/10; Nos. 1029-1030, 1032, 1035-1036, 8/1; No. 1033-1034, 8/25.
Forgeries exist.

Inverted Surcharge

1029a	A82	10c on $4000	175.00
1030a	A82	10c on $6000	375.00
1031a	A82	10c on $20,000	210.00
1032a	A82	10c on $2,000,000	225.00
1033a	A82	20c on $500,000	300.00
1034a	A82	20c on $1,000,000	300.00

Allegory of Election A102

1951, Mar. 20   Engr.   Unwmk.
Perf. 12x12½, Imperf.
Without Gum

1037	A102	40c carmine	15.00	2.00
a.		Horiz. pair, imperf. btwn.	85.00	
1038	A102	$1 dp blue	35.00	4.00
1039	A102	$1.60 purple	60.00	5.00
1040	A102	$2 brown	85.00	5.00
		Nos. 1037-1040 (4)	195.00	16.00

Souvenir Sheet
Imperf

1041	A102	$2 dp blue grn	575.00	400.00

Adoption of local self-government in Taiwan.

Design A97 Surcharged — A103

Surcharge in Various Colors
1951, July 19   *Perf. 12½*
Without Gum

1042	A103	$5 green (R Br)	110.00	12.50
1043	A103	$10 green (Bk)	225.00	14.00
1044	A103	$20 green (R)	950.00	40.00
1045	A103	$50 green (P)	1,600.	100.00
		Nos. 1042-1045 (4)	2,885.	166.50

Farmer and Scroll Announcing Tax Reduction — A104

1952, Jan. 1   Without Gum   Perf. 14

1046	A104	20c red orange	11.00	1.50
1047	A104	40c dk green	15.00	2.75
1048	A104	$1 brown	26.00	6.50
1049	A104	$1.40 dp blue	42.50	4.50
1050	A104	$2 dk gray	120.00	40.00
1051	A104	$5 brown car	160.00	16.00
	Nos. 1046-1051 (6)		374.50	71.25

Land tax reduction of 37.5% in Taiwan.
Value, imperf. set, $1,100.

Pres. Chiang Kai-shek, Flag and Followers A105

Flag in Violet Blue and Carmine

1952, Mar. 1   Unwmk.   Perf. 14
Without Gum

1052	A105	40c rose car	16.00	.50
a.		Vert. pair, imperf. btwn.	150.00	
1053	A105	$1 dp green	30.00	2.25
1054	A105	$1.60 brown org	62.50	1.10
a.		Horiz. pair, imperf. btwn.	320.00	
1055	A105	$2 brt blue	125.00	19.00
1056	A105	$5 violet brn	145.00	5.00
	Nos. 1052-1056 (5)		378.50	27.85

2nd anniv. of Chiang Kai-shek's return to the presidency.
Value, imperf. set, $495.
See Nos. 1064-1069.

Nos. 975-976, 978-979 Surcharged in Black

1952, Aug. 1   Perf. 12½

1057	A94	3c on 4c bl grn	6.25	5.25
1058	A94	3c on 10c dp lil	6.25	5.25
a.		Inverted surcharge		
1059	A94	3c on 20c blue	8.75	7.50
1060	A94	3c on 50c dk brn	10.00	8.75
	Nos. 1057-1060 (4)		31.25	26.75

Forgeries exist.

Geese Type of 1949 with Value Omitted Surcharged

1952, Dec. 8

1061	A97	$10 green (P)	100.00	16.00
1062	A97	$20 green (R)	300.00	27.50
1063	A97	$50 green (Bk)	2,750.	750.00
	Nos. 1061-1063 (3)		3,150.	793.50

Chiang Type of 1952 Redrawn
Perf. 12½

1953, Mar. 1   Engr.   Unwmk.
Without Gum

Flag in Dark Blue & Carmine

1064	A105	10c red orange	5.00	1.50
1065	A105	20c green	1.05	1.50
1066	A105	40c rose pink	15.00	2.00
1067	A105	$1.40 blue	45.00	3.25
1068	A105	$2 brown	120.00	6.50
1069	A105	$5 rose violet	180.00	17.50
	Nos. 1064-1069 (6)		366.05	32.25

Chiang Kai-shek's return to presidency, 3rd anniv.
Many differences in redrawn design. Value, imperf. set, $495.

Nos. 1020, 1014, 1016 and 1022 Surcharged in Various Colors

1953   Rouletted

1070	A101	3c on $1 ultra (C)	2.00	.50
1070A	A101	10c on 15c org yel (G) ('54)	7.50	1.05
1071	A101	10c on 30c cl (Bl)	4.00	1.40
1072	A101	20c on $1.60 bl (Bk)	4.50	1.50
	Nos. 1070-1072 (4)		18.00	4.45

Chinese characters and ornamental device at bottom differ on each value.
Issued: No. 1071, 2/1; No. 1070, 5/25; No. 1072, 6/13; No. 1070A, 7/16.

Nurse & Patients — A106

Cross in Red, Burelage Color in Italics

1953, July 1   Litho.   Perf. 12½
Without Gum

1073	A106	40c brown, *buff*	15.00	2.00
1074	A106	$1.60 blue, *bl*	35.00	2.00
1075	A106	$2 green, *yel*	55.00	2.25
1076	A106	$5 red org, *org*	95.00	10.00
	Nos. 1073-1076 (4)		200.00	16.25

Chinese Anti-Tuberculosis Association.

Chiang Kai-shek — A107

1953, Oct. 31   Engr.   Without Gum

1077	A107	10c dk brown	5.75	.25
1078	A107	20c lilac	5.75	.25
1079	A107	40c dp green	5.75	.25
1080	A107	50c dp pink	8.00	.45
1081	A107	80c brown bis	22.00	2.00
1082	A107	$1 dp olive grn	10.00	.25
1083	A107	$1.40 dp blue	10.00	.25
1084	A107	$1.60 dp carmine	10.00	.25
1085	A107	$1.70 apple grn	10.00	1.10
1086	A107	$2 brown	12.00	.25
1087	A107	$3 dark blue	200.00	9.00
1088	A107	$4 aqua	12.00	.70
1089	A107	$5 red orange	18.00	.70
1090	A107	$10 dk green	80.00	4.00
1091	A107	$20 dk brn lake	100.00	10.00
a.		Souvenir folder	600.00	
	Nos. 1077-1091 (15)		509.25	29.70

67th birthday of Pres. Chiang Kai-shek.
No. 1091a contains Nos. 1077-1091 imperf, arranged in 3 sheets of 5 stamps each.

Silo Highway Bridge — A108

$1.60 and $5, Silo bridge, side view.
Without Gum
Various Frames

1954, Jan. 28   Unwmk.   Perf. 12½

1092	A108	40c vermilion	20.00	3.00
1093	A108	$1.60 blue violet	100.00	3.00
1094	A108	$3.60 sepia	75.00	9.00
1095	A108	$5 magenta	175.00	24.00
a.		Souvenir folder	2,100.	
	Nos. 1092-1095 (4)		370.00	39.00

Opening of Silo bridge, 1st anniversary.
No. 1095a contains one sheet of 4 containing Nos. 1092-1095 imperforate. Beware of stapled folders.

Forest of Evergreens — A109

1954, Mar. 12   Perf. 12x12½
Without Gum

1096	A109	40c shown	17.00	1.50
1097	A109	$10 Nursery	126.50	10.00

Issued to publicize forest conservation.

Runner — A110

1954, Mar. 29   Without Gum

1098	A110	40c dp ultra	14.00	2.00
1099	A110	$5 carmine	100.00	10.00

11th Youth Day, Mar. 29, 1954.

Globe, Bridge and Ship — A111

1954, Oct. 21   Perf. 12
Without Gum

1100	A111	40c red orange	15.00	1.00
1101	A111	$5 deep blue	17.50	4.50

2nd Overseas Chinese Day, Oct. 21, 1954.

Ex-Prisoner with Broken Chains — A112

Designs: $1, Ex-prisoner with torch and flag, UN emblem. $1.60, Torch and date.

1955, Jan. 23

1102	A112	40c blue green	2.50	.65
a.		Vert. pair, imperf. btwn.	150.00	

1103	A112	$1 sepia	18.50	5.00
1104	A112	$1.60 lake	18.50	4.25
	Nos. 1102-1104 (3)		39.50	9.90

Honoring Chinese who fought on the side of the North Korean army, who, when released January 23, 1954, chose to return to the Republic of China.

Nos. 1019-1021, 1017 Surcharged in Brown, Blue or Green

a

b

c

1955   Rouletted

1105	A101(a)	3c on $1 (Br)	2.75	.50
1106	A101(b)	10c on 80c (Bl)	3.75	.50
1107	A101(b)	10c on $1.50 (Bl)	3.75	.50
1108	A101(c)	20c on 40c (G)	4.50	.85
	Nos. 1105-1108 (4)		14.75	2.35

Issued: No. 1105, 1108, 2/18; Nos. 1106-1107, 8/1.

Hand Planting Evergreen Tree — A113

Design: $50, Seedling and map of Taiwan.

1955, Apr. 1   Perf. 12
Without Gum

1109	A113	$20 dp carmine	32.50	1.25
1110	A113	$50 blue	80.00	5.75

Issued to publicize forest conservation.

Chiang Kai-shek, Flags, Building A114

1955, May 20   Engr.   Perf. 12
Without Gum
1111	A114	20c olive	4.50	.40
1112	A114	40c blue green	4.00	.40
1113	A114	$2 car rose	10.75	1.25
1114	A114	$7 dp ultra	17.00	2.00
a.		Souv. sheet of 4, #1111-1114, imperf.	325.00	200.00
		Nos. 1111-1114 (4)	36.25	4.05

First anniversary of Pres. Chiang Kai-shek's re-election.
No. 1114a is perf. 12 at right edge of sheet. Value is for sheet with right selvage.

Armed Forces Emblem — A115

1955, Sept. 3   Without Gum
1115	A115	40c dk blue	4.75	.50
1116	A115	$2 org ver	17.00	1.50
1117	A115	$7 bl grn	27.50	1.75
a.		Sheet of 3, #1115-1117, imperf.	700.00	500.00
		Nos. 1115-1117 (3)	49.25	3.75

Armed Forces Day, Sept. 3.
No. 1117a is perf. 12 at right edge of sheet. Value is for sheet with right selvage.

Nos. 1017, 1018 and C64 Surcharged in Magenta

1955, Sept. 16   Typo.   Rouletted
1118	A101	20c on 40c red org	5.00	.40
1119	A101	20c on 50c choc	5.00	.40
1120	AP6	20c on 60c dp blue	7.00	.50
		Nos. 1118-1120 (3)	17.00	1.30

Flags of UN and China A116

1955, Oct. 24   Engr.   Perf. 11½
Without Gum
1121	A116	40c dk blue	3.50	.55
1122	A116	$2 dk car rose	6.75	1.10
1123	A116	$7 slate green	11.50	1.90
		Nos. 1121-1123 (3)	21.75	3.55

10th anniv. of the UN, Oct. 24, 1955.

> **Catalogue values for unused stamps in this section, from this point to the end of the section, are for Never Hinged items.**

Pres. Chiang Kai-shek — A117

1955, Oct. 31   Photo.   Perf. 13½
1124	A117	40c dk bl, red & brn	6.00	.60
1125	A117	$2 grn, red & dk bl	12.75	2.00
1126	A117	$7 brn, red & grn	19.00	3.00
a.		Souv. sheet of 3, #1124-1126, imperf.	180.00	180.00
		Nos. 1124-1126 (3)	37.75	5.60

69th birthday of Pres. Chiang Kai-shek.
No. 1126a is perf. 12 at right edge of sheet. Value is for sheet with right selvage.

Birthplace of Sun Yat-sen — A118

1955, Nov. 12   Engr.   Perf. 12
Without Gum
1127	A118	40c blue	3.25	.45
1128	A118	$2 red brown	8.00	1.00
1129	A118	$7 rose lake	10.00	2.00
		Nos. 1127-1129 (3)	21.25	3.45

90th anniversary, birth of Sun Yat-sen.

No. 959a Surcharged in Bright Green

1956, Feb. 10   Litho.   Rouletted
1130	A96	20c on orange	.60	.25

See No. 1213.

China Map and Transportation Methods — A119

Wmk. 281
1956, Mar. 20   Engr.   Perf. 12
Without Gum
1131	A119	40c dk carmine	2.00	.25
1132	A119	$1 intense blk	4.00	.65
1133	A119	$1.60 chocolate	5.50	.45
1134	A119	$2 dk green	8.75	1.00
		Nos. 1131-1134 (4)	20.25	2.35

60th anniv. of the founding of the modern Chinese postal system.

Souvenir Sheets
Imperf
1135	A119	$2 magenta	60.00	30.00
1136	A119	$2 red	60.00	30.00

Exhib. for the 60th anniv. of the modern Chinese postal system, Mar. 20, 1956.

Children at Play — A120

1956, Apr. 4   Unwmk.   Perf. 12
Without Gum
1137	A120	40c emerald	1.75	.25
1138	A120	$1.60 dk blue	3.50	.50
1139	A120	$2 dk carmine	5.75	1.00
		Nos. 1137-1139 (3)	11.00	1.75

Children's Day, Apr. 4, 1956.

Early and Modern Locomotives A121

1956, June 9   Wmk. 281 Vert.
Without Gum
1140	A121	40c rose car	4.25	.40
1141	A121	$2 blue	6.00	.65
1142	A121	$8 green	10.00	1.75
		Nos. 1140-1142 (3)	20.25	2.80

75th anniversary of Chinese Railroads.

Pres. Chiang Kai-shek
A122   A123

A124

Various Portraits of Chiang
Perf. 14½x13½, 14½ (A123), 13½x14½
1956, Oct. 31   Photo.   Unwmk.
1143	A122	20c red orange	4.50	.25
1144	A122	40c carmine rose	6.75	.25
1145	A123	$1 brt ultra	9.00	.30
1146	A123	$1.60 red lilac	11.50	.25
1147	A124	$2 red brown	16.00	.50
1148	A124	$8 brt grnsh blue	35.00	.85
		Nos. 1143-1148 (6)	82.75	2.40

70th birthday of Pres. Chiang Kai-shek.

Types of Special Delivery, Air Post and Registration Stamps of 1949 Surcharged in Black or Maroon

a   b

c

1956   Unwmk.   Litho.   Rouletted
Without Gum
1150	SD2(a)	3c red violet	1.25	.25
a.		Perf. 12½	3.50	.30
1151	AP5(b)	3c blue green (M)	1.25	.25
1152	R2(c)	10c bright red	1.25	.25
		Nos. 1150-1152 (3)	3.75	.75

Issued: No. 1150, 4/25; No. 1151, 11/11; No. 1152, 12/25.

Telecommunications Emblem and Radio Tower — A125

Wmk. 281
1956, Dec. 28   Engr.   Perf. 12
Without Gum
1153	A125	40c deep ultra	1.60	.25
1154	A125	$1.40 carmine	2.25	.25
1155	A125	$1.60 dark green	3.25	.25
1156	A125	$2 chocolate	4.25	.40
		Nos. 1153-1156 (4)	11.35	1.15

Chinese telegraph service, 75th anniv.

Map of China — A126

Pin Perf., Perf. 12x12½
1957   Litho.   Wmk. 281
Without Gum
1157	A126	3c brt blue	.90	.25
1158	A126	10c violet	1.40	.25
1159	A126	20c red orange	.90	.25
1160	A126	40c rose red	1.75	.25

Unwmk.
1161	A126	$1 orange brown	2.50	.25
1162	A126	$1.60 green	3.75	.25
		Nos. 1157-1162 (6)	11.20	1.50

Map inscription reads: "Recovery of Mainland."
See Nos. 1177-1182.

Mother Instructing Mencius — A127

Design: $3, Mother tattooing Yueh Fei.

Without Gum
Unwmk.
1957, May 12   Engr.   Perf. 12
1163	A127	40c green	1.50	.25
1164	A127	$3 redsh brown	2.75	.40

Issued to honor Mother's Day, 1957.

Badge of Chinese Boy Scouts — A128

1957, Aug. 11   Without Gum
1165	A128	40c lilac	.80	.25
1166	A128	$1 green	1.75	.50
1167	A128	$1.60 dk blue	2.50	.25
		Nos. 1165-1167 (3)	5.05	1.00

Cent. of the birth of Lord Baden-Powell and to publicize the World Scout Jubilee Jamboree, England, Aug. 1-12.

Globe, Radio Tower and Microphone A129

1957, Sept. 16   Without Gum
1168	A129	40c vermilion	.60	.25
1169	A129	50c brt rose lilac	1.00	.25
1170	A129	$3.50 dark blue	1.75	.55
		Nos. 1168-1170 (3)	3.35	1.05

30th anniv. of Chinese broadcasting.

Map of Taiwan — A130

1957, Oct. 26   Without Gum
1171	A130	40c blue green	3.25	.40
1172	A130	$1.40 lt ultra	6.25	1.75
1173	A130	$2 gray	8.50	1.90
		Nos. 1171-1173 (3)	18.00	4.05

Start of construction on the Cross Island Highway, Taiwan.

Freighter "Hai Min" and River Boat "Kiang Foo" — A131

**1957, Dec. 16   Engr.   *Perf. 12*
Without Gum**
1174	A131	40c deep ultra	.75	.25
1175	A131	80c rose lake	1.50	.95
1176	A131	$2.80 vermilion	2.25	1.40
		Nos. 1174-1176 (3)	4.50	2.60

85th anniv. of the establishment of the China Merchants Steam Navigation Co.

Type of 1957
Pin Perf., Perf. 12x12½
**1957, Dec. 25   Typo.   Unwmk.
Without Gum
Dark Blue Frames**
1177	A126	3c brt blue	.30	.25
1178	A126	10c violet	.55	.25
1179	A126	20c brick red	.85	.25
1180	A126	40c rose red	1.00	.25
1181	A126	$1 dp org brn	3.25	.25
1182	A126	$1.60 dp green	4.00	.30
		Nos. 1177-1182 (6)	9.95	1.55

Stamps with bars obliterating the face value are specimens.

Butterfly — A132

Various Insects in Natural Colors
Perf. 13½
1958, Mar. 20   Unwmk.   Photo.
1183	A132	10c pale grn, grn & blk	1.25	.50
1184	A132	40c lem, pink, grn & blk	1.25	.50
1185	A132	$1 yel grn & mar	2.25	.60
1186	A132	$1.40 yel, org & blk	3.25	.75
1187	A132	$1.60 pale brn & dk pur	4.75	.90
1188	A132	$2 brt yel, org & blk	5.75	1.25
		Nos. 1183-1188 (6)	18.50	4.50

Mme. Chiang Kai-shek Orchid — A133

Orchids: 20c, Formosan Wilson, horiz. $1.40, Klotzsch. $3, Fitzgerald, horiz.

Orchids in Natural Colors
1958, Mar. 20
1189	A133	20c chocolate	2.25	.40
1190	A133	40c purple	2.50	.40
1191	A133	$1.40 dk vio brn	4.50	.60
1192	A133	$3 dark blue	6.25	1.10
		Nos. 1189-1192 (4)	15.50	2.50

World Health Organization Emblem — A134

**1958, May 28   Engr.   *Perf. 12*
Without Gum**
1193	A134	40c dark blue	.50	.25
1194	A134	$1.60 brick red	.65	.25
1195	A134	$2 deep red lilac	.85	.40
		Nos. 1193-1195 (3)	2.00	.90

10th anniv. of the WHO.

President's Mansion, Taipei — A135

Wmk. 323
**1958, Sept. 20   Engr.   *Perf. 12*
Without Gum**
1196	A135	$10 blue green	16.00	.30
a.		Granite paper	12.00	.30
1197	A135	$20 car rose	24.00	.50
a.		Granite paper	20.00	.50
1198	A135	$50 red brown	60.00	2.00
1199	A135	$100 dk blue	95.00	7.50
		Nos. 1196-1199 (4)	195.00	10.30

Issued: Nos. 1196a, 1197a, 5/24/63.
See Nos. 1349-1351. For surcharge see No. J131.

Taiwan Farm Scene A136

**1958, Oct. 1   Unwmk.
Without Gum**
1200	A136	20c emerald	1.25	.25
1201	A136	40c black	1.50	.25
1202	A136	$1.40 brt magenta	2.75	.25
1203	A136	$3 ultra	4.50	.75
		Nos. 1200-1203 (4)	10.00	1.50

10th anniversary of the Joint Commission on Rural Reconstruction.

Pres. Chiang Kai-shek A137

1958, Oct. 31   Photo.   *Perf. 13½*
1204	A137	40c multicolored	1.25	.45

Pres. Chiang Kai-shek on his 72nd birthday.

UNESCO Building, Paris A138

**1958, Nov. 3   Engr.   *Perf. 12*
Without Gum**
1205	A138	20c dark blue	.35	.25
1206	A138	40c green	.50	.25
1207	A138	$1.40 orange ver	.70	.40
1208	A138	$3 red lilac	1.25	.55
		Nos. 1205-1208 (4)	2.80	1.45

UNESCO Headquarters in Paris opening, Nov. 3.

Flame from Liberty Torch Encircling Globe — A139

**1958, Dec. 10   Unwmk.
Without Gum**
1209	A139	40c green	.25	.25
1210	A139	60c gray brown	.30	.25
1211	A139	$1 carmine	.50	.25
1212	A139	$3 ultra	.75	.40
		Nos. 1209-1212 (4)	1.80	1.15

10th anniversary of the signing of the Universal Declaration of Human Rights.

No. 959a Surcharged in Bright Green

Rouletted
**1958, Dec. 11   Litho.   Unwmk.
Without Gum**
1213	A96	20c on orange	.55	.25

Ballot Box, Scales and Constitution — A140

**1958, Dec. 25   Engr.   *Perf. 12*
Without Gum**
1214	A140	40c green	1.25	.25
1215	A140	50c dull purple	1.75	.25
1216	A140	$1.40 car rose	2.00	.25
1217	A140	$3.50 dk blue	3.50	.75
		Nos. 1214-1217 (4)	8.50	1.50

Adoption of the constitution, 10th anniv.

Chu Kwang Tower, Quemoy — A141

**1959-60   Wmk. 323   Litho.   *Perf. 12*
Without Gum**
1218	A141	3c orange	.50	.25
1218A	A141	5c lt yel grn ('60)	.60	.25
1219	A141	10c lilac	.70	.25
1220	A141	20c ultra	.90	.25
1221	A141	40c brown	1.10	.25
1222	A141	50c bluish grn	1.40	.25
1223	A141	$1 rose red	1.50	.25
1224	A141	$1.40 yel grn	2.10	.25
1225	A141	$2 gray grn	2.75	.25
1226	A141	$2.80 rose pink	4.00	.25
1227	A141	$3 slate blue	4.25	.25
		Nos. 1218-1227 (11)	19.80	2.75

See Nos. 1270-1283.

ILO Emblem and Headquarters, Geneva — A142

**1959, June 15   Engr.   *Perf. 12*
Without Gum**
1228	A142	40c blue	.40	.25
1229	A142	$1.60 dk brown	.50	.25
1230	A142	$3 brt blue grn	.75	.25
1231	A142	$5 orange ver	1.25	.50
		Nos. 1228-1231 (4)	2.90	1.25

40th anniversary of the ILO.

Bugler and Tents A143

**1959, July 8   Unwmk.
Without Gum**
1232	A143	40c carmine	.95	.25
1233	A143	50c dark blue	1.10	.25
1234	A143	$5 green	1.90	.55
		Nos. 1232-1234 (3)	3.95	1.05

10th World Boy Scout Jamboree, Makiling National Park, Philippines, July 17-26.

Inscribed Stone, Mt. Tai-wu, Quemoy — A144

Map of Taiwan Straits A145

**1959, Sept. 3   Engr.   *Perf. 12*
Without Gum**
1235	A144	40c brown	.90	.25
1236	A145	$1.40 ultra	1.00	.25
1237	A145	$2 green	1.75	.25
1238	A144	$3 dark blue	2.10	.30
		Nos. 1235-1238 (4)	5.75	1.05

Defense of Quemoy and Matsu islands. For overprints see Nos. 1258-1259.

Pigeons Circling Globe A146

1959, Oct. 4   Without Gum
1239	A146	40c blue	.45	.25
1240	A146	$1 rose carmine	.80	.25
1241	A146	$2 gray brown	1.10	.25
1242	A146	$3.50 red orange	1.40	.50
		Nos. 1239-1242 (4)	3.75	1.25

Intl. Letter Writing Week, Oct. 4-10.

National Taiwan Science Hall, Taipei — A147

1959, Nov. 12   Photo.   *Perf. 13x13½*
1243	A147	40c shown	1.40	.25
1244	A147	$3 Front view	2.75	.70

Emblem
A148

1959, Dec. 7   Engr.   Perf. 12
Without Gum
1245	A148	40c blue green	.40	.25
1246	A148	$1.60 red lilac	.70	.25
1247	A148	$3 orange	1.10	.60
		Nos. 1245-1247 (3)	2.20	1.10

Intl. Confederation of Free Trade Unions, 10th anniv.

Sun Yat-sen, Lincoln and Flags
A149

1959, Dec. 25   Photo.   Perf. 13½, 12   Unwmk.
1248	A149	40c multicolored	.50	.25
1249	A149	$3 multicolored	1.25	.60

Issued to honor Sun Yat-sen and Abraham Lincoln as "Leaders of Democracy."

Mailman on Motorcycle Delivering Night Mail — A150

Postal Launch
A151

1960, Mar. 20   Engr.   Perf. 11½
Without Gum
1250	A150	$1.40 dk violet brn	1.50	.25
1251	A151	$1.60 ultra	1.50	.25

Issued to publicize the Prompt Delivery Service.

WRY Uprooted Oak Emblem — A152

1960, Apr. 7   Photo.   Perf. 13
1252	A152	40c blk, red brn & emer	.75	.25
1253	A152	$3 blk, red org & grn	1.40	.35

World Refugee Year, 7/1/59-6/30/60.

Cross Island Highway, Taiwan — A153

Design: $1, $2, Road through tunnel, vert.

Perf. 11½
1960, May 9   Engr.   Unwmk.
Without Gum
1254	A153	40c green	1.25	.25
1255	A153	$1 dk blue	2.50	.30
1256	A153	$2 brown vio	2.50	.30
1257	A153	$3 brown	3.75	.40
a.		Souv. sheet of 2, #1255, 1257, wmk. 323, imperf.	250.00	140.00
		Nos. 1254-1257 (4)	10.00	1.25

Opening of the Cross Island Highway, Taiwan.

Red Overprint on Nos. 1237-1238
Chinese and English: "Welcome U.S. President Dwight D. Eisenhower 1960"

1960, June 18   Unwmk.   Perf. 12
1258	A145	$2 green	1.40	.30
a.		Inverted overprint	2,250.	2,250.
1259	A144	$3 dk blue	1.75	.45

Eisenhower's visit to China, June 18, 1960.

Phonopost — A154

1960, June 27   Without Gum
1260	A154	$2 red orange	1.75	.40

Phonopost Service of the Chinese armed forces.

Two Horses and Groom, by Han Kan — A155

Paintings from Palace Museum, Taichung: $1, Two Riders, by Wei Yen. $1.60, Flowers and Birds by Hsiao Yung, vert. $2, Pair of Mandarin Ducks by Monk Hui Ch'ung.

1960, Aug. 4   Photo.   Perf. 13
1261	A155	$1 ol gray, blk & brn	4.00	.55
1262	A155	$1.40 bis brn, blk & fawn	8.00	1.00
1263	A155	$1.60 multicolored	9.00	1.75
1264	A155	$2 beige, blk & gray grn	14.00	3.25
		Nos. 1261-1264 (4)	35.00	6.55

Chinese paintings, 7th-11th centuries.
For other painting types with large straight numerals in the upper corners and large Chinese characters on the side see A186, A241 and A285.

Youth Corps Flag and Summer Activities — A156

Design: $3, similar to 50c, horiz.

1960, Aug. 20   Engr.   Perf. 12
Without Gum
1265	A156	50c slate green	.50	.25
1266	A156	$3 copper brown	1.10	.45

Summer activities of China Youth Corps.

Reforestation
A157

$2, Protection of forest. $3, Timber industry.

1960, Aug. 29   Photo.   Perf. 13½x13
1267	A157	$1 multicolored	1.60	.25
1268	A157	$2 multicolored	2.25	.80
1269	A157	$3 multicolored	3.25	.60
a.		Souvenir sheet of 3	29.00	22.50
		Nos. 1267-1269 (3)	7.10	1.65

Fifth World Forestry Congress, Seattle, Washington, Aug. 29-Sept. 10.
No. 1269a contains Nos. 1267-1269 assembled as a triptych, 65½x40mm and imperf., but with simulated black perforations.

Chu Kwang Tower, Quemoy — A158

1960-61   Wmk. 323   Litho.   Perf. 12
Without Gum
1270	A158	3c lt red brown	.50	.25
1271	A158	40c pale violet	.50	.25
1272	A158	50c orange ('61)	.80	.25
1273	A158	60c rose lilac	1.00	.25
1274	A158	80c pale green	1.10	.25
1275	A158	$1 gray grn ('61)	1.25	.25
1276	A158	$1.20 gray olive	1.25	.25
1277	A158	$1.50 ultra	1.50	.25
1278	A158	$2 car rose ('61)	1.75	.25
1279	A158	$2.50 pale blue	1.90	.25
1280	A158	$3 bluish green	2.00	.25
1281	A158	$3.20 lt red brown	1.75	.25
1282	A158	$3.60 vio blue ('61)	3.75	.30
1283	A158	$4.50 vermilion	7.00	.35
		Nos. 1270-1283 (14)	26.05	3.65

For surcharges see Nos. J132-J134.

Without Gum
1962-64   Granite Paper
1270a	A158	3c light red brown	.75	.25
1270B	A158	10c emer ('63)	2.25	.25
1271a	A158	40c pale violet	.75	.25
1274a	A158	80c pale green	.75	.25
1275a	A158	$1 gray grn ('63)	12.00	.25
1278a	A158	$2 carmine rose	6.00	.25
1281a	A158	$3.20 red brn ('64)	15.00	.25
1282A	A158	$4 brt blue grn	15.00	.25
1283a	A158	$4.50 vermilion	21.00	.50
		Nos. 1270a-1283a (9)	73.50	2.50

Two types of No. 1271a: I. Seven lines in "0" of "40". II. Eight lines in "0."

Sports — A159

Perf. 12½
1960, Oct. 25   Photo.   Unwmk.
1284	A159	50c Diving	1.25	.25
1285	A159	80c Discus thrower	1.00	.25
1286	A159	$2 Basketball	2.50	.30
1287	A159	$2.50 Soccer	2.75	.55
1288	A159	$3 Hurdling	4.00	.25
1289	A159	$3.20 Runner	5.25	.80
		Nos. 1284-1289 (6)	16.75	2.90

Bronze Wine Container, 1751-1111 B.C. — A160

Ancient Chinese Art Treasures: $1, Cauldron, 1111-771 B.C. $1.20, Porcelain vase, 960-1126 A.D. $1.50, Perforated tube, 1111-771 B.C. $2, Jug in shape of monk's cap, 1368-1661 A.D. $2.50, Jade flower vase, 1368-1661, A.D.

1961   Photo.   Perf. 13
1290	A160	80c lt ol, blk & dk vio	3.00	.25
1291	A160	$1 sal, bl & blk	5.75	.35
1292	A160	$1.20 yel, brn & ultra	9.00	.50
1293	A160	$1.50 lil, bl & sep	7.00	1.10
1294	A160	$2 pale grn, dk grn & red brn	10.00	.70
1295	A160	$2.50 grnsh bl & dk vio	15.00	1.25
		Nos. 1290-1295 (6)	49.75	4.15

Issue dates: Nos. 1290, 1292, 1295, Feb. 1. Nos. 1291, 1293-1294, May 1.

Flat Bowl, 1111-771 B.C. — A161

80c, Palace perfumer, 1662-1911. $1, Corn vase, 770-221 B.C. $2, Jade tankard, 960-1126 A.D. $4, Glazed washer, 1127-1279 A.D. $4.50, Jade chimera, 8 B.C.-206 A.D.

1961
1296	A160	80c pink, brn & bl & yel	2.25	.30
1297	A160	$1 cit, blk & brn	6.00	.60
1298	A160	$1.50 sal & ind	7.00	1.25
1299	A160	$2 bl, blk & rose	14.50	.75
1300	A161	$4 red, blk & bluish gray	17.00	1.25
1301	A161	$4.50 grnsh bl, blk & brn	35.00	3.00
		Nos. 1296-1301 (6)	81.75	7.15

Issued: Nos. 1296-1298, 8/15; Nos. 1299-1301, 9/15.

1962

Designs: 80c, Topaz twin wine vessels, 1662-1911 A.D. $1, Squat pouring vase, 1751-1111 B.C. $2.40, Vase, 1368-1661 A.D. $3, Wine vase, 1751-1111 B.C. $3.20, Covered porcelain jar, 1662-1911 A.D. $3.60, Perforated disc, 206 B.C.-8 A.D.

1302	A160	80c crim, blk & ocher	2.00	.25
1303	A160	$1 blue & vio blk	2.50	.25
1304	A160	$2.40 hn brn, blk & bl	20.00	1.00
1305	A160	$3 blue, blk & pink	22.50	.90
1306	A160	$3.20 ultra, lt grn & red	20.00	.90
1307	A160	$3.60 yel, blk & brn	35.00	1.25
		Nos. 1302-1307 (6)	102.00	4.55

Issue dates: Nos. 1303-1304, 1307, Jan. 15. Nos. 1302, 1305-1306, Feb. 15.

Farmer with Mechanized Plow — A162

1961, Feb. 4   Engr.   Perf. 12
Without Gum
1308 A162 80c rose violet   1.40 .25
1309 A162 $2 green   3.25 .50
1310 A162 $3.20 vermilion   5.00 .35
   Nos. 1308-1310 (3)   9.65 1.10
   1961 agricultural census.

Madame Chiang Kai-shek and League Emblem — A163

Unwmk.
1961, Mar. 8   Photo.   Perf. 13
Portrait in Black
1311 A163 80c lt grn & car rose   2.10 .30
1312 A163 $1 yel grn & car rose   4.00 .60
1313 A163 $2 org brn & car rose   4.00 .70
1314 A163 $3.20 lil & car rose   6.50 1.40
   Nos. 1311-1314 (4)   16.60 3.00

10th anniversary of the Chinese Women's Anti-Aggression League.

Spiny Lobster and Mail Order Service Emblem — A164

1961, Mar. 20   Engr.   Perf. 11½
Without Gum
1315 A164 $3 slate green   5.50 .40

Issued to publicize the mail order service for consumer goods.

Jeme Tien-yow and Pataling Tunnel — A165

$2, Jeme Tien-yow & 1909 locomotive.

1961, Apr. 26   Perf. 11½
Without Gum
1316 A165 80c lilac   1.50 .25
1317 A165 $2 black, horiz.   3.50 .60

Centenary of the birth of Jeme Tien-yow, builder of the Peking-Kalgan railroad.

Map of China inscribed: "Recovery of the Mainland" — A166

Pres. Chiang Kai-shek — A167

1961, May 20   Photo.   Perf. 13½
1318 A166 80c multicolored   2.50 .25
1319 A167 $2 multicolored   5.00 1.25
   a. Souvenir sheet of 2   22.50 22.50

1st anniversary of Pres. Chiang Kai-shek's 3rd term inauguration.
No. 1319a contains one each of Nos. 1318-1319, imperf. with simulated perforations. Without gum.

Convair 880-M, Biplane of 1921 and Flag — A168

1961, July 1   Perf. 13x12½
1320 A168 $10 multicolored   4.50 1.40

40th anniversary of civil air service.

Sun Yat-sen and Chiang Kai-shek — A169

Flag and Map of China — A170

Perf. 13½
1961, Oct. 10   Unwmk.   Photo.
1321 A169 80c gray, lt brn & sl   1.60 .25
1322 A170 $5 gray, ultra, red & beige 4.25 1.60
   a. Souvenir sheet of 2   16.00 16.00

50th anniv. of the Republic of China. No. 1322a contains one each of Nos. 1321-1322, imperf. with simulated perforations. No gum.

Green Lake — A171

Lotus Pond A172

Taiwan Scenery: $2, Sun-Moon Lake. $3.20, Wulai waterfalls.

Perf. 13½x14, 14x13½
1961, Oct. 31   Unwmk.
1323 A171 80c multicolored   4.00 .25
1324 A172 $1 multicolored   9.00 .90
1325 A172 $2 multicolored   12.00 .70
1326 A171 $3.20 multicolored 16.00 1.25
   Nos. 1323-1326 (4)   41.00 3.10

Oil Refinery — A173

Designs: $1.50, Steel works. $2.50, Aluminum plant. $3.20, Fertilizer plant, horiz.

1961, Nov. 14   Perf. 11½
1327 A173 80c multicolored   2.00 .25
1328 A173 $1.50 multicolored 3.50 .80
1329 A173 $2.50 multicolored 5.00 .70
1330 A173 $3.20 multicolored 7.25 .65
   Nos. 1327-1330 (4)   17.75 2.40

Chinese industrial development and the Golden Jubilee Convention of the Chinese Institute of Engineers, Nov. 13-16.

Atomic Reactor, Tsing-Hwa University A174   Atomic Reactor in Operation A175

Design: $3.20, Atomic symbol and laboratory, Tsing-Hwa, horiz.

1961-62   Photo.   Perf. 12½
1331 A174 80c multicolored   2.25 .25
1332 A175 $2 multicolored   5.00 1.40
1333 A175 $3.20 multicolored 5.50 1.25
   Nos. 1331-1333 (3)   12.75 2.90

Inauguration on Apr. 13, 1961, of the 1st Chinese atomic reactor at the National Tsing-Hwa University Institute of Nuclear Science. Issued: 80c, 12/2; $2, $3.20, 3/20/62.

Microwave Reflector and Telegraph Wires — A176

Design: $3.20, Microwave parabolic antenna and mountains, horiz.

1961, Dec. 28   Perf. 12½
1334 A176 80c multicolored   1.50 .25
1335 A176 $3.20 multicolored 3.00 .80

80th anniv. of Chinese telecommunications.

Mechanical Postal Equipment and Twine Tying Machine — A176a

Wmk. 323
1962, Mar. 20   Engr.   Perf. 11½
Without Gum
1336 A176a 80c chocolate   1.50 .45

Yu Shan Observatory A177   Observation Balloon, Earth and Cumulus Clouds A178

Design: $1, Map showing route of typhoon Pamela, Sept. 1961, horiz.

1962   Without Gum
1337 A177 80c brown   .95 .25
1338 A178 $1 bluish black   1.90 .30
1339 A178 $2 green   2.50 .65
   Nos. 1337-1339 (3)   5.35 1.20

Issue dates: 80c, $2, Mar. 23; $1, May 7. World Meteorological Day, Mar. 23.

Child Receiving Milk, UN Emblem A179

1962, Apr. 4   Without Gum
1340 A179 80c rose red   .85 .25
1341 A179 $3.20 green   2.50 .50
   a. Souvenir sheet of 2 16.00 4.50

15th anniv. of UNICEF. No. 1341a contains one each of Nos. 1340-1341 imperf. with simulated perforations.

Malaria Eradication Emblem — A180

Unwmk.
1962, Apr. 7   Photo.   Perf. 13
1342 A180 80c dk bl, red & lt grn   .60 .25
1343 A180 $3.60 brn, pink & grn   1.60 1.00

WHO drive to eradicate malaria.

Yu Yu-jen — A181

1962, Apr. 24   Perf. 13
1344 A181 80c gray, blk & pink   2.00 .25

Issued to honor Yu Yu-jen, newspaper reporter, revolutionary leader and co-worker of Sun Yat-sen, on his 84th birthday.

Cheng Ch'eng-kung (Koxinga) — A182

1962, Apr. 29
1345 A182 80c deep claret   2.00 .25
1346 A182 $2 dark green   3.50 .55

300th anniversary (in 1961) of the recovery of Taiwan from the Dutch by Koxinga.

Emblem of Intl. Cooperative Alliance — A183   Clasped Hands Across Globe — A184

Wmk. 323
1962, July 7   Engr.   Perf. 12
Without Gum

1347	A183	80c brown	.90	.25
1348	A184	$2 violet	2.00	.45

Intl. Cooperative Movement and 40th Intl. Cooperative Day, July 7, 1962.

Mansion Type of 1958
1962, July 20   Without Gum

1349	A135	$5 gray green	2.75	.25
1350	A135	$5.60 violet	3.75	.25
1351	A135	$6 orange	3.50	.25
	Nos. 1349-1351 (3)		10.00	.75

1963   Granite Paper

1349a	A135	$5 gray green	3.50	.25
1350a	A135	$5.60 violet	4.00	.25
1351a	A135	$6 orange	5.50	.25
	Nos. 1349a-1351a (3)		13.00	.75

"Art and Science" — A185

$2, "Education," book and UNESCO emblem, horiz. $3.20, "Communications," globes, horiz.

1962, Aug. 28   Wmk. 323   Perf. 12
Without Gum

1352	A185	80c lilac rose	.60	.25
1353	A185	$2 rose claret	1.50	.40
1354	A185	$3.20 yellow green	1.75	.30
	Nos. 1352-1354 (3)		3.85	.95

UNESCO activities in China.

Emperor T'ai Tsung, T'ang Dynasty, 627-649
A186

Emperors: $2, T'ai Tsu, Sung dynasty, 960-975. $3.20, T'ai Tsu, Yuan dynasty (Genghis Khan), 1206-27. $4, T'ai Tsu, Ming dynasty, 1368-98.

1962, Sept. 20   Photo.   Unwmk.

1355	A186	80c multicolored	25.00	3.00
1356	A186	$2 multicolored	90.00	7.00
1357	A186	$3.20 multicolored	150.00	8.00
1358	A186	$4 multicolored	260.00	21.00
	Nos. 1355-1358 (4)		525.00	39.00

Lions International Emblem A187

1962, Oct. 8   Perf. 13½

1359	A187	80c multicolored	1.25	.25
1360	A187	$3.60 multicolored	2.50	.80
a.		Souvenir sheet of 2	18.00	9.00

45th anniv. of Lions Intl. No. 1360a contains one each of Nos. 1359-1360, imperf. with simulated perforations.

Pole Vaulting — A188

Shooting A189

1962, Oct. 25   Unwmk.   Perf. 13

1361	A188	80c multicolored	1.00	.25
1362	A189	$3.20 multicolored	2.25	.40

Sports meet.

Young Farmers and 4-H Emblem — A190

Design: $3.20, 4-H emblem and rice.

Wmk. 323
1962, Dec. 7   Engr.   Perf. 12
Without Gum

1363	A190	80c carmine	.75	.25
1364	A190	$3.20 green	2.25	.65
a.		Souvenir sheet of 2	18.00	11.00

10th anniv. of the 4-H Club in China. No. 1364a contains one each of Nos. 1363-1364, imperf. with simulated perforations.

Flag, Liner of China Merchants' Steam Navigation Co. — A191

Design: $3.60, Company's Pacific navigation chart and freighter, horiz.

Perf. 13½
1962, Dec. 16   Unwmk.   Photo.

1365	A191	80c multicolored	1.60	.25
1366	A191	$3.60 multicolored	4.25	1.00

90th anniversary of the China Merchants' Steam Navigation Co., Ltd.

Farm Woman, Tractor and Plane Dropping Food over Mainland — A192

Perf. 12½
1963, Mar. 21   Unwmk.   Photo.

1367	A192	$10 multicolored	4.00	1.00

FAO "Freedom from Hunger" campaign.

Torch, Young Couple and Martyrs' Monument, Canton A193

Wmk. 323
1963, Mar. 29   Engr.   Perf. 11½
Without Gum

1368	A193	80c purple	1.00	.25
1369	A193	$3.20 green	2.00	.40

Issued for the 20th Youth Day.

Swallows, Pagoda and AOPU Emblem — A194

Designs: $2, Northern gannet, horiz. $6, Japanese crane and pine.

Unwmk.
1963, Apr. 1   Photo.   Perf. 13

1370	A194	80c multicolored	5.00	.75
1371	A194	$2 multicolored	7.00	.65
1372	A194	$6 multicolored	11.00	2.10
	Nos. 1370-1372 (3)		23.00	3.50

1st anniversary of the formation of the Asian-Oceanic Postal Union, AOPU.

Refugee Girl (Li Ying) and Map of China — A195

Refugees Fleeing Mainland A196

Wmk. 323
1963, June 27   Engr.   Perf. 11½
Without Gum

1373	A195	80c bluish black	1.40	.25
1374	A196	$3.20 dp claret	3.00	.30

1st anniv. of the evacuation of Chinese mainland refugees from Hong Kong to Taiwan. Designs from photographs of refugees.

Nurse and Red Cross A197

Design: $10, Globe and Red Cross.

Perf. 12½
1963, Sept. 1   Unwmk.   Photo.

1375	A197	80c black & carmine	6.50	.30
1376	A197	$10 slate, gray & car	7.75	2.75

Centenary of International Red Cross.

Basketball Player, Stadium and Asian Cup — A198

$2, Hands reaching for ball and Asian cup.

Wmk. 323
1963, Nov. 20   Engr.   Perf. 12
Without Gum

1377	A198	80c lilac rose	1.25	.25
1378	A198	$2 violet	2.40	.80

The 2nd Asian Basketball Championship, Taipei, Nov. 20.

UN Emblem, Torch and Men — A199

Scales and Men of Various Races A200

1963, Dec. 10   Wmk. 323   Perf. 11½
Without Gum

1379	A199	80c brt green	.80	.30
1380	A200	$3.20 maroon	1.50	.65

Universal Declaration of Human Rights, 15th anniversary.

Village and Orchids A201   "Kindle the Fire of Conscience" A202

Perf. 13½x13
1963, Dec. 17   Photo.   Unwmk.

1381	A201	40c multicolored	3.50	.50
1382	A202	$4.50 multicolored	5.50	2.25

Contribution of the Good-People-Good-Deeds campaign to improve ethical standards.

Sun Yat-sen and Book, "Three Principles of the People" A203

1963, Dec. 25   Perf. 13

1383	A203	$5 blue & multi	10.00	1.50

"Land-to-the-Tillers" program, 10th anniv. An 80c was prepared but not issued.

Torch — A204

Hands Unchained — A205

Wmk. 323
1964, Jan. 23   Engr.   Perf. 11½
Without Gum

1384	A204	80c red orange	.60	.25
1385	A205	$3.20 indigo	2.75	.35

Liberty Day, 10th anniversary.

Broadleaf
Cactus — A206

Designs: $1, Crab cactus. $3.20, Nopalx-
ochia. $5, Grizzly bear cactus.

Perf. 12½
1964, Feb. 27   Unwmk.   Photo.
Plants in Original Colors
1386 A206   80c dp plum &
                    fawn   4.50   .25
1387 A206 $1 dk blue & car   7.75   .90
1388 A206 $3.20 green   11.50   .25
1389 A206 $5 lilac & yellow   12.50 1.10
       Nos. 1386-1389 (4)   36.25 2.50

Wu Chih-
hwei — A207

Wmk. 323
1964, Mar. 25   Engr.   Perf. 11½
Without Gum
1390 A207   80c black brown   1.75   .25

Centenary of the birth of Wu Chih-hwei
(1865-1953), politician and leader of the
Kuomintang.

Chu Kwang Tower,
Quemoy — A208

Perf. 13x12½
1964-66   Wmk. 323   Litho.
Granite Paper; Without Gum
1391 A208   3c sepia   .25   .25
1392 A208   5c brt yel grn
                    ('65)   .25   .25
1393 A208   10c yellow grn   .25   .25
1394 A208   20c slate grn ('65) .25   .25
1395 A208   40c rose red   .25   .25
1396 A208   50c brown   .25   .25
1397 A208   80c orange ('65)   .25   .25
1398 A208 $1 violet ('65)   .25   .25
1399 A208 $1.50 brt lilac ('66) 2.50 .25
1400 A208 $2 lilac rose   2.50   .25
1401 A208 $2.50 ultra ('65)   2.50   .25
1402 A208 $3 slate   2.50   .30
1403 A208 $3.20 brt blue   5.00   .25
1404 A208 $4 brt green   5.75   .25
       Nos. 1391-1404 (14)   20.50 3.55

Nurses
Holding
Candles
A209

Florence Nightingale
and Student
Nurse — A210

1964, May 12   Engr.   Perf. 11½
Without Gum
1406 A209   80c violet blue   1.40   .25
1407 A210 $4 red   3.50   .50

Issued for Nurses Day.

Shihmen
Reservoir
A211

Designs: $1, Irrigation system. $3.20, Main
dam and power plant. $5, Spillway.

Perf. 12½
1964, June 14   Unwmk.   Photo.
1408 A211   80c multicolored   2.25   .25
1409 A211 $1 multicolored   3.75   .45
1410 A211 $3.20 multicolored   7.00   .55
1411 A211 $5 multicolored   10.00 1.40
       Nos. 1408-1411 (4)   23.00 2.65

Completion of Shihmen Reservoir.

15th Century Ship,
Modern
Liner — A212

Wmk. 323
1964, July 11   Engr.   Perf. 11½
Without Gum
1412 A212   80c rose red   1.25   .25
1413 A212 $3.60 brt green   1.90   .35

China's 10th Navigation Day.

Bananas
A213

Unwmk.
1964, July 25   Photo.   Perf. 14
1414 A213   80c shown   10.00 1.00
1415 A213 $1 Oranges   20.00 2.00
1416 A213 $3.20 Pineapple   23.50 2.00
1417 A213 $4 Watermelon   37.50 5.00
       Nos. 1414-1417 (4)   91.00 10.00

Artillery,
Warships, Jet
Fighters
A214

Wmk. 323
1964, Sept. 3   Engr.   Perf. 11½
Without Gum
1418 A214   80c dk blue   1.60   .25
1419 A214 $6 violet brown   4.25   .60

Issued for the 10th Armed Forces Day.

Unisphere, Flags of
China and
U.S. — A215

Chinese
Pavilion, NY
World's
Fair — A216

1964, Sept. 10   Photo.   Unwmk.
1420 A215   80c violet & multi   2.75   .25
1421 A216 $5 blue & multi   6.25   .90

NY World's Fair, 1964-65. See Nos. 1450-
1451.

Cowboy Carrying
Calf, and
Ranch — A217

Wmk. 323
1964, Sept. 24   Engr.   Perf. 11½
Without Gum
1422 A217 $2 brown lake   1.60   .25
1423 A217 $4 dark violet blue 3.25   .80

Animal Protection Week, Sept. 24-30.

Bicycling — A218

Sports: $1, Runner. $3.20, Gymnast on
rings. $10, High jump.

1964, Oct. 10   Without Gum
1424 A218   80c violet blue   1.05   .25
1425 A218 $1 rose red   1.75   .25
1426 A218 $3.20 dull blue grn 2.25   .40
1427 A218 $10 lilac   4.00 2.00
       Nos. 1424-1427 (4)   9.05 2.90

18th Olympic Games, Tokyo, Oct. 10-25.

Xu Guangqi — A219

1964, Nov. 8   Engr.   Perf. 11½
Without Gum
1428 A219   80c indigo   2.75   .25

Issued to honor Xu Guangqi (1562-1633),
scholar and statesman.

Pharmaceutical
Industry — A220

Textile
Industry
A221

$2, Chemical industry. $3.60, Cement
industry.

1964, Nov. 11   Photo.   Unwmk.
1429 A220   40c multi   2.75   .25
1430 A221 $1.50 multi   3.50   .70
1431 A220 $2 multi   5.50   .50
1432 A221 $3.60 multi   6.25 1.10
       Nos. 1429-1432 (4)   18.00 2.55

Dr. Sun Yat-
sen — A222

1964, Nov. 24   Engr.   Wmk. 323
Without Gum
1433 A222   80c green   2.00   .30
1434 A222 $3.60 purple   5.25 1.00

Founding of the Kuomintang by Sun Yat-
sen, 70th anniversary.

Eleanor Roosevelt
and Scales of
Justice — A223

Unwmk.
1964, Dec. 10   Photo.   Perf. 13
1435 A223 $10 violet & brown   2.10   .40

Issued to honor Eleanor Roosevelt (1884-
1962) on the 16th anniversary of the Universal
Declaration of Human Rights.

Scales, Code Book
and Plum
Blossom — A224

Wmk. 323
1965, Jan. 11   Engr.   Perf. 11½
Without Gum
1436 A224   80c carmine rose   .55   .25
1437 A224 $3.20 dull slate grn 1.10   .65

The 20th Judicial Day.

Rotary Emblem and
Mainspring — A225

1965, Feb. 23   Wmk. 323   Perf. 11½
Without Gum
1438 A225 $1.50 vermilion   .75   .25
1439 A225 $2 emerald   .90   .25
1440 A225 $2.50 blue   1.25   .40
       Nos. 1438-1440 (3)   2.90   .90

Rotary International, 60th anniversary.

Double Carp
Design — A226

Wmk. 323
1965, Mar. 29   Engr.   Perf. 11½
Granite Paper; Without Gum
1441 A226 $5 purple   12.50 1.25
1442 A226 $5.60 dp blue   21.00 2.00
1443 A226 $6 brown   19.00 1.25
1444 A226 $10 lilac rose   32.00 1.25
1445 A226 $20 rose car   35.00 2.00

1446	A226	$50 green	42.50	4.50
1447	A226	$100 crim rose	52.50	7.50
		Nos. 1441-1447 (7)	214.50	19.75

New dies used to reprint Nos. 1444-1447, 8/20/67. Remainders of Nos. 1441-1447 issued with gum, 11/1/71.

Madame Chiang
Kai-shek — A227

1965, Apr. 17   Photo.   Unwmk.

| 1448 | A227 | $2 multicolored | 18.00 | 1.00 |
| 1449 | A227 | $6 salmon & multi | 32.50 | 4.00 |

Chinese Women's Anti-Aggression League, 15th anniversary.

Unisphere and Chinese Pavilion — A228

"100 Birds Paying Homage to Queen Phoenix" and Unisphere — A229

1965, May 8

| 1450 | A228 | $2 blue & multi | 30.00 | 1.50 |
| 1451 | A229 | $10 red, ocher & bis | 35.00 | 3.00 |

New York World's Fair, 1964-65.

ITU Emblem, Old and New Communication Equipment A230

Design: $5, similar to 80c, vert.

Perf. 13½x13, 13x13½

1965, May 17   Photo.   Unwmk.

| 1452 | A230 | 80c multicolored | .80 | .25 |
| 1453 | A230 | $5 multicolored | 2.40 | .75 |

Centenary of the ITU.

Red Sea Bream A231

Fish: 80c, White pomfret. $2, Skipjack, vert. $4, Moonfish.

1965, July 1   Perf. 13

1454	A231	40c multicolored	2.25	.25
1455	A231	80c multicolored	3.50	.40
1456	A231	$2 multicolored	7.75	1.40
1457	A231	$4 multicolored	13.50	2.00
		Nos. 1454-1457 (4)	27.00	4.05

Issued for Fishermen's Day.

Confucius — A232

Portraits: $2.50, Yueh Fei. $3.50, Wen Tien-hsiang. $3.60, Mencius.

Wmk. 323

1965-66   Engr.   Perf. 11½

Without Gum

1458	A232	$1 deep carmine	4.50	.35
1459	A232	$2.50 black brown	3.00	.35
1460	A232	$3.50 dark red	6.50	.75
1461	A232	$3.60 dark blue	7.75	.90
		Nos. 1458-1461 (4)	21.75	2.35

The $2.50 and $3.50 have colored background.
Forgeries of No. 1461 exist.
Issued: Nos. 1458, 1461, 9/28/65; Nos. 1459-1460, 9/3/66.
See Nos. 1507-1508, design A251.

ICY Emblem — A233

Design: $6, ICY emblem, horiz.

Unwmk.

1965, Oct. 24   Photo.   Perf. 13

| 1462 | A233 | $2 brn, blk & gold | 1.60 | .25 |
| 1463 | A233 | $6 brt grn, red & gold | 3.75 | 1.40 |

International Cooperation Year, 1965.

Street Crossing, Traffic Light — A234

Wmk. 323

1965, Nov. 1   Engr.   Perf. 11½

Without Gum

| 1464 | A234 | $1 brown violet | 1.50 | .55 |
| 1465 | A234 | $4 crimson rose | 3.00 | 1.10 |

Issued to publicize traffic safety.

Sun Yat-sen — A235

Designs: $4, Dr. Sun Yat-sen, portrait at right. $5, Sun Yat-sen and flags, horiz.

Perf. 13½

1965, Nov. 12   Unwmk.   Photo.

1466	A235	$1 multicolored	3.50	.25
1467	A235	$4 multicolored	1.10	1.00
1468	A235	$5 multicolored	13.00	2.50
		Nos. 1466-1468 (3)	17.60	3.75

Children with New Year's Firecrackers A236

Dragon Dance, "Dragon Playing Ball" A237

1965, Dec. 1   Photo.   Perf. 13

| 1469 | A236 | $1 multi | 5.50 | .30 |
| 1470 | A237 | $4.50 multi | 12.50 | 1.10 |

Lien Po from "Marshal and Prime Minister Reconciled" — A238

Facial Paintings for Chinese Operas: $3, Kuan Yü from "Reunion at Ku City." $4, Gen. Chang Fei from "The Battle of Chang Pan Hill." $6, Buddha from "The Flower-Scattering Angel."

1966, Feb. 15   Unwmk.   Perf. 11½

1471	A238	$1 olive & multi	10.75	1.00
1472	A238	$3 multicolored	20.00	2.00
1473	A238	$4 multicolored	38.00	4.00
1474	A238	$6 ver & multi	40.00	6.00
		Nos. 1471-1474 (4)	108.75	13.00

Labels with a similar appearance to these stamps exist. These labels have the numbers 1 to 20 in the upper right corner, but lack the "00."

Postal Service Emblem Held by Carrier Pigeon — A239

Stone, Mt. Tai-wu, Quemoy, and Mailman A240

postal service emblem and: $3, Postal Museum. $4, Mailman climbing symbolic slope.

1966, Mar. 20   Photo.   Perf. 12½

1475	A239	$1 green & multi	1.75	.25
1476	A240	$2 multicolored	3.50	.30
1477	A240	$3 multicolored	4.25	.40
1478	A239	$4 multicolored	8.75	2.25
		Nos. 1475-1478 (4)	18.25	3.20

China postal service, 70th anniversary.

Fishing on a Snowy Day, "Five Dynasties" (907-960) A241

Paintings from Palace Museum: $3.50, Calves on the Plain, Sung artist (960-1126). $4.50, Winter landscape, Sung artist (960-1126). $5, Magpies, by Lin Ch'un, Southern Sung dynasty (1127-1279).

1966, May 20   Photo.   Perf. 13

1479	A241	$2.50 blk, brn & red	11.50	.50
1480	A241	$3.50 bis brn, blk & gray	30.00	.75
1481	A241	$4.50 blk, buff & sl	42.50	1.90
1482	A241	$5 multicolored	55.00	2.75
		Nos. 1479-1482 (4)	139.00	5.90

Inauguration of Pres. Chiang Kai-shek for a 4th term.

Dragon Boat Race A242

Lion Dance — A243

$4, Lady Chang O flying to the Moon.

1966   Unwmk.

1483	A242	$2.50 multi	5.50	.40
1484	A242	$4 multi	10.00	.50
1485	A243	$6 multicolored	20.00	1.00
		Nos. 1483-1485 (3)	35.50	1.90

Dragon Boat, Mid-Autumn and Lunar New Year Festivals. Issued: $2.50, 6/23; $4, 9/29; $6, 11/26.

Flags of China and Argentina A244

1966, July 9   Photo.   Perf. 13

| 1486 | A244 | $10 multicolored | 4.25 | .60 |

Argentina's Independence, 150th anniv.

Lin Sen — A245

Wmk. 323

1966, Aug. 1   Engr.   Perf. 11½

Without Gum

| 1487 | A245 | $1 dk brown | 2.00 | .25 |

Centenary of the birth of Lin Sen (1867-1943), Chairman of the Nationalist Government of China (1931-43).

Flying Geese — A246

1966-67   Perf. 11½ Rough

Granite Paper; Without Gum

1496	A246	$3.50 brown	1.10	.40
1497	A246	$4 vermilion	1.05	.40
1498	A246	$4.50 brt green	1.90	.45
1499	A246	$5 rose lilac	1.10	.40
1500	A246	$5.50 yel grn ('67)	2.25	.40
1501	A246	$6 brt blue	2.50	.50
1502	A246	$6.50 violet	2.25	.45
1503	A246	$7 black	1.25	.40
1504	A246	$8 car rose ('67)	1.90	.40
		Nos. 1496-1504 (9)	15.30	3.80

The $4.50, $5, $6, $7 and $8 were reissued with gum in 1970-71.

Pres. Chiang Kai-shek in Chung San Robe — A247

$5, Chiang Kai-shek in marshal's uniform.

Unwmk.

1966, Oct. 31		**Photo.**		**Perf. 13**	
1505	A247	$1	multicolored	1.90	.30
1506	A247	$5	multicolored	6.25	1.60

Chiang Kai-shek's inauguration for a fourth term as president, May 20, 1966.

Famous Men Type of 1965-66 with Frame Line

Portraits: No. 1507, Tsai Yuan-pei (1868-1940), educator. No. 1508, Chiu Ching (1875-1907), woman educator and revolutionist.

1967	**Wmk. 323**	**Engr.**		**Perf. 11½**	
		Without Gum			
1507	A232	$1	violet blue	2.25	.25
1508	A232	$1	black	2.25	.25

Issue dates: No. 1507, Jan. 11. No. 1508, July 15.

No. 1507 is on granite paper.

Motorized Mailman and Microwave Station — A248

"Transportation" and Radar Weather Station — A249

Unwmk.

1967, Mar. 15		**Photo.**		**Perf. 13**	
1511	A248	$1	multicolored	1.40	.25
1512	A249	$5	multicolored	2.50	.90

Issued to publicize the progress in communication and transportation services.

Pres. Chiang Kai-shek and Chinese Flag — A250

Design: $4, Different frame.

1967, May 20		**Litho.**		**Perf. 13**	
1513	A250	$1	multicolored	1.90	.90
1514	A250	$4	multicolored	3.00	.90

First anniversary of President Chiang Kai-shek's 4th-term inauguration.

Chu Yuan, 332-295 B.C. — A251

Portraits: $2, Li Po (705-760). $2.50, Tu Fu (712-770). $3, Po Chu-i (772-846).

Granite Paper; Without Gum
Wmk. 323

1967, June 12		**Engr.**		**Perf. 11½**	
1515	A251	$1	black	1.10	.25
1516	A251	$2	brown	3.50	.25
1517	A251	$2.50	brown blk	4.75	.45
1518	A251	$3	grnsh black	7.00	.45
	Nos. 1515-1518 (4)			16.35	1.40

Issued for Poets' Day.
See design A232.

Hotei, Wood Carving — A252

Handicrafts: $2.50, Vase and plate. $3, Dolls. $5, Palace lanterns.

Perf. 11½

1967, Aug. 12		**Unwmk.**		**Photo.**	
1519	A252	$1	gray & multi	3.00	.65
1520	A252	$2.50	multi	4.00	1.00
1521	A252	$3	multi	5.00	1.65
1522	A252	$5	multi	6.75	3.50
	Nos. 1519-1522 (4)			18.75	6.80

Taiwan handicraft industry.

World Map — A253

Granite Paper; Without Gum
Wmk. 323

1967, Sept. 25		**Engr.**		**Perf. 11½**	
1523	A253	$1	vermilion	.45	.25
1524	A253	$5	blue	1.10	.50

1st Conference of the World Anti-Communist League, WACL, Taipei, Sept. 25-29.

Players on Stilts: "The Fisherman and the Woodcutter" A254

Unwmk.

1967, Oct. 10		**Photo.**		**Perf. 13**	
1525	A254	$4.50	multi	1.90	.45

Issued for the 56th National Day.

Maroon Oriole — A255

Formosan Birds: $1, Formosan barbet, vert. $2.50, Formosan green pigeon. $3, Formosan blue magpie. $5, Crested serpent eagle, vert. $8, Mikado pheasants.

1967, Nov. 25		**Photo.**		**Perf. 11**	
		Granite Paper			
1526	A255	$1	multi	4.00	.25
1527	A255	$2	multi	5.50	.40
1528	A255	$2.50	multi	6.75	.50
1529	A255	$3	multi	8.00	.60
1530	A255	$5	multi	9.50	.70
1531	A255	$8	multi	11.50	1.25
	Nos. 1526-1531 (6)			45.25	3.70

Chung Hsing Pagoda — A256

Buddha, Changhua A257

Designs: $2.50, Seashore, Yeh Liu Park. $5, National Palace Museum, Taipei.

Unwmk.

1967, Dec. 10		**Photo.**		**Perf. 13**	
1532	A256	$1	multi	1.50	.25
1533	A257	$2.50	multi	4.00	.50
1534	A257	$4	multi	5.00	.60
1535	A257	$5	multi	5.75	.90
	Nos. 1532-1535 (4)			16.25	2.25

Issued for International Tourist Year 1967.

China Park, Manila, and Flags — A258

1967, Dec. 30				**Perf. 13½**	
1536	A258	$1	multicolored	.65	.25
1537	A258	$5	multicolored	2.25	.65

Sino-Philippine Friendship Year 1966-67.

Sun Yat-sen Building, Yangmingshan
A259   A259a

Perf. 13x12½

1968-75		**Litho.**		**Wmk. 323**	
		Granite Paper			
1538	A259	5c	lt brown	.60	.25
1539	A259	10c	grnsh black	.60	.25
1540	A259	50c	brt rose lilac	.60	.25
1541	A259	$1	vermilion	.60	.25
1542	A259	$1.50	emerald	1.10	.70
1543	A259	$2	plum	1.05	.25
1544	A259	$2.50	blue	1.25	.25
1545	A259	$3	grnsh blue	1.40	.25
	Nos. 1538-1545 (8)			7.20	2.45

See Nos. 1702-1709. For overprints see Nos. 1723-1725.

Coil Stamps

Perf. 13 Horiz.

		Photo.		**Unwmk.**	
1546	A259a	$1	carmine rose	.55	.25
1547	A259a	$1	vermilion	.55	.25

Issued: 50c, $1, $2.50, 1/23/68; No. 1546, 3/20/70; No. 1547, 1/28/75; others 7/11/68.
Inscription on No. 1546 is in color with white background. On No. 1547 it is white with colored background.

Harvesting Sugar Cane — A260

Unwmk.

1968, Mar. 1		**Photo.**		**Perf. 13**	
1548	A260	$1	olive & multi	1.75	.25
1549	A260	$4	multicolored	3.00	.45

Jade Cabbage, 1662-1911 — A261

Ancient Art Treasures: $1.50, Jade battle axe. $2, Porcelain flower bowl, 960-1126 A.D., horiz. $2.50, Cloisonné enamel vase, 1723-1736 A.D. $4, Agate flower holder in shape of finger citrus, 1662-1911 A.D., horiz. $5, Sacrificial kettle, 1111-771 B.C.

1968, Mar. 29		**Unwmk.**		**Perf. 13**	
1550	A261	$1	rose & multi	2.25	.25
1551	A261	$1.50	blue & multi	3.25	.50
1552	A261	$2	blue & multi	3.50	.25
1553	A261	$2.50	dull rose & multi	4.25	.50
1554	A261	$4	pink & multi	5.50	.60
1555	A261	$5	blue & multi	6.50	.70
	Nos. 1550-1555 (6)			25.25	2.80

For similar artifact designs inscribed "Republic of China," with single-color denominations in slanted numerals and the cents underlined, see types A276, A291, A323, A336, A384, A395, A411.
Artifact designs with denominations in outlined numerals begin with type A439.

View of City in Cathay (1) — A262

Views: No. 1557, City and wall of Forbidden City (2). No. 1558, Wall at right, bridge at left (3). No. 1559, Queen's ship landing at left (4). No. 1560, Palace (5). $5, City wall and gate. $8, Suburb around Great Bridge. Design from scroll "A City in Cathay," painted 1736.

1968, June 18		**Photo.**		**Perf. 13½**	
		Size: 50x29mm			
1556	A262	$1	multicolored	2.25	.40
1557	A262	$1	multicolored	2.25	.40
1558	A262	$1	multicolored	2.25	.40
1559	A262	$1	multicolored	2.25	.40
1560	A262	$1	multicolored	2.25	.40
a.	Strip of 5, #1556-1560			10.00	10.00
		Size: 60x31mm			
		Perf. 13x13½			
1561	A262	$1	multicolored	12.00	2.10
1562	A262	$8	multicolored	21.00	2.75
	Nos. 1556-1562 (7)			44.25	6.85

See Nos. 1610-1614. For similar designs see types A281, A299, A326, A343.

Entrance Gate, Taroko Gorge A263

$8, Sun Yat-sen Building, Yangmingshan.

1968, Feb. 12		**Photo.**		**Perf. 13**	
1563	A263	$5	multicolored	1.75	.35
1564	A263	$8	multicolored	3.00	.40

The 17th Annual Conference of the Pacific Area Travel Association.

Vice President Chen Cheng — A264

1968, Mar. 5
1565 A264 $1 brown & multi 1.60 .25
Vice President Chen Cheng (1898-1965).

Flying Geese — A265

Wmk. 323
1968, Mar. 20   Litho.   Perf. 12
Granite Paper
1566 A265 $1 vermilion 9.00 .25
Souvenir Sheet
Imperf
1567 A265 $3 green 11.00 3.50
90th anniv. of Chinese postage stamps. No. 1567 contains one stamp with simulated perforations.

WHO Emblem and "20" — A266

1968, Apr. 7   Engr.   Perf. 12
Granite Paper
1568 A266 $1 green .45 .25
1569 A266 $5 scarlet 1.25 .65
20th anniv. of WHO.

Symbolic Water Cycle — A267

Wmk. 323
1968, June 6   Litho.   Perf. 11½
Granite Paper
1570 A267 $1 green & org .45 .25
1571 A267 $4 brt blue & multi 1.40 .25
Hydrological Decade (UNESCO) 1965-74.

Broadcasting to Mainland China — A268

Dual Carriers for FM Broadcasting A269

Wmk. 323
1968, Aug. 1   Litho.   Perf. 12
Granite Paper
1572 A268 $1 bl, vio bl & gray .55 .25
1573 A269 $4 lt ultra & ver 1.25 .25
40th anniv. of the Broadcasting Corp. of China, and the inauguration of frequency modulation broadcasting.

Human Rights Flame — A270

1968, Sept. 3   Granite Paper
1574 A270 $1 multicolored .60 .25
1575 A270 $5 multicolored 1.50 .25
International Human Rights Year 1968.

Crop Improvement and Extension Work — A271

Wmk. 323
1968, Sept. 30   Litho.   Perf. 12
Granite Paper
1576 A271 $1 yel, bister & dk brn .45 .25
1577 A271 $5 yel, emer & dk grn 1.75 .50
Joint Commission on Rural Reconstruction, 20th anniversary.

Javelin — A272

Designs: $2.50, Weight lifting. $5, Pole vault, horiz. $8, Woman hurdling, horiz.

Unwmk.
1968, Oct. 12   Photo.   Perf. 13
1578 A272 $1 multi .55 .25
1579 A272 $2.50 multi .80 .25
1580 A272 $5 multi 1.25 .25
1581 A272 $8 pink & multi 1.90 .35
Nos. 1578-1581 (4) 4.50 1.10
19th Olympic Games, Mexico City, 10/12-27.

Pres. Chiang Kai-shek and Whampoa Military Academy — A273

Designs: $2, Pres. Chiang Kai-shek reviewing forces of the Northern Expedition. $2.50, Suppression of bandits, reconstruction work and New Life Movement emblem. $3.50, Marco Polo Bridge near Peking and victory parade, Nanking. $4, Original copy of Constitution of Republic of China. $5, Nationalist Chinese flag flying over mainland China.

1968, Oct. 31   Perf. 11½x12
1582 A273 $1 multi .75 .30
1583 A273 $2 multi 1.00 .30
1584 A273 $2.50 multi 1.40 .45
1585 A273 $3.50 multi 1.75 .60
1586 A273 $4 multi 2.25 1.00
1587 A273 $5 multi 3.75 1.25
Nos. 1582-1587 (6) 10.90 3.90
Chiang Kai-shek's achievements for China.

Cock — A274

1968, Nov. 12   Litho.   Perf. 12
Granite Paper
1588 A274 $1 pink & multi 17.00 1.00
1589 A274 $4.50 lilac & multi 40.00 6.00
Issued for use on New Year's greetings.

Flag — A275

1968, Dec. 25   Wmk. 323   Perf. 12½
Granite Paper
1590 A275 $1 multicolored .70 .25
1591 A275 $5 lt blue & multi 1.00 .75
Constitution of the Republic of China, 20th anniversary.

Jade Belt Buckle, 1662-1911 — A276

Ancient Art Treasures: $1.50, Yellow jade vase, 960-1126 A.D., vert. $2, Cloisonne enamel square teapot, 1662-1911 A.D. $2.50, Kuei, sacrificial bronze vessel, 722-481 B.C. $4, Heavenly ball vase, 1368-1661 A.D., vert. $5, Gourd-shaped vase, 1662-1911 A.D., vert.

Unwmk.
1969, Jan. 15   Photo.   Perf. 13
1592 A276 $1 dl rose & multi 1.10 .25
1593 A276 $1.50 rose & multi 2.00 .25
1594 A276 $2 brt rose & multi 2.50 .25
1595 A276 $2.50 lt blue & multi 2.75 .60
1596 A276 $4 tan & multi 3.00 .80
1597 A276 $5 pale blue & multi 3.00 1.00
Nos. 1592-1597 (6) 14.35 3.15

Servicemen and Savings Emblem A277

Wmk. 323
1969, Feb. 1   Engr.   Perf. 12
Granite Paper
1598 A277 $1 dull red brown .35 .25
1599 A277 $4 deep blue 1.00 .55
Military Savings Program, 10th anniv.

Ti (Flute) A278

Musical Instruments: $2.50, Sheng (13 bamboo pipes connected at the base). $4, P'i p'a (lute). $5, Cheng (zither).

Unwmk.
1969, Mar. 16   Photo.   Perf. 13
1600 A278 $1 buff & multi .55 .30
1601 A278 $2.50 lt ap grn & multi 1.25 .40
1602 A278 $4 pink & multi 1.60 .45
1603 A278 $5 grnsh bl & multi 2.25 .60
Nos. 1600-1603 (4) 5.65 1.75

Sun Yat-sen Building and Kuomintang Emblem A279

1969, Mar. 29   Litho.   Perf. 13½
1604 A279 $1 multicolored .70 .25
10th Natl. Cong. of the Chinese Nationalist Party (Kuomintang), Mar. 29. A $2.50 stamp portraying Sun Yat-sen and Chiang Kai-shek was prepared but not issued.

Double Carp Design — A280

Perf. 13½x12½
1974   Engr.   Wmk. 323
Granite Paper
1606 A280 $10 dark blue 2.50 .40
1607 A280 $20 dark brown 5.25 .40
1608 A280 $50 green 8.50 .75
1609 A280 $100 bright red 10.75 1.40
Nos. 1606-1609 (4) 27.00 2.95

1969   Perf. 11½
1606a A280 $10 3.25 .35
1607a A280 $20 4.25 .35
1608a A280 $50 11.00 .45
1609a A280 $100 17.00 .90
Nos. 1606a-1609a (4) 35.50 2.05
The 1969 issue is 27mm high; 1974, 28mm. See No. 1980.

Bridal Procession — A281

Designs: No. 1610, Musicians and standard bearer from bridal procession. $2.50, Emigrant farm family in oxcart. $5, Art gallery. $8, Roadside food stands. Designs from scroll "A City in Cathay," painted in 1736.

Perf. 13½
1969, May 20   Unwmk.   Photo.
1610 A281 $1 multi 1.25 .35
1611 A281 $1 multi 1.25 .35
a. Pair, #1610-1611 2.75 2.75
1612 A281 $2.50 multi 4.00 1.00
1613 A281 $5 multi 4.25 .75
1614 A281 $8 multi 7.25 1.25
Nos. 1610-1614 (5) 18.00 3.70

ILO Emblem A282

Wmk. 323
1969, June 15   Engr.   Perf. 11½
Granite Paper
1615 A282 $1 dark blue .70 .25
1616 A282 $8 dark carmine 1.50 .55
ILO, 50th anniversary.

Family at Dinner Table and Dressing A283

Designs: $2.50, Housecleaning and obeying traffic rules. $4, Recreation (music, fishing, basketball) and education.

Wmk. 323

1969, July 15   Engr.   Perf. 11½
1617	A283	$1 brick red	.25	.25
1618	A283	$2.50 blue	.70	.35
1619	A283	$4 green	.80	.45
		Nos. 1617-1619 (3)	1.75	1.05

Model Citizen's Life Movement.

Pupils in Laboratory and Playing — A284

Design: $1, $5, Pupils with book and various school activities, horiz.

Granite Paper

1969, Sept. 1   Wmk. 323   Perf. 11½
1620	A284	$1 brt red	.25	.25
1621	A284	$2.50 brt green	.75	.30
1622	A284	$4 dk blue	1.00	.30
1623	A284	$5 brown	1.40	.55
		Nos. 1620-1623 (4)	3.40	1.40

Free 9-year education system, 1st anniv.

Wild Flowers and Pheasants, by Lu Chih (Ming) A285

Paintings: $2.50, Bamboo and birds, Sung dynasty. $5, Flowers and Birds, Sung dynasty. $8, Cranes and Flowers, by G. Castiglione, S.J. (1688-1766).

1969, Oct. 9   Photo.   Perf. 13½
1624	A285	$1 multi	1.40	.35
1625	A285	$2.50 multi	3.50	.45
1626	A285	$5 multi	8.50	.75
1627	A285	$8 multi	11.50	1.10
		Nos. 1624-1627 (4)	24.90	2.65

Golden Scepter Rose — A286

Roses: $1, "Charles Mollerin," called black rose. $5, Peace. $8, Josephine Bruce.

1969, Oct. 31   Litho.   Perf. 14
1628	A286	$1 lt vio & multi	1.25	.25
1629	A286	$2.50 lt bl & multi	3.75	.25
1630	A286	$5 dl org & multi	4.75	.35
1631	A286	$8 ap grn & multi	4.50	.70
		Nos. 1628-1631 (4)	14.25	1.55

Rocket and Radar Station — A287

Wmk. 323

1969, Nov. 21   Engr.   Perf. 11½
| 1632 | A287 | $1 rose claret | 1.50 | .25 |

The 30th Air Defense Day.

Symbol of International Cooperation A288

1969, Nov. 25
| 1633 | A288 | $1 rose claret | .35 | .25 |
| 1634 | A288 | $5 green | 1.10 | .35 |

5th General Assembly of the Asian Parliamentary Union, Taipei, Nov. 24-28.

Pekingese — A289

1969, Dec. 1   Litho.   Perf. 12
Granite Paper
| 1635 | A289 | 50c red & multi | 2.00 | .50 |
| 1636 | A289 | $4.50 green & multi | 10.00 | 2.00 |

Issued for use on New Year's greetings.

Satellite, Earth Station and Map of Taiwan A290

1969, Dec. 28   Unwmk.   Photo.   Perf. 13
1637	A290	$1 brown & multi	.45	.25
1638	A290	$5 vio blue & multi	1.60	.35
1639	A290	$8 purple & multi	2.25	.65
		Nos. 1637-1639 (3)	4.30	1.25

Inauguration of the Communication Satellite Earth Station at Chin-Shan-Li, Dec. 28.

Agate Grinding Stone, 1662-1911 A291

Ancient Art Treasures: $1, Carved lacquer ware vase, 1662-1911, vert. $2, White jade Chin-li-chih melons, 1662-1911. $2.50, Black jade shepherd and ram, 206 B.C.-220 A.D. $4, Chien-lung twin porcelain vase, 1736-1796, vert. $5, Ju porcelain vase with 3 bulls, 960-1126, vert.

1970, Jan. 23
1640	A291	$1 lt grnsh bl & multi	.75	.25
1641	A291	$1.50 pale bl & multi	1.40	.25
1642	A291	$2 green & multi	1.60	.25
1643	A291	$2.50 pink & multi	2.75	.35
1644	A291	$4 ol bis & multi	3.00	.45
1645	A291	$5 ultra & multi	4.00	.80
		Nos. 1640-1645 (6)	13.50	2.35

Hsuan Chuang — A292

Chu Hsi — A293

Design: $2.50, Hua To.

1970   Wmk. 323   Engr.   Perf. 11½
Granite Paper
1646	A292	$1 car rose	.70	.25
1647	A293	$2.50 blue grn	1.10	.25
1648	A293	$4 blue	1.75	.45
		Nos. 1646-1648 (3)	3.55	.95

Issued in memory of Hsuan Chuang (602-664), who propagated Buddhism in China; Chu Hsi (1130-1200), who developed Neo-Confucianism, and Hua To (3rd century A.D.) physician and surgeon.
Issued: $2.50, 3/17; others, 2/20.

EXPO '70 Pavilion, Emblem and Flags of Participants A294

Design: $5, Chinese pavilion, EXPO '70 emblem, exhibition and Chinese flags.

1970, Mar. 13   Unwmk.   Photo.   Perf. 13
| 1649 | A294 | $5 org red & multi | .70 | .25 |
| 1650 | A294 | $8 lt blue & multi | 1.75 | .70 |

EXPO '70 International Exhibition, Osaka, Japan, Mar. 15-Sept. 13.

Nimbus III and WMO Emblem A295

Design: $1, Agricultural meteorological station and tropical landscape, vert.

Perf. 14x13½, 13½x14
1970, Mar. 23   Litho.   Wmk. 323
Granite Paper
| 1651 | A295 | $1 green & multi | .55 | .25 |
| 1652 | A295 | $8 blue & multi | 1.00 | .65 |

10th Annual World Meteorological Day.

Martyrs' Shrine, Taipei A296

Shrine's Gate A297

1970, Mar. 29   Unwmk.   Photo.   Perf. 13
| 1653 | A296 | $1 multicolored | .70 | .25 |
| 1654 | A297 | $8 multicolored | 1.75 | .65 |

Completion of the Martyrs' Shrine in Northern Taipei, dedicated to the memory of 72 young revolutionaries who died Mar. 29, 1911.

Yueh Fei Fighting for Lost Territories A298

Characters from Chinese Operas: $2.50, Emperor Shun and stepmother. $5, The Lady Warrior Chin Liang-yu. $8, Kuan Yu and groom.

1970, May 4   Unwmk.   Perf. 13½
1655	A298	$1 multi	1.10	.25
1656	A298	$2.50 multi	2.75	.55
1657	A298	$5 multi	3.75	.65
1658	A298	$8 multi	5.75	.80
		Nos. 1655-1658 (4)	13.35	2.25

A299

Three Horses Playing — A300

Horses: No. 1659, Barren tree at right. No. 1660, Horse standing in river. No. 1661, Tree trunk in lower left corner. No. 1662, Trees in left background. No. 1663, shown. $8, Groom roping horses. Designs from scroll "One Hundred Horses" by Lang Shih-ning (Giuseppe Castiglione, 1688-1766).

Perf. 13½
1970, June 18   Unwmk.   Photo.
1659	A299	$1 multi	1.00	.25
1660	A299	$1 multi	1.00	.25
1661	A299	$1 multi	1.00	.25
1662	A299	$1 multi	1.00	.25
1663	A299	$1 multi	1.00	.25
a.		Strip of 5, #1659-1663	8.00	8.00
1664	A300	$5 bister & multi	9.75	2.00
1665	A300	$8 dl yel & multi	11.50	3.00
		Nos. 1659-1665 (7)	26.25	6.25

Lai-tsu Amusing his Old Parents — A301

Chinese Fairy Tales: No. 1667, Man disguised as deer, and hunters. No. 1668, Boy cooling his father's bed. No. 1669, Boy fishing through ice. No. 1670, Son reunited with old mother. No. 1671, Emperor tasting mother's medicine. No. 1672, Boy saving oranges for mother. No. 1673, Boy saving father from tiger.

Wmk. 323

1970, July 10   Litho.   Perf. 13½
Granite Paper
1666	A301	10c red & multi	.25	.25
1667	A301	10c car rose & multi	.25	.25
1668	A301	10c lt vio & multi	.25	.25
1669	A301	10c gray & multi	.25	.25
1670	A301	10c emerald & multi	.25	.25
1671	A301	50c bister & multi	.45	.25
1672	A301	$1 sky blue & multi	.65	.35
1673	A301	$1 dp blue & multi	.55	.45
		Nos. 1666-1673 (8)	2.90	2.30

See Nos. 1726-1733.

Man's First Step onto Moon — A302

$1, Pres. Chiang Kai-shek's message brought to the moon. $5, Neil A. Armstrong, Michael Collins, Edwin E. Aldrin, Jr., and moon, horiz.

Perf. 13½x13, 13x13½

1970, July 21		Photo.	Unwmk.	
1674	A302	$1 yellow & multi	1.00	.25
1675	A302	$5 lt yel grn & multi	1.60	.45
1676	A302	$8 blue & multi	2.75	.70
		Nos. 1674-1676 (3)	5.35	1.40

1st anniv. of man's 1st landing on the moon.

Asian Productivity Year Symbol A303

Wmk. 323

1970, Aug. 18		Litho.	Perf. 13½	

Granite Paper

1677	A303	$1 emerald & multi	.65	.25
1678	A303	$5 blue & multi	1.25	.40

Issued to publicize Asian Productivity Year.

Flags of China and UN — A304

1970, Sept. 19		Wmk. 323	Perf. 12	

Granite Paper

1679	A304	$5 blue, car & blk	1.75	.65

25th anniversary of the United Nations.

Postal Zone Map — A305

Postal Code Emblem A306

1970, Oct. 8			Litho.	
1680	A305	$1 lt blue & multi	.90	.25
1681	A306	$2.50 green & multi	1.10	.40

Issued to publicize the postal code system.

Eleventh Month Scroll — A307

Designs: A scroll series, "Activities of the 12 Months," painted on silk by a group of painters of the Ch'ien Lung court (1736-1796). Chinese number in parenthesis at right of denomination tells month.

Jan., Feb., Mar.

（一）（二）（三）

Perf. 13½x13

1970-71		Photo.	Unwmk.	
1682	A307	$1 multi	2.25	.40
1683	A307	$2.50 multi	5.00	1.00
1684	A307	$5 multi	8.50	1.40

Apr., May, June

（四）（五）（六）

1685	A307	$1 multi	2.25	.40
1686	A307	$2.50 multi	5.00	1.00
1687	A307	$5 multi	8.50	1.40

July, Aug., Sept.

（七）（八）（九）

1688	A307	$1 multi	2.25	.40
1689	A307	$2.50 multi	5.00	1.00
1690	A307	$5 multi	8.50	1.40

Oct., Nov., Dec.

（十）（一十）（二十）

1691	A307	$1 multi	2.25	.40
1692	A307	$2.50 multi	5.00	1.00
1693	A307	$5 multi	8.50	1.40
		Nos. 1682-1693 (12)	63.00	11.20

Issued: Nos. 1691-1693, 10/21/70; Nos. 1682-1684, 1/14/71; Nos. 1685-1687, 4/26/71; Nos. 1688-1690, 8/27/71.

Family at Home A308

$4, Family of 5 going on an excursion, vert.

Perf. 13½x14, 14x13½

1970, Nov. 11		Litho.	Wmk. 323	

Granite Paper

1694	A308	$1 multicolored	.70	.25
1695	A308	$4 yel grn & multi	1.50	.35

Issued to publicize family planning.

Piggy Bank — A309

1970, Dec. 1			Perf. 12½x12	

Granite Paper

1696	A309	50c multi	3.25	.25
1697	A309	$4.50 blue & multi	5.00	.90

Issued for use on New Year's greetings.

Tibia Fusus Shells A310

Rare Taiwan Shells: $2.50, Harpeola kurodai. $5, Conus stupa kuroda. $8, Entemnotrochus rumphii.

1971, Feb. 25			Perf. 13x13½	
1698	A310	$1 vio & multi	.50	.25
1699	A310	$2.50 multi	1.90	.25
1700	A310	$5 org & multi	2.40	.45
1701	A310	$8 grn & multi	3.25	.65
		Nos. 1698-1701 (4)	8.05	1.60

Sun Yat-sen Building, Yangmingshan A311

Perf. 13½x12½

1971		Litho.	Wmk. 323	

Granite Paper

1702	A311	5c brown	.25	.25
1703	A311	10c dk gray	.25	.25
1704	A311	50c brt rose lilac	.95	.25
1705	A311	$1 vermilion	1.00	.25
1706	A311	$1.50 ultra	1.10	.25
1707	A311	$2 plum	1.25	.25
1708	A311	$2.50 emerald	1.40	.25
1709	A311	$3 aqua	1.90	.30
		Nos. 1702-1709 (8)	8.10	2.05

Passbook and Postal Savings Certificate A312

$4, People and hand dropping coin into bank.

Perf. 13½x14

1971, Mar. 20		Litho.	Wmk. 323	
1712	A312	$1 yel grn & multi	.65	.25
1713	A312	$4 ver & multi	1.50	.30

Publicizing Chinese Postal Savings Service.

Cooperation Emblem, Farmers — A313

Design: $8, Chinese teaching rice farming to Africans, horiz.

Unwmk.

1971, May 20		Photo.	Perf. 13	
1714	A313	$1 multicolored	.65	.25
1715	A313	$8 multicolored	1.40	.70

Sino-African Technical Cooperation Committee, 10th anniversary.

Rock Monkey — A314

Taiwan Animals: $2, White-face flying squirrel. $3, Chinese pangolin. $5, Formosan sika deer. $2, $3, $5 are horiz.

1971, June 25			Perf. 11½	
1716	A314	$1 gold & multi	.40	.25
1717	A314	$2 gold & multi	1.25	.25
1718	A314	$3 gold & multi	1.75	.30
1719	A314	$5 gold & multi	2.50	.50
		Nos. 1716-1719 (4)	5.90	1.30

Pitcher — A315

Designs: $2.50, Players at base, horiz. $4, Batter and catcher.

1971, July 29		Photo.	Perf. 13	
1720	A315	$1 multi	.30	.25
1721	A315	$2.50 multi	.50	.25
1722	A315	$4 multi	.90	.25
		Nos. 1720-1722 (3)	1.70	.75

Pacific Regional competition for the 1971 Little League World Series.

Nos. 1541, 1544-1545 Overprinted in Magenta or Red

Perf. 13x12½

1971, Sept. 9		Litho.	Wmk. 323	

Granite Paper

1723	A259	$1 vermilion (M)	.30	.25
1724	A259	$2.50 blue (R)	.60	.25
1725	A259	$3 grnsh blue (R)	.60	.25
		Nos. 1723-1725 (3)	1.50	.75

Chinese victory in 1971 Little League World Series, Williamsport, Pa., Aug. 24.

Fairy Tale Type of 1970

Chinese Fairy Tales (Filial Piety): No. 1726, Birds and elephant helping in rice field. No. 1727, Son gathering mulberries for mother. No. 1728, Son gathering firewood. No. 1729, Son, mother and bandits. No. 1730, Son carrying heavy burden. 50c, Son digging for bamboo shoots in winter. No. 1732, Man and wife working as slaves. No. 1733, Father, son and carriage.

1971, Sept. 22			Perf. 13½	

Granite Paper

1726	A301	10c dp org & multi	.25	.25
1727	A301	10c lilac & multi	.25	.25
1728	A301	10c ocher & multi	.25	.25
1729	A301	10c dp car & multi	.25	.25
1730	A301	10c lt ultra & multi	.25	.25
1731	A301	50c multicolored	.30	.25
1732	A301	$1 emerald & multi	.80	.25
1733	A301	$1 lt red brn & multi	.80	.25
		Nos. 1726-1733 (8)	3.15	2.00

Flag of China, "Double Ten" and Anniversary Emblems A316

Designs (Flag of China and): $2.50, National anthem. $5, Gen. Chiang Kai-shek. $8, Sun Yat-sen.

1971, Oct. 10		Photo.	Perf. 13	
1734	A316	$1 orange & multi	.40	.25
1735	A316	$2.50 multi	1.05	.25
1736	A316	$5 green & multi	1.25	.30
1737	A316	$8 olive & multi	1.25	.30
		Nos. 1734-1737 (4)	3.95	1.15

60th National Day.

Bird in Flight (AOPU Emblem) A317

Perf. 13½x14

1971, Nov. 8		Litho.	Wmk. 323	
1738	A317	$2.50 yellow & multi	.70	.25
1739	A317	$5 orange & multi	.90	.25

Asian-Oceanic Postal Union Executive Committee Session, Taipei, Nov. 8-15.

"White Frost Hawk," by Lang Shih-ning
A318

Dog Series I

Designs: $2, "Star-Glancing Wolf." $2.50, "Golden-Winged Face." $5, "Young Black Dragon." $8, "Young Gray Dragon."

Designs from painting series "Ten Prized Dogs," by Lang Shih-ning (Giuseppe Castiglione, 1688-1766).

Perf. 13½x13

			Litho.	**Unwmk.**
1971, Nov. 16				
1740	A318	$1 Facing left	.70	.25
1741	A318	$2 Lying down	1.00	.25
1742	A318	$2.50 Scratching	1.25	.30
1743	A318	$5 Facing right	3.00	.50
1744	A318	$8 Looking back	5.00	1.00
		Nos. 1740-1744 (5)	10.95	2.30

Dog Series II

Designs: $1, "Black with Snow-white Paws." $2, "Yellow Leopard." $2.50, "Flying Magpie." $5, "Heavenly Lion." $8, "Mottled Tiger."

1972, Jan. 12				
1745	A318	$1 Facing right	2.00	.25
1746	A318	$2 Walking	3.50	.25
1747	A318	$2.50 Sleeping	5.00	.30
1748	A318	$5 Facing left	10.00	.50
1749	A318	$8 Sitting	22.50	1.00
		Nos. 1745-1749 (5)	43.00	2.30

Squirrels — A319

Perf. 13½x12½

				Wmk. 323
1971, Dec. 1				
1750	A319	Block of 4	5.00	3.50
a.		50c in UL corner	.90	.25
b.		50c in UR corner	.90	.25
c.		50c in LL corner	.90	.25
d.		50c in LR corner	.90	.25
1751	A319	Block of 4	20.00	5.00
a.		$4.50 in UL corner	4.50	.60
b.		$4.50 in UR corner	4.50	.60
c.		$4.50 in LL corner	4.50	.60
d.		$4.50 in LR corner	4.50	.60

New Year 1972.

Flags of China and Jordan
A320

1971, Dec. 16 — **Perf. 13½**

Granite Paper

1752	A320	$5 multicolored	1.60	.25

50th anniversary of the founding of the Hashemite Kingdom of Jordan.

Cargo Ship "Hai King" — A321

$7, Ocean liner & map of Pacific Ocean, vert.

1971, Dec. 16			**Perf. 12½**	
1753	A321	$4 grn, dk bl & red	.70	.45
1754	A321	$7 ocher & multi	1.10	.55

China Merchants Steam Navigation Co., cent.

Downhill Skiing, Olympic Rings
A322

$5, Cross-country skiing. $8, Giant slalom.

			Perf. 13½	
1972, Feb. 3				
1755	A322	$1 org, blk & bl	.30	.25
1756	A322	$5 yel grn, dp org & blk	.70	.25
1757	A322	$8 red, gray & blk	.80	.25
		Nos. 1755-1757 (3)	1.80	.75

11th Winter Olympic Games, Sapporo, Japan, Feb. 3-13.

Vase, 18th Century — A323

Porcelain Series I

Porcelain Masterworks of Ching Dynasty: $2, Covered jar. $2.50, Pitcher. $5, Vase with 5 openings and dragon design. $8, Covered jar with children design.

Perf. 11½

			Photo.	**Unwmk.**
1972, Mar. 20				
1758	A323	$1 violet & multi	.70	.25
1759	A323	$2 plum & blue	1.50	.25
1760	A323	$2.50 org ver & bl	2.25	.25
1761	A323	$5 bis brn & bl	2.50	.45
1762	A323	$8 sl grn & multi	3.75	.45
		Nos. 1758-1762 (5)	10.70	1.65

See Nos. 1812-1821, 1864-1868.

Nine Flying Doves
A324

Perf. 13½x14

			Litho.	**Wmk. 323**
1972, Apr. 1				
1763	A324	$1 lt blue & blk	.55	.25
1764	A324	$5 lt violet & blk	1.60	.30

Asian-Oceanic Postal Union, 10th anniv.

"Dignity with Self-reliance" — A325

Perf. 13½x12½

			Litho.	**Wmk. 323**
1972-75				
1765	A325	5c brown & yel	.25	.25
1766	A325	10c blue & org	.25	.25
1767	A325	20c cl & yel grn ('75)	.25	.25
1768	A325	50c lil & lil rose	.25	.25
1769	A325	$1 red & brt bl	.30	.25
1770	A325	$1.50 yel & dk bl	.40	.25
1771	A325	$2 maroon & org	.60	.25
1772	A325	$2.50 emer & ver	1.50	.25
1773	A325	$3 red & lt grn	1.10	.25
		Nos. 1765-1773 (9)	4.90	2.25

Souvenir Sheet

Imperf

1775	A325	Sheet of 2	5.00	2.25

No. 1775 commemorates ROCPEX '72 Philatelic Exhibition, Taipei, Oct. 24-Nov. 2. It contains 2 stamps similar to Nos. 1771 and 1773 with simulated perforations.

Issued: $1, $1.50, $2, $3, 5/20/72; 5c, 10c, 50c, $2.50, No. 1775, 10/24/72; 20c, 1975. For overprints see Nos. 1787-1790.

Emperor Shih-tsung's Procession — A326

Messengers on Horseback — A327

Designs from scrolls depicting Emperor Shih-tsung's (reigned 1522-1566) journey to and from tombs at Cheng-tien. No. 1776 shows land journey departure and is designed from right to left. No. 1779 shows return trip by boat and is designed from left to right. The 5 stamps of Nos. 1776 and 1780 are numbered 1 to 5 in Chinese (see illustrations with Nos. 1682-1686 for numerals).

			Photo.	**Unwmk.**	**Perf. 13½**
1972					
1776		Strip of 5		3.50	3.00
a.	A326	$1 shown (1)		.55	.35
b.	A326	$1 Seven carriages (2)		.55	.35
c.	A326	$1 Carriage drawn by 23 horses (3)		.55	.35
d.	A326	$1 Procession (4)		.55	.35
e.	A326	$1 Emperor under 2 canopies (5)		.55	.35
1777	A327	$2.50 shown		2.25	.50
1778	A327	$5 Guards with flags, fans & spears		3.00	.50
1779	A327	$8 Sedan chair carried by 28 men		6.00	.60
1780		Strip of 5		3.50	3.00
a.	A326	$1 Three barges (1)		.55	.35
b.	A326	$1 Procession, sedan chairs (2)		.55	.35
c.	A326	$1 Two barges with trunks (3)		.55	.35
d.	A326	$1 Procession on land (4)		.55	.35
e.	A326	$1 Procession, 2 sedan chairs (5)		.55	.35
1781	A326	$2.50 Courtiers at city welcoming Emperor		2.25	.40
1782	A327	$5 Orchestra on horseback		3.00	.40
1783	A326	$8 Barges		3.75	.50
		Nos. 1776-1783 (8)		27.25	8.90

Issue dates: No. 1776-1779, June 14; Nos. 1780-1783, July 12.

First Day Covers — A328   Magnifying Glass, Tongs, Gauge — A329

Design: $2.50, Sun Yat-sen stamp of 1971 (type A311) under magnifying glass.

Wmk. 323

			Engr.	**Perf. 12**
1972, Aug. 9				
1784	A328	$1 dk vio blue	.25	.25
1785	A328	$2.50 brt green	.25	.25
1786	A329	$8 scarlet	.55	.25
		Nos. 1784-1786 (3)	1.05	.75

Promotion of philately. Printed in sheets of 40. Each sheet contains 4 blocks of 10 stamps surrounded by margins with inscriptions.

Nos. 1768-1770, 1772 Overprinted in Dark Blue or Red

Perf. 13½x12½

			Litho.	**Wmk. 323**
1972, Sept. 9				
1787	A325	$1 red & brt bl (DB)	.25	.25
1788	A325	$1.50 yel & dk bl (R)	.40	.25
1789	A325	$2 mar & org (R)	.55	.25
1790	A325	$3 red & lt grn (DB)	.60	.25
		Nos. 1787-1790 (4)	1.80	1.00

China's championship victories in the Little League World Series, Gary, Ind., and in the Senior League World Series, Williamsport, Pa., Aug. 1972.

Emperor Yao (2357-2258 B.C.) — A330

Rulers: $4, Emperor Shun (ruled 2255-2208 B.C.). $4.50, Yu, the Great (ruled 2205-2198 B.C.). $5, King T'ang (ruled 1783-1754 B.C.). $5.50, King Wen (ruled 1171-1122 B.C.). $6, King Wu (ruled 1121-1114 B.C.). $7, Chou Kung (died 1105 B.C.). $8, Confucius (551-479 B.C.).

			Engr.	**Perf. 12**
1972-73				
		Granite Paper		
1791	A330	$3.50 dk blue	.40	.25
1792	A330	$4 rose red	.60	.25
1793	A330	$4.50 bluish lil	.80	.25
1794	A330	$5 brt green	.40	.25
1795	A330	$5.50 dp claret ('73)	1.25	.25
1796	A330	$6 dp org ('73)	1.10	.25
a.		Perf. 13½x12½ ('76)	1.10	.30
1797	A330	$7 sepia ('73)	1.10	.25
a.		Perf. 13½x12½ ('76)	1.10	.30
1798	A330	$8 indigo ('73)	1.25	.25
a.		gray, perf. 13½x12½ ('76)	1.75	.35
		Nos. 1791-1798 (8)	6.90	2.00

In the first printing, Nos. 1791-1794, 1796-1798 measure 32mm high. In a 1974 reissue they are 33mm.

Mountain Climbing — A331

Designs (China Youth Corps emblem and): $2.50, Skiing (skiers forming circle). $4, Diving. $8, Parachute jumping.

Unwmk.

			Photo.	**Perf. 12**
1972, Oct. 31				
1800	A331	$1 green & multi	.25	.25
1801	A331	$2.50 blue & multi	.50	.25
1802	A331	$4 orange & multi	.75	.25
1803	A331	$8 multicolored	1.25	.25
		Nos. 1800-1803 (4)	2.75	1.00

China Youth Corps, 20th anniversary.

JCI Emblem A332

			Litho.	**Wmk. 323**
1972, Nov. 12				
1804	A332	$1 multicolored	.25	.25
1805	A332	$5 orange & multi	.40	.25
1806	A332	$8 multicolored	.70	.40
		Nos. 1804-1806 (3)	1.35	.90

27th Junior Chamber International (JCI) World Congress, Taipei, Nov. 12-19.

Electronic Mail
Sorter — A333

Plane, Ship and
Pier — A334

Progress of Communications System on
Taiwan: $5, Highway overpass over railroad.

Wmk. 323

1972, Nov. 12	Engr.	Perf. 11½
1807 A333 $1 red	.25	.25
1808 A334 $2.50 blue	.50	.25
1809 A334 $5 dk violet brn	1.10	.35
Nos. 1807-1809 (3)	1.85	.85

Cow and Calf
(Parental
Love) — A335

1972, Dec. 1	Litho.	Perf. 12
1810 A335 50c red & blk	2.75	.30
1811 A335 $4.50 yel, red & brn	4.25	.90

New Year 1973. Printed in sheets of 80,
divided into 4 panes of 20, separated by vertical and horizontal gutters 2 rows wide. 20 red
chops meaning "Happy New Year" are printed
in the gutters.

Porcelain Type of 1972 and

Stem Bowl
with
Dragons
A336

Porcelain Series II

Porcelain Masterworks of Ming Dynasty: $1,
Covered vase with fruits and flowers. $2, Vase
with ornamental and floral design. $2.50, Vase
imitating ancient bronze. $5, Flask with flowers
of 4 seasons. $8, Garlic head vase.

1973	Photo.	Perf. 11½
1812 A323 $1 gray & multi	1.10	.25
1813 A323 $2 lt brn & multi	1.60	.25
1814 A323 $2.50 brt grn & multi	2.25	.25
1815 A323 $5 ultra & multi	2.40	.35
1816 A323 $8 olive & multi	3.50	.60
Nos. 1812-1816 (5)	10.85	1.70

Porcelain Series III

Ming Porcelain: $2, Refuse container with
dragons. $2.50, Covered jar with lotus. $5,
Covered jar with horses. $8, Bowl with figures
of immortals.

1817 A336 $1 gray & multi	1.10	.25
1818 A336 $2 lt vio & multi	1.60	.25
1819 A336 $2.50 dk red & multi	2.25	.25
1820 A336 $5 blue & multi	2.40	.35
1821 A336 $8 dp org & multi	3.50	.60
Nos. 1817-1821 (5)	10.85	1.70

Issued: Nos. 1812-1816, 1/10; Nos. 1817-
1821, 3/24.
See Nos. 1864-1868.

Oyster Fairy and Fisherman's
Dance — A337

$1, Kicking shuttlecock, vert. $5, Rowing
boat over land. $8, Old man carrying young
lady, vert.

1973, Feb. 7	Photo.	Perf. 11½
	Granite Paper	
1822 A337 $1 multicolored	.70	.25
1823 A337 $4 Shown	1.10	.25
1824 A337 $5 multicolored	1.25	.25
1825 A337 $8 multicolored	1.40	.40
Nos. 1822-1825 (4)	4.45	1.15

Chinese folklore popular entertainment.

Bamboo
Boat
A338

Taiwanese Handicrafts: $2.50, Painted mar-
ble vase, vert. $5, Painted glass plate. $8,
Doll, bridegroom carrying bride on back, vert.

Perf. 13½x14½, 14½x13½

1973, Mar. 9		Photo.
1826 A338 $1 multi	.25	.25
1827 A338 $2.50 multi	.85	.25
1828 A338 $5 multi	1.25	.25
1829 A338 $8 multi	1.75	.40
Nos. 1826-1829 (4)	4.10	1.15

Federation Emblem,
Cargo Hook,
Crane — A339

Emblem,
Tractor, New
Buildings
A340

Wmk. 323

1973, Apr. 2	Litho.	Perf. 12½
1830 A339 $1 salmon & multi	.40	.25
1831 A340 $5 blue & blk	.75	.25

12th convention of International Federation
of Asian and Western Pacific Contractors
Association, Taipei, Apr. 2-10.

Pres. Chiang Kai-
shek, Flag of
China — A341

Design: $4, like $1 with different border.

Unwmk.

1973, May 20	Photo.	Perf. 12
1832 A341 $1 yellow & multi	.75	.25
1833 A341 $4 dk grn & multi	1.10	.50

First anniversary of Pres. Chiang Kai-shek's
inauguration for a fifth term.

Lin Tse-hsü — A342

Wmk. 323

1973, June 3	Engr.	Perf. 12
1834 A342 $1 sepia	.75	.25

Lin Tse-hsü (1785-1850), Governor of
Hunan and Kwantung, who destroyed large
quantity of opium at Humen, Kwantung, June
3, 1839.

Willows and Palace Gate in the
Morning — A343

Lady Watering
Peonies,
Stone
Ornament
A344

Design from scroll "Spring Morning in the
Han Palace," by Chiu Ying. The five stamps of
No. 1835 are numbered 1 to 5 and the five
stamps of No. 1838 are numbered 6-10 in Chinese (see illustrations with Nos. 1682-1691 for
numerals). The stamps are numbered and
listed from right to left.

1973	Photo.	Unwmk.	Perf. 11½
	Granite Paper		
1835	Strip of 5	3.00	3.00
a.	A343 $1 shown (1)	.40	.25
b.	A343 $1 Ladies feeding peacocks (2)	.40	.25
c.	A343 $1 Lady watering peonies (3)	.40	.25
d.	A343 $1 Pear tree in bloom (4)	.40	.25
e.	A343 $1 Lady musicians (5)	.40	.25
1836 A344 $5 shown		2.25	.60
1837 A344 $8 Lady musicians		3.50	1.00
1838	Strip of 5	3.00	3.00
a.	A343 $1 Ladies playing go (6)	.40	.25
b.	A343 $1 Various games (7)	.40	.25
c.	A343 $1 Talking and playing music (8)	.40	.25
d.	A343 $1 Artist painting portrait (9)	.40	.25
e.	A343 $1 Sentries guarding wall (10)	.40	.25
1839 A344 $5 Ladies playing go		2.25	.60
1840 A344 $8 Girl chasing butterfly		3.50	1.00
Nos. 1835-1840 (6)		17.50	9.20

Issued: Nos. 1835-1837, 6/20; Nos. 1838-
1840, 7/18.

Fan, Bamboo Design, by Hsiang Te-
hsin — A345

Designs: Painted fans, Ming dynasty.

Perf. 12½x13

1973, Aug. 15	Photo.	Wmk. 368
1841 A345 $1 bister & multi	.50	.25
1842 A345 $2.50 bister & multi	.95	.25
1843 A345 $5 bister & multi	1.75	.35
1844 A345 $8 bister & multi	2.75	.50
Nos. 1841-1844 (4)	5.95	1.35

See Nos. 1934-1937.

Little League
Emblem — A346

Wmk. 370

1973, Sept. 9	Litho.	Perf. 13½
1845 A346 $1 yel, car & dk bl	.90	.25
1846 A346 $4 yel, grn & dk bl	1.60	.35

Chinese victory in Little League Twin Championships, Gary, Ind., and Williamsport, Pa.

INTERPOL
Emblem — A347

Wmk. 370

1973, Sept. 11	Litho.	Perf. 12
1847 A347 $1 blue & org	.25	.25
1848 A347 $5 green & org	.70	.25
1849 A347 $8 magenta & org	1.00	.40
Nos. 1847-1849 (3)	1.95	.90

Intl. Criminal Police Organization, 50th anniv.

Ch'iu Feng-
chia — A348

Wmk. 323

1973, Oct. 5	Engr.	Perf. 11½
1850 A348 $1 violet black	.70	.25

2nd meeting of overseas Hakkas, Taipei,
Oct. 5-7, and to honor Ch'iu Feng-chia (1864-
1912), Hakka scholar, poet and revolutionist.

Tsengwen
Reservoir
A349

Tsengwen
Dam — A350

Perf. 13½

1973, Oct. 31	Photo.	Unwmk.
1851	Strip of 3	.90	.70
a.	A349 $1 Upper shore	.25	.25
b.	A349 $1 shown	.25	.25
c.	A349 $1 Lower shore	.25	.25

Perf. 12x11½

1852 A350 $5 shown	.65	.30
1853 A350 $8 Spillway	1.00	.60
Nos. 1851-1853 (3)	2.55	1.60

Inauguration of Tsengwen Reservoir. No.
1851 printed in sheets of 15.

Tiger — A351

Wmk. 370

1973, Dec. 1	Litho.	Perf. 12½
1854 A351 50c multi	1.10	.25
1855 A351 $4.50 multi	2.00	.50

New Year 1974.

"Snow-dotted Eagle," by Lang Shih-ning — A352

No. 1857, "Comfortable Ride." No. 1858, "Red Flower Eagle." No. 1859, "Cloud-running Steed." No. 1860, "Sky-running steed." $2.50, "Red Jade Seat." $5, "Thunderclap Steed." $8, "Arabian Champion." Designs from painting series "Ten Prized Horses," by Lang Shih-ning (Giuseppe Castiglione, 1688-1766).

1973	Litho.	Unwmk.	Perf. 13	
1856	A352	50c shown	.75	.25
1857	A352	$1 Pinto, blk tail	1.00	.35
1858	A352	$1 Facing left	1.00	.35
1859	A352	$1 Facing right	1.00	.35
1860	A352	$1 Pinto, white tail	1.00	.35
a.		Horiz. or vert. strip of 4, #1857-1860	5.00	4.00
1861	A352	$2.50 Palomino	2.25	.60
1862	A352	$5 Grazing	3.75	1.00
a.		Souvenir sheet of 4	40.00	17.00
1863	A352	$8 Brown stallion	6.00	1.25
		Nos. 1856-1863 (8)	16.75	4.50

No. 1862a contains 4 stamps with simulated perforations similar to Nos. 1856-1857, 1861-1862.
Issued: 50c, $2.50, $5, 11/21; others 12/21.

Porcelain Types of 1972-73
Porcelain Series IV

Porcelain Masterworks of Sung Dynasty: $1, Vase. $2, Three-tiered vase. $2.50, Lotus-shaped bowl. $5, Incense burner. $8, Incense burner on stand.

1974, Jan. 16	Photo.	Perf. 11½	
1864	A323	$1 ultra & multi	.60	.25
1865	A336	$2 multicolored	1.10	.25
1866	A336	$2.50 red & multi	1.40	.25
1867	A336	$5 lilac & multi	1.60	.25
1868	A336	$8 green & multi	1.60	.50
		Nos. 1864-1868 (5)	6.30	1.50

Juggler — A353

Design: $8, Magician producing dishes from his robe, horiz.

1974, Feb. 6	Photo.	Perf. 11½	
1869	A353	$1 yellow & multi	.70	.25
1870	A353	$8 yellow & multi	1.60	.25

Taroko Gorge, Hualien — A354

Designs: $2.50, Luce Chapel, Tunghai University. $5, Tzu En Pagoda, Sun Moon Lake. $8, Goddess of Mercy, Keelung.

1974, Mar. 22	Photo.	Perf. 12	
1871	A354	$1 multi	.50	.25
1872	A354	$2.50 multi	1.10	.25
1873	A354	$5 multi	1.40	.25
1874	A354	$8 multi	2.00	.25
		Nos. 1871-1874 (4)	5.00	1.00

Taiwan landmarks.

Fighting Cocks (Brass) A355

Designs: $2.50, Grapes and bowl with fruit (imitation jade). $5, Fisherman (wood carving), vert. $8, Basket with plastic roses, vert.

Perf. 13½x14½, 14½x13½

1974, Apr. 10			
1875	A355	$1 bl grn & multi	.30	.25
1876	A355	$2.50 brown & multi	.70	.25
1877	A355	$5 crimson & multi	1.00	.25
1878	A355	$8 multicolored	2.10	.40
		Nos. 1875-1878 (4)	4.10	1.15

Taiwanese handicraft products.

Sun Yat-sen Memorial Hall — A356

Taiwan landmarks: $2.50, Reaching-moon Tower, Cheng Ching Lake. $5, Orchid Island (boats). $8, Penghu Interisland Bridge.

1974, May 15	Photo.	Perf. 11½	
		Granite Paper		
1879	A356	$1 blue & multi	.30	.25
1880	A356	$2.50 blue & multi	.70	.25
1881	A356	$5 blue & multi	.90	.25
1882	A356	$8 blue & multi	1.25	.25
		Nos. 1879-1882 (4)	3.15	1.00

Pres. Chiang and Gate of Whampoa Military Academy A357

Marching Cadets and Entrance Gate — A358

Wmk. 323

1974, June 16	Engr.	Perf. 11½	
1883	A357	$1 carmine rose	.45	.25
1884	A358	$14 violet blue	.90	.40

50th anniversary of the founding of the Whampoa Military Academy.

Long-distance Runner and Olympic Rings — A359

$8, Women's relay race, Olympic rings.

1974, June 23	Litho.	Perf. 12½	
1885	A359	$1 blue, blk & red	.30	.25
1886	A359	$8 pink, blk & red	1.00	.40

80th anniv. of Intl. Olympic Committee.

The Boy Wang Ch'i Fighting Invaders — A360

Folk Tales: No. 1888, T'i Ying pleading for her father before the Emperor. No. 1889, Wen Yen-po flushing out ball caught in tree. No. 1890, Boy Wang Hua returning gold piece he found. No. 1891, Pu Shih, a rich sheep raiser and benefactor. No. 1892, K'ung Yung as a child choosing smallest pear. No. 1893, Tung Yu studying. No. 1894, Szu Ma-kuang saving playmate from drowning in water jar.

1974, July 15	Wmk. 370	Perf. 13½	
1887	A360	50c olive & multi	.35	.25
1888	A360	50c ultra & multi	.35	.25
1889	A360	50c ocher & multi	.35	.25
1890	A360	50c red brn & multi	.35	.25
a.		Block of 4, #1887-1890	1.40	1.40
1891	A360	$1 green & multi	.75	.40
1892	A360	$1 lilac & multi	.75	.40
1893	A360	$1 blue & multi	.75	.40
1894	A360	$1 car & multi	.75	.40
a.		Block of 4, #1891-1894	3.00	3.00
		Nos. 1887-1894 (8)	4.40	2.60

For similar designs see A380, A427, A456, A495.

Myrtle, by Wei Sheng — A361

Silk Fan Paintings, Sung Dynasty (960-1279 A.D.): $2.50, Cabbage and Insects, by Hsu Ti. $5, Hibiscus, Cat and Dog, by Li Ti. $8, Pomegranate and Birds, by Wu Ping. Fans from National Palace Museum.

Perf. 13x12½

1974, Aug. 14	Photo.	Wmk. 368	
1895	A361	$1 multi	.25	.25
1896	A361	$2.50 multi	.85	.25
1897	A361	$5 multi	1.40	.25
1898	A361	$8 multi	2.00	.50
		Nos. 1895-1898 (4)	4.50	1.25

See Nos. 1950-1953.

Battle at Marco Polo Bridge, July 7, 1937 A362

Wmk. 370

1974, Sept. 3	Litho.	Perf. 13½	
1899	A362	$1 multicolored	.45	.25

Souvenir Sheet
Wmk. 323
Without Gum; Granite Paper

1900		Sheet of 8	9.00	9.00
a.		A362 $1, single stamp	.80	.80

20th Armed Forces Day. No. 1900 commemorates Armed Forces Stamp Exhibition, Sun Yat-sen Memorial Hall, Sept. 3-9.

Chrysanthemum A363

Designs: Various chrysanthemums.

		Unwmk.		
1974, Sept. 30	Photo.	Perf. 12		
		Granite Paper		
1901	A363	$1 lilac & multi	.25	.25
1902	A363	$2.50 multi	.70	.25
1903	A363	$5 orange & multi	.95	.25
1904	A363	$8 multi	1.60	.35
		Nos. 1901-1904 (4)	3.50	1.10

Rep. of China Pavilion, EXPO Emblem A364

Map of Fair Grounds, Chinese Flag A364a

Wmk. 370

1974, Oct. 10	Litho.	Perf. 13	
1905	A364	$1 multi	.25	.25
1906	A364a	$8 multi	.70	.40

EXPO '74, Spokane, Wash., May 4-Nov. 4. Theme, "Preserve the Environment."

Steel Mill, Kaohsiung A365

Taichung Harbor A366

Designs: $1, Taiwan North Link Railroad and map. $2, Oil refinery. $2.50, Electric train. $3.50, Taoyuan International Airport. $4, Taiwan North-South Highway and map. $4.50, Kaohsiung shipyard. $5, Su-ao Port.

Perf. 13x12½, 12½x13

1974, Oct. 31		Wmk. 323	
1907	A365	50c lilac, yel & brn	.25	.25
1908	A365	$1 green & org	.25	.25
1909	A365	$2 blue & yel	.25	.25
1910	A365	$2.50 emer & org	.25	.25
1911	A366	$3 ocher & ultra	.25	.25
1912	A366	$3.50 sl grn & yel	.25	.25
1913	A366	$4 brown & yel	.25	.25
1914	A366	$4.50 ver & bl	.35	.25
1915	A366	$5 sepia & dk bl	.35	.25
		Nos. 1907-1915 (9)	2.45	2.25

Major construction projects.
See Nos. 2009-2017, 2068-2076. For overprints see Nos. 2064-2065, 2112-2113.

Agaricus Bisporus A367

Edible Mushrooms: $2.50, Pleurotus ostreatus. $5, Dictyophora indusiata. $8, Flammulina velutipes.

Perf. 11½

1974, Nov. 15	Unwmk.	Photo.	
1916	A367	$1 multi	.55	.25
1917	A367	$2.50 multi	.55	.25
1918	A367	$5 multi	1.00	.25
1919	A367	$8 multi	1.25	.30
		Nos. 1916-1919 (4)	3.35	1.05

9th Intl. Scientific Congress on the Cultivation of Edible Fungi, Taipei, Nov. 1974.

Batters and World Map — A368

Pitcher and Championship Banners — A369

Wmk. 323

1974, Nov. 24   Litho.   Perf. 13½
1920 A368 $1 multicolored   .90 .25
1921 A369 $8 multicolored   .80 .35

China's victory in 1974 Little League Baseball World Series Triple Championships.

Rabbit — A370

Wmk. 323

1974, Dec. 10   Photo.   Perf. 12½
1922 A370 50c orange & multi   .60 .25
1923 A370 $4.50 brown & multi   2.10 .30

New Year 1975.

Acrobat with Iron Rod — A371

$5, Two acrobats spinning tops, horiz.

Granite Paper

1975, Jan. 15   Unwmk.   Perf. 11½
1924 A371 $4 yellow & multi   .90 .40
1925 A371 $5 yellow & multi   1.40 .45

Children Watching Puppet Show — A372

Ceremonial New Year Greetings — A373

Designs from scroll "Festivals for the New Year," by Ting Kuan-p'eng. Nos. 1926a-1926e are numbered 1-5 in Chinese.
$5, Children buying firecrackers. $8, Children and man with trained monkey.

1975, Feb. 25   Photo.   Perf. 11½
Granite Paper
1926   Strip of 5   3.75 2.50
a.   A372 $1 Ceremonial New
       Year Greetings (1)   .55 .25
b.   A372 $1 Man with trained
       monkey (2)   .55 .25
c.   A372 $1 Crowd and musi-
       cians (3)   .55 .25

d.   A372 $1 Picnic under a tree
       (4)   .55 .25
e.   A372 $1 shown (5)   .55 .25
1927 A373 $2.50 shown   2.50 .30
1928 A373 $5 multi   3.00 .55
1929 A373 $8 multi   5.25 .90
       Nos. 1926-1929 (4)   14.50 4.25

Sun Yat-sen Memorial Hall, Taipei A374

Sun Yat-sen's Handwriting — A375

Sun Yat-sen, Bronze Statue in Memorial Hall — A376

Sun Yat-sen Memorial Hall, St. John's University, NY A377

Perf. 13½x14, 14x13½

1975, Mar. 12   Litho.
1930 A374 $1 green & multi   .25 .25
1931 A375 $4 yel grn & multi   .55 .25
1932 A376 $5 yellow & multi   .80 .25
1933 A377 $8 gray & multi   1.10 .30
       Nos. 1930-1933 (4)   2.70 1.05

Dr. Sun Yat-sen (1866-1925), statesman and revolutionary leader.

Fan Type of 1973 Inscribed "Landscape" (1st Character, 2nd Row)

Painted fans, Ming Dynasty. Second row of inscription gives design description.

Perf. 12½x13

1975, Apr. 16   Photo.   Wmk. 368
1934 A345 $1 bister & multi   .30 .25
1935 A345 $2.50 bister & multi   .95 .25
1936 A345 $5 bister & multi   2.00 .35
1937 A345 $8 bister & multi   2.25 .55
       Nos. 1934-1937 (4)   5.50 1.40

Yuan-chin coin, 1122-221 B.C. — A378

Ancient Chinese Coins: $4, Pan-liang, 221-207 B.C. $5, Five chu, 206 B.C.-220 A.D. $8, Five chu, 502-557 A.D.

The Cloth-bag Monk, by Chang Hung (1577-1668) A379

Chinese Paintings: $4, Lao-tzu Riding Buffalo, by Chao Pu-chih (1053-1110). $5, Portrait of Shih-te, by Wang Wen (1497-1576). $8, Splashed-ink Immortal, by Liang K'ai (early 13th century).

Perf. 11½

1975, June 18   Photo.   Unwmk.
Granite Paper
1942 A379 $2 blk, buff & ver   .75 .25
1943 A379 $4 blk, gray & red   1.75 .25
1944 A379 $5 blk, yel & ver   2.75 .40
1945 A379 $8 tan, red & blk   3.75 .60
       Nos. 1942-1945 (4)   9.00 1.50

Chu Yin Reading by the Light of Fireflies — A380

Folk Tales: No. 1947, Hua Mu-lan going to war for her father. No. 1948, King Kou Chien tasting gall. $5, Chou Ch'u killing tiger.

Perf. 14x13½

1975, July 16   Litho.   Wmk. 368
1946 A380 $1 olive & multi   .25 .25
1947 A380 $2 bis brn & multi   .40 .25
1948 A380 $2 lt grn & multi   .60 .25
1949 A380 $5 blue & multi   1.40 .30
       Nos. 1946-1949 (4)   2.65 1.05

See Nos. 2108-2111.

Cherry-Apple Blossoms, by Lin Ch'un — A381

Silk Fan Paintings, Sung Dynasty: $2, Spring Blossoms and Butterfly, by Ma K'uei. $5, Monkeys and Deer, by I Yüan-chih. $8, Tame Sparrow among Bamboo.

Perf. 13x12½

1975, Aug. 15   Litho.   Wmk. 323
1950 A381 $1 multicolored   .30 .25
1951 A381 $2 multicolored   1.10 .25
1952 A381 $5 multicolored   1.50 .40
1953 A381 $8 multicolored   3.00 .80
       Nos. 1950-1953 (4)   5.90 1.70

See Nos. 2001-2004.

Wmk. 323

1975, May 20   Litho.   Perf. 13
1938 A378 $1 salmon & multi   .25 .25
1939 A378 $4 yellow & multi   .95 .25
1940 A378 $5 dl yel & multi   1.10 .25
1941 A378 $8 lt vio & multi   1.75 .25
       Nos. 1938-1941 (4)   4.05 1.00

Gen. Chang Tzu-chung (1891-1940) A382

No. 1955, Maj. Gen. Kao Chih-hong (1908-37). No. 1956, Capt. Sha Shih-chiun (1896-1938). No. 1957, Maj. Gen. Hsieh Chin-yuan (1905-41). No. 1958, Lt. Yen Hai-wen (1916-37). No. 1959, Lt. Gen. Tai An-lan (1905-42).

Wmk. 323

1975, Sept. 3   Engr.   Perf. 12
1954 A382 $2 carmine   .25 .25
1955 A382 $2 sepia   .25 .25
1956 A382 $2 dull green   .25 .25
1957 A382 $5 violet black   .30 .25
1958 A382 $5 violet blue   .30 .25
1959 A382 $5 dark blue   .30 .25
       Nos. 1954-1959 (6)   1.65 1.50

Martyrs of the resistance fight against Japan.

Lotus Pond with Willows, by Madame Chiang — A383

Paintings by Madame Chiang Kai-shek: $5, Sun Breaks through Mountain Clouds. $8, A Pair of Pine Trees. $10, Fishing and Farming.

Perf. 13½

1975, Oct. 31   Litho.   Unwmk.
1960 A383 $2 multicolored   1.00 .25
1961 A383 $5 multicolored   2.25 .30
1962 A383 $8 multicolored   3.25 .40
1963 A383 $10 multicolored   4.50 .75
       Nos. 1960-1963 (4)   11.00 1.70

For similar design see type A404.

Cauldron with Phoenix Handles, 481-221 B.C. A384

Ancient Bronzes: $2, Rectangular cauldron, 1122-722 B.C., vert. $8, Flat jar, 481-221 B.C. $10, 3-legged wine vessel, 1766-1122 B.C., vert.

1975, Nov. 12   Photo.   Perf. 12
1964 A384 $2 pink & multi   .25 .25
1965 A384 $5 lt blue & multi   .85 .25
1966 A384 $8 yellow & multi   1.10 .25
1967 A384 $10 lilac & multi   1.25 .30
       Nos. 1964-1967 (4)   3.45 1.05

For similar design see type A395. No. 1964 has 7 Chinese characters at left, No. 2005 has 4. No. 1967 has 4 characters at left, No. 2008 has 5.

Dragon, Nine-Dragon Wall, Peihai — A385

Wmk. 323

1975, Dec. 1   Litho.   Perf. 12½
1968 A385 $1 orange & multi   .75 .30
1969 A385 $5 green & multi   1.50 .90

New Year 1976.

Techi Dam — A386

Design: $10, Panoramic view of Techi Dam.

1975, Dec. 17   Unwmk.   Perf. 13½
1970 A386 $2 green & multi   .25 .25
1971 A386 $10 blue & multi   .55 .45

Completion of Techi Dam, Tachia River.

Biathlon and Olympic Rings — A387

Olympic Rings and: $5, Luge. $8, Skiing.

1976, Jan. 15   Litho.   Perf. 13½
1972 A387 $2 blue & multi   .35 .25
1973 A387 $5 blue & multi   .65 .25
1974 A387 $8 blue & multi   1.00 .25
    Nos. 1972-1974 (3)   2.00 .75

12th Winter Olympic Games, Innsbruck, Austria, Feb. 4-15.

Chin, Oldest Chinese Instrument A388

Musical Instruments: $5, Se, c. 2900 B.C. $8, Standing kong-ho (harp). $10, Sleeping kong-ho.

1976, Feb. 11   Unwmk.   Perf. 14
1975 A388 $2 yellow & multi   .35 .25
1976 A388 $5 orange & multi   .55 .25
1977 A388 $8 grnsh bl & multi   .80 .25
1978 A388 $10 multicolored   1.25 .30
    Nos. 1975-1978 (4)   2.95 1.05

For similar design see Type A407.

Double Carp Type of 1969
Perf. 13½x12½
1976, Dec. 15   Engr.   Unwmk.
1980 A280 $14 carmine rose   2.25 .30

Mail Collecting A389

Mail Sorting — A390

Postal Service, 80th Anniv.: $8, Mail transport. $10, Mail delivery.

Wmk. 323
1976, Mar. 20   Litho.   Perf. 13½
1984 A389 $2 yellow & multi   .30 .25
1985 A390 $5 green & multi   .55 .30
1986 A390 $8 blue & multi   .80 .30
1987 A389 $10 orange & multi   1.00 .40
    a.   Souv. sheet of 4, #1984-1987 12.50 9.00
    Nos. 1984-1987 (4)   2.65 1.25

Pres. Chiang Kai-shek A391

People Paying Homage — A392

No. 1990, Pres. Chiang lying in state. No. 1991, Hearse leaving funeral chapel. $5, People along funeral route. $8, Spirit tablet in Tzuhu Guest House. $10, Tzuhu Guest House, Pres. Chiang's burial place.

1976, Apr. 4
1988 A391 $2 gray & multi   .25 .25
1989 A392 $2 gray & multi   .25 .25
1990 A392 $2 gray & multi   .25 .25
1991 A392 $2 gray & multi   .25 .25
1992 A392 $5 gray & multi   .40 .25
1993 A392 $8 gray & multi   .40 .25
1994 A392 $10 gray & multi   .50 .35
    Nos. 1988-1994 (7)   2.30 1.85

Pres. Chiang Kai-shek (1887-1975), first death anniversary.

Flags of China and US — A393

Wmk. 323
1976, May 29   Litho.   Perf. 13½
1995 A393 $2 multicolored   .25 .25
1996 A393 $10 yellow & multi   .80 .40

American Bicentennial.

Coin, 12th Century B.C. — A394

Bronze Shovel Coins (pu): $5, Pointed-feet coin, 481-221 B.C. $8, Round-feet coin, 722-481 B.C. $10, Square-feet coin, 3rd-2nd centuries B.C.

1976, June 16
1997 A394 $2 salmon & multi   .25 .25
1998 A394 $5 lt blue & multi   .65 .25
1999 A394 $8 gray & multi   1.05 .30
2000 A394 $10 multicolored   1.60 .40
    Nos. 1997-2000 (4)   3.55 1.20

Fan Painting Type of 1975
Silk Fan Paintings, Sung Dynasty: $2, Hibiscus, by Li Tung. $5, Lilies, by Lin Ch'un. $8, Deer and Pine, by Mou Chung-fu. $10, Quail and Wild Flowers, by Li An-chung.

Perf. 13x12½
1976, July 14   Litho.   Wmk. 323
2001 A381 $2 multicolored   .75 .25
2002 A381 $5 multicolored   1.75 .25
2003 A381 $8 multicolored   2.25 .30
2004 A381 $10 multicolored   3.50 .40
    Nos. 2001-2004 (4)   8.25 1.20

Cauldron, Shang Dynasty — A395

Ancient Bronzes: $5, 3-legged cauldron, Chou Dynasty (1122-722 B.C.). $8, Wine container, Chou Dynasty. $10, Wine vessel with spout, Shang Dynasty (1766-1122 B.C.).

1976, Aug. 25   Photo.   Perf. 11½
Granite Paper
2005 A395 $2 rose & multi   .25 .25
2006 A395 $5 lt blue & multi   .95 .25
2007 A395 $8 yellow & multi   1.40 .25
2008 A395 $10 lilac & multi   1.50 .30
    Nos. 2005-2008 (4)   4.10 1.05

Construction Types of 1974
Designs: $1, Taiwan North Link railroad and map. $2, Railroad electrification. $3, Taichung Harbor. $4, Taiwan North-South Highway and map. $5, Steel Mill, Kaohsiung. $6, Taoyuan International Airport. $7, Kao-hsiung shipyard. $8, Oil refinery. $9, Su-ao Port.

Perf. 13½x12½, 12½x13½
1976   Litho.   Wmk. 323
2009 A365 $1 carmine & grn   .25 .25
2010 A365 $2 orange & multi   .25 .25
2011 A366 $3 violet & multi   .25 .25
2012 A366 $4 carmine & multi   .25 .25
2013 A365 $5 green & brn   .25 .25
2014 A366 $6 brown & multi   .40 .25
2015 A366 $7 brown & multi   .50 .25
2016 A365 $8 carmine & grn   .60 .25
2017 A366 $9 olive & blue   .70 .25
    Nos. 2009-2017 (9)   3.45 2.25

Chiang Kai-shek and Mother A396

Sun Yat-sen and Chiang Kai-shek at Canton Station — A397

Design: $5, Chiang Kai-shek, portrait.

1976, Oct. 31   Litho.   Perf. 13½
2023 A396 $2 multicolored   .35 .25
2024 A396 $5 multicolored   .80 .25
2025 A397 $10 multicolored   1.10 .40
    Nos. 2023-2025 (3)   2.25 .90

Pres. Chiang Kai-shek, 90th anniv. of birth.

Flags of Kuomintang and China A398

Sun Yat-sen and Chiang Kai-shek A399

1976, Nov. 12   Perf. 13½x14
2026 A398 $2 multicolored   .25 .25
2027 A399 $10 multicolored   .65 .45
    a.   Souv. sheet of 2, #2026-2027 4.50 4.50

11th National Kuomintang Cong., Taipei.

Brazen Serpent — A400

1976, Dec. 15   Wmk. 323   Perf. 12½
2028 A400 $1 red, lilac & gold   .75 .25
2029 A400 $5 plum, yel & gold   1.75 .25

New Year 1977.

Bird and Plum Blossoms, by Ch'en Hung-shou A401

Chinese Paintings: $8, "Wintry Days" (pine), by Yang Wei-chen. $10, Rock and Bamboo, by Hsia Ch'ang.

Perf. 11½
1977, Jan. 12   Photo.   Unwmk.
Granite Paper
2030 A401 $2 multicolored   1.00 .25
2031 A401 $8 multicolored   3.00 .25
2032 A401 $10 multicolored   3.75 .40
    Nos. 2030-2032 (3)   7.75 .90

Black-naped Orioles — A402

Birds of Taiwan: $8, Common Kingfisher. $10, Chinese pheasant-tailed jacana.

1977, Feb. 16   Litho.
2033 A402 $2 multicolored   .55 .25
2034 A402 $8 multicolored   1.10 .25
2035 A402 $10 multicolored   2.00 .35
    Nos. 2033-2035 (3)   3.65 .85

See Nos. 2163-2165.

Census Emblem, Industry and Commerce A403

Perf. 13½
1977, Mar. 16   Litho.   Unwmk.
2036 A403 $2 red & multi   .25 .25
2037 A403 $10 purple & multi   .80 .40

Industry and Commerce Census.

Green Mountains Rising into Clouds, by Madame Chiang — A404

Landscapes, by Madame Chiang Kai-shek: $5, Boat in the Beauty of Spring. $8, Scholar beside Waterfall. $10, Water Rises to Meet the Bridge.

Perf. 11½

1977, Mar. 31	Unwmk.		Photo.
Granite Paper			
2038	A404	$2 multi	.55	.25
2039	A404	$5 multi	2.25	.25
2040	A404	$8 multi	2.75	.50
2041	A404	$10 multi	3.00	.60
	Nos. 2038-2041 (4)		8.55	1.60

League Emblem — A405

1977, Apr. 18	Litho.		Perf. 12½
2042	A405	$2 carmine & multi	.25	.25
2043	A405	$10 green & multi	.80	.65

10th World Anti-Communist League Conference.

Blood Donation — A406

Design: $2, Donating blood, horiz.

1977, May 5	Wmk. 323		Perf. 13½
2044	A406	$2 red & black	.25	.25
2045	A406	$10 red & black	.80	.65

Blood donation movement.

San-hsien A407

Musical Instruments: $5, Tung-hsiao (bamboo flute). $8, Yang-chin (butterfly harpsichord). $10, Pai-hsiao (pipes). Background shows musician playing instrument.

1977, June 21	Unwmk.		Photo.
			Perf. 14
2046	A407	$2 multicolored	.35	.25
2047	A407	$5 multicolored	.60	.25
2048	A407	$8 multicolored	.80	.25
2049	A407	$10 multicolored	1.00	.30
	Nos. 2046-2049 (4)		2.75	1.05

Idea Leuconoe — A408

Protected Butterflies: $4, Hebomoia glaucippe formosana. $6, Stichophthalma

howqua formosana. $10, Atrophaneura horishana.

1977, July 20	Litho.		Perf. 13½
2050	A408	$2 ver & multi	.40	.25
2051	A408	$4 lt grn & multi	.90	.25
2052	A408	$6 lt bl & multi	1.40	.40
2053	A408	$10 yellow & multi	1.75	.50
	Nos. 2050-2053 (4)		4.45	1.40

National Palace Museum A409

Temple — A410

Children's Drawings: $2, Sea Goddess Festival. $4, Boats on Shore of Lan-yu.

Wmk. 323

1977, Aug. 27	Litho.		Perf. 13½
2054	A409	$1 multicolored	.25	.25
2055	A409	$2 multicolored	.25	.25
2056	A409	$4 multicolored	.40	.25
2057	A410	$5 multicolored	.50	.25
	Nos. 2054-2057 (4)		1.40	1.00

8th Exhib. of World School Children's Art.

Carved Lacquer Plate, Wan-li Ware A411

Ancient Carved Lacquer Ware: $5, Bowl, Ching dynasty. $8, Round box, Ming dynasty. $10, Four-tiered box, Ching dynasty.

Perf. 13x14

1977, Sept. 28	Photo.		Wmk. 368
2058	A411	$2 multicolored	.40	.25
2059	A411	$5 multicolored	.85	.25
2060	A411	$8 multicolored	1.75	.25
2061	A411	$10 multicolored	1.50	.30
	Nos. 2058-2061 (4)		4.50	1.05

Lions International, Emblem and Activities — A412

Unwmk.

1977, Oct. 8	Litho.		Perf. 13
2062	A412	$2 multicolored	.25	.25
2063	A412	$10 multicolored	.55	.35

Intl. Association of Lions Clubs, 60th anniv.

Nos. 2069 and 2075 Overprinted in Claret

Perf. 13½x12½

1977, Sept. 9	Litho.		Unwmk.
2064	A365	$2 orange & multi	.25	.25
2065	A365	$8 carmine & grn	.60	.30

Little League baseball championship.

Chinese Quality Mark — A413

Perf. 13x12½

1977, Oct. 14	Litho.		Unwmk.
2066	A413	$2 red & multi	.50	.25
2067	A413	$10 blue & multi	2.00	.30

International Standardization Day.

**Construction Types of 1974
Redrawn: Numerals Outlined**

Designs as 1976 Issue.

Perf. 13½x12½, 12½x13½

1977	Litho.		Unwmk.
	Granite Paper		
2068	A365	$1 car & dp grn	.25	.25
2069	A365	$2 ver & multi	.25	.25
2070	A366	$3 violet & multi	.25	.25
2071	A366	$4 carmine & multi	.25	.25
2072	A365	$5 green & multi	.30	.25
2073	A366	$6 sepia & multi	.30	.25
2074	A366	$7 sepia & multi	.35	.25
2075	A365	$8 red lil & multi	.40	.25
2076	A366	$9 olive & multi	.40	.25
	Nos. 2068-2076 (9)		2.75	2.25

Numerals are in solid color on Nos. 1907-1915, 2009-2017; in outline on Nos. 2068-2076.

For overprints see Nos. 2064-2065, 2112-2113.

Man and Heart — A414

Perf. 13½x12½

1977, Nov. 12	Litho.		Wmk. 323
2077	A414	$2 multicolored	.25	.25
2078	A414	$10 multicolored	.80	.40

Physical health, cardiac care.

White Stallion — A415

New Year 1978: $5, Two horses, horiz. Designs from painting "100 Horses," by Lang Shih-ning.

Perf. 12½

1977, Dec. 1	Unwmk.		Litho.
2079	A415	$1 red & multi	.50	.25
2080	A415	$5 emerald & multi	1.50	.55

First Page of Constitution A416

Pres. Chiang Accepting Constitution, 1946 — A417

1977, Dec. 25	Litho.		Perf. 13½
2081	A416	$2 multicolored	.25	.25
2082	A417	$10 multicolored	.80	.30

30th anniversary of the Constitution.

Knife Coin with 3 Characters, 403-221 B.C. — A418

Designs: Ancient knife coins.

1978, Jan. 18	Wmk. 323		Perf. 13½
2083	A418	$2 salmon & multi	.40	.25
2084	A418	$5 lt blue & blk	.90	.25
2085	A418	$8 lt gray & multi	1.00	.25
2086	A418	$10 tan & multi	1.25	.30
	Nos. 2083-2086 (4)		3.55	1.05

China No. 1 and Flag of China — A419

Designs: $5, No. 464 (Sun Yat-sen). $10, No. 1204 (Chiang Kai-shek).

1978, Feb. 21	Litho.		Perf. 13½
2087	A419	$2 brown & multi	.55	.25
2088	A419	$5 blue & multi	.70	.25
2089	A419	$10 orange & multi	1.00	.40
a.	Souv. sheet of 3, #2087-2089	11.00	5.00
	Nos. 2087-2089 (3)		2.25	.90

Centenary of Chinese postage stamps.

Sun Yat-Sen Memorial Hall A420

China Nos. 2079 and 2 — A421

Perf. 14x12½, 12½x14

1978, Mar. 20			Wmk. 323
2090	A420	$2 multicolored	.25	.25
2091	A421	$10 multicolored	.50	.35

ROCPEX '78 Phil. Exhib., Taipei, Mar. 20-29.

Chiang Kai-shek with Revolutionary Army — A422

Pres. Chiang Kai-shek (1887-1975); $2, as young man, 1912, vert. $8, Making speech at Mt. Lu, July 17, 1937. $10, Reviewing Armed Forces on National Day, 1956, and Chinese flags, vert.

1978, Apr. 5   Wmk. 323   Perf. 13½

2092	A422	$2 violet & multi	.30	.25
2093	A422	$5 green & multi	.50	.25
2094	A422	$8 blue & multi	.75	.40
2095	A422	$10 vio blue & multi	1.00	.50
		Nos. 2092-2095 (4)	2.55	1.40

Nuclear Reactor and Plant — A423

Perf. 13½x12½

1978, Apr. 26   Unwmk.

2096	A423	$10 multicolored	.70	.25

First nuclear power plant on Taiwan.

Poem by Wen Cheng-ming (1470-1559) A424

Chinese Calligraphy: $2, Letter by Wang Hsi-chih (307-365). $4, Eulogy by Chu Sui-liang (596-658). $8, From Autobiography of Huai-su, Tang Dynasty. $10, Poem by Ch'ang Piao, Sung Dynasty.

1978, May 20   Wmk. 323   Perf. 13½

2097	A424	$2 multicolored	.85	.25
2098	A424	$4 multicolored	3.50	.25
2099	A424	$6 multicolored	3.50	.50
2100	A424	$8 multicolored	3.75	.30
2101	A424	$10 multicolored	5.00	.55
		Nos. 2097-2101 (5)	16.60	1.85

Head and Dao Cancer Fund Emblem — A425

1978, June 15   Litho.   Perf. 13½

2102	A425	$2 red, org & ol	.25	.25
2103	A425	$10 dk & lt bl & grn	.70	.35

Cancer prevention.

Carved Lacquer Vase, Ming Dynasty — A426

Ancient Carved Lacquer Ware: $2, Box with dragon and cloud design, Ch'ing dynasty, horiz. $5, Double box on legs, Ch'ing dynasty, horiz. $8, Round box with peonies, Ming dynasty, horiz.

1978, July 12

2104	A426	$2 gray olive & multi	.40	.25
2105	A426	$5 gray olive & multi	.50	.25
2106	A426	$8 gray olive & multi	.75	.25
2107	A426	$10 gray olive & multi	1.05	.30
		Nos. 2104-2107 (4)	2.70	1.05

Tsu Ti Practicing with his Sword — A427

Folk Tales: No. 2109, Pan Ch'ao, diplomat and governor. No. 2110, Tien Tan's "Fire Bull Battle." $5, Liang Hung-yu, a general's wife, who served as drummer in battle.

Wmk. 323

1978, Aug. 16   Litho.   Perf. 13½

2108	A427	$1 multicolored	.25	.25
2109	A427	$2 bister & multi	.55	.25
2110	A427	$2 gray & multi	.90	.25
2111	A427	$5 multicolored	1.25	.25
		Nos. 2108-2111 (4)	2.95	1.00

For similar designs see types A456, A495.

Nos. 2071 & 2073 Overprinted in Red

1978, Sept. 9   Perf. 12½x13

2112	A366	$4 multicolored	.30	.25
2113	A366	$6 multicolored	.75	.30

Triple championships won by Chinese teams in Little League World Series. "1978" overprint on $4 at left, on $6 at right.

Ixias Pyrene A428

Protected Butterflies: $4, Euploea sylvestor swinhoei. $6, Cyrestis thyodamas formosana. $10, Byasa polyeuctes termessus.

1978, Sept. 20

2114	A428	$2 multicolored	.55	.25
2115	A428	$4 multicolored	.70	.25
2116	A428	$6 multicolored	1.05	.30
2117	A428	$10 multicolored	2.75	.45
		Nos. 2114-2117 (4)	5.05	1.25

Scout Symbols — A429

1978, Oct. 5   Litho.   Perf. 13½

2118	A429	$2 multicolored	.40	.25
2119	A429	$10 multicolored	.65	.30

5th Chinese Boy Scout Jamboree, Cheng Ching Lake, Oct. 5-12.

Tropical Tomatoes — A430

Design: $10, Tropical tomatoes, horiz.

1978, Oct. 23   Wmk. 323

2120	A430	$2 multicolored	.30	.25
2121	A430	$10 multicolored	1.25	.40

International Symposium on Tropical Tomatoes, Taiwan, Oct. 23-28.

Sino-Saudi Bridge A431

Design: $6, Buttresses of bridge, flags of Taiwan and Saudi Arabia, horiz.

1978, Oct. 31

2122	A431	$2 multicolored	.35	.25
2123	A431	$6 multicolored	1.40	.30

Completion of Sino-Saudi Bridge over Cho-Shui River.

National Flag — A432

1978-80   Perf. 13½

2124	A432	$1 red & dk bl, I	.25	.25
a.		Bklt. pane of 16 ($5, $6, $8, $10, 3 $1, 9 $2)	7.75	
b.		Type II		.25
2125	A432	$2 red & dk bl, I	.25	.25
a.		Bklt. pane of 15 + label	11.50	
b.		Type II		.25
2126	A432	$3 yel grn & multi ('80)	.30	.25
2127	A432	$4 bis & multi ('80)	.35	.25
2128	A432	$5 dk grn & multi, I	.25	.25
a.		Type II		.25
2129	A432	$6 brn org & multi	.30	.25
2130	A432	$7 dk brn & multi ('80)	.35	.25
2131	A432	$8 dk grn & multi, I	.45	.25
a.		Type II		.45
2132	A432	$10 brt bl & multi ('79)	.60	.25
2133	A432	$12 brt rose lil & multi ('80)	.60	.25
		Nos. 2124-2133 (10)	3.70	2.50

Two types exist: I. Second line (red) below flag is same width as blue line. II. Second line is a hairline, notably thinner. The $3, $4, $7 and $12 were issued only in type II; $6, $10, Nos. 2134, 2124a, only in type I.
Nos. 2129-2133 have colorless inscriptions and denomination in a panel of solid color.
Nos. 2124a, 2125a have selvage inscribed in blue. 1980 printings are in green or red.

Coil Stamp

1980, Jan. 15   Perf. 12 Horiz.

2134	A432	$2 multicolored	.25	.25

See Nos. 2288-2300. For overprints see Nos. 2540-2541.

Three Rams, by Emperor Hsuan-tsung A433

Wmk. 323

1978, Dec. 1   Litho.   Perf. 12½

2135	A433	$1 multicolored	.30	.25
2136	A433	$5 multicolored	1.75	.40

New Year 1979.

Taoyuan International Airport — A434

$10, Passenger terminal, control tower.

1978, Dec. 31   Perf. 13½

2137	A434	$2 multi	.40	.25
2138	A434	$10 multi, horiz.	.70	.40

Completion of Taoyuan Intl. Airport.

Oracle Bones and Inscription, 1766-1123 B.C. — A435

Antiquities and Inscriptions: $5, Lehchi cauldron, 722-481 B.C. $8, Small seal (turtle), 206 B.C.-8 A.D. $10, Inscribed stone tablet, 175-183 A.D.

1979, Jan. 17

2139	A435	$2 multicolored	.60	.25
2140	A435	$5 multicolored	1.25	.30
2141	A435	$8 multicolored	2.25	.50
2142	A435	$10 multicolored	2.25	.65
		Nos. 2139-2142 (4)	6.35	1.70

Origin and development of Chinese characters.

Chihkan Tower, 1653 A436

Taiwan Scenery: $5, Shrine of Confucius, 1665. $8, Shrine of Koxinga, 1661. $10, Eternal Castle and moat.

1979, Feb. 11   Litho.   Perf. 13½

2143	A436	$2 multicolored	.40	.25
2144	A436	$5 multicolored	.85	.25
2145	A436	$8 multicolored	1.10	.25
2146	A436	$10 multicolored	2.10	.25
		Nos. 2143-2146 (4)	4.45	1.00

Children Playing on Winter Day, Sung Dynasty — A437

1979, Mar. 8

2147	A437	Block of 4	14.00	9.25
a.		$5 in UL corner	3.50	.55
b.		$5 in UR corner	3.50	.55
c.		$5 in LL corner	3.50	.55
d.		$5 in LR corner	3.50	.55
e.		Souvenir sheet of 4, #2147, imperf.	27.50	16.00

No. 2147e has simulated perforations.

Lu Hao-tung — A438

Perf. 13x12½

1979, Mar. 29   Engr.   Wmk. 323

2148	A438	$2 blue	.50	.25

Lu Hao-tung (1868-1895), revolutionist.

Yellow Jade Brush Holder — A439

Ancient Brush Washers: $5, White jade, Ming Dynasty. $8, Dark green jade, Ch'ing Dynasty. $10, Bluish jade, Ch'ing Dynasty. All horiz.

Granite Paper
Unwmk.

1979, Apr. 12   Photo.   Perf. 12

2149	A439	$2 multicolored	.25	.25
2150	A439	$5 multicolored	1.10	.25
2151	A439	$8 multicolored	1.50	.35
2152	A439	$10 multicolored	2.10	.50
		Nos. 2149-2152 (4)	4.95	1.35

For similar artifacts designs with single-color background and denominations in outlined numerals with the cents, see types A453, A469, A489, A523, A547, A582.

A440   A440a

Plum Blossoms, Natl. Flower

Perf. 13½x12½

1979-92   Engr.   Wmk. 323
Granite Paper

2153	A440	$10 dk blue	1.60	.25
a.		Plain paper ('88)	2.50	.30
2154	A440	$20 brown	2.00	.25
b.		Plain paper ('87)	3.50	.60
2154A	A440	$40 brt car, plain paper ('85)	2.00	.25
2155	A440	$50 dull green	4.25	.25
a.		Plain paper ('87)	5.00	.55
2156	A440	$100 vermilion	6.00	.90
e.		Plain paper ('92)	6.00	3.25

Perf. 14x13½

2156A	A440a	$300 pur & red org ('83)	16.00	3.25
c.		Plain paper ('91)	18.00	3.25
2156B	A440a	$500 ver & brn ('82)	24.00	5.50
d.		Plain paper ('91)	26.00	5.50
		Nos. 2153-2156B (7)	55.85	10.65

Issued: Nos. 2156Ac, 2156Bd, May 1; No. 2156e, Jan. 7

City Houses and Garden — A441

Design: $10, Rural landscape, horiz.

Perf. 13x12½, 12½x13

1979, June 5   Litho.

2157	A441	$2 multicolored	.25	.25
2158	A441	$10 multicolored	.75	.35

Protection of the Environment.

Bankbook and Computer Department A442

Designs: $2, Children at counter, vert. $5, People standing in line, vert. $10, Hand putting coin in savings bank, symbolic tree.

1979, July 1   Wmk. 323   Perf. 13½

2159	A442	$2 multicolored	.30	.25
2160	A442	$5 multicolored	.45	.25
2161	A442	$8 multicolored	.65	.25
2162	A442	$10 multicolored	.80	.25
		Nos. 2159-2162 (4)	2.20	1.00

Postal savings, 60th anniversary.

Bird Type of 1977

Birds of Taiwan: $2, Swinoe's pheasant. $8, Steere's babbler. $10, Formosan yuhina.

1979, Aug. 8   Perf. 11½

2163	A402	$2 multicolored	.50	.25
2164	A402	$8 multicolored	1.25	.25
2165	A402	$10 multicolored	1.40	.35
		Nos. 2163-2165 (3)	3.15	.85

Rowland Hill, Penny Black A443

Perf. 13½x13

1979, Aug. 27   Litho.   Wmk. 323

2166	A443	$10 multicolored	1.25	.35

Sir Rowland Hill (1795-1879), originator of penny postage.

Jar with Rope Design, Shang Dynasty — A444

Ancient Chinese Pottery: $5, Two-handled jar, Shang dynasty. $8, Red jar with "ears," Han dynasty. $10, Green glazed jar, Han dynasty.

1979, Sept. 12   Perf. 13½

2167	A444	$2 multicolored	.45	.25
2168	A444	$5 multicolored	1.40	.25
2169	A444	$8 multicolored	2.50	.25
2170	A444	$10 multicolored	2.75	.30
		Nos. 2167-2170 (4)	7.10	1.05

Children and IYC Emblem — A445

1979, Sept. 28   Litho.   Perf. 13½

2171	A445	$2 multicolored	.35	.25
2172	A445	$10 multicolored	.70	.35

International Year of the Child.

Trade Symbols, Competition Emblem A446

1979, Dec. 9   Litho.   Perf. 13½

2173	A446	$2 blue & multi	.25	.25
2174	A446	$10 green & multi	.80	.35

10th National Vocational Training Competition, Taichung, Dec. 9.

Trees on a Winter Plain, by Li Ch'eng A447

Paintings: $5, Bamboo, Wen T'ung. $8, Old tree, bamboo and rock, by Chao Meng-fu. $10, Twin Pines, by Li K'an.

1979, Nov. 21

2175	A447	$2 multicolored	.60	.25
2176	A447	$5 multicolored	1.25	.25
2177	A447	$8 multicolored	3.00	.40
2178	A447	$10 multicolored	4.25	.50
		Nos. 2175-2178 (4)	9.10	1.40

Monkey — A448

1979, Dec. 1   Perf. 12½

2179	A448	$1 yellow & multi	1.40	.25
2180	A448	$6 tan & multi	3.00	.50

New Year 1980.

Rotary Emblem and "75" — A449

Rotary Intl., 75th Anniv.: $12, Anniv. emblem.

1980, Feb. 23   Litho.   Perf. 13½

2181	A449	$2 multicolored	.35	.25
2182	A449	$12 multi, vert.	.80	.35

Mt. Hohuan A450

Taiwan Landscapes (East-West Cross-Island Highway): $2, Tunnel of Nine Turns, vert. $12, Bridge, Tien Hsiang, vert.

1980, Mar. 1   Wmk. 323

2183	A450	$2 multicolored	.30	.25
2184	A450	$8 multicolored	1.00	.25
2185	A450	$12 multicolored	1.60	.35
		Nos. 2183-2185 (3)	2.90	.85

A451

1980, Mar. 29   Engr.   Perf. 13½x12½
Granite Paper

2186	A451	$2 red brown	.55	.25

Shih Chien-Ju (1879-1900), revolutionist.

A452

$2, Chung-cheng Memorial Hall. $8, Quotation. $12, Bronze statue.

1980, Apr. 4   Litho.   Perf. 13½

2187	A452	$2 multicolored	.25	.25
2188	A452	$8 multicolored	.50	.25
2189	A452	$12 multicolored	.60	.50
		Nos. 2187-2189 (3)	1.35	1.00

Chiang Kai-shek (1887-1975).

Melon-shaped Jade Brush Washer, Ming Dynasty — A453

Jade Pottery: $2, Jar with dragons, Sung dynasty, vert. $8, Monk's alms bowl, Ch'ing dynasty. $10, Yellow jade brush washer, Ch'ing dynasty.

1980, May 20   Photo.   Perf. 12
Granite Paper

2190	A453	$2 multicolored	.45	.25
2191	A453	$5 multicolored	.90	.25
2192	A453	$8 multicolored	1.60	.25
2193	A453	$10 multicolored	2.00	.30
		Nos. 2190-2193 (4)	4.95	1.05

Energy Conservation A454

1980, July 15   Litho.   Perf. 13½

2194	A454	$2 multicolored	.25	.25
2195	A454	$12 multicolored	.80	.40

A455

T'ang Dynasty pottery.

1980, Aug. 18   Litho.   Perf. 13½

2196	A455	$2 Soldier	.45	.25
2197	A455	$5 Roosters	1.40	.25
2198	A455	$8 Horse	1.90	.25
2199	A455	$10 Camel	2.25	.30
		Nos. 2196-2199 (4)	6.00	1.05

A456

Folk Tales: $1, Grinding mortar into a nee-dle. No. 2201, Confucius Returning Lost Arti-cle (shown). No. 2202, Wen Tien-hsiang in jail. $5, Sending coal in snow.

Perf. 14x13½

1980, Sept. 23   Litho.   Wmk. 323
2200 A456 $1 multicolored   .25   .25
2201 A456 $2 multicolored   .30   .25
2202 A456 $2 multicolored   .80   .25
2203 A456 $5 multicolored   1.10   .30
   Nos. 2200-2203 (4)   2.45 1.05

Railroad Electrification A457

No. 2205, Taichung Harbor. No. 2206, Chiang Kai-shek Airport. No. 2207, Steel Mill. No. 2208, Sun Yat-sen Freeway. No. 2209, Nuclear power plant. No. 2210, Petrochemical plants. No. 2211, Su-ao Harbor. No. 2212, Kaohsiung shipyard. No. 2213, North link railroad.

1980, Oct. 10   Perf. 13½x14
2204 A457 $2 shown   .50   .25
2205 A457 $2 multicolored   .50   .25
2206 A457 $2 multicolored   .50   .25
2207 A457 $2 multicolored   .50   .25
2208 A457 $2 multicolored   .50   .25
2209 A457 $2 multicolored   .50   .25
2210 A457 $2 multicolored   .50   .25
2211 A457 $2 multicolored   .50   .25
2212 A457 $2 multicolored   .50   .25
2213 A457 $2 multicolored   .50   .25
   a. Souv. sheet of 10, #2204-2213   9.50 9.50
   b. Block of 10, #2204-2213   4.50 4.50
   Nos. 2204-2213 (10)   5.00 2.50

Completion of major construction projects.

10th National Savings Day — A458

$2, Ancient coin and coin banks.

Wmk. 323
1980, Oct. 25   Litho.   Perf. 13½
2214 A458 $2 multicolored   .55   .25
2215 A458 $12 shown   1.10   .40

Landscape, by Ch'iu Ying, Ming Dynasty — A459

1980, Nov. 12   Litho.   Perf. 13½
2216 A459 Block of 4   10.75 5.25
   a. $5 in UL corner   2.50   .40
   b. $5 in UR corner   2.50   .40
   c. $5 in LL corner   2.50   .40
   d. $5 in LR corner   2.50   .40
   e. Souvenir sheet, imperf. 16.00 14.50

No. 2216e has simulated perforations.

Cock — A460

1980, Dec. 1   Perf. 12½
2217 A460 $1 multicolored   .90   .25
2218 A460 $6 multicolored 2.75   .35
   a. Souv. sheet, 2 each #2217-2218 11.50 11.50

New Year 1981.

Faces, Flag, Census Form — A461

1980, Dec. 13   Perf. 13½
2219 A461 $2 shown   .25   .25
2220 A461 $12 Buildings, horiz. 1.00 .40

1980 population and housing census.

TIROS-N Satellite — A462

Design: $10, Central weather bureau, horiz.

1981, Jan. 28   Litho.   Perf. 13½
2221 A462 $2 multicolored   .35   .25
2222 A462 $10 multicolored 1.00   .40

Completion of meteorological satellite ground station, Taipei.

"Happiness" A463

New Year 1981 (Calligraphy): No. 2224, Wealth. No. 2225, Longevity. No. 2226, Joy.

1981, Feb. 3   Perf. 13½x12½
2223 A463 $5 multi, 5 at B   1.00   .25
2224 A463 $5 multi, 5 at R   1.00   .25
2225 A463 $5 multi, 5 at L   1.00   .25
2226 A463 $5 multi, 5 at T   1.00   .25
   a. Block of 4, #2223-2226 4.50 1.75

International Year of the Disabled — A464

1981, Feb. 19   Litho.   Perf. 13½
2227 A464 $2 multicolored   .25   .25
2228 A464 $12 multicolored .70   .25

Mt. Ali — A465

1981, Mar. 1
2229 A465 $2 shown   .30   .25
2230 A465 $7 Oluanpi Beach   1.00   .25
2231 A465 $12 Sun Moon Lake   1.60   .30
   Nos. 2229-2231 (3)   2.90   .80

A $2 multicolored stamp for the 12th National Kuomintang Congress at Taipei was prepared for release Mar. 29, 1981, but not issued. It showed Sun Yat-sen, Chiang Kai-shek, flags of China and the Kuomintang and a map of China.

Children in Forest A467

Children's Day: Drawings.

1981, Apr. 4
2233 A467 $1 multicolored   .25   .25
2234 A467 $2 multicolored   .25   .25
2235 A467 $5 multicolored   .25   .25
2236 A467 $7 multicolored   .30   .25
   Nos. 2233-2236 (4)   1.05 1.00

Chiang Kai-shek Memorial Hall — A468

1981, Apr. 5   Perf. 12½x13½
2237 A468 20c bluish lilac   .25   .25
   a. Photo. ('87)   .25   .25
2238 A468 40c crim rose   .25   .25
   a. Photo. ('87)   .25   .25
2239 A468 50c dull red brn   .25   .25
   a. Photo. ('88)   .25   .25
   Nos. 2237-2239 (3)   .75   .75

Chiang Kai-shek (1887-1975). See Nos. 2601-2603.

Cloisonne Enamel Brush Washer, 15th Cent. A469

Cloisonne Enamel: $5, Ritual vessel, 15th cent., vert. $8, Plate, 17th cent. $10, Vase, Ming Dynasty, vert.

1981, May 20   Photo.   Perf. 12
Granite Paper
2240 A469 $2 multicolored   .50   .25
2241 A469 $5 multicolored   1.10   .25
2242 A469 $8 multicolored   1.25   .25
2243 A469 $10 multicolored 1.60   .30
   Nos. 2240-2243 (4)   4.45 1.05

For similar enamelware stamps see Nos. 2318-2321, 2348-2351, 2410-2413.

Early & Modern Locomotives A470

Wmk. 323
1981, June 9   Litho.   Perf. 12½
2244 A470 $2 shown   .45   .25
2245 A470 $14 Trains, horiz. 1.60 .40

Railroad service centenary.

Linnaeus Crab — A471

1981, June 14   Perf. 13½
2246 A471 $2 De Haan crab, horiz. .30   .25
2247 A471 $5 shown   .60   .25
2248 A471 $8 Miers crab, horiz.   .95   .25
2249 A471 $14 Rathbun crab   1.75   .30
   Nos. 2246-2249 (4)   3.60 1.05

Central Weather Bureau, 40th Anniv. — A472

1981, July 1   Litho.   Perf. 13½
2250 A472 $2 multicolored   .30   .25
2251 A472 $14 multicolored 1.25   .40

Scene from The Cowherd and the Weaving Maid — A473

Designs: Scenes from the Cowherd and the Weaving Maid.

1981, Aug. 6   Litho.   Perf. 13½x14
2252 A473 $2 multicolored   .50   .25
2253 A473 $4 multicolored   .80   .25
2254 A473 $8 multicolored   1.50   .25
2255 A473 $14 multicolored 2.25   .50
   Nos. 2252-2255 (4)   5.05 1.25

First Lasography Exhibition — A474

Lasography Designs.

1981, Aug. 15   Perf. 13½
2256 A474 $2 multicolored   .25   .25
2257 A474 $5 multicolored   .30   .25
2258 A474 $8 multicolored   .65   .25
2259 A474 $14 multicolored 1.10   .50
   Nos. 2256-2259 (4)   2.30 1.25

Soccer Players — A475

1981, Sept. 9   Litho.   Perf. 13½
2260 A475 $5 multicolored   .50   .25
2261 A475 $5 multicolored   .50   .25
   a. A475 Pair, #2260-2261 1.10   .65

Sports Day.

A477

70th Anniv. of Republic: No. 2263, Eastward Expedition (soldiers on Hill). No. 2264, Northward Expedition (Chiang on horse). No. 2265, Resistance War with Japan (Chiang, fist raised). No. 2266, Suppression of Communist Rebels (Battle scene). No. 2267, Counteroffensive and unification. $8, Chiang Kai-shek. $14, Sun Yat-sen.

1981, Oct. 10   *Perf. 13½*

2262	A477	$2 multicolored	.25	.25
2263	A477	$2 multicolored	.25	.25
2264	A477	$2 multicolored	.25	.25
2265	A477	$2 multicolored	.25	.25
2266	A477	$3 multicolored	.25	.25
2267	A477	$2 multicolored	.25	.25
2268	A477	$8 multicolored	.45	.25
2269	A477	$14 multicolored	1.00	.45
a.		Souv. sheet of 8, #2262-2269	9.00	3.50
		Nos. 2262-2269 (8)	2.95	2.20

No. 2269a issued Oct. 25.

ROCPEX TAIPEI '81 Intl. Philatelic Exhibition, Taipei, Oct. 25-Nov. 2 — A478

1981, Oct. 25

2270	A478	$2 multicolored	.25	.25
2271	A478	$14 multicolored	.50	.25

Nos. 2269a, 2270-2271 overprinted with four characters meaning "Best of Show" were not valid for postage. They were inserted in a special "ROCPEX" book, edition of 10,000. Value $25.

Boys Playing Games (#2272a) — A479

Designs: a.-j. "One Hundred Boys," Sung Dynasty scroll (each stamp is numbered from 1 to 10 in Chinese. See illustrations with Nos. 1682-1691 for numerals.) Two strips of 5 each in continuous design.

1981, Nov. 12

2272		Block of 10	16.50	16.50
a.-e.	A479	$2 single (top row)	1.50	.25
f.-j.	A479	$2 single (bottom row)	1.50	.25

New Year 1982 (Year of the Dog) — A480

Wmk. 323

1981, Dec. 1   *Litho.*   *Perf. 12½*

2273	A480	$1 multicolored	1.25	.25
2274	A480	$10 multicolored	2.00	.40
a.		Souv. sheet, 2 ea #2273-2274	13.50	5.00

Information Week, Dec. 6-12 — A481

1981, Dec. 7   *Perf. 14x13½*

2275	A481	$2 multicolored	.55	.25

Telecommunications Centenary — A482

1981, Dec. 28   *Perf. 14x13½, 13½x14*

2276	A482	$2 Telephone, vert.	.25	.25
2277	A482	$3 Old, new phones	.25	.25
2278	A482	$8 Submarine cable	.40	.25
2279	A482	$18 Computers, vert.	.55	.30
		Nos. 2276-2279 (4)	1.45	1.05

Floral Arrangement A483

Various floral arrangements in Ming vases.

Wmk. 323

1982, Jan. 23   *Litho.*   *Perf. 13½*

2280	A483	$2 multicolored	.25	.25
2281	A483	$3 multicolored	.35	.25
2282	A483	$8 multicolored	.75	.25
2283	A483	$18 multicolored	1.75	.50
		Nos. 2280-2283 (4)	3.10	1.25

Compare with designs A559, A584.

The Ku Cheng Reunion — A484

Designs: Opera scenes.

Wmk. 323

1982, Feb. 15   *Litho.*   *Perf. 13½*

2284	A484	$2 multicolored	.55	.25
2285	A484	$3 multicolored	1.75	.25
2286	A484	$4 multicolored	1.90	.25
2287	A484	$18 multicolored	3.50	.60
		Nos. 2284-2287 (4)	7.70	1.35

Flag Type of 1978
Value Colorless in Colored Panel

1981   *Litho.*   *Perf. 13½*

Panel Color

2288	A432	$1	dk blue	.30	.25
2289	A432	$1.50	lt olive	.30	.25
2290	A432	$2	dk olive bis	.30	.25
2291	A432	$3	red	.30	.25
2292	A432	$4	blue	.30	.25
2293	A432	$5	sepia	.30	.25
2294	A432	$6	orange	.40	.25
2295	A432	$7	green	.60	.25
2296	A432	$8	magenta	.75	.25
2297	A432	$9	olive grn	.95	.25
2298	A432	$10	dk purple	1.10	.25
2299	A432	$12	lilac	1.25	.25
2300	A432	$14	dk green	1.25	.30
			Nos. 2288-2300 (13)	8.10	3.30

Second line (red) below flag is a hairline, notably thinner.
For overprints see Nos. 2540-2541.

Robert Koch — A485

Wmk. 323

1982, Mar. 24   *Litho.*   *Perf. 13½*

2309	A485	$2 multicolored	.25	.25

Tubercle Bacillus centenary.

Cheng Shih-liang, Revolutionary A486

1982, Mar. 29   *Engr.*   *Perf. 13½x12½*
Granite Paper

2310	A486	$2 carmine rose	.25	.25

Children's Day A487

Designs: Various children's drawings.

1982, Apr. 4   *Litho.*

2311	A487	$2 multi, vert.	.40	.25
2312	A487	$3 multicolored	.60	.25
2313	A487	$5 multicolored	.80	.25
2314	A487	$8 multicolored	.80	.25
		Nos. 2311-2314 (4)	2.60	1.00

Dentists' Day A488

$2, Tooth, boy. $3, Flossing, brushing. $10, Examination.

1982, May 4   *Litho.*   *Perf. 13½*

2315	A488	$2 multicolored	.30	.25
2316	A488	$3 multicolored	.60	.25
2317	A488	$10 multicolored	1.10	.30
		Nos. 2315-2317 (3)	2.00	.80

Champleve Enamel Cup and Saucer, 18th Cent. A489

Painted Enamelware: $5, Cloisonne gold-plated duck Ch'ien-lung period (1736-1795), vert. $8, Incense burner, K'ang-hsi period (1662-1722). $12, Cloisonne pitcher, Ch'ien-lung period, vert.

1982, May 20   *Photo.*   *Perf. 12*
Granite Paper

2318	A489	$2 multicolored	.40	.25
2319	A489	$5 multicolored	.80	.25
2320	A489	$8 multicolored	2.00	.25
2321	A489	$12 multicolored	2.75	.25
		Nos. 2318-2321 (4)	5.95	1.00

See Nos. 2348-2351.

Poets' Day — A490

Tang Dynasty Poetry Illustrations (618-906): $2, Spring Dawn, by Meng Hao-Jan. $3, On Looking for a Hermit and Not Finding Him, by Chia Tao. $5, Summer Dying, by Liu Yu-Hsi. $18, Looking at the Snow Drifts on South Mountain, by Tsu Yung. Chinese characters are to the left of the denominations on Nos. 2322-2325, Nos. 2396-2399 have no characters to the left of the denominations.

Wmk. 323

1982, June 25   *Litho.*   *Perf. 13½*

2322	A490	$2 multicolored	2.25	.25
2323	A490	$3 multicolored	4.00	.35
2324	A490	$5 multicolored	6.25	.75
2325	A490	$18 multicolored	14.50	1.50
		Nos. 2322-2325 (4)	27.00	2.85

See Nos. 2352-2355.

5th World Women's Softball Championship, Taipei, July 1-12 — A491

1982, July 2

2326	A491	$2 lt grn & multi	.65	.25
2327	A491	$18 tan & multi	1.25	.40

Scouting Year A492

$2, Crossing bridge, Baden-Powell. $18, Emblem, camp.

1982, July 18

2328	A492	$2 multicolored	.25	.25
2329	A492	$18 multicolored	.70	.40

Stamp in Tongs A493

$18, Album stamps magnified.

1982, Aug. 9

2330	A493	$2 shown	.65	.25
2331	A493	$18 multicolored	1.40	.40

Carved Lion, Tsu Shih Temple — A494

Tsu Shih Temple of Sanhsia Architecture: $3, Lion brackets, horiz. $5, Sub-lintels. $18, Tiled roof, horiz.

1982, Sept. 1   Litho.   Perf. 13½
2332 A494 $2 multicolored   .40   .25
2333 A494 $3 multicolored   .55   .25
2334 A494 $5 multicolored   1.25   .25
2335 A494 $18 multicolored   1.75   .40
    Nos. 2332-2335 (4)   3.95 1.15

Hsun Kuan Saving
Hsiang-cheng
City — A495

Designs: Scenes from The Thirty-Six Examples of Filial Piety, Folk Tale collection by Wu Yen-huan.

1982, Oct. 15   Perf. 14x13½
2336 A495 $1 multicolored   .25   .25
2337 A495 $2 multicolored   .50   .25
2338 A495 $3 multicolored   .70   .25
2339 A495 $5 multicolored   .80   .25
    Nos. 2336-2339 (4)   2.25 1.00

30th Anniv.
of China
Youth
Corps
A496

$2, Riding. $3, Raising flag, vert. $18, Mountain climbing.

1982, Oct. 31
2340 A496 $2 multicolored   .25   .25
2341 A496 $3 multicolored   .25   .25
2342 A496 $18 multicolored   .60   .40
    Nos. 2340-2342 (3)   1.10   .90

Seated Lohan
(Buddhist
Saint) — A497

Paintings of Lohan, Hanging Scrolls by Liu Sung-nien, 13th cent.

Perf. 13x12½
1982, Nov. 12   Litho.   Wmk. 323
2343 A497 $2 multicolored   1.25   .25
2344 A497 $3 multicolored   3.00   .25
2345 A497 $18 multicolored   7.75   .85
  a. Souv. sheet, #2343-2345   27.50 13.00
    Nos. 2343-2345 (3)   12.00 1.35

No. 2345a comes overprinted in red in the sheet margins. Value, unused $18, Used $12.

New Year 1983
(Year of the
Boar) — A498

1982, Dec. 1   Perf. 12½
2346 A498 $1 multicolored   1.60   .25
2347 A498 $10 multicolored   2.75   .45
  a. Souv. sheet, 2 ea #2346-
      2347   14.50 6.50

Enamelware Type of 1982

Designs: $2, Square basin, Ch'ing Dynasty (1644-1911). $3, Vase, Ch'ien-lung period (1736-1795). $4, Tea pot, Ch'ien-lung period. $18, Elephant vase, Ch'ing Dynasty.

1983, Jan. 5   Photo.   Perf. 12
Granite Paper
2348 A489 $2 multi   .50   .25
2349 A489 $3 multi, vert.   .70   .25
2350 A489 $4 multi   1.25   .25
2351 A489 $18 multi, vert.   2.00   .50
    Nos. 2348-2351 (4)   4.45 1.25

Poetry Illustration Type of 1982

Sung Dynasty Poetry: $2, Seeing the Flowers Fade Away. $3, River. $5, Freckled with Clouds is the Azure Sky. $11, Yielding Fine Fragrance in the Snow. Nos. 2352-2355 vert.

Wmk. 323
1983, Feb. 10   Perf. 13½
2352 A490 $2 multicolored   1.40   .25
2353 A490 $3 multicolored   5.25   .35
2354 A490 $5 multicolored   7.50   .50
2355 A490 $11 multicolored   11.00   .60
    Nos. 2352-2355 (4)   25.15 1.70

Mt. Jade, Taiwan — A499

$2, Wawa Valley, vert. $3, University Pond, vert.

1983, Mar. 1
2356 A499 $2 multicolored   .70   .25
2357 A499 $3 multicolored   1.10   .25
2358 A499 $18 shown   1.75   .50
    Nos. 2356-2358 (3)   3.55 1.00

400th Anniv. of
Arrival of Matteo
Ricci (1552-1610),
Italian Missionary
A500

Perf. 14x13½
1983, Apr. 3   Litho.   Wmk. 323
2359 A500 $2 Globe   .45   .25
2360 A500 $18 Great Wall   1.40   .35

Mandarin
Phonetic
Symbols,
70th
Anniv. — A501

$2, Wu Ching-heng, inventor. $18, Children writing.

Wmk. 323
1983, May 22   Litho.   Perf. 13½
2361 A501 $2 multicolored   .45   .25
2362 A501 $18 multicolored   1.40   .30

Scenes from Lady
White Snake
Fairytale — A502

1983, June 15   Perf. 14x13½
2363 A502 $2 multicolored   .60   .25
2364 A502 $3 lt blue & multi   1.10   .25
2365 A502 $3 orange & multi   1.10   .25
2366 A502 $18 multicolored   1.25   .50
    Nos. 2363-2366 (4)   4.05 1.25

A503

Various bamboo carved objects: $2, Bamboo jug. $3, Tao-t'ieh motif vase. $4, Landscape sculpture. $18, Brush holder, Ming dynasty.
    Nos. 2367-2369 Ch'ing dynasty.

Wmk. 323
1983, July 14   Litho.   Perf. 13½
2367 A503 $2 multicolored   .75   .25
2368 A503 $3 multicolored   .90   .25
2369 A503 $4 multicolored   1.05   .25
2370 A503 $18 multicolored   2.25   .40
    Nos. 2367-2370 (4)   4.95 1.15

A504

Wmk. 323
1983, Aug. 5   Litho.   Perf. 13½
2371 A504 $2 Globe   .55   .25
2372 A504 $18 Emblem   .80   .35

World Communications Year.

Fishing
Industry
(Local Fish)
A505

$2, Epinephelus tauvina. $18, Saurida undosquamis.

1983, Aug. 20
2373 A505 $2 multicolored   .60   .25
2374 A505 $18 multicolored   2.25   .35

40th Journalists'
Day — A506

1983, Sept. 1
2375 A506 $2 multicolored   .55   .25

Views of
Mongolia and
Tibet — A507

1983, Sept. 15
2376 A507 $2 Village   .55   .25
2377 A507 $3 Potala Palace   1.00   .25
2378 A507 $5 Sheep grazing   1.10   .25
2379 A507 $11 Camel caravan   1.75   .40
    Nos. 2376-2379 (4)   4.40 1.15

2nd East
Asian Bird
Protection
Conference,
Oct. — A508

$2, Lanius cristatus, vert. $18, Butastur indicus.

1983, Oct. 8   Litho.   Perf. 13½
2380 A508 $2 multicolored   .65   .25
2381 A508 $18 multicolored   2.50   .40

A509

Plum Blossoms, photography by Hu Ch'ung-hsien.

1983, Oct. 31   Litho.   Perf. 14x13½
2382 A509 $2 multicolored   .35   .25
2383 A509 $3 multi, diff.   .65   .25
2384 A509 $5 multi, diff.   .70   .25
2385 A509 $11 multi, diff.   1.00   .30
    Nos. 2382-2385 (4)   2.70 1.05

A510

$2, JCI and Congress emblems. $18, Globe and emblems, horiz.

1983, Nov. 6   Perf. 13x13½, 13½x13
2386 A510 $2 multicolored   .25   .25
2387 A510 $18 multicolored   .90   .40

Jaycees Intl., 38th World Congress, Taipei.

8th Asian-Pacific Cardiology
Congress — A511

$18, Electrocardiogram.

1983, Nov. 27   Litho.   Perf. 13½
2388 A511 $2 shown   .30   .25
2389 A511 $18 multicolored   1.10   .65

New Year 1984
(Year of the
Rat) — A512

1983, Dec. 1   Litho.   Perf. 12½
2390 A512 $1 multicolored   1.75   .70
2391 A512 $10 multicolored   4.00   .45
  a. Souv. sheet, 2 each #2390-
      2391   30.00 9.00

Literacy Week
A513

$18, Modern family, vert.

1983, Dec. 17   Litho.   *Perf. 13½*
2392 A513 $2 shown   .35 .25
2393 A513 $18 multicolored   1.10 .55

World Freedom Day
A514

$2, Korean War Patriots. $18, Intl. support.

1984, Jan. 23   Litho.   *Perf. 13½*
2394 A514 $2 multicolored   .35 .25
2395 A514 $18 multicolored 1.40 .35

Drama Day — A515

Yuan Dynasty Poetry Illustrations by Tien-shih Lin (Poems by): $2, Kuan Yun-shih. $3, Po Pu. $5, Chang Ko-chiu. $18, Shang Cheng-shu. (See note with Nos. 2322-2325.)

1984, Feb. 15   *Perf. 13½*
2396 A515 $2 multicolored   1.90   .35
2397 A515 $3 multicolored   3.75   .45
2398 A515 $5 multicolored   6.50   .65
2399 A515 $18 multicolored 10.00 1.40
     Nos. 2396-2399 (4)   22.15 2.75

A516

A517

A518

Arbor Day — A519

1984, Mar. 12   Litho.   *Perf. 13½x14*
2400 A516 $2 multicolored   .90 .25
2401 A517 $2 multicolored   .90 .25
2402 A518 $2 multicolored   .90 .25
2403 A519 $2 multicolored   .90 .25
  a. Block of 4, #2400-2403 5.00 3.25

Lin Chueh-min — A520

1984, Mar. 29   Engr.   *Perf. 13x12½*
Granite Paper
2404 A520 $2 dark green   .25 .25

Central News Agency, 60th Anniv. — A521

$2, Emblem. $10, Emblem, satellite, dish antenna.

Perf. 14x13½
1984, Apr. 1   Litho.   Wmk.
2405 A521 $2 multicolored   .25 .25
2406 A521 $10 multicolored .70 .45

God of Longevity — A522

Paintings by Chang Ta-chien (1899-1983): $2, Five Auspicious Tokens. $18, Lotus Blossoms in Ink Splash.

Wmk. 323
1984, Apr. 20   Litho.   *Perf. 11½*
2407 A522 $2 multicolored   1.50 .25
2408 A522 $5 multicolored   4.00 .25
2409 A522 $18 multicolored 6.00 .50
     Nos. 2407-2409 (3)   11.50 1.00

Ch'ing Dynasty Enamelware A523

$2, Cup, pot, plate, horiz. $3, Wine jug. $4, Teapot. $18, Candle holder.

1984, May 20   Photo.   *Perf. 12*
Granite Paper
2410 A523 $2 multicolored   .40 .25
2411 A523 $3 multicolored   .80 .25
2412 A523 $4 multicolored 1.25 .25
2413 A523 $18 multicolored 1.60 .45
     Nos. 2410-2413 (4)   4.05 1.20

China Airlines World-wide Service Inauguration A524

1984, May 31   Litho.   *Perf. 13½x14*
2414 A524 $2 Jet circling globe .25 .25
2415 A524 $7 Globe, jet   .50 .25
2416 A524 $11 New York City   .65 .30
2417 A524 $18 Amsterdam   .85 .45
     Nos. 2414-2417 (4)   2.25 1.25

30th Navigation Day A525

Perf. 13½x13
1984, July 11   Litho.   Wmk. 323
2418 A525 $2 Container ship 1.10 .25
2419 A525 $18 Oil tanker   2.10 .35

1984 Summer Olympics — A526

Perf. 13½x14, 14x13½
1984, June 23
2420 A526 $2 Judo, horiz.   .30 .25
2421 A526 $5 Archery   .50 .65
2422 A526 $18 Swimming, horiz.   1.00 .80
     Nos. 2420-2422 (3)   1.80 1.70

Alpine Plants — A527

$2, Gentiana arisanensis. $3, Epilobium nankotaizanense. $5, Adenophora uehatae. $18, Aconitum fukutomei.

1984, Aug. 8   *Perf. 13*
2423 A527 $2 multi   .50 .25
2424 A527 $3 multi 1.00 .25
2425 A527 $5 multi 1.40 .25
2426 A527 $18 multi 2.00 .50
     Nos. 2423-2426 (4) 4.90 1.25

The Eighteen Scholars, Sung Dynasty Hanging Scroll — A528

$2, Playing instruments. $3, Playing chess. $5, Practicing calligraphy. $18, Painting.

Wmk. 323
1984, Aug. 20   *Perf. 13*
2427 A528 $2 multicolored   2.40 .25
2428 A528 $3 multicolored   4.75 .35
2429 A528 $5 multicolored   7.00 .50
2430 A528 $18 multicolored 16.00 1.00
     Nos. 2427-2430 (4)   30.15 2.10

Athletics Day — A529

1984, Sept. 9
2431 $5 Two players   .90 .25
2432 $5 One player   .90 .25
  a. A529 Pair, #2431-2432   2.00 .90

A531

1984, Sept. 9
2433 A531 $10 "20," map of Asia .70 .25
Asian-Pacific Parliamentarians' Union, 20th anniv.

A532

1984, Oct. 10   Litho.   *Perf. 12½*
2434 A532 $2 No. 1458   .25 .25
2435 A532 $5 No. 296   .60 .25
2436 A532 $18 Museum   .90 .50
  a. Souv. sheet of 3, #2434-2436 9.00 2.25
     Nos. 2434-2436 (3)   1.75 1.00
Postal Museum opening.

Flag, Alliance Emblem — A533

1984, Oct. 16   *Perf. 13½*
2437 A533 $2 multicolored   .45 .25

Grand Alliance for China's Reunification Under the Three Principles of the People Convention, Taipei, Oct. 16-17.

Veteran's Assistance A534

1984, Nov. 1   Litho.   *Perf. 13½*
2438 A534 $2 Vignettes   .45 .25

Pine Tree A535

Bamboo A535a

Plum Tree — A535b

1984-88
2439 A535 $2 multicolored   .25 .25
2440 A535a $8 multicolored .75 .25
2441 A535b $10 pale yellow bister background .80 .25
  a. Grayish tan background .40 .25
     Nos. 2439-2441 (3)   1.80 .75

Issued: Nos. 2439-2440, 2441a, 11/12; No. 2441,1/12/88.

See Nos. 2495-2503, 3303.

A536

1984, Dec. 1   **Perf. 12x12½**
2442 A536 $1 multicolored   1.10   .25
2443 A536 $10 multicolored   3.00   .30
  a.   Min. sheet, 2 ea #2442-2443   7.75   3.50

New Year 1985 (Year of the Ox).

Scales, Legal Codes — A537

1985, Jan. 11   **Litho.**   **Perf. 13½**
2444 A537 $5 multicolored   .65   .25

Judicial Day 1985.

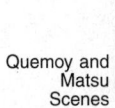

Quemoy and Matsu Scenes A538

$2, Ku-kang Lake, Quemoy. $5, Kuang-hai Stone, Quemoy. $8, Sheng-li Reservoir, Matsu. $10, Tung-chu Lighthouse, Matsu.

1985, Jan. 23   **Litho.**   **Perf. 13½x14**
2445 A538 $2 multicolored   .30   .25
2446 A538 $5 multicolored   .80   .25
2447 A538 $8 multicolored   1.05   .25
2448 A538 $10 multicolored   1.40   .25
  Nos. 2445-2448 (4)   3.55   1.00

Sir Robert Hart (1835-1911) A539

1985, Feb. 15   **Litho.**   **Perf. 14x13½**
2449 A539 $2 No. 1   .45   .25

Inspector General of Chinese Customs, 1863-1908, and founder of the Chinese Postal Service.

Lo Fu-hsing (1886-1914) A540

1985, Feb. 24   **Perf. 13x13½**
2450 A540 $2 multicolored   .45   .25

Tsou Jung (1882-1905) A541

1985, Mar. 29   **Engr.**   **Perf. 13½x12½**
Granite Paper
2451 A541 $3 green   .45   .25

Chung-cheng Memorial Hall Main Gate — A542

$8, Tzuhu Memorial. $10, Chiang Kai-shek, vert.

1985, Apr. 5   **Litho.**   **Perf. 13**
2452 A542 $2 shown   .30   .25
2453 A542 $8 multicolored   1.10   .25
2454 A542 $10 multicolored   1.25   .30
  Nos. 2452-2454 (3)   2.65   .80

Tenth death anniv. of Chiang Kai-shek.

A543

1985, May 8   **Litho.**   **Perf. 13½**
2455 A543 $2 Carnation   1.00   .25
2456 A543 $2 Day lily   1.00   .25
  a.   Pair, #2455-2456   2.50   .80

Mother's Day.

Tunnel to Chi-chin Island — A544

1985, May 18
2457 A544 $5 multicolored   .70   .25

Kaohsiung Cross-Harbor Tunnel, 1st anniv.

Girl Scouts, 75th Anniv. — A545

Wmk. 323
1985, June 1   **Litho.**   **Perf. 13½**
2458 A545 $2 multicolored   .25   .25
2459 A545 $18 multicolored   2.00   .30

The Book of Odes, Confucius A545a

1985, June 22   **Litho.**   **Wmk. 323**
2460 A545a $2 Spring   1.25   .25
2461 A545a $5 Summer   2.40   .25
2462 A545a $8 Fall   4.75   .30
2463 A545a $10 Winter   6.00   .50
  Nos. 2460-2463 (4)   14.40   1.30

Fruit — A546

Perf. 13½x14
1985, July 5   **Litho.**   **Wmk. 323**
2464 A546 $2 Wax Jambo   .70   .25
2465 A546 $3 Guava   1.25   .25
2466 A546 $5 Carambola   1.40   .25
2467 A546 $8 Litchi nut   1.50   .30
  Nos. 2464-2467 (4)   4.85   1.05

Ch'ing Dynasty (1644-1911) Ivory Carvings — A547

$2, Dragon Boat. $3, Landscape. $5, Melon, water container. $18, Brush holder, vert.

1985, July 18   **Wmk. 323**   **Perf. 13½**
2468 A547 $2 multicolored   .25   .25
2469 A547 $3 multicolored   .60   .25
2470 A547 $5 multicolored   .90   .25
2471 A547 $18 multicolored   1.10   .35
  Nos. 2468-2471 (4)   2.85   1.10

T'ang Dynasty (618-907) Aristocrat — A548

Designs: $5, Sung Dynasty (960-1280) palace woman. $8, Yuan Dynasty (1280-1368) aristocrat. $11, Ming Dynasty (1368-1644) aristocrat.

1985, Aug. 1   **Wmk. 323**   **Perf. 13½**
2472 A548 $2 multicolored   .55   .25
2473 A548 $5 multicolored   1.75   .25
2474 A548 $8 multicolored   2.50   .25
2475 A548 $11 multicolored   3.00   .30
  Nos. 2472-2475 (4)   7.80   1.05

4th Asian Conf. on Costume, Aug. 3.
In the 2 rows of Chinese characters above the denomination, the right row has 3 characters and a dot on Nos. 2472-2475, 4 characters and a dot on Nos. 2549-2552. Nos. 2605-2608, 2660-2663 have solid black numerals.
See Nos. 2549-2552, 2605-2608, 2660-2663, 2721-2724, 2794-2797.

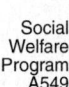

Social Welfare Program A549

Perf. 13½x14
1985, Aug. 15   **Wmk. 323**
2476 A549 $2 Heart, bird feeding young   .45   .25

Historic Sites A550

$2, Taipei North Gate. $5, San Domingo Fort, Tamsui. $8, Lung Shun Temple, Lukang. $10, Confucius Temple, Changhua.

Wmk. 323
1985, Sept. 3   **Litho.**   **Perf. 13½**
2477 A550 $2 multicolored   .25   .25
2478 A550 $5 multicolored   .65   .25
2479 A550 $8 multicolored   .85   .25
2480 A550 $10 multicolored   1.10   .25
  Nos. 2477-2480 (4)   2.85   1.00

Bonsai — A551

Perf. 13½x14
1985, Sept. 22   **Wmk. 323**
2481 A551 $2 Oak   .35   .25
2482 A551 $5 Five-leaf pine   .75   .25
2483 A551 $8 Lohan pine   1.00   .25
2484 A551 $18 Banyan   1.50   .50
  Nos. 2481-2484 (4)   3.60   1.25

Trade Shows — A552

Taipei World Trade Center and show emblems: a, Sporting goods. b, Toys and gifts. c, Electronics. d, Machinery. Se-tenant in continuous design.

1985, Oct. 5   **Perf. 13½**
2485 A552 Strip of 4   3.50   1.25
  a.-d. $2 any single   .75   .25

Scenes of Modern Taiwan, Map, Flag A553

$18, Chiang Kai-shek, Triumphal Arch.

1985, Oct. 25
2486 A553 $2 shown   1.00   .25
2487 A553 $18 multicolored   2.00   .70

Defeat of Japanese army, end of World War II, and return of Taiwan to control of the Republic, 40th anniv.

7th Asian Conference on Mental Retardation A554

1985, Nov. 8   **Perf. 14x13½**
2488 A554 $2 multicolored   .40   .25
2489 A554 $11 multicolored   1.50   .30

Sun Yat-sen and Birthplace
A555

1985, Nov. 12   **Perf. 13½**
2490 A555 $2 multicolored .40 .25
2491 A555 $18 multicolored 1.75 .40

Postal Life Insurance, 50th Anniv. — A556

1985, Dec. 1
2492 A556 $2 multicolored .45 .25

New Year 1986 (Year of the Tiger) — A557

1985, Dec. 1   **Perf. 12½**
2493 A557 $1 multicolored .60 .25
2494 A557 $10 multicolored 2.00 .35
   a.   Min. sheet, 2 ea #2493-2494 11.00 3.25

Flora Types of 1984

1986, Jan. 10   **Litho.**   **Perf. 13½**
2495 A535 $1 multicolored .25 .25
2496 A535a $11 multicolored .65 .25
2497 A535b $18 multicolored .90 .25

1988, Feb. 12
2498 A535 $1.50 multicolored .25 .25
2499 A535a $7.50 multicolored .65 .25
2500 A535b $16 multicolored 1.25 .30

No. 2500 has value expressed in dollars and cents. For surcharge, see No. 3303.

1989, Feb. 24
2501 A535 $3 multicolored .25 .25
2502 A535a $16.50 multicolored 1.25 .30
2503 A535b $21 multicolored 1.60 .35
   Nos. 2495-2503 (9) 7.05 2.45

Cultural Renaissance Movement — A558

Painting: Hermit Anglers on a Mountain Stream, Ming Dynasty, 1386-1644. Continuous design. (Each stamp is numbered from 1 to 5 in Chinese. See illustrations with Nos. 1682-1691 for numerals.)

1986, Jan. 28   **Litho.**   **Perf. 13½**
2507   Strip of 5 9.00 7.00
   a.-e.   A558 $2 any single 1.50 .25

See No. 2604.

Floral Arrangements
A559

Wmk. 323
1986, Feb. 20   **Litho.**   **Perf. 13½**
2517 A559 $2 denom. UL .35 .25
2518 A559 $5 denom. UR .75 .25
2519 A559 $8 shown .85 .25
2520 A559 $10 denom. UL 1.25 .25
   Nos. 2517-2520 (4) 3.20 1.00

Compare with designs A483, A584.

Natl. Postal Service, 90th Anniv.
A560

$2, Unloading express mail at airport. $5, Motorcycle delivery. $8, Technological innovations. $10, Electronic sorting machine.

1986, Mar. 20
2521 A560 $2 multi .25 .25
2522 A560 $5 multi, vert. .35 .25
2523 A560 $8 multi, vert. .55 .25
2524 A560 $10 multi .65 .25
   a.   Souv. sheet of 4, #2521-2524 5.75 2.55
   Nos. 2521-2524 (4) 1.80 1.00

Chen Tien-hua (1875-1905), Revolutionary
A561

1986, Mar. 29   **Engr.**   **Perf. 13½x12½**
Granite Paper
2525 A561 $2 violet .55 .25

Yushan Natl. Park
A562

1986, Apr. 10   **Litho.**   **Perf. 13½**
2526 A562 $2 multicolored .50 .25
2527 A562 $5 multi, diff. 1.25 .25
2528 A562 $8 multi, diff. 1.60 .25
2529 A562 $10 multi, diff. 2.00 .30
   Nos. 2526-2529 (4) 5.35 1.05

Power Plants
A563

1986, Apr. 29
2530 A563 $2 Hydro-electric .30 .25
2531 A563 $8 Thermo-electric .80 .25
2532 A563 $10 Nuclear 1.10 .25
   Nos. 2530-2532 (3) 2.20 .75

Economic prosperity through energy development.

Paintings by P'u Hsin-yu (1896-1963)
A564

1986, May 22   **Perf. 11½**
2533 A564 $2 Bird 1.75 .25
2534 A564 $8 Landscape 3.50 .30
2535 A564 $10 Woman in forest 5.50 .35
   Nos. 2533-2535 (3) 10.75 .90

Asian Productivity Org., 25th Anniv. — A565

1986, June 3   **Perf. 13x13½**
2536 A565 $2 multicolored .25 .25
2537 A565 $11 multicolored 1.00 .30

Natl. Productivity Center, 30th anniv.

Coral-reef Fish
A566

Designs: a, Chrysiptera starcki. b, Chelmon rostratus. c, Chaetodon xanthurus. d, Chaetodon quadrimaculatus. e, Chaetodon meyeri. f, Genicanthus semifasciatus. g, Genicanthus semifasciatus. h, Pomacanthus annularis. i, Lienardella fasciata. j, Balistapus undulatus.

1986, June 27   **Perf. 13½**
2538   Block of 10 6.50 4.00
   a.-j.   A566 $2 any single .60 .25

Protection of Intellectual Property Rights — A567

1986, June 12
2539 A567 $2 Macaw 1.40 .25

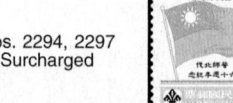

Nos. 2294, 2297 Surcharged

1986, July 9   **Litho.**   **Perf. 13½**
2540 A432 $2 on $6 multi .25 .25
2541 A432 $8 on $9 multi .55 .25

60th Anniv. of northward expedition by the national revolutionary army.

Bridges
A568

$2, Tzu Mu, 1965. $5, Chang Hung, 1968. $8, Kuan Fu, 1977. $10, Kuan Tu, 1983.

1986, July 30
2542 A568 $2 multicolored .45 .25
2543 A568 $5 multicolored 1.10 .25
2544 A568 $8 multicolored 1.40 .25
2545 A568 $10 multicolored 2.00 .25
   Nos. 2542-2545 (4) 4.95 1.00

Love between Liang Shanpo and Chu Yingtai, Folk Tale — A569

Cartoons by Huang Mu-ts'un: a, Yingtai disguised to go to school. b, Yingtai and Shanpo meet in class. c, The friends at pond. d, Yingtai summoned home for arranged marriage. e, Yingtai and Shanpo ascend to heaven as butterflies (each stamp is numbered from 1 to 5 in Chinese. See illustrations with Nos. 1682-1691 for numerals.)

1986, Aug. 12   **Perf. 12½**
2546   Strip of 5 4.00 2.00
   a.-e.   A569 $5 any single .60 .25

Social Awareness Campaign
A570

1986, Sept. 12   **Litho.**   **Perf. 13½**
2547 A570 $2 Rainbow, children .30 .25
2548 A570 $8 Children, adults .70 .25

Folk Costumes — A571

Designs: $2, Shang Dynasty (1766-1122 B.C.) aristocrat. $5, Warring States (403-221 B.C.) aristocrat. $8, Later Han Dynasty (A.D. 25-221) empress. $10, Flying ribbons gown, Wei and Tsin Dynasties (A.D. 221-420) aristocrat.

1986, Sept. 23   **Litho.**   **Perf. 13½**
2549 A571 $2 multicolored .85 .25
2550 A571 $5 multicolored 1.40 .25
2551 A571 $8 multicolored 1.75 .25
2552 A571 $10 multicolored 2.75 .25
   Nos. 2549-2552 (4) 6.75 1.00

Ch'ing Dynasty Ju-i Scepters
A572

$2, White jade. $3, Red coral. $4, Redwood and gems. $18, Gilded wood.

1986, Oct. 10   **Photo.**   **Perf. 14x14½**
2553 A572 $2 multicolored .25 .25
2554 A572 $3 multicolored .45 .25
2555 A572 $4 multicolored .60 .25
2556 A572 $18 multicolored 1.60 .40
   Nos. 2553-2556 (4) 2.90 1.15

See Nos. 2582-2585.

Chiang Kai-shek
A573

Portrait and: $5, Map and flag. $8, Emblem. $10, Flags on globe.

1986, Oct. 31   Litho.   Perf. 13½
2557	A573	$2 multicolored	.25	.25
2558	A573	$5 multicolored	.85	.25
2559	A573	$8 multicolored	1.10	.25
2560	A573	$10 multicolored	1.40	.25
a.		Souv. sheet of 4, #2557-2560	9.00	2.50
		Nos. 2557-2560 (4)	3.60	1.00

Cultural Heritage A574

Architecture: $2, Chin-Kuang Fu land development and defense fund building, 1826. $5, Erh-sha-wan Gun Emplacement, Keelung, 1841, restored 1979. $8, Fort Hsi T'ai, 1886. $10, Matsu Temple, Peng-hu, renovated 1563-1624.

1986, Nov. 14   Litho.   Perf. 13½
2561	A574	$2 multicolored	.40	.25
2562	A574	$5 multicolored	.95	.25
2563	A574	$8 multicolored	1.10	.25
2564	A574	$10 multicolored	1.40	.30
		Nos. 2561-2564 (4)	3.85	1.05

New Year 1987 (Year of the Hare) — A575

1986, Dec. 1   Perf. 12½
2565	A575	$1 dl pink & multi	.50	.25
2566	A575	$10 pale grn & multi	2.25	.30
a.		Souv. sheet, 2 each #2565-2566	14.50	3.50

Kenting, 1st Natl. Park A576

1987, Jan. 8   Litho.   Perf. 13½
2567	A576	$2 Garden	.45	.25
2568	A576	$5 Shore rocks	1.10	.25
2569	A576	$8 Shore and hill	1.40	.25
2570	A576	$10 Shore and rocks, diff.	2.00	.30
		Nos. 2567-2570 (4)	4.95	1.05

Folk Art — A577

Puppets: $2, Hand puppet. $5, Marionette. $18, Shadow puppet.

1987, Feb. 12   Litho.   Perf. 14x13½
2571	A577	$2 multicolored	.35	.25
2572	A577	$5 multicolored	1.00	.25
2573	A577	$18 multicolored	1.75	.40
		Nos. 2571-2573 (3)	3.10	.90

Speedpost A578

1987, Mar. 20   Litho.   Perf. 14x13½
| 2574 | A578 | $2 multicolored | .35 | .25 |
| 2575 | A578 | $18 multicolored | 1.25 | .40 |

Stamp Day.

Wu Yueh (1878-1905), Revolutionary A579

1987, Mar. 29   Engr.   Perf. 13½x12½
| 2576 | A579 | $2 orange | 1.10 | .25 |

Landscapes Painted by Madame Chiang Kai-shek — A580

$2, Singing Creek with Bamboo Orchestra. $5, Mountains Draped in Clouds. $8, Vista of Tranquility. $10, Mountains after a Snowfall.

1987, Apr. 10   Litho.   Perf. 13½
2577	A580	$2 blk, buff & ver	.45	.25
2578	A580	$5 blk, buff & ver	1.25	.25
2579	A580	$8 blk, buff & ver	2.75	.30
2580	A580	$10 blk, buff & ver	3.75	.45
		Nos. 2577-2580 (4)	8.20	1.25

Stone Sculptures — A581

Designs: a, Head of a Bodhisattva, sandstone, Northern Wei Dynasty (386-534). b, Standing Buddha, limestone, Northern Ch'i Dynasty (550-577). c, Head of a Bodhisattva, sandstone, T'ang Dynasty (618-907). d, Seated Buddha, alabaster, T'ang Dynasty.

1987, Apr. 23
| 2581 | | Strip of 4 | 3.50 | 2.25 |
| *a.-d.* | | A581 $5 any single | .70 | .30 |

No. 2581a shows seven Chinese characters at left; No. 2581c shows five.

Ju-i Scepters, Ch'ing Dynasty A582

$2, Silver and gems. $3, Gold and gems. $4, Gilded, jade and inlaid gems. $18, Gilded, inlaid malachite.

1987, May 7   Photo.   Perf. 14x14½
2582	A582	$2 multicolored	.55	.25
2583	A582	$3 multicolored	1.40	.25
2584	A582	$4 multicolored	2.10	.25
2585	A582	$18 multicolored	3.00	.45
		Nos. 2582-2585 (4)	7.05	1.20

Feitsui Reservoir Inauguration A583

$2, Reservoir. $18, Hsintien Stream, reservoir.

1987, June 6   Litho.   Perf. 13½x14
| 2586 | A583 | $2 multicolored | .45 | .25 |
| 2587 | A583 | $18 multicolored | 1.75 | .45 |

Flower Arrangements by Huang Yung-ch'uan A584

$8, Flowers in brown vase.

1987, June 19   Perf. 13½
2588	A584	$2 denom. LL	.25	.25
2589	A584	$5 denom. LL	.70	.25
2590	A584	$8 denom. UR	.90	.25
2591	A584	$10 denom. UR	1.00	.25
		Nos. 2588-2591 (4)	2.85	1.00

Compare with designs A483, A559.

Lions Club Intl. 70th Annual Convention, Taipei — A585

1987, July 1
| 2592 | A585 | $2 multicolored | .30 | .25 |
| 2593 | A585 | $18 multicolored | 1.40 | .50 |

Sino-Japanese War, 50th Anniv. — A586

$1, Battle front. $2, Chiang Kai-shek giving speech. $5, Public donating funds. $6, Troops marching. $8, Signing of peace treaty. $18, Parade.

1987, July 7   Perf. 14x13½
2594	A586	$1 multicolored	.25	.25
2595	A586	$2 multicolored	.40	.25
2596	A586	$5 multicolored	.45	.25
2597	A586	$6 multicolored	.60	.25
2598	A586	$8 multicolored	.85	.25
2599	A586	$18 multicolored	1.00	.40
		Nos. 2594-2599 (6)	3.55	1.65

Wang Yun-wu (1888-1979), Lexicographer A587

1987, Aug. 14   Perf. 13½
| 2600 | A587 | $2 gray black | .55 | .25 |

Memorial Hall Type of 1981
Perf. 12½x13½
1987, Sept. 24   Photo.
2601	A468	10c lake	.25	.25
2602	A468	30c brt green	.25	.25
2603	A468	60c brt blue	.25	.25
		Nos. 2601-2603 (3)	.75	.75

A588

Cultural Renaissance Movement — A589

Scroll, 1543, by Weng Chen-ming (1470-1559), a copy of Chao Po-su's *Red Cliff*. Nos. 2604a-2604e and 2604f-2604j are printed in continuous designs. (Each stamp is numbered from 1 to 10 in Chinese. See illustrations with Nos. 1682-1691 for numerals.)

1987, Sept. 22   Engr.   Perf. 13½
2604		Block of 10	13.50	13.50
a.-e.		A588 $3 any single	1.00	.25
f.-j.		A589 $3 any single	1.00	.25

Folk Costumes — A590

$1.50, Han woman, early Ch'ing Dynasty (1644-1911). $3, Wife of a Ch'ing Dynasty Manchu Bannerman. $7.50, Urban woman wearing Manchu ch'i-p'ao dress, c. 1912. $18, Short jacket over long skirt, c. 1920.

1987, Oct. 2   Litho.
2605	A590	$1.50 multicolored	1.25	.25
2606	A590	$3 multicolored	1.50	.25
2607	A590	$7.50 multicolored	1.75	.25
2608	A590	$18 multicolored	2.10	.50
		Nos. 2605-2608 (4)	6.60	1.25

Nos. 2605-2608 have 3 groups of 2 smaller Chinese characters above denomination. Nos. 2660-2663 have 2 groups of 2 and 4 characters.

A591

$3, Ta Chen Tian temple, Taichung. $18, Confucius.

1987, Nov. 12   Perf. 13½x14
| 2609 | A591 | $3 multicolored | .45 | .25 |
| 2610 | A591 | $18 multicolored | 1.75 | 1.10 |

Intl. Symposium on Confucianism, Taipei, Nov. 12-17.

A592

1987, Dec. 1   Perf. 12½
2611	A592	$1.50 multicolored	.60	.25
2612	A592	$12 multicolored	2.50	.45
a.		Souv. sheet, 2 ea #2611-2612	11.00	2.50

New Year 1988 (Year of the Dragon).

Constitution, 40th Anniv. — A593

1987, Dec. 25   Litho.   Perf. 13½
2613	A593	$3 multicolored	.25	.25
2614	A593	$16 multi, diff.	1.10	.55

Prevent Hypertension Campaign A594

1988, Jan. 8   Perf. 12½x13½
2615	A594	$3 multicolored	.45	.25

Fruit Tree Blossoms — A595

No. 2616, Prunus mume. No. 2617, Prunus armeniaca. No. 2618, Prunus persica.
No. 2619, Paeonia suffruticosa. No. 2620, Punica granatum. No. 2621, Nelumbo nucifera.
No. 2622, Impatiens balsamina. No. 2623, Osmanthus fragrans. No. 2624, Chrysanthemum morifolium.
No. 2625, Hibiscus mutabilis. No. 2626, Camellia japonica. No. 2627, Narcissus tazetta.

Wmk. 323
1988, Feb. 4   Litho.   Perf. 13½
2616	A595	$3 multi	1.50	.25
2617	A595	$7.50 multi	1.75	.30
2618	A595	$12 multi	2.25	.50
a.		Min. sheet of 3, #2616-2618	22.50	22.50

Wmk. 323
1988, May 5   Litho.   Perf. 13½
2619	A595	$3 multi	.45	.25
2620	A595	$7.50 multi	1.40	.30
2621	A595	$12 multi	1.60	.50
a.		Min. sheet of 3, #2619-2621	13.50	13.50

Wmk. 323
1988, Aug. 9   Litho.   Perf. 13½
2622	A595	$3 multi	.40	.25
2623	A595	$7.50 multi	1.25	.30
2624	A595	$12 multi	1.50	.50
a.		Min. sheet of 3, #2622-2624	12.00	12.00

Wmk. 323
1988, Nov. 7   Litho.   Perf. 13½
2625	A595	$3 multi	.40	.25
2626	A595	$7.50 multi	1.75	.30
2627	A595	$12 multi	2.10	.50
a.		Min. sheet of 3, #2625-2627	12.50	12.50
		Nos. 2616-2627 (12)	16.35	4.20

Tourism Day — A596

Folk art: $3, Modeled dough figurines. $7.50, Blown sweet-malt sugar candy. $16, Sugar paintings.

Perf. 13½x14
1988, Mar. 2   Litho.   Wmk. 323
2628	A596	$3 multicolored	.75	.30
2629	A596	$7.50 multicolored	1.50	.45
2630	A596	$16 multicolored	2.75	1.05
		Nos. 2628-2630 (3)	5.00	1.80

A597

Perf. 13½x12½
1988, Mar. 29   Engr.   Wmk. 323
2631	A597	$3 brown	.40	.25

Hsu Hsi-lin (1873-1907), hero of the revolution.

A598

$1.50, Biotechnology. $3, Energy resources. $7, Immunization. $7.50, Automation. $10, Telecommunications. $12, Laser technology. $16, Micro-optics. $16.50, Agricultural research.

1988   Litho.   Perf. 13½
2632	A598	$1.50 multicolored	.25	.25
2633	A598	$3 multicolored	.30	.25
2634	A598	$7 multicolored	.45	.25
2635	A598	$7.50 multicolored	.45	.25
2636	A598	$10 multicolored	.60	.40
2637	A598	$12 multicolored	.65	.40
2638	A598	$16 multicolored	.95	.65
2639	A598	$16.50 multicolored	1.25	.65
		Nos. 2632-2639 (8)	4.90	3.10

Industrialization by technological development. Issued: $3, $7.50, $10, $16, Apr. 22; others, May 9.

Police Day A599

Wmk. 323
1988, June 15   Litho.   Perf. 13½
2640	A599	$3 Traffic control	.25	.25
2641	A599	$12 Rescue operations	.80	.40

Amphibians A600

$1.50, Microhyla butleri. $3, Rana taipehensis. $7.50, Microhyla inornata. $16, Rhacophorus smaragdinus.

1988, July 8   Perf. 13½x14
2642	A600	$1.50 multicolored	1.10	.25
2643	A600	$3 multicolored	1.75	.25
2644	A600	$7.50 multicolored	2.25	.35
2645	A600	$16 multicolored	3.00	.75
		Nos. 2642-2645 (4)	8.10	1.60

China Broadcasting Corp. (BBC), 60th Anniv. — A601

Wmk. 323
1988, Aug. 1   Litho.   Perf. 13½
2646	A601	$3 multicolored	.45	.25

Victory at the Battle of Kinmen, 30th Anniv. A602

Designs: $1.50, Chiang Kai-shek and artillery commander. $3, With troops. $7.50, Cannon. $12, Tanks.

1988, Aug. 23
2647	A602	$1.50 multicolored	.40	.25
2648	A602	$3 multicolored	.50	.25
2649	A602	$7.50 multicolored	.55	.25
2650	A602	$12 multicolored	.80	.40
		Nos. 2647-2650 (4)	2.25	1.15

Sports Promotion — A603

Nos. 2651-2652, Basketball. Nos. 2653-2654, Baseball.

1988, Sept. 9
2651		$5 Players	.90	.25
2652		$5 Players	.90	.25
a.		A603 Pair, #2651-2652	1.90	1.10
2653		$5 Batter	.90	.25
2654		$5 Catcher	.90	.25
a.		A603 Pair, #2653-2654	1.90	1.10
		Nos. 2651-2654 (4)	3.60	1.00

Nos. 2652a, 2654a have continuous designs.

Yangmingshan Natl. Park — A604

$1.50, Volcanic crater. $3, Lake. $7.50, Tatun Volcanic Range. $16, Dormant volcano.

1988, Sept. 16
2655	A604	$1.50 multicolored	.25	.25
2656	A604	$3 multicolored	.45	.25
2657	A604	$7.50 multicolored	.85	.25
2658	A604	$16 multicolored	1.60	.55
		Nos. 2655-2658 (4)	3.15	1.30

Lofty Mount Lu, a Hanging Scroll, 1467, By Shen Chou (1427-1509) — A605

Painting details: a, UL. b, UR. c, LL. d, LR.

Wmk. 323
1988, Oct. 19   Litho.   Perf. 11½
2659	A605	Block of 4	7.00	5.00
a.-d.		$5 any single	1.50	.35

Folk Costumes — A606

Designs: $2, Shang Dynasty (1766-1122 B.C.) nobleman. $3, Warring States (403-221) B.C.) ruler. $7.50, Wei-Chin Period (221-420) official. $12, Northern Dynasties (502-581) official.

Perf. 13½x14
1988, Nov. 23   Litho.   Wmk. 323
2660	A606	$2 multicolored	.50	.25
2661	A606	$3 multicolored	.85	.25
2662	A606	$7.50 multicolored	1.75	.35
2663	A606	$12 multicolored	2.40	.55
		Nos. 2660-2663 (4)	5.50	1.40

Nos. 2721-2724 have groups of 2 and 6 Chinese characters above denomination; Nos. 2660-2663 groups of 2 and 4; Nos. 2794-2797 groups of 1 and 5.

A607

1988, Dec. 1   Perf. 12½
2664	A607	$2 multicolored	.55	.25
2665	A607	$13 multicolored	4.25	.60
a.		Souv. sheet, 2 each #2664-2665	14.50	14.50

New Year 1989 (Year of the Snake).

A608

Wmk. 323
1989, Jan. 4   Litho.   Perf. 13½
2666	A608	$3 black	.55	.25

Tai Ch'uan-hsien (1890-1949), party leader.

Pres. Chiang Ching-kuo (1910-88) A609

1989, Jan. 13
2667	A609	$3 shown	.25	.25
2668	A609	$6 Suffrage	.40	.25
2669	A609	$7.50 Industry	.60	.30
2670	A609	$16 Children	.95	.65
		Nos. 2667-2670 (4)	2.20	1.45

Ni Ying-tien (1884-1910), Revolution Leader — A610

Perf. 13½x12½
1989, Mar. 28   Engr.   Wmk. 323
2671 A610 $3 black   .45 .25

Stop Smoking — A611

Perf. 13½x12½
1989, Apr. 7   Litho.   Wmk. 323
2672 A611 $3 multicolored   .45 .25

Lighthouses — A612

75c, Mu Tou Yu. $2, Lu Tao. $2.25, Pen Chia Yu. $3, Pitou Chiao. $4.50, Tungyin Tao. $6, Chilai Pi. $7, Fukwei Chiao. $7.50, Hua Yu. $9, Oluan Pi. $10, Kaohsiung. $10.50, Yuweng Tao. $12, Tungchu Tao. $13, Yeh Liu. $15, Tungchi Yu. $16.50, Chimei Yu.

1989-91   Perf. 13½
2673 A612 75c multi   .40 .25
2674 A612 $2 multi   .40 .25
2675 A612 $2.25 multi   .40 .25
2676 A612 $3 multi   .60 .25
2677 A612 $4.50 multi   .75 .25
2678 A612 $6 multi   .80 .25
2679 A612 $7 multi   .90 .35
2680 A612 $7.50 multi   .95 .35
2681 A612 $9 multi   1.00 .25
2682 A612 $10 multi   1.05 .45
2683 A612 $10.50 multi   1.10 .35
2683A A612 $12 multi   1.60 .55
2683B A612 $13 multi   2.00 .45
2683C A612 $15 multi   2.10 .80
2684 A612 $16.50 multi   2.40 .75
     Nos. 2673-2684 (15)   16.45 5.80

Issued: $7, $15, 5/19/90; $6, $12, 1/9/91; $2, $3, $10, $16.50, 5/20/91; others, 1989.
See Nos. 2811-2823.

1st Natl. Wealth Survey A613

1989, May 18   Litho.   Perf. 13½
2685 A613 $3 multicolored   .30 .25

Ch'u Ts'u Collection of Poems, 722-481 B.C. — A614

Designs: $3, Man overlooking fields. $7.50, Man, woman on path. $12, Man holding staff. $16, Man, stallion, stone gate. Excerpts: $3, "I once tended nine fields of orchids; Also I had planted a hundred rods of melilotus" (Li Sao). $7.50, "No grief is greater than parting of the living; No joy is more than making new friends" (Chiu Ko, shao ssu ming). $12, "Since my heart is straight and good, Why should I be

chagrined at living remote and neglected?" (Chiu Chang, she chiang). $16, "The steed will not gallop itself into servitude; The phoenix has no appetite for slave food." (Chiu Pien).

1989, June 7   Photo.   Perf. 11½x12
Granite Paper
2686 A614 $3 multicolored   .45 .25
2687 A614 $7.50 multicolored   1.10 .45
2688 A614 $12 multicolored   2.10 .70
2689 A614 $16 multicolored   2.50 1.00
     Nos. 2686-2689 (4)   6.15 2.40

Compare with types A629, A663. Nos. 2686-2689 have two Chinese characters near denomination. Nos. 2725-2728 have groups of 3 and 4 characters.

Taipei Subway Inauguration — A615

$3, Subway tunnel. $16, Entering underground.

1989, June 27   Litho.   Perf. 13½
2690 A615 $3 multicolored   .40 .25
2691 A615 $16 multicolored   1.75 .90

A616

A616a

A616b

A616c

Butterflies A616c

$2, Graphium sarpedon connectens. $3, Papilo memnon heronus. $7.50, Princeps demoleus libanius. $9, Pachliopa aristolochiae interpositas.

Wmk. 323
1989, July 14   Perf. 13½
2692 A616 $2 multicolored   .45 .25
2693 A616a $3 multicolored   .85 .30
2694 A616b $7.50 multicolored   2.00 .40
2695 A616c $9 multicolored   2.50 .50
     Nos. 2692-2695 (4)   5.80 1.45

Compare with design A627.

Ch'ing Dynasty Teapots from I-Hsing of Kiangsu, 1644-1911 A617

1989, July 28   Perf. 13½x14
2696 A617 $2 multicolored   .30 .25
2697 A617 $3 multi, diff.   .90 .25
2698 A617 $12 multi, diff.   2.25 .50
2699 A617 $16 multi, diff.   2.25 .70
     Nos. 2696-2699 (4)   5.70 1.70

For stamps with teapot designs and solid black denominations see Nos. 2760-2764.

Intl. Seminar on Fan Chung-yen (989-1052), Military Leader and Civil Service Reformer — A618

Perf. 14x13½
1989, Sept. 1   Litho.   Wmk. 323
2700 A618 $12 multicolored   1.25 .55

Autumn Colors on the Ch'iao and Hua Mountains, 14th Cent., by Ch'iao Meng-fu A619

a, Right side of mountain, trees. b, Trees, left side of mountain. c, House, trees. d, shown.

Wmk. 323
1989, Oct. 5   Litho.   Perf. 13½
2701 Strip of 4   10.00 4.75
  a.-d. A619 $7.50 any single   2.25 .55

Social Welfare A619a

1989, Nov. 3   Litho.   Perf. 13½
2701E A619a $3 multicolored   .45 .25

Taroko Natl. Park — A620

Designs: $2, Marble gorge, Liwu River. $3, Hohuan Mountain. $12, Waterfall, Cirque of Nanhu. $16, Chingshui Cliff.

Wmk. 323
1989, Nov. 28   Litho.   Perf. 13½
2702 A620 $2 multicolored   .25 .25
2703 A620 $3 multicolored   .45 .35
2704 A620 $12 multicolored   1.00 .55
2705 A620 $16 multicolored   1.25 .70
     Nos. 2702-2705 (4)   2.95 1.85

New Year 1990 (Year of the Horse) — A621

1989, Dec. 1   Perf. 12½
2706 A621 $2 multicolored   .45 .25
2707 A621 $13 multicolored   1.75 .80
  a. Souv. sheet, 2 ea #2706-2707 8.00 3.00

Yu Lu — A622

Men Shen, "guardian spirits" (likenesses of legendary beings placed on residence doors at the new year): No. 2708, Yu Lu. No. 2709, Shen Shu. No. 2710, Wei-ch'ih Ching-te. No. 2711, Ch'in Shu-pao.

Wmk. 323
1990, Jan. 19   Litho.   Perf. 13½
2708 A622 $3 shown   1.25 .25
2709 A622 $3 "$3" at LR   1.25 .25
  a. Pair, #2708-2709   2.50 2.00
2710 A622 $7.50 "$7.50" at LL   3.00 .50
2711 A622 $7.50 "$7.50" at LR   3.00 .50
  a. Pair, #2710-2711   6.00 5.00
     Nos. 2708-2711 (4)   8.50 1.50

Nos. 2709a, 2711a have continuous designs.

A623

Scenery — A624

Designs: $2, Lishan House, Pear Mountain. $18, Tayu Pass, Tayuling, vert.

Wmk. 323
1990, Feb. 10   Litho.   Perf. 13½
2712 A623 $2 multicolored   .50 .25
2713 A624 $18 multicolored   2.00 1.00

Labor Insurance System, 40th Anniv. — A625

1990, Mar. 1
2714 A625 $3 multicolored   .60 .25

Liquefied Natural Gas A626

$3, Terminal, Yung-an Hsiang of Kaohsiung. $16, Container ship, map, refinery.

1990, Mar. 31   Litho.   Perf. 13½
2715 A626 $3 multi   .50 .25
2716 A626 $16 multi, vert.   1.50 .65

A627

A627a

A627b

Butterflies
A627c

$2, Salatura genutia. $3, Hypolimnas misippus. $7.50, Pieris canidia. $9, Precis almana.

1990, Apr. 20

2717	A627	$2 multicolored	.45	.25
2718	A627a	$3 multicolored	.45	.25
2719	A627b	$7.50 multicolored	1.25	.35
2720	A627c	$9 multicolored	1.75	.45
		Nos. 2717-2720 (4)	3.90	1.30

Compare with design A616.

Folk
Costumes — A628

$2, Official, Sui & T'ang Dynasties (589-907). $3, Official, T'ang & Sung Dynasties (618-1280). $7.50, Royal guardsman, Chin & Yuan Dynasties (1115-1368). $12, Highest ranking civil official, Ming Dynasty (1368-1644).

1990, May 10   Litho.   Perf. 13½

2721	A628	$2 multicolored	.35	.25
2722	A628	$3 multicolored	.75	.25
2723	A628	$7.50 multicolored	1.50	.30
2724	A628	$12 multicolored	1.60	.55
		Nos. 2721-2724 (4)	4.20	1.35

See note after No. 2663.

Yueh Fu
Classical
Poetry
A629

Lyrics from Tzu-yeh folk songs, Six Dynasties (222-589): $3, Spring Song at Midnight. $7.50, Summer Song at Midnight. $12, Autumn Song at Midnight. $16, Winter Song at Midnight.

Wmk. 323

1990, June 27   Litho.   Perf. 11½
Granite Paper

2725	A629	$3 shown	.50	.25
2726	A629	$7.50 Couple, river	1.25	.35
2727	A629	$12 Washing clothes, river	3.00	.55
2728	A629	$16 River in winter	4.25	.80
		Nos. 2725-2728 (4)	9.00	1.95

Compare with designs A614 and A663.

Bonsai
A630

Designs: $3, Pinus thunbergii parl. $6.50, Ehretia microphylla lamk. $12, Buxus harlandii hance. $16, Celtis sinensis pers.

1990, July 20   Litho.   Perf. 13½

2729	A630	$3 multicolored	.30	.25
2730	A630	$6.50 multicolored	.70	.30
2731	A630	$12 multicolored	1.00	.70
2732	A630	$16 multicolored	1.50	.80
		Nos. 2729-2732 (4)	3.50	2.05

Snuff
Bottles — A631

$3, Bamboo stem shaped. $6, Peony motif. $9, Amber. $16, White jade.

1990, Aug. 9

2733	A631	$3 multicolored	.40	.25
2734	A631	$6 multicolored	.75	.30
2735	A631	$9 multicolored	1.05	.45
2736	A631	$16 multicolored	2.10	.80
		Nos. 2733-2736 (4)	4.30	1.80

Formosan
Firecrest
A632

$3, Laughing thrush. $7.50, White-eared sibia. $16, Yellow tit.

1990, Aug. 20   Litho.   Perf. 13½

2737	A632	$2 shown	.40	.25
2738	A632	$3 multicolored	.40	.25
2739	A632	$7.50 multicolored	1.00	.25
2740	A632	$16 multicolored	2.25	.60
		Nos. 2737-2740 (4)	4.05	1.35

Sports — A633

1990, Sept. 8   Litho.   Perf. 13½

2741	A633	$2 Sprint	.30	.25
2742	A633	$3 Long jump	.30	.25
2743	A633	$7 Pole vault	1.10	.30
2744	A633	$16 High hurdle	1.50	.60
		Nos. 2741-2744 (4)	3.20	1.40

Flying
Tigers, 50th
Anniv.
A634

1990, Sept. 26   Litho.   Perf. 13½

2745	A634	$3 multicolored	1.25	.25

Children's
Drawings
A635

1990, Oct. 9

2746	A635	$2 Cat	.30	.25
2747	A635	$3 Peacocks	.30	.25
2748	A635	$7.50 Chickens	.90	.30
2749	A635	$12 Cattle	1.40	.50
		Nos. 2746-2749 (4)	2.90	1.30

National
Theater
A636

Photo. & Engr.

1990, Oct. 30   Perf. 13½

2750	A636	$3 shown	.40	.25
2751	A636	$12 Natl. concert hall	1.60	.80

A637

Ancient money.

1990, Nov. 5   Litho.   Perf. 13x13½

2752	A637	$2 Shell	.40	.25
2753	A637	$3 Oyster	.40	.25
2754	A637	$6.50 Bone	.60	.35
2755	A637	$7.50 Jade	.80	.40
2756	A637	$9 Bronze	.90	.50
		Nos. 2752-2756 (5)	3.10	1.75

A638

1990, Dec. 1   Perf. 12½

2757	A638	$2 multicolored	.70	.25
2758	A638	$13 multicolored	2.75	.80
a.		Souv. sheet, 2 ea #2757-2758	9.50	2.50

New Year 1991 (Year of the Sheep).

Hu Shih (1891-
1962),
Educator — A639

Wmk. 323

1990, Dec. 17   Engr.   Perf. 13½

2759	A639	$3 purple	.50	.25

Teapots,
Natl. Palace
Museum
A640

Teapots: $2, Blue phoenix, Ming Dynasty. $3, Dragon handle and spout, Ming Dynasty. $9, Blue landscape, flowered top, Ch'ing Dynasty. $12, Rectangular, passion flower motif, Ch'ing Dynasty. $16, Rectangular, flower motif, Ch'ing Dynasty.

1991, Jan. 18   Photo.   Perf. 12
Granite Paper

2760	A640	$2 yel, blk & blue	.40	.25
2761	A640	$3 brt yel grn & blk	.60	.40
2762	A640	$9 pink & multi	1.00	.60
2763	A640	$12 violet & multi	1.40	.80
2764	A640	$16 lt blue & multi	1.60	1.20
		Nos. 2760-2764 (5)	5.00	3.25

God of Happiness
A641

God of
Joy — A642

No. 2766, God of Wealth. No. 2768, God of Longevity.

1991, Feb. 7   Litho.   Perf. 13½

2765	A641	$3 shown	.60	.25
2766	A641	$3 multi	.60	.25
2767	A642	$7.50 shown	1.40	.30
2768	A642	$7.50 multi	1.40	.30
		Nos. 2765-2768 (4)	4.00	1.10

Perf. 13½ Vert.

2765a	A641	$3	1.50	.25
2766a	A641	$3	1.50	.25
2767a	A642	$7.50	1.50	.25
2768a	A642	$7.50	1.50	.25
b.		Bklt. pane of 8, 2 each #2765a-2768a + label	14.00	

Native
Plants
A643

Designs: $2, Petasites formosanus. $3, Heloniopsis acutifolia. $7.50, Disporum shimadai. $9, Viola nagasawai.

1991, Mar. 12   Litho.   Perf. 13½

2769	A643	$2 multicolored	.40	.25
2770	A643	$3 multicolored	.50	.25
2771	A643	$7.50 multicolored	.80	.30
2772	A643	$9 multicolored	.90	.35

1991, June 12

Designs: $2, Gaultheria itoana. $3, Lysionotus montanus. $7.50, Leontopodium microphyllum. $9, Gentiana flavo-maculata.

2773	A643	$2 multicolored	.30	.25
2774	A643	$3 multicolored	.50	.25
2775	A643	$7.50 multicolored	1.25	.30
2776	A643	$9 multicolored	1.50	.35

1991, Sept. 12

Designs: $3.50, Rosa transmorrisonensis. $5, Impatiens devolii. $9, Impatiens uniflora. $12, Impatiens tayemonii.

2777	A643	$3.50 multicolored	.50	.25
2778	A643	$5 multicolored	.70	.25
2779	A643	$9 multicolored	1.25	.35
2780	A643	$12 multicolored	1.50	.45

1991, Dec. 12

Designs: $3.50, Kalanchoe garambiensis. $5, Pieris taiwanensis. $9, Pleione formosana. $12, Elaeagnus oldhamii.

2781	A643	$3.50 multicolored	.50	.25
2782	A643	$5 multicolored	.70	.25
2783	A643	$9 multicolored	.90	.60
2784	A643	$12 multicolored	1.25	.70
		Nos. 2769-2784 (16)	13.45	5.40

Hsiung Cheng-Chi (1887-1910), Revolutionary A644

1991, Mar. 28   Engr.   Perf. 13½x12½

2785	A644	$3 blue	.50	.25

Republic of China, 80th Anniv. A645

$3, Agriculture. $7.50, Science & technology. $12, Cultural activities. $16, Transportation.

1991, Mar. 28   Litho.   Perf. 13½

2786	A645	$3 multicolored	.40	.25
2787	A645	$7.50 multicolored	.80	.40
2788	A645	$12 multicolored	1.40	.70
2789	A645	$16 multicolored	1.60	.90
		Nos. 2786-2789 (4)	4.20	2.25

Children's Toys — A646

No. 2790, Bamboo pony. No. 2791, Woven-grass grasshopper. No. 2792, Top. No. 2793, Pinwheels.

1991, Apr. 20   Litho.   Perf. 13½

2790	A646	$3 multicolored	.50	.30
2791	A646	$3 multicolored	.50	.30
2792	A646	$3 multicolored	.50	.30
2793	A646	$3 multicolored	.50	.30
a.		Souv. sheet of 4, #2790-2793	8.00	5.00
		Nos. 2790-2793 (4)	2.00	1.20

See Nos. 2840-2843. Compare with designs A676, A696.

Perf. 13½ Vert.

2790a	A646	$3	1.25	.30
2791a	A646	$3	1.25	.30
2792a	A646	$3	1.25	.30
2793b	A646	$3	1.25	.30
c.		Bklt. pane, 2 each #2790a-2793b + label	10.00	
		Nos. 2790a-2793b (4)	5.00	1.20

Folk Costumes — A647

Ch'ing Dynasty (1644-1911): $2, Winter court hat, Mang robe. $3, Summer court hat, surcoat. $7.50, Winter overcoat. $12, Common hat, traveling robe.

1991, June 29   Litho.   Perf. 13½

2794	A647	$2 multicolored	.50	.25
2795	A647	$3 multicolored	.65	.25
2796	A647	$7.50 multicolored	1.60	.30
2797	A647	$12 multicolored	2.25	.45
		Nos. 2794-2797 (4)	5.00	1.25

See note after No. 2663.
Nos. 2794-2797 have groups of one and five Chinese characters.

Traffic Safety Year A648

$7.50, Don't drink & drive.

1991, July 17   Litho.   Perf. 13½

2798	A648	$3 shown	.30	.25
2799	A648	$7.50 multicolored	.90	.35

Cloisonne Enamel Lions, Ch'ing Dynasty (1644-1911) A649   A649a

1991, July 20   Litho.   Perf. 12½

2800	A649	yel grn & multi	.70	.25
2801	A649a	violet & multi	2.75	.75
		Nos. 2800-2801 (2)	3.45	1.00

No. 2800 paid basic domestic rate, No. 2801 paid basic express mail rate on date of issue.

Fruits — A650

1991, Aug. 10   Litho.   Perf. 14x13½

2802	A650	$3 Strawberry	.40	.25
2803	A650	$7.50 Grapes	.70	.50
2804	A650	$9 Mango	.90	.60
2805	A650	$16 Sugar apple	1.50	.90
		Nos. 2802-2805 (4)	3.50	2.25

Birds — A651

Designs: a, Myiophoneus insularis. b, Cinclus pallasii. c, Aix galericulata. d, Nycticorax nycticorax. e, Egretta garzetta. f, Rhyacornis fuliginosus. g, Enicurus scouleri. h, Motacilla cinerea. i, Alcedo atthis. j, Motacilla alba.

1991, Aug. 24   Perf. 13½

2806		Block of 10	7.00	4.00
a.-j.		A651 $5 any single	.50	.30

Outdoor Activities A652

1991, Sept. 27   Wmk. 323   Perf. 13½

2807	A652	$2 Rock climbing	.30	.25
2808	A652	$3 Fishing	.40	.25
2809	A652	$7.50 Bird watching	.85	.35
2810	A652	$10 Playing in water	1.25	.50
		Nos. 2807-2810 (4)	2.80	1.35

Intl. Federation of Camping and Caravaning, 1991 Rally.

**Lighthouse Type of 1989
Inscription Panel in Blue**

1991-92   Perf. 13½

2811	A612	50c like #2683C	.30	.25
2812	A612	$1 like #2674	.40	.25
2813	A612	$3.50 like #2678	.50	.25
2814	A612	$5 like #2679	.60	.25
a.		Booklet pane of 10	7.00	
2815	A612	$7 like #2676	.60	.25
2816	A612	$9 like #2681	.90	.35
2817	A612	$10 like #2682	1.10	.40
2818	A612	$12 like #2683A	1.25	.50
a.		$12 Bklt. pane of 5 + label	7.00	
2819	A612	$13 like #2675	1.25	.50
2820	A612	$19 like #2680	1.90	.80
2821	A612	$20 like #2683B	2.00	.80
2822	A612	$26 like #2683	2.10	1.10
2823	A612	$28 like #2684	2.10	1.10
		Nos. 2811-2823 (13)	15.00	6.80

Issued: 50c, $3.50, $5, $12, 10/2; No. 2818a, 9/26/92; $1, $19, $20, 3/2/92; $26, $28, 5/20/92; $7, $9, $10, $13, 8/21/92.

Peacocks by Lan Shih-ning (Giuseppe Castiglione, 1688-1768) A653

$20, Peacock spreading tail feathers.

Perf. 12x11½

**1991, Oct. 30   Photo.   Unwmk.
Granite Paper**

2826	A653	$5 multicolored	.80	.50
2827	A653	$20 multicolored	3.00	1.00
a.		Souvenir sheet of 1	6.00	5.00

New Year 1992 (Year of the Monkey) — A654

Wmk. 323

1991, Nov. 30   Litho.   Perf. 12½

2828	A654	$3.50 orange & multi	.40	.25
2829	A654	$13 tan & multi	1.50	.60
a.		Souv. sheet, 2 ea #2828-2829	6.00	2.00

Chinese Books A655

$3.50, Scroll. $5, Fold bindings. $9, Butterfly bindings. $15, String bindings.

Wmk. 323

1992, Jan. 17   Litho.   Perf. 13½

2830	A655	$3.50 multicolored	.30	.25
2831	A655	$5 multicolored	.50	.25
2832	A655	$9 multicolored	.90	.35
2833	A655	$15 multicolored	1.50	.65
		Nos. 2830-2833 (4)	3.20	1.50

Good Fortune and Satisfaction A656

Five Blessings Upon the House — A657

Nienhwa paintings: No. 2835, Peace in the Wake of Firecrackers. No. 2837, An Abundance for Every Year.

1992, Jan. 27   Litho.   Perf. 13½

2834	A656	$5 multicolored	.40	.25
2835	A656	$5 multicolored	.40	.25
2836	A657	$12 multicolored	1.10	.60
2837	A657	$12 multicolored	1.10	.60
a.		Bklt. pane, 2 each #2834-2837 + label	10.00	
		Nos. 2834-2837 (4)	3.00	1.70

Lunar New Year.

A658

Lunar New Year: a, like #2664. b, like #2611. c, like #2565. d, like #2493. e, like #2442. f, like #2390. g, like #2346. h, like #2273. i, like #2217. j, like #2828. k, like #2757. l, like #2706.

Wmk. 323

1992, Feb. 18   Litho.   Perf. 12½

2838	A658	$5 Block of 12, #a.-l., ver & multi	6.50	3.00
m.		Sheet of 12, #2838a-2838 l	6.75	3.25

A659

Trees: a, Chamaecyparis formosensis. b, Chamaecyparis taiwanensis. c, Calocedrus formosana. d, Cunninghamia konishii. e, Taiwania crypto- merioides.

1992, Mar. 12   Perf. 13½

2839	A659	$5 Strip of 5, #a.-e.	3.50	1.50

Children's Toys Type of 1991

1992, Apr. 29   Litho.   Perf. 13½

2840	A646	$5 Walking on iron pots	.70	.25
a.		Perf. 13½ vert.	.70	.25
2841	A646	$5 Chopstick gun	.70	.25
a.		Perf. 13½ vert.	.70	.25
2842	A646	$5 Hoop rolling	.70	.25
a.		Perf. 13½ vert.	.70	.25
2843	A646	$5 Grass fighting	.70	.25
a.		Sheet of 4, #2840-2843	5.75	5.75
b.		As "a," imperf. (simulated perfs), red inscription in sheet margin	11.50	11.50
c.		Perf. 13½ vert.	.70	.25
d.		Bklt. pane, 2 each #2840a-2842a, 2843c + label	5.75	
		Nos. 2840-2843 (4)	2.80	1.00

Issue date: No. 2843b, May 15.

A660

Mother and son in: $3.50, Spring. $5, Summer. $9, Autumn. $10, Winter.

Wmk. 323

1992, May 9	Litho.		**Perf. 13½**	
2844	A660	$3.50 multicolored	.35	.25
2845	A660	$5 multicolored	.70	.25
2846	A660	$9 multicolored	1.25	.40
2847	A660	$10 multicolored	1.40	.45
	Nos. 2844-2847 (4)		3.70	1.35

Parent-child relationships.

A661

Glassware Decorated with Enamel — Vases: $3.50, Faceted, decorated with bats and longevity characters. $5, Double-lobed, with children at play. $7, Flowered. $17, Tutoring scene.

Wmk. 323

1992, June 25	Litho.		**Perf. 13½**	
Background colors				
2848	A661	$3.50 pink	.30	.25
2849	A661	$5 green	.45	.25
2850	A661	$7 bister	.70	.30
2851	A661	$17 blue	2.00	.70
	Nos. 2848-2851 (4)		3.45	1.50

Stone Lion of Lugouqiao A662

Various stone lions.

Wmk. 323

1992, July 7	Engr.		**Perf. 13½**	
2852	A662	$5 olive grn & pur	.60	.25
2853	A662	$5 blue & brown	.60	.25
2854	A662	$12 org & olive grn	1.40	.50
2855	A662	$12 purple & black	1.40	.50
	Nos. 2852-2855 (4)		4.00	1.50

Compare with designs A614, A629, A663.

Ku Shih Classical Poetry — A663

Excerpts: $3.50, "Flesh and body are as closely linked as leaves to a tree." $5, "Once a man and woman get married, conjugal love will last forever without doubt." $9, "Man takes pains to uphold virtue." $15, "Tartar horses lean toward the northern wind."

1992, Aug. 8		Litho.		
2856	A663	$3.50 Children playing near tree	.30	.25
2857	A663	$5 Man & woman	.70	.25
2858	A663	$9 Couple near stream	1.25	.35
2859	A663	$15 Horse, tree	1.75	.60
	Nos. 2856-2859 (4)		4.00	1.45

Life in the Countryside A664

Scenes of temple fair: a, Two women, man beating drum, crowd. b, Vendor with basket. c, People playing musical instruments. d, Man with food cart. e, Women with umbrella, basket.

Wmk. 323

1992, Sept. 22	Litho.		**Perf. 11½**	
2860	A664	$5 Strip of 5, #a.-e.	5.00	3.50

Silk Tapestries A665

Ming Dynasty Silk Tapestry Drawing on Life: $5, Two Birds Perched on a Red Camellia Branch. $12, Two Birds Playing on a Peach Branch.

1992, Oct. 9	Litho.		**Perf. 11½**	
Granite Paper				
2861	A665	$5 multicolored	.70	.25
2862	A665	$12 multicolored	1.90	.60
a.	Sheet of 2, #2861-2862		3.00	1.00

Chinese Opera A666

Actors, props: $3.50, Nin Hsiang-ju's carting to a party from "The General and Premier." $5, Hsao En rowing a boat from "The Lucky Pearl." $9, Wang Chao-chun making peace with the frontier from "Chao-chun Serves as an Envoy." $12, Scene with red sedan chair from "Escort to the Wedding."

Wmk. 323

1992, Oct. 21	Litho.		**Perf. 13½**	
2863	A666	$3.50 multicolored	.30	.25
2864	A666	$5 multicolored	.65	.25
2865	A666	$9 multicolored	1.05	.40
2866	A666	$12 multicolored	1.00	.55
	Nos. 2863-2866 (4)		3.00	1.45

Alishan Forest Railway — A667

1992, Nov. 5			**Perf. 11½**	
2867	A667	$5 Steam engine	.70	.25
2868	A667	$15 Diesel engine	1.50	.65

Endangered Mammals of Taiwan A668

Designs: a, Lutra lutra chinensis. b, Pteropus dasymallus formosus. c, Neofelis nebulosa brachyurus. d, Selenarctos thibetanus formosanus.

Perf. 11½x12

1992, Nov. 25	Photo.		**Unwmk.**	
Granite Paper				
2869	A668	$5 Block of 4, #a.-d.	3.50	1.50

New Year 1993 (Year of the Rooster) — A669

Design: $13, Rooster facing left.

Wmk. 323

1992, Dec. 1	Litho.		**Perf. 12½**	
2870	A669	$3.50 red & multi	.50	.25
a.	Perf. 13½ vert.		.50	.25
2871	A669	$13 pur & multi	1.25	.45
a.	Souv. sheet, 2 ea #2870-2871		4.00	4.00
b.	As "a" with added inscription in border		4.00	4.00
c.	Bklt. pane, 5 ea #2870-2871		9.25	
d.	Perf. 13½ vert.		1.25	.50
e.	Booklet pane, 6 each #2870a, 2871d + label		10.75	

Inscription on No. 2871b reads "Philippine Stamp Exhibition 1992-Taipei" in English and Chinese.

Johann Adam Schall von Bell (1592-1666), Astronomer and Missionary — A670

1992 Dec. 10			**Perf. 11½**	
2872	A670	$5 multicolored	1.00	.25

Traditional Nienhwas of Window Frames — A671

Wmk. 323

1993, Jan. 7	Litho.		**Perf. 11½**	
Background Color				
2873	A671	$5 brt green	.25	.25
2874	A671	$5 red lilac	.25	.25
2875	A671	$12 yellow	.65	.40
2876	A671	$12 red	.65	.40
	Nos. 2873-2876 (4)		1.80	1.30

Lunar New Year.

Perf. 13½ Vert.

2873a	A671	$5	1.00	.45
2874a	A671	$5	1.00	.45
2875a	A671	$12	1.00	.45
2876a	A671	$12	1.00	.45
b.	Booklet pane, 2 each #2873a-2876a + label		9.00	

Nos. 2873a-2876a are 29x43mm.

Traditional Crafts A672

$3.50, Clip & paste moldings. $5, Lanterns. $9, Pottery jars. $15, Oil paper umbrella.

1993, Jan. 16

2877	A672	$3.50 multi	.30	.25
2878	A672	$5 multi	.40	.25
2879	A672	$9 multi	.80	.40
2880	A672	$15 multi	1.25	.65
	Nos. 2877-2880 (4)		2.75	1.55

Chinese Creation Story — A673

Designs: $3.50, Pan Gu's creation of the universe, vert. $5, Pan Gu transmitted himself into all creatures. $9, Nu Wa created human beings with pestled earth. $19, Nu Wa mended sky with smelted stone, vert.

1993, Feb. 6	**Perf. 12x11½, 11½x12**			
2881	A673	$3.50 multicolored	.30	.25
2882	A673	$5 multicolored	.50	.25
2883	A673	$9 multicolored	.90	.45
2884	A673	$19 multicolored	1.75	1.40
	Nos. 2881-2884 (4)		3.45	2.55

Lucky Animals — A674

$3.50, Mandarin duck. $5, Chinese unicorn. $10, Deer. $15, Crane.

Wmk. 323

1993, Mar. 2	Litho.		**Perf. 13½**	
2885	A674	$3.50 multi	.30	.25
2886	A674	$5 multi	.45	.25
2887	A674	$10 multi	.90	.50
2888	A674	$15 multi	1.40	1.25
	Nos. 2885-2888 (4)		3.05	2.25

See Nos. 2920-2923.

Water Plants — A675

$5, Nymphaea x hybrida. $9, Nuphar shimadai. $12, Eichhornia crassipes.

1993, Mar. 12			**Perf. 11½**	
2889	A675	$5 multicolored	.60	.25
2890	A675	$9 multicolored	1.00	.40
2891	A675	$12 multicolored	1.25	.50
	Nos. 2889-2891 (3)		2.85	1.15

A676

No. 2892, Sandbag tossing. No. 2893, Bamboo dragonfly twisting. No. 2894, Rubber band skipping. No. 2895, Waist-strength dueling.

1993   Litho.   Wmk. 323   Perf. 11½
2892	A676	$5 multicolored	.50	.30
2893	A676	$5 multicolored	.50	.30
2894	A676	$5 multicolored	.50	.30
2895	A676	$5 multicolored	.50	.30
a.		Souv. sheet, #2892-2895	3.25	3.25
b.		As "a," with green & black inscriptions in border	3.25	3.25
c.		As "a," with red inscription in border	3.25	3.25
		Nos. 2892-2895 (4)	2.00	1.20

Inscriptions on No. 2895b read "AUSTRALIAN STAMP EXHIBITION 1993-TAIPEI" in Chinese and English.

Inscription on No. 2895c reads "Chinese Stamp Exhibition-Thailand" in Chinese.

Nos. 2895b-2895c each have perforations extending into the margin at top (No. 2895c) or bottom (No. 2895b).

Issue dates: Nos. 2892-2895, 2895a, Apr. 20; No. 2895b, Apr. 23; No. 2895c, Apr. 30.

Perf. 13½ Vert.
2892a	A676	$5	1.00	.30
2893a	A676	$5	1.00	.30
2894a	A676	$5	1.00	.30
2895d	A676	$5	1.00	.30
e.		Bklt. pane, 2 each #2892a-2894a, 2895d + label	8.50	

A677

Yangtze River
A678

Designs: No. 2896, Source on Ching-Kang-Chang Plateau. No. 2897, Abrupt bend, Chinsha River. No. 2898, Narrow waterway, Roaring Tiger Gorge, Chinsha River. No. 2899, Sheer cliffs, Chuntang Gorge. $9, Three Small Gorges (Dragon Gate, Pawu, and Titsui).

Perf. 13x13½
1993, May 15   Litho.   Wmk. 323
2896	A677	$3.50 shown	.30	.25
2897	A677	$3.50 multicolored	.30	.25
2898	A678	$5 shown	.55	.25
2899	A677	$5 multicolored	.55	.25
2900	A677	$9 multicolored	1.05	.40
		Nos. 2896-2900 (5)	2.75	1.40

Environmental Protection
A679   A680

Children's paintings: $5, No More Noise Pollution, by Yen Chao-min. $17, Clothing My Hometown with Green, by Hu Hui-chun.

Perf. 12½x13½, 13½x12½
1993, June 5
2901	A679	$5 multicolored	.50	.30
2902	A680	$17 multicolored	1.50	1.25

Ch'eng-hua Porcelain, Natl. Palace Museum
A681

Cups decorated in tou-ts'ai: $3.50, Human figures. $5, Chickens. $7, Flowers and fruits. $9, Dragon.

1993, June 30   Perf. 12
2903	A681	$3.50 multicolored	.30	.25
2904	A681	$5 multicolored	.55	.30
2905	A681	$7 multicolored	.75	.50
2906	A681	$9 multicolored	.90	.80
		Nos. 2903-2906 (4)	2.50	1.85

Vocational Training
A682

$3.50, Graphic artist. $5, Computer operator. $9, Carpenter. $12, Welder.

Wmk. 323
1993, July 24   Litho.   Perf. 12½
2907	A682	$3.50 multicolored	.30	.25
2908	A682	$5 multicolored	.40	.30
2909	A682	$9 multicolored	.75	.60
2910	A682	$12 multicolored	1.05	.90
		Nos. 2907-2910 (4)	2.50	2.05

Parent-Child Relationship
A683

Silhouettes: $3.50, Adult carrying child on shoulders. $5, Father playing flute for daughter. $9, Father teaching daughter. $10, Father, adult son enjoying wildlife.

Wmk. 323
1993, Aug. 4   Litho.   Perf. 11½
Background Color
2911	A683	$3.50 tan	.30	.25
2912	A683	$5 green	.45	.30
2913	A683	$9 lilac	.95	.70
2914	A683	$10 red brown	1.10	.80
		Nos. 2911-2914 (4)	2.80	2.05

Souvenir Sheet

Taipei '93, Asian Intl. Philatelic Exhibition — A684

Enjoying Antiques, by Tu Chin, 15th cent: a, Man carrying stick. b, Man selecting antiques from table. c, Man seated in chair. d, Two people at table.

Perf. 12x11½
1993, Aug. 14   Photo.   Unwmk.
Granite Paper
2915	A684	$5 Sheet of 4, #a.-d.	3.75	3.00

Persimmon   Loquat
A685   A686

1993, Sept. 10   Litho.   Perf. 12½
2916	A685	$5 shown	.50	.30
2917	A685	$5 Peach	.50	.30
2918	A686	$12 shown	1.25	.90
2919	A686	$12 Papaya	1.25	.90
		Nos. 2916-2919 (4)	3.50	2.40

Lucky Animals Type of 1993
Wmk. 323
1993, Sept. 29   Litho.   Perf. 13½
2920	A674	$1 Blue dragon	.30	.30
2921	A674	$2.50 White tiger	.30	.30
2922	A674	$9 Linnet	.85	.56
2923	A674	$19 Black tortoise	1.75	1.10
		Nos. 2920-2923 (4)	3.20	2.20

Taiwan Area Games, Taoyuan — A687

Designs: a, Taekwondo. b, Pommel horse.

Wmk. 323
1993, Oct. 20   Litho.   Perf. 12½
2924	A687	$5 Pair, #a.-b.	1.25	.80

Stone Lions — A688

Stone lions from: $3.50, Taipei New Park. $5, Hsinchu City Council. $9, Hsinchu City God Temple. $12, Fort Providentia, Tainan.

1993, Oct. 30
2925	A688	$3.50 multicolored	.30	.30
2926	A688	$5 multicolored	.45	.30
2927	A688	$9 multicolored	.90	.55
2928	A688	$12 multicolored	1.25	.75
		Nos. 2925-2928 (4)	2.90	1.90

Syrmaticus Mikado
A689

Designs: a, Hatchling. b, Mother with chicks. c, Immature female, male. d, Adult female, male (profile, showing plumage).

Perf. 11½
1993, Nov. 17   Photo.   Unwmk.
Granite Paper
2929	A689	$5 Strip of 4, #a.-d.	2.75	2.00

New Year 1994 (Year of the Dog) — A690

Design: $13, Dog facing left.

Wmk. 323
1993, Dec. 1   Litho.   Perf. 12½
2930	A690	$3.50 red & multi	.30	.30
a.		Perf. 13½ vert.	.30	.30
b.		As "a," bklt. pane of 12 + label	3.75	
2931	A690	$13 green & multi	1.40	.70
a.		Souv. sheet, 2 ea #2930-2931	3.75	2.00
b.		As "a," overprinted in red	3.75	2.00

No. 2931b is inscribed in Chinese for Kaohsiung Kuo-kuang Stamp Exhibition-1993, and has additional perforations extending into top and bottom margins.

Asian Vegetable Research and Development Center, 20th Anniv. — A691

$13, Researchers in field.

1993, Dec. 7
2932	A691	$5 shown	.40	.30
2933	A691	$13 multicolored	1.40	.90

Formation of Constitutional Court — A692

Wmk. 323
1994, Jan. 11   Litho.   Perf. 12½
2934	A692	$5 multicolored	.50	.30

Paper Making — A693

Designs: No. 2935, Cutting bamboo. No. 2936, Cooking bamboo. No. 2937, Pouring syrup into wooden panel. No. 2938, Stacking panel. No. 2939, Drying paper.

1994, Jan. 24   Perf. 12x12½
2935	A693	multicolored	.30	.25
2936	A693	$3.50 multicolored	.30	.25
2937	A693	$5 multicolored	.60	.25
2938	A693	$5 multicolored	.60	.25
2939	A693	$12 multicolored	1.25	.80
		Nos. 2935-2939 (5)	3.05	1.80

See Nos. 2993-2997, 3071-3075, 3098-3102, 3174-3177.

Flowers — A694

$5, Clivia miniata. $12, Cymbidium sinense. $19, Primula malacoides.

1994, Feb. 17   Perf. 12½
2940	A694	$5 multicolored	.40	.30
2941	A694	$12 multicolored	1.25	.80
2942	A694	$19 multicolored	1.90	1.40
		Nos. 2940-2942 (3)	3.55	2.50

Kinmen Wind Lion Lords — A695

Various Wind Lion Lords.

1994, Mar. 18   Litho.   Perf. 12½
2943	A695	$5 green & multi	.50	.30
2944	A695	$9 yellow & multi	.80	.50
2945	A695	$12 org yel & multi	1.25	.70
2946	A695	$17 blue & multi	1.50	1.00
		Nos. 2943-2946 (4)	4.05	2.50

Children at Play — A696

No. 2947, Playing with paper boat. No. 2948, Fighting with water gun. No. 2949, Throwing paper airplane. No. 2950, Playing "train" with rope.

Wmk. 323
1994, Apr. 2   Litho.   Perf. 12½
2947	A696	$5 multicolored	.50	.30
2948	A696	$5 multicolored	.50	.30
2949	A696	$5 multicolored	.50	.30

2950 A696 $5 multicolored .50 .30
    a. Souv. sheet, #2947-2950 2.75 1.50
    Nos. 2947-2950 (4) 2.00 1.20

Perf. 13½ Vert.

2947a A696 $5 .50 .30
2948a A696 $5 .50 .30
2949a A696 $5 .50 .30
2950b A696 $5 .50 .30
    c. Bklt. pane, 2 ea #2947a-2949a,
      2950b + label 4.50 1.50
    Nos. 2947a-2950b (4) 2.00 1.20

A697

Life in the countryside: $5, Playing chess. $10, Playing musical instruments. $12, Telling stories. $19, Drinking tea.

Wmk. 323

1994, Apr. 25 **Litho.** **Perf. 12½**
2951 A697 $5 multicolored .40 .30
2952 A697 $10 multicolored 1.00 .60
2953 A697 $12 multicolored 1.25 .85
2954 A697 $19 multicolored 1.90 1.25
    Nos. 2951-2954 (4) 4.55 3.00

A698

Mother, baby birds: $5, Malay bittern. $7, Little tern, horiz. $10, Common noddy, horiz. $12, Muller's barbet.

1994, May 7
2955 A698 $5 multicolored .40 .35
2956 A698 $7 multicolored .70 .40
2957 A698 $10 multicolored 1.10 .70
2958 A698 $12 multicolored 1.25 .75
    Nos. 2955-2958 (4) 3.45 2.20

A699

Protection of Intellectual Property Rights: $5, Palm-shaped book. $15, Human head, computer disk.

Wmk. 323

1994, May 28 **Litho.** **Perf. 12½**
2959 A699 $5 multicolored .60 .30
2960 A699 $15 multicolored 1.60 .90

A700

Designs: $5, Care for Lost Children. $17, Care for the aged.

1994, June 11
2961 A700 $5 multicolored .30 .25
2962 A700 $17 multicolored 1.10 .75

Intl. Olympic Committee, Cent. — A701

1994, June 23
2963 A701 $5 shown .50 .30
2964 A701 $15 Sporting events 1.50 .90

A702

Shei-pa Natl. Park: $5, Tapachienshan. $7, Shei-san Landslide Scar. $10, Holy Ridge. $17, Shiah-tsuei Lake.

Wmk. 323

1994, July 1 **Litho.** **Perf. 12½**
2965 A702 $5 multicolored .55 .30
2966 A702 $7 multicolored .70 .45
2967 A702 $10 multicolored 1.10 .60
2968 A702 $17 multicolored 1.75 1.10
    Nos. 2965-2968 (4) 4.10 2.45

A703

$5, Portrait of Chien Mu (b. 1895), educator.

1994, July 30 **Perf. 11½x12**
2969 A703 $5 multicolored .50 .30

Intl. Year of the Family A704

$5, Rainbow, window. $15, Globe, house.

1994, Aug. 25 **Perf. 11½**
2970 A704 $5 multicolored .50 .30
2971 A704 $15 yel & multi 1.50 .90

Invention Myths — A705

Designs: $5, Sueirenjy digging wood to obtain fire. $10, Fushijy drawing Pa-Kua. $12, Shennungjy making agricultural tools. $15, Tsang-jier creating written characters.

1994, Sept. 17 **Photo.** **Perf. 11½**
Granite Paper
2972 A705 $5 multicolored .50 .30
2973 A705 $10 multicolored 1.05 .65
2974 A705 $12 multicolored 1.25 .90
2975 A705 $15 multicolored 1.60 1.05
    Nos. 2972-2975 (4) 4.40 2.90

A706

Design: $5, Dr. Lin Yutang, linguist, writer, 100th birthday.

Wmk. 323

1994, Oct. 8 **Litho.** **Perf. 12½**
2976 A706 $5 multicolored .50 .30

A707

$5, Cheng Ho's ship. $17, Chart, ship, Cheng Ho.

1994, Oct. 17
2977 A707 $5 multicolored .50 .30
2978 A707 $17 multicolored 1.50 .90

World Trade Week.

Sun Yat-sen, Founding of Kuomintang, Cent. — A708

Design: $19, Democratic elections, factories, economic development.

Wmk. 323

1994, Nov. 24 **Litho.** **Perf. 12½**
2979 A708 $5 multicolored .50 .30
2980 A708 $19 multicolored 1.75 1.10

A709

1994, Nov. 29
2981 A709 $3.50 Facing right .40 .30
    a. Perf. 13½ vert. .40 .30
    b. As "a," booklet pane of 6 2.50
      Complete booklet, 2 #2981b +
      label 5.00
2982 A709 $13 Facing left 1.40 .90
    a. Souv. sheet, 2 ea #2981-2982 3.50 2.40

New Year 1995 (Year of the Boar).

A710

$5, Portrait. $15, Greeting farm family.

1994, Dec. 24 **Litho.** **Perf. 12½**
2983 A710 $5 multicolored .50 .30
2984 A710 $15 multicolored 1.50 .90

Pres. Yen Chia-kan, 1st death anniv.

Horse's Back Roofline A711

Swallow's Tail Roofline — A711a

Talisman (Stove & Bowl) Roofline — A711b

Cylinder-Shaped Brick Roofline — A711c

Traditional Architecture: Roof lines.

Perf. 12½x12

1995, Jan. 10 **Litho.** **Wmk. 323**
2985 A711 $5 multicolored .45 .30
2986 A711a $5 multicolored .45 .30
2987 A711b $12 multicolored 1.25 .75
2988 A711c $19 multicolored 1.90 1.25
    Nos. 2985-2988 (4) 4.05 2.60

See Nos. 3079-3082, 3113-3116, 3187-3190, 3235-3238.

Ancient Chinese Engravings — A712

Various floral designs.

1995, Jan. 24 **Perf. 13½**
Denomination in Black
2989 A712 $3.50 multicolored .30 .25
2990 A712 $5 multicolored .60 .30
2991 A712 $19 multicolored 1.75 1.25
2992 A712 $26 multicolored 2.75 1.75
    Nos. 2989-2992 (4) 5.40 3.55

See Nos. 3018-3021, 3044-3047, 3076-3078, 3178-3181, 3221-3226, 3254-3256, 3299-3300.

Ancient Skills Type of 1994

Methods of irrigation: No. 2993, Water wheel. No. 2994, Gear-driven bucket lift. $5, Pedal-powered hoist. $12, Hand-cranked hoist. $13, Using pole with counter-weight to raise bucket.

Perf. 12x11½

1994, Feb. 14 **Litho.** **Wmk. 323**
2993 A693 $3.50 multicolored .30 .25
2994 A693 $3.50 multicolored .30 .25
2995 A693 $5 multicolored .50 .30
2996 A693 $12 multicolored 1.25 .85
2997 A693 $13 multicolored 1.40 .95
    Nos. 2993-2997 (5) 3.75 2.60

Beauties on an Outing, by Lee Gong-lin — A713

a, Two riders. b, Rider on black horse, woman with child on horse. c, Three riders. d, One rider.

Unwmk.
1995, Mar. 3 **Photo.** **Perf. 12**
Granite Paper
2998 A713 $9 Strip of 4, #a.-d. 4.00 2.50
    e. Souv. sheet, #2998b-2998c 2.00 1.25

No. 2998 is a continuous design.

Natl. Health Insurance Plan — A714

Perf. 11½x12½

1995, Mar. 1 **Litho.** **Wmk. 323**
2999 A714 $12 multicolored 1.25 .80

Flowers — A715

$5, Lilium speciosum. $12, Haemanthus multiflorus. $19, Hyacinthus orientalis.

1995, Mar. 20   Litho.   Perf. 12½
3000	A715	$5 multicolored	.40	.30
3001	A715	$12 multicolored	.90	.75
3002	A715	$19 multicolored	1.90	1.25
	Nos. 3000-3002 (3)		3.20	2.30

Chinese Calligraphy A716

Cold Food Observance, poem by Su Shih, red inscriptions at: a, Lower left. b, Middle. c, Upper right. d, Right half of design.

1995, Apr. 6   Perf. 13½
3003	Strip of 4	4.00	2.50
a.-d.	A716 $5 any single	.50	.30

Paintings by Tsou I Kuei's — A717

1995, May 5   Photo.   Die Cut
Self-Adhesive
3004	A717	$5 Red peony	.60	.25
3005	A717	$5 Pink peony	.60	.25
a.	Bklt. pane, 9 ea #3004-3005		10.75	

By its nature, No. 3005a is a complete booklet. The peelable backing serves as a booklet cover.

Campaign Against Illegal Drugs — A718

$15, Arm, hypodermic needle.

Wmk. 323
1995, June 1   Perf. 12½
3006	A718	$5 shown	.50	.30
3007	A718	$15 multicolored	1.25	.90

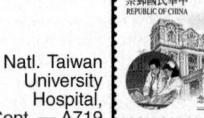

Natl. Taiwan University Hospital, Cent. — A719

Designs: $5, Medical treatment, old hospital. $19, Medical research, new hospital.

1995, June 20
3008	A719	$5 multicolored	.70	.30
3009	A719	$19 multicolored	1.75	1.25

East Coast Scenes A720

Designs: No. 3010, Green hills above Chichi Bay. No. 3011, Rocky promontory, Shihyuesan. $12, Changhong Bridge.

Wmk. 323
1995, July 1   Litho.   Perf. 12½
3010	A720	$5 multicolored	.50	.30
3011	A720	$5 multicolored	.50	.30
3012	A720	$12 multicolored	1.25	.80
3013	A720	$15 multicolored	1.75	1.10
	Nos. 3010-3013 (4)		4.00	2.50

Oncorhynchus Masou Formosanus A721

Designs: $5, Mating. $7, Female digging a spot to lay eggs. $10, Hatching of fry. $17, Fry swimming in river.

Perf. 14x14½
1995, July 27   Litho.   Unwmk.
3014	A721	$5 multicolored	.50	.30
3015	A721	$7 multicolored	.75	.50
3016	A721	$10 multicolored	.95	.75
3017	A721	$17 multicolored	1.75	1.25
	Nos. 3014-3017 (4)		3.95	2.80

Ancient Chinese Engraving Type

Various pictures of birds on tree branches.

Wmk. 323
1995, Aug. 18   Litho.   Perf. 13½
Denomination in Black
3018	A712	$2.50 multicolored	.35	.35
3019	A712	$7 multicolored	.80	.45
3020	A712	$13 multicolored	1.40	1.00
3021	A712	$28 multicolored	3.50	2.00
	Nos. 3018-3021 (4)		6.05	3.80

Marine Life — A722

No. 3022, Tubastraea aurea. No. 3023, Chromodoris elizabethina. $5, Spirobranchus gigateus. $17, Himerometra magnipinna.

Wmk. 323
1995, Sept. 7   Litho.   Perf. 12½
3022	A722	$3.50 multicolored	.35	.30
3023	A722	$3.50 multicolored	.35	.30
3024	A722	$5 multicolored	.65	.40
3025	A722	$17 multicolored	1.90	1.00
	Nos. 3022-3025 (4)		3.25	2.00

Louis Pasteur (1822-95) — A723

1995, Sept. 20
3026	A723	$17 multicolored	2.00	1.00

Natl. Palace Museum, 70th Anniv. A724

Designs: No. 3027, Painting, "Strange Peaks and Myriad Trees." No. 3028, Greenish blue porcelain vase, vert. $5, Bronze X Fu-K'uei Ting vessel, vert. $26, Calligraphy of quatrain in seven-character verse, "The Fragrance of Flowers."

Perf. 12x11½, 11½x12
1995, Oct. 9   Photo.   Unwmk.
3027	A724	$3.50 multicolored	.30	.25
3028	A724	$3.50 multicolored	.30	.25
3029	A724	$5 multicolored	.65	.40
3030	A724	$26 multicolored	2.40	1.50
	Nos. 3027-3030 (4)		3.50	2.25

A725

End of World War II, 50th Anniv.: $5, Chinese soldiers in battle. $19, Flag, outline map of Taiwan, presidential mansion.

Perf. 11½x12
1995, Oct. 24   Litho.   Wmk. 323
3031	A725	$5 multicolored	.60	.25
3032	A725	$19 multicolored	1.90	.65
a.	Souvenir sheet, #3031-3032		2.50	.90

A726

Sea Turtles: No. 3033, Chelonia mydas. No. 3034, Caretta caretta. No. 3035, Lepidochelys olivacea. No. 3036, Eretmochelys imbricata.

Wmk. 323
1995, Nov. 10   Litho.   Perf. 12½
3033	A726	$5 multicolored	.70	.25
3034	A726	$5 multicolored	.70	.25
3035	A726	$5 multicolored	.70	.25
3036	A726	$5 multicolored	.70	.25
	Nos. 3033-3036 (4)		2.80	1.00

Taiwan Agricultural Research Institute, Cent. — A727

Perf. 12x11½
1995, Nov. 22   Litho.   Wmk. 323
3037	A727	$5 In rice field	.75	.25
3038	A727	$28 In anthurium field	2.50	.90

New Year 1996 (Year of the Rat) — A728

Designs: $3.50, $13, Different stylized rats.

Wmk. 323
1995, Dec. 1   Litho.   Perf. 12½
3039	A728	$3.50 pink & multi	.30	.25
a.	Perf. 13½ vert.		.30	.25
b.	As "a," booklet pane of 6		1.60	
	Complete booklet, 2 #3039b + gutter		3.25	
3040	A728	$13 olive & multi	.90	.45
a.	Souv. sheet, 2 ea #3039-3040		3.75	1.10

Traditional Wedding Ceremony A729

Designs: $5, Escorting bride. $12, Kowtowing Heaven, Earth, and ancestors. $19, Seated in bridal chamber.

1996, Jan. 10
3041	A729	$5 multicolored	.40	.25
3042	A729	$12 multicolored	1.25	.50
3043	A729	$19 multicolored	2.25	.75
	Nos. 3041-3043 (3)		3.90	1.50

Ancient Chinese Engraving Type

Various pictures of fruit.

Wmk. 323
1996, Jan. 25   Litho.   Perf. 13½
Denomination in Black
3044	A712	$9 multicolored	.90	.40
3045	A712	$12 multicolored	1.25	.65
3046	A712	$15 multicolored	1.50	.75
3047	A712	$17 multicolored	1.75	.85
	Nos. 3044-3047 (4)		5.40	2.65

Scenic Dwelling at Chü-Ch'ü, by Wang Meng, Yüan Dynasty — A730

Denominations: a, UL. b, UR. c, LL. d, LR.

Perf. 12½x12
1996, Feb. 15   Litho.   Unwmk.
3048	A730	Block of 4, #a.-d.	4.00	3.00
a.-d.	$5 any single		.85	.75

A731

Flowers: $5, Bougainvillea spectabilis. $12, Wisteria sinensis. $19, Merremia tuberosa.

1996, Mar. 8   Unwmk.   Perf. 12½
3049	A731	$5 multicolored	.50	.25
3050	A731	$12 multicolored	1.25	.60

Wmk. 323
3051	A731	$19 multicolored	1.75	.90
	Nos. 3049-3051 (3)		3.50	1.75

A732

Chinese Postal Service, Cent.: $5, Mailboxes. $9, Instruments of measurement. $12, Methods of mail transport. $13, Computers, plastic card.

Wmk. 323
1996, Mar. 20   Litho.   Perf. 13½
3052	A732	$5 multicolored	.55	.25
3053	A732	$9 multicolored	.90	.50
3054	A732	$12 multicolored	1.05	.60
3055	A732	$13 multicolored	1.25	.70
a.	Souvenir sheet #3052-3055		3.75	1.90
	Nos. 3052-3055 (4)		3.75	2.05

Natl. Chiao Tung University, Cent. — A733

Wmk. 323
1996, Apr. 8   Litho.   Perf. 12½
3056	A733	$19 multicolored	1.75	.90

Penghu Natl. Scenic Areas — A734

No. 3057, Chimei Giant Lion. No. 3058, Chipei Beach. $12, Tungpan Yu. $17, Tingkou Yu.

1996, May 1
3057	A734	$5 multicolored	.40	.25
3058	A734	$5 multicolored	.40	.25
3059	A734	$12 multicolored	1.10	.45
3060	A734	$17 multicolored	1.60	.65
		Nos. 3057-3060 (4)	3.50	1.60

Tzu-Chi Buddhist Compassionate Relief Foundation — A735

$5, Hand holding people. $19, Lotus blossom, sick person.

Wmk. 323
1996, May 11   Litho.   Perf. 13
3061	A735	$5 multicolored	.50	.30
3062	A735	$19 multicolored	2.75	1.00

First Democratic Presidential Election A736

New Pres., Vice Pres. and: $3.50, Natl. flag. $5, Presidential office building. $13, Development of Asia-Pacific Operations Hub project. $15, Greeting people at fair.

1996, May 20   Wmk. 323   Perf. 12½
3063	A736	$3.50 multicolored	.30	.25
3064	A736	$5 multicolored	.55	.25
3065	A736	$13 multicolored	1.25	.50
3066	A736	$15 multicolored	1.40	.55
a.		Souvenir sheet, #3063-3066	3.50	1.40
		Nos. 3063-3066 (4)	3.50	1.55

South China Sea Archipelago A737

Outline map of region, Interior Dept. monuments on: $5, Pratas Isl. $17, Itu Aba Isl.

1996, June 5   Wmk. 323   Perf. 12½
3067	A737	$5 multicolored	.50	.25
3068	A737	$17 multicolored	1.75	.65
a.		Souvenir sheet, #3067-3068	1.65	.85

Modern Olympic Games, Cent. — A738

$5, Gymnast, cyclist. $15, Early Greek athletes.

Perf. 12½x12
1996, June 22   Litho.   Wmk. 323
3069	A738	$5 multicolored	.60	.25
3070	A738	$15 multicolored	1.60	.55

Ancient Skills Type of 1994

Manufacturing silk: No. 3071, Feeding silkworms. No. 3072, Picking out cocoons. $7, Reeling raw silk. $10, Degumming raw silk. $13, Weaving silk.

1996, July 5   Perf. 12
3071	A693	$5 multicolored	.50	.25
3072	A693	$5 multicolored	.50	.25
3073	A693	$7 multicolored	.60	.30

3074	A693	$10 multicolored	1.00	.60
3075	A693	$13 multicolored	1.40	.90
		Nos. 3071-3075 (5)	4.00	2.10

Ancient Chinese Engraving Type
1996, Aug. 5   Perf. 13½
Denomination in Black
3076	A712	$1 Bamboo	.50	.25
3077	A712	$10 Orchid	.90	.60
3078	A712	$20 Plum tree branch	2.00	1.00
		Nos. 3076-3078 (3)	3.40	1.85

A738a

A738b

A738c

Column and Beam Construction — A738d

Perf. 12x11½
1996, Aug. 22   Litho.   Wmk. 323
3079	A738a	$5 Tou-kung (lion)	.55	.30
3080	A738b	$5 Chiue-ti	.55	.30
3081	A738c	$10 Bu-tong	1.00	.50
3082	A738d	$19 Dye-tou	1.90	.90
		Nos. 3079-3082 (4)	4.00	2.00

Motion Pictures, Cent. — A739

Chinese movies: No. 3083, Princess Iron Fan, first full-length animated film, 1941. No. 3084, Chin Shan Bi Xie, 1957. $5, Oyster Girl, 1964. $19, City of Sadness, 1989.

1996, Sept. 17   Litho.   Perf. 12½x12
3083	A739	$3.50 multicolored	.30	.25
3084	A739	$3.50 multicolored	.30	.25
3085	A739	$5 multicolored	.60	.25
3086	A739	$19 multicolored	1.75	.70
		Nos. 3083-3086 (4)	2.95	1.45

Winning Pictures from Children's Stamp Design Contest A740

Denomination triangle color, location: a, Red, LR. b, Red, LL. c, Green, LR. d, Green, LL. e, Pink, LL. f, Red, UR. g, Red, UL. h, Green, UR. i, Green, UL. j, Pink, UL. k, Purple, LR. l, Purple, LL. m, Tan, LR. n, Tan, LL. o, Pink, LR. p, Purple, UR. q, Purple, UL. r, Tan, UR. s, Tan, UL. t, Pink, UR.

Perf. 12½x12
1996, Oct. 9   Litho.   Unwmk.
3087	A740	$5 Sheet of 20, #a.-t.	15.00	6.00

A741

Ancient Chinese paintings: $5, Autumn Scene with Wild Geese. $7, Reeds and Wild Geese. $13, Wild Geese Gathering on a Shore of Reeds. $15, Wild Geese on a Bank in Autumn.

1996, Oct. 21   Photo.   Perf. 12
Granite Paper
3088	A741	$5 multicolored	.55	.25
3089	A741	$7 multicolored	.70	.25
3090	A741	$13 multicolored	1.25	.50
3091	A741	$15 multicolored	1.50	.55
a.		Souv. sheet, #3088-3091	4.50	2.00
		Nos. 3088-3091 (4)	4.00	1.55

10th Asian Intl. Philatelic Exhib., Taipei '96.

A742

Designs: $5, Computerized letters, numbers, bar coding. $26, Globe, graph line.

Perf. 12½x12
1996, Nov. 1   Litho.   Wmk. 323
3092	A742	$5 multicolored	.60	.30
3093	A742	$26 multicolored	2.75	1.40

Merchant's Day, 50th Anniv.

A743

Caring for the Handicapped: $5, Woman in wheelchair working at computer. $19, Handicapped child painting picture.

Wmk. 323
1996, Nov. 15   Litho.   Perf. 12½
3094	A743	$5 multicolored	.70	.30
3095	A743	$19 multicolored	1.75	.90

A744

1996, Dec. 2
3096	A744	$3.50 gray & multi	.40	.25
a.		Perf. 13½ vert.		.25
b.		As "a," booklet pane of 6	2.40	
		Complete booklet, 2 #3096b + gutter	4.80	
3097	A744	$13 blue & multi	1.60	.55
a.		Souv. sheet, 2 ea #3096-3097	4.00	1.50
b.		As "a," overprinted	4.00	1.50

New Year 1997 (Year of the Ox). No. 3097b overprinted in red lilac in sheet margin with Chinese inscription for Kaohsiung Intl. Stamp Exhibition for Chinese Postal Service cent.

Ancient Skills Type of 1994

Making porcelain: No. 3098, Pounding stone, looking at bottom of bowl. No. 3099, Painting, shaping. $7, Painting. $10, Glazing. $13, Firing.

Perf. 11½x12
1997, Jan. 15   Litho.   Wmk. 323
3098	A693	$5 multicolored	.50	.25
3099	A693	$5 multicolored	.50	.25
3100	A693	$7 multicolored	.80	.25
3101	A693	$10 multicolored	1.00	.40
3102	A693	$13 multicolored	1.25	.50
		Nos. 3098-3102 (5)	4.05	1.65

Carp Encircled By Dragons — A745

Perf. 13x12½
1997, Feb. 14   Engr.   Wmk. 323
3103	A745	$50 carmine	5.00	2.50
3104	A745	$60 dark blue	6.00	3.00
3105	A745	$70 red orange	7.00	3.50
3106	A745	$100 olive green	10.00	5.00
		Nos. 3103-3106 (4)	28.00	14.00

See Nos. 3131-3132, 3252-3253, 3369-3370, 3426, 3871, 4312.

Feb. 28, 1947 Rebellion, 50th Anniv. — A746

Perf. 12x11½
1997, Feb. 28   Litho.   Wmk. 323
3107	A746	$19 Memorial	1.75	.90

Woody Plants — A747

$5, Rhododendron x mucronatum. $12, Hibiscus rosa-sinensis. $19, Hydrangea macrophylla.

Wmk. 323
1997, Mar. 12   Litho.   Perf. 12½
3108	A747	$5 multicolored	.60	.30
3109	A747	$12 multicolored	1.40	.60
3110	A747	$19 multicolored	2.00	.90
		Nos. 3108-3110 (3)	4.00	1.80

Water Resource Protection
A748   A749

1997, Mar. 22   Perf. 12½
3111	A748	$5 multicolored	.60	.30
3112	A749	$19 multicolored	2.00	.90

A749a   A749b

A749c

Traditional
Architecture —
A749d

Carp Type

1997, July 3   Engr.   Perf. 13
3131 A745 $300 vio & dark
         blue   30.00 15.00
3132 A745 $500 dk red & mag 45.00 25.00

horse. $5, "The Flaming Mountain," people
fighting, fire in background. $20, "The Cobweb
Cave," man using pole to fight, spider in
cobweb.

1997, Sept. 24   Photo.   Perf. 11½x12
Granite Paper
3146 A758 $3.50 multicolored   .50   .30
3147 A758 $3.50 multicolored   .50   .30
3148 A758 $5 multicolored   .60   .40
3149 A758 $20 multicolored   1.60 .80
     Nos. 3146-3149 (4)   3.20 1.80

vase of flowers. No. 3160, "All is Lucky," bowl
of fruit, vase with branch of fruit blossoms.

Perf. 11½x12
1998, Jan. 23   Litho.   Wmk. 323
Background Color
3157 A763 $5 pink   .50   .25
3158 A763 $5 beige   .50   .25
 a.   Pair, 3157-3158   1.00   .30
3159 A763 $12 light yellow .90   .35
3160 A763 $12 tan   .90   .35
 a.   Pair, #3159-3160   1.80   .70
     Nos. 3157-3160 (4)   2.80 1.20

Perf. 12x12½
1997, Apr. 9   Litho.   Wmk. 323
3113 A749a $5 Door   .50   .30
3114 A749b $5 Gable wall   .50   .30
3115 A749c $10 Carved brick 1.25 .60
3116 A749d $19 Column dragon 1.75 .80
     Nos. 3113-3116 (4)   4.00 2.00

Electronic
Industry's Use
of Integrated
Circuits
A754

$5, Integrated circuit for computer & tele-
communications industry. $26, Wafer linked to
portable computer, cellular phone, electronic
synthesizer.

1997, July 16   Litho.   Perf. 12½x12
3133 A754 $5 multicolored   .60   .30
3134 A754 $26 multicolored 2.75 1.25

Opening of
Second
Northern
Freeway
A759

Designs: $5, Bitan Bridge crossing, Shin-
dian River. $19, Hsinchu interchange.

Wmk. 323
1997, Aug. 26   Litho.   Perf. 13
3150 A759 $5 multicolored   .60   .25
3151 A759 $19 multicolored 1.75 .80

A764

Herbaceous Flowers: $5, Gaillardia
pulchella. $12, Kalanchoe blossfeldiana. $19,
Portulaca oleracea.

Wmk. 323
1998, Mar. 1   Litho.   Perf. 12½
3161 A764 $5 multicolored   .40   .25
3162 A764 $12 multicolored .80   .50
3163 A764 $19 multicolored 1.75 .80
     Nos. 3161-3163 (3)   2.95 1.55

Insects — A750

Designs: $5, Dorcus formosanus. $7, Phyl-
lophorina kotoshoensis. $10, Troides magel-
lanus. $17, Megacrania tsudai.

1997, Apr. 25   Photo.   Perf. 11½
Granite Paper
3117 A750 $5 multicolored   .50   .30
3118 A750 $7 multicolored   .80   .40
3119 A750 $10 multicolored 1.10 .60
3120 A750 $17 multicolored 1.75 .90
     Nos. 3117-3120 (4)   4.15 2.20

Chinese
Martial
Arts — A755

Various stances in martial arts.

Wmk. 323
1997, Aug. 8   Litho.   Perf. 13
3135 A755 $5 shown   .50   .30
3136 A755 $5 multi, vert.   .50   .30
3137 A755 $9 multi, vert.   .80   .40
3138 A755 $19 multi, vert. 1.75 .80
     Nos. 3135-3138 (4)   3.55 1.80

Illustrations
from Ching
Dynasty
Bird
Manual
A760

Various birds.

1997, Oct. 9   Photo.   Perf. 11½
Granite Paper
3152 A760 $5 Sheet of 20, #a.-
          t.   12.00 9.50

Compare with Nos. 3268-3269.

Emperor Shih-
tzu, on Hunting
Expedition, by
Liu Kuan-tao
A765

$5, Horseman drawing bow. $19, Emperor
Shih-tzu leading hunting party on horseback.

1998, Mar. 20   Photo.   Perf. 12
Granite Paper
3164 A765 $5 multicolored 1.00   .25
Size: 64x40mm
3165 A765 $5 multicolored 2.00   .60
 a.   Souvenir sheet, #3164-3165 3.00 1.25

No. 3165a is a continuous design.

Minerals
A751

Wmk. 323
1997, May 8   Litho.   Perf. 13
3121 A751 $5 Aragonite   .50   .30
3122 A751 $5 Alunite   .50   .30
3123 A751 $12 Enargite   1.25 .60
3124 A751 $19 Hokutolite   1.75 .80
     Nos. 3121-3124 (4)   4.00 2.00

Sports — A757

1997, Sept. 9   Perf. 12½
3143 A757 $5 Badminton   .50   .30
3144 A757 $12 Bowling   1.25 .60
3145 A757 $19 Tennis   1.60 .90
     Nos. 3143-3145 (3)   3.35 1.80

Pres.
Chiang
Ching-kuo
(1910-88)
A762

1998, Jan. 13   Engr.   Perf. 13½
3155 A762 $5 Portrait, vert. .50 .30
Perf. 11½
3156 A762 $19 shown   1.25 .90

Children's
Folk
Rhymes
A766

No. 3166, "A Frog Has One Mouth." No.
3167, "A Little Mouse Climbs an Oil Lamp."
$12, "Fireflies." $19, "Egrets."

Wmk. 323
1998, Apr. 4   Litho.   Perf. 11½
3166 A766 $5 multicolored   .50   .30
3167 A766 $5 multicolored   .50   .30
3168 A766 $12 multicolored .75   .60
3169 A766 $19 multicolored 1.75 .80
     Nos. 3166-3169 (4)   3.50 2.00

Nanyashan
Outlook
A752

No. 3126, Pitou coastline. No. 3127, Stone
pillars, Nanya. No. 1328, Tsaoling trail.

1997, May 31   Perf. 12½
3125 A752 $5 shown   .55   .25
3126 A752 $5 multicolored   .55   .25
3127 A752 $12 multicolored 1.25 .60
3128 A752 $19 multicolored 1.25 .60
     Nos. 3125-3128 (4)   3.60 1.70

Chinese Classical
(Yuan)
Opera — A756

Designs: No. 3139, Chang Shen playing
musical instrument, Tsuei Ying-ying listening
outside, from "Hsi Hsiang Chi." No. 3140,
Kuan Gung standing on ferry and holding
large knife, enemies in distance, from "Dan
Daw Huei." $12, Abduction of Wang Chao-juin
on horseback, from "Han Guong Chiou." $15,
Emperor Tang Ming Huang envisioning concu-
bine, Makueibo, from "Wu Tong Yu."

1997, Aug. 22
3139 A756 $5 multicolored   .50   .30
3140 A756 $5 multicolored   .50   .30
3141 A756 $12 multicolored 1.00 .50
3142 A756 $15 multicolored 1.50 .70
     Nos. 3139-3142 (4)   3.50 1.80

Ming Dynasty
Novel "Journey to
the
West" — A758

Episodes from novel: No. 3146, "Palm of
Buddha," man making inscription while holding
pole. No. 3147, "The pilgrimage of T'ang
Monk," characters traveling west, one on

A763

Common Chinese Expressions of Good For-
tune, designs: No. 3157, "Happy Occasion of
Abundance," fish, vase with pictures of sun
and sea. No. 3158, "Harmonious Union as
One," flower with two blooms. No. 3159,
"Honor and Wealth," flowers growing in pot,

Copyright
Law in
Taiwan,
70th Anniv.
A767

1998, Apr. 30
3170 A767 $19 multicolored 1.75 .80

A753

Around-The-Island Railway System: $5,
Cliffs at Chingshuei, Northern Loop Line. $28,
Southbound train passing through tunnel,
Central Mountain area.

Wmk. 323
1997, June 12   Litho.   Perf. 13½
3129 A753 $5 multicolored   .70   .30
3130 A753 $28 multicolored 2.40 .90

1997, Dec. 1   Litho.   Perf. 12½
3153 A761 $3.50 pink & multi .30   .25
 a.   Perf. 14 vert.   .30   .25
 b.   As "a," booklet pane of 6 1.90
      Complete booklet, 2 #3153b +
      gutter   3.80
3154 A761 $13 yellow & multi 1.00   .45
 a.   Souv. sheet, 2 ea #3153-3154 2.60 1.10

New Year 1998
(Year of the
Tiger) — A761

A768

Portraits of Mythological Character, Chung K'uei: $5, Making ghosts work for him, from Kung Kai's "Chung K'uei Moving," Song Dynasty. $20, Dancing beside small ghost, from "An Auspicious Occasion," Ming Dynasty.

1998, May 15   Photo.   Perf. 11½
Granite Paper

3171	A768	$5 multicolored	1.25	.25
3172	A768	$20 multicolored	2.25	.80

A769
Wmk. 323

1998, May 25   Litho.   Perf. 11½

3173	A769	$15 multicolored	1.25	.60

Intl. Law Assoc., 125th anniv.

Ancient Skills Type of 1994

Ships and methods of transport, horiz.: $5, Grain barge. $7, Six-oared boat. $10, One-wheeled carriage. $13, Southern Chinese one-man push cart.

1998, June 10   Perf. 12x11½

3174	A693	$5 multicolored	.50	.25
3175	A693	$7 multicolored	.60	.25
3176	A693	$10 multicolored	.80	.30
3177	A693	$13 multicolored	1.00	.40
	Nos. 3174-3177 (4)		2.90	1.20

Ancient Chinese Engravings Type of 1995 Redrawn with Chinese Inscription Reading Left to Right

Various floral designs. Denominations do not include two zeros.

Wmk. 323

1998, July 8   Litho.   Perf. 13½
Denomination in Red

3178	A712	$7 like #2989	.55	.30
3179	A712	$19 like #2990	1.60	.75
3180	A712	$20 like #2991	1.75	.85
3181	A712	$26 like #2992	2.10	1.05
	Nos. 3178-3181 (4)		6.00	2.95

Novel, "Red Chamber Dream," by Tsao Hsueh-chin
A770

Scenes from love story: No. 3182, Chia Pao-yu visits the garden (with group of women). No. 3183, Lin Tai-yu buries flowers (with hoe). $5, Hsueh Pao-chai plays with butterflies. $20, Shih Hsiang-yun in a drunken sleep (on bench).

1998, July 16   Perf. 11x11½

3182	A770	$3.50 multicolored	.25	.25
3183	A770	$3.50 multicolored	.25	.25
3184	A770	$5 multicolored	.40	.25
3185	A770	$20 multicolored	1.60	.75
	Nos. 3182-3185 (4)		2.50	1.50

20th Asia Pacific Jamboree, 8th Taiwan Jamboree — A771

1998, Aug. 5   Litho.   Perf. 11

3186	A771	$5 Emblem	.30	.25
3186A	A771	$5 Tents	.30	.25
b.	Pair, #3186-3186A		1.00	.50

Traditional Architecture Type of 1995

Terraces set on raised platforms: No. 3187, Spirit way (carved stone ramp between two staircases). No. 3188, Octagonal base of a column. $10, Carved cornerstone. $19, Carved stone drainage spout.

Perf. 11½x12

1998, Aug. 26   Wmk. 323

3187	A711	$5 multi, vert.	.50	.25
3188	A711	$5 multi, vert.	.50	.25
3189	A711	$10 multi, vert.	.80	.30
3190	A711	$19 multi, vert.	1.25	.55
	Nos. 3187-3190 (4)		3.05	1.35

Sports Stamps — A772

Table tennis: No. 3191, Player awaiting serve. No. 3192, Player serving.
Rugby: No. 3193, Two players. No. 3194, Three players.

Wmk. 323

1998, Sept. 9   Litho.   Perf. 11½
Denomination Color

3191		$5 green	.40	.25
3192		$5 red	.40	.25
a.	A772 Pair, #3191-3192		.80	.30
3193		$7 red	.50	.25
3194		$7 blue	.50	.25
a.	A772 Pair, #3193-3194		1.00	.40
	Nos. 3191-3194 (4)		1.80	1.00

Chinese Fables A773

Designs: No. 3195, "A Frog in a Well." No. 3196, "The Fox Borrows the Tiger's Ferocity." $12, "Adding Legs to a Drawing of a Snake." $19, "The Snipe and the Clam are at a Deadlock."

Wmk. 323

1998, Sept. 25   Perf. 11½

3195	A773	$5 multicolored	.50	.30
3196	A773	$5 multicolored	.50	.30
3197	A773	$12 multicolored	1.00	.50
3198	A773	$19 multicolored	1.50	.70
	Nos. 3195-3198 (4)		3.50	1.80

Kinmen National Park A774

No. 3199, Taiwushan mountain area. No. 3200, Kunningtou Cliff, beach. $12, Teyueh Tower, Huang Hui-huang's house, Shuitou village. $19, Putou Beach, Liehyu Coast.

1998, Oct. 16

3199	A774	$5 multicolored	.50	.30
3200	A774	$5 multicolored	.50	.30
3201	A774	$12 multicolored	1.10	.50
3202	A774	$19 multicolored	1.75	.70
	Nos. 3199-3202 (4)		3.85	1.80

Birds — A775

Spizaetus nipalensis: No. 3203, On tree branch. No. 3204, In flight.
Spilornis cheela: No. 3205, On tree branch. No. 3206, In flight.
Ictinaetus malayensis: No. 3207, On tree branch. No. 3208, In flight.
Milvus migrans: No. 3209, Perched on rock. No. 3210, In flight.

1998, Oct. 30   Litho.   Perf. 11½

3203		$5 multicolored	.40	.25
3204		$5 multicolored	.40	.25
a.	A775 Pair, #3203-3204		.80	.30
3205		$5 multicolored	.40	.25
3206		$5 multicolored	.40	.25
a.	A775 Pair, #3205-3206		.80	.30
3207		$10 multicolored	.80	.30
3208		$10 multicolored	.80	.30
a.	A775 Pair, #3207-3208		1.60	.60
3209		$10 multicolored	.80	.30
3210		$10 multicolored	.80	.30
a.	A775 Pair, #3209-3210		1.60	.60
	Nos. 3203-3210 (8)		4.80	2.20

Ancient Jade Carvings A776

No. 3211, 2 men mining jade on a mountain. No. 3212, Mountain with 2 pavilions, stream. $7, Figures washing an elephant. $26, Mountain, trees, men.

Perf. 11½x12, 12x11½

1998, Nov. 13   Photo.
Granite Paper

3211	A776	$5 multi	.40	.30
3212	A776	$5 multi, vert.	.40	.30
3213	A776	$7 multi	.60	.30
3214	A776	$26 multi, vert.	2.00	1.00
a.	Souvenir sheet, #3211-3214		4.50	2.00

New Year 1999 (Year of the Rabbit)
A777   A778

Wmk. 323

1998, Dec. 2   Litho.   Perf. 12½

3215	A777	$3.50 multicolored	.40	.25
b.	Perf. 14 vert.		.40	.25
b.	As "a," booklet pane of 6		2.50	
	Complete bklt., 2 #3215b + gutter		5.00	
3216	A778	$13 multicolored	1.40	.40
a.	Souv. sheet, 2 ea #3215-3216		4.00	2.50
b.	As "a," ovptd. in margin, perf. 12½x11¾		4.00	2.50

No. 3216b was issued 1/30/99 and is inscribed in sheet margin, "ALLIANCE '99 INT'L. FAIR OF PRODUCTS & TRAVEL / Jan. 30-Feb. 1, 1999" and four lines of Chinese text.

Common Expressions of Good Fortune — A779

Expressions, designs: No. 3217, "To have prosperous descendants," gourd on a vine. No. 3218, "A good marriage that soon brings sons," pair of Mandarin ducks, lotus flowers, seeds. No. 3219, "Prosperity from start to finish," egret, flowers. No. 3220, "Reunion and abundance," fish surrounded by flowers.

Perf. 11½x12

1999, Jan. 6   Litho.   Wmk. 323

3217	A779	$5 multicolored	.50	.25
3218	A779	$5 multicolored	.50	.25
3219	A779	$12 multicolored	1.00	.50
3220	A779	$12 multicolored	1.00	.50
	Nos. 3217-3220 (4)		3.00	1.50

Ancient Chinese Engravings Type of 1995 Redrawn with Chinese Inscription Reading Left to Right; No Zeros

Various pictures of birds on tree branches, bamboo and orchid.

1999, Jan. 20   Perf. 13½
Denomination in Red

3221	A712	$1 like #3018	.25	.25
3222	A712	$3.50 like #3019	.30	.25
3223	A712	$5 like #3020	.40	.25
3224	A712	$10 like #3021	.75	.35
3225	A712	$12 like #3076	1.00	.40
3226	A712	$28 like #3077	2.25	1.10
	Nos. 3221-3226 (6)		4.95	2.60

Indoor Potted Plants — A781

$5, Sinningia speciosa. $12, Saintpaulia x hybrida. $19, Anthurium scherzerianum.

Perf. 12½

1999, Feb. 10   Photo.   Unwmk.

3228	A781	$5 multicolored	.40	.25
3229	A781	$12 multicolored	.90	.40
3230	A781	$19 multicolored	1.60	.80
	Nos. 3228-3230 (3)		2.90	1.45

Ancient Chinese Painting, "Joy in Peacetime" A782

No. 3231, Woman holding child, boy with small elephant. No. 3232, Boy carrying lantern, crane on leash, people under tree. $7, Family, children playing with toy animals on wheels. $26, Women in front of steps, children playing with toys, boy on edge of balcony.

1999, Mar. 2   Photo.   Perf. 12
Granite Paper

3231	A782	$5 multicolored	.40	.25
3232	A782	$5 multicolored	.40	.25
3233	A782	$7 multicolored	.55	.30
3234	A782	$26 multicolored	1.75	.80
a.	Souvenir sheet, #3231-3234		2.00	1.75
	Nos. 3231-3234 (4)		3.10	1.55

A782a   A782b

A782c

Traditional
Architecture —
A782d

Decorative features: No. 3235, Hanging cylinder with carving of woman and deer. No. 3236, Taishi screen. $10, Xuanyu (decorative element on gable). $19, Wood carving.

1999, Mar. 20   Litho.   Wmk. 323

3235	A782a	$5 multicolored	.40	.25
3236	A782b	$5 multicolored	.40	.25
3237	A782c	$10 multicolored	.75	.30
3238	A782d	$19 multicolored	1.50	.60
		Nos. 3235-3238 (4)	3.05	1.40

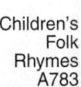
Children's
Folk
Rhymes
A783

Titles: No. 3239, "Baby Sleep." No. 3240, "Be Brave." $12, "Rock, Rock, Rock." $19, "Buggie Flies."

Perf. 11½x11

1999, Apr. 2   Litho.   Unwmk.

3239	A783	$5 multicolored	.50	.25
3240	A783	$5 multicolored	.50	.25
3241	A783	$12 multicolored	1.00	.35
3242	A783	$19 multicolored	1.40	.55
		Nos. 3239-3242 (4)	3.40	1.40

Taiwan's
Aboriginal
Culture
A784

Celebrations wearing traditional costumes: a, Dancing in row, mountain in background, Atayal Ancestor Festival. b, People wearing hip bells, Saisiat Festival of the Dwarfs. c, Standing arm in arm in circle, Bunun eight-part contrapuntal vocals. d, Row of people standing inside building, Tsou Victory Festival. e, Group outside before large display board, Rukai Harvest Festival. f, Holding bamboo poles in air, Paiwan "Maleveq" Bamboo Festival. g, Men walking while holding millet leaves in air, Puyuma Harvest Ceremony. h, Women dancing in row, tree in background, Ami Harvest Ceremony. i, Holding boat in air, Yami Boat Ceremony.

Block of 9

1999, Apr. 22   Perf. 13

3243	A784	$5 #a.-i. + label	6.00	5.50

No. 3243 was issued in sheets of 2 blocks + 2 labels. The labels contain the upper and lower halves of Taiwan. The lower block of 9 is in reverse order.

Intl. Council
of Nurses,
Cent.
A785

1999, May 12   Litho.   Perf. 11½

3244	A785	$5 shown	.50	.25
3245	A785	$17 Nurse, world map	1.40	.50

Chinese Classical
Opera — A786

Legends of the Ming Dynasty: No. 3246, Fan Li watching Hsi-shih wash yarn, "Wuan Sha Chi." No. 3247, Tsai Pochieh, Niu looking at moon, Chao Waniang with pipa (stringed instrument) on her back, "The Story of a Pipa." $12, Hung Funu surprising Li Ching, "The Story of Hung Fu." $15, Jueilan setting up incense table, "Paiyueh Pavilion."

1999, May 27   Perf. 13

3246	A786	$5 multicolored	.45	.25
3247	A786	$6 multicolored	.50	.25
3248	A786	$12 multicolored	1.10	.35
3249	A786	$15 multicolored	1.40	.45
a.		Souvenir sheet, #3246-3249	3.50	1.75
b.		As "a," imperf., with added inscription	3.50	1.75
		Nos. 3246-3249 (4)	3.45	1.30

No. 3249b was issued 7/23 and is inscribed in sheet margin with exhibition emblem, two lines of Chinese text and "TAIPEI INTERNATIONAL STAMP EXHIBITION 1999 (INVITATIONAL)."

New
Taiwan
Dollar, 50th
Anniv.
A787

1999, June 15   Perf. 11½

3250	A787	$5 Coins	.50	.25
3251	A787	$25 Currency	2.00	.75

Carp Type of 1997 Redrawn With Denominations at Right

1999, July 1   Engr.   Perf. 13½x12½

3252	A745	$50 green	4.00	3.00
3253	A745	$100 brown	9.00	4.00

Ancient Chinese Engravings Type of 1995 Redrawn with Chinese Inscription Reading Left to Right

Perf. 13½

1999, July 15   Litho.   Unwmk.

Denomination in Red

3254	A712	50c like #3044	.25	.25
3255	A712	$6 like #3045	.50	.25
3256	A712	$15 like #3046	1.75	.75
		Nos. 3254-3256 (3)	2.50	1.25

Father's
Day
A788

Designs: $5, Children with large present, silhouette of their father. $25, Father teaching son how to ride bicycle, girl.

1999, Aug. 8   Perf. 11½

3257	A788	$5 multicolored	.50	.30
3258	A788	$25 multicolored	2.00	1.25

Chinese
Gourmet
Food
A789

Dish, region: a, Peony lobster, Taiwan. b, "Buddha Jumps the Wall" steamed seafood (with blue & white teapot, bowl), Fukien. c, Hors d'oeuvres shaped as star, Canton. d, "Dongpo Pork" (on yellow plate, bowl), Kiangsu and Chekiang. e, "Stewed Fish Jaws" (surrounded by strawberries, pineapple), Shanghai. f, "Beggar's Chicken" (with napkin), Hunan. g, "Carp Jumping over Dragon's

Gate," Szechwan. h, "Peking Duck" (in footed dish), Beijing.

1999, Aug 20   Litho.   Unwmk.

3259	A789	$5 Block of 8, #a.-h.	3.25	1.60

Outdoor
Activities — A790

1999, Sept. 9   Perf. 11¼x11½

3260	A790	$5 Diving	.40	.30
3261	A790	$6 Rafting	.50	.40
3262	A790	$10 Surfing	.90	.50
3263	A790	$25 Windsurfing	2.25	.50
		Nos. 3260-3263 (4)	4.05	1.70

Taiwanese
Opera
A791

$5, Stage, audience. $6, Dressing room. $10, Actress, tents. $25, Actress as clown.

1999, Oct. 15   Litho.   Perf. 11½x11¼

3264	A791	$5 multicolored	.40	.30
3265	A791	$6 multicolored	.50	.40
3266	A791	$10 multicolored	.90	.50
3267	A791	$25 multicolored	2.25	.80
		Nos. 3264-3267 (4)	4.05	2.00

Illustrations
from Ching
Dynasty
Bird Manual
A792

No. 3268, Yellow-headed parrot. No. 3269, Blue-winged parrotlet (4 characters at LL). $12, African gray parrot (5 characters at UL). $25, King parrot (5 characters at UL).

1999, Nov. 11   Litho.   Perf. 11½

3268	A792	$5 multicolored	.50	.30
3269	A792	$5 multicolored	.50	.30
3270	A792	$12 multicolored	1.25	.50
3271	A792	$25 multicolored	2.40	1.10
		Nos. 3268-3271 (4)	4.65	2.20

Compare with No. 3152.
See Nos. 3316-3319, 3379-3381, 3510-3512.

New Year 2000 (Year of the Dragon)
A793   A794

1999, Dec. 1   Litho.   Perf. 12½

3272	A793	$3.50 multicolored	.30	.25
a.		Perf. 13¼ vert.	.30	.25
b.		As "a," booklet pane of 6	1.60	
		Complete booklet, 2 #3272b + gutter	3.50	
3273	A794	$13 multicolored	1.00	.40
a.		Souv. sheet, 2 ea #3272-3273	2.50	1.50

Millennium
A795

No. 3274, ROCSAT-1. No. 3275, Deer. $12, Train. $15, Dove, St. Peter's Basilica.

1999, Dec. 31   Litho.   Perf. 11½

3274	A795	$5 multicolored	.50	.30
3275	A795	$5 multicolored	.50	.30
3276	A795	$12 multicolored	1.10	.50
3277	A795	$15 multicolored	1.40	.70
a.		Souvenir sheet of 4, #3274-3277, perf. 12	3.50	1.75
b.		Souvenir sheet of 4, #3274-3277, imperf.	3.50	1.80

Taipei 2000 Stamp Exhibition (No. 3277b). No. 3277b has simulated perforations.

Calligraphy
Tools
A796

Designs: No. 3278, "Colored Cloud Dragon" writing brushes of Ming Emperor Chia-Ching. No. 3279, "Imperial Dragon Fragrance" ink stick of Ming Emperor Lung-Ching, vert. $7, "Clear Heart House" calligraphic work by Tsai Hsiang, Sung Dynasty, vert. $26, Celadon toad inkstone, Sung Dynasty.

2000, Jan. 12   Photo.   Perf. 11¾
Granite Paper

3278	A796	$5 multicolored	.40	.30
3279	A796	$5 multicolored	.50	.30
3280	A796	$7 multicolored	.65	.40
3281	A796	$26 multicolored	2.40	1.00
		Nos. 3278-3281 (4)	3.95	2.00

Opening of
Second
Southern
Freeway
A797

Designs: $5, $25, Kaoping River bridge. $12, Interchange.

2000, Feb. 2   Litho.   Perf. 13x13¼

3282	A797	$5 multi	.60	.30
3283	A797	$12 multi	1.20	.50

Souvenir Sheet
Perf. 12

3284	A797	$25 multi	2.50	1.25

No. 3284 contains one 80x30mm stamp.

Seasons
A798

Spring — No. 3285: a, Buds on tree. b, Farmer plowing. c, Cranes. d, Farmers planting. e, Basket of offerings to dead ancestors. f, Farmer's clothing.
Summer — No. 3286: a, Rice seedlings. b, Water wheel. c, Ripened rice. d, Cicada on tree. e, Palm leaf fan. f, Watermelons.
Autumn — No. 3287: a, Farmers in field. b, Granary. c, Dew on grass. d, Reddened maple leaves. e, Leafless tree. f, Hoarfrost on leaves.
Winter — No. 3288: a, Jar on table. b, Snow-covered pine trees. c, Snow-covered mountains. d, Bowl of rice balls. e, Snow-covered plum blossoms. f, House and village.

2000, Feb. 3   Perf. 11¾

3285		Strip of 6	3.00	2.25
a.-f.	A798	$5 multicolored	.40	.25
3286		Strip of 6	3.00	2.25
a.-f.	A798	$5 multicolored	.40	.25
3287		Strip of 6	3.00	2.25
a.-f.	A798	$5 multicolored	.40	.25
3288		Strip of 6	3.00	2.25
a.-f.	A798	$5 multicolored	.40	.25
		Nos. 3285-3288 (4)	12.00	9.00

Issued: No. 3285, 2/3; No. 3286, 5/5; No. 3287, 8/4; No. 3288, 11/3.

Soochow University, Cent. A799

Designs: $5 School gate. $25, Justice statue at Law School.

2000, Mar. 16   **Perf. 13x13¼**
3289	A799	$5 multi	.50	.30
3290	A799	$25 multi	2.40	1.25

Novel "The Romance of the Three Kingdoms" A800

No. 3291, Gathering of Liu Bei, Guan Yu and Chang Fei. No. 3292, Guan Yu reading. $5, Three visits to the thatched cottage. $20, Filling boats with straw for making arrows.

2000, Apr. 12   **Litho.**   **Perf. 11½**
3291	A800	$3.50 multi	.60	.30
3292	A800	$3.50 multi	.60	.30
3293	A800	$5 multi	.80	.40
3294	A800	$20 multi	1.75	.70
a.		Souv. sheet, #3291-3294, perf. 12	3.75	3.25
		Nos. 3291-3294 (4)	3.75	1.70

Inauguration of New President and Vice-president — A801

a, Pres. Chen Shui-bian, Vice-pres. Lu Hsiu-lien. b, Presidential Office Building.

2000, May 20   **Litho.**   **Perf. 11¾**
3295	A801	$5 Pair, #a-b	.75	.30
c.		Souvenir sheet, 2 #3295	2.50	1.00

Tropic of Cancer Monuments A802

2000, June 21   **Perf. 13**
3296	A802	$5 Hsialiao	.40	.30
3297	A802	$12 Wuho	1.25	.60
3298	A802	$25 Chingpu	2.25	1.10
		Nos. 3296-3298 (3)	3.90	2.00

Ancient Chinese Engravings Type of 1995 Redrawn with Chinese Inscription Reading Left to Right

2000, July 5   **Litho.**   **Perf. 13½**
Denomination in Red
3299	A712	$32 like #3046	2.75	1.75
3300	A712	$34 like #3078	3.25	1.75

Sacred Trees — A803

Designs: $5, Taiwan Giant, Miaoli County. $39, Sleeping Moon, Chiayi County.

2000, July 20   **Litho.**   **Perf. 11¼x11½**
3301	A803	$5 multi	.40	.30
3302	A803	$39 multi	1.50	1.50

No. 2499 Surcharged in Red
2000, Aug. 24   **Litho.**   **Perf. 13½**
3303	A535a	$3.50 on $7.50 multi	.75	.30

Poisonous Plants — A804

Designs: No. 3304, $5, Lycoris radiata. No. 3305, $5, Cerbera manghas. $12, Abrus precatorius. $20, Nerium indicum.

2000, Sept. 8   **Litho.**   **Perf. 13**
3304-3307	A804	Set of 4	4.25	2.00

Sept. 21, 1999 Earthquake, 1st Anniv. — A805

Designs: $5, Map, seismograph reading. $12, Rescue workers. $25, Earthquake preparedness.

2000, Sept. 21   **Perf. 11¼x11½**
3308-3310	A805	Set of 3	4.25	2.00

Dragonflies A806

Designs: Nos. 3311, 3315a, $5, Lamelligomphus formosanus. Nos. 3312, 3315b, $5, Anotogaster sieboldii, vert. Nos. 3313, 3315c, $12, Trithemis festiva, vert. Nos. 3314, 3315d, $12, Neurothemis ramburii.

2000, Oct. 11   **Perf. 13**
3311-3314	A806	Set of 4	3.50	1.50

Souvenir Sheet
Stamps Without White Margins
Perf. 11¾
3315	A806	Sheet of 4, #a-d	3.50	1.50

Bird Manual Type of 1999

No. 3316, $5, Corn bunting (2 characters at UR). No. 3317, $5, Brambling (3 characters at UL). $12, Bali mynah (3 characters at LR). $25, Indian grackle (2 characters at LR).

2000, Oct. 26   **Perf. 11½**
3316-3319	A792	Set of 4	4.50	2.00

Compare No. 3317 with No. 3378.

Tamkang University, 50th Anniv. A807

$5, Palace Lamp Boulevard, classroom buildings. $25, Maritime Museum, Scroll Plaza.

2000, Nov. 8   **Perf. 13**
3320-3321	A807	Set of 2	3.00	1.50

A808

New Year 2001 (Year of the Snake) — A809

2000, Dec. 1   **Perf. 12½**
3322	A808	$3.50 multi	.50	.25
a.		Perf. 13¼ vert.	.50	.25
b.		As "a," booklet pane of 6	3.00	
		Booklet, 2 #3322b + gutter	6.00	
3323	A809	$13 multi	1.25	.40
a.		Souv. sheet, 2 ea #3322-3323	3.50	1.50
b.		As "a," with added marginal inscription in red	3.50	1.50

Added marginal inscription of No. 3323b reads in Chinese "Turn-of-the-Century Intl. Stamp Exhibition, Kaohsiung / Dec. 25, 2000-Jan. 3, 2001" in red.
Issued: No. 3323b, 12/25/00.

Establishment of Trade Links with People's Republic of China — A810

Ships in Taiwan Strait and: $9, Building. $25, Obelisk.

2001, Jan. 1   **Litho.**   **Perf. 11½**
3324-3325	A810	Set of 2	3.00	2.50

A811

Common Chinese expressions of good fortune: No. 3326, $5, "Marital bliss," twin lotus blossoms on one stalk (pink background). No. 3327, $5, "Success in one's career," longan, lichee and walnuts (light green background). No. 3328, $12, "Producing many offspring," split pomegranates (buff background). No. 3329, $12, "Growing old together with wealth and high position," bulbuls flying around peonies (light orange background).

2001, Jan. 2   **Perf. 11¾x12¼**
3326-3329	A811	Set of 4	3.00	2.50

See Nos. 3404-3407.

Zodiac Signs A812

Designs: No. 3330, $5, Aquarius. No. 3331, $12, Gemini. No. 3332, $25, Libra. No. 3333, $5, Capricorn. No. 3334, $12, Taurus. No. 3335, $25, Virgo. No. 3336, $5, Aries. No. 3337, $12, Leo. No. 3338, $25, Sagittarius. No. 3339, $5, Pisces. No. 3340, $12, Cancer. No. 3341, $25, Scorpio.

2001   **Perf. 12**
3330-3341	A812	Set of 12	18.00	12.00

Values are for stamps with surrounding selvage.
Issued: Nos. 3330-3332, 2/14. Nos. 3333-3335, 4/20. Nos. 3336-3338, 7/25. Nos. 3339-3341, 11/8.

Fruit — A813

$1, Plums. $3.50, Tangerines. $5, Apples. $7, Pears. $12, Guavas. $20, Longans. $25, Cantaloupes. $40, Grapefruit.

2001-05   **Litho.**   **Perf. 12½x13¼**
3342	A813	$1 multi	.25	.25
3343	A813	$3.50 multi	.35	.25
a.		"Republic of China" 12½mm long ('05)	.35	.25
3344	A813	$5 multi	.45	.25
3345	A813	$7 multi	.65	.25
3346	A813	$12 multi	1.05	.65
3347	A813	$20 multi	1.60	1.00
a.		"Republic of China" 12½mm long ('05)	1.60	.85
3348	A813	$25 multi	2.00	1.05
3349	A813	$40 multi	3.75	3.25
		Nos. 3342-3349 (8)	10.10	6.95

Issued: $5, $7, $12, $25, 2/23. $1, $3.50, $20, $40, 8/23. No. 3343a, 3347a, 5/16/05.
"Republic of China" on Nos. 3343 and 3347 is 12mm long and is in taller letters.
See Nos. 3408-3411, 3472-3475.

Mount Jade A814

Designs: No. 3350, $5, Main peak (shown). No. 3351, $5, Western peak, flowers in foreground. $12, Northern peak. $25, Eastern peak.

2001, Mar. 8   **Litho.**   **Perf. 11½x11¼**
3350-3353	A814	Set of 4	4.50	3.75

Compare Type A814 with Types A834-A837, A855-A858.

Children's Rhymes A815

Designs: No. 3354, $5, Little Ball (blue background). No. 3355, $5, Point to the Water Vat (pink background). $12, Pangolin. $25, Shake and Stamp.

2001, Apr. 4
3354-3357	A815	Set of 4	4.50	3.75

Buddhist Statues — A816

Designs: $5, Sakyamuni Buddha, Northern Wei Dynasty. $9, Seated Buddha, Tang Dynasty. $12, Mahavairocana Buddha, Sung Dynasty.

2001, May 11   **Perf. 11¼x11½**
3358-3360	A816	Set of 3	2.50	2.00
3360a		Souvenir sheet, #3358-3360, perf. 12	2.50	2.50

Agricultural Implements — A817

Designs: $5, Rice wind drum. $7, Plow. $10, Bamboo rice baskets. $25, Coir rainwear.

2001, May 25   **Perf. 11½x11¼**
3361-3364 A817   Set of 4   4.50 3.75

Dr. George Leslie Mackay (1844-1901) A818

2001, June 1   **Perf. 11¼x11½**
3365 A818 $25 multi   2.25 2.00

2001 Kiwanis International Convention A819

Designs: $5, Girl, Earth. $25, Mother and child, map.

2001, June 22   **Perf. 13**
3366-3367 A819   Set of 2   2.50 2.00

Kites — A820

No. 3368: a, Dragon. b, Phoenix. c, Tiger. d, Fish.

2001, July 13   **Perf. 11¼x11½**
3368   Horiz. strip of 4   2.00 1.60
a.-d. A820 $5 Any single   .45 .80

Carp Encircled by Dragons Type of 1997 With Denominations at Right
2001, Aug. 3   **Engr.**   **Perf. 13**
Size: 25x33mm
3369 A745 $300 red vio & dk bl   20.00 10.00
3370 A745 $500 red & brown   45.00 20.00

Rapid Transit A821

Designs: $5, Train, transit system emblem. $12, Passengers in station, fare card. $25, Chientan Station.

2001, Aug. 14   **Litho.**   **Perf. 13**
3371-3372 A821   Set of 2   1.75 1.00
Souvenir Sheet
Perf. 11¾
3373 A821 $25 multi   2.75 1.50
No. 3373 contains one 85x42mm stamp.

Fables — A822

Designs: No. 3374, $5, Now Three, Now Four (man and monkeys). No. 3375, $5, Selling the All-Penetrating Sword and Unyielding Shield (men watching man with sword and shield). $12, Waiting by the Tree for the Rabbit. $25, An Old Fool Moves Mountains.

2001, Sept. 6   **Litho.**   **Perf. 11½**
3374-3377 A822   Set of 4   3.75 3.00

Bird Manual Type of 1999 and

Siberian Rubythroat A823

Designs: No. 3379, Waxwing (3 characters at UR). $12, White-rumped munia (2 characters at R). $25, Great barbet (3 characters at LL).

2001, Sept. 28   **Litho.**   **Perf. 11½**
3378 A823 $5 shown   .60 .40
3379 A792 $5 multi   .60 .40
3380 A792 $12 multi   1.10 .60
3381 A792 $25 multi   2.00 1.60
Nos. 3378-3381 (4)   4.30 3.00

Republic of China, 90th Anniv. A824

Designs: No. 3382, $5, Terminal, Chiang Kai-shek Intl. Airport. No. 3383, $5, Electronic products made in Republic of China. $12, Dancers at National Theater. $15, Dolphins.

2001, Oct. 9   **Litho.**   **Perf. 11½**
3382-3385 A824   Set of 4   3.25 2.50

2001 National Games — A825

Athletes and: $5, Torch. $25, Map.

2001, Oct. 18   **Litho.**   **Perf. 12½**
3386-3387 A825   Set of 2   2.50 2.00

34th Baseball World Cup A826

Emblem, map and: No. 3388, $5, Pitcher. No. 3389, $5, Batter. $12, Catcher. $20, Runner sliding.

2001, Oct. 30   **Perf. 11½**
3388-3391 A826   Set of 4   3.75 3.00
3391a   Souvenir sheet, #3388-3391, perf. 12   3.75 3.00

Puppet Theater A827

Designs: $5, Mozhaonu, from "Thunder Storm." $6, Taiyangnu, from "Rising Winds, Surging Clouds." $10, Kuangdao, from "Thunder Crazy Sword." $25, Chin Chia-chien, from "Thunder Golden Light."

2001, Nov. 16   **Litho.**   **Perf. 11½**
3392-3395 A827   Set of 4   4.50 3.00

National Defense Medical Center, Cent. A828

Designs: $5, Medical students, old medical school building. $25, Doctors, new medical school building.

2001, Nov. 23   **Perf. 13**
3396-3397 A828   Set of 2   2.50 2.00

New Year 2002 (Year of the Horse) — A829

Horse and: $3.50, Clouds. $13, Flowers.

2001, Dec. 3   **Litho.**   **Perf. 12½**
3398 A829 $3.50 multi   .50 .30
a.   Perf. 13¾ vert.   .50 .30
b.   Booklet pane, 12 #3398a   4.50
   Booklet, #3398b   5.00
3399 A829 $13 multi   1.50 1.00
a.   Souvenir sheet, 2 each #3398-3399   4.00 2.50

Paul Cardinal Yu Pin (1901-78) — A830

2001, Dec. 7   **Perf. 11½**
3400 A830 $25 multi   2.25 .90
a.   Souvenir sheet of 1, perf. 12   2.25 1.60

Greetings A831

No. 3401: a, Pink chrysanthemums, red background. b, White lilies, red background. c, Pink flowers, yellow background. d, Red orange flowers, yellow background. e, Pink flowers, green background. f, Coral roses, blue green background. g, Star and wreath, blue background. h, Poinsettias, blue background. i, Red violet flowers, purple background. j, Yellow flowers, purple background.

2001, Dec. 12   **Perf. 12½**
3401   Sheet of 10 + 10 labels   4.50 3.00
a.-j. A831 $5 Any single   .45 .30

Labels could be personalized for an additional fee.
Sheets with blank (unprinted) labels were not released.

Fu Hsing Kang College, 50th Anniv. A832

Designs: $5, Students with flags. $25, Tower, administration building, statue of students.

2002, Jan. 4   **Perf. 11½**
3402-3403 A832   Set of 2   2.50 2.00

Expressions of Good Fortune Type of 2001

Designs: No. 3404, $5, "Continuously produce good offspring," lotus and sweet osmanthus flowers in a vase (gradiated pink background). No. 3405, $5, "A high, moral gentleman," orchid and sweet osmanthus in containers (gradiated green background). No. 3406, $12, "A hall full of the rich and famous," flowering crabapple in a vase (gradiated orange background). No. 3407, $12, "Safe and peaceful in all seasons," roses in vase (gradiated purple background).

2002, Jan. 16   **Perf. 11¾x12¼**
3404-3407 A811   Set of 4   3.50 3.00

Fruit Type of 2001

2002-05   **Litho.**   **Perf. 12½x13¼**
3408 A813 $6 Avocados   .45 .25
3409 A813 $10 Lichees   .90 .35
a.   "Republic of China" 12½mm long ('05)   .75 .35
3410 A813 $17 Dates   1.50 .60
a.   "Republic of China" 12½mm long ('05)   1.25 .65
3411 A813 $32 Passion fruit   2.75 1.05
a.   "Republic of China" 12½mm long ('05)   2.50 1.25
Nos. 3408-3411 (4)   5.60 2.25

Issued: Nos. 3408-3411, 2/8/02; 3409a, 3410a, 3411a, 5/16/05.
"Republic of China" on Nos. 3409-3411 is 12mm long and is in taller letters.

Folk Traditions A833

Designs: No. 3412, $5, Release of sky lanterns (orange background). No. 3413, $5, Fireworks display (blue background). $10, Matsu procession (lilac background). $20, Dragon boat race (pink background).

2002, Feb. 26   **Litho.**   **Perf. 12½**
3412-3415 A833   Set of 4   4.00 3.00
See Nos. 3440-3443.

Winter, Mount Hsueh A834

North Ridge, Mount Hsueh A835

Autumn, Mount Hsueh A836

Glacial Cirques, Mount Hsueh A837

2002, Mar. 20   *Perf. 11½*

3416	A834	$5 multi	.40 .40
3417	A835	$5 multi	.40 .40
3418	A836	$12 multi	1.00 .90
3419	A837	$25 multi	2.00 1.75
		Nos. 3416-3419 (4)	3.80 3.45

Compare with Types A814, A855-A858.

Novel "The Romance of the Three Kingdoms" — A838

Designs: No. 3420, $3.50, Three heroes battling Lu Bu (warriors on horseback). No. 3421, $3.50, To the rescue of his master's family (one warrior on horseback). $5, Scraping away the poison from the bone (medicinal bleeding). $20, Playing a lute to make the enemy retreat (horseman and gate).

2002, Apr. 4

3420-3423	A838	Set of 4	5.00 2.10
a.		Souvenir sheet, #3420-3423, perf. 12	5.00 5.00

Endangered Bird Thalasseus Bernsteini — A839

No. 3424: a, Two birds in flight. b, Bird in flight heading left. c, Bird landing on rock carrying fish. d, Bird on rock with beak open. e, Adult feeding chick. f, Bird diving. g, Bird landing with bill open. h, Bird standing on rock, looking left. i, Adult with chick. j, Adult on nest. $25, Bird in flight.

2002, May 15   **Litho.**   *Perf. 11½*

3424	A839	$5 Sheet of 10, #a-j	5.00 4.00

Souvenir Sheet
Perf. 12

3425	A839	$25 multi	3.00 2.00

No. 3424 contains ten 40x30mm stamps.

Dragon & Carp Type of 1997 Redrawn With Denomination at Right

2002, June 5   **Engr.**   *Perf. 13¼x12½*

3426	A745	$80 brown	6.00 3.50

Porcelain Bowls — A840

Ching Dynasty bowls depicting: No. 3427, $5, Peacock (salmon background). No. 3428, $5, Lotus flowers (blue green background). $7, Peonies. $32, Sparrows and bamboo.

2002, June 21   **Litho.**   *Perf. 11½*

3427-3430	A840	Set of 4	4.25 3.75

Flowers — A841

Designs: $5, Matthiola incana. $12, Gardenia jasminoides. $25, Michelia figo.

2002, July 5   *Perf. 13*

3431-3433	A841	Set of 3	3.25 1.50

Cetaceans — A842

Designs: No. 3434, $5, Megaptera novaeangliae, whaling ship. No. 3435, $5, Tursiops truncatus, people on shore attracting cetacean. $10, Orcinus orca, boat following cetaceans. $25, Grampus griseus, people rescuing beached dolphin.

2002, July 25   **Litho.**   *Perf. 11½x11¼*

3434-3437	A842	Set of 4	4.50 1.75
a.		Souvenir sheet, #3434-3437, perf. 12	4.50 3.25

Intl. Paralympic Committee World Table Tennis Championships — A843

Player: No. 3438, $5, On crutches. No. 3439, $5, In wheelchair.

2002, Aug. 13   *Perf. 11½x11¼*

3438-3439	A843	Set of 2	1.25 .80

Folk Traditions Type of 2002

Designs: No. 3440, $5, Launching of water lanterns (green background). No. 3441, $5, Snatching flags for good luck (yellow background). $10, Worship of the just (blue background). $20, Burning the Prince's boat (red orange background).

2002, Aug. 22   *Perf. 12½*

3440-3443	A833	Set of 4	3.25 2.75

Republic of China – Vatican City Diplomatic Relations, 60th Anniv. — A844

Designs: $5, Chinese and Vatican flags, Chinese Presidential building, St. Peter's Basilica. $17, Flags, doves, Celso Cardinal Costantini.

2002, Sept. 20   *Perf. 11½x11¼*

3444-3445	A844	Set of 2	2.00 1.25

Bird Manual Type of 1999 and

White-rumped Munia — A845

Designs: No. 3446, $5, Vernal hanging parrot (3 characters at LL). $12, White-headed greenfinch (4 characters at LL). $25, Yunnan greenfinch (2 characters at UL).

2002, Oct. 9

3446	A792	$5 multi	.50 .40
3447	A845	$5 multi	.50 .40
3448	A792	$12 multi	.90 .80
3449	A792	$25 multi	1.90 1.75
		Nos. 3446-3449 (4)	3.80 3.35

Taiwanese Opera — A846

Designs: $5, Liang Shan-po and Chu Ying-tai. $6, Hsueh Ting-shan and Fan Li-hua. $10,

---

Hsueh Ping-kuei and Wang Pao-chuan. $25, The Living Buddha Chikung.

2002, Oct. 25

3450-3453	A846	Set of 4	3.50 1.50

Koalas — A847

Designs: No. 3454, $5, Adult with cub. No. 3455, $5, Adult on branch. $9, Adult with head on branch. $21, Adult with cub, diff.

2002, Nov. 15   *Perf. 11¼x11½*

3454-3457	A847	Set of 4	3.50 1.60
a.		Souvenir sheet, #3454-3457, perf. 12	3.50 2.75

Knots — A848

Nos. 3458-3459 — Various knots (Denomination, denomination color and background color): a, UL, orange, light orange. b, UL, purple, yellow. c, UL, green, light green. d, UL, yellow, light blue. e, UL, blue, pink. f, UR, orange, light orange. g, UR, red violet, yellow. h, UR, blue, light green. i, UR, yellow, light blue. j, UR, red violet, pink.

No. 3460 (yellow denominations, olive green background): a, Like #3458a. b, Like #3458b. c, Like #3458c, d, #3458d. e, Like #3458e. f, Like #3458f. g, Like #3458g. h, Like #3458h. i, Like #3458i. j, Like #3458j.

2002, Nov. 22   **Litho.**   *Perf. 12½*

3458		Block of 10	2.25 1.20
a.-j.	A848	$3.50 Any single	.25 .25
k.		Sheet of 10 #3458f + 10 attached labels	.25 .25
l.		Sheet of 10 #3458g + 10 attached labels	12.00 12.00
m.		Sheet of 10 #3458h + 10 attached labels	12.00 12.00
n.		Sheet of 10 #3458i + 10 attached labels	12.00 12.00
o.		Sheet of 10 #3458j + 10 attached labels	12.00 12.00
p.		Sheet , #3458a-3458j + 10 attached labels	12.00 12.00
q.		Sheet, #3458a, 3458b, 3458d, 3458f, 3458g, 3458i + 6 attached labels ('04)	12.00 12.00
3459		Block of 10	3.50 1.75
a.-j.	A848	$5 Any single	.35 .25
k.		Sheet of 10 #3459a + 10 attached labels	12.50 12.50
l.		Sheet of 10 #3459b + 10 attached labels	12.50 12.50
m.		Sheet of 10 #3459c + 10 attached labels	12.50 12.50
n.		Sheet of 10 #3459d + 10 attached labels	12.50 12.50
o.		Sheet of 10 #3459e + 10 attached labels	12.50 12.50
p.		Sheet of 10 #3459f + 10 attached labels	12.50 12.50
q.		Sheet of 10 #3459g + 10 attached labels	12.50 12.50
r.		Sheet of 10 #3459h + 10 attached labels	12.50 12.50
s.		Sheet of 10 #3459i + 10 attached labels	12.50 12.50
t.		Sheet of 10 #3459j + 10 attached labels	12.50 12.50
3460		Block of 10	17.50 8.50
a.-j.	A848	$25 Any single	1.75 .80
k.		Sheet of 10 #3460a + 10 attached labels	24.00 24.00
l.		Sheet of 10 #3460b + 10 attached labels	24.00 24.00
m.		Sheet of 10 #3460c + 10 attached labels	24.00 24.00
n.		Sheet of 10 #3460d + 10 attached labels	24.00 24.00
o.		Sheet of 10 #3460e + 10 attached labels	24.00 24.00
p.		Sheet, #3460a-3460j + 10 attached labels	24.00 24.00
		Nos. 3458-3460 (3)	23.25 11.45

Nos. 3458k-3458p sold for $185 each; Nos. 3459k-3459u for $200 each; Nos. 3460k-3460p for $400 each. Labels, which were personalized, were separated from stamps on Nos. 3458k-3458p, 3459k-3459u, 3460k-3460p by vertical rows of simulated perforations.

No. 3458q sold for $141 and has labels, which could be personalized, that are separated from the stamps by simulated perforations. Issued 9/30/04.

New Year 2003 (Year of the Ram) — A849

Designs: $3.50, Yellow ram. $13, Red ram.

2002, Dec. 2   **Litho.**   *Perf. 12¼*

3461	A849	$3.50 multi	.40 .25
a.		Perf. 12¼ Vert.	.40 .25
b.		As "a," booklet pane of 6	2.25
		Booklet, 2 #3461b	5.25
3462	A849	$13 multi	1.10 .40
a.		Souvenir sheet, 2 each #3461-3462	3.00 1.50
b.		As "a," with Chinese text in red in L & R sheet margins	3.00 1.50

Issued: No. 3462b, 1/1/03. Chinese text in left and right sheet margins on No. 3462b commemorates the establishment of Chunghwa Post Co., Ltd.

Street Scene on a Summer Day, by Chen Cheng-po — A850

Girl in the White Dress, by Li Mei-shu — A851

Courtyard with Banana Trees, by Liao Chi-chun — A852

Sunrise, by Kuo Po-chuan — A853

Perf. 11½x11¼, 11¼x11½

2002, Dec. 6

3463	A850	$5 multi	.40 .25
3464	A851	$5 multi	.40 .25
3465	A852	$12 multi	.75 .30
3466	A853	$20 multi	1.60 .55
		Nos. 3463-3466 (4)	3.15 1.35

Admission to World Trade Organization, 1st Anniv. — A854

2003, Jan. 1   **Litho.**   *Perf. 11½x11¼*

3467	A854	$17 multi	2.75 1.10

Spring on Wuyen Peak — A855

Glacial Cirques, Mt. Nanhu
A856

Mt. Nanhu
A857

Snow on Mt. Chungyang Chien
A858

2003, Jan. 23

3468	A855	$5 multi	.40	.25
3469	A856	$5 multi	.40	.25
3470	A857	$12 multi	.90	.35
3471	A858	$25 multi	1.60	.70
	Nos. 3468-3471 (4)		3.30	1.55

Compare with Types A814, A834-A837.

Fruit Type of 2001

2003-05		**Litho.**	**Perf. 12½x13¼**	
3472	A813	$9 Rose apples	.60	.25
a.	"Republic of China" 12½mm long ('05)		.60	.30
3473	A813	$13 Kumquats	.90	.40
3474	A813	$15 Lemons	1.10	.45
a.	"Republic of China" 12½mm long ('05)		.95	.50
3475	A813	$34 Coconuts	2.00	1.00

Issued: Nos. 3472-3475, 2/14/03; 3472a, 3474a, 5/16/05.

"Republic of China" on Nos. 3472 and 3474 is 12mm long and is in taller letters.

Love — A859

Hearts and: No. 3476, $5, Woman tending to man in wheelchair. No. 3477, $5, Family. $10, Landscape. $25, Girl and dogs.

2003, Mar. 20   **Perf. 11¼x11½**
3476-3479 A859   Set of 4   3.50   2.50

Puppet Theater
A860

Designs: No. 3480, $5, *Journey to the West* performed on outdoor stage. No. 3481, $5, Puppets on television. $10, *Mysteries of the Wolf Castle* performed at the National Opera House. $25, Screening of movie, *Legend of the Sacred Stone*.

2003, Apr. 3   **Perf. 11½x11¼**
3480-3483 A860   Set of 4   3.50   2.50

Merops Philippinus
A861

Designs: Nos. 3484, 3488a, $5, Foraging. Nos. 3485, 3488b, $5, Roosting. Nos. 3486,

3488c, $10, Bathing. Nos. 3487, 3488d, $20, Feeding chick.

2003, May 8   **Perf. 12½**
With White Frame
3484-3487 A861   Set of 4   3.00   2.25
Souvenir Sheet
Without White Frame
3488 A861   Sheet of 4, #a-d   3.00   2.25

No. 3488 contains four 33x25mm stamps.

Furniture — A862

Designs: No. 3489, $5, Wash basin stand. No. 3490, $5, Canopy bed. $12, Taishi chair. $20, Pahsien table.

2003, May 22   **Perf. 11¼x11½**
3489-3492 A862   Set of 4   3.25   1.50

Folktale "Eight Immortals Cross the Sea" — A863

Immortal: No. 3493, $5, Riding catfish. No. 3494, $5, On donkey. $10, Holding fan. $25, In brown robe.

2003, June 12
3493-3496 A863   Set of 4   3.50   1.50

See Nos. 3535-3538.

Moths
A864

Designs: No. 3497, $5, Antitrygodes divisaria perturbata. No. 3498, $5, Vamuna virilis. $12, Sinna extrema. $20, Thyas juno.

2003, June 26   **Perf. 11½x11¼**
3497-3500 A864   Set of 4   3.25   1.50

Dragonflies
A865

Designs: Nos. 3501, 3505a, $5, Acisoma panorpoides panorpoides. Nos. 3502, 3505b, $5, Sympetrum eroticu ardens, vert. Nos. 3503, 3505c, $10, Anax parthenope julius. Nos. 3504, 3505d, $17, Rhyothemis variegata arria, vert.

2003, July 25   **Perf. 12½**
With White Frames
3501-3504 A865   Set of 4   3.25   1.50
Souvenir Sheet
Without White Frames
Perf. 11¾
3505 A865   Sheet of 4, #a-d   3.25   1.50

Stamp size: Nos. 3505a, 3505c, 33x25mm; Nos. 3505b, 3505d, 25x33mm.

Greetings
A866

No. 3506: a, Cranes. b, Wood carving and red plate. c, Fish and coin. d, Bamboo. e, Wood carving of bird.

No. 3507: a, Vase with tasseled rope. b, Like #3506a. c, Like #3506b. d, Three brown containers. e, Like #3508. f, Dragon. g, Like #3506c. h, Like #3506d. i, Horse and rider. j, Like #3506e.

No. 3508, Vase with flowers.

2003, Aug. 9   **Perf. 12½**

3506		Horiz. strip of 5	1.25	.65
a.-e.	A866 $3.50 Any single		.25	.25
f.	Sheet of 10 #3506a+ 10 attached labels		12.00	12.00
g.	Sheet of 10 #3506b+ 10 attached labels		12.00	12.00
h.	Sheet of 10 #3506c + 10 attached labels		12.00	12.00
i.	Sheet of 10 #3506d + 10 attached labels		12.00	12.00
j.	Sheet of 10 #3506e + 10 attached labels		12.00	12.00
k.	Sheet, 2 each #3506a-3506e + 10 attached labels		12.00	12.00
3507		Block of 10	3.50	1.75
a.-j.	A866 $5 Any single		.35	.25
k.	Sheet of 10 #3507a + 10 attached labels		12.50	12.50
l.	Sheet of 10 #3507b + 10 attached labels		12.50	12.50
m.	Sheet of 10 #3507c + 10 attached labels		12.50	12.50
n.	Sheet of 10 #3507d + 10 attached labels		12.50	12.50
o.	Sheet of 10 #3507e + 10 attached labels		12.50	12.50
p.	Sheet of 10 #3507f + 10 attached labels		12.50	12.50
q.	Sheet of 10 #3507g + 10 attached labels		12.50	12.50
r.	Sheet of 10 #3507h + 10 attached labels		12.50	12.50
s.	Sheet of 10 #3507i + 10 attached labels		12.50	12.50
t.	Sheet of 10 #3507j + 10 attached labels		12.50	12.50
u.	Sheet, #3507a-3507j + 10 attached labels		12.50	12.50
v.	Sheet, #3507d, 3507e, 3507f, 3507g, 3507h, 3507j + 6 attached labels ('04)		9.00	9.00
3508	A866 $12 multi		.85	.45
a.	Sheet of 10 #3508 + 10 attached labels		17.00	17.00
	Nos. 3506-3508 (3)		5.60	2.85

Nos. 3506f-3506k sold for $185 each; Nos. 3507k-3507u for $200 each; No. 3508a for $270 each. Labels, which were personalized, were separated from stamps on Nos. 3506f-3506k, 3507k-3507u, 3508a by vertical rows of simulated perforations.

No. 3507v sold for $150 and has labels, which could be personalized, that are separated from the stamps by simulated perforations. Issued 5/30/04.

Bird Manual Type of 1999 and

White-throated Laughing Thrush — A867

Designs: No. 3510, Great mynah (2 characters at LR). $12, Yellow-legged buttonquail (3 characters at UL). $25, Crested lark (4 characters at L).

Perf. 11½x11¼				
2003, Sept. 10			**Litho.**	
3509	A867	$5 multi	.40	.25
3510	A792	$5 multi	.40	.25
3511	A792	$12 multi	.90	.35
3512	A792	$25 multi	1.75	.75
	Nos. 3509-3512 (4)		3.45	1.60

Chungshan Park, Taichung
A868

Tourist attractions: No. 3514, $5, Dongshan River Bridge, Ilan. $11, Badlands, Tianliao. $20, Sansiantai, Chenggong.

2003, Oct. 28   **Litho.**   **Perf. 11½**
3513-3516 A868   Set of 4   3.00   1.25

Chungshan Park, cent. (No. 3513).

Veterans Day, 25th Anniv.
A869

Veterans Affairs Commission insignia and: $5, Veterans building Central Cross-Island Highway. $25, Veterans, homes and hospital for veterans.

2003, Oct. 31
3517-3518 A869   Set of 2   2.00   .90

The Back Yard, by Lu Tie-jhou — A870

A Gold Mine Tower: Jioufen, by Lin Ke-gong — A871

Leisurely, by Chen Jin — A872

East Gate, by Li Ze-fan
A873

2003, Nov. 20

3519	A870	$5 multi	.40	.25
3520	A871	$5 multi	.40	.25
3521	A872	$10 multi	.75	.30
3522	A873	$20 multi	1.50	.60
	Nos. 3519-3522 (4)		3.05	1.40

New Year 2004 (Year of the Monkey) — A874

Monkey holding fruit: $3.50, With tail. $13, In hand.

2003, Dec. 1			**Perf. 12¼**	
3523-3524	A874	Set of 2	1.40	.70
3523a		Perf. 12¼ vert.	.35	.25
3524a		Sheet, 2 each #3523-3524	2.50	1.60
3523b		Booklet pane, 12 #3523a	6.50	
		Complete booklet, #3523b	7.25	

Springs
A875

Designs: No. 3525, $5, Yangmingshan Hot Springs, fumaroles (light orange background). No. 3526, $5, Suao Cold Springs, Nanfangao Bridge (light blue background). $10, Guanziling Murky Hot Spring, Shuei Huo Tong Yuan. $25, Green Island Seabed Hot Springs, Green Island Lighthouse.

2003, Dec. 14   **Perf. 13**
3525-3528 A875 Set of 4   3.50 1.50
3528a Souvenir sheet, #3525-3528   3.50 2.00

Completion of Highway 3 — A876

Designs: $5, Jhonggang Interchange. $25, Cingshuei Service Area.
$20, Cingshuei Service Area, diff.

2004, Jan. 8   **Litho.**   **Perf. 12½**
3529-3530 A876 Set of 2   2.25 .90
Souvenir Sheet
Perf. 11½x11¼
3531 A876 $20 multi   1.50 1.25
No. 3531 contains one 80x30mm stamp.

Flowers — A877

Designs: No. 3532, $5, Lilium formosanum. No. 3533, $5, Hippeastrum x hybridum. $12, Fressia x hybrida.

2004, Jan. 17   **Perf. 12¼**
3532-3534 A877 Set of 3   1.75 .70
3534a Souvenir sheet, #3532-3534, perf. 13   1.75 1.25
3534b As "a," with Taiwan Flower Expo emblem and text added in margin   1.75 1.25

Eight Immortals Cross the Sea Type of 2003

Immortal: No. 3535, $5, With crane and flute. No. 3536, $5, With lotus flower. $10, Holding stick, wearing red robe. $25, Carrying flower basket.

2004, Feb. 25   **Perf. 11¼x11½**
3535-3538 A863 Set of 4   3.50 1.50

Red Cross Society, Cent. — A878

No. 3539: a, Heart, stylized people with arms raised. b, Heart, stylized people doing Red Cross activities.

2004, Mar. 9   **Perf. 11¼x11½**
3539 A878 $5 Horiz. pair, #a-b   1.00 .50

A Young Girl From Lu Kai, by Yan Shui-long
A879

Old Street in Taipei, by Yang San-lang
A880

Happy Farmers, by Lee Shih-chiao
A881

Fish Shop, by Liu Chi-hsiang
A882

Perf. 11¼x11½, 11½x11¼
2004, Mar. 25
3540 A879 $5 multi   .40 .25
3541 A880 $5 multi   .40 .25
3542 A881 $10 multi   .80 .30
3543 A882 $20 multi   1.40 .60
   Nos. 3540-3543 (4)   3.00 1.40

Butterflies
A883

Designs: No. 3544, $5, Parantica sita niphonica. No. 3545, $5, Choaspes benjaminii formosanus. $17, Junonia almana. $20, Artipe eryx horiella.

2004, Apr. 21   **Perf. 11½x11¼**
3544-3547 A883 Set of 4   3.50 1.50

Yijhen Folk Art Performers
A884

Designs: No. 3548, $5, Eight Generals (buff background). No. 3549, $5, Song Jiang Battle Array (grayish blue background). $11, Drum Dance. $25, Stilt walkers.

2004, May 11
3548-3551 A884 Set of 4   3.50 1.50

Inauguration of Pres. Chen Shiu-bian and Vice-President Hsiu-lien Annette Lu — A885

No. 3552 — President, Vice-President and: a, Map of Taiwan, flag, crowd. b, Map of People's Republic of China and Taiwan, handshake, flowers. c, Buildings, crowd. d, Train, highway, buildings.
$12, President, Vice-President, buildings, train, highway.

2004, May 20   **Perf. 12½**
3552 Horiz. strip of 4   1.75 .70
a.-d. A885 $5 Any single   .40 .25
Souvenir Sheet
Perf. 12
3553 A885 $12 multi   1.50 1.25
No. 3553 contains one 80x30mm stamp.

Opening of Movie, *Harry Potter and the Prisoner of Azkaban* — A886

No. 3554: a, $5, Harry, messenger owl Hedwig, with letter. b, $5, Hedwig, rose background. c, $5, Harry riding Hippogriff. d, $5, Hippogriff, green background. e, $5, Harry, Monster Book of Monsters. f, $25, Crookshanks the Cat.
No. 3555: a, $5, Harry playing quidditch. b, $5, Harry playing quidditch, Dementors. c, $5, Harry and Hermoine riding Hippogriff. d, $5, Harry holding wand, Hogwarts. e, $5, Harry practicing Patronus Charm to repel Dementors. f, $25, Harry thrusting wand.

2004, June 4   **Perf. 12**
Sheets of 6, #a-f
3554-3555 A886 Set of 2   10.00 6.00

Postal administrators said that Nos. 3554-3555 would not be not sold directly to customers at foreign addresses. The sheets were made available abroad through Canada Post's philatelic agency, and also were sent to foreign standing order customers.

Old Train Stations
A887

Designs: No. 3556, $5, Keelung Station, rickshaws. No. 3557, $5, Taipei Station, automobile. $15, Hsinchu Station, ox and cart. $25, Taichung Station, wagons.

2004, June 9   **Perf. 13½x13¾**
3556-3559 A887 Set of 4   3.50 1.50
Compare Type A887 with Types A926-A929.

Iron Fort, Nangan Island
A888

Cinbi, Beigan Island
A889

Fujheng, Tungchu Island
A890

Lienyuyikeng, Tungyin Island — A891

2004, July 1   **Litho.**   **Perf. 11½x11¼**
3560 A888 $5 multi   .40 .25
3561 A889 $5 multi   .40 .25
3562 A890 $9 multi   .70 .25
3563 A891 $25 multi   1.90 .75
   Nos. 3560-3563 (4)   3.40 1.50
Matsu National Scenic Area.

Crabs
A892

Designs: No. 3564, $3.50, Uca formosensis. No. 3565, $3.50, Uca borealis. $5, Uca arcuata. $25, Uca lactea.

2004, July 21
3564-3567 A892 Set of 4   2.50 1.10

Souvenir Sheet

Listening to the Lute, Attributed to Li Sung — A893

No. 3568: a, $5, Lute player. b, $25, Scholar and woman.

2004, Aug. 6   **Perf. 12**
3568 A893 Sheet of 2, #a-b   2.50 2.50

Souvenir Sheet

Taipei 2005 Intl. Stamp
Exhibition — A894

No. 3569: a, $5, Sun Moon Lake. b, $25, Mt.
Ali.

2004, Aug. 27   *Perf. 11½x11¼*
3569   A894   Sheet of 2, #a-b   3.00   3.00

Intl. Day of
Peace
A895

2004, Sept. 21   *Perf. 12¼x11¾*
3570   A895 $15 multi   1.25   .55

Souvenir Sheets

Hello Kitty — A896

No. 3571, oval stamps: a, $5, Dear Daniel,
donuts. b, $15, Hello Kitty, Taipei 101 Building.
No. 3572, rectangular stamps: a, $5, Hello
Kitty, bird, horiz. b, $15, Dear Daniel, Fisher-
man's Wharf, Danshuei.

2004, Sept. 24   *Perf.*
3571   A896   Sheet of 2, #a-b   1.75   1.25
          Perf. 12
3572   A896   Sheet of 2, #a-b   1.75   1.25

Sayings With Numbers Greeting Stamps

One Sea
of Smooth
Sailing
A897

Two Lions
Bring
Good
Fortune
A898

Three Goats of
Auspiciousness — A899

Safety in
All Four
Seasons
A900

Five
Blessings
at the
Door
A901

Six is Silky
Smooth
A902

Married for
Seven
Lives
A903

Eight
Immortals
Wish for
Your
Perfection
A904

Nine
Means
Success
A905

Ten is All
Around
Perfection
A906

2004, Oct. 10   *Perf. 12½*
3573   Block of 10   3.25   1.10
   a.   A897 $3.50 multi   .30   .25
   b.   A898 $3.50 multi   .30   .25
   c.   A899 $3.50 multi   .30   .25

   d.   A900 $3.50 multi   .30   .25
   e.   A901 $3.50 multi   .30   .25
   f.   A902 $3.50 multi   .30   .25
   g.   A903 $3.50 multi   .30   .25
   h.   A904 $3.50 multi   .30   .25
   i.   A905 $3.50 multi   .30   .25
   j.   A906 $3.50 multi   .30   .25

Changed Colors

3574   Block of 10   4.25   1.50
   a.   A897 $5 multi   .40   .25
   b.   A898 $5 multi   .40   .25
   c.   A899 $5 multi   .40   .25
   d.   A900 $5 multi   .40   .25
   e.   A901 $5 multi   .40   .25
   f.   A902 $5 multi   .40   .25
   g.   A903 $5 multi   .40   .25
   h.   A904 $5 multi   .40   .25
   i.   A905 $5 multi   .40   .25
   j.   A906 $5 multi   .40   .25
   k.   Sheet, #3574a-3574j + 10 at-
      tached labels ('04)   11.00   11.00

No. 3574k sold for $170 and has labels,
which could be personalized, that are separated from the stamps by simulated perforations. Issued 10/10/04.

Kaohsiung
Medical
University.
50th Anniv.
A907

Designs: No. 3575, $5, University gate and
buildings. No. 3576, $5, Building, researcher,
beaker, mosquito and snake.

2004, Oct. 16   *Perf. 12½*
3575-3576   A907   Set of 2   1.00   .50

Main Peak,
Mt. Cilai
A908

North
Peak, Mt.
Cilai
A909

South
Peak, Mt.
Cilai
A910

Grasslands, Mt. Cilai — A911

2004, Oct. 16   *Perf. 11½x11¼*
3577   A908 $5 multi   .35   .25
3578   A909 $5 multi   .35   .25
3579   A910 $12 multi   .95   .35
3580   A911 $25 multi   1.90   .75
    Nos. 3577-3580 (4)   3.55   1.60

Sports In Which Taiwanese Athletes
Won Medals At 2004 Summer
Olympics
A912

Designs: No. 3581, $5, Women's
Taekwondo. No. 3582, $5, Men's Taekwondo,
vert. $9, Archery. $12, Athletes on winner's
platform, vert.

Perf. 11¼x11½, 11½x11¼
2004, Oct. 22
3581-3584   A912   Set of 4   2.50   1.25

Platalea
Minor
A913

Designs: No. 3585, $2.50, Pair in flight. No.
3586, $2.50, Pair standing on one leg. $15,
With wings spread. $25, Foraging for food.
$20, Birds in water.

2004, Oct. 30   *Perf. 13½x13¼*
3585-3588   A913   Set of 4   3.50   1.65
         Souvenir Sheet
3589   A913 $20 multi   2.25   1.00

No. 3589 contains one 80x30mm stamp.

Pres. Yen Chia-
kan (1905-93)
A914

2004, Nov. 5   *Perf. 13¼x13½*
3590   A914 $12 multi   1.10   .45

New Year 2005
(Year of the
Cock) — A915

Designs: $3.50, Cock on lantern. $13, Lanterns, cock
$5, Cock, hen and chick, horiz.

2004, Nov. 10   *Perf. 12¼x11¾*
3591-3592   A915   Set of 2   1.25   .90
        Souvenir Sheet
        Perf. 11¾x11¼
3593   A915 $5 multi   .60   .45

No. 3593 contains one 46x26mm stamp.

Prefectural
Hall,
Chiayi
A916

East Gate,
Chiayi
A917

2004, Nov. 20   *Perf. 13½x13¼*
3594   A916 $5 multi   .50   .30
3595   A917 $5 multi   .50   .30

Chiayi, 300th anniv.

Embroidered Squares for Ching Dynasty Civil Official Court Dresses — A918

Designs: No. 3596, $3.50, Manchurian crane (orange background). No. 3597, $3.50, Golden pheasant (green background). $5, Peacock. $25, Goose.

2005, Jan. 20 Litho. Perf. 11½x11¼
3596-3599 A918 Set of 4 2.40 1.25
See Nos. 3727-3730.

Greetings A919

No. 3600 — Cartoon balloon with various keyboard characters creating faces and backgrounds with: a, Hands. b, Envelopes. c, Hearts. d, Flowers.

2005, Jan. 31 Perf. 12½
3600 Horiz. strip of 4 1.60 .85
a.-d. A919 $5 Any single .40 .25
e. Sheet, #3600a-3600d + 4 attached labels 11.50 11.50

No. 3600e sold for $140 and has labels, which could be personalized, that are separated from the stamps by simulated perforations. Sheets exist with various arrangements of stamps and positions of labels respective to the stamps (at left, above or below).

Rotary International, Cent. — A920

Rotary emblem and: $5, Map of Taiwan. $12, Dove.

2005, Feb. 23 Perf. 13½x13¼
3601-3602 A920 Set of 2 1.25 1.00

Mangroves A921

Designs: No. 3603, $3.50, Kandelia obovata. No. 3604, $3.50, Rhizophora stylosa. No. 3605, $5, Avicennia marina. No. 3606, $5, Lumnitzera racemosa.

2005, Mar. 10 Perf. 11½x11¼
3603-3606 A921 Set of 4 1.25 1.00

Longshan Temple, Mengjia A922

Lin Ben Yuan Garden, Banciao A923

Designs: $13, Chaotain Temple, Beigang. $15, Fort Anping, Tainan.

2005, Mar. 18
3607 A922 $5 multi .35 .25
3608 A923 $5 multi .35 .25
3609 A923 $13 multi .85 .40
3610 A923 $15 multi .95 .45
Nos. 3607-3610 (4) 2.50 1.35

Souvenir Sheet

Taipei 2005 Intl. Stamp Exhibition — A924

No. 3611: a, $5, Wood carving, Mandarin Ducks Playing in a Lotus Pond. b, $25, Hand puppets, horiz.

2005, Apr. 19 Perf. 12
3611 A924 Sheet of 2, #a-b 3.00 3.00

Coral Reef Fish A925

Designs: No. 3612, $5, Rhinomuraena quaesita. No. 3613, $5, Pomacanthus semicirculatus. $12, Forcipiger flavissimus. $25, Pterois volitans.

2005, May 16 Perf. 11½x12
3612-3615 A925 Set of 4 3.50 1.75
a. Sheet, 2 each #3612-3615 7.00 7.00

Changhua Train Station, 1918 A926

Chiayi Train Station, 1933 A927

Tainan Train Station, 1936 A928

Kaohsiung Train Station, 1941 A929

2005, June 9 Perf. 13½x13¾
3616 A926 $5 multi .40 .25
3617 A927 $5 multi .40 .25
3618 A928 $15 multi 1.10 .50
3619 A929 $25 multi 1.75 .80
Nos. 3616-3619 (4) 3.65 1.80
Compare with type A887.

Novel "The Romance of the Three Kingdoms" A930

Designs: No. 3620, $3.50, Mayhem in the Fengyi Pavilion (man and woman near pavilion railing). No. 3621, $3.50, Deterring the Enemy in Changban (horse and rider on bridge). $5, Releasing Tsao Tsao (rider on horse near flag). $20, A Trick in the Bag (man in bed holding bag).

Perf. 11½x11¼
2005, June 23 Litho.
3620-3623 A930 Set of 4 2.50 2.00
3623a Souvenir sheet, #3620-3623 2.50 2.00

Lifeline Suicide Prevention Hotline — A931

2005, July 1 Perf. 12x11½
3624 A931 $12 multi 1.25 .90

Albert Einstein's Theory of Relativity, Cent. — A932

2005, July 1
3625 A932 $15 multi 1.25 .60

Souvenir Sheets

Mickey Mouse — A933

No. 3626: a, $5, At ship's wheel, in Steamboat Willie. b, $25, As wizard, in Fantasia.

No. 3627: a, $5, Holding sword, in The Prince and the Pauper. b, $25, With Pluto, in Mickey's Twice Upon a Christmas.

2005, Aug. 3 Perf. 12
Sheets of 2, #a-b
3626-3627 A933 Set of 2 4.00 2.00

Rooster-shaped Wine Vessel — A934

2005, Aug. 19 Perf. 11¼x11½
3628 A934 $15 multi .95 .45
a. Sheet of 6, perf. 12 5.75 3.00
Taipei 2005 Intl. Stamp Exhibition.

Souvenir Sheets

A935

A936

A937

A938

A939

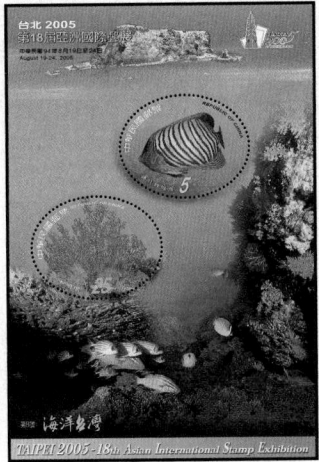

Taipei 2005 Intl. Stamp
Exhibition — A940

No. 3629: a, $5, Green Island and shoreline.
b, $25, Formosan rock monkey.
No. 3630: a, $5, Microscope. b, $25, DNA
double helices, vert.
No. 3631: a, $5, Flowers. $25, Fruit.
No. 3632: a, $5, Ear Shooting Ceremony,
vert. b, $25, Dragon boat in race.
No. 3633: a, $5, Bowl of food and ladle. b,
$25, Rice cakes.
No. 3634: a, $5, Royal empress angelfish, b,
$25, Red horny coral.

		2005		**Perf.**
3629	A935	Sheet of 2, #a-b	2.50	.95

Perf. 13½x13, 13x13½

| 3630 | A936 | Sheet of 2, #a-b | 2.50 | .95 |

Perf. 13½

| 3631 | A937 | Sheet of 2, #a-b | 2.50 | .95 |

Perf. 13¼x13½, 13½x13¼

| 3632 | A938 | Sheet of 2, #a-b | 2.50 | .95 |

Perf. 12

| 3633 | A939 | Sheet of 2, #a-b | 2.50 | .95 |

Perf.

| 3634 | A940 | Sheet of 2, #a-b | 2.50 | .95 |
| | | Nos. 3629-3634 (6) | 15.00 | 5.70 |

Issued: No. 3629, 8/19; No. 3630, 8/20; No.
3631, 8/21; No. 3632, 8/22; No. 3633, 8/23;
No. 3634, 8/24. No. 3629 contains two 38mm
diameter stamps. No. 3634 contains two
43x33mm oval stamps.

Novel, "Journey
to the
West" — A941

Designs: No. 3635, $3.50, Stone Monkey
(monkeys at waterfall). No. 3636, $3.50, Bud-
dhist Baby in the River. $5, Making a Pass at
Chang E. $20, Taming the Monster of the
River of Flowing Sands.

		2005, Sept. 15	**Perf. 11¼x11½**
3635-3638	A941	Set of 4	2.40 1.90

Souvenir Sheet

Kaohsiung 2005 Intl. Stamp
Exhibition — A942

No. 3639: a, $5, Loyalty and Filial Piety, by
Cian Syuan, vert. b, Gilt scepter.

Perf. 13¼x13½, 13½x13¼

		2005, Oct. 7		
3639	A942	Sheet of 2, #a-b	2.00	2.00

Souvenir Sheets

A943

Opening of Movie, *Harry Potter and
the Goblet of Fire* — A944

No. 3640: a, $5, Triwizard Cup. b, $5, Harry
and Hungarian Horntail. c, $5, Golden Egg. d,
$5, Harry swimming. e, $5, Harry summoning
Firebolt with wand. f, $25, Harry and Triwizard
Cup.
No. 3641: a, $5, Hungarian Horntail. b, $5,
Harry on Firebolt. c, $5, Voldemort's snake,
Nagini. d, $5, Grindylows. e, $5, Dumbledore's
phoenix, Fawkes. f, $25, Merchieftainess.

		2005, Nov. 18	**Perf. 12**
3640	A943	Sheet of 6, #a-f	5.00 2.50
3641	A944	Sheet of 6, #a-f	5.00 2.50

New Year 2006
(Year of the
Dog) — A945

Designs: $3.50, Dog at left. $13, Dog at
lower right.
$12, Three dogs, horiz.

		2005, Dec. 1	**Perf. 12¼x11¾**
3642-3643	A945	Set of 2	1.25 1.00
		Souvenir Sheet	

Perf. 11¾x11¼

| 3644 | A945 | $12 multi | | 1.25 .70 |

No. 3644 contains one 46x26mm stamp.

Pets — A946

Designs: $3.50, Siberian husky. $5, Golden
retriever. $12, Himalayan cat. $25, Scottish
fold cat.

Perf. 13½x12½

		2005, Dec. 22		**Litho.**

Country Name in Green

3645	A946	$3.50 multi	.30	.25
3646	A946	$5 multi	.40	.25
3647	A946	$12 multi	.80	.35
3648	A946	$25 multi	1.50	.75
		Nos. 3645-3648 (4)	3.00	1.60

See Nos. 3652-3655, 3685-3688 3712-3715.

Tea Ceremony — A947

No. 3649: a, Preparation of tea set (dull
orange panel). b, Placing of tea leaves in pot
(lemon panel). c, Pouring hot water over pots
and cups (light green panel). d, Drying of pot
and pouring of tea (blue geen panel). e, Smell-
ing and drinking of tea (gray blue panel).

		2006, Jan. 26	**Perf. 13½**
3649	A947	Horiz. strip of 5	2.00 1.00
a.-e.		$5 Any single	.40 .25

Taipei 101
Building — A948

Designs: $5, In day. $12, At night.

		2006, Feb. 23	**Perf. 12**
3650-3651	A948	Set of 2	1.25 .70

Pets Type of 2005

Designs: $2.50, Labrador retriever. $7, St.
Bernard. $10, Siamese cat. $32, Persian cat.

		2006, Mar. 8	**Perf. 13½x12½**

Country Name in Blue

3652	A946	$2.50 multi	.25	.25
3653	A946	$7 multi	.45	.25
3654	A946	$10 multi	.60	.30
3655	A946	$32 multi	2.00	1.00
		Nos. 3652-3655 (4)	3.30	1.80

See Nos. 3712-3715.

King Penguins
A949

Aptenodytes patagonicus: No. 3656, $5,
Adult and juvenile. No. 3657, $5, Courtship.
$9, Swimming and diving, horiz. $12, Gliding
and preening, horiz.
$15, Colony, horiz.

Perf. 11¼x11½, 11½x11¼

		2006, Mar. 26	
3656-3659	A949	Set of 4	2.40 2.00
		Souvenir Sheet	

Perf. 12

| 3660 | A949 | $15 multi | | 1.60 1.00 |

No. 3660 contains one 80x30mm stamp.

Miniature Sheet

Children's Art — A950

No. 3661 — Winning drawings in children's stamp design competition: a, Birds with black bills. b, People with red faces. c, Pheasants. d, Chinese celebration. e, Fishing boats and catch. f, People with large flowers and fruit. g, Man painting Chinese lantern. h, Bridge and ducks. i, Train. j, Bees and flowers. k, People with black faces. l, Boy on ladder. m, People and chickens. n, Ring of people around dancers and musicians. o, People and large lions. p, Two cats. q, People and cow. r, Whale and fish. s, People with white faces bending backwards. t, Bus.

2006, Apr. 4 **Perf. 11½**
3661 A950 $5 Sheet of 20, #a-t 6.50 3.50

Fireflies
A951

Designs: No. 3662, $5, Pyrocoelia analis. No. 3663, $5, Diaphanes citrinus. No. 3664, $5, Diaphanes niveus. No. 3665, $5, Diaphanes formosus.

2006, May 25 **Perf. 13½x13¼**
3662-3665 A951 Set of 4 1.60 .75

Souvenir Sheet

Completion of Nangang to Suao Section of National Expressway 5 — A952

2006, June 16 **Litho.** **Perf. 11½**
3666 A952 $12 multi 1.50 .80

Souvenir Sheets

Winnie the Pooh — A953

No. 3667: a, $5, Winnie the Pooh pushing Piglet in wheelbarrow. b, $25, Winnie the Pooh, Piglet and Tigger floating in inner tube. No. 3668: a, $5, Winnie the Pooh and Piglet running in autumn. b, $25, Winnie the Pooh and Tigger ice fishing.

2006, June 21 **Perf. 12**
Sheets of 2, #a-b
3667-3668 A953 Set of 2 4.00 2.00

Tourism Greeting Stamps A954

Designs: Nos. 3669a, 3670a, Satchel and cliff. Nos. 3669b, 3670b, Camera and boat. Nos. 3669c, 3670c, Notebook, pen and bridge. No. 3669d, 3670d, Sailboat and rock. No. 3669e, 3670e, Heart and train.

2006, June 30 **Perf. 12½**
3669 Horiz. strip of 5 1.50 .55
a.-e. A954 $3.50 Any single .30 .30
f. Sheet, 2 each #3669a-3669e, + 5 labels 7.00
3670 Horiz. strip of 5 2.00 .80
a.-e. A954 $5 Any single .40 .25
f. Sheet, 2 each #3670a-3670e, + 5 labels 7.00

Nos. 3669f and 3670f each sold for $100. Labels could be personalized.

Fish
A955

Designs: No. 3671, $5, Amphiprion ocellaris. No. 3672, $5, Zanclus cornutus. No. 3673, $12, Coris gaimard. No. 3674, $12, Oxycirrhites typus.

2006, July 14 **Perf. 11½**
3671-3674 A955 Set of 4 2.40 2.00
3674a Miniature sheet, 2 each #3671-3674, perf. 11½x12 4.75 4.75

A956

Sung Dynasty Calligraphy and Painting — A957

Designs: $5, Poem by Huang T'ing-chien. $9, Calligraphy on silk, by Mi Fu. Nos. 3677, 3679a, $12, Detail of magpie in flight, from Magpies and Hare, by Ts'ui Po. Nos. 3678, 3679b, $15, Detail of magpie on branch, from Magpies and Hare.

2006, Aug. 4 **Perf. 11½**
Denominations in Black
3675-3678 A956 Set of 4 2.75 1.40
Souvenir Sheet
Denominations in Black and Orange
Perf. 12½
3679 A957 Sheet of 2, #a-b 2.25 1.10

Dragonflies
A958

Designs: Nos. 3680, 3684a, $5, Crocothemis servilia servilia. Nos. 3681, 3684b, $5, Orthetrum, pruinosum neglectum, vert. Nos. 3682, 3684c, $12, Diplacodes trivialis, vert. No. 3683, 3684d, $12, Orthetrum sabina sabina.

Perf. 13x13¼, 13¼x13
2006, Aug. 16 **With White Frames**
3680-3683 A958 Set of 4 2.40 2.00
Souvenir Sheet
Without White Frames
Perf. 11¾
3684 A958 Sheet of 4, #a-d 2.40 2.00

Pets Type of 2005

Designs: $1, Yorkshire terrier. $9, Pomeranian. $15, Abyssinian cat. $20, Norwegian Forest cat.

2006, Aug. 30 **Perf. 13½x12½**
Country Name in Blue
3685 A946 $1 multi .25 .25
3686 A946 $9 multi .55 .25
3687 A946 $15 multi .90 .45
3688 A946 $20 multi 1.25 .60
Nos. 3685-3688 (4) 2.95 1.55

Aerial Activities — A959

Designs: No. 3689, $3.50, Paragliding. No. 3690, $3.50, Hang gliding, horiz. $12, Ultralight aircraft, horiz. $15, Parasailing.

2006, Sept. 15 **Perf. 13½**
3689-3692 A959 Set of 4 2.75 1.50

Pitta Nympha — A960

Designs: Nos. 3693, 3697a, $5, On branch. Nos. 3694, 3697b, $5, In flight, horiz. Nos. 3695, 3697c, $10, With young at nest, horiz. Nos. 3696, 3697d, $10, With insect in beak.

Perf. 13¼x13, 13x13¼
2006, Sept. 30 **With White Frames**
3693-3696 A960 Set of 4 2.25 1.10
Souvenir Sheet
Without White Frames
Perf. 11¾
3697 A960 Sheet of 4, #a-d 2.25 1.10

Cetaceans A961

Designs: No. 3698, $5, Stenella attenuata. No. 3699, $5, Stenella longirostris. $10, Feresa attenuata. $15, Physeter macrocephalus.

Perf. 13x12 Syncopated
2006, Oct. 18 **Litho.**
3698-3701 A961 Set of 4 2.50 1.50
3701a Souvenir sheet, #3698-3701 2.50 1.50

Flowers
A962

Designs: No. 3702, $5, Ludwigia octovalvis. No. 3703, $5, Hygrophila pogonocalyx, vert. $12, Titanotrichum oldhamii, vert.

2006, Nov. 8 **Perf. 11½**
3702-3704 A962 Set of 3 1.60 .80

Scenic Areas A963

Designs: No. 3705, $5, Jhongshan Building, Yangmingshan National Park. No. 3706, $5, Taroko Gorge, vert. $9, Queen's Head Rock, vert. $12, Sun Moon Lake.

2006, Nov. 11 **Perf. 12½**
3705-3708 A963 Set of 4 2.25 1.10

A964

New Year 2007 (Year of the Pig) — A965

Designs: $3.50, Pig on drum. $13, Pig and drums.

2006, Dec. 1 **Perf. 12¼x11¾**
3709-3710 A964 Set of 2 1.25 .60
Souvenir Sheet
Perf. 11½x11¼
3711 A965 $12 multi 1.25 .60

Pets Type of 2005

Designs: 50c, Border collie. $13, Beagle. $17, American Shorthair cat. $34, Maine Coon cat.

2006, Dec. 18 **Perf. 13½x12½**
Country Name in Green
3712 A946 50c multi .25 .25
3713 A946 $13 multi .80 .40
3714 A946 $17 multi 1.10 .55
3715 A946 $34 multi 2.10 1.10
Nos. 3712-3715 (4) 4.25 2.30

Inauguration of High Speed Rail Line — A966

No. 3716: a, 700T Series train. b, Hsinchu Station.

2006, Dec. 25 **Perf. 11½**
3716 A966 $12 Horiz. pair, #a-b 1.50 .75

Orchids — A967

Designs: $3.50, Phaius tankervilleae. $5, Spiranthes sinensis. $12, Vanda x hybrida. $25, Cattleya sp.

2007, Jan. 10	**Litho.**	**Perf. 13½x12½**		
3717	A967	$3.50 multi	.25	.25
3718	A967	$5 multi	.30	.25
3719	A967	$12 multi	.75	.35
3720	A967	$25 multi	1.50	.75
	Nos. 3717-3720 (4)		2.80	1.60

See Nos. 3751-3754, 3768-3771.

Ching Dynasty Jewelry A968

Designs: No. 3721, $5, Earrings. No. 3722, $5, Hairpin. $12, Fingernail guard. $25, Ring.

2007, Jan. 17		**Perf. 11½**		
3721-3724	A968	Set of 4	3.00	1.50

Valentine's Day — A969

Heart and faces in: $5, White. $20, Red.

2007, Feb. 6				
3725-3726	A969	Set of 2	1.50	.75

Embroidered Squares Type of 2005

Embroidered squares for Ching Dynasty military officials: No. 3727, $3.50, Cilin (light green background). No. 3728, $3.50, Lion (light orange background). $5, Leopard (bright orange background). $25, Tiger (light blue background).

2007, Feb. 16		**Perf. 11½x11¼**		
3727-3730	A918	Set of 4	2.25	1.10

Feb. 28, 1947 Massacre Memorial Museum A970

2007, Feb. 28				
3731	A970	$5 multi	4.00	.25

Bridges A971

Designs: No. 3732, $5, Kanjin Bridge, Taoyuan (green panel). No. 3733, $5, Fusing Bridge, Luofu (purple panel). $12, MacArthur Second Bridge, Taipei. $15, Dajhih Bridge, Taipei.

2007, Apr. 12	**Litho.**	**Perf. 11½x12**		
3732-3735	A971	Set of 4	2.25	1.10

See Nos. 3808-3811.

Lesser Panda A972

Panda: No. 3736, $5, Eating bamboo. No. 3737, $5, Resting on rock. No. 3738, $10, Walking near tree, vert. No. 3739, $10, Scratching on rock, vert. $12, Two pandas, vert.

Perf. 11½x11¼, 11¼x11½

2007, Apr. 25				
3736-3739	A972	Set of 4	1.90	.95

Souvenir Sheet

Perf. 12

3740	A972	$12 multi	.75	.35

No. 3740 contains one 40x50mm stamp.

Dharma Drum Mountain Intl. Buddhist Educational Complex — A973

Chung Tai Chan Monastery A974

Fo Guang Shan Monastery A975

Tzu Chi Foundation Building — A976

2007, May 24		**Perf. 13¼x13**		
3741	A973	$5 multi	.30	.25
3742	A974	$5 multi	.30	.25
3743	A975	$5 multi	.30	.25
3744	A976	$5 multi	.30	.25
	Nos. 3741-3744 (4)		1.20	1.00

Dahlia and Butterflies A977

Iris and Butterfly A978

Clematis and Ladybugs A979

Tung Blossom and Butterflies A980

Rose and Butterfly A981

Sunflower and Insects — A982

Bird-of-Paradise Flower and Butterfly A983

Lotus and Butterflies A984

English Daisies and Dragonfly A985

Balloon Flower and Dragonfly A986

2007, May 28		**Perf. 12½**		
3745		Block of 10	2.10	1.10
a.	A977	$3.50 multi	.25	.25
b.	A978	$3.50 multi	.25	.25
c.	A979	$3.50 multi	.25	.25
d.	A980	$3.50 multi	.25	.25
e.	A981	$3.50 multi	.25	.25
f.	A982	$3.50 multi	.25	.25
g.	A983	$3.50 multi	.25	.25
h.	A984	$3.50 multi	.25	.25
i.	A985	$3.50 multi	.25	.25
j.	A986	$3.50 multi	.25	.25

Changed Colors

3746		Block of 10	3.00	1.50
a.	A977	$5 multi	.30	.25
b.	A978	$5 multi	.30	.25
c.	A979	$5 multi	.30	.25
d.	A980	$5 multi	.30	.25
e.	A981	$5 multi	.30	.25
f.	A982	$5 multi	.30	.25
g.	A983	$5 multi	.30	.25
h.	A984	$5 multi	.30	.25
i.	A985	$5 multi	.30	.25
j.	A986	$5 multi	.30	.25

Food Preparation Implements — A987

Designs: No. 3747, $5, Rice bucket and shelf (light blue background). No. 3748, $5, Steamer (green background). No. 3749, $12, Rice baskets (tan background). No. 3750, $12, Dinnerware (lilac background).

2007, June 28		**Perf. 11½x11¼**		
3747-3750	A987	Set of 4	2.10	1.10

Orchids Type of 2007 Inscribed "Taiwan" Instead of "Republic of China"

Designs: $1, Paphiopedilum sp. $2.50, Phalaenopsis aphrodite. $10, Dendrobium sp. $32, Oncidium x hybridum.

2007, July 12		**Perf. 13½x12½**		
3751	A967	$1 multi	.25	.25
3752	A967	$2.50 multi	.25	.25
3753	A967	$10 multi	.60	.30
3754	A967	$32 multi	2.00	1.00
	Nos. 3751-3754 (4)		3.10	1.80

End of Martial Law, 20th Anniv. — A988

2007, July 15		**Perf. 11¼x11½**		
3755	A988	$12 multi	.75	.35

Fish A989

Designs: No. 3756, $5, Nemateleotris magnifica. No. 3757, $5, Balistoides conspicillum. $12, Paracanthurus hepatus. $25, Cetoscarus bicolor.

2007, July 27		**Perf. 11½x11¼**		
3756-3759	A989	Set of 4	5.50	1.60

Chiang Wei-shui (1890-1931), Political and Social Leader — A990

2007, Aug. 6	**Engr.**	**Perf. 11¼x11½**		
3760	A990	$25 brown	1.50	.75

Taiwan - African Heads of State Summit, Taipei A991

2007, Sept. 9	**Litho.**	**Perf. 11½x11¼**		
3761	A991	$12 multi	.90	.55

Top right corner (above A987 listing):

h.	A984	$5 multi	.30	.25
i.	A985	$5 multi	.30	.25
j.	A986	$5 multi	.30	.25

Miniature Sheet

Eighteen Scholars of T'ang, by
Emperor Hui-tsung. — A992

No. 3762 — Various portions of painting
numbered: a, (10-5), 36x30mm. b, (10-4),
51x30mm. c, (10-3), 43x30mm. d, (10-2),
45x30mm. e, (10-1), 43x30mm. f, (10-10),
43x30mm. g, (10-9), 51x30mm. h, (10-8),
43x30mm. i, (10-7), 45x30mm. j, (10-6),
36x30mm.

2007, Sept. 21   **Perf. 13¼**
3762 A992   Sheet of 10   3.00   1.50
  a.-j. $5 Any single   .30   .25

Doves — A993

2007, Sept. 28   **Perf. 11¼x11½**
3763 A993 $5 multi   .60   .30

Portions of the design were applied by a
thermographic process producing a shiny,
raised effect.

Shells
A994

Designs: No. 3764, $5, Marchia loebbeckei.
No. 3765, $5, Harpa major. No. 3766, $12,
Epitonium scalare. No. 3767, $12, Cypraea
aurantium.

2007, Oct. 11   Litho.   **Perf. 11½x11¼**
3764-3767 A994   Set of 4   2.10   1.10

Orchids Type of 2007 Inscribed "Taiwan" Instead of "Republic of China"

Designs: $7, Ascocentrum sp. $9, Arundina
graminifolia. $15, Vanda teres. $20, Epidendrum sp.

2007, Oct. 24   **Perf. 13½x12½**
3768 A967 $7 multi   .45   .25
3769 A967 $9 multi   .55   .30
3770 A967 $15 multi   .95   .45
3771 A967 $20 multi   1.25   .60
     Nos. 3768-3771 (4)   3.20   1.60

Birds — A995

Designs: $3.50, Pericrocotus solaris. $5,
Parus varius. $12, Luscinia calliope. $25,
Phoenicurus auroreus.

2007, Nov. 3
3772 A995 $3.50 multi   .25   .25
3773 A995 $5 multi   .30   .25
3774 A995 $12 multi   .75   .35
3775 A995 $25 multi   1.60   .80
     Nos. 3772-3775 (4)   2.90   1.65

See Nos. 3792-3795, 3819-3822, 3845-3848.

Outdoor
Activities — A996

Designs: No. 3776, $5, Speed walking. No.
3777, $5, Cycling. $12, Skateboarding. $25,
Rollerblading.

2007, Nov. 9   **Perf. 11½**
3776-3779 A996   Set of 4   3.00   1.50

Scouting, Cent. — A997

2007, Nov. 28   **Perf. 12½**
3780 A997 $12 multi   .75   .35

A998

New Year 2008 (Year of the
Rat) — A999

2007, Dec. 3   **Perf. 12½x11¾**
3781 A998 $3.50 Rat at left   .30   .25
3782 A998 $13 Rat at right   .90   .40

Souvenir Sheet
Perf. 12½
3783 A999 $12 multi   1.25   .60

Democracy
Movement
Leaders
A1000

Designs: No. 3784, Lei Chen (1897-1979),
publisher. No. 3785, Fu Jheng (1927-91), editor. No. 3786, Kuo Yu Shing (1908-85), politician. No. 3787, Huang Hsin Chieh (1928-99),
politician.

2007, Dec. 10   Engr.   **Perf. 11½**
3784 A1000 $5 brown   .30   .25
3785 A1000 $5 green   .30   .25
3786 A1000 $5 claret   .30   .25
3787 A1000 $5 brown black   .30   .25
     Nos. 3784-3787 (4)   1.20   1.00

Liou Family Compound,
Shangfangliao — A1001

Lin Family Mansion, Banciao — A1002

Li Teng-fang Compound,
Dasi — A1003

Siao Family Compound,
Jiadong — A1004

2008, Jan. 23   Litho.   **Perf. 12**
3788 A1001 $5 multi   .30   .25
3789 A1002 $5 multi   .30   .25
3790 A1003 $5 multi   .30   .25
3791 A1004 $12 multi   .75   .40
     Nos. 3788-3791 (4)   1.65   1.15

Birds Type of 2007

Designs: $1, Dicrurus aeneus. $2.50,
Lanius schach. $10, Dendrocitta formosae.
$32, Pycnonotus sinensis.

2008, Jan. 30   **Perf. 13½x12½**
3792 A995 $1 multi   .25   .25
3793 A995 $2.50 multi   .25   .25
3794 A995 $10 multi   .65   .30
3795 A995 $32 multi   2.00   1.00
     Nos. 3792-3795 (4)   3.15   1.80

A1005

Puppet Theater — A1006

No. 3796: a, Mirror Man, denomination at
UL. b, Old Oddball, denomination at UR.
No. 3797: a, Shih Yan-wun, denomination at
UL. b, Dragon Lady of the Bitter Sea, denomination at UR.

2007, Feb. 4   **Perf. 11½**
3796 A1005 $5 Horiz. pair, #a-b   .65   .30
3797 A1006 $5 Horiz. pair, #a-b   .65   .30
  c.   Souvenir sheet, #3796-3797,
     perf. 11½x11   1.30   .60

Syrmaticus Mikado — A1007

Litho. & Engr.
2008, Mar. 7   **Perf. 12**
3798 A1007 $25 multi   1.75   .85

Taipei 2008 Intl.
Stamp
Exhibition
A1008

Paintings: $5, Plum Blossoms and Solitary
Bird, by Pien Wen-chin. $9, Apricot Blossoms
and Peacocks, by Lu Chi. $13, Wild Duck by a
Brook, by Ch'en Lin. $15, Bamboo and Shrike,
by Li An-chung.

2008, Mar. 7   Litho.   **Perf. 12½**
3799-3802 A1008   Set of 4   2.75   1.40
3802a   Souvenir sheet, #3799-3802,
     perf. 12½ syncopated   2.75   1.40

Miniature Sheets

A1009

Characters From Animated Film,
"Finding Nemo" — A1010

No. 3803: a, Turtles (32mm diameter). b,
Dory (26x34mm). c, Bubbles (32mm diameter). d, Nemo (34x26mm). e, Pearl (32mm
diameter).
No. 3804 (all stamps 32mm diameter): a,
Sheldon. b, Squirt. c, Tad. d, Nemo. e, Peach.

**Perf. 13x13½ (#3803b), 13½x13
(#3803d)**
2008, Apr. 3
3803 A1009 $5 Sheet of 5, #a-e   1.75   .85
3804 A1010 $5 Sheet of 5, #a-e   1.75   .85

Cactus
Flowers — A1011

Designs: No. 3805, $5, Hylocerus undatus. No. 3806, $5, Thelocactus bicolor. $12, Rhipsalidopsis gaertneri.

2008, Apr. 30 Litho. Perf. 11¼x11½
3805-3807 A1011 Set of 3 1.50 .75

Bridges Type of 2007 Inscribed "Taiwan"

Designs: No. 3808, $5, Wurih Bridge, Taichung. No. 3809, $5, Jilu Bridge, Nantou, at night. $12, Shueiyun Bridge, Shueili. $15, Sindong Bridge, Miaoli.

2008, May 12 Perf. 11½x11¼
3808-3811 A971 Set of 4 2.50 1.25

A1012

A1013

A1014

Inauguration of President Ma Ying-jeou and Vice-president Vincent C. Siew — A1015

2008, May 20 Perf. 13½x13¼
3812 A1012 $5 multi .35 .25
3813 A1013 $5 multi .35 .25
3814 A1014 $13 multi .85 .45
3815 A1015 $15 multi 1.00 .50
a. Miniature sheet, #3812-3815, perf. 12 2.60 1.40
Nos. 3812-3815 (4) 2.55 1.45

 Yellow Tiger Flag A1016

Portrait of Jheng Cheng-gong A1017

2008, May 29 Perf. 12½
Stamps With White Frames
3816 A1016 $5 multi .35 .25
3817 A1017 $25 multi 1.75 .85
Souvenir Sheet Perf. 13½
Stamps Without White Frames
3818 Sheet of 2 2.10 1.10
a. A1016 $5 multi .35 .25
b. A1017 $25 multi 1.75 .85

National Taiwan Museum, cent.

Birds Type of 2007
Designs: $7, Streptopelia orientalis. $15, Passer montanus. $20, Pica pica. $34, Zosterops japonicus.

2008, June 5 Perf. 13½x12½
3819 A995 $7 multi .50 .25
3820 A995 $15 multi 1.00 .50
3821 A995 $20 multi 1.40 .70
3822 A995 $34 multi 2.25 1.10
Nos. 3819-3822 (4) 5.15 2.55

Stag Beetles — A1018

Designs: No. 3823, $5, Neolucanus swinhoei. No. 3824, $5, Dorcus schenklingi. $10, Lucanus datunensis. $12, Cyclommatus asahinai.

2008, June 5 Perf. 12¼
3823-3826 A1018 Set of 4 2.10 1.10

Shells A1019

Designs: No. 3827, $5, Murex troscheli. No. 3828, $5, Lambis chiragra. $12, Spondylus regius. No. 3830, $12, Cymatium pyrum.

2008, July 9 Litho. Perf. 13½
3827-3830 A1019 Set of 4 2.25 1.10

Urocissa Caerulea A1020

Designs: Nos. 3831, 3835a, $5, Adults feeding hatchlings in nest. Nos. 3832, 3835b, $5, Bird holding snake in beak. Nos. 3833, 3835c, $12, Bird in flight. Nos. 3834, 3835d, $12, Bird on branch with spread wings.

2008, July 9 Perf. 13x13¼
Stamps With White Frames
3831-3834 A1020 Set of 4 2.25 1.10
Souvenir Sheet
Stamps Without White Frames Perf. 11¾
3835 A1020 Sheet of 4, #a-d 2.25 1.10
No. 3835 contains four 34x25mm stamps.

Miniature Sheet

A Hundred Deers, by Ignace Sichelbart — A1021

No. 3836 — Parts of painting numbered: a, 8-1 (45x38mm). b, 8-2 (55x38mm). c, 8-3 (45x38mm). d, 8-4 (43x38mm). e, 8-5 (37x38mm). f, 8-6 (43x38mm). g, 8-7 (43x38mm). h, 8-8 (65x38mm).

2008, July 16 Perf. 13¼
3836 A1021 Sheet of 8, #a-h 2.60 1.40
a.-h. $5 Any single .30 .25

Items From Aboriginal Culture — A1022

Designs: $5, Paiwan earthenware pot. No. 3838, $12, Ami lover's bag (orange background). No. 3839, $12, Rukai men's headdress (green background). $25, Bunun men's neck ornament.

2008, Aug. 1 Perf. 11¼x11½
3837-3840 A1022 Set of 4 3.50 1.75

Miniature Sheet

Yimin Festival — A1023

No. 3841: a, Erection of lantern poles. b, Bowl of congee, spoon, flowers. c, Sinpu Yimin Temple, horiz. d, Pig competition, horiz.

2008, Aug. 20 Litho. Perf. 12½
3841 A1023 $5 Sheet of 4, #a-d 1.25 .65

New Year 2009 (Year of the Ox) — A1024

Designs: $3.50, Head of ox. $13, Ox. $12, Ox in water, horiz.

2008, Dec. 1 Perf. 12¼x11¾
3842-3843 A1024 Set of 2 1.00 .50
Souvenir Sheet Perf. 11¾x11¼
3844 A1024 $12 multi .75 .35
No. 3844 contains one 50x30mm stamp.

Birds Type of 2007 Inscribed "Republic of China (Taiwan)"
Designs: 50c, Rostratula benghalensis. $9, Turdus poliocephalus. $13, Amaurornis phoenicurus. $17, Cettia acanthizoides.

2009, Jan. 15 Perf. 13½x12½
3845 A995 50c multi .25 .25
3846 A995 $9 multi .55 .25
3847 A995 $13 multi .80 .40
3848 A995 $17 multi 1.00 .50
Nos. 3845-3848 (4) 2.60 1.40

Giant Pandas in Taipei Zoo A1025

Designs: $5, Tuan Tuan on log bridge. $9, Yuan Yuan eating. $25, Tuan Tuan and Yuan Yuan.

2009, Jan. 20 Perf. 11½x11¼
3849-3850 A1025 Set of 2 .85 .40
Souvenir Sheet Perf. 12
3851 A1025 $25 multi 1.50 1.00
No. 3851 contains one 50x40mm stamp.

Ceremonial Objects A1026

Designs: No. 3852, $5, Gift basket with handle, two women in background. No. 3853, $5, Wooden box, men carrying box in background. No. 3854, $12, Bridal sedan chair, wedding procession in background. No. 3855, $12, Candlesticks, bride and groom holding incense sticks in background.

2009, Feb. 10 Perf. 11½x11¼
3852-3855 A1026 Set of 4 2.25 1.10

Shells A1027

Designs: No. 3856, $5, Strombus sinuatus. No. 3857, $5, Hydatina amplustre. $12, Cymatium hepaticum. No. 3859, $12, Mitra mitra.

2009, Feb. 26 Perf. 13½
3856-3859 A1027 Set of 4 2.25 1.10

Flowers — A1028

Designs: $3.50, Lantana camara. $5, Murraya paniculata. $12, Tabebuia chrysantha. $25, Hibiscus sabdariffa.

2009, Mar. 12 Perf. 13½x12½
3860 A1028 $3.50 multi .25 .25
3861 A1028 $5 multi .30 .25
3862 A1028 $12 multi .75 .35
3863 A1028 $25 multi 1.50 .75
Nos. 3860-3863 (4) 2.80 1.60
See Nos. 3890-3893, 3905-3908, 3934-3937.

Opening of Red and Orange Lines of Kaohsiung Mass Rapid Transit System A1029

Train and: $5, Central Park Station. $25, World Games Station.

2009, Apr. 7 Perf. 11½x11¼
3864-3865 A1029 Set of 2 2.00 1.00

A1030

Pres. Chiang Ching-kuo (1910-88) — A1031

Pres. Chiang: No. 3866, $5, Wearing hat (gray panel). No. 3877, $5, Wearing suit and tie (dull purple panel). $10, Holding cane (blue panel), horiz. $12, Holding baby (brown panel), horiz.

Perf. 11¼x11½, 11½x11¼
2009, Apr. 13
3866-3869 A1030 Set of 4   1.90 .95
Souvenir Sheet
3870 A1031 $25 shown   1.60 .75

Carp Encircled By Dragons Type of 1997 With Denominations at Lower Right and Inscribed "Republic of China (Taiwan)"
2009, May 20 Engr.   Perf. 13¼x12½
3871 A745 $50 blue   3.25 1.60

Miniature Sheet

Butterflies — A1032

No. 3872: a, $5, Papilio xuthus (butterfly cutout at LL). b, $5, Troides aeacus formosanus (butterfly cutout at LR). c, $12, Graphium agamemnon (butterfly cutout at UL). d, $12, Papilio paris nakaharai (butterfly cutout at UR).

2009, June 25 Litho.   Perf. 11½x12
3872 A1032 Sheet of 4, #a-d   2.10 1.10

2009 World Games, Kaohsiung — A1033

Designs: $5, Kaohsiung Arena and World Games mascots Kao Mei and Syong Ge. $12, Main Stadium and World Games emblem.

2009, July 16   Perf. 12
3873-3874 A1033 Set of 2   1.10 .55
3874a   Souvenir sheet, #3873-3874   1.10 .55

Ancient Art Treasures — A1034

Designs: No. 3875, $5, Two Qing Dynasty gold gourds. No. 3876, $5, Gold bowl used by Emperor Qianlong. No. 3877, $12, Mughal Empire inlaid round urn. No. 3878, $12, Qing Dynasty gilt ewer.

2009, July 20   Perf. 12¼
3875-3878 A1034 Set of 4   2.10 1.10
3878a   Souvenir sheet, #3875-3878, perf. 12¼x11¾   2.10 1.10

Sites in Kinmen — A1035

Designs: $5, Guningtou. $9, Zhaishan Tunnel. No. 3881, $10, Interior of Qingtian Hall. No. 3882, $10, Lake Taihu.

2009, July 29   Perf. 12½
3879-3882 A1035   Set of 4   2.10 1.10

Paintings by Lin Yu-shan (1907-2004) — A1036

No. 3883: a, $5, On the Way Home. b, $25, Two Heads of Cattle.

2009, Aug. 7   Litho.   Perf. 12½x12
3883 A1036   Horiz. pair, #a-b, + central label   1.90 .95

Nursery Rhymes — A1037

Designs: No. 3884, $5, Little Girl and Her Doll (blue denomination). No. 3885, $5, Kingdom of Dolls (king and soldier on horses, yellow denomination). No. 3886, $5, Train, horiz. (red denomination). No. 3887, $5, Thunder Shower, horiz. (fish, fireflies, lotus flower, denomination in orange).

2009, Aug. 26   Perf. 12¼
3884-3887 A1037   Set of 4   1.25 .60

21st Summer Deaflympics, Taipei — A1038

Designs: $5, Badminton, running. $25, Taekwondo, tennis.

2009, Sept. 5   Perf. 11½
3888-3889 A1038   Set of 2   1.90 .95

Flowers Type of 2009
Designs: $1, Calliandra emarginata. $2.50, Bombax ceiba. $10, Delonix regia. $32, Spathodea campanulata.

2009, Oct. 14   Litho.   Perf. 13½x12½
3890 A1028 $1 multi   .25 .25
3891 A1028 $2.50 multi   .25 .25
3892 A1028 $10 multi   .65 .30
3893 A1028 $32 multi   2.00 1.00
  Nos. 3890-3893 (4)   3.15 1.80

Greetings A1039

No. 3894: a, Necklace (orange background). b, Gift boxes (pink background). c, Bouquet of roses (yellow background). d, Lollipop and candy (light blue background). e, Balloons (orange red background). f, Champagne flutes (blue violet background). g, Hearts (yellow green background). h, Cake and strawberry

(red background). i, Sparklers (red violet background). j, Four-leaf clover (green background).
No. 3895: a, Necklace (orange red background). b, Gift boxes (yellow green background). c, Bouquet of roses (pink background). d, Lollipop and candy (yellow background). e, Balloons (red background). f, Champagne flutes (red violet background). g, Hearts (orange background). h, Cake and strawberry (green background). i, Sparklers (blue background). j, Four-leaf clover (yellow background).

2009, Nov. 12   Perf. 12½
3894   Block of 10   2.50 1.25
a.-j. A1039 $3.50 Any single   .25 .25
3895   Block of 10   3.00 1.50
a.-j. A1039 $5 Any single   .30 .25

Nos. 3894 and 3895 were each printed in sheets containing two blocks + 5 labels.

Ferns — A1040

Designs: $5, Asplenium nidus. $9, Cyathea spinulosa. $12, Cyathea lepifera. $25, Cibotium taiwanense.

2009, Nov. 26   Perf. 11¼x11½
3896-3899 A1040   Set of 4   3.25 1.60
3899a   Souvenir sheet, #3896-3899   3.25 1.60
  See Nos. 4060-4063.

A1041

New Year 2010 (Year of the Tiger) — A1042

Tiger at: $3.50, Left. $13, Right.

2009, Dec. 1   Perf. 12¼x12½
3900-3901 A1041   Set of 2   1.10 .55
Souvenir Sheet
Perf. 12½
3902 A1042 $12 multi   .75 .35

Anti-Corruption Day — A1043

Background color: $5, Light blue. $25, Lilac.

2009, Dec. 9   Litho.   Perf. 11½
3903-3904 A1043   Set of 2   1.90 .95

Flowers Type of 2009
Designs: $7, Michelia champaca. $15, Duranta repens. $20, Ixora chinensis. $34, Lagerstroemia speciosa.

2010, Jan. 20   Perf. 13½x12½
3905 A1028 $7 multi   .45 .25
3906 A1028 $15 multi   .95 .45
3907 A1028 $20 multi   1.25 .65
3908 A1028 $34 multi   2.25 1.10
  Nos. 3905-3908 (4)   4.90 2.45

Lin An-tai Historical Home, Taipei — A1044

Li Family Compound, Luzhou — A1045

Lin Family Compound, Wufeng — A1046

Xiaoyun Villa, Shengang — A1047

2010, Feb. 9   Perf. 13½x13¼
3909 A1044 $5 multi   .35 .25
3910 A1045 $5 multi   .35 .25
3911 A1046 $5 multi   .35 .25
3912 A1047 $12 multi   .75 .35
  Nos. 3909-3912 (4)   1.80 1.10

Little Taiwan, Qimei Islet A1048

Whale Arch, Xiaomen Islet A1049

Scenery of Penghu Islands: No. 3914, Basalt rocks, Xiaomen Islet. No. 3916, Heart-shaped stone weir, Qimei Islet.

2010, Feb. 24   Perf. 13½
3913 A1048 $5 shown   .35 .25
3914 A1048 $5 multi   .35 .25
3915 A1049 $10 shown   .65 .30
3916 A1049 $10 multi   .65 .30
  Nos. 3913-3916 (4)   2.00 1.10

Bridges A1050

Designs: No. 3917, $5, Jinde Bridge, Dong-gang (shown). No. 3918, $5, Qigu River Bridge, Tainan. No. 3919, $12, Anyi Bridge,

Tainan. No. 3920, $12, Wangyue Bridge, Tainan (blue bridge at night).

2010, Mar. 10 **Perf. 11½**
3917-3920 A1050 Set of 4 2.25 1.10

Mushrooms
A1051

Designs: Nos. 3921, 3925a, $5, Dictyphora multicolor. Nos. 3922, 3925b, $5, Pleurotus salmoneostramineus. Nos. 3923, 3925c, $12, Pseudocolus fusiformis. Nos. 3924, 3925d, $12, Coprinus disseminatus.

2010, Mar. 25 **Perf. 13**
Stamps With White Frames
3921-3924 A1051 Set of 4 2.25 1.10
Miniature Sheet
Stamps Without White Frames
Perf. 11¾
3925 A1051 Sheet of 4, #a-d 2.25 1.10

Crabs
A1052

Designs: No. 3926, $5, Cardisoma carnifex. No. 3927, $5, Scandarma lintou. $10, Sesarmops intermedius. $25, Gecarcoidea lalandii.

2010, Apr. 15 **Perf. 11½**
3926-3929 A1052 Set of 4 3.00 1.50

Scenes From *The Romance of the Three Kingdoms*
A1053

Designs: No. 3930, $3.50, Shooting an Arrow at the Halberd Beside the Gate of the Camp (shown). No. 3931, $3.50, Commenting on Heroes Over Wine. $5, Zhou Yu's Anger at Being Tricked by Zhuge Liang Three Times. $20, Holding Meng Huo Captive Seven Times.

2010, Apr. 29 **Perf. 11½**
3930-3933 A1053 Set of 4 2.10 1.10
3933a Sheet of 4, #3930-3933, perf. 12 2.10 1.10

Flowers Type of 2009

Designs: 50c, Bauhinia variegata. $9, Euphorobia milii. $13, Brunfelsia hopeana. $17, Plumeria rubra.

2010, May 12 Litho. **Perf. 13½x12½**
3934 A1028 50c multi .25 .25
3935 A1028 $9 multi .55 .30
3936 A1028 $13 multi .80 .40
3937 A1028 $17 multi 1.10 .55
Nos. 3934-3937 (4) 2.70 1.50

Long-horned Beetles
A1054

Designs: 75c, Erythrus formosanus. $2.50, Rosalia formosa conviva. $5, Aphrodisium faldermannii yuagii. $25, Anoplophora horsfieldi tonkinensis.

2010, May 21 **Perf. 12½x13½**
3938 A1054 75c multi .25 .25
3939 A1054 $2.50 multi .25 .25
3940 A1054 $5 multi .30 .25
3941 A1054 $25 multi 1.60 .80
Nos. 3938-3941 (4) 2.40 1.55

See Nos. 3976-3979, 4027-4030, 4134-4137.

Girl Scouts, Cent. — A1055

Emblems and: $5, Two doves, stylized globe. $25, Dove, ribbon hearts.

2010, June 1 **Perf. 12½**
3942-3943 A1055 Set of 2 1.90 .95

Souvenir Sheet

Water Buffaloes, Sculpture by Huang Tu-shui (1895-1930) — A1056

Litho. & Embossed
2010, June 22 **Perf. 11½x11¼**
3944 A1056 $25 multi 1.60 .80

A1057

Scenes From Novel "Journey to the West" — A1058

Designs: No. 3945, Complete Enlightenment. No. 3946, Sun Wukong Wreaks Havoc in Heaven. $12, Dreaming of Beheading the Jing River Dragon King. $25, Stealing the Ginseng Fruits.

2010, July 7 Litho. Perf. 11¼x11½
3945 A1057 $5 multi .35 .25
3946 A1058 $5 multi .35 .25
3947 A1058 $12 multi .75 .35
3948 A1058 $25 multi 1.60 .80
Nos. 3945-3948 (4) 3.05 1.65

Compare with Nos. 4003-4006.

Lighthouses
A1059

Designs: No. 3949, $5, Chilung Tao Lighthouse (denomination in yellow). No. 3950, $5, Wenkan Tui Lighthouse (denomination in blue). $10, Paisha Chia Lighthouse (denomination in lilac), horiz. $25, Liuchiu Yu Lighthouse (denomination in light green), horiz.

Perf. 11¼x11½, 11½x11¼
2010, July 28
3949-3952 A1059 Set of 4 3.00 1.50
See Nos. 4160-4163.

Modern Taiwanese Paintings — A1060

No. 3953: a, $5, Bamboo Grove in Early Summer, by Tsai Yun-yan. b, $25, Pear Espalier, by Lu Yun-sheng.

2010, Aug. 9 **Perf. 12x12½**
3953 A1060 Horiz. pair, #a-b, + central label 1.90 .95

Souvenir Sheet

Nine Elders of Mt. Hsiang, by Unknown Painter — A1061

No. 3954: a, $5, Servant and elders playing game (35mm diameter). b, $25, Three elders and dancer (35mm diameter). c, $25, Elders in bamboo grove (37x29mm oval stamp).

2010, Sept. 9 **Perf.**
3954 A1061 Sheet of 3, #a-c 3.50 1.75

Stamps Depicting Educators
A1062

Designs: $5, Republic of China No. 1648 (Chu Hsi). $25, Republic of China No. 1798 (Confucius).

Perf. 11¼x11½
2010, Sept. 28 **Litho.**
3955-3956 A1062 Set of 2 1.90 .95

Shells
A1063

Designs: No. 3957, $5, Thatcheria mirabilis. No. 3958, $5, Tibia martinii. No. 3959, $12, Stellaria solaris. No. 3960, $12, Rapa rapa.

2010, Oct. 4 **Perf. 11½x11¼**
3957-3960 A1063 Set of 4 2.25 1.10

Bridges
A1064

Designs: No. 3961, $5, Lizejian Bridge, Yilan (shown). No. 3962, $5, Taroko Bridge, Hualien. $12, Hongye Bridge, Taitung. $15, Pudu Bridge, Hualien.

2010, Oct. 20
3961-3964 A1064 Set of 4 2.50 1.25

National Taipei University of Technology, Cent. — A1065

No. 3965: a, $5, Building, old gate. b, $25, Sixth Instructional Building, Technology Building, new gate.

2010, Nov. 1 **Perf. 12½**
3965 A1065 Horiz. pair, #a-b 2.00 1.00

A1066

A1067

A1068

A1069

A1070

A1071

A1072

A1073

A1074

A1075

A1076

A1077

A1078

A1079

A1080

A1081

A1082

A1083

A1084

2010, Nov. 6   Litho.   Perf. 13½x13¼

3966		Sheet of 9	3.25	1.60
a.	A1066	$5 multi	.35	.25
b.	A1067	$5 multi	.35	.25
c.	A1068	$5 multi	.35	.25
d.	A1069	$5 multi	.35	.25
e.	A1070	$5 multi	.35	.25
f.	A1071	$5 multi	.35	.25
g.	A1072	$5 multi	.35	.25
h.	A1073	$5 multi	.35	.25

| i. | A1074 | $5 multi | .35 | .25 |

Perf. 13¼x13½

3967		Sheet of 10	3.50	1.75
a.	A1075	$5 multi	.35	.25
b.	A1076	$5 multi	.35	.25
c.	A1077	$5 multi	.35	.25
d.	A1078	$5 multi	.35	.25
e.	A1079	$5 multi	.35	.25
f.	A1080	$5 multi	.35	.25
g.	A1081	$5 multi	.35	.25
h.	A1082	$5 multi	.35	.25
i.	A1083	$5 multi	.35	.25
j.	A1084	$5 multi	.35	.25

Taipei International Flora Expo.

Qing Dynasty Gilt Copper Censers A1085

Censer with: No. 3968, $5, Turquoise inlays (shown). No. 3969, $5, Lotus flower designs. $10, Glass and enamel inlays. $25, White jade, turquoise and glass inlays.

2010, Nov. 18   Perf. 11½

3968-3971	A1085	Set of 4	3.00	1.50
3971a		Souvenir sheet of 4,		
		#3968-3971, perf. 12	3.00	1.50

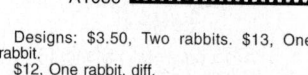

New Year 2011 (Year of the Rabbit) A1086

Designs: $3.50, Two rabbits. $13, One rabbit. $12, One rabbit, diff.

2010, Dec. 1   Perf. 12¼

3972-3973	A1086	Set of 2	1.10	.55

Souvenir Sheet   Perf. 12½

3974	A1086	$12 multi	.80	.40

No. 3974 contains one 61x37mm stamp.

Miniature Sheet

Fireworks Displays — A1087

No. 3975: a, $5, Double Tenth Day display, Taipei (30x30mm). b, $5, New Year's display at Taipei 101 Building (24x48mm). c, $25, Lantern Festival display, Kaohsiung (30x30mm). d, $25, Dragon Boat Festival display, Longtan (24x48mm).

Litho. With Hologram

2011, Jan. 1   Perf. 13¼

3975	A1087	Sheet of 4, #a-d	4.25	2.10

Long-horned Beetles Type of 2010

Designs: $1, Aeolesthes oenochrous. $3.50, Doliops similis. $10, Thermistis taiwanensis. $32, Dorysthenes pici.

2011, Jan. 26   Litho.   Perf. 12½x13½

3976	A1054	$1 multi	.25	.25
3977	A1054	$3.50 multi	.25	.25
3978	A1054	$10 multi	.70	.35
3979	A1054	$32 multi	2.25	1.10
		Nos. 3976-3979 (4)	3.45	1.95

Valentine's Day — A1088

Quick response code and: $5, Outline of heart. $25, Heart.

2011, Feb. 14   Perf. 12½

3980-3981	A1088	Set of 2	2.10	1.10

Values are for stamps with surrounding selvage.

Fish A1089

Designs: No. 3982, $5, Candidia barbatus. No. 3983, $5, Opsariichthys pachycephalus. $12, Spinibarbus hollandi. $25, Squalidus banarescui.

2011, Mar. 18   Perf. 13½x13¼

3982-3985	A1089	Set of 4	3.25	1.60

Miniature Sheet

Butterflies — A1090

No. 3986: a, $5, Euploea eunice hobsoni (butterfly cutout at LL). b, $5, Euploea sylvester swinhoei (butterfly cutout at LR). c, $12, Euploea tulliolus koxinga (denomination at LL). d, $12, Euploea mulciber barsine (denomination at LR).

2011, Apr. 8   Perf. 12½x12

3986	A1090	Sheet of 4, #a-d	2.40	1.25

National Tsing Hua University, Cent. A1091

Designs: $5, Second campus gate, old library building. $25, Current campus gate, Humanities and Social Sciences Building.

2011, Apr. 20   Perf. 12½

3987-3988	A1091	Set of 2	2.10	1.10

Alpine Flowers — A1092

Designs: No. 3989, $5, Gentiana scabrida var. punctulata. No. 3990, $5, Euphrasia transmorrisonensis. No. 3991, $10, Clematis montana, horiz. No. 3992, $10, Cypripedium formosanum, horiz.

2011, May 16   Perf. 12

3989-3992	A1092	Set of 4	2.10	1.10

A Singularly Harmonious Vibration — A1093

Double Happiness A1094

Blessings From the Three Stars A1095

Four is for Everything Goes as One Wishes A1096

Bumper Crops of All Five Grains A1097

Spring in All Six Directions A1098

Seven is for a Match Made in Heaven A1099

The Eight Immortals Wish for Your Longevity A1100

Nine Similes and Three
Abundances — A1101

Ten
Complete
A1102

No. 3993 — Color of denomination: a, Blue
green. b, Pink. c, Gray. d, Orange red. e, Red
violet. f, Red. g, Blue gray. h, Purple. i, Green.
j, Olive green.
No. 3994 — Color of denomination: a, Olive
green. b, Gray. c, Pink. d, Purple. e, Red. f,
Blue gray. g, Orange red. h, Green. i, Red
violet. j, Blue green.

2011, May 27		Perf. 12½	
3993	Block of 10	2.50	1.25
a.	A1093 $3.50 multi	.25	.25
b.	A1094 $3.50 multi	.25	.25
c.	A1095 $3.50 multi	.25	.25
d.	A1096 $3.50 multi	.25	.25
e.	A1097 $3.50 multi	.25	.25
f.	A1098 $3.50 multi	.25	.25
g.	A1099 $3.50 multi	.25	.25
h.	A1100 $3.50 multi	.25	.25
i.	A1101 $3.50 multi	.25	.25
j.	A1102 $3.50 multi	.25	.25
3994	Block of 10	3.50	1.75
a.	A1093 $5 multi	.35	.25
b.	A1094 $5 multi	.35	.25
c.	A1095 $5 multi	.35	.25
d.	A1096 $5 multi	.35	.25
e.	A1097 $5 multi	.35	.25
f.	A1098 $5 multi	.35	.25
g.	A1099 $5 multi	.35	.25
h.	A1100 $5 multi	.35	.25
i.	A1101 $5 multi	.35	.25
j.	A1102 $5 multi	.35	.25

Sea Slugs
A1103

Designs: No. 3995, $5, Mexichromis multi-
tuberculata. No. 3996, $5, Chromodoris wil-
lani. $12, Gymnodoris ceylonica. $25, Glos-
sodoris averni.

2011, June 8		Perf. 12½	
3995-3998	A1103 Set of 4	3.25	1.60

Owls — A1104

Designs: No. 3999, $5, Asio otus. No. 4000,
$5, Otus sunia. $10, Strix aluco. $25,
Glaucidium brodiei.

2011, July 7 Engr.	Perf. 12¾x12½	
3999-4002	A1104 Set of 4	3.25 1.60

See Nos. 4051-4054, 4122-4125.

Swindling
Treasures
A1105

Red
Boy — A1106

Crossing the
River on a
Turtle's
Back — A1107

Achieving
Nirvana — A1108

2011, July 21		Litho.	
4003	A1105 $5 multi	.35	.25
4004	A1106 $5 multi	.35	.25
4005	A1107 $12 multi	.85	.40
4006	A1108 $25 multi	1.75	.85
	Nos. 4003-4006 (4)	3.30	1.75

Scenes from Novel "Journey to the West."
Compare with Nos. 3945-3948.

Atayal Facial
Tattoos
A1109

2011, Aug. 1		Perf. 12½	
4007	A1109 $25 multi	1.75	.85

Souvenir Sheet

Scroll Painting, "Nine Elders of Mt.
Hsiang" — A1110

No. 4008: a, $5, Three elders and attendant
at game table. b, $25, Three elders and three
attendants dancing. c, $25, Two elders read-
ing, attendant, tree in foreground.

2011, Sept. 9		Perf. 13½x13¼	
4008	A1110 Sheet of 3, #a-c	3.75	1.90

National
Palace
Museum
A1111

Taipei 101
Building
A1112

Sun Moon
Lake
A1113

Yushan
(Jade
Mountain)
A1114

Alishan
A1115

Love River,
Kaohsiung
A1116

Beach,
Kenting
A1117

Day Lilies
in
Liushidan
Mountains
A1118

Taroko
National
Park
A1119

Jiufen
A1120

2011, Sept. 27		Perf. 12½	
4009	Block of 10	2.50	1.25
a.	A1111 $3.50 multi	.25	.25
b.	A1112 $3.50 multi	.25	.25
c.	A1113 $3.50 multi	.25	.25
d.	A1114 $3.50 multi	.25	.25
e.	A1115 $3.50 multi	.25	.25
f.	A1116 $3.50 multi	.25	.25
g.	A1117 $3.50 multi	.25	.25
h.	A1118 $3.50 multi	.25	.25
i.	A1119 $3.50 multi	.25	.25
j.	A1120 $3.50 multi	.25	.25
4010	Block of 10	3.50	1.75
a.	A1111 $5 multi	.35	.25
b.	A1112 $5 multi	.35	.25
c.	A1113 $5 multi	.35	.25
d.	A1114 $5 multi	.35	.25
e.	A1115 $5 multi	.35	.25
f.	A1116 $5 multi	.35	.25
g.	A1117 $5 multi	.35	.25
h.	A1118 $5 multi	.35	.25
i.	A1119 $5 multi	.35	.25
j.	A1120 $5 multi	.35	.25

Travel destinations. Nos. 4009 and 4010
were each printed in sheets containing two
blocks + 5 labels.

A1121

Republic of China, Cent. — A1122

No. 4011: a, Flag of Republic of China, Sun
Yat-sen, doves over buildings. b, Presidential
Office Building, bananas, pineapple, sugar
cane. c, Building, highway bridge, airplane,
ship. d, Train, silicon wafers, satellite dish. No.
4012, Flag of Republic of China, Presidential
Office Building, Sun Yat-sen.

Perf. 12½x13¼ Syncopated

2011, Oct. 10		Litho.	
4011	Horiz. strip of 4	3.25	1.60
a.-b.	A1121 $5 Either single	.35	.25
c.	A1121 $10 multi	.65	.35
d.	A1121 $25 multi	1.75	.85

**Souvenir Sheet
Litho. With Foil Application
Perf. 13¼**

| 4012 | A1122 $25 multi | 1.75 | .85 |

The syncopation between Nos. 4011a and
4011b is a rectangle, and oval between Nos.
4011b and 4011c and 4011c and 4011d.

Plum Blossoms
A1123

Perf. 13¼x13½

2011, Oct. 10	Litho. & Engr.	
4013	A1123 $100 multi	6.75 3.25

No. 4013 was printed in sheets of 10 + 8
labels.

Scouting in
China,
Cent. — A1124

Scout and: $5, City. $12, Mountain, horiz.

Perf. 12¾x12½, 12½x12¾

2011, Nov. 1		Litho.	
4014-4015	A1124 Set of 2	1.25	.60

Railway Branch Lines — A1125

No. 4016: a, $5, Shalun Branch Line (denomination in pink). b, $5, Jiji Branch Line (denomination in orange). c, $12, Neiwan Branch Line (denomination in blue). d, $12, Liujia Branch Line (denomination in pink). e, $15, Pingxi Branch Line.

2011, Nov. 12				Perf. 12½	
4016		Vert. strip of 5		3.50	1.75
a.-b.	A1125 $5 Either single			.35	.25
c.-d.	A1125 $12 Either single			.80	.40
e.	A1125 $15 multi			1.00	.50

New Year 2012 (Year of the Dragon) A1126

Designs: $3.50, Two dragons. $13, Dragon facing left. $12, Dragon facing right.

2011, Dec. 1			Perf. 13	
4017-4018	A1126	Set of 2	1.10	.55

Souvenir Sheet
Perf. 12½

4019	A1126 $12 multi		.80	.40

No. 4019 contains one 64x40mm stamp.

Souvenir Sheet

Alishan Forest Railway, Cent. — A1127

No. 4020: a, $5, Diesel engine, tunnel. b, $25, Steam engine.

2011, Dec. 25			Perf. 12½x12¾	
4020	A1127	Sheet of 2, #a-b	2.00	1.00

Berries — A1128

Designs: $3.50, Actinidia callosa. $5, Synsepalum dulcificum. $12, Solanum americanum. $25, Solanum verbascifolium.

2012, Jan. 12			Perf. 13¼x12½	
4021	A1128 $3.50 multi		.25	.25
4022	A1128 $5 multi		.35	.25
4023	A1128 $12 multi		.85	.40
4024	A1128 $25 multi		1.75	.85
	Nos. 4021-4024 (4)		3.20	1.75

See Nos. 4084-4087, 4106-4109, 4164-4167..

A1129

Roses — A1130

No. 4025: a, Rose. b, Rose, stem and leaves. $32, Two roses.

Litho. & Embossed

2012, Feb. 10			Perf. 14½	
4025	A1129	Horiz. pair + central label	2.60	1.25
a.	$12 multi		.85	.40
b.	$25 multi		1.75	.85

Souvenir Sheet
Litho.
Perf.

4026	A1130 $32 multi		2.25	1.10

No. 4026 is impregnated with a rose scent.

Long-horned Beetles Type of 2010

Designs: $7, Leptura formosomontana formosomontana. $12, Pyrestes curticornis. $15, Anaglyptus meridionalis. $20, Anoplophora albopicta.

2012, Mar. 9	Litho.		Perf. 12½x13½	
4027	A1054 $7 multi		.50	.25
4028	A1054 $12 multi		.85	.40
4029	A1054 $15 multi		1.00	.50
4030	A1054 $20 multi		1.40	.70
	Nos. 4027-4030 (4)		3.75	1.85

Mushrooms A1131

Designs: Nos. 4031, 4035a, $5, Amanita rubrovolvata. Nos. 4032, 4035b, $5, Entoloma murraii. Nos. 4033, 4035c, $12, Geastrum sessile. Nos. 4034, 4035d, $12, Clavulinopsis miyabeana.

2012, Mar. 23			Perf. 13¼x13	
4031-4034	A1131	Set of 4	2.40	1.25

Souvenir Sheet
Stamps Without White Frames
Perf. 12¾x13

4035	A1131	Sheet of 4, #a-d	2.40	1.25

No. 4035 contains four 26x34mm stamps.

Fish A1132

Designs: No. 4036, $5, Formosania lacustre. No. 4037, $5, Tanakia himantegus. $12, Channa asiatica. $25, Sinogastromyzon puliensis.

2012, Apr. 11			Perf. 12½x13¼	
4036-4039	A1132	Set of 4	3.25	1.60

Scenes From Novel "Outlaws of the Marsh" A1133

Designs: No. 4040, $5, Demons Released (denomination at LL). No. 4041, $5, Slaying the Tiger on Jingyang Ridge (denomination at LR). $10, Mountain God Temple on a Stormy Night. $25, Knocking the Lord of the West Dead.

2012, Apr. 25			Perf. 12½x12¾	
4040-4043	A1133	Set of 4	3.25	1.60

See Nos. 4110-4113.

"A Match Made in Heaven" A1134

"One Child After Another" A1135

Congratulatory greetings: $5, "The Hall is Packed with Wealth and Riches." $12, "A Family Experinces Two Joys."

2012, May 4			Perf. 13	
4044	A1134 $3.50 multi		.25	.25
4045	A1135 $3.50 multi		.25	.25
4046	A1135 $5 multi		.35	.25
4047	A1135 $12 multi		.80	.40
	Nos. 4044-4047 (4)		1.65	1.15

Booklet Stamp
Perf. 13½ Vert.

4048	A1135 $5 multi		.35	.25
a.	Booklet pane of 12		4.25	
	Complete booklet, #4048a		4.25	

Inauguration of President Ma Ying-jeou and Vice President Wu Den-yih — A1136

No. 4049 — President, Vice president and: a, Flag and Presidential Palace. b, Taipei 101 building, train, ship and airplane. c, Children, dancers, National Theater. d, Map of Taiwan, stylized globe. $32, President, Vice President, flag, Presidential Palace, plum blossoms, horiz.

2012, May 20			Perf. 13¼x13½	
4049		Horiz. strip of 4	2.40	1.25
a.-b.	A1136 $5 Either single		.35	.25
c.-d.	A1136 $12 Either single		.80	.40

Souvenir Sheet
Perf. 13½x13¼

4050	A1136 $32 multi		2.25	1.10

No. 4050 contains one 80x30mm stamp.

Owls Type of 2011

Designs: No. 4051, $5, Asio flammeus. No. 4052, $5, Otus spilocephalus. $10, Strix leptogrammica. $25, Ninox scutulata.

2012, June 6	Engr.		Perf. 12¾x12½	
4051-4054	A1104	Set of 4	3.00	1.50

Festivals A1137

Designs: No. 4055, $5, Chinese New Year (fireworks and calligraphic couplets). No.

4056, $5, Lantern Festival (lanterns and sandals). $10, Dragon Boat Festival (herb sachets and covered wine containers). $25, Mid-autumn Festival (Jade Hare, Lady Chang'e, moon cakes).

2012, June 20	Litho.		Perf. 12½	
4055-4058	A1137	Set of 4	3.00	1.50

Miniature Sheet

Bees and Wasps — A1138

No. 4059: a, $5, Phimenes flavopictus. b, $5, Xanthopimpla pedator. c, $5, Vespa ducalis. d, $10, Apis mellifera. e, $10, Xylocopa tranquebarorum. f, $10, Apis cerana.

2012, July 12			Perf. 13	
4059	A1138	Sheet of 6, #a-f	3.00	1.50

Ferns Type of 2009

Designs: No. 4060, $5, Polystichum lepidocaulon. No. 4061, $5, Bolbitis heteroclita. $10, Adiantum malesianum, horiz. $25, Asplenium prolongatum, horiz.

Perf. 12¾x12½, 12½x12¾

2012, July 25				
4060-4063	A1040	Set of 4	3.00	1.50
4063a		Sheet of 4, #4060-4063, perf. 12, + label	3.00	1.50

Familial Bonds A1139

Silhouettes of: $5, Father and daughter. $7, Mother and son. $10, Mother, father and child. $12, Grandparents and child.

2012, Aug. 24			Perf. 12½x13¼	
4064-4067	A1139	Set of 4	2.40	1.25

Miniature Sheet

Teas and Tourist Attractions — A1140

No. 4068: a, Baozhong tea, Pinglin Tea Museum (bright yellow frame). b, Tieguanyin tea, Maokong Funicular (yellow orange frame). c, Black tea, Sun Moon Lake Wharf (orange frame). d, Oolong tea, Alishan Forest train (bister frame). e, Oriental Beauty tea, Emei Lake Suspension Bridge (red brown frame).

2012, Sept. 12			Perf. 12½	
4068	A1140	$10 Sheet of 5, #a-e	3.50	1.75

Nos. 4068a-4068e each have a cut-out of a teapot under the denomination.

Cotton Rose — A1141

Bird-of-Paradise Flower — A1142

Clary Sage — A1143

Dancing Lady Orchid — A1144

Zinnia — A1145

Marigold A1146

Chinese Hibiscus — A1147

Fragrant Olive — A1148

Flowering Crab Apple — A1149

Hydrangea A1150

2012, Sept. 28		Perf. 13¼	
4069	Block of 10	2.50	1.25
a.	A1141 $3.50 multi	.25	.25
b.	A1142 $3.50 multi	.25	.25
c.	A1143 $3.50 multi	.25	.25
d.	A1144 $3.50 multi	.25	.25
e.	A1145 $3.50 multi	.25	.25
f.	A1146 $3.50 multi	.25	.25
g.	A1147 $3.50 multi	.25	.25
h.	A1148 $3.50 multi	.25	.25
i.	A1149 $3.50 multi	.25	.25
j.	A1150 $3.50 multi	.25	.25
4070	Block of 10	3.50	1.75
a.	A1141 $5 multi	.35	.25
b.	A1142 $5 multi	.35	.25
c.	A1143 $5 multi	.35	.25
d.	A1144 $5 multi	.35	.25
e.	A1145 $5 multi	.35	.25
f.	A1146 $5 multi	.35	.25

g.	A1147 $5 multi	.35	.25
h.	A1148 $5 multi	.35	.25
i.	A1149 $5 multi	.35	.25
j.	A1150 $5 multi	.35	.25

Miniature Sheets

A1151

Characters From *Toy Story* — A1152

No. 4071: a, $5, Mr. Pricklepants, Peas-in-a-Pod (40x30mm). b, $5, Aliens (35mm diameter). c, $5, Trixie, Buttercup (40x30mm). d, $12, Lotso-Huggin Bear (30x40mm). e, $12, Woody (35mm diameter).

No. 4072: a, $5, Woody on Bullseye (35mm diameter). b, $5, Rex (35mm diameter). c, $5, Hamm (35mm diameter). d, $12, Buzz Lightyear (35mm diameter). e, $12, Jessie (30x40mm).

Serpentine Die Cut (round stamps), Serpentine Die Cut 14x13½ (horiz. stamps), Serpentine Die Cut 13½x14 (vert. stamps)

2012, Oct. 23		Self-Adhesive	
4071	A1151	Sheet of 5, #a-e	2.75 1.40
4072	A1152	Sheet of 5, #a-e	2.75 1.40

Protected Mammals A1153

Designs: No. 4073, $5, Paguma larvata taivana. No. 4074, $5, Mustela nivalis formosana. $10, Martes flavigula chrysospila. $25, Viverricula indica pallida.

2012, Nov. 7 Litho.		Perf. 12½x13¼	
4073-4076	A1153	Set of 4	3.25 1.60

A1154

Three Friends and a Hundred Birds, by Pien Wen-chin (c. 1356-c. 1428) — A1155

No. 4077 — Details from painting of various birds in tree: a, $5. b, $10. c, $12. $70, Entire painting.

2012, Nov. 22		Perf. 13¼x13	
4077	A1154	Sheet of 3, #a-c	1.90 .95

Souvenir Sheet
Silk-Faced Paper
Perf. 14x14¼

4078	A1155	$70 multi	5.00 2.50

New Year 2013 (Year of the Snake) A1156

Designs: $3.50, Two snakes. $13, Snake, head at left.
$12, Snake, head at right.

2012, Dec. 3		Perf. 13	
4079-4080	A1156	Set of 2	1.25 .60

Souvenir Sheet
Perf. 12½

4081	A1156	$12 multi	.85 .45

No. 4081 contains one 64x40mm stamp.

Marine Life — A1157

No. 4082: a, $10, Eurypharynx pelecanoides. b, $10, Bufoceratias shaoi. c, $12, Argyropelecus aculeatus. d, $12, Regalecus glesne.
$25, Histioteuthis celetaria pacifica, vert.

Litho., Litho. With Foil Application (#4082c)

2012, Dec. 12		Perf. 14x13¼	
4082	A1157	Sheet of 4, #a-d	3.00 1.50

Souvenir Sheet
Perf. 13¼x14

4083	A1157	$25 multi	1.75 .85

Berries Type of 2012

Designs: $2.50, Rhodomyrtus tomentosa. $7, Ardisia squamulosa. $10, Hylocereus undatus. $32, Mahonia japonica.

2013, Jan. 17 Litho.		Perf. 13¼x12½	
4084	A1128	$2.50 multi	.25 .25
4085	A1128	$7 multi	.50 .25
4086	A1128	$10 multi	.70 .35
4087	A1128	$32 multi	2.25 1.10
		Nos. 4084-4087 (4)	3.70 1.95

Chinese Dishes — A1158

No. 4088 — Chopsticks and: a, Kung Pao Chicken, bowl of rice, spoon. b, Mud Crab with Glutinous Rice Cake, cup of green tea, salt shaker. c, Three-cup Chicken, bowl of sauce, salt shaker. d, Hakka Stir-fry, bowl of rice, salt shaker.

2013, Jan. 31		Perf. 13¼x13	
4088	A1158	$5 Horiz. strip of 4, #a-d	1.40 .70

Compare with Type A1176.

St. Valentine's Day — A1159

Designs: $12, Colored roses. $25, White roses.

Litho. & Embossed

2013, Feb. 4		Perf. 13¼x13½	
4089-4090	A1159	Set of 2	2.50 1.25
4090a		Souveneir sheet of 2, #4089-4090	2.50 1.25

Grain Farming — A1160

Designs: $5, Oryza sativa. $7, Setaria italica. $10, Zea mays. $25, Triticum aestivum.

2013, Mar. 5	Litho.	Perf. 12½	
4091-4094	A1160	Set of 4	3.25 1.60

A1161

A1162

A1163

A1164

A1165

Qing Dynasty Embroidery — A1166

2013, Mar. 20   Litho.   Perf. 14

4095	A1161	$10 multi	.70	.35
4096	A1162	$10 multi	.70	.35
4097	A1163	$10 multi	.70	.35
4098	A1164	$10 multi	.70	.35
4099	A1165	$10 multi	.70	.35
	Nos. 4095-4099 (5)		3.50	1.75

Litho. & Embossed With Foil Application
Souvenir Sheet
Silk-Faced Paper
Perf. 13x13¼

4100	A1166	$100 multi	6.75	3.50

Children at Play — A1167

Children: No. 4101, $5, Carrying lantern. No. 4102, $5, Flying paper airplanes. No. 4103, $5, With pinwheels. No. 4104, $5, With spinning top. No. 4105, $5, With hand puppets.

2013, Apr. 2   Litho.   Perf. 12½

4101-4105	A1167	Set of 5	1.75	.85
4105a		Booklet pane of 10, 2 each #4101-4105, perf. 12½ on 3 sides	3.50	—
		Complete booklet, #4105a	3.50	

See Nos. 4168-4172.

Berries Type of 2012

Designs: $1, Ribes formosanum. $15, Garcinia subelliptica. $17, Coffea arabica. $20, Smilax oreata.

2013, Apr. 17   Perf. 13¼x12½

4106	A1128	$1 multi	.25	.25
4107	A1128	$15 multi	1.00	.50
4108	A1128	$17 multi	1.25	.60
4109	A1128	$20 multi	1.40	.70
	Nos. 4106-4109 (4)		3.90	2.05

Capturing Daming Prefecture by Ruse A1168

Heavenly Inscriptions on Stele A1169

Lianshan Outlaws Granted Imperial Amnesty A1170

Successful Expedition Against Liao Empire A1171

2013, May 10   Perf. 12½x12¾

4110	A1168	$5 multi	.35	.25
4111	A1169	$5 multi	.35	.25
4112	A1170	$10 multi	.70	.35
4113	A1171	$25 multi	1.75	.85
	Nos. 4110-4113 (4)		3.15	1.70

Scenes from novel "Outlaws of the Marsh." Compare with Nos. 4040-4043.

Congratulations — A1172

Designs: No. 4114, $3.50, Tropical fish. No. 4115, $3.50, Swans. No. 4116, $5, Penguins. No. 4117, $5, Mandarin ducks.

2013, May 22   Perf. 12½

4114-4117	A1172	Set of 4	1.25	.60

Values are for stamps with surrounding selvage.

Herbs — A1173

Designs: No. 4118, $5, Mentha x piperita. No. 4119, $5, Rosmarinus officinalis. $12, Salvia elegans. $15, Artemisia indica.

2013, June 11

4118-4121	A1173	Set of 4	2.50	1.25

See Nos. 4179-4182, 4244-4247.

Owls Type of 2011

Designs: No. 4122, $5, Otus lettia. No. 4123, $5, Tyto longimembris. $10, Ketupa flavipes. $25, Otus elegans botelensis.

2013, June 26   Engr.

4122-4125	A1104	Set of 4	3.00	1.50

Vases — A1174

Designs: $12, Ming Dynasty vase with "One Hundred Deer" design. $25, Qing Dynasty vase with "One Hundred Boys" design.

2013, July 10   Litho.

4126-4127	A1174	Set of 2	2.50	1.25
4127a		Souvenir sheet of 2, #4126-4127	2.50	1.25

Mushrooms A1175

Designs: Nos. 4128, 4132a, $5, Ramaria botrytis. Nos. 4129, 4132b, $5, Morchella elata. Nos. 4130, 4132c, $12, Gomphus floccosus. Nos. 4131, 4132d, $12, Aleuria aurantia.

2013, July 24   Perf. 12½
Stamps With White Frames

4128-4131	A1175	Set of 4	2.25	1.10

Souvenir Sheet
Stamps Without White Frames
Perf. 12½x13

4132	A1175	Sheet of 4, #a-d	2.25	1.10

No. 4132 contains four 26x34mm stamps.

Chinese Dishes — A1176

No. 4133 — Chopsticks and: a, Stinky tofu, condiment bowl at UL. b, Taiwanese meatball, two sauce bottles at UL. c, Oyster omelet, teapot and condiment bowl at UL. d, Braised pork rice, salt and pepper shakers at UL.

2013, Aug. 16   Perf. 13¼x13

4133	A1176	$5 Horiz. strip of 4, #a-d	1.40	.70

Compare with Type A1158.

Long-horned Beetles Type of 2010

Designs: No. 4134, Parandra lanyuana. No. 4135, Bunothorax takasagoensis. $10, Oplatocera mandibulata. $25, Cyrtoclytus kusumai.

2013, Aug. 28   Perf. 12½x13½

4134	A1054	$5 multi	.35	.25
4135	A1054	$5 multi	.35	.25
4136	A1054	$10 multi	.70	.35
4137	A1054	$25 multi	1.75	.85
	Nos. 4134-4137 (4)		3.15	1.70

Soong May-ling (Madame Chiang) (1898-2003), First Lady — A1177

2013, Sept. 12   Perf. 12¾x12½

4138	A1177	$12 multi	.80	.40

A1178

Emperor Gaozong Era Artifacts — A1179

No. 4139: a, Qing Dynasty gourd-shaped vase. b, Qing Dynasty carved red lacquer bowl, horiz. c, Northern Song Dyanasty plate with celadon glaze, horiz. d, Qing Dynasty jade bear-shaped vessel.

$25, Qing Dynasty New Year's silk tapestry scroll.

2013, Oct. 8   Litho.   Perf. 12

4139	A1178	Sheet of 4 + label	2.50	1.25
a.		$5 multi	.35	.25
b.-c.		$10 Either single	.65	.30
d.		$12 multi	.85	.40

Souvenir Sheet
Perf. 12¾x12½

4140	A1179	$25 multi	1.75	.85

Presidential Office Building, Taipei — A1180

Sun Yat-sen Memorial Hall, Taipei — A1181

National Palace Museum, Taipei — A1182

Taipei 101 Building — A1183

Chiang Kai-shek Memorial Hall, Taipei — A1184

Jiufen — A1185

Alishan — A1186

Qingshui Cliff — A1187

Queen's Head Rock Formation A1188

Sun Moon Lake — A1189

2013, Oct. 22 Litho. Perf. 13¼

4141		Block of 6	2.10	1.10
a.	A1180	$5 multi	.35	.25
b.	A1181	$5 multi	.35	.25
c.	A1182	$5 multi	.35	.25
d.	A1183	$5 multi	.35	.25
e.	A1184	$5 multi	.35	.25
f.	A1185	$5 multi	.35	.25
4142		Block of 4	3.50	1.60
a.	A1186	$12 multi	.85	.40
b.	A1187	$12 multi	.85	.40
c.	A1188	$12 multi	.85	.40
d.	A1189	$12 multi	.85	.40

Bicycle Paths — A1190

Bicyclist on: No. 4143, $5, Yangguang Bridge on Xindian River Bicycle Path, New Taipei City (pale orange panel). No. 4144, $5, Bali Zuoan Bicycle Path, New Taipei City (pink panel). No. 4145, $10, Sankeng Bicycle Path, Taoyuan (green panel). No. 4146, $10, Hsinchu Coast Bicycle Path (yellow panel).

2013, Nov. 8 Litho. Perf. 13¼x13
Stamp + Label

4143-4146	A1190	Set of 4	2.10	1.10

Dragon and Phoenix — A1191

2013, Nov. 15 Engr. Perf. 13¼x12½

4147	A1191	$50 car & rose	3.50	1.75

Qing Dynasty Bowl, 1723-35 A1192

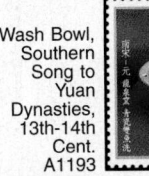

Wash Bowl, Southern Song to Yuan Dynasties, 13th-14th Cent. A1193

Ming Dynasty Jar With Lid, 1465-87 A1194

12th Cent. Ding Ware Pillow A1195

Ming Dynasty Flower Holder A1196

Qing Dynasty Covered Box, 1874-1908 A1197

Qing Dynasty Jadeite Cabbage and Insects Figurine A1198

Ru Ware Warming Bowl, 11th-12th Cent. A1199

Qing Dynasty Stone With Meat Design A1200

Western Zhoud Dynasty Mao-gong Ding (Ritual Vessel) A1201

2013, Nov. 22 Litho. Perf. 12½

4148		Block of 6	2.10	1.10
a.	A1192	$5 multi	.35	.25
b.	A1193	$5 multi	.35	.25
c.	A1194	$5 multi	.35	.25
d.	A1195	$5 multi	.35	.25
e.	A1196	$5 multi	.35	.25
f.	A1197	$5 multi	.35	.25
4149		Block of 4	3.50	1.60
a.	A1198	$12 multi	.85	.40
b.	A1199	$12 multi	.85	.40
c.	A1200	$12 multi	.85	.40
d.	A1201	$12 multi	.85	.40

Items in National Palace Museum.

New Year 2014 (Year of the Horse) A1202

Designs: $3.50, Horse with leg lifted. $13, Horse leaping. $12, Two leaping horses.

2013, Dec. 2 Litho. Perf. 13

4150-4151	A1202	Set of 2	1.10	.55

Souvenir Sheet
Perf. 12½

4152	A1202	$12 multi	.85	.40

No. 4152 contains one 64x40mm stamp.

Corals A1203

Designs: $3.50, Dendronephthya gigantea. $5, Pavona cactus. $10, Acropora granulosa. $15, Melithaea ochracea.

2014, Jan. 8 Litho. Perf. 12½x13¼

4153-4156	A1203	Set of 4	2.25	1.10

See Nos. 4257-4260, 4308-4311.

Chinese Desserts — A1204

No. 4157: a, Pineapple-filled shortcrust pastries, orange shopping bag and box. b, Mochi, green shopping bag and box. c, Sun cakes, red shopping bag and box. d, Egg yolk pastries, rose lilac shopping bag and box.

2014, Jan. 22 Litho. Perf. 13¼x13

4157	A1204	$5 Horiz. strip of 4, #a-d	1.40	.70

Lophura Swinhoii — A1205

No. 4158: a, Immature male. b, Head of mature male. c, Chicks. d, Hen and chick. $25, Male and female.

Perf. 12½x13¼

2014, Feb. 20 Litho.

4158	A1205	Block of 4	2.25	1.25
a.-b.		$5 Either single	.35	.25
c.		$10 multi	.65	.35
d.		$12 multi	.80	.40

Souvenir Sheet
Perf. 13½

4159	A1205	$25 multi	1.75	.85

No. 4159 contains one 80x50mm stamp.

Lighthouses Type of 2010

Designs: No. 4160, $5, Fangyuan Lighthouse (denomination in rose), horiz. No. 4161, $5, Chamu Yu Lighthouse (denomination in blue), horiz. $10, Lanyu Lighthouse (denomination in purple), horiz. $25, Sandiaojiao Lighthouse (denomination in yellow), horiz.

2014, Mar. 6 Litho. Perf. 12½x12¾

4160-4163	A1059	Set of 4	3.00	1.50

Berries Type of 2012

Designs: No. 4164, Lycium chinense. No. 4165, Dianella ensifolia. $15, Ampelopsis brevipedunculata var. hancei. $34, Diplocylos palmatus.

Perf. 13¼x12½

2014, Mar. 27 Litho.

4164	A1128	$5 multi	.35	.25
4165	A1128	$5 multi	.35	.25
4166	A1128	$15 multi	1.00	.50
4167	A1128	$34 multi	2.25	1.10
	Nos. 4164-4167 (4)		3.95	2.10

Children at Play Type of 2013

Designs: No. 4168, $5, Boy on hobby horse. No. 4169, $5, Children playing with bamboo helicopters. No. 4170, $5, Child flying kite. No. 4171, $5, Children playing marbles. No. 4172, $5, Children with Lion Dance costumes.

2014, Apr. 2 Litho. Perf. 12½

4168-4172	A1167	Set of 5	1.75	.85
4172a		Booklet pane of 10, 2 each #4168-4172, perf. 12½ on 3 sides	3.50	—
		Complete booklet, #4172a	3.50	

Children at Play Bathing a Buddha, Scroll Painting by Su Hanchen A1206

Children Playing in an Autumn Garden, Scroll Painting by Su Hanchen A1207

Children Playing in Summer, Scroll Painting by Unknown Artist — A1208

Children Playing in Autumn, Scroll Painting by Unknown Artist — A1209

Children Painting in Winter, Scroll Painting by Unknown Artist — A1210

2014, Apr. 30   Litho.   Perf. 13¼x12½

4173	A1206	$5 multi	.35	.25
4174	A1207	$5 multi	.35	.25
4175	A1208	$10 multi	.70	.35
4176	A1209	$10 multi	.70	.35
4177	A1210	$12 multi	.80	.40
	Nos. 4173-4177 (5)		2.90	1.60

"The Swan Goose Carries a Message" — A1211

Perf. 13½x13¼

2014, May 9   Litho. & Engr.
4178 A1211 $9 multi   .60 .30
See People's Republic of China No. 4189.

Herbs Type of 2013

Designs: $3.50, Foeniculum vulgare. $5, Perilla frutescens. $12, Lavandula angustifolia. $25, Ocimum basilicum.

2014, June 11   Litho.   Perf. 12½
4179-4182 A1173 Set of 4   3.00 1.50

Souvenir Sheet

Electrification of the Hua-tung Railway — A1212

No. 4183: a, $5, Trains in Hualien Station. b, $12, Train and Kecheng bridge. c, $25, Train exiting Shanli Tunnel.

Perf. 12½x12¾
2014, June 28   Litho.
4183 A1212 Sheet of 3, #a-c   3.00 1.50

Cuichi Pond A1213

Tunlu Pond A1214

Designs: $10, Qicai Lake. $12, Jiaming Lake.

2014, July 17   Litho.   Perf. 13¼

4184	A1213	$5 multi	.35	.25
4185	A1214	$5 multi	.35	.25
4186	A1214	$10 multi	.70	.35
4187	A1214	$12 multi	.80	.40
	Nos. 4184-4187 (4)		2.20	1.25

National Taiwan Library, Cent. — A1215

2014, Aug. 9   Litho.   Perf. 12½
4188 A1215 $12 multi   .80 .40

Jugang Tower and Residential Buildings, Kinmen — A1216

Wentai Pagoda and Buildings, Kinmen — A1217

2014, Aug. 28   Litho.   Perf. 12½
4189   Horiz. pair   1.10 .65
 a. A1216 $5 multi   .35 .25
 b. A1217 $12 multi   .80 .40

Kinmen County, cent.

Miniature Sheet

Museums — A1218

No. 4190: a, $5, National Taiwan Museum of Fine Arts (modern building with lawn), Taichung. b, $5, National Taiwan Museum, Taipei (building with 6 pillars). c, $5, National Museum of Taiwan Literature (building with domes at sides). d, $5, National Museum of Taiwan History (building with solar panels). e, $12, National Palace Museum, vert.

2014, Sept. 10   Litho.   Perf. 12½
4190 A1218 Sheet of 5, #a-e, +
            4 labels   2.10 1.10

Blue and White Porcelain A1219

Designs: $5, Qing Dynasty dish with floral design. $10, Ming Dynasty jar with peony design. $12, Ming Dynasty jar with dragon design. $20, Qing Dynasty vase depicting women.
$25, Qing Dynasty plate with bird and flowers design, horiz.

Litho. & Embossed
2014, Sept. 19   Perf. 13¾x13½
4191-4194 A1219 Set of 4   3.25 1.60
Souvenir Sheet
Perf. 13½x13¾
4195 A1219 $25 multi   1.75 .85

Miniature Sheet

Taipei 2015 Asian International Stamp Exhibition — A1220

No. 4196: a, $5, Pink azalea blossoms in spring, Mt. Hehuan. b, $5, Tung trees in summer, Pingxi Railway. c, $10, Maple trees in autumn, Wuling Farm. d, $25, Cherry blossoms in winter, Mt. Xue.

2014, Oct. 3   Litho.   Perf. 12½
4196 A1220 Sheet of 4, #a-d, +
            4 labels   3.00 1.50

Miniature Sheet

Taipei Zoo, Cent. — A1221

No. 4197: a, $5, Formosan serow (30x40mm). b, $5, Formosan pangolin (40x30mm). c, $10, Asian elephant (55x38mm). d, $10, Formosan black bear (30x40mm). e, $12, Bengal tiger (55x38mm). f, $12, Giant pandas (38x55mm).

Perf. 13¼x12½, 12½x13¼
2014, Oct. 16   Litho.
4197 A1221 Sheet of 6, #a-f   3.50 1.75

Scenes From Novel "The Dream of Red Mansions," by Cao Xueqin A1222

Designs: No. 4198, $5, Women standing around seated man. No. 4199, $5, Woman and five men looking at garden. $10, Visit of Yuanchun at Lantern Festival. $25, Baochai chasing butterflies.

2014, Oct. 27   Litho.   Perf. 13x13½
4198-4201 A1222 Set of 4   3.00 1.50
See Nos. 4228-4231, 4304-4307.

Flowers in Koji Pottery Vases — A1223

Large vases with: No. 4202, $5, Peonies (yellow green panel). No. 4203, $5, Lotuses (blue panel). $10, Chrysanthemums (orange panel). $25, Camellias (pink lilac panel).

2014, Nov. 14   Litho.   Perf. 13½
4202-4205 A1223 Set of 4   3.00 1.50

Bride and Groom In Chinese Attire A1224

Bride and Groom in Western Attire A1225

Bride and groom with: No. 4206, Red ribbon. No. 4207, Angels and flowers. No. 4208, Red streamer and bow. No. 4209, Hearts and horses.

2014, Nov. 21   Litho.   Perf. 12½
4206	A1224	$3.50 multi	.25	.25
4207	A1225	$3.50 multi	.25	.25
4208	A1224	$5 multi	.35	.25
4209	A1225	$5 multi	.35	.25
	Nos. 4206-4209 (4)		1.20	1.00

New Year 2015 (Year of the Ram) — A1226

Designs: $3.50, Bright pink ram. $13, Purple ram. $12, Two rams.

2014, Dec. 1   Litho.   Perf. 13
4210-4211	A1226	Set of 2	1.10	.55

Souvenir Sheet   Perf. 12½
4212	A1226	$12 multi	.80	.40

No. 4212 contains one 64x40mm stamp.

Archaeological Treasures From Yin Ruins — A1227

No. 4213: a, Marble figurine depicting owl, rose brown background. b, Cauldron with handles, light blue background. c, Oracle bone, rose brown background. d, Mask for horse with turquoise inlays, gray blue background. e, Figurine of human head with crest, light blue background. f, Anthropomorphic figurine with tiger's head, rose brown background. g, Wine container with detachable cap, gray blue background. h, Deer skull with inscriptions, rose brown background.

2014, Dec. 10   Litho.   Perf. 12½
4213	A1227	Block of 8	4.25	2.10
a.-d.		$5 Any single	.25	.25
e.-h.		$12 Any single	.80	.40
i.		Souvenir sheet of 8, #4213a-4213h + 4 labels	4.25	2.10

Jellyfish — A1228

Designs: $5, Pelagia noctiluca. $7, Physophora hydrostatica. $10, Mastigias papua. $12, Cyanea capillata.

2015, Jan. 8   Litho.   Perf. 13¼x13
4214-4217	A1228	Set of 4	2.25	1.10

Legumes A1229

Designs: $5, Arachis hypogaea. $7, Vigna angularis. $10, Glycine max. $25, Vigna radiata.

2015, Jan. 28   Litho.   Perf. 13¼x12½
4218-4221	A1229	Set of 4	3.00	1.50

Animals — A1230

Nos. 4222 and 4223: a, Rabbits. b, Squirrels. c, Dogs. d, Bears. e, Elephants. f, Cats. g, Deer. h, Sheep. i, Zebras. j, Giraffes.

2015, Feb. 12   Litho.   Perf. 13¼
4222		Block of 10	2.50	1.25
a.-j.	A1230	$3.50 Any single	.25	.25
4223		Block of 10	3.50	1.75
a.-j.	A1230	$5 Any single	.35	.25

Bo Le Appraises the Horse A1231

The Ambition of a Swan A1232

Adept With Both the Pen and the Sword A1233

Tiny Blade of Grass and Spring Sun A1234

Perf. 12½x12¾

2015, Mar. 20   Litho.
4224	A1231	$5 multi	.35	.25
4225	A1232	$5 multi	.35	.25
4226	A1233	$5 multi	.35	.25
4227	A1234	$5 multi	.35	.25
	Nos. 4224-4227 (4)		1.40	1.00

Chinese idioms.

Daiyu Burying the Flowers A1235

Tanchun Starting a Poetry Club A1236

Grandmother Liu Touring Daguanyuan — A1237

Miaoyu Tasting Tea A1238

2015, Mar. 30   Litho.   Perf. 13x13¼
4228	A1235	$5 multi	.35	.25
4229	A1236	$5 multi	.35	.25
4230	A1237	$10 multi	.65	.30
4231	A1238	$25 multi	1.60	.80
	Nos. 4228-4231 (4)		2.95	1.60

Scenes from "The Dream of Red Mansions," by Cao Xueqin. Compare with Nos. 4198-4201, 4304-4307.

Teresa Teng (1953-95), Singer — A1239

Various photographs of Teng with panel color of: $5, Pink. $9, Orange. $13, Dull rose. $15, Lilac.

2015, Apr. 15   Litho.   Perf. 12½
4232-4235	A1239	Set of 4	2.75	1.40

Control Yuan Building, Cent. — A1240

2015, Apr. 24   Litho.   Perf. 13¼
4236	A1240	$25 multi	1.75	.85

Taipei 2015 Intl. Stamp Exhibition — A1241

No. 4237: a, Dragon. b, Geese.

2015, Apr. 24   Litho.   Perf. 14
4237	A1241	Horiz. pair + central label	2.10	1.10
a.		$5 multi	.35	.25
b.		$25 multi	1.75	.85
c.		Souvenir sheet of 4, 2 each #4237a-4237b, perf. 13¼x13½ syncopated	4.25	2.25

Black-faced Spoonbills on Zengwen River — A1242

Black-winged Stilt, Sicao Wetlands A1243

2015, Apr. 25   Litho.   Perf. 14
4238	A1242	$10 multi	.65	.30
4239	A1243	$25 multi	1.75	.85
a.		Horiz. pair, #4238-4239, + central label	2.40	1.25
b.		Vert. pair, #4238-4239, no label	2.40	1.25

Taipei 2015 Intl. Stamp Exhibition. Nos 4238-4239 were printed in sheets of 16 (8 of each stamp) + 9 labels.

A1244

Taipei 2015 Intl. Stamp Exhibition — A1245

No. 4240: a, Family, child playing with blocks. b, Family on bicycle.
No. 4241: a, Family, child playing with blocks at left, on bicycle at right. b, Family, child playing with blocks at right, on bicycle at left.

2015, Apr. 26   Litho.   Perf. 12¾x12½
4240	A1244	Horiz. pair + central label	2.10	1.10
a.		$5 multi	.35	.25
b.		$25 multi	1.75	.85

Souvenir Sheet
4241	A1245	Sheet of 2	3.50	1.75
a.-b.		$25 Either single	1.75	.85

Taipei 2015 Intl. Stamp Exhibition — A1246

No. 4242: a, Sky Lantern Festival, Pingxi. b, Xiao Liuqiu coral island.

2015, Apr. 27   Litho.   Perf. 14
4242	A1246	Horiz. pair + central label	2.60	1.25
a.		$12 multi	.80	.40
b.		$25 multi	1.75	.85

Taipei 2015 Intl. Stamp Exhibition — A1247

No. 4243 — Scroll paintings: a, Literary Gathering, by Emperor Huizong. b, Elegant Gathering in the Western Garden, by Zhao Mengfu.

2015, Apr. 28   Litho.   Perf. 13¼x12½
4243 A1247   Horiz. pair + central label   2.40 1.25
a. $9 multi   .60 .30
b. $25 multi   1.75 .85
c.   Souvenir sheet of 2, #4243a-4243b, + label   2.40 1.25

Herbs Type of 2013

Designs: $3.50, Allium schoenoprasum. $5, Borago officinalis. $12, Tropaeolum majus. $25, Chamaemelum nobile.

2015, June 11   Litho.   Perf. 12½
4244-4247 A1173   Set of 4   3.00 1.50

Liberation of Taiwan in World War II, 70th Anniv. — A1248

Designs: No. 4248, $3.50, Soldiers carrying flags. No. 4249, $3.50, Farm woman holding sheaf of rice, Shimen Reservoir. No. 4250, $5, People cheering Chiang Kai-shek, horiz. No. 4251, $5, Crowd in plaza celebrating Taiwan Retrocession Day, 1963, horiz.

2015, July 7   Litho.   Perf. 12½
4248-4251 A1248   Set of 4   1.10 .55

A1249

Prehistoric Artifacts — A1250

Designs: $5, Frog-shaped jade ornament. $7, Jade tubes. $9, Circular jade bangle. $12, String of jade beads. $20, Jade earring.

2015, Aug. 21   Litho.   Perf. 12½
4252-4255 A1249   Set of 4   2.10 1.10
Souvenir Sheet
4256 A1250 $20 multi   1.25 .60

Corals Type of 2014

Designs: $3.50, Montipora foliosa. $5, Sarcophyton ehrenbergi. $10, Ellisella robusta. $15, Stylaster gracilis.

2015, Sept. 10   Litho.   Perf. 12½
4257-4260 A1203   Set of 4   2.10 1.10

A1251

Paintings by Giuseppe Castiglione (Lang Shining) — A1252

Designs: No. 4261, $5, Gathering of Auspicious Signs (flowers in vase). No. 4262, $5, Long-haired Dog Beneath Blossoms. No. 4263, $9, Ayusi Sweeping Bandits with a Lance, horiz. No. 4264, $9, Cochin Lemur, horiz.
No. 4265 — Golden Pheasant in Spring: a, $12. b, $70.

2015, Oct. 8   Litho.   Perf. 13¼
4261-4264 A1251   Set of 4   1.75 .85
Souvenir Sheet
Silk-Faced Paper
4265 A1252   Sheet of 2, #a-b   5.00 2.50

Sun Yat-sen (1866-1925), First President of Republic of China — A1253

Various depictions of Sun Yat-sen: $5, $12, horiz.

2015, Nov. 12   Litho.   Perf. 12½
4266-4267 A1253   Set of 2   1.10 .55

Rail Tourism — A1254

Designs: $5, Yuli-Taitung Summer Formosa train, railroad bridge. $10, South Link Line train, bridge near coast. $15, Jiji Line Evolution No. 1001 train, bicyclists.

2015, Nov. 25   Litho.   Perf. 13x13¼
4268-4270 A1254   Set of 3   1.90 .95

New Year 2016 (Year of the Monkey) A1255

Designs: $3.50, Monkey facing right. $13, Monkey facing left. $12, Two monkeys.

2015, Dec. 1   Litho.   Perf. 13
4271-4272 A1255   Set of 2   1.00 .50
Souvenir Sheet
Perf. 12½
4273 A1255 $12 multi   .75 .35

No. 4273 contains one 64x40mm stamp.

A1256

Opening of National Palace Museum Southern Branch — A1257

Designs: $5, Right-spiraling conch, Qing dynasty. $10, Jade bowl with handles and lid. $12, Hanging scroll with deities Good Fortune, Wealth and Long Life.
No. 4277: a, Board from Tibetan Kangyar with text and two deities. b, Board from Tibetan Kangyar with five deities.

Perf. 14¼x14½
2015, Dec. 10   Litho.
4274-4276 A1256   Set of 3   1.75 .85
Souvenir Sheet
Perf. 14¾
4277 A1257 $25 Sheet of 2, #a-b 3.00 1.50

Souvenir Sheets

Fan With Verse in Calligraphy by Wen Zhengming (1470-1559) — A1258

2016, Jan. 13   Litho.   Perf. 13½
4278 A1258 $25 multi   1.50 .75
Litho. With Bamboo Veneer Affixed
4279 A1258 $80 multi   4.75 2.40

Fruit — A1259

Designs: $1, Atemoyas. $2.50, Papayas. $5, Lychees. $15, Dates.

2016, Jan. 28   Litho.   Perf. 12½x13½
4280 A1259 $1 multi   .25 .25
4281 A1259 $2.50 multi   .25 .25
4282 A1259 $5 multi   .30 .25
4283 A1259 $15 multi   .90 .45
    Nos. 4280-4283 (4)   1.70 1.20

Churches — A1260

Designs: No. 4284, $5, Church of St. Joseph, Jinlun (with "Kiokai ni Santo Yosef" sign). No. 4285, $5, Holy Family Church,

Taipei. No. 4286, $12, Minor Basilica of the Immaculate Conception, Wanjin. No. 4287, $12, Cathedral of the Holy Rosary, Kaohsiung, vert.

2016, Feb. 4   Litho.   Perf. 13¼
4284-4287 A1260   Set of 4   2.10 1.10

Souvenir Sheet

Chinese Postal Service, 120th Anniv. — A1261

No. 4288 — Mailbox and: a, $5, Bicycle. b, $12, Motorcycle.

2016, Mar. 18   Litho.   Perf. 13
4288 A1261   Sheet of 2, #a-b   1.10 .55

Tree Peonies — A1262

Peach Blossoms A1263

Herbaceous Peonies — A1264

Flowering Crab Apple and Magnolia Blossoms A1265

Corn Poppies and Fringed Iris — A1266

Yellow Prickly Roses and Peonies — A1267

Carnations A1268

Cherries and Grosbeaks A1269

Perf. 13¼x12½

2016, Mar. 29			Litho.	
4289	A1262	$5 multi	.30	.25
4290	A1263	$5 multi	.30	.25
4291	A1264	$7 multi	.45	.25
4292	A1265	$9 multi	.55	.30
4293	A1266	$10 multi	.65	.30
4294	A1267	$10 multi	.65	.30
4295	A1268	$12 multi	.75	.35
4296	A1269	$12 multi	.75	.35
	Nos. 4289-4296 (8)		4.40	2.35

Paintings by Giuseppe Castiglione (1688-1766).

Miniature Sheet

Taitung County — A1270

No. 4297: a, $5, Footbridge, Sanxiantai. b, $5 People watching hot air balloons over Luye Highlands. c, $10, Fishing boat, Lanyu Island. d, $12, National Museum of Prehistory, Taitung.

2016, Apr. 20	Litho.	Perf. 12½x12¾		
4297	A1270	Sheet of 4, #a-d	2.00	1.00

Tea Grinding, by Liu Songnian (1174-1224) A1271

Lu Tong Brewing Tea, by Qian Xuan (1235-1305) A1272

Tasting Tea, by Wen Zhengming (1470-1559) A1273

2016, May 5		Litho.	Perf. 12¾	
4298	A1271	$5 multi	.30	.25
4299	A1272	$15 multi	.95	.45
4300	A1273	$25 multi	1.60	.80
	Nos. 4298-4300 (3)		2.85	1.50

South China Sea Peace Initiative A1274

No. 4301: a, Map of South China Sea, memorial plaque, Taiping Island. b, Taiping Lighthouse. c, Solar panels, Taiping Island National Monument and flags. d, Trail, goat and chickens.

2016, May 5	Litho.	Perf. 12½x12¾		
4301		Horiz. strip of 4	2.60	1.40
a.	A1274	$5 multi	.30	.25
b.	A1274	$9 multi	.55	.30
c.	A1274	$13 multi	.80	.40
d.	A1274	$15 multi	.95	.45

Pixelated Faces — A1275

Line-Drawn Faces — A1276

No. 4302 — Images of newly-elected Pres. Tsai Ing-wen and Vice-president Chen Chien-jen with background colors of: a, Light gray brown. b, Orange. c, Brownish gray. d, Turquoise.
$32, 20 pixelated faces.

2016, May 20	Litho.	Perf. 12½		
4302		Strip of 4	2.10	1.10
a.	A1275	$5 multi	.30	.25
b.	A1276	$5 multi	.30	.25
c.	A1275	$12 multi	.75	.35
d.	A1276	$12 multi	.75	.35

Souvenir Sheet
Perf. 12½x12¾

4303	A1275	$32 multi	2.00	1.00

No. 4303 contains one 80x30mm stamp.

Xiangling Studies Poetry A1277

White Snow and Pink Plum Blossoms A1278

Qingwen Repairs a Coat A1279

Lantern Festival Feast A1280

2016, June 29		Litho.	Perf. 14	
4304	A1277	$5 multi	.30	.25
4305	A1278	$5 multi	.30	.25
4306	A1279	$10 multi	.65	.30
4307	A1280	$25 multi	1.60	.80
	Nos. 4304-4307 (4)		2.85	1.60

Scenes from "The Dream of Red Mansions," by Cao Xueqin. Compare with Nos. 4198-4201, 4228-4231.

Corals Type of 2014

Designs: $3.50, Euphyllia ancora. $5, Fungia (Pleuractis) taiwanensis. $10, Scleronephthya gracillimum. $15, Anella mollis.

2016, July 14	Litho.	Perf. 12½x13¼		
4308-4311	A1203	Set of 4	2.10	1.10

Carp Encircled by Dragons Type of 1997 With Denomination at Right and Inscribed "Republic of China (Taiwan)"

2016, Aug. 3	Engr.	Perf. 13¼x12½		
4312	A745	$100 dk purple	6.25	3.25

Fruit Type of 2016

Designs: $7, Tomatoes. $17, Guavas. $25, Persimmons. $34, Pineapple.

Perf. 12½x13½

2016, Aug. 17			Litho.	
4313	A1259	$7 multi	.45	.25
4314	A1259	$17 multi	1.10	.55
4315	A1259	$25 multi	1.60	.80
4316	A1259	$34 multi	2.25	1.10
	Nos. 4313-4316 (4)		5.40	2.70

A1281

A1282

A1283

A1284

A1285

A1286

A1287

A1288

A1289

Seals — A1290

Perf. 13½x12½

2016, Sept. 14			Litho.	
4317		Block of 10	2.50	1.25
a.	A1281	$3.50 multi	.25	.25
b.	A1282	$3.50 multi	.25	.25
c.	A1283	$3.50 multi	.25	.25
d.	A1284	$3.50 multi	.25	.25
e.	A1285	$3.50 multi	.25	.25
f.	A1286	$3.50 multi	.25	.25
g.	A1287	$3.50 multi	.25	.25
h.	A1288	$3.50 multi	.25	.25
i.	A1289	$3.50 multi	.25	.25
j.	A1290	$3.50 multi	.25	.25
4318		Block of 10	3.00	1.50
a.	A1281	$5 multi	.30	.25
b.	A1282	$5 multi	.30	.25
c.	A1283	$5 multi	.30	.25
d.	A1284	$5 multi	.30	.25
e.	A1285	$5 multi	.30	.25
f.	A1286	$5 multi	.30	.25
g.	A1287	$5 multi	.30	.25
h.	A1288	$5 multi	.30	.25
i.	A1289	$5 multi	.30	.25
j.	A1290	$5 multi	.30	.25

Hu Shih (1891-1962), Writer and Diplomat A1291

Chien Shih-Liang (1908-83), Chemist — A1292

Wu Ta-You (1907-2000), Physicist A1293

2016, Sept. 28		Engr.	Perf. 12½	
4319	A1291	$5 slate blue	.30	.25
4320	A1292	$5 red violet	.30	.25
4321	A1293	$5 brown	.30	.25
	Nos. 4319-4321 (3)		.90	.75

Past presidents of Academia Sinica.

Balloon and Bicyclist — A1294

Bird and Open Box — A1295

2016, Oct. 21 Litho. *Perf. 14*
4322 A1294 $5 multi .35 .25
4323 A1295 $25 multi 1.60 .80
Souvenir Sheet
Litho. & Embossed With Foil Application
4324 Sheet of 2 4.00 2.00
a. A1294 $32 multi 2.00 1.00
b. A1295 $32 multi 2.00 1.00

PhilaTaipei 2016 World Stamp Exhibition, Taipei.

PhilaTaipei 2016 World Stamp Exhibition, Taipei — A1296

No. 4325: a, Yushan, Sun Moon Lake, butterfly, dragon boat. b, Map of Taiwan, birds, Taipei 101 Building, 85 Sky Tower, Kaohsiung.

Perf. 14 Syncopated
2016, Oct. 21 Litho.
4325 A1296 Horiz. pair 3.00 1.40
a. $13 gold & multi .85 .40
b. $32 gold & multi 2.00 1.00

A1297

PhilaTaipei 2016 World Stamp Exhibition, Taipei A1298

2016, Oct. 22 Litho. *Perf. 13½*
4326 A1297 $9 multi .60 .30
4327 A1298 $25 multi 1.60 .80

Souvenir Sheet

PhilaTaipei 2016 World Stamp Exhibition, Taipei — A1299

No. 4328: a, Animals and birds in tree (64x40mm). b, Fish and marine life in ocean (50x30mm).

2016, Oct. 22 Litho. *Perf. 14*
4328 A1299 Sheet of 2 3.00 1.50
a. $15 multi .95 .50
b. $32 multi 2.00 1.00

PhilaTaipei 2016 World Stamp Exhibition, Taipei — A1300

No. 4329 — Little Yam: a, Mailing letter. b, Holding opened envelope.

2016, Oct. 22 Litho. *Perf. 13¼x12¾*
4329 A1300 Horiz. pair + central label 2.00 1.00
a. $5 multi .35 .25
b. $25 multi 1.60 .80

Souvenir Sheet

PhilaTaipei 2016 World Stamp Exhibition, Taipei — A1301

No. 4330: a, Bird carrying flower (39x30mm heart-shaped). b, Person, flowers, hearts (30x40mm).

Perf. ($17), Perf. 12¾x12½ ($25)
2016, Oct. 22 Litho.
4330 A1301 Sheet of 2 2.75 1.40
a. $17 multi 1.10 .55
b. $25 multi 1.60 .80

Souvenir Sheet

Traveler at Shanyin County, Fan Painting by Lan Ying (c. 1585-1664) — A1302

2016, Oct. 24 Litho. *Perf. 14*
4331 A1302 $25 multi 1.60 .80

SEMI-POSTAL STAMPS

SP1

Red or Blue Surcharge
1920, Dec. 1 Unwmk. *Perf. 14, 15*
B1 SP1 1c on 2c green 5.00 2.00
B2 SP1 3c on 4c scar (B) 8.00 3.00
B3 SP1 5c on 6c gray 12.00 6.00
Nos. B1-B3 (3) 25.00 10.00

The surcharge represents the actual franking value. The extra cent helped victims of the 1919 Yellow River flood.

War Refugees SP2

Black Surcharge
1944, Oct. 10 Engr. *Perf. 12*
B4 $2 +$2 on 50c + 50c 2.00 2.00
B5 $4 +$4 on 8c + 8c 2.00 2.00
B6 $5 +$5 on 21c + 21c 2.00 2.00
B7 $6 +$6 on 28c + 28c 4.00 4.00
B8 $10 +$10 on 33c + 33c 5.00 5.00
B9 $20 +$20 on $1 + $1 6.00 6.00
a. Sheet of 6, #B4-B9 85.00 60.00
Nos. B4-B9 (6) 21.00 21.00

The borders of each stamp differ slightly in design. The surtax was for war refugees.
Nos. B4-B8 exist without surcharge, but were not regularly issued.

Great Wall of China — SP4

1948, July 5 Litho. *Perf. 14, Imperf.*
Without Gum
Cross in Carmine
B11 SP4 $5000 + $2000 vio .50 2.50
B12 SP4 $10,000 + $2000 brn .50 2.50
B13 SP4 $15,000 + $2000 gray .50 2.50
a. Cross omitted
Nos. B11-B13 (3) 1.50 7.50

The surtax was for anti-tuberculosis work. Fakes of B13a exist with cross chemically removed. No genuine used copies are known.

Republic of China (Taiwan)

Chinese Refugee Family — SP5

1954, Oct. 1 Engr. *Perf. 12*
Without Gum
B14 SP5 40c + 10c dp bl 25.00 5.00
B15 SP5 $1.60 + 40c lil rose 67.50 26.00
B16 SP5 $5 + $1 red 125.00 110.00
Nos. B14-B16 (3) 217.50 141.00

The surtax was used to aid in the evacuation of Chinese from North Viet Nam.

Catalogue values for unused stamps in this section, from this point to the end of the section, are for Never Hinged items.

Sept. 21, 1999 Earthquake Relief — SP6

a, Damaged buildings, map, rescue workers. b, Hands, heart, earthquake fault.

1999, Nov. 1 Litho. *Imperf.*
Sheet of 2
B17 SP6 $25 +$25, #a.-b. 9.00 9.00

No. B17 has simulated perforations.

Souvenir Sheet

Typhoon Morakot Relief — SP7

No. B18: a, Map of Taiwan surrounded by clouds, rescuers and rafts. b, House, construction equipment and workers.

2009, Oct. 9 Litho. *Imperf.*
B18 SP7 $25 +$25 Sheet of 2, #a-b 7.00 7.00

No. B18 has simulated perforations.

AIR POST STAMPS

Curtiss "Jenny" over Great Wall (Bars of Republic flag on tail) — AP1

Unwmk.
1921, July 1 Engr. *Perf. 14*
C1 AP1 15c bl grn & blk 50.00 50.00
C2 AP1 30c scar & blk 50.00 50.00
C3 AP1 45c dull vio & blk 50.00 50.00
C4 AP1 60c dk blue & blk 65.00 65.00
C5 AP1 90c ol grn & blk 72.50 72.50
Nos. C1-C5 (5) 287.50 287.50

(Nationalist sun emblem on tail) — AP2

1929, July 5
C6	AP2	15c blue grn & blk	10.00	3.00
C7	AP2	30c dk red & blk	15.00	5.00
C8	AP2	45c dk vio & blk	24.00	10.00
C9	AP2	60c dk blue & blk	27.50	12.00
C10	AP2	90c ol grn & blk	27.50	18.00
		Nos. C6-C10 (5)	104.00	48.00

Junkers F-13 over Great Wall AP3

1932-37
C11	AP3	15c gray grn	.70	.45
C12	AP3	25c orange ('33)	5.00	2.00
C13	AP3	30c red	10.00	2.50
C14	AP3	45c brown vio	1.00	.45
C15	AP3	50c dk brown ('33)	1.00	.45
C16	AP3	60c dk blue	1.00	.45
C17	AP3	90c olive grn	1.00	.60
C18	AP3	$1 yellow grn ('33)	1.50	.45
C19	AP3	$2 brown ('37)	1.50	.80
C20	AP3	$5 brown car ('37)	4.00	3.00
		Nos. C11-C20 (10)	26.70	12.15

See #C21-C40. For surcharges and overprints see #C41-C52, C54-C60, 9N111-9N114, 9NC1-9NC7, Szechwan C1, C3-C6, Sinkiang C5-C19.

Type of 1932-37, with secret mark

1932-37 Issue, Lower part of left character joined

Secret Mark, 1940-41 Issue, Separated

Perf. 12, 12½, 12½x13, 13
1940-41   **Wmk. 261**
C21	AP3	15c gray green	1.00	.60
C22	AP3	25c yellow org	1.25	.80
C23	AP3	30c red	1.00	.60
a.		Vert. pair, imperf. between	500.00	
C24	AP3	45c dull rose vio ('41)	1.00	.60
C25	AP3	50c brown	1.00	.60
C26	AP3	60c dp blue ('41)	1.00	.60
C27	AP3	90c olive ('41)	1.00	.70
C28	AP3	$1 apple grn ('41)	1.00	.70
C29	AP3	$2 lt brown ('41)	1.00	.70
C30	AP3	$5 lake	2.50	1.20
		Nos. C21-C30 (10)	11.75	7.10

Unwmk.
Perf. 12½, 13, 13½
C31	AP3	15c gray green ('41)	.70	.30
C32	AP3	25c lt orange ('41)	.70	.30
C33	AP3	30c lt red ('41)	.70	.30
C34	AP3	45c lt rose vio ('41)	.70	.45
C35	AP3	50c brown	.70	.60
C36	AP3	60c blue ('41)	.70	.60
C37	AP3	90c lt olive ('41)	.70	.60
C38	AP3	$1 apple grn ('41)	.70	.70
C39	AP3	$2 lt brown ('41)	3.00	1.50
C40	AP3	$5 lake ('41)	2.00	1.25
		Nos. C31-C40 (10)	10.60	6.60

For surcharges see note following No. C20.

Nos. C11 and C12 Surcharged

1946, May 2   Unwmk.   Perf. 14
C41	AP3	$53 on 15c	1.50	*1.25*
C42	AP3	$73 on 25c	2,000.	—

Forgeries of No. C42 exist.

On Nos. C23, C21, C22, C29 and C30
Perf. 13, 13x12, 12½
Wmk. 261
C43	AP3	$23 on 30c red	.70	.70
C44	AP3	$53 on 15c gray grn	20.00	25.00
C45	AP3	$73 on 25c yel org	.70	.70
C46	AP3	$100 on $2 lt brown	1.25	.50
C47	AP3	$200 on $5 lake	.70	.70
		Nos. C43-C47 (5)	23.35	27.60

On Nos. C33, C31, C32, C39 and C40
Perf. 13, 13x12, 13x12½, 12½
Unwmk.
C48	AP3	$23 on 30c lt red	.60	1.00
a.		Inverted surcharge	450.00	
b.		"2300" omitted	50.00	
c.		Last character (kuo) of surch. omitted	120.00	
C49	AP3	$53 on 15c gray grn	.60	1.00
a.		Horiz. pair, imperf. btwn.	1,500.	675.00
C50	AP3	$73 on 25c lt org	.60	1.50
a.		Inverted surcharge	1,200.	
C51	AP3	$100 on $2 lt brn	.60	.60
C52	AP3	$200 on $5 lake	.60	.40
a.		Inverted surcharge	500.00	
		Nos. C48-C52 (5)	3.00	4.50

The surcharges on Nos. C41-C52 represent Chinese natl. currency and were applied at Shanghai.

Douglas DC-4 over Sun Yat-sen Mausoleum, Nanking — AP4

1946, Sept. 10   Litho.   Perf. 14
Without Gum
C53	AP4	$27 blue	.65	1.00

For surcharges see Nos. C61, Szechwan C2.

No. C23 Surcharged in Black

Perf. 13x12
1948, May 18   Wmk. 261
C54	AP3	$10,000 on 30c red	.60	1.00

Same, in Black or Carmine, on Nos. C33, C32, C37, C36, C18 and C38
Unwmk.
Perf. 12½, 13x12½, 14
C55	AP3	$10,000 on 30c lt red	.60	.75
C56	AP3	$20,000 on 25c lt org	.60	.75
C57	AP3	$30,000 on 90c lt ol (C)	.60	1.00
C58	AP3	$50,000 on 60c blue (C)	.60	1.00
C59	AP3	$50,000 on $1 yel grn (C) (#C18)	175.00	150.00
C60	AP3	$50,000 on $1 ap grn (C) (#C38)	.60	.90

No. C53 Surcharged in Black

Perf. 14
C61	AP4	$10,000 on $27 bl	.75	3.00
		Nos. C54-C61 (8)	179.35	158.40

Douglas DC-4 and Arrow — AP5

Perf. 12½
1949, May 2   Unwmk.   Litho.
Without Gum
C62	AP5	blue green	7.00	7.00
a.		Rouletted	12.00	17.50

See note after No. 959.
For overprints see Taiwan No. C1, Fukien No. C1, Kansu No. C1, PRC Nos. 26, 102.

Revenue Stamp Overprinted in Blue

1949, May   Engr.   Perf. 14
C63	A95	$100 olive green	125.00	110.00

See note after No. 962.

Republic of China (Taiwan)

Cheng Ch'eng-kung (Koxinga) — AP6

Rouletted
1950, Sept. 26   Unwmk.   Typo.
Without Gum
C64	AP6	60c deep blue	14.00	7.00

For surcharge see No. 1120.

Plane over City Gate, Taipei — AP7

Jet Planes above Chung Shan Bridge — AP8

Two Doves Near Koxinga Shrine — AP9

1954   Engr.   Perf. 11½
Without Gum
C65	AP7	$1 dk brown	11.00	1.00
a.		Vert. pair, imperf. btwn.		200.00
C66	AP8	$1.60 olive blk	14.00	.80
a.		Vert. pair, imperf. btwn.	140.00	
b.		Horiz. pair, imperf. btwn.	100.00	110.00
C67	AP9	$5 grnsh blue	20.00	1.75
		Nos. C65-C67 (3)	45.00	3.55

Issued: No. C66, 8/14; Nos. C65, C67, 9/1.

No. C67 Surcharged in Red
1958, Dec. 11   Without Gum
C68	AP9	$3.50 on $5 grnsh bl	4.00	1.50

Sea Gull — AP10

1959, Mar. 20   Photo.   Perf. 13
C69	AP10	$8 blue, gray & blk	5.50	.40

Sabre Jets in Bomb Burst Formation — AP11

Plane Formations: $2, Loop, horiz. $5, Diamond formation passing over grounded plane, horiz.

1960, Feb. 29   Unwmk.   Perf. 13
C70	AP11	$1 multicolored	6.50	.50
C71	AP11	$2 multicolored	6.00	.50
C72	AP11	$5 multicolored	10.00	.50
		Nos. C70-C72 (3)	22.50	1.60

Issued to honor the Chinese Air Force and the "Thunder Tiger" aerobatic team.

Jet Airliner over Pitan Bridge AP12

Designs: $6, Jet over Tropic of Cancer monument, Kiai, vert. $10, Jet over Lion Head mountain, Sinchu, vert.

1963, Aug. 14   Photo.   Perf. 13
C73	AP12	$2.50 multi	7.25	.25
C74	AP12	$6 multi	12.50	.40
C75	AP12	$10 multi	16.00	.65
		Nos. C73-C75 (3)	35.75	1.30

Boeing 727 over Chilin Pavilion, Grand Hotel — AP13

Design: $8, Boeing 727 over National Palace Museum, Taipei.

1967, Apr. 1   Unwmk.   Perf. 13
C76	AP13	$5 multicolored	3.75	.25
C77	AP13	$8 multicolored	5.50	.50

Wild Geese Flying over Mountains — AP14

Wild Geese flying over: $5, The sea. $8, The land, horiz.

1969, Aug. 14   Photo.   Perf. 13
C78	AP14	$2.50 multicolored	3.00	.25
C79	AP14	$5 multicolored	4.75	.45
C80	AP14	$8 multicolored	5.75	.60
		Nos. C78-C80 (3)	13.50	1.30

Presidental Palace and Tzu-Ch'iang Squadron AP15

$7, China Airlines jet. $12, China flag, jet.

1980, June 18   Litho.   Perf. 13½

C81	AP15	$5 shown	.25	.25
C82	AP15	$7 multicolored	.70	.30
C83	AP15	$12 multicolored	1.00	.50
	Nos. C81-C83 (3)		1.95	1.05

Civil Aeronautics Administration, 37th Anniv. — AP16

Jet Airliners over: $7, Chiang Kai-shek Intl. Airport, vert. $11, Chung Cheng Memorial Hall. $18, Sun Yat-sen Memorial Hall.

Perf. 14x13½, 13½x14

1984, Jan. 20   Litho.

C84	AP16	$7 multicolored	.50	.25
C85	AP16	$11 multicolored	.80	.40
C86	AP16	$18 multicolored	1.00	.60
	Nos. C84-C86 (3)		2.30	1.25

Airplane AP17

1987, Aug. 4   Litho.   Perf. 13½

C87	AP17	$9 multicolored	.60	.40
C88	AP17	$14 multicolored	.95	.55
C89	AP17	$18 multicolored	1.25	.65
	Nos. C87-C89 (3)		2.80	1.60

SPECIAL DELIVERY STAMPS

Used values of Nos. E1-E8 are for mailer's receipts. Complete unused strips of four are exceptionally scarce because the first section (#1) was to remain in the P.O. booklet.

The mailer received the righthand section (#4), usually canceled, as a receipt. The middle two sections were canceled and attached to the letter. Upon arrival at the destination P.O. they were canceled again, usually on the back, with the righthand copy (#3) retained by that P.O. The lefthand copy (#2) was signed by the recipient and returned to the original P.O. as evidence of delivery. Sections 2 and 3 usually are thin or badly damaged.

Unused strips of three (#2-4) can be found of Nos. E3-E8.

Design: Dragon in irregular oval. Stamp 8x2½ inches, divided into four parts by perforation or serrate rouletting.

"Chinese Imperial Post Office" in lines, repeated to form the background which is usually lighter in color than the rest of the design. **Dragon's head facing downward Background with period after "POSTOFFICE."**

No Date

1905   Unwmk.   Perf. 11

| E1 | 10c grass green | 12,000. | 500.00 |

Serrate Roulette in Black

| E2 | 10c deep green | 15,000. | 500.00 |

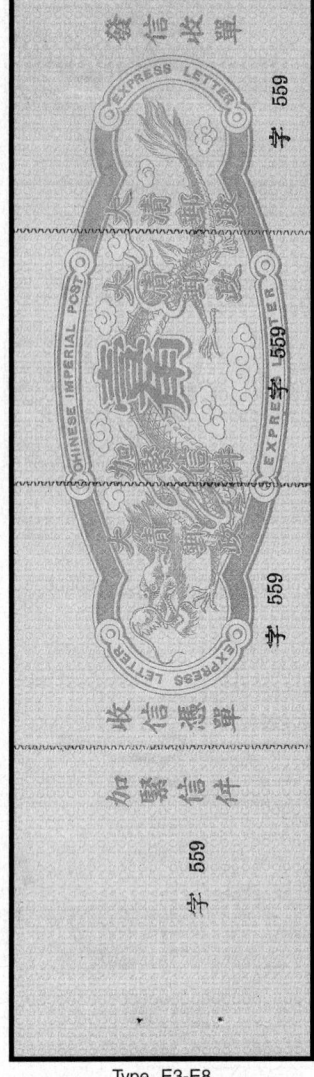

Type, E3-E8

Dragon's head facing forward Background with no period after "POSTOFFICE"

1907-10   No Date

| E3 | 10c light bluish green | 2,000. | 250.00 |

Background with date at bottom

1909-11

| E4 | 10c grn (Feb. 1909) | 1,750. | 200.00 |
| E5 | 10c bl grn (Jan. 1911) | 1,600. | 150.00 |

"IMPERIAL POST OFFICE" in serifed letters repeated to form the background. No Date, No Border Background of 30 or 28 lines

1912

| E6 | 10c green (30 lines) | 1,400. | 130.00 |
| a. | 28 lines | 1,600. | 800.00 |

Background of 35 lines of sans-serif letters Colored Border

| E8 | 10c green | 1,600. | 190.00 |

On No. E8 the medallion in the third section has Chinese characters in the background instead of the usual English inscriptions. E6 and E8 occur with many types of four-character overprints reading "Republic of China," applied locally but unofficially at various post offices.

Type, E9, E10

Design: Wild Goose. Stamp 7½x2¾ inches, divided into five parts. **"CHINESE POST OFFICE" in sans-serif letters, repeated to form the background of 28 lines. With border. Serrate Roulette in Black**

1913

| E9 | 10c green | 900.00 | 110.00 |

Unused values for Nos. E9-E10 are for complete strips of five parts. Used values are for single parts.

"CHINESE POST OFFICE" in antique letters, forming a background of 29 or 30 lines. No border.

1914   Serrate Roulette in Green

| E10 | 10c green | 325.00 | 50.00 |

On No. E9 the background is in sans-serif capitals, the Chinese and English inscriptions are on white tablets and the serial numbers are in black.

On No. E10 the background is in antique capitals and extends under the inscriptions. The serial numbers are in green.

NOTE:

In February, 1916, the Special Delivery Stamps were demonetized and became merely receipts without franking value. To mark this, four of the five sections of the stamp had the letters A, B, C, D either handstamped or printed on them.

SD1

1941   Unwmk.   Typo.   Rouletted Without Gum

| E11 | SD1 | ($2) car & yel | 35.00 | 32.50 |

Motorcycle Messenger — SD2

1949, July   Litho.   Perf. 12½ Without Gum

| E12 | SD2 | red violet | 9.00 | 20.00 |
| a. | Rouletted | | 12.00 | 21.00 |

See note after No. 959.
For surcharge and overprints see Nos. 1150, Taiwan E1, Fukien E1.

Revenue Stamp Overprinted in Purple Brown

1949   Without Gum

| E13 | A95 | $10 grnsh gray | 55.00 | 55.00 |

See note after No. 962.

REGISTRATION STAMPS

R1

1941   Unwmk.   Typo.   Rouletted Without Gum

| F1 | R1 | ($1.50) green & buff | 21.00 | 21.00 |

Mountain Scene — R2

1949, July   Litho.   Perf. 12½ Without Gum

| F2 | R2 | carmine | 10.00 | 15.00 |
| a. | Rouletted | | 12.00 | 18.00 |

See note after No. 959.
For surcharge and overprints see Nos. 1152, Taiwan F1, Fukien F1, PRC 103.

Revenue Stamp Overprinted in Carmine

1949

| F3 | A95 | $50 dark blue | 35.00 | 24.00 |

See note after No. 962.

POSTAGE DUE STAMPS

Regular Issue of 1902-03 Overprinted in Black

D1

1904		Unwmk.	Perf. 14 to 15	
J1	A17	½c chocolate	14.00	6.00
J2	A17	1c ocher	14.00	5.00
J3	A17	2c scarlet	17.00	6.00
J4	A17	4c red brn	18.00	7.00
J5	A17	5c salmon	20.00	12.00
J6	A17	10c dk blue grn	33.00	20.00
a.		Vert. pair, imperf. btwn.	2,000.	2,000.
		Nos. J1-J6 (6)	116.00	56.00

1904			Engr.	
J7	D1	½c blue	7.00	4.00
a.		Horiz. pair, imperf. btwn.	3,000.	2,000.
J8	D1	1c blue	12.00	4.00
J9	D1	2c blue	12.00	4.00
a.		Horiz. pair, imperf. btwn.	2,000.	1,800.
J10	D1	4c blue	15.00	6.00
J11	D1	5c blue	18.00	7.00
J12	D1	10c blue	20.00	9.00
J13	D1	20c blue	50.00	12.00
J14	D1	30c blue	70.00	40.00
		Nos. J7-J14 (8)	204.00	86.00

Arabic numeral of value at left on Nos. J12-J14.

1911				
J15	D1	1c brown	25.00	18.00
J16	D1	2c brown	40.00	32.50

The ½c, 4c, 5c and 20c in brown exist but were not issued as they arrived in China after the downfall of the Ching dynasty.

Issues of 1904 Overprinted in Red

1912				
J19	D1	½c blue	700.	1,000.
J20	D1	4c blue	900.	1,100.
J21	D1	5c blue	1,000.	1,100.
J22	D1	10c blue	1,500.	1,100.
J23	D1	20c blue	3,000.	3,200.
J24	D1	30c blue	3,000.	3,200.

Nos. J15-J16 exist with this overprint, but were not regularly issued.

Nos. J1-J14 Overprinted in Red

1912				
J25	D1	½c blue	5.00	3.00
J26	D1	1c brown	6.00	3.00
a.		Horiz. pair, imperf. btwn.	3,000.	3,000.
b.		Inverted overprint	550.00	550.00
J27	D1	2c brown	8.00	4.00
J28	D1	4c blue	15.00	6.00
J29	D1	5c blue	275.00	300.00
J30	D1	5c brown	20.00	10.00
a.		Inverted overprint	320.00	340.00
J31	D1	10c blue	25.00	13.00
J32	D1	20c blue	27.00	17.00
J33	D1	30c blue	35.00	30.00
		Nos. J25-J33 (9)	416.00	386.00

Issues of 1904 Overprinted in Black

1912				
J34	D1	½c blue	15.00	10.00
J35	D1	½c brown	8.00	3.00
J36	D1	1c brown	8.00	3.00
a.		Inverted overprint	350.00	350.00
J37	D1	2c brown	10.00	5.00
J38	D1	4c blue	20.00	9.50
J39	D1	5c brown	27.50	14.00
a.		Horiz. pair, imperf. btwn.	3,800.	3,800.
J40	D1	10c blue	45.00	27.50
J41	D1	20c brown	65.00	100.00
J42	D1	30c blue	75.00	65.00
		Nos. J34-J42 (9)	273.50	237.00

D4

Printed by Waterlow & Sons

1913, May			Perf. 14, 15	
J43	D4	½c blue	3.00	1.50
a.		Horiz. pair, imperf. btwn.	4,000.	3,000.
J44	D4	1c blue	3.50	1.50
J45	D4	2c blue	5.00	3.00
J46	D4	4c blue	8.00	3.00
J47	D4	5c blue	12.00	6.00
J48	D4	10c blue	17.50	8.00
J49	D4	20c blue	27.50	13.00
J50	D4	30c blue	35.00	15.00
		Nos. J43-J50 (8)	111.50	51.00

Printed by the Chinese Bureau of Engraving & Printing

1915		Re-engraved	Perf. 14	
J51	D4	½c blue	3.00	1.00
J52	D4	1c blue	3.75	.65
J53	D4	2c blue	4.00	.65
J54	D4	4c blue	5.00	.75
J55	D4	5c blue	7.00	1.50
J56	D4	10c blue	11.00	2.50
J57	D4	20c blue	17.50	8.00
J58	D4	30c blue	50.00	20.00
		Nos. J51-J58 (8)	101.25	35.05

In the upper part of the stamps of type D4 there is an ornament of five marks like the letter "V". Below this is a curved label with an inscription in Chinese characters. On the 1913 stamps there are two complete background lines between the ornament and the label. The 1915 stamps show only one unbroken line at this place. There are other minute differences in the engraving of the stamps of the two issues.

D5

1932			Perf. 14	
J59	D5	½c orange	.60	.30
J60	D5	1c orange	.60	.30
J61	D5	2c orange	.60	.30
J62	D5	4c orange	.60	.30
J63	D5	5c orange	1.50	1.50
J64	D5	10c orange	2.00	2.00
J65	D5	20c orange	2.75	3.00
J66	D5	30c orange	4.00	4.00
		Nos. J59-J66 (8)	12.65	11.70

See Nos. J69-J79. For surcharges see Nos. 1NJ1, 9NJ1-9NJ4.

Regular Stamps of 1939 Overprinted in Black or Red

1940				
J67	A57	$1 henna & dk brn (Bk)	8.00	25.00
J68	A57	$2 dl bl & org brn (R)	12.00	25.00

Type of 1932
Printed by The Commercial Press, Ltd.

Perf. 12½, 12½x13, 13

1940-41			Engr.	
J69	D5	½c yellow orange	.80	1.00
J70	D5	1c yellow orange	.80	1.00
J71	D5	2c yel org ('41)	.80	1.00
J72	D5	4c yellow orange	.80	1.00
J73	D5	5c yel org ('41)	1.20	1.00
J74	D5	10c yel org ('41)	.80	1.00
J75	D5	20c yel org ('41)	.80	1.00
J76	D5	30c yellow orange	.80	1.00
J77	D5	50c yellow orange	1.00	1.00
J78	D5	$1 yellow orange	1.20	1.00
J79	D5	$2 yellow orange	1.50	2.00
		Nos. J69-J79 (11)	10.50	12.00

For surcharge see No. 1NJ1.

D6

Thin Paper Without Gum

1944		Typo.	Perf. 13	
J80	D6	10c bluish green	.80	3.00
J81	D6	20c light chalky blue	.80	3.00
J82	D6	40c dull rose	.80	3.00
J83	D6	50c bluish green	.80	3.00
J84	D6	60c dull blue	.80	3.00
J85	D6	$1 dull rose	.80	2.00
J86	D6	$2 lilac brown	.80	2.00
		Nos. J80-J86 (7)	5.60	19.00

D7

1945		Without Gum	Unwmk.	
J87	D7	$2 rose carmine	.80	2.00
J88	D7	$6 rose carmine	.80	2.00
J89	D7	$8 rose carmine	.80	2.00
J90	D7	$10 rose carmine	.80	2.00
J91	D7	$20 rose carmine	.80	2.00
J92	D7	$30 rose carmine	1.00	2.00
		Nos. J87-J92 (6)	5.00	12.00

For surcharges see Nos. J102-J109.

D8

Thin Paper Without Gum

1947		Litho.	Perf. 14	
J93	D8	$50 plum	.80	2.00
J94	D8	$80 plum	.80	2.00
J95	D8	$100 plum	.80	2.00
J96	D8	$160 plum	.80	2.00
J97	D8	$200 plum	.80	2.00
J98	D8	$400 violet brown	.80	2.00
J99	D8	$500 violet brown	.80	2.00
a.		Vert. pair, imperf. between	80.00	
J100	D8	$800 violet brown	.80	2.00
J101	D8	$2000 violet brown	.80	2.00
		Nos. J93-J101 (9)	7.20	18.00

Type of 1945, Redrawn Surcharged in Black

		Without Gum Deep claret		
1948		Engr.	Perf. 13½x14	
J102	D7	$1000 on $20	.70	2.50
J103	D7	$2000 on $30	.70	2.50
J104	D7	$3000 on $50	.70	2.50
J105	D7	$4000 on $100	.70	2.00
J106	D7	$5000 on $200	.70	2.00
J107	D7	$10,000 on $300	.70	1.00
J108	D7	$20,000 on $500	.70	1.00
J109	D7	$30,000 on $1000	.70	1.00
		Nos. J102-J109 (8)	5.60	14.50

There are many differences in the redrawn design.

No. 627 Surcharged in Black

1949			Perf. 12	
J110	A72	1 (c) on $40 org	.70	10.00
J111	A72	2 (c) on $40 org	.70	10.00
J112	A72	5 (c) on $40 org	.70	10.00
J113	A72	10 (c) on $40 org	.70	10.00
J114	A72	20 (c) on $40 org	.70	10.00
J115	A72	50 (c) on $40 org	.70	10.00
J116	A72	$1 on $40 org	.70	10.00
J117	A72	$2 on $40 org	.70	10.00
J118	A72	$5 on $40 org	1.00	10.00
J119	A72	$10 on $40 org	1.00	5.00
		Nos. J110-J119 (10)	7.60	95.00

Republic of China (Taiwan)

No. 438 Surcharged in Green or Black

1951		Unwmk.	Perf. 12½	
J120	A47	40c on 40c org (G)	18.00	24.00
J121	A47	80c on 40c org (Bk)	18.00	24.00

Revenue Stamps Surcharged in Various Colors

1953		Unwmk.	Perf. 12½, 14	
		Without Gum		
J122	A95	10c on $50 dk bl (O)	18.00	4.50
J123	A95	20c on $100 ol grn (Dk Br)	18.00	4.50
J124	A95	40c on $20 org brn (Dk Bl)	20.00	1.50
J125	A95	80c on $500 sl grn (Dk Bl)	30.00	2.50
J126	A95	$1 on $30 dk vio (G)	30.00	8.25
		Nos. J122-J126 (5)	116.00	21.25

D9

1956		Unwmk. Litho.	Perf. 12½	
		Without Gum		
J127	D9	20c rose car, & lt bl	1.25	.25
J128	D9	40c green & buff	1.75	.25
J129	D9	80c brown & gray	3.50	.40
J130	D9	$1 ultra & pink	4.00	.40
		Nos. J127-J130 (4)	10.50	1.30

No. 1197 Surcharged in Dark Violet

Wmk. 323

1961, Dec. 28		Engr.	Perf. 12	
		Without Gum		
J131	A135	$5 on $20 car rose	1.75	.50

Nos. 1274, 1282-1283 Surcharged in Black, Carmine Rose or Blue

1964-65			Litho.	
J132	A158	10c on 80c pale grn (CR) ('65)	.25	.25
J133	A158	20c on $3.60 vio bl ('65)	.30	.25
J134	A158	40c on $4.50 ver (B) ('65)	.65	.25
		Nos. J132-J134 (3)	1.20	.75

D10

1966-76   Wmk. 323   *Perf. 12½*
Granite Paper; Without Gum

J135	D10	10c dk brn & lil	.25	.25
J136	D10	20c blue & yel	.40	.25
J137	D10	50c vio bl & lt bl ('70)	.65	.25
J138	D10	$1 purple & sal	.50	.25
J139	D10	$2 grn & lt bl	.65	.25
J140	D10	$5 red & sal	1.25	.30
a.		$5 org red & pale yel	1.25	.30
J141	D10	$10 lil rose & pink ('76)	22.50	1.00
		Nos. J135-J141 (7)	26.20	2.55

The 50c, $10 and No. J140a are gummed. The $1 and $2 were reissued with gum in 1968 and 1973 respectively. No. J140a and the $10 are on ordinary paper.

> Catalogue values for unused stamps in this section, from this point to the end of the section, are for Never Hinged items.

D11

1984-88   Litho.   *Perf. 12½*

J142	D11	$1 rose & violet	.25	.25
J143	D11	$2 yellow & blue	.25	.25
J144	D11	$3 pale grn & brt rose lil	.25	.25
J145	D11	$5 blue & yellow	.25	.25
J146	D11	$5.50 rose lil & brt blue	.40	.35
J147	D11	$7.50 bis yel & dp vio	.60	.45
J148	D11	$10 yel & lil rose	.50	.30
J149	D11	$20 sky blue & citron	1.60	1.25
		Nos. J142-J149 (8)	4.10	3.35

Issued: $3, $5.50, $7.50, $20, Apr. 1, 1988; others, Mar. 15, 1984.

D12

1998, Sept. 30   Litho.   *Perf. 12½*
Background Color

J150	D12	50c orange yellow	.25	.25
J151	D12	$1 pink	.25	.25
J152	D12	$2 deep pink	.25	.25
J153	D12	$5 yellow green	.40	.25
J154	D12	$10 blue	.75	.30
J155	D12	$20 green	1.60	.60
		Nos. J150-J155 (6)	3.50	1.90

Lotus Flower, Peach, Bats, Coins and Chinese Characters — D13

Perf. 12½x12¼

2008, Nov. 12   Litho.
Denomination Color

J156	D13	$1 dark red	.25	.25
J157	D13	$3 green	.25	.25
J158	D13	$5 olive green	.30	.25
J159	D13	$10 purple	.60	.30
J160	D13	$20 bister	1.25	.60
		Nos. J156-J160 (5)	2.65	1.65

Type of 2008
Die Cut Perf. 22

2015, Oct. 28   Litho.
Self-Adhesive
Denomination Color

J161	D13	50c red brown	.25	.25
J162	D13	$2 dark blue	.25	.25

PARCEL POST STAMPS

PP1

PP2

PP3

1945-48   Unwmk.   Engr.   *Perf. 13*
Without Gum

Q1	PP1	$500 green	12.00	1.00
Q2	PP1	$1000 blue	12.00	1.00
Q3	PP1	$3000 rose red	22.50	1.60
Q4	PP1	$5000 brown	150.00	30.00
Q5	PP1	$10,000 lil gray	270.00	50.00
Q6	PP1	$20,000 red org	5,000.	
		Nos. Q1-Q5 (5)	466.50	83.60

No. Q6 was prepared but not issued.
For surcharges see People's Republic of China Nos. 5LQ1-5LQ2, 5LQ27-5LQ28.

Perf. 12½

Q7	PP2	$3000 red org	30.00	2.00
Q8	PP2	$5000 dk blue	40.00	2.00
Q9	PP2	$10,000 violet	45.00	5.00
Q10	PP2	$20,000 dk red	50.00	5.00

Perf. 13½

Q11	PP3	$1000 org yel	9.00	1.50
Q12	PP3	$3000 bl grn	9.00	1.50
Q13	PP3	$5000 red org	9.00	1.50
Q14	PP3	$7000 dl blue	9.00	1.50
Q15	PP3	$10,000 car rose	10.00	2.00
Q16	PP3	$30,000 olive	10.00	2.00
Q17	PP3	$50,000 indigo	10.00	2.00
Q18	PP3	$70,000 org brn	14.00	4.00
Q19	PP3	$100,000 dp plum	14.00	4.00

Denomination Tablet Without Inner Frame

Q20	PP3	$200,000 dk grn	18.50	4.00
Q21	PP3	$300,000 pink	18.50	4.00
Q22	PP3	$500,000 vio brn	18.50	4.00
Q23	PP3	$3,000,000 sl bl	20.00	7.00
Q24	PP3	$5,000,000 lilac	20.00	7.00
Q25	PP3	$6,000,000 ol gray	22.00	10.00
Q26	PP3	$8,000,000 scar	22.00	11.00
Q27	PP3	$10,000,000 sage grn	25.00	14.00
		Nos. Q11-Q27 (17)	258.50	81.00

Zeros for "cents" omitted on Nos. Q23-Q27.
See Taiwan Nos. Q1-Q5. For surcharges see Nos. 883-885, Northeastern Provinces Q1, Szechwan Q1, People's Republic of China 3LQ1-3LQ9, 5LQ3-5LQ16, 5LQ29-5LQ30.

#Q11-Q15, Q23-Q24 Surcharged in Black or Carmine (#Q35)

1949   Unwmk.   *Perf. 13½*

Q32	PP3	$10 on $3000	5.00	1.00
Q33	PP3	$20 on $5000	5.00	1.00
Q34	PP3	$50 on $10,000	5.00	1.00
Q35	PP3	$100 on $3,000,000	8.00	2.00
Q36	PP3	$200 on $5,000,000	12.00	2.00
Q37	PP3	$500 on $1000	22.50	.25
Q38	PP3	$1000 on $7000	22.50	.30
		Nos. Q32-Q38 (7)	80.00	7.55

5 characters in each line on Nos. Q33-Q38.

MILITARY STAMPS

No. 454 Overprinted in Dull Red

1943-44   Unwmk.   *Perf. 12*
M1	A59	8c turquoise green	6.00	9.00

Nos. 383, 453-454 Overprinted in Red or Black

6mm between characters
Perf. 14, 12½

M2	A57	8c olive green	6.00	9.00
a.		8mm between characters	6.00	9.00
M3	A59	8c red orange (B)	550.00	
M4	A59	8c turquoise green	12.00	10.00

Forgeries of No. M3 abound.

No. 493 Overprinted in Red

Perf. 13

M5	A62	16c dull olive brn	11.00	9.00
a.		Perf. 10½-11	300.00	

No. M5 overprinted in black is a proof.

Stamps of 1942-44 Overprinted in Carmine or Black

M6	A62	50c sage grn (C)	6.00	7.00
M7	A62	$1 rose lake	8.00	9.00
M8	A62	$1 dull green	8.00	9.00
M9	A62	$2 dk bl grn (C)	10.00	14.00
M10	A62	$2 dk vio brn ('44)	200.00	150.00
		Nos. M6-M10 (5)	232.00	189.00

Nos. 383 and 357 Overprinted in Red

1944   *Perf. 12, 14*

M11	A57	8c olive green	6.00	10.00
a.		Right character inverted	1,000.	
M12	A57	16c olive gray	90.00	90.00

Anti-Aircraft Guns — M1

1945, Jan. 1   Typo.   *Perf. 12½*
Thin Paper Without Gum

M13	M1	rose	3.00	10.00

For overprints see Northeastern Provinces Nos. M2-M3.

TAIWAN

(Formosa)

100 Sen = 1 Yen
100 Cents = 1 Dollar

Stamps and Types of Japan (Taiwan) Overprinted in Black

Stamps Divided by Lines of Colored Dashes
Values in Sen and Yen

1945   Unwmk.   Litho.   *Imperf.*
Without Gum

1	A1	3s carmine	2.50	10.00
2	A1	5s blue grn	2.50	2.00
3	A1	10s pale blue	2.50	.55
a.		Inverted overprint	375.00	
b.		Double overprint	375.00	
4	A1	30s dk brown	14.00	10.00
5	A1	40s violet	14.00	7.00
6	A1	50s gray brn	10.00	5.00
7	A1	1y olive grn	10.00	5.00

Same Overprint on Types of Japan

8	A99	5y gray grn	24.00	18.00
9	A100	10y brown vio	45.00	45.00
a.		Inverted overprint	375.00	
		Nos. 1-9 (9)	126.50	102.55

The basic stamps of this issue were prepared by Japanese authorities for Taiwan use before the end of World War II when the island reverted to Chinese control. They are printed on crude buff or white wove paper. The overprint translates: "For Use in Taiwan, Chinese Republic."

A second overprinting of Nos. 2-3 was made with a different font.

China, Nos. 728-731, Srchd. in Black

1946   Without Gum   *Perf. 14*

10	A75	70s on $20 green	3.50	5.50
a.		Inverted surcharge	1,200.	
11	A75	1y on $30 blue	3.50	5.50
12	A75	2y on $50 dk brn	3.50	5.75
13	A75	3y on $100 car	3.75	5.75
		Nos. 10-13 (4)	14.25	22.50

Convening of the Chinese Natl. Assembly.

China Issues and Types of 1940-1946 Srchd. in Black — a

Perf. 12½, 12½x13, 13, 13x12½, 14
1946-47
Nos. 18, 23-28 Without Gum

14	A46	2s on 2c dp bl	.80	1.50
15	A48	5s on 5c dl red org	.80	1.00
16	A39	10s on 4c pale vio	.80	1.50
17	A48	30s on 15c brn car	.80	1.00
18	A73	50s on $20 car	.80	1.00
19	A37	65s on $20 brt yel grn	1.00	2.00
20	A47	1y on 20c lt bl	.80	2.00
a.		Inverted surcharge	950.00	
21	A37	1y on $30 choc	1.00	1.75
22	A37	2y on $50 red org	1.50	2.00
23	A73	3y on $100 dk car	.80	2.00
24	A73	5y on $200 ol grn	.80	2.00
25	A73	10y on $500 brt bl	.80	1.50
26	A73	20y on $700 red brn	1.00	1.00
27	A73	50y on $1000 rose lake	2.00	1.50
28	A73	100y on $3000 blue	2.75	1.60
		Nos. 14-28 (15)	16.45	23.35

The bottom line of the surcharge expresses the new value and consists of 2, 3 or 4 characters.
Nos. 14, 18-19, 21-28 issued in 1947.

Same Surcharge on China No. 412

1947		**Wmk. 261**		**Perf. 13**
28A	A48	30s on 15c brn car	135.00	150.00

Type of China, 1946, with additional inscription on both sides of head

1947		**Unwmk.**	**Engr.**	**Perf. 11, 11½**
29	A74	70c carmine	3.50	4.75
30	A74	$1 green	3.50	4.75
31	A74	$2 vermilion	3.50	4.75
32	A74	$3 yel grn	3.50	4.75
33	A74	$7 yel org	3.50	4.75
34	A74	$10 magenta	3.50	4.75
		Nos. 29-34 (6)	21.00	28.50

60th birthday of Chiang Kai-shek.

Type of China, 1947, with additional inscription above value

1947				**Perf. 14**
35	A76	50c deep green	3.50	5.50
36	A76	$3 deep blue	3.50	5.50
37	A76	$7.50 carmine	3.50	5.50
38	A76	$10 light brown	3.50	5.50
39	A76	$20 deep claret	3.50	5.50
		Nos. 35-39 (5)	17.50	27.50

First anniversary of return of Chinese National Government to Nanking.

Dr. Sun Yat-sen — A3

1947, July 10			**Without Gum**	
40	A3	$1 dk brown	1.00	2.50
41	A3	$2 org brn	1.20	2.00
42	A3	$3 blue grn	1.20	2.00
43	A3	$5 vermilion	2.50	2.75
44	A3	$9 deep blue	1.00	1.20
45	A3	$10 brt rose car	1.00	.80
46	A3	$20 deep green	.85	.70
47	A3	$50 rose lilac	.85	.60
48	A3	$100 blue	.85	.60
49	A3	$200 dark red	.85	.60
		Nos. 40-49 (10)	11.30	13.75

The 30c gray and $7.50 orange were not regularly issued without surcharge. Value for the two stamps, $450.

See Nos. 63-68. For overprint and surcharges see Nos. 51-53, 69-73, 102, J10-J17.

Type of 1947 Surcharged in Black — b

1948		**Unwmk.**		**Perf. 14**
51	A3	$25 on $100 blue	2.50	3.00
52	A3	$500 on $7.50 org	6.75	3.50
53	A3	$1000 on 30c gray	14.00	9.00
		Nos. 51-53 (3)	23.25	15.50

Stamps of China, 1943-48, Surcharged Type "a" in Black or Carmine

1948-49			**Perf. 12½, 14**	
		Without Gum		
54	A73	$5 on $70 red org (#639)	1.00	2.50
55	A62	$10 on $3 dk yel (#555)	4.50	3.50
56	A82	$10 on $150 dk bl (C) (#745)	1.20	1.75
57	A82	$20 on $250 dp lil (C) (#746)	1.10	1.20
58	A67	$100 on $20 car (#592)	1,600.	—
59	A82	$1000 on $20,000 rose pink ('49) (#788)	6.50	3.50
		Nos. 54-59 (6)	1,614.	12.45

The bottom line of the surcharge expresses the new value and consists of 2 or 3 characters.

Forgeries of No. 58 abound.

Type of 1947

1949		**Engr.**		**Perf. 14**
63	A3	$25 olive grn	1.20	1.00
64	A3	$5000 ocher	10.00	2.00
65	A3	$10,000 apple grn	10.00	5.00
66	A3	$20,000 ol bister	10.00	2.00
67	A3	$30,000 indigo	10.00	2.00
68	A3	$40,000 violet brn	9.00	2.00
		Nos. 63-68 (6)	50.20	17.00

For overprint and surcharges see Nos. 101, 103, J12.

No. 42 and type of 1947 Surcharged Type "b" in Black, Carmine Violet or Red Violet

1949				
69	A3	$300 on $3 bl grn	1.75	1.00
70	A3	$1000 on $3 bl grn (C)	3.00	1.00
71	A3	$2000 on $3 bl grn (V)	2.50	1.00
72	A3	$3000 on $3 bl grn (RV)	12.00	4.25
73	A3	$3000 on $7.50 org	120.00	5.50
		Nos. 69-73 (5)	139.25	12.75

For overprints see Nos. J10-J11.

Stamps of China, 1940-47, Surcharged Type "a" in Black or Carmine
Perf. 12½, 13x13½, 14

74	A39	$2 on 2½c rose lil (#424)	.80	.80
75	A72	$5 on $40 org (#627)	1.00	2.00
76	A73	$5 on $50 pur (C) (#638)	1.00	1.50
77	A73	$5 on $100 dk car (#640)	1.25	.80
78	A57	$20 on 2c ol grn (#368)	1.00	1.75
81	A63	$100 on $20 rose (#571)	1.10	.50
82	A67	$200 on $10 dk bl (C) (#591)	8.00	1.75
84	A57	$500 on $30 dl vio (#521)	18.00	5.00
86	A62	$800 on $4 red brn (#504)	15.00	6.00
87	A67	$5000 on $10 dk bl (#591)	18.00	5.00
88	A67	$10,000 on $20 car (#592)	18.00	4.00
89	A82	$200,000 on $3000 bl (C) (#750)	900.00	50.00
		Nos. 74-89 (12)	983.15	79.10

Northeastern Provinces No. 47, Surcharged in Green, Red Violet, Black or Blue

1949-50				
91	A2	2c on $44 (G)	62.50	6.00
92	A2	5c on $44 (RV) ('50)	57.50	7.00
a.		Violet surcharge	85.00	11.50
93	A2	10c on $44 (RV) ('50)	75.00	6.00
94	A2	20c on $44 (Bk) ('50)	100.00	7.00
a.		Double surcharge	200.00	
95	A2	30c on $44 (Bl) ('50)	110.00	14.00
96	A2	50c on $44 (Bl) ('50)	130.00	17.00
		Nos. 91-96 (6)	535.00	57.00

There were two printings of Nos. 91-93, with minor differences.

China 959a, Overprinted in Black

Overprint 15mm Wide

1949		**Unwmk.**	**Rouletted 9½**	
97	A96	orange	5.50	1.75

China Nos. 567, 498 and 640 Surcharged Type "a" in Black

1948-49		**Unwmk.**	**Perf. 12½, 13, 14**	
98	A63	$20 on $3 red	3.50	2.50
99	A62	$50 on 50c sage grn	3.75	5.00
a.		Perf. 11	50.00	75.00
100	A73	$600 on $100 dk car	6.50	3.50
		Nos. 98-100 (3)	13.75	11.00

Bottom line of surcharge consists of 3 characters.

No. 99 has two settings of surcharge: I. Spacing 10mm between rows of characters. II. Spacing 12mm.

#67, 47 and 68 Surcharged in Violet (#101) or Black

1949				**Perf. 14**
101	A3	2c on $30,000 ind	52.50	30.00
102	A3	10c on $50 rose lil	52.50	6.75
103	A3	10c on $40,000 vio brn	125.00	30.00
		Nos. 101-103 (3)	230.00	66.75

Numerals slightly larger on Nos. 101-103.
For similar surcharges on China type A82 see China Nos. 1025-1036.

AIR POST STAMP

China No. C62a, Overprinted in Black

Overprint 15mm Wide

1949		**Unwmk.**	**Rouletted 9½**	
C1	AP5	blue green	2.50	2.50

SPECIAL DELIVERY STAMP

China No. E12a, Overprinted in Black

Overprint 12½mm Wide

1950		**Unwmk.**	**Rouletted 9½**	
E1	SD2	red violet	10.00	4.50

REGISTRATION STAMP

China No. F2a, Overprinted in Black

Overprint 12mm Wide

1950		**Unwmk.**	**Rouletted 9½**	
F1	R2	carmine	10.00	4.50

POSTAGE DUE STAMPS

D1

		Unwmk.		
1948, Feb. 10		**Litho.**		**Perf. 14**
		Without Gum		
J1	D1	$1 blue	2.50	5.00
J2	D1	$3 blue	2.50	5.75
J3	D1	$5 blue	2.50	5.75
J4	D1	$10 blue	2.50	7.75
J5	D1	$20 blue	2.50	4.75
		Nos. J1-J5 (5)	12.50	29.00

Nos. J1-J4 Surcharged in Carmine

1948, Dec. 4				
J6	D1	$50 on $1 blue	24.00	13.00
J7	D1	$100 on $3 blue	24.00	13.00
J8	D1	$300 on $5 blue	24.00	13.00
J9	D1	$500 on $10 blue	24.00	13.00
		Nos. J6-J9 (4)	96.00	52.00

Nos. 70, 72 and 64 Handstamped in Violet

1949, Aug. 5				
J10	A3	$1000 on $3 bl grn	35.00	22.00
J11	A3	$3000 on $3 bl grn	54.00	29.00
J12	A3	$5000 ocher	120.00	70.00
		Nos. J10-J12 (3)	209.00	121.00

No. 48 Surcharged in Various Colors

1950				
J13	A3	4c on $100 bl (Br)	12.00	10.00
J14	A3	10c on $100 bl (RV)	22.50	26.00
J15	A3	20c on $100 bl (Bk)	10.00	22.50
J16	A3	40c on $100 bl (C)	47.50	90.00
J17	A3	$1 on $100 bl (Bl)	35.00	47.50
		Nos. J13-J17 (5)	127.00	196.00

PARCEL POST STAMPS

Type of China, Parcel Post Stamps of 1945-48 With Added Inscription

1949		**Unwmk.**	**Engr.**	**Perf. 14**
Q1	PP3	$100 bluish grn	265.00	1.00
Q2	PP3	$300 rose car	265.00	1.00
Q3	PP3	$500 olive green	265.00	1.00
Q4	PP3	$1000 slate	265.00	1.00
Q5	PP3	$3000 deep plum	265.00	1.00
		Nos. Q1-Q5 (5)	1,325.	5.00

Chinese characters in lower corners have colorless background; denomination tablet in color.

OCCUPATION STAMPS

Issued Under Japanese Occupation

Unused values for Japanese occupation issues are for never hinged examples.

Canceled Stamps

Postally used stamps of the Japanese occupation generally have heavy, smudgy cancels.

Kwangtung

China No. 297 Overprinted in Black

1942		**Unwmk.**		**Perf. 12½**
1N1	A37	2c olive green	8.00	8.00
a.		Inverted overprint	120.00	165.00

Same Overprint in Red or Black on Stamps of China, 1939-41

Perf. 12½, 14

1N2	A57	3c dl cl (#350)	2.75	2.75
1N3	A57	8c ol grn (#383)	2.75	2.75
1N4	A57	10c grn (#354) (R)	2.50	2.75
1N5	A57	10c grn (#384) (R)	3.50	3.50
1N6	A57	16c ol gray (#357)	7.50	7.25
1N7	A57	30c scar (#385)	4.00	3.00
1N8	A57	50c dk bl (#386) (R)	5.00	9.00
1N9	A57	$1 org brn & sep (#387)	10.00	10.00
1N10	A57	$2 dp bl & yel brn (#388)	12.00	9.50
1N11	A57	$5 red & sl grn (#389)	15.00	10.00
1N12	A57	$10 dk grn & dl pur (#390)	30.00	20.00
1N13	A57	$20 rose lake & dk bl (#391)	13.00	13.00

Same Overprint on China Nos. 422 and 433

Perf. 12½

1N14	A40	1c orange	2.00	2.40
a.		Inverted overprint	87.50	80.00
1N15	A47	20c lt blue	4.00	5.00

Same Overprint on Stamps of China, 1941

Perf. 12

1N16	A59	1c orange	4.50	4.50
1N17	A59	5c green	2.50	4.50
1N18	A59	8c turq green	2.75	3.75
1N19	A59	10c brt green	3.25	3.75
1N20	A59	17c olive	4.00	6.00
1N21	A59	30c scarlet	6.00	7.00
1N22	A59	50c dark blue	4.00	4.00
		Nos. 1N1-1N22 (22)	149.00	142.40

Stamps of China, 1939-41 Overprinted in Black

1942 Perf. 12½, 14

1N23	A57	2c olive grn (#368)	1.50	2.00
1N24	A57	3c dl claret (#350)	1.50	2.00
1N25	A57	5c olive grn (#352)	1.50	1.25
1N26	A57	8c olive grn (#353)	300.00	—
1N27	A57	8c olive grn (#369)	1.00	1.00
1N28	A57	10c green (#354)	1.50	2.00
1N29	A57	16c ol gray (#357)	1.50	3.00
1N30	A57	25c dk bl (#358)	2.00	4.00
1N31	A57	30c scarlet (#385)	2.50	3.00
1N32	A57	50c dk blue (#386)	2.25	2.75
1N33	A57	$1 org brn & sep (#387)	13.00	17.00
1N34	A57	$2 dp bl & yel brn (#388)	13.00	14.00
1N35	A57	$5 red & sl grn (#389)	14.00	17.00
1N36	A57	$10 dk grn & dl pur (#390)	20.00	20.00
1N37	A57	$20 rose lake & dk bl (#391)	14.00	27.50
		Nos. 1N23-1N25,1N27-1N37 (14)	89.25	116.50

No. 1N26 is valued in fine condition.

Same Overprint on China Nos. 397-401

1942 Wmk. 261 Perf. 14

1N38	A57	$1 org brn & sep	10.00	9.00
1N39	A57	$2 dp bl & yel brn	9.00	13.00
1N40	A57	$5 red & sl grn	11.00	14.00
1N41	A57	$10 dk grn & dl pur	22.50	26.50
1N42	A57	$20 rose lake & dk bl	22.50	24.00
		Nos. 1N38-1N42 (5)	75.00	86.50

Same Overprint on Stamps of China, 1941

1942 Unwmk. Perf. 12

1N43	A59	2c brt ultra	1.00	2.00
1N44	A59	5c green	1.00	2.00
1N45	A59	8c red org	2.00	3.00
1N46	A59	8c turq grn	2.00	3.00
1N47	A59	10c brt green	2.00	5.00
1N48	A59	17c olive	2.00	5.00
1N49	A59	25c rose vio	2.00	4.00
1N50	A59	30c scarlet	2.00	3.00
1N51	A59	50c dk blue	3.00	3.00
1N52	A59	$1 brn & blk	7.00	8.00
1N53	A59	$2 bl & blk	7.00	8.75
1N54	A59	$5 scar & blk	13.00	13.00

1N55	A59	$10 grn & blk	17.00	17.00
1N56	A59	$20 rose vio & blk	11.00	20.00
		Nos. 1N43-1N56 (14)	72.00	96.75

China Nos. 354 and 369 Surcharged in Black

1945 Unwmk. Perf. 12½

1N57	A57	$200 on 10c grn	200.00	110.00
1N58	A57	$400 on 8c ol grn	200.00	110.00

China No. 422 Surcharged in Black

1945

1N59	A40	$400 on 1c org	750.00	600.00

Forgeries exist.

OCCUPATION POSTAGE DUE STAMPS

China, No. J79 Surcharged Diagonally with New Value Between Parallel Lines in Black

1945 Unwmk. Perf. 12½

1NJ1	D5	$100 on $2 yel org	825.00	900.00
a.		Inverted surcharge	1,100.	1,100.

MENG CHIANG (Inner Mongolia)

Nos. 297-298, 301-303 Overprinted

Characters 4mm High — I

Characters 5mm High — II

1941 Engr. Unwmk.

2N1	A37	2c #297, I	3.00	2.00
a.		Type II	2.00	2.00
2N2	A37	4c #298, II	55.00	
a.		Type I	60.00	55.00
2N3	A37	15c #301, I	6.00	5.50
a.		Type II	45.00	6.00
2N4	A37	20c #302, II	11.00	8.75
a.		Type I	12.00	16.00
2N5	A37	25c #303, II	12.00	14.00
a.		Type I	92.50	92.50
		Nos. 2N1-2N5 (5)	87.00	30.25

For surcharge see No. 2N116.

On Nos. 312, 314, 318, 321

1941 Perf. 14

2N6	A39	½c #312, I	14.00	17.50
a.		Type I	47.50	
2N7	A39	2½c #314, II	5.00	3.75
a.		Type I	8.75	8.75
2N8	A45	13c #318, II	7.50	6.00
a.		Type I	120.00	110.00
2N9	A48	30c #321, II	87.50	92.50
		Nos. 2N6-2N9 (4)	114.00	119.75

On Stamps of 1939-41

1941 Perf. 12½

2N10	A57	2c #368, II	2.40	3.00
2N11	A57	3c #350, II	1.00	1.00
a.		Type I	2.00	2.00
2N12	A57	5c #352, II	2.10	2.50
a.		Type I	2.75	6.00
2N13	A57	8c #353, I	3.00	3.00
a.		Type II	2.00	2.00
2N14	A57	8c #369, II	20.00	11.00
2N15	A57	10c #354, II	3.00	2.25
2N16	A57	16c #357, II	6.00	6.00

2N17	A57	$1 #359, II	30.00	25.00
a.		#347, I	440.00	440.00
b.		#347, I	87.50	80.00
2N18	A57	$5 #361, II	100.00	92.50
		Nos. 2N10-2N18 (9)	167.00	145.25

For surcharges see Nos. 2N117, 2N119.

On Stamps of 1940 with Secret Marks

1941 Unwmk. Perf. 14

2N19	A57	5c #382, II	2.50	2.00
2N20	A57	8c #383, I	4.00	3.25
a.		Type II	55.00	
2N21	A57	10c #384, II	2.25	2.00
a.		Type I	4.00	4.00
2N22	A57	30c #385, II	3.00	4.00
a.		Type I	5.00	5.00
2N23	A57	50c #386, II	9.00	7.25
a.		Type I	7.25	7.25
2N24	A57	$1 #387, I	22.50	17.50
a.		Type II	30.00	29.00
2N25	A57	$2 #388, I	30.00	22.50
a.		Type II	35.00	32.50
2N26	A57	$5 #389, I	42.50	45.00
a.		Type II	87.50	
2N27	A57	$10 #390, I	87.50	87.50
a.		Type I	87.50	87.50
2N28	A57	$20 #391, I	120.00	120.00
a.		Type I	120.00	110.00
		Nos. 2N19-2N28 (10)	323.25	311.00

For surcharge see No. 2N120.

On Stamps of 1940 with Secret Marks

1941 Wmk. 261 Perf. 14

2N29	A57	10c #394, II	4.50	4.50
2N30	A57	30c #395, II	6.00	6.00
a.		Type I	120.00	110.00
2N31	A57	50c #396, II	8.00	9.00
		Nos. 2N29-2N31 (3)	18.50	19.50

On Stamps of 1940-41 (Martyrs) with Secret Marks

Perf. 12½, 13 & Compound

1941 Wmk. 261

2N32	A39	½c #402, II	12.00	14.00
2N33	A40	1c #403, II	3.00	2.00
a.		Type I	5.00	3.50
2N34	A39	2½c #405, I	80.00	72.50
a.		Type II	80.00	80.00
2N35	A48	3c #406, II	6.00	4.00
2N36	A46	10c #410, II	12.50	12.50
a.		Type I	21.00	
2N37	A46	17c #413, II	62.50	—
a.		Type I	80.00	80.00
2N38	A40	25c #416, II	8.00	10.00
2N39	A48	30c #418, II	72.50	77.50
a.		Type I	77.50	87.50
2N40	A47	40c #419, II	8.50	7.00
a.		Type I	14.50	13.00
2N41	A40	50c #420, I	13.00	14.00
a.		Type II	60.00	

Unwmk.

2N42	A39	½c #421, II	2.00	3.00
a.		Type I	5.00	5.00
2N43	A40	1c #422, I	2.00	2.00
a.		Type II	4.25	3.50
2N44	A46	2c #423, II	8.50	6.00
2N45	A48	3c #425, II	4.00	3.50
a.		Type I	5.00	4.00
2N46	A39	4c #426, II	2.00	2.00
2N47	A45	8c #428, II	19.00	
a.		Type I	100.00	
2N48	A46	10c #429, II	24.00	24.00
a.		Type II	72.50	
2N49	A45	13c #430, II	8.00	7.25
a.		Type I	24.00	
2N50	A48	15c #431, II	5.00	5.00
2N51	A46	17c #432, II	5.00	5.00
a.		Type I	7.25	6.00
2N52	A47	20c #433, II	5.00	5.00
a.		Type I	6.00	7.00
2N53	A45	21c #434, II	5.00	5.00
2N54	A40	25c #435, I	6.00	8.00
2N55	A46	28c #436, II	5.00	7.00
2N56	A40	50c #439, II	21.50	18.00
a.		Type I	18.00	19.00
		Nos. 2N42-2N56 (15)	122.00	100.75

For surcharges see Nos. 2N114-2N115, 2N118, 2N121-2N122.

China Nos. 297-298, 302 Surcharged in Black

1942 Unwmk. Perf. 12½, 13

2N57	A37	1c on 2c ol grn	55.00	55.00
2N58	A37	2c on 4c grn	14.00	14.00
2N59	A37	10c on 20c ultra	85.00	42.50
		Nos. 2N57-2N59 (3)	154.00	111.50

Same, on China No. 313

Perf. 14

2N60	A40	½c on 1c org	62.50	19.50

Same, on Stamps of China, 1938-41

Perf. 12½

2N61	A57	1c on 2c (#368)	2.00	1.25
2N62	A57	4c on 8c (#353)	14.00	13.00
a.		Inverted surcharge	47.50	
2N63	A57	4c on 8c (#369)	6.00	7.00
2N64	A57	5c on 10c (#354)	3.00	3.00
2N65	A57	8c on 16c (#357)	11.00	7.00
2N66	A57	50c on $1 (#359)	15.00	17.50
a.		On No. 347	220.00	220.00
b.		On No. 344	660.00	—
2N67	A57	$1 on $2 (#360)	87.50	72.50
		Nos. 2N61-2N67 (7)	138.50	121.25

No. 2N66b was issued without gum.

Same, on Stamps of China, 1940

Perf. 14

2N68	A57	4c on 8c (#383)	3.00	1.50
2N69	A57	15c on 30c (#385)	10.00	10.00
a.		Inverted surcharge	55.00	55.00
2N70	A57	25c on 50c (#386)	10.00	10.00
2N71	A57	50c on $1 (#387)	30.00	18.00
2N72	A57	$1 on $2 (#388)	30.00	18.00
2N73	A57	$5 on $10 (#390)	75.00	62.50
2N74	A57	$10 on $20 (#391)	140.00	110.00
		Nos. 2N68-2N74 (7)	298.00	230.00

Same, on China No. 395

1942 Wmk. 261 Perf. 14

2N75	A57	15c on 30c scar	140.00	100.00

Same, on China Nos. 418 and 419

Perf. 12½, 13

2N76	A48	15c on 30c brn car	47.50	47.50
2N77	A47	20c on 40c org	20.00	13.50
		Nos. 2N75-2N77 (3)	207.50	161.00

Same, on Stamps of China, 1940-41

1942 Unwmk.

2N78	A40	½c on 1c org	3.00	3.00
2N79	A39	2c on 4c pale vio	6.00	6.00
2N80	A47	10c on 20c lt bl	6.00	6.00
2N81	A47	20c on 40c org	17.50	14.50
2N82	A40	25c on 50c grn	24.00	24.00
		Nos. 2N78-2N82 (5)	56.50	53.50

Same Surcharge on "New Peking" Prints

Perf. 14

2N83	A37	1c on 2c ol grn	14.50	25.00
2N84	A37	2c on 4c grn	1.40	1.00
2N85	A46	5c on 10c dl vio	5.00	9.00
2N86	A57	8c on 16c ol gray	2.00	2.75
2N87	A47	10c on 20c red brn	5.00	7.25
2N88	A48	15c on 30c brn car	4.00	4.00
2N89	A47	20c on 40c org	9.00	10.00
2N90	A40	25c on 50c grn	6.00	6.00
2N91	A57	50c on $1 org brn & sep	8.50	14.50
2N92	A57	$1 on $2 dp bl & org brn	40.00	45.00
2N93	A57	$5 on $10 dk grn & dl pur	60.00	80.00
		Nos. 2N83-2N93 (11)	155.40	204.50

The "New Peking" printings were made by the Chinese Bureau of Engraving and Printing for use in Japanese controlled areas of North China. They are on thin, poor quality paper, with dull gum or without gum and there are slight alterations in the designs.

Dragon-Carved Pillar and Doves — A1

Wmk. Characters in Circle in Sheet

1943 Engr. Perf. 12xPin-perf. 12

2N94	A1	4f deep orange	4.00	4.00
2N95	A1	8f dark blue	5.00	4.00

5th anniv. of the Inner Mongolia post and telegraph service.

The watermark, which is 40mm in diameter and covers four stamps, occurs three times in the sheet.

Mining Coal — A2

1943 Unwmk. Photo. Perf. 12

2N96	A2	4f Prus green	4.00	5.00
2N97	A2	8f brown red	4.00	5.00

2nd anniv. of the "Greater East Asia War."

Flying Horse — A3   Yun Wang — A4

1944 Perf. 12½x12, 12x12½

2N98	A3	4f rose	3.00	5.00
2N99	A4	8f dull blue	3.00	5.00

5th anniv. of the founding of the Federal Autonomous Government of Mongolia, Sept. 1, 1939.

Industrial Plant — A5

1944, Dec. 8 Photo. Perf. 12x12½

2N100	A5	8f red brown	4.00	6.00

3rd anniv. of the "Greater East Asia War" and to encourage production increase.

New Peking Printings of 1942 Overprinted in Black

1945 Unwmk. Engr. Perf. 14
Without Gum

2N101	A37	2c olive grn	12.00	—
2N102	A37	4c dull grn	20.00	—
2N103	A37	5c green	21.00	27.50
2N104	A57	$1 org brn & sep	6.00	8.00
2N105	A57	$2 dp bl & org brn	15.00	19.00
2N106	A57	$5 red & grnsh blk	50.00	50.00

Same Overprint on New Peking Printings of Martyrs Issue

2N107	A40	1c orange	2.00	2.00
2N108	A45	8c dp orange	3.00	3.00
2N109	A46	10c dl violet	3.00	3.00
2N110	A47	20c red brown	3.00	3.00
2N111	A48	30c brown car	3.00	3.00
2N112	A47	40c orange	2.00	2.00
2N113	A40	50c green	8.00	8.00

For surcharges see Nos. 2N123-2N127.

Stamps of Meng Chiang, 1941, Surcharged in Red or Black

50c   10c

$1

1945

2N114	A39	10c on ½c ol blk (#2N42, II, R)	4.00	4.00
a.		On #2N42a, I	7.25	8.00
2N115	A40	10c on 1c org (#2N43a, II, R)	2.00	2.00
a.		Without secret mark (China #422a)	40.00	40.00
b.		On #2N43, I	3.00	3.50
2N116	A37	50c on 2c ol grn (#2N1a, II, B)	18.00	35.00
a.		On #2N1, I	18.00	35.00
2N117	A57	50c on 2c ol grn (#2N10, II, B))	1.40	2.00
2N118	A39	50c on 4c pale vio (#2N46, II, R)	2.00	2.00
2N119	A57	50c on 5c grn (#2N12, II, R)	1.00	1.10
a.		On #2N12a, II	12.50	12.50
2N120	A57	50c on 5c grn (#2N19, II, R)	1.50	2.10

Nos. 2N114-2N120 (7) 29.90 48.20

Same Surcharge on #2N32, 2N33

1945 Wmk. 261

2N121	A39	10c on ½c ol blk, II (R)	29.00	35.00
2N122	A40	10c on 1c orange, II (R)	6.00	6.00
a.		On #2N33a, I	35.00	—

Same Surcharge on Nos. 2N107, 2N101-2N103 and 2N108

1945 Unwmk.

2N123	A40	10c on 1c org (R)	2.00	2.00
2N124	A37	50c on 2c ol grn (Bk)	5.00	5.00
2N125	A37	50c on 4c dl grn (R)	10.00	10.00
2N126	A37	50c on 5c green	1.00	2.00
2N127	A45	$1 on 8c dp org (R)	4.00	6.00

Nos. 2N123-2N127 (5) 22.00 25.00

NORTH CHINA
Honan
Nos. 297-298, 301-303 Overprinted

I   II

1941 Engr. Unwmk.

3N1	A37	2c #297, II	18.00	18.00
a.		Type I	30.00	30.00
3N2	A37	4c #298, I	12.00	7.25
		Type II	32.50	32.50
3N3	A37	15c #301, I	3.00	3.00
a.		Type II	40.00	3.00
3N4	A37	20c #302, I	11.00	8.00
3N5	A37	25c #303, II	24.00	24.00

Nos. 3N1-3N5 (5) 68.00 60.25

1941 Perf. 14

3N6	A39	½c #312, I	3.00	3.50
		Type II	40.00	
3N7	A39	2½c #314, I	4.00	3.00
		Type II	4.00	3.00
3N8	A45	13c #318, II	4.00	4.00
		Type I	100.00	100.00
3N9	A48	30c #321, II	18.00	18.00
3N10	A47	40c #322, II	100.00	100.00

Nos. 3N6-3N10 (5) 129.00 127.50

On Stamps of 1939-41

1941 Perf. 12½

3N11	A57	2c #368, II	2.00	2.00
3N12	A57	3c #350, I	2.00	2.00
		Type II	3.00	2.00
3N13	A57	5c #352, II	4.00	2.00
a.		Type I	2.40	2.40
3N14	A57	8c #353, II	4.00	2.00
a.		Type I	3.00	1.50
3N15	A57	10c #354, II	6.00	4.25
3N16	A57	16c #357, II	2.50	3.00
3N17	A57	$1 #359, II	20.00	20.00
a.		Type I	325.00	325.00
b.		On #347, I	80.00	75.00
3N18	A57	$5 #361, II	80.00	80.00

Nos. 3N11-3N18 (8) 120.50 115.25

For overprints see Nos. 3N56, 3N58, 3N61.

On Stamps of 1940 with Secret Marks

1941 Unwmk. Perf. 14

3N20	A57	5c #382, II	4.00	3.00
3N21	A57	8c #383, II	4.00	1.00
3N22	A57	10c #384, II	6.00	2.00

3N23	A57	30c #385, I	9.00	9.00
		Type II	15.00	11.00
3N24	A57	50c #386, I	6.00	6.00
		Type II	18.00	17.00
3N25	A57	$1 #387, I	12.00	15.00
		Type II	80.00	80.00
3N26	A57	$2 #388, I	18.00	18.00
		Type II	24.00	24.00
3N27	A57	$5 #389, I	40.00	29.00
		Type II	62.50	57.50
3N28	A57	$10 #390, I	65.00	62.50
		Type I	195.00	195.00
3N29	A57	$20 #391, I	125.00	140.00
		Type I	125.00	140.00

Nos. 3N20-3N29 (10) 289.00 285.50

On Stamps of 1940 with Secret Marks

1941 Wmk. 261 Perf. 14

3N30	A57	5c #392, II	24.00	14.50
3N31	A57	5c #393, II	15.00	10.00
3N32	A57	30c #395, II	32.50	29.00
3N33	A57	50c #396, II	75.00	67.50

Nos. 3N30-3N33 (4) 146.50 121.00

On Stamps of 1940-41 (Martyrs) with Secret Marks

Perf. 12½, 13 & Compound

1941 Wmk. 261

3N34	A39	½c #402, II	3.00	3.50
3N35	A40	1c #403, II	3.00	2.00
		Type I	5.00	3.00
3N36	A39	2½c #405, II	18.00	17.00
3N37	A46	10c #410, II	20.00	18.50
		Type I	35.00	35.00
3N38	A45	13c #411, II	5.00	5.00
3N39	A46	17c #413, II	6.00	5.00
		Type I	13.00	9.00
3N40	A40	25c #416, II	7.50	5.00
3N41	A47	40c #419, II	9.00	6.00
		Type I	20.00	20.00

Nos. 3N34-3N41 (8) 71.50 62.00

Unwmk.

3N42	A39	½c #421, II	4.00	2.00
a.		Type I	6.00	4.50
3N43	A40	1c #422, I	3.00	2.50
a.		Type II	6.00	4.50
3N44	A46	2c #423, I	15.00	15.00
3N45	A48	3c #425, I	2.50	2.50
3N46	A39	4c #426, II	4.00	4.00
3N47	A46	10c #429, II	50.00	50.00
3N48	A45	13c #430, II	5.50	3.50
		Type I	30.00	25.00
3N49	A48	15c #431, II	4.50	4.50
3N50	A46	17c #432, II	6.00	4.50
		Type I	20.00	20.00
3N51	A47	20c #433, II	6.00	4.00
		Type I	62.50	50.00
3N52	A45	21c #434, II	7.50	5.00
3N53	A40	25c #435, I	8.00	7.00
3N54	A46	28c #436, II	5.00	5.00

Nos. 3N42-3N54 (13) 121.00 109.50

For overprints see Nos. 3N55, 3N59.

Overprinted in Red

1942

3N55	A39	4c #3N46	6.00	6.00
3N56	A57	8c #3N14	50.00	40.00
3N57	A57	8c #369, II	25.00	21.00

Nos. 3N55-3N57 (3) 81.00 67.00

The fall of Singapore.

Overprinted in Red

1942

3N58	A57	2c #3N11	15.00	15.00
3N59	A39	4c #3N46	20.00	25.00
3N60	A57	8c #369, II	72.50	72.50
3N61	A57	8c #3N14	65.00	72.50

Nos. 3N58-3N61 (4) 172.50 185.00

Formation of Manchukuo, 10th anniv.

Hopei

On Stamps of 1940-41 (Martyrs) with Secret Marks

I   II

1941 Engr. Unwmk.

4N1	A37	2c #297, II	4.00	3.00
a.		Type I	11.00	11.00
4N2	A37	4c #298, I	4.50	4.50
		Type II	85.00	
4N3	A37	15c #301, II	5.00	3.00
		Type I	4.25	4.00
4N4	A37	20c #302, II	37.50	35.00
4N5	A37	25c #303, II	35.00	8.75
a.		Type I	95.00	90.00

Nos. 4N1-4N5 (5) 86.00 54.25

On Nos. 312, 314, 318, 321

1941 Perf. 14

4N6	A39	½c #312, II	3.00	2.00
		Type I	10.00	10.00
4N7	A39	2½c #314, II	4.00	4.00
		Type I	4.00	2.00
4N8	A45	13c #318, II	5.00	4.00
		Type I	5.00	4.00
4N9	A48	30c #321, II	7.00	7.00

Nos. 4N6-4N9 (4) 19.00 15.00

On Stamps of 1939-41

1941 Perf. 12½

4N10	A57	2c #368, II	5.00	3.00
4N11	A57	2c #349, II	3.00	2.00
4N12	A57	3c #350, II	5.00	2.00
a.		Type I	3.00	2.00
4N13	A57	5c #352, II	3.00	2.00
a.		Type I	3.50	2.00
4N14	A57	8c #353, II	2.00	1.00
a.		Type I	2.00	1.60
4N15	A57	8c #369, II	6.00	3.75
4N16	A57	10c #354, II	3.00	1.00
4N17	A57	16c #357, II	4.00	2.00
4N18	A57	$1 #359, II	175.00	165.00
a.		On #347, I	250.00	
4N19	A57	$2 #360, II	62.50	55.00
a.		Type I	65.00	55.00
4N20	A57	$5 #361, II	65.00	65.00
a.		Type II	65.00	75.00
4N21	A57	$10 #362, II	200.00	200.00
4N22	A57	$20 #363, II	450.00	450.00

Nos. 4N10-4N22 (13) 983.50 951.75

For overprints see Nos. 4N66-4N68, 4N70.

On Stamps of 1940 with Secret Marks

1941 Unwmk. Perf. 14
Type II

4N24	A57	5c #382	2.00	1.00
4N25	A57	8c #383	2.00	1.00
4N26	A57	10c #384	6.00	3.00
4N27	A57	30c #385	4.00	3.00
4N28	A57	50c #386	4.00	3.00
4N29	A57	$1 #387	10.00	6.00
4N30	A57	$2 #388	45.00	20.00
4N31	A57	$5 #389	55.00	50.00
4N32	A57	$10 #390	65.00	55.00
4N33	A57	$20 #391	75.00	72.50

Nos. 4N24-4N33 (10) 268.00 214.50

For overprints see Nos. 4N65, 4N71.

Type I

4N24a	A57	5c	2.00	1.50
4N25a	A57	8c	70.00	70.00
4N26a	A57	10c	3.00	2.40
4N28a	A57	50c	6.00	3.00
4N29a	A57	$1	11.00	6.00
4N30a	A57	$2	60.00	32.50
4N31a	A57	$5	55.00	55.00
4N32a	A57	$10	45.00	65.00
4N33a	A57	$20	110.00	110.00

Nos. 4N24a-4N33a (9) 347.00 345.40

On Stamps of 1940 with Secret Marks

1941 Wmk. 261 Perf. 14

4N34	A57	5c #392, II	3.00	2.00
4N35	A57	5c #393, II	2.00	2.00
4N36	A57	10c #394, II	4.00	2.00
4N37	A57	30c #395, II	10.00	10.00
a.		Type I	15.00	14.00
4N38	A57	50c #396, II	5.00	5.00

Nos. 4N34-4N38 (5) 24.00 16.00

On Stamps of 1940-41 (Martyrs) with Secret Marks

Perf. 12½, 13 & Compound

1941 Wmk. 261

4N39	A39	½c #402, II	3.00	3.00
4N40	A40	1c #403, I	2.50	2.00
		Type II	3.00	3.00
4N41	A46	2c #404, II	4.00	2.00
4N42	A39	2½c #405, II	5.00	4.00
4N43	A48	3c #406, II	4.00	3.00

4N44 A46 10c #410, II 5.00 4.00
a. Type I 6.00 5.00
4N45 A45 13c #411, II 4.00 4.00
4N46 A46 17c #413, II 5.00 3.50
a. Type I 4.25 4.25
4N47 A40 25c #416, II 7.50 5.00
4N48 A48 30c #418, II 30.00 22.50
a. Type I 50.00 50.00
4N49 A47 40c #419, II 6.00 4.00
a. Type I 6.00 5.75
Nos. 4N39-4N49 (11) 76.00 57.00

Unwmk.

4N50 A39 ½c #421, II 3.00 2.00
a. Type I 4.00 2.25
4N51 A40 1c #422, II 4.00 2.00
a. Type I 5.00 2.00
4N52 A46 2c #423 4.00 2.00
4N53 A48 3c #425, I 4.00 2.00
a. Type II 5.50 4.25
4N54 A39 4c #426, II 4.50 2.50
4N55 A45 8c #428, II 4.00 2.50
a. Type I 5.00 3.50
4N56 A46 10c #429, II 5.00 3.00
4N57 A45 13c #430, I 5.00 4.00
a. Type II 4.50 4.50
4N58 A48 15c #431, II 9.00 5.75
4N59 A46 17c #432, II 8.00 5.00
a. Type I 8.00 6.00
4N60 A47 20c #433, II 6.00 4.00
a. Type I 6.00 5.00
4N61 A45 21c #434, II 6.00 5.00
4N62 A40 25c #435, I 6.00 5.00
a. Type II 5.00 5.00
4N63 A46 28c #436, II 5.00 4.00
Nos. 4N50-4N63 (14) 73.50 48.75

For overprints see Nos. 4N64, 4N69.

Honan Singapore Overprint in Red

1942

4N64 A39 4c #4N54 5.00 6.00
4N65 A57 8c #4N25 8.00 10.00
4N66 A57 8c #4N14 12.00 14.00
4N67 A57 8c #4N15 12.00 15.00
Nos. 4N64-4N67 (4) 37.00 45.00

Honan Anniv. of Manchukuo Overprint in Red

1942

4N68 A57 2c #4N10 16.00 17.00
4N69 A39 4c #4N54 7.00 8.25
4N70 A57 8c #4N14 90.00 90.00
4N71 A57 8c #4N25 15.00 17.00
Nos. 4N68-4N71 (4) 128.00 132.25

Shansi

Nos. 297-298, 301, 303 Overprinted

I

II

1941 Engr. Unwmk.

5N1 A37 2c #297, II 65.00 65.00
a. Type I 87.50 55.00
5N2 A37 4c #298, I 50.00 62.50
a. Type II 125.00 165.00
5N3 A37 15c #301, II 5.25 6.75
a. Type I 9.00 11.00
5N4 A37 25c #303, II 9.00 13.50
a. Type I 62.50 67.50
Nos. 5N1-5N4 (4) 129.25 147.75

On Nos. 312, 314, 318, 321

1941 *Perf. 14*

5N5 A39 ½c #312, II 55.00 55.00
a. Type I 4.00 4.00
5N6 A39 2½c #314, II 3.00 3.00
a. Type I 4.00 4.00
5N7 A45 13c #318, II 6.00 4.00
a. Type I 240.00 240.00
5N8 A48 30c #321, II 15.00 12.00
Nos. 5N5-5N8 (4) 79.00 74.00

On Stamps of 1939-41

1941 *Perf. 12½*

5N9 A57 2c #368, II 2.40 2.00
5N10 A57 3c #350, II 2.00 2.00
a. Type I 15.00 15.00
5N11 A57 5c #352, II 7.00 3.50
a. Type I 7.50 5.00
5N12 A57 8c #353, II 1.50 1.50
a. Type I 4.00 3.50
5N13 A57 8c #369, II 42.50 25.00
5N14 A57 10c #354, II 17.00 8.00
5N15 A57 16c #357, II 7.50 5.00
5N16 A57 $1 #359, II 20.00 17.00
5N17 A57 $2 #360, II 50.00 50.00
5N18 A57 $5 #361, II 40.00 57.50
Nos. 5N9-5N18 (10) 189.90 171.50

For overprints see Nos. 5N62-5N64, 5N66-5N67.

On Stamps of 1940 with Secret Marks

1941 Unwmk. *Perf. 14*

5N19 A57 5c #382, II 3.00 2.00
5N20 A57 8c #383, II 3.00 2.00
5N21 A57 10c #384, I 6.00 2.00
a. Type II 32.50 5.00
5N22 A57 30c #385, II 9.00 4.00
a. Type I 7.50 3.00
5N23 A57 50c #386, I 7.50 5.00
a. Type II 5.75 5.75
5N24 A57 $1 #387, I 18.00 14.00
a. Type II 45.00 37.50
5N25 A57 $2 #388, II 40.00 25.00
a. Type I 25.00 25.00
5N26 A57 $5 #389, II 32.50 32.50
a. Type I 97.50 97.50
5N27 A57 $10 #390, II 70.00 70.00
a. Type I 75.00 75.00
5N28 A57 $20 #391, II 70.00 70.00
a. Type I 125.00 135.00
Nos. 5N19-5N28 (10) 259.00 226.50

For overprints see Nos. 5N61, 5N68.

On Stamps of 1940 with Secret Marks

1941 Wmk. 261 *Perf. 14*

5N29 A57 5c #392, II 6.00 3.00
5N30 A57 5c #393, II 3.00 2.00
5N31 A57 10c #394, II 6.00 3.00
5N32 A57 30c #395, I 37.50 80.00
5N33 A57 50c #396, I 15.00 11.00
Nos. 5N29-5N33 (5) 67.50 99.00

On Stamps of 1940-41 (Martyrs) with Secret Marks

Perf. 12½, 13 & Compound

1941 Wmk. 261

5N34 A39 ½c #402, II 3.00 3.00
5N35 A40 1c #403, II 3.00 2.00
a. Type I 3.00 2.00
5N36 A46 2c #404, II 7.50 5.00
5N37 A39 2½c #405, I 9.00 10.50
5N38 A46 10c #410, I 9.75 9.75
5N39 A45 13c #411, II 6.00 5.00
5N40 A46 17c #413, I 47.50 32.50
5N41 A40 25c #416, II 5.00 5.00
5N42 A48 30c #418, I 150.00 150.00
a. Type II 150.00 150.00
5N43 A47 40c #419, II 6.00 6.00
a. Type I 37.50 37.50
5N44 A40 50c #420, II 7.50 7.50
a. Type I 42.50 42.50
Nos. 5N34-5N44 (11) 254.25 236.25

Unwmk.

5N45 A39 ½c #421, II 3.00 3.75
a. Type I 5.25 5.75
5N46 A40 1c #422, I 4.50 3.00
a. Type II 3.00 3.00
5N47 A46 2c #423, II 4.00 4.00
5N48 A48 3c #425, I 11.00 9.00
5N49 A39 4c #426, II 5.00 5.00
5N50 A45 8c #428, I 17.00 15.00
a. Type II 35.00 21.00
5N51 A46 10c #429, I 50.00 50.00
a. Type II 57.50 57.50
5N52 A45 13c #430, I 30.00 20.00
a. Type II 22.50 22.50
5N53 A48 15c #431, II 6.75 6.75
5N54 A46 17c #432, II 6.00 6.00
a. Type I 6.00 5.50
5N55 A47 20c #433, II 7.50 6.00
a. Type I 7.50 4.00
5N56 A45 21c #434, II 6.00 6.00
5N57 A40 25c #435, I 9.00 5.00
5N58 A46 28c #436, II 7.50 6.00
5N59 A40 50c #439, II 17.00 15.00
Nos. 5N45-5N59 (15) 184.25 160.50

For overprints see Nos. 5N60, 5N65.

Honan Singapore Overprint in Red

1942

5N60 A39 4c #5N49 6.00 7.00
5N61 A57 8c #5N20 18.00 22.50
5N62 A57 8c #5N12 18.00 18.00
5N63 A57 8c #5N13 50.00 55.00
Nos. 5N60-5N63 (4) 92.00 102.50

Honan Anniv. of Manchukuo Overprint in Red

1942

5N64 A57 2c #5N9 18.00 17.00
5N65 A39 4c #5N49 13.50 17.00
5N66 A57 8c #5N12 50.00 62.50
5N67 A57 8c #5N13 72.50 85.00
5N68 A57 8c #5N20 55.00 55.00
Nos. 5N64-5N68 (5) 209.00 236.50

Shantung

Nos. 297-298, 301-303 Overprinted

I

II

1941 Engr. Unwmk.

6N1 A37 2c #297, II 2.50 2.00
a. Type I 5.00 5.00
6N2 A37 4c #298, II 8.00 7.25
a. Type I 9.25 8.00
6N3 A37 15c #301, II 3.00 2.50
a. Type I 4.00 3.50
6N4 A37 20c #302, II 6.00 5.00
6N5 A37 25c #303, II 12.00 7.25
a. Type I 265.00 225.00
Nos. 6N1-6N5 (5) 31.50 24.00

On Nos. 312, 314, 318

1941 *Perf. 14*

6N6 A39 ½c #312, II 3.00 2.00
a. Type I 3.00 2.00
6N7 A39 2½c #314, II 3.00 2.10
a. Type I 4.50 2.00
6N8 A45 13c #318, II 6.00 3.00
a. Type I 40.00 25.00
Nos. 6N6-6N8 (3) 12.00 7.10

On Stamps of 1939-41

1941 *Perf. 12½*

6N9 A57 2c #349, II 3.00 2.00
6N10 A57 2c #368, II 2.00 2.00
6N11 A57 3c #350, II 2.00 2.00
a. Type I 3.00 1.50
6N12 A57 5c #352, II 3.50 2.00
a. Type I 3.00 1.50
6N13 A57 8c #353, II 3.00 2.00
a. Type I 2.00 1.00
6N14 A57 8c #369, II 2.00 2.00
6N15 A57 10c #354, II 3.50 2.00
6N16 A57 16c #357, II 5.50 7.50
6N17 A57 $1 #359, II 27.00 13.00
a. Type I 425.00 425.00
b. On No. 347, I 62.50 57.50
6N18 A57 $5 #361, II 60.00 55.00
Nos. 6N9-6N18 (10) 111.50 89.50

For overprints see Nos. 6N62, 6N64-6N65, 6N67-6N68.

On Stamps of 1940 with Secret Marks

1941 Unwmk. *Perf. 14*

6N20 A57 5c #382, II 2.00 1.25
6N21 A57 8c #383, II 3.00 1.00
a. Type I 3.00 1.50
6N22 A57 10c #384, II 3.00 2.00
6N23 A57 30c #385, II 4.00 2.00
a. Type I 7.00 7.50
6N24 A57 50c #386, I 8.00 6.75
a. Type II 9.00 8.00
6N25 A57 $1 #387, II 9.00 5.00
a. Type I 24.00 22.50
6N26 A57 $2 #388, II 18.00 15.00
a. Type I 24.50 27.50
6N27 A57 $5 #389, II 30.00 30.00
a. Type I 42.50 40.00
6N28 A57 $10 #390, II 67.50 67.50
a. Type I 72.50 72.50
6N29 A57 $20 #391, II 97.50 97.50
a. Type I 100.00 125.00
Nos. 6N20-6N29 (10) 242.00 228.00

For overprints see Nos. 6N63, 6N69.

On Stamps of 1940 with Secret Marks

1941 Wmk. 261 *Perf. 14*

6N30 A57 5c #392, II 3.00 2.00
6N31 A57 5c #393, II 3.00 2.00
6N32 A57 10c #394, II 10.00 8.00
6N33 A57 30c #395, II 7.50 7.00
a. Type I 25.00 25.00
6N34 A57 50c #396, II 10.00 4.25
a. Type I 12.00 11.50
Nos. 6N30-6N34 (5) 33.50 23.25

On Stamps of 1940-41 (Martyrs) with Secret Marks

Perf. 12½, 13 & Compound

1941 Wmk. 261

6N35 A39 ½c #402, II 4.50 3.00
6N36 A40 1c #403, II 4.50 2.00
a. Type I 3.00 2.00
6N37 A39 2½c #405, II 25.00 17.00
6N38 A46 10c #410, I 11.00 4.00
6N39 A45 13c #411, II 10.00 5.00
6N40 A46 17c #413, II 5.00 5.00
a. Type I 11.00 11.00
6N41 A40 25c #416, II 7.50 5.00
6N42 A48 30c #418, I 60.00 37.50
6N43 A47 40c #419, II 6.00 6.00
a. Type I 37.50 37.50
6N44 A40 50c #420, II 12.00 9.00
Nos. 6N35-6N44 (10) 145.50 93.50

Unwmk.

6N45 A39 ½c #421, II 4.00 2.00
a. Type I 7.50 4.25
6N46 A40 1c #422, II 3.00 2.00
a. Type I 3.25 3.25
b. On No. 422a, II 97.50 97.50
6N48 A46 2c #423, II 5.00 2.50
6N49 A48 3c #425, I 6.00 5.00
a. Type II 5.00 6.75
6N50 A39 4c #426, II 5.00 3.00
6N51 A45 8c #428, II 4.00 3.50
a. Type I 40.00 40.00
6N52 A46 10c #429, I 15.00 15.00
6N53 A45 13c #430, I 6.00 4.50
a. Type II 4.50 4.50
6N54 A48 15c #431, II 5.00 5.00
6N55 A46 17c #432, II 5.00 4.00
a. Type I 5.00 5.00
6N56 A47 20c #433, II 6.00 4.50
a. Type I 6.75 6.75
6N57 A45 21c #434, II 9.00 5.00
6N58 A40 25c #435, I 7.00 5.75
6N59 A46 28c #436, II 5.00 4.00
6N60 A40 50c #439, II 55.00 55.00
Nos. 6N45-6N60 (15) 140.00 120.75

For overprints see Nos. 6N61, 6N66.

Honan Singapore Overprint in Red

1942

6N61 A39 4c #6N50 5.00 5.00
6N62 A57 8c #6N13 24.50 30.00
6N63 A57 8c #6N21 30.00 24.50
6N64 A57 8c #6N14 40.00 40.00
Nos. 6N61-6N64 (4) 99.50 99.50

Honan Anniv. of Manchukuo Overprint in Red

1942

6N65 A57 2c #6N10 9.00 9.00
6N66 A39 4c #6N50 11.00 11.00
6N67 A57 8c #6N13 40.00 30.00
6N68 A57 8c #6N14 65.00 72.50
6N69 A57 8c #6N21 32.50 37.50
Nos. 6N65-6N69 (5) 157.50 160.00

Supeh

Nos. 297-298, 301-302 Overprinted

I

II

1941 Engr. Unwmk.

7N1 A37 2c #297, I 24.00 13.00
a. Type II 27.50 15.00
7N2 A37 4c #298, I 100.00 57.50
a. Type II 110.00
7N3 A37 15c #301, II 8.00 6.00
a. Type I 6.00 6.00
7N4 A37 20c #302, II 15.00 6.00
Nos. 7N1-7N4 (4) 147.00 82.50

On Nos. 312, 314, 318

1941 *Perf. 14*

7N5 A39 ½c #312, I 4.50 4.25
7N6 A39 2½c #314, II 6.00 4.00
a. Type I 5.50 4.00
7N7 A45 13c #318, II 6.00 5.00
a. Type I 160.00 160.00
Nos. 7N5-7N7 (3) 16.50 13.25

On Stamps of 1939-41

1941 *Perf. 12½*

7N8 A57 2c #368, II 5.50 3.00
7N9 A57 3c #350, II 5.50 3.00
a. Type I 24.50 24.50
7N10 A57 5c #352, II 6.00 4.00
a. Type I 7.50 4.00
7N11 A57 8c #353, I 6.00 4.00
a. Type II 8.00 4.00
7N12 A57 8c #369, II 50.00 42.50
7N13 A57 10c #354, II 9.00 5.00
7N14 A57 16c #357, II 9.00 5.00
7N15 A57 $1 #359, II 18.00 18.00
a. On No. 347, I 210.00 210.00
Nos. 7N8-7N15 (8) 109.00 84.50

For overprints see Nos. 7N56-7N58, 7N60-7N61.

On Stamps of 1940 with Secret Marks

1941 Unwmk. *Perf. 14*

7N17 A57 5c #382, II 7.50 4.00
7N18 A57 8c #383, II 6.00 2.00
7N19 A57 10c #384, I 7.50 4.25
a. Type II 4.25 4.25
7N20 A57 30c #385, I 8.00 5.00
a. Type II 12.00 9.00
7N21 A57 50c #386, II 8.00 5.50
a. Type I 12.00 7.00

7N22	A57	$1 #387, I		45.00	30.00
a.		Type II		40.00	50.00
7N23	A57	$2 #388, II		29.00	29.00
a.		Type I		32.50	40.00
7N24	A57	$5 #389, I		50.00	50.00
a.		Type II		100.00	100.00
7N25	A57	$10 #390, I		80.00	80.00
a.		Type II		90.00	90.00
7N26	A57	$20 #391, II		100.00	100.00
a.		Type I		100.00	110.00
		Nos. 7N17-7N26 (10)		341.00	309.75

On Stamps of 1940 with Secret Marks

1941 Wmk. 261 Perf. 14

7N27	A57	10c #394, II		9.00	6.00
7N28	A57	30c #395, I		25.00	17.00
7N29	A57	50c #396, I		18.00	18.50
		Nos. 7N27-7N29 (3)		52.00	41.50

On Stamps of 1940-41 (Martyrs) with Secret Marks

Perf. 12½, 13 & Compound

1941 Wmk. 261

7N30	A39	½c #402, II		5.75	5.75
7N31	A40	1c #403, I		7.00	4.00
a.		Type II		6.00	3.50
7N32	A46	2c #404, II		6.00	3.00
7N33	A39	2½c #405, I		40.00	32.50
7N34	A46	10c #410, II		32.50	19.50
7N35	A45	13c #411, II		12.00	6.75
7N36	A46	17c #413, II		9.00	5.75
a.				100.00	100.00
7N37	A40	25c #416, II		10.00	6.00
7N38	A48	30c #418, I		25.00	14.50
7N39	A47	40c #419, II		10.00	6.00
a.				15.00	9.00
7N40	A40	50c #420, I		100.00	100.00
		Nos. 7N30-7N40 (11)		257.25	203.75

Unwmk.

7N41	A39	½c #421, II		6.00	4.25
a.		Type I		9.00	5.75
7N42	A40	1c #422, II		4.50	2.00
7N43	A46	2c #423, I		14.50	14.50
7N44	A48	3c #425, I		9.00	5.00
7N45	A39	4c #426, II		11.00	11.00
7N46	A46	10c #429, II		50.00	50.00
7N47	A45	13c #430, II		9.00	7.50
7N48	A48	15c #431, II		7.50	7.00
7N49	A46	17c #432, II		8.00	8.00
7N50	A47	20c #433, II		12.00	6.75
a.		Type I		12.00	7.00
7N51	A45	21c #434, II		12.00	6.75
7N52	A40	25c #435, II		12.00	7.00
a.		Type I		18.00	18.00
7N53	A46	28c #436, II		6.75	6.75
		Nos. 7N41-7N53 (13)		162.25	137.00

For overprints see Nos. 7N55, 7N59.

Honan Singapore Overprint in Red

1942

7N54	A37	4c #298, II		95.00	110.00
7N55	A39	4c #7N45		7.50	13.00
7N56	A57	8c #7N11a		40.00	40.00
7N57	A57	8c #7N12		24.00	20.00
		Nos. 7N54-7N57 (4)		166.50	183.00

Honan Anniv. of Manchukuo Overprint in Red

1942

7N58	A57	2c #7N8		17.00	24.50
7N59	A39	4c #7N45		30.00	17.00
7N60	A57	8c #7N11a		115.00	130.00
7N61	A57	8c #7N12		100.00	97.50
		Nos. 7N58-7N61 (4)		262.00	269.00

North China

For use in Honan, Hopei, Shansi, Shantung and Supeh (Northern Kiangsu)

Stamps of China, 1931-37 Surcharged North China (Hwa Pei) and Half of Original Value

1942 Unwmk. Perf. 14, 12½

8N1	A40	½c on 1c (#313)		2.00	2.50
8N2	A37	1c on 2c (#297)		.75	1.10
8N3	A37	2c on 4c (#298)		1.50	1.25
8N4	A45	4c on 8c (#316)		150.00	

Same Surcharge on Stamps of 1938-41

Perf. 12½

8N5	A57	1c on 2c (#349)		5.00	8.50
8N6	A57	1c on 2c (#368)		.50	.30
8N7	A57	4c on 8c (#353)		2.10	1.25
8N8	A57	4c on 8c (#369)		.60	.35
8N9	A57	5c on 10c grn		.65	.50

8N10	A57	8c on 16c ol gray		2.00	.80
8N11	A57	50c on $1 (#359)		8.00	8.00
8N12	A57	50c on $1 (#344)		575.00	575.00
8N13	A57	50c on $1 (#347)		110.00	110.00
8N14	A57	$1 on $2 (#360)		12.50	12.50
8N15	A57	$1 on $2 (#345)		40.00	32.50
8N16	A57	$1 on $2 (#348)		155.00	155.00

No. 8N12 was issued without gum.
For overprint see No. 8N58.

Same Surcharge on China Nos. 383-388, 390-391

Perf. 14

8N17	A57	4c on 8c ol grn		.80	.65
8N18	A57	5c on 10c grn		1.25	2.00
8N19	A57	15c on 30c scar		1.50	1.25
a.		Inverted surcharge		80.00	80.00
8N20	A57	25c on 50c dk bl		2.00	1.75
8N21	A57	50c on $1 brn & sep		4.50	4.50
8N22	A57	$1 on $2 dp bl & yel brn		5.75	5.75
8N23	A57	$5 on $10 dk grn & dl pur		50.00	50.00
8N24	A57	$10 on $20 rose lake & dk bl		50.00	60.00
		Nos. 8N17-8N24 (8)		115.80	125.90

For overprint see No. 8N55.

Same Surcharge on China Nos. 394-396

Wmk. 261

8N25	A57	5c on 10c grn		1.00	1.50
8N26	A57	15c on 30c scar		3.50	5.00
8N27	A57	25c on 50c dk bl		1.50	1.50
		Nos. 8N25-8N27 (3)		6.00	8.00

Same Surcharge on Stamps of 1940-41

1942 Wmk. 261 Perf. 12½, 13

8N28	A40	½c on 1c org		.30	.25
8N29	A46	1c on 2c dp bl		2.50	2.50
8N30	A46	4c on 8c dp grn		20.00	24.50
8N31	A46	5c on 10c dl vio		3.00	3.00
8N32	A48	15c on 30c brn car		9.75	9.75
8N33	A47	20c on 40c org		5.75	2.50
8N34	A40	25c on 50c grn		5.75	5.00
		Nos. 8N28-8N34 (7)		47.05	47.50

Unwmk.

8N35	A40	½c on 1c org (#422)		.30	.25
a.		½c on 1c org (#422a)		37.00	37.00
8N36	A46	1c on 2c dp bl		1.40	1.40
8N37	A39	2c on 4c pale vio		1.00	.85
8N38	A45	4c on 8c dp grn		1.25	2.00
8N39	A46	5c on 10c dl vio		3.00	3.00
8N40	A47	10c on 20c lt bl		3.75	.75
8N41	A47	20c on 40c org		.40	.40
8N42	A40	25c on 50c grn		32.50	32.50
		Nos. 8N35-8N42 (8)		47.20	41.75

Same Surcharge on "New Peking" Prints

Perf. 14

8N43	A37	1c on 2c ol grn		.35	.25
8N44	A37	2c on 4c dl grn		.90	.25
a.		Inverted surcharge		42.50	
8N45	A45	4c on 8c dp grn		.65	.25
8N46	A37	8c on 16c ol gray		.35	.25
8N47	A47	10c on 20c red brn		1.75	1.50
8N48	A48	15c on 30c brn car		.85	.85
8N49	A47	20c on 40c org		2.10	.50
a.		Inverted surcharge		55.00	
8N50	A40	25c on 50c grn		1.75	1.50
8N51	A57	50c on $1 org brn & sep		3.50	3.50
8N52	A57	$1 on $2 dp bl & org brn		5.75	3.50
8N53	A57	$5 on $10 dk grn & dl pur		24.50	24.50
		Nos. 8N43-8N53 (11)		42.45	36.85

See note after No. 2N93. For overprints see #8N54, 8N56-8N57, 8N59.

Nos. 8N44, 8N17 and 8N46 with Additional Overprint in Red

1943 Unwmk. Perf. 14

8N54	A37	2c on 4c dl grn		.30	1.00
8N55	A57	4c on 8c ol grn		1.50	1.75
8N56	A57	8c on 16c ol gray		1.50	3.00
		Nos. 8N54-8N56 (3)		3.30	5.75

Return of the Foreign Concessions to China.

Nos. 8N44, 8N8 and 8N46 with Additional Overprint in Red

1943, Aug. 15 Perf. 14, 12½

8N57	A37	2c on 4c dl grn		.55	.85
8N58	A57	4c on 8c ol grn		.45	1.00
8N59	A57	8c on 16c ol gray		.50	.85
		Nos. 8N57-8N59 (3)		1.50	2.70

North China Postal Service, 5th anniv.

Stamps of China, 1934-41, Overprinted in Black

1943, Nov. 1

8N60	A40	1c org (#313)		.85	.85
8N61	A40	1c org (#422)		.85	.75
8N62	A57	10c grn (#354)		.50	.45
8N63	A57	$2 dp bl & yel brn (#388)		30.00	30.00
8N64	A57	$5 red & grnsh blk (#361)		24.00	20.00
8N65	A57	$5 red & sl grn (#389)		9.75	9.75
8N66	A57	$10 dk grn & dl pur (#390)		14.50	14.50
8N67	A57	$20 rose lake & dk bl (#391)		90.00	110.00
		Nos. 8N60-8N67 (8)		170.45	186.30

Same Overprint on "New Peking" Prints

8N68	A40	1c orange		.30	.25
8N69	A37	2c olive grn		.30	.75
8N70	A37	4c dull green		.30	1.50
8N71	A37	5c green		.60	.75
8N72	A57	9c olive grn		.35	.60
8N73	A46	10c dl violet		.35	.75
8N74	A57	16c olive gray		.30	.45
8N75	A57	18c olive gray		.30	.45
8N76	A47	20c henna		.50	.60
8N77	A40	30c brown car		.45	.45
8N78	A47	40c brt orange		.45	.75
a.		Inverted overprint		42.50	42.50
8N79	A57	50c green		2.50	2.50
8N80	A57	$1 org brn & sep		4.25	1.25
8N81	A57	$2 bl & org brn		2.50	2.20
8N82	A57	$5 red & sl grn		5.00	7.50
8N83	A57	$10 dk grn & dl pur		9.00	9.00
8N84	A57	$20 rose lake & dk bl		10.00	12.50
		Nos. 8N68-8N84 (17)		37.45	42.25

See note after No. 2N93. For overprints see Nos. 8N85-8N90, 8N95-8N106.

Nos. 8N70 and 8N62 with Additional Overprint in Red

1944, Jan. 9

8N85	A37	4c dull green		.35	1.05
8N86	A57	10c green		.35	.75

1st anniv. of the declaration of war against the Allies by North China.

Nos. 8N72, 8N75, 8N79 and 8N80 with Additional Overprint in Red

1944, Mar. 30

8N87	A57	9c olive green		.80	1.50
8N88	A57	18c olive gray		3.50	3.00
8N89	A40	50c green		5.75	7.50
8N90	A57	$1 org brn & sepia		2.10	3.00
a.		Red overprint inverted		37.00	37.00
		Nos. 8N87-8N90 (4)		12.15	15.00

North China Political Council, 4th anniv.

Shanghai-Nanking Nos. 9N101-9N104 Surcharged North China (Hwa Pei) and New Value in Red or Black

a   b

c

d

1944 Perf. 12½x12, 12x12½

8N91	OS1 (a)	9c on 50c org		1.40	1.75
8N92	OS1 (b)	18c on $1 grn		1.50	2.10
a.		Double surcharge		37.00	37.00
8N93	OS2 (c)	36c on $2 dp bl (R)		1.75	2.10
8N94	OS2 (d)	90c on $5 car rose		2.10	2.50
		Nos. 8N91-8N94 (4)		6.75	8.45

Nos. 8N72, 8N75, 8N79 and 8N80 Overprinted in Red or Blue

1944, Aug. 15

8N95	A57	9c olive grn		3.55	1.50
8N96	A57	18c olive gray		1.10	3.00
8N97	A40	50c green		2.20	2.10
8N98	A57	$1 org brn & sep (Bl)		3.50	4.00
		Nos. 8N95-8N98 (4)		10.35	10.60

6th anniv. of the General P.O. Dept. of North China.

North China Nos. 8N76, 8N79-8N81 Overprinted in Blue or Black

1944, Dec. 5

8N99	A47	20c henna (Bl)		3.00	3.50
8N100	A40	50c green (Bl)		3.00	3.50
8N101	A57	$1 org brn & sep (Bl)		5.75	6.75
8N102	A57	$2 bl & org brn		5.75	1.75
		Nos. 8N99-8N102 (4)		13.50	15.50

Death of Wang Ching-wei, puppet ruler of China.

North China Nos. 8N76, 8N79-8N81 Overprinted in Red or Black

1945

8N103	A47	20c henna		3.00	4.00
8N104	A40	50c green (R)		9.00	9.00
8N105	A57	$1 org brn & sep		3.25	3.50
8N106	A57	$2 bl & org brn		5.75	2.00
		Nos. 8N103-8N106 (4)		21.00	18.50

2nd anniv. of the declaration of war.

Shanghai-Nanking Nos. 9N105-9N106 Surcharged in Red

1945　　　　**Perf. 12x12½**
8N107	OS3	50c on $3 lt org	.65	.85
8N108	OS3	$1 on $6 blue	.65	.85

Return of the foreign concessions in Shanghai.

Dragon Pillar — OS1

Designs: $2, Long Bridge and White Pagoda. $5, Tower in Imperial City. $10, Marble Boat, Summer Palace.

1945　Unwmk.　Litho.　Perf. 14
Various Papers
8N109	OS1	$1 dull yellow	1.50	1.50
8N110	OS1	$2 deep blue	.30	1.50
8N111	OS1	$5 sage green	3.00	.75
8N112	OS1	$10 dull green	.50	1.10
		Nos. 8N109-8N112 (4)	5.30	4.85

North China Political Council, 5th anniv.

Dr. Sun Yat-sen — OS2

Various Papers

1945　　　　　　**Without Gum**
8N113	OS2	$1 bister	.30	.25
8N114	OS2	$2 dark blue	1.10	.35
8N115	OS2	$5 fawn	2.50	2.50
8N116	OS2	$10 sage green	2.50	1.40
8N117	OS2	$20 dull violet	2.50	1.75
8N118	OS2	$50 brown	50.00	57.50
		Nos. 8N113-8N118 (6)	58.90	63.75

Nos. 8N113-8N118 without "Hwa Pei" overprint are proofs.

Wutai Mountain, Shansi — OS3

Designs: $10, Kaifeng Iron Pagoda. $20, International Bridge, Tientsin. $30, Taishan Mountain, Shantung. $50, General Post Office, Peking.

Various Papers

1945, Aug. 15　　　**Without Gum**
8N119	OS3	$5 gray green	.30	1.05
8N120	OS3	$10 dull brown	.75	1.05
8N121	OS3	$20 dull purple	.55	1.50
8N122	OS3	$30 slate blue	1.10	1.50
8N123	OS3	$50 carmine	3.25	3.00
		Nos. 8N119-8N123 (5)	5.95	8.10

North China Postal Directorate, 7th anniv.

SHANGHAI AND NANKING

China Nos. 299-303 Surcharged

a　　　　　　　b

Surcharged Type "b"

1942-45　Unwmk.　Perf. 12½, 13½
9N1	A37	$6 on 5c green	.90	1.25
9N2	A37	$20 on 15c scar	.45	.90
9N3	A37	$500 on 15c dk grn	.30	1.25
9N4	A37	$1000 on 20c ultra	3.50	3.50
9N5	A37	$1000 on 25c ultra	3.50	3.50
		Nos. 9N1-9N5 (5)	8.65	10.40

A $1000 on 20c ultramarine, No. 293, exists.

Surcharged Type "a" (Nos. 9N6-9N10) or Type "b" (Nos. 9N11-9N40) on Type A57 Stamps of 1939-41
Perf. 12½
9N6	25c on 5c (#352)		2.50	4.00
9N7	30c on 2c (#368)		.25	.30
9N8	50c on 5c (#350)		.30	.35
9N9	50c on 5c (#352)		.30	.30
9N10	50c on 8c (#353)		.30	.45
9N11	$1 on 8c (#353)		.30	.25
9N12	$1 on 8c (#369)		14.50	14.50
9N13	$1 on 15c (#356)		.30	.25
9N14	$1.30 on 16c (#357)		.30	.50
9N15	$1.50 on 15c (#356)		.30	.50
9N16	$2 on 5c (#352)		1.40	1.40
9N17	$2 on 10c (#354)		.30	.35
9N18	$3 on 15c (#356)		.30	.35
9N19	$4 on 16c (#357)		.50	.30
9N20	$5 on 15c (#356)		.30	.30
9N21	$5 on 15c (#351)		.75	1.75
a.	Perf. 14 (#371)		62.50	62.50
9N22	$6 on 5c (#352)		.30	.45
9N23	$6 on 8c (#353)		.50	1.25
9N24	$6 on 8c (#369)		990.00	990.00
9N25	$6 on 10c (#354)		.30	.30
9N26	$10 on 10c (#354)		.30	.35
9N27	$10 on 16c (#357)		.60	.30
9N28	$20 on 15c (#350)		.30	.50
9N29	$20 on 15c (#355)		1.40	3.00
9N30	$20 on 15c (#356)		.50	.50
9N31	$20 on $2 (#360)		1.75	3.50
9N32	$100 on 3c (#350)		.60	.50
9N33	$500 on 8c (#353)		3.00	5.50
9N34	$500 on 8c (#369)		42.50	57.50
9N35	$500 on 10c (#354)		3.00	4.25
9N36	$500 on 15c (#355)		1.50	3.00
9N37	$500 on 15c (#356)		1.25	2.50
9N38	$500 on 16c (#357)		1.50	5.00
9N39	$1000 on 25c (#358)		1.50	3.00
9N40	$2000 on $5 (#361)		1.75	3.00
	Nos. 9N1-9N23,9N25-9N40 (39)		94.10	130.65

Nos. 381-391 (Type A57) Surcharged with Type "b"
Perf. 14
9N41	$1 on 8c ol grn		.30	.35
9N42	$1.70 on 30c scar		.35	.75
a.	Perf. 12½		4.00	4.00
9N43	$2 on 5c ol grn		.50	1.50
9N44	$2 on $1 org brn & sep		1.25	3.00
9N45	$3 on 8c ol grn		.75	.75
a.	$3 on 8c olive green (#383a)		42.50	42.50
b.	"3" with flat top		.50	.50
9N46	$6 on 5c grn		.50	.60
9N47	$6 on 5c grn		.50	1.00
9N48	$6 on 8c ol grn		.45	.85
9N49	$10 on 10c grn		.50	2.50
a.	Perf. 12½		2.50	7.50
9N50	$20 on $2 dp bl & yel brn		1.50	1.50
9N51	$50 on 30c scar		.90	1.00
9N52	$50 on 50c dk bl		.80	.80
9N53	$50 on $5 red & sl grn		1.10	1.10
9N54	$50 on 20 rose lake & dk bl		2.50	3.00
9N55	$100 on $10 dk grn & dl pur		2.00	2.00
9N56	$200 on $20 rose lake & dk bl		.75	1.25
9N57	$500 on 8c ol grn		13.50	16.00
a.	$500 on 8c ol grn (#383a)		30.50	30.00
9N58	$500 on 10c grn		3.00	4.25
9N59	$1000 on 30c scar		2.50	3.50
9N60	$1000 on 50c dk bl		1.25	1.75
9N61	$1000 on $2 dp bl & yel brn		3.00	9.75
9N62	$2000 on $5 red & sl		1.50	2.00

China Nos. 392-395 and 399-401 (Type A57) Surcharged with Type "b"
1942-45	**Wmk. 261**		**Perf. 14**	
9N63	$2 on $1 org brn & sep, perf. 12½		1.00	1.75
9N64	$6 on 5c grn		.50	1.05
9N65	$6 on 5c ol grn		1.40	2.00
9N66	$50 on $5 red & sl grn		.85	1.25
a.	Numeral tablet violet		1.00	1.25
9N67	$100 on $10 dk grn & dl pur		.50	.75
9N68	$200 on $20 rose lake & dk bl		.60	.75
9N69	$500 on 10c grn		2.50	3.00
9N70	$1000 on 30c scar		3.50	4.00
9N71	$5000 on $10 dk grn & dl pur, perf. 12½		8.00	9.75
a.	Perf. 14		125.00	125.00
	Nos. 9N41-9N71 (31)		58.25	83.50

Nos. 9N63 and 9N71 were not issued without surcharge. A $50 on 30c scarlet exists.

Same Surch. on Stamps of 1940-41
Perf. 12½, 13
Wmk. 261
9N72	A46	$30 on 2c dp bl	150.00	150.00

A $7.50 on ½c and a $15 on 1c are known.

Unwmk.
9N73	A39	$7.50 on ½c ol blk	2.50	3.00
9N74	A40	$15 on 1c org	.35	1.50
a.		Without secret mark	62.50	62.50
9N75	A46	$30 on 2c dp bl	1.40	2.00
9N76	A40	$200 on 1c org	.30	.35
9N77	A45	$200 on 8c dp org	.85	1.25
		Nos. 9N73-9N77 (5)	5.40	8.10

Surcharged Type "a" (Nos. 9N78-9N81) or Type "b" (Nos. 9N82-9N96) on Type A59 Stamps of 1941
Perf. 12
9N78	5c on ½c sepia		.25	.35
9N79	10c on 1c orange		.25	.35
9N80	20c on 1c orange		.25	.50
9N81	40c on 5c green		.25	.50
9N82	$5 on 5c green		.25	.35
9N83	$10 on 10c brt grn		.25	.35
9N84	$50 on ½c sepia		.25	.35
9N85	$50 on 1c orange		.45	.50
9N86	$50 on 17c olive		.45	.60
9N87	$200 on 5c green		.45	.50
9N88	$200 on 8c turq grn		.30	.30
9N89	$200 on 8c red org		.45	.75
9N90	$500 on $5 scar & blk		.50	.50
9N91	$1000 on 8c grn		.45	.65
9N92	$1000 on 25c rose vio		.50	.65
9N93	$1000 on 30c scarlet		1.25	.65
9N94	$1000 on $2 bl & blk		1.25	1.25
9N95	$1000 on $10 grn & blk		.50	.65
9N96	$2000 on $5 scar & blk		1.25	1.25
	Nos. 9N78-9N96 (19)		9.50	11.00

Stamps of China 1939-41 Surcharged in Red or Blue

1943　Unwmk.　Perf. 12, 12½
9N97	A57	25c on 5c grn	.25	1.50
9N98	A59	50c on 8c red org (Bl)	.25	.60
9N99	A57	$1 on 16c ol gray	.25	1.75
9N100	A59	$2 on 50c dk bl	.25	.60
		Nos. 9N97-9N100 (4)	1.00	4.45

Return of the foreign concessions in Shanghai.

Wheat and Cotton — OS1

Purple Mountain, Nanking OS2

Perf. 12½x12, 12x12½
1944		**Engr.**	**Unwmk.**	
9N101	OS1	50c orange	.90	1.10
9N102	OS1	$1 green	.90	1.10
9N103	OS2	$2 deep blue	.90	1.10
9N104	OS2	$5 carmine rose	.90	1.10
		Nos. 9N101-9N104 (4)	3.60	4.40

Puppet government at Nanking, 4th anniv. For surcharges see Nos. 8N91-8N94, 9N107-9N110.

Map of Foreign Concessions in Shanghai — OS3

1944　　　　　　**Perf. 12x12½**
9N105	OS3	$3 lt orange	.90	1.10
9N106	OS3	$6 blue	.90	1.10

1st anniversary of the return of the foreign concessions in Shanghai.
For surcharges see Nos. 8N107-8N108.

Nos. 9N101-9N104 Surcharged in Black with Type "b"
1945, Mar. 30
9N107	OS1	$15 on 50c orange	.90	1.10
9N108	OS1	$30 on $1 green	.90	1.10
9N109	OS2	$60 on $2 dp blue	.90	1.10
9N110	OS2	$200 on $5 car rose	.90	1.10
		Nos. 9N107-9N110 (4)	3.60	4.40

China Nos. C31, C32, C36 and C38 Srchd. in Red, Green, Orange or Carmine

1945　　　　　　**Perf. 12½, 13**
9N111	AP3	$150 on 15c (R)	.45	.90
9N112	AP3	$250 on 25c (G)	.45	.90
9N113	AP3	$60 on 50c (O)	.45	.90
9N114	AP3	$1,000 on $1 (C)	.45	.90
		Nos. 9N111-9N114 (4)	1.80	3.60

Issue as air raid precaution propaganda.

AIR POST STAMPS

China Nos. C35 and C38 Surcharged in Black

The surcharges on Nos. 9NC1-9NC7 were in Japanese currency because all air mail then was carried by Japanese planes.

The surcharges translate: (10c) "Airmail fee for postcard within the nation has been paid." (20c) "Airmail fee for letter within the nation has been paid."

1941　Unwmk.　Perf. 12½
9NC1	AP3	10(s) on 50c brown	.55	.40
9NC2	AP3	20(s) on $1 apple grn	.90	.90

Two types of surcharge exist on No. 9NC1.

Similar Surcharge on No. C28
1941　Wmk. 261　Perf. 13
9NC3	AP3	20(s) on $1 ap grn	18.00	18.00

Nos. C37 and C39 Surcharged

The surcharges translate: (18c and 25c) "Airmail fee for postcard to Japan has been paid." (35c) "Airmail fee for letter to Japan has been paid."

1941　Unwmk.　Perf. 12½, 13
9NC4	AP3	18(s) on 90c lt olive	.55	.60
9NC5	AP3	25(s) on 90c lt olive	.45	.60
9NC6	AP3	35(s) on $2 lt brown	.45	.60
		Nos. 9NC4-9NC6 (3)	1.45	1.80

No. 9NC6 with Additional Surcharge in Red
Perf. 12½
9NC7	AP3	60(s) on 35(s) on $2	.45	.55

POSTAGE DUE STAMPS

Postage Due Stamps of China 1932 Surcharged in Black

1945		**Unwmk.**		**Perf. 14**
9NJ1	D5	$1 on 2c org	.90	1.75
9NJ2	D5	$2 on 5c org	.90	1.75
9NJ3	D5	$5 on 10c org	.90	1.75
9NJ4	D5	$10 on 20c org	.90	3.00
		Nos. 9NJ1-9NJ4 (4)	3.60	8.25

Northeastern Provinces

With the end of World War II and the collapse of Manchukuo, the Northeastern Provinces reverted to China. In many Manchurian towns and cities, the Manchukuo stamps were locally handstamped in ideograms: "Republic of China," "China Postal Service" or "Temporary Use for China." A typical example is shown above.

Dr. Sun Yat-sen — A1

Black Surcharge

1946, Feb.		**Unwmk.**	**Typo.**	**Perf. 14**
1	A1	50c on $5 red	.35	1.40
2	A1	50c on $10 green	.90	2.10
3	A1	$1 on $10 green	.35	1.75
4	A1	$2 on $20 brown vio	.35	1.40
5	A1	$4 on $50 brown	.35	1.10
		Nos. 1-5 (5)	2.30	7.75

The two characters at left express the new value.

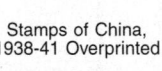

Stamps of China, 1938-41 Overprinted

1946, Apr.		**Perf. 12½, 13, 13½, 14**		
6	A40	1c org (#422)	.35	3.75
7	A48	3c dp yel brn (#425)	.35	3.75
8	A48	5c dl red org (#427)	.35	4.75
9	A57	10c grn (#354)	.35	3.75
10	A57	10c grn (#384)	.35	3.75
11	A47	20c lt bl (#433)	.35	3.75
a.		Horiz. pair, imperf. btwn	100.00	
		Nos. 6-11 (6)	2.10	23.50

Dr. Sun Yat-sen — A2

1946, July		**Engr.**		**Perf. 14**
		Without Gum		
12	A2	5c lake	.35	3.50
13	A2	10c orange	.35	3.50
14	A2	20c yel grn	.35	3.50
15	A2	25c blk brn	.35	3.50
16	A2	50c red org	.35	2.75

17	A2	$1 blue	.35	2.25
18	A2	$2 dk vio	.35	2.75
19	A2	$2.50 indigo	.35	3.50
20	A2	$3 brown	.35	2.75
21	A2	$4 org brn	.35	3.50
22	A2	$5 dk grn	.35	2.75
23	A2	$10 crimson	.35	1.75
24	A2	$20 olive	.35	1.40
25	A2	$50 blue vio	.40	1.00
		Nos. 12-25 (14)	4.95	38.90

Two types of $4, $10, $20 and $50: I- Character *kuo* directly left of sun emblem is open at upper and lower left corners of "box." Diagonal stroke from top center to lower right has no hook at bottom. II- Character is closed at left corners. Diagonal stroke has hook at bottom.

See Nos. 47-52, 61-63. For surcharges see Nos. M1, Taiwan 91-96, People's Republic of China 35-48, 3L37-3L52, 3L55-3L66, 3L71-3L75.

China Nos. 728-731 Surcharged in Black

1946				
26	A75	$2 on $20 green	.35	3.25
27	A75	$3 on $30 blue	.35	3.25
28	A75	$5 on $50 dark brown	.35	3.25
29	A75	$10 on $100 carmine	.35	3.25
		Nos. 26-29 (4)	1.40	13.00

Convening of Chinese National Assembly.

Type of China, 1946, with added inscriptions on both sides of head

1947		**Engr.**	**Perf. 11, 11½**	
30	A74	$2 carmine	.65	4.00
31	A74	$3 green	1.10	4.00
32	A74	$5 vermilion	1.10	4.00
33	A74	$10 yel grn	1.10	4.00
34	A74	$20 yel org	1.40	4.00
35	A74	$30 magenta	1.40	4.00
		Nos. 30-35 (6)	6.75	24.00

60th birthday of Chiang Kai-shek.

Type of China, 1947, with additional inscription above value

1947		**Unwmk.**	**Engr.**	**Perf. 14**
36	A76	$2 deep green	.65	2.00
37	A76	$4 deep blue	.65	2.00
38	A76	$6 carmine	.65	2.00
39	A76	$10 lt brown	.65	2.00
40	A76	$20 deep claret	.65	2.00
		Nos. 36-40 (5)	3.25	10.00

First anniversary of return of Chinese National Government to Nanking.

China Nos. 644 to 646 and 634 Surcharged in Black

1947		**Perf. 12½, 14**		
41	A73	$100 on $1000 rose lake	1.10	4.25
42	A73	$300 on $3000 bl	1.10	4.25
43	A73	$500 on $5000 dp grn & ver	.55	5.00
44	A37	$500 on $30 choc	1.00	4.25
		Nos. 41-44 (4)	3.75	17.75

Type of 1946

1947		**Engr.**		**Perf. 14**
		Without Gum		
47	A2	$44 dk car rose	40.00	57.50
48	A2	$100 dp grn	.35	.70
49	A2	$200 rose brn	.35	1.40
50	A2	$300 bluish grn	.35	2.75
51	A2	$500 rose car	.35	.70
52	A2	$1000 dp orange	.35	.60
		Nos. 47-52 (6)	41.75	63.65

For surcharges see note following No. 25.

Stamps and Types of 1946-47 Surcharged in Black or Red

1948		**Unwmk.**		**Perf. 14**
53	A2	$1500 on 20c yel grn	.90	4.50
54	A2	$3000 on $1 blue	.45	5.00
55	A2	$4000 on 25c blk brn (R)	.45	4.00
56	A2	$8000 on 50c red org	.45	3.25
57	A2	$10,000 on 10c org	.55	3.25
58	A2	$50,000 on $109 dk grn (R)	1.00	6.25
59	A2	$100,000 on $65 dl grn	.90	6.25
60	A2	$500,000 on $22 gray (R)	1.50	6.25
		Nos. 53-60 (8)	6.20	38.75

Type of 1946

1947, Nov. 5			**Without Gum**	
61	A2	$22 gray	80.00	85.00
62	A2	$65 dull green	80.00	100.00
63	A2	$109 dark green	85.00	100.00
		Nos. 61-63 (3)	245.00	285.00

For surcharges see note following No. 25.

POSTAGE DUE STAMPS

D1

1947		**Unwmk.**	**Engr.**	**Perf. 14**
		Without Gum		
J1	D1	10c dark blue	.55	7.75
J2	D1	20c dark blue	.55	7.75
J3	D1	50c dark blue	.55	5.75
J4	D1	$1 dark blue	.25	4.25
J5	D1	$2 dark blue	.25	5.50
J6	D1	$5 dark blue	.25	5.50
		Nos. J1-J6 (6)	2.40	36.50

Nos. J4-J6 are known on paper with the papermaker's watermark, "COSMOS BOND."

Nos. J1 to J3 Surcharged in Red

1948				
J7	D1	$10 on 10c dark blue	.35	9.00
J8	D1	$20 on 20c dark blue	.35	9.00
J9	D1	$50 on 50c dark blue	.35	9.00
		Nos. J7-J9 (3)	1.05	27.00

The surcharge reads "Changed to . . . dollars." Characters at the left express the new value and vary on each denomination.

MILITARY STAMPS

No. 16 Surcharged in Black

1947		**Unwmk.**		**Perf. 14**
M1	A2	$44 on 50c red org	11.00	40.00

The surcharge reads: "Army Post. Temporarily for 44 dollars."

China No. M13 Overprinted in Black

Thin Paper Without Gum
Perf. 12½

M2	M1	rose	2.75	18.00

China No. M13 Overprinted in Black

M3	M1	rose	62.50	62.50

PARCEL POST STAMP

China No. Q25 Surcharged in Black

1948		**Unwmk.**	**Engr.**	**Perf. 13½**
		Without Gum		
Q1	PP3	$500,000 on $5,000,000		
		lil		180.00

Used value is for CTO.

The use of this handstamp from Anhwei has not been verified.

FUKIEN PROVINCE

Stamps of China, 1945-49, Surcharged

1949		**Engr.**		**Perf. 14**
		Without Gum		
1	A82	1c on $500 bl grn	10.00	6.25
2	A82	1c on $7000 lt red brn	15.00	22.50
3	A82	2c on $2,000,000 ver	5.00	6.75
4	A82	2½c on $50,000 dp bl	35.00	35.00
5	A73	4c on $100 dk car	4.50	4.50
6	A73	10c on $200 ol grn	7.25	9.00
7	A82	10c on $3000 bl	5.50	4.50
8	A82	10c on $4000 gray	7.25	10.75
9	A82	10c on $6000 rose lil	4.50	6.25
10	A82	10c on $100,000 dl grn	5.75	6.75
11	A82	10c on $1,000,000 cl	5.75	6.25
12	A82	40c on $200,000 brn vio	9.00	10.00
		Nos. 1-12 (12)	114.50	128.50

The surcharge on No. 2 is handstamped and in slightly larger characters.

Issue dates: No. 2, May 10; others, June.

China Nos. 973, 975-978 Overprinted

1949, June Litho. Perf. 12½, 13
13	A94	1c apple grn	18.00	5.50
14	A94	4c blue green	5.50	2.00
15	A94	10c deep lilac	55.00	27.50
16	A94	16c orange red	11.00	*27.50*
17	A94	20c blue	55.00	27.50
		Nos. 13-17 (5)	144.50	90.00

Same Overprint on China No. 959
1949, July Litho. Perf. 12½
18	A96	orange	72.50	72.50

Same Overprint on Fukien Nos. 1, 3-4, 8, 11 in Black or Red
1949, June Engr. Perf. 14
19	A82	1c on $500 bl grn	150.00	150.00
20	A82	2c on $2,000,000 ver	55.00	55.00
21	A82	2½c on $50,000 dp bl	90.00	90.00
22	A82	10c on $4000 gray	37.50	37.50
23	A82	10c on $1,000,000 cl	145.00	145.00
		Nos. 19-23 (5)	477.50	477.50

AIR POST STAMP
China #C62 Overprinted as #13-17
1949, July Litho. Perf. 12½
C1	AP5	blue green	72.50	37.50

SPECIAL DELIVERY STAMP
China #E12 Overprinted as #13-17
1949, July Litho. Perf. 12½
E1	SD2	red violet	50.00	35.00

REGISTRATION STAMP
China #F2 Overprinted as #13-17
1949, July Litho. Perf. 12½
F1	R2	carmine	50.00	35.00

HUNAN PROVINCE

China No. 640 Surcharged

1949, May Engr. Perf. 14
1	A73	on $100 dk car	14.50	8.50

The first printing of surcharge on No. 1 is in smaller characters.

China Nos. 797, 788, 750, 747 Surcharged

1949, May Engr. Perf. 14
2	A82	1c on $2,000,000 ver	27.50	27.50
3	A82	2c on $20,000 rose pink	27.50	27.50
4	A82	5c on $3000 blue	35.00	40.00
5	A82	10c on $500 blue grn	30.00	27.50
		Nos. 2-5 (4)	120.00	122.50

AIR POST STAMP

China No. 790 Surcharged

1949, May Engr. Perf. 14
C1	A82	On $40,000 green	22.50	*24.00*

SPECIAL DELIVERY STAMP
China No. 637 Surcharged as No. F1 in Red
1949, May Engr. Perf. 14
E1	A73	On $30 dark blue	27.50	27.50

REGISTRATION STAMP

China No. 754 Surcharged

1949, May Engr. Perf. 14
F1	A82	On $7000 lt red brn	27.50	27.50

HUPEH PROVINCE

China Type A95 Surcharged

1949, May Litho.
1	A95	1c on $20 red brn	67.50	67.50
2	A95	10c on $20 red brn	67.50	67.50

KANSU PROVINCE

China No. 959 Handstamped in Purple

1949, Aug. Litho. Perf. 12½
1	A96	orange	*1,100.*

AIR POST STAMP
Same Handstamp Overprinted on China No. C62 in Red
1949, Aug. Litho. Perf. 12½
C1	AP5	blue green	*1,100.*

Counterfeits exist.

KIANGSI PROVINCE

China Nos. 789-791 Surcharged

1949 Engr. Perf. 14
1	A82	On $30,000 choc	57.50	55.00
2	A82	On $40,000 green	57.50	55.00
3	A82	On $50,000 dp bl	57.50	55.00
		Nos. 1-3 (3)	172.50	165.00

AIR POST STAMP
Similar Surcharge on China No. 754
1949 Engr. Perf. 14
C1	A82	On $7000 lt red brn	62.50	62.50

Third and fourth characters in right column of surcharge read "Air Mail" in Chinese on No. C1, "Registered" on Nos. F1-F2.

SPECIAL DELIVERY STAMP
Similar Surcharge on China No. 750
1949 Engr. Perf. 14
E1	A82	On $3000 blue	67.50	45.00

See note below No. C1.

REGISTRATION STAMPS
Similar Surcharge on China Nos. 747 and 754
1949 Engr. Perf. 14
F1	A82	On $500 bl grn	67.50	45.00
F2	A82	On $7000 lt red brn	67.50	55.00

KWANGSI PROVINCE

China Nos. 811 and 818 Also Surcharged in Red

1949, May 21 Typo.
6	A62	5c on $20,000 on 10c dp grn	30.00	30.00
7	A62	5c on $40,000 on 20c dk ol grn	67.50	67.50

China Stamps of 1946-48 Surcharged in Black or Red

a   b

1949 Engr. Perf. 14
Type "a" Surcharge
8	A82	½c on $500,000 lil rose	40.00	27.50
9	A82	1c on $200,000 brn vio	35.00	12.00
10	A82	2c on $300,000 yel grn	120.00	72.50
11	A73	5c on $3000 blue	35.00	20.00
12	A82	5c on $3000 blue	18.00	11.00
13	A82	5c on $40,000 grn	35.00	20.00

Type "b" Surcharge
14	A82	13c on $50,000 dp bl (R)	25.00	16.00
15	A82	13c on $50,000 dp bl	100.00	25.00
16	A82	17c on $7000 lt red brn	27.50	27.50
17	A82	21c on $100,000 dl grn	32.50	29.00
		Nos. 8-17 (10)	468.00	260.50

SHENSI PROVINCE

China Nos. 747, 750 Surcharged

1949, May Engr. Perf. 14
1	A82	On $500 bl grn	45.00	45.00
2	A82	On $3000 blue	45.00	45.00

AIR POST STAMP
Similar Surcharge on China No. 754
1949, May Engr. Perf. 14
C1	A82	On $7000 lt red brn	55.00	55.00

SPECIAL DELIVERY STAMP
Similar Surcharge on China No. 746 in Red
1949, May Engr. Perf. 14
E1	A82	On $250 dp lil	62.50	62.50

REGISTRATION STAMPS
Similar Surcharge on China Nos. 626, 637 in Red
1949, May Typo. Perf. 12
F1	A72	on $30 dp bl	62.50	62.50
F2	A73	on $30 dk bl	55.00	55.00

SZECHWAN PROVINCE

Re-engraved Issue of China, 1923, Overprinted

1933 Unwmk. Perf. 14
1	A29	1c orange	11.00	1.00
2	A29	5c claret	11.00	1.40
3	A30	50c deep green	32.50	6.75
		Nos. 1-3 (3)	54.50	9.15

The overprint reads "For use in Szechwan Province exclusively."

Same on Sun Yat-sen Issue of 1931-37
Type II
1933-34 Perf. 12½
4	A37	2c olive grn	2.00	1.00
5	A37	5c green	22.50	2.40
6	A37	15c dk green	7.75	3.50
7	A37	15c scar ('34)	9.00	12.00
8	A37	25c ultra	7.50	1.75
9	A37	$1 org brn & dk brn	22.50	4.00
10	A37	$2 bl & org brn	55.00	6.75
11	A37	$5 dl red & blk	125.00	37.50
		Nos. 4-11 (8)	251.25	68.90

Same on Martyrs Issue of 1932-34
1933 Perf. 14
12	A39	½c black brn	.80	.80
13	A40	1c orange	1.25	.55
14	A39	2½c rose lilac	3.50	3.75
15	A48	3c deep brown	3.00	3.00
16	A45	8c brown org	1.75	1.50

17	A46	10c dull violet	4.50	.55
18	A45	13c blue green	5.00	1.00
19	A46	17c brown olive	5.50	1.40
20	A47	20c brown red	8.50	1.00
21	A48	30c brown violet	6.75	1.00
22	A47	40c orange	18.00	1.40
23	A40	50c green	37.50	2.10
		Nos. 12-23 (12)	96.05	18.05

Stamps of China, 1947-48, Surcharged

1949   **Engr.**   **Perf. 14**

24	A82	on $150 dk bl	72.50	55.00
25	A82	on $250 dp lil	72.50	55.00
26	A82	on $500 bl grn	21.00	12.50
27	A82	on $1000 red	55.00	42.50
28	A82	on $2000 ver	21.00	9.50
29	A82	on $3000 blue	21.00	9.50
30	A82	on $4000 gray	21.00	9.50
31	A82	on $5000 dk brn	62.50	62.50
32	A82	on $6000 rose lil	21.00	21.00
33	A82	on $7000 lt red brn	55.00	45.00
34	A82	on $10,000 dk bl & car	30.50	16.00
35	A82	on $20,000 rose pink	22.50	16.00
36	A82	on $30,000 choc	29.00	22.50
37	A82	on $50,000 grn & dk bl	29.00	25.00
38	A82	on $50,000 dp bl	29.00	22.50
39	A82	on $100,000 dl yel & ol	29.00	22.50
40	A82	on $100,000 dl grn	29.00	25.00
41	A82	on $200,000 vio brn & dp bl	29.00	22.50
42	A82	on $200,000 brn vio	29.00	22.50
43	A82	on $300,000 sep & org brn	40.00	27.50
44	A82	on $300,000 yel grn	55.00	40.00
45	A82	on $500,000 dk Prus grn & sep	29.00	22.50
46	A82	on $1,000,000 claret	55.00	40.00
47	A82	on $2,000,000 ver	29.00	27.50
48	A82	on $3,000,000 ol bis	29.00	27.50
49	A82	on $5,000,000 ultra	110.00	67.50
		Nos. 24-49 (26)	1,026.	769.00

Several of Nos. 24-49 exist with inverted surcharge and a few with bottom character of left row repeated in right row, same position. Counterfeits exist.

China No. 737 Surcharged in Black

1949   **Perf. 12½**

50	A77	2c on $500 ol grn	40.00	55.00

China No. 975 Handstamp Surcharged in Purple

1949   **Litho.**

51	A94	2½c on 4c bl grn	55.00	40.00

AIR POST STAMPS

China Nos. C55-C58, C60-C61 Surcharged

Perf. 12½, 13x12½, 14

1949, July   **Unwmk.**

C1	AP3	On $10,000 on 30c	9.00	9.00
a.		On #C54		500.00
C2	AP4	On $10,000 on $27	14.50	20.00
a.		Second surcharge inverted	250.00	
b.		On #C53	125.00	
C3	AP3	On $20,000 on 25c	14.50	16.00
C4	AP3	On $30,000 on 90c	16.00	27.50
C5	AP3	On $50,000 on 60c	125.00	155.00
C6	AP3	On $50,000 on $1	17.00	24.00
		Nos. C1-C6 (6)	196.00	251.50

REGISTRATION STAMPS

Stamps of China, 1944-47, Surcharged

Engraved; Typographed (A72)

1949   **Perf. 12, 13, 14**

F1	A64	On $100 yel brn	77.50
F2	A72	On $100 dk brn	77.50
F3	A64	On $200 dk grn	155.00
F4	A72	On $200 brn vio	72.50
F5	A73	On $200 ol grn	77.50
F6	A73	On $500 brt bl grn	155.00
F7	A73	On $700 red brn	275.00
F8	A73	On $5000 dp grn & ver	120.00
		Nos. F1-F8 (8)	1,010.

PARCEL POST STAMP

China No. Q10 Surcharged

1949   **Engr.**   **Perf. 12½**

Q1	PP2	1c on $20,000 dk red	—	—

TSINGTAU PROVINCE

China Nos. 890, 903, 900, 894 Handstamp Surcharged in Purple (#1-2), Blue (#3) or Red (#4)

Engraved; Lithographed

1949, May   **Perf. 14, 12½**

1	A94	1c on $100 org brn	100.00	90.00
2	A94	4c on $5000 lt bl	100.00	90.00
3	A94	6c on $500 rose lil	100.00	90.00
4	A94	10c on $1000 bl	100.00	90.00
		Nos. 1-4 (4)	400.00	360.00

YUNNAN PROVINCE

Stamps of China, 1923-26, Overprinted

The overprint reads "For exclusive use in the Province of Yunnan." It was applied to prevent stamps being purchased in the depreciated currency of Yunnan and used elsewhere.

1926   **Unwmk.**   **Perf. 14**

1	A29	½c blk brn	1.10	.35
2	A29	1c orange	1.75	.35
3	A29	1½c violet	3.75	4.25
4	A29	2c yellow grn	2.75	.50
5	A29	3c blue green	2.75	.35
6	A29	4c olive grn	3.50	.50
7	A29	5c claret	3.50	.50
8	A29	6c red	5.25	1.25
9	A29	7c violet	5.50	1.90
10	A29	8c brown org	4.75	1.40
11	A29	10c dark blue	3.00	.30
12	A30	13c brown	1.75	1.90
13	A30	15c dark blue	1.75	1.90
14	A30	16c olive grn	3.50	1.90
15	A30	20c brown red	8.50	3.25
16	A30	30c brown vio	5.25	5.75
17	A30	50c deep green	5.50	5.75
18	A31	$1 org brn & sep	20.50	14.00
19	A31	$2 blue & red brn	35.00	14.00
20	A31	$5 red & slate	240.00	260.00
		Nos. 1-20 (20)	359.35	320.10

Unification Issue of China, 1929, Overprinted in Red

1929   **Perf. 14**

21	A35	1c brown org	2.25	2.25
22	A35	4c olive grn	3.75	5.75
23	A35	10c dark blue	12.00	9.00
24	A35	$1 dark red	120.00	90.00
		Nos. 21-24 (4)	138.00	107.00

Similar Overprint in Black on Sun Yat-sen Mausoleum Issue Characters 15½-16mm apart

25	A36	1c brown orange	2.25	2.25
26	A36	4c olive grn	2.25	3.75
27	A36	10c dark blue	9.00	8.50
28	A36	$1 dark red	77.50	67.50
		Nos. 25-28 (4)	91.00	81.75

London Print Issue of China, 1931-37, Overprinted

1932-34   **Unwmk.**   **Perf. 12½**

Type I (double circle)

29	A37	1c orange	4.00	2.75
30	A37	2c olive grn	5.00	5.50
31	A37	4c green	3.25	5.50
32	A37	20c ultra	3.25	3.00
33	A37	$1 org brn & dk brn	50.00	55.00
34	A37	$2 bl & org brn	82.50	85.00
35	A37	$5 dl red & blk	250.00	295.00
		Nos. 29-35 (7)	398.00	451.75

Type II (single circle)

36	A37	2c olive grn	26.00	26.00
37	A37	4c green	17.00	10.75
38	A37	5c green	15.00	10.00
39	A37	15c dk green	8.00	8.75
40	A37	15c scar ('34)	8.00	10.00
41	A37	25c ultra	11.00	11.50
42	A37	$1 org brn & dk brn	67.50	67.50
43	A37	$2 bl & org brn	125.00	125.00
44	A37	$5 dl red & blk	260.00	260.00
		Nos. 36-44 (9)	537.50	529.50

Nos. 36-39, 41-44 were overprinted in London as well as in Peking. The London overprints are 11mm in length; the Peking overprints are 12mm in length. There are other minor differences. Value of London overprints is significantly more than the Peking overprints, which are valued above.

Tan Yuan-chang Issue of China, 1933, Overprinted

1933   **Perf. 14**

45	A49	2c olive green	1.75	1.75
46	A49	5c green	3.00	2.40
47	A49	25c ultra	5.25	5.50
48	A49	$1 red	80.00	65.00
		Nos. 45-48 (4)	90.00	74.65

Martyrs Issue of China, 1932-34, Overprinted

1933

49	A39	½c blk brown	1.75	1.60
50	A40	1c orange	3.50	2.75
51	A39	2½c rose lilac	4.00	4.50
52	A48	3c deep brown	6.25	2.25
53	A45	8c brown org	2.75	2.75
54	A46	10c dull vio	4.00	4.50
55	A45	13c blue grn	2.50	1.10
56	A46	17c brn olive	12.50	12.50
57	A47	20c brown red	3.25	3.25
58	A48	30c brown vio	10.00	10.00
59	A47	40c orange	47.50	47.50
60	A40	50c green	47.50	47.50
		Nos. 49-60 (12)	145.50	140.20

China No. 324 was overprinted with characters arranged vertically, like Sinkiang No. 114, but was not issued.

China Stamps of 1945-49 Surcharged in Black or Blue

Engraved; Lithographed; Typographed

1949   **Perf. 12, 12½, 14**

61	A82	1c on $200,000 brn vio	19.00	19.00
62	A82	1.2c on $40,000 grn	19.00	21.00
63	A94	6c on $200 red org	19.00	19.00
64	A94	10c on $20,000 org	19.00	21.00
65	A94	12c on $50 dk Prus grn (Bl)	19.00	19.00
66	A72	12c on $50 grnsh gray (Bl)	19.00	19.00
67	A72	12c on $200 brn vio (Bl)	19.00	21.00
68	A94	30c on $20 vio brn	19.00	19.00
69	A82	$1.20 on $100,000 dl grn	30.00	35.00
		Nos. 61-69 (9)	182.00	193.00

China No. 888 and 630 Surcharged

1949   **Engr.**   **Perf. 14**

70	A94	4c on $20 vio brn	360.00	225.00

         Typo.   **Perf. 12**

71	A72	12c on $200 brn vio	310.00	200.00

MANCHURIA

Kirin and Heilungkiang Issue

Stamps of China,
1923-26, Overprinted

The overprint reads: "For use in Ki-Hei District" the two names being abbreviated.

The intention of the overprint was to prevent the purchase of stamps in Manchuria, where the currency was depreciated, and their resale elsewhere.

1927		Unwmk.	Perf. 14	
1	A29	½c black brn	1.90	.35
2	A29	1c orange	1.90	.35
3	A29	1½c violet	2.50	1.90
4	A29	2c yellow grn	2.50	1.90
5	A29	3c blue grn	1.75	.75
6	A29	4c olive grn	.85	.35
7	A29	5c claret	1.75	.35
8	A29	6c red	2.50	1.90
9	A29	7c violet	5.25	1.90
10	A29	8c brown org	3.50	1.90
11	A29	10c dk blue	1.90	.50
12	A30	13c brown	4.00	3.00
13	A30	15c dk blue	4.00	3.00
14	A30	16c olive grn	4.00	2.75
15	A30	20c brown red	6.00	3.50
16	A30	30c brown vio	8.75	3.50
17	A30	50c dp green	12.00	4.25
18	A31	$1 org brn & sep	26.00	8.75
19	A31	$2 bl & red brn	70.00	19.00
20	A31	$5 red & slate	325.00	325.00
		Nos. 1-20 (20)	486.05	384.90

Several values of this issue exist with inverted overprint, double overprint and in pairs with one overprint omitted. These "errors" were not regularly issued. Forgeries also exist.

Chang Tso-lin
Stamps of 1928
Overprinted in Red
or Blue

1928			Perf. 14	
21	A34	1c brown org (R)	2.75	1.75
22	A34	4c olive grn (R)	1.75	1.75
23	A34	10c dull blue (R)	5.00	3.75
24	A34	$1 red (Bl)	50.00	45.00
		Nos. 21-24 (4)	59.50	52.25

Unification Issue of China, 1929, Overprinted in Red as in 1928

1929				
25	A35	1c brown orange	2.00	2.00
26	A35	4c olive green	3.75	3.25
27	A35	10c dark blue	13.00	12.00
28	A35	$1 dark red	110.00	100.00
		Nos. 25-28 (4)	128.75	117.75

Similar Overprint in Black on Sun Yat-sen Mausoleum Issue of China Characters 15-16mm apart

1929			Perf. 14	
29	A36	1c brown orange	2.25	2.50
30	A36	4c olive green	2.75	3.00
31	A36	10c dark blue	8.50	5.25
32	A36	$1 dark red	85.00	65.00
		Nos. 29-32 (4)	98.50	75.75

SINKIANG

Stamps of China,
1913-19, Overprinted
in Black or Red

The first character of overprint is ½mm out of alignment, to the left, and the overprint measures 16mm.

1915		Unwmk.	Perf. 14	
1	A24	½c black brn	1.75	.95
2	A24	1c orange	1.75	.70
3	A24	2c yellow grn	2.40	1.25
4	A24	3c slate grn	2.40	.65
5	A24	4c scarlet	4.75	1.10
6	A24	5c rose lilac	3.50	.95
7	A24	6c gray	6.50	2.75
8	A24	7c violet	6.50	8.50
9	A24	8c brown orange	5.50	5.50
10	A24	10c dark blue	5.50	2.75
11	A25	13c brown	6.50	3.50
12	A25	16c olive grn	13.00	9.25
13	A25	20c brown red	13.00	7.25
14	A25	30c brown violet	14.50	11.00
15	A25	50c deep green	40.00	18.50
16	A26	$1 ocher & blk (R)	145.00	62.50
a.		Second & third characters of overprint transposed	70,000.	
		Nos. 1-16 (16)	272.55	137.10

Stamps of China,
1913-19, Overprinted
in Black or Red

The five characters of overprint are correctly aligned and measure 15½mm.

1916-19				
17	A24	½c black brn	2.00	2.40
18	A24	1c orange	3.25	1.75
19	A24	1½c violet	4.50	4.00
20	A24	2c yellow grn	3.25	1.75
21	A24	3c slate grn	5.50	.70
22	A24	4c scarlet	5.50	1.25
23	A24	5c rose lilac	5.50	.90
24	A24	6c gray	8.00	1.25
25	A24	7c violet	8.00	11.00
26	A24	8c brown org	8.75	8.50
27	A24	10c dark blue	8.75	1.25
28	A25	13c brown	4.75	8.00
29	A25	15c brown	6.00	8.50
30	A25	16c olive grn	5.50	4.00
31	A25	20c brown red	4.50	3.00
32	A25	30c brown vio	6.75	6.00
33	A25	50c deep green	9.25	5.50
34	A26	$1 ocher & blk (R)	29.00	11.00
35	A26	$2 dk bl & blk (R)	27.50	12.00
36	A26	$5 scar & blk (R)	110.00	37.50
37	A26	$10 yel grn & blk (R)	275.00	175.00
38	A26	$20 yel & blk (R)	1,435.	875.00
		Nos. 17-38 (22)	1,976.	1,180.

For overprint see No. C4.

China Nos.
243-246
Overprinted

1921			Perf. 14	
39	A27	1c orange	1.75	1.75
40	A27	3c blue green	3.50	3.50
41	A27	6c gray	13.50	13.50
42	A27	10c blue	80.00	80.00
		Nos. 39-42 (4)	98.75	98.75

Constitution Issue
of China, 1923,
Overprinted

1923				
43	A32	1c orange	1.55	1.55
44	A32	3c blue green	6.50	6.50
45	A32	4c red	9.75	9.75
46	A32	10c blue	27.50	27.50
		Nos. 43-46 (4)	45.30	45.30

Stamps of China, 1923-26, Overprinted as in 1916-19, in Black or Red

1924		Re-engraved		
47	A29	½c black brn	1.50	3.00
48	A29	1c orange	1.50	1.25
49	A29	1½c violet	2.75	5.00
50	A29	2c yellow grn	4.25	1.40
51	A29	3c blue grn	4.25	1.25
52	A29	4c gray	4.25	6.75
53	A29	5c claret	1.40	.90
54	A29	6c red	7.50	2.75
55	A29	7c violet	8.50	7.50
56	A29	8c org brn	17.00	15.00
57	A29	10c dark blue	6.75	1.90
58	A30	13c red brown	6.00	8.50
59	A30	15c deep blue	8.75	6.75
60	A30	16c olive grn	10.00	9.75
61	A30	20c brown red	8.50	6.25
62	A30	30c brown vio	9.75	6.75
63	A30	50c deep green	10.00	6.75
64	A31	$1 org brn & sep (R)	18.00	8.50
65	A31	$2 bl & red brn (R)	40.00	12.00
66	A31	$5 red & slate (R)	95.00	19.00
67	A31	$10 grn & claret (R)	300.00	170.00
68	A31	$20 plum & bl (R)	425.00	325.00
		Nos. 47-68 (22)	990.65	626.05

See #69, 114. For overprints see #C1-C3.

Same Overprint on China No. 275

1926				
69	A29	4c olive green	5.50	5.50

Chang Tso-lin
Stamps of China,
1928, Overprinted
in Red or Blue

1928			Perf. 14	
70	A34	1c brn org (R)	1.75	1.75
71	A34	4c ol grn (R)	2.75	2.75
72	A34	10c dull bl (R)	6.50	6.50
73	A34	$1 red (Bl)	55.00	55.00
		Nos. 70-73 (4)	66.00	66.00

Unification Issue of China, 1929, Overprinted in Red as in 1928

1929				
74	A35	1c brown org	2.75	2.75
75	A35	4c olive grn	4.75	4.75
76	A35	10c dk blue	11.50	11.50
77	A35	$1 dk red	90.00	90.00
		Nos. 74-77 (4)	109.00	109.00

Similar Overprint in Black on Sun Yat-sen Mausoleum Issue of China Characters 15mm apart

1929			Perf. 14	
78	A36	1c brown org	2.25	2.25
79	A36	4c olive grn	3.50	3.50
80	A36	10c dark blue	8.00	8.00
81	A36	$1 dark red	95.00	95.00
		Nos. 78-81 (4)	108.75	108.75

Stamps of Sun Yat-sen
Issue of 1931-37
Overprinted

1932		Type I	Perf. 12½	
82	A37	1c orange	1.75	4.00
83	A37	2c olive grn	4.25	5.75
84	A37	4c green	2.50	6.50
85	A37	20c ultra	4.00	8.25
86	A37	$1 org brn & dk brn	12.00	20.00
87	A37	$2 bl & org brn	35.00	42.50
88	A37	$5 dl red & blk	40.00	60.00
		Nos. 82-88 (7)	99.50	147.00

No. 83 was overprinted in Shanghai in 1938. The overprint differs in minor details.

1932-38			Type II	
89	A37	2c olive grn	.45	2.00
90	A37	4c green	1.25	4.00
91	A37	5c green	.80	4.00
92	A37	15c dk green	1.10	4.00
93	A37	15c scar ('37)	1.10	4.00
93A	A37	20c ultra ('38)	.80	2.75
94	A37	25c ultra	1.25	4.00
95	A37	$1 org brn & dk brn	9.50	11.00
96	A37	$2 bl & org brn	20.00	32.50
97	A37	$5 dl red & blk	40.00	65.00
		Nos. 89-97 (10)	76.25	133.25

Nos. 89, 90 and 94 were overprinted in London, Peking and Shanghai. Nos. 92, 95-97 exist with London and Peking overprints. Nos. 91 and 93 exist with Peking and Shanghai overprints. No. 93A is a Shanghai overprint. The overprints differ in minor details.

Tan Yuan-chang Issue of China, 1933, Overprinted as in 1928

1933			Perf. 14	
98	A49	2c olive grn	3.75	3.75
99	A49	5c green	4.75	4.75
100	A49	25c ultra	15.00	15.00
101	A49	$1 red	75.00	65.00
		Nos. 98-101 (4)	98.50	88.50

Stamps of China
Martyrs Issue of 1932-
34 Overprinted

1933-34				
102	A39	½c black brown	.25	3.50
103	A40	1c orange	1.10	4.25
104	A39	2½c rose lilac	.25	3.25
105	A48	3c deep brown	.25	3.25
106	A45	8c brown orange	.75	3.50
107	A46	10c dull violet	.25	3.25
108	A45	13c blue green	.25	4.50
109	A46	17c brown olive	.25	2.50
110	A47	20c brown red	1.10	6.50
111	A48	30c brown violet	.40	4.50
112	A47	40c orange	.60	3.25
113	A40	50c green	.70	2.50
		Nos. 102-113 (12)	6.15	44.75

Nos. 102-113 were originally overprinted in Peking. In 1938, Nos. 103-105, 108-112 were overprinted in Shanghai. The two overprints differ in minor details. No. 105, Shanghai overprint, is scarce. Value $35.

China No. 324 Overprinted as in 1916-19

1936			Perf. 14	
114	A29	6c brown	20.00	20.00

Stamps of China, 1939-40 Overprinted in Black
Type III

1940-45		Unwmk.	Perf. 12½	
115	A57	2c olive green	.85	1.00
116	A57	3c dull claret ('41)	.25	1.50
117	A57	5c green	.25	1.50
118	A57	5c olive green	.25	1.50
119	A57	8c olive green ('41)	.25	.75
120	A57	10c green ('41)	.25	1.10
121	A57	15c scarlet	.55	2.50
122	A57	16c olive gray ('41)	.40	1.00
123	A57	25c dark blue	.55	2.75
124	A57	$1 hn & dk brn (type II)	6.25	11.00
125	A57	$2 dp bl & org brn (type I)	4.50	11.00
126	A57	$5 red & grnsh blk	26.00	32.50
		Nos. 115-126 (12)	40.35	68.10

			Perf. 14	
		With Secret Marks		
127	A57	8c ol grn (#383a)	1.10	1.65
a.		On #383	19.00	22.50
128	A57	10c green ('41)	10.00	13.00
129	A57	30c scarlet ('45)	.30	1.10
130	A57	50c dk blue ('45)	.55	1.75
131	A57	$1 org brn & sep	.55	2.25
132	A57	$2 dp bl & org brn	.55	2.25
133	A57	$5 red & sl grn	.65	3.75
134	A57	$10 dk grn & dl pur	1.90	2.75
135	A57	$20 rose lake & dk bl	3.50	5.50
		Nos. 127-135 (9)	19.10	34.00

Wmk. Character Yu (Post) (261)
Perf. 14

1936				
136	A57	5c olive green	.30	2.50
137	A57	10c green	.35	3.75
138	A57	30c scarlet	.35	5.00
139	A57	50c dark blue	.45	2.50
		Nos. 136-139 (4)	1.45	13.75

Martyrs Issue, 1940-
41, Overprinted in
Black

Perf. 12, 12½, 13, 13x12, 13½x13

1941-45			Wmk. 261	
140	A40	1c orange	.35	2.40
141	A39	2½c rose lilac	.35	4.50
142	A45	8c dp org ('45)	5.75	12.00
143	A46	10c dull vio	.45	3.00
144	A45	13c dp yel grn	1.00	5.50
145	A46	17c brown olive	1.00	5.25
146	A40	25c red vio ('45)	2.00	7.25
147	A47	40c orange ('45)	3.50	9.25
		Nos. 140-147 (8)	14.40	49.15

Unwmk.

148	A39	½c olive blk	.35	3.25
149	A40	1c orange ('45)	.35	2.40
150	A46	2c dp blue ('45)	3.25	3.75
151	A48	3c dp yel brn	.35	4.50
152	A39	4c pale vio ('45)	.35	4.50
153	A45	8c dp orange	.35	5.50
154	A45	13c dp yel grn ('45)	.65	4.00
155	A48	15c brn car ('45)	.35	4.00
156	A46	17c brn ol ('45)	1.00	4.00
157	A47	20c lt blue ('45)	.35	3.25
158	A45	21c ol brn ('45)	1.25	4.50
159	A46	28c olive ('45)	1.45	5.50
160	A47	40c orange ('45)	3.00	14.00
161	A40	50c green ('45)	2.00	7.00
		Nos. 148-161 (14)	15.05	70.65

Stamps of China,
1942-43 Overprinted
in Carmine, Black or
Red

1944   Without Gum   Perf. 12½, 13

162	A62	10c dp grn (C)	1.75	7.75
163	A62	20c dk ol grn (C)	2.00	7.75
164	A62	25c violet brn	.30	8.50
165	A62	30c dk orange	.95	9.00
166	A62	40c red brown	.30	8.50
167	A62	50c sage green	.30	5.00
a.		Perf. 11	16.00	24.00
168	A62	$1 rose lake	3.75	5.00
169	A62	$1 dull green	.30	8.50
170	A62	$1.50 dp bl (C)	.30	9.50
171	A62	$2 dk bl grn (R)	2.40	7.00
172	A62	$3 yellow	.30	12.00
173	A62	$5 cerise	2.40	11.00
		Nos. 162-173 (12)	15.05	99.50

For surcharges see Nos. 194-195.

Same Overprint on Stamps of China, 1942-43, in Black

1944-46   Imperf.

174	A57	$10 red brown	140.00	125.00
175	A57	$20 rose red	6.75	17.00
176	A57	$30 dull vio	5.00	17.00
177	A57	$40 rose red	5.00	17.00
178	A57	$50 blue ('46)	1,080.	1,170.
179	A57	$100 orange brn	14.50	22.50

Perf. 13½

180	A57	$4 dp blue	2.00	13.50
181	A57	$5 lilac gray	3.50	13.50
182	A57	$10 red brn	3.50	13.50
183	A57	$20 blue grn	2.00	15.00
184	A57	$20 rose red	140.00	140.00
185	A57	$30 dull vio	4.00	17.00
186	A57	$40 rose	4.00	16.00
187	A57	$50 blue	4.50	17.00
188	A57	$100 orange brn	160.00	140.00
		Nos. 174-177,179-188 (14)	494.75	584.00

Beware of trimmed examples of Nos. 182
and 187 offered as Nos. 174 and 178.

Nos. 162 and 164
Surcharged in Black

1944, Aug. 1

194	A62	12c on 10c dp grn	9.00	27.50
195	A62	24c on 25c brn vio	9.00	27.50

Stamps of China,
1940-41, Overprinted
in Black at Chengtu,
Szechwan

1943

196	A57	10c green (#354)	25.00	30.00
197	A47	20c lt blue (#433)	25.00	30.00

Wmk. 261   Perf. 14

198	A57	50c dk blue (#396)	25.00	30.00

China Nos. 565 and
567 Overprinted in
Black

1945   Unwmk.   Perf. 12½

200	A63	40c brown red	.45	20.00
201	A63	$3 red	.45	18.00

China Nos. 640-642,
788, 751, 753
Surcharged in Black or
Red

1949   Engr.   Perf. 14

202	A73	1c on $100 dk car	29.00	35.00
203	A73	3c on $200 ol grn (R)	29.00	35.00
204	A73	5c on $500 brt bl grn (R)	29.00	35.00
205	A82	10c on $20,000 rose pink	25.00	30.00
206	A82	50c on $4000 gray (R)	100.00	100.00
207	A82	$1 on $6000 rose lil	110.00	110.00
		Nos. 202-207 (6)	322.00	345.00

AIR POST STAMPS

Sinkiang Nos. 53, 57,
59, 32 Overprinted in
Red

1932-33   Unwmk.   Perf. 14

C1	A29	5c claret ('33)	400.00	290.00
C2	A29	10c dark blue ('33)	400.00	225.00
C3	A30	15c deep blue	2,700.	775.00
C4	A25	30c brown violet	1,170.	990.00

Counterfeits exist of Nos. C1-C4.

Air Post Stamps of China, 1932-37 Handstamped in Dull Red

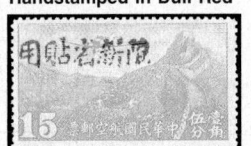

1942

C5	AP3	15c gray green	7.25	9.00
C6	AP3	25c orange	425.00	375.00
C7	AP3	30c red	15.50	27.50
C8	AP3	45c brown vio	11.00	18.00
C9	AP3	50c dk brown	45.00	50.00
C10	AP3	60c dk blue	11.00	21.00
C11	AP3	90c olive grn	57.50	80.00
C12	AP3	$1 yellow grn	12.00	20.00
		Nos. C5-C12 (8)	584.25	600.50

Same Handstamped Overprint on Air Post Stamps of China, 1940-41 in Dull Red

1942   Wmk. 261   Perf. 12½, 13, 13½

C13	AP3	15c gray green	6.75	15.00
C14	AP3	25c yellow orange	6.75	17.00

1942   Unwmk.

C15	AP3	25c light orange	6.75	13.50
C16	AP3	30c light red	6.75	13.50
C17	AP3	50c brown	9.00	15.00
C18	AP3	$2 light brown	42.50	42.50
C19	AP3	$5 lake	42.50	42.50
		Nos. C15-C19 (5)	107.50	127.00

Twelve values exist with this overprint in
black. Their status has not been determined.
Inverted overprints exist in both red and black.

Official Perforated Characters

For use on official mail, various Sinkiang stamps were perforated with an
arrangement of four Chinese characters
("For Official Business Only"). These
include Nos. 1-38, 47-69, 114.

OFFICES IN TIBET

12 Pies = 1 Anna
16 Annas = 1 Rupee

Stamps of China,
Issues of 1902-10,
Surcharged

1911   Unwmk.   Perf. 12 to 16

1	A17	3p on 1c ocher	27.50	45.00
a.		Inverted surcharge	3,500.	
2	A17	½a on 2c grn	27.50	45.00
3	A17	1a on 4c ver	27.50	45.00
4	A17	2a on 7c mar	27.50	45.00
5	A17	2½a on 10c ultra	35.00	55.00
6	A18	3a on 16c ol grn	70.00	80.00
a.		Large "S" in "Annas"	1,250.	
7	A18	4a on 20c red brn	70.00	80.00
8	A18	6a on 30c rose red	125.00	140.00
9	A18	12a on 50c yel	325.00	400.00
10	A19	1r on $1 red & pale rose	900.00	900.00
11	A19	2r on $2 red & yel	1,620.	1,800.
		Nos. 1-11 (11)	3,255.	3,635.

Beware of fake overprints.

PEOPLE'S REPUBLIC OF CHINA

'pē-pəls ri-'pə-blik of 'chī-nə

LOCATION — Eastern Asia
GOVT. — Communist Republic
POP. — 1,339,724,852 (2010 est.)
CAPITAL — Beijing (Peking)

The communists completed their conquest of all mainland China in 1949. They established the Central Government and General Postal Administration in Peking. They ordered all but two regions to stop selling regional issues by June 30, 1950, extending validity one year from that date. The Northeast and Port Arthur-Dairen regions were exempted because their currency had a different value. These two regions stopped using separate issues at the end of 1950. Thereafter unified issues were used throughout mainland China.

On July 1, 1997 Hong Kong returned to Chinese control as an administrative district. Hong Kong stamps issued under Chinese rule will continue to be listed under "Hong Kong."

Reprints

After currency revaluation Mar. 1, 1955, reprints were prepared and put on sale by the Philatelic Agency in order to supply stocks of exhausted issues for collectors. Minor differences in design or paper distinguish the reprints. They are of commemorative and special issues up to the gymnastics set of 1952. Reprints are less expensive. Values are for original issues. Reprint distinctions are footnoted.

Used Stamps

Most used stamps before 1970 exist primarily canceled to order. Postally used stamps generally sell for ½ the unused value.

Beginning in 1987 the PRC stopped furnishing quantities of used stamps to the philatelic market. When available, used stamps of these issues sell for the same or more than unused stamps.

PRC Issue Numbers

Commemorative issues, beginning in 1949, and special issues, beginning in 1951, bear 4 numbers in lower margin: 1. Issue number. 2. Total of stamps in set. 3. Position of stamp in set. 4. Cumulative number of stamp (usually in parenthesis). A fifth number, the year of issue, was added in 1952.

The numbering system varies at times, with all numbers omitted on Scott 938-1046.

In certain sets listings include parenthetically the position-in-set number. During some periods these parentheses in listings hold the stamp's cumulative number. Issue numbers are noted when one or more designs are not illustrated.

Gum

All stamps to the beginning of 1960 were issued without gum, except as noted. After that date, most stamps have gum, which is translucent and almost invisible. Catalogue values are for stamps with fresh, untoned paper and gum. Stamps with toned paper or gum sell for approximately 20% to 50% less. All issues are unwatermarked, unless otherwise noted.

100 fen = 1 yuan ($)

Catalogue values for unused stamps in this country are for Never Hinged items, beginning with Scott 487 in the regular postage section, Scott B1 in the semipostal section.

Syncopated Perforations

Type A (1st stamp No. 2880): On the two shorter sides, an oval hole equal in width to three holes is centered.

Lantern and Gate of Heavenly Peace — A1

Original   Reprint

Reprints have altered ornament on lantern base. On originals, it is a full oval; on reprints, only a partial circle. Value, set: unused $12; used $3.

1949, Oct. 8   Litho.   Perf. 12½

1	A1	$30 blue	8.00	6.50
2	A1	$50 rose red	9.00	6.50
3	A1	$100 green	11.50	6.50
4	A1	$200 maroon	11.50	6.50
		Nos. 1-4 (4)	40.00	26.00

1st session of Chinese People's Consultative Political Conference. See Nos. 1L121-1L124.

Globe and Hand Holding Hammer — A2

Original   Reprint

Reprints show heavier shading on index finger and thumb. Value, set $8 unused or $3 used.

1949, Nov. 16

5	A2	$100 carmine	25.00	9.00
6	A2	$300 slate green	25.00	9.00
7	A2	$500 dark blue	25.00	9.00
		Nos. 5-7 (3)	75.00	27.00

Asiatic and Australasian Congress of the World Federation of Trade Unions, Peking. The $100, imperf., is of dubious status. See Nos. 1L133-1L135.

Conference Hall, Peking — A3

Mao Tse-tung on Rostrum A4

Original   Reprint

Nos. 8-9: First character in top inscription shows a square, reprints an oblong.
Nos. 10-11: Originals have heavy cross-hatching and lines which touch back of head and top of rostrum. Reprints have lighter lines which do not touch head or top of rostrum. Reprints, value set $25 unused, $9 used.

1950, Feb. 1   Engr.   Perf. 14

8	A3	$50 red	12.50	8.00
9	A3	$100 blue	12.50	8.00
10	A4	$300 red brown	14.00	11.00
11	A4	$500 green	20.00	17.50
		Nos. 8-11 (4)	59.00	44.50

Chinese People's Consultative Political Conference. See Nos. 1L136-1L139.

Gate of Heavenly Peace (actual size) — A5

First Issue: Top line of shading broken at right.

1950, Feb. 10   Litho.   Perf. 12½

12	A5	$200 green	15.00	2.25
13	A5	$300 brown red	1.00	1.25
14	A5	$500 red	1.00	.60
15	A5	$800 orange	100.00	1.75
16	A5	$1000 dull violet	4.00	.75
17	A5	$2000 olive	19.00	2.75
18	A5	$5000 brt pink	1.00	2.25
19	A5	$8000 blue	.75	20.00
20	A5	$10,000 brown	1.00	2.75
		Nos. 12-20 (9)	142.75	34.35

1950, June 9   Typo.

Second Issue: Top line of shading extends to frame line at right.

21	A5	$1000 dull violet	1.75	1.25
22	A5	$3000 red brown	1.50	1.00
23	A5	$10,000 brown	1.00	1.25
		Nos. 21-23 (3)	4.25	3.50

Other Gate of Heavenly Peace issues are illustrated where they are listed. See A10, A13, A14 and A42 for similar designs.
For similar types with Chinese characters in upper right corner see Northeast China A28, A29, Port Arthur & Darien A11, North China A8.

China Nos. 959, C62, E12, F2 Surcharged in Blue, Black, Green or Red

Rouletted, Perf. 12½ (#27, 29)
1950, Mar.   Litho.

24	SD2	$100 on red vio (Bl)	.70	2.25
a.		Perf. 12½	7.50	3.25
25	R2	$200 on red (Bk)	3.00	1.75
a.		Perf. 12½	52.50	3.25
26	AP5	$300 on bl grn (Bk)	.50	1.25
a.		Perf. 12½	1.10	1.25
27	A96	$500 on org (Gr)	.75	.50
a.		Perf. 14	60.00	50.00
28	A96	$800 on org (R)	4.00	1.00
a.		Perf. 12½	30.00	4.00
b.		Perf. 14	850.00	75.00
29	A96	$1000 on org (Bk)	.50	.50
a.		Perf. 14	.50	.50
		Nos. 24-29 (6)	9.45	7.25

Harvesters with Ox — A6

1950, May

30	A6	$20,000 on $10,000 red	575.00 110.00

No. 30 is surcharged on an unissued stamp of East China. Value, without surcharge (unissued) $1,500.

Flag, Mao Tse-tung, Gate of Heavenly Peace — A7

Original   Reprint

Originals have a single curved line in jacket button, reprints have an extra dot in button. Value, set unused $42.50 used $16.

1950, July 1   Perf. 14
Yellow Stars

31	A7	$800 green & red	50.00	15.00
32	A7	$1000 brn & red	75.00	20.00
33	A7	$2000 dk brn & red	90.00	20.00
34	A7	$3000 dk blue & red	130.00	30.00
		Nos. 31-34 (4)	345.00	85.00

Inauguration of the People's Republic, Oct. 1, 1949. See Nos. 1L150-1L153.

Sun Yat-sen Stamps of Northeastern Provinces Surcharged in Red, Black or Blue

1950, July 1   Engr.

35	A2	$50 on 20c yel grn	10.00	7.00
36	A2	$50 on 25c blk brn	5.00	5.00
37	A2	$50 on 50c red org (Bk)	2.25	3.00
38	A2	$100 on $2.50 ind	1.50	2.50
39	A2	$100 on $3 brn (Bk)	2.50	5.00
40	A2	$100 on $4 org brn, Type II (Bl)	4.00	10.00
a.	Type I		800.00	275.00
41	A2	$100 on $5 dk grn (Bk)	7.00	3.75
42	A2	$100 on $10 crim, Type II (Bl)	35.00	12.00
a.	Type I		7,500.	
43	A2	$400 on $20 ol, Type II (Bl)	70.00	47.50
a.	Type I		1,000.	300.00
44	A2	$400 on $44 dk car rose (Bl)	3.50	8.50
45	A2	$400 on $65 dl grn (Bk)	135.00	75.00
46	A2	$400 on $100 dp grn	27.50	11.00
47	A2	$400 on $200 rose brn (Bk)	70.00	21.00
48	A2	$400 on $300 bluish grn	90.00	27.50
		Nos. 35-48 (14)	463.25	238.75

Flying Geese Type of China Surcharged in Red, Blue, Green, Brown or Black

1950, Aug. 1   Perf. 12½, Imperf.

49	A97	$50 on 10c dk bl (R)	.25	.40
50	A97	$100 on 16c ol, imperf. (Bl)	.35	.45
51	A97	$100 on 50c dl grn, imperf. (R)	.35	.35
52	A97	$200 on $1 org (G)	.45	.30
53	A97	$200 on $2 bl (Br)	6.25	.90
54	A97	$400 on $5 car rose (Bk)	.50	.50
55	A97	$400 on $10 bl grn (Bk)	.45	1.50
56	A97	$400 on $20 pur (Bk)	1.10	2.75
		Nos. 49-56 (8)	9.70	7.15

Dove of Peace, by Picasso — A8

1950, Aug. 1   Engr.   Perf. 14
57	A8	$400 brown	27.50	7.00
58	A8	$800 green	27.50	7.00
59	A8	$2000 blue	47.50	12.00
		Nos. 57-59 (3)	102.50	26.00

World Peace Campaign. See Nos. 1L154-1L156.
Paper of originals appears bright under ultraviolet lamp. That of reprints looks dull. Value, set unused $8.50 used $4.

Chinese Flag and "1" — A9

$800

Original   Reprint

Reprints are a brighter red, leaves beside "1" are gray brown instead of reddish brown. On the $800 the arrangement of dots in background differs in relationship to large star. Value, set unused $25 used $10.

1950   Engr. & Litho.
Flag in Red & Yellow
60	A9	$100 purple	37.50	13.00
61	A9	$400 red brown	40.00	15.00
62	A9	$800 green	50.00	11.00
63	A9	$1000 lt olive	85.00	20.00
64	A9	$2000 blue	90.00	42.50
		Nos. 60-64 (5)	302.50	101.50

1st anniv. of the Chinese People's Republic.
Size of $800: 38x46mm; others 26x32mm.
Issue dates: No. 62, Oct. 1; others Oct. 31.
See Nos. 1L157-1L161.

Gate of Heavenly Peace (actual size) — A10

Third Issue: Cloud almost touches character at upper left. Cloud breaks inner frame line at top.

1950   Litho.
65	A10	$100 lt grnsh bl	35.00	11.00
66	A10	$200 green	240.00	19.00
67	A10	$300 dk carmine	2.50	5.00
68	A10	$400 grnsh gray	7.00	4.00
69	A10	$500 carmine	1.25	3.50
70	A10	$800 orange	7.00	1.00
71	A10	$2000 gray olive	3.00	2.25
		Nos. 65-71 (7)	295.75	45.75

Issued: $800, 10/8; $500, $2000, 12/1; others, 10/6.

"Communication" and Map of China — A11

Original   Reprint

Originals have 3 lines below horizontal bar (2nd character); reprints have four. Value, set unused $3.25, used $1.50.

1950, Nov. 1   Litho.
72	A11	$400 green & brn	35.00	11.00
73	A11	$800 carmine & grn	40.00	9.00

First All-China Postal Conference, Peking.
See Nos. 1L162-1L163.

Stalin and Mao Tse-tung — A12

1950, Dec. 1   Engr.   Perf. 14
74	A12	$400 red	21.00	12.00
75	A12	$800 dp green	21.00	10.00
76	A12	$2000 dk blue	32.50	12.00
		Nos. 74-76 (3)	74.50	34.00

Signing of Sino-Soviet Treaty of Friendship, Alliance and Mutual Assistance. See Nos. 1L176-1L178.
Paper of originals appears bright under ultraviolet lamp. That of reprints looks dull. Value, set unused $18.50, used $7.

East China Issue of 1949
Surcharged in Red, Black, Brown or Blue

Train and Postal Runner — A12a

1950, Dec.   Litho.   Perf. 12½
77	A12a	$50 on $10 dp ultra (R)	.30	.30
78	A12a	$100 on $15 org ver (Bk)	.30	.30
a.		$100 on $15 red (Bk), perf. 14	1.00	.85
79	A12a	$300 on $50 car (Bk)	.40	.30
80	A12a	$400 on $1600 vio bl (Br)	2.50	1.00
81	A12a	$400 on $2000 brn vio (Bl)	1.00	.70
		Nos. 77-81 (5)	4.50	2.60

East China Issue of 1949
Surcharged in Red or Black

Chairman Mao — A12b

1950, Dec.
82	A12b	$50 on $10 ultra (R)	.45	.25
83	A12b	$100 on $15 ver (Bk)	.60	.30
84	A12b	$400 on $2000 grn (Bk)	2.25	.90
		Nos. 82-84 (3)	3.30	1.45

(actual size) — A13

Fourth Issue: Similar to 3rd issue, but large cloud does not break inner frame line at top.

1950-51   Litho.
85	A13	$100 lt blue	.80	1.75
86	A13	$200 dull green	10.00	4.25
87	A13	$300 dull lilac	.65	5.00
88	A13	$400 gray grn	8.00	1.50
89	A13	$500 carmine	.75	1.50
90	A13	$800 orange	70.00	6.25
a.		Imperf., pair		
91	A13	$1000 violet	1.00	2.75
92	A13	$2000 olive	270.00	7.00
93	A13	$3000 brown	.90	5.50
94	A13	$5000 pink	.90	4.50
		Nos. 85-94 (10)	363.00	40.00

Issued: $200, $300, $500, $800, $2000, $5000, 12/22/50; others 6/8/51.

(actual size) — A14

Fifth Issue: Colored network on surface in salmon.

1951, Jan. 18   Engr.   Perf. 14
95	A14	$10,000 brown	2.50	32.50
96	A14	$20,000 olive	3.50	14.00
97	A14	$30,000 green	80.00	100.00
98	A14	$50,000 violet	100.00	50.00
99	A14	$100,000 scar	2,500.	325.00
100	A14	$200,000 blue	3,250.	650.00
		Nos. 95-100 (6)	5,936.	1,172.

Unit Issue of China Surcharged

1951, May 2   Litho.   Perf. 12½
101	SD2	$5 on rose lilac	3.75	3.25
102	AP5	$10 on brt grn	2.25	3.25
103	R2	$15 on red	1.50	1.75
104	A96	$25 on orange	1.50	1.75
		Nos. 101-104 (4)	9.00	10.00

Issued for use in Northeast China, but available for use throughout China. Nos. 101-104 rouletted were sold for philatelic purposes only. Value, set unused $10, used $8.

Chairman Mao Tse-tung — A15

1951, July 1   Engr.   Perf. 14
105	A15	$400 chestnut	10.00	6.50
106	A15	$500 deep green	12.00	6.50
107	A15	$800 crimson	14.50	6.50
		Nos. 105-107 (3)	36.50	19.50

Chinese Communist Party, 30th anniv.
Reprints are on whiter, thinner and harder paper. Value, set unused $21.50, used $12.

Picasso Dove — A16

1951, Aug. 15   Perf. 12½
108	A16	$400 orange brn	25.00	13.00
109	A16	$800 blue grn	25.00	13.00
110	A16	$1000 dull vio	25.00	13.00
		Nos. 108-110 (3)	75.00	39.00

Reprints are perf 14. Value, set unused $30, used $9.50.

Remittance Stamp of China
Surcharged in Carmine or Black

(same size) — A17

Engraved, Commercial Press
1951, Sept.   Perf. 12½
111	A17	$50 on $2 bl grn (C)	1.50	1.00

Rouletted 9½
Typo., Kang Hwa Printing Co.
112	A17	$50 on $2 gray bl (C)	4.25	5.25
113	A17	$50 on $5 red org (Bk)	1.50	1.50
114	A17	$50 on $50 gray (C)	5.00	5.25

Perf. 13
Lithographed, Central Trust Co.
115	A17	$50 on $50 gray blk (C)	1.00	1.00

Perf. 11½x10
Lithographed, Chung Hwa Book Co.
116	A17	$50 on $50 gray (C)	3.00	1.25
a.		Perf. 11½	2.00	1.25
		Nos. 111-116 (6)	16.25	15.25

National Emblem — A18

Engraved; Background Network
Lithographed in Yellow
1951, Oct. 1   Perf. 14
117	A18	$100 Prus blue	12.50	7.00
118	A18	$200 brown	12.50	7.00
119	A18	$400 orange	12.50	7.00
120	A18	$500 green	17.50	7.00
121	A18	$800 carmine	18.50	7.00
		Nos. 117-121 (5)	73.50	35.00

Reprints exist but are difficult to distinguish; paper whiter, and colors slightly brighter. Value, set unused or used $20.

Rough Perfs
Rough perforations are normal on many early issues. These include Nos. 122-123, 136-140, 155-176, 239-240, 299-300, 453-456, 467-482, 629-634, 684-707, 737-745 and probably others.

Lu Hsun and Quotation A19

Original

Reprint

Reprints have dot in triangle at lower right; no dot in original. Value, set unused $6.50, used $2.25.

1951, Oct. 19   Litho.   Perf. 12½
122 A19 $400 lilac   11.00 6.00
123 A19 $800 green   15.00 6.00

15th anniversary of the death of Lu Hsun (1881-1936), writer.

Peasant Uprising, Chintien — A20

Design: Nos. 126-127, Coin of Taiping Regime and decrees of peasant government.

Original

Reprint

Reprints of Nos. 124-125 have additional short stroke at upper left.

Original

Reprint

Reprints of Nos. 126-127 have two short strokes on scale near tail of right dragon on coin. Value, Nos. 124-127 unused $10, used $4.25.

1951, Dec. 15   Engr.   Perf. 14
124 A20 $400 green   15.00 7.00
125 A20 $800 scarlet   12.00 7.00
126 A20 $800 orange   12.00 7.00
127 A20 $1000 deep blue   20.00 7.00
　　Nos. 124-127 (4)   59.00 28.00

Centenary of Taiping Peasant Rebellion.

Old and New Methods of Agriculture — A21

Original

Reprint

One short horizontal line between legs of plower; 2 lines in reprints. Value, set unused $9.50, used $4.

1952, Jan. 1
128 A21 $100 scarlet   10.00 6.50
129 A21 $200 bright blue   10.00 6.50
130 A21 $400 deep brown   10.00 6.50
131 A21 $800 green   10.00 6.50
　　Nos. 128-131 (4)   40.00 26.00

Agrarian reform.

Potala Monastery, Lhasa — A22

Nos. 134-135, Farmer plowing with yaks.

1952, Mar. 15   Perf. 12½
132 A22 $400 vermilion   15.00 7.00
133 A22 $800 claret   15.00 7.00
134 A22 $800 blue grn   15.00 7.00
135 A22 $1000 dull vio   15.00 7.00
　　Nos. 132-135 (4)   60.00 28.00

Liberation of Tibet.

Reprints, perf 14, have a small Chinese character at lower left of the vignette which is missing in the original. Value, set unused $22, used $7.

Children of Four Races — A23

1952, Apr. 12   Litho.
136 A23 $400 dull grn   1.50 .35
137 A23 $800 vio blue   1.75 .45

Intl. Child Protection Conf., Vienna.

Hammer and Sickle on Numeral 1 — A24

Labor Day: No. 139, Dove rising from worker's hand. No. 140, Dove, hammer, wheat & chimneys.

1952, May 1
138 A24 $800 scarlet   2.50 .40
139 A24 $800 blue grn   2.50 .40
140 A24 $800 orange brn   2.50 .40
　　Nos. 138-140 (3)   7.50 1.20

Physical Exercises — A25

Stamps printed in blocks of four for each color, each block representing a specific setting-up exercise; exercises coincided with a national radio program. Where exercise positions are identical within the block, the serial number in the LL margin of each stamp (and in parenthesis in the listings below) is the only means of differentiation.

1952, June 20
141 A25   Block of 4   140.00 50.00
a. $400 vermilion (1)   8.00 4.00
b. $400 vermilion (2)   8.00 4.00
c. $400 vermilion (3)   8.00 4.00
d. $400 vermilion (4)   8.00 4.00
142 A25   Block of 4   140.00 50.00
a. $400 blue (5)   8.00 4.00
b. $400 blue (6)   8.00 4.00
c. $400 blue (7)   8.00 4.00
d. $400 blue (8)   8.00 4.00
143 A25   Block of 4   140.00 50.00
a. $400 brown red (9)   8.00 4.00
b. $400 brown red (10)   8.00 4.00
c. $400 brown red (11)   8.00 4.00
d. $400 brown red (12)   8.00 4.00
144 A25   Block of 4   140.00 50.00
a. $400 yellow green (13)   8.00 4.00
b. $400 yellow green (14)   8.00 4.00
c. $400 yellow green (15)   8.00 4.00
d. $400 yellow green (16)   8.00 4.00
145 A25   Block of 4   140.00 50.00
a. $400 red orange (17)   8.00 4.00
b. $400 red orange (18)   8.00 4.00
c. $400 red orange (19)   8.00 4.00
d. $400 red orange (20)   8.00 4.00
146 A25   Block of 4   140.00 50.00
a. $400 dull blue (21)   8.00 4.00
b. $400 dull blue (22)   8.00 4.00
c. $400 dull blue (23)   8.00 4.00
d. $400 dull blue (24)   8.00 4.00
147 A25   Block of 4   140.00 50.00
a. $400 orange (25)   8.00 4.00
b. $400 orange (26)   8.00 4.00
c. $400 orange (27)   8.00 4.00
d. $400 orange (28)   8.00 4.00
148 A25   Block of 4   140.00 50.00
a. $400 dull purple (29)   8.00 4.00
b. $400 dull purple (30)   8.00 4.00
c. $400 dull purple (31)   8.00 4.00
d. $400 dull purple (32)   8.00 4.00
149 A25   Block of 4   140.00 50.00
a. $400 yellow bister (33) 8.00 4.00
b. $400 yellow bister (34) 8.00 4.00
c. $400 yellow bister (35) 8.00 4.00
d. $400 yellow bister (36) 8.00 4.00
150 A25   Block of 4   140.00 50.00
a. $400 sky blue (37)   8.00 4.00
b. $400 sky blue (38)   8.00 4.00
c. $400 sky blue (39)   8.00 4.00
d. $400 sky blue (40)   8.00 4.00
　　Nos. 141-150 (10)   1,400. 500.00

Originals are on thin gray paper, colors darker. Reprints on thicker white paper, colors brighter. Value, set of blocks unused $52.50, used $47.50.

Hunting, Wei Dynasty, A.D. 386-580 A26

Designs from Murals in Cave Temples at Tunhuang, Kansu Province: No. 152, Lady attendants, Sui Dynasty, 581-617 A.D. No. 153, Gandharvas (mythology), Tang Dynasty, 618-906. No. 154, Dragon, Tang Dynasty.

1952, July 1   Engr.
151 A26 $800 slate green (1)   2.25 .55
152 A26 $800 chocolate (2)   2.25 .55
a.   Vert. pair, imperf. between 360.00
153 A26 $800 indigo (3)   2.25 .55
154 A26 $800 dk vio (4)   2.25 .55
　　Nos. 151-154 (4)   9.00 2.20

"Glorious Mother Country," 1st series.

Marco Polo Bridge, near Peking A27

Designs: No. 156, Cavalry passing through Great Wall. No. 157, Departure of New Fourth Army. No. 158, Mao Tse-tung and Gen. Chu Teh planning counter-attack.

1952, July 7   Litho.   Perf. 14
155 A27 $800 brt blue   3.75 .50
156 A27 $800 blue grn   3.75 .50
157 A27 $800 plum   3.75 .50
158 A27 $800 scarlet   3.75 .50
　　Nos. 155-158 (4)   15.00 2.00

15th anniversary of war against Japan.

Soldier, Sailor & Airman — A28

No. 160, Soldier and Tanks. No. 161, Sailor & warships. No. 162, Airman & planes.

1952, Aug. 1   Engr.   Perf. 12½
159 A28 $800 carmine   2.50 .50
160 A28 $800 deep green   2.50 .50
161 A28 $800 purple   2.50 .50
162 A28 $800 orange brown 2.50 .50
　　Nos. 159-162 (4)   10.00 2.00

25th anniv. of People's Liberation Army.

Huai River Sluice Dam — A29

No. 164, Train on the Chengtu-Chungking Railway. No. 165, Oil refinery and derricks in the Northwest. No. 166, Mechanized state farm.

1952, Oct. 1   Perf. 14
163 A29 $800 dk violet   3.00 .60
164 A29 $800 red   3.00 .60
165 A29 $800 dk vio brn   3.00 .60
166 A29 $800 dp green   3.00 .60
　　Nos. 163-166 (4)   12.00 2.40

"Glorious Mother Country," 2nd series.

Doves and Globe A30

Designs: Nos. 167-168, Picasso dove over Pacific, vert. $2500, as No. 169.

1952, Oct. 2   Perf. 14
167 A30 $400 maroon   2.00 .35
168 A30 $800 red   2.00 .35
169 A30 $800 brown orange 2.00 .35
170 A30 $2500 deep green   2.00 .55
　　Nos. 167-170 (4)   8.00 1.60

Peace Conf. of the Asian and Pacific Regions.

Volunteers on the March — A31

No. 172, Chinese peasants loading supplies. No. 173, Volunteers attacking across river. No. 174, Meeting of Chinese & Korean troops.

1952, Oct. 25
171 A31 $800 blue green (1)   3.50 .40
172 A31 $800 vermilion (2)   3.50 .40
173 A31 $800 violet (3)   3.50 .40
174 A31 $800 lake brown (4)   3.50 .40
　　Nos. 171-174 (4)   14.00 1.60

2nd anniv. of Chinese Volunteers in Korea.

Woman Textile Worker A32

Design: No. 176, Farm woman with sickle.

1953, Mar. 10
175 A32 $800 carmine   1.75 .40
176 A32 $800 emerald   1.75 .40

International Women's Day.

Textile Worker — A33

$200, Shepherdess. $250, Stone lion. $800, Lathe operator. $1600, Coal miners. $2000, Corner tower of Forbidden City, Peking.

1953   Litho.   Perf. 14, 12½ ($250)

177	A33	$50 magenta	1.00	.25
178	A33	$200 emerald	1.50	.45
179	A33	$250 ultra	5.00	2.75
180	A33	$800 blue grn	1.00	.25
181	A33	$1600 gray	1.00	.50
182	A33	$2000 red org	2.00	.35
		Nos. 177-182 (6)	11.50	4.55

Issued: Nos. 177-181, Mar. 25; No. 182, May 23.

Karl Marx — A34

1953, May 20   Engr.   Perf. 14

183	A34	$400 dk brown	2.75	.50
184	A34	$800 slate grn	2.75	.50

135th anniv. of the birth of Karl Marx.

Workers and Banners — A35

1953, June 25

185	A35	$400 Prus blue	2.25	.40
186	A35	$800 carmine	2.25	.40

7th All-China Trade Union Congress.

Picasso Dove — A36

1953, July 25

187	A36	$250 blue grn	1.75	.40
188	A36	$400 orange brn	2.25	.45
189	A36	$800 purple	3.00	.65
		Nos. 187-189 (3)	7.00	1.50

World Peace.

Groom, Wei Dynasty, 386-580 A37

Scenes from Tunhuang Murals: No. 191, Court Players, Wei Dynasty. No. 192, Battle Scene, Sui Dynasty, 581-617. No. 193, Ox-drawn palanquin, Tang Dynasty, 618-906.

1953, Sept. 1

190	A37	$800 dp green (1)	2.00	.50
191	A37	$800 red org (2)	2.00	.50
192	A37	$800 Prus blue (3)	2.00	.50
193	A37	$800 carmine (4)	2.00	.50
		Nos. 190-193 (4)	8.00	2.00

"Glorious Mother Country," 3rd series.

Stalin and Mao on Kremlin Terrace A38

Statue of Stalin at Volga-Don Canal — A39

Designs: No. 195, Lenin proclaiming Soviet power. No. 197, Stalin as orator.

1953, Oct. 5

194	A38	$800 green (1)	2.50	1.25
195	A38	$800 carmine (2)	2.50	1.25
196	A39	$800 brt blue (3)	3.50	1.25
197	A39	$800 org brn (4)	4.50	2.00
		Nos. 194-197 (4)	13.00	5.75

Russian October Revolution, 35th anniv.

Stamps in same designs with two additional characters meaning "Soviet" in the single-line Chinese inscription, and in different colors, were unofficially released at several small post offices in Hunan, Fukien and Canton areas in February, 1953, but were withdrawn after only a small number had been sold. Value, set $30,000. unused, $12,000 canceled.

Compass, 3rd Century B.C. A40

No. 199, Seismoscope, later Han Dynasty. No. 200, Drum cart to measure distance, Chin Dynasty. No. 201, Armillary sphere, Ming Dynasty.

1953, Dec. 1

198	A40	$800 indigo (1)	2.50	.90
199	A40	$800 dk green (2)	2.50	.90
200	A40	$800 dk blue (3)	2.50	.90
201	A40	$800 choc (4)	2.50	.90
		Nos. 198-201 (4)	10.00	3.60

Major inventions by ancient and medieval Chinese scientists.

"Glorious Mother Country," 4th series.

Francois Rabelais — A41

Designs: $400, Jose Marti, Cuban revolutionary. $800, Chu Yuan (350-275 B.C.), philosopher. $2200, Nicolaus Copernicus, astronomer.

1953, Dec. 30

202	A41	$250 slate grn (3)	1.80	.40
203	A41	$400 brown blk (4)	1.80	.40
204	A41	$800 indigo (1)	1.80	.40
205	A41	$2200 choc (2)	1.80	.40
		Nos. 202-205 (4)	7.20	1.60

(same size) Gate of Heavenly Peace — A42

Sixth Issue: Inscription at upper right.

1954, Apr. 16   Litho.

206	A42	$50 carmine	.50	.30
207	A42	$100 lt blue	.50	.30
208	A42	$200 green	.50	.25
209	A42	$250 ultra	3.75	.80
210	A42	$400 gray grn	1.00	.25
211	A42	$800 orange	.50	.25
212	A42	$1600 gray	.50	.65
213	A42	$2000 olive	1.25	.50
		Nos. 206-213 (8)	8.50	3.30

Textile Plant, Harbin — A43

Designs: $200, Tangku Harbor. $250, Tien-shui-Lanchow railroad bridge, Kansu Province. $400, Heavy machine-building plant, Taiyuan, Shansi. No. 218, Automatic blast, furnace, Anshan, Manchuria. No. 219, Fushun open-cut coal mine. $2000, Automatic power plant, Northeast. $3200, Prospecting in Tayeh district, Hupeh.

1954, May 1   Engr.

214	A43	$100 brown olive	1.50	1.00
215	A43	$200 blue green	3.00	1.00
216	A43	$250 violet	1.50	.50
217	A43	$400 black	1.50	1.00
218	A43	$800 claret	1.50	.50
219	A43	$800 indigo	1.50	.50
220	A43	$2000 red	2.00	.50
221	A43	$3200 dark brown	2.00	1.00
		Nos. 214-221 (8)	14.50	6.00

Economic progress.

Lenin — A44

$400, Lenin and Stalin Monument, Gorki, horiz. $2000, Lenin proclaiming Soviet power.

1954, June 30

222	A44	$400 deep green	2.00	1.50
223	A44	$800 dark brown	3.00	1.25
224	A44	$2000 deep carmine	3.50	1.00
		Nos. 222-224 (3)	8.50	3.75

30th anniversary of the death of Lenin.

Pottery Vessels, Neolithic Period, 2000 B.C. — A45

Archeological Treasures: No. 226, Stone clime, Shang Dynasty, c. 1200 B.C. No. 227, Kuo Chi Tsu-pai bronze basin, Middle Chou Dynasty, 816 B.C. No. 228, Lacquered box and wine cup, Warring States Period, 403-221 B.C.

1954, Aug. 25

225	A45	$800 brown	1.90	.40
226	A45	$800 indigo	1.90	.40
227	A45	$800 Prus bl	1.90	.40
228	A45	$800 dk car	1.90	.40
		Nos. 225-228 (4)	7.60	1.60

"Glorious Mother Country," 5th series.

Pipe Production, Anshan Steel Mill — A46

Design: $800, Rolling mill, Anshan.

1954, Oct. 1

229	A46	$400 Prus green	3.25	.60
230	A46	$800 vio brown	3.25	.60

Stalin Statue, by Tomsky — A47

Designs: $800, Stalin portrait. $2000, Stalin viewing hydroelectric plant.

1954, Oct. 15   Size: 21x45mm

231	A47	$400 black	1.50	.70

Size: 26x37mm

232	A47	$800 black brown	2.50	.70

Size: 42x26mm

233	A47	$2000 deep red	4.00	.95
		Nos. 231-233 (3)	8.00	2.35

First anniversary of the death of Stalin.

Exhibition Building, Peking — A48

1954, Nov. 7

234	A48	$800 brown, cream	35.00	7.00
a.		Size: 53½x24mm	45.00	11.00

Russian Economic and Cultural Exhibition, Peking. No. 234 measures 52½x24½mm.

Apprentices and Lathe — A49

Progress in Technology: $800, Heavy machinery and workers.

1954, Dec. 15

235	A49	$400 dk olive grn	3.25	.50
236	A49	$800 bright red	3.25	.60

Woman Worker Voting — A50

People Celebrating Opening of Congress — A51

1954, Dec. 30

237	A50	$400 deep claret	2.50	.75
238	A51	$800 bright red	3.75	1.00

First National Congress.

Flags, Worker and Woman Holding
Constitution — A52

1954, Dec. 30
239 A52 $400 brown, *buff*   2.50   .40
240 A52 $800 brt red, *yel*   4.00   .60

Adoption of Constitution.

High-tension
Pylon — A53

1955, Feb. 25
241 A53 $800 dk Prus bl   6.00   1.10

Development of electric power.

Factory
Health
Workers
and Red
Cross
A54

1955, June 25   Engr.; Cross Typo.
242 A54 8f dp grn & red   16.00 2.50

50th anniversary of Chinese Red Cross.

Stalin and
Mao in
Kremlin
A55

Soviet Specialist
and Chinese
Worker — A56

1955, July 25   Engr.
243 A55   8f brown red   17.50 1.00
244 A56 20f olive blk   25.00 2.75

5th anniv. of Sino-Soviet Friendship Treaty.

Chang Heng (78-
139),
Astronomer — A57

Portraits of Scientists: No. 246, Tsu Chung-
chih (429-500), mathematician. No. 247,
Chang Sui (683-727), astronomer. No. 248, Li
Shih-chen (1518-1593), physician and
pharmacologist.

1955, Aug. 25   Perf. 14
245 A57 8f sepia, *buff*   5.00   1.00
  a.   Min. sheet, sepia, *white*   60.00 18.00
246 A57 8f dp grn, *buff*   5.00   1.00
  a.   Min. sheet, deep green, *white* 60.00 18.00
247 A57 8f black, *buff*   5.00   1.00
  a.   Min. sheet, blk, *white*   60.00 18.00
248 A57 8f claret, *buff*   5.00   1.00
  a.   Min. sheet, claret, *white* 60.00 18.00
       Nos. 245-248 (4)   20.00   4.00

Miniature sheets contain one imperf. stamp.

Steel
Pouring
Ladle
A58

No. 250, High tension line (2). No. 251,
Mechanized coal mining (3). No. 252, Tank
cars and derricks (4). No. 253, Heavy machine
shop (5). No. 254, Soldier on guard (6). No.
255, Spinning machine (7). No. 256, Workers
discussing 5-year plan (8). No. 257, Combine
harvester (9). No. 258, Milk production (10).
No. 259, Dam (11). No. 260, Pottery industry
(12). No. 261, Truck (13). No. 262, Ship at
dock (14). No. 263, Geological survey (15).
No. 264, Higher education (16). No. 265, Family (17). No. 266, Workers' rest home (18).

1955-56   Litho.
Position-in-set number in ( )
249 A58 8f shown (1)   3.75   .75
250 A58 8f multicolored   3.75   .75
251 A58 8f multicolored   3.75   .75
252 A58 8f multicolored   3.75   .75
253 A58 8f multicolored   3.75   .75
254 A58 8f multicolored   3.75   .75
255 A58 8f multicolored   3.75   .75
256 A58 8f multicolored   3.75   .75
257 A58 8f multicolored   3.75   .75
258 A58 8f multicolored   3.75   .75
259 A58 8f multicolored   3.75   .75
260 A58 8f multi ('56)   3.75   .75
261 A58 8f multicolored   3.75   .75
262 A58 8f multicolored   3.75   .75
263 A58 8f multicolored   3.75   .75
264 A58 8f multicolored   3.75   .75
265 A58 8f multicolored   3.75   .75
266 A58 8f multi ('56)   3.75   .75
       Nos. 249-266 (18)   67.50 13.50

1st 5 Year Plan. Issued: Nos. 249-257, 10/1;
Nos. 258-259, 261-265, 12/15; Nos. 260, 266,
2/24/56.

Lenin — A59

1955, Dec. 15   Engr.   Perf. 14
267 A59   8f dk blue grn   21.00 1.50
268 A59 20f dk rose car   26.00 2.50

85th anniversary of the birth of Lenin.

Engels — A60

1955, Dec. 15
269 A60   8f deep orange   20.00 1.50
270 A60 20f brown   30.00 2.50

135th anniversary of the birth of Friedrich
Engels (1820-1895), German socialist.

Storming Lu Ting Bridge — A61

Crossing Great
Snow Mountains
A62

1955, Dec. 30
271 A61 8f dark red   19.00   1.00
272 A62 8f dark blue   27.50   3.25

Long March of Chinese Communist army,
20th anniversary.

Miner — A63   Gate of Heavenly
                     Peace — A64

Designs: 1f, Machinist. 2f, Airman. 2½f,
Nurse. 4f, Soldier. 8f, Steel worker. 10f, Scientist. 20f, Farm woman. 50f, Sailor.

1955-56   Litho.   Perf. 14
273 A63 ½f orange brn   1.75   .35
274 A63   1f purple   1.75   .35
275 A63   2f green   2.50   .35
276 A63 2½f blue ('56)   4.00   .35
277 A63   4f gray olive   2.50   .35
278 A63   8f red org (Peking
             printing)   4.00   .75
  a.   Perf. 12½ (Shanghai printing) 400.00 55.00
279 A63 10f claret ('56)   20.00   .40
280 A63 20f dp blue   7.25   .50
281 A63 50f gray   6.50   .60
       Nos. 273-281 (9)   50.25   4.00

                    Engr.
282 A64 $1 claret ('56)   2.50   .40
283 A64 $2 sepia ('55)   4.25   .40
284 A64 $5 indigo ('56)   8.00   .70
285 A64 $10 dp org ('56)   13.00   7.00
286 A64 $20 gray vio ('56) 16.00 20.00
       Nos. 282-286 (5)   43.75 28.50

Nos. 282-286 are the 7th Gate Issue. Used
values for Nos. 282-286 are for postally used
examples.

Trucks, Mountains, Highway
Map — A65

Suspension Bridge
over Tatu
River — A66

No. 289, 1st truck arriving in Lhasa, & the
Potala.

1956, Mar. 10   Engr.
287 A65 4f dp blue   3.00   .75
288 A66 8f dk brown   2.25   .50
289 A65 8f carmine   2.25   .50
       Nos. 287-289 (3)   7.50   1.75

Completion of Sikang-Tibet and Chinghai-
Tibet Highways.

Summer
Palace
and
Marble
Boat
A67

Famous Views of Imperial Peking: No. 291,
Peihai Park with Jade Belt Marble Bridge. No.
292, Gate of Heavenly Peace. No. 293, Temple of Heaven. No. 294, Great Throne Hall,
Forbidden City.

1956-57
290 A67 4f car rose (1)   9.00   1.00
291 A67 4f blue grn (2)   9.00   1.00
292 A67 8f red org (3) ('57) 9.00 1.00
293 A67 8f Prus blue (4)   9.00   1.00
294 A67 8f yellow brn (5)   9.00   1.00
       Nos. 290-294 (5)   45.00 5.00

Issued: No. 292, 2/20/57; others, 6/15/56.
No. 292 exists with sun rays in background.
Values: unused, $250,000; used, $80,000.

Salt
Making
A68

Designs: No. 296, Dwelling of the Eastern
Han period. No. 297, Duck hunting and harvesting. No. 298, Carriage crossing bridge.

1956, Oct. 1
295 A68 4f gray olive   2.00   .35
296 A68 4f slate blue   2.00   .35
297 A68 8f gray brown   2.00   .35
298 A68 8f sepia   2.00   .35
       Nos. 295-298 (4)   8.00   1.40

Murals, Tung Han Dynasty, 250 B.C.-220
A.D., found near Chengtu.

Ancient
Coins and
"Save"
A69

1956, Oct. 1
299 A69 4f yellow brown   8.00   1.25
300 A69 8f rose red   13.00 1.25

Promotion of saving.

Gate of Heavenly
Peace — A70

1956, Nov. 10
301 A70   4f dk green   11.00   .55
302 A70   8f brt red   15.00   .80
303 A70 16f dk carmine   25.00   .90
       Nos. 301-303 (3)   51.00 2.25

8th National Congress of the Communist
Party of China.

Sun Yat-sen — A71

1956, Nov. 12

304	A71	4f brown, *cream*	21.00	1.75
305	A71	8f dp blue, *cream*	30.00	3.00

90th anniversary of birth of Sun Yat-sen.

Weight Lifting — A72

1957, Mar. 20   Litho.   *Perf. 12½*

Hibiscus red and green; inscription brown

306	A72	4f Shot put (2)	3.00	.25
307	A72	4f shown (5)	3.00	.25
308	A72	8f Track (1)	3.00	.75
309	A72	8f Soccer (3)	3.00	.50
310	A72	8f Bicycling (4)	3.00	.75
		Nos. 306-310 (5)	15.00	2.50

First National Workers' Sports Meeting.

Truck Factory No. 1, Changchun — A73

China's truck industry: 8f, Trucks rolling off assembly line.

1957, May 1   Engr.   *Perf. 14*

311	A73	4f light brown	2.75	.55
312	A73	8f slate green	3.75	.60

Nanchang Uprising — A74

No. 314, Mao and Chu Teh at Chingkanshan. No. 315, Crossing Yellow River. No. 316, Liberation of Nanking, 4/23/49.

1957

313	A74	4f blk vio (1)	30.00	3.00
314	A74	4f slate grn (2)	30.00	2.50
315	A74	8f red brn (3)	30.00	2.50
316	A74	8f dp blue (4)	30.00	2.00
		Nos. 313-316 (4)	120.00	10.00

People's Liberation Army, 30th anniv. Issued: Nos. 313, 315, 8/10; No. 314, 8/30; No. 316, 12/30.

Congress Emblem — A75

1957, Sept. 30

317	A75	8f chocolate	8.00	1.00
318	A75	22f indigo	10.00	1.00

4th Intl. Trade Union Cong., Leipzig, 10/4-15.

Yangtze River Bridge A76

20f, Road leading to and over bridge.

1957, Oct. 1

319	A76	8f scarlet	2.00	.60
320	A76	20f slate blue	5.00	.60

Completion of Yangtze River Bridge at Wuhan.

Fireworks over Kremlin — A77

Designs: 8f, Hammer and sickle over globe and broken chain. 20f, Stylized dove and olive branch. 22f, Hands of three races holding book with Marx and Lenin. 32f, Star and pylon.

1957, Nov. 7

321	A77	4f brt red	4.00	.75
322	A77	8f chocolate	5.00	.75
323	A77	20f dp green	9.00	.75
324	A77	22f red brown	11.00	1.25
325	A77	32f dp blue	22.50	2.00
		Nos. 321-325 (5)	51.50	5.50

40th anniv. of Russian October Revolution.

Map of Yellow River Basin A78

No. 327, Sanmen Gorge dam & powerhouse. No. 328, Ocean liner on Yellow River. No. 329, Dam, irrigation canals & tree-bordered fields.

1957, Dec. 30

326	A78	4f deep orange (1)	16.00	1.75
327	A78	4f deep blue (2)	16.00	2.00
328	A78	8f deep lake (3)	27.50	2.25
329	A78	8f blue green (4)	27.50	2.50
		Nos. 326-329 (4)	87.00	8.50

Yellow River control plan.

Old Man and Young Drummer — A79

1957, Dec. 30   Litho.

330	A79	8f shown (1)	2.25	.30
331	A79	8f Plowman (2)	2.25	.30
332	A79	8f Woman planting tree (3)	2.25	.30
333	A79	8f Harvest (4)	2.25	.30
		Nos. 330-333 (4)	9.00	1.20

Agricultural cooperation.

Train on Bridge, Ship and Train — A80

Designs (Congratulatory Banner and): 4f, Crane, dove and flowers. 8f, Crane with hot ingots, cotton bolls and wheat.

1958, Jan. 30   Engr.

334	A80	4f emer, *cream*	2.25	1.50
335	A80	8f red, *cream*	2.25	1.50
336	A80	16f ultra, *cream*	2.25	1.50
		Nos. 334-336 (3)	6.75	4.50

Fulfillment of First Five-Year Plan.

Sungyu Pagoda, Honan — A81

Ancient Pagodas: No. 338, Chienhsun Pagoda, Yunnan. No. 339, Sakyamuni Pagoda, Shansi. No. 340, Flying Rainbow Pagoda, Shansi.

1958, Mar. 15   Engr.

337	A81	8f sepia (1)	4.75	.60
338	A81	8f Prus blue (2)	4.75	.40
339	A81	8f maroon (3)	4.75	.60
340	A81	8f dp green (4)	4.75	.80
		Nos. 337-340 (4)	19.00	2.40

Trilobite, Kaoli — A82

Designs: 8f, Lufeng dinosaur. 16f, Choukoutien sino-megaceros.

1958, Apr. 15

341	A82	4f blue	2.75	.40
342	A82	8f sepia	4.00	.40
343	A82	16f slate green	3.25	.40
		Nos. 341-343 (3)	10.00	1.20

Prehistoric animals of China.

Heroes Monument A83

1958, May 1

344	A83	8f scarlet	37.50	4.00
a.		Souvenir sheet, imperf.	*225.00*	90.00

Unveiling of People's Heroes Monument, Peking. No. 344a issued May 30.

Karl Marx — A84

Design: 22f, Marx Speaking to German Workers' Educational Association, London, painting by Zhukow.

1958, May 5

345	A84	8f chocolate	18.00	1.50
346	A84	22f dk green	22.50	3.00

Karl Marx (1818-83), 140th birth anniv.

Cogwheels and Factories — A85

1958, May 25

347	A85	4f brt grnsh bl	25.00	2.00
348	A85	8f red lilac	27.50	3.00

8th All-China Trade Union Cong., Peking.

Dove over Globe — A86

1958, June 1

349	A86	8f violet blue	7.00	1.50
350	A86	20f blue green	15.00	3.00

4th Congress of the Intl. Democratic Women's Federation, Vienna, June 1958.

Mother and Child — A87

Children's Day: No. 352, Watering sunflowers. No. 353, Playing hide-and-seek. No. 354, Sailing toy boat.

1958, June 1   Litho.

351	A87	8f green & multi (1)	22.50	2.00
352	A87	8f green & multi (2)	22.50	2.00
353	A87	8f green & multi (3)	22.50	2.00
a.		Red omitted	—	
354	A87	8f green & multi (4)	22.50	2.00
		Nos. 351-354 (4)	90.00	8.00

Kuan Han-ching A88

Designs (Operas): 4f, "Dream of Butterflies." 20f, "The Riverside Pavilion."

1958, June 20   Engr.

355	A88	4f indigo, cr	27.50	2.00
356	A88	8f brown, cr	32.50	4.00
357	A88	20f black, cr	47.50	2.00
a.		Souvenir sheet of 3, *ivory*	400.00	125.00
		Nos. 355-357 (3)	107.50	8.00

700th anniversary of publication of works of Kuan Han-ching (1210-1280), dramatist. No. 357a contains 3 imperf. stamps similar to Nos. 355-357. Size: 130x100mm. Issued June 28.

Planetarium A89

20f, Telescope and stars over Peking.

1958, June 25

358	A89	8f dk green	8.00	2.00
359	A89	20fr indigo	11.00	2.50

First Chinese planetarium, Peking.

Marx and
Engels — A90

8f, Cover of 1st edition of the Communist Manifesto.

1958, July 1
360 A90 4f dk red vio   28.00 3.00
361 A90 8f Prus blue   32.50 1.75

110th anniversary of publication of the Communist Manifesto.

Wild Goose and
Broadcasting
Tower — A91

1958, July 10
362 A91 4f ultra   16.00 3.50
363 A91 8f deep green   20.00 1.75

1st Conference of the Ministers of Posts and Telecommunications of Socialist Countries, Moscow, Dec. 3-17, 1957.

Peony and
Doves — A92

8f, Olive branch with ribbon & clouds. 22f, Atomic energy symbol over factories.

1958, July 20
364 A92 4f red   18.00 3.00
365 A92 8f green   14.00 2.50
366 A92 22f red brown   26.00 4.75
    Nos. 364-366 (3)   58.00 10.25

Congress for Disarmament and International Cooperation, Stockholm, July 17-22.

Bronze Weather
Vane — A93

Designs: No. 368, Weather balloon. No. 369, Typhoon tower and weather map of Asia.

1958, Aug. 25
367 A93 8f yel bis & blk (1)   2.00 .40
368 A93 8f blue & blk (2)   2.00 .40
369 A93 8f brt grn & blk (3)   2.00 .40
    Nos. 367-369 (3)   6.00 1.20

Meteorological services in ancient and modern China.

"5" Encircling IUS
Emblem — A94

1958, Sept. 4
370 A94 8f rose lilac   22.50 2.00
371 A94 22f dp blue grn   35.00 3.50

Intl. Union of Students, 5th Cong., Peking, 9/4-13.
Nos. 370-371 exist with incorrect inscription. Values: No. 370, unused $15,000; used $3,000; No. 370, unused $160,000; used $120,000.

Telegraph
Building,
Peking
A95

1958, Sept. 29
372 A95 4f greenish black   5.25 .75
373 A95 8f rose red   5.25 .75

Opening of Telegraph Building, Peking.

Exhibition
Emblem and
Exhortation
A96

Designs: No. 375, Dragon over clouds signifying "aiming high." No. 376, Flying horses, signifying "great leap forward" in production.

1958, Oct. 1
374 A96 8f slate grn (1)   18.00 1.25
375 A96 8f rose car (2)   18.00 1.25
376 A96 8f red brown (3)   18.00 1.75
    Nos. 374-376 (3)   54.00 4.25

National Exhibition of Industry and Communications, Peking.

Worker and
Excavator
A97

Design: 8f, Completed dam and pylon.

1958, Oct. 25
377 A97 4f dark brown   3.25 .50
378 A97 8f deep Prussian blue   5.25 .50

13 Ming Tombs Reservoir completion.

Sputnik 3 in
Orbit — A98

Designs: 4f, Sputnik over armillary sphere. 10f, Trajectories of 3 Sputniks over earth.

1958, Oct. 30
379 A98 4f scarlet   6.00 .75
380 A98 8f dp violet bl   6.00 1.00
381 A98 10f dp green   8.00 2.00
    Nos. 379-381 (3)   20.00 3.75

Anniversary of first earth satellite launched by the USSR.

Chinese
and North
Korean
Soldiers
A99

Designs: No. 383, Chinese soldier embracing Korean woman. No. 384, Chinese girl presenting flowers to returning soldier.

1958, Nov. 20
382 A99 8f brt purple (1)   6.00 1.00
383 A99 8f chestnut (2)   6.00 .60
384 A99 8f rose car (3)   6.00 .60
    Nos. 382-384 (3)   18.00 2.20

Return of the Chinese Volunteers from Korea.

Forest and
Mountains
A100

Afforestation: No. 386, Mounted forest patrol. No. 387, Mechanized lumbering, horiz. No. 388, Tree-planting: "Turning the Country Green," horiz.

1958, Dec. 15
385 A100 8f dp blue grn (1)   4.00 .85
386 A100 8f slate grn (2)   4.00 .85
387 A100 8f dk purple (3)   4.00 .85
388 A100 8f indigo (4)   4.00 .85
    Nos. 385-388 (4)   16.00 3.40

Peony — A101

Designs: 3f, Lotus. 5f, Chrysanthemums.

1958, Sept. 25   **Litho.**
389 A101 1½f lilac rose   3.50 .75
390 A101 3f blue grn   11.00 2.25
391 A101 5f dp orange   2.00 .45
    Nos. 389-391 (3)   16.50 3.45

Atomic
Reactor
A102

1958, Dec. 30   **Engr.**
392 A102 8f shown   15.00 1.75
393 A102 20f Cyclotron   22.50 2.50

Inauguration of China's first atomic reactor and cyclotron, Peking.

Children Launching
Model
Planes — A103

8f, Gliders over trees. 10f, Parachutists descending. 20f, Small monoplanes in mid-air.

1958, Dec. 30
394 A103 4f carmine   1.50 .50
395 A103 8f dp slate grn   2.00 .50
396 A103 10f dk brown   2.75 .50
397 A103 20f Prus blue   3.50 .50
    Nos. 394-397 (4)   9.75 2.00

Sports-aviation publicity.

Camel Carrying
Load — A104

Designs: No. 399, Pomegranates. No. 400, Rooster. No. 401, Theatrical figure.

1959, Jan. 1
398 A104 8f vio & blk (1)   17.50 .90
399 A104 8f dp bl grn & blk (2)   17.50 .90
400 A104 8f red & blk (3)   17.50 .90
401 A104 8f dp bl & blk (4)   17.50 .90
    Nos. 398-401 (4)   70.00 3.60

Paper cut-outs (folk art).

Red Flag, Mao
and
Workers — A105

Designs: 8f, Traditional and modern blast furnaces. 10f, Steel works and workers.

1959
402 A105 4f brt red   27.50 1.50
403 A105 8f lake   27.50 1.75
404 A105 10f deep red   32.50 2.00
    Nos. 402-404 (3)   87.50 5.25

"Great Leap Forward" in steel production. Issue dates: 4f, 8f, Feb. 19; 10f, May 25.

Women Workers
and Atomic
Model — A106

Design: 22f, Chinese and Soviet women holding banners dated "3.8."

1959, Mar. 8
405 A106 8f emerald, cr   2.75 .50
406 A106 22f magenta, cr   3.75 .50

International Women's Day.

Natural History
Museum
A107

1959, Apr. 1
407 A107 4f greenish blue   2.75 .75
408 A107 8f olive brown   2.75 .75

Opening of Museum of Natural History, Peking.

Wheat — A108

Designs on Chinese Flag: No. 410, Rice. No. 411, Cotton bolls. No. 412, Soybeans, rapeseed and peanuts.

1959, Apr. 25
409 A108 8f red (1)   2.50 .50
410 A108 8f red (2)   2.50 .50
411 A108 8f red (3)   2.50 .50
412 A108 8f red (4)   2.50 .50
    a.   Block of 4, #409-412   45.00 8.00

Successful harvest, 1958.

A109

Designs: 4f, Marx, Lenin and workers. 8f, Black, yellow and white fists holding banner. 22f, Steel workers parading with banners dated "5.1."

1959, May 1

413	A109	4f ultra	5.00	1.50
414	A109	8f red	9.00	1.25
415	A109	22f emerald	18.00	2.00
		Nos. 413-415 (3)	32.00	4.75

International Labor Day.

A110

8f, Peking airport. 10f, Plane loading on runway.

1959, June 20

416	A110	8f lilac & blk	22.50	2.50
417	A110	10f ol gray & blk	30.00	2.00

Opening of new Peking Airport.

Students with Marx-Lenin Banners A111

Design: 8f, Workers with banners of Mao.

1959, July 1   Photo.   Perf. 11x11½

418	A111	4f gray, red & dk brn	27.50	11.00
419	A111	8f bis, red & dk brn	50.00	7.50

40th anniv. of the May 4th students' uprising.

Frederick Joliot-Curie — A112

22f, Three races, dove and olive branch.

1959, July 25   Engr.   Perf. 11½

420	A112	8f violet brn	9.00	2.00
421	A112	22f dk violet	18.00	3.00

10th anniv. of the World Peace Movement.

Stamp Printing Plant, Peking A113

1959, Aug. 15   Perf. 11x11½

422	A113	8f dp blue grn	14.00	1.75

Sino-Czechoslovak cooperation in stamp production.

Table Tennis — A114

1959, Aug. 30   Litho.   Perf. 14

423	A114	4f black & blue	7.50	.75
424	A114	8f black & red	6.50	.75

25th World Table Tennis Championships, Dortmund, German Democratic Republic.

Soviet Space Rocket — A115

1959, Sept. 10   Photo.   Perf. 11½

425	A115	8f Prus bl, red & blk	22.00	3.00

Launching of first Russian space rocket, Jan. 2, 1959.

Backyard Steel Production — A116

Designs: No. 426, Sun rising over "industry and agriculture." No. 428, Farming. No. 429, Trade. No. 430, Education. No. 431, Militia. No. 432, Communal dining. No. 433, Nursery. No. 434, Care for the aged. No. 435, Health services. No. 436, Flutist; culture and sports. No. 437, Flower symbolizing unity of industry, agriculture, trade, education and armed forces.

Position-in-set number in ( ).

1959, Sept. 25   Engr.

426	A116	8f rose (1)	4.75	.65
427	A116	8f violet brn (2)	4.75	.65
428	A116	8f dp orange (3)	4.75	.65
429	A116	8f slate grn (4)	4.75	.65
430	A116	8f dp blue (5)	4.75	.65
431	A116	8f olive (6)	4.75	.65
432	A116	8f indigo (7)	4.75	.65
433	A116	8f lilac rose (8)	4.75	.65
434	A116	8f gray blk (9)	4.75	.65
435	A116	8f emerald (10)	4.75	.65
436	A116	8f dk violet (11)	4.75	.65
437	A116	8f red (12)	4.75	.65
		Nos. 426-437 (12)	57.00	7.80

First anniversary of Peoples' Communes.

Mao and Gate of Heavenly Peace — A117

Designs: No. 439, Marx, Lenin and Kremlin. 22f, Dove over globe.

Perf. 11½ x 11

1959, Sept. 28   Photo.

With Gum

438	A117	8f lt brown & red	55.00	3.50
439	A117	8f dull blue & red	25.00	2.00
440	A117	22f blue grn & red	25.00	5.00
		Nos. 438-440 (3)	105.00	10.50
		Set, never hinged	170.00	

National Emblem A118

1959, Oct. 1   Litho.   Perf. 14

441	A118	4f pale grn, red & gold	10.00	2.00
442	A118	8f gray, red & gold	12.00	2.00
443	A118	10f lt blue, red & gold	18.50	3.50
444	A118	20f pale brn, red & gold	30.00	4.50
		Nos. 441-444 (4)	70.50	12.00

Blast Furnaces — A119

No. 446, Large coal mine. No. 447, Planer. Wuhan heavy machinery plant. No. 448, Wuhan Yangtze River Bridge. No. 449, Combine harvester. No. 450, Hsinankiang hydroelectric station. No. 451, Spinning machine. No. 452, Kirin chemical fertilizer plant.

Engraved and Photogravure

1959, Oct. 1   Perf. 11½ x 11

With Gum

445	A119	8f brown & rose red (1)	4.00	1.25
446	A119	8f brown & gray (2)	4.00	1.25
447	A119	8f brown & yel brn (3)	4.00	1.25
448	A119	8f brown & stl bl (4)	4.00	1.25
449	A119	8f brown & org (5)	4.00	1.25
450	A119	8f brown & ol (6)	4.00	1.25
451	A119	8f brown & bl grn (7)	4.00	1.25
452	A119	8f brown & vio (8)	4.00	1.25
		Nos. 445-452 (8)	32.00	10.00
		Set, never hinged	62.50	

Celebration at Gate of Heavenly Peace — A120

Designs: 10f, Workers and factory, vert. 20f, People rejoicing, vert.

1959, Oct. 1   Litho.   Perf. 14

453	A120	8f cream & multi	9.00	3.00
454	A120	10f cream & multi	17.50	3.25
455	A120	20f cream & multi	20.00	5.00
		Nos. 453-455 (3)	46.50	11.25

Mao Proclaiming Republic — A121

1959, Oct. 1   Engr.

456	A121	20f deep carmine	240.00	65.00

Nos. 438-456 commemorate 10th anniversary of the Proclamation of the People's Republic of China.

A122

Designs: No. 457, Pioneers' emblem. No. 458, Pioneer Bugler. No. 459, Schoolgirl. No. 460, Girl using rain gauge. No. 461, Boy planting tree. No. 462, Girl figure skater.

1959, Nov. 10   Photo.   Perf. 11½

457	A122	4f red yel & blk (1)	11.00	.90
458	A122	4f Prus bl & red (2)	11.00	.90
459	A122	8f brn & red (3)	11.00	.90
460	A122	8f dk bl & red (4)	11.00	.90
461	A122	8f red & grn (5)	11.00	.90
462	A122	8f mag & red (6)	11.00	.90
		Nos. 457-462 (6)	66.00	5.40

10th anniversary of the Young Pioneers. Black inscription on No. 457 engraved.

A123

4f, Exhibition emblem, communications symbols. 8f, Exhibition emblem & chimneys.

1959, Dec. 1   Engr.

463	A123	4f dark blue	2.50	.50
464	A123	8f red	3.00	.50

Exhibition of Industry and Communications, Peking.

Palace of Nationalities A124

Engraved, Frame Lithographed

1959, Dec. 10   Perf. 14

465	A124	4f red & blk	12.00	1.00
466	A124	8f brt grn & blk	16.00	1.50

Inauguration of the Cultural Palace of Nationalities, Peking.

Athletes' Monument and Track — A125

Sports: No. 468, Parachuting. No. 469, Marksmanship. No. 470, Diving. No. 471, Table tennis. No. 472, Weight lifting. No. 473, High jump. No. 474, Rowing. No. 475, Track. No. 476, Basketball. No. 477, Traditional Chinese fencing. No. 478, Motorcycling. No. 479, Gymnastics. No. 480, Bicycling. No. 481, Horsemanship. No. 482, Soccer.

1959, Dec. 28   Litho.

467	A125	8f bis, blk & gray (1)	7.00	.85
468	A125	8f dl bl, blk & gray (2)	7.00	.85
469	A125	8f red brn & blk (3)	7.00	.85
470	A125	8f grn, blk & brn (4)	7.00	.85
471	A125	8f brt grn, blk, brn & gray (5)	7.00	.85
472	A125	8f gray, blk & brn (6)	7.00	.85
473	A125	8f dl bl, blk & brn (7)	7.00	.85
474	A125	8f Prus grn, blk & brn (8)	7.00	.85
475	A125	8f org, blk & brn (9)	7.00	.85
476	A125	8f dl vio, blk & brn (10)	7.00	.85
477	A125	8f lt ol, blk & brn (11)	7.00	.85
478	A125	8f bl, blk & gray (12)	7.00	.85
479	A125	8f gray bl, blk, grn, & bl (13)	7.00	.85
480	A125	8f gray, blk, brn, & vio (14)	7.00	.85
481	A125	8f red org, blk, brn, & gray (15)	7.00	.85
482	A125	8f lt gray, blk, brn, & red (16)	7.00	.85
		Nos. 467-482 (16)	112.00	13.60

First National Sports Meeting, Peking.

Wheat and Main Pavilion A126

Designs (Pavilion and): 8f, Meteorological symbols. 10f, Domestic animals. 20f, Fish.

1960, Jan. 20 Engr. & Litho.
Cream Background

483	A126	4f black & org	1.75	.50
484	A126	8f black & dull bl	1.75	.50
485	A126	10f black & org brn	1.75	.50
486	A126	20f black & grnsh bl	1.75	.50
		Nos. 483-486 (4)	7.00	2.00

Opening of the National Agricultural Exhibition Halls, Peking.

With Gum
From No. 487 onward all stamps were issued with gum except as noted.

> Catalogue values for unused stamps in this section, from this point to the end of the section, are for Never Hinged items.

Conference Hall, Tsunyi A127

Designs: 8f, Mao addressing conference. 10f, Crossing Chinsha River.

Engraved (4f, 10f); Photogravure (8f)

1960, Jan. 25			Perf. 11x11½	
487	A127	4f violet & blue	50.00	9.00
488	A127	8f red & multi	70.00	5.50
489	A127	10f slate green	110.00	11.00
		Nos. 487-489 (3)	230.00	25.50

25th anniversary of the Communist Party Conference at Tsunyl.

Clara Zetkin (1857-1933) A128

8f, Mother, child and dove. 10f, Woman tractor driver. 22f, Women of three races.

1960, Mar. 8 Photo. Perf. 11½x11

490	A128	4f black & multi	6.00	.50
491	A128	8f black & multi	10.00	.75
492	A128	10f black & multi	11.00	1.00
493	A128	22f black & multi	14.00	2.00
		Nos. 490-493 (4)	41.00	4.25

50th anniv. of International Women's Day.

Chinese and Russian Workers — A129

Designs: 8f, Chinese and Russian flags. 10f, Chinese and Russian soldiers.

1960, Mar. 10

494	A129	4f dk brown	27.50	5.00
495	A129	8f red, yel & blk	37.50	2.00
496	A129	10f dp brown	47.50	8.00
		Nos. 494-496 (3)	112.50	15.00

10th anniv. of Sino-Soviet Treaty of Friendship. Black inscription engraved on No. 495.

Flags of Hungary and China A130

Design: 8f, Parliament Building, Budapest.

1960, Apr. 4 Perf. 11 x 11½

497	A130	8f yel, blk, red & grn	52.50	7.00
498	A130	8f blue, red & blk	57.50	7.00

15th anniv. of the liberation of Hungary.

Lenin Speaking — A131

Designs: 8f, Portrait of Lenin. 20f, Lenin talking with Smolny Palace guard.

Engraved (4f, 20f); Engraved and Photogravure (8f)

1960, Apr. 22			Perf. 11½ x 11	
499	A131	4f violet brn	26.00	1.50
500	A131	8f org red & blk	32.50	2.75
501	A131	20f dk brown	42.50	3.50
		Nos. 499-501 (3)	101.00	7.75

90th anniversary of the birth of Lenin.

Lunik 2, Moon and Russian Arms — A132

Design: 10f, Lunik 3 over moon.

1960, Apr. 30 Engr. Perf. 11½

502	A132	8f red	10.00	1.75
503	A132	10f green	14.00	1.75

Russian space flights.

Pioneers and Flags of Czechoslovakia and China — A133

View of Prague with Charles Bridge A134

Perf. 11½x11; 11x11½

1960, May 9			Photo.	
504	A133	8f yellow & multi	40.00	6.00
505	A134	8f deep green	40.00	6.00

Liberation of Czechoslovakia, 15th anniv.

Nostril Bouquet A135

Various goldfish: No. 507, Black-back dragon eye (2). No. 508, Bubble eye (3). No. 509, Red tiger head (4). No. 510, Pearl scale (5). No. 511, Blue dragon eye (6). No. 512, Skyward eye (7). No. 513, Red cap (8). No. 514, Purple cap (9). No. 515, Red head (10). No. 516, Red and white dragon eye (11). No. 517, Red dragon eye (12).

1960, June 1 Perf. 11x11½

506	A135	4f shown (1)	42.50	5.00
507	A135	4f multi	42.50	5.00
508	A135	4f multi	42.50	5.00

509	A135	4f multi	42.50	5.00
510	A135	8f multi	95.00	5.00
511	A135	8f multi	60.00	5.00
512	A135	8f multi	60.00	5.00
513	A135	8f multi	30.00	7.50
514	A135	8f multi	30.00	7.50
515	A135	8f multi	30.00	7.50
516	A135	8f multi	70.00	7.50
517	A135	8f multi	40.00	12.00
		Nos. 506-517 (12)	585.00	77.00

Unused values for Nos. 506-517 are for examples with untoned gum.

Sow with Litter A136

No. 519, Pig being inoculated. No. 520, Pigs. No. 521, Pig and mechanized feeding. No. 522, Pig and bales.

1960, June 15

518	A136	8f red & blk (1)	47.50	8.50
519	A136	8f dp grn & blk (2)	47.50	8.50
520	A136	8f lil rose & blk (3)	47.50	8.50
521	A136	8f lt yel grn & blk (4)	47.50	8.50
522	A136	8f org & blk (5)	47.50	8.50
		Nos. 518-522 (5)	237.50	42.50

Flag Inscribed "Serving the Workers" — A137

Design: 8f, Inscribed stone seal.

1960, July 30 Photo. Perf. 11½x11

523	A137	4f lt grn, red, pink & brn	45.00	4.00

Photogravure & Engraved

524	A137	8f pale bl, red & bis	57.50	6.00

3rd Natl. Cong. for Literature and Arts, Peking.

Flowers, Flags of North Korea and China — A138

Design: 8f, Flying horse of Korea.

1960, Aug. 15 Photo.

525	A138	8f red & multi	47.50	7.00
526	A138	8f ultra, red & indigo	60.00	10.00

15th anniversary of the liberation of Korea.

Railroad Station, Peking — A139

Design: 10f, Train arriving at station.

1960, Aug. 30 Perf. 11½

527	A139	8f blue, cream & brn	45.00	14.00
528	A139	10f bluish grn, cr & ind	65.00	15.00

Opening of new Peking Railroad Station.

Girls and Flags of North Viet Nam and China A140

Lake of the Returning Sword, Hanoi — A141

1960, Sept. 2 Perf. 11x11½, 11½x11

529	A140	8f red & multi	18.00	3.00
530	A141	8f red, gray grn & gray	18.00	3.00

15th anniversary of the Democratic Republic of North Viet Nam.

Worker and Fresh-air Installation — A142

Designs: No. 532, Exterminator. No. 533, Window cleaning. No. 534, Medical examination of child. No. 535, Physical exercise.

1960, Sept. 10 Perf. 11½

531	A142	8f black & orange (1)	11.00	1.00
532	A142	8f indigo & slate (2)	11.00	1.00
533	A142	8f brown & blue (3)	11.00	1.00
534	A142	8f maroon & ocher (4)	11.00	1.00
535	A142	8f indigo & brt grn (5)	11.00	1.00
		Nos. 531-535 (5)	55.00	5.00

National health campaign.

Great Hall of the People — A143

Design: 10f, Inside view.

1960, Oct. 1

536	A143	8f yellow & multi	45.00	15.00
537	A143	10f brown & multi	65.00	17.00

Completion of the Great Hall of the People, Peking.

Dr. Norman Bethune — A144

No. 539, Dr. Bethune operating on a soldier.

Photo. (No. 538); Engr. (No. 539)

1960, Nov. 20			Perf. 11½x11	
538	A144	8f red & multi	22.50	3.00
539	A144	8f sepia	22.50	2.00

Dr. Norman Bethune (1890-1939), Canadian surgeon with 8th Route Army.

Engels Addressing Congress at The Hague — A145

1960, Nov. 28   **Engr.**
540 A145 8f shown   45.00 2.75

Photo.
541 A145 10f Portrait of Engels   50.00 7.50

140th anniversary of the birth of Friedrich Engels (1820-1895), German Socialist.

"Hwang Shi Ba" — A146

1960-61   **Photo.**
Various Chrysanthemums in Natural Colors

542 A146 4f bl gray (1)	22.50	2.50
543 A146 4f pink (2)	22.50	2.50
544 A146 8f dk gray (3)	25.00	2.50
545 A146 8f dp blue (4)	25.00	2.50
546 A146 8f green (5)	25.00	2.50
547 A146 8f magenta (6)	25.00	2.50
548 A146 8f olive (7)	25.00	2.50
549 A146 8f grnsh bl (8)	25.00	2.50
550 A146 10f gray (9)	30.00	3.50
551 A146 10f choc (10)	30.00	3.50
552 A146 20f dp blue (11)	50.00	4.00
553 A146 20f brt red (12)	50.00	4.00
554 A146 22f olive bis (13)	100.00	9.00
555 A146 22f carmine (14)	100.00	9.00
556 A146 30f grnsh gray (15)	100.00	11.00
557 A146 30f brt pink (16)	70.00	7.00
558 A146 35f dp green (17)	70.00	10.00
559 A146 52f brt lilac rose (18)	70.00	20.00
Nos. 542-559 (18)	865.00	101.00

Issued: Nos. 548-550, 557-559, 12/10/60; Nos. 545-547, 554-556, 1/18/61; Nos. 542-544, 2/24/61.

Freighter — A147

1960, Dec. 15   **Perf. 11½**
Without Gum
560 A147 8f deep blue   11.50 2.00

1st 10,000-ton Chinese-built freighter, launching.

Pantheon, Paris — A148

Design: 8f, Proclamation of the Commune.

Engraved and Photogravure
1961, Mar. 18   **Perf. 11½x11**
561 A148 8f gray blk & red   37.50 5.75
562 A148 8f brown & red   37.50 6.75

90th anniversary of the Paris Commune.

Championship Symbol and Jasmine — A149

Designs: 10f, Table tennis racket and ball; Temple of Heaven. 20f, Table tennis match. 22f, Peking workers' gymnasium.

1961, Apr. 5   **Photo.**   **Perf. 11**
563 A149 8f multicolored	7.50	.75
564 A149 10f multicolored	8.50	1.00
565 A149 20f multicolored	9.50	1.50
566 A149 22f multicolored	11.00	2.00
a. Souv. sheet, #563-566	750.00	600.00
Nos. 563-566 (4)	36.50	5.25

26th World Table Tennis Championships, Peking.

Jeme Tien-yow — A150

Design: 10f, Train and tunnel, Peking-Changchow Railroad.

1961, June 20   **Perf. 11½x11**
567 A150 8f ol grn & blk   7.00 1.00
568 A150 10f org brn & brn   22.50 3.50

Centenary of the birth of Jeme Tien-yow, railroad construction engineer.

Congress Building, Shanghai — A151

Designs: 8f, August 1st Building, Nanchang. 10f, Provisional Central Government Office, Juikin. 20f, Pagoda Hill, Yenan. 30f, Gate of Heavenly Peace, Peking.

1961, July 1   **Perf. 11½**
569 A151 4f gold, red & cl	47.50	5.00
570 A151 8f gold, red & bl grn	47.50	3.00
571 A151 10f gold, red & yel brn	57.50	5.00
572 A151 20f gold, red & ul-tra	85.00	7.00
573 A151 30f gold, red & org red	90.00	17.50
Nos. 569-573 (5)	327.50	37.50

40th anniv. of the Chinese Communist Party.

August 1 Building, Nanchang — A152

3f, 4f, 5f, Trees & Sha Cho Pa Building, Juikin. 8f, 10f, 20f, Pagoda Hill, Yenan. 22f, 30f, 50f, Gate of Heavenly Peace, Peking.

1961-62   **Perf. 11**
Engr.
Without Gum
Size: 24x16mm

574 A152 1f vio blue	16.00	.75
575 A152 1½f maroon	37.50	2.75
576 A152 2f indigo	19.00	1.25
577 A152 3f dull vio	55.00	3.50
578 A152 4f green	4.25	.70
579 A152 5f gray	4.25	.45
580 A152 8f sepia	4.25	.40
581 A152 10f brt lil rose	11.00	.40
582 A152 20f grnsh bl	3.25	.40
583 A152 22f brown	2.00	.40
584 A152 30f blue	3.25	.40
585 A152 50f vermilion	3.25	.40
Nos. 574-585 (12)	163.00	11.80

Issued: 1f, 1½f, 5f, 7/20/62; others 7/20/61.
See Nos. 647-654, 1059-1064.

Flowers, Flags of Mongolia and China A153

Design: 10f, Parliament, Ulan Bator, and statue of Sukhe Bator.

1961, July 11   **Photo.**   **Perf. 11x11½**
586 A153 8f crim, ultra & yel   120.00 15.00
587 A153 10f orange, blk & yel   160.00 25.00

40th anniv. of the Mongolian People's Republic.

Military Museum — A154

Photo. & Engr.
1961, Aug. 1   **Perf. 11½**
588 A154 8f gray bl, brn & grn   80.00 3.00
   a. Inscribed series "(229)" (error)   150.00 14.00
589 A154 10f gray, blk & grn   85.00 3.50

Opening of the People's Revolutionary Military Museum.

Uprising at Wuchang A155

Sun Yat-sen — A156

Perf. 11x11½, 11½x11
1961, Oct. 10   **Photo.**
590 A155 8f gray & blk   50.00 4.00
591 A156 10f tan & black   70.00 4.50

50th anniversary of the 1911 Revolution.

Donkey — A157

Designs: 8f, 10f, 20f, 22f, Horses; 30f, 50f, Camels. Ceramic statuettes from Tang Dynasty (618-906) graves.

1961, Nov. 10   **Perf. 11½x11**
Statuettes in Original Colors

592 A157 4f dull blue	18.00	2.25
593 A157 8f gray green	18.00	2.25
594 A157 8f dp purple	18.00	2.25
595 A157 10f dp blue	18.00	2.25
596 A157 20f olive	18.00	2.25
597 A157 22f blue grn	25.00	3.50
598 A157 30f red brown	40.00	5.00
599 A157 50f slate	40.00	5.00
Nos. 592-599 (8)	195.00	24.75

Rejoicing Tibetans — A158

Designs: 8f, Woman sower. 10f, Celebration of bumper crop. 20f, People's representatives. 30f, Tibetan children.

1961, Nov. 25
600 A158 4f brn & ocher	37.50	3.00
601 A158 8f brn & lt bl grn	30.00	3.00
602 A158 10f brn & yel	47.50	3.00
603 A158 20f brn & rose	100.00	6.00
604 A158 30f brn & bluish gray	125.00	9.00
Nos. 600-604 (5)	340.00	24.00

Rebirth of the Tibetan people.

Lu Hsun — A159

1962, Feb. 26
605 A159 8f red brown & blk   5.00 1.50

80th anniv. of the birth of Lu Hsun, writer.

An Chi Bridge, Chao Hsien — A160

Bridges of Ancient China: 8f, Pao Tai, Soochow. 10f, Chu Pu, Kwan Hsien. 20f, Chen Yang, San Kiang.

1962, May 15   **Perf. 11**
606 A160 4f dk gray blue	5.00	.80
607 A160 8f dp green	5.00	.80
608 A160 10f brown	20.00	2.50
609 A160 20f grnsh blue	10.00	2.00
Nos. 606-609 (4)	40.00	6.10

Tu Fu — A161

4f, Tu Fu memorial pavilion, Chengtu.

1962, May 25   **Perf. 11½x11**
610 A161 4f ol bis & blk   60.00 2.25
611 A161 8f grnsh bl & blk   70.00 4.00

Poet Tu Fu, 1,250th anniversary of birth.

Cranes and Bamboo — A162

10f, Two cranes in flight. 20f, Crane on rock.

1962, June 10

612	A162	8f tan & multi	20.00	2.00
613	A162	10f blue & multi	37.50	4.00
614	A162	20f bister & multi	50.00	5.50
		Nos. 612-614 (3)	107.50	11.50

"The Sacred Crane," from paintings by Chen Chi-fo.

Cuban Soldier and Flag A163

Designs: 10f, Sugar cane worker. 22f, Militiaman and woman.

1962, July 10　　　　**Perf. 11x11½**

615	A163	8f car, rose & blk	35.00	5.00
616	A163	10f green & blk	60.00	8.00
617	A163	22f ultra & blk	140.00	35.00
		Nos. 615-617 (3)	235.00	48.00

Support of Cuba.

Torch and Map of Algeria — A164

Design: 22f, Algerian soldiers and flag.

1962, July 10　　　　**Perf. 11½x11**

618	A164	8f dp brown & red org	3.00	1.25
619	A164	22f ocher & dp brn	8.00	1.75

Support of Algeria.

Mei Lan-fang — A165

Designs (Mei Lan-fang in Women's Roles): No. 621, Beating drum. No. 622, With fan. 10f, Lady Yu with swords. 20f, With bag. 22f, Heavenly Maiden, horiz. 30f, With spinning wheel, horiz. 50f, Kneeling, horiz. $3, Scene from opera "Drunken Beauty."

1962　　**Perf. 11½x11, 11x11½**

620	A165	4f tan & multi	200.00	40.00
621	A165	8f tan & multi	140.00	14.00
622	A165	8f gray & multi	140.00	14.00
623	A165	10f gray & multi	200.00	14.00
624	A165	20f lt grn & multi	200.00	27.50
625	A165	22f cream & multi	275.00	42.50
626	A165	30f lt blue & multi	275.00	50.00
627	A165	50f buff & multi	275.00	50.00
		Nos. 620-627 (8)	1,705.	252.00

Souvenir Sheet
Perf. 11

628	A165	$3 brown & multi	15,000.	5,000.

Stage art of Mei Lan-fang, actor.
Issued: 4f, 8f, 10f, 8/8; $3, 9/15; others 9/1.
Nos. 620-627 exist imperf. Value, set unused $6,500, used $2,000.
No. 628 contains one 48x58mm stamp and almost always has some faults. Values above are for fault-free examples. Value for No. 628 with small faults, unused $8,500. Excellent forgeries exist.

Flower Drum Dance, Han — A166

Folk Dances: 8f, Ordos, Mongolia. 10f, Catching shrimp, Chuang. 20f, Friend, Yi. 30f, Fiddle dance, Tibet. 50f, Tambourine dance, Uighur.
Cumulative numbers 246-251 at lower right.

1962, Oct. 15　Litho.　Perf. 12½
Without Gum

629	A166	4f cream & multi	2.75	.60
630	A166	8f cream & multi	2.75	.60
631	A166	10f cream & multi	2.75	.60
632	A166	20f cream & multi	3.50	1.00
633	A166	30f cream & multi	5.50	1.50
634	A166	50f cream & multi	7.00	2.00
		Nos. 629-634 (6)	24.25	6.30

See Nos. 696-707.

Soldiers Storming Winter Palace — A167

Design: 8f, Lenin leading soldiers, vert.

1962, Nov. 7　Photo.　Perf. 11½

635	A167	8f black & red	75.00	6.00
636	A167	20f slate grn & red	160.00	13.00

45th anniversary of the Russian Revolution.

Monument and Map of Albania — A168

Design: 10f, Albanian flag and Girl Pioneer.

1962, Nov. 28　　　Perf. 11½x11

637	A168	8f Prus blue & sepia	4.00	1.25
638	A168	10f red, yel, & blk	5.50	1.25

50th anniversary of Albanian independence.

Tsai Lun, Inventor of Papermaking A169

Designs: No. 640, Paper making. No. 641, Sun Szu-miao, physician. No. 642, Writing medical treatise. No. 643, Shen Ko, geologist. No. 644, Making field notes. No. 645, Kuo Shou-chin, astronomer. No. 646, Astronomical instrument.
Cumulative numbers 297-304 at lower right.

1962, Dec. 1　　　　Perf. 11½x11

639	A169	4f multicolored	9.00	1.00
640	A169	4f multicolored	9.00	1.00
641	A169	8f multicolored	11.00	1.25
642	A169	8f multicolored	11.00	1.25
643	A169	10f multicolored	11.00	3.50
644	A169	10f multicolored	11.00	3.50
645	A169	20f multicolored	21.00	6.00
646	A169	20f multicolored	21.00	6.00
		Nos. 639-646 (8)	104.00	23.50

Scientists of ancient China.

No. 639 exists with an extra character in the inscription. Value, unused $12,500, used $2,500.

Building Type of 1961

Designs: 1f, 2f, Building, Nanchang. 3f, 4f, Trees and Sha Cho Pa Building. 8f, 10f, 20f, Pagoda Hill, Yenan. 30f, Gate of Heavenly Peace, Peking.

1962, Jan.　Litho.　Rough Perf. 12½
Size: 21x16mm
Without Gum

647	A152	1f ultra	.80	.25
648	A152	2f greenish gray	.80	.25
649	A152	3f violet gray	.80	.25
650	A152	4f green	.80	.25
651	A152	8f dk olive, perf. 14	1.75	.25
b.		Perf. 11x11½	9.00	
652	A152	10f brt rose lilac	3.75	.30
653	A152	20f slate blue	3.75	.65
654	A152	30f dull blue	4.25	.65
		Nos. 647-654 (8)	16.70	2.75

Tank Monument, Havana A170

Crowd in Peking — A171

Designs: No. 656, Cuban revolutionaries. No. 658, Crowd in Havana. No. 659, Cuban soldier. No. 660, Castro and Cuban flag.

Perf. 11½, 11x11½
1963, Jan. 1　　　　Photo.

655	A170	4f red & blk brn	55.00	2.50
656	A170	4f green & blk	55.00	2.50
657	A171	8f dull red & brn	90.00	6.00
658	A171	8f dull red & brn	110.00	12.50
659	A170	10f ocher & blk	100.00	15.00
660	A170	10f red, blue & blk	115.00	55.00
		Nos. 655-660 (6)	525.00	93.50

4th anniversary of the Cuban revolution.

Green Dragontail — A172

No. 661, Tibetan clouded yellow (1). No. 662, Tritailed glory (2). No. 663, Neumogeni jungle queen (3). No. 664, Washan swordtail (4). No. 665, Striped ringlet (5). No. 667, Dilunulated peacock (7). No. 668, Yamfly (8). No. 669, Golden kaiser-i-hind (9). No. 670, Mushaell hairstreak (10). No. 671, Yellow orange-tip (11). No. 672, Great jay (12). No. 673, Striped punch (13). No. 674, Hainan violet-beak (14). No. 675, Omeiskipper (15). No. 676, Philippines birdwing (16). No. 677, Richtofenis red apollo (17). No. 678, Blue-banded king crow (18). No. 679, Solskyi copper (19). No. 680, Yunnan clipper (20).

1963　　　Without Gum　　Perf. 11

661	A172	4f multi	12.00	1.75
662	A172	4f multi	12.00	1.75
663	A172	4f multi	12.00	1.75
664	A172	4f multi	12.00	1.75
665	A172	4f multi	12.00	1.75
666	A172	8f shown (6)	13.50	1.75
667	A172	8f multi	13.50	1.75
668	A172	8f multi	13.50	1.75
669	A172	8f multi	13.50	1.75
670	A172	8f multi	13.50	1.75
671	A172	10f multi	20.00	2.50
672	A172	10f multi	20.00	2.50
673	A172	10f multi	20.00	2.50
674	A172	10f multi	20.00	2.50
675	A172	10f multi	20.00	2.50
676	A172	20f multi	25.00	5.00
677	A172	20f multi	25.00	5.00
678	A172	22f multi	25.00	5.00

679	A172	30f multi	30.00	10.00
680	A172	50f multi	30.00	10.00
		Nos. 661-680 (20)	362.50	65.00

Issued: Nos. 666-675, July 15; others Apr. 5.

Karl Marx — A173

Designs: No. 682, "Workers of the World, Unite" on cover of first edition of Communist Manifesto. No. 683, Marx and Engels.

1963, May 5　　　　Perf. 11½
Without Gum

681	A173	8f black, gold & sal (1)	25.00	3.50
682	A173	8f gold & red (2)	25.00	3.50
683	A173	8f gold & choc (3)	25.00	3.50
		Nos. 681-683 (3)	75.00	10.50

145th anniversary of birth of Karl Marx (1818-1883), German political philosopher.

Child with Top — A174

Child: No. 685, eating berries. No. 686, as traffic policeman. No. 687, with windmill. No. 688, listening to caged cricket. No. 689, with sword. No. 690, embroidering. No. 691, with umbrella. No. 692, playing with sand. No. 693, playing table tennis. No. 694, learning to add. No. 695, with kite.

1963, June 1　Litho.　Perf. 12½
Without Gum
Multicolored Designs

684	A174	4f grnsh gray (1)	5.00	.60
685	A174	4f tan (2)	5.00	.60
686	A174	8f gray (3)	5.00	.60
687	A174	8f blue (4)	5.00	.60
688	A174	8f tan (5)	5.00	.60
689	A174	8f dp gray (6)	5.00	1.00
690	A174	8f citron (7)	5.00	1.00
691	A174	8f gray (8)	5.00	1.00
692	A174	10f green (9)	7.50	1.75
693	A174	10f violet (10)	7.50	1.75
694	A174	20f bister (11)	14.00	3.00
695	A174	20f green (12)	14.00	3.00
		Nos. 684-695 (12)	83.00	15.10

Children's Day. Value, imperf set unused $300, used $150.

Dance Type of 1962

Folk Dances: 4f, Weavers' dance, Puyi. 8f, Kazakh. 10f, Olunchun. 20f, Labor dance, Kaochan. 30f, Reed pipe dance, Miao. 50f, Fan dance, Korea.
Cumulative numbers 261-266 at lower right.

1963, June 15　　　　Perf. 12½
Without Gum

696	A166	4f cream & multi	3.00	.40
697	A166	8f cream & multi	3.00	.50
698	A166	10f cream & multi	4.00	.60
699	A166	20f cream & multi	5.00	1.75
700	A166	30f cream & multi	5.00	1.75
701	A166	50f cream & multi	8.00	3.25
		Nos. 696-701 (6)	28.00	8.25

1963, June 30　　　　Without Gum

Folk Dances: 4f, "Wedding Ceremony," Yu. 8f, "Encircling Mountain Forest," Pai. 10f, Long drum dance, Yao. 20f, Third day of the third month dance, Li. 30f, Knife dance, Kawa. 50f, Peacock dance, Thai.

Cumulative numbers 279-284 at lower right.

702	A166	4f cream & multi	3.00	.40
703	A166	8f cream & multi	3.00	.50
704	A166	10f cream & multi	3.00	.60
705	A166	20f cream & multi	6.00	1.25
706	A166	30f cream & multi	6.00	1.25
707	A166	50f cream & multi	6.00	1.25
	Nos. 702-707 (6)		27.00	5.25

Giant Panda Eating Apples — A175

Designs: No. 709, Giant panda eating bamboo shoots. 10f, Two pandas, horiz.

1963, Aug. 5 Photo. Perf. 11½x11
Size: 28x38mm

708	A175	8f pale blue & blk	35.00	2.50
709	A175	8f pale blue & blk	55.00	7.50

Size: 50x29mm
Perf. 11½

710	A175	10f olive & blk	37.50	2.50
	Nos. 708-710 (3)		127.50	12.50

Value, imperf set unused $300, used $130.

Table Tennis Player — A176

No. 712, Trophies won by Chinese team.

1963, Sept. 10 Engr. Perf. 11½

711	A176	8f dk olive grn	27.50	2.50
712	A176	8f brown	27.50	2.50

27th World Table Tennis Championships.

Snub-nosed Langur — A177

Designs: 10f, Two monkeys playing. 22f, Two monkeys grooming.

1963, Sept. 23 Photo. Perf. 11½x11

713	A177	8f gray & multi	18.00	1.75
714	A177	10f gray & multi	18.00	1.75
715	A177	22f gray & multi	32.50	7.25
	Nos. 713-715 (3)		68.50	10.75

Value, imperf set unused $300, used $100.

Jade-green Screen Mountain — A178

Hwang Shan Landscapes (Yellow Mountains), Anhwei Province: No. 717, "Guests Welcoming Pines" (2). No. 718, Pines and

Rock Behind the Sea (3). No. 719, Terrace of Keeping Cool (4). No. 720, Mount of Heavenly Capital (5). No. 721, Mount of Scissors (6). No. 722, Forest of Ten Thousand Pines (7). No. 723, "Brush Blooming in Dream" (8). No. 724, Mount of Lotus Flower (9). No. 725, Cumulus Cloud over West Sea (10). No. 726, Old Pines of Hwang Shan (11). No. 727, "Watching the Clouds over West Sea" (12). No. 728, Mount of Stalagmites (13). No. 729, "Stone Monkey Watching the Sea" (14). No. 730, Forest of Lions (15). No. 731, Three Fairy Tales of Pen Lai (16).
Nos. 724-731 horiz.

Engraved and Photogravure
1963, Oct. 15 Perf. 11½

716	A178	4f shown (1)	35.00	5.00
717	A178	4f multi	35.00	5.00
718	A178	4f multi	35.00	5.00
719	A178	4f multi	35.00	5.00
720	A178	8f multi	27.50	4.50
721	A178	8f multi	27.50	4.50
722	A178	8f multi	27.50	4.50
723	A178	8f multi	27.50	4.50
724	A178	10f multi	57.50	8.50
725	A178	10f multi	57.50	8.50
726	A178	10f multi	57.50	8.50
727	A178	10f multi	57.50	8.50
728	A178	20f multi	75.00	11.00
729	A178	22f multi	75.00	11.00
730	A178	30f multi	150.00	35.00
731	A178	50f multi	150.00	50.00
	Nos. 716-731 (16)		930.00	179.00

Soccer Player — A179

Athletes and Banners — A180

No. 733, Discus, women's. No. 734, Diving, men's. No. 735, Gymnastics, women's.

Engraved and Photogravure
1963, Nov. 17 Perf. 11

732	A179	8f gray, red & blk (1)	18.00	1.75
733	A179	8f gray, ultra & blk (2)	18.00	1.75
734	A179	8f lt grn, brn & blk (4)	18.00	1.75
735	A179	8f gray, lil rose & blk (5)	18.00	1.75

Photo.
Perf. 11½

736	A180	10f red & multi (3)	60.00	5.50
	Nos. 732-736 (5)		132.00	12.50

Games of the Newly Emerging Forces, Djakarta.

Clay Rooster and Goat — A181

Chinese Folk Toys: No. 738, Cloth camel. No. 739, Cloth tigers. No. 740, Clay ox and rider. No. 741, Cloth rabbit, wooden doll, clay roosters. No. 742, Straw rooster. No. 743, Cloth donkey and bird. No. 744, Clay lion. No. 745, Cloth tiger and tumbler doll.

1963, Dec. 10 Litho. Perf. 11½
Toys Multicolored; Without Gum

737	A181	4f bister (1)	2.00	.80
738	A181	4f gray (4)	2.00	.80
739	A181	4f lt blue (7)	2.00	.80
740	A181	8f bister (2)	2.00	.80
741	A181	8f gray (5)	2.00	.80
742	A181	8f lt blue (8)	2.00	.80
743	A181	10f bister (3)	4.00	.80
744	A181	10f gray (6)	4.00	.80
745	A181	10f lt blue (9)	4.00	.80
	Nos. 737-745 (9)		24.00	7.20

Armed Vietnamese Family — A182

Liberation of South Viet Nam: No. 747, Militia with Vietnamese flag.

1963, Dec. 20 Photo. Perf. 11½x11

746	A182	8f tan, blk & red	9.00	1.50
747	A182	8f red & multi	9.00	1.50

Flags of Cuba and China — A183

Design: No. 749, Boy waving Cuban flag.

1964, Jan. 1

748	A183	8f red, yel, bl & ind	65.00	6.50
749	A183	8f multicolored	65.00	6.50

5th anniversary of the liberation of Cuba.

Woman Driving Tractor — A184

Woman of the People's Commune: No. 751, harvesting. No. 752, picking cotton. No. 753, picking fruit. No. 754, reading book. No. 755, on guard duty.

1964, Mar. 8

750	A184	8f ol, pink & brn (1)	5.00	1.00
751	A184	8f brn yel & org (2)	5.00	1.00
752	A184	8f gray & multi (3)	5.00	1.00
753	A184	8f black, org & bl (4)	5.00	1.00
754	A184	8f green & multi (5)	5.00	2.00
755	A184	8f lilac & multi (6)	5.00	2.00
	Nos. 750-755 (6)		30.00	8.00

Chinese and African Men A185

Design: No. 757, African drummer.

1964, Apr. 12 Photo. Perf. 11

756	A185	8f red & multi	4.75	.90
757	A185	8f black & dk brn	4.75	.90

African Freedom Day.

Marx, Engels, Lenin and Stalin — A186

Design: No. 759, Banners and workers.

1964, May 1 Perf. 11½

758	A186	8f gold, red & blk	52.50	7.00
759	A186	8f gold, red & blk	52.50	7.00

Labor Day.

Orchard, Yenan A187

Yenan, Shrine of the Chinese Revolution: No. 761, Central Auditorium, Yang Chia Ling. No. 762, Mao's office and residence. No. 763, Auditorium, Wang Chia Ping. No. 764, Border Region Assembly Hall. No. 765, Pagoda Hill and Bridge.

1964, July 1 Photo. Perf. 11x11½

760	A187	8f multicolored (1)	11.00	2.00
761	A187	8f multicolored (2)	11.00	2.00
762	A187	8f multicolored (3)	11.00	2.00
763	A187	8f multicolored (4)	11.00	2.00
764	A187	8f multicolored (5)	11.00	2.00
765	A187	52f multicolored (6)	85.00	17.50
	Nos. 760-765 (6)		140.00	27.50

Map and Flag of Viet Nam — A188

1964, July 20 Perf. 11½

766	A188	8f multicolored	50.00	5.00

Victory in South Viet Nam.

Alchemist's Glowing Crucible — A189

No. 768, Night-shining jade (2). No. 769, Purple Kuo's cap (3). No. 770, Chao pink (4). No. 771, Yao yellow (5). No. 772, Twin beauty (6). No. 773, Ice-veiled ruby (7). No. 774, Gold-sprinkled Chinese ink (8). No. 775, Cinnabar jar (9). No. 776, Lan Tien jade (10). No. 777, Imperial robe yellow (11). No. 778, Hu red (12). No. 779, Pea green (13). No. 780, Wei purple (14). No. 781, Intoxicated celestial peach (15).
No. 782, Glorious crimson & great gold pink.

1964, Aug. 5 Perf. 11½x11

767	A189	4f shown (1)	15.00	1.50
768	A189	4f multi	15.00	1.50
769	A189	8f multi	9.00	1.50
770	A189	8f multi	9.00	1.50
771	A189	8f multi	9.00	1.50
772	A189	8f multi	9.00	1.50
773	A189	8f multi	9.00	1.50
774	A189	10f multi	15.00	1.50
775	A189	10f multi	15.00	1.50
776	A189	10f multi	15.00	1.50
777	A189	10f multi	15.00	1.50
778	A189	10f multi	15.00	1.50
779	A189	20f multi	60.00	14.00
780	A189	43f multi	90.00	20.00
781	A189	52f multi	150.00	30.00
	Nos. 767-781 (15)		450.00	82.00

Souvenir Sheet
Perf. 11½
Without Gum

782	A189	$2 multi	2,200.	800.00

No. 782 contains one 48x59mm stamp.

Wine
Cup — A190

Sacrificial bronze vessels of Yin dynasty, prior to 1050 B.C.: No. 784, Ku beaker (2). No. 785, Kuang wine urn (3). No. 786, Chia wine cup (4). No. 787, Tsun wine vessel (5). No. 788, Yu wine urn (6). No. 789, Tsun wine vessel (7). No. 790, Ceremonial cauldron (8).

Engraved and Photogravure

				1964, Aug. 25	**Perf. 11½x11**
783	A190	4f shown (1)		11.00	1.50
784	A190	4f multi		11.00	1.50
785	A190	8f multi		10.00	1.50
786	A190	8f multi		10.00	1.50
787	A190	10f multi		22.50	1.75
788	A190	10f multi		22.50	1.75
789	A190	20f multi		40.00	4.25
790	A190	20f multi		40.00	4.25
		Nos. 783-790 (8)		167.00	18.00

Grain
Harvest — A191

Designs: No. 792, Students planting trees. No. 793, Study period. No. 794, Scientific experimentation.

			1964, Sept. 26	**Photo.**
791	A191	8f multicolored (1)	7.00	1.00
792	A191	8f multicolored (2)	7.00	1.00
793	A191	8f multicolored (3)	7.00	1.00
794	A191	8f multicolored (4)	7.00	1.00
		Nos. 791-794 (4)	28.00	4.00

Youth helping in agriculture.

Marx, Engels,
Trafalgar Square,
London — A192

		1964, Sept. 28	**Perf. 11½**
795	A192	8f red, gold & red brn	125.00	25.00

Centenary of the First International.

Gold Ink

Stamps with gold ink often show some tarnishing. Values are for untarnished gold color. Tarnished stamps will sell for less.

People with
Banners — A193

No. 797, Gate of Heavenly Peace and Chinese flag. No. 798, People with banners, facing left.

1964, Oct. 1

796	A193	8f cream & multi (1)	37.50	5.50
797	A193	8f cream & multi (2)	37.50	5.50
798	A193	8f cream & multi (3)	37.50	5.50
a.		Souvenir sheet of 3	2,900.	1,250.
b.		Strip of 3, #796-798	275.00	80.00
		Nos. 796-798 (3)	112.50	16.50

15th anniv. of the People's Republic.
No. 798a contains No. 798b in continuous design without separating perfs. No. 798a almost always has disturbed gum, with interleaving paper sticking to it, or tarnished gilt. Such examples sell for considerably less than the very fine example valued above.
Values for No. 798b are for an unfolded strip.

Oil
Derricks — A194

Oil industry: 4f, Geological surveyors and truck, horiz. 8f, "Christmas tree" and extraction accessories. 10f, Oil refinery. 20f, Tank cars, horiz.

1964, Oct. 1

799	A194	4f lt blue & multi	70.00	8.00
800	A194	8f shown	110.00	15.00
801	A194	8f lilac & multi	60.00	6.50
802	A194	10f slate & multi	60.00	6.50
803	A194	20f brown & multi	140.00	25.00
		Nos. 799-803 (5)	440.00	61.00

Albanian
and
Chinese
Flags
A195

10f, Enver Hoxha and Albanian coat of arms.

		1964, Nov. 29	**Perf. 11x11½**
804	A195	8f red & multi	30.00	10.00
805	A195	10f red, yel & blk	45.00	18.00

20th anniv. of the liberation of Albania.

Power Dam
Construction
A196

No. 807, Installation of turbogenerator rotor. No. 808, Main dam. 20f, Pylon.

		1964, Dec. 15	**Perf. 11½**
806	A196	4f multicolored	65.00	10.00
807	A196	8f multicolored	55.00	5.00
808	A196	8f multicolored	90.00	5.00
809	A196	20f multicolored	165.00	27.50
		Nos. 806-809 (4)	375.00	47.50

Hsin An Kiang Dam and hydroelectric power station.

Fertilizer Industry — A197

Chemical Industry: No. 811, Plastics. No. 812, Medicines. No. 813, Rubber. No. 814, Insecticides. No. 815, Industrial acids. No. 816, Industrial alkaloids. No. 817, Synthetic fibers.

		1964, Dec. 30	**Photo. & Engr.**
810	A197	8f red & blk (1)	9.00	1.50
811	A197	8f yel grn & blk (2)	9.00	1.50
812	A197	8f brown & blk (3)	9.00	1.50
813	A197	8f lilac rose & blk (4)	9.00	1.50
814	A197	8f blue & blk (5)	9.00	1.50
815	A197	8f orange & blk (6)	9.00	1.50
816	A197	8f violet & blk (7)	9.00	1.50
817	A197	8f brt green & blk (8)	9.00	1.50
		Nos. 810-817 (8)	72.00	12.00

Mao Studying Map — A198

Mao Tse-
tung — A199

Design: No. 819, Victory at Lushan Pass.

		1965, Jan. 31	**Photo.**	**Perf. 11**
818	A198	8f red & multi	85.00	22.50
819	A198	8f red & multi	85.00	22.50
			Perf. 11½x11	
820	A199	8f gold & multi	120.00	30.00
		Nos. 818-820 (3)	290.00	75.00

Tsunyi Conference, 30th anniversary.

Conference Hall,
Bandung — A200

No. 822, Asians and Africans applauding.

		1965, Apr. 18	**Perf. 11½x11**
821	A200	8f cream & multi	3.75	.75
822	A200	8f cream & multi	3.75	.75

10th anniversary of the Bandung, Indonesia, Conference, Apr. 1955.

Lenin — A201

1965, Apr. 25   **Perf. 11½**

823	A201	8f red, choc & salmon	25.00	5.00

95th anniversary of the birth of Lenin.

Chinese
Player — A202

No. 825, European woman (2). No. 826, Chinese woman (3). No. 827, European man (4).

		1965, Apr. 25	**Perf. 11½**
824	A202	8f shown (1)	.70	.35
825	A202	8f multi	.70	.35
826	A202	8f multi	.70	.35
827	A202	8f multi	.70	.35
a.		Block of 4, #824-827	9.00	4.50

28th World Table Tennis Championships, Ljubljana, Yugoslavia, Apr. 15-25.

Climbers on Mt.
Minya
Konka — A203

Mountain Climbers: No. 829, on Muztagh Ata. No. 830, on Mt. Jolmo Lungma (Mt. Everest). No. 831, Women camping on Kongur Tiubie Tagh. No. 832, on Shisha Pangma.

		1965, May 25	**Photo. & Engr.**
828	A203	8f blue, blk & ol (1)	15.00	1.75
829	A203	8f blue, blk & ol (2)	15.00	1.75
830	A203	8f ultra, blk & gray (3)	15.00	1.75
831	A203	8f lt bl, blk & yel gray (4)	15.00	1.75
832	A203	8f ultra, blk & gray (5)	15.00	1.75
		Nos. 828-832 (5)	75.00	8.75

Chinese mountaineering achievements, 1957-64.

Marx and
Lenin — A204

		1965, June 21 Photo.	**Perf. 11½x11**
833	A204	8f red, yel & blk	22.50	4.00

Postal Ministers' Congress, Peking.

Tseping
Valley
A205

Chingkang Mountains, Cradle of the Chinese Revolution: No. 835, San Wan Tsun (2). No. 836, Octagon Bldg., Mao Ping (3). No. 837, River and Bridge at Lung Shih (4). No. 838, Ta Ching Tsun (5). No. 839, Bridge across the Lung Yuan (6). No. 840, Hwang Yang Mountain (7). No. 841, Chingkang peaks (8).

1965, July 1   **Perf. 11x11½**

834	A205	4f shown (1)	30.00	7.50
835	A205	8f multi	30.00	2.50
836	A205	8f multi	25.00	2.50
837	A205	8f multi	25.00	2.50
838	A205	8f multi	25.00	2.50

839	A205	10f multi	50.00	2.50
840	A205	10f multi	50.00	10.00
841	A205	52f multi	40.00	17.50

Nos. 834-841 (8)   275.00 47.50

Soldiers with Books — A206

No. 843, Soldiers reading Little Red Books (2). No. 844, With shell and artillery (3). No. 845, Rifle instruction (4). No. 846, Sewing jacket (5). No. 847, Bayonet charge (6). No. 848, With Banner (7). No. 849, Military band (8).

1965, Aug. 1   Perf. 11½
Without Gum

842	A206	8f shown (1)	40.00	6.00
843	A206	8f multi	40.00	6.00
844	A206	8f multi	40.00	6.00
845	A206	8f multi	40.00	6.00
846	A206	8f multi	40.00	6.00
847	A206	8f multi	40.00	10.00
848	A206	8f multi	40.00	10.00
849	A206	8f multi	40.00	10.00

Nos. 842-849 (8)   320.00 60.00

People's Liberation Army. Nos. 846-849 vertical.

"Welcome to Peking" — A207

No. 851, Chinese and Japanese young men. No. 852, Chinese and Japanese girls. No. 853, Musical entertainment. No. 854, Emblem of meeting.

1965, Aug. 25   Perf. 11½x11

850	A207	4f yellow & multi	2.00	1.00
851	A207	8f pink & multi	2.00	1.00
852	A207	8f multicolored	2.50	1.00
853	A207	10f yellow & multi	4.00	2.00
854	A207	22f lt blue & multi	9.00	3.00

Nos. 850-854 (5)   19.50 8.00

Chinese-Japanese Youth Meeting, Peking.

North Vietnamese Soldier — A208

Designs: No. 856, Soldier with guns. No. 857, Soldier giving victory salute.

1965, Sept. 2   Perf. 11½x11

855	A208	8f red & red brn (1)	4.00	1.10
856	A208	8f red & blk (2)	4.00	1.10
857	A208	8f red & vio brn (3)	4.00	1.10

Perf. 11½

858	A209	8f black & red (4)	6.00	1.50

Nos. 855-858 (4)   18.00 4.80

Struggle of the people of Viet Nam.

Mao Tse-tung at His Desk — A210

Crossing Yellow River A211

Victory Monument A212

Design: No. 862, Recruits in cart.

1965, Sept. 3   Perf. 11

859	A210	8f red & multi (1)	55.00	15.00

Perf. 11x11½, 11½x11

860	A211	8f red & dk grn (2)	37.50	3.75
861	A212	8f red & dk brn (3)	37.50	3.75
862	A211	8f red & dk grn (4)	37.50	3.75

Nos. 859-862 (4)   167.50 26.25

20th anniversary of victory over Japan.

2nd National Games — A213

National Games Opening Ceremonies — A214

Perf. 11½x11, 11 (A214)
1965, Sept. 28

863	A213	4f Soccer (1)	16.00	1.50
864	A213	4f Archery (2)	16.00	1.50
865	A213	8f Javelin (3)	16.00	1.50
866	A213	8f Gymnastics (4)	16.00	1.50
867	A213	8f Volleyball (5)	16.00	1.50
868	A214	10f shown (6)	40.00	3.75
869	A213	10f Bicyling (7)	45.00	3.50
870	A213	20f Diving (8)	50.00	6.00
871	A213	22f Hurdles (9)	50.00	6.00
872	A213	30f Weight lifting (10)	60.00	14.00
873	A213	43f Basketball (11)	60.00	14.00

Nos. 863-873 (11)   385.00 54.75

Government Building — A215

1½f, 5f, 22f, Gate of Heavenly Peace. 2f, 8f, 30f, People's Hall. 3f, 10f, 50f, Military Museum.

1965-66   Perf. 11½x11
Without Gum

874	A215	1f brown	.35	.30
875	A215	1½f red lilac	.45	.30
876	A215	2f green	.45	.30
877	A215	3f blue grn	.50	.30
878	A215	4f brt blue	.60	.30
879	A215	5f vio brn ('66)	1.75	.30
880	A215	8f rose red	.75	.30
881	A215	10f gray olive	1.60	.30
882	A215	20f violet	1.75	.30
883	A215	22f orange	1.75	.30
884	A215	30f yellow grn	3.50	.40
885	A215	50f dp blue ('66)	10.00	2.50

Nos. 874-885 (12)   23.45 5.90

Textile Workers — A216

No. 887, Machine shop (2). No. 888, Welder (3). No. 889, Students (4). No. 890, Militia (5).

1965, Nov. 30

886	A216	8f shown (1)	27.50	3.00
887	A216	8f multicolored	27.50	3.00
888	A216	8f multicolored	27.50	3.00
889	A216	8f multicolored	27.50	3.00
890	A216	8f multicolored	27.50	3.00

Nos. 886-890 (5)   137.50 15.00

Women workers.

Soccer — A217

Children's Sports: No. 892, Racing. No. 893, Tobogganing and skating. No. 894, Gymnastics. No. 895, Swimming. No. 896, Rifle practice. No. 897, Jumping rope. No. 898, Table tennis.

1966, Feb. 25   Perf. 11

891	A217	4f emer & multi (1)	1.50	.45
892	A217	4f yel brn & multi (2)	1.50	.45
893	A217	8f blue & multi (3)	1.50	.45
894	A217	8f yellow & multi (4)	1.50	.55
895	A217	8f grnsh bl & multi (5)	1.50	.55
896	A217	8f green & multi (6)	1.50	.55
897	A217	10f org & multi (7)	4.50	1.25
898	A217	52f grnsh gray & multi (8)	14.00	5.75

Nos. 891-898 (8)   27.50 10.00

Mobile Transformer A218

New Industrial Machinery: No. 900, Electron microscope, vert. No. 901, Lathe. No. 902, Vertical boring and turning machine, vert. No. 903, Gear-grinding machine. No. 904, Hydraulic press. No. 905, Milling machine. No. 906, Electron accelerator, vert.

Perf. 11x11½, 11½x11
1966, Mar. 30   Photo. & Engr.

899	A218	4f yellow & blk (1)	30.00	2.75
900	A218	8f blk & lt ultra (2)	30.00	1.75
901	A218	8f sal pink & blk (3)	30.00	1.75
902	A218	8f olive & blk (4)	30.00	1.75
903	A218	8f rose lil & blk (5)	30.00	1.75
904	A218	10f gray & blk (6)	40.00	7.50
905	A218	10f bl grn & blk (7)	40.00	9.50
906	A218	22f lilac & blk (8)	47.50	7.00

Nos. 899-906 (8)   277.50 33.75

Military and Civilian Workers A219

Women in Various Occupations: No. 908, Train conductor. No. 909, Red Cross worker. No. 910, Kindergarten teacher. No. 911, Road sweeper. No. 912, Hairdresser. No. 913, Bus conductor. No. 914, Traveling saleswoman. No. 915, Canteen worker. No. 916, Rural mail carrier.

1966, May 10   Perf. 11x11½

907	A219	8f red & multi (1)	2.75	1.10
908	A219	8f pale grn & multi (2)	2.75	1.10
909	A219	8f yellow & multi (3)	2.75	1.10
910	A219	8f green & multi (4)	2.75	1.10
911	A219	8f salmon & multi (5)	2.75	1.10
912	A219	8f pale bl & bl (6)	2.75	1.10
913	A219	8f yellow & multi (7)	2.75	1.10
914	A219	8f tan & multi (8)	2.75	1.10
915	A219	8f yel grn & multi (9)	2.75	1.10
916	A219	8f green & multi (10)	2.75	1.10

Nos. 907-916 (10)   27.50 11.00

Statue "Thunderstorm" — A220

22f, Open book and association emblem.

1966, June 27   Perf. 11

917	A220	8f red & black	10.00	3.00
918	A220	22f red, gold & yel	20.00	4.50

Afro-Asian Writers' Assoc. Conf., Peking.

Sun Yat-sen — A221

1966, Nov. 12   Perf. 11½x11

919	A221	8f sepia & lt buff	85.00	27.50

Birth centenary of Sun Yat-sen.

Athletes Holding Portrait of Mao — A222

Two Women Athletes with Little Red Book A223

No. 921, Athletes holding Little Red Books. No. 923, Athletes reading Mao texts.

1966, Dec. 31   Perf. 11

920	A222	8f red & multi (1)	75.00	14.00
921	A222	8f red & multi (2)	55.00	14.00

Perf. 11x11½

922	A223	8f blue & multi (3)	70.00 15.00
923	A223	8f blue & multi (4)	70.00 15.00
		Nos. 920-923 (4)	270.00 58.00

1st Athletic Games of the New Emerging Nations.

Appreciation of Lu Hsun by Mao — A224

Designs: No. 925, Portrait of Lu Hsun. No. 926, Lu Hsun's handwriting (3 vert. rows).

Engr. & Photo.; Photo. (#925)
1966, Dec. 31　　　*Perf. 11½*

924	A224	8f red & black (1)	75.00 20.00
925	A224	8f red & multi (2)	110.00 20.00
926	A224	8f red & black (3)	75.00 20.00
		Nos. 924-926 (3)	260.00 60.00

Lu Hsun, Revolutionary writer (1881-1936).

"Be Resolute ...," by Mao Tse-tung — A225

Designs: No. 928, Drilling crew fighting natural gas fire, horiz. No. 929, Attempt to close fire-engulfed valve.

Sizes: Nos. 927, 929, 26x38mm; No. 928, 49x29mm

Perf. 11½x11, 11½ (No. 928)
1967, Mar. 10　　　Photo.

927	A225	8f red, gold & blk	57.50 16.00
928	A225	8f brick red & blk	57.50 16.00
929	A225	8f brick red & blk	57.50 16.00
		Nos. 927-929 (3)	172.50 48.00

Heroic oil well firefighters.

Liu Ying-chun A226

No. 931, With book by Mao (2). No. 932, Holding bridle of horse (3). No. 933, With film slide (4). No. 934, Lecturing (5). No. 935, Fatal attempt to stop runaway horse (6).

1967, Mar. 25　　　*Perf. 11½x11*

930	A226	8f shown (1)	55.00 16.00
931	A226	8f multi	55.00 16.00
932	A226	8f multi	55.00 16.00
933	A226	8f multi	55.00 16.00
934	A226	8f multi	55.00 16.00
935	A226	8f multi	55.00 16.00
		Nos. 930-935 (6)	330.00 96.00

In memory of soldier Liu Ying-chun, hero.

Third 5-Year Plan — A227

Design: No. 936, Banners, 3 workers and male soldier facing right (industrial growth). No. 937, Banners, 3 workers and female militia member facing left (agricultural growth).

1967, Apr. 15　　　*Perf. 11*

936	A227	8f red & multi	85.00 18.00
937	A227	8f red & multi	85.00 18.00

Third Five-Year Plan.

Mao Tse-tung — A228

Thoughts of Mao — A229

1967, Apr. 20　　　*Perf. 11½*

938	A228	8f red & multi	125.00 50.00

Red & Gold

939	A229	8f 39 characters	90.00 50.00
940	A229	8f 50 characters	90.00 50.00
941	A229	8f 39 characters in 6 lines	90.00 50.00
942	A229	8f 53 characters	90.00 50.00
943	A229	8f 46 characters	90.00 50.00
a.		Strip of 5, #939-943	1,200. 550.00

Gold & Red

944	A229	8f 41 characters	135.00 90.00
945	A229	8f 49 characters	135.00 90.00
946	A229	8f 35 characters	135.00 90.00
947	A229	8f 22 characters	135.00 90.00
948	A229	8f 29 characters	135.00 90.00
a.		Strip of 5, #944-948	2,250. 750.00
		Nos. 938-948 (11)	1,250. 750.00

Thoughts of Mao Tse-tung.
Values for Nos. 943a and 948a are for unfolded strips without tarnishing. Strips with folds and/or tarnishing sell for much less.

For Nos. 938-1046, beware of forgeries, removed cancels and repairs. No numbers appear below design on Nos. 938-1046.

Gate of Heavenly Peace and Text from C. C. P. Communique Praising Mao — A230

Mao and Lin Piao A231

No. 950, Mao and poem. No. 951, Mao among people of various races. No. 952, Mao facing left and Red Guards with books. No. 953, Mao with upraised right hand. No. 955, Mao leaning on rail, horiz. 10f, Mao and Lin Piao in discussion, horiz.

Engraved and Photogravure
1967　　　*Perf. 11x11½*

Size: 36x56mm

949	A230	4f yel, red & mar	120.00 40.00

Photo.

950	A230	8f yel, brn, & red	100.00 40.00
951	A230	8f yel, red & multi	100.00 40.00
952	A230	8f yel, red & multi	100.00 40.00

Size: 36x50mm, 50x36mm
Perf. 11

953	A231	8f black & multi	140.00 40.00
954	A231	8f black & multi	375.00 160.00
955	A231	8f lt blue & multi	110.00 40.00
956	A231	10f black & multi	375.00 160.00
		Nos. 949-956 (8)	1,420. 560.00

"Mao Tse-tung Our Great Teacher."
Issued: Nos. 949-953, 5/1; Nos. 954-956, 9/20.

Mao Text (4 lines) — A232

Parade of Supporters — A233

Design: No. 958, Mao text (5 lines).

Engraved and Photogravure
1967, May 23　　　*Perf. 11½*

957	A232	8f black, red & yel	325.00 125.00
958	A232	8f black, red & yel	325.00 150.00

Photo.
Perf. 11

959	A233	8f multicolored	325.00 150.00
		Nos. 957-959 (3)	975.00 425.00

25th anniversary of Mao Tse-tung's "Talks on Literature and Art" in Yenan.

A stamp was prepared in August 1967 for the 50th anniversary of the Autumn Harvest March. It was not issued, but a few examples have entered the marketplace. It depicts Mao Tse-tung on the left and Lin Piao on the right, against a blue sky. A cut example comprising the right half of the stamp was sold in a Jan. 2010 Hong Kong auction for the equivalent of U.S. $285,000. Presumably, an intact example would sell for far more.

Mao Tse-tung — A234

1967　　　Engr.　　　*Perf. 11*

960	A234	4f brown	50.00 25.00
961	A234	8f carmine	180.00 45.00
962	A234	35f dk brown	30.00 11.50
963	A234	43f vermilion	35.00 11.50
964	A234	52f carmine	40.00 15.00
		Nos. 960-964 (5)	335.00 108.00

46th anniv. of Chinese Communist Party. Issue dates: 8f, July 1; others Sept.

Mao, "Sun of the Revolution" — A235

No. 966, Mao and people of various races.

1967, Oct. 1　　　*Perf. 11½x11*

965	A235	8f multicolored	72.50 35.00
966	A235	8f multicolored	160.00 45.00

People's Republic of China, 18th anniv.

"September 9" — A236

"Huichang" A237

"Peitaiho"
A238

Reply to Comrade Kuo Mo-jo — A239

Mao Tse-tung Writing Poems — A240

Poems by Mao: No. 967, "The Long March." No. 968, "Liupanshan." No. 969, shown. No. 970, "The Cave of the Fairies." No. 971, "Snow." No. 972, "Lushan Pass." No. 975, "Conquest of Nanking." No. 976, "The Yellow Crane Pavilion." No. 977, "Swimming." No. 979, "Changsha."

1967-68   Photo.   Perf. 11
Size: 79x18½mm

967	A236	4f 9 characters, UL panel	125.00	90.00
968	A236	4f 11 characters, UL panel	125.00	30.00

Size: 60x24mm
Perf. 11½

969	A236	8f shown, 10 characters in UL panel	90.00	45.00
970	A236	8f 21 characters in UL panel	115.00	45.00
971	A236	8f 11 characters in UL panel	100.00	60.00
972	A236	8f 9 characters in UL panel	100.00	60.00

Size: 29x50mm

973	A237	8f shown	600.00	140.00
974	A238	8f shown	775.00	225.00
975	A238	8f 3 rows in bottom panel	525.00	150.00
976	A238	8f 2 rows in bottom panel	275.00	140.00

Size: 52x38mm
Perf. 11

977	A239	8f 3 short vert. rows, at left of poem	400.00	145.00
978	A239	10f shown	60.00	30.00
979	A239	10f undivided text	130.00	30.00
980	A240	10f red, yel & multi	130.00	45.00
		Nos. 967-980 (14)	3,550.	1,235.

Issued: Nos. 969-970, 980, 10/1; Nos. 973-974, 977, 5/20/68; others 7/20/68.

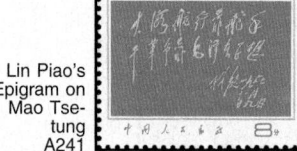

Lin Piao's Epigram on Mao Tsetung
A241

1967, Dec. 26   Photo.   Perf. 11x11½
981 A241 8f red & gold   45.00 15.00

Mao and Parade of Artists — A242

"Raid on White Tiger Regiment" — A243

"Red Detachment of Women" — A244

No. 983, "The Red Lantern," vert. No. 985, "Shachiapang" (women & soldier). No. 986, "On the Dock". No. 987, "Taking Bandits' Fort". No. 989, "The White-haired Girl". No. 990, Mao with Orchestra & Chorus (50x36mm).

1968   Perf. 11½x11; 11 (983, 990)

982	A242	8f shown (56x36mm)	130.00	25.00
983	A242	8f multi	130.00	30.00
984	A243	8f multi	130.00	35.00
985	A243	8f multi	130.00	35.00
986	A243	8f multi	130.00	35.00
987	A243	8f multi	130.00	35.00
988	A244	8f shown	180.00	65.00
989	A244	8f multi	130.00	50.00
990	A242	8f multi	130.00	40.00
		Nos. 982-990 (9)	1,220.	350.00

Mao's direction for revolutionary literature and art. Issued: Nos. 982-987, Jan. 30; Nos. 988-990, May 1.

"Unite still more closely . . ." — A245

1968, May 31   Photo.   Perf. 11
991 A245 8f red, gold & red brn   265.00 80.00

Mao Tse-tung's statement of support of Afro-Americans.

Statement about Cultural Revolution
A246

Directives of Chairman Mao: No. 993, Experiences of Revolutionary Committee. No. 994, Leadership role of Revolutionary Committee. No. 995, Basic principle of reform. No. 996, Purpose of Cultural Revolution.

1968, July 20   Photo.   Perf. 11½
No. of Lines Over Signature

992	A246	8f shown	475.00	250.00
993	A246	8f 5	475.00	250.00
994	A246	8f 4½	475.00	250.00
995	A246	8f 4	475.00	250.00
996	A246	8f 8	475.00	250.00
a.		Strip of 5, #992-996	5,250.	2,100.
		Nos. 992-996 (5)	2,375.	1,250.

Value for No. 996a is for an unfolded strip.

Lin Piao's Statement, July 26, 1965 — A247

1968, Aug. 1   Engr. & Photo.
997 A247 8f red, gold & blk   37.50 10.00

Chinese People's Liberation Army, 41st anniv.

Mao Tse-tung Going to An Yuan, 1921
A248

1968, Aug. 1   Perf. 11x11½
998 A248 8f multicolored   180.00 50.00

Shade varieties include varying amount of red in clouds.

An 8f stamp was prepared in Sept. 1968, showing black writing on a red background, regarding Chairman Mao's inscriptions to Japanese Labor Friends. It was not issued, but a few examples have reached the marketplace. Value, *$175,000.*

Directive of Chairman Mao — A249

1968, Nov. 30   Perf. 11½
999 A249 8f red & blk brn   225.00 50.00

China Map, Worker, Farmer and Soldier
999A

1968, Nov.   Photo.   Perf. 11½x11
999A A249a 8f red, bl & bis   135,000. 80,000.

Map inscribed: "The entire nation is red." Issued in Canton and quickly withdrawn because Taiwan appears white instead of red.
No. 999A most often is found repaired. Values are for sound, unrepaired examples. Counterfeits exist.

Two values were prepared to celebrate the Great Victory of the Cultural Revolution but were not issued, although a few examples have entered the marketplace. Values for sound stamps: 8f, Mao Tse-tung and Lin Piao, $300,000; 8f, map and workers, $1,150,000.

Woman, Miner and Soldier Holding Little Red Book
A250

1968, Dec. 26   Perf. 11x11½
1000 A250 8f multicolored   65.00 15.00

Canceled-to-order
From about this point on stamps are valued postally used.

Yangtze Bridge, Nanking
A251

Road across Bridge — A252

No. 1003, Side view. 10f, Aerial view.

Lithographed,
Perf. 11½x11 (A251);
Photogravure,
Perf. 11½ (A252)

1969 — Without Gum

1001	A251	4f multicolored	8.00	3.00
1002	A252	8f multicolored	68.00	10.00
1003	A252	8f multicolored	20.00	6.00
1004	A251	10f multicolored	6.00	3.00
		Nos. 1001-1004 (4)	102.00	22.00

Inauguration of Yangtze Bridge at Nanking on Dec. 29, 1968.

Singer and Pianist
A253

(Piano Music from the Opera, "The Red Lantern"): No. 1006, Woman singer and pianist.

1969, Aug.　Photo.　Perf. 11x11½
Without Gum

1005	A253	8f multicolored	25.00	12.50
1006	A253	8f multicolored	110.00	18.50

Harvest
A254

No. 1008, Two harvesters. No. 1009, Harvesters with Little Red Books. No. 1010, Red Cross Worker examining baby.

1969, Oct.　Without Gum

1007	A254	4f shown	15.00	3.50
a.		Brown omitted	50.00	50.00
1008	A254	8f multi	70.00	9.00
1009	A254	8f multi	90.00	20.00
1010	A254	10f multi	10.00	4.00
		Nos. 1007-1010 (4)	185.00	36.50

Agriculture students.

Armed Forces and Slogan — A255

Guarding the Coast — A256

Designs: No. 1013, 43f, Snow patrol, vert.

1969, Oct.　Without Gum　Perf. 11½

1011	A255	8f red & multi	60.00	16.00
a.		Bayonets omitted	300.00	85.00
1012	A256	8f blue & multi	15.00	5.00
1013	A256	8f blue & multi	15.00	5.00
1014	A256	35f black & multi	12.00	5.00
1015	A256	43f black & multi	15.00	7.50
		Nos. 1011-1015 (5)	117.00	38.50

Defense of Chen Pao-tao (Damansky Islands) in Ussuri River.

Farm Woman
A257

Designs: 8f, Foundry worker. 10f, Soldier.

1969, Dec.　Perf. 10; 11½
Without Gum

1016	A257	4f ver & dk pur	2.50	.75
a.		Perf 11½	7.50	1.50

1017	A257	8f ver & dk brn	3.00	.75
a.		Perf 11½	4.50	1.50
1018	A257	10f ver & blk	5.00	1.50
a.		Perf 11½		900.00
		Nos. 1016-1018 (3)	10.50	3.00

Perforation

Nos. 1016-1018 and some succeeding issues bear two kinds of perforation: clean (Peking) and rough (Shanghai).

Building — A258

Communist Party Building, Shanghai
A259

Agriculture Building, Canton — A260

Foundry Worker — A261

Type I

Two types of 8f Gate of Heavenly Peace:
I — Strong, definite halo around sun.
II — Halo missing, white shades gradually into red.
No. 1022, 1929 Party Day House, Pu Tien. No. 1023, Mao's Home and Office, Yunnan. No. 1024, Woman Tractor Driver. No. 1025, Gate of Heavenly Peace. No. 1026, Heroes Monument. No. 1027, Pagoda Hill, Yenan. No. 1028, Gate of Heavenly Peace (no sun). No. 1029, Monument, Tsu Ping. No. 1030, Conference Hall, Tsunyi. No. 1031, Highway ('72). No. 1032, Shao Shan Village, Birthplace of Mao. No. 1033, Conference Hall. No. 1034, Chingkang Peaks. No. 1035, as 4f, different view. No. 1036, People's Hall, Peking.

1969-72　Photo.　Perf. 10, 11½
Without Gum

1019	A258	1f shown	.40	.30
1020	A259	1½f shown	1.50	1.00
a.		Perf. 11½	8.00	4.00
1021	A260	2f shown	.40	.30
1022	A260	3f multi	1.00	.30
1023	A260	4f multi	.55	.30
1024	A261	5f multi	2.50	.75
1025	A260	8f multi, type II	.90	.40
a.		Type I	2.50	1.25
1026	A259	8f multi	3.50	1.50
a.		Perf. 11½	7.50	3.50
1027	A260	8f multi	7.50	3.25
1028	A260	8f multi	1.00	.40
1029	A260	10f multi	1.00	.40
1030	A259	20f multi	5.50	1.75
a.		Perf. 11½	22.50	5.50
1031	A260	20f multi	2.00	.55
1032	A260	22f multi	2.00	.60
1033	A260	35f multi	2.50	.60
1034	A260	43f multi	3.50	.70
1035	A259	50f multi	2.00	.50
1036	A260	52f multi	6.00	.85
1037	A261	$1 shown ('70)	12.00	1.75
		Nos. 1019-1037 (19)	55.75	16.20

Kin Hsün-hua
A262

1970, Jan.　Without Gum　Perf. 11½

1045	A262	8f red & black	32.50	17.50
a.		8f red & gray brown	40.00	15.00

Death of Kin Hsün-hua in Kirin border flood.

Mounted Patrol — A263

1970, Aug. 1　Without Gum

1046	A263	8f yel grn & multi	22.50	9.00

People's Liberation Army, 43rd anniv.

Commemorative stamps from Nos. 1047 to 1142 and 1211-1214, carry a cumulative number in parentheses at lower left and the year at lower right. Where such numbers help to identify, they are quoted in parentheses.

Cpl. Yang Tse-jung — A264

Ensemble
A265

No. 1048, Armed guards (2). No. 1049, Yang leaping through forest (3). No. 1051, Yang in folk costume (5). No. 1052, Four actors (6).

1970, Aug. 1　Perf. 11½x11, 11x11½
Without Gum

1047	A264	8f shown (1)	40.00	10.00
1048	A264	8f multi	12.50	3.50
1049	A264	8f multi	20.00	6.00
1050	A265	8f shown (4)	75.00	13.00
1051	A265	8f multi	15.00	3.75
1052	A265	8f multi	20.00	8.00
		Nos. 1047-1052 (6)	182.50	44.75

Scenes from opera "Taking Tiger Mountain by Strategy." Nos. 1048, 1052, horizontal.

Frontier Guard
A266

1971, Jan.　Litho.　Perf. 10
Without Gum

1053	A266	4f multicolored	6.00	1.75
a.		Perf. 11½	5.50	1.75
b.		Perf. 11½x10	5.00	2.75
c.		Perf. 10x11½	5.75	3.25

Banner of the Commune
A267

Street Battle, Paris, 1871
A268

10f, Proclamation of the Commune. 22f, Rally.

Perf. 11½x11, 11x11½
1971, Mar. 18　Litho. & Engr.
Without Gum

1054	A267	4f sal & multi	40.00	18.00
1055	A268	8f ver, pink & brn	240.00	50.00
1056	A267	10f ver, pink & dk brn	15.00	11.00
1057	A268	22f ver, pink & dk brn	11.00	10.00
		Nos. 1054-1057 (4)	306.00	89.00

Centenary of the Paris Commune.

Redrawn Building Type of 1961

Designs: 2f, 3f, August 1 building, Nanchang. 4f, 52f, Gate of Heavenly Peace, Peking. 10f, 20f, Pagoda Hill, Yenan.

1971, July 1　Litho.　Perf. 11x11½
Size: 21x16mm
Without Gum

1059	A152	2f slate green	2.00	.75
1060	A152	3f sepia	3.00	1.25
1061	A152	4f brt pink	5.00	2.00
1062	A152	10f brt rose lil	1.50	1.25
1063	A152	20f dk blue grn	3.75	1.25
1064	A152	52f orange	2.50	3.00
		Nos. 1059-1064 (6)	17.75	9.50

Paper of Nos. 1059-1064 is white. That of Nos. 647-654 is toned.

Communist Party Building, Shanghai — A269

People and Factories — A270

Designs: No. 1068, Peasant Movement Training Institute. No. 1069, Ching Kang Peaks. No. 1070, Conference Building, Tsunyi. No. 1071, Pagoda Hill, Yenan. No. 1073, People and People's Hall, Peking. No. 1074, People and Pagoda Hill, Yenan. 22f, Gate of Heavenly Peace, Peking.

1971, July 1   Photo.   Perf. 11½
Red and Gold Frame
Without Gum

1067	A269	4f vermilion (12)	25.00	5.00
1068	A269	4f brt grn (13)	25.00	5.00
1069	A269	8f grnsh bl & red (14)	32.50	5.00
1070	A269	8f ol blk (15)	40.00	5.00
1071	A269	8f bis, grn & red (16)	40.00	5.00
1072	A270	8f yel, red & multi (18)	40.00	8.00
1073	A270	8f yel, red & multi (19)	40.00	8.00
1074	A270	8f yel, red & multi (20)	40.00	8.00
a.		Strip of 3, #1072-1074	220.00	75.00
1075	A269	22f red, gold & brn (17)	20.00	9.00
		Nos. 1067-1075 (9)	302.50	58.00

50th anniv. of the Chinese Communist Party. No. 1073 has date of 1921-1971 at top. No. 1074a has a continuous design and is valued as an unfolded strip.

Chinese Welcome A271

No. 1077, Chinese & African players. No. 1078, Chinese & African girl players. 43f, Games' emblem.

1971, Nov. 3   Litho.   Perf. 11½
Without Gum

1076	A271	8f lil rose & multi	22.50	5.75
1077	A271	8f lt yellow & multi	22.50	5.75
1078	A271	8f dk grn & multi	22.50	5.75
1079	A271	43f grn, gold & org	85.00	16.00
		Nos. 1076-1079 (4)	152.50	33.25

Afro-Asian Table Tennis Games, Peking.

Enver Hoxha — A272

No. 1081, Party's birthplace. No. 1082, Albanian flag. 52f, Albanian partisans, horiz.

1971, Nov. 3   Photo.   Perf. 11
Without Gum

1080	A272	8f Prus blue & multi	32.50	7.00
1081	A272	8f buff & multi	20.00	6.00
1082	A272	8f red, yel & multi	20.00	6.00
1083	A272	52f lt blue & multi	35.00	9.00
		Nos. 1080-1083 (4)	107.50	28.00

30th anniversary of the founding of Albanian Communist Party.

Yenan Pagoda and 1942 Meeting House A273

No. 1085, Uniformed choir (34). No. 1086, "Brother & Sister" (35). No. 1087, Outdoor performance (36). No. 1088, "The Red Signal Lantern" (37). No. 1089, Dancer from "The Red Company of Women" (38).

1972, May 23   Photo.   Perf. 11
Without Gum

1084	A273	8f shown (33)	25.00	7.50
1085	A273	8f multi	25.00	7.50
1086	A273	8f multi	25.00	7.50
1087	A273	8f multi	25.00	7.50
1088	A273	8f multi	25.00	7.50
1089	A273	8f multi	25.00	7.50
		Nos. 1084-1089 (6)	150.00	45.00

30th anniversary of the publication of the Discussions on Literature and Art at the Yenan Forum.

Various Ball Games — A274

Workers' Gymnastics A275

No. 1092, Tug of war (41). No. 1093, Mountain climbers and tents (42). No. 1094, Children diving & swimming (43).

1972, June 10

1090	A274	8f shown (39)	45.00	4.00
1091	A275	8f shown (40)	22.50	4.00
1092	A275	8f multi	22.50	4.00
1093	A275	8f multi	20.00	4.00
1094	A275	8f multi	22.50	4.00
		Nos. 1090-1094 (5)	132.50	20.00

10th anniversary of Mao Tse-tung's edict on physical culture.

Ocean Freighter Fenglei — A276

No. 1096, Tanker Taching No. 30 (30). No. 1097, Cargo-passenger ship Changzeng (31). No. 1098, Dredger Xienfeng (32).

1972, July 10   Photo.   Perf. 11½
Without Gum

1095	A276	8f shown (29)	70.00	11.00
1096	A276	8f multi	20.00	9.00
1097	A276	8f multi	20.00	9.00
1098	A276	8f multi	47.50	11.00
		Nos. 1095-1098 (4)	157.50	40.00

Table Tennis Players' Welcome A277

No. 1099, Championship emblem, vert. (45). No. 1101, Table tennis (47). No. 1102, Women from different countries, vert. (48).

1972, Sept. 2   Perf. 11½x11, 11x11½
Without Gum

1099	A277	8f multi	12.50	5.00
1100	A277	8f shown (46)	35.00	5.00
1101	A277	8f multi	22.50	5.00
1102	A277	22f multi	20.00	6.00
		Nos. 1099-1102 (4)	90.00	21.00

First Asian table tennis championships.

Wang Chin-hsi — A278

Engraved and Photogravure
1972, Dec. 25   Perf. 11½x11

1103	A278	8f multicolored (44)	65.00	25.00

Wang Chin-hsi, the Iron Man, fighter for the working class.

Workers on Cliffs along Canal — A279

No. 1105, Canal flowing through tunnel (50). No. 1106, Bridge (51). No. 1107, Canal along cliffs (52).

1972, Dec. 30

1104	A279	8f multi (49)	30.00	7.00
1105	A279	8f multicolored	30.00	7.00
1106	A279	8f multicolored	40.00	10.00
1107	A279	8f multicolored	40.00	10.00
		Nos. 1104-1107 (4)	140.00	34.00

Construction of Red Flag Canal, Linhsien county, Honan.

Giant Panda — A280

Designs: Pandas in various positions. The 8f stamps are horizontal.

Perf. 11½x11, 11x11½
1973, Jan. 15   Photo.
Designs in Black and Red

1108	A280	4f lt yel grn (61)	9.00	8.00
1109	A280	8f buff (59)	9.00	6.00
1110	A280	8f lt tan (60)	9.00	6.00
1111	A280	10f pale grn (58)	100.00	18.00
1112	A280	20f pale bl gray (57)	50.00	10.00
1113	A280	43f pale lil (62)	15.00	14.00
		Nos. 1108-1113 (6)	192.00	62.00

Woman Coal Miner — A281

No. 1115, Committee member (64). No. 1116, Telephone line worker (65).

1973, Mar. 8   Photo.   Perf. 11½x11

1114	A281	8f shown (63)	28.00	6.00
1115	A281	8f multi	20.00	7.00
1116	A281	8f multi	20.00	6.00
		Nos. 1114-1116 (3)	68.00	19.00

Intl. Working Women's Day. Designs are after paintings from an exhib. for 30th anniv. of the Yenan Forum on Literature and Art.

Dancing Girl — A282

No. 1118, Musician, boy (87). No. 1119, Girl with scarf (88). No. 1120, Boy with tambourine (89). No. 1121, Girl with drum (90).

1973, June 1   Photo.   Perf. 11

1117	A282	8f shown (86)	3.25	1.75
1118	A282	8f multi	3.25	1.75
1119	A282	8f multi	3.25	1.75
1120	A282	8f multi	3.25	1.75
1121	A282	8f multi	3.25	1.75
a.		Strip of 5, #1117-1121	60.00	22.50
		Nos. 1117-1121 (5)	16.25	8.75

Values for No. 1121a are for an unfolded strip.

Tournament Emblem — A283

No. 1123, Visitors from Asia, Africa and Latin America arriving by plane (92). No. 1124, Woman player (93). No. 1125, African, Asian & Latin American women (94).

1973, Aug. 25   Photo.   Perf. 11½

1122	A283	8f multi (91)	18.00	3.00
1123	A283	8f multicolored	14.00	3.00
1124	A283	8f multicolored	14.00	3.00
1125	A283	22f multicolored	14.00	3.00
		Nos. 1122-1125 (4)	60.00	12.00

Asian, African and Latin American Table Tennis Friendship Invitational Tournament.

The White-haired Girl — A284

Designs: Scenes from the ballet "The White-haired Girl." Nos. 1126, 1129 vert.

1973, Sept. 25   Photo.   Perf. 11½

1126	A284	8f multi (53)	40.00	12.00
1127	A284	8f multi (54)	50.00	12.00
1128	A284	8f multi (55)	40.00	12.00
1129	A284	8f multi (56)	45.00	12.00
		Nos. 1126-1129 (4)	175.00	48.00

Fair Building, Canton — A285

1973, Oct. 15   Photo.   Perf. 11

1130	A285	8f multicolored (95)	27.50	3.00

Export Commodities Fall Fair, Canton.

Teapot with Blue Phoenix Design — A286

Excavated Works of Art: No. 1132, Silver pot with horse design. No. 1133, Black pottery horse. No. 1134, Woman, clay figurine. No. 1135, Carved stone pillar base. No. 1136, Galloping bronze horse. No. 1137, Bronze inkwell (toad). No. 1138, Bronze lamp, Chang Hsin Palace. No. 1139, Bronze tripod. No. 1140, Square bronze pot. 20f, Bronze wine vessel. 52f, Painted red clay tripod.

1973, Nov. 20   Perf. 11½

1131	A286	4f ol bis & multi (66)	5.50	.75
1132	A286	4f ver & multi (67)	5.50	.75
1133	A286	8f yel grn & multi (68)	4.50	.75
1134	A286	8f brt rose & multi (69)	4.50	.75
1135	A286	8f lt vio & multi (70)	4.50	.75
1136	A286	8f yel bis & multi (71)	4.50	.75
1137	A286	8f lt bl & multi (72)	4.50	.75
1138	A286	8f gray & multi (73)	4.50	.75
1139	A286	10f yel bis & multi (74)	4.50	.75
1140	A286	10f dp org & multi (75)	4.50	.75
1141	A286	20f lil & multi (76)	9.00	2.00
1142	A286	52f grn & multi (77)	14.50	4.00
		Nos. 1131-1142 (12)	70.50	13.50

Marginal Markings

Marginal inscriptions on stamps of 1974-91 start at lower left with "J" for commemoratives and "T" for "special issues," followed by three numbers indicating (a) set sequence for the year, (b) total of stamps in set, and (c) number of stamp within set. At right appears the year date. Listings include the "c" number parenthetically. The "a" number is included only when it will help identify stamps not illustrated.

Example: T26 (6-3), the 3rd stamp of 6 from the 26th special set. Set numbers and or positions will be shown only when they help identify a stamp. An illustrated single stamp set will not have these numbers in the listings.

Woman Gymnast — A287

Designs: No. 1144, Gymnast on rings. No. 1145, Aerial split over balance beam, woman. No. 1146, Gymnast on parallel bars. No. 1147, Uneven bars, woman. No. 1148, Gymnast on horse. T.1.

1974, Jan. 1   Photo.   Perf. 11½x11

1143	A287	8f lt grn & multi (1)	10.00	3.50
1144	A287	8f lt vio & multi (2)	10.00	3.50
1145	A287	8f lt blue & multi (3)	10.00	3.50
1146	A287	8f sal & multi (4)	12.50	4.50
1147	A287	8f yel & multi (5)	10.00	4.50
1148	A287	8f lil rose & multi (6)	12.50	4.50
		Nos. 1143-1148 (6)	65.00	24.00

Girls Twirling Bamboo Diabolos — A288

Designs: No. 1149, Lion Dance, vert. No. 1150, Handstand on chairs, vert. No. 1152, Men balancing jar. No. 1153, Plate spinning, vert. No. 1154, Twirling umbrella, vert. T.2.

1974, Jan. 21   Perf. 11

1149	A288	8f brn & multi (1)	7.00	2.75
1150	A288	8f Prus bl & multi (2)	7.00	2.75
1151	A288	8f lilac & multi (3)	10.00	2.75
1152	A288	8f dull bl & multi (4)	7.00	2.75
1153	A288	8f ol grn & multi (5)	7.00	2.75
1154	A288	8f gray & multi (6)	10.00	2.75
		Nos. 1149-1154 (6)	48.00	16.50

Traditional acrobatics.

Shao Shan — A289

Site of 1st National Communist Party Congress — A289a

Peasant Movement Institute, Kwangchow — A289b

Headquarters of Nanchang Uprising — A289c

Great Hall of the People, Beijing — A289d

View of Wen Chia Shih — A289e

Tien An Men, Beijing — A289f

Tzeping in Chingkang Mountains — A289g

Site of Kutien Meeting — A289h

Tsunyi Conference Site — A289i

Yenan (bridge) — A289j

Hsi Pai Ho, Communist Party Meeting Site — A289k

Fairy Cave, Lushan — A289l

Monument to People's Heroes — A289m

Transportation by Railroad — A289n

Trucks on Mountain Road — A289o

1973-74   Litho.   Perf. 11
Without Gum

1163	A289	1f sl grn & pale grn	.65	.35
1164	A289a	1½f car & buff	.65	.35
1165	A289b	2f dk blue & pale grn	.70	.35
1166	A289c	3f dk ol & yel	.70	.35
1167	A289d	4f red & yel	1.00	.35
1168	A289e	5f brn & lt yel	.80	.35
1169	A289f	8f dull mag & buff	.80	.35
a.		Perf. 11½x12	15.00	
1170	A289g	10f blue & buff	.80	.40
1171	A289h	20f dk red & buff	1.50	.40
1172	A289i	22f vio & lt yel	5.00	1.90
1173	A289j	35f mar & lt yel	3.50	1.75
1174	A289k	43f red brn & buff	4.50	2.00
1175	A289l	50f dk blue & pink	3.00	.50
1176	A289m	52f sepia & buff	3.00	.50

Photogravure & Engraved

1177	A289n	$1 multicolored ('73)	5.00	1.25
1178	A289o	$2 multicolored	6.00	1.25
		Nos. 1163-1178 (16)	37.60	12.40

Capital Stadium — A290

Design: 8f, Hotel Peking.

1974, Dec. 1   Photo.   Perf. 11
Without Gum

1179	A290	4f black & yel grn	.75	.25
1180	A290	8f black & ultra	.60	.25

"Veteran Secretary" — A291   Well Diggers — A292

Designs: Nos. 1183-1186 horizontal. T.3.

1974, Apr. 20   Photo.   Perf. 11

1181	A291	8f shown (1)	4.00	2.25
1182	A292	8f shown (2)	4.00	2.25
1183	A291	8f Spring hoeing (3)	5.00	2.25
1184	A291	8f Farmers (4)	5.00	2.25
1185	A292	8f Farm (5)	5.00	2.25
1186	A291	8f Bumper crops (6)	5.00	2.25
		Nos. 1181-1186 (6)	28.00	13.75

Paintings by farmers of Huhsien County, shown at exhibition in Peking.

Mailman on Motorcycle — A293

1974, May 15   Photo.   Perf. 11

1187	A293	8f shown (1)	10.00	4.50
1188	A293	8f People of the world (2)	10.00	3.50
1189	A293	8f Great Wall (3)	15.00	3.50
		Nos. 1187-1189 (3)	35.00	11.50

Centenary of the UPU. J.1.

Barefoot Doctor Inoculating Children A294

Designs (Barefoot Doctors): No. 1191, Crossing stream at night to reach patient, vert. No. 1192, Gathering herbs, vert. No. 1193, Acupuncture treatment for farmer in the field.

Perf. 11x11½, 11½x11
1974, June 26   Photo.

1190	A294	8f multicolored (82)	15.00	2.00
1191	A294	8f multicolored (83)	20.00	3.00
1192	A294	8f multicolored (84)	17.50	2.00
1193	A294	8f multicolored (85)	15.00	2.00
		Nos. 1190-1193 (4)	67.50	9.00

Steel Worker Wang Chin-hsi — A295

No. 1195, Workers studying Mao's writings around campfire. No. 1196, Drilling for oil in winter. No. 1197, Scientific industrial management. No. 1198, Oil derricks and farms. T.4.

1974, Sept. 30   Photo.   Perf. 11

1194	A295	8f multi (5-1)	6.00	1.50
1195	A295	8f multi (5-2)	5.50	1.50
1196	A295	8f multi (5-3)	5.50	1.50
1197	A295	8f multi (5-4)	5.50	1.50
1198	A295	8f multi (5-5)	6.00	1.50
		Nos. 1194-1198 (5)	28.50	7.50

Workers of Taching as examples of achievement.

Members of Tachai Commune — A296

No. 1200, Farmers leveling mountains and fields in winter. No. 1201, Scientific farming. No. 1202, Trucks carrying surplus harvest. No. 1203, Young workers with banner. T.5.

1974, Sept. 30

1199	A296	8f multi (5-1)	5.00	1.50
1200	A296	8f multi (5-2)	5.00	1.50
1201	A296	8f multi (5-3)	5.00	1.50
1202	A296	8f multi (5-4)	6.00	1.50
1203	A296	8f multi (5-5)	6.00	1.50
		Nos. 1199-1203 (5)	27.00	7.50

Farmers of Tachai as examples of achievement.

Arms of Republic and Members of
Ethnic Groups — A297

1974, Oct. 1
1204 A297 8f multi (1-1)   37.50   8.50

Taching Steel
Worker — A298

Designs: No. 1206, Tachai farm woman. No.
1207, Soldier, planes and ships. J.3.

1974, Oct. 1
1205 A298 8f multi (3-1)   4.50   2.00
1206 A298 8f multi (3-2)   4.50   2.00
1207 A298 8f multi (3-3)   4.50   2.00
  a.   Strip of 3, #1205-1207   25.00 12.00

People's Republic of China, 25th anniv.
Values for No. 1207a are for an unfolded
strip.

Export Commodities Fair Building,
Canton — A299

1974, Oct. 15
1208 A299 8f multicolored   12.00   2.00

Chinese Export Commodities Fair, Canton.

Guerrillas'
Monument,
Permet,
Albania — A300

Albanian Patriots
and Coat of
Arms — A301

1974, Nov. 29   Photo.   Perf. 11½x11
1209 A300 8f multicolored   8.50   2.00
1210 A301 8f multicolored   8.50   2.00

Albania's liberation, 30th anniversary.

Water-cooled Generator — A302

Industrial Products: No. 1212, Motorized
rice sprouts transplanter. No. 1213, Universal
cylindrical grinding machine. No. 1214, Open-
air rock drill, vert. All dated 1973.

Photogravure and Engraved
1974, Dec. 23   Perf. 11
1211 A302 8f vio & multi (78)   75.00 11.00
1212 A302 8f yel grn & multi
         (79)   100.00 25.00
1213 A302 8f ver & multi (80)   75.00 11.00
1214 A302 8f blue & multi
         (81)   150.00 25.00
  Nos. 1211-1214 (4)   400.00 72.00

Congress Delegates — A303

Designs: No. 1216, Red flags, constitution
and flowers. No. 1217, Worker, farmer and
soldier, agriculture and industry.

1975, Jan. 25   Photo.   Perf. 11½
1215 A303 8f gold & multi (3-
         1)   16.00   4.00
1216 A303 8f gold & multi (3-
         2)   20.00   4.00
1217 A303 8f gold & multi (3-
         3)   25.00 10.00
  Nos. 1215-1217 (3)   61.00 18.00

Fourth National People's Congress, Peking.

Teacher Studying Revolutionary
Works — A304

No. 1219, Teacher, children and horse. No.
1220, Outdoors class. No. 1221, Class held in
boat. T.9.

1975, Mar. 8   Photo.   Perf. 11
1218 A304 8f multi (4-1)   17.50   5.00
1219 A304 8f multi (4-2)   27.50   6.00
1220 A304 8f multi (4-3)   20.00   5.00
1221 A304 8f multi (4-4)   17.50   4.00
  Nos. 1218-1221 (4)   82.50 20.00

Rural women teachers and for International
Working Women's Day.

"Broadsword," Encounter
Position — A305

No. 1223, Exercise with 2 swords (woman).
No. 1224, Graceful boxing (woman). No. 1225,
Man leaping with spear. No. 1226, Woman
holding fighting staff. 43f, 2 women with
spears against man with 3-section staff.

1975, June 10   Photo.   Perf. 11x11½
Size: 39x29mm
1222 A305 8f (6-1)   6.00   2.25
1223 A305 8f (6-2)   7.00   2.25
1224 A305 8f (6-3)   5.00   2.25
1225 A305 8f (6-4)   5.00   2.25
1226 A305 8f (6-5)   6.00   2.25
Size: 59x29mm
1227 A305 43f red & multi (6-
         6)   12.00   8.00
  Nos. 1222-1227 (6)   41.00 19.25

Wushu ("Kung Fu"), self-defense exercises.
Tête bêche in sheets of 50 (5x10). Value, set
of pairs $120.

Mass Judgment
and
Criticisms — A306

No. 1229, Brigade leader writing wall newspaper. No. 1230, Study and criticism on battlefield, horiz. No. 1231, Former "slave" led into
battle by criticism of Lin Piao and Confucius,
horiz. T.8.

Perf. 11½x11, 11x11½
1975, Aug. 20   Photo.
1228 A306 8f red & multi (4-
         1)   20.00   4.00
1229 A306 8f red & multi (4-
         2)   20.00   4.00
1230 A306 8f red & multi (4-
         3)   18.50   4.00
1231 A306 8f red & multi (4-
         4)   20.00   4.00
  Nos. 1228-1231 (4)   78.50 16.00

Campaign to encourage criticism of Lin Piao
and Confucius.

Athletes Studying Theory of
Dictatorship of Proletariat — A307

3rd National Sports Meet: No. 1232,
Women athletes leading parade, vert. No.
1234, Women volleyball players. No. 1235,
Runner, soldier, farmer and worker, vert. No.
1236, Young athlete and various sports. No.
1237, Athletes of various races and horse
race. 35f, Children and diving tower, vert. J.6.

1975, Sept. 12   Photo.   Perf. 11½
1232 A307 8f multi (7-1)   4.50   1.00
1233 A307 8f multi (7-2)   8.50   1.00
1234 A307 8f multi (7-3)   18.50   2.00
1235 A307 8f multi (7-4)   4.50   1.00
1236 A307 8f multi (7-5)   4.50   1.00
1237 A307 8f multi (7-6)   4.50   1.00
1238 A307 35f multi (7-7)   4.50   3.00
  Nos. 1232-1238 (7)   49.50 10.00

Mountaineers
A308

Mt. Everest
A309

Design: No. 1240, Mountaineers raising
Chinese flag on summit, horiz. T.15.

1975   Photo.   Perf. 11½x11, 11x11½
1239 A308 8f multi (3-2)   2.50   1.00
1240 A308 8f multi (3-3)   2.50   1.00
1241 A309 43f multi (3-1)   4.00   1.25
  Nos. 1239-1241 (3)   9.00   3.25

Chinese Mt. Everest expedition.

Agricultural Workers with
Book — A310

No. 1243, Workers carrying load. No. 1244,
Woman driving harvester combine. J.7.

1975, Oct. 1   Perf. 11½
1242 A310 8f multi (3-1)   9.00   1.75
1243 A310 8f multi (3-2)   9.00   1.75
1244 A310 8f multi (3-3)   13.00   1.75
  Nos. 1242-1244 (3)   31.00   5.25

National Conference to promote learning
from Tachai's achievements in agriculture.

Girl Giving Boy
Red
Scarf — A311

Designs (Children): No. 1246, Putting up
wall posters criticizing Lin Piao and Confucius.
No. 1247, Studying. No. 1248, Harvesting.
52f, Physical training. T.14.

1975, Dec. 1   Photo.   Perf. 11½
1245 A311 8f multi (5-1)   4.00   1.25
1246 A311 8f multi (5-2)   4.00   1.25
1247 A311 8f multi (5-3)   4.00   1.25
1248 A311 8f multi (5-4)   4.00   1.25
1249 A311 52f multi (5-5)   8.00   2.50
  Nos. 1245-1249 (5)   24.00   7.50

Moral, intellectual and physical progress of
Chinese children.

Woman
Plowing
Rice Field
A312

No. 1251, Mechanized rice planting. No.
1252, Drainage and irrigation. No. 1253,
Woman spraying insecticide over cotton field.
No. 1254, Combine. T.13.

1975, Dec. 15   Perf. 11
1250 A312 8f multi (5-1)   7.00   1.75
1251 A312 8f multi (5-2)   7.00   1.75
1252 A312 8f multi (5-3)   5.00   1.75
1253 A312 8f multi (5-4)   5.00   1.75
1254 A312 8f multi (5-5)   5.00   1.75
  Nos. 1250-1254 (5)   29.00   8.75

Priority program of farm mechanization.

Farmland and Irrigation Canal — A313

Designs of Nos. 1255-1270 numbered J.8.:
No. 1256, Irrigation canal (16-2). No. 1257,
Fertilizer plant (16-3). No. 1258, Textile plant
(16-4). No. 1259, Anshan Iron and Steel Co.
(16-5). No. 1260, Coal freight trains (16-6).
No. 1261, Hydroelectric station (16-7). No.
1262, Ship building (16-8). No. 1263, Oil
industry (16-9). No. 1264, Pipe line and port
(16-10). No. 1265, Train on viaduct (16-11).
No. 1266, Scientific research (16-12). No.
1267, Classroom (16-13). No. 1268, Health
Center (16-14). No. 1269, Apartment houses
(16-15). No. 1270, Department store (16-16).

1976   Photo.   Perf. 11½
1255 A313 8f shown (16-1)   8.00   2.25
1256 A313 8f multi   8.00   2.25
1257 A313 8f multi   15.00   2.25
1258 A313 8f multi   8.00   2.25

1259 A313 8f multi	8.00	2.25
1260 A313 8f multi	10.00	2.25
1261 A313 8f multi	10.00	2.25
1262 A313 8f multi	10.00	2.25
1263 A313 8f multi	10.00	2.25
1264 A313 8f multi	10.00	2.25
1265 A313 8f multi	10.00	2.25
1266 A313 8f multi	8.00	2.25
1267 A313 8f multi	24.00	5.50
1268 A313 8f multi	8.00	2.25
1269 A313 8f multi	8.00	2.25
1270 A313 8f multi	24.00	5.50
Nos. 1255-1270 (16)	179.00	42.50

Nos. 1255-1270 commemorate fulfillment of 4th Five-year Plan.

Issued: Nos. 1255-1259, 2/20; Nos. 1260-1264, 4/9; Nos. 1265-1270, 6/12.

Heart Surgery with Acupuncture Anesthesia — A314

Operating Room and: No. 1272, Man driving tractor with severed arm restored. No. 1273, Man exercising broken arm in cast. No. 1274, Patient threading needle after cataract operation. T.12.

1976, Apr. 9	**Photo.**	**Perf. 11½**
1271 A314 8f brn & multi (4-1)	8.00	2.00
1272 A314 8f yel grn & multi (4-2)	15.00	3.00
1273 A314 8f bl grn & multi (4-3)	8.00	1.75
1274 A314 8f vio bl & multi (4-4)	8.00	1.75
Nos. 1271-1274 (4)	39.00	8.50

Achievements in medical and health services.

Students in May 7 School — A315

Designs: No. 1276, Students as farm workers. No. 1277, Production brigade. J.9.

1976, May 7	**Photo.**	**Perf. 11½**
1275 A315 8f multi (3-1)	12.00	2.00
1276 A315 8f multi (3-2)	5.00	2.00
1277 A315 8f multi (3-3)	11.00	2.00
Nos. 1275-1277 (3)	28.00	6.00

Chairman Mao's May 7 Directive, 10th anniv.

Mass Training in Swimming — A316

No. 1279, Swimmers crossing Yangtze River. No. 1280, Swimmers walking into the surf. J.10.

1976, July 16	**Photo.**	**Perf. 11½**
	Size: 47x27mm	
1278 A316 8f multi (3-1)	8.00	2.00
	Size: 35x27mm	
1279 A316 8f multi (3-2)	8.00	2.00
1280 A316 8f multi (3-3)	8.00	2.00
Nos. 1278-1280 (3)	24.00	6.00

Chairman Mao's swim in Yangtze River, 10th anniversary.

Workers, Peasants and Soldiers Going to College — A317

No. 1282, Classroom. No. 1283, Instruction on construction site. No. 1284, Computer room. No. 1285, Graduates returning home. T.18.

1976, Sept. 6	**Photo.**	**Perf. 11½**
1281 A317 8f multi (5-1)	10.00	2.50
1282 A317 8f multi (5-2)	11.00	2.50
1283 A317 8f multi (5-3)	13.00	3.50
1284 A317 8f multi (5-4)	13.00	3.50
1285 A317 8f multi (5-5)	11.00	2.50
Nos. 1281-1285 (5)	58.00	14.50

Success of proletarian education system.

Power Line Repair by Woman — A318

No. 1287, Insulator repair. No. 1288, Cherry picker. No. 1289, Transformer repair. T.16.

1976, Sept. 15		
1286 A318 8f multi (4-1)	9.00	1.75
1287 A318 8f multi (4-2)	9.00	1.75
1288 A318 8f multi (4-3)	6.00	1.75
1289 A318 8f multi (4-4)	6.00	1.75
Nos. 1286-1289 (4)	30.00	7.00

Maintenance of high power lines.

Lu Hsun A319

No. 1291, Lu Hsun sick, writing in bed. No. 1292, Lu Hsun with worker, soldier and peasant. J.11.

	Photo. & Engr.	
1976, Oct. 19		**Perf. 11x11½**
1290 A319 8f multi (3-1)	5.00	2.00
	Photo.	
1291 A319 8f multi (3-2)	14.00	3.50
1292 A319 8f multi (3-3)	7.50	2.00
Nos. 1290-1292 (3)	26.50	7.50

Lu Hsun (1881-1936), writer and revolutionary leader.

Old Farmer Tying Towel on Student's Head — A320

Designs: No. 1294, Student teaching farm woman, horiz. No. 1295, Students climbing mountain for new water resources. No. 1296, Student testing wheat, horiz. 10f, Student feeding lamb. 20f, Frontier guards, horiz. T.17.

1976, Dec. 22	**Photo.**	**Perf. 11½**
1293 A320 4f multi (6-1)	4.50	.75
1294 A320 8f multi (6-2)	4.50	.85
1295 A320 8f multi (6-3)	4.50	.85
1296 A320 8f multi (6-4)	10.00	3.00
1297 A320 10f multi (6-5)	7.00	.85
1298 A320 20f multi (6-6)	8.00	2.50
Nos. 1293-1298 (6)	38.50	8.80

Students' efforts to help poor country people.

Mao's Home, Shaoshan — A321

Shaoshan, Mao's birthplace: No. 1300, School building. No. 1301, Farmers' Association building. 10f, Railroad station. T.11.

1976, Dec. 26		**Perf. 11**
1299 A321 4f multi (4-1)	3.50	1.50
1300 A321 8f multi (4-2)	3.50	1.50
1301 A321 8f multi (4-3)	6.25	1.50
1302 A321 10f multi (4-4)	3.50	1.50
Nos. 1299-1302 (4)	16.75	6.00

Chou En-lai — A322

No. 1304, Chou giving report at 10th Party Congress. No. 1305, Chou with Wang Chin-hsi, famous oil worker, horiz. No. 1306, Chou with people of Tachai, 1973, horiz. J.13.

1977, Jan. 8	**Photo.**	**Perf. 11½**
1303 A322 8f multi (4-1)	3.75	1.25
1304 A322 8f multi (4-2)	5.00	1.25
1305 A322 8f multi (4-3)	3.75	1.25
1306 A322 8f multi (4-4)	10.00	1.25
Nos. 1303-1306 (4)	22.50	5.00

Premier Chou En-lai (1898-1976), a founder of Chinese Communist Party, 1st death anniversary.

Liu Hu-lan, an Inspiration A323

Liu Hu-lan, Chinese heroine: No. 1307, Liu Hu-lan monument. No. 1308, Mao Tse-tung quotation: "A great life-a glorious death." J.12.

1977, Jan. 31		
1307 A323 8f multi (3-1)	16.00	4.00
1308 A323 8f multi (3-2)	5.00	2.00
1309 A323 8f multi (3-3)	5.00	2.00
Nos. 1307-1309 (3)	26.00	8.00

Uprising in Taiwan A324

Design: 10f, Gate of Heavenly Peace, Peking; Sun Moon Lake, Taiwan, Taiwanese people holding PRC flag. J.14.

1977, Feb. 28	**Photo.**	**Perf. 11**
1310 A324 8f multi (2-1)	9.00	1.25
1311 A324 10f multi (2-2)	11.00	1.75

Uprising of the people of Taiwan, 2/28/47.

Sharpshooters — A325

Militia Women: No. 1313, Women horseback riders. No. 1314, Underground defense tunnel. T.10.

1977, Mar. 8		**Perf. 11½**
1312 A325 8f multi (3-1)	7.00	3.00
1313 A325 8f multi (3-2)	7.00	3.00
1314 A325 8f multi (3-3)	10.00	3.00
Nos. 1312-1314 (3)	24.00	9.00

Coal Mining — A326

Export (Loading Railroad Car onto Ship) — A326b

Sheepherding — A326a

Hydroelectric Station — A326d

Forestry — A326c

Fishery — A326e

Combine in Field — A326f

Steel Production — A326h

Textiles — A326j

Radio Tower, Mail Truck — A326g

Trucks on Mountain Road — A326i

Tractor Assembly Line — A326k

Offshore Oil
Rigs, Birds,
Setting Sun —
A326l

Railroad Bridge,
Yangtze Gorge
— A326m

No numbers.

1977		Photo.	Perf. 11½	
1315	A326	1f yel grn, red & blk	.45	.30
1316	A326a	1½f bl grn, yel grn & brn	.50	.30
1317	A326b	2f org, bl & blk	.50	.30
1318	A326c	3f ol & dk grn	.60	.30
1319	A326d	4f lil, org & blk	.85	.30
1320	A326e	5f lt ol & ultra	.85	.30
1321	A326f	8f red & yel	.85	.30
1322	A326g	10f lt grn, org & bl	.85	.30
1323	A326h	20f org, yel & bl	.95	.30
1324	A326i	30f bl, gray grn & blk	1.25	.30
1325	A326j	40f multicolored	1.40	.35
1326	A326k	50f cit, red & blk	1.25	.35
1327	A326l	60f pur, lt & dk org	1.25	.45
1328	A326m	70f blue & multi	2.00	.75
		Nos. 1315-1328 (14)	13.55	4.90

Nos. 1316, 1317 and 1325 exist imperf.
Value, pair each $1,000.

Address by
Party
Committee
A327

Designs: No. 1330, Planting new rice fields.
No. 1331, Farmers reading wall newspaper.
No. 1332, Land reclamation. T.22.

1977, Apr. 9   **Perf. 11x11½**

1329	A327	8f multi (4-1)	4.50	1.00
1330	A327	8f multi (4-2)	4.50	1.00
1331	A327	8f multi (4-3)	4.50	1.00
1332	A327	8f multi (4-4)	4.50	1.00
		Nos. 1329-1332 (4)	18.00	4.00

Building Tachai-type communities throughout China.

Worker at Microphone — A328

Designs: No. 1334, Drilling for oil during
snowstorm. No. 1335, Crowd advancing under
Red banner. No. 1336, Workers, industrial
complex, rocket blast-off. J.15.

1977, Apr. 25   **Perf. 11**

1333	A328	8f multi (4-1)	7.00	1.25
1334	A328	8f multi (4-2)	7.00	1.25
1335	A328	8f multi (4-3)	7.00	1.25
1336	A328	8f multi (4-4)	7.00	1.25
		Nos. 1333-1336 (4)	28.00	5.00

Conference on learning from Taching workers in industry.

Mongolians
Hailing
Anniversary
A329

10f, Iron and steel complex, iron ore train.
20f, Cattle grazing in improved pasture. J.16.

1977, May 1   **Perf. 11x11½**

1337	A329	8f multi (3-1)	5.00	.75
1338	A329	10f multi (3-2)	1.50	.55
1339	A329	20f multi (3-3)	3.00	1.00
		Nos. 1337-1339 (3)	9.50	2.30

30th anniversary of Inner Mongolian Autonomous Region.

1877 Flag of
Romania and
Oak
Leaves — A330

Mihai Viteazu
Memorial (16th
Century
Hero) — A331

10f, Battle of Smirdan, by N. Grigorescu.
J.17.

1977, May 9   **Photo.**   **Perf. 11**

1340	A330	8f multi (3-1)	5.00	1.25
1341	A331	10f multi (3-2)	1.00	1.00
1342	A331	20f multi (3-3)	1.00	1.00
		Nos. 1340-1342 (3)	7.00	3.25

Centenary of Romanian independence.

Yenan "Let
100
Flowers
Bloom"
A332

No. 1344, Hammer, sickle, gun & flowers;
"Proletarian revolutionary literature will prosper." J.18.

1977, May, 23

1343	A332	8f grn, red & gold	1.75	.65
1344	A332	8f lt brn, red & gold	1.75	.65

Yenan Forum on Literature & Art, 35th anniv.

Zhu De — A333

Designs: No. 1346, Zhu De, last address to
Congress. No. 1347, Zhu De at his desk,
horiz. No. 1348, Zhu De on horseback as
commander of Red Army. J.19.

1977, July 6   **Photo.**   **Perf. 11½**

1345	A333	8f multi (4-1)	1.50	.45
1346	A333	8f multi (4-2)	1.50	.45
1347	A333	8f multi (4-3)	2.00	.55
1348	A333	8f multi (4-4)	2.00	.55
		Nos. 1345-1348 (4)	7.00	2.00

Zhu De (1886-1976), Commander of Red
Army, Chairman of National People's
Congress.

Military under
Mao's
Banner — A334

No. 1350, Red Flag, Soldiers, Chingkang
Mountains. No. 1351, Guerrilla fighters
returning to base. No. 1352, Guerrillas crossing Yangtze. No. 1353, National defense. J.20.

1977, Aug. 1

1349	A334	8f multi (5-1)	7.00	1.50
1350	A334	8f multi (5-2)	3.50	1.50
1351	A334	8f multi (5-3)	5.50	1.50
1352	A334	8f multi (5-4)	5.50	1.50
1353	A334	8f multi (5-5)	4.00	1.50
		Nos. 1349-1353 (5)	25.50	7.50

Liberation Army Day, 50th anniversary of
People's Army.

Gate of Heavenly Peace, People and
Red Flags — A335

Designs: No. 1355, People marching under
Red Flag with Mao's portrait. No. 1356, People marching under Red Flag with hammer
and sickle. J.23.

1977, Aug. 22   **Photo.**   **Perf. 11½x11**

1354	A335	8f multi (3-1)	15.00	4.00
1355	A335	8f multi (3-2)	15.00	4.00
1356	A335	8f multi (3-3)	15.00	4.00
		Nos. 1354-1356 (3)	45.00	12.00

11th National Congress of the Communist
Party of China.

Chairman
Mao — A336

Designs (Mao Portraits): No. 1358, as
young man in Shansi. No. 1359, addressing
Communist Party in Plenary Session. No.
1360, Proclaiming People's Republic at Gate
of Heavenly Peace. No. 1361, at airport with
Chou En-lai and Zhu De, horiz. No. 1362,
Reviewing Army as old man. J.21.

1977, Sept. 9   **Photo.**   **Perf. 11½**

1357	A336	8f multi (6-1)	4.00	1.25
1358	A336	8f multi (6-2)	4.00	1.25
1359	A336	8f multi (6-3)	4.00	1.25
1360	A336	8f multi (6-4)	4.00	1.25
1361	A336	8f multi (6-5)	6.00	1.25
1362	A336	8f multi (6-6)	4.00	1.25
		Nos. 1357-1362 (6)	26.00	7.50

Mao-Tse-tung (1893-1976), first death
anniversary.

Mao Memorial Hall — A337

Completion of Mao Memorial Hall: No.
1364, Chairman Hua's inscription. J.22.

1977, Sept. 9

1363	A337	8f lt ultra & multi	5.00	1.50
1364	A337	8f lt grn, tan & gold	7.50	2.25

Tractors Moving Drilling Tower — A338

No. 1366, Shui Pow Tsi oil well and women
workers. No. 1367, Construction of oil pipe

line, Taching, and silos. No. 1368, Tung Fang
Hung oil refinery, Peking. No. 1369, Taching
oil loaded into tanker in harbor. 20f, Off-shore
drilling platform "Pohai No. 1." T.19.

1978, Jan. 31   **Photo.**   **Perf. 11**

1365	A338	8f multi (6-1)	2.00	.75
1366	A338	8f multi (6-2)	2.00	.75
1367	A338	8f multi (6-3)	2.00	.75
1368	A338	8f multi (6-4)	4.00	.75
1369	A338	8f multi (6-5)	4.00	.75
1370	A338	20f multi (6-6)	4.00	2.00
		Nos. 1365-1370 (6)	18.00	5.75

Development of Chinese oil industry.

"Army Teaching Militia" — A339

No. 1372, "Army helping with rice planting."
T.23.

1978, Feb. 5   **Photo.**   **Perf. 11**

1371	A339	8f multi (2-1)	4.50	1.25
1372	A339	8f multi (2-2)	4.50	1.25

Army and people working as a family.

Red Flags, Mao
Tse-tung — A340

Constitution and
Red
Flags — A341

No. 1375, Atom symbol over symbols of
agriculture & industry. All designs include
Great Hall of the People, Peking, & flowers.
J.24.

1978, Feb. 26

1373	A340	8f multi (3-1)	4.00	.85
1374	A341	8f multi (3-2)	4.00	.85
1375	A340	8f multi (3-3)	4.00	.85
		Nos. 1373-1375 (3)	12.00	2.55

5th National People's Congress.

Mao's Eulogy for
Lei Feng — A342

Lei Feng,
Studying Mao's
Works — A343

No. 1377, Chairman Hua's thoughts (5
lines). J.26.

1978, Mar. 5

1376	A342	8f gold & red (3-1)	8.00 2.00
1377	A342	8f gold & red (3-2)	8.00 2.00
1378	A343	8f multicolored (3-3)	8.00 2.00
		Nos. 1376-1378 (3)	24.00 6.00

Lei Feng (1940-1962), communist fighter; 15th anniversary of Chairman Mao's eulogy "Learn from Comrade Lei Feng."

Hsiang Ching-yu — A344

Yang Kai-hui — A345

1978, Mar. 8

1379	A344	8f multi (2-1)	4.00 1.00
1380	A345	8f multi (2-2)	4.00 1.00

Hsiang Ching-yu, pioneer of Women's Movement, executed 1928; Yang Kai-hui, communist fighter, executed 1930. J.27.

A346

A346a

A346b

No. 1381, Conference emblem. No. 1382, Banners symbolizing industry, agriculture, defense & science. No. 1383, Red flag, atom symbol & globe. J.25.

1978, Mar. 18   Litho.   Perf. 11½x11

1381	A346	8f gold & red (3-1)	3.00	.90
1382	A346a	8f multi (3-2)	3.00	.90
1383	A346b	8f multi (3-3)	3.00	.90
a.		Souvenir sheet of 3	400.00	180.00
		Nos. 1381-1383 (3)	9.00	2.70

Natl. Science Conf. No. 1383a contains Nos. 1381-1383 with simulated perforations. Sold for 50f.

Release of Weather Balloon A347

Weather Observations: No. 1385, Radar station, typhoon watch. No. 1386, Computer, weather maps. No. 1387, Local weather observers. No. 1388, Rockets intercepting hail clouds. T.24.

1978, Apr. 25   Photo.   Perf. 11x11½

1384	A347	8f multi (5-1)	1.50 .70
1385	A347	8f multi (5-2)	1.50 .70
1386	A347	8f multi (5-3)	1.50 .70
1387	A347	8f multi (5-4)	1.50 .70
1388	A347	8f multi (5-5)	1.50 .70
		Nos. 1384-1388 (5)	7.50 3.50

Galloping Horse — A348

Designs: Galloping Horses, by Hsu Peihung (1895-1953). 40f, 50f, 60f, 70f, $5, horiz. T.28.

1978, May 5   Perf. 11½x11, 11x11½

1389	A348	4f multi (10-1)	3.00 1.00
1390	A348	8f multi (10-2)	3.00 1.00
1391	A348	8f multi (10-3)	3.00 1.00
1392	A348	10f multi (10-4)	4.00 1.00
1393	A348	20f multi (10-5)	4.00 1.00
1394	A348	30f multi (10-6)	8.50 2.00
1395	A348	40f multi (10-7)	6.50 1.75
1396	A348	50f multi (10-8)	25.00 3.00
1397	A348	60f multi (10-9)	8.00 2.00
1398	A348	70f multi (10-10)	7.00 2.00
		Nos. 1389-1398 (10)	72.00 15.75

Souvenir Sheet

1399	A348	$5 multicolored	525.00 190.00

No. 1399 contains one stamp showing 4 horses, size: 89x39mm.

Children Playing Soccer — A349

Designs: No. 1401, Children on the beach. No. 1402, Little girls dancing. No. 1403, Children taking long walks. 20f, Children exercising for good health. T.21.

Size: 22x27mm

1978, June 1   Perf. 11½

1400	A349	8f multi (5-2)	1.00 .50
1401	A349	8f multi (5-3)	1.00 .50
1402	A349	8f multi (5-4)	1.00 .50
1403	A349	8f multi (5-5)	1.00 .50

Size: 48x28mm

1404	A349	20f multi (5-1)	1.25 .80
		Nos. 1400-1404 (5)	5.25 2.80

Build up your health while young.

Synthetic Fiber Feeder A350

Designs: No. 1406, Drawing out threads. No. 1407, Weaving. No. 1408, Dyeing and printing. No. 1409, Finished products. T.25.

1978, June 15   Photo.   Perf. 11½

1405	A350	8f multi (5-1)	1.00 .60
1406	A350	8f multi (5-2)	1.00 .60
1407	A350	8f multi (5-3)	1.00 .60
1408	A350	8f multi (5-4)	1.00 .60

1409	A350	8f multi (5-5)	1.00 .60
a.		Strip of 5, #1405-1409	11.00 11.00
		Nos. 1405-1409 (5)	5.00 3.00

Chemical fiber industry. No. 1409a has continuous design. No. 1409a is valued as an unfolded strip. Folded strips sell for less.

Conference Emblem A351

"Develop Economy and Ensure Supplies" A352

1978, June 20   Perf. 13

1410	A351	8f multi (2-1)	1.75 .55
1411	A352	8f multi (2-2)	1.75 .55

Natl. Conf. on Learning from Taching and Tachai in Finance and Trade. J.28.

New Pastures, Mongolia — A353

Designs: No. 1413, Kazakh shepherds selecting sheep for breeding. No. 1414, Mechanized shearing of sheep, Tibet. T.27.

1978, June 30   Photo.   Perf. 11½

1412	A353	8f multi (3-1)	3.00 .80
1413	A353	8f multi (3-2)	3.00 .80
1414	A353	8f multi (3-3)	3.00 .80
		Nos. 1412-1414 (3)	9.00 2.40

Learning from Tachai in developing animal husbandry and new pastoral areas.

Coke Oven — A354

Iron and Steel Industry: No. 1416, Iron furnace. No. 1417, Pouring steel. No. 1418, Steel rolling. No. 1419, Finished iron and steel products. T.26.

1978, July 22

1415	A354	8f multi (5-1)	2.25 .50
1416	A354	8f multi (5-2)	2.25 .50
1417	A354	8f multi (5-3)	2.25 .50
1418	A354	8f multi (5-4)	2.25 .50
1419	A354	8f multi (5-5)	2.25 .50
		Nos. 1415-1419 (5)	11.25 2.50

Iron Fist to Prevent Revisionism A355

No. 1421, "Carrying forward revolutionary tradition." No. 1422, "Strenuous training in military skills to wipe out enemy." T.32.

1978, Aug. 1   Photo.   Perf. 11½

1420	A355	8f multi (3-1)	3.50 .70
1421	A355	8f multi (3-2)	3.50 .70
1422	A355	8f multi (3-3)	3.50 .70
		Nos. 1420-1422 (3)	10.50 2.10

"Learn from Hard-boned 6th Company." (A military unit since 1939).

Jug in Shape of Sheep — A356

Arts and Crafts: 4f, Giant lion (toy; horiz.). No. 1425, Rhinoceros (lacquer ware; horiz.). 10f, Cat (embroidery). 20f, Bag (weaving; horiz.). 30f, Teapot in shape of peacock (cloisonné). 40f, Plate with lotus, and swan-shaped box (lacquer ware; horiz.). 50f, Dragon flying in sky (ivory). 60f, Sun rising (jade; horiz.). 70f, Flight to human world (ivory). $3, Flying fairies (arts and crafts; horiz.). T.29.

1978, Aug. 26

1423	A356	4f multi (10-1)	.95 .45
1424	A356	8f multi (10-2)	.95 .45
1425	A356	8f multi (10-3)	.95 .45
1426	A356	10f multi (10-4)	.95 .55
1427	A356	20f multi (10-5)	.95 .55
1428	A356	30f multi (10-6)	2.00 .80
1429	A356	40f multi (10-7)	2.50 1.10
1430	A356	50f multi (10-8)	6.00 2.75
1431	A356	60f multi (10-9)	3.50 2.75
1432	A356	70f multi (10-10)	3.50 1.60
		Nos. 1423-1432 (10)	22.25 11.45

Souvenir Sheet

1433	A356	$3 multi	300.00 175.00

No. 1433 contains one 85x36mm stamp.

Women, Atom Symbol, Rocket and Wheat A357

1978, Sept. 8   Photo.   Perf. 11

1434	A357	8f multicolored	2.00 1.00

4th National Women's Congress.

Ginseng — A358

Medicinal Plants: No. 1436, Horn of plenty. No. 1437, Blackberry lily. No. 1438, Balloon-flower. 55f, Rhododendron dauricum. T.30.

1978, Sept. 15

1435	A358	8f multi (5-1)	1.00 .35
1436	A358	8f multi (5-2)	1.00 .35
1437	A358	8f multi (5-3)	1.00 .35
1438	A358	8f multi (5-4)	1.00 .35
1439	A358	55f multi (5-5)	4.00 1.25
		Nos. 1435-1439 (5)	8.00 2.65

Flag, Wheat, Cogwheel, Plane, Atom Symbols — A359

1978, Oct. 11   Photo.   Perf. 11

1440	A359	8f multicolored	3.50 1.00

9th National Trade Union Congress.

Youth League Emblem A360

1978, Oct. 16
1441 A360 8f multicolored 3.50 1.00

10th Natl. Communist Youth League Cong.

Chinese and Japanese Girls Exchanging Gifts A361

Great Wall and Mt. Fuji A362

1978, Oct. 22
1442 A361 8f multicolored 1.50 .75
1443 A362 55f multicolored 2.50 1.50

Signing of Sino-Japanese Peace and Friendship Treaty.

Moslem, Chinese and Mongolian People — A363

No. 1445, Loading coal at Holan Mountain. 10f, Irrigated rice fields & boxthorn. J.29.

1978, Oct. 25
1444 A363 8f multi (3-1) 2.50 1.00
1445 A363 8f multi (3-2) 2.50 1.00
1446 A363 10f multi (3-3) 3.00 1.00
    Nos. 1444-1446 (3) 8.00 3.00

20th anniversary of founding of Ningsia Moslem Autonomous Region.

Chinsha River Bridge, West Szechuan A364

Highway Bridges: No. 1448, Hsinhong bridge, Wuhsi. No. 1449, Chiuhsikou bridge, Fengdu. No. 1450, Chinsha River bridge, West Szechuan. 60f, Shangyeh bridge, Sanmen. $2, Hsiang-kiang River bridge. T.31.

1978, Nov. 1   Photo.   Perf. 11½x11
1447 A364 8f multi (5-1) 1.50 .40
1448 A364 8f multi (5-2) 1.50 .40
1449 A364 8f multi (5-3) 1.50 .40
1450 A364 8f multi (5-4) 1.50 .40
1451 A364 60f multi (5-5) 3.00 1.25
    Nos. 1447-1451 (5) 9.00 2.85

Souvenir Sheet
1452 A364 $2 multi 300.00 160.00

No. 1452 contains one 86x37mm stamp.

Mechanical Transplanting of Rice Seedlings A365

Paintings: No. 1454, Spraying fields. No. 1455, Seed selection. No. 1456, Trade. No. 1457, Delivery of public grain in city. T.34.

1978, Nov. 30   Perf. 11½
1453 A365 8f multi (5-1) 3.00 1.50
1454 A365 8f multi (5-2) 3.00 1.50
1455 A365 8f multi (5-3) 3.00 1.50
1456 A365 8f multi (5-4) 3.00 1.50
1457 A365 8f multi (5-5) 3.00 1.50
    a. Strip of 5, #1453-1457 22.50 16.50

Agricultural progress. No. 1457a has a continuous design. Value is for unfolded strip. Folded strips are worth less.

Dancers and Fireworks — A366

Designs: No. 1459, Industry, vert. 10f, Agriculture, vert. J.33.

1978, Dec. 11   Photo.   Perf. 11
1458 A366 8f multi (3-1) 4.00 1.00
1459 A366 8f multi (3-2) 3.00 1.00
1460 A366 10f multi (3-3) 1.50 1.00
    Nos. 1458-1460 (3) 8.50 3.00

20th anniversary of Kwangsi Chuang Autonomous Region.

Miners with Pneumatic Drill A367

Mine Development: 4f, Old Tibetan peasant reporting to surveyor. 10f, Open-cut mining with power shovel. 20f, Loaded electric train in pit. T.20.

1978, Dec. 29   Photo. & Engr.
1461 A367 4f multi (4-1) 2.50 1.00
1462 A367 8f multi (4-2) 3.50 1.75
1463 A367 10f multi (4-3) 2.50 1.00
1464 A367 20f multi (4-4) 2.50 1.00
    Nos. 1461-1464 (4) 11.00 4.75

A368

Golden Pheasants: 4f, Roosting on rock. 8f, In flight. 45f, Seeking food. T.35.

1979, Jan. 25   Photo.   Perf. 11½
1465 A368 4f multi (3-1) 2.00 1.00
1466 A368 8f multi (3-2) 2.50 2.00
1467 A368 45f multi (3-3) 4.00 3.00
    Nos. 1465-1467 (3) 8.50 6.00

Albert Einstein, Equation — A369

1979, Mar. 14   Photo.   Perf. 11½x11
1468 A369 8f multi 2.50 1.25

Phoenix Battling Monster, Praying Woman A370

60f, Man riding dragon to heaven. Designs from silk paintings found in Changsha tomb, Warring States Period (475-221 B.C.). T.33.

1979, Mar. 29   Perf. 11
1469 A370 8f multi (2-1) 2.50 1.50
1470 A370 60f multi (2-2) 3.50 1.50

Summer Palace — A371

Photo., Photo. & Engr. ($5)
1979-80   Perf. 13
1471 A371 $1 Pagoda ('80) .80 .35
1472 A371 $2 Shown 1.50 .70
1473 A371 $5 Temple, Beihai Park 4.50 1.50
    Nos. 1471-1473 (3) 6.80 2.55

Issued: $2, June 16, 1979.

Hammer and Sickle "51" and Bars from "International" — A372

1979, May 1   Photo.   Perf. 11
1474 A372 8f multicolored 2.00 1.00

International Labor Day, 90th anniv.

"Tradition of May 4th Movement" A373

Young Woman, Rocket, Antenna, Nuclear Reactor A374

1979, May 4
1475 A373 8f multicolored 1.25 .65
1476 A374 8f multicolored 1.25 .65

60th anniversary of May 4th Movement.

IYC Emblem, Children Holding Balloons — A375

Children of Three Races, IYC Emblem — A376

1979, May 25   Perf. 11½
1477 A375 8f multicolored 1.75 1.00
1478 A376 60f multicolored 11.00 4.50

International Year of the Child.

Great Wall in Spring A377

Designs (The Great Wall): No. 1480, in summer. No. 1481, in autumn. 60f, in winter. $2, Guard tower. T.38.

1979, June 25   Photo.   Perf. 11
1479 A377 8f multi (4-1) 2.00 .95
1480 A377 8f multi (4-2) 2.00 .95
1481 A377 8f multi (4-3) 2.00 1.00
1482 A377 60f multi (4-4) 10.00 4.50
    Nos. 1479-1482 (4) 16.00 7.40

Souvenir Sheet
1483 A377 $2 multi 140.00 70.00

For overprint see No. 1492.

Roaring Tiger — A379

Manchurian Tiger: 8f, Two young tigers. 60f, Tiger at rest. T.40.

1979, July 20   Perf. 11½x11
1484 A379 4f multi (3-1) 3.50 1.00
1485 A379 8f multi (3-2) 2.00 1.00
1486 A379 60f multi (3-3) 3.00 1.75
    Nos. 1484-1486 (3) 8.50 3.75

Mechanical Harvesting — A380

Work of the Communes: No. 1488, Forestry. No. 1489, Raising ducks. No. 1490, Women weaving baskets. 10f, Fishing. T.39.

1979, Aug. 10   **Perf. 11½**

1487	A380	4f multi (5-1)	6.00	2.00
1488	A380	8f multi (5-2)	3.25	1.00
1489	A380	8f multi (5-3)	3.25	1.00
1490	A380	8f multi (5-4)	3.25	1.00
1491	A380	10f multi (5-5)	4.00	1.75
		Nos. 1487-1491 (5)	19.75	6.75

No. 1483 Overprinted with Gold Inscription and "1979"
Souvenir Sheet

1979, Aug. 25   **Photo.**   **Perf. 11**

1492	A377	$2 multicolored	600.00	200.00

31st International Stamp Exhibition, Riccione, Italy. J41 (1-1).
Forged overprints exist.

Games Emblem, Sports — A381

No. 1494, Soccer, badminton, high jump, speed skating. No. 1495, Fencing, skiing, gymnastics, diving. No. 1496, Motorcycling, table tennis, basketball, archery. No. 1497, Emblem only. J.43.

1979, Sept. 15   **Perf. 11½x11**

1493	A381	8f multi (4-1)	1.00	.80
1494	A381	8f multi (4-2)	1.00	.80
1495	A381	8f multi (4-3)	1.00	.80
1496	A381	8f multi (4-4)	1.00	.80
a.		Block of 4, #1493-1496	6.00	4.00

Souvenir Sheet
Perf. 11½

1497	A381	$2 multi, vert.	85.00	45.00

4th National Games. Size of stamp in No. 1497: 22x26mm.

Flag and Rainbow — A382

Design: No. 1499, Flag and mountains.

1979, Oct. 1   **Photo.**   **Perf. 11½**

1498	A382	8f multicolored	2.25	1.00
1499	A382	8f multicolored	5.00	1.50

National Emblem — A383

1979, Oct. 1   **Photo.**   **Perf. 11½**

1500	A383	8f multicolored	4.00	1.50

Souvenir Sheet

1501	A383	$1 multicolored	80.00	32.50

Dancers — A384

Designs: Nos. 1503-1505, various dances. J.47.

1979, Oct. 1   **Photo.**   **Perf. 11½**

1502	A384	8f multi (4-1)	.85	.40
1503	A384	8f multi (4-2)	.85	.40
1504	A384	8f multi (4-3)	.85	.40
1505	A384	8f multi (4-4)	.85	.40
a.		Block of 4, #1502-1505	7.00	5.00

Tractor, Aerial Crop Spraying, Irrigation — A385

No. 1507, Gear, computers. No. 1508, Rocket, submarine, jets. No. 1509, Atom symbol. J.48.

1979, Oct. 1   **Photo.**   **Perf. 11½**

1506	A385	8f multi (4-1)	2.50	.90
1507	A385	8f multi (4-2)	2.50	.90
1508	A385	8f multi (4-3)	1.50	.80
1509	A385	8f multi (4-4)	2.00	.80
		Nos. 1506-1509 (4)	8.50	3.40

National Anthem A386

1979, Oct. 1   **Engr.**   **Perf. 11**

1510	A386	8f multicolored	11.00	2.00

Exhibition Emblem — A387

1979, Oct. 3

1511	A387	8f multicolored	1.25	.90

Junior National Scientific and Technological Exhibition.

Children Flying Model Planes — A388

No. 1513, Girls and microscope. No. 1514, Children and telescope. No. 1515, Boy catching butterflies. No. 1516, Girl taking meteorological readings. No. 1517, Boys sailing model boat. No. 1518, Girl with book. T.41.

1979, Oct. 3

1512	A388	8f multi (6-1)	1.50	.70
1513	A388	8f multi (6-2)	1.50	.70
1514	A388	8f multi (6-3)	1.50	.70
1515	A388	8f multi (6-4)	1.50	.70
1516	A388	8f multi (6-5)	1.50	.70
1517	A388	60f multi (6-6)	7.00	3.00
		Nos. 1512-1517 (6)	14.50	6.50

Souvenir Sheet
Perf. 11

1518	A388	$2 multi	1,600.	900.00

Study Science from Childhood. No. 1518 contains one stamp, size: 90x40mm.

Yu Shan Mountain A389

Taiwan Landscapes: No. 1520, Sun and Moon Lake. No. 1521, Chihkan Tower. No. 1522, Suao-Hualien Highway. 55f, Tian Xiang Falls. 60f, Banping Mountain. T.42.

1979, Oct. 20   **Photo.**   **Perf. 11x11½**

1519	A389	8f multi (6-1)	1.50	.85
1520	A389	8f multi (6-2)	1.50	.85
1521	A389	8f multi (6-3)	1.50	.85
1522	A389	8f multi (6-4)	1.50	.85
1523	A389	55f multi (6-5)	4.00	1.50
1524	A389	60f multi (6-6)	11.00	3.00
		Nos. 1519-1524 (6)	21.00	7.90

Arts Symbols A390

8f, Seals and modernization symbols. J.39.

1979, Oct. 30

1525	A390	4f multicolored	1.25	.65
1526	A390	8f multicolored	2.00	.85

4th Natl. Cong. of Literary and Art Workers.

Train in Tunnel A391

Railroads: No. 1528, Mountain bridge. No. 1529, Freight train. T.36.

1979, Oct. 30   **Photo. & Engr.**

1527	A391	8f multi (3-1)	3.00	1.00
1528	A391	8f multi (3-2)	3.00	1.25
1529	A391	8f multi (3-3)	3.00	1.50
		Nos. 1527-1529 (3)	9.00	3.75

Chrysanthemum Petal — A392

Camellias: No. 1531, Lion head. No. 1532, Camellia chryantha. 10f, Small osmanthus leaf. 20f, Baby face. 30f, Cornelian. 40f, Peony camellia. 50f, Purple gown. 60f, Dwarf rose. 70f, Willow leaf spinel pink. $2, Red jewelry. T.37.

1979, Nov. 10   **Photo.**   **Perf. 11x11½**

1530	A392	4f multi (10-1)	5.25	1.00
1531	A392	8f multi (10-2)	1.75	.65
1532	A392	8f multi (10-3)	1.75	.65
1533	A392	10f multi (10-4)	1.75	.65
1534	A392	20f multi (10-5)	1.75	1.00
1535	A392	30f multi (10-6)	14.00	3.00
1536	A392	40f multi (10-7)	2.75	1.25
1537	A392	50f multi (10-8)	1.50	1.00
1538	A392	60f multi (10-9)	3.25	1.00
1539	A392	70f multi (10-10)	3.50	1.00
		Nos. 1530-1539 (10)	37.25	11.20

Souvenir Sheet
Perf. 11½x11

1540	A392	$2 multi	240.00	140.00

No. 1540 contains one 86x36mm stamp.

No. 1540 Overprinted and Numbered in Gold in Margin
Souvenir Sheet

1979, Nov. 10

1541	A392	$2 multicolored	450.00	160.00

People's Republic of China Phil. Exhib., Hong Kong, 1979. J42 (1-1).
Forged overprints exist.

Norman Bethune Treating Soldier — A393

Design: 70f, Bethune statue.

1979, Nov. 12

1542	A393	8f multi (2-2)	1.50	.45
1543	A393	70f multi (2-1)	4.50	2.00

Dr. Norman Bethune, 40th death anniv. J.50.

Central Archives Hall A394

Intl. Archives Weeks: No. 1545, Gold archive cabinet, vert. 60f, Pavilion. J.51.

Perf. 11x11½, 11½x11
1979, Nov. 26   **Photo.**

1544	A394	8f multi (3-1)	2.00	1.00
1545	A394	8f multi (3-2)	2.00	1.00
1546	A394	60f multi (3-3)	11.00	2.25
		Nos. 1544-1546 (3)	15.00	4.25

Monkey King in Waterfall Cave — A395

Monkey King, Scenes from Pilgrimage to the West (Novel): No. 1548, Fighting Necha, son of Prince Li. No. 1549, In Mother Queen's peach orchard. No. 1550, In the alchemy furnace. 10f, Subduing the white bone demon. 20f, With palm leaf fan. 60f, In cobweb cave. 70f, Walking on scripture-seeking route. T.43.

1979, Dec. 1   **Perf. 11½x11**

1547	A395	8f multi (8-1)	5.00	1.75
1548	A395	8f multi (8-2)	5.00	1.75
1549	A395	8f multi (8-3)	5.00	1.75
1550	A395	8f multi (8-4)	5.00	1.75
1551	A395	10f multi (8-5)	7.00	1.75
1552	A395	20f multi (8-6)	7.00	1.75
1553	A395	60f multi (8-7)	30.00	10.00
1554	A395	70f multi (8-8)	18.00	6.00
		Nos. 1547-1554 (8)	82.00	26.50

Stalin Delivering Speech A396

Joseph Stalin (1879-1953): No. 1555, Portrait of Stalin, vert. J.49.

Perf. 11x11½, 11½x11
1979, Dec. 21   **Engr.**

1555	A396	8f brown (2-1)	1.25	1.00
1556	A396	8f black (2-2)	1.75	1.00

A397

No. 1557, Peony (16-1). No. 1558, Squirrels and grapes (16-2). No. 1559, Crabs candle and wine (16-3). No. 1560, Tadpoles in mountain spring (16-4). No. 1561, Chicks (16-5). No. 1562, Lotus (16-6). No. 1563, Red plum (16-7). No. 1564, Kingfisher (16-8). No. 1565, Bottle gourd (16-9). No. 1566, Voice of autumn (16-10). No. 1567, Wisteria (16-11). No. 1568, Chrysanthemums (16-12). No. 1569, Shrimp (16-13). No. 1570, Litchi (16-14). No. 1571, Cabbages, mushrooms (16-15). No. 1572, Peaches (16-16).

No. 1573, Hyacynth.

1980		Photo.	Perf. 11½	
1557	A397	4f multi	2.50	1.00
1558	A397	4f multi	2.50	1.00
1559	A397	8f multi	2.00	.75
1560	A397	8f multi	2.00	.75
1561	A397	8f multi	2.00	.75
1562	A397	8f multi	2.00	.75
1563	A397	8f multi	2.00	.75
1564	A397	8f multi	2.00	.75
1565	A397	10f multi	5.00	1.75
1566	A397	20f multi	5.00	1.75
1567	A397	30f multi	6.00	2.00
1568	A397	40f multi	30.00	8.00
1569	A397	50f multi	7.50	2.00
1570	A397	55f multi	7.50	3.00
1571	A397	60f multi	37.50	8.00
1572	A397	70f multi	15.00	5.00
	Nos. 1557-1572 (16)		130.50	38.00

Souvenir Sheet

1573	A397	$2 multi	250.00	125.00

Qi Baishi paintings. Issued: Nos. 1557-1560, 1569-1572, 1/15; others, 5/20. No. 1573 contains one 37½x61mm stamp. T. 44.

A398

Opera Masks: No. 1574, Meng Liang Mask from Hongyang Cave Opera. No. 1575, Li Kui, from Black Whirlwind. No. 1576, Huang Gai, from Meeting of Heroes. No. 1577, 10f, Lu Zhishen, from Wild Boar Forest. 20f, Lian Po, from Reconciliation between the General and Minister. 60f, Zhang Fei, from Reed Marsh. 70f, Dou Erdun, from Stealing the Emperor's Horse, T. 45.

1980, Jan. 25			Perf. 11½x11	
1574	A398	4f multi (8-1)	4.25	1.25
1575	A398	4f multi (8-2)	25.00	5.50
1576	A398	8f multi (8-3)	3.00	1.25
1577	A398	8f multi (8-4)	3.00	1.75
1578	A398	10f multi (8-5)	4.00	1.75
1579	A398	20f multi (8-6)	4.00	1.75
1580	A398	60f multi (8-7)	7.00	3.00
1581	A398	70f multi (8-8)	8.00	4.00
	Nos. 1574-1581 (8)		58.25	20.25

A set of eight similar to Nos. 1574-1581 was prepared but not issued in 1964. The unissued stamps are dated "1964" in the bottom margin. Sound examples appear rarely in the marketplace and sell for $125,000 or more.

Speed Skating, Olympic Rings — A399

Olympic Rings and: No. 1582, Chinese flag. No. 1584, Figure skating. 60f, Downhill skiing. J.54.

1980, Feb. 13			Perf. 11½	
1582	A399	8f multi (4-1)	2.25	.70
1583	A399	8f multi (4-2)	2.25	.70
1584	A399	8f multi (4-3)	2.25	.70
1585	A399	60f multi (4-4)	8.00	3.00
	Nos. 1582-1585 (4)		14.75	5.10

13th Winter Olympic Games, Lake Placid, NY, Feb. 12-24.

Monkey, New Year — A400

Engraved and Photogravure

1980, Feb. 15			Perf. 11½	
1586	A400	8f multicolored	1,750.	550.00

Excellent forgeries of No. 1586 exist.

Clara Zetkin — A401

Photogravure & Engraved

1980, Mar. 8			Perf. 11½x11	
1587	A401	8f black & yellow	2.50	1.10

International Working Women's Day, 70th anniv., founded by Clara Zetkin (1857-1933).

Orchard A402

Afforestation: 8f, Trees lining highway. 10f, Aerial seeding. 20f, Trees surrounding factory. T.48.

1980, Mar. 12			Perf. 11x11½	
1588	A402	4f multi (4-1)	3.25	.75
1589	A402	8f multi (4-2)	3.25	.75
1590	A402	10f multi (4-3)	1.50	.55
1591	A402	20f multi (4-4)	1.50	.55
	Nos. 1588-1591 (4)		9.50	2.60

Apsaras, Symbols of Modernization — A403

1980, Mar. 15			Photo.	Perf. 11½	
1592	A403	8f multicolored		2.75	1.40

2nd National Conference of the Scientific and Technical Association of China.

Mail Transport (T.49) — A404

1980, Mar. 20			Perf. 11x11½	
1593	A404	2f Ship (4-1)	1.75	1.50
1594	A404	4f Bus (4-2)	5.50	2.00
1595	A404	8f Train (4-3)	4.75	2.00
1596	A404	10f Jet (4-4)	3.75	2.25
	Nos. 1593-1596 (4)		15.75	7.75

Forgeries exist.

Lungs, Heart, Cigarette, WHO Emblem — A405

1980, Apr. 7			Perf. 11½x11	
1597	A405	8f shown (2-1)	2.00	.60
1598	A405	60f Faces (2-2)	14.00	3.50

Fight against cigarette smoking. J.56.

Statue of Chien Chen (688-763) — A406

Loan to China by Japan of statue of Chien Chen (Jian Zhen), Buddhist missionary to Japan (754-763): No. 1600, Chien Chen Memorial Hall, Yangchou, horiz. 60f, Chien Chen's ship, horiz. His name in Japan is Ganjin. J.55.

1980, Apr. 13			Perf. 11x11½, 11½x11	
1599	A406	8f multi (3-1)	4.00	1.10
1600	A406	8f multi (3-2)	4.00	1.10
1601	A406	60f multi (3-3)	35.00	7.75
	Nos. 1599-1601 (3)		43.00	9.95

Lenin's 110th Birthday — A407

Photogravure and Engraved

1980, Apr. 22			Perf. 11½x11	
1602	A407	8f multicolored	3.00	1.10

Swallow Chick Kite — A408

Kites. T.50: No. 1604, Slender-swallow (4-2). No. 1605, Semi-slender swallow (4-3). No. 1606, Dual swallows (4-4).

1980, May 10			Photo.	Perf. 11½	
1603	A408	8f shown (4-1)		5.50	1.75
1604	A408	8f multi		5.50	1.75
1605	A408	8f multi		5.50	1.75
1606	A408	70f multi		30.00	6.25
	Nos. 1603-1606 (4)			46.50	11.50

Hare Running from Fallen Papaya A409

1980, June 1			Photo.	Perf. 11x11½	
1607		Strip of 4 + label		17.50	17.50
a.	A409	8f shown (4-1)		2.00	1.60
b.	A409	8f Hare fox, monkey running away (4-2)		2.00	1.60
c.	A409	8f Lion instructing animals (4-3)		2.00	1.60
d.	A409	8f Discovery of fallen papaya (4-4)		2.00	1.60
e.		Bklt. pane, 2 #1607		500.00	
		Complete booklet		900.00	

Gu Dong fairy tale. T.51.
Beware of complete booklets of No. 1607e with forged booklet covers.

Terminal Building, Jets — A410

1980, June 20			Perf. 11½	
1608	A410	8f Shown (2-1)	4.00	1.25
1609	A410	10f Runways, jets (2-2)	4.00	1.25

Peking Intl. Airport opening. T.47.

Sika Stag — A411

8f, Doe and fawn (3-2). 60f, Herd (3-3).

1980, July 18			Photo.	Perf. 11½	
1610	A411	4f Shown (3-1)		2.25	1.40
1611	A411	8f multi		2.25	1.40
1612	A411	60f multi		11.00	5.25
	Nos. 1610-1612 (3)			15.50	8.05

T.52.

White Lotus — A412

No. 1614, Rose-tipped snow (4-2). No. 1615, Buddha's seat (4-3). No. 1616, Variable charming face (4-4).
No. 1617, Fresh lotus on rippling water.

1980, Aug. 4				
1613	A412	8f Shown (4-1)	5.00	2.00
1614	A412	8f multi	5.00	2.00
1615	A412	8f multi	5.00	2.00
1616	A412	70f multi	55.00	8.00
	Nos. 1613-1616 (4)		70.00	14.00

Souvenir Sheet

1617	A412	$1 multi	300.00	140.00

No. 1617 contains one 48x88mm stamp. T.54.

Pearl Cave, Sword-cut Stone
Sculptures — A413

Guilin Landscapes: No. 1619, Three mountains, distant views. No. 1620, Nine-horse fresco hill. No. 1621, Egrets around aged banyan. No. 1622, Western hills at sunset, vert. No. 1623, Moonlight on Lijiang River, vert. 60f, Springhead, ancient ferry, vert. 70f, Scenic path, Yangshue, vert. T.53.

1980, Aug. 30		Photo.	Perf. 11½	
1618	A413	8f multi (8-1)	2.00	1.00
1619	A413	8f multi (8-2)	2.00	1.00
1620	A413	8f multi (8-3)	2.00	1.00
1621	A413	8f multi (8-4)	2.00	1.00
1622	A413	8f multi (8-5)	2.00	1.00
1623	A413	8f multi (8-6)	2.00	1.00
1624	A413	60f multi (8-7)	20.00	4.00
1625	A413	70f multi (8-8)	25.00	5.00
		Nos. 1618-1625 (8)	57.00	15.00

Entrance
Gate and
Good
Fairies
A414

Great Wall,
Symbols of
Chicago,
San
Francisco
and New
York
A415

1980, Sept. 13		Photo.	Perf. 11x11½	
1626	A414	8f multicolored	2.00	.90
1627	A415	70f multicolored	14.00	3.75

Exhibitions of the People's Republic of China in San Francisco, Chicago and New York, Sept.-Dec. Sheets of 12 were sold only at the US exhibitions at increasing prices. Value, set of two sheets of 12, $1,500.

Romanian Flag,
Warrior and
Scroll — A416

1980, Sept. 20		Photo.	Perf. 11½x11	
1628	A416	8f multicolored	2.75	1.50

2050th anniv. of Dacia, 1st independent Romanian state.

UNESCO Exhibition of Drawings and
Paintings (J.60) — A417

No. 1629, Sea of Clouds, by Liu Haisu (3-1). No. 1630, Oriole and Magnolia, by Yu Feian, vert., (3-2). No. 1631, Camels, by Wu Zuoren (3-3).

1980, Oct. 8			Perf. 11½	
1629	A417	8f multi	2.00	.80
1630	A417	8f multi	2.00	.80
1631	A417	8f multi	2.00	.80
		Nos. 1629-1631 (3)	6.00	2.40

Scenes from Tarrying Garden
(T.56) — A418

No. 1632, Quxi Tower (4-1). No. 1633, Yuancui Pavilion (4-2). No. 1634, Hanbi Shanfang (4-3). No. 1635, Guanyun Peak (4-4).

1980, Oct. 25		Photo.	Perf. 11½	
1632	A418	8f multi	7.00	4.00
1633	A418	8f multi	7.00	4.00
1634	A418	10f multi	11.00	4.00
1635	A418	60f multi	60.00	17.50
		Nos. 1632-1635 (4)	85.00	29.50

Xu Guangqi
(1562-1633),
Agronomist
A419

Scientists of Ancient China: No. 1637, Li Bing, hydraulic engineer, 3rd century B.C. No. 1638, Jia Sixie, agronomist, 5th century. 60f, Huang Daopo, textile expert, 13th century. J.58.

Photogravure and Engraved

1980, Nov. 20			Perf. 11½x11	
1636	A419	8f multi (4-1)	6.50	2.00
1637	A419	8f multi (4-2)	6.50	2.00
1638	A419	8f multi (4-3)	6.50	2.00
1639	A419	60f multi (4-4)	40.00	11.00
		Nos. 1636-1639 (4)	59.50	17.00

Shooting, Olympic
Rings — A420

1980, Nov. 26			Photo.	
1640	A420	4f shown (5-1)	2.25	.45
1641	A420	8f Gymnastics (5-2)	2.25	.45
1642	A420	8f Diving (5-3)	2.25	.45
1643	A420	10f Volleyball (5-4)	2.25	.75
1644	A420	60f Archery (5-5)	14.00	2.75
		Nos. 1640-1644 (5)	23.00	4.85

Return to International Olympic Committee, 1st anniversary. J.62.

Chinese
River
Dolphin
A421

Photogravure & Engraved

1980, Dec. 25			Perf. 11x11½	
1645	A421	8f shown (2-1)	2.00	.50
a.		Booklet pane of 6	50.00	
1646	A421	60f Dolphins (2-2)	8.00	1.75
a.		Booklet pane of 1	50.00	

Stamps from No. 1645a have straight edges on top or bottom.

Cock — A422

Photogravure & Engraved

1981, Jan. 5			Perf. 11½	
1647	A422	8f multicolored	32.50	6.00
a.		Booklet pane of 12	275.00	
		Complete booklet	300.00	

New Year 1981.
Stamps from booklet pane have straight edges on top or bottom.

Early
Morning in
Xishuang
Bana (T.55)
A423

No. 1649, Dai mountain village (6-2). No. 1650, Rainbow over Lanchang River (6-3). No. 1651, Ancient temple vert. (6-4). No. 1652, Moonlit night, vert. (6-5). No. 1653, Phoenix tree, vert. (6-6).

Perf. 11x11½, 11½x11

1981, Jan. 20			Photo.	
1648	A423	4f shown (6-1)	8.00	1.50
1649	A423	4f multi	3.00	.75
1650	A423	8f multi	3.00	.75
1651	A423	8f multi	3.00	.75
1652	A423	8f multi	3.00	.75
1653	A423	60f multi	15.00	3.50
		Nos. 1648-1653 (6)	35.00	8.00

Flower Basket
Palace
Lantern — A424

Designs: Palace lanterns. T.60.

1981, Feb. 19		Photo.	Perf. 11½	
1654	A424	4f multi (6-1)	2.00	1.00
1655	A424	8f multi (6-2)	2.00	1.00
1656	A424	8f multi (6-3)	2.00	1.00
1657	A424	8f multi (6-4)	2.00	1.00
1658	A424	20f multi (6-5)	4.50	3.50
1659	A424	60f multi (6-6)	25.00	7.50
		Nos. 1654-1659 (6)	37.50	15.00

Crossing
River,
Scene from
Marking the
Gunwale
A425

Scenes from Marking the Gunwale fable. T.59: No. 1660, Text (5-1). No. 1662, Dropping sword in water (5-3). No. 1663, Marking gunwale (5-4). No. 1664, Searching for sword (5-5).

1981, Mar. 10		Photo.	Perf. 11x11½	
1660	A425	8f multi	2.00	1.25
1661	A425	8f shown (5-2)	2.00	1.25
1662	A425	8f multi	2.00	1.25
1663	A425	8f multi	2.00	1.25
1664	A425	8f multi	2.00	1.25
a.		Bklt. pane, 2 each #1660-1664		
		Complete booklet, #1664a	55.00	
b.		Strip of 5, #1660-1664	16.00	10.00

Chinese
Juniper
A426

Designs: Miniature landscapes. T.61: No. 1665, Chinese elm, vert. (6-1). No. 1666, Juniper, vert. (6-2). No. 1667, Maidenhair tree, vert. (6-3). No. 1669, Persimmon (6-5). No. 1670, Juniper (6-6).

1981, Mar. 31			Perf. 11½	
1665	A426	4f multi	3.25	1.40
1666	A426	8f multi	2.25	1.10
1667	A426	8f multi	2.25	1.10
1668	A426	10f shown (6-4)	2.25	1.10
1669	A426	20f multi	2.25	1.25
1670	A426	60f multi	14.00	4.25
		Nos. 1665-1670 (6)	26.25	10.20

Vase with Tiger-shaped
Handles — A427

Cizhou Kiln Ceramic Pottery: 4f, Vase with 2 tigers, Song Dynasty. No. 1672, Black glazed jar, Jin Dynasty. No. 1673, Amphora. No. 1674, Jar with 2 phoenixes (Yuan Dynasty). 10f, Flat flask, Yuan Dynasty. T.62.

1981, Apr. 15		Photo.	Perf. 11½x11	
1671	A427	4f multi, vert. (6-1)	1.50	.80
1672	A427	8f multi (6-2)	1.50	.80
1673	A427	8f multi, vert. (6-3)	1.50	.80
1674	A427	8f multi (6-4)	1.50	.80
1675	A427	10f multi (6-5)	1.50	.80
1676	A427	60f multi (6-6)	7.50	3.50
		Nos. 1671-1676 (6)	15.00	7.50

Panda and
Colored
Stamps — A428

1981, Apr. 29		Photo.	Perf. 11½x11	
1677	A428	8f shown (2-1)	.45	.30
1678	A428	60f Boat, bird (2-2)	3.00	1.60
a.		Booklet pane (8 #1677, souv. sheet with 1677-1678)	20.00	
		Complete booklet, #1678a	22.50	

Qinchuan
Steer
A429

Cattle Breeds: No. 1680, Binhu buffalo. No. 1681, Yak. No. 1682, Black and white dairy cows. 10f, Pasture red cow. 55f, Simmental cross-breed. T.63.

1981, May 5			Perf. 11x11½	
1679	A429	4f multi (6-1)	1.75	1.00
1680	A429	8f multi (6-2)	2.75	1.25
1681	A429	8f multi (6-3)	2.50	1.25
1682	A429	8f multi (6-4)	2.00	1.00
1683	A429	10f multi (6-5)	2.00	1.00
1684	A429	55f multi (6-6)	3.00	1.00
		Nos. 1679-1684 (6)	14.00	6.50

Mail Delivery
Slogan — A430

1981, May 9			Perf. 11	
1685	A430	8f multicolored	1.25	.30

13th World Telecommunications
Day — A431

1981, May 17   **Perf. 11½x11**
1686 A431 8f multicolored   1.50   .35

Construction
Worker — A432

No. 1688, Miner (4-2). No. 1689, Children
crossing street (4-3). No. 1690, Farm worker
(4-4).

1981, May 20   **Perf. 11½**
1687 A432 8f shown (4-1)   1.40   .55
1688 A432 8f multi   1.40   .55
1689 A432 8f multi   1.40   .55
1690 A432 8f multi   1.40   .55
       Nos. 1687-1690 (4)   5.60 2.20

National Safety Month. J.65.

Telephone
Building,
Peking — A433

1981, June 5   Engr.   Perf. 11½x11
1691 A433 8f violet brown   1.25   .65

Swaythling Cup,
Men's Team Table
Tennis — A434

36th World Table Tennis Championships
Victory — No. 1692: a, St. Bride Vase, men's
singles (7-3). b, Iran Cup, men's doubles (7-4).
c, G. Geist Prize, women's singles (7-5). d,
W.J. Pope Trophy, women's doubles (7-6). e,
Heydusek Prize, mixed doubles (7-7). No.
1694, Marcel Corbillon Cup, women's team.
Nos. 1693-1694 printed in sheets of 16 (8
each) + 2 labels. J.71.

1981, June 30 Photo.   Perf. 11½x11
1692   Strip of 5   6.50 3.75
  a.-e.   A434 8f multi   .45   .25
1693 A434 20f multi (7-1)   1.75   .85
1694 A434 20f multi (7-2)   1.75   .85

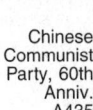

Chinese
Communist
Party, 60th
Anniv.
A435

1981, July 1   Photo.   Perf. 11x11½
1695 A435 8f multicolored   1.50   .60

Hanpo
Pass,
Lushan
Mountains
(T.67)
A436

No. 1696, Five-veteran Peak, vert. (7-1). No.
1698, Yellow Dragon Pool, vert. (7-3). No.
1699, Sunlit Peak (7-4). No. 1700, Three-layer
Spring, vert. (7-5). No. 1701, Stone and pines
(7-6). No. 1702, Dragon-head Cliff, vert. (7-7).

Photogravure & Engraved
1981, July 20   **Perf. 12½x12**
1696 8f multi   3.00   .70
1697 8f shown (7-2)   3.00   .70
1698 8f multi   3.00   .70
1699 8f multi   3.00   .70
1700 8f multi   3.00   .70
1701 8f multi   3.00   .70
1702 60f multi   30.00 5.00
      Nos. 1696-1702 (7)   48.00 9.20

Tremella
Fuciformis
A437

Edible mushrooms. T.66: No. 1704, Dictyophora indusiata (6-2). No. 1705, Hericium
erinaceus (6-3). No. 1706, Russula rubra (6-
4). No. 1707, Lentinus edodes (6-5). No. 1708,
Agaricus bisporus (6-6).

1981, Aug. 6   Photo.   Perf. 11½
1703 A437 4f shown (6-1)   1.00   .50
1704 A437 8f multi   1.00   .50
1705 A437 8f multi   1.00   .50
1706 A437 8f multi   1.00   .50
1707 A437 10f multi   1.00   .50
1708 A437 70f multi   8.00 2.25
      Nos. 1703-1708 (6)   13.00 4.75

Quality Month
(J.66) — A438

1981, Sept. 1   Photo.   Perf. 11½x11
1709 A438 8f Silver medal (2-1)   2.50   .55
1710 A438 8f Gold medal (2-2)   2.50   .55

Lunan Stone
Forest,
Yunn — A439

Designs: Views of limestone formations,
Lunan Stone Forest. Nos. 1711-1713 horiz.
T.64.

1981, Sept. 18   **Perf. 11½**
1711 A439 8f multi (5-1)   1.50   .60
1712 A439 8f multi (5-2)   1.50   .60
1713 A439 8f multi (5-3)   1.50   .60
1714 A439 10f multi (5-4)   1.50   .60
1715 A439 70f multi (5-5)   14.00 4.75
      Nos. 1711-1715 (5)   20.00 7.15

Lu Xun,
Writer, Birth
Centenary
(J.67)
A440

1981, Sept. 25
1716 A440 8f shown (2-1)   2.25   .40
1717 A440 20f Portrait (diff.) (2-2) 3.50 1.50

Sun Yat-
sen and
Text
A441

70th Anniv. of 1911 Revolution: No. 1719,
72 Martyrs Grave, Huang Hua Gang. No.
1720, Hubei Provincial Government Headquarters, 1911. J.68.

1981, Oct. 10   Photo.   Perf. 11x11½
1718 A441 8f multi (3-1)   2.00   .45
1719 A441 8f multi (3-2)   2.00   .45
1720 A441 8f multi (3-3)   2.00   .45
      Nos. 1718-1720 (3)   6.00 1.35

Asian Conference of Parliamentarians
on Population and Development,
Peking, Oct. 27 (J.73) — A442

1981, Oct. 27   Perf. 11½x11, 11x11½
1721 A442 8f Tree, vert. (2-1)   .75   .30
1722 A442 70f shown (2-2)   1.40   .75

Xishuang
Banna — A443

Mt. Hua —
A443a

Mt. Tai —
A443b

Huang Guo Shu
Falls — A443c

Hainan Island —
A443d

Tiger Hill,
Suzhou —
A443e

Great Wall —
A443f

Immense Forest
— A443g

Mt. Tian —
A443h

Grassland, Inner
Mongolia —
A443i

Stone Forest —
A443j

Banping Mountain
— A443k

Mt. Qomolangma
— A443l

Seven-Star Crag
— A443m

Three Gorges,
Changjiang River
— A443n

Guilin landscape
— A443o

Mt. Huangshan
— A443p

Nos. 1731-1739 are horizontal.

**Perf. 11¼, 13x13¼ (#1726, 1729),
13¼x13 (#1731)**

1981-83   **Engr.**
1723 A443   1f blue green   .25   .25
1724 A443a 1½f red orange   .25   .25
1725 A443b 2f gray green   .25   .25
1726 A443c 3f red brown   .30   .25
1727 A443d 4f purple   .30   .25
1728 A443e 5f brown   .35   .25
1729 A443f 8f blue   .35   .25
1730 A443g 10f purplish brn   .35   .25
1731 A443h 20f blue green   .35   .25
1732 A443i 30f light brown   .35   .25
1733 A443j 40f blue black   .45   .25
1734 A443k 50f violet   .60   .25
1735 A443l 70f greenish blk   .75   .40
1736 A443m 80f rose lake   .85   .55
1737 A443n $1 violet black   1.00 .60
1738 A443o $2 green   1.75 1.25
1739 A443p $5 Prussian blue   4.00 2.25
      Nos. 1723-1739 (17)   12.50 8.05

Issued: Nos. 1737-1739, 10/9/82; Nos.
1732, 1734-1736 4/1/83.

Photo.

Perf. 11½

1726a	A443	3f tan & brown	.25	.25
1727a	A443	4f pink & purple	.25	.25
1727b		Perf. 11½x11	10.00	10.00
1729a	A443	8f blue	.35	.25
1730a	A443	10f dark brown	.55	.40
1731a	A443	20f blue green	1.25	.75
	Nos. 1726a-1731a (5)		2.65	1.90

Nos. 1727a, 1729a, 1730a exist tagged. Values 10-15% higher.

Cowrie Shell and Shell-shaped Coin — A444

Ancient Coins. T.65.

Photogravure and Engraved

1981, Oct. 29   Perf. 11½x11

1740	A444	4f shown (8-1)	1.50	.50
1741	A444	4f Shovel (8-2)	1.50	.50
1742	A444	8f Shovel, diff. (8-3)	1.50	.50
1743	A444	8f Shovel, diff. (8-4)	2.00	.50
1744	A444	8f Knife (8-5)	2.00	.50
1745	A444	8f Knife (8-6)	2.00	.50
1746	A444	60f Knife, diff. (8-7)	9.00	2.50
1747	A444	70f Gong (8-8)	12.00	3.00
	Nos. 1740-1747 (8)		31.50	8.50

See Nos. 1765-1772.

A445

1981, Nov. 10   Photo.   Perf. 11½x11

1748	A445	8f multicolored	1.00	.40

Intl. Year of the Disabled.

A446

Twelve Beauties, from The Dream of Red Mansions, by Cao Xueqin: No. 1749, Daiyu (12-1). No. 1750, Baochai (12-2). No. 1751, Yuanchun (12-3). No. 1752, Yingchun (12-4). No. 1753, Tanchun (12-5). No. 1754, Xichun (12-6). No. 1755, Xiangyuh (12-7). No. 1756, Liwan (12-8). No. 1757, Xifeng (12-9). No. 1758, Sister Qiao (12-10). No. 1759, Keqing (12-11). No. 1760, Miaoyu (12-12). No. 1761, Baoyu, Daiyu.

1981-82   Photo.   Perf. 11

1749	A446	4f multi	5.00	.95
1750	A446	4f multi	3.00	.95
1751	A446	8f multi	4.00	1.50
1752	A446	8f multi	3.00	1.00
1753	A446	8f multi	3.00	1.00
1754	A446	8f multi	3.00	1.00
1755	A446	8f multi	3.00	1.25
1756	A446	10f multi	3.00	1.25
1757	A446	20f multi	3.00	1.25
1758	A446	30f multi	5.00	1.75
1759	A446	40f multi	22.50	6.00
1760	A446	80f multi	8.00	2.75
	Nos. 1749-1760 (12)		65.50	20.65

Souvenir Sheet

1761	A446	$2 multi	260.00	120.00

No. 1761 contains one 59x39mm stamp. Issued: Nos. 1749, 1751, 1753, 1755, 1757, 1759, 1761, 11/20/81; others, 4/24/82. T.69.

A447

8f, Girl playing (2-1). 20f, Girl holding trophy (2-2).

1981, Dec. 21   Photo.

1762	A447	8f multi	.60	.30
1763	A447	20f multi	1.10	.55

Women's team victory in 3rd World Cup Volleyball Championship (J.76).

A448

Photogravure & Engraved

1982, Jan. 5   Perf. 11½

1764	A448	8f multicolored	6.00	2.00
a.		Booklet pane of 10 + label	30.00	
		Complete booklet, #1764a	32.50	32.50

New Year 1982 (Year of the Dog). Stamps from No. 1764a have straight edges at top or bottom.

Coin Type of 1981

No. 1765, Guilian mask (8-1). No. 1766, Shu shovel (8-2). No. 1767, Xia zhuan shovel (8-3). No. 1768, Han Dan shovel (8-4). No. 1769, Knife (8-5). No. 1770, Ming knife (8-6). No. 1771, Jin hua knife (8-7). No. 1772, Yi Liu Hua coin (8-8).

1982, Feb. 12

1765	A444	4f multi	1.10	.55
1766	A444	4f multi	1.10	.55
1767	A444	8f multi	1.10	.55
1768	A444	8f multi	1.10	.55
1769	A444	8f multi	1.10	.55
1770	A444	8f multi	1.10	.70
1771	A444	70f multi	4.00	2.00
1772	A444	80f multi	5.00	2.50
	Nos. 1765-1772 (8)		15.60	7.95

T.71.

Nie Er (1912-1935), Natl. Anthem Composer — A449

1982, Feb. 15   Perf. 11x11½

1773	A449	8f multicolored	2.00	.50

Intl. Drinking Water and Sanitation Decade, 1981-1990 A450

1982, Mar. 1   Perf. 11½x11

1774	A450	8f multicolored	1.00	.50

TB Bacillus Centenary A451

1982, Mar. 24   Perf. 11x11½

1775	A451	8f multicolored	1.50	.50

Fire Control (T.76) — A452

No. 1776, Water hoses (2-1). No. 1777, Chemical extinguisher (2-2).

1982, May 8   Photo.   Perf. 11½x11

1776	A452	8f multicolored	1.50	.50
1777	A452	8f multicolored	1.50	.50

Syzygy of the Nine Planets, Mar. 10 and May 16 — A453

1982, May 16   Perf. 11½

1778	A453	8f multicolored	2.00	.60

Medicinal Herbs — A454

No. 1779, Hemerocallis flava (6-1). No. 1780, Fritillaria unibracteata (6-2). No. 1781, Aconitum carmichaeli (6-3). No. 1782, Lilium brownii (6-4). No. 1783, Arisaema (6-5). No. 1784, Paeonia lactiflora (6-6). No. 1785, Iris tectorum maxim.

1982, May 20   Perf. 11½x11

1779	A454	4f multi	.65	.45
1780	A454	8f multi	.65	.45
1781	A454	8f multi	.65	.45
1782	A454	10f multi	1.40	.65
1783	A454	20f multi	1.75	.75
1784	A454	70f multi	5.25	1.50
	Nos. 1779-1784 (6)		10.35	4.25

Souvenir Sheet

1785	A454	$2 multi	27.50	17.50

No. 1785 contains one 89x39mm stamp. Nos. 1779-1784 numbered T.72.

Soong Ching Ling (1893-1981), Sun Yat-sen's Widow — A455

8f, Addressing Consultative Conf. (2-1). 20f, Portrait (2-2).

1982, May 29   Perf. 11½

1786	A455	8f multi	1.00	.45
1787	A455	20f multi	4.00	1.40

J.82.

Sable (T.68) A456

1982, June 20   Photo.   Perf. 11½

1788	A456	8f shown (2-1)	1.25	.50
1789	A456	80f Sable, diff. (2-2)	5.00	3.50
a.		Bklt. pane of 8, 6 8f plus sheetlet of 2 (8f, 80f)	37.50	
		Complete booklet, #1789a	44.00	

A457

1982, June 30   Perf. 11½x11

1790	A457	8f multicolored	1.75	.40

Natl. census, July 1.

A458

1982, July 25   Photo.   Perf. 11½x11

1791	A458	8f multicolored	1.40	.40

2nd UN Conference on Peaceful Uses of Outer Space, Vienna, Aug. 9-21.

Strolling in Autumn Woods, by Shen Zhou, Ming Dynasty — A459

Fan Paintings (Ming or Qing Dynasty): No. 1793, Jackdaw on Withered Tree, by Tang Yin. No. 1794 Bamboo and Sparrows, by Zhou Zhimian. 10f, Writing Poem under Pine, by Chen Hongshou and Bai Han. 20f, Chrysanthemums, by Yun Shouping, Qing. 70f, Birds, Crape Myrtle and Chinese Parasol, by Wang Wu, Qing. T.77.

1982, July 31   Perf. 11½

1792	A459	4f multi (6-1)	3.00	.80
1793	A459	8f multi (6-2)	1.25	.70
1794	A459	8f multi (6-3)	1.25	.70
1795	A459	10f multi (6-4)	2.00	.70
1796	A459	20f multi (6-5)	2.00	.80
1797	A459	70f multi (6-6)	6.00	2.25
	Nos. 1792-1797 (6)		15.50	5.95

A460

1982, Aug. 25   **Perf. 11½x11**
1798   A460   8f multicolored   .80   .35
60th anniv. of Chinese Geological Society.

A461

1982, Aug. 25   Photo.   Perf. 11½x11
1799   A461   4f Orpiment (4-1)   .75   .30
1800   A461   8f Stibnite (4-2)   .75   .30
1801   A461   10f Cinnabar (4-3)   1.50   .30
1802   A461   20f Wolframite (4-4)   1.50   .55
    Nos. 1799-1802 (4)   4.50   1.45

T.73.

Souvenir Sheet

Messenger, Tomb Mural, Jiayu Pass,
Wei-Jin Period — A462

1982, Aug. 25
1803   A462 $1 multicolored   27.50   12.00
All-China Philatelic Federation, 1st Cong.

12th Natl.
Communist Party
Congress
A463

1982, Sept. 1   **Perf. 11½**
1804   A463   8f multicolored   1.75   .45

Hoopoe — A464

No. 1806, Swallows (5-2). No. 1807, Oriole
(5-3). No. 1808, Chickadees (5-4). No. 1809,
Woodpecker (5-5).
No. 1810, Cuckoos.

1982, Sept. 10   **Perf. 11½x11**
1805   A464   8f shown (5-1)   1.25   .40
1806   A464   8f multi   1.25   .40
1807   A464   8f multi   1.25   .40

1808   A464   20f multi   3.25   .80
1809   A464   70f multi   9.00   3.25
    Nos. 1805-1809 (5)   16.00   5.25
Souvenir Sheet
1810   A464 $2 multi   52.50   18.50
No. 1810 contains one 56x36mm stamp.
T.79.

Japan-China
Relations
Normalization, 10th
Anniv. — A465

Flower Paintings: 8f, Plum blossoms, by
Guan Shanyue. 70f, Hibiscus, by Xiao
Shufang. J.84.

1982, Sept. 29   **Perf. 11**
1811   A465   8f multi (2-1)   1.25   .30
1812   A465   70f multi (2-2)   2.50   .95

World Food
Day — A466

1982, Oct. 16   **Perf. 11½**
1813   A466   8f multicolored   1.25   .40

Guo Morou
(1892-1978),
Acad. of Sciences
Pres. — A467

Designs: Portraits. J.87.

1982, Nov. 16   Photo.   Perf. 11½x11
1814   A467   8f multi (2-1)   .60   .30
1815   A467   20f multi (2-2)   1.50   .50

Bodhisattva, 11th
Cent.
Sculpture — A468

Liao Dynasty Buddha Sculptures, Lower
Huayan Monastery. T.74.

1982, Nov. 19   **Perf. 11**
1816   A468   8f multi (4-1)   1.25   .40
1817   A468   8f multi (4-2)   1.25   .40
1818   A468   8f multi (4-3)   1.75   .40
1819   A468   70f multi (4-4)   4.50   2.75
    Nos. 1816-1819 (4)   8.75   3.95
Souvenir Sheet
Perf. 11x11½
1820   A468 $2 multicolored   55.00   20.00
No. 1820 contains one 36x55mm stamp.

Dr. D.S.
Kotnis,
Indian
Physician in
8th Army
(J.83)
A469

Perf. 11½x11, 11x11½
1982, Dec. 9   Photo.
1821   A469   8f Portrait, vert. (2-1)   .55   .25
1822   A469   70f Riding horse (2-2)   2.25   1.50

11th
Communist
Youth
League
Natl.
Congress
A470

1982, Dec. 20   **Perf. 11x11½**
1823   A470   8f multicolored   1.50   .50

Bronze Wine
Container — A471

Western Zhou Dynasty Bronze (1200-771
B.C.): No. 1825, Three-legged cooking pot.
No. 1826, Food bowl. No. 1827, Three-legged
cooking pot (diff.). No. 1828, Animal-shaped
wine container. 10f, Wine container with lid.
20f, Round food bowl. 70f, Square wine
container. T.75.

Photogravure & Engraved
1982, Dec. 25   **Perf. 11**
1824   A471   4f multi (8-1)   1.75   .80
1825   A471   4f multi (8-2)   1.75   .80
1826   A471   8f multi (8-3)   1.75   .80
1827   A471   8f multi (8-4)   3.00   1.25
1828   A471   8f multi (8-5)   1.75   .80
1829   A471   10f multi (8-6)   2.75   .80
1830   A471   20f multi (8-7)   3.50   1.50
1831   A471   70f multi (8-8)   17.50   4.50
    Nos. 1824-1831 (8)   33.75   11.25

A472

1983, Jan. 5   **Perf. 11½**
1832   A472   8f multicolored   20.00   4.50
   a.   Booklet pane of 12   50.00   70.00
     Complete booklet, #1832a   70.00
New Year 1983 (Year of the Pig).
Stamps from No. 1832a have straight edges
at top or bottom and sell for less as singles
than No. 1832.

A473

Stringed Instruments (T.81).

1983, Jan. 20   Perf. 11½x11, 11x11½
1833   A473   4f Konghou (5-1)   3.75   1.25
1834   A473   8f Ruan (5-2)   3.75   1.25
1835   A473   8f Qin, horiz. (5-3)   3.75   1.25
1836   A473   10f Piba (5-4)   3.75   1.25
1837   A473   70f Sanxian (5-5)   29.00   8.00
    Nos. 1833-1837 (5)   44.00   13.00

A474

No. 1838, Memorial Tower, Zhengzhou (2-
1). No. 1839, Monument, Jiangan (2-2).

1983, Feb. 7   Photo.   Perf. 11½x11
1838   A474   8f multi   .80   .40
1839   A474   8f multi   1.00   .40
60th Anniv. of Peking-Hankow Railroad
Workers' Strike (J.89).

The
Western
Chamber,
Traditional
Opera, by
Wang Shifu
(1271-1368)
A475

Scenes from the opera.

1983, Feb. 21   Photo.   Perf. 11x11½
1840   A475   8f multi (4-1)   3.50   2.00
1841   A475   8f multi (4-2)   3.50   2.00
1842   A475   10f multi (4-3)   6.00   2.50
1843   A475   80f multi (4-4)   27.50   7.50
    Nos. 1840-1843 (4)   40.50   14.00
Souvenir Sheet
Photogravure and Engraved
Perf. 12
1844   A475 $2 multicolored   120.00   60.00
No. 1844 contains one 27x48mm stamp.
T.82.

Karl Marx (1818-
1883)
(J.90) — A476

8f, Portrait (2-1). 20f, Making speech (2-2).

Photogravure & Engraved
1983, Mar. 14   **Perf. 11½x11**
1845   A476   8f multicolored   .60   .35
1846   A476   20f multicolored   1.25   .55

Tomb of the
Yellow
Emperor
(T.84)
A477

8f, Tomb, vert. (3-1). 10f, Hall of Founder of
Chinese Culture (3-2). 20f, Cypress tree, vert.
(3-3).

Photogravure & Engraved

1983, Apr. 5   **Perf. 11½**
1847	A477	8f multi	1.50	.75
1848	A477	10f multi	2.00	.75
1849	A477	20f multi	3.25	1.10
	Nos. 1847-1849 (3)		6.75	2.60

World Communications Year — A478

1983, Apr. 28   **Photo.**   **Perf. 11½**
1850	A478	8f multicolored	1.50	.60

Male Chinese Alligator (T.85) — A479

20f, Female, hatching eggs (2-2).

Photogravure & Engraved

1983, May 24   **Perf. 11**
1851	A479	8f shown (2-1)	1.10	.55
1852	A479	20f multicolored	1.90	.90

Kitten, by Tan Arxi — A480

Various children's drawings. T.86.

1983, June 1   **Perf. 11½x11**
1853	A480	8f multi (4-1)	.50	.30
1854	A480	8f multi (4-2)	.50	.30
1855	A480	8f multi (4-3)	.50	.30
1856	A480	8f multi (4-4)	.50	.30
	Nos. 1853-1856 (4)		2.00	1.20

6th Natl. People's Congress (J.94) A481

8f, Hall (2-1). 20f, Natl. anthem score (2-2).

1983, June 6   **Perf. 11x11½**
1857	A481	8f multicolored	1.25	.50
1858	A481	20f multicolored	3.25	.90

Terra Cotta Figures, Qin Dynasty (221-207 BC) A482

No. 1859, Soldiers (4-1). No. 1860, Heads (4-2). No. 1861, Soldiers, horses (4-3). No. 1862, Excavation site (4-4).
No. 1863, Soldier leading horse.

1983, June 30
1859	A482	8f multi	1.10	.70
1860	A482	8f multi	1.10	.70
1861	A482	10f multi	1.75	.85

1862	A482	70f multi	5.00	3.25
a.	Bklt. pane of 8 (#1859, 3 #1860, 3 #1861, #1862)		35.00	25.00
	Nos. 1859-1862 (4)		8.95	5.50

Souvenir Sheet
1863	A482	$2 multi	55.00	32.50
a.	Booklet pane of 1		55.00	
	Complete booklet, #1862a, #1863a		95.00	65.00

No. 1863 contains one 59x39mm stamp. T.88.

A483

Female roles in Peking opera (T.87) — 4f, Sun Yujiao (8-1). No. 1865, 8f, Chen Miaochang (8-2). No. 1866, 8f, Bai Suzhen (8-3). No. 1867, 8f, Sister Thirteen (8-4). 10f, Qin Xianglian (8-5). 20f, Yang Yuhuan (8-6). 50f, Cui Yingying (8-7). 80f, Mu Guiying (8-8).

1983, July 20   **Photo.**   **Perf. 11**
1864	A483	4f multi	2.75	.95
1865	A483	8f multi	2.75	.95
1866	A483	8f multi	2.75	.95
1867	A483	8f multi	2.75	.95
1868	A483	10f multi	2.75	.95
1869	A483	20f multi	2.75	.95
1870	A483	50f multi	15.00	4.00
1871	A483	80f multi	20.00	6.50
	Nos. 1864-1871 (8)		51.50	16.20

A484

Paintings by Liu Lingcang: No. 1872, Li Bai (4-1). No. 1873, Du Fu (4-2). No. 1874, Han Yu (4-3). No. 1875, Liu Zongyuan (4-4).

1983, Aug. 10   **Photo.**   **Perf. 11½**
1872	A484	8f multi	2.25	.45
1873	A484	8f multi	2.25	.45
1874	A484	8f multi	2.25	.45
1875	A484	70f multi	13.00	3.50
	Nos. 1872-1875 (4)		19.75	4.85

Poets and philosophers of ancient China (J.92).

5th Natl. Women's Congress — A485

1983, Sept. 1   **Photo.**   **Perf. 11½**
1876	A485	8f multicolored	1.25	.40

5th National Games (J.93) — A486

No. 1877, Emblem (6-1). No. 1878, Gymnast (6-2). No. 1879, Badminton (6-3). No. 1880, Diving (6-4). No. 1881, High jump (6-5). No. 1882, Wind surfing (6-6).

1983, Sept. 16   **Photo.**   **Perf. 11½**
1877	A486	4f multi	.85	.35
1878	A486	8f multi	.85	.35
1879	A486	8f multi	.85	.35
1880	A486	8f multi	.85	.35
1881	A486	20f multi	1.50	.40
1882	A486	70f multi	5.50	2.25
	Nos. 1877-1882 (6)		10.40	4.05

Family Planning (T.91) A487

No. 1883, One child (2-1). No. 1884, Cultivated land (2-2).

1983, Sept. 19   **Perf. 11x11½**
1883	A487	8f multicolored	.60	.30
1884	A487	8f multicolored	.60	.30

10th Intl. Trade Union Congress — A488

1983, Oct. 18   **Litho.**   **Perf. 11½**
1885	A488	8f multicolored	.90	.40

Mute Swans (T.83) A489

Cygnus Olor: No. 1886, One swan (4-1). No. 1887, Two swans (4-2). No. 1888, Four swans (4-3). No. 1889, Six swans (4-4).

Perf. 11x11½ on 3 sides

1983, Nov. 18   **Photo.**
1886	A489	8f multi	.35	.30
1887	A489	8f multi	1.40	.55
1888	A489	10f multi	1.40	.55
1889	A489	80f multi	3.00	1.90
a.	Booklet pane, 7 #1886, 1 each #1887-1889		30.00	20.00
	Complete booklet, #1889a		55.00	27.50
	Nos. 1886-1889 (4)		6.15	3.30

A490

Various photos. J.96.

1983, Nov. 24   **Photo.**   **Perf. 11½**
1890	A490	8f multi (4-1)	1.40	.50
1891	A490	8f multi (4-2)	1.40	.50
1892	A490	8f multi (4-3)	1.40	.50
1893	A490	8f multi (4-4)	1.40	.50
	Nos. 1890-1893 (4)		5.60	2.00

85th birth anniv. of Liu Shaoqi, political leader.

A491

1983, Nov. 29   **Photo.**   **Perf. 11½**
1894	A491	8f No. 117 (2-1)	.55	.30
1895	A491	20f No. 4L1 (2-2)	.75	.40

CHINAPEX '83 Natl. Philatelic Exhibition (J.99).

A492

Various portraits. J.97.

1983, Dec. 26   **Photo.**   **Perf. 11½**
1896	A492	8f 1925 (4-1)	1.25	.35
1897	A492	8f 1945 (4-2)	1.25	.35
1898	A492	10f 1952 (4-3)	5.75	1.00
1899	A492	20f 1961 (4-4)	3.50	.60
	Nos. 1896-1899 (4)		11.75	2.30

90th birth anniv. of Mao Tse-tung.

A493

Photogravure and Engraved

1984, Jan. 5   **Perf. 11½**
1900	A493	8f multicolored	7.00	2.50
a.	Booklet pane of 12		80.00	30.00
	Complete booklet, #1900a		110.00	92.50

New Year 1984 (Year of the Rat). Stamps from No. 1900a have straight edge at top or bottom.

Beauties Wearing Flowers — A494

Portions of painting by Zhou Fang (Tang Dynasty). T.89.

1984, Mar. 24   **Photo.**   **Perf. 11**
1901	A494	8f multi (3-1)	1.75	.40
1902	A494	10f multi (3-2)	2.75	.60
1903	A494	70f multi (3-3)	8.50	3.00
	Nos. 1901-1903 (3)		13.00	4.00

Souvenir Sheet
1904	A494	$2 Entire painting	180.00	55.00

No. 1904 contains one 162x40mm stamp.

Chinese Roses (T.93) — A495

No. 1905, Spring of Shanghai (6-1). No. 1906, Rosy Dawn of Pujiang River (6-2). No. 1907, Pearl (6-3). No. 1908, Black whirlwind (6-4). No. 1909, Yellow flower in battlefield (6-5). No. 1910, Blue Phoenix (6-6).

1984, Apr. 20	Photo.	Perf. 11½	
1905	A495	4f multi	.90	.30
1906	A495	8f multi	.90	.30
1907	A495	8f multi	.90	.30
1908	A495	10f multi	.90	.35
1909	A495	20f multi	2.00	.45
1910	A495	70f multi	4.50	1.40
	Nos. 1905-1910 (6)		10.10	3.10

Ren Bishi (1904-50), Statesman
A496

1984, Apr. 30		Perf. 11½x11
1911	A496	8f multicolored	.75	.30

Crested Ibis (T.94)
A497

1984, May 15	Photo.	Perf. 11x11½
1912	A497	8f Flying (3-1)	.80	.25
1913	A497	8f Wading (3-2)	.80	.25
1914	A497	80f Perching (3-3)	2.50	1.50
	Nos. 1912-1914 (3)		4.10	2.00

Chinese Red Cross Society, 80th Anniv. — A498

1984, May 29		Perf. 11½
1915	A498	8f multicolored	.85	.30

Gezhou Dam, Yangtze River (T.95) — A499

8f, Dam (3-1). 10f, Bridge, vert. (3-2). 20f, Lock Gate #2 (3-3).

1984, June 15		Photo.
1916	A499	8f multi	.50	.35
1917	A499	10f multi	.75	.40
1918	A499	20f multi	1.60	.75
	Nos. 1916-1918 (3)		2.85	1.50

Zhuo Zheng Garden, Suzhou (T.96) — A500

No. 1919, Inverted Image Tower (4-1). No. 1920, Loquat Garden (4-2). No. 1921, Water Court, Xiao Cang Lang (4-3). No. 1922, Yuanxiang Hall, Yiyu Study (4-4).

Photogravure & Engraved

1984, June 30		Perf. 11½x11
1919	A500	8f multi	.75	.45
1920	A500	8f multi	.75	.45
1921	A500	10f multi	.85	.45
1922	A500	70f multi	2.25	1.50
	Nos. 1919-1922 (4)		4.60	2.85

1984 Summer Olympics A501

No. 1923, Shooting (6-1). No. 1924, High jump (6-2). No. 1925, Weight lifting (6-3). No. 1926, Gymnastics (6-4). No. 1927, Volleyball (6-5). No. 1928, Diving (6-6). No. 1929, Athletes, rings.

1984, July 28	Photo.	Perf. 11½
1923	A501	4f multi	.35	.25
1924	A501	8f multi	.40	.25
1925	A501	8f multi	.40	.25
1926	A501	10f multi	.45	.25
1927	A501	20f multi	.50	.35
1928	A501	80f multi	1.25	.40
	Nos. 1923-1928 (6)		3.35	1.70

Souvenir Sheet

1929	A501	$2 multi	14.00	7.00

No. 1929 contains one 61x38mm stamp. J.103.

Calligraphy — A502

Artworks by Wu Changshuo. T.98: No. 1931, A Pair of Peaches (8-2). No. 1932, Lotus (8-3). No. 1933, Wisteria (8-4). No. 1934, Peony (8-5). No. 1935, Chrysanthemum (8-6). No. 1936, Plum Blossom (8-7). No. 1937, Seal Cutting (8-8).

1984, Aug. 27	Photo.	Perf. 11½
1930	A502	4f shown (8-1)	.90	.35
1931	A502	4f multi	.90	.35
1932	A502	8f multi	2.00	.35
1933	A502	8f multi	.80	.35
1934	A502	8f multi	8.00	2.00
1935	A502	10f multi	1.75	.60
1936	A502	20f multi	2.00	.60
1937	A502	70f multi	4.75	2.00
	Nos. 1930-1937 (8)		21.10	6.60

Luanhe River Water Diversion Project (T.97) — A503

Perf. 11½x11, 11 (#1939)
1984, Sept. 11		Photo.
1938	A503	8f multi (3-1)	.40	.30
1939	A503	10f multi, horiz. (3-2)	.40	.30
1940	A503	20f multi (3-3)	.60	.40
	Nos. 1938-1940 (3)		1.40	1.00

Chinese-Japanese Youth (J.104) — A504

1984, Sept. 24	Photo.	Perf. 11½
1941	A504	8f Neighbors (3-1)	.35	.30
1942	A504	20f Planting tree (3-2)	.55	.30
1943	A504	80f Dancing (3-3)	1.10	.70
	Nos. 1941-1943 (3)		2.00	1.30

People's Republic, 35th Anniv. (J.105) — A505

No. 1944, Engineer (5-1). No. 1945, Farm woman (5-2). No. 1946, Scientist (5-4). No. 1947, Soldier (5-5). No. 1948, Cranes (5-3).

1984, Oct. 1	Photo.	Perf. 11½x11
Size: 26x35mm		
1944	A505	8f multi	.45	.30
1945	A505	8f multi	.45	.30
1946	A505	8f multi	.45	.30
1947	A505	8f multi	.45	.30
Size: 36x48mm		
Perf. 11		
1948	A505	20f multi	2.25	1.00
	Nos. 1944-1948 (5)		4.05	2.20

110th Birth Anniv. of Chen Jiageng (J.106) A506

8f, Chen Jiageng (2-1). 80f, Jimei School (2-2).

1984, Oct. 21	Photo.	Perf. 12½x12
1949	A506	8f multi	.65	.25
1950	A506	80f multi	2.10	.40

The Maiden's Study A507

Scenes from The Peony Pavilion, by Tang Xianzu. T.99: No. 1952, In the dreamland (4-2). No. 1953, Du Liniang drawing self-portrait (4-3). No. 1954, Married to Liu Mengmai (4-4). No. 1955, Playing in the garden.

Photogravure & Engraved

1984, Oct. 30		Perf. 11
1951	A507	8f shown (4-1)	.75	.50
1952	A507	8f multi	.75	.50
1953	A507	20f multi	1.60	.90
1954	A507	70f multi	3.25	2.60
	Nos. 1951-1954 (4)		6.35	4.50

Souvenir Sheet
Perf. 11½

1955	A507	$2 multi	45.00	25.00

No. 1955 contains one 90x60mm stamp.

Emei Shan Mountain Scenery (T.100) — A508

No. 1956, Baoguo Temple (6-1). No. 1957, Leiyin Temple (6-2). No. 1958, Hongchun Lawn (6-3). No. 1959, Elephant bath (6-4). No. 1960, Woyun Temple (6-5). No. 1961, Shining Cloud Sea at Jinding (6-6).

1984, Nov. 16		Perf. 11
1956	A508	4f multi	1.10	.55
1957	A508	8f multi	.75	.40
1958	A508	8f multi	.45	.45
1959	A508	10f multi	1.00	.55
1960	A508	20f multi	2.00	1.25
1961	A508	80f multi	6.00	2.75
	Nos. 1956-1961 (6)		11.30	5.95

A509

Portraits: 8f, During the Long March (3-1). 10f, At 7th Natl. Party Congress (3-2). 20f, In motorcade (3-3).

1984, Dec. 15	Photo.	Perf. 11½x11
1962	A509	8f multi	.35	.35
1963	A509	10f multi	.45	.40
1964	A509	20f multi	.65	.40
	Nos. 1962-1964 (3)		1.45	1.15

Former party secretary Ren Bishi (1904-50).

Flower Arrangement A510

1984, Dec. 25		Perf. 11
1965	A510	8f multi	.75	.40

Chinese insurance industry.

New Year 1985 (Year of the Ox) — A511

Photogravure & Engraved

1985, Jan. 5		Perf. 11½
1966	A511	8f T.102	2.25	.55
a.	Bklt. pane of 4 + 8 plus label		24.00	12.00
	Complete booklet, #1966a		35.00	

Stamps from No. 1966a have straight edge at top or bottom.

Zunyi Meeting, 50th Anniv. — A512

Paintings: 8f, The Zunyi Meeting, by Liu Xiangping. 20f, The Red Army Successfully Arrived in Northern Shaanxi, by Zhao Yu. J.107.

1985, Jan. 15   Photo.   Perf. 11x11½

| 1967 | A512 | 8f multi (2-1) | 1.10 | .40 |
| 1968 | A512 | 20f multi (2-2) | 1.90 | .80 |

A513

Lantern Folk Festival: No. 1969, Lotus of Good Luck. No. 1970, Auspicious dragon and phoenix. No. 1971, A hundred flowers blossoming. 70f, Prosperity and affluence. T.104.

1985, Feb. 28   Perf. 11½

1969	A513	8f multi (4-1)	1.60	.55
1970	A513	8f multi (4-2)	1.60	.55
1971	A513	8f multi (4-3)	1.60	.55
1972	A513	70f multi (4-4)	5.00	1.60
		Nos. 1969-1972 (4)	9.80	3.25

A514

1985, Mar. 8

| 1973 | A514 | 20f multicolored | .80 | .45 |

UN Decade for Women (1976-85).

Mei (Prunus mume) (T.103) — A515

No. 1974, Green calyx (6-1). No. 1975, Pendant mei (6-2). No. 1976, Contorted dragon (6-3). No. 1977, Cinnabar (6-4). No. 1978, Versicolor mei (6-5). No. 1979, Apricot mei (6-6).

No. 1980, Duplicate and condensed fragrance mei.

1985, Apr. 5   Perf. 11

1974	A515	8f multi	1.10	.35
1975	A515	8f multi	1.10	.35
1976	A515	8f multi	1.10	.35
1977	A515	10f multi	2.10	.35
1978	A515	20f multi	3.25	.75
1979	A515	80f multi	8.25	2.25
		Nos. 1974-1979 (6)	16.90	4.40

Souvenir Sheet
Perf. 11½

| 1980 | A515 | $2 multi | 45.00 | 25.00 |

No. 1980 contains one 93x52mm stamp.

Huizo Guild Hall, Guangzhou — A516

1985, May 1   Photo.   Perf. 11

| 1981 | A516 | 8f multi | .80 | .40 |

All-China Fed. of Trade Unions.

Intl. Youth Year A517

1985, May 4   Photo.

| 1982 | A517 | 20f multicolored | 1.00 | .35 |

A518

Paintings of giant pandas: 8f, 20f, 50f, 80f, by Han Meilin; $3, by Wu Zuoren. T.106.

1985, May 24   Perf. 11½

1983	A518	8f multi (4-1), vert.	1.25	.35
1984	A518	20f multi (4-2)	1.50	.40
1985	A518	50f multi (4-3), vert.	1.50	.50
1986	A518	80f multi (4-4)	4.00	.70
		Nos. 1983-1986 (4)	8.25	1.95

Souvenir Sheet
Perf. 11x11½

| 1987 | A518 | $3 multi, vert. | 5.25 | 3.00 |
| a. | | Ovptd. in sheet margin | 8.00 | |

No. 1987 contains one 39x59mm stamp.
No. 1987a ovptd. in sheet margin with panda hologram, PJZ-4 and horizontal Chinese inscription in gold. Issued 10/9/96.
No. 1987a was sold in a mount affixed to a small card.

Xian Xinghai (1905-1945), Composer A519

Design: Bust, by Cao Chongen and music from The Yellow River Cantata.

1985, June 13   Photo.   Perf. 11½x11

| 1988 | A519 | 8f multicolored | 1.10 | .45 |

Agnes Smedley, 1892-1950 (3-1) — A520

American journalists: 20f, Anna Louise Strong, 1885-1970 (3-2). 80f, Edgar Snow, 1905-1972 (3-3). J.112.

1985, June 25

1989	A520	8f multicolored	.35	.30
1990	A520	20f multicolored	.45	.30
1991	A520	80f multicolored	.90	.60
		Nos. 1989-1991 (3)	1.70	1.20

Zheng He's West Seas Expedition, 580th Anniv. — A521

No. 1992, Portrait of the navigator. No. 1993, Peace envoy. 20f, Trade, cultural exchange. 80f, Honored for navigational feats. J.113.

1985, July 11   Perf. 11½

1992	A521	8f multi (4-1)	.55	.30
1993	A521	8f multi (4-2)	.55	.30
1994	A521	20f multi (4-3)	1.10	.45
1995	A521	80f multi (4-4)	2.60	.90
		Nos. 1992-1995 (4)	4.80	1.95

Xu Beihong, 1895-1953, Painter (J.114) A522

8f, Self-portrait (2-1), vert.

1985, July 19   Perf. 11½x11, 11x11½

| 1996 | A522 | 8f multicolored | .50 | .30 |
| 1997 | A522 | 20f shown (2-2) | 1.10 | .40 |

A523

Designs: 8f, Lin Zexu, 1785-1850, statesman, patriot. 80f, Burning opium at Humen, bas-relief.

1985, Aug. 30   Perf. 11

| 1998 | A523 | 8f multi (2-1) | .45 | .35 |

Size: 51x22mm

| 1999 | A523 | 80f multi (2-2) | 1.25 | .45 |

Lin Zexu's ban of the opium trade catalyzed the Anglo-Chinese Opium Wars. J.115.

A524

8f, Prosperity (3-1). 10f, Celebration (3-2). 20f, Abundant Harvest (3-3).

1985, Sept. 1   Perf. 11½x11

2000	A524	8f multi	.65	.30
2001	A524	10f multi	.85	.35
2002	A524	20f multi	1.75	.55
		Nos. 2000-2002 (3)	3.25	1.20

Tibet Autonomous Region, 20th anniv. (J.116).

End of World War II, 40th Anniv. A525

Woodcuts by Wu Biduan: 8f, The Chinese Army Rose Against the Japanese Agressors at Logouqiao (2-1). 80f, The Eighth Route Army and Militia Fought Around the Great Wall (2-2). J.117.

1985, Sept. 3   Perf. 11

| 2003 | A525 | 8f multi | .50 | .30 |
| 2004 | A525 | 80f multi | .95 | .55 |

2nd Natl. Worker's Games, Sept. 8-15, Beijing A526

Competitors from various events and: 8f, Men's bicycling (2-1). 20f, Women hurdlers (2-2). J.118.

1985, Sept. 8   Perf. 11x11½

| 2005 | A526 | 8f multi | .75 | .65 |
| 2006 | A526 | 20f multi | 1.10 | .90 |

Xinjiang Uygur Autonomous Region, 30th Anniv. (J.119) A527

8f, Oasis in the Gobi, woman (3-1). 10f, Oil field, Lake Tianchi (3-2). 20f, Tianshan pasture, woman (3-3).

1985, Oct. 1   Photo.   Perf. 11½

2007	A527	8f multi	.35	.35
2008	A527	10f multi	.40	.35
2009	A527	20f multi	.70	.40
		Nos. 2007-2009 (3)	1.45	1.10

Size of No. 2008, 60x30mm.

1st Natl. Youth Games, Oct. 6-15, Zhengzhou (J.121) — A528

8f, Girls' track & field (2-1). 20f, Boys' basketball (2-2).

1985, Oct. 6   Perf. 11½x11

| 2010 | A528 | 8f multi | .40 | .30 |
| 2011 | A528 | 20f multi | .65 | .55 |

Forbidden City Main Buildings — A529

1985, Oct. 10   Perf. 11½

2012	A529	8f multi (4-1)	.35	.30
2013	A529	8f multi (4-2)	.35	.30
2014	A529	20f multi (4-3)	.35	.30
2015	A529	80f multi (4-4)	.70	.70
a.		Vert. strip of 4, #2012-2015	2.75	2.75

Palace Museum, 60th anniv. J.120.

Zou Taofen (1895-1935), Journalist (J.122) — A530

1985, Nov. 5   Perf. 11½x11

2016	A530	8f Portrait (2-1)	.35	.35
2017	A530	20f Epitaph by Zhou Enlai (2-2)	.35	.35
a.		Pair, #2016-2017	1.00	.90

December 9th
Revolution, 50th
Anniv. — A531

1985, Dec. 9 *Perf. 11½*
2018 A531 8f Memorial Pavilion .90 .30

New Year
1986 — A532

Photogravure & Engraved
1986, Jan. 5 *Perf. 11½*
2019 A532 8f multicolored 1.10 .50
a. Bklt. pane of 4 + 8 with label
btwn 5.50
Complete booklet, #2019a 20.00

Natl. Space
Industry — A533

4f, 1st experimental satellite. No. 2021,
Recoverable satellite. No. 2022, Underwater
rocket launch. 10f, Rocket launch. 20f, Earth
satellite receiver. 70f, Satellite trajectory diagram. T.108.

1986, Feb. 1 Photo.
2020 A533 4f multi (6-1) .65 .35
2021 A533 8f multi (6-2) .65 .35
2022 A533 8f multi (6-3) .65 .35
2023 A533 10f multi (6-4) .65 .40
2024 A533 20f multi (6-5) 1.50 .40
2025 A533 70f multi (6-6) 3.25 .80
Nos. 2020-2025 (6) 7.35 2.65

Dong Biwu (1886-
1975), Party
Founder
(J.123) — A534

Photogravure and Engraved
1986, Mar. 5 *Perf. 11½x11*
2026 A534 8f 1975 (2-1) .90 .30
2027 A534 20f 1945 (2-2) 1.10 .65

Lin Boqu (1886-
1960), Party
Leader
(J.124) — A535

1986, Mar. 20
2028 A535 8f shown (2-1) .65 .30
2029 A535 20f Lin standing (2-2) .85 .50

Marshal He Long (1896-1969),
Revolution Leader (J.126) — A536

20f, On horseback (2-2).

1986, Mar. 22 *Perf. 11x11½*
2030 A536 8f shown (2-1) 1.00 .30
2031 A536 20f multicolored 1.25 .45

Halley's
Comet — A537

1986, Apr. 11 Photo. *Perf. 11½*
2032 A537 20f dk bl & gray 1.00 .30

White
Crane
(T.110)
A538

8f, Two cranes (3-1). 10f, One flying (3-2),
vert. 70f, Four cranes (3-3), vert.
$2, Flock.

1986, May 22 *Perf. 11x11½, 11½x11*
2033 A538 8f multi .90 .30
2034 A538 10f multi .90 .30
2035 A538 70f multi 2.40 .75
Nos. 2033-2035 (3) 4.20 1.35

Souvenir Sheet
2036 A538 $2 multi 9.00 4.50
No. 2036 contains one 116x25mm stamp.

Li Weihan (1896-1984), Party Leader
(J.127) — A539

1986, June 2 *Perf. 11x11½*
2037 A539 8f Portrait (2-1) .50 .30
2038 A539 20f Writing (2-2) .65 .50

Intl. Peace
Year
A540

1986, June 16 *Perf. 11*
2039 A540 8f multi 1.00 .30

Mao Dun (1896-1981), Writer
(J.129) — A541

1986, July 4 *Perf. 11x11½*
2040 A541 8f Portrait (2-1) .50 .30
2041 A541 20f Portrait, diff. (2-2) .65 .50

Wang Jiaxiang (1906-1974), Party
Leader (J.130) — A542

1986, Aug. 15
2042 A542 8f Portrait (2-1) .50 .30
2043 A542 20f Portrait, diff. (2-2) .65 .50

Teacher's
Day
A543

1986, Sept. 10 *Perf. 11*
2044 A543 8f multi 1.00 .30

Magnolia
Liliflora
(T.111)
A544

No. 2045, Blossom (3-1). No. 2046, Two
blossoms (3-2). No. 2047, Blossom, diff. (3-3).
No. 2048, Three blossoms.

1986, Sept. 23 *Perf. 11x11½*
2045 A544 8f multi .45 .40
2046 A544 8f multi .45 .40
2047 A544 70f multi 2.60 2.40
Nos. 2045-2047 (3) 3.50 3.20

Souvenir Sheet
2048 A544 $2 multi 13.50 8.00
No. 2048 contains one 132x70mm stamp.

Inner
Mongolia — A545

Tibet — A545a

Northeastern
China — A545b

Hunan — A545c

So. Yangtze
River — A545d

Beijing —
A545e

Yunnan —
A545f

Shanghai —
A545g

Anhui — A545h

No. Shaanxi —
A545i

Sichuan —
A545j

Taiwan —
A545k

Fujian — A545l

Zhejiang — A545m

Folk Houses.

Perf. 13x13½, 11x11½, (1½f, 3f, #2057-2062)
1986, Apr. 1 Photo.
2049 A545 1f multi .25 .25
2050 A545a 1½f multi .25 .25
2051 A545b 2f multi .25 .25
2052 A545c 3f multi .25 .25
2053 A545d 4f multi .25 .25
2054 A545e 8f multi .25 .25
2055 A545f 10f multi .25 .25
2056 A545g 20f multi .25 .25
2057 A545h 30f multi .30 .25
2058 A545i 40f multi .40 .30
2059 A545j 50f multi .60 .40
2060 A545k 90f multi .80 .55
2061 A545l $1 multi .85 .65
2062 A545m $1.10 multi .90 .75
Nos. 2049-2062 (14) 5.85 4.90

Issue dates: 3f, Dec. 25; 4f, $1, Oct. 15; 20f,
50f, Sept. 10; 40f, Nov. 15; others, Apr. 1.
Postal forgeries of No. 2056 exist.
See Nos. 2198-2204.

1989-90 Photo.
2055a Perf. 11x11½ ('89) 1.00 1.00
2056a Perf. 11x11½ ('89) 1.50 1.00
2057a Perf. 13x13½ ('90) .65 .35
2058a Perf. 13x13½ ('90) 9.00 4.50
2059a Perf. 13x13½ ('89) 1.10 .60
2061a Perf. 13x13½ ('90) 2.25 1.25
Nos. 2055a-2061a (6) 15.50 8.70

Souvenir Sheet

All-China Philatelic Federation, 2nd
Congress — A546

1986, Oct. 17 Litho. *Perf. 11½*
2063 A546 $2 Jade lion 8.50 3.50

Leaders of the 1911 Revolution (J.132) A547

1986, Oct. 10 Photo. Perf. 11x11½
2064 A547 8f Sun Yat-sen (3-1) 1.00 .40
2065 A547 10f Huang Xing (3-2) 1.40 .80
2066 A547 40f Zhang Taiyan (3-3) 3.00 1.60
Nos. 2064-2066 (3) 5.40 2.80

Souvenir Sheet

Sun Yat-sen (1866-1925) — A548

1986, Nov. 12 Perf. 11½
2067 A548 $2 multicolored 16.00 6.50

Marshal Zhu De (1886-1976) (J.134) — A549

Designs: 20f, Orating.

1986, Dec. 1 Engr. Perf. 11½x11
2068 A549 8f sepia (2-1) 2.75 .35
2069 A549 20f myrtle grn (2-2) 5.00 .55

Sports of Ancient China A550

Stone carvings. T.113: No. 2070, Archery (4-1), vert. No. 2071, Weiqi (4-2). No. 2072, Golf (4-3). No. 2073, Soccer (4-4), vert..

Perf. 11½x11, 11x11½
1986, Dec. 20 Photo.
2070 A550 8f multi .65 .35
2071 A550 8f multicolored .65 .35
2072 A550 10f multicolored .95 .45
2073 A550 50f multicolored 4.00 2.00
Nos. 2070-2073 (4) 6.25 3.15

A551

Photogravure & Engraved
1987, Jan. 5 Perf. 11½
2074 A551 8f blk, dk pink & yel grn 1.40 .45
a. Bklt. pane of 4 + 8 + label 16.00 —
Complete booklet, #2074a 30.00

New Year 1987 (Year of the Hare).

A552

8f, Traveling (3-1). 20f, Cave writing (3-2). 40f, Mountain climbing (3-3).

1987, Feb. 20 Photo. Perf. 11½
2075 A552 8f multi .75 .35
2076 A552 20f multi 2.50 1.40
2077 A552 40f multi 4.50 2.25
Nos. 2075-2077 (3) 7.75 4.00

Xu Xiake (1587-1621), Ming Dynasty geographer (J.136).

Birds of Prey (T.114) — A553

No. 2078, Kite (4-1). No. 2079, Sea eagle (4-2), vert. No. 2080, Vulture (4-3), vert. No. 2081, Buzzard (4-4).

1987, Mar. 20
2078 A553 8f multi .60 .40
2079 A553 8f multi .60 .40
2080 A553 10f multi .95 .40
2081 A553 90f multi 6.00 1.40
Nos. 2078-2081 (4) 8.15 2.60

Liao Zhongkai (1877-1925), National Party Leader (J.137) — A554

20f, Liao, He Xiangning (2-2).

1987, Apr. 23 Perf. 11½x11
2082 A554 8f shown (2-1) 1.00 .30
2083 A554 20f multi 2.00 .35

Kites (T.115) — A555

No. 2084, Hawk (4-1). No. 2085, Dragon (4-2). No. 2086, Symbolic octagon (4-3). No. 2087, Phoenix (4-4).

1987, Apr. 1
2084 A555 8f multi .75 .35
2085 A555 8f multi .75 .35
a. Pair, #2084-2085 2.75 2.25

2086 A555 30f multi 2.00 .95
2087 A555 30f multi 2.00 .95
a. Pair, #2086-2087 5.25 4.00
Nos. 2084-2087 (4) 5.50 2.60

Nos. 2085a, 2087a have continuous designs.

A556

Portraits of Ye Jianying (1897-1986), central committee vice chairman (J.138).

1987, Apr. 28
2088 A556 8f multi (3-3) 1.00 .40
2089 A556 10f multi (3-2) 1.50 .50
2090 A556 30f multi (3-1) 5.50 1.90
Nos. 2088-2090 (3) 8.00 2.80

Caves of the Thousand Buddhas, Dunhuang, Gansu Province — A557

Wall Paintings: 8f, Worshipping Bodhisattvas, Northern Liang Dynasty. 10f, Deer King Jataka, Northern Wei Dynasty. 20f, Heavenly Musicians, Northern Wei Dynasty. 40f, Flying Devata, Northern Wei Dynasty. $2, Mahasattva Jataka. T.116.

1987, May 20 Perf. 11½
2091 A557 8f multi (4-1) .55 .30
2092 A557 10f multi (4-2) .65 .35
2093 A557 20f multi (4-3) 1.75 .85
2094 A557 40f multi (4-4) 3.00 1.40
Nos. 2091-2094 (4) 5.95 2.90

Souvenir Sheet
2095 A557 $2 multi 27.50 15.00

No. 2095 contains one 92x73mm stamp. See Nos. 2149-2152, 2283-2286, 2407-2411, 2505-2508, 2704-2707.

Children's Day Festival A558

Children's drawings: No. 2096, Happy Holiday, by Yan Qinghui, age 7. No. 2097, Peace and Happiness, by Liu Yuan, age 7. T.117.

1987, June 1 Perf. 12½x12
2096 A558 8f shown (2-1) 1.25 .25
2097 A558 8f multi, vert. (2-2) 1.60 .45

Rural Development A559

No. 2098, Village, southeast China (4-1). No. 2099, Market (4-2). No. 2100, Dairy industry (4-3). No. 2101, Theater (4-4).

1987, June 25 Perf. 11½
2098 A559 8f multi .60 .45
2099 A559 8f multi .60 .45
2100 A559 10f multi .85 .60
2101 A559 20f multi 1.75 1.25
Nos. 2098-2101 (4) 3.80 2.75

Nos. 2099-2100 horiz. T.118.

Postal Savings Bank Inauguration A560

1987, July 1
2102 A560 8f multicolored 2.00 .35

Esperanto Language Movement, Cent. — A561

1987, July 26
2103 A561 8f lt olive grn, blk & brt blue 1.75 .40

People's Liberation Army, 60th Anniv. (J.140) A562

No. 2104, Flag, Great Wall (4-1). No. 2105, Rocket launch, soldier, village (4-2). No. 2106, Submarine, sailor (4-3). No. 2107, Aircraft, pilot (4-4).

1987, Aug. 1 Perf. 11
2104 A562 8f multi .75 .35
2105 A562 8f multi .75 .35
2106 A562 10f multi 1.75 .40
2107 A562 30f multi 2.50 .65
Nos. 2104-2107 (4) 5.75 1.75

Intl. Year of Shelter for the Homeless A563

1987, Aug. 20 Perf. 11
2108 A563 8f gray, dk car rose & blk 1.00 .30

Chinese Art Festival, Sept. 5-25, Beijing — A564

1987, Sept. 5 Perf. 11
2109 A564 8f brt red, gold & blk 3.00 .40

Fairy Tales — A565

4f, Pan Gu inventing the universe. No. 2111, Nu Wa creating man. No. 2112, Yi shooting nine suns. 10f, Chang'e flying to the moon. 20f, Kua Fu pursuing the sun. 90f, Jing Wei filling the sea. T.120.

1987, Sept. 25 Perf. 11½
2110 A565 4f multi (6-1) .55 .30
2111 A565 8f multi (6-2) .65 .30
2112 A565 8f multi (6-3) .65 .30
2113 A565 10f multi (6-4) .80 .30

2114	A565	20f multi (6-5)	1.10	.50
2115	A565	90f multi (6-6)	2.50	1.50
		Nos. 2110-2115 (6)	6.25	3.20

Communist Party of China, 13th Natl. Congress
A566

1987, Oct. 25 — *Perf. 11*

2116	A566	8f multicolored	1.25	.50

Yellow Crane Tower (T.121)
A567

No. 2118, Yue Yang Tower (4-2). No. 2119, Teng Wang Pavilion (4-3). No. 2120, Peng Lai Pavilion (4-4).

1987, Oct. 30

2117	A567	8f shown (4-1)	.50	.25
2118	A567	8f multi	.50	.30
2119	A567	10f multi	.65	.45
2120	A567	90f multi	3.75	3.50
a.		Min. sheet of 4, #2117-2120	17.00	10.00
		Nos. 2117-2120 (4)	5.40	4.50

No. 2120a sold for $1.50.

6th Natl. Games (J.144) — A568

No. 2121, Pole vault (4-1). No. 2122, Softball (4-2). No. 2123, Weight lifting (4-3). No. 2124, Diving (4-4).

1987, Nov. 20 — *Perf. 11½x11*

2121	A568	8f multi	.35	.25
2122	A568	8f multi	.35	.25
2123	A568	30f multi	.60	.35
2124	A568	50f multi	1.00	.55
		Nos. 2121-2124 (4)	2.30	1.40

Souvenir Sheet

Bronze Bells from the Tomb of Marquis Yi of the Zeng State (c. 433 B.C.), Hubei Province — A569

1987, Dec. 10 — *Litho.* — *Imperf.*

2125	A569	$3 multicolored	9.50	4.50

Classic Literature — A570

Outlaws of the Marsh: 8f, Shi Jin practicing martial arts. 10f, Sagacious Lu, the "Tattooed Monk," uprooting a willow tree. 30f, Lin Chong seeking shelter from snow storm at the Mountain Spirit Temple. 50f, Song Jiang helps Ward Chief Chao Gai flee. $2, Outlaws of the Marsh capture treasures. T.123.

1987, Dec. 20 — *Photo.* — *Perf. 11*

2126	A570	8f multi (4-1)	.60	.25
2127	A570	10f multi (4-2)	.80	.25
2128	A570	30f multi (4-3)	2.50	.70
2129	A570	50f multi (4-4)	3.50	1.50
		Nos. 2126-2129 (4)	7.40	2.70

Souvenir Sheet
Perf. 11½x11

2130	A570	$2 multi	30.00	16.00

No. 2130 contains one 90x60mm stamp.
See Nos. 2216-2219, 2373-2377, 2449-2452, 2822-2826, 2889-2893.

New Year 1988 (Year of the Dragon) — A571

Photo. & Engr.

1988, Jan. 5 — *Perf. 11½*

2131	A571	8f multicolored	3.25	.55
a.		Bklt. pane of 4 + 8 with label between	38.00	—
		Complete booklet, #2131a	55.00	

Cai Yuanpei (1868-1940), Education Reformer ((J.145) — A572

1988, Jan. 11 — *Photo.* — *Perf. 11½x11*

2132	A572	8f shown (2-1)	.70	.25
2133	A572	20f Seated (2-2)	1.10	.50

Tao Zhu (1908-1969), Party Leader (J.146) — A573

1988, Jan. 16 — *Perf. 11x11½*

2134	A573	8f shown (2-1)	1.25	.30
2135	A573	20f Tao, diff. (2-2)	1.60	.55

Folklore (T.125)
A574

1988, Feb. 10

2136	A574	8f shown (4-1)	.45	.25
2137	A574	10f multi, diff. (4-2)	.60	.25
2138	A574	20f multi, diff. (4-3)	.75	.40
2139	A574	30f multi, diff. (4-4)	1.50	.70
		Nos. 2136-2139 (4)	3.30	1.60

A575

1988, Mar. 25 — *Photo.* — *Perf. 11½*

2140	A575	8f multicolored	1.00	.30

7th Natl. People's Congress.

A576

8f, Wuzhi Mountain (4-1). 10f, Wanquan River (4-2). 30f, "End of the Earth" (4-3). $1.10, "Deer Turning Its Head" (4-4).

1988, Apr. 20 — *Photo.* — *Perf. 11½*

2141	A576	8f multi	.50	.25
2142	A576	10f multi	.65	.25
2143	A576	30f multi	.90	.30
2144	A576	$1.10 multi	1.20	.50
		Nos. 2141-2144 (4)	3.25	1.30

Establishment of Hainan Province (J.148).

Modern Scientists
A577

Designs: 8f, Li Siguang, geologist. 10f, Zhu Kezhen, meteorologist and geographer. 20f, Wu Youxun, physicist. 30f, Hua Luogeng, mathematician. J.149.

1988, Apr. 28 — *Perf. 11x11½*

2145	A577	8f multi (4-1)	.55	.25
2146	A577	10f multi (4-2)	.65	.25
2147	A577	20f multi (4-3)	.85	.30
2148	A577	30f multi (4-4)	1.50	.60
		Nos. 2145-2148 (4)	3.55	1.40

Wall Paintings Type of 1987

Caves of the Thousand Buddhas, Dunhuang, Gansu Province: No. 2149, Hunting, Western Wei Dynasty. No. 2150, Fishing, Western Wei Dynasty. 10f, Farming, Northern Zhou Dynasty. 90f, Building a Pagoda, Northern Zhou Dynasty. T.126.

1988, May 25 — *Perf. 11½x11*

2149	A557	8f multi (4-1)	.55	.25
2150	A557	8f multi (4-2)	.55	.25
2151	A557	10f multi (4-3)	.75	.30
2152	A557	90f multi (4-4)	2.60	.75
		Nos. 2149-2152 (4)	4.45	1.55

Environmental Protection — A578

No. 2153, Soil (4-1). No. 2154, Air (4-2). No. 2155, Water (4-3). No. 2156, Prevent noise pollution (4-4).

1988, June 5 — *Photo.* — *Perf. 11*

2153		8f multi	.55	.30
2154		8f multi	.55	.30
2155		8f multi	.55	.30
2156		8f multi	.55	.30
a.	A578	Block of 4, #2153-2156	4.25	1.75

Souvenir Sheet

China Nos. 1-3 — A579

Photo. & Engr.

1988, July 2 — *Perf. 13*

2157	A579	$3 multicolored	11.00	7.00

Postage stamps of China, 110th anniv.

11th Asian Games (in 1990), Beijing (J.151)
A580

8f, Emblem (2-1). 30f, Character trademark (2-2).

1988, July 20 — *Photo.* — *Perf. 11x11½*

2158	A580	8f multi	.35	.25
2159	A580	30f multi	.75	.45

See No. 2300a.

Signing of the Sino-Japanese Peace Treaty, 10th Anniv. (J.152) — A581

1988, Aug. 12 — *Photo.* — *Perf. 11*

2160	A581	8f Peony (2-1)	.30	.25
2161	A581	$1.60 Sakura (2-2)	.90	.50
a.		Pair, #2160-2161	3.25	1.50

Achievements in Construction — A582

Designs: 8f, Coal-loading wharf, Ch'in-huang-tao Port. 10f, Ethylene refinery, Qilu. 20f, Pao-shan steel plant, Shanghai. 30f, Central Television Broadcasting Station. T.128.

1988, Sept. 2 — *Photo.* — *Perf. 11*

2162	A582	8f multi (4-1)	.50	.25
2163	A582	10f multi (4-2)	.75	.30
2164	A582	20f multi (4-3)	.90	.35
2165	A582	30f multi (4-4)	1.00	.45
		Nos. 2162-2165 (4)	3.15	1.35

See Nos. 2221-2224, 2279-2282, 2354-2357.

Mt. T'ai Shan, Shantung Province
(T.130) — A583

8f, T'ai Shan Temple (4-1). 10f, Ladder to Heaven (4-2). 20f, Daguang peak (4-3). 90f, Sun-watching peak (4-4).

1988, Sept. 14   **Photo. & Engr.**
2166	A583	8f multi	.40	.25
2167	A583	10f multi	.50	.40
2168	A583	20f multi	.90	.50
2169	A583	90f multi	3.75	1.40
		Nos. 2166-2169 (4)	5.55	2.55

Liao Chengzhi (1908-1983), Party Leader (J.153) — A584

1988, Sept. 25   **Photo.**   **Perf. 11½x11**
2170	A584	8f shown (2-1)	.40	.25
2171	A584	20f Writing (2-2)	.75	.45

Marshal Peng Dehuai (1898-1974), Party Leader (J.155) — A585

20f, Peng in uniform (2-2).

1988, Oct. 24   **Photo.**   **Perf. 11x11½**
2172	A585	8f shown (2-1)	.45	.25
2173	A585	20f multi	1.25	.60

1st Natl. Farmers' Games (J.154) A586

1988, Oct. 9   **Photo.**   **Perf. 11½**
2174	A586	8f Cycling (2-1)	.35	.25
2175	A586	20f Javelin (2-2)	.65	.40

Literary Masterpieces — A587

The Romance of the Three Kingdoms, by Luo Guanzhong, 14th cent.: No. 2176, Three heroes' sworn brotherhood (4-1). No. 2177, Battle between Lu Bu and the heroes, vert. (4-2). No. 2178, Struggle between man and woman at Fengyi Pavilion (4-3). No. 2179, Two noblemen, vert. (4-4). No. 2180, Guan Yu's battle through five passes. T.131.

Perf. 11½x11, 11x11½
1988, Nov. 25   **Photo.**
2176	A587	8f multicolored	.40	.25
2177	A587	8f multicolored	.40	.30
2178	A587	30f multicolored	1.10	.60
2179	A587	50f multicolored	1.40	1.00
		Nos. 2176-2179 (4)	3.30	2.15

Souvenir Sheet
Perf. 11
2180	A587	$3 multicolored	27.50	14.50

See Nos. 2310-2313, 2403-2406, 2539-2543.

Intl Volunteers' Day — A588

1988, Dec. 5   **Photo.**   **Perf. 11**
2181	A588	20f multicolored	1.00	.30

A589

Milu, *Elaphurus davidianus* (T.132).

1988, Dec. 20   **Photo.**   **Perf. 11½x11**
2182	A589	8f Buck (2-1)	1.10	.25
2183	A589	40f Herd (2-2)	3.00	2.00

Exist imperf. Value, pairs each $6.50.

Orchids (T.129) — A590

8f, Da yi pin (4-1). 10f, Dragon (4-2). 20f, Large phoenix tail (4-3). 50f, Silver-edged black (4-4).
Red lotus petal.

1988, Dec. 25   **Perf. 12**
2184	A590	8f multi	.70	.30
2185	A590	10f multi	.85	.35
2186	A590	20f multi	1.10	.45
2187	A590	50f multi	1.40	.95
a.		Strip of 4, #2184-2187	6.50	3.75
		Nos. 2184-2187 (4)	4.05	2.05

Souvenir Sheet
Perf. 11½x11
2188	A590	$2 multi	15.00	8.00

No. 2188 contains one 55x37mm stamp.

A591

Grotto Statuary: $2, Buddha. $5, Warrior, Longmen Grotto, Henan. $10, Goddess. $20, Woman and birds.

Photo & Engr.
1988-89   **Perf. 11½x11**
2189	A591	$2 buff & reddish blk	1.40	.30
2190	A591	$5 buff & grnh blk	1.75	.65

2191	A591	$10 buff & brn blk	2.75	1.25
a.		Souv. sheet of 1, buff & sep	20.00	
2192	A591	$20 buff & indigo	6.75	2.50
		Nos. 2189-2192 (4)	12.65	4.70

Issued: $2, 11/30; $5, 8/10; $10, 10/15; $20, 10/20.

No. 2191a released on Oct. 12, 1989, for the China Natl. Philatelic Exhibition and the 40th anniv. of the People's Republic.

Nos. 2189-2192, 2191a are almost always found with small ink spots on the stamps. Values are for stamps in this condition.

A592

Photo. & Engr.
1989, Jan. 5   **Perf. 11½**
2193	A592	8f multicolored	3.25	.30
a.		Bklt. pane of 4+8 with label between	17.50	
		Complete booklet, #2193a	26.00	

New Year 1989 (Year of the Snake). Stamps from No. 2193a have one or two straight edges and sell for less as singles than No. 2193.

Qu Qiubai (1899-1935), Party Leader (J.157) — A593

1989, Jan. 29   **Photo.**   **Perf. 11x11½**
2194	A593	8f multi (2-1)	.45	.35
2195	A593	20f multi, diff. (2-2)	.75	.55

Brown-eared Pheasant, *Crossoptilon mantchuricum* (T.134) — A594

1989, Feb. 21   **Perf. 11½**
2196	A594	8f multi (2-1)	.45	.25
2197	A594	50f multi, diff. (2-2)	.80	.40

Folk Houses Type of 1986
1989-91   **Photo.**   **Perf. 13x13½**
2198	A545	5f Shandong	.25	.25
2199	A545	15f Guangxi	.25	.25
2200	A545	25f Ningxia	.30	.25
2201	A545	80f Shanxi	.60	.25
2202	A545	$1.30 Qinghai	.60	.40
2203	A545	$1.60 Guizhou	.75	.40
2204	A545	$2 Jiangxi	1.00	.40
		Nos. 2198-2204 (7)	3.75	2.20

Issued: 5f, 6/10/91; 15f, 11/25/90; 25f, 11/10/90; 80f, 9/20/90; $1.30, $1.60, 3/10/89; $2, 4/25/91.

Silk Painting Excavated from Han Tomb No. 1 at Mawangdui, Changsha (T.135)
A595

8f, In the Heavens (3-1). 20f, On the Earth, vert. (3-2). 30f, In the Netherworld, vert. (3-3). $5, Entire painting.

1989, Mar. 25   **Photo.**   **Perf. 11x11½**
2208	A595	8f multi	.55	.25
a.		Perf. 11½	5.50	5.50
2209	A595	20f multi	.55	.25
a.		Perf. 11½	5.50	5.50

2210	A595	30f multi	.55	.25
a.		Perf. 11½	5.50	5.50
		Nos. 2208-2210 (3)	1.65	.75

Textured Paper, Without Gum
Size: 90x165mm
Imperf
2211	A595	$5 multi	4.50	3.25

Prevention and Resistance of Cancer (T.136) — A596

20f, Woman's thermogram (2-2).

1989, Apr. 7   **Litho.**   **Perf. 12**
2212	A596	8f shown (2-1)	.35	.25
2213	A596	20f multicolored	.65	.30

May Fourth Movement, 70th Anniv. (J.158) A597

1989, May 4   **Photo.**   **Perf. 11**
2214	A597	8f Bas-relief	.60	.30

Interparliamentary Union, Cent. — A598

1989, June 29   **Photo.**   **Perf. 11x11½**
2215	A598	20f multi	.80	.30

Literature Type of 1987

Outlaws of the Marsh: 8f, Wu Song slaying a tiger on Jingyang Ridge. 10f, Qin Ming dodging arrows. 20f, Hua Rong shooting a wild goose on Mt. Liangshan. $1.30, Li Kui fighting Zhang Shun from a junk. T.138.

1989, July 25   **Photo.**   **Perf. 11**
2216	A570	8f multi (4-1)	.30	.25
2217	A570	10f multi (4-2)	.30	.25
2218	A570	20f multi (4-3)	.40	.35
2219	A570	$1.30 multi (4-4)	.75	.50
		Nos. 2216-2219 (4)	1.75	1.35

Asia-Pacific Telecommunity, 10th Anniv. — A599

1989, Aug. 4   **Litho.**   **Perf. 12**
2220	A599	8f multi	.55	.25

Type of 1988

Achievements in Engineering and Construction: 8f, Beijing Intl. Telecommunications Building, vert. 10f, Xi Qu Coal Mine, Gu Jiao, Shanxi Province. 20f, Long Yang Gorge Hydroelectric Power Station, Qinghai Province. 30f, Da Yao Shan Tunnel of the Guangzhou-Heng Yang Railway. T.139.

1989, Aug. 10   **Photo.**   **Perf. 11**
2221	A582	8f multi (4-1)	.30	.25
2222	A582	10f multi (4-2)	.30	.25
2223	A582	20f multi (4-3)	.30	.30
2224	A582	30f multi (4-4)	.35	.30
		Nos. 2221-2224 (4)	1.25	1.10

Mt. Huashan — A601

Designs: 8f, Five prominent peaks. 10f, View from atop Huashan. 20f, 1000-foot precipice. 90f, Blue Dragon Ridge. T.140.

1989, Aug. 25   Photo. & Engr.
2225	A601	8f multi (4-1)	.40	.25
2226	A601	10f multi (4-2)	.50	.25
2227	A601	20f multi (4-3)	.60	.35
2228	A601	90f multi (4-4)	1.35	.55
		Nos. 2225-2228 (4)	2.85	1.40

Modern Art — A602

Paintings: 8f, *The Fable of the White Snake,* by Ye Qianyu. 20f, *Li River in Fine Rain,* by Li Keran. 50f, *Marching Together,* by Wu Zuoren. T.141

1989, Sept. 1   Photo.
2229	A602	8f multi (3-1)	.50	.25
2230	A602	20f multi (3-2)	.60	.25
2231	A602	50f multi (3-3)	1.25	.40
		Nos. 2229-2231 (3)	2.35	.90

People's Political
Conference
A603

1989, Sept. 21   Perf. 12
2232	A603	8f No. 2	.80	.30

A604

Confucius (551-479 B.C.) — A605

Designs: 8f, The lecture in the Apricot Temple, Qufu. $1.60, Confucius riding in an ox cart. J.162.

1989, Sept. 28   Photo.   Perf. 11
2233	A604	8f shown (2-1)	1.00	.40
2234	A604	$1.60 multi (2-2)	3.00	1.00

**Souvenir Sheet
Without Gum**

Litho.   Imperf.
2235	A605	$3 multicolored	6.00	4.25

A606

Gate of Heavenly Peace — A607

1989, Oct. 1   Photo.   Perf. 11x11½
2236	A606	8f shown (4-1)	.30	.25
2237	A606	10f Flowers (4-2)	.35	.25
2238	A606	20f Five stars (4-3)	.45	.25
2239	A606	40f Construction (4-4)	.75	.25
		Nos. 2236-2239 (4)	1.85	1.00

**Souvenir Sheet
Without Gum**

Litho.   Imperf.
2240	A607	$3 shown	4.00	2.25

PRC, 40th anniv. J.163.

Photography,
Sesquicentennial — A608

1989, Oct. 15   Photo.   Perf. 11
2241	A608	8f multicolored	.75	.30

Li Dazhao (1889-1927), Party Leader
(J.164) — A609

1989, Oct. 29   Photo.   Perf. 11
2242	A609	8f Li, soldiers (2-1)	.75	.30
a.		Perf. 11½	6.00	6.00
2243	A609	20f Li, text (2-2)	1.25	.30
a.		Perf. 11½	6.00	6.00

Positron
Collider
Produced
in Beijing
A610

1989, Nov. 1   Perf. 11
2244	A610	8f multicolored	.90	.60

Rocket
Defense
A611

Designs: 4f, Transporting 3 rockets. 8f, Disassembled rocket on transport. 10f, Launch, vert. 20f, Stage separation in space. T.143.

1989, Nov. 15   Litho.   Perf. 12
2245	A611	4f multicolored (4-1)	.35	.30
2246	A611	8f multicolored (4-2)	.50	.35
2247	A611	10f multicolored (4-3)	.65	.40
2248	A611	20f multicolored (4-4)	.85	.55
		Nos. 2245-2248 (4)	2.35	1.60

A612

Views of West Lake (T.144) — A613

1989, Nov. 25   Photo.   Perf. 11x11½
2249	A612	8f multi (4-1)	.50	.30
2250	A612	10f multi, diff. (4-2)	.65	.30
2251	A612	30f multi, diff. (4-3)	.85	.35
2252	A612	40f multi, diff. (4-4)	1.10	.40
		Nos. 2249-2252 (4)	3.10	1.35

**Souvenir Sheet
Perf. 11½x11**
2253	A613	$5 multicolored	8.00	2.50

11th Asian
Games
A614

Various stadiums. J.165.

1989, Dec. 15   Perf. 11x11½
2254	A614	8f multi (4-1)	.30	.25
2255	A614	10f multi (4-2)	.30	.25
2256	A614	30f multi (4-3)	.30	.25
2257	A614	$1.60 multi (4-4)	.55	.40
		Nos. 2254-2257 (4)	1.45	1.15

See Nos. 2295-2300.

A615

Photo & Engr.

1990, Jan. 5   Perf. 11½
2258	A615	8f multicolored	1.60	.35
a.		Bklt. pane of 12 + 4 labels	20.00	—
		Complete booklet, #2258a	22.00	
b.		As. No. 2258, perf. 11½x11	16.00	16.00

New Year 1990 (Year of the Horse). Stamps from No. 2258a have straight edges at top or bottom and sell for less as singles than No. 2258.

Narcissus
(T.147) — A616

1990, Feb. 10   Photo.   Perf. 11x11½
2259	A616	8f multi (4-1)	.25	.25
2260	A616	20f multi, diff. (4-2)	.30	.30
2261	A616	30f multi, diff. (4-3)	.45	.30
2262	A616	$1.60 multi, diff. (4-4)	.55	.40
		Nos. 2259-2262 (4)	1.55	1.25

Norman Bethune (1890-1939),
Surgeon (J.166) — A617

Litho. & Engr.

1990, Mar. 3   Perf. 11x11½
2263	A617	8f In Canada (2-2)	.30	.25
2264	A617	$1.60 In China (2-1)	.60	.50
a.		Pair, #2263-2264	1.60	1.25

See Canada Nos. 1264-1265.

Intl. Women's
Day — A618

1990, Mar. 8   Photo.   Perf. 11½x11
2265	A618	20f multicolored	.60	.30

Afforestation (T.148) — A619

8f, Bird, flora (4-1). 10f, Buildings (4-2). 20f, Great Wall, forest, (4-3). 30f, Bushes, evergreens (4-4).

1990, Mar. 12   Perf. 11
2266	A619	8f multi	.30	.25
2267	A619	10f multi	.30	.25
2268	A619	20f multi	.45	.25
2269	A619	30f multi	.55	.25
		Nos. 2266-2269 (4)	1.60	1.00

Pottery
(T.149) — A620

1990, Apr. 10   Litho.   Perf. 12
2270	A620	8f multi (4-1)	.25	.25
2271	A620	20f multi (4-2)	.30	.25
2272	A620	30f multi (4-3)	.50	.30
2273	A620	50f multi (4-4)	.65	.30
		Nos. 2270-2273 (4)	1.70	1.10

Li Fuchun (1900-1975), Party Leader
(J.168) — A621

1990, May 22 Photo. *Perf. 11x11½*
2274 A621   8f shown   .40   .30
2275 A621 20f In uniform (2-2)   .60   .35

Bronze
Head — A622

Bronze treasures from Emperor Qin Shi
Huang Mausoleum: 50f, Horse head. $5,
Chariots. T.151.

1990, June 20 Photo. *Perf. 11½x11*
2276 A622   8f shown (2-1)   .45   .25
2277 A622 50f multicolored (2-2)   .75   .35

Miniature Sheet
Size: 141x79mm

2278 A622 $5 multicolored   9.50 4.50

Achievements Type of 1988

Designs: 8f, 2nd automobile factory. 10f,
Yizheng Joint Corporation of Chemical Fiber
Industry. 20f, Shengli Oil Field. 30f, Qinshan
Nuclear Power Station. T.152.

1990, June 30 Litho. *Perf. 12*
2279 A582   8f shown (4-1)   .30   .25
2280 A582 10f multicolored (4-2)   .30   .25
2281 A582 20f multicolored (4-3)   .45   .25
2282 A582 30f multicolored (4-4)   .60   .30
      Nos. 2279-2282 (4)   1.65 1.05

Wall Paintings Type of 1987

8f, Flying Devatas. 10f, Worshipping
Bodhisatva. 30f, Savior Avolokitesvara. 50f,
Indra. T.150.

1990, July 10   *Perf. 11½x11*
2283 A557   8f multi (4-1)   .30   .25
2284 A557 10f multi, vert. (4-2)   .30   .25
2285 A557 30f multi, vert. (4-3)   .40   .30
2286 A557 50f multi (4-4)   .80   .40
      Nos. 2283-2286 (4)   1.80 1.20

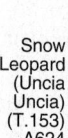

Snow
Leopard
(Uncia
Uncia)
(T.153)
A624

1990, July 20 Photo. *Perf. 11½*
2287 A624   8f multicolored (2-1)   .45   .25
2288 A624 50f multicolored (2-2)   .80   .30

Chinese
Soviet Post
Stamp of
1931
A625

Design: 20f, Chinese Red Post issue of
West Fukien, 1929. J.169.

1990, Aug. 1 Litho. *Perf. 12*
2289 A625   8f multi (2-1)   .40   .25
2290 A625 20f multi, diff. (2-2)   .80   .25

Zhang Wentian (1900-1990)
(J.170) — A626

1990, Aug. 30   *Perf. 11x11½*
2291 A626   8f shown (2-1)   .35   .25
2292 A626 20f multi, diff. (2-2)   .75   .25

Intl. Literacy
Year — A627

1990, Sept. 8   *Perf. 11½x11*
2293 A627 20f multicolored   .75   .30

Chinese
Films — A628

1990, Sept. 21 Litho. *Perf. 11*
2294 A628 20f multicolored   .90   .25

11th Asian
Games,
Beijing
(J.172)
A629

4f, Running (6-1). 8f, Gymnastics (6-2). 10f,
Karate (6-3). 20f, Volleyball (6-4). 30f, Swimming (6-5). $1.60, Shooting (6-6).

1990, Sept. 22   *Perf. 11x11½*
2295 A629   4f multi   .25   .25
2296 A629   8f multi   .25   .25
2297 A629 10f multi   .30   .25
2298 A629 20f multi   .30   .25
2299 A629 30f multi   .40   .30
2300 A629 $1.60 multi   .90   .65
  a.   Souv. sheet of 12, #2158-
       2159, 2254-2257, 2295-
       2300   9.00 6.00
      Nos. 2295-2300 (6)   2.40 1.95

Souvenir Sheet

Sportphilex '90, Beijing — A629a

1990, Sept. 21 Litho. *Perf. 11½*
2300B A629a $10 multi   22.50 11.00
  No. 2300B exists imperf. Value, $700.

Modern
Scientists
A630

Designs: 8f, Lin Qiaozhi, obstetrician. 10f,
Zhang Yuzhe, astronomer. 20f, Hou Debang,
chemist. 30f, Ding Ying, agronomist. J.173.

1990, Oct. 10 Litho. *Perf. 12*
2301 A630   8f multicolored (4-1)   .45   .25
2302 A630 10f multicolored (4-2)   .45   .25
2303 A630 20f multicolored (4-3)   .80   .25
2304 A630 30f multicolored (4-4)   .85   .25
      Nos. 2301-2304 (4)   2.55 1.00

Mt. Hengshan — A631

Designs: 8f, Towering Temple. 10f, South
Sacred Mountain. 20f, Forested mountainside.
50f, Imposing Zhurong Peak. T.155.

Photo. & Engr.
1990, Nov. 5   *Perf. 11*
2305 A631   8f multicolored (4-1)   .50   .30
2306 A631 10f multicolored (4-2)   .70   .30
2307 A631 20f multicolored (4-3) 1.00   .35
2308 A631 50f multicolored (4-4) 1.60   .45
      Nos. 2305-2308 (4)   3.80 1.40

  See Nos. 2342-2345. 2628-2631.

Souvenir Sheet

China Philatelic Federation, 3rd
Congress — A632

1990, Nov. 28   *Perf. 11½x11*
2309 A632 $2 multicolored   5.50 4.00

  Two types of No. 2309 exist. Either two or
three of the horizontal bars in seventh character from top right are connected at left side.
Value for No. 2309 is for the first type. Examples with three bars connected, value $7.

Literature Type of 1988

Romance of the Three Kingdoms by Luo
Guanzhong: No. 2310, Night Attack on
Wuchao. No. 2311, Making Three Calls at the
Thatched Cottage. 30f, Rescuing the Master
Single-handedly. 50f, Turning the Changban
Bridge Upside Down. T.157.

1990, Dec. 10 Photo. *Perf. 11½x11*
2310 A587 20f multicolored (4-1)   .30   .25
2311 A587 20f multi, vert. (4-2)   .30   .25
2312 A587 30f multicolored (4-3)   .35   .30
2313 A587 50f multi, vert. (4-4)   .55   .35
      Nos. 2310-2313 (4)   1.50 1.15

Han Xizai's Night Revels by Gu
Hongzhong — A633

Designs: a, Guests enjoying food, music (5-
1). b, Music and dance (5-2). c, Hand washing
(5-3). d, Musicians (5-4). e, Guests departing
(5-5). T.158.

1990, Dec. 20 Litho. *Perf. 12*
2314   Strip of 5   5.00 3.25
  a.-e. A633 50f any single   .70   .40

New Year 1991
(Year of the
Sheep) — A634

Photo. & Engr.
1991, Jan. 5   *Perf. 11½*
2315 A634 20f multicolored   2.50   .50
  a.   Bklt. pane of 12 + label 17.50   —
       Complete booklet, #2315a 19.00

  Stamps from No. 2315a have straight edges
at top or bottom and sell for less as singles
than No. 2315.

Dujiangyan Irrigation Project — A635

Designs: 20f, Yuzui, flood control. 50f,
Feishayan, drainage. 80f, Baopingkou, water
volume control. T.156.

1991, Feb. 20 Photo. *Perf. 11½x11*
2316 A635 20f multicolored   .55   .25
2317 A635 50f multicolored   1.25   .50
2318 A635 80f multicolored   2.25   .90
      Nos. 2316-2318 (3)   4.05 1.65

A636

1991, Mar. 18
2319 A636 20f multicolored   .75   .30

  Paris Commune, 120th anniv.

A637

1991, Apr. 20   Photo.   Perf. 10
2320	A637	20f multi (2-1)	.45	.30
a.		Perf. 11½x11	1.50	.90

Perf. 11½x11
2321	A637	50f Child & adult hands (2-2)	.55	.30

Family planning (T.160).

Horned Animals (T.161)
A638

No. 2322, Saiga tatarica (4-1). No. 2323, Budorcas taxicolor (4-2). No. 2324, Ovis ammon (4-3). No. 2325, Capra ibex (4-4).

1991, May 10   Perf. 11x11½
2322	A638	20f multi	.30	.25
2323	A638	20f multi	.30	.25
a.		Perf. 11	7.00	7.00
2324	A638	50f multi	.50	.30
a.		Perf. 11	17.50	17.50
2325	A638	$2 multi	.75	.35
		Nos. 2322-2325 (4)	1.85	1.15

No. 2322 exists imperf. Value, pair $140.

A639

25f, Song and dance (2-1). 50f, Golden bridge (2-2).
$2, PRC No. 132, cranes.

1991, May 23   Photo.   Perf. 11
2326	A639	25f multi	.45	.30
2327	A639	50f multi	.70	.35

Souvenir Sheet
2328	A639	$2 multi	15.00	5.00

Occupation of Tibet, 40th anniv. (J.176).

A640

1991, June 22   Perf. 11½x11
2329	A640	20f multicolored	.60	.30

Antarctic Treaty, 30th anniv.

Rhododendrons — A641

Varieties of rhododendrons. T.162: No. 2330, Delavayi (8-1). No. 2331, Molle (8-2). No. 2332, Simsii (8-3). No. 2333, Fictolacteum

(8-4). No. 2334, Agglutinatum, vert. (8-5). No. 2335, Fortunei, vert. (8-6). No. 2336, Giganteum, vert. (8-7). No. 2337, Rex, vert. (8-8).
$5, Wardii.

1991, June 25   Litho.   Perf. 12
2330	A641	10f multi	.40	.25
2331	A641	15f multi	.40	.25
2332	A641	20f multi	.40	.25
2333	A641	20f multi	.40	.30
2334	A641	50f multi	.80	.30
2335	A641	80f multi	1.25	.40
2336	A641	90f multi	1.40	.60
2337	A641	$1.60 multi	2.50	.75
		Nos. 2330-2337 (8)	7.55	3.10

Souvenir Sheet
Perf. 11½
2338	A641	$5 multi	11.50 8.50

No. 2338 contains one 80x40mm stamp.

Chinese Communist Party, 70th Anniv. (J.178)
A642

50f, Hammer and sickle (2-2).

1991, July 1   Photo.   Perf. 11x11½
2339	A642	20f shown (2-1)	1.00	.30
2340	A642	50f multicolored	1.50	.50

Peasant Uprising, 209B.C.
A643

1991, July 7
2341	A643	20f brown	.60 .25

Mt. Hengshan Type of 1990

Designs: No. 2342, Monastery on mountainside. No. 2343, Snow-covered mountain top. 55f, Inscription carved into mountainside. 80f, Hidden monastery. T.163.

Photo. & Engr.
1991, July 20   Perf. 11
2342	A631	20f multi (4-1)	.30	.25
2343	A631	20f multi (4-2)	.30	.25
2344	A631	55f multi (4-3)	.70	.30
2345	A631	80f multi (4-4)	.95	.45
		Nos. 2342-2345 (4)	2.25	1.25

Intl. Union for Quaternary Research, 13th Conf.
A644

1991, Aug. 2   Photo.   Perf. 11x11½
2346	A644	20f multicolored	.70	.30
a.		Perf. 11½	13.00	13.00

Chengde Mountain Resort — A645

Ch'ing Dynasty Royal Gardens: 15f, Pine valleys. 20f, Mid-lake pavilion. 90f, Islet, maple trees. $2, Chengde Royal Summer Resort. T.164.

1991   Perf. 11½x11
2347	A645	15f multi (3-1)	.30	.25
2348	A645	20f multi (3-2)	.40	.30
2349	A645	90f multi (3-3)	.90	.60
		Nos. 2347-2349 (3)	1.60	1.15

Souvenir Sheet
2350	A645	$2 multicolored	6.50 3.75

No. 2350 contains one 90x40mm stamp.
Issue dates: $2, Aug. 19; others, Aug. 10.

A646

Chen Yi, (b. 1901), party leader (J.181).

1991, Aug. 26   Photo.   Perf. 11½x11
2351	A646	20f shown (2-1)	.50	.25
2352	A646	50f Verse (2-2)	.90	.40

A647

1991, Sept. 14
2353	A647	80f Disaster relief	.55 .30

Achievements Type of 1988

20f, Luoyang glassworks. 25f, Urumchi chemical fertilizer project. 55f, Dalian expressway, Shenyang. 80f, Xichang satellite launching center. T.165.

1991, Sept. 20   Litho.   Perf. 12
2354	A582	20f multi (4-1)	.30	.25
2355	A582	25f multi (4-2)	.30	.30
2356	A582	55f multi (4-3)	.65	.35
2357	A582	80f multi (4-4)	.75	.45
		Nos. 2354-2357 (4)	2.00	1.35

Revolutionary Heroes — A648

Designs: No. 2358, Xu Xilin (1873-1907). No. 2359, Qiu Jin (1879-1907). No. 2360, Song Jiaoren (1882-1913). J.182.

Perf. 10 (#2358), 11x11½
1991, Oct. 10   Photo.
2358	A648	20f shown (3-1)	.85	.40
a.		Perf. 11x11½	5.00	1.50
2359	A648	20f multi (3-2)	.60	.30
2360	A648	20f multi (3-3)	.60	.30
		Nos. 2358-2360 (3)	2.05	1.00

Jingdezhen Chinaware A649

Designs: 15f, Glazed wine pot and warming bowl, Song Dynasty, vert. No. 2362, Porcelain vase, Yuan Dynasty, vert. No. 2363, Jar, Ming Dynasty. 25f, Porcelain vase, Ch'ing Dynasty, vert. 50f, Modern underglazed plate, vert. $2, Modern octagonal eggshell bowl, T.166.

Perf. 11¼x11½, 11½x11¼ (#2363, 2366)
1991, Oct. 11   Photo.
2361	A649	15f multi (6-1)	.40	.25
2362	A649	20f multi (6-2)	.40	.25
2363	A649	20f multi (6-3)	.40	.25
2364	A649	25f multi (6-4)	.40	.25
2365	A649	50f multi (6-5)	.40	.30
2366	A649	$2 multi (6-6)	1.00	.50
		Nos. 2361-2366 (6)	3.00	1.80

Perf. 11¼x11, 11x11¼ (#2363a, 2366a)
1991
2361a	A649	15f multi	.55	.25
2362a	A649	20f multi	.55	.25
2363a	A649	20f multi	.55	.25
2364a	A649	25f multi	.55	.30
2365a	A649	50f multi	.55	.30
2366a	A649	$2 multi	1.00	.55
		Nos. 2361a-2366a (6)	3.75	1.90

Tao Xingzhi, Educator, Birth Cent. (J.183) — A650

50f, Wearing robe (2-2).

1991, Oct. 18   Litho.   Perf. 12
2367	A650	20f shown (2-1)	.40	.25
2368	A650	50f multicolored	.60	.35

Xu Xiangqian, Revolutionary Leader, 90th Birth Anniv. (J.184) — A651

1991, Nov. 8   Perf. 11x11½
2369	A651	20f shown (2-1)	.45	.30
2370	A651	50f In uniform (2-2)	.65	.40

1st Women's Soccer World Championships, Guangdong Province (J.185) — A652

Designs: 50f, Woman kicking soccer ball.

1991, Nov. 16   Perf. 11½x11
2371	A652	20f red & multi (2-1)	.40	.30
2372	A652	50f grn & multi (2-2)	.50	.35

Literature Type of 1987

Outlaws of the Marsh: 20f, Dai Zong sends a false letter from Liangshan Marsh. No. 2374, Ten feet of steel alone captures Stumpy Tiger Wang. No. 2375, Mistress Gu breaks open the jail in Dengzhou to rescue the Xie Brothers. 90f, Sun Li offers a plan to attack Zhu Family manor. $3, Mount Liangshan gallants raid the execution grounds. T.167.

1991, Nov. 19   Perf. 11
2373	A570	20f multi (4-1)	.30	.25
2374	A570	25f multi (4-2)	.40	.30
2375	A570	25f multi (4-3)	.45	.35
2376	A570	90f multi (4-4)	1.60	.55
		Nos. 2373-2376 (4)	2.75	1.45

Souvenir Sheet
Perf. 11x11½
2377	A570	$3 multicolored	10.00 5.50

No. 2377 contains one 60x90mm stamp.

Beginning with No. 2378 stamps are inscribed "CHINA" and are numbered chronologically with the year followed by the number of the set. Additional numbers in parentheses indicate the number and position of each stamp in a set. We will note these only when helpful in identifying stamps.

New Year 1992, Year of the Monkey
A653   A654

20f, Monkey, peach. 50f, Magpies, plum branches.

Photo. & Engr.

1992, Jan. 25   *Perf. 11½*
2378 A653 20f multicolored   .40 .30
2379 A654 50f multicolored   .70 .35

Storks — A655

1992, Feb. 20 Photo.   *Perf. 11x11½*
2380 A655 20f Ciconia nigra   .30 .25
2381 A655 $1.60 Ciconia ciconia   .80 .45

Conifers — A656

Designs: 20f, Metasequoia glyptostroboides. 30f, Cathaya argyrophylla. 50f, Taiwania flousiana. 80f, Abies beshanzuensis.

1992, Mar. 10 Litho.   *Perf. 12½*
2382 A656 20f multicolored   .30 .25
2383 A656 30f multicolored   .30 .25
2384 A656 50f multicolored   .35 .30
2385 A656 80f multicolored   .55 .35
   Nos. 2382-2385 (4)   1.50 1.15

Marine Life A660

20f, Pagrosomus major. 25f, Penaeus chinesis. 50f, Chlamys farreri. 80f, Laminaria japonica.

1992, Apr. 15 Photo.   *Perf. 11*
2386 A660 20f multi   .25 .25
2387 A660 25f multi   .25 .25
2388 A660 50f multi   .35 .25
2389 A660 80f multi   .40 .25
   Nos. 2386-2389 (4)   1.25 1.05

Publication of "Discussions on Literature and Art at the Yenan Forum," 50th Anniv. — A661

1992, May 23 Photo.   *Perf. 11½x11*
2390 A661 20f org, blk & red   .90 .30

A662

1992, June 5   Litho.   *Perf. 12*
2392 A662 20f multicolored   .95 .30
   UN Conf. on Human Development, 20th anniv.

A663

Insects: 20f, Coccinella septempunctata. 30f, Sympetrum croceolum. 50f, Chrysopa septempunctata. $2, Tenodera aridifolia sinensis.

1992, June 28
2393 A663 20f multicolored   .30 .25
2394 A663 30f multicolored   .35 .30
2395 A663 50f multicolored   .40 .35
2396 A663 $2 multicolored   1.10 .55
   Nos. 2393-2396 (4)   2.15 1.45

1992 Summer Olympics, Barcelona A664

20f, Basketball, vert. 25f, Women's gymnastics. 50f, Women's diving. 80f, Weight lifting, vert. $5, Runners.

1992, July 25   Photo.   *Perf. 11*
2397 A664 20f multi   .30 .25
2398 A664 25f multi   .35 .25
2399 A664 50f multi   .40 .25
2400 A664 80f multi   .50 .35
   Nos. 2397-2400 (4)   1.55 1.15

Souvenir Sheet

2401 A664 $5 multicolored   2.75 2.25
   No. 2401 contains one 54x40mm stamp.

Intl. Space Year — A665

1992, Aug. 18   Litho.   *Perf. 12*
2402 A665 20f multicolored   .80 .30

Literature Type of 1988

Romance of the Three Kingdoms by Luo Guanzhong: 20f, Verbal battle with scholars. 30f, Goading Sun Quan with sarcasm, vert. 50f, Jiang Gan stealing the letter. $1.60, Gathering arrows with straw-covered boats, vert.

Perf. 11½x11, 11x11½

1992, Aug. 25   Photo.
2403 A587 20f multi   .30 .25
2404 A587 30f multi   .35 .30
2405 A587 50f multi   .40 .35
2406 A587 $1.60 multi   .85 .45
   Nos. 2403-2406 (4)   1.90 1.35

Wall Paintings Type of 1987

20f, Bodhisattva, vert. 25f, Musical performance, vert. 55f, Flight of a dragon. 80f, Envoy to the western regions. $5, Avalokitesvara-Bodhisattva, vert.

1992, Sept. 15   *Perf. 11*
2407 A557 20f multicolored   .30 .25
2408 A557 25f multicolored   .35 .30
2409 A557 55f multicolored   .40 .35
2410 A557 80f multicolored   .65 .40
   Nos. 2407-2410 (4)   1.70 1.30

Souvenir Sheet

   Perf. 11½
2411 A557 $5 multicolored   3.00 2.25
   No. 2411 contains one 52x70mm stamp.

Normalization of Diplomatic Relations Between China and Japan, 20th Anniv. — A666

20f, Cranes, Great Wall of China, Mt. Fuji. $2, Japanese, Chinese children, dove.

1992, Sept. 29 Photo.   *Perf. 11x11½*
2412 A666 20f multicolored   .25 .25
2413 A666 $2 multicolored   .95 .55

A667

Statue of Mazu, Chinese Goddess of the Sea.

1992, Oct. 4   Litho.   *Perf. 12*
2414 A667 20f multicolored   .60 .30

A667a

1992, Oct. 12 Photo.   *Perf. 11½x11*
2414A A667a 20f multicolored   1.50 .30
   14th Chinese Communist Party Congress.

Jiao Yulu (1922-1964), Communist Party Leader — A668

1992, Oct. 28   Litho.   *Perf. 12*
2415 A668 20f multicolored   .60 .30

Famous Men A669

Designs: 20f, Xiong Qinglai, mathematician. 30f, Tang Feifan, microbiologist. 50f, Zhang Xiaoqian, physician. $1, Liang Sicheng, architect.

1992, Nov. 20
2416 A669 20f multicolored   .30 .25
2417 A669 30f multicolored   .35 .25
2418 A669 50f multicolored   .45 .30
2419 A669 $1 multicolored   .80 .35
   Nos. 2416-2419 (4)   1.90 1.15

Luo Ronghuan, Leader of People's Army, 90th Anniv. of Birth A670

1992, Nov. 26 Photo.   *Perf. 11x11½*
2420 A670 20f In dress uniform   .45 .30
2421 A670 50f In field uniform   .75 .40

Constitution of the People's Republic of China, 10th Anniv. — A671

1992, Dec. 4   *Perf. 11½x11*
2422 A671 20f multicolored   .80 .30

Liu Bocheng, Leader of People's Army, Birth Cent. A672

Designs: 20f, In dress uniform. 50f, During period of Long March, vert.

1992, Dec. 4   *Perf. 11x11½, 11½x11*
2423 A672 20f multicolored   .45 .30
2424 A672 50f multicolored   .75 .40

Quingtian Stone Carvings — A673

10f, Spring. 20f, Chinese sorghum. 40f, Harvest. $2, Blooming flowers, full moon.

1992, Dec. 15   Litho.   *Perf. 12*
2425 A673 10f multicolored   .25 .25
2426 A673 20f multicolored   .25 .25
2427 A673 40f multicolored   .30 .25
2428 A673 $2 multicolored   .50 .30
   Nos. 2425-2428 (4)   1.30 1.05

New Year 1993 (Year of the Rooster)
A674   A675

Photo. & Engr.

1993, Jan. 5   *Perf. 11½*
2429 A674 20f red & black   .50 .25
2430 A675 50f red, white & blk   .70 .30

Madam Song Quingling, Chinese Communist Leader, Birth Cent. A676

1993, Jan. 20 Photo. Perf. 11x11½
2431 A676 20f Portrait .35 .30
a. Perf. 11 5.00 5.00
2432 A676 $1 With children .65 .45
a. Perf. 11 5.00 5.00

No. 2431 exists imperf. Value, pair $140.

Camelus Bactrianus Ferus A677

1993, Feb. 20 Litho. Perf. 12
2433 A677 20f shown .30 .25
2434 A677 $1.60 Adult, young .70 .35

8th Natl. People's Congress A678

1993, Mar. 15 Litho. Perf. 12
2435 A678 20f multicolored .80 .30

A679

Game of Weiqi (Go): 20f, Painting of players of ancient times. $1.60, Game board showing Chinese-style position.

1993, Apr. 30 Litho. Perf. 12
2436 A679 20f multi .30 .25
2437 A679 $1.60 multi .60 .40

A680

20th Cent. Revolutionaries: 20f, Li Jishen (1885-1959), horiz. 30f, Zhang Lan (1872-1955). 50f, Shen Junru (1875-1963). $1, Huang Yanpei (1878-1965), horiz.

1993, May 15 Litho. Perf. 12
2438 A680 20f multi .30 .25
2439 A680 30f multi .30 .25
2440 A680 50f multi .35 .30
2441 A680 $1 multi .50 .35
Nos. 2438-2441 (4) 1.45 1.15

See Nos. 2483-2486.

A681

1993, May 9 Photo. Perf. 12
2442 A681 50f Runner (2-1) .35 .25
2443 A681 50f Mascot (2-2) .35 .25
a. Pair, #2442-2443 .85 .75

First East Asian Games. No. 2443a printed in continuous design.

A682

Bamboo: 20f, Phyllostachys nigra. 30f, Phyllostachys aureosulcata spectabilis. 40f, Bambusa ventricosa. $1, Pseudosasa amabilis. $5, Phyllostachys heterocycla pubescens, horiz.

1993, June 15 Litho. Perf. 12½
2444 A682 20f multi .35 .25
2445 A682 30f multi .45 .25
2446 A682 40f multi .55 .30
2447 A682 $1 multi .75 .35
Nos. 2444-2447 (4) 2.10 1.15

Souvenir Sheet
Photo.
Perf. 11
2448 A682 $5 multicolored 3.00 2.25
a. As #2448, added inscription 7.50 7.50

No. 2448 contains one 54x40mm stamp.
No. 2448a is inscribed in sheet margin with hologram of panda at left, Chinese inscription for CHINA '96 and PJZ-3 at bottom, and flag and tagged security emblem at right. Soaking in water may affect the hologram. Issued: May 10, 1996.

Literature Type of 1987

Outlaws of the Marsh: 20f, Chai Jin is trapped in Gaotang. 30f, Shi Qian steals armor. 50f, Xu Ning teaches how to use barbed lance. $2, Shi Xiu leaps from building to rescue condemned man from execution.

1993, Aug. 20 Photo. Perf. 11
2449 A570 20f multi .35 .25
2450 A570 30f multi .40 .25
2451 A570 50f multi .55 .30
2452 A570 $2 multi 1.00 .45
Nos. 2449-2452 (4) 2.30 1.25

Changbai Mountains — A683

1993, Sept. 3 Perf. 11½x11
2453 A683 20f Tianchi .25 .25
2454 A683 30f Alpine tundra .30 .25
2455 A683 50f Waterfall .35 .30
2456 A683 $1 Mixed forest .45 .35
Nos. 2453-2456 (4) 1.35 1.15

Seventh Natl. Games — A684

1993, Sept. 4
2457 A684 20f multicolored .75 .30

Longmen Grottoes — A685

Designs: 20f, Rocana, Ancestor Worshipping Temple. 30f, Sakyamuni, Middle Binyang Cave, Northern Wei. 50f, Maharaja, devas treading on Yaksha. $1, Bodhisattva at the left side of Rocana, Guyang Cave, Northern Wei. $5, Ancestor Worshipping Temple.

1993, Sept. 5 Litho. Perf. 12
2458 A685 20f multi .30 .25
2459 A685 30f multi .35 .25
2460 A685 50f multi .50 .30
2461 A685 $1 multi .95 .45
Nos. 2458-2461 (4) 2.10 1.25

Souvenir Sheets
2462 A685 $5 multicolored 3.00 3.00
a. Overprinted in gold 10.00 6.50
b. Overprinted in silver 6.00 4.00

No. 2462 contains one 120x40mm stamp.
Overprint in margin of No. 2462a includes Chinese characters and "PJZ-1." Bangkok '95 (No. 2462a). No. 2462a sold for $6.
No. 2462a exists with serial number inscribed in sheet margin. The same number is inscribed on Thailand No. 1615b. These were sold as a set. Value for the two sheets with matching numbers, $26.50.
Sheet margin of No. 2462b contains silver lettering in Chinese for Thailand stamp exhibition and "PJZ-7." No. 2462b exists with serial number inscribed in sheet margin. Value: $11.50.
Issued: No. 2462a, 8/95; No. 2462b, 12/5/97.

Honey Bees A686

10f, Queen and two bees. 15f, Extracting nectar. 20f, Two Zhonghua bees. $2, Two bees in flight.

1993, Sept. 21 Photo. Perf. 11½
2463 A686 10f multi .30 .25
a. Perf. 11x11½ 5.00 5.00
2464 A686 15f multi .30 .25
a. Perf. 11x11½ 5.00 5.00
2465 A686 20f multi .30 .30
2466 A686 $2 multi .75 .50
Nos. 2463-2466 (4) 1.65 1.30

Lacquerware — A687

1993, Oct. 20 Photo. Perf. 12
2467 A687 20f Bowl .25 .25
2468 A687 30f Duck .30 .25
2469 A687 50f Round tray .35 .25
2470 A687 $1 Lidded box .40 .30
Nos. 2467-2470 (4) 1.30 1.05

Paintings, by Zheng Banqiao — A688

Designs: 10f, Bamboo, rock on fan. No. 2472, Orchard. No. 2473, Orchard, bamboo, rock on scroll, vert. 30f, Bamboo, rock on scroll, vert. 50f, Vase and chrysanthemums. $1.60, Chinese calligraphy on fan.

1993, Nov. 22 Litho. Perf. 12½
2471 A688 10f multi (6-1) .30 .25
2472 A688 20f multi (6-2) .30 .25
2473 A688 20f multi (6-3) .30 .25
2474 A688 30f multi (6-4) .40 .30
2475 A688 50f multi (6-5) .40 .30
2476 A688 $1.60 multi (6-6) .60 .35
Nos. 2471-2476 (6) 2.30 1.70

No. 2476 exists imperf. Value, pair $240.

A689

1993, Nov. 26 Perf. 12
2477 A689 20f multicolored .60 .30

Yang Hucheng, birth cent.

Mao Tse-tung (1893-1976) A690

$1, Portrait, seated.
$5, Standing by Great Wall.

1993 Photo. Perf. 11½
2478 A690 20f shown 1.75 .35
2479 A690 $1 multicolored 4.75 .55

Souvenir Sheet
2480 A690 $5 multicolored 4.00 3.00
a. Overprinted in gold in margin 7.50 6.00

No. 2480 contains one 48x58mm stamp.
No. 2480a sold for $8.
No. 2478 exists imperf. Value, pair $350.
Issued: $5, 11/16; 20f, $1, 12/26; No. 2480a, 4/9/99.

New Year 1994 (Year of the Dog)
A691 A692

1994, Jan. 5 Photo. Perf. 11½
2481 A691 20f multi .45 .25
2482 A692 50f yel, red & blk .65 .35

20th Cent. Revolutionaries Type

Designs: No. 2483, Chen Qiyou, horiz. No. 2484, Chen Shutong. No. 2485, Ma Xulun. No. 2486, Xu Deheng, horiz.

1994, Feb. 25 Litho. Perf. 12
2483 A680 20f blk & brn (4-1) .35 .30
2484 A680 20f blk & brn (4-2) .35 .30
2485 A680 50f blk & brn (4-3) .40 .30
2486 A680 50f blk & brn (4-4) .40 .30
Nos. 2483-2486 (4) 1.50 1.20

Sturgeon — A693

20f, Huso dauricus. 40f, Acipenser sinensis. 50f, Psephurus gladius. $1, Acipenser dabryanus.

1994, Mar. 18   Litho.   Perf. 12½

2487	A693	20f multi	.40	.25
2488	A693	40f multi	.45	.25
2489	A693	50f multi	.55	.30
2490	A693	$1 multi	.75	.40
		Nos. 2487-2490 (4)	2.15	1.20

Afforestation Campaign — A694

Designs: 15f, Sand dunes. 20f, Flowers on sand dune. 40f, Forest of poplars. 50f, Oasis.

1994, Apr. 21   Litho.   Perf. 12

2491	A694	15f multi	.25	.25
2492	A694	20f multi	.30	.25
2493	A694	40f multi	.35	.25
2494	A694	50f multi	.40	.30
		Nos. 2491-2494 (4)	1.30	1.05

Teapots — A695

Style of teapot: 20f, Round, three-legged. 30f, Square, four-legged. 50f, Eight diagrams. $1, Round-eared.

1994, May 5   Litho.   Perf. 12

2495	A695	20f multi	.30	.25
2496	A695	30f multi	.35	.25
2497	A695	40f multi	.40	.30
2498	A695	$1 multi	.85	.35
		Nos. 2495-2498 (4)	1.90	1.15

Huangpu Military School, 70th Anniv. A696

1994, June 16   Litho.   Perf. 12

2499	A696	20f multicolored	.65	.30

Intl. Olympic Committee, Cent. A697

1994, June 23

2500	A697	20f multicolored	.60	.25

Ancient Chinese Writers — A698

Designs: 20f, Tao Yuanming holding basket of flowers. 30f, Cao Zhi holding sword at side. 50f, Si Maqian writing on scroll. $1, Qu Yuan walking away with sword under arm.

1994, June 25

2501	A698	20f multi	.25	.25
2502	A698	30f multi	.30	.25
2503	A698	50f multi	.35	.30
2504	A698	$1 multi	.55	.35
		Nos. 2501-2504 (4)	1.45	1.15

Wall paintings Type of 1987

10f, Flying Devata. 20f, Vimalakirti. 50f, Z. Yichao on the march. $1.60, Sorceresses.

1994, July 16   Photo.   Perf. 11

2505	A557	10f multi	.25	.25
2506	A557	20f multi	.30	.25
2507	A557	50f multi	.35	.30
2508	A557	$1.60 multi	.55	.35
		Nos. 2505-2508 (4)	1.45	1.15

Zhaojun's Marriage to Xiongnu — A699

1994, Aug. 25   Photo.   Perf. 11½x11

2509	A699	20f Zhaojun	.35	.30
2510	A699	50f Leaving home	.65	.35

Souvenir Sheet
Perf. 11½

2511	A699	$3 Wedding	3.25	3.25

No. 2511 contains one 85x46mm stamp.

Sixth Far East and South Pacific Games for the Disabled, Beijing — A700

1994, Sept. 4   Litho.   Perf. 12

2512	A700	20f multicolored	1.00	.25

Wulingyuan State Forest Park — A701

20f, South Gate to Heaven. 30f, Shentangwan. 50f, No. One Bridge. $1, Writing-brush Peak. $3, Picturesque corridor.

1994, Sept. 25   Litho.   Perf. 12

2513	A701	20f multi, vert.	.35	.25
2514	A701	30f multi, vert.	.45	.30
2515	A701	50f multi	.55	.40
2516	A701	$1 multi	.90	.50
		Nos. 2513-2516 (4)	2.25	1.45

Souvenir Sheet
Perf. 11½x12

2517	A701	$3 multicolored	3.25	2.75

No. 2517 contains one 50x36mm stamp.

Wuyi Mountains — A702

Designs: a, Jade-girl Peak (4-1). b, Nine-bend Brook (4-2). c, Guadun Village (4-3). d, Alpine Grassland (4-4).

1994, Sept. 30   Perf. 12

2518	Strip of 4	2.00	1.50
a.-d.	A702 50f any single	.40	.25

No. 2518 exists imperf. Value, $225.

Listening to the Rapids, by Fu Baoshi (1904-65) A703

Paintings: No. 2520, Appreciating a Painting. No. 2521, Dadi's Thatched Hut. 40f, Playing the Ruan. 50f, At Hupao. $1, The Road to Shanyin.

1994, Oct. 5

2519	A703	10f multi (6-1)	.30	.25
2520	A703	20f multi (6-2)	.30	.25
2521	A703	20f multi (6-3)	.30	.25
2522	A703	40f multi (6-4)	.35	.30
2523	A703	50f multi (6-5)	.50	.35
2524	A703	$1 multi (6-6)	.90	.40
		Nos. 2519-2524 (6)	2.65	1.80

Cranes — A704

20f, Whooping crane. $2, Black-necked crane.

Photo. & Engr.
1994, Oct. 9   Perf. 11x11½

2528	A704	20f multi	.35	.25
2529	A704	$2 multi	.65	.50

See US Nos. 2867-2868.

Souvenir Sheet

UPU, 120th Anniv. — A705

1994, Oct. 9   Litho.   Perf. 12

2530	A705	$3 multicolored	3.00	2.00
a.	Ovptd. in sheet margin		4.00	3.00

No. 2530a ovptd. in sheet margin with UPU hologram, vertical Chinese inscription in gold. Issued: July 18, 1996.

Gorges of Yangtze River — A706

Designs: 10f, Baidicheng. No. 2532, Qutang Gorge. No. 2533, Wuxia Gorge. 30f, Goddess Peak. 50f, Xiling Gorge. $1, Qu Yuan Memorial Temple.
$5, The Three Gorges.

1994, Nov. 4   Photo.   Perf. 12

2531	A706	10f multi (6-1)	.30	.25
2532	A706	20f multi (6-2)	.30	.25
2533	A706	20f multi (6-3)	.30	.25
2534	A706	30f multi (6-4)	.30	.25
2535	A706	50f multi (6-5)	.35	.30
2536	A706	$1 multi (6-6)	.40	.35
		Nos. 2531-2536 (6)	1.95	1.65

Souvenir Sheet
Perf. 11½x11

2537	A706	$5 multicolored	3.50	2.75

No. 2537 contains one 116x35mm stamp.

Souvenir Sheet

All-China Philatelic Federation, 4th Congress — A707

1994, Nov. 17   Litho.   Perf. 11

2538	A707	$3 multicolored	2.25	1.50

Literature Type of 1988

Romance of the Three Kingdoms by Luo Guanzhong: 20f, Composing a poem with a lance in hands. 30f, Liu Bei's marriage, vert. 50f, Overwhelming Xiaoyaojin with prowess. $1, Campsites burned, vert.
$5, Fierce battle at Chibi.

Perf. 11½x11, 11x11½

1994, Nov. 24   Photo.

2539	A587	20f multicolored	.25	.25
2540	A587	30f multicolored	.30	.25
2541	A587	50f multicolored	.35	.30
2542	A587	$1 multicolored	.40	.35
		Nos. 2539-2542 (4)	1.30	1.15

Souvenir Sheet
Perf. 11

2543	A587	$5 multicolored	5.25	4.00

No. 2543 contains one 158x36mm stamp.

Special Economic Zones A708

Designs: a, Shenzhen (5-1). b, Zhuhai (5-2). c, Shantou (5-3). d, Xiamen (5-4). e, Hainan (5-4).

1994, Dec. 10   Litho.   Perf. 12

2544	A708	50f Strip of 5, #a.-e.	3.50	2.00

Pagodas of
Ancient
China — A709

Designs: No. 2545, Dayan Pagoda, Cien
Temple. No. 2546, Zhenguo Pagoda, Kaiyuan
Temple. 50f, Liuhe Pagoda, Kaihua Temple.
$2, Youguo Temple.

Photo. & Engr.

1994, Dec. 15		**Perf. 11½x11**	
2545	20f tan, brn & blk (4-1)	.30	.25
2546	20f tan, brn & blk (4-2)	.35	.25
2547	50f tan, brn & blk (4-3)	.40	.25
2548	$2 tan, brn & blk (4-4)	.75	.30
a.	Souvenir sheet of 4, #2545-2548	5.00	4.50
	Nos. 2545-2548 (4)	1.80	1.05

No. 2548a sold for $5.

New Year 1995 (Year of the Boar)
A711   A712

Photo. & Engr.

1995, Jan. 5		**Perf. 11½**	
2550	A711 20f multicolored	.75	.25
2551	A712 50f multicolored	.85	.30

Winter
Scenes
A713

Designs: 20f, Snow willows, Cold River. 50f,
Ice & snow on jade trees, vert.

1995, Jan. 12	**Litho.**	**Perf. 12**	
2552	A713 20f multicolored	.35	.25
2553	A713 50f multicolored	.65	.30

Mt. Dinghushan — A714

Designs: 15f, Topographical map. No. 2555,
Stream flowing down from mountain. No.
2556, Buildings on mountain side. $2.30, Sil-
ver pheasants.

1995, Feb. 15	**Litho.**	**Perf. 12½**	
2554	A714 15f multi (4-1)	.30	.25
2555	A714 20f multi (4-2)	.45	.30
2556	A714 20f multi (4-3)	.45	.30
2557	A714 $2.30 multi (4-4)	1.25	.35
	Nos. 2554-2557 (4)	2.45	1.20

World Summit for Social Development,
Copenhagen — A715

1995, Mar. 6	**Photo.**	**Perf. 11x11½**	
2558	A715 20f multicolored	3.00	.40

Owls — A716

1995, Mar. 22	**Photo.**	**Perf. 11½**	
2559	A716 10f Eagle owl	.40	.30
2560	A716 20f Long-eared owl	.50	.30
2561	A716 50f Snowy owl	.65	.40
2562	A716 $1 Grass owl	1.25	.50
	Nos. 2559-2562 (4)	2.80	1.50

Sweet
Osmanthus
A717

No. 2563, Thunbergii (4-1). No. 2564,
Latifolius (4-2). No. 2565, Aurantiacus (4-3).
No. 2566, Semperflorens (4-4).

1995, Apr. 14	**Litho.**	**Perf. 12**	
2563	A717 20f multicolored	.35	.25
2564	A717 20f multicolored	.35	.25
2565	A717 50f multicolored	.45	.30
2566	A717 $1 multicolored	.90	.45
	Nos. 2563-2566 (4)	2.05	1.25

A souvenir sheet of 4, Nos. 2563-2566,
exists, both perf and imperf. Value, perf $5.,
imperf. $75.

43rd World Table Tennis
Championships, Tianjin — A718

1995, May 1	**Litho.**	**Perf. 12**	
2567	A718 20f Athlete	.35	.25
2568	A718 50f Arena	.55	.30
a.	Souv. sheet of 2, #2567-2568	20.00	14.00

No. 2568a sold for $7. Issued 8/14/95.

Spring Outing — A719

Designs: No. 2569, Group riding horses.
No. 2570, Three riding horses.

1995, May 23	**Litho.**	**Perf. 12**	
2569	A719 50f multi (2-1)	.75	.35
2570	A719 50f multi (2-2)	.75	.35
a.	Pair, #2569-2570	2.75	1.25

No. 2570a is a continuous design.

Shadow
Play — A720

Various costumed characters.

1995, June 8	**Photo.**	**Perf. 12x12½**	
2571	A720 20f multi (4-1)	.30	.25
2572	A720 40f multi (4-2)	.30	.25
2573	A720 50f multi (4-3)	.40	.30
2574	A720 50f multi (4-4)	.40	.30
	Nos. 2571-2574 (4)	1.40	1.10

Highway Interchanges, Beijing — A721

1995, June 20	**Photo.**	**Perf. 11½x11**	
2575	A721 20f Siyuan	.30	.25
2576	A721 30f Tianningsi	.35	.25
2577	A721 50f Yuting	.40	.25
2578	A721 $1 Anhui	.55	.30
	Nos. 2575-2578 (4)	1.60	1.05

Diplomatic Relations Between China &
Thailand, 20th Anniv. — A722

No. 2579, Elephants walking right into
water. No. 2580, Elephants walking left into
water.

1995, July 1			
2579	A722 $1 multi (2-1)	.35	.30
2580	A722 $1 multi (2-2)	.35	.30
a.	Pair, #2579-2580	1.00	.85

No. 2580a is a continuous design.

Taihu
Lake
A723

Lake scenes: No. 2581, Yellow trees. No.
2582, Structures on bank, boats, hills. No.
2583, Structures across inlet. No. 2584, Red
trees, home. 230f, Winter scene. 500f, Houses
on cliff, lighthouse.

1995, July 20	**Photo.**	**Perf. 11½**	
2581	A723 20f multi (5-1)	.25	.25
2582	A723 20f multi (5-2)	.30	.25
2583	A723 50f multi (5-3)	.45	.30
2584	A723 50f multi (5-4)	.45	.30
2585	A723 230f multi (5-5)	1.10	.70
	Nos. 2581-2585 (5)	2.55	1.80

Souvenir Sheet
Perf. 11

2586	A723 500f multicolored	3.50	2.75
a.	Ovptd. in sheet margin	8.50	7.00

No. 2586 contains one 90x60mm stamp
with continuing design.

No. 2586a issued 3/24/97. Gold overprint in
sheet margin contains an emblem, Chinese
inscription saying "Hong Kong Returns to
China" and "PJZ-5."

Posts of
Ancient
China
A724

1995, Aug. 17	**Photo.**	**Perf. 12**	
2587	A724 20f Yucheng	.35	.25
2588	A724 50f Jimingshan	.55	.30

Shaolin
Temple,
1500th
Anniv.
A725

No. 2589, Entrance (4-1). No. 2590, Pagoda
Forest (4-2). No. 2591, Martial arts (4-3). No.
2592, Historical rescue (4-4).

1995, Aug. 30			
2589	A725 20f multicolored	.60	.25
2590	A725 20f multicolored	.60	.25
2591	A725 50f multicolored	.70	.30
2592	A725 100f multicolored	1.50	.50
	Nos. 2589-2592 (4)	3.40	1.30

Cultural Relics of
Tibet — A726

20f, Jar. 30f, Casque. 50f, Celestial motion
chart. 100f, Pearl mandala.

1995, Sept. 1			
2593	A726 20f multicolored	.25	.25
2594	A726 30f multicolored	.30	.25
2595	A726 50f multicolored	.35	.25
2596	A726 100f multicolored	.40	.30
	Nos. 2593-2596 (4)	1.30	1.05

Wildlife
A727

1995, Sept. 1		**Perf. 11x11½**	
2597	A727 20f Koalas	.30	.25
2598	A727 $2.90 Pandas	1.10	.85

See Australia No. 1459.

End of
World War
II, 50th
Anniv.
A728

10f, July 7th event. No. 2600, Victory at
Taier village. No. 2601, Soldier, hundred-regi-
ment battle. No. 2602, Guerrilla war. No. 2603,
Troops on parade, joining forces at Mangyo.
60f, Aircraft donated by Chinese living abroad.
No. 2605, Taiwan recovered. No. 2606, Japanese surrender aboard USS Missouri.

1995, Sept. 3			
2599	A728 10f multi (8-1)	.25	.25
2600	A728 20f multi (8-2)	.30	.25
2601	A728 20f multi (8-3)	.30	.25
2602	A728 20f multi (8-4)	.35	.30
2603	A728 50f multi (8-5)	.35	.30
2604	A728 60f multi (8-6)	.40	.35
2605	A728 100f multi (8-7)	.55	.40
2606	A728 100f multi (8-8)	.55	.40
	Nos. 2599-2606 (8)	3.05	2.50

4th World
Conference
on Women,
Beijing
A729

Symbols of: 15f, Equality. 20f, Development.
50f, Peace. 60f, Friendship.

1995, Sept. 4 — Perf. 12

2607	A729	15f multi	.25 .25
2608	A729	20f multi	.30 .25
2609	A729	35f multi	.35 .25
2610	A729	60f multi	.40 .30
	Nos. 2607-2610 (4)		1.30 1.05

The Great Wall — A730

230f, Shanhaiguan Pass. 290f, Jinshanling.

1995, Oct. 5 — Photo. — Perf. 12½

2611	A730	60f shown	.25 .25
2612	A730	230f multicolored	.75 .30
2613	A730	290f multicolored	.95 .35
	Nos. 2611-2613 (3)		1.95 .90

See Nos. 2755, 2792-2795, 2907-2910, 2934-2941, 2952-2955.

Jiuhua Mountains A731

10f, Sunrise at Peak Terrace, horiz. No. 2615, Hall of Meditation. No. 2616, Temple of Bodhisattva, horiz. No. 2617, Sunset at Zhiyuan, horiz. No. 2618, Great Rock. No. 2619, Phoenix Pine, horiz.

1995, Oct. 9 — Perf. 12

2614	A731	10f multi (6-1)	.30 .25
2615	A731	20f multi (6-2)	.30 .25
2616	A731	20f multi (6-3)	.30 .25
2617	A731	50f multi (6-4)	.40 .30
2618	A731	50f multi (6-5)	.40 .30
2619	A731	290f multi (6-6)	1.25 .45
	Nos. 2614-2619 (6)		2.95 1.80

Motion Pictures, Cent. A732

Projector and: 20f, Black and white film. 50f, Color film.

1995, Oct. 13

2620	A732	20f blue & black	.35 .25
2621	A732	50f multicolored	.65 .30

UN, 50th Anniv. A733

Designs: 20f, UN flag, Headquarters. 50f, Stylized flags, UN emblem, "50."

1995, Oct. 24 — Litho.

2622	A733	20f multi	.50 .25
2623	A733	50f multi	1.25 .30

Sanqing Mountains — A734

No. 2624, Good Fortune Land. No. 2625, Sichun Goddess. 50f, Bodhisattva Enjoys Music. 100f, Huge Boa out of Mountain.

1995, Nov. 1 — Photo. — Perf. 12

2624	A734	20f multi (4-1)	.30 .25
2625	A734	20f multi (4-2)	.30 .25
2626	A734	50f multi, vert. (4-3)	.35 .25
2627	A734	100f multi, vert. (4-4)	.45 .40
	Nos. 2624-2627 (4)		1.40 1.15

Mt. Hengshan Type of 1990

Songshan Mountains: 20f, Ancient Temple of Mount Song. 50f, Moon waiting at Songmen Gate. 60f, Shaolin Temple. $1, Panorama view of Mt. Song.

Photo. & Engr.

1995, Nov. 10 — Perf. 11

2628	A631	20f multi	.30 .25
2629	A631	50f multi	.40 .25
2630	A631	60f multi	.50 .30
2631	A631	$1 multi	1.10 .40
	Nos. 2628-2631 (4)		2.30 1.20

Scenic Views of Hong Kong — A735

Designs: 20f, Victoria Harbor. 50f, Central Plaza at night. 60f, Hong Kong Cultural Center. 290f, Repulse Bay.

1995, Nov. 28 — Photo. — Perf. 12

2632	A735	20f multi	.25 .25
2633	A735	50f multi	.30 .25
2634	A735	60f multi	.35 .30
2635	A735	290f multi	1.10 .40
	Nos. 2632-2635 (4)		2.00 1.20

No. 2635 exists imperf. Value, pair $140.

Sun Zi's Art of War — A736

Drawings depicting: No. 2637, Discussing strategy. 30f, Capturing Ying. 50f, Battle at Ailing. 100f, Meeting of sovereigns, Huangchi.

1995, Dec. 4 — Perf. 11x11½

2636	A736	20f multi (5-1)	.30 .25
2637	A736	20f multi (5-2)	.30 .25
2638	A736	30f multi (5-3)	.40 .30
2639	A736	50f multi (5-4)	.50 .35
2640	A736	100f multi (5-5)	1.00 .45
	Nos. 2636-2640 (5)		2.50 1.60

New Year 1996 (Year of the Rat) A737 A738

Photo. & Engr.

1996, Jan. 5 — Perf. 11½

2641	A737	20f multi	.80 .25
2642	A738	50f multi	1.75 .40

3rd Asian Winter Games A739

No. 2643, Speed skating. No. 2644, Ice hockey. No. 2645, Figure skating. No. 2646, Skiing.

1996, Feb. 4 — Litho. — Perf. 12

2643	A739	50f multi (4-1)	.30 .25
2644	A739	50f multi (4-2)	.30 .25
2645	A739	50f multi (4-3)	.30 .25
2646	A739	50f multi (4-4)	.30 .25
a.	Block of 4, #2643-2646		1.50 1.00

China/Korea Submarine Fiber Optic Cable System — A740

1996, Feb. 8 — Litho. — Perf. 12

2647	A740	20f multicolored	.60 .25

First day covers are dated 12/15/95. See Korea No. 1863.

Shenyang Imperial Palace — A741

Designs: No. 2648, Buildings, denomination UL. No. 2649, Buildings, denomination LR.

1996, Mar. 18 — Photo. — Perf. 12

2648	A741	50f multi (2-1)	.35 .25
2649	A741	50f multi (2-2)	.35 .25
a.	Pair, Nos. 2648-2649		1.00 .75

China Post, Cent. A742

Post Office buildings: 10f, Tianjin Posts Bureau. 20f, Beijing Postal Administration. 50f, Directorate of Posts of China. 100f, Beijing postal hub.
500f, China #78-85.

1996, Mar. 20 — Perf. 11½

2650	A742	10f multi	.30 .25
2651	A742	20f multi	.45 .25
2652	A742	50f multi	.50 .30
2653	A742	100f multi	.65 .40
	Nos. 2650-2653 (4)		1.90 1.20

Souvenir Sheet
Perf. 11

2654	A742	500f multicolored	5.50 4.75

No. 2654 contains one 89x59mm stamp.

Huang Binhong, Artist — A743

No. 2655, Calligraphy. No. 2656, Landscape. 40f, Qingcheng Mts. No. 2658, View from Xiing. No. 2659, Colored landscape. 230f, Flowers.

1996, Apr. 5 — Perf. 11½

2655	A743	20f multi (6-1)	.30 .25
2656	A743	20f multi (6-2)	.30 .25
2657	A743	40f multi (6-3)	.50 .30
2658	A743	50f multi (6-4)	.60 .30
2659	A743	50f multi (6-5)	.60 .35
2660	A743	230f multi (6-6)	2.40 .55
	Nos. 2655-2660 (6)		4.70 2.00

Aircraft — A744

1996, Apr. 17 — Perf. 12

2661	A744	20f F-8 (4-1)	.30 .25
2662	A744	50f A-5 (4-2)	.55 .30
2663	A744	50f Yun-7 (4-3)	.55 .30
2664	A744	100f Yun-12 (4-4)	.90 .45
	Nos. 2661-2664 (4)		2.30 1.30

Potted Landscapes — A745

Nos. 2665-2666, Lijing & Divine Peak. Nos. 2667-2668, Melting Snow & Eagle Rock. Nos. 2668-2669, Manch & Rosy Clouds.

1996, Apr. 18

2665	A745	20f multi (6-1)	.25 .25
2666	A745	20f multi (6-2)	.25 .25
a.	Pair, #2665-2666		.75 .60
2667	A745	50f multi (6-3)	.35 .25
2668	A745	50f multi (6-4)	.35 .25
a.	Pair, #2667-2668		1.00 .80
2669	A745	100f multi (6-5)	.50 .40
2670	A745	100f multi (6-6)	.50 .40
a.	Pair, #2669-2670		1.60 1.40
	Nos. 2665-2670 (6)		2.20 1.80

Iron Trees — A746

No. 2671, Cycas revoluta. No. 2672, Cycas panzhihuaensis. 50f, Cycas pectinata. 230f, Cycas multipinnata.

1996, May 2 — Litho. — Perf. 12

2671	A746	20f multi (4-1)	.30 .25
2672	A746	20f multi (4-2)	.30 .25
2673	A746	50f multi (4-3)	.35 .25
2674	A746	230f multi (4-4)	.80 .40
	Nos. 2671-2674 (4)		1.75 1.15

Nos. 2671-2674 exist imperf. Value, set of pairs $325.

China-San Marino Relations, 25th Anniv. A747

No. 2675, Great Wall of China (2-1). No. 2676, Mt. Titano (2-2).

1996, May 6 — Photo. — Perf. 12

2675	A747	100f multi	.40 .30
2676	A747	100f multi	.40 .30
a.	Pair, #2675-2676		1.00 .80

See San Marino Nos. 1356-1357.

Artifacts from Hemudu Ruins — A748

Designs: 20f, Agricultural tool. 50f, Pile to support building. 100f, Paddles for boats. 230f, Bird and sun carved in wood.

1996, May 12 Litho. *Perf. 12*
2677	A748	20f multi	.30	.25
2678	A748	50f multi	.35	.25
2679	A748	100f multi	.40	.30
2680	A748	230f multi	.85	.40
		Nos. 2677-2680 (4)	1.90	1.20

Souvenir Sheet

CHINA '96, 9th Asian Intl. Philatelic
Exhibition — A749

1996, May 18 *Perf. 11½x12*
2681	A749	500f multicolored	6.25	4.25
a.		Overprint in gold	8.50	7.50

No. 2681 exists imperf. Value, $18.
Overprint in margin of No. 2681a includes
Chinese characters, Shanghai '97 exhibition
emblem, and "PJZ-6." Issued in 1998.

Children's
Activities
A750

Designs: 20f, Singing, playing musical
instruments. 30f, Pushing child in wheelchair,
holding umbrella. 50f, Placing flag on South
Pole, penguins. 100f, Planting tree.

1996, June 1 *Perf. 12*
2682	A750	20f multi	.25	.25
2683	A750	30f multi	.30	.25
2684	A750	50f multi	.35	.25
2685	A750	100f multi	.45	.30
		Nos. 2682-2685 (4)	1.35	1.05

Modern Olympic
Games,
Cent. — A751

1996, June 23 Photo. *Perf. 12*
2686	A751	20f multicolored	.85	.30

Protection
of Land
A752

Stylized designs representing: 20f, Making
use of land. 50f, Protection of farmland.

1996, June 25 *Perf. 11x11½*
2687	A752	20f multi	.40	.25
2688	A752	50f multi	.60	.30

A753

Military
Terraces — A754

1996, July 9 Litho. *Perf. 12*
2689	A753	20f multi	.40	.25
2690	A754	50f multi	.60	.30

Vehicles — A755

No. 2691, Red Flag, 4-door limousine. No.
2692, Dongfeng, stake truck. 50f, Jiefang, 4-
door truck. 100f, Beijing, canvas-topped jeep.

1996, July 15 Photo. *Perf. 12*
2691	A755	20f multi (4-1)	.30	.25
2692	A755	20f multi (4-2)	.30	.25
2693	A755	50f multi (4-3)	.40	.25
2694	A755	100f multi (4-4)	.60	.35
		Nos. 2691-2694 (4)	1.60	1.10

New Tangshan Built Following 1976
Earthquake — A756

No. 2695, Farm cottages (4-1). No. 2696,
Factory (4-2). No. 2697, Street (4-3). No.
2698, Port (4-4).

1996, July 28 *Perf. 11½*
2695	A756	20f multi	.25	.25
2696	A756	50f multi	.35	.25
2697	A756	50f multi	.35	.25
2698	A756	100f multi	.45	.30
		Nos. 2695-2698 (4)	1.40	1.05

30th Intl. Geological
Conference — A757

1996, Aug. 4 Litho. *Perf. 12*
2699	A757	20f multicolored	.70	.30

Tianchi Lake, Tianshan
Mountains — A758

20f, High mountain lake. No. 2701, Splendid
Waterfalls. No. 2702, Snow-capped peaks.
100f, Lakeside scenery.

1996, Aug. 8
2700	A758	20f multi (4-1)	.25	.25
2701	A758	50f multi, vert. (4-2)	.35	.25
2702	A758	50f multi, vert. (4-3)	.35	.25
2703	A758	100f multi (4-4)	.50	.30
		Nos. 2700-2703 (4)	1.45	1.05

Wall Paintings Type of 1987

10f, Illustration of Mount Wutai. 20f, King of
Khotan, vert. 50f, Savior Avalokitesvara. 100f,
Worshipping Bodhisattvas. $5, Thousand Arm Avalokitesvara.

1996, Aug. 15 Photo. *Perf. 11*
2704	A557	10f multi, vert.	.30	.25
2705	A557	20f multi	.35	.25
2706	A557	50f multi	.40	.30
2707	A557	100f multi	.60	.40
		Nos. 2704-2707 (4)	1.65	1.20

Souvenir Sheet
2708	A557	500f multicolored	6.25	4.00

No. 2708 contains one 46x102mm stamp.

Mausoleums of
Western
Xia — A759

Designs: No. 2709: Mausoleum terrace. No.
2710, Ornament on Divine Gate. 50f, Stele.
100f, Stele remnant, Shouling.

1996, Aug. 22 Photo. *Perf. 11½*
2709	A759	20f multi (4-1)	.25	.25
2710	A759	20f multi (4-2)	.25	.25
2711	A759	50f multi (4-3)	.35	.25
2712	A759	100f multi (4-4)	.50	.30
		Nos. 2709-2712 (4)	1.35	1.05

Railways in China — A760

Designs: 15f, Datong-Quinhuangdao Railway. 20f, Lanzhou-Xinjiang Two-Track Railway. 50f, Beijing-Kowloon Railway. 100f, Beijing Western Railway Station

1996, Sept. 1
2713	A760	15f multi	.40	.25
2714	A760	20f multi	.60	.25
2715	A760	50f multi	.60	.30
2716	A760	100f multi	1.25	.55
		Nos. 2713-2716 (4)	2.85	1.35

A761

Chinese Archives: No. 2717, Archives on
tortoise shells, Shang Dynasty. No. 2718,
Archives on wood slips, Han Dynasty. 50f, Iron
scrolls, Ming Dynasty. 100f, Books of Ch'ing
Dynasty.

1996, Sept. 2 Litho. *Perf. 12*
2717	A761	20f multi (4-1)	.60	.25
2718	A761	20f multi (4-2)	.60	.25
2719	A761	20f multi (4-3)	.80	.25
2720	A761	100f multi (4-4)	1.75	.45
		Nos. 2717-2720 (4)	3.75	1.25

A762

1996, Sept. 10 *Perf. 12*
2721	A762	20f Portrait	.45	.25
2722	A762	50f In uniform	.75	.35

Ye Ting (1896-1946), co-founder of Chinese
People's Liberation Army.

96th Conference of Inter-Parliamentary
Union — A763

1996, Sept. 16 *Perf. 11½*
2723	A763	20f multi	.80	.25

Shanghai — A764

No. 2724, Communication (6-1). No. 2725,
Lujiazui (6-2). No. 2726, Jinqiao (6-3). No.
2727, Zhanghiang (6-4). No. 2728, Wai-
gaoqiao (6-5). No. 2729, Residential (6-6).
No. 2730, Panoramic view.

Photo. & Engr.
1996, Sept. 21 *Perf. 11½*
2724	A764	10f multicolored	.25	.25
2725	A764	20f multicolored	.35	.25
2726	A764	20f multicolored	.40	.25
2727	A764	50f multicolored	.45	.30
2728	A764	60f multicolored	.50	.30
2729	A764	100f multicolored	.90	.35
		Nos. 2724-2729 (6)	2.85	1.70

Souvenir Sheet
Perf. 11
2730	A764	500f multicolored	7.50	6.50
a.		Margin ovptd.	18.00	10.00

No. 2730 contains one 90x45mm stamp.
No. 2730a issued 10/20/01. It is inscribed in
margin with multicolored emblems and gold
"PJZ-14," "APEC CHINA 2001," and Chinese
characters.

Space Navigation — A765

1996, Oct. 7 Litho. *Perf. 12*
2731	A765	20f Rocket lift-off	.45	.25
2732	A765	100f Satellite in orbit	.65	.35

Singapore Waterfront — A766

Design: 290f, Panmen, Suzhou, China.

1996, Oct. 9		**Photo.**	**Perf. 11½**	
2733	A766	20f multi	.30	.25
2734	A766	290f multi	1.00	.40

See Singapore Nos. 768-769.

Victory of Long March, 60th Anniv. — A767

Designs: 20f, Red Army through Marshland. 50f, Reunion of Three Armies.

1996, Oct. 22		**Litho.**	**Perf. 12**	
2735	A767	20f multi	.60	.35
2736	A767	50f multi	1.20	.60

Colored Sculpture of Tianjin A768

Designs: 20f, The Two Immortals. No. 2738, Making Candy. No. 2739, Returning from Fishing. 100f, Xi Chun in Painting.

1996, Nov. 5		**Photo.**	**Perf. 11½**	
2737	A768	20f multi (4-1)	.25	.25
2738	A768	50f multi (4-2)	.30	.25
2739	A768	50f multi (4-3)	.30	.25
2740	A768	100f multi (4-4)	.35	.30
		Nos. 2737-2740 (4)	1.20	1.05

Hong Kong A769

20f, Bank of China. 40f, Container Terminal. 60f, Kai Tak Airport. 290f, Stock Exchange.

1996, Dec. 19		**Litho.**	**Perf. 12**	
2741	A769	20f multi (4-1)	.25	.25
2742	A769	40f multi (4-2)	.30	.25
2743	A769	60f multi (4-3)	.40	.25
2744	A769	290f multi (4-4)	1.25	.35
		Nos. 2741-2744 (4)	2.20	1.10

Nos. 2741-2744 exist imperf. Value, set of pairs $700.

Visit China — A770

1997, Jan. 1			
2745	A770	50f multi	1.00 .25

A771

1997, Jan. 1				
2746	A771	50f multicolored	1.00	.25

First natl. agricultural census.

New Year 1997 (Year of the Ox)
A772   A773

		Photo. & Engr.		
1997, Jan. 5			**Perf. 11½**	
2747	A772	50f multi (2-2)	.75	.30
2748	A773	150f multi (2-1)	1.75	.60

Paintings by Pan Tianshou (1897-1971) A774

No. 2749, Pines on the Yellow Mountain. No. 2750, Rosy Clouds of Dawn. No. 2751, Clearing Up after Mould Rains. No. 2752, Chrysanthemum and Bamboo. No. 2753, Sleeping Cat. No. 2754, A Corner of Lingyan Brook.

1997, Mar. 14		**Photo.**	**Perf. 11½**	
2749	A774	50f multi (6-1)	.30	.25
2750	A774	50f multi (6-2)	.30	.25
2751	A774	100f multi (6-3)	.75	.35
2752	A774	100f multi (6-4)	.75	.35
2753	A774	150f multi (6-5)	1.40	.40
2754	A774	150f multi (6-6)	1.40	.40
		Nos. 2749-2754 (6)	4.90	2.00

Great Wall Type of 1995

1997, Apr. 1		**Photo.**	**Perf. 13x12**	
2755	A730	50f multicolored	.25	.25

A776

Tea: No. 2756, People forming circle beside tea tree. No. 2757, Statue of tea sage. No. 2758, Tea utensils, horiz. No. 2759, Painting of tea party, horiz.

1997, Apr. 8		**Litho.**	**Perf. 12**	
2756	A776	50f multi (4-1)	.50	.25
2757	A776	50f multi (4-2)	.50	.25
2758	A776	150f multi (4-3)	.90	.40
2759	A776	150f multi (4-4)	.90	.40
		Nos. 2756-2759 (4)	2.80	1.30

A777

Stylized designs depicting: No. 2760, Celebration. No. 2761, Unity (group of people), horiz. 200f, Advance (horses running), horiz.

1997, May 1		**Photo.**	**Perf. 11½**	
2760	A777	50f multi (3-1)	.35	.25
2761	A777	50f multi (3-2)	.35	.25
2762	A777	200f multi (3-3)	.95	.35
		Nos. 2760-2762 (3)	1.65	.85

Inner Mongolia Autonomous Region, 50th anniv.

Pheasants A778

Designs: 50f, Chinese copper pheasant. 540f, Common pheasant.

		Litho. & Engr.		
1997, May 9			**Perf. 11½x11**	
2763	A778	50f multi (2-1)	.35	.25
2764	A778	540f multi (2-2)	2.25	.90

See Sweden Nos. 2225-2226.

Dong Architecture A779

No. 2765, Zengchong Drum Tower. No. 2766, Bai'er Drum Tower. No. 2767, Wind and Rain Bridge over the River, horiz. No. 2768, Wind and Rain Bridge in the Field, horiz.

1997, June 2		**Litho.**	**Perf. 12**	
2765	A779	50f multi (4-1)	.25	.25
2766	A779	50f multi (4-2)	.25	.25
a.		Pair, #2765-2766	.75	.60
2767	A779	150f multi (4-3)	.50	.30
2768	A779	150f multi (4-4)	.50	.30
a.		Pair, #2767-2768	1.25	1.10
		Nos. 2765-2768 (4)	1.50	1.10

Maiji Grottoes — A780

Statues: No. 2769, Buddha and Xieshi Bodhisattva. No. 2770, Xieshi Bodhisattva and his disciple. 100f, Maid. No. 2772, Buddha. No. 2773, Xieshi Bodhisattva. 200f, Provider.

1997, June 13				
2769	A780	50f multi (6-1)	.30	.25
2770	A780	50f multi (6-2)	.30	.25
2771	A780	100f multi (6-3)	.40	.25
2772	A780	150f multi (6-4)	.55	.30
2773	A780	150f multi (6-5)	.55	.30
2774	A780	200f multi (6-6)	.70	.35
		Nos. 2769-2774 (6)	2.80	1.70

A780a

A781

Texts surrounded by flowers: 50f, Sino-British Joint Declaration. 150f, Basic Law of the Hong Kong Special Adminstrative Region. 800f, Deng Xiaoping.

1997, July 1		**Litho.**	**Perf. 12**	
2774A	A780a	50f multi (2-1)	.35	.25
2774B	A780a	150f multi (2-2)	.95	.65
		Souvenir Sheets		
2774C	A781	800f multi	4.25	3.50
d.		Overprinted in sheet margin	7.00	5.00
		Litho. (stamp) & Embossed (margin)		
		Perf. 13½		
2775	A781	$50 gold & multi	45.00	45.00
a.		Overprinted in margin	47.50	47.50

Deng Xiaoping (1904-97), return of Hong Kong to China.

No. 2775 was released in special souvenir folder.

No. 2744C exists imperf. Value, $500.

No. 2774Cd contains gold Chinese inscription for Hong Kong's Return Exhibition Tour, emblem, and "PJZ-8" in sheet margin. Issued: 6/19/98.

Overprint in margin on No. 2775a is Chinese inscription, "2000-1" and "(2-1)J." Issued: 1/1/00.

Ancient Temples of Wutai Mountain — A782

Designs: 40f, Taihuai Township. No. 2777, Nanchan Temple. No. 2778, Foguang Temple. No. 2779, Xiantong Temple. No. 2780, Bodhisattva Summit. 200f, Zhenhai Temple.

1997, July 26		**Litho.**	**Perf. 12**	
2776	A782	40f multi (6-1)	.25	.25
2777	A782	50f multi (6-2)	.30	.25
2778	A782	50f multi (6-3)	.30	.25
2779	A782	150f multi (6-4)	.55	.30
2780	A782	150f multi (6-5)	.55	.30
2781	A782	200f multi (6-6)	.70	.35
		Nos. 2776-2781 (6)	2.65	1.70

Chinese People's Liberation Army, 70th Anniv. — A783

No. 2782, Land Force. No. 2783, Naval Force. No. 2784, Air Force. No. 2785, Strategic Missile Troops. 200f, Joint military maneuvers.

1997, Aug. 1				
2782	A783	50f multi (5-1)	.45	.30
2783	A783	50f multi (5-2)	.45	.30
2784	A783	50f multi (5-3)	.45	.30
2785	A783	50f multi (5-4)	.45	.30
2786	A783	200f multi (5-5)	2.00	.90
		Nos. 2782-2786 (5)	3.80	2.10

Shoushan Stone Carvings A784

Designs: No. 2787, "Rhythm of Autumn," vert. No. 2788, "Rhinoceros under Sunshine,", vert. No. 2789, "Jade's Fragrance," (basket of fruit). No. 2790, "Drunken Joy."
800f, Qianlong's Chain Seals.

1997, Aug. 17   Litho.   Perf. 12
2787	A784	50f multi (4-1)	.30	.25
2788	A784	50f multi (4-2)	.30	.25
2789	A784	150f multi (4-3)	.55	.30
2790	A784	150f multi (4-4)	.55	.30
		Nos. 2787-2790 (4)	1.70	1.10

Souvenir Sheet
| 2791 | A784 | 800f multi | 5.00 | 4.50 |

No. 2791 contains one 60x60mm stamp.

Great Wall Type of 1995
Gates: 30f, Huangyaguan. 100f, Badaling. 150f, Joyongguan. 200f, Zijingguan.

1997, Sept. 1   Photo.   Perf. 13x12
2792	A730	30f yellow & black	.25	.25
2793	A730	100f vermilion & black	.40	.25
2794	A730	150f green & black	.55	.25
2795	A730	200f red & black	.70	.30
		Nos. 2792-2795 (4)	1.90	1.05

Communist Party of China, 15th Natl. Congress A785

1997, Sept. 12   Litho.   Perf. 12
| 2796 | A785 | 50f multicolored | 1.00 | .40 |

A786

No. 2797, China Rose. No. 2798, New Zealand Monthly Rose.

1997, Oct. 9   Photo.   Perf. 11½
2797		150f multi (2-1)	.65	.30
2798		150f multi (2-2)	.65	.30
a.		A786 Pair, #2797-2798	1.90	1.50

See New Zealand Nos. 1469-1470.

Eighth Natl. Games A788

1997, Oct. 12   Litho.   Perf. 12
2799	A788	50f Athletes (2-1)	.35	.25
2800	A788	150f Stadium)2-2)	.65	.40
a.		Souv. sheet, #2799-2800	5.25	4.00

No. 2800a sold for 300f.

Temple of Heaven, Beijing — A789

No. 2801, Hall of Prayers for Bumper Harvests. No. 2802, Imperial Vault of Heaven. No. 2803, Circular Mound Altar. No. 2804, Fasting Palace.

1997, Oct. 16   Litho.   Perf. 12
2801	A789	50f multi (4-1)	.35	.25
2802	A789	50f multi (4-2)	.35	.25
a.		Pair, #2801-2802	.85	.75
2803	A789	150f multi (4-3)	.55	.30
2804	A789	150f multi (4-4)	.55	.30
a.		Pair, #2803-2804	1.40	1.10
		Nos. 2801-2804 (4)	1.80	1.10

Mt. Huangshan — A790

a, Mt. Huangshan at sunrise (8-1). b, Xihai Peaks (8-2). c, Flying Rock in surging clouds (8-3). d, Beihai in drifting clouds (8-4). e, Yuping Peak (8-5). f, Mystical stone (8-6). g, Tiandu Peak over clouds (8-7). h, Fabled Abode of Immortals (8-8).

1997, Oct. 20   Photo.   Perf. 11½
Sheet of 8 + Label
| 2805 | A790 | 200f #a.-h. | 12.00 | 9.00 |

Nos. 2805d, 2805e are each 36x46mm.
22nd UPU Congress, Beijing, 1999.

City Wall of Xi'an A791

Designs: No. 2806, Surrounding tower. No. 2807, Arrow Tower. No. 2808, Watch Tower. No. 2809, Corner Tower.

1997, Oct. 24   Litho.   Perf. 12
2806	A791	50f multi (4-1)	.30	.25
2807	A791	50f multi (4-2)	.30	.25
2808	A791	150f multi (4-3)	.55	.35
2809	A791	150f multi (4-4)	.55	.35
		Nos. 2806-2809 (4)	1.70	1.20

Three Gorges Dam Project on Yangtze River — A792

No. 2810, New channel being opened to navigation. No. 2811, Damming Yangtze River.

1997, Nov. 8   Photo.   Perf. 11½
2810	A792	50f multi (2-1)	.35	.25
2811	A792	50f multi (2-2)	.35	.25
a.		Pair, #2810-2811	1.00	.75

Macao Landmarks — A793

50f, Ma Kok Temple. 100f, Lin Fong Temple. 150f, St. Paul's Ruins. 200f, Guia Lighthouse.

1997, Nov. 11   Litho.   Perf. 12
2812	A793	50f multi (4-1)	.25	.25
2813	A793	100f multi (4-2)	.40	.25
2814	A793	150f multi (4-3)	.50	.35
2815	A793	200f multi (4-4)	.65	.40
		Nos. 2812-2815 (4)	1.80	1.25

Steel Production Exceeds 100 Million Tons in 1996 A794

50f, Ancient method of producing steel. 150f, Modern mill, pouring steel from smelter.

1997, Nov. 25
| 2816 | A794 | 50f multi (2-1) | .40 | .25 |
| 2817 | A794 | 150f multi (2-2) | .90 | .40 |

Telecommunications — A795

Stylized designs: No. 2818, Digital transmissions. No. 2819, Computer, "X-changing" data. No. 2820, Computer receiving signals, Chinese landmarks. No. 2821, Cellular phone transmission, man's head.

1997, Dec. 10
2818	A795	50f multi (4-1)	.30	.25
2819	A795	50f multi (4-2)	.30	.25
2820	A795	150f multi (4-3)	.55	.35
2821	A795	150f multi (4-4)	.55	.35
		Nos. 2818-2821 (4)	1.70	1.20

Literature Type of 1987
Outlaws of the Marsh: 40f, Huyan Zhuo coaxes Guan Sheng in a moonlit night. No. 2823, Lu Junyi captures Shi Wengong. No. 2824, Yan Qing defeats sky supporting pillar. 150f, Thunderbolt defeats Imperial Army.
800f, Heroes of Mount Liangshan take seats in order of rank.

1997, Dec. 22   Photo.   Perf. 11
2822	A570	40f multi (4-1)	.30	.25
2823	A570	50f multi (4-2)	.35	.30
2824	A570	50f multi (4-3)	.35	.30
2825	A570	150f multi (4-4)	.80	.40
		Nos. 2822-2825 (4)	1.80	1.25

Souvenir Sheet
| 2826 | A570 | 800f multicolored | 3.50 | 3.25 |

No. 2826 contains one 60x90mm stamp.

New Year 1998 (Year of the Tiger)
A796   A797

Photo. & Engr.
1998, Jan. 5   Perf. 11½
| 2827 | A796 | 50f multi (2-1) | .60 | .25 |
| 2828 | A797 | 150f multi (2-2) | 1.40 | .40 |

Gardens of Lingnan — A798

1998, Jan. 18   Litho.   Perf. 12
2829	A798	50f Keyaun (4-1)	.30	.25
2830	A798	50f Liangyuan (4-2)	.30	.25
2831	A798	100f Qinghui (4-3)	.40	.30
2832	A798	200f Yuyin Villa (4-4)	.70	.35
		Nos. 2829-2832 (4)	1.70	1.15

Deng Xiaoping (1904-97) — A799

No. 2833, At middle age. No. 2834, During Liberation War. No. 2835, With Mao Tse-tung. 100f, As Chairman of Central Military Commission. 150f, Making speech on 35th anniversary of People's Republic. 200f, Making speech, hand raised, 1992.

1998, Feb. 19   Photo.   Perf. 11½
2833	A799	50f multi (6-1)	.50	.25
2834	A799	50f multi (6-2)	.50	.25
2835	A799	50f multi (6-3)	.50	.25
2836	A799	100f multi (6-4)	.75	.30
2837	A799	150f multi (6-5)	1.00	.40
2838	A799	200f multi (6-6)	1.25	.55
		Nos. 2833-2838 (6)	4.50	2.00

Chinese People's Police — A800

Designs: 40f, Golden shield. No. 2840, Blitz operation. No. 2841, Cooperation between police and people. 100f, Traffic control. 150f, Fire police. 200f, Border guards.

1998, Feb. 28   Litho.   Perf. 12
2839	A800	40f multi (6-1)	.25	.25
2840	A800	50f multi (6-2)	.30	.25
2841	A800	50f multi (6-3)	.30	.25
2842	A800	100f multi (6-4)	.40	.30
2843	A800	150f multi (6-5)	.55	.30
2844	A800	200f multi (6-6)	.70	.35
		Nos. 2839-2844 (6)	2.50	1.70

A801

1998, Mar. 5
| 2845 | A801 | 50f multi (1-1) | 1.00 | .25 |

Ninth Natl. People's Congress, Beijing.

A802

Chou En-lai (1898-1976), Communist Party leader: No. 2846, In military uniform on horse. No. 2847, As First Premier, walking. No. 2848, As diplomat wearing lei. No. 2849, Standing and applauding.

1998, Mar. 5   Photo.   Perf. 11½
2846	A802	50f multi (4-1)	1.00	.25
2847	A802	50f multi (4-2)	1.00	.25
2848	A802	150f multi (4-3)	1.40	.50
2849	A802	150f multi (4-4)	1.40	.50
		Nos. 2846-2849 (4)	4.80	1.50

Nine-Village Valley — A803

Designs: No. 2850, Fangcao Lake. No. 2851, Wuhua Lake. No. 2852, Shuzheng Waterfalls. No. 2853, Nuorilang Waterfalls. No. 2854, Long Lake.

1998, Mar. 26 Litho. Perf. 12
2850 A803 50f multi (4-1) .30 .25
2851 A803 50f multi (4-2) .30 .25
2852 A803 150f multi (4-3) .50 .35
2853 A803 150f multi (4-4) .50 .35
Nos. 2850-2853 (4) 1.60 1.20

Souvenir Sheet
2854 A803 800f multicolored 3.25 3.00
No. 2854 contains one 93x52mm stamp.

Dai Architecture — A804

No. 2855, Building on stilts. No. 2856, Well. No. 2857, Pavilion. No. 2858, Pagoda.

1998, Apr. 12 Photo. Perf. 11½
2855 A804 50f multi (4-1) .30 .25
2856 A804 50f multi (4-2) .30 .25
2857 A804 150f multi (4-3) .55 .35
2858 A804 150f multi (4-4) .55 .35
Nos. 2855-2858 (4) 1.70 1.20

Construction, Hainan Special Economic Zone — A805

No. 2859, Urban construction, Haikou. No. 2860, Economic development zone, Yangpu. No. 2861, Phoenix Intl. Airport, Sanya. No. 2862, Natl. tourism and resort zone, Yalongwan.

1998, Apr. 13 Litho. Perf. 12
2859 A805 50f multi (4-1) .25 .25
2860 A805 50f multi (4-2) .25 .25
  a. Pair, #2859-2860 .75 .65
2861 A805 150f multi (4-3) .55 .30
2862 A805 150f multi (4-4) .55 .30
  a. Pair, #2861-2862 1.25 1.00
Nos. 2859-2862 (4) 1.60 1.10

Ancient Academies — A806

Designs: No. 2863, Yingtian. No. 2864, Songyang. No. 2865, Yuelu. No. 2866, Bailu.

1998, Apr. 29
2863 A806 50f multi (4-1) .30 .25
2864 A806 50f multi (4-2) .30 .25
2865 A806 150f multi (4-3) .55 .35
2866 A806 150f multi (4-4) .55 .35
Nos. 2863-2866 (4) 1.70 1.20

Beijing University, Cent. A807

1998, May 4 Litho. Perf. 12
2867 A807 50f multicolored 1.00 .25

22nd UPU Congress, Beijing A808

50f, Emblem (2-1). 540f, Emblem, vert. (2-2).

1998, May 15 Litho. Perf. 12
2868 A808 50f multicolored .25 .25
2869 A808 540f multicolored 1.75 .85

Shennongjia Nature Reserve — A809

No. 2870, Mountain peaks. No. 2871, River, gorge. No. 2872, Primitive forest. No. 2873, Grasslands.

1998, June 6
2870 A809 50f multi (4-1) .30 .25
2871 A809 50f multi (4-2) .30 .25
2872 A809 150f multi (4-3) .55 .35
2873 A809 150f multi (4-4) .55 .35
Nos. 2870-2873 (4) 1.70 1.20

Chongqing — A810

1998, June 18 Litho. Perf. 12
2874 A810 50f Great Hall (2-1) .40 .25
2875 A810 150f Port (2-2) .70 .45

Xilinguole Grassland — A811

Designs: No. 2876, Sheep grazing, sheep herders. No. 2877, Cattle grazing, flowers. 150f, Poplar and birch forest, deer. 800f, Xilinguole River Bend.

1998, June 24
2876 A811 50f multi (3-1) .30 .25
2877 A811 50f multi (3-2) .30 .25
2878 A811 150f multi (3-3) .55 .35
Nos. 2876-2878 (3) 1.15 .85

Souvenir Sheet
2879 A811 800f multicolored 3.25 3.00
No. 2879 contains one 56x36mm stamp.

Paintings, by He Xiangning (1878-1972) — A812

50f, Tiger (3-1). 100f, Lion, vert. (3-2). 150f, Plum blossom, vert. (3-3).

Perf. 12½ Syncopated Type A (2 Sides)
1998, June 27 Photo.
2880 A812 50f multi .50 .25
2881 A812 100f multi .80 .35
2882 A812 150f multi 1.00 .50
Nos. 2880-2882 (3) 2.30 1.10

Jingpo Lake — A813

Views of lake: No. 2883, Bridge, houses on cliff, boat. No. 2884, Islands, boats at shore. No. 2885, Boat, island. No. 2886, Waterfalls.

1998, Aug. 15 Litho. Perf. 12
2883 A813 50f multi (4-1) .30 .25
2884 A813 50f multi (4-2) .30 .25
2885 A813 50f multi (4-3) .30 .25
2886 A813 50f multi (4-4) .30 .25
  a. Strip of 4, #2883-2886 1.50 1.25

Würzburg Palace — A814

Puning Temple, Chengde — A815

1998, Aug. 20 Litho. Perf. 12
2887 A814 50f multi (2-1) .35 .25
2888 A815 540f multi (2-2) 1.90 1.40
See Germany Nos. 2012-2013.

Literature Type of 1987
Romance of the Three Kingdoms: No. 2889, Liu Bei finds a guardian for his heir at Baidi City. No. 2890, Zhuge Liang leads his army home, vert. 100f, Death of Zhuge Liang. 150f, Three Kingdoms united under the reign of Jin, vert.
800f, The Stratagem of Empty City.

1998, Aug. 26 Photo. Perf. 11½
2889 A570 50f multi (4-1) .25 .25
2890 A570 50f multi (4-2) .25 .25
2891 A570 100f multi (4-3) .40 .35
2892 A570 150f multi (4-4) .60 .55
Nos. 2889-2892 (4) 1.50 1.40

Souvenir Sheet
2893 A570 800f multicolored 7.25 4.25
No. 2893 contains one 158x37mm stamp.

Flood Victims Relief — A816

1998, Sept. 10 Photo. Perf. 13x13½
2894 A816 50f + 50f label .60 .40

The Louvre, France A817

Design: 200f, Hall of Heavenly Peace, Imperial Palace, China.

1998, Sept. 12 Photo. Perf. 13x13½
2895 A817 50f multi (2-1) .35 .25
2896 A817 200f multi (2-2) .85 .55
See France Nos. 2669-2670.

Cliff Paintings of Helan Mountains — A818

50f, Human face (3-1). 100f, Hunting (3-2). 150f, Ox (3-3).

1998, Sept. 23 Litho. Perf. 12
2897 A818 50f multi .30 .25
2898 A818 100f multi .40 .35
2899 A818 150f multi .55 .45
Nos. 2897-2899 (3) 1.25 1.05

Longquan Pottery and Porcelain — A819

Designs: No. 2900, Vase with five spouts. No. 2901, Vase with phoenix ears. No. 2902, Double gourd vase. 150f, Ewer.

1998, Oct. 13
2900 A819 50f multi (4-1) .30 .25
2901 A819 50f multi (4-2) .30 .25
2902 A819 50f multi (4-3) .30 .25
2903 A819 150f multi (4-4) .65 .50
Nos. 2900-2903 (4) 1.55 1.25

Mausoleum of Yandi A820

Designs: 50f, Meridian Gate. 100f, Saluting Pavilion. 150f, Tomb.

1998, Oct. 28 Litho. Perf. 12
2904 A820 50f multi (3-1) .25 .25
2905 A820 100f multi (3-2) .35 .30
2906 A820 150f multi (3-3) .50 .40
  a. Souvenir sheet, #2904-2906 2.40 2.00
Nos. 2904-2906 (3) 1.10 .95

Great Wall Type of 1995

10f, Jiumenko Pass. 300f, Niagziguan Pass. 420f, Pianguan Pass. 500f, Bianjing Tower.

1998, Nov. 1   Photo.   Perf. 13x12

2907	A730	10f apple grn & blk	.25	.25
2908	A730	300f olive & black	1.00	.75
2909	A730	420f brn org & blk	1.50	1.00
2910	A730	500f blue, blk & brn	1.75	1.25
		Nos. 2907-2910 (4)	4.50	3.25

Major Campaigns in Liberation War — A821

No. 2911, Making plans. No. 2912, Conquering Jinzhou. No. 2913, Battle in Huaihai. No. 2914, Liberating Beijing. 150f, People moving supplies.

1998, Nov. 14   Litho.   Perf. 12

2911	A821	50f red & multi (5-1)	.55	.25
2912	A821	50f gray & multi (5-2)	.55	.25
2913	A821	50f org yel & multi (5-3)	.55	.25
2914	A821	50f org & multi (5-4)	.55	.25
2915	A821	150f brn org & multi (5-5)	1.25	.75
		Nos. 2911-2915 (5)	3.45	1.75

Liu Shaoqi (1898-1969), Communist Party Leader — A822

Various portraits.

1998, Nov. 24   Photo.   Perf. 11½

2916	A822	50f multi (4-1), vert.	.35	.25
2917	A822	50f multi (4-2), vert.	.35	.25
2918	A822	50f shown (4-3)	.35	.25
2919	A822	150f multi (4-4)	1.10	.50
		Nos. 2916-2919 (4)	2.15	1.25

Chillon Castle, Lake Geneva A823

Bridge 24, Slender West Lake, Yangzhou A824

1998, Nov. 25   Perf. 11x11½

2920	A823	50f multi (2-1)	.35	.25
2921	A824	540f multi (2-2)	1.90	1.40

See Switzerland Nos. 1037-1039.

Lingqu Canal — A825

No. 2922, Dam. No. 2923, Bridge over canal, vert. 150f, Boat approaching lock, vert.

1998, Dec. 1   Litho.   Perf. 12

2922	A825	50f multi (3-1)	.30	.25
2923	A825	50f multi (3-2)	.30	.25
2924	A825	150f multi (3-3)	.60	.45
		Nos. 2922-2924 (3)	1.20	.95

Buildings in Macao — A826

Designs: 50f, Building complex, Nanwan. 100f, Friendship Bridge. 150f, Macao Stadium. 200f, Macao Intl. Airport.

1998, Dec. 12   Litho.   Perf. 12

2925	A826	50f multi (4-1)	.25	.25
2926	A826	100f multi (4-2)	.40	.30
2927	A826	150f multi (4-3)	.55	.40
2928	A826	200f multi (4-4)	.70	.60
		Nos. 2925-2928 (4)	1.90	1.55

11th Communist Party Congress, 20th Anniv. — A827

50f, Deng Xiaoping (2-1). 150f, Handbill, buildings (2-2).

1998, Dec. 18

2929	A827	50f multicolored	.65	.25
2930	A827	150f multicolored	1.25	.45

Fish of the Coral Reef A828

a, Pomacanthus imperator (8-1). b, Plectropomus maculatus (8-2). c, Chaetodon plebeius (8-3). d, Chaetodon chrysurus (8-4), vert. e, Heniochus acuminatus (8-5), vert. f, Lutjanus sebae (8-6). g, Balistoides conspicillum (8-7). h, Pygoplites diancanthus (8-8).

1998, Dec. 22   Perf. 11½
Sheet of 8

2931	A828	200f #a.-h. + label	6.00	6.00
	i.	As No. 2931, with margin ovptd. in gold	10.00	10.00

UPU, 22nd Congress, Beijing '99 World Philatelic Exhibition.
Nos. 2931d-2931e are each 40x49mm.
No.2931i issued 7/15/00. No. 2931i inscribed in margin in gold "PJZ-12", "1997-1999" and Chinese characters. Inscription for best philatelic item from 1997-99.

New Year 1999 (Year of the Rabbit)
A829   A830

50f, Stylized rabbit (2-1). 150f, Symbol for rabbit (2-2).

Photo. & Engr.
1999, Jan. 5   Perf. 11½

2932	A829	50f multicolored	1.00	.25
2933	A830	150f multi	1.50	.50

Great Wall Type of 1995

5f, Hushan Section. 20f, Shanhaiguan Pass. 40f, Jinshanling Section. 80f, Mutianyu Section. 270f, Pingxingguan Pass. 320f, Desheng Pass. 440f, Yanmen Pass. 540f, Zhenbei Tower.

1999, Mar. 1   Photo.   Perf. 13x12

2934	A730	5f bl, blk & bl grn	.25	.25
2935	A730	20f vio & blk	.40	.25
2936	A730	40f pink & blk	.45	.30
2937	A730	80f grn, blk & ol	.60	.40
2938	A730	270f grn, blk & brn	1.50	.65
2939	A730	320f vio, blk & bwn	2.00	1.10
2940	A730	440f red brn, blk & bwn	3.75	2.00
2941	A730	540f blue & black	3.50	1.50
		Nos. 2934-2941 (8)	12.45	6.45

Stone Carvings of the Han Dynasty A831

No. 2942, Plowing fields with oxen. No. 2943, Group weaving. No. 2944, Three figures dancing in front of fire. No. 2945, Horses, carriage. No. 2946, Group in assassination attempt. No. 2947, Goddess Chang'e.

1999, Mar. 16   Perf. 12

2942	A831	50f dark green & blk	.25	.25
2943	A831	50f brown & blk	.25	.25
2944	A831	50f dark blue & blk	.25	.25
2945	A831	150f dark brown & blk	.55	.45
2946	A831	150f brown olive & blk	.55	.45
2947	A831	150f dark purple & blk	.55	.45
		Nos. 2942-2947 (6)	2.40	2.10

A832

Chinese Ceramics (Porcelain from the Jun Kiln): 80f, Halberd-shaped cup. 100f, Cup. 150f, Dual-handled stove. 200f, Dual-handled vase with base.

1999, Apr. 8   Photo.   Perf. 11½

2948	A832	80f multi (4-1)	.30	.25
2949	A832	100f multi (4-2)	.40	.30
2950	A832	150f multi (4-3)	.60	.45
2951	A832	200f multi (4-4)	.85	.60
		Nos. 2948-2951 (4)	2.15	1.60

Great Wall Type of 1995

Designs: 60f, Huanghua Tower. $10, Huama section. $20, Sanguankou Pass. $50 Jiayuguan Pass.

1999, May 1   Photo.   Perf. 13x12

2952	A730	60f multicolored	.30	.30

Size: 28x22mm
Perf. 11½
Photo. & Engr.

2953	A730	$10 multicolored	4.00	3.00
2954	A730	$20 multicolored	8.00	5.75
2955	A730	$50 multicolored	17.50	14.50
		Nos. 2952-2955 (4)	29.80	23.55

A833

1999, May 1   Litho.   Perf. 12

2956	A833	80f shown (2-1)	.40	.25
2957	A833	200f Tree (2-2)	.80	.55

Kunming World Horticultural Fair.

Red Deer A834

1999, May 18   Litho.   Perf. 11x11½

2958	A834	80f Bucks	.35	.25
2959	A834	80f Does	.35	.25
a.		Pair, #2958-2959	.80	.70

See Russia No. 6514.

Beauty of Putuo Mountain — A835

No. 2960, Puji Temple (6-1). No. 2961, Nantian Gate, vert. (6-2). No. 2962, 100-step Sand (6-3). No. 2963, Pantuo Rock (6-4). No. 2964, Fanyin Cave, vert. (6-5). No. 2965, Fayu Temple (6-6).

1999, June 3   Litho.   Perf. 12

2960	A835	30f multicolored	.25	.25
2961	A835	60f multicolored	.30	.25
2962	A835	60f multicolored	.30	.25
2963	A835	80f multicolored	.35	.30
2964	A835	80f multicolored	.35	.30
2965	A835	280f multicolored	.95	.75
		Nos. 2960-2965 (6)	2.50	2.10

Fang Zhimin (1899-1935), Revolutionary A836

1999, Aug. 21   Photo.   Perf. 11¼

2966	A836	80f Close-up (2-1)	.50	.35
2967	A836	80f Standing (2-2)	.50	.35

Souvenir Sheet

China 1999 World Philatelic Exhibition — A837

1999, Aug. 21   Perf. 11½x11¼

2968	A837	800f multicolored	4.50	4.00

Exists overprinted in upper corners in gold. Value, $10.

A838

22nd UPU Congress — A839

Congress sites: 80f, 1st, Bern. 540f, 22nd, Beijing.
800f, Inscription by Pres. Jiang Zemin.

1999, Aug. 23   Litho.   Perf. 12
2969 A838 80f multi (2-1)   .35   .25
2970 A838 540f multi (2-2)   2.00 1.40

Souvenir Sheet
Perf. 12¼
2971 A839 800f multicolored   5.50 5.00

UPU, 125th
Anniv. — A840

1999, Sept. 7   Litho.   Perf. 12
2972 A840 80f multicolored   .65   .35

Intl. Year of the
Elderly — A841

1999, Sept. 9
2973 A841 80f multicolored   .80   .25

Chinese People's Political Consultative
Conference, 50th Anniv. — A842

60f, Building (2-1). 80f, Mao Zedong, vert.
(2-2).

1999, Sept. 21
2974 A842 60f multi   .75   .25
2975 A842 80f multi   2.00   .35

Ethnic Groups in China — A843

Designs (stamp number following "56-" at
LR): a, Han (1). b, Mongols (2). c, Hui (3). d,
Tibetans (4). e, Uygurs (5) f, Miao (6). g, Yi (7).
h, Zhuang (8). i, Bouyei (9). j, Koreans (10). k,
Manchu (11). l, Dongs (12). m, Yao (13). n, Bai
(14). o, Tujia (15). p, Hani (16). q, Kazak (17).
r, Dai (18). s, Li (19). t, Lisu (20). u, Va (21). v,
She (22). w, Gaoshan (23). x, Lahu (24). y,
Shui (25). z, Dongxiang (26). aa, Naxi (27).
ab, Jingpo (28). ac, Kirgiz (29). ad, Tu (30). ae,
Daur (31). af, Mulam (32). ag, Qiang (33). ah,
Blang (34). ai, Salas (35). aj, Maonan (36). ak,
Gelao (37). al, Xibe (38). am, Achang (39). an,
Pumi (40). ao, Tajiks (41). ap, Nu (42). aq,
Uzbeks (43). ar, Russians (44). as, Ewenki
(45). at, De'ang (46). au, Bonan (47). av,
Yugur (48). aw, Jing (49). ax, Tartars (50). ay,
Drung (51). az, Oroqen (52). ba, Hezhe (53).
bb, Moiba (54). bc, Lhoba (55). bd, Jino (56).

1999, Oct. 7   Photo.   Perf. 13¼
2976 A843 80f Sheet of 56,
            #a.-bd.   22.50 18.00

Mountains — A844

1999, Oct. 5   Perf. 11½x11¼
2977 A844 80f Lushan (2-1)   .55   .30
2978 A844 80f Kuryongyon (2-2)   .55   .30

Project Hope,
10th
Anniv. — A845

1999, Oct. 30   Photo.   Perf. 11½
2979 A845 80f multi   .75   .30

Scientific and Technological
Achievements — A846

Designs: No. 2980, Cambrian era fossil. No.
2981, Underwater robot. No. 2982, Best result
of Goldbach conjecture, vert. No. 2983, 2.16m
telescope, vert.

1999, Nov. 1   Litho.   Perf. 12
2980 A846 80f multi (4-1)   .60   .30
2981 A846 80f multi (4-2)   .60   .30
  a. Pair, #2980-2981   4.25 2.00
2982 A846 80f multi (4-3)   .60   .30
2983 A846 80f multi (4-4)   .60   .30
  a. Pair, #2982-2983   4.25 2.00
      Nos. 2980-2983 (4)   2.40 1.20

Li Lisan (1899-
1967), Minister of
Labor — A847

No. 2984, As young man (2-1). No. 2985,
Wearing glasses (2-2).

1999, Nov. 19   Photo.   Perf. 11½
2984 A847 80f multi   .50   .30
2985 A847 80f multi   .50   .30

Return of Macao to China — A848

Designs: 80f, Sino-Portuguese declaration,
flower. 150f, Basic Law of Macao Special
Administrative Region, Great Wall.
800f, $50, Deng Xiaoping.

1999-2000   Photo.   Perf. 11¾x11½
2986 A848 80f multi (2-1)   .55   .30
2987 A848 150f multi (2-2)   .75   .50

Souvenir Sheets
Perf. 13
2988 A848 800f multi   4.25 3.75

Litho. (stamp) & Embossed (margin)
Perf. 12
2989 A848 $50 multi   15.00 15.00
  a. Overprinted in margin   37.50 37.50

No. 2988 contains one 60x50mm stamp
with star-shaped perforations in the corners.
Overprint in margin on No. 2989a is Chinese inscription, "2000-1" and "(2-2)J."
Issued: No. 2989a, 1/1/00; others, 12/20/99.

Nie Rongzhen
(1899-1992),
Military
Leader — A849

1999, Dec. 29   Litho.   Perf. 12
2990 A849 80f In uniform (2-1)   .75   .30
2991 A849 80f Seated (2-2)   .75   .30

Millennium — A850

No. 2992, Sun Yat-sen, #590. No. 2993,
#2214. No. 2994, #2339. No. 2995, #2601.
No. 2996, Mao Zedong, #456. 200f, #2248.
260f, #2730. 280f, Deng Xiaoping, #2774C.

1999, Dec. 31   Litho.   Perf. 12
2992 A850 60f multi (8-1)   .30   .25
2993 A850 60f multi (8-2)   .30   .25
2994 A850 80f multi (8-3)   .40   .25
2995 A850 80f multi (8-4)   .40   .25
2996 A850 80f multi (8-5)   .40   .25
2997 A850 200f multi (8-6)   .85   .40
2998 A850 260f multi (8-7)   .95   .50
2999 A850 280f multi (8-8)   1.10   .60
      Nos. 2992-2999 (8)   4.70 2.75

New Year 2000
(Year of the
Dragon) — A851

80f, Dragon (2-1). $2.80, Rising sun (2-2).

Photo. & Engr.
2000, Jan. 5   Perf. 11½x11¾
3000 A851 80f multi   10.00   .90
3001 A851 $2.80 multi   15.00 1.40

A852

Spring Festival: No. 3002, Welcoming the
Spring Festival. No. 3003, Bidding farewell to
outgoing year. $2.80, Offering sacrifices to
god of land.
$8, Family reunion, horiz.

2000, Jan. 29   Photo.   Perf. 11¼
3002 A852 80f multi (3-1)   .75   .25
3003 A852 80f multi (3-2)   .75   .25
3004 A852 $2.80 multi (3-3)   2.50   .80
      Nos. 3002-3004 (3)   4.00 1.30

Souvenir Sheet
Perf. 11¼x11
3005 A852 $8 multi   6.00 6.00
  a. Ovptd. in sheet margin   8.50 8.50

No. 3005 contains one 90x60mm stamp.
No. 3005a contains gold Chinese inscription
for New Century Philatelic Exhibition, "2000,"
and "PJZ-11" in sheet margin. Issued: 4/28.

A853

Wildlife.

2000, Feb. 25   Photo.   Perf. 13¼x13
3006 A853 Sheet of 10 + 2 la-
            bels   8.00 8.00
  a. 30f Nipponia nippon   .25   .25
  b. 60f Teinopalpus aureus   .25   .25
  c. 80f Ailuropoda melanoleuca   .30   .25
  d. $1 Crossoptilon manichuricum .35   .25
  e. $1.50 Acipenser sinensis   .50   .35
  f. $2 Rhinopithecus roxellanae .65   .45
  g. $2.60 Lipotes vexillifer   .85   .60
  h. $2.80 Grus japonensis   .90   .65
  i. $3.70 Panthera tigris   1.25   .85
  j. $5.40 Alligator sinensis   1.90 1.40

Cultural
Relics — A854

Designs; 60f, Neolithic Age jade dragon. No. 3008, Dragon-shaped ornament. No. 3009, Carved tile with dragon. No. 3010, Copper mirror with dragon. No. 3011, Bronze dragon. $2.80, Dragon on sandalwood throne.

		2000, Mar. 7	Litho.	Perf. 12	
3007	A854	60f multi (6-1)		1.00	.25
3008	A854	80f multi (6-2)		1.50	.40
3009	A854	80f multi (6-3)		1.50	.40
3010	A854	80f multi (6-4)		1.50	.40
3011	A854	80f multi (6-5)		1.50	.40
3012	A854	$2.80 multi (6-6)		5.00	2.50
		Nos. 3007-3012 (6)		12.00	4.35

Yangtze River Highway Bridges — A855

2000, Mar. 26	Litho.	Perf. 12	
3013	A855	80f Wanxian (4-1)	.45	.30
3014	A855	80f Huangshi (4-2)	.45	.30
3015	A855	80f Tongling (4-3)	.45	.30
3016	A855	$2.80 Jiangyin (4-4)	1.75	.75
		Nos. 3013-3016 (4)	3.10	1.65

Landscapes in Dali — A856

Designs: No. 3017, Cangshan Mountain and Erhai Lake. No. 3018, Pagodas at Chongsheng Temple. No. 3019, Jizu Mountain. $2.80, Shibao Mountain.

Perf. 11¾x11½

2000, Apr. 19	Photo.		
3017	A856	80f multi (4-1)	.30	.25
3018	A856	80f multi (4-2)	.30	.25
3019	A856	80f multi (4-3)	.30	.25
3020	A856	$2.80 multi (4-4)	1.00	.70
		Nos. 3017-3020 (4)	1.90	1.45

Legend of Mulan — A857

Mulan: No. 3021, Weaving cloth. No. 3022, Joining army. No. 3023, On expedition. No. 3024, Returning home.

2000, Apr. 30	Litho.	Perf. 12	
3021	A857	80f multi (4-1)	.35	.30
3022	A857	80f multi (4-2)	.35	.30
3023	A857	80f multi (4-3)	.35	.30
3024	A857	80f multi (4-4)	.35	.30
a.		Strip, #3021-3024	2.50	2.50

Taer Lamasery A858

No. 3025, Good Luck Treasure Pagoda. No. 3026, Big Golden Tile Palace. No. 3027, Big Scripture Hall. $2.80, Banqen residence.

2000, May 5

3025	A858	80f multi (4-1)	.35	.30
3026	A858	80f multi (4-2)	.35	.30
3027	A858	80f multi (4-3)	.35	.30
3028	A858	$2.80 multi (4-4)	1.00	.75
		Nos. 3025-3028 (4)	2.05	1.65

Cai Chang and Li Fuchun A859

2000, May 22			
3029	A859	80f multi	.90	.30

Stampin' the Future Children's Stamp Design Contest Winners — A860

Various children's drawings: No. 3030, 30f, (8-1). No. 3031, 60f, (8-2). No. 3032, 60f, (8-3). No. 3033, 80f, (8-4). No. 3034, 80f, (8-5). No. 3035, 80f, (8-6). $2.60, (8-7). $2.80, (8-8).

Perf. 11½x11¼

2000, June 1	Photo.	
3030-3037	A860	Set of 8	3.75	2.50

Chen Yun (1905-95), Statesman A861

No. 3038, 80f, As a young man (4-1). No. 3039, 80f, In uniform, vert. (4-2). No. 3040, 80f, In black jacket, vert. (4-3). $2.80, As old man (4-4).

Perf. 13x13¼, 13¼x13

2000, June 13		
3038-3041	A861	Set of 4	2.75	1.50

Pots A862

Designs: No. 3042, 80f, Wine vessel (2-1). No. 3043, 80f, Horse milk pot (2-2).

2000, June 28	Litho.	Perf. 12	
3042-3043	A862	Set of 2	1.00	.50

See Kazakhstan No. 305.

Laoshan Mountain — A863

No. 3044, 80f, Huge Peak (4-1). No. 3045, 80f, Yangkou Bay (4-2). No. 3046, 80f, Beijiu Lake (4-3). $2.80, Taiqing Palace (4-4).

Perf. 11½x11¼

2000, July 15	Photo.	
3044-3047	A863	Set of 4	2.00	1.75
3047a		Souvenir sheet, #3044-3047	6.00	6.00

Souvenir Sheet

All-China Philatelic Federation, Fifth Congress — A864

2000, July 18	Litho.	Perf. 12	
3048	A864	$8 multi	6.00	5.50
a.		Margin ovptd. in gold	8.50	7.50

No. 3048a issued 9/21/01. It is inscribed in margin in gold "PJZ-13," "2001," with Chinese characters and Nanjing 2001 Philatelic Exhibition mascot.

Small Carp Leap Through Dragon Gate Legend — A865

No. 3049: a, Grandma Carp tells a story (5-1). b, Small Carp look for Dragon Gate (5-2). c, Help from Uncle Crab (5-3). d, Small Carp leap through Dragon Gate (5-4). e, Aunt Swallow passes on a letter (5-5).

2000, Aug. 8	Photo.	Perf. 11½	
3049	A865	80f Horiz. strip of 5, #a-e	2.75	2.40
f.		Booklet pane, #3049 + 2 labels, perf. 12	11.00	
		Booklet, #3049f	12.50	

Shenzhen Special Economic Zone — A866

No. 3050: a, 80f, Financial Center district (5-1). b, 80f, China Intl. Exhibition Center (5-2). c, 80f, Yantian Harbor area (5-3). d, 80f, Shenzhen Bay tourist area (5-4). e, $2.80, Shekou industrial district (5-5).

2000, Aug. 26	Litho.	Perf. 12	
3050	A866	Horiz. strip of 5, #a-e	2.75	2.50

2000 Summer Olympics, Sydney — A867

2000, Sept. 15	Photo.	Perf. 13¼x13	
3051	A867	$8 multi	4.25	4.25
a.		Sheet of 2	50.00	50.00

No. 3051a issued 10/31/00.

Beaches — A868

a, Coconuts Bay, PRC (2-1). b, Varadero Beach, Cuba (2-2).

2000, Sept. 26	Litho.	Perf. 12	
3052	A868	Pair	.90	.75
a.-b.		80f Any single	.85	.25

See Cuba Nos. 4108-4109.

Masks and Puppets A869

No. 3053, Tan background (2-1). No. 3054, Violet blue background (2-2).

2000, Oct. 9	Photo.	Perf. 13x13½	
3053-3054	A869	80f Set of 2	1.00	.60

See Brazil Nos. 2767-2768.

Relics from the Tomb of Prince Jing of Zhongshan — A870

No. 3055, 80f, Eternal Fidelity palace lamp (4-1). No. 3056, 80f, Bronze pot (4-2). No. 3057, 80f, Boshan incense burner (4-3). $2.80, Cup (4-4).

2000, Oct. 20		Perf. 13½x13¼	
3055-3058	A870	Set of 4	2.25	1.75

Ancient Thinkers — A871

No. 3059, 60f, Confucius (6-1). No. 3060, 80f, Mencius (6-2). No. 3061, 80f, Lao Zi (6-3). No. 3062, 80f, Zhuang Zi (6-4). No. 3063, 80f, Mo Zi (6-5). $2.80, Xun Zi (6-6).

Photo. & Engr.

2000, Nov. 11		Perf. 11¼x11	
3059-3064	A871	Set of 6	9.50	3.00

Test of Shenzhou Spacecraft, 1st Anniv. — A872

No. 3065: a, Launch (2-1). b, In orbit (2-2).

2000, Nov. 20	Photo.	Perf. 11½	
3065	A872	Pair	5.00	4.00
a.-b.		80f Any single	1.00	.35
c.		Sheet, 6 #3065	45.00	45.00

World Meteorological Organization, 50th Anniv. — A873

Designs: No. 3066, 80f, Weather satellite (4-1). No. 3067, 80f, Weather measuring equipment on Qinghai-Tibetan Plateau (4-2). No. 3068, 80f, Weather-predicting computer (4-3). $2.80, Airplane for cloud seeding (4-4).

2000, Nov. 22	Litho.	Perf. 12	
3066-3069	A873	Set of 4	2.00	1.50

Flowers — A874

No. 3070, 80f, Scarlet kaffir lily (4-1). No. 3071, 80f, Noble clivia (4-2). No. 3072, 80f, Golden striated lily (4-3). $2.80, White kaffir lily (4-4).

Perf. 11¼x11½
2000, Dec. 12 **Photo.**
3070-3073 A874 Set of 4 3.25 1.75
3073a Souv. sheet, #3070-3073 6.00 6.00

Ancient Bells — A875

No. 3074, 80f, Jingshu bell (4-1). No. 3075, 80f, Su chime bell (4-2). No. 3076, 80f, Jingyun bell (4-3). $2.80, Qianlong bell (4-4).

2000, Dec. 31 **Perf. 11¼x11½**
3074-3077 A875 Set of 4 2.25 1.60

Advent of New Millennium
A876

Designs: 60f, Sun, moon, date, time, building (5-1). No. 3079, 80f, Dove, Earth (5-2). No. 3080, 80f, Map, leaf, infant's hands (5-3). No. 3081, 80f, Circuitboard, head, Earth, horiz. (5-4). $2.80, Moon, stars, sundial (5-5).

2001, Jan. 1 **Litho.** **Perf. 12**
3078-3082 A876 Set of 5 5.00 2.00

New Year 2001 (Year of the Snake) — A877

Snake and: 80f, Flower (2-1). $2.80, Chinese character for snake (2-2).

Photo. & Engr.
2001, Jan. 5 **Perf. 11½x11¾**
3083 A877 80f multi 2.75 .75
a. Sheet of 6 17.50 17.50
3084 A877 $2.80 multi 3.25 1.25
a. Sheet of 6 24.00 24.00

Clown Roles in Peking Opera — A878

Designs: No. 3085, 80f, Tang Qin (6-1). No. 3086, 80f, Lin Lihua (6-2). No. 3087, 80f, Gao Lishi (6-3). No. 3088, 80f, Jiang Gan (6-4). No.

3089, 80f, Yang Xiangwu (6-5). $2.80, Shi Qian (6-6).

2001, Feb. 15 **Photo.** **Perf. 11½x11**
3085-3090 A878 Set of 6 2.75 2.00

Wildlife — A879

2001, Mar. 16 **Perf. 13¼x13**
3091 Sheet of 10 + 2 labels 10.00 9.00
a. A879 30f Budorcas taxicolor .25 .25
b. A879 60f Psephurus gladius .40 .40
c. A879 60f Elaphurus davidianus .40 .40
d. A879 80f Acipenser dabryanus .50 .50
e. A879 80f Capra ibex .50 .50
f. A879 80f Haliaeetus pelagicus .50 .50
g. A879 80f Camelus bactrianus .50 .50
h. A879 $1 Uncia uncia .65 .65
i. A879 $2.60 Martes zibellina 1.75 1.75
j. A879 $5.40 Saiga tatarica 3.50 3.50

Ancient Towns — A880

Designs: No. 3092, 80f, Zhouzhuang, Kunshan (6-1). No. 3093, 80f, Tongli, Wujiang (6-2). No. 3094, 80f, Wuzhen, Tongxiang (6-3). No. 3095, 80f, Nanxun, Huzhou (6-4). No. 3096, 80f, Luzhi, Wuxian (6-5). $2.80, Xitang, Jiashan (6-6).

2001, Apr. 7 **Photo.** **Perf. 11½x11¼**
3092-3097 A880 Set of 6 2.75 2.50
3097a Booklet pane, #3092-3097 + 6 labels 9.00
Booklet, #3097a 11.50

Strange Stories From a Chinese Studio, by Pu Songling
A881

Designs: 60f, Ying Ning (4-1). No. 3099, 80f, A Bao (4-2). No. 3100, 80f, Mask of Evildoer (4-3). $2.80, Stealing Peach (4-4). $8, Taoist Priest from Laoshan.

2001, Apr. 21 **Perf. 11½**
3098-3101 A881 Set of 4 2.25 2.00
Souvenir Sheet
Perf. 13½x13
3102 A881 $8 multi 10.00 10.00
No. 3102 contains one 90x60mm stamp.

Yongle Temple Murals
A882

No. 3103: a, Lady Queen Mother (4-1). b, Jade Lady Presenting Treasure (4-2). c, Celestial Worthy of the East (4-3). d, Venus and Mercury (4-4).

2001, May 5 **Litho.** **Perf. 12**
3103 Horiz. strip of 4 2.50 2.50
a. A882 60f multi .30 .25
b.-c. A882 80f Any single .40 .35
d. A882 $2.80 multi 1.10 .95

Mount Wudang — A883

Designs: 60f, Nanyan Hall (3-1). No. 3105, 80f, Zixiao Temple (3-2). No. 3106, 80f, Taizi Slope (3-3). $8, Golden Crown in spring.

Perf. 11¼x11½
2001, May 26 **Photo.**
3104-3106 A883 Set of 3 2.50 1.10
Souvenir Sheet
Perf. 12¼x12½
3107 A883 $8 multi + label 7.00 7.00
No. 3107 contains one 47x71mm stamp.

Ancient Chinese Receptacles
A884

Designs: No. 3108, 80f, Earthenware vase. No. 3109, 80f, Porcelain coffee pot.

2001, June 12 **Perf. 11¼x11½**
3108-3109 A884 Set of 2 1.00 .60
See Belgium Nos. 1858-1859.

Dragon Boat Festival
A885

Designs: No. 3110, Dragon boat race (3-1). No. 3111, Making Zongzi (3-2). $2.80, Expelling five poisons (3-3).

2001, June 25 **Photo.** **Perf. 13x13½**
3110 A885 80f multi .50 .30
a. Sheet of 9 9.50 —
3111 A885 80f multi .50 .30
a. Sheet of 9 9.50 —
3112 A885 $2.80 multi 1.25 1.00
a. Sheet of 9 32.50 —
Nos. 3110-3112 (3) 2.25 1.60
Nos. 3110-3112 each issued in sheets of 40.

Early Leaders of the Communist Party — A886

Designs: No. 3113, 80f, Wang Jinmei (5-1). No. 3114, 80f, Zhao Shiyan (5-2). No. 3115, 80f, Deng Enming (5-3). No. 3116, 80f, Cai Hesen (5-4). No. 3117, 80f, He Shuheng (5-5).

2001, June 28 **Perf. 11¼x11**
3113-3117 A886 Set of 5 3.50 2.00

Communist Party, 80th Anniv.
A887

2001, July 1 **Photo.** **Perf. 13x13¼**
3118 A887 80f multi 2.00 .40
a. Sheet of 8 40.00 —
No. 3118 issued in sheets of 40.

Emblem of 2008 Summer Olympics, Beijing — A888

2001, July 14 **Perf. 13x13¼**
3119 A888 80f multi + label .90 .60
a. Sheet of 36 + 39 labels 40.00 —
No. 3119 printed in sheets of 12 stamp + label pairs with one large central label. See Hong Kong No. 940, Macao No. 1067.
No. 3119a contains 12 each of No. 3119, Hong Kong No. 940 (with different adjacent label), and Macao No. 1067 (with different adjacent label).

Waterfalls
A889

Designs: No. 3120, 80f, Yinlianzhuitan (3-1). No. 3121, 80f, Doupotang, horiz. (3-2). No. 3122, 80f, Dishuitan (3-3). $8, Huangguoshu.

Perf. 12¼x12, 12x12¼
2001, July 22 A889 Set of 3 **Litho.**
3120-3122 A889 Set of 3 1.50 1.00
Souvenir Sheet
Perf. 12
3123 A889 $8 multi 7.00 7.00
No. 3123 contains one 40x60mm stamp.

Beidaihe Beach — A890

Designs: 60f, Pigeon Nest (4-1). No. 3125, 80f, Zhonghai Beach (4-2). No. 3126, 80f, Lianfeng Hill (4-3). $2.80, Tiger Stone (4-4).

2001, Aug. 5 **Litho.** **Perf. 12**
3124-3127 A890 Set of 4 2.00 1.75

21st Universiade
A891

Emblem, "2001" and: 60f, Concentric circles (3-1). 80f, Runners (3-2). $2.80, Hemispheres of globe (3-3).

2001, Aug. 22   **Litho.**
3128-3130 A891   Set of 3   1.75 1.40
3129a   Sheet of 20 +20 labels   22.50

No. 3129a exists with different margin designs.

Sheets of four No. 3129 plus four labels were not placed on sale but were included with 2001 year sets. Uncut sheets containing two of these sheets also exist.

Datong River Diversion Project — A892

Designs: No. 3131, 80f, Sluice gates (4-1). No. 3132, 80f, Xianming Gorge water pipeline (4-2). No. 3133, 80f, Tunnel (4-3). $2.80, Zhuanglang River Aqueduct (4-4).

2001, Aug. 26
3131-3134 A892   Set of 4   2.25 1.75

Wuhu Bridge — A893

View from: 80f, Shore (2-1). $2.80, Roadway (2-2).

Photo. & Engr.
2001, Sept. 20   **Perf. 11½x11¼**
3135-3136 A893   Set of 2   1.60 1.25

Orchids
A894

Designs: No. 3137, 80f, Paphiopedilum malipoense (4-1). No. 3138, 80f, Paphiopedilum dianthum (4-2). No. 3139, 80f, Paphiopedilum markianum (4-3). $2.80, Paphiopedilum appletonianum (4-4).

2001, Sept. 28   **Photo.**   **Perf. 12½**
3137-3140 A894   Set of 4   2.25 2.00
3140a   Souvenir sheet, #3137-   6.00
      3140

Ancient Gold Masks — A895

Designs: No. 3141, 80f, Mask of San Xing Dui (2-1). No. 3142, 80f, Funerary mask of King Tutankhamun, Egypt (2-2).

2001, Oct. 12   **Perf. 11¾x11½**
3141-3142 A895   Set of 2   2.25 1.25

See Egypt Nos. 1807-1808.

People's Republic of China as 2001 Asia-Pacific Economic Cooperation Head — A896

2001, Oct. 20   **Litho.**   **Perf. 12**
3143 A896 80f multi   .90 .35

Souvenir Sheet

Ertan Hydroelectric Plant — A897

2001, Oct. 20   **Litho.**   **Perf. 12¼**
3144 A897 $8 multi   3.75 3.75

Horses, Zhaoling Mausoleum A898

Horse: a, Facing right, galloping (6-1). b, Facing right, galloping, diff. (6-2). c, Facing right, walking (6-3). d, With attendant (6-4). e, Facing left, walking (6-5). f, Facing left, galloping (6-6).

2001, Oct. 28   **Photo.**   **Perf. 12**
Fawn Background

3145   Horiz. strip of 6   3.50 3.00
  a.   A898 60f multi   .30 .25
  b.-e.   A898 80f multi   .40 .30
  f.   A898 $2.80 multi   1.00 .90
  g.   Sheet, 2 each #3145a-3145c,
      white background, photo. &
      embossed   16.00 —
  h.   Sheet, 2 each #3145d-3145f,
      white background, photo. &
      embossed   16.00 —

Sailing Ships — A899

No. 3146: a, Chinese junk, 13th cent. (2-1). b, Portuguese caravel, 15th cent. (2-2).

2001, Nov. 8   **Perf. 13x13¼**
3146 A899 80f Horiz. pair, #a-b   1.40 1.00

See Portugal No. 2454.

9th Natl. Games — A900

No. 3147: a, 80f, Diving (2-1). b, $2.80, Volleyball (2-2).

2001, Nov. 11   **Litho.**   **Perf. 12**
3147 A900   Horiz. pair, #a-b   1.50 1.50
  c.   Souvenir sheet, #3147   3.75 3.75

Liupan Shan Mountains — A901

Various landscapes: No. 3148, 80f (4-1). No. 3149, 80f (4-2). No. 3150, 80f (4-3). $2.80, (4-4).

Photo. & Engr.
2001, Nov. 24   **Perf. 11¼x11½**
3148-3151 A901   Set of 4   2.25 2.00

Xiu Xian and the White Snake — A902

Designs: No. 3152, Women, umbrella (4-1). No. 3153, Three men (4-2). No. 3154, Man with sword, man with bowl (4-3). $2.80, Women on bridge (4-4).

Perf. 11½, 11½x11 (#3153-3154)
2001, Dec. 5   **Photo.**
3152 A902   80f multi   .40 .30
  a.   Booklet pane of 1   1.10 —
3153 A902   80f multi   .40 .30
  a.   Booklet pane of 1   1.10 —
3154 A902   80f multi   .40 .30
  a.   Booklet pane of 1   1.10 —
3155 A902 $2.80 multi   1.25 .90
  a.   Booklet pane of 1   4.00 —
     Booklet, #3152a-3155a   7.50
   Nos. 3152-3155 (4)   2.45 1.80

Admission to World Trade Organization A903

2001, Dec. 11   **Photo.**   **Perf. 13¼x13**
3156 A903 80f multi   1.40 1.25

Koxinga's Recovery of Taiwan from the Dutch, 340th Anniv. — A904

Koxinga and: No. 3157, 80f, Warriors, ships (3-1). No. 3158, 80f, Warriors, horse (3-2). $2.80, People, trees (3-3).

Perf. 11½x11¼
2001, Dec. 13   **Photo.**
3157-3159 A904   Set of 3   2.00 1.75

Souvenir Sheet

Qinhai - Tibet Railway — A905

2001, Dec. 29   **Perf. 13¼**
3160 A905 $8 multi   5.00 5.00

New Year 2002 (Year of the Horse) — A906

Designs: 80f, Ceramic horse (2-1). $2.80, Flowers, Chinese symbol for horse (2-2).

Photo. & Engr.
2002, Jan. 5   **Set of 2**   **Perf. 11½**
3161-3162 A906   Set of 2   5.50 2.75

Nos. 3161-3162 each exist in a miniature sheet of six. Value, each $20.

Art of Badashanren (1626-1705) A907

Designs: 60f, Two Eagles (6-1). No. 3164, 80f, Pine Tree (6-2). No. 3165, 80f, Lotus Flowers (6-3). 80f, Chysanthemum in Vase (6-4). $2.60, Two Magpies on a Rock (6-5). $2.80, Landscape After Dong Yuan (6-6).

Perf. 11¼x11½
2002, Jan. 20   **Photo.**
3163-3168 A907   Set of 6   4.25 4.00

Environmental Protection — A908

Designs: 5f, Keeping birth rate low. 10f, Forest conservation. 30f, Conservation of mineral resources. 60f, Preventing air pollution. 80f, Conservation of water. $1.50, Conservation of ocean resources.

Perf. 12¾x13¼ Syncopated
2002   **Photo.**
3169 A908   5f multi   .25 .25
3170 A908   10f multi   .30 .25
3171 A908   30f multi   .30 .25
3172 A908   60f multi   .35 .25
3173 A908   80f multi   .40 .25
3174 A908 $1.50 multi   .75 .40
   Nos. 3169-3174 (6)   2.35 1.65

Issued: 10f, 60f, 2/1; others, 4/1. See Nos. 3334-3335.

Birds — A909

Designs: 80f, Yellow-bellied tragopan. $1, Biddulph's ground jay. $2, Taiwan blue magpies. $4.20, Alashan redstart. $5.40, Kozlov's bunting.

2002   **Perf. 13¼**
3175 A909   80f multi   .40   .30
  a.   Booklet pane of 10 +2 labels   4.00
        Booklet, #3175a   4.00
3176 A909 $1 multi   .50   .35
3177 A909 $2 multi   .90   .65
3178 A909 $4.20 multi   1.60 1.25
3179 A909 $5.40 multi   2.00 1.50
      Nos. 3175-3179 (5)   5.40 4.05

Issued: 80f, $1, $2, 2/1; Nos. 3178, 3179, 4/1. No. 3175a, 12/7.
See Nos. 3336-3337, 3547-3548.

Flowers — A910

No. 3180: a, Camellia nitidissima (2-1). b, Couroupita guianensis (2-2).

2002, Feb. 5   **Perf. 13¼x13**
3180 A910   80f Horiz. pair, #a-b   1.10   .85
      See Malaysia Nos. 861-864.

Musical Instruments A911

Designs: 60f, Yaqin (5-1). No. 3182, 80f, Erhu (5-2). No. 3183, 80f, Banhu (5-3). No. 3184, 80f, Satar (5-4). $2.80, Matouqin (5-5).

2002, Feb. 23   **Litho.**   **Perf. 12**
3181-3185 A911   Set of 5   2.75 2.00

Souvenir Sheet

The Royal Carriage, by Yan Liben — A912

2002, Mar. 16   **Photo.**
3186 A912 $8 multi   12.00 9.00

Song Dynasty Pottery and Porcelain from Ruyao Kilns A913

Designs: 60f, Wine vessel (4-1). No. 3188, 80f, Three-legged basin (4-2). No. 3189, 80f, Bowl (4-3). $2.80, Dish (4-4).

2002, Mar. 30   **Litho.**
3187-3190 A913   Set of 4   2.50 2.00

Strange Stories from a Chinese Studio, by Pu Songling A914

No. 3191: a, 60f, Xi Fangping (4-1). b, 80f, Pianpian (4-2).
No. 3192: a, 80f, Tian Qilang (4-3). b, $2.80, Bai Qiulian (4-4).

2002, Apr. 21   **Photo.**   **Perf. 11½**
3191 A914   Vert. pair, #a-b   1.00   .90
3192 A914   Horiz. pair, #a-b   1.60 1.25

Qianshan Mountain — A915

No. 3193: a, Wuliang Taoist Temple (4-1). b, Maitreya Peak (4-2). c, Longquan Temple (4-3). d, Terrace of Immortals (4-4).

2002, Apr. 26   **Perf. 12**
3193 A915   Horiz. strip of 4   2.25 2.00
  a.-c.   80f Any single   .30   .25
  d. $2.80 multi   .90   .70

Ancient City of Lijiang — A916

Designs: No. 3194, 80f, Sifang Street (3-1). No. 3195, 80f, Stream, vert. (3-2). $2.80, House of Naxi people (3-3).

2002, May 1   **Perf. 11½**
3194-3196 A916   Set of 3   4.25 2.00
  a.   Souvenir sheet, #3194-3196 5.50 5.00

No. 3196a sold for $6.60.

Ruyi (Good Luck Symbol) — A917

2002, May 10   **Litho.**   **Perf. 12**
3197 A917 80f multi + label   .60   .30

Exists in miniature sheet of 4 + 4 vert. labels (value $6) and in sheet of 16 + 16 horiz. labels (value $20).

Stamps with Attached Labels

Starting with No. 3197, stamps listed as having attached labels are known to have been issued in dozens of different sheets having various margin and label designs, various numbers of stamps and labels in the sheets, and different stamp and label combinations. Little information has been made available about these sheets, and all seem to have been sold for prices significantly above face value. Labels on these sheets do not seem to have been personalizable with personal photos but have illustrations with approved designs.

2002 World Cup Soccer Championships, Japan and Korea — A918

No. 3198: a, 80f, Player (2-1). b, $2.80, Players (2-2).

2002, May 16   **Photo.**   **Perf. 12¼**
3198 A918   Horiz. pair, #a-b   1.50 1.25

A souvenir sheet containing People's Republic of China No. 3198, Hong Kong Nos. 978a-978b and Macao 1091a-1091b exists, and sold for premium over face value. Value $17.50.

Lighthouses A919

Nautical charts and: No. 3199, 80f, Maota Pagoda Lighthouse (5-1). No. 3200, 80f, Jiangxin Pagoda Lighthouses (5-2). No. 3201, 80f, Huaniaoshan Lighthouse (5-3). No. 3202, 80f, Laotieshan Lighthouse (5-4). No. 3203, 80f, Lin'gao Lighthouse (5-5).

Photo. & Engr.
2002, May 18   **Perf. 11½x11**
3199-3203 A919   Set of 5   2.25 1.50

Yellow River Dams A920

Designs: No. 3204, 80f, Lijia Gorge (4-1). No. 3205, 80f, Liujia Gorge (4-2). No. 3206, 80f, Qingtong Gorge (4-3). No. 3207, 80f, Sanmen Gorge (4-4). $8, Xiaolangdi, vert.

2002, June 8   **Photo.**   **Perf. 12**
3204-3207 A920   Set of 4   1.60 1.25

Souvenir Sheet
Perf. 13x13¼
3208 A920 $8 multi   3.50 3.00

No. 3208 contains one 40x60mm stamp.

Dazu Stone Carvings — A921

Designs: No. 3209, 80f, Avalokitesvara of the Sun and Moon, North Mountain (4-1). No. 3210, 80f, Samantabhadra, North Mountain (4-2). No. 3211, 80f, Three Avatamasaka Sages, Holy Summit Mountain (4-3). No. 3212, 80f, Statue in Cave of the Three Emperors, Stone Gate Mountain (4-4). $8, Avalokitesvara of a Thousand Hands, Holy Summit Mountain.

2002, June 18   **Litho.**   **Perf. 12**
3209-3212 A921   Set of 4   1.40 1.00

Souvenir Sheet
Photo.
Perf. 13x13¼
3213 A921 $8 multi   3.25 2.75

No. 3213 contains one 40x60mm stamp.

Desert Flowers A922

No. 3214: a, Ammopiptanthus mongolicus (4-1). b, Calligonum rubicandum (4-2). c, Hedysarum scoparium (4-3). d, Tamarix leptostachys (4-4).

2002, June 29 Photo.   Perf. 13x13¼
3214   Vert. strip of 4   1.75 1.50
  a.-c.   A922 80f Any single   .35   .25
  d.   A922 $2 multi   .70   .60

Antarctic Scenes A923

Designs: No. 3215, 80f, Penguins (3-1). No. 3216, 80f, Aurora Australis (3-2). $2, Bird, Grove Mountains (3-3).

2002, July 15   **Litho.**   **Perf. 12**
3215-3217 A923   Set of 3   1.75 1.25

Qinghai Lake — A924

Designs: No. 3218, 80f, Lake shore (3-1). No. 3219, 80f, Birds on rock (3-2). $2.80, View of lake and birds (3-3).

2002, July 20
3218-3220 A924   Set of 3   1.75 1.40

Early Communist Party Leaders — A925

Designs: No. 3221, 80f, Huang Gonglue (1898-1931) (5-1). No. 3222, 80f, Xu Jishen (1901-31) (5-2). No. 3223, 80f, Cai Shengxi (1906-32) (5-3). No. 3224, 80f, Wei Baqun (1894-1932) (5-4). No. 3225, 80f, Liu Zhidan (1903-36) (5-5).

2002, Aug. 1   **Photo.**
3221-3225 A925   Set of 5   3.25 2.00

Launch of First Manned Chinese Spacecraft A962

No. 3314: a, 80f, Astronaut, Shenzhou spacecraft (2-1). b, $2, Yang Liwei, flag (2-2).

2003, Oct. 16   **Perf. 13x13¼**
3314 A962   Pair, #a-b   11.50 7.50

A booklet containing No. 3314, Hong Kong No. 1062 and Macao No. 1128 exists. The booklet sold for a premium over face value. Value, $20.

Folktale of Liang Shanbo and Zhu Yingtai — A963

Designs: No. 3315, 80f, Zhu Yingtai, disguised as a man, and Liang Shanbo become sworn brothers at Caoqiao (5-1). No. 3316, 80f, Classmates for three years (5-2). No. 3317, 80f, Bidding farewell (5-3). No. 3318, 80f, Sad parting on the terrace (5-4). $2, Turning into butterflies (5-5).

2003, Oct. 18   **Perf. 12**
3315-3319 A963   Set of 5   3.00 1.75

A booklet containing booklet panes of 1 of each of Nos. 3315-3319 exists. Value, $7.50. A sheet exists containing 2 each of Nos. 3315-3319. Value, $25.

China 2003 Intl. Stamp Exhibition, Mianyang A964

2003, Nov. 20   **Photo.**   **Perf. 13¼**
3320 A964   80f multi   1.00 .60

World AIDS Day — A965

2003, Dec. 1   **Perf. 11¼x11**
3321 A965   80f multi   2.00 1.00

Mao Zedong (1893-1976) — A966

Mao: No. 3322, 80f, Seated in folding chair (4-1). No. 3323, 80f, Standing (4-2). No. 3324,

80f, Seated on bench (4-3). No. 3325, 80f, Seated at desk (4-4).

Litho. & Engr.
2003, Dec. 6   **Perf. 12**
3322-3325 A966   Set of 4   16.00 9.00

A sheet exists containing 2 each of Nos. 3322-3325 in se-tenant strips of 4. Value, $100.

Bronze Objects of Eastern Zhou Dyansty — A967

Designs: No. 3326, 60f, Square plate with turtle and fish patterns (8-1). No. 3327, 60f, Gui of the Duke of Qin (handled bowl with lid) (8-2). No. 3328, 80f, Iron-footed tripod of the King of Zhongshan (8-3). No. 3329, 80f, Gourd-shaped ladle of Yi, the Marquis of Zeng (8-4). No. 3330, 80f, Divine animal wine vessel, vert. (8-5). No. 3331, 80f, Wine vessel with phoenix pattern, vert. (8-6). $1, Square pot with lotus and cranes design, vert. (8-7). $2, Tripod with a dragon-shaped handle, vert. (8-8).

Perf. 11½x11¼, 11¼x11½
2003, Dec. 13   **Photo. & Engr.**
3326-3333 A967   Set of 8   6.25 3.00

A sheet of 8 No. 3328 exists. Value, $45.

Environmental Protection Type of 2002

Designs: 50f, Prevention and control of desertification. $4.50, Protection of biodiversity.

Perf. 12¾x13¼ Syncopated
2004, Jan. 1   **Photo.**
3334 A908   50f multi   .35 .35
3335 A908 $4.50 multi   1.50 .90

Bird Type of 2002

Designs: $5, Yellow-bellied tit. $6, Yunnan nuthatch.

2004, Jan. 1   **Perf. 13¼**
3336 A909 $5 multi   1.75 1.60
3337 A909 $6 multi   2.00 1.90

New Year 2004 (Year of the Monkey) A968

2004, Jan. 5   **Perf. 13 Syncopated**
3338 A968   80f multi   2.50 1.25
   a.   Booklet pane of 10   25.00
       Complete booklet, #3338a   27.00

Sheets of 4 and sheets of 6 exist. Value, set $70.

Taohuawu New Year Pictures — A969

Designs: No. 3339, 80f, Feelings of Pipa (4-1). No. 3340, 80f, Kylin Bringing a Son (4-2). No. 3341, 80f, Liu Hai Playing with the Golden Toad (4-3). $2, Ten Beauties Playing Football (4-4).

2004, Jan. 14   **Litho.**   **Perf. 12**
3339-3342 A969   Set of 4   1.50 1.25
3342a   Souvenir sheet, #3339-3342   7.00 5.50

A sheet of 2 each of Nos. 3339-3342 in se-tenant blocks of 4 exists. Value, $12.

Deng Yingchao (1904-92), Communist Party Leader — A970

No. 3343: a, Holding book. b, Portrait.

2004, Feb. 4   **Litho. & Engr.**
3343 A970   80f Vert. pair, #a-b   1.25 1.25

Suzhou Industrial Park, 10th Anniv. A971

2004, Mar. 1   **Photo.**   **Perf. 13x13¼**
3344 A971   80f multi   1.00 .50

See Singapore No. 1084.

Red Cross Society, Cent. — A972

2004, Mar. 10   **Perf. 11¼x11**
3345 A972   80f multi   .70 .35

Stories Explaining Chinese Idioms A973

Idioms: No. 3346, 80f, Trying to learn the Handan walk (4-1). No. 3347, 80f, Lord Ye's love for dragon (4-2). No. 3348, 80f, Filling a position in a Yu band (4-3). No. 3349, 80f, When the snipe and the clam grapple (4-4).

Perf. 12½x13¼ Syncopated
2004, Apr. 2
3346-3349 A973   Set of 4   1.75 1.25

A sheet of 2 each of Nos. 3346-3349 in se-tenant strips of 4 exists. Value, $15.

Peacocks — A974

Designs: No. 3350, 80f, Blue peacock (2-1). No. 3351, 80f, Albino peacock, vert. (2-2). $6, Green peacocks.

2004, Apr. 13   **Perf. 12¾**
3350-3351 A974   Set of 2   .80 .60

Souvenir Sheet
Perf. 13¼x13
3352 A974 $6 multi   4.00 3.25

No. 3352 contains one 60x40mm stamp

Nanxi River — A975

No. 3353: a, River and mountain (4-1). b, Tree and boat in foreground, mountains in background (4-2). c, Rocks, boat in river (4-3). d, Boat, spit of land with trees (4-4).

2004, Apr. 24   **Photo.**   **Perf. 12¾**
3353   Horiz. strip of 4   2.00 1.60
   a.   A975 60f multi   .30 .25
   b.-c.   A975 80f Either single   .40 .30
   d.   A975 $2 multi   .75 .55

Danxia Mountain — A976

Designs: 60f, Sengmao Peak (4-1). No. 3355, 80f, Xianlong Lake (4-2). No. 3356, 80f, Chahu Peak (4-3). $2, Jinjiang River (4-4).

2004, May 1   Litho. & Engr.   Perf. 12
3354-3357 A976   Set of 4   1.75 1.40

Economic and Technological Development Zones, 20th Anniv. — A977

2004, May 4   **Litho.**
3358 A977   80f multi   .80 .50

Exists in a sheet of 8 stamps + 8 labels. Value, $6.

Hometowns of Returned Chinese — A978

Designs: No. 3359, 80f, Xinglong Overseas Chinese Farm (4-1). No. 3360, 80f, Jinan University (4-2). No. 3361, 80f, Fuqing Rongqiao Development Zone (4-3). No. 3362, 80f, Kaiping (4-4).

2004, May 15   Photo.   Perf. 11x11¼
3359-3362 A978   Set of 4   1.40 1.10

Sima Guang Breaking the Vat — A979

Designs: No. 3363, 80f, Sima Guang falling into water (3-1). No. 3362, 80f, Breaking vat (3-2). No. 3363, $2, Rescued (3-3).

2004, June 1   **Perf. 12**
3363-3365 A979   Set of 3   1.40 1.25
   A sheet of 2 each of Nos. 3363-3365 exists. Value, $18.

Scenes of Villages of Southern Anhui Province A980

Designs: No. 3366, 80f, Archway (4-1). No. 3367, 80f, Old buildings (4-2). No. 3368, 80f, Buildings on South Lake (4-3). No. 3369, 80f, Moon Pond (4-4).

Photo. & Engr.
2004, June 25   **Perf. 11x11¼**
3366-3369 A980   Set of 4   1.40 1.25

Liu Yi Delivering a Letter — A981

Designs: No. 3370, 80f, Dragon Princess asking Liu Yi to deliver a letter (4-1). No. 3371, 80f, Delivering letter to Dongting Lake (4-2). No. 3372, 80f, Family reunion (4-3). $2, Couple embracing (4-4).

2004, July 17 Photo.   **Perf. 13¼x13**
3370 A981   80f multi   .35 .30
   a.   Booklet pane of 1   .75 —
3371 A981   80f multi   .35 .30
   a.   Booklet pane of 1   .75 —
3372 A981   80f multi   .35 .30
   a.   Booklet pane of 1   .75 —
3373 A981 $2 multi   .75 .30
   a.   Booklet pane of 1   2.00 —
    Complete booklet, #3370a-3373a   4.50
   Nos. 3370-3373 (4)   1.80 1.20
   Complete booklet sold for $6.

Souvenir Sheet

Eight Immortals Crossing the Sea — A982

2004, July 30   **Perf. 12 Syncopated**
3374 A982 $6 multi   4.50 4.00

Peony — A983

2004, July 31   **Litho.**   **Perf. 12¾**
3375 A983   80f multi + label   .65 .45
   Perf 12¾ examples come from a sheet containing four examples with labels below the stamps that also contain four No. 3261. The sheetlet sold for $15. Value, $17.50.

2004 Summer Olympics, Athens — A984

Olympic rings and: No. 3376, 80f, Parthenon, Athens (2-1). No. 3377, 80f, Hall of Good Harvest, Temple of Heaven, Beijing.

2004, Aug. 13   **Photo.**   **Perf. 12¾**
3376-3377 A984   Set of 2   1.00 1.00
   Perf. 12¾ examples come from a sheet containing four examples with labels below the stamps that also contain four No. 3261. The sheetlet sold for $15. Value, $17.50.
   See Greece Nos. 2124-2125.

Deng Xiaoping (1904-97), Chinese Leader — A985

Designs: No. 3378, 80f, Walking (2-1). No. 3379, 80f, Saluting, horiz. (2-2). $6, Seated.

2004, Aug. 22   **Perf. 12 Syncopated**
3378-3379 A985   Set of 2   2.00 1.10
Souvenir Sheet
Perf. 13 Syncopated
3380 A985 $6 multi   3.50 3.25
   No. 3380 contains one 47x57mm stamp.

South China Tiger A986

Designs: 80f, Head (2-1). $2, Adult and young (2-2).

2004, Aug. 23   **Litho.**   **Perf. 12**
3381-3382 A986   Set of 2   1.40 1.10
   A sheet of 4 each of Nos. 3381-3382 in setenant pairs exists. Value, $17.50.

People's Congress, 50th Anniv. — A987

Designs: No. 3383, 80f, Congress members arriving at Huairentang Hall of Zhongnanhai (2-1). No. 3384, 80f, Interior of Great Hall of the People (2-2).

2004, Sept. 15   **Perf. 13¼**
3383-3384 A987   Set of 2   1.25 1.00
   A sheet containing 3 pairs of Nos. 3383-3384 exists. Value, $15.

Bloodstone Seals A988

No. 3385: a, 80f, Seal of Emperor Qianlong (2-1). b, $2, Seal of Emperor Jiaqing (2-2).

Litho. & Embossed
2004, Sept. 17   **Perf. 13x13¼**
3385 A988   Pair, #a-b   1.50 1.10

Celery Wormwood A989

Designs: No. 3386, 80f, Purple flowers (4-1). No. 3387, 80f, Blue flowers (4-2). No. 3388, 80f, Red flowers (4-3). $2, Yellow flowers (4-4).

2004, Sept. 19   **Photo.**   **Perf. 13¼x13**
3386-3389 A989   Set of 4   1.75 1.50
   A sheet containing 2 strips of 3386-3389 exists. Value, $15.

Chinese and Romanian Handicrafts A990

Designs: No. 3390, 80f, Drum with tigers and birds, China (2-1). No. 3391, 80f, Cucuteni pottery jar, Romania (2-2).

2004, Sept. 22   **Perf. 13 Syncopated**
3390-3391 A990   Set of 2   1.10 1.00
   A sheet containing 4 pairs of Nos. 3390-3391 exists.
   See Romania No. 4668.

National Symbols A991

Designs: No. 3392, 80f, Flag (2-1). No. 3393, 80f, Arms, vert. (2-2).

Perf. 13¼x13 Syncopated, 13x13¼ Syncopated
2004, Sept. 30
3392-3393 A991   Set of 2   3.00 2.50
   A sheet of 4 self-adhesive examples of both Nos. 3392 and 3393 was included in a souvenir folder sold only at the International Stamp and Coin Expo in Beijing in 2004. Value, $35.

Landscapes of Chinese Borderlands — A992

Designs: No. 3394, 80f, Forest, Xing'an Mountains (12-1). No. 3395, 80f, Lake in Yalu River Basin (12-2). No. 3396, 80f, Reefs in Yellow Sea (12-3). No. 3397, 80f, Zhoushan Archipelago (12-4). No. 3398, 80f, Coast of Taiwan (12-5). No. 3399, 80f, Xisha Islands (12-6). No. 3400, 80f, Karst landscape, Southern Guangxi (12-7). No. 3401, 80f, Rain forest, Southern Yunnan (12-8). No. 3402, 80f, Mt. Qomolangma (12-9). No. 3403, 80f, Pamirs (12-10). No. 3404, 80f, Badain Jaran Desert (12-11). No. 3405, 80f, Hulun Buir Steppe (12-12).

2004, Oct. 1   **Perf. 12¾**
3394-3405 A992   Set of 12   3.75 3.00
3405a   Sheet of 12, #3394-3405 + central label   10.00 7.50

Buildings in China and Spain — A993

Designs: No. 3406, 80f, Jinmao Tower, China (2-1). No. 3407, 80f, Park Guell, Spain.

2004, Oct. 8   **Perf. 13¼x13**
3406-3407 A993   Set of 2   1.25 .90
   See Spain Nos. 3319-3320.

Miniature Sheet

The Festival of Pure Brightness on the River, by Zhang Zeduan — A994

No. 3408 — Various details from painting: a, 60f, Trees (9-1). b, 80f, Trees, people on horseback (9-2). c, 80f, Buildings, boats on river (9-3). d, 80f, Buildings, boats on river, diff. (9-4). e, 80f, Bridge (9-5). f, 80f, Buildings, boats on river (9-6). g, 80f, Buildings (9-7). h, $1, Tower (9-8). i, $2, Intersection (9-9).

Litho. & Engr.
2004, Oct. 18   **Perf. 12**
3408 A994   Sheet of 9, #a-i   18.00 15.00

Phoenix — A995

2004, Nov. 1   **Litho.**   **Perf. 12¾**
3409 A995   80f multi + label   .80 .30
   A sheet of 4 No. 3409 + label exists. Value, $6.
   A sheet of 10 serpentine die cut 12¼ self-adhesive stamps like No. 3409 + 10 labels depicting Snoopy for 25 yuan. Value, $15.

Pavilions — A996

Designs: No. 3410, 80f, Aiwan (4-1). No. 3411, 80f, Pipa (4-2). No. 3412, 80f, Lan (4-3). No. 3413, 80f, Zuiweng (4-4).

2004, Nov. 6 **Photo.** *Perf. 13¼x13*
3410-3413 A996 Set of 4 1.40 .90
A sheet of 2 each of Nos. 3410-3413 exists. Value, $13.

Ancient Calligraphy A997

Designs: No. 3414, 80f, Yiying stele (4-1). No. 3415, 80f, Zhangqian stele (4-2). No. 3416, 80f, Caoquan stele (4-3). No. 3417, 80f, Shimen song (4-4).

Photo. & Engr.
2004, Dec. 5 *Perf. 11¼x11*
3414-3417 A997 Set of 4 2.50 .90
A sheet of 2 each of Nos. 3414-3417 exists. Value, $10.

New Year 2005 (Year of the Rooster) A998

Perf. 13 Syncopated
2005, Jan. 5 **Photo.**
3418 A998 80f multi 1.00 .35
a. Booklet pane of 10 10.00 —
Complete booklet, #3418a 10.00
No. 3418 exists in sheets of 4 and 6. Value, $17 each.

Tarim-Baihe Gas Pipeline — A999

No. 3419: a, 80f, Derrick (2-1). b, $3, Pipes (2-2).

2005, Jan. 8 **Litho.** *Perf. 12*
3419 A999 Horiz. pair, #a-b 2.00 1.25

Historic Structures in Taiwan A1000

No. 3420: a, North Gate, Taipei City Wall (5-1). b, Confucian Temple (5-2). c, Longshan Temple, Lugang (5-3). d, Erkunshen Cannon Fort, Tainan (5-4). e, Matsu Temple, Penghu (5-5).

Perf. 13 Syncopated
2005, Jan. 30 **Litho. & Engr.**
3420 Vert. strip of 5 2.25 1.75
a.-d. A1000 80f Any single .30 .25
e. A1000 $1.50 multi .60 .45

Yangjiabu New Year Woodprints A1001

Designs: No. 3421, 80f, Door God (4-1). No. 3422, 80f, Abundance for year (4-2). No. 3423, 80f, Good news on New Year's Day (4-3). No. 3424, 80f, Goddess strewing flowers from heaven (4-4).

2005, Feb. 1 **Litho.** *Perf. 13¼x13*
3421-3424 A1001 Set of 4 1.50 .95
3424a Souvenir sheet, #3421-3424 4.50 2.50
No. 3424a sold for $4.80. A miniature sheet containing 2 of each stamp exists. Value, $12.

Magnolias A1002

Designs: No. 3425, 80f, Magnolia dennudata (4-1). No. 3426, 80f, Magnolia delavayi (4-2). No. 3427, 80f, Magnolia grandiflora (4-3). No. 3428, 80f, Magnolia liliflora (4-4).

2005, Mar. 5 **Photo.** *Perf. 13x13¼*
3425-3428 A1002 Set of 4 2.50 1.10

Great Wall of China — A1003

2005, Apr. 1 **Litho.** *Perf. 12¾*
3429 A1003 80f multi + label .60 .30
See note following No. 3462. See No. 3846A.

Earth Day — A1004

2005, Apr. 22 **Photo.** *Perf. 13¼*
3430 A1004 80f multi .80 .30
A ring of syncopated perforations surrounds the vignette.

Jigong Mountains A1005

No. 3431: a, Mountain at daybreak (4-1). b, Garden in clouds (4-2). c, Moon Pond (4-3). d, Black Dragon Waterfall (4-4).

Perf. 12½ Syncopated
2005, Apr. 28 **Litho.**
3431 Horiz. strip of 4 1.50 1.25
a.-d. A1005 80f Any single .35 .25

All-China Federation of Trade Unions, 80th Anniv. — A1006

2005, May 1 *Perf. 12*
3432 A1006 80f multi 3.50 .40

Paintings of Flower Arrangements A1007

Designs: No. 3433, 80f, Magnolia Flowers, by Chen Hongshou (2-1). No. 3434, 80f, Flower Vase in a Window Niche, by Ambrosius Bosschaert the Elder (2-2).

Perf. 12½ Syncopated
2005, May 18 **Photo.**
3433-3434 A1007 Set of 2 1.25 .50
See Liechtenstein Nos. 1315-1316.

Dalian Bay Area Views — A1008

No. 3435: a, Tiger Beach (4-1). b, Bangchui Island (4-2). c, Golden Pebble Beach (4-3). d, Lushunkou (4-4).

2005, May 21 *Perf. 12¾ Syncopated*
3435 Horiz. strip of 4 1.50 1.25
a.-d. A1008 80f Any single .35 .25

Fudan University, Cent. A1009

Litho., Engr. & Embossed
2005, May 27 *Perf. 12*
3436 A1009 80f multi .80 .25

Hans Christian Andersen (1805-75), Author A1010

No. 3437 — Fairy tales by Andersen: a, The Emperor's New Clothes (5-1). b, The Little Mermaid (5-2). c, Thumbelina (5-3). d, The Little Match Girl (5-4). e, The Ugly Duckling (5-5).

Perf. 13¼ Syncopated
2005, June 1 **Photo.**
3437 Horiz. strip of 5 2.00 1.40
a.-e. A1010 60f Any single .30 .25
f. Booklet pane of 1, #3437a .50 —
g. Booklet pane of 1, #3437b .50 —
h. Booklet pane of 1, #3437c .50 —
i. Booklet pane of 1, #3437d .50 —
j. Booklet pane of 1, #3437e .50 —
Complete booklet, #3437f-3437j 5.00
The complete booklet sold for $6.
A sheet of ten serpentine die cut 10 self-adhesive stamps containing two of each of the designs of Nos. 3437a-3437e and ten labels exists. Value, $12.

Voyages of Admiral Zheng He, 600th Anniv. — A1011

No. 3438: a, Admiral Zheng He (3-1). b, Building, map of voyages (3-2). c, Compass, drawing of ship (3-3) $6, Ship, horiz.

2005, June 28 **Litho.**
3438 Horiz. strip of 3 1.50 1.00
a.-c. A1011 80f Any single .30 .25
Souvenir Sheet
3439 A1011 $6 multi 3.00 2.50
No. 3439 contains one 70x50mm stamp.

Nantong Museum — A1012

No. 3440: a, Southern Hall (2-1). b, Central Hall (2-2).

Photo. & Engr.
2005, July 16 *Perf. 12½x12¾*
3440 A1012 80f Horiz. pair, #a-b 1.10 .75

Xianghai National Nature Reserve — A1013

Designs: No. 3441, 80f, Red-crowned cranes in nest (4-1). No. 3442, 80f, Three birds in flight, trees (4-2). No. 3443, 80f, Birds at lake (4-3). No. 3444, 80f, Eagles flying above steppe (4-4).

2005, July 30 **Photo.** *Perf. 12¾*
3441-3444 A1013 Set of 4 1.50 .90

Miniature Sheet

People's Army Generals — A1014

No. 3445: a, Yang Jingyu (5-1). b, Zuo Quan (5-2). c, Peng Xuefeng (5-3). d, Luo Binghui (5-4). e, Guan Xiangying (5-5).

2005, Aug. 1   **Perf. 12**
3445 A1014 80f Sheet of 10, 2
    each #a-e   7.00   4.75

End of World War II, 60th
Anniv. — A1015

No. 3446: a, Soldiers with machine guns (4-1). b, Bugler (4-2). c, Soldier holding gun, troops landing in Normandy (4-3). d, Conquering Berlin (4-4).
$6, Dove, vert.

Perf. 12¾ Syncopated
2005, Aug. 15   **Litho.**
3446 A1015 80f Block of 4, #a-d   1.50   .90
Souvenir Sheet
Photo.
Perf. 12¾
3447 A1015 $6 multi   3.00   2.00

Tibet Autonomous Region, 40th
Anniv. — A1016

2005, Aug. 26   **Photo.**   **Perf. 13¼**
3448 A1016 80f multi   1.00   .30

Chinese Motion
Pictures,
Cent. — A1017

2005, Aug. 28   **Litho.**   **Perf. 12¾x13**
3449 A1017 80f multi   .70   .25

Exists in a sheet of 8 stamps + 8 labels.

"Five Happinesses Arrive" — A1018

2005, Sept. 16   **Perf. 12¾**
3450 A1018 80f multi + label   1.00   .35

See note following No. 3462.

Fanjing
Mountain
Nature
Reserve
A1019

No. 3451: a, Golden Summit (4-1). b, Mushroom Rock (4-2). c, Forest (4-3). d, Heiwan River (4-4).

2005, Sept. 18   **Photo.**   **Perf. 13x13¼**
3451   Horiz. strip of 4   1.75   1.40
    a.-d.   A1019 80f Any single   .35   .25

Farm
Technology
A1020

Sheep and: No. 3452, 80f, Chinese water wheel (2-1). No. 3453, 80f, Dutch windmill (2-2).

2005, Sept. 22   **Perf. 12**
3452-3453 A1020   Set of 2   1.40   .50

See Netherlands Nos. 1203-1204.

Miniature Sheet

People's Liberation Army
Generals — A1021

No. 1021: a, Su Yu (10-1). b, Xu Haidong (10-2). c, Huang Kecheng (10-3). d, Chen Geng (10-4). e, Tan Zheng (10-5). f, Xiao Jinguang (10-6). g, Zhang Yunyi (10-7). h, Luo Ruiqing (10-8). i, Wang Shusheng (10-9). j, Xu Guangda (10-10).

Litho. & Engr.
2005, Sept. 27   **Perf. 13¼x13**
3454 A1021 80f Sheet of 10, #a-j   4.75   3.25

Miniature Sheet

Goddess of the River Luo, by Gu
Kaizhi — A1022

Various painting details with width of: a, 50mm (10-1). b, 50mm (10-2). c, 60mm (10-3). d, 40mm (10-4). e, 60mm (10-5). f, 60mm (10-6). g, 60mm (10-7). h, 50mm (10-8). i, 40mm (10-9). j, 50mm (10-10).

2005, Sept. 28   **Perf. 12**
3455 A1022 80f Sheet of 10,
    #a-j   12.00   8.50

Xinjiang Uygur Autonomous Region,
50th Anniv. — A1023

No. 3456: a, Male dancers and musicians (3-1). b, Male and female dancers (3-2). c, Women carrying plates of food (3-3).

Perf. 12x12½ Syncopated
2005, Oct. 1   **Litho.**
3456 A1023   Horiz. strip of 3   1.25   1.00
   a.-c.   80f Any single   .30   .25

Souvenir Sheet

10th National Games, Jiangsu
Province — A1024

2005, Oct. 12   **Photo.**   **Perf. 12¾**
3457 A1024 $6 multi   2.50   2.00

Wild Cats
A1025

Designs: No. 3458, 80f, Panthera pardus orientalis (2-1). No. 3459, 80f, Puma concolor (2-2).

2005, Oct. 13   **Photo.**   **Perf. 13x13¼**
3458-3459 A1025   Set of 2   1.20   .50

See Canada Nos. 2122-2123.

"Be Safe Every Year" — A1026

2005, Nov. 6   **Litho.**   **Perf. 13¼**
3460 A1026 80f red & blk + label 3.50   1.00

A serpentine die cut 10 self-adhesive stamp of type A1026 exists. Value, $22.50.

Relics From Chengtoushan
Archaeological Site — A1027

2005, Nov. 6   **Photo.**   **Perf. 12½**
3461 A1027 80f multi   .70   .25

"Beam With Delight" — A1028

2005, Nov. 11   **Litho.**   **Perf. 12¾**
3462 A1028 80f multi + label   1.10   .25

A sheet of 2 each of Nos. 3429, 3450 and 3462 exists. Value, $6.

2008 Summer
Olympics,
Beijing — A1029

Designs: No. 3463, Beijing Olympics emblem, Olympic rings (6-1).
No. 3464 — Beijing Olympic mascots with emblem on chest: a, Beibei (6-2). b, Jingjing (6-3). c, Huanhuan (6-4). d, Yingying (6-5). e, Nini (6-6).
No. 3465: a, Like #3463. b, Like #3464a. c, Like #3464b. d, Like #3464c. e, Like #3464d. f, Like #3464e.

2005, Nov. 12   **Photo.**   **Perf. 13¼x13**
3463 A1029 80f multi   .50   .25
3464 A1029 80f Horiz. strip of
    5, #a-e   11.00   8.50
Self-Adhesive
Serpentine Die Cut 11¾
3465 A1029 80f Sheet, 2 each
    #a-f   40.00   40.00

A sheet of 5 30x30mm stamps with the Beijing Olympics emblem and Olympic rings was issued in 2008. Value, $15.

New Year
2006 (Year of
the Dog)
A1030

Perf. 13 Syncopated
2006, Jan. 5   **Photo.**
3466 A1030 80f multi   1.00   .25
  a.   Sheet of 6   10.00   7.25
  b.   Booklet pane of 10   5.00
       Complete booklet, #3466b   6.00

A sheet of 4 exists that was a giveaway for standing-order customers. Value, $9.

Wuqiang New
Year Woodprints
A1031

Designs: No. 3467, 80f, Being Safe All Year Round (4-1). No. 3468, 80f, Five Blessings Approach Your Door (4-2). No. 3469, 80f, Flower of Prosperity Blossoms (4-3). No. 3470, 80f, Lion Rolling the Embroidered Ball (4-4).

Litho. & Engr.
2006, Jan. 22   **Perf. 12**
3467-3470 A1031   Set of 4   1.75   1.00
3470a   Souvenir sheet, #3467-3470   4.50   2.50
3470b   Souvenir sheet, 2 each
    #3467-3470   9.00   6.00

Lanterns
A1032

Designs: No. 3471, 80f, Fish lantern (5-1). No. 3472, 80f, Chinese white cabbage lantern (5-2). No. 3473, 80f, Lotus lantern (5-3). No. 3474, 80f, Dragon and phoenix lantern (5-4). $1.50, Butterfly lantern (5-5).

2006, Feb. 12 Photo. Perf. 13¼x13
3471-3475 A1032 Set of 5 4.50 2.50
3475a Sheet, 2 each #3471-3475 12.00 6.00

Abolition of Agricultural Tax — A1033

Perf. 13½ Syncopated
2006, Feb. 22
3476 A1033 80f multi 7.00 1.25

Lijiang River — A1034

No. 3477: a, Yangdi (4-1). b, Langshi. c, Huangbu (4-3). d, Xingping (4-4).

2006, Feb. 25 Perf. 12¾
3477 A1034 Horiz. strip of 4 3.75 1.75
a.-d. 80f Any single .60 .25

Relic Plants — A1035

Designs: No. 3478, 80f, Ginkgo biloba (4-1). No. 3479, 80f, Glyptostrobus pensilis (4-2). No. 3480, 80f, Davidia involucrata (4-3). No. 3481, 80f, Liriodendron chinense (4-4).

Perf. 12x12¼ Syncopated
2006, Mar. 12 Litho.
3478-3481 A1035 Set of 4 5.00 1.50

Dogs
A1036

Designs: Nos. 3482, 3486a, 80f, Pekingese (4-1). Nos. 3483, 3486b, 80f, Pug, vert. (4-2). Nos. 3484, 3486c, 80f, Chow chow (4-3). Nos. 3485, 3486d, 80f, Tibetan mastiff, vert. (4-4).

Perf. 13¼ Syncopated
2006, Mar. 19 Litho. & Engr.
3482-3485 A1036 Set of 4 2.00 1.40

Self-Adhesive
Serpentine Die Cut 11¾ on 2 Sides
3486 A1036 80f Sheet, 2 each
#3486a-3486d 11.00 *7.00*

Qingcheng Mountain
A1037

Designs: 60f, Remote mountain gate (4-1). No. 3488, 80f, Winding path (4-2). No. 3489, 80f, Ancient temple (4-3). No. 3490, 80f, Spring (4-4).

2006, Apr. 12 Perf. 13¼ Syncopated
3487-3490 A1037 Set of 4 3.50 1.50

Statues in Yungang Grottoes — A1038

Designs: No. 3491, 80f, Sakyamuni (4-1). No. 3492, 80f, Bodhisattva (4-2). No. 3493, 80f, Head of Bodhisattva (4-3). No. 3494, 80f, Xieshi Bodhisattva (4-4).
$6, Sakyamuni, diff.

Perf. 13¼x13½ Syncopated
2006, Apr. 13 Photo.
3491-3494 A1038 Set of 4 5.00 1.00

Souvenir Sheet
Perf. 13 Syncopated
3495 A1038 $6 multi 3.50 3.00
No. 3495 contains one 40x60mm stamp.

Tianzhu Mountain — A1039

Designs: 60f, Green Dragon Mountain Stream (4-1). No. 3497, 80f, Taoist Practice Terrace (4-2). No. 3498, 80f, Sanzu Temple (4-3). No. 3499, 80f, Qingtian Peak (4-4).

2006, Apr. 22 Perf. 11½x11¼
3496-3499 A1039 Set of 4 2.50 1.00

Scientists
A1040

Designs: No. 3500, 80f, Liang Xi (1883-1958), forester (4-1). No. 3501, 80f, Mao Yisheng (1896-1989), civil engineer (4-2). No. 3502, 80f, Yan Jici (1900-96), physicist (4-3). No. 3503, 80f, Zhou Peiyuan (1902-93), physicist (4-4).

Litho. & Engr.
2006, May 13 Perf. 12
3500-3503 A1040 Set of 4 6.25 2.25

Lighthouses — A1041

No. 3504: a, Dagu Lighthouse (4-1). b, Guishan Island Lighthouse (4-2). c, Wusongkou Lighthouse (4-3). d, Mulantou Lighthouse (4-4).

2006, May 22 Photo. Perf. 12¾
3504 A1041 Horiz. strip of 4 3.25 2.25
a.-d. 80f Any single .50 .25

Chinese Space Program, 50th Anniv. — A1042

No. 3505: a, Geospace Double Star Exploration (2-1). b, Shenzhou 6 (2-2).

Perf. 12x11¼ Syncopated
2006, June 8 Litho.
3505 A1042 80f Horiz. pair, #a-b 2.25 1.25

Silver and Gold Objects — A1043

Designs: No. 3506, 80f, Jeeweled Qing Dynasty cup, China (2-1). No. 3507, 80f, Tankard with Biblical designs, by Peter Rohde, Poland.

2006, June 20 Photo. Perf. 13¼x13
3506-3507 A1043 Set of 2 2.00 .65
See Poland No. 3829.

Olympic Rings and Emblem of 2008 Summer Olympics, Beijing — A1043a

2006, June 23 Litho. Perf. 12
3507A A1043a 80f multi + label 1.25 .45

Printed in sheets of 15 stamps + 15 labels, sheets of 5 stamps + 5 labels, sheets of 4 stamps + 4 labels to right of stamps, sheets of 4 stamps + 4 labels below stamps, and sheets of 8 stamps + 8 labels. Value, set of 5 sheets $50.

Early Communist Leaders
A1044

Designs: No. 3508, 80f, Gao Junyu (1896-1925) (5-1). No. 3509, 80f, Wang Hebo (1882-1927) (5-2). No. 3510, 80f, Su Zhaozheng (1885-1929) (5-3). No. 3511, 80f, Peng Pai (1896-1929) (5-4). No. 3512, 80f, Deng Xhongxia (1894-1933) (5-5).

2006, June 30 Litho. & Engr.
3508-3512 A1044 Set of 5 *30.00 17.50*

Opening of Qinghai-Tibet Railway — A1045

Designs: No. 3513, 80f, Bridge across Kekexili, antelopes (3-1). No. 3514, 80f, Train crossing Danggula Mountains, cattle (3-2). No. 3515, 80f, Lhasa Railway Station, birds (3-3).

Perf. 12½x12 Syncopated
2006, July 1 Litho.
3513-3515 A1045 Set of 3 7.25 2.50

Kanasi Nature Reserve — A1046

Designs: No. 3516, 80f, Kanasi Lake (4-1). No. 3517, 80f, Crouching Dragon Bend (4-2). No. 3518, 80f, Celestial Bend (4-3). No. 3519, 80f, Moon Bend (4-4).

2006, July 8 Photo. Perf. 12¾
3516-3519 A1046 Set of 4 6.50 2.25

Earthquake Protection and Damage Mitigation
A1047

2006, July 26 Perf. 13½x13
3520 A1047 80f multi 4.25 .75

2008 Summer Olympics, Beijing — A1048

Designs: Nos. 3521, 3525a, 60f, Basketball (4-1). Nos. 3522, 3525b, 80f, Fencing (4-2). Nos. 3523, 3525c, Sailing (4-3). Nos. 3524, 3525d, $3, Gymnastics (4-4).

2006, Aug. 8 Photo. Perf. 13¼x13
3521-3524 A1048 Set of 4 3.25 2.00

Self-Adhesive
Serpentine Die Cut 11¾
3525 A1048 Sheet of 8, 2
each #a-d 16.00 *11.00*

Portions of the designs of Nos. 3525a-3525d were applied by a thermographic process, producing a shiny, raised effect.

Treasures of the Study — A1049

Designs: No. 3526, 80f, Brushes (4-1). No. 3527, 80f, Ink (4-2). No. 3528, 80f, Paper (4-3). No. 3529, 80f, Ink stone (4-4).

Perf. 12x12½ Syncopated
2006, Sept. 10　　　**Litho.**
3526-3529　A1049　Set of 4　8.00　3.00

A sheet of 2 each of Nos. 3526-3529 exists. Value, $60.

All-China Federation of Returned Overseas Chinese, 50th Anniv. A1050

Perf. 12½x12 Syncopated
2006, Sept. 25
3530　A1050　80f multi　　　1.00　.30

Musical Instruments — A1051

Designs: No. 3531, 80f, Seven-stringed qin, China (2-1). No. 3532, 80f, Bösendorfer piano, Austria (2-2).

Perf. 13x12½ Syncopated
2006, Sept. 26　　　**Litho.**
3531-3532　A1051　Set of 2　2.50　.60

See Austria Nos. 2066-2067.

Chinese Export Commodities Fair — A1052

Perf. 13½x13¼ Syncopated
2006, Oct. 15　　　**Photo.**
3533　A1052　80f multi　　　1.00　.25

Long March, 70th Anniv. — A1053

Designs: No. 3534, 80f, Setting Out (4-1). No. 3535, 80f, Zunyi Conference (4-2). No. 3536, 80f, Speedily Occupy the Luding Bridge (4-3). No. 3537, 80f, The Red Army Through the Marshland (4-4).
$6, Reunion.

2006, Oct. 22　　　**Perf. 13x13¼**
3534-3537　A1053　Set of 4　3.75　1.75
Souvenir Sheet
3538　A1053　$6 multi　　　4.50　3.75

No. 3538 contains one 80x50mm stamp. A souvenir sheet of one of No. 3535 exists. No. 3538 exists imperf.

Dialogue With ASEAN, 15th Anniv. A1054

Perf. 12½x12 Syncopated
2006, Oct. 30　　　**Litho.**
3539　A1054　80f multi　　1.50　.30

"Enjoying Prosperity Year After Year" A1055

"Happy New Year" — A1055a

Perf. 12¾ Syncopated
2006, Nov. 1　　　**Photo.**
3540　A1055　80f multi　　.30　.25
3541　A1055a　$3 multi　　1.10　.85

A souvenir sheet containing Nos. 3540-3541 exists. Value, $12.
See note following No. 3628. See Nos. 3708a, 3869b, 3978a, 4238a, 4326a.

Beijing Summit of Forum on China-Africa Cooperation — A1056

2006, Nov. 3　**Litho.**　**Perf. 13¼**
3542　A1056　80f multi　　1.25　.25

Buildings Associated With Dr. Sun Yat-sen (1826-1925) A1057

Designs: No. 3543, 80f, Sun Yat-sen Villa (4-1). No. 3544, 80f, Mausoleum (4-2). No. 3545, 80f, Sun Yat-sen Memorial Hall (4-3). No. 3546, 80f, Sun Yat-sen University (4-4).

Perf. 13¼ Syncopated
2006, Nov. 12　　**Litho. & Engr.**
3543-3546　A1057　Set of 4　5.00　1.75

Birds Type of 2002

Designs: 40f, Chinese monal pheasant. $1.20, Taiwan yuhinas.

Perf. 13½ Syncopated
2006, Nov. 15　　　**Photo.**
3547　A909　40f multi　　.30　.25
3548　A909　$1.20 multi　　.45　.35

Heavenly Steed, Silk Roll Painting — A1058

No. 3549: a, Horse and rider. b, People looking at horse.

2006, Dec. 3　**Photo.**　**Perf. 12¾**
3549　A1058　$1.20 Horiz. pair,
　　　#a-b　　2.00　1.25

Wu Lanfu (1906-88), Politician A1059

2006, Dec. 23　　**Perf. 13¼x13**
3550　A1059　$1.20 multi　11.50　4.00

Trains — A1060

Designs: No. 3551, $1.20, Locomotive, blue background (4-1). No. 3552, $1.20, Locomotive, red brown background (4-2). No. 3553, $1.20, Box car (4-3). No. 3554, $1.20, Log cars and gateway (4-4).
$6, Locomotive and city skyline.

2006, Dec. 28　　**Perf. 13x13¼**
3551-3554　A1060　Set of 4　27.50　12.00
Souvenir Sheet
Perf. 13¼x13
3555　A1060　$6 multi　16.00　12.00

No. 3555 contains one 90x40mm stamp.

China Post, 110th Anniv. — A1061

Perf. 12x11½ Syncopated
2006, Dec. 30　　　**Litho.**
3556　A1061　$1.20 multi　1.50　.60

A sheet containing 6 No. 3556 exists. Value, $8.50.

New Year 2007 (Year of the Pig) — A1062

Perf. 13 Syncopated
2007, Jan. 5　　　**Photo.**
3557　A1062　$1.20 multi　1.00　.35
　　a.　Souvenir sheet of 6　12.00　6.00
　　b.　Booklet pane of 10　6.00　—
　　　　Complete booklet, #3557b　6.25

A sheet containing 4 No. 3557 exists. Value, $12.50.

6th Asian Winter Games — A1063

Perf. 12x12½ Syncopated
2007, Jan. 28　　　**Litho.**
3558　A1063　$1.20 multi　2.00　.35

Shiwan Pottery Figurines A1064

Designs: No. 3559, $1.20, Ta Xue Xun Mei (2-1). No. 3560, $1.20, Wang Zhaojun Chu Sai (2-2).

2007, Feb. 3　**Photo.**　**Perf. 13¼x13**
3559-3560　A1064　Set of 2　1.00　.65
3560a　　Miniature sheet, 4 each
　　　　#3559-3560　8.00　3.50

"Divine Birds of the Sun" — A1065

2007, Feb. 9　**Litho.**　**Perf. 12**
3561　A1065　$1.20 multi + label　.65　.35

Printed in sheets of 6 + 6 labels (value, $11), 8 + 8 labels and 15 + 15 labels (value, $20).

Mianzhu New Year Woodcuts A1066

Designs: No. 3562, $1.20, Zuo Zuo Ti Dao (4-1). No. 3563, $1.20, Mu Guiying (4-2). No. 3564, $1.20, Shuang Xi Tong Zi (4-3). No. 3565, $1.20, Zhang Xian She Gou (4-4).

Perf. 12x11½ Syncopated
2007, Feb. 10　　**Litho. & Engr.**
3562-3565　A1066　Set of 4　2.25　1.50
3565a　　Souvenir sheet of 4, #3562-3565　3.00　2.50
3565b　　Miniature sheet of 8, 2 each
　　　　#3562-3565　10.00　8.00

A lithographed sheet similar to No. 3565b on a textured silk-faced paper exists.

Beijing Opera — A1067

Designs: 80f, Lin Xiangru (6-1). No. 3567, $1.20, Song Shijie (6-2). No. 3568, $1.20, Zhou Yu (6-3). No. 3569, $1.20, Xu Xian (6-4). No. 3570, $1.20, Gao Chong (6-5). No. 3571, $1.20, Ren Tanghui (6-6).

2007, Mar. 10　**Photo.**　**Perf. 13¼x13**
3566-3571　A1067　Set of 6　2.75　2.00

Postal Savings Bank — A1068

2007, Mar. 20   **Perf. 12¾**
3572 A1068 $1.20 multi   .65   .35
    a.   Miniature sheet of 8   9.00   4.50

Writings of
Li Keran
A1069

Designs: No. 3573, $1.20, Man viewing waterfall (6-1). No. 3574, $1.20, Mountains with red-leaved trees (6-2). No. 3575, $1.20, People looking at scroll (6-3). No. 3576, $1.20, Crane flying above man under tent (6-4). No. 3577, $1.20, Cattle and driver in pond (6-5). No. 3578, $1.20, Raining in Jiangnan (6-6).

Perf. 13x13¼ Syncopated
2007, Mar. 26
3573-3578 A1069   Set of 6   4.50   2.25

Modern
Chinese
Drama,
Cent.
A1070

Perf. 13 Syncopated
2007, Apr. 6   **Litho.**
3579 A1070 $1.20 multi   .60   .35

Yangzhou Garden — A1071

No. 3580: a, He Garden (3-1). b, Ge Garden (3-2). c, Xu Garden (3-3).

Perf. 12x11½ Syncopated
2007, Apr. 8
3580 A1071   Horiz. strip of 3   1.75   1.40
    a.-c. $1.20 Any single   .50   .35

Dances — A1072

Designs: No. 3581, $1.20, Dragon dance (2-1). No. 3582, $1.20, Lion dance (2-2).

2007, Apr. 13   **Litho.**   **Perf. 12¾x13**
3581-3582 A1072   Set of 2   1.40   .70
    See Indonesia No. 2100.

Torch Relay for 2008 Summer
Olympics, Beijing — A1073

2007, Apr. 27   **Perf. 12**
3583 A1073 $1.20 multi + label   1.75   .60
    a.   Sheet of 4 + 4 labels   3.00   2.50

Inner Mongolia Autonomous Region,
60th Anniv. — A1074

Designs: No. 3584, $1.20, Horsemen, wrestlers, archer (2-1). No. 3585, $1.20, Seven women (2-2).

Perf. 12½x12 Syncopated
2007, May 1
3584-3585 A1074   Set of 2   1.00   .70
3585a   Souvenir sheet, #3584-3585   2.75   2.25

Mausoleums of
Qing Emperors
A1075

Designs: No. 3586, $1.20, Zhaoling Mausoleum (3-1). No. 3587, $1.20, Xiaoling Mausoleum (3-2). No. 3588, Tailing Mausoleum (3-3).

2007, May 12   **Photo.**   **Perf. 12¾**
3586-3588 A1075   Set of 3   1.25   1.00

Tongji
University,
Cent.
A1076

2007, May 20   *Perf. 12½ Syncopated*
3589 A1076 $1.20 multi   .60   .40

Kong Rong and Pears — A1077

Nos. 3590 and 3591: a, Denomination at LL (2-1). b, Denomination at LR (2-2).

2007, June 1   **Perf. 13¼x13**
3590 A1077 $1.20 Horiz. pair,
        #a-b   1.00   .85

Self-Adhesive
Booklet Stamps
Serpentine Die Cut 11¾

3591 A1077 $1.20 Horiz. pair,
        #a-b   .85   .85
    c.   Booklet pane, 4 #3591   5.00

Chongqing — A1078

No. 3592: a, City skyline (2-1). b, City and highway interchange (2-2).

Perf. 12x11½ Syncopated
2007, June 8   **Litho.**
3592 A1078 $1.20 Horiz. pair,
        #a-b   1.10   .90

Wudalianchi Natl. Park — A1079

No. 3593: a, Heilong Mountain (3-1). b, Sanchi Pool (3-2). c, Sea of Rock (3-3).

2007, June 19   **Photo.**   **Perf. 12¾**
3593 A1079   Horiz. strip of 3   1.75   1.25
    a.-c. $1.20 Any single   .45   .35

Return
of Hong
Kong,
10th
Anniv.
A1080

Designs: No. 3594, $1.20, Flags of People's Republic of China and Hong Kong, doves, monument (3-1). No. 3595, $1.20, "CEPA" and stylized buildings (3-2). No. 3596, $1.20, Hong Kong buildings, bridge (3-3).

Perf. 13¼x12¾ Syncopated
2007, July 1
3594-3596 A1080   Set of 3   1.40   1.00
    A souvenir sheet containing Nos. 3594-3596 and Hong Kong No. 1275 sold for $12.95 in Hong Kong currency. Value, $27.50.

Pres. Yang
Shangkun (1907-
98)
A1081

Designs: No. 3597, $1.20, Standing in uniform (2-1). No. 3598, $1.20, Seated at desk, horiz. (2-2).

Perf. 11½x11, 11x11½
2007, July 5   **Photo. & Engr.**
3597-3598 A1081   Set of 2   3.25   .85

Nanji Islands Marine
Reserve — A1082

Shells and: No. 3599, $1.20, Sanpanwei (3-1). No. 3600, $1.20, Longchuanjiao (3-2). No. 3601, $1.20, Dashaao (3-3).

Perf. 12¾x12½ Syncopated
2007, July 10   **Photo.**
3599-3601 A1082   Set of 3   1.60   1.00

Emblem of People's Liberation
Army — A1083

2007, July 15   **Litho.**   **Perf. 12**
3602 A1083 $1.20 multi + label   1.25   .45

Souvenir Sheet

All-China Philatelic Federation, 6th
Congress — A1084

Perf. 12½ Syncopated
2007, July 28   **Litho. & Engr.**
3603 A1084 $6 multi   3.75   2.25
    A sheet of 2 No. 3603 exists. Value, $9.

People's
Liberation Army,
80th
Anniv. — A1085

Designs: No. 3604, $1.20, Soldiers saluting (4-1). No. 3605, $1.20, Soldier carrying sack (4-2). No. 3606, $1.20, Soldier with rifle (4-3). No. 3607, $1.20, Soldiers wearing UN Peacekeeper berets (4-4).

Perf. 13¼x12½ Syncopated
2007, Aug. 1   **Photo.**
3604-3607 A1085   Set of 4   3.25   2.00
    A sheet of eight (two each Nos. 3604-3607) exists. Value, $10.

Olympic
Sports — A1086

Designs: Nos. 3608, 3614a, $1.20, Diving (6-1). Nos. 3609, 3614b, $1.20, Shooting (6-2). Nos. 3610, 3614c, $1.20, Athletics (6-3). Nos. 3611, 3614d, $1.20, Volleyball (6-4). Nos. 3612, 3614e, $1.20, BMX bicycling (6-5). Nos. 3613, 3614f, $1.20, Weight lifting (6-6).

2007, Aug. 8   **Photo.**   **Perf. 13¼x13**
3608-3613 A1086   Set of 6   3.50   2.25
3613a   Sheet of 10, #3521-3524,
        3608-3613, + label   12.00   12.00

Self-Adhesive
Serpentine Die Cut 11¾

3614   Miniature sheet of 12, 2
        each #a-f   18.50
    a.-f.   A1086 $1.20 Any single   .40   .30
    No. 3613a sold for $18.60.

Tengchong Volcano Area — A1087

Designs: No. 3615, $1.20, Rehai (3-1). No. 3616, $1.20, Volcanoes, vert. (3-2). No. 3617, $1.20, Shenzhu Valley, vert. (3-3).

Perf. 12x12½ Syncopated, 12½x12 Syncopated

2007, Aug. 18
3615-3617 A1087 Set of 3   1.50 1.00

Nos. 3615-3617 were printed together in a sheet of 15 stamps + a horizontal label. The first row consists of the label and 2 No. 3615; the second row, 3 No. 3615; the third row, 5 No. 3616; and the fourth row, 5 No. 3617.

Jin Hu — A1088

No. 3618: a, Da Chibi (2-1). b, Maoer Mountain (2-2).

Perf. 12¾ Syncopated

2007, Sept. 2   Litho.
3618 A1088 $1.20 Horiz. pair,
   #a-b   1.10 .95

2007 Women's Soccer World Cup, People's Republic of China A1089

2007, Sept. 10   Photo.   **Perf. 13¼**
3619 A1089 $1.20 multi   1.10 .75

Values are for stamps with surrounding selvage.

2007 World Summer Special Olympics, Shanghai — A1090

2007, Oct. 2   **Perf. 13¼**
3620 A1090 $1.20 multi   .70 .40

Historic Sites in Three Gorges Reservoir Area — A1091

Designs: No. 3621, $1.20, Zhang Fei Temple (4-1). No. 3622, $1.20, Shibaozhai Village, vert. (4-2). No. 3623, $1.20, Ancient Dachang, vert. (4-3). No. 3624, $1.20, Quyuan's Grave (4-4).

Perf. 13¼ Syncopated

2007, Oct. 13   Litho. & Engr.
3621-3624 A1091 Set of 4   2.00 1.50

17th Natl. Communist Party Congress — A1092

Designs: No. 3625, $1.20, Memorial for First Natl. Communist Party Congress (2-1). No. 3626, $1.20, Site of Second Plenary Session of the Seventh Central Committee. $6, Dove and monument.

Perf. 13¼x13 Syncopated

2007, Oct. 15   Photo.
3625-3626 A1092 Set of 2   2.75 1.00

Souvenir Sheet

Perf. 13¼x13

3627 A1092 $6 multi   5.00 3.25

No. 3627 contains one 60x40mm stamp. A souvenir sheet of 2 of Nos. 3625-3626 exists. Value, $50.

"Happiness" A1093

Perf. 12¾ Syncopated

2007, Nov. 1   Photo.
3628 A1093 $1.20 multi   .45 .40

A sheet containing Nos. 3628, 3541 and four labels exists. Value, $14.

Ancient Calligraphy A1094

Designs: No. 3629, $1.20, Proclamation (6-1). No. 3630, $1.20, Zhang Menglong Stele (6-2). No. 3631, $1.20, Inscription for Sweet Spring at Jiucheng Palace (6-3). No. 3632, $1.20, Preface for Sacred Religion at Wild Goose Pagoda (6-4). No. 3633, $1.20, Yan Qinli Stele (6-5). No. 3634, $1.20, Mysterious Pagoda Stele (6-6).

Perf. 12x11½ Syncopated

2007, Nov. 5   Litho.
3629-3634 A1094 Set of 6   3.25 2.25

A sheet containing 2 each of lithographed and embossed examples of Nos. 3629-3634 exists. Value, $10.

Mountains — A1095

Designs: No. 3635, $1.20, Mount Gongga, People's Republic of China (2-1). No. 3636, $1.20, Popocatepetl, Mexico (2-2).

Perf. 12¾ Syncopated

2007, Nov. 22
3635-3636 A1095 Set of 2   2.25 .75

See Mexico Nos. 2561-2562.

Launch of China's First Lunar Probe A1096

2007, Nov. 26   Litho. & Embossed
3637 A1096 $1.20 multi   3.75 1.75

Emblem of Expo 2010, Shanghai A1097

Mascot of Expo 2010 — A1098

Perf. 11½ Syncopated

2007, Dec. 19   Litho.
3638 A1097 $1.20 multi   .60 .45
  a.   Booklet pane of 1   .70
3639 A1098 $1.20 multi   .60 .45
  a.   Booklet pane of 1   .70
  b.   Booklet pane of 10, 5 each
     #3638-3639   7.00
     Complete booklet, #3638a,
     3639a, 3639b   7.00

Venues at 2008 Summer Olympics, Beijing — A1099

Designs: 80f, China Agricultural University Gymnasium (6-1). No. 3641, $1.20, Laoshan Mountain Bike Course (6-2). No. 3642, $1.20, National Indoor Stadium (6-3). No. 3643, $1.20, Beijing University Gymnasium (6-4). No. 3644, $1.20, National Aquatics Center (6-5). No. 3645, $3, Qingdao Olympic Sailing Center (6-6). $6, National Stadium.

2007, Dec. 20   Photo.   **Perf. 13x13¼**
3640-3645 A1099 Set of 6   3.50 2.75

Souvenir Sheet

Perf. 13

3646 A1099 $6 multi   5.75 4.00

No. 3646 contains one pentagonal 65x62mm stamp. A self-adhesive sheet of 2 each of Nos. 3640-3645 exists. Value, $12.

New Year 2008 (Year of the Rat) A1100

Perf. 12¾ Syncopated

2008, Jan. 5   Photo.
3647 A1100 $1.20 multi   .80 .40
  a.   Booklet pane of 10   8.00
     Complete booklet, #3647a   8.00

Miniature sheets containing 4 and 6 stamps exist. Value, each $11.

Zhuxian New Year Woodprints A1101

Designs: No. 3648, $1.20, Gate guardian (4-1). No. 3649, $1.20, Woman lecturing son (4-2). No. 3650, $1.20, Come back with fruitful result (4-3). No. 3651, $1.20, Chivalrous women (4-4).

2008, Jan. 15   Photo.   **Perf. 13¼x13**
3648-3651 A1101   Set of 4   1.75 1.50
3651a   Souvenir sheet of 4,
     #3648-3651   3.00 2.25

No. 3651a sold for $7.20. A miniature sheet containing two each of Nos. 3648-3651 exists. Value, $7.50.

Beijing Opera Characters A1102

Designs: 80f, Zhang Fei (6-1). No. 3653, $1.20, Cao Cao (6-2). No. 3654, $1.20, Bao Zheng (6-3). No. 3655, $1.20, Lian Po (6-4). No. 3656, $1.20, Xu Yanzhao (6-5). No. 3657, $1.20, Yang Yansi (6-6).

Perf. 12x11½ Syncopated

2008, Feb. 23   Litho.
3652-3657 A1102 Set of 6   3.00 2.25

Miniature Sheet

Birds — A1103

No. 3658: a, Urocissa caerulea (6-1). b, Emberiza koslowi (6-2). c, Tragopan caboti (6-3). d, Garrulax sukatschewi (6-4). e, Chrysolophus pictus (6-5). f, Podoces biddulphi (6-6).

2008, Feb. 28   Photo.   **Perf. 13¼x13**
3658 A1103 $1.20 Sheet of 6,
   #a-f   5.00 3.25

11th National People's Congress — A1104

2008, Mar. 5
3659 A1104 $1.20 multi   .65 .40

Olympic Torch Relay — A1105

Designs: $1.20, Lighting of torch in Greece, mascot holding torch (2-1). $3, Torch, torch bearer, vert. (2-2).

2008, Mar. 5   Photo.   Perf. 13¼
3660-3661 A1105   Set of 2   2.00 1.25
3661a   Souvenir sheet, #3660-
              3661   9.00 4.50

No. 3661a sold for $6.30. A sheet containing 4 self-adhesive examples each of Nos. 3660-3661 exists. Value, $15.

Suzhou-Nantong Yangtze River Bridge — A1106

No. 3662 — Denomination at: a, Left (2-1). b, Right (2-2).

2008, Apr. 12   Perf. 13¼
3662 A1106 $1.20 Horiz. pair,
               #a-b   1.10   .90

Boao Forum For Asia — A1107

No. 3663: a, Dongyu Island (2-1). b, Forum venue (2-2).

Perf. 12x11½ Syncopated
2008, Apr. 13   Litho.
3663 A1107 $1.20 Horiz. pair,
               #a-b   1.10   .90

Qiandao Lake — A1108

No. 3664 — Islands with denomination at: a, Left (2-1). b, Right (2-2).

2008, Apr. 16   Perf. 12¾ Syncopated
3664 A1108 $1.20 Horiz. pair,
               #a-b   1.10   .90
   c.   Souvenir sheet, #3664   3.25 2.75
         No. 3664c sold for $3.60.

A1109

Olympic Expo, Beijing — A1110

2008, Apr. 30 Photo. Perf. 11¼x11
3665 A1109 $1.20 multi   .75   .40

Litho.
Perf. 12½
3666 A1110 $1.20 multi   .75   .40

A circle of perforations surrounds the circular design on No. 3665.

Summer Palace — A1111

Designs: No. 3667, $1.20, Shiqikong Bridge (6-1). No. 3668, $1.20, Corridor (6-2). No. 3669, $1.20, Boat (6-3). No. 3670, $1.20, Garden of Harmonious Pleasures (6-4). No. 3671, $1.20, Yudai Bridge (6-5). No. 3672, $1.20, Houhu Lake (6-6).
$6, Tower of the Fragrance of Buddha, vert.

Litho. & Engr.
2008, May 10   Perf. 12
3667-3672 A1111   Set of 6   3.25 2.10
Souvenir Sheet
Perf. 12x11¾
3673 A1111 $6 multi   3.00 2.00

No. 3673 contains one 50x62mm stamp.

Cao Chong Weighs the Elephant A1112

Cao Chong: Nos. 3674, 3676, $1.20, Marking water level on boat carrying elephant (2-1). Nos. 3675, 3677, $1.20, Replacing elephant with weighable objects (2-2).

2008, June 1   Photo.   Perf. 13x13¼
3674-3675 A1112   Set of 2   1.00 1.00
Booklet Stamps
Self-Adhesive
Serpentine Die Cut 11¾
3676-3677 A1112   Set of 2   .85   —
3677a   Booklet pane of 8, 4 each
              #3676-3677   3.50   —
         Complete booklet, #3677a   4.00

Temples A1113

Designs: No. 3678, $1.20, White Horse Temple, China (2-1). No. 3679, $1.20, Maha Bodhi Temple, India (2-2).

2008, June 6   Perf. 13¼x13
3678-3679 A1113   Set of 2   1.25   .75
         See India No. 2246.

Development on the Taiwan Strait — A1114

Designs: No. 3680, $1.20, Minjiang River development (4-1). No. 3681, $1.20, Port of Xiamen (4-2). No. 3682, $1.20, Exhibition Hall

---

(4-3). No. 3683, $1.20, Fujian-Taiwan Kinship Museum (4-4).

2008, June 18   Perf. 12¾
3680-3683 A1114   Set of 4   1.75 1.50
A sheet containing 2 each of Nos. 3680-3683 + 1 label exists. Value, $7.

Second Land Survey — A1115

Designs: No. 3684, $1.20, Satellite, rural land survey (2-1). No. 3685, $1.20, Theodolite, urban land survey (2-2).

Perf. 12¾x12½
2008, June 25   Litho.
3684-3685 A1115   Set of 2   .85   .75

Qiuci Grotto Murals A1116

Designs: No. 3686, $1.20 Heavenly Kings (4-1). No. 3687, $1.20, Bodhisattva (4-2). No. 3688, $1.20, Flying Apsaras, horiz. (4-3). No. 3689, $1.20, Maitreya Preaching, horiz. (4-4).

2008, July 6   Photo.   Perf. 13¼
3686-3689 A1116   Set of 4   2.00 1.50

General Qi Jiguang (1528-88) A1117

Qi Jiguang: No. 3690, $1.20, Standing (2-1). No. 3691, $1.20, On horse (2-2).

Perf. 12x12½ Syncopated
2008, July 19   Litho.
3690-3691 A1117   Set of 2   1.25   .90

Opening of 2008 Summer Olympics, Beijing — A1118

2008, Aug. 8   Photo.   Perf. 13¼
3692 A1118 $1.20 multi   2.25   .50

A sheet of 8 self-adhesive stamps similar to No. 3692 exists. Value, $11. A sheet of 8 stamps with a holographic background exists. Value, $35.

Olympex 2008 Philatelic Exhibition, Beijing — A1119

Designs: No. 3693, $1.20, Greece #127 (2-1). No. 3694, $1.20, Portugal #RA14 (2-2). $6, Greece #127, gold medal and mascots of 2004 Summer Olympics.

2008, Aug. 8   Photo.   Perf. 13¼x13
3693-3694 A1119   Set of 2   1.75   .85
Souvenir Sheet
Litho.
Perf.
3695 A1119 $6 multi   4.50 3.50

No. 3695 contains one 56mm diameter stamp. No. 3695 exists on silk paper. Value, $20.

2008 Summer Olympics Gold Medal A1119a

2008, Aug. 9   Litho.   Perf. 12
3695A A1119a $1.20 multi + la-
                 bel   4.00 4.00

Labels could be personalized. No. 3695A was printed in sheets of various sizes, with many sheets having pre-printed labels depicting Olympic athletes.

Closing of 2008 Summer Olympics A1120

Designs: No. 3696, $1.20, National Stadium, Beijing (4-1). No. 3697, $1.20, Tower, Forbidden City, Beijing (4-2). No. 3698, $1.20, Millennium Wheel, London (4-3). No. 3699, $1.20, Tower of London (4-4).

2008, Aug. 24   Photo.   Perf. 13¼
3696-3699 A1120   Set of 4   4.00 2.25

A sheet containing 3 self-adhesive examples each of Nos. 3696-3699 exists. Value, $11.

China Central Television, 50th Anniv. A1121

Perf. 13½x13 Syncopated
2008, Sept. 2
3700 A1121 $1.20 multi   .85   .40

Emblem of 2008 Paralympic Games, Beijing — A1122

Paralympic Games Mascot — A1123

2008, Sept. 6   **Perf. 13¼x13**
3701 A1122 $1.20 multi   .75 .40
3702 A1123 $1.20 multi   .75 .40

University of Science and Technology, 50th Anniv. — A1124

Perf. 12x11¼ Syncopated
2008, Sept. 20   **Litho.**
3703 A1124 $1.20 multi   1.50 .40

Ningxia Hui Autonomous Region, 50th Anniv. — A1125

No. 3704: a, Windmills (3-1). b, Trees and wildlife in desert (3-2). c, People holding flower bouquets (3-3).

Perf. 13¼x12¾ Syncopated
2008, Sept. 23   **Photo.**
3704 A1125   Horiz. strip of 3   1.40 1.25
   a.   80f multi   .25 .25
   b.-c. $1.20 Either single   .45 .35

Airports — A1126

No. 3705: a, Beijing Capital International Airport (3-1). b, Shanghai Pudong International Airport (3-2). c, Guangzhou Baiyun International Airport (3-3).

2008, Sept. 28   **Perf. 12¾**
3705   Vert. strip of 3   2.00 1.50
   a.-c.   A1126 $1.20 Any single   .45 .35

Guangxi Zhuang Autonomous Region, 50th Anniv. — A1127

No. 3706: a, Dancers (3-1). b, Building (3-2). c, Port (3-3).

Perf. 12¾ Syncopated
2008, Oct. 18   **Litho.**
3706 A1127   Horiz. strip of 3   1.25 1.25
   a.   80f multi   .25 .25
   b.-c. $1.20 Either single   .45 .35

Happy New Year Type of 2006 and

"Blossom of Fortune" A1128

Perf. 11¾ Syncopated
2008, Oct. 9   **Litho.**
3707 A1128 $1.20 multi   .50 .35
Souvenir Sheet
3708   Sheet of 2, #3707, 3708a   12.00 8.00
   a.   A1055a $3 gold & multi   6.25 6.25

Seventh Asia-Europe Meeting, Beijing — A1129

Perf. 12x11¼ Syncopated
2008, Oct. 24
3709 A1129 $1.20 multi   .80 .40
   a.   Miniature sheet of 12   6.75 6.75

"Harmony" — A1130

2008, Dec. 3   **Perf. 12**
3710 A1130 $1.20 multi + label   .50 .40

Expo 2010, Shanghai — A1131

2008, Dec. 13   **Perf. 12**
3711 A1131 $1.20 multi + label   .60 .45
Compare with Type A1097.

A1132

Reform in China, 30th Anniv. — A1133

Perf. 12x11¼ Syncopated
2008, Dec. 18   **Litho.**
3712 A1132 $1.20 multi   1.00 .60
   a.   Miniature sheet of 8   5.00 5.00
Souvenir Sheet
Photo.
Perf.
3713 A1133 $6 multi + label   3.75 3.75
  A sheet containing 2 examples of No. 3713 exists. Value, $35.

New Year 2009 (Year of the Ox) — A1134

Perf. 13 Syncopated
2009, Jan. 5   **Photo.**
3714 A1134 $1.20 multi   1.00 .45
   a.   Miniature sheet of 6   17.00 5.00
   b.   Booklet pane of 10   8.00
     Complete booklet, #3714b   8.50
A sheet of 4 No. 3714 exists. Value, $7.

Bo Yibo (1908-2007), Politician A1135

Bo Yibo: No. 3715, $1.20, Standing (2-1). No. 3716, $1.20, Seated, horiz. (2-2).

2009, Jan. 15   **Perf. 13¼x13, 13x13¼**
3715-3716 A1135   Set of 2   1.25 .90

Zhangzhou New Year Woodprints A1136

Designs: No. 3717, $1.20, Lion holding a sword in mouth (4-1). No. 3718, $1.20, The coming flood of wealth, vert. (4-2). No. 3719, $1.20, Goddess sending children, vert. (4-3). No. 3720, $1.20, Rat marrying off its daughter (4-4).

2009, Jan. 18   **Perf. 12**
3717-3720 A1136   Set of 4   1.75 1.50
3720a   Souvenir sheet, #3717-3720 + label   2.50 2.50
3720b   Miniature sheet of 8, 2 each #3717-3720   4.50 4.50

A1137

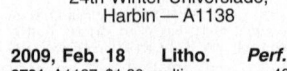

A1138

24th Winter Universiade, Harbin — A1138

2009, Feb. 18   **Litho.**   **Perf. 12¾**
3721 A1137 $1.20 multi   .40 .40
3722 A1138 $1.20 multi   .40 .40

Electric Power Grid Construction — A1139

No. 3723: a, Power station (3-1). b, Transmission towers and power lines (3-2). c, Light bulb, city skyline (3-3).

Perf. 12x12½ Syncopated
2009, Feb. 24
3723 A1139 $1.20   Horiz. strip of 3, #a-c   1.25 1.25

Paintings by Shi Tao (1642-1707) A1140

No. 3724: a, Chaohu Lake (30x55mm) (6-1). b, Enjoying Fountain Sound (25x55mm) (6-2). c, Double Chrysanthemums (30x55mm) (6-3). d, Plum Blossoms and Bamboo (25x55mm) (6-4). e, Horse and its Owner (30x55mm) (6-5). f, Lotus (25x55mm) (6-6).

2009, Mar. 22   **Perf. 12½x13**
3724   Horiz. strip of 6   5.50 2.75
   a.   A1140 80f multi   .35 .25
   b.-f.   A1140 $1.20 Any single   .65 .45

A1141

China 2009 World Stamp Exhibition, Luoyang — A1142

Designs: No. 3725, $1.20, Vase (2-1). No. 3726, $1.20, Jar with stopper (2-2). $6, National Beauty and Heavenly Fragrance.

Perf. 12¾ Syncopated
2009, Apr. 10   **Litho. & Embossed**
3725-3726 A1141   Set of 2   1.10 .85
Souvenir Sheet
Litho.
Perf. 13 Syncopated
3727 A1142 $6 multi   4.50 3.50
Nos. 3725 and 3726 both exist in sheets of 4. Value, set $6.50.
No. 3727 exists in a sheet of 2. Value, $16.

China at World Expos A1143

Scenes from Expos from: No. 3728, $1.20, 1904, 1915, 1926, 1933 (red panel) (4-1). No. 3729, $1.20, 1982, 1982 (brown panel) (4-2). No. 3730, $1.20, 1999 (green panel) (4-3). No. 3731, $1.20, 2010 (blue panel) (4-4).

Perf. 13¼x12¾ Syncopated

2009, May 1			Photo.
3728-3731	A1143	Set of 4	2.00 2.00
3731a		Miniature sheet of 8, 2 each #3728-3731	7.00 7.00

Fenghuang — A1144

No. 3732: a, North Gate (3-1). b, Rainbow Bridge (3-2). c, Street (3-3).

Perf. 12¾ Syncopated

2009, May 23			Litho.
3732	A1144	Horiz. strip of 3	1.25 1.25
a.-c.		$1.20 Any single	.40 .35

Children's Art — A1145

Designs: Nos. 3733, 3737, 80f, Love for the Motherland (yellow orange panel) (4-1). Nos. 3734, 3738, $1.20, Happy Life, horiz. (red panel) (4-2). Nos. 3735, 3739, $1.20, Peace Lovers (blue panel) (4-3). Nos. 3736, 3740, $1.20, Enthusiasm for Science, horiz. (green panel) (4-4).

Perf. 13¼x13, 13x13¼

2009, June 1			Photo.
3733-3736	A1145	Set of 4	1.60 1.40

Booklet Stamps
Self-Adhesive
Serpentine Die Cut 12

3737-3740	A1145	Set of 4	1.40 1.40
3740a		Booklet pane of 8, 2 each #3737-3740	3.00

Hangzhou Bay Bridge — A1146

No. 3741: a, Bridge. b, Marine platform.

2009, June 18		Litho.	Perf. 12
3741	A1146	$1.20 Horiz. pair, #a-b	1.00 .80

Li Xiannian (1909-92), People's Republic of China President A1147

Designs: No. 3742, $1.20, Wearing army uniform and cap (3-1). No. 3743, $1.20, Wearing gray suit with collar buttoned (3-2). No. 3744, $1.20, Wearing gray suit and eyeglasses (3-3).

2009, June 23		Photo.	Perf. 13¼x13
3742-3744	A1147	Set of 3	1.50 1.25

A1148

16th Asian Games, Guangzhou — A1149

2009, June 30		Photo.	Perf. 13¼
3745	A1148	$1.20 multi	.60 .50
3746	A1149	$1.20 multi	.60 .50

A sheet containing four each of Nos. 3745-3746 exists.

Great Hall of the People — A1150

Designs: No. 3747, East Gate (2-1). No. 3748, Great Auditorium (2-2).

2009, July 18		Litho.	Perf. 13¼x12½
3747	A1150	$1.20 multi	.55 .45
3748	A1150	$1.20 multi	.55 .45
a.		Booklet pane of 2, #3747-3748	1.10 —
b.		Booklet pane of 8, 4 each #3747-3748	4.50 —
		Complete booklet, #3748a, 3748b	4.50

Sanjiangyuan Nature Reserve — A1151

No. 3749: a, Geladandong (3-1). b, Eling Lake (3-2). c, Dza Chu (3-3).

Perf. 13¼x12½ Syncopated

2009, July 25			Photo.
3749	A1151	Horiz. strip of 3	1.40 1.25
a.-c.		$1.20 Any single	.40 .35

Flag, 60th Anniv. — A1152

2009, Aug. 2		Litho.	Perf. 13¼
3750	A1152	$1.20 multi + label	.80 .60

A souvenir sheet of 4 No. 3750 + one label exists.

Labrang Lamasery A1153

No. 3751: a, Grand Sutra Hall (2-1). b, Gongtang Pagoda (2-2).

Perf. 13x12¾ Syncopated

2009, Aug. 2			
3751	A1153	$1.20 Vert. pair, #a-b	.80 .80

Stork Tower A1154

Golden Gate A1155

2009, Aug. 14			Photo.
3752	A1154	$1.20 multi	.55 .40
3753	A1155	$1.20 multi	.55 .40

A1156

Huang Long Scenic Area — A1157

Designs: No. 3754, $1.20, Guest Welcome Ponds (3-1). No. 3755, $1.20, Waterfall (3-2). No. 3756, $1.20, Erdao Lake (3-3). $6, Five-color Ponds.

2009, Aug. 27			Perf. 12¾
3754-3756	A1156	Set of 3	1.25 1.10

Souvenir Sheet
Perf. 13¼x12¾ Syncopated

3757	A1157	$6 multi	2.25 2.25

A miniature sheet containing 2 each of Nos. 3754-3756 exists. Value, $6.

National Library of China — A1158

Books and: No. 3758, $1.20, Old building (2-1). No. 3759, $1.20, Modern building (2-2).

2009, Sept. 9   Perf. 13¼ Syncopated

3758-3759	A1158	Set of 2	1.10 1.10

Miniature Sheet

Tang Poems — A1159

No. 3760: a, $1.20, Downstream to Jiangling, by Il Bai (boat near rocks) (6-1). b, $1.20, A View of Taishan Mountain, by Du Fu (mountains) (6-2). c, $1.20, The Song of Pipa, by Bai Juyi (musician) (6-3). d, $1.20, To One Unnamed, by Li Shangyin (book) (6-4). e, $1.50, Looking at the Moon and Thinking of One Far Away, by Zhang Jiulin (Moon) (6-5). f, $3, On the Stork Tower, by Wang Zhihuan (Stork Tower) (6-6).

Litho., Engr. & Silk-screened
Perf. 12¾x13¼ Syncopated

2009, Sept. 13			
3760	A1159	Sheet of 6, #a-f	6.50 6.50

Lanzhoui University, Cent. A1160

Perf. 13x12½ Syncopated

2009, Sept. 17		Litho.	
3761	A1160	$1.20 multi	.55 .50

Chinese People's Political Consultative Conference, 60th Anniv. — A1161

Flowers and: No. 3762, $1.20, Conference emblem (2-1). No. 3763, $1.20, Conference venue, horiz. (2-2).

Perf. 13¼ Syncopated

2009, Sept. 17			
3762-3763	A1161	Set of 2	1.10 1.10

A1162

Beijing-Hangzhou Grand
Canal — A1163

Designs: No. 3764, $1.20, Lantern Lighting
Pagoda (6-1). No. 3765, $1.20, Boats and
Tianhou Temple (6-2). No. 3766, $1.20, Shan-
shan Guild Hall (6-3). No. 3767, $1.20, Qingji-
ang Water Gate (6-4). No. 3768, $1.20, Boats
and Wenfeng Pagoda (6-5). No. 3769, $1.20,
Gongchen Bridge (6-6).
$6, Canal.

Perf. 13x13¼ Syncopated
2009, Sept. 26   A1162   Photo.
3764-3769   A1162   Set of 6   3.25 2.10
Souvenir Sheet
Perf. 13¼ Syncopated
3770   A1163 $6 multi   3.00 3.00

A1164

People's Republic of China, 60th
Anniv. — A1165

Designs: No. 3771, $1.20, Marchers (4-1).
No. 3772, $1.20, Tractors pulling floats bear-
ing Chinese symbols (4-2). No. 3773, $1.20,
Flag, emblems of Macao and Hong Kong (4-
3). No. 3774, $1.20, Olympic rings and torch
(4-4).
$6, Flag.

Perf. 13x12½ Syncopated
2009, Oct. 1
3771-3774   A1164   Set of 4   1.80 1.50
Souvenir Sheet
Perf. 13¼x13½ Syncopated
3775   A1165 $6 multi   4.25 3.50
A miniature sheet containing two each of
Nos. 3771-3774 exists.

National Day Parade — A1166

Designs: No. 3776, $1.20, Infantry Group
(red background) (4-1). No. 3777, $1.20, Army
and 2nd Artillery Group (green background)
(4-2). No. 3778, $1.20, Navy Equipment
Group (blue background) (4-3). No. 3779,
$1.20, Air Group (orange background) (4-4).

Perf. 13¼x12½ Syncopated
2009, Oct. 1
3776-3779   A1166   Set of 4   2.25 2.00
A miniature sheet containing two each of
Nos. 3776-3779 exists. Value, $9.

"Music" — A1167

2009, Sept. 29   Litho.   Perf. 12
3780   A1167 $1.20 multi + label   .75 .35
See Stamps With Attached Labels note
after No. 3197.

"Happiness With the Spring" — A1168

2009, Oct. 9   Perf. 13 Syncopated
3781   A1168 $1.20 multi   .75 .35
A souvenir sheet containing Nos. 3781 and
3708a exists.

A1169

11th National
Games,
Shandong
A1170

Perf. 13¼x13 Syncopated
2009, Oct. 16
3782   A1169 $1.20 multi   .35 .35
3783   A1170 $1.20 multi   .35 .35
a.   Souvenir sheet, #3782-3783   1.25 1.25
No. 3783a sold for $3.60.

Ancient
Academies
A1171

Designs: No. 3784, $1.20, Stone Drum
Academy (4-1). No. 3785, $1.20, Anding
Academy (4-2). No. 3786, $1.20, Ehu Acad-
emy (4-3). No. 3787, $1.20, Dongpo Academy
(4-4).

Perf. 13¼ Syncopated
2009, Nov. 15   Photo.
3784-3787   A1171   Set of 4   1.40 1.40
A souvenir sheet containing two each of
Nos. 3784-3787 exists.

Guangji Bridge — A1172

No. 3788: a, Building at left on shore,
bridge, ships (3-1). b, Ships, central part of
bridge (3-2). c, Bridge, building at right on
shore (3-3).

Perf. 12¾ Syncopated
2009, Nov. 16   Litho.
3788   A1172   Horiz. strip of 3   1.10 1.10
a.-c. $1.20 Any single   .35   .35

Ma Lianliang
(1901-66), Opera
Performer, in
Kong Ming
Borrows the East
Wing — A1173

Ma Lianliang in
Zhao the
Orphan — A1174

Perf. 13¼x13½ Syncopated
2009, Nov. 28   Photo.
3789   A1173 $1.20 multi   .50 .35
3790   A1174 $1.20 multi   .50 .35

Return of
Macao to
China,
10th
Anniv.
A1175

Doves and: No. 3791, $1.20, Golden Lotus
sculpture, flags of People's Republic of China
and Macao (3-1). No. 3792, $1.20, "CEPA,"
buildings (3-2). $1.50, Bridge, buildings (3-3).

Perf. 13¼x13 Syncopated
2009, Dec. 20
3791-3793   A1175   Set of 3   1.25 1.25
3793a   Souvenir sheet, #3791-3793,
        Macao #1302a-1302c   2.40 2.40
See Macao Nos. 1302-1303. No. 3793a was
not offered for sale in Macao.

16th Asian Games,
Guangzhou — A1176

2009, Dec. 25   Litho.   Perf. 12
3794   A1176 $1.20 multi + label   1.00 .40
Compare with Type A1148. See Stamps
With Attached Labels note after No. 3197.

Gutian Conference, 80th
Anniv. — A1177

Perf. 13¼x13 Syncopated
2009, Dec. 28
3795   A1177 $1.20 multi   .80 .35

Ballet Dancers in
Red Detachment
of
Women — A1178

Designs: No. 3796, $1.20, Dancer in red (2-
1). No. 3797, $1.20, Dancers in blue (2-2).

2010, Jan. 1   Photo.   Perf. 13¼
3796-3797   A1178   Set of 2   2.75 1.00

New Year
2010 (Year of
the Tiger)
A1179

2010, Jan. 5   Perf. 12¾ Syncopated
3798   A1179 $1.20 multi   1.00 .40
a.   Booklet pane of 10   4.00
     Complete booklet, #3798a   5.00
No. 3798 exists in sheets of 4 and 6.

Gen. Song Renqiong (1909-
2005) — A1180

Designs: No. 3799, $1.20, Wearing cap (2-
1). No. 3800, $1.20, Reading book (2-2).

Perf. 13 Syncopated
2010, Jan. 8   Litho.
3799-3800   A1180   Set of 2   1.00 .70

Expo 2010, Shanghai — A1181

Designs: 80f, Expo Center (4-1). No. 3802,
$1.20, China Pavilion (4-2). No. 3803, $1.20,
Expo Performance Center (4-3). $3, Theme
Pavilion (4-4).
$6, Shanghai Expo Park, vert.

Perf. 13¼x13 Syncopated
2010, Jan. 21   Photo.
3801-3804   A1181   Set of 4   2.00 2.00

Souvenir Sheet

Perf. 13x12¾ Syncopated

3805 A1181 $6 multi 5.50 4.50

No. 3805 contains one 30x75mm stamp. A sheet containing two each of Nos. 3801-3804 exists. A sheet containing two examples of No. 3805 exists.

Liangping New Year Woodprints A1182

Designs: No. 3806, $1.20, Gate god (4-1). No. 3807, $1.20, Stealing the immortal grass (4-2). No. 3808, $1.20, Peace leads to happiness (4-3). No. 3809, $1.20, Exiting the pass with a stolen token (4-4).

2010, Feb. 6   Perf. 13¼x13

3806-3809 A1182	Set of 4	1.40	1.40
3809a	Souvenir sheet, #3806-3809 + label	2.50	2.50
3809b	Souvenir sheet of 8, 2 each #3806-3809 on fabric-faced paper	10.00	8.00
3809c	As "b," plain paper	6.25	6.25

No. 3809a sold for $7.20.

Intl. Women's Day, Cent. — A1183

Perf. 13¼x13 Syncopated

2010, Mar. 8

3810 A1183 $1.20 multi .... .50 .40

Dwelling in Fuchun Mountains, Painting by Huang Gongwang — A1184

No. 3811 — Various parts of painting with inscription: a, (6-1). b, (6-2). c, (6-3). d, (6-4). e, (6-5). f, (6-6).

2010, Mar. 20   Perf. 13¼

3811 A1184	Block of 6	17.50	15.00
a.-d.	$1.20 Any single	.60	.35
e.	$1.50 multi	.75	.50
f.	$3 multi	1.25	.95

Tomb Sweeping Festival — A1185

Designs: No. 3812, $1.20, Ancestor worship (3-1). No. 3813, $1.20, Spring outing (3-2). No. 3814, $1.20, Planting willows (3-3).

Perf. 13¼x13½ Syncopated

2010, Apr. 5   Litho.

3812-3814 A1185 Set of 3 ...... 1.10 1.10

A sheet containing three each of Nos. 3812-3814 exists.

Idioms — A1186

Designs: No. 3815, $1.20, The foolish old man removes the mountains (4-1). No. 3816, $1.20, Sleeping on brushwood and tasting gall (4-2). No. 3817, $1.20, Mao Sui recommending himself (4-3). No. 3818, $1.20, Rising to practice swordplay upon hearing the rooster crow (4-4).

Perf. 13¼x13½ Syncopated

2010, Apr. 18   Photo.

3815-3818 A1186 Set of 4 ...... 1.40 1.40

Opening of Expo 2010, Shanghai A1187

2010, May 1   Perf. 13¼ Syncopated

3819 A1187 $1.20 multi .... 1.00 .40

A sheet of six exists.

A1188

A1189

Ancient Calligraphy — A1190

No. 3820 — Preface to the Orchid Pavilion: a, Denomination at right (6-1). b, Denomination at left (6-2).
No. 3821 — Poems Composed During the Cold Food Festival in Huangzhou: a, Denomination at right (6-3). b, Denomination at left (6-4).
No. 3822 — Elegiac Lament for My Nephew: a, Denomination at right (6-5). b, Denomination at left (6-6).

2010, May 15   Perf. 13x13¼

3820 A1188	$1.20 Horiz. pair, #a-b	.70	.70
3821 A1189	$1.20 Horiz. pair, #a-b	.70	.70
3822 A1190	$1.20 Horiz. pair, #a-b	.70	.70
	Nos. 3820-3822 (3)	2.10	2.10

A sheet containing two each Nos. 3820-3822 exists.

Tenth Global Travel and Tourism Summit, Beijing — A1191

2010, May 25   Perf. 13¼ Syncopated

3823 A1191 $1.20 multi .... 3.50 .50

Wen Yanbo's Ball Goes Into Hole in Tree A1192

Wen Yanbo Retrieves Ball With Water A1193

2010, June 1   Perf. 13 Syncopated

3824 A1192	$1.20 multi	.35	.35
3825 A1193	$1.20 multi	.35	.35
a.	Booklet pane of 2, #3824-3825	.70	—
b.	Booklet pane of 8, 4 each #3824-3825	3.00	—
	Complete booklet, #3825a, 3825b	4.00	

A1194

Environmental Protection A1195

Perf. 13¼x13½ Syncopated

2010, June 5

3826 A1194	$1.20 multi	1.25	.40
3827 A1195	$1.20 multi	1.25	.40

Kunqu Opera — A1196

Designs: No. 3828, $1.20, Washing the Silken Gauze (3-1). No. 3829, $1.20, The Peony Pavilion (3-2). No. 3830, $1.20, The Palace of Long Life (3-3).

Perf. 13¼ Syncopated

2010, June 12   Photo.

3828-3830 A1196 Set of 3 ...... 1.10 1.10

A miniature sheet containing 3 each of Nos. 3828-3830 exists.

Pearl River Scenes — A1197

Designs: No. 3831, $1.20, Five Goats Statue, Guangzhou (4-1). No. 3832, $1.20, Guangzhou Center for the Performing Arts (4-2). No. 3833, $1.20, Guangzhou skyline (4-3). No. 3834, $1.20, Guangzhou Intl. Convention and Exhibition Center (4-4).

Perf. 13¼x13 Syncopated

2010, June 28

3831-3834 A1197	Set of 4	1.40	1.40
3834a	Souvenir sheet of 8, 2 each #3831-3834	4.75	4.75

Loulan — A1198

Designs: No. 3835, $1.20, Ruins of Buddhist stupa (2-1). No. 3836, $1.20, Ruins of building (2-2).

2010, July 3   Litho.

3835-3836 A1198 Set of 2 ...... .70 .70

Maritime Day — A1199

Perf. 13½x13 Syncopated

2010, July 11   Photo.

3837 A1199 $1.20 multi .... .80 .35

Composers — A1200

Designs: No. 3838, $1.20, Johann Sebastian Bach (1685-1750) (4-1). No. 3839, $1.20, Joseph Haydn (1732-1809) (4-2). No. 3840, $1.20, Wolfgang Amadeus Mozart (1756-91) (4-3). $4.50, Ludwig van Beethoven (1770-1827) (4-4).

Perf. 13¼x12¾ Syncopated

2010, July 25   Litho. & Engr.

3838-3841 A1200 Set of 4 ...... 2.40 2.40

Legend of the Cowherd and the Weaving Maid — A1201

Designs: No. 3842, Dress-linked affection (4-1). No. 3843, Happy lovers (4-2). No. 3844, Carrying children to chase wife (4-3). No. 3845, Heavenly reunion (4-4).

Perf. 13¼x13¾ Syncopated

2010, Aug. 16				**Photo.**	
3842	A1201	$1.20 multi		.40	.35
a.		Booklet pane of 1 + 5 labels		.60	—
3843	A1201	$1.20 multi		.40	.35
a.		Booklet pane of 1 + 5 labels		.60	—
3844	A1201	$1.20 multi		.40	.35
a.		Booklet pane of 1 + 5 labels		.60	—
3845	A1201	$1.20 multi		.40	.35
a.		Booklet pane of 1 + 5 labels		.60	—
		Complete booklet, #3842a-3845a		3.00	
		Nos. 3842-3845 (4)		1.60	1.40

Complete booklet sold for $8.

2010 Asian Para Games, Guangzhou — A1202

2010, Sept. 3			**Perf. 13**	
3846	A1202	$1.20 multi	.80	.35

Values are for stamp with adjacent selvage.

Great Wall Type of 2005

2010, Sept. 3	**Litho.**		**Perf. 12**	
3846A	A1003	$1.20 multi + label	5.00	5.00

See note following No. 3462.

A1203

Shangri-La (Zhongdian) — A1204

Designs: No. 3847, $1.20, Songzanlin Lamasery (4-1). No. 3848, $1.20, Napa Lake and grassland (4-2). No. 3849, $1.20, Pudacuo National Park (4-3). No. 3850, $1.20, Dukezong (4-4). $6, Meili Snow Mountain.

Perf. 13¼x13 Syncopated

2010, Sept. 13				
3847-3850	A1203	Set of 4	1.50	1.50
Souvenir Sheet				
Perf. 13¼x13¾ Syncopated				
3851	A1204	$6 multi	2.50	1.90

Confucius and Buildings — A1205

No. 3852: a, $1.20, Confucius and temple (3-1). b, $1.20, Family home of Confucius (3-2). c, $3, Cemetery of Confucius (3-3).

Perf. 13¼ Syncopated

2010, Sept. 28			**Litho.**	
3852	A1205	Horiz. strip of 3, #a-c	2.00	1.60
d.		Souvenir sheet, #3852a-3852c	3.00	3.00

Huai River Water Control Project — A1206

Designs: No. 3853, $1.20, Nanwan Reservoir (4-1). No. 3854, $1.20, Linhuaigang Water Control Project (4-2). No. 3855, $1.20, Huai River Outflow Project (4-3). No. 3856, $1.20, Nansi Lake Water Control Project (4-4).

Perf. 12¾x13 Syncopated

2010, Oct. 14				
3853-3856	A1206	Set of 4	1.50	1.50

Flora — A1207

Drawings of: No. 3857, $1.20, Plum blossom (4-1). No. 3858, $1.20, Orchid (4-2). No. 3859, $1.20, Bamboo (4-3). No. 3860, $1.20, Chrysanthemums (4-4).

2010, Oct. 18		**Perf. 13¼ Syncopated**		
3857-3860	A1207	Set of 4	2.50	1.50
3860a		Souvenir sheet of 8, 2 each #3857-3860	20.00	15.00

Zhu Xi (Chu Hsi) (1130-1200), Philosopher A1208

Designs: No. 3861, $1.20, Portrait of Zhu Xi (2-1). No. 3862, $1.20, Zhu Xi, student and horse (2-2).

Perf. 13¼x13½ Syncopated

2010, Oct. 22		**Litho. & Engr.**		
3861-3862	A1208	Set of 2	1.00	.75

2010 Asian Games, Guangzhou A1209

Designs: 80f, Badminton (6-1). No. 3864, $1.20, Wushu (6-2). No. 3865, $1.20, Hurdles (6-3). No. 3866, $1.20, Equestrian (6-4). No. 3867, $1.20, Dragon boat racing (6-5). $3, Weiqi (6-6).

Perf. 13¼ Syncopated

2010, Nov. 12			**Photo.**	
3863-3868	A1209	Set of 6	2.60	2.60
3868a		Sheet of 12, 2 each #3863-3868	8.00	8.00

Souvenir Sheet

New Year 2011 — A1210

No. 3869: a, $1.20, Chinese lantern, calendar for February 2011. b, $3, Like #3541, with copper frame.

Serpentine Die Cut 12¼

2010, Oct. 9	**Self-Adhesive**	**Litho.**		
3869	A1210	Sheet of 2, #a-b, + 13 labels	4.75	4.75

Traditional Chinese Medicine Stores — A1211

Designs: No. 3870, $1.20, Tongren Tang (4-1). No. 3871, $1.20, Huqing Yu Tang (4-2). No. 3872, $1.20, Lei Yongshang (4-3). No. 3873, $1.20, Chen Liji (4-4).

Perf. 13¼ Syncopated

2010, Nov. 20			**Photo.**	
3870-3873	A1211	Set of 4	1.50	1.50

High-speed Train — A1212

Perf. 13¼x12¾ Syncopated

2010, Dec. 7			**Photo.**	
3874	A1212	$1.20 multi	1.50	.80

Chinese Capital Markets A1213

Bar graph and: No. 3875, $1.20, Bull, computers at capital market (2-1). No. 3876, $1.20, City, satellite dish, train (2-2).

Perf. 13¼ Syncopated

2010, Dec. 12			**Litho.**	
3875-3876	A1213	Set of 2	1.75	1.25
3876a		Souvenir sheet of 8, 4 each #3875-3876	30.00	20.00

New Year 2011 (Year of the Rabbit) A1214

Perf. 13 Syncopated

2011, Jan. 5			**Photo.**	
3877	A1214	$1.20 multi	.80	.60
a.		Booklet pane of 10	8.00	
		Complete booklet, #3877a	8.00	
b.		Souvenir sheet of 6	12.50	10.00

A souvenir sheet containing 4 No. 3877 exists.

Fengxiang New Year Woodprints A1215

Designs: No. 3878, $1.20, General Yuchi Jingde (4-1). No. 3879, $1.20, Fortune boy (4-2). No. 3880, $1.20, Beauties (4-3). No. 3881, $1.20, Fortune flower vase (4-4).

Perf. 13¼x13¾ Syncopated

2011, Jan. 10			**Litho.**	
3878-3881	A1215	Set of 4	1.50	1.50

Sheet of eight containing two each Nos. 3878-3881 on plain and fabric-faced paper exist.

Early Leaders of the Communist Party of China — A1216

Designs: No. 3882, $1.20, Chen Yannian (1898-1927) (5-1). No. 3883, $1.20, Zhang Tailei (1898-1927) (5-2). No. 3884, $1.20, Luo Yinong (1902-28) (5-3). No. 3885, $1.20, Yun Daiying (1895-1931) (5-4). No. 3886, $1.20, Xiang Ying (1898-1941) (5-5).

2011, Feb. 21				
3882-3886	A1216	Set of 5	1.90	1.90

Liangzhu Jade — A1217

Designs: No. 3887, $1.20, Cong (carved block of jade) (2-1). No. 3888, $1.20, Bi (ring of jade) (2-2).

2011, Mar. 8			**Photo.**	
3887-3888	A1217	Set of 2	.75	.75

Scenes From "The Scholars," Novel by Wu Jingzi — A1218

Designs: 80f, Lotus painter Wang Mian (6-1). No. 3890, $1.20, Fanjin passing the Imperial exam (6-2). No. 3891, $1.20, Two lamp wicks (6-3). No. 3892, $1.20, Ma Er tours West Lake (6-4). No. 3893, $1.20, Mr. and Mrs. Du Shaoqing (6-5). No. 3894, $1.20,

Shen Qunzhi selling writings by Sheli Bridge (6-6).

2011, Mar. 21
3889-3894 A1218 Set of 6 2.10 2.10
A sheet of 12 containing two each of Nos. 3889-3894 exists.

Chinese Calligraphy A1219

Designs: No. 3895, $1.20, Pingfu Tie, by Lu Ji (4-1). No. 3896, $1.20, Chuyue Tie, by Wang Xizhi (4-2). No. 3897, $1.20, Gushi Si Tie, by Zhangxu (4-3). No. 3898, $1.20, Zixu Tie, by Huaisu (4-4).

2011, Apr. 15 Perf. 13¼ Syncopated
3895-3898 A1219 Set of 4 1.50 1.50
A sheet of eight containing two each Nos. 3895-3896, printed on rice paper exists.

Military Aircraft — A1220

Designs: No. 3899, $1.20, J-10 fighter (3-1). No. 3900, $1.20, JH-7 fighter (3-2). No. 3901, $1.20, AC313 helicopter (3-3).

Perf. 13¼x12¾ Syncopated
2011, Apr. 17 Litho.
3899-3901 A1220 Set of 3 1.50 1.25

World Reading Day A1221

2011, Apr. 23 Perf. 13 Syncopated
3902 A1221 $1.20 multi .60 .50

Tsinghua University, Cent. A1222

2011, Apr. 24 Litho. & Embossed
3903 A1222 $1.20 multi .80 .50

Expo 2011, Xi'an — A1223

Designs: $1.20, Emblem (2-1). $3, Mascot (2-2).

Perf. 13¼x13¾ Syncopated
2011, Apr. 28 Photo.
3904-3905 A1223 Set of 2 1.40 1.40

26th Summer Universiade, Shenzhen — A1224

No. 3906: a, $1.20, Emblem (50x30mm, 4-1). b, $1.20, Mascot (30x30mm, 4-2). No. 3907: a, $1.20, Shenzhen Universiade Sports Center (50x30mm, 4-3). b, $3, Torch, Chinese and English text (30x30mm, 4-4).

2011, May 4 Litho. Perf. 13¼
Horiz. Pairs, #a-b
3906-3907 A1224 Set of 2 2.10 2.10
3907a Sheet of 8 2 each #3906a-3906b, 3907a-3907b 6.50 5.50

Cloud Brocade A1225

Designs: No. 3908, $1.20, Dragon (3-1). No. 3909, $1.20, Crane insignia of first-rank civil official (3-2). No. 3910, $1.20, Fish (Double happiness, 3-3).

Perf. 13¼x12¾
2011, May 10 Photo.
3908-3910 A1225 Set of 3 1.50 1.25
3910a Souvenir sheet of 3, #3908-3910, + 3 labels 5.50 3.50

Emblem of Communist Party of China — A1226

2011, May 21 Litho. Perf. 13¼
3911 A1226 $1.20 multi + label 1.00 .75
See Stamps With Attached Labels note after No. 3187.

Liberation of Tibet, 60th Anniv. — A1227

Designs: No. 3912, $1.20, Potala Palace, Chinese soldiers, Tibetans and livestock (3-1). No. 3913, $1.20, Airplane over building, dancers (3-2). No. 3914, $1.20, Building, dancers (3-3).

Perf. 13¼x13¾ Syncopated
2011, May 23 Photo.
3912-3914 A1227 Set of 3 1.50 1.25

Scientists A1228

Designs: No. 3915, $1.20, Bei Shizhang (1903-2009), biologist (4-1). No. 3916, $1.20, Qian Xuesen (1911-2009), rocket scientist (4-

2). No. 3917, $1.20, Hou Xianglin (1912-2008), chemical engineer (4-3). No. 3918, $1.20, Qian Sanqiang (1913-92), nuclear physicist (4-4).

Perf. 13x12¾ Syncopated
2011, May 25 Set of 4 1.50 1.50
3915-3918 A1228

Ming and Qing Dynasty Furniture — A1230

No. 3919: a, 80f, Qing Dynasty rosewood-embedded copper dragon throne (6-1). b, $1.20, Ming Dynasy pearwood folding chair (6-2).
No. 3920: a, $1.20, Ming Dynasty pearwood official's armchair with carved Chinese characters (6-3). b, $1.20, Ming Dynasty pearwood armchair with carved dragons (6-4).
No. 3921: a, $1.20, Qing Dynasty rosewood-embedded marble armchair (6-5). b, $1.20, Ming Dynasty marble-embedded rosewood drum stool (6-6).

Perf. 13¼x13¾ Syncopated
2011, June 20 Litho.
3919 A1230 Horiz. pair, #a-b .65 .65
  c. Booklet pane, #3919a-3919b + 2 labels .90 —
3920 A1230 $1.20 Horiz. pair, #a-b .75 .75
  c. Booklet pane, #3920a-3920b + 2 labels 1.10 —
3921 A1230 $1.20 Horiz. pair, #a-b .75 .75
  c. Booklet pane, #3921a-3921b + 2 labels 1.10 —
  d. Booklet pane, #3919a-3919b, 3920a-3920b, 3921a-3921b 3.25 —
      Complete booklet, #3919c, 3920c, 3921c, 3921d 6.50
  Nos. 3919-3921 (3) 2.15 2.15

A1231

Communist Party of China, 90th Anniv. — A1232

Flag of the Communist Party of China and: No. 3922, $1.20, People and building (6-1). No. 3923, $1.20, Soldiers and monument (6-2). No. 3924, $1.20, Sculpture and building (6-3). No. 3925, $1.20, City skyline, sculpture of bull (6-4). No. 3926, $1.20, City skyline and modern building (6-5). No. 3927, $1.20, Beijing National Stdium, Chinese Pavilion, Shanghai (6-6).
$6, Flag of the Communist Party of China.

2011, June 22 Photo. Perf. 13¼
3922-3927 A1231 Set of 6 2.50 2.50
3924a Sheet of 6, 2 each #3922-3924 8.75 8.75
3927a Sheet of 6, 2 each #3925-3927 8.75 8.75
Souvenir Sheet
Perf. 13¼x13
3928 A1232 $6 multi 3.50 2.75

Opening of Beijing-Shanghai High Speed Railway — A1233

Perf. 13¼x12¾ Syncopated
2011, June 30
3929 A1233 $1.20 multi 1.75 .90

Cycling — A1234

Designs: No. 3930, $1.20, Cyclists on bike path (2-1). No. 3931, $1.20, Cyclists racing (2-2).

2011, July 2 Litho.
3930-3931 A1234 Set of 2 1.00 .80

Folk Vocal Arts — A1235

Designs: No. 3932, $1.20, Xiangsheng (4-1). No. 3933, $1.20, Singer with drum (4-2). No. 3934, $1.20, Pingtan (4-3). No. 3935, $1.20, Performer in black robe (4-4).

2011, July 8 Perf. 13¼ Syncopated
3932-3935 A1235 Set of 4 1.50 1.50
3935a Sheet of 8, 4 each #3932-3935 9.50 9.50

Chinese Culture Abroad — A1236

No. 3936: a, Chinese Festival, London Eye (4-1). b, Chinese Benevolent Association sculpture and building, Buddhist temple, modern building (4-2). c, Chinatown, Transamerica Pyramid, San Francisco (4-3). d, Chinese school building, mountain (4-4).

Perf. 13¼x13¾ Syncopated
2011, July 10
3936 Horiz. strip of 4 2.60 2.60
  a.-c. A1236 $1.20 Any single .40 .40
  d. A1236 $4.50 multi 1.40 1.40

Cargo Ships — A1237

No. 3937: a, Cosco Asia container ship (4-1). b, Xinsheng Hai bulk transport ship (4-2).

Perf. 13¼x12¾ Syncopated

2011, Aug. 8			**Photo.**
3937	A1237	$1.20 Horiz. pair, #a-b	1.00 .85

Peonies — A1238

Lilies — A1239

Sunflowers — A1240

Chinese Rose — A1241

Carnations — A1242

Camellias — A1243

Azalea Flowers — A1244

Lotus Flowers — A1245

Plum Blossoms — A1246

Magnolia Blossoms — A1247

2011, Sept. 1		Litho.	**Perf. 12**
3938	A1238	$1.20 multi + label	.65 .50
3939	A1239	$1.20 multi + label	.65 .50
3940	A1240	$1.20 multi + label	.65 .50
3941	A1241	$1.20 multi + label	.65 .50
3942	A1242	$1.20 multi + label	.65 .50
3943	A1243	$1.20 multi + label	.65 .50
3944	A1244	$1.20 multi + label	.65 .50
3945	A1245	$1.20 multi + label	.65 .50
3946	A1246	$1.20 multi + label	.65 .50
3947	A1247	$1.20 multi + label	.65 .50
		Nos. 3938-3947 (10)	6.50 5.00

See Stamps With Attached Labels note after No. 3197.

Traditional Games of Ethnic Minorities A1248

No. 3948, $1.20: a, Men in board shoe race (4-1). b, Women with bamboo poles (4-2). No. 3949, $1.20: a, Top spinning (4-3). b, Stilt racing (4-4).

Perf. 13x12¾ Syncopated

2011, Sept. 10			**Photo.**
Vert. Pairs, #a-b			
3948-3949	A1248	Set of 2	1.50 1.50

A1249

Lord Guan Yu (?-219) — A1250

Lord Guan Yu: No. 3950, $1.20, On horse (2-1). No. 3951, $1.20, Seated, reading annals (2-2).

Perf. 13x13¼ Syncopated

2011, Sept. 12			
3950-3951	A1249	Set of 2	2.75 1.00

Souvenir Sheet

Perf. 13¼x13 Syncopated

3952	A1250	$6 multi	6.50 6.00

A limited edition souvenir sheet of 6 containing three each Nos. 3950-3951 exists.

Details From the Scroll of the 87 Immortals A1251

Various details with stamps numbered: No. 3953, $1.20, (6-1). No. 3954, $1.20, (6-2). No. 3955, $1.20, (6-3). No. 3956, $1.20, (6-4). $1.50, (6-5). $3, (6-6).

Perf. 13¼ Syncopated

2011, Sept. 26			Litho.
3953-3958	A1251	Set of 6	3.00 3.00
3958a		Booklet pane of 6, #3953-3958	4.00 —
		Complete booklet, #3958a	6.50

A1252

Chinese Revolution, Cent. — A1253

Designs: No. 3959, $1.20, Wuchang Uprising (2-1). No. 3960, $1.20, Revolution leaders (2-2).

$6, Dr. Sun Yat-sen (1866-1925), leader of revolution.

Perf. 13¼x13 Syncopated

2011, Oct. 10			**Photo.**
3959-3960	A1252	Set of 2	1.00 .85
3960a		Sheet of 8, 4 each #3959-3960	8.00 7.00

Souvenir Sheet

Perf. 13¼x12¾ Syncopated

3961	A1253	$6 multi	2.00 2.00

A1254

Rebuilding Efforts After May 12, 2008 Sichuan Earthquake — A1255

Designs: No. 3962, $1.20, Clock, rebuilt town (4-1). No. 3963, $1.20, Sculpture, rebuilt sections of ancient town (4-2). No. 3964, $1.20, Sculpture, buildings (4-3). No. 3965, $1.20, Flag, sculpture, rebuilt village (4-4). $6, Rebuilt town, sculpture, wind generators.

Perf. 13¼ Syncopated

2011, Oct. 13			Litho.
3962-3965	A1254	Set of 4	1.50 1.50

Souvenir Sheet

Perf. 13 Syncopated

3966	A1255	$6 multi	2.00 2.00

A1256

Tianjin Binhai New Area — A1257

Building and: No. 3967, $1.20, New downtown (3-1). No. 3968, $1.20, Yujiabao Financial District (3-2). No. 3969, $1.20, Map of National Animation Industry Park (3-3). $6, Port, crane, container ship.

Perf. 13¼x12¾ Syncopated

2011, Oct. 21			**Photo.**
3967-3969	A1256	Set of 3	1.25 1.25

Souvenir Sheet

Perf. 13x13¾ Syncopated

3970	A1257	$6 multi	1.90 1.90

A1258

China 2011 Intl. Philatelic Exhibition, Wuxi — A1259

Designs: No. 3971, $1.20, Flat-sided container with spout and handle (2-1). No. 3972, $1.20, A-fu (2-2). $6, Yu Zhuang Qiu, by Ni Zan.

Perf. 13¼x13¾ Syncopated
2011, Oct. 10
3971-3972 A1258 Set of 2 .75 .75
3972a Sheet of 8, 4 each #3971-3972 + label 6.50 6.50

Souvenir Sheet
Perf. 13¼x13 Syncopated
3973 A1259 $6 multi 1.90 1.90

Xinhua News Agency, 80th Anniv. A1260

Various buildings: No. 3974, $1.20, Red electric wave (4-1). No. 3975, $1.20, Anti-Japanese War (4-2). No. 3976, $1.20, War of Liberation (4-3). No. 3977, $1.20, Going global (4-4).

Perf. 13¼ Syncopated
2011, Nov. 7 Litho.
3974-3977 A1260 Set of 4 1.50 1.50

Bird on Branch A1261

2011, Oct. 9 **Perf. 11¾ Syncopated**
3978 A1261 $1.20 multi .40 .40
a. Souvenir sheet of 2, #3708a, 3978 3.75 3.75

Armillary Spheres A1262

Designs: No. 3980, $1.20, Simplified armillary sphere built by Guo Shoujing, 1276 (2-1). No. 3981, $1.20, Equatorial armillary sphere built by Tycho Brahe, 1595 (2-2).

Perf. 13¼x12¾ Syncopated
2011, Dec. 10 Litho. & Engr.
3980-3981 A1262 Set of 2 1.00 .90
See Denmark Nos. 1576-1577.

New Year 2012 (Year of the Dragon) A1263

Perf. 12¾ Syncopated
2012, Jan. 5 Photo.
3982 A1263 $1.20 multi 1.50 1.00
a. Booklet pane of 10 15.00
Complete booklet, #3982a 16.00

Limited edition sheets of 4 and 6 stamps exist.

Bank of China, Cent. — A1264

Designs: $1.20, Old bank building (2-1). $1.50, Modern bank building (2-2).

2012, Feb. 5 **Perf. 13 Syncopated**
3983-3984 A1264 Set of 2 3.50 2.00

Emblem and Building of Zhonghua Book Company A1265

Perf. 13¼x13¾ Syncopated
2012, Feb. 23 Litho.
3985 A1265 $1.20 multi .70 .50

Diplomatic Relations Between People's Republic of China and Israel, 20th Anniv. — A1266

Designs: No. 3986, $1.20, Waxwing, five-pointed star (2-1). No. 3987, $1.20, White dove, Star of David (2-2).

2012, Mar. 20 Litho. & Embossed
3986-3987 A1266 Set of 2 2.50 1.50
See Israel Nos. 1923-1924.

Asian-Pacific Postal Union, 50th Anniv. — A1267

2012, Apr. 1 Photo. **Perf. 13x13¼**
3988 A1267 $1.20 multi .80 .80

Musicians A1268

Designs: No. 3989, $1.20, Xiao Youmei (1884-1940) (4-1). No. 3990, $1.20, Liu Tianhua (1895-1932) (4-2). No. 3991, $1.20, He Lvting (1903-99) (4-3). No. 3992, $1.20, Ma Sicong (1912-87) (4-4).

2012, Apr. 15 **Perf. 13 Syncopated**
3989-3992 A1268 Set of 4 1.60 1.60

Chinese Characters A1269

Embellished character for: No. 3993, $1.20, Good luck (fu) (4-1). No. 3994, $1.20, Richness (lu) (4-2). No. 3995, $1.20, Longevity (shou) (4-3). No. 3996, $1.20, Happiness (xi) (4-4).

Litho With Foil Application
2012, Apr. 27
3993-3996 A1269 Set of 4 4.50 2.50
3996a Souvenir sheet of 8, 2 each #3993-3996 13.00 13.00

Communist Youth League, 90th Anniv. A1270

Designs: 80f, Building, flag of Youth League (2-1). $1.20, Emblem, Great Wall of China, boy and girl (2-2).

Perf. 13x12¾ Syncopated
2012, May 4 Photo.
3997-3998 A1270 Set of 2 .65 .65
3998a Souvenir sheet of 8, 4 each #3997-3998 4.50 4.50

International Nurses Day — A1271

2012, May 12
3999 A1271 $1.20 multi .40 .40

Nanjing University, 110th Anniv. — A1272

Perf. 13¼x13¾ Syncopated
2012, May 20 Litho.
4000 A1272 $1.20 multi .40 .40

Flowers and: No. 4001, $1.20, Former building of Chinese Communist Party Central Committee (2-1). No. 4002, $1.20, National Performing Arts Center, Beijing (2-2).

2012, May 23 Photo.
4001-4002 A1273 Set of 2 1.00 .80

Tables — A1274

No. 4003: a, Ming Dynasty pear wood drawing table (50x30mm) (4-1). b, Qing Dynasty square pear wood table (40x30mm) (4-2).
No. 4004: a, Ming Dynasty pear wood incense stand with base (40x30mm) (4-3). b, Ming Dynasty rock wood table (50x30mm) (4-4).

Perf. 13¼x13 Syncopated
2012, June 9 Litho. & Embossed
4003 A1274 $1.20 Horiz. pair, #a-b .75 .75
c. Booklet pane of 1 #4003a + 2 labels .40 —
d. Booklet pane of 1 #4003b + 2 labels .40 —
4004 A1274 $1.20 Horiz. pair, #a-b .75 .75
c. Booklet pane of 1 #4004a + 2 labels .40 —
d. Booklet pane of 1 #4004b + 2 labels .40 —
e. Booklet pane of 8, #4003a-4003b, 4004a-4004b 1.50 —
Complete booklet, #4003c, 4003d, 4004c, 4004d, 4004e 3.25

Third Asian Beach Games, Haiyang A1275

Designs: No. 4005, $1.20, Beach volleyball (3-1). No. 4006, $1.20, Inline skating (3-2). No. 4007, $1.20, Waterskiing (3-3).

Perf. 13¼ Syncopated
2012, June 16 Photo.
4005-4007 A1275 Set of 3 1.25 1.25

Rocket Launch and Spacecraft — A1276

2012, June 25 Litho. **Perf. 12**
4008 A1276 $1.20 multi + label .40 .40

See Stamps With Attached Labels note after No. 3197.

Places in People's Republic of China — A1277

Designs: No. 4009, $1.20, Jingangshan Mountain (6-1). No. 4010, $1.20, Ruijin (6-2). No. 4011, $1.20, Zunyi (6-3). No. 4012, $1.20, Huining (6-4). No. 4013, $1.20, Yan An (6-5). No. 4014, $1.20, Xibaipo (6-6).

Perf. 13¼x12¾ Syncopated
2012, June 30   **Litho. & Engr.**
4009-4014   A1277   2.25   2.25
4014a   Sheet of 12, 2 each #4009-
     4014   5.75   5.75

Full Coverage in
Insurance
Systems
A1278

Perf. 13¼x13¾ Syncopated
2012, July 1   **Photo.**
4015   A1278 $1.20 gold & red   1.50   .75

Emblem of Chinese Olympic
Committee — A1279

2012, July 17   **Litho.**   **Perf. 12**
4016   A1279 $1.20 multi + label   1.00   .70
See Stamps With Attached Labels note
after No. 3197.

National Museum and
Stamps — A1280

No. 4017 — Museum and: a, $1.20, People's Republic of China #787. b, $3, People's Republic of China #790.

Perf. 13¼ Syncopated
2012, July 8   **Litho. & Engr.**
4017   A1280   Horiz. pair, #a-b   1.40   1.40

2012 Summer
Olympics,
London
A1281

Designs: No. 4018, $1.20, Soccer (4-1). No. 4019, $1.20, Tennis (4-2). No. 4020, $1.20, Equestrian (4-3). No. 4021, $1.20, Hurdles (4-4).

Perf. 13¼x13 Syncopated
2012, July 27   **Photo.**
4018-4021   A1281   Set of 4   1.50   1.50
4021a   Sheet of 8, 2 each #4018-
     4021   6.25   6.25

Generals
A1282

Designs: No. 4022, $1.20, Zhao Bosheng (1897-1933) (5-1). No. 4023, $1.20, Duan Dechang (1904-33) (5-2). No. 4024, $1.20,

Xie Zichang (1897-1935) (5-3). No. 4025, $1.20, Zeng Zhongsheng (1900-35) (5-4). No. 4026, $1.20, Dong Zhentang (1895-1937) (5-5).

Perf. 13¼x13¾ Syncopated
2012, Aug. 1
4022-4026   A1282   Set of 5   1.90   1.90

A1283

Silk Road — A1284

Designs: No. 4027, $1.20, Buildings, figurines of camel and man (4-1). No. 4028, $1.20, Building, horse figurine (4-2). No. 4029, $1.20, Mountains, pitcher (4-3). No. 4030, $1.20, Cliff buildings, horse and rider figurine (4-4).

Perf. 13¼x12¾ Syncopated
2012, Aug. 1
4027-4030   A1283   Set of 4   1.50   1.50
4030a   Sheet of 8, 2 each #4027-
     4030   7.25   7.25
Souvenir Sheet
Perf. 13¼ Syncopated
4031   A1284 $6 shown   1.90   1.90

Liu
Sanjie — A1285

Designs: No. 4032, $1.20, Song fairy (4-1). No. 4033, $1.20, Singing, horiz. (4-2). No. 4034, $1.20, Couple with embroidered ball, horiz. (4-3). No. 4035, $1.20, Riding a carp to heaven (4-4).

Perf. 13¼x13½ Syncopated, 13
Syncopated
2012, Aug. 23
4032-4035   A1285   Set of 4   1.50   1.50
4032a   Booklet pane of 1   .65   —
4033a   Booklet pane of 1   .65   —
4034a   Booklet pane of 1   .65   —
4035a   Booklet pane of 1   .65   —
    Complete booklet, #4032-4035a   2.60

Complete booklet sold for $8.

Hetian
Jade
A1286

Designs: No. 4036, $1.20, Figurine of dragon (4-1). No. 4037, $1.20, Bi with grain design, vert. (4-2). No. 4038, $1.20, Cup on plate (4-3). No. 4039, $1.20, Figurine of children washing elephant, vert. (4-4).

Litho. & Embossed
2012, Aug. 28   **Perf. 12**
4036-4039   A1286   Set of 4   1.50   1.50
4039a   Souvenir sheet of 4,
     #4036-4039 + label   2.40   2.40

A1287

Sanxingdui Bronze Relics — A1288

Designs: No. 4040, $1.20, Mask (2-1). No. 4041, $1.20, Statue of person kneeling (2-2). $6, Statue of person standing.

Perf. 13¼x13½ Syncopated
2012, Sept. 26   **Litho.**
4040-4041   A1287   Set of 2   .80   .80
Souvenir Sheet
Perf. 13x13¼
4042   A1288 $6 multi   1.90   1.90

Miniature Sheet

Song Poetry — A1289

No. 4043: a, 80f, Sand of Silk Washing, by Yan Shu (6-1). b, $1.20, Meditating on the Past at Chibi, by Su Shi (6-2). c, $1.20, Fairy of the Magpie Bridge, by Qin Guan (6-3). d, $1.20, A Twig of Plum Blossoms (6-4). e, $1.20, Ode to the Plum Blossom, by Lu You (6-5). f, $3, This Unconstrained Poem to Chen Tongfu, by Xin Qiji (6-6).

Perf. 13x13¼ Syncopated
2012, Aug. 31
4043   A1289   Sheet of 6, #a-f   3.75   3.75

Yanbian Culture — A1290

Designs: No. 4044, $1.20, Harvest Dance (3-1). No. 4045, $1.20, Dancers (3-2). No. 4046, $1.20, Hymn for harmony (3-3).

Perf. 13¼x13 Syncopated
2012, Sept. 3   **Photo.**
4044-4046   A1290   Set of 3   1.25   1.25
4046a   Sheet of 9, 3 each #4044-
     4046   3.75   3.75

Qin Dynasty Liye Bamboo
Slips — A1291

No. 4047: a, Multiplication table, denomination at UL (2-1). b, Calendar, denomination at UR (2-2).

Perf. 13¼ Syncopated
2012, Sept. 13
4047   A1291 $1.20 Horiz. pair,
     #a-b   .80   .80

"Good
Fortune"
A1292

Perf. 11¾ Syncopated
2012, Oct. 9   **Litho.**
4048   A1292 $1.20 multi   .40   .40
a.   Souvenir sheet of 2, #3708a,
     4048   1.90   1.90

Porcelain Objects From Dehua
Kiln — A1293

No. 4049, $1.20: a, Three-legged pot with dragon decoration (4-1). b, Vase with handles (4-2).
No. 4050, $1.20: a, Seated Guanyin figurine (4-3). b, Bodhidharma figurine (4-4).

Perf. 13¼ Syncopated
2012, Oct. 20   **Photo.**
     Horiz. Pairs, #a-b
4049-4050   A1293   Set of 2   1.60   1.60

History of Merchants — A1294

Designs: No. 4051, $1.20, Steamship, 1872 (3-1). No. 4052, $1.20, Shekou skyline (3-2). $1.50, Hong Kong skyline (3-3).

Perf. 13¼x13 Syncopated
2012, Oct. 26   Litho.
4051-4053 A1294   Set of 3   1.25 1.25
4053a   Souvenir sheet of 6, 2
      each #4051-4053   4.75 4.75

A1295

18th National Congress of Chinese Communist Party — A1296

No. 4054: a, Rocket launch (2-1). b, Great Wall of China (2-2).

Perf. 13¼ Syncopated
2012, Nov. 8   Photo.
4054 A1295 $1.20 Horiz. pair,
     #a-b   .80 .80
Souvenir Sheet
Perf. 13 Syncopated
4055 A1296 $6 multi   2.00 2.00
A sheet containing four No. 4054 exists.

Bridges — A1297

Designs: No. 4056, $1.20, Taizhou Yangtze River Bridge (2-1). No. 4057, $1.20, Bosporus Bridge, Istanbul, Turkey (2-2).

Perf. 13¼x13 Syncopated
2012, Nov. 26   Litho.
4056-4057 A1297   Set of 2   .80 .80
     See Turkey No. 3319.

Auditing — A1298

No. 4058: a, Three-legged pot, bas-relief (4-1). b, Imperial Chinese chop (4-2). c, Auditing document of Communist era with red circular seal, building, star, hammer and sickle (4-3). d, Modern auditing documents, building (4-4).

Perf. 13 Syncopated
2012, Nov. 30   Photo.
4058 A1298   Horiz. strip of 4   1.60 1.60
a.-d. $1.20 Any single   .40 .40

Confucius Institute — A1299

No. 4059: a, $1.20, Stylized dove and globe (2-1). b, $3, Panda (2-2).

2012, Dec. 1
4059 A1299   Horiz. pair, #a-b   1.40 1.40

Constitution of People's Republic of China, 30th Anniv. — A1300

Perf. 13½x13¼ Syncopated
2012, Dec. 4   Litho.
4060 A1300 $1.20 multi   .40 .40

New Year 2013 (Year of the Snake) A1301

Perf. 12¾ Syncopated
2013, Jan. 5   Photo.
4061 A1301 $1.20 multi   .40 .40
a.   Booklet pane of 10   8.75
     Complete booklet, #4061a   8.75
A limited edition sheet of 6 stamps exists.

Offshore Oil Exploration — A1302

Designs: No. 4062, $1.20, Exploration ship (3-1). No. 4063, $1.20, Offshore drilling rig (3-2). $3, Production ship (3-3).

Perf. 13¼x13 Syncopated
2013, Jan. 18
4062-4064 A1302   Set of 3   1.75 1.75

Heart and Flowers — A1303

2013, Feb. 28   Litho.   Perf. 12
4065 A1303 $1.20 multi + label   .40 .40
See Stamps With Attached Labels note after No. 3197.

Lanterns — A1304

2013, Mar. 3
4066 A1304 $1.20 multi + label   .40 .40
See Stamps With Attached Labels note after No. 3197.

12th National People's Congress A1305

Perf. 13¼x13½ Syncopated
2013, Mar. 5   Photo.
4067 A1305 $1.20 multi   .40 .40
a.   Souvenir sheet of 6   4.50 4.50

Mao Zedong's Instruction to Follow Examples of Comrade Lei Feng, 50th Anniv. — A1306

Lei Feng (1940-62), model soldier: 80f, Holding gun (4-1). No. 4069, $1.20, Studying book (4-2). No. 4070, $1.20, Polishing object (4-3). No. 4071, $1.20, Holding baby (4-4).

Perf. 13¼ Syncopated
2013, Mar. 5   Litho. & Engr.
4068-4071 A1306   Set of 4   1.40 1.40
4071a   Sheet of 8, 2 each #4068-
     4071   5.50 5.50

Party School of the Central Committee, 80th Anniv. A1307

Perf. 13 Syncopated
2013, Mar. 13   Litho.
4072 A1307 $1.20 multi   .40 .40

Peach Blossoms A1308

Various peach blossoms in decorative frames: No. 4073, 80f, (12-1). No. 4074, 80f, (12-2). No. 4075, $1.20, (12-3). No. 4076, $1.20, (12-4). No. 4077, $1.20, (12-5). No. 4078, $1.20, (12-6). No. 4079, $1.20, (12-7). No. 4080, $1.20, (12-8). No. 4081, $1.20, (12-9). No. 4082, $1.20, (12-10). No. 4083, $1.20, (12-11). $1.50, (12-12).

Perf. 13¼x13 Syncopated
2013, Mar. 16   Photo.
4073-4084 A1308   Set of 12   4.50 4.50
4078a   Sheet of 12, 2 each #4073-
     4078   5.50 5.50
4084a   Sheet of 12, 2 each #4079-
     4084   6.50 6.50

World Water Day — A1309

2013, Mar. 22
4085 A1309 $1.20 multi   .40 .40

Painting of Women Producing Silk — A1310

Details from painting: No. 4086, $1.20, Women beating silk in basin (3-1). No. 4087, $1.20, Women working silk thread (3-2). No. 4088, $1.20, Women pulling silk cloth (3-3). $6, Entire painting.

Perf. 13 Syncopated
2013, Apr. 13   Litho.
4086-4088 A1310   Set of 3   1.25 1.25
Souvenir Sheet
Perf. 13½ Syncopated
4089 A1310 $6 multi   2.00 2.00
No. 4089 contains one 59x37mm stamp.

Cloisonné Ware — A1311

Designs: 80f, Yuan Dynasty three-legged pot (6-1). No. 4091, $1.20, Ming Dynasty container (6-2). No. 4092, $1.20, Qing Dynasty Zun vessel (6-3). No. 4093, $1.20, Qing Dynasty pot with spout and handle (6-4). No. 4094, $1.20, Hanging vase with handle (6-5). $3, Ming Dynasty bottle vase (6-6).

Perf. 13¼x13½ Syncopated
2013, Apr. 21
4090-4095 A1311   Set of 6   3.00 3.00
4095a   Sheet of 12, 2 each #4090-
     4095   7.75 7.75

Souvenir Sheet

7th Congress of All-China Philatelic Federation — A1312

2013, Apr. 25   Litho. & Embossed
4096 A1312 $6 multi   2.00 2.00

Earthquake Relief A1313

Perf. 13x12½ Syncopated
2013, May 3   Photo.
4097 A1313 $1.20 multi   7.50 7.50

Mother's Day — A1314

Litho. With Foil Application
Perf. 13x12¾ Syncopated
2013, May 11
4098　A1314　$1.20 multi　　　.40　.40

Galloping Horse — A1315

2013, May 19　Litho.　Perf. 12
4099　A1315　$1.20 multi + label　.40　.40
See Stamps With Attached Labels note after No. 3197.

Town Scenes A1316

Designs: No. 4100, $1.20, Qiantong (8-1). No. 4101, $1.20, Laitan (8-2). No. 4102, $1.20, Heping (8-3). No. 4103, $1.20, Jingziuan (8-4). No. 4104, $1.20, Heshun (8-5). No. 4105, $1.20, Tangjiawan (8-6). No. 4106, $1.20, Lizhuang (8-7). No. 4107, $1.20, Jingsheng (8-8).

Perf. 13¼x12¾ Syncopated
2013, May 19　Litho. & Engr.
4100-4107　A1316　Set of 8　3.25　3.25

Zhangjiajie Tianzi Mountain A1317

Xiapu Beaches A1318

Qilian Yu Island Group, Paracel Islands A1319

Panjin Red Beach A1320

Longsheng Terraced Fields A1321

Fields and Irrigation Canals, Xinghua A1322

Perf. 13x12¾ Syncopated
2013, May 19　　　Photo.
4108　A1317　80f multi　　　.25　.25
4109　A1318　80f multi　　　.25　.25
4110　A1319　$1.20 multi　　.40　.40
4111　A1320　$1.20 multi　　.40　.40
4112　A1321　$1.50 multi　　.50　.50
4113　A1322　$3 multi　　　1.00　1.00
　　　Nos. 4108-4113 (6)　　2.80　2.80

Tadpoles and Pond Life A1323

No. 4114 — Tadpoles and: a, Shrimp. b, Goldfish. c, Crab. d, Turtles. e, Frog.

Perf. 13x12½ Syncopated
2013, June 1　　　Photo.
4114　　Horiz. strip of 5　1.90　1.90
　a.　A1323 80f multi　　　.25　.25
　b.-e.　A1323 $1.20 Any single　.40　.40
　f.　Booklet pane of 5, #4114a-
　　　4114e　　　　　　1.90　—
　　Complete booklet, #4114f　1.90

Gold and Bronze Statues of Buddha — A1324

Buddha statue from: 80f, Five Dynasties period (6-1). No. 4116, $1.20, Song Dynasty (6-2). No. 4117, $1.20, Ming Dynasty (6-3). No. 4118, $1.20, Ming Dynasty, diff. (6-4). No. 4119, $1.20, Ming Dynasty, diff. (6-5). No. 4120, $1.20, Ming Dynasty, diff. (6-6).
$6, Five Buddha statues.

Perf. 13¼ Syncopated
2013, June 16　　　Litho.
4115-4120　A1324　Set of 6　2.25　2.25
Souvenir Sheet
Perf. 13 Syncopated
4121　A1324　$6 multi　　　2.00　2.00
No. 4121 contains one 74x83mm stamp.

Four Arts of Chinese Scholars A1325

Designs: No. 4122, $1.20, Scholar playing a qin (4-1). No. 4123, $1.20, Scholars playing game of Go (4-2). No. 4124, $1.20, Scholars learning calligraphy (4-3). No. 4125, $1.20, Scholar and wall painting (4-4).

Longhu Mountain — A1326

Perf. 13¼ Syncopated
2013, July 13　　　Litho.
4122-4125　A1325　Set of 4　1.60　1.60

No. 4126: a, Elephant Trunk Hill (3-1). b, Rocks of Immortals (3-2). c, Zhengyi Taoist Abbey (3-3).
$6, Longhu Mountain and lake, horiz.

Perf. 13¼ Syncopated
2013, July 27　　　Photo.
4126　A1326　$1.20 Horiz. strip of
　　　3, #a-c　　　　1.25　1.25
Souvenir Sheet
Perf. 13x13½ Syncopated
4127　A1326　$6 multi　　　2.00　2.00

Ship — A1327

Stars — A1328

Knot — A1329

Painting of Bamboo — A1330

Die Cut Perf. 12¾ Syncopated
2013, Aug. 8　　　Photo.
Self-Adhesive
4128　A1327　80f multi　　　.25　.25
Die Cut Perf. 13¼x13 Syncopated
4129　A1328　$1.20 multi　　.40　.40
4130　A1329　$2.40 multi　　.80　.80
4131　A1330　$3 multi　　　1.00　1.00
　　　Nos. 4128-4131 (4)　2.45　2.45

Mascot of 2014 Youth Olympic Games, Nanjing — A1331

2013, Aug. 15　Litho.　Perf. 12
4132　A1331　$1.20 multi + label　.40　.40
See Stamps With Attached Labels note after No. 3197.

China-ASEAN Expo, 10th Anniv. — A1332

Perf. 13¼x12¾ Syncopated
2013, Aug. 15　　　Photo.
4133　A1332　$1.20 multi　　.40　.40

Cats A1333

Cat breed: No. 4134, $1.20, Chinese Li Hua (4-1). No. 4135, $1.20, Maine Coon (4-2). No. 4136, $1.20, Abyssinian, vert. (4-3). No. 4137, $1.20, Exotic shorthair, vert. (4-4).

Perf. 13 Syncopated, 13¼x13¾ Syncopated (#4136-4137)
2013, Aug. 18　Litho. & Engr.
4134-4137　A1333　Set of 4　1.60　1.60

Sun and Peonies — A1334

2013, Aug. 26　Litho.　Perf. 12
4138　A1334　$1.20 multi + label　.40　.40
See Stamps with Attached Labels note after No. 3197.

12th National Games, Liaoning — A1335

Designs: No. 4139, $1.20, Rhythmic gymnastics (2-1). No. 4140, $1.20, Fencing (2-2).

Perf. 13¼x13 Syncopated
2013, Aug. 31　　　Litho.
4139-4140　A1335　Set of 2　.80　.80
4140a　　Souvenir sheet of 2,
　　　#4139-4140　　　1.40　1.40

Wei Guoqing (1913-89), Political and Military Leader — A1336

Wei Guoqing: No. 4141, $1.20, Wearing army cap (2-1). No. 4142, $1.20, Without cap (2-2).

Perf. 13¼x13¾ Syncopated
2013, Sept. 2　Litho.
4141-4142　A1336　Set of 2　.80　.80

Yu Yuan Garden, Shanghai — A1337

Designs: 80f, Zigzag Bridge and Mid-lake Pavilion (4-1). No. 4144, $1.20, Grand Rockery (4-2). No. 4145, $1.20, Yuan-yu Building (4-3). No. 4146, $1.20, Exquisite Jade Rock (4-4).

Perf. 13¼x12¾ Syncopated
2013, Sept. 7   Litho. & Engr.
4143-4146 A1337 Set of 4   1.50 1.50

Nanhua Temple — A1338

No. 4147: a, Cao Xi Gate (4-1). b, Mahavira Hall (4-2). c, Ling Zhao Pagoda (4-3). d, Liu Zu Hall (4-4).

Perf. 13¼x13 Syncopated
2013, Sept. 7   Photo.
4147   Horiz. strip of 4   1.60 1.60
a.-d. A1338 $1.20 Any single   .40   .40

Poets — A1339

Designs: No. 4148, $1.20, Jia Yi (200 B.C.-168 B.C.) (4-1). No. 4149, $1.20, Sima Xiangru (179 B.C.-118 B.C.) (4-2). No. 4150, $1.20, Yang Xiong (53 B.C.-18 A.D.) (4-3). No. 4151, $1.20, Ban Gu (32-92) (4-4).

Perf. 13¼ Syncopated
2013, Sept. 15   Photo.
4148-4151 A1339 Set of 4   1.60 1.60

Table Tennis — A1340

Players: No. 4152, $1.20, Woman (2-1). No. 4153, $1.20, Man (2-2).

Perf. 13½x13 Syncopated
2013, Sept. 27   Photo.
4152-4153 A1340 Set of 2   .80   .80
See Sweden No. 2715.

Chinese Technical Achievements — A1341

Designs: 80f, Rendezvous of Shenzhou and Tiangong spacecraft (4-1). No. 4155, $1.20, Beidou Navigation Satellite System (4-2). No. 4156, $1.20, Liaoning Aircraft Carrier (4-3). No. 4157, $1.20, Jiaolong Manned Submersible (4-4).

Perf. 13x12¾ Syncopated
2013, Sept. 29   Photo.
4154-4157 A1341 Set of 4   1.50 1.50
4157a   Souvenir sheet of 4,
          #4154-4157   1.50 1.50

Fish and Flowers A1342

Perf. 12¾x12 Syncopated
2013, Oct. 9   Litho.
4158 A1342 $1.20 multi   .40   .40
a.   Souvenir sheet of 2, #3708a,
      4158, perf. 11¾ syncopated 2.50 2.50

Tenth China Art Festival A1343

Perf. 13¼x13 Syncopated
2013, Oct. 11   Litho.
4159 A1343 $1.20 multi   .40   .40

Xi Zhongxun (1913-2002), Communist Party Official — A1344

Xi Zhnongxun: No. 4160, $1.20, As young man in military uniform (2-1). No. 4161, $1.20, As older man (2-2).

Perf. 13¼x13½ Syncopated
2013, Oct. 15   Litho. & Engr.
4160-4161 A1344 Set of 2   .80   .80

21st Intl. Congress of Supreme Audit Institutions, Beijing — A1345

No. 4162: a, Congress emblem, Gate of Heavenly Peace (2-1). b, Emblem of Intl. Organization of Supreme Audit Institutions, Great Wall of China (2-2)

Perf. 13¼ Syncopated
2013, Oct. 22   Litho.
4162 A1345 $1.20 Horiz. pair,
            #a-b   .80   .80

Hybrid Rice — A1346

No. 4163: a, Seed production (2-1). b, Stalk of rice, rice bowl (2-2).

2013, Oct. 25 Litho. *Perf. 13¼x13¾*
4163 A1346 $1.20 Horiz. pair,
            #a-b   .80   .80

Mao Zedong (1893-1976), Chairman of People's Republic of China — A1347

Various paintings of Mao Zedong: No. 4164, $1.20, With boats in background (4-1). No. 4165, $1.20, With opened overcoat (4-2). No. 4166, $1.20, With arm extended, vert. (4-3). No. 4167, $1.20, Watching waves come ashore (4-4).

Perf. 13¼ Syncopated
2013, Nov. 16   Litho.
4164-4167 A1347 Set of 4   1.60 1.60

Wuhan University, 120th Anniv. A1348

Perf. 13 Syncopated
2013, Nov. 29   Litho.
4168 A1348 $1.20 multi   .40   .40

Chinese Junk — A1349

2013, Nov. 22 Litho. *Perf. 12*
4169 A1349 $1.20 multi + label .40 .40
See Stamps With Attached Labels note under No. 3197.

First Moon Landing by Chinese Space Vehicles — A1350

No. 4170: a, $1.20, Chang'e 3 Lander (2-1). b, $1.50, Yutu Moon Rover (2-2).

Perf. 13¼x13 Syncopated
2014, Jan. 1   Photo.
4170 A1350 Horiz. pair, #a-b .90   .90

New Year 2014 (Year of the Horse) A1351

Perf. 12¾ Syncopated
2014, Jan. 5   Photo.
4171 A1351 $1.20 multi   .40   .40
a.   Booklet pane of 10   4.00
      Complete booklet, #4171a 4.00

Diplomatic Relations Between France and People's Republic of China, 50th Anniv. — A1352

Desings: No. 4172, $1.20, Qinhuai River, Nanjing (2-1). No. 4173, $1.20, Seine River, Paris (2-2).

Perf. 13x12½ Syncopated
2014, Jan. 27   Litho. & Engr.
4172-4173 A1352 Set of 2   .80   .80
See France Nos. 4587-4588.

Birds of Prey — A1353

Designs: No. 4174, $1.20, Aquila heliaca (4-1). No. 4175, $1.20, Circus cyaneus, horiz. (4-2). No. 4176, $1.50, Accipiter gentilis, horiz. (4-3). No. 4177, $1.50, Falco tinnunculus (4-4).

Perf. 12¾ Syncopated (vert. stamps), 13x12½ Syncopated
2014, Feb. 23   Litho. & Engr.
4174-4177 A1353 Set of 4   1.75 1.75

Bathing Horses, by Zhao Mengfu (1254-1322) — A1354

No. 4179: a, 7 horses and rider. (50x38mm) (3-1). b, 5 horses, 3 riders, 3 grooms, Chinese text (57x38mm) (3-2). c, 2 horses, 2 men (50x38mm) (3-3).
$6, Entire painting.

Perf. 13¼ Syncopated
2014, Mar. 1   Litho.
4178   Horiz. strip of 3   1.40 1.40
a.-b. A1354 $1.20 Either single .40 .40
c.   A1354 $1.50 multi   .50   .50
          Souvenir Sheet
     Perf. 13½x14 Syncopated
4179 A1354 $6 multi   2.00 2.00
No. 4179 contains one 153x31mm stamp.

Strengthening of Consumer Rights in China — A1355

Designs: No. 4180, $1.20, Scales, book and Consumer Rights Day emblem (2-1). No. 4181, $1.20, Hands, bowl, shirt, house, steering wheel. (2-2).

Perf. 13¼x13¾ Syncopated
2014, Mar. 15   Litho.
4180-4181 A1355 Set of 2   .80   .80

Internet Life — A1356

Designs: No. 4182, $1.20, Internet icons, man and woman touching hands (4-1). No. 4183, $1.20, Computer screen, mouse, man pushing shopping cart with Internet icons (4-2). No. 4184, $1.20, Hand holding smart phone showing picture of man on laptop computer (4-3). $1.50, Clouds with Internet icons, people on hills (4-4).

Perf. 13¼x13½ Syncopated
2014, Apr. 20   **Photo.**
4182-4185 A1356   Set of 4   1.75   1.75

Theme Pavilion and Emblem A1357

Botanical Pavilion and Mascot A1358

Perf. 13 Syncopated
2014, Apr. 25   **Photo.**
4186 A1357 $1.20 multi (2-1)   .40   .40
4187 A1358 $1.20 multi (2-2)   .40   .40

Intl. Horticultural Exposition, Qingdao.

Chinese People's Association for Friendship With Foreign Countries, 60th Anniv. — A1359

Perf. 13¼ Syncopated
2014, May 3   **Litho.**
4188   A1359 $1.20 multi   .40   .40

Wild Goose Delivering Letters — A1360

Perf. 13¼x13 Syncopated
2014, May 10   **Litho. & Engr.**
4189 A1360 $1.20 multi   .40   .40

See Republic of China No. 4178.

Buddhist Art — A1361

Designs: No. 4190, $1.20, Sakyamuni Buddha (4-1). No. 4191, $1.20, Amitayus Buddha (4-2). No. 4192, $1.20, Green Tara (4-3). No. 4193, $1.20, White Tara (4-4). $6, Sahasra-bhuja Sahasra-netra Avalokitesvara.

Perf. 13¼x13 Syncopated
2014, May 18   **Litho.**
4190-4193 A1361   Set of 4   1.60   1.60
Souvenir Sheet
Perf. 13x13¼ Syncopated
4194 A1361 $6 multi   1.90   1.90
No. 4194 contains one 66x108mm stamp.

Birds in Bamboo Forest — A1362

2014, May 28   **Litho.**   **Perf. 12**
4195 A1362 $1.20 multi + label   .40   .40
See Stamps With Attached Labels note after No. 3197.

Premiere of Animated Movie *The Monkey King* — A1363

Designs: No. 4196, 80f, Monkey King seeking weapon in Dragon King's palace (6-1). No. 4197, 80f, Horses in water and in flight (6-2). No. 4198, $1.20, Monkey King, other monkeys, banner (6-3). No. 4199, $1.20, Monkey King in peach tree (6-4). No. 4200, $1.20, Monkey King in battle (6-5). No. 4201, $1.20, Monkey King breaking picture frame (6-6).

Perf. 13¼x12¾ Syncopated
2014, June 1   **Photo.**
4196-4201 A1363   Set of 6   2.10   2.10
4201a   Booklet pane of 6, #4196-
          4201   2.10   —
          Complete booklet, #4201a   2.10

Huangpu Military Academy, 90th Anniv. — A1364

Perf. 13¼x12¾ Syncopated
2014, June 16   **Litho. & Engr.**
4202 A1364 $1.20 multi   .40   .40

The Dream of Red Mansions, Novel by Cao Xueqin A1365

Scenes from novel: No. 4203, $1.20, Lady Dowager sends for her motherless granddaughter (4-1). No. 4204 $1.20, Confounded monk ends a confounding case (4-2). No. 4205, $1.20, Grandmother Liu saw Madam Phoenix first (4-3). $1.50, Baoyu recognizes the gold locket (4-4). $6, Spirit of Baoyu.

Perf. 13 Syncopated
2014, June 21   **Photo.**
4203-4206 A1365   Set of 4   1.75   1.75
Souvenir Sheet
4207 A1365 $6 multi   2.00   2.00
No. 4207 contains one 45x70mm stamp. Compare with Nos. 4375-4379.

Huangmei Opera — A1366

Designs: 80f, A Happy Marriage with a Fairy (3-1). No. 4209, $1.20, Royal Son-in-law (3-2). No. 4210, $1.20, Collecting Grass for Pig (3-3).

Perf. 13¼ Syncopated
2014, July 6   **Litho.**
4208-4210 A1366   Set of 3   1.10   1.10

Fruit — A1367

Designs: No. 4211, $1.20, Apples (4-1). No. 4212, $1.20, Peaches (4-2). No. 4213, $1.50, Pomegranates (4-3). No. 4214, $1.50, Kumquats (4-4).

Perf. 13¼x13 Syncopated
2014, July 15   **Litho.**
4211-4214 A1367   Set of 4   1.75   .75

2014 Youth Olympic Games, Nanjing — A1368

Perf. 13¼x13½ Syncopated
2014, Aug. 16   **Litho.**
4215 A1368 $1.20 multi   .40   .40

Basin — A1369

2014, Aug. 20   **Litho.**   **Perf. 12**
4216 A1369 $1.20 multi + label   .40   .40
See Stamps With Attached Labels note after No. 3197.

Deng Xiaoping (1904-97), Leader of People's Republic of China A1370

Deng Xiaoping: No. 4217, $1.20, In military uniform, Red Army flag (4-1). No. 4218, $1.20, At lectern, United Nations Building and flag (4-2). No. 4219, $1.50, Reading speech, microphones, teapot, flag of Chinese Communist Party (4-3). No. 4220, $1.50, With extended arm, flag of People's Republic of China (4-4)

Perf. 13 Syncopated
2014, Aug. 22   **Litho.**
4217-4220 A1370   Set of 4   1.75   1.75

Zhuge Liang (181-234), Chancellor of Shu Han — A1371

Designs: No. 4221, $1.20, Zhuge Liang standing (2-1). No. 4222, $1.20, Zhuge Liang writing (2-2). $6, Zhuge Liang standing, diff.

Perf. 13¼ Syncopated
2014, Aug. 28   **Litho.**
4221-4222 A1371   Set of 2   .80   .80
Souvenir Sheet
4223 A1371 $6 multi   2.00   2.00
No. 4223 contains one 38x62mm stamp.

Teacher's Day — A1372

Designs: $1.20, Candles in hot-air balloon basket, eyeglasses and book on desk (2-1). $1.50, Tree with symbols of education, stylized faces (2-2).

Perf. 13¼x13¾ Syncopated
2014, Sept. 10   **Photo.**
4224-4225 A1372   Set of 2   .90   .90

Miniature Sheet

Yangtze River — A1373

No. 4226: a, $1.20, River running through mountains (9-1). b, $1.20, River passing Chongqing (9-2). c, $1.20, Three Gorges (9-3). d, $1.20, Hubei and Hunan (9-4). e, $1.20, Mount Lu and Jiujiang River (9-5). f, $1.20, Yellow Mountain (9-6). g, $1.50, Bridges over river (9-7). h, $1.50, River passing towns (9-8). i, $3, River running into sea (9-9).

Perf. 13¼x12¾ Syncopated

2014, Sept. 13			Photo.
4226 A1373	Sheet of 9, #a-i	4.50	4.50

People's Congress, 60th Anniv. — A1374

60th anniv. emblem and: No. 4227, $1.20, Building and people (2-1). No. 4228, $1.20, Great Hall of the People and flags (2-2).

Perf. 12¾x12½ Syncopated

2014, Sept. 15			Litho.
4227-4228 A1374	Set of 2	.80	.80

National Rejuvenation — A1375

Ribbons and: 80f, Buildings, flags and ship (4-1). No. 4230, $1.20, Buildings, construction cranes, harvesters (4-2). No. 4231, $1.20, China Central Television Building, Ferris wheel, buildings, dancers (4-3). No. 4232, $1.20, Ethnic dancers and musicians, buildings (4-4).

Perf. 13 Syncopated

2014, Sept. 20			Photo.
4229-4232 A1375	Set of 4	1.50	1.50
4232a	Souvenir sheet of 4, #4229-4232	1.50	1.50

Filial Piety — A1376

Designs: No. 4233, $1.20, Yu Shun, elephants and birds (4-1). No. 4234, $1.20, Wife of Jiang Shi holding tray with bowl and plate, carp jumping from spring (4-2). No. 4235, $1.50, Hua Mulan with spear on horseback (4-3). No. 4236, $1.50, Sun Simao studying medicine (4-4).

Perf. 13¼ Syncopated

2014, Sept. 30			Litho. & Engr.
4233-4236 A1376	Set of 4	1.75	1.75

A1377

A1378

Xinjiang Production and Construction Corps, 60th Anniv. — A1379

Perf. 13 Syncopated

2014, Oct. 7			Litho.
4237	Horiz. strip of 3	1.25	1.25
a.	A1377 $1.20 multi	.40	.40
b.	A1378 $1.20 multi	.40	.40
c.	A1379 $1.20 multi	.40	.40

Calabash — A1380

Perf. 12¾ Syncopated

2014, Oct. 9			Litho.
4238 A1380	$1.20 multi	.40	.40
a.	Souvenir sheet of 2, #3869b (perf. 12 syncopated), #4238	1.40	1.40

Scientists A1381

Designs: No. 4239, $1.20, Wang Ganchang (1907-98), nuclear physicist (6-1). No. 4240, $1.20, Zhou Jiuzhang (1907-68), spacecraft engineer (6-2). No. 4241, $1.20, Guo Yonghuai (1909-68), physicist (6-3). No. 4242, $1.20, Deng Jiaxian (1924-86), nuclear physicist (6-4). No. 4243, $1.20, Zhu Guangya (1924-2011), nuclear physicist (6-5). No. 4244, $1.20, Wang Xuan (1937-2006), computer scientist (6-6).

Perf. 13¼ Syncopated

2014, Oct. 16			Photo.
4239-4244 A1381	Set of 6	2.40	2.40

Sail Your Dreams — A1382

2014, Oct. 31	Litho.		Perf. 13¼
4245 A1382	$1.20 multi + label	.40	.40

See Stamps With Attached Labels note after No. 3197.

Meeting of Leaders of Asia-Pacific Economic Cooperation, Beijing — A1383

2014, Nov. 10	Litho.		Perf. 13¼x13
4246 A1383	$1.20 multi	.40	.40

10th China Intl. Aviation and Aerospace Exhibition — A1384

No. 4247: a, Helicopter, airplanes, city skyline (2-1). b, Space Station, rockets, astronaut (2-2).

2014, Nov. 11	Litho.		Perf. 13¼x13
4247 A1384	$1.20 Horiz. pair, #a-b	.80	.80

Chinese Character for "Congratulations" — A1385

2014, Nov. 12	Litho.		Perf. 12
4248 A1385	$1.20 multi + label	.40	.40

See Stamps With Attached Labels note after No. 3197.

Chinese Arctic and Antarctic Research Expeditions, 30th Anniv. — A1386

No. 4249: a, $1.20, Map of Antarctica, research expedition station, buildings, penguins (2-1). b, $1.50, Map of Arctic region, ship, buildings and polar bears (2-2).

Perf. 13x12¾ Syncopated

2014, Nov. 20			Litho.
4249 A1386	Vert. pair, #a-b	.90	.90

Double Happiness — A1387

2014, Dec. 1	Litho.		Perf. 13¼x13
4250 A1387	$3 multi	1.00	1.00

Values are for stamp with surrounding selvage.

Miniature Sheet

Yuan Dramatic Works — A1388

No. 4251: a, 80f, Sand and Sky — Autumn Thoughts, by Ma Zhiyuan (6-1). b, $1.20, Sheep on the Slope — Meditation on the Past at Tong Pass, by Zhang Yanghao (6-2). c, $1.20, Dou E Yuan, by Guan Hanqing (6-3). d, $1.20, Over the Wall, by Bai Pu (6-4). e, $1.50, The Orphan of Zhao, by Ji Junxiang (6-5). f, $3, Premature Death of a Beautiful Young Girl, by Zheng Guangzu (6-6).

Litho. & Engr.			
2014, Dec. 1			Perf. 13¼
4251 A1388	Sheet of 6, #a-f	3.00	3.00

New Year 2015 (Year of the Ram) A1389

Perf. 13 Syncopated

2015, Jan. 5			Photo.
4252 A1389	$1.20 multi	.40	.40
a.	Booklet pane of 10	4.00	—
	Complete booklet, #4252a	4.00	

Greeting Chinese New Year A1390

Perf. 13 Syncopated

2015, Jan. 10			Litho.
4253 A1390	$1.20 multi	.40	.40

Zunyi Conference, 80th Anniv. — A1391

Designs: No. 4254, $1.20, Conference site (2-1). No. 4255, $1.20, Conference participants (2-2).

Perf. 13¼x13 Syncopated

2015, Jan. 15			Litho.
4254-4255 A1391	Set of 2	.80	.80

24 Solar Terms — A1392

No. 4256: a, Beginning of Spring (children and flowers) (6-1). b, Rain water (fisherman and birds). (6-2). c, Waking of insects (cowherd and bulls) (6-3). d, Spring equinox (boy on bull) (6-4). e, Pure brightness (kite flying) (6-5). f, Grain rain (women tending to vegetables on racks, rabbits) (6-6).

Perf. 13 Syncopated
2015, Feb. 4　　　　　　　　　　Photo.
4256 A1392 $1.20 Block of 6, #a-
　　　　　f　　　　　　　　2.40 2.40
Values are for stamps with surrounding selvage.

Court Ladies Swinging Fans, by Zhou Fang — A1393

No. 4257 — Painting details numbered: a, (3-1). b, (3-2). c, (3-3).
$6, Entire painting.

Perf. 13¼x13 Syncopated
2015, Mar. 22　　　　　　　　　Litho.
4257　　Horiz. strip of 3　　　1.40 1.40
　a.-b.　A1393 $1.20 Either single　.40　.40
　c.　A1393 $1.50 multi　　　　　.50　.50
Souvenir Sheet
Perf. 12¾x12½ Syncopated
4258 A1393 $6 multi　　　　　2.00 2.00
No. 4258 contains one 157x28mm stamp.

Writers — A1394

Designs: No. 4259, $1.20, Tang Xianzu (1550-1616) (6-1). No. 4260, $1.20, Feng Menglong (1574-1645) (6-2). No. 4261, $1.20, Pu Songling (1640-1715) (6-3). No. 4262, $1.20, Hong Sheng (1645-1704) (6-4). No. 4263, $1.20, Kong Shangren (1648-1718) (6-5). No. 4264, $1.20, Cao Xueqin (c.1715-c.1763) (6-6).

Perf. 13 Syncopated
2015, Apr. 4　　　　　　Litho. & Engr.
4259-4264 A1394　Set of 6　　2.40 2.40

Slender West Lake — A1395

Designs: No. 4265, $1.20, Lotus Bridge (3-1). No. 4266, $1.20, Twenty-four Bridge (3-2). $1.50, White Pagoda (3-3).

Perf. 13¼x13 Syncopated
2015, Apr. 18　　　　　Litho. & Engr.
4265-4267 A1395　Set of 3　　1.25 1.25

Scenes from *Journey to the West*, by Wu Cheng'en — A1396

Designs: No. 4268, $1.20, Great sage equalling heaven (4-1). No. 4269, $1.20, Sun Wukong surrendered to Buddha (4-2). No. 4270, $1.50, Tang monk makes vows to go to the West (4-3). No. 4271, $1.50, Tang monk disciples Monkey King (4-4).
$6, Making havoc in heaven.

Perf. 13¼ Syncopated
2015, May 3　　　　　　　　　Litho.
4268-4271 A1396　Set of 4　　1.75 1.75
Souvenir Sheet
Photo.
Perf. 13¼x13 Syncopated
4272 A1396 $6 multi　　　　　2.00 2.00

Vacation Activities A1397

Designs: 80f, Man taking photograph. $1.20, Family in automobile on bridge. $3, Backpacking.

Die Cut Perf. 12½ Syncopated
2015, May 19　　　　　　　　Photo.
Self-Adhesive
4273 A1397　80f multi　　　　.25　.25
4274 A1397　$1.20 multi　　　.40　.40
4275 A1397　$3 multi　　　　1.00 1.00
　Nos. 4273-4275 (3)　　　1.65 1.65

World Metrology Day — A1398

Perf. 13¼x12¾ Syncopated
2015, May 20　　　　　　　　Litho.
4276 A1398 $1.20 multi　　　　.40　.40

Ships — A1399

Designs: No. 4277, $1.20, Space tracking ship (4-1). No. 4278, $1.20, Liquified natural gas tanker (4-2). No. 4279, $1.20, Floating Production Storage and Offloading ship (4-3). $1.50, Guided missile destroyer (4-4).

Perf. 13¼x12¾ Syncopated
2015, June 3　　　　　　　　Litho.
4277-4280 A1399　Set of 4　　1.75 1.75

World Environment Day — A1400

Perf. 13¼x12¾ Syncopated
2015, June 5　　　　　　　　Photo.
4281 A1400 $1.20 multi　　　　.40　.40

Father's Day — A1401

Litho. With Foil Application
Perf. 13¼x13 Syncopated
2015, June 13
4282 A1401 $1.20 multi　　　.40　.40

Rainbows, Hearts and Gift Box — A1402

2015, June 18　　Litho.　Perf. 13¼
4283 A1402 $1.20 multi + label　.40　.40
See Stamps With Attached Labels note after No. 3197.

Mickey Mouse — A1403

2015, June 20　　Litho.　　Perf. 12
4284 A1403 $1.20 multi　　　.40　.40
See Stamps With Attached Labels note after No. 3197.

Qiantang River Tidal Bores — A1404

No. 4285: a, Crossing bores (3-1). b, Spectators watching wave (3-2). c, Spectators watching reverse bore (3-3).

Perf. 13¼x12¾ Syncopated
2015, July 1　　　　　Litho. & Engr.
4285　　Horiz. strip of 3　　　1.40 1.40
　a.-b.　A1404 $1.20 Either single　.40　.40
　c.　A1404 $1.50 multi　　　　.50　.50

Peace Dove — A1405

2015, July 3　　Litho.　　Perf. 13¼
4286 A1405 $1.20 multi + label　.40　.40
See Stamps With Attached Labels note after No. 3197.

Qingyuan Mountain — A1406

Designs: 80f, Sky Lake (3-1). No. 4288, $1.20, Rock carvings (3-2). No. 4289, $1.20, Statue of Lao Zi (3-3).

Perf. 13¼x12¾ Syncopated
2015, July 18　　　　　Litho. & Engr.
4287-4289 A1406　Set of 3　　1.10 1.10

Stylized Athletes — A1407

2015, July 20　　Litho.　Perf. 13¼
4290 A1407 $1.20 multi + label　.40　.40
See Stamps With Attached Labels note after No. 3197.

Happiness of the People A1408

Buildings and: 80f, Fruit sellers, machine (4-1). No. 4292, $1.20, Bus, medical care (4-2). No. 4293, $1.20, Automobile, person in wheelchair, voters (4-3). No. 4294, $1.20, Ferris wheel, tai chi, woman pushing baby carriage (4-4).

Perf. 13x12¾ Syncopated
2015, July 25　　　　　　　　Photo.
4291-4294 A1408　Set of 4　　1.40 1.40
4294a　　Souvenir sheet of 4,
　　　　　#4291-4294　　　　1.40 1.40

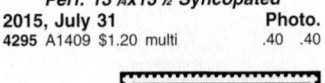

Awarding of 2022 Winter Olympics to Beijing — A1409

Perf. 13¼x13½ Syncopated
2015, July 31　　　　　　　　Photo.
4295 A1409 $1.20 multi　　　　.40　.40

Lord Bao (999-1062), Government Official A1410

Designs: No. 4296, $1.20, Lord Bao throwing inkstone into water (2-1). No. 4297, $1.20, Case of Chen Shimei (2-2).
$6, Lord Bao seated.

Perf. 13¼ Syncopated
2015, Aug. 8   **Photo.**
4296-4297 A1410   Set of 2   .75 .75

Souvenir Sheet

Perf. 13¼x13½ Syncopated
4298 A1410 $6 multi   1.90 1.90

No. 4298 contains one 60x67mm stamp.

Mandarin Ducks
A1411

Perf. 13x12¾ Syncopated
2015, Aug. 20   **Litho. & Engr.**
4299 A1411 $1.20 multi   .40 .40

Lunar Exploration by China — A1412

2015, Aug. 20   **Litho.**   **Perf. 13¼**
4300 A1412 $1.20 multi + label   .40 .40

See Stamps With Attached Labels note after No. 3197.

Miniature Sheet

Yellow River — A1413

No. 4301: a, $1.20, Beginning of river (9-1). b, $1.20, Nine Bays (9-2). c, $1.20, River bend in Hinterland (9-3). d, $1.20, Great bend (9-4). e, $1.20, River approaching Hukou Waterfalls (9-5). f, $1.20, Hukou Waterfalls and Sanjing (9-6). g, $1.50, Helou area (9-7). h, $1.50, Zhongshou Plain (9-8). i, $3, Mountains and buildings in foreground (9-9).

Perf. 13¼x12¾ Syncopated
2015, Aug. 23   **Photo.**
4301 A1413   Sheet of 9, #a-i   4.25 4.25

Tibet Autonomous Region, 50th Anniv. — A1414

No. 4302: a, Tibetans, symbols of Tibet, cranes and mountains (3-1). b, Tibetans, doves, buildings (3-2). c, Tibetan family, house, symbols of Tibet (3-3).

Perf. 13¼x12¾ Syncopated
2015, Sept. 1   **Photo.**
4302   Horiz. strip of 3   1.25 1.25
a.-c.   A1414 $1.20 Any single   .40 .40

Victory in World War II, 70th Anniv. — A1415

Soldiers and: No. 4303, 80f, September 18 Memorial Museum (13-1). No. 4304, 80f,

Northeast China Revolutionary Martyrs Memorial Hall (13-2). No. 4305, $1.20, Museum of the War of Chinese People's Resistance Against Japanese Aggression (13-3). No. 4306, $1.20, Shanghai Songhu Anti-Japanese War Memorial Hall (13-4). No. 4307, $1.20, Museum of Victims in the Nanjing Massacre by Japanese Invaders (13-5). No. 4308, $1.20, Taierzhuang Campaign Memorial Hall (13-6). No. 4309, $1.20, Yan'an Revolutionary Memorial Hall (13-7). No. 4310, $1.20, Memorial Hall of Former Site of the Eighth Route Army Headquarters (13-8). No. 4311, $1.20, Hundred Regiments Offensive Memorial Hall (13-9). No. 4312, $1.20, Pingxingguan Victory Memorial Hall (13-10). No. 4313, $1.20, Museum of Tunnel Warfare at Ranzhuang (13-11). No. 4314, $1.20, New Fourth Army Memorial Hall (13-12). No. 4315, $1.20, Memorial Hall of Anti-Japanese War in Western Yunnan (13-13).
$6, Statue of soldier with sword, vert.

Perf. 13¼x13 Syncopated
2015, Sept. 3   **Photo.**
4303-4315 A1415   Set of 13   4.75 4.75

Souvenir Sheet
4316 A1415 $6 multi   1.90 1.90

No. 4316 contains one 50x60mm stamp.

Flying Fairies — A1416

2015, Sept. 9   **Litho.**   **Perf. 13¼**
4317 A1416 $1.20 multi   .40 .40

See Stamps With Attached Labels note after No. 3197.

Birthday Cake — A1417

2015, Sept. 10   **Litho.**   **Perf. 12**
4318 A1417 $1.20 multi   .40 .40

See Stamps With Attached Labels note after No. 3197.

Synthetic Crystalline Bovine Insulin, 50th Anniv. A1418

Perf. 13x12¾ Syncopated
2015, Sept. 17   **Photo.**
4319 A1418 $1.20 multi   .40 .40

10th International Garden Expo, Wuhan — A1419

Designs: $1.20, Buildings (2-1). $1.50, Buildings, diff. (2-2).

Perf. 13x12¾ Syncopated
2015, Sept. 25   **Photo.**
4320-4321 A1419   Set of 2   .85 .85

United Nations, 70th Anniv. — A1420

Designs: $1.20, United Nations emblem, stylized dove (2-1). $1.50, United Nations Headquarters, arrows (2-2).

Perf. 13¼x13 Syncopated
2015, Sept. 26   **Litho.**
4322-4323 A1420   Set of 2   .85 .85

Xianjiang Production and Construction Corps, 60th Anniv. — A1421

No. 4324: a, Building, wind generators, airplane, train, bridge (3-1). b, Agricultural products, city skyline, airplane, bridge over river, doves, farm community (3-2). c, Dancers (3-3).

Perf. 13¼x13 Syncopated
2015, Oct. 1   **Photo.**
4324   Horiz. strip of 3   1.25 1.25
a.-c.   A1421 $1.20 Any single   .40 .40

Tianjin University, 120th Anniv. A1422

Perf. 13x12¾ Syncopated
2015, Oct. 2   **Photo.**
4325 A1422 $1.20 multi   .40 .40

Good Fortune and Longevity A1423

Perf. 12¾ Syncopated
2015, Oct. 9   **Litho.**
4326 A1423 $1.20 multi   .40 .40
a.   Souvenir sheet of 2, #3969b
       (perf. 12¾), 4326   1.40 1.40

Palace Museum — A1424

Designs: No. 4327, $1.20, Meridian Gate (4-1). No. 4328, $1.20, Hall of Supreme Harmony (4-2). No. 4329, $1.50, Corner Tower (4-3). No. 4330, $1.50, Gate of Heavenly Purity (4-4).

Perf. 13¼x12 Syncopated
2015, Oct. 10   **Litho.**
Stamp + Label
4327-4330 A1424   Set of 4   1.75 1.75

Poets — A1425

Designs: No. 4331, $1.20, Du Fu (712-70) (4-1). No. 4332, $1.20, Su Dongpo (1037-1101) (4-2). No. 4333, $1.20, Bai Juyi (772-846) (4-3). No. 4334, $1.20, Cao Zhi (192-232) (4-4).

Perf. 13¼ Syncopated
2015, Nov. 12   **Litho. & Engr.**
4331-4334 A1425   Set of 4   1.50 1.50

Delivery of First ARJ21 Airplane to Chengdu Airlines — A1426

Perf. 13¼x13 Syncopated
2015, Nov. 28   **Photo.**
4335 A1426 $1.20 multi   .40 .40

Chinese Values A1427

Designs: No. 4336, $1.20, Bird's nest (importance of family) (3-1). No. 4337, $1.20, Ox (dreams and spirit, 47x28mm) (3-2). $1.50, Child daydreaming (unity of personal and national dreams) (3-3).

Perf. 13 Syncopated, 13¼x13 Syncopated (#4337)
2015, Nov. 29   **Photo.**
4336-4338 A1427   Set of 3   1.25 1.25

New Year 2016 (Year of the Monkey) A1428

Designs: No. 4339, $1.20, Monkey with peach (2-1). No. 4340, $1.20, Three monkeys (2-2).

Perf. 13 Syncopated
2016, Jan. 5   **Litho. & Engr.**
4339-4340 A1428   Set of 2   .75 .75
4340a   Booklet pane of 10, 5 each
           #4339-4340   7.50 —
           Complete booklet, #4340a 7.50

Children Celebrating Chinese New Year A1429

Perf. 13 Syncopated
2016, Jan. 10   **Litho.**
4341 A1429 $1.20 multi   .40 .40

Paintings by Liu Haisu (1896-1994) — A1430

Designs: No. 4342, $1.20, Land So Rich in Beauty (3-1). No. 4343, $1.20, Ink Lotus (3-2). $1.50, Yellow Mountain Renzi Waterfall (3-3).

Litho. (#4342), Photo. (#4343), Litho. & Engr. (#4344)

2016, Mar. 16   Perf. 13 Syncopated
4342-4344   A1430   Set of 3   1.25   1.25

China Post, 120th Anniv. — A1431

Designs: No. 4345, $1.20, Mailbox, post office, statue of postman on horse, bicycle (4-1). No. 4346, $1.20, All-day automated kiosk, modern post office interior (4-2). No. 4347, $1.20, Airplane, parcel sorting conveyors, mail van (4-3). No. 4348, $1.20, Automated savings bank kiosks, credit cards (4-4).

Perf. 13¼x13 Syncopated
2016, Mar. 20   Litho.
4345-4348   A1431   Set of 4   1.50   1.50

Painting of Gaoyi Tu, by Sun Wei — A1432

No. 4349: a, Right side of painting (47x35mm) (3-1). b, Center of painting (62x35mm) (3-2). c, Left side of painting (47x35mm) (3-3).
$6, Entire painting.

Perf. 13¼ Syncopated
2016, Apr. 2   Photo.
4349   Horiz. strip of 3   1.25   1.25
   a.-b.   A1432 $1.20 Either single   .40   .40
   c.   A1432 $1.50 multi   .45   .45
Souvenir Sheet
Perf. 13½x13¾ Syncopated
4350   A1432 $6 multi   1.90   1.90
No. 4350 contains one 134x35mm stamp.

Jiaotong University, 120th Anniv. — A1433

Perf. 13½ Syncopated
2016, Apr. 8   Photo.
4351   A1433 $1.20 multi   .40   .40

Song Ci (1186-1249), Forensic Medicine Expert — A1434

Song Ci, Scribe and Child — A1435

Perf. 13½ Syncopated
2016, Apr. 13   Litho. & Engr.
4352   A1434 $1.20 multi   .40   .40
4353   A1435 $1.50 multi   .45   .45

Nationwide Reading A1436

Perf. 13¼x13½ Syncopated
2016, Apr. 23   Litho.
4354   A1436 $1.20 multi   .40   .40

A1437

Tangshan International Horticulture Exposition — A1438

Perf. 13 Syncopated
2016, Apr. 29   Litho.
4355   A1437 $1.20 multi   .40   .40
4356   A1438 $1.50 multi   .45   .45

24 Solar Terms — A1439

No. 4357: a, Beginning of summer (woman, butterflies and flowers) (6-1). b, Lesser fullness of grain (woman at loom) (6-2). c, Grain in beard (man in rice paddy) (6-3). d, Summer solstice (crouching children and flowers) (6-4). e, Lesser heat (man and goat near water wheel) (6-5). f, Greater heat (children looking at scroll under vines) (6-6).

Perf. 13 Syncopated
2016, May 5   Photo.
4357   A1439 $1.20 Block of 6, #a-
      f   2.25   2.25
Values are for stamps with surrounding selvage.

Scientists A1440

Designs: No. 4358, $1.20, Ding Wenjiang (1887-1936), geologist (4-1). No. 4359, $1.20, Jin Shanbao (1895-1997), agronomist (4-2). No. 4360, $1.20, Ye Qisun (1898-1977), physicist (4-3). No. 4361, $1.20, Ye Duzheng (1916-2013), meteorologist (4-4).

Perf. 13¼ Syncopated
2016, May 8   Litho. & Engr.
4358-4361   A1440   Set of 4   1.50   1.50

Snow-covered Landscape — A1441

Wanfeng Peaks Forest A1442

Sand Lake A1443

Xixi National Wetland Park A1444

Perf. 13x12¾ Syncopated
2016, May 12   Photo.
4362   A1441   40f multi   .25   .25
4363   A1442 $1 multi   .30   .30
4364   A1443 $2 multi   .60   .60
4365   A1444 $4.20 multi   1.25   1.25
    Nos. 4362-4365 (4)   2.40   2.40

Ancient Chinese Towns — A1445

Designs: No. 4366, $1.20, Zhentong (6-1). No. 4367, $1.20, Qiliping (6-2). No. 4368, $1.20, Qingyan (6-3). No. 4369, $1.20, Zhujiajiao (6-4). No. 4370, $1.20, Sanhe (6-5). No. 4371, $1.20, Huangyao (6-6).

Perf. 13¼x12¾ Syncopated
2016, May 19   Litho. & Engr.
4366-4371   A1445   Set of 6   2.25   2.25

Cultural Heritage Day — A1446

No. 4372 — Inscription on emblem: a, $1.20, China Intangible Cultural Heritage (2-1). b, $1.50, China Cultural Heritage (2-2).

Perf. 13¼x13½ Syncopated
2016, June 11   Litho.
4372   A1446   Horiz. pair, #a-b   .85   .85

Opening of Shanghai Disney Resort — A1447

Designs: $1.20, Mickey and Minnie Mouse (2-1). $1.50, Tinker Bell, Enchanted Storybook Castle (2-2).

Perf. 13¼x13 Syncopated
2016, June 16   Photo.
4373-4374   A1447   Set of 2   .85   .85
  4374a   Souvenir sheet of 2,
       #4373-4374   1.25   1.25
No. 4374a sold for $4.

A1448

The Dream of Red Mansions, Novel by Cao Xueqin — A1449

Scenes from novel: No. 4375, $1.20, Xifeng abuses her power (4-1). No. 4376, $1.20, Lingguan writes on the ground (4-2). No. 4377, $1.20, Qingwen, the maid, tearing the fan (4-3). $1.50, Baoyu receives a flogging (4-4).
$6, Rong-guo House makes itself ready for an important visitor.

Perf. 13 Syncopated
2016, June 18   Photo.
4375-4378   A1448   Set of 4   1.60   1.60
Souvenir Sheet
4379   A1449 $6 multi   1.90   1.90
Compare with Nos. 4203-4207.

Longxing Temple, Zhengding — A1450

Designs: $1.20, Moni Hall (2-1). $1.50, Dabei Pavilion (2-2).

Perf. 13¼x13 Syncopated

2016, June 26			Litho.	
4380-4381	A1450	Set of 2	.85	.85

Pass the Flame — A1451

2016, July 8   Litho.   Perf. 13¼

4382	A1451	$1.20 multi + label	.40	.40

See Stamps With Attached Labels note after No. 3197.

Artifacts From Ruins of Yin — A1452

No. 4383: a, 80f, Oracle bone with inscription (3-1). b, $1.20, Bronze ware (3-2). c, $1.50, Jadeware (3-3)

Perf. 11¾ Syncopated

2016, July 13			Litho. & Engr.	
4383	A1452	Horiz. strip of 3, #a-c	1.10	1.10

Red-billed Leiothrix A1455

Perf. 13x12¾ Syncopated

2016, Aug. 9			Litho. & Engr.	
4390	A1455	$1.20 multi	.40	.40

Miniature Sheet

Great Wall of China — A1456

No. 4391: a, $1.20, Shanhai Pass and Old Dragon Head (9-1). b, $1.20, Hushan Great Wall (9-2). c, $1.20, Jinshanling, Jiumenkou and Huangyaguan (9-3). d, $1.20, Gubeikou, Huanghuacheng, Mutianyu, Badaling and Juyongguan (9-4). e, $1.20, Zijingguan, Pingxingguan, Niangziguan, Yanmenguan, Deshengkou and Bianjinlou (9-5). f, $1.20, Pianguan (9-6). g, $1.50, Zhenbeitai and Huamachi (9-7). h, $1.50, Sanguankou (9-8). i, $3, Yumenguan and Jiayuguan (9-9).

Perf. 13¼x12¾ Syncopated

2016, Aug. 20			Litho. & Engr.	
4391	A1456	Sheet of 9, #a-i	4.00	4.00

G20 Summit, Hangzhou — A1457

Perf. 13¼x13 Syncopated

2016, Aug. 27			Photo.	
4392	A1457	$1.20 multi	.40	.40

Full Moon on Mid-Autumn Night — A1458

Perf. 13¼ Syncopated

2016, Aug. 28			Litho.	
4393	A1458	$1.20 multi	.40	.40

Microperforations surround the Moon in the vignette.

SEMI-POSTAL STAMPS

> Catalogue values for unused stamps in this section are for Never Hinged items.

Girl Holding Ball — SP1

1984, Feb. 16		Photo.	Perf. 11½	
B1	SP1	8f + 2f shown (2-1)	1.25	.30
B2	SP1	8f + 2f Boy, panda (2-2)	1.25	.30

Surtax for China Children's Fund. T.92.

Hands Reading Braille — SP2

No. B4, Sign language, lip reading. No. B5, Artificial limb. No. B6, Handicapped person in wheelchair.

1985, Mar. 15		Photo.	Perf. 11½	
B3	SP2	8f + 2f shown (4-1)	1.00	.60
B4	SP2	8f + 2f multi (4-2)	1.00	.60
B5	SP2	8f + 2f multi (4-3)	1.00	.60
B6	SP2	8f + 2f multi (4-4)	1.00	.60
		Nos. B3-B6 (4)	4.00	2.40

Surtax for China Welfare Fund. T.105.

Children (T.137) SP3

No. B7, Friends. No. B8, Penguins. No. B9, Bird, Moon, Sun. No. B10, Girl, boy playing ball.

1989, June 1		Litho.	Perf. 12	
B7	SP3	8f +4f multi (4-1)	.25	.25
B8	SP3	8f +4f multi (4-2)	.25	.25
B9	SP3	8f +4f multi (4-3)	.25	.25
B10	SP3	8f +4f multi (4-4)	.25	.25
a.		Strip of 4, #B7-B10	1.50	1.50

Intl Children's Day, 40th anniv., and 10th Intl. Year of the Child. Surtax for China Children's Fund.

Sichuan Earthquake Relief — SP4

2008, May 20		Photo.	Perf. 13x13¼	
B11	SP4	$1.20 + $1 multi + label	18.00	4.00

AIR POST STAMPS

Mail Plane and Temple of Heaven — AP1

1951, May 1   Engr.   Perf. 12½
Without Gum

C1	AP1	$1000 carmine	1.00	.40
C2	AP1	$3000 green	1.00	.40
C3	AP1	$5000 orange	1.00	.40
a.		Pair, imperf. between	600.00	—
C4	AP1	$10,000 vio brn & grn	3.00	1.00
C5	AP1	$30,000 dk bl & brn	24.00	4.25
		Nos. C1-C5 (5)	30.00	6.45

Planes at Airport — AP2

Designs: 28f, Plane over winding mountain highway. 35f, Plane over railroad yard. 52f, Plane over ship.

1957-58		Without Gum	Perf. 14	
C6	AP2	16f indigo	16.00	1.00
C7	AP2	28f olive black	16.00	1.00
C8	AP2	35f slate	16.00	5.00
C9	AP2	52f Prus blue ('58)	16.00	2.00
		Nos. C6-C9 (4)	64.00	9.00

POSTAGE DUE STAMPS

Grain and Cogwheel — D1

1950, Sept. 1		Typo.	Perf. 12½	
		Without Gum		
J1	D1	$100 steel blue	.25	.25
J2	D1	$200 steel blue	.25	.25
J3	D1	$500 steel blue	.25	.25
J4	D1	$800 steel blue	25.00	1.00
J5	D1	$1000 steel blue	.45	.40
J6	D1	$2000 steel blue	.70	.40
J7	D1	$5000 steel blue	.70	.60
J8	D1	$8000 steel blue	.70	1.00
J9	D1	$10,000 steel blue	2.00	2.00
		Nos. J1-J9 (9)	30.30	6.15

D2

1954, Aug. 18		Litho.	Perf. 14	
		Without Gum		
J10	D2	$100 red	1.50	.25
J11	D2	$200 red	.75	.25
J12	D2	$500 red	1.50	.25
J13	D2	$800 red	.60	.25
J14	D2	$1600 red	.75	.25
		Nos. J10-J14 (5)	5.10	1.25

MILITARY STAMP

Red Star, 8-1 in Center — M1

1953, Aug.   Litho.   Perf. 14
Without Gum

M1	M1	$800 yel, org & red	300.00	125.00

This stamp also was printed in deep purple, orange & red (value, $3,000.), and blue, orange & red (value, $240,000). These were not issued.

While it has been assumed for many years that each color was for a separate branch of the armed forces (army, air force and navy), there is no documentation to support that theory. Quantities printed also do not correspond to the number of servicemen in each branch.

M2

1995		Litho.	Perf. 12	
M4	M2	20f multicolored	6.50	2.00

NORTHEAST CHINA

The Northeast Liberation Area included the provinces of Liaoning, Kirin, Jehol and Heilungkiang, the area generally known as Manchuria under the Japanese. The first post war issues were local overprints on stamps of Manchukuo. In early 1946, a Ministry of Posts and Telegraphs served the areas already liberated, and in August, 1946, a Communications Committee of the Political Council was established. In June, 1947, these postal services were subordinated to the Harbin General Post Office, and this was extended to Changchun on Oct. 22, 1948, and to Mukden on Nov. 4, 1948. It was rapidly extended to cover all Manchuria.

Rough Perfs
Rough perforations are normal on most regional issues.

All Stamps Issued without Gum

Mao Tse-tung
A1   A2

1946, Feb. Unwmk. Litho. *Perf. 11*

1L1	A1	$1 violet	22.50	12.00
1L2	A2	$2 vermilion	2.50	1.00
1L3	A2	$5 orange	2.75	1.00
a.		Booklet pane of 6	250.00	
1L4	A2	$10 blue	3.00	1.25
a.		Booklet pane of 6	250.00	
		Nos. 1L1-1L4 (4)	30.75	15.25

Value, imperf set $125.
For surcharges see Nos. 1L20-1L23, 1L49-
1L50, 1L89, 1L91, 1L93.

Map of China,
Lion, Hyena
and Chiang
Kai-shek — A3

1946, Dec. 12 *Perf. 10½*

1L5	A3	$1 violet	2.25	1.50
1L6	A3	$2 orange	2.25	1.50
1L7	A3	$5 org brn	7.50	7.00
1L8	A3	$10 lt grn	12.00	10.00
a.		Imperf., pair	60.00	
		Nos. 1L5-1L8 (4)	24.00	20.00

10th anniversary of the capture of Chiang
Kai-shek at Sian.

Railroad
Workers,
Chengchow
A4

1947, Feb. 7 *Perf. 10½*

1L9	A4	$1 pink	2.00	2.00
1L10	A4	$2 dull grn	2.00	2.00
1L11	A4	$5 pink	3.50	2.25
1L12	A4	$10 dull grn	7.00	5.50
		Nos. 1L9-1L12 (4)	14.50	11.75

24th anniversary of the Chengchow railroad
workers' strike and massacre.

Women (Worker,
Soldier and
Farmer) — A5

Wmk. Chinese Characters in Sheet
1947, Mar. 8 *Perf. 10½x11*

1L13	A5	$5 brick red	5.00	2.00
1L14	A5	$10 brown	5.00	2.00

International Women's Day, March 8.
Exists imperf.

Same Overprinted
in Green
("Northeast Postal
Service")

1947, Mar. 18

1L15	A5	$5 brick red	9.50	6.00
1L16	A5	$10 brown	9.50	6.00

Exists imperf.

Children
Carrying
Banner — A6

1947, Apr. 4 *Perf. 11x10½*
Granite Paper

1L17	A6	$5 rose red	7.00	5.00
1L18	A6	$10 lt green	12.00	9.50
1L19	A6	$30 orange	17.50	11.00
		Nos. 1L17-1L19 (3)	36.50	25.50

Children's Day.

Nos. 1L1-1L2
Surcharged in Red,
Brown, Black, Blue or
Green

1947, Apr. Unwmk. *Perf. 11*

1L20	A1	$50 on $1 vio (R)	30.00	32.50
a.		Brown surcharge	30.00	32.50
1L21	A2	$50 on $2 ver	30.00	32.50
a.		Brown surcharge	30.00	32.50
1L22	A1	$100 on $1 vio	30.00	32.50
a.		Green surcharge	30.00	32.50
1L23	A2	$100 on $2 ver (Bl)	30.00	32.50
a.		Green surcharge	30.00	32.50
		Nos. 1L20-1L23 (4)	120.00	130.00

Farmer and
Worker — A7

Wmk. Chinese Characters in Sheet
1947, May 1 *Perf. 10½x11*
Granite Paper

1L24	A7	$10 orange red	6.00	6.00
1L25	A7	$30 ultra	10.00	10.00
1L26	A7	$50 gray green	6.50	6.50
		Nos. 1L24-1L26 (3)	22.50	22.50

Labor Day. Value, imperf. pairs, set $425.

Ax Severing
Chain — A8

1947, May 4 *Perf. 11*

1L27	A8	$10 brt green	8.00	8.00
1L28	A8	$30 brown	8.00	8.00
1L29	A8	$50 violet	10.00	10.00
		Nos. 1L27-1L29 (3)	26.00	26.00

28th anniversary of the students' revolt at
Peking University against the 1918 peace
treaty. Value, imperf. pairs, set $525.

Workers with Banner: "Oppose
Imperialist Aggression" — A9

1947, May 30 *Perf. 10½x11*
Banner in Red

1L30	A9	$2 brt lilac	7.50	8.00
1L31	A9	$5 brt green	7.50	8.00
1L32	A9	$10 yellow	9.50	9.00
1L33	A9	$20 violet	9.00	8.50
1L34	A9	$30 red brown	9.00	8.50
1L35	A9	$50 dk blue	12.00	8.50
1L36	A9	$100 brown	15.00	8.50
a.		Souvenir sheet of 7	375.00	
		Nos. 1L30-1L36 (7)	69.50	59.00

22nd anniversary of the Shanghai-Nanking
Road incident. No. 1L36a is on granite paper
and contains 7 imperf. stamps similar to Nos.
1L30-1L36. Size: 215x158mm. Value, imperf.
pairs, ordinary paper, set $1,300.

Mao and Communist Flag — A10

1947, July 1 *Perf. 10½x11*

1L37	A10	$10 red	20.00	24.00
1L38	A10	$30 brt lilac	20.00	24.00
1L39	A10	$50 rose brn	60.00	65.00
1L40	A10	$100 vermilion	70.00	80.00
		Nos. 1L37-1L40 (4)	170.00	193.00

26th anniversary of the founding of the Chinese Communist Party.

Hand Holding
Rifle — A11

1947, July 7 *Perf. 10½*

1L41	A11	$10 orange	10.00	12.00
1L42	A11	$30 green	10.00	12.00
1L43	A11	$50 dull blue	15.00	14.00
1L44	A11	$100 brown	20.00	18.00
a.		Souvenir sheet of 4	475.00	400.00
		Nos. 1L41-1L44 (4)	55.00	56.00

10th anniversary of the start of Sino-Japanese War. No. 1L44a contains 4 imperf.
stamps similar to Nos. 1L41-1L44. Size:
149x107mm.
Exist imperf. Value, set of pairs $1,100.

White Mountain
and Black
Water,
Northeast
China — A12

Wmk. Zigzag Lines (141)
1947, Aug. 15 *Perf. 10½*

1L45	A12	$10 brown org	5.50	8.50
1L46	A12	$30 lt ol grn	5.50	8.50
1L47	A12	$50 blue grn	17.50	16.00
1L48	A12	$100 sepia	27.50	22.50
		Nos. 1L45-1L48 (4)	56.00	55.50

2nd anniversary of the reoccupation of
Northeast China and the surrender of Japan.
Exist imperf. Value, set of pairs $700.

Nos. 1L1-1L2
Surcharged in Black,
Red, Green or Blue

1947, Aug. 29 Unwmk. *Perf. 11*

1L49	A1	$5 on $1 vio	40.00	40.00
a.		Red surcharge	40.00	40.00
b.		Green surcharge	40.00	40.00
1L50	A2	$10 on $2 ver	40.00	40.00
a.		Blue surcharge	40.00	40.00
b.		Green surcharge	40.00	40.00

Map of
Manchuria — A13

1947, Sept. 18 Unwmk.
White Paper

1L51	A13	$10 gray green	7.00	10.00
1L52	A13	$20 rose lilac	7.00	10.00
1L53	A13	$30 black brown	13.00	10.00
1L54	A13	$50 carmine	13.00	10.00
		Nos. 1L51-1L54 (4)	40.00	40.00

16th anniversary of Japanese attack on
Mukden, Sept. 18, 1931.

Northeast
Political
Council
Offices — A14

1947, Oct. 10 *Perf. 10½*

1L55	A14	$10 yel orange	50.00	50.00
1L56	A14	$20 rose red	50.00	50.00
1L57	A14	$100 brown	110.00	110.00
		Nos. 1L55-1L57 (3)	210.00	210.00

35th anniversary of the founding of the Chinese Republic.

Mao Tse-tung (Value
figures
repeated) — A15

1947, Oct. 10 White Paper *Perf. 11*

1L58	A15	$1 brown	3.50	1.50
1L59	A15	$5 gray green	2.50	1.50
1L60	A15	$10 brt green	18.00	9.00
1L61	A15	$15 bluish lilac	18.00	9.00
1L62	A15	$20 brt rose	1.00	1.50
1L63	A15	$30 green	1.00	2.00
1L64	A15	$50 black brown	25.00	13.50
1L65	A15	$90 blue	6.50	4.00
		Nos. 1L58-1L65 (8)	75.50	42.00

Newsprint

1L66	A15	$100 red		.80
a.		White paper	8.00	5.00
1L67	A15	$500 red orange	40.00	17.50
a.		White paper	32.50	30.00

Type A22 resembles A15, but has "YUAN" at
upper right.
The $1, $90 were also printed on newsprint.
See footnote following No. 1L72.
See Nos. 1L68-1L72. For surcharges see
Nos. 1L84-1L88, 1L90, 1L92, 1L94.

White Paper

1947, Nov. Redrawn

1L68	A15	$50 lt grn	1.00	1.50
1L69	A15	$150 red org, wmkd.		
		Chinese charac-		
		ters	2.25	1.50
a.		Unwatermarked	2.75	
1L70	A15	$250 bluish lil	.90	1.50
a.		Wmkd. Chinese characters	1.25	1.50

Nos. 1L69 and 1L69a exist in same sheet.

1947, Dec. Unwmk. Newsprint

1L71	A15	$300 green	55.00	30.00
1L72	A15	$1000 yellow	1.50	1.50
a.		White paper	1.50	1.50
		Nos. 1L68-1L72 (5)	60.65	36.00

Panel below portrait 8½x3mm on Nos.
1L68-1L70; 7x3mm on No. 1L58-1L67. Nos.
1L68-1L70 have different ornamental border.
Nos. 1L71-1L72 without zeros for cents.
For surcharges see Nos. 1L90, 1L92, 1L94.

Hand Holding
Torch — A16

1947, Dec. 12 Unwmk. *Perf. 11*
White Paper

1L73	A16	$30 rose red	17.50	17.50
1L74	A16	$90 dk bl	19.00	17.50
1L75	A16	$150 green	21.00	17.50
		Nos. 1L73-1L75 (3)	57.50	52.50

11th anniversary of the capture of Chiang
Kai-shek at Sian.

Tomb of Gen. Li
Chao-lin — A17

1948, Mar. 9 Unwmk. *Perf. 10½x11*
1L76 A17 $30 green   24.00 24.00
 a. Granite paper, wmkd.   24.00 24.00
1L77 A17 $150 vio gray   24.00 24.00
 a. Granite paper, wmkd.   24.00 24.00
2nd anniversary of the assassination of
Gen. Li Chao-lin, Commander of 3rd Army.

Globe and
Banner — A18

Wmk. Chinese Characters in Sheet
1948, May 1   *Perf. 11x10½*
1L78 A18 $50 red   17.00 13.00
1L79 A18 $150 green   9.50 20.00
1L80 A18 $250 lilac   9.50 40.00
 Nos. 1L78-1L80 (3)   36.00 73.00
Labor Day.

Student, Torch
and
Banner — A19

1948, May 4 Unwmk. *Perf. 10½x11*
Granite paper
1L81 A19 $50 green   21.00 20.00
1L82 A19 $150 brown   21.00 25.00
1L83 A19 $250 red   25.00 30.00
 Nos. 1L81-1L83 (3)   67.00 75.00
Youth Day, May 4.

Nos. 1L58, 1L61,
1L59, 1L63, 1L65,
1L2-1L4, 1L68-1L69,
1L71 Srchd. in Black,
Blue, Red or Green

1948-49   *Perf. 11*
1L84 A15 $100 on $1   75.00 90.00
 a. Blue surcharge   50.00 50.00
1L85 A15 $100 on $15   28.00 28.00
 a. Blue surcharge   50.00 50.00
1L86 A15 $300 on $5 (R)   55.00 42.50
1L87 A15 $300 on $30 (R)   20.00 20.00
1L88 A15 $300 on $90 (R)   15.00 15.00
1L89 A2 $500 on $2   12.00 12.00
1L90 A15 $500 on $50 (R,
                        '49)   30.00 25.00
1L91 A2 $1500 on $5 (Bl)   12.00 10.00
1L92 A15 $1500 on $150
                     (G; '49)   25.00 25.00
 a. Blue surcharge   50.00 50.00
1L93 A2 $2500 on $10 (R)   15.00 15.00
1L94 A15 $2500 on $300
                        ('49)   20.00 20.00
 Nos. 1L84-1L94 (11)   307.00 302.50

Crane
Operator — A20

Wmk. Chinese Characters in Sheet
1948, May   *Perf. 11*
1L95 A20 $100 red & pink   4.50   2.00
1L96 A20 $300 vio brn & yel   7.50   2.75
1L97 A20 $500 bl & grn   11.00   3.50
 Nos. 1L95-1L97 (3)   23.00   8.25
6th All-China Labor Conference, Harbin.

Farmer, Worker and
Soldier
Saluting — A21

1948, Dec. 3 Unwmk. *Perf. 11x10½*
White paper
1L98 A21 $500 vermilion   17.50 16.00
1L99 A21 $1500 brt grn   20.00 18.00
1L100 A21 $2500 brown   32.50 30.00
 Nos. 1L98-1L100 (3)   70.00 64.00
Liberation of Northeast China.
Values for Nos. 1L98-1L100 are for fine
stamps.

Mao Tse-tung
("YUAN" at upper
right) — A22

1949, Feb.   *Perf. 11*
1L101 A22 $300 olive   .90   1.25
1L102 A22 $500 orange   8.50   9.00
1L103 A22 $1500 bl grn   .90   1.25
1L104 A22 $4500 brown   .90   1.25
1L105 A22 $6500 dk bl   .90   1.25
 Nos. 1L101-1L105 (5)   12.10 14.00
See type A15. For surcharges see Nos.
1L126-1L129, 1L131-1L132.

Workers, Globe
and Flag — A23

1949, May 1   *Perf. 11½*
1L106 A23 $1000 red & dl bl   .65   1.10
1L107 A23 $1500 red & pale
                          bl   .65   1.10
1L108 A23 $4500 rose & ol
                         brn   .85   1.10
1L109 A23 $6500 dl org & grn   .85   1.10
1L110 A23 $10,000 mar & ultra   4.00   4.25
 Nos. 1L106-1L110 (5)   7.00   8.65
Labor Day.

Fields and
Factories — A24

1949   *Perf. 10, 11*
1L111 A24 $5000 Prus bl   7.75   5.25
1L112 A24 $10,000 org brn   .60   1.75
1L113 A24 $50,000 green   .90   2.50
1L114 A24 $100,000 violet   1.25 13.00
 Nos. 1L111-1L114 (4)   10.50 22.50
Production in agriculture and industry.

Workers with
Flags — A25

1949, July 1   *Perf. 11*
1L115 A25 $1500 vio, lt bl & red 1.50   2.25
1L116 A25 $4500 dk brn, lt bl &
                         ver   1.50   2.25
1L117 A25 $6500 gray, lt bl &
                    rose red   3.25   5.50
 Nos. 1L115-1L117 (3)   6.25 10.00
28th anniversary of the founding of the Chinese Communist Party.

Heroes' Monument,
Harbin — A26

1949, Aug. 15   *Perf. 11½x11*
1L118 A26 $1500 brick red   1.50   3.25
1L119 A26 $4500 yel grn   2.00   3.25
1L120 A26 $6500 lt blue   4.00   3.25
 Nos. 1L118-1L120 (3)   7.50   9.75
4th anniversary of the Reoccupation, and
the surrender of Japan.

"Northeast Postal Service"
The following commemorative issues
are similar to those of the People's
Republic of China, with the 4 characters
shown added in different sizes and various arrangements.
Reprints were also issued similar to
those of the PRC.

Chinese Lantern Type of PRC, 1949
1949, Sept. 12 Litho. *Perf. 12½*
1L121 A1 $1000 dp blue   35.00 11.00
1L122 A1 $1500 scarlet   35.00 13.00
1L123 A1 $3000 green   65.00 17.50
1L124 A1 $4500 maroon   65.00 17.50
 Nos. 1L121-1L124 (4)   200.00 59.00
Reprints exist. Value, set $14.

Factory — A27

1949, Oct.   *Perf. 11x10½*
1L125 A27 $1500 orange   1.50   1.75
For surcharge see No. 1L130.

Nos. 1L101, 1L103-
1L105, 1L125
Surcharged in Black
or Green

1949, Nov. 20
1L126 A22 $2000 on $300   37.50 17.00
1L127 A22 $2000 on
                 $4500
                    (G)   50.00 40.00
1L128 A22 $2500 on
                 $1500   .70   7.50
1L129 A22 $2500 on
                 $6500   37.50 35.00
1L130 A27 $5000 on
                 $1500   .60   2.00
1L131 A22 $20,000 on
                 $4500   .40   7.00
1L132 A22 $35,000 on $300   .50 11.00
 Nos. 1L126-1L132 (7)   127.20 119.50

Globe and Hammer Type of PRC
1949, Nov. 15   *Perf. 12½*
1L133 A2 $5000 crimson   650.00 250.00
1L134 A2 $20,000 dp
                  green   950.00 275.00
1L135 A2 $35,000 vio blue   1,250. 325.00
 Nos. 1L133-1L135 (3)   2,850. 850.00
*Reprints, value; Nos. 1L133-1L134, each
$2; No. 1L135, $575.*

**Mao and Conference Hall Types of
PRC**
1950, Feb. 1   *Perf. 14*
1L136 A3 $1000 vermilion   35.00 29.00
1L137 A3 $1500 dp blue   35.00 29.00
1L138 A4 $5000 dk vio
                     brn   60.00 45.00
1L139 A4 $20,000 green   60.00 55.00
 Nos. 1L136-1L139 (4)   190.00 158.00
Reprints exist. Value, set $13.

Gate of Heavenly
Peace — A28

1950   *Perf. 10½*
Narrow horizontal shading
1L140 A28 $500 olive   2.00   .60
1L141 A28 $1000 orange   2.25   .60
1L142 A28 $1000 lil rose   4.00   .60
1L143 A28 $2000 gray grn   1.75   .35
1L144 A28 $2500 yellow   4.50   .35
1L145 A28 $5000 dp org   35.00   .35
1L146 A28 $10,000 brn org   2.50   .65
1L147 A28 $20,000 vio brn   1.50   .35
1L148 A28 $35,000 dp blue   1.50   .45
1L149 A28 $50,000 brt grn   22.50 1.00
 Nos. 1L140-1L149 (10)   77.50 5.30
See A29.

Flag and Mao Type of PRC
1950, July 1   *Perf. 14*
Yellow Stars
1L150 A7 $5000 grn & red   200.00 115.00
1L151 A7 $10,000 brn & red   225.00 115.00
1L152 A7 $20,000 dk brn &
                      red   225.00 115.00
1L153 A7 $30,000 dk vio bl
                     & red   375.00 150.00
 Nos. 1L150-1L153 (4)   1,025. 495.00
Reprints exist. Value, set $55.

Picasso Dove Type of PRC
1950, Aug. 1 Engr.   *Perf. 14*
1L154 A8 $2500 brown   16.00 20.00
1L155 A8 $5000 green   21.00 20.00
1L156 A8 $20,000 blue   28.00 20.00
 Nos. 1L154-1L156 (3)   65.00 60.00
Reprints exist. Value, set $6.

Flag Type of PRC
1950, Oct. 1   Engr. & Litho.
Flag in Red & Yellow
1L157 A9 $1000 purple   175.00 40.00
1L158 A9 $2500 org brn   190.00 42.50
1L159 A9 $5000 dp grn   200.00 55.00
1L160 A9 $10,000 olive   210.00 57.50
1L161 A9 $20,000 blue   250.00 95.00
 Nos. 1L157-1L161 (5)   1,025. 290.00
Size of No. 1L159: 38x47mm, others
26x33mm.
Reprints exist. Value, set $40.

Postal Conference Type of PRC
1950, Nov. 1   Litho.
1L162 A11 $2500 grn & dp org   45.00 20.00
1L163 A11 $5000 car & grn   45.00 20.00
 Reprints exist. Value, set, $5.

Gate of Heavenly
Peace — A29

1950-51   *Perf. 10½*
Wide horizontal shading
1L164 A29 $5000 orange   15.00 11.00
1L165 A29 $30,000 scarlet   9.00 20.00
1L166 A29 $100,000 violet   16.00 24.00
Wmk. Zigzag Lines (141)
1L167 A29 $250 brown   1.75   2.50
1L168 A29 $500 olive   1.75   2.50
1L169 A29 $1000 lil rose   2.00   4.00
1L170 A29 $2000 dl grn ('51)   3.00   4.00
1L171 A29 $2500 yellow   1.75   4.00
1L172 A29 $5000 orange   3.75   4.00
1L173 A29 $10,000 brn org
                        ('51)   2.50   4.00
1L174 A29 $12,500 maroon   1.75   4.00
1L175 A29 $20,000 dp brn
                        ('51)   2.75   7.50
 Nos. 1L164-1L175 (12)   61.00 91.50
A $50,000 green was prepared, but not
issued. Value $200.

Stalin and Mao Tse-tung Type of PRC
Unwmk.

1950, Dec. 1	**Engr.**		**Perf. 14**
1L176	A12	$2500 red	24.00 17.50
1L177	A12	$5000 dp green	29.00 17.50
1L178	A12	$20,000 dk blue	29.00 17.50
Nos. 1L176-1L178 (3)			82.00 52.50

Reprints exist. Value, set $16.

NORTHEAST CHINA PARCEL POST STAMPS

Locomotive — PP1

1951	**Litho.**	**Perf. 10½**
1LQ1	$100,000 purple	500.00
	Imperf	
1LQ2	$300,000 brown	1,350.
1LQ3	$500,000 grnsh bl	2,000.
1LQ4	$1,000,000 ver	3,750.

Value, Nos. 1LQ2-1LQ4 perf. 10½, $2,650.
For similar type see North China PP1.

PORT ARTHUR AND DAIREN

The Liaoning Postal Administration was established on April 1, 1946, in accordance with the Sino-Soviet Treaty, but was renamed one week later the Port Arthur and Dairen Postal Administration. On Apr. 3, 1947, it was combined with telecommunications and renamed the Kwantung Post and Telegraph General Administration.

On May 1, 1949, the name was again changed to Port Arthur and Dairen Post and Telegraph Administration. Postal tariffs were based on local currency and both Manchukuo and Japanese stamps were overprinted for use.

Gum

Nos. 2L1-2L35, 2L37-2L55 and 2L62-2L66 were issued with gum.

Manchukuo Nos. 162 and 94 Handstamp Surcharged in Violet ("Liaoning Post")

1946, Mar. 15			
2L1	A19	20f on 30f buff	72.50 72.50
2L2	A18	1y on 12f org	37.50 37.50

Same Surcharge on Japan Nos. 260, 337, 195, 244, 263, 342 in Violet, Red or Black

1946, Apr. 1			
2L3	A85	20f on 3s grn (V)	19.50 21.00
2L4	A151	1y on 17s gray vio (R)	16.00 18.00
2L5	A57	5y on 6s car	30.00 27.50
2L6	A57	5y on 6s crim	30.00 27.50
2L7	A88	5y on 6s org	22.00 20.00
2L8	A154	15y on 40s dk vio	110.00 125.00
Nos. 2L1-2L8 (8)			337.50 349.00

Surcharge sideways on Nos. 2L5-2L6.

Japan Nos. 260 and 263 Surcharged

1946, Apr.			
2L9	A85	1y on 3s grn	—
2L10	A88	5y on 6s org	—

Sha Ho Kow (suburb of Dairen) issue. The status of this issue is in question.

Manchukuo Nos. 84, 88 and 98 Handstamp Surcharged in Green, Red or Black

1946, May 1			
2L11	A16	1y on 1f red brn (G)	18.00 24.00
2L12	A18	5y on 4f lt ol grn	24.00 32.50
2L13	A19	15y on 30f chnt brn	52.50 62.50
Nos. 2L11-2L13 (3)			94.50 119.00

Transfer of postal administration and Labor Day.

Manchukuo Nos. 159, 86 and 94 Surcharged in Green, Red or Black

1946, July 7			
2L14	A17	1y on 6f crim rose (G)	11.50 20.00
2L15	A17	5y on 2f lt grn (R)	52.50 85.00
2L16	A18	15y on 13f dp org	110.00 110.00
Nos. 2L14-2L16 (3)			174.00 215.00

Outbreak of war with Japan, 9th anniv.

Manchukuo Nos. 94, 84 and 158 Surcharged in Black, Green or Red

1946, Aug. 15			
2L17	A18	1y on 12f dp org	22.50 27.50
2L18	A16	5y on 1f red brn (G)	52.50 50.00
2L19	A10	15y on 5f gray blk (R)	110.00 100.00
Nos. 2L17-2L19 (3)			185.00 177.50

Surrender of Japan, first anniversary.

Manchukuo Nos. 159, 94 and 86 Surcharged in Green, Black or Red

1946, Oct. 10			
2L20	A17	1y on 6f crim rose (G)	32.50 30.00
2L21	A18	5y on 12f dp org	57.50 55.00
2L22	A17	15y on 2f lt grn (R)	110.00 100.00
Nos. 2L20-2L22 (3)			200.00 185.00

35th anniversary of Chinese revolution.

Manchukuo Nos. 84, 159 and 94 Surcharged in Black, Green or Blue

1946, Oct. 19			
2L23	A16	1y on 1f red brn	50.00 50.00
2L24	A17	5y on 6f crim rose (G)	100.00 100.00
2L25	A18	15y on 12f dp org (Bl)	135.00 135.00
Nos. 2L23-2L25 (3)			285.00 285.00

10th anniversary of the death of Lu Hsun (1881-1936), writer.

Manchukuo Nos. 86, 159 and 95 Surcharged in Red, Green or Black

1947, Feb. 20			
2L26	A17	1y on 2f lt grn (R)	85.00 85.00
2L27	A17	5y on 6f crim rose (G)	175.00 175.00
2L28	A18	15y on 13f dk red brn	325.00 325.00
Nos. 2L26-2L28 (3)			585.00 585.00

29th anniversary of the Red (USSR) Army.

Manchukuo Nos. 86, 159 and 162 Surcharged in Red, Green or Black

1947, May 1			
2L29	A17	1y on 2f lt grn (R)	24.00 24.00
2L30	A17	5y on 6f crim rose (G)	67.50 65.00
2L31	A19	15y on 30f buff	110.00 100.00
Nos. 2L29-2L31 (3)			201.50 189.00

Labor Day.

Manchukuo Nos. 86, 88, 98 and 162 Surcharged ("Kwantung Postal Service, China")

1947, Sept. 15			
2L32	A17	5y on 2f lt grn	40.00 40.00
2L33	A18	15y on 4f lt ol grn	65.00 62.50
2L34	A19	20y on 30f red brn	100.00 95.00
2L35	A19	20y on 30f buff	110.00 100.00
Nos. 2L32-2L35 (4)			315.00 297.50

Manchukuo Nos. 86 and 159 Surcharged in Red and Green

Sacred Golden Kite (same size) — A1

1948, Feb. 20			
2L36	A17	10y on 2f lt grn (R)	150.00 150.00
2L37	A17	20y on 6f crim rose (G)	190.00 190.00
2L38	A1	100y on bl & red brn	800.00 800.00

30th anniversary of the Red (USSR) Army. No. 2L38 is on an ungummed label for the 2600th anniv. of the Japanese Empire.

Japan No. 260 and Manchukuo Nos. 84, 86 and 88 Surcharged in Red, Blue or Black

1948, July			
2L39	A85	5y on 3s grn (R)	125.00 125.00
2L40	A16	10y on 1f red brn (Bl)	250.00 250.00
2L41	A17	50y on 2f lt grn (R)	500.00 500.00
2L42	A18	100y on 4f lt ol grn (R)	900.00 900.00

Smaller Characters on Bottom Line

2L43	A17	10y on 2f lt grn (R)	300.00 250.00
2L44	A16	50y on 1f red brn	350.00 300.00

Stamps of Manchukuo Nos. 84, 86 and 88 Surcharged in Blue, Red or Black

1948, Nov. 1			
2L45	A16	10y on 1f red brn (Bl)	275.00 600.00
2L46	A17	50y on 2f lt grn (R)	450.00 600.00
2L47	A18	100y on 4f lt ol grn	1,100. 600.00

31st anniversary of the Russian Revolution.

Manchukuo Nos. 86 and 161 Surcharged in Red or Green

1948, Nov. 15			
2L48	A17	10y on 2f lt grn	1,050. 1,050.
2L49	A17	50y on 20f brn (G)	1,200. 1,200.

Kwantung Agricultural and Industrial Exhibition.

Manchukuo Nos. 86, 88 and 161 Surcharged in Red, Black or Green

1949, Jan.			
2L50	A17	20y on 2f lt grn (R)	500.00
2L51	A18	50y on 4f lt ol grn	700.00
2L52	A17	100y on 20f brn (G)	700.00

Without Gum

From No. 2L56 onward all stamps were issued without gum except as noted.

Farmer and Worker — A2   Train and Ship — A3

Ship at Dock (No. 2L55) — A4

(No. 2L56)

1949	**Litho.**		**Perf. 11, 11½**
2L53	A2	5y pale grn	3.00 5.00
2L54	A3	10y orange	20.00 20.00
2L55	A4	50y vermilion	22.50 22.50
2L56	A4	50y red (redrawn)	24.00 24.00
Nos. 2L53-2L56 (4)			69.50 71.50

Issue dates: No. 2L56, July 7; others Apr. 1.
For surcharges see Nos. 2L62-2L66.

Worker, Flag and Means of Transport
A5

1949, May 1   *Perf. 11*
2L57 A5 10y rose pink   55.00 55.00
   a.   10y vermilion   75.00 75.00

Labor Day. No. 2L57a is from a worn plate.

Mao Tse-tung and Red Flag — A6

1949, July 1
2L59 A6 50y red   45.00 45.00

28th anniversary of the founding of the Chinese Communist Party.

Heroes Monument, Dairen — A7

1949, Sept.
2L60 A7 10y red, bl & olive   45.00 45.00
   a.   10y red, blue & pale blue   100.00 85.00

4th anniversary of victory over Japan and opening of the Dairen Industrial Fair.

Nos. 2L53-2L54 Surcharged in Red or Black

a   b

c

1949, Sept.   **With Gum**
2L62 A2(a)   7y on 5y (R)   40.00 40.00
2L63 A2(a)   7y on 5y   40.00 40.00
2L64 A2(b)   50y on 5y (R)   95.00 95.00
2L65 A3(b)   100y on 10y   500.00 400.00
2L66 A3(c)   500y on 10y (R)   650.00 475.00
   Nos. 2L62-2L66 (5)   1,325. 1,050.

Size of surcharge on No. 2L63: 16x19mm.

A 500y on 5y, red surcharge "c," and a 500y on 10y orange, surcharge "b" were prepared but not issued.

Stalin and Lenin — A8

1949, Nov. 7   *Perf. 11x11½*
2L68 A8 10y dl bl grn (shades)   100.00 65.00

32nd anniversary of the Russian Revolution.

Workers Saluting Mao, Star and Flag — A9

1949, Nov. 16   *Perf. 11*
2L69 A9 35y dk bl, red, & yel   110.00 75.00

Founding of the People's Republic of China.

Stalin — A10

1949, Dec. 20   *Perf. 11½*
2L70 A10 20y dull magenta   90.00 110.00
2L71 A10 35y rose red   90.00 110.00

70th birthday of Stalin.

Gate of Heavenly Peace — A11

1950, Mar. 10   **Typo.**   *Perf. 10½*
2L72 A11 10y Prus blue   425.00 400.00
2L73 A11 20y dull grn   225.00 150.00
2L74 A11 35y red   15.00 20.00
2L75 A11 50y deep pur   15.00 25.00
2L76 A11 100y lilac rose   55.00 55.00
   Nos. 2L72-2L76 (5)   735.00 650.00

NORTH CHINA

The North China Liberation Area included the provinces of Hopeh, Chahar, Shansi and Suiyuan. The original postal service, begun in the Shansi-Hopeh-Chahar Border Area in December, 1937, became the North China Postal and Telegraph Administration in May, 1949.

All Stamps Issued without Gum Except as Noted

Large Victory Issue

Cavalry Man Holding Nationalist Flag — A1

Wmk. Wavy Lines
1946, Mar.   *Perf. 10½*
Granite Paper
Size: 34½x42mm
3L1 A1 $1 red brown   4.50 4.50
   a.   Newsprint   10.00 12.00
3L2 A1 $2 gray grn   4.50 4.50
3L3 A1 $4 vermilion   5.00 5.00
3L4 A1 $5 vio brn   16.00 6.00
3L5 A1 $8 vio bl   16.00 6.00
3L6 A1 $10 dp car   5.00 5.00
3L7 A1 $12 yellow   15.00 15.00
3L8 A1 $20 lt green   34.00 34.00
   Nos. 3L1-3L8 (8)   100.00 80.00

Defeat of Japan.

Small Victory Issue
Perf. 10½x10, 9½ rough
1946, May   **Unwmk.**
Granite paper
Size: 20x21mm
3L9 A1 $1 red org   1.60 2.25
3L10 A1 $2 green   2.50 2.25
3L11 A1 $3 lt lilac   4.75 8.50
3L12 A1 $5 dull pur   6.25 .40
3L13 A1 $8 dk blue   13.50 17.50
3L14 A1 $10 rose red   2.50 4.50
3L15 A1 $15 purple   77.50 67.50
3L16 A1 $20 green   4.75 6.25
3L17 A1 $30 brt grnsh bl   4.00 7.25
3L18 A1 $40 brt rose lilac   4.75 3.25
3L19 A1 $50 brown   36.00 .75
3L20 A1 $60 myrtle green   67.50 1.60

Wmk. Wavy Lines
3L21 A1 $100 orange   9.00 4.50
3L22 A1 $200 dull blue   12.00 4.50
3L23 A1 $500 rose   57.50 70.00
   Nos. 3L9-3L23 (15)   304.10 201.00

North China Postal and Telegraph Administration

Charging Infantrymen A2   Agriculture and Industry A3

1949, Jan.   **Unwmk.**   *Imperf.*
White Paper
3L24 A2   50c brown lake   3.50 3.00
3L25 A2 $1 Prussian blue   3.50 3.50
Newsprint
3L26 A2 $2 apple green   3.50 3.50
3L27 A2 $3 dull violet   3.50 3.50
3L28 A2 $5 brown   3.50 3.50
3L29 A3 $6 deep rose   3.50 1.25
   a.   White paper   3.50 3.50
3L30 A2 $10 blue grn   1.25 2.00
3L31 A2 $12 dp car   3.75 4.50
   Nos. 3L24-3L31 (8)   26.00 23.75

No. 3L29 issued in Peking, others in Tientsin.

Remittance Stamps of China Surcharged

A4

壹
$1

叁
$3

1949, Jan.   **Engr.**   *Perf. 13*
Small Central Characters
3L32 A4   50c on $50 brn blk   3.25 3.50
3L33 A4 $1 on $50 gray blk   5.50 2.75
3L34 A4 $3 on $50 gray   5.50 2.50
Large Central Characters
3L35 A4   50c on $50 blk   2.50 1.60
3L36 A4 $6 on $20 dk vio brn   7.50 1.60
   Nos. 3L32-3L36 (5)   24.25 11.95

Issued in Tientsin.
For surcharges see Nos. 3LQ10-3LQ21.

Sun Yat-sen Type A2 of Northeastern Provinces and China No. 640 Srchd. in Black, Red, Green or Blue

#3L37-3L45,   #3L46, 3L51,
3L47-3L50,   3L53
3L52

c

Type "b," bottom character of left vertical row (yuan) differs. Type "c," top character of right vertical row differs.

1949, Mar. 7   *Perf. 14*
3L37 A2   50c on 5c lake   .85 2.75
3L38 A2 $1 on 10c org   .85 2.25
3L39 A2 $2 on 20c yel grn   80.00 25.00
3L40 A2 $3 on 50c red org   .85 1.75
3L41 A2 $4 on $5 dk grn   9.50 2.25
3L42 A2 $6 on $10 crim   2.75 2.25
3L43 A2 $10 on $300 bluish grn   6.00 3.25
3L44 A2 $12 on $1 bl   4.00 3.25
3L45 A2 $18 on $3 brn   7.00 1.75
3L46 A2 $20 on 50c red org (Bl)   2.75 1.50
3L47 A2 $20 on $20 ol, II   5.50 4.50
   a.   Type I   20.00 13.50
3L48 A2 $30 on $2.50 ind (R)   7.00 4.00
3L49 A2 $40 on 25c blk brn (R)   9.00 6.25
3L50 A2 $50 on $109 dk grn (R)   17.50 9.00
3L51 A2 $80 on $1 bl (R)   22.50 4.50
3L52 A2 $100 on $65 dl grn (R)   30.00 9.00
3L53 A73 $100 on $100 dk car, surch. 16mm wide (Bl)   30.00 3.25
   a.   Surcharge 14mm wide   30.00 10.00

1949, Apr.
3L55 A2 (c) $2 on 20c yel grn   1.75 3.25
3L56 A2 (c) $3 on 50c red org   .85 2.25
3L57 A2 (c) $4 on $5 dk grn   7.00 4.25
3L58 A2 (c) $6 on $10 crim, I   4.50 4.25
   a.   Type II   15.00 10.00
3L59 A2 (c) $12 on $1 blue   1.75 1.75

d   e

1949, Apr.   **Type "d"**
3L60 A2 $1 on 25c blk grn (G)   .50 1.25
3L61 A2 $10 on $300 bluish grn (R)   13.00 5.75
3L62 A2 $20 on 50c red org (G)   26.00 25.00
3L63 A2 $20 on $20 ol (R)   11.00 4.25
3L64 A2 $40 on 25c blk brn (R)   11.00 5.00
3L65 A2 $50 on $109 dk grn, surch. 15mm wide (R)   13.00 13.00
   a.   Surcharge 13mm wide   30.00 30.00
3L66 A2 $80 on $1 bl (R)   8.00 5.00

Type "d" On Stamps on China
3L67 A73 $100 on $100 dk car (G)   65.00 35.00
3L68 A73 $300 on $700 red brn (Bl)   20.00 12.50
3L69 A82 $500 on $500 bl grn (R)   20.00 4.50
3L70 A82 $3000 on $3000 bl (R)   20.00 8.25

Type "e" On Stamps of Northeastern Provinces
1949, Aug.
3L71 A2 $10 on $10 crim, II (Bl)   8.00 3.50
   a.   Type I   12.50 12.00
3L72 A2 $30 on 20c yel grn (R)   8.00 2.25
3L73 A2 $50 on $44 dk car rose (Bl)   8.00 1.25
3L74 A2 $100 on $3 brn (Bl)   14.00 6.50
3L75 A2 $200 on $4 org brn, II (Bl)   40.00 24.00
   a.   Type I   1,100. 450.00

On China No. 754 in Blue
3L76 A82 $10 on $7000 lt red brn   12.50 8.50
   Nos. 3L37-3L76 (39)   549.90 269.25

Overprints on Nos. 3L71 and 3L76 have 2 characters in center row.

Farmer and Worker
on Globe — A5

1949, May 1   Engr.   Perf. 14

3L77	A5	$20 crimson	9.50	9.50
3L78	A5	$40 dark blue	9.50	9.50
3L79	A5	$60 brown org	9.50	9.50
3L80	A5	$80 dk green	9.50	9.50
3L81	A5	$100 purple	9.50	9.50
		Nos. 3L77-3L81 (5)	47.50	47.50

Labor day. Exists imperf. Value, set $50.
Also issued in blocks of 4, imperf between.
Value, unused or used, $17.50.

Mao Tse-tung
(Chinese
Numeral) — A6

Mao Tse-tung
(Arabic
Numeral) — A7

1949, July 1   Perf. 14

3L82	A6	$10 red	8.00	5.00
3L83	A7	$20 dk blue	2.00	3.50
3L84	A6	$50 orange	13.00	5.50
3L85	A7	$80 dk green	5.50	5.00
3L86	A6	$100 purple	10.00	2.75
3L87	A7	$120 olive	2.00	5.00
3L88	A6	$140 vio brn	10.00	6.50
		Nos. 3L82-3L88 (7)	50.50	33.25

28th anniv. of the founding of the Chinese
Communist Party. Value, imperf, set $150.

Gate of Heavenly
Peace — A8

1949, Nov. 26   Litho.   Perf. 12½

3L89	A8	$50 orange	1.00	7.00
3L90	A8	$100 crimson	.50	2.00
3L91	A8	$200 green	2.00	2.00
3L92	A8	$300 rose brn	15.00	4.50
3L93	A8	$400 blue	15.00	4.50
3L94	A8	$500 brown	15.00	2.50
3L95	A8	$700 violet	8.00	7.00
		Nos. 3L89-3L95 (7)	56.50	29.50

Farmers and
Factory — A9

1949, Dec.   Engr.   Perf. 14

3L96	A9	$1000 orange	19.00	6.00
3L97	A9	$3000 dark blue	1.00	1.50
3L98	A9	$5000 crimson	1.00	2.75
3L99	A9	$10,000 red brown	1.00	5.75
		Nos. 3L96-3L99 (4)	22.00	16.00

NORTH CHINA PARCEL POST STAMPS

Parcel Post Stamps of China Nos. Q23-Q27 (Type PP3) Srchd. in Red, Black (#3LQ6-3LQ9) or Blue (#3LQ2)

a   b

c

1949, June

Surcharged Type "a"

3LQ1	$300 on $6,000,000	55.00
3LQ2	$400 on $8,000,000	55.00
3LQ3	$500 on $10,000,000	55.00
3LQ4	$800 on $5,000,000	55.00
3LQ5	$1000 on $3,000,000	75.00

Surcharged Type "b"

3LQ6	$500 on $3,000,000	75.00
3LQ7	$1000 on $5,000,000	90.00

Surcharged Type "c"

3LQ8	$5000 on $8,000,000	225.00
3LQ9	$5000 on $10,000,000	300.00
	Nos. 3LQ1-3LQ9 (9)	985.00

Nos. 3LQ8-3LQ9 have large numerals
unboxed.

Remittance Stamps of China (like North China Type A4) Surcharged in Black or Red

a   b

Peking Surcharge "a"

1949, June   Litho.   Perf. 13

3LQ10	$6 on $5 ver	11.00	3.50
3LQ11	$20 on $50 gray	11.00	3.50
3LQ12	$50 on $20 dk vio brn	11.00	3.50
3LQ13	$100 on $10 ol grn	11.00	7.00

Tientsin Surcharge "b"

Engr.   Perf. 14

3LQ14	$20 on $1 brn org	14.00	6.00
a.	Perf. 12½	22.50	7.50
3LQ15	$30 on $2 dk grn	14.00	5.00
a.	Red surcharge	22.50	11.00
3LQ16	$30 on $10 ol grn	125.00	42.50
3LQ17	$100 on $10 gray grn (R)	14.50	6.00

Litho.
Perf. 13

3LQ18	$50 on $5 red	14.00	6.00

Engr.
Perf. 14

3LQ19	$20 on $1 org brn	40.00	17.00

Perf. 12½

3LQ20	$100 on $10 yel grn (R)	65.00	30.00

Typo.
Roulette 9½

3LQ21	$30 on $2 bl grn (R)	50.00	20.00

The surcharge on No. 3LQ19 is without first
and last lines.
Nos. 3LQ14, 3LQ14a, 3LQ15, 3LQ15a,
3LQ16-3LQ17, 3LQ19-3LQ20 issued with
gum.

Locomotive — PP1

1949, Nov.   Engr.   Perf. 14

3LQ22	PP1	$500 crim	17.50	17.50
3LQ23	PP1	$1000 dp		
		bl	175.00	50.00
3LQ24	PP1	$2000 green	250.00	75.00
3LQ25	PP1	$5000 dp		
		ol	350.00	125.00
3LQ26	PP1	$10,000 org	650.00	250.00
3LQ27	PP1	$20,000 red		
		brn	1,400.	750.00
3LQ28	PP1	$50,000 brn		
		pur	3,000.	1,200.
		Nos. 3LQ22-3LQ28 (7)	5,843.	2,468.

NORTHWEST CHINA

The Northwest China Liberation Area
consisted of the provinces of Sinkiang,
Tsinghai, Ningsia and the western part
of Shensi. The area was first established as the Shensi-Kansu-Ningsia
Border Area in October, 1936, after the
Long March to Yenan. Remote Sinkiang
was not included until late 1949.

All Stamps Issued without Gum

Pagoda on
Yenan Hill — A1

1945, Mar.   Litho.   Imperf.

4L1	A1	$1 green	26.00
4L2	A1	$5 dk blue	150.00
4L3	A1	$10 rose red	25.00
4L4	A1	$50 dull pur	30.00
4L5	A1	$100 yel org	55.00
		Nos. 4L1-4L5 (5)	286.00

Rouletted 9

4L1a	*A1*	*$1*	95.00
4L2a	*A1*	*$5*	160.00
4L3a	*A1*	*$10*	100.00

First issue; denomination in Chinese and
Arabic. Heavy shading at top of vignette. Columns at sides.
See types A2, A3 and A4. For surcharges
see Nos. 4L6-4L10, 4L23.

Nos. 4L1-4L2 Surcharged in Red

a   b

c   d

1946, Nov.

4L6	A1	(a) $30 on $1 grn	35.00
4L7	A1	(b) $30 on $1 grn	160.00
a.		Rectangular lower left character	1,000.
4L8	A1	(c) $30 on $1 grn	20.00
4L9	A1	(b) $60 on $1 grn	2,500.
4L10	A1	(d) $90 on $5 dk bl	37.50

Surcharge on Nos. 4L7a is type "b" as illustrated. Surcharge on No. 4L7 differs from "b,"
having lower left character as in type "a."
Surcharge on No. 4L9 the upper left
surcharge character differs from that shown in
"b."

Pagoda on
Yenan Hill — A2

1948, June

4L11	A2	$100 buff	175.00
4L12	A2	$300 rose pink	8.00
4L13	A2	$500 red	8.50
4L14	A2	$1000 blue	8.00
4L15	A2	$2000 yel grn	24.00
4L16	A2	$5000 dull pur	22.50
		Nos. 4L11-4L16 (6)	246.00

Second issue; denominations in Chinese
only. Many shades and proofs exist.
For surcharge see No. 4L24.

Pagoda on
Yenan Hill
(same
size) — A3

1948, Dec.

4L17	A3	10c yel org	2.00
4L18	A3	20c lemon	2.00
4L19	A3	$1 dk blue	2.00
4L20	A3	$2 vermilion	2.00
4L21	A3	$5 pale bl grn	11.00
4L22	A3	$10 violet	18.00
		Nos. 4L17-4L22 (6)	37.00

Third issue; ornamental border at sides.
Many shades exist.

Nos. 4L2 and 4L13
Surcharged in Red or
Black

1949, Jan.

4L23	A1	$1 on $5 dk bl	80.00	80.00
4L24	A2	$2 on $500 red	40.00	40.00

Pagoda on
Yenan Hill — A4

1949, May 1

4L25	A4	50c yel to olive	.85	2.00
4L26	A4	$1 dl bl to indigo	.85	2.00
4L27	A4	$3 ol yel to org yel	.85	2.00
4L28	A4	$5 blue green	2.25	3.00
a.	Upper left character as on #4L25			
4L29	A4	$10 vio to dp vio	7.50	9.00
4L30	A4	$20 pink to rose red	13.50	22.00
		Nos. 4L25-4L30 (6)	25.80	38.00

Fourth issue; light shading at top of vignette,
columns without ornaments at sides. Many
shades exist.

China Nos. 959, F2
and E12 Overprinted
("People's Post,
Shensi")

1949, June 13   Engr.   Perf. 12½

4L31	A96	orange	25.00	16.00
4L32	R2	carmine	35.00	35.00
4L33	SD2	red vio	35.00	35.00
		Nos. 4L31-4L33 (3)	95.00	86.00

Stamps of China, Sun
Yat-sen Type A94 of
1949, Overprinted in
Black or Red
("People's Post,
Shensi")

Lithographed; Engraved

1949, July 1   **Perf. 14, 12½**

4L34	$10 green (887)	1.25	1.25
4L35	$20 vio brn (888)	1.25	2.25
4L36	$20 vio brn (896)	1.25	1.25
4L37	$50 dk Prus grn (889; R)	6.00	5.25
4L38	$50 grn (951)	6.00	5.25
4L39	$100 org brn (890)	14.50	6.25
4L40	$500 ros lil (892)	20.00	6.25
4L41	$1000 dp bl (952; R)	27.50	15.00
4L42	$2000 vio (902;R)	30.00	18.00
4L43	$5000 car (953)	45.00	37.50
4L44	$10,000 car (954)	80.00	75.00
	Nos. 4L34-4L44 (11)	232.75	173.25

Kansu-Ningsia-Tsinghai Area, Lanchow Overprints

China Nos. 959a, F2 and E12 Overprinted ("People's Post, Kansu")

1949, Oct.   **Engr.**   *Rouletted*

4L45	A96	orange	22.50	22.50

     Perf. 12½

4L46	R2	carmine	32.50	32.50
4L47	SD2	red vio	32.50	32.50
	Nos. 4L45-4L47 (3)		87.50	87.50

Stamps of China, Sun Yat-sen Type A94 of 1949, Overprinted ("People's Post, Kansu")

Engraved; Lithographed

1949, Oct.   **Perf. 14, 12½**

4L48	$10 grn (887)	2.25	2.25
4L49	$20 vio brn (888)	2.25	3.25
4L50	$50 dk Prus grn (889)	5.25	8.25
4L51	$100 org brn (890)	3.50	3.25
4L52	$100 dk org brn (898)	5.25	6.00
4L53	$200 red org (891)	6.50	5.25
4L54	$500 rose lil (892)	6.50	5.25
4L55	$1000 blue (894)	3.50	3.25
4L56	$1000 dp bl (901)	6.50	7.50
4L57	$2000 vio (902)	11.00	15.00
4L58	$5000 lt bl (903)	22.00	27.50
4L59	$10,000 sepia (904)	30.00	37.50
4L60	$20,000 ap orn (905)	60.00	72.50
	Nos. 4L48-4L60 (13)	164.50	196.75

No. 4L54-4L60 exist with wider spaced overprints.

China Nos. 959, F2 and 791-792 Surcharged in Black or Red ("People's Post, Sinkiang")

1949, Oct.

4L61	A96	$1 on org	12.00	13.50
4L62	R2	$3 on car	18.00	20.00
4L63	A82	10c on $50,000 dp bl (R)	40.00	40.00
4L64	A82	$1.50 on $100,000 dl grn (R)	80.00	80.00
	Nos. 4L61-4L64 (4)		150.00	153.50

Northwest People's Post

Mao Tse-tung — A5   Great Wall — A6

1949, Oct. 15   **Litho.**   *Imperf.*

4L65	A5	$50 rose	7.00	3.75
a.	$200 cliche in $50 plate	225.00	

4L66	A6	$100 dark blue	1.75	2.00
4L67	A5	$200 orange	6.50	6.00
4L68	A6	$400 sepia	12.00	7.50
	Nos. 4L65-4L68 (4)	27.25	19.25

EAST CHINA

The East China Liberation Area included the provinces of Shantung, Kiangsu, Chekiang, Anhwei and Fukien. The original postal service established in Shantung in 1941, became the East China Posts and Telegraph General Office in July, 1948.

All Stamps Issued without Gum

Mao Tse-tung — A1

1948, Mar.   **Litho.**   **Perf. 10½**

5L1	A1	$50 yel org	2.00	1.75
5L2	A1	$100 dp rose	6.00	3.00
5L3	A1	$200 dk vio bl	6.00	3.00
5L4	A1	$300 brt grn	7.50	3.00
5L5	A1	$500 dp blue	2.50	3.00
5L6	A1	$800 vermilion	7.50	2.50
5L7	A1	$1000 dk blue	12.00	12.00
5L8	A1	$5000 rose	30.00	30.00
5L9	A1	$10,000 dp car	75.00	75.00
	Nos. 5L1-5L9 (9)	148.50	133.25

Many varieties, including unissued imperforates exist.

Transportation and Tower — A2

Perf. 9 to 11 and compound

1949, Apr.   **Litho.**

5L10	A2	$1 yel grn	.95	.25
5L11	A2	$2 blue grn	.60	.25
5L12	A2	$3 dull red	.60	.25
5L13	A2	$5 pale brn (ovpt. 4x4mm)	.60	.25
a.	Without overprint		65.00	65.00
b.	Overprint 3x3mm		1.25	1.00
c.	As "b," purple overprint		65.00	
5L14	A2	$10 ultra	.90	.25
5L15	A2	$13 brt vio	.60	.25
5L16	A2	$18 brt blue	.60	.25
5L17	A2	$21 vermilion	.90	.25
5L18	A2	$30 gray	.60	.60
5L19	A2	$50 crimson	2.25	1.50
5L20	A2	$100 olive	27.50	22.00
	Nos. 5L10-5L20 (11)	36.10	26.10

Seventh anniv. of Shantung Communist Postal Administration. The overprint on the $5, character "yu" meaning "Posts," obliterates Japanese flag on tower, erroneously included in design. Value, imperfs. of Nos. 5L10-5L12, 5L13c, 5L14-5L20 on different paper, set $150.

Train and Postal Runner (1949.2.7) — A3

1949, Apr.   **Litho.**   **Perf. 8 to 11**

5L21	A3	$1 brt emer	.25	1.50
5L22	A3	$2 blue grn	.25	1.50
5L23	A3	$3 dk red	.25	1.50
5L24	A3	$5 brown	.35	2.00
5L25	A3	$10 ultra	.60	2.25
5L26	A3	$13 brt vio	.35	1.75
5L27	A3	$18 brt blue	.35	1.75
5L28	A3	$21 vermilion	3.50	4.00
5L29	A3	$30 slate	.35	2.25
5L30	A3	$50 crimson	.45	2.25
5L31	A3	$100 olive	2.00	3.50
	Nos. 5L21-5L31 (11)	8.70	24.25

7th anniv. of Shantung P. O., Feb. 7. Imperf. sets were sold by the Philatelic Dept., Tientsin P.O. Value $40. See Nos. 5L69-5L76. For surcharges see People's Republic of China Nos. 77-81.

Mao, Soldiers, Map — A4

Perf. 9½ to 11 and comp.

1949, Apr.

5L32	A4	$1 brt emer	.40	.25
5L33	A4	$2 blue grn	.40	.25
5L34	A4	$3 dull red	.40	.25
5L35	A4	$5 brown	.40	.25
5L36	A4	$10 ultra	.60	.25
5L37	A4	$13 brt vio	.60	.40
5L38	A4	$18 brt blue	.60	.40
5L39	A4	$21 vermilion	.60	.40
5L40	A4	$30 gray	.60	.50
5L41	A4	$50 crimson	.60	.50
5L42	A4	$100 olive	6.75	5.00
	Nos. 5L32-5L42 (11)	11.95	8.45

Victory of Hwai-Hai (Hwaiying and Haichow). Imperf. sets were sold by the Philatelic Dept., Tientsin P.O. Value, set $100.

Stamps of China, Sun Yat-sen Type of 1949, Surcharged in Red or Black

(Nanking) — a   (Wuhu) — b

1949, May 4   **Engr.**   **Perf. 12½**

5L43	A94 (a)	$1 on $10 grn (895, R)	1.00	.75
a.	Perf. 13		3.25	3.00
5L44	A94 (a)	$3 on $20 vio brn (896)	3.00	1.50
a.	Perf. 13		3.00	4.50
b.	Perf. 14		5.75	5.50
c.	Surcharge inverted		200.00	

Sun Yat-sen Type A94 Surcharged Type "b"

Lithographed, Engraved

1949, May   **Perf. 12½, 14**

5L45	$30 on $1000 dp bl (901)	10.00	7.50
5L46	$30 on $1000 bl (894)	10.00	7.50
5L47	$50 on $200 org red (899)	10.00	7.50
5L48	$100 on $5000 lt bl (903)	22.50	20.00
5L49	$300 on $10,000 sep (904, R)	67.50	60.00
5L50	$500 on $200 org red (899)	100.00	85.00
	Nos. 5L45-5L50 (6)	220.00	187.50

Many varieties exist.

China Nos. 913a and 913 Srchd. in Blue, Green, Black or Red, (East China)

1949, May   **Litho.**   **Perf. 12½**

5L51	A95	$5 on 50c on $20 brn, II (B)	17.50	16.00
a.	Green surcharge		100.00	100.00
5L52	A95	$10 on 50c on $20 brn, II	17.50	16.00
5L53	A95	$20 on 50c on $20 red brn, II (R)	17.50	16.00
a.	Type I (R)		21.00	21.00
	Nos. 5L51-5L53 (3)	52.50	48.00

Stamps of China, Sun Yat-sen Type of 1949, Srchd. in Black or Red, (Hangchow)

Engr., Litho. (No. 5L57)

1949, June 25   **Perf. 14, 12½**

5L54	A94	$1 on $1 org (886)	4.00	4.00
5L55	A94	$3 on $20 vio brn (896, R)	2.00	2.00
5L56	A94	$5 on $100 org brn (890)	7.50	7.50
5L57	A94	$5 on $100 dk org brn (898)	5.00	5.00

Maps of Shanghai and Nanking — A5

1949, May 30   **Litho.**   **Perf. 8½ to 11**

5L60	A5	$1 orange ver	.30	3.50
5L61	A5	$2 blue green	.30	3.50
5L62	A5	$3 brt violet	.40	3.50
5L63	A5	$5 violet brn	.40	.50
5L64	A5	$10 ultra	.40	1.00
5L65	A5	$30 slate	.40	3.00
5L66	A5	$50 carmine	.40	3.00
5L67	A5	$100 olive	.40	1.00
5L68	A5	$500 orange	15.00	8.00
	Nos. 5L60-5L68 (9)	18.00	27.00

Liberation of Shanghai and Nanking. Many shades, paper and perforation varieties and imperfs. exist.

Train and Postal Runner Type Dated "1949"

1949, July 1950, Feb.   **Perf. 12½, 14**

5L69	A3	$10 dp ultra	.25	.25
5L70	A3	$15 orange ver	.25	.45
a.	$15 red, perf. 14		.50	.30
5L71	A3	$30 slate green	.25	.25
a.	Perf. 12½		.50	.50
5L72	A3	$50 carmine	.25	.50
5L73	A3	$60 bl grn, perf. 14	.25	1.50
5L74	A3	$100 ol, perf. 14	8.00	2.00
5L75	A3	$1600 vio bl ('50)	.90	4.00
5L76	A3	$2000 brn vio ('50)	1.00	4.00
	Nos. 5L69-5L76 (8)	11.15	12.95

Chu Teh, Mao, Troops with Flags — A7

1949, Aug. 17   **Perf. 12½**

5L77	A7	$70 orange	.40	.35
5L78	A7	$270 crimson	.50	.35
5L79	A7	$370 emerald	.60	.50
5L80	A7	$470 vio brn	1.00	.60
5L81	A7	$570 blue	.50	.50
	Nos. 5L77-5L81 (5)	3.00	2.30

22nd anniv. of the People's Liberation Army. For similar type see Southwest China A1.

Mao Tse-tung — A8

1949, Oct.

5L82	A8	$10 dk blue	8.00	15.00
5L83	A8	$15 vermilion	10.00	15.00
5L84	A8	$70 brown	.50	.50
5L85	A8	$100 vio brn	.50	.50
5L86	A8	$150 orange	.50	.50
5L87	A8	$200 grnsh gray	.50	.50
5L88	A8	$500 gray bl	.50	.50
5L89	A8	$1000 rose	.50	.50
5L90	A8	$2000 emerald	.50	.50
	Nos. 5L82-5L90 (9)	21.50	33.50

For surcharges see People's Republic of China Nos. 82-84.

Stamps of China, Sun Yat-sen Type of 1949 Surcharged in Black or Red

1949, Nov.   **Litho.**   **Perf. 12½**

5L91	A94	$400 on $200 org red (899)	22.50	1.50
5L92	A94	$1000 on $100 grnsh gray (897, R)	2.25	.70
5L93	A94	$1200 on $100 dk org brn (898)	.30	1.50

East China Liberation Area

5L58	A94	$10 on $50 dk Prus grn (889, R)	24.00	24.00
5L59	A94	$13 on $10 grn (895)	2.75	2.75
	Nos. 5L54-5L59 (6)	45.25	45.25

5L94	A94	$1600 on $20,000 ap grn (905)	.30	3.00
5L95	A94	$2000 on $1000 dp bl (952,R)	.30	.75
a.		Perf. 14	45.00	25.00
		Nos. 5L91-5L95 (5)	25.65	7.45

EAST CHINA PARCEL POST STAMPS

Parcel Post Stamps of China 1945-48 Surcharged, (Shantung)

1949, Aug. 1		**Engr.**	**Perf. 13**	
5LQ1	PP1	$200 on $500 grn	*10.00*	8.00
5LQ2	PP1	$500 on $1000 bl	30.00	18.00
		Type PP3	**Perf. 13½**	
5LQ3		$200 on $200,000 dk grn	32.50	16.00
5LQ4		$200 on $10,000,000 sage grn	32.50	14.00
5LQ5		$500 on $7000 dl bl	65.00	40.00
5LQ6		$500 on $50,000 indigo	12.00	10.00
5LQ7		$1000 on $10,000 car rose	12.00	10.00
5LQ8		$1000 on $100,000 dk rose brn	37.50	18.00
5LQ9		$1000 on $300,000 pink	12.00	10.00
5LQ10		$1000 on $500,000 vio brn	90.00	45.00
5LQ11		$1000 on $8,000,000 org ver	15.00	12.00
5LQ12		$2000 on $5,000,000 dl vio	30.00	30.00
5LQ13		$2000 on $6,000,000 brn blk	55.00	35.00
5LQ14		$3000 on $30,000 ol	60.00	35.00
5LQ15		$3000 on $70,000 org brn	30.00	24.00
5LQ16		$5000 on $3,000,000 dl bl	90.00	52.50
		Nos. 5LQ1-5LQ16 (16)	613.50	377.50

China Type A97, No. 987 Surcharged

$200 $500
$1000 $2000
$5000 $10,000

1949, Sept. 7		**Litho.**	**Perf. 12½**	
5LQ17		$200 on $10	35.00	15.00
5LQ18		$500 on $10	35.00	15.00
5LQ19		$1000 on $10	35.00	15.00
5LQ20		$2000 on $10	50.00	32.50
5LQ21		$5000 on $10	75.00	45.00
5LQ22		$10,000 on $10	150.00	75.00
		Nos. 5LQ17-5LQ22 (6)	380.00	202.50

Flying Geese Type of China, 1949, and China Nos. 984-986 Surcharged in Red or Black

1950, Jan. 28				
5LQ23	A97	$5000 on 10c bl vio (R)	30.00	25.00
5LQ24	A97	$10,000 on $1 brn org	45.00	40.00
5LQ25	A97	$20,000 on $2 bl	75.00	70.00
5LQ26	A97	$50,000 on $5 car rose	130.00	130.00
		Nos. 5LQ23-5LQ26 (4)	280.00	265.00

Parcel Post Stamps of China Type PP3, Nos. Q1-Q2, Q12-Q13 Surcharged in Red or Black

1950, Jan. 28		**Engr.**	**Perf. 13, 13½**	
5LQ27		$5000 on $500 grn (R)	.75	15.00
5LQ28		$10,000 on $1000 bl (R)	80.00	65.00
5LQ29		$20,000 on $3000 bl grn	140.00	110.00
5LQ30		$50,000 on $5000 org red	7.50	75.00
		Nos. 5LQ27-5LQ30 (4)	228.25	265.00

CENTRAL CHINA

The Central Chinese Liberation Area included the provinces of Honan, Hupeh, Hunan and Kiangsi. The area was established between August and September, 1949, following the occupation of Hankow by Red Army forces.

All Stamps Issued without Gum

Hupeh Postal and Telegraph Administration

Stamps of China, Sun Yat-sen Type A94 of 1949, Surcharged ("Chinese P.O., Temporary Use")

Engraved; Lithographed

1949, June 4		**Perf. 14, 12½**		
		Thin parallel lines		
6L1		$1 on $200 red org (891)	4.00	4.50
6L2		$6 on $10,000 sep (904)	4.00	4.50
6L3		$15 on $1 org (886)	4.00	4.50
6L4		$30 on $100 org brn (890)	7.50	6.00
6L5		$30 on $100 dk org brn (898)	4.00	4.50
6L6		$50 on $20 vio brn (896)	25.00	14.00
6L7		$80 on $1000 dp bl (901)	5.50	5.00
		Thick parallel lines		
6L8		$1 on $200 red org (891)	7.00	7.00
6L9		$3 on $5000 lt bl (903)	3.50	4.00
6L10		$10 on $500 rose lil (892)	3.50	4.00
6L11		$10 on $500 rose lil (900)	5.25	5.75
6L12		$50 on $20 vio brn (888)	7.00	7.50
6L13		$50 on $20 vio brn (896)	4.00	5.00
6L14		$80 on $1000 bl (894)	6.50	5.00
6L15		$80 on $1000 dp bl (901)	27.00	16.00
6L16		$100 on $50 dk Prus grn (903)	5.00	6.00
		Nos. 6L1-6L16 (16)	122.75	103.25

Kiangsi Postal and Telegraph Administration.

Central Trust Revenue Stamps of China Surcharged ("People's Post, Kiangsi")

(same size) — A1

$30

$60

1949, July				
6L48	A4	$110 org brn	1.00	1.25
6L49	A4	$130 violet	5.00	3.00
6L50	A4	$200 dp org	.50	.50
6L51	A4	$290 rose	1.75	1.25
6L52	A4	$370 dk bl	1.75	1.25
6L53	A4	$500 lt bl, I	7.50	1.50
a.		$500 blue, II	20.00	7.00
6L54	A4	$1000 dull red, II	20.00	8.00
a.		$1000 dark red, I	27.50	8.00

1949, June 20		**Engr.**	**Perf. 12½**	
6L17	A1	$3 on $30 pur	2.50	3.00
6L18	A1	$15 on $15 red org	7.00	3.00
6L19	A1	$30 on $50 dk bl	7.00	3.00
6L20	A1	$60 on $50 dk bl	7.00	3.00
6L21	A1	$130 on $15 red org	4.00	3.00

The $15 surcharge has 3 characters in left vertical row, the $130 surcharge has 5.

Same Surcharge on Sun Yat-sen Issues of China, 1945-49

Engraved, Lithographed

		Perf. 14, 12½		
6L22	A82	$1 on $250 dp lil (746)	6.50	6.50
6L23	A94	$5 on $1000 dp bl (901)	6.50	6.50
6L24	A94	$5 on $2000 vio (902)	6.50	6.50
6L25	A94	$5 on $5000 lt bl (903)	3.50	4.00
6L26	A94	$10 on $1000 bl (894)	6.50	6.50
6L27	A82	$20 on $4000 gray	4.50	4.00
6L28	A73	$30 on $100 dk car	6.50	6.50
6L29	A82	$30 on $20,000 rose pink	4.50	4.00
6L30	A94	$80 on $500 rose lil (900)	4.00	4.00
6L31	A94	$100 on $1000 dp bl (901)	3.50	4.00
6L32	A82	$200 on $250 dp lil	4.50	4.50
		Nos. 6L17-6L32 (16)	84.50	72.00

Central China Posts and Telegraph Administration

Farmer, Soldier and Worker
A2   A3

I — Top white line of square character (yuan) at upper left does not touch left vertical stroke. No gap in shading between soldier's feet.

II — Top line connects with left vertical stroke. Gap in shading between feet.

Perf. 10 to 11½ & Comp.				
1949				**Litho.**
6L33	A2	$1 orange	10.00	5.00
6L34	A2	$3 brn org	6.00	5.00
6L35	A2	$6 emerald	7.50	5.00
6L36	A3	$7 yel brn	1.00	3.00
6L37	A3	$10 brn org	.25	.35
6L38	A3	$14 brn org	35.00	27.50
6L39	A2	$15 ultra	2.00	2.50
6L40	A2	$30 grn, type I	.25	.40
a.		Type II	.80	.70
6L41	A3	$35 gray bl	25.00	25.00
6L42	A2	$50 rose vio	12.00	12.00
6L43	A3	$70 dp grn	.70	.25
6L44	A2	$80 pink	.90	3.00
6L45	A3	$100 brn org	.80	2.00
6L46	A3	$220 rose red	4.00	2.00
		Nos. 6L33-6L46 (14)	105.40	93.00

Nos. 6L33 and 6L34 exist imperf. Value, each $13.50.

For surcharges & overprints see Nos. 6L63-6L65, 6L66-6L73, 6L75, 6L90-6L98, 6L100-6L108.

Star Enclosing Map of Hankow Area — A4

Two types of $500:
I — Thick numerals of "500." No period after "500."
II — Thin numerals and period.

Two types of $1000:
I — No period after "1000."
II — Period after "1000."

6L55	A4	$5000 brown	5.00	5.00
6L56	A4	$10,000 brt pink	6.00	6.00
		Nos. 6L48-6L56 (9)	48.50	21.75

For surcharges and overprints see Nos. 6L74, 6L76-6L81, 6L99, 6L109.

Hankow River Customs Building
A5

River Wall, Wuchang — A6

Design: $290, $370, River scene, Hanyang.

1949, Aug. 16			**Perf. 11**	
6L57	A5	$70 green	3.00	2.00
6L58	A5	$220 crimson	3.00	2.00
6L59	A5	$290 brown	3.00	2.00
6L60	A5	$370 brt blue	3.00	2.00
6L61	A6	$500 purple	7.00	3.00
6L62	A6	$1000 vermilion	7.00	2.00
		Nos. 6L57-6L62 (6)	26.00	13.00

Liberation of Hankow, Wuchang and Hanyang.
Exist imperf. About the same value.
For overprints see Nos. 6L82-6L87.

Nos. 6L35, 6L39 and 6L40 Surcharged in Red ("Honan Renminbi Currency")

1949, July				
6L63	A2	$7 on $6 emer	7.00	7.00
6L64	A2	$14 on $15 ultra	7.50	7.50
6L65	A2	$70 on $30 grn	9.00	10.00
		Nos. 6L63-6L65 (3)	23.50	24.50

Surcharge shown is for $70. The $7 has 5 characters in left column and no bottom line.

Issues of 1949 Overprinted ("Honan Renminbi Currency")

1949, Aug.				
6L66	A2	$3 brn org	.95	.90
6L67	A2	$7 yel brn	.95	.90
6L68	A2	$10 bl grn	1.90	1.90
6L69	A3	$14 org brn	1.90	3.00
6L70	A2	$30 yel grn (6L40a)	2.00	3.00
6L71	A3	$35 gray bl	.95	5.00
6L72	A2	$50 rose vio	7.00	5.00
6L73	A2	$70 dp grn	2.00	3.75
6L74	A4	$110 org brn	7.00	7.00
6L75	A3	$220 rose red	6.00	6.00
6L76	A4	$290 brown	10.00	10.00
6L77	A4	$370 blue	10.00	10.00
6L78	A4	$500 bl, II	12.00	14.00
6L79	A4	$1000 dk red, I	25.00	30.00
6L80	A4	$5000 brown	100.00	110.00
6L81	A4	$10,000 brt pink	200.00	225.00
		Nos. 6L66-6L81 (16)	383.65	431.45

Width of the overprint varies slightly.

Nos. 6L57-6L62 Overprinted ("Honan Renminbi Currency")

1949, Aug.   **Perf. 11**

6L82	A5	$70 green	2.50	3.00
6L83	A5	$220 crimson	4.00	4.25
6L84	A5	$290 brown	4.00	4.25
6L85	A5	$370 brt bl	6.00	6.50
6L86	A5	$500 purple	6.00	6.50
6L87	A6	$1000 vermilion	8.00	8.50
		Nos. 6L82-6L87 (6)	30.50	33.00

Width of overprint on Nos. 6L82-6L85, 7mm; on Nos. 6L86-6L87, 12mm.
Exist imperf. About the same value.

Changchow Issue Surcharged in Red ("Honan Renminbi Currency")

(same size) Mao Tsetung — A7

1949, Sept.   **Perf. 10**

6L88	A7	$290 on $30 yel grn	30.00	32.50
6L89	A7	$370 on $30 yel grn	37.50	50.00

Issues of 1949 Surcharged

1950, Jan.

6L90	A2	$200 on $1	.55	1.75
6L91	A2	$200 on $3	3.00	1.60
6L92	A2	$200 on $6	.55	1.75
6L93	A3	$200 on $7	3.00	1.60
6L94	A3	$200 on $14	3.00	1.60
6L95	A3	$200 on $35	3.25	2.40
6L96	A2	$200 on $70	3.00	1.60
6L97	A2	$200 on $80	3.00	1.60
6L98	A3	$200 on $220	3.00	1.60
6L99	A4	$200 on $370	.50	1.75
6L100	A2	$300 on $70	.50	2.50
6L101	A2	$300 on $80	.50	1.75
6L102	A3	$300 on $220	.25	1.75
6L103	A3	$1200 on $3	27.50	27.50
6L104	A3	$1200 on $7	5.25	5.00
6L105	A3	$1200 on $14	7.00	6.75
6L106	A2	$2100 on $1	35.00	35.00
6L107	A2	$2100 on $6	35.00	35.00
6L108	A3	$2100 on $35	10.00	9.00
6L109	A4	$5000 on $370	4.50	4.50
		Nos. 6L90-6L109 (20)	148.35	146.00

Two types of surcharge exist, differing in spacing of characters in top row.

CENTRAL CHINA PARCEL POST STAMPS

Star and Map of Hankow — PP1

1949, Nov.   **Litho.**   **Perf. 11, 11½**

6LQ1	PP1	$5000 brown	4.50	5.75
6LQ2	PP1	$10,000 scarlet	19.00	17.00
6LQ3	PP1	$20,000 dk sl grn	9.50	18.00
6LQ4	PP1	$50,000 vermilion	5.00	35.00
		Nos. 6LQ1-6LQ4 (4)	38.00	75.75

SOUTH CHINA

The South China Liberation Area included the provinces of Kwangtung and Kwangsi and Hainan Island. The South China Postal and Telegraph Administration was organized on or about Nov. 4, 1949.

All Stamps Issued without Gum

Pearl River Bridge, Canton — A1

1949, Nov. 4   **Litho.**   **Imperf.**

7L1	A1	$10 green	.85	.50
7L2	A1	$20 sepia	.85	.50
7L3	A1	$30 violet	.85	.50
7L4	A1	$50 carmine	.85	.50
7L5	A1	$100 ultramarine	1.50	.50
		Nos. 7L1-7L5 (5)	4.90	2.50

For surcharges see Nos. 7L19-7L23.

China Nos. 993-995 With Additional Overprint in Red ("Liberation of Swatow")

1949, Nov. 9

7L6	A94	2½c on $500 rose lil (993)	35.00	35.00
a.		Handstamped	80.00	80.00
7L7	A94	2½c on $500 rose lil (994)	40.00	40.00
a.		Handstamped	95.00	95.00
7L8	A94	15c on $10 grn (995)	50.00	50.00
a.		Handstamped	175.00	175.00

On Unit Issues of China, 1949

7L9	A96	org (959)	19.00	12.50
7L10	AP5	bl grn (C62)	24.00	27.50
7L11	SD2	red vio (E12)	24.00	27.50
7L12	R2	car (F2)	40.00	40.00

On Sun Yat-sen and Flying Geese Issues of China

7L13	A94	2c on $10 (974)	150.00	200.00
7L14	A94	4c bl grn (975)	300.00	400.00
7L15	A94	10c dp lil (976)	20.00	20.00
7L16	A94	20c bl (978)	40.00	32.50
7L17	A97	$1 brn org (984)	45.00	30.00
7L18	A97	$10 bl grn (987)	450.00	400.00
		Nos. 7L6-7L18 (13)	1,217.	1,303.

Forgeries exist of Nos. 7L13-7L14, 7L18.

Nos. 7L1-7L3 Surcharged in Red or Green

1950, Jan.

7L19	A1	$300 on $30 vio (R)	2.50	2.00
7L20	A1	$500 on $20 brn (R)	2.50	3.00
7L21	A1	$800 on $30 vio (G)	3.00	4.00
7L22	A1	$1000 on $10 gray grn (R)	3.50	3.00
7L23	A1	$1000 on $20 brn (R)	3.50	2.25
		Nos. 7L19-7L23 (5)	15.00	14.25

SOUTHWEST CHINA

The Southwest China Liberation Area included the provinces of Kweichow, Szechwan, Yunnan, Sikang and Tibet. The Southwest Postal and Telegraph Administration was organized on or about Nov. 15, 1949 after the liberation of Kweiyang, capital of Kweichow Province.

All Stamps Issued without Gum

Chu Teh, Mao and Troops — A1

1949, Dec.   **Litho.**   **Perf. 12½**

8L1	A1	$10 deep blue	4.00	4.25
8L2	A1	$20 rose claret	.45	2.00
8L3	A1	$30 dp org	.60	2.00
8L4	A1	$50 gray grn	1.00	2.00
8L5	A1	$100 carmine	.90	1.50
8L6	A1	$200 blue	1.25	1.50
8L7	A1	$300 bl vio	1.50	1.50

8L8	A1	$500 dk gray	3.00	2.50
8L9	A1	$1000 pale pur	11.00	6.00
8L10	A1	$2000 green	20.00	20.00
8L11	A1	$5000 orange	57.50	60.00
		Nos. 8L1-8L11 (11)	101.20	103.75

For surcharges and overprints see Nos. 8L21-8L29, 8L40-8L47, 8L55.

China Nos. 974-975, 984, 986-987 Surcharged ("Kweichow People's Post")

1949, Dec. 1   **Perf. 12½**

8L12	A94	$20 on 2c org	8.00	10.00
8L13	A94	$50 on 4c bl grn	12.00	12.00
8L14	A97	$100 on $1 brn org	20.00	15.00
8L15	A97	$400 on $5 car rose	40.00	45.00
8L16	A97	$2000 on $10 bl grn	140.00	95.00
		Nos. 8L12-8L16 (5)	220.00	177.00

Map of China, Flag Planted in Southwest A2

1950, Jan.   **Litho.**   **Perf. 9 to 11½**

8L17	A2	$20 dark blue	1.25	2.50
8L18	A2	$30 green	2.75	2.50
8L19	A2	$50 red	1.75	3.50
8L20	A2	$100 brown	2.75	3.50
		Nos. 8L17-8L20 (4)	8.50	12.00

Liberation of the Southwest.
For surcharges see Nos. 8L30-8L39, 8L56-8L59.

Nos. 8L5-8L6 Surcharged

No. 8L22

$300

$1200

$1500

$2000

    Perf. 12½

8L21	A1	$300 on $100 car	3.50	4.00
8L22	A1	$500 on $100 car	3.50	4.00
8L23	A1	$1200 on $100 car	7.00	7.00
8L24	A1	$1500 on $200 bl	7.00	7.00
8L25	A1	$2000 on $200 bl	11.00	10.00
		Nos. 8L21-8L25 (5)	32.00	32.00

Nos. 8L5-8L6 Overprinted ("East Szechwan")

1950, Jan.

8L26	A1	$100 carmine	9.00	9.00
8L27	A1	$200 blue	9.00	9.00

Nos. 8L5-8L6 Handstamp Surcharged

1950, Jan.

8L28	A1	$1200 on $100 car	15.00	27.50
8L29	A1	$1500 on $200 bl	40.00	27.50

Many varieties, including wide and narrow settings, exist.

Nos. 8L17-8L20 Surcharged in Black or Red

$60

$150

$300

$1500

$3000

$5000

$10,000

$20,000

$50,000

1950   *Perf. 9 to 11½*

8L30	A2	$60 on $30	12.00	9.00
8L31	A2	$150 on $30	12.00	9.00
8L32	A2	$300 on $20 (R)	2.00	4.00
8L33	A2	$300 on $30	12.00	9.00
8L34	A2	$1500 on $100	72.50	22.50
8L35	A2	$3000 on $50	7.75	22.50
8L36	A2	$5000 on $50	3.50	22.50
8L37	A2	$10,000 on $50	120.00	42.50
8L38	A2	$20,000 on $50	4.00	42.50
8L39	A2	$50,000 on $50	5.75	60.00
		Nos. 8L30-8L39 (10)	251.50	243.50

Nos. 8L5-8L7 Overprinted ("West Szechwan")

1950, Jan.   *Perf. 12½*

8L40	A1	$100 carmine	22.50	24.00
8L41	A1	$200 pale blue	30.00	32.50
8L42	A1	$300 blue violet	40.00	42.50
		Nos. 8L40-8L42 (3)	92.50	99.00

Nos. 8L4-8L7 Surcharged

No. 8L43

No. 8L44

No. 8L45

No. 8L46

No. 8L47

1950, Jan.

8L43	A1	$500 on $100	8.75	8.75
a.		Narrow spacing	70.00	60.00
8L44	A1	$800 on $100	8.75	8.75
8L45	A1	$1000 on $50	11.00	11.00
8L46	A1	$2000 on $200	22.50	27.50
8L47	A1	$3000 on $300	35.00	45.00
		Nos. 8L43-8L47 (5)	86.00	101.00

Two lines of surcharge 7mm apart on No. 8L43, 4mm on No. 8L43a.

China Nos. 975 and 977 Surcharged

No. 8L48   No. 8L50

Perf. 12½, 13 or Compound

1950, Jan.

8L48	A94	$100 on 4c	7.50	13.50
8L49	A94	$200 on 4c	12.00	22.50
8L50	A94	$800 on 16c	67.50	67.50
8L51	A94	$1000 on 16c	300.00	375.00
		Nos. 8L48-8L51 (4)	387.00	478.50

Unit Issue of China Overprinted ("Southwest People's Post")

1950, Jan.   **Engr.**   *Rouletted*

8L52	A96	orange	150.00	175.00
a.		Perf. 12½	225.00	250.00

Perf. 12½

8L53	SD2	red violet	225.00	250.00
8L54	R2	carmine	225.00	250.00
		Nos. 8L52-8L54 (3)	600.00	675.00

On No. 8L54, space between overprint columns is 3mm and right column is raised to height of left.

Nos. 8L3, 8L17-8L20 Surcharged in Black or Red

1950, Mar.   *Perf. 12½, 9 to 11½*

8L55	A1	$800 on $30	45.00	45.00
8L56	A2	$1000 on $50	9.00	12.00
8L57	A2	$2000 on $100	13.50	18.00
8L58	A2	$4000 on $20 (R)	35.00	40.00
8L59	A2	$5000 on $30	55.00	55.00
		Nos. 8L55-8L59 (5)	157.50	170.00

CHRISTMAS ISLAND

ˈkris-məs ˈī-lənd

LOCATION — In the Indian Ocean, 230 miles south of Java
GOVT. — A territory of Australia
AREA — 52 sq. mi.
POP. — 2,373 (1999 est.)

Australia took over Christmas Island from Singapore in 1958.

> **Catalogue values for all unused stamps in this country are for Never Hinged items.**

Queen Elizabeth II — A1

Engr.; Name and Value Typo. in Black

1958, Oct. 15   **Unwmk.**   *Perf. 14½*

1	A1	2c yellow orange	.45	.80
2	A1	4c brown	.55	.35
3	A1	5c lilac	.55	.50
4	A1	6c dull blue	1.75	.35
5	A1	8c gray brown	3.25	.50
6	A1	10c violet	2.50	.35
7	A1	12c carmine rose	3.50	2.00
8	A1	20c ultramarine	2.50	2.00
9	A1	50c yellow green	3.50	2.00
10	A1	$1 greenish blue	3.75	2.00
		Nos. 1-10 (10)	22.30	10.85
		Set, hinged	11.00	

Map of Island — A2   Island Scene — A3

4c, Moonflower. 5c, Robber crab. 8c, Phosphate train. 10c, Crane loading phosphate. 12c, Flying fish cove. 20c, Loading ship. 50c, Frigate bird. $1, Yellow-billed tropic bird.

Perf. 14x14½, 14½x14

1963, Aug. 28   **Engr.**

11	A2	2c orange	1.00	.55
12	A2	4c red brown	.40	.35
13	A2	5c rose lilac	.40	.35
14	A3	6c slate	.35	.45
15	A2	8c black	2.00	.45
16	A2	10c violet	.35	.25
17	A3	12c dull red	.30	.40
18	A3	20c dark blue	1.00	.35
19	A3	50c green	1.25	.35

Size: 35x21mm

20	A3	$1 orange yellow	1.75	.45
		Nos. 11-20 (10)	8.80	3.85
		Set, hinged	6.50	

"Simpson and His Donkey" by Wallace Anderson — A3a

1965, Apr. 14   **Photo.**   *Perf. 13½x13*

21	A3a	10c brt grn, sepia & blk	.55	1.25

ANZAC issue. See note after Australia No. 387.

Moorish Goddess A4

Fish: 1c, Golden striped grouper. 3c, Forceps fish. 4c, Queen triggerfish. 5c, Regal angelfish. 9c, Surgeonfish. 10c, Turkeyfish. 15c, Saddleback butterflyfish. 20c, Clown butterflyfish. 30c, Ghost pipefish. 50c, Lined surgeonfish. $1, Meyer's butterflyfish.

1968-70   **Photo.**   *Perf. 13½*

22	A4	1c multicolored	.55	.55
23	A4	2c multicolored	.75	.25
24	A4	3c multicolored	.75	.35
25	A4	4c multicolored	.75	.25
a.		Dark blue ("4c") omitted	3,000.	
26	A4	5c multicolored	.75	.30
27	A4	9c multicolored	.75	.60
28	A4	10c multicolored	.75	.30
29	A4	15c multicolored	6.50	3.00
30	A4	20c multicolored	1.75	.90
31	A4	30c multicolored	6.50	3.00
32	A4	50c multicolored	2.50	2.50
33	A4	$1 multicolored	2.50	2.50
		Nos. 22-33 (12)	24.80	14.50
		Set, hinged	16.00	

Issued: 15c, 30c, 12/14/70; others, 5/6/68.

Christmas Issues

"Hark the Herald Angels Sing" — A5

1969, Nov. 10   **Photo.**   *Perf. 13½*

34	A5	5c dk blue, gold, buff & red	.35	.35

A6

3c, The Ansidei Madonna, by Raphael. 5c, Virgin and Child, by Morando.

1970, Oct. 26   **Photo.**   *Perf. 14x14½*

35	A6	3c gold & multi	.25	.25
36	A6	5c silver & multi	.25	.25

A7

5c, Adoration of the Shepherds, Seville School. 20c, Adoration of the Shepherds, by Guido Reni.

1971, Oct. 4

37	A7	6c black & multi	.50	.50
38	A7	20c dark blue & multi	1.15	1.15

"Flying Fish," 1887 — A8

Ships and Map of Christmas Island: 1c, "Eagle," 1714. 2c, "Redpole," 1890. 3c, "Hoi Houw," 1959. 4c, "Pigot," 1771. 5c, "Valetta," 1968. 7c, "Asia," 1805. 8c, "Islander," 1929-60. 9c, "Imperieuse," 1888 (incorrectly inscribed "Imperious"). 10c, "Egeria," 1887. 20c, "Thomas," 1615. 25c, "Gordon," 1864. 30c, "Cygnet," 1688. 35c, "Triadic," 1958. 50c, "Amethyst," 1857. $1, "Royal Mary," 1643.

1972-73   **Photo.**   *Perf. 14½x13½*

39	A8	1c yel green & multi	.30	.55
40	A8	2c lt red brn & multi	.35	.65
41	A8	3c dp rose & multi	.35	.70
42	A8	4c multicolored	.45	.70
43	A8	5c multicolored	.45	.70
44	A8	6c lilac & multi	.45	.70
45	A8	7c lt green & multi	.45	.70
46	A8	8c blue & multi	.50	.70
47	A8	9c org & multi	.75	.65
48	A8	10c lem & multi	.45	.50
49	A8	20c tan & multi	.50	.80
50	A8	25c multi & multi	.60	1.60
51	A8	30c multicolored	.75	1.00
52	A8	35c tan & multi	.80	1.00
53	A8	50c ultra & multi	.90	1.60
54	A8	$1 yellow & multi	1.25	1.90
		Nos. 39-54 (16)	9.30	14.45

Issued: 6c, 7c, 8c, 20c, 2/5/72; 1c, 2c, 3c, $1, 6/5/72; 4c, 5c, 9c, 50c, 2/6/73; 10c, 25c, 30c, 35c, 6/4/73.

A9   A9a
"Peace"   "Joy"

1972, Oct. 2   **Litho.**   *Perf. 14½*

55	A9	3c black & multi	.50	.50
56	A9a	3c black & multi	.50	.50
a.		Pair, #55-56	1.25	1.25
57	A9	7c black & multi	.65	.65
58	A9a	7c black & multi	.65	.65
a.		Pair, #57-58	1.50	1.50
		Nos. 55-58 (4)	2.30	2.30

Mother and Child, Christmas Island Map — A10

1973, Oct. 2 Photo. Perf. 14½x13½
59 A10 7c blue & multi .60 .60
60 A10 25c brt green & multi 1.75 1.75
Christmas.

Mother and Child with Star and Cross — A11

1974, Oct. 2 Photo. Perf. 13½x14½
61 A11 7c black & lilac rose .55 .55
62 A11 30c black & yellow 1.60 2.00
Christmas.

Flight into Egypt — A12

1975, Oct. 2 Photo. Perf. 14½x13½
63 A12 10c gold, black & yel .40 .40
64 A12 35c gold, vio blk & rose .90 1.25
Christmas.

Star of Bethlehem and Dove
A13   A14

1976, Oct. 2 Photo. Perf. 13½
65 A13 10c red & multi .25 .35
66 A14 10c red & multi .25 .35
a. Pair, #65-66 .90 1.50
67 A13 35c blue & multi .40 .55
68 A14 35c blue & multi .40 .55
a. Pair, #67-68 1.10 1.75
Nos. 65-68 (4) 1.30 1.80
Christmas.

Andrew Clunies-Ross (first settler) A15

Famous Visitors: 1c, William Dampier, explorer, buccaneer. 2c, Capt. Willem de Vlamingh, Dutch explorer. 3c, Vice Adm. John F. L. P. Maclear, Royal Navy. 4c, John Murray, oceanographer, scientist. 5c, Adm. Pelham Aldrich and crew collecting specimen. 7c, Joseph Jackson Lister, naturalist, and arenga listeri plant. 8c, Adm. William Henry May. 9c, Henry Nicholas Ridley, botanist. 10c, George Clunies-Ross, pioneer phosphate miner. 20c, Capt. Joshua Slocum. 45c, Charles William Andrews, zoologist, and frigate birds. 50c, Karl Richard Hanitsch, zoologist, and fruit pigeon. 75c, Victor W. W. Saunders Purcell, Sinologist. $1, Fam Choo Beng, educator. $2, Harold Spencer-Jones, astronomer.

1977-78 Photo. Perf. 14x13½
69 A15 1c multicolored .25 .80
70 A15 2c multicolored .25 .90
71 A15 3c multicolored .25 .90
72 A15 4c multicolored .25 .90
73 A15 5c multicolored .30 .40
74 A15 6c multicolored .30 .70
75 A15 7c multicolored .30 .45
76 A15 8c multicolored .30 .75
77 A15 9c multicolored .35 1.75
78 A15 10c multicolored .30 .55
79 A15 20c multicolored .35 .70
80 A15 45c multicolored .65 .45
81 A15 50c multicolored .90 2.00
82 A15 75c multicolored .70 1.25
83 A15 $1 multicolored .80 1.25
84 A15 $2 multicolored 1.30 2.00
Nos. 69-84 (16) 7.55 15.75

Issued: 1c, 6c, 9c, $1, 4/30/77; 2c, 3c, 4c, $2, 2/22/78; 5c, 7c, 45c, 50c, 5/31/78; 8c, 10c, 20c, 75c, 9/1/78.

Australian Arms, Map of Christmas Island — A16

1977, June 2 Litho. Perf. 14½x13½
85 A16 45c multicolored .50 .50
25th anniv. of reign of Elizabeth II.

Souvenir Sheet

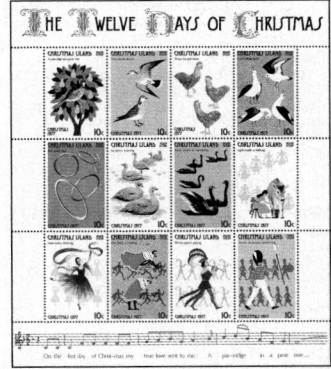

The Twelve Days of Christmas — A17

Twelve Days of Christmas: a, Partridge in a pear tree. b, 2 turtle doves. c, 3 French hens. d, 4 calling birds. e, 5 gold rings. f, 6 geese. g, 7 swans. h, 8 maids a-milking. i, 9 ladies dancing. j, 10 lords a-leaping. k, 11 pipers piping. l, 12 drummers drumming.

Unwmk.
1977, Oct. 20 Litho. Perf. 14
86 A17 Sheet of 12 1.50 2.00
a.-l. 10c, any single .25 .25
m. Wmk. 373 ('78) 2.75 3.75
Christmas.

Common Design Types pictured following the introduction.

Elizabeth II Coronation Anniversary
Common Design Types
Souvenir Sheet

1978, Apr. 21 Litho. Perf. 15
87 Sheet of 6 3.50 4.00
a. CD326 45c White swan of Bohun .55 .60
b. CD327 45c Elizabeth II .55 .60
c. CD328 45c Abbott's booby .55 .60

No. 87 contains 2 se-tenant strips of Nos. 87a-87c, separated by horizontal gutter with commemorative and descriptive inscriptions.

Souvenir Sheet

The Song of Christmas — A18

Song of Christmas: a, Christ Child. b, Herald angels. c, Redeemer. d, Israel. e, Star. f, Three Wise Men. g, Manger. h. "All He stands for." i, "Shepherds came."

1978, Oct. 2 Litho. Perf. 14
88 A18 Sheet of 9 1.50 1.75
a.-i. 10c single stamp .25 .25
Christmas. Each stamp design incorporates one letter of "Christmas."

IYC Emblem, Oriental Children — A19

Design: IYC emblem and children of different races holding hands, continuous design.

1979, Apr. 20 Litho. Perf. 14
89 Strip of 5 1.50 2.25
a.-e. A19 20c single stamp .25 .45
International Year of the Child.

Rowland Hill and No. 25 — A20

Sir Rowland Hill (1795-1879), originator of penny postage, and Christmas Island stamps: a, #1. b, #11. c, #21. d, #25. e, #34.

1979, Aug. 27 Litho. Perf. 13x13½
90 Strip of 5 1.10 1.75
a.-e. A20 20c any single .25 .40

Three Kings Bearing Gifts — A21

Christmas: 55c, Virgin and Child, globe.

1979, Oct. 22 Litho. Perf. 14x14½
91 A21 20c multicolored .25 .30
92 A21 55c multicolored .45 .70

25 Years of Golf — A22

1980, Feb. 12 Litho. Perf. 14½x14
93 A22 20c shown .35 .55
94 A22 55c Clubhouse .95 1.40

Surveyor, Phosphate Industry A23

No. 96, Drilling for samples. No. 97, Sample analysis. No. 98, Mine planning. No. 99, Jungle clearing. No. 100, Overburden removal. No. 101, Open cut mining. No. 102, Restoration. No. 103, Screening and stockpiling. No. 104, Loading train. No. 105, Rail transport. No. 106, Drying. No. 107, Crushing. No. 108, Pipeline. No. 109, Bulk storage. No. 110, Loading ship.

1980-81 Litho. Perf. 14x14½
95 A23 15c shown .25 .25
96 A23 22c multicolored .25 .25
97 A23 40c multicolored .30 .30
98 A23 55c multicolored .45 .45
99 A23 15c multicolored .25 .25
100 A23 22c multicolored .25 .25
101 A23 40c multicolored .30 .30
102 A23 55c multicolored .45 .45
103 A23 22c multicolored .30 .30
104 A23 28c multicolored .35 .35
105 A23 40c multicolored .45 .45
106 A23 60c multicolored .55 .55
107 A23 22c multicolored .30 .30
108 A23 28c multicolored .35 .35
109 A23 40c multicolored .45 .45
110 A23 60c multicolored .55 .55
Nos. 95-110 (16) 5.80 5.80

Issued: Nos. 96-98, 5/5/80; Nos. 99-102, 7/14/80; Nos. 103-106, 2/9/81; Nos. 107-110, 5/4/81.

Souvenir Sheet

Christmas — A24

1980, Oct. 6 Litho. Perf. 13½x13
111 A24 Sheet of 6 1.60 2.25
a. 15c Angel .25 .35
b. 22c Virgin and child .25 .35
c. 60c Angel .30 .35
d. 15c Angel holding soldier .25 .35
e. 22c Kneeling woman and man .25 .35
f. 60c Chinese, Indian, European children .30 .35

Christmas. No. 111 contains 2 strips of 3 (Nos. 111a-111c and 111d-111f) with gutter between.

Cryptoblepharus Egeriae — A25

Reptiles: 30c, Emoia nativitata. 40c, Lepidodactylus listeri. 60c, Cyrtodactylus nov.

1981, Aug. 10 Litho. Perf. 13x13½
112 A25 24c shown .25 .25
113 A25 30c multicolored .30 .30
114 A25 40c multicolored .45 .45
115 A25 60c multicolored .55 .55
Nos. 112-115 (4) 1.55 1.55

Souvenir Sheet

Christmas — A26

1981, Oct. 19   Litho.   Perf. 14½x14
116	A26	Sheet of 4	1.60	2.00
a.		18c Angels, star	.25	.30
b.		24c Nativity	.25	.35
c.		40c Children praying to Jesus	.50	.60
d.		60c Children praying	.55	.75

Reef Heron
A27

2c, Noddies. 3c, Glossy swiftlet. 4c, Imperial pigeon. 5c, Christmas Isld. silvereyes. 10c, Thrush. 25c, Silver bosunbird. 30c, Christmas Isld. emerald doves. 40c, Brown boobies. 50c, Red-footed boobies. 65c, Christmas Isld. frigatebird. 75c, Golden bosunbirds. 80c, Nankeen kestrel, vert. $1, Christmas Isld. hawk owl, vert. $2 Goshawk, vert. $4 Abbott's boobies, vert.

1982-83   Litho.   Perf. 14
117	A27	1c shown	.65	.25
118	A27	2c multicolored	.65	.25
119	A27	3c multicolored	.65	.75
120	A27	4c multicolored	.65	.75
121	A27	5c multicolored	.80	.95
122	A27	10c multicolored	.65	.75
123	A27	25c multicolored	1.00	.75
124	A27	30c multicolored	.70	.75
125	A27	40c multicolored	.70	.60
126	A27	50c multicolored	.70	.60
127	A27	65c multicolored	.70	.60
128	A27	75c multicolored	.85	.75
129	A27	80c multicolored	1.00	2.00
130	A27	$1 multicolored	2.00	2.25
131	A27	$2 multicolored	1.75	4.00
132	A27	$4 multicolored	2.75	3.00
		Nos. 117-132 (16)	16.20	19.00

Issued: 1c, 2c, 25c $4, 3/8; 3c, 4c, 10c, $2, 6/14; 40c, 50c, 65c, 75c, 8/23; 5c, 30c, 80c, $1, 2/21/83.

Christmas — A28

Paper sculptures.

1982, Oct. 18   Litho. & Embossed
135	A28	27c Joseph	.30	.30
136	A28	50c Angel	.40	.40
137	A28	75c Mary, Baby Jesus	.50	.65
a.		Strip of 3, #135-137	1.30	1.60

25th Anniv. of Boat Club — A29

Designs: Various boating activities.

Perf. 14x14½, 14½x14

1983, May 2   Litho.
138	A29	27c multicolored	.30	.30
139	A29	35c multicolored	.30	.30
140	A29	50c multi, horiz.	.45	.45
141	A29	75c multi, horiz.	.45	.45
		Nos. 138-141 (4)	1.50	1.50

25th Anniv. of Australian Territory A30

24c, Maps. golden bosun bird, kangaroo. 30c, Map, flag. 85c, Boeing 727, maps.

1983, Oct. 1   Litho.   Perf. 14
142	A30	24c multicolored	.70	.45
143	A30	30c multicolored	.80	.80
144	A30	85c multicolored	1.60	2.00
		Nos. 142-144 (3)	3.10	3.25

Christmas — A31

Designs: Christmas candles.

1983, Oct. 31   Litho.   Perf. 13½x13
145	A31	24c multicolored	.25	.30
146	A31	30c multicolored	.35	.50
147	A31	85c multicolored	.75	1.50
		Nos. 145-147 (3)	1.35	2.30

Red Land Crab — A32

30c, Feeding. 40c, Migration. 55c, Developmental stages. 85c, Adult female, young.

1984, Feb. 20   Litho.   Perf. 14x14½
148	A32	30c multicolored	.30	.30
149	A32	40c multicolored	.40	.40
150	A32	55c multicolored	.40	.40
151	A32	85c multicolored	.80	.80
		Nos. 148-151 (4)	1.90	1.90

Local Fungi — A33

30c, Leucocoprinus fragilissimus. 40c, Microporus xanthopus. 45c, Trogia anthidepas. 55c, Haddowia longipes. 85c, Phillipsia domingensis.

1984, Apr. 30   Perf. 13½x14½
152	A33	30c multicolored	.45	.45
153	A33	40c multicolored	.50	.50
154	A33	45c multicolored	.65	.65
155	A33	55c multicolored	.75	.75
156	A33	85c multicolored	.95	.95
		Nos. 152-156 (5)	3.30	3.30

Cricket on Christmas Isld., 25th Anniv. A34

1984, July 23   Litho.   Perf. 14
157	A34	30c Runout	.50	.75
158	A34	40c Catch at point	.55	1.00
159	A34	55c Batsman	.65	1.25
160	A34	85c Batsman hitting	.75	1.50
		Nos. 157-160 (4)	2.45	4.50

Souvenir Sheet

Christmas; Ausipex '84 A35

1984, Sept. 21   Litho.   Perf. 13½
161		Sheet of 3 + 3 labels	2.60	2.60
a.		A35 30c Father Christmas arriving	.45	.45
b.		A35 55c Distributing gifts	.75	.75
c.		A35 85c Waving good-bye	1.25	1.25

Crabs A36

No. 162, Birgus latro. No. 163, Cardiosoma hirtipes. No. 164, Gecarcoidea natalis. No. 165, Ocypode ceratophthalma. No. 166, Ceonobita rugosa. No. 167, Metasesarma rousseauxi. No. 168, Coenobita brevimana. No. 169, Geograpsus stormi. No. 170, Grapsus tenuicrustatus. No. 171, Geograpsus grayi. No. 172, Ocypode cordimana. No. 173, Geograpsus crinipes.

1985   Litho.   Perf. 13x13½
162	A36	30c multicolored	1.00	.90
163	A36	30c multicolored	1.00	.90
164	A36	33c multicolored	1.10	1.00
165	A36	40c multicolored	1.10	1.00
166	A36	45c multicolored	1.10	1.25
167	A36	45c multicolored	1.25	1.50
168	A36	55c multicolored	1.25	1.50
169	A36	60c multicolored	1.75	1.75
170	A36	60c multicolored	2.25	2.50
171	A36	85c multicolored	2.50	2.50
172	A36	90c multicolored	2.50	3.25
173	A36	90c multicolored	3.00	4.00
		Nos. 162-173 (12)	19.80	22.05

Issued: 30c, 40c, 55c, 85c, 1/30; Nos. 163, 166, 169, 172, 4/29; Nos. 164, 167, 170, 173, 7/22.

Once in Royal David's City — A37

Songs: 33c, While Shepherds Watched Their Flocks by Night. 45c, Away in a Manger. 60c, We Three Kings of Orient Are. 90c, Hark! The Herald Angels Sing.

1985, Oct. 28   Litho.   Perf. 14x14½
174	A37	27c multicolored	.80	1.25
175	A37	33c multicolored	.90	1.40
176	A37	45c multicolored	1.10	1.50
177	A37	60c multicolored	1.20	1.60
178	A37	90c multicolored	1.30	1.75
a.		Strip of 5, #174-178	6.75	9.00
		Nos. 174-178 (5)	5.30	7.50

Christmas.

Halley's Comet A38

33c, Over island. 45c, Edmond Halley. 60c, Over phosphate shipping. 90c, Over Flying Fish Cove.

1986, Apr. 30   Litho.   Perf. 14
179	A38	33c multicolored	.40	.70
180	A38	45c multicolored	.50	1.10
181	A38	60c multicolored	.75	2.10
182	A38	90c multicolored	1.10	1.90
		Nos. 179-182 (4)	2.75	6.40

Indigenous Flowers — A39

1986, June 30   Litho.   Perf. 14
183	A39	33c Ridley's orchid	.85	.55
184	A39	45c Hanging flower	.60	.85
185	A39	60c Hoya	.60	1.50
186	A39	90c Sea hibiscus	.70	2.00
		Nos. 183-186 (4)	2.75	4.90

Royal Wedding Issue, 1986
Common Design Type

Designs: 33c, Couple in Buckingham Palace garden. 90c, Andrew operating helicopter.

1986, July 23   Litho.   Perf. 14½x14
187	CD338	33c multicolored	.45	.45
188	CD338	90c multicolored	1.00	1.75

Christmas A40

Santa Claus at Christmas Island: 30c, Speedboating. 36c, At the beach. 55c, Fishing. 70c, Golfing. $1, Sleeping in hammock.

1986, Sept. 30   Litho.   Perf. 13x13½
189	A40	30c multicolored	.80	.60
190	A40	36c multicolored	.95	.60
191	A40	55c multicolored	1.40	1.50
192	A40	70c multicolored	2.50	3.50
193	A40	$1 multicolored	2.50	4.00
		Nos. 189-193 (5)	8.15	10.20

Visiting Ships, Cent. A41

1987, Jan. 21   Perf. 14½
194	A41	36c Flying Fish	1.00	.80
195	A41	90c Egeria	1.90	2.50

Wildlife A42

1c, Blind snake. 2c, Blue-tailed skink. 3c, Insectivorous bat. 5c, Green cricket. 10c, Christmas Is. fruit bat. 25c, Gecko. 30c, Praying mantis. 36c, Hawk owl. 40c, Bull-mouth helmet shell. 41c, Nudibranch. 50c, Textile cone shell. 65c, Brittle-stars. 75c, Royal angelfish. 90c, Christmas Is. white butterfly. $1, Mimic butterfly. $2, Shrew. $5, Green turtle.

1987-89   Litho.   Perf. 14
196	A42	1c multicolored	.40	.90
197	A42	2c multicolored	.40	.90
198	A42	3c multicolored	.75	.90
199	A42	5c multicolored	1.10	.90
200	A42	10c multicolored	.90	.90
201	A42	25c multicolored	.90	1.00
202	A42	30c multicolored	1.00	1.25
203	A42	36c multicolored	2.25	1.75
204	A42	40c multicolored	1.50	2.75
204A	A42	41c multi ('89)	3.25	1.00
205	A42	50c multicolored	1.60	2.75
206	A42	65c multicolored	1.00	1.25
207	A42	75c multicolored	1.00	1.75
208	A42	90c multicolored	3.25	3.00
209	A42	$1 multicolored	3.25	3.00
210	A42	$2 multicolored	3.25	6.50

211 A42 $5 multicolored 4.00 *6.50*
  a. Sheet of 16, #196-204,
    205-211 47.50 47.50
  Nos. 196-211 (17) 29.80 37.00

Issued: 1c, 2c, 25c, $5, 3/25; 3c, 10c, 36c, $2, 6/24; 40c, 50c, 65c, 75c, 8/26; 5c, 30c, 90c, $1, 3/1/88; 41c, 9/1/89.
Stamps contained in No. 211a inscribed "1988" at bottom.
For overprint see Nos. 246-247.

Souvenir Sheet

Santa Claus Delivering
Presents — A43

1987, Oct. 7   **Litho.**   **Perf. 13½**
212 A43 Sheet of 4 5.50 5.50
  a. 30c multicolored .60 .60
  b. 37c multicolored .65 .65
  c. 90c multicolored 1.75 1.75
  d. $1 multicolored 1.90 1.90

Christmas. Nos. 212a-212d printed in a continuous design.

Australia
Bicentennial
A44

Designs: a, First Fleet sighted by 5 Aboriginals on land. b, Four Aboriginals on land, one in canoe. c, Ships entering bay, kangaroos. d, Europeans land. e, Flag raising.

1988, Jan. 26   **Litho.**   **Perf. 13**
213 Strip of 5 10.00 10.00
  a.-e. A44 37c any single 1.75 1.75

Nos. 213a-213e printed in a continuous design. See Cocos Islands No. 172.

Annexation of the
Island,
Cent. — A45

37c, Capt William Henry May. 53c, Annexation ceremony. 95c, HMS Imperieuse. $1.50, Building cairn of stones.

1988, June 8   **Litho.**   **Perf. 14½**
214 A45 37c multicolored .65 .65
215 A45 53c multicolored .90 .90
216 A45 95c multicolored 1.50 1.50
217 A45 $1.50 multicolored 2.00 2.00
  Nos. 214-217 (4) 5.05 5.05

Settlement of
Christmas
Is.,
Cent. — A46

Transportation: 37c, Horse and cart, 1910. 55c, Phosphate mining, 1910. 70c, Steam locomotive, 1914. $1, Arrival of first aircraft, 1957.

1988, Aug. 24   **Litho.**   **Perf. 14½**
218 A46 37c multicolored .95 .55
219 A46 53c multicolored 1.40 .75
220 A46 70c multicolored 1.40 1.00
221 A46 $1 multicolored 2.25 1.60
  Nos. 218-221 (4) 6.00 3.90

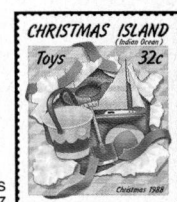

Christmas
Presents — A47

32c, Bucket, shovel, boat. 39c, Snorkeling equipment. 90c, Toy soldier, doll, stuffed animals. $1, Race car, truck, plane.

1988, Nov. 15   **Perf. 14x14½**
222 A47 32c multicolored .50 .50
223 A47 39c multicolored .60 .60
224 A47 90c multicolored 1.25 1.25
225 A47 $1 multicolored 1.50 1.00
  Nos. 222-225 (4) 3.85 3.35

Chinese
New
Year — A48

1989, Jan. 31   **Perf. 14½**
226 A48 39c Good harvest .70 .70
227 A48 70c Prosperity 1.00 1.00
228 A48 90c Good fortune 1.25 1.25
229 A48 $1 Progress 1.50 1.50
  Nos. 226-229 (4) 4.45 4.45

Sir John Murray (1841-1914),
Oceanographer — A49

39c, Portrait. 80c, Murray Hill (map). $1, Murray's equipment. $1.10, HMS Challenger.

1989, Mar. 16   **Perf. 14½x14**
230 A49 39c multicolored .70 .70
231 A49 80c multicolored 1.25 1.25
232 A49 $1 multicolored 1.60 1.60
233 A49 $1.10 multicolored 1.90 1.90
  Nos. 230-233 (4) 5.45 5.45

Malay-Hari Raya
Folk
Celebration — A50

39c, Children. 55c, Tambourine player. 80c, Girl. $1.10, Minaret.

1989, May 31   **Perf. 14**
234 A50 39c multicolored .50 .50
235 A50 55c multicolored .85 .85
236 A50 80c multicolored 1.10 1.10
237 A50 $1.10 multicolored 1.75 1.75
  Nos. 234-237 (4) 4.20 4.20

Ferns — A51

41c, Huperzia phlegmaria. 65c, Asplenium polydon. 80c, Davallia denticulata. $1.10, Asplenium nidus.

1989, Aug. 16
238 A51 41c multicolored .90 .90
239 A51 65c multicolored 1.25 1.25
240 A51 80c multicolored 1.40 1.25
241 A51 $1.10 multicolored 2.10 2.10
  Nos. 238-241 (4) 5.65 5.50

Christmas — A52

Biblical scenes: 36c, Joseph. 41c, Manger. 80c, Shepherds see star. $1.10, Magi riding camels.

1989, Oct. 4   **Litho.**   **Perf. 14½x15**
242 A52 36c multicolored .65 .55
243 A52 41c multicolored .70 .60
244 A52 80c multicolored 1.75 .90
245 A52 $1.10 multicolored 1.90 1.25
  Nos. 242-245 (4) 5.00 3.30

Nos. 204A
and 209
Overprinted

1989, Oct. 18   **Litho.**   **Perf. 14**
246 A42 41c multicolored *1.40* .60
247 A42 $1 multicolored *4.75* 1.40

STAMPSHOW '89, Melbourne.
No. 247 is dated "1989."

1st Sighting of
Christmas Is., 375th
Anniv. — A53

Sightings of the island: 41c, John Milward, master of the British East India ship *Thomas*, 1615. $1.10, William Mynors, captain of *Royal Mary*, 1643.

1990, Jan. 31   **Litho.**   **Perf. 14x15**
248 A53 41c multicolored 2.00 .50
249 A53 $1.10 multicolored 2.40 1.50

Transport
Through the
Ages — A55

1c, Phosphate transport. 2c, Phosphate train. 3c, Rail car, vert. 5c, Road train. 10c, Trishaw, vert. 15c, Terex. 25c, Long bus. 30c, Passenger rake, vert. 40c, Passenger barge, vert. 50c, Kolek canoe. 65c, Flying doctor, ambulance. 75c, Tradestore van. 90c, Vintage truck. $1, Water tanker. $2, Traction engine. $5, Steam locomotive, flat car.

Perf. 14x13½, 13½x14
1990   **Litho.**   **Unwmk.**
254 A55 1c multicolored .25 .25
255 A55 2c multicolored .45 .45
256 A55 3c multicolored .30 .30
257 A55 5c multicolored .50 .50
258 A55 10c multicolored .45 .45
259 A55 15c multicolored .75 .75
260 A55 25c multicolored .40 .40
261 A55 30c multicolored .40 .40
262 A55 40c multicolored .45 .45
263 A55 50c multicolored .65 .65
264 A55 65c multicolored 3.75 1.75
265 A55 75c multicolored 1.75 1.75
266 A55 90c multicolored 1.75 1.75
267 A55 $1 multicolored 1.90 1.90
268 A55 $2 multicolored 2.50 2.50
269 A55 $5 multicolored 3.50 3.75
  Nos. 254-269 (16) 19.75 18.00

Issued: 1c, 3c, 10c, 25c, 30c, 40c, 50c, $5, Apr. 18; others, Aug. 22.

World Wildlife
Fund — A56

Abbott's boobies (*Sula abbotti*): 20c, Adult (facing left). 29c, Adult (facing right). No. 273, Adults, nest, hatchling. No. 274a, Adult landing on tree branch. No. 274b, Adult resting on branch. No. 274c, Adult, young in nest.

Perf. 14x14½
1990, June 6   **Litho.**   **Unwmk.**
270 A56 10c shown 1.25 1.25
271 A56 20c multicolored 1.75 1.75
272 A56 29c multicolored 2.00 2.00
273 A56 41c multicolored 3.25 3.25
  Nos. 270-273 (4) 8.25 8.25

Souvenir Sheet
Perf. 14½
274 Sheet of 3 8.25 8.25
  a.-c. A56 41c any single 2.50 2.50
  d. Overprinted in purple 13.50 13.50
  e. Overprinted in green 17.50 17.50

No. 274d overprint reads "WORLD STAMP EXHIBITION / AUCKLAND, NEW ZEALAND, 24 AUGUST-2 SEPTEMBER 1990."
No. 274e overprint reads "BIRDPEX '90 National Philatelic Exhibition / University of Canterbury Christchurch NZ 6-9 Dec 1990 / In Conjunction / With The 20th International Ornithological Congress" and Bird's head.
Issued: No. 274d, Aug. 24; No. 274e, Dec. 6.

Centenary of Visit by Botanist Henry
Ridley — A57

1990, July 11   **Litho.**   **Perf. 14½**
275 A57 41c No. 77 .85 *.90*
276 A57 75c Ridley, vert. 1.30 *2.00*

Christmas
A58

Flowers: 38c, Corymborkus veratrifolia. 43c, Hoya aldrichii. 80c, Quisqualis indica. $1.20, Barringtonia racemosa.

1990, Oct. 3   **Litho.**   **Perf. 14½**
294 A58 38c multicolored 1.00 1.00
295 A58 43c multicolored 1.30 1.10
296 A58 80c multicolored 2.10 2.25
297 A58 $1.20 multicolored 3.00 *3.75*
  Nos. 294-297 (4) 7.40 8.10

1st Phosphate
Mining Lease,
Cent. — A59

1991, Feb. 13   **Litho.**   **Perf. 14½**
298 A59 43c Freighter 1.15 1.15
299 A59 43c Loading rail cars 1.15 1.15
300 A59 85c Shay locomotive 1.30 1.30
301 A59 $1.20 Bucket shovel 1.90 1.90
302 A59 $1.70 Reforestation 2.25 2.25
  a. Strip of 5, #298-302 8.00 8.00
  Nos. 298-302 (5) 7.75 7.75

Island Police Force — A60

No. 303, Community relations. No. 304, Traffic control. 90c, Customs and quarantine. $1.20, Search and rescue.

1991, Apr. 17	Litho.		Perf. 14½	
303	A60	43c multicolored	1.75	1.75
304	A60	75c multicolored	1.75	1.75
305	A60	90c multicolored	2.50	2.50
306	A60	$1.20 multicolored	3.25	3.25
a.		Souvenir sheet of 4, #303-306	9.25	9.25
		Nos. 303-306 (4)	9.25	9.25

Maps — A61

75c, Goos Atlas, 1666. $1.10, Apres De Manevillette, 1745. $1.20, Comberford, 1667.

1991, June 19	Litho.		Perf. 14	
307	A61	43c shown, 1991	1.10	1.10
308	A61	75c multicolored	2.10	2.10
309	A61	$1.10 multicolored	2.75	2.75
310	A61	$1.20 multicolored	3.00	3.00
		Nos. 307-310 (4)	8.95	8.95

Trees A62

43c, Bruguiera gymnorrhiza. 70c, Syzygium operculatum. 85c, Ficus microcarpa. $1.20, Arenga listeri.

1991, Aug. 21	Litho.		Perf. 14	
311	A62	43c multicolored	1.25	1.25
312	A62	70c multicolored	1.75	1.75
313	A62	85c multicolored	2.00	2.00
314	A62	$1.20 multicolored	2.25	2.25
		Nos. 311-314 (4)	7.25	7.25

Christmas A63

Drawings of "What Christmas Means to Me" by: No. 315a, S'ng Yen Luiw. b, Liew Ann Nee. c, Foo Pang Chuan. d, Too Lai Peng. e, Jesamine Wheeler. 43c, Ho Puay Ha. $1, Ng Hooi Hua. $1.20, Yani Kawi.

1991, Oct. 2			Perf. 14½	
315		Strip of 5	4.25	4.25
a.-e.		A63 38c any single	.75	.75
316	A63	43c multicolored	.85	.70
317	A63	$1 multicolored	1.90	1.90
318	A63	$1.20 multicolored	2.10	2.10
		Nos. 315-318 (4)	9.10	8.95

A64

War Time Evacuation, 50th Anniv.: No. 319, Conference to decide upon evacuation. No. 320, Europeans awaiting barge. $1.05, Barge

approaching waiting ship. $1.20, Remaining population waving to TSS Islander.

1992, Feb. 19	Litho.		Perf. 14½	
319	A64	45c multicolored	1.25	1.25
320	A64	45c multicolored	1.25	1.25
321	A64	$1.05 multicolored	2.60	2.60
322	A64	$2.75 multicolored	2.75	2.75
		Nos. 319-322 (4)	7.85	7.85

Shells — A65

5c, Cypraea tigris. 10c, Cypraea caput-serpentis. 15c, Lambis scorpius. 20c, Chlamys pallium. 25c, Engina mendicaria. 30c, Drupa ricinus. 40c, Distorsio reticulata. 45c, Turbo petholatus. 50c, Cantharus pulcher. 60c, Conus capitaneus. 70c, Turbo lajonkairii. 80c, Lambis chiragra. 90c, Angaria delphinus. $1, Vasum ceramicum. $2, Tonna perdix. $5, Drupa rubusidaea.

1992	Litho.		Perf. 15x14½	
326	A65	5c multicolored	.60	.90
327	A65	10c multicolored	.90	.80
328	A65	15c multicolored	1.40	.80
329	A65	20c multicolored	1.40	.80
330	A65	25c multicolored	1.40	.80
331	A65	30c multicolored	1.40	.80
332	A65	40c multicolored	1.40	.80
333	A65	45c multicolored	1.75	.90
334	A65	50c multicolored	1.75	.90
335	A65	60c multicolored	2.25	1.00
336	A65	70c multicolored	2.75	1.25
337	A65	80c multicolored	2.75	1.75
338	A65	90c multicolored	2.75	2.00
339	A65	$1 multicolored	2.75	2.10
340	A65	$2 multicolored	2.00	3.50
341	A65	$5 multicolored	5.00	5.00
		Nos. 326-341 (16)	32.25	24.60

Issued: 10c, 20c, 30c, 45c, 60c, 80c, $1, $2, 4/15; 5c, 15c, 25c, 40c, 50c, 70c, 90c, $5, 8/19.

For overprint see No. 348.

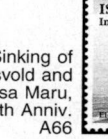

Sinking of Eidsvold and Nissa Maru, 50th Anniv. A66

Designs: 45c, Eidsvold hit by torpedo. 80c, Eidsvold sinking. $1.05, Nissa Maru hit by torpedo. $1.20, Nissa Maru sinking.

1992, June 17	Litho.		Perf. 14x13½	
343	A66	45c multicolored	2.25	2.25
344	A66	80c multicolored	3.00	3.00
345	A66	$1.05 multicolored	3.50	3.50
346	A66	$1.20 multicolored	3.75	3.75
		Nos. 343-346 (4)	12.50	12.50

Christmas — A67

Coastline, booby birds: a, 40c, Plants on shore, birds. b, 40c, Birds, rocks offshore. c, 45c, Birds on shore. d, $1.05, Birds in flight, coastline. e, $1.20, Forest, rocky coastline.

1992, Oct. 7	Litho.		Perf. 14½	
347	A67	Strip of 5, #a.-e.	7.00	9.00

No. 341 Ovptd. in Red Violet

1992, Sept. 1	Litho.		Perf. 15x14½	
348	A65	$5 on #342	11.00	8.75

Kuala Lumpur Philatelic Exhibition.

Starting with No. 349, Christmas Island stamps are valid for postage on items mailed in Australia and Australian stamps are valid on items posted on Christmas Island.

Seabirds — A68

Designs: a, Abbott's booby. b, Christmas Island frigatebird. c, Common noddy. d, Golden bosunbird. e, Brown booby.

1993, Mar. 4	Litho.		Perf. 14½x14	
349	A68	45c Strip of 5, #a.-e.	3.75	4.25
f.		Souvenir sheet of 5, #a.-e.	4.00	4.50
g.		As "f," overprinted	9.00	9.00
h.		As "f," overprinted	7.00	7.00

No. 349g Ovptd. in Gold in sheet margin with Taipei '93 emblem and: "ASIAN INTERNATIONAL INVITATION STAMP EXHIBITION / TAIPEI '93" in Chinese and English.

No. 349h Ovptd. in Gold in Sheet Margin with "INDOPEX '93 / 6TH ASIAN INTERNATIONAL PHILATELIC EXHIBITION 1993 / PAMERAN INTERNASIONAL PENGUMPULAN / KEENAM DI ASIA TAHUN 1993" and show emblem.

Issued: No. 349g, 4/93; No. 349h, 5/29/93.

Scenic Views — A69

1993, June 1			Perf. 14x14½	
350	A69	85c Dolly Beach	1.75	1.75
351	A69	95c Blow holes	2.10	2.10
352	A69	$1.05 Merrial Beach	2.25	2.25
353	A69	$1.20 Rain forest	2.50	2.50
		Nos. 350-353 (4)	8.60	8.60

Christmas — A70

40c, Turtle on beach. 45c, Crabs, wave. $1, Frigatebird, rainforest.

1993, Sept. 2	Litho.		Perf. 14½x14	
354	A70	40c multicolored	1.25	1.25
355	A70	45c multicolored	1.25	1.25
356	A70	$1 multicolored	2.50	2.50
		Nos. 354-356 (3)	5.00	5.00

Naming of Christmas Island, 350th Anniv. — A71

1993, Dec. 1	Litho.		Perf. 14x14½	
357	A71	$2 multicolored	3.75	3.75

New Year 1994 (Year of the Dog) — A72

1994, Jan. 20	Litho.		Perf. 14x14½	
358	A72	45c shown	1.25	1.50
359	A72	45c Pekingese	1.25	1.50
a.		Pair, #358-359	3.00	4.00
b.		Souvenir sheet of 1, #359a	4.00	4.00
c.		As "b," overprinted	4.75	4.75
d.		As "b," overprinted	7.75	7.75
e.		As "b," overprinted	8.00	8.00
f.		As "b," overprinted	15.50	15.50

No. 359c Ovptd. in gold in sheet margin with dog and "Melbourne / STAMP & COIN SHOW / 11-13 February 1994;" No. 359d with "HONG KONG '94 STAMP EXHIBITION" and show emblem; No. 359e with "Canberra /Stamp Show '94 / 19-21 March / 1994" and show emblem; No. 359f with "QUEENSLAND STAMP & COIN SHOW 1994 / JUNE 11, 12, 13."

Issued: No. 359c, 2/11/94; No. 359d, 2/18/94; No. 359e, 3/19/94; No. 359f, 1995.

Christmas Island Railway Steam Locomotives A73

85c, Locomotive No. 4. 95c, Locomotive No. 9. $1.20, Locomotive No. 1.

1994, May 19	Litho.		Perf. 14x14½	
360	A73	85c multicolored	2.00	2.00
361	A73	95c multicolored	2.25	2.25
362	A73	$1.20 multicolored	2.60	2.60
		Nos. 360-362 (3)	6.85	6.85

Orchids — A74

a, Brachypeza archytas. b, Thelasis capitata. c, Corymborkis veratrifolia. d, Flickingeria nativitatis. e, Dendrobium crumenatum.

1994, Aug. 16	Litho.		Perf. 14½x14	
363	A74	45c Strip of 5, #a.-e.	7.00	7.00

Christmas A75

1994, Sept. 8	Litho.		Perf. 14x14½	
364	A75	40c Angel	.70	.60
365	A75	45c Wise man	.90	.60
366	A75	85c Bethlehem	1.50	1.50
		Nos. 364-366 (3)	3.10	2.70

New Year 1995 (Year of the Boar) — A76

Design: 85c, Stylized boar, diff.

1995, Jan. 12	Litho.		Perf. 14x14½	
367	A76	45c shown	.80	.80
368	A76	85c multicolored	1.40	1.40
a.		Souvenir sheet, #367-368	3.00	3.00
b.		As "a," overprinted	7.00	7.00
c.		As "a," overprinted	15.00	15.00

No. 368b ovptd. in gold in sheet margin with outline of boar and: "STAMP & COIN FAIR / ROYAL EXHIBITION BUILDING / MELBOURNE VIC. 3000 . 10-12 FEB 1995."

No. 368c ovptd. in sheet margin with Taiwan flag and map of Australia with flag, and also

Chinese characters, dates and "STAMP TAI-WAN, SYDNEY, / AUSTRALIA MAY 20-28 1995."

Christmas Island Golf Course, 40th Anniv. — A77

1995, May 11   Litho.   Perf. 14
369 A77 $2.50 multicolored   6.00 6.00

Christmas A78

Santa Claus riding great frigatebird: 40c, Reading map. 45c, Dropping presents. 80c, Waving.

1995, Sept. 14   Litho.   Perf. 14x14½
370 A78 40c multicolored   .90 .75
371 A78 45c multicolored   1.00 .75
372 A78 80c multicolored   1.50 1.50
     Nos. 370-372 (3)   3.40 3.00

End of World War II, 50th Anniv. — A79

No. 373a, RAAF reconnaissance flight, 1945. No. 373b, Arrival of HMS Rother, 1945.

Litho. & Engr.
1995, Oct. 12   Perf. 14x14½
373   Pair   2.75 2.75
  a.-b. A79 45c any single   1.00 1.00

Angelfish A80

1995, Oct. 12   Litho.
374 A80 75c Lemonpeel   1.25 1.75
375 A80 $1 Emperor   1.90 2.50
     See also Nos. 381-387.

New Year 1996 (Year of the Rat) A81

Litho. with Foil Application
1996, Jan. 9   Perf. 14x14½
376 A81 45c Facing right   1.25 1.25
377 A81 45c Facing left   1.25 1.25
  a.   Pair, #376-377   3.00 3.00
  b.   Souvenir sheet, #377a   3.75 3.75
  c.   As "b," overprinted   10.00 10.00

No. 377c overprinted in gold in sheet margin "STAMP AND COIN FAIR / MELBOURNE / 23-25 February 1996."

Fish — A82

20c, Pinktail triggerfish. 30c, Longnose file-fish. 45c, Princess anthias. 85c, Green moon wrasse. 90c, Spotted boxfish. 95c, Moorish idol. $1.20, Glass bigeye.

1996-97   Litho.   Perf. 14x14½
381 A82 20c multicolored   .40 .40
382 A82 30c multicolored   .60 .50
383 A82 45c multicolored   .90 .50
384 A82 85c multicolored   1.75 2.00
385 A82 90c multicolored   1.00 1.00
386 A82 95c multicolored   1.75 1.75
387 A82 $1.20 multicolored   2.25 3.25
     Nos. 381-387 (7)   8.65 9.40

Issued: 20c, 30c, 45c, 90c, 4/18/96; 85c, 95c, $1.20, 7/17/97.

Birds — A83

1996, July 11   Litho.   Perf. 14½x14
399 A83 45c White-eye   1.25 1.25
400 A83 85c Hawk-owl   2.00 2.00

Christmas A84

Sailing ships, words from Christmas carol: 40c, "I Saw Three Ships." 45c, "Come sailing in." 80c, "On Christmas day in the morning."

1996, Sept. 12   Litho.   Perf. 14
401 A84 40c multicolored   1.00 .75
402 A84 45c multicolored   1.10 .90
403 A84 80c multicolored   1.60 1.60
     Nos. 401-403 (3)   3.70 3.25

Exploration of Australian Coast & Christmas Island by Willem de Vlamingh, 300th Anniv. — A85

"Portrait of a Dutch Navigator," by Jan Verkolje.

1996, Oct. 27   Litho.   Perf. 14
404 A85 45c multicolored   1.25 1.25

No. 404 was issued se-tenant with Australia No. 1571 (No. 1571a). Value, pair $4.

New Year 1997 (Year of the Ox) — A86

Constellation and: No. 405, Ox facing right. No. 406, Ox facing left.

Litho. with Foil Application
1997, Jan. 6   Perf. 14x14½
405 A86 45c multicolored   1.00 1.00
406 A86 45c multicolored   1.00 1.00
  a.   Pair, #405-406   2.75 2.75
  b.   Souvenir sheet, #405-406   3.00 3.00

Christmas A87

Santa on Christmas Island: 40c, Reading letters. 45c, Making toys. 80c, In sleigh.

1997, Sept. 11   Litho.   Perf. 14x14½
407 A87 40c multicolored   .65 .65
408 A87 45c multicolored   .75 .75
409 A87 80c multicolored   1.75 1.75
     Nos. 407-409 (3)   3.15 3.15

New Year 1998 (Year of the Tiger) — A88

Litho. with Foil Application
1998, Jan. 5   Perf. 14x14½
410 A88 45c shown   1.25 1.25
411 A88 45c Looking backward   1.25 1.25
  a.   Pair, #410-411   3.00 3.00
  b.   Souvenir sheet of 2, #410-411   3.50 3.50

Marine Life — A89

Designs: a, 5c, Frigatebird. b, 5c, Ambon chromis, denomination LR. c, 5c, Ambon chromis, denomination LL. d, 5c, Pink anemonefish, denomination, UR. e, 5c, Pink anemonefish, denomination LL. f, 10c, Eastern reef egret. g, 10c, Whitelined cod. h, 10c, Pyramid butterfly fish. i, 10c, Dusky parrotfish. j, 10c, Spotted garden eel. k, 25c, Sooty tern. l, 25c, Scissortail sergeant. m, 25c, Thicklip wrasse. n, 25c, Blackaxil chromis. o, 25c, Orange anthias. p, 45c, Brown booby. q, 45c, Green turtle. r, 45c, Pink anemonefish. s, 45c, Blue sea star. t, 45c, Kunie's chromodoris.

1998, Mar. 12   Litho.   Perf. 14
412 A89 45c Sheet of 20, #a.-t.   10.00 10.00

Tree Flowers of Christmas — A90

1998, Sept. 3   Litho.   Perf. 14½x14
413 A90 40c Orchid tree   .80 .80
414 A90 80c Flame tree   1.60 1.60
415 A90 95c Sea hibiscus   1.60 1.60
     Nos. 413-415 (3)   4.00 4.00

New Year 1999 (Year of the Rabbit) A91

Litho. with Foil Application
1999, Jan. 14   Perf. 14x14½
416 A91 45c shown   1.00 1.00
417 A91 45c Rabbit looking left   1.00 1.00
  a.   Pair, #416-417   2.75 2.75
  b.   Souvenir sheet, #417a   3.25 3.25

Festivals on Christmas Island — A92

Children's drawings: No. 418, Carrying balloons in parade, by Fong Jason. No. 419, Giant crab, by Siti Zanariah Zainal. 85c, Children at night, by Tan Diana, vert. $1.20, Green mosque, tree, by Anwar Ramian, vert.

1999, July 15   Litho.   Perf. 14x14½
418 A92 45c multicolored   .75 .75
419 A92 45c multicolored   .75 .75
  a.   Pair, #418-419   1.75 1.75

Perf. 14½x14
420 A92 85c multicolored   1.00 1.00
421 A92 $1.20 multicolored   1.75 1.75
     Nos. 418-421 (4)   4.25 4.25

Christmas A93

Designs: 40c, Santa Claus in hammock. 45c, Santa, birds, crab, lizard, cake. 95c, Santa, booby-drawn sleigh.

1999, Sept. 9   Litho.   Perf. 14x14½
422 A93 40c multicolored   .95 .80
423 A93 45c multicolored   1.10 .95
424 A93 95c multicolored   1.75 1.75
     Nos. 422-424 (3)   3.80 3.50

New Year 2000 (Year of the Dragon) A94

Litho. with Foil Application
2000, Jan. 13   Perf. 14x14½
425 A94 45c shown   1.10 1.10
426 A94 45c Dragon facing left   1.10 1.10
  a.   Pair, #425-426   3.00 3.00
  b.   Souvenir sheet, #426a   3.50 3.50

Faces of Christmas Island — A95

Ordinary people: a, Yeow Jian Min, without shirt. b, Ida Chin, with blue shirt. c, Ho Tak Wah, old man. d, Thomas Faul and James Neill. e, Siti Sanniah Kawi, with striped blouse.

2000, Apr. 13   Litho.   Perf. 14½x14
427 A95 45c Strip of 5, #a.-e.   4.75 4.75

Christmas — A96

No. 428: a, We three kings of Orient are. b, Bearing gifts we traverse afar. 45c, Star of wonder, star of night.

2000, Sept. 5   Litho.   Perf. 14½x14
428   Pair   1.90 1.90
  a.-b. A96 40c Any single   .60 .60
429 A96 45c multi   .60 .60

New Year 2001 (Year of the Snake) A97

Snake color: 45c, Green. $1.35, Silver.

Litho. with Foil Application
2001, Jan. 8   **Perf. 14x14½**
430-431 A97   Set of 2   3.00   3.00
   a.   Souvenir sheet, #430-431   4.00   *4.00*

Fungi — A98

Designs: $1, Chaetocalathus semisupinus. $1.50, Pycnoporus sanguineus.

2001, Oct. 25   Litho.   **Perf. 14x14½**
432-433 A98   Set of 2   4.00   4.00

New Year
2002 (Year of the Horse) — A99

Zodiac
Animals and Their Chinese Characters
A100

Designs: 45c, Purple horse. $1.35, Gold horse.
No. 436: a, Rat. b, Ox. c, Tiger. d, Rabbit. e, Dragon. f, Snake. g, Horse. h, Sheep. i, Monkey. j, Cock. k, Dog. l, Boar.

Litho. With Gold Foil Application
2002, Jan. 8   **Perf. 14x14½**
434-435 A99   Set of 2   3.00   3.00
   a.   Souvenir sheet, #434-435   4.00   *4.00*
436   Sheet of 14, #a-l,
      #435a   12.00   12.00
   a.-d.   A100 5c Any single   .55   .55
   e.-h.   A100 15c Any single, orange
      background   .60   .60
   i.-l.   A100 25c Any single, orange
      background   .65   .65

See Nos. 442, 447, 451, 456, 462-463.

Worldwide Fund for Nature
(WWF) — A101

Christmas Island birds — No. 437: a, Imperial pigeon. b, Hawk owl.
$1, Goshawk. $1.50, Thrush.

2002, May 1   Litho.   **Perf. 14½x14**
437 A101   45c Horiz. pair, #a-b   1.60   1.60
438 A101 $1 multi   1.60   1.60
439 A101 $1.50 multi   2.75   2.75
    Nos. 437-439 (3)   5.95   5.95

Zodiac Animals Type of 2002 and

New Year
2003 (Year of the Ram)
A102

Designs: 50c, Yellow and orange ram. $1.50, Blue ram.
No. 442: a, Rat. b, Ox. c, Tiger. d, Rabbit. e, Dragon. f, Snake. g, Horse. h, Sheep. i, Monkey. j, Cock. k, Dog. l, Boar.

Litho. With Gold Foil Application
2003, Jan. 7   **Perf. 14x14½**
440-441 A102   Set of 2   3.50   3.50
   a.   Souvenir sheet, #440-441   4.00   *4.00*
442   Sheet of 14, #a-l,
      #441a   12.00   12.00
   a.-d.   A100 10c Any single, red violet background   .50   .50
   e.-h.   A100 15c Any single, red violet background   .60   .60
   i.-l.   A100 25c Any single, red violet background   .70   .70

See No. 463.

Christmas — A103

Designs: 45c, Arrival of Santa Claus on whale shark. 50c, Santa giving gifts to red crabs.

2003, Oct. 31   Litho.   **Perf. 14½x14**
443-444 A103   Set of 2   3.00   3.00

Zodiac Animals Type of 2002 and

New Year
2004 (Year of the Monkey)
A104

Designs: 50c, Yellow and orange monkey. $1.45, Red orange monkey, lotus flower.
No. 447: a, Rat. b, Ox. c, Tiger. d, Rabbit. e, Dragon. f, Snake. g, Horse. h, Sheep. i, Monkey. j, Cock. k, Dog. l, Boar.

Litho. With Gold Foil Application
2004, Jan. 6   **Perf. 14x14½**
445-446 A104   Set of 2   4.50   4.50
   446a   Souvenir sheet, #445-446   5.50   5.50
447   Sheet of 14, #a-l,
      #446a   12.00   12.00
   a.-d.   A100 10c Any single, light and dark blue background   .50   .50
   e.-h.   A100 15c Any single, light and dark blue background   .60   .60
   i.-l.   A100 25c Any single, light and dark blue background   .70   .70

No. 446a exists with a 2004 Hong Kong Stamp Expo overprint in sheet margin in red. This sheet was sold at the show and was sold at some post offices in Australia, but not on Christmas Island. Value: *$15.*
See No. 463.

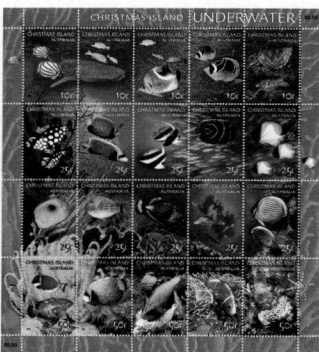

Marine Life — A105

No. 448: a, Two butterflyfish, rear of whale shark. b, Three striped fish, front of whale shark. c, Four fish. d, Two fish. e, Two green turtles. f, Two triggerfish (polka dots), red coral at LL. g, Two fish with thin horizontal stripes with yellow tails. h, Two fish with thick vertical stripes. i, Black and white fish. j, Three fish. k, Yellow fish with black spot, blue fish, red coral, yellow coral. l, Striped fish, clam. m, Black fish, small red fish. n Red fish, divers. o, Two striped fish, red coral under denomination. p, Blue and yellow fish, red and white spotted fish, yellow coral. q, Blue and yellow fish, yellow coral, sea anemones. r, Three blue fish with orange spots. s, Sea anemone and two anemonefish. t, Nudibranch, red coral and starfish.

2004, July 13   Litho.   **Perf. 14½x14**
448 A105   Sheet of 20   11.00   11.00
   a.-e.   10c Any single   .25   .25
   f.-o.   25c Any single   .45   .45
   p.-t.   50c Any single   .95   .95

Zodiac Animals Type of 2002 and

New Year
2005 (Year of the Cock)
A106

Designs: 50c, Cock, spirals at right. $1.45, Cock, spirals at right.
No. 451: a, Rat. b, Ox. c, Tiger. d, Rabbit. e, Dragon. f, Snake. g, Horse. h, Sheep. i, Monkey. j, Cock. k, Dog. l, Boar.

Litho. With Gold Foil Application
2005, Jan. 4   **Perf. 14x14½**
449-450 A106   Set of 2   4.50   4.50
   450a   Souvenir sheet, #449-450   4.50   4.50
   450b   As "a," with Taipei 2005 emblem overprinted in margin   5.00   5.00
451   Sheet of 14, #a-l,
      #450a   14.00   14.00
   a.-d.   A100 10c Any single, red and yellow background   .45   .45
   e.-h.   A100 15c Any single, red and yellow background   .45   .45
   i.-l.   A100 25c Any single, red and yellow background   .65   .65

See No. 463.

Christmas
A107

Santa Claus, birds and: 45c, Palm tree, presents. 90c, Sleigh, crabs.

2005, Nov. 1   Litho.   **Perf. 14¼x14**
452 A107   45c multi   1.25   1.25
   a.   Booklet pane of 4   5.00
453 A107   90c multi   2.25   2.25

No. 452a exists with two different margins. These two panes were issued in a booklet that also contained three examples of Australia No. 2423a. The entire booklet sold for $9.95.

Zodiac Animals Type of 2002 and

New Year
2006 (Year of the Dog)
A108

Designs: 50c, Purple dog. $1.45, Copper dog.
No. 456: a, Rat. b, Ox. c, Tiger. d, Rabbit. e, Dragon. f, Snake. g, Horse. h, Sheep. i, Monkey. j, Cock. k, Dog. l, Boar.

Litho. With Copper Foil Application
2006, Jan. 5   **Perf. 14x14½**
454-455 A108   Set of 2   3.25   3.25
   455a   Souvenir sheet, #454-455   3.25   3.25
456   Sheet of 14, #a-l,
      #455a   9.00   9.00
   a.-d.   A100 10c Any single, brown and yellow background   .30   .30
   e.-h.   A100 15c Any single, brown and yellow background   .35   .35
   i.-l.   A100 25c Any single, brown and yellow background   .50   .50

See No. 463.

Buildings — A109

Designs: 50c, Mosque. $1.45, Tai Jin House.
No. 458: a, Tai Pak Kong Temple. b, Soon Tian Temple.

2006, June 13   Litho.   **Perf. 14½x14**
457 A109   50c multi   1.25   1.25
458 A109 $1 Horiz. pair, #a-b   4.50   4.50
459 A109 $1.45 multi   3.25   3.25
    Nos. 457-459 (3)   9.00   9.00

Zodiac Animals Types of 1996-2006 and

New Year
2007 (Year of the Boar)
A110

Zodiac
Animals
A111

Designs: Nos. 460, 463l. 50c, Boar facing right. $1.45, Boar facing left.
No. 462: a, Rat. b, Ox. c, Tiger. d, Rabbit. e, Dragon. f, Snake. g, Horse. h, Sheep. i, Monkey. j, Cock. k, Dog. l, Boar.

Litho. With Copper Foil Application
2007, Jan. 9   **Perf. 14x14½**
460-461 A110   Set of 2   4.25   4.25
   461a   Souvenir sheet, #460-461   4.25   4.25
462   Sheet of 14, #a-l,
      #461a   10.00   10.00
   a.-d.   A100 10c Any single, multicolored background   .25   .25
   e.-h.   A100 15c Any single, multicolored background   .30   .25
   i.-l.   A100 25c Any single, multicolored background   .50   .50

Self-Adhesive
Serpentine Die Cut 12¼ Syncopated (#463a-463l), Serpentine Die Cut (#463m)
463   Sheet of 13   19.00
   a.   A81 50c Like #376   1.10   1.10
   b.   A86 50c Like #405   1.10   1.10
   c.   A88 50c Like #410   1.10   1.10
   d.   A91 50c Like #416   1.10   1.10
   e.   A94 50c Like #425   1.10   1.10
   f.   A97 50c Like #430   1.10   1.10
   g.   A99 50c Like #434   1.10   1.10
   h.   A102 50c Like #440   1.10   1.10
   i.   A104 50c Like #445   1.10   1.10
   j.   A106 50c Like #449   1.10   1.10
   k.   A108 50c Like #454   1.10   1.10
   l.   A110 50c Like #460   1.10   1.10
   m.   A111 $1 multi   3.00   3.00
   n.   Booklet pane, 2 each #463a-463b   4.00
   o.   Booklet pane, 2 each #463c-463f   4.00
   p.   Booklet pane, 2 each #463e-463f   4.00
   q.   Booklet pane, 2 each #463g-463h   4.00
   r.   Booklet pane, 2 each #463i-463j   4.00
   s.   Booklet pane, 2 each #463k-463l   4.00
    Complete booklet, #463n-463s   25.00

Complete booklet sold for $12.95.

Christmas
A112

Santa Claus: 45c, In boat. 50c, Hoisted by crane. $1.10, On beach.

2007, Nov. 1   Litho.   **Perf. 14x14½**
464-466 A112   Set of 3   4.00   4.00

New Year 2008
(Year of the Rat) — A113

Designs: 50c, Rat. $1.45, Chinese character for "rat."
No. 469: a, Rat, diff. b, Ox. c, Dragon. d, Snake. e, Tiger. f, Rabbit. g, Horse. h, Pig. i, Goat. j, Monkey. k, Rooster. l, Dog.

Litho. With Foil Application

2008, Jan. 8   **Perf. 14**

467	A113	50c multi	1.00	1.00
a.		Perf. 14¾x14	7.00	7.00

Perf. 14¾x14

468	A113	$1.45 multi	2.75	2.75
a.		Souvenir sheet, #467a, 468	3.75	3.75
b.		As "a," with Olympex emblem in margin	3.75	3.75
469		Sheet of 14, #467a, 468, 469a-469l	11.00	11.00
a.-d.	A113	10c Any single	.25	.25
e.-h.	A113	15c Any single	.35	.35
i.-l.	A113	25c Any single	.50	.50
m.		Booklet pane of 4, #469a, 469b, 2 #468	6.75	—
n.		Booklet pane of 4, #469e, 469f, 2 #467a	2.75	—
o.		Booklet pane of 4, #469c, 469d, 2 #467a	2.75	—
p.		Booklet pane of 4, #469g, 469i, 2 #467a	3.00	—
q.		Booklet pane of 4, #469j, 469k, 2 #467a	3.25	—
r.		Booklet pane of 4, #469h, 469l, 2 #467a	3.00	—
		Complete booklet, #469m-469r	22.00	

Complete booklet sold for $10.95. Issued: No. 468b, 8/8. See Nos. 512g, 546d.

Territorial Status of Christmas Island, 50th Anniv. A114

No. 470: a, Gecarcoidea natalis. b, Papasula abbotti. c, Asplenium listeri. $1.45, Seal of Union of Christmas Island Workers. $2.45, Christmas Island flag.

2008, June 10   **Litho.**   **Perf. 14¼**

470		Horiz. strip of 3	3.75	3.75
a.-c.	A114	50c Any single	1.00	1.00
471	A114	$1.45 multi	3.50	3.50
472	A114	$2.45 multi	5.50	5.50
		Nos. 470-472 (3)	12.75	12.75

Christmas — A115

Designs: Nos. 473, 475, 50c, Christmas tree, bird, crabs and shells. Nos. 474, 476, $1.20, Crabs with gifts and Christmas lights.

2008, Oct. 31   **Litho.**   **Perf. 14½x14**

473-474	A115	Set of 2	3.00	3.00

Serpentine Die Cut 11¼ Syncopated

Self-Adhesive

475	A115	50c multi	1.00	1.00
a.		Booklet pane of 10	10.00	

Booklet Stamp

476	A115	$1.20 multi	2.00	2.00
a.		Booklet pane of 5	10.00	

No. 475 was also printed in sheets of 10.

Christmas With Personalized Picture — A116

Designs as before.

Serpentine Die Cut 11½x11¼ Syncopated

2008, Oct. 31   **Litho.**

Self-Adhesive

477	A116	50c multi	4.00	4.00
478	A116	$1.20 multi	7.00	7.00

Nos. 477-478 each were sold in sheets of 20 and have personalized pictures and a

---

straight edge at right, and lack separations between the stamp and the personalized photo. Sheets of 20 of No. 477 sold for $23, and No. 478 sold for $37.

New Year 2009 (Year of the Ox) — A117

Designs: 55c, Rat. $1.65, Chinese character for "ox."

No. 481: a, Rat. b, Ox, diff. c, Dragon. d, Snake. e, Tiger. f, Rabbit. g, Horse. h, Pig. i, Goat. j, Monkey. k, Rooster. l, Dog.

Litho. With Foil Application

2009, Jan. 8   **Perf. 14¾x14**

479	A117	55c multi	.90	.90
480	A117	$1.65 multi	2.75	2.75
a.		Souvenir sheet, #479-480	4.00	4.00
481		Sheet of 14, #479-480, 481a-481l	13.00	13.00
a.-d.	A117	10c Any single	.30	.30
e.-h.	A117	20c Any single	.35	.35
i.-l.	A117	25c Any single	.50	.50
m.		Booklet pane of 4, #481b, 481e, 2 #480	6.50	—
n.		Booklet pane of 4, #481c, 481f, 2 #479	2.75	—
o.		Booklet pane of 4, #481d, 481g, 2 #479	2.75	—
p.		Booklet pane of 4, #481i, 481j, 2 #479	3.00	—
q.		Booklet pane of 4, #481k, 481l, 2 #479	3.00	—
r.		Booklet pane of 4, #481a, 481h, 2 #479	2.75	—
		Complete booklet, #481m-481r	21.00	

No. 479 was issued in a sheet of 9 + 9 labels that could be personalized and removed. The sheet sold for $15.95. Gutter strips of 10 of No. 484 exist with five labels forming a picture featuring the 12 Zodiac animals.

Complete booklet sold for $12.95. See Nos. 512h, 546e.

Christmas — A118

2009, Nov. 2   **Litho.**   **Perf. 14¾x14**

482	A118	$1.25 multi	3.25	3.25

Booklet Stamp

Self-Adhesive

Serpentine Die Cut 11¼ Syncopated

483	A118	$1.25 multi	3.25	3.25
a.		Booklet pane of 5	16.50	

New Year 2010 (Year of the Tiger) — A119

Designs: 55c, Tiger. $1.65, Chinese character for "tiger."

No. 486: a, Rat. b, Ox. c, Dragon. d, Snake. e, Tiger, diff. f, Rabbit. g, Horse. h, Pigs. i, Goat. j, Monkey. k, Rooster. l, Dog.

Litho. With Foil Application

2010, Jan. 12   **Perf. 14¾x14**

484	A119	55c multi	1.25	1.25
485	A119	$1.65 multi	3.25	3.25
a.		Souvenir sheet, #484-485	5.50	5.50
486		Sheet of 14, #484-485, 486a-486l	14.50	14.50
a.-d.	A119	10c Any single	.30	.30
e.-h.	A119	20c Any single	.40	.40
i.-l.	A119	25c Any single	.55	.55
m.		Booklet pane of 4, #486e, 486f, 2 #485	8.00	—
n.		Booklet pane of 4, #486c, 486d, 2 #484	3.25	—
o.		Booklet pane of 4, #486g, 486i, 2 #484	4.00	—
p.		Booklet pane of 4, #486j, 486k, 2 #484	4.00	—
q.		Booklet pane of 4, #486a, 486l, 2 #484	4.00	—
r.		Booklet pane of 4, #486a, 486b, 2 #484	3.25	—
		Complete booklet, #486m-486r	23.00	

Complete booklet sold for $12.95. A sheet of 13 self-adhesive stamps containing a round $1 stamp depicting a flower and stamps similar to Nos. 467, 479, 484, 486c, 486d, 486f, 486g, 486h, 486i, 486j, 486k, 486l, sold for $9.95.

No. 484 was issued in a sheet of 9 + 9 labels that could be personalized and removed. The sheet sold for $15.95. Gutter strips of 10 of No. 484 exist with five labels forming a picture featuring the 12 Zodiac animals.

A sheet containing lithographed versions of Nos. 486a-486l and 12 labels that could not be personalized sold for $10. See Nos. 512i, 546f.

Worldwide Fund for Nature (WWF) A120

No. 487 — Christmas Island frigatebird: a, Adult on nest. b, Adults and chick at nest.
No. 488 — Christmas Island frigatebird: a, Chick and adult at nest. b, Adult in flight.

2010, Aug. 17   **Litho.**   **Perf. 14¼**

487		Horiz. pair	4.25	4.25
a.-b.	A120	60c Either single	1.60	1.25
488		Horiz. pair	9.75	9.75
a.-b.	A120	$1.80 Either single	4.25	2.75
c.		Souvenir sheet, #487a-487b, 488a-488b	14.00	14.00

Christmas — A121

Golden bosunbird: 60c, Carrying gift. $1.30, Flying away from gift on beach.

2010, Nov. 1   **Litho.**   **Perf. 14¾x14**

489	A121	60c multi	2.25	2.25
490	A121	$1.30 multi	4.50	4.50

Booklet Stamp

Self-Adhesive

Serpentine Die Cut 11¼ Syncopated

491	A121	60c multi	2.25	2.25
a.		Booklet pane of 10	22.50	
491B	A121	$1.30 multi	4.50	4.25
c.		Booklet pane of 5	22.50	

New Year 2011 (Year of the Rabbit) — A122

Designs: 60c, Rabbit. $1.80, Chinese character for "rabbit."

No. 494: a, Rat. b, Ox. c, Dragon. d, Snake. e, Tiger. f, Rabbit, diff. g, Horse. h, Pig. i, Goat. j, Monkey. k, Rooster. l, Dog.

Litho. With Foil Application

2011, Jan. 11   **Perf. 14¾x14**

492	A122	60c multi	1.25	1.25
493	A122	$1.80 multi	3.75	3.75
a.		Souvenir sheetof 2, #492-493	5.50	5.50
494		Sheet of 14, #492-493, 494a-494l	13.00	13.00
a.-d.	A122	15c Any single	.30	.30
e.-h.	A122	20c Any single	.40	.40
i.-l.	A122	25c Any single	.50	.50
m.		Booklet pane of 4, #494a, 494b, 2 #492	3.75	—
n.		Booklet pane of 4, #494e, 494f, 2 #492	4.00	—

---

o.		Booklet pane of 4, #494g, 494i, 2 #492	4.25	—
p.		Booklet pane of 4, #494h, 494l, 2 #492	4.25	—
q.		Booklet pane of 4, #494j, 494k, 2 #492	4.25	—
r.		Booklet pane of 4, #494c, 494d, 2 #493	9.75	—
		Complete booklet, #494m-494r	31.00	

Complete booklet sold for $14.95. A sheet of 12 containing Nos. 494a-494l + 12 labels that could not be personalized sold for $15.95. See Nos. 512j, 546g.

Crabs — A123

No. 495: a, Red crab. b, Robber crab.
No. 496: a, Jackson's crab. b, Blue crab.

2011, June 7   **Litho.**   **Perf. 14¾x14**

495	A123	60c Horiz. pair, #a-b	4.00	4.00
496	A123	$1.20 Horiz. pair, #a-b	7.50	7.50

Christmas A124

Santa Claus: 55c, Giving cracker to crab. $1.50, In water holding flippers.

2011, Oct. 31   **Perf. 14x14¾**

497	A124	55c multi	1.75	1.75
498	A124	$1.50 multi	4.00	4.00

Booklet Stamps

Self-Adhesive

Serpentine Die Cut 11¼ Syncopated

499	A124	55c multi	1.75	1.75
a.		Booklet pane of 10	17.50	
500	A124	$1.50 multi	4.00	4.00
a.		Booklet pane of 5	20.00	

New Year 2012 (Year of the Dragon) — A125

Designs: 60c, Dragon. $1.80, Chinese character for "dragon."

No. 503: a, Rat. b, Ox. c, "Dragon" in circle. d, Snake. e, Tiger. f, Rabbit. g, Horse. h, Pig. i, Goat. j, Monkey. k, Rooster. l, Dog.

Litho. with Foil Application

2012, Jan. 10   **Perf. 14¾x14**

501	A125	60c multi	1.40	1.40
502	A125	$1.80 multi	4.00	4.00
a.		Souvenir sheet of 2, #501-502	5.50	5.50
b.		As "a," with 2012 Beijing Intl. Stamp & Coin Expo overprint in sheet margin in gold	5.00	5.00
503		Sheet of 14, #501-502, 503a-503l	11.00	11.00
a.-d.	A125	15c Any single	.35	.35
e.-h.	A125	20c Any single	.45	.45
i.-l.	A125	25c Any single	.55	.55
m.		Booklet pane of 4, #503c, 503d, 2 #502	8.75	—
n.		Booklet pane of 4, #503g, 503i, 2 #501	4.00	—
o.		Booklet pane of 4, #503j, 503k, 2 #501	4.00	—
p.		Booklet pane of 4, #503h, 503l, 2 #501	4.00	—
q.		Booklet pane of 4, #503a, 503b, 2 #501	3.50	—
r.		Booklet pane of 4, #503e, 503f, 2 #501	3.75	—
		Complete booklet, #503m-503r	28.00	

Complete booklet sold for $12.95.
Issued: No. 502b, 11/2.
See Nos. 512k, 546h.

Ferns
A126

No. 504: a, Tectaria devexa. b, Asplenium listeri.

No. 505: a, Bolbitis heteroclita. b, Pteris tripartita.

2012, May 1   Litho.   Perf. 14x14¾
504	Horiz. pair	3.00	3.00
a.-b.	A126 60c Either single	1.25	1.25
505	Horiz. pair	6.00	6.00
a.-b.	A126 $1.20 Either single	2.50	2.50

Christmas — A127

Designs: 55c, Sand sculpture of Santa Claus, frigatebirds, turtle and crabs. $1.60, Santa Claus decorating sand sculpture of Christmas tree, starfish, crabs, bird.

2012, Nov. 1   Perf. 14¾x14
506	A127 55c multi	1.50	1.50
507	A127 $1.60 multi	3.75	3.75
a.	Souvenir sheet of 2, #506-507	5.25	5.25

**Booklet Stamp
Self-Adhesive**

Serpentine Die Cut 11¼ Syncopated
508	A127 $1.60 multi	3.75	3.75
a.	Booklet pane of 5	19.00	

New Year Types of 2008-12 and

New Year 2013
(Year of the
Snake) — A128

Rat and
Apples — A129

Flower
A130

Designs: No. 509, 60c, Snake. $1.80, Chinese character for "snake."

No. 511: a, Rat and apples. b, Ox and cherries. c, Dragon and tomatoes. d, Snake amd eggs. e, Tiger and fish. f, Rabbit and oranges. g, Horse and bananas. h, Boar and spinach. i, Goat and onions. j, Monkey and grapes. k, Rooster and pumpkins. l, Dog and milk bottles.

No. 512: a, Like No 511g. b, Like No. 511h. c, Like No. 511i. d, Like No. 511j. e, Like No. 511k. f, Like No. 511l. g, Rat with purple foil. h, Ox with purple foil. i, Tiger with purple foil. j, Rabbit with purple foil. k, Dragon with purple foil. l, Like No. 509.

Litho. With Foil Application
2013, Jan. 13   Perf. 14¾x14
509	A128 60c multi	1.25	1.25
510	A128 $1.80 multi	3.75	3.75
a.	Souvenir sheet of 2, #509-510	5.25	5.25
b.	As "a," with emblem overprinted in gold in sheet margin	4.75	4.75
511	Sheet of 14, #509-510, 511a-511l	10.00	10.00
a.-d.	A129 15c Any single	.30	.30
e.-h.	A129 20c Any single	.40	.40
i.-l.	A129 25c single	.55	.55
m.	Booklet pane of 4, #511d, 511g, 2 #510	9.00	—
n.	Booklet pane of 4, #511i, 511j, 2 #509	4.00	—
o.	Booklet pane of 4, #511k, 511l, 2 #509	4.00	—
p.	Booklet pane of 4, #511a, 511h, 2 #509	3.50	—
q.	Booklet pane of 4, #511b, 511e, 2 #509	3.50	—
r.	Booklet pane of 4, #511c, 511f, 2 #509	3.50	—
	Complete booklet, #511m-511r	27.50	

Issued: No. 510b, 9/26. China International Collection Expo (No. 510b).

Self-Adhesive

Serpentine Die Cut 12¼, Serpentine Die Cut (#512m)
512	Sheet of 13	25.00	
a.-b.	A129 20c Either single	.70	.70
c.-f.	A129 25c Any single	.90	.90
g.	A113 50c pur & multi	1.75	1.75
h.	A117 55c pur & multi	2.00	2.00
i.	A119 55c pur & multi	2.00	2.00
j.	A122 60c pur & multi	2.10	2.10
k.	A125 60c pur & multi	2.10	2.10
l.	A128 60c pur & multi	2.10	2.10
m.	A130 $1 pur & multi	3.75	3.75

Complete booklet sold for $12.95. No. 512 sold for $9.95.
See Nos. 546i.

Fish — A131

No. 513: a, Cocos angelfish. b, Ladder wrasse.
$1.20, Redtooth triggerfish. $1.80, Redstriped pigfish.

2013, May 21   Litho.   Perf. 14x14¾
513	Horiz. pair	2.50	2.50
a.-b.	A131 60c Either single	1.25	1.25
514	A131 $1.20 multi	2.50	2.50
515	A131 $1.80 multi	3.50	3.50
	Nos. 513-515 (3)	8.50	8.50

Flowering Shrubs — A132

No. 516: a, Colubrina pedunculata. b, Abutilon listeri.
No. 517: a, Urena lobata var. sinuata. b, Indigofera hirsuta.
No. 518, Like No. 516a. No. 519, Like No. 516b.

2013, June 18   Perf. 14¾x14
516	A132 60c Horiz. pair, #a-b	2.40	2.40
517	A132 $1.20 Horiz. pair, #a-b	4.50	4.50

**Booklet Stamps
Self-Adhesive**

Serpentine Die Cut 11¼ Syncopated
518	A132 60c multi	1.25	1.25
519	A132 60c multi	1.25	1.25
a.	Booklet pane of 10, 5 each #518-519	16.00	

Christmas
A133

Designs: 55c, Santa Claus riding on frigatebird. $1.80, Frigatebird and crab in balloon gondola.

2013, Nov. 1   Litho.   Perf. 14x14¾
520	A133 55c multi	1.10	1.10
521	A133 $1.80 multi	3.50	3.50
a.	Souvenir sheet of 2, #520-521	5.00	5.00

**Booklet Stamps
Self-Adhesive**

Serpentine Die Cut 11¼ Syncopated
522	A133 $1.80 multi	3.50	3.50
a.	Booklet pane of 5	20.00	

Litho. With Foil Application
523	A133 $1.80 multi	3.50	3.50
a.	Booklet pane of 10	40.00	

New Year 2014
(Year of the
Horse) — A134

Designs: 60c, Horse. $1.80, Chinese character for "horse."

No. 526: a, Rat. b, Ox. c, Dragon. d, Snake. e, Tiger. f, Rabbit. g, Horse, diff. h, Pig. i, Goat. j, Monkey. k, Rooster. l, Dog.

Litho. With Foil Application
2014, Jan. 7   Perf. 14¾x14
524	A134 60c multi	1.10	1.10
525	A134 $1.80 multi	3.25	3.25
a.	Souvenir sheet of 2, #524-525	4.50	4.50
526	Sheet of 14, #524-525, 526a-526l	8.75	8.75
a.-d.	A134 15c Any single	.25	.25
e.-h.	A134 20c Any single	.35	.35
i.-l.	A134 25c Any single	.45	.45
m.	Booklet pane of 4, #526g, 526i, 2 #525	7.75	—
n.	Booklet pane of 4, #526j, 526k, 2 #524	3.25	—
o.	Booklet pane of 4, #526h, 526l, 2 #524	3.25	—
p.	Booklet pane of 4, #526a, 526b, 2 #524	3.00	—
q.	Booklet pane of 4, #526e, 526f, 2 #524	3.25	—
r.	Booklet pane of 4, #526c, 526d, 2 #524	3.00	—
	Complete booklet, #526m-526r	23.50	

Complete booklet sold for $12.95. See No. 546j.

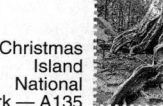

Christmas
Island
National
Park — A135

Designs: No. 527a, Forest. No. 527b, Beach. $1.40, Sea cliffs. $2.10, Wetlands.

2014, June 17   Litho.   Perf. 14x14¾
527	Horiz. pair	3.00	3.00
a.-b.	A135 70c Either single	1.40	1.40
528	A135 $1.40 multi	2.75	2.75
529	A135 $2.10 multi	4.00	4.00
	Nos. 527-529 (3)	9.75	9.75

Red Crab
Migration
A136

Designs: 70c, Red crab. $2.10, Red crabs migrating.

2014, Aug. 12   Litho.   Perf. 14x14¾
530-531	A136 Set of 2	5.25	5.25

Christmas — A137

Designs: 65c, Crab offering gift to Santa Claus. $1.80, Crab holding gift-wrapped coconut.

2014, Oct. 31   Litho.   Perf. 14¾x14
532	A137 65c multi	1.25	1.25
533	A137 $1.80 multi	3.25	3.25
a.	Souvenir sheet of 2, #532-533	4.50	4.50

**Booklet Stamps
Self-Adhesive**

Serpentine Die Cut 11¼ Syncopated
534	A137 65c multi	1.25	1.25
a.	Booklet pane of 10 + 10 etiquettes	12.50	
535	A137 $1.80 multi	3.25	3.25
a.	Booklet pane of 5	16.50	

New Year 2015
(Year of the
Goat) — A138

Designs: 70c, Goat. $2.10, Chinese character for "goat."

No. 538: a, Rat. b, Ox. c, Dragon. d, Snake. e, Goat, diff. f, Monkey. g, Rooster. h, Dog. i, Tiger. j, Rabbit. k, Horse. l, Pig.

Litho. With Foil Application
2015, Jan. 8   Perf. 14¾x14
536	A138 70c multi	1.10	1.10
537	A138 $2.10 multi	3.25	3.25
a.	Souvenir sheet of 2, #536-537	4.50	4.50
538	Sheet of 14, #536-537, 538a-538l	9.00	9.00
a.-d.	A138 15c Any single	.25	.25
e.-h.	A138 25c Any single	.40	.40
i.-l.	A138 30c Any single	.50	.50
m.	Booklet pane of 4, #538e, 538f, 2 #537	8.00	—
n.	Booklet pane of 4, #538g, 538h, 2 #536	3.25	—
o.	Booklet pane of 4, #538a, 538l, 2 #536	3.25	—
p.	Booklet pane of 4, #538b, 538i, 2 #536	3.25	—
q.	Booklet pane of 4, #538c, 538j, 2 #536	3.25	—
r.	Booklet pane of 4, #538d, 538k, 2 #536	3.25	—
	Complete booklet, #538m-538r	24.50	

Complete booklet sold for $14.95. See No. 546k.

Christmas — A139

Designs: 65c, Waterfall, Christmas tree made of red crabs. $1.80, Red crabs, snowman made of turtle and coconut.

2015, Oct. 30   Litho.   Perf. 14¾x14
539	A139 65c multi	.95	.95
540	A139 $1.80 multi	2.60	2.60
a.	Souvenir sheet of 2, #539-540	3.75	3.75

**Booklet Stamps
Self-Adhesive**

Serpentine Die Cut 11¼ Syncopated
541	A139 $1.80 multi	2.60	2.60
a.	Booklet pane of 5	13.00	

Litho. With Foil Application
542	A139 65c multi	.95	.95
a.	Booklet pane of 10	9.50	

New Year Types of 2008-15 and

New Year 2016
(Year of the
Monkey) — A140

Peach
A141

Designs: $1, Monkey. $3, Chinese character for "monkey."

No. 545: a, Rat. b, Rabbit. c, Goat. d, Dog. e, Ox. f, Dragon. g, Monkey, diff. h, Pig. i, Tiger. j, Snake. k, Horse. l, Rooster.

Litho. With Foil Application
2016, Feb. 3   **Perf. 14¾x14**

543	A140	$1 multi	1.50 1.50
544	A140	$3 multi	4.50 4.50
a.		Souvenir sheet of 2, #543-544	6.00 6.00
545		Sheet of 14, #543-544, 545a-545l	12.00 12.00
a.-d.	A140	20c Any single	.30 .30
e.-h.	A140	30c Any single	.45 .45
i.-l.	A140	50c Any single	.75 .75
m.		Booklet pane of 4, #543, 544, 545a, 545e	6.75
n.		Booklet pane of 4, #545b, 545i, 2 #543	4.25
o.		Booklet pane of 4, #545f, 545j, 2 #543	4.25
p.		Booklet pane of 4, #543, 544, 545c, 545k	7.25
q.		Booklet pane of 4, #545g, 545l, 2 543	4.25
r.		Booklet pane of 4, #545d, 545h, 2 #543	3.75
		Complete booklet, #545m-545r	30.50

Self-Adhesive
Serpentine Die Cut 12¼ Syncopated, Serpentine Die Cut (#546m)

546		Sheet of 13	14.50
a.	A140	20c Like #545d	.35 .35
b.	A140	30c Like #545h	.50 .50
c.	A140	50c Like #545l	.85 .85
d.	A113	50c Rat	.85 .85
e.	A117	55c Ox	.90 .90
f.	A119	55c Tiger	.90 .90
g.	A122	60c Rabbit	1.00 1.00
h.	A125	60c Dragon	1.00 1.00
i.	A128	60c Snake	1.00 1.00
j.	A134	60c Horse	1.00 1.00
k.	A136	70c Goat	1.10 1.10
l.	A140	$1 Like #543	1.60 1.60
m.	A141	$2 multi	3.25 3.25

Complete booklet sold for $20.95. No. 546 sold for $9.95.

With Personalized Photo at Right Like Type A116
Litho. With Foil Application
Serpentine Die Cut 11½x11¼ Syncopated
Self-Adhesive

547	A140	$1 gold & multi	2.40 2.40

No. 547 was printed in a sheet of 20 and has personalized pictures and a straight edge at right and lack separations between the stamp and the personalized photo. Sheets of 20 sold for $33 each.

Robber Crab — A142

Various depictions of crab with denomination in: No. 548a, Greenish yellow. No. 548b, Turquoise green. $2, Red.

2016, Apr. 26   **Litho.**   **Perf. 14x14¾**

548		Horiz. pair	3.00 3.00
a.-b.	A142	$1 Either single	1.50 1.50
549	A142	$2 multi	3.00 3.00

Shells A143

No. 550: a, Lambis scorpius. b, Tectus niloticus.
No. 551: a, Conus canonicus. b, Tridacna squamosa.

2016, Aug. 23   **Litho.**   **Perf. 14x14¾**

550		Horiz. pair	3.00 3.00
a.-b.	A143	$1 Either single	1.50 1.50
551		Horiz. pair	6.00 6.00
a.-b.	A143	$2 Either single	3.00 3.00

Christmas — A144

Birds and: 65c, Santa Claus in sleigh. $1.80, Rudolph, the red-nosed reindeer.

2016, Oct. 31   **Litho.**   **Perf. 14¾x14**

552	A144	65c multi	1.00 1.00
553	A144	$1.80 multi	2.75 2.75
a.		Souvenir sheet of 2, #552-553	3.75 3.75

Booklet Stamps
Self-Adhesive
Serpentine Die Cut 11¼ Syncopated

554	A144	$1.80 multi	2.75 2.75
a.		Booklet pane of 5	14.00

Litho. With Foil Application

555	A144	65c multi	1.00 1.00
a.		Booklet pane of 10 + 10 etiquettes	10.00

CILICIA

sə-'li-sh̄ē-ə

LOCATION — A territory of Turkey, in Southeastern Asia Minor
GOVT. — Former French occupation
AREA — 6,238 sq. mi.
POP. — 383,645
CAPITAL — Adana

British and French forces occupied Cilicia in 1918 and in 1919 its control was transferred to the French. Eventually part of Cilicia was assigned to the French Mandated Territory of Syria but by the Lausanne Treaty of 1923 which fixed the boundary between Syria and Turkey, Cilicia reverted to Turkey.

40 Paras = 1 Piaster

Issued under French Occupation

Numbers in parentheses are those of basic Turkish or French stamps.

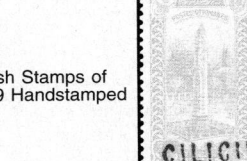

Turkish Stamps of 1913-19 Handstamped
CILICIE

Perf. 11½, 12, 12½, 13½
1919   **Unwmk.**
On Pictorial Issue of 1913

2	A24	2pa red lilac (254)	9.00 9.00
a.		Inverted overprint	20.00 20.00
b.		Double overprint	30.00 30.00
3	A25	4pa dk brn (255)	7.25 7.25
a.		Inverted overprint	20.00 20.00
b.		Double overprint	22.50 22.50
4	A27	6pa dk blue (257)	27.50 20.00
a.		Inverted overprint	32.50 32.50
b.		Double overprint	50.00 50.00
5	A32	1¾pi slate & red brn (262)	8.75 8.75
a.		Inverted overprint	20.00 20.00
b.		Double overprint	22.50 22.50

On Issue of 1915

6	A17	1pi blue (300)	3.75 3.75
a.		Inverted overprint	10.00 10.00
b.		Double overprint	10.00 10.00
c.		In pair with unovptd. stamp	20.00 20.00
7	A21	20pa car rose (318)	13.50 12.00
a.		Inverted overprint	20.00 20.00
b.		Double overprint	35.00 35.00
9	A22	20pa car rose (330)	35.00 32.50
a.		Inverted overprint	45.00 45.00
b.		Double overprint	45.00 45.00

On Commemorative Issue of 1916

9A	A41	5pa grn (345)	130.00 92.50
10	A41	20pa ultra (347)	7.25 7.25
a.		Double overprint	15.00 15.00
11	A41	1pi vio & blk (348)	9.50 9.50
a.		Double overprint	27.50 27.50
b.		Perf 12½	9.50 9.50
c.		In pair with unovptd. stamp	19.00 19.00
12	A41	5pi yel brn & blk (349)	4.00 4.00
a.		Double overprint	7.50 7.50

On Issue of 1916-18

13	A44	10pa grn (424)	8.75 8.75
a.		Perf 11½ (424a)	8.75 8.75
b.		Double overprint	24.00 24.00
14	A47	50pa ultra (428)	45.00 35.00
a.		Perf 11½ (428a)	45.00 35.00
b.		Double overprint	90.00 90.00
15	A51	25pi car, straw (434)	8.75 8.75
16	A52	50pi car (437)	8.75 8.75
17	A52	50pi ind (438)	32.50 32.50

On Issue of 1917

18	A53	5pi on 2pa Prus blue (547)	15.00 15.00
a.		Perf 11½ (547c)	15.00 15.00

On Issue of 1919

19	A47	50pa ultra (555)	40.00 32.50
a.		Perf 11½ (555a)	40.00 32.50
b.		Double overprint	80.00 80.00
20	A48	2pi org brn & indigo (556)	40.00 32.50
21	A49	5pi pale bl & blk (557a)	40.00 32.50
a.		Perf 11½ (557)	40.00 32.50
b.		Perf 11½x12½ (557b)	40.00 32.50

On Newspaper Stamp of 1916

22	A10	5pa on 10pa gray grn (P137)	4.75 4.75
d.		Inverted overprint	11.00 11.00
e.		Double overprint	14.00 14.00

On Semi-Postal Stamps of 1915

22A	A21	20pa car rose (B8)	92.50 80.00
22B	A21	1pi ultra (B9)	2,250. 1,700.
22C	A21	1pi ultra (B13)	1,900. 1,200.

On Semi-Postal Stamps of 1916

23	A17	1pi bl (B19)	10.50 10.50
a.		Inverted overprint	16.00 16.00
b.		Double overprint	16.00 16.00
c.		Perf 11½	25.00 25.00
24	A21	20pa car rose (B28)	3.75 3.75
a.		Inverted overprint	7.50 7.50
b.		Double overprint	10.00 10.00
25	A21	1pi ultra (B29)	8.75 8.75
a.		Inverted overprint	15.00 15.00
b.		Double overprint	25.00 25.00

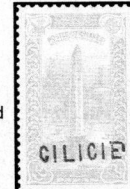

Turkish Stamps of 1913-18 Handstamped
CILICIE

1919   **On Pictorial Issue of 1913**

31	A24	2pa red lil (254)	4.00 4.00
a.		Inverted overprint	8.00 8.00
b.		Double overprint	12.00 12.00
c.		In pair with unovptd. stamp	16.00 16.00
32	A25	4pa dk brn (255)	15.00 15.00
a.		Inverted overprint	22.00 22.00
b.		Double overprint	40.00 40.00

On Issue of 1915

33	A17	1pi blue (300)	13.50 13.50
a.		Inverted overprint	20.00 20.00
b.		Double overprint	35.00 35.00
34	A22	20pa car rose (330)	5.00 5.00
a.		Inverted overprint	9.50 9.50
b.		Double overprint	15.00 15.00
c.		In pair with unovptd. stamp	20.00 20.00

On Commemorative Issue of 1916

35	A41	20pa ultra (347)	15.00 15.00
a.		Inverted overprint	30.00 30.00
b.		Perf 12½ (347a)	15.00 15.00
36	A41	1pi vio & blk (348)	3.25 3.25
a.		Inverted overprint	6.50 6.50
b.		Perf 12½ (348a)	3.25 3.25

On Issue of 1917

40	A53	5pi on 2pa Prus bl (547)	13.50 13.50
a.		Perf 11½ (547c)	13.50 13.50

On Newspaper Stamp of 1916

41	A10	5pa on 10pa gray grn (P137)	27.50 27.50
a.		Inverted overprint	50.00 50.00
b.		In pair with unovptd. stamp	60.00 60.00

On Semi-Postal Stamp of 1915

41A	A21	20pa car rose (B8)	210.00 150.00

On Semi-Postal Stamps of 1916

42	A17	1pi blue (B19)	6.50 6.50
a.		Inverted overprint	12.00 12.00
b.		Double overprint	13.00 13.00
c.		Perf 12 (B19a)	8.00 8.00
d.		Perf 12x13¼ (B19b)	8.00 8.00
43	A21	20pa car rose (B28)	3.25 3.25
a.		Inverted overprint	8.00 8.00
b.		Double overprint	9.00 9.00
		Nos. 31-43 (11)	316.50 256.50

Turkish Stamps of 1913-19 Handstamped
Cilicie

1919   **On Pictorial Issue of 1913**

51	A24	2pa red lil (254)	11.00 11.00
a.		Inverted overprint	16.00 16.00
b.		Double overprint	25.00 25.00
c.		In pair with unovptd. stamp	40.00 40.00
52	A25	4pa dk brn (255)	3.75 3.75
a.		Inverted overprint	7.50 7.50
b.		Double overprint	10.00 10.00

On Issue of 1915

53	A17	1pi blue (300)	5.50 5.50
a.		Inverted overprint	11.00 11.00
b.		Double overprint	15.00 15.00
55	A22	5pa ocher (328)	40.00 35.00
a.		Double overprint	80.00 80.00
56	A22	20pa car rose (330)	4.00 4.00
a.		Inverted overprint	8.00 8.00
b.		Double overprint	12.00 12.00
c.		In pair with unovptd. stamp	17.50 17.50

On Commemorative Issue of 1916

57	A41	20pa ultra (347)	4.00 4.00
a.		Inverted overprint	8.00 8.00
b.		Double overprint	12.00 12.00
c.		Double overprint, one inverted	9.50 9.50
d.		In pair with unovptd. stamp	17.50 17.50
58	A41	1pi vio & blk (348)	3.75 3.75
a.		Inverted overprint	7.50 7.50
b.		Double overprint	10.00 10.00
59	A41	5pi yel brn & blk (349)	12.00 12.00
a.		Inverted overprint	18.00 18.00
b.		Double overprint	24.00 24.00

On Issue of 1916

59A	A17	1pi blue (372)	— —

On Issue of 1916-18

60	A43	5pa org (421)	45.00 40.00
a.		Inverted overprint	70.00 70.00
b.		Perf 11½ (421a)	45.00 40.00
61	A46	1pi dl vio (426)	13.50 13.50
a.		Inverted overprint	21.00 21.00
b.		Double overprint	35.00 35.00
63	A52	50pi green, straw (439)	35.00 27.50

On Issue of 1917

64	A53	5pi on 2pa Prus bl (547)	32.50 27.50
a.		Double overprint	75.00 75.00
b.		Perf 11½ (421a)	32.50 27.50

On Newspaper Stamp of 1916

65	A10	5pa on 10pa gray grn (P137)	8.75 8.75
a.		Inverted overprint	13.50 13.50
b.		Double overprint	24.00 24.00

On Semi-Postal Stamp of 1915

65A	A21	20pa car rose (B8)	1,200. 850.00

On Semi-Postal Stamps of 1916

66	A17	1pi blue (B19)	30.00 30.00
a.		Inverted overprint	55.00 55.00
67	A19	20pa car (B26)	13.50 13.50
a.		Inverted overprint	17.50 17.50
68	A21	20pa car rose (B28)	180.00 92.50
69	A21	20pa car rose (B31)	8.00 8.00
a.		Inverted overprint	15.00 15.00
b.		Double overprint	22.50 22.50
69C	A21	1pi ultra (401)	110.00 80.00
		Nos. 51-69C (20)	1,760. 1,270.

Turkey No. 424 Handstamped
T.E.O. Cilicia

1919

71	A44	10pa green (420)	9.50 9.50
a.		Inverted overprint	17.50 17.50
b.		Double overprint	25.00 25.00
c.		Perf 11½ (420a)	11.00 11.00

"T.E.O." stands for "Territoires Ennemis Occupés."

Turkish Stamps of 1913-19 Overprinted in Black, Red or Blue
T.B.O. Cilicie

In this setting there are various broken and wrong font letters and the letter "i" is sometimes replaced by a "t."

1919   **On Pictorial Issue of 1913**

75	A30	1pi blue (R) (260)	4.75 4.75
a.		Inverted overprint	11.00 11.00
b.		Double overprint	11.00 11.00

c.	Double overprint, one inverted		20.00	20.00

On Issue of 1915

76	A21	20pa car rose (318)	8.75	8.75

On Commemorative Issue of 1916

76A	A41	5pa grn (345)	200.00	110.00
77	A41	20pa ultra (347)	13.50	13.50
a.		Inverted overprint	20.00	20.00
b.		Double overprint	30.00	30.00
c.		Perf 12½ (347a)	13.50	13.50
78	A41	1pi vio & blk (348)	24.00	24.00
a.		Inverted overprint	35.00	35.00
b.		Double overprint	60.00	60.00
c.		Double overprint, one inverted	65.00	65.00

On Issue of 1916-18

79	A43	5pa org (Bl) (421)	4.75	4.75
a.		Inverted overprint	9.50	9.50
b.		Double overprint	13.00	13.00
c.		Double overprint, one inverted	11.00	11.00
d.		Perf 11½ (421a)	4.75	4.75
80	A44	10pa grn (424)	8.75	8.75
a.		Inverted overprint	16.00	16.00
b.		Double overprint	22.50	22.50
c.		Double overprint, one inverted	20.00	20.00
d.		Perf 11½ (424a)	8.75	8.75
81	A45	20pa dp rose (Bk) (425)	27.50	27.50
a.		Double overprint	60.00	60.00
82	A45	20pa dp rose (Bl) (425)	1.00	1.00
a.		Inverted overprint	5.50	5.50
b.		Double overprint	8.00	8.00
c.		Double overprint, one inverted	10.00	10.00
83	A48	2pi org brn & indigo (429)	1.60	1.60
a.		Double overprint	5.50	5.50
b.		Perf 11½ (429a)	1.60	1.60
83C	A49	5pi pale blue & black (R) (430)	1.60	1.60
a.		Inverted overprint	9.50	9.50
b.		Double overprint	9.50	9.50
c.		Double overprint, one inverted	12.00	12.00
d.		Perf 11½ (430a)	1.60	1.60
84	A51	25pi car, *straw* (434)	5.50	5.50
a.		Inverted overprint	15.00	15.00
b.		Double overprint	20.00	20.00
c.		Double overprint, one inverted	13.50	13.50
85	A52	50pi grn, *straw* (439)	92.50	87.50
a.		Inverted overprint	150.00	150.00
b.		Double overprint	150.00	150.00
c.		Double overprint, one inverted	160.00	160.00

On Issue of 1917

85A	A53	5pi on 2pa Prus bl (547)	—	
86	A53	5pi on 2pa Prus bl (548)	13.50	13.50
a.		Perf 11½ (548c)	13.50	13.50

On Newspaper Stamps of 1916-19

87	A10	5pa on 10p gray grn (P137)	2.25	2.25
a.		Inverted overprint	5.50	5.50
b.		Double overprint	7.00	7.00
c.		Double overprint, one inverted	13.50	13.50
88	A21	5pa on 2pa ol grn (P173)	1.00	1.00
a.		Inverted overprint	5.50	5.50
b.		Double overprint	7.00	7.00
c.		Double overprint, one inverted	6.50	6.50

On Semi-Postal Stamps of 1915-17

90	A21	20pa car rose (B28)	8.75	8.75
a.		Double overprint	16.00	16.00
91	A41	10pa car (B42)	3.25	3.25
a.		Inverted overprint	7.25	7.25
b.		Double overprint	9.00	9.00
c.		Double overprint, one inverted	12.00	12.00
d.		Perf 12½ (B42b)	3.25	3.25
92	A11	10pa on 20pa vio brn (B38)	3.25	3.25
a.		Inverted overprint	9.50	9.50
b.		Double overprint	12.00	12.00
c.		Double overprint, one inverted	14.00	14.00
93	SP1	10pa red vio (B46)	2.50	2.50
a.		Overprint sideways	8.00	8.00

It is understood that the newspaper and semi-postal stamps overprinted "Cilicie" were used as ordinary postage stamps.

A1

1920		Blue Surcharge	*Perf. 11½*	
98	A1	70pa on 5pa red	2.40	2.40
a.		Double surcharge	40.00	40.00
b.		Triple surcharge	240.00	
c.		Inverted surcharge	35.00	35.00
d.		Double overprint, one inverted	45.00	45.00
e.		In pair with unovptd. stamp	110.00	
99	A1	3½pi on 5pa red	3.00	2.75
a.		Se-tenant with No. 98, horiz. pair	120.00	120.00
b.		As "a," inverted surcharge	240.00	240.00
c.		Double surcharge	40.00	40.00
d.		Inverted surcharge	35.00	35.00
d.		Double surcharge, one inverted	45.00	45.00

Nos. 98-99 exist with a variety of surcharge misspellings. For detailed listings, see the *Scott Classic Specialized Catalogue*.

French Offices in Turkey No. 26 Surcharged

1920			*Perf. 14x13½*	
100	A3	20pa on 10c rose red (I)	2.00	2.00
a.		"PARAS" omitted	72.50	72.50

Three types of "20" exist on No. 100: I, "2" bold; II "2" faint; III, "0" distinctly taller than "2." See the *Scott Classic Specialized Catalogue of Stamps and Covers* for detailed listings.

Stamps of France, 1900-17, Surcharged

1920				
101	A16	5pa on 2c vio brn	1.60	1.60
102	A22	10pa on 5c green	2.00	2.00
103	A22	20pa on 10c red	4.00	4.00
104	A22	1pi on 25c blue	2.75	2.25
105	A20	2pi on 15c gray green	12.00	12.00
106	A18	5pi on 40c red & gray bl	26.00	26.00
107	A18	10pi on 50c bis brn & lav	32.50	32.50
108	A18	50pi on 1fr claret & ol grn	180.00	180.00
109	A18	100pi on 5fr dk bl & buff	900.00	900.00
		Nos. 101-109 (9)	1,161.	1,160.

Nos. 106 to 109 surcharged in four lines. "O.M.F." stands for "Occupation Militaire Francaise."

1917 Stamps of France Surcharged

No. 110

No. 115

1920				
110	A16	5pa on 2c vio brn (109b)	13.00	
111	A22	10pa on 5c grn (110b)	13.00	
b.		Double surcharge	75.00	
c.		On ordinary paper (110)	19.00	
112	A22	20pa on 10c red (162)	9.75	
a.		Inverted surcharge	75.00	
b.		Double surcharge	67.50	
113	A22	1pi on 25c bl (168d)	6.00	
114	A20	2pi on 15c gray grn (139c)	27.00	

115	A18	5pi on 40c red & gray bl (121)	50.00	
116	A18	20pi on 1fr claret & ol grn (125)	190.00	
a.		"O.M.F. Cilicie" omitted	625.00	
b.		Double surcharge	625.00	
		Nos. 110-116 (7)	308.75	

On Nos. 115 and 116 "SAND. EST" is placed vertically. "Sand. Est" is an abbreviation of Sandjak de l'Est (Eastern County).
Nos. 110-116 were prepared for use, but never issued.

Stamps of France, 1900-17, Surcharged

First Setting: 1.75-2mm spacing between "Cilicie" and figures of value

1920				
117	A16	5pa on 2c vio brn	1.25	1.25
a.		Inverted surcharge	32.50	27.50
b.		"Cililie"	35.00	35.00
c.		Surcharge 5pi (error)	60.00	60.00
h.		Double surcharge	35.00	35.00
119	A22	10pa on 5c grn	1.50	1.50
a.		Inverted surcharge	30.00	26.00
b.		Surch. 5pa (error), upright	55.00	55.00
c.		Surch. 5pa (error), invtd.	75.00	67.50
121	A22	20pa on 10c red	1.75	1.75
a.		Inverted surcharge	32.50	27.50
b.		Surch. 10pa (error), upright	60.00	60.00
c.		Surch. 10pa (error), invtd.	80.00	72.50
f.		Surch. 10pa (error)	35.00	35.00
g.		Double surcharge, one inverted	47.50	47.50
122	A22	1pi on 25c blue	2.00	2.00
a.		Double surcharge	72.50	72.50
b.		Inverted surcharge	55.00	52.50
123	A20	2pi on 15c gray green	2.25	2.25
a.		Double surcharge	45.00	45.00
b.		Inverted surcharge	35.00	32.50
c.		Double surcharge, one inverted	55.00	55.00
124	A18	5pi on 40c red & gray blue	4.00	4.00
a.		Double surcharge	65.00	65.00
b.		Inverted surcharge	40.00	40.00
e.		"PIASRTES"	72.50	72.50
125	A18	10pi on 50c bis brn & lav	12.50	12.50
a.		Double surcharge	60.00	60.00
b.		Inverted surcharge	55.00	47.50
c.		First "S" in "PIASTRES" inverted	110.00	110.00
e.		"PIASRTES"	72.50	72.50
126	A18	50pi on 1fr clar & ol grn	17.50	17.50
a.		Double surcharge	130.00	
b.		Double surcharge	180.00	
e.		"PIASRTES"	87.50	
127	A18	100pi on 5fr dk bl & buff	45.00	45.00
a.		Inverted surcharge	180.00	
d.		"PIASRTES"	925.00	
		Nos. 117-127 (9)	87.75	87.75

This surcharge has "O.M.F." in thicker letters than the preceding issues.
There were two printings of this surcharge, which may be distinguished by the spacing between "Cilicie" and figures of value. See the *Scott Classic Specialized Catalogue of Stamps and Covers* for detailed listings.
For overprints see Nos. C1-C2.

AIR POST STAMPS

Nos. 123 and 124 Handstamped

			Perf. 14x13½	
1920, July 15			**Unwmk.**	
C1	A20	2pi on 15c gray grn	*9,250.*	9,250.
C2	A18	5pi on 40c red & gray blue	*9,500.*	9,500.
a.		"PIASRTES"		

A very limited number of Nos. C1 and C2 were used on two air mail flights between Adana and Aleppo. At a later date impressions from a new handstamp were struck "to oblige" on stamps of the regular issue of 1920 (Nos. 123, 124, 125 and 126) that were in stock at the Adana Post Office.

Counterfeits exist.

POSTAGE DUE STAMPS

Turkish Postage Due Stamps of 1914 Handstamped

Handstamped

1919			**Unwmk.**	*Perf. 12*	
J1	D1	5pa claret		22.00	22.00
a.		Inverted overprint		35.00	35.00
b.		Double overprint		50.00	50.00
J2	D2	20pa red		22.50	22.50
a.		Inverted overprint		35.00	35.00
b.		Double overprint		50.00	50.00
J3	D3	1pi dark blue		35.00	35.00
a.		Inverted overprint		50.00	50.00
J4	D4	2pi slate		45.00	45.00
a.		Inverted overprint		65.00	65.00
		Nos. J1-J4 (4)		124.50	124.50

Handstamped

J5	D1	5pa claret	26.00	26.00
a.		Inverted overprint	40.00	40.00
b.		Double overprint	55.00	55.00
J6	D2	20pa red	30.00	30.00
a.		Inverted overprint	45.00	45.00
b.		Double overprint	60.00	60.00
J7	D3	1pi dark blue	35.00	35.00
a.		Inverted overprint	47.50	47.50
J8	D4	2pi slate	35.00	35.00
a.		Inverted overprint	47.50	47.50
		Nos. J5-J8 (4)	126.00	126.00

Handstamped

J9	D1	5pa claret	22.00	22.00
a.		Inverted overprint	32.50	32.50
b.		Double overprint	32.50	32.50
J10	D2	20pa red	22.50	22.50
a.		Inverted overprint	32.50	32.50
b.		Double overprint	35.00	35.00
J11	D3	1pi dark blue	35.00	35.00
a.		Inverted overprint	47.50	47.50
J12	D4	2pi slate	22.00	22.00
a.		Inverted overprint	32.50	32.50
		Nos. J9-J12 (4)	101.50	101.50

Postage Due Stamps of France Surcharged

1921				
J13	D2	1pi on 10c choc	11.00	11.00
a.		Inverted overprint	130.00	
J14	D2	2pi on 20c olive grn	11.00	11.00
a.		Inverted overprint	130.00	
J15	D2	3pi on 30c red	11.00	11.00
a.		Inverted overprint	92.50	
J16	D2	4pi on 50c vio brn	10.50	10.50
a.		Inverted overprint	92.50	
		Nos. J13-J16 (4)	43.50	43.50

COCHIN CHINA

'kō-chən 'chī-nə

LOCATION — The southernmost state of French Indo-China in the Cambodian Peninsula.
GOVT. — French Colony
AREA — 26,476 sq. mi.
POP. — 4,615,968
CAPITAL — Saigon

100 Centimes = 1 Franc

Surcharged in Black on Stamps of French Colonies

a

b

c

1886-87		Unwmk.		Perf. 14x13½	
1	A9(a)	5c on 25c yel, straw		225.00	120.00
2	A9(b)	5c on 2c brn, buff		40.00	32.50
3	A9(b)	5c on 25c yel, straw		32.50	27.50
a.		Inverted surcharge		275.00	275.00
4	A9(c)	5c on 25c blk, rose ('87)		60.00	47.50
a.		Double surch., one of type b		3,750.	2,750.
b.		Triple surch., two of type b		—	—
c.		Inverted surcharge		375.00	375.00
d.		Double surch., both type "a"		2,750.	3,250.
e.		Triple surch., types "a," "b" and "c"			8,750.
		Nos. 1-4 (4)		357.50	227.50

1888

5	A9	15c on half of 30c brn, bis	125.00

No. 5 was prepared but not issued.
The so-called Postage Due stamps were never issued.
Stamps of Cochin China were superseded by those of Indo-China in 1892.

COCOS ISLANDS

'kō-kəs 'ī-ləndz

(Keeling Islands)

LOCATION — Indian Ocean, 1,330 miles northwest of Australia, 580 miles southwest of Java
GOVT. — A territory of Australia
AREA — 6 sq. mi.
POP. — 670 (1994)

Of 27 small coral islands making up two atolls, two islands are inhabited. Cocos Islands stamps are also valid within Australia.

12 Pence = 1 Shilling
100 Cents = 1 Dollar (1969)

Copra Industry — A1

Super Constellation A2

Map of Islands — A3

Designs: 1sh, Coco palms. 2sh, Sailboat (dukong). 2sh3p, Fairy tern.

Perf. 14½

1963, June 11		Unwmk.		Engr.	
1	A1	3p dk red brown		1.25	1.25
2	A2	5p vio blue		1.50	.85
3	A3	8p red		1.75	1.25
4	A1	1sh green		1.75	.85
5	A3	2sh dull purple		7.00	2.50
6	A2	2sh3p green		13.00	4.00
		Nos. 1-6 (6)		26.25	10.70
		Set, hinged		13.00	

"Simpson and His Donkey" by Wallace Anderson — A3a

1965, Apr. 14	Photo.	Perf. 13½x13		
7	A3a	5p brt grn, sepia & blk	.85	.85

ANZAC issue. See note after Australia No. 387.

Nos. 8-31 are valid for postage in Australia.

Turbo Lajonkairii — A4

Blenny — A5

Designs: 2c, Tridacna crocea (shell). 3c, Tridacna derasa (shell). 5c, Porites cocosensis (coral). 6c, Flyingfish. 10c, Banded rail (bird). 15c, Java sparrow. 20c, Red-tailed tropic bird. 30c, Sooty tern. 50c, Eastern reef heron. $1, Great frigate bird.

Perf. 13½

1969, July 9		Unwmk.	Photo.	
Size: 21½x27mm, 26½x22mm				
8	A4	1c multicolored	.30	.55
9	A4	2c multicolored	1.00	.70
10	A5	3c multicolored	.40	.25
11	A5	4c multicolored	.30	.45
a.		Salmon omitted	2,000.	
12	A5	5c multicolored	.35	.30
13	A5	6c multicolored	.60	.65
14	A5	10c multicolored	.75	.75
15	A5	15c multicolored	.90	.30
16	A5	20c multicolored	.75	.30
17	A5	30c multicolored	.75	.30
18	A4	50c multicolored	.90	.50
Size: 21½x34mm				
19	A4	$1 multicolored	2.00	1.25
		Nos. 8-19 (12)	9.00	6.30

"Dragon" — A6

"Juno" — A7

Perf. 13½x13, 13x13½

1976, Mar. 29			Photo.	
20	A6	1c shown	.30	.30
21	A7	2c shown	.30	.30
22	A7	5c "Beagle"	.30	.30
23	A7	10c "Sydney"	.35	.35
24	A7	15c "Emden"	.55	.55
25	A6	20c "Ayesha"	.55	.55
26	A6	25c "Islander"	.55	.55
27	A6	30c "Cheshire"	.55	.55
28	A7	35c "Jukung"	.55	.55
29	A7	40c "Scotia"	.55	.55
30	A6	50c "Orontes"	.70	.70
31	A6	$1 Royal Yacht "Gothic"	.90	.90
		Nos. 20-31 (12)	6.15	6.15

Historic ships.

Flag, Southern Cross, Islands' Map — A8

Council Emblem, Sailboat A9

1979, Sept. 3	Litho.	Perf. 15½		
32	A8	20c multicolored	.35	.35
33	A9	50c multicolored	.55	.75

Inauguration of Cocos Islands' postal service (20c), and establishment of Cocos Islands Council (50c).

Forcipiger Flavissimus A10

Fish: 2c, Chaetodon ornatissimus. 5c, Anthias. 10c, Meyer's coralfish. 15c, Halichoeres. 20c, Amphiprion clarkii. 22c, Balistapus undulatus. 25c, Maori wrasse. 28c, Macropharyngodon meleagris. 30c, Chaetodon madagascariensis. 35c, Centropyge colini. 40c, Bodianus axillaris. 50c, Corisgaimardi. 55c, Spotted wrasse. 60c, Epinephelus tauvina. $1, Paracanthurus hepatus. $2, Striped butterflyfish.

1979-80			Litho.	Perf. 15½
34	A10	1c multicolored	.25	1.00
35	A10	2c multicolored	.25	.35
36	A10	5c multicolored	.35	1.10
37	A10	10c multi ('80)	.25	1.00
38	A10	15c multicolored	.30	.35
39	A10	20c multicolored	.40	.35
40	A10	22c multi ('80)	.35	.35
41	A10	25c multi ('80)	.40	1.00
42	A10	28c multi ('80)	.35	.35
43	A10	30c multicolored	.50	.45
44	A10	35c multi ('80)	.55	1.25
45	A10	40c multi ('80)	.65	.55
46	A10	50c multicolored	.85	.75
47	A10	55c multi ('80)	.60	1.10
48	A10	60c multi ('80)	.70	.75
49	A10	$1 multicolored	1.15	2.25
50	A10	$2 multi ('80)	2.25	2.75
		Nos. 34-50 (17)	10.15	15.70

Sailboats in Lagoon A11

Christmas: 25c, Yachts and seagulls, vert.

1979, Oct. 22	Litho.	Perf. 15½		
51	A11	25c multicolored	.40	.30
52	A11	55c multicolored	.60	.70

Star of Bethlehem, Map of Cocos Islands A12

Christmas (Map of Cocos Islands and): 28c, Three kings. 60c, Nativity.

1980, Oct. 22	Litho.	Perf. 13½x13		
53	A12	15c multicolored	.25	.25
54	A12	28c multicolored	.30	.30
55	A12	60c multicolored	.70	.70
		Nos. 53-55 (3)	1.25	1.25

Flag and Arms of Great Britain — A13

Australian Territory Status, 25th Anniv. (British Flag and Arms of Past Administrators): No. 57, Ceylon, 1878, 1942-1946. No. 58, Straits Settlements, 1886. No. 59, Singapore, 1946. No. 60, Australia (flag), 1955.

1980, Nov. 24	Litho.	Perf. 13½x13		
56	A13	22c multicolored	.25	.25
57	A13	22c multicolored	.25	.25
58	A13	22c multicolored	.25	.25
59	A13	22c multicolored	.25	.25
60	A13	22c multicolored	.25	.25
a.		Strip of 5, Nos. 56-60	1.75	1.75

Eye of the Wind, Map of Cocos Islands — A14

28c, Expedition routes, horiz. 35c, Francis Drake, Golden Hinde. 60c, Prince Charles, Eye of the Wind.

1980, Dec. 18		Perf. 13x13½, 13½x13		
61	A14	22c shown	.35	.35
62	A14	28c multicolored	.35	.35
63	A14	35c multicolored	.35	.35
64	A14	60c multicolored	.60	.60
		Nos. 61-64 (4)	1.65	1.65

Operation Drake circumnavigation.

Livestock in Quarantine A15

22c, Aerial view of station. 60c, Livestock, diff.

1981, May 12	Litho.	Perf. 13½x13		
65	A15	22c multicolored	.30	.30
66	A15	45c shown	.40	.40
67	A15	60c multicolored	.70	.70
		Nos. 65-67 (3)	1.40	1.40

West Island Quarantine Station opening.

Catalina Guba II A16

Inauguration of Air Service to Indian Ocean: No. 69, Avro Lancastrian. No. 70, Douglas DC4 Skymaster, Lockheed Constellation. No. 71, Lockheed Electra. No. 72, Boeing 727.

1981, June 23   Litho.   Perf. 13½x13

68	A16	22c multicolored	.30	.30
69	A16	22c multicolored	.30	.30
70	A16	22c multicolored	.30	.30
71	A16	22c multicolored	.30	.30
72	A16	22c multicolored	.30	.30
a.		Strip of 5, #68-72	1.75	1.75

Prince Charles and Lady Diana — A17

1981, July 29   Litho.   Perf. 13½x13

73	A17	24c multicolored	.25	.25
74	A17	60c multicolored	.70	.70

Royal Wedding.

Angels We Have Heard on High — A18

Christmas: Carols: 30c, Shepherds Why this Jubilee. 60c,

1981, Oct. 22   Photo.   Perf. 13½x13

75	A18	18c shown	.30	.30
76	A18	30c multicolored	.35	.35
77	A18	60c multicolored	.45	.45
		Nos. 75-77 (3)	1.10	1.10

Sesquicentennial of Charles Darwin's Visit — A19

1981, Dec. 28   Litho.   Perf. 13½x13

78	A19	24c Coral	.30	.30
79	A19	45c Darwin, coral	.40	.40
80	A19	60c Beagle, coral	.55	.55
		Nos. 78-80 (3)	1.25	1.25

Souvenir Sheet

81		Sheet of 2	1.00	1.00
a.	A19	24c Atoll	.45	.45
b.	A19	24c Atoll, diff.	.45	.45

125th Anniv. of Annexation to the British Dominions A20

1982, Mar. 31   Litho.   Perf. 13½x14

82	A20	24c Queen Victoria	.30	.30
83	A20	45c British flag	.50	.50
84	A20	60c Capt. Fremantle	.60	.60
		Nos. 82-84 (3)	1.40	1.40

Scouting Year — A21

Perf. 13½x14, 14x13½

1982, July 21   Litho.

85	A21	27c Baden-Powell	.40	.40
86	A21	75c Emblem, map, vert.	.90	.90

Macroglossum Corythus — A22

1c, Presic villida, vert. 2c, Cephonodes picus. 10c, Chasmina candida, vert. 20c, Nagia linteola. 25c, Eublemma rivula, vert. 30c, Eurrhyparodes tricoloralis, vert. 35c, Hippotion boerhaviae. 40c, Euploea core corinna, vert. 45c, Psara hipponalis. 50c, Danaus chrysippus. 55c, Hypolimas misippus, vert. 60c, Spodoptera litura, vert. $1, Achaea janata, vert. $2, Hippotion velox. $3, Utetheisa pulchelloides.

1982, Sept. 6

87	A22	1c multicolored	1.00	.65
88	A22	2c multicolored	.40	.50
89	A22	5c shown	1.50	.80
90	A22	10c multicolored	.40	.50
91	A22	20c multicolored	.40	.60
92	A22	25c multicolored	.40	.70
93	A22	30c multicolored	.40	.60
94	A22	35c multicolored	1.75	.80
95	A22	40c multicolored	.40	.75
96	A22	45c multicolored	.50	.75
97	A22	50c multicolored	.60	1.40
98	A22	55c multicolored	.55	.90
99	A22	60c multicolored	.60	1.75
100	A22	$1 multicolored	2.25	2.75
101	A22	$2 multicolored	1.50	2.75
102	A22	$3 multicolored	2.00	2.50
		Nos. 87-102 (16)	14.65	18.70

Christmas A23

1982, Oct. 25   Perf. 13x13½

104	A23	21c Holy Family	.25	.25
105	A23	35c Angel	.30	.30
106	A23	75c Flight into Egypt	.90	.90
		Nos. 104-106 (3)	1.45	1.45

Christmas — A24

The Birth of Christ: a, God Will Look After Us; b, Our Baby King Jesus; c, Your Saviour is Born; d, Wise Men Followed the Star; e, And Worship the Lord.

1983, Oct. 31   Litho.   Perf. 14x13½

107	A24	Strip of 5	1.50	1.50
a.-e.		24c any single	.25	.25

Cocos-Malay Culture — A25

Festive Occasions: 45c, Hari Raya. 75c, Melenggok dance. 85c, Wedding.

1984, Jan. 27   Litho.   Perf. 14x13½

108	A25	45c multicolored	.50	.40
109	A25	75c multicolored	.75	.65
110	A25	85c multicolored	.90	.75
		Nos. 108-110 (3)	2.15	1.80

75th Anniv. of Barrel Mail (1909-1955) A26

Designs: 35c, Mail distribution, Direction Isld. 55c, Jukongs retrieving barrels from ocean liner. 70c, Morea receiving outgoing barrel mail, 1909. $1, Barrel mail recovery.

1984, Apr. 20   Litho.   Perf. 13½x14

111	A26	35c multicolored	.55	.55
112	A26	55c multicolored	.95	.95
113	A26	70c multicolored	1.10	1.10
		Nos. 111-113 (3)	2.60	2.60

Souvenir Sheet

114	A26	$1 multicolored	2.25	2.25

375th Anniv. of Islands' Discovery — A27

30c, Capt. William Keeling. 65c, The Hector. 95c, Astrolabe. $1.10, Map, 1666.

1984, July 10   Litho.   Perf. 14x13½

115	A27	30c multicolored	.70	.55
116	A27	65c multicolored	1.40	1.25
117	A27	95c multicolored	1.75	1.60
118	A27	$1.10 multicolored	2.00	1.90
		Nos. 115-118 (4)	5.85	5.30

AUSIPEX '84 — A28

45c, Malay Settlement, Home Island. 55c, West Island Air Strip, settlement. $2, Jukong ships racing, Melbourne Exhibition Center.

1984, Sept. 21   Litho.   Perf. 13½

119	A28	45c multicolored	.65	.55
120	A28	55c multicolored	.70	.70

Souvenir Sheet

121	A28	$2 multicolored	3.00	3.00

Christmas A29

1984, Oct. 31   Litho.   Perf. 13½

122	A29	24c Fish	.40	.40
123	A29	35c Butterfly	.60	.60
124	A29	55c Bird	1.00	1.00
		Nos. 122-124 (3)	2.00	2.00

Souvenir Sheet

Act of Self-Determination — A30

Integration with Australia: a, Australians welcoming Cocos islanders. b, Australian flag over the islands.

1984, Nov. 30   Litho.   Perf. 13½x14

125	A30	Sheet of 2	2.50	2.50
a.-b.		30c any single	1.10	1.10

Crafts — A31

1985, Jan. 30   Perf. 14x13½

126	A31	30c Boat building	.55	.35
127	A31	45c Blacksmith	.80	.50
128	A31	55c Woodcarving	1.15	.80
		Nos. 126-128 (3)	2.50	1.65

Cable-laying Ships — A32

1985, Apr. 24   Perf. 13½x14

129	A32	33c Scotia	1.45	1.00
130	A32	65c Anglia	2.25	1.60
131	A32	80c Patrol	2.25	2.75
		Nos. 129-131 (3)	5.95	5.35

Birds A33

33c, Redfooted booby, vert. 60c, Nankeen night heron. $1, Buff-banded rail.

1985, July 17   Perf. 13½

132	A33	33c multicolored	2.50	2.50
133	A33	60c multicolored	2.75	2.75
134	A33	$1 multicolored	3.00	3.00
a.		"Block" of 3, #132-134	9.00	9.00

Nos. 132-134 printed in a continuous design.

Seashells A34

1c, Trochus maculatus. 2c, Smaragdia rangiana. 3c, Chama. 4c, Cypraea moneta. 5c, Drupa morum. 10c, Conus miles. 15c, Terebra maculata. 20c, Fragum fragum. 30c, Turbo lajonkairii. 33c, Mitra fissurata. 40c, Lambis lambis. 50c, Tridacna squamosa. 60c, Cypraea histrio. $1, Phillidia varicosa. $2, Halgerda tessellata. $3, Harminoea cymbalum.

1985-86   Litho.   Perf. 13½x14

135	A34	1c multicolored	.65	1.10
136	A34	2c multicolored	.65	1.10
137	A34	3c multicolored	.65	1.10
138	A34	4c multicolored	1.10	1.10
139	A34	5c multicolored	.65	1.10
140	A34	10c multicolored	.75	1.75
141	A34	15c multicolored	2.25	1.50
142	A34	20c multicolored	2.25	1.75
143	A34	30c multicolored	2.25	1.75
144	A34	33c multicolored	2.25	1.75
145	A34	40c multicolored	2.25	1.75
146	A34	50c multicolored	2.25	2.25
147	A34	60c multicolored	2.25	2.75
148	A34	$1 multicolored	3.25	3.25
149	A34	$2 multicolored	3.25	3.25
150	A34	$3 multicolored	3.75	3.75
		Nos. 135-150 (16)	30.45	31.00

Issue dates: 1c, 5c, 33c, $1, Sept. 18. 2c, 3c, 10c, $3, Jan. 29, 1986. 15c-30c, 40c, Apr. 30, 1986. 4c, 50c, 60c, $2, July 30, 1986.
For surcharges see Nos. 225, 228-229, 231-233.

Souvenir Sheet

Christmas — A35

a, Star LR. b, Star LL. c, Star UR. d, Star UL.

1985, Oct. 30   Perf. 13½x14

151	A35	Sheet of 4	3.00	3.00
a.-d.		27c any single	.75	.75

Darwin's Visit to the Islands — A36

33c, Charles Darwin. 60c, Map of voyage. $1, HMS Beagle.

1986, Apr. 1   Litho.   Perf. 14x13½
152	A36	33c multicolored	.75	.75
153	A36	60c multicolored	1.40	2.00
154	A36	$1 multicolored	2.00	2.75
		Nos. 152-154 (3)	4.15	5.50

Christmas A37

30c, Coconut palm, holly. 90c, Shell, ornament. $1, Tropical fish, bell.

1986, Oct. 20   Litho.   Perf. 13½x14
155	A37	30c multicolored	.70	.70
156	A37	90c multicolored	2.50	2.50
157	A37	$1 multicolored	2.50	2.50
		Nos. 155-157 (3)	5.70	5.70

Sailboats A38

a, Jukong. b, Ocean racers. c, Sarimanok. d, Ayesha. No. 158 has a continuous design.

1987, Jan. 28
158	Strip of 4	6.00	6.00
a.-d.	A38 36c any single	1.15	1.15

Island Views — A39

70c, Direction Island. 90c, West Island. $1, Golf course, Cocos.

1987, Apr. 8
159	A39	70c multicolored	2.00	1.75
160	A39	90c multicolored	2.75	3.00
161	A39	$1 multicolored	3.25	3.50
		Nos. 159-161 (3)	8.00	8.25

Communications — A40

1987, July 29   Litho.   Perf. 13½x14
162	A40	70c Radio	1.50	1.50
163	A40	75c Air service	1.60	1.60
164	A40	90c Satellite	1.90	1.90
165	A40	$1 Airmail	2.25	2.25
		Nos. 162-165 (4)	7.25	7.25

Industries A41

1987, Sept. 16
166	A41	45c Batik printing	1.40	1.40
167	A41	65c Boat building	1.90	1.90
168	A41	75c Copra production	2.25	2.25
		Nos. 166-168 (3)	5.55	5.55

Industrial activities of the Cocos Malay people.

Christmas — A42

30c, Peace on Earth. 90c, Unity. $1, Goodwill Towards All.

1987, Oct. 28   Perf. 14x13½
169	A42	30c multicolored	.45	.45
170	A42	90c multicolored	1.25	1.25
171	A42	$1 multicolored	1.75	1.75
		Nos. 169-171 (3)	3.45	3.45

Australia Bicentennial A43

Arrival of the First Fleet, Sydney Cove, Jan. 1788: a, Five aboriginals on shore. b, Four aboriginals on shore, one in canoe. c, Ships entering bay, kangaroos. d, Europeans land, white cranes. e, Flag raising.

1988, Jan. 26   Litho.   Perf. 13
172	Strip of 5	10.00	10.00
a.-e.	A43 37c any single	1.25	1.25

No. 172 has a continuous design. See Christmas Is. No. 213.

Life Cycle of the Coconut — A44

1988, Apr. 13   Litho.   Perf. 14x13½
173	A44	37c Flower	.65	.65
174	A44	65c Small nut stage	1.25	1.25
175	A44	90c Mature nuts	1.45	1.45
176	A44	$1 Seedlings	1.90	1.90
a.		Souvenir sheet of 4, #173-176	7.50	7.50
		Nos. 173-176 (4)	5.25	5.25

For surcharge see No. O1.

Cocos Postage Stamps, 25th Anniv. A45

Litho. & Engr.
1988, June 15   Perf. 15x14
177	A45	37c No. 1	1.25	.85
178	A45	55c No. 4	1.50	1.25
179	A45	65c No. 2	1.75	1.75
180	A45	70c No. 3	2.00	2.00
181	A45	90c No. 5	2.25	2.75
182	A45	$1 No. 6	2.50	3.00
		Nos. 177-182 (6)	11.25	11.60

For overprint and surcharge see Nos. 216, 236.

Flowering Plants — A46

1c, Pisonia grandis. 2c, Cocos nucifera. 5c, Morinda citrifolia. 10c, Cordia subcordata. 30c, Argusia argentea. 37c, Calophyllum inophyllum. 40c, Barringtonia asiatica. 50c, Caesalpinia bonduc. 90c, Terminalia catappa. $1, Pemphis acidula. $2, Scaevola sericea. $3, Hibiscus tiliaceus.

1988-89   Litho.   Perf. 14x13½
183	A46	1c multicolored	.55	1.00
184	A46	2c multicolored	.55	1.00
185	A46	5c multicolored	1.10	1.10
186	A46	10c multicolored	.75	1.10
189	A46	30c multicolored	1.10	1.60
190	A46	37c multicolored	1.60	1.40
191	A46	40c multicolored	1.10	1.60
192	A46	50c multicolored	1.40	3.25
194	A46	90c multicolored	2.00	5.00
195	A46	$1 multicolored	2.00	2.75
197	A46	$2 multicolored	2.50	3.00
198	A46	$3 multicolored	3.75	4.50
		Nos. 183-198 (12)	18.40	27.30

Issued: 1c, 5c, 37c, $3, 7/29; 2c, 10c, 30c, $2, 1/18/89; 40c, 50c, 90c, $1, 4/19/89. For self-adhesive sheet of 3 see No. 217.

Souvenir Sheet

1988, July 30
199	A46	$3 like No. 198	9.00	9.00

SYDPEX '88.

Christmas A47

1988, Oct. 12   Litho.   Perf. 13½x14
200	A47	32c multicolored	.90	.90
201	A47	90c multicolored	2.10	2.10
202	A47	$1 multicolored	2.50	2.50
		Nos. 200-202 (3)	5.50	5.50

1st Aerial Survey of the Indian Ocean Air Route, 50th Anniv. — A48

40c, P.G. Taylor, pilot. 70c, Guba II seaplane and crew. $1, Guba II landing off Direction Island. $1.10, Unissued 5sh stamp of Australia, 1939.

1989, July 19   Litho.   Perf. 14x13½
203	A48	40c multicolored	1.00	1.00
204	A48	70c multicolored	1.60	1.60
205	A48	$1 multicolored	2.25	2.25
206	A48	$1.10 multicolored	2.50	2.50
		Nos. 203-206 (4)	7.35	7.35

Jukong, Traditional Sailing Vessel of the Cocos Malay People — A49

1989, Oct. 18   Litho.   Perf. 14x13½
207	A49	35c multicolored	1.10	1.10
208	A49	80c multicolored	2.50	2.50
209	A49	$1.10 multicolored	3.50	3.50
		Nos. 207-209 (3)	7.10	7.10

Christmas.

Naval Engagement of the HMAS Sydney and the German Raider SMS Emden, 75th Anniv. — A50

Designs: 40c, HMAS Sydney. 70c, SMS Emden. $1, Steam launch belonging to the Emden. $1.10, HMAS Sydney and naval crest.

1989, Nov. 9   Litho.   Perf. 13½x14
210		Strip of 4 + label	7.25	7.50
a.	A50	40c multicolored	.65	.65
b.	A50	70c multicolored	1.25	1.25
c.	A50	$1 multicolored	1.75	1.75
d.	A50	$1.10 multicolored	1.90	1.90
e.		Souvenir sheet of 4, #210a-210d	10.00	10.00

Crabs — A52

45c, Xanthid. 75c, Ghost. $1, Red-backed mud crab. $1.30, Coconut, vert.

1990, May 31   Litho.   Perf. 14½
212	A52	45c multicolored	1.40	1.40
213	A52	75c multicolored	2.50	2.50
214	A52	$1 multicolored	2.75	2.75
215	A52	$1.30 multicolored	3.50	3.50
		Nos. 212-215 (4)	10.15	10.15

No. 180 Ovptd. in Red

Litho. & Engr.
1990, Aug. 24   Perf. 15x14
216	A45	70c gray, black & red	12.00	12.00

Flowering Plants Type of 1988

1990, Aug. 24   Photo.   Rouletted 9½
Self-Adhesive
217		Sheet of 3	12.00	12.00
a.	A46	10c like No. 186	.40	.40
b.	A46	90c like No. 194	2.75	2.75
c.	A46	$2 like No. 197	6.00	6.00

World Stamp Exhibition, New Zealand 1990. Nos. 217a-217c inscribed 1990.

Explorers and Their Ships A54

45c, Capt. Keeling, Hector, 1609. 75c, Capt. Fitzroy, Beagle, 1836. $1, Capt. Belcher, Samarang, 1846. $1.30, Capt. Fremantle, Juno, 1857.

1990, Aug. 24   Litho.   Perf. 14½
218	A54	45c violet brown	1.60	1.75
219	A54	75c pale bl & vio brn	2.75	3.75
220	A54	$1 pale yel & vio brn	3.25	5.00
221	A54	$1.30 buff & vio brn	5.25	7.50
a.		Souv. sheet of 4, #218-221, imperf.	11.00	11.00
		Nos. 218-221 (4)	12.85	18.00

Christmas — A55

1990, Dec. 12　Litho.　Rouletted 5

222	A55	40c Star at left	1.40	1.40
a.		Bklt. pane of 10 + 2 labels	27.50	
223	A55	70c Star in center	2.50	2.50
a.		Bklt. pane, 4 #222, 2 #223 + 6 labels	35.00	
224	A55	$1.30 Star at right	5.00	5.00
		Nos. 222-224 (3)	8.90	8.90

**Nos. 140, 141, 143, 146-147, 179
Surcharged in Blue or Black**

No. 225

No. 228

No. 229

No. 231

No. 232

No. 233

No. 236

Litho., Litho. & Engr.

1990-91　　　Perf. 13½x14, 15x14

225	A34	(1c) on 30c #143	6.50	6.50
228	A34	(43c) on 10c #140	47.50	47.50
229	A34	(43c) on 10c #140	19.00	19.00
231	A34	70c on 60c #147 (bk)	10.00	10.00
232	A34	80c on 50c #146 (bk)	10.00	10.00
233	A34	$1.20 on 15c #141 (bk)	10.00	10.00
236	A45	$5 on 65c #179	45.00	45.00
		Nos. 225-236 (7)	148.00	148.00

Issued: No. 236, 11/11; No. 228, 12/18; Nos. 225, 229, 231-233, 1/1991.

Beaded Sea
Star — A56

75c, Feather star. $1, Slate pencil urchin. $1.30, Globose sea urchin.

1991, Feb. 28　Litho.　Perf. 14½

237	A56	45c shown	1.25	1.25
238	A56	75c multicolored	1.75	1.75
239	A56	$1 multicolored	2.50	2.50
240	A56	$1.30 multicolored	3.00	3.00
		Nos. 237-240 (4)	8.50	8.50

Hari
Raya — A57

1991, Mar.　Litho.　Perf. 14½

241	A57	45c multicolored	1.25	1.25
242	A57	75c multi, diff.	1.90	1.90
243	A57	$1.30 multi, diff.	3.50	3.50
		Nos. 241-243 (3)	6.65	6.65

Christmas — A58

1991, Nov. 6　Litho.　Perf. 15½

244	A58	38c Child praying	1.00	1.00
245	A58	43c Child sleeping	1.25	1.25
246	A58	$1 Child singing	2.50	2.50
247	A58	$1.20 Child in wonder	3.25	3.25
		Nos. 244-247 (4)	8.00	8.00

Souvenir Sheet

248		Sheet of 4	8.50	8.50
a.		A58 38c Two children	.95	.95
b.		A58 43c Three girls	1.05	1.05
c.		A58 $1 Boy, two girls	2.50	2.50
d.		A58 $1.20 Boy, girl	2.75	2.75

Nos. 248a-248d are in a continuous design depicting a children's choir.

Crustaceans
A59

Designs: 5c, Lybia tessellata. 10c, Pilodius areolatus. 20c, Trizopagurus strigatus. 30c, Lophozozymus pulchellus. 40c, Thalamitoides quadridens. 45c, Calcinus elegans, vert. 50c, Clibarius humilis. 60c, Trapezia rufopunctata, vert. 80c, Pylopaguropsis magnimanus, vert. $1, Trapezia ferruginea, vert. $2, Trapezia guttata, vert. $3, Trapezia cymodoce, vert.

1992　　Litho.　Perf. 14½

249	A59	5c multicolored	1.20	1.75
250	A59	10c multicolored	1.20	1.75
251	A59	20c multicolored	1.20	1.75
252	A59	30c multicolored	1.25	3.00
253	A59	40c multicolored	1.40	3.00
254	A59	45c multicolored	1.50	3.00
255	A59	50c multicolored	1.50	4.00
256	A59	60c multicolored	1.75	4.00
257	A59	80c multicolored	2.10	4.00
258	A59	$1 multicolored	2.75	4.00
259	A59	$2 multicolored	5.50	5.50
260	A59	$3 multicolored	8.50	8.50
		Nos. 249-260 (12)	29.85	44.25

Issued: 10c, 30c, 50c, 80c, $1, $2, 8/11; others, 2/28.

Discovery of
America, 500th
Anniv. — A60

1992, May 22　Litho.　Perf. 14½

261	A60	$1.05 multicolored	4.00	4.00

Buff-banded Rail — A61

No. 262: a, 10c, Bird looking for food. b, 15c, Adult with chick. c, 30c, Two adults eating. d, 45c, Adult with eggs, hatchling.
No. 263: a, 45c, Two birds, one in water. b, 85c, Chick in nest. c, $1.20, Bird's head.

1992, June 18　Litho.　Perf. 14

262	A61	Strip of 4, #a.-d.	6.00	6.00

Souvenir Sheet

263	A61	Sheet of 3, #a.-c.	7.50	7.50

World Wildlife Fund (No. 262).

World War II,
50th
Anniv. — A62

45c, Royal Air Force Spitfire fighters. 85c, Japanese bombing of Kampong. $1.20, Sunderland reconnaissance flying boat.

1992, Oct. 13　Litho.　Perf. 14½

264	A62	45c multicolored	1.90	1.90
265	A62	85c multicolored	3.50	3.50
266	A62	$1.20 multicolored	4.75	4.75
		Nos. 264-266 (3)	10.15	10.15

Festive
Season — A63

40c, Storm waves on reef edge. 80c, Direction Island. $1, Moorish idols among coral.

1992, Nov. 10　Litho.　Perf. 15x14½

267	A63	40c multicolored	1.50	1.50
268	A63	80c multicolored	2.75	2.75
269	A63	$1 multicolored	3.50	3.50
		Nos. 267-269 (3)	7.75	7.75

Corals — A64

45c, Lobophyllia hemprichii. 85c, Pocillopora eydouxi. $1.05, Fungia scutaria. $1.20, Sarcophyton sp.

1993, Jan. 28　Litho.　Perf. 14½

270	A64	45c multicolored	.90	.90
271	A64	85c multicolored	1.60	1.60
272	A64	$1.05 multicolored	2.25	2.25
273	A64	$1.20 multicolored	2.75	2.75
		Nos. 270-273 (4)	7.50	7.50

A65

Island Currency Tokens: 45c, 5r token, 1968. 85c, Island scene token, 1968. $1.05, 150r token, 1977. $1.20, Token, 1910.

1993, Mar. 30　Litho.　Perf. 15x14½

274	A65	45c multicolored	1.40	1.40
275	A65	85c multicolored	2.25	2.25
276	A65	$1.05 multicolored	3.00	3.00
277	A65	$1.20 multicolored	3.75	3.75
		Nos. 274-277 (4)	10.40	10.40

A66

Education: 5c, Primary classroom activities. 45c, Secondary studies. 85c, Crafts, traditional basket weaving. $1.05, Office staff, higher education. $1.20, Marine officers, coxswain's training.

1993, June 1　Litho.　Perf. 14½

278	A66	5c multicolored	.95	.95
279	A66	45c multicolored	1.50	1.50
280	A66	85c multicolored	2.50	2.50
281	A66	$1.05 multicolored	2.75	2.75
282	A66	$1.20 multicolored	3.25	3.25
		Nos. 278-282 (5)	10.95	10.95

Air-Sea
Rescue
Service
A67

45c, Men in lifeboat. 85c, Westwind Seascan. $1.05, R.J. Hawke inter-island ferry.

1993, Aug. 17　Litho.　Perf. 14½

283	A67	45c multicolored	2.00	2.00
284	A67	85c multicolored	3.00	3.00
285	A67	$1.05 multicolored	4.00	4.00
a.		Souvenir sheet of 3, #283-285	12.00	12.00
		Nos. 283-285 (3)	9.00	9.00

A limited printing exists of No. 285a with Taipei '95 overprint. Value, $110.

Festive
Season — A68

1993, Oct. 24　Litho.　Perf. 14½

286	A68	40c pink & multi	1.50	1.50
287	A68	80c blue & multi	3.00	3.00
288	A68	$1 yellow & multi	4.00	4.00
		Nos. 286-288 (3)	8.50	8.50

From No. 289 on, Cocos Island stamps are valid for postage in Australia.

Map and Reef
Life — A69

Reef triggerfish — No. 289: a, Two fish, purple coral (b). b, Three fish. c, Two fish, red coral (e). e, One fish.
Green turtles — No. 290: a, Eggs, turtles. b, Two turtles (c). c, Group of baby turtles. d, Baby turtle. e, Fish, large turtle.
Pyramid butterflyfish — No. 291: a, Three fish. b, Two small, one large fish, coral (c). c, One small, one large fish, coral (d). d, Three fish, coral (e). e, Coral, one fish.
Junkongs sailing craft — No. 292: a, One boat, red sail. b, Two boats, one blue & white sail, one red sail. c, One boat, yellow sail. d, Two boats sailing away. e, Two boats, one red sail, one white & blue sail.

1994, Feb. 17 Litho. Perf. 14½x14
289	A69	5c Strip of 5, #a.-e.	1.40	1.75
290	A69	10c Strip of 5, #a.-e.	1.75	2.25
291	A69	20c Strip of 5, #a.-e.	2.25	3.00
292	A69	45c Strip of 5, #a.-e.	5.25	5.75
f.		Sheet of 20, #289-292	11.00	14.50

No. 292 also produced in sheets of 20.

Puppets — A70

1994, June 16 Litho. Perf. 14½x14
293	A70	45c Prabu Abjasa	.95	.95
294	A70	90c Prabu Pandu	1.75	1.75
295	A70	$1 Judistra	1.90	1.90
296	A70	$1.35 Abimanju	2.50	2.50
		Nos. 293-296 (4)	7.10	7.10

Christmas A71

1994, Oct. 31 Litho. Perf. 14x14½
297	A71	40c Angel	.80	.80
298	A71	45c Wise man	1.00	1.00
299	A71	80c Bethlehem	1.60	1.60
		Nos. 297-299 (3)	3.40	3.40

Seabirds A72

45c, White-tailed tropicbird, masked booby. 85c, Great frigatebird, white tern.

1995, Mar. 16 Litho. Perf. 14x14½
300	A72	45c multicolored	.80	.80
301	A72	85c multicolored	1.60	1.60
a.		Souvenir sheet of 2, #300-301	3.00	3.00
b.		As "a," overprinted	7.75	7.75

No. 301b ovptd. in gold in sheet margin with Jakarta '95 exhibition emblem and: "8th Asian International Philatelic Exhibition / PAMERAN FILATELI INTERNASIONAL ASIA VIII."
No. 301b issued 8/19/95.

Insects — A73

No. 302: a, Yellow crazy ant. b, Aedes mosquito. c, Hawk moth. d, Scarab beetle. e, Lauxaniid fly.
$1.20, Common eggfly butterfly.

1995, July 13 Litho. Perf. 14½x14
302	A73	45c Strip of 5, #a.-e.	6.00	6.00
303	A73	$1.20 multicolored	2.75	2.75

Fish — A74

Designs: 5c, Redspot wrasse. 30c, Gilded triggerfish. 40c, Saddled butterflyfish. 45c, Ringeyed hawkfish. 75c, Orangespine unicornfish. 80c, Blue tang. 85c, Humpback wrasse. 90c, Threadfin butterflyfish. $1, Bluestripe snapper. $1.05, Longnosed butterflyfish. $1.20, Freckled hawkfish. $2, Powder blue surgeonfish.

1995-97 Litho. Perf. 14x14½
304	A74	5c multicolored	.40	.40
305	A74	30c multicolored	.60	.60
306	A74	40c multicolored	.95	.95
307	A74	45c multicolored	1.10	1.10
308	A74	75c multicolored	1.60	1.60
309	A74	80c multicolored	1.75	1.75
310	A74	85c multicolored	1.75	1.75
311	A74	90c multicolored	2.00	2.00
312	A74	$1 multicolored	2.25	2.25
313	A74	$1.05 multicolored	2.25	2.25
314	A74	$1.20 multicolored	3.00	3.00
315	A74	$2 multicolored	5.25	5.25
		Nos. 304-315 (12)	22.90	22.90

Issued: 40c, 80c, $1.05, 11/1/95; 30c, 45c, 85c, $2, 8/8/96; 5c, 75c, 90c, $1, $1.20, 8/14/97.
See Nos. 327-329, 335.

Festive Season — A75

Designs: 45c, Greeting others, asking forgiveness. 75c, Drum beaters celebrate Hari Raya Puasa. 85c, Sharing food with friends.

1996, Feb. 19 Litho. Perf. 14
316	A75	45c multicolored	.80	.80
317	A75	75c multicolored	1.90	1.90
318	A75	85c multicolored	2.25	2.25
		Nos. 316-318 (3)	4.95	4.95

Animals Imported Into Australia Through Cocos Islands Quarantine Station — A76

45c, Black rhinoceros. 50c, Alpacas. $1.05, Boran cattle. $1.20, Ostrich.

1996, June 13 Litho. Perf. 14½x14
319	A76	45c multicolored	1.40	1.40
320	A76	50c multicolored	1.60	1.60
321	A76	$1.05 multicolored	2.75	2.75
322	A76	$1.20 multicolored	3.75	3.75
		Nos. 319-322 (4)	9.50	9.50

A77

Festive Season: 45c, Tambourine, dancing on shore, bird. 75c, Woman clapping, sailboats racing. 85c, Fish, night scene on beach.

1997, Jan. 6 Litho. Perf. 14½x14
323	A77	45c multicolored	.95	.95
324	A77	75c multicolored	1.50	1.50
325	A77	85c multicolored	1.90	1.90
		Nos. 323-325 (3)	4.35	4.35

A78

Children's drawings: a, Gift package. b, Mosque. c, Cocos Malay woman. d, Island scene. e, Two dancers.

1998, Jan. 22 Litho. Perf. 14
326	A78	45c Strip of 5, #a.-e.	4.75	4.75

Festive Season.

Fish Type of 1995

Designs: 70c, Crowned squirrelfish. 95c, Sixstripe wrasse. $5, Goldback anthias.

1998, Aug. 13 Litho. Perf. 14x14½
327	A74	70c multicolored	1.25	1.25
328	A74	95c multicolored	1.50	1.50
329	A74	$5 multicolored	8.25	8.25
		Nos. 327-329 (3)	11.00	11.00

Jukong Boats, Hari Raya Festival — A79

a, Women placing items in leaves, people along beach. b, Two women, boats along beach. c, Flowers, man in boat. d, Palm trees, two men, man in boat. e, Two people in boat.

1999, Feb. 11 Litho. Perf. 14½x14
330	A79	45c Strip of 5, #a.-e.	4.75	4.75

Flora and Fauna — A80

a, 45c, Two birds on tree branch. b, 25c, Bird in flight. c, 10c, Sailboat with sail down. d, 5c, Sailboat with red sails. e, 45c, Two birds in flight. f, 25c, Butterflies. g, 10c, School of fish. h, 5c, School of fish swimming left, coral. i, 45c, Red hibiscus flower. j, 25c, Three birds in flight. k, 10c, Two moorish idols. l, 5c, Turtles. m, 45c, Butterfly, flowers. n, 25c, Moth with wings folded, flowers. o, 10c, Two gold fish. p, 5c, Various fish swimming right. q, 45c, Yellow hibiscus. r, 25c, Butterfly on flowers. s, 10c, Two birds in flight. t, 5c, Large fish, coral.

1999, June 17 Litho. Perf. 14½x14
331	A80	Sheet of 20, #a.-t.	17.00	17.00

Faces of Cocos Islands A81

Ordinary people: a, Ratma Anthoney, with white shirt. b, Nakia Haji Dolman, with multicolored head covering. c, Muller Eymin, with white head covering. d, Courtney Press, with flowered outfit. e, Mhd Abu-Yazid, with blue shirt with stripes.

2000, Apr. 13 Litho. Perf. 14x14½
332	A81	45c Strip of 5, #a.-e.	5.00	5.00

Worldwide Fund for Nature — A82

No. 333: a, Purple crab. b, Little nipper crab. No. 334: a, Horn-eyed ghost crab. b, Smooth-banded ghost crab.

2000, June 20 Litho. Perf. 14x14¾
333	A82	5c Pair, #a-b	1.10	1.10
334	A82	45c Pair, #a-b	2.25	2.25

Fish Type of 1995

No. 335: a, Wideband fusilier. b, Striped surgeonfish. c, Orangeband surgeonfish. d, Indo-Pacific sergeant.

2001, Feb. 8 Litho. Perf. 14x14½
335		Block of 4	5.00	5.00
a.-d.	A74	45c Any single	.90	.90

Turtles — A83

No. 336: a, Loggerhead. b, Hawksbill. c, Leatherback. d, Green.

2002, Oct. 1 Litho. Perf. 14x14½
336	A83	Block of 4	5.50	5.50
a.-d.		45c Any single	1.00	1.00

Shore Birds — A84

No. 337: a, Eastern reef egret. b, Sooty tern. c, Ruddy turnstone. d, Whimbrel.

2003, June 17
337		Horiz. strip of 4	7.50	7.50
a.-d.	A84	50c Any single	1.45	1.45

Royal Visit, 50th Anniv. — A85

Queen Elizabeth II and: No. 338a, Cocos Malay musicians. No. 338b, Royal Yacht Gothic. $1, Clunies Ross (Oceania) House. $1.45, Dignitary presenting model of Malay jukong.

2004, Mar. 16
338	A85	50c Horiz. pair, #a-		
		b	2.75	2.75
339	A85	$1 multi	2.75	2.75
340	A85	$1.45 multi	4.00	4.00
a.		Souvenir sheet, #338a, 338b, 339, 340	10.00	10.00
b.		As "a," with 2004 World Stamp Championship emblem ovptd. in gold in margin	10.00	10.00
		Nos. 338-340 (3)	9.50	9.50

No. 340b issued 8/28.

Worldwide Fund for Nature (WWF) — A86

Designs: No. 341a, Blacktip reef shark. No. 341b, Gray reef sharks. $1, Blacktip reef sharks. $1.45, Gray reef shark.

2005, Jun 21 Perf. 14½x14
341	A86	50c Horiz. pair, #a-		
		b	3.50	3.50
342	A86	$1 multi	3.50	3.50
343	A86	$1.45 multi	5.00	5.00
		Nos. 341-343 (3)	12.00	12.00

Wildlife — A87

No. 344: a-e, Various birds. f-t, Various fish and marine life.

2006, June 13			**Perf. 14¾x14**	
344	A87	Sheet of 20	21.00	21.00
a.-e.		10c Any single	.50	.50
f.-o.		25c Any single	.80	.80
p.-t.		50c Any single	1.75	1.75

Mollusks — A88

Designs: No. 345a, Oriental moonsnail. No. 345b, Perly nautilus. $1, Partridge tun. $1.45, Giant clam.

2007, Mar. 20			**Perf. 14x14½**	
345	A88	50c Horiz. pair, #a-		
		b	3.50	3.50
346	A88	$1 multi	3.50	3.50
347	A88	$1.45 multi	5.50	5.50
		Nos. 345-347 (3)	12.50	12.50

Birds — A89

No. 345, a, Black-winged stilt. b, Chinese pond heron. $1, White-breasted waterhen, horiz. $1.45, Saunders' tern, horiz.

2008, Feb. 26			**Perf. 14**	
348	A89	50c Horiz. pair, #a-		
		b	3.50	3.50
349	A89	$1 multi	3.50	3.50
350	A89	$1.45 multi	5.00	5.00
		Nos. 348-350 (3)	12.00	12.00

History of Cocos Islands — A90

No. 351: a, Sighting of islands by Captain William Keeling, 1609. b, Visit of Charles Darwin, 1836. $1.10, Control of islands by Clunies Ross family, 1827-1978. $1.65, Australian territory, 1955.

2009, Apr. 21			**Perf. 14¼**	
351	A90	55c Horiz. pair, #a-		
		b	3.50	3.50
352	A90	$1.10 multi	3.50	3.50
353	A90	$1.65 multi	5.50	5.50
		Nos. 351-353 (3)	12.50	12.50

Flowers — A91

No. 354: a, Ipomoea pes-caprae. b, Hibiscus tiliaceus.
No. 355: a, Suriana maritima. b, Morinda citrifolia.

2010, Sept. 15		**Litho.**	**Perf. 14¾x14**	
354	A91	60c Horiz. pair, #a-b	2.40	2.40
355	A91	$1.20 Horiz. pair, #a-b	4.75	4.75

Boats — A92

Designs: 60c, Jukongs. $1.20, Small boat. $1.80, Glass-bottom boat, horiz. $3, Yacht, horiz.

		Perf. 14¾x14, 14x14¾		
				Litho.
356	A92	60c multi	1.25	1.25
357	A92	$1.20 multi	2.40	2.40
358	A92	$1.80 multi	3.75	3.75
359	A92	$3 multi	6.00	6.00
		Nos. 356-359 (4)	13.40	13.40

Miniature Sheet

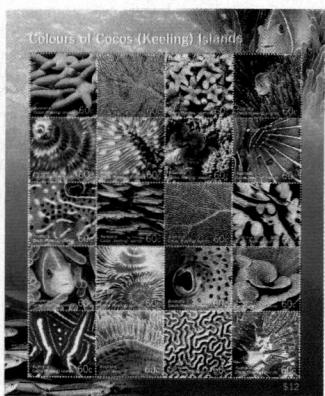

Marine Life — A93

No. 360: a, Sea cucumbers with red coloring. b, Fan coral with breaks at right. c, Sea cucumbers with purple coloring. d, Pink anemonefish in sea anemone. e, Christmas tree worm, tip at upper left. f, Mushroom coral. g, Giant clam. h, Fin of Spotted lionfish. i, Eye of Scribbled filefish (brown and blue fish). j, School of Neon fusiliers. k, Fan coral (intact). l, Nudibranch. m, Pink anemonefish in sea anemone, close-up. n, Christmas tree worms. o, Eye of Foster's hawkfish (pink and red fish). p, Foliaceous coral. q, Durban dancing shrimp. r, Magnificent sea anemone. s, Brain coral. t, Crown of thorns sea star.

2011, Sept. 6			**Perf. 14¼**	
360	A93	Sheet of 20	25.00	25.00
a.-t.		60c Any single	1.25	1.25

A sheet of 9 stamps containing stamps similar to Nos. 360a, 360b, 360d, 360e, 360j, 360l, 360m, 360n, and 360t but with glossy varnish was sold only with a set of nine gift cards for $9.99.

Colorful Skies Over Cocos Islands A94

Skies over: 60c, Pier. $1.20, Rocks in water. $1.80, Beach. $3, Palm trees.

2012, May 22			**Perf. 14x14¾**	
361-364	A94	Set of 4	13.00	13.00

Butterflies — A95

No. 365: a, Meadow argus. b, Common crow.
No. 366: a, Australian painted lady. b, Varied eggfly.

2012, Aug. 2				
365	A95	Horiz. pair	2.50	2.50
a.-b.		60c Either single	1.25	1.25
366	A95	Horiz. pair	5.25	5.25
a.-b.		$1.20 Either single	2.60	2.60

Cocos Islands Postage Stamps, 50th Anniv. — A96

Designs: 5c, Sea turtle and underwater photographer. 60c, Man in outrigger canoe. $1, Sailboarder. $1.20, Coconut. $2, Egret.

2013, June 4			**Perf. 14¾x14**	
367-371	A96	Set of 5	9.25	9.25
371a		Souvenir sheet of 5, #367-371	9.25	9.25

A booklet containing five of No. 368 was produced locally and in very limited quantities.

Barrel Mail — A97

Designs: 60c, Men and barrels in ocean, cover franked with Australia #213. $3, Men on shore signaling ship, cover franked with Australia #166 and 236.

2013, Aug. 6		**Litho.**	**Perf. 14¼**	
372-373	A97	Set of 2	6.50	6.50

Historical Cocos Islands Maps — A98

Designs: No. 374a, 17th cent. map with natives at right. No. 374b, Map from 18th cent. with French inscriptions. $1.40, Map from 19th cent. $2.10, Map from 20th cent.

2014, June 24		**Litho.**	**Perf. 14¼**	
374		Horiz. pair	2.80	2.80
a.-b.		A98 70c Either single	1.40	1.40
375	A98	$1.40 multi	2.75	2.75
376	A98	$2.10 multi	4.00	4.00
		Nos. 374-376 (3)	9.55	9.55

Battle of the Cocos Islands, Cent. — A99

Warships: 70c, HMAS Sydney. $3.50, SMS Emden.

2014, Oct. 14		**Litho.**	**Perf. 14¼**	
377-378	A99	Set of 2	7.25	7.25

Worldwide Fund for Nature (WWF) — A100

Birds: No. 379, 70c, Herald petrels. No. 380, 70c, Oriental pratincoles. No. 381, 70c, Little curlews. No. 382, 70c, Indian yellow-nosed albatrosses.

2015, Apr. 22		**Litho.**	**Perf. 14¼**	
379-382	A100	Set of 4	4.50	4.50

A101

Uninhabited Islands — A102

No. 383: a, Pulu Klapa Satu (green water in foreground). b, Pulu Maraya (white beach in foreground).
No. 384: a, Pulu Blan Madar (at twilight). b, Pulu Beras (at midday).

2015, Aug. 25		**Litho.**	**Perf. 14¾x14**	
383	A101	Horiz. pair	2.00	2.00
a.-b.		70c Either single	1.00	1.00
384	A102	Horiz. pair	4.00	4.00
a.-b.		$1.40 Either single	2.00	2.00

Dolphins A103

Designs: No. 385, $1, Common dolphin. No. 386, $1, Indo-Pacific bottlenose dolphin. No. 387, $1, Spinner dolphin.

2016, May 17		**Litho.**	**Perf. 14x14¾**	
385-387	A103	Set of 3	4.50	4.50

A104

Art — A105

Nos. 388 and 389 — Various works with denomination at: a, UL. b, UR.

2016, Oct. 18		**Litho.**	**Perf. 14x14¾**	
388	A104	Horiz. pair	3.25	3.25
a.-b.		$1 Either single	1.60	1.60

389	A105	Horiz. pair	6.50	6.50
a.-b.		$2 Either single	3.25	3.25
c.		Souvenir sheet of 4, #388a, 388b, 389a, 389b	9.75	9.75

OFFICIAL STAMP

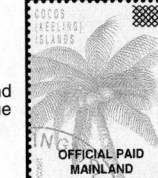

No. 175 Ovptd. and
Srchd. in Dark Blue

1991, Jan. 25   Litho.   Perf. 14x13½
O1 A44 (43c) on 90c multi   110.00

No. O1 was not sold to the public unused. Used value is for a canceled-to-order example. Mint examples exist in the marketplace. Value, $250.

COLOMBIA

kə-'ləm-bē-ə

LOCATION — On the northwest coast of South America, bordering on the Caribbean Sea and the Pacific Ocean
GOVT. — Republic
AREA — 456,535 sq. mi.
POP. — 39,309,422 (1999 est.)
CAPITAL — Bogota

In 1810 the Spanish Viceroyalty of New Granada gained its independence and with Venezuela and Ecuador formed the State of Greater Colombia. In 1832 this state split into three independent units as Venezuela, Ecuador and the Republic of New Granada. The name of the country has been, successively, Granadine Confederation (1858-61), United States of New Granada (1861), United States of Colombia (1861-65), and the Republic of Colombia (1885 to date).

100 Centavos = 1 Peso

> **Catalogue values for unused stamps in this country are for Never Hinged items, beginning with Scott 594 in the regular postage section, Scott B1 in the semipostal section, Scott C200 in the airpost section, Scott CE1 in the airpost special delivery section, Scott E2 in the special delivery section, and Scott RA33 in the postal tax section.**

In the earlier days many towns did not have handstamps for canceling and stamps were canceled with pen and ink. Pen cancellations, therefore, do not indicate fiscal use. (Postage stamps were not used for revenue purposes.) Used values for Nos. 1-128 are for stamps with illegible manuscript cancels or handstamp cancels of Bogota or Medellin. Stamps with legible manuscript or other handstamped town-name cancels sell for more.

Fractions of many Colombian stamps of both early and late issues are found canceled, their use to pay postage having been tolerated even though forbidden by the postal laws and regulations. Many are known to have been made for philatelic purposes.

Watermarks

Wmk. 116 — Crosses and Circles

Wmk. 127 — Quatrefoils

Wmk. 194 — Multiple Curvilinear Triangles

Wmk. 229 — Wavy Lines

Wmk. 255 — Wavy Lines and C Multiple

Wmk. 331 — REPUBLICA DE COLOMBIA

Wmk. 334 — Rectangles

Wmk. 346 — Parallel Curved Lines

Stamps inscribed "Colombia" that show the Panama Canal area were used in Panama and can be found in Vol. 5.

Granadine Confederation

Coat of Arms — A1

Type A1 — Asterisks in frame. Wavy lines in background.
Type A2 — Diamond-shaped ornaments in frame. Straight lines in background. Numerals larger.

1859   Unwmk.   Litho.   *Imperf.*
Wove Paper

1	A1	2½c green	120.00	120.00
a.		2½c yellow green	120.00	120.00
2	A1	5c blue	140.00	87.50
a.		Tête bêche pair	4,500.	7,250.
b.		"50" instead of "5"		7,500.
3	A1	5c violet	375.00	120.00
a.		Tête bêche pair	6,000.	6,000.
b.		"50" instead of "5"		15,000.
4	A1	10c red brown	140.00	80.00
a.		10c buff	140.00	80.00
6	A1	20c blue	120.00	67.50
a.		20c gray blue	120.00	67.50
b.		Se-tenant with 5c		
c.		Tête bêche pair	40,000.	32,500.
7	A1	1p carmine	72.50	120.00
a.		1p rose	110.00	150.00
8	A1	1p rose, *bluish*	350.00	

The 10c green is an essay.
Reprints of No. 7 are in brown rose or brown red. Wavy lines of background are much broken; no dividing lines between stamps.

Coat of Arms — A2

1860   Laid Paper

9	A2	5c lilac	325.00	210.00

Wove Paper

10	A2	5c gray lilac	85.00	65.00
a.		5c lilac	85.00	65.00
11	A2	10c yellow buff	85.00	55.00
a.		Tête bêche pair	7,000.	7,000.
12	A2	20c blue	210.00	140.00

United States of New Granada

Arms of New Granada — A3

1861

13	A3	2½c black	1,450.	400.00
14	A3	5c yellow	400.00	175.00
a.		5c buff	400.00	175.00
16	A3	10c blue	1,250.	175.00
17	A3	20c red	500.00	475.00
18	A3	1p pink	1,250.	375.00

There are 54 varieties of the 5c, 20c, and 1 peso.
Forgeries exist of Nos. 13-18.

United States of Colombia

Coat of Arms — A4

1862

19	A4	10c blue	250.00	125.00
20	A4	20c red	4,500.	725.00
21	A4	50c green	250.00	175.00
22	A4	1p red lilac	600.00	175.00
23	A4	1p red lil, *bluish*	5,500.	1,750.

No. 23 is on a thinner, coarser wove paper than Nos. 19-22.

Coat of Arms — A5

1863

24	A5	5c orange	100.00	65.00
a.		Star after "Cent"	110.00	72.50
25	A5	10c blue	175.00	24.00
a.		Period after "10"	200.00	30.00
26	A5	20c red	225.00	75.00
a.		Star after "Cent"	250.00	82.50
b.		Transfer of 50c in stone of 20c	18,500.	5,500.

Bluish Paper

28	A5	10c blue	175.00	32.50
a.		Period after "10"	190.00	35.00
29	A5	50c green	210.00	75.00
a.		Star after "Cent"	210.00	77.50

Ten varieties of each.

Coat of Arms — A6

1864   Wove Paper

30	A6	5c orange	60.00	37.50
a.		Tête bêche pair	475.00	400.00
31	A6	10c blue	55.00	15.00
a.		Period after 10	55.00	15.00
32	A6	20c scarlet	100.00	55.00
33	A6	50c green	85.00	55.00
34	A6	1p red violet	350.00	175.00

Two varieties of each.

Arms of Colombia
A7   A9

A8

1865

35	A7	1c rose	10.00	10.00
a.		bluish pelure paper	30.00	21.00
36	A8	2½c black, *lilac*	21.00	14.00
37	A9	5c yellow	47.50	20.00
a.		5c orange	47.50	20.00
38	A9	10c violet	67.50	4.50
39	A9	20c blue	67.50	20.00
40	A9	50c green	120.00	52.50
41	A9	50c grn (small figures)	120.00	52.50
42	A9	1p vermilion	125.00	18.00
a.		1p rose red	125.00	18.00
b.		Period after "PESO"	150.00	20.00

Ten varieties of each of the 5c, 10c, 20c, and 50c, and six varieties of the 1 peso. No. 36 was used as a carrier stamp.

A10   A11   A12

A13   A14

A15   A16

1866   White Wove Paper

45	A10	5c orange	72.50	27.50
46	A11	10c lilac	17.00	5.25
a.		Pelure paper	21.00	11.50
47	A12	20c light blue	42.50	21.00
a.		Pelure paper	67.50	52.50
48	A13	50c green	17.00	13.00
49	A14	1p rose red, *bluish*	92.50	32.50
a.		1p vermilion	92.50	52.50
51	A15	5p blk, *green*	500.00	210.00
52	A16	10p blk, *vermilion*	350.00	200.00

There are several varieties of the 1 peso having the letters "U," "N," "S" and "O" smaller.

A17   A18

A19   A20

A21

TEN CENTAVOS:

Type I — "B" of "COLOMBIA" over "V" of "CENTAVOS".

Type II — "B" of "COLOMBIA" over "VO" of "CENTAVOS."

ONE PESO:

Type I — Long thin spear heads. Diagonal lines in lower part of shield.

Type II — Short thick spear heads. Horizontal and a few diagonal lines in lower part of shield.

Type III — Short thick spear heads. Crossed lines in lower part of shield. Ornaments at each side of circle are broken. (See No. 97.)

1868

53	A17	5c orange	67.50	52.50
54	A18	10c lilac (I)	4.25	1.10
a.		10c red violet (I)	4.25	1.10
b.		10c lilac (II)	4.25	1.10
c.		10c red violet (II)	4.25	1.10
d.		Printed on both sides	7.50	2.50
55	A19	20c blue	3.00	1.25
56	A20	50c yellow green	3.50	2.40
57	A21	1p ver (II)	4.25	2.10
a.		Tête beche pair	140.00	100.00
b.		1p rose red (I)	60.00	27.50
c.		1p rose red (II)	4.00	2.10
		Nos. 53-57 (5)	82.50	59.35

See Nos. 83-84, 96-97.

Counterfeits or reprints.

10c — There is a large white dot at the upper left between the circle enclosing the "X" and the ornament below.

50c — There is a shading of dots instead of dashes below the ribbon with motto. There are crossed lines in the lowest section of the shield instead of diagonal or horizontal ones.

1p — The ornaments in the lettered circle are broken. There are crossed lines in the lowest section of the shield. These counterfeits, or reprints, are on white paper, wove and laid, on colored wove paper and in fancy colors.

A22

Two varieties

1869-70   Wove Paper

59	A22	2½c black, *violet*	4.75	2.50
a.		Laid paper ('70)	325.00	250.00
b.		Laid batonné paper ('70)	30.00	24.00

Nos. 59, 59a, 59b were used as carrier stamps.

Counterfeits, or reprints, are on magenta paper wove or ribbed.

A23   A24

1870   Wove Paper

62	A23	5c orange	2.00	1.25
a.		5c yellow	2.00	1.25
63	A24	25c black, *blue*	16.00	13.00

See No. 89.

In the counterfeits, or reprints, of No. 63, the top of the "2" of "25" does not touch the down stroke. The counterfeits are on paper of various colors.

A25   A26

5 pesos — The ornament at the left of the "C" of "Cinco" cuts into the "C," and the shading of the flag is formed of diagonal lines.

10 pesos — The stars have extra rays between the points, and the central part of the shield has some horizontal lines of shading at each end.

Surface Colored, Chalky Paper

1870

64	A25	5p blk, *green*	100.00	67.50
65	A26	10p blk, *vermilion*	120.00	67.50

See Nos. 77-79, 125-126.

A27   A28

A29

TEN CENTAVOS:

Type I — "S" of "CORREOS" 2½mm high. First "N" of "NACIONALES" small.

Type II — "S" of "CORREOS" 2mm high. First "N" of "NACIONALES" wide.

1871-74   Thin Porous Paper

66	A27	1c green ('72)	3.50	3.50
67	A27	1c rose ('73)	3.50	3.50
a.		1c carmine ('73)	3.50	3.50
68	A28	2c brown	1.60	1.60
a.		2c red brown	1.60	1.60
69	A29	10c vio (I) ('74)	2.50	2.50
a.		10c lilac (I) ('74)	2.50	2.50
b.		10c violet (II) ('74)	2.50	2.50
c.		10c lilac (II) ('74)	2.50	2.50
d.		As #69, laid paper ('72)	140.00	140.00
e.		As "b," laid paper ('72)	140.00	140.00
		Nos. 66-69 (4)	11.10	11.10

Counterfeits or reprints.

1c — The outer frame of the shield is broken near the upper left corner and the "A" of "Colombia" has no cross-bar.

2c — There are scratches across "DOS" and many white marks around the letters on the large "2." The counterfeits, or reprints, are on white wove and bluish white laid paper.

Condor — A30

Liberty Head

A31   A32

5 pesos, redrawn — The ornament at the left of the "C" only touches the "C," and the shading of the flag is formed of vertical and diagonal lines.

10 pesos, redrawn — The stars are distinctly five pointed, and there is no shading in the central part of the shield.

1877   Wove Paper

73	A30	5c purple	7.25	2.10
a.		5c lilac	7.25	2.10
74	A31	10c bister brown	3.50	.90
a.		10c red brown	3.50	.90
b.		10c violet brown	3.50	.90
75	A32	20c blue	4.25	1.40
a.		20c violet blue	25.00	3.50
77	A26	10p blk, *rose*	120.00	67.50
78	A25	5p blk, *lt grn,* redrawn	42.50	32.50
79	A26	10p blk, *rose,* redrawn	17.00	2.75
a.		10p blk, *dark rose,* redrawn	17.00	2.75
		Nos. 73-79 (6)	194.50	107.15

Stamps of the issues of 1871-77 are known with private perforations of various gauges, also with sewing machine perforation.

In the counterfeits, or reprints, of the 5 pesos the ornament at the left of the "C" of "Cinco" is separated from the "C" by a black line.

In the counterfeits, or reprints, of the 10 pesos the outer line of the double circle containing "10" is broken at the top, below "OS" of "Unidos," and the vertical line of shading contained in the double circle are very indistinct. There is a colorless dash below the loop of the "P" of "Pesos."

1876-79   Laid Paper

80	A30	5c lilac	85.00	65.00
81	A31	10c brown	47.50	2.75
82	A32	20c blue	100.00	67.50
83	A20	50c green ('79)	97.50	65.00

84	A21	1p pale red (II) ('79)	62.50	15.00
		Nos. 80-84 (5)	392.50	215.25

1879   Wove Paper

89	A24	25c green	32.50	32.50

1881   Blue Wove Paper

93	A30	5c violet	20.00	13.00
a.		5c lilac	20.00	13.00
94	A31	10c brown	12.00	2.50
95	A32	20c blue	12.00	3.75
96	A20	50c yellow green	12.50	7.50
97	A21	1p ver (III)	17.00	7.50
		Nos. 93-97 (5)	73.50	34.25

For types of 1p, see note over No. 53.

Reprints of the 10c and 20c are much worn. On the 10c the letters "TAVOS" of "CENTAVOS" often touch. On the 20c the letters "NT" of "VEINTE" touch and the left arm of the "T" is too long. Reprints of the 25c, 50c and 1p have the characteristics previously described. The reprints are on white wove or laid paper, on colored papers, and in fancy colors. Stamps on green paper exist only as reprints.

A34   A35

A36

1 centavo — The period before "UNION" is round and there are rays between the stars and the condors.

2 centavos — The "2's" and "C's" in the corners are placed upright.

5 centavos — The last star at the right almost touches the frame.

10 centavos — The letters of the inscription are thin; there are rays between the stars and the condor.

1881   White Wove Paper   Imperf.

103	A34	1c green	5.00	4.00
104	A35	2c vermilion	2.10	1.60
a.		2c rose	2.50	1.60
106	A34	5c blue	5.00	1.60
b.		Printed on both sides		
107	A36	10c violet	4.25	1.25
108	A34	20c black	4.75	2.00
		Nos. 103-108 (5)	21.10	10.45

The stamps of this issue are found with perforations of various gauges, also sewing machine perforation, all of which are unofficial. See Nos. 112, 114-115.

Liberty Head — A37

1881   Imperf.

109	A37	1c blk, *green*	3.50	5.00
110	A37	2c blk, *lilac rose*	3.50	5.00
111	A37	5c blk, *lilac*	8.50	1.75
		Nos. 109-111 (3)	15.50	11.75

Nos. 109 to 111 are found with regular or sewing machine perforation, unofficial.

Reprints:

1c — The top line of the stamp and the top frame extend to the left. 2c — There is a curved line over the scroll below the "AV" of "CENTAVOS."

5c — There are scratches across the "5" in the upper left corner. All three values were reprinted on the three colors of paper of the originals.

A37a

Redrawn

1 centavo — The period before "UNION" is square and the rays between the stars and the condor have been wholly or partly erased.

2 centavos — The "2's" and "C's" in the corners are placed diagonally.

5 centavos — The last star at the right touches the wing of the condor.

10 centavos — The letters of the inscription are thick; there are no rays under the stars; the last star at the right touches the wing of the condor and this wing touches the frame.

1883   Imperf.

112	A34	1c green	4.75	4.25
113	A37a	2c rose	2.10	1.75
114	A34	5c blue	4.00	1.00
a.		5c ultramarine	4.00	1.00
b.		Printed on both sides, reverse ultra	25.00	20.00
115	A36	10c violet	5.00	1.40
		Nos. 112-115 (4)	15.85	8.40

The stamps of this issue are found with regular or sewing machine perforation, privately applied.

A38   A39

1883   Perf. 10½, 12, 13½

116	A38	1c gray grn, *grn*	1.00	1.00
a.		Imperf., pair	5.00	5.00
117	A39	2c red, *rose*	1.00	1.25
a.		2c org red, *rose*	1.00	1.25
b.		2c red, *buff*	12.00	12.00
c.		Imperf., pair (#117 or 117a)	7.75	7.75
d.		"DE LOS" in very small caps	15.00	15.00
118	A38	5c blue, *bluish*	2.50	1.50
a.		5c dk bl, *bluish*	2.50	1.90
b.		5c blue	3.25	2.50
c.		Imperf., pair (#118 or 118a)	7.75	7.75
d.		As "b," imperf., pair	12.00	12.00
119	A39	10c org, *yel*	1.25	1.40
a.		"DE LOS" in large caps	60.00	26.00
b.		Imperf., pair	16.00	16.00
120	A39	20c vio, *lilac*	1.40	1.40
a.		Imperf., pair	16.00	16.00
122	A38	50c brn, *buff*	3.00	3.25
a.		Perf. 12	3.00	3.25
123	A38	1p claret, *bluish*	5.50	1.90
a.		Imperf., pair	16.00	16.00
		Nos. 116-123 (7)	15.65	11.70

Redrawn Types of 1877

1883 (?)   Perf. 10½, 12

125	A25	5p orange brown	10.00	6.00
126	A26	10p black, *gray*	10.00	7.25

1886   Perf. 10½, 11½, 12

127	A38	5p brown, *straw*	10.00	5.50
a.		Imperf., pair	32.50	32.50
128	A38	10p black, *rose*	10.00	5.50
a.		Imperf., pair	32.50	32.50

Republic of Colombia

A40   Simón Bolívar — A41

Pres. Rafael Núñez — A42

1886   Perf. 10½ and 13½

129	A40	1c grn, *grn*	1.75	.70
a.		Imperf., pair	6.75	6.75
130	A41	5c blue, *bl*	1.75	.40
a.		5c ultra, *blue*	1.75	.40
b.		Imperf., pair (#130)	6.75	6.75
131	A42	10c orange	3.50	.70
a.		Imperf., pair	9.25	9.25
b.		Pelure paper	4.50	1.00
		Nos. 129-131 (3)	7.00	1.80

Gen. Antonio
Jose de Sucre
Alcala — A43

Gen. Antonio
Nariño — A44

1887

133	A43	2c org red, *rose*	2.25	1.00
a.		2c orange red, *yellowish*	6.00	6.00
b.		2c orange red	7.25	7.25
c.		Imperf., pair (#133)	10.00	10.00
134	A44	20c pur, *grysh*	3.00	1.10
a.		Imperf., pair	8.50	8.50
b.		Pelure paper	3.50	2.25

Impressions of No. 134 on white, blue or greenish blue paper were not regularly issued.

Arms — A45

1888

135	A45	50c brn, *buff*	1.75	*1.90*
a.		Imperf., pair	6.00	6.00
136	A45	1p claret, *bluish*	8.00	2.10
137	A45	1p claret	3.50	1.60
138	A45	5p org brn	8.50	6.50
139	A45	5p black	14.50	9.50
140	A45	10p black, *rose*	21.00	6.75
		Nos. 135-140 (6)	57.25	28.35

See Nos. 155, 158-159.

Nariño — A46

1889

141	A46	20c pur, *grayish*	1.90	1.25
a.		Imperf., pair	9.25	9.25

Impressions on white, blue or greenish blue paper were not regularly issued.

A47

A48

A49

A50

A51

1890-91   *Perf. 10½, 13½, 11*

142	A47	1c grn, *grn*	1.90	1.60
143	A48	2c org red, *rose*	.95	.95
144	A49	5c bl, *grnsh bl*	1.40	.40
a.		5c deep blue, *blue*	1.40	.40
b.		Imperf., pair	5.50	5.50
146	A50	10c brn, *yel*	1.00	.40
a.		10c brown, *buff*	1.00	.40
147	A51	20c vio, pelure paper	3.50	*3.50*
		Nos. 142-147 (5)	8.75	6.85

A52

A52a

A53

A53a

A54

Perf. 10½, 12, 13½, 14 to 15½

1892-99   Ordinary Paper

148	A47	1c red, *yel*	.85	.40
149	A52	2c red, *rose*	42.50	42.50
150	A52	2c green	.50	.30
a.		2c yellow green	.50	.30
151	A49	5c blk, *buff*	13.00	.35
152	A52a	5c org brn, *pale buff*	1.00	.30
a.		5c red brown, *salmon* ('97)	1.00	.30
153	A50	10c bis brn, *rose*	.75	.40
		10c brown, *brownish*	2.00	1.60
154	A53	20c brn, *bl*	.75	.40
a.		20c red brown, *blue*	.75	.40
b.		20c yel brn, *grnsh bl* ('97)	5.50	13.00
c.		20c brown, *buff* ('97)	19.00	13.00
155	A45	50c vio, *vio*	1.25	.75
156	A53a	50c red vio, *vio* ('99)	1.75	
157	A54	1p bl, *grnsh*	2.10	.90
a.		1p blue, *buff*	2.10	.90
158	A45	5p red, *pale rose*	8.50	3.25
159	A45	10p blue	16.00	3.25
a.		Thin, pale rose paper	27.50	7.25
		Nos. 148-159 (12)	88.95	
		Nos. 148-155,157-159 (11)	52.80	

Type A53a is a redrawing of type A45. The letters of the inscriptions are slightly larger and the numerals "50" slightly smaller than in type A45.

The 20c brown on white paper is believed to be a chemical changeling.

Nos. 148, 150-152a, 153-155, 157, 159 exist imperf. Value per pair, $6-9.

A56

1899

162	A56	1c red, *yellow*	.70	.35
163	A56	5c red brn, *sal*	.70	.35
164	A56	10c brn, *lil rose*	2.00	.95
165	A56	50c blue, *lilac*	1.40	1.25
		Nos. 162-165 (4)	4.80	2.90

Cartagena Issues

A57

1899   Blue Overprint   *Imperf.*

167	A57	5c red, *buff*	30.00	30.00
a.		Sewing machine perf.	30.00	30.00
168	A57	10c ultra, *buff*	30.00	30.00
a.		Sewing machine perf.	30.00	30.00

Nos. 167 and 167a differ slightly from the illustration.

Bolivar No. 55 Overprinted with 7 Parallel Wavy Lines and

A58

A59

A60

A61

Perf. 14 (#169), Sewing Machine Perf.

1899   Purple Overprint

169	A18	1c black	60.00	60.00
170	A58	1c brn, *buff*	20.00	20.00
a.		Altered from 10c	30.00	30.00
171	A59	2c blk, *buff*	20.00	20.00
a.		Altered from 10c	30.00	30.00
172	A60	5c mar, *grnsh bl*	18.00	18.00
a.		Perf. 12	18.00	18.00
b.		Without overprint	10.50	10.50
173	A61	10c red, *sal*	18.00	18.00
a.		Perf. 12	18.00	18.00
		Nos. 169-173 (5)	136.00	136.00

Types A58 and A59 illustrate Nos. 170a and 171a, which were made from altered plates of the 10c (No. 168). Nos. 170 and 171 were made from altered plate of the 5c denomination (No. 167), show part of the top flag of the "5" and differ slightly from the illustrations.

Nos. 170-173 exist imperf. Values about same as perf.

A62

1900   Purple Overprint   *Imperf.*

174	A62	5c red	25.00	25.00
a.		Perf. 12	35.00	35.00

A63

A64

"Gobierno Provisorio" at Top

1900   Litho.   *Perf. 12 Vertically*

175	A63	1c (ctvo) blk, *bl grn*	47.50	8.00
a.		"cvo."	120.00	14.50
b.		"cvos."	47.50	8.00
c.		"centavo"	55.00	47.50
176	A63	2c black	26.00	6.00
177	A63	5c blk, *pink*	26.00	6.00
a.		Name at side (V)	62.50	9.00
178	A63	10c blk, *pink*	26.00	6.00
a.		Name at side (V)	62.50	9.00
179	A63	20c blk, *yellow*	47.50	8.00
a.		Name at side (G)	92.50	12.00
		Nos. 175-179 (5)	173.00	34.00

"Gobierno Provisional" at Top Name at Side in Black or Green

1900

180	A64	1c (ctvo.) blk, *bl grn*	47.50	8.00
a.		"centavo"	125.00	47.50
181	A64	2c blk, *bl grn*	30.00	5.00
182	A64	5c blk (G)	30.00	5.00
a.		"ctvos." smaller	47.50	9.00
183	A64	10c blk, *pink*	30.00	5.00
184	A64	20c blk, *yel* (G)	47.50	8.00
		Nos. 180-184 (5)	185.00	31.00

Issues of the rebel provisional government in Cucuta.

A65

A66

Purple Overprint

1901   *Sewing Machine Perf.*

185	A65	1c black	1.00	1.00
a.		Without overprint	2.25	2.25
b.		Double overprint	2.50	2.50
c.		Imperf., pair	2.50	2.50
d.		Inverted overprint	1.25	1.25
186	A66	2c blk, *rose*	1.00	1.00
a.		Imperf., pair	2.50	2.50
b.		Without overprint	2.25	2.25
c.		Double overprint	2.50	2.50

A67

A68

1901   Rose Overprint

187	A67	1c blue	1.00	1.00
a.		Imperf., pair	4.00	4.00
188	A68	2c brown	1.00	1.00
a.		Imperf., pair	4.00	4.00
b.		Without overprint	1.00	1.00

A69

A70

Sewing Machine or Regular Perf. 12, 12½

1902   Magenta Overprint

189	A69	5c violet	2.25	2.25
a.		Without overprint	2.25	2.25
b.		Double overprint	2.25	2.25
c.		Imperf., pair	4.75	4.75
190	A70	10c yel brn	2.25	2.25
a.		Double overprint	2.25	2.25
b.		Imperf., pair	4.75	4.75
c.		Without overprint	2.25	2.25
d.		Printed on both sides	3.25	3.25

A71

A72

1902   Magenta Overprint

191	A71	5c yel brn	2.25	2.25
a.		Without overprint	2.10	2.10
b.		Imperf., pair	6.00	6.00
192	A71	10c black	1.75	1.75
a.		Without overprint	1.50	1.50
b.		Imperf., pair	9.00	9.00
193	A72	20c maroon	5.50	4.50
b.		Imperf., pair	15.00	15.00
		Nos. 191-193 (3)	9.50	8.50

Nos. 191-193 exist tête bêche. Value of 10c and 20c, each $15.

Washed examples of Nos. 167-174, 185-193 are offered as "without overprint."

Barranquilla Issues

Magdalena
River — A75

Iron Quay at
Sabanilla — A76

La Popa
Hill — A77

1902-03   *Imperf.*

194	A75	2c green	1.60	1.60
195	A75	2c dk bl	1.60	1.60
196	A75	2c rose	22.50	22.50
197	A76	10c scarlet	1.10	1.10
198	A76	10c orange	13.00	13.00
199	A76	10c rose	1.75	1.75
200	A76	10c maroon	1.90	1.90
201	A76	10c claret	1.90	1.90
202	A77	20c violet	3.50	3.50
a.		Laid paper		9.50
203	A77	20c dl bl	9.50	9.50
204	A77	20c dl bl, *pink*	125.00	125.00
205	A77	20c car rose	20.00	20.00
		Nos. 194-205 (12)	203.35	203.35

Sewing Machine Perf. and Perf. 12

194a	A75	2c green	9.50	9.50
195a	A75	2c dark blue	9.50	9.50
196a	A75	2c carmine	47.50	47.50
197a	A76	10c scarlet	4.75	4.75
198a	A76	10c orange	35.00	35.00
199a	A76	10c rose	6.50	6.50
200a	A76	10c maroon	6.50	6.50
201a	A76	10c claret	6.00	6.00
202b	A77	20c purple	.70	.70
c.		20c lilac	.70	.70
203a	A77	20c dull blue	9.50	9.50
204a	A77	20c dull blue, *rose*	150.00	150.00
205b	A77	20c carmine rose	72.50	72.50
		Nos. 194a-205b (12)	357.95	357.95

See Nos. 240-245.

Cruiser
"Cartagena" — A78

Bolívar — A79

General Próspero
Pinzón — A80

A81   A82

1903-04   *Imperf.*

209	A78	5c blue	2.75	2.75
210	A79	5c bister	4.50	4.50
211	A79	50c yellow	3.75	3.75
212	A79	50c green	4.50	4.50
213	A79	50c scarlet	4.50	4.50
214	A79	50c carmine	4.50	4.50
a.		50c rose	4.50	4.50
215	A79	50c pale brown	4.50	4.50
216	A80	1p yellow brn	1.60	1.60
217	A80	1p rose	2.50	2.50
218	A80	1p blue	2.50	2.50
219	A80	1p violet	25.00	25.00
220	A81	5p claret	5.50	5.50
221	A81	5p pale brown	8.00	8.00
222	A81	5p blue green	7.50	7.50
223	A82	10p pale green	7.75	7.75
224	A82	10p claret	25.00	25.00
		Nos. 209-224 (16)	114.35	114.35

Nos. 216 and 217 measure 20½x26½mm
and No. 218, 18x24mm. Stamps of this issue
exist with forged perforations.

Perf. 12

209a	A78	5c blue	9.50	9.50
210a	A78	5c bister	9.50	9.50
211a	A79	50c yellow	9.50	9.50
b.		50c orange	25.00	25.00
212a	A79	50c green	25.00	25.00
213a	A79	50c scarlet	11.50	11.50
214a	A79	50c rose	11.50	11.50

215a	A79	50c pale brown	11.50	11.50
216a	A80	1p yellow brown	5.25	5.25
217a	A80	1p rose	7.50	7.50
218a	A80	1p blue	9.50	9.50
219a	A80	1p violet	62.50	62.50
220a	A81	5p claret	20.00	20.00
221a	A81	5p pale brown	22.50	22.50
222a	A81	5p blue green	22.50	22.50
223a	A82	10p pale green	30.00	30.00
224a	A82	10p claret	77.50	77.50
		Nos. 209a-224a (16)	345.25	343.25

Laid Paper   *Imperf.*

240	A76	10c dk bl, *lil*	6.25	6.25
241	A76	10c dk bl, *bluish*	3.75	3.75
242	A76	10c dk bl, *brn*	3.75	3.75
243	A76	10c dk bl, *sal*	9.25	9.25
244	A76	10c dk bl, *grnsh bl*	5.00	5.00
245	A76	10c dk bl, *dp rose*	3.75	3.75
		Nos. 240-245 (6)	31.75	31.75

Perf. 12

240a	A76	10c dk bl, *lilac*	13.50	13.50
241a	A76	10c dk bl, *bluish*	9.25	9.25
242a	A76	10c dk bl, *brn*	9.25	9.25
243a	A76	10c dk bl, *salmon*	72.50	72.50
244a	A76	10c dk bl, *grnsh bl*	20.00	20.00
245a	A76	10c dk bl, *deep rose*	9.25	9.25
		Nos. 240a-245a (6)	133.75	133.75

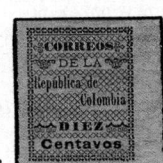

A82a

Imperf., Sewing Machine Perf.

1902   **Typeset**

255	A82a	10c black, *rose*	3.50	3.50
256	A82a	20c blk, *orange*	2.50	2.50

This issue was printed in either Cali or
Popayan.

Medellin Issue

A83

1902

257	A83	1c grn, *straw*	.35	.50
258	A83	2c salmon, *rose*	.35	.50
259	A83	5c dp bl, *grnsh*	.35	.50
260	A83	10c pale brn, *straw*	.35	.50
261	A83	20c pur, *rose*	.45	.50
262	A83	50c dl rose, *grnsh*	2.25	3.00
263	A83	1p blk, *yellow*	4.50	6.75
264	A83	5p slate, *blue*	35.00	35.00
265	A83	10p dk brn, *rose*	22.50	22.50
		Nos. 257-265 (9)	66.10	69.75

For overprint see No. L8.

Imperf., Pairs

257a	A83	1c	11.00	11.00
258a	A83	2c	11.00	11.00
259a	A83	5c	11.00	11.00
260a	A83	10c	11.00	11.00
261a	A83	20c	11.00	11.00
262a	A83	50c	11.00	11.00
263a	A83	1p	27.50	27.50
264a	A83	5p	80.00	80.00
265a	A83	10p	50.00	50.00

Regular Issue

A84   A85

A86   A87

A88   A89

A90   A91

A92

1902   *Imperf.*

266	A84	2c blk, *rose*	.25	.25
267	A85	4c red, *grn*	.25	.25
268	A86	5c grn, *grn*	.25	.25
269	A87	10c blk, *pink*	.25	.25
c.		10c blk, rose	1.10	1.10
270	A88	20c brn, *buff*	.25	.25
271	A89	50c dk grn, *rose*	1.40	1.40
272	A90	1p pur, *buff*	.60	.60
273	A91	5p grn, *bl*	4.25	4.25
274	A92	10p grn, *pale grn*	13.00	6.50
		Nos. 266-274 (9)	20.50	14.00

For overprint see No. H4.

Sewing Machine Perf.

266a	A84	2c blk, *rose*	1.90	1.90
267a	A85	4c red, *grn*	1.60	1.60
268a	A86	5c grn, *grn*	1.90	1.90
269a	A87	10c blk, *pink*	1.90	1.90
270a	A88	20c brn, *buff*	3.25	2.50
271a	A89	50c dk grn, *rose*	6.50	5.25
272a	A90	1p pur, *buff*	7.75	6.50
273a	A91	5p grn, *blue*	35.00	35.00
274a	A92	10p grn, *pale grn*	65.00	65.00
		Nos. 266a-274a (9)	124.80	121.55

1903   **Perf. 12**

266b	A84	2c blk, *rose*	1.40	1.40
269b	A87	10c blk, *pink*	1.60	1.60
270b	A88	20c brn, *buff*	1.60	1.60
272b	A90	1p pur, *buff*	3.25	3.25
273b	A91	5p grn, *blue*	27.50	27.50
274b	A92	10p grn, *pale grn*	52.50	45.00
		Nos. 266b-274b (6)	87.85	80.35

1903   *Imperf.*

284	A85	4c blue, *grn*	.35	.35
285	A86	5c blue, *blue*	.35	.35
286	A88	20c blue, *buff*	.35	.35
288	A89	50c blue, *rose*	1.75	1.75
		Nos. 284-288 (4)	2.80	2.80

Sewing Machine Perf.

284a	A85	4c blue, *grn*	2.25	1.75
285a	A86	5c blue, *blue*	2.25	1.75
286a	A88	20c blue, *buff*	3.25	2.50
288a	A89	50c blue, *rose*	6.50	5.75
		Nos. 284a-288a (4)	14.25	11.75

Perf. 12

284b	A85	4c blue, *grn*	2.50	2.50
285b	A86	5c blue, *blue*	2.50	2.50
286b	A88	20c blue, *buff*	3.50	3.50
288b	A89	50c blue, *rose*	9.75	9.75
		Nos. 284b-288b (4)	18.25	18.25

A93

1904   **Pelure Paper**   *Imperf.*

303	A93	½c yellow brn	1.10	1.10
304	A90	1c blue green	1.10	1.10
a.		1c yellow green	1.10	1.10
306	A84	2c blue	.90	.65
307	A86	5c carmine	1.00	1.00
308	A87	10c violet	1.10	.90
		Nos. 303-308 (5)	5.20	4.75

For overprint see No. H13.

1904   **Perf. 13**

303a	A93	½c yellow brown	4.25	4.25
304b	A90	1c blue green	5.50	5.00
c.		1c yellow green	7.50	7.00
306a	A84	2c blue	2.50	2.50

Perf. 12

307a	A86	5c carmine	2.25	2.25
308a	A87	10c violet	2.25	2.25
		Nos. 303a-308a (5)	16.75	16.25

A94   A95

Pres. José Manuel
Marroquín — A96

**Imprint: "Lit. J.L.Arango Medellin.
Col."**

1904   **Wove Paper**   **Perf. 12**

314	A94	½c yellow	.85	.25
315	A94	1c green	.85	.25
316	A94	2c rose	.85	.25
317	A94	5c blue	1.40	.25
318	A94	10c violet	1.75	.25
319	A94	20c black	1.75	.25
320	A95	1p brown	19.00	3.00
321	A96	5p red & blk, *yel*	60.00	60.00
322	A96	10p bl & blk, *grnsh*	60.00	60.00
		Nos. 314-322 (9)	146.45	124.50

Redrawn

314a	A94	½c	.85	.25
315a	A94	1c	.85	.25
316a	A94	2c	.85	.25
317a	A94	5c	1.40	.25
319a	A94	20c	1.75	.25
		Nos. 314a-319a (5)	5.70	1.25

Imperf., Pairs

314b	A94	½c	3.25	3.25
315b	A94	1c	2.50	2.50
316b	A94	2c	3.25	3.25
317b	A94	5c	3.25	3.25
318a	A94	10c	4.25	4.25
319b	A94	20c	7.75	7.75
320a	A95	1p	65.00	65.00
		Nos. 314b-320a (7)	89.25	89.25

On the redrawn types, the imprint is close to
the base of the design instead of being spaced
from it. On the redrawn 2c and 5c, the lower
end of the vertical white line below "OR" of
"CORREOS" forms a hook which turns to the
right instead of to the left as in the originals.
See Nos. 325-330. For surcharges see Nos.
351-354, L1-L7, L9-L13, L15-L25.

A97

100p has different frame.

1903   *Imperf.*

323	A97	50p org yel, *pale pink*	92.50	92.50
324	A97	100p dk bl, *dk rose*	77.50	77.50

Imprint: "Lit. Nacional"

Perf. 10, 13, 13½ and Compound

1908

325	A94	½c orange	.85	.25
a.		½c yellow	.85	.25
b.		Imperf., pair	2.50	1.90
b.		Without imprint	5.25	5.25
326	A94	1c yel grn	.75	.25
a.		Without imprint	.75	.25
d.		Imperf., pair	4.00	3.25
327	A94	2c red	.75	.25
a.		2c carmine	.75	.25
b.		Imperf., pair	4.00	3.25
328	A94	5c blue	.60	.25
a.		Imperf., pair	4.25	5.25

329	A94	10c violet	50.00	1.00
330	A94	20c gray blk	50.00	1.00
		Nos. 325-330 (6)	102.95	3.00

The above stamps may be easily distinguished from those of 1904 by the perforation, by the height of the design, 24mm instead of 23mm, and by the "Lit. Nacional" imprint.

Camilo Torres
A99

Policarpa
Salavarrieta
A100

Bolívar Demanding
Liberation of
Slaves — A105

Designs: 2c, Nariño. 5c, Bolívar. 10c, Francisco José de Caldas. 20c, Francisco de Paula Santander. 10p, Bolívar Resigning.

1910, Aug.		**Engr.**		***Perf. 12***
331	A99	½c violet & blk	.50	.30
a.		Center inverted	425.00	425.00
332	A100	1c deep green	.40	.25
333	A100	2c scarlet	.40	.25
334	A100	5c deep blue	1.25	.45
335	A100	10c plum	10.00	5.00
336	A100	20c black brn	15.00	5.50
337	A105	1p dk violet	85.00	25.00
338	A105	10p claret	325.00	250.00
		Nos. 331-338 (8)	437.55	286.75

Colombian independence centenary.

Caldas
A107

Monument to
Battle of
Boyacá
A113

View of
Cartagena
A114

Coat of Arms
A118

Designs: 1c, Torres. 2c, Narino. 4c, Santander. 5c, Bolivar. 10c, Jose Maria Cordoba. 1p, Sucre. 2p, Rufino Cuervo. 5p, Antonio Ricaurte y Lozano.

1917		**Engr.**		***Perf. 14***
339	A107	½c bister	.35	.25
340	A107	1c green	.30	.25
341	A107	2c car rose	.30	.25
342	A107	4c violet	.90	.30
343	A107	5c dull blue	3.00	.25
344	A107	10c gray	3.00	.25
345	A113	20c red	1.50	.25
346	A114	50c carmine	1.75	.25
347	A107	1p brt blue	12.00	.40
348	A107	2p orange	13.50	.45
349	A107	5p gray	40.00	11.00
350	A118	10p dk brown	47.50	11.50
		Nos. 339-350 (12)	124.10	25.40

The 1c, 5c, 10c, 50c, 2p, 5p and 10p also exist perf. 11½ and 11½ compounded with 14.

Litho. varieties of Nos. 343, 345 and 346 are counterfeits made to defraud the government. Imperforate examples of Nos. 339-350 are not known to have been regularly issued.

See Nos. 373-374, 400-405. For overprints and surcharges see Nos. 369-370, 377, 409-410, 440, C1, O3, O5-O9.

Nos. 318-319, 329-330
Surcharged in Red

1918			**On Issue of 1904**	
351	A94	½c on 20c black	1.25	.35
352	A94	3c on 10c violet	3.00	.60
		On Issue of 1908		
353	A94	½c on 20c gray blk	10.00	6.25
354	A94	3c on 10c violet	15.00	5.00
		Nos. 351-354 (4)	29.25	12.20

Nos. 351-354 inclusive exist with surcharge reading up or down. On one stamp in each sheet the letter "S" in "Especie" is omitted. All denominations exist with a small zero before the decimal in the surcharge.

A119

1918		**Litho.**		***Perf. 13½***
358	A119	3c red	.95	.25
a.		Imperf., pair	5.00	5.00

A120

1920		**Engr.**		***Perf. 14***
359	A120	3c red, org	.40	.25
a.		Imperf., pair	3.75	3.75

See No. 371-372. For surcharge see No. 453.

A121

A122

A123

Perf. 10, 13½ and Compound				
1920-21				**Litho.**
360	A121	½c yellow	1.40	.50
361	A121	1c green	.85	.25
362	A121	2c red	.65	.25
363	A122	3c green	.65	.25
a.		3c yellow green	.65	.25
364	A121	5c blue	1.25	.25
365	A121	10c violet	6.00	1.50
366	A121	20c deep green	6.75	4.00
367	A123	50c dark red	8.50	4.00
		Nos. 360-367 (8)	26.05	11.00

The tablet with "PROVISIONAL" was added separately to each design on the various lithographic stones and its position varies slightly on different stamps in the sheet. For some values there were two or more stones, on which the tablet was placed at various angles. Nos. 360-366 exist imperf.
See No. 375.

No. 342 Surcharged in Red

a

(15mm wide)
— b

1921				
369	A107	(a) 3c on 4c violet	.95	.25
a.		Double surcharge	15.00	
370	A107	(b) 3c on 4c violet	3.75	2.00
		See No. 377.		

Types of 1917-21

1923-24		**Engr.**		***Perf. 13½***
371	A120	1½c chocolate	1.25	.60
372	A120	3c blue	.50	.25
373	A107	5c claret ('24)	3.00	.25
374	A107	10c blue	9.25	.50
		Litho.		
375	A121	10c dark blue	12.50	7.25
		Nos. 371-375 (5)	26.50	8.85

No. 342 Surcharged in Red

(18mm wide)

1924				
377	A107	3c on 4c vio	3.75	1.50
a.		Double surcharge	15.00	
b.		Double surch., one invtd.	15.00	
c.		With added surch. "3cs." in red		

A124

1924-25		**Litho.**	***Perf. 10, 10x13½***	
379	A124	1c red	.85	.25
380	A124	3c dp blue ('25)	.85	.25

Exist imperf. Value, each pair $6.25.

A125

A126

Black, Red or Green Srch. & Ovpt.
Imprint of Waterlow & Sons

1925			***Perf. 14, 14½***	
382	A125	1c on 3c bis brn	.70	.25
383	A126	4c violet (R)	.50	.25
a.		Inverted surcharge	8.75	8.75

Imprint of American Bank Note Co.
Perf. 12

384	A125	1c on 3c bis brn	7.50	6.25
a.		Inverted surcharge	19.00	19.00
385	A126	4c violet (G)	.50	.30
a.		Inverted overprint	9.50	9.50
		Nos. 382-385 (4)	9.20	7.05

Correos
Provisional

Revenue stamps of basic types A125 and A126 were handstamped as above in violet or blue by the Cali post office in 1925, but were not authorized by the government. Denominations so overprinted are 1c, 2c, 3c, 4c and 5c.

A127

A128

Perf. 10, 13½x10

1926		**Litho.**	**Wmk. 194**	
395	A127	1c gray green	.50	.25
396	A128	4c deep blue	.55	.25

Exist imperf. Value, each pair $5.

Types of 1917 and

Sabana
Station — A129

1926-29		**Unwmk. Engr.**	***Perf. 14***	
400	A107	4c deep blue	.50	.25
401	A118	8c dark blue	.60	.25
402	A107	30c olive bister	6.00	.70
403	A129	40c brn & yel brn	9.25	1.25
404	A107	5p violet	9.25	.90
a.		Perf. 11 ('29)	12.00	1.00
405	A118	10p green	15.00	2.50
a.		Perf. 11 ('29)	30.00	4.75
		Nos. 400-405 (6)	40.60	5.85

For surcharges & overprint see Nos. 409-410, O4.

Death of
Bolívar
A130

1930, Dec. 17			***Perf. 12½***	
408	A130	4c dk blue & blk	.60	.35

Cent. of the death of Simón Bolívar. See Nos. C80-C82.

Nos. 400 and 402
Surcharged in Red or
Dark Blue

1932, Jan. 20			***Perf. 14***	
409	A107	1c on 4c dp bl (R)	.30	.25
a.		Inverted surcharge	5.25	5.25
410	A107	20c on 30c ol bis	10.00	.70
a.		Inverted surcharge	21.00	
b.		Double surcharge	21.00	

Emerald
Mine — A131

Oil
Wells — A132

Coffee Cultivation
A133

Platinum
Mine — A134

Gold
Mining — A135

Christopher
Columbus — A136

**Imprint: "Waterlow & Sons Ltd.
Londres"**

1932		Wmk. 229	Perf. 12½	
411	A131	1c green	.60	.25
412	A132	2c red	.60	.25
413	A133	5c brown	.70	.25
414	A134	8c blue blk	4.75	.60
415	A135	10c yellow	3.50	.25
416	A136	20c dk blue	10.00	.40
		Nos. 411-416 (6)	20.15	2.00

See Nos. 441-442, 464-466a, 517. For surcharges see Nos. 455, 527, O1, O10-O11, O13, RA30.

Pedro de
Heredia — A137

Perf. 11½

1934, Jan. 10		Unwmk.	Litho.	
417	A137	1c dark green	3.00	.80
418	A137	5c chocolate	3.75	.65
419	A137	8c dark blue	3.00	.80
		Nos. 417-419 (3)	9.75	2.25

Cartagena, 400th anniv. See Nos. C111-C114.

Coffee
Picking — A138

1934, Dec.		Engr.	Perf. 12	
420	A138	5c brown	3.00	.25

Soccer — A139   Condor — A145

Allegory of Olympic Games at
Barranquilla — A140

Foot Race
A141

Tennis
A142

Pier at
Puerto
Colombia
A143

View of the
Bay
A144

Designs: 4c, Discus Thrower. 10c, Hurdling. 15c, Athlete in stadium. 18c, Baseball. 24c, Swimming. 50c, View of Barranquilla. 1p, Post and Telegraph Building. 2p, Monument to Flag. 5p, Coat of Arms.

1935, Jan. 26		Litho.	Perf. 11½	
421	A139	2c bluish grn & buff	1.60	.50
422	A139	4c deep green	1.60	.50
423	A140	5c dk brn & yel	1.60	.50
a.		Horiz. pair, imperf. btwn.	240.00	
424	A141	7c dk carmine	3.00	1.75
425	A142	8c blk & pink	2.50	2.50
426	A141	10c brown & bl	3.50	1.75
427	A143	12c indigo	4.25	3.00
428	A141	15c bl & red brn	7.25	5.50
429	A141	18c dk vio & buff	10.00	8.25
430	A144	20c purple & grn	8.50	7.00
431	A144	24c bluish grn & ultra	8.50	6.75
432	A144	50c ultra & buff	13.00	10.00
433	A144	1p drab & blue	120.00	62.50
434	A145	2p dull grn & gray	140.00	110.00
435	A145	5p pur blk & bl	475.00	500.00
436	A145	10p black & gray	550.00	575.00
		Nos. 421-436 (16)	1,350.	1,296.

3rd Natl. Olympic Games, Barranquilla. Counterfeits of 10p exist.

Oil
Wells — A155   Gold
Mining — A157

Imprint: "American Bank Note Co."

1935, Mar.		Unwmk. Engr.	Perf. 12	
437	A155	2c carmine rose	.45	.25
439	A157	10c deep orange	25.00	.25

See Nos. 468, 470, 498, 516. For surcharge and overprints see Nos. 496, 596, O2.

No. 347 Surcharged in
Black

1935, Aug.			Perf. 14	
440	A107	12c on 1p brt bl	4.75	1.50

**Types of 1932
Imprint: "Lit. Nacional Bogotá"**

1935-36		Litho.	Perf. 11, 11½, 12½	
441	A131	1c lt green	.25	.25
a.		Imperf., pair	4.25	
442	A133	5c brown ('36)	.70	.25
a.		Imperf., pair	4.75	4.00

For overprints and surcharges, see Nos. 527, O1.

Bolívar
A159   Tequendama
Falls
A160

Wmk. Wavy Lines. (229)

1937		Engr.	Perf. 12½	
443	A159	1c deep green	.25	.25
a.		Perf. 14	.25	.25
444	A160	12c deep blue	3.25	1.10

See No. 570. For surcharges and overprints see Nos. 454, 456, C231, C326, O12.

Soccer Player
A161   Discus
Thrower
A162

Runner — A163

1937, Jan. 4		Photo.	Unwmk.	
445	A161	3c lt green	1.40	.85
446	A162	10c carmine rose	3.75	1.75
447	A163	1p black	35.00	26.00
		Nos. 445-447 (3)	40.15	28.60

National Olympic Games, Manizales. For surcharge see No. 452.

Exposition
Palace — A164

Stadium at
Barranquilla
A165   Monument to
the Colors
A166

1937, Jan. 4				
448	A164	5c violet brown	2.75	.40
449	A165	15c blue	6.75	4.50
450	A166	50c orange brn	19.00	9.75
		Nos. 448-450 (3)	28.50	14.65

Barranquilla National Exposition.

Stamps of 1926-37
Surcharged in Black

1937-38		Unwmk.	Perf. 12½	
452	A161	1c on 3c lt grn	1.00	1.00
a.		Inverted surcharge	2.25	2.25
453	A118	5c on 8c dk bl	.50	.45
a.		Inverted surcharge	2.25	2.25

Wmk. 229

454	A160	2c on 12c dp bl	.50	.40
455	A134	5c on 8c bl blk	.60	.65
a.		Invtd. surcharge	2.00	2.00
456	A160	10c on 12c dp bl ('38)	5.50	1.00
a.		Dbl. surcharge	11.00	11.00
		Nos. 452-456 (5)	8.10	3.50

Calle del
Arco — A168   Entrance to
Church of the
Rosary — A169

Arms of Bogotá
A170   Gonzálo
Jiménez de
Quesada
A171

Bochica
A172   Santo Domingo
Convent
A173

Mass of the Conquistadors — A174

1938, July 27		Unwmk.	Perf. 12½	
457	A168	1c yellow green	.25	.25
458	A169	2c scarlet	.25	.25
459	A170	5c brown blk	.35	.25
460	A171	10c brown	.75	.40
461	A172	15c brt blue	3.75	1.60
462	A173	20c brt red vio	3.75	1.60
463	A174	1p red brown	50.00	29.00
		Nos. 457-463 (7)	59.10	33.35

Bogotá, 400th anniversary.

**Types of 1932
Imprint: "Litografía Nacional
Bogotá"**

1938, Dec. 5		Litho.	Perf. 10½, 11	
464	A132	2c rose	1.00	.35
465	A135	10c yellow	2.50	.35
466	A136	20c dull blue	10.00	1.25
a.		20c dark blue, perf. 12½ ('44)	62.50	6.25
		Nos. 464-466 (3)	13.50	1.95

Types of 1935 and

Bolívar
A175   Coffee Picking
A176

Arms of
Colombia
A177   Christopher
Columbus
A178

Caldas
A179

Sabana Station
A180

Imprint: "American Bank Note Co."

Wmk. 255

1939, Mar. 3		**Engr.**	**Perf. 12**	
467	A175	1c green	.25	.25
468	A155	2c car rose	.25	.25
469	A176	5c dull brown	.25	.25
470	A157	10c deep orange	.50	.25
471	A177	15c dull blue	1.75	.25
472	A178	20c violet blk	19.00	.25
473	A179	30c olive bister	5.50	.35
474	A180	40c bister brn	17.00	3.75
	Nos. 467-474 (8)		44.50	5.60

See Nos. 497-499, 515, 518, 574. For surcharges and overprints see Nos. 506-507, 520-522, 596, RA26, RA47.

Gen.
Santander
A181

Allegory
A182

Gen.
Santander
A183

Statue at
Cúcuta
A184

Birthplace of
Santander
A185

Church at
Rosario
A186

Paya — A187

Bridge at
Boyacá — A188

Death of General
Santander
A189

Invasion of the
Liberators
A190

Perf. 13x13½, 13½x13

1940, May 6		**Engr.**	**Wmk. 229**	
475	A181	1c olive green	.25	.25
476	A182	2c dk carmine	.50	.35
477	A183	5c sepia	.25	.25
478	A184	8c carmine	1.75	1.75
479	A185	10c orange yel	.80	.60
480	A186	15c dark blue	2.10	1.40
481	A187	20c green	2.75	2.10
482	A188	50c violet	6.50	6.00

483	A189	1p deep rose	20.00	20.00
484	A190	2p orange	65.00	65.00
	Nos. 475-484 (10)		99.90	97.70

Death of General Francisco Santander, cent.

Tobacco Plant
A194

Gen.
Santander
A195

Garcia
Rovira — A196

R.
Galan — A197

Antonio Sucre — A198

1940-43	**Engr.**	**Wmk. 255**	**Perf. 12**	
488	A194	8c rose car & grn	1.25	.65
489	A195	15c dp blue ('43)	1.25	.25
490	A196	20c slate ('41)	4.75	.50
491	A197	40c brown bis ('41)	2.75	.50
492	A198	1p black	5.00	1.25
	Nos. 488-492 (5)		15.00	3.15

See Nos. 500, 554. For overprint see No. RA28.

Arms of
Palmira — A199

Unwmk.

1942, July 4		**Litho.**	**Perf. 11**	
493	A199	30c claret	5.50	.65

8th Natl. Agricultural Exposition, held at Palmira.

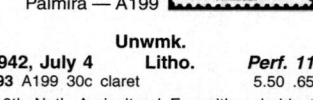

Paradise of
Isaacs,
Palmira — A200

1942, July 4

494	A200	50c lt blue grn	5.50	.85

Issued in honor of the writer, Jorge Isaacs.

Signing Treaty of
the Wisconsin
A201

1942, Nov. 21   **Perf. 10½**

495	A201	10c dull orange	3.75	.50
a.	"2. XI.1902" instead of "21. XI. 1902"		22.50	25.00
b.	Perf. 12		6.00	6.00

40th anniv. of the signing of the Treaty of the Wisconsin, Nov. 21, 1902.

No. 470 Surcharged
in Black

1944   **Wmk. 255**   **Perf. 12**

496	A157	5c on 10c dp org	.25	.25

Counterfeits exist of No. 496 with inverted or double surcharge.

Types of 1935-41 and

National
Shrine — A202

San Pedro
Alejandrino
A203

Imprint: "Columbian Bank Note Co."

1944-45	**Unwmk.**	**Engr.**	**Perf. 11**	
497	A175	1c green	.25	.25
498	A155	2c rose	.25	.25
499	A176	5c dull brown	.25	.25
500	A196	20c gray black	3.75	.75
501	A202	30c dl ol grn ('45)	2.25	1.25
502	A203	50c rose	2.25	1.25
	Nos. 497-502 (6)		9.00	4.00

No. 499
Surcharged in
Black

1944, Oct.

506	A176	1c on 5c dull brn	.25	.25
507	A176	2c on 5c dull brn	.25	.25

Nos. 506 and 507 exist with inverted or double surcharge, created by favor.

Flag — A204

Arms — A205

Murillo Toro — A206

Hospital of
St. John of
God
A207

Virrey Solis
A208

1944, Oct. 10   **Litho.**

508	A204	2c ultra & bis	.25	.25
a.	Sheet of 18		15.00	
b.	Imperf., pair		15.00	
509	A205	5c ultra & bis	.25	.25
a.	Sheet of 22		18.00	
b.	Imperf., pair		15.00	
510	A206	20c blk & bluish grn	.80	.80
a.	Sheet of 8		16.00	
b.	Imperf., pair		22.50	
511	A207	40c blk & red	3.50	3.50
a.	Sheet of 4		26.00	
512	A208	1p blk & red	9.50	9.50
a.	Sheet of 2		30.00	
	Nos. 508-512 (5)		14.30	14.30

Souvenir Sheet

Perf. 11x11½ All Around, Stamps Imperf.

513	Sheet of 5, #508-512	25.00	40.00
	Never hinged		40.00

75th anniv. of Gen. Benevolent Assoc. of Cundinamarca.

Nos. 508-513 were printed in composite sheets containing one each of Nos. 508a, 509a, 510a, 511a and 512a, and two of 513. Fifty of these were presented to government officials.

Murillo
Toro — A210

1944, Nov. 10   **Perf. 11**

514	A210	5c lt brown	.30	.25

Types of 1932-39 and

San Pedro
Alejandrino
A211

Imprint: "Litografia Nacional Bogota"

1944		**Litho.**	**Perf. 12½**	
515	A175	1c dp green	.25	.25
a.	1c olive green		.35	.25
b.	Imperf., pair		1.75	1.75
516	A155	2c dk carmine	.25	.25
a.	Imperf., pair		1.75	1.75
517	A135	10c yellow org	3.50	.45
518	A179	30c gray olive	12.00	1.75
a.	Imperf., pair		35.00	
519	A211	50c rose	12.00	5.25
	Nos. 515-519 (5)		28.00	7.95

No. 469
Overprinted in
Green, Blue or
Red

Wmk. 255

1945, July 19		**Engr.**	**Perf. 12**	
520	A176	5c dull brn (G)	.40	.25
521	A176	5c dull brn (R)	.40	.25
522	A176	5c dull brn (Bl)	.40	.25
	Nos. 520-522 (3)		1.20	.75

Portraits are Joseph Stalin, Franklin D. Roosevelt and Winston Churchill.
Nos. 520-522 exist with overprint inverted. Value, $20 each.

Clock Tower,
Cartagena — A212

1945, Nov. 15

523	A212	50c olive black	4.25	1.60

For overprints see Nos. 543-544.

Sierra Nevada of Santa Marta A213

Designs: 30c, Seaplane Tolima. 50c, San Sebastian Fort, Cartagena.

Unwmk.

			1945, Dec. 14	**Litho.**	**Perf. 11**
524	A213	20c light green	2.00	1.40
525	A213	30c pale blue	2.00	1.40
526	A213	50c salmon pink	2.00	1.40
		Nos. 524-526 (3)	6.00	4.20

25th anniv. of the 1st airmail service in America, according to the inscription, but earlier services are known to have existed.

No. 442 Surcharged in Black

			1946, Mar. 8	**Perf. 11x11½, 12½**
527	A133	1c on 5c brown	.25	.25
a.	Inverted surcharge		.90	

Gen. Antonio Jose de Sucre — A216

Wmk. 255

			1946, Apr. 16	**Engr.**	**Perf. 12**
		Size: 19x26½mm		
528	A216	1c brn & turq grn	.25	.25
529	A216	2c vio & rose car	.25	.25
		Size: 23x31mm		
530	A216	5c sepia & blue	.25	.25
531	A216	9c dk grn & red	.50	1.60
532	A216	10c ultra & org	.40	.50
533	A216	20c blk & dp org	.40	.50
534	A216	30c brn red & grn	.55	.35
535	A216	40c ol blk & red vio	.55	.40
536	A216	50c dp brn & vio	.55	.40
		Nos. 528-536 (9)	3.70	4.50

Map of South America — A217

Unwmk.

			1946, June 7	**Litho.**	**Perf. 11**
537	A217	15c ultra	.50	.50
a.	Imperf., pair		4.00	

National Observatory — A218

1946, Aug.

538	A218	5c fawn	.25	.25
a.	Imperf., pair		6.00	

See No. 565.

Andrés Bello — A219

Wmk. 255

			1946, Sept. 3	**Engr.**	**Perf. 12**
539	A219	3c sepia	.25	.25
540	A219	10c orange	.40	.35
541	A219	15c slate black	.45	.35
		Nos. 539-541,C145 (4)	1.35	1.20

Bello (1781-1865), poet and educator.

Joaquín de Cayzedo y Cuero — A220

			1946, Sept. 20	**Wmk. 229**	**Perf. 12½**
542	A220	2p bluish green	3.50	1.25

See No. 568. For surcharge see No. 613.

Type of 1945, Overprinted in Black or Green

			1946, Dec. 6	**Wmk. 255**	**Perf. 12**
543	A212	50c red (Bk)	1.50	2.75
a.	Double overprint		25.00	
544	A212	50c red (G)	1.50	2.75
a.	Double overprint		25.00	

5th Central American and Caribbean Championship Games.

Coffee — A221

Engraved and Lithographed

			1947, Jan. 10	**Wmk. 229**	**Perf. 12½**
545	A221	5c multicolored	.30	.25

Colombian Orchid: Masdevallia Nycterina A222

Designs (Orchids): 2c, Miltonia vexillaria. No. 548, Cattleya chocoensis. No. 549, Odontoglossum crispum. No. 550, Cattleya dowiana aurea. 10c, Cattleya labiata trianae.

			1947, Feb. 7	**Wmk. 255**	**Perf. 12**
546	A222	1c multicolored	.25	.25
547	A222	2c multicolored	.25	.25
548	A222	5c multicolored	.60	.25
549	A222	5c multicolored	.60	.25
550	A222	5c multicolored	.60	.25
551	A222	10c multicolored	.90	.35
		Nos. 546-551 (6)	3.20	1.60

Antonio Nariño — A228

Alberto Urdaneta y Urdaneta — A229

Perf. 12½

			1947, May 9	**Litho.**	**Unwmk.**
552	A228	5c blue, *grnsh*	.25	.25
553	A229	10c red brn, *grnsh*	.30	.25
		Nos. 552-553,C146-C147 (4)	1.40	1.20

4th Pan-American Press Congress, 1946.

Sucre Type of 1940

			1947	**Wmk. 255**	**Engr.**	**Perf. 12**
554	A198	1p violet	2.75	1.25

José Celestino Mutis and José Jerónimo Triana A230

Miguel A. Caro and Rufino J. Cuervo — A231

			1947	**Wmk. 229**	**Perf. 12½**
555	A230	25c olive green	.50	.40
556	A231	3p dark purple	4.00	3.75

See Nos. 567, 569. For surcharge see No. 610.

Metropolitan Cathedral, Plaza Bolívar, Bogotá — A232

National Capitol A233

Ministry of Foreign Affairs A234

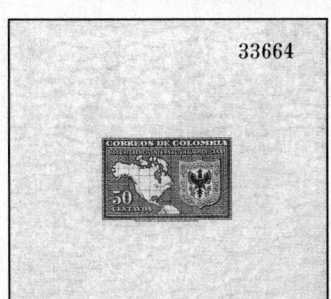

A235

			1948, Apr. 2		
557	A232	5c black brown	.25	.25
558	A233	10c orange	.40	.55
559	A234	15c dark blue	.40	.55
		Nos. 557-559,C148-C149 (5)	2.20	2.50

Miniature Sheet

Imperf

560	A235	50c slate	2.00	1.60

9th Pan-American Conf., Bogotá.

No. RA5A Overprinted in Black

			1948	**Unwmk.**	**Perf. 12½**
		Without Gum		
561	PT3	1c yellow orange	.25	.25

The letter "C" is the initial of "CORREOS."

Nos. RA33, RA24 and RA25 Overprinted in Black

			1948	**Wmk. 255**	**Perf. 12.**
562	PT6	1c olive	.25	.25
563	PT6	2c green	.25	.25
564	PT6	20c brown	.25	.25
		Nos. 562-564 (3)	.75	.75

Nos. 561-564 exist with inverted and double overprints.

Observatory Type of 1946

Unwmk.

			1948, June 30	**Litho.**	**Perf. 11**
565	A218	5c blue	.25	.25

Simón Bolívar — A236

Wmk. 255

			1948, May 29	**Engr.**	**Perf. 12**
566	A236	15c green	.40	.25

Types of 1946-47

			1948	**Unwmk.**	**Perf. 12½**
567	A230	25c green	.25	.25
568	A220	2p dp green	.55	.25
569	A231	3p dp red violet	.55	.35
		Nos. 567-569 (3)	1.35	.85

Falls Type of 1937

			1948		**Wmk. 229**
570	A160	10c red	.25	.25

For overprints see Nos. C231, C326.

Carlos Martinez Silva — A237

Perf. 13½

			1948, Dec. 21	**Unwmk.**	**Litho.**
571	A237	40c carmine	.40	.25

Juan de Dios Carrasquilla A238

1949, May 20   Wmk. 229   Perf. 12½
572 A238 5c bister   .25   .25
75th anniv. of the foundation of the Colombian Soc. of Agriculture.

Julio Garavito Armero — A239

Wmk. 229
1949, Apr. 24   Engr.   Perf. 12
573 A239 4c green   .35   .25
Issued to honor Julio Garavito Armero (1865-1920), mathematician.

Coffee Type of 1939
Imprint: "American Bank Note Co."
1949, Aug. 4   Wmk. 255
574 A176 5c blue   .25   .25

Arms of Colombia — A240

1949, Oct. 7   Unwmk.   Perf. 13
575 A240 15c blue   .25   .25
Issued to honor the new Constitution. See Nos. C164-C165.

Shield and Tree — A241

1949, Oct. 13   Wmk. 229   Perf. 12½
576 A241 5c olive   .25   .25
4th anniv. of Colombia's 1st Forestry Cong. and propaganda for the government's reforestation program.

Francisco Javier Cisneros — A242

1949, Dec. 15   Photo.   Unwmk.
577 A242 50c red vio & yel   .75   .60
578 A242 50c green & vio   .75   .60
579 A242 50c brown & lt bl   .75   .60
      Nos. 577-579 (3)   2.25   1.80
50th anniv. (in 1948) of the death of Francisco Javier Cisneros.

Masdevallia Chimaera A243

Odontoglossum Crispum — A244

Eastern Hemisphere — A245

Designs: 3c, Cattleya labiata trianae. 4c, Masdevallia nycterina. 5c, Cattleya dowiana aurea. 11c, Miltonia vexillaria. 18c, Santo Domingo post office.

1950, Aug. 22   Photo.   Perf. 13
580 A243 1c brown   .25   .25
581 A244 2c violet   .25   .25
582 A243 3c rose lilac   .25   .25
583 A243 4c emerald   .30   .25
584 A243 5c red orange   .50   .25
585 A244 11c red   1.50   1.50
586 A244 18c ultra   2.50   .50
      Nos. 580-586 (7)   5.55   3.25

Miniature Sheet
Imperf
587 A245 50c orange yel   3.50   3.50
75th anniv. (in 1949) of the UPU. See No. C199. For surcharge see No. C232.

Antonio Baraya — A246

Perf. 12½
1950, Nov. 27   Unwmk.   Engr.
588 A246 2c red   .25   .25

Colombian Farm A247

1950, Dec. 28   Photo.   Perf. 11½
589 A247 5c dp car & buff   .25   .25
590 A247 5c bl grn & gray   .25   .25
591 A247 5c vio bl & gray   .25   .25
      Nos. 589-591 (3)   .75   .75
Issued to publicize rural life.

Arms of Bogotá A248

Arms of Colombia A249

Perf. 12x12½
1950, Dec. 28   Engr.   Wmk. 255
592 A248 5p deep green   2.00   1.50
593 A249 10p red orange   6.00   2.00

> Catalogue values for unused stamps in this section, from this point to the end of the section, are for Never Hinged items.

Map and Badge — A250

Perf. 12½x13
1951, Jan. 30   Photo.   Unwmk.
594 A250 20c red, yel & bl   .60   .25
60th anniversary (in 1947) of the formation of the Colombian Society of Engineers.

Guillermo Valencia — A251

1951, Oct. 20   Engr.   Perf. 13x13½
595 A251 25c black   1.20   .25
Issued to honor Guillermo Valencia (1873-1943), newspaper founder, governor of Cauca, presidential candidate, author.

No. 468 Overprinted in Black

1951, Dec. 11   Wmk. 255   Perf. 12
596 A155 2c carmine rose   .30   .25
Issued to publicize the reversion of the Mares oil concession to Colombia.

Nicolas Osorio — A252

No. 598, Pompilio Martinez. No. 599, Ezequiel Uricoechea. No. 600, Jose M. Lombana.

Perf. 11½
1952, Aug. 6   Unwmk.   Engr.
Various Frames
597 A252 1c deep blue   .25   .25
598 A252 1c deep blue   .25   .25
599 A252 1c deep blue   .25   .25
600 A252 1c deep blue   .25   .25
      Nos. 597-600 (4)   1.00   1.00
Nos. 597-600 were printed in a single sheet containing four panes of twenty-five each, separated by double rows of ornamental tabs. Although inscribed "sobretasa," the stamps were for ordinary postage.

Types of Postal Tax Stamps of 1945-50 and

Communications Building
A253   A253a

1952   Perf. 12
601 A253 5c ultra   .35   .25
Wmk. 255
602 PT10 20c brown   10.00   4.50
603 PT6 25c dk gray   42.50 42.50
604 PT10 25c blue green   1.00   .25
605 A253a 50c orange yel   25.00 13.00
606 A253a 1p rose carmine   2.50   .30
607 A253a 2p lilac rose   25.00   9.75
608 A253a 2p violet   3.00   .65
      Nos. 601-608 (8)   109.35 71.20
Although inscribed "sobretasa," Nos. 601-608 were issued for ordinary postage.
For surcharges see Nos. 612, RA48.

Cathedral of Manizales — A254

Perf. 11½
1952, Oct. 10   Photo.   Unwmk.
609 A254 23c blue & gray blk   .50   .25
Centenary of city of Manizales.
For surcharge see No. 619.

No. 555 Surcharged in Blue

1952, Oct. 30   Wmk. 229   Perf. 12½
610 A230 15c on 25c olive green   .45   .25
Latin American Siderurgical Conf., 1952. See No. C226.

Queen Isabella I and Monument A255

Perf. 12½
1953, Mar. 10   Unwmk.   Engr.
611 A255 23c blue & black   .95   .70
5th cent. of the birth of Queen Isabella I of Spain.
For surcharge see No. 693.

Nos. 606 and 568 Surcharged with New Values in Dark Blue
1953, Oct. 19   Wmk. 255
612 A253a 40c on 1p rose car   1.60   .25
613 A220 50c on 2p dp green   1.60   .25

Manuel Ancizar A256

Portraits: 23c, José Jeronimo Triana. 30c, Manuel Ponce de Leon. 1p, Agustin Codazzi.

Perf. 12½x13
1953, Nov.   Engr.   Unwmk.
Frames in Black

614	A256	14c rose red	.70 .65
615	A256	23c ultra	.60 .25
616	A256	30c chocolate	.45 .25
617	A256	1p emerald	.45 .25
		Nos. 614-617 (4)	2.20 1.40

Cent. (in 1950) of the establishment of the Chorographic Commission. For surcharges and overprint see Nos. 620, 687, 690, 692, C284.

Murillo Toro and Map — A257

Black Surcharge
Engraved and Lithographed
1953, Dec. 12   Wmk. 255   Perf. 12
618 A257 5c on 5p multi   .40 .25

2nd Natl. Phil. Exhib., Bogotá, Dec. 1953. See No. C237.

Nos. 609 and 614 Surcharged with New Value or New Value and Ornaments
1953   Unwmk.   Perf. 11½, 12½x13
619 A254 5c on 23c (C)   .40 .25
620 A256 5c on 14c (Bk)   .40 .25

No. 614 surcharged "CINCO" in blue is listed as No. 687.

Symbolical of St. Francis Receiving Christ's Wounds — A258

1954, Apr. 23   Photo.   Perf. 11½
621 A258 5c sepia & green   .40 .25

400th anniversary of the establishment of Colombia's first Franciscan community.

Soldier, Map and Arms A259

1954, June 13   Engr.   Perf. 13
622 A259 5c dull blue   .25 .25

1st anniv. of the assumption of the presidency by Gen. Gustavo Rojas Pinilla. See Nos. 255, 637a.

Sports Emblem — A260

Design: 10c, Stadium and athlete holding arms of Colombia.

1954, July 18   Unwmk.
623 A260 5c deep blue   .50 .25
624 A260 10c red   .85 .25
     Nos. 623-624,C256-C257 (4) 3.65 1.10

7th Natl. Athletic Games, Cali, July 1954.

History Academy Seal — A261

1954, July 24
625 A261 5c ultra & green   .30 .25

50th anniversary (in 1952) of the Colombian Academy of History.

Convent and Cell of St. Peter Claver — A262

1954, Sept. 9
627 A262 5c dark green   .25 .25
a.   Souvenir sheet   8.00 12.00

300th anniv. of the death of St. Peter Claver. No. 627a contains one stamp similar to No. 627, but printed in greenish black. Sheet size: 121x129½mm. See Nos. C258-C258a.

Mercury — A263

1954, Oct. 29
628 A263 5c orange   .55 .25
     Nos. 628,C259-C260 (3) 1.65 .75

1st Intl. Fair and Exhibition, Bogota, 1954.

Tapestry Madonna A264

College Cloister A265

Designs: 10c, Brother Cristobal de Torres. 20c, College chapel and arms.

Perf. 12½x11½, 11½x12½
1954, Dec. 6
629 A264 5c orange & blk   .40 .25
630 A264 10c blue   .40 .25
631 A265 15c violet brn   .40 .25
632 A265 20c black & brn   1.00 .35
a.   Souvenir sheet   12.00 16.00
     Nos. 629-632,C263-C266 (8) 6.80 2.80

Founding of the Senior College of Our Lady of the Rosary, Bogota, 300th anniv. (in 1953). No. 632a contains four stamps similar to Nos. 629-632, but printed in different colors: 5c yellow and black, 10c green, 15c dull violet, 20c black and light-blue.

Steel Mill — A266

1954, Dec. 12   Perf. 12½x13
633 A266 5c ultra & blk   .30 .25

Issued to mark the opening of the Paz del Rio steel mill, October 1954. See No. C267.

José Marti — A267

1955, Jan. 28   Perf. 13½x13
634 A267 5c deep carmine   .25 .25

Centenary of the birth of José Marti (1853-1895), Cuban patriot. See No. C268.

Arms, Flags and Soldiers Building Bridge A268

1955, Mar. 23   Perf. 12½
635 A268 10c claret   .30 .25

Issued to honor Colombian soldiers who served in Korea, 1951-53. See Nos. 637a, C269.

Fleet Emblem — A269

M. S. City of Manizales and New York Skyline A270

1955, Apr. 12   Unwmk.
636 A269 15c deep green   .25 .25
637 A270 20c violet   .45 .25
a.   Souvenir sheet   9.50 12.00
     Nos. 636-637,C270-C271 (4) 2.00 1.15

Grand-Colombian Merchant Fleet. No. 637a contains four stamps similar to Nos. 622, 635-637, but printed in different colors: 5c blue, 10c dark carmine, 15c green, 20c purple.

Hotel Tequendama and Church of San Diego — A271

1955, May 16   Photo.   Perf. 11½x12
638 A271 5c blue   .25 .25

See No. C273.

Bolivar's Country Estate, Bogotá A272

1955, Sept. 28   Engr.   Perf. 12½
639 A272 5c deep ultra   .25 .25

50th anniv. of Rotary Intl. See No. C274.

Belalcazar, Jiménez de Quesada and Balboa A273

Caravels and Columbus A274

5c, San Martin, Bolivar and Washington.

Engraved and Photogravure
1955, Oct. 29   Perf. 13x12½
640 A273 2c yel grn & brn   .50 .25
641 A273 5c brt bl & brn   .50 .25
642 A274 23c lt ultra & blk .55 .25
a.   Souvenir sheet   24.00 24.00
     Nos. 640-642,C275-C280 (9) 29.85 15.00

7th Cong. of the Postal Union of the Americas and Spain, Bogota, Oct. 12-Nov. 9, 1955. No. 642a contains one each of Nos. 640-642, printed in slightly different shades.

José Eusebio Caro — A275

1955, Nov. 29   Engr.   Perf. 13½x13
643 A275 5c brown   .25 .25

José Eusebio Caro (1817-53), poet. See No. C281.

Departmental Issue

Map — A276

View of San Andres Harbor — A277

Cattle at Waterhole
A278

Designs: 2c, Docks, Atlantico. 3c, "Industry," Antioquia. 4c, Cartagena Harbor, Bolivar. No. 647, Steel Mill, Boyaca. No. 648, Cattle, Cordoba. No. 649, Map. No. 650, San Andres Harbor. No. 651, Cacao picker, Cauca. 10c, Coffee picker, Caldas. 15c, Salt Mine Chapel, Zipaquira, Cundinamarca. 20c, Tropical plants and map, Choco. 23c, Harvester, Huila. 25c, Banana plantation, Magdalena. 30c, Gold mining, Nariño. 40c, Tobacco plantation, Santander. 50c, Oil wells, North Santander. 60c, Cotton plantation, Tolima. 1p, Sugar industry, Cauca. 3p, Amazon river at Leticia, Amazonas. 5p, Windmills and panoramic view, La Guajira. 10p, Rubber plantation, Vaupes.

Perf. 13½x13, 13x13½, 13
Engr.; Engr. & Litho.

		1956		Unwmk.
		Various Frames		
644	A277	2c car & grn	.25	.25
645	A276	3c brn vio & blk	.25	.25
646	A277	4c grn & blk	.25	.25
647	A276	5c dk brn & bl	.25	.25
648	A277	5c ol & dk vio brn	.30	.25
649	A276	5c bl & blk	.25	.25
650	A277	5c car & grnsh bl	.25	.25
651	A277	5c ol grn & red brn	.25	.25
652	A276	10c org & blk	.40	
653	A276	15c ultra & blk	.25	.25
654	A276	20c dk brn & bl	.25	.25
655	A277	23c ultra & ver	.30	.25
656	A277	25c ol grn & blk	.30	.25
657	A277	30c ultra & brn	.25	.25
658	A277	40c dl pur & red brn	.25	.25
659	A277	50c dk grn & blk	.25	.25
660	A277	60c pale brn & grn	.25	.25
661	A278	1p mag & grnsh bl	1.90	.25
662	A278	2p grn & red brn	2.75	.25
663	A278	3p car & blk	4.25	.50
664	A278	5p brn & lt ultra	7.50	1.00
665	A276	10p red brn & grn	20.00	6.00
		Nos. 644-665 (22)	40.95	12.25

Nos. 645, 647, 649, 652-654 measure 27x32mm, No. 665 27x37mm. See Nos. 681-684, 685, 688-689. For surcharges and overprints see Nos. 685, 688-689, C289, C312.

Columbus and Proposed Lighthouse
A279

1956, Oct. 12   Photo.   Perf. 12
666 A279 3c gray black   .50 .25
Issued in honor of Christopher Columbus. See Nos. C285, C306.

Altar of St. Elizabeth and Tomb of Jimenez de Quesada
A280

1956, Nov. 19   Unwmk.
667 A280 5c red lilac   .25 .25
7th cent. of St. Elizabeth of Hungary, patron saint of Sante Fé de Bogotá. See No. C286.

St. Ignatius of Loyola — A281

1956, Nov. 26   Engr.   Perf. 12½x13
668 A281 5c blue   .25 .25
400th anniv. of the death of St. Ignatius of Loyola. See No. C287. For overprint see No. C324.

Javier Pereira — A282

1956, Dec. 28   Unwmk.   Perf. 12
669 A282 5c blue   .25 .25
Issued to honor 167-year-old Javier Pereira. See No. C288.

Emblem and Dairy Farm
A283

Designs: 2c, Emblem and tractor. 5c, Emblem, coffee and corn.

1957, Mar. 5   Photo.   Perf. 14x13½
670 A283 1c lt ol grn   .25 .25
671 A283 2c lt brn   .25 .25
672 A283 5c lt bl   .25 .25
    Nos. 670-672,C292-C296 (8) 3.35 2.60
Agrarian Savings Bank of Colombia, 25th anniv.
For overprint see No. C322.

Arms of Military Academy and Gen. Rafael Reyes
A284

Design: 10c, Arms and Academy.

1957, July 20   Engr.   Perf. 12½
673 A284 5c blue   .25 .25
674 A284 10c orange   .40 .25
  a. Souv. sheet of 2   22.50 22.50
    Nos. 673-674,C299-C300 (4) 1.40 1.00
50th anniv. of the Colombian Military Academy.
No. 674a contains one each of Nos. 673-674 in slightly different shades.
For overprints see Nos. C328, C312.

Statue of José Matias Delgado — A285

1957, Sept. 16   Photo.   Perf. 12
675 A285 2c rose brn   .25 .25
Issued in honor of Jose Matias Delgado, liberator of El Salvador. See No. C301.

Santo Michelena, Marcos y Crespo, P. Alcantara Herran and UPU Monument
A286

1957, Oct. 10   Unwmk.
676 A286 5c green   .25 .25
677 A286 10c gray   .30 .25
    Nos. 676-677,C302-C303 (4) 1.25 1.00
Intl. Letter Writing Week and 14th UPU Cong.

St. Vincent de Paul and Children — A287

1957, Oct. 18
678 A287 1c dark olive green   .25 .25
Colombian Society of St. Vincent de Paul, cent. See No. C304. For overprint see No. C323.

Fencer
A288

1957, Nov. 22   Photo.   Perf. 12
679 A288 4c lilac   .25 .25
3rd South American Fencing Championship. See No. C305. For overprint see No. C332.

Francisco José de Caldas and Hypsometer — A289

1958, May 12   Unwmk.   Perf. 12
680 A289 10c black   .25 .25
    Nos. 680,C309-C310 (3) 1.40 .75
International Geophysical Year, 1957-58.

Departmental Issue
Type of 1956
Designs as before.

1958   Engr.   Perf. 13
681 A276 3c ultra & brn   .25 .25
682 A276 3c ol grn & pur   .25 .25
683 A276 10c grn & brn   .25 .25
684 A276 10c dk bl & brn   .25 .25
    Nos. 681-684 (4) 1.00 1.00

Nos. 646, C291, 614, 653, 655, 616, C308, 615 and 611 Surcharged with New Value, and Old Value Obliterated, or Overprinted in Dark Blue or Green

Perf. 12½, 12½x13, 13
1958-59   Unwmk.
685 A277 2c on 4c grn & blk   .25 .25
686 AP48 5c dp plum & multi ('59)   .25 .25
687 A256 5c on 14c blk & rose red ("CINCO") ('59)   .30 .30
688 A276 5c on 15c ultra & blk   .25 .25
689 A277 5c on 23c ultra & ver (G)   .25 .25

690 A256 5c on 30c blk & choc ("CINCO")   .25 .25
691 AP40 10c on 25c rose vio   .25 .25
692 A256 20c on 23c blk & ultra (G) ("VEINTE") ('59)   .30 .25
693 A255 20c on 23c bl & blk ('59)   .30 .25
    Nos. 685-693 (9) 2.40 2.30
On No. 686 the words "Correo Extra Rapido" are obliterated in dark blue.

Father Rafael Almanza and Church of San Diego, Bogota
A290

1958, Oct. 23   Photo.   Perf. 14x13
695 A290 10c purple   .25 .25
    Nos. 695,C313-C314 (3) .80 .75
For overprint see No. C336.

Msgr. R. M. Carrasquilla and Church
A291

1959, Jan. 22   Perf. 14x13
696 A291 10c dk red brn   .25 .25
    Nos. 696,C315-C316 (3) 1.30 .75
Cent. of the birth of Msgr. R. M. Carrasquilla (1857-1930), rector of Our Lady of the Rosary Seminary, Bogotá. For overprints see Nos. C335, C341.

Miss Universe 1959 — A292

1959, June 26   Photo.   Perf. 11½
697 A292 10c multi   .80 .25
    Nos. 697,C317-C318 (3) 50.05 49.15
Luz Marina Zuluaga, Miss Universe, 1959. For overprint see No. C342.

Jorge Eliecer Gaitan — A293

1959, July 28   Engr.   Perf. 12x13½
698 A293 10c on 3c gray bl (Bl)   .25 .25
699 A293 30c rose vio   .45 .25
    Nos. 698-699,C319-C320 (4) 4.20 3.50
Issued in honor of Jorge Eliecer Gaitan (1898-1948), lawyer and politician.
No. 698 exists without blue surcharge.

Gen. Francisco de Paula Santander — A294

Designs: Nos. 701, 703, Simon Bolivar.

1959   Litho.   Wmk. 331   Perf. 12½
700 A294 5c brown & yel   .25 .25
701 A294 5c ultra & bl   .25 .25
702 A294 10c gray & grn   .25 .25
703 A294 10c gray & red   .25 .25
    Nos. 700-703,C389 (5) 4.50 1.45

Capitol, Bogota A295

1959
704 A295 2c dk bl & red brn .25 .25
705 A295 3c blk brn & lilac .25 .25

Stamp of 1859 and Mail Transport by Mule — A296

Designs (various stamps of 1859 and): 10c, Mail boat on the Magdalena river. 15c, as 5c. 25c, Train.

Unwmk.
1959, Dec. 1   Photo.   Perf. 12
709 A296 5c org & grn .25 .25
710 A296 10c rose cl & bl .25 .25
711 A296 15c car rose & grn .40 .40
712 A296 25c bl & red brn .50 .50
 Nos. 709-712,C351-C354 (8) 5.90 4.15
Centenary of Colombian postage stamps.

Two-Toed Sloth — A297

Designs: 10c, Alexander von Humboldt. 20c, Spider monkey.

1960, Feb. 12   Perf. 12
713 A297 5c grnsh bl & brn .25 .25
714 A297 10c blk & dp car .25 .25
715 A297 20c cit & gray brn .25 .25
 Nos. 713-715,C357-C359 (6) 8.10 5.40
Cent. of the death of Alexander von Humboldt (1769-1859), German naturalist and geographer.
For overprint and surcharge see Nos. C411, C413.

Anthurium Andreanum A298

Flower: 20c, Espeletia grandiflora.

1960, May 10
716 A298 5c multi .85 .25
717 A298 20c brn, yel & gray ol .85 .25
 Nos. 716-717,C360-C370 (13) 17.85 18.30
See Nos. C420-C425. For overprint see No. C412.

Lincoln Statue, Washington A299

Wmk. 331
1960, June 10   Litho.   Perf. 10½
718 A299 20c rose lil & blk .35 .25
 Nos. 718,C375-C376 (3) 2.15 1.50

Florero House, Cradle of the Republic A300

Arms of Santa Cruz de Mompox — A301

Design: 5c, First coins of Republic.

Unwmk.
1960, July 19   Photo.   Perf. 12
719 A301 5c grn & ocher .25 .25
720 A300 20c ol bis & mar .25 .25
721 A301 20c multi .25 .25
 Nos. 719-721,C377-C385 (12) 7.90 6.05
Colombia's independence, 150th anniv.

St. Isidore and Farm Animals — A302

Design: 20c, Nativity by Gregorio de Arce Vasquez y Ceballos.

1960, Sept. 26   Perf. 12
722 A302 10c multi .25 .25
723 A302 20c multi .25 .25
 Nos. 722-723,C387 (3) .75 .75
St. Isidore the Farmer, patron saint of the rural people.
See Nos. 747, C388, C439-C440.

UN Headquarters and Emblem A303

Wmk. 331
1960, Oct. 24   Litho.   Perf. 11
724 A303 20c blk & pink .25 .25

Souvenir Sheet
Imperf
725 A303 50c dk brn, brt grn & blk 4.00 4.00
15th anniversary of the United Nations.

Pan-American Highway through Colombia — A304

1961, Mar. 7 Unwmk. Perf. 10½x11
726 A304 20c brn & grnsh bl .75 .70
 Nos. 726,C390-C393 (5) 3.75 3.50
8th Pan-American Highway Congress, Bogota, May 20-29, 1960.

Alfonso Lopez — A305

1961, Mar. 22   Photo.   Perf. 12½
727 A305 10c brt rose & brn .25 .25
728 A305 20c vio & brn .25 .25
 Nos. 727-728,C394-C395 (4) 1.35 1.00
Alfonso Lopez (1886-1959), President of Colombia. See No. C396.

Cauca River Bridge, Cali A306

Page from Resolutions of Confederated Cities — A307

1961-62   Perf. 12½x13, 13½x13
729 A306 10c red brn, bl, grn & red ('62) .25 .25
730 A307 20c pale brn & blk .25 .25
 Nos. 729-730,C397-C401 (7) 3.75 2.45
50th anniversary (in 1960) of the Department of Valle del Cauca.

View of Cucuta and Arms A308

No. 732, Arms of Ocana and Pamplona.

1961, Aug. 29   Perf. 13x13½
731 A308 20c bl, blk, yel & red .25 .25
732 A308 20c ocher, ultra & red .25 .25
 Nos. 731-732,C402-C403 (4) 1.45 1.00
50th anniv. (in 1960) of the Department of North Santander.

Arms of Popayan — A309

Designs: No. 734, Arms of Barranquilla. No. 735, Arms of Bucaramanga.

Perf. 12½x13
1961, Oct. 10   Unwmk.
Arms in Multicolor
733 A309 10c blue & silver .25 .25
734 A309 20c blue & yellow .25 .25
735 A309 20c blue & gold .25 .25
 Nos. 733-735,C404-C408 (8) 3.20 2.00
Issued to honor Atlantico Department.

Basketball A310

1961, Dec. 16 Litho. Perf. 13½x14
736 A310 20c shown .25 .25
737 A310 20c Runners .25 .25
738 A310 20c Boxers .50 .25
739 A310 25c Soccer .25 .25
 Nos. 736-739,C414-C418 (9) 4.35 2.65
4th Bolivarian Games, Barranquilla, 1961.

Colombian Anti-Malaria Emblem — A311

Design: 50c, Malaria eradication emblem and mosquito in swamp.

1962, Apr. 12   Unwmk.   Perf. 12
740 A311 20c lt bis & red .25 .25
741 A311 50c bis & ultra .30 .25
 Nos. 740-741,C426-C428 (5) 6.45 6.15

Engineers Society Emblem — A312

1962, June 12 Photo. Perf. 11½x12
742 A312 10c multi .25 .25
 Nos. 742,C429-C432 (5) 3.70 3.55
Colombian Society of Engineers, 75th anniv.

Flags of American Nations — A313

1962, June 28   Perf. 13
Flags in National Colors
743 A313 25c blk & org ver .25 .25
Souvenir Sheet
744 A313 2.50p blk & yel 5.75 5.75
70th anniv. of the founding of the Organization of American States.
See No. C433.

Woman Casting Ballot and Statue of Policarpa Salavarrieta — A314

Perf. 12x12½
1962, July 20   Litho.   Wmk. 229
745 A314 10c lt bl, gray & blk .25 .25
Issued to publicize women's political rights.
See Nos. 752, C434, C448-C450.

Scouts at Campfire and Tents — A315

Perf. 11½x12

1962, July 28　Photo.　Unwmk.
746　A315　10c brt grnsh bl & brn　.30　.30
　　Nos. 746,C435-C438 (5)　9.30　7.40

Colombian Boy Scouts, 30th anniv.

St. Isidore Type of 1960 Redrawn

1962, Aug. 28　　　　Perf. 12
747　A302　10c pink & multi　.25　.25
　　Nos. 747,C439-C440 (3)　5.00　5.00

The frame on No. 747 is solid color with white inscription similar to type AP82.

Railroad Map of Colombia — A316

1962, Sept. 28　　　　Perf. 12½
748　A316　10c blk, gray, grn & red　.25　.25
　　Nos. 748,C441-C444 (5)　7.75　5.50

Progress of Colombian railroads and the completion of the Atlantic Line from Santa Marta to Bogota.

Post Horn — A317

Perf. 13½x14

1962, Oct. 18　Litho.　Wmk. 346
749　A317　20c dull gray vio & blk　.25　.25
　　Nos. 749,C445-C446 (3)　.90　.75

50th anniv. of the founding of the Postal Union of the Americas and Spain, UPAE.

"Virgin of the Rock" — A318

1963, Mar. 11　　　　Wmk. 346
750　A318　60c multi　.25　.25

Vatican II, the 21st Ecumenical Council of the Roman Catholic Church. See No. C447.

Red Cross Centenary Emblem — A319

1963, May 1　　　　Perf. 12x12½
751　A319　5c olive bister & red　.25　.25

Centenary of International Red Cross.

Women's Rights Type of 1962

1963, July 11　　　　Wmk. 346
752　A314　5c org, gray & blk　.25　.25
　　Nos. 752,C448-C450 (4)　1.30　1.00

Manuel Mejia J. and Flag of National Coffee Growers Assn. A320

Perf. 12½x13

1965, Feb. 10　Engr.　Unwmk.
753　A320　25c rose & blk　.25　.25
　　Nos. 753,C464-C466 (4)　6.50　1.15

Manuel Mejia J. (1887-1958), banker and manager of the National Coffee Growers Association.

Julio Arboleda (1817-62), Writer, Soldier and Statesman A321

1966, Mar. 9　Litho.　Perf. 14x13½
754　A321　5c lt brn, lt yel grn & blk　.30　.25

Spanish Galleon, 16th Century A322

History of Maritime Mail: 15c, Rio Hacha brigantine, 1850. 20c, Uraba canoe. 40c, Magdalena River steamship and barge, 1900. 50c, Modern motor ship and sea gull.

1966, June 16　Photo.　Unwmk.
755　A322　5c org & multi　.40　.25
756　A322　15c car rose, blk & brn　.40　.25
757　A322　20c brt grn, org & blk　.40　.25
758　A322　40c dp bl & multi　.50　.25
759　A322　50c pale bl & multi　1.25　.60
　　Nos. 755-759 (5)　2.95　1.60

Plumed Hogfish A323

Design: 10p, Bat ray and brittle starfish.

1966, Aug. 25　Photo.　Perf. 12½x13
760　A323　80c multi　.25　.25
761　A323　10p multi　8.25　5.25
　　Nos. 760-761,C481-C483 (5)　27.75　20.15

Arms of Venezuela, Colombia and Chile A324

1966, Oct. 11　Litho.　Perf. 14x13½
762　A324　40c yel & multi　.25　.25
　　Nos. 762,C484-C485 (3)　.95　.75

Visits of Eduardo Frei and Raul Leoni, presidents of Chile and Venezuela.

Camilo Torres, 1766-1816, Lawyer — A325

Portraits: 60c, Jorge Tadeo Lozano (1771-1816), naturalist. 1p, Francisco Antonio Zea (1776-1822), naturalist and politician.

Perf. 13½x14

1967, Jan. 18　Litho.　Unwmk.
763　A325　25c vio & bis　.30　.25
764　A325　60c dk red brn & bis　.30　.25
765　A325　1p grn & bis　.50　.25
　　Nos. 763-765,C486-C487 (5)　1.90　1.25

Issued to honor famous men of Colombia.

Map of South America and Arms A326

1967, Feb. 2　Litho.　Perf. 14x13½
766　A326　40c multi　.30　.25
767　A326　60c multi　.30　.25
　　Nos. 766-767,C488 (3)　1.10　.75

Declaration of Bogota for cooperation and world peace, signed by Colombia, Chile, Ecuador, Peru and Venezuela.

Monochaetum Orchid and Bee — A327

Orchid: 2p, Passiflora vitifolia and butterfly.

1967, May 23　Litho.　Perf. 14
768　A327　25c multi　.35　.25
769　A327　2p multi　2.50　1.50
　　Nos. 768-769,C489-C491 (5)　9.60　3.15

1st Natl. Orchid Exhib. and the Topical Phil. Flora and Fauna Exhib., Medellin, Apr. 1967.

Lions Emblem — A328

1967, July 12　Litho.　Perf. 13½x14
770　A328　10p multi　3.50　2.00

50th anniv. of Lions Intl. See No. C492.

SENA Emblem — A329

Lithographed and Embossed
1967, Sept. 20　　　　Unwmk.
771　A329　5p gold, brt grn & blk　1.50　.25

10th anniv. of Natl. Apprenticeship Service, SENA. See No. C494.

Gold Diadem in Calima Style — A330

Pre-Columbian Art: 3p, Gold statuette, ornamental globe and bird, horiz.

Perf. 13½x14, 14x13½

1967, Oct. 13　　　　Photo.
772　A330　1.60p brt rose lil, gold & brn　.95　.25
773　A330　3p dk bl, gold & brn　1.25　.40
　　Nos. 772-773,C495-C497 (5)　20.85　11.40

Meeting of the UPU Committee of Postal Studies, Bogota, Oct., 1967.

Radar Installation A331

1p, Map of communications network.

1968, May 14　Litho.　Perf. 13½x14
774　A331　50c brt yel grn, blk & org brn　.25　.25
775　A331　1p multi　.35　.25
　　Nos. 774-775,C498-C499 (4)　1.15　1.00

20th anniv. of the National Telecommunications Service (TELECOM).

The Eucharist — A332

1968, June 6　Litho.　Perf. 13½x14
776　A332　60c multi　.25　.25
　　Nos. 776,C500-C501 (3)　.80　.75

39th Eucharistic Cong., Bogotá, 8/18-25.

St. Augustin, by Gregorio Vasquez — A333

Designs: 60c, The Gathering of Manna, by Gregorio Vasquez. 1p, The Marriage of the Virgin, by Baltazar de Figueroa. 5p, Jeweled monstrance, c. 1700. 10p, Pope Paul VI, painting by Roman Franciscan nuns.

1968, Aug. 13   Photo.   Perf. 13

777	A333	25c multicolored	.25	.25
778	A333	60c multicolored	.25	.25
779	A333	1p multicolored	.25	.25
780	A333	5p multicolored	.80	.25
781	A333	10p multicolored	1.60	.45
a.		Souvenir sheet of 2	4.00	4.00

Nos. 777-781,C502-C506 (10) 10.70 5.20

39th Eucharistic Congress. Bogotá, Aug. 18-25. No. 781a contains two imperf. stamps similar to Nos. 780-781.

Pope Paul VI — A334

1968, Aug. 22   Litho.   Perf. 13½x14

782	A334	25c multi	.30	.25

Nos. 782,C507-C509 (4) 1.30 1.00

Visit of Pope Paul VI to Colombia, 8/22-24.

Arms of National University — A335

1968, Oct. 29   Litho.   Perf. 13½x14

783	A335	80c multi	.40	.25

Centenary of the founding of the National University. See No. C510.

Stamp of Antioquia, 1868 — A336

1968, Nov. 20   Litho.   Perf. 12x12½

784	A336	30c emer & bl	.30	.25

Souvenir Sheet

785	A336	5p lt olive & blue	3.75	3.75

Cent. of the 1st postage stamps of Antioquia and the 7th Natl. Phil. Exhib., Medellin, Nov. 20-29.

Institute Emblem — A337

1969, Mar. 5   Litho.   Perf. 13½x14

786	A337	20c multi	.35	.25

25th anniv. (in 1967) of the Inter-American Agricultural Sciences Institute. See No. C511.

Battle of Boyaca (Detail), by José Maria Espinosa — A338

Design: 30c, Army of liberation crossing Pisba Pass, by Francisco Antonio Caro.

1969, July 24   Litho.   Perf. 13½x14

787	A338	20c gold & multi	.35	.25
788	A338	30c gold & multi	.35	.25

Nos. 787-788,C517 (3) 1.70 .85

Fight for independence, sesquicentennial.

"Poverty" A339

1970, Mar. 1   Litho.   Perf. 14

789	A339	30c bl & multi	.35	.25

Colombian Institute for Family Welfare and 10th anniv. of the Children's Rights Law.

Greek Mask and Pre-Columbian Symbol of Literary Contest — A340

1970, Sept. 12   Litho.   Perf. 14x13½

790	A340	30c dk brn, red org & ocher	.25	.25

3rd Latin American Theatrical Festival of the Universities, Manizales, Sept. 12-20.

Colombian Stamps, Envelope and Emblem A341

1970, Sept. 24   Litho.   Perf. 14x13½

791	A341	2p brt bl & multi	.30	.25

Issued to publicize Philatelic Week.

Arms of Ibague and Discobolus A342

1970, Oct. 13

792	A342	80c buff, emer & sepia	.25	.25

9th National Games in Ibague.

St. Theresa, by Baltazar de Figueroa — A343

1970, Oct. 28   Litho.   Perf. 13½x14

793	A343	2p multi	.50	.25

Elevation of St. Theresa (1515-1582), to Doctor of the Church. See No. C568. For overprint see No. C568.

Casa Cural A344

1971, May 20   Litho.   Perf. 14x13½

794	A344	1.10p multi	.30	.25

Fourth centenary (in 1970) of the founding of Guacari, Valle. See No. 809.

Dancers and Music, Currulao — A345

1p, Chicha Maya dancers and music.

1971   Litho.   Perf. 13½x14

795	A345	1p pink & multi	.35	.25
796	A345	1.10p lt bl & multi	.35	.25

Souvenir Sheets
Imperf

797		Sheet of 3	6.00	6.00
a.	A345	2.50p Napanga	.65	.65
b.	A345	2.50p Joropo	.65	.65
c.	A345	5p Guabina	1.25	1.25
798		Sheet of 3	6.00	6.00
a.	A345	4p Bambuco	1.00	1.00
b.	A345	4p Cumbia	1.00	1.00
c.	A345	4p Currulao	1.00	1.00

Issued: No. 795, 12/20; No. 796, 8/5; Nos. 797-798, 8/10.

Constitutional Assembly, by Delgado A346

1971, Oct. 2   Perf. 14

801	A346	80c multi	.25	.25

Sequicentennial of Gran Colombian Constitutional Assembly in Rosario del Cucuta. See No. C589. For overprint see No. C589.

Arrows Emblem — A347

1972, Feb. 24   Perf. 13½x14

802	A347	60c blk & gray	.30	.25

Inter-Governmental Committee on European Migration, 20th anniversary.

Student and World Map A348

1972, Mar. 15   Perf. 14x13½

803	A348	1.10p lt grn & brn	.25	.25

20th anniv. of ICETEX, an organization which furnishes financial help for educational purposes and for technical studies abroad.

UN Emblem, Soldier and Frigate A349

1972, Apr. 7

804	A349	1.20p lt bl & multi	.25	.25

Colombian Battalion in Korea, 20th anniv.

Mother Francisca Josefa del Castillo — A350

1972, Apr. 6   Perf. 13½x14

805	A350	1.20p brn & multi	.25	.25

Tercentenary (in 1971) of the birth of Mother Francisca Josefa del Castillo, Poor Clare abbess and writer.

Handicraft A351

1972, Apr. 11

806	A351	1.10p multi	.35	.25

Nos. 806,C569-C571 (4) 1.55 1.00

Colombian artisans.

Maxillaria
Triloris — A352

1972, Apr. 20
807 A352 20p green & multi 7.25 .75
10th Natl. Phil. Exhib., Medellin.

Emeralds — A353

1972, June 16 Litho. Perf. 13½x14
808 A353 1.10p multi 1.25 .25

Type of 1971
Design: Antonio Nariño House.

1972, June 17 Perf. 14x13½
809 A344 1.10p multi .60 .25
4th centenary, town of Leyva.

San Andres and
Providencia
Islands — A354

1972, June 24 Perf. 13½x14
810 A354 60c bl & multi .25 .25
Sesquicentennial of annexation by Colombia of San Andres and Providencia Islands.

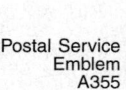

Postal Service
Emblem — A355

1972, Nov. 15 Litho. Perf. 12½x12
811 A355 1.10p emerald .25 .25

Family
A356

1972, Nov. 23
812 A356 60c orange .25 .25
Social progress.

Radio League
Emblem — A357

1973, Apr. 6 Litho. Perf. 12x12½
813 A357 60c lt bl, ultra & red .25 .25
40th anniversary of the Colombian Radio Amateurs' League.

Human Figure,
Tamalameque
A358

Excavated Ceramic Artifacts: 1p, Winged urn, Tairona. 1.10p, Jug, Muisca.

1973, June 15 Litho. Perf. 13½x14
814 A358 60c lt bl & multi .40 .25
815 A358 1p org & multi .80 .25
816 A358 1.10p vio bl & multi .50 .25
Nos. 814-816,C583-C586 (7) 7.25 2.75

Antonio Nariño,
by José M.
Espinosa — A359

1973, Dec. 13 Litho. Perf. 13½x14
817 A359 60c multi .25 .25
Sesquicentennial of the death of General Antonio Nariño (1765-1823).

Child — A360

1973, Dec. 17
818 A360 1.10p multi .25 .25
National Campaign for Children's Welfare.

Symbols of
Financial
Controls
A361

1973, Dec. 20 Litho. Perf. 14x13½
819 A361 80c ultra, ocher & blk .25 .25
50th anniv. of Comptroller-general's Office.

Mother Laura
Montoya — A362

1974, June 18 Litho. Perf. 13½x14
820 A362 1p multi .25 .25
Mother Laura Montoya (1874-1949), founder and Mother Superior of the Missionaries of Mary Immaculata and St. Catherine of Siena.

Runner and
Games'
Emblem — A363

1974, July 18 Litho. Perf. 14x13½
821 A363 2p ver, yel & brn .35 .25
10th National Games, Pereira.

José
Rivera
A364

1974, Aug. 3 Litho. Perf. 14x13½
822 A364 10p grn & multi 1.40 .25
50th anniv. of the publication of "La Voragine" (The Whirlpool) by José Eustasio Rivera.

Abstract
Pattern — A365

1974, Oct. 24 Litho. Perf. 13½x14
823 A365 1.10p multi .25 .25
Cent. of Natl. Insurance Co. See No. C610.

Train Emerging
from
Tunnel — A366

1974, Nov. 27 Litho. Perf. 13½x14
824 A366 1.10p multi .25 .25
Centenary of the Antioquia railroad.

Boy, Puppy and
Soccer
Ball — A367

Christmas: 1p, Girl with racket and kitten.

1974, Dec. 9
825 A367 80c multi .25 .25
826 A367 1p multi .25 .25

A368

1975, Apr. 11 Litho. Perf. 14x13½
827 A368 80c Gold Animal .45 .25
828 A368 1.10p Gold necklace .45 .25
Nos. 827-828,C621-C622 (4) 6.65 1.35
Pre-Columbian Sinu culture artifacts. For surcharge see No. 840.

Guglielmo
Marconi — A369

1975, June 2 Litho. Perf. 13½x14
829 A369 3p multi .30 .25
Birth centenary of Guglielmo Marconi (1874-1937), Italian electrical engineer and inventor.

Santa Marta
Cathedral — A370

1975, July 26
830 A370 80c multi .30 .25
400th anniv. of Santa Marta City. See No. C623.

Rafael
Nuñez — A371

1975, Sept. 28 Litho. Perf. 13½x14
831 A371 1.10p multi .30 .25
Rafael Nunez (1825-1894), philosopher, poet, political leader, birth sesquicentenary. For surcharge see No. 848.

Arms of
Medellin — A372

1975-79 Perf. 13½x14, 12 (1.20p)
832 A372 1p shown .40 .25
833 A372 1.20p Ibagué .35 .25
834 A372 1.20p Tunja .25 .25
835 A372 1.50p Cucuta .55 .25
836 A372 1.50p Cartagena .25 .25
836A A372 4p Sogamoso 1.00 .25
837 A372 5p Popayan .50 .25

838	A372	5p Barranquilla	.55	.25
839	A372	10p San Gil	1.00	.25
839A	A372	10p Socorro	1.00	.25
		Nos. 832-839A (10)	5.85	2.50

1p for the tercentenary of Medellin; No. 835, the cent. of Cucuta's reconstruction.
Issued: 1p, 11/4; No. 835, 11/29; No. 836, 2/10/76; No. 833, 7/30/76; No. 834, 12/2076; No. 837, 8/30/77; No. 838, 9/20/77; 10p, 8/9/79; 4p, 9/14/79.
See Nos. 905-913, C818. For surcharge see No. 849.

No. 827 Surcharged

1975   **Perf. 14x13½**
840 A368 1.20p on 80c multi   .35 .25

Purace Indians, Cauca — A373

1976, Nov. 10   Litho.   Perf. 13½x14
841 A373 1.50p multi   .25 .25

Callicore A374

5p, Morpho (butterfly). 20p, Anthurium.

1976, Nov. 17   **Perf. 12**
842 A374 3p multicolored   .90 .25
843 A374 5p multicolored   1.50 .25
844 A374 20p multicolored   4.25 1.00
   Nos. 842-844 (3)   6.65 1.50

Rotary Emblem — A375

1976, Dec. 3   Litho.   Perf. 12
845 A375 1p multicolored   .25 .25
Rotary Club of Colombia, 50th anniversary.

Declaration of Independence, by John Trumbull — A376

1976, Dec. 21   Litho.   Perf. 12
846 A376 Strip of 3   10.00 11.50
  a.-c.   30p any single   2.75 2.00
American Bicentennial. No. 846 printed in sheets of 4 triptychs.

Policeman with Dog — A377

1976, Dec. 29   **Perf. 13½x14**
847 A377 1.50p multicolored   .25 .25
Honoring the National Police.
For surcharge see No. 850.

Nos. 831, 834, 847 Surcharged in Light Brown
1977, June   Litho.   Perf. 13½x14, 12
848 A371 2p on 1.10p multi   .40 .25
849 A372 2p on 1.20p multi   .25 .25
850 A377 2p on 1.50p multi   .25 .25
   Nos. 848-850 (3)   .90 .75

Souvenir Sheet

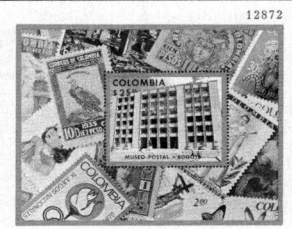

Postal Museum, Bogota — A378

1977, July 27   Litho.   Perf. 14
855 A378 25p multi   3.50 3.50
Postal Museum, Bogota.

Mother and Child — A379

1977-78   Litho.   Perf. 12
856 A379 2p multi   .25 .25
857 A379 2.50p multi ('78)   1.75 .25
National good nutrition plan.
Issue dates: 2p, Aug. 30; 2.50p, Jan. 26.

Jacana and Eichhornia A380

20p, Mayan cotinga and pyrostegia venusta.

1977, Sept. 6   Litho.   Perf. 14
858 A380 10p multicolored   2.50 .25
859 A380 20p multicolored   4.00 .50
   Nos. 858-859,C644-C647 (6)   10.20 1.75

Fidel Cano, by Francisco Cano — A381

1977, Sept. 16   **Perf. 14**
860 A381 4p multicolored   .25 .25
90th anniversary of El Espectador, newspaper founded by Fidel Cano.

Abacus and Alphabet — A382

1977, Sept. 16   **Perf. 13½x14**
861 A382 3p multicolored   .25 .25
Popular education.

Cattleya Triannae — A383

1978-79   Litho.   Perf. 12
862 A383 2.50p multi   .75 .25
863 A383 3p multi ('79)   .75 .25
Issue dates: 2.50p, Apr. 18. 3p, May 10.

Sprinting and Games Emblem A384

Sports: a, sprinting. b, basketball. c, baseball. d, boxing. e. bicycling. f, fencing. g, soccer. h, gymnastics. i, judo. j, weight lifting. k, wrestling. l, swimming. m, tennis. n, target shooting. o, volleyball. p, water polo.

1978, June 27   Litho.   Perf. 14
868   Sheet of 16   29.00 29.00
  a.-p.   A384 10p, any single   1.25 .25
13th Central American and Caribbean Games, Medellin.

"Sigma 2" by Alvaro Herrán A385

1978, June 30
869 A385 8p multicolored   .55 .25
Chamber of Commerce, Bogota, centenary.

Gen. Tomás Cipriano de Mosquera (1778-1878), Statesman A386

1978, Oct. 6   Litho.   Perf. 12
870 A386 6p multicolored   .45 .25

Anthurium Narinenses — A387

1979, July 23   **Perf. 12**
871 A387 3p red & multi   .30 .25
872 A387 3p purple & multi   .30 .25
873 A387 3p rose & purple   .30 .25
874 A387 3p white & multi   .30 .25
  a.   Block of 4, #871-874   2.50 2.50

Gen. Rafael Uribe, by Acevedo Bernal — A388

1979, Oct. 31   Litho.   Perf. 12
875 A388 8p multicolored   .50 .25
Gen. Uribe, statesman, 60th death anniv.

Village, by Leonor Alarcon — A389

1979, Nov. 22   **Perf. 14**
876 A389 15p multicolored   1.60 .60
Community Work Boards, 20th anniversary.

Introduction of Color Television A390

1980, Mar. 4   Litho.   Perf. 14
877 A390 5p multicolored   .60 .25

Bullfight, Arms of Cali A391

1980, Mar. 25
878 A391 5p multicolored   .70 .25
Cali Tourist Festival, 12/25/79-1/2/80.

"Learn to Write" — A392

a, shown. b, "a." c, "b." d, "c." e, "ch." f, "d." g, "e." h, "f." i, "g." j, "h." k, "i." l, "j." m, "k." n, "l." o, "ll." p, "m." q, "n." r, "ñ." s, "o." t, "p." u, "q." v, "r." w, "s." x, "t." y, "u." z, "v." aa, "w." ab, "x." ac, "y." ad, "z."

1980, Apr. 25   Litho.   Perf. 12½
879   Block of 30   27.50 27.50
  a.-ad.   A392 4p any single   .75 .25
Each stamp shows letter of alphabet and corresponding animal or subject. Issued in sheets of 90 (10x9).

Villavicencio Festival — A393

Design: 9p, Vallenato festival.

1980 **Litho.** **Perf. 14**
880 A393 5p multicolored .55 .25
881 A393 9p multicolored .55 .25
  Issue dates: 5p, July 15; 9p, June 17.

Gustavo Uribe Ramirez and Tree A394

1980, Aug. 5 **Litho.** **Perf. 12**
882 A394 10p multicolored 1.10 .25
  Gustavo Uribe Ramirez (1893-1968), ecologist.

Narino Palace (Former Presidential Residence) — A395

1980, Sept. 19 **Litho.** **Perf. 14**
883 A395 5p multicolored .70 .25

Monument to First Pioneers of 1819, Armenia A396

1980, Oct. 14
884 A396 5p multicolored .60 .25

11th National Games, Neiva — A397

1980, Nov. 28 **Perf. 13½x14**
885 A397 5p multicolored .60 .25

Fight against Cancer — A398

1980, Dec. 9
886 A398 10p multicolored .50 .25

Xavier University Law Faculty, 50th Anniversary A399

1980, Dec. 16 **Litho.** **Perf. 14½**
887 A399 20p multicolored .85 .30

Death of Bolivar — A400

1980, Dec. 17 **Perf. 12**
888 A400 25p multicolored 1.25 .60
  Simon Bolivar, death sesquicentennial. See No. C696.

José Maria Obando, President of Colombia A401

  115th Anniv. of Constitution (Former Presidents): b, Jose Hilario Lopez. c, Manuel Murillo Toro. d, Santiago Perez. e, Rafael Reyes. f, Carlos E. Restrepo. g, Jose Vicente Concha. h, Miguel Abadia Mendez. i, Eduardo Santos. j, Mariano Ospina Perez.

1981, June 9 **Litho.** **Perf. 12**
889 Strip of 10 6.00
  a.-j. A401 5p multicolored .50 .25

1981, Sept. 23 **Litho.** **Perf. 12**
  Designs: a, Rafael Nunez (1825-94). b, Marco Fidel Suarez (1855-1927). c, Pedro Nel Ospina (1858-1927). d, Enrique Olaya Herrera (1880-1937). e, Alfonso Lopez Pumarejo (1886-1959). f, Aquileo Parra (1825-1900). g, Santos Gutierrez (1820-72). h, Tomas Cipriano de Mosquera (1789-1878). i, Mariano Ospina Rodriguez. j, Pedro Alcantara Herran (1800-72).

890 Strip of 10 50.00
  a.-j. A401 7p multicolored 3.50 .50

1981, Aug. 11 **Litho.** **Perf. 12**
  Designs like No. 889.
891 Strip of 10 55.00
  a.-j. A401 7p multicolored 4.00 1.00

1981, Nov. 11 **Litho.** **Perf. 12**
  Designs: a, Manuel Maria Mallarino. b, Santos Acosta. c, Eustorgio Salgar. d, Julian Trujillo. e, Francisco Javier Zaldua. f, Guillermo Leon Valencia. g, Laureano Gomez. h, Manuel A. Sanclemente. i, Miguel Antonio Caro. j, Jose Eusebio Otalora.
892 Strip of 10 32.50
  a.-j. A401 7p multicolored 2.50 .40

1981, Dec. 15 **Litho.** **Perf. 12**
  Designs: a, Ruben Piedrahita Arango. b, Jorge Holguin. c, Ramon Gonzalez Valencia. d, Jose Manuel Marroquin. e, Carlos Holguin. f, Bartolome Calvo. g, Sergio Camargo. h, Jose Maria Rojas Garrido. i, J.M. Campo Serrano. j, Eliseo Payan.
893 Strip of 10 25.00
  a.-j. A401 7p multicolored 1.75 .30

1982, May 3 **Perf. 12**
  Designs: a, Simon Bolivar. b, Francisco de Paula Santander. c, Joaquin Mosquera. d, Domingo Caicedo. e, Jose Ignacio de Marquez. f, Roberto Urdaneta Arbelaez. g, Carlos

Lozano y Lozano. h, Guillermo Quintero Calderon. i, Jose de Obaldia. j, Juan de Dios Aranzazu.
894 Strip of 10 14.50
  a.-j. A401 7p multicolored 1.40 .25
  See No. 1110, 1329.

Jose Maria Villa and West Bridge over Cauca River A404

1981, Nov. 25 **Litho.** **Perf. 14x13½**
895 A404 60p multicolored 1.50 .30

Agrarian, Mineral and Industrial Credit Bank, 50th Anniv. — A405

1981, Dec. 9 **Litho.** **Perf. 14**
896 A405 15p multicolored .50 .25

Los Nevados Park — A406

1981, Dec. 10 **Litho.** **Perf. 13½x14**
897 A406 20p multicolored .70 .25

Girl Sitting on Fence — A407

1982, Feb. 22 **Litho.** **Perf. 12½x12**
898 Strip of 3 5.00 5.00
  a. A407 30p shown 1.10 .40
  b. A407 30p Girl, basket 1.10 .40
  c. A407 30p Boy, wheelbarrow 1.10 .40

Floral Bouquet — A408

  Various floral arrangements (background): a, Flowers in vase (gray). b, Roses (red). c, Daisies (green). d, Roses (blue). e, Assorted (red). f, Yellow & orange flowers (green). g, Assorted (lilac). h, Roses (gray). i, Pink flowers (green). j, Flowers in basket (gray).

1982, July 28
900 Strip or block of 10 17.00 17.00
  a.-j. A408 7p, any single 1.75 .30

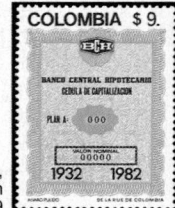

Hipotecario Bank, 50th Anniv. — A409

1982, July 29 **Perf. 14**
901 A409 9p black & green .50 .25

St. Thomas Aquinas (1225-1274) A410

  Paintings by Zurbaran.

1982 **Litho.** **Perf. 12**
902 A410 5p multicolored .40 .25
903 A410 5p St. Teresa of Avila .40 .25
904 A410 5p St. Francis of Assisi .40 .25
  Nos. 902-904 (3) 1.20 .75
  Issued: No. 902, 8/6; No. 903, 9/28; No. 904, 10/4.

Arms Type of 1975

  No. 905, Buga. No. 906, San Juan de Pasto. No. 907, Rionegro. No. 908, Santa Fe de Bogota. No. 909, Santiago de Cali. No. 910, Honda. No. 911, Cartago. No. 912, Antioquia ('86).

1982-90 **Litho.** **Perf. 14, 12 (50p)**
905 A372 10p .40 .25
906 A372 10p multicolored 1.25 .25
907 A372 16p multicolored .70 .25
908 A372 20p multicolored 1.00 .25
909 A372 20p multicolored .30 .25
910 A372 23p multicolored .75 .25
911 A372 55p multicolored .70 .25
912 A372 55p multicolored 1.00 .25
  Nos. 905-912 (8) 6.10 2.00
  Issued: 16p, 23p, No. 905, 12/7; No. 908, 3/1/83; No. 906, 4/12/83; No. 909, 7/25/86; 55p, 8/5/86; 50p, 5/30/90.
  See No. C818.

Gabriel Marquez, 1982 Nobel Prize, Literature — A412

1982, Dec. 10 **Perf. 13½x14**
917 A412 7p gray & green .25 .25
  See Nos. C731-C732.

Public Education Bicentenary (Society of Mary for Education) A413

1983, May 6
918 A413 9p gold & blk .40 .25

José Maria Espinosa Prieto, Painter — A414

1983, June 3   **Perf. 12**
919 A414 9p Self-portrait, 1860   .40   .25

250th Anniv. of City of Cucuta — A415

1983, June 23   **Litho.**   **Perf. 12**
920 A415 9p multicolored   .35   .25

Porfirio Barba-Jacob (1883-1942), Poet — A416

1983, July 29   **Litho.**   **Perf. 13½x14**
921 A416 9p Portrait   .35   .25

Simon Bolivar, 200th Birth Anniv. A417

1983, July 24   **Perf. 12**
922 A417 9p multicolored   .30   .25
See Nos. C736-C737.

Royal Spanish Botanical Expedition, 200th Anniv. — A418

No. 923, Cinchona lancefolia. No. 924, Passiflora laurifolia. No. 925, Cinchona cordiflora.

1983, Aug. 18   **Perf. 14**
923 A418 9p multicolored   .25   .25
924 A418 9p multicolored   .25   .25
925 A418 60p multicolored   1.75   .50
   Nos. 923-925,C738-C740 (6)   6.25   1.90

Dawn in the Andes, by Alejandro Obregon A420

1983, Oct. 5   **Litho.**   **Perf. 12**
928 A420 20p multicolored   .50   .25
See No. C741.

Francisco de Paula Santander (1792-1840), General — A421

1984, Mar. 6   **Litho.**   **Perf. 14½x14**
929 A421 12p light olive green   .30   .25
930 A421 12p pale carmine   .30   .25
931 A421 12p light ultra   .30   .25
   Nos. 929-931 (3)   .90   .75

Admiral Jose Prudencio Padilla (1784-1831) — A423

1984, May 17   **Litho.**   **Perf. 12**
933 A423 10p multicolored   .40   .25

Luis Antonio Calvo (1882-1945) Composer — A424

1984, July 26
934 A424 18p multicolored   .40   .25

Diego Fallon (1834-1905), Educator, Musician, Poet — A425

1984, Aug. 31   **Perf. 12**
935 A425 20p multicolored   .45   .25

Candelario Obeso (1849-1884), Writer — A426

1984, Sept. 4   **Perf. 14x13½**
936 A426 20p multicolored   .45   .25

Site of Marandua, Future City A427

1984, Sept. 28   **Perf. 12**
937 A427 15p multicolored   .35   .25
See No. C744.

Christmas 1984 A428

Nativity and Children Playing, by Jose Uriel Sierra, Age 7.

1984, Dec. 14
938 A428 12p multicolored   .35   .25
See No. C746.

Dr. Luis Eduardo Lopez, Education Minister A429

1984, Dec. 21
939 A429 22p multicolored   .45   .25

Maria Concepcion Loperena de Fernandez de Castro, Independence War Heroine — A430

1985, Jan. 6
940 A430 12p multicolored   .35   .25

Gonzalo Mejia (1885-1956) — A431

12p, Portrait, biplane, camera.

1985, Feb. 25
941 A431 12p multicolored   .45   .25
Aviation, motion picture and meat exporting industrialist.

Self-portrait with Wife — A432

1985, Feb. 25
942 A432 37p multicolored   .80   .30
Pedro Nel Gomez (1899-1984), painter. See No. C748.

Fauna A433

No. 943, Hydrochaeris hydrochaeris. No. 944, Felis pardalis. No. 945, Tremarctos ornatus, vert. No. 946, Tapirus pinchaque.

1985   **Perf. 14**
943 A433 12p multicolored   .50   .30
    Perf. 13
944 A433 15p multicolored   .50   .25
945 A433 15p multicolored   .50   .25
946 A433 20p multicolored   .85   .30
   Nos. 943-946,C758 (5)   3.85   1.35

Carlos Gardel (1890-1935), Entertainer A434

15p, Portrait, Fokker F-31 Trimotor.

1985, June 23   **Perf. 14**
947 A434 15p multicolored   .30   .25

Camina Literacy Program — A435

1985, Nov. 25   **Perf. 13½x14**
948 A435 15p Tree, alphabet   .30   .25

Christmas 1985 A436

1985, Dec. 4   **Litho.**   **Perf. 13**
949 A436 15p multicolored   .40   .25
Rafael Pombo Children's Foundation. See No. C755.

Eduardo Carranza (b. 1913), Poet — A437

1986, Feb. 13
950 A437 18p multicolored   .30   .25

Colombian Free University, Cent. — A438

1986, Feb. 14
951 A438 18p multicolored   .30 .25

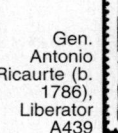

Gen. Antonio Ricaurte (b. 1786), Liberator A439

1986, May 7   Litho.   Perf. 13
952 A439 18p Leiva birthplace   .30 .25

Jose Asuncion Silva (1865-1896), Poet, and Scene from Nocturno — A440

1986, May 30   Litho.   Perf. 12
953 A440 18p multicolored   .30 .25

Fernando Gomez Martinez (1897-1985), Journalist — A441

1986, June 19
954 A441 24p multicolored   .30 .25

Santiago de Cali, 450th Anniv. A442

1986, July 25   Litho.   Perf. 13
955 A442 25p La Merced   .30 .25

A443

Monsignor Jose Vicente Castro Silva (1885-1968), rector of the Mayor del Rosario School: portrait by Ricardo Gomez.

1986, Aug. 4   Litho.   Perf. 12
956 A443 20p multicolored   .35 .25

Natl. University — A444

1986, Oct. 14   Litho.   Perf. 12
957 A444 40p multicolored   .60 .40
  Faculties: Fine Arts, cent., and Architecture, 50th anniv.

Rafael Maya (1897-1980), Poet, and Salamanca University Entrance — A445

1986, Oct. 15
958 A445 25p multicolored   .35 .25
  See No. C772.

Condor in Flight — A446   Inia goefrenis A446a

  No. 962, Inia goeffrensis. No. 963, Procyon cancrivorus. No. 964, Monachus tropicalis. No. 965, Pteronura brasiliensis. No. 966, Trichechus manatus. No. 967, Odocoileus virginianus. No. 968, Trogon personatus personatus. Nos. 962-968 horiz.

1986-89   Litho.   Perf. 12
959 A446 20p ultra   .35 .25
960 A446 25p ultra ('87)   .50 .25
        Perf. 14½x14, 14x14½
961 A446a 30p grn ('87)   .50 .25
962 A446a 30p dull vio ('87)   .50 .25
              Engr.
            Wmk. 334
963 A446a 35p chest brn
                    ('88)   .75 .25
964 A446a 35p dark grn ('88)   .75 .25
965 A446a 40p deep org
                    ('88)   .75 .25
966 A446a 40p gray ('88)   .85 .25
967 A446a 40p tan ('89)   .85 .25
968 A446a 45p dark vio ('88)   .85 .25
        Nos. 959-968 (10)   6.65 2.50

  Issued: 20p, 11/6; 25p, 5/25; No. 961, 6/8; No. 962, 12/24; No. 963, 8/6; No. 964, 9/20; No. 965, 9/20; No. 966, 11/29; No. 967, 4/29; No. 968, 12/16.
  See Nos. 996-1001, C778-C781.

A447

1987, Jan. 29   Unwmk.   Perf. 12
969 A447 25p multicolored   .50 .25
  Pedro Uribe Mejia (1886-1972), pioneer of Colombian coffee industry.

Santa Barbara Church — A448

1987, May 3   Perf. 13½x13
970 A448 500p multicolored   5.50 1.75
  Mompox, 450th anniv.

Writers A449

  Portraits and scenes from works: 70p, Jorge Isaacs (1837-1895), novelist, and scene from Maria. 90p, Aurelio Martinez Mutis (1884-1954), poet, and scene from La Epopeya del Condor.

1987   Perf. 12
971 A449 70p multicolored   .90 .25
972 A449 90p multicolored   1.25 .40
  Issue dates: 70p, July 28. 90p, Sept. 2.

A450

Social Security & Communications.

1987   Litho.   Perf. 13½x13
973 A450 35p multicolored   .40 .25

A451

Natl. Anthem, Cent.: Score, lyricist Rafael Nunez and composer Oreste Sindici. Dated 1987.

1988, May 25   Litho.   Perf. 12
974 A451 70p multicolored   .80 .25

Human Rights — A452

        Perf. 14½x14, 14x14½
1988-89   Engr.
975 A452 30p Life   .35 .25
976 A452 35p Suffrage   .35 .25
977 A452 40p Association, horiz.   .45 .25
978 A452 45p Culture, horiz.   .45 .25
        Nos. 975-978 (4)   1.50 1.00
  Issued: 30p, 35p, 5/12; 40p, 7/1; 45p, 10/27/89.
  See Nos. C797, C807.

Pasto, 450th Anniv. A453

1988, May 20   Litho.   Perf. 12
979 A453 60p Cathedral, Pasto   .70 .35
        Dated 1987.

Bogota Aqueduct and Sewage System, Cent. — A454

1988, May 20
980 A454 100p Waterfall   1.25 .35

Maria Currea de Aya (1888-1985), Women's Rights Activist — A455

1988, May 27
981 A455 80p multicolored   .95 .25

A456

Sailfish, Istiophorus Americanus.

        Perf. 14x13½
1988, July 19   Engr.   Wmk. 334
982 A456 (A) dark blue   4.25 2.25
983 A456 (B) Prus blue   1.25 .40
  At the time of issue, No. 982 was sold for 400p and No. 983 for 100p. See type A486.

A457

              Unwmk.
1988, Aug. 10   Litho.   Perf. 12
984 A457 120p multicolored   1.25 .35
  San Bartolome College, founded in 1604.

Jorge Alvarez Lleras (1885-1952), Engineer and Director of the Natl. Astronomical Observatory — A458

1988, Aug. 17
985 A458 90p multicolored   1.00 .45

Pres. Eduardo
Santos (1888-
1974)
A459

1988, Aug. 30
986 A459 80p multicolored   .85 .25

Andres
Bello
Seminary
A460

Unwmk.
1988, Dec. 27 Litho. Perf. 12
987 A460 115p multicolored   1.25 .25

Adpostal,
25th Anniv.
A461

1989, May 3
988 A461 45p multicolored   .40 .25

Military
Leaders — A462

*Bolivar and Santander at the Los
Llanos Campaign — A463*

1989 Litho. Perf. 12
989 A462 40p Santander   .60 .25
990 A462 40p Bolivar   .60 .25
991 A463 45p multicolored   .60 .25
  Nos. 989-991 (3)   1.80 .75

  Liberation campaign, 170th anniv.
  Issued: No. 989, 8/25; No. 990, 7/25; 45p,
8/7.

From Boyaca to Santa Fe — A464

1989, Aug. 7 Litho. Perf. 12
992   45p multicolored   1.50 .45
993   45p multicolored   1.50 .45
  a. A464 Pair, #992-993   4.00 2.00

  Liberation campaign, 170th anniv.

Liberation Campaign Triptych — A466

  Designs: a, Gen. Santander, liberation
force. b, Simon Bolivar riding mount. c, Insurgent cavalry.

Unwmk.
1989, Aug. 7 Litho. Perf. 13
994 A466 Strip of 3   4.50 1.75
  a.-c. 45p any single   1.25 .55

  Liberation Campaign, 170th anniv.

Tunja,
450th
Anniv.
A467

1989, Aug. 8 Perf. 12
995 A467 45p multicolored   .40 .25

Fauna Type of 1988

  Designs: No. 996, Harpia harpyja, horiz. No.
997, Urocyon cinereoargenteus. No. 998,
Dendrobates histrionicus. No. 1000,
Phenacosaurus indenenae. No. 1001,
Cebuella pygmaea. No. 1002, Eurypyga
helias, horiz.

Perf. 14½x14, 14x14½
1989-90 Engr. Wmk. 334
996 A446a 45p black   1.00 .25
997 A446a 50p blue gray   .60 .25
998 A446a 50p deep claret   .40 .25
999 A446a 55p red brown   .85 .25
1000 A446a 60p brown   .60 .25
1001 A446a 60p org brown   .60 .25
  Nos. 996-1001 (6)   4.05 1.50

  Issued: 45p, 9/7; Nos. 997, 1000, 3/1/90;
No. 998, 4/25; 55p, 8/18; No. 1001, 8/6.

City of Armenia,
Cent. — A468

1989, Aug. 30 Unwmk. Perf. 12
1011 A468 135p multicolored   1.25 .80

Espeletia
Hartwegiana
A469

1990, Mar. 28 Litho. Perf. 12
1012 A469 60p multicolored   .35 .25

Gen. Francisco De Paula Santander
(1792-1840) — A470

1990, May 6 Perf. 14x13½
1013 A470 50p multicolored   .40 .25
  Nos. 1013,C823-C827 (6)   3.80 2.75
  See Nos. 1046-1047.

General
Santander Police
Academy, 50th
Anniv. — A471

1990, May 16 Perf. 12
1014 A471 60p multicolored   .40 .25

Department
of La
Guajira
A473

1990, July 1 Perf. 12
1016 A473 60p multicolored   .60 .25

Ceiba
Pentandra
A474

1990, July 15 Litho. Perf. 12
1017 A474 60p multicolored   .50 .25

Tibouchina
lepidota — A475

1990, Aug. 8 Litho. Perf. 12
1018 A475 70p multicolored   .90 .25

Ceroxylon
quindiuense
A476

Unwmk.
1990, Aug. 28 Litho. Perf. 14
1019 A476 70p multicolored   .50 .25

St. John
Bosco — A477

1990, Sept. 28 Perf. 12
1020 A477 60p multicolored   .60 .25
  Salesian Order in Colombia, cent.

A478

1991, Mar. 28 Litho. Perf. 12
1021 A478 70p multicolored   .50 .25
  Miraculous Christ, Pilgrimage Church of
Buga.

Moths and
Butterflies
A479

  No. 1022, Callithea philotima. No. 1023,
Anaea syene, vert. No. 1024, Thecla coronata,
vert. No. 1025, Agrias amydon. No. 1026,
Morpho rhetenor. No. 1027, Heliconius
longarenus.

1991, Apr. 18 Litho. Perf. 14
1022 A479 70p multicolored   .90 .25
1023 A479 70p multicolored   .90 .25
1024 A479 80p multicolored   1.10 .25
1025 A479 80p multicolored   1.20 .25
1026 A479 170p multicolored   2.50 .35
1027 A479 190p multicolored   2.50 .35
  Nos. 1022-1027 (6)   9.10 1.70

  Nos. 1025-1027 are airmail.

New
Constitution
A480

1991, July 4 Litho. Perf. 14
1028 A480 70p multicolored   .40 .25

A481

1991, July 19 Perf. 12
1029 A481 80p multicolored   .40 .30
  Pres. Dario Echandia Olaya (1897-1989).
See No. 1042.

A482

1991, Aug. 7
1030 A482 70p multicolored .35 .25
Col. Antanasio Girardot (1791-1813).

A483

1991, Aug. 15 Litho. Perf. 14
1031 A483 80p multicolored .50 .25
Luis Carlos Galan Sarmiento (1943-1989), political reformer.

A484

Pre-Columbian Artifacts: 80p, Statue of cat god. No. 1033, Pitcher from tomb of high official. No. 1034, Statue with two heads. 210p, Flying fish, horiz.

1991, Aug. 24 Perf. 12
1032 A484 80p multicolored .75 .25
1033 A484 90p multicolored .90 .25
1034 A484 90p multicolored .90 .25
1035 A484 210p multicolored 2.00 .30
Nos. 1032-1035 (4) 4.55 1.05
Nos. 1034-1035 are airmail.

Colonial Architecture A485

80p, Cloister of St. Augustine, Tunja. No. 1037, Community Bridge, Chia. No. 1038, Roadside Chapel, Pamplona. 190p, Church of Immaculate Conception, Bogota.

1991 Litho. Perf. 12
1036 A485 80p multi .75 .25
1037 A485 90p multi 1.25 .25
1038 A485 90p multi, vert. 1.00 .30
1039 A485 190p multi, vert. 2.00 .35
Nos. 1036-1039 (4) 5.00 1.15
Issue dates: No. 1037, Sept. 9; others, Sept. 27. Nos. 1038-1039 are airmail.

Istiaphorus Americanus A486

1991, Sept. 3 Perf. 14
1040 A486 830p multicolored 6.50 1.50

Colombian Police Force, Cent. A487

1991, Oct. 12 Perf. 12
1041 A487 80p multicolored .60 .25

President Type of 1991
Pres. Alberto Lleras Camargo (1906-1990)

1991, Nov. 5
1042 A481 80p multicolored .45 .25

Sogamoso City Hall — A489

1991, Dec. 17 Litho. Perf. 12
1043 A489 80p multicolored .50 .25

A490

Designs: No. 1044, Diana Turbay Quintero (1950-91), journalist. No. 1045, Indalecio Lievano Aguirre (1917-82), diplomat.

1992 Litho. Perf. 14
1044 A490 80p multicolored .45 .25
1045 A490 80p multicolored .45 .25
Issued: No. 1044, Jan. 24; No. 1045, Apr. 21.

Santander Type of 1990 and

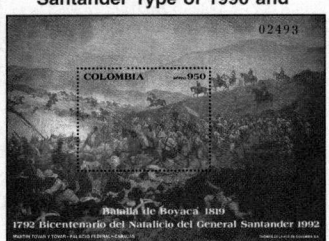

Battle of Boyaca — A491a

1992, Apr. 2 Perf. 14
Size: 26x37mm
1046 A470 80p Monument .50 .30
1047 A470 190p Portrait 1.25 .70
Souvenir Sheet
Perf. 13½x14
1047A A491a 950p multicolored 6.50 6.50
Nos. 1047-1047A are airmail. Gen. Francisco de Paula Santander, bicent. of birth.

A492

Ministers of Justice: 100p, Enrique Low Murtra (1939-91). 110p, Rodrigo Lara Bonilla (1946-84).

1992, Apr. 30 Litho. Perf. 12
1048 A492 100p multicolored .70 .30
1049 A492 110p multicolored .80 .30

A493

1992, May 18 Perf. 14
1050 A493 110p multicolored .75 .40
15th natl. games, Barranquilla.

Wildlife — A494

No. 1051, Oroaetus icidori. No. 1052, Tremarctos ornatus.

1992, Apr. 14 Litho. Perf. 12
1051 A494 (B) multicolored 1.90 .80
1052 A494 (A) multicolored 9.00 3.50
Nos. 1051-1052 had face values of 200p and 950p respectively on date of issue.

Endangered Species A495

No. 1053, Crocodylus acatus. No. 1054, Vultur gryphus, vert.

1992, Aug. 4
1053 A495 100p multicolored 1.25 .40
1054 A495 100p multicolored 1.25 .40

A496

1992, Aug. 24 Litho. Perf. 14
1055 A496 100p multicolored .60 .30
1056 A496 110p multicolored .60 .30
Maria Lopez de Escobar, founder of the House of the Mother and Child. No. 1056 is airmail.

A497

1992, Sept. 23 Litho. Perf. 12
1057 A497 100p multicolored .50 .30
Conference of First Ladies of the Americas and Caribbean, Cartagena.

Recycling — A498

1992, Oct. 9 Litho. Perf. 12
1058 A498 100p multicolored .50 .30

Discovery of America, 500th Anniv. — A499

Paintings: 100p, Zenaida, by Ana Mercedes Hoyos. No. 1060, Estudio Para 1/500, by Beatriz Gonzalez. No. 1061, Blue Eagle, by Alejandro Obregon. 230p, Cantileo, by Luis Luna. 260p, Corn, by Antonio Caro. 400p, Grand Curtain, by Luis Caballero. 440p, Homage to Guatavita, by Alejandro Obregon.

1992, Oct. 5 Litho. Perf. 13½x14
1059 A499 100p multicolored .50 .30
1060 A499 110p multicolored .50 .30
1061 A499 110p multicolored .50 .30
1062 A499 230p multicolored 1.25 .70
1063 A499 260p multicolored 1.50 .80
Nos. 1059-1063 (5) 4.25 2.40
Souvenir Sheets
Perf. 12
1064 A499 400p multicolored 3.00 3.00
1065 A499 440p multicolored 3.00 3.00
Nos. 1061-1063 are airmail.

World Post Day — A500

1992, Oct. 19 Litho. Perf. 12
1066 A500 (B) multicolored 1.20 .65
No. 1066 had face value of 200p on day of issue.

Christmas — A501

Children's paintings of: 100p, Nativity scene. 110p, Adoration of the Magi.

1992, Nov. 20 Litho. Perf. 12
1067 A501 100p multicolored .60 .30
1068 A501 110p multicolored .60 .30
No. 1068 is airmail.

Three Musicians, by Fernando Botero
A502

1993, Feb. 5   **Litho.**   **Perf. 12**
1069 A502 (B) multicolored   1.25   .80
    No. 1069 had a face value of 250p on day of issue.

Lions Intl. Campaign Against Amblyopia
A503

1993, Mar. 26   **Perf. 14**
1070 A503 100p multicolored   .50   .30

Holy Week in Popayan
A504

1993, Apr. 5   **Perf. 14x13½**
1071 A504 (B) multicolored   1.25   .80
    No. 1071 had a face value of 250p on day of issue.

A505

1993, Apr. 7   **Perf. 12**
1072 A505 (B) multicolored   1.25   .80
    Pan American Health Org., 90th anniv.
    No. 1072 had a face value of 250p on day of issue.

A506

1993, Apr. 14
1073 A506 (B) multicolored   1.25   .80
    Franciscans of Mary Immaculate, cent. No. 1073 had a face value of 250p on day of issue.

A507

1993, Apr. 22   **Litho.**   **Perf. 14**
1074 A507 (B) multicolored   1.25   .80
    EXFILBO '93, 18th Natl. Philatelic Exhibition. No. 1074 had a face value of 250p on day issue.

Guillermo Cano, writer — A508

1993, July 2   **Litho.**   **Perf. 12**
1075 A508 250p multicolored   1.50   .75

Human Rights
A509

    Rights: a, 150p, Of prisoners. b, 150p, Of the elderly. c, 200p, Of the infirm. d, 200p, Of children. e, 220p, Of women. f, 220p, Of the poor. g, 460p, To clean environment. h, 520p, Of indigenous people.
    Painting: 800p, Peace, Rights, and Freedom, by Alfredo Vivero, vert.

1993, June 10   **Perf. 14**
1076 A509   Block of 8, #a.-h.   12.00 7.50
    Souvenir Sheet
1077 A509 800p multicolored   5.50 5.50
    Nos. 1076e-1076h are airmail.

Amazon Region of Colombia — A510

    No. 1078a, Parrot. No. 1078b, Anaconda. No. 1079a, Victoria regia. No. 1079b, Flor ipecacuana. 880p, Map, native, horiz.

1993   **Litho.**   **Perf. 12**
1078 A510 150p Pair, #a.-b.   1.75 1.25
1079 A510 220p Pair, #a.-b.   2.50 1.50
    Souvenir Sheet
1080 A510 880p multicolored   5.00 5.00
    Nos. 1079-1080 are airmail.

Famous People — A511

    Designs: a, 150p, Alberto Pumarejo (1893-1970). b, 150p, Lorencita Villegas de Santos (1892-1960). c, 200p, Meliton Rodriguez (1875-1942). d, 200p, Tomas Carrasquilla (1858-1940).

1993   **Litho.**   **Perf. 14x13½**
1081 A511   Block of 4, #a.-d.   4.00 2.75

Christmas — A512

1993, Nov. 30   **Perf. 12**
1082 A512 200p Holy Family   .95   .60
1083 A512 220p Shepherd   1.60 1.10
    No. 1083 is airmail.

Tourism
A513

    Designs: No. 1084a, San Andres Providence. b, Cocuy Natl. Park. c, Lake Cocha. d, Waterfalls, Serrania de la Macarena. 250p, Lake Otun. No. 1086a, Chicamocha River. b, Sierra Nevada de Santa Marta mountains. 520p, Penol Reservoir.

1993, Dec. 1   **Litho.**   **Perf. 12**
1084 A513 220p Block of 4, #a.-d.   4.50 3.00
1085 A513 250p multicolored   1.25   .75
1086 A513 460p Pair, #a.-b.   4.75 3.00
1087 A513 520p multicolored   2.75 1.50
    Nos. 1084-1087 (4)   13.25 8.25
    Nos. 1084, 1086-87 are airmail.

A514

1993, Dec. 21   **Litho.**   **Perf. 14**
1088 A514 150p multicolored   .60   .40
    Natl. Museum, 170th anniv.

Marie Poussepin
A515

1994, Jan. 25   **Litho.**   **Perf. 14**
1089 A515 300p multicolored   1.50   .80

A516

    Birds: 180p, Ognorhynchus icterotis. 240p, Rallus semiplumbeus. 270p, Semnornis ramphastinus. 560p, Anas cyanoptera.

1994, Mar. 4
1090 A516 180p multi   1.40   .40
1091 A516 240p multi   1.60   .55
1092 A516 270p multi, horiz.   2.00   .70
1093 A516 560p multi, horiz.   4.00 1.40
    Nos. 1090-1093 (4)   9.00 3.05
    Nos. 1092-1093 are airmail.

A517

1994, Apr. 11   **Litho.**   **Perf. 14**
1094 A517 300p multicolored   1.25   .80
    Air Force, 75th anniv.

Latin American Presidential Summit, Cartagena
A518

1994, June 14   **Litho.**   **Perf. 14**
1095 A518 300p shown   1.00   .65
1096 A518 630p Flags   2.10 1.60
    No. 1096 is airmail.

1994 World Cup Soccer Championships, US — A519

    World Cup Trophy and: 180p, Soccer player, Colombian flag. 270p, Two players with ball. 560p, Soccer ball, Colombian flag, vert. 1110p, Soccer player offering hand to another.

1994, May 26 — **Perf. 12**
1097 A519 180p multicolored .80 .40
1098 A519 270p multicolored 1.20 .55
1099 A519 560p multicolored 2.50 1.40
Nos. 1097-1099 (3) 4.50 2.35
Souvenir Sheet
1100 A519 1110p multicolored 7.00 7.00
Nos. 1098-1099 are airmail.

Ricardo Rendon (1894-1931), Artist — A520

1994, June 30 **Litho.** **Perf. 12**
1101 A520 240p black 1.40 .65

1993 Census — A521

1994, Aug. 12 **Perf. 14**
1102 A521 240p multicolored 1.10 .45

Ministry of Communications Inravision, 30th Anniv. — A522

1994, Aug. 3
1103 A522 180p multicolored 1.00 .50

Intl. Year of the Family A523

1994, Sept. 1 **Litho.** **Perf. 14**
1104 A523 300p multicolored 1.25 .65

America Issue — A524

Methods of mail delivery: 270p, Horse, bicycle. 300p, Men holding stamps showing truck, ship, plane.

1994, Oct. 18 **Litho.** **Perf. 13**
1105 A524 270p multicolored 1.60 .65
1106 A524 300p multicolored 2.40 .70
No. 1105 is airmail.

Colombian Society of Engineers, Cent. A525

1994, Oct. 20 **Litho.** **Perf. 12**
1107 A525 180p multicolored .75 .40

Christmas A526

1994, Nov. 22 **Litho.** **Perf. 13½x13**
1108 A526 270p Magi .95 .65
1109 A526 300p Holy family 1.10 .70
No. 1108 is airmail.

Former President Type of 1981
Miniature Sheet of 20
Designs: a, Jose Miguel Pey. b, Jorge Tadeo Lozano. c, Antonio Narino. d, Camilo Torres. e, Jose Fernandez Madrid. f, Jose Maria del Castillo y Rada. g, Custodio Garcia Rovira. h, Antonio Villavicencio. i, Liborio Mejia. j, Rafael Urdaneta. k, Juan Garcia del Rio. l, Jose Maria Melo. m, Tomas Herrera. n, Froilan Largacha. o, Salvador Camacho Roldan. p, Ezequiel Hurtado. q, Dario Echandia Olaya. r, Alberto Lleras Camargo. s, Gustavo Rojas Pinilla. t, Carlos Lleras Restrepo.

1995, Apr. 4 **Litho.** **Perf. 12**
1110 A401 270p #a.-t. 35.00 35.00

World Offroad Bicycle Championships, Melgar — A527

1995, Mar. 30 **Perf. 14**
1111 A527 400p multicolored 1.60 .90

A528

1995, Oct. 12 **Litho.** **Perf. 12**
1112 A528 220p multicolored 1.00 .45
Gen. Jose Maria Obando (1795-1861), President.

A529

1995, Nov. 28 **Perf. 14**
1113 A529 400p Clean air 1.50 .75
1114 A529 400p Clean water 1.50 .75
Preserve the environment. America issue.

Christmas A530

Stained glass windows: 220p, Flight into Egypt. 330p, Nativity.

1995, Dec. 18 **Perf. 12**
1115 A530 220p multicolored .75 .40
1116 A530 330p multicolored 1.10 .65
No. 1116 is airmail.

Bogotá to Boyacá World Cycling Championship — A531

1995, Oct. 4 **Litho.** **Perf. 12**
1117 A531 400p multicolored 1.75 .75

León De Greiff (1895-1976), Poet — A532

1996, May 2 **Litho.** **Perf. 12**
1118 A532 400p black 1.40 .60

Mosquera Courtyard, Natl. Capitol A533

1996, July 18 **Litho.** **Perf. 14**
1119 A533 400p multicolored 1.50 .60

Medellin Rapid Transit System A534

1996, July 2 **Perf. 12**
1120 A534 500p multicolored 2.00 .90

A535

1996, June 20
1121 A535 500p multicolored 1.60 .75
Community of St. John of God in Colombia, 400th anniv.

A536

Arms: a, Santa Maria la Antigua del Darien. b, San Sebastian de Mariquita. c, Villa de la Marinilla. d, Villa of Santa Cruz of Mompox.

1996, June 25
1122 A536 400p Block of 4,
#a.-d. 5.00 5.00
e. As "d," inscribed AEREO 15.00 15.00
f. Block of 4, #1122a-1122c, 1122e 20.00 20.00
Issued in sheets of 16 stamps.

1996 Summer Olympic Games, Atlanta — A537

1996, July 16
1123 A537 500p multicolored 2.00 .75

SAYCO (Colombian Authors and Composers Society), 50th Anniv. — A538

1996, Aug. 17 **Litho.** **Perf. 12**
1124 A538 400p multicolored 1.50 .60

Exfilbo '96, 20th Natl. Philatelic Exhibition A539

Jewelry from Gold Museum, Bogotá.

1996, Oct. 19 **Litho.** **Perf. 12**
1125 A539 400p multicolored 1.50 .60

Souvenir Sheet

Founders Theater, Manizales, 30th Anniv. — A540

Drop curtain: a, Eagle, people watching man drawing on ground, vert. b, People, animals on hillside.

1996, Oct. 28   *Perf. 14*
1126 A540 4000p #a.-b.   30.00 30.00

Christmas
A541

No. 1127, Mailman handing woman letter. No. 1128, Woman reading letter, mailman holding bundle of mail.

1996, Nov. 22
1127 A541 400p multicolored   1.75 .40
1128 A541 400p multicolored   1.75 .40
No. 1128 is airmail.

America
Issue — A542

No. 1129, Men's costume. No. 1130, Women's costume.

1996, Nov. 29   *Perf. 12*
1129 A542 500p multicolored   1.75 .60
1130 A542 500p multicolored   1.75 .60

Historical Landmarks — A543

a, Cemetery, Santa Cruz of Mompox. b, Carved face, San Agustin Archaeological Park. c, Entrance, Palace of the Inquisition, Cartagena de Indias. d, Inside ruins, Tierradentro Archaeological Park.

1996, Dec. 6   *Perf. 14*
1131 A543 400p Block of 4,
    #a.-d.   10.00 10.00

Alvaro Gomez
Hurtado (1919-95), Politician, Writer — A544

1997, Mar. 18   Litho.   *Perf. 12*
1132 A544 400p multicolored   1.50 .75

Bogotá
Journalists
Assoc.,
50th Anniv.
A545

1997, July 10   Litho.   *Perf. 12*
1133 A545 400p multicolored   1.50 .40

Natl. Festival of Porro — A546

1997, June 26   *Perf. 13½x14*
1134 A546 400p multicolored   1.50 .40

Pres. Virgilio
Barco (1921-97) — A547

1997, Nov. 27   Litho.   *Perf. 14*
1135 A547 500p multicolored   1.75 .40

Colombia in
Peace
A548

500p, Children playing. 1100p, Children dancing.

1997, Dec. 30   Litho.   *Perf. 12*
1136 A548 500p multicolored   1.40 .40
1137 A548 1100p multicolored   3.00 .90
No. 1137 is airmail.

America
Issue
A549

500p, Postman by day. 1100p, Postman by night.

1997, Dec. 30
1138 A549 500p multicolored   2.00 .50
1139 A549 1100p multicolored   4.00 1.25
No. 1139 is airmail.

Jorge Eliecer
Gaitan (1903-48),
Politician — A550

1998, Apr. 24   Litho.   *Perf. 14*
1140 A550 500p multicolored   1.75 .80

Free
University,
75th Anniv.
A551

1998, July 1   Litho.   *Perf. 14*
1141 A551 500p black & red   2.75 .75

Santander
Industrial
University, 50th
Anniv. — A552

1998, May 14   *Perf. 12*
1142 A552 500p multicolored   1.75 .80

City of Manizales, 150th
Anniv. — A553

1998, July 24   Litho.   *Perf. 12*
1143 A553 500p multicolored   2.75 .75

A554

Pre-Columbian art, agency: a, Tairona, Bank of the Republic. b, Malagana, Controller General. c, Quimbaya, Bank Superintendent.

1998, July 24
1144 A554 500p Strip of 3, #a.-c. 7.50 7.50
Natl. financial agencies, 70th anniv.

A555

1998, Aug. 21   *Perf. 14*
1145 A555 500p multicolored   2.75 .80
Pres. Misael Pastrana Borrero (1923-97).

University
of the
Andes,
50th Anniv.
A556

1998, Sept. 28
1146 A556 500p multicolored   2.25 .80

Christmas
A557

Designs: 500p, Woman kneeling down to get water with bowl, cherubs in sky. No. 1148a, Magi. No. 1148b, Nativity scene.

1998, Nov. 19   Litho.   *Perf. 14*
1147 A557 500p multicolored   1.25 .75
1148 A557 1000p Pair, #a.-b.   4.75 3.25
No. 1148 is airmail.

A558

Emblems of Colombian Academies: a, Language. b, Medicine. c, Law. d, History. e, Science. f, Ecomonics. g, Religion.

1998, Dec. 15   *Perf. 12*
    Sheet of 7 + Label
1149 A558 500p #a.-g.   14.00 14.00

A559

1999, Apr. 16   *Perf. 14*
1150 A559 1000p multicolored   2.25 1.00
Gen. José Hilario López.

Famous
Women — A559a

America Issue: 600p, Soledad Román de Nuñez. 1200p, Bertha Herández de Ospina.

1999, Mar. 25   Litho.   *Perf. 12*
1151 A559a 600p multicolored   1.50 .50
1152 A559a 1200p multicolored   3.00 1.00
No. 1152 is airmail.

Turtles — A560

a, Chelonia mydas. b, Dermochelys coriacea. c, Eretmochelys imbricata.

1999, Apr. 16 *Perf. 14*
1153 A560 1300p Strip of 3, #a.-c. 13.00 13.00

Dr. Eduardo Zuleta Angel, Diplomat (b. 1899) — A561

1999, Sept. 9 Litho. *Perf. 12*
1154 A561 600p multicolored 1.40 .45

Pamplona, 450th Anniv. A562

1999 Litho. *Perf. 12*
1155 A562 1000p multicolored 2.75 .75

Sovereign Military Order of Malta, 900th Anniv. — A563

1999, June 24 *Perf. 14*
1156 A563 1200p multicolored 4.00 1.25

Japanese Immigration to Colombia — A564

Designs: a, Red at right. b, Red at left.

1999, May 12 *Perf. 13½x14*
1157 A564 1300p Pair, #a.-b. 6.00 6.00

Pan American Games, Winnipeg, Manitoba — A565

Designs: a, Flag, Olympic rings. b, Runner facing right. c, Weight lifter facing left. d, Cyclist facing right. e, Shooter facing left. f, Roller skater facing right. g, Runner facing left. h, Weight lifter facing right. i, Cyclist facing left. j, Shooter facing right. k, Roller skater facing left. l, Like "a," with lilac vertical line under "12."

1999, July 23 Litho. *Perf. 14*
1158 A565 1200p Sheet of 12, #a.-l. 30.00 30.00

Luis A. Robles (b. 1849) — A566

1999, Oct. 27
1159 A566 600p multi 1.10 .40

Manufacture of Aspirin, Cent. A567

1999, Dec. 1 *Perf. 12¾*
1160 A567 600p multi 1.10 .40
Value is for stamp with surrounding selvage.

UPU, 125th Anniv. A568

1999, Oct. 29 *Perf. 14¼*
1161 A568 1000p "125" 1.75 .75
1162 A568 1300p "1874-1999" 2.75 1.00

Inter-American Development Bank, 40th Anniv. — A569

Abstract art: a, "Colombia" in yellow. b, "Colombia" in red.

1999, Nov. 19 *Perf. 14x14¼*
1163 A569 1000p Pair, #a.-b. 3.50 1.40

America Issue, A New Millennium Without Arms — A570

a, Stylized hands. b, Large flower at LR.

1999, Nov. 9 *Perf. 14*
1164 A570 1200p Pair, #a.-b. 4.25 1.90

Christmas — A571

a, Holy Family, animals. b, Angel, Magi.

1999, Nov. 29 *Perf. 13½x14*
1165 A571 600p Pair, #a.-b. 2.25 .90

Millennium — A572

Designs: a, Nude man, flag, dove. b, Globe, rainbow, "2000."

2000, Jan. 3 *Perf. 14*
1166 A572 1000p Pair, #a.-b. 4.00 4.00

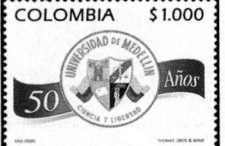

University of Medellin, 50th Anniv. A573

2000, Feb. 1 Litho. *Perf. 14*
1167 A573 1000p multi 1.50 .65

Father José Rafael Faría Bermúdez (1896-1979) A574

2000, Mar. 6 Litho. *Perf. 14*
1168 A574 1300p multi 1.75 .90

2000 Summer Olympics, Sydney A575

2000, Apr. 21
1169 A575 1000p multi 1.75 .75

Popayán Religious Music Festival A576

2000, July 7
1170 A576 1000p multi 1.90 .65

America Issue, Campaign Against AIDS A577

2000, Sept. 19 Litho. *Perf. 14x13½*
1171 A577 1000p multi 4.00 1.60

Radio Station HJCK, 50th Anniv. — A578

2000, Sept. 28 Litho. *Perf. 14*
1172 A578 1000p multi 1.50 .65

Birth Registration A579

2000, Nov. 14 Litho. *Perf. 14¼*
1173 A579 1000p multi 1.50 .60

Paintings A580

No. 1174: a, Archangel, by Fernando Botero. b, Gypsy Woman With Tamourine, by Jean-Baptiste-Camille Corot. c, Vera Sergine Renoir, by Renoir. d, Man on Horse, by Botero. e, Mother Superior, by Botero. f, A Town, by Botero. g, Flowers, by Botero. h, Cézanne, by Botero. i, Patio, by Botero. j, Absinthe Drinker in Grenelle, by Toulouse-Lautrec. k, A Little Valley, by Corot. l, The Studio, by Botero.

2001, Jan. 31 *Perf. 12*
1174 Sheet of 12 15.00 15.00
  a.-l. A580 650p Any single .95 .45

Children's Day — A581

2001, Mar. 15   **Litho.**   **Perf. 14**
1175 A581 1100p multi   3.75 1.40

Abolition of Slavery, 150th Anniv. — A582

2001, May 21   **Litho.**   **Perf. 14¼x14**
1176 A582 1100p multi   3.75 1.40

Discovery of Magdalena River, 500th Anniv. — A583

2001, June 13   **Litho.**   **Perf. 14**
1177 A583 1100p multi   3.75 1.40

Copa America Soccer Tournament A584

2001, July 18   **Litho.**   **Perf. 12¾**
1178 A584 1900p multi   5.25 1.75

Values are for examples with surrounding selvage.

America Issue — Los Katios Natl. Park, UNESCO World Heritage Site — A585

2001, Aug. 17   **Perf. 13¾x14**
1179 A585 2100p multi   7.50 3.00

Year of Dialogue Among Civilizations A586

2001, Oct. 9   **Perf. 14**
1180 A586 650p multi   2.50 .80

Reclining Woman, by Fernando Botero — A587

2001, Oct. 23   **Perf. 14¼**
1181 A587 1100p multi   4.00 1.40

Christmas A588

2001, Nov. 19   **Perf. 14**
1182 A588 1100p multi   4.00 1.40

National Beauty Pageant — A589

Flag, Miss Colombia Vanesa A. Mendoza Bustos and: a, Cartagena de Indias. b, St. Francis of Assisi Cathedral, Quibdo.

2002, Jan. 22   **Perf. 14x14¼**
1183 A589 800p Horiz. pair, #a-b   3.00 1.00

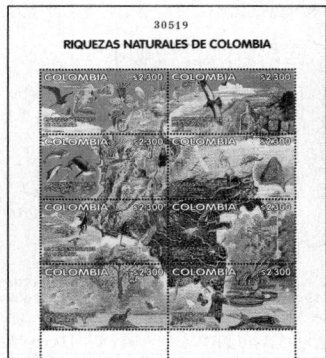

Natural Riches of Colombia — A590

Parts of map of Colombia, various wildlife and/or natives and: a, Bird and clouds at left. b, Turtle at upper left. c, Fish and whales at left. d, Man on horse at center. e, Volcano at upper left. f, Red and blue parrots at right. g, Flamingos at left. h, Snake at lower left.

2002, Feb. 1   **Perf. 14¼x14**
1184 A590 2300p Sheet of 8, #a-h   45.00 45.00

Children's Day — A591

2002, Feb. 18   **Perf. 12**
1185 A591 1400p multi   2.50 1.10

New Emblem of Adpostal — A592

2002, Mar. 7   **Perf. 14**
1186 A592 800p multi   1.60 .60

7th South American Games A593

2002, Jan. 7
1187 A593 2100p multi   3.00 1.25

Oxyura Jamaicensis A594

2002, Apr. 30   **Litho.**   **Perf. 12**
1188 A594 3900p multi   6.50 3.00

Souvenir Sheet

Frogs — A595

No. 1189: a, 7200p, Hyla crepitans. b, 7600p, Dendrobates histrionicus.

2002, Apr. 30   **Perf. 13¾x14**
1189 A595 Sheet of 2, #a-b   21.00 21.00

Souvenir Sheet

Butterflies — A596

No. 1190: a, Dryas iulia. b, Dryadula phaetusa, vert.

2002, Apr. 30   **Perf. 12**
1190 A596 13,700p Sheet of 2, #a-b   37.50 37.50

Foundation for Reconstructive Surgery, 25th Anniv. — A597

2002, May 24   **Perf. 14**
1191 A597 1000p multi   1.60 .60

Pre-Columbian Art — A598

No. 1192, 800p: a, Nariño pectoral. b, Nariño disc.
No. 1193, 1400p: a, Calima diadem. b, Calima pectoral.
No. 1194, 2100p: a, Anthropomorphic Tairona pectoral. b, Round Tairona pectoral.

2002, June 7   **Perf. 13½x14**
     Horiz. Pairs, #a-b
1192-1194 A598 Set of 3   15.00 15.00

Surgical Society of Bogota San José Hospital, Cent. — A599

No. 1195: a, Early doctors and nurse. b, Hospital.

2002, July 22   **Perf. 14**
1195 A599 800p Horiz. pair, #a-b 2.75 2.75

Consuelo Araújo Noguera (1940-2001), Assassinated Former Minister of Culture — A600

2002, Aug. 1
1196 A600 1400p multi   2.50 1.00

Union Network International A601

2002, Aug. 12
1197 A601 1000p multi   1.60 .65

America Issue — Youth, Education and Literacy — A602

No. 1198: a, Person reading book. b, Letters amd words.

2002, Oct. 9
1198 A602 2500p Horiz. pair, #a-b   7.00 6.00

Christmas
A603

2002, Nov. 6   **Litho.**   ***Perf. 14x13¾***
1199   A603   800p multi   2.00   .65

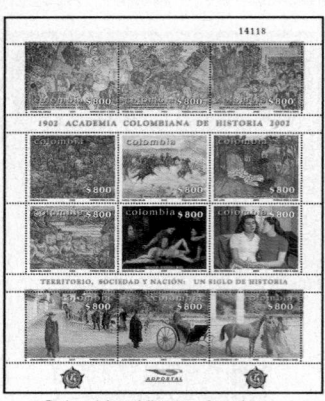

Colombian History Academy,
Cent. — A604

No. 1200: a, Mural scene with Simon Bolivar at UR. b, Mural scene with horsemen at top. c, Mural scene with man with outstretched arms at UL. d, Cafetal, 1956. e, Batalla de Palonegro, 1905. f, Tigre Cazando Sabanera, 1963. g, El Barqueo, 1936. h, Colombia Asesinada, 1902. i, Dos Mujeres, 1951. j, Bearded man at left, Plaza de Santander. k, Carriage, Plaza de Santander. l, Horse, man and woman, Plaza de Santander.

2002, Nov. 19   ***Perf. 13¾x14***
1200   A604   800p   Sheet of 12,
       #a-l   22.50   22.50

Peace
Treaty
Ending War
of 1,000
Days, Cent.
A605

2002, Nov. 21   ***Perf. 14x13¾***
1201   A605   1600p multi   3.50   1.10

Carnival
A606

No. 1202: a, shown. b, Participants holding masks on sticks. c, Participants on float.

2003, Jan. 4   ***Perf. 14***
1202   Horiz. strip of 3   6.50   6.50
   a.-b.   A606 1000p Either single   1.25   1.25
   c.   A606 1200p multi   1.60   1.60

Printed in sheets of 3 horizontal strips and 2 horiz. strips of 3 labels.

Articulated
Bus, Bogota
A607

2003, Mar. 13   ***Perf. 12***
1203   A607   1000p multi   1.60   .70

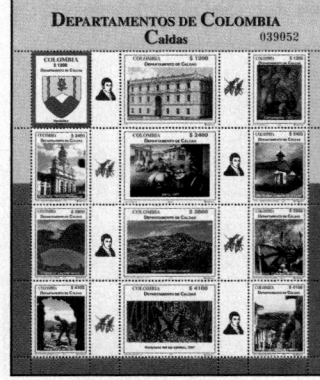

Departments — A608

No. 1204 — Caldas Department: a, 1200p, Arms. b, 1200p, Government office building, Manizales, horiz. c, 1200p, Campesinos, 1957. d, 2400p, Church, Salamina. e, 2400p, Neira, 1997, horiz. f, 2400p, Enea Chapel, Manizales. g, 2800p, Laguna Verde, Villamaria. h, 2800p, Aguadas, horiz. i, 2800p, Devil's carnival, Riosucio. j, 4100p, Miner, Marmato. k, 4100p, Mariposas del Eje Cafetero, 2001, horiz. l, 4100p, Pacora.

No. 1205, 1000p — Huila Department: a, Arms. b, Government office building, Neiva, horiz. c, La Gaitana. d, Bordones Waterfall, Isnos. e, San Agustín World Heritage Archaeological Park, horiz. f, Lavapatas Spring, San Agustín. g, La Tatacoa Desert, Villavieja. h, Liberty tree, Gigante, horiz. i, Sombrero maker, Suaza. j, Nuestra Señora de los Dolores Church, Aipe. k, Paisaje, horiz. l, Dancers.

No. 1206 — 2400p: a, Historic center of Barichara. b, Ophthalmologic Foundation of Santander, Bucaramanga, horiz. c, Girón. d, Santander Industrial University Intl. Piano Festival, 20th anniv. emblem. e, Petroleum Christ Statue, refinery, Barrancabermeja, horiz. f, Church, San Andrés. g, Gustavo Cote Uribe (1918-94), writer. h, Chamber of Commerce, Bucaramanga, horiz. i, Carnival of Eastern Colombia, Bucaramanga. j, Historic center of Albania. k, Chicamocha River Canyon, Cepitá, horiz. l, Entreguerras.

Sheets of 12, #a-l, + 8 labels

2003   ***Perf. 12***
1204   A608   Caldas   42.50   42.50
1205   A608   Huila   17.50   17.50
1206   A608   Santander   35.00   35.00

Issued: No. 1204, Apr. 11. No. 1205, June 29. No. 1206, July 22. Size of horiz. stamps: 46x37mm.

See Nos. 1224-1226, 1246, 1265-1267, 1273, 1288-1289, 1316, 1335-1336, 1359, 1377, 1393, 1430.

Fish and Coral of
the Rosario
Islands — A609

2003, Jan. 16   **Litho.**   ***Perf. 12***
1207   A609   1000p multi   3.25   .85

Hapalopsittaca
Fuertesi — A610

2003, June 13
1208   A610   1000p multi   3.25   .85

Souvenir Sheets

Orchids — A611

No. 1209 — 2400p: a, Masdevallia ignea. b, Miltoniopsis vexillaria.
No. 1210 — 2800p: a, Odontoglossum crispum, horiz. b, Masdevallia macrura.
No. 1211, vert. — 5000p: a, Cimbidium. b, Oncidium obryzatum.
No. 1212 — 7000p: a, Cattleya dowiana. b, Cattleya trianaei (49x49mm).

Sheets of 2, #a-b

Perf. 14¼, 13¾x14 (#1212b)
2003, June 13
1209-1212   A611   Set of 4   50.00   50.00

Tejo,
National
Sport
A612

No. 1213: a, Players, tree in foreground (49x39mm). b, Players, light poles (49x39mm). c, Cacique Turmeque.

2003, July 25   ***Perf. 12***
1213   Horiz. strip of 3   10.00   10.00
   a.-c.   A612 2400p Any single   2.25   1.40

America Issue — A613

Flora and fauna: a, Denomination at UR. b, Denomination at LR.

2003, Oct. 9   **Litho.**   ***Perf. 12***
1214   A613   1600p Vert. pair, #a-b   5.00   5.00

Printed in sheets of four pairs and four labels.

Souvenir Sheet

Colombia Libraries National Reading
Plan — A614

No. 1215: a, 1200p, Building. b, 4100p, Building, diff.

2003, Oct. 30   **Litho.**   ***Perf. 12***
1215   A614   Sheet of 2, #a-b   8.00   8.00

General Ramón
Arturo Rincón
Quiñones (1922-
75) — A615

2003, Oct. 31
1216   A615   1000p multi   1.75   .50

Souvenir Sheet

Administrative Security Deparment,
50th Anniv. — A616

2003, Oct. 31
1217   A616   4100p multi   6.00   6.00

Armed
Forces
A617

No. 1218 — Arms and mottos: a, General Command of Military Forces. b, National Army. c, National Navy. d, Air Force. e, Colombian Forces in Korea, 50th anniv.

2003, Nov. 7
1218   Vert. strip of 5   8.00   8.00
   a.-e.   A617 1200p Any single   1.10   .60

Christmas — A618

No. 1219: a, Good Shepherd, sheep. b, Tree, comet, airplane, rabbit. c, Rabbits, dog. d, Automobile, angel, reindeer, horse. e, Sheep, woman with basket, swan, house. f, Branch with leaves, horse and rider, duck, Indian with bow and arrow.

2003, Dec. 2   **Litho.**   ***Perf. 12***
1219   Block of 6   9.00   9.00
   a.-f.   A618 1000p Any single   1.10   .65

Colombia and the Eldorado Legend — A619

No. 1220: a, Print of Eldorado ceremony, by Teodoro De Bry, 1595. b, Watercolor painting of Lake Guatavita, by M. María Paz, 1855. c, Watercolor painting of Lake Guatavita, by Gonzalo Ariza, 1984. d, Print of Lake Guatavita, by A. Humboldt Thibault and F. Schoell, 1813. e, Photo of Lake Guatavita, by Fernando Urbina Rangel, 1983. f, Print of Lake Guatavita, by Eustacio Barreto, 1883.

No. 1221 — Muisca raft: a, 1700p, Front. b, 2000p, Back, vert.

2004, Mar. 10
1220	A619	2800p Sheet of 6, #a-f, + 3 labels	13.00	13.00

Souvenir Sheet
1221	A619	Sheet of 2, #a-b	3.00	3.00

Locomotives — A620

No. 1222, 1100p: a, 2-8-2. b, 4-8-0.
No. 1223, 1300p: a, 2-6-2. b, 4-6-2.

2004, Mar. 19   Horiz. Pairs, #a-b
1222-1223	A620	Set of 2	13.50	13.50

Nos. 1222-1223 each printed in sheets of four pairs and two pairs of labels.

Departments Type of 2003

No. 1224, 1100p — Nariño Department: a, Galeras Volcano, San Juan de Pasto, horiz. b, Statue of Gen. Antonio Nariño. c, Nariño Government Building, San Juan de Pasto, horiz. d, Farm, Catambuco, horiz. e, Nuestra Señora de las Lajas Sanctuary, Ipiales. f, Sandoná city center, horiz. g, Gallery of Mirrors, horiz. h, Barnizadores de Pasto Chorography Commission. i, Golden palms, horiz. j, El Morro, Tumaco, horiz. k, Virgen de la Playa Sanctuary, San Pablo. l, Festival of Whites and Blacks, horiz.

No. 1225, 2000p — Tolima Department: a, Nevado del Tolima, horiz. b, Tolima arms. c, Ambalema, horiz. d, Bowls, La Chamba, horiz. e, Natural Bridge, Icononzo. f, Hermitage, Mariquita, horiz. g, Matachos, horiz. h, Prison, Ibagué. i, Alberto Castilla Conservatory Room, horiz. j, Fishermen, Magdalena River, horiz. k, Cacique Calarcá. l, Tolima Art Museum, Ibagué.

No. 1226, 3000p — Chocó Department: a, Coat of Arms. b, Quibdó skyline, horiz. c, Indian girls. d, San Pacho Fiesta. e, Carrasquilla College, Quibdó, horiz. f, Houses, Nóvita. g, Canoe on San Juan River. h, Women grinding corn meal, horiz. i, Nuestra Senora del Rosario Church, Condoto. j, Utría Bay. k, Bellavista Church, Bojayá, horiz. l, Goldsmith, Acandi.

Horiz. stamps are 46x37mm.

Sheets of 12, #a-l, +8 labels
2004	Litho.		Perf. 13¾x14	
1224	A608	Nariño	10.50	10.50
1225	A608	Tolima	18.00	18.00
1226	A608	Chocó	30.00	30.00
	Nos. 1224-1226 (3)		58.50	58.50

Issued: No. 1224, 8/5; No. 1225, 4/16. No. 1226, 11/17.

Maloka Science and Technology Center A621

2004, July 6   Litho.   Perf. 12¾
1227	A621	1100p multi	1.25	1.25

Values are for stamps with surrounding selvage.

2004 Summer Olympics, Athens — A622

2004, Aug. 5   Perf. 13¾x14
1228	A622	4400p multi	3.75	3.75

Natl. Association of Contractors, 60th Anniv. A623

No. 1229: a, Denomination in white. b, Denomination in black.

2004, Aug. 5   Perf. 14x13¾
1229		Pair	4.50	4.50
a.-b.	A623	2800p Either single	2.25	2.25

Printed in sheets containing 6 pairs and one large central label.

FIFA (Fédération Internationale de Football Association), Cent. — A624

2004, Aug. 25   Perf. 13¼x14
1230	A624	3500p multi	3.00	3.00

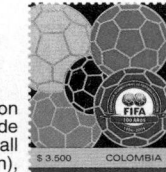

Women's Citizenship, 50th Anniv. — A625

2004, Sept. 24   Perf. 14
1231	A625	15,000p multi	13.00	13.00

Fair and Expositions Corporation, 50th Anniv. — A626

2004, Oct. 14   Perf. 13½x13
1232	A626	1300p multi	1.25	1.25

Colombian Radio Announcers Association, 50th Anniv. — A627

2004, Oct. 21   Perf. 14
1233	A627	1700p multi	1.60	1.60

17th National Games — A628

2004, Dec. 10   Litho.   Perf. 12¾
1234	A628	7000p multi + label	6.25	6.25

Printed in sheets of 4 + 5 labels.

America Issue — Environmental Conservation — A629

Designs: No. 1235, 5000p, Whale, Gorgona National Nature Park. No. 1236, 5000p, Hammerhead sharks, Malpelo Flora and Fauna Sanctuary.

2004, Dec. 14   Perf. 14
1235-1236	A629	Set of 2	9.00	9.00

Miniature Sheet

Christmas — A630

No. 1237 — Inscriptions: a, Jesús en la mansion de su padre. b, Eterna sumision a Dios. c, Jesús desciende al seno de su madre. d, Aceptacion de milagro divino. e, La ilusion de Maria. f, Voluntad divina en manos del emperador. g, Paciencia, expectativa y anhelo. h, Belén: Humilde hospedaje. i, Nacimiento, la faz de Dios encarnado.

2004, Dec. 15
1237	A630	2800p Sheet of 9, #a-i	32.50	32.50

Pre-Columbian Gold Artifacts From Gold Museum — A631

No. 1238, 1200p: a, Tumaco ear covering. b, Zenú nose ring.
No. 1239, 1800p: a, Cauma nose ring. b, Tierradentro bracelet.

Pairs, #a-b

2005, Jan. 21   Perf. 12x12½
1238-1239	A631	Set of 2	5.25	5.25

Issued: No. 1238, 1/21; No. 1239, 3/28.

Rotary International, Cent. — A632

2005, Feb. 23   Perf. 13½x14
1240	A632	3100p multi	2.75	2.75

Souvenir Sheet

Butterflies — A633

No. 1241: a, Protographium tyastes panamensis. b, Dismorphia zaela laura. c, Actinote ozomene.

2005, June 7   Litho.   Perf. 14¼
1241	A633	4600p Sheet of 3, #a-c	13.00	13.00

FENALCO (Natl. Federation of Retailers), 60th Anniv. A634

2005, June 10   Perf. 14
1242	A634	1200p multi	1.10	1.10

Souvenir Sheets

Department Centenaries — A635

No. 1243, 3100p: a, Map of Caldas Department. b, Map of Colombia highlighting Caldas.
No. 1244, 3700p: a, Map of Huila Department. b, Map of Colombia highlighting Huila.
No. 1245, 4200p: a, Map of Atlantico Department. b, Map of Colombia highlighting Atlantico.

Sheets of 2, #a-b

2005, June		**Perf. 14x13½**
1243-1245	A635	Set of 3 25.00 25.00

Departments Type of 2003

No. 1246 — San Andrés y Providencia Department: a, Aerial view of San Andrés, horiz. b, Arms. c, Aerial view of Johnny Cay, horiz. d, Cayo Cangrejo, horiz. e, Artisan. f, Culture House, San Andrés, horiz. g, Morgan Head, Santa Catalina Island, horiz. h, Island view. i, Ensenada, San Andrés, horiz. j, Island architecture, horiz. k, Baptist Church, San Andrés. l, Aerial view of Providencia and Santa Catalina Islands.
Horiz. stamps are 46x37mm.

2005, July 20		**Perf. 13¾x14**
1246	A608	1200p Sheet of 12,
		#a-l 13.00 13.00

Bogota Botanical Gardens — A636

2005, Aug. 5		**Perf. 14**
1247	A636	1400p multi 1.25 1.25

15th Bolivarian Games — A637

2005, Aug. 11		**Perf. 13¾x14**
1248	A637	3500p multi 3.25 3.25

Association of Graduates of the University of the Andes, 50th Anniv. A638

2005, Sept. 14		**Perf. 14**
1249	A638	2000p multi 1.75 1.75

Intl. Day of Ozone Layer Protection A639

2005, Sept. 16		
1250	A639	2000p multi 1.75 1.75

Souvenir Sheet

Publication of Don Quixote, 400th Anniv. — A640

No. 1251 — Paintings of Miguel de Cervantes by: a, Ricardo Rendón Bravo. b, Eduardo Ramírez Villamizar, vert. c, Santiago Martínez Delgado, vert.

Perf. 13½x14 (#1251a), 14x13½

2005, Oct. 25		
1251	A640	1300p Sheet of 3, #a-c 3.50 3.50

Colpatria Bank, 50th Anniv. A641

2005, Nov. 2		**Perf. 14x13½**
1252	A641	1200p multi 1.10 1.10

Arms of City of Facatativá A642

2005, Oct. 30		Litho. **Perf. 14**
1253	A642	1800p multi 1.75 1.75

Latin Union, 50th Anniv. — A643

2005, Dec. 1		**Perf. 13½x14**
1254	A643	5000p multi 4.75 4.75
		Printed in sheets of 4.

Souvenir Sheet

America Issue, Fight Against Poverty — A644

2005, Nov. 30		**Perf. 14x13½**
1255	A644	Sheet of 2 #1255a 9.50 9.50
a.		5000p Single stamp 4.75 4.75

Souvenir Sheet

Escuela de Lanceros (Military School), 50th Anniv. — A645

2005, Nov. 30		**Perf. 14**
1256	A645	Sheet of 2 #1256a 19.00 19.00
a.		10,000p Single stamp 9.50 9.50

Christmas A646

2005, Dec. 9		**Perf. 14**
1257	A646	3100p multi 3.00 3.00
		Printed in sheets of 7.

Colombian Journalism A647

2006, Feb. 9		Litho.
1258	A647	2000p multi 1.90 1.90

St. Francis Xavier (1506-52) A648

2006, Apr. 7		
1259	A648	4500p multi 3.75 3.75

Pope John Paul II (1920-2005) A649

2006, Apr. 4		
1260	A649	4800p multi 3.75 3.75

Souvenir Sheet

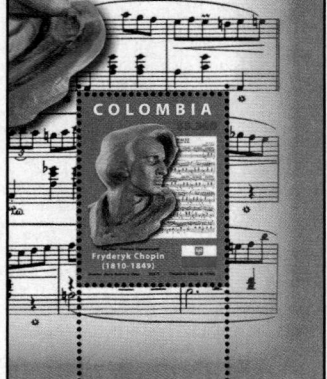

Frederic Chopin (1810-49), Composer — A650

2006, May 25		**Perf. 13½x13**
1261	A650	5300p multi 5.00 5.00
		Printed in sheets of 4.

Gold Artifacts Type of 2005

No. 1262: a, Quimbaya striated lime receptacle with handles. b, Quimbaya thin lime receptacle.

2006, Jan. 26		**Perf. 12x12½**
1262	A631	1500p Pair, #a-b 3.50 3.50

Italian Cultural Institute of Bogota, 50th Anniv. — A651

No. 1263: a, Lute at lower left. b, Violin at lower right.

2006, Feb. 23		**Perf. 14**
1263	A651	1300p Horiz. pair, #a-b 2.25 2.25

Souvenir Sheet

Rayo Museum, 25th Anniv. — A652

No. 1264: a, Artwork in blue, white, red, yellow and black. b, Artwork in white, blue, tan and black.

2006, Jan. 21		**Perf. 13½x13**
1264	A652	Sheet, 2 each #a-b 4.50 4.50
a.-b.		1300p Either single 1.10 1.10

Departments Type of 2003

No. 1265 — Valle del Cauca Department: a, Mapping Commission drawing of Cali, horiz. b, Arms of Valle del Cauca. c, Arms and panoramic view of Sevilla, horiz. d, Calima Lake, El Darién, horiz. e, La Ermita, Santiago de Cali. f, Port of Buenaventura, horiz. g, Railroad station, Palmira, horiz. h, Sugar cane. i, Salsa dancers, Cali, horiz. j, El Paraiso Museum, El Cerrito, horiz. k, Basilica, Buga. l, Aerial view of Valle del Cauca, horiz.

No. 1266 — Boyacá Department: a, Plaza de Bolivar, Tunja, horiz. b, Arms of Boyacá. c, Mapping Commission drawing of Campo de Boyacá, horiz. d, Bolivar Monument, Campo de Boyacá, horiz. e, Altar of the Virgin of Chiquinquirá. f, Panoramic view of Garagoa, horiz. g, Plaza de los Libertadores, Duitama, horiz. h, Emeralds. i, Plaza Mayor, Villa de Leyva, horiz. j, Sierra Nevada del Cocuy, horiz. k, Temple of the Sun, Sogamoso. l, El Salitre Farm, Paipa, horiz.

No. 1267 — Quindío Department: a, Quindío Pass, 1836, horiz. b, Quimbaya culture sculpture. c, Coffee plantation house, Quimbaya, horiz. d, Coffee bean picker, Pijao, horiz. e, Valle de Cocora, Salento. f, Botanical Gardens, Calarca, horiz. g, La Estación Metropolitan Cultural Center, Armenia, horiz. h, Monument and government building, Armenia. i, Free Cemetery, Circasia, horiz. j, Aerial view of Buenavista, horiz. k, San José Temple, Génova. l, Founding of Armenia, horiz.

Horizontal stamps are 46x37mm.

Sheets of 12, #a-l, + 8 labels

2006			**Perf. 13½x14**	
1265 A608	1300p	Valle del Cauca	13.00	13.00
1266 A608	2000p	Boyacá	20.00	20.00
1267 A608	3300p	Quindío	32.50	32.50
Nos. 1265-1267 (3)			65.50	65.50

20th Central American and Caribbean Games A653

2006, July 15	**Litho.**		**Perf. 14**	
1268 A653	2000p multi		1.75	1.75

Pres. Alberto Lleras Camargo (1906-90) — A654

Denominations: a, 1300p. b, 3300p.

2006, Dec. 6	**Litho.**		**Perf. 14x13¾**	
1269 A654	Horiz. pair, #a-b + alternating labels		4.25	4.25

Souvenir Sheet

America Issue, Energy Conservation — A655

No. 1270: a, Left hand. b, Right hand.

2006, Dec. 28		**Perf. 12**	
1270 A655	5000p Sheet of 2, #a-b	9.50	9.50

Christmas — A656

Denominations: a, 1300p. b, 3300p.

2006, Dec. 13		**Perf. 13¾x14**	
1271 A656	Vert. pair, #a-b	4.25	4.25

General José Maria Cordova Military School, Cent. — A657

2007, May 30		**Perf. 14**	
1272 A657	10,000p multi	11.00	11.00

Departments Type of 2003

No. 1273 — Sucre Department: a, Coat of arms. b, St. Francis of Assisi Cathedral, Sincelejo, horiz. c, Palm trees, Tolú. d, Cattle, Sucre. e, Bull ring, Sincelejo, horiz. f, Church, Corozal. g, Musical score of "Fiesta en Corraleja." h, Painting of fandango dancers, horiz. i, Fisherman, Caimito. j, Palm trees, Sincelejo. k, Cane weaver, Sampués, horiz. l, Hammocks, Morroa.

Horizontal stamps are 46x37mm.

Sheet of 12, #a-l, + 8 Labels

2007, May 30		**Perf. 12**	
1273 A608	3300p Sucre	42.50	42.50

Miniature Sheet

Scouting, Cent. — A658

No. 1274: a, International and Colombian Scouting emblems, Scouts with Lord Robert Baden-Powell. b, Emblem of 21st World Scout Jamboree, Colombian Scouting emblem, children's drawing of Colombian scout. c, Scouting emblem, Lord Robert Baden-Powell. d, International and Colombian Scouting emblems, animal track.

2007, June 26		**Perf. 14**	
1274 A658	1500p Sheet of 8, 2 each #a-d, + central label	12.50	12.50

Souvenir Sheet

El Espectador Newspaper, 120th Anniv. — A659

No. 1275: a, Newspaper from 1887. b, Paperboy, horiz.

2007, June 28		**Perf. 12**	
1275 A659	4500p Sheet of 2, #a-b	9.25	9.25

Pan American Games, Rio de Janeiro — A660

2007, July 9		**Perf. 14**	
1276 A660	3700p multi	3.75	3.75

Fourth Spanish Language Intl. Congress — A661

2007, June 25		
1277 A661	5300p multi + label	5.25 5.25

Caja de Compensación Familiar, 50th Anniv. — A662

2007, Oct. 10	**Litho.**	**Perf. 14**	
1278 A662	3500p multi	3.75	3.75

Colombian Association of Engineers, 50th Anniv. A663

2007, Oct. 17		
1279 A663	1400p multi	1.40 1.40

Bogota Honors and Awards — A664

No. 1280: a, 2007 UNESCO World Book Capital. b, Venice Biennale Golden Lion Award

for Architecture. c, 2007 Latin American Cultural Capital.

2007, Oct. 23			
1280 A664	3700p Horiz. strip of 3, #a-c	11.00	11.00

Minuto de Dios, 50th Anniv. A665

2007, Nov. 22		
1281 A665	1600p multi	1.60 1.60

Christmas A666

2007, Nov. 27		
1282 A666	3300p multi	3.25 3.25

America Issue, Education For All — A667

2007, Dec. 13		
1283 A667	3500p multi	3.50 3.50

Pres. Carlos Lleras Restrepo (1908-94) A668

2008, Apr. 8	**Litho.**	**Perf. 12**	
1284 A668	1400p multi	1.60	1.60

Colombian Friendship With Japan, Cent. A669

2008, May 22		**Perf. 14**	
1285 A669	5200p multi	6.25	6.25

New Emblem of Postal Network of Colombia A670

2008, May 28		
1286 A670	2100p multi	2.50 2.50

Compare with Type A685.

National Institute for the Blind, 50th Anniv. A671

Litho. & Embossed
2008, June 10
1287 A671 1400p multi 1.75 1.75

Departments Type of 2003
No. 1288 — Antioquia Department: a, Medellín skyline, horiz. b, Arms of Antioquia. c, Necoclí, horiz. d, Silleteros Parade, horiz. e, Purse. f, Rafael Uribe Uribe Palace of Culture, horiz. g, Molas, horiz. h, Lipaugus weberi. i, Waterfall, Támesis, horiz. j, Coffee cups, horiz. k, Santa Fé de Antioquia Church. l, Orquide-orama, Medellín Botanical Gardens, horiz.
No. 1289 — Amazonas Department: a, Departmental emblem. b, Monkey, Isla de los Micos, horiz. c, Victoria Regia water lily. d, Butterfly, Puerto Nariño. e, Indigenous child, horiz. f, Caiman. g, Beaded mask. h, Dolphin, horiz. i, Amazonas landscape. j, Flower. k, Fisherman casting net, horiz. l, Fruits at Plaza de Mercado, Puerto Leticia.
Horizontal stamps are 50x40mm.

Sheets of 12, #a-l, + 8 labels
2008 Litho. Perf. 13¾x14
1288 A608 1500p Antioquia 15.00 15.00
Perf. 12
1289 A608 1600p Amazonas 22.00 22.00
Issued: No. 1288, 10/22; No. 1289, 7/18.

Battle of Maracaibo Lake, 185th Anniv. — A672

2008, July 30 Perf. 12
1290 A672 3900p multi 4.50 4.50

Treaty of Amity and Commerce Between Colombia and Switzerland, Cent. — A673

2008, July 31 Perf. 14
1291 A673 5200p multi 6.00 6.00

2008 Summer Olympics, Beijing — A674

2008, Aug. 1
1292 A674 5000p multi 5.75 5.75
Souvenir Sheet
1293 A674 10,000p multi 11.50 11.50

Aguadas, Bicent. — A675

2008, Aug. 15
1294 A675 3500p multi 3.75 3.75

Accordion Festival, Villanueva A676

2008, Sept. 25
1295 A676 5600p multi 6.00 6.00

Pres. Alfonso López Michelsen (1913-2007) A677

2008, Oct. 8
1296 A677 5100p multi 4.50 4.50

Miniature Sheet

Ministry of Communications, 85th Anniv. — A678

No. 1297 — Arms of Colombia and: a, Stylized person, emblem for Government Online program. b, Children, emblem for Computers for Education progam, vert. c, Girl with "@" balloon, campaign for clean Internet. d, Emblem for Compartel, vert.

2008, Oct. 29
1297 A678 1500p Sheet of 4, #a-d 5.00 5.00

Episcopal Conference of Colombia, Cent. — A679

2008, Nov. 6
1298 A679 1500p multi 1.40 1.40

18th Carlos Lleras Restrepo National Games A680

2008, Nov. 21
1299 A680 1500p multi 1.40 1.40

Natl. Department of Planning, 50th Anniv. A681

2008, Dec. 9
1300 A681 1500p multi 1.40 1.40

Christmas A682

Adoration of the Shepherds, by Gregorio Vásquez de Arce y Ceballos: a, 1400p. b, 3500p.

2008, Dec. 12
1301 A682 Vert. pair, #a-b 4.50 4.50

Miniature Sheet

Luis Angel Arango Library, 50th Anniv. — A683

No. 1302 — Open book with: a, Ship page and "B." b, Sun page and "L." c, Dove page and "a." d, Face page and "A."

2008, Dec. 16 Perf. 13¾x14
1302 A683 1300p Sheet of 4, #a-d 4.75 4.75

America Issue, National Festivals — A684

Paintings: No. 1303, 1400p, November 11, 1811, Absolute Independence of Cartagena, by Cecilia Porras. No. 1304, 1400p, Liberty Indian, by unknown artist, vert.

2008, Dec. 29 Perf. 13¾x14, 14x13¾
1303-1304 A684 Set of 2 2.50 2.50

4-72 Colombia Postal Network Emblem — A685

Designs: 200p, Emblem on blue background with red frame. 400p, Emblem against blue background, and three arrows against red, blue and yellow backgrounds. 500p, Emblem against white background with blue frame. 600p, Emblem and map of Colombia.

2009, Mar. 1 Litho. Perf. 14
1305-1308 A685 Set of 4 1.40 1.40

Souvenir Sheet

Cali Philatelic Club, 70th Anniv. — A686

No. 1309: a, Necklace with flower-shaped pendant. b, Miltoniopsis roezlii, vert.

2009, Mar. 12 Perf. 12
1309 A686 2000p Sheet of 2, #a-b 7.50 7.50

Inter-America Development Bank, 50th Anniv. — A687

2009, Mar. 27
1310 A687 3700p multi 3.25 3.25

President Julio César Turbay (1916-2005) — A688

2009, Apr. 1 Perf. 14x13½
1311 A688 1700p multi 1.40 1.40
Printed in sheets of 9 + 6 labels.

Naval School for Non-Commissioned Officers, Barranquilla, 75th Anniv. — A689

2009, Apr. 17   **Perf. 14**
1312 A689 4000p multi   3.50 3.50

Colombian War School, Cent. A690

2009, May 8   **Perf. 12**
1313 A690 5500p multi   5.50 5.50

President Guillermo León Valencia (1909-71) A691

2009, May 27
1314 A691 4200p multi   4.25 4.25

Fight of July 20, 1810, by Julián Rubiano Chávez A692

2009, June 25   **Perf. 12**
1315 A692 1700p multi   1.75 1.75

Departments Type of 2003
Miniature Sheet
No. 1316 — La Guajira Department: a, Arms of La Guajira. b, Francisco el Hombre, mural in La Guajira Cultural Center, horiz. c, Waterfall, Montes de Oca. d, Phoenicopterus ruber. e, Domingueka, Kogui village, horiz. f, Cape of La Vela. g, Majayuts (Wayuu women). h, Riohacha Cathedral, horiz. i, Cardinalis phoeniceus. j, Aloe vulgaris. k, Caesalpinia coriaria, horiz. l, Wayuu mochilas (bags).
Horizontal stamps are 50x40mm.

Sheet of 12, #a-l, + 8 Labels
2009, July 24   Litho.   Perf. 12
1316 A608 1700p La Guajira   21.00 21.00

Miniature Sheet

Heliconia Varieties — A693

No. 1317: a, Heliconia stricta. b, Heliconia rostrata. c, Heliconia wagneriana. d, Heliconia orthotricha. e, Heliconia psittacorum.

2009, Aug. 14   Litho.   Perf. 12
1317 A693 2000p Sheet of 5, #a-e, + 5 labels   10.00 10.00

Miniature Sheet

First Colombian Postage Stamps, 150th Anniv. — A694

No. 1318: a, Colombia #1. b, Colombia #6. c, Colombia #4. d, Colombia #3. e, Colombia #7. f, Map of Colombia and text on gray background.
10,000p, Like No. 1318f with blue background.

2009, Aug. 25   Perf. 12
1318 A694 4000p Sheet of 6, #a-f   24.00 24.00
Souvenir Sheet
1319 A694 10,000p multi   10.00 10.00

America Issue, Traditional Games — A695

No. 1320 — Chaza player: a, Bare-handed. b, Holding racquet.

2009, Oct. 13   Litho.   Perf. 14
1320 A695 5000p Horiz. pair, #a-b   10.00 10.00

Rafael Uribe Uribe (1859-1914), General — A696

2009, Oct. 20
1321 A696 1500p multi   1.50 1.50

Madrid Town Hall A697

2009, Nov. 13
1322 A697 10,000p multi   10.50 10.50
Madrid, Cundinamarca Department, 450th anniv.

Miniature Sheet

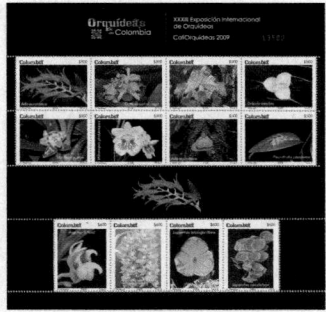

Orchids — A698

No. 1323: a, 500p, Ada aurantiaca (many flowers). b, 500p, Cattleya patinii cogn. c, 500p, Cattleya schroderae. d, 500p, Dracula amaliae. e, 500p, Huntleya gustavi. f, 500p, Miltoniopsis phalaenopsis. g, 500p, Ada aurantiaca (one flower). h, 500p, Pleurothallis casapensis. i, 600p, Anguloa cliftonii, vert. j, 600p, Cycnoche barthriorum, vert. k, 600p, Lepanthes telipogoniflora, vert. l, 600p, Lepanthes calodictyon, vert.

2009, Nov. 20
1323 A698 Sheet of 12, #a-l   6.50 6.50
33rd Intl. Orchid Exposition, Cali.

Miniature Sheet

Independence, Bicent. — A699

No. 1324: a, Bishop Andrés Rosillo y Meruelo (1758-1835). b, Josè Félix de Restrepo (1760-1832), statesman. c, Camilo Torres Tenorio (1766-1816), President of the Congress. d, Bishop Juan Fernández de Sotomayor (1777-1849). e, Antonio Villavicencio y Berástegui (1775-1816), President of the United Provinces of New Granada. f, Juan de Dios Morales (1767-1810), governmental minister and revolutionary. g, José María Carbonel (1778-1816), revolutionary agitator. h, Antonio Morales Galavís (1784-1852), military commander. i, José Ramón de Leyva (1747-1816), military commander. j, Nicolás Mauricio de Omaña, priest, lawyer.

2009, Nov. 24
1324 A699 6000p Sheet of 10, #a-j   65.00 65.00

Christmas A700

2009, Nov. 27   Perf. 12
1325 A700 5000p multi   6.50 6.50

Souvenir Sheet

Campaign for a Mine-free World — A701

2009, Dec. 3   Perf. 14
1326 A701 20,000p multi   22.50 22.50

Winning Designs in Stamp Design Contest — A702

No. 1327: a, Abstract face, by Vito. b, Collage, by Caracha. c, People holding hands, by D. Bueno.

2009, Dec. 15
1327 A702 1800p Horiz. strip of 3, #a-c   7.50 7.50

Miniature Sheet

Famous People — A703

No. 1328: a, Mercedes Abrego (1770-1813), spy. b, Gerardo Molina R. (1906-91), politician. c, Virginia Gutiérrez (1922-99), social anthropologist. d, María Mercedes Carranza (1945-2003), poet. e, Gonzalo Arango (1931-76), poet. f, Adolfo Mejía (1905-76), composer. g, General Benjamín Herrera (1853-1924). h, César Uribe Piedrahita (1896-1951), medical writer. i, Emilio Robledo (1875-1962), medical educator. j, Luis Duque Gómez (1916-2000), archaeologist. k, Enrique A. Becerra (1883-1954), jurist. l, Hugo Escobar Sierra (1927-2003), politician.

2010, Jan. 28   **Perf. 13½x14**
1328 A703 4000p Sheet of 12,
#a-l   60.00 60.00

Presidents Type of 1981
Miniature Sheet

No. 1329 — Presidents, coup leaders and other leaders of Colombia: a, Virgilio Barco Vargas. b, Julio César Turbay Ayala. c, Alfonso López Michelsen. d, Misael Pastrana Borrero. e, Carlos Lemos Simmonds. f, Victor Mosquera Chaux. g, Indalecio Liévano Aguirre. h, Rafael Azuero Manchola. i, Gabriel París Gordillo. j, Deogracias Fonseca. k, Rafael Navas Pardo. l, Luis Ernesto Ordóñez. m, Diego Euclides de Angulo. n, Clímaco Calderón Reyes. o, Andrés Cerón Serrano. p, Ignacio Gutiérrez Vergara. q, Juan José Nieto Gil. r, Rufino Cuervo. s, Manuel Rodríguez Torices. t, José Joaquín Camacho.

2010, Jan. 28   **Perf. 14**
1329   Sheet of 20   47.50 47.50
a.-t. A401 1900p Any single   2.00   2.00

Ninth South American Games, Medellin — A704

2010, Feb. 18
1330 A704 5800p multi   8.00 8.00

Pope John Paul II (1920-2005) — A705

2010, Feb. 19   **Perf. 13x13¼**
1331 A705 4400p multi   5.50 5.50

Miniature Sheet

Endangered Birds — A706

No. 1332: a, Crax alberti. b, Ognorhynchus icterotis. c, Hapalopsittaca fuertesi. d, Amazilia castaneiventris. e, Rallus semiplumbeus. f, Coeligena prunellei. g, Grallaria gigantea. h, Bangsia aureocincta. i, Hypopyrrhus pyrohypogaster.

2010, Apr. 6   **Perf. 13¼x13**
1332 A706 1900p Sheet of 9,
#a-i   22.50 22.50

Souvenir Sheet

Expo 2010, Shanghai — A707

2010, May 7   **Perf. 13¾x14**
1333 A707 5000p multi   6.00 6.00

Miniature Sheet

Discovery of San Andrés, Providencia and Santa Catalina Archipelago, 500th Anniv. — A708

No. 1334: a, San Andrés Island. b, Providencia and Santa Catalina Islands. c, Quitasueño Keys. d, Bolivar Key. e, Roncador Keys. f, Bajo Nuevo Keys. g, Serranilla Keys. h, Serrana Keys. i, Alburquerque Keys.

2010, June 12   **Litho.**   **Perf. 14**
1334 A708 5900p Sheet of 9,
#a-i, + 3 labels   85.00 85.00

Departments Type of 2003

No. 1335 — Guainía Department: a, Arms of Guainía. b, Princess Inírida Monument, horiz. c, Egretta alba. d, Cerro Mavicure. e, Canoe on Inírida River, horiz. f, Curripaco baskets. g, Guacamaya superba. h, Confluence of the Guaviare and Inírida Rivers, horiz. i, Remanso. j, Cualé Rapids. k, Children from Paujil, horiz. l, Coco Petroglyphs.

No. 1336 — Atlántico Department: a, Arms of Atlántico. b, Palacio de la Cultura, Barranquilla, horiz. c, Tubará rock paintings. d, Fluvicola pica. e, Julio Flórez Museum, Usiacurí, horiz. f, Tocagua Marsh, Luruaco. g, Bull's head carnival mask. h, San Antonio de Padua Church, Soledad, horiz. i, Tabebuya rosea. j, Iraca Palm handicrafts. k, Pier at Puerto Colombia, horiz. l, Customs House, Barranquilla.

Horiz. stamps are 50x40mm.

Sheets of 12, #a-l, + 8 labels

2010   **Perf. 12x12½**
1335 A608   600p Guainía   15.00 15.00
1336 A608 2000p Atlántico   35.00 35.00
Issued: No. 1335, 7/24; No. 1336, 6/15.

Gonzalo Jiménez de Quesada Police Academy A709

2010, June 24   **Perf. 14**
1337 A709 2000p multi   2.50 2.50

Bambuco National Pageant and Folklore Festival, Neiva, 50th Anniv. — A710

2010, June 22   **Perf. 13¼x13**
1338 A710 4200p multi   5.50 5.50

Admiral Padilla Naval Academy A711

2010, July 3   **Perf. 14**
1339 A711 500p multi   4.00 4.00

Miniature Sheet

Norte de Santander Department, Cent. — A712

No. 1340: a, Map of Norte de Santander Department. b, Government building. c, Estoraques Nature Area. d, Catatumbo River. e, Santa Ana de Ocaña Cathedral. f, Santa Clara de Pamplona Cathedral.

2010, July 14   **Litho.**
1340 A712 6000p Sheet of 6,
#a-f   47.50 47.50

Teresa Pizarro de Angulo (c. 1930-2000), National Beauty Pageant Director — A713

2010, Aug. 3
1341 A713 5900p multi   8.00 8.00

Pinillos National College, Bicent. (in 2009) A714

2010, Aug. 27   **Litho.**   **Perf. 14**
1342 A714 4000p multi   5.25 5.25

America Issue, National Symbols — A715

No. 1343: a, Colombian flag. b, Colombian coat of arms.

2010, Oct. 12   **Perf. 13½x14**
1343 A715 2100p Horiz. pair, #a-b   6.50 6.50

Medellin Institute of Fine Arts, Cent. A716

2010, Oct. 19   **Perf. 14x13¾**
1344 A716 4400p multi   5.50 5.50

Miniature Sheet

Valle del Cauca Department, Cent. — A717

No. 1345: a, Map of Valle del Cauca Department. b, Sula granti. c, Overo Chapel. d, Pance River, Farallones Park. e, Ilama Culture vessel. f, Sonso Lake, Buga.

2010, Nov. 18   **Perf. 14**
1345 A717 4000p Sheet of 6,
#a-f   32.50 32.50

Colombia National Ballet, 50th Anniv. — A718

2010, Nov. 22
1346 A718 1200p multi   6.00 6.00

Christmas A719

2010, Nov. 23   **Perf. 13x13¼**
1347 A719 5000p multi   6.50 6.50

Eduardo Caballero Calderón (1910-93), Writer A720

2010, Dec. 1   **Perf. 14**
1348 A720 3000p multi   4.00 4.00

Miniature Sheet

Independence, Bicent. — A721

No. 1349 — Various paintings depicting scenes from towns declaring independence in 1810: a, Caratgena. b, Mompox. c, Pamplona. d, Socorro. e, Santa Marta. f, Chocó. g, Popayán. h, Cali. i, Tunja. j, Santa Fé de Bogotá. k, Santa Fé de Antioquia. l, Pore.

2010, Oct. 22 — **Perf. 13½x14**
1349 A721 2000p Sheet of 12.
#a-l   32.50 32.50

Radio Station HJCK, Bogota A722

2011, Feb. 10 — **Perf. 14**
1350 A722 600p multi   1.50 1.50

4-72 Colombia Postal Network Emblem and "Es Tu Correo!" — A723

Frame Color
Serpentine Die Cut 12½
2011, Mar. 22 — **Self-Adhesive**
1351 A723 10,000p blue   13.50 13.50
1352 A723 20,000p red   27.50 27.50

El Catolicismo Newspaper, 162nd Anniv. — A724

2011, Mar. 30 — **Perf. 13x13¼**
1353 A724 1700p multi   2.75 2.75

Souvenir Sheet

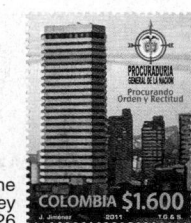

Biological Diversity — A725

2011, Apr. 11 — **Perf. 13**
1354 A725 6100p multi   10.00 10.00

Office of the Attorney General — A726

2011, May 10 — **Perf. 14**
1355 A726 1600p multi   3.00 3.00

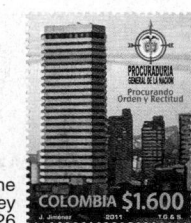

Under-20 World Cup Soccer Championships, Colombia A727

2011, July 21 Litho. — **Perf. 13¼x13**
1356 A727 2000p multi   3.25 3.25

Rufino José Cuervo (1844-1911), Writer — A728

2011, July 27 — **Perf. 14**
1357 A728 5000p multi   8.00 8.00

Alfonso López Pumarejo National Carabiniers School, 50th Anniv. — A729

2011, Aug. 9 — **Perf. 14**
1358 A729 2100p multi   3.25 3.25

Departments Type of 2003
Miniature Sheet

No. 1359 — Norte de Santander Department: a, Arms of Norte de Santander. b, Virgin of Torcoroma and church, horiz. c, Locomotive. d, Sculpture of Barí Indian. e, Laguna Brava and Sisavita Complex, horiz. f, Southern tamandua, El Bojoso Reserve. g, Clock Tower, Cucuta. h, Street in La Play de Belén, horiz. i, Historic church, Rosario. j, Piedras Negras National Park. k, Pamplona University, horiz. l, Páramo de Guerrero.
Horiz. stamps are 46x37mm.

Sheet of 12, #a-l, + 8 labels
2011, Aug. 25 — **Perf. 13¼x13**
1359 A608 3000p Norte de
      Santander   55.00 55.00

Souvenir Sheet

Intl. Year of Forests — A730

2011, Aug. 30 — **Perf. 14**
1360 A730 6200p multi   10.00 10.00

Miniature Sheet

Heroines of Independence — A731

No. 1361: a, Manuela Beltrán Archila. b, Manuela Cañizares. c, Manuela Sanz de Santamaría. d, Policarpa Salvarrieta. e, Matilde Anaray. f, Juana Velasco de Gallo. g, Simona Amaya. h, Antonia Santos. i, Simona Duque de Alzate. j, Manuela Sáenz de Thorne.

2011, Sept. 12 — **Perf. 13x13¼**
1361 A731 1500p Sheet of 10,
     #a-j   24.00 24.00

Intl. Year of People of African Descent — A732

2011, Oct. 12 — **Perf. 13¼x13**
1362 A732 5000p multi   8.00 8.00

2011 Pan American Games, Guadalajara, Mexico — A733

2011, Oct. 19 — **Perf. 14**
1363 A733 600p multi   1.00 1.00

Souvenir Sheet

Postal Union of the Americas, Spain and Portugal (UPAEP), Cent. — A734

2011, Nov. 11
1364 A734 1800p multi   3.00 3.00

Bolívar House, Bucaramanga — A735

2011, Nov. 15 — **Perf. 13x13¼**
1365 A735 1200p multi   2.00 2.00

Declaration of Independence of Cartagena, 200th Anniv. — A736

2011, Nov. 26 — **Perf. 14**
1366 A736 6000p multi   9.00 9.00

Emblem of United Nations AIDS Program A737

2011, Dec. 1
1367 A737 1900p multi   3.25 3.25

Mailbox — A738

2011, Dec. 2 — **Litho.**
1368 A738 500p multi   1.25 1.25
     America issue.

Christmas A739

2011, Dec. 2
1369 A739 1600p multi   2.75 2.75

Souvenir Sheet

El Tiempo Newspaper, Cent. — A740

2011, Dec. 13　　　**Perf. 13x13¼**
1370 A740 4000p multi　　　6.50 6.50

2012 Summer
Olympics,
London — A741

No. 1371: a, Swimming, fencing, wrestling. b, Equestrian, running, cycling. c, Judo, boxing, weight lifting. d, Shot put, soccer, tennis.

2012, Mar. 6　　　**Perf. 14x14¼**
1371　Horiz. strip of 4　20.00 20.00
a.-d.　A741 3000p Any single　4.00　4.00
Nos. 1371a-1371d were printed in sheets of 8 containing two of each stamp.

National Police
Magazine,
Cent. — A742

2012, Mar. 23　　　**Perf. 14**
1372 A742 2000p multi　　　3.50 3.50

National Police
Symphony,
Cent. — A743

2012, Mar. 23
1373 A743 6400p multi　　　11.00 11.00

Diplomatic Relations Between
Colombia and South Korea, 50th
Anniv. — A744

No. 1374: a, Ginseng flowers and root. b, Coffee bush and beans.

2012, May 1　　　**Perf. 13x13¼**
1374 A744 600p Horiz. pair, #a-b 2.50 2.50
See South Korea No. 2379.

Souvenir Sheet

Neiva, 400th Anniv. — A745

2012, May 4　　　**Perf. 14**
1375 A745 4000p multi　　　6.50 6.50

Souvenir Sheet

Rehabilitation Center for Blind Adults,
50th Anniv. — A746

2012, June 3　　　**Litho. & Embossed**
1376 A746 6000p multi　　　10.00 10.00

Departments Type of 2003
Miniature Sheet

No. 1377 — Cauca Department: a, Arms of Cauca. b, Puracé National Park, horiz. c, Gorgona National Park. d, Samanea saman. e, Laguna Grande de la Magdalena, horiz. f, Niña Maria de Caloto icon. g, Street in San Sebastian. h, Nuestra Señora de la Asuncion Cathedral, Popayán, horiz. i, Battle of Bajo Palacé. j, Tierradentro National Archaeological Park. k, San Andrés Church, Pisimbalá, horiz. l, Megaptera novaeangliae.
Horiz. stamps are 46x37mm.

Sheet of 12, #a-l, + 8 labels
2012, July 24　Litho.　Perf. 12x12½
1377 A608 1200p Cauca　　24.00 24.00

Miniature Sheet

Famous Men — A747

No. 1378: a, Diego de Torres y Moyachoque (1549-90), Turmequé cacique. b, Pantaleón Germán Ribón (1774-1816), military leader. c, Cayetano Betancur (1910-82), philosopher. d, Luis Bermúdez (1912-94), composer.

2012, Aug. 16　　　**Perf. 13¼**
1378 A747 4600p Sheet of 4,
　　　　#a-d　　30.00 30.00

Rafael Pombo (1833-1912), Writer of
Children's Literature — A748

2012, Aug. 23　　　**Perf. 13x13¼**
1379 A748 2100p multi + label　3.50 3.50

Voceadores de
Prensa, Painting
by Débora
Arango Pérez
(1907-2005)
A749

2012, Aug. 28　　　**Perf. 14**
1380 A749 2400p multi　　　4.00 4.00

19th National
Games and 3rd
Paranational
Games — A750

2012, Sept. 5
1381 A750 1500p multi　　　2.75 2.75

Art by
Omar Rayo
A751

No. 1382 — Art with stripes of: a, White, black and red. b, White, black and yellow. c, White, green, yellow, red and blue.

2012, Sept. 20　　　**Perf. 13x13¼**
1382　Horiz. strip of 3　　5.00 5.00
a.-c.　A751 1000p Any single　1.50 1.50

Jorge Palacios Preciado
(1940-2003),
Historian — A752

2012, Sept. 29
1383 A752 500p multi　　　.85　.85

Plaza
Mayor,
Leyva
A753

2012, Oct. 4
1384 A753 4500p multi　　　8.50 8.50
First Congress of the United Provinces of
New Granada, Bicent.

Souvenir Sheet

MITOS Y LEYENDAS

America Issue, Myths and
Legends — A754

No. 1385: a, El Hojarasquin. b, El Ribiel and El Tesoro de Morgan.

2012, Oct. 9
1385 A754 4000p Sheet of 2,
　　　　#a-b　　13.00 13.00

Fedepalma
(National
Federation of Oil
Palm Growers),
50th
Anniv. — A755

2012, Oct. 24　　　**Perf. 14**
1386 A755 6000p multi　　　9.50 9.50

Gen. Francisco de Paula
Santander (1792-
1840) — A756

2012, Nov. 16　　　**Perf. 13¼**
1387 A756 1000p multi　　　1.75 1.75

Christmas
A757

2012, Dec. 14　　　**Perf. 14**
1388 A757 2500p multi　　　4.25 4.25

Medals
Won at
2012
Summer
Olympics,
London
A758

2012, Dec. 18　　　**Perf. 13**
1389 A758 1800p multi　　　4.00 4.00
A souvenir sheet containing one 30,000p stamp depicting medals won at the 2012 Summer Olympics was produced in limited quantities.

Miniature Sheet

Bicentenario de Proclamación de las Constituciones de Socorro, Cundinamarca, Tunja, Antioquia, Cartagena de Indias y Neiva.

08241

Proclamation of State Constitutions, 200th Anniv. — A759

No. 1391 — Seals of state of: a, Socorro. b, Cundinamarca. c, Tunja. d, Antioquia. e, Cartagena de Indias. f, Neiva.

Litho. & Embossed
2012, Dec. 19   **Perf. 13¼x13**
1391 A759 500p Sheet of 6, #a-f 5.00 5.00

Renaming of Los Hermanos National Park After Gloria Valencia de Castaño (1927-2011), Television Personality — A760

2013, Apr. 29   **Litho.**
1392 A760 1800p multi + label 2.00 2.00

Departments Type of 2003
Miniature Sheet

No. 1393 — Cundinamarca Department: a, Arms of Cundinamarca. b, Tequendama Falls, Soacha, horiz. c, Poster commemorating bicentennial of Cundinamarca's independence. d, Basilica del Santo Cristo, Ubaté. e, Salt Cathedral, Zipaquirá, horiz. f, Ironworks, Pacho. g, Lagunas del Cerro, Machetá. h, Cliffs, Suesca, horiz. i, St. John the Baptist Parish Church, San Juan de Rioseco. j, Chapel, Siecha. k, Bridge of the Commoners, Chía, horiz. l, Versalles Falls, Guaduas.
Horiz. stamps are 46x37mm.

2013, July 16   **Perf. 13¼x13**
Sheet of 12, #a-l, + 8 labels
1393 A608 2100p Cundinamarca 27.00 27.00

2013 World Games, Cali — A761

2013, July 26   **Litho.**   **Perf. 14**
1394 A761 2200p multi + label 2.40 2.40

Deportivo Independiente Medellín Soccer Team, Cent. — A762

2013, July 28   **Perf. 14x13½**
1395 A762 4500p multi 4.75 4.75

Town of Río de Oro, 355th Anniv. — A763

2013, Aug. 1   **Perf. 13½x14**
1396 A763 800p multi .85 .85

Alfonso Palacio Rudas (1912-96), Politician — A764

2013, Aug. 9   **Litho.**
1397 A764 7000p multi 7.50 7.50

Soledad Acosta de Samper (1833-1913), Writer — A765

2013, Sept. 3   **Perf. 13¼x13**
1398 A765 2500p multi 2.60 2.60

Campaign Against Crime A766

2013, July 19   **Litho.**   **Perf. 14x13½**
1399 A766 2000p multi 2.25 2.25

Aspects of Life of Coffee Pickers — A767

2013, July 30   **Litho.**   **Perf. 14½x14¼**
1400 A767 2000p multi 2.25 2.25

Discovery of the Pacific Ocean by Vasco Núñez de Balboa, 500th Anniv. — A768

2013, Sept. 9   **Litho.**   **Perf. 13½x14**
1401 A768 1400p multi 1.50 1.50

Pres. Alfonso López Michelsen (1913-2007) A769

2013, Sept. 9   **Litho.**   **Perf. 13½x14**
1402 A769 2500p multi 2.60 2.60

Christmas A770

2013, Nov. 26   **Litho.**   **Perf. 14x13½**
1403 A770 3500p multi 3.75 3.75

Pereira, 150th Anniv. (in 2013) A771

2014, Mar. 13   **Litho.**   **Perf. 13x13¼**
1404 A771 2500p multi 2.60 2.60

Gimnasio Moderno, Bogota, Cent. A772

2014, Mar. 18   **Litho.**   **Perf. 13x13¼**
1405 A772 800p multi .85 .85

Jaguar Mask — A773

2014, May 13   **Litho.**   **Perf. 13½**
1406 A773 7200p multi + label 7.75 7.75

Artisans of Colombia, 50th anniv. No. 1406 was printed in sheets of 4 + 4 labels.

Souvenir Sheet

2014 World Cup Soccer Championships, Brazil — A774

No. 1407: a, Soccer ball. b, Emblem of the Colombian Soccer Federation, vert.

2014, May 23   **Litho.**   **Perf. 13¾**
1407 A774 2600p Sheet of 2, #a-b 5.50 5.50
  c. Booklet pane of 2, #1407a-1407b 10.00 —
     Complete booklet, 5 #1407c 50.00

Issued: No. 1407c, 7/8. Each example of No. 1407c in the complete booklet has a different pane margin. These pane margins differ from the sheet margin on No. 1407.

Official Journal, 150th Anniv. A775

2014, Oct. 9   **Litho.**   **Perf. 13x13¼**
1408 A775 1300p multi 1.25 1.25

4-72 Colombia Postal Network Emblem and Text — A776

Serpentine Die Cut 12¼x12¾
2014, Aug. 25   **Litho.**
Self-Adhesive
Frame Color
1409 A776 10,000p blue 10.50 10.50
1410 A776 20,000p red 21.00 21.00

Scouting in Colombia, Cent. (in 2013) — A777

2014, Nov. 22   **Litho.**   **Perf. 13¼x13**
1411 A777 3000p multi 2.60 2.60

Fanny Mikey (c. 1930-2008), Founder of Bogota Ibero-American Theater Festival — A778

2014, Dec. 2   **Litho.**   **Perf. 13¼x13**
1412 A778 500p multi .45 .45

Christmas — A779

Perf. 13½x13¼
2014, Dec. 10   **Litho.**
1413 A779 100p multi .25 .25

Augusto Ramirez Ocampo (c. 1934-2011), Politician — A780

2014, Dec. 23   **Litho.**   **Perf. 13¼x13**
1414 A780 1000p multi .85 .85

Gabriel García Márquez (1927-2014), 1982 Nobel Literature Laureate — A781

2015, July 14   Litho.   Perf. 13¼x13
1415 A781   200p multi   .25   .25

Souvenir Sheet
Imperf
1416 A781   10,000p multi   7.00 7.00

No. 1416 contains one 45x56mm stamp.

Fauna — A782

Designs: 200p, Allobates juanii. 500p, Eriocnemis mirabilis. 1000p, Diglosa gloriosissima. 2000p, Crocodylus intermedius. 5000p, Ateles hybridus. 10,000p, Phyllobates terribilis. 20,000p, Batrachemys dahli.

Serpentine Die Cut 12¾
2015, July 14   Litho.
Self-Adhesive
1417 A782   200p multi   .25   .25
1418 A782   500p multi   .35   .35
1419 A782   1000p multi   .70   .70
1420 A782   2000p multi   1.40   1.40
1421 A782   5000p multi   3.50   3.50
1422 A782   10,000p multi 7.00   7.00
1423 A782   20,000p multi 14.00 14.00
   Nos. 1417-1423 (7)   27.20 27.20

20th National and 4th Paranational Games, Chocó and Tolima — A783

2015, Nov. 7   Litho.   Perf. 13¼x13
1424 A783   5000p multi + label   3.25 3.25

Souvenir Sheet
Litho. & Embossed With Foil Application
Perf. 13
1425 A783   12,000p gold & multi   7.75 7.75

No. 1425 contains one 40x52mm stamp.

Manuel Mejía Vallejo (1923-89), Writer — A784

Serpentine Die Cut 12¾
2015, Nov. 12   Litho.
Self-Adhesive
1426 A784   20,000p multi   13.00 13.00

Paulina Vega Dieppa, 2014 Miss Universe — A785

2015, Nov. 14   Litho.   Perf. 13¼x13
1427 A785   20,000p multi   13.00 13.00

National Police School of Criminal Investigation, Cent. (in 2014) — A786

2015, Dec. 10   Litho.   Perf. 13¼x13
1428 A786   1000p multi   .65   .65

Christmas A787

2015, Dec. 11   Litho.   Perf. 13¼x13
1429 A787   10,000p multi   6.25 6.25

Departments Type of 2003
Miniature Sheet

No. 1430 — Risaralda Department: a, Arms of Risaralda. b, Cathedral of Our Lady of Poverty, Pereira, horiz. c, Pseudoscada lavinia. d, Santa Rosa de Cabal Thermal Springs. e, House of Culture, Marsella, horiz. f, Immaculate Mary Church, Marsella. g, Magnolia wolfii. h, Emberá-Chamí women, horiz. i, Dosquebradas Viaduct. j, Alouatta seniculus. k, Oxypogon stubelii, horiz. l, Old Railway Station, Pereira.
Horiz. stamps are 46x37mm.

2015, Dec. 14   Litho.   Perf. 13¼x13
Sheet of 12, #a-l, + 8 labels
1430 A608   100p Risaralda   .75   .75

SEMI-POSTAL STAMP

Catalogue values for unused stamps in this section are for Never Hinged items.

Girl Giving First Aid — SP1

Perf. 13½x14
1966, Apr. 26   Litho.   Unwmk.
B1 SP1   5c + 5c multicolored   .25   .25
Issued for the Red Cross.

AIR POST STAMPS

No. 341 Overprinted

1919   Unwmk.   Perf. 14
C1   A107   2c car rose   3,500.   1,700.
 a.   Numerals "1" with serifs   7,250.   4,250.

Used for the first experimental flight from Barranquilla to Puerto Colombia, 6/18/19. Values are for faulty stamps.

Issued by Compania Colombiana de Navegacion Aerea

From 1920 to 1932 the internal airmail service of Colombia was handled by the Compania Colombiana de Navegacion Aerea (1920) and the Sociedad Colombo-Alemana de Transportes Aéreos, known familiarly as "SCADTA" (1920-1932).
These organizations, under government contracts, operated and maintained their own post offices and issued stamps which were the only legal franking for airmail service during this period, both in the internal and international mails. All letters had to bear government stamps as well.

Woman and Boy Watching Plane — AP1

Designs: No. C3, Clouds and small biplane at top. No. C4, Tilted plane viewed close-up from above. No. C5, Flier in plane watching biplane. No. C6, Lighthouse. No. C7, Fuselage and tail of biplane. No. C8, Condor on cliff. No. C9, Plane at rest; pilot foreground. No. C10, Ocean liner.

1920, Feb.   Unwmk.   Litho.   Imperf.
Without Gum
C2   AP1   10c multi   3,000. 1,875.
C3   AP1   10c multi   3,800. 1,875.
C4   AP1   10c multi   4,600. 1,875.
C5   AP1   10c multi   3,500. 1,875.
C6   AP1   10c multi   3,000. 1,875.
C7   AP1   10c multi   11,000. 3,800.
C8   AP1   10c multi   6,000. 3,000.
C9   AP1   10c multi   3,500. 1,875.
C10 AP1   10c multi   4,600. 2,750.

Nos. C2-C10 were overprinted on the nine lighter-colored varieties of a set of 18 publicity labels produced by the Curtiss Co. for inclusion with packs of cigarettes. These labels were printed setenant, in panes of 18 (3x6). Value for the set of 18 values without overprint: $4,000.

Flier in Plane Watching Biplane — AP2

1920, Mar.
C11   AP2   10c green   60.00 92.50

Four other 10c stamps, similar to No. C11, have two designs showing plane, mountains and water. They are printed in deep green or light brown red. Some authorities state that these four were not used regularly.

Issued by Sociedad Colombo-Alemana de Transportes Aereos (SCADTA)

Seaplane over Magdalena River — AP3

1920-21   Litho.   Perf. 12
C12   AP3   10c yellow ('21)   60.00 47.50
C13   AP3   15c blue ('21)   65.00 52.50
C14   AP3   30c blk, *rose*   30.00 16.00
C15   AP3   30c rose ('21)   60.00 45.00
C16   AP3   50c pale green   60.00 47.50
   Nos. C12-C16 (5)   275.00 208.50

For surcharges see Nos. C17-C24, C36-C37.

No. C16 Handstamp Surcharged in Violet or Black

a

b

c

d

e

f

g

1921

C17	AP3 (a)	10c on 50c	1,250.	1,200.
C18	AP3 (b)	10c on 50c	1,250.	1,200.
C19	AP3 (c)	10c on 50c	1,250.	1,200.
C20	AP3 (b)	30c on 50c	925.	625.
C21	AP3 (d)	30c on 50c	925.	625.
C22	AP3 (e)	30c on 50c	1,850.	1,450.
C23	AP3 (f)	30c on 50c	1,850.	1,450.
C24	AP3 (g)	30c on 50c	1,850.	1,450.

No. C16 with Typewritten Surcharge in Red

1921

C24A	AP3	10c on 50c	—	1,500.
C24B	AP3	30c on 50c		

Plane over
Magdalena
River — AP4

Plane over
Bogota
Cathedral
AP5

1921   *Perf. 11½*

C25	AP4	5c orange yellow	4.50	4.00
C26	AP4	10c slate green	2.10	1.50
C27	AP4	15c orange brown	2.10	1.60
C28	AP4	20c red brown	4.50	2.10
a.		Horiz. pair, imperf. vert.	210.00	
C29	AP4	30c green	2.10	1.10
C30	AP4	50c blue	3.25	1.25
C31	AP4	60c vermilion	85.00	32.50
C32	AP5	1p gray black	22.50	5.00
C33	AP5	2p rose	42.50	20.00
C34	AP5	3p violet	125.00	72.50
C35	AP5	5p olive green	325.00	300.00
		Nos. C25-C35 (11)	618.55	441.55

Exist imperf.
For surcharge see No. C52.

Nos. C16 and C12 Handstamp Surcharged

h

i

1921-22   *Perf. 12*

C36	AP3 (h)	20c on 50c	3,750.	2,500.
C37	AP3 (i)	30c on 10c	850.	575.

Seaplane over
Magdalena
River — AP6

Plane over
Bogota
Cathedral
AP7

1923-28   **Wmk. 116**   *Perf. 14x14½*

C38	AP6	5c orange yellow	1.75	.25
C39	AP6	10c green	1.75	.25
C40	AP6	15c carmine	1.75	.25
C41	AP6	20c gray	1.75	.25
C42	AP6	30c blue	1.75	.25
C43	AP6	40c purple ('28)	12.50	8.00
C44	AP6	50c green	2.10	.25
C45	AP6	60c brown	3.25	.25
C46	AP6	80c olive grn ('28)	32.50	30.00
C47	AP7	1p black	14.50	3.25
C48	AP7	2p red orange	21.00	6.00
C49	AP7	3p violet	37.50	25.00
C50	AP7	5p olive green	67.50	32.50
		Nos. C38-C50 (13)	199.60	106.50

For surcharges and overprints see Nos.
C51, C53-C54, CF1.

Nos. C41 and C31 Surcharged in Carmine and Dark Blue

No. C51   No. C52

1923

C51	AP6	30c on 20c gray (C)	92.50	57.50
C52	AP4	30c on 60c ver	85.00	37.50

Nos. C41-C42
Overprinted in Black

1928   **Wmk. 116**   *Perf. 14x14½*

C53	AP6	20c gray	80.00	62.50
C54	AP6	30c blue	80.00	62.50

Goodwill flight of Lt. Benjamin Mendez from
New York to Bogota.

Magdalena
River and
Tolíma
Volcano
AP8

Columbus' Ship and
Plane
AP9

1929, June 1   **Wmk. 127**   *Perf. 14*

C55	AP8	5c yellow org	1.25	.25
C56	AP8	10c red brown	1.25	.25
C57	AP8	15c deep green	1.25	.25
C58	AP8	20c carmine	1.25	.25
C59	AP8	30c gray blue	1.25	.25
C60	AP8	40c dull violet	1.25	.25
C61	AP8	50c dk olive grn	2.50	.25
C62	AP8	60c orange brown	3.75	.25
C63	AP8	80c green	11.00	3.25
C64	AP9	1p blue	12.00	2.50
C65	AP9	2p brown orange	18.00	5.75
C66	AP9	3p pale rose vio	42.50	18.00
C67	AP9	5p olive green	100.00	37.50
		Nos. C55-C67 (13)	197.25	69.00

For surcharges and overprints see Nos.
C80-C95, CF2, CF4.

For International Airmail

AP10   AP11

1929, June 1   **Wmk. 127**   *Perf. 14*

C68	AP10	5c yellow org	6.25	7.25
C69	AP10	10c red brown	1.25	3.00
C70	AP10	15c deep green	1.25	3.00
C71	AP10	20c carmine	1.25	3.75
C72	AP10	25c violet blue	1.25	.85
C73	AP10	30c gray blue	1.25	.95
C74	AP10	50c dk olive grn	1.25	1.90
C75	AP10	60c brown	2.50	3.00
C76	AP11	1p blue	5.50	7.25
C77	AP11	2p red orange	8.50	10.00
C78	AP11	3p violet	100.00	100.00
C79	AP11	5p olive green	125.00	140.00
		Nos. C68-C79 (12)	255.25	280.95

This issue was sold abroad for use on corre-
spondence to be flown from coastal to interior
points of Colombia. Cancellations are those of
the country of origin rather than Colombia.
For overprint see No. CF3.

Nos. C63, C66 and C64 Surcharged in Black

m

n

1930, Dec. 15

C80	AP8(m)	10c on 80c	7.25	7.25
C81	AP9(n)	20c on 3p	13.50	13.50
C82	AP9(n)	30c on 1p	17.00	13.50
		Nos. C80-C82 (3)	37.75	*34.25*

Simon Bolivar (1783-1830).

Colombian Government Issues
Nos. C55-C67 Overprinted in Black

o

p

1929, June 1   **Wmk. 127**

1932, Jan. 1   **Typo.**   *Perf. 14*

C83	AP8(o)	5c yellow org	10.00	10.00
C84	AP8(o)	10c red brown	2.25	.60
C85	AP8(o)	15c deep green	3.75	3.75
C86	AP8(o)	20c carmine	1.90	.35
C87	AP8(o)	30c gray blue	1.90	.60
C88	AP8(o)	40c dull violet	2.50	1.25
C89	AP8(o)	50c dk ol grn	5.00	3.75
C90	AP8(o)	60c orange brn	4.25	3.75
C91	AP8(o)	80c green	17.00	17.00
C92	AP9(p)	1p blue	14.50	12.00
C93	AP9(p)	2p brown org	37.50	35.00
C94	AP9(p)	3p pale rose vio	77.50	65.00
C95	AP9(p)	5p olive green	125.00	*140.00*
		Nos. C83-C95 (13)	303.05	293.05

Coffee   Gold
AP12   AP16

Designs: 10c, 50c, Cattle. 15c, 60c, Petroleum. 20c, 40c, Bananas. 3p, 5p, Emerald.

1932-39   **Wmk. 127**   **Photo.**   *Perf. 14*

C96	AP12	5c org & blk brn	.90	.25
C97	AP12	10c lake & blk	1.00	.25
C98	AP12	15c bl grn & vio	.50	.25
C99	AP12	15c ver & vio blk ('39)	4.00	.25
C100	AP12	20c car & ol blk	.85	.25
C101	AP12	20c turq grn & ol blk ('39)	4.25	.35
C102	AP12	30c dk bl & blk brn	2.40	.25
C103	AP12	40c dk vio & ol bis	1.10	.25
C104	AP12	50c dk grn & brnsh blk	6.75	1.50
C105	AP12	60c dk brn & blk vio	1.40	.25
C106	AP12	80c grn & blk brn	9.50	2.00
C107	AP16	1p dk bl & ol bis	10.00	1.25
C108	AP16	2p org brn & ol bis	16.00	2.75
C109	AP16	3p dk vio & emer	26.00	7.25
C110	AP16	5p gray blk & emer	57.50	21.00
		Nos. C96-C110 (15)	142.15	38.10

For overprint see No. CF5.

Nos. C104, C106-C108 Surcharged

a

b

1934, Jan. 5

C111	AP12(a)	10c on 50c	4.50	4.50
C112	AP12(a)	15c on 80c	6.25	6.25
C113	AP16(b)	20c on 1p	6.50	6.50
C114	AP16(b)	30c on 2p	7.25	7.25
		Nos. C111-C114 (4)	24.50	24.50

400th anniversary of Cartagena.

Nos. C100 and C103 Surcharged in Black or Carmine

1939, Jan. 15

C115	AP12	5c on 20c (Bk)	.35	.35
C116	AP12	5c on 40c (C)	.35	.25
C117	AP12	15c on 20c (Bk)	1.50	.50
a.		Double surcharge	12.00	
b.		Pair, one with dbl. surch.	14.00	
c.		Inverted surcharge	12.00	12.00

No. CF5 Surcharged in Black

C118	AP12	5c on 20c	.70	.70
		Nos. C115-C118 (4)	2.90	1.80

Nos. C102-C103
Surcharged in Black or
Red

1940, Oct. 20

C119	AP12	15c on 30c	1.25	.50
a.		Inverted surcharge	12.00	
C120	AP12	15c on 40c (R)	2.00	.75
a.		Double surcharge	12.00	

Pre-Columbian
Monument — AP18

Proclamation of
Independence — AP22

Designs: 10c, 40c, Symbol of Legend of El Dorado. 15c, 50c, Spanish Fortifications, Cartagena. 20c, 60c, Colonial Bogotá. 2p, 5p, National Library, Bogota.

Unwmk.

1941, Jan. 28   Engr.   Perf. 12

C121	AP18	5c gray black	.25	.25
C122	AP18	10c yellow org	.25	.25
C123	AP18	15c carmine rose	.25	.25
C124	AP18	20c yellow grn	.35	.25
a.		Horiz. pair, imperf. vert.	87.50	
C125	AP18	30c deep blue	.35	.25
C126	AP18	40c rose lake	1.40	.25
C127	AP18	50c turq green	1.40	.25
C128	AP18	60c sepia	1.40	.25
C129	AP18	80c olive blk	3.25	.40
C130	AP22	1p blue & blk	4.00	.50
C131	AP22	2p red org & blk	8.00	2.00
C132	AP22	3p violet & blk	16.00	6.50
C133	AP22	5p lt green & blk	40.00	20.00
		Nos. C121-C133 (13)	76.90	31.40

See Nos. C151-C163, C217-C225. For overprints see Nos. C175-C198, C200-C216, C226, C290.

San Sebastian Fort,
Cartagena — AP24

National
Capitol,
Bogotá
AP27

Designs: 5c, 20c, 50c, San Sebastian Fort, Cartagena. 10c, 30c, 60c, Tequendama Waterfall. 15c, 40c, 80c, Bay of Santa Maria.

Unwmk.

1945, Nov. 3   Litho.   Perf. 11

C134	AP24	5c blue gray	.25	.25
C135	AP24	10c yellow org	.25	.25
C136	AP24	15c rose	.25	.25
C137	AP24	20c lt yel grn	.30	.25
C138	AP24	30c ultra	.30	.25
C139	AP24	40c claret	.50	.25
C140	AP24	50c bluish grn	.55	.25

C141	AP24	60c lt vio brn	2.25	.80
C142	AP24	80c dk slate grn	3.50	.80
C143	AP27	1p dk blue	5.00	.75
C144	AP27	2p red orange	7.00	2.50
		Nos. C134-C144 (11)	20.15	6.60

Part-perforate varieties exist for all denominations except 80c.

Imperf., Pairs

C134a	AP24	5c	8.50
C135a	AP24	10c	8.50
C136a	AP24	15c	8.50
C137a	AP24	20c	8.50
C138a	AP24	30c	8.50
C139a	AP24	40c	8.50
C140a	AP24	50c	8.50
C141a	AP24	60c	8.50
C142a	AP24	80c	10.50
C143a	AP27	1p	17.50
C144a	AP27	2p	60.00

Bello Type of Regular Issue, 1946
Wmk. 255

1946, Sept. 3   Engr.   Perf. 12

C145	A219	5c deep blue	.25	.25

Francisco José de   Manuel del
Caldas   Socorro
AP29   Rodriguez
                        AP30

Perf. 12½

1947, May 9   Litho.   Unwmk.

C146	AP29	5c dp bl, *grnsh*	.35	.25
C147	AP30	10c red org, *grnsh*	.50	.45

4th Pan-American Press Congress (1946).

Chancellery Patio — AP31

Capitol,
Patio
Rafael
Nunez
AP32

AP33

1948, Apr. 2   Engr.   Wmk. 229

C148	AP31	5c dark brown	.25	.25
C149	AP32	15c deep blue	.90	.90

Miniature Sheet
Imperf

C150	AP33	50c brown	1.90	1.90

9th Pan-American Conference, Bogotá.

Types of 1941

1948, July 21   Unwmk.   Perf. 12

C151	AP18	5c orange yel	.25	.25
C152	AP18	10c scarlet	.25	.25
C153	AP18	15c deep blue	.25	.25
C154	AP18	20c violet	.25	.25
C155	AP18	30c yellow grn	.35	.25
C156	AP18	40c gray	.40	.25
C157	AP18	50c rose lake	.40	.25
C158	AP18	60c olive gray	.70	.25

C159	AP18	80c red brn	.85	.25
C160	AP22	1p ol grn & vio brn	1.50	.30
C161	AP22	2p dp grn & brt bl	2.50	.65
C162	AP22	3p rose car & blk	5.50	3.75
C163	AP22	5p lt brn & turq grn	14.00	7.00
		Nos. C151-C163 (13)	27.20	13.95

"Air Week" 5c Blue

The War and Air Department issued a 5c blue stamp in May, 1949, to publicize Air Week (Semana de Aviacion). This stamp had no franking value and its use was optional during May 16-23.

Justice and
Liberty — AP34

Design: 10c, Liberty holding tablet of laws.

1949, Oct. 7   Unwmk.   Perf. 13

C164	AP34	5c blue green	.25	.25
C165	AP34	10c orange	.25	.25

Issued to honor the new Constitution.

Wing — AP35

For Domestic Postage

1950, June 22   Litho.   Perf. 12

C166	AP35	5c org yel	.25	.30
C167	AP35	10c brown red	.35	.30
C168	AP35	15c lt blue	.40	.40
C169	AP35	20c lt green	.60	.95
C170	AP35	30c lilac gray	1.50	*2.40*
C171	AP35	60c chocolate	1.90	*3.50*

With Network as in Parenthesis

C172	AP35	1p gray (buff)	14.00	*16.00*
C173	AP35	2p bl (pale grn)	14.00	*20.00*
C174	AP35	5p red brn (red brn)	40.00	*60.00*
		Nos. C166-C174 (9)	73.00	*103.85*

No. C172 was issued both with and without network.

Nos. C151-C157 and
C160-C163
Overprinted in Black

1950, July 18

C175	AP18	5c orange yel	.25	.25
C176	AP18	10c scarlet	.25	.25
C177	AP18	15c deep blue	.25	.25
C178	AP18	20c violet	.25	.25
C179	AP18	30c yellow green	.30	.25
C180	AP18	40c gray	2.50	.80
C181	AP18	50c rose lake	.75	.40
C182	AP22	1p ol grn & vio brn	4.00	4.50
C183	AP22	2p dp grn & brt bl	7.50	6.00
C184	AP22	3p rose car & blk	10.00	16.00
C185	AP22	5p lt brn & turq grn	35.00	52.50
		Nos. C175-C185 (11)	61.05	81.45

Nos. C151-C163
Overprinted in Black

1950, July 12

C186	AP18	5c orange yel	.25	.25
C187	AP18	10c scarlet	.25	.25
C188	AP18	15c deep blue	.25	.25
C189	AP18	20c violet	.25	.25
C190	AP18	30c yellow green	.25	.25
C191	AP18	40c gray	.55	.25
C192	AP18	50c rose lake	.55	.25
C193	AP18	60c olive gray	.85	.25
C194	AP18	80c red brown	1.25	.50
C195	AP22	1p ol grn & vio brn	1.50	.70
C196	AP22	2p dp grn & brt bl	4.50	2.40
C197	AP22	3p rose car & blk	10.00	12.00
C198	AP22	5p lt brn & turq grn	30.00	35.00
		Nos. C186-C198 (13)	50.45	52.60

On Nos. C175-C198, "L" stands for LANSA, "A" for AVIANCA.

UPU Type
Miniature Sheet

Unwmk.

1950, Aug. 22   Photo.   Imperf.

C199	A245	50c gray	3.50	3.50

75th anniv. (in 1949) of the UPU.

> Catalogue values for unused stamps in this section, from this point to the end of the section, are for Never Hinged items.

Types of 1941
Overprinted at Lower
Right in Black

Unwmk.

1951, Sept. 15   Engr.   Perf. 12

C200	AP18	40c orange yel	1.60	1.00
C201	AP18	50c ultra	2.10	1.40
C202	AP18	60c gray	1.60	1.00
C203	AP18	80c car rose	1.50	1.00
C204	AP22	1p red org & red brn	6.00	6.00
C205	AP22	2p rose car & bl	7.25	7.25
C206	AP22	3p choc & emer	18.00	20.00
C207	AP22	5p org & gray	47.50	52.50
		Nos. C200-C207 (8)	85.55	90.15

Types of 1941
Overprinted at Lower
Right in Black

1951-54

C208	AP18	40c orange yel	5.50	.55
C209	AP18	50c ultra	16.00	.65
C210	AP18	60c gray	4.50	.55
a.		Overprint centered	4.50	.55
C211	AP18	80c car rose	1.00	.35
C212	AP22	1p red org & red brn	4.75	.50
C213	AP22	1p ol grn & vio brn ('54)	7.00	.95

C214 AP22 2p rose car & bl 4.75 .70
C215 AP22 3p choc & emer 8.75 2.10
C216 AP22 5p org & gray 16.00 2.25
Nos. C208-C216 (9) 68.25 8.60

All values except the 2p and 3p exist without overprint.

Types of 1941
1952, May 10 Engr.
C217 AP18 5c ultra .50 .25
C218 AP18 10c ultra .50 .25
C219 AP18 15c ultra .50 .25
C220 AP18 20c ultra .90 .40
C221 AP18 30c ultra 2.50 .95

Color Change
C222 AP18 5c car rose .50 .25
C223 AP18 10c car rose .50 .25
C224 AP18 20c car rose .95 .25
C225 AP18 30c car rose 2.00 .55
Nos. C217-C225 (9) 8.85 3.40

Type of 1941 Surcharged in Blue

1952, Oct. 30
C226 AP18 70c on 80c car rose 1.75 .80
Latin American Siderurgical Conf., 1952.

Type of Postal Tax Stamps, 1948-50, Nos. 602 and 604 Surcharged or Overprinted in Black

1953 Wmk. 255 Perf. 12
C227 PT10 5c on 8c blue .25 .25
C228 PT10 15c on 20c brown .30 .25
C229 PT10 15c on 25c bl grn 1.60 .25
C230 PT10 25c blue green .90 .25
Nos. C227-C230 (4) 3.05 1.00

Many varieties of overprint or surcharge exist on Nos. C227-C231.

No. 570 Overprinted in Blue

1953, Aug. Wmk. 229 Perf. 12½
C231 A160 10c red .25 .25

"Extra Rapido"
Stamps inscribed "Extra Rapido" are for use on domestic airmail carried by airlines other than AVIANCA.

No. 585 Surcharged and Overprinted in Dark Blue

1953 Unwmk. Perf. 13
C232 A244 5c on 11c red .50 .35

Capitol and Arms — AP37

Revenue Stamps Overprinted "Correo Extra-Rapido"
Gray Security Paper
1953 Wmk. 255 Engr. Perf. 12
C233 AP37 1c on 2c green .25 .25
C234 AP37 50c red orange .25 .25

AP38

Real Estate Tax Stamps Ovptd. "Correo Extra-Rapido" in Black or Carmine
1953
C235 AP38 5c red orange .25 .25
C236 AP38 20c brown (C) .30 .25

On 20c, overprint is at bottom of stamp and two lines of ornaments cover real estate tax inscription at top.

Castillo y Rada and Map — AP39

Real Estate Tax Stamp Surcharged "Correo Aereo, II Exposicion Filatelica Nacional, Bogota Dicbre 1953, 15 Centavos"
1953, Dec. 12 Engr. & Litho.
C237 AP39 15c on 10p multi .50 .35
2nd Natl. Philatelic Exhib., Bogota, Dec. 1953.

No. RA45 Overprinted in Black

1953
C238 PT10 10c purple .25 .25

Galeras Volcano — AP40

Retreat of San Diego — AP41

Designs: No. C241, Las Lajas Shrine, Narino. No. C242, 50c, Bolivar monument. 20c, 80c, Ruiz mountain, Manizales. 40c, George Isaacs monument, Cali. 60c, Mono Fountain, Tunja. 1p, Stadium, Medellin. 2p, Pastelillo Fort, Cartagena. 3p, Santo Domingo University gate. 5p, Las Lajas Shrine. 10p, Map of Colombia.

Perf. 13½x13, 13
1954, Jan. 15 Engr. Unwmk.
C239 AP40 5c dp red vio .25 .25
C240 AP41 10c black .25 .25
C241 AP40 15c red orange .25 .25
C242 AP40 15c car rose .25 .25
C243 AP40 20c brown .25 .25
C244 AP40 30c brown org .25 .25
C245 AP40 40c blue .25 .25
C246 AP40 50c dk violet brn .35 .25
C247 AP40 60c dk brown .40 .25
C248 AP40 80c red brown .55 .25

Size: 37x27mm
Center in Black
C249 AP41 1p deep blue 3.25 .25
C250 AP41 2p dark green 4.75 .40
C251 AP41 3p carmine rose 11.00 1.40

Size: 38x32mm, 32x38mm
C252 AP41 5p dk grn & red brn 14.50 3.50
C253 AP40 10p gray grn & red org 20.00 7.50
Nos. C239-C253 (15) 56.55 15.55

See Nos. C307-C308. For surcharges and overprints see Nos. 691, C321, C325, C330, C333-C334, C343-C346.

Condor Carrying Shield AP42

Inscribed: "Correo Extra-Rapido"
1954, Apr. 23 Litho. Perf. 12½
C254 AP42 5c lilac rose .95 .40
For overprint see No. RA53.

Soldier-Map-Arms Type
1954, June 13 Engr. Perf. 13
C255 A259 15c carmine .40 .25
See No. C271a.

Games Type
Design: 20c, Stadium and Athlete holding arms of Colombia.
1954, July 18
C256 A260 15c chocolate .70 .25
C257 A260 20c deep blue green 1.60 .35

Church of St. Peter Claver, Cartagena AP45

1954, Sept. 9
C258 AP45 15c brown .40 .25
a. Souvenir sheet 8.00 12.00
St. Peter Claver, 300th death anniv.
No. C258a contains one stamp similar to No. C258, but printed in red brown.

Mercury Type
1954, Oct. 29
C259 A263 15c deep blue .55 .25

Inscribed "Extra Rapido"
C260 A263 50c scarlet .55 .25

Archbishop Manuel José Mosquera, Death Cent. — AP47

Inscribed: "Correo Extra Rapido"
1954, Nov. 17
C261 AP47 2c yellow green .25 .25

Virgin of Chiquinquira — AP48

Inscribed: "Correo Extra Rapido"
1954, Dec. 4 Engr. & Litho.
C262 AP48 5c org brn & multi .25 .25
See No. C291. For overprint see No. 686.

College Types
Designs: 20c, Brother Cristobal de Torres. 50c, College chapel and arms.
Perf. 12½x11½, 11½x12½
1954, Dec. 6 Engr. Unwmk.
C263 A264 15c orange & blk .50 .25
C264 A264 20c ultra .85 .25
C265 A265 25c dark brown .85 .25
C266 A265 50c black & car 2.40 .95
a. Souvenir sheet 12.00 16.00
Nos. C263-C266 (4) 4.60 1.70

No. C266a contains four stamps similar to Nos. C263-C266, but printed in different colors: 15c red and black, 20c pale purple, 25c brown, 50c black and olive green.

Steel Mill Type
1954, Dec. 12 Perf. 12½x13
C267 A266 20c green & blk 1.75 .60

Marti Type
1955, Jan. 28 Perf. 13½x13
C268 A267 15c deep green .30 .25

Korean Veterans Type
1955, Mar. 23 Perf. 12½
C269 A268 20c dark green .55 .25

Merchant Fleet Types
1955, Apr. 12 Perf. 12½
C270 A269 25c black .40 .25
C271 A270 50c dark green .90 .40
a. Souvenir sheet 9.50 12.00

No. C271a contains 4 stamps similar to Nos. C255, C269-C271, but printed in different colors; 15c lilac red, 20c olive, 25c bluish black, 50c bluish green.

Marco Fidel Suarez (1855-1927), Pres. 1918-21 — AP56

Inscribed: "Correo Extra Rapido"
1955, April 23 Perf. 13
C272 AP56 10c deep blue .25 .25

Hotel-Church Type
1955, May 16 Photo. Perf. 11½x12
C273 A271 15c rose brown .40 .25

Rotary Type
Unwmk.
1955, Oct. 17 Engr. Perf. 13
C274 A272 15c dk carmine rose .40 .25

Atahualpa, Tisquesuza and Montezuma AP59

Ferdinand the Catholic and Queen Isabella I AP60

Designs: 15c, O'Higgins, Santander and Sucre. 20c, Marti, Hidalgo and Petion. 1p, Artigas, Solano Lopez and Murillo. 2p, Abdon Calderon, Baron de Rio Branco and José de La Mar.

1955, Oct. 12 Engr. & Photo.
Inscribed: "Extra Rapido"
C275 AP59 2c dk brn & blk .45 .25
C276 AP60 5c dk brn & yel .45 .25

Regular Air Post
C277 AP59 15c rose car & blk .55 .25
C278 AP59 20c pale brn & blk .85 .25
a. Souvenir sheet of 2 30.00 30.00

Inscribed: "Extra Rapido"
C279 AP60 1p ol gray & brn 15.00 7.50
C280 AP60 2p violet & blk 11.00 5.75
Nos. C275-C280 (6) 28.30 14.25

7th Cong. of the Postal Union of the Americas and Spain, Bogota, Oct. 12-Nov. 9, 1955.

No. C278a contains one each of Nos. C277-
C278 printed in different shades.

Caro Type
1955, Nov. 29   Engr.   Perf. 13½x13
C281 A275 15c gray green   .40 .25

University of
Salamanca
AP62

Inscribed: "Extra Rapido"
1955, Nov. 29   Unwmk.   Perf. 13
C282 AP62 20c dark brown   .25 .25
University of Salamanca, 7th centenary.

Type of Postal Tax Stamp of 1948-50 Surcharged

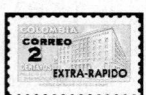

1956   Wmk. 255   Engr.   Perf. 12
C283 PT10 2c on 8c blue   .25 .25

No. 617
Overprinted in
Black

1956   Unwmk.   Perf. 12½x13
C284 A256 1p black & emerald   .40 .25

Columbus Type
1956, Oct. 11   Photo.   Perf. 12
C285 A279 15c intense blue   .65 .25
See No. C306.

St. Elizabeth Type
1956, Nov. 19
C286 A280 15c red brown   .50 .25

St. Ignatius Type
1956, Nov. 26   Engr.   Perf. 12½x13
C287 A281 5c brown   .25 .25

Javier
Pereira — AP63

1956, Dec. 28   Unwmk.   Perf. 12
C288 AP63 20c rose carmine   .25 .25
Issued to honor 167-year-old Javier Pereira.

No. 649 and Type
of 1941
Overprinted in
Red

1957   Perf. 13½x13
C289 A276 5c blue & black   7.50 3.25
Perf. 12
C290 AP22 5p orange & gray   11.00 7.50
The overprint measures 14mm.

Virgin Type of 1954
Engraved and Lithographed
1957, May 23   Unwmk.   Perf. 13
C291 AP48 5c dp plum & multi   .25 .25

Bank Type
No. C292, 20c, Emblem, cow, horse & herd.
10c, Emblem & tractor. 15c, Emblem, coffee &
corn. No. C293, Emblem & dairy farm.

1957   Photo.   Perf. 14x13½
C292 A283 5c chocolate   .25 .25
C293 A283 5c orange   .25 .25
C294 A283 10c green   .70 .45
C295 A283 15c black   .40 .25
C296 A283 20c dull red   1.00 .65
  Nos. C292-C296 (5)   2.60 1.85
No. C292 is inscribed "Extra Rapido."
Issued: No. C292, 3/5; others 5/23.

Cyclist
AP64

1957, July 6   Unwmk.   Perf. 12
C297 AP64 2c brown   .25 .25
C298 AP64 5c ultra   .25 .25
Seventh Bicycle Tour of Colombia.

Academy Type
Designs: 15c, Coat of arms and Gen. Rafael Reyes. 20c, Coat of arms and Academy.

1957, July 20   Engr.   Perf. 12½
C299 A284 15c rose carmine   .30 .25
C300 A284 20c brown   .45 .25

Delgado Type
1957, Sept. 15   Photo.   Perf. 12
C301 A285 10c slate blue   .25 .25

UPU Type
1957, Oct. 10
C302 A286 15c dark red brown   .30 .25
C303 A286 25c dark blue   .40 .25

St. Vincent de Paul Type
1957, Oct. 18
C304 A287 5c rose brown   .25 .25

Fencing Type
1957, Nov. 23   Perf. 12
C305 A288 20c dark red brown   .40 .30

Columbus Type Inscribed "Extra Rapido"
1958, Jan. 8   Unwmk.   Perf. 12
C306 A279 3c dark green   .25 .25

Scenic Type
Design: 25c, Las Lajas Shrine.
1958, June 20   Engr.   Perf. 13
C307 AP40 25c dark blue   .30 .25
C308 AP40 25c rose violet   .30 .25

IGY Type
1958, May 12   Photo.   Perf. 12
C309 A289 25c green   .50 .25
Inscribed "Extra Rapido"
C310 A289 1p purple   .65 .25

No. 659
Ovptd. in
Carmine

1958, Oct. 16   Engr.   Perf. 13
C312 A277 50c dk green & blk   .50 .25

Almanza Type
1958, Oct. 23   Photo.   Perf. 14x13
C313 A290 25c dark gray   .30 .25
Inscribed "Extra Rapido"
C314 A290 10c olive green   .25 .25

Carrasquilla Type
1959, Jan. 22   Photo.   Perf. 14x13
C315 A291 25c carmine rose   .25 .25
C316 A291 1p dark blue   .80 .25

Miss Universe Type
1959, June 26   Unwmk.   Perf. 11½
C317 A292 1.20p multicolored   1.75 1.40
C318 A292 5p multicolored   47.50 47.50

Gaitan Type
Inscribed and
Surcharged in Black
or Blue

1959, July 28   Engr.   Perf. 12x13½
C319 A293 2p on 1p black   1.75 1.50
C320 A293 2p on 1p black (Bl)   1.75 1.50
The 1p black, type A293, exists without
surcharge.

No. C247
Surcharged in
Dark Blue

1959, Aug. 24   Unwmk.   Perf. 13
C321 AP40 50c on 60c dk brown   1.75 .40

Regular
and Air
Post Issues
of 1948-59
Ovptd. in
Black or
Red

1959-60
C322 A283 5c orange   .35   .25
C323 A287 5c rose brn
               ('60)   .50   .50
C324 A281 5c brown (R)   .40   .30
C325 AP41 10c black   .25   .25
  a.   Double overprint   2.50 2.50
C326 A160 10c red, #C231   .40   .25
  a.   Double overprint   1.40 1.40
C328 A284 15c rose car   .25   .25
  a.   Inverted overprint   3.00 3.00
C330 AP40 20c brown   .25   .25
  a.   Double overprint   1.40 1.40
C331 A284 20c brown   .25   .25
C332 A288 20c dk red brn
               ('60)   .25   .25
C333 AP40 25c rose vio
               ('60)   .25   .25
C334 AP40 25c dark blue   .25   .25
C335 A291 25c car rose   .25   .25
C336 A290 25c dark gray   .25   .25
C338 AP40 30c brown org   .25   .25
C340 AP40 50c on 60c dk
               brn   .40   .25
C341 A291 1p dark brown   .95   .25
  a.   Double overprint   2.50 2.50
C342 A292 1.20p brn, ultra,
               car & ol   1.50   .80
C343 AP41 2p dk grn & blk   2.00   .25
C344 AP41 3p car rose &
               blk   6.00   .25
C345 AP41 5p dk grn &
               red brn   8.00 1.10
  a.   Double overprint   10.00 10.00
  b.   Inverted overprint   10.00 10.00
C346 AP40 10p gray grn &
               red org   10.00 2.25
  Nos. C322-C346 (21)   33.00 9.20
Issued following agreement between the
Colombian government and AVIANCA to unify
the air postage used on all mail carried by
AVIANCA.
Vertical overprint on Nos. C342 and C346.

Airmail
Stamp
of 1919 and
Planes
AP66

60c, Nos. C349a, C350a, Planes of 1919
and 1959. Nos. C349b, C350b, Stamp of 1919
and Planes.

Unwmk.
1959, Dec. 5   Photo.   Perf. 12
C347 AP66 35c lt bl, blk & red   .65   .25
C348 AP66 60c yel grn & gray   1.10   .75
Souvenir Sheets
C349   Sheet of 2   12.00 12.00
  a.   AP66 1p orange & gray   2.00 1.50
  b.   AP66 1p lilac, gray & red 2.00 1.50
Inscribed "Extra Rapido"
1960, May 17
C350   Sheet of 2   12.00 12.00
  a.   AP66 1.50p red orange &
         gray   2.00 1.50
  b.   AP66 1.50p olive, gray &
         rose   2.00 1.50
Nos. C347-C350 for the 40th anniv. of air
post service and of the AVIANCA company.

Type of Regular Issue and

1859 Stamp and
Seaplane
AP67

Designs (various stamps of 1859 and): 10c,
Map of Colombia. 25c, Pres. Mariano Ospina.
1.20p, Plane over mountains.

1959, Dec. 1   Photo.   Perf. 12
C351 A296 25c choc & red   .50   .35
C352 AP67 50c ver & ultra   1.25   .65
C353 AP67 1.20p yel grn & car   2.50 1.50
Inscribed "Extra Rapido"
C354 A296 10c lemon & vio   .25   .25
  Nos. C351-C354 (4)   4.50 2.75

Souvenir Sheet

Tête Bêche 5c Stamps of
1859 — AP68

Wmk. 331
1959, Dec. 23   Litho.   Imperf.
C355 AP68 5p blue, pink   19.00 19.00
Cent. of Colombian postage stamps.
No. C355 exists with inscription "VALOR
$5.10" instead of "VALOR $5."

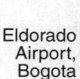

Eldorado
Airport,
Bogota
AP69

1960, Jan. 5   Wmk. 331   Perf. 12½
C356 AP69 35c black & ocher   .65   .25
C356A AP69 60c ver & gray   .75   .45
Inscribed "Extra Rapido"
C356B AP69 1p Prus bl & gray   1.25   .70
  Nos. C356-C356B (3)   2.65 1.40

Ant Bear
AP70

1.30p, Armadillo. 1.45p, Parrot fish.

Unwmk.

1960, Feb. 12		**Photo.**	*Perf. 12*	
C357	AP70	35c sepia	1.60	.25
C358	AP70	1.30p rose car & dk brn	3.00	2.40
C359	AP70	1.45p lt bl, bl & yel	2.75	2.00
		Nos. C357-C359 (3)	7.35	4.65

Alexander von Humboldt, German naturalist and geographer (1769-1859).

Flower Type

Nos. C360, C362, C366, Passiflora mollissima. Nos. C361, C364, C367, Odontoglossum luteo purpureum. Nos. C363, C369, Anthurium andreanum. Nos. C365, C370, Stanhopea tigrina. No. C368, Espeletia grandiflora.

1960, May 10		**Photo.**	*Perf. 12*	
		Flowers in Natural Colors		
C360	A298	5c dark blue	.25	.25
C361	A298	35c maroon	.55	.25
C362	A298	60c dark blue	1.10	.70
C363	A298	1.45p dark brown	1.25	1.10
		Inscribed "Extra Rapido"		
C364	A298	5c maroon	.25	.25
C365	A298	10c brown	.25	.25
C366	A298	1p dark blue	2.50	3.00
C367	A298	1p maroon	2.50	3.00
C368	A298	1p brown	2.50	3.00
C369	A298	1p brown	2.50	3.00
C370	A298	1p brown	2.50	3.00
		Nos. C360-C370 (11)	16.15	17.80

See Nos. C420-C425.

Fleeing Family and Uprooted Oak Emblem AP71

Perf. 10, 11

1960, May 24		**Litho.**	**Wmk. 331**	
C371	AP71	60c bl grn & gray	.40	.25

World Refugee Year, 7/1/59-6/30/60.

Souvenir Sheet

Pan-American Highway Through Colombia — AP72

1960, May 28		**Litho.**	*Imperf.*	
C372	AP72	2.50p brn & aqua	7.50	7.50

8th Pan-American Highway Congress, Bogota, May 20-29.

Lincoln Type

1960, June 6			*Perf. 10½*	
C375	A299	40c dl red brn & blk	1.40	1.00
C376	A299	60c rose red & blk	.40	.25

Type of Regular Issue and

Joaquin Camacho, Jorge Tadeo Lozano and Jose Miguel Pey AP73

Flag, Coins and Arms of Mompox and Cartagena — AP74

No. C378, Arms of Cartagena. 35c, 1.45p, Colombian flag. 60c, Andres Rosillo, Antonio Villavicencio and Joaquin Caicedo. 1p, Manuel de Bernardo Alvarez and Joaquin Gutierrez. 1.20p, Jose Antonio Galan statue. 1.30p, Front page of newspaper La Bagatela, 1811. 1.65p, Antonia Santos, Jose Acevedo y Gomez and Liborio Mejia.

Unwmk.

1960, July 20		**Photo.**	*Perf. 12*	
C377	AP73	5c lilac & brn	.25	.25
C378	A301	5c dp bl grn & multi	.25	.25
C379	AP73	35c multicolored	.25	.25
C380	AP73	60c red brn & grn	.45	.25
C381	AP73	1p ver & sl grn	1.10	.70
C382	A301	1.20p ultra & ind	1.10	.70
C383	AP73	1.30p orange & blk	1.10	.70
C384	AP73	1.45p multicolored	1.40	1.10
C385	AP73	1.65p green & brn	1.25	1.10
		Nos. C377-C385 (9)	7.15	5.30

Souvenir Sheet
Stamps Inscribed "Extra Rapido"

C386	AP74	Sheet of 4	7.50	7.50
a.		50c deep claret & multi	1.00	1.00
b.		50c green & multi	1.00	1.00
c.		1p brown olive, yel, blue & car	1.00	1.00
d.		1p lilac & gray	1.00	1.00

150th anniv. of Colombia's independence.

St. Isidore Type

Designs: 35c, No. C388a, St. Isidore and farm animals. No. C388b, Nativity.

Unwmk.

1960, Sept. 26		**Photo.**	*Perf. 12*	
C387	A302	35c multicolored	.25	.25

Souvenir Sheet
Stamps Inscribed "Extra Rapido"

C388	A302	Sheet of 2	10.00	10.00
a.		1.50p multicolored	3.00	3.00
b.		1.50p multicolored	3.00	3.00

See Nos. C439-C440.

Type of Regular Issue, 1959

Wmk. 331

1960, Nov. 23		**Litho.**	*Perf. 12½*	
C389	A294	35c Bolivar	3.50	.45

Pan-American Highway Type

1961, Mar. 7	**Unwmk.**		*Perf. 10½x11*	
C390	A304	10c rose lil & emer	.75	.70
C391	A304	20c ver & lt bl	.75	.70
C392	A304	30c black & emer	.75	.70
		Inscribed "Extra Rapido"		
C393	A304	10c dk blue & emer	.75	.70
		Nos. C390-C393 (4)	3.00	2.80

8th Pan-American Highway Congress, Bogota, May 20-29, 1960.

Lopez Type

1961, Mar. 22		**Photo.**	*Perf. 12½*	
C394	A305	35c blue & brown	.60	.25
		Inscribed "Extra Rapido"		
C395	A305	10c emerald & brn	.25	.25
		Souvenir Sheet		
C396	A305	1p lilac & brn	6.00	6.00

Brother Damian and San Francisco Church, Cali AP75

Designs: 10c, View of Cali, vert. No. 398, Emblem of University del Valle, vert. 1.30p, Fine Arts School, Cali. 1.45p, Agricultural College, Palmira.

		Perf. 13x13½, 13½x13		
1961, Aug. 17		**Photo.**	**Unwmk.**	
C397	AP75	35c vio brn & ol	.40	.25
C398	AP75	35c olive & grn	.40	.25
C399	AP75	1.30p sepia & pink	1.10	.50
C400	AP75	1.45p multicolored	1.10	.70
		Inscribed: "Extra Rapido"		
C401	AP75	10c brn & red grn	.25	.25
		Nos. C397-C401 (5)	3.25	1.95

50th anniv. (in 1960) of the department of Valle del Cauca.

View of Cucuta AP76

10c, Church of the Rosary, Cucuta, vert.

1961, Aug. 29				
C402	AP76	35c brn ol & grn	.70	.25
		Inscribed: "Extra Rapido"		
C403	AP76	10c dk brn & gray grn	.25	.25

50th anniv. (in 1960) of the department of North Santander.

Old and New Ships of Barranquilla AP77

Arms and View of San Gil — AP78

Hotel, Popayan AP79

Statue of Christ in Procession AP80

Design: 1.45p, View of Velez.

		Perf. 12½x13, 13x12½		
1961, Oct. 10		**Photo.**	**Unwmk.**	
C404	AP77	35c gold & bl	.55	.25
C405	AP78	35c bl grn, yel & red	.55	.25
C406	AP79	35c car & brn	.55	.25
C407	AP78	1.45p brown & grn	.55	.25
		Inscribed: "Extra Rapido"		
C408	AP80	10c brown & yel	.25	.25
		Nos. C404-C408 (5)	2.45	1.25

Types of Regular and Air Post
Souvenir Sheets

Designs, No. C409: 35c, Barranquilla arms. 40c, Popayan arms. c, Arms and view of San Gil. d, Holy Week in Popayan.

No. C410: a, Old and new ships at Barranquilla. b, Hotel, Popayan. c, Bucaramanga arms. d, Holy Week in Popayan.

C409		Sheet of 4	12.00	12.00
a.		A309 35c gold & multi	1.00	1.00
b.		A309 40c gold & multi	1.00	1.00
c.		AP78 1p blue, yellow & red	2.00	2.00

d.		AP80 1p car rose & yellow	2.00	2.00
		Stamps Inscribed: "Extra Rapido"		
C410		Sheet of 4	12.00	12.00
a.		AP77 50c gold & car rose	1.50	1.50
b.		AP79 50c gold & blue	1.50	1.50
c.		A309 50c pink & multi	1.50	1.50
d.		AP80 50c blue & yellow	1.50	1.50

Nos. C404-C408 are in honor of the Atlantico Department. Nos. C409-C410 are in honor of the Departments of Atlantico, Cauca and Santander.

Nos. 713, 716 and 715 Overprinted and Surcharged

1961, Sept.			*Perf. 12*	
C411	A297	5c grnsh bl & brn	.25	.25
C412	A298	5c multicolored	.25	.25
C413	A297	10c on 20c cit & gray brn	.25	.25
		Nos. C411-C413 (3)	.75	.75

"Aereo" in script on No. C412.
See Nos. C420-C425.

Sports Type

Designs: No. C414, Women divers. No. C415, Tennis, mixed doubles. 1.45p, No. C419b, Baseball. No. C417, Torch bearer. Nos. C418, C419a, Bolivar statue and flags of six participating nations. No. C419c, Soccer. No. C419d, Basketball.

1961, Dec. 16		**Litho.**	*Perf. 13½x14*	
C414	A310	35c ultra, yel & brn	.75	.25
C415	A310	35c car, yel & brn	.75	.25
C416	A310	1.45p Prus grn, yel & brn	1.10	.65
		Inscribed: "Extra Rapido"		
C417	A310	10c car lake, yel & brn	.25	.25
C418	A310	10c ol, yel, bl & red	.25	.25
		Nos. C414-C418 (5)	3.10	1.65
		Souvenir Sheet		
		Stamps Inscribed: "Extra Rapido"		
		Imperf		
C419		Sheet of 4	8.00	8.00
a.		A310 50c multi	.60	.60
b.		A310 50c multi	.60	.60
c.		A310 1p multi	1.25	1.25
d.		A310 1p multi	1.25	1.25

Flower Type of 1960

5c, Passiflora mollissima. 10c, Espeletia grandiflora. 20c, 2p, Odontoglossum luteo purpureum. 25c, Stanhopea tigrina. 60c, Anthurium Andreanum.

Unwmk.

1962, Jan. 30		**Photo.**	*Perf. 12*	
		Flowers in Natural Colors		
C420	A298	5c gray	.25	.25
C421	A298	10c gray blue	.25	.25
C422	A298	20c rose lilac	.25	.25
C423	A298	25c citron	.30	.25
C424	A298	60c light brown	.30	.25
		Inscribed "Extra Rapido"		
C425	A298	2p salmon pink	2.75	1.25
		Nos. C420-C425 (6)	4.10	2.50

Anti-Malaria Type

Designs: 40c, Colombian anti-malaria emblem. 1p, 1.45p, Malaria eradication emblem and mosquito in swamp.

1962, Apr. 12		**Litho.**	*Perf. 12*	
C426	A311	40c yellow & red	.25	.25
C427	A311	1.45p gray & ultra	.65	.40
		Inscribed "Extra Rapido"		
C428	A311	1p yel grn & ultra	5.00	5.00
		Nos. C426-C428 (3)	5.90	5.65

WHO drive to eradicate malaria.

Type of Regular Issue, 1962 and

Abelardo Ramos and Engineering School, Cauca — AP81

Designs: 10c, Miguel Triana, Andres A. Arroyo and Monserrate shrine with cable cars. 15c, Diodoro Sanchez and first meeting place of Engineers Society. 2p, Engineers Society emblem.

1962, June 12 Photo. Perf. 11½x12
C429	AP81	5c blue & dp rose	.25	.25
C430	AP81	10c green & sepia	.25	.25
C431	AP81	15c lilac & sepia	.45	.30

Inscribed: "Extra Rapido"
C432	A312	2p blk, yel, red & bl	2.50	2.50
		Nos. C429-C432 (4)	3.45	3.30

75th anniv. of the founding of the Colombian Soc. of Engineers and 6th Natl. Cong. of Engineers.

American States Type

1962, June 28 Photo. Perf. 13

Flags in National Colors
C433	A313	35c black & blue	.35	.25

Women's Rights Type

Perf. 12x12½

1962, July 20 Litho. Wmk. 229
C434	A314	35c buff, gray & blk	.25	.25
		See Nos. C448-C450.		

Scout Type

Designs: 15c, No. C438, Scouts at campfire and tents. 40c and No. C437, Girl Scouts.

Perf. 11½x12

1962, July 26 Photo. Unwmk.
C435	A315	15c brown & rose	.30	.25
C436	A315	40c dp cl & pink	.40	.30
C437	A315	1p blue & buff	.80	.55

Inscribed "Extra Rapido"
C438	A315	1p purple & yel	7.50	6.00
		Nos. C435-C438 (4)	9.00	7.10

Nos. C435 and C438 for 30th anniv. of the Colombian Boy Scouts. Nos. C436 and C437 for the 25th anniv. of the Girl Scouts.

Nativity by Gregorio Vasquez AP82

Design: 2p, St. Isidore, similar to type A302.

Inscribed "Extra Rapido"
Unwmk.

1962, Aug. 28 Photo. Perf. 12
C439	AP82	10c gray & multi	.25	.25
C440	AP82	2p gray & multi	4.50	4.50
		See Nos. C387-C388.		

Type of Regular Issue, 1962 and

Pres. Aquileo Parra and Magdalena River Bridge AP83

Design: 5c, Locomotives of 1854 and 1961. 10c, Railroad map of Colombia.

1962, Sept. 28 Photo. Perf. 12½
C441	AP83	5c sep & slate grn	.25	.25
C442	A316	10c multicolored	.25	.25

Engr.
C443	AP83	1p dull pur & brn	2.00	.25

Inscribed: "Extra Rapido."
C444	AP83	5p bl, brn & dl grn	5.00	4.50
		Nos. C441-C444 (4)	7.50	5.25

Progress of Colombian railroads and completion of the Atlantic Line from Santa Maria to Bogota.

UPAE Type

Designs: 50c, Map of Americas and carrier pigeon. 60c, Post horn.

Perf. 13½x14

1962, Oct. 18 Litho. Wmk. 346
C445	A317	50c slate grn & gold	.40	.25
C446	A317	60c gold & plum	.25	.25

Pope John XXIII AP84

1963, Mar. 11
C447	AP84	60c gold, red brn, buff & red	.40	.25

Vatican II, the 21st Ecumenical Council of the Roman Catholic Church.

Women's Rights Type of 1962

Perf. 12x12½

1963-64
C448	A314	5c sal, gray & blk ('64)	.25	.25
C449	A314	45c pale grn, gray & blk	.40	.25
C450	A314	45c brt pink, gray & blk	.40	.25
		Nos. C448-C450 (3)	1.05	.75

Games Emblem — AP85

1963, Aug. 12 Perf. 13x14
C451	AP85	20c gray & multi	.25	.25
C452	AP85	80c buff & multi	.25	.25

South American Athletic Championships (22nd for men, 12th for women), Cali, June 30-July 7.

Bolivar Statue by Arenas-Betancourt — AP86

Perf. 14x13½

1963, Aug. 30 Unwmk.
C453	AP86	1.90p olive bis & blue	.25	.25

Centenary of the city of Pereira.
For surcharge see No. C574.

Tennis Player — AP87

1963, Oct. 11 Perf. 13½x14
C454	AP87	55c multicolored	.25	.25

30th South American Tennis Championships, Medellin, Oct. 3-13.

Pres. John F. Kennedy and Alliance for Progress Emblem AP88

1963, Dec. 17 Litho. Perf. 14x13½
C455	AP88	10c multicolored	.25	.25

President John F. Kennedy (1917-1963).

Church of the True Cross, National Pantheon, Bogota — AP89

2p, Christ of the Martyrs, bell and tomb.

Perf. 13½x14

1964, Mar. 10 Photo. Unwmk.
C459	AP89	1p multicolored	.25	.25
C460	AP89	2p multicolored	.35	.25

View of Cartagena AP90

1964, Mar. 18 Litho. Perf. 14x13½
C461	AP90	3p vio, bl, ocher & brn	1.40	.60

Cartagena's independence in 1811, Simon Bolivar's visit in 1812 and the siege of 1815.

Eleanor Roosevelt AP91

1964, Nov. 10 Photo. Perf. 12
C462	AP91	20c ol & dl red brn	.25	.25

Eleanor Roosevelt (1884-1962).

Alberto Castilla and Score of "El Bunde" AP92

1964, Nov. 10 Unwmk.
C463	AP92	30c ol bis & Prus grn	.25	.25

Department of Tolima and Maestro Alberto Castilla (1878-1937) who in 1906 founded the Tolima Conservatory of Music in Ibague.

Mejia Type

Mejia portrait and: 45c, Women picking coffee. 5p, Mules carrying coffee bags. 10p, Loading coffee on freighter "Manuel Mejia."

1965, Feb. 10 Engr. Perf. 12½x13
C464	A320	45c brown & blk	.25	.25
C465	A320	5p gray grn & blk	2.50	.25
C466	A320	10p ultra & blk	3.50	.40
		Nos. C464-C466 (3)	6.25	.90

ITU Emblem AP93

1965, Oct. 25 Photo. Perf. 12
C467	AP93	80c Prus bl, lt bl & red	.25	.25

Cent. of the ITU.

Cattleya Truanae — AP94

1965, Oct. 3 Litho. Perf. 13½x14
C468	AP94	20c yellow & multi	1.00	.40

Fifth Philatelic Exhibition.

Cent. of the Telegraph in Colombia — AP95

No. C469, Pres. Manuel Murillo Toro statue, telegraph and orbits. No. C470, Telegraph and satellites over South America, horiz.

1965, Nov. 1 Perf. 13½x14, 14x13½
C469	AP95	60c multicolored	.25	.25
C470	AP95	60c multicolored	.25	.25

Junkers F-13 Seaplane, 1920 AP96

History of Colombian Aviation: 10c, Dornier Wal, 1924. 20c, Dornier Mercur, 1926. 50c, Trimotor Ford, 1932. 60c, De Havilland biplane, 1930. 1p, Douglas DC-4, 1947. 1.40p, Douglas DC-3, 1944. 2.80p, Superconstellation 1049, 1951. 3p, Boeing 720B jet, 1961.

Perf. 14x13½

1965-66 Photo. Unwmk.
C471	AP96	5c multicolored	.25	.25
C472	AP96	10c multicolored	.25	.25
C473	AP96	20c multicolored	.25	.25
C474	AP96	50c multicolored	.25	.25
C475	AP96	60c multicolored	.40	.25
C476	AP96	1p multicolored	.75	.25
C477	AP96	1.40p multicolored	.90	.25
C478	AP96	2.80p multicolored	1.60	.60
C479	AP96	3p multicolored	2.40	.85
		Nos. C471-C479 (9)	7.05	3.20
		Nos. C471-C479,CE4 (10)	7.60	3.45

Issued: 5c, 60c, 3p, 12/13/65; 10c, 1p, 1.40p, 7/15/66; 20c, 50c, 2.80p, 12/14/66.

Automobile Club Emblem and Car on Road AP97

1966, Feb. 16   Litho.   Perf. 14x13½
C480 AP97 20c multicolored   .25 .25

25th anniv. (in 1965) of the Automobile Club of Colombia.

Fish Type

Fish: 2p, Flying fish. 2.80p, Queen angelfish. 20p, King mackerel.

1966, Aug. 25   Photo.   Perf. 12½x13
C481 A323 2p multicolored   .50 .25
C482 A323 2.80p multicolored 1.25 .90
C483 A323 20p multicolored 17.50 13.50
Nos. C481-C483 (3)   19.25 14.65

Coat of Arms Type

1966, Oct. 11   Litho.   Perf. 14x13½
C484 A324 1p ultra & multi   .40 .25
C485 A324 1.40p red & multi   .30 .25

Portrait Type

80c, Father Felix Restrepo Mejia, S.J. (1887-1965), theologian, scholar. 1.70p, José Joaquin Casas (1866-1951), educator, diplomat.

Perf. 13½x14
1967, Jan. 18   Litho.   Unwmk.
C486 A325 80c dk bl & bis   .30 .25
C487 A325 1.70p blk & bis   .50 .25

Declaration of Bogota Type

1967, Feb. 2   Litho.   Perf. 14x13½
C488 A326 3p multicolored   .50 .25

See note after No. 767.

Orchid Type

Orchids: 1p, Cattleya dowiana aurea, vert. 1.20p, Masdevallia coccinea, vert. 5p, Catasetum macrocarpum and bee.

1967, May 23   Litho.   Perf. 14
C489 A327 1p multicolored   1.00 .25
C490 A327 1.20p multicolored .75 .25
C491 A327 5p multicolored   5.00 .90
a. Souv. sheet of 3, #C489-C491   17.50 17.50
Nos. C489-C491 (3)   6.75 1.40

Lions Type

1967, July 12   Litho.   Perf. 13½x14
C492 A328 25c multicolored   .25 .25

"First Caesarean Section" by Grau AP98

Perf. 14x13½
1967, Sept. 7   Litho.   Unwmk.
C493 AP98 80c multicolored   .25 .25

Issued to publicize the 6th Congress of Colombian Surgeons, Bogota, Sept. 25.

SENA Type

Lithographed and Embossed
1967, Sept. 20   Perf. 13½x14
C494 A329 2p gold, ver & blk   .50 .25

Pre-Columbian Art Type

Designs: 30c, Bird pectoral. 5p Ornamental pectoral. 20p, Pitcher.

1967, Oct. 13   Photo.   Perf. 13½x14
C495 A330 30c ver, gold & brn   .40 .25
C496 A330 5p red, gold & brn   3.25 .50
a. Souvenir sheet of 2   12.00 12.00
C497 A330 20p vio, gold & brn   15.00 10.00
Nos. C495-C497 (3)   18.65 10.75

No. C496a also commemorates the 6th Natl. Phil. Exhib. No. C496a contains 2 imperf. stamps in changed colors similar to Nos. C495-C496 (30c has green background and 5p maroon background).

Telecommunications Type

Designs: 50c, Signal lights. 1p, Early Bird satellite, Southern Cross and radar.

Perf. 13½x14
1968, May 14   Litho.   Unwmk.
C498 A331 50c blk, ver & emer   .25 .25
C499 A331 1p ultra, yel & gray   .30 .25

Eucharist Type

1968, June 6   Litho.   Perf. 13½x14
C500 A332 80c rose lil, red, yel & blk   .25 .25
C501 A332 3p bl, red, yel & blk   .30 .25

Eucharistic Congress Type

Designs: 80c, The Last Supper, by Gregorio Vasquez, horiz. 1p, St. Francis Xavier Preaching, by Gregorio Vasquez. 2p, The Dream of the Prophet Elias, by Gregorio Vasquez. 3p, Monstrance, c. 1700. 20p, Pope Paul VI, painting by Roman Franciscan nuns.

1968, Aug. 13   Photo.   Perf. 13
C502 A333 80c multicolored   .25 .25
C503 A333 1p multicolored   .40 .25
C504 A333 2p multicolored   .45 .25
C505 A333 3p lil & multi   .95 .25
C506 A333 20p gold & multi   5.50 2.75
Nos. C502-C506 (5)   7.55 3.75

Shrine of the Eucharist, Bogota AP99

1.20p, Pope Paul VI giving blessing and Papal arms. 1.80p, Cathedral of Bogota.

Perf. 14x13½, 13½x14
1968, Aug. 22   Litho.
C507 AP99 80c multi   .30 .25
C508 AP99 1.20p multi, vert.   .30 .25
C509 AP99 1.80p multi, vert.   .40 .25
Nos. C507-C509 (3)   1.00 .75

Visit of Pope Paul VI to Colombia.

Computer Symbols — AP100

1968, Oct. 29   Litho.   Perf. 13½x14
C510 AP100 20c buff, car & grn   .25 .25

Cent. of the Natl. University and the 1st Data Processing Cong. in 1967 at the University.

Agriculture Institute Type

1968, Mar. 5   Litho.   Perf. 13½x14
C511 A337 1p gray & multi   .25 .25

Microscope and Pen — AP101

1969, Mar. 24   Litho.   Perf. 14
C512 AP101 5p blk, yel, ver & pur 2.40 .35

20th anniv. (in 1968) of the University of the Andes.

Alexander von Humboldt and Andes AP102

1969, May 3   Litho.   Perf. 14x13½
C513 AP102 1p grn & brn   .65 .35

Alexander von Humboldt (1769-1859), German naturalist and traveler.

Map of Colombia, Amphibian Plane and Letter AP103

Design: 1.50p, No. C516b, Globe, letter, and jet of Avianca airlines.

1969, June 18   Litho.   Perf. 14x13½
C514 AP103 1p multi   .45 .25
C515 AP103 1.50p multi   .65 .25

Souvenir Sheet
Imperf
C516   Sheet of 2   7.50 7.50
a. AP103 5p green & multi   1.00 1.00
b. AP103 5p violet & multi 1.00 1.00

50th anniv. of the 1st air post flight in Colombia. No. C516 also for 8th Natl. Philatelic Exhibition, EXFILBA 69, Barranquilla, June 18-22. No. C516 contains 2 stamps in the designs of the 1p and 1.50p.

Independence Type

2.30p, Simon Bolivar, José Antonio Anzoategui, Francisco de Paula Santander and victorious army entering Bogota, 9/18/1819; painting by Ignacio Castillo Cervantes.

1969, July 24   Litho.   Perf. 13½x14
C517 A338 2.30p gold & multi 1.00 .35

Social Security Emblem — AP104

1969, Oct. 29   Litho.   Perf. 13½x14
C518 AP104 20c emer & blk   .25 .25

20th anniv. of the Colombian Institute of Social Security.

Neurosurgeons' Congress Emblem — AP105

1969, Oct. 29
C519 AP105 70c vio, red & yel   .50 .30

Issued to publicize the 13th Congress of Latin-American Neurosurgeons, Bogota.

Junkers F-13 AP106

Nos. C521, C522b, Globe with airlines from Bogota & Boeing jet. No. C522a, like No. C520.

1969, Nov. 28   Litho.   Perf. 14x13½
C520 AP106 2p grn & multi   .75 .25
C521 AP106 3.50p ultra & multi 1.40 .50

Souvenir Sheet
Imperf
C522   Sheet of 2   7.50 7.50
a. AP106 3.50p lt grn & multi   .75 .75
b. AP106 5p ultra & multi   1.00 1.00

50th anniv. of AVIANCA; No. C522 also publicizes the 1st Interamerican Phil. Exhib., Bogota, Nov. 28-Dec. 7.
No. C522 contains 2 imperf. stamps.

Child Mailing Letter — AP107

Christmas: 1.50p, Praying child and gifts.

1969, Dec. 16   Litho.   Perf. 13½x14
C523 AP107 60c ocher & multi   .80 .25
C524 AP107 1p multicolored   .85 .25
C525 AP107 1.50p multicolored 1.10 .25
Nos. C523-C525 (3)   2.75 .75

Radar Station and Pre-Columbian Head — AP108

1970, Mar. 25   Litho.   Perf. 14x13½
C526 AP108 1p dl grn, blk & brick red   .30 .25

Issued to publicize the opening of the communications satellite earth station at Chocontá in Cundinamarca Province.

Emblem of Colombian Youth Sports Institute — AP109

2.30p, Games' emblem (dove and 3 rings).

1970, Apr. 6   Litho.   Perf. 13½x14
C527 AP109 1.50p dk ol grn, yel & blk   .30 .25
C528 AP109 2.30p red & multi   .40 .25

9th Natl. Youth Games, Ibague, July 10-20.

Art Exhibition Emblem — AP110

1970, Apr. 30   Litho.   Perf. 13½x14
C529 AP110 30c multicolored   .25 .25

2nd Biennial Art Exhib., Medellin, 6/1-7/14.

Eduardo Santos, Rural and Urban Buildings AP111

1970, June 18   Litho.   Perf. 14x13½
C530 AP111 1p grn, yel & blk   .25 .25
Issued to commemorate the founding (in 1939) of the Territorial Credit Institute.

UN Emblem, Scales and Dove — AP112

1970, June 26   Perf. 13½x14
C531 AP112 1.50p dk bl, lt bl & yel .25 .25
25th anniversary of United Nations.

EXFILCA Emblem — AP113

1970, Nov.   Litho.   Perf. 13½x14
C532 AP113 10p bl, gold & blk   5.00 .25
EXFILCA 70, 2nd Interamerican Philatelic Exhib., Caracas, Venezuela, Nov. 27-Dec. 6.

Mother Juana Ruperta in Napanga Costume and Music by Efrain Orozco — AP114

Designs: 1p, Dancers from Eastern Plains and music by Alejandro Wills. No. C535, Guabina man, woman and folk song. No. C536, Bambuco man and woman, and music. No. C537, Man and woman dancing the Cumbia, and music.

1970-71   Litho.   Perf. 13½x14
C533 AP114 60c dp lil rose & multi   .70 .25
C534 AP114 1p ultra & multi   .65 .25
C535 AP114 1.30p bl & multi   .75 .25
C536 AP114 1.30p emer & multi ('71)   .90 .25
C537 AP114 1.30p lil & multi ('71)   .65 .25
 Nos. C533-C537 (5)   3.65 1.25

Athlete and Games Emblem — AP115

Design: 2p, Games emblem.

1971, Mar. 11
C542 AP115 1.50p multicolored   .90 .90
C543 AP115 2p blk, org & grn   .80 .55
6th Pan-American Games, Cali, 7/30-8/13.

Gilberto Alzate Avendano AP116

1971, Apr. 29   Litho.   Perf. 14x13½
C544 AP116 1p bl & multi   .60 .25
Avendano (1910-60), journalist, popular leader.

Commemorative Medal — AP117

Lithographed and Embossed
1971, June 21   Perf. 14x13½
C545 AP117 1p slate grn & gold   .60 .30
Centenary (in 1970) of the Bank of Bogota.

Olympic Center — AP118

Soccer — AP119

Designs (Games Emblem and): Nos. C546-C546C, Olympic Center. No. 547, Soccer. No. C548, Wrestling. No. C549, Bicycling. No. C550, Volleyball. No. C551, Diving (women). No. C552, Fencing. No. C553, Sailing. No. C554, Equestrian. No. C555, Jumping. No. C556, Rowing. No. C557, Cali emblem. No. C558, Basketball (women). No. C559, Stadium. No. C560, Baseball. No. C561, Hockey. No. C562, Weight lifting. No. C563, Medals. No. C564, Boxing. No. C565, Gymnastics (women). No. C566, Sharpshooting.

1971, July 16   Litho.   Perf. 13½x14
Multicolored and Emblem Color:
C546 AP118 1.30p yellow   1.50 .30
C546A AP118 1.30p green   1.50 .30
C546B AP118 1.30p blue   1.50 .30
C546C AP118 1.30p carmine   1.50 .30
C547 AP119 1.30p emerald   1.50 .30
C548 AP119 1.30p lilac   1.50 .30
C549 AP119 1.30p blue   1.50 .30
C550 AP119 1.30p carmine   1.50 .30
C551 AP119 1.30p blue   1.50 .30
C552 AP119 1.30p carmine   1.50 .30
C553 AP119 1.30p blue   1.50 .30
C554 AP119 1.30p gray   1.50 .30
C555 AP119 1.30p green   1.50 .30
C556 AP119 1.30p blue   1.50 .30
C557 AP118 1.30p orange   1.50 .30
C558 AP119 1.30p carmine   1.50 .30
C559 AP118 1.30p light blue   1.50 .30
C560 AP119 1.30p plum   1.50 .30
C561 AP119 1.30p yel grn   1.50 .30
C562 AP119 1.30p pink   1.50 .30
C563 AP118 1.30p deep org   1.50 .30
C564 AP119 1.30p plum   1.50 .30
C565 AP119 1.30p lilac rose   1.50 .30
C566 AP119 1.30p green   1.50 .30
 a. Sheet of 25, #C546-C566   60.00 60.00
6th Pan American Athletic Games, Cali. No. C546B appears twice in sheet.

Battle of Carabobo, by Martin Tovar y Tovar — AP120

1971, Nov. 25   Litho.   Perf. 13½x14
C567 AP120 1.50p multicolored 1.25 .25
Sesquicentennial of the Battle of Carabobo.

St. Theresa Type Overprinted

1972   Litho.   Perf. 13½x14
C568 A343 2p multicolored   .30 .25
See note after No. 793.

Vendor — AP121

Designs: 50c, Woman wearing shawl, and woven shawl. 3p, Fruit vendor (puppet).

1972, Apr. 11   Litho.   Perf. 13½x14
C569 AP121 50c multicolored   .35 .25
C570 AP121 1p multicolored   .35 .25
C571 AP121 3p multicolored   .50 .25
 Nos. C569-C571 (3)   1.20 .75
Colombian artisans.

Mormodes Rolfeanum AP122

1972, Apr. 20   Perf. 14x13½
C572 AP122 1.30p multicolored   .75 .25
7th World Orchidology Congress, Medellin.

Congo Grande Dancer — AP123

1972, June 21   Litho.   Perf. 13½x14
C573 AP123 1.30p multicolored   .60 .25
International Carnival of Barranquilla.

No. C453 Surcharged in Brown

1972, Oct. 5   Litho.   Perf. 14x13½
C574 AP86 1.30p on 1.90p   .75 .25

Laureano Gomez, by Ridriguez Cubillos — AP124

No. C576, Guillermo Leòn Valencia Muñoz.

1972   Perf. 13½x14
C575 AP124 1.30p multicolored   .25 .25
C576 AP124 1.30p multicolored   .25 .25
Laureano Gomez (1898-1966), Guillermo Leon Valencia Munoz (1909-71), Presidents of Colombia.
 Issued: No. C575, 10/17; No. C576, 11/28.

Benito Juarez — AP125

1972, Dec. 12   Perf. 13½x14
C577 AP125 1.50p multicolored   .25 .25
Benito Juarez (1806-1872), revolutionary leader and president of Mexico.

Rebecca Fountain AP126

1972, Dec. 19   Litho.
C578 AP126 80c multicolored   .70 .45
C579 AP126 1p multicolored   .65 .25

"Bucaramanga" — AP127

1972, Dec. 22   Perf. 14x13½
C580 AP127 5p multicolored   1.00 .25
Founding of Bucaramanga, 350th anniv.

Xavier University AP128

1973, May 8   Litho.   Perf. 14x13½
C581 AP128 1.30p lt grn & sep   .30 .25
C582 AP128 1.50p lt bl & sep   .30 .25
350th anniversary of the founding of Xavier University in Bogotá.

Ceramic Type

Excavated Ceramic Artifacts: 1p, Winged urn, Tairona. 1.30p, Woman and child, Sinu. 1.70p, Two-headed figure, Quimbaya. 3.50p, Man, Tumaco.

1973   Litho.   Perf. 13½x14
C583 A358   1p multicolored   1.75 1.20
C584 A358 1.30p multicolored   .90 .25
C585 A358 1.70p multicolored   1.00 .25
C586 A358 3.50p multicolored   1.90 .30
  Nos. C583-C586 (4)   5.55 2.00
Issue dates: 1p, Oct. 11; others, June 15.

Battle of Maracaibo, by Manuel F. Rincon AP129

1973, July 24   Litho.   Perf. 14x13½
C587 AP129 10p bl & multi   2.50 .25
Battle of Maracaibo, sesquicentennial.

Bank Emblem AP130

1973, Oct. 1   Litho.   Perf. 14x13½
C588 AP130 2p multicolored   .30 .25
50th anniv. of the Bank of the Republic.

No. 801 Overprinted "AEREO"

1973, Oct. 11   Perf. 14
C589 A346 80c multicolored   .30 .25

Pres. Pedro Nel Ospina, by Coroleano Leudo — AP131

1973, Nov. 9   Perf. 13½x14
C590 AP131 1.50p multicolored   .25 .25
50th anniversary of the Ministry of Communications founded under Pres. Ospina.

Arms of Toro — AP132

1973, Dec. 1
C591 AP132   1p multicolored   .25 .25
Founding of Toro, Valle del Cauca, 4th cent.

Bolivar, Battle of Bombona AP133

1973, Dec. 7   Litho.   Perf. 14x13½
C592 AP133 1.30p multicolored   .25 .25
Sesquicentennial (in 1972) of the Battle of Bombona.

Nicolaus Copernicus AP134

1974, Feb. 19   Litho.   Perf. 13½x14
C593 AP134 2.50p multicolored   .70 .25
500th anniversary of the birth of Nicolaus Copernicus (1473-1543), Polish astronomer.

Andes, Map of South America AP135

1974, May 11   Litho.   Perf. 14
C594 AP135 2p multicolored   .50 .25
Meeting of Communications Ministers of Members of the Andean Group, Cali, May 7-11, 1974.

Television Set AP136

1974, July 16   Litho.   Perf. 14x13½
C595 AP136 1.30p org, blk & brn   .25 .25
20th anniversary of Colombian television and 10th anniversary of INRAVISION, the National Institute of Radio and Television.

Championship Emblem — AP137

1974, Aug. 5   Litho.   Perf. 14x13½
C596 AP137 4.50p multicolored   .40 .25
2nd World Swimming Championships, Cali.

Condor — AP138

1974, Aug. 28   Perf. 14
C597 AP138 1.50p multicolored   .25 .25
Bank of Colombia centenary.

UPU Envelope AP139

1974, Sept. 9   Litho.   Perf. 14
C598 AP139 20p multicolored   3.00 .30
Centenary of Universal Postal Union.

Symbol of Flight — AP140

1974, Sept.   Perf. 12x12½
C599 AP140 20c olive   .25 .25

Gen. José Maria Cordoba — AP141

1974, Oct. 14   Litho.   Perf. 13½x14
C609 AP141 1.30p multicolored   .25 .25
Sesquicentennial of the Battles of Junin and Ayacucho.

Insurance Type

Design: 3p, Abstract pattern.

1974, Oct. 24   Litho.   Perf. 13½x14
C610 A365 3p multicolored   .30 .25

White-tailed Trogon, Letter — AP142

Designs (UPU Letter and): 1.30p, Keelbilled Toucan, horiz. 2p, Peruvian cock-of-the-rock, horiz. 2.50p, Scarlet macaw.

Perf. 13½x14, 14x13½

1974, Nov. 14
C611 AP142   1p multicolored   1.10 .25
C612 AP142 1.30p multicolored   1.10 .25
C613 AP142   2p multicolored   1.75 .25
C614 AP142 2.50p multicolored   1.75 .25
  Nos. C611-C614 (4)   5.70 1.00
Centenary of Universal Postal Union. For surcharge see No. C656.

Forest No. 1, by Roman Roncancio — AP143

Boy with Thorn in Finger, by Gregorio Vazquez AP144

Paintings: 3p, Women Fruit Vendors, by Miguel Diaz Vargas (1886-1956). 5p, Annunciation, Santafereña School, 17th-18th cent.

Perf. 13½x14, 14x13½

1975, Mar. 12   Litho.
C615 AP143 2p multicolored   .75 .25
C616 AP144 3p multicolored   .50 .25
C617 AP144 4p multicolored   .65 .25
C618 AP144 5p multicolored   1.10 .25
  Nos. C615-C618 (4)   3.00 1.00
Modern and Colonial Colombian paintings.

Trees and Lake AP145

Design: 6p, Victoria regia, Amazon River.

1975, Mar. 12   Perf. 14x13½
C619 AP145 1p yellow & multi   .25 .25
C620 AP145 6p yellow & multi   .60 .25
Nature conservation of trees and Amazon Region.

Gold Treasure Type

Designs: 2p, Nose pendant. 10p, Alligator-shaped staff ornament.

1975, Apr. 11   Litho.   Perf. 14x13½
C621 A368 2p grn, gold & brn   1.00 .25
C622 A368 10p multicolored   4.75 .60

El Rodadero, Santa Maria AP146

1975, July 26   Litho.   Perf. 14x13½
C623 AP146 2p multicolored   .25 .25
400th anniversary of Santa Marta City.

AP147

1975, Aug. 31   Litho.   Perf. 13½x14
C624 AP147   4p multicolored   .25   .25
Intl. Women's Year 1975. Maria de Jesus Paramo de Collazos founded 1st normal school for women in Bucaramanga in 1875.

"Sugar Cane" — AP148

1976, Mar. 12   Litho.   Perf. 13½x14
C625 AP148   5p blk & grn   1.25   .25
4th Congress of Latin-American and Caribbean sugar-exporting countries, Cali, 3/8-12.

View of Bogota — AP149

1976, July 2   Litho.   Perf. 12
C626 AP149   10p shown   1.25   .90
C627 AP149   10p Barranquilla   1.25   .90
C628 AP149   10p Cali   1.25   .90
C629 AP149   10p Medellin   1.25   .90
   a.   Block of 4, #C626-C629   6.00   6.00
Habitat, UN Conf. on Human Settlements, Vancouver, Canada, May 31-June 11.

University Emblem and "90" — AP150

1976, Aug. 6   Litho.   Perf. 13½x14
C630 AP150   5p lt blue & multi   .50   .25
Univ. of Colombia day school, 90th anniv.

Miguel Samper — AP151

1976, Oct. 29   Litho.   Perf. 13½x14
C631 AP151   2p multicolored   .25   .25
Samper (1825-99), economist and writer.

Telephone, 1895 — AP152

1976, Nov. 2
C632 AP152   3p multicolored   .25   .25
Centenary of first telephone call by Alexander Graham Bell, Mar. 10, 1876.

747 Jumbo Jet AP153

1976, Dec. 3   Litho.   Perf. 12
C633 AP153   2p multicolored   .25   .25
Inauguration of 747 jumbo jet service by Avianca.
For surcharge see No. C636.

Convent, Church and Plaza de San Francisco — AP154

1976, Dec. 29   Litho.   Perf. 14
C634 AP154   6p multicolored   .50   .25
150th anniv. of the Congress of Panama.

Souvenir Sheet

Bank of the Republic Emblem — AP155

1977, June 6   Litho.   Perf. 14
C635 AP155   25p multicolored   13.00   13.00
Opening of Philatelic Museum of Medellin under auspices of Banco de la Republica.

No. C633 Surcharged in Light Brown

1977, June   Litho.   Perf. 12
C636 AP153   3p on 2p multi   .25   .25

Coffee — AP156

1977-78   Litho.   Perf. 12½
C640 AP156   3p multi   .50   .25
C641 AP156   3.50p multi ('78)   .50   .25
Colombian coffee.

Coffee Grower, Pack Mule — AP157

1977, Aug. 9   Litho.   Perf. 13½x14
C642 AP157   10p multicolored   .50   .25
National Federation of Coffee Growers, 50th anniversary.

Beethoven and 9th Symphony AP158

1977, Aug. 17
C643 AP158   8p multicolored   1.25   .25
Sesquicentennial of the death of Ludwig van Beethoven (1770-1827).

Bird Type

Tropical Birds and Plants: No. C644, Woodpecker and Meriania. C645, Purple gallinule and water lilies. No. C646, Xipholaena punicea and Cochlospermum orinocense. No. C647, Crowned flycatcher and Jacaranda copaia.

1977, Sept. 6   Litho.   Perf. 14
C644 A380   5p multicolored   .75   .25
C645 A380   5p multicolored   .75   .25
C646 A380   10p multicolored   1.10   .25
C647 A380   10p multicolored   1.10   .25
   Nos. C644-C647 (4)   3.70   1.00

Games' Emblem — AP159

1977, Sept. 9   Perf. 12x12½
C648 AP159   6p multicolored   .25   .25
13th Central American and Caribbean Games, Medellin, 1978.

La Cayetana, by Enrique Grau AP160

No. C650, Water Nymphs, by Beatriz Gonzalez.

1977, Sept. 13   Perf. 14x13½
C649 AP160   8p multicolored   .80   .25
C650 AP160   8p multicolored   .80   .25
Women's suffrage, 20th anniversary.

Judge Francisco Antonio Moreno, by Joaquin Gutierrez AP161

Design: 25p, Viceroy Manuel de Guirior.

1977, Sept. 13   Perf. 12
C651 AP161   20p multicolored   1.60   .75
C652 AP161   25p multicolored   2.40   1.10
Bicentenary of National Library.

Federico Lleras Acosta — AP162

1977, Sept. 27   Litho.   Perf. 14
C653 AP162   5p multicolored   .30   .25
Dr. Federico Lleras Acosta, veterinarian and bacteriologist; birth centenary.

Cauca University Arms — AP163

1977, Oct. 14
C654 AP163   5p multicolored   .30   .25
Sesquicentennial of the University of Cauca.

CUDECOM Building, Bogota AP164

1977, Oct. 14
C655 AP164   1.50p multicolored   .25   .25
Colombian Society of Engineers, 90th anniv.

No. C612 Surcharged with New Value and Bars in Brown

1977, Dec. 3   Litho.   Perf. 14x13½
C656 AP142   2p on 1.30p multi   .30   .25

Lost City, Tayrona Culture — AP165

1978, Apr. 18   Litho.   Perf. 12½
C657 AP165   3.50p multicolored   .25   .25

Creator of Energy, by Arenas Betancourt AP166

1978, Apr. 25   *Perf. 12*
C658 AP166 4p blue & multi   .25   .25
   Sesquicentennial of Antioquia University Law School.

Column of the Slaves — AP167

1978, May 9
C659 AP167 2.50p multicolored   .25   .25
   Sesquicentennial of Ocana Convention (meeting of various political groups).

Statue of Catalina, Cartagena AP168

1978, May 30   **Litho.**   *Perf. 12*
C660 AP168 4p blk & lt bl   .25   .25
   Sesquicentennial of University of Cartagena.

Gold Pendant, Tolima — AP169

1978, July 11   **Litho.**   *Perf. 12x12½*
C661 AP169 3.50p multicolored   .25   .25

Apotheosis of Spanish Language, by Luis Alberto Acuña — AP170

1978, Aug. 9   *Perf. 14*
C662 AP170   Strip of 3   4.75   4.75
   a.-c.   11p, any single   1.10   1.10
   Millennium of Spanish language.

Presidential Guard — AP171

1978, Aug. 16   *Perf. 13½x14*
C663 AP171 9p multicolored   .45   .45
   Presidential Guard Battalion, 50th anniv.

Figure, Muisca Culture — AP172

1978, Sept. 12   **Litho.**   *Perf. 12½*
C664 AP172 3.50p multicolored   .30   .25

Apse of Carmelite Church — AP173

1978, Oct. 12   *Perf. 13*
C665 AP173 30p multicolored   2.75   .40
   Souvenir Sheet
   Perf. 13½x14
C666 AP173 50p multicolored   3.75   3.75
   ESPAMER '78 Philatelic Exhibition, Bogota, Oct. 12-21.

Owl, Gold Ornament, Calima — AP174

   No. C669, Gold frog, Quimbaya culture. No. C670, Gold nose pendant, Tairona, horiz.

1978-80   **Litho.**   *Perf. 12½*
C667 AP174 3.50p multi   .40   .25
C668 AP174 4p multi ('79)   .25   .25
C669 AP174 4p multi ('79)   .40   .25
C670 AP174 5p multi ('80)   .60   .25
   Nos. C667-C670 (4)   1.65   1.00

Virgin and Child, by Gregorio Vasquez — AP175

1978, Nov. 28   *Perf. 13½x14*
C671 AP175 2.50p multicolored   .25   .25
   Christmas 1978.

Bull Ring, Cathedral, Manizales AP176

1979, Jan. 6   **Litho.**   *Perf. 14*
C672 AP176 7p multicolored   .80   .25
   Manizales Fair.

Children Playing Hopscotch, and IYC Emblem — AP177

   No. C674, Child at blackboard and UNESCO emblem. No. C675, The Paper Collector, by Omar Gordillo, and UN emblem.

1979, July 19   *Perf. 13½x14, 14x13½*
C673 AP177 8p multi   .40   .30
C674 AP177 12p multi, horiz.   .55   .45
C675 AP177 12p multi   .55   .45
   Nos. C673-C675 (3)   1.50   1.20
   International Year of the Child.

Rio Prado Hydroelectric Station — AP178

1979, Aug. 24   *Perf. 13½x14*
C676 AP178 5p multicolored   .80   .25

Tomb, 6th Century — AP179

1979, Sept. 25   **Litho.**   *Perf. 14*
C677 AP179 8p multicolored   .80   .35
   San Augustin Archaeological Park.

Gonzalo Jimenez de Quesada, by C. Leudo AP180

1979, Oct. 11   *Perf. 12*
C678 AP180 20p multicolored   3.50   1.50
   Gonzalo Jimenez de Quesada (1500-1579), Spanish conquistador.

Hill, Penny Black, Colombia No. 1 — AP181

1979, Oct. 23   *Perf. 13½x14*
C679 AP181 15p multicolored   .90   .25
   Sir Rowland Hill (1795-1879), originator of penny postage.

Amazon Region — AP182

   Tourism: 14p, San Fernando Fortress.

1979   **Litho.**   *Perf. 13½x14*
C680 AP182 7p multicolored   .60   .25
C681 AP182 14p multicolored   1.60   .75
   Issue dates: 7p, Nov. 16; 14p, Nov. 9.
   See Nos. C717-C719.

AP183

   Creche Sculptures: No. C682, Three Kings and soldiers. No. C683, Nativity. No. C684, Shepherds.

1979, Nov. 30   *Perf. 12*
C682 AP183 3p multicolored   1.50   1.10
C683 AP183 3p multicolored   1.50   1.10
C684 AP183 3p multicolored   1.50   1.10
   a.   Strip of 3, #C682-C684   4.50   3.50
   Christmas 1979.

AP184

   Magdalena Bridge, Avianca emblem.

1979, Dec. 5   *Perf. 14*
C685 AP184 15p multicolored   .70   .25
   Barranquilla, 350th anniversary; Avianca National Airline, 60th anniversary.

AP185

Boy Playing Flute, by Judith Leyster.

1980, Feb. 15   **Perf. 13½x14**
C686 AP185 6p multicolored   .60 .25
2nd Intl. Music Competition, Ibague, Dec. 1979.

Gen. Antonio José de Sucre, 150th Death Anniversary AP186

1980, Feb. 15 **Litho.** **Perf. 12½x12**
C687 AP186 12p multicolored   .60 .25

The Watchman, by Edgar Negret AP187

1980, Feb. 26   **Perf. 12x12½**
C688 AP187 25p multicolored   2.50 1.40

Virgin Mary, by Real del Sarte, 1929 AP188

1980, May 23 **Litho.** **Perf. 14x13½**
C689 AP188 12p multicolored   .60 .25
Apparition of the Virgin Mary to Sister Catalina Labouri Gontard, 150th anniv.

San Gil Produce Market, by Luis Roncancio — AP189

1980, May 27   **Perf. 13½x14**
C690 AP189 12p multicolored   .70 .25

Pres. Enrique Olaya Herrera, by Miguel Diaz Vargas — AP190

1980, Oct. 28 **Litho.** **Perf. 12**
C691 AP190 20p multicolored   1.25 .40
Enrique Olaya Herrera (1880-1936), president, 1930-1934.

The Boy Fishing in a Bucket AP191

Christmas (Christmas Stories by Rafael Pombo): No. C693, The Frog and the Mouse. No. C694, The Seven Lives of the Cat.

1980, Nov. 21 **Litho.** **Perf. 14½**
C692 AP191 4p multicolored   .25 .25
C693 AP191 4p multicolored   .25 .25
C694 AP191 4p multicolored   .25 .25
    Nos. C692-C694 (3)   .75 .75

28th World Golf Cup, Cajica — AP192

1980, Dec. 9 **Litho.** **Perf. 13½x14**
C695 AP192 30p multicolored   4.50 3.00

Bolivar Type

Simon Bolivar Death Sesquicentennial: 6p, Portrait, last words to Colombia, vert.

1980, Dec. 17   **Perf. 12**
C696 A400 6p multicolored   .80 .45

St. Peter Claver Holding Cross AP193

1981, Jan. 13   **Perf. 14½**
C697 AP193 15p multicolored   .70 .30
St. Peter Claver (1580-1654), helped American Indians.

Sculptured Bird, San Augustin AP194

Archaeological Finds: No. C699, Funeral chamber, Tierradentro. No. C700, Chamber hallway, Tierradentro. No. C701, Statue of man, San Augustin.

1981, May 12 **Litho.** **Perf. 14**
C698 AP194 7p multicolored   1.00 .25
C699 AP194 7p multicolored   1.00 .25
C700 AP194 7p multicolored   1.00 .25
C701 AP194 7p multicolored   1.00 .25
    a.   Block of 4, #C698-C701   5.00 5.00
    See Nos. C707-C710D.

Child with Hobby Horse, by Fernando Botero — AP195

4th Biennial Arts show, Medellin: 20p, Square Abstract, by Omar Rayo. 25p, Flowers, by Alejandro Obregon.

1981, May 15   **Perf. 12**
C702 AP195 20p multicolored   1.25 .25
C703 AP195 25p multicolored   1.40 .40
C704 AP195 50p multicolored   2.50 .75
    Nos. C702-C704 (3)   5.15 1.40

8th South American Swimming Championships, Medellin — AP196

1981, June 5
C705 AP196 15p multicolored   .60 .25

Santamaria Bull Ring, 50th Anniv. — AP197

1981, June 9 **Litho.** **Perf. 12**
C706 AP197 30p multicolored   3.25 1.75

Quimbaya Culture — AP197a

1981, Sept. 23 **Litho.** **Perf. 14**
Yellow Background
C707 9p Man   1.00 .25
C708 9p Seated man   1.00 .25
C709 9p Seal, print   1.00 .25
C710 9p Jug   1.00 .25
    e.   AP197a Block of 4, #C707-C710   5.00 3.50

Calima Culture — AP197b

No. C710A, Anthropomorphic container. No. C710B, Jar. No. C710C, Anthropomorphic jar. No. C710D, Urn.

1981, Dec. 17   **White Background**
C710A 9p multicolored   1.50 .25
C710B 9p multicolored   1.50 .25
C710C 9p multicolored   1.50 .25
C710D 9p multicolored   1.50 .25
    f.   AP197b Block of 4, #C710A-C710D   9.00 9.00

Fruit AP198

1981, Nov. 3 **Litho.** **Perf. 14**
C711   Block of 6   24.00 20.00
    a.-f. AP198 25p, any single   3.50 1.50

Revolt of the Comuneros, 200th Anniv. — AP199

1981, Nov. 21 **Litho.** **Perf. 12**
C712 AP199 20p multicolored   .90 .40

Jose Manuel Restrepo, Historian, 1775?-1860? AP200

1981, Dec. 1 **Litho.** **Perf. 12**
C713 AP200 35p multicolored   1.40 .75

Andres Bello, 1780?-1865 AP201

1981, Dec. 11 **Litho.** **Perf. 12**
C714 AP201 18p multicolored   .70 .25

Colombia's Admission to UPU, 100th Anniv. AP202

30p, No. 103. 50p, Hemispheres, Nos. 104-108.

1981	**Litho.**		**Perf. 12**	
C715	AP202	30p multicolored	1.25	.35

Size: 100x70mm

Imperf

C716	AP202	50p multicolored	4.75	4.75

Issued: No. C715, Dec. 18. No. C716, Dec. 28.

Tourism Type of 1979

No. C717, Solano Bay. No. C718, Tota Lake, Boyaca. No. C719, Corrales, Boyaca.

1982	**Litho.**		**Perf. 12**	
C717	AP182	20p multicolored	.60	.25
C718	AP182	20p multicolored	.60	.25
C719	AP182	20p multicolored	.60	.25
	Nos. C717-C719 (3)		1.80	.75

Issued: No. C717, 6/2; others, 6/16.

1982 World Cup — AP202a

Players and team emblems: a, "America." b, "A. B." c, "Cali." d, "C." e, "C/D." f, "Junior F.B.C." g, "D/M." h, Stadium. i, "M." j, "Club Atletico Nacional." k, "D/P." l, "Quindio." m, "Santa Fe." n, "T." o, "Santa Marta."

1982, June 21			**Perf. 14**	
C720		Sheet of 15	10.00	6.75
	a.-o.	AP202a 9p, any single	.70	.30

Bogota Gun Club Centenary AP202b

1982, July 16			**Perf. 12**	
C721	AP202b	20p multicolored	.70	.25

Gold Crocodile Figure, Tairona Culture AP202c

Tairona Culture Exhibit, Gold Museum: Various figures. Nos. C723-C727 vert.

1982, July 28

Gold, Black and

C722	AP202c	25p light brown	2.75	.95
C723	AP202c	25p bright pink	2.75	.95
C724	AP202c	25p green	2.75	.95
C725	AP202c	25p dark blue	2.75	.95
C726	AP202c	25p violet	2.75	.95
C727	AP202c	25p red	2.75	.95
	Nos. C722-C727 (6)		16.50	5.70

Government Buildings, Pereira — AP203

1982, Aug. 4	**Litho.**		**Perf. 12**	
C728	AP203	35p multicolored	1.25	.40

Biplane in Flight, by Edgar Antonio Bustos AP204

1982, Aug. 5			**Perf. 14**	
C729	AP204	18p multicolored	.60	.25

American Air Forces Cooperation System.

Magdalena River AP205

1982, Oct. 21	**Litho.**		**Perf. 12**	
C730	AP205	30p multicolored	1.40	.75

Marquez Type

1982, Dec. 10			**Perf. 13½x14**	
C731	A412	25p gray & blue	.70	.25
C732	A412	30p gray & brown	1.00	.25

San Andres Archipelago — AP206

1983, Apr. 9	**Litho.**		**Perf. 12**	
C733	AP206	25p Liberty Fort	.60	.25

Opening of Las Gaviotas (The Seagulls) Ecological Center, Bogota — AP207

1983, June 1			**Litho.**	
C734	AP207	12p multicolored	.40	.25

50th Anniv. of Radio Amateurs League AP208

1983, June 11			**Perf. 14x13½**	
C735	AP208	12p multicolored	.30	.25

Bolivar Type

1983, July 24			**Perf. 12**	
C736	A417	30p multicolored	.80	.25
C737	A417	100p multicolored	2.50	1.75

Botanical Exhibition Type

No. C738, Begonia guaduensis. No. C739, Chinchona ovaliflora. No. C740, Begonia urticae.

1983, Aug. 18			**Perf. 14**	
C738	A418	12p multicolored	.55	.25
C739	A418	12p multicolored	.55	.25
C740	A418	40p multicolored	2.90	.40
	Nos. C738-C740 (3)		4.00	.90

Cartagena, 450th Anniv. — AP208a

12p, Customs Square. 35p, Historic sites, Cartagena.

1983, Sept. 9	**Litho.**		**Perf. 12**	
C740A	AP208a	12p multi	.50	.25
C740B	AP208a	35p multi	1.25	.30

Painting Type

1983, Oct. 5	**Litho.**		**Perf. 12**	
C741	A420	30p multicolored	2.00	.50

Scouting Year — AP209

1983, Oct. 24				
C742	AP209	12p multicolored	.25	.25

Coffee Beans — AP210

1984, Mar. 28	**Litho.**		**Perf. 14½x14**	
C743	AP210	14p multicolored	.25	.25

Marandua City Type

1984, Sept. 28			**Perf. 12**	
C744	A427	30p multicolored	.75	.25

AP211

1984, Nov. 2				
C745	AP211	45p multicolored	.90	.25

45th Cong. of Americanists, Bogota, 1985.

Christmas Type

1984, Dec. 14				
C746	A428	14p multicolored	.35	.25

AP212

Design: Dove, map and flags of Colombia, Mexico, Costa Rica and Venezuela.

1985, Feb. 15				
C747	AP212	40p multicolored	.90	.30

Contadora Group of Latin American countries.

Gomez Type

1985, Feb. 25				
C748	A432	40p multicolored	.95	.30

Birds — AP213

14p, Dryocopus lineatus nuperus. 20p, Xiphorhynchus picus. 50p, Eriocnemis cupreoventris. 55p, Momotus momota.

1985

C749	AP213	14p multicolored	.80	.30
C750	AP213	20p multicolored	1.50	.30
C751	AP213	50p multicolored	3.50	1.00
C752	AP213	55p multicolored	4.50	1.25
	Nos. C749-C752 (4)		10.30	2.85

Issued: 14p, 4/12; 20p, 50p, 8/6; 55p, 8/29.

AP214

1985, July 15				
C753	AP214	20p multicolored	.30	.25

Admiral Padilla Naval School, 50th anniv.

1985 Census AP215

1985, Oct. 15			**Perf. 12**	
C754	AP215	20p multicolored	.40	.25

Christmas Type

1985, Dec. 4	**Litho.**		**Perf. 13**	
C755	A436	20p Girl, Christmas tree	.40	.25

Alfonso Lopez Pumarejo (1886-1959), President, 1934-38, 1942-45 — AP216

1986, Jan. 31				
C756	AP216	24p multicolored	.35	.25

Coffee Berries, Natl. Cycling Team AP217

1986, Feb. 4
C757 AP217 60p multicolored 1.25 .75
Natl. Coffee Producers Assoc. sponsorship of natl. cycling team, 25th anniv.

Fauna Type of 1985
1986, Feb. 18
C758 A433 50p Pudu mephis-
tophiles 1.50 .25

World Communications Day — AP218

1986, May 17   Litho.   Perf. 13
C759 AP218 50p multicolored .65 .25

Intl. Peace Year — AP219

1986, June 13   Litho.   Perf. 13
C760 AP219 55p multicolored 1.00 .45

AP220

24p, Portrait, papal arms. 55p, Portrait, Medellin cathedral, horiz. 60p, Blessing crowd, horiz.
200p, Praying, Madonna of Bogota.

1986, July 1   Litho.   Perf. 13
C761 AP220 24p multicolored 1.00 .25
C762 AP220 55p multicolored 1.00 .25
C763 AP220 60p multicolored 1.00 .25
    Nos. C761-C763 (3) 3.00 .75
Souvenir Sheet
C764 AP220 200p multicolored 4.50 3.50
Visit of Pope John Paul II.
Nos. C762-C763 each printed in sheets of 20 with se-tenant labels picturing religious symbols.

AP221

1986, July 15   Perf. 12
C765 AP221 25p multicolored .30 .25
Enrique Santos Montejo (1886-1971), journalist.

Bach, Handel and Schutz, Composers AP222

1986, July 17   Perf. 13
C766 AP222 70p Bach 1.50 .40
C767 AP222 100p Text, music 2.00 .55

Salesian Order Education in Colombia, Cent. AP223

1986, July 23   Perf. 12
C768 AP223 25p De La Salle,
founder .35 .25

Completion of Coal Mining Complex, El Cerrejon AP224

1986, July 29   Litho.   Perf. 12
C769 AP224 55p multi 1.25 .75

AP225

Natl. Constitution, Cent. — AP226

25p, The Five Signators, by R. Vasquez, detail, & Bogota Cathedral. 200p, Pres. Nunez & Miguel Antonio Caro, Natl. Council of Delegates chairman, & Presidential Palace, constitution.

1986, Aug. 5   Litho.   Perf. 14
C770 AP225 25p multi .35 .25
Souvenir Sheet
Perf. 12
C771 AP226 200p multi 3.00 3.00

Poet Type
Federico Garcia Lorca (1898-1936), poet, and birthplace, Fuentevaqueros, Granada, Spain.

1986, Sept. 26   Litho.   Perf. 12
C772 A445 60p multi .90 .50

Gratitude for Intl. Aid after the Armero Mudslide Disaster AP227

1986, Nov. 13
C773 AP227 50p multi 1.00 .75

Christmas AP228

Wood sculpture: Virgin Mestiza, Nerina.

1986, Dec. 19   Litho.   Perf. 12
C774 AP228 25p multi .35 .25

The Apotheosis of Popayan, by Ephrain Martinez Zambrano (1898-1956) — AP229

1987, Jan. 13
C775 100p Popayan riding horse 2.50 1.25
C776 100p Onlookers 2.50 1.25
    a. AP229 Pair, #C775-C776 5.00 3.50

AP230

1987, Mar. 16   Litho.   Perf. 12
C777 AP230 30p multi .50 .25
The Conversion of St. Augustine of Hippo, 1600th anniv.

Type of 1987
30p, Phoenicopterus ruber. 35p, Pseudemys scripta, horiz. No. C780, Crax alberti. No. C781, Symphysodon aequifasciatum, horiz.

Perf. 14½x14, 14x14½
1987-89   Wmk. 334
C778 A446a 30p lake .35 .25
C779 A446a 35p dark red brn .40 .25
C780 A446a 45p dark blue gray .30 .25
C781 A446a 45p blue .30 .25
    Nos. C778-C781 (4) 1.35 1.00

Issue dates: 30p, June 8. 35p, Dec. 24. No. C780, Dec. 6, 1988. No. C781, June 23, 1989.

AP231

Perf. 13½x13
1987, Apr. 10   Unwmk.
C783 AP231 25p multi .30 .25
Natl. University School of Mining, Medellin, cent.

Purebred Horses AP232

1987, June 17   Perf. 12
C784 AP232 60p White horse 1.25 .30
C785 AP232 70p Black horse 1.25 .30

El Espectador Newspaper, Cent. AP233

Design: Frontispieces from 1887, 1915, 1948, 1974 and portraits of founder Don Fidel Cano, editors Don Luis Cano, Luis Gabriel Cano Isaza and Alfonso Cano Isaza.

1987, July 24   Perf. 12½x12
C786 AP233 60p multi .85 .25

Intl. Year of Shelter for the Homeless AP234

1987, Sept. 21   Perf. 14
C787 AP234 60p multi .50 .25

Flags AP235

1987, Nov. 27   Litho.   Perf. 13x13½
C788 AP235 80p multi 1.00 .30
Ist Meeting of the eight Latin-American Presidents, Acapulco, Nov.

Christmas
AP236

1987, Dec. 8   **Litho.**   **Perf. 14**
C789   AP236   30p multi   .45   .25

Rural Telephone System AP237

1988, Feb. 4   **Litho.**   **Perf. 14**
C790   AP237   70p multi   .80   .30

Founding of Bogota, 450th Anniv. — AP238

1988, Apr. 11   **Litho.**   **Perf. 12**
C791   AP238   70p multi   .90   .25

Bogota, 450th Anniv. AP238a

80p, Modern district, vert. 90p, Colonial district.

Unwmk.
1988, July 1   **Litho.**   **Perf. 12**
C792   AP238a   80p multi   .75   .25
C793   AP238a   90p multi   .85   .30

Gold Artifacts AP239

Artifacts in the Gold Museum: 70p, Mask. 80p, Two-headed human figure inside a circle, Muisca tribe. 90p, Ritual figure of the Quimbaya.

1988   **Perf. 12**
C794   AP239   70p multi   .90   .50
C795   AP239   80p multi   1.00   .60
C796   AP239   90p multi   1.40   .75
    Nos. C794-C796 (3)   3.30   1.85

Issue dates: 70p, May 13; 80p, 90p, Oct. 7.

Human Rights Type
Perf. 14x14½
1988, July 1   **Engr.**   **Wmk. 334**
C797   A452   40p Communication, horiz.   .40   .25

AP240

1988, Sept. 28   **Litho.**   **Perf. 12**
C798   AP240   80p multi   .90   .25

Zipa Tisquesusa (d. 1538), Chibcha Indian leader during revolt against Spanish Conquistadors.

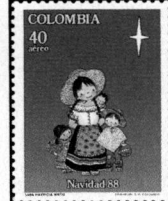

Christmas AP241

1988, Nov. 23   **Litho.**   **Perf. 12**
C799   AP241   40p multi   .60   .25

Agustin Nieto Caballero (1889-1975), Educator — AP242

Unwmk.
1989, Mar. 18   **Litho.**   **Perf. 12**
C800   AP242   100p multi   .90   .50

Pres. Laureano Gomez (1889-1965) AP243

1989, Mar. 29
C801   AP243   45p multi   .45   .25

Intl. Coffee Organization — AP244

1989, Apr. 3
C802   AP244   110p multi   1.00   .50

12th Session of the UN Commission on Human Rights — AP245

1989, Apr. 28
C803   AP245   100p multi   1.00   .40

French Revolution, Bicent. AP246

1989, June 29   **Litho.**
C804   AP246   100p multi   .90   .40

PHILEXFRANCE '89 — AP247

a, Bananas, tropical fruits. b, Fruits, flowers. c, Birds, animals. d, Precious gems, metals and mineral resources. e, View of fields, Colombian carrying produce basket. f, Waterfall. g, Fish, coast.

1989   **Litho.**   **Perf. 14**
C805   AP247   Pane of 7   17.50   17.50
   a.-g.   110p any single   1.75   .40

No. C805 printed in sheets containing panes of 7, rouletted between.

Souvenir Sheet

Los Lanceros, by R. Arenas Betancur — AP248

1989   **Litho.**   **Perf. 12**
C806   AP248   250p multicolored   2.25   1.25

Human Rights Type
Perf. 14½x14
1989, Aug. 18   **Engr.**   **Wmk. 334**
C807   A452   55p Family   .40   .25

Natl. Anti-Drugs Campaign AP249

Unwmk.
1989, Aug. 23   **Litho.**   **Perf. 12**
C808   AP249   115p multicolored   .90   .25

America Issue AP250

UPAE emblem and artifacts or customs of pre-Columbian peoples: 115p, Quimbaya, Calima or Tolima gold smiths. 130p, Potter and Sinu ceramic figurine.

1989   **Perf. 12**
C809   AP250   115p multicolored   1.25   .40
C810   AP250   130p multicolored   1.25   .60

Issue dates: 115p, Oct. 12; 130p, Aug. 23.

Joaquin Quijano Mantilla (1878-1944), Journalist — AP251

1989, Sept. 29   **Perf. 12**
C811   AP251   170p multicolored   1.50   .50

Arts and Crafts in Barro-Raquira AP252

1989   **Litho.**   **Perf. 12**
C812   AP252   55p multicolored   .40   .25
    Christmas.

Boeing 767 AP253

1989, Dec. 5   **Litho.**   **Perf. 12**
C813   AP253   130p multicolored   1.25   .30

Bolivar Installed at the Congress of Angostura, by Tito Salas — AP254

1989, Dec. 12
C814   AP254   130p multicolored   1.10   .50
    Creation of the Republic, 1819.

Fathers of the Nation Leaving the Constitutional Convention AP255

1989, Dec. 12
C815   AP255   130p shown   1.10   .50
C816   AP255   130p Arms   1.10   .50
C817   AP255   130p Temple of the Rosary   1.10   .50
    Nos. C815-C817 (3)   3.30   1.50

Constitution of the Republic, 1821.

Arms Type of Regular Issue, 1982
1990, Mar. 1   **Litho.**   **Perf. 12**
C818   A372   60p Velez   .30   .25

Presidential Summit, Cartagena AP256

130p, Plaza de la Aduana.

1990, Feb. 15 Litho. *Perf. 12*
C819 AP256 130p multi .55 .25

Colombian National Radio, 50th Anniv. — AP257

1990, Feb. 16 Litho. *Perf. 12*
C820 AP257 150p multicolored 1.00 .25

Teresa Cuervo Borda (1889-1976), Art Historian — AP258

1990, Mar. 28 Litho. *Perf. 12*
C821 AP258 60p multicolored .35 .25

Second Latin American Theater Festival, Bogota — AP259

1990, Apr. 10
C822 AP259 150p buff, tan & gold 1.00 .25

Santander Type

No. C823, Santander holding the Constitution. No. C824, Central Cemetery, Bogota and National Pantheon. No. C825, Santander, as organizer of public education. No. C826, "Postman of New Granada" (Man and burro) by Joseph Brown and Jose Maria del Castillo, horiz. 500p, Santander on death bed.

1990, May 6 *Perf. 14x13½*
C823 A470 60p multicolored .30 .25
C824 A470 60p multicolored .30 .25
C825 A470 70p multicolored .40 .25
C826 A470 70p multicolored .40 .25
Nos. C823-C826 (4) 1.40 1.00

Souvenir Sheet
Perf. 12
C827 A470 500p multi 2.00 1.50
No. C827 contains one 54x40mm stamp.

First Postage Stamp, 150th Anniv. AP260

1990, May 6 *Perf. 14*
C828 AP260 150p multicolored .80 .40

Trans-Caribbean Fiber Optic Cable — AP261

1990, May 19 *Perf. 12*
C829 AP261 150p multicolored 1.25 .40

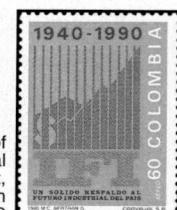

Institute of Industrial Development, 25th Anniv. — AP262

1990, May 22
C830 AP262 60p multicolored .40 .25

Souvenir Sheet

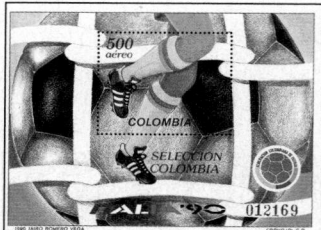

World Cup Soccer Championships, Italy — AP263

1990, June 8
C831 AP263 500p multicolored 4.50 3.50

AP264

1990, June 27
C832 AP264 130p multicolored .80 .25
Organization of American States, cent.

AP265

1990, July 26
C833 AP265 170p multicolored 1.25 .50
Museum of Gold, 50th Anniv.

Dolphins, Marine Birds AP266

170p, Jungle fauna, vert.

1990, Oct. 12 Litho. *Perf. 12*
C834 AP266 150p shown 2.50 .25
C835 AP266 170p multi 2.50 .25

AP267

1990, Nov. 16 Litho. *Perf. 12*
C836 AP267 70p multicolored .50 .25
Monastery of Our Lady of Las Lajas.

AP268

1991, Feb. 8 Litho. *Perf. 12*
C837 AP268 170p multicolored 1.00 .50
Newspaper Publishing, 200th Anniv.

Christmas AP269

1990, Nov. 1 Litho. *Perf. 12*
C838 AP269 70p multicolored .60 .25

AP270

Whales and Dolphins: 80p, Megaptera novaeangliae, breaching. 170p, Megaptera novaeangliae, diving. 190p, Inia geoffrensis, Sotalia fluviatilis, horiz.

1991, May 31 Litho. *Perf. 14*
C839 AP270 80p multicolored 1.25 .25
C840 AP270 170p multicolored 2.75 .30
C841 AP270 190p multicoloed 3.25 .30
Nos. C839-C841 (3) 7.25 .85

America Issue AP271

190p, Ship arriving in New World.

1991, Oct. 11 Litho. *Perf. 14*
C842 AP271 90p shown .60 .30
C843 AP271 190p multi 1.25 .50

Adoration of the Magi — AP272

1991, Dec. 20 Litho. *Perf. 14*
C844 AP272 90p multicolored .60 .30
Christmas.

Country Flags — AP273

1991, Dec. 2
C845 AP273 190p multi 1.10 .50
Fifth summit of Latin American presidents.

AP274

1992, Feb. 8 Litho. *Perf. 12*
C846 AP274 210p multicolored 1.25 .60
8th UNCTAD Conference, Cartagena.

Proclamation of New Constitution, July 4, 1991 — AP275

1991, Nov. 27 Litho. *Perf. 14*
C847 AP275 90p multicolored .40 .25

Export Products AP276

90p, Flowers. 210p, Fruits, vegetables, horiz.

1992, Mar. 11 *Perf. 12*
C848 AP276 90p multi .60 .30
C849 AP276 210p multi 1.40 .65

Copyright Protection AP277

1992, Apr. 13   Litho.   Perf. 12
C850 AP277 190p multicolored   1.50 .60

1992 Summer Olympics AP278

1992, June 4   Litho.   Perf. 14
C851 AP278 110p multicolored   .75 .30

Earth Summit '92 — AP279

a, Tree, mountain landscape. b, Birds in tree.

1992, June 2   Litho.   Perf. 14
C852 A279 230p Pair, #a.-b.   2.75 2.00

America Issue AP280

Paintings: 230p, Discovery of America by Christopher Columbus, by Salvador Dali. 260p, Magical America, Myth and Legend, by Alfredo Vivero.

1992, July 22   Perf. 14x13½
C853 AP280 230p multicolored   1.75 .70
C854 AP280 260p multicolored   2.00 .75

McDonnell Douglas MD83 AP281

1992, Sept. 22   Litho.   Perf. 12
C855 AP281 110p multicolored   .50 .30

Curtain of Colon Theatre AP282

1992, Oct. 12   Litho.   Perf. 12
C856 AP282 230p multicolored   1.25 .65

Gloria Lara, 1938-82 — AP283

1992, Nov. 27   Litho.   Perf. 12
C857 AP283 230p multicolored   1.25 .65

AP284

1993, June 7   Litho.   Perf. 12
C858 AP284 220p multicolored   1.25 .60

1993 American Soccer Cup, Ecuador.

Intl. Year of Indigenous People — AP285

1993, July 1   Perf. 14
C859 AP285 460p multicolored   2.50 1.25

South American Eliminations for 1994 World Cup Soccer Championships, US — AP286

1993, July 31   Litho.   Perf. 12
C860 AP286 220p multicolored   1.75 .60

AP287

America Issue (Endangered species): a, 220p, Saguinus oedipus. b, 220p, Porphyrula martinica. c, 460p, Rupicola peruviana. d, 520p, Trichecus manatus.

1993, Oct. 19   Litho.   Perf. 12
C861 AP287 Block of 4, #a.-d.   7.50 7.50

AP288

1994, Mar. 21   Litho.   Perf. 12
C862 AP288 630p multicolored   3.25 1.75

Intl. Decade for Natural Disaster Reduction.

Beatification of Josemaria Escriva de Balaguer — AP289

1994, May 17   Litho.   Perf. 13½x14
C863 AP289 560p multicolored   2.50 1.40

First Airmail Delivery, 75th Anniv. AP290

Design: 270p, William Knox Martin, airplane over Port Colombia, 1919.

1994, July 29   Litho.   Perf. 14
C864 AP290 270p multicolored   1.25 .55

Natl. Institute of Medical Law & Forensic Sciences, 80th Anniv. AP291

1994, Oct. 27   Litho.   Perf. 12
C865 AP291 560p multicolored   2.25 1.25

Sociedad Colombo-Alemana de Transportes Aereos (SCADTA), 75th Anniv. — AP292

1995, Jan. 2   Litho.   Perf. 12
C866 AP292 330p No. C15   1.10 .50

Flora and Fauna — AP293

Iguana iguana: No. C867a, Facing right. b, Facing left.
Rain forest: No. C868a, Nuts on branch, flowers. b, Waterfall, hanging red flower.

1995, Jan. 17
C867 AP293 650p Pair, #a.-b.   6.50 6.50
C868 AP293 750p Pair, #a.-b.   6.50 6.50

Nos. C867-C868 are continuous designs.

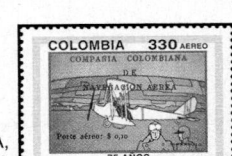

SCADTA, 75th Anniv. AP294

1995, Mar. 30   Litho.   Perf. 14
C869 AP294 330p No. C9   1.50 .75

FAO, 50th Anniv. AP295

1995, Apr. 25   Litho.   Perf. 13x13½
C870 AP295 750p multicolored   3.50 1.75

Andres Bello Organization, 25th Anniv. — AP296

1995, Apr. 27   Perf. 13½x13
C871 AP296 650p multicolored   2.50 1.25

Colombian Firefighters, Cent. — AP297

1995, May 5   Perf. 12
C872 AP297 330p multicolored   1.50 .75

Fenalco, 50th Anniv. — AP298

1995, May 25   Perf. 13½
C873 AP298 330p multicolored   1.25 .65

UN, 50th Anniv. — AP299

1995, June 21   Perf. 12
C874 AP299 750p multicolored   3.00 1.50

First Pacific Ocean Games — AP300

1995, June 23
C875 AP300 750p multicolored 3.00 1.50

11th Summit of Non-Aligned Countries, Cartagena — AP302

1995, Oct. 13 **Litho.** *Perf. 12*
C877 AP302 650p multicolored 2.75 1.25

Motion Pictures, Cent. AP303

Design: 330p, Charlie Chaplin and Jackie Coogan in "The Kid," Estela López Pomareda in "Maria," first Colombian feature length film.

1995, Oct. 19 *Perf. 14*
C878 AP303 330p black & sepia 1.50 .75

AP304

1995, Nov. 23 *Perf. 12*
C879 AP304 650p multicolored 2.10 1.00
Andes Development Corporation (CAF), 25th Anniv.

AP305

Fight against illegal drug trafficking: No. C880, Locating illegally grown plants. No. C881, Hands in handcuffs, horiz.

1995, Nov. 21 *Perf. 14*
C880 AP305 330p multicolored .70 .45
C881 AP305 330p multicolored .70 .45

Miniature Sheet of 16

Myths and Legends — AP306

Madre-Monte: a.-d.
La Llorona: e.-h.
El Mohán: i.-l.
Hombre Caimán: m.-p.
Background color changes from top to bottom rows. Top row is blue. Row 2 is blue green. Row 3 is green. Row 4 is lilac. Each design comes in all four colors.

1995, Dec. 6
C882 AP306 750p #a.-p. 40.00 40.00
See No. C886.

José Asunción Silva (1865-96), Poet AP307

1996, Apr. 23 **Litho.** *Perf. 12*
C883 AP307 400p multicolored 1.25 .75

Isla de Providencia AP308

1996, Apr. 25 *Perf. 14*
C884 AP308 800p multicolored 2.75 1.40

Policarpa Salavarrieta (1796-1817), Patriot — AP309

1996, Apr. 26
C885 AP309 900p multicolored 3.00 1.50

Myths and Legends Type

Designs: a, Kogui Creation. b, Yonna Wayu. c, Jaguar Man. d, Master of the Animals.

1996, Aug. 12 **Litho.** *Perf. 13½x14*
C886 AP306 900p Block of 4,
  #a.-d. 13.00 13.00

Metropolitan Basilica, Medellin AP310

1996, July 12
C887 AP310 400p multicolored 1.10 .55

National Archives Building AP311

1996, July 30 **Litho.** *Perf. 14*
C888 AP311 400p multicolored 1.25 .60

CERLALC, 25th Anniv. AP312

1996, Aug. 16 **Litho.** *Perf. 12*
C889 AP312 800p multicolored 2.75 1.25
UNESCO.

Pioneers in Petroleum Industry — AP313

a, Jorge Isaacs, pumping oil. b, Francisco Burgos Rubio, refinery at night. c, Diego Martínez Camargo, derrick. d, Prisciliano Cabrales Lora, off-shore drilling. e, Manuel María Palacio, oil tanker loading offshore. f, Roberto De Mares, refinery, lake. g, General Virgilio Barco Maldonado, men positioning equipment. h, Roustabout, "ECOPETROL" emblem.

1996, Sept. 5 **Litho.** *Perf. 13½x14*
C890 AP313 800p Block of 8,
  #a.-h. 20.00 20.00

Colombian Golf Federation, 50th Anniv. AP314

1996, Sept. 19 **Litho.** *Perf. 12*
C891 AP314 400p multicolored 2.25 .60

Covenant for the Children AP315

1997, Feb. 28 **Litho.** *Perf. 14*
C892 AP315 400p multicolored 2.00 .75

AP316

1997, Apr. 25 *Perf. 12*
C893 AP316 800p multicolored 4.00 1.75
Motion pictures in Colombia, cent.

AP317

1997, May 13 **Litho.** *Perf. 12*
C894 AP317 400p multicolored 2.00 .75
Social Security Institute, 50th anniv.

Ericsson in Colombia, Cent. — AP318

1997, May 22 *Perf. 13½x14*
C895 AP318 900p multicolored 4.50 2.00

Bogotá Colonial Bldg., Home of Natl. Mint and Numismatic Museum — AP319

1997, July 10 *Perf. 12*
C896 AP319 800p multicolored 3.00 1.40

Phytelephas Seemannii — AP320

1997, July 23 *Perf. 13½x14*
C897 AP320 900p multicolored 3.00 .90

Cordoba
Cattle Fair
AP321

1997, June 21 *Perf.* **14**
C898 AP321 400p multicolored 1.50 .45

Personalities — AP322

No. C899: a, Cacique Gaitana, 16th cent., Indian resistance leader. b, Josefa Acevedo de Gómez (1803-61), writer. c, Domingo Bioho (d. 1621), black leader. d, Soledad Acosta de Samper (1831-1913), historian. e, Maria Cano Márquez (1897-1967), popular leader. f, Manuel Quintín Lame (1880-1967), native leader. g, Ezequiel Uricoechea (1834-80), linguist, naturalist. h, Juan Rodríguez Freyle (1566-1642), colonial reporter. i, Gerardo Reichel-Dolmatoff (1912-94), archaeologist. j, Ramón de Zubiría (1922-95), writer, educator. k, Esteban Jaramillo (1874-1947), economist. l, Pedro Fermín de Vargas (1762-c. 1810), economist.

No. C900: a, Luis Carlos "el tuerto" López (1879-1950), poet. b, Aurelio Arturo (1906-74), poet. c, Enrique Pérez Arbeláez (1896-1972), botanist. d, José Maria González Benito (1843-1903), mathematician, astronomer. e, José Manuel Rivas Sacconi (1917-91), diplomat. f, Eduardo Lemaitre Román (1914-94), historian. g, Diójenes Arrieta (1848-93), politician. h, Gabriel Turbay Abunader (1901-47), politician, diplomat. i, Guillermo Echavarría Misas (1888-1985), aviation pioneer. j, Juan Friede Alter (1901-90), historian. k, Fabio Lozano Torrijos (1865-1947), diplomat. l, Lino de Pombo (1797-1862), engineer, diplomat.

Sheets of 12

1997, Dec. 19 Litho. *Perf.* **13½x14**
C899 AP322 500p #a.-l. 22.50 22.50
C900 AP322 500p #a.-l. 22.50 22.50

Colombian Society of Orthopedic Surgery and Traumatology, 50th Anniv. — AP323

1997 *Perf.* **12**
C901 AP323 1000p multicolored 3.00 1.00

AP324

1998, Apr. 30 Litho. *Perf.* **14**
C902 AP324 1000p multicolored 3.00 .80
Organization of American States, 50th anniv.

AP325

1998, May 22
C903 AP325 1000p bl & org 3.00 .80
4th Bolivar Philatelic Exhibition, Santa Fe de Bogota.

World Health Organization, 50th Anniv. — AP326

1998, Apr. 7 *Perf.* **12**
C904 AP326 1100p multicolored 3.00 1.00

1998 World Cup Soccer Championships, France — AP327

Stylized designs: a, Foot. b. Soccer ball. c, Hand.

1998, June 9 Litho. *Perf.* **14**
C905 AP327 1100p Strip of 3,
#a.-c. 12.00 12.00

Intl. Year of the Ocean — AP328

1998, May 22 *Perf.* **12**
C906 AP328 1100p ARC Gloria 3.50 .95

Myths and Legends — AP329

Designs: a, Bochica. b, Chimingagua. c, Bachue and Huitica.

Perf. **13¼x12¾**
1998, Nov. 27 **Litho.**
C907 AP329 1000p Strip of 3,
#a.-c. 15.00 15.00

AIR POST SPECIAL DELIVERY STAMPS

Catalogue values for unused stamps in this section are for Never Hinged items.

Post Horn and Wings APSD1

Unwmk.
1958, May 19 Litho. *Perf.* **12**
CE1 APSD1 25c dk bl & red .55 .25

No. CE1
Ovptd. in
Red

1959
CE2 APSD1 25c dk bl & red .50 .25

Jet Plane and Envelope — APSD2

1963, Oct. 4 *Perf.* **14**
CE3 APSD2 50c red & blk .25 .25

Aviation Type
80c, Boeing 727 jet, 1966.

Perf. **14x13½**
1966, Dec. 14 Photo. Unwmk.
CE4 AP96 80c crim & multi .55 .25

AIR POST REGISTRATION STAMPS

Issued by Sociedad Colombo-Alemana de Transportes Aereos (SCADTA)

No. C41 Overprinted in Red

1923 Wmk. 116 *Perf.* **14x14½**
CF1 AP6 20c gray 4.75 1.10

No. C58 Overprinted in Black

1929 Wmk. 127 *Perf.* **14**
CF2 AP8 20c carmine 8.00 7.00
Same Overprint on No. C71
CF3 AP10 20c carmine 6.50 6.00

Colombian Government Issues

No. C86 Overprinted in Black

1932
CF4 AP8 20c carmine 6.50 6.00

No. C100 Overprinted

CF5 AP12 20c car & ol blk 6.00 1.25
For surcharge see No. C118.

SPECIAL DELIVERY STAMPS

Special Delivery
Messenger — SD1

1917 Unwmk. Engr. *Perf.* **14**
E1 SD1 5c dark green 60.00 150.00

Catalogue values for unused stamps in this section, from this point to the end of the section, are for Never Hinged items.

SD2

1987, July 31 Litho. *Perf.* **14**
E2 SD2 25p emerald & ver .30 .30
E3 SD2 30p emerald & ver .35 .35

REGISTRATION STAMPS

R1   R2

1865 Unwmk. Litho. *Imperf.*
F1 R1 5c black 87.50 47.50
F2 R2 5c black 110.00 50.00

R3   R4

Vertical Lines in Background
1870 **White Paper**
F3 R3 5c black 3.00 2.50
F4 R4 5c black 3.00 2.50
Horizontal Lines in Background
F5 R3 5c black 10.00 8.50
F6 R4 5c black 3.00 2.50
Nos. F3-F6 (4) 19.00 16.00

Reprints of Nos. F3 to F6 show either crossed lines or traces of lines in background.

R5

1881 *Imperf.*
F7 R5 10c violet 60.00 52.50
  a. Sewing machine perf. 67.50 60.00
  b. Perf. 11 75.00 62.50

R6

1883 **Perf. 12, 13½**
F8 R6 10c red, *orange* 2.00 *2.50*

R7

1889-95 **Perf. 12, 13½**
F9 R7 10c red, *grysh* 9.50 4.50
F10 R7 10c red, *yelsh* 9.50 4.50
F11 R7 10c dp brn, *rose buff* 2.00 1.60
    ('95)
F12 R7 10c yel brn, *lt buff* ('92) 2.00 1.60
    Nos. F9-F12 (4) 23.00 12.20
    Nos. F9-F12 exist imperf.

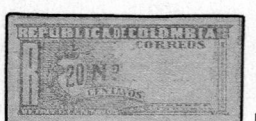

R9

1902 **Imperf.**
F13 R9 20c red brown, *blue* 1.60 1.60
  a. Sewing machine perf. 4.75 4.75
  b. Perf. 12 4.75 4.75

Medellin Issue

R10

1902 **Laid Paper** **Perf. 12**
F16 R10 10c blk vio 15.00 15.00
  a. Wove paper 21.00 21.00

Regular Issue
Imperf

1903
F17 R9 20c blue, *blue* 1.60 1.60
  a. Sewing machine perf. 4.75 4.75
  b. Perf. 12 4.75 4.75

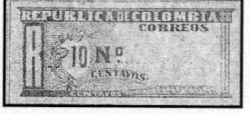

R11

1904 **Pelure Paper** **Imperf.**
F19 R11 10c purple 3.75 3.75
  a. Sewing machine perf. 5.00 3.75
  b. Perf. 12 6.25 5.00

R12

Imprint: "J. L. Arango"

1904 **Wove Paper** **Perf. 12**
F20 R12 10c purple 2.50 .60
  a. Imperf., pair 7.75 7.75

Imprint: "Lit. Nacional"

1909 **Perf. 10, 14, 10x14, 14x10**
F21 R12 10c purple 2.75 .85
  a. Imperf., pair 6.25 6.25
For overprints see Nos. LF1-LF4.

Execution at Cartagena in
1816 — R13

1910, July 20 **Engr.** **Perf. 12**
F22 R13 10c red & black 21.00 *90.00*
Centenary of National Independence.

Pier at Puerto Colombia — R14

Tequendama Falls — R15

Perf. 11, 11½, 14, 11½x14
1917, Aug. 25
F23 R14 4c green & ultra .55 *3.50*
  a. Center inverted 575.00 575.00
F24 R15 10c deep blue 8.00 *.60*

R16

1925 **Litho.** **Perf. 10x13½**
F25 R16 (10c) blue 4.25 1.90
  a. Imperf., pair 15.00 12.50
  b. Perf. 13½x10 7.50 5.00

ACKNOWLEDGMENT OF RECEIPT STAMPS

AR1

1893 **Unwmk.** **Litho.** **Perf. 13½**
H1 AR1 5c ver, *blue* 4.75 4.75

1894 **Perf. 12**
H2 AR1 5c vermilion 4.50 *5.00*

AR2

1902-03 **Imperf.**
H3 AR2 10c blue, *blue* 3.50 5.00
  a. 10c, blue, *greenish blue* 3.50 5.00
  b. Sewing machine perf. 3.50 5.00
  c. Perf. 12 3.50 5.00

The handstamp "AR" in circle is believed to be a postmark.

AR2a

Purple Handstamp
1903 **Imperf.**
H4 AR2a 10c black, *pink* 25.00 25.00

AR3

1904 **Pelure Paper** **Imperf.**
H12 AR3 5c pale blue 10.50 10.50
  a. Perf. 12 10.50 10.50

No. 307 Overprinted
in Black, Green or
Violet

H13 A86 5c carmine 17.50 17.50

AR4

1904 **Perf. 12**
H16 AR4 5c blue 3.25 2.75
  a. Imperf., pair 8.75 8.75
For overprints see Nos. LH1-LH2.

General José
Acevedo y
Gómez — AR5

1910, July 20 **Engr.**
H17 AR5 5c orange & green 7.00 *17.50*
Centenary of National Independence.

Sabana Station
AR6

Map of
Colombia
AR7

1917 **Perf. 14**
H18 AR6 4c bister brown 5.50 *6.00*
H19 AR7 5c orange brown 5.50 *4.50*
  a. Imperf., pair 14.00

LATE FEE STAMPS

LF1

1886 **Unwmk.** **Litho.** **Perf. 10½**
I1 LF1 2½c blk, *lilac* 4.00 3.25
  a. Imperf., pair 15.00 15.00

LF2

1892 **Perf. 12, 13½**
I2 LF2 2½c dk bl, *rose* 3.50 2.50
  a. Imperf., pair 15.00
I3 LF2 2½c ultra, *pink* 3.50 2.50

LF3

1902 **Imperf.**
I4 LF3 5c purple, *rose* 1.00 1.00
  a. Perf. 12 2.10 2.10

LF4

1914 **Perf. 10, 13½**
I6 LF4 2c vio brown 5.00 5.00
I7 LF4 5c blue green 5.00 4.25

Overprints illustrated above are
unauthorized and of private origin.

POSTAGE DUE STAMPS

These are not, strictly speaking, postage due stamps but were issued to cover an additional fee, "Sobreporte," charged on mail to foreign countries with which Colombia had no postal conventions.

D1

D2

D3

1866   Unwmk.   Litho.   *Imperf.*

J1	D1	25c black, *blue*	80.00	55.00
J2	D2	50c black, *yellow*	55.00	*80.00*
J3	D3	1p black, *rose*	160.00	*125.00*
		Nos. J1-J3 (3)	295.00	260.00

DEPARTMENT STAMPS

These stamps are said to be for interior postage, to supersede the separate issues for the various departments.

Regular Issues
Handstamped in Black,
Violet, Blue or Green —
a

On Stamps of 1904

1909   Unwmk.   *Perf. 12*

L1	A94	½c yellow	2.50	2.50
a.		Imperf., pair	7.50	7.50
L2	A94	1c yel grn	3.75	2.50
L3	A94	2c red	5.50	3.75
a.		Imperf., pair	15.00	15.00
L4	A94	5c blue	6.25	4.00
L5	A94	10c violet	8.75	8.75
L6	A94	20c black	14.00	14.00
L7	A95	1p brown	22.50	21.00

On Stamp of 1902

L8	A83	10p dk brn, *rose*	25.00	25.00
		Nos. L1-L8 (8)	88.25	81.50

On Stamps of 1908
Perf. 10, 13, 13½ and Compound

L9	A94	½c orange	2.90	2.90
a.		Imperf., pair	7.50	7.50
L10	A94	1c green	5.00	5.00
a.		Without imprint	6.25	6.25
L11	A94	2c red	5.50	5.50
a.		Imperf., pair	15.00	15.00
L12	A94	5c blue	5.50	5.50
a.		Imperf., pair	15.00	15.00
L13	A94	10c violet	8.75	8.75

On Tolima Stamp of 1888
Perf. 10½

L14	A23	1p red brn	27.50	27.50
		Nos. L9-L14 (6)	55.15	55.15

Regular Issues
Handstamped — b

On Stamps of 1904
Perf. 12

L15	A94	½c yellow	2.50	2.50
L16	A94	1c yellow grn	4.25	4.25
L17	A94	2c red	7.50	7.50
L18	A94	5c blue	7.50	7.50
L19	A94	10c violet	10.00	10.00
L20	A94	20c black	14.00	14.00
L21	A94	1p brown	25.00	25.00
		Nos. L15-L21 (7)	70.75	70.75

On Stamps of 1908
Perf. 10, 13, 13½

L22	A94	½c orange	2.75	2.75
L23	A94	1c yellow grn	7.75	7.75
L24	A94	2c red	6.25	6.25
a.		Imperf., pair	15.00	15.00
L25	A94	5c light blue	7.50	7.50
		Nos. L22-L25 (4)	24.25	24.25

The handstamps on Nos. L1-L25 are, as usual, found inverted and double.

DEPARTMENT REGISTRATION STAMPS

**Registration Stamps of 1904
Handstamped like Nos. L1-L25**

1909   Unwmk.   *Perf. 12*

LF1	R12 (a)	10c purple	30.00	30.00
LF2	R12 (b)	10c purple	30.00	30.00

On Registration Stamp of 1909
Perf. 10, 13

LF3	R12 (a)	10c purple	30.00	30.00
LF4	R12 (b)	10c purple	30.00	30.00
		Nos. LF1-LF4 (4)	120.00	120.00

Nos. LF1-LF4 exist imperf. Value per pair, $125.

DEPARTMENT ACKNOWLEDGMENT OF RECEIPT STAMPS

Acknowledgment of
Receipt Stamp of 1904
Hstmpd.

1909   Unwmk.   *Perf. 12*

LH1	AR4 (a)	5c blue	30.00	30.00
a.		Imperf., pair	125.00	
LH2	AR4 (b)	5c blue	30.00	30.00
a.		Imperf., pair	125.00	

LOCAL STAMPS FOR THE CITY OF BOGOTA

A1

Pelure Paper

1889   Unwmk.   Litho.   *Perf. 12*

LX1	A1	½c black	1.10	1.10
a.		Imperf., pair	7.25	7.25

Impressions on bright blue and blue-gray paper were not regularly issued.

A2

White Wove Paper

1896   *Perf. 12, 13½*

LX2	A2	½c black	1.10	1.10

A3

1903   *Imperf.*

LX3	A3	10c black, *pink*	7.25	1.40
a.		Perf. 12	7.25	1.40

OFFICIAL STAMPS

Stamps of 1917-1937 Overprinted in Black or Red

a

b

1937   Unwmk.   *Perf. 11, 12, 13½*

O1	A131 (a)	1c green	.25	.25
O2	A157 (a)	10c dp org	.25	.25
O3	A107 (b)	30c olive bis	2.10	1.00
O4	A129 (b)	40c brn & yel brn	1.60	.80
O5	A114 (b)	50c car	1.60	.80
O6	A107 (b)	1p lt blt	13.00	5.50
O7	A107 (b)	2p org	15.00	6.50
O8	A107 (b)	5p gray	47.50	*52.50*
O9	A118 (b)	10p dk brn	110.00	*125.00*

Wmk. 229
Perf. 12½

O10	A132 (a)	2c red	.25	.25
O11	A133 (a)	5c brn	.25	.25
O12	A160 (a)	12c dp bl (R)	1.00	.50
O13	A136 (a)	20c dk bl (R)	1.60	.80
		Nos. O1-O13 (13)	194.40	194.40

Tall, wrong font "I's" in OFICIAL exist on all stamps with "a" overprint.

POSTAL TAX STAMPS

"Greatest Mother"
PT1

Perf. 11½

1935, May 27   Unwmk.   Litho.

RA1	PT1	5c olive blk & scar	4.00	1.25

Required on all mail during Red Cross Week in 1935 (May 27-June 3) and in 1936.

Mother and Child — PT2

Perf. 10½, 10½x11

1937, May 24   Unwmk.

RA2	PT2	5c red	2.75	.90

Required on all mail during Red Cross Week. The tax was for the Red Cross.

Ministry of Posts and Telegraphs Building — PT3

1939-45   Litho.   *Perf. 10½, 12½*

RA3	PT3	¼c dp bl	.25	.25
RA3A	PT3	¼c dk vio brn ('45)	.25	.25
RA4	PT3	½c pink	.25	.25
RA5	PT3	1c violet	.30	.25
RA5A	PT3	1c yel org ('45)	1.75	.70
RA6	PT3	2c pck grn	.55	.25
RA7	PT3	20c lt brn	4.50	1.50
		Nos. RA3-RA7 (7)	7.85	3.45

Obligatory on all mail. The tax was for the construction of the new Communications Building.

The 25c of type PT3 and PT4 were not usable on postal matter.

For overprint see No. 561.

Ministry of Posts and Telegraphs Building — PT4

1940, Jan. 20   Engr.   Wmk. 229

RA8	PT4	¼c ultra	.25	.25
RA9	PT4	½c carmine	.25	.25
RA10	PT4	1c violet	.25	.25
RA11	PT4	2c bl grn	.30	.25
RA12	PT4	20c brown	1.25	.25
		Nos. RA8-RA12 (5)	2.30	1.25

See note after No. RA7. See No. RA18.

"Protection" — PT5

1940, Apr. 25   Wmk. 255   *Perf. 12*

RA13	PT5	5c rose carmine	.30	.25

See No. RA17.

Postal Tax Stamps
of 1939 Surcharged
in Black

1943   Unwmk.   *Perf. 10½*

RA14	PT3	½c on 1c violet	.25	.25
a.		Inverted surcharge	2.00	
RA15	PT3	½c on 2c pck grn	.25	.25
RA16	PT3	½c on 20c lt brn	.25	.25
		Nos. RA14-RA16 (3)	.75	.75

**Types of 1940
Imprint: "Litografia Colombia
Bogota S.A."**

1944   Litho.   *Perf. 11*

RA17	PT5	5c dark rose	.40	.25

Imprint: "Lito-Colombia Bogota-Colombia"

RA18	PT4	¼c ultra	.25	.25

Ministry of Posts and Telegraphs Building — PT6

1945-48   Wmk. 255   Engr.   *Perf. 12*

RA19	PT6	¼c ultra	.25	.25
RA20	PT6	¼c sepia ('46)	.25	.25
RA21	PT6	½c car rose	.25	.25
RA22	PT6	½c dp mag ('46)	.25	.25
RA23	PT6	1c vio ('46)	.25	.25
RA23A	PT6	1c red org ('46)	.25	.25
RA24	PT6	2c grn ('46)	.25	.25
RA25	PT6	20c brn ('47)	7.50	.30
a.		20c red brown ('48)	.70	.25
		Nos. RA19-RA25 (8)	9.25	2.05

These stamps were obligatory on all mail. The surtax was for the construction of the new Communications Building. See Nos. 603, RA33. For overprints see Nos. 562-564.

No. 469
Overprinted in
Carmine

1946, May 25

RA26	A176	5c dull brown	.45	.25

The surtax was for the Red Cross.

Ministry of Posts
and Telegraphs
Building — PT7

1946   Unwmk.   Litho.   *Perf. 11*

RA27	PT7	3c blue	.25	.25

No. 490 Overprinted in Carmine

1947   Wmk. 255   Perf. 12
RA28 A196 20c gray black   5.25 2.90

Arms of Colombia and Red Cross — PT8

Perf. 12½
1947, Sept.   Unwmk.   Engr.
RA29 PT8 5c car lake   .25 .25

The surtax of Nos. RA29 and RA40 was for the Red Cross. See No. RA40.

No. 466 Overprinted in Carmine

RA30 A136 20c dark blue   32.50 20.00

> Catalogue values for unused stamps in this section, from this point to the end of the section, are for Never Hinged items.

Type of 1945
1947   Wmk. 255   Engr.   Perf. 12
RA33 PT6 1c olive bister   .30 .25

Black Surcharge — PT9

1948   Unwmk.   Litho.   Perf. 11
RA36 PT9 1c on 5c lt brn   .30 .25
RA37 PT9 1c on 10c lt vio   .30 .25
RA38 PT9 1c on 25c red   .30 .25
RA39 PT9 1c on 50c ultra   .30 .25
Nos. RA36-RA39 (4)   1.20 1.00

Type of 1947
1948   Perf. 10½
RA40 PT8 5c vermilion   .25 .25

Ministry of Posts and Telegraphs Building — PT10

1948-50   Wmk. 255   Engr.   Perf. 12
RA41 PT10 1c rose car ('49)   .30 .25
RA42 PT10 2c green ('50)   .30 .25
RA43 PT10 3c blue   .30 .25
RA44 PT10 5c gray   .30 .25
RA45 PT10 10c purple   .30 .25
Nos. RA41-RA45 (5)   1.50 1.25

A 25c stamp of type PT10 was for use on telegrams, later for regular postage. See Nos. 602, 604. For overprints and surcharge see Nos. C227-C230, C238, C283, RA51.

Mother and Child — PT11

Dark Blue Surcharge
Unwmk.
1950, May 25   Litho.   Perf. 11
RA46 PT11 5c on 2c gray, red, blk & yel   1.25 .40
a.   "195" instead of "1950"   2.50 2.50
b.   Top bar and "19" of "1950" omitted   2.50 2.50

Marginal perforations omitted, creating 26 straight-edged stamps in each sheet of 44. Surtax for Red Cross.

No. 574 Overprinted in Black

1950, May 26   Wmk. 255   Perf. 12
RA47 A176 5c blue   .25 .25
a.   Inverted overprint   8.00

Telegraph Stamp Surcharged in Black

RA48 A253a 8c on 50c org yel   .25 .25

Fiscal stamps of type A253a were available for postal use after May 9, 1952. See Nos. 605-608.

Arms and Cross — PT12

Bartolome de Las Casas Aiding Youth — PT13

Perf. 12½
1951, May   Unwmk.   Engr.
RA49 PT12 5c red   .25 .25
RA50 PT13 5c carmine   .25 .25

The surtax was for the Red Cross.

No. RA43 Surcharged in Black

1951   Wmk. 255   Perf. 12
RA51 PT10 1c on 3c blue   .25 .25

Type of 1951
Engraved; Cross Lithographed
1953   Unwmk.   Perf. 12½
RA52 PT13 5c grn & car   .35 .25

Surtax of Nos. RA52-RA60 for the Red Cross.

No. C254 Overprinted in Carmine

1954
RA53 AP42 5c lilac rose   2.00 .90

St. Peter Claver Offering Gifts to Slaves — PT14

Engraved; Cross Typographed
1955, May 2   Unwmk.   Perf. 13
RA54 PT14 5c dp plum & red   .30 .25

Death of St. Peter Claver, 300th anniv.

Jean Henri Dunant and Santiago Samper Brush PT15

Photo.; Red Cross & "Cruz Roja" Engr.
1956, June 1   Unwmk.   Perf. 13
RA55 PT15 5c brown & red   .45 .25

Nurses and Ambulances PT16

1958, June 2   Photo.   Perf. 12
RA56 PT16 5c gray & red   .25 .25

St. Louisa de Marillac and Church PT17

No. RA58, Henri Dunant and battle scene.

1960, Sept. 1   Litho.   Perf. 11
RA57 PT17 5c brown & rose   .30 .25
RA58 PT17 5c vio blue & rose   .30 .25

No. RA57 for 3rd cent. of the Sisters of Charity. No. RA58 for cent. (in 1959) of the Red Cross idea.

Manuelita de la Cruz — PT18

1961, Nov. 2   Engr.   Perf. 13
RA59 PT18 5c dull pur & red   .25 .25
RA60 PT18 5c brown & red   .25 .25

Issued in memory of Red Cross Nurse Manuelita de la Cruz, who died in the line of duty during the floods of 1955. Obligatory on domestic mail for a month.

Red Cross Worker, Patient — PT19

1965, Apr. 30   Photo.   Perf. 12
RA61 PT19 5c blue gray & red   .25 .25

Obligatory on domestic mail during May.

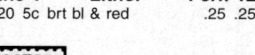

Nurse's Cap — PT20

1967, June 1   Litho.   Perf. 12
RA62 PT20 5c brt bl & red   .25 .25

Red Cross — PT21

1969, July 1   Litho.   Perf. 12x12½
RA63 PT21 5c vio bl & red   .25 .25

Child Care — PT22

1970, July 1   Litho.   Perf. 12½x12
RA64 PT22 5c light bl & red   .25 .25

ANTIOQUIA

ant-ē-'ō-kē-ə

Originally a State, now a Department of the Republic of Colombia. Until the revolution of 1885, the separate states making up the United States of Colombia were sovereign governments in their own right. On August 4, 1886, the National Council of Bogotá, composed of two delegates from each state, adopted a new constitution which abolished the sovereign rights of states, which then became departments with governors appointed by the President of the Republic. The nine original states represented at the Bogotá Convention retained some of their previous rights, as management of their own finances, and all issued postage stamps until as late as 1904. For Panama's issues, see Panama Nos. 1-30.

Coat of Arms
A1   A2

A3   A4

Wove Paper

1868		Unwmk.	Litho.	Imperf.
1	A1	2½c blue	1,000.	750.
2	A2	5c green	750.	575.
3	A3	10c lilac	3,000.	1,000.
4	A4	1p red	675.	750.

Reprints of Nos. 1, 3 and 4 are on a bluish white paper and all but No. 3 have scratches across the design.

A5   A6
A7   A8
A9   A10

1869

5	A5	2½c blue	3.75	3.25
6	A6	5c green	5.50	5.00
7	A7	5c green	5.50	5.00
8	A8	10c lilac	7.25	3.50
9	A9	20c brown	7.25	3.50
10	A10	1p rose red	14.50	13.00
a.		1p vermilion	27.50	25.00
		Nos. 5-10 (6)	43.75	33.25

Reprints of Nos. 7, 8 and 10 are on a bluish white paper; reprints of Nos. 5 and 10a on white paper. The 10c blue is believed to be a reprint.

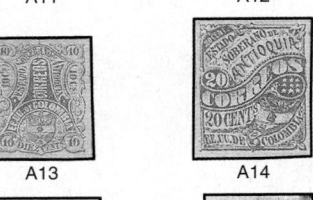

A11   A12
A13   A14
A15   A16
A17   A18

1873

12	A11	1c yellow grn	5.25	4.00
a.		1c green	5.25	4.00
13	A12	5c green	8.75	6.50
14	A13	10c lilac	25.00	21.00
15	A14	20c yellow brn	8.75	7.50
a.		20c dark brown	8.75	7.50

16	A15	50c blue	2.00	1.75
17	A16	1p vermilion	3.75	3.00
18	A17	2p black, *yellow*	8.75	8.00
19	A18	5p black, *rose*	65.00	55.00

A19   A20

Liberty Head
A21   A22

Pedro Justo
Berrio — A23

1875-85

20	A19	1c blk, *grn*, un-glazed ('76)	1.60	2.40
a.		Glazed paper	2.60	3.25
b.		1c blk, *lt grn*, laid paper ('85)	3.75	3.50
21	A19	1c black ('76)	1.10	1.00
a.		Laid paper	160.00	110.00
22	A19	1c bl grn ('85)	2.50	4.00
23	A19	1c red lil, laid paper ('85)	2.50	4.00
24	A20	2½c blue	2.50	1.90
a.		Pelure paper ('78)	1,500.	1,100.
25	A21	5c green	16.00	14.50
a.		Laid paper	160.00	87.50
26	A22	5c green	16.00	14.50
a.		Laid paper	160.00	87.50
27	A23	10c lilac	25.00	21.00
a.		Laid paper	160.00	125.00
28	A20	10c vio, pelure paper ('78)	900.00	675.00

Arms — A24   Liberty — A25

A26   A27

1878-85

29	A24	2½c blue, pelure paper	2.75	2.50
30	A24	2½c green ('83)	2.50	2.10
a.		Laid paper ('83)	80.00	55.00
31	A24	2½c blk, *buff* ('85)	7.25	6.50
32	A25	5c green ('83)	4.50	4.00
a.		Pelure paper	32.50	27.50
b.		Laid paper ('82)	40.00	13.00
33	A25	5c violet ('83)	9.50	7.50
a.		5c blue violet ('83)	9.50	7.50
34	A26	10c vio, laid paper ('82)	190.00	65.00
35	A26	10c scar ('83)	2.50	2.10
a.		Tete beche pair	110.00	110.00
36	A27	20c brown ('83)	4.50	4.00
a.		Laid paper ('82)	6.00	5.50

A28   A29

Liberty — A30

1883-85

37	A28	5c brown	5.25	3.50
a.		Laid paper	225.00	87.50
38	A28	5c green ('85)	140.00	45.00
a.		Laid paper ('85)	160.00	75.00
39	A28	5c yel, laid paper ('85)	5.50	4.50
40	A29	10c bl grn, laid paper	5.50	4.75
41	A29	10c bl ('85)	5.50	4.50
42	A29	10c lil, laid paper ('85)	12.00	7.50
a.		Wove paper ('85)	125.00	80.00
43	A30	20c bl, laid paper ('85)	4.50	4.00

Coat of Arms — A31

1886		A31		Wove Paper	
55	A31	1c grn, *pink*	.65	.55
56	A31	2½c blk, *orange*	.65	.55
57	A31	5c ultra, *buff*	2.00	1.75
a.		5c blue, *buff*	3.25	3.25
58	A31	10c rose, *buff*	1.75	1.60
a.		Transfer of 50c in stone of 10c	140.00	140.00
59	A31	20c dk vio, *buff*	1.75	1.60
61	A31	50c yel brn, *buff*	3.25	2.75
62	A31	1p yel, *grn*	5.25	4.50
63	A31	2p green, *vio*	5.25	4.50
		Nos. 55-63 (8)	20.55	17.80

1887-88

64	A31	1c red, *vio*	.50	.45
65	A31	2½c lil, *pale lil*	.50	.60
66	A31	5c car, *buff*	.65	.65
67	A31	5c red, *grn*	3.75	1.75
68	A31	10c brn, *grn*	.65	.80
		Nos. 64-68 (5)	6.05	4.25

Medellin Issue

A32   A33

A34

1888			Typeset	
69	A32	2½c blk, *yellow*	16.00	14.50
70	A33	5c blk, *yellow*	8.75	7.50
71	A34	5c red, *yellow*	5.25	4.50
		Nos. 69-71 (3)	30.00	26.50

Two varieties of No. 69, six of No. 70 and ten of No. 71.

A35

1889

72	A35	2½c red	8.00	6.75

Ten varieties including "eentavos."

Regular Issue

Coat of Arms — A36

1889			Litho.	Perf. 13½	
73	A36	1c blk, *rose*	.25	.25
74	A36	2½c blk, *blue*	.25	.25
75	A36	5c blk, *yellow*	.30	.30
76	A36	10c blk, *green*	.30	.30
		Nos. 73-76 (4)	1.10	1.10

A37   A38

A39   A40

Coat of Arms — A41

1890

78	A37	20c blue	1.40	1.40
79	A38	50c vio brn	2.50	2.50
a.		Transfer of 20c in stone of 50c	95.00	95.00
80	A38	50c green	2.25	2.25
81	A39	1p red	2.00	2.00
82	A40	2p blk, *mag*	14.50	14.50
83	A41	5p blk, *org red*	22.50	22.50
		Nos. 78-83 (6)	45.15	45.15

Nos. 73-76, 82-83 exist imperf.

The so-called "errors" of Nos. 73 to 76, printed on paper of wrong colors, are essays or, possibly, reprints. They exist perforated and imperforate.

See No. 96.

A42   A43
A44   A45

1890			Typeset	Perf. 14	
84	A42	2½c blk, *buff*	2.25	2.25
85	A43	5c blk, *orange*	2.25	2.25
86	A44	10c blk, *buff*	7.00	7.00
87	A44	10c blk, *rose*	9.00	9.00
88	A45	20c blk, *orange*	9.00	9.00
		Nos. 84-88 (5)	29.50	29.50

20 varieties of the 5c, 10 each of the other values.

A46

1892		Litho.		Perf. 13½
89	A46	1c brn, *brnsh*	.40	.40
90	A46	2½c pur, *lil*	.40	.40
92	A46	5c blk, *gray*	1.10	.55
a.		Transfer of 2½c in stone of 5c	200.00	
		Nos. 89-92 (3)	1.90	1.35

1893				
93	A46	1c blue	.25	.25
94	A46	2½c green	.40	.40
95	A46	5c vermilion	.25	.25
96	A36	10c pale brown	.25	.25
		Nos. 93-96 (4)	1.15	1.15

A47

1896				Perf. 14
97	A47	2c gray	.25	.25
98	A47	2c lilac rose	.25	.25
99	A47	2½c brown	.25	.25
100	A47	2½c steel blue	.25	.25
101	A47	3c orange	.25	.25
102	A47	3c olive grn	.25	.25
103	A47	5c green	.25	.25
104	A47	5c yellow buff	.30	.30
105	A47	10c brown vio	.55	.55
106	A47	10c violet	.55	.55
107	A47	20c brown org	1.40	1.40
108	A47	20c blue	1.40	1.40
109	A47	50c gray brn	1.40	1.40
110	A47	50c rose	1.40	1.40
111	A47	1p blue & blk	17.50	17.50
112	A47	1p rose red & blk	17.50	17.50
113	A47	2p orange & blk	55.00	55.00
114	A47	2p dk grn & blk	55.00	55.00
115	A47	5p red vio & blk	95.00	95.00
116	A47	5p purple & blk	95.00	95.00
		Nos. 97-116 (20)	343.75	343.75

#115-116 with centers omitted are proofs.

General José María
Córdoba — A48

1899				Perf. 11
117	A48	½c grnsh bl	.25	.25
118	A48	1c slate blue	.25	.25
119	A48	2c slate brown	.25	.25
120	A48	3c red	.25	.25
121	A48	4c bister brown	.25	.25
122	A48	5c green	.25	.25
123	A48	10c scarlet	.25	.25
124	A48	20c gray violet	.25	.25
125	A48	50c olive bister	.25	.25
126	A48	1p greenish blk	.25	.25
127	A48	2p olive gray	.25	.25
		Nos. 117-127 (11)	2.75	2.75

Numerous part-perf. and imperf. varieties of Nos. 117-127 exist.

Used values for Nos. 117-127 are for favor-canceled stamps with oval cancels in violet. Postally used examples are valued at $1.75 each.

A49   A50

A50a

1901		Typeset		Perf. 12
128	A49	1c red	.25	.25
129	A50	1c ultra	.65	.65
130	A50	1c bister	.65	.65
130A	A50a	1c dull red	.65	.65
130B	A50a	1c ultra	4.50	4.50
		Nos. 128-130B (5)	6.70	6.70

Eight varieties of No. 128, four varieties of Nos. 129-130B.

A51   A52

Atanasio   Dr. José Félix
Girardot   Restrepo
A53   A54

1902		Litho.		Wove Paper
131	A51	1c brt rose	.25	.25
a.		Laid paper	.65	.65
b.		Imperf., pair	2.75	
132	A51	2c blue	.25	.25
a.		Transfer of 3c in stone of 2c	6.00	6.00
133	A51	3c green	.25	.25
a.		Imperf., pair	5.00	
134	A51	4c dull violet	.25	.25
135	A52	5c rose red	.25	.25
136	A53	10c rose lilac	.25	.25
a.		Small head	5.75	5.75
b.		10c rose	.25	.25
137	A53	20c gray green	.25	.25
138	A53	30c brt rose	.25	.25
139	A53	40c blue	.25	.25
140	A53	50c brn, *yel*	.25	.25
		Laid Paper		
141	A54	1p purple & blk	.80	.80
142	A54	2p rose & blk	.80	.80
143	A54	5p sl bl & blk	1.50	1.50
		Nos. 131-143 (13)	5.60	5.60

1903				Wove Paper
143A	A51	1c blue	.25	.25
144	A51	2c violet	.25	.25
a.		Imperf.	3.00	

A55   A56

A57

Designs: 1p, Francisco Antonio Zea. 2p, Custodio Garcia Rovira. 3p, La Pola (Policarpa Salavarrieta). 4p, J. M. Restrepo. 5p, José Fernández Madrid. 10p, Juan del Corral.

1903-04				
145	A55	4c yellow brn	.35	.30
146	A55	5c blue	.35	.30
147	A56	10c yellow	.35	.30
148	A56	20p purple	.35	.30
149	A56	30c brown	.90	.85
150	A56	40c green	.90	.85
151	A56	50c rose	.35	.30
152	A57	1p olive gray	.90	.85
153	A57	2p purple	.90	.85
154	A57	3p dark blue	.90	.85
155	A57	4p dull red	1.50	1.50
156	A57	5p red brown	4.50	2.10
157	A57	10p scarlet	9.25	5.25
		Nos. 145-157 (13)	21.50	14.60

Nos. 145-146, 151, 153-157 exist imperf. Value of pairs, $4 to $5.

Manizales Issue

Stamps of these designs are local private post issues.

OFFICIAL STAMPS Stamps of 1903-04 with overprint "OFICIAL" were never issued.

REGISTRATION STAMPS

R1

1896		Unwmk.	Litho.	Perf. 14
F1	R1	2½c rose	1.25	1.25
F2	R1	2½c dull blue	1.25	1.25

Córdoba
R2

R3

1899				Perf. 11
F3	R2	2½c dull blue	.25	.25
F4	R3	10c red lilac	.25	.25

R4

1902				Perf. 12
F5	R4	10c purple, *blue*	.30	.30
a.		Imperf.	—	

ACKNOWLEDGMENT OF RECEIPT STAMPS

AR1

1902-03		Unwmk.	Litho.	Perf. 12
H1	AR1	5c black, *rose*	1.10	1.10
H2	AR1	5c slate ('03)	.35	.35

LATE FEE STAMPS

Córdoba — LF1

1899		Unwmk.	Litho.	Perf. 11
I1	LF1	2½c dark green	.30	.30
a.		Imperf., pair	3.00	

LF2

1901		Typeset		Perf. 12
I2	LF2	2½c red violet	.80	.80
a.		2½c purple	.80	.80

LF3

1902				Litho.
I3	LF3	2½c violet	.25	.25

City of Medellin

Stamps of the designs shown were not issued by any governmental agency but by the Sociedad de Mejoras Publicas.

BOLIVAR

bə-'lē-ˌvär

Originally a State, now a Department of the Republic of Colombia. (See Antioquia.)

A1

1863-66		Unwmk.	Litho.	Imperf.
1	A1	10c green	1,200.	600.00
a.		Five stars below shield	2,500.	2,400.
2	A1	10c red ('66)	27.50	30.00
a.		Diagonal half used as 5c on cover		120.00
b.		Five stars below shield	80.00	72.50
3	A1	1p red	6.75	7.75

Fourteen varieties of each. Counterfeits of Nos. 1 and 1a exist.

Coat of Arms
A2   A3

A4

A5

1873
4	A2	5c blue	7.25	7.25
5	A3	10c violet	7.25	7.25
6	A4	20c yellow green	32.50	32.50
7	A5	80c vermilion	65.00	65.00
		Nos. 4-7 (4)	112.00	112.00

A6

A7

A8

1874-78
8	A6	5c blue	27.50	14.00
9	A7	5c blue ('78)	8.00	7.25
10	A8	10c violet ('77)	4.00	3.75
		Nos. 8-10 (3)	39.50	25.00

Bolívar — A9

Dated "1879"

1879 White Wove Paper Perf. 12½
11	A9	5c blue	.30	.30
a.		Imperf., pair	.90	
12	A9	10c violet	.25	.25
13	A9	20c red	.30	.30
a.		20c green (error)	11.00	11.00

Bluish Laid Paper
15	A9	5c blue	.30	.30
a.		Imperf., pair	2.25	
16	A9	10c violet	1.60	1.60
a.		Imperf., pair	4.50	
17	A9	20c red	.40	.40
a.		Imperf., pair	2.00	
		Nos. 11-17 (6)	3.15	3.15

Stamps of 80c and 1p on white wove paper and 1p on bluish laid paper were prepared but not placed in use.

Dated "1880"

1880 White Wove Paper Perf. 12½
19	A9	5c blue	.30	.30
a.		Imperf., pair	1.60	
20	A9	10c violet	.40	.40
a.		Imperf., pair	1.60	
21	A9	20c red	.40	.40
a.		20c green (error)	14.00	14.00
23	A9	80c green	2.50	2.50
24	A9	1p orange	2.75	2.75
a.		Imperf., pair	5.50	
		Nos. 19-24 (5)	6.35	6.35

Bluish Laid Paper
25	A9	5c blue	.30	.30
a.		Imperf., pair	1.40	
26	A9	10c violet	2.50	2.50
27	A9	20c red	.40	.40
a.		Imperf., pair	3.00	
28	A9	1p orange	450.00	
a.		Imperf.	*475.00*	

A11

A12

A13

A15

A16

Dated "1882"
White Wove Paper

1882 Perf. 12, 16x12
29	A11	5c blue	.35	.35
30	A12	10c lilac	.25	.25
31	A13	20c red	.35	.35
33	A15	80c green	.65	.65
34	A16	1p orange	.65	.65
		Nos. 29-34 (5)	2.25	2.25

Nos. 29, 30 and 34 are known imperforate. They are printer's waste and were not issued through post offices.

A17

1882 Engr. Perf. 12
35	A17	5p blue & rose red	.65	.65
a.		Imperf., pair	5.25	
b.		Perf. 16	8.00	6.75
c.		Perf. 14	6.75	6.75
36	A17	10p brown & blue	1.75	1.75
a.		Imperf., pair	8.75	
b.		Perf. 16	7.25	6.00
c.		Rouletted	8.75	8.75

Dated "1883"

1883 Litho. Perf. 12, 16x12
37	A11	5c blue	.25	.25
a.		Imperf., pair	1.00	
b.		Perf. 12	12.00	2.40
38	A12	10c lilac	.30	.30
39	A13	20c red	.30	.30
41	A15	80c green	.30	.30
42	A16	1p orange	1.60	1.60
a.		Perf. 16x12	2.25	2.25
		Nos. 37-42 (5)	2.75	2.75

1884 Dated "1884"
43	A11	5c blue	.30	.30
a.		Perf. 12	16.00	16.00
44	A12	10c lilac	.25	.25
45	A13	20c red	.25	.25
a.		Perf. 12	8.00	8.00
47	A15	80c green	.30	.35
a.		Perf. 12	4.00	4.00
48	A16	1p orange	.30	.30
		Nos. 43-48 (5)	1.40	1.45

1885 Dated "1885"
49	A11	5c blue	.25	.25
50	A12	10c lilac	.25	.25
51	A13	20c red	.25	.25
53	A15	80c green	.25	.25
54	A16	1p orange	.30	.30
		Nos. 49-54 (5)	1.30	1.30

The note after No. 34 will also apply to imperforate stamps of the 1884-85 issues.

A18

1891 Perf. 14
55	A18	1c black	.30	.30
56	A18	5c orange	.30	.30
a.		Imperf., pair	.90	
57	A18	10c carmine	.30	.30
58	A18	20c blue	.65	.65

59	A18	50c green	.95	.95
60	A18	1p purple	.95	.95
		Nos. 55-60 (6)	3.45	3.45

For overprint see Colombia No. 169.

Bolívar
A19

José Fernández Madrid
A20

Manuel Rodriguez Torices
A21

José María García de Toledo
A22

1903 Laid Paper Imperf.
62	A19	50c dk bl, *pink*	.65	.65
a.		Bluish paper	.65	.65
63	A19	50c sl grn, *pink*	.65	.65
a.		Rose paper	2.25	2.25
b.		Greenish blue paper	3.25	3.25
c.		Yellow paper	4.50	4.50
d.		Brown paper	4.50	4.50
e.		Salmon paper	8.00	8.00
64	A19	50c pur, *pink*	2.25	2.25
a.		White paper	4.50	4.50
b.		Brown paper	4.50	4.50
c.		Greenish blue paper	4.50	4.50
d.		Lilac paper	4.50	4.50
e.		Rose paper	4.00	4.00
f.		Yellow paper	4.50	4.50
g.		Salmon paper	6.50	6.50
h.		As "a," wove paper	9.75	9.75
65	A20	1p org, *sal*	.65	.65
a.		Yellow paper	5.00	5.00
b.		Greenish blue paper	16.00	16.00
66	A20	1p gray grn, *lil*	1.60	1.60
a.		Yellow paper	7.00	7.00
b.		Salmon paper	8.00	8.00
c.		Green paper	8.00	8.00
d.		White wove paper	12.00	
67	A21	5p car rose, *lil*	.65	.65
a.		Brown paper	1.25	1.25
b.		Yellow paper	1.25	1.25
c.		Greenish blue paper	5.00	5.00
d.		Bluish paper	6.50	6.50
e.		Salmon paper	8.00	8.00
f.		Rose paper	9.75	9.75
68	A22	10p dk bl, *bluish*	1.40	1.40
a.		Greenish blue paper	1.40	1.40
b.		Rose paper	8.00	8.00
c.		Salmon paper	8.00	8.00
d.		Yellow paper	8.00	8.00
e.		Brown paper	9.00	9.00
f.		Lilac paper	12.00	12.00
g.		White paper	9.75	9.75
69	A22	10p pur, *grnsh bl*	3.75	3.75
a.		Bluish paper	8.00	8.00
b.		Rose paper	7.25	7.25
c.		Yellow paper	8.00	8.00
d.		Brown paper	8.00	8.00
		Nos. 62-69 (8)	11.60	11.60

Sewing Machine Perf.
Laid Paper
70	A19	50c dk bl, *pink*	1.10	1.10
a.		Bluish paper	1.10	1.10
71	A19	50c sl grn, *pink*	2.25	2.25
72	A19	50c pur, *grnsh bl*	4.50	4.50
a.		White paper	4.50	4.50
b.		White wove paper	8.00	
73	A20	1p org, *sal*	2.25	2.25
74	A20	1p gray grn, *lil*	9.75	9.75
a.		Yellow paper	9.75	9.75
75	A21	5p car rose, *yel*	1.75	1.75
a.		Lilac paper	4.50	4.50
b.		Brown paper	4.50	4.50
c.		Bluish paper	6.00	6.00
d.		White wove paper	9.75	
76	A22	10p dk bl, *grnsh bl*	5.00	5.00
a.		Bluish paper	7.50	7.50
b.		Yellow paper	9.75	9.75
c.		As "b," wove paper	12.00	
77	A22	10p pur, *grnsh bl*	7.50	7.50
a.		Bluish paper	13.00	13.00
b.		Rose paper	8.50	8.50
c.		Yellow paper	13.00	13.00
		Nos. 70-77 (8)	34.10	34.10

José María del Castillo y Rada — A23

Manuel Anguiano — A24

Pantaleón C. Ribón — A25

1904 Sewing Machine Perf.
89	A23	5c black	.25	.25
90	A24	10c brown	.25	.25
91	A25	20c red	.30	.30
92	A25	20c red brown	.65	.65
		Nos. 89-92 (4)	1.45	1.45

Imperf., pairs
89a	A23	5c black	4.00	4.00
90a	A24	10c brown	3.00	3.00
91a	A25	20c red	7.25	7.25
92a	A25	20c red brown	7.25	7.25

A26

A27

A28

1904 Imperf.
93	A26	½c black	.65	.65
a.		Tête bêche pair	3.75	3.75
94	A27	1c blue	1.25	1.25
95	A28	2c purple	1.40	1.40
		Nos. 93-95 (3)	3.30	3.30

REGISTRATION STAMPS

Simón Bolívar — R1

White Wove Paper
Perf. 12½, 16x12
1879		**Unwmk.**		**Litho.**
F1	R1	40c brown	.75	.75

Bluish Laid Paper
F2	R1	40c brown	.75	.75
a.		Imperf., pair	3.50	

Dated "1880"
1880			**White Wove Paper**	
F3	R1	40c brown	.35	.35

Bluish Laid Paper
F4	R1	40c brown	.75	.75
a.		Imperf., pair	3.50	

Bolivar

Simón Bolívar — R2

Dated "1882" to "1885"
White Wove Paper

1882-85			**Perf. 16x12**	
F5	R2	40c brown (1882)	.35	.35
F6	R2	40c brown (1883)	.30	.30
F7	R2	40c brown (1884)	.30	.30
F8	R2	40c brown (1885)	.30	.30
		Nos. F5-F8 (4)	1.25	1.25

		Perf. 12		
F5a	R2	40c	19.00	
F6a	R2	40c	16.00	
F7a	R2	40c	16.00	
F8a	R2	40c	16.00	
		Nos. F5a-F8a (4)	67.00	

R3

1903		**Laid Paper**	**Imperf.**	
F9	R3	20c orange, *rose*	.65	.65
a.		Salmon paper	1.25	1.25
b.		Greenish blue paper	6.50	6.50
		Sewing Machine Perf.		
F10	R3	20c orange, *rose*	2.75	2.75
a.		Salmon paper	2.75	2.75
b.		Greenish blue paper	6.50	6.50

R4

1904		**Wove Paper**		
F11	R4	5c black	3.25	3.25

ACKNOWLEDGMENT OF RECEIPT STAMPS

AR1

1903	**Unwmk.**	**Litho.**	**Imperf.**	
		Laid Paper		
H1	AR1	20c org, *rose*	2.75	2.75
a.		Yellow paper	1.40	1.40
b.		Greenish blue paper	5.50	5.50
H2	AR1	20c dk bl, *yel*	2.25	2.25
a.		Brown paper	3.75	3.75
b.		Rose paper	2.75	2.75
c.		Salmon paper	7.50	7.50
d.		Greenish blue paper	7.50	7.50
		Sewing Machine Perf.		
H3	AR1	20c org, *grnsh bl*	6.75	6.75
a.		Yellow paper	7.75	7.75
H4	AR1	20c dk bl, *yel*	7.75	7.75
a.		Lilac paper	7.75	7.75
		Nos. H1-H4 (4)	19.50	19.50

AR2

1904		**Wove Paper**		
H5	AR2	2c red	1.25	1.25

LATE FEE STAMPS

LF1

1903	**Unwmk.**	**Litho.**	**Imperf.**	
		Laid Paper		
I1	LF1	20c car rose, *bluish*	.65	.65
I2	LF1	20c pur, *bluish*	.65	.65
a.		Rose paper	2.25	2.25
b.		Brown paper	2.25	2.25
c.		Lilac paper	2.25	2.25
d.		Yellow paper	7.00	7.00
		Sewing Machine Perf.		
I3	LF1	20c car rose, *bluish*	3.75	3.75
I4	LF1	20c pur, *bluish*	3.75	3.75
a.		Rose paper	6.50	6.50
b.		Lilac paper	6.50	6.50
c.		Yellow paper	12.00	12.00
		Nos. I1-I4 (4)	8.80	8.80

BOYACA

bō-yä-cä

Originally a State, now a Department of the Republic of Colombia. (See Antioqua.)

Diego Mendoza Pérez — A1

1902	**Unwmk.**	**Litho.**	**Perf. 13½**	
		Wove Paper		
1	A1	5c blue green	.80	.80
a.		Bluish paper	95.00	95.00
b.		Imperf., pair	16.00	16.00
		Laid Paper		
		Perf. 12		
2	A1	5c green	110.00	110.00

Coat of Arms
A2　　　A3

Gen. Próspero Pinzón — A4　　　A5

Monument of Battle of Boyacá — A6

President José Manuel Marroquin — A7

1903		**Litho.**	**Imperf.**	
4	A2	10c dark gray	.30	.30
5	A3	20c red brown	.35	.35
6	A5	1p red	3.25	3.25
a.		1p claret	3.75	3.75
8	A6	5p black, *rose*	1.25	1.25
a.		5p black, *buff*	12.00	12.00
9	A7	10p black, *buff*	1.25	1.25
a.		10p black, *rose*	12.00	12.00
b.		As "a," tête bêche pair	24.00	
		Nos. 4-9 (5)	6.40	6.40
		Perf. 12		
10	A2	10c dark gray	.35	.35
11	A3	20c red brown	.40	.40
12	A4	50c green	.35	.35
13	A4	50c dull blue	2.50	2.50
14	A5	1p red	.35	.35
a.		1p claret	3.00	3.00
16	A6	5p black, *rose*	11.00	11.00
a.		5p black, *buff*	9.50	9.50
17	A7	10p black, *buff*	1.10	1.10
a.		10p black, *rose*	11.00	11.00
b.		Tête bêche pair	12.00	12.00
		Nos. 10-17 (7)	16.05	16.05

Statue of Bolívar — A8

1904				
18	A8	10c orange	.25	.25
a.		Imperf., pair	3.75	3.75

CAUCA

Stamps of these designs were issued by a provincial post between 1879(?) and 1890.

Stamps of this design are believed to be of private origin and without official sanction.

Items inscribed "No hay estampillas" (No stamps available) and others inscribed "Manuel E. Jiménez" are considered by specialists to be receipt labels, not postage stamps.

CUNDINAMARCA

kün-di-nə-'mär-kə

Originally a State, now a Department of the Republic of Colombia.

(See Antioquia.)

Coat of Arms
A1　　　A2

1870	**Unwmk.**	**Litho.**	**Imperf.**	
1	A1	5c blue	5.25	5.25
2	A2	10c red	16.00	16.00

The counterfeits, or reprints, show traces of the cuts made to deface the dies.

A3　　　A4

A5　　　A6

1877-82				
3	A3	10c red ('82)	3.50	3.50
a.		Laid paper ('77)	4.50	4.50
4	A4	20c green ('82)	7.50	7.50
a.		Laid paper ('77)	12.00	12.00
7	A5	50c purple ('82)	8.25	8.25
8	A6	1p brown ('82)	12.00	12.00
		Nos. 3-8 (4)	31.25	31.25

A7　　　Redrawn

1884				
10	A7	5c blue	.80	.80
11	A7	5c blue (redrawn)	.80	.80
a.		Tête bêche pair	80.00	80.00

The redrawn stamp has no period after "COLOMBIA."

A8　　　A9

A10

A11

1883   **Typeset**

13	A8	10c black, *yellow*	14.00	14.00
14	A9	50c black, *rose*	14.00	14.00
15	A10	1p black, *brown*	37.50	37.50
16	A11	2r black, *green*	2,200.	

Typeset varieties exist: 4 of the 10c, 2 each of 50c and 1p.

Some experts doubt that No. 16 was issued. The variety without signature and watermarked "flowers" is believed to be a proof. Forgeries exist.

A12

1886   **Litho.**

17	A12	5c blue	.80	.80
18	A12	10c red	5.00	5.00
19	A12	10c red, *lilac*	2.75	2.75
20	A12	20c green	4.25	4.25
a.		20c yellow green	5.00	5.00
21	A12	50c purple	5.50	5.50
22	A12	1p orange brown	5.75	5.75
		Nos. 17-22 (6)	24.05	24.05

Nos. 17 to 22 have been reprinted. The colors are aniline and differ from those of the original stamps. The impression is coarse and blurred.

A13   A14

A15   A16

A17   A18

A19   A20

A21

1904   **Perf. 10½, 12**

23	A13	1c orange	.25	.25
24	A14	2c gray blue	.25	.25
25	A15	3c rose	.35	.35
26	A16	5c olive grn	.35	.35
27	A16	10c pale brn	.35	.35
28	A17	15c pink	.35	.35
29	A18	20c blue, *grn*	.35	.35
30	A18	20c blue	.60	.60
31	A19	40c blue	.60	.60
32	A19	40c blue, *buff*	21.00	21.00
33	A20	50c red vio	.60	.60
34	A21	1p gray grn	.60	.60
		Nos. 23-34 (12)	25.65	25.65

     Imperf

23a	A13	1c orange	.75	.75
24a	A14	2c blue	.75	.75
b.		2c slate	6.50	6.50
25a	A15	3c rose	.90	.90
26a	A15	5c olive green	1.60	1.60
27a	A16	10c pale brown	2.00	2.00
28a	A17	15c pink	.50	.50
29a	A18	20c blue, *green*	2.00	2.00
30a	A18	20c blue	2.00	2.00
31a	A19	40c blue	.70	.70
32a	A19	40c blue, *buff*	21.00	21.00
33a	A20	50c red violet	.70	.70
34a	A21	1p gray green	.70	.70
		Nos. 23a-34a (12)	33.60	33.60

REGISTRATION STAMPS

R1

1883   **Unwmk.**   **Imperf.**

F1	R1	black, *orange*	17.00	17.00

R2

1904   **Perf. 12**

F2	R2	10c bister	.85	.85
a.		Imperf.	3.75	3.75

INSURED LETTER STAMP

IL1

1883   **Imperf.**
Thin Paper with Vertical Mesh

G1	IL1	20c blk, *emerald grn*	80.00	120.00

Magdalena

Items inscribed "No hay estampillas" (No stamps available) are considered by specialists to be not postage stamps but receipt labels.

Panama

Issues of Panama as a state and later Department of Colombia are listed with the Republic of Panama issues (Nos. 1-30).

SANTANDER

sän-ˌtän-'de͟ə͟r

Originally a State, now a Department of the Republic of Colombia.
(See Antioquia.)

Coat of Arms
A1   A2

1884   **Unwmk.**   **Litho.**   **Imperf.**

1	A1	1c blue	.30	.30
a.		1c gray blue	.50	.50
2	A2	5c red	.50	.50
3	A2	10c bluish purple	1.90	1.90
a.		Tête bêche pair		
		Nos. 1-3 (3)	2.70	2.70

No. 2 exists unofficially perforated 14.

A3

1886   **Imperf.**

4	A3	1c blue	.90	.90
5	A3	5c red	.30	.30
6	A3	10c red violet	.50	.50
a.		10c deep violet	.50	.50
b.		Inscribed "CINCO CENTAVOS"	26.00	26.00
		Nos. 4-6 (3)	1.70	1.70

The numerals in the upper corners are omitted on No. 5, while on No. 6 there are no numerals in the side panels. No. 6 exists unofficially perforated 12.

A4

1887

7	A4	1c blue	.25	.25
a.		1c ultramarine	1.75	1.75
8	A4	5c red	1.75	1.75
9	A4	10c violet	5.50	5.50
		Nos. 7-9 (3)	7.50	7.50

A5   A6

A7

1889   **Perf. 11½ and 13½**

10	A5	1c blue	.35	.35
11	A6	5c red	1.25	1.25
12	A7	10c purple	.45	.45
a.		Imperf., pair	16.00	20.00
		Nos. 10-12 (3)	2.05	2.05

A8

1892   **Perf. 13½**

13	A8	5c red, *rose buff*	1.00	1.00

A9

1895-96

14	A9	5c brown	.70	.70
15	A9	5c yel grn ('96)	.70	.70

A10   A11

A12

1899   **Perf. 10**

16	A10	1c black, *green*	.35	.35
17	A11	5c black, *pink*	.35	.35

      Perf. 13½

18	A12	10c blue	.70	.70
a.		Perf. 12	1.00	1.00
		Nos. 16-18 (3)	1.40	1.40

A13

1903   **Imperf.**

19	A13	50c red	.60	.60
a.		50c rose	.60	.60
b.		"SANTENDER"	2.50	2.50
c.		"Corrcos"	2.50	2.50
d.		"Corceos"	2.50	2.50
e.		Tête bêche pair	4.75	4.75
f.		Pair, one without overprint	2.75	2.75

The overprint "Correos de Departmento Bucaramanga" on the 50c red revenue stamp has been proved to be a cancellation.

A14   A15

Arms   Locomotive
A16   A17

A18   A19

A20

1904   **Imperf.**

22	A14	5c dark green	.25	.25
a.		5c yellow green	.40	.40
24	A15	10c rose	.25	.25
25	A16	20c brown violet	.25	.25
26	A17	50c yellow	.25	.25
27	A18	1p black	.25	.25
28	A19	5p dark blue	.35	.35
29	A20	10p carmine	.40	.40
		Nos. 22-29 (7)	2.00	2.00

1905

30	A14	5c pale blue	.45	.45
31	A15	10c red brown	.45	.45
32	A16	20c yellow green	.45	.45
33	A17	50c red violet	.60	.60
34	A18	1p dark blue	.60	.60
35	A19	5p pink	.60	.60
36	A20	10p red	1.60	1.60
		Nos. 30-36 (7)	4.75	4.75

Provisional.
Correos de Santander.
Medio centavo
A21

1907			Imperf.	
37	A21	½c on 50c rose	.80	1.60

City of Cucuta

Stamps of these and similar designs on white and yellow paper, with and without surcharges of ½c, 1c or 2c, are believed to have been produced without government authorization.

TOLIMA

tə-lē-mə

Originally a State, now a Department of the Republic of Colombia. (See Antioquia.)

A1

1870	Unwmk.	Typeset	Imperf.	
	White Wove Paper			
1	A1	5c black	62.50	62.50
2	A1	10c black	75.00	75.00
a.	Vert. se-tenant pair		1,500.	1,500.

Printed from two settings. Setting I, ten types of 5c. Setting II, six types of 5c and four types of 10c.

	Blue Laid Batonné Paper			
3	A1	5c black		950.00
	Buff Laid Batonné Paper			
4	A1	5c black	150.00	100.00
	Blue Wove Paper			
5	A1	5c black	70.00	45.00
	Blue Vertically Laid Paper			
6	A1	5c black	110.00	70.00
a.	Paper with ruled blue vertical lines			
	Blue Horizontally Laid Paper			
7	A1	5c black	100.00	75.00
	Blue Quadrille Paper			
8	A1	5c black	150.00	80.00

Ten varieties each of Nos. 3-5 and 7; 20 varieties each of Nos. 6 and 8.

Official imitations were made in 1886 from new settings of the type. There are only 2 varieties of each value. They are printed on blue and white paper, wove, batonné, laid, etc.

A2　　　　　　A3

A4　　　　　　A5

Yellowish White Wove Paper

1871		Litho.	Imperf.	
9	A2	5c deep brown	2.25	2.25
a.	5c red brown		2.25	2.25
b.	Value reads "CINGO"		40.00	40.00

10	A3	10c blue	6.25	6.25
11	A4	50c green	8.00	8.00
12	A5	1p carmine	13.00	13.00
	Nos. 9-12 (4)		29.50	29.50

The 5p stamps, type A2, are bogus varieties made from an altered die of the 5c.

The 10c, 50c and 1 peso stamps have been reprinted on bluish white wove paper. They are from new plates and most copies show traces of fine lines with which the dies had been defaced. Reprints of the 5c have a large cross at the top. The 10c on laid batonné paper is known only as a reprint.

A6　　　　　　A7

A8　　　　　　A9

1879				
	Grayish or White Wove Paper			
14	A6	5c yellow brown	.45	.45
a.	5c purple brown		.45	.45
15	A7	10c blue	.50	.50
16	A8	50c green, *bluish*	.50	.50
a.	White paper		1.60	1.60
17	A9	1p vermilion	2.25	2.25
a.	1p carmine rose		9.00	9.00
	Nos. 14-17 (4)		3.70	3.70

A10

1883			Imperf.	
18	A6	5c orange	.45	.45
19	A7	10c vermilion	.95	.95
20	A10	20c violet	1.50	1.50
	Nos. 18-20 (3)		2.90	2.90

Coat of Arms — A12

1884			Imperf.	
23	A12	1c gray	.25	.25
24	A12	2c rose lilac	.25	.25
a.	2c slate		.25	.25
25	A12	2 ½c dull orange	.25	.25
26	A12	5c brown	.25	.25
27	A12	10c blue	.35	.35
a.	10c slate		.25	.25
28	A12	20c lemon	.35	.35
a.	Laid paper		5.00	5.00
29	A12	25c black	.30	.30
30	A12	50c green	.30	.30
31	A12	1p vermilion	.40	.40
32	A12	2p violet	.60	.60
a.	Value omitted		30.00	30.00
33	A12	5p yellow	.40	.40
34	A12	10p lilac rose	1.10	1.10
a.	Laid paper		30.00	30.00
b.	10p gray		175.00	
	Nos. 23-34 (12)		4.80	4.80

A13　　　　　　A14

Condor with Long Wings Touching Flagstaffs
A15　　　　　　A16

1886		Litho.	Perf. 10½, 11	
	White Paper			
36	A13	5c brown	1.40	1.40
a.	5c yellow brown		1.40	1.40
b.	Imperf., pair		17.50	
37	A14	10c blue	3.75	3.75
a.	Imperf., pair		17.50	
38	A15	50c green	3.25	3.25
a.	Imperf., pair		17.50	
39	A16	1p vermilion	2.75	2.75
a.	Imperf., pair		26.00	
	Nos. 36-39 (4)		11.15	11.15

No. 38 has been reprinted in pale gray green, perforated 10½, and No. 39 in bright vermilion, perforated 11½. The impressions show many signs of wear.

Lilac Tinted Paper

36c	A13	5c orange brown	12.50	12.50
37b	A14	10c blue	12.50	12.50
38b	A15	50c green	9.25	9.25
39b	A16	1p vermilion	8.25	8.25
	Nos. 36c-39b (4)		42.50	42.50

A17　　　　　　A18

Items similar to A15 and A16 but with condor with long wings and upper flagstaffs omitted are forgeries.

Condor with Short Wings
A19　　　　　　A20

1886		**White Paper**	Perf. 12	
44	A19	1c gray	6.25	6.25
45	A17	2c rose lilac	6.50	6.50
46	A18	2 ½c dull org	19.00	19.00
47	A19	5c brown	8.50	8.00
48	A20	10c blue	8.00	8.00
49	A20	20c lemon	6.50	6.50
a.	Tête bêche pair		275.00	275.00
50	A20	25c black	6.25	6.25
51	A20	50c green	3.75	3.75
52	A20	1p vermilion	5.00	4.25
53	A20	2p violet	7.25	7.25
b.	Tête bêche pair		190.00	190.00
54	A20	5p orange	13.00	13.00
55	A20	10p lilac rose	7.50	7.50
	Nos. 44-55 (12)		97.50	96.25

Imperf., Pairs

44a	A19	1c		17.00
47a	A19	5c		29.00
48a	A20	10c		29.00
52a	A20	1p		21.00
53a	A20	2p		26.00
54a	A20	5p		40.00
55a	A20	10p		17.00

A23

1888			Perf. 10½	
62	A23	5c red	.25	.25
63	A23	10c green	.30	.30
64	A23	50c blue	.75	.75
65	A23	1p red brown	1.90	1.90
	Nos. 62-65 (4)		3.20	3.20

For overprint see Colombia No. L14.

1895			Perf. 12, 13½	
66	A23	1c blue, *rose*	.25	.25
67	A23	2c grn, *lt grn*	.25	.25
68	A23	5c red	.25	.25
69	A23	10c green	.50	.50
70	A23	20c blue, *yellow*	.30	.30
71	A23	1p brown	2.10	2.10
	Nos. 66-71 (6)		3.65	3.65

Imperf., Pairs

62a	A23	5c		8.75
63a	A23	10c		12.00
64a	A23	50c	14.50	14.50
65a	A23	1p		21.00
66a	A23	1c		21.00
67a	A23	2c		21.00
70a	A23	20c		24.00

"No Hay Estampillas"
Items inscribed "No hay estampillas" (No stamps available) are considered by specialists to be not postage stamps but receipt labels.

"Honda Issue"
This item seems to be of private origin.

A24　　　　　　A25

A26　　　　　　A27

A28　　　　　　A29

A30　　　　　　A31

Sewing Machine or Regular Perf. 12

1903-04			Litho.	
79	A24	4c black, *green*	.25	.25
80	A25	10c dull blue	.25	.25
81	A26	20c orange	.50	.50
82	A27	50c black, *rose*	.25	.25
a.	50c black, *buff*		.25	.25
84	A28	1p brown	.25	.25
85	A29	2p gray	.25	.25
86	A30	5p red	.25	.25
a.	Tête bêche pair		8.00	12.00

87	A31	10p black, *blue*	.25	.25
a.		10p black, *light green*	.25	.25
b.		10p black, *grn, glazed*	3.75	3.75
		Nos. 79-87 (8)	2.25	2.25

Imperf

79a	A24	4c black, *green*	.25	.25
80a	A25	10c dull blue	.25	.25
81a	A26	20c orange	1.25	1.25
82b	A27	50c black, *rose*	1.75	1.75
c.		50c black, *buff*	1.75	1.75
84a	A28	1p brown	.25	.25
85a	A29	2p gray	.25	.25
86b	A30	5p red	.25	.25
c.		Tête bêche pair	12.00	16.00
87c	A31	10p black, *blue*	2.50	2.50
d.		Tête bêche pair		
e.		10p black, *light green*	3.75	3.75
f.		10p black, *green, glazed*	19.00	19.00
		Nos. 79a-87c (8)	6.75	6.75

COMORO ISLANDS

ˈkä-mə-ˌrō ˈī-ləndz

LOCATION — In Mozambique Channel between Madagascar and Mozambique
GOVT. — Republic
AREA — 838 sq. mi.
POP. — 562,723 (1999 est.)
CAPITAL — Moroni

The Comoro Archipelago consists of the islands of Mayotte, Anjouan, Grand Comoro (Grande Comore) and Moheli, which issued their own stamps as French protectorates or colonies from 1887-1914. The archipelago was attached to Madagascar from 1914 to 1946, when it became a separate French territory. In July 1975, Anjouan, Grand Comoro and Moheli united to declare independence as the State of Comoro. Mayotte remained French.

100 Centimes = 1 Franc

> Catalogue values for all unused stamps in this country are for Never Hinged items.

Anjouan Bay — A2

Comoro Woman Grinding Grain — A3

Moroni Mosque on Grand Comoro A4

1950		Unwmk.	Engr.	Perf. 13	
30	A2	10c blue		.30	.50
31	A2	50c green		.30	.50
32	A2	1fr dk ol brn		.40	.50
33	A3	2fr brt grn		.75	.50
34	A3	5fr purple		1.10	.75
35	A3	6fr vio brn		1.25	1.10
36	A4	7fr red		1.10	.75
37	A4	10fr dk grn		1.25	1.00
38	A4	11fr dp ultra		1.50	1.25
		Nos. 30-38 (9)		7.95	6.85

Imperforates

Most Comoro Islands stamps exist imperforate in issued and trial colors, and also in small presentation sheets in issued colors.

Common Design Types pictured following the introduction.

Military Medal Issue
Common Design Type

1952		Engraved and Typographed		
39	CD101	15fr multi	50.00	40.00

Mosque of Ouani, Anjouan — A5

Coelacanth A6

1952-54			Engr.	
40	A5	15fr dark brown	2.00	1.75
41	A5	20fr red brown	4.00	3.50
42	A6	40fr aqua & indigo ('54)	25.00	18.00
		Nos. 40-42 (3)	31.00	23.25

FIDES Issue
Common Design Type

Design: 9fr, Women at water pump.

1956		Unwmk.	Perf. 13x12½	
43	CD103	9fr dp vio	2.25	1.60

Human Rights Issue
Common Design Type

1958		Engr.	Perf. 13	
44	CD105	20fr ol grn & dk bl	11.00	11.00

Flower Issue
Common Design Type

1959		Photo.	Perf. 12½x12	
45	CD104	10fr Colvillea	5.50	4.50

View of Dzaoudzi and Radio Symbol A8

Comoro radio station: 25fr, Radio tower and radio waves over Islands.

1960, Dec. 23		Engr.	Perf. 13	
46	A8	20fr maroon, vio bl & grn	1.75	1.25
47	A8	25fr ultra, brn & grn	2.00	1.00

Harpa Conoidalis — A9

Sea Shells: 50c, Cypraecassis rufa. 2fr, Murex ramosus. 5fr, Turbo marmoratus. 20fr, Pterocera scorpio. 25fr, Charonia tritonis.

1962, Jan. 13			Photo.	

Shells in Natural Colors

48	A9	50c lilac & brn	1.25	1.25
49	A9	1fr yel & red	1.25	1.25
50	A9	2fr pale grn & pink	2.75	2.75
51	A9	5fr yel & grn	3.25	3.25

52	A9	20fr salmon & brn	11.50	11.50
53	A9	25fr bister & pink	16.00	16.00
		Nos. 48-53,C5-C6 (8)	81.00	71.00

Wheat Emblem and Globe A10

1963, Mar. 21		Engr.	Perf. 13	
54	A10	20fr choc & dk grn	5.50	4.50

FAO "Freedom from Hunger" campaign.

Red Cross Centenary Issue
Common Design Type

1963, Sept. 2		Unwmk.	Perf. 13	
55	CD113	50fr emer, gray & car	9.50	7.00

Human Rights Issue
Common Design Type

1963, Dec. 10			Engr.	
56	CD117	15fr dk red & yel grn	9.50	7.50

Tobacco Pouch — A13

Designs: 4fr, Censer. 10fr, Carved lamp.

1963, Dec. 27			Perf. 13	

Size: 22x36mm

57	A13	3fr multi	.80	.80
58	A13	4fr org, dp cl & sl grn	1.10	1.10
59	A13	10fr org brn, dk red brn & grn	2.00	2.00
		Nos. 57-59,C8-C9 (5)	18.90	12.65

Philatec Issue
Common Design Type

1964, Mar. 31				
60	CD118	50fr dk bl, red & grn	4.50	4.00

Grand Comoro Canoe — A14

Design: 30fr, Boutre felucca.

Size: 22x37mm

1964, Aug. 7		Photo.	Perf. 13x12½	
61	A14	15fr multi	3.00	2.50
62	A14	30fr lt grn & multi	5.50	4.50
		Nos. 61-62,C10-C11 (4)	20.00	11.25

Spiny Lobster — A15

Designs: 12fr, Hammerhead shark, horiz. 20fr, Turtle, horiz. 25fr, Merou fish.

1965, Dec. 20		Engr.	Perf. 13	
63	A15	1fr grn, lil & ocher	1.25	.75
64	A15	12fr org red, slate & gray	2.75	1.60
65	A15	20fr org, red & bl grn	4.00	1.75
66	A15	25fr bl grn, dk brn & red	7.00	3.25
		Nos. 63-66 (4)	15.00	7.35

Hotel Itsandra, Moroni A16

Design: 15fr, Lake Salé, Grand Comoro.

1966, Dec. 19		Photo.	Perf. 12½x13	
67	A16	15fr multi	1.10	.70
68	A16	25fr multi	1.25	.70
		Nos. 67-68,C18-C19 (4)	16.35	9.65

Comoro Sunbird A17

Birds: 10fr, Malachite kingfisher. 15fr, Rothschild's fody. 30fr, Cuckoo-roller.

1967, June 20		Photo.	Perf. 12½x13	

Size: 36x23mm

69	A17	2fr ocher & multi	2.75	1.50
70	A17	10fr lil & multi	4.50	2.00
71	A17	15fr yel grn & multi	6.50	3.00
72	A17	30fr pink & multi	13.50	6.50
		Nos. 69-72,C20-C21 (6)	50.75	27.50

For surcharge see No. 133.

WHO Anniversary Issue
Common Design Type

1968, May 4		Engr.	Perf. 13	
73	CD126	40fr grn, vio & dp car	2.75	2.00

Surgeonfish A19

Design: 25fr, Imperial angelfish.

1968, Aug. 1		Engr.	Perf. 13	

Size: 36x22mm

74	A19	20fr vio bl, yel & red brn	3.50	3.50
75	A19	25fr Prus bl, dk bl & org	4.25	4.25
		Nos. 74-75,C23-C24 (4)	25.75	17.00

For surcharge & overprint see Nos. C52, C74.

Human Rights Year Issue
Common Design Type

1968, Aug. 10		Engr.	Perf. 13	
76	CD127	60fr brn, grn & org	3.50	3.50

Msoila Prayer Rug and Praying Man — A20

Each stamp shows a different prayer position.

1969, Feb. 27		Engr.	Perf. 13	
77	A20	20fr bl grn, rose red & pur	1.40	.95
78	A20	30fr pur, rose red & bl grn	1.60	1.40
79	A20	45fr rose red, pur & bl grn	3.00	1.75
		Nos. 77-79 (3)	6.00	4.10

Vanilla Flower A21

Design: 15fr, Flower of ylang-ylang tree. 25fr, Poinsettia (country name at upper left).

1969-70   Photo.   *Perf. 12½x13*
Size: 36x23mm

80	A21	10fr multi	1.25	.60
81	A21	15fr multi	1.75	.80
82	A21	25fr multi ('70)	4.25	1.50
		Nos. 80-82,C26-C28 (6)	28.50	16.90

Issued: Nos. 80-81, 3/20. No. 82, 3/5.

ILO Issue
Common Design Type

1969, Nov. 24   Engr.   *Perf. 13*

83	CD131	5fr org, emerald & gray	1.25	.75

UPU Headquarters Issue
Common Design Type

1970, May 20   Engr.   *Perf. 13*

84	CD133	65fr pur, bl grn & red brn	5.50	2.00

Chiromani Costume, Anjouan — A22

25fr, Bouiboui costume, Grand Comoro.

1970, Oct. 30   Photo.   *Perf. 12½x13*

85	A22	20fr grn, yel & red	1.60	.80
86	A22	25fr brn, yel & dk bl	1.90	1.10

Friday Mosque — A23

1970, Dec. 18   Engr.   *Perf. 13*

87	A23	5fr rose car, grn & grnsh bl	.75	.75
88	A23	10fr dp lil, grn & vio	1.00	.75
89	A23	40fr cop red, grn & dp brn	1.75	1.40
		Nos. 87-89 (3)	3.50	2.90

Great White Egret — A24

Birds: 10fr, Comoro pigeon. 15fr, Green-backed heron. 25fr, Comoro blue pigeon. 35fr, Humbolt's flycatcher. 40fr, Allen's gallinule.

1971, Mar. 12   Photo.   *Perf. 12½x13*

90	A24	5fr multi	1.50	.80
91	A24	10fr yel & multi	2.00	.80
92	A24	15fr bl & multi	3.25	1.75
93	A24	25fr org & multi	4.75	2.00
94	A24	35fr yel grn & multi	6.50	2.50
95	A24	40fr gray & multi	8.00	3.25
		Nos. 90-95 (6)	26.00	11.10

For overprint see No. 145.

Pyrostegia Venusta — A25

Flowers: 3fr, Dogbane, horiz. 20fr, Frangipani.
Size: 22x36mm, 36x22mm

1971, July 19   Photo.   *Perf. 13*

96	A25	1fr ver & grn	.95	.85
97	A25	3fr yel, grn & red	1.40	1.00
98	A25	20fr ver & grn	3.50	2.50
		Nos. 96-98,C37-C38 (5)	17.35	11.50

For surcharges see Nos. 131-132, C75, C83.

Lithograph Cone A26

Sea Shells: 10fr, Pacific lettered cone. 20fr, Aulicus cone. 35fr, Polita nerita. 60fr, Snakehead cowrie.

1971, Oct. 4

99	A26	5fr lt ultra & multi	1.25	1.00
100	A26	10fr multi	1.75	1.40
101	A26	20fr vio & multi	3.75	2.25
102	A26	35fr lt bl & multi	7.25	2.75
103	A26	60fr lt vio & multi	9.50	3.50
		Nos. 99-103 (5)	23.50	10.90

For surcharge see No. 150.

De Gaulle Issue
Common Design Type

Designs: 20fr, Gen. de Gaulle, 1940. 35fr, Pres. de Gaulle, 1970.

1971, Nov. 9   Engr.   *Perf. 13*

104	CD134	20fr dk car & blk	4.00	2.50
105	CD134	35fr dk car & blk	5.00	3.25

Louis Pasteur, Slides, Microscope A27

1972, Aug. 2

106	A27	65fr indigo, org, & ol brn	5.50	4.75

Sesquicentennial of the birth of Louis Pasteur (1822-1895), chemist.

Type of Air Post Issue 1971

Designs: 10fr, View of Goulaivoini. 20fr, Bay, Mitsamiouli. 35fr, Gate and fountain, Foumbouni. 50fr, View of Moroni.

1973, June 28   Photo.   *Perf. 13*

107	AP10	10fr bl & multi	1.00	.30
108	AP10	20fr grn & multi	1.50	.75
109	AP10	35fr bl & multi	2.50	1.25
110	AP10	50fr bl & multi	2.75	1.75
		Nos. 107-110,C53 (5)	17.25	10.55

For overprint see No. 143.

Bank of Madagascar and Comoros — A28

Buildings in Moroni: 15fr, Post and Telecommunications Administration. 20fr, Prefecture.

1973, July 10   Photo.   *Perf. 13x12½*

111	A28	5fr multi	.65	.55
112	A28	15fr multi	.90	.80
113	A28	20fr multi	1.25	1.00
		Nos. 111-113 (3)	2.80	2.35

For surcharge see No. 134.

Salimata Hamissi Mosque A29

20fr, Zaouiyat Chaduli Mosque, vert.

Perf. 12½x13, 13x12½

1973, Oct. 20   Photo.

114	A29	20fr multi	1.25	.95
115	A29	35fr multi	2.10	1.25

For surcharges see Nos. 135, 138.

Cheikh Mausoleum A30

Design: 50fr, Mausoleum of President Said Mohamed Cheikh (different view).

1974, Mar. 16   Engr.   *Perf. 13*

116	A30	35fr grn, ol brn & blk	1.60	1.10
117	A30	50fr grn, ol brn & blk	2.50	1.25

For surcharge see No. 140.

Koran Stand, Anjouan A31

Designs: 15fr, Carved combs, vert. 20fr, 3-legged table, vert. 75fr, Sugar press.

1974, May 10   Photo.   *Perf. 12½x13*

118	A31	15fr emer & multi	1.25	.60
119	A31	20fr grn & multi	1.40	.65
120	A31	35fr multi	2.25	1.10
121	A31	75fr multi	4.50	2.00
		Nos. 118-121 (4)	9.40	4.35

For overprints and surcharges see Nos. 137, 141, 149.

UPU Emblem, Symbolic Postmark A32

1974, Oct. 9   Engr.   *Perf. 13x12½*

122	A32	30fr multi	2.00	1.75

Centenary of Universal Postal Union.
For surcharge see No. 155.

Bracelet A33

1975, Feb. 28   Engr.   *Perf. 13*

123	A33	20fr shown	1.10	.95
124	A33	35fr Diadem	1.90	1.25
125	A33	120fr Saber	5.00	3.25
126	A33	135fr Dagger	7.00	4.00
		Nos. 123-126 (4)	15.00	9.45

For surcharges see Nos. 136, 142, 151, 154.

Mohani Village, Moheli — A34

50fr, Djoezi Village, Moheli. 55fr, Chirazi tombs.

1975, May 26   Photo.   *Perf. 13*

127	A34	30fr vio bl & multi	2.00	1.00
128	A34	50fr Prus bl & multi	3.25	1.50
129	A34	55fr grn & multi	3.50	2.50
		Nos. 127-129 (3)	8.75	5.00

For overprints and surcharge see Nos. 139, 146, 148.

Scuba Diver Photographing Coelacanth — A35

1975, June 27   Engr.   *Perf. 13*

130	A35	50fr multi	8.25	5.75

1975 coelacanth expedition.
For overprint see No. 147.

STATE OF COMORO

In 1978 the islands' name became the Federal and Islamic Republic of the Comoros.

Issues of 1971-75 Srchd. and Ovptd. with Bars and: "ETAT COMORIEN" in Black, Silver or Red

Tambourine Player — A36

No. 153, Women dancers & tambourine players.

Printing & Perforations as Before, Photogravure (A36)

1975   *Perf. 13 (A36)*

131	A25	5fr on 1fr	.40	.25
132	A25	5fr on 3fr	.40	.25
133	A17	10fr on 2fr	1.25	.50
134	A28	15fr on 20fr (R)	.80	.25
135	A29	15fr on 20fr (S)	.80	.25
136	A33	15fr on 20fr	.80	.25
137	A31	20fr	1.00	.25
138	A29	25fr on 35fr	1.00	.25
139	A34	30fr	1.00	.60
140	A30	30fr on 35fr	1.00	.30
141	A31	30fr on 35fr	1.00	.30
142	A33	30fr on 35fr	1.00	.60
143	AP10	35fr	1.25	.75
144	SP2	35fr on 35fr + 10fr	1.25	.75
145	A24	40fr	2.75	1.50
146	A34	50fr	1.90	1.90
147	A35	50fr	2.50	1.25
148	A34	50fr on 55fr (S)	1.90	.95
149	A31	75fr	2.00	.55
150	A26	75fr on 60fr (S)	4.00	2.00
151	A33	100fr on 120fr	2.50	.90
152	A36	100fr bl & multi	3.25	1.75
153	A36	100fr on 150fr (S)	2.50	.90
154	A26	200fr on 135fr	6.00	2.40
155	A32	500fr on 30fr	12.00	6.75
		Nos. 131-155 (25)	54.25	26.40

Nos. 152-153 exist without overprint or surcharge. Value, each $90.
No. 155 exists with red surcharge. Value $12.

Litho. & Embossed "Gold Foil" Stamps

These stamps generally are of a different design format than the rest of the issue. Since there is a commemorative inscription tieing them to the issue a separate illustration is not being shown.

Apollo-Soyuz — A37

Spacecraft and astronauts: 10fr, Soyuz lift-off, Alexei A. Leonov and Valeri N. Kubasov, vert. 30fr, Apollo lift-off, Thomas P. Stafford, Vance D. Brand, Donald K. Slayton, vert. 50fr, Meeting in space. 100fr, Chairman Brezhnev, President Ford talking with astronauts and cosmonauts. 200fr, Spacecraft preparing to dock. 400f, Return to Earth. 500fr, Spacecraft, mission emblems. 1500fr, Apollo-Soyuz crew. No. 164, Preparing to dock, diff.

1975, Dec. 15   Litho.   Perf. 13½

156	A37	10fr multicolored	.40	.25
157	A37	30fr multicolored	.50	.25
158	A37	50fr multicolored	.70	.55
159	A37	100fr multicolored	1.00	.60
160	A37	200fr multicolored	2.00	1.25
161	A37	400fr multicolored	4.00	2.50
		Nos. 156-161 (6)	8.60	5.40

Litho. & Embossed
Size: 45x45mm

162	A37	1500fr gold & multi	17.50	—

Souvenir Sheets
Litho.

163	A37	500fr multicolored	4.50	1.75

Litho. & Embossed

164	A37	1500fr gold & multi	17.50	—

Nos. 159-164 are airmail. No. 163 contains one 64x44mm stamp. No. 164 contains one 45x45mm stamp.

No. 162 exists in a souvenir sheet of 1. Value $50.

For overprints see Nos. 477-478.

A38

American Revolution, Bicent. — A39

Designs: 15fr, Lewis and Clark, Blackfoot Indian. 25fr, John C. Fremont, Kit Carson, Indian dancer. 35fr, Daniel Boone, Buffalo Bill Cody, wagon train. 40fr, Richard E. Egan, Johnny Frey, Pony Express. 75fr, Henry Wells, William G. Fargo, stagecoach. 400fr, Frontiersman, Indian. 500fr, Leland Stanford, Thomas C. Dunant, transcontinental railroad. 1000fr, George Washington, winter at Valley Forge. 1500fr, John Paul Jones, ship.

1976, Jan. 15   Litho.

165	A38	15fr multicolored	.25	.25
166	A38	25fr multicolored	.45	.25
167	A38	35fr multicolored	.75	.35
168	A38	40fr multicolored	.85	.45
169	A38	75fr multicolored	1.50	.60
170	A38	500fr multicolored	6.25	2.50
		Nos. 165-170 (6)	10.05	4.40

Litho. & Embossed

171	A39	1000fr gold & multi	13.50	—

Souvenir Sheets
Litho.

172	A38	400fr multicolored	5.50	1.75

Litho. & Embossed

173	A39	1500fr gold & multi	16.50	—

Nos. 170-173 are airmail. See Nos. 230, 232 and note after No. 479.

No. 171 exists in a souvenir sheet of 1. Value $55.

1976 Winter Olympics, Innsbruck — A40

5fr, Women's figure skating. 30fr, Slalom skiing. 35fr, Speed skating. 50fr, Downhill skiing. 200fr, Ski jumping. 400fr, Cross country skiing. No. 180, 1000fr, Downhill skier, hockey. 500fr, Hockey. No. 182, 1000fr, Olympic Rings.

1976, Mar. 30   Litho.

174	A40	5fr multicolored	.25	.25
175	A40	30fr multicolored	.25	.25
176	A40	35fr multicolored	.50	.25
177	A40	50fr multicolored	.65	.50
178	A40	200fr multicolored	2.10	1.00
179	A40	400fr multicolored	4.50	1.25
		Nos. 174-179 (6)	8.25	3.50

Litho. & Embossed
Size: 56x35mm

180	A40	1000fr multicolored	13.00	—

Souvenir Sheets
Litho.

181	A40	500fr multicolored	8.00	1.75

Litho. & Embossed

182	A40	1000fr multicolored	11.00	—

Nos. 178-182 are airmail. Nos. 181-182 contain one 58x35mm stamp. For overprint see No. 471.

No. 162 exists in a souvenir sheet of 1. Value $45.

1976 Summer Olympics, Montreal — A41

20fr, Runner, Athens, 1896. 25fr, Sprints. 40fr, High jump, Paris, 1900. 75fr, High jump. 100fr, Women stretching, St. Louis, 1904. 500fr, Uneven parallel bars. 400fr, Olympic Stadium, Montreal.

1976, Mar. 30   Litho.

183	A41	20fr multicolored	.25	.25
184	A41	25fr multicolored	.35	.25
185	A41	40fr multicolored	.50	.25
186	A41	75fr multicolored	1.00	.45
187	A41	100fr multicolored	1.10	.50
188	A41	500fr multicolored	6.00	1.75
		Nos. 183-188 (6)	9.20	3.45

Souvenir Sheet

189	A41	400fr multicolored	4.50	1.25

Nos. 187-189 are airmail.
For overprint see No. 476.

Fairy Tales — A42

15fr, Hansel & Gretel. 30fr, Alice in Wonderland. 35fr, Pinocchio. 40fr, Good Little Henry. 50fr, Peter and the Wolf. 400fr, Thousand and One Nights.

1976, June 28

190	A42	15fr multicolored	.25	.25
191	A42	30fr multicolored	.50	.25
192	A42	35fr multicolored	.65	.25
193	A42	40fr multicolored	.65	.25
194	A42	50fr multicolored	1.00	.25
195	A42	400fr multicolored	6.50	2.00
		Nos. 190-195 (6)	9.55	3.25

No. 195 is airmail. Nos. 190-191, 193, 195 are vert.

Invention of Telephone, Cent. — A43

Designs: 10fr, A. G. Bell, 1st telephone. 25fr, Charles Bourseul, Paris-London phone service, 1891. 75fr, Philipp Reis, telephone operators. 100fr, Earth to Moon to Earth communications. 200fr, Satellite. 400fr, Ship-to-Satellite communications. No. 201, Satellite in orbit, antenna. No. 203, Global communications.

1976, July 1

196	A43	10fr multicolored	.25	.25
197	A43	25fr multicolored	.35	.25
198	A43	75fr multicolored	1.00	.30
199	A43	100fr multicolored	1.40	.50
200	A43	200fr multicolored	2.25	.90
201	A43	500fr multicolored	5.50	1.75
		Nos. 196-201 (6)	10.75	3.95

Souvenir Sheets

202	A43	400fr multicolored	7.00	1.75
203	A43	500fr multicolored	7.00	1.75

Nos. 199-203 are airmail. Nos. 202-203 contain a 73x44mm stamp. For overprint see No. 472.

Comoro Flag, Map and Government Buildings — A44

1976, Nov. 18   Litho.   Perf. 13½

204	A44	30fr multi	.75	.30
205	A44	50fr multi	1.50	.30

1st anniversary of independence.
For overprints and surcharges see Nos. 353-372.

Viking Probe to Mars — A45

Designs: 5fr, Nicolaus Copernicus, rocket launch. 10fr, Albert Einstein, Carl Sagan, Thomas Young, horiz. 25fr, Viking probe orbiting Mars. 35fr, Discovery of America by Vikings, horiz. 100fr, Flag, Viking landing on Mars. 500fr, Viking emblem, surface of Mars, horiz. 400fr, Viking probe. No. 212, Wagon train, frontiersman, rocket launch. No. 214, Viking on Martian surface, robotic shovel.

1976, Nov. 23

206	A45	5fr multicolored	.25	.25
207	A45	10fr multicolored	.25	.25
208	A45	25fr multicolored	.35	.25
209	A45	35fr multicolored	.35	.25
210	A45	100fr multicolored	1.25	.40
211	A45	500fr multicolored	7.00	1.50
		Nos. 206-211 (6)	9.45	2.90

Litho. & Embossed
Size: 57x39mm

212	A45	1500fr gold & multi	14.00	—

Souvenir Sheets
Litho.

213	A45	400fr multicolored	5.00	1.50

Litho. & Embossed

214	A45	1500fr gold & multi	15.00	—

American Revolution, bicentennial. Nos. 211-214 are airmail. No. 213 contains one 60x42mm stamp.

No. 212 exists in a souvenir sheet of 1. Value $50.

UN Postal Administration, 25th Anniv. — A46

Designs: 15fr, UN #24, irrigating field. 30fr, UN #43, doctor, nurse. 50fr, UN #162, mother holding child. 75fr, UN #42, communications satellite in orbit. 200fr, UN #32, Concorde, Zeppelin. 400fr, UN #18, cargo plane. 500fr, People passing letters around globe.

1976, Nov. 25   Litho.

215	A46	15fr multicolored	.25	.25
216	A46	30fr multicolored	.30	.25
217	A46	50fr multicolored	.60	.30
218	A46	75fr multicolored	.80	.30
219	A46	200fr multicolored	2.50	1.00
220	A46	400fr multicolored	5.00	2.00
		Nos. 215-220 (6)	9.45	4.10

Souvenir Sheet

221	A46	500fr multicolored	5.00	2.00

Nos. 219-221 are airmail. No. 221 contains one 57x40mm stamp. For overprints see Nos. 282-284, 473.

Comoro Flag, UN Headquarters and Emblem — A47

1976, Nov. 25

222	A47	40fr multicolored	1.40	.30
223	A47	50fr multicolored	1.90	.40

1st anniv. of UN membership.

Type of 1976 and

US Bicentennial — A48

Civil War Battles: 10fr, Fort Sumter, Lincoln. 30fr, Bull Run, Gen. P.G.T. Beauregard, vert. 50fr, Antietam, Gen. Joseph E. Johnston. 100fr, Gettysburg, Gen. Meade. 200fr, Chattanooga, Gen. Sherman, vert. 400fr, Appomattox, Gen. Pickett. 500fr, Surrender at Appomattox, Generals Lee and Grant. 1000fr, Lincoln, battlefield. No. 230, Pres. Kennedy, lunar lander.

1976, Dec. 30   Litho.

224	A48	10fr multicolored	.25	.25
225	A48	30fr multicolored	.30	.25
226	A48	50fr multicolored	.65	.25
227	A48	100fr multicolored	1.10	.45
228	A48	200fr multicolored	2.50	.80
229	A48	400fr multicolored	5.00	1.50
		Nos. 224-229 (6)	9.80	3.50

Litho. & Embossed
Size: 61x51mm

230	A39	1500fr gold & multi	17.00	—

Souvenir Sheets
Litho.

231	A48	500fr multicolored	6.50	1.75

Litho. & Embossed

232	A39	1000fr gold & multi	9.50	—

American Revolution bicentennial. Nos. 227-232 are airmail. No. 231 contains one 60x42mm stamp.

No. 230 exists in a souvenir sheet of 1. Value $50.

Endangered Species — A49

15fr, Andean condor, vert. 20fr, Australian tiger cat. 35fr, Leopard, vert. 40fr, White rhinoceros. 75fr, Nyala, vert. 400fr, Orangutan. 500fr, Lemur, vert.

1976, Dec. 30   **Litho.**

233	A49	15fr multicolored	.30	.25
234	A49	20fr multicolored	.65	.25
235	A49	35fr multicolored	1.00	.25
236	A49	40fr multicolored	1.25	.45
237	A49	75fr multicolored	3.00	.55
238	A49	400fr multicolored	8.00	1.50
		Nos. 233-238 (6)	14.20	3.25

Souvenir Sheet

239	A49	500fr multicolored	7.00	1.75

Nos. 238-239 airmail. No. 239 contains one 40x58mm stamp.
See note after No. 479.

Endangered Species — A50

10fr, Wolf. 30fr, Aye-aye. 40fr, Cephalopus zebra. 50fr, Giant tortoise. 200fr, Ocelot. 400fr, Penguin.
500fr, Sumatran tiger.

1977, Apr. 14

240	A50	10fr multicolored	.25	.25
241	A50	30fr multicolored	.45	.25
242	A50	40fr multicolored	.90	.30
243	A50	50fr multicolored	1.00	.30
244	A50	200fr multicolored	3.00	.75
245	A50	400fr multicolored	6.50	1.50
		Nos. 240-245 (6)	12.10	3.35

Souvenir Sheet

246	A50	500fr multicolored	8.00	1.50

Nos. 244-246 airmail. No. 246 contains one 58x40mm stamp.

Giffard Airship, 1851 and Paris-St. Germain Train, 1837, France — A51

Airships & Locomotives: 25fr, Santos-Dumont's airship, 1906, Brazilian Tander 120FIN, Brazil. 50fr, Astra, 1914, Trans-Siberian Express, 1905, Russia. 75fr, R.34, 1919, Southern Belle, 1910, Great Britain. 200fr, Navy airship, Pacific Class locomotive, 1930, US. No. 252, Hindenburg, Rheingold Express, 1933, Germany. No. 253, Graf-Zeppelin, 1928, Nord-Express Type 231, 1925, Germany.

1977, Apr. 14

247	A51	20fr multicolored	.30	.25
248	A51	25fr multicolored	.30	.25
249	A51	50fr multicolored	.75	.25

250	A51	75fr multicolored	1.10	.25
251	A51	200fr multicolored	2.75	.60
252	A51	500fr multicolored	6.25	1.60
		Nos. 247-252 (6)	11.45	3.20

Souvenir Sheet

253	A51	500fr multi, horiz.	6.00	2.00

Nos. 251-253 are airmail. No. 253 contains one 58x39mm stamp.

Nobel Prize, 75th Anniv. — A52

Nobel Prize winners: 30fr, Medicine. 40fr, Physics. 50fr, Literature. 100fr, Physics. 200fr, Chemistry. vert. 75fr, Peace.
500fr, Nobel medal.

1977, July 7

254	A52	30fr multicolored	.75	.25
255	A52	40fr multicolored	.75	.25
256	A52	50fr multicolored	1.25	.25
257	A52	100fr multicolored	3.25	.25
258	A52	200fr multicolored	5.50	.75
259	A52	400fr multicolored	12.50	1.25
		Nos. 254-259 (6)	24.00	3.00

Souvenir Sheet

260	A52	500fr multicolored	5.50	1.75

Nos. 258-260 are airmail.
See note after No. 479.

Peter Paul Rubens, 400th Birth Anniv. — A53

Portraits: 20fr, Portrait of the Artist's Daughter, Clara. 25fr, Suzanne Fourment. 50fr, Toilet of Venus, (detail). 75fr, Ceres (detail). 200fr, Young Woman with Blonde Braided Hair. No. 266, Helene Fourment in her Wedding Dress. No. 267, Self-portrait.

1977, July 7

261	A53	20fr multicolored	.25	.25
262	A53	25fr multicolored	.30	.25
263	A53	50fr multicolored	.65	.25
264	A53	75fr multicolored	1.10	.30
265	A53	200fr multicolored	2.50	.60
266	A53	500fr multicolored	6.25	1.50
		Nos. 261-266 (6)	11.05	3.15

Souvenir Sheet

267	A53	500fr multicolored	5.50	1.75

Nos. 265-267 are airmail.
See note after No. 479.

Fish A54

30fr, Swordfish. 40fr, Gaterin. 50fr, Sea scorpion. 100fr, Chaetodon lunula. 200fr, Amphiprion. 400fr, Tetrodon.
500fr, Coelacanth.

1977, Nov. 21

268	A54	30fr multicolored	.50	.25
269	A54	40fr multicolored	1.00	.25
270	A54	50fr multicolored	1.75	.25
271	A54	100fr multicolored	3.25	.45

272	A54	200fr multicolored	4.00	.75
273	A54	400fr multicolored	7.50	1.50
		Nos. 268-273 (6)	18.00	3.45

Souvenir Sheet

274	A54	500fr multicolored	8.00	2.00

Nos. 272-274 airmail. No. 274 contains one 52x47mm stamp.

Space Exploration — A55

30fr, Jupiter lander. 50fr, Voyager probe, Uranus. vert. 75fr, Pioneer probe, Venus. 100fr, Space shuttle, vert. 200fr, Viking III, Mars. 400fr, Apollo-Soyuz, vert.
500fr, Allegory of the Sun.

1977, Nov. 21

275	A55	30fr multicolored	.30	.25
276	A55	40fr multicolored	.60	.25
277	A55	75fr multicolored	1.00	.25
278	A55	100fr multicolored	1.10	.40
279	A55	200fr multicolored	2.50	.60
280	A55	400fr multicolored	5.00	1.25
		Nos. 275-280 (6)	10.50	3.00

Souvenir Sheet

281	A55	500fr multicolored	5.00	1.75

Nos. 279-281 airmail. No. 281 contains one 52x42mm stamp.

No. 219 Overprinted in One Line in Gold, Silver or Red
"Paris-New-York - 22 Nov. 1977"

1977, Nov. 22

282	A46	200fr multicolored	5.00	2.75
283	A46	200fr multicolored (S)	30.00	—
284	A46	200fr multicolored (R)	10.00	—
		Nos. 282-284 (3)	45.00	2.75

Birds — A56

15fr, Porphyrula alleni. 20fr, M. superciliosus. 35fr, Alcedo vintsioides johannae. 40fr, Terpsiphone. 75fr, Nectarinia comorensis. 400fr, Egretta alba.
500fr, Foudia eminentissima, horiz.

1978, Feb. 6

285	A56	15fr multicolored	.35	.25
286	A56	20fr multicolored	.50	.25
287	A56	35fr multicolored	.70	.30
288	A56	40fr multicolored	1.00	.40
289	A56	75fr multicolored	2.00	.50
290	A56	400fr multicolored	8.00	2.25
		Nos. 285-290 (6)	12.55	3.95

Souvenir Sheet

291	A56	500fr multicolored	7.50	1.75

Nos. 290-291 are airmail. For overprint and surcharges see Nos. 444-448.

World Cup Soccer Championships, Argentina — A57

Designs: 30fr, Greece, 5th. cent. B.C. 50fr, Brittany, 19th cent. 75fr, London, 14th cent. 100fr, Italy, 18th cent. 200fr, England, 19th cent. 400fr, English Cup match, 1891. 500fr,

English Cup final, 1962. No. 298, Player, satellite. No. 300, Players.

1978, Feb. 6

292	A57	30fr multicolored	.30	.25
293	A57	50fr multicolored	.60	.25
294	A57	75fr multicolored	.75	.30
295	A57	100fr multicolored	1.10	.40
296	A57	200fr multicolored	2.50	.60
297	A57	400fr multicolored	5.00	1.25
		Nos. 292-297 (6)	10.25	3.05

Litho. & Embossed
Size: 60x42mm

298	A57	1000fr gold & multi	11.00	—

Souvenir Sheets
Litho.

299	A57	500fr multicolored	6.00	1.75

Litho. & Embossed

300	A57	1000fr gold & multi	10.00	4.00

Nos. 296-300 are airmail. No. 300 contains one 60x42mm stamp. No. 298 exists in a souvenir sheet of 1. Value $50.
For overprints and surcharges see Nos. 402-408, 449-453.

Composers — A58

30fr, J.S. Bach. 40fr, W.A. Mozart. 50fr, Berlioz. 100fr, Verdi. 200fr, Tchaikovsky. 400fr, George Gershwin.
500fr, Beethoven.

1978, Apr. 5   **Litho.**

301	A58	30fr multicolored	.90	.25
302	A58	40fr multicolored	1.10	.25
303	A58	50fr multicolored	1.50	.30
304	A58	100fr multicolored	3.00	.30
305	A58	200fr multicolored	4.50	.60
306	A58	400fr multicolored	9.00	1.25
		Nos. 301-306 (6)	20.00	2.95

Souvenir Sheet

307	A58	500fr multicolored	9.00	1.75

Nos. 305-307 are airmail. For overprints and surcharges see Nos. 454-458.

Albrecht Durer, 450th Death Anniv. — A59

Portraits: 20fr, Oswolt Krel. 25fr, Elspeth Tucher. 50fr, Hieronymus Holzschuher. 75fr, Young Woman. 200fr, Emperor Maximilian I. No. 313, Young Woman, (detail). No. 314, Self-portrait.

1978, Apr. 5

308	A59	20fr multicolored	.25	.25
309	A59	25fr multicolored	.30	.25
310	A59	50fr multicolored	.65	.30
311	A59	75fr multicolored	1.00	.30
312	A59	200fr multicolored	2.50	.60
313	A59	500fr multicolored	6.00	1.60
		Nos. 308-313 (6)	10.70	3.30

Souvenir Sheet

314	A59	500fr multicolored	5.50	1.75

Nos. 312-314 airmail. No. 314 contains one 42x52mm stamp. See note after No. 479.

Issues Not Valid for Postage

The government changed in May 1978. A number of sets that had not been issued seem to have been invalid for postage until they were overprinted with the new country name. These are a set of 9 for the 25th anniv. of Elizabeth's coronation, a set of 7 for butterflies, a set of 6 for the 10th Intl. Communications Year, a set of 7 for the history of aviation, a set of 9 for Rubens, and a set of 9 for Durer.

These sets, unoverprinted, exist both mint and cancelled to order. They are no scarcer than the previous listed issues.

See note after No. 479.

Islamic Republic
Nos. 204-205 Surcharged and Overprinted with 3 Lines and: "République / Fédérale / et Islamique / des Comores"

1978, July 24   Litho.   Perf. 13½

353	A44	30fr multi	1.75	—
354	A44	40fr on 30fr multi	1.75	—
355	A44	50fr multi	1.75	—
356	A44	100fr on 50fr multi	1.75	—
		Nos. 353-356 (3)	1.50	

Nos. 353 and 355 were also overprinted to commemorate World Cup Soccer winner; Albrecht Dürer; Railroad anniversary; Voyager I and II; 1980 Olympic Games; World Cup Soccer, Espana '82.

Nos. 353, 355 Overprinted

1978, July 25   Litho.   Perf. 13½

357	A44	30fr multi	8.50	—
358	A44	50fr multi	12.50	—

Coronation of Queen Elizabeth II, 25th anniv.

Nos. 353, 355 Overprinted

1978, July 26   Litho.   Perf. 13½

359	A44	30fr multi	6.00	—
360	A44	50fr multi	9.00	—

Birth of Capt. James Cook, 250th anniv.

Nos. 353, 355 Overprinted

1978, July 31   Litho.   Perf. 13½

365	A44	30fr multi	6.00	—
366	A44	50fr multi	10.00	—

Intl. Civil Aviation Organization.

Nos. 353, 355 Overprinted

1978, Aug. 3   Litho.   Perf. 13½

371	A44	30fr multi	7.00	—
372	A44	50fr multi	8.00	—

Intl. Year of the Child (in 1979).

Europe-Africa A66

Various satellites or spacecraft.

1978, Dec. 16

386	A66	10fr multicolored	.25	.25
387	A66	25fr multicolored	.25	.25
388	A66	35fr multicolored	.40	.25
389	A66	50fr multicolored	.65	.25
390	A66	100fr multicolored	1.10	.60
391	A66	500fr multicolored	5.50	1.25
		Nos. 386-391 (6)	8.15	2.85

Souvenir Sheet

392	A66	500fr multicolored	5.50	1.75

Nos. 390-392 airmail. No. 392 contains one 61x40mm stamp.

Sir Rowland Hill — A67

20fr, Saxony #1. 30fr, Netherlands #1. 40fr, Great Britain #2. 75fr, US #2. 200fr, France #33. 400fr, Basel #3L1. 1500fr, British Guiana #13.

500fr, Moheli, Mayotte, Anjouan, Grand Comoro #1. No. 401, 1500fr, Hill, Mauritius #3.

1978, Dec. 16

393	A67	20fr multi	.25	.25
394	A67	30fr multi	.30	.25
395	A67	40fr multi	.60	.25
396	A67	75fr multi	.75	.30
397	A67	200fr multi	2.10	.60
398	A67	400fr multi	4.50	1.25
		Nos. 393-398 (6)	8.50	2.90

Litho. & Embossed
Size: 39x58mm

399	A67	1500fr multi	13.00	—

Souvenir Sheets
Litho.

400	A67	500fr multi	5.50	1.75

Litho. & Embossed

401	A67	1500fr multi	13.00	—

Nos. 397-401 are airmail. No. 400 contains one 57x49mm stamp. No. 401 contains one 58x39mm stamp.
No. 399 exists in a souvenir sheet of 1. Value $40.

Nos. 292-297, 299 Ovptd. in Black & Silver

1978, Dec. 16

402	A57	30fr multicolored	.30	.25
403	A57	50fr multicolored	.60	.25
404	A57	75fr multicolored	.90	.25
405	A57	100fr multicolored	1.10	.45
406	A57	200fr multicolored	2.25	.60
407	A57	400fr multicolored	4.75	1.25
		Nos. 402-407 (6)	9.90	3.05

Souvenir Sheet

408	A57	500fr multicolored	5.50	1.25

Nos. 406-407 are airmail.
Exists with Country name in red on silver. Value approx. triple those of overprints in black.

Galileo and Voyager I — A68

Exploration of Solar System: 30fr, Kepler and Voyager II. 40fr, Copernicus and Voyager I, 100fr, Huygens and Voyager II. 200fr, William Herschel and Voyager II. 400fr, Urbain Leverrier and Voyager II. 500fr, Voyagers I and II, symbolic solar system.

1979, Feb. 19   Litho.   Perf. 13

409	A68	20fr multi	.25	.25
410	A68	30fr multi	.30	.25
411	A68	40fr multi	.50	.25
412	A68	100fr multi	1.10	.25
413	A68	200fr multi	1.90	.50
414	A68	400fr multi	4.00	1.00
		Nos. 409-414 (6)	8.05	2.50

Souvenir Sheet

415	A68	500fr multi	5.00	1.50

Nos. 413-415 airmail.

Philidor, Anderssen, Steinitz and King — A69

100fr, Chess pieces and board, Venetian chess player. 500fr, Chess Grand Masters Alekhine, Spassky, Fischer, and bishop.

1979, Feb. 19

416	A69	40fr multi	.50	.25
417	A69	100fr multi	1.00	.25
418	A69	500fr multi	5.00	1.50
		Nos. 416-418 (3)	6.50	2.00

Chess Grand Masters. No. 418 airmail.

Nos. 419-425 are reserved for Summer Olympics set of 6 with one souvenir sheet, released Mar. 28, 1979. Values: set, unused $7; set, used $3; souvenir sheet, unused $6; souvenir sheet, used $3.

Charaxes Defulvata — A71

Fauna: 50fr, Leptosomus discolor. 75fr, Bee eater.

1979, Apr. 10   Litho.   Perf. 12½

426	A71	30fr multi	1.75	.30
427	A71	50fr multi	4.50	1.00
428	A71	75fr multi	6.50	2.00
		Nos. 426-428 (3)	12.75	3.30

Otto Lilienthal and Glider — A72

History of Aviation: No. 430, Wright brothers and Flyer A. No. 431, Louis Bleriot and Bleriot XI. 100fr, Claude Dornier and Dornier-

Wal hydrofoil. 200fr, Charles Lindbergh and Spirit of St. Louis.

1979, May 2   Perf. 13
Black Overprint and Surcharge

429	A72	30fr multi	.50	.50
430	A72	50fr multi	.80	.80
431	A72	50fr on 75fr multi	.80	.80
432	A72	100fr multi	1.60	1.60
433	A72	200fr multi	2.50	2.50
		Nos. 429-433 (5)	6.20	6.20

No. 433 airmail.
For unoverprinted stamps see note after No. 314.

Papilio Dardanus Cenea A73

Butterflies: 15fr, Papilio dardanus. 30fr, Chrysiridia croesus. 50fr, Precis octavia. 75fr, Bunaea alcinoe.

1979, May 2
Black Overprint and Surcharge

434	A73	5fr on 20fr multi	.25	.25
435	A73	15fr multi	.35	.25
436	A73	30fr multi	.70	.45
437	A73	50fr multi	1.40	.95
438	A73	75fr multi	2.25	1.50
		Nos. 434-438 (5)	4.95	3.40

For unoverprinted stamps see note after No. 314.

Man Reading Proclamation — A74

No. 439, Coronation coach. No. 440, Drummer. No. 441, With crown, orb, scepter. No. 443, St. Edward's Crown.

1979, May 2   Litho.   Perf. 13½
Black Surcharge and Overprint

439	A74	5fr on 25fr multi	.25	.25
440	A74	10fr multi	.30	.30
441	A74	50fr on 40fr multi	.70	.70
442	A74	50fr on 200fr shown	1.10	1.10
443	A74	100fr multi	1.40	1.40
		Nos. 439-443 (5)	3.75	3.75

No. 442 is airmail.
For unoverprinted stamps see note after No. 314.

Nos. 285-289 (Birds) Overprinted or Surcharged like A72-A74

1979, May 2   Litho.   Perf. 13

444	A56	15fr multi	.30	.30
445	A56	30fr on 35fr multi	.70	.70
446	A56	50fr on 20fr multi	1.25	1.25
447	A56	50fr on 40fr multi	1.25	1.25
448	A56	200fr on 75fr multi	4.00	4.00
		Nos. 444-448 (5)	7.50	7.50

Nos. 292-296 (Soccer) Overprinted or Surcharged like A72-A74

1979, May 2   Litho.   Perf. 13

449	A57	1fr on 100fr multi	.25	.25
450	A57	2fr on 75fr multi	.25	.25
451	A57	3fr on 30fr multi	.25	.25
452	A57	50fr multi	.90	.55
453	A57	200fr multi	2.25	2.25
		Nos. 449-453 (5)	3.90	3.55

No. 453 airmail.

Nos. 301-305 (Composers) Overprinted or Surcharged like A72-A74

1979, May 2   Perf. 13½

454	A58	5fr on 100fr multi	.25	.25
455	A58	30fr multi	1.25	1.25
456	A58	40fr multi	1.75	1.75

457 A58 50fr multi 2.25 2.25
458 A58 50fr on 200fr multi 3.50 3.50
   Nos. 454-458 (5) 9.00 9.00
   No. 458 airmail.

Intl. Year of the Child — A75

Intl. Year of the Child emblem and: 20fr, Astronaut on moon, child in astronaut costume. 30fr, Luger, child with snowboard. 40fr, Woman from Dürer painting, child practicing Chinese calligraphy. 100fr, Steam locomotive, child with toy train. 200fr, Adults and children playing soccer. 400fr, Olympic rower, child in rowboat.

500fr, Karl Benz, boy in toy car, horiz.

No. 465A, Louis Blériot, child with remote-control airplane, horiz.

No. 465B, Capt. James Cook, child with teddy bear and toy gun, horiz.

1979, May 30   Litho.   Perf. 13½
459 A75 20fr multi .25 .25
460 A75 30fr multi .30 .25
461 A75 40fr multi .40 .25
462 A75 100fr multi 1.00 .35
463 A75 200fr multi 2.00 .50
464 A75 400fr multi 4.00 1.10
   Nos. 459-464 (6) 7.95 2.70
Souvenir Sheet
465 A75 500fr multi 5.75 2.75
Litho. & Embossed
Size: 51x42mm
465A A75 1500fr gold & multi 13.50 —
Souvenir Sheet
Perf. 13¼
465B A75 1500fr gold & multi 13.50 —
   Nos. 463-465A are airmail. Nos. 465 and 465B each contain one 51x42mm stamp.

Litchi Nuts — A76

1979, June 15   Litho.   Perf. 12½
466 A76 60fr shown 1.00 .30
467 A76 70fr Papayas 1.25 .45
468 A76 100fr Avocados 1.40 .55
469 A76 125fr Bananas 1.90 .90
   Nos. 466-469 (4) 5.55 2.20
   For surcharges see Nos. 515, 533.

Basketball Players — A77

1979, Aug. 28   Litho.   Perf. 13
470 A77 200fr multi 2.50 1.40
   Indian Ocean Olympics.

Nos. 176, 198, 218, 187, 159-160 and Type A78 Overprinted in Black

Nimbus Weather Satellite — A78

No. 475, Apollo-Soyuz. No. 479, Molniya.

Printing & Perfs. as Before, Litho.
(A78)
1979, Sept. 15   Perf. 13 (A78)
471 A40 35fr multi .70 .70
472 A43 75fr multi 1.50 1.50
473 A46 75fr multi 1.50 1.50
474 A78 75fr multi 1.50 1.50
475 A78 100fr multi 2.10 2.10
476 A41 100fr multi 2.10 2.10
477 A37 100fr multi 2.10 2.10
478 A37 200fr multi 4.25 4.25
479 A78 200fr multi 4.25 4.25
   Nos. 471-479 (9) 20.00 20.00
   Nos. 476-479 airmail.
   For type A78 see note after No. 314.

Nos. 166-167, 169, 235-236, 257, 262, 309, 311, the unissued Rubens set (4 values) and Durer set (5 values) exist with this overprint, supposedly also issued Sept. 15. Value, set of 18 $12.

Dugout on Beach A80

Anjouan Puppet — A81

1980, Jan. 4   Litho.   Perf. 13
498 A80 60fr multi 1.00 .25
499 A81 100fr multi 1.50 .45
   For surcharge see No. 534.

Sultan Said Ali — A82

1980, Feb. 20   Perf. 12½x13
500 A82 40fr shown .75 .25
501 A82 60fr Sultan Ahmed 1.00 .25

Sherlock Holmes, Doyle — A83

1980, Feb. 25   Perf. 12½
502 A83 200fr multi 4.75 1.75
   Sir Arthur Conan Doyle (1859-1930), writer.
   For surcharge see No. 513.

Grand Mosque, Holy Ka'aba, Mecca — A84

1980, Mar. 12   Perf. 13x12½
503 A84 75fr multi 1.00 .40
   Hegira, 1350th anniv.
   For surcharge see No. 514.

Year of the Holy City of Jerusalem A85

1980, Mar. 12   Perf. 13x13½
504 A85 60fr multi 1.00 .40

Kepler, Copernicus and Pluto — A86

1980, Apr. 30   Litho.   Perf. 12½
505 A86 400fr multi 4.50 2.25
   Discovery of Pluto, 50th anniversary.
   For surcharge see No. 531.

Muscle System, Avicenna — A87

1980, Apr. 30   Engr.   Perf. 13
506 A87 60fr multi 1.00 .40
   Avicenna, Arab physician, birth millennium.

Soccer Players — A88

World Cup Soccer 1982; Various soccer scenes. 60fr, 150fr, 500fr, vert.

1981, Feb. 20   Litho.   Perf. 12½
507 A88 60fr multi .65 .25
508 A88 75fr multi .75 .25
509 A88 90fr multi 1.25 .25
510 A88 100fr multi 1.10 .45
511 A88 150fr multi 1.90 .60
   Nos. 507-511 (5) 5.65 1.80
Souvenir Sheet
512 A88 500fr multi 5.00 1.50
   For overprints & surcharge see Nos. 532, 555-560.

Nos. 502-503, 469 Surcharged

and

Merops Superciliosus A89

Red, Black or Blue Surcharge
Perf. 12½, 13x12½ (No. 514)
1981, Feb.   Litho.
513 A83 15fr on 200fr multi .50 .50
514 A84 20fr on 75fr multi .50 .50
515 A76 40fr on 125fr multi (Bk) 1.50 1.50
516 A89 60fr on 75fr multi (Bl) 3.00 3.00
   Nos. 513-516 (4) 5.50 5.50

A90

Space Exploration: 50fr, Apollo program, vert. 75fr, 100fr, 500fr, Columbia space shuttle.

1981, July 13   Litho.   Perf. 14
517 A90 50fr multi .60 .25
518 A90 75fr multi .75 .25
519 A90 100fr multi 1.25 .30
520 A90 450fr multi 6.00 1.50
   Nos. 517-520 (4) 8.60 2.30
Souvenir Sheet
521 A90 500fr multi 5.00 1.50
   For overprints and surcharges see Nos. 599, 804F.

Prince Charles and Lady Diana,
Buckingham Palace — A91

200fr, Highwood House. 450fr, Carnarvon
Castle.

1981, Sept. 1   Litho.   Perf. 14½
522 A91 125fr shown   1.00   .30
523 A91 200fr multicolored   1.50   .60
524 A91 450fr multicolored   3.50 1.25
  a.   Souvenir sheet of 3   6.50 2.00
        Nos. 522-524 (3)   6.00 2.15

Royal wedding. No. 524a contains Nos.
522-524 in changed colors.
For overprints see Nos. 551-553.

Official Stamp Flag Type
1981, Oct.   Litho.   Perf. 13
526 O1   5fr multi   .25   .25
527 O1 15fr multi   .25   .25
528 O1 25fr multi   .30   .25
529 O1 35fr multi   .40   .25
530 O1 75fr multi   .75   .35
        Nos. 526-530 (5)   1.95 1.35

Nos. 505, 509, 468, 499 Surcharged

1981, Nov.   Litho.   Perf. 12½
531 A86   5fr on 400fr multi   .40   .40
532 A88 20fr on 90fr multi   .80   .80
533 A76 45fr on 100fr multi   2.00   .25
534 A81 45fr on 100fr multi   2.00   .25
        Nos. 531-534 (4)   5.20 1.70

75th Anniv. of Grand Prix — A92

Winners and their Cars: 20fr, Mercedes,
1914. 50fr, Delage, 1925. 75fr, Rudi Caracci-
ola, 1926. 90fr, Stirling Moss, 1955. 150fr,
Maserati, 1957.
500fr, Changing wheels, vert.

1981, Dec. 28   Litho.   Perf. 12½
535 A92   20fr multicolored   .30   .25
536 A92   50fr multicolored   .65   .25
537 A92   75fr multicolored   .90   .25
538 A92   90fr multicolored   1.10   .35
539 A92 150fr multicolored   1.60   .45
        Nos. 535-539 (5)   4.55 1.55

Souvenir Sheet
Perf. 13
540 A92 500fr multicolored   6.00 1.75

For overprint see No. 600.

Scouting
Year — A93

1982, Jan. 5   Perf. 12½
541 A93   50fr Climbing rocks   .60   .25
542 A93   75fr Boating   .85   .25
543 A93 250fr Sailing   3.00   .90
544 A93 350fr Sailing, diff.   3.75 1.10
        Nos. 541-544 (4)   8.20 2.50

Souvenir Sheet
Perf. 13
545 A93 500fr Baden-Powell   6.50 1.75

For overprint see No. 601.

21st Birthday of Princess of
Wales — A94

Various portraits of Princess Diana.

1982, July 1   Litho.   Perf. 14
546 A94 200fr multi   2.00   .60
547 A94 300fr multi   3.25   .90

Souvenir Sheet
548 A94 500fr multi   5.00 1.50

Johannes
von Goethe
(1749-1832)
A95

1982, July
549 A95   75fr multi   .75   .25
550 A95 350fr multi   3.75   .90

Nos. 522-524a Overprinted in Blue

1982, July 31   Perf. 14½
551 A91 125fr multi   1.50   .60
552 A91 200fr multi   2.50   .90
553 A91 450fr multi   4.50 2.00
  a.   Souvenir sheet of 3   7.50 7.50
        Nos. 551-553 (3)   8.50 3.50

Birth of Prince William of Wales, June 21.

**Nos. 507-512 Overprinted with
Finalists and Score in Red**
1982, Sept. 20   Litho.   Perf. 12½
555 A88   60fr multi   .65   .25
556 A88   75fr multi   .75   .35
557 A88   90fr multi   1.00   .45
558 A88 100fr multi   1.10   .45
559 A88 150fr multi   1.40   .60
        Nos. 555-559 (5)   4.90 2.10

Souvenir Sheet
560 A88 500fr multi   5.00 1.50

Italy's victory in 1982 World Cup.

Paintings by
Norman
Rockwell
A96

1982, Oct. 11   Litho.   Perf. 14
561 A96   60fr 1931   .65   .25
562 A96   75fr 1925   .70   .25
563 A96 100fr 1922   1.25   .25
564 A96 150fr 1919   1.40   .55
565 A96 200fr 1924   2.00   .60
566 A96 300fr 1918   3.50 1.00
        Nos. 561-566 (6)   9.50 2.90

Sultans of Anjouan — A97

30fr, Said Mohamed Sidi, vert. 60fr, Ahmed
Abdallah, vert. 75fr, Salim. 300fr, Sidi,
Abdallah.

1982, Dec.   Perf. 12½x13, 13x12½
567 A97   30fr multicolored   .40   .25
568 A97   60fr multicolored   .75   .25
569 A97   75fr multicolored   1.00   .25
570 A97 300fr multicolored   3.50 1.40
        Nos. 567-570 (4)   5.65 2.15

Landscapes — A98

1983, Sept. 30   Litho.   Perf. 13
571 A98   60fr D'Ziani Lake   .75   .30
572 A98 100fr Sunset   1.25   .45
573 A98 175fr Anjouan, vert. 2.00   .75
574 A98 360fr Itsandra   4.00 1.25
575 A98 400fr Anjouan, diff. 5.00 1.60
        Nos. 571-575 (5)   13.00 4.35

For surcharge see No. 815S.

Woman
from Moheli
A99

1983, Oct. 17   Litho.   Perf. 12½x13
576 A99   30fr shown   .45   .25
577 A99   45fr Woman, diff.   .65   .25
578 A99   50fr Man from Mayotte .70   .25
        Nos. 576-578 (3)   1.80   .75

Horses — A100

1983, Nov. 30   Litho.   Perf. 13
579 A100   75fr Arabian   .70   .25
580 A100 100fr Anglo-Arabian 1.00   .30
581 A100 125fr Lippizaner   1.20   .40
582 A100 150fr Tennessee   1.50   .50
583 A100 200fr Appaloosa   2.00   .70
584 A100 300fr Pure English   3.00 1.00
585 A100 400fr Clydesdale   4.00 1.25
586 A100 500fr Andalusian   5.00 1.50
        Nos. 579-586 (8)   18.40 5.90

Double
Portrait, by
Raphael
A101

200fr, Girl, fresco detail. 300fr, St. George
Killing Dragon. 400fr, Balthazar Castiglione.

1983, Dec. 30   Litho.   Perf. 13
587 A101 100fr shown   1.25   .45
588 A101 200fr multicolored   2.50   .80
589 A101 300fr multicolored   3.25   .90
590 A101 400fr multicolored   5.50 1.25
        Nos. 587-590 (4)   12.50 3.40

For surcharges see Nos. 703, 800E, 815M.

Ships and Automobiles — A102

No. 591, William Fawcett. No. 592, De Dion,
1885. No. 593, Lightning. No. 594, Benz Victoria, 1893. No. 595, Rapido. No. 596, Columbia
Electric, 1901. No. 597, Sindia. No. 598, Fiat,
1902.

1984, Oct. 9   Litho.   Perf. 12½
591 A102 100fr multi   1.25   .30
592 A102 100fr multi   1.50   .30
593 A102 150fr multi   1.90   .45
594 A102 150fr multi   2.25   .60
595 A102 200fr multi   2.50   .75
596 A102 200fr multi   3.00   .75
597 A102 350fr multi   4.50 1.00
598 A102 350fr multi   5.00 1.10
        Nos. 591-598 (8)   21.90 5.25

For surcharge see No. 812Q.

**Nos. 521, 540, 545, C126, C131
Ovptd. in Black, Blue, Red or Gold**

No. 599

No. 600

No. 601

No. 603

No. 599, '85 / HAMBOURG (Bk). No. 600, TSUKUBA EXPO '85 (Bl). No. 601, ARGENTINA '85/BUENOS AIRES (R). No. 602, Rome, ITALIA '85 emblem (R). No. 603, OLYM - PHILEX/ '85 / LAUSANNE (G).

1985, Mar. 11   **Perf. 14, 13**
Souvenir Sheets

599	A90	500fr multi	5.00 5.00
600	A92	500fr multi	5.00 5.00
601	A93	500fr multi	5.00 5.00
602	AP31	500fr multi	5.00 5.00
603	AP32	500fr multi	5.00 5.00
		Nos. 599-603 (5)	25.00 25.00

Nos. 602-603 airmail.

Victor Hugo (1802-1885), Author, Pantheon, Paris — A103

Anniversaries and events: 200fr, IYY, Jules Verne (1828-1905), author. 300fr, IYY, Mark Twain (1835-1910), author. 450fr, Queen Mother, 85th birthday, vert. 500fr, Statue of Liberty, cent., vert.

1985, May 27   **Litho.**   **Perf. 13**

604	A103	100fr multi	1.25 .30
605	A103	200fr multi	2.25 .60
606	A103	300fr multi	3.50 .90
607	A103	450fr multi	5.00 1.25
608	A103	500fr multi	6.00 1.50
		Nos. 604-608 (5)	18.00 4.55

For surcharges see Nos. 704, 800A.

Sea Shells — A104

75fr, Lambis chiragra. 125fr, Strombe lentifinosum. 200fr, Tonna gala. 300fr, Cymbium glans. 450fr, Lambis crocata.

1985, Oct. 23   **Perf. 14**

609	A104	75fr multicolored	1.00 .25
610	A104	125fr multicolored	1.40 .35
611	A104	200fr multicolored	2.25 .60
612	A104	300fr multicolored	3.50 .90
613	A104	450fr multicolored	5.50 1.40
		Nos. 609-613 (5)	13.65 3.50

Comoros Admission to UN, 10th Anniv. — A105

1985, Nov. 12   **Litho.**   **Perf. 13x12½**

614	A105	5fr multi	.25 .25
615	A105	30fr multi	.30 .25
616	A105	75fr multi	.90 .25
617	A105	125fr multi	1.40 .50
618	A105	400fr multi	4.50 1.50
		Nos. 614-618 (5)	7.35 2.75

For surcharge see No. 800F.

Moroni Rotary Club, 20th Anniv. — A106

1985, Nov. 30   **Perf. 13**

619	A106	25fr multi	.40 .25
620	A106	75fr multi	.90 .40
621	A106	125fr multi	1.10 .45
622	A106	500fr multi	4.00 2.00
		Nos. 619-622 (4)	6.40 3.10

Mushrooms — A107

75fr, Boletus edulis. 125fr, Sarcoscypha coccinea. 200fr, Hypholoma fasciculare. 350fr, Astraeus hygrometricus. 500fr, Armillariella mellea.

1985, Dec. 24   **Perf. 13½**

623	A107	75fr multicolored	1.00 .30
624	A107	125fr multicolored	1.20 .45
625	A107	200fr multicolored	2.25 .60
626	A107	350fr multicolored	4.00 .90
627	A107	500fr multicolored	5.50 1.50
		Nos. 623-627 (5)	13.95 3.75

For surcharge see No. 815R.

Health Year A108

25fr, Pediatric examination. 100fr, Weighing child. 200fr, Immunization.

1986, Oct. 2   **Litho.**   **Perf. 15x14½**

628	A108	25fr multicolored	.35 .25
629	A108	100fr multicolored	1.50 .60
630	A108	200fr multicolored	2.75 1.25
		Nos. 628-630 (3)	4.60 2.10

For surcharge see No. 705.

Musical Instruments A109

1986, Dec. 24   **Litho.**   **Perf. 13**

631	A109	75fr Ndzoumara	.90 .40
632	A109	125fr Ndzedze	1.25 .60
633	A109	210fr Gaboussi	2.10 .90
634	A109	500fr Ngoma	6.00 1.75
		Nos. 631-634 (4)	10.25 3.65

For surcharges see Nos. 796P, 796T, 800L, 815A.

Role of Women in National Development — A110

75fr, Working fields. 125fr, Harvesting crops, vert. 1000fr, Basketweaving.

1987, Mar. 7   **Perf. 13**

635	A110	75fr multi	.55 .30
636	A110	125fr multi	1.10 .50
637	A110	1000fr multi	10.00 3.50
		Nos. 635-637 (3)	11.65 4.30

Service Organizations — A111

Emblems and activities: 75fr, Nos. 642, Kiwanis or 643c, Rotary Intl. for child survival. 125fr, Nos. 641, Kiwanis or 643b, Lions Intl. for aid to the handicapped. 210fr, No. 643a, Kiwanis helping poor and homeless children.

1988   **Litho.**   **Perf. 13½**

638	A111	75fr dk bl, lt bl & multi	.75 .30
639	A111	125fr dk brn, lt brn & multi	1.40 .45
640	A111	210fr org, yel & multi	2.25 .75
641	A111	425fr red, pink & multi	4.50 1.75
642	A111	500fr bl, yel & multi	6.00 2.00
643		Strip of 3	13.00 6.00
a.	A111	210fr grn, lt grn & multi	2.10 .75
b.	A111	425fr pur, pink & multi	4.50 1.75
c.	A111	500fr red, orange & multi	6.00 2.00
		Nos. 638-643 (6)	27.90 11.25

For surcharges see Nos. 654-656, 815B, 815W.

A112

1988 Olympics, Calgary and Seoul — A113

75fr, Women's figure skating. 100fr, Running. 125fr, Women's speed skating. 150fr, Equestrian. 350fr, Two-man luge. 400fr, Biathlon. 500fr, Pole vault. 600fr, Soccer.
No. 652, Women's downhill skiing, satellite. No. 653, Track, satellite.

1988   **Litho.**   **Perf. 13½**

644	A112	75fr multicolored	.65 .25
645	A112	100fr multicolored	1.00 .30
646	A112	125fr multicolored	1.00 .40
647	A112	150fr multicolored	1.50 .50
648	A112	350fr multicolored	3.25 .90
649	A112	400fr multicolored	4.00 1.40
650	A112	500fr multicolored	4.00 1.25
651	A112	600fr multicolored	6.00 1.50
		Nos. 644-651 (8)	21.40 6.50

Souvenir Sheets

652	A113	750fr multicolored	7.75 1.50
653	A113	750fr multicolored	7.75 1.50

Nos. 649 and 651-653 are airmail.
For surcharges see Nos. 800C, 800M, 815V.

No. 643 and Service Organization Types Surcharged

No. 655, like #643b. No. 656, like #643c.

1988, July 18   **Litho.**   **Perf. 13½**

654		Strip of 3	5.50 5.00
a.	A111	75fr on 210fr #643a	.65 .45
b.	A111	200fr on 425fr #643b	1.75 .90
c.	A111	300fr on 500fr #643c	2.75 1.25
655	A111	125fr on 425fr pur, lt pur & multi, blk letters	1.10 .60
656	A111	400fr on 500fr car, pink & multi	3.75 2.00
		Nos. 654-656 (3)	10.35 7.60

Nos. 655-656 not issued without surcharge.

Discovery of America, 500th Anniv. (in 1992) — A114

Designs: 75fr, Christopher Columbus, Santa Maria. 125fr, Martin Alonzo Pinzon (c. 1441-1493), Pinta. 150fr, Vicente Yanez Pinzon (c. 1460-1523), Nina. 250fr, Search for Cipango, legendary rich islands off the coast of Asia. 375fr, Santa Maria shipwrecked. 450fr, Preparing for 4th voyage. 750fr, Samana Cay landing.

1988, Apr. 18   **Litho.**   **Perf. 13½**

657	A114	75fr multi	.65 .25
658	A114	125fr multi	1.10 .30
659	A114	150fr multi	1.50 .45
660	A114	250fr multi	2.10 .75
661	A114	375fr multi	3.75 1.00
662	A114	450fr multi	4.50 1.25
		Nos. 657-662 (6)	13.60 4.00

Souvenir Sheet

663	A114	750fr multi, horiz.	7.75 1.50

Nos. 661-663 airmail. No. 663 contains one 42x30mm stamp.
For surcharges see Nos. 702, 815D.

1992 Summer Olympics, Barcelona A115

1988, Apr. 18
664	A115	75fr Discus, vert.	.60	.25
665	A115	100fr shown	.90	.30
666	A115	125fr Cycling	1.25	.35
667	A115	150fr Wrestling	1.50	.50
668	A115	375fr Basketball, vert.	3.75	1.00
669	A115	600fr Tennis, vert.	6.00	1.25
		Nos. 664-669 (6)	14.00	3.65

Souvenir Sheet
670	A115	750fr Marathon, vert.	7.75	1.50

Nos. 668-670 are airmail.

Famous Men — A116

Rotary Intl. — A117

150fr, Yuri Gagarin (1934-68), USSR, cosmonaut. 300fr, Jean-Henri Dunant, Red Cross founder. 400fr, Roger Clemens, baseball player. 500fr, Garry Kasparov, USSR, 1985 world chess champion. 600fr, Paul Harris, US, Rotary founder. 750fr, Neil Armstrong walking on the Moon, John F. Kennedy. No. 678, The Thinker by Rodin, Rotary Intl. emblem.

1988, Dec. 6   Litho.   Perf. 13½
671	A116	150fr multi	1.75	.50
672	A116	300fr multi	1.75	.50
673	A116	400fr multi	1.75	.50
674	A116	500fr multi	1.75	.50
675	A116	600fr multi	1.75	.50
a.		Souv. sheet of 5, #671-675 + label	10.00	—
		Nos. 665-669 (5)	18.40	3.50

Litho. & Embossed
676	A117	1500fr gold & multi	15.00	—

Souvenir Sheets
Litho.
677	A116	750fr multi	7.75	1.50

Litho. & Embossed
678	A117	1500fr gold & multi	15.00	—

Intl. Red Cross, 125th anniv. (300fr), Rotary Intl. (600fr, Nos. 676, 678). Nos. 674-678 are airmail.
Nos. 672-673 exist in souv. sheets of 1.
No. 676 exists in a souvenir sheet of 1. Value $42.50.

Inventors and Sportsmen A118

Portraits and modes of transportation: Designs: 75fr, Alain Prost, F-1 McLaren-Honda. 125fr, George Stephenson and locomotive *Borsig of 1935*. 500fr, Ettore Bugatti (1881-1947), 1939 Bugatti Aravis Type 57. 600fr, Rudolf Diesel (1858-1913) and V200 BB diesel-electric locomotive. 750fr, Dennis Conner, captain of the *Stars and Stripes*, winner of the 1987 America's Cup. No. 684, Michael Fay, patron of the *New Zealand*, an entry in the America's Cup. No. 685, Enzo Ferrari and 1989 Ferrari Formula 1, horiz.

1988, Dec. 27   Litho.   Perf. 13½
679	A118	75fr multi	.75	.45
680	A118	125fr multi	1.25	.25
681	A118	500fr multi	5.00	1.25
682	A118	600fr multi	6.00	1.25
683	A118	750fr multi	7.00	1.25
684	A118	1000fr multi	10.00	1.25
		Nos. 679-684 (6)	30.00	5.70

Souvenir Sheet
685	A118	1000fr multi	10.00	1.50

Nos. 683-685 are airmail.
Nos. 679-684 exist in souv. sheets of 1.

Scouts, Butterflies and Birds — A119

Scouts involved in various activities and species: 50fr, Gathering specimens, *Papilio nireus aristophontes oberthur* female. 75fr, Studying specimen and male. 150fr, Cooking out, *Charaxes fulvescens separanus poulton*. 375fr, Picking mushrooms, *Lonchura cuculatus*. 450fr, Examining specimen, *Charaxes castor comoranus rothschild*. 500fr, Identifying specimen, *Zosterops maderaspatana*. 750fr, Studying specimens, *Foudia omissa* and *Charaxes paradoxa lathy* female. No. 692, Photographing specimen, *Junonia rhadama*. No. 694, Examining specimen, *Agapornis cana cana*.

1989   Litho.
686	A119	50fr multi	.50	.25
687	A119	75fr multi	.60	.25
688	A119	150fr multi	1.40	.30
689	A119	375fr multi	4.00	.75
690	A119	450fr multi	4.75	1.00
691	A119	500fr multi	5.75	1.25
		Nos. 686-691 (6)	17.00	3.80

Litho. & Embossed
692	A119	1500fr gold & multi	16.00	—

Souvenir Sheets
Litho.
693	A119	750fr multi	10.00	1.50

Litho. & Embossed
694	A119	1500fr gold & multi	13.00	—

Nos. 690-694 are airmail. Issue dates: Nos. 692, 694, May 15; others, Mar. 15.
No. 692 exists in a souvenir sheet of 1. Value $42.50.
For surcharges see Nos. 800D, 815T.

Gold Medalists of the 1988 Summer Olympics A120

Communication satellites, various equestrians and their mounts: 75fr, Nicole Uphoff, West Germany, individual dressage, and Aussat K3. 150fr, Pierre Durand, France, individual jumping, and Brazilsat. 375fr, Janos Martinek, Hungary, individual modern pentathlon, and ECS 4. 600fr, Mark Todd, New Zealand, individual three-day event, and Olympus. 750fr, Team jumping, West Germany, and satellite. No. 699, Pierre Durand, France, individual show jumping. No. 701, Nicole Uphoff, West Germany, individual dressage.

1989, Apr. 10   Litho.   Perf. 13½
695	A120	75fr multi	.65	.25
696	A120	150fr multi	1.25	.35
697	A120	375fr multi	3.00	.75
698	A120	600fr multi	5.00	1.25
		Nos. 695-698 (4)	9.90	2.60

Litho. & Embossed
699	A120	1500fr gold & multi	16.00	—

Souvenir Sheets
Litho.
700	A120	750fr multi	6.75	1.50

Litho. & Embossed
701	A120	1500fr gold & multi	13.00	—

No. 701 contains one 39x38mm stamp. Nos. 698-701 are airmail.

No. 699 exists in a souvenir sheet of 1. Value $45.
For surcharges see Nos. 796Q, 804I.

Nos. 660, 588, 605 and 630 Surcharged
1989   Litho.   Perfs. as Before
702	A114	25fr on 250fr #660	.40	.25
703	A101	150fr on 200fr #588	1.50	.50
704	A103	150fr on 200fr #605	1.50	.50
705	A108	150fr on 200fr #630	1.50	.50
		Nos. 702-705 (4)	4.90	1.75

1992 Summer Olympics, Barcelona A121

1989, Apr. 26   Litho.   Perf. 13½
706	A121	75fr Running	.65	.25
707	A121	150fr Soccer	1.25	.40
708	A121	300fr Tennis	2.50	.60
709	A121	375fr Baseball	3.25	.80
710	A121	500fr Pommel horse	4.00	1.00
711	A121	600fr Table tennis	5.00	1.25
		Nos. 706-711 (6)	16.65	4.30

Souvenir Sheet
712	A121	750fr Equestrian	6.75	1.50

Nos. 710-712 are airmail.
For surcharges see Nos. 796J, 796K, 800J, 812R.

Dr. Joseph-Ignace Guillotin (1738-1814) — A122

French Revolution, Bicent.: 150fr, French artillery, Gen. Francois-Christophe Kellermann (1735-1820). 375fr, Royalist insurgents & leader, Jean Cottereau (1757-94). 600fr, King Louis XVI (1774-92), troops. 1000fr, Storming of the Bastille & Jacques Necker, statesman (1732-1804). No. 717, Lafayette, Mounier, Sieyes & Declaration of the Rights of Man and Citizen. No. 719, Robespierre & St. Just before the Convention on 9 Thermidor.

1989, Oct. 25   Litho.   Perf. 13½
713	A122	75fr multicolored	.70	.25
714	A122	150fr multicolored	1.25	.35
715	A122	375fr multicolored	3.00	.60
716	A122	600fr multicolored	5.00	1.25
		Nos. 713-716 (4)	9.95	2.45

Litho. & Embossed
717	A122	1500fr gold & multi	13.00	—

Souvenir Sheets
Litho.
718	A122	1000fr multicolored	8.50	1.75

Litho. & Embossed
719	A122	1500fr gold & multi	13.00	

Philexfrance 1989. No. 716-719 are airmail.
No. 714 incorrectly inscribed "Francois-Etienne."
Nos. 713-716 exist in souvenir sheets of 1.
No. 717 exists in a souvenir sheet of 1. Value $22.
For surcharges see Nos. 796B, 800W, 804J.

Airport Pavilion A124

Designs: 10fr, 25fr, Airport pavilion. 50fr, 75fr, 150fr, Federal Assembly.

World Cup Soccer Championships, Italy — A125

1990, Apr. 1   Litho.   Perf. 13
722	A124	5fr brn, org & brt red	.25	.25
723	A124	10fr brn, org & brt bl	.25	.25
724	A124	25fr brn, org & brt grn	.25	.25
725	A124	50fr blk & brt red	.45	.25
726	A124	75fr blk & brt bl	.75	.30
727	A124	150fr blk & grn	1.40	.60
		Nos. 722-727 (6)	3.35	1.90

Players from: 50fr, Brazil. 75fr, England. 100fr, Federal Republic of Germany. 150fr, Belgium. 375fr, Italy. 600fr, Argentina. 750fr, Argentina and Italy.

1990   Litho.   Perf. 13½
728	A125	50fr multicolored	.45	.25
729	A125	75fr multicolored	.65	.30
730	A125	100fr multicolored	.80	.35
731	A125	150fr multicolored	1.10	.45
732	A125	375fr multicolored	3.00	1.00
733	A125	600fr multicolored	5.00	1.25
		Nos. 728-733 (6)	11.00	3.60

Litho. & Embossed
734	A125	1500fr gold & multi	13.00	5.00

Souvenir Sheets
Litho.
735	A125	750fr multicolored	6.75	1.50

Litho. & Embossed
736	A125	1500fr gold & multi	13.00	—

Nos. 732-736 are airmail.
No. 734 exists in a souvenir sheet of 1. Value $22.50.
For surcharges see Nos. 796L, 796O, 804K.

Telecom '91 A125a

75fr, Emblem, vert.

1990, Oct. 29   Litho.   Perf. 13½
736A	A125a	75fr multi	1.00	.60
736B	A125a	150fr shown	2.00	1.25

Nos. 736A-736B exist imperf.

A126

Designs: 75fr, Hubble Space Telescope placed in orbit. 150fr, Pope John Paul II, Pres. Gorbachev meet Dec. 3, 1989. 200fr, Kevin Mitchell, San Francisco Giants, Natl. League Most Valuable Player, 1989. 250fr, De Gaulle, France, and Adenauer, West Germany, meet in Sept. 1962. 300fr, Cassini probe to Titan, 2002. 375fr, Bullet train and Concorde, France. 450fr, Garry Kasparov, World Chess Champion. 500fr, Paul Harris (1868-1947), founder of Rotary Intl.

1990, Nov. 26   Litho.   Perf. 13½
737	A126	75fr sil & multi	.75	.25
738	A126	150fr sil & multi	1.50	.40
739	A126	200fr sil & multi	2.00	.40
740	A126	250fr sil & multi	2.50	.40
741	A126	300fr sil & multi	3.00	.50
742	A126	375fr sil & multi	3.75	.65
743	A126	450fr sil & multi	4.50	1.00
744	A126	500fr sil & multi	5.25	.75
		Nos. 737-744 (8)	23.25	4.35

Nos. 743-744 are airmail.

No. 737-744 exist in souv. sheets of 1. Value, set of 8 $50.

For surcharges see Nos. 796A, 796R, 800I, 804A, 804L, 815E, 815U.

A127

Winter Olympics participants: 75fr, Edi Reinalter, Switzerland, slalom, 1948. 100fr, Canadian hockey team, 1924. 375fr, Gratia Van der Oye, women's slalom, Holland, 1936. 600fr, Heikki Hasu, Finland, combined cross country and ski jumping, 1948. 750fr, Helene Engelman & Alfred Berger, Austria, pairs figure skating, 1924. No. 751, Speed skater, horiz. No. 751A, Luge, horiz.

1990, Dec. 10

746	A127	75fr multicolored	.60	.25
747	A127	100fr multicolored	.75	.30
748	A127	375fr multicolored	3.50	1.00
749	A127	600fr multicolored	6.00	1.25
		Nos. 746-749 (4)	10.85	2.80

Souvenir Sheet

750	A127	750fr multicolored	7.00	1.50

Litho. & Embossed

751	A127	1500fr gold & multi	16.00	—

Souvenir Sheet

751A	A127	1500fr gold & multi	15.00	—

1992 Winter Olympics, Albertville. Nos. 748-751A are airmail. No. 750 contains one 36x41mm stamp.

No. 751 exists in a souvenir sheet of 1. Value $22.

For surcharges see Nos. 796M, 800K, 804M, 812S.

A128

Ground station, Moroni Volo-Volo.

1991, May 17   Litho.   Perf. 13½

752	A128	75fr multicolored	1.00	.25
753	A128	150fr multicolored	1.60	.45
754	A128	225fr multicolored	2.40	.75
755	A128	300fr multicolored	3.50	1.00
756	A128	500fr multicolored	5.50	1.25
		Nos. 752-756 (5)	14.00	3.70

For surcharge see No. 815N.

Indian Ocean Conference — A129

1991, June 17

757	A129	75fr multicolored	.50	.25
758	A129	150fr multicolored	1.40	.75
759	A129	225fr multicolored	2.00	1.00
		Nos. 757-759 (3)	3.90	2.00

World War II, 50th Anniv. A130

Actors, Films: 150fr, Errol Flynn, Objective Burma. 300fr, Henry Fonda, The Longest Day. 450fr, Humphrey Bogart, Sahara.

1991, Aug. 5

760	A130	150fr sil & multi	1.75	.45
761	A130	300fr sil & multi	3.25	.75
762	A130	450fr sil & multi	5.00	.90
		Nos. 760-762 (3)	10.00	2.10

No. 762 is airmail. Nos. 760-762 exist in souvenir sheets of 1. Value, set of 3 $15.

For surcharges see Nos. 796D, 800H, 804B, 804G.

A131

De Gaulle and: 125fr, Battle of Koufra. 375fr, Battle of Britain. 500fr, Battle of Monte Cassino. 1000fr, Airplanes. 1500fr, De Gaulle at podium.

1991, Aug. 5   Litho.   Perf. 13½

763	A131	125fr multi	1.50	.30
764	A131	375fr multi	3.00	.75
765	A131	500fr multi	5.00	.90
		Nos. 763-765 (3)	9.50	1.95

Souvenir Sheet

766	A131	1000fr multi	12.00	2.00

Litho. & Embossed

767	A132	1500fr gold & multi	16.00	—

Nos. 765-767 are airmail. No. 767 exists in souvenir sheet of 1. Value $20.

For surcharges see Nos. 796G, 804N, 816I.

Charles de Gaulle A132

Anniversaries and Events — A133

Designs: 100fr, Satellite Columbus in polar orbit. 150fr, Gandhi. 250fr, Jean-Henri Dunant. 300fr, Wolfgang Amadeus Mozart. 375fr, Brandenburg Gate. 400fr, Konrad Adenauer. 450fr, Elvis Presley. 500fr, Ferdinand von Zeppelin.

1991, Nov. 18   Litho.   Perf. 13½

768	A133	100fr multicolored	1.25	.30
769	A133	150fr multicolored	1.60	.35
770	A133	250fr multicolored	2.50	.60
771	A133	300fr multicolored	3.00	.60
772	A133	375fr multicolored	4.25	.90
773	A133	400fr multicolored	5.00	.90
774	A133	450fr multicolored	5.50	.90
a.		Souv. sheet, #771, 774		
775	A133	500fr multicolored	5.50	1.00
a.		Souv. sheet, #772-773, 775		
		Nos. 768-775 (8)	28.60	5.65

Nobel Peace Prize, 90th anniv. (No. 770). Mozart, bicent. of death (No. 771). Brandenburg Gate, bicent. (No. 772). Konrad Adenauer, 25th anniv. of death (No. 773). Elvis Presley, 15th anniv. of death (in 1992) (No. 774). Count Zeppelin, 75th anniv. of death (in 1992) (No. 775).

Nos. 774-775 are airmail. Nos. 768-775 exist in souvenir sheets of 1. Value, set $50.

For surcharges see Nos. 796F, 796H, 800G, 804C, 804O, 815F, 815O, 816J.

Mushrooms — A134

75fr, Cepe comestible. 150fr, Geastre en etoile. 600fr, Pezize ecarlate.

1992, Mar. 23   Litho.   Perf. 13½

776	A134	75fr multicolored	.80	.40
777	A134	150fr multicolored	1.50	.60
778	A134	600fr multicolored	6.00	1.50
		Nos. 776-778 (3)	8.30	2.50

No. 778 is airmail. Nos. 776-778 exist imperf. and in souvenir sheets of one. Values, imperf set $12; set of souvenir sheets $10.

Shells A135

125fr, Conus textile. 150fr, Cypraecassis rufa. 500fr, Leporicypraea mappa. 750fr, Nautilus pompilius.

1992, Mar. 23

779	A135	125fr multicolored	1.60	.50
780	A135	150fr multicolored	1.75	.65
781	A135	500fr multicolored	6.00	1.90
		Nos. 779-781 (3)	9.35	3.05

Souvenir Sheet

782	A135	750fr multicolored	10.50	2.00

Nos. 781-782 are airmail. Nos. 779-781 exist imperf. and in souvenir sheets of one. Values, imperf set $15; set of souvenir sheets $12. No. 782 exists imperf. Value, $12.

For surcharges see Nos. 800N, 816K.

Space Programs A136

Designs: 75fr, Mercury rocket, chimpanzee Ham, US. 125fr, Mars Observer, US. No. 785, Veronica rocket, cat Felix, France. No. 786, Mars rover, US, Mars car, USSR. 500fr, Phobos project, USSR. 600fr, Sputnik II, dog Laika, USSR. 1000fr, Viking, US, vert.

1992, Mar. 30   Litho.   Perf. 13½

783	A136	75fr multicolored	1.25	.25
784	A136	125fr multicolored	1.75	.30
785	A136	150fr multicolored	2.25	.70
786	A136	150fr multicolored	2.10	.70
787	A136	500fr multicolored	6.50	1.25
a.		Souv. sheet, #784, 786-787		

788	A136	600fr multicolored	7.75	1.40
a.		Souv. sheet, #783, 785, 788		
		Nos. 783-788 (6)	21.60	4.60

Souvenir Sheet

789	A136	1000fr multicolored	13.00	2.25

Nos. 787-789 are airmail. Nos. 783-788 exist imperf. and in souvenir sheets of one. Values: imperf set, $32.50; set of souvenir sheets, $25. No. 789 contains one 30x42mm stamp.

For surcharges see Nos. 800O, 804Q.

Voyages of Discovery A137

Designs: 75fr, Space shuttle Endeavour, sailing ship Endeavour, Capt. Cook. 100fr, Satellite, sailing ship Golden Hinde, Sir Francis Drake. 150fr, ISO observation satellite, sailing ship Susan Constant, John Smith. 225fr, Probe B, sailing ship Discovery, Robert F. Scott. 375fr, Magellan probe over Venus, sailing ship, Ferdinand Magellan. 500fr, Newton probe, sailing ship Sao Gabriel, Vasco da Gama.

1000fr, Hermes-Columbus space shuttle, Columbus and his fleet.

1992, May 28   Litho.   Perf. 13½

790	A137	75fr multicolored	1.25	.25
791	A137	100fr multicolored	1.40	.30
792	A137	150fr multicolored	2.25	.45
793	A137	225fr multicolored	2.75	.75
794	A137	375fr multicolored	5.25	1.00
795	A137	500fr multicolored	6.00	1.25
a.		Souvenir sheet of 6, #790-795	15.00	7.00
		Nos. 790-795 (6)	18.90	4.00

Souvenir Sheet

796	A137	1000fr multicolored	13.00	2.25

Nos. 794-796 are airmail. Nos. 790-795 exist imperf. in souvenir sheets of one. Values: imperf sets $35; set of souvenir sheets $45.

For surcharges see Nos. 796E, 800P, 804P.

Various Stamps Surcharged

a — (Obliterator of dots)

Methods and Perfs as Before

1992-95

796A	A126	10fr on 300fr #741	—	
796B	A122	15fr on 375fr #715	—	
796C	AP41	25fr on 210fr #C164	—	
796D	A130	25fr on 300fr #761	—	
796E	A137	25fr on 375fr #794	—	
796F	A133	35fr on 400fr #773	—	
796G	A131	50fr on 375fr #764	—	
796H	A133	50fr on 375fr #772	—	
796I	AP34	50fr on 475fr #C138	—	
796J	A121	75fr on 300fr #708	—	—
796K	A121	75fr on 375fr #709	—	
796L	A125	75fr on 375fr #732	—	
796M	A127	75fr on 375fr #748	—	
796N	AP42	75fr on 600fr #C170	—	
796O	A125	100fr on 375fr #732	—	
796P	A109	150fr on 210fr #633	—	
796Q	A120	150fr on 375fr #697	—	—
796R	A126	150fr on 375fr #742	—	
796S	AP40	150fr on 450fr #C162	—	
796T	A109	150fr on 500fr #634	—	
796U	AP42	150fr on 500fr #C169	—	

No. 796J exists with quadruple surcharge.

No. 796Q exists with inverted surcharge and with double surcharge, one inverted.

Organization of
African Unity,
30th
Anniv. — A138

1993, Feb. 15   Litho.   Perf. 13½x13
797 A138 25fr blue & multi   .25   .25
798 A138 50fr pink & multi   .50   .25

Perf. 12
799 A138 75fr green & multi   1.40   .45
800 A138 150fr vermilion & multi   2.25 1.00
   Nos. 797-800 (4)   4.40 1.95

Various Stamps Surcharged

b — (Bar
obliterator)

Methods and Perfs as Before
1992-95
800A A103 50fr on 450fr #607   —
  x.   Zero in surcharge thin at top
       and bottom
800B AP47 75fr on 800fr
         #C192   —
800C A112 100fr on 350fr #648   —
800D A119 100fr on 375fr #689   —
  g.   Zero in surcharge thin at top
       and bottom
  y.   150fr on 375fr #689 (error)
800E A101 100fr on 400fr #590   —
800F A105 100fr on 400fr #618   —
  h.   Zero in surcharge thin at top
       and bottom
800G A133 100fr on 400fr #773   —
  i.   Zero in surcharge thin at top
       and bottom
800H A130 125fr on 450fr #762   —
800I A126 150fr on 250fr #740   —
800J A121 150fr on 375fr #709   —
  z.   Zero in surcharge thin at top
       and bottom
800K A127 150fr on 375fr #748   —
  a.   Zero in surcharge thin at top
       and bottom
800L A109 150fr on 500fr #634   —
  k.   Zero in surcharge thin at top
       and bottom
800M A112 150fr on 500fr #650   —
  b.   Zero in surcharge thin at top
       and bottom
800N A135 150fr on 500fr #781   —
800O A136 150fr on 500fr #787   —
800P A137 150fr on 500fr #795   —
  c.   Zero in surcharge thin at top
       and bottom
800Q AP41 150fr on 500fr
         #C165   —
  d.   Zero in surcharge thin at top
       and bottom
800R AP44 150fr on 500fr
         #C177   —
  l.   Zero in surcharge thin at top
       and bottom
  m.   Denomination above oblitera-
       tor
  n.   As "l," denomination above
       obliterator
800S AP45 150fr on 500fr
         #C181   —
  e.   Zero in surcharge thin at top
       and bottom
800T AP42 150fr on 500fr
         #C185   —
  o.   Zero in surcharge thin at top
       and bottom
800U AP47 150fr on 500fr
         #C191   —
800V AP50 150fr on 500fr
         #C212   —
  p.   Zero in surcharge thin at top
       and bottom
800W A122 150fr on 600fr #716   —

Surcharge on No. 800W is sideways reading
top to bottom. Nos. 800B and 800F exist with
inverted surcharge. Nos. 800F, 800R, 800W,
and perhaps other values exist with misplaced
surcharge.
No. 800F exists with zeros in surcharge in
different sizes.

1994 World Cup
Soccer
Championships,
U.S. — A139

1993, May 12   Litho.   Perf. 13x12½
801 A139 25fr red & multi   .25   .25
802 A139 75fr brown & multi   .65   .30
803 A139 100fr blue & multi   1.40   .40
804 A139 150fr green & multi   1.60   .60
   Nos. 801-804 (4)   3.90 1.55

Various Stamps Surcharged Type "b" in Black or Red
Methods and Perfs as Before
1992-95
804A A126 200fr on 300fr #741   —
  s.   Zero in surcharge thin at top
       and bottom
804B A130 200fr on 300fr #761   —
804C A133 200fr on 300fr #771   —
  w.   Zero in surcharge thin at top
       and bottom
804D AP45 200fr on 300fr
         #C180   —
  x.   Zero in surcharge thin at top
       and bottom
804E AP47 200fr on 300fr
         #C190   —
  t.   Zero in surcharge thin at top
       and bottom
804F A90   200fr on 450fr #520   —
  u.   Overprint right side up
  y.   Overprint right side up, zero in
       surcharge thin at top and
       bottom
804G A130 200fr on 450fr #762   —
  a.   Zero in surcharge thin at top
       and bottom
  b.   As "a," two obliterators
804H AP40 200fr on 450fr
         #C162   —
  c.   Zero in surcharge thin at top
       and bottom
804I A120 225fr on 375fr #697   —
804J A122 225fr on 375fr #715   —
804K A125 225fr on 375fr #732   —
804L A126 225fr on 375fr #742   —
804M A127 225fr on 375fr #748   —
  v.   "f" in surcharge omitted
804N A127 225fr on 375fr #764   —
804O A133 225fr on 375fr #772   —
804P A137 225fr on 375fr #794   —
804Q A136 225fr on 500fr #787   —

Red Surcharge
804R AP40 200fr on 300fr
         #C161   —

Surcharge on No. 804F is inverted.
No. 804D exists with "020fr" surcharge. Nos.
804D and 804F exists with zeroes in
surcharge in different sizes.

Intl. Telecommunications Day — A140

1993, May 17
805 A140 50fr red & multi   .40   .25
806 A140 75fr blue & multi   .65   .30
807 A140 100fr green & multi   1.10   .40
808 A140 150fr black & multi   1.60   .60
   Nos. 805-808 (4)   3.75 1.55

Miniature Sheet

Prehistoric Animals — A141

Designs: a, 75fr, Edaphosaurus. b, 75fr,
Moschops. c, 75fr, Sauroctonus. d, 75fr,
Ornitholestes. e, 75fr, Kentrosaurus. f, 75fr,
Compsognathus. g, 75fr, Styracosaurus. h,
75fr, Acanthopholis. i, 150fr, Edmontonia. j,
150fr, Struthiomimus. k, 450fr,
Dromiceiomimus. l, 450fr, Iguanodon. m,
150fr, Diatryma. n, 150fr, Uintatherium. o,
525fr, Synthetoceras. p, 525fr, Euryapteryx.
1200fr, Tyrannosaurus rex.

1994, Apr. 5   Litho.   Perf. 13½
809 A141 Sheet of 16, #a.-p.   22.50 9.00

Souvenir Sheet
810 A141 1200fr multicolored   13.00 3.00

No. 810 is airmail and contains one
42x60mm stamp.

Miniature Sheets

Flora — A142

No. 811a: 75fr, Hibiscus syriacus. b, 75fr,
Anacardier. c, 75fr, Suillus lutens. d, 150fr,
Pyrostegia venusta. e, 150fr, Manioc. f, 150fr,
Lycogala epidendron. g, 525fr, Allamanda
cathartica. h, 525fr, Cacao. i, 525fr, Clathrus
ruber.
Butterflies, insects: No. 812a, 75fr, Colotis
zoe. b, 150fr, Acherontia atropos. c, 450fr,
Danaus chrysippus. d, 75fr, Charaxes
comoranus. e, 150fr, Euchloron megaera. f,
450fr, Papilio phorbanta. g, 75fr, Hypurgus
ova. h, 150fr, Onthophagus catta. i, 450fr,
Echinosoma bolivari.

1994, May 24   Litho.   Perf. 13½
811 A142 Sheet of 9   16.00 5.50
  j.   Souvenir sheet of 3, #811a,
       811d, 811g   16.00 5.00
  k.   Souvenir sheet of 3, #811b,
       811e, 811h   16.00 5.00
  l.   Souvenir sheet of 3, #811c,
       811f, 811i   16.00 5.00
812 A142 Sheet of 9, #a.-i.   15.00 5.00
  j.   Souv. sheet of 3, #812a-812c 16.00 5.00
  k.   Souv. sheet of 3, #812d-812f 16.00 5.00
  l.   Souv. sheet of 3, #812g-812i 16.00 5.00

For surcharges see No. 826F.

Independence, 20th Anniv. — A142a

Designs: 100fr, 200fr, 300fr, Maps of Grand
Comoro, Moheli, Mayotte and Anjouan.

1995 (?)   Litho.   Perf. 13x12¾
812M A142a 100fr multi   —
812N A142a 200fr multi   —
812O A142a 300fr multi   —

For surcharge see No. 826M.

Various Stamps Surcharged in Gold

c — (Wide numerals, obliterator of
small sqares in grid)

Methods and Perfs as Before
1996, Dec.
812P AP40 200fr on 300fr
         #C161   —
812Q A102 200fr on 350fr #598   —
812R A121 200fr on 375fr #709   —
  v.   "2" same size as "0"
812S A127 200fr on 375fr #748   —
812T AP31 200fr on 400fr
         #C125   —
812U AP44 200fr on 500fr
         #C177   —

Size of numerals and obliteration grids
varies.

A143

Diana, Princess of Wales (1961-97): Various portraits.

1997, Dec. 15   Litho.   Perf. 14
813 A143 150fr Sheet of 12,
         #a.-l.   10.00 4.00
814 A143 375fr Sheet of 6,
         #a.-f.   12.00 5.00

Souvenir Sheet
815 A143 1000fr multicolored   5.50 2.25

Various Stamps Surcharged Type "c" in Black
Methods and Perfs as Before
1996, Dec.
815A A109 200fr on 210fr #633   —
815B A111 200fr on 210fr #640   —
815C AP41 200fr on 210fr
         #C164   —
815D A114 200fr on 250fr #660   —
815E A126 200fr on 250fr #740   —
815F A133 200fr on 250fr #770   —
815G AP30 200fr on 250fr
         #C116   —
815H AP38 200fr on 250fr
         #C151   —
815I AP38 200fr on 250fr
         #C152   —
  x.   Pair, #815H-815I + label
815J AP42 200fr on 250fr
         #C168   —
815K AP42 200fr on 250fr
         #C184   —
815L AP28 200fr on 260fr
         #C110   —
815M A101 200fr on 300fr #589   —
  y.   With gold obliterator over old
       value
815N A128 200fr on 300fr #755   —
815O A133 200fr on 300fr #771   —

815P AP31 200fr on 300fr
#C124   —
815Q AP37 200fr on 300fr
#C150   —
815R A107 200fr on 350fr #626   —
815S A98 200fr on 360fr #574   —
815T A119 200fr on 375fr #689   —
815U A126 200fr on 375fr #742   —
815V A112 200fr on 400fr #649   —
815W A111 200fr on 425fr #641   —

Size of surcharge numerals and obliteration grid varies. Black surcharge on No. 815My is misplaced. No. 815Q exists with misplaced surcharge that is faintly tripled, a surcharge with thinner zeroes, and a pair containing No. C150 next to No. 815Q with misplaced surcharge that is faintly tripled and has thinner zeroes. No. 815W exists with an inverted surcharge and with a double surcharge, one inverted.

Mother Teresa (1910-97) — A144

1997, Dec. 15   Litho.   Perf. 14
816 A144 200fr multicolored   1.50 1.00

No. 816 was issued in sheets of 9.

Aromatic Plants — A144a

Designs: 25fr, 50fr, 1000fr, Piper nigrum. 100fr, 125fr, 200fr, Cinnamomum ceylanicum. 300fr, Syzigium aromaticum. 500fr, Myristica fragrans.

1997, Dec. 15   Litho.   Perf. 14
816A A144a 25fr multi   —
816B A144a 50fr multi   —
816C A144a 100fr multi   —
816D A144a 125fr multi   —
816E A144a 200fr multi   —
816F A144a 300fr multi   —
816G A144a 500fr multi   —
816H A144a 1000fr multi   —

**Various Stamps Surcharged Type
"c" in Black**

Methods and Perfs as Before

1996, Dec.
816I A131 200fr on 500fr #765   — —
816J A133 200fr on 500fr #775   — —
816K A135 200fr on 500fr #781   — —
816L AP42 200fr on 500fr
#C169   — —
816M AP42 200fr on 600fr
#C185   — —
816N AP42 200fr on 600fr
#C170   —
816O AP42 200fr on 600fr
#C186   — —

Size of surcharge and obliteration grid varies.

**Vertical Pairs from No. B4
Surcharged with Silver Bar to
Obliterate Surtax**

Methods and Perfs as before.

1996, Dec.
816P   Surcharged pair of
#B4a, B4e   —
t. SP3 200fr on 200fr+10fr Galileo   —
u. SP3 200fr on 200fr+10fr Planet
A & 3 stars   —
816Q   Surcharged pair of
#B4b, B4f   —
v. SP3 200fr on 200fr+10fr Copernicus   —
w. SP3 200fr on 200fr+10fr ICE   —
816R   Surcharged pair of
#B4c, B4g   —
x. SP3 200fr on 200fr+10fr Kepler   —
y. SP3 200fr on 200fr+10fr Planet
A & 5 stars   —
816S   Surcharged pair of
#B4d, B4h   —
z. SP3 200fr on 200fr+10fr Halley   —
aa. SP3 200fr on 200fr+10fr Vega   —

A full sheet of Nos. 816P-816S is not known to exist.

Cats
A145

Designs, vert: 75fr, Silver banded. 150fr, Lac de Van. 200fr, European short hair. No. 820, 200fr, Somali. No. 821, 375fr, Japanese bobtail. No. 822, 375fr, Egyptian mau.
No. 823, each 375fr: a, Poupée de chiffon. b, Maine coon. c, Norwegian forest cat. d, Persian. e, Droop-eared. f, Marbled American short hair.
No. 824, each 375fr: a, Manx. b, Cashmere. c, British shorthair. d, Cornish rex. e, American curl. f, Ocicat.
No. 825, 1500fr, Silver-chocolate Somali. No. 826, 1500fr, Chocolate Persian, vert.

1998, June 3   Litho.   Perf. 14
817-822 A145 Set of 6   7.50 7.50

Sheets of 6
823-824 A145 Set of 2   24.00 24.00

Souvenir Sheets
825-826 A145 Set of 2   17.50 6.00

**No. C215D Surcharged Type "c" in
Red or Black**

Methods and Perfs as Before

1997 (?)
826A AP52a 100fr on 225fr   — —
826B AP52a 200fr on 225fr   — —
826C AP52a 200fr on 225fr (Bk) —
826D AP52a 500fr on 225fr   —
826E AP52a 600fr on 225fr   —

Size of surcharge numerals varies. No. 826B exists with inverted surcharge, No. 826C exists with double surcharge.

No. 811 Surcharged on Six Stamps

d — (Obliterator of Triangles and Wavy Lines)

Methods and Perfs as Before

1998 (?)
826F   Sheet of 9   —
g. A142 200fr on 150fr Pyrostegia
venusta   —
h. A142 200fr on 150fr Manioc   —
i. A142 200fr on 150fr Lycogala epidendron   —
j. A142 200fr on 525fr Allamanda
cathartica   —
k. A142 200fr on 525fr Cacao   —
l. A142 200fr on 525fr Clathrus
ruber   —

The three 75fr stamps on the sheet received no surcharge.

No. 812O Surcharged

e — (Obliterator of Bars, Dots, and Semicircles)

Methods and Perfs as Before

1998 (?)
826M A142a 100fr on 300fr   —

Size of surcharge numerals varies.

Marine
Life
A146

No. 827, each 150fr: a, Pomacanthus imperator. b, Cephalopholis miniata. c, Diver. d, Nautilus pompilius. e, Sphyraena barracuda. f, Manta birostris. g, Lutjanus sebae. h, Chaetodonplus duboulayi. i, Amphiprion bicinctus.
No. 828, vert , each 150fr: a, Istiophorus platypterus. b, Sterna fuscata. c, Larus pipixcan. d, Hippocampus kuda. e, Amphiprion ocellaris (2 fish). f, Octopus vulgaris. g, Chaetodon striatus. h, Actini aquina. i, Acanthurus leucosternon.
No. 829: a, Diomedea exulans. b, Delphinus delphis. c, Sailboat. d, Sphyrna zygaena. e, Loligo forbesi. f, Galeocerdo cuvieri. g, Pomacanthus imperator, diff. h, Amphiprion ocellaris (1 fish). i, Forcipiger flavissimus. j, Electrophorus electricus. k, Dermochelys coriaoea. l, Asterias rubens.
No. 830, 1500fr, Mastigias papua, vert. No. 831, 1500fr, Sepia officinalis. No. 832, 1500fr, Zancius canescens.

1998, Aug. 10   Litho.   Perf. 14

Sheets of 9 or 12
827-828 A146 Set of 2   13.00 13.00
829 A146 200fr #a.-l.   12.00 12.00

Souvenir Sheets
830-832 A146 Set of 3   22.50 22.50

Nos. 830-832 each contain one 51x38mm or 38x51mm stamp.

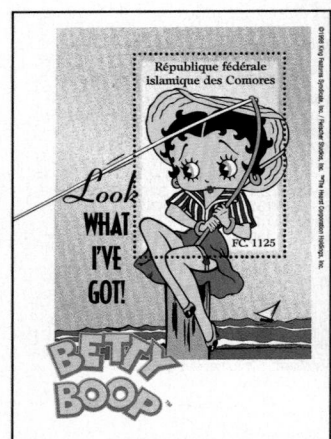

Betty Boop — A146a

No. 832A: b, Wearing hula skirt, dancing. c, With dog, wearing blue dress, in pink heart. d, Wearing polka dot dress. e, In bathtub. f, Face in red heart. g, Holding top hat. h, With flamingos. i, With dog, Wearing red dress, blue ribbon. j, Wearing hula skirt, on surf board. 1125fr, With fishing pole.

1998   Litho.   Perf. 13¼
832A A146a 300fr Sheet of
9, #b-j   16.00 16.00

Souvenir Sheet
832K A146a 1125fr multi   7.00 7.00

No. 832A contains nine 35x41mm stamps.

Popeye — A146b

No. 832L: m, Wimpy. n, Popeye, Olive Oyl, ship's wheel. o, Swee'Pea. p, Head of Popeye. q, Popeye. r, Head of Olive Oyl. s, Jeep. t, Olive Oyl. u, Brutus.
No. 832V, 1125fr, Popeye with spinach can. No. 832W, 1125fr, Like #832Ln, horiz.

1998
832L A146b 450fr Sheet of 9,
#m-u   24.00 24.00

Souvenir Sheets
832V-832W A146b Set of 2   14.00 14.00

No. 832L contains nine 35x51mm stamps, No. 832W contains one 60x50mm stamp.

Coelacanth — A147

World Wildlife Fund: a, Swimming right, colored background. b, Swimming right, white background. c, In net. d, Swimming left.
No. 833E: f, Like #833a. g, Like #833d. h, Like #833c. i, Like #833b.

1998
833 A147 200fr Strip of 4, #a-
d   6.00 6.00
833E A147 375fr Sheet of 4, #f-i 37.50

No. 833 was issued in sheets of 3 vertical strips.
No. 833E exists imperf. Value $45.

I Love Lucy — A147a

No. 833F, vert. — Lucy: g, With black ribbon in hair. h, Wearing burlap sack. i, With trapeze in mouth. j, With one arm raised. k, On telephone. l, Wearing red and white apron. m, Wearing bright green dress. n, Wearing blue dress. o, With fishing gear.
1125fr, With Ricky, with fishing gear.

1998   Litho.   Perf. 13¼
833F A147a 250fr Sheet of
9, #g-o   13.00 13.00

Souvenir Sheet
833P A147a 1125fr multi   7.00 7.00

No. 833F contains nine 35x51mm stamps.

Diana, Princess of Wales (1961-97) — A148

Nos. 834-835, 835J, Various portraits.
No. 836, 1125fr, Wearing scarf, green dress. No. 837, 1125fr, Wearing black and white hat and outfit.

1998 Litho. Perf. 13½
Sheets of 9

834	A148	250fr #a.-i.	13.00 13.00
835	A148	350fr #a-i.	18.00 18.00
835J	A148	450fr #k.-s.	24.00 24.00

Souvenir Sheets

836-837	A148	Set of 2	13.00 13.00

Nos. 835, 835J contain 42x51mm stamps. Nos. 836-837 each contain one 42x60mm stamp.

Entertainers
A149

No. 838: Various portraits of Grace Kelly (Princess Grace of Monaco) (1929-92). No. 839: Various portraits of Frank Sinatra (1915-98).

1998 Sheets of 9

838	A149	300fr #a.-i.	16.00 16.00
839	A149	500fr #a.-i.	26.50 26.50

Classic Automobiles — A150

No. 840, each 150fr: a, 1936 Jaguar SS. b, 1939 Lincoln Continental. c, 1903 Mercedes. d, 1936 MG-TA. e, 1946 Oldsmobile Custom Cruiser 98. f, 1933 Pontiac. g, 1940 Rolls-Royce Silver Ghost 40/50. h, 1950 Studebaker Starlight Coupe. i, 1932 Ford V8.
No. 841, each 150fr: a, 1927 Alfa Romeo RLSS. b, 1933 DuPont Model G. c, Bentley Speed Six. d, 1932 Cadillac 355. e, 1955 Corvette. f, 1934 Chrysler Airflow. g, Buick Coupe deVille. h, Model T Ford. i, 1920 Duesenberg Model A.
No. 842, 1500fr, Rolls-Royce Phantom II Continental. No. 843, 1500fr, 1927 Daimler Double Six.

1998, Oct. 29 Litho. Perf. 14
Sheets of 9

840-841	A150	Set of 2	13.00 13.00

Souvenir Sheets

842-843	A150	Set of 2	17.00 17.00

Birds — A151

No. 844, 75fr, Macareux moine. No. 845, 75fr, Calliste à tête verte. No. 846, 150fr, Soutmanga de la reine Christine. No. 847, 150fr, Rale d'eau. No. 848, 200fr, Lophophore replendissant. No. 849, 200fr, Francolin noir. No. 850, 375fr, Mesia à oreillonis argentes. No. 851, 375fr, Mérion splendide.
No. 852: a, Canard plongeur austral. b, Garrot a ceil d'or. c, Harle huppé. d, Canard colvert. e, Canard branchu. f, Sarcelle elegante.
No. 853: a, Emérillon. b, Nyctale de tengmalm. c, Aigle royal d, Kétoupa malais. e, Caracara. f, Chouette à lunettes.
No. 854, Jacana du mexique. No. 855, Toucan de cuvier.

1999, Jan. 23 Litho. Perf. 14

844-851	A151	Set of 8	8.50 8.50

Sheets of 6, #a-f

852-853	A151	375fr Set of 2	22.50 22.50

Souvenir Sheets

854-855	A151	1500fr Set of 2	16.00 16.00

Fauna
A152

No. 856, vert, each 150fr: a, Giraffa camaloprdalis. b, Macaca fusata. c, Loxodonta africana. d, Ovis dalli. e, Phoenicopterus ruber. f, Orcinus orca. g, Ursus horribilis. h, Lemur catta.
No. 857, vert, each 150fr: a, Pongo pygmaeus. b, Ceratotherium simum. c, Ailuropoda melanoleuca. d, Tursiops truncartus. e, Felis caracel. g, Eudyptes chrysocome. h, Bison bison. i, Panthera uncia.
No. 858, vert, each 150fr: a, Phascolarctos cinereus. b, Ammotragus levia. c, Hippopotamus amphibius. d, Saimiri boliviensis. e, Acinonyx jubatus. f, Gorilla gorilla. g, Branta sandvicensis. h, Thalarctos maritimus.
No. 859, each 150fr: a, Panthera tigris. b, Phoca groenlandica. c, Acipenser sturio. d, Lepidochelys kempii. e, Ailuropoda melanoleuca. f, Isurus oxyrinchus. g, Chelydra serpentina. h, Eretmochelys imbricata.
Each 1500fr: No. 860: Pan troglodytes, vert. No. 861, Panthera tigris altaica, vert. No. 862, Oryx gazella, vert. No. 863, Hippotigris zebra. No. 864, Diceros bicornis. No. 865, Panthera leo. No. 866, Amazona viridgenalis. No. 867, Pygoscelis papua, vert.

1999, Jan. 25 Sheets of 8

856-859	A152	Set of 4	25.00 25.00

Souvenir Sheets

860-867	A152	Set of 8	65.00 65.00

Fish
A153

No. 868, 75fr, Pomacantus imperator. No. 869, 75fr, Heniochus intermedium. No. 870, 150fr, Mirolaprichthys. No. 871, 150fr, Pomacanthus paru. No. 872, 375fr, Ostzacion tuberculatus. No. 873, 375fr, Colisa calia.
No. 874, each 150fr: a, Coris aygula. b, Chromis caeruleys. c, Euxiphipops navarchus. d, Pseudobalistes fuscus. e, Zebrasoma flavescens. f, Mycteroperca urba. g, Zenphelus flavocaeruleus. h, Equetus lanceolatus. i, Acanthurus leucostemon.
No. 875, each 150fr: a, Chaetodon tinkeri. b, Ostzaciidae. c, Seatophagus argus. d, Adioryx coruscus. e, Pygoplites diacanthus. f, Paracanthurus hepatus. g, Chaetodon plebius. h, Lythrypnus dalli. i, Myrichthys oculatus.
Each 1500fr: No. 876, Amphiprion percula. No. 877, Cymnothorne undulatus.

1998, Oct.-Nov. Litho. Perf. 14

868-873	A153	Set of 6	7.00 7.00

Sheets of 9

874-875	A153	Set of 2	14.00 14.00

Souvenir Sheets

876-877	A153	Set of 2	16.00 16.00

Marine
Life — A154

No. 878, 75fr, Tubastrea aurea. No. 879, 75fr, Condylachtis gigantea. No. 880, 150fr, Paracanthurus hepatus. No. 881, 150fr, Balistoides conspicillum. No. 882, 200fr, Diodon holocanthus. No. 883, 200fr, Sebastes rubrivintus. No. 884, 375fr, Trygonorhina fasciata. No. 885, 375fr, Phocoenoides dalli.
No. 886, each 150fr: a, Epinephelus guttatus. b, Diademichthys lineatus. c, Plotosus lineatus. d, Rhinomuraena quaesita. e, Zanclus cornutus. f, Persephona punctata. g, Murex pecten. h, Tetrosomus gibbosus.
No. 887, each 150fr: a, Lythrypnus dalli. b, Premnas biaculeatus. c, Pseudanthias tuka. d, Capros aper. e, Balistoides conspicillum. f, Oreaster reticulatus. g, Octopus joubini. h, Fasciolaris tulipa.
Each 1500fr: No. 888, S. picturatus. No. 889, Megaptera novaeangliae.

1999

878-885	A154	Set of 8	8.50 8.50

Sheets of 8

886-887	A154	Set of 2	17.00 17.00

Souvenir Sheets

888-889	A154	Set of 2	19.00 19.00

Prehistoric Animals — A155

No. 890, each 150fr: a, Meganeura. b, Archaeopteryx. c, Peteinosaurus. d, Eudimorphodon. e, Brachiosaurus. f, Gallimimus. g, Tarbosaurus. h, Parasaurolophus. i, Sauropelta. j, Herrarasaurus. k, Stegosaurus. l, Lambeosaurus.
No. 891, each 150fr: a, Ramphorhinchus. b, Quetzalcoatlus. c, Pterodactylus. d, Pteranodon. e, Dimorphodon. f. Camarasaurus. g, Tenontosaurus. h, Protoceratops. i, Coelurosaurus. j, Mixosaurus. k, Ceresiosaurus. l, Sharovipteryx.
Each 1500fr: No. 892, Ceratosaurus. No. 893, Mesosaurus. No. 894, Megazostrodon. No. 895, Diatryma.

1999 Sheets of 12

890-891	A155	Set of 2	19.00 19.00

Souvenir Sheets

892-895	A155	Set of 4	32.50 32.50

Prehistoric Animals, Lemurs and Butterflies — A156

Prehistoric animals — No. 895A — Prehistoric sea creatures: b, Eurhinodelphis. c, Stenopterygius. d, Ichthyosaurus. e, Pakicetus. f, Xenacanthus. g, Zygorhiza. h, Basilosaurus. i, Mesosaurus. j, Cetotherium.
No. 896: a, Elasmosaurus (b). b, Quetzalcoatl (c). c, Mesadactylus (b). d, Dimorphodon (e). e, Rhamphorhynchus (c, d, f, i). f, Pteranodon (c, i). g, Pterodactylus (h). h, Eudimorphodon (i). i, Ornithodesmus (g, h).
Lemurs — No. 897: a, Haplorhinien primitif. b, Aye aye (c, e, f). c, Lemur vari. d, Indri. e, Makis varis (f, i). f, Potto. g, Lemur catta. h, Lemur macaos. i, Microcebe souris.
Butterflies — No. 898: a, Charaxes nobilis. b, Charaxes eupale. c, Charaxes brutus. d, Lobobunea turlini. e, Papilio nobilis. f, Athletes gigas. g, Papilio antimachus. h, Epiphora albida. i, Papilio zalmoxis.

1998 Sheets of 9 Perf. 13¼x13½

895A	A156	150fr #b-j	6.50 6.50
896	A156	200fr #a.-i.	9.75 9.75
897	A156	250fr #a.-i.	12.00 12.00
898	A156	300fr #a.-i.	14.50 14.50

See Nos. 928-933.

A157

Endangered Species — A157a

Designs: 75fr, Galago crassicaudatus. 150fr, Vulpes vulpes. 200fr, Anomalurus pusillus. 375fr, Loxodonta africana, vert.

Primates, Nos. 903a-903c, Various views of Pan troglodytes. Nos. 903d-903f, Various views of gorilla gorilla. Nos. 903g-903i, Various views of pongo pygmaeus.
No. 904, each 375fr: a, Tragelaphus strepsiceros. b, Capra hircus. c, Egretta alba. d, Tockus flavirostris.
No. 905, each 150fr: a, Boletus edulis. b, Suillus grevillei. c, Boletinus cavipes. d, Morchella esculenta. e, Morchella conica. f, Clitocybe dealbata. g, Hygrocybe nigrescens. h, Clitocybe geotropa. i, Lepiota cristata.
No. 906, each 375fr: a, Pelecanus occidentalis. b, Orcinus orca. c, Delphinus delphis. d, Iguana iguana.
No. 907: a, Panthera tigris altaica. b, Camelus bactrianus. c, Canus lupus. d, Cuon alpinus. e, Rangifer tarandus dawsoni. f, Gulo gulo.
Each 1500fr: No. 908, Loxodonta africana, vert. No. 909, Ursus thibetanus.

Perf. 14, 14½x14 (#904-906)
1999, Jan. 25 Litho.

899-902	A157	Set of 4	4.50 4.50
903	A157	150fr Sheet of 9, #a.-i.	8.00 8.00

Sheets of 4

904-906	A157a	Set of 3	24.00 24.00

Sheet of 6

907	A157	375fr #a.-f.	12.00 12.00

Souvenir Sheets

908-909	A157	Set of 2	16.00 16.00

Mushrooms
A158   A159

No. 910, 75fr, Russula xerampelina. No. 911, 75fr, Catathelasma imperiale. No. 912, 150fr, Cortinarius violaceus. No. 913, 150fr, Cortinarius camphoratus. No. 914, 200fr, Rozites caperata. No. 915, 200fr, Coprinus picaceus. No. 916, 375fr, Coprinus cromatus. No. 917, 375fr, Russula cavipes.
No. 918, each 150fr: a, Boletus edulis. b, Suillus grevillei. c, Boletinus cavipes. d, Morchella esculenta. e, Morchella conica. f, Clitocybe dealbata. g, Hygrocybe nigrescens. h, Clitocybe geotropa. i, Lepiota cristata.
No. 919, each 150fr: a, Amanita citrina. b, Amanita phalloides. c, Cortinarius praestans. d, Phallus impudicus. e, Cortinarius bicolor. f, Cortinarius renidens. g, Lactarius torminosus. h, Boletus satanas. i, Cystolepiota bucknalii.
No. 920, each 375fr: a, Amanita muscaria. b, Coprinus comatus. c, Clitocybe odora. d, Cantharellus cibarius. e, Mycena epipterygia. f, Marasmius oreades.
No. 921, each 375fr: a, Boletus edulis. b, Laccaria laccata. c, Agaricus campestris. d, Hypholoma fasciculare. e, Lepiota procera. f, Russula aurata.
Each 1500fr: No. 922, Ramaria aurea, horiz. No. 923, Panellus serotinus. No. 924,

Macrolepiota procera. No. 925, Amanita muscaria. No. 926, Hebeloma crustuliniforme. No. 927, Lepiota molybdites.

1999		Litho.	Perf. 14	
910-917	A158	Set of 8	8.50	8.50
Sheets of 9				
918-919	A158	Set of 2	14.00	14.00
Sheets of 6				
920-921	A159	Set of 2	24.00	24.00
Souvenir Sheets				
922-925	A158	Set of 4	32.50	32.50
926-927	A159	Set of 2	16.00	16.00

Raptors — A160

No. 927A — Birds: b, Souimanga royal. c, Martin-pecheur huppe. d, Pie-grieche. e, Barbican a tete roughe. f, Beau-marquet. g, Rollier a poitrine lilas. h, Pintade vulturine. i, Grenadier. j, Outarde korhaon.
No. 928: a, Sparrow hawk. b, Red-tailed buzzard. c, Dark kite. d, African fish eagle. e, Bald eagle. f, Fawn-colored vulture. g, Peregrine falcon. h, Osprey. i, Harpie eagle.
Dinosaurs — No. 929: a, Dilophosaurus. b, Megalosaurus. c, Ceratosaurus. d, Coelophysis. e, Tyrannosaurus. f, Deinonychus. g, Allosaurus. h, Stegosaurus. i, Albertosaurus.
Gems — No. 930: a, Ruby. b, Liroconite. c, Emerald. d, Euclase. e, Diamond. f, Chrysoberyl. g, Plancheite. h, Kasolite. i, Indigolite.
Meteorites — No. 931: a, Martian. b, Antarctic. c, C2 Chondrite. d, Archondrite. e, Octaedrite moyenne. f, Iron. g, Tektite. h, Chondrite olivine. i, Iron, diff.
Mushrooms — No. 932: a, Paxillus atrotomentosus. b, Craterellus cornucopioides. c, Boletus satanas. d, Clavaria truncata. e, Phallus impudicus. f, Scleroderma aurantiacum. g, Amanita citrina. h, Catathe lasma. i, Inocybe fastigiata.
1125fr, Wulfenite.

1998		**Sheets of 9**	Perf. 13¼x13½	
927A	A160	175fr #b-j	8.00	8.00
928	A160	200fr #a.-i.	9.75	9.75
929	A160	250fr #a.-i.	11.50	11.50
930	A160	375fr #a.-i.	17.50	17.50
931	A160	400fr #a.-i.	19.00	19.00
932	A160	400fr #a.-i.	19.00	19.00
Souvenir Sheet				
933	A160	1125fr multicolored	5.75	5.75

No. 933 contains one 36x51mm stamp.
Captions on Nos. 928e and 928h are transposed.
See Nos. 896-898.

"Illegal" Stamps

Comoro Islands postal officials have declared as "illegal" the following items:
Muhammad Ali, sheet of nine 300fr stamps (previously No. 934);
Muhammad Ali, 1125fr souvenir sheet (previously No. 935);
Babe Ruth, sheet of nine 375fr stamps;
Babe Ruth, two 1125fr souvenir sheets;
Ocean Life, sheet of nine stamps with values of 100, 150, 250, 300, 350, 400, 450, and 500fr;
Horses, sheet of nine stamps with values of 100, 150, 250, 300, 350, 400, 450, and 500fr;
Pandas, sheet of nine stamps with values of 100, 150, 250, 300, 350, 400, 450, and 500fr;
Flora and Fauna: 25fr Harpe costata, 25fr Hibiscus, 50fr Volute lapponica, 50fr Tournesol de Comoros, 100fr Ghetonia mydas, 125fr Octopus vulgaris, 150fr Ylang ylang, 300fr Coelacanth, 300fr Tellina variegata.
Famous People: 250fr, Willy Messerschmitt, Messerschmitt BF-109G-6/R6. 300fr, Louis Pasteur, rabies vaccine administered to Joseph Meister. 350fr, Dr. Albert Schweitzer. 400fr, Ferdinand von Zeppelin, flying Zeppelin. 475fr, Henri Dunant, Nobel Prize. 500fr, Albert Einstein, Gravity Probe B. 550fr, Ayrton Senna, race car. 600fr, Pope John Paul II. 750fr, Iranian Pres. Mohammad Khatami, Pope John Paul II. 800fr, Crew of Apollo 11. 1125fr souvenir sheet, Lindbergh, Spirit of St. Louis.

Submarines — A161

No. 934: a, USS Salt Lake City, US. b, Le Terrible, France. c, Amethyste, France.

1999		Litho.	Perf. 13¼	
934	A161	150fr Sheet of 3, #a-c	3.00	3.00

Automobiles — A161a

No. 935: a, Cadillac Eldorado, Cadillac Series 62, US. b, Aston Martin DB2 IV Mark III, Austin Healey. c, Alfa Romeo Superlegera, Alfa Romeo Giuletta.
1125fr, Aston Martin DB5.

1999				
935	A161a	200fr Sheet of 3, #a-c	3.50	3.50
Souvenir Sheet				
935D	A161a	1125fr multi	7.00	7.00

No. 935D contains one 51x30mm stamp.

Motorcycles — A162

No. 935E: f, Honda NR. g, Christian Leliard and motorcycle. h, Joe S. Wright and motorcycle.

1999				
935E	A162	250fr Sheet of 3, #f-h	4.50	4.50

Helicopters — A162a

No. 936: a, Westland Wessex. b, MIL MI-8. c, Sikorsky 5-76 Spirit.

1999				
936	A162a	300fr Sheet of 3, #a-c	5.50	5.50

Dogs and Sleds — A163

No. 937: a, Alaskan malamute, US. b, Greenlandic. c, Siberian husky.

1999				
937	A163	400fr Sheet of 3, #a-c	7.00	7.00

Airplanes A164

No. 938: a, Tupolev Tu-160. b, Lockheed F-117A. c, Rafale C.01.
No. 939: a, Ilyshin Il-76. b, Boeing E-3. c, Concorde.
1125fr, Concorde, diff.

1999		Litho.	Perf. 13¼	
		Sheets of 3		
938	A164	375fr #a.-c.	6.50	6.50
939	A164	450fr #a.-c.	8.00	8.00
Souvenir Sheet				
940	A164	1125fr mulicolored	7.00	7.00

No. 940 contains one 50x30mm stamp.

Trains A165

No. 941: a, Series E. b, Series 9100. c, Kitson-Still I-C-I.
No. 942: a, HST 125. b, TGV. c, RTG.
1125fr, Sereis DD40AX.

1999		Litho.	Perf. 13¼	
		Sheets of 3		
941	A165	400fr #a.-c.	7.25	7.25
942	A165	500fr #a.-c.	9.00	9.00
Souvenir Sheet				
943	A165	1125fr mulicolored	7.00	7.00

No. 943 contains one 50x30mm stamp.

Space Achievements — A166

No. 944: a, Shuttles Discovery, Buran. b, Ariane V. c, John Glenn, Saturn V.
No. 945: a, Valentina Tereshkova, Soyuz 9. b, Dogs Laika, Bielka. c, Yuri Gagarin, Vostok 1.
1125fr, Space Shuttle Discovery, John Glenn.

1999		Litho.	Perf. 13¼	
		Sheets of 3		
944	A166	500fr #a.-c.	9.00	9.00
945	A166	600fr #a.-c.	11.00	11.00
Souvenir Sheet				
946	A166	1125fr multi	7.00	7.00

No. 946 contains one 51x30mm stamp.

Teams in 1998 World Cup Soccer Tournament — A167

Players in 1998 World Cup Soccer Tournament — A168

No. 947, 150fr: a, Italy. b, Chile, c, Cameroun. d, Austria. e, Netherlands. f, Belgium. g, South Korea. h, Mexico.
No. 948, 250fr: a, Brazil. b, Scotland. c, Morocco. d, Norway. e, Spain. f, Nigeria. g, Paraguay. h, Bulgaria.
No. 949, 300fr: a, France. b, South Africa. c, Saudi Arabia. d, Denmark. e, Germany. f, United States. g, Yugoslavia. h, Iran.
No. 950, 500fr: a, England. b, Colombia. c, Romania. d, Tunisia. e, Argentina. f, Croatia. g, Jamaica. h, Japan.
No. 951, 350fr: a, Desailly, French flag. b, Ronaldo, Brazilian flag. c, Suker, Croatian flag. d, Kluivert, Netherlands flag. e, French players, World Cup trophy. f, Brazilian player (yellow and green shirt). g, Croatian player (checked shirt). h, Netherlands player (orange shirt).

1998		Litho.	Perf. 13x13½	
		Sheets of 8, #a-h		
947-950	A167	Set of 4	50.00	50.00
951	A168	multi	14.50	14.50

Trucks — A169

No. 952: a, Truck with ornamentation over cab. b, Blue truck. c, Green truck. d, Yellow truck.

1999		Litho.	Perf. 13¼	
952	A169	350fr Sheet of 4, #a-d	—	—

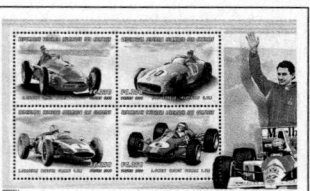

Automobile Racing, Chess, Tennis and Table Tennis, Fishing and Diving — A170

No. 953, 250fr — Automobile racing: a, Giuseppe Farina and Alfa 1500. b, Juan Fangio and Mercedes 2.5L. c, Jack Brabham and Cooper Climax 2.5L. d, Jim Clark and Lotus Climax 1.5L.
No. 954, 300fr — Chess players: a, Garry Kasparov. b, Akiba Rubinstein. c, Max Euwe. d, Mikhail Botvinnik.
No. 955, 375fr — Fishing and diving: a, Shark fishing. b, Sport fishing. c, Diver, back half of shark. d, Diver, front half of shark.
No. 956, 500fr — Chess players: a, Bent Larsen. b, José Raúl Capablanca. c, Boris Spassky. d, Bobby Fischer.

No. 957, 600fr — Tennis and table tennis: a, Female tennis player. b, Male table tennis player. c, Female table tennis player. d, Male tennis player.

No. 958, 1125fr — Chess players: a, Samuel Reshevsky. b, Vassili Smyslov.

No. 959, 1125fr — Fishing and diving: a, Sport fishing, diff. b, Divers and marine life.

No. 960, 1125fr — Tennis and table tennis: a, Male table tennis player, diff. b, Women tennis players.

1999   *Perf. 13¼*
Sheets of 4, #a-d
953-957   A170   Set of 5   47.50 47.50
Souvenir Sheets of 2, #a-b
958-960   A170   Set of 3   21.00 21.00

Nos. 816E, 816G Surcharged

Methods and Perfs. As Before
2001, June 16
963   A144a   100fr on 500fr multi   —   —
964   A144a   125fr on 200fr multi   —   —

Traditional Costumes A171

Designs: 125fr, Woman. No. 966, 150fr, No. 969, 300fr, Woman, diff. No. 967, 150fr, No. 968, 300fr, Man.

2002, Apr. 8   Litho.   *Perf. 13¼x13*
965-969   A171   Set of 5   8.50 8.50

Flowers — A172

Designs: 50fr, Cananga odorata. 600fr, Vanilla planifolia.

2003, Oct. 9
970-971   A172   Set of 2   5.25 5.25

Marine Mammals A173

Designs: 75fr, Peponocephala electra. 1000fr, Megaptera novaeangliae.

2003, Oct. 9   *Perf. 13x13¼*
972-973   A173   Set of 2   9.00 9.00

Wood Handicrafts A174

Designs: 100fr, Carved door. 300fr, Candleholder.

2003, Oct. 9   *Perf. 13¼x13*
974-975   A174   Set of 2   3.25 3.25

Orchids — A175

Orchid color: 50fr, White. 75fr, Yellow. 100fr, Mauve. 600fr, Red.

2003, Oct. 9
976-979   A175   Set of 4   6.50 6.50

Diplomatic Relations Between Comoro Islands and People's Republic of China, 30th Anniv. — A176

No. 980: a, 125fr, Chinese President Hu Jintao and Comoro Islands President Azali Assoumani, country flags. b, 125fr, Coelacanth, Worldwide Fund for Nature emblem, country arms. c, 300fr, Comoros Islands Broadcasting Center, country arms. d, 600fr, Comoros Islands People's Palace, country flags.

2006, Jan. 1   Litho.   *Perf. 12*
980   A176   Block of 4, #a-d   5.75 5.75

Comoro Islands postal officials have declared as "illegal" the following items:
Impressionist Paintings, sheet of five 500fr stamps.
Paintings in the Louvre, six different sheets of two 500fr stamps.
American Actors and Actresses, four different sheets of four 350fr stamps.
European Astronauts, three souvenir sheets of one 500fr stamp.
Disneyland, 50th anniv., souvenir sheet of one 500fr stamp.

Léopold Sédar Senghor (1906-2001), First President of Senegal — A177

Perf. 13x13¼, 13¼x13
2007, June 1   Litho.
980E   A177   125fr pur & blk   —
981   A177   125fr grn & multi   .70   .70
982   A177   125fr yel & multi, vert.   .70   .70
983   A177   300fr grn & blk   1.75   1.75
983A   A177   300fr blue & multi
984   A177   300fr red vio & blk, vert.   1.75   1.75
985   A177   350fr pur & multi, vert.   2.00   2.00
986   A177   500fr brn & blk, vert.   2.75   2.75
     Nos. 981-983, 984-986 (7)   9.65 9.65
     Dated 2006.

Medicinal Plants — A178

Designs: 75fr, Cymbopogon citratus. 125fr, Ocimum suave. 150fr, Aloe molucaca. 250fr, Like 75fr. 300fr, Like 150fr. 500fr, Like 125fr.

2007, June 1   *Perf. 13¼x13*
987-992   A178   Set of 6   7.75 7.75

A179

Transportation and Space — A180

No. 993 — Military aircraft and flags: a, 125fr, B-24 Liberator, U.S. flag. b, 150fr, Mitsubishi G4-M3, Japanese flag. c, 225fr, Petlyakov Pe-2, Russian flag. d, 300fr, Savoia-Marchetti SM-79, Italian flag. e, 400fr, Nakajima Ki84, Japanese flag. f, 1000fr, Dornier Do-335, German flag.
3000fr, Mitsubishi A6M5, Japanese flag.

2008, Oct. 1   *Perf. 13x13¼*
993   A179   Sheet of 6, #a-f   12.50 12.50
Souvenir Sheet
Perf. 13¼ Syncopated
994   A180   3000fr multi   17.00 17.00

Medical Vehicles

No. 995 — Red Cross flag and: a, 125fr, English ambulance. b, 150fr, ASLAV-A, Australia. c, 225fr, Red Cross vehicle, U.S. d, 300fr, Devon Air Ambulance helicopter, United Kingdom. e, 400fr, USNS Mercy. f, 1000fr, Medical worker on motorcycle, Hong Kong.
3000fr, M1133 Medical evacuation vehicle, U.S.

2008, Oct. 1   *Perf. 13x13¼*
995   A179   Sheet of 6, #a-f   12.50 12.50
Souvenir Sheet
Perf. 13¼ Syncopated
996   A180   3000fr multi   17.00 17.00

Submarines

No. 997: a, 125fr, Nautilus, 1800. b, 150fr, Brandtaucher, 1850. c, 225fr, Pioneer, 1861. d, 300fr, Flach, 1866. e, 400fr, Ictineo I 1858. f, 1000fr, Resurgam, 1878.
3000fr, Turtle, 1776.

2008, Oct. 1   *Perf. 13x13¼*
997   A179   Sheet of 6, #a-f   12.50 12.50
Souvenir Sheet
Perf. 13¼ Syncopated
998   A180   3000fr multi   17.00 17.00

U.S. High Speed Trains

No. 999 — Acela Express and U.S. landmarks: a, 125fr, Hollywood sign. b, 150fr, Golden Gate Bridge. c, 225fr, World Trade Center. d, 300fr, Statue of Liberty. e, 400fr, San Francisco skyline. f, 1000fr, White House.
3000fr, U.S. Capitol.

2008, Oct. 1   *Perf. 13x13¼*
999   A179   Sheet of 6, #a-f   12.50 12.50
Souvenir Sheet
Perf. 13¼ Syncopated
1000   A180   3000fr multi   17.00 17.00

Chinese High Speed Trains

No. 1001 — Maglev, flag of People's Republic of China, and Chinese landmarks: a, 200fr, Xian. b, 250fr, Tea house. c, 350fr, Pudong. d, 450fr, Great Wall of China. e, 500fr, Potala Palace. f, 1000fr, Gate of Heavenly Peace.
3000fr, Great Wall of China, diff.

2008, Oct. 1   *Perf. 13x13¼*
1001   A179   Sheet of 6, #a-f   15.50 15.50
Souvenir Sheet
Perf. 13¼ Syncopated
1002   A180   3000fr multi   17.00 17.00

Japanese High Speed Trains

No. 1003 — Shinkansen, Japanese flag, and Japanese landmarks: a, 200fr, Amanohashidate. b, 250fr, Itsukushima Shrine. c, 350fr, Umeda Sky Building, Osaka. d, 450fr, Buildings in Shiodome. e, 500fr, Temple in Kyoto. f, 1000fr, Himeji Castle.
3000fr, Minato Mirai 21.

2008, Oct. 1   *Perf. 13x13¼*
1003   A179   Sheet of 6, #a-f   15.50 15.50
Souvenir Sheet
Perf. 13¼ Syncopated
1004   A180   3000fr multi   17.00 17.00

Automobiles

No. 1005: a, 200fr, 1886 Daimler. b, 250fr, 1906 Renault GP. c, 350fr, 1923 Ford Model T. d, 450fr, 1954 Mercedes Benz 300 SL. e, 500fr, 1988 Ferrari Testarossa. f, 1000fr, 2007 Bugatti Veyron.
3000fr, 2007 Lamborghini Murcielago LP640 Versace.

2008, Oct. 1   *Perf. 13x13¼*
1005   A179   Sheet of 6, #a-f   15.50 15.50
Souvenir Sheet
Perf. 13¼ Syncopated
1006   A180   3000fr multi   17.00 17.00

Airplanes and Airports

No. 1007 — Airplane at airport and flag: a, 200fr, Changri Airport, Singapore flag. b, 250fr, John F. Kennedy Airport, New York, and U.S. flag. c, 350fr, Frankfort Airport, German flag. d, 450fr, Narita Airport, Tokyo, Japanese flag. e, 500fr, Beijing Airport, flag of People's Republic of China. f, 1000fr, Schiphol Airport, Amsterdam, Netherlands flag.
3000fr, 2007 Heathrow Airport, London, British flag.

2008, Oct. 1   *Perf. 13x13¼*
1007   A179   Sheet of 6, #a-f   15.50 15.50
Souvenir Sheet
Perf. 13¼ Syncopated
1008   A180   3000fr multi   17.00 17.00

Mars Probes

No. 1009 — Mars and: a, 200fr, Spirit. b, 250fr, Mars Polar. c, 350fr, Viking. d, 450fr, Mars Climate. e, 500fr, Phoenix. f, 1000fr, Sojourner.
3000fr, Mariner 3.

2008, Oct. 1   *Perf. 13x13¼*
1009   A179   Sheet of 6, #a-f   15.50 15.50
Souvenir Sheet
Perf. 13¼ Syncopated
1010   A180   3000fr multi   17.00 17.00

Ocean Liners

No. 1011: a, 200fr, Titanic. b, 250fr, Golden Princess. c, 350fr, Mauretania. d, 450fr, MS Queen Victoria. e, 500fr, Queen Elizabeth 2. f, 1000fr, Queen Mary 2.
3000fr, Pacific Princess.

2008, Oct. 1   *Perf. 13x13¼*
1011   A179   Sheet of 6, #a-f   15.50 15.50
Souvenir Sheet
Perf. 13¼ Syncopated
1012   A180   3000fr multi   17.00 17.00

Postal Vehicles

No. 1013: a, 125fr, English postal van, carrier pigeon with letter, British flag. b, 150fr, Swiss postal bus, Horn, Swiss flag. c, 225fr, Spanish postal truck, posthorn, Spanish flag. d, 300fr, Swedish postal truck, carrier pigeon with letter, Swedish flag. e, 400fr, Israeli postal van, carrier pigeon with letter, Israeli flag. f, 1000fr, German postal buses, post horn, German flag.

3000fr, Hungarian postal van, posthorn, Hungarian flag.

2009, Jan. 5   *Perf. 13x13¼*
1013 A179   Sheet of 6, #a-f   12.50 12.50
Souvenir Sheet
Perf. 13¼ Syncopated
1014 A180 3000fr multi   16.50 16.50
Dated 2008.

Subway Trains

No. 1015: a, 125fr, Beijing train and system map, Forbidden City, flag of People's Republic of China. b, 150fr, London train and system map, Big Ben, British flag. c, 225fr, Paris train and system map, Eiffel Tower, French flag. d, 300fr, Tokyo train and system map, Tokyo Tower, Japanese flag. e, 400fr, New York train and system map, Statue of Liberty, U.S. flag. f, 1000fr, Moscow train and system map, Red Square, Russian flag.

3000fr, Madrid train and system map, Statue of Bear and Tree, Spanish flag.

2009, Jan. 5   *Perf. 13x13¼*
1015 A179   Sheet of 6, #a-f   12.50 12.50
Souvenir Sheet
Perf. 13¼ Syncopated
1016 A180 3000fr multi   16.50 16.50
Dated 2008.

German High Speed Trains

No. 1017 — ICE, flag of Germany and: a, 125fr, Cologne Cathedral. b, 150fr, Neuschwanstein Castle. c, 225fr, Göltsch Viaduct. d, 300fr, Kaiser Wilhelm Memorial Church, Berlin. e, 400fr, Brandenburg Gate. f, 1000fr, Eltz Castle.

3000fr, Brandenburg Gate, diff.

2009, Jan. 5   *Perf. 13x13¼*
1017 A179   Sheet of 6, #a-f   12.50 12.50
Souvenir Sheet
Perf. 13¼ Syncopated
1018 A180 3000fr multi   16.50 16.50
Dated 2008.

French High Speed Trains

No. 1019 — TGV, flag of France and: a, 125fr, Notre Dame Cathedral, Paris. b, 150fr, Louvre Museum. c, 225fr, Hôtel de Ville, Paris. d, 300fr, Eiffel Tower. e, 400fr, Moulin Rouge. f, 1000fr, Arc de Triomphe.

3000fr, Eiffel Tower, diff.

2009, Jan. 5   *Perf. 13x13¼*
1019 A179   Sheet of 6, #a-f   12.50 12.50
Souvenir Sheet
Perf. 13¼ Syncopated
1020 A180 3000fr multi   16.50 16.50
Dated 2008.

Fire Trucks

No. 1021: a, 125fr, Zuk, Poland. b, 150fr, Isuzu Forward, Japan. c, 225fr, Pegaso 7217, Spain. d, 300fr, A LF 16/12, Germany. e, 400fr, WPFD Engine 3, U.S. f, 1000fr, Scientific Support Truck, United Kingdom.

3000fr, Palm Beach fire truck, U.S.

2009, Jan. 5   *Perf. 13x13¼*
1021 A179   Sheet of 6, #a-f   12.50 12.50
Souvenir Sheet
Perf. 13¼ Syncopated
1022 A180 3000fr multi   16.50 16.50
Dated 2008.

Sailing Ships and Lighthouses

No. 1023 — Various lighthouses and: a, 125fr, Lettie G, 1893. b, 150fr, Maple Leaf, 1904. c, 225fr, Etoile, 1930. d, 300fr, Brigantine St. Lawrence, 1952. e, 400fr, Cuauhtemoc, 1982. f, 1000fr, Royal clipper, 2001.

3000fr, Belle Poule, 1834.

2009, Jan. 5   *Perf. 13x13¼*
1023 A179   Sheet of 6, #a-f   12.50 12.50
Souvenir Sheet
Perf. 13¼ Syncopated
1024 A180 3000fr multi   16.50 16.50
Dated 2008.

Airplanes

No. 1025: a, 125fr, Airbus A380. b, 150fr, Concorde F-BTSD. c, 225fr, Concorde G-BOAC. d, 300fr, Airbus A380, diff. e, 400fr, Airbus A380, diff. f, 1000fr, Concorde F-BVFC.
3000fr, Concorde F-BTSD, diff.

2009, Jan. 5   *Perf. 13x13¼*
1025 A179   Sheet of 6, #a-f   12.50 12.50
Souvenir Sheet
Perf. 13¼ Syncopated
1026 A180 3000fr multi   16.50 16.50
Dated 2008.

Antique Automobiles

No. 1027: a, 200fr, 1893 Duryea. b, 250fr, 1897 Oldsmobile. c, 350fr, 1896 Ford. d, 450fr, 1903 Vauxhall. e, 500fr, 1886 Daimler Maybach. f, 1000fr, 1906 Haynes.
3000fr, 1904 Mercedes Simplex.

2009, Jan. 5   *Perf. 13x13¼*
1027 A179   Sheet of 6, #a-f   15.00 15.00
Souvenir Sheet
Perf. 13¼ Syncopated
1028 A180 3000fr multi   16.50 16.50
Dated 2008.

Combat Vehicles

No. 1029: a, 200fr, Jino Motors truck, South Korea. b, 250fr, PTU, Singapore. c, 350fr, BRDM, Russia. d, 450fr, KRAZ AVC-30, Ukraine. e, 500fr, Avalanche truck, Russia. f, 1000fr, Fahd 240/30, Egypt.
3000fr, 1904 Humber Flying Pig MK2, FV1611, Great Britain.

2009, Jan. 5   *Perf. 13x13¼*
1029 A179   Sheet of 6, #a-f   15.00 15.00
Souvenir Sheet
Perf. 13¼ Syncopated
1030 A180 3000fr multi   16.50 16.50
Dated 2008.

Motorcycles and Their Inventors

No. 1031: a, 200fr, 1885 Daimler, Karl Benz. b, 250fr, 1901 NSU, Christian Schmidt. c, 350fr, 1920 Excelsior 20R, William G. Henderson. d, 450fr, 1914 Indian V-Twin, Oscar Hedstrom. e, 500fr, 1927 Böhmerland, Albin Hugo Liebisch. f, 1000fr, 1923 BMW R32, Max Friz.
3000fr, 1905 Scott, Alfred Angus Scott.

2009, Jan. 5   *Perf. 13x13¼*
1031 A179   Sheet of 6, #a-f   15.00 15.00
Souvenir Sheet
Perf. 13¼ Syncopated
1032 A180 3000fr multi   16.50 16.50
Dated 2008.

A181

Birds and Lighthouses, Famous People   A182

No. 1033: a, 125fr, Alopochen aegyptiacus, El Montaza Lighthouse, Egypt. b, 150fr, Larus dominicanus, Agulhas Lighthouse, South Africa. c, 225fr, Gavia stellata, Europa Point Lighthouse, Gibraltar. d, 300fr, Oceanites oceanicus, Ilha do Goa Lighthouse, Mozambique. e, 400fr, Thalassarche cauta, Walvis Bay Lighthouse, Namibia. f, 1000fr, Pelecanus rufescens, Bwene Lighhouse, Tanzania.

3000fr, Phaethon aethereus, Lagos Lighthouse, Nigeria.

2009, Jan. 7   *Perf. 13x13¼*
1033 A181   Sheet of 6, #a-f   12.50 12.50
Souvenir Sheet
Perf. 13¼ Syncopated
1034 A182 3000fr multi   16.50 16.50
Dated 2008.

Scouting Centenary (in 2007)

No. 1035 — Robert Baden-Powell, Scouting emblem and: a, 125fr, Two Scouts saluting. b, 150fr, Two Scouts reading map. c, 225fr, Two Scouts standing with book. d, 300fr, Three Scouts looking at plant. e, 400fr, Two Scouts standing. f, 1000fr, Scouts and tent.

3000fr, Scouts practicing first aid.

2009, Jan. 7   *Perf. 13x13¼*
1035 A181   Sheet of 6, #a-f   12.50 12.50
Souvenir Sheet
Perf. 13¼ Syncopated
1036 A182 3000fr multi   16.50 16.50
Dated 2008.

Medical Pioneers

No. 1037: a, 125fr, Sir Humphry Davy. b, 150fr, Robert Koch. c, 225fr, Emil Adolf von Behring. d, 300fr, Louis Pasteur. e, 400fr, Sir Frederick Banting. f, 1000fr, Sir Alexander Fleming.

3000fr, Jean Henri Dunant.

2009, Jan. 7   *Perf. 13x13¼*
1037 A181   Sheet of 6, #a-f   12.50 12.50
Souvenir Sheet
Perf. 13¼ Syncopated
1038 A182 3000fr multi   16.50 16.50
Dated 2008.

Classical Composers

No. 1039: a, 125fr, Joseph Haydn. b, 150fr, Louis Hector Berlioz. c, 225fr, Franz Schubert. d, 300fr, Ludwig van Beethoven. e, 400fr, Franz Liszt. f, 1000fr, Johannes Brahms.

3000fr, Wolfgang Amadeus Mozart.

2009, Jan. 7   *Perf. 13x13¼*
1039 A181   Sheet of 6, #a-f   12.50 12.50
Souvenir Sheet
Perf. 13¼ Syncopated
1040 A182 3000fr multi   16.50 16.50
Dated 2008.

Ornithologists

No. 1041: a, 125fr, John James Audubon and Corvus cristatus. b, 150fr, John Gould and Trogon ambiguus. c, 225fr, Audubon and Columba migratoria. d, 300fr, Gould and Tanager darwinii. e, 400fr, Audubon and Corvus corax. f, 1000fr, Gould and Astrapia nigra.

3000fr, Gould, Audubon, two birds.

2009, Jan. 7   *Perf. 13x13¼*
1041 A181   Sheet of 6, #a-f   12.50 12.50
Souvenir Sheet
Perf. 13¼ Syncopated
1042 A182 3000fr multi   16.50 16.50
Dated 2008.

Paleontologists

No. 1043: a, 125fr, Barnum Brown and Archaeopteryx. b, 150fr, Thomas Condon and Gallimimus. c, 225fr, Robert Broom and Irritator. d, 300fr, William Buckland and Dimorphodon. e, 400fr, Edward Drinker Cope and Parasaurolophus. f, 1000fr, Edwin H. Colbert and Allosaurus.

3000fr, Roy Chapman Andrews and fossil dinosaur egg.

2009, Jan. 7   *Perf. 13x13¼*
1043 A181   Sheet of 6, #a-f   12.50 12.50
Souvenir Sheet
Perf. 13¼ Syncopated
1044 A182 3000fr multi   16.50 16.50
Dated 2008.

Humanists

No. 1045: a, 125fr, Miriam Makeba and Nelson Mandela. b, 150fr, Mahatma Gandhi. c, 225fr, Mother Teresa. d, 300fr, Yassir Arafat. e, 400fr, Shirin Ebadi. f, 1000fr, Mohammed El-Baradei.

3000fr, Dr. Martin Luther King, Jr.

2009, Jan. 7   *Perf. 13x13¼*
1045 A181   Sheet of 6, #a-f   12.50 12.50
Souvenir Sheet
Perf. 13¼ Syncopated
1046 A182 3000fr multi   16.50 16.50
Dated 2008.

Aviators

No. 1047: a, 125fr, Edward Rickenbacker. b, 150fr, Jimmy Doolittle. c, 225fr, Beryl Markham. d, 300fr, Elinor Smith. e, 400fr, Antoine de Saint-Exupéry. f, 1000fr, Charles Lindbergh.

3000fr, Wiley Post.

2009, Jan. 7   *Perf. 13x13¼*
1047 A181   Sheet of 6, #a-f   12.50 12.50
Souvenir Sheet
Perf. 13¼ Syncopated
1048 A182 3000fr multi   16.50 16.50
Dated 2008.

Astronauts and Cosmonauts

No. 1049: a, 125fr, Yuri Gagarin and Vostok 1. b, 150fr, Neil Armstrong and Apollo 11. c, 225fr, Alan Shepard, Jr. and Apollo 14. d, 300fr, Valentina Tereshkova and Vostok 6. e, 400fr, Pavel Popovich and Soyuz 14. f, 1000fr, John Glenn and Mercury 6.

3000fr, Yang Liwei and Shenzhou 5.

2009, Jan. 7   *Perf. 13x13¼*
1049 A181   Sheet of 6, #a-f   12.50 12.50
Souvenir Sheet
Perf. 13¼ Syncopated
1050 A182 3000fr multi   16.50 16.50
Dated 2008.

Mineralogists

No. 1051: a, 200fr, Ignacy Domeyko and sulfur. b, 250fr, James Dwight Dana and barite. c, 350fr, William Niven and rhodochrosite. d, 450fr, George Kunz and legrandite. e, 500fr, Waldemar Brogger and pyrite. f, 1000fr, Otto von Abich and rutile.

3000fr, Max von Laue and calcite.

2009, Jan. 7   *Perf. 13x13¼*
1051 A181   Sheet of 6, #a-f   15.00 15.00
Souvenir Sheet
Perf. 13¼ Syncopated
1052 A182 3000fr multi   16.50 16.50
Dated 2008.

Entomologists

No. 1053: a, 200fr, Nathan Banks and Nymphalis antiopa. b, 250fr, Louis Agassiz and Apatura ilia. c, 350fr, Henry Walter Bates and Gonepterix rhamni. d, 450fr, Per Olof Christopher Aurivillus and Biston betularius. e, 500fr, John Henry Comstock and Parnassius apollo. f, 1000fr, Jean Henri Fabre and Acronicta aceris.

3000fr, William Kirby and Acherontia atropos.

2009, Jan. 7   *Perf. 13x13¼*
1053 A181   Sheet of 6, #a-f   15.00 15.00
Souvenir Sheet
Perf. 13¼ Syncopated
1054 A182 3000fr multi   16.50 16.50
Dated 2008.

Mycologists

No. 1055: a, 200fr, Charles Horton Peck and Chroogomphus vinicolor. b, 250fr, Michel Adanson and Macrolepiota procera. c, 350fr, Miles Joseph Berkeley and Paxillus involutus. d, 450fr, Andrea Cesalpino and Tricholoma flavovirens. e, 500fr, Eduard Fischer and Phallus impudicus. f, 1000fr, Charles Edwin Bessey and Armillariella mellea.

3000fr, Peter Adolph Karsten and Marasmius oreades.

2009, Jan. 7   *Perf. 13x13¼*
1055 A181   Sheet of 6, #a-f   15.00 15.00
Souvenir Sheet
Perf. 13¼ Syncopated
1056 A182 3000fr multi   16.50 16.50
Dated 2008.

Explorers

No. 1057: a, 200fr, Ferdinand Magellan. b, 250fr, Vasco da Gama. c, 350fr, Christopher Columbus. d, 450fr, James Cook. e, 500fr, Marco Polo. f, 1000fr, Amerigo Vespucci.
3000fr, Columbus, diff.

2009, Jan. 7 *Perf. 13x13¼*
1057 A181 Sheet of 6, #a-f 15.00 15.00
Souvenir Sheet
Perf. 13¼ Syncopated
1058 A182 3000fr multi 16.50 16.50
Dated 2008.

David Livingstone

No. 1059 — Livingstone, map of Africa, and: a, 200fr, Livingstone with compass. b, 250fr, Lion attacking man. c, 350fr, Livingstone with rifle. d, 450fr, Men reading newspapers, African man and boy. e, 500fr, Livingstone with daughter. f, 1000fr, Livingstone reading book to Africans.
3000fr, Meeting Henry M. Stanley.

2009, Jan. 7 *Perf. 13x13¼*
1059 A181 Sheet of 6, #a-f 15.00 15.00
Souvenir Sheet
Perf. 13¼ Syncopated
1060 A182 3000fr multi 16.50 16.50
Dated 2008.

Nobel Peace Prize Recipients

No. 1061: a, 200fr, Jane Addams, 1931, and peace marchers. b, 250fr, Nelson Mandela, 1993, and globe. c, 350fr, Kofi Annan, 2001, United Nations emblem and dove. d, 450fr, Mother Teresa, 1979, and children. e, 500fr, Aung San Suu Kyi, 1991, Burmese children. f, 1000fr, Wangari Muta Maathai, 2004, globe and dove.
3000fr, Dr. Albert Schweitzer, 1952, map of Africa, Red Cross, hands.

2009, Jan. 7 *Perf. 13x13¼*
1061 A181 Sheet of 6, #a-f 15.00 15.00
Souvenir Sheet
Perf. 13¼ Syncopated
1062 A182 3000fr multi 16.50 16.50
Dated 2008.

World Chess Champions

No. 1063: a, 200fr, Boris Spassky. b, 250fr, Bobby Fischer. c, 350fr, Anatoly Karpov. d, 450fr, Garry Kasparaov. e, 500fr, Vladimir Kramnik. f, 1000fr, Viswanathan Anand.
3000fr, Tigran Petrosian.

2009, Jan. 7 *Perf. 13x13¼*
1063 A181 Sheet of 6, #a-f 15.00 15.00
Souvenir Sheet
Perf. 13¼ Syncopated
1064 A182 3000fr multi 16.50 16.50
Dated 2008.

Vincent Van Gogh

No. 1065 — Self-portraits and: a, 200fr, Vincent's Bedroom in Arles. b, 250fr, Olive Trees and the Alpilles in the Background. c, 350fr, Wheat Field with Cypresses. d, 450fr, The Night Café in the Place Lamartine in Arles. e, 500fr, The Red Vineyard. f, 1000fr, Starry Night.
3000fr, Starry Night over the Rhone.

2009, Jan. 7 *Perf. 13x13¼*
1065 A181 Sheet of 6, #a-f 15.00 15.00
Souvenir Sheet
Perf. 13¼ Syncopated
1066 A182 3000fr multi 16.50 16.50
Dated 2008.

70th Birthday of Romy Schneider

No. 1067 — Schneider and scenes from her films: a, 200fr, Le Trio Infernal, 1974. b, 250fr, Adorable Sinner, 1959. c, 350fr, Ludwig, 1972. d, 450fr, Sissi: The Young Empress, 1956. e, 500fr, César and Rosalie, 1972. f, 1000fr, Max and the Junkmen, 1971.
3000fr, Christine, 1958.

2009, Jan. 7 *Perf. 13x13¼*
1067 A181 Sheet of 6, #a-f 15.00 15.00
Souvenir Sheet
Perf. 13¼ Syncopated
1068 A182 3000fr multi 16.50 16.50
Dated 2008.

A183

Mushrooms and Fauna — A184

No. 1069 — Mushrooms: a, 125fr, Amanita caesarea. b, 150fr, Amanita pantherina. c, 225fr, Pleurotus eryngii. d, 300fr, Amanita rubescens. e, 400fr, Boletus edulis. f, 1000fr, Pluteus leoninus.
3000fr, Amanita phalloides.

2009, Mar. 2 *Perf. 13x13¼*
1069 A183 Sheet of 6, #a-f 11.50 11.50
Souvenir Sheet
Perf. 13¼ Syncopated
1070 A184 3000fr multi 15.50 15.50

Camels

No. 1071: a, 125fr, Camelus dromedarius. b, 150fr, Camelus bactrianus. c, 225fr, Camelus bactrianus, diff. d, 300fr, Camelus dromedarius, diff. e, 400fr, Camelus dromedarius, diff. f, 1000fr, Camelus bactrianus, diff.
3000fr, Two Camelus bactrianus.

2009, Mar. 2 *Perf. 13x13¼*
1071 A183 Sheet of 6, #a-f 11.50 11.50
Souvenir Sheet
Perf. 13¼ Syncopated
1072 A184 3000fr multi 15.50 15.50

Gorillas

No. 1073: a, 125fr, Gorilla gorilla gorilla. b, 150fr, Gorilla gorilla. c, 225fr, Gorilla beringei graueri. d, 300fr, Gorilla beringei beringei. e, 400fr, Gorilla beringei beringei. f, 1000fr, Gorilla gorilla diehli.
3000fr, Gorilla gorilla, diff.

2009, Mar. 2 *Perf. 13x13¼*
1073 A183 Sheet of 6, #a-f 11.50 11.50
Souvenir Sheet
Perf. 13¼ Syncopated
1074 A184 3000fr multi 15.50 15.50

Dogs

No. 1075: a, 125fr, Aidi. b, 150fr, Africanis. c, 225fr, Sloughi. d, 300fr, Basenji. e, 400fr, Boerboel. f, 1000fr, Azawakh.
3000fr, Rhodesian ridgeback.

2009, Mar. 2 *Perf. 13x13¼*
1075 A183 Sheet of 6, #a-f 11.50 11.50
Souvenir Sheet
Perf. 13¼ Syncopated
1076 A184 3000fr multi 15.50 15.50

Beetles

No. 1077: a, 125fr, Trachelophorus giraffa. b, 150fr, Cicindela campestris. c, 225fr, Leptinotarsa decemlineata (light blue frame). d, 300fr, Gelastocoris oculatus (light blue frame). e, 400fr, Scarites guineensis. f, 1000fr, Goliathus albosignatus.
3000fr, Staphylinus olens.

2009, Mar. 2 *Perf. 13x13¼*
1077 A183 Sheet of 6, #a-f 11.50 11.50
Souvenir Sheet
Perf. 13¼ Syncopated
1078 A184 3000fr multi 15.50 15.50

Bees and Wasps

No. 1079: a, 125fr, Chrysis ignita. b, 150fr, Megarhyssa macrurus. c, 225fr, Leptinotarsa decemlineata (yellowish green frame). d, 300fr, Gelastorcoris oculatus (yellowish green frame). e, 400fr, Parazumia symmorpha. f, 1000fr, Pteromalus puparum.
3000fr, Sphex ichneumoneus.

2009, Mar. 2 *Perf. 13x13¼*
1079 A183 Sheet of 6, #a-f 11.50 11.50
Souvenir Sheet
Perf. 13¼ Syncopated
1080 A184 3000fr multi 15.50 15.50

Fish

No. 1081: a, 125fr, Latimeria chalumnae. b, 150fr, Synanceia verrucosa. c, 225fr, Scorpaena scrofa. d, 300fr, Periophthalmus argentilineatus. e, 400fr, Lophius americanus. f, 1000fr, Pristis microdon.
3000fr, Narcine brasiliensis.

2009, Mar. 2 *Perf. 13x13¼*
1081 A183 Sheet of 6, #a-f 11.50 11.50
Souvenir Sheet
Perf. 13¼ Syncopated
1082 A184 3000fr multi 15.50 15.50

Shells and Lighthouses

No. 1083: a, 125fr, Pleurotomaria fricana and Hood Point Lighthouse. b, 150fr, Patella ferruginea and Swakopmund Lighthouse. c, 225fr, Tectus pyramis and Cape Columbine Lighthouse. d, 350fr, Monodonta turbinata and Seal Point Lighthouse. e, 400fr, Mesalia opalina and Moroni Lighthouse. f, 1000fr, Cypraea diliculum and Cape Agulhas Lighthouse.
3000fr, Ranella olearia and Umhlanga Rocks Lighthouse.

2009, Mar. 2 *Perf. 13x13¼*
1083 A183 Sheet of 6, #a-f 11.50 11.50
Souvenir Sheet
Perf. 13¼ Syncopated
1084 A184 3000fr multi 15.50 15.50

Cats

No. 1085: a, 200fr, Sokoke. b, 250fr, Abyssinian. c, 350fr, Egyptian Mau. d, 450fr, Sokoke, diff. e, 500fr, Abyssinian, diff. f, 1000fr, Egyptian Mau, diff.
3000fr, Felis nigripes.

2009, Mar. 2 *Perf. 13x13¼*
1085 A183 Sheet of 6, #a-f 14.50 14.50
Souvenir Sheet
Perf. 13¼ Syncopated
1086 A184 3000fr multi 15.50 15.50

Owls

No. 1087: a, 200fr, Otus pembaensis. b, 250fr, Ptilopsis granti. c, 350fr, Tyto alba. d, 450fr, Asio otus. e, 500fr, Strix woodfordii. f, 1000fr, Tyto soumagnei.
3000fr, Bubo africanus.

2009, Mar. 2 *Perf. 13x13¼*
1087 A183 Sheet of 6, #a-f 14.50 14.50
Souvenir Sheet
Perf. 13¼ Syncopated
1088 A184 3000fr multi 15.50 15.50

Kingfishers

No. 1089: a, 200fr, Megaceryle maxima. b, 250fr, Alcedo atthis. c, 350fr, Halcyon senegalensis. d, 450fr, Ipsidina picta. e, 500fr, Todiramphus chloris. f, 1000fr, Alcedo cristata.
3000fr, Halcyon malimbica.

2009, Mar. 2 *Perf. 13x13¼*
1089 A183 Sheet of 6, #a-f 14.50 14.50
Souvenir Sheet
Perf. 13¼ Syncopated
1090 A184 3000fr multi 15.50 15.50

Butterflies

No. 1091: a, 200fr, Crenis pechuelli. b, 250fr, Charaxes zingha. c, 350fr, Taenaris catops turdula. d, 450fr, Danaus chrysippus alcippus. e, 500fr, Anaea cyanae. f, 1000fr, Epiphile orea negrina.
3000fr, Cithaeria aurora.

2009, Mar. 2 *Perf. 13x13¼*
1091 A183 Sheet of 6, #a-f 14.50 14.50
Souvenir Sheet
Perf. 13¼ Syncopated
1092 A184 3000fr multi 15.50 15.50

Dolphins

No. 1093: a, 200fr, Stenella coeruleoalba. b, 250fr, Stenella attenuata. c, 350fr, Sousa plumbea. d, 450fr, Stenella longirostris. e, 500fr, Tursiops truncatus. f, 1000fr, Lissodelphis peronii.
3000fr, Lagenorhynchus cruciger.

2009, Mar. 2 *Perf. 13x13¼*
1093 A183 Sheet of 6, #a-f 14.50 14.50
Souvenir Sheet
Perf. 13¼ Syncopated
1094 A184 3000fr multi 15.50 15.50

Frogs

No. 1095: a, 200fr, Xenopos laevis. b, 250fr, Astyloternus robustus. c, 350fr, Mantella aurantiaca. d, 450fr, Rana goliath. e, 500fr, Pyxicephalus adspersus. f, 1000fr, Breviceps mossambicus.
3000fr, Phrynomantis bifasciatus.

2009, Mar. 2 *Perf. 13x13¼*
1095 A183 Sheet of 6, #a-f 14.50 14.50
Souvenir Sheet
Perf. 13¼ Syncopated
1096 A184 3000fr multi 15.50 15.50

Prehistoric Animals

No. 1097: a, 200fr, Heterodontosaurus. b, 250fr, Malawisaurus. c, 350fr, Carnotaurus. d, 450fr, Rhamphorhynchus. e, 500fr, Ouranosaurus. f, 1000fr, Herrerasaurus.
3000fr, Abrictosaurus.

2009, Mar. 2 *Perf. 13x13¼*
1097 A183 Sheet of 6, #a-f 14.50 14.50
Souvenir Sheet
Perf. 13¼ Syncopated
1098 A184 3000fr multi 15.50 15.50

SEMI-POSTAL STAMPS

Anti-Malaria Issue
Common Design Type
Perf. 12½x12

1962, Apr. 7 **Engr.** **Unwmk.**
B1 CD108 25fr + 5fr brt pink 4.00 4.00
WHO drive to eradicate malaria.

Nurse Feeding Infant — SP1

1967, July 3 **Engr.** *Perf. 13*
B2 SP1 25fr + 5fr multi 3.25 3.25
For the Red Cross.

Mother and Child — SP2

1974, Aug. 10 **Engr.** *Perf. 13*
B3 SP2 35fr + 10fr red & dk brn 2.75 2.75
For the Red Cross.
For surcharge see No. 144.

Space Achievements SP3

World Philatelic Programs emblems (stamp collecting or Halley's Comet) and astronomer or satellite: a, Galileo. b, Copernicus. c, Kepler. d, Halley. e, *Planet A*, Japan, and 3 stars. f, *ICE*, US. g, *Planet A*, 5 stars. h, *Vega*, USSR.

Miniature Sheet

1988   Litho.   Perf. 13½
B4   Sheet of 8   15.00 15.00
  a.-h. SP3 200fr +10fr multi   1.50 1.50
   See No. C193.
   For surcharges see Nos. 816P-816S.

AIR POST STAMPS

Comoro Village — AP1

Comoro Men and Moroni Mosque — AP2

Design: 200fr, Mosque of Ouani, Anjouan.

1950-54   Unwmk.   Engr.   Perf. 13
C1   AP1 50fr grn & red brn   4.50 1.40
C2   AP2 100fr dk brn & red   6.75 1.75
C3   AP1 200fr dk grn, rose brn
      & pur ('54)   26.00 9.50
    Nos. C1-C3 (3)   37.25 12.65

Liberation Issue
Common Design Type

1954, June 6
C4   CD102 15fr sepia & red   35.00 20.00

Madrepora Fructicosa
AP3

100fr, Coral, shells and sea anemones.

1962, Jan. 13   Photo.   Perf. 12½x13
C5   AP3 100fr multi   15.00 15.00
C6   AP3 500fr multi   30.00 20.00

Telstar Issue
Common Design Type

1962, Dec. 5   Engr.   Perf. 13
C7   CD111 25fr dp vio, dl pur &
      red lil   5.00 3.00

Type of Regular Issue
Unwmk.

1963, Dec. 27   Engr.   Perf. 13
Size: 26½x48mm
C8   A13 65fr Baskets   5.00 3.50
C9   A13 200fr Pendant   10.00 5.25

Boat Type of Regular Issue

1964, Aug. 7   Photo.   Perf. 13
Size: 27x48mm
C10 A14 50fr Mayotte pirogue   4.50 1.75
C11 A14 85fr Schooner   7.00 2.50

Olympic Torch
and
Boxers — AP4

1964, Oct. 10   Engr.   Perf. 13
C12 AP4 100fr red brn, dk brn &
      gray grn   7.50 7.50
  18th Olympic Games, Tokyo, Oct. 10-25.

Order of Star of
Grand
Comoro — AP5

1964, Dec. 10   Photo.   Perf. 13
C13 AP5 500fr multi   17.50 15.00

ITU Issue
Common Design Type

1965, May 17   Photo.   Perf. 13
C14 CD120 50fr gray, grnsh bl
      & ol   20.00 10.00

French Satellite A-1 Issue
Common Design Type

Designs: 25fr, Diamant rocket and launching installations. 30fr, A-1 satellite.

1966, Jan. 17   Engr.   Perf. 13
C15 CD121 25fr dk pur & ultra   4.50 4.50
C16 CD121 30fr dk pur & ultra   6.00 6.00
  a. Strip of 2, #C15-C16 + label 11.00 11.00

French Satellite D-1 Issue
Common Design Type

1966, May 16   Engr.   Perf. 13
C17 CD122 30fr dk grn, org &
      brn   4.00 4.00

Old Gun Battery, Dzaoudzi — AP6

200fr, Ksar Castle, Mutsamudu, vert.

1966, Dec. 19   Photo.   Perf. 13
C18 AP6 50fr multi   5.00 2.50
C19 AP6 200fr multi   9.00 5.75

Bird Type of Regular Issue

Birds: 75fr, Madagascar paradise flycatchers. 100fr, Blue-cheeked bee eaters.

1967, June 20   Photo.   Perf. 13
C20 A17 75fr yel grn & multi   10.50 6.50
C21 A17 100fr lt bl & multi   13.00 8.00

Woman
Skier — AP7

1968, Apr. 29   Engr.   Perf. 13
C22 AP7 70fr brt grn, lt bl & choc 6.50 4.75
  10th Winter Olympic Games, Grenoble, France, Feb. 6-18, 1968.

Fish Type of Regular Issue

50fr, Moorish idol. 90fr, Diagramma lineatus.

1968, Aug. 1   Engr.   Perf. 13
Size: 47½x27mm
C23 A19 50fr plum blk & yel   8.00 4.00
C24 A19 90fr brt grn, yel & gray
      grn   10.00 5.25
  For surcharge & overprint see Nos. C52, C74.

Swimmer, Butterfly Stroke — AP8

1969, Jan. 27   Photo.   Perf. 12½
C25 AP8 65fr ver, grnsh bl & blk 5.25 3.50
  19th Olympic Games, Mexico City, 10/12-27.

Flower Type of Regular Issue

50fr, Heliconia sp. 85fr, Tuberose. 200fr, Orchid (angraecum eburneum).

1969, Mar. 20   Photo.   Perf. 13
Size: 27x48mm
C26 A21 50fr multi, vert.   4.75 3.50
C27 A21 85fr multi, vert.   5.50 4.50
C28 A21 200fr multi, vert.   11.00 6.00
    Nos. C26-C28 (3)   21.25 14.00

Concorde Issue
Common Design Type

1969, Apr. 17   Engr.
C29 CD129 100fr pur & brn
      org   24.00 16.00

View of EXPO,
Globe and
Moon — AP9

90fr, Geisha, map of Japan & EXPO emblem.

1970, Sept. 13   Photo.   Perf. 13
C30 AP9 60fr slate & multi   4.50 2.40
C31 AP9 90fr multi   5.50 3.25
  EXPO '70 International Exposition, Osaka, Japan, Mar. 15-Sept. 13.

Sunset over Mutsamudu — AP10

Map of Archipelago — AP11

Designs: 20fr, Sada Village, Mayotte. 65fr, Old Iconi Palace, Grand Comoro. 85fr, Nioumatchoua Island, Moheli.

1971, May 3   Photo.   Perf. 13
C32 AP10 15fr dk bl & multi   1.20 .65
C33 AP10 20fr multi   1.75 .80
C34 AP10 65fr grn & multi   3.75 1.60
C35 AP10 85fr bl & multi   5.50 2.50

Engr.
C36 AP11 100fr brn red, grn &
      vio bl   7.50 5.50
    Nos. C32-C36 (5)   19.70 11.05
  See Nos. 107-110, C45-C49, C53, C62-C64. For overprints & surcharges see Nos. 143, C69, C71, C73, C76-C77, C79-C80, C82, C84.

Flower Type of Regular Issue

Flowers: 60fr, Hibiscus schizopetalus. 85fr, Acalypha sanderii.

1971, July 19   Photo.   Perf. 13
Size: 27x48mm
C37 A25 60fr grn, ver & yel   5.00 2.40
C38 A25 85fr grn, red & yel   6.50 4.75
  For surcharge see No. C75.

Mural, Moroni Airport — AP12

Designs: 85fr, Mural in Arrival Hall, Moroni Airport. 100fr, View of Moroni Airport.

1972, Mar. 30   Photo.   Perf. 13
C39 AP12 65fr gray & multi   2.00 .85
C40 AP12 85fr gray & multi   2.25 1.20

Engr.
C41 AP12 100fr brn, bl & slate
      grn   4.00 2.10
    Nos. C39-C41 (3)   8.25 4.15
  New airport in Moroni.

Eiffel Tower and Moroni Telephone Exchange — AP13

75fr, Frenchman and Comoro Islander talking on telephone, radio tower and beacons.

1972, Apr. 24
C42 AP13 35fr dl red & gray   1.25 .85
C43 AP13 75fr dk car, vio & bl   2.25 .95
  First radio-telephone connection between France and Comoro Islands.

Underwater Spear-fishing — AP14

1972, July 5   Engr.   Perf. 13
C44 AP14 70fr vio bl, brt grn &
            mar   8.75 5.50
For surcharge see No. C78.

Types of 1971
Designs: 20fr, Cape Sima. 35fr, Bambao Palace. 40fr, Domoni Palace. 60fr, Gomajou Peninsula. 100fr, Map of Anjouan Island.

1972, Nov. 15   Photo.
C45 AP10 20fr brn & multi   .90   .65
C46 AP10 35fr dk grn & multi   1.20   .80
C47 AP10 40fr bl & multi   1.75   .95
C48 AP10 60fr grnsh blk &
            multi   2.50 1.60
Engr.
C49 AP11 100fr mar, bl & sl
            grn   13.50 7.25
     Nos. C45-C49 (5)   19.85 11.25

Pres. Said
Mohamed Cheikh
(1904-70)
AP15

1973, Mar. 16   Photo.   Perf. 13
C50 AP15 20fr multi   1.25   .80
C51 AP15 35fr multi   1.60 1.00
For overprints see Nos. C70, C72.

No. C24 Surcharged

1973, Apr. 30   Engr.   Perf. 13
C52 A19 120fr on 90fr multi   13.00 7.25
Intl. Commission for Coelacanth Studies.

Map of
Grand
Comoro
AP16

1973, June 28   Engr.   Perf. 13
C53 AP16 135fr vio, bl & dk brn 9.50 6.50
See Nos. C65, C68. For surcharges see Nos. C90-C92.

Karthala
Volcano
AP17

1973, July 16   Photo.   Perf. 13x12½
C54 AP17 120fr multi   7.50 5.50
Eruption of Karthala, Sept. 1972.
For surcharge see No. C89.

Armauer G.
Hansen — AP18

Design: 150fr, Nicolaus Copernicus (1473-1543), Polish astronomer.

1973, Sept. 5   Engr.   Perf. 13
C55 AP18 100fr brn, dk bl & sl
            grn   7.00 3.50
C56 AP18 150fr grnsh bl, vio bl &
            choc   8.00 5.25
Cent. of the discovery of the Hansen bacillus, the cause of leprosy.
For overprint & surcharge see Nos. C81, C93.

Pablo Picasso (1881-1973) — AP19

1973, Sept. 30   Photo.
C57 AP19 200fr blk & multi   12.00 9.75
Souvenir Sheet
C58 AP19 100fr blk & multi   16.00 14.50
For overprint see No. C87.

Order of the Star
of
Anjouan — AP20

1974, Jan. 7   Photo.   Perf. 13
C59 AP20 500fr brn, bl & gold   13.00 9.50
For overprint see No. C95.

Said Omar ben
Soumeth — AP21

135fr, Grand Mufti Said Omar, horiz.

1974, Jan. 31   Perf. 13x13½, 13½x13
C60 AP21 135fr blk & multi   4.50 2.75
C61 AP21 200fr blk & multi   5.50 3.50
For overprint & surcharge see Nos. C85, C88.

Types of 1971-73
Designs (Views on Mayotte): 20fr, Moya Beach. 35fr, Chiconi. 90fr, Port Mamutzu. 120fr, Map of Mayotte.

1974, Aug. 31   Photo.   Perf. 13
C62 AP10 20fr bl & multi   1.20   .95
C63 AP10 35fr grn & multi   2.50 2.00
C64 AP10 90fr multi   6.25 3.50
Engr.
C65 AP16 120fr ultra & grn   9.00 5.50
     Nos. C62-C65 (4)   18.95 11.95

Jet Take-off — AP22

1975, Jan. 10   Engr.   Perf. 13
C66 AP22 135fr multi   7.25 4.75
First direct route Moroni-Hahaya-Paris.
For surcharge see No. C86.

Rotary Emblem, Meeting House,
Map — AP23

1975, Feb. 23   Photo.   Perf. 13
C67 AP23 250fr multi   10.50 7.25
Rotary Intl., 70th anniv., Moroni Rotary Club, 10th anniv.
For surcharge see No. C94.

Map Type of 1973
Design: 230fr, Map of Moheli, horiz.

1975, May 26   Engr.   Perf. 13
C68 AP16 230fr ocher, ol grn &
            bl   11.00 8.00

STATE OF COMORO
Issues of 1968-75 Surcharged and
Overprinted in Black, Silver, Red or
Orange

1975   Printing & Perfs. as Before
C69 AP10 10fr on 20fr #C62   .60   .25
C70 AP15 20fr (S)   1.00   .25
C71 AP10 30fr on 35fr (R)
            #C63   1.00   .25
C72 AP15 35fr (S)   1.25   .75
C73 AP10 40fr (O)   1.50   .75
C74 A19 50fr   2.50 1.25
C75 A25 75fr on 60fr   2.00 1.10
C76 AP10 75fr on 60fr   2.00 1.10

C77 AP10 75fr on 65fr (O)   2.00 1.10
C78 AP14 75fr on 70fr   2.50 1.25
C79 AP11 100fr #C36   4.00 2.00
C80 AP11 100fr #C49   4.00 2.00
C81 AP18 100fr   4.00 2.00
C82 AP10 100fr on 85fr (O)   2.50 1.50
C83 A25 100fr on 85fr   2.50 1.50
C84 AP10 100fr on 90fr   2.50 1.50
C85 AP21 100fr on 135fr (S)   2.50 1.50
C86 AP22 100fr on 135fr   3.00 2.00
C87 AP19 200fr (S)   8.00 4.00
C88 AP21 200fr (S)   6.00 3.50
C89 AP17 200fr on 120fr   8.00 4.00
C90 AP16 200fr on 120fr   6.00 3.50
C91 AP16 200fr on 135fr   6.00 3.50
C92 AP16 200fr on 230fr   6.00 3.50
C93 AP18 400fr on 150fr   10.00 5.25
C94 AP23 400fr on 250fr   10.00 5.25
C95 AP20 500fr   12.00 7.25
     Nos. C69-C95 (27)   113.35 61.80

See postage section for airmail stamps that are part of joint postage/airmail sets.

Rotary
Emblem,
Landscape
AP26

1979, July 31   Litho.   Perf. 13x12½
C107 AP26 400fr multi   7.00 3.00
Rotary International.

IYC Emblem,
Mother and
Child — AP27

1979, July 31   Perf. 13x13½
C108 AP27 250fr multi   3.50 3.50
Intl. Year of the Child. See No. CB1. For surcharges see Nos. C121, C202.

Dimadjou
Dispensary,
Map of
Southern
Africa,
Emblem
AP28

260fr, Globe, Concorde, emblem.

1980, Feb. 23   Litho.   Perf. 12½
C109 AP28 100fr shown   1.25   .40
C110 AP28 260fr multicolored   3.00 1.00
Rotary International, 75th anniv. and Moroni Rotary Club, 15th anniv. (100fr).
For surcharges see Nos. 815L, C119-C120.

First Transatlantic Flight, 50th
Anniversary — AP29

1980, May 30   Litho.   Perf. 13
C111 AP29 200fr multi   3.50 1.75

No. C111 Surcharged in Blue

1981, Feb.   **Litho.**   *Perf. 13*
C112 AP29 30fr on 200fr multi   1.00   .35

The Dove and the Rainbow, by
Picasso — AP30

Picasso Birth Centenary: 70fr, Still Life on a
Sideboard. 150fr, Studio with Plaster Head.
250fr, Bowl and Pot, vert. 500fr, The Red
Tablecloth.

1981, June 30   **Litho.**   *Perf. 12½*
C113 AP30 40fr multi   .55   .25
C114 AP30 70fr multi   .95   .25
C115 AP30 150fr multi   1.90   .50
C116 AP30 250fr multi   3.25   .70
C117 AP30 500fr multi   6.25 1.50
    Nos. C113-C117 (5)   12.90 3.20

For surcharges see Nos. 815G, C118.

Nos. C114, C109-C110, CB1 Srchd.

1981, Nov.   **Litho.**   *Perf. 12½, 13*
C118 AP30 10fr on 70fr multi   .40   .40
C119 AP28 10fr on 100fr multi   .80   .80
C120 AP28 50fr on 260fr multi   2.00   .25
C121 AP27 50fr on 200fr+30fr
         multi   2.00   .25
    Nos. C118-C121 (4)   5.20 1.70

Manned Flight Bicentenary — AP31

Balloons: 100fr, Montgolfiere, 1783. 200fr,
Lunardi, 1784. 300fr, Blanchard and Jeffries,
1785. 400fr, Giffard, 1852, horiz.
500fr, Paris Siege. 1870.

1983, Apr. 20   **Litho.**   *Perf. 13*
C122 AP31 100fr multicolored   1.00   .30
C123 AP31 200fr multicolored   1.90   .50
C124 AP31 300fr multicolored   3.25   .90
C125 AP31 400fr multicolored   4.50 1.25
    Nos. C122-C125 (4)   10.65 2.95

Souvenir Sheet

C126 AP31 500fr multicolored   5.50 1.50

For overprints and surcharges see Nos.
602, 812T, 815P.

Pre-Olympic Year Sailing — AP32

150fr, Type 470, pink and yellow sail. 200fr,
Flying Dutchman. 300fr, Type 470, white sails.
400fr, Finn.
500fr, Soling.

1983, June 30   **Litho.**   *Perf. 13*
C127 AP32 150fr multi   1.50   .40
C128 AP32 200fr multi   2.25   .50
C129 AP32 300fr multi   3.25   .90
C130 AP32 400fr multi   4.75 1.00
    Nos. C127-C130 (4)   11.75 2.80

Souvenir Sheet

C131 AP32 500fr multi   5.50 1.50

For overprint and surcharge see Nos. 603,
C206.

1984 Summer Olympics — AP33

60fr, Basketball, 2 players. 100fr, Basketball, 6 players. 165fr, Basketball, 4 players.
175fr, Baseball catcher, horiz. 200fr, Baseball,
horiz.
500fr, Basketball, diff.

1984, July 10   **Litho.**   *Perf. 13*
C132 AP33 60fr multicolored   .50   .25
C133 AP33 100fr multicolored   .90   .40
C134 AP33 165fr multicolored   1.50   .65
C135 AP33 175fr multicolored   1.60   .65
C136 AP33 200fr shown   1.90   .80
    Nos. C132-C136 (5)   6.40 2.75

Souvenir Sheet

C137 AP33 500fr multicolored   8.00 1.50

Nos. C132-C134 vert.

Development
Conference
AP34

475fr, Tools for development.

1984, July 2   **Litho.**   *Perf. 13*
C138 AP34 475fr multi   5.50 2.00

For surcharge see No. 796I.

Audubon Bicentenary — AP35

100fr, Hirundo rustica, vert. 125fr, Icterus
galbula, vert. 150fr, Buteo lineatus. 500fr,
Sphyropieus varius.

1985, Jan. 15   **Litho.**   *Perf. 13*
C139 AP35 100fr multicolored   1.25   .40
C140 AP35 125fr multicolored   1.50   .50
C141 AP35 150fr multicolored   2.00   .60
C142 AP35 500fr multicolored   5.25 2.00
    Nos. C139-C142 (4)   10.00 3.50

Moroni Port Missile Defense — AP36

No. C146, Ngome Ntsoudjini Scout troop.

1985, May 20   **Litho.**   *Perf. 13x12½*
C145 AP36 200fr multi   3.00 1.25
C146 AP36 200fr multi   3.00 1.25
   a.   Pair, #C145-C146 + label   6.00 6.00

PHILEXAFRICA '85, Lome.
For surcharges see Nos. C207-C208.

Natl. Flag, Sun,
Outline Map of
Islands — AP37

1985, July 6
C147 AP37 10fr multi   .30   .25
C148 AP37 15fr multi   .30   .25
C149 AP37 125fr multi   2.25   .60
C150 AP37 300fr multi   5.50 1.50
    Nos. C147-C150 (4)   8.35 2.60

Natl. independence, 10th anniv.
For surcharge see No. 815Q.

Runners — AP38

1985, Nov. 12
C151 AP38 250fr shown   2.75 1.75
C152 AP38 250fr Mining   2.75 1.75
   a.   Pair, #C151-C152 + label   6.00 6.00

PHILEXAFRICA '85, Lome, Togo, 11/16-24.
For surcharges see Nos. 815H-815I, C204-
C205.

Air Transport Union, UTA, 50th
Anniv. — AP39

25fr, F-AOUL seaplane. 75fr, Camel driver,
DC-8. 100fr, Noratlas and Heron DC-4s. 125fr,
UTA cargo plane. 1000fr, Aircraft, 1935-1985.

1985, Dec. 30   **Litho.**   *Perf. 13*
C153 AP39 25fr multi   .25   .25
C154 AP39 75fr multi   .75   .30
C155 AP39 100fr multi   1.10   .40
   a.   Souv. sheet of 3, #C153-
       C155, perf. 12½   3.50 2.25
C156 AP39 125fr multi   1.40   .60

Size: 40x52mm
Perf. 12½x13
C157 AP39 1000fr multi   12.00 6.00
   a.   Souv. sheet of 2, #C156-
       C157, perf. 12½   13.00 8.00
    Nos. C153-C157 (5)   15.50 7.55

Halley's Comet — AP40

Comets, astronomers and probes: 125fr,
Edmond Halley, Giotto probe. 150fr,
Giacobini-Zinner, 1959. 225fr, Encke, 1961.
300fr, Bradfield, 1980. 450fr, Planet A probe.

1986, Mar. 7   *Perf. 13*
C158 AP40 125fr multi   1.25   .45
C159 AP40 150fr multi   1.50   .50
C160 AP40 225fr multi   2.50   .90
C161 AP40 300fr multi   3.00 1.25
C162 AP40 450fr multi   5.00 1.75
    Nos. C158-C162 (5)   13.25 4.85

For surcharges see Nos. 796S, 804H,
804R, 812P.

1986 World Cup Soccer
Championships, Mexico — AP41

Various soccer plays.

1986, June 11   **Litho.**   *Perf. 13*
C163 AP41 125fr multi   1.25   .45
C164 AP41 210fr multi   2.25   .80
C165 AP41 500fr multi   5.50 2.00
C166 AP41 600fr multi   6.00 2.25
    Nos. C163-C166 (4)   15.00 5.50

For surcharges see Nos. 796C, 800Q, 815C.

Tennis at the
1988 Summer
Olympics — AP42

Various players.

1987, Jan. 28   **Litho.**   *Perf. 13½*
C167 AP42 150fr multi   1.75   .45
C168 AP42 250fr multi   3.00   .75
C169 AP42 500fr multi   5.50 1.50
C170 AP42 600fr multi   6.75 1.75
    Nos. C167-C170 (4)   17.00 4.45

For overprints and surcharges see Nos.
796N, 796U, 815J, 816L, 816N, C183-C186,
C203.

World Wildlife Fund — AP43

Various pictures of the mongoose lemur.

1987, Feb. 18   *Perf. 13*

C171	AP43	75fr multi, vert.	2.50	.50
C172	AP43	100fr multi	3.50	.75
C173	AP43	125fr multi	5.50	1.00
C174	AP43	150fr multi	6.50	1.25
		Nos. C171-C174 (4)	18.00	3.50

1988
Winter
Olympics,
Calgary
AP44

150fr, Slalom. 225fr, Ski jumping. 500fr, Women's giant slalom. 600fr, Luge.

1987, Apr. 10   Litho.   *Perf. 13½*

C175	AP44	150fr multi	1.25	.45
C176	AP44	225fr multi	2.25	.75
C177	AP44	500fr multi	5.50	1.60
C178	AP44	600fr multi	6.00	2.25
		Nos. C175-C178 (4)	15.00	5.05

For surcharges see Nos. 800R, 812U.

AP45

Aviation
History
AP46

Designs: 200fr, Inventors Didier Daurat and Raymond Vanier with 1935 Air Blue F-ANR1. 300fr, Farman biplane, 1st scheduled airmail delivery, Paris-LeMans-St. Nazaire, Aug. 17, 1918. 500fr, Bleriot aircraft, 1st scheduled airmail delivery, Villacoublay-Vendome-Poitiers-Pauillac, Oct. 15, 1913. 1000fr, Henri Pequet and his aircraft, Feb. 18, 1911.

1987, Dec. 29   Litho.   *Perf. 13*

C179	AP45	200fr multi	2.25	.65
C180	AP45	300fr multi	3.25	1.00
C181	AP45	500fr multi	5.50	1.60

         Perf. 12½x13

C182	AP46	1000fr multi	11.00	2.25
		Nos. C179-C182 (4)	22.00	5.50

Airmail history exposition, Allahabad.
For surcharges see Nos. 800S, 804D.

Nos. C167-C170 Ovptd. in Red for 1988 Olympic Tennis Champions

Overprint includes name of athlete and "Medaille d'or / Seoul" or "Medaille / d'argent / Seoul."

1988, Nov.   Litho.   *Perf. 13½*

C183	AP42	"Miloslav Mecir / (Tchec.)"	1.25	.75
C184	AP42	"Tim Mayotte / (U.S.A.)"	1.90	1.40
C185	AP42	"Steffi Graf / (R.F.A.)"	5.00	2.75
C186	AP42	"Gabriela Sabatini / (Argentine)"	6.00	3.75
		Nos. C183-C186 (4)	14.15	8.65

For surcharges see Nos. 800T, 815K, 816M, 816O.

Early Aviators and Aircraft — AP47

100fr, Alberto Santos-Dumont (1873-1932), & *Bagatelle,* 1st documented power flight in Europe, Oct. 23, 1906. 150fr, Wright Brothers & *Flyer A.* 200fr, Louis Bleriot (1872-1936) & *Bleriot XI,* 1st crossing of the English Channel in a heavier-than-air craft, July 25, 1909. 300fr, Henri Farman (1874-1958) & Voisin biplane, 1st fixed-route 1-kilometer circular flight, Jan. 13, 1908. 500fr, Gabriel (1880-1973) & Charles (1882-1912) Voisin, established 1st biplane factory (1908), & Voisin biplane. 800fr, Roland Garros (1888-1918), 1st trans-Mediterranean flight, Sept. 23, 1913.

1988, Dec. 7   Litho.   *Perf. 13*

C187	AP47	100fr pur	.90	.45
C188	AP47	150fr brt lil rose	1.60	.60
C189	AP47	200fr blk	2.00	.90
C190	AP47	300fr dark yel org	3.00	.90
C191	AP47	500fr dark blue	5.00	1.50
C192	AP47	800fr lt olive grn	7.50	3.00
		Nos. C187-C192 (6)	20.00	7.35

For surcharges see Nos. 800B, 800U, 804E, C209.

Souvenir Sheet

Space Achievements — AP48

Design: World Philatelic Programs stamp collecting emblem, Soviet satellite and Edmond Halley.

1988   Litho.   *Perf. 13½*

C193	AP48	750fr multi	8.00	1.50

Nos. C108, C168,
C151-C152, C128,
C145-C146 and
C189 Surcharged

1989   Litho.   *Perfs. as Before*

C202	AP27	5fr on 250fr #C108	.25	.25
C203	AP42	25fr on 250fr #C168	.25	.25
C204	AP38	50fr on 250fr #C151	.50	.25
C205	AP38	50fr on 250fr #C152	.50	.25
a.		Pair, #C204-C205 + label	1.25	1.25
C206	AP32	150fr on 200fr #C128	1.40	.60
C207	AP36	150fr on 200fr #C145	1.40	.60
C208	AP36	150fr on 200fr #C146	1.40	.60
a.		Pair, #C207-C208 + label	6.00	6.00
C209	AP47	150fr on 200fr #C189	1.40	.60
		Nos. C202-C209 (8)	7.10	3.40

World Cup Soccer, Championships,
Italy — AP50

Various soccer plays and map of Italy.

1990, June   Litho.   *Perf. 13*

C210	AP50	75fr multicolored	.60	.30
C211	AP50	150fr multicolored	1.40	.60
C212	AP50	500fr multicolored	4.25	1.90
C213	AP50	1000fr multicolored	8.75	4.00
		Nos. C210-C213 (4)	15.00	6.80

For surcharge see No. 800V.

Souvenir Sheet

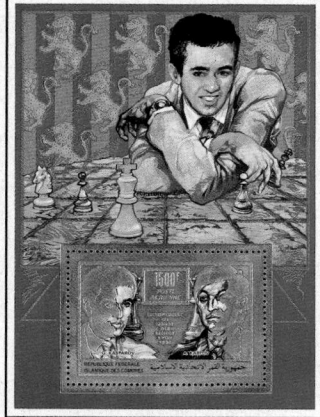

Garry Kasparov, Anatoly Karpov,
Russian Chess Champions — AP51

Litho. & Embossed

1991, Aug. 5   *Perf. 13½*

C214	AP51	1500fr gold & multi	12.00	—

World Chess Championships.

1992
Summer
Olympics,
Barcelona
AP52

Litho. & Embossed

1992, July 28   *Perf. 13½*

C215	AP52	1500fr gold & multi	26.50	12.00

Sculpted Table —
AP52a

1994 (?)   Litho.   *Perf. 13¼x13½*
        Background Color

C215A	AP52a	15fr blue	—	—
C215B	AP52a	75fr green	—	—
C215C	AP52a	100fr pink	—	—
C215D	AP52a	225fr orange	—	—

For surcharges see Nos. 826A-826E.

Sea
Turtles
AP53

1995   Litho.   *Perf. 13½x13¼*
       Frame Color

C216	AP53	10fr blue	25.00	25.00
C217	AP53	25fr pink	—	—
C218	AP53	30fr green	25.00	25.00
C219	AP53	50fr lilac	50.00	50.00

No. C215A
Surcharged in
Blue Violet

      Perf. 13¼x13½

2001, June 16   Litho.

C220	AP52a	300fr on 15fr	—	—

AIR POST SEMI-POSTAL STAMP

Type of Air Post 1979

Design: IYC emblem, mother and son.

1979, July 31   Photo.   *Perf. 13½x13*

CB1	AP27	200fr + 30fr multi	3.50	3.50

International Year of the Child.
For surcharge see No. C121.

POSTAGE DUE STAMPS

Anjouan Mosque — D1

1950   Unwmk.   Engr.   *Perf. 14x13*

J1	D1	50c deep green	1.20	.95
J2	D1	1fr black brown	1.20	1.00

Coelacanth — D2

1954

J3	D2	5fr dk brown & green	1.10	1.00
J4	D2	10fr gray & red brown	1.50	1.50
J5	D2	20fr indigo & blue	2.75	2.50
		Nos. J3-J5 (3)	5.35	5.00

Hibiscus
D3

2fr, Pineapple, vert. 5fr, White butterfly. 10fr, Chameleon. 15fr, Blooming banana, vert. 20fr, Orchids. 30fr, Allamanda cathartica. 40fr, Cashews, vert. 50fr, Custard apple, vert. 100fr, Breadfruit. 200fr, Vanilla. 500fr, Ylang ylang.

1977, Nov. 19   Litho.   *Perf. 13½*

J6	D3	1fr shown	.35	.25
J7	D3	2fr multicolored	.35	.25
J8	D3	5fr multicolored	.35	.25
J9	D3	10fr multicolored	.35	.25
J10	D3	15fr multicolored	.35	.25
J11	D3	20fr multicolored	.35	.25
J12	D3	30fr multicolored	.50	.25
J13	D3	40fr multicolored	.95	.25
J14	D3	50fr multicolored	1.10	.25
J15	D3	100fr multicolored	2.10	.75
J16	D3	200fr multicolored	4.50	.95
J17	D3	500fr multicolored	10.75	1.50
		Nos. J6-J17 (12)	22.00	5.45

OFFICIAL STAMPS

Comoro
Flag — O1

Perf. 13x12½

1979-85   Litho.   Unwmk.

O1	O1	5fr multi	.25	.25
O2	O1	10fr multi	.25	.25
O3	O1	20fr multi	.25	.25
O4	O1	30fr multi	.50	.25
O5	O1	40fr multi	.65	.25
O6	O1	60fr multi ('80)	.60	.25
O7	O1	75fr multi ('85)	.40	.25
O8	O1	100fr multi	1.25	.60
		Nos. O1-O8 (8)	4.15	2.35

See Nos. 526-530.

Pres. Said
Mohamed Cheikh
(1904-1970) — O2

1980-85

O9	O2	100fr multi	1.00	.40
O10	O2	125fr multi ('85)	2.00	1.50
O11	O2	400fr multi	3.00	1.25
		Nos. O9-O11 (3)	6.00	3.15

CONGO, DEMOCRATIC REPUBLIC

ˌde-mə-ˈkra-tik ri-ˈpə-blik of ˈkäŋ‿gō

LOCATION — Central Africa
GOVT. — Republic
AREA — 895,348 sq. mi. (estimated)
POP. — 22,480,000 (est. 1971)
CAPITAL — Kinshasa (Leopoldville)

Congo was an independent state, founded by Leopold II of Belgium, until 1908 when it was annexed to Belgium as a colony. Congo became an independent republic in 1960. The name was changed to Republic of Zaire, Oct. 28, 1971. In 1998 some issues again used the name Congo Democratic Republic. See Zaire in Vol. 6 for later issues.

100 Centimes = 1 Franc
100 Sengi = 1 Li-Kuta,
100 Ma-Kuta = 1 Zaire (1967)

Catalogue values for all unused stamps in this country are for Never Hinged items.

Belgian Congo Flower
Issue of 1952-53
Overprinted or
Surcharged

Perf. 11½

1960, June 30   Photo.   Unwmk.
Flowers in Natural Colors
Size: 21x25½mm
Granite Paper

323	A86	10c dp plum & ocher		
324	A86	10c on 15c red & yel grn	.25	.25
325	A86	20c grn & gray	.25	.25
326	A86	40c grn & sal	.25	.25
327	A86	50c on 60c bl grn & pink	.25	.25

328	A86	50c on 75c dp plum & gray	.25	.25
329	A86	1fr car & yel	.30	.25
330	A86	1.50fr vio & ap grn	.30	.25
331	A86	2fr ol grn & buff	.30	.25
332	A86	3fr ol grn & pink	.45	.25
333	A86	4fr choc & lil	1.50	1.00
334	A86	5fr dp plum & lt bl grn	.55	.25
335	A86	6.50fr dk car & lil	.70	.25
336	A86	8fr grn & lt yel	.80	.30
337	A86	10fr dp plum & pale ol	1.50	.30
338	A86	20fr vio bl & dl sal	3.50	.80

Nos. 324, 327-328 exist without "CONGO" overprint but with surcharge, also without surcharge but with "CONGO." Inverted and double overprints exist. Values from $10 to $50 each.

Belgian Congo
Flower Issue of
1952-53 Overprinted
or Surcharged

Size: 22x32mm

339	A86	50fr dp plum & gray bl	19.00	6.00
340	A86	100fr grn & buff	45.00	10.00
		Nos. 323-340 (18)	75.40	21.40

Belgian Congo
Nos. 306-317,
Ovptd. or
Srchd. in Red,
Blue, Black or
Brown

341	A92	10c bl & brn (R)	.25	.25
342	A93	20c red org & sl (Bl)	.25	.25
343	A92	40c brn & bl (Bk)	.25	.25
344	A93	50c brt ultra, red & sep (R)	.25	.25
345	A92	1fr brn, grn & blk (Br)	.25	.25
346	A93	1.50fr blk & org yel (R)	.25	.25
347	A92	2fr crim, blk & brn (Bl)	.45	.25
348	A93	3.50fr on 3fr blk, gray & lil rose (Bk)	.65	.25
349	A92	5fr brn, dk brn & brt grn (Br)	.85	.25
350	A93	6.50fr bl, brn & org yel (R)	1.00	.25
a.		Black overprint	1.75	.60
351	A92	8fr org brn, ol bis & lil (Br)	1.25	.40
352	A93	10fr multi (R)	1.60	.60
		Nos. 341-352 (12)	7.30	3.50

Inverted and double overprints exist. Values from $15 to $20 each.

Same Overprint on Belgian Congo No. 318

1960

353	A94	50c gldn brn, ocher & red brn	1.00	1.00

Same Overprint and Surcharge of New Value on Belgian Congo Nos. 321-322

Inscription in French

354	A95	3.50fr on 3fr gray & red	1.00	.70

Inscription in Flemish

355	A95	3.50fr on 3fr gray & red	1.00	1.00
		Nos. 353-355 (3)	3.00	2.40

Nos. 353-355 are known with inverted overprints. Value, each $10.

Map of
Congo
A93a

1960   Photo.   Perf. 11½

356	A93a	20c brown	.25	.25
357	A93a	50c rose red	.25	.25
358	A93a	1fr green	.25	.25
359	A93a	1.50fr red brn	.25	.25
360	A93a	2fr rose car	.25	.25
361	A93a	3.50fr lilac	.25	.25
362	A93a	5fr brt bl	.25	.25
363	A93a	6.50fr gray	.25	.25

364	A93a	10fr orange	.50	.25
365	A93a	20fr ultra	.90	.25
		Nos. 356-365 (10)	3.40	2.50

Congo's Independence.
Nos. 356-365 exist imperf. Value, set unused $25.
For overprints see Nos. 371-380.

Flag, People
and Broken
Chain — A94

1961, Jan. 4   Unwmk.   Perf. 11½
Flag in Blue and Yellow

366	A94	2fr rose vio	.25	.25
367	A94	3.50fr vermilion	.25	.25
368	A94	6.50fr yel brn	.25	.25
369	A94	10fr brt grn	.35	.25
370	A94	20fr car rose	.50	.30
		Nos. 366-370 (5)	1.60	1.30

Signing of the Independence Agreement by Belgium, Jan. 4, 1959.

Nos. 356-365 Overprinted in Blue, Black or Red: "Conference Coquilhatville Avril Mai 1961"

1961

371	A93a	20c brn (Bl)	1.75	1.75
372	A93a	50c rose red (Bk)	1.75	1.75
373	A93a	1fr grn (R)	1.75	1.75
374	A93a	1.50fr red brn (Bl)	1.75	1.75
375	A93a	2fr rose car (Bk)	1.75	1.75
376	A93a	3.50fr lil (Bl)	1.75	1.75
377	A93a	5fr brt bl (R)	1.75	1.75
378	A93a	6.50fr gray (R)	1.75	1.75
379	A93a	10fr org (Bk)	1.75	1.75
380	A93a	20fr ultra (R)	1.75	1.75
		Nos. 371-380 (10)	17.50	17.50

Coquilhatville Conf., Apr.-May, 1961.
Nos. 371-380 exist with inverted overprints. Value $15 each.

Pres. Joseph
Kasavubu — A95

Kasavubu and
Map of
Congo — A96

10fr-100fr, Kasavubu in uniform and map.

Perf. 11½

1961, June 30   Unwmk.   Photo.
Portrait and Inscription in Dark Brown

381	A95	10c yellow	.25	.25
382	A95	20c dp rose	.25	.25
383	A95	40c bl grn	.25	.25
384	A95	50c salmon	.25	.25
385	A95	1fr lilac	.25	.25
386	A95	1.50fr lt brn	.25	.25
387	A95	2fr brt grn	.25	.25
388	A96	3.50fr rose pink	.25	.25
389	A96	5fr gray	6.50	.25
390	A96	6.50fr ultra	1.00	.25
391	A96	8fr olive	1.00	.25
392	A95	10fr lt vio	2.25	.80
393	A95	20fr orange	2.25	.25
394	A95	50fr lt bl	3.75	.35
395	A95	100fr apple green	6.25	.55
		Nos. 381-395 (15)	25.00	4.70

First anniversary of independence.
Exists imperf. Value, set $70.

Nos. 381-387, 389 and 392 Overprinted: "REOUVERTURE du PARLEMENT JUILLET 1961"

1961
Portrait and Inscription in Dark Brown

396	A95	10c yellow	.25	.25
397	A95	20c dp rose	.25	.25
398	A95	40c bl grn	.25	.25
399	A95	50c salmon	.55	.35
400	A95	1fr lilac	.55	.35

401	A95	1.50fr lt brn	1.50	1.00
402	A95	2fr brt grn	1.50	1.00
403	A96	5fr gray	1.50	1.00
404	A95	10fr lt vio	1.50	1.00
		Nos. 396-404 (9)	7.85	5.45

Congolese parliament re-opening, 7/1961.
Nos. 396-404 exist with inverted overprints. Value $9 each.

Dag Hammarskjold
and Map of Africa
with Congo — A97

1962, Jan. 20   Photo.   Perf. 11½
Gray Background

405	A97	10c dk brn	.25	.25
406	A97	20c Prus bl	.25	.25
407	A97	30c brown	.25	.25
408	A97	40c dk bl	.25	.25
409	A97	50c brn red	.25	.25
410	A97	3fr ol grn	5.00	2.00
411	A97	6.50fr dk vio	1.50	.35
412	A97	8fr red brn	1.75	.50
		Nos. 405-412 (8)	9.50	4.10

Souvenir Sheets
Imperf

413	A97	25fr blk brn	10.00	10.00
a.		Overprint in green	4.50	4.50

Dag Hammarskjold, Sec. Gen. of the UN, 1953-61.
Nos. 405-412 exist imperf. Value, set unused $20.
No 413a is overprinted "30 Juin 1962" on stamp and "2eme Anniversaire de l'Independance" on sheet margin. Issued June 30, 1962.
For overprints see Nos. 417-424.

Malaria Eradication
Emblem and
Mosquito — A98

1962, June 15   Granite Paper

414	A98	1.50fr yel, blk & dk red	.25	.25
415	A98	2fr yel grn, brn & bl grn	.30	.25
416	A98	6.50fr ultra, blk & mar	.40	.25
		Nos. 414-416 (3)	.95	.75

WHO drive to eradicate malaria.
Nos. 414-416 exist imperf. Value, set unused $2.

Nos. 405-412
Overprinted in Blue,
Purple, Black or
Carmine

1962, Oct. 15   Gray Background

417	A97	10c dk brn (Bl)	.25	.25
418	A97	20c Prus bl (P)	.25	.25
419	A97	30c brn (Bk)	.25	.25
420	A97	40c dk bl (C)	.25	.25
421	A97	50c brn red (Bl)	2.50	1.00
422	A97	3fr ol grn (P)	.25	.25
423	A97	6.50fr dk vio (Bk)	.25	.25
424	A97	8fr red brn (C)	.40	.25
		Nos. 417-424 (8)	4.40	2.75

Reorganization of Adoula administration.
Inverted overprints exist. Value, $8.00 each.

Canceled to Order
Starting in 1963, values in the used column are for "canceled to order" stamps. Postally used examples sell for much more.

A99

1963, Jan. 28   Engr.   Perf. 10½x13
425	A99	2fr dull purple	1.50	1.00
426	A99	4fr red	.25	.25
427	A99	7fr dark blue	.25	.25
428	A99	20fr slate green	.50	.25
		Nos. 425-428 (4)	2.50	1.75

Congo's 1st participation at the UPU Cong., New Delhi, Mar. 1963.
Nos. 425-428 exist imperf. Value, set unused $20.
An imperf sheet containing No. 428 in brown exists. Value $30.
For overprints see Nos. 468-471.

Shoebill — A100

Birds: 10c, Pelicans. 20c, Crested guinea fowl, horiz. 30c, Openbill. 40c, White-bellied storks, horiz. 2fr, Marabou. 3fr, Greater flamingos, horiz. 4fr, Congolese peacock. 5fr, Hartlaub ducks, horiz. 6fr, Secretary bird. 7fr, Black-casqued hornbill, horiz. 8fr, Sacred ibis and nest. 10fr, Crowned crane, horiz. 20fr, Saddle-bill stork, horiz.

1963   Unwmk.   Photo.   Perf. 11½
429	A100	10c pink, ultra & ocher	.25	.25
430	A100	20c rose red, bl & blk	.25	.25
431	A100	30c grn, ocher & blk	.25	.25
432	A100	40c gray, org & blk	.25	.25
433	A100	1fr brn, emer & gray	.25	.25
434	A100	2fr gray, red & ind	3.25	.60
435	A100	3fr ol grn, blk & rose	.25	.25
436	A100	4fr car rose, vio bl & grn	.25	.25
437	A100	5fr lake, lt bl & blk	.45	.25
438	A100	6fr pur, yel & blk	3.50	.60
439	A100	7fr bl grn, blk & ind	.55	.25
440	A100	8fr yel, org & blk	.65	.25
441	A100	10fr bl, blk & rose	.65	.25
442	A100	20fr cit, red & blk	1.20	.25
		Nos. 429-442 (14)	12.00	4.20

Nos. 429-442 exist imperf. Value, set unused $50.
Nos. 436 and 438 exist in imperf sheets of one. Value, each $40.

Cinchona Ledgeriana — A101

Red Cross Nurse — A102

10c, 30c, 5fr, Strophanthus sarmentosus.

Perf. 12½x13½, 13½x12½
1963, May 25   Engr.   Unwmk.
Cross in Red
443	A101	10c vio & dl grn	.25	.25
444	A101	20c magenta & bl	.25	.25
445	A101	30c grn & org	.25	.25
446	A101	40c bl & vio	.25	.25
447	A101	5fr ol & rose claret	.25	.25
448	A101	7fr org & blk	.25	.25
449	A102	9fr gray olive & red	.25	.25
450	A102	20fr purple & red	2.50	1.00
		Nos. 443-450 (8)	4.25	2.75

International Red Cross centenary.

Nos. 443-450 exist imperf. Value, set unused $15.
A souvenir sheet of three contains imperf. 5fr, 7fr, and 20fr stamps similar to Nos. 447, 448 and 450, but in changed colors. Size: 109x75mm. Value $30.

Men Joining Hands and Map of Congo — A103

1963, June 29   Photo.   Perf. 11½
451	A103	4fr multi	1.25	.50
452	A103	5fr multi	.25	.25
453	A103	9fr multi	.25	.25
454	A103	12fr multi	.35	.25
		Nos. 451-454 (4)	2.10	1.25

Issued to celebrate national reconciliation.
Nos. 451-454 exist imperf. Value, set unused $10.

Bulldozer and Kabambare Sewer, Leopoldville — A104

Designs: 30c, 5fr, 12fr, Excavator and blueprint. 50c, 9fr, Building Ituri road.

1963, July 1   Engr.   Unwmk.
455	A104	20c multi	.25	.25
456	A104	30c multi	.25	.25
457	A104	50c multi	.25	.25
458	A104	3fr multi	1.50	.60
459	A104	5fr multi	.25	.25
460	A104	9fr multi	.25	.25
461	A104	12fr multi	.25	.25
		Nos. 455-461 (7)	3.00	2.10

Issued to publicize aid to Congo by the European Economic Community.
Nos. 455-461 exist imperf. Value, set unused $20.

Leopoldville Airport N'Djili — A105

5fr, 7fr, 50fr, Tail assembly and airport.

1963, Nov. 30   Photo.   Perf. 11½
462	A105	2fr gray, yel & red brn	.25	.25
463	A105	5fr mag, vio & yel	.25	.25
464	A105	6fr bl, yel & dk brn	1.75	.60
465	A105	7fr multi	.25	.25
466	A105	30fr lil, yel & ol	.40	.25
467	A105	50fr multi	.65	.30
		Nos. 462-467 (6)	3.55	1.90

Issued to publicize Air Congo.
Nos. 462-467 exist imperf. Value, set unused $15.
For surcharge see No. 606.

Nos. 425-428 Overprinted with Silver Frame on Three Sides and Black Inscription: "15e anniversaire / 10 DECEMBRE 1948 / DROITS DE L'HOMME / 10 DECEMBRE 1963"
Engraved and Typographed
1963, Dec. 10   Perf. 10½x13
468	A99	2fr dull purple	.25	.25
469	A99	4fr red	.25	.25
470	A99	7fr dark blue	.25	.25
471	A99	20fr slate green	.35	.25
		Nos. 468-471 (4)	1.10	1.00

Universal Declaration of Human Rights, 15th anniv.
Nos. 468-471 exist with side date panels transposed ("1963" at left, "1948" at right). Value, each $15.

Laboratory Technician and Atomic Emblem A106

1.50fr, 60fr, University. 8fr, 75fr, First African nuclear reactor. 25fr, 100fr, University and crest.

1964, Feb. 1   Photo.   Perf. 14x12½
472	A106	50c multi	.25	.25
473	A106	1.50fr multi	.25	.25
474	A106	8fr multi	3.00	2.75
475	A106	25fr multi	.25	.25
476	A106	30fr multi	.35	.25
477	A106	60fr multi	.60	.35
478	A106	75fr multi	.70	.60
479	A106	100fr multi	1.25	1.00
a.		Souv. sheet of 3	7.00	7.00
		Nos. 472-479 (8)	6.65	5.70

Lovanium University, Leopoldville, 10th anniv.
No. 479a contains 3 imperf. multicolored stamps: 20fr, design as 50c; 30fr, as 8fr; 100fr.
Nos. 472-479 exist imperf. Value, set unused $25.

Belgian Congo Issues of 1952-59 Overprinted "REPUBLIQUE DU CONGO" and Surcharged in Black on Overprinted Metallic Panels
1964   Perf. 11½
480	A93	1fr on 20c red org & sl (#307)	.25	.25
481	A86	2fr on 1.50fr (#273)	11.00	3.75
482	A93	5fr on 6.50fr (#315)	.80	.25
483	A86	6fr on 6.50fr (#278)	1.10	.35

Republic Issues of 1960-61 Surcharged in Black on Overprinted Metallic Rectangles or Ovals
484	A86	1fr on 6.50fr (#335)	.25	.25
485	A93	1fr on 20c (#342)	.25	.25
486	A86	2fr on 1.50fr (#330)	.25	.25
487	A95	3fr on 20c (#382)	.55	.25
488	A95	4fr on 40c (#383)	.55	.25
489	A93	5fr on 6.50fr ("Congo" red) (#350)	.80	.25
a.		"Congo" black	.80	.25
490	A93a	6fr on 6.50fr (#363)	.80	.25
491	A93a	7fr on 20c (#356)	.80	.25
		Nos. 480-491 (12)	17.40	6.60

Pole Vault A107

7fr, 20fr, Javelin, vert. 8fr, 100fr, Hurdling.

Perf. 11½
1964, July 13   Unwmk.   Photo.
Granite Paper
492	A107	5fr gray, dk brn & car	.25	.25
493	A107	7fr rose, vio & emer	.95	.35
494	A107	8fr org, yel, red brn & vio bl	.25	.25
495	A107	10fr bl, vio brn & mag	.25	.25
496	A107	20fr gray grn, red brn & ver	.25	.25
497	A107	100fr lil, dk brn & grn	.95	.25
a.		Souv. sheet of 3	10.00	10.00
		Nos. 492-497 (6)	2.90	1.60

18th Olympic Games, Tokyo, Oct. 10-25. No. 497a contains 3 imperf. stamps (20fr orange & dark brown, pole vault; 30fr citron and dark brown, hurdling; 100fr dull green and dark brown, javelin). Sheet issued Sept. 10.
Nos. 492-497 exist imperf. Value, set unused $40.

National Palace, Leopoldville — A108

1964, Sept. 15   Granite Paper
498	A108	50c lil rose & bl	.25	.25
499	A108	1fr bl & lil rose	.25	.25
500	A108	2fr brn red & vio	.25	.25
501	A108	3fr emer & red	.25	.25

502	A108	4fr org & vio bl	.25	.25
503	A108	5fr gray vio & emer	.25	.25
504	A108	6fr sep & org	.25	.25
505	A108	7fr gray ol & red brn	.25	.25
506	A108	8fr rose red & vio bl	2.00	.30
507	A108	9fr vio bl & rose red	.25	.25
508	A108	10fr brn ol & grn	.25	.25
509	A108	20fr bl & brn org	.25	.25
510	A108	30fr dk car rose & grn	.25	.25
511	A108	40fr ultra & dk car rose	.35	.25
512	A108	50fr brn org & grn	.40	.25
513	A108	100fr slate & ver	.85	.25
		Nos. 498-513 (16)	6.60	4.05

Nos. 498-513 exist imperf. Value, set unused $25.
For overprints and surcharges see Nos. 574-577, 593-598, 609-615, 670-671, 673-674, 676-677, 680, 684-687.

Pres. John F. Kennedy (1917-63) A109

1964, Dec. 8   Photo.   Perf. 13½
514	A109	5fr dk bl & blk	.25	.25
515	A109	6fr rose claret & blk	.25	.25
516	A109	9fr brn & blk	.25	.25
517	A109	30fr pur & blk	.55	.25
518	A109	40fr dl grn & blk	3.50	1.00
519	A109	60fr red brn & blk	1.20	.35
		Nos. 514-519 (6)	6.00	2.35

Souvenir Sheet
| 520 | A109 | 150fr blk & mar | 6.50 | 6.50 |

Nos. 514-519 exist imperf. Value, set unused $60. No. 520 exists imperf. Value, unused $60.

Rocket and Unisphere — A110

Engraved and Typographed
1965, Mar. 1   Unwmk.   Perf. 12
521	A110	50c lil & blk	.25	.25
522	A110	1.50fr bl & lil	.25	.25
523	A110	2fr red brn & brt grn	.25	.25
524	A110	10fr grn & dk red	1.00	.55
525	A110	18fr vio bl & brn	.35	.25
526	A110	27fr rose red & grn	.35	.25
527	A110	40fr gray & org	.35	.25
		Nos. 521-527 (7)	2.80	2.05

New York World's Fair, 1964-65.
Nos. 521-527 exist imperf. Value, set unused $20.

Basketball A111

6fr, 40fr, Soccer, horiz. 15fr, 60fr, Volleyball.

1965, Apr.   Photo.   Perf. 13½
528	A111	5fr blk, grnsh bl & ocher	.25	.25
529	A111	6fr blk, bl gray & crim	.25	.25
530	A111	15fr blk, org & yel grn	.25	.25
531	A111	24fr blk, rose lil & brt grn	.40	.25
532	A111	40fr blk, brt grn & ultra	2.00	.70
533	A111	60fr blk, bl & red lil	.70	.25
		Nos. 528-533 (6)	3.85	1.95

First African Games, Leopoldville, Mar. 31-Apr. 7, 1965.
Nos. 528-533 exist imperf. Value, set unused $15.
For surcharges see Nos. 604-605.

Earth and
Satellites
A112

Designs: 9fr, 15fr, 20fr, 40fr, Satellites at
left, globe at right.

Perf. 14x14½

1965, June 28   Photo.   Unwmk.
534	A112	6fr blk, sal & vio	.25 .25
535	A112	9fr blk, lt grn & gray	.25 .25
536	A112	12fr org, gray & blk	.25 .25
537	A112	15fr grn, ultra & blk	.25 .25
538	A112	18fr blk, lt grn & gray	1.50 .40
539	A112	20fr blk, sal & vio	.25 .25
540	A112	30fr grn, ultra & blk	.25 .25
541	A112	40fr org, gray & blk	.35 .25
		Nos. 534-541 (8)	3.35 2.15

Cent. of the ITU.
Nos. 534-541 exist imperf. Value, set
unused $30.

Congolese
Paratrooper
and
Parachutes
A113

1965, July 5   Perf. 13x14
542	A113	5fr brt bl & brn	.25 .25
543	A113	6fr org & brn	.25 .25
544	A113	7fr br grn & brn	.40 .25
545	A113	9fr brt pink & brn	.25 .25
546	A113	18fr lem & brn	.25 .25
		Nos. 542-546 (5)	1.40 1.25

Fifth anniversary of independence.
Nos. 542-546 exist imperf. Value, set
unused $15.

Matadi Harbor and ICY
Emblem — A114

ICY Emblem and: 8fr, 25fr, Katanga mines.
9fr, 60fr, Tshopo Dam, Stanleyville.

1965, Oct. 25   Photo.   Perf. 13x14
547	A114	6fr ultra, blk & yel	.25 .25
548	A114	8fr org red, blk & bl	.25 .25
549	A114	9fr bl grn, blk & brn org	.25 .25
550	A114	12fr car rose, blk & gray	1.00 .35
551	A114	25fr ol, blk & rose red	.25 .25
552	A114	60fr gray, blk & org	.65 .25
		Nos. 547-552 (6)	2.65 1.60

International Cooperation Year, 1965.
Nos. 547-552 exist imperf. Value, set
unused $20.
For overprints and surcharges see Nos.
559-560, 607-608.

Soldiers
Giving First
Aid — A115

The Army Serving the Country: 7fr, Bridge
building. 9fr, Feeding child. 19fr, Maintenance
of telegraph lines. 20fr, House building. 30fr,
Soldier and flag. (19fr, 20fr, 30fr, vert.)

Perf. 12½x13, 13x12½

1965, Nov. 17
553	A115	5fr sal, brn & red	.25 .25
554	A115	7fr yel & grn	.25 .25
555	A115	9fr ol & brn	.25 .25
556	A115	19fr brt grn & brn	1.10 .60
557	A115	20fr lt bl & brn	.30 .25
558	A115	30fr multi	.50 .25
		Nos. 553-558 (6)	2.65 1.85

See Nos. 582-586.
Nos. 553-558 exist imperf. Value, set
unused $15.
For surcharges see Nos. 602, 678-679, 683.

Nos. 551-552 Overprinted with UN Emblem and "6e Journée Météorologique Mondiale / 23.3.66." on Metallic Strip

1966, Mar. 23   Photo.   Perf. 13x14
559	A114	25fr ol & blk	1.40 .55
560	A114	60fr gray & blk	1.40 .65

6th World Meteorological Day.
Nos. 559-560 exist imperf. Value, set
unused $10.

Woman's Head and Goat — A116

10fr, Sculptured heads. 12fr, Sitting figure
and two heads, vert. 53fr, Figure with earrings
and kneeling woman with bowl, vert.

Perf. 11½x13, 13x11½

1966, Apr. 23   Litho.   Unwmk.
561	A116	10fr red, blk & gray	.25 .25
562	A116	12fr grn, blk & bl	.25 .25
563	A116	15fr dp bl, blk & lil	.30 .25
564	A116	53fr dp rose, blk & vio bl	1.50 1.10
		Nos. 561-564 (4)	2.30 1.85

Intl. Negro Arts Festival, Dakar, Senegal,
Apr. 1-24.
Nos. 561-564 exist imperf. Value, set
unused $15.

Pres. Joseph Desiré Mobutu and
Fishing Industry
A117

Pres. Mobutu and: 4fr, Pyrethrum harvest.
6fr, Building industry. 8fr, Winnowing rice.
10fr, Cotton harvest. 12fr, Banana harvest.
15fr, Coffee harvest. 24fr, Pineapple harvest.
No. 573a, Pres. Mobutu without cap, and men
rolling up sleeves.

1966, May 1   Photo.   Perf. 11½
565	A117	2fr dk brn & dk bl	.25 .25
566	A117	4fr brn & org	.25 .25
567	A117	6fr dk brn & ol	.75 .60
568	A117	8fr dk brn & brt grnsh bl	.25 .25
569	A117	10fr dk brn & brn red	.25 .25
570	A117	12fr dk brn & vio	.25 .25
571	A117	15fr dk brn & lt ol grn	.25 .25
572	A117	24fr dk brn & lil rose	.25 .25
		Nos. 565-572 (8)	2.50 2.35

Souvenir Sheet
Perf. 11x11½
573		Sheet of 4	2.25 2.25
a.	A117	15fr brn, black & ultra	.50 .50

Lt. Gen. Joseph Desiré Mobutu, Pres. of
Congo, and publicizing the "Back to Work"
campaign.
Nos. 565-572 exist imperf. Value, set
unused $15. No. 573 exists imperf. Value,
unused $10.
For surcharges see Nos. 601, 603, 616,
619-624, 672, 675, 681-682.

Nos. 510-
513
Overprinted

1966, June 13   Perf. 11½
574	A108	30fr dk car rose & grn	1.10 1.10
575	A108	40fr ultra & dk car rose	1.20 1.20
576	A108	50fr brn org & grn	1.40 1.40
577	A108	100fr slate & ver	1.40 1.40
		Nos. 574-577 (4)	5.10 5.10

Inauguration of WHO Headquarters, Geneva.

Soccer Player — A118

30fr, 2 soccer players. 50fr, 3 soccer players. 60fr, Jules Rimet Cup, soccer ball &
globe.

1966, July 25   Photo.   Perf. 14
578	A118	10fr ocher, vio & brt grn	.25 .25
579	A118	30fr brt rose lil, vio & ap grn	.45 .25
580	A118	50fr ap grn, Prus bl & tan	1.50 1.00
581	A118	60fr brt grn, dk brn & gold	1.50 .50
		Nos. 578-581 (4)	3.70 2.00

World Cup Soccer Championship, Wembley, England, July 11-30.
Nos. 578-581 exist imperf. Value, set
unused $15.
For overprints see Nos. 587-590.

Army Type of 1965

The Army Serving the Country: 2fr, Soldiers
giving first aid. 6fr, Feeding child. 10fr, House
building, vert. 18fr, Bridge building. 24fr, Soldier and flag, vert.

1966, Aug. 8   Perf. 12½x13, 13x12½
582	A115	2fr ver, ind & red	.25 .25
583	A115	6fr ultra red brn	.25 .25
584	A115	10fr yel grn & red brn	.75 .50
585	A115	18fr car rose & vio	.25 .25
586	A115	24fr multi	.25 .25
		Nos. 582-586 (5)	1.75 1.50

Nos. 582-586 exist imperf. Value, set
unused $10.

#578-581 Overprinted in Black ("a"), Carmine or Green ("b"): "FINALE / ANGLETERRE-ALLEMAGNE / 4-2"

1966, Nov. 14   Photo.   Perf. 14
587	A118	10fr pair, B and C	.60 .60
588	A118	30fr pair, B and C	2.25 2.00
589	A118	50fr pair, B and C	3.50 2.50
590	A118	60fr pair, B and C	4.50 3.75
		Nos. 587-590 (4)	10.85 8.85

England's victory in the World Soccer Cup
Championship. The two colors of the overprint
alternate in the sheets.

Souvenir Sheets

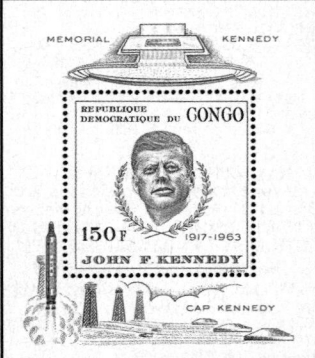

Pres. John F. Kennedy — A119

1966, Dec. 28   Engr.   Perf. 13
591	A119	150fr brown	22.50 17.50
592	A119	150fr slate	22.50 17.50

Issued in memory of Pres. John F. Kennedy. No. 591 has slate green, No. 592 deep
orange marginal design. Two imperf. sheets
exist: 150fr brown with violet blue margin and
150fr slate with lilac margin. Size: 65x76mm.
Values, $20 each.

Nos. 498-
503
Surcharged
in Black,
Red or
Maroon
and

Map of Africa, Torch — A120

1967, Sept. 11   Photo.   Perf. 11½
593	A108	1k on 2fr	.25 .25
a.		Inverted overprint	5.00
594	A108	3k on 5fr	.25 .25
595	A108	5k on 4fr	.35 .25
596	A108	6.60k on 1fr (R)	.50 .25
a.		Inverted overprint	5.00
597	A108	9.60k on 50c	.70 .30
a.		Inverted overprint	5.00
598	A108	9.80k on 3fr (M)	.75 .50
		Nos. 593-598 (6)	2.80 1.80

Souvenir Sheet
599	A120	50k grnsh bl, blk & red	2.50 2.50

4th meeting of the Org. for African Unity,
Kinshasa (Leopoldville), Sept. 9-11.
No. 599 exists imperf. Value, unused $15.
No. 599 in other colors was not a postal
issue.

Souvenir Sheet

Horn Blower and EXPO
Emblem — A121

1967, Sept. 28   Engr.   Perf. 11½
600	A121	50k dk brn	3.50 3.50

EXPO '67, International Exhibition, Montreal, Apr. 28-Oct. 27, 1967.
No. 600 exists imperf. Value, unused $15.

Nos. 565-566 and 582 Overprinted: "NOUVELLE CONSTITUTION 1967" and Surcharged with New Value on Metallic Panel in Magenta or Brown
Perf. 11½, 12½x13

1967, Oct. 9   Photo.
601	A117	4k on 2fr (M)	.25 .25
602	A115	5k on 2fr (B)	.45 .25
603	A117	21k on 4fr (M)	1.50 .90
		Nos. 601-603 (3)	2.20 1.40

Promulgation of the Constitution, June 4,
1967.

Nos. 528 and 530 Surcharged with New Value and Overprinted: "1ers Jeux Congolais / 25/6 au 2/7/1967 / Kinshasa"

1967, Oct. 16   Photo.   Perf. 13½
604	A111	1k on 5fr multi	.35 .25
605	A111	9.60k on 15fr multi	.75 .50

First Congolese Games, Kinshasa, June 25-
July 2, 1967.

No. 465 Surcharged with New Value and Overprinted: "1er VOL BAC / ONE ELEVEN / 14/5/67"

1967, Oct. 16   **Perf. 11½**
606 A105 9.60k on 7fr mul   1.20 .25
1st flight of the BAC 111 in the service of Air Congo, May 14, 1967.

Nos. 547 and 549 Surcharged in Red or Black: "JOURNÉE MONDIALE / DE L'ENFANCE / 8-10-67"

1968, Feb. 10 Photo.   Perf. 13x14
607 A114 1k on 6fr (R)   .35 .25
608 A114 9k on 9fr (R)   1.00 .70
Intl. Children's Day. The surcharge is on a rectangle printed in metallic ink.

Nos. 498, 504 and 501 Surcharged in Blue or Red: "Année Internationale / du Tourisme 24-10-1967"

1968, Feb. 10   **Perf. 11½**
609 A108 5k on 50c lil rose & bl (Bl)   .45 .25
610 A108 10k on 6fr sepia & org (R)   .65 .55
611 A108 15k on 3fr emer & red (R)   1.00 1.00
     Nos. 609-611 (3)   2.10 1.80
International Tourist Year. The surcharge is on a rectangle printed in metallic ink.

Nos. 500, 498 and 502 Surcharged in Black, Violet Blue or Gold

1968, July   Photo.   Perf. 11½
612 A108 1k on 2fr   .30 .25
613 A108 2k on 50c (VBl)   .45 .25
614 A108 2k on 50c (G)   .45 .25
615 A108 9.60k on 4fr   2.00 1.10
     Nos. 612-615 (4)   3.20 1.85
The surcharge on No. 612 consists of a black rectangle and new denomination in upper right corner; the surcharge on No. 613 has a violet blue rectangle with denomination printed in white on it; on No. 614 the rectangle is gold and the denomination black; on No. 615 the rectangle is black and the denomination white.

No. 565 Surcharged in White on Black Rectangle

1968, Oct.   Photo.   Perf. 11½
616 A117 10k on 2fr dk brn & dk bl   .70 .25

Leopard
A122

1968, Nov. 5   Litho.   Perf. 10½
617 A122 2k brt grnsh bl & blk   .30 .25
618 A122 9.60k red & blk   1.50 .25
Nos. 617-618 exist imperf. Value, set unused $10.

Mobutu Type of 1966 Surcharged

1968, Dec. 20   Photo.   Perf. 11½
619 A117 15s on 2fr sep & brt bl   .25 .25
620 A117 1k on 6fr sep & brn   .25 .25
621 A117 3k on 10fr sep & emer   .25 .25
622 A117 5k on 12fr sep & org   .35 .25
623 A117 20k on 15fr sep & brt grn   1.25 .50
624 A117 50k on 24fr sep & brt lil   3.25 1.50
     Nos. 619-624 (6)   5.60 3.00

Human Rights Flame — A123

1968, Dec. 30   **Perf. 12½x13**
625 A123 2k lt ultra & brt grn   .25 .25
626 A123 9.60k grn & dp car   .75 .30
627 A123 10k brt lil & brn   .75 .35
628 A123 40k org brn & pur   2.50 1.25
     Nos. 625-628 (4)   4.25 2.15
International Human Rights Year.
Nos. 625-628 exist imperf. Value, set unused $15.

Type of 1968 Overprinted in Gold

1969, Jan. 27 Photo. Perf. 12½x13
629 A123 2k ap grn & red brn   .25 .25
630 A123 9.60k rose & emer   .75 .30
631 A123 10k gray & ultra   .75 .35
632 A123 40k grnsh bl & pur   2.50 1.25
     Nos. 629-632 (4)   4.25 2.15
4th summit meeting of OCAM (Organisation Communitee Afrique et Malgache), Kinshasa, Jan. 27.
Nos. 629-632 exist imperf. Value, set unused $15.

Kinshasa Fair Emblem and Cotton Boll — A124

Fair Emblem and: 6k, Copper. 9.60k, Coffee. 9.80k, Diamond. 11.60k, Oil palm fruits.

1969, May 2   Photo.   Perf. 12½x13
633 A124 2k brt pur, gold & red lil   .25 .25
634 A124 6k grn, gold & bl grn   .95 .50
635 A124 9.60k brn, gold & lt brn   1.25 .40
636 A124 9.80k ultra & gold   1.40 .60
637 A124 11.60k hn brn, gold & brn   1.60 .90
     Nos. 633-637 (5)   5.45 2.65
Kinshasa Fair, Limete, June 30-July 21.
Nos. 633-637 exist imperf. Value, set unused $25.

Fair Entrance, Emblem — A125

Fair Emblem and: 3k, Gecomin Mining Co. Pavilion. 10k, Administration Building. 25k, Pavilion of the Organization for African Unity.

1969, June 30   Photo.   Perf. 11½
Granite Paper
638 A125 2k brt rose lil & gold   .25 .25
639 A125 3k blue & gold   .25 .25
640 A125 10k lt ol grn & gold   .80 .40
641 A125 25k copper red & gold   1.80 1.00
     Nos. 638-641 (4)   3.10 1.90
Kinshasa Fair, Limete, June 30-July 21.
Nos. 638-641 exist imperf. Value, set unused $15.

Congo Arms — A126   Pres. Mobutu — A127

1969, July-Sept.   Litho.   Perf. 14
642 A126 10s org & blk   .25 .25
643 A126 15s ultra & blk   .25 .25
644 A126 30s brt grn & blk   .25 .25
645 A126 60s brt rose lil & blk   .25 .25
646 A126 90s dp bister & blk   .25 .25
     Perf. 13
647 A127 1k sky bl & multi   .25 .25
648 A127 2k org & multi   .25 .25
649 A127 3k multi   .30 .25
650 A127 5k brt rose & multi   .40 .25
651 A127 6k ultra & multi   .40 .25
652 A127 9.60k multi   .75 .40
653 A127 10k lt lil & multi   1.00 .50
654 A127 20k yel & multi   1.75 1.00
655 A127 50k multi   5.00 2.50
656 A127 100k fawn & multi   10.00 6.00
     Nos. 642-656 (15)   21.35 12.90
Nos. 642-656 exist imperf. Value, set unused $25.

Well Driller, by Oscar Bonnevalle — A128

Paintings: 4k, Preparation of cocoa, by Jean Van Noten. 8k, Dock workers, by Constantin Meunier. 10k, Poultry shop, by Henri Evenepoel. 15k, Steel industry, by Constantin Meunier.

Perf. 13x14, 14x13 (8k)
1969, Dec. 15   **Litho.**
     Size: 41x41mm
657 A128 3k multi   .25 .25
658 A128 4k multi   .25 .25
     Size: 28x41mm
659 A128 8k multi   .50 .30
     Size: 41x41mm
660 A128 10k multi   .75 .40
661 A128 15k multi   1.50 .70
     Nos. 657-661 (5)   3.25 1.90
50th anniv. of the ILO.
Nos. 657-661 exist imperf. Value, set unused $15.

Souvenir Sheet

Adoration of the Kings, by Rubens — A129

1969, Dec.   Engr.   Perf. 13
662 A129 50k red lilac   5.50 5.50
Issued for Christmas 1969.
No. 662 exists imperf. Value, unused $9.

Pres. Mobutu, Map and Flag of Congo A130

1970, June 30   Litho.   Perf. 13½x13
663 A130 10s multi   .25 .25
664 A130 90s pur & multi   .25 .25
665 A130 1k brn & multi   .25 .25
666 A130 2k multi   .25 .25
667 A130 7k multi   .35 .25
668 A130 10k multi   .55 .25
669 A130 20k multi   1.25 .60
     Nos. 663-669 (7)   3.15 2.10
10th anniversary of independence.
Nos. 663-669 exist imperf. Value, set unused $12.

Issues of 1964-1966 Surcharged

Perf. 11½, 12½x13, 13x12½
1970, Sept. 24   **Photo.**
670 A108 10s on 1fr (#499)   .25 .25
671 A108 20s on 2fr (#500)   .25 .25
672 A117 20s on 3fr (#565)   1.00 .50
673 A108 30s on 3fr (#501)   .25 .25
674 A108 40s on 4fr (#502)   .25 .25
675 A117 40s on 4fr (#566)   1.00 .50
676 A108 60s on 7fr (#505)   3.00 1.75
677 A108 90s on 9fr (#507)   3.00 1.75
678 A115 90s on 9fr (#555)   .60 .40
679 A115 1k on 7fr (#554)   .60 .40
680 A108 1k on 6fr (#504)   .25 .25
681 A117 1k on 12fr (#570)   2.75 1.75
682 A117 2k on 24fr (#572)   1.25 .50
683 A115 2k on 24fr (#586)   1.25 .50
684 A108 3k on 30fr (#510)   2.25 1.25
685 A108 4k on 40fr (#511)   .50 .25
686 A108 5k on 50fr (#512)   9.00 5.00
687 A108 10k on 100fr (#513)   2.25 1.25
     Nos. 670-687 (18)   29.95 17.05

Telecommunications Building, Geneva — A131

Designs: 2k, 6.60k, UPU Headquarters, Bern. 9.80k, 10k, 11k, UN Headquarters, NY.

1970, Oct. 24   Photo.   Perf. 11½
688 A131 1k pink & grn   .25 .25
689 A131 2k org & grn   .25 .25
690 A131 6.60k grnsh bl & rose car   .40 .25
691 A131 9.60k yel & vio bl   .50 .35
692 A131 9.80k lt ultra & brn   .50 .35
693 A131 10k lt pur & brn   .50 .35
694 A131 11k rose & brn   .70 .45
     Nos. 688-694 (7)   3.10 2.25
ITU; new UPU Headquarters, Bern; 25th anniv. of the UN.
Nos. 688-694 exist imperf. Value, set unused $35.

Pres. Mobutu, Congolese Flag and Arch — A132

1970, Nov. 24   Litho.   Perf. 13
695 A132 2k yel & multi   .25 .25
696 A132 10k bl & multi   1.00 .50
697 A132 20k red & multi   2.50 1.50
     Nos. 695-697 (3)   3.75 2.25
Fifth anniversary of new government.
Nos. 695-697 exist imperf. Value, set unused $6.

Apollo 11 in Flight
A133

Designs: 2k, Astronaut and spacecraft on moon. 7k, Pres. Mobutu decorating astronauts' wives. 10k, Pres. Mobutu with Neil A. Armstrong, Col. Edwin E. Aldrin, Jr. and Lt. Col. Michael Collins. 30k, Armstrong, Aldrin and Collins in space suits.

1970, Dec. 24   **Perf. 13x13½**
698	A133	1k bl & blk	.30	.25
699	A133	2k brt pur & blk	.50	.25
700	A133	7k dl org & blk	1.50	.85
701	A133	10k rose red & blk	2.00	1.25
702	A133	30k grn & blk	5.50	3.50
		Nos. 698-702 (5)	9.80	6.10

Visit of US Apollo 11 astronauts and their wives to Kinshasa.
Nos. 698-702 exist imperf. Value, set unused $25.

Metopodontus Savagei — A134

Designs: Various insects of Congo.

1971, Jan. 25   **Photo.**   **Perf. 11½**
703	A134	10s dl rose & multi	.75	.30
704	A134	20s gray & multi	.75	.30
705	A134	90s multi	.75	.30
706	A134	1k citron & multi	.75	.30
707	A134	2k gray grn & multi	.75	.30
708	A134	3k lt vio & multi	1.75	.60
709	A134	5k bl & multi	5.00	2.00
710	A134	10k multi	7.00	2.50
711	A134	30k grn & multi	16.00	6.75
712	A134	40k ocher & multi	25.00	10.00
		Nos. 703-712 (10)	58.50	23.35

Colotis Protomedia — A135

Various butterflies and moths of Congo.

1971, Feb. 24
713	A135	10s lt ultra & multi	.75	.35
714	A135	20s choc & multi	.75	.35
715	A135	70s dp org & multi	.75	.35
716	A135	1k vio bl & multi	.75	.35
717	A135	3k multi	1.75	.60
718	A135	5k dk grn & multi	4.75	1.50
719	A135	10k multi	6.25	2.00
720	A135	15k emer & multi	11.00	3.50
721	A135	25k yel & multi	17.50	4.50
722	A135	40k multi	24.00	11.00
		Nos. 713-722 (10)	68.25	24.50

Nos. 713-722 exist imperf. Value, set unused $75.

UN Emblem, Racial Unity — A136

1971, Mar. 21   **Photo.**   **Perf. 11½**
723	A136	1k lt grn & multi	.25	.25
724	A136	4k gray & multi	.25	.25
725	A136	5k lt lil & multi	.40	.25
726	A136	10k lt bl & multi	.90	.35
		Nos. 723-726 (4)	1.80	1.10

Intl. year against racial discrimination.
Nos. 723-726 exist imperf. Value, set unused $12.

Hypericum Bequaertii
A137

Flowers: 4k, Dissotis brazzae. 20k, Begonia wollastonii. 25k, Cassia alata.

1971, May 24   **Litho.**   **Perf. 14**
727	A137	1k multi	1.00	.25
728	A137	4k multi	1.75	.45
729	A137	20k multi	9.25	2.50
730	A137	25k multi	12.00	3.25
		Nos. 727-730 (4)	24.00	6.45

Nos. 727-730 exist imperf. Value, set unused $30.

Obelisk at N'sele, Pres. Mobutu A138

1971, May 20   **Photo.**   **Perf. 11½**
731	A138	4k gold & multi	.55	.25

4th anniversary of the People's Revolutionary Movement.
No. 731 exists imperf. Value, unused $6.

Radar Station A139

Designs: 1k, Waves. 6k, Map of Africa with telecommunications network.

1971, June 25   **Photo.**   **Perf. 11½**
732	A139	1k rose & multi	.25	.25
733	A139	3k yel & multi	.55	.35
734	A139	6k lt bl & multi	1.40	1.00
		Nos. 732-734 (3)	2.20	1.60

3rd World Telecommunications Day, May 17 (1k); opening of satellite telecommunications ground station, Kinshasa, June 30 (3k); Pan-African telecommunication system (6k).
Nos. 732-734 exist imperf. Value, set unused $15.

Grass Monkeys A140

Designs: 20s, Moustached monkeys, vert. 70s, De Brazza's monkeys. 1k, Yellow baboons. 3k, Pygmy chimpanzee, vert. 5k, Mangabeys, vert. 10k, Owlfaced monkeys. 15k, Diana monkeys. 25k, Black-and-white colobus, vert. 40k, L'Hoest's monkeys, vert.

1971, Aug.
735	A140	10s vio & multi	.75	.35
736	A140	20s lt bl & multi	.75	.35
737	A140	70s ocher & multi	1.25	.45
738	A140	1k gray & multi	1.25	.45
739	A140	3k rose & multi	2.00	1.00
740	A140	5k brn & multi	4.50	2.50
741	A140	10k multi	8.75	4.75
742	A140	15k multi	14.00	6.50
743	A140	25k brt bl & multi	23.50	11.00
744	A140	40k red & multi	32.50	16.00
		Nos. 735-744 (10)	89.25	43.35

Nos. 735-744 exist imperf. Value, set unused $120.

Hotel Inter-Continental, Kinshasa — A141

1971, Oct. 2   **Photo.**   **Perf. 13**
745	A141	2k silver & multi	.25	.25
746	A141	12k gold & multi	.55	.25

Nos. 745-746 exist imperf. Value, set unused $6.

Man Reading A142

Designs: 2.50k, Open book and abacus. 7k, Five letters surrounding symbolic head.

1971, Oct. 24
747	A142	50s multi	.25	.25
748	A142	2.50k multi	.25	.25
749	A142	7k multi	1.40	1.00
		Nos. 747-749 (3)	1.90	1.50

Fight against illiteracy.

Nos. 747-749 exist imperf. Value, set unused $10.
Succeeding issues are listed in Vol. 6 under Zaire. Beginning in 1998, Zaire reverted to using the Congo name, at least temporarily. Until the situation is resolved, the current stamps inscribed "Congo" will be listed under Zaire.

SEMI-POSTAL STAMPS

Women Carrying Food, Wheat Emblem, and Tractor SP22

1963, Mar. 21   **Photo.**   **Perf. 14x13**
B48	SP22	5fr + 2fr multi	.25	.25
B49	SP22	9fr + 4fr multi	.45	.25
B50	SP22	12fr+ 6fr multi	.50	.25
B51	SP22	20fr+ 10fr multi	2.25	1.75
		Nos. B48-B51 (4)	3.45	2.50

FAO "Freedom from Hunger" campaign.
Nos. B48-B51 exist imperf. Value, set unused $30.
No. B51 exists in an imperf sheet of one, in light and dark violet. Value $30.

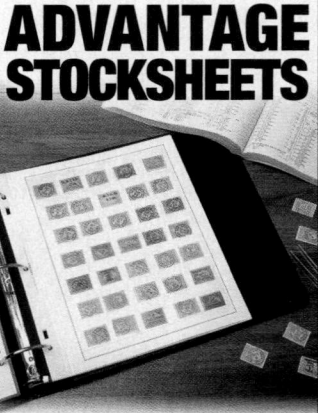

CONGO, PEOPLE'S REPUBLIC

'pē-pəls ri-'pə-blik of

'kän͡ɟₔgō

(ex-French)

LOCATION — West Africa at equator
GOVT. — Republic
AREA — 132,046 sq. mi.
POP. — 2,716,814 (1999 est.)
CAPITAL — Brazzaville

The former French colony of Middle Congo became a member state of the French Community on November 28, 1958, and achieved independence on August 15, 1960. For some years before 1958, the colony was joined with three other French territories to form French Equatorial Africa. Issues of Middle Congo (1907-1933) are listed under that heading.

100 Centimes = 1 Franc

Catalogue values for all unused stamps in this country are for Never Hinged items.

Allegory of
New
Republic
A7

1959 Unwmk. Engr. Perf. 13
89 A7 25fr brn, dp clar, org & ol .75 .25
1st anniv. of the proclamation of the Republic.

Imperforates

Most stamps of the Republic of the Congo exist imperforate in issued and trial colors, and also in small presentation sheets in issued colors.

Common Design Types pictured following the introduction.

C.C.T.A. Issue
Common Design Type
1960 Unwmk. Perf. 13
90 CD106 50fr dl grn & plum 1.00 1.00

President Fulbert
Youlou — A8

1960
91 A8 15fr grn, blk & car .35 .35
92 A8 85fr indigo & car 2.00 .45

Flag, Map and UN
Emblem — A9

1961, Mar. 11 Perf. 13
Flag in Green, Yellow & Red
93 A9 5fr vio brn & dk bl .25 .25
94 A9 20fr org & dk bl .45 .25
95 A9 100fr grn & dk bl 2.00 .80
Nos. 93-95 (3) 2.70 1.30
Congo's admission to United Nations.

Rainbow
Runner
A10

Fish: 50c, 3fr, Rainbow runner. 1fr, 2fr, Sloan's viperfish. 5fr, Hatchet fish. 10fr, A deep-sea fish.

1961, Nov. 28 Engr.
96 A10 50c brn, ol grn & sal .30 .25
97 A10 1fr bl grn & sepia .30 .25
98 A10 2fr ultra, sep & dk grn .30 .25
99 A10 3fr dk bl, grn & salmon .45 .30
100 A10 5fr red brn, grn & blk .70 .30
101 A10 10fr blue & red brn 1.40 .45
Nos. 96-101 (6) 3.45 1.80

Brazzaville
Market — A11

1962, Mar. 23 Unwmk. Perf. 13
102 A11 20fr blk, red & grn .80 .25

Abidjan Games Issue
Common Design Type
20fr, Boxing. 50fr, Running, finish line.

1962, July 21 Photo. Perf. 12½x12
103 CD109 20fr car, brt pink, brn
& blk .45 .25
104 CD109 50fr car, brt pink, brn
& blk .90 .30
Nos. 103-104,C7 (3) 3.85 1.80

African-Malgache Union Issue
Common Design Type
1962, Sept. 8
105 CD110 30fr multicolored 1.50 .50

Waves
Around
Globe
A11a

Design: 100fr, Orbit patterns around globe.

1963, Sept. 19 Perf. 12½
106 A11a 25fr org, grn & ultra .75 .30
107 A11a 100fr lt red brn, bl &
plum 1.75 .90
Issued to publicize space communications.

King Makoko's
Collar — A12

Unwmk.
1963, Oct. 21 Engr. Perf. 13
108 A12 10fr showm .45 .25
109 A12 15fr Kebekebe mask .60 .25

UNESCO
Emblem,
Scales and
Tree
A12a

1963, Dec. 10 Unwmk. Perf. 13
110 A12a 25fr grn, dk bl & brn .80 .30
15th anniv. of the Universal Declaration of Human Rights.

Barograph
and WMO
Emblem
A12b

1964, Mar. 23 Engr.
111 A12b 50fr grn, red brn & ultra 1.50 .60
Fourth World Meteorological Day.

Mechanic with
Machine — A13

1964, Apr. 8
112 A13 20fr grnsh bl, mag & dk
brn .80 .30
Training of technicians.

Corn and
Tools
A14

1964, Apr. 24 Unwmk. Perf. 13
113 A14 80fr brn, grn & brn car 1.60 .60
Importance of manual labor.

Diaboua
Ballet
A15

Kébékébé
Dance — A16

1964, May 8 Engr.
114 A15 30fr multicolored 1.25 .30
115 A16 60fr multicolored 2.25 .65

Carved
Figure — A17

1964, May 22
116 A17 50fr brn red & sepia 1.50 .55

Classroom
A18

1964, May 26
117 A18 25fr dk brn, red & blue .80 .30
Issued to publicize education.

Type of Air Post Issue, 1963, Inscribed

1964, Aug. 15 Photo. Perf. 13x12
118 AP5 20fr lt bl, red, ocher, dk
brn & grn .80 .25
1st anniv. of the revolution and Natl. Feast Day, Aug. 15.

Fire Squid
A19

15fr, Johnson's deep-sea angler (fish).

1964, Oct. 20 Engr. Perf. 13
119 A19 2fr ver, lt grn & brn .80 .50
120 A19 15fr vio, lt ol grn & dp cl 2.75 1.50

Cooperation Issue
Common Design Type
1964, Nov. 7 Unwmk. Perf. 13
121 CD119 25fr car, brt grn & dk
brn .80 .35

Communications Emblems — A20

1965, Jan. 1 Litho. Perf. 12½x13
122 A20 25fr ol, red brn & blk .80 .25
Issued to commemorate the establishment of the national postal administration.

Sitatunga — A21   Dancer on
Stilts — A22

Design: 20fr, Elephant, horiz.

1965, Mar. 15 Engr. Perf. 13
123 A21 15fr redsh brn, dl grn &
bl 1.00 .40
124 A21 20fr blk, dp bl & sl grn 1.00 .40
125 A22 85fr lil & multi 3.50 1.50
Nos. 123-125 (3) 5.50 2.30

Pres. Alphonse
Massamba-Debat
A23

1965-66   Photo.   Perf. 12x12½
126 A23 20fr dk brn, grn & yel   .40 .25
127 A23 25fr brn, bl grn, emer &
             blk ('66)   .40 .25
128 A23 30fr brn, bl grn, org & blk
             ('66)   .70 .25
        Nos. 126-128 (3)   1.50 .75

Soccer
Player
A24

Designs: 25fr, Games' emblem (map of
Africa and runners). 50fr, Field ball player.
85fr, Runner. 100fr, Bicyclist.

1965, July 17   Photo.   Perf. 12½
             Size: 28x28mm
129 A24 25fr blk, red, yel & grn   .50 .30
             Size: 34x34mm
130 A24 40fr yel grn & multi   .70 .45
131 A24 50fr red & multi   .70 .45
132 A24 85fr blk & multi   1.25 .65
133 A24 100fr yel & multi   1.75 .75
    a.   Min. sheet of 5, #129-133   7.50 7.50
        Nos. 129-133 (5)   4.90 2.60

1st African Games, Brazzaville, July 18-25.

Arms of
Congo — A25

1965, Nov. 15   Litho.   Perf. 12½x13
134 A25 20fr multicolored   .80 .25

Cooperative
Village
A26

30fr, Gymnastic drill team with streamers.

1966, Feb. 18   Perf. 12½x13
135 A26 25fr multicolored   .80 .25
136 A26 30fr multicolored   .80 .30

Sculptured
Mask — A27

Designs: 30fr, Weaver, painting. 85fr,
String instrument, painting, horiz.

Perf. 13x12½, 12½x13
1966, Apr. 9   Photo.
137 A27 30fr multicolored   .70 .30
138 A27 85fr multicolored   1.90 .70
139 A27 90fr multicolored   2.25 1.00
        Nos. 137-139 (3)   4.85 2.00
    Intl. Negro Arts Festival, Dakar, Senegal,
4/1-24.

Men and
Clocks
A28

1966, Apr. 15   Perf. 12½x12
140 A28 70fr pale brn, ocher &
             dk brn   1.60 .50
    Introduction of the shorter work day (less
lunch time, earlier quitting time).

WHO Headquarters, Geneva — A29

1966, May 3   Photo.   Perf. 12½x13
141 A29 50fr org yel, vio & bl   1.50 .50
    Inauguration of the WHO Headquarters,
Geneva.

Church of St. Peter
Claver — A30

1966, June 15   Photo.   Perf. 13x12½
142 A30 70fr multicolored   1.50 .40

Women's
Basketball — A31

Sport: 1fr, Women's volleyball, horiz. 3fr,
Women's field ball, horiz. 5fr, Athletes of various races. 10fr, Torch bearer. 15fr, Soccer
and gold medal of First African Games.

1966, July 15   Engr.   Perf. 13
143 A31 1fr ultra, choc & ol   .25 .25
144 A31 2fr choc, grn & bl   .25 .25
145 A31 3fr dk grn, dk car &
             choc   .25 .25
146 A31 5fr slate, emer & choc   .30 .25
147 A31 10fr dl bl, dk grn & vio   .55 .25
148 A31 15fr vio, car & choc   .75 .30
        Nos. 143-148 (6)   2.35 1.55

Jules Rimet
Cup and
Globe
A32

1966, July 15   Photo.   Perf. 12½x12
149 A32 30fr brt red, gold, blk &
             bl   1.25 .45
    8th World Soccer Cup Championship, Wem-
bley, England, July 11-30.

Savorgnan
de Brazza
School
A33

1966, Sept. 15 Photo. Perf. 12½x12
150 A33 30fr dk pur, grn, yel &
             blk   .80 .25

Pointe-Noire Railroad Station — A34

1966, Oct. 15   Engr.   Perf. 13
151 A34 60fr grn, red & brn   1.50 .60

Student with
Microscope — A35

1966, Nov. 28   Engr.   Perf. 13
152 A35 90fr brn, grn & ind   1.50 .70
        20th anniv. of UNESCO.

Balumbu
Mask — A36

Masks: 10fr, Kuyu. 15fr, Bakwélé. 20fr,
Batéké.

1966, Dec. 12   Engr.   Perf. 13
153 A36 5fr car rose & dk brn   .45 .25
154 A36 10fr Prus bl & brn   .50 .25
155 A36 15fr sep, dl org & dk bl   .60 .25
156 A36 20fr dp bl & multi   .80 .25
        Nos. 153-156 (4)   2.35 1.00

Order of the
Revolution and
Map — A37

Learning
the
Alphabet
A38

Design: 45fr, Harvesting and loading sugar
cane, and sugar mill.

Perf. 12x12½, 12½x12
1967, Mar. 15   Photo.
157 A37 20fr org & multi   .80 .30
158 A38 25fr blk, ocher & dk car   .80 .35
159 A38 45fr yel grn & lt bl   1.50 .30
        Nos. 157-159 (3)   3.10 .95

    Issued to honor the members of the Order
of the Revolution (20fr); to publicize the literacy campaign (25fr); to publicize, sugar production (45fr).

Mahatma
Gandhi — A39

1967, Apr. 21   Engr.   Perf. 13
160 A39 90fr blue & black   2.25 .75
    Issued in memory of Mohandas K. Gandhi
(1869-1948), Hindu nationalist leader.

"Elegant
Lady" — A40

Dolls: 10fr, Fruit vendor   25fr, Woman
pounding saka-saka. 30fr, Mother and child.

1967, June   Photo.   Perf. 13x12½
161 A40 5fr gold & multi   .25 .25
162 A40 10fr yel grn & multi   .45 .25
163 A40 25fr lt ultra & multi   .50 .25
164 A40 30fr multicolored   .60 .25
        Nos. 161-164 (4)   1.80 1.00

ITY
Emblem,
Village and
Waterfall
A41

1967, July 5   Engr.   Perf. 13
165 A41 60fr rose cl, org & ol grn   .90 .40
    Issued for International Tourist Year, 1967.

Europafrica Issue

Symbols of
Cooperation — A42

1967, July 20 Photo. Perf. 12x12½
166 A42 50fr multicolored   .90 .30

Arms of
Brazzaville — A43

1967, Aug. 15   Litho.   Perf. 12½x13
167 A43 30fr yel & multi   .80 .35
    Fourth anniversary of the revolution.

UN Emblem, Dove
and People — A44

1967, Oct. 24 Photo. Perf. 13x12½
168 A44 90fr bl, dk brn, red brn & yel 1.75 .60
Issued for United Nations Day, Oct. 24.

Boy and UNICEF Emblem — A45

1967, Dec. 11 Engr. Perf. 13
169 A45 90fr mar, blk & ultra 1.75 .60
21st anniv. of UNICEF.

Albert Luthuli, Dove and Globe A46

1968, Jan. 29 Engr. Perf. 13
170 A46 30fr brt grn & ol bis .80 .35
Albert Luthuli (1899-1967) of South Africa, winner of 1960 Nobel Peace Prize.

Arms of Pointe Noire — A47

1968, Feb. 20 Litho. Perf. 12½x13
171 A47 10fr brt pink & multi .80 .30

Motherhood — A48

1968, May 25 Engr. Perf. 13
172 A48 15fr dk car rose, sky bl & blk .80 .30
Issued for Mother's Day.

Mayombe Viaduct — A49

1968, June 24
173 A49 45fr mar, slate grn & bl 2.00 .45

A50

5fr, Daimler, 1889. 20fr, Berliet, 1897. 60fr, Peugeot, 1898. 80fr, Renault, 1900. 85fr, Fiat, 1902.

1968, July 29 Photo. Perf. 13x12½
174 A50 5fr multi .45 .25
175 A50 20fr multi .90 .30
176 A50 60fr multi 1.75 .40
177 A50 80fr multi 2.75 .70
178 A50 85fr multi 3.25 .90
Nos. 174-178,C67-C68 (7) 17.85 6.05

Tanker, Refinery and Map of Area Served — A50a

1968, July 30 Perf. 12½
179 A50a 30fr multicolored .80 .30
Issued to commemorate the opening of the Port Gentil (Gabon) Refinery, June 12, 1968.

WHO Emblem and Tree of Life — A51

1968, Nov. 28 Engr. Perf. 13
180 A51 25fr dk grn, red & dp lil .80 .30
20th anniv. of WHO.

Development Bank Issue
Common Design Type
1969, Sept. 10 Engr. Perf. 13
181 CD130 25fr car rose, grn & ocher .40 .25
182 CD130 30fr bl, grn & ocher .40 .25

Bicycle A52

Bicycles & Motorcycles: 75fr, Hirondelle. 80fr, Folding bicycle. 85fr, Peugeot. 100fr, Excelsior Manxman. 150fr, Norton. 200fr, Brough Superior "Old Bill." 300fr, Matchless and N.L.G.-J.A.P.S.

1969, Oct. 6 Engr. Perf. 13
183 A52 50fr multicolored 1.25 .30
184 A52 75fr multicolored 1.50 .30
185 A52 80fr multicolored 1.75 .40
186 A52 85fr multicolored 2.00 .50
187 A52 100fr multicolored 3.00 .85
188 A52 150fr multicolored 4.00 1.00
189 A52 200fr multicolored 5.25 1.75
190 A52 300fr multicolored 9.50 2.75
Nos. 183-190 (8) 28.25 7.85

Mayombe Train and Tourist Year Emblem A53

40fr, Train and Mbamba Tunnel, vert.

Perf. 13x12½, 12½x13
1969, Oct. 20 Photo.
191 A53 40fr multicolored 2.40 .40
192 A53 60fr multicolored 4.00 .65
Issued for African Tourist Year.

Loutete Cement Works A54

Loutete Cement Works: 15fr, Mixing tower, vert. 25fr, Cable transport, vert. 30fr, General view of plant.

1969, Dec. 10 Engr. Perf. 13
193 A54 10fr dk gray, rose cl & dk ol .25 .25
194 A54 15fr Prus bl, red brn & pur .50 .25
195 A54 25fr mar, brn & Prus bl .60 .25
196 A54 30fr vio brn, ultra & blk .70 .25
a. Min. sheet of 4, #193-196 2.75 2.75
Nos. 193-196 (4) 2.05 1.00

ASECNA Issue
Common Design Type
1969, Dec. 12
197 CD132 100fr dull brown 2.00 .40
Nos. 197 (1) 2.00 .40

Pineapple Harvest and ILO Emblem A55

30fr, Worker at lathe and ILO emblem.

1969, Dec. 20 Engr. Perf. 13
198 A55 25fr bl, olive & brn .60 .25
199 A55 30fr rose red, choc & slate .85 .35
50th anniv. of the ILO.

SOTEXCO Textile Plant, Kinsoundi A56

20fr, Women in spinnery. 25fr, Hand-printing textiles. 30fr, Checking woven cloth.

1970, Jan. 20
200 A56 15fr grn, blk & lil .45 .25
201 A56 20fr plum, car & sl grn .45 .25
202 A56 25fr bl, slate & brn .60 .25
203 A56 30fr gray, car rose & brn .60 .25
Nos. 200-203 (4) 2.10 1.00

Hotel Cosmos, Brazzaville A57

1970, Jan. 30
204 A57 90fr slate grn, bl & red brn 1.40 .50

The status of the three sets for Kennedy, etc., Summer Olympics, and Baroque paintings is not certain.

Linzolo Church — A58

Diosso Gorge A59

Design: 90fr, Foulakari waterfall.

1970 Engr. Perf. 13
205 A58 25fr multicolored .80 .25
206 A59 70fr multicolored 1.50 .30
207 A59 90fr multicolored 2.25 .40
Nos. 205-207 (3) 4.55 .95
Issue dates: 25fr, Feb. 10; others, Feb. 25.

Volvaria Esculenta — A60

Mushrooms: 10fr, Termitomyces entolomoides. 15fr, Termitomyces microcarpus. 25fr, Termitomyces aurantiacus. 30fr, Termitomyces mammiformis. 50fr, Tremella fuciformis.

1970, Mar. 31 Photo. Perf. 13
208 A60 5fr multicolored 6.75 1.00
209 A60 10fr multicolored 9.00 1.40
210 A60 15fr multicolored 13.50 2.00
211 A60 25fr multicolored 22.50 4.00
212 A60 30fr multicolored 32.50 5.75
213 A60 50fr multicolored 70.00 10.00
Nos. 208-213 (6) 154.25 24.15

Laying Coaxial Cable A61

Design: 30fr, Full view of rail car; 3 cable layers on railway roadbed.

1970, Apr. 30 Engr. Perf. 13
214 A61 25fr dk brn & multi 1.00 .30
215 A61 30fr brn & multi 1.25 .60
Issued to publicize the laying of the coaxial cable linking Brazzaville and Pointe Noire. For surcharges see Nos. 263-264.

UPU Headquarters Issue
Common Design Type
1970, May 20
216 CD133 30fr dk pur, gray & mag .80 .25

Mother Feeding Child — A62

Design: 90fr, Mother nursing infant.

1970, May 30 Photo.
217 A62 85fr vio bl & multi 1.00 .30
218 A62 90fr lil & multi 1.10 .40
Issued for Mother's Day.

Dag Hammarskjold, UN Emblem — A63

UN Emblem and: No. 220, Trygve Lie, horiz. No. 221, U Thant, horiz.

1970, June 20 Engr. Perf. 13
219 A63 100fr scar, dk red & dk pur 1.40 .80
220 A63 100fr dk red, ultra & ind 1.40 .80

221	A63	100fr grn, emer & dk red	1.40	.80
a.		Souv. sheet of 3, #219-221	5.50	5.50
		Nos. 219-221 (3)	4.20	2.40

25th anniv. of the UN and to honor its Secretaries General.

Brillantaisia Vogeliana A64

Sternotomis Variabilis — A65

Plants and Beetles: 2fr, Plectranthus decurrens. 3fr, Myrianthemum mirabile. 5fr, Connarus griffonianus. 15fr, Chelorrhina polyphemus. 20fr, Metopodontus savagei.

Perf. 12½x12, 12x12½

1970, June 30   Photo.

222	A64	1fr dk grn & multi	.70	.25
223	A64	2fr multicolored	.70	.25
224	A64	3fr indigo & multi	.70	.25
225	A64	5fr lemon & multi	1.40	.25
226	A65	10fr lilac & multi	2.25	.40
227	A65	15fr orange & multi	3.25	.40
228	A65	20fr multicolored	3.25	.60
		Nos. 222-228 (7)	12.25	2.40

For surcharge see No. 288.

Stegosaurus — A66

Prehistoric Fauna: 20fr, Dinotherium, vert. 60fr, Brachiosaurus, vert. 80fr, Arsinoitherium.

1970, July 20

229	A66	15fr dl grn, ocher & red brn	1.75	.30
230	A66	20fr lt bl & multi	3.50	.65
231	A66	60fr lt bl & multi	6.25	.95
232	A66	80fr lt bl & multi	8.00	1.75
		Nos. 229-232 (4)	19.50	3.65

Mikado 141, 1932 A67

Locomotives: 60fr, Steam locomotive 130+032, 1947. 75fr, Alsthom BB 1100, 1962. 85fr, Diesel BB BB 302, 1969.

1970, Aug. 20   Engr.   *Perf. 13*

233	A67	40fr mag, bl grn & blk	2.75	.80
234	A67	60fr blk, bl & grn	3.25	.90
235	A67	75fr red, bl & blk	4.50	1.25
236	A67	85fr car, sl grn & ocher	7.50	1.75
		Nos. 233-236 (4)	18.00	4.70

Cogniauxia Padolaena — A68

Tropical Flowers: 2fr, Celosia cristata. 5fr, Plumeria acutifolia. 10fr, Bauhinia variegata. 15fr, Poinsettia. 20fr, Thunbergia grandiflora.

1971, Feb. 10   Photo.   *Perf. 12x12½*

237	A68	1fr lil & multi	.25	.25
238	A68	2fr yel & multi	.25	.25
239	A68	5fr ultra & multi	.25	.25
240	A68	10fr yel & multi	1.10	.25
241	A68	15fr multicolored	1.60	.30
242	A68	20fr dk red & multi	2.75	.40
		Nos. 237-242 (6)	6.20	1.70

Green Night Adder — A69

Reptiles: 10fr, African Egg-eating snake, horiz. 15fr, Flap-necked chameleon. 20fr, Nile crocodile, horiz. 25fr, Rock python, horiz. 30fr, Gaboon viper. 40fr, Brown house snake, horiz. 45fr, Jameson's mamba.

Perf. 12x12½, 12½x12

1971, June 26   Photo.

243	A69	5fr multicolored	.40	.25
244	A69	10fr multicolored	.40	.25
245	A69	15fr multicolored	1.40	.25
246	A69	20fr multicolored	2.25	.25
247	A69	25fr grn & multi	3.00	.35
248	A69	30fr multicolored	3.75	.75
249	A69	40fr bis & multi	4.25	.95
250	A69	45fr multicolored	5.75	1.00
		Nos. 243-250 (8)	21.20	4.05

Pseudimbrasia Deyrollei — A70

Caterpillars: 15fr, Bunaea alcinoe, vert. 20fr, Epiphora vacuna ploetzi. 25fr, Imbrasia eblis. 30fr, Imbrasia dione, vert. 40fr, Holocera angulata.

1971, July 3   *Perf. 13*

251	A70	10fr ver, blk & grn	1.00	.25
252	A70	15fr multicolored	1.50	.30
253	A70	20fr yel grn, blk & ocher	2.25	.40
254	A70	25fr multicolored	3.50	.60
255	A70	30fr red, blk & yel	5.00	.90
256	A70	40fr bl, blk & org	6.75	1.25
		Nos. 251-256 (6)	20.00	3.70

Boy Scout — A70a

Scouts, Lord Baden-Powell — A70b

Designs: c, Scout facing left. d, Scout facing forward. e, Lord Baden-Powell.

Embossed on Metallic Foil

1971, July 14   *Die Cut Perf. 10½*

256A	A70a	90fr Block of 4, #b.-e, silver	12.00	12.00
256F	A70b	1000fr gold	30.00	30.00

No. 256F is airmail.

Cymothoe Sangaris A71

Butterflies and Moths: 40fr, Papilio dardanus, vert. 75fr, Iolaus timon. 90fr, Papilio phorcas, vert. 100fr, Euchloron megaera.

1971, Oct. 15   *Perf. 12½x12, 12x12½*

257	A71	30fr yel & multi	1.75	.40
258	A71	40fr grn & multi	3.25	.65
259	A71	75fr multicolored	5.25	1.25
260	A71	90fr multicolored	7.00	1.90
261	A71	100fr ultra & multi	9.50	2.50
		Nos. 257-261 (5)	26.75	6.70

Black and White Men Working Together — A72

1971, Oct. 30   *Perf. 13x12½*

262	A72	50fr org & multi	1.60	.50

Intl. Year Against Racial Discrimination.

Nos. 214-215 Surcharged

1971, Nov. 18   Engr.   *Perf. 13*

263	A61	30fr on 25fr multicolored	.65	.30
264	A61	40fr on 30fr multicolored	.95	.35

Inauguration of cable service between Brazzaville and Pointe Noire. Words of surcharge arranged differently on No. 264.

Map of Congo — A73

1971, Dec. 31   Photo.   *Perf. 12½x13*

265	A73	30fr bl & multi	.35	.25
266	A73	40fr yel grn & multi	.45	.25
267	A73	100fr gray & multi	1.10	.40
		Nos. 265-267 (3)	1.90	.90

"Labor, Democracy, Peace."

Lion — A74

2fr, African elephants. 3fr, Leopard. 4fr, Hippopotamus. 5fr, Gorilla, vert. 20fr, Potto. 30fr, De Brazza's monkey. 40fr, Pygmy chimpanzee, vert.

1972, Jan. 31   Engr.   *Perf. 13*

268	A74	1fr grn & multi	.35	.25
269	A74	2fr dk red & multi	.50	.25
270	A74	3fr red brn & multi	.80	.25
271	A74	4fr vio & multi	1.00	.25
272	A74	5fr brn & multi	1.10	.25
273	A74	20fr org & multi	2.75	.35
274	A74	30fr ocher & multi	3.50	.45
275	A74	40fr Prus bl & multi	5.25	.75
		Nos. 268-275 (8)	15.25	2.80

WHO, 25th Anniv. — A75

Perf. 12½x13, 13x12½

1973, June 30   Typo.

276	A75	40fr WHO Emblem	.65	.25
277	A75	50fr WHO emblem, horiz.	.95	.25

Kronenbourg Brewery — A76

Brewery Trademark and: 40fr, Laboratory. 75fr, Vats and controls. 85fr, Automatic control room. 100fr, Pressure room. 250fr, Bottling plant.

1973, July 15   Engr.   *Perf. 13*

278	A76	30fr red & multi	.50	.25
279	A76	40fr red & multi	.60	.25
280	A76	75fr red & multi	1.20	.30
281	A76	85fr red & multi	1.75	.40
282	A76	100fr red & multi	1.90	.55
283	A76	250fr red & multi	3.75	1.00
		Nos. 278-283 (6)	9.70	2.75

Kronenbourg Brewery, Brazzaville.

Golwe Locomotive, 1935 — A77

Locomotives: 40fr, Diesel, 1935. 75fr, Diesel Whitcomb, 1946. 85fr, Diesel CC200.

1973, Aug. 1   Engr.   *Perf. 13*

284	A77	30fr indigo & multi	2.00	.50
285	A77	40fr vio bl & multi	3.00	.85
286	A77	75fr multicolored	4.25	1.50
287	A77	85fr multicolored	5.50	2.75
		Nos. 284-287 (4)	14.75	5.60

No. 225 Srchd. and Ovptd. in Ultramarine

1973, Aug. 16   Photo.   *Perf. 12½x12*

288	A64	100fr on 5fr multicolored	1.75	.60

African solidarity in drought emergency.

African Postal Union Issue
Common Design Type

1973, Sept. 12   Engr.   *Perf. 13*

289	CD137	100fr bl grn, vio & brn	1.60	.80

Bees,
Beehive,
Honeycomb
A78

1973, Dec. 10   Engr.   Perf. 13
290 A78 30fr sl grn, dk red & bl   1.10 .25
291 A78 40fr sl bl, sl grn & lt grn   1.50 .25
"Work and economy."

Family, UN
and FAO
Emblems
A79

40fr, Grain, emblems. 100fr, Grain, emblems, vert.

1973, Dec. 10
292 A79 30fr dk car & dk brn   .50 .25
293 A79 40fr dk grn, yel & ind   .60 .25
294 A79 100fr grn, brn & org   1.40 .40
    Nos. 292-294 (3)   2.50 .90

World Food Program, 10th anniversary.

Amilcar Cabral,
Cattle and
Child — A80

1974, July 15   Engr.   Perf. 13
295 A80 100fr multicolored   1.60 .60

First death anniversary of Amilcar Cabral (1924-1973), leader of anti-Portuguese guerrilla activity in Portuguese Guinea.

Félix
Eboué,
Cross of
Lorraine
A81

1974, Aug. 31   Litho.   Perf. 13
296 A81 30fr bl & multi   .80 .30
297 A81 40fr brt pink & multi   1.60 .60

Félix A. Eboué (1884-1944), Governor of Chad, first colonial governor to join Free French in WWII, 30th death anniversary.

Pineapples
A82

1974, Nov. 12
298 A82 30fr shown   .60 .30
299 A82 30fr Bananas   .70 .30
300 A82 30fr Safous   .70 .30
301 A82 40fr Avocados   1.25 .30
302 A82 40fr Mangos   1.25 .30
303 A82 40fr Papaya   1.25 .30
304 A82 40fr Orange   1.25 .30
    Nos. 298-304 (7)   7.00 2.10

Charles de Gaulle and Conference
Building — A83

1974, Nov. 25   Engr.   Perf. 13
305 A83 100fr multicolored   5.00 1.90

Brazzaville Conference, 25th anniversary.

George Stephenson and Various
Locomotives — A84

1974, Dec. 15
306 A84 75fr slate grn & ol   4.00 1.00

George Stephenson (1781-1848), English inventor and railroad founder.

UDEAC Issue

Presidents and Flags of Cameroun,
CAR, Congo, Gabon and Meeting
Center — A84a

1974, Dec. 8   Photo.   Perf. 13
307 A84a 40fr gold & multi   .65 .25
    See note after Cameroun No. 595.
    See No. C195.

Irish Setter
A85

1974, Dec. 15   Photo.   Perf. 13x13½
308 A85 30fr shown   1.25 .30
309 A85 40fr Borzoi   1.50 .30
310 A85 75fr Pointer   3.25 .75
311 A85 100fr Great Dane   4.50 .80
    Nos. 308-311 (4)   10.50 2.15

1974, Dec. 15

Designs: Cats.
312 A85 30fr Havana chestnut   1.25 .30
313 A85 40fr Red Persian   1.50 .30
314 A85 75fr Blue British   3.50 .75
315 A85 100fr African serval   5.00 .80
    Nos. 312-315 (4)   11.25 2.15

Labor Party
Flags and
People
A86

40fr, Hands holding flowers and tools.

1974, Dec. 31   Engr.   Perf. 13x12½
316 A86 30fr red & multi   .65 .25
317 A86 40fr red & multi   .95 .25

5th anniversary of Congolese Labor Party and of introduction of red flag.

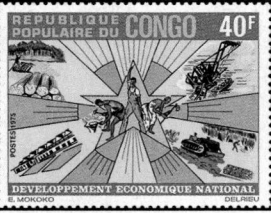

Symbols of Development — A87

U Thant and UN Headquarters — A88

Paul G.
Hoffman
and UN
Emblem
A89

Perf. 13x12½, 12½x13
1975, Feb. 28   Litho.
318 A87 40fr multicolored   .80 .35
319 A88 50fr light blue & multi   .80 .35
320 A89 50fr yellow & multi   .80 .35
    Nos. 318-320 (3)   2.40 1.05

National economic development.

Map of China and Mao Tse-
tung — A90

1975, Mar. 9   Engr.   Perf. 13
321 A90 75fr multicolored   5.50 1.50

25th anniv. of the PRC.

Woman
Breaking
Bonds,
Women's
Activities,
Map of
Congo
A91

1975, June 20   Litho.   Perf. 12½
322 A91 40fr gold & multi   .80 .35

Revolutionary Union of Congolese Women, URFC, 10th anniversary.

CARA Soccer Team — A92

Design: 40fr, Team captain and manager receiving trophy, vert.

1975, July 15   Litho.   Perf. 12½
323 A92 30fr multicolored   .65 .25
324 A92 40fr multicolored   .95 .25

CARA team, winners of African Soccer Cup 1974.

Citroen, 1935 — A93

Designs: Early autombiles.

1975, July 17   Perf. 12
325 A93 30fr shown   1.10 .40
326 A93 40fr Alfa Romeo, 1911   1.35 .40
327 A93 50fr Rolls Royce, 1926   1.75 .55
328 A93 75fr Duryea, 1893   3.50 .70
    Nos. 325-328 (4)   7.70 2.05

Tipoye Transport — A94

1975, Aug. 5
329 A94 30fr shown   .90 .40
330 A94 40fr Dugout canoe   1.00 .65

Traditional means of transportation.

Raising Red Flag — A95

1975, Aug. 15
331 A95 30fr shown   .80 .25
332 A95 40fr National Conference   .80 .25

2nd anniv. of installation of popular power (30fr) and 3rd anniv. of Natl. Conf. (40fr).

Line
Fishing — A96

Traditional Fishing: 30fr, Trap fishing, horiz. 60fr, Spear fishing. 90fr, Net fishing, horiz.

1975, Aug. 31	**Litho.**	***Perf. 12***	
333	A96	30fr multicolored	.80	.25
334	A96	40fr multicolored	.80	.30
335	A96	60fr multicolored	1.25	.50
336	A96	90fr multicolored	2.50	1.00
		Nos. 333-336 (4)	5.35	2.05

Woman Pounding "Foufou" — A97

Household Tasks: No. 338, Woman chopping wood. 40fr, Woman preparing manioc, horiz.

1975, Sept. 5				
337	A97	30fr multicolored	.60	.25
338	A97	30fr multicolored	.60	.25
339	A97	40fr multicolored	.90	.25
		Nos. 337-339 (3)	2.10	.75

Musical Instruments A98

1975, Sept. 20			***Perf. 12½***	
340	A98	30fr Esanga	.75	.25
341	A98	40fr Kalakwa	1.25	.25
342	A98	60fr Likembe	1.50	.30
343	A98	75fr Ngongui	2.00	.40
		Nos. 340-343 (4)	5.50	1.20

Dzeke (Congolese) Shell Money — A99

Ancient Money: No. 346, like No. 344. Nos. 345, 347, Okengo, Congolese, iron bar. 40fr, Gallic coin, c. 60 B.C. 50fr, Roman denarius, 37 B.C. 60fr, Danubian coin, 2nd cent. B.C. 85fr, Greek stater, 4th cent. B.C.

1975-76		**Engr.**	***Perf. 13***	
344	A99	30fr red & multi	.60	.25
345	A99	30fr vio & multi	.60	.25
346	A99	35fr ol & multi	.90	.25
347	A99	35fr dk car rose & multi	.90	.25
348	A99	40fr Prus bl & brn	.90	.25
349	A99	50fr Prus bl & ol	1.00	.30
350	A99	60fr dk grn & brn	1.25	.35
351	A99	85fr mag & sl grn	2.10	.45
		Nos. 344-351 (8)	8.25	2.35

Nos. 346-347 inscribed "1976" and issued Mar. 1976; others issued Oct. 5, 1975.

Moschops — A100

Pre-historic Animals: 70fr, Tyrannosaurus. 95fr, Cryptocleidus. 100fr, Stegosaurus.

1975, Oct. 15		**Litho.**	***Perf. 13***	
352	A100	55fr multicolored	2.25	.30
353	A100	75fr multicolored	3.25	.35
354	A100	95fr multicolored	5.75	.75
355	A100	100fr multicolored	8.00	1.25
		Nos. 352-355 (4)	19.25	2.65

Albert Schweitzer (1875-1965), Medical Missionary — A101

1975, Oct. 15			**Engr.**	
356	A101	75fr ol, brn & red	1.50	.40

Alexander Fleming A102

Designs: No. 358, André Marie Ampère. No. 359, Clement Ader.

1975, Nov. 15		**Engr.**	***Perf. 13***	
357	A102	60fr brn, grn & blk	1.60	.45
358	A102	95fr blk, red & grn	2.50	.65
359	A102	95fr red, blue & indigo	2.50	.65
		Nos. 357-359 (3)	6.60	1.75

Fleming (1881-1955), developer of penicillin; Ampère (1775-1836), physicist; Ader (1841-1925), aviation pioneer.

UN Emblem "ONU" and "30" — A103

1975, Dec. 20		**Engr.**	***Perf. 13***	
360	A103	95fr car, ultra & grn	1.60	.50

United Nations, 30th anniversary.

Women's Broken Chain — A104

Design: 60fr, Equality between man and woman, globe, IWY emblem.

1975, Dec. 20			***Perf. 12½***	
361	A104	35fr mag, ocher & gray	.90	.25
362	A104	60fr ultra, brn & blk	1.75	.50

International Women's Year, 1975.

Pres. Marien Ngouabi, Flag and Workers — A105

Echo of the P.C.T. A106

1975, Dec. 31		***Perf. 12½x12, 13x12½***		
363	A105	30fr multicolored	.55	.25
364	A106	35fr multicolored	.65	.25

6th anniversary of the Congolese Labor Party (P.C.T.). See No. C215.

A.G. Bell and 1876 Telephone A107

1976, Apr. 25		**Litho.**	***Perf. 12½x13***	
365	A107	35fr yel, brn & org brn	.65	.25

Cent. of 1st telephone call by Alexander Graham Bell, Mar. 10, 1876. See No. C229.

Women Selling Fruit and Vegetables A108

1976, Sept. 19		**Litho.**	***Perf. 12½x13***	
366	A108	35fr shown	.50	.25
367	A108	60fr Market scene	1.20	.30

Congolese Coiffure — A109

Designs: Various women's hair styles.

1976, Oct. 10		**Litho.**	***Perf. 13***	
368	A109	35fr multicolored	.55	.25
369	A109	60fr multicolored	.90	.25
370	A109	95fr multicolored	1.40	.35
371	A109	100fr multicolored	1.60	.40
		Nos. 368-371 (4)	4.45	1.25

Pole Vault, Map of Central Africa A110

95fr, Long jump and map of Central Africa.

1976, Oct. 25			***Perf. 12½***	
372	A110	60fr yel & multi	.70	.25
373	A110	95fr yel & multi	1.25	.40
		Nos. 372-373, C230-C231 (4)	6.45	2.50

Gold medalists, 1st Central African Games, Yaoundé, July 27-30, 1975.

Antelope A111

1976, Oct. 27		**Litho.**	***Perf. 12½***	
		Size: 36x36mm		
374	A111	5fr shown	.55	.25
375	A111	10fr Buffalos	.65	.25
376	A111	15fr Hippopotamus	1.00	.30
377	A111	20fr Wart hog	2.00	.35
378	A111	25fr Elephants	2.25	.40
		Nos. 374-378 (5)	6.45	1.55

1976, Dec. 8		**Size: 26x36mm**		

Birds — 5fr, Saddle-bill storks. 10fr, Malachite kingfisher. 20fr, Crowned cranes.

379	A111	5fr multicolored	1.00	.25
		Size: 36x36mm		
380	A111	10fr multicolored	1.25	.25
381	A111	20fr multicolored	2.00	.60
		Nos. 379-381 (3)	4.25	1.10

Bicycling, Map of Participants A112

1976, Dec. 21		**Photo.**	***Perf. 12½x13***	
382	A112	35fr shown	.35	.25
383	A112	60fr Fieldball	.60	.25
384	A112	80fr Running	1.00	.35
385	A112	95fr Soccer	1.25	.40
		Nos. 382-385 (4)	3.20	1.25

First Central African Games, Libreville, Gabon, June-July 1976.

Heliotrope A113

Flowers: 5fr, Water lilies. 15fr, Bird-of-paradise flower.

1976, Dec. 23		**Photo.**	***Perf. 12½x13***	
386	A113	5fr multicolored	.25	.25
387	A113	10fr multicolored	.35	.25
388	A113	15fr multicolored	.60	.25
		Nos. 386-388 (3)	1.20	.75

Torch and Olive Branches A114

1976, Dec. 25		**Litho.**	***Perf. 12½x13***	
389	A114	35fr multicolored	.80	.25

National Pioneer Movement.

The Spirit of '76 — A115

125fr, Pulling down George III statue. 150fr, Battle of Princeton. 175fr, Generals of Revolutionary War. 200fr, Burgoyne's surrender at Saratoga. 500fr, Battle of Lexington.

1976, Dec. 29   Litho.   Perf. 14
390	A115	100fr multicolored	1.00	.25
391	A115	125fr multicolored	1.10	.35
392	A115	150fr multicolored	1.60	.40
393	A115	175fr multicolored	2.00	.50
394	A115	200fr multicolored	2.25	.60
		Nos. 390-394 (5)	7.95	2.10

Souvenir Sheet
395	A115	500fr multicolored	5.75	1.50

American Bicentennial.

Dugout Canoe Race A116

Design: 60fr, 2-man dugout canoes.

1977, Mar. 27   Litho.   Perf. 13x13½
396	A116	35fr multicolored	.60	.25
397	A116	60fr multicolored	1.00	.35

Dugout canoe races on Congo River.

Lilan Goua A117

Fresh-water Fish: 15fr, Liko ko. 25fr, Liyan ga. 35fr, Mbessi. 60fr, Mongandza.

1977, June 15   Litho.   Perf. 12½
398	A117	10fr multicolored	.75	.25
399	A117	15fr multicolored	.90	.25
400	A117	25fr multicolored	1.25	.25
401	A117	35fr multicolored	2.00	.30
402	A117	60fr multicolored	3.50	.45
		Nos. 398-402 (5)	8.40	1.50

Traditional Headdress — A118

1977, June 30   Litho.   Perf. 12½
403	A118	35fr shown	.45	.30
404	A118	60fr Leopard cap	.90	.35

See Nos. C234-C235.

Bondjo Wrestling A119

40fr, 50fr, Bondjo wrestling, diff. 40fr, horiz.

1977, July 15
405	A119	25fr multicolored	.50	.25
406	A119	40fr multicolored	.60	.25
407	A119	50fr multicolored	.70	.30
		Nos. 405-407 (3)	1.80	.80

"Schwaben" LZ 10, 1911 — A120

Zeppelins: 60fr, "Viktoria Luise." LZ 11, 1913. 100fr, LZ 120. 200fr, LZ 127. 300fr, "Graf Zeppelin II" LZ 130.

1977, Aug. 5   Litho.   Perf. 11
408	A120	40fr multicolored	.50	.25
409	A120	60fr multicolored	.75	.25
410	A120	100fr multicolored	1.25	.30
411	A120	200fr multicolored	2.50	.60
412	A120	300fr multicolored	4.00	.95
		Nos. 408-412 (5)	9.00	2.35

History of the Zeppelin. Exist imperf. See No. C236.

Coat of Arms and Rising Sun A121

1977, Aug. 15
413	A121	40fr multicolored	.80	.25

14th anniversary of the revolution.

Victor Hugo and The Hunchback of Notre Dame — A122

Designs (Hugo and): 60fr, Les Miserables. 100fr, Les Travailleurs de la Mer (octopus).

1977, Aug. 20   Engr.   Perf. 13
414	A122	35fr multicolored	.75	.30
415	A122	60fr multicolored	1.00	.30
416	A122	100fr multicolored	1.90	.45
		Nos. 414-416 (3)	3.65	1.05

Victor Hugo (1802-1885), French novelist.

Mao Tsetung A123

Lithographed; Gold Embossed
1977, Sept. 9   Perf. 12x12½
417	A123	400fr red & gold	16.00	8.00

Chairman Mao Tse-tung (1893-1976), Chinese Communist leader, 1st death anniv.

Peter Paul Rubens A124

1977, Sept. 20   Gold Embossed
418	A124	600fr gold & lt bl	10.00	6.00

Peter Paul Rubens (1577-1640), painter.

Child Leading Blind Woman Across Street A125

1977, Oct. 22   Litho.   Perf. 12½x13
419	A125	35fr multicolored	.80	.25

World Health Day: To see is life.

Paul Kamba and Records A126

1977, Oct. 29
420	A126	100fr multicolored	1.60	.50

Paul Kamba (1912-1950), musician.

Trajan Vuia and Flying Machine — A127

Designs: 75fr, Louis Bleriot and plane. 100fr, Roland Garros and plane. 200fr, Charles Lindbergh and Spirit of St. Louis. 300fr, Tupolev Tu-144. 500fr, Lindbergh and Spirit of St. Louis over ship in Atlantic.

1977, Nov. 18   Litho.   Perf. 14
421	A127	60fr multicolored	.60	.25
422	A127	75fr multicolored	.90	.25
423	A127	100fr multicolored	1.10	.30
424	A127	200fr multicolored	2.25	.50
425	A127	300fr multicolored	3.25	.70
		Nos. 421-425 (5)	8.10	2.00

Souvenir Sheet
426	A127	500fr multicolored	5.75	1.25

History of aviation.

Elizabeth II and Prince Philip A128

Design: 300fr, Elizabeth II wearing Crown.

1977, Dec. 21
427	A128	250fr multicolored	2.25	.65
428	A128	300fr multicolored	2.75	.70

Reign of Queen Elizabeth II, 25th anniv. See No. C239. For overprints see Nos. 468-469, C244.

King Baudouin A129

Design: No. 430, Charles de Gaulle.

1977, Dec. 21
429	A129	200fr multicolored	2.25	.65
430	A129	200fr multicolored	2.25	.65

King Baudouin of Belgium and Charles de Gaulle, president of France.

Ambete Sculpture A130

Congolese art: 85fr, Babembe sculpture.

1978, Feb. 18   Engr.   Perf. 13
431	A130	35fr lt brn & multi	.65	.25
432	A130	85fr lt grn & multi	1.50	.45

St. Simon, by Rubens A131

Rubens Paintings: 140fr, Duke of Lerma. 200fr, Madonna and Saints. 300fr, Rubens and his Wife Helena Fourment. 500fr, Farm at Laeken.

1978, Mar. 7   Litho.   Perf. 13½x14
433	A131	60fr gold & multi	.60	.25
434	A131	140fr gold & multi	1.50	.30
435	A131	200fr gold & multi	2.25	.45
436	A131	300fr gold & multi	3.50	.65
		Nos. 433-436 (4)	7.85	1.65

Souvenir Sheet
437	A131	500fr gold & multi	6.00	1.40

Peter Paul Rubens, 400th birth anniv.

Pres. Ngouabi and
Microphones — A132

60fr, Ngouabi at his desk, horiz. 100fr,
Portrait.

Perf. 12½x13, 13x12½

1978, Mar. 18   Litho.
438 A132 35fr multicolored   .45 .25
439 A132 60fr multicolored   .50 .25
440 A132 100fr multicolored   .90 .40
     Nos. 438-440 (3)   1.85 .90
Pres. Marien Ngouabi, 1st death anniv.

Ferenc Puskas and Argentina '78
Emblem — A133

Players and Emblem: 75fr, Giacinto
Facchetti. 100fr, Bobby Moore. 200fr, Ray-
mond Kopa. 300fr, Pele. 500fr, Franz
Beckenbauer.

1978, Apr. 4   **Perf. 14x13½**
441 A133 60fr multicolored   .60 .25
442 A133 75fr multicolored   .70 .25
443 A133 100fr multicolored   1.10 .25
444 A133 200fr multicolored   2.25 .55
445 A133 300fr multicolored   3.25 .75
     Nos. 441-445 (5)   7.90 2.05

Souvenir Sheet

446 A133 500fr multicolored   6.25 1.25
11th World Cup Soccer Championship,
Argentina, June 1-25.
For overprints see Nos. 481-486.

Pearl S. Buck and Chinese
Women — A134

Nobel Prize winners: 75fr, Fridtjof Nansen,
refugees and Nansen passport. 100fr, Henri
Bergson, book and flame. 200fr, Alexander
Fleming and Petri dish. 300fr, Gerhart
Hauptmann and book. 500fr, Henri Dunant
and Red Cross Station.

1978, Apr. 29
447 A134 60fr multicolored   .60 .25
448 A134 75fr multicolored   .70 .25
449 A134 100fr multicolored   1.10 .30
450 A134 200fr multicolored   2.00 .50
451 A134 300fr multicolored   2.75 .60
     Nos. 447-451 (5)   7.15 1.90

Souvenir Sheet

452 A134 500fr multicolored   6.00 1.40

African
Buffalos
A135

Endangered animals and Wildlife Fund
Emblem: 35fr, Okapi, vert. 85fr, Rhinoceros.
150fr, Chimpanzee, vert. 200fr, Hippopotamus. 300fr, Buffon's kob, vert.

1978   **Perf. 14½**
453 A135 35fr multicolored   1.25 .45
454 A135 60fr multicolored   1.75 .55
455 A135 85fr multicolored   4.25 .85
456 A135 150fr multicolored   6.00 1.25
457 A135 200fr multicolored   8.00 1.75
458 A135 300fr multicolored 15.00 2.50
     Nos. 453-458 (6)   36.25 7.35
Issue dates: 35fr, Aug. 11; others, July 11.

Emblem, Young
People, Gun and
Fist — A136

1978, July 28   **Perf. 12½**
459 A136 35fr multicolored   .80 .30
11th World Youth Festival, Havana, 7/28-8/5.

Pyramids and Camels — A137

Seven Wonders of the Ancient World: 50fr,
Hanging Gardens of Babylon. 60fr, Statue of
Zeus, Olympia. 95fr, Colossus of Rhodes.
125fr, Mausoleum of Halicarnassus. 150fr,
Temple of Artemis, Ephesus. 200fr, Light-
house, Alexandria. 300fr, Map of Eastern
Mediterranean showing locations. 50fr, 60fr,
95fr, 125fr, 200fr, vertical.

1978, Aug. 12   Litho.   **Perf. 14**
460 A137 35fr multicolored   .50 .25
461 A137 50fr multicolored   .60 .25
462 A137 60fr multicolored   .75 .25
463 A137 95fr multicolored   1.00 .30
464 A137 125fr multicolored 1.25 .45
465 A137 150fr multicolored 1.75 .55
466 A137 200fr multicolored 2.25 .75
467 A137 300fr multicolored 3.25 1.00
     Nos. 460-467 (8)   11.35 3.80

Nos. 427-428 Overprinted in Silver

No. 468

No. 469

1978, Sept.   Litho.   **Perf. 14**
468 A128 250fr multicolored   2.25 .90
469 A128 300fr multicolored   2.75 1.25
25th anniversary of coronation of Queen
Elizabeth II. See No. C244.

Kwame Nkrumah and Map of
Africa — A138

1978, Sept. 23 Litho. Perf. 13x12½
470 A138 60fr multicolored   .80 .40
Nkrumah (1909-72), Pres. of Ghana.

Wild Boar Hunt — A139

Local hunting and fishing: 50fr, Fish smoking. 60fr, Hunter with spears and dog, vert.

1978   Litho.   **Perf. 12**
471 A139 35fr multicolored   2.00 .25
472 A139 50fr multicolored   .80 .25
473 A139 60fr multicolored   2.75 .25
     Nos. 471-473 (3)   5.55 .75
Issue dates: 35fr, 60fr, Oct. 5; 50fr, Oct. 10.

View of Kalchreut, by Dürer — A140

Paintings by Dürer: 150fr, Elspeth Tucher,
vert. 250fr, "The Great Piece of Turf," vert.
350fr, Self-portrait, vert.

1978, Nov. 23   Litho.   **Perf. 14**
474 A140 65fr multicolored   .60 .25
475 A140 150fr multicolored 1.40 .35
476 A140 250fr multicolored 2.25 .65
477 A140 350fr multicolored 3.50 .90
     Nos. 474-477 (4)   7.75 2.15
Albrecht Dürer (1471-1528), German painter.

Basketmaker
A141

Productive Labor: 90fr, Woodcarver. 140fr,
Women hoeing field.

1978, Nov. 18   Litho.   **Perf. 12½**
          Size: 25x36mm
478 A141 85fr multicolored   .90 .40
479 A141 90fr multicolored   1.00 .40
          Size: 27x48mm
           Perf. 12
480 A141 140fr multicolored 1.50 .65
     Nos. 478-480 (3)   3.40 1.45

Nos. 441-446 Overprinted in Silver

a

b

c

d

e

f

1978, Nov.   **Perf. 14x13½**
481 A133 (a) 60fr multicolored   .65 .25
482 A133 (b) 75fr multicolored   .75 .35
483 A133 (c) 100fr multicolored 1.05 .45
484 A133 (d) 200fr multicolored 2.10 .65
485 A133 (e) 300fr multicolored 3.00 1.00
     Nos. 481-485 (5)   7.55 2.70

Souvenir Sheet

486 A133 (f) 500fr multicolored 6.00 2.40
Winners, World Soccer Cup Championships
1962-1978.

Heart and Charts
A142

1978, Dec. 16   Engr.   Perf. 13
487 A142 100fr multicolored   1.60 .50
Fight against hypertension.

Party Emblem and Road — A143

1978, Dec. 31   Litho.   Perf. 12½x12
488 A143 60fr multicolored   .65 .25
Congolese Labor Party, 9th anniversary.

Capt. Cook, Polynesians and House — A144

Capt. James Cook (1728-1779): 150fr, Island scene. 250fr, Polynesian longboats. 350fr, Capt. Cook's ships off Hawaii.

1979, Jan. 16   Perf. 14½
489 A144 65fr multicolored   .70 .25
490 A144 150fr multicolored   1.75 .35
491 A144 250fr multicolored   2.75 .60
492 A144 350fr multicolored   3.50 1.00
    Nos. 489-492 (4)   8.70 2.20

Pres. Marien Ngouabi — A145

1979, Mar. 18   Litho.   Perf. 12
493 A145 35fr multicolored   .35 .25
494 A145 60fr multicolored   .50 .25
Assassination of President Ngouabi, 2nd anniv.

"1979," IYC Emblem, Child
A146

A146a

1979, Apr. 30   Litho.   Perf. 12½x13
495 A146 45fr multicolored   .45 .25
496 A146 75fr multicolored   .90 .35
Souvenir Sheet
Perf. 14½
496A A146a 250fr multicolored   2.75 1.00
International Year of the Child.
Issued: 45fr, 75fr, Apr. 30; 250fr, Sept. 5.

Pottery Vases and Solanum — A147

Design: 150fr, Mail runner, Concorde, train, UPU emblem, envelope.

1979, June 8   Litho.   Perf. 13
497 A147 60fr multicolored   1.75 .60
Engr.
498 A147 150fr multicolored   3.50 1.25
Philexafrique II, Libreville, Gabon, June 8-17. Nos. 497, 498 each printed in sheets of 10 with 5 labels showing exhibition emblem.

Rowland Hill, Diesel Locomotive, Germany No. 78 — A148

Designs (Rowland Hill and): 100fr, Old steam locomotive and France No. B10. 200fr, Diesel locomotive and US No. 245. 300fr, Steam locomotive and England-Australia First Aerialpost vignette, 1919. 500fr, Electric train, Concorde and Middle Congo No. 75.

1979, June 30   Perf. 14
499 A148 65fr multicolored   .60 .25
500 A148 100fr multicolored   1.00 .25
501 A148 200fr multicolored   2.25 .50
502 A148 300fr multicolored   3.00 .75
    Nos. 499-502 (4)   6.85 1.75
Souvenir Sheet
503 A148 500fr multicolored   5.75 1.25
Sir Rowland Hill (1795-1879), originator of penny postage.

Salvador Allende, Flags, Demonstrators — A149

1979, July 21   Litho.   Perf. 12½
504 A149 100fr multicolored   1.60 .50
Salvador Allende, president of Chile.

Old Man Telling Stories — A150

1979, July 28
505 A150 45fr multicolored   .80 .25
Story telling as education.

Handball Players
A151

75fr, Players and ball. 250fr, Pres. Ngouabi, cup on map of Africa, player.

1979, July 31   Litho.   Perf. 12½
Size: 40x30mm, 30x40mm
506 A151 45fr multi   .60 .25
507 A151 75fr multi, vert.   1.00 .25
Size: 22x40mm
Perf. 12x12½
508 A151 250fr multicolored   2.75 1.00
Marien Ngouabi Handball Cup.

Map and Flag of Congo — A152

1979, Aug. 15
509 A152 50fr multicolored   .80 .25
16th anniversary of revolution.

Souvenir Sheet

Virgin and Child, by Dürer — A153

1979, Aug. 13   Perf. 13½
510 A153 500fr red brn & lt grn   6.50 2.50
Albrecht Dürer (1471-1528), German engraver and painter.

Bach and Contemporary Instruments — A155

No. 512, Albert Einstein, astronauts on moon.

1979, Sept. 10   Perf. 13½
511 A155 200fr multicolored   2.25 .75
512 A155 200fr multicolored   2.25 .75

Yoro Fishing Port
A156

1979, Sept. 26   Litho.   Perf. 12½
513 A156 45fr shown   .65 .25
514 A156 75fr Port at night   .95 .35

Mukukulu Dam — A157

1979, Oct. 5   Perf. 12½x12
515 A157 20fr multicolored   .60 .25
516 A157 45fr multicolored   1.10 .30

Emblem, Control Tower, Jets
A158

1979, Dec. 12   Litho.   Perf. 12½
517 A158 100fr multicolored   1.60 .50
ASECNA (Air Safety Board), 20th anniv.

Congolese Labor Party, 10th Anniversary
A159

1979, Dec. 31
518 A159 45fr multicolored   .80 .25

Post Office, 15th Anniv. — A160

1980, Mar. 30   Litho.   Perf. 12½
519 A160 45fr multicolored   .60 .25
520 A160 95fr multicolored   1.10 .30

Visit of Pope John Paul II — A161

1980, May 5
521 A161 100fr multicolored   3.50 1.00

Rotary International, 75th
Anniversary — A162

1980, May 10　　Litho.　　Perf. 12½
522 A162 150fr multicolored　　　　1.50 .50

Pointe
Noire
Foundry
A163

1980, June 18　　Litho.　　Perf. 12½
523 A163 30fr shown　　　　　.30 .25
524 A163 35fr Different view　　　.50 .25

Claude Chappe, Tower — A164

1980, June 21　　Litho.　　Perf. 12½
525 A164 200fr multicolored　　　2.50 1.00
　Claude Chappe (1763-1805), French
engineer.

Mossaka Harbor — A165

1980, June 23
532 A165 45fr shown　　　　　.60 .25
533 A165 90fr Different view　　1.10 .25

Papilio Dardanus
(Front and
Back) — A167

　15fr, Kalima aethiops. 20fr, Papilio
demodocus. 60fr, Euphaedra. 90fr,
Hypolimnas misippus.
　300fr, Charaxes smaragdalis.

1980, July 12　　Litho.　　Perf. 12½
534 A167 　5fr shown　　　　　.60 .30
　a.　Perf. 12½x13　　　　　1.60 1.60
535 A167 　15fr multicolored　　1.40 .30
　a.　Perf. 12½x13　　　　　2.00 2.00
536 A167 　20fr multicolored　　1.40 .40
　a.　Perf. 12½x13　　　　　2.40 2.40
537 A167 　60fr multicolored　　3.25 .75
538 A167 　90fr multicolored　　6.50 1.00
　Nos. 534-538 (5)　　　　13.15 2.75
Souvenir Sheet
539 A167 300fr multicolored　　10.00 17.00

July 31st Hospital — A168

1980, July 31
540 A168 45fr multicolored　　　.80 .25

Human Rights
Emblem,
People — A169

　500fr, Man breaking chain.

1980, Aug. 2
541 A169 350fr shown　　　　2.75 1.00
542 A169 500fr multicolored　　4.50 1.50
　Human Rights Convention, 32nd anniv.

Citizens
and
Congolese
Arms
A170

　95fr, Dove on flag, fists, vert. 150fr, Dove
holding Congolese arms.

1980, Aug. 15　　　　　Perf. 12½
543 A170 75fr shown　　　　　.70 .30
544 A170 95fr multicolored　　　.90 .30
545 A170 150fr multicolored　　1.50 .60
　Nos. 543-545 (3)　　　　　3.10 1.20
　August 13-15th Revolution, 17th anniv.

Coffee and Cocoa
Trees on Map of
Congo — A171

　Coffee and Cocoa Day: 95fr, Branches,
map of Congo.

1980, Aug. 18　　　　　Perf. 13½x13
546 A171 45fr multicolored　　　.60 .25
547 A171 95fr multicolored　　1.10 .40

Logging
A172

1980, Aug. 28
548 A172 70fr shown　　　　　.80 .30
549 A172 75fr Wood transport　　.80 .30

Pres. Neto of
Angola, 1st
Death
Anniv. — A173

1980, Sept. 11
550 A173 100fr multicolored　　　.90 .30

Lark — A174

　Designs: Birds.

1980, Sept. 17
551 A174 　45fr multi, horiz.　　.90　.30
552 A174 　75fr multi, horiz.　1.10　.30
553 A174 　90fr multi, horiz.　1.40　.35
554 A174 150fr multicolored　2.25　.50
555 A174 200fr multicolored　3.00 1.00
556 A174 250fr multicolored　3.50 1.25
　a　Souv. sheet of 6, #551-556　22.50 17.50
　Nos. 551-556 (6)　　　　12.15 3.70

World
Tourism
Conference,
Manila, Sept.
27 — A175

1980, Sept. 27　　Litho.　　Perf. 13½x13
557 A175 100fr multicolored　　　.90 .35

First Day of School Term — A176

1980, Oct. 2　　Photo.　　Perf. 13
558 A176 50fr multicolored　　　.70 .25

First House in Brazzaville — A177

　Brazzaville Centenary: 65fr, First native village. 75fr, Old Town Hall, 1912. 150fr, View
from bank of Bacongo, 1912. 200fr, Meeting
of explorer Savorgnan de Brazza and chief
Makoko, 1880.

1980, Oct. 3　　Litho.　　Perf. 12½
559 A177 　45fr multicolored　　.50　.25
560 A177 　65fr multicolored　　.70　.30
561 A177 　75fr multicolored　1.00　.40
562 A177 150fr multicolored　1.75　.65
563 A177 200fr multicolored　2.25 1.00
　Nos. 559-563 (5)　　　　6.20 2.60

Boys on Bank of Congo River — A178

1980, Oct. 30
564 A178 80fr shown　　　　　.85 .25
565 A178 150fr Djoue Bridge　　1.90 .40

Revolutionary Stadium and
Athletes — A179

1980, Nov. 20　　　　Perf. 13x12½
566 A179 60fr multicolored　　　.80 .25

Rebuilt
Railroad
Bridge over
Congo
River
A180

1980, Nov. 29　　　　Perf. 13x13½
567 A180 75fr multicolored　　　.90 .30

Mangoes,
Loudima
Fruit Packing
Station
A181

1980, Dec. 2　　　　　Perf. 13
568 A181 10fr shown　　　　　.25 .25
569 A181 25fr Oranges　　　　.50 .25
570 A181 40fr Citrons　　　　.60 .25
571 A181 85fr Mandarins　　1.10 .30
　Nos. 568-571 (4)　　　　2.45 1.05

African Postal
Union, 5th
Anniversary
A182

1980, Dec. 24　　　　　Perf. 13½
572 A182 100fr multicolored　　　.90 .30

Moungouni
Earth
Satellite
Station
A183

1980, Dec. 30　　　　　Perf. 12½
573 A183 75fr multicolored　　　.80 .25

Hertzian Wave Communication,
Brazzaville — A184

1980, Dec. 30   *Perf. 12½x12*
574 A184 150fr multicolored   1.60 .40

1980 African Handball Champion
Team — A185

100fr, Receiving cup, vert.

Perf. 12½x13, 13x12½
1981, Jan. 26   **Litho.**
575 A185 100fr multicolored   1.25 .35
576 A185 150fr shown   1.50 .60

Pres. Denis Sassou-Nguesso — A186

1981, Feb. 5   **Litho.**   *Perf. 12½*
577 A186 45fr multicolored   .45 .25
578 A186 75fr multicolored   .60 .25
579 A186 100fr multicolored   .90 .25
    Nos. 577-579 (3)   1.95 .75

Luna 17, 1970. — A187

Space Conquest: 150fr, Space shuttle in orbit. 200fr, Shuttle, space station. 300fr, Shuttle, landing field. 500fr, Shuttle lift-off.

1981, May 4   **Litho.**   *Perf. 14x13½*
580 A187 100fr multicolored   1.00 .25
581 A187 150fr multicolored   1.40 .40
582 A187 200fr multicolored   2.00 .55
583 A187 300fr multicolored   2.75 .80
    Nos. 580-583 (4)   7.15 2.00
    Souvenir Sheet
584 A187 500fr multicolored   5.00 1.40
    For overprint see No. 725.

Fight Against
Apartheid — A188

1981, May 5   **Litho.**   *Perf. 12½*
585 A188 100fr deep blue   .90 .25

Twin Palm Tree
of
Louingui — A189

1981, May 22   *Perf. 12x12½*
586 A189 75fr multicolored   1.00 .25

13th World Telecommunications
Day — A190

1981, June 6   *Perf. 12½*
587 A190 120fr multicolored   1.50 .50

Rubber
Extraction — A191

1981, June 27   *Perf. 13*
588 A191 50fr shown   .60 .25
589 A191 70fr Sap draining   .90 .30

Intl. Year of
the
Disabled
A192

1981, June 29   **Engr.**
590 A192 45fr multicolored   .60 .25
    See No. B7.

Bird Trap — A194

Designs: Animal traps. 10fr vert.

1981, July
596 A194 5fr multicolored   .90 .25
597 A194 10fr multicolored   .90 .25
598 A194 15fr multicolored   1.40 .25
599 A194 20fr multicolored   1.40 .25

600 A194 30fr multicolored   2.00 .25
601 A194 35fr multicolored   2.00 .30
    Nos. 596-601 (6)   8.60 1.55

Mausoleum of King Maloango — A195

150fr, Mausoleum, portrait.

1981, July 4   **Litho.**   *Perf. 12½*
602 A195 75fr shown   .70 .25
603 A195 150fr multicolored   1.25 .40

Prince
Charles
and
Lady
Diana,
Coach
A196

Royal wedding: Couple and coaches.

1981, Sept. 1   **Litho.**   *Perf. 14½*
604 A196 100fr multicolored   1.00 .25
605 A196 200fr multicolored   2.00 .55
606 A196 300fr multicolored   3.25 .80
    Nos. 604-606 (3)   6.25 1.60
    Souvenir Sheet
607 A196 400fr multicolored   4.00 1.10

World Food
Day — A197

1981, Oct. 16   **Litho.**   *Perf. 13½x13*
608 A197 150fr multicolored   1.75 .55

12th World
UPU Day
A198

1981, Oct. 24   **Engr.**   *Perf. 13x12½*
609 A198 90fr multicolored   .90 .25

Royal
Guard
A199

1981, Oct. 31   **Litho.**   *Perf. 12½x13*
610 A199 45fr multicolored   .90 .25

Eradication of
Manioc
Beetle — A200

1981, Nov. 18   **Litho.**   *Perf. 12½*
611 A200 75fr multicolored   1.20 .25

Natl. Red
Cross — A201

10fr, Bandaging patient. 35fr, Treating child.
60fr, Drawing well water.

1981, Nov. 18   *Perf. 13*
612 A201 10fr multicolored   .30 .25
613 A201 35fr multicolored   .50 .25
614 A201 60fr multicolored   .80 .25
    Nos. 612-614 (3)   1.60 .75

Giant
Baobab
("Tree of
Savorgnan
de Brazza")
A202

1981, Dec. 19   **Litho.**   *Perf. 13*
615 A202 45fr multicolored   .90 .25
616 A202 75fr multicolored   1.25 .30

Fetish
Figure — A203

Designs: Various carved figures.

1981, Dec. 19   *Perf. 12½*
617 A203 15fr multicolored   .30 .25
   a.   Perf. 12½x13   .30 .25
618 A203 25fr multicolored   .40 .25
   a.   Perf. 12½x13   .40 .25
619 A203 45fr multicolored   .50 .25
620 A203 50fr multicolored   .60 .25
   a.   Perf. 12½x13   .60 .35
621 A203 60fr multicolored   .70 .25
    Nos. 617-621 (5)   2.50 1.25

Caves of
Bangou
A204

1981, Dec. 29   *Perf. 13x13½*
622 A204 20fr multicolored   .45 .25
623 A204 25fr multicolored   .45 .25

King Makoko and His Queen, Ivory
Sculptures by R. Engongodzo — A205

25fr, Woman, facing right, vert. 35fr,
Woman, facing left, vert.

Perf. 13½x13, 13x13½

1982, Feb. 27			Litho.	
624	A205	25fr multicolored	.35	.25
625	A205	35fr multicolored	.45	.25
626	A205	100fr shown	1.00	.30
		Nos. 624-626 (3)	1.80	.80

George Stephenson (1781-1848) and
Inter City 125, Gt. Britain — A206

Locomotives: 150fr, Sinkansen Bullet Train,
Japan. 200fr, Advanced Passenger Train, Gt.
Britain. 300fr, TGV-001, France.

1982, Mar. 2		Litho.	Perf. 12½	
627	A206	100fr multicolored	1.00	.25
628	A206	150fr multicolored	1.60	.40
629	A206	200fr multicolored	2.25	.55
630	A206	300fr multicolored	3.25	.80
		Nos. 627-630 (4)	8.10	2.00

Scouting
Year
A207

100fr, Looking through binoculars. 150fr,
Reading map. 200fr, Helping woman. 300fr,
Crossing rope bridge. 500fr, Hiking, horiz.

1982, Apr. 13		Litho.	Perf. 13	
631	A207	100fr multicolored	1.25	.25
632	A207	150fr multicolored	1.50	.40
633	A207	200fr multicolored	2.25	.55
634	A207	300fr multicolored	3.25	.80
		Nos. 631-634 (4)	8.25	2.00
		Souvenir Sheet		
635	A207	500fr multicolored	5.00	1.75

For overprint see No. 726.

Franklin
Roosevelt
A208

1982, June 12		Litho.	Perf. 13	
636	A208	150fr shown	1.75	.60
637	A208	250fr Washington	2.75	.85
638	A208	350fr Goethe	3.75	1.10
		Nos. 636-638 (3)	8.25	2.55

21st Birthday of Princess Diana,
July 1 — A209

1982, June 12			Perf. 14	
639	A209	200fr Candles	2.00	.55
640	A209	300fr "21"	2.75	.80
		Souvenir Sheet		
641	A209	500fr Diana	5.00	1.40

5-Year
Plan, 1982-
1986
A210

60fr, Road construction. 100fr, Communications, vert. 125fr, Operating room equipment,
vert. 150fr, Hydroelectric power, vert.

Perf. 13x12½, 12½x13

1982, June 19				
642	A210	60fr multicolored	.80	.25
643	A210	100fr multicolored	1.25	.30
644	A210	125fr multicolored	1.60	.35
645	A210	150fr multicolored	1.75	.40
		Nos. 642-645 (4)	5.40	1.30

ITU Plenipotentiary Conference,
Nairobi — A211

1982, June 26			Perf. 13	
646	A211	300fr multicolored	3.00	.90

Nos. 604-607 Overprinted in Blue

1982, July 30			Perf. 14½	
647	A196	100fr multicolored	.90	.30
648	A196	200fr multicolored	1.75	.60
649	A196	300fr multicolored	2.75	1.00
		Nos. 647-649 (3)	5.40	1.90
		Souvenir Sheet		
650	A196	400fr multicolored	3.50	2.50

Birth of Prince William of Wales, June 21.

Nutrition
Campaign
A212

1982, July 24		Litho.	Perf. 12½	
651	A212	100fr multicolored	1.40	.25

WHO African Headquarters,
Brazzaville — A213

1982, July 24		Litho.	Perf. 12½	
652	A213	125fr multicolored	1.60	.45

TB Bacillus Centenary — A214

1982, Aug. 7			Perf. 12½x12	
653	A214	250fr Koch, bacillus	3.25	1.10

Pres. Sassou-Nguesso and 1980
Simba Prize — A215

1982, Oct. 20		Litho.	Perf. 13	
654	A215	100fr multicolored	.90	.30

Turtles — A216

Various turtles and tortoises.

1982, Dec. 1				
655	A216	30fr multicolored	.90	.25
656	A216	45fr multicolored	1.50	.30
657	A216	55fr multicolored	1.60	.40
		Nos. 655-657 (3)	4.00	.95

Boy Gathering
Coconuts — A217

1982, Dec. 11				
658	A217	100fr multicolored	1.40	.30

Nest in Tree
Trunk — A218

75fr, Nests in palm tree. 100fr, Woven nest
on thorn branch.

1982, Dec. 29			Perf. 12½	
659	A218	40fr shown	1.00	.25
660	A218	75fr multicolored	1.60	.25
661	A218	100fr multicolored	2.50	.40
		Nos. 659-661 (3)	5.10	.90

Hertzian Wave Communication
Network — A219

1982, Dec. 30			Perf. 13x12½	
662	A219	45fr multicolored	.45	.25
663	A219	60fr multicolored	.50	.25
664	A219	95fr multicolored	.90	.30
		Nos. 662-664 (3)	1.85	.80

30th Anniv. of
Customs
Cooperation
Council — A220

1983, Jan. 26		Litho.	Perf. 12½x13	
665	A220	100fr Headquarters	.90	.30

Mausoleum of Pres. Marien
Ngouabi — A221

1983, Feb. 8			Perf. 13	
666	A221	60fr multicolored	.50	.25
667	A221	80fr multicolored	.80	.25

Ironsmiths — A222

1983			Perf. 12½	
668	A222	45fr shown	.80	.25
669	A222	150fr Weaver, vert.	1.50	.50

Issue dates: 45fr, Mar. 5; 150fr, Feb. 24.

Carved Chess Pieces, by R. Engongonzo — A223

Various pieces.

1983, Feb. 26   *Perf. 13*
670 A223 40fr multicolored   .40 .25
671 A223 60fr multicolored   1.00 .25
672 A223 95fr multicolored   2.00 .50
    Nos. 670-672 (3)   3.40 1.00

Easter 1983 A224

Raphael drawings: 200fr, Transfiguration study. 300fr, Deposition from Cross, horiz. 400fr, Christ in Glory.

1983, Apr. 20   **Litho.**   *Perf. 13*
673 A224 200fr multicolored   2.00 .50
674 A224 300fr multicolored   3.25 .65
675 A224 400fr multicolored   4.50 .85
    Nos. 673-675 (3)   9.75 2.00

Seashells A225

1983   **Litho.**   *Perf. 15x14*
675A A225 25fr multicolored   150.00 65.00
676 A225 35fr multicolored   1.25 .30
677 A225 65fr multicolored   1.60 .35
    Dated 1982.

A226

Various traditional combs.

1983, May   *Perf. 14*
678 A226 30fr multicolored   .35 .25
679 A226 70fr multicolored   .90 .25
680 A226 85fr multicolored   1.00 .25
    Nos. 678-680 (3)   2.25 .75

A227

Litho. & Engr.
1983, Aug. 10   *Perf. 12½x13*
681 A227 60fr multicolored   .65 .25
682 A227 100fr multicolored   .95 .30
    20th anniv. of revolution.

Centenary of the Arrival of Christian Missionaries — A228

Churches and Clergymen: 150fr, A. Carrie, Church of the Sacred Heart, Loango, vert. 250fr, Msgr. Augouard; St. Louis, Liranga; St. Joseph, Linzolo.

1983, Aug. 23   *Perf. 12½*
683 A228 150fr multicolored   1.60 .40
684 A228 250fr multicolored   2.75 .70

Local Flowers — A229

5fr, Liana thunderaie, vert. 15fr, Bougainvillea. 20fr, Anthurium, vert. 45fr, Allamanda. 75fr, Hibiscus, vert.

1984, Jan. 20   **Litho.**   *Perf. 12½*
685 A229 5fr multicolored   .25 .25
686 A229 15fr multicolored   .35 .25
687 A229 20fr multicolored   .50 .25
688 A229 45fr multicolored   1.00 .25
689 A229 75fr multicolored   1.40 .30
    Nos. 685-689 (5)   3.50 1.30

35th Anniv. of World Peace Council A230

1984, Mar. 31   **Litho.**   *Perf. 13x12½*
690 A230 50fr multicolored   .45 .25
691 A230 100fr multicolored   .90 .30

Anti-Nuclear Arms Campaign A231

1984, May 31   **Litho.**   *Perf. 12x12½*
692 A231 200fr Explosion, victims   1.75 .50

Agriculture Day A232

10fr, Rice. 15fr, Pineapples. 60fr, Manioc, vert. 100fr, Palm tree, map, vert.

    Perf. 13x13½, 13½x13
1984, June 30   **Litho.**
693 A232 10fr multicolored   .25 .25
694 A232 15fr multicolored   .25 .25
695 A232 60fr multicolored   .60 .25
696 A232 100fr multicolored   1.10 .35
    Nos. 693-696 (4)   2.20 1.10

Congress Palace — A233

1984, July 27   *Perf. 13*
697 A233 60fr multicolored   .60 .25
698 A233 100fr multicolored   1.00 .30
    Chinese-Congolese cooperation.

CFCO-Congo Railways, 50th Anniv. — A234

10fr, Loulombo Station. 25fr, Les Bandas Chinese Labor Camp. 125fr, "50". 200fr, Administration building.

1984, July 30   *Perf. 13½*
699 A234 10fr multicolored   .35 .25
700 A234 25fr multicolored   .60 .25
701 A234 125fr multicolored   2.75 .70
702 A234 200fr multicolored   6.25 1.00
    Nos. 699-702 (4)   9.95 2.20

Locomotives — A235

Ships on the Congo River — A236

No. 703, CC 203. No. 704, Tugboat. No. 705, BB 103. No. 706, Pusher tugboat. No. 707, BB-BB 301. No. 708, Dredger. No. 709, BB 420 L'Eclair. No. 710, Cargo ship.

1984, Aug. 24   *Perf. 12½*
703 A235 100fr multi   1.10 .35
704 A236 100fr multi   1.10 .35
705 A235 150fr multi   1.60 .50
706 A236 150fr multi   1.60 .50
707 A235 300fr multi   3.25 1.10
708 A236 300fr multi   3.25 1.10
709 A235 500fr multi   5.25 1.75
710 A236 500fr multi   5.25 1.75
    Nos. 703-710 (8)   22.40 7.40

World Fisheries Year A237

5fr, Basket of fish. 20fr, Net fishermen in boat. 25fr, School of fish. 40fr, Net fisherman. 55fr, Trawler

1984, Oct. 16   *Perf. 13½*
711 A237 5fr multicolored   .50 .25
712 A237 20fr multicolored   .80 .25
713 A237 25fr multicolored   .80 .25
714 A237 40fr multicolored   1.25 .30
715 A237 55fr multicolored   2.25 .35
    Nos. 711-715 (5)   5.60 1.40

Anti-polio Campaign A238

250fr, Disabled men, hand. 300fr, Target, disabled women, horiz.

1984, Oct. 30
716 A238 250fr multicolored   2.75 .90
717 A238 300fr multicolored   3.25 1.00

M'Bamou Palace Hotel, Brazzaville A239

1984, Dec. 15   *Perf. 14½*
718 A239 60fr multicolored   .50 .25
719 A239 100fr multicolored   1.00 .30

Fauna A240

1984, Dec.   *Perf. 15x14½*
720 A240 30fr Pangolin   2.50 .75
721 A240 70fr Bat   5.50 1.50
722 A240 85fr Civet cat   6.75 2.00
    Nos. 720-722 (3)   14.75 4.25

Congo River Logging A241

60fr, Log raft, crew hut. 100fr, Tugboat pushing logs.

1984, Dec.   *Perf. 13½x13*
723 A241 60fr multicolored   .60 .25
724 A241 100fr multicolored   1.25 .35

Nos. 584, 635 Ovptd. in Black or Green
Souvenir Sheets

TSUKUBA EXPO '85

ITALIA '85 emblem, ROME

1985, Mar. 8　　　　　**Perf. 14x13½, 13**
725 A187 500fr multi　　　　　5.75　4.50
726 A207 500fr multi　　　　　5.75　4.50
　　　　See Nos. C336-C337.

Zonocerus Variegatus — A242

1985, Mar. 15　　　　　**Perf. 13**
727 A242 125fr multicolored　　　1.75　.35

Burial of a Teke Chief — A243

1985, Apr. 30　　　　　**Perf. 12½**
728 A243 225fr multicolored　　　2.25　.75

Edible Fruit A244

5fr, Trichoscypha acuminata, vert. 10fr, Aframomum africanum. 125fr, Gambeya lacuurtiana. 150fr, Landolphia jumelei.

Perf. 13½, 13 (#732A), 13½x13¼ (#732B)

1985, June 15
729　A244　5fr multicolored　　　.25　.25
730　A244　10fr multicolored　　　.25　.25
730A A244　90fr like #730　　　1.40　.40
731　A244　125fr multicolored　　1.75　.55
732　A244　150fr multicolored　　1.75　.55
732A A244　205fr like #731　　　—　—
732B A244　300fr Like #732　　　—　—

Sizes: No. 729, 22x36mm, Nos. 731, 732A, 36x22mm.
Nos. 730A, 732A, 732B inscribed "Congo" only.
For overprints, see Nos. 1155, 1170, 1183-1185.
Compare type A244 with type A352.

Lions Club Intl., 30th Anniv. — A245

250fr, Flag, District 403B.

1985, June 25　　　　　**Perf. 12½**
733 A245 250fr multicolored　　　2.75　.70

Russian Soldier, Kremlin, Fall of Berlin A246

1985, July 27　　　　　**Perf. 12**
734 A246 60fr multicolored　　　.80　.25

Defeat of Nazi Germany, end of World War II, 40th anniv.

Lady Olave Baden-Powell, Girl Guides Founder — A247

Anniversaries and events: 150fr, Girl Guides, 75th anniv. 250fr, Jacob Grimm, fabulist; Sleeping Beauty. 350fr, Johann Sebastian Bach, composer; European Music Year, St. Thomas Church organ, Leipzig. 450fr, Queen Mother, 85th birthday, vert. 500fr, Statue of Liberty, cent., vert.

1985, Aug. 26　　　　　**Perf. 13**
735 A247 150fr multicolored　　1.60　.50
736 A247 250fr multicolored　　2.25　.90
737 A247 350fr multicolored　　3.00　1.25
738 A247 450fr multicolored　　3.75　1.60
739 A247 500fr multicolored　　5.00　2.00
　　　Nos. 735-739 (5)　　　15.60　6.25

PHILEXAFRICA '85, Lome, Togo, Nov. 16-24 — A248

No. 741, Airport, postal van.

1985, Oct. 10　　　　　**Perf. 13x12½**
740 A248 250fr shown　　　　2.75　1.00
741 A248 250fr multicolored　　2.75　1.00
　a.　Pair, #740-741 + label　　6.50　6.50

Mushrooms — A249

100fr, Coprinus, vert. 150fr, Cortinarius. 200fr, Armillariella mellea. 300fr, Dictyophora. 400fr, Crucibulum vulgare.

1985, Dec. 14　**Litho.**　**Perf. 13**
742 A249 100fr multicolored　　1.50　.35
743 A249 150fr multicolored　　2.25　.50
744 A249 200fr multicolored　　3.00　.85
745 A249 300fr multicolored　　4.00　1.25
746 A249 400fr multicolored　　6.00　1.50
　　　Nos. 742-746 (5)　　　16.75　4.45

Arbor Day — A250

60fr, Planting sapling. 200fr, Map, lifecycle diagram.

1986, Mar. 6　　　　　**Perf. 13½**
747 A250 60fr multicolored　　　.45　.25
748 A250 200fr multicolored　　1.90　.90

Children's Hoop Races — A251

1986, Apr. 30　　　　　**Perf. 12½**
749 A251 5fr Two boys　　　　.30　.25
750 A251 10fr One boy　　　　.30　.25
751 A251 60fr Three boys, horiz.　.80　.25
　a.　Souvenir sheet of 3, #749-751　2.00　1.75
　　　Nos. 749-751 (3)　　　1.40　.75

Intl. Environment Day — A252

60fr, Garbage disposal. 125fr, Dumping garbage.

1986, June 5　**Litho.**　**Perf. 13½**
752 A252 60fr multicolored　　　.60　.25
753 A252 125fr multicolored　　1.20　.45

A253

Traditional Modes of Transporting Goods: 5fr, Basket on head, child in sling carrier. 10fr, Child in carrier on hip, large basket strapped to forehead. 60fr, Man carrying load on shoulder.

1986, July 15　**Litho.**　**Perf. 13x12½**
754 A253 5fr multicolored　　　.30　.25
755 A253 10fr multicolored　　　.30　.25
756 A253 60fr multicolored　　　.80　.40
　　　Nos. 754-756 (3)　　　1.40　.90

Mission of the Sisters of St. Joseph of Cluny, Cent. A254

1986, Aug. 19　**Litho.**　**Perf. 12½x13**
757 A254 230fr multicolored　　2.75　1.25

A255

1986, Aug. 30　**Litho.**　**Perf. 13½**
758 A255 40fr multicolored　　　.45　.25
759 A255 60fr multicolored　　　.55　.25
760 A255 100fr multicolored　　1.00　.30
　　　Nos. 758-760 (3)　　　2.00　.85

UNESCO intl. communications development program.

Intl. Peace Year — A256

1986, Sept. 15　**Litho.**　**Perf. 13½**
761 A256 100fr multicolored　　　.90　.30

World Food Day A257

75fr, Food staples. 120fr, Mother feeding child.

1986, Oct. 16
762 A257 75fr multicolored　　　.80　.25
763 A257 120fr multicolored　　1.25　.40

UN Child Survival Campaign A258

Mothers, children and pinwheels in various designs.

1986, Oct. 27
764 A258 15fr multi, vert.　　　.25　.25
765 A258 30fr multicolored　　　.25　.25
766 A258 70fr multi, vert.　　　.70　.30
　　　Nos. 764-766 (3)　　　1.20　.80

A258a

1986, Dec. 5　**Litho.**　**Perf. 12x12½**
766A A258a 100fr multicolored　　1.50　.35

27th Soviet Communist Party congress.

A259

1987, Feb. 10   Litho.   Perf. 13½
767 A259 30fr multicolored   .25   .25
768 A259 45fr multicolored   .45   .25
769 A259 75fr multicolored   .70   .25
770 A259 120fr multicolored   1.10   .35
      Nos. 767-770 (4)   2.50 1.10

Election of President Sassou-Nguesso, head of the Organization of African States.

Traditional Wedding
A260

1987, Feb. 18   Litho.   Perf. 12½x13
771 A260 5fr multicolored   .25   .25
772 A260 15fr multicolored   .25   .25
773 A260 20fr multicolored   .25   .25
      Nos. 771-773 (3)   .75   .75

The Blue Lake — A261

1987, July 16   Perf. 12½
774 A261 5fr multicolored   .25   .25
775 A261 15fr multicolored   .25   .25
776 A261 75fr multicolored   1.00   .30
777 A261 120fr multicolored   1.25   .40
      Nos. 774-777 (4)   2.75 1.20

Pres. Marien Ngouabi — A262

1987, July 16   Perf. 13
778 A262 75fr multicolored   .75   .30
779 A262 120fr multicolored   1.25   .40

Tenth death anniv.

Congress of African Scientists — A263

1987, Sept. 10   Perf. 13x12½
780 A263 15fr multicolored   .25   .25
781 A263 90fr multicolored   .70   .30
782 A263 230fr multicolored   2.00   .80
      Nos. 780-782 (3)   2.95 1.35

4th African Games, Nairobi — A264

1987, Oct. 30   Perf. 12½
783 A264 75fr multicolored   .75   .40
784 A264 120fr multicolored   1.25   .60

Raoul Follereau (1903-1977), Philanthropist — A265

1987, Oct. 20   Perf. 13½
785 A265 120fr multicolored   1.50   .60

Cure leprosy.

FAO, 40th Anniv. — A266

1987, Nov. 17   Perf. 12½
786 A266 300fr multicolored   2.75 1.10

Anti-Apartheid Campaign
A267

Nelson Mandela
A268

Perf. 13½x15, 14½x15
1987, Sept. 21   Litho.
787 A267 60fr multicolored   .60   .25
788 A268 240fr multicolored   2.40   .75

Natl. UNICEF Vaccination Campaign
A269

30fr, Inoculating adults, horiz. 500fr, Inoculating children, horiz.

Perf. 13½x14½, 14½x13½
1987, Sept. 28
789 A269 30fr multicolored   .25   .25
790 A269 45fr shown   .50   .25
791 A269 500fr multicolored   5.25 2.00
      Nos. 789-791 (3)   6.00 2.50

No. 791 is airmail.

Africa Fund — A270

1987, Sept. 28   Perf. 13½x15
792 A270 25fr multicolored   .30   .25
793 A270 50fr multicolored   .65   .25
794 A270 70fr multicolored   .80   .25
      Nos. 792-794 (3)   1.75   .75

Self-sufficiency in Food Production by the Year 2000 — A271

1987, Nov. 20   Litho.   Perf. 13½
795 A271 20fr multicolored   .25   .25
796 A271 55fr multicolored   .60   .25
797 A271 100fr multicolored   1.10   .35
      Nos. 795-797 (3)   1.95   .85

Simon Kimbangu (b. 1887), Founder of the Church of Christ on Earth — A272

75fr, Kimbangu, vert. 120fr, Kimbangu, parrot, vert. 240fr, Kimbanguist Church, Nkamba.

1987, Nov. 28   Perf. 12½
798 A272 75fr multicolored   .70   .30
799 A272 120fr multicolored   1.10   .40
800 A272 240fr multicolored   2.75 1.00
a.   Souvenir sheet of 3, #798-
      800   5.75 5.00
      Nos. 798-800 (3)   4.55 1.70

October Revolution, Russia, 70th Anniv. — A273

Lenin inspecting revolutionary troops, Red Square, from an unspecified painting.

1988, Feb. 19   Litho.   Perf. 12½x12
801 A273 75fr multicolored   2.10   .60
802 A273 120fr multicolored   3.00 1.00

African Writers Opposing Apartheid — A274

1988, Apr. 6   Litho.   Perf. 13½
803 A274 15fr multicolored   .25   .25
804 A274 60fr multicolored   .50   .25
805 A274 75fr multicolored   .80   .30
      Nos. 803-805 (3)   1.55   .80

For overprint see No. 1157.

Intl. Fund for Agricultural Development (IFAD), 10th Anniv. — A275

1988, Apr. 30
806 A275 240fr multicolored   2.25   .85

Invention of the Telegraph by Samuel Morse, 150th Anniv. (in 1987) — A276

1988, Apr. 28
807 A276 90fr Morse, vert.   .90   .30
808 A276 120fr shown   1.10   .40

A277

5fr, Eucalyptus trees, Brazzaville. 10fr, Stop cutting down trees.

1988, Sept. 20   Litho.   Perf. 13½
809 A277 5fr multicolored   .30   .25
810 A277 10fr multicolored   .50   .25

Fight against desertification.

A278

Campaigns: No. 812, Return to the Land Campaign (farming). 120fr, Self-sufficiency in food production.

1988, Aug. 12   Litho.   Perf. 13½
811 A278 75fr shown   .75   .30
812 A278 75fr multicolored   .75   .30
813 A278 120fr multicolored   .90   .40
      Nos. 811-813 (3)   2.40 1.00

Congo Revolution, 25th anniv.

Yoro Fishing Village
A279

1988, Sept. 1
814 A279 35fr shown   .45   .25
815 A279 40fr Liberty Place   .45   .25

Intl. Day for the Fight Against AIDS
A280

75fr, Emblem. 180fr, Modified UN emblem, campaign emblem.

1988, Dec. 1   Litho.   Perf. 13½
816 A280 60fr shown   .45   .25
817 A280 75fr multicolored   .70   .25
818 A280 180fr multicolored   1.75   .60
      Nos. 816-818 (3)   2.90 1.10

Natl. Committee for the Fight Against AIDS and Evangelical Anglican Church of Congo anti-AIDS campaign.

February 5 Movement, 10th Anniv. A281

75fr, Rally. 120fr, Pres. Sassou-Nguesso, natl. achievements.

1989, Apr. 21 Litho. Perf. 13½
819 A281 75fr multicolored .75 .30
820 A281 120fr multicolored 1.00 .40

UN Declaration of Human Rights, 40th Anniv. (in 1988) A282

1989, May 19 Perf. 13
821 A282 120fr multicolored .90 .40
822 A282 350fr multicolored 2.75 1.20

Marien Nguabi, Founder of Congo Labor Party A282a

1989, July 31 Litho. Perf. 12½x13
822A A282a 240fr red & yellow 2.25 .75

Red Cross and Red Crescent Societies, 125th Anniv. A283

120fr, Dunant, emblem, Congo Red Cross.

1989, Sept. 19 Litho. Perf. 13
823 A283 75fr shown 1.20 .40
824 A283 120fr multicolored 1.40 .65
No. 824 is airmail.

Organization of African Unity, 25th Anniv. — A284

1989, Oct. 19 Litho. Perf. 12½
825 A284 120fr multicolored 1.10 .40

African Development Bank, 25th Anniv. — A285

1989, Dec. 22 Litho. Perf. 12½x13
826 A285 75fr multicolored .80 .35
827 A285 120fr multicolored 1.10 .40

WHO, 40th Anniv. (in 1988) A286

75fr, Blood donation, vert.

1989, Dec. 28 Litho. Perf. 12½
828 A286 60fr shown .75 .35
829 A286 75fr multicolored .90 .50
See Nos. 846-847 for overprints.

Congo Labor Party (PCT), 20th Anniv. — A287

1989, Dec. 22 Litho. Perf. 13x12½
830 A287 75fr multicolored .75 .35
831 A287 120fr multicolored 1.10 .40

Cacti A288

35fr, Opuntia phaeacantha discata. 40fr, Opuntia ficus indica. 60fr, Opuntia erinacea. 75fr, Opuntia rufida. 120fr, Opuntia leptocaulis.
220fr, Opuntia compresa.

Perf. 12½x13, 13x12½
1989, Nov. 22
832 A288 35fr multicolored .35 .25
833 A288 40fr multicolored .50 .25
834 A288 60fr multicolored .90 .25
835 A288 75fr multicolored 1.25 .30
836 A288 120fr multicolored 1.75 .45
Nos. 832-836 (5) 4.75 1.50

Souvenir Sheet
Perf. 12½
837 A288 220fr multicolored 5.00 2.10
Nos. 832-833, 835 and 837 vert. No. 837 contains one 32x40mm stamp.

1992 Winter Olympics, Albertville A289

1989, Dec. 22 Perf. 12½
838 A289 75fr Ice dancing .60 .25
839 A289 80fr Nordic skiing .60 .30
840 A289 100fr Speed skating .90 .35

841 A289 120fr Luge 1.10 .45
842 A289 200fr Alpine skiing 1.75 .70
843 A289 240fr Ice hockey 2.25 .85
844 A289 400fr Ski jumping 3.25 1.40
Nos. 838-844 (7) 10.45 4.30

Souvenir Sheet
Perf. 13
845 A289 500fr Bobsled 4.50 2.40
No. 845 contains one 32x40mm stamp.

Nos. 828-829 Ovptd. in 3 or 5 Lines

1989, Dec. 28 Perf. 12½
846 A286 60fr multicolored .75 .45
847 A286 75fr multicolored .90 .60
Health care for everyone.

Intl. Literacy Year — A290

1990, June 26 Litho. Perf. 13½
848 A290 75fr bl, blk & yel .80 .35

Birds A291

Designs: 25fr, Tourterelle des bois. 50fr, Fauvette pitchou, vert. 70fr, Faucon crecerelle, vert. 150fr, Perroquet gris, vert.

1990, July 10
849 A291 25fr multicolored .35 .25
850 A291 50fr multicolored .70 .30
851 A291 70fr multicolored 1.10 .55
852 A291 150fr multicolored 2.10 1.25
Nos. 849-852 (4) 4.25 2.35

Dance Masks — A292

1990, July 24 Perf. 13
853 A292 120fr Mondo 1.10 .40
854 A292 360fr Bapunu 3.50 1.25
855 A292 400fr Kwele 4.00 1.50
Nos. 853-855 (3) 8.60 3.15
For overprints see Nos. 1172, 1173.

Flowering Plants — A293

30fr, Tournesol (sunflower). 45fr, Cassia alata, horiz. 75fr, Oeillette (opium poppy). 90fr, Acalypha sanderil.

1990, Sept. 15 Litho. Perf. 12½
856 A293 30fr multicolored .25 .25
857 A293 45fr multicolored .45 .25
858 A293 75fr multicolored .70 .25
859 A293 90fr multicolored 1.00 .35
Nos. 856-859 (4) 2.40 1.10

1992 Summer Olympics, Barcelona — A294

100fr, Street scene, vert. 200fr, Sailing, diff. 240fr, Marketplace. 350fr, Harbor. 500fr, Monument, vert.
750fr, Cathedral, vert.

1990, June 28 Litho. Perf. 13½
860 A294 100fr multicolored .70 .30
861 A294 150fr shown .95 .35
862 A294 200fr multicolored 1.20 .40
863 A294 240fr multicolored 1.50 .55
864 A294 350fr multicolored 2.40 .75
865 A294 500fr multicolored 3.25 .90
Nos. 860-865 (6) 10.00 3.25

Souvenir Sheet
866 A294 750fr multicolored 5.50 3.50
Nos. 864-865 airmail. Nos. 860-865 exist in miniature sheets of 1.

Royal Necklaces A295

1990, Aug. 18 Litho. Perf. 13½
867 A295 75fr shown .75 .35
868 A295 100fr Necklace, diff. 1.00 .60

Boy Scouts Observing Nature A296

Scout: 35fr, Photographing butterfly, Euphaedra eusimoides. 40fr, Picking mushrooms, Armillaria mellea. 75fr, Drawing butterfly, Palla decius. 80fr, Using magnifying glass, Kallima ansorgei. 500fr, Using microscope, Cortinarius speciocissimus. 600fr, Feeding butterfly, Graphium illyris. No. 874B, Photographing butterfly, Berberia plistonax, horiz. 750fr, Photographing mushrooms, Volvariella bombycina. No. 875A, Examining mushrooms, Coprinus domesticus.

1991, June 8 Litho. Perf. 13½
869 A296 35fr multicolored .50 .25
870 A296 40fr multicolored .60 .25
871 A296 75fr multicolored .80 .25
872 A296 80fr multicolored 1.00 .25
873 A296 500fr multicolored 4.50 1.25

874	A296	600fr multicolored		4.50	1.25
a.		Min. sheet of 4, #869, 871-872, 874		8.50	3.75
		Nos. 869-874 (6)		11.90	3.50

Litho. & Embossed

874B	A296	1500fr gold & multi		*32.50*	—

Souvenir Sheets

Litho.

875	A296	750fr multicolored		5.25	2.25

Litho. & Embossed

875A	A296	1500fr gold & multi		14.00	—

Nos. 869-874 exist in souvenir sheets of 1.
Nos. 873-875 are airmail.

Medicinal Plants — A297

Designs: 15fr, Ocimum viride. 20fr, Kalanchoe pinnata, vert. 30fr, Euphorbia hirta. 60fr, Catharanthus roseus, vert. 75fr, Bidens pilosa, vert. 100fr, Brillantaisia patula, vert. 120fr, Cassia occidentalis, vert.

1991, Jan. 30   Litho.   Perf. 11½

876	A297	15fr multicolored		.30	.25
877	A297	20fr multicolored		.30	.25
878	A297	30fr multicolored		.30	.25
879	A297	60fr multicolored		.60	.25
880	A297	75fr multicolored		.80	.35
881	A297	100fr multicolored		1.20	.55
882	A297	120fr multicolored		1.25	.75
		Nos. 876-882 (7)		4.75	2.65

Mushrooms A298

30fr, Amanita rubescens. 45fr, Catathelasma imperiale. 75fr, Amanita caesarea. 90fr, Boletus regius. 120fr, Pluteus cervinus. 150fr, Boletus chrysenteron. 200fr, Agaricus arvensis.

350fr, Boletus versipellis, horiz.

1991, Mar. 25   Litho.   Perf. 13

883	A298	30fr multi		.35	.25
883A	A298	45fr multi		.50	.25
883B	A298	75fr multi		.90	.25
883C	A298	90fr multi		1.10	.25
883D	A298	120fr multi		1.35	.40
883E	A298	150fr multi		1.75	.60
883F	A298	200fr multi		2.50	.75
		Nos. 883-883F (7)		8.45	2.75

Souvenir Sheet

Perf. 12½

883G	A298	350fr multi		8.00	3.00

No. 883G contains one 40x32mm stamp.

Trains — A298a

Designs: 60fr, Dr-16, Finland. 75fr, TGV, France. 120fr, S350, Italy. 200fr, DE24000, Turkey. 250fr, DE1024, Germany.

1991, Apr. 10   Litho.   Perf. 12½x12¼

883H	A298a	60fr multi		.65	.25
883I	A298a	75fr multi		.70	.30
883J	A298a	120fr multi		1.25	.45
883K	A298a	200fr multi		2.25	.75
883L	A298a	250fr multi		3.25	1.00

Dated 1990.

African Tourism Year — A299

1991, Apr. 15   Litho.   Perf. 13½

884	A299	75fr shown		.80	.35
885	A299	120fr Zebra, map		1.20	.60

Allegory of New Republic — A300

1991, May 13   Litho.   Perf. 13

888	A300	15fr blue		.25	.25
889	A300	30fr brt grn		.25	.25
890	A300	60fr org yel		.40	.25
891	A300	75fr brt pink		.55	.30
892	A300	120fr dk brown		1.00	.45
		Nos. 888-892 (5)		2.45	1.50

Trans-Siberian Railroad, Cent. — A301

1991, June 6   Litho.   Perf. 13

899	A301	120fr Map		1.50	.50
900	A301	240fr Map, train		3.00	1.20

Telecom 91 — A302

1991, June 29   Litho.   Perf. 13

901	A302	75fr multicolored		.75	.30
902	A302	120fr multi, vert.		1.25	.60

6th World Forum and Exposition on Telecommunications, Geneva, Switzerland.

Insects — A303

1991, July 2   Perf. 12½

903	A303	75fr Peanut beetle		1.00	.25
904	A303	120fr Centaur, horiz.		1.40	.45
905	A303	200fr Coffee beetle		2.25	.75
906	A303	300fr Goliath beetle		3.50	1.50
		Nos. 903-906 (4)		8.15	2.95

Water conservation A304

1991, July 16   Litho.   Perf. 12½

907	A304	75fr multicolored		.80	.35

Amnesty Intl., 30th Anniv. A305

Designs: 40fr, Candle, sun, vert. 75fr, "30," broken chains, vert.

1991, Aug. 13   Perf. 13½

908	A305	40fr multicolored		.35	.25
909	A305	75fr multicolored		.60	.25
910	A305	80fr multicolored		.70	.35
		Nos. 908-910 (3)		1.65	.85

Congo Postage Stamps, Cent. — A306

75fr, Similar to French Congo #1. 120fr, Similar to French Congo #35. 240fr, Similar to Congo Republic #89. 500fr, Similar to French Congo #1, 35 and Congo Republic #89.

Litho. & Engr.

1991, Aug.   Perf. 13x13½

911	A306	75fr beige & dk grn		.80	.30
912	A306	120fr beige, dk grn & brn		1.10	.45
913	A306	240fr multicolored		2.25	1.10
914	A306	500fr multicolored		4.50	2.00
a.		Strip of 4, #911-914		10.00	9.00

Ducks A307

75fr, Anas acuta. 120fr, Somateria mollissima, vert. 200fr, Anas clypeata, vert. 240fr, Anas platyrhynchos.

1991, Aug. 8   Litho.   Perf. 12½

915	A307	75fr multicolored		1.25	.30
916	A307	120fr multicolored		1.50	.45
917	A307	200fr multicolored		2.00	.75
918	A307	240fr multicolored		3.50	1.00
		Nos. 915-918 (4)		8.25	2.50

Automobiles and Space — A308

Designs: 35fr, Ferrari 512S by Pininfarina. 40fr, Vincenzo Lancia, Lancia Stratos by Bertone. 75fr, Maybach Zeppelin type 12, Wilhelm Maybach. 80fr, Mars Observer, 1992. 500fr, Magellan probe surveying Venus. 600fr, Magnification of Sun, Ulysses probe. 750fr, Crew of Apollo 11.

1991, Aug. 23   Litho.   Perf. 13½

919	A308	35fr multicolored		.30	.25
920	A308	40fr multicolored		.30	.25
921	A308	75fr multicolored		.60	.30
922	A308	80fr multicolored		.65	.30
923	A308	500fr multicolored		4.25	2.25
924	A308	600fr multicolored		5.00	2.50
		Nos. 919-924 (6)		11.10	5.85

Souvenir Sheet

925	A308	750fr multicolored		6.50	3.50

Nos. 923-925 are airmail. No. 925 contains one 60x42mm stamp. Nos. 919-921 exist in souvenir sheets of 1.

Butterflies A309

75fr, Petit bleu. 120fr, Charaxe. 240fr, Papillon feuille, vert. 300fr, Papillon de l'oranger, vert.

1991, Aug. 31   Perf. 11½

926	A309	75fr multi		1.20	.30
927	A309	120fr multi		1.50	.50
928	A309	240fr multi		2.10	.80
929	A309	300fr multi		3.75	1.00
		Nos. 926-929 (4)		8.55	2.60

For overprints see Nos. 1156, 1165.

Celebrities and Organizations — A310

Designs: 100fr, Bo Jackson, baseball and football player. 150fr, Nick Faldo, golfer. 200fr, Rickey Henderson, Barry Bonds, baseball players. 240fr, Garry Kasparov, World Chess Champion. 300fr, Starving child, Lions and Rotary Clubs emblems. 350fr, Wolfgang Amadeus Mozart. 400fr, De Gaulle, Churchill. 500fr, Jean-Henri Dunant, founder of Red Cross. 750fr, De Gaulle, vert.

1991, Sept. 2   Perf. 13½

930	A310	100fr multicolored		1.00	.40
931	A310	150fr multicolored		1.40	.60
932	A310	200fr multicolored		2.00	.80
933	A310	240fr multicolored		2.75	.95
934	A310	300fr multicolored		3.00	1.25
935	A310	350fr multicolored		3.75	1.40
936	A310	400fr multicolored		4.50	1.60
937	A310	500fr multicolored		5.00	2.00
		Nos. 930-937 (8)		23.40	9.00

Souvenir Sheet

938	A310	750fr multicolored		8.00	3.50

Nos. 936-938 are airmail. No. 938 contains one 35x50mm stamp.
For overprint, see No. 1199.

Gen. Charles de Gaulle in Africa — A311

120fr, De Gaulle, Free French flag, vert. 240fr, De Gaulle, Appeal of Brazzaville, 1940.

1991, Sept. 2   Perf. 13½x13, 13x13½

939	A311	75fr multicolored		.90	.40
940	A311	120fr multicolored		1.25	.60
941	A311	240fr multicolored		2.40	1.20
		Nos. 939-941 (3)		4.55	2.20

A312

Paintings — A313

1991, Oct. 12   *Perf. 11½*
942 A312 75fr multicolored   .75   .35
943 A313 120fr multicolored   1.10   .45

Discovery of America, 500th Anniv. (in 1992) — A314

20fr, Portrait of Christopher Columbus by Sebastian Del Pombo. 35fr, Portrait of Columbus. 40fr, Portrait of Columbus facing right. 55fr, Santa Maria. 75fr, Nina. 150fr, Pinta. 200fr, Arms & signature of Columbus.

1991, May 30   *Perf. 13*
944 A314 20fr multicolored   .40   .25
945 A314 35fr multicolored   .40   .25
946 A314 40fr multicolored   .50   .35
947 A314 55fr multicolored   .65   .35
948 A314 75fr multicolored   .95   .35
949 A314 150fr multicolored   1.75   .85
950 A314 200fr multicolored   2.25   1.00
    Nos. 944-950 (7)   6.90 3.40

Primates A315

30fr, Cercopithecus diana. 45fr, Pan troglodytes. 60fr, Theropithecus gelada. 75fr, Papio hamadryas. 90fr, Macaca nemestrina. 120fr, Gorilla gorilla. 240fr, Mandrillus sphinx. 250fr, Gorilla gorilla.

1991, Dec. 13   **Litho.**   *Perf. 13*
951 A315 30fr multicolored   .35   .25
952 A315 45fr multicolored   .45   .25
953 A315 60fr multicolored   .85   .25
954 A315 75fr multicolored   1.00   .35
955 A315 90fr multicolored   1.20   .50
956 A315 120fr multicolored   1.60   .50
957 A315 240fr multicolored   3.50   .75
    Nos. 951-957 (7)   8.95 2.85

Souvenir Sheet
958 A315 250fr multicolored   4.25 1.50

Nos. 953-958 are vert.

Anniversaries and Events A316

Designs: 50fr, Launching of Sputnik II with dog, Laika, 1957. 75fr, Mahatma Gandhi and Martin Luther King, Jr. 1964. 120fr, Launching of Meteosat and ERS-1 over Europe and Africa. 240fr, Maybach Zeppelin automobile and Ferdinand von Zeppelin, 75th death anniversary. 300fr, Konrad Adenauer, 25th death anniversary and opening of the Brandenburg Gate, 1989. 500fr, Pope John Paul II's visit to Africa. 600fr, Elvis Presley, American entertainer.

1992, Feb. 4   **Litho.**   *Perf. 13½*
959 A316 50fr multicolored   .75   .25
960 A316 75fr multicolored   .75   .25
961 A316 120fr multicolored   1.25   .45
962 A316 240fr multicolored   2.75   .85
963 A316 300fr multicolored   2.50   .80
964 A316 500fr multicolored   5.25 1.40
   a.   Souvenir sheet of 3, #960, 963-964   11.50 5.75
    Nos. 959-964 (6)   13.25 4.00

Souvenir Sheet
965 A316 600fr multicolored   6.00 2.40

Nos. 959-964 exist in souvenir sheets of 1. Nos. 962, 964-965 are airmail. For Overprint, see No. 1166.

Explorers A317

Genoa '92: 75fr, Juan de la Cosa, nautical chart. 95fr, Martin Alonso Pinzon, astrolabe. 120fr, Alonso de Ojeda, hour glass. 200fr, Vicente Yanez Pinzon, sun dial. 250fr, Bartholomew Columbus, quadrant.

400fr, Columbus, flag, horiz.

1992, Oct. 21   **Litho.**   *Perf. 13*
966 A317 75fr multicolored   1.00   .30
967 A317 95fr multicolored   1.20   .30
968 A317 120fr multicolored   1.90   .30
969 A317 200fr multicolored   2.75   .40
970 A317 250fr multicolored   3.75   .50
    Nos. 966-970 (5)   10.60 1.80

Souvenir Sheet
971 A317 400fr multi   14.00 14.00

Birds — A318

Designs: 60fr, Sagittarius serpentarius. 75fr, Ephippiorhynchus senegalensis. 120fr, Bugeranus carunculatus. 200fr, Ardea melanocephala. 250fr, Phoenicopterus ruber roseus.

400fr, Balearica regulorum.

1992, Oct. 21
972 A318 60fr multicolored   .70   .25
973 A318 75fr multicolored   .80   .25
974 A318 120fr multicolored   1.10   .30
975 A318 200fr multicolored   2.00   .40
976 A318 250fr multicolored   2.75   .50
    Nos. 972-976 (5)   7.35 1.70

Souvenir Sheet
977 A318 400fr multicolored   4.00 1.00

For overprint, see No. 1191.

Wild Cats — A319

45fr, Panthera leo. 60fr, Panthera tigris. 75fr, Lynx lynx. 95fr, Caracal caracal. 250fr, Leopardus pardalis.

500fr, Acinonyx jubatus.

1992, Nov. 21   **Litho.**   *Perf. 13*
978 A319 45fr multicolored   .50   .50
979 A319 60fr multicolored   .60   .60
980 A319 75fr multicolored   .70   .70

981 A319 95fr multicolored   .80   .80
982 A319 250fr multicolored   2.25 2.25
    Nos. 978-982 (5)   4.85 4.85

Souvenir Sheet
983 A319 400fr multicolored   4.50 1.75

No. 983 contains one 32x40mm stamp.

1992 Winter Olympics, Albertville — A320

Gold medalists: 150fr, N. Mishkutyonok, A. Dmitriev, pairs figure skating, Unified team. 200fr, I. Appelt, H. Winkler, G. Haldacher, T. Schroll, 4-man bobsled, Austria. 500fr, Gunda Niemann, speed skating, Germany. 600fr, Bjorn Daehlie, cross-country skiing, Norway. 750fr, Alberto Tomba, giant slalom, Italy.

1992, Dec. 21   **Litho.**   *Perf. 13½*
984 A320 150fr multicolored   1.25   .40
985 A320 200fr multicolored   1.75   .50
986 A320 500fr multicolored   4.00 1.10
987 A320 600fr multicolored   6.00 1.00
    Nos. 984-987 (4)   13.00 3.00

Souvenir Sheet
988 A320 750fr multicolored   7.00 2.00

Nos. 986-988 are airmail. No. 988 contains one 35x50mm stamp. Name on No. 987 spelled incorrectly.

1992 Summer Olympics, Barcelona A321

Barcelona landmarks, Olympic event: 75fr, Steeple of La Sagrada Familia, baseball. 100fr, The Muse, Palace of Music, running. 150fr, Cupola interior, long jump. 200fr, St. Paul Hospital, pole vault. 400fr, Sculpture, by Miro, shot put. 500fr, Galley, Maritime Museum, table tennis. 750fr, La Sagrada Familia, tennis.

1992, Dec. 21
989 A321 75fr multicolored   .80   .25
990 A321 100fr multicolored   1.00   .30
991 A321 150fr multicolored   1.25   .40
992 A321 200fr multicolored   2.00   .65
993 A321 400fr multicolored   3.50   .65
994 A321 500fr multicolored   4.50 1.00
    Nos. 989-994 (6)   13.05 3.25

Souvenir Sheet
995 A321 750fr multicolored   7.00 1.50

Nos. 993-995 are airmail.

Christmas A321a

Paintings: 95fr, The Madonna of the Grand Duke, by Raphael. 120fr, Virgin and Child, by Francesco Mazzo. 200fr, The Madonna with a Book, by Botticelli. 250fr, The Madonna Carondelet, by Fra Bartolommeo. 400fr, Madonna and Child, by Raphael.

1992, Dec. 20   **Litho.**   *Perf. 12½*
995A A321a 95fr multicolored   1.25   .30
995B A321a 120fr multicolored   —   —
995C A321a 200fr multicolored   2.75   .75
995D A321a 250fr multicolored   3.25 1.25
    Nos. 995A-995D (4)   7.25 2.30

Souvenir Sheet
995E A321a 400fr multicolored   4.50 1.90

Nos. 995A-995E were not available until late 1993. For overprint, see No. 1192.

Birds of Prey — A322

1993, Jan. 15   **Litho.**   *Perf. 12½x13*
996 A322 45fr Charognard   .65   .25
997 A322 75fr Vulture   2.00   .30
998 A322 120fr Eagle   2.50   .65
    Nos. 996-998 (3)   5.15 1.20

A323

Traditional ceramics: 45fr, Liloko. 75fr, Mbeya. 120fr, Jug with ladles, Mbeya.

1993, Dec. 21   **Litho.**   *Perf. 13½*
999 A323 45fr multicolored   .60   .30
1000 A323 75fr multicolored   1.20   .50
1001 A323 120fr multicolored   1.75   .85
    Nos. 999-1001 (3)   3.55 1.65

1994 World Cup Soccer Championships, United States — A324

Design: 75fr, Player stretching to kick ball. 95fr, Goalie diving to stop ball. 120fr, Player stretching to kick ball. 200fr, Player kicking. 250fr, Goalie catching ball. 400fr, Players competing for ball.

1993, Jan. 15   **Litho.**   *Perf. 12¾*
1002 A324 75fr multi   1.40   .80
1003 A324 95fr multi   1.45 1.10
1004 A324 120fr multi   2.40 1.40
1005 A324 200fr multi   3.50 2.10
1006 A324 250fr multi   4.00 2.75
    Nos. 1002-1006 (5)   12.75 8.15

Souvenir Sheet
Perf. 12½
1007 A324 400fr multi   6.00 4.00

No. 1007 contains one 40x32mm stamp.

Wild Animals A325

Designs: 60fr, Damaliscus lunatus. 75fr, Gazella granti. 95fr, Equus quagga. 120fr, Panthera pardus. 200fr, Syncerus caffer. 250fr, Hippopotamus ambibius. 300fr, Necrosyrtes monachu. 350fr, Panthera leo.

1993, Feb. 20   Litho.   *Perf. 13*
1008	A325	60fr multicolored	.75	.25
1009	A325	75fr multicolored	1.25	.25
1010	A325	95fr multicolored	1.40	.30
1011	A325	120fr multicolored	1.90	.30
1012	A325	200fr multicolored	3.25	.40
1013	A325	240fr multicolored	4.00	.40
1014	A325	300fr multicolored	4.75	.40
1015	A325	250fr multicolored	5.50	.75
a.		Sheet of 8, #1008-1015	20.00	20.00
		Nos. 1008-1015 (8)	22.80	3.05

No. 1015a is a continuous design.

Wild Flowers — A326

Designs: 75fr, Hibiscus schizopetalus. 95fr, Pentas lanceolata. 120fr, Ricinus communis. 200fr, Delonix regia. 250fr, Stapelia gigantea.

1993, May 20   Litho.   *Perf. 12½*
1016	A326	75fr multicolored	.85	.30
1017	A326	95fr multicolored	1.10	.40
1018	A326	120fr multicolored	2.25	.50
1019	A326	200fr multicolored	3.75	1.00
1020	A326	250fr multicolored	4.50	1.60
		Nos. 1016-1020 (5)	12.45	3.80

Deep Sea Submersibles A327

75fr, Transport PC-1202. 95fr, J. Sea Link 1. 120fr, Nemo. 200fr, Robot. 250fr, Alvin. 400fr, Star III.

1993, June 25
1021	A327	75fr multi	1.25	.50
1022	A327	95fr multi	1.60	.75
1023	A327	120fr multi	2.00	1.00
1024	A327	200fr multi	3.00	1.50
1025	A327	250fr multi	3.75	2.00
		Nos. 1021-1025 (5)	11.60	5.75

Souvenir Sheet
1026	A327	400fr multi	8.00	4.00

No. 1026 contains one 32x40mm stamp.

1996 Summer Olympic Games, Atlanta A329

Designs: 50fr, Equestrian. 75fr, Cycling. 120fr, Sailing. 240fr, shown. 300fr, Hurdles. 500fr, Women's basketball. 750fr, Running.

1993, Apr. 26   Litho.   *Perf. 13½*
1030-1035	A329	Set of 6	15.00	4.00
1035a		Sheet of 6, #1030-1035	17.50	6.00

Souvenir Sheet
1036	A329	750fr multicolored	6.50	1.50

Nos. 1030-1036 exist imperf. Nos. 1030-1035 exist in souvenir sheets of 1.

Brasiliana '93 — A330

Birds: 75fr, Vidua whydah. 95fr, Vidua regia. 120fr, Steganura paradisea. 200fr, Vidua macroura. 250fr, Anthreptes platura. 400fr, Coliuspasser macrourus, horiz.

1993, July 15   Litho.   *Perf. 12x12½*
1037-1041	A330	Set of 5	11.00 11.00

Souvenir Sheet
1042	A330	400fr multicolored	11.00 11.00

Prehistoric Animals — A331

75fr, Ichthyostega. 95fr, Archaeopteryx. 120fr, Brachiosaurus. 200fr, Tyrannosaurus. 250fr, Pteranodon, vert. 400fr, Brontosaurus.

1993, Aug. 20   Litho.   *Perf. 13*
1043	A331	75fr multicolored	1.00	1.00
1044	A331	95fr multicolored	1.25	1.25
1045	A331	120fr multicolored	1.60	1.60
1046	A331	200fr multicolored	2.50	2.50
1047	A331	250fr multicolored	3.50	3.50
		Nos. 1043-1047 (5)	9.85	9.85

Souvenir Sheet
1048	A331	400fr multicolored	6.50	6.50

No. 1048 contains one 32x40mm stamp.

Powered Flight, 90th Anniv. — A332

Designs: 75fr, Wilbur Wright, Model B airplane, vert. 95fr, Orville Wright and Model B biplane, vert. 120fr, First flight by Orville Wright. 200fr, Flight at Kitty Hawk. 250fr, Wright Brothers and airplane.

   Perf. 12¼x12½, 12½x12¼
1993, Dec. 17   Litho.
1049	A332	75fr multi	.65	.65
1050	A332	95fr multi	.85	.85
1051	A332	120fr multi	.95	.95
1052	A332	200fr multi	1.75	1.75
1053	A332	250fr multi	2.25	2.25
		Nos. 1049-1053 (5)	6.45	6.45

Evolution of the Elephant A333

25fr, Palaeomastodon. 45fr, Mammut. 50fr, Amebelodon. 75fr, Platybelodon. 120fr, Mammuthus.

1994, June 20   Litho.   *Perf. 12½*
1054	A333	25fr multicolored	.75	.30
1055	A333	45fr multicolored	1.25	.50
1056	A333	50fr multicolored	1.45	.50
1057	A333	75fr multicolored	2.25	.80
1058	A333	120fr multicolored	3.50	1.40
		Nos. 1054-1058 (5)	9.20	3.50

Protection of Nature — A335

Designs: 50fr, Choeropsis liberiensis. 90fr, Hyemoschus aquaticus. 205fr, Taurotragus euryceros, vert. 300fr, Redunca redunca, vert.

1994, Aug. 27   Litho.   *Perf. 12½*
1063	A335	50fr multicolored	.50	.35
1064	A335	90fr multicolored	.80	.35
1065	A335	205fr multicolored	1.90	1.10
1066	A335	300fr multicolored	2.75	1.60
		Nos. 1063-1066 (4)	5.95	3.40

For overprint see No. 1167.

Seaplanes — A336

Designs: 30fr, Cant Z-505, Italy. 45fr, Martin Mariner PBM-3, US. No. 1069, E-59, Russia. No. 1070, Short Sunderland, Great Britain. No. 1071, Martin Mars XPB2M-1, US. 400fr, Boeing 314, US.

1994, Sept. 2   Litho.   *Perf. 12½*
1067	A336	30fr multicolored	.40	.25
1068	A336	45fr multicolored	.50	.25
1069	A336	90fr multicolored	1.00	.40
1070	A336	90fr multicolored	1.00	.40
1071	A336	90fr multicolored	1.00	.40
		Nos. 1067-1071 (5)	3.90	1.70

Souvenir Sheet
1071A	A336	400fr multicolored	5.00	2.50

No. 1071A contains one 40x32mm stamp.

Intl. Year of the Family — A337

205fr, African map, child. 300fr, Family, native huts.

1995, Jan. 28   Litho.   *Perf. 12½*
1072	A337	90fr shown	.75	.40
1073	A337	205fr multicolored	1.60	1.00
1074	A337	300fr multicolored	2.50	1.50
		Nos. 1072-1074 (3)	4.85	2.90

For overprint see No. 1168.

Insects — A338

1994, July 24   Litho.   *Perf. 12½*
1075	A338	90fr Tarantula	1.90	.40
1076	A338	205fr Spider	4.50	1.10
1077	A338	240fr Ladybug	5.00	1.25
		Nos. 1075-1077 (3)	11.40	2.75

Souvenir Sheet
1078	A338	400fr Bee	4.75	2.00

Costumes — A338a

1995   Litho.   *Perf. 12¾x12½*
1078A	A338a	90fr M'Bochi	.90	.60
1078B	A338a	205fr Téké	1.50	.90
1078C	A338a	500fr Loango	3.50	1.50
		Nos. 1078A-1078C (3)	5.90	3.00

Rotary Intl., 90th Anniv. A339

Designs: 90fr, Polio victim. No. 1080, Playing ball with children. No. 1081, Children with food. 300fr, Delivering polio vaccine. 1500fr, Paul Harris, Rotary emblem.

1996, Feb. 6   Litho.   *Perf. 14*
1079	A339	90fr multicolored	.60	.25
1080	A339	205fr multicolored	1.25	.50
1081	A339	205fr multicolored	1.25	.50
1082	A339	300fr multicolored	1.60	.60
		Nos. 1079-1082 (4)	4.70	1.85

Souvenir Sheet
1083	A339	1500fr multicolored	5.00	3.25

For overprint, see Mo. 1201.

18th World Scout Jamboree, The Netherlands — A340

Designs: No. 1084, Handshake. No. 1085, Scout helping another with arm sling. 205fr, Saving life in water. 300fr, Lord Baden-Powell. 1000fr, Scout salute.

1996, Feb. 6   Litho.   *Perf. 14*
1084	A340	90fr multicolored	.60	.25
1085	A340	90fr multicolored	.60	.25
1086	A340	205fr multicolored	1.25	.40
1087	A340	300fr multicolored	1.75	.50
		Nos. 1084-1087 (4)	4.20	1.40

Souvenir Sheet
1088	A340	1000fr multicolored	4.50	2.10

1998 World Cup Soccer Tournament A340a

Various players. Denominations: 90fr, 150fr, 205fr, 300fr, 400fr, 500fr. No. 1088G, 100fr, Player's legs.

1996   Litho.   *Perf. 12¾*
1088A-1088F	A340a	Set of 6	5.00 5.00

Souvenir Sheet
   Perf. 13¼x13
1088G	A340a	1000fr multi	3.00 3.00

No. 1088G contains one 40x31mm stamp.

Antique Automobiles — A341

90fr, 1936 Armstrong Siddeley Twelve. 150fr, 1935 Aston Martin Mark II. 205fr, 1938 Morris 8. 300fr, 1955-62 MG Series MGA. 400fr, 1932 SS1. 500fr, 1938 Alvis 25 SB.

1996, Apr. 30	Litho.		Perf. 12½x12	
1089	A341	90fr multicolored	.40	.25
1090	A341	150fr multicolored	.65	.40
1091	A341	205fr multicolored	.85	.50
1092	A341	300fr multicolored	1.25	.75
1093	A341	400fr multicolored	1.75	1.00
1094	A341	500fr multicolored	2.10	1.25
	Nos. 1089-1094 (6)		7.00	4.15

Domestic Cats — A342

90fr, Persian. 150fr, Siamese. 205fr, Norwegian forest. 300fr, Exotic shorthair. 400fr, Maine coon. 500fr, Red abyssinian. 1000fr, Turkish Angora.

1996, Mar. 10			Perf. 13x12½	
1095	A342	90fr multicolored	.40	.25
1096	A342	150fr multicolored	.65	.40
1097	A342	205fr multicolored	.90	.50
1098	A342	300fr multicolored	1.35	.75
1099	A342	400fr multicolored	1.75	1.00
1100	A342	500fr multicolored	2.25	1.25
	Nos. 1095-1100 (6)		7.30	4.15

Souvenir Sheet

1101	A342	1000fr multicolored	3.00	2.50

No. 1101 contains one 32x40mm stamp.

1996 Summer Olympic Games, Atlanta A343

90fr, Fencing, vert. 150fr, Archery, vert. 205fr, Basketball, vert. 300fr, Baseball, vert. 400fr, Volleyball. 500fr, 2-man kayak. 1000fr, Judo, vert.

1996		Perf. 13x12½, 12½x13		
1102	A343	90fr multi	.50	.25
1103	A343	150fr multi	.80	.40
1104	A343	205fr multi	1.10	.55
1105	A343	300fr multi	1.60	.80
1106	A343	400fr multi	2.25	1.10
1107	A343	500fr multi	2.50	1.25
	Nos. 1102-1107 (6)		8.75	4.35

Souvenir Sheet

1108	A343	1000fr multi	5.25	2.50

No. 1108 contains one 32x40mm stamp.

Flowers — A344

Designs: 90fr, Nerium oleander. 150fr, Eucaliptus globulus. 205fr, Centaurea cyanus. 300fr, Coffea arabica. 400fr, Hibiscus sabdariffa. 500fr, Cassia angustifolia.

1996, May 10		Perf. 12½		
1109	A344	90fr multicolored	.40	.25
1110	A344	150fr multicolored	.65	.40
1111	A344	205fr multicolored	.90	.55
1112	A344	300fr multicolored	1.25	.80
1113	A344	400fr multicolored	1.75	1.10
1114	A344	500fr multicolored	2.00	1.25
	Nos. 1109-1114 (6)		6.95	4.35

Mother Carrying Baby — A345

1996		Litho.	Perf. 13	
1115	A345	40fr blue	4.00	2.00
1116	A345	50fr violet brown	5.00	2.50
1117	A345	90fr orange	9.00	4.50
1118	A345	100fr green blue	10.00	5.00
1119	A345	115fr gray	11.00	5.50
1120	A345	205fr brown	20.00	10.00
	Nos. 1115-1120 (6)		59.00	29.50

It has been stated that this set was not issued.
See Nos. 1145-1150.
For overprints, see Nos. 1159, 1185A.

A346

1996, Aug. 31		Litho.	Perf. 13½	
1121	A346	90fr orange & multi	.50	.30
1122	A346	205fr green & multi	1.25	.75

Investiture of Pres. Pascal Lissouba, 4th anniv.

Owls — A347

1996, Mar. 29		Perf. 14½		
1123	A347	90fr Tyto alba	.70	.25
1124	A347	205fr Bubo poensis	1.50	.50
1125	A347	300fr Scotopelia peli	2.40	.90
1126	A347	500fr Asio capensis	3.50	1.50
	Nos. 1123-1126 (4)		8.10	3.15

Military Aircraft — A348

Designs: 90fr, Vought-Sikorsky Vindicator SB2U-1. 150fr, Grumman Wildcat F4F-3. 205fr, North American SNJ-2. 300fr, Brewster Bermuda. 400fr, Blackburn Skua 1. 500fr, Mitsubishi Type 98-1.
1000fr, P-40 Warhawk (Flying Tigers).

1996, June 24	Litho.		Perf. 12½x12	
1127	A348	90fr multicolored	.35	.25
1128	A348	150fr multicolored	.60	.30
1129	A348	205fr multicolored	.80	.50
1130	A348	300fr multicolored	1.20	.75
1131	A348	400fr multicolored	1.60	1.00
1132	A348	500fr multicolored	2.00	1.25
	Nos. 1127-1132 (6)		6.55	4.05

Souvenir Sheet
Perf. 13

1133	A348	1000fr multicolored	4.00	2.50

No. 1133 contains one 32x40mm stamp.

Aquatic Flowers — A348a

Design: 90fr, Cyrtosperma senegalense.

1996, July 3	Litho.	Perf. 14x14¼		
1133A	A348a	90fr multi	.70	.50

An additional stamp was issued in this set. The editors would like to examine it.

Crocodilians A348b

205fr, Nile crocodile. 255fr, Gavial. 300fr, Caiman.

1996, July 16	Litho.		Perf. 14	
1133C	A348b	205fr multi	1.25	.90
1133D	A348b	255fr multi	1.60	1.00
1133E	A348b	300fr multi	1.90	1.00
	Nos. 1133C-1133E (3)		4.75	2.90

United Nations, 50th Anniv. — A348c

1996		Litho.	Perf. 12½	
1133F	A348c	300fr multi	—	—

Arctocebus Calabarensis A349

a, 90fr, With young. b, 205fr, Touching leaf. c, 300fr, Climbing to left. d, 255fr, Walking on branch.

1998, June 3	Litho.	Perf. 14		
1134	A349	Strip of 4, #a.-d.	5.00	5.00

No. 1134 issued in sheets of 12 stamps. World Wildlife Fund.

Endangered Species — A350

No. 1135, Kabus defassa, vert. No. 1136, Caphalophus sylvicutor. 205fr, Potamochoerus porcus. 300fr, Tragelaplus spekei.

1996		Litho.	Perf. 14	
1135	A350	90fr multi	.55	.25
1136	A350	90fr multi, vert.	.55	.25
1137	A350	205fr multi, vert.	1.10	.45
1138	A350	300fr multi	1.60	.65
	Nos. 1135-1138 (4)		3.80	1.60

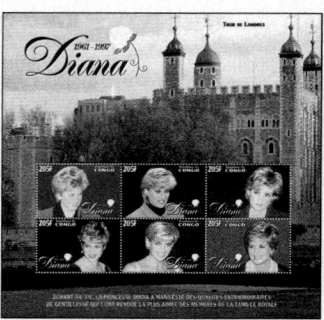

Diana, Princess of Wales (1961-97) — A351

Nos. 1139-1141: Various portraits with white rose.
Diana, rose, famous people in sheet margin: 750fr, Henry Kissinger, vert. No. 1143, Mother Teresa, vert. No. 1144, Hillary Clinton, vert.

1998, Aug. 31	Litho.	Perf. 14		
Sheets of 6				
1139	A351	205fr #a.-f.	5.50	2.00
1140	A351	255fr #a.-f., vert.	7.00	2.75
1141	A351	300fr #a.-f., vert.	8.00	3.00
Souvenir Sheets				
1142	A351	750fr multicolored	3.00	3.00
1143-1144	A351	1000fr each	5.00	5.00

Stamps of Type A345 inscribed only "Congo" ovptd.

1998		Litho.	Perf. 13	
1145	A345	40fr blue		8.00
1146	A345	50fr violet brown		8.00
1147	A345	90fr orange		8.00
1148	A345	100fr green blue	—	8.00
1149	A345	115fr gray		8.00
1150	A345	205fr brown		8.00
	Nos. 1145-1150 (6)			48.00

A352

Designs: 90fr, Aframomum africanum. 205fr, Gambeya lacuurtiana (37x24mm). 300fr, Landolphia jumeli.

Perf. 13½x13¼, 13 (#1152)

1998			Litho.	
1151	A352	90fr multi		10.00
1152	A352	205fr multi		10.00
1153	A352	300fr multi		10.00
	Nos. 1151-1153 (3)			30.00

No. 1153 has denomination in yellow.

No. 732A Overprinted

No. 929 Overprinted

1998		Litho.	Perf. 13	
1155	A244	205fr multi	—	—
1156	A309	300fr multi	—	—

An additional stamp was issued in this set. The editors would like to examine them.

Nos. 732B, 804, 854, 855, 929, 963, 1066, 1074, 1118, 1133D Ovptd. Like

and

A355

Perfs. as before, Perf. 14 (#1164), Perf. 13½x13¼ (#1170)
Methods as before, Litho. (#1164, 1170)

1998

1157	A274	60fr multi (#804)	
1159	A345	100fr green blue (#1118)	
1164	A348b	255fr multi (#1133D)	
1165	A309	300fr multi (#929)	
1166	A316	300fr multi (#963)	—
1167	A335	300fr multi (#1066)	—
a.		Overprint reading horizontally	
1168	A337	300fr multi (#1074)	
1169	A355	300fr multi	
1170	A244	300fr multi (#732B)	—
a.		Overprint reading horizontally	
1172	A292	360fr multi (#854)	—
1173	A292	400fr multi (#855)	

Numbers have been reserved for additional overprinted stamps. Overprint reads horizontally on Nos. 1157, 1159, 1166, 1169, 1172 and 1173, vertically reading down on Nos. 1164, 1167, 1168 and 1170, and vertically reading up on No. 1165. No. 1170 has white denomination.

The editors would like to see examples of No. 1169 without the overprint.

1998 World Cup Soccer Championships, France — A358

Designs: 90fr, Netherlands, 4th place. 205fr, Croatia, bronze medal. 300fr, Brazil, silver medal. 500fr, France, gold medal.

1998, Nov. 16   Litho.   Perf. 13x13¼
1175-1178 A358 Set of 4   12.00 5.00

Masks — A359

90fr, Kwele wood mask. 150fr, Kwele wood mask. No. 1181, Teke/Tsangui wood mask. No. 1182, Kuyu wood mask.

Perf. 13¼x13½

1998, Nov. 20			**Litho.**	
1179	A359	90fr multicolored	.90	.40
1180	A359	150fr multicolored	1.20	.70
1181	A359	205fr multicolored	1.20	1.00
1182	A359	205fr multicolored	1.20	1.00
		Nos. 1179-1182 (4)	4.50	3.10

No. 732B Overprinted

Type I — Unserifed Upper and Lower Case Letters, 7x3mm

Type II — Serifed Upper and Lower Case Letters, 12x3mm

Type III — Upper Case Letters, 9x2mm

Methods and Perfs as Before
1999 ?

1183	A244	300fr multi (I)	— —
1184	A244	300fr multi (II)	— —
1185	A244	300fr multi (III)	— —

No. 1119 Overprinted Like No. 1149 But With Wider "G" In Overprint Method and Perf. As Before
1999 ?
1185A A345 115fr gray   —

Nos. 934, 975, 995B, 1082, C342-C343 Overprinted Like No. 1157 and

A359a

Methods as Before, Litho. (#1204)
1999 ?   Perf. as Before, 12½ (#1204)

1187	AP120	200fr multi (#C342)	— —
1188	AP120	200fr multi (#C343)	— —
a.		Horiz. pair, #1187-1188, + central label	
1191	A318	200fr multi (#975)	— —
1192	A321a	200fr multi (#995B)	— —
1199	A310	300fr multi (#934)	— —
1201	A339	300fr multi (#1082)	— —
1204	A359a	300fr multi	— —

The editors would like to see examples of No. 1204 without the overprint. Overprint reads horizontally on No. 1204, horizontally and inverted on Nos. 1187-1188, vertically reading down on Nos. 1191 and 1199, and vertically reading up on Nos. 1192 and 1201.

PhilexFrance 99 — A360

Design: 205fr, Raffia cloth with tassels. 300fr, Woven raffia cloth.

1999, July 2   Litho.   Perf. 13x13¼
1211 A360 205fr multi   2.00 1.00
1212 A360 300fr multi   2.50 1.50

First French Postage Stamp, 150th Anniv. — A361

Litho. With Hologram
1999   Perf. 13x13¼
1213 A361 300fr multi   2.50 2.50

Central African Economic and Monetary Community Week — A363

Designs: 90fr, Map and flags. 205fr, Map and circle of flags.

1999   Litho.   Perf. 14½
1227 A363 90fr multi   — 5.00
1228 A363 205fr multi   —

Additional stamps may exist in this set. The editors would like to examine any examples.

Third Pan-African Music Festival — A364

Designs: 120fr, Emblem. 270fr, Map of Africa with drummers.

2001, Aug. 4   Litho.   Perf. 13½x13
1229-1230 A364 Set of 2   3.25 3.25

Independence, 40th Anniv. — A365

Designs: 90fr, Dove, vine, map, hands, people. 205fr, Tools, clasped and opened hands, map.

2001, Nov. 15   Litho.   Perf. 13¼x13
1231-1232 A365 Set of 2   30.00 —

Birds — A366

Designs: 90fr, Egretta garzetta. No. 1234, Ardea cenerea. No. 1234A, Egretta garzetta (white bird). .205fr, Ardea purpurea. No. 1235, Ciconia nigra. No. 1235A, Ciconia ciconia

2001   Perf. 13¼

1233	A366	90fr multi	— —
1234	A366	120fr multi	— —
1234A	A366	120fr multi	— —
1234B	A366	205fr multi	— —
1235	A366	270fr multi	— —
1235A	A366	270fr multi	— —

Type of A345 Inscribed "REPUBLIQUE DU CONGO" Overprinted "LEGAL" Like No. 1145
2001 ?   Litho.   Perf. 13
1236 A345 90fr blue   — —

Fruit — A367

Designs: 40fr, Mbila esobe. 50fr, Ikami. 70fr, Tsia, vert. 80fr, Bamou. 120fr, Malombo. 270fr, Ntondolo, vert.

2002, June 25   Litho.   Perf. 13½
1237-1242 A367 Set of 6

Birds — A368

Designs: 40fr, Calao (hornbill). 80fr, Cigogne blanche (white stork). 120fr, Grue cendrée (gray crane). 270fr, Marabout.

2002, July 23   Perf. 13½x13
1243-1246 A368 Set of 4   — —

Elephants A369

Designs; 120fr, Mammoth. 270fr, Elephant on savannah, horiz. 350fr, Elephant, horiz. 500fr, Forest elephant near lake.

Perf. 13¼x13, 13x13¼
2003, June 20   Set of 4   — —
1247-1250 A369

Flowers — A370

Designs: 120fr, Muflier (antirrhinum). 270fr, Pivoine (peony). 400fr, Petunia. 600fr, Mauve (mallow), horiz.

2003, July 6   Set of 4   6.50 6.50
1251-1254 A370

Moringa Olifera — A371

Highlighted portion: 30fr, Bark. 70fr, Root. 90fr, Leaves. 115fr, Seeds and open pod. 120fr, Flowers. 360fr, Pod.

2005, Feb. 3   Litho.   Perf. 13¼x13
1255-1260 A371   Set of 6   5.00 5.00
      Dated 2004.

Fruits — A372

Designs: 120fr, Custard apple. 200fr, Tangerine. 270fr, Guava. 360fr, Grapefruit.

2005, July 13   Litho.   Perf. 13½
1261-1264 A372   Set of 4   7.25 7.25

Albert Einstein (1879-1955), Physicist — A373

2005, Aug. 17   Litho.   Perf. 13¼x13
1265 A373 400fr multi   4.25 4.25

A374

2005, Oct. 3   Perf. 13¼x13
1266 A374 120fr multi   1.10 1.10
**   Perf. 13½x13¼**
1267 A375 360fr multi   3.25 3.25

Brazzaville, 125th Anniv. — A375

Pope Benedict XVI — A376

Pope Benedict XVI: 360fr, Waving. 500fr, Holding crucifix.

2005, Nov. 28   Perf. 13¼x13½
1268-1269 A376   Set of 2   4.25 3.75

Coat of Arms — A377

Colors: 30fr, Dark brown. 40fr, Red. 50fr, Bister brown. 60fr, Dark green.

2006, Jan. 4   Litho.   Perf. 13½
1270-1273 A377   Set of 4   — —

Denis Sassou-Nguesso, President of African Union — A378

2006, Mar. 14   Litho.   Perf. 13x13¼
1274 A378 500fr multi   2.40 2.40

Léopold Sédar Senghor (1906-2001), First President of Senegal — A379

2006, May 15
1275 A379 360fr multi   1.75 1.75

Animals — A380

Designs: 40fr, Crocodile. 50fr, Pangolin, horiz. 60fr, Lizard, horiz. 120fr, Cat, horiz.

2006   Litho.   Perf. 13¼x13, 13x13¼
1276-1279 A380   Set of 4   5.00 2.50

World Religion Day — A381

2007   Perf. 13½x13
1280 A381 120fr multi   1.20 1.00

Opening of Pierre Savorgnan de Brazza Memorial, Brazzaville A382

Memorial and: 120fr, Statue. 500fr, Photo of Savorgnan de Brazza. 1000fr, Statue, diff.

2008   Perf. 13¼
1281-1283 A382   Set of 3   7.00 7.00

Protestant Evangelization in Congo, Cent. — A382a

2009   Litho.   Perf. 13x13¼
1283A A382a 360fr multi

A383

Pan-African Postal Union, 30th Anniv. — A384

2010   Litho.   Perf. 13½x13¼
1284 A383 120fr multi   1.00 1.00
1285 A384 360fr multi   3.00 3.00

President and Flag of Republic of Congo A386

President and Flag of People's Republic of Congo A387

President Denis Sassou-Nguesso and Flag of Republic of Congo — A388

President: No. 1287, Abbé Fulbert Youlou (1917-72). No. 1288, Alphonse Massamba-Débat (1921-77). No. 1289, Joachim Yhombi-Opango. No. 1290, Denis Sassou-Nguesso. No. 1291, Pascal Lissouba.

2010   Litho.   Perf. 13½
1287 A386 270fr multi   — —
1288 A386 270fr multi   — —
1289 A387 270fr multi   — —
1290 A387 270fr multi   — —
1291 A386 270fr multi   — —
1292 A388 270fr multi   — —

Republic of Congo, 50th anniv. Additional stamps may exist in this set. The editors would like to examine any examples.

15th Francophonie Summit, Dakar — A389

Designs: 120fr, Building, Pres. Denis Sassou-Nguesso. 360fr, Conferees on sofa.

2014   Litho.   Perf. 13¼x13
1293 A389 120fr multi   — —
1294 A389 360fr multi   — —

11th African Games, Brazzaville — A390

2015   Litho.   Perf. 13¼x13
1295 A390 200fr multi   — —

SEMI-POSTAL STAMPS

Anti-Malaria Issue
Common Design Type

1962, Apr. 7   Engr.   Perf. 12½x12
B3   CD108 25fr + 5fr bister   1.40 1.00

Freedom from Hunger Issue
Common Design Type

1963, Mar. 21   Unwmk.   Perf. 13
B4   CD112 25fr + 5fr vio bl, bl
           grn & brn   1.40 1.00

Boy Suffering from Sleeping Sickness SP1

Fight Against Communicable Diseases; 40fr+5fr, Examination, treatment, vert.

1981, June 6   Litho.   Perf. 13
B5   SP1 40fr + 5fr multi   .60 .25
B6   SP1 65fr + 10fr multi   1.00 .30

IYD Type of 1981

1981, June 29   Perf. 12½
B7   A192 75fr + 5fr multi   .90 .35

AIR POST STAMPS

Olympic Games Issue
French Equatorial Africa No. C37
Surcharged in Red Like Chad No. C1

1960   Unwmk.   Engr.   Perf. 13
C1   AP8 250fr on 500fr grnsh
          blk, blk & sl   8.00 8.00
   17th Olympic Games, Rome, 8/25-9/11.

Helicrysum Mechowiam — AP1

Flowers: 200fr, Cogniauxia podolaena. 500fr, Thesium tencio.

1961, Sept. 28   Engr.   Perf. 13
C2 AP1 100fr grn, lil & yel   2.90 1.60
C3 AP1 200fr bl grn, yel & brn   4.75 2.40
C4 AP1 500fr brn red, yel & sl grn   14.50 6.00
Nos. C2-C4 (3)   22.15 10.00

Air Afrique Issue
Common Design Type

1961, Nov. 25   Unwmk.   Perf. 13
C5 CD107 50fr lil rose, sl grn & grn   1.75 .90

Loading Timber, Pointe-Noire Harbor — AP2

1962, June 8   Photo.   Perf. 12½x12
C6 AP2 50fr multicolored   1.50 .90
Opening of the Intl. Fair and Exhib., Pointe-Noire, June 8-11.

Abidjan Games — AP3

1962, July 21   Perf. 12x12½
C7 AP3 100fr Basketball   2.50 1.25

Costus Spectabilis AP4

Design: 250fr, Mountain acanthus.

1963   Unwmk.   Perf. 13
C8 AP4 100fr multicolored   4.00 1.75
C9 AP4 250fr multicolored   8.00 3.25
Issued: 100fr, 8/9; 250fr, 11/4.

Brazzaville City Hall and Pres. Fulbert Youlou — AP4a

1963, Aug.   Photo.   Perf. 13x12
C10 AP4a 100fr multicolored   150.00 125.00

African Postal Union Issue
Common Design Type

1963, Sept. 8   Perf. 12½
C13 CD114 85fr pur, ocher & red 1.40 .75

Air Afrique Issue, 1963
Common Design Type
Perf. 13x12

1963, Nov. 19   Unwmk.   Photo.
C14 CD115 50fr multicolored   1.60 .60

Liberty Place, Brazzaville — AP5

1963, Nov. 28
C15 AP5 25fr multicolored   1.00 .40
See No. 118.

Europafrica Issue
Common Design Type

1963, Nov. 30   Perf. 12x13
C16 CD116 50fr gray, yel & dk brn   1.60 1.00

Timber Industry — AP6

1964, May 12   Engr.   Perf. 13
C17 AP6 100fr grn, brn red & blk 2.50 1.10

Chiefs of State Issue

Map and Presidents of Chad, Congo, Gabon and CAR AP6a

1964, June 23   Photo.   Perf. 12½
C18 AP6a 100fr multicolored   1.60 1.00
See note after Central African Republic No. C19.

Europafrica Issue

Sunburst, Wheat, Cogwheel and Globe — AP7

1964, July 20   Perf. 12x13
C19 AP7 50fr yel, Prus bl & mar 1.60 .75
See note after Cameroun No. 402.

Hammer Thrower, Olympic Flame and Stadium — AP8

50fr, 100fr, vert.

1964, July 30   Engr.   Perf. 13
C20 AP8 25fr shown   .40 .30
C21 AP8 50fr Weight lifter   .75 .60
C22 AP8 100fr Volleyball   1.60 1.10
C23 AP8 200fr High jump   3.00 2.25
a.   Min. sheet of 4, #C20-C23   7.25 7.25
Nos. C20-C23 (4)   5.75 4.25
18th Olympic Games, Tokyo, 10/10-25/64.

Communications Symbols — AP8a

1964, Nov. 2   Litho.   Perf. 12½x13
C24 AP8a 25fr dl rose & dk brn   .80 .45
See note after Chad No. C19.

Town Hall, Brazzaville — AP9

1965, Jan. 30   Photo.   Perf. 12½
C25 AP9 100fr multicolored   1.10 .75

Coupling Hooks — AP10

1965, Feb. 27   Photo.   Perf. 13x12
C26 AP10 50fr multicolored   1.40 .75
Economic Europe-Africa Association.

Breguet Dial Telegraph, ITU Emblem and Telstar — AP11

1965, May 17   Engr.   Perf. 13
C27 AP11 100fr dk bl, ocher & brn   2.25 .75
Cent. of the ITU.

Pope John XXIII (1881-1963), St. Peter's Cathedral — AP12

Perf. 12½x13
1965, June 26   Photo.   Unwmk.
C28 AP12 100fr gldn brn & multi 1.50 .75

Pres. John F. Kennedy — AP13

Portraits: 25fr on 50fr, Patrice Lumumba, premier of Congo Republic (ex-Belgian). 50fr, Sir Winston Churchill. 80fr, Barthélémy Boganda, premier of Central African Republic.

1965, June   Perf. 12½
C29 AP13 25fr on 50fr dk brn & red   .50 .40
a.   Surcharge omitted   35.00 35.00
C30 AP13 50fr dk brn & yel grn   1.00 1.00
C31 AP13 80fr dk brn & bl   1.75 1.50
C32 AP13 100fr dk brn & org yel   2.60 2.25
a.   Min. sheet of 4, #C29-C32   6.25 6.25
Nos. C29-C32 (4)   5.85 5.15

A second miniature sheet contains one each of Nos. C29a, C30-C32. Value, $50.
Issued: 25fr, 80fr, 6/25; 50fr, 100fr, No. C32a, 6/26.

Log Rolling — AP14

1965, Aug. 14   Engr.   Perf. 13
C33 AP14 50fr grn, brn & red brn 1.60 .75
Issued to publicize national unity.

World Map and Symbols of Agriculture and Industry — AP15

1965, Oct. 18   Engr.   Perf. 13
C34 AP15 50fr dk bl, blk, brn & org   1.40 .90
International Cooperation Year, 1965.

Abraham Lincoln — AP16

1965, Dec. 15   Photo.   Perf. 13
C35 AP16 90fr pink & multi   1.40 .60
Centenary of death of Abraham Lincoln.

Charles de Gaulle, Torch and Map of
Africa — AP17

1966, Feb. 28　　Engr.　　Perf. 13
C36　AP17　500fr dk red, dk grn
　　　　　　　　　& dk red brn　30.00 26.00
22nd anniv. of the Brazzaville Conf.

D-1 Satellite over
Brazzaville
Space Tracking
Station — AP18

1966, May 15　　Engr.　　Perf. 13
C37　AP18　150fr blk, dl red & bl
　　　　　　　　　grn　　　　　　2.25 1.25

Grain, Atom
Symbol and Map
of Africa and
Europe — AP19

1966, July 20　　Photo.　　Perf. 12x13
C38　AP19　50fr multicolored　　.90　.75
See note after Gabon No. C46.

Pres. Massamba-Debat and
President's Palace — AP20

3rd anniv. of the Revolution: 30fr,
Robespierre and storming of the Bastille. 50fr,
Lenin and storming of the Winter Palace.

1966, Aug. 15　　Photo.　　Perf. 12x12½
C39　AP20　25fr multicolored　　.45　.30
C40　AP20　30fr multicolored　　.65　.30
C41　AP20　50fr multicolored　1.60　.50
　a.　　Souv. sheet of 3, #C39-C41　2.25　2.25
　　　Nos. C39-C41 (3)　　　2.70　1.10

Air Afrique Issue, 1966
Common Design Type
1966, Aug. 31　　Photo.　　Perf. 13
C42　CD123　30fr lilac, lemon & blk　1.00　.25

Dr. Albert Schweitzer — AP21

1966, Sept. 4　　Photo.　　Perf. 12½
C43　AP21　100fr red, blk, bl & lil　2.25 1.25
Issued to honor Dr. Albert Schweitzer
(1875-1965), medical missionary.

Crab, Microscope
and
Pagoda — AP22

1966, Dec. 26　　Photo.　　Perf. 13
C44　AP22　100fr multicolored　1.75 1.00
9th Intl. Anticancer Cong., Tokyo. 10/23-29.

AP23

Birds: 50fr, Social Weaver. 75fr, European
Bee-eater. 100fr, Lilac-breasted roller. 150fr,
Regal sunbird. 200fr, Crowned cranes. 250fr,
Secretary bird. 300fr, Knysna touraco.

1967　　　Photo.　　Perf. 13
C45　AP23　50fr multicolored　1.60　.75
C46　AP23　75fr multicolored　3.25 1.00
C47　AP23　100fr multicolored　3.25 1.00
C48　AP23　150fr multicolored　4.25 2.25
C49　AP23　200fr multicolored　7.50 2.50
C50　AP23　250fr multicolored　9.50 3.00
C51　AP23　300fr multicolored　13.50 5.00
　　　Nos. C45-C51 (7)　　42.85 15.50
Issued: Nos. C45-C47, 2/13; others, 6/20.

Shackled
Hands
AP24

1967, May 24　　Photo.　　Perf. 12½x13
C52　AP24　500fr multicolored　8.00 3.00
Issued for African Liberation Day.

Sputnik 1, Explorer 6 and
Earth — AP25

Space Craft: 75fr, Ranger 6, Lunik 2 and
moon. 100fr, Mars 1, Mariner 4 and Mars.
200fr, Gemini, Vostok and earth.

1967, Aug. 1　　Engr.　　Perf. 13
C53　AP25　50fr multicolored　　.60　.30
C54　AP25　75fr multicolored　1.10　.35
C55　AP25　100fr multicolored　1.60　.60
C56　AP25　200fr multicolored　2.75 1.50
　　　Nos. C53-C56 (4)　　6.05 2.75
Space explorations.

African Postal Union Issue, 1967
Common Design Type
1967, Sept. 9　　Engr.　　Perf. 13
C57　CD124　100fr ver, ol & emer　1.60　.60

Boy Scouts, Tents and Jamboree
Emblem — AP26

Design: 70c, Borah Peak, Idaho; tents,
Scout sign and Jamboree emblem.

1967, Sept. 29
C58　AP26　50fr multicolored　　.80　.30
C59　AP26　70fr multicolored　1.20　.50
12th Boy Scout World Jamboree, Farragut
State Park, ID, Aug. 1-9.

Sikorsky S-43 and Map of
Africa — AP27

1967, Oct. 2　　Photo.　　Perf. 13
C60　AP27　30fr multicolored　　.75　.30
30th anniv. of the 1st airmail connection by
Aeromaritime Lines from Casablanca to
Pointe-Noire.

Men of Four Races Dancing on
Globe — AP28

1968, Feb 8　　Engr.　　Perf. 13
C61　AP28　70fr dk brn, ultra & em-
　　　　　　　　　er　　　　　　1.50　.60
Friendship among peoples.

The Oath of the Horatii, by Jacques
Louis David — AP29

Paintings: 25fr, On the Barricades, by Delacroix. No. C63, Grandfather and Grandson, by
Ghirlandajo, vert. No. C64, The Demolition of
the Bastille, by Hubert Robert. 200fr, Negro
Woman Arranging Peonies, by Jean F. Bazille.

1968　　Photo.　　Perf. 12x12½, 12½x12
C62　AP29　25fr multicolored　1.75　.35
C63　AP29　30fr multicolored　　.90　.30
C64　AP29　30fr multicolored　1.75　.50
C65　AP29　100fr multicolored　2.25　.90
C66　AP29　200fr multicolored　5.00 1.75
　　　Nos. C62-C66 (5)　11.65 3.80
Issue dates: Nos. C62, C64, Aug. 15. Nos.
C63, C65-C66, Mar. 20.
See Nos. C78-C81, C111-C115.

Early Automobile Type
1968, July 29　　Photo.　　Perf. 13x12½
C67　A50　150fr Ford, 1915　　3.50 1.75
C68　A50　200fr Citroen, 1922　5.25 1.75

Europafrica Issue

Square Knot — AP30

1968, July 20　　Photo.　　Perf. 13
C69　AP30　50fr multicolored　1.50　.50
5th anniv. of the economic agreement
between the European Economic Community
and the African and Malgache Union.

Martin Luther
King, Jr. — AP31

1968, Aug. 5　　　　Perf. 12½
C70　AP31　50fr lt grn, Prus grn &
　　　　　　　　　blk　　　　　　1.60　.40

Robert F.
Kennedy — AP32

1968, Sept. 30　　Photo.　　Perf. 13x12½
C71　AP32　50fr dp car, ap grn & blk　.85　.40

Running — AP33

Olympic Rings and: 20fr, Soccer, vert. 60fr, Boxing, vert. 85fr, High jump.

1968, Dec. 27   Engr.   Perf. 13
C72 AP33 5fr emer, brt bl &
　　　　　choc　　　　　　　.25　.25
C73 AP33 20fr dk bl, brn & dk
　　　　　grn　　　　　　　.45　.25
C74 AP33 60fr mar, brt grn &
　　　　　choc　　　　　　　.90　.60
C75 AP33 85fr blk, car rose &
　　　　　choc　　　　　　1.75　.85
　　Nos. C72-C75 (4)　　3.35　1.95

19th Olympic Games, Mexico City, 10/12-27.

PHILEXAFRIQUE Issue

G. De Gueidan, by Nicolas de Largillière AP34

1968, Dec. 30   Photo.   Perf. 12½
C76 AP34 100fr pink & multi　2.75　1.75

Issued to publicize PHILEXAFRIQUE, Philatelic Exhibition, in Abidjan, Feb. 14-23. Printed with alternating pink label.
See Nos. C89-C93.

2nd PHILEXAFRIQUE Issue
Common Design Type

Design: 50fr, Middle Congo No. 72 and Pointe-Noire harbor.

1969, Feb. 14   Engr.   Perf. 13
C77 CD128 50fr car rose, sl grn
　　　　　& bis brn　　　　2.00　1.75

Painting Type of 1968

Paintings: 25fr, Battle of Rivoli, by Carle Vernet. 50fr, Battle of Marengo, by Jacques Augustin Pajou. 75fr, Battle of Friedland, by Horace Vernet. 100fr, Battle of Jena, by Charles Thevenin.

1969, May 20   Photo.   Perf. 12x12½
C78 AP29 25fr vio bl & multi　1.25　.45
C79 AP29 50fr cop red & multi　1.75　.80
C80 AP29 75fr grn & multi　　3.00　1.10
C81 AP29 100fr brn & multi　5.00　1.40
　　Nos. C78-C81 (4)　　11.00　3.75

Bicentenary of birth of Napoleon I.

Ernesto Ché Guevara — AP35

1969, June 10   Photo.   Perf. 12½
C82 AP35 90fr brn, org & blk　1.60　.50

Issued in memory of Ernesto Ché Guevara (1928-1967), Cuban revolutionist.

Doll, Train and Space Toy — AP36

1969, June 20   Engr.   Perf. 13
C83 AP36 100fr mag, org & gray　1.75　.75
International Toy Fair, Nuremberg, Germany.

Europafrica Issue

Ribbon Tied Around Bar — AP37

1969, Aug. 5   Photo.   Perf. 13x12
C84 AP37 50fr bl grn, lil & blk　.90　.35
See note after Chad No. C11.

Souvenir Sheet

Armstrong, Aldrin and Collins — AP38

Design: No. C85b, Blast-off from Moon.

Embossed on Gold Foil
1969, Sept. 15   Imperf.
C85 AP38 1000fr #a-b　　40.00　37.50
See note after Algeria No. 427. No. C85 contains one each of Nos. C85a and C85b with simulated perforations.

Painter, Poto-Poto School — AP39

150fr, Sculpture lesson (man, infant and sculpture). 200fr, Potter working on vase.

1970, Feb. 20   Engr.   Perf. 13
C86 AP39 100fr multicolored　2.25　.60
C87 AP39 150fr multicolored　3.00　.95
C88 AP39 200fr multicolored　3.75　1.75
　　Nos. C86-C88 (3)　　9.00　3.30

Painting Type (Philexafrique)

Paintings: 150fr, Child with Cherries, by John Russell. 200fr, Erasmus, by Hans Holbein the Younger. 250fr, "Silence" (head), by Bernardino Luini. 300fr, Scene from the Massacre of Scio, by Delacroix. 500fr, The Capture of Constantinople by the Crusaders, by Delacroix.

1970   Photo.   Perf. 12½
C89 AP34 150fr lil & multi　4.50　1.50
C90 AP34 200fr multicolored　5.75　1.75
C91 AP34 250fr brn & multi　6.25　2.25
C92 AP34 300fr multicolored　8.00　3.25
C93 AP34 500fr brn & multi　13.50　4.50
　　Nos. C89-C93 (5)　　38.00　13.25

Aurichalcite — AP40

1970, Mar. 20
C94 AP40 100fr shown　　5.25　1.75
C95 AP40 150fr Dioptase　8.00　2.50

Lenin — AP41

1970, June 25   Photo.   Perf. 12½
C96 AP41 45fr shown　　1.00　.35
C97 AP41 75fr Lenin, seated　1.75　.50

Centenary of the birth of Lenin (1870-1924), Russian communist leader.

Karl Marx — AP42

Design: No. C99, Friedrich Engels.

1970, July 10   Engr.   Perf. 13
C98 AP42 50fr emer, dk brn & dk
　　　　　red　　　　　　1.40　.35
C99 AP42 50fr ultra, dk brn & dk
　　　　　red　　　　　　1.40　.35

Karl Marx (1818-1883) and Friedrich Engels (1820-1895), German socialist writers.

Otto Lilienthal's Glider, 1891 — AP43

Designs: 50fr, "Spirit of St. Louis," Lindbergh's first transatlantic solo flight, 1927. 70fr, Sputnik 1, first satellite in space. 90fr, First man on the moon, Apollo 11, 1969.

1970, Sept. 5   Engr.   Perf. 13
C100 AP43 45fr dp car, bl & ol
　　　　　bis　　　　　　1.00　.30
C101 AP43 50fr emer, sl grn &
　　　　　brn　　　　　　1.00　.35
C102 AP43 70fr brt bl, ol bis &
　　　　　dp car　　　　1.25　.50
C103 AP43 90fr brn, bl & ol gray　1.90　.75
　　Nos. C100-C103 (4)　　5.15　1.90

Forerunners of space exploration.

Saint on Horseback AP44

Designs from Stained Glass Windows, Brazzaville Cathedral: 150fr, Saint with staff. 250fr, The Elevation of the Host, from rose window.

1970, Dec. 10   Photo.   Perf. 12½
C104 AP44 100fr multicolored　1.25　.50
C105 AP44 150fr multicolored　1.75　.85
C106 AP44 250fr multicolored　3.00　1.75
　　a.　Souv. sheet of 3, #C104-C106　6.75　6.75
　　Nos. C104-C106 (3)　　6.00　3.10

Christmas 1970.

Marilyn Monroe and NYC — AP45

Portraits: 150fr, Martine Carol and Paris. 200fr, Erich von Stroheim and Vienna. 250fr, Sergei Eisenstein and Moscow.

1971, Mar. 16   Engr.   Perf. 13
C107 AP45 100fr brt grn, red
　　　　　brn & ultra　　7.00　.50
C108 AP45 150fr brn, brt lil &
　　　　　ultra　　　　7.00　.75
C109 AP45 200fr choc & ultra　7.00　1.10
C110 AP45 250fr brn, brn
　　　　　vio & ultra　7.00　1.25
　　Nos. C107-C110 (4)　28.00　3.60

History of motion pictures.

Painting Type of 1968

Paintings: 100fr, Christ Carrying Cross, by Paolo Veronese. 150fr, Christ on the Cross, Burgundian School, 1500, vert. 200fr, Descent from the Cross, by Rogier van der Weyden. 250fr, Christ Laid in the Tomb, Flemish School, 1500, vert. 500fr, Resurrection, by Hans Memling, vert.

1971, Apr. 26   Photo.   Perf. 13
C111 AP29 100fr green & multi　1.75　.75
C112 AP29 150fr green & multi　2.75　.90
C113 AP29 200fr green & multi　4.00　1.10
C114 AP29 250fr green & multi　4.50　1.60
C115 AP29 500fr green & multi　10.00　3.00
　　Nos. C111-C115 (5)　23.00　7.35

Easter 1971.

Map of Africa and Telecommunications System — AP46

1971, June 18   Photo.   Perf. 12½
C116 AP46 70fr bl, gray & dk brn　.80　.30
C117 AP46 85fr bl, lil rose & dk
　　　　　brn　　　　　1.25　.35
C118 AP46 90fr grn, yel & dk brn　1.60　.70
　　Nos. C116-C118 (3)　　3.65　1.35

Pan-African telecommunications system.

Globe and Waves — AP47

1971, June 19
C119 AP47 65fr lt bl & multi   .80   .30
3rd World Telecommunications Day.

Japanese Mask
and Play — AP48

Design: 150fr, Japanese and African
women, symbolic leaves.

1971, June 28   Engr.   Perf. 13
C120 AP48 75fr lil, blk & mag   1.00   .70
C121 AP48 150fr dk brn, brn red
                                 & red lil   1.60 1.10
PHILATOKYO '71 International Stamp Exhi-
bition, Tokyo, Apr. 20-30.

13th World Boy Scout Jamboree,
Japan, gold foil 1000fr airmail and silver
foil souv. sheet of four 90fr, issued July
14. Values: 1000fr single, $30; sheet of
four, $13.

Olympic Torch
and
Rings — AP49

350fr, Olympic rings and various sports.

1971, July 20   Engr.   Perf. 13
C122 AP49 150fr multi   1.90   .95
C123 AP49 350fr multi, horiz.   4.50 2.50
Pre-Olympic Year, 1971.

Scout Emblem, Japanese Dragon and
African Carved Canoe — AP50

Designs (Boy Scout Emblem and): 90fr,
Japanese mask and African boy, vert. 100fr,
Japanese woman and African drummer, vert.
250fr, Congolese mask.

1971, Aug. 25
C124 AP50 85fr multicolored   1.10   .30
C125 AP50 90fr multicolored   1.25   .35
C126 AP50 100fr multicolored   1.60   .45
C127 AP50 250fr multicolored   3.25   .90
   Nos. C124-C127 (4)   7.20 2.00
13th Boy Scout World Jamboree, Asagiri
Plain, Japan, Aug. 2-10.

Olympic Rings and Running — AP51

Designs (Olympic Rings and): 85fr, Hurdles. 90fr, Weight lifting, boxing, discus, running, javelin. 100fr, Wrestling. 150fr, Boxing.

1971, Sept. 30
C128 AP51 75fr plum, bl & dk
                           brn   .75   .35
C129 AP51 85fr scar, sl & dk
                           brn   .85   .35
C130 AP51 90fr vio bl & dk brn   1.10   .60
C131 AP51 100fr brn & slate   1.40   .60
C132 AP51 150fr grn, red & dk
                           brn   2.40 1.00
   Nos. C128-C132 (5)   6.50 2.90
75th anniv. of the 1st modern Olympic
Games.

Congo No. C36 and de
Gaulle — AP52

Design: No. C135, Charles de Gaulle.

1971, Nov. 9
C133 AP52 500fr slate grn &
                           multi   18.00 15.00

Pres. Marien
Ngouabi's Tribute
to de
Gaulle — AP53

**Lithographed; Gold Embossed
Perf. 12½**
C134 AP53 1000fr gold, grn
                      & red   27.50 20.00
C135 AP53 1000fr gold, grn
                      & red   27.50 20.00
a.   Pair, #C134-C135   55.00 55.00
Charles de Gaulle (1890-1970), president of
France.

African Postal Union Issue, 1971
Common Design Type
Design: 100fr, Allegory of Congo Republic
(woman) and UAMPT Building, Brazzaville.

1971, Nov. 13   Photo.   Perf. 13x13½
C136 CD135 100fr bl & multi   1.60   .75

Flag of Congo Republic and
"Revolution" — AP54

1971, Nov. 30
C137 AP54 100fr red & multi   1.75   .60
8th anniversary of revolution.

Workers and Flag — AP55

40fr, Flag of Congo Republic and sun.

1971, Dec. 31   Photo.   Perf. 13x12½
C138 AP55 30fr multicolored   .75   .30
C139 AP55 40fr red & multi   1.50   .50
2nd anniv. of founding of Congolese Labor
Party (No. C138), and adoption of red flag
(No. C139).

Book Year
Emblem — AP56

1972, June 3   Litho.   Perf. 12½
C140 AP56 50fr red, grn & yel   1.00   .40
International Book Year 1972.

Congolese Soccer Team — AP57

No. C142, Captain of winning team and cup,
vert.

1973, Feb. 22   Photo.   Perf. 13
C141 AP57 100fr ultra, red & blk 1.50   .75
C142 AP57 100fr red, yel & blk   1.50   .75

Girl Holding Bird,
Environment
Emblem — AP58

1973, Mar. 5   Engr.
C143 AP58 85fr org, slate grn &
                           bl   1.75   .90
UN Conference on Human Environment,
Stockholm, Sweden, June 5-16, 1972.

Miles Davis
AP59

Designs: 140fr, Ella Fitzgerald. 160fr,
Count Basie. 175fr, John Coltrane.

1973, Mar. 5   Photo.   Perf. 13x13½
C144 AP59 125fr multicolored   3.50   .95
C145 AP59 140fr multicolored   3.50 1.00
C146 AP59 160fr multicolored   4.50 1.50
C147 AP59 175fr multicolored   4.50 1.50
   Nos. C144-C147 (4)   16.00 4.95
Black American jazz musicians.

Olympic Rings, Hurdling — AP60

150fr, Pole vault, vert. 250fr, Wrestling.

1973, Mar. 15   Engr.   Perf. 13
C148 AP60 100fr shown   1.10   .60
C149 AP60 150fr multi   1.75   .90
C150 AP60 250fr multi   2.75 1.50
   Nos. C148-C150 (3)   5.60 3.00
20th Olympic Games, Munich, 8/26-9/11/72.

Refinery and Storage Tanks,
Djéno — AP61

Designs: 230fr, Off-shore drilling platform,
vert. 240fr, Workers assembling drill, vert.
260fr, Off-shore drilling installation.

1973, Mar. 20
C151 AP61 180fr red, bl & indi-
                           go   3.25 1.50
C152 AP61 230fr red, bl & blk   4.00 1.50
C153 AP61 240fr red, ind & brn   4.50 1.60
C154 AP61 260fr red, bl & blk   7.25 2.25
   Nos. C151-C154 (4)   19.00 6.85
Oil installations, Pointe-Noire.

Astronauts, Landing Module and Lunar
Rover on Moon — AP62

1973, Mar. 31
C155 AP62 250fr multicolored   4.00 1.75
Apollo 17 US moon mission, 12/7-19/72.

ITU Emblem,
Symbols of
Communications
AP63

1973, May 24   Engr.   Perf. 13
C156 AP63 120fr multicolored   2.25   .90
5th International Telecommunications Day.

White Horse, by Delacroix — AP64

Designs: Paintings by Eugene Delacroix.

1973, June 30   Photo.   Perf. 13
C157 AP64 150fr shown   2.25 1.50
C158 AP64 250fr Lion sleeping 5.00 2.40
C159 AP64 300fr Lion and tiger 5.25 2.50
    Nos. C157-C159 (3)   12.50 6.40
        See Nos. C169-C171.

Copernicus and Heliocentric
System — AP65

1973, June 30   Engr.
C160 AP65 50fr multicolored   1.00 .45
    500th anniversary of the birth of Nicolaus
Copernicus (1473-1543), Polish astronomer.

Plane, Ship, Rocket, Village, Sun and
Clouds — AP66

1973, July
C161 AP66 50fr red & multi   1.60 .60
    Cent. of intl. meteorological cooperation.

Pres. Marien
Ngouabi — AP67

1973, Aug. 12   Photo.   Perf. 13
C162 AP67 30fr multicolored   .35 .25
C163 AP67 40fr aqua & multi   .45 .25
C164 AP67 75fr red & multi   1.00 .35
    Nos. C162-C164 (3)   1.80 .85
    10th anniversary of independence.

Stamps,
Album,
African
Woman
AP68

No. C167, Stamps in shape of map of
Congo, album, globe. No. C168, Like 30fr.

1973, Aug. 12
C165 AP68 30fr pur & multi   1.90 .30
C166 AP68 40fr multicolored   .25 .25
C167 AP68 100fr dk brn & multi 3.75 .80
C168 AP68 100fr ocher & multi .90 .40
    Nos. C165-C168 (4)   6.80 1.75

Nos. C165, C168 for the 10th anniv. of the
revolution, Nos. C166-C167 the Intl. Philatelic
Exhib., Brazzaville.

**Painting Type of 1973 Inscribed
"EUROPAFRIQUE"**

Details from "Earth and Paradise," by Jan
Brueghel, the Elder: No. C169, Spotted hyena.
No. C170, Leopard and lion. No. C171, Ele-
phant and creatures.

1973, Oct. 10   Photo.   Perf. 13
C169 AP64 100fr multi   3.00 1.50
C170 AP64 100fr multi   3.00 1.50
C171 AP64 100fr multi   3.00 1.50
    Nos. C169-C171 (3)   9.00 4.50

US and Russian Spacecraft
Docking — AP69

Design: 80fr, US and USSR spacecraft
docked in space and emblems of 1975 joint
space mission.

1973, Oct. 15   Engr.   Perf. 13
C172 AP69 40fr bl, red & brn   .50 .35
C173 AP69 80fr red, grn & bl   1.10 .50
Planned joint US and Soviet space missions.
For overprint see No. C251.

UPU Monument, Satellites, Big
Dipper — AP70

1973, Nov. 20   Engr.   Perf. 13
C174 AP70 80fr vio bl & lt bl 1.60 .50
    Universal Postal Union Day.

Astronauts Working in Space — AP71

40fr, Spacecraft & Skylab docking in space.

1973, Nov. 30
C175 AP71 30fr ultra, sl grn & choc .65 .25
C176 AP71 40fr mag, org & sl grn   .95 .25
    Skylab, first space laboratory.

Goalkeeper,
Soccer — AP72

Design: 100fr, Soccer player kicking ball.

1973, Dec. 20
C177 AP72 40fr sl grn, sepia &
        brn   .75 .25
C178 AP72 100fr pur, red & slate
        grn   1.90 .75
    World Soccer Cup, Munich, 1974.

John F.
Kennedy
(1917-1963)
AP73

1973, Dec. 20   Photo.   Perf. 12½
C179 AP73 150fr ultra, gold & blk 1.75 .90

Runners — AP74

1973, Dec. 20   Engr.   Perf. 13
C180 AP74 40fr sl grn, red &
        brn   .60 .25
C181 AP74 100fr red, sl grn, &
        brn   1.75 .75
    2nd African Games, Lagos, Nigeria.

Flag over Map of
Congo — AP75

1973, Dec. 31   Photo.
C182 AP75 40fr dp grn & multi .80 .25
    4th anniversary of Congolese Labor Party
and of the Congo Red Flag.

Soccer and
Games
Emblem — AP76

1974, June 20   Photo.   Perf. 13
C183 AP76 250fr multicolored   3.75 1.90
    World Cup Soccer Championship, Munich,
June 13-July 7.

Astronauts Yuri A. Gagarin and Alan
B. Shepard — AP77

Designs: 30fr, Space, globe, Russian and
American flags with names of astronauts who
perished in space. 100fr, Alexei Leonov and
Neil A. Armstrong in space and on moon.

1974, June 30   Engr.   Perf. 13
C184 AP77 30fr red, ultra & brn   .45 .25
C185 AP77 40fr red, bl & brn   .70 .25
C186 AP77 100fr car, grn & brn   1.60 .90
    Nos. C184-C186 (3)   2.75 1.40
        For overprint see No. C254.

Soccer Game
Superimposed on
Ball — AP78

1974, July 31   Photo.   Perf. 13
C187 AP78 250fr multicolored   3.50 1.75
    Germany's victory in World Cup Soccer
Championship.

Link-up Emblem,
Stages of Link-
up — AP79

300fr, Spacecraft docking over globe.

1974, Aug. 8   Engr.   Perf. 13
C188 AP79 200fr pur, bl & red 2.25 1.10
C189 AP79 300fr multi, horiz. 3.50 1.50
    Russo-American space cooperation.
For overprint see No. C255.

Symbols of Communications, UPU
Emblem — AP80

1974, Aug. 10
C190 AP80 500fr blk & red   6.75 3.00
    Centenary of Universal Postal Union.
For surcharge see No. C194.

Lenin and Pendulum Trace
Pattern — AP81

1974, Sept. 16   Engr.   Perf. 13
C191 AP81 150fr multicolored   2.10 1.10
    Lenin (1870-1924).

Churchill
and Order
of the
Garter
AP82

Marconi and Wireless Telegraph AP83

1974, Oct. 1　Litho.　Perf. 13
C192 AP82 200fr lt grn & multi　2.50 1.25
C193 AP83 200fr lt ultra & multi　2.50 1.25

No. C190 Srchd. in Violet Blue with New Value, 2 Bars and "9 OCTOBER 1974"

1974, Oct. 9
C194 AP80 300fr on 500fr multi　4.25 2.75
Universal Postal Union Day.

UDEAC Issue

Presidents and Flags of Cameroun, CAR, Gabon and Congo — AP83a

1974, Dec. 8　Photo.　Perf. 13
C195 AP83a 100fr gold & multi　1.60 .50
See note after Cameroun No. 595.

Regatta at Argenteuil, by Monet — AP84

Impressionist Paintings: 40fr, Seated Dancer, by Degas. 50fr, Girl on Swing, by Renoir. 75fr, Girl with Straw Hat, by Renoir. All vertical.

1974, Dec. 15
C196 AP84 30fr gold & multi　1.50 .35
C197 AP84 40fr gold & multi　2.00 .35
C198 AP84 50fr gold & multi　2.75 .50
C199 AP84 75fr gold & multi　3.25 .80
　Nos. C196-C199 (4)　9.50 2.00

National Fair AP85

1974, Dec. 20
C200 AP85 30fr multicolored　.95 .35
National Fair, Aug. 24-Sept. 8.

Flags of Participating Nations, Map of Africa — AP86

1974, Dec. 20　　　Perf. 13
C201 AP86 40fr ultra & multi　.80 .45
Conference of Chiefs of State of Central and East Africa, Brazzaville, Aug. 31-Sept. 2.

"Five Weeks in a Balloon," by Jules Verne AP87

Design: 50fr, "Around the World in 80 Days," by Jules Verne.

1975, June 30　Litho.　Perf. 12½
C202 AP87 40fr multicolored　1.40 .50
C203 AP87 50fr multicolored　1.75 1.00
Jules Verne (1828-1905), French science fiction writer, 70th death anniversary.

Paris-Brussels Train, 1890 — AP88

Design: 75fr, Santa Fe, 1880.

1975, June 30
C204 AP88 50fr ocher & multi　2.00 .75
C205 AP88 75fr lt bl & multi　4.25 .90

Soyuz and Apollo-Soyuz Emblem — AP89

Design: 100fr, Apollo and emblem.

1975, July 20　Litho.　Perf. 12½
C206 AP89 95fr org, blk & mag　1.25 .50
C207 AP89 100fr vio, bl & blk　1.40 .60
Apollo Soyuz space test project (Russo-American space cooperation), launching July 15; link-up, July 17.
For overprints see Nos. C252-C253.

Bicycling and Montreal Olympic Emblem — AP90

Designs (Montreal Olympic Emblem and): 40fr, Boxing, vert. 50fr, Basketball, vert. 95fr, High jump. 100fr, Javelin. 150fr, Running.

Perf. 12½x13, 13x12½
1975, Oct. 30　　　　　Photo.
C208 AP90 40fr multicolored　.50 .25
C209 AP90 50fr red & multi　.60 .25
C210 AP90 85fr bl & multi　1.00 .35
C211 AP90 95fr org & multi　1.10 .45
C212 AP90 100fr multicolored　1.40 .50
C213 AP90 150fr multicolored　1.75 .80
　Nos. C208-C213 (6)　6.35 2.60
Pre-Olympic Year 1975.

Map of Africa, Sports and Flags — AP91

1975, Dec. 20　Litho.　Perf. 12½
C214 AP91 30fr multicolored　.80 .35
1st African Games, Brazzaville, 10th anniv.

Workers and Flag — AP92

1975, Dec. 31　Litho.　Perf. 12½
C215 AP92 60fr multicolored　1.10 .25
Congolese Labor Party (P.C.T.), 6th anniv.

Alphonse Fondere — AP93

Historic Ships: 5fr, like 30fr. 10fr, 40fr, Hamburg, 1839. 15fr, 50fr, Gomer, 1831. 20fr, 60fr, Great Eastern, 1858. 95fr, J.M. White II, 1878.

1976　　　Engr.　　Perf. 13
C216 AP93 5fr multicolored　.25 .25
C217 AP93 10fr multicolored　.25 .25
C218 AP93 15fr multicolored　.30 .25
C219 AP93 20fr multicolored　.50 .25
C220 AP93 30fr multicolored　.75 .25
C221 AP93 40fr multicolored　1.00 .35
C222 AP93 50fr multicolored　1.25 .50
C223 AP93 60fr multicolored　1.75 .60
C224 AP93 95fr multicolored　2.50 1.00
　Nos. C216-C224 (9)　8.55 3.70
　Issued: Nos. C216-C219, May; Nos. C220-C224, Mar. 7.

Europafrica Issue

Peasant Family, by Louis Le Nain — AP94

Paintings: 80fr, Boy with Top, by Jean B. Chardin. 95fr, Venus and Aeneas, by Nicolas Poussin. 100fr, The Rape of the Sabine Women, by Jacques Louis David.

1976, Mar. 20　Litho.　Perf. 12½
C225 AP94 60fr gold & multi　1.25 .45
C226 AP94 80fr gold & multi　1.40 .70
C227 AP94 95fr gold & multi　1.90 .70
C228 AP94 100fr gold & multi　2.10 .85
　Nos. C225-C228 (4)　6.65 2.70
Nos. C225-C228 printed in sheets of 8 stamps and horizontal gutter with commemorative inscription.

Telephone Type of 1976

1976, Apr. 25　Litho.　Perf. 12½x13
C229 A107 60fr pink, mar & crim　.90 .30

Sports Type of 1976

Designs: 150fr, Runner and map of Central Africa. 200fr, Discus and map.

1976, Oct. 25　　　　Perf. 12½
C230 A110 150fr multicolored　1.75 .75
C231 A110 200fr multicolored　2.75 1.10

Map of Africa, Flag and OAU Headquarters AP95

1976, Dec. 16　Typo.　Perf. 13x14
C232 AP95 60fr multicolored　.80 .35
13th anniv. of the Organization for African Unity.

Europafrica Issue

Map of Europe and Africa — AP96

1977, June 28　Litho.　Perf. 13
C233 AP96 75fr multicolored　.90 .45

Headdress Type of 1977

1977, June 30　　　　Perf. 12½
Designs: 250fr, Two straw caps. 300fr, Beaded cap.
C234 A118 250fr multicolored　2.75 1.50
C235 A118 300fr multicolored　3.00 1.75

Zeppelin Type of 1977
Souvenir Sheet

Design: 500fr, LZ 127 over US Capitol.

1977, Aug. 5　Litho.　Perf. 11
C236 A120 500fr multicolored　6.75 2.00
No. C236 exists imperf.

Checkerboard
AP97

1977, Aug. 20   Engr.   Perf. 13
C237 AP97 60fr red & blk   .90 .35
Lomé Convention on General Agreement on Tariffs and Trade (GATT).

Newton, Intelsat Satellite and Classical "Planets" — AP98

1977, Aug. 25
C238 AP98 140fr multicolored   2.00 .90
Isaac Newton (1642-1727), natural philosopher and mathematician.

Elizabeth II Type of 1977
Souvenir Sheet
Design: 500fr, Royal family on balcony.

1977, Dec. 21   Litho.   Perf. 14
C239 A128 500fr multicolored   5.75 1.75
For overprint see No. C244.

Mallard
AP99

Birds: 75fr, Purple heron, vert. 150fr, Reed warbler, vert. 240fr, Hoopoe, vert.

1978, May 22   Perf. 13x12½, 12½x13
C240 AP99 65fr multicolored   1.40 .50
C241 AP99 75fr multicolored   1.40 .50
C242 AP99 150fr multicolored   3.50 1.00
C243 AP99 240fr multicolored   5.50 1.75
   Nos. C240-C243 (4)   11.80 3.75

No. C239 Overprinted in Silver:
"ANNIVERSAIRE DU /
COURONNEMENT / 1953-1978"

1978, Sept.   Litho.   Perf. 14
Souvenir Sheet
C244 A128 500fr multicolored   4.50 3.00
25th anniv. of coronation of Elizabeth II.

Philexafrique II-Essen Issue
Common Design Types
No. C245, Leopard and Congo No. C243. No. C246, Eagle and Wurttemberg No. 1.

1978, Nov. 1   Litho.   Perf. 12½
C245 CD138 100fr multicolored   2.00 1.10
C246 CD139 100fr multicolored   2.00 1.10
  a.   Pair, #C245-C246   7.00 7.00

Map of Africa,
Satellites
AP100

1978, Nov. 25   Engr.   Perf. 13
C247 AP100 100fr multicolored   1.60 .50
Pan-African Telecommunications Network, PANAFTEL.

Map of Africa and
People — AP101

1979, Aug. 2   Litho.   Perf. 12½
C248 AP101 45fr multicolored   .50 .25
C249 AP101 75fr multicolored   .85 .40
5th Conference of Panafrican Youth Movement, Brazzaville, Aug. 2-7.

Abala
Peasant
Woman
AP102

1979, Aug. 20
C250 AP102 150fr multicolored   1.75 .90

Nos. C173, C206-C207, C186, C189
Overprinted

No. C251

No. C252

Perf. 13, 12½
1979, Nov. 5   Engr., Litho.
C251 AP69 80fr multicolored   1.00 .90
C252 AP89 95fr multicolored   1.10 1.00
C253 AP89 100fr multicolored   1.10 1.00
C254 AP77 100fr multicolored   1.10 1.00
C255 AP79 300fr multicolored   3.00 2.75
   Nos. C251-C255 (5)   7.30 6.65
Apollo 11 moon landing, 10th anniversary.

Runner, Olympic Rings — AP103

Pre-Olympic Year: 100fr, Boxing. 200fr, Fencing. 300fr, Soccer. 500fr, Moscow '80 emblem.

1979   Litho.   Perf. 13½
C256 AP103 65fr multi   .60 .25
C257 AP103 100fr multi   .95 .25
C258 AP103 200fr multi, vert.   1.90 .50
C259 AP103 300fr multi   2.75 .75
C260 AP103 500fr multi, vert.   4.75 1.25
   Nos. C256-C260 (5)   10.95 3.00

Cross-Country
Skiing — AP104

Lake Placid '80 Emblem and: 60fr, Slalom. 200fr, Ski jump, 350fr, Downhill skiing, horiz. 500fr, Woman skier.

1979, Dec   Perf. 14½
Size: 24x42mm, 42x24mm
C261 AP104 40fr multicolored   .45 .25
C262 AP104 60fr multicolored   .60 .25
C263 AP104 200fr multicolored   1.90 .45
C264 AP104 350fr multicolored   3.50 .90
Size: 31½x46½mm
Perf. 14
C265 AP104 500fr multicolored   4.50 1.40
   Nos. C261-C265 (5)   10.95 3.25
13th Winter Olympic Games, Lake Placid, NY, Feb. 12-24, 1980.

Nos. C261-C265
Overprinted in
Black

40fr, Zimiatov. 60fr, Moser-Proell. 200fr, Tomanen. 350fr, Stock. 500fr, Stenmark-Wenzel.

1980, Apr. 28
C266 AP104 40fr multi   .45 .25
C267 AP104 60fr multi   .60 .25
C268 AP104 200fr multi   1.90 .75
C269 AP104 350fr multi   3.50 1.25
C270 AP104 500fr multi   4.75 1.90
   Nos. C266-C270 (5)   11.20 4.40

Long Jump, Olympic Rings — AP105

1980, May 2   Litho.   Perf. 14½
C271 AP105 75fr multi, vert.   .90 .25
C272 AP105 150fr multi   1.40 .30
C273 AP105 250fr multi, vert. 2.25 .50
C274 AP105 350fr multi, vert. 3.25 .70
   Nos. C271-C274 (4)   7.80 1.75
Souvenir Sheet
C275 AP105 500fr multi   5.00 1.60
22nd Summer Olympic Games, Moscow, July 19-Aug. 3.
For overprints see Nos. C292-C296.

Stadium, Mascot, Madrid Club
Emblem — AP106

Stadium, Mascot and Club Emblem: 75fr, Zaragoza. 100fr, Madrid Athletic Club. 150fr, Valencia. 175fr, Spain. 250fr, Barcelona.

1980, June 23   Litho.   Perf. 14x13½
C276 AP106 60fr multicolored   .60 .25
C277 AP106 75fr multicolored   .60 .25
C278 AP106 100fr multicolored   1.00 .25
C279 AP106 150fr multicolored   1.40 .35
C280 AP106 175fr multicolored   1.60 .50
   Nos. C276-C280 (5)   5.20 1.60
Souvenir Sheet
C281 AP106 250fr multicolored   2.75 1.25
World Soccer Cup 1982.
For overprints see Nos. C298-C303.

Adoration of the Shepherds — AP107

Rembrandt Paintings: 100fr, The Burial. 200fr, Christ at Emmaus. 300fr, Annunciation, vert. 500fr, Crucifixion, vert.

1980, July 4   Perf. 12½
C282 AP107 65fr multicolored   .55 .25
C283 AP107 100fr multicolored   .85 .50
C284 AP107 200fr multicolored   1.75 .60
C285 AP107 300fr multicolored   2.50 .85
C286 AP107 500fr multicolored   4.50 1.50
   Nos. C282-C286 (5)   10.15 3.75

Albert Camus (1913-1960),
Writer — AP108

Design: 150fr, Jacques Offenbach (1819-1880), composer, vert.

1980, July 5   Engr.   Perf. 13
C287 AP108 100fr multicolored   1.25 .50
C288 AP108 150fr multicolored   2.25 1.25

Raffia Dancing Skirts — AP109

Traditional Dancing Costumes: 300fr, Tam-tam dancers, vert. 350fr, Masks.

1980, Aug. 6   Litho.   *Perf. 13½*

C289	AP109	250fr multicolored	2.75	.95
C290	AP109	300fr multicolored	3.25	1.50
C291	AP109	350fr multicolored	4.00	1.90
	Nos. C289-C291 (3)		10.00	4.35

Nos. C271-C275
Overprinted

75fr, Dombrowki (RDA), 150fr, Saneiev (URSS), 250fr, Simeoni (IT), 350fr, Thompson (GB)

1980, Nov. 14   Litho.   *Perf. 14½*

C292	AP105	75fr multicolored	.70	.30
C293	AP105	150fr multicolored	1.40	.60
C294	AP105	250fr multicolored	2.25	.90
C295	AP105	350fr multicolored	3.25	1.50
	Nos. C292-C295 (4)		7.60	3.30

Souvenir Sheet

C296	AP105	500fr multicolored	5.00	4.00

The Studio by Picasso — AP109a

150fr, Landscape. 200fr, Cannes Studio. 300fr, Still Life. 500fr, Still Life, diff.

1981, July 4   *Perf. 12½*

C296A	AP109a	100fr shown	1.10	.50
C296B	AP109a	150fr multi	1.60	.75
C296C	AP109a	200fr multi	2.10	1.00
C296D	AP109a	300fr multi	3.75	1.50
C296E	AP109a	500fr multi	6.25	2.50
	Nos. C296A-C296E (5)		14.80	6.25

1st Seminar on Petroleum, Gas and
Energy Alternatives, Brazzaville
AP109b

45fr, Emblem, oil platform, other energy sources. 100fr, Emblem, map, oil platforms. 150fr, Map, other energy sources. 200fr, Maps of Africa, Congo, oil worker.

1981   Litho.   *Perf. 12½*

C296F	AP109b	45fr multi	20.00	13.00
C296G	AP109b	75fr multi	32.50	19.00
C296H	AP109b	100fr multi	45.00	27.50
C296I	AP109b	150fr multi	65.00	40.00
C296J	AP109b	200fr multi	90.00	50.00
	Nos. C296F-C296J (5)		252.50	149.50

1350th Anniv. of
Mohamed's
Death at
Medina — AP110

400fr, Medina Mosque minaret.

1982, July 17   Litho.   *Perf. 13*

C297	AP110	400fr multi	3.75	1.75

Nos. C276-C281 Overprinted in
Black on Silver

No. C298

No. C299

No. C300

No. C301

No. C302

1982, Oct. 7   Litho.   *Perf. 14x13½*

C298	AP106	60fr multicolored	.55	.25
C299	AP106	75fr multicolored	.65	.30
C300	AP106	100fr multicolored	1.00	.45
C301	AP106	150fr multicolored	1.60	.60
C302	AP106	175fr multicolored	1.75	.60
	Nos. C298-C302 (5)		5.55	2.20

Souvenir Sheet

C303	AP106	250fr multicolored	2.50	1.90

50th Anniv. of Amelia Earhart's
Transatlantic Flight — AP111

1982, Dec. 4   Engr.   *Perf. 13*

C304	AP111	150fr multicolored	1.75	.75

Wind
Surfing
AP112

Various wind surfing scenes, 1984 Olympic Games, 100fr, 300fr, 400fr vert.

1983, June 4   Litho.   *Perf. 13*

C305	AP112	100fr multicolored	.90	.25
C306	AP112	200fr multicolored	1.75	.50
C307	AP112	300fr multicolored	2.75	.70
C308	AP112	400fr multicolored	3.50	1.00
	Nos. C305-C308 (4)		8.90	2.45

Souvenir Sheet

C309	AP112	500fr multicolored	5.00	2.50

For overprint see No. C336.

Manned
Flight
Bicentenary
AP113

Various balloons: 100fr, Montgolfiere, 1783. 200fr, Flesselles, 1784. 300fr, Auguste Piccard, 1931. 400fr, Don Piccard. 500fr, Mail transport balloon, 1870.

1983, June 7

C310	AP113	100fr multicolored	1.10	.25
C311	AP113	200fr multicolored	2.10	.40
C312	AP113	300fr multicolored	3.00	.60
C313	AP113	400fr multicolored	4.50	.90
	Nos. C310-C313 (4)		10.70	2.15

Souvenir Sheet

C314	AP113	500fr multicolored	5.75	1.60

For overprint see No. C337.

Christmas
1983
AP114

Various Virgin and Child Paintings by Botticelli.

1984, Jan. 21   Litho.   *Perf. 13*

C315	AP114	150fr multicolored	1.25	.50
C316	AP114	350fr multicolored	3.00	1.10
C317	AP114	500fr multicolored	4.50	1.50
	Nos. C315-C317 (3)		8.75	3.10

Vase of
Flowers, by
Manet
(1832-83)
AP115

Paintings: 200fr, Small Holy Family, by Raphael. 300fr, La Belle Jardiniere, by Raphael. 400fr, Virgin of Loretto, by Raphael. 500fr, Portrait of Richard Wagner (1813-83), by Giuseppe Tivoli.

1984, Feb. 24   Litho.   *Perf. 13*

C318	AP115	100fr multicolored	.90	.30
C319	AP115	200fr multicolored	1.90	.70
C320	AP115	300fr multicolored	2.75	1.00
C321	AP115	400fr multicolored	3.75	1.40
C322	AP115	500fr multicolored	5.00	1.50
	Nos. C318-C322 (5)		14.30	4.90

1984 Summer Olympics — AP116

1984, Mar. 31   *Perf. 13*

C323	AP116	45fr Judo, vert.	.45	.25
C324	AP116	75fr Judo, diff.	.70	.25
C325	AP116	150fr Wrestling	1.40	.50
C326	AP116	175fr Fencing	1.60	.60
C327	AP116	350fr Fencing, diff.	3.25	1.10
	Nos. C323-C327 (5)		7.40	2.70

Souvenir Sheet

C328	AP116	500fr Boxing	5.00	2.50

1984 Summer Olympic Gold
Medalists — AP117

Sailing/yachting: 100fr, Stephan Van Den Berg, Netherlands, Windglider Class. 150fr, US, Soling Class. 200fr, Spain, 470 Class. 500fr, US, Flying Dutchman Class.

1984, Dec. 18   Litho.   *Perf. 13*

C329	AP117	100fr multi, vert.	1.00	.45
C330	AP117	150fr multi	1.40	.65
C331	AP117	200fr multi	2.00	.90
C332	AP117	500fr multi, vert.	4.50	2.25
	Nos. C329-C332 (4)		8.90	4.25

Virgin and Child, by Giovanni Bellini
(c. 1430-1516) — AP118

Religious paintings: 100fr, Holy Family, by Andrea del Sarto (1486-1530). 400fr, Virgin with Angels, by Cimabue (c. 1240-1302).

1985, Feb. 12   Litho.   *Perf. 13*

C333	AP118	100fr multi, vert.	.80	.45
C334	AP118	150fr multi	1.60	.90
C335	AP118	400fr multi, vert.	3.00	1.75
	Nos. C333-C335 (3)		5.40	3.10

Christmas 1984.

Nos. C309, C314 Ovptd. with
Exhibition in Blue or Green

Overprint are: No. C336, OLYMPHILEX '85 / LAUSANNE (B). No. C337, MOPHILA '85 / HAM - BURG (G).

1985, Mar. 8   *Perf. 13*

Souvenir Sheets

C336	AP112	500fr multicolored	5.00	4.00
C337	AP113	500fr multicolored	5.00	4.00

Audubon Birth Bicentenary — AP119

Illustrations of North American bird species by Audubon: 100fr, Passiformes fringillidae, vert. 150fr, Eudocimus ruber, vert. 200fr, Buteo jamaicensis. 350fr, Camptorhynchus labradorius.

1985, Apr. 11   **Perf. 13½**
C338	AP119	100fr multicolored	1.00	.45
C339	AP119	150fr multicolored	1.50	.65
C340	AP119	200fr multicolored	1.90	.90
C341	AP119	350fr multicolored	3.75	1.50
		Nos. C338-C341 (4)	8.15	3.50

PHILEXAFRICA '85, Lome — AP120

Youths in public service activities: No. C342, Community health care. No. C343, Agriculture.

1985, May 20   **Perf. 13**
C342	AP120	200fr multicolored	2.50	1.50
C343	AP120	200fr multicolored	2.50	1.50
a.		Pair, #C342-C343 + label	6.00	6.00

For overprints see Nos. 1187-1188.

Admission to UN, 25th Anniv. — AP121

1985, Aug. 13
| C344 | AP121 | 190fr multicolored | 1.75 | .75 |

Rainbow, emblem AP122

1985, Oct. 25   **Perf. 12½**
| C345 | AP122 | 180fr multicolored | 1.60 | .65 |

UN, 40th Anniv.

Christmas — AP123

Paintings: 100fr, The Virgin and the Infant Jesus, by David. 200fr, Adoration of the Magi, by Hieronymus Bosch (1450-1516). 400fr, Virgin and Child, by Van Dyck.

1985, Dec. 20   **Perf. 13**
C346	AP123	100fr multicolored	.90	.35
C347	AP123	200fr multicolored	1.90	.75
C348	AP123	400fr multicolored	3.50	1.75
		Nos. C346-C348 (3)	6.30	2.85

Nos. C346-C347 vert.

Halley's Comet — AP124

125fr, Halley, comet. 150fr, West's Comet, 1976. 225fr, Ikeya Seki's Comet, 1965. 300fr, Trajectory diagram. 350fr, Comet, Vega probe.

1986, Feb. 17
C349	AP124	125fr multicolored	1.00	.50
C350	AP124	150fr multicolored	1.25	.60
C351	AP124	225fr multicolored	1.75	.90
C352	AP124	300fr multicolored	2.25	1.25
C353	AP124	350fr multicolored	2.75	1.50
		Nos. C349-C353 (5)	9.00	4.75

Nos. C350-C351 vert.

Cosmos-Frantel Hotel — AP125

1986, May 1   **Perf. 13½**
| C354 | AP125 | 250fr multicolored | 2.50 | .90 |

1986 World Cup Soccer Championships, Mexico — AP126

Various soccer plays.

1986, July 22   **Litho.**   **Perf. 13**
C355	AP126	150fr multicolored	1.25	.60
C356	AP126	250fr multicolored	2.00	1.00
C357	AP126	440fr multicolored	3.75	1.75
C358	AP126	600fr multicolored	6.50	2.50
		Nos. C355-C358 (4)	13.50	5.85

Air Africa, 25th Anniv. — AP127

1986, Nov. 29   **Litho.**   **Perf. 13½**
| C359 | AP127 | 200fr multicolored | 2.00 | .75 |

1988 Winter Pre-Olympics, Calgary — AP128

150fr, Downhill skiing. 250fr, Bobsled. 440fr, Women's cross-country skiing. 600fr, Ski jumping.

1986, Dec. 15   **Perf. 13**
C360	AP128	150fr multicolored	1.25	.60
C361	AP128	250fr multicolored	2.25	.95
C362	AP128	440fr multicolored	4.00	1.50
C363	AP128	600fr multicolored	5.75	2.40
		Nos. C360-C363 (4)	13.25	5.45

Nos. C361-C362 vert.

Christmas AP129

Paintings by Rogier van der Weyden (c.1399-1464): 250fr, Virgin and Child. 440fr, The Nativity. 500fr, Virgin with Carnation.

1986, Dec. 23   **Perf. 13½**
C364	AP129	250fr multicolored	2.25	1.00
C365	AP129	440fr multicolored	4.25	1.75
C366	AP129	500fr multicolored	4.50	2.10
		Nos. C364-C366 (3)	11.00	4.85

Crocodiles, World Wildlife Fund — AP130

75fr, Osteolaemus tetraspis. 100fr, Crocodylus cataphractus. 125fr, Osteolaemus tetraspis, diff. 150fr, Crocodylus cataphractus, diff.

1987, Jan. 22   **Perf. 13**
C367	AP130	75fr multicolored	2.25	1.10
C368	AP130	100fr multicolored	2.75	1.25
C369	AP130	125fr multicolored	3.50	1.75
C370	AP130	150fr multicolored	4.00	3.00
		Nos. C367-C370 (4)	12.50	7.10

1988 Summer Olympics, Seoul — AP131

1987, July 11   **Litho.**   **Perf. 13**
C371	AP131	100fr Backstroke	.90	.35
C372	AP131	200fr Freestyle	1.75	.75
C373	AP131	300fr Breaststroke	2.75	1.10
C374	AP131	400fr Butterfly	3.50	1.40
		Nos. C371-C374 (4)	8.90	3.60

Souvenir Sheet
| C375 | AP131 | 750fr Start of event | 6.75 | 3.50 |

Launch of Sputnik, First Artificial Satellite, 30th Anniv. — AP132

1987, June 5   **Perf. 12½x12**
| C376 | AP132 | 60fr multicolored | .50 | .25 |
| C377 | AP132 | 240fr multicolored | 2.25 | 1.10 |

Butterflies — AP133

75fr, Precis epicleli. 120fr, Deilephila nerii. 450fr, Euryphene senegalensis. 550fr, Precis almanta.

1987, Sept. 4   **Perf. 12½**
C378	AP133	75fr multicolored	1.20	.30
C379	AP133	120fr multicolored	2.00	.45
C380	AP133	450fr multicolored	6.00	1.75
C381	AP133	550fr multicolored	8.00	2.40
		Nos. C378-C381 (4)	17.20	4.90

Coubertin, Eternal Flame and Greece No. 125 — AP134

Cameo portrait, athletes and stamps: 120fr, Runners, France No. 198. 350fr, Congo Republic No. C22, hurdler. 600fr, High jump, Congo Republic No. C75.

1987, Nov. 4
C382	AP134	75fr shown	.80	.30
C383	AP134	120fr multicolored	1.10	.45
C384	AP134	350fr multicolored	3.50	1.25
C385	AP134	600fr multicolored	5.25	2.10
		Nos. C382-C385 (4)	10.65	4.10

Pierre de Coubertin (1863-1937), promulgator of the modern Olympics.

Arrival of Schweitzer in Lambarene, 75th Anniv. — AP135

1988, Apr. 17   Litho.   Perf. 12½
C386 AP135 240fr multicolored   2.75 1.25

Dr. Albert Schweitzer (1875-1965), Nobel Peace Prize winner of 1952, founded Lambarene Hospital, Gabon, in 1913.

1988 Summer Olympics, Seoul — AP136

Pentathlon: 75fr, Swimming. 170fr, Cross-country running, vert. 200fr, Shooting. 600fr, Equestrian. 700fr, Fencing.

1988, June 10   Litho.   Perf. 13
C387 AP136 75fr multicolored   .70 .25
C388 AP136 170fr multicolored   1.60 .60
C389 AP136 200fr multicolored   1.75 .70
C390 AP136 600fr multicolored   5.00 2.00
    Nos. C387-C390 (4)   9.05 3.55

Souvenir Sheet
C391 AP136 750fr multicolored   6.75 3.75

Elimination Matches, 1990 World Cup Soccer Championships — AP137

Various athletes and cities in Italy.

1989, June 15   Litho.   Perf. 13
C392 AP137 75fr Bari   .60 .30
C393 AP137 120fr Rome   1.00 .45
C394 AP137 500fr Florence   4.75 1.90
C395 AP137 550fr Naples   5.25 2.00
    Nos. C392-C395 (4)   11.60 4.65

PHILEXFRANCE '89 — AP138

Paintings: 300fr, Storming of the Bastille, July 14, 1789, from a gouache by J.P. Houel. 400fr, Eiffel Tower, by G. Seurat.

1989, June 22
C396 AP138 300fr multicolored   2.75 1.10
C397 AP138 400fr multicolored   3.75 1.50

French revolution, bicent. (300fr); Eiffel Tower, cent. (400fr).

First Moon Landing, 20th Anniv. AP139

Man's first step on the Moon: No. C398, Astronaut on ladder. No. C399, Conducting experiments on the Moon's surface.

1989, June 22
C398 AP139 400fr multicolored   3.75 1.50
C399 AP139 400fr multicolored   3.75 1.50

World Cup Soccer Championships, Italy — AP140

Various soccer plays and architecture.

1990, June 8   Litho.   Perf. 13
C400 AP140 120fr multicolored   1.00 .50
C401 AP140 240fr multicolored   2.10 .95
C402 AP140 500fr multicolored   4.25 2.00
C403 AP140 600fr multicolored   5.25 2.40
    Nos. C400-C403 (4)   12.60 5.85

Pan African Postal Union, 10th Anniv. AP141

1991, Jan. 10   Litho.   Perf. 13½
C404 AP141 60fr shown   .55 .25
C405 AP141 120fr Emblem   1.00 .50

1992 Winter Olympics, Albertville AP142

120fr, Ice hockey. 300fr, Speed skating. 1500fr, Slalom skiing.

1991, June 8   Litho.   Perf. 13½
C406 AP142 120fr multi   1.40 .60
C407 AP142 300fr multi   3.00 1.50

Litho. & Embossed
C408 AP142 1500fr multi   15.00 15.00

Numbers have been reserved for souvenir sheets in this set.

1992 Summer Olympics, Barcelona AP143

No. C411, Equestrian. No. C412, Long jump.

Litho. & Embossed
1992, Dec. 21   Perf. 13½
C411 AP143 1500fr gold & multi   16.00 16.00

Souvenir Sheet
C412 AP143 1500fr gold & multi   21.00 21.00

Anniversaries AP144

Designs: 90fr, Victor Schoelcher, missionary, death cent. 205fr, Martin Luther King, civil rights reformer, 25th death anniv. 300fr, Claude Chappe (1763-1805), bicent. of visual telegraph.

1993   Litho.   Perf. 14
C413 AP144 90fr multicolored   1.00 .50
C414 AP144 205fr multicolored   2.50 1.25
C415 AP144 300fr multicolored   3.50 1.75
    Nos. C413-C415 (3)   7.00 3.50

1994 Winter Olympics, Lillehammer AP145

400fr, Ice dancing. 600fr, Ice hockey. 750fr, Downhill skiing.

1993, Apr. 26   Litho.   Perf. 13
C416 AP145 400fr multicolored   4.00 1.40
C417 AP145 600fr multicolored   7.50 1.75

Souvenir Sheet
C418 AP145 750fr multicolored   8.00 4.00

Nos. C416-C417 exist in imperf. souvenir sheets of 1. Nos. C416-C418 exist imperf.

AIR POST SEMI-POSTAL STAMPS

Hathor Pillar — SPAP1

1964, Mar. 9   Unwmk.   Engr.   Perf. 13
CB1 SPAP1 10fr + 5fr vio & chnt   .90 .50
CB2 SPAP1 25fr + 5fr org brn & slate grn   1.10 .70
CB3 SPAP1 50fr + 5fr slate grn & brn red   2.25 1.60
    Nos. CB1-CB3 (3)   4.25 2.80

UNESCO world campaign to save historic monuments in Nubia.

POSTAGE DUE STAMPS

Messenger — D6

MH. 1521 Broussard Plane — D7

Early Transportation: 1fr, Litter. 2fr, Canoe. 5fr, Bicyclist. 10fr, Steam locomotive. 25fr, Seaplane.

1961, Dec. 4   Unwmk.   Engr.   Perf. 11
J34 D6 50c ultra, ol bis & red   .25 .25
  a. Pair, #J34, J40   .25
J35 D6 1fr red brn, red & grn   .25 .25
  a. Pair, #J35, J41   .30
J36 D6 2fr grn, ultra & brn   .25 .25
  a. Pair, #J36, J42   .40
J37 D6 5fr pur & gray brn   .25 .25
  a. Pair, #J37, J43   .50
J38 D6 10fr bl, grn & chocolate   .70 .70
  a. Pair, #J38, J44   1.40 1.40
J39 D6 25fr bl, dk grn & dk brn   1.60 1.60
  a. Pair, #J39, J45   3.25

Modern transportation: 1fr, Land Rover. 2fr, River boat transporting barge. 5fr, Trailer-truck. 10fr, Diesel locomotive. 25fr, Boeing 707 jet plane.

J40 D7 50c ultra, olive bis & red   .25 .25
J41 D7 1fr red & grn   .25 .25
J42 D7 2fr ultra, grn & brn   .25 .25
J43 D7 5fr pur & gray brn   .25 .25
J44 D7 10fr dk grn & chocolate   .70 .70
J45 D7 25fr bl, dk grn & sepia   1.60 1.60
    Nos. J34-J45 (12)   6.60 6.60

Pairs printed tête bêche, se-tenant at the base.

Flowers — D8

Flowers: 2fr, Phaeomeria magnifica. 5fr, Millettia laurentii. 10fr, Tuberose. 15fr, Pyrostegia venusta. 20fr, Hibiscus.

1971, Mar. 25   Photo.   Perf. 12x12½
J46 D8 1fr multi   .35 .35
J47 D8 2fr multi   .45 .45
J48 D8 5fr pink & multi   .55 .55
J49 D8 10fr dk grn & multi   .70 .70
J50 D8 15fr multi   1.10 1.10
J51 D8 20fr multi   1.40 1.40
    Nos. J46-J51 (6)   4.55 4.55

Flowers and Fruit — D9

5fr, Passiflora quadrangulares. 10fr, Cannaceae, vert. 15fr, Ananas comosus, vert.

1986, June 5   Litho.   Perf. 13

J52	D9	5fr multicolored	.25	.25
J53	D9	10fr multicolored	.45	.45
J54	D9	15fr multicolored	.55	.55
		Nos. J52-J54 (3)	1.25	1.25

OFFICIAL STAMPS

Coat of Arms — O1

Perf. 14x13

			Unwmk.	Typo.
1968-70				
O1	O1	1fr multi ('70)	.25	.25
O2	O1	2fr multi ('70)	.25	.25
O3	O1	5fr multi ('70)	.25	.25
O4	O1	10fr multi ('70)	.25	.25
O5	O1	25fr emer & multi	.45	.25
O6	O1	30fr red & multi	.60	.25
O7	O1	50fr multi ('70)	1.10	.50
O8	O1	85fr multi ('70)	2.25	.90
O9	O1	100fr multi ('70)	2.75	1.10
O10	O1	200fr multi ('70)	3.75	2.00
		Nos. O1-O10 (10)	11.90	6.00

COOK ISLANDS

ˈkuk ˈī-ləndz

(Rarotonga)

LOCATION — South Pacific Ocean, northeast of New Zealand
GOVT. — Internal self-government, linked to New Zealand
AREA — 91 sq. mi.
POP. — 19,103 (1996)
CAPITAL — Avarua

Fifteen islands in Northern and Southern groups extend over 850,000 square miles of ocean.

Separate stamp issues used by Aitutaki (1903-32 and 1972 onward) and Penrhyn Islands (1902-32 and 1973 onward). Niue is included geographically, but administered separately. It continues to issue separate stamps.

12 Pence = 1 Shilling
20 Shillings = 1 Pound
100 Cents = 1 Dollar (1967)

Catalogue values for unused stamps in this country are for Never Hinged items, beginning with Scott 127 in the regular postage section, Scott B1 in the semipostal section, Scott C1 in the air post section, Scott CB1 in the air post semi-postal section and Scott O16 in the official section.

For more detailed listings for classic issues of Cook Islands, see the Scott *Classic Specialized Catalogue of Stamps and Covers 1840-1940.*

Watermarks

Wmk. 61 — Single-lined N Z and Star Close Together

Wmk. 62 — Single-lined N Z and Star Wide Apart

Wmk. 253 — Multiple N Z and Star

A1

1892   Unwmk.   Typo.   Perf. 12½
Toned Paper

1	A1	1p black	35.00	30.00
2	A1	1½p violet	50.00	45.00
a.		Imperf. pair	19,000.	
3	A1	2½p blue	47.50	45.00
4	A1	10p carmine	160.00	150.00
		Nos. 1-4 (4)	292.50	270.00

White Paper

5	A1	1p black	35.00	30.00
a.		Vert. pair, imperf. between	11,000.	
6	A1	1½p violet	50.00	45.00
7	A1	2½p blue	47.50	45.00
8	A1	10p carmine	160.00	150.00
		Nos. 5-8 (4)	292.50	270.00

Nos. 1-8 were printed in sheets of 60 (6x10), from a setting of six slightly different cliches.

Queen Makea Takau — A2

1893-94   Wmk. 62   Perf. 12x11½

9	A2	1p brown	50.00	55.00
10	A2	1p blue ('94)	13.00	2.50
11	A2	1½p brt violet	19.00	8.50
12	A2	2½p rose	55.00	27.50
13	A2	5p olive gray	24.00	16.00
14	A2	10p green	85.00	57.50
		Nos. 9-14 (6)	246.00	167.00

Wrybill (Torea) — A3

1898-1900   Perf. 11

15	A3	½p blue ('00)	6.50	15.00
a.		"d" omitted at upper right	1,750.	
16	A2	1p brown	32.50	21.00
17	A2	1p blue	6.00	5.50
18	A2	1½p violet	19.00	7.50
19	A3	2p chocolate ('00)	15.00	8.50
20	A2	2½p car rose ('00)	25.00	13.00
21	A2	5p olive gray	30.00	21.00
22	A3	6p red violet ('00)	24.00	29.00
23	A2	10p green	26.00	57.50
24	A3	1sh car rose ('00)	57.50	57.50
		Nos. 15-24 (10)	241.50	235.50

No. 17 Surcharged in Black

1899

25	A2	½p on 1p blue	40.00	50.00
a.		Double surcharge	1,000.	1,200.
b.		Inverted surcharge	1,200.	1,100.

No. 16 Overprinted in Black

1901

26	A2	1p brown	210.00	160.00
a.		Inverted overprint	2,400.	1,900.
c.		Double overprint	1,900.	1,900.

Some single stamps were overprinted by favor. Other varieties could exist. Forgeries exist.

Types of 1893-98

1902   Unwmk.

27	A3	½p green	10.00	10.00
a.		Vert. pair, imperf. horiz.	1,400.	
28	A2	1p rose	16.00	21.00
29	A2	2½p dull blue	15.00	25.00
		Nos. 27-29 (3)	41.00	56.00

1902   Wmk. 61   Perf. 11

30	A3	½p green	4.25	3.75
31	A2	1p rose	4.75	3.50
32	A2	1½p brt violet	4.75	10.00
33	A3	2p chocolate	11.00	12.00
a.		Figures of value omitted	2,750.	3,600.
b.		Perf. 11x14	2,600.	
34	A2	2½p dull blue	4.50	8.25
35	A2	5p olive gray	42.50	57.50
36	A3	6p purple	37.50	32.50
37	A2	10p blue green	55.00	120.00
38	A3	1sh car rose	55.00	82.50
a.		Perf. 11x14	3,000.	
		Nos. 30-38 (9)	219.25	330.00

1909-19   Perf. 14, 14x14½, 14½x14

39	A3	½p green, perf 14½x14 ('11)	13.00	9.50
a.		½p dp grn, perf 14 ('15)	42.50	17.50
b.		As "a," wmk upright	14.00	22.50
40	A2	1p red, wmk. sideways ('09)	15.00	5.00
41	A2	1½p purple, perf 14x15 ('16)	21.00	4.75
42	A3	2p dp brown ('19)	6.00	57.50
43	A2	10p dp green ('18)	40.00	110.00
44	A3	1sh car rose ('19)	32.50	110.00
		Nos. 39-44 (6)	127.50	296.75

Nos. 39-40 are on both ordinary and chalky paper; Nos. 41-44 on chalky paper.

New Zealand Stamps of 1909-19 Surcharged in Dark Blue or Red

1919   Typo.   Perf. 14x15

48	A43	½p yel green (R)	.45	1.25
a.		Pair, one without surcharge		
49	A42	1p carmine	1.25	5.00
50	A47	1p brown org (R)	.60	.90
51	A43	2p yellow (R)	1.75	2.00
52	A43	3p chocolate	3.25	15.00

Engr.   Perf. 14x14½

53	A44	2½p dull blue (R)	2.75	2.50
54	A45	3p violet brown	3.00	2.00
55	A45	4p purple	2.25	4.25
56	A44	4½p dark green	2.25	9.50
57	A45	6p car rose	2.00	5.50
58	A44	7½p red brown, perf 14x13½	2.10	6.50
59	A44	9p ol green (R)	3.75	17.50
60	A45	1sh vermilion	3.25	30.00
		Nos. 48-60 (13)	28.65	101.90

The Polynesian surcharge restates the denomination of the basic stamp.

Landing of Capt. Cook A4

Avarua Waterfront A5

Capt. James Cook — A6

Palm — A7

Houses at Arorangi — A8

Avarua Harbor — A9

1920   Unwmk.   Engr.   Perf. 14

61	A4	½p green & black	4.75	30.00
62	A5	1p car & black	5.50	30.00
a.		Center inverted	875.00	
63	A6	1½p blue & black	10.00	10.00
64	A7	3p red brn & blk	2.50	6.50
65	A8	6p org & red brn	4.25	10.00
66	A9	1sh vio & black	8.00	20.00
a.		Center inverted	875.00	
		Nos. 61-66 (6)	35.00	106.50

The stamps overprinted or inscribed "Rarotonga" were used throughout the Cook Islands.

For surcharges see Nos. 78, 79.

New Zealand Postal-Fiscal Stamps of 1906-13 Overprinted in Red or Dark Blue — a

Perf. 14, 14½, 14x14½

			Typo.	Wmk. 61
1921				
67	PF1	2sh blue (R)	32.50	65.00
68	PF1	2sh6p brown	22.50	60.00
69	PF1	5sh green (R)	32.50	77.50
70	PF1	10sh claret	90.00	140.00
71	PF2	£1 rose	150.00	260.00
		Nos. 67-71 (5)	327.50	602.50

Types of 1920 Issue

1924-26   Engr.   Perf. 14

72	A4	½p yel grn & black	5.25	10.00
73	A5	1p carmine & black	7.00	2.50

Issued: ½p, May 13, 1926; 1p, Nov. 10, 1924.

New Zealand Stamps of 1926 Overprinted in Red

1926-28   Typo.   Perf. 14, 14½x14

74	A56	2sh blue ('27)	19.00	47.50
a.		2sh dark blue	12.00	47.50
75	A56	3sh violet ('28)	19.00	50.00

Rarotongan Chief (Te Po) — A10

Avarua Harbor — A11

1927, Oct. 15   Engr.   Perf. 14

76	A10	2½p dk bl & red brn	8.00	29.00
77	A11	4p dull vio & bl grn	13.00	20.00

No. 63 Surcharged in Red

1931 — Unwmk.

78	A6	2p on 1½p blue & blk	11.00	4.75

Same Surcharge on Type of 1920
Wmk. 61

79	A6	2p on 1½p blue & blk	5.50	13.00

No. 79 was not issued without surcharge.

New Zealand Postal-Fiscal Stamps of 1931-32 Overprinted Type "a" in Blue or Red

1931, Nov. 12 — Typo.

80	PF5	2sh6p dp brown (Bl)	16.00	26.00
81	PF5	5sh green (R)	27.50	65.00
82	PF5	10sh dk car (Bl)	45.00	110.00
83	PF5	£1 pink (Bl) ('32)	125.00	200.00
		Nos. 80-83 (4)	213.50	401.00

See Nos. 103-108, 124A-126C.

Landing of Capt. Cook — A12

Capt. James Cook — A13

Double Canoe — A14

Islanders Unloading Ship — A15

View of Avarua Harbor — A16

R.M.S. Monowai — A17

King George V — A18

Unwmk.
1932, Mar. 16 — Engr. — Perf. 13
Center in Black

84	A12	½p deep green	4.00	19.00
a.		Perf. 14	32.50	105.00
85	A13	1p brown lake	7.75	5.25
a.		Center inverted	9,500.	9,500.
b.		Perf. 14	17.50	32.50
86	A14	2p brown	3.50	8.75
a.		Perf. 14	10.00	24.00
87	A15	2½p dark ultra	27.50	70.00
b.		Perf. 14	20.00	65.00

Perf. 14

88	A16	4p ultra	12.00	65.00
a.		Perf. 13	32.50	75.00
b.		Perf. 14x13	35.00	130.00
89	A17	6p orange	5.00	17.50
a.		Perf. 13	30.00	57.50
90	A18	1sh deep violet	24.00	26.00
		Nos. 84-90 (7)	83.75	211.50

Nos. 84 to 90 were available for postage in Aitutaki, Penrhyn and Rarotonga and replaced the special issues for those islands.

Inverted centers of the ½p (value $1,000), 1p (value $550), and 2p (value $3,500) are from printers waste.

1933-36 — Wmk. 61 — Perf. 14

91	A12	½p dp grn & blk	1.20	5.25
92	A13	1p dk car & black ('35)	1.50	2.40
93	A14	2p brn & blk ('36)	1.75	.60
94	A15	2½p dk ultra & blk	1.75	2.50
95	A16	4p blue & black	1.75	.60
96	A17	6p org & blk ('36)	2.00	2.50
97	A18	1sh dp vio & black ('36)	27.50	42.50
		Nos. 91-97 (7)	37.45	56.35

See Nos. 116-121.

Silver Jubilee Issue

Types of 1932 Overprinted in Black or Red

Perf. 13½x14
1935, May 7

98	A13	1p dk car & brn red	.65	1.50
99	A15	2½p dk ultra & bl (R)	2.00	3.50
100	A17	6p dull org & green	7.00	7.00
		Nos. 98-100 (3)	9.65	12.00
		Set, never hinged	16.00	

The vertical spacing of the overprint is wider on No. 100.

New Zealand Stamps of 1926 Overprinted in Black — b

1936, July 15 — Typo. — Perf. 14

101	A56	2sh blue	15.00	50.00
102	A56	3sh violet	16.00	80.00

1931-35 New Zealand Postal-Fiscal Stamps Ovptd. Type "b" in Black or Red

1932-36

103	PF5	2sh6p brown ('36)	47.50	110.00
104	PF5	5sh grn (R) ('36)	52.50	130.00
105	PF5	10sh dk car ('36)	92.50	250.00
106	PF5	£1 pink ('36)	125.00	275.00
107	PF5	£3 lt grn (R)	500.00	900.00
108	PF5	£5 dk blue (R)	250.00	400.00
		Nos. 103-108 (6)	1,068.	2,065.

Issue dates: Mar. 1932, July 15, 1936.

New Zealand Stamps of 1937 Overprinted in Black

Perf. 14x13½
1937, June 1 — Engr. — Wmk. 253

109	A78	1p rose carmine	.25	.25
110	A78	2½p dark blue	.25	.25
111	A78	6p vermilion	.35	.30
		Nos. 109-111 (3)	.85	.80
		Set, never hinged	2.25	

King George VI A19

Village and Palms A20

Coastal Scene with Canoe — A21

1938, May 2 — Wmk. 61 — Perf. 14

112	A19	1sh dp violet & blk	6.00	13.00
113	A20	2sh dk red brn & blk	12.00	16.00
114	A21	3sh yel green & blue	32.50	40.00
		Nos. 112-114 (3)	50.50	69.00
		Set, never hinged	90.00	

See Nos. 122-124.

Mt. Ikurangi behind Avarua — A22

1940, Sept. 2 — Engr. — Wmk. 253

115	A22	3p on 1½p violet & blk	.80	.70

Issued only with surcharge. Stamps without surcharge are from the printer's archives. Value $275.

Types of 1932-38

Engr. — Perf. 14
1944-46

116	A12	½p dk ol grn & blk ('45)	1.00	4.50
117	A13	1p dk car & blk ('45)	1.50	1.25
118	A14	2p brn & blk ('46)	.90	7.00
119	A15	2½p dk bl & blk ('45)	.60	2.00
120	A16	4p blue & black	2.50	15.00
121	A17	6p org & black	1.00	2.50
122	A19	1sh dp vio & blk	1.00	3.50
123	A20	2sh dk red brn & blk	27.50	50.00
124	A21	3sh yel green & blue ('45)	25.00	40.00
		Nos. 116-124 (9)	61.00	125.75
		Set, never hinged	100.00	

New Zealand Nos. AR76, AR78, AR86 and Type of 1931 Postal-Fiscal Stamps Overprinted Type "b" in Black or Red

1943-50 — Wmk. 253 — Typo. — Perf. 14

124A	PF5	2sh6p brn ('51)	37.50	37.50
125	PF5	5sh green (R)	8.25	37.50
126	PF5	10sh dp pink ('51)	42.50	100.00
126A	PF5	£1 pink ('54)	42.50	110.00
126B	PF5	£3 lt grn (R) ('53)	40.00	175.00
126C	PF5	£5 dk bl (R) ('54)	200.00	400.00
		Nos. 124A-126C (6)	370.75	860.00

Values for Nos. 124A-126C are for the second printing with watermarks inverted.

Set, never hinged 550.00

For surcharges see Nos. 192-194.

> **Catalogue values for unused stamps in this section, from this point to the end of the section, are for Never Hinged items.**

Peace Issue
New Zealand Nos. 248, 250, 254 and 255 Overprinted in Black or Blue

c

d

Perf. 13x13½, 13½x13
1946, June 1 — Engr.

127	A94 (c)	1p emerald	.30	.25
128	A96 (d)	2p rose vio (Bl)	.35	.35
129	A100(c)	6p org red & red brn	.80	.70
130	A101(c)	8p brn lake & blk (Bl)	.55	.55
		Nos. 127-130 (4)	2.00	1.85

Ngatangiia Channel, Rarotonga A23

Capt. James Cook Statue and Map of Cook Islands — A24

Designs: 1p, Cook and map of Hervey Isls. 2p, Rev. John Williams, his ship Messenger of Peace, and map of Rarotonga. 3p, Aitutaki map and palms. 5p, Mail plane landing at Rarotonga airport. 6p, Tongareva (Penrhyn) scene. 8p, Islander's house, Rarotonga. 2sh, Thatched house, mat weaver. 3sh, Steamer Matua offshore.

Perf. 13½x13, 13x13½
1949, Aug.1 — Engr. — Wmk. 253

131	A23	½p brown & violet	.25	1.25
132	A23	1p green & orange	3.00	3.00
133	A23	2p carmine & brn	1.75	3.00
134	A23	3p ultra & green	4.50	1.75
135	A23	5p purple & grn	5.00	1.25
136	A23	6p car rose & blk	5.25	2.25
137	A23	8p orange & olive	.65	2.25
138	A24	1sh chocolate & bl	3.50	3.00
139	A24	2sh rose car & brn	5.00	11.00
140	A24	3sh bl grn & lt ultra	17.50	27.50
		Nos. 131-140 (10)	46.40	56.25

For surcharge see No. 147.

Coronation Issue
Type of New Zealand

1953, May 25 — Photo. — Perf. 14x14½

145	A113	3p brown	1.25	1.25
146	A114	6p slate black	1.40	1.40

No. 135 Surcharged in Black

1960, Apr. 1 — Engr. — Perf. 13½x13

147	A23	1sh6p on 5p purple & grn	.70	.55

Tiare Maori — A25

Fishing God — A26

Frangipani — A26a

Fairy Tern — A26b

Hibiscus — A26c

Bonito — A26d

Oranges — A26e

Queen Elizabeth II — A27

Island Scene
A28

Administration building, Mangaia —
A28a

Ship in Rarotonga Harbor — A28b

Perf. 13½x13, 13x13½
Litho.; Engr.; (1sh6p)
1963, June 4

148	A25	1p multicolored	.60	.70
149	A26	2p multicolored	.25	.65
150	A26a	3p multicolored	.55	.55
151	A26b	5p multicolored	6.25	2.00
152	A26c	6p multicolored	.80	.60
153	A26d	8p blue & dark blue	3.50	1.40
154	A26e	1sh orange & green	.80	.75
155	A27	1sh6p violet	2.25	2.00
156	A28	2sh gray & brown	1.60	1.25
157	A28a	3sh emer & black	1.60	1.90
158	A28b	5sh ultra & brown	13.00	5.25
		Nos. 148-158 (11)	31.20	17.05

For overprints and surcharges see Nos. 167-169, 179-181, 183-184, 186-190.

Solar Eclipse and Palm Tree — A29

1965, May 31 Litho.   Perf. 13x13½

159	A29	6p black, lt blue & yel	.30 .30

Observation of the solar eclipse on Manuae Island, May 30, 1965. Exists imperf.
For surcharge see No. 185.

Flag of New Zealand and Map of Cook Islands
A30

Designs: 10p, London Missionary Society Church and graveyard. 1sh, Reading of Proclamation of Cession, Oct. 8, 1900, and Queen Elizabeth II. 1sh9p, Nikao School and flag of New Zealand.

Perf. 13½x13
1965, Sept. 16 Litho.   Wmk. 253

160	A30	4p blue & red	.25 .25
161	A30	10p multicolored	.25 .25
162	A30	1sh multicolored	.25 .25
163	A30	1sh9p multicolored	.45 .45
		Nos. 160-163 (4)	1.20 1.20

Establishment of internal self-government.
For surcharges see Nos. 182, 191.

**Nos. 160-162 and 156-158
Overprinted in Red**

1966, Jan. 24   Litho.   Wmk. 253

164	A30	4p blue & red	1.10 .30
165	A30	10p multicolored	2.00 .50
a.		Inverted overprint	275.00
166	A30	1sh multicolored	2.00 .85
a.		Inverted overprint	200.00
167	A28	2sh gray & brown	2.00 1.25
168	A28	3sh emer & black	2.00 1.25
169	A28	5sh ultra & brown	2.25 1.75
		Nos. 164-169 (6)	11.35 5.90

Statesman and WWII leader.
Lower case "l" instead of "1" in "1874" in overprint exists on all. Value set, $70.

Adoration of the Wise Men, by Fra Angelico — A31

Paintings: 2p, Nativity, by Hans Memling, vert. 4p, Adoration of the Wise Men, by Velazquez. 10p, Adoration of the Wise Men, by Hieronymus Bosch. 1sh6p, Adoration of the Shepherds, by Jose Ribera, vert.

Perf. 13x14½, 14½x13
1966, Nov. 28   Photo.   Unwmk.

170	A31	1p multicolored	.25 .25
171	A31	2p multicolored	.25 .25
172	A31	4p multicolored	.25 .25
173	A31	10p multicolored	.30 .30
174	A31	1sh6p multicolored	.40 .40
		Nos. 170-174 (5)	1.45 1.45

Christmas. Issued in sheets of 6 with ornamental gold border.

Perf. 13x12, 12x13

170a	A31	1p	.50 .85
171a	A31	2p	16.00 14.00
172a	A31	4p	1.25 1.25
173a	A31	10p	2.75 6.00
174a	A31	1sh6p	42.50 8.50
		Nos. 170a-174a (5)	63.00 30.60

Tennis and Queen Elizabeth
A32

Sport: 1p, Women's basketball and Games' emblem. 4p, Boxing and team emblem. 7p, Soccer and Queen Elizabeth II.

1967, Jan. 12   Perf. 13½

175	A32	½p brt olive & multi	.25 .25
176	A32	1p brt blue & multi	.25 .25
177	A32	4p purple & multi	.25 .25
178	A32	7p red & multi	.25 .25
		Nos. 175-178, C10-C11 (6)	1.50 1.50

Second South Pacific Games, Noumea, New Caledonia, Dec. 8-18, 1966.

Nos. 148-155, 157-161 Surcharged with New Value or Black or Red

Pair (#181b), with Type I on left (#181) and Type II on right (#181a)

1967

179	A25	1c on 1p	.35 1.75
180	A26	2c on 2p	.25 .25
181	A25	2½c on 3p (I)	.25 .25
a.		Type II	.25 .25
b.		Pair, #181 and #181a	.35 .45

182	A30	3c on 4p	.25 .25
183	A26	4c on 5p	7.25 .40
184	A25	5c on 6p	.25 .25
185	A29	5c on 6p	4.00 1.25
186	A26	7c on 8p	.25 .25
187	A26	10c on 1sh	.25 .25
188	A27	15c on 1sh6p (R)	1.60 1.10
189	A28	30c on 3sh (R)	22.50 7.00
190	A28	50c on 5sh (R)	3.25 2.00
191	A30	$1 on 10p (R)	14.50 5.50
		Nos. 179-191 (13)	54.95 20.50

Issued: 2c, 2½c, 3c, 5c, 7c, 10c, 4/3; others 5/4.
No. 191 is surcharged "10/ $1.00" and 3 bars over old value.
Numerous varieties of surcharge include wrong-font "c," thin numerals, etc.

**Nos. 126A, 126B and 126C
Surcharged in Red
Wmk. 253**

Stamp of 1892, Village and Queen Victoria
A33

1967, June 6   Typo.   Perf. 14

192	PF5	$2 on £1 pink	70.00 100.00
193	PF5	$6 on £3 lt green	175.00 200.00
194	PF5	$10 on £5 dk blue	200.00 225.00
		Nos. 192-194 (3)	445.00 525.00

Frequently found with stained gum.

Designs: 3c (4p), PO, Rarotonga, and Elizabeth II. 8c (10p), View of Avarua, Rarotonga, and 10p stamp of 1892. 18c (1sh9p), Map of Cook Islands, DC-3, S.S. Moana Roa and Capt. Cook.

Perf. 13½
1967, July 3   Photo.   Unwmk.

195	A33	1c (1p) multi	.25 .25
196	A33	3c (4p) multi	.25 .25
197	A33	8c (10p) multi	.30 .30
198	A33	18c (1sh9p) multi	1.10 .80
a.		Souvenir sheet of 4, #195-198	2.75 2.75
		Nos. 195-198 (4)	1.90 1.60

75th anniv. of the 1st Cook Islands stamps. Issued in sheets of 8 stamps and 1 label with inscription in yellow margin.

Hibiscus — A34

Elizabeth II
A35

Elizabeth II and Flowers — A36

Flowers: 1c, Rose of Sharon. 2c, 15c, Frangipani. 2½c, Butterfly pea. 3c, Suva queen and Queen Elizabeth II. 4c, Water lily. 5c, Bauhania. 6c, Yellow hibiscus. 8c, Alamanda and Queen Elizabeth II. 9c, Stephanotis. 10c, Flamboyant poinciana. 20c, Thunbergia. 25c, Canna lily and Queen Elizabeth II. 30c, Poinsettia. 50c, Gardenia.
The $4 exists with "FOUR DOLLARS" in two widths: type 1, 32½mm; type 2, 33½mm.

1967-69   Photo.   Perf. 14x13½

199	A34	½c gold & multi	.30 .25
200	A34	1c gold & multi	.30 .25
201	A34	2c gold & multi	.30 .25
202	A34	2½c gold & multi	.55 .25
203	A34	3c gold & multi	.60 .25
204	A34	4c *Walter Lily*	.90 1.25
205	A34	4c *Water Lily*	2.25 2.00
206	A34	5c gold & multi	.40 .25
207	A34	6c gold & multi	.45 .25
208	A34	8c gold & multi	.45 .25
209	A34	9c gold & multi	.45 .25
210	A34	10c gold & multi	.45 .25
211	A34	15c gold & multi	.45 .25
212	A34	20c gold & multi	5.00 1.50
213	A34	25c gold & multi	.90 .45
214	A34	30c gold & multi	.75 .55
215	A34	50c gold & multi	1.10 .55
216	A35	$1 gold & multi	2.40 .60
217	A35	$2 gold & multi	5.50 .90
218	A36	$4 multi, type 2 ('68)	2.25 4.00
a.		Type 1	40.00 55.00
219	A36	$6 multi ('68)	2.25 5.00
219A	A36	$8 multi ('69)	6.25 12.00
220	A36	$10 multi ('68)	4.25 11.00
		Nos. 199-220 (23)	38.50 42.55

Nos. 199-220 (except No. 204) were reprinted in 1970/71 with the fluorescent printing described below. Value, set: unused $60; used $40.
For surcharges see Nos. 290-291, 305-309, B1-B13, B17-B18, B20. For overprints see Nos. 277-283, 302-304, 315, 351-356, O1-O15.

Fluorescence

Since 1968 a number of stamps have been issued with a "fluorescent security underprinting" in a multiple coat of arms pattern. Some issues have this underprint, some do not.
Stamps issued both with and without the underprint are Nos. 199-203, 205-220, 283, 290-291.
From Nos. 292-296 onward, all stamps have this underprint unless otherwise noted.

Ia Orana Maria, by Gauguin
A37

Gauguin Paintings: 3c, Riders on the Beach. 5c, Still Life with Flowers. 8c, Whispered Words. 15c, Maternity. 22c, Why Are You Angry?

1967, Oct. 23   Photo.   Perf. 13½

221	A37	1c gold & multi	.25 .25
222	A37	3c gold & multi	.25 .25
223	A37	5c gold & multi	.25 .25
224	A37	8c gold & multi	.25 .25
225	A37	15c gold & multi	.30 .25
226	A37	22c gold & multi	.40 .40
a.		Souvenir sheet of 6, #221-226	2.75 2.75
		Nos. 221-226 (6)	1.70 1.65

Nos. 221-226 are printed in sheets of 6 (3x2).
For surcharge see No. B3.

Holy Family by Rubens — A38

Paintings: 3c, Adoration of the Magi, by Albrecht Durer. 4c, The Lucca Madonna, by Jan Van Eyck. 8c, Adoration of the Shepherds, by Jacopo da Bassano. 15c, Nativity, by El Greco. 25c, Madonna and Child, by Antonio Allegri da Correggio.

1967, Dec. 4   **Perf. 12x13**

227	A38	1c gold & multi	.25	.25
228	A38	3c gold & multi	.25	.25
229	A38	4c gold & multi	.25	.25
230	A38	8c gold & multi	.25	.25
231	A38	15c gold & multi	.25	.25
232	A38	25c gold & multi	.30	.30
		Nos. 227-232 (6)	1.55	1.55

Christmas.

Capt. Cook and
Matavai Bay,
Tahiti, by
Sydney
Parkinson
A39

1c, Ships off Huahine Island, Tahiti, by John & James Clevely. 2c, town & harbor of Kamchatka, by John Webber, & Queen Elizabeth II. 4c, "The Ice Islands" (Antarctica), by William Hodges.

1968, Sept. 12   **Photo.**   **Perf. 13**

233	A39	½c gold & multi	.25	.25
234	A39	1c gold & multi	.25	.25
235	A39	2c gold & multi	.25	.25
236	A39	4c gold & multi	.25	.25
		Nos. 233-236,C12-C15 (8)	3.20	3.20

Bicent. of Capt. Cook's 1st voyage of discovery. Printed in sheets of 10 stamps and 2 labels (3x4). Labels show portraits of Elizabeth II and Cook.

Gymnast
A40

1968, Oct. 21

237	A40	1c Sailing	.25	.25
238	A40	5c shown	.25	.25
239	A40	15c High jump	.25	.25
240	A40	20c Woman diver	.30	.25
241	A40	30c Bicyclist	.55	.25
242	A40	50c Woman hurdler	.45	.30
		Nos. 237-242 (6)	2.05	1.55

19th Olympic Games, Mexico City, Oct. 12-27. Printed in sheets of 10 stamps and 2 labels (3x4).

Virgin and Child,
by Titian — A41

Paintings: 4c, Holy Family, by Raphael. 10c, Madonna of the Rosary, by Murillo. 20c, Adoration of the Magi, by Memling. 30c, Adoration of the Magi, by Ghirlandajo.

1968, Dec. 2   **Photo.**   **Perf. 13**

243	A41	1c gold & multi	.25	.25
244	A41	4c gold & multi	.25	.25
245	A41	10c gold & multi	.25	.25
246	A41	20c gold & multi	.25	.25
247	A41	30c gold & multi	.30	.30
a.		Souv. sheet, #243-247 + label	1.75	1.75
		Nos. 243-247 (5)	1.30	1.30

Issued in sheets of 6 (2x3).

Training
on
Ropeway
A42

Designs: ½c, Boy Scouts cooking over campfire. 5c, Training with signal flags, and Queen Elizabeth II. 10c, Planting a tree. 20c, Erecting a hut. 30c, Lord Baden-Powell, lake and mountains (visit to Rarotonga in 1935).

1969, Feb. 6   **Photo.**   **Perf. 13½**

248	A42	½c multicolored	.25	.25
249	A42	1c multicolored	.25	.25
250	A42	5c multicolored	.25	.25
251	A42	10c multicolored	.25	.25
252	A42	20c multicolored	.25	.25
253	A42	30c multicolored	.35	.35
		Nos. 248-253 (6)	1.60	1.60

5th Natl. Boy Scout Jamboree, Christchurch, New Zealand, Jan. 2-12.
Issued in sheets of 10 stamps and 2 labels (4x3).

A43

No. 254a, Soccer. No. 254b, Pole vault. No. 255a, Weight lifting. No. 255b, Basketball, Elizabeth II. No. 256a, Long jump. No. 256b, Tennis. No. 257a, Running. No. 257b, Javelin, Elizabeth II. No. 258a, Boxing. No. 258b, Golf.

       Perf. 13½x13

1969, July 7   **Photo.**   **Unwmk.**

254	A43	½c Pair, #a.-b.	.40	.40
255	A43	1c Pair, #a.-b.	.40	.40
256	A43	4c Pair, #a.-b.	1.20	1.20
257	A43	10c Pair, #a.-b.	1.60	1.60
258	A43	15c Pair, #a.-b.	3.00	3.00
c.		Souv. sheet, #254-258 + 2 labels	7.75	7.50
		Nos. 254-258 (5)	6.60	6.60

3rd South Pacifc Games, Port Moresby, Papua and New Guinea, Aug. 13-23.
Issued in sheets of 10.

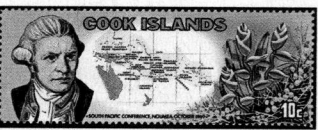

Map of Cook Islands and Capt.
Cook — A44

Map of Cook Islands and: 5c, Premier Albert Henry of Cook Islands. 25c, Coat of arms of New Zealand. 30c, Queen Elizabeth II.

1969, Oct. 8   **Photo.**   **Perf. 13**

264	A44	5c red & multi	.35	.35
265	A44	10c lemon & multi	1.00	.50
266	A44	25c green & multi	.50	.50
267	A44	30c blue & multi	.50	.50
		Nos. 264-267 (4)	2.35	1.85

South Pacific Conf., Noumea, Oct. 1969.

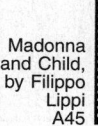

Madonna
and Child,
by Filippo
Lippi
A45

Paintings: 4c, Holy Family, by Baccio della Porta. 10c, Madonna and Child, by Anton Raphael Mengs. 20c, Madonna and Child, by Le Maitre de Flemalle. 30c, Madonna and Child by Correggio.

1969, Nov. 21   **Photo.**   **Perf. 13½**

268	A45	1c buff & multi	.25	.25
269	A45	4c buff & multi	.25	.25
270	A45	10c buff & multi	.25	.25
271	A45	20c buff & multi	.25	.25

272	A45	30c buff & multi	.25	.25
a.		Souv. sheet, #268-272 + label	1.50	1.50
		Nos. 268-272 (5)	1.25	1.25

Issued in sheets of 8 stamps, one label with portrait of Queen Elizabeth II.

Resurrection of
Christ, by
Raphael — A46

The Resurrection of Christ by: 8c, Dirk Bouts. 20c, Albert Altdorfer, 25c, Murillo.

1970, Mar. 12   **Photo.**   **Perf. 13½**
      Size: 25½x56mm

273	A46	4c gold & multi	.25	.25
274	A46	8c gold & multi	.25	.25
275	A46	20c gold & multi	.25	.25
276	A46	25c gold & multi	.25	.25
a.		Souv. sheet, #273-276 + 2 labels	1.40	1.40
		Nos. 273-276 (4)	1.00	1.00

Easter 1970.
Printed in sheets of 8 stamps and a label (3x3) showing portrait of Queen Elizabeth II and name of painting and painter.
See Nos. 316-318.

Nos. 205, 208,
211-212, 214,
217 Overprinted

1970, Apr.   **Perf. 14x13½**

277	A34	4c gold & multi	.30	.30
278	A34	8c gold & multi	.30	.30
279	A34	15c gold & multi	.30	.30
280	A34	20c gold & multi	.40	.40
281	A34	30c gold & multi	.30	.30
282	A35	$2 gold & multi	1.25	1.25

**No. 218 Overprinted: "KIA ORANA /
APOLLO 13 /ASTRONAUTS"**

283	A36	$4 gold & multi	2.50	2.50
		Nos. 277-283 (7)	5.35	5.35

Splashdown of Apollo 13 west of Rarotonga, Apr. 17, 1970.
Issued: Nos. 277-282, 4/17; $4, 4/30.
Values for No. 283 is for stamps with fluorescence.
Stamps without fluorescence: Value, mint $32.50, used $50.

Queen Elizabeth II, Prince Philip,
Princess Anne and Prince
Charles — A47

Design: 30c, Wedgwood bust of Capt. Cook and "Endeavour." $1, Royal visit commemorative coin, obverse and reverse.

1970, June 12   **Photo.**   **Perf. 13½**

284	A47	5c gold & multi	.90	.30
285	A47	30c gold & multi	2.25	1.50
286	A47	$1 gold & multi	3.00	3.00
a.		Souv. sheet, #284-286 + label	9.75	9.75
		Nos. 284-286 (3)	6.15	4.80

Visit of the British royal family.

**Nos. 284-286 Overprinted in Silver
or Black: "Fifth Anniversary Self-
Government August 1970"**

1970, Aug. 27   **Photo.**   **Perf. 13½**

287	A47	5c gold & multi (S)	.60	.25
288	A47	30c gold & multi	1.10	.50
289	A47	$1 gold & multi	1.50	1.25
		Nos. 287-289 (3)	3.20	2.00

5th anniv. of self-government. The overprint on No. 287 is arranged in one line around 3 sides of the design; the overprint on Nos. 288-289 is in 3 horizontal lines.

Nos. 219A-220 Surcharged

1970, Nov. 11   **Photo.**   **Perf. 14x13½**

290	A36	$4 on $8 gold & multi	3.50	3.50
291	A36	$4 on $10 multi	2.50	2.50

In each sheet of 15, 3 stamps have 2 surcharged bars instead of one.
Nos. 290-291 without fluorescence: Value, mint $70, used $85.

Nativity
A48

Illuminations from 14th Century Robert de Lisle Psalter: 4c, Angel and shepherds. 10c, The Circumcision. 20c, The Adoration of the Kings. 30c, The Presentation at the Temple.

1970, Nov. 30   **Photo.**   **Perf. 13½**

292	A48	1c gold & multi	.25	.25
293	A48	4c gold & multi	.25	.25
294	A48	10c gold & multi	.25	.25
295	A48	20c gold & multi	.25	.25
296	A48	30c gold & multi	.25	.25
a.		Souv. sheet, #292-296 + label	1.50	1.50
		Nos. 292-296 (5)	1.25	1.25

Christmas.
Issued in sheets of 5 stamps and a label (3x2) showing portrait of Queen Elizabeth II and source of design.

Nos. 214-215
Overprinted

1971

296B	A34	30c +20c multi	.40	.60
296C	A34	50c +20c multi	1.25	2.00

Issued: 30c, 2/25; 50c, 3/8.
Nos. 296B-296C were issued to prepay regular postage plus the fee of a private carrier who had contracted to deliver mail within the United Kingdom during a postal strike. The strike ended on March 8, and these stamps were withdrawn March 12.

Queen Elizabeth II and Prince
Philip — A49

Designs: 4c, Royal family at Balmoral. 10c, Prince Philip sailing. 15c, Prince Philip as polo player. 25c, Prince Philip and royal yacht.

1971, Mar. 11   Litho.   Perf. 13½

297	A49	1c brt blue & multi	.25	.25
298	A49	4c brt blue & multi	.30	.30
299	A49	10c brt blue & multi	.85	.85
300	A49	15c brt blue & multi	1.00	1.00
301	A49	25c brt blue & multi	1.60	1.60
a.		Souv. sheet, #297-301 + 2 labels	5.50	5.50
		Nos. 297-301 (5)	4.00	4.00

Visit of Prince Philip, Duke of Edinburgh to Rarotonga, Feb. 27, 1971. Printed in sheets of 10 stamps and 2 labels showing Queen Elizabeth II commemorative coin and a portrait of Prince Philip.

Nos. 210, 213-214 Overprinted

1971, Sept. 8   Photo.   Perf. 14x13½

302	A34	10c gold & multi	.50	.50
303	A34	25c gold & multi	.50	.50
304	A34	30c gold & multi	.50	.50
		Nos. 302-304 (3)	1.50	1.50

4th South Pacific Games, Papeete, French Polynesia, Sept. 8-19. See Nos. B8-B13.

Nos. 202, 205, 208-209 and 211 Surcharged with New Value and Three Bars

1971, Oct. 20

305	A34	10c on 2½c multi	.25	.25
306	A34	10c on 4c multi	.25	.25
307	A34	10c on 8c multi	.25	.25
308	A34	10c on 9c multi	.25	.25
309	A34	10c on 15c multi	.25	.25
		Nos. 305-309 (5)	1.25	1.25

Madonna and Child, by Bellini — A50

Christmas: Paintings of the Madonna and Child, by Giovanni Bellini.

1971, Nov. 30   Perf. 13½

310	A50	1c gold & multi	.25	.25
311	A50	4c gold & multi	.25	.25
312	A50	10c gold & multi	.30	.30
313	A50	20c gold & multi	.40	.30
314	A50	30c gold & multi	.55	.40
a.		Souv. sheet, #310-314 + label	2.25	2.25
		Nos. 310-314 (5)	1.75	1.50

See No. B14.

No. 216 Overprinted: "SOUTH PACIFIC / COMMISSION / FEB. 1947-1972"

1972, Feb. 17   Photo.   Perf. 14x13½

315	A35	$1 gold & multi	.80	.80

South Pacific Commission, 25th anniv.

Easter Type of 1970

Illuminations from 14th century Robert de Lisle Psalter: 5c, St. John. 10c, Christ crucified. 30c, Virgin Mary.

1972, Mar. 6   Photo.   Perf. 13½
Size: 21x68mm

316	A46	5c gold & multi	.25	.25
317	A46	10c gold & multi	.25	.25
318	A46	30c gold & multi	.30	.30
a.		Souvenir sheet of 3, #316-318	1.00	1.00
		Nos. 316-318 (3)	.80	.80

Printed in sheets of 12.
For surcharges see Nos. B15-B16, B19.

Rocket over Moon — A51

No. 319a, Shown. No. 319b, Earth over moon. No. 320a, Landing module and astronaut. No. 320b, Astronaut collecting moon rocks. No. 321a, Earth and rocket over moon. No. 321b, Lunar rover and astronaut. No. 322a, Helicopter over raft in Pacific. No. 322b, Capsule and parachutes.

1972, Apr. 17

319	A51	5c Pair, #a.-b.	.25	.25
320	A51	10c Pair, #a.-b.	.50	.50
321	A51	25c Pair, #a.-b.	1.40	1.40
322	A51	30c Pair, #a.-b.	1.60	1.60
c.		Souvenir sheet of 8	6.00	6.00
		Nos. 319-322 (4)	3.75	3.75

Apollo moon explorations.
No. 322c contains Nos. 319-322 arranged in 2 blocks of 4 divided by a map showing splashdown area of Apollo X, XII and XIII.
For surcharges see Nos. B21-B24.

High Jump, Olympic Rings — A52

1972, June 26

327	A52	10c shown	.30	.30
328	A52	25c Running	.55	.55
329	A52	30c Boxing	.55	.55
a.		Souv. sheet, #327-329 + label	2.00	2.00
		Nos. 327-329 (3)	1.40	1.40

20th Olympic Games, Munich, Aug. 26-Sept. 10. Sheets of 8 stamps and label. See No. B29.

Rest on Flight to Egypt, by Caravaggio — A53

Paintings: 5c, Virgin of the Swallows, by Guercino. 10c, Virgin with Green Cushion, by Andrea Solario. 20c, Virgin and Child, by Lorenzo di Credi. 30c, Virgin and Child, by Giovanni Bellini.

1972, Oct. 11   Photo.   Perf. 13½

330	A53	1c gold & multi	.25	.25
331	A53	5c gold & multi	.35	.25
332	A53	10c gold & multi	.45	.25
333	A53	20c gold & multi	.55	.30
334	A53	30c gold & multi	.90	.40
a.		Souv. sheet, #330-334 + label	4.00	4.00
		Nos. 330-334 (5)	2.50	1.45

Christmas. See No. B30.

Princess Elizabeth and Prince Philip — A54

Designs: 5c, Wedding ceremony, Westminster Abbey. 15c, Bridal portrait. 30c, Official wedding picture of royal family.

1972, Nov. 20   Size: 29x40mm

335	A54	5c silver & multi	.25	.25
336	A54	10c silver & multi	.35	.35

Size: 40x40mm

337	A54	15c silver & multi	.40	.40

Size: 66x40mm

338	A54	30c silver & multi	.55	.55
		Nos. 335-338 (4)	1.55	1.55

25th anniversary of the marriage of Queen Elizabeth II and Prince Philip.
Nos. 335-337 printed in sheets of 8 stamps and one label; No. 338 in sheets of 6.

1c Coin with Queen Elizabeth II and Taro Leaf — A55

Queen Elizabeth II Coins: 2c, Pineapples. 5c, Hibiscus. 10c, Oranges. 20c, Fairy terns. 50c, Bonito. $1, Tangaroa, Polynesian god of creation, vert.

1973, Mar. 15   Photo.   Perf. 13x13½
Size: 37x24mm

339	A55	1c dp car, blk & gold	.25	.25
340	A55	2c blue, blk & gold	.25	.25
341	A55	5c green, blk & gold	.25	.25

Size: 46x30mm

342	A55	10c vio, blue, blk & sil	.25	.25
343	A55	20c dk green, blk & sil	.35	.35
344	A55	50c dp car, black & sil	.60	.60

Size: 32x54½mm

345	A55	$1 blue, blk & silver	.80	.80
		Nos. 339-345 (7)	2.75	2.75

Coinage commemorating silver wedding anniversary of Queen Elizabeth II.
Printed in sheets of 20 stamps and label showing Westminster Abbey.

"Noli me Tangere," by Titian — A56

Paintings: 10c, Descent from the Cross, by Rubens. 30c, The Lamentation of Christ, by Dürer.

1973, Apr. 9

346	A56	5c gold & multi	.25	.25
347	A56	10c gold & multi	.30	.30
348	A56	30c gold & multi	.35	.35
a.		Souvenir sheet of 3, #346-348	1.00	1.00
		Nos. 346-348 (3)	.90	.90

Easter. Printed in sheets of 15 stamps and one label.
See Nos. 378-380, B31-B33, B39-B41.

Queen Elizabeth II in Coronation Regalia — A57

1973, June 1   Photo.   Perf. 14x13½

349	A57	10c gold & multi	.75	.75

Souvenir Sheet
Perf. 13½x14½

350	A57	50c gold & multi	3.00	3.00

20th anniv. of the coronation of Queen Elizabeth II. No. 349 printed in sheets of 5 stamps and one label.

Nos. 206, 208, 210, 212-214 Overprinted: "TENTH ANNIVERSARY / CESSATION OF / NUCLEAR TESTING / TREATY"

1973, July 25   Photo.   Perf. 14x13½

351	A34	5c gold & multi	.25	.25
352	A34	8c gold & multi	.25	.25
353	A34	10c gold & multi	.25	.25
354	A34	20c gold & multi	.25	.25
355	A34	25c gold & multi	.25	.25
356	A34	30c gold & multi	.25	.25
		Nos. 351-356 (6)	1.50	1.50

Nuclear Test Ban Treaty, 10th anniv. and as protest against French nuclear testing on Mururoa atoll.

Tipairua — A58

Historic South Pacific sailing vessels.

1973, Sept. 17   Photo.   Perf. 13½x13

357	A58	½c shown	.25	.25
358	A58	1c Wa'a Kaulua	.25	.25
359	A58	1½c Tainui	.25	.25
360	A58	5c War canoe	.40	.25
361	A58	10c Pahi	.50	.35
362	A58	15c Amatasi	.85	.85
363	A58	25c Vaka	1.25	1.25
		Nos. 357-363 (7)	3.75	3.45

Annunciation A59

Designs from 15th Century Prayer Book: 5c, The Visitation. 10c, Adoration of the Shepherds. 20c, Adoration of the Kings. 30c, Slaughter of the Innocents.

1973, Oct. 30   Photo.   Perf. 13x13½

364	A59	1c multicolored	.25	.25
365	A59	5c multicolored	.25	.25
366	A59	10c multicolored	.25	.25
367	A59	20c multicolored	.25	.25
368	A59	30c multicolored	.25	.25
a.		Souv. sheet, #364-368 + label	.90	.90
		Nos. 364-368 (5)	1.25	1.25

Christmas. See Nos. B34-B38.

Princess Anne — A60

30c, Mark Phillips. 50c, Princess and Mark Phillips.

1973, Nov. 14   Photo.   Perf. 14

369	A60	25c shown	.25	.25
370	A60	30c multicolored	.30	.25
371	A60	50c multicolored	.35	.25
a.		Souv. sheet, #369-371 + label	1.00	1.00
		Nos. 369-371 (3)	.90	.85

Wedding of Princess Anne and Capt. Mark Phillips.

Running and Games Emblem A61

1c, Diving. 3c, Boxing. 10c, Weight lifting. 30c, Bicycling. 50c, Discobolus.

1974, Jan. 24　Photo.　Perf. 14

372	A61	1c multi, vert.	.25	.25
373	A61	3c multi, vert.	.25	.25
374	A61	5c multi	.25	.25
375	A61	10c multi	.25	.25
376	A61	30c multi	.50	.50
		Nos. 372-376 (5)	1.50	1.50

Souvenir Sheet

| 377 | A61 | 50c multi, vert. | 1.25 | 1.25 |

10th British Commonwealth Games, Christchurch, New Zealand, Jan. 24-Feb. 2. No. 377 contains one stamp 35x45mm.

Easter Type of 1973 Dated "1974"

Paintings: 5c, Jesus Carrying Cross, by Raphael. 10c, Jesus in the Arms of God, by El Greco. 30c, Descent from the Cross, by Caravaggio.

1974, Mar. 25　　　　Perf. 13½x13

378	A56	5c gold & multi	.25	.25
379	A56	10c gold & multi	.25	.25
380	A56	30c gold & multi	.30	.30
a.		Souvenir sheet of 3, #378-380	1.25	1.25
		Nos. 378-380 (3)	.80	.80

Easter. See Nos. B39-B41.

Phallicium Glaucum A62

Queen Elizabeth II — A63

Queen and Shells — A64

Cook Islands sea shells: 1c, Vasum turbinellus. 1 ½c, Corculum cardissa. 2c, Terebellum terebellum. 3c, Aulica vespertilio. 4c, Strombus gibberulus. 5c, Cymatium pileare. 6c, Cyprae caputserpentis. 8c, Bursa granularis. 10c, Tenebra muscaria. 15c, Mitra mitra. 20c, Natica alapillonis roding. 25c, Gloripallium pallium. 30c, Conus miles. 50c, Conus textile. 60c, Oliva sericea roding.

The designs of the 2c, 5c, 10c, 30c include portrait of Queen Elizabeth II.

1974-75　　　Photo.　　Perf. 13½

381	A62	½c shown	.30	.30
382	A62	1c multicolored	.30	.30
383	A62	1½c multicolored	.30	.30
384	A62	2c multicolored	.30	.30
385	A62	3c multicolored	.40	.30
386	A62	4c multicolored	.45	.30
387	A62	5c multicolored	.50	.30
388	A62	6c multicolored	.50	.30
389	A62	8c multicolored	.60	1.50
390	A62	10c multicolored	.60	.40
391	A62	15c multicolored	.65	.30
392	A62	20c multicolored	.90	.30
393	A62	25c multicolored	.95	2.00
394	A62	30c multicolored	1.00	.40
395	A62	50c multicolored	7.00	3.25
396	A62	60c multicolored	7.50	3.25
397	A63	$1 shown	2.50	3.50
398	A63	$2 multi ('75)	2.50	2.75

Perf. 14x13½

399	A64	$4 multi ('75)	3.50	5.50
400	A64	$6 multi ('75)	11.00	5.50
401	A64	$8 multi ('75)	12.50	9.00
402	A64	$10 multi ('75)	18.00	6.50
		Nos. 381-402 (22)	72.25	46.55

Issued: 50c, 60c, $1, 8/26; $2, 1/27; $4, 3/17; $6, 4/29; $8, 5/30; $10, 6/30; others, 5/17.

For surcharges & overprints see Nos. 488-498, 526-528, 991, O16-O26, O30-O31.

Soccer Player and Map of Oceania A65

50c, Munich stadium & map of Oceania. $1, Soccer player, Munich stadium & World Cup.

1974, July 5　　Photo.　　Perf. 13½
Size: 31x29mm

403	A65	25c multicolored	.30	.30
404	A65	50c multicolored	.40	.40

Size: 68x28½mm

405	A65	$1 multicolored	.75	.75
a.		Souvenir sheet of 3, #403-405	1.50	1.50
		Nos. 403-405 (3)	1.45	1.45

World Cup Soccer Championship, Munich, June 13-July 7. Nos. 403-405 printed in sheets of 8 and commemorative label.

$2.50 Capt. Cook Silver Coin — A66

Commemorative Silver Coins: $7.50, $7.50 coin with Queen Elizabeth II on obverse; Capt. Cook, map of Islands and "Resolution" on reverse. $2.50 coin shows "Resolution," "Adventure" and globe on reverse.

1974, July 22　　Photo.　　Perf. 14

406	A66	$2.50 sil, vio & blk	10.00	6.75
407	A66	$7.50 grn, sil & blk	20.00	15.00
a.		Souvenir sheet of 2, #406-407	37.50	37.50

Bicentenary of Capt. Cook's 2nd voyage of discovery. Nos. 406-407 printed in sheets of 5 and commemorative label.

Cook Islands Nos. 1, 49, 62, 66, 77 — A67

Stamps of Cook Islands: 25c, DC-3 over old Rarotonga landing strip, and No. 19. 30c, Rarotonga Post Office, UPU emblem and No. 65. 50c, UPU emblem and Nos. 1, 19, 49, 62, 65-66 and 77.

1974, Sept. 16　Photo.　Perf. 13½x14

408	A67	10c gold & multi	.25	.25
409	A67	25c gold & multi	.35	.35
410	A67	30c gold & multi	.40	.40
411	A67	50c gold & multi	.75	.75
a.		Souv. sheet, #408-411, perf. 13½	1.60	1.60
		Nos. 408-411 (4)	1.75	1.75

Cent. of UPU. Nos. 408-411 printed in sheets of 8 and commemorative label.

Virgin and Child, with St. John, by Raphael — A68

Paintings: 5c, Holy Family, by Andrea del Sarto. 10c, Nativity, by Correggio. 20c, Holy Family, by Rembrandt. 30c, Nativity, by Van der Weyden.

1974, Oct. 15　　Photo.　　Perf. 13½

412	A68	1c multicolored	.25	.25
413	A68	5c multicolored	.25	.25
414	A68	10c multicolored	.25	.25
415	A68	20c multicolored	.40	.40
416	A68	30c multicolored	.55	.55
a.		Souv. sheet, #412-416 + label	1.75	1.75
		Nos. 412-416 (5)	1.70	1.70

Christmas 1974. Nos. 412-416 printed in sheets of 15 and one label showing Queen Elizabeth II.

See Nos. B42-B46.

Churchill and Blenheim Palace A69

Sir Winston Churchill (1874-1965) and: 10c, Parliament. 25c, Chartwell. 30c, Buckingham Palace. 50c, St. Paul's Cathedral.

1974, Nov. 20　　Photo.　　Perf. 14

417	A69	5c violet & multi	.25	.25
418	A69	10c maroon & multi	.25	.25
419	A69	25c dk blue & multi	.30	.30
420	A69	30c brown & multi	.40	.40
421	A69	50c multicolored	.75	.75
a.		Souv. sheet, #417-421 + label	2.25	2.25
		Nos. 417-421 (5)	1.95	1.95

Nos. 417-421 printed in sheets of 5 stamps and one label showing $100 commemorative gold coin.

Vasco Nunez de Balboa — A70

5c, Ferdinand Magellan & route around South America. 10c, Juan Sebastian de Elcano & ship. 25c, Andres de Urdaneta & ship. 25c, Miguel Lopez de Legaspi & ship.

1975, Feb. 3　　　　　Perf. 13½

422	A70	1c multicolored	.25	.25
423	A70	5c multicolored	.65	.25
424	A70	10c multicolored	1.25	.30
425	A70	25c multicolored	2.00	.90
426	A70	30c multicolored	2.25	1.00
		Nos. 422-426 (5)	6.40	2.70

16th century explorers of the Pacific Ocean.

Apollo and Apollo-Soyuz Emblem — A71

Apollo-Soyuz Emblem &: No. 427b, Soyuz. No. 428a, Aleksei A. Leonov & Valery N. Kubasov. No. 428b, Donald K. Slayton, Vance D. Brand & Thomas P. Stafford. No. 429a, Cosmonaut inside Soyuz capsule. No. 429b, American astronauts inside Apollo capsule.

1975, July 15　　Photo.　　Perf. 13½

427	A71	25c Pair, #a.-b.	.80	.80
428	A71	30c Pair, #a.-b.	.90	.90
429	A71	50c Pair, #a.-b.	1.25	1.25
c.		Souvenir sheet of 6, #427-429	2.75	2.75
		Nos. 427-429 (3)	2.95	2.95

Apollo Soyuz space test project (Russo-American space cooperation), launching July 15; link-up, July 17. Printed sheets of 18 stamps and 2 labels showing flags.

$100 Gold Commemorative Coin — A72

1975, Aug. 8　Photo.　Perf. 13½x13

433	A72	$2 gold & dp violet	3.50	3.25

Bicentenary of the completion of Capt. Cook's second voyage of discovery.

Cook Islands' Flag, Map of Islands and New Zealand A73

Prime Minister Sir Albert Henry — A74

Design: 25c, View of Rarotonga and flag.

1975, Aug. 8　　Perf. 13½x13, 13x13½

434	A73	5c gold & multi	.40	.25
435	A74	10c gold & multi	.50	.25
436	A73	25c gold & multi	1.25	.50
		Nos. 434-436 (3)	2.15	1.00

Tenth anniversary of self-government.

Virgin and Child, 15th Century, Flemish — A75

Paintings: 10c, Madonna in the Field, by Raphael. 15c, Holy Family, by Raphael. 20c, Adoration of the Shepherds, by J. B. Mayno. 35c, Annunciation, by Murillo.

1975, Dec. 1　　Photo.　　Perf. 13½

437	A75	6c gold & multi	.25	.25
438	A75	10c gold & multi	.25	.25
439	A75	15c gold & multi	.30	.30
440	A75	20c gold & multi	.30	.30
441	A75	35c gold & multi	.45	.45
a.		Souv. sheet, #437-441 + label	1.60	1.60
		Nos. 437-441 (5)	1.55	1.55

Christmas. See Nos. B47-B51.

Descent from the Cross, by Raphael A76

Paintings: 15c, Pieta, by Veronese. 35c, Pieta, by El Greco.

1976, Mar. 29   Photo.   Perf. 13½
442	A76	7c gold & multi	.25	.25
443	A76	15c gold & multi	.50	.50
444	A76	35c gold & multi	.80	.80
a.		Souvenir sheet of 3, #442-444	1.75	1.75
		Nos. 442-444 (3)	1.55	1.55

Easter. Nos. 442-444 printed in sheets of 20 with label showing Queen Elizabeth II. See Nos. B52-B54.

Benjamin Franklin and "Resolution" — A77

Designs: $2, Capt. James Cook and "Resolution." $3, Cook, "Resolution" and Franklin.

1976, May 29   Photo.   Perf. 13½
445	A77	$1 gold & multi	3.75	2.50
446	A77	$2 gold & multi	7.75	5.50

Souvenir Sheet
Perf. 13
447	A77	$3 gold & multi	11.50	6.50

American Bicentennial. No. 447 contains one stamp 73x31mm. Nos. 445-446 printed in sheets of 5 and corner label with Franklin's request to assist Capt. Cook.
For overprint see No. O29.

Nos. 445-447 Overprinted "Royal Visit July 1976"
1976, July 6   Photo.   Perf. 13½
448	A77	$1 gold & multi	2.25	1.75
449	A77	$2 gold & multi	6.00	5.25

Souvenir Sheet
Perf. 13
450	A77	$3 gold & multi	7.50	6.75

Visit of Queen Elizabeth II and Prince Philip to the United States.

High Hurdles — A78

15c, Field hockey. 30c, Fencing. 35c, Soccer.

1976, July 22   Perf. 13½
451	A78	7c Pair, #a.-b.	.40	.40
452	A78	15c Pair, #a.-b.	.50	.50
453	A78	30c Pair, #a.-b.	.90	.90
454	A78	35c Pair, #a.-b.	1.10	1.10
c.		Souvenir sheet of 8, #451-454	3.50	3.50
		Nos. 451-454 (4)	2.90	2.90

21st Olympic Games, Montreal, Canada, 7/17-8/1. Printed in sheets of 10 stamps + 2 labels.

The Visitation — A80

Designs: 10c, Virgin and Child. 15c, Adoration of the Shepherds. 20c, Adoration of the Kings. 35c, Holy Family. After painted Renaissance altar sculptures.

1976, Oct. 12   Photo.   Perf. 14x13½
459	A80	6c gold & multi	.25	.25
460	A80	10c gold & multi	.25	.25
461	A80	15c gold & multi	.25	.25
462	A80	20c gold & multi	.25	.25
463	A80	35c gold & multi	.25	.25
a.		Souv. sheet, #459-463 + label	1.25	1.25
		Nos. 459-463 (5)	1.25	1.25

Christmas. Nos. 459-463 printed in sheets of 20 with label showing Queen Elizabeth II. See Nos. B55-B59.

$5 Silver Coin, 1976 — A81

1976, Nov. 15   Photo.   Perf. 13½
464	A81	$1 multicolored	2.00	1.50

National Wildlife and Conservation Day. Issued in sheets of 5 stamps and commemorative label. See Nos. 502, 536.

A82

No. 465a, Crown. No. 465b, Elizabeth II in Coronation Vestments. No. 466a, Westminster Abbey. No. 466b, Coach in procession. No. 467a, Queen and Prince Philip after coronation. No. 467b, Investiture of Sir Albert Henry, Premier of Cook Islands, 1974.

1977, Feb. 7   Photo.   Perf. 13½x13
465	A82	25c Pair, #a.-b.	.40	.40
466	A82	50c Pair, #a.-b.	.75	.75
467	A82	$1 Pair, #a.-b.	1.25	1.25
c.		Souv. sheet, #465-467, perf. 13	2.75	2.75
		Nos. 465-467 (3)	2.40	2.40

Reign of Queen Elizabeth II, 25th anniv. Printed in sheets of 8.
For overprints see No. O27.

Crucifixion, by Rubens — A83

Paintings by Rubens: 15c, Christ Between the Thieves. 35c, Descent from the Cross.

1977, Mar. 28   Photo.   Perf. 14x13½
471	A83	7c gold & multi	.40	.40
472	A83	15c gold & multi	.50	.50
473	A83	35c gold & multi	1.00	1.00
a.		Souv. sheet, #471-473, perf 13	2.00	2.00
		Nos. 471-473 (3)	1.90	1.90

Easter 1977, and 400th birth anniv. of Peter Paul Rubens (1577-1640), Flemish painter. Nos. 471-473 printed in sheets of 24 stamps and corner label with portrait of Queen Elizabeth II and description. See Nos. B60-B62.

Virgin and Child, by Memling — A84

Virgin and Child by: 10c, Hans Memling. 15c, Geertgen Tot Sin Jans. 20c, Carlo Crivelli. 35c, School of Henry Blex.

1977, Oct. 3   Photo.   Perf. 13½
474	A84	6c gold & multi	.25	.25
475	A84	10c gold & multi	.25	.25
476	A84	15c gold & multi	.25	.25
477	A84	20c gold & multi	.35	.35
478	A84	35c gold & multi	.55	.55
a.		Souv. sheet, #474-478 + label	1.60	1.60
		Nos. 474-478 (5)	1.65	1.65

Christmas. Nos. 474-478 printed in sheets of 24 and label. See Nos. B63-B67.

$5-silver Coin, 1977 — A85

1977, Nov. 15   Photo.   Perf. 13½
479	A85	$1 silver & multi	2.00	.95

National Wildlife Conservation Day. No. 479 issued in sheets of 5 and one label.

Capt. Cook, by Nathaniel Dance and "Resolution" — A86

$1, "Capt. Cook Landing at Owyhee" and Capt. Cook. $2, Cook Islands $200 commemorative coin, 1978, and Cook Monument, Hawaii, 1825.

1978, Jan. 20   Litho.   Perf. 13½
480	A86	50c gold & multi	.80	.80
481	A86	$1 gold & multi	1.25	1.25
482	A86	$2 gold & multi	2.50	2.50
a.		Souvenir sheet of 3, #480-482	4.75	4.75
		Nos. 480-482 (3)	4.55	4.55

Bicentennial of Capt. Cook's arrival in Hawaii.
Nos. 480-482 issued in sheets of 5 with corner label showing ship off Hawaiian coast.
For overprints see Nos. 499-501a.

Pieta, by Rogier van der Weyden A87

Paintings, National Gallery, London: 35c, Burial of Jesus, by Michelangelo. 75c, Jesus at Emmaus, by Caravaggio.

1978, Mar. 20   Photo.   Perf. 13½x13
483	A87	15c gold & multi	.30	.30
484	A87	35c gold & multi	.50	.50
485	A87	75c gold & multi	.75	.75
a.		Souv. sheet, #483-485 + label	1.25	1.25
		Nos. 483-485 (3)	1.55	1.55

Easter. Nos. 483-485 printed in sheets of 5 and corner label showing National Gallery. See Nos. B68-B70.

Souvenir Sheets

Coronation of Queen Elizabeth II, 25th anniv. — A88

1978, June 6   Photo.   Perf. 13
486	A88	Sheet of 4 + 2 labels	1.30	1.30
a.		50c Queen Elizabeth II	.30	.30
b.		50c Lion of England	.30	.30
c.		50c Imperial State Crown	.30	.30
d.		50c Tangaroa figure	.30	.30
487	A88	Sheet of 4 + label	1.55	1.30
a.		70c like 486a	.30	.30
b.		70c Scepter with Cross	.30	.30
c.		70c St. Edward's Crown	.30	.30
d.		70c Rarotongan staff god	.30	.30
e.		Souv. sheet of 8, #486a-487d + label	2.50	2.50

Coronation of Queen Elizabeth II, 25th anniv.

Nos. 381, 383, 388-389, 393-396 Srchd. in Silver, Black or Gold

1978, Nov. 10   Photo.   Perf. 13½
488	A62	5c on 1½c multi (S)	.25	.25
489	A62	7c on ½c multi	.25	.25
490	A62	10c on 6c multi (G)	.40	.40
491	A62	10c on 8c multi (G)	.40	.40
492	A62	15c on ½c multi	.65	.60
493	A62	15c on 25c multi (S)	.65	.60
494	A62	15c on 30c multi	.65	.60
495	A62	15c on 50c multi (S)	.65	.60
496	A62	15c on 60c multi (G)	.65	.60
497	A62	17c on ½c multi	.80	.80
498	A62	17c on 15c multi (S)	.80	.80
		Nos. 488-498 (11)	6.15	5.90

See Nos. 526-528.

Nos. 480-482a Overprinted in Black on Silver Panel

1978, Nov. 13   Litho.   Perf. 13½
499	A86	50c gold & multi	1.00	1.00
500	A86	$1 gold & multi	1.50	1.50
501	A86	$2 gold & multi	2.25	2.25
a.		Souvenir sheet of 3, #499-501	15.00	15.00
		Nos. 499-501 (3)	4.75	4.75

250th anniv. of Capt. Cook's birth. Similar overprint in 4 lines was applied to labels. Label of No. 501a overprinted only with dates 1728, 1978.

Coin Type of 1976

$1, $5 Silver coin, 1978 (Polynesian warbler).

1978, Nov. 15   Photo.   Perf. 13½
502	A81	$1 multicolored	1.60	1.60

National Wildlife and Conservation Day. Sheets of 24 containing 4 panes of 6.

A89

Virgin and Child by: 15c, Rogier van der Weyden. 17c, Carlo Crivelli. 35c, Murillo.

1978, Dec. 8   Photo.   Perf. 13
503	A89	15c multicolored	.35	.35
504	A89	17c multicolored	.45	.45
505	A89	35c multicolored	.75	.75
a.		Souvenir sheet of 3, #503-505	1.60	1.60
		Nos. 503-505 (3)	1.55	1.55

Christmas. See Nos. B71-B73.

A90

Descent from the Cross, by Gaspar de Crayer (Details): 10c, Pieta. 12c, St. John. 15c, Mary Magdalene. 20c, Cherubs.

1979, Apr. 5   Photo.   Perf. 13
506	A90	10c multicolored	.25	.25
507	A90	12c multicolored	.25	.25
508	A90	15c multicolored	.25	.25
509	A90	20c multicolored	.50	.50
		Nos. 506-509 (4)	1.25	1.25

Easter. See No. B74.

A91

20c, Capt. Cook, by John Weber. 30c, Resolution, by Henry Roberts. 35c, Endeavour. 50c, Death of Capt. Cook, by George Carter.

1979, July 23   Photo.   Perf. 14x13½
510	A91	20c multicolored	.40	.40
511	A91	30c multicolored	.55	.55
512	A91	35c multicolored	.65	.65
513	A91	50c multicolored	.80	.80
a.		Souvenir sheet of 4	2.50	2.50
		Nos. 510-513 (4)	2.40	2.40

Capt. Cook (1728-1779), explorer. No. 513a contains 4 stamps similar to Nos. 510-513 with black frames.

Sir Rowland Hill, Originator of Penny Postage — A92

No. 514a, Postrider. No. 514b, Stagecoach. No. 514c, Automobile. No. 514d, Streamlined train. No. 515a, Cap-Horniers, sailing ship. No. 515b, River steamer. No. 515c, Liner Deutschland. No. 515d, Liner United States. No. 516a, Balloon Neptune. No. 516b, Junkers F13. No. 516c, Graf Zeppelin. No. 516d, Concorde.

1979, Sept. 10   Perf. 14½
514	A92	30c Block of 4, #a.-d.	1.00	1.00
515	A92	35c Block of 4, #a.-d.	1.10	1.10
516	A92	50c Block of 4, #a.-d.	1.60	1.60
e.		Souv. sheet of 12, #514-516	4.00	4.00
		Nos. 514-516 (3)	3.70	3.70

Nos. 381, 383, 396 Srchd. in Gold or Silver

1979, Sept. 12   Photo.   Perf. 13½
526	A62	6c on ½c multi	.25	.25
527	A62	10c on 1½c multi (S)	.25	.25
528	A62	15c on 60c multi	.25	.25
		Nos. 526-528 (3)	.75	.75

Nos. 526-528 have 3 thick bars of equal length over old value.

Girl and Baby, IYC Emblem — A93

IYC Emblem and: 50c, Boy playing tree drum. 65c, Children dancing.

1979, Oct. 10   Perf. 13
529	A93	30c multicolored	.25	.25
530	A93	50c multicolored	.35	.35
531	A93	65c multicolored	.45	.45
		Nos. 529-531 (3)	1.05	1.05

See No. B75.

Apollo 11 Emblem — A94

50c, Apollo 11 crew, lunar map. 60c, Astronaut walking on moon. 65c, Splashdown.

1979, Nov. 7   Perf. 14
532	A94	30c multicolored	.30	.30
533	A94	50c multicolored	.50	.50
534	A94	60c multicolored	.60	.60
535	A94	65c multicolored	.70	.70
a.		Souv. sheet, #532-535, perf. 13	2.50	2.50
		Nos. 532-535 (4)	2.10	2.10

Apollo 11 moon landing, 10th anniv.

Coin Type of 1976

$1, $5 Silver coin, 1979 (Rarotonga fruit dove).

Perf. 13½x14½
1979, Nov. 15   Photo.
536	A81	$1 multicolored	1.75	1.75

National Wildlife and Conservation Day.

Christmas Tree Ornaments — A95

Christmas (Flowers and): 10c, Star. 12c, Bells and candle. 15c, Ancestral statue.

1979, Dec. 14   Perf. 14
537	A95	6c multicolored	.25	.25
538	A95	10c multicolored	.25	.25
539	A95	12c multicolored	.25	.25
540	A95	15c multicolored	.25	.25
		Nos. 537-540,B76-B79 (8)	2.00	2.00

See also Nos. C16-C19, CB1-CB4.

A96

Bible illustrations by Gustave Dore, 1833-1883: No. 541a, Flagellation. No. 541b, Jesus Wearing Crown of Thorns. No. 542a, Jesus Mocked. No. 542b, Jesus Falls. No. 543a, The Crucifixion. No. 543b, Descent from the Cross.

1980, Mar. 31   Perf. 13
541	A96	20c Pair, #a.-b.	.50	.50
542	A96	30c Pair, #a.-b.	.70	.70
543	A96	35c Pair, #a.-b.	.80	.80
		Nos. 541-543 (3)	2.00	2.00

Easter. See Nos. 553, B80-B83.

Doves with Olive Branch, Rotary Emblem A97

1980, May 27   Photo.   Perf. 14
547	A97	30c shown	.35	.35
548	A97	35c Flowers	.40	.40
549	A97	50c Flags, globe	.55	.55
		Nos. 547-549 (3)	1.30	1.30

Rotary Intl., 75th anniv. See No. B87.

Easter Type of 1980 and

New Zealand No. 1 — A98

No. 550a, Postrider. No. 550b, Coach. No. 550c, Automobile. No. 550d, Train.
New Zealand #2 and: No. 551a, Sailing ship. No. 551b, River steamer. No. 551c, Transatlantic liner (facing left). No. 551d, Transatlantic liner (facing right).
New Zealand #3 and: No. 552a, 1870-71 mail balloon. No. 552b, 1919 plane. No. 552c, Graf Zeppelin. No. 552d, Concorde.

1980, Aug. 22   Photo.   Perf. 14
550	A98	30c Block of 4, #a.-d.	1.25	1.00
551	A98	35c Block of 4, #a.-d.	1.60	1.25
552	A98	50c Block of 4, #a.-d.	2.25	1.40
e.		Souvenir sheet of 12	6.25	5.50
		Nos. 550-552 (3)	5.10	3.65

Souvenir Sheet
Perf. 13
553	A96	Sheet of 6, #541-543	2.50	1.50

ZEAPEX '80, New Zealand Intl. Stamp Exhib., Auckland, Aug. 23-31. No. 552e contains four each of Nos. 550-552 arranged horizontally (4x3). No. 553 has black on gold overprint: "ZEAPEX / '80 / Auckland / +10c" in margin.

Queen Mother Elizabeth, 80th Birthday — A99

1980, Sept. 22   Photo.   Perf. 13
554	A99	50c multicolored	.75	.75

Souvenir Sheet
555	A99	$2 multicolored	1.50	1.50

No. 554 issued in sheets of 9 (3x3).

Johannes Kepler, Spacecraft — A100

Designs: Nos. 556a, 559a, Kepler, spacecraft (diff.). No. 556b, Kepler, Apollo Command Module, moon. No. 559b, Kepler, lunar rover, astronaut on moon. Nos. 557a-558b, Jules Verne, various scenes from From Earth to Moon, vert.

1980, Nov. 7   Photo.   Perf. 13
556	A100	12c Pair, #a-b	1.00	1.00
557	A100	20c Pair, #a-b	1.00	1.00
558	A100	30c Pair, #a-b	1.10	1.10
c.		Souvenir sheet, #557-558	2.25	2.25
559	A100	50c Pair, #a-b	2.00	2.00
c.		Souv. sheet, #556, 559	3.00	3.00
		Nos. 556-559 (4)	5.10	5.10

Death anniversaries of Johannes Kepler, German astronomer and Jules Verne, French science fiction writer.

Burning Bush Coral — A101

Daisy Coral — A102

Nos. 564a, 570a, 576a, Siphonogorgia. Nos. 564b, 570b, 576b, Pavona practorta. Nos. 564c, 570c, 576c, Stylaster echinatus. Nos. 564d, 570d, 576d, Tubastraea. Nos. 565a, 571a, 577a, Millepora alcicornis. Nos. 565b, 571b, 577b, Junceella gemmaea. Nos. 565c, 571c, 577c, Fungia fungites. Nos. 565d, 571d, 577d, Heliofungia actiniformis. Nos. 566a, 572a, 578a, Distichopora violacea. Nos. 566b, 572b, 578b, Stylaster. Nos. 566c, 572c, 578c, Gonipora. Nos. 566d, 572d, 578d, Caulastraea echinulata. Nos. 567a, 573a, 579a, Ptilosarcus gurneyi. Nos. 567b, 573b, 579b, Stylophora pistillata. Nos. 567c, 573c, 579c, Melithaea squamata. Nos. 567d, 573d, 579d, Porites andrewsi. Nos. 568a, 574a, 580a, Lobophyllia bemprichii. Nos. 568b, 574b, 580b, Palauastrea ramosa. Nos. 568c, 574c, 580c, Bellonella indica. Nos. 568d, 574d, 580d, Pectinia alcicornis. Nos. 569a, 575a, 581a, Sarcophyton digitatum. Nos. 569b, 575b, 581b, Melithaea albitincta. Nos. 569c, 575c, 581c, Plerogyra sinuosa. Nos. 569d, 575d, 581d, Dendrophyllia gracilis.

1980-82   *Perf. 13½x13*
Strips of 4 (#564-575) or Blocks of 4 (#576-581)

564	A101	1c #a.-d.	.60	.60
565	A101	3c #a.-d.	.65	.65
566	A101	4c #a.-d.	.70	.70
567	A101	5c #a.-d.	.75	.75
568	A101	6c #a.-d.	.80	.80
569	A101	8c #a.-d.	.85	.85
570	A101	10c #a.-d.	.90	.90
571	A101	12c #a.-d.	1.00	1.00
572	A101	15c #a.-d.	1.10	1.10
573	A101	20c #a.-d.	1.25	1.25
574	A101	25c #a.-d.	1.40	1.40
575	A101	30c #a.-d.	1.75	1.75
576	A101	35c #a.-d.	1.90	1.90
577	A101	50c #a.-d.	2.50	2.50
578	A101	60c #a.-d.	2.75	2.75
579	A101	70c #a.-d.	7.00	7.00
580	A101	80c #a.-d.	7.50	7.50
581	A101	$1 #a.-d.	8.00	8.00

Perf. 14x13½

582	A102	$2 like #566c	8.00	3.25
583	A102	$3 like #565d	10.00	3.25
584	A102	$4 like #567b	4.00	10.00
585	A102	$6 like #564c	6.00	15.00
586	A102	$10 like #569b	22.50	27.50
		Nos. 564-586 (23)	91.90	100.40

Issued: 1-8c, 11/21/80; 10-30c, 12/19/80; 35-60c, 3/16/81; 70c, 80c, 4/13/81; $1, 5/20/81; $2, $3, 11/27/81; $4, $6, 1/11/82; $10, 3/5/82.

For surcharges see Nos. 710-714, 716, 738, 740, 811-815, 953-954, 956-957, 959, 961-962, 964, 978-979, 984-986, B109-B111, O50-O53. For overprints see Nos. 992, 1049.

Annunciation, 13th Century Prayerbook Illustration — A102a

1980, Dec. 1   **Photo.**   *Perf. 14*

652	A102a	15c shown	.25	.25
653	A102a	30c Visitation	.30	.30
654	A102a	40c Nativity	.40	.40
655	A102a	50c Epiphany	.50	.50
a.		Souvenir sheet of 4, #652-655	1.35	1.35
		Nos. 652-655 (4)	1.45	1.45

Christmas. See Nos. B88-B91.

Crucifixion, 12th Cent. Prayerbook Illustration — A103

1981, Apr. 10   *Perf. 14*

656	A103	15c shown	.25	.25
657	A103	25c Placing in Tomb	.35	.35
658	A103	40c Marys at the Tomb	.50	.50
		Nos. 656-658 (3)	1.10	1.10

Easter. See Nos. B92-B95.

Prince Charles and Lady Diana — A104

1981, July 29   **Photo.**   *Perf. 14*

659	A104	$1 Charles	.50	.50
660	A104	$2 shown	1.25	1.25
a.		Souv. sheet of 2, #659-660	2.00	2.00

Royal Wedding. Issued in sheets of 4. For overprints and surcharges see Nos. 679-680, 715, 835, 980-981, B97-B98.

Soccer Players — A105

Designs: Various soccer players.

1981, Oct 20   **Photo.**   *Perf. 14*

661	A105	20c Pair, #a.-b.	.80	.80
662	A105	30c Pair, #a.-b.	1.00	1.00
663	A105	35c Pair, #a.-b.	1.40	1.40
664	A105	50c Pair, #a.-b.	1.75	1.75
		Nos. 661-664 (4)	4.95	4.95

ESPANA '82 World Cup Soccer Championships. See No. B96.

Virgin and Child, by Rubens — A107

Christmas: Rubens Paintings: 15c, Coronation of St. Catherine. 40c, Adoration of the Shepherds. 50c, Adoration of the Kings.

1981, Dec. 14   **Photo.**   *Perf. 14x13½*

669	A107	8c shown	.45	.25
670	A107	15c multicolored	.55	.25
671	A107	40c multicolored	1.00	1.00
672	A107	50c multicolored	1.25	1.25
		Nos. 669-672 (4)	3.25	2.75

Souvenir Sheets

1982, Jan. 18

673	A107	75c +5c like #669	.85	.85
674	A107	75c +5c like #670	.85	.85
675	A107	75c +5c like #671	.85	.85
676	A107	75c +5c like #672	.85	.85

Surtax was for school children. See No. B99.

21st Birthday of Princess Diana — A108

No. 677a, 21st Birthday. No. 677b, 1 July 1982. No. 678a, Wedding portrait. No. 678b, 1 July 1982. No. 678cd, $1.25, No. 678ce, $2.50, both inscribed "21st Birthday / 1 July 1982."

1982, June 21   **Photo.**   *Perf. 14*

677	A108	$1.25 Pair, #a.-b.	3.50	3.50
678	A108	$2.50 Pair, #a.-b.	4.00	4.00
c.		Souv. sheet of 2, #d.-e.	6.25	6.25

Issued in sheets of 4. See Nos. 681-682. For surcharges and overprints see Nos. 739-740, 833-834, 982.

Nos. 659-660a Overprinted

No. 680cd, $1; No. 680ce, $2, both inscribed "21 JUNE 1982 ROYAL BIRTH."

1982, July 12

679	A104	$1 Pair, #a.-b.	1.75	1.75
680	A104	$2 Pair, #a.-b.	4.00	4.00
c.		Souv. sheet of 2, #d.-e.	4.25	4.25

Issued in sheets of 4. For surcharges see Nos. 987-988.

Design A108 Inscribed

No. 682cd, $1.25; No. 682ce, $2.50, both inscribed "Royal Birth / June 1982."

1982, Aug. 3

681	A108	$1.25 Pair, #a.-b.	2.50	2.50
682	A108	$2.50 Pair, #a.-b.	5.00	5.00
c.		Souv. sheet of 2, #d.-e.	5.50	5.50

Issued in sheets of 4.

Serenade, by Norman Rockwell (1894-1978) A109

10c, The Hikers. 20c, The Doctor and the Doll. 30c, Home From Camp.

1982, Sept. 10   **Photo.**   *Perf. 14*

683	A109	5c shown	.25	.25
684	A109	10c multicolored	.25	.25
685	A109	20c multicolored	.25	.25
686	A109	30c multicolored	.25	.25
		Nos. 683-686 (4)	1.00	1.00

Christmas A110

Princess Diana Holding Prince William. Various Details from Virgin with Garlands, by Rubens.

1982, Nov. 30   **Photo.**   *Perf. 14*

687	A110	35c multicolored	1.40	.75
688	A110	48c multicolored	2.00	1.50
689	A110	60c multicolored	2.25	1.75
690	A110	$1.70 multicolored	3.00	5.00
		Nos. 687-690 (4)	8.65	9.00

Souvenir Sheets
Perf. 13½

691		Sheet of 4	6.50	6.50
a.		A110 60c like 35c	1.50	1.50
b.		A110 60c like 48c	1.50	1.50
c.		A110 60c like #689	1.50	1.50
d.		A110 60c like $1.70	1.50	1.50
692		A110 75c + 5c like 35c	1.75	1.75
693		A110 75c + 5c like 48c	1.75	1.75
694		A110 75c + 5c like 60c	1.75	1.75
695		A110 75c + 5c like $1.70	1.75	1.75

No. 691 contains 4 stamps (27x32mm., showing only painting details) plus 2 labels showing Diana and William. Nos. 692-695 show Diana and William (27x39mm), multicolored margins show painting details. Surtax was for child welfare.

Commonwealth Day — A111

No. 696a, Tangaroa statue. No. 696b, Rarotonga oranges. No. 696c, Rarotonga Airport. No. 696d, Prime Minister Thomas Davis.

1983, Mar. 14   **Photo.**   *Perf. 14*

696	A111	60c Block of 4, #a.-d.	2.75	2.75

For overprints see No. O46.

Scouting Year — A112

36c, Camping. 48c, Rope swing. 60c, Tree planting.

1983, Apr. 5   **Photo.**   *Perf. 13x13½*

700	A112	12c Pair, #a.-b.	.90	.90
701	A112	36c Pair, #a.-b.	1.25	1.25
702	A112	48c Pair, #a.-b.	1.75	1.75
703	A112	60c Pair, #a.-b.	2.75	2.75
		Nos. 700-703 (4)	6.65	6.65

Souvenir Sheet of 8

704		#a.-d.	7.00	7.00

No. 704 contains one each of Nos. 700-703 with 2c surtax.

Nos. 700-704 Overprinted

1983, July 4   **Photo.**   *Perf. 13x13½*

705	A112	12c Pair, #a.-b.	1.25	1.25
706	A112	36c Pair, #a.-b.	1.75	1.75
707	A112	48c Pair, #a.-b.	2.25	2.25
708	A112	60c Pair, #a.-b.	3.00	3.00
		Nos. 705-708 (4)	8.25	8.25

Souvenir Sheet of 8

709	A112	#a.-d.	6.50	6.50

Nos. 569, 572, 574-575, 579, 587, 660 Surcharged in Black or Gold

No. 710a

No. 712a

No. 715

No. 716

Perf. 13½x13, 14x13½, 14

1983, Aug. 12   **Photo.**

Strips of 4, #a.-d. (#710-713) or
Block of 4, #a.-d. (#714)

710	A101	18c on 8c #569	2.75	2.75
711	A101	36c on 15c #572	4.25	4.25
712	A101	36c on 30c #575	4.50	4.50
713	A101	48c on 25c #574	6.00	6.00
714	A101	72c on 70c #579	10.00	10.00
715	A104	96c on $2 #660		
		(G)	7.50	5.00
716	A102	$5.60 on $6 #585		
		(G)	20.00	18.00
	Nos. 710-716 (7)		55.00	50.50

A114

A115

1983, Sept. 9   **Perf. 14**

732	Pair		1.00	1.00
a.	A114 6c Gt. Britain		.50	.50
b.	A115 6c Cook Islds. Group Federal flag		.50	.50
733	Pair		1.25	1.25
a.	A114 12c Raratonga ensign		.60	.60
b.	A115 12c New Zealand		.60	.60
734	Pair		1.50	1.50
a.	A114 15c Cook Islds, 1973-79		.70	.70
b.	A115 15c Cook Islds, 1983		.70	.70
c.	Souvenir sheet of 6, #732-734		2.00	2.00
735	Pair		1.50	1.50
a.	A114 20c like #732a		.70	.70
b.	A115 20c like #732b		.70	.70
736	Pair		1.60	1.60
a.	A114 30c like #733a		.75	.75
b.	A115 30c like #733b		.75	.75
737	Pair		1.75	1.75
a.	A114 35c like #734a		.85	.85
b.	A115 35c like #734b		.85	.85
c.	Souvenir sheet of 6, #735-737		3.50	3.50
	Nos. 732-737 (6)		8.60	8.60

Nos. 732-737 have different background landscapes; Nos. 735-737 airmail with silver background. Nos. 734c, 737c perf. 13½.

Nos. 576, 586, 678 Surcharged in
Black or Gold

Perf. 13½x13, 14x13½, 14

1983, Aug. 30   **Photo.**

Block of 4, #a.-d.

738	A101	36c on 35c #576	4.25	4.25
	Pair, #a.-b. (#739)			
739	A108	96c on $2.50		
		#678 (G)	5.50	5.50
740	A102	$5.60 on $10 #586		
		(G)	20.00	18.00
	Nos. 738-740 (3)		29.75	27.75

Satellite Earth
Station — A116

Designs: Various satellites in orbit.

1983, Oct. 10   **Litho.**   **Perf. 13½**

744	A116	36c multicolored	.75	.75
745	A116	48c multicolored	1.00	1.00
746	A116	60c multicolored	1.25	1.25
747	A116	96c multicolored	1.75	1.75
	Nos. 744-747 (4)		4.75	4.75

Souvenir Sheet

748	A116	$2 multicolored	3.50	3.50

World Communications Year.

Christmas
A117

Raphael Paintings: 12c, La Belle Jardiniere. 18c, Madonna and Child with Five Saints. 36c, Madonna and Child with Saint John. 48c, Madonna of the Fish. 60c, Madonna of the Baldacchino.

1983   **Photo.**   **Perf. 14**

749	A117	12c multicolored	.75	.75
750	A117	18c multicolored	1.00	1.00
751	A117	36c multicolored	1.50	1.50
752	A117	48c multicolored	1.90	1.90
753	A117	60c multicolored	2.50	2.50
	Nos. 749-753 (5)		7.65	7.65

Souvenir Sheets

Perf. 13½

754		Sheet of 5	3.00	3.00
a.	A117 12c + 3c like #749		.25	.25
b.	A117 18c + 3c like #750		.25	.25
c.	A117 36c + 3c like #751		.50	.50
d.	A117 48c + 3c like #752		.65	.65
e.	A117 60c + 3c like #753		.85	.85
755	A117 85c + 5c like #749		1.20	1.20
756	A117 85c + 5c like #750		1.20	1.20
757	A117 85c + 5c like #751		1.20	1.20
758	A117 85c + 5c like #752		1.20	1.20
759	A117 85c + 5c like #753		1.20	1.20

Nos. 749-753 issued in sheets of 5 + label. Surtax was for children's charities.
Issued: Nos. 749-754, Nov. 14; others, Dec. 9.

Manned Flight
Bicent. — A118

Various balloons: 36c, 1st manned flight, 1783. 48c, Ascent of Adorne, Strasbourg, 1784. 60c, 1785. 72c, Man on horse, 1785. 96c, Godard's aerial acrobatics, 1850. $2.50, Blanchard & Jefferies, 1785.

1984, Jan. 16   **Photo.**   **Perf. 13**

760	A118	36c multicolored	.70	.70
761	A118	48c multicolored	.85	.85
762	A118	60c multicolored	.95	.95
763	A118	72c multicolored	1.10	1.10
764	A118	96c multicolored	1.25	1.25
	Nos. 760-764 (5)		4.85	4.85

Souvenir Sheets

765	A118	$2.50 multicolored	3.25	3.25
766		Sheet of 5	4.75	4.75
a.	A118 36c + 5c like 36c		.60	.60
b.	A118 48c + 5c like 48c		.70	.70
c.	A118 60c + 5c like 60c		1.05	1.05
d.	A118 72c + 5c like 72c		1.20	1.20
e.	A118 96c + 5c like 96c		1.60	1.60

No. 765 contains 1 stamp 30x48mm, perf. 13½.

Save the
Whales
Campaign
A119

10c, Cuvier's beaked whale. 18c, Risso's dolphin. 20c, True's beaked whale. 24c, Long-finned pilot whale. 30c, Narwhal. 36c, Beluga whale. 42c, Common dolphin. 48c, Commerson's dolphin. 60c, Bottle-nosed dolphin. 72c, Sowerby's whale. 96c, Common porpoise. $2, Boutu.

1984, Feb. 10   **Photo.**   **Perf. 13**

767	A119	10c multicolored	.55	.55
768	A119	18c multicolored	.75	.75
769	A119	20c multicolored	.85	.85
770	A119	24c multicolored	.90	.90
771	A119	30c multicolored	1.00	1.00
772	A119	36c multicolored	1.25	1.25
773	A119	42c multicolored	1.50	1.50
774	A119	48c multicolored	1.60	1.60
775	A119	60c multicolored	1.75	1.75
776	A119	72c multicolored	2.25	2.25
777	A119	96c multicolored	2.50	2.50
778	A119	$2 multicolored	3.50	3.50
	Nos. 767-778 (12)		18.40	18.40

1984 Summer
Olympics
A120

Posters of Various Summer Olympics: 18c, Athens, 1896. 24c, Paris, 1900. 36c, St. Louis, 1904. 48c, London, 1948. 60c, Tokyo, 1964. 72c, Berlin, 1936. 96c, Rome, 1960. $1.20, Los Angeles, 1932.
72c, 96c, $1.20 airmail.

1984, Mar. 8   **Photo.**   **Perf. 13½**

779	A120	18c multicolored	.45	.45
780	A120	24c multicolored	.50	.55
781	A120	36c multicolored	.60	.60
782	A120	48c multicolored	.70	.70
783	A120	60c multicolored	.80	.80
784	A120	72c multicolored	.90	.90
785	A120	96c multicolored	1.00	1.00
786	A120	$1.20 multicolored	1.25	1.25
	Nos. 779-786 (8)		6.20	6.25

For overprints see Nos. 826-828.

Coral — A121

and

Nos. 582-586 Surcharged

1c, Siphonogorgia. 2c, Millepora alcicornis. 3c, Distichopora violacea. 5c, Ptilosarcus gurneyi. 10c, Lobophyllia bemprichii. 12c, Sarcophyton digitatum. 14c, Pavona praetorta. 18c, Junceela gemmacea. 20c, Stylaster. 24c, Stylophora pistillata. 30c, Palauastrea ramosa. 36c, Melithaea albitincta. 40c, Stylaster echinatus. 42c, Fungia fungites. 48c, Gonipora. 50c, Melithaea squamata. 52c, Bellonella indica. 55c, Plerogyra sinuosa. 60c, Tubastraea. 70c, Heliofungia actinformis. 85c, Caulastraea echinulata. 96c, Porites andrewsi. $1.10, Pectinia alcicornis. $1.20, Dendrophyllia gracilis.

1984   *Perf. 13½x13*

787	A121	1c multi	.25	.50
788	A121	2c multi	.25	.25
789	A121	3c multi	.30	.30
790	A121	5c multi	.30	.30
791	A121	10c multi	.30	.30
792	A121	12c multi	.30	.30
793	A121	14c multi	.40	.30
794	A121	18c multi	.55	.35
795	A121	20c multi	.65	.35
796	A121	24c multi	.75	.35
797	A121	30c multi	.90	.35
798	A121	36c multi	1.00	.40
799	A121	40c multi	1.10	.40
800	A121	42c multi	1.25	.40
801	A121	48c multi	1.25	.40
802	A121	50c multi	1.25	.40
803	A121	52c multi	1.30	.40
804	A121	55c multi	1.40	.60
805	A121	60c multi	1.50	.60
806	A121	70c multi	2.00	.60
807	A121	85c multi	2.00	1.25
808	A121	96c multi	2.00	1.50
809	A121	$1.10 multi	2.00	1.75
810	A121	$1.20 multi	2.50	2.50

Perf. 14x13½

Size: 59½x38½mm

811	A102	$3.60 on $2 #582	5.75	5.75
812	A102	$4.20 on $3 #583	6.25	6.25
813	A102	$5 on $4 #584	6.50	6.50
814	A102	$7.20 on $6 #585	9.00	9.00
815	A102	$9.60 on $10		
		#586	11.00	11.00
	Nos. 787-815 (29)		64.00	53.35

Issued: Nos. 787-801, 3/23; Nos. 802-810, 5/15; Nos. 811-813, 6/28; No. 814, 7/20; No. 815, 8/10.
For surcharges & overprints see Nos. 948-952, 955, 958, 960, 963, 965-967, B105-B108, O32-O45.

Nos. 784-786 Overprinted With
Winners

No. 826

No. 827

Decathlon
Daley Thompson
Great Britain

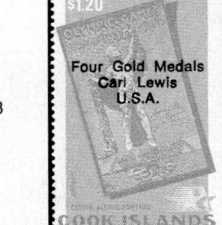

No. 828

Four Gold Medals
Carl Lewis
U.S.A.

1984, Aug. 24   Photo.   Perf. 13½

826	A120	72c multicolored	.75	.75
827	A120	96c multicolored	1.10	1.10
828	A120	$1.20 multicolored	1.75	1.75
		Nos. 826-828 (3)	3.60	3.60

1984 Summer Olympics. Nos. 826-828 airmail.

AUSIPEX '84 — A123

36c, Captain Cook's cottage. 48c, The Endeavour. 60c, Cook's landing. $2, Portrait, by John Webber.

1984, Sept. 20

829	A123	36c multicolored	1.75	1.50
830	A123	48c multicolored	2.50	2.50
831	A123	60c multicolored	2.60	2.75
832	A123	$2 multicolored	3.00	3.00
a.		Souv. sheet, #829-832, 90c ea	8.50	8.50
b.		Sheet of 4, STAMPEX '86 emblem	8.00	8.00
		Nos. 829-832 (4)	9.85	9.75

No. 832b issued Aug. 4, 1986, for STAMPEX '86, Adelaide, Aug. 4-10; margin ovptd. with exhibition emblem, stamp picturing James Cook ovptd. with gold circle and black "Stampex 86 / Adelaide."

Nos. 677-678 Ovptd. & Surcharged in Gold

No. 659 Ovptd. & Surcharged in Silver

1984, Oct. 15   Photo.   Perf. 14

833	A108	$1.25 Pair, #a.-b.	1.75	1.75
834	A108	$2.50 Pair, #a.-b.	4.50	4.50
835	A104	$3 on $1 No. 659	3.25	3.25
		Nos. 833-835 (3)	9.50	9.50

Nos. 833-835 printed in sheets of 4 stamps.

A124

Christmas (Paintings): 36c, Virgin on Throne with Child, by Giovanni Bellini (c. 1430-1516). 48c, Virgin and Child, 15th century, artist unknown. 60c, Virgin and Child with Saints, by Alvise Vivarini (c. 1446-1505). 96c, Virgin and Child with Angels, by Hans Memling (c. 1435-1494). $1.20, Adoration of the Magi, by Giovanni Tiepolo (1696-1770).

1984

838	A124	36c multicolored	1.25	.85
839	A124	48c multicolored	1.50	.95
840	A124	60c multicolored	2.00	2.00
841	A124	96c multicolored	2.50	2.50
842	A124	$1.20 multicolored	3.00	3.00
		Nos. 838-842 (5)	10.25	9.30

Souvenir Sheets

Perf. 13½

843		Sheet of 5	4.25	4.25
a.	A124	36c +5c like #838	.50	.50
b.	A124	48c +5c like #839	.65	.65
c.	A124	60c +5c like #840	.75	.75
d.	A124	96c +5c like #841	1.10	1.10
e.	A124	$1.20 +5c like #842	1.25	1.25
844	A124	95c + 5c like #838	1.25	1.25
845	A124	95c + 5c like #839	1.25	1.25
846	A124	95c + 5c like #840	1.25	1.25
847	A124	95c + 5c like #841	1.25	1.25
848	A124	95c + 5c like #842	1.25	1.25

Surtax of No. 843 for children's organizations, of Nos. 844-848 for youth education.
Issued: Nos. 838-843, 11/21; Nos. 844-848, 12/10.

A125

Illustrations of North American bird species by artist, naturalist John J. Audubon: 30c, Downy woodpecker. 55c, Black-throated blue warbler. 65c, Yellow-throated warbler. 75c, Chestnut-sided warbler. 95c, Dickcissel. $1.15, White-crowned sparrow. $1.30, Red-cockaded woodpecker. $2.80, Seaside sparrow. $5.30, Zenaida dove.

1985, Apr. 23   Perf. 13x13½

849	A125	30c multicolored	1.25	1.25
850	A125	55c multicolored	2.00	2.00
851	A125	65c multicolored	2.25	2.25
852	A125	75c multicolored	2.50	2.50
853	A125	95c multicolored	2.75	2.75
854	A125	$1.15 multicolored	3.00	3.00
		Nos. 849-854 (6)	13.75	13.75

Souvenir Sheets

855	A125	$1.30 multicolored	2.00	2.00
856	A125	$2.80 multicolored	3.50	3.50
857	A125	$5.30 multicolored	7.50	7.50

Audubon birth bicentenary.

Locomotives — A126

20c, Kingston Flyer, New Zealand. 55c, Class 640, Italy. 65c, Gotthard, Switzerland. 75c, Union Pacific 6900, US. 95c, Super Continental, Canada. $1.15, TGV, France. $2.20, Flying Scotsman, U.K. $3.40, Orient Express, Europe.

1985, May 14   Litho.   Perf. 14x13½

858	A126	20c multicolored	.25	.25
859	A126	55c multicolored	.35	.35
860	A126	65c multicolored	.45	.45
861	A126	75c multicolored	.50	.50
862	A126	95c multicolored	.60	.60
863	A126	$1.15 multicolored	.65	.65
864	A126	$2.20 multicolored	1.00	1.00
865	A126	$3.40 multicolored	1.25	1.25
		Nos. 858-865 (8)	5.05	5.05

Intl. Youth
Year — A127

Paintings: 55c, Helena Fourment, by Rubens. 65c, Vigee-Lebrun and Daughter, by Elizabeth Vigee-Lebrun (1755-1842). 75c, On the Terrace, by Renoir. $1.30, Young Mother Sewing, by Mary Cassatt (1845-1926).

1985, June 6   Photo.   Perf. 13x13½

866	A127	55c multicolored	2.75	2.75
867	A127	65c multicolored	3.25	3.25
868	A127	75c multicolored	3.75	3.75
869	A127	$1.30 multicolored	6.00	6.00
		Nos. 866-869 (4)	15.75	15.75

Souvenir Sheet

870		Sheet of 4	8.75	8.75
a.	A127	55c + 10c like #866	1.25	1.25
b.	A127	65c + 10c like #867	1.50	1.50
c.	A127	75c + 10c like #868	2.00	2.00
d.	A127	$1.30 + 10c like #869	3.25	3.25

Surtax for youth organizations.

Queen Mother,
85th Birthday
A128

Portraits: 65c, Lady Elizabeth, 1908, by Mable Hankey. 75c, Duchess of York, 1923, by Savely Sorine. $1.15, Duchess of York, 1925, by Philip De Laszlo. $2.80, $5.30, Queen Elizabeth, 1938, by Sir Gerald Kelly.

1985, June 28

871	A128	65c multi	.55	.55
872	A128	75c multi	.65	.65
873	A128	$1.15 multi	1.00	1.00
874	A128	$2.80 multi	1.50	1.50
874A		Sheet of 4 ('86)	6.00	6.00
b.-e.		A128 55c, like #871-874	1.40	1.40
		Nos. 871-874A (5)	9.70	9.70

Souvenir Sheet

875	A128	$5.30 multi	4.50	4.50

Nos. 871-874 printed in sheets of four.
No. 874A issued 8/4/86, for 86th birthday.
For surcharges see Nos. B114, B116, B122, B134, B140.

A129

Portraits of prime ministers: 30c, Albert Henry, 1965-78. 50c, Sir Thomas Davis, 1978-83. 65c, Geoffrey Henry, 1983.

1985, July 29

876	A129	30c multicolored	1.00	1.00
877	A129	50c multicolored	1.50	1.50
878	A129	65c multicolored	2.00	2.00
		Nos. 876-878 (3)	4.50	4.50

Souvenir Sheet

879		Sheet of 3	3.75	3.75
a.	A129	55c like #876	1.20	1.20
b.	A129	55c like #877	1.20	1.20
c.	A129	55c like #878	1.20	1.20

Self-government, 20th anniv.

A130

1985, July 29   Perf. 14

880	A130	55c Golf	4.00	4.00
881	A130	65c Rugby	4.25	4.25
882	A130	75c Tennis	5.25	5.25
		Nos. 880-882 (3)	13.50	13.50

Souvenir Sheet

883		Sheet of 3	11.50	11.50
a.	A130	55c + 10c like #880	3.25	3.25
b.	A130	65c + 10c like #881	3.25	3.25
c.	A130	75c + 10c like #882	3.25	3.25

South Pacific Mini Games, Rarotonga, July 31-Aug. 10. Surtax for the benefit of the Mini Games.

A131

Seahorse & conf. emblems: 55c, South Pacific Bureau for Economic Cooperation. 65c, No. 887b, South Pacific Forum. 75c, No. 887c, Pacific Islands Conf.

1985, July 29   Perf. 14

884	A131	55c blk, scar & gold	1.25	1.25
885	A131	65c blk, vio & gold	1.40	1.40
886	A131	75c blk, brt grn & gold	1.50	1.50
		Nos. 884-886 (3)	4.15	4.15

Souvenir Sheet

887		50c Sheet of 3, #a.-c.	2.50	2.50

Pacific islands conf., Rarotonga, 7/30-8/10.

A132

Virgin and Child paintings by Botticelli: 55c, Madonna of the Magnificent. 65c, Madonna with Pomegranate. 75c, Madonna with Child & Six Angels. 95c, Madonna & Child with St. John.

1985

888	A132	55c multicolored	1.60	1.60
889	A132	65c multicolored	2.10	2.10
890	A132	75c multicolored	2.50	2.60
891	A132	95c multicolored	3.25	3.25
		Nos. 888-891 (4)	9.45	9.55

Souvenir Sheets

Perf. 13½

892	A132	$2.75 Sheet of 4	6.00	6.00
a.	A132	50c like #888	1.25	1.25
b.	A132	50c like #889	1.25	1.25
c.	A132	50c like #890	1.25	1.25
d.	A132	50c like #891	1.25	1.25

Imperf

893	A132	$1.20 like #888	1.75	1.75
894	A132	$1.45 like #889	2.00	2.00
895	A132	$2.20 like #890	3.25	3.25
896	A132	$2.75 like #891	3.50	3.50

Christmas. Issue dates: Nos. 888-892, Nov. 18; Nos. 893-896, Dec. 9.

Halley's
Comet — A133

Paintings: 55c, No. 902a, The Eve of the Deluge, by John Martin (1789-1854). 65c, No. 902b, Lot and His Daughters, by Lucas van Leyden (1494-1533). 75c, No. 902c, Auspicious Comet, 1587, anonymous. $1.25, No. 902d, Events Following Charles I, by Herman Saftleven (1609-1658). $2, No. 902e, Ossian Receiving Napoleonic Officers, by Anne Louis Girodet-Trioson (1764-1824). $4, Halley's Comet over the Thames, 1759, by Samuel Scott (1702-1772).

1986, Mar. 13   Photo.   Perf. 14

897	A133	55c multicolored	1.25	1.25
898	A133	65c multicolored	1.50	1.50
899	A133	75c multicolored	1.75	1.75
900	A133	$1.25 multicolored	2.25	2.25
901	A133	$2 multicolored	3.50	3.50
	Nos. 897-901 (5)		10.25	10.25

Souvenir Sheets
Perf. 13½

902		Sheet of 5 + label	6.00	6.00
a.-e.	A133 70c, each single		1.10	1.10
903	A133	$4 multicolored	7.50	7.50

For surcharges see Nos. B113, B115, B117, B123, B129.

Elizabeth II, 60th
Birthday — A134

Various portraits.

1986, Apr. 21   Perf. 13x13½

904	A134	95c multi	1.10	1.10
905	A134	$1.25 multi	1.25	1.25
906	A134	$1.50 multi	1.60	1.60
	Nos. 904-906 (3)		3.95	3.95

Souvenir Sheets

907	A134	$1.10 like #904	2.00	2.00
908	A134	$1.95 like #905	3.50	3.50
909	A134	$2.45 like #906	4.75	5.75

For surcharges see Nos. 972-974, B118, B124, B127, B136-B137, B139.

AMERIPEX '86 — A135

Designs: $1, US No. 1, The Resolution, Rarotonga. $1.50, Downtown Chicago. $2, No. 398, Benjamin Franklin, The Resolution.

1986, May 21   Photo.   Perf. 14

910	A135	$1 multi	3.50	3.50
911	A135	$1.50 multi	5.25	5.25
912	A135	$2 multi	6.75	6.75
	Nos. 910-912 (3)		15.50	15.50

For surcharges see Nos. B119, B128, B130.

Statue of Liberty,
Cent. — A136

1986, July 4

913	A136	$1 Head	1.00	1.00
914	A136	$1.25 Torch	1.25	1.25
915	A136	$2.75 Liberty Is.	2.75	2.75
	Nos. 913-915 (3)		5.00	5.00

For surcharges see Nos. B120, B125, B132.

Wedding of
Prince Andrew
and Sarah
Ferguson — A137

1986, July 23

916	A137	$1 Sarah Ferguson	.80	.80
917	A137	$2 Prince Andrew	1.60	1.60

Size: 60x33½mm
Perf. 13½x13

918	A137	$3 Couple	2.40	2.40
	Nos. 916-918 (3)		4.80	4.80

Nos. 916-918 each printed in sheets of 4.
For surch. see Nos. 975-977, B121, B131, B135.

Christmas
A138

Paintings by Rubens: 55c, No. 922a, The Holy Family. $1.30, No. 922b, Virgin with Garland. $2.75, No. 922c, Adoration of Magi.

1986, Nov. 17   Litho.   Perf. 13½

919	A138	55c multi	1.40	1.40
920	A138	$1.30 multi	3.25	3.25
921	A138	$2.75 multi	6.50	6.50
	Nos. 919-921 (3)		11.15	11.15

Souvenir Sheets

922		Sheet of 3	14.00	14.00
a.-c.	A138 $2.40, any single		4.50	4.50
923	A138	$6.40 multi	15.00	15.00

No. 922 contains 3 stamps 38½x49mm.
For surcharges see Nos. B100-B104, B112, B126, B133, B138, B141.

Stamps of 1980-84 Surcharged in Black

Strips of 4, #a.-d. (#953, 954, 956, 957) or
Blocks of 4, #a.-d. (#959, 961, 962, 964)

1987, Feb.   Litho.   Perfs. as before

948	A121	5c on 1c #787	.25	.25
949	A121	5c on 2c #788	.25	.25
950	A121	5c on 3c #789	.25	.25
951	A121	5c on 12c #792	.25	.25
952	A121	5c on 14c #793	.25	.25
953	A101	10c on 15c #572	.55	.55
954	A101	10c on 25c #574	.55	.55
955	A121	18c on 24c #796	.25	.25
956	A101	18c on 12c #571	1.10	1.10
957	A101	18c on 20c #573	1.10	1.10
958	A121	55c on 52c #803	.90	.90
959	A101	55c on 35c #576	3.25	3.25
960	A101	65c on 42c #800	1.00	1.00
961	A101	65c on 50c #577	4.50	4.50
962	A101	65c on 60c #578	4.50	4.50
963	A101	75c on 48c #801	1.25	1.25
964	A101	75c on 70c #579	4.50	4.50
965	A121	95c on 96c #808	1.50	1.50
966	A121	95c on $1.10 #809	1.50	1.50
967	A121	95c on $1.20 #810	1.50	1.50

Stamps of 1981-86 Surcharged in Black (A102), Black and Gold (#968-970, A137) or Gold (#971, A134, A104, A108)

968	A123	$1.30 on 36c #829	1.90	1.90
969	A123	$1.30 on 48c #830	1.90	1.90
970	A123	$1.30 on 60c #831	1.90	1.90
971	A123	$1.30 on $2 #832	1.90	1.90
972	A134	$2.80 on 95c #904	4.25	4.25
973	A134	$2.80 on $1.25 #905	4.25	4.25
974	A134	$2.80 on $1.50 #906	4.25	4.25
975	A137	$2.80 on $1 #916	4.25	4.25
976	A137	$2.80 on $2 #917	4.25	4.25
977	A137	$2.80 on $3 #918	4.25	4.25
978	A102	$6.40 on $4 #584	7.50	7.50
979	A102	$7.20 on $6 #585	8.50	8.50
980	A104	$9.40 on $1 #659	11.00	11.00
981	A104	$9.40 on $2 #660	11.00	11.00

Pair, #a.-b.

982	A108	$9.40 on $2.50 #678	22.00	22.00
	Nos. 948-982 (35)		122.30	122.30

Issued: 5c, Nos. 955, 958, 960, 963, 95c, $6.40, $7.20, 2/10; 10c, Nos. 956-957, 959, 961-962, 964, 2/11; $12.30, $2.80, $9.40, 2/12.
For surcharge see No. B111.

Stamps of 1980-82 Surcharged in Black (A102) or Gold (A104)

No. 984

No. 989

Perfs. as before
1987, June 17   Photo.

984	A102	$2.80 on $2 #582	2.75	2.75
985	A102	$5 on $3 #583	4.75	4.75
986	A102	$9.40 on $10 #586	8.50	8.50

Pairs, #a.-b.

987	A104	$9.40 on $1 #679	17.00	17.00
988	A104	$9.40 on $2 #680	17.00	17.00
	Nos. 984-988 (5)		50.00	50.00

Souvenir Sheet

989	A104	$9.20 on #680c	15.00	15.00

Nos. 399 and 584 Ovptd. in Black on Gold Bar

1987, Nov. 20   Photo.   Perf. 14x13½

991	A64	$4 on #399	4.00	4.00
992	A102	$4 on #584	4.00	4.00

Christmas — A139

The Holy Family, religious paintings by Rembrandt in European museums: $1.25, No. 996a, The Louvre, Paris. $1.50, No. 996b, $6, The Holy Family with Angels, The Hermitage, Leningrad. $1.95, No. 996c, The Alte Pinakothek, Munich.

1987, Dec. 7   Photo.   Perf. 13½

993	A139	$1.25 multi	2.50	2.50
994	A139	$1.50 multi	3.50	3.50
995	A139	$1.95 multi	4.50	4.50
	Nos. 993-995 (3)		10.50	10.50

Souvenir Sheets

996		Sheet of 3	8.50	8.50
a.-c.	A139 $1.15 any single		2.50	2.50

Perf. 13x13½

997	A139	$6 multi	11.00	11.00

Size of Nos. 996a-996c: 49½x38½mm. No. 997 contains 1 stamp 39½x31½mm.

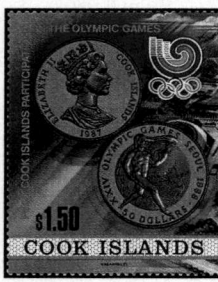

1988 Summer Olympics, Seoul A140

Designs: a, Cook Islands commemorative silver coin (obverse and reverse) issued on Aug. 20, 1987, for the '88 Summer Games. b, Seoul Olympic Park, torch and emblem. c, Steffi Graf, women's tennis champion, and '88 gold medal.

1988, Apr. 26   Photo.   Perf. 13½x14

998		Strip of 3	15.00	15.00
a.-c.	A140 $1.50 multicolored		5.00	5.00

Souvenir Sheet
Perf. 13½

999	A140	$10 multi	15.00	15.00

Participation of national athletes in the Olympics for the first time, introduction of tennis as an Olympic gold-medal event.
No. 999 contains one stamp 114x47mm combining the designs of Nos. 998a-998c.

Nos. 998-999 Overprinted

a-c

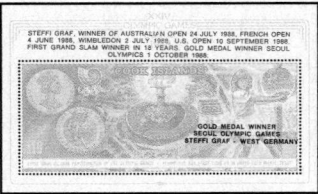

d

1988, Oct. 12   Photo.   Perf. 13½x14

| 1000 | | Strip of 3 | 12.00 | 12.00 |
| a.-c. | A140 | $1.50 multicolored | 4.00 | 4.00 |

Souvenir Sheet
Perf. 13½

| 1001 | A140(d) | $10 on No. 999 | 16.00 | 16.00 |

Christmas
A141

Paintings by Albrecht Durer: 70c, Virgin and Child. 85c, Virgin and Child, diff. 95c, Virgin and Child, diff. $1.25, Virgin and Child, diff. $6.40, The Nativity.

1988, Nov. 11   Perf. 13½

1002	A141	70c multi	2.75	2.75
1003	A141	85c multi	3.25	3.25
1004	A141	95c multi	3.75	3.75
1005	A141	$1.25 multi	5.00	5.00
		Nos. 1002-1005 (4)	14.75	14.75

Souvenir Sheet

| 1006 | A141 | $6.40 multi | 12.00 | 12.00 |

No. 1006 contains one stamp 45x60mm.

Scene and Left Half of Mission Emblem
A142

1st Moon Landing, 20th Anniv. — A144

No. 1007a, Launch vehicle in space. No. 1007b, *Eagle* landing on Moon. No. 1008a, Astronaut descending ladder. No. 1008b, Astronaut on Moon. No. 1009a, Seismic experiment. No. 1009b, Solar wind experiment. No. 1010a, Liftoff from Moon. No. 1010b, Splashdown and recovery.
The "b" stamps have the right half of the emblem.

1989, July 14   Photo.   Perf. 13

1007	A142	40c Pair, #a.-b.	3.00	3.00
1008	A142	55c Pair, #a.-b.	4.50	4.50
1009	A142	65c Pair, #a.-b.	5.00	5.00
1010	A142	75c Pair, #a.-b.	5.50	5.50
		Nos. 1007-1010 (4)	18.00	18.00

Souvenir Sheet

| 1011 | A144 | $4.20 Armstrong and Aldrin | 8.75 | 8.75 |

Printed with continuous designs.

World Wildlife Fund
A145

Endangered bird species: 15c, $1, Pomarea dimidiata. 20c, $1.25, Pomarea dimidiata (two). 65c, $1.50, Ptilinopus rarotongensis (two). 70c, $1.75, Ptilinopus rarotongensis.

1989, Oct. 4   Photo.   Perf. 13½x13

1016	A145	15c multicolored	1.40	1.40
1017	A145	20c multicolored	2.00	2.00
1018	A145	65c multicolored	5.50	5.50
1019	A145	70c multicolored	6.25	6.25
		Nos. 1016-1019 (4)	15.15	15.15

Souvenir Sheets
Without WWF Emblem
Perf. 13½

1020	A145	$1 like 15c	2.75	2.75
1021	A145	$1.25 like 20c	3.25	3.25
1022	A145	$1.50 like 65c	3.75	3.75
1023	A145	$1.75 like 70c	4.25	4.25

World Wildlife Fund. Nos. 1020-1023 are airmail and contain one 52x34mm stamp; decorative margins continue the designs.
For overprints see Nos. C24-C27.

Christmas — A146

Details of *Adoration of the Magi*, by Rubens: 70c, Witnesses. 85c, Madonna. 95c, Christ child. $1.50, Attendant. $6.40, Entire painting.

1989, Nov. 24   Photo.   Perf. 13½x13

1024	A146	70c multicolored	1.60	1.60
1025	A146	85c multicolored	1.75	1.75
1026	A146	95c multicolored	2.10	2.10
1027	A146	$1.50 multicolored	3.25	3.25
		Nos. 1024-1027 (4)	8.70	8.70

Souvenir Sheet
Perf. 13½

| 1028 | A146 | $6.40 multicolored | 15.00 | 15.00 |

No. 1028 contains one 45x60mm stamp.

Religious History
A147

70c, John Williams, LMS Mission Church. 85c, Bernardine Castanie, Roman Catholic Church. 95c, Osborne J.P. Widstoe, Church of Jesus Christ of Latter Day Saints. $1.60, J.E. Caldwell, Seventh Day Adventist Church.

1990, Feb. 19   Photo.   Perf. 13½x13

1029	A147	70c multicolored	1.00	1.00
1030	A147	85c multicolored	1.20	1.20
1031	A147	95c multicolored	1.40	1.40
1032	A147	$1.60 multicolored	2.40	2.40
		Nos. 1029-1032 (4)	6.00	6.00

Souvenir Sheet
Perf. 13½

1033		Sheet of 4	7.00	7.00
a.	A147	90c like 70c	1.50	1.50
b.	A147	90c like 85c	1.50	1.50
c.	A147	90c like 95c	1.50	1.50
d.	A147	90c like $1.60	1.50	1.50

No. 1033 contains 4 36x36mm stamps.

Penny Black, 150th Anniv. — A148

Paintings: 85c, No. 1038a, *Woman Writing a Letter,* by Gerard Terborch (1617-1681). $1.15, No. 1038b, *Portrait of George Gisze,* by Hans Holbein the Younger. $1.55, No. 1038c, *Portrait of Mrs. John Douglas,* by Thomas Gainsborough. $1.85, No. 1038d, *Portrait of a Gentleman,* by Albrecht Durer.

1990, May 2   Photo.   Perf. 13½

1034	A148	85c multicolored	1.40	1.40
1035	A148	$1.15 multicolored	2.00	2.00
1036	A148	$1.55 multicolored	2.60	2.60
1037	A148	$1.85 multicolored	3.25	3.25
		Nos. 1034-1037 (4)	9.25	9.25

Souvenir Sheet

| 1038 | | Sheet of 4 | 13.00 | 13.00 |
| a.-d. | A148 | $1.05 any single | 3.00 | 3.00 |

The margin of No. 1038 pictures the Stamp World '90 emblem and Great Britain #1-2.

1992 Olympics
A149

Designs: a. Summer Games, Barcelona (runners). b. Eternal flame, commemorative coin obverse (Queen Elizabeth II) and reverse (athletes). c. Winter Games, Albertville (skier).

1990, June 15   Photo.   Perf. 14

| 1039 | | Strip of 3 | 18.00 | 18.00 |
| a.-c. | A149 | $1.85 any single | 6.00 | 6.00 |

Queen Mother, 90th Birthday
A150

1990, July 20   Photo.   Perf. 13½

| 1040 | A150 | $1.85 multicolored | 6.50 | 6.50 |

Souvenir Sheet

| 1041 | A150 | $6.40 multicolored | 13.00 | 13.00 |

Christmas
A151

Paintings: 70c, Adoration of the Magi by Memling. 85c, The Holy Family by Lotto. 95c, Madonna and Child with Saints John and Catherine by Titian. $1.50, The Holy Family by Titian. $6.40, Madonna and Child Enthroned, Surrounded by Saints by Vivarini.

1990, Nov. 29   Litho.   Perf. 14

1042	A151	70c multicolored	1.75	1.75
1043	A151	85c multicolored	2.40	2.40
1044	A151	95c multicolored	2.50	2.50
1045	A151	$1.50 multicolored	3.75	3.75
		Nos. 1042-1045 (4)	10.40	10.40

Souvenir Sheet

| 1046 | A151 | $6.40 multicolored | 15.00 | 15.00 |

For overprints and surcharges see Nos. 1251, 1254, 1257-1258.

1992 Olympic Games — A152

1991, Feb. 12   Perf. 13½

| 1047 | A152 | $6.40 multicolored | 15.00 | 15.00 |

Discovery of America 500th Anniv. (in 1992) — A153

1991, Feb. 14   Photo.   Perf. 13½x13

| 1048 | A153 | $1 multicolored | 4.25 | 4.25 |

No. 586 Ovptd. "65th BIRTHDAY" in Gold

1991, Apr. 22   Litho.   Perf. 14x13½

| 1049 | A102 | $10 multicolored | 18.00 | 18.00 |

Christmas
A154

Paintings: 70c, Adoration of the Child, by Delle Notti (Gerrit van Honthorst). 85c, Birth of the Virgin, by Murillo. $1.15, Adoration of the Shepherds, by Rembrandt. $1.50, Adoration of the Shepherds, by Le Nain. $6.40, Madonna and Child, by Fra Filippo Lippi, vert.

1991, Nov. 12   Litho.   Perf. 14

1050	A154	70c multicolored	1.00	1.00
1051	A154	85c multicolored	3.00	3.00
1052	A154	$1.15 multicolored	4.25	4.25
1053	A154	$1.50 multicolored	5.75	5.75
		Nos. 1050-1053 (4)	14.00	14.00

Souvenir Sheet

| 1054 | A154 | $6.40 multicolored | 15.00 | 15.00 |

For overprints and surcharges see Nos. 1252-1253, 1255-1256.

Marine Life — A155

A155a

5c, Red-breasted maori wrasse. 10c, Blue sea star. 15c, Black & gold angelfish. 20c, Spotted pebble crab. 25c, Black-tipped cod. 30c, Spanish dancer. 50c, Royal angelfish. 80c, Squirrel fish. 85c, Red pencil sea urchin. 90c, Red-spot rainbow fish. $1, Black-lined maori wrasse. $2, Longnose butterflyfish. $3, Red-spot rainbow fish. $5, Blue sea star. $7, Royal angelfish. $10, Spotted pebble crab. $15, Red pencil sea urchin.

1992-94   Litho.   Perf. 14½x13½

1058	A155	5c multi	.40	.40
1059	A155	10c multi	.40	.40
1062	A155	15c multi	.40	.40
1064	A155	20c multi	.50	.50

1065	A155	25c multi	.55	.55
1066	A155	30c multi	.65	.65
1071	A155	50c multi	1.10	1.10
1076	A155	80c multi	1.75	1.75
1077	A155	85c multi	1.75	1.75
1078	A155	90c multi	1.75	1.75
1080	A155	$1 multi	2.00	2.00
1081	A155	$2 multi	3.75	3.75
1082	A155a	$3 multi	4.50	4.50
1083	A155a	$5 multi	8.00	8.00
1085	A155a	$7 multi	12.00	12.00
1087	A155a	$10 multi	17.00	17.00
1089	A155a	$15 multi	25.00	25.00
		Nos. 1058-1089 (17)	81.50	81.50

Issued: 85c, 90c, $1, $2, 3/23/92; $3, $5, 10/25/93; $7, 12/6/93; $10, 1/31/94; $15, 9/9/94; others, 1/22/92.

See Nos. 1154-1176 for stamps with buff border. For overprints see Nos. O54-O68.

Endangered Wildlife — A156

$1.15 each: No. 1095, Tiger. No. 1096, Asiatic elephant. No. 1097, Grizzly bear. No. 1098, Black rhinoceros. No. 1099, Chimpanzee. No. 1100, Asian bighorn. No. 1101, Heavisides dolphin. No. 1102, Eagle owl. No. 1103, Bee hummingbird. No. 1104, Feliseoncolor cougar. No. 1105, European otter. No. 1106, Red kangaroo.

1992		**Litho.**	**Perf. 14**
1095-1106	A156	Set of 12	20.00 20.00

Issued: No. 1095, 4/6; No. 1096, 4/7; No. 1097, 4/8; No. 1098, 4/9; No. 1099, 4/10; No. 1100, 4/11; No. 1101, 7/13; No. 1102, 7/14; No. 1103, 7/15; No. 1104, 7/16; No. 1105, 7/17; No. 1106, 7/18.

See Nos. 1119-1124, 1134-1138.
For surcharges see Nos. 1239-1250.

Discovery of America, 500th Anniv. — A157

1992, May 22		**Litho.**	**Perf. 14x14½**
1107	A157	$6 multicolored	9.00 9.00

Souvenir Sheet
Perf. 15x14

1107A	A157	$10 Coming ashore	10.50 10.50

Issued: No. 1107, 5/22. No. 1107A, 9/21.
No. 1107A contains one 40x30mm stamp.

1992 Summer Olympics, Barcelona — A158

Designs: No. 1108a, $50 coin, soccer players. b, Flags of Spain, Cook Islands, Barcelona medal. c, $10 coin, basketball players. No. 1109a, Runners. b, $10, $50 coins. c, Cyclists. $6.40, Javelin.

1992, July 24		**Litho.**	**Perf. 13**
1108	A158	$1.75 Strip of 3,	
		#a.-c.	9.00 9.00
1109	A158	$2.25 Strip of 3,	
		#a.-c.	11.00 11.00

Souvenir Sheet

1110	A158	$6.40 multicolored	19.00 19.00

6th Festival of Pacific Arts, Rarotonga A159

80c, UNESCO poster. 85c, $1, $1.75, Different carvings of Rarotongan fertility god, Tangaroa.

1992, Oct. 16		**Litho.**	**Perf. 15x14**
1111	A159	80c multicolored	1.75 1.75
1112	A159	85c multicolored	2.00 2.00
1113	A159	$1 multicolored	2.40 2.40
1114	A159	$1.75 multicolored	3.75 3.75
		Nos. 1111-1114 (4)	9.90 9.90

For overprints see Nos. 1231-1234.

ROYAL VISIT

Overprinted in Black

1992, Oct. 16

1115	A159	80c on #1111	2.10 2.10
1116	A159	85c on #1112	2.50 2.50
1117	A159	$1 on #1113	2.50 2.50
1118	A159	$1.75 on #1114	4.75 4.75
		Nos. 1115-1118 (4)	11.85 11.85

Endangered Wildlife Type of 1992

No. 1119, Jackass penguin. No. 1120, Asian lion. No. 1121, Peregrine falcon. No. 1122, Persian fallow deer. No. 1123, Key deer. No. 1124, Alpine ibex.

1992		**Litho.**	**Perf. 14**
1119	A156	$1.15 multicolored	1.75 1.75
1120	A156	$1.15 multicolored	1.75 1.75
1121	A156	$1.15 multicolored	1.75 1.75
1122	A156	$1.15 multicolored	1.75 1.75
1123	A156	$1.15 multicolored	1.75 1.75
1124	A156	$1.15 multicolored	1.75 1.75
		Nos. 1119-1124 (6)	10.50 10.50

Issued: No. 1119, 11/2; No. 1120, 11/3; No. 1121, 11/4; No. 1122, 11/5; No. 1123, 11/6; No. 1124, 11/7.

Christmas A160

Paintings by El Parmigianino: 70c, Worship of Shepherds. 85c, $6.40, Virgin with Long Neck. $1.15, Virgin with Rose. $1.90, St. Margaret's Virgin.

1992, Nov. 20		**Litho.**	**Perf. 13½**
1125	A160	70c multicolored	1.00 1.00
1126	A160	85c multicolored	1.60 1.60
1127	A160	$1.15 multicolored	2.10 2.10
1128	A160	$1.90 multicolored	3.75 3.75
		Nos. 1125-1128 (4)	8.45 8.45

Souvenir Sheet

1129	A160	$6.40 multicolored	12.50 12.50

No. 1129 contains one 36x47mm stamp.

Queen Elizabeth II's Accession to the Throne, 40th Anniv. — A161

Various portraits of Queen Elizabeth II.

1992, Dec. 10		**Litho.**	**Perf. 14**
1130	A161	80c multicolored	1.25 1.25
1131	A161	$1.15 multicolored	2.00 2.00
1132	A161	$1.50 multicolored	3.25 3.25
1133	A161	$1.95 multicolored	4.50 4.50
		Nos. 1130-1133 (4)	11.00 11.00

Endangered Wildlife Type of 1992

No. 1134, English mandrill. No. 1135, Gorilla. No. 1136, Vanessa atlanta. No. 1137, Sichuan takin. No. 1138, Ring tailed lemur.

1993		**Litho.**	**Perf. 14**
1134	A156	$1.15 multicolored	2.00 2.00
1135	A156	$1.15 multicolored	2.00 2.00
1136	A156	$1.15 multicolored	2.00 2.00
1137	A156	$1.15 multicolored	2.00 2.00
1138	A156	$1.15 multicolored	2.00 2.00
		Nos. 1134-1138 (5)	10.00 10.00

Issued: No. 1134, 2/1; No. 1135, 2/2; No. 1136, 2/3; No. 1137, 2/4; No. 1138, 2/5.

Coronation of Queen Elizabeth II, 40th Anniv. — A162

Designs: $1, Coronation ceremony. $2, Coronation portrait. $3, Queen, family on balcony, Buckingham Palace.

1993, June 2		**Litho.**	**Perf. 14**
1139	A162	$1 multicolored	2.25 2.25
1140	A162	$2 multicolored	4.75 4.75
1141	A162	$3 multicolored	7.00 7.00
		Nos. 1139-1141 (3)	14.00 14.00

Christmas A163

Paintings: 70c, Virgin with Child, by Filippo Lippi. 85c, Bargellini Madonna, by Lodovico Carracci. $1.15, Virgin of the Curtain, by Raphael. $2.50, Holy Family, by Il Bronzino. $4, Saint Zachary Virgin, by Il Parmigianino.

1993, Nov. 8		**Litho.**	**Perf. 14**
1142	A163	70c multicolored	1.00 1.00
1143	A163	85c multicolored	1.40 1.40
1144	A163	$1.15 multicolored	1.75 1.75
1145	A163	$2.50 multicolored	3.50 3.50

Size: 32x47mm
Perf. 13½

1146	A163	$4.00 multicolored	6.25 6.25
		Nos. 1142-1146 (5)	13.90 13.90

1994 Winter Olympics, Lillehammer — A164

1994, Feb. 11		**Litho.**	**Perf. 13½x14**
1147	A164	$5 multicolored	10.00 10.00

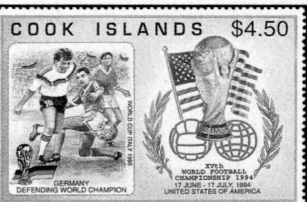

1994 World Cup Soccer Championships, US — A165

1994, June 17		**Litho.**	**Perf. 14**
1148	A165	$4.50 multicolored	8.00 8.00

First Manned Moon Landing, 25th Anniv. — A166

Apollo 11 emblem and: No. 1149a, First step onto Moon, US flag. No. 1149b, Astronaut carrying experiment packs on Moon. No. 1150a, Astronaut, US flag. No. 1150b, Flag, reflection shown in astronaut's visor.

1994, July 20			
1149	A166	$2.25 Pair, #a.-b. + label	9.00 9.00
1150	A166	$2.25 Pair, #a.-b. + label	9.00 9.00

Living Reef Type of 1992

1994, Oct. 24		**Litho.**	**Perf. 14½x13½**
		Size: 41x31mm	
		Buff & Multicolored	
1154	A155	5c like #1058	.50 .50
1158	A155	15c like #1062	.50 .50
1160	A155	20c like #1064	.60 .60
1161	A155	25c like #1065	.65 .65
1162	A155	30c like #1066	.75 .75
1167	A155	50c like #1071	1.40 1.40
1172	A155	80c like #1076	2.25 2.25
1173	A155	85c like #1077	2.40 2.40
1174	A155	90c like #1078	2.50 2.50
1176	A155	$1 like #1080	2.75 2.75
		Nos. 1154-1176 (10)	14.30 14.30

Miniature Sheet

The Return of Tommy Tricker — A167

Scenes from film: a, Three people in canoe. b, Traditional dancers. c, Couple walking on beach. d, Aerial view of island. e, Girls performing hand gestures. f, Girls walking along sand bar.

1994, Nov. 23		**Litho.**	**Perf. 14**
1191	A167	85c Sheet of 6, #a.-f.	9.50 9.50

See No. 1213.

Christmas — A168

Paintings: No. 1192a, The Virgin and Child, by Morales. b, Adoration of Kings, by Gerard David. c, Adoration of Kings, by Vinc Foppa. d, The Madonna & Child with St. Joseph & Infant Baptist, by Baroccio.

No. 1193a, Madonna with Iris, in style of Durer. b, Adoration of Shepherds, by Le Nain. c, The Virgin and Child, by follower of Leonardo. d, The Mystic Nativity, by Botticelli.

1994, Nov. 30   Litho.   Perf. 14
1192 A168 85c Block of 4, #a.-d.   6.75 6.75
1193 A168 $1 Block of 4, #a.-d.   7.75 7.75

Robert Louis Stevenson (1850-94),
Writer — A169

Adventure scenes from books: a, "Treasure Island." b, "David Balfour." c, "Dr. Jekyll and Mr. Hyde." d, "Kidnapped."

1994, Dec. 12   Perf. 14x15
1194 A169 $1.50 Block of 4,
        #a.-d.   14.00 14.00

UN, 50th Anniv. — A170

$4.50, FAO, 50th anniv.

1995   Litho.   Perf. 13x13½
1195 A170 $4.75 multicolored   6.25 6.25
                Perf. 13½
1196 A170 $4.50 multicolored   6.75 6.75
    Each issued in sheets of 4.
    Issued: $4.75, 7/17; $4.50, 10/12.

Queen Mother, 95th Birthday — A172

1995, Aug. 31
1197 A172 $5 multicolored   12.00 12.00

End of World War II, 50th
Anniv. — A173

Designs: a, German surrender, Rheims. b, Japanese surrender, Tokyo Bay.

1995, Sept. 4   Perf. 13
1198 A173 $3.50 Pair, #a.-b.   22.00 22.00
No. 1198 was issued in sheets of 4 stamps.

Year of the
Sea Turtle
A174

Designs: 85c, Green turtle in water. $1, Hawksbill turtle in water. $1.75, Green turtle nesting. $2.25, Hawksbill turtle hatchlings leaving nest.

1995, Nov. 20   Litho.   Perf. 14
1199 A174 85c multicolored   2.00 2.00
1200 A174 $1 multicolored   2.75 2.75
1201 A174 $1.75 multicolored 4.25 4.25
1202 A174 $2.25 multicolored 5.75 5.75
    Nos. 1199-1202 (4)   14.75 14.75

1996
Summer
Olympics,
Atlanta
A175

1996, Jan. 12   Litho.   Perf. 14
1203 A175 85c Discus   1.40 1.40
1204 A175 $1 Torch bearer 1.75 1.75
1205 A175 $1.50 Sprinting   2.60 2.60
1206 A175 $1.85 Gymnastics   3.50 3.50
1207 A175 $2.10 Archery   4.00 4.00
1208 A175 $2.50 Javelin   4.50 4.50
    Nos. 1203-1208 (6)   17.75 17.75

Queen Elizabeth
II, 70th
Birthday — A176

Designs: $1.90, No. 1212a, In blue hat, coat. $2.25, No. 1212b, Wearing tiara. $2.75, No. 1212c, In robes of Order of the Garter.

1996, June 21   Litho.   Perf. 14
1209 A176 $1.90 multicolored 3.00 3.00
1210 A176 $2.25 multicolored 4.00 4.00
1211 A176 $2.75 multicolored 4.50 4.50
    Nos. 1209-1211 (3)   11.50 11.50
                Sheet of 3
1212 A176 $2.50 #a.-c. + label 14.00 14.00
Nos. 1209-1211 were issued in sheets of 4.

**"The Return of Tommy Tricker"
Type of 1994**

No. 1213a-1213f, like #1191a-1191f.

1997, Aug. 28   Litho.   Perf. 14
1213 A167 90c Sheet of 6,
        #a.-f.   9.50 9.50

**Nos. 1213a-1213f Overprinted in
Silver**

a

b

1997, Sept. 12   Litho.   Perf. 14
1214 A167 90c Sheet 6, #a.-f.   9.00 9.00
    Nos. 1214a, 1214d-1214e are overprinted type "a"; Nos. 1214b-1214c, 1214f type "b."

Butterflies
A177

5c, Lampides boeticus (female). 10c, Vanessa atalanta. 15c, Lampides boeticus (male). 20c, Papilio godeffroyi. 25c, Danaus hamata. 30c, Xois sesara. 50c, Vagrans egista. 70c, Parthenos sylvia. 80c, Hyblaea sanguinea. 85c, Melanitis leda. 90c, Ascalapha odorata. $1, Precis villida. $1.50, Parthenos sylvia. $2, Lampides boeticus. $3, Precis villida. $4, Melanitis leda. $5, Vagrans egista. $7, Hyblaea sanguinea. $10, Vanessa atalanta. $15, Papilio godeffroyi.

1997-98   Litho.   Perf. 13
1215 A177   5c multi   .25   .25
1216 A177 10c multi   .25   .25
1217 A177 15c multi   .25   .25
1218 A177 20c multi   .30   .30
1219 A177 25c multi   .35   .35
1220 A177 30c multi   .35   .35
1221 A177 50c multi   .55   .55
1222 A177 70c multi   .80   .80
1223 A177 80c multi   .95   .95
1224 A177 85c multi   .95   .95
1225 A177 90c multi   1.00 1.00
1226 A177 $1 multi   1.10 1.10
                Perf. 13½
              Size: 41x25mm
1226A A177 $1.50 multi   1.60 1.60
1226B A177 $2 multi   2.25 2.25
1226C A177 $3 multi   3.25 3.25
1226D A177 $4 multi   4.75 4.75
1226E A177 $5 multi   5.50 5.50
1226F A177 $7 multi   8.50 8.50
1226G A177 $10 multi   11.50 11.50
1226H A177 $15 multi   15.00 15.00
    Nos. 1215-1226H (20) 59.45 59.45

    Issued: 5c, 10c, 15c, 20c, 25c, 30c, 50c, 70c, 10/22/97; 80c, 85c, 90c, $1, 11/12/97; $1.50, $2, $3, 3/11/98; $4, $5, 6/19/98; $7, $10, 9/18/98; $15, 11/13/98.
    For surcharges, see Nos. 1259-1264.

Queen Elizabeth II and Prince Philip,
50th Wedding Anniv.
A178

1997, Nov. 20   Perf. 14
1227 A178 $2 multicolored   3.00 3.00
                Souvenir Sheet
1228 A178 $5 like #1227,
        close-up   9.00 9.00
    No. 1228 is a continuous design.

Diana, Princess of
Wales (1961-
97) — A179

1998, Mar. 18   Litho.   Perf. 14
1229 A179 $1.15 shown   1.50 1.50
                Souvenir Sheet
1230 A179 $3.50 like #1229   5.25 5.25
No. 1229 was issued in sheets of 5 + label.
    See No. B142.

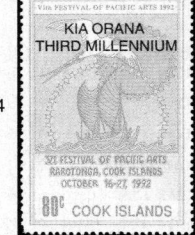

Nos. 1111-1114
Ovptd.

**Printing Methods and Perfs as
before**

1999, Dec. 31
1231 A159 80c on #1111   1.25 1.25
1232 A159 85c on #1112   1.25 1.25
1233 A159 $1 on #1113   1.50 1.50
1234 A159 $1.75 on #1114 2.50 2.50
    Nos. 1231-1234 (4)   6.50 6.50

Queen Mother, 100th Birthday — A180

No. 1235: a, As child. b, As young woman. c, Wearing green hat. d, Wearing tiara.

2000, Oct. 20   Litho.   Perf. 14
1235 A180 $4.50 Sheet of 4,
        #a-d   18.00 18.00
                Souvenir Sheet
1236 A180 $6 Wearing blue
        hat   5.50 5.50

2000 Summer Olympics,
Sydney — A181

No. 1237: a, Ancient runner. b, Track and field. c, Ancient archery. d, Archery.

2000, Nov. 14
1237 A181 $1.75 Sheet of 4,
        #a-d   9.00 9.00
                Souvenir Sheet
1238 A181 $3.90 Torch bearer 4.50 4.50

Nos. 1095-1106 Surcharged in Gold

2001, Apr. 30	**Litho.**		***Perf. 14***	
1239	A156	80c on $1.15 #1101	1.25	1.25
1240	A156	80c on $1.15 #1102	1.25	1.25
1241	A156	80c on $1.15 #1103	1.25	1.25
1242	A156	80c on $1.15 #1104	1.25	1.25
1243	A156	80c on $1.15 #1105	1.25	1.25
1244	A156	80c on $1.15 #1106	1.25	1.25
1245	A156	90c on $1.15 #1095	1.25	1.25
1246	A156	90c on $1.15 #1096	1.25	1.25
1247	A156	90c on $1.15 #1097	1.25	1.25
1248	A156	90c on $1.15 #1098	1.25	1.25
1249	A156	90c on $1.15 #1099	1.25	1.25
1250	A156	90c on $1.15 #1100	1.25	1.25
	Nos. 1239-1250 (12)		15.00	15.00

Nos. 1042-1045, 1050-1053 Surcharged or Overprinted in Black or Gold

2002, Nov. 11	**Litho.**		***Perf. 14***	
1251	A151	20c on 70c #1042	.25	.25
1252	A154	20c on 70c #1050	.25	.25
1253	A154	80c on $1.15 #1052 (G)	1.50	1.50
1254	A151	85c #1043	1.60	1.60
1255	A151	85c #1051	1.60	1.60
1256	A154	90c on $1.50 #1053	1.75	1.75
1257	A151	95c #1044	1.90	1.90
1258	A151	$1 on $1.50 #1045	2.25	2.25
	Nos. 1251-1258 (8)		11.10	11.10

Nos. 1226A-1226F Surcharged

Methods and Perfs As Before
2003, June 30

1259	A177	20c on $1.50 #1226A	.30	.30
1260	A177	80c on $2 #1226B	1.00	1.00
1261	A177	85c on $3 #1226C	1.25	1.25
1262	A177	85c on $4 #1226D	1.25	1.25
1263	A177	90c on $5 #1226E	1.50	1.50
1264	A177	90c on $7 #1226F	1.50	1.50
	Nos. 1259-1264 (6)		6.80	6.80

Obliterator on Nos. 1260-1264 is a Moai head.

United We Stand — A182

2003, Sept. 30	**Litho.**	***Perf. 14***	
1265	A182 90c multi	3.00	3.00

Printed in sheets of 4.

2004 Summer Olympics, Athens A183

Designs: 40c, Poster for 1992 Barcelona Olympics. 60c, Pancration, horiz. $1, Cycling, horiz. $2, Gold medal, 1936 Berlin Olympics.

2004, Sept. 29	**Litho.**		***Perf. 14¼***	
1266-1269	A183	Set of 4	6.50	6.50

Worldwide Fund for Nature (WWF) — A184

Birds of Suwarrow National Park: 80c, Cook Islands reed warblers. 90c, Mangaia kingfishers. $1.15, Rarotonga starlings. $1.95, Atiu swiftlets.

2005, June 13	**Litho.**		***Perf. 14***	
1270-1273	A184	Set of 4	6.50	6.50

Each stamp printed in sheets of 4.

Pope John Paul II (1920-2005) — A185

2005, Nov. 11			
1274	A185 $1.35 multi	2.75	2.75

Printed in sheets of 5 + label.

A186

A187

A188

Designs: 5c, Black-lined Maori wrasse. 10c, Blue lorikeets. 20c, Daisy coral. 30c, Ocean sunfish. 40c, Female Lampides boeticus butterfly. 50c, Rarotonga starlings.

No. 1285: a, Mangaia kingfishers. b, Cook Islands reef warblers. c, Rarotonga starlings, diff. d, Matiu swiftlets.

No. 1286: a, Male Lampides boeticus. b, Vagrans egista. c, Melantis leda. d, Female Lampides boeticus, diff.

No. 1287: a, Daisy coral, diff. b, Hydroid coral. c, Sea star. d, Smooth sea star.

No. 1288: a, Black-tipped cod. b, Red spot rainbow fish. c, Black-lined Maori wrasse, diff. d, Fish (incorrectly identified as Smooth sea star).

No. 1289: a, Three Ocean sunfish, Latin name at LL. b, Three Ocean sunfish, large clump of seaweed, Latin name at LR. c, Two Ocean sunfish, diver. d, Three Ocean sunfish, small clump of seaweed at top, Latin name at LR.

No. 1290: a, Blue lorikeets on palm branch. b, Blue lorikeets in tree hollow. c, Blue lorikeets and white flowers. d, Blue lorikeets and pink flowers.

No. 1291 — Queen Elizabeth II and: a, Hawksbill turtle. b, Leatherback turtle. c, Green turtle. d, Olive ridley turtle.

No. 1292 — Queen Elizabeth II and: a, Sowerby's whales. b, Cuvier's beaked whales. c, Bottle-nosed dolphin. d, Commerson's dolphins.

$7.50, Queen Elizabeth II, fish and marine life. $10, Queen Elizabeth II, butterflies and flowers. $15, Queen Elizabeth II and birds.

Illustrations A187 and A188 reduced.

2007		**Litho.**	***Perf. 13¼***	
1279	A186	5c multi	.25	.25
1280	A186	10c multi	.25	.25
1281	A186	20c multi	.30	.30
1282	A186	30c multi	.45	.45
1283	A186	40c multi	.60	.60
1284	A186	75c multi	.75	.75
		Size: 48x27mm		
		Perf. 14x14¾		
1285		Block of 4	4.75	4.75
a.-d.	A186	80c Any single	1.10	1.10
1286		Block of 4	5.25	5.25
a.-d.	A186	90c Any single	1.25	1.25
1287		Block of 4	5.75	5.75
a.-d.	A186	$1 Any single	1.40	1.40
1288		Block of 4	6.50	6.50
a.-d.	A186	$1.10 Any single	1.60	1.60
1289		Block of 4	7.00	7.00
a.-d.	A186	$1.20 Any single	1.75	1.75
1290		Block of 4	11.50	11.50
a.-d.	A186	$2 Any single	2.75	2.75
		Perf. 13¾		
1291		Block of 4	19.00	19.00
a.-d.	A187	$3 Any single	4.75	4.75
1292		Block of 4	31.00	31.00
a.-d.	A187	$5 Any single	7.75	7.75
		Perf. 13¼		
1293	A188	$7.50 multi	12.00	12.00
1294	A188	$10 multi	15.50	15.50
1295	A188	$15 multi	24.00	24.00
	Nos. 1279-1295 (17)		144.85	144.85

Issued: Nos. 1279-1290, 3/20; No. 1291, 10/10; No. 1292, 11/13; Nos. 1293-1295, 12/10.

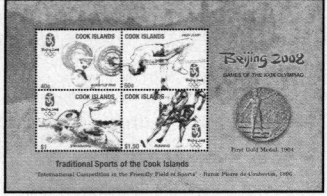

2008 Summer Olympics, Beijing — A189

No. 1296: a, 40c, Weight lifting. b, 60c, High jump. c, $1, Swimming. d, $1.50, Running.

2008, July 28	**Litho.**		***Perf. 14¾x14***	
1296	A189	Sheet of 4, #a-d	5.25	5.25

Pacific Mini-Games, Rarotonga A190

Designs: 20c, Shot put and discus. 80c, High jump. 90c, Weight lifting. $3, Running.

2009, Sept. 21	**Litho.**		***Perf. 13¾***	
1297-1300	A190	Set of 4	7.25	7.25
1300a		Souvenir sheet, #1297-1300	7.25	7.25

Nos. 1297-1300 Ovptd. in Gold with Names of Winners

Overprint text: 20c, Daniel Kilama / New Caledonia / Men's Discus Throw / 27th Sept. 2009. 80c, Johanna Sui / Tahiti / Women's High Jump / 24th Sept. 2009. 90c, Yukio Peter / Nauru / 84kg Clean & Jerk / 1st Oct. 2009. $3, Niko Verekauta / Fiji / Men's 100 metres / 24th Sept. 2009.

2009, Oct. 21	**Litho.**		***Perf. 13¾***	
1301-1304	A190	Set of 4	7.25	7.25
1304a		Souvenir sheet, #1301-1304	7.25	7.25

Flowers — A191

Designs: 10c, Catharanthus roseus. 20c, Ixora casei. 30c, Hibiscus rosa-sinensis cultivar. 40c, Heliconia psittacorum. 50c, Hibiscus schizopetalus, vert. 70c, Alpinia purpurata, vert. 80c, Bougainvillea spectabilis, vert. 90c, Hibiscus rosa-sinensis. $1, Nymphaea capensis. $1.10, Euphorbia pulcherrima. $1.20, Impatiens walleriana. $2, Anthurium andraeanum. $3, Chrysanthemum cultivar. $4, Acalypha pendula, vert. $5, Heliconia rostrata, vert. $7.50, Tagetes patular cultivar. $10, Phalaenopsis cultivar. $20, Catharanthus roseus, diff.

2010, Sept. 10	**Litho.**		***Perf. 13¾***	
		Sizes: 60x37mm, 37x60mm		
1305	A191	10c multi	.25	.25
1306	A191	20c multi	.30	.30
1307	A191	30c multi	.45	.45
1308	A191	40c multi	.60	.60
1309	A191	50c multi	.75	.75
1310	A191	70c multi	1.00	1.00
1311	A191	80c multi	1.25	1.25
1312	A191	90c multi	1.40	1.40
1313	A191	$1 multi	1.50	1.50
1314	A191	$1.10 multi	1.60	1.60
1315	A191	$1.20 multi	1.75	1.75
1316	A191	$2 multi	3.00	3.00
1317	A191	$3 multi	4.50	4.50
1318	A191	$4 multi	5.75	5.75
1319	A191	$5 multi	7.25	7.25
1320	A191	$7.50 multi	11.00	11.00

1321	A191	$10 multi		14.50	14.50
1322	A191	$20 multi		29.00	29.00
		Nos. 1305-1322 (18)		85.85	85.85

See Nos. 1328-1337, 1388-1389.
For overprints see Nos. O70-O117.

ANZAC
Day
A192

Designs: 80c, Girl Guides in parade. 90c, Boy Scouts in parade. $1.10, Monument, vert. $1.20, Cook Islands flag, vert.
No. 1327: a, Church interior. b, Church exterior.

Perf. 14¾x14¼, 14¼x14¾
2010, Sept. 14

1323-1326		Set of 4		6.00	6.00

Souvenir Sheet

1327	A192	$3 Sheet of 2, #a-b		9.00	9.00

For overprints, see Nos. 1391-1400.

Flower Type of 2010 in Smaller Sizes

Designs as before.

2010, Oct. 27   Litho.   Perf. 14
Sizes: 42x28mm, 28x42mm

1328	A191	10c multi		.25	.25
1329	A191	20c multi		.30	.30
1330	A191	30c multi		.50	.50
1331	A191	50c multi		.80	.80
1332	A191	$1 multi		1.25	1.25
1333	A191	90c multi		1.50	1.50
1334	A191	$1 multi		1.60	1.60
1335	A191	$1.10 multi		1.75	1.75
1336	A191	$1.20 multi		1.90	1.90
1337	A191	$2 multi		3.25	3.25
		Nos. 1328-1337 (10)		13.10	13.10

For surcharges, see Nos. 1437-1445.

Expo
2010,
Shanghai
A193

Designs: 80c, Anthurium flower. 90c, Angelfish. $1.10, Fish near ocean floor. $1.20, Coconuts.
$6, Palm tree and ocean, vert.

2010, Oct. 27   Perf. 14¾x14¼

1338-1341	A193	Set of 4		6.50	6.50

Souvenir Sheet
Perf. 14¼

1342	A193	$6 multi		9.75	9.75

No. 1342 contains one 38x50mm stamp.

Miniature Sheet

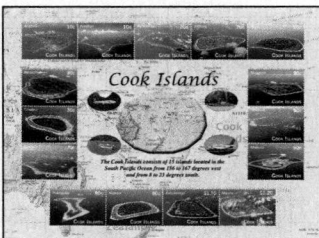

Aerial Views of Islands — A194

No. 1343: a, 10c, Aitutaki. b, 10c, Penrhyn. c, 20c, Palmerston. d, 20c, Mitiaro. e, 30c, Rarotonga. f, 30c, Takutea. g, 50c, Atiu. h, 70c, Suwarrow. i, 80c, Pukapuka. j, 80c, Nassau. k, 90c, Mangaia. l, 90c, Manihiki. m, 90c, Manuae. n, $1.10, Rakahanga. o, $1.20, Mauke.

2010, Nov. 8   Perf. 14

1343	A194	Sheet of 15, #a-o		14.00	14.00

Service of Queen Elizabeth II and Prince Philip — A195

Designs: 80c, Queen Elizabeth II. 90c, Queen and Prince Philip. $1, Queen and Prince Philip, diff. $1.10, Queen and Prince Philip, diff. $1.20, Queen and Prince Philip, diff. $1.50, Prince Philip.
$6.60, Queen and Prince Philip, diff.

2010, Dec. 6   Litho.   Perf. 13¼

1344-1349	A195	Set of 6		9.75	9.75
1349a		Sheet of 6, #1344-1349, + 3 labels		9.75	9.75

Souvenir Sheet

1350	A195	$6.60 multi		10.00	10.00

Worldwide Fund for Nature (WWF) — A196

Rimatara lorikeet: 80c, Pair on flower. 90c, In flight. $2.40, On branch. $3.60, Trio at nest.

2010, Dec. 9   Litho.   Perf. 14

1351-1354	A196	Set of 4		11.50	11.50

A197

Engagement of Prince William and Catherine Middleton — A198

Designs: Nos. 1355, 1358a, 1360, Middleton. Nos. 1356, 1358b, 1361, Prince in military uniform.
No. 1357: a, Prince in military uniform. b, Prince playing polo. c, Middleton, fence. d, Prince, man and woman in background. e, Middleton, woman in background. f, Couple, Prince at left. g, Middleton with black hat. h, Prince. i, Couple, Middleton at left. j, Hands of couple, engagement ring.
$8.10, Couple, Prince in uniform at left.

2011, Jan. 14   Perf. 14

1355	A197	$2.40 multi		3.75	3.75
1356	A197	$3.60 multi		5.50	5.50

Miniature Sheets

1357	A198	10c Sheet of 10, #a-j		1.60	1.60

Perf. 13¾x13½

1358	A197	Sheet of 2, #a-b		9.25	9.25

Souvenir Sheets
Perf. 14¼

1359	A197	$8.10 multi		12.50	12.50
1360	A197	$11 multi		17.00	17.00
1361	A197	$11 multi		17.00	17.00
		Nos. 1359-1361 (3)		46.50	46.50

No. 1358 contains two 28x44mm stamps. Nos. 1359-1361 each contain one 38x50mm stamp.

Peonies — A199

No. 1362: a, 80c, Pink peonies (30x40mm). b, 90c, Purple peony (30x30mm). c, $1.10, Peach peonies (30x30mm). d, $1.20, Pink peony (30x30mm).
$8.10, Red peony.

2011, Apr. 8   Litho.   Perf. 14¾

1362	A199	Sheet of 4, #a-d		6.25	6.25

Souvenir Sheet

1363	A199	$8.10 multi		13.00	13.00

No. 1363 contains one 70x60mm stamp.

Wedding of Prince William and Catherine Middleton A200

Designs: 20c, Couple, Prince at right. 30c, Westminster Abbey. 80c, Couple, Prince at left.

2011, Apr. 29   Perf. 13¼

1364-1366	A200	Set of 3		2.10	2.10
1366a		Souvenir sheet of 3, #1364-1366		2.10	2.10

Rarotonga Tourism — A201

Designs: 10c, Whale breaching ocean's surface near boat. 20c, Palm trees, boat. 30c, Starfish. 50c, Palm trees near ocean. 70c, Crab. 80c, Cook Islands flag on boat. 90c, Airplane, windsurfer. $1, Trees near beach. $1.10, Cliffs, airplane. $1.20, Palm trees near beach. $1.50, Goat. $2, Chicken. $3, Island and beach. $4, Fish. $5, Aerial view of Rarotonga. cruise ship.

2011, July 22   Litho.   Perf. 14

1367	A201	10c multi		.25	.25
1368	A201	20c multi		.35	.35
1369	A201	30c multi		.50	.50
1370	A201	50c multi		.85	.85
1371	A201	70c multi		1.25	1.25
1372	A201	80c multi		1.40	1.40
1373	A201	90c multi		1.50	1.50
1374	A201	$1 multi		1.75	1.75
1375	A201	$1.10 multi		1.90	1.90
1376	A201	$1.20 multi		2.00	2.00
1377	A201	$1.50 multi		2.50	2.50
1378	A201	$2 multi		3.50	3.50
1379	A201	$3 multi		5.00	5.00
1380	A201	$4 multi		6.75	6.75
1381	A201	$5 multi		8.50	8.50
a.		Sheet of 15, #1367-1381		38.00	38.00
		Nos. 1367-1381 (15)		38.00	38.00

National Environment Service A202

Designs: 80c, Bristle-thighed curlew. 90c, Fiddler crab. $1.10, Taro plant and flower. $1.20, Wetlands flora.

2011, Oct. 21   Perf. 13¾

1382-1385	A202	Set of 4		6.50	6.50

Nos. 1382-1385 each were printed in sheets of 4.

Souvenir Sheets

Stamps at Work — A203

No. 1386: a, $1.10, Quick response code. b, $5, Emblem for Wetlands for Healthy Islands.
No. 1387: a, $1.10, Quick response code, text and website address. b, $5, Damage from 2011 Japan tsunami.

2011, Oct. 21   Perf. 15x14¼
Sheets of 2, #a-b

1386-1387	A203	Set of 2		19.50	19.50

Twenty percent of the sales of No. 1387 were donated to Japan tsunami relief efforts.

Flowers Type of 2010 With Head of Queen Elizabeth II Added at Lower Right

Designs: $26.90, Plumeria rubra. $31.10, Hypolimnas bolina.

2011, Oct. 25   Perf. 14¼x15
Size: 44x29mm

1388	A191	$26.90 multi		42.50	42.50
1389	A191	$31.10 multi		50.00	50.00

Christmas
A204

No. 1390: a, Five gold rings. b, Six geese a laying. c, Seven swans a swimming. d, Eight maids a milking.

2011, Dec. 23   Litho.   Perf. 13¼

1390		Horiz. strip of 4		13.00	13.00
a.	A204	$1.10 multi		1.75	1.75
b.	A204	$1.20 multi		1.90	1.90
c.	A204	$2.10 multi		3.50	3.50
d.	A204	$3.60 multi		5.75	5.75
e.		Souvenir sheet of 4, #1390a-1390d		13.00	13.00

Nos. 1323-1327 Overprinted in Gold or Silver

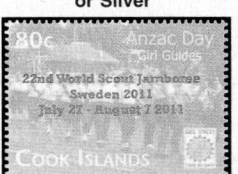

Methods and Perfs As Before
2012, Jan. 10

1391	A192	80c On No. 1323 (G)		1.40	1.40
1392	A192	80c On No. 1323 (S)		1.40	1.40
1393	A192	90c On No. 1324 (G)		1.50	1.50

1394	A192	90c On No. 1324 (S)	1.50	1.50
1395	A192	$1.10 On No. 1325 (G)	1.90	1.90
1396	A192	$1.10 On No. 1325 (S)	1.90	1.90
1397	A192	$1.20 On No. 1326 (G)	2.00	2.00
1398	A192	$1.20 On No. 1326 (S)	2.00	2.00
	Nos. 1391-1398 (8)		13.60	13.60

Souvenir Sheets of 2, #a-b

1399	A192	$3 On No. 1327 (G)	10.00	10.00
1400	A192	$3 On No. 1327 (S)	10.00	10.00

Overprint reads up on Nos. 1395-1398.

Beatification of Pope John Paul II — A205

No. 1401: a, $3, Pope Benedict XVI. b, $3.30, Pope John Paul II.

2012, Jan. 10   Litho.   Perf. 13¾

1401	A205	Horiz. pair, #a-b	10.50	10.50

No. 1401 was printed in sheets containing two pairs.

Reign of Queen Elizabeth II, 60th Anniv. — A206

Queen Elizabeth II: 80c, Wearing tiara. 90c, Wearing red hat. $1, Wearing tiara, diff. $1.10, Wearing gray hat. $1.20, With dog. $1.50, Wearing aquamarine dress. $6.60, Wearing aquamarine dress, diff.

2012, Feb. 6   Perf. 13¼

1402-1407	A206	Set of 6	11.00	11.00
1407a		Souvenir sheet of 6, #1402-1407, + 3 labels	11.00	11.00

Souvenir Sheet

1408	A206	$6.60 multi	11.00	11.00

Worldwide Fund for Nature (WWF) — A207

Designs: 90c, Partula assimilis. $1.20, Libera fraterncula. $1.50, Lamprocystis globosa. $2.70, Sinployea peasei.

2012, Apr. 11   Perf. 14

1409-1412	A207	Set of 4	10.00	10.00
1412a		Sheet of 16, 4 each #1409-1412	40.00	40.00

2012 Summer Olympics, London — A208

Designs: 80c, Swimming. 90c, Map of South Pacific, Great Britain and Ireland. $2, Sailing.

2012, June 22   Perf. 13¾

1413-1415	A208	Set of 3	6.00	6.00
1415a		Souvenir sheet of 3, #1413-1415	6.00	6.00
1415b		Souvenir sheet of 6, 2 each #1413-1415	12.00	12.00

Miniature Sheets

43rd Pacific Islands Forum, Rarotonga — A209

No. 1416 — Flag of: a, Canada. b, People's Republic of China. c, European Union. d, France. e, India. f, Indonesia. g, Italy. h, Japan. i, Republic of Korea. j, Malaysia. k, Philippines. l, Thailand. m, United Kingdom. n, United States.

No. 1417 — Flag of: a, Australia. b, Cook Islands. c, Fiji. d, Kiribati. e, Micronesia. f, Nauru. g, New Zealand. h, Niue. i, Palau. j, Papua New Guinea. k, Marshall Islands. l, Samoa. m, Solomon Islands. n, Tonga. o, Tuvalu. p, Vanuatu.

2012, Aug. 22   Perf. 14

1416	A209	90c Sheet of 14, #a-n	21.00	21.00
1417	A209	90c Sheet of 16, #a-p	24.00	24.00

Adoration of the Magi, by Giotto di Bondone A210

Entry into Jerusalem, by Giotto A211

Lamentation, by Giotto — A212

Kiss of Judas, by Giotto A213

Life of Mary Magdalene - Raising of Lazarus, by Giotto A214

Death of Mary, by Giotto A215

Perf. 14¾x14¼

2012, Nov. 16   Litho.
Stamps With White Frames

1418		Horiz. pair	2.80	2.80
a.	A210	80c multi	1.40	1.40
b.	A211	80c multi	1.40	1.40
1419		Horiz. pair	3.00	3.00
a.	A212	90c multi	1.50	1.50
b.	A213	90c multi	1.50	1.50
1420		Horiz. pair	10.00	10.00
a.	A214	$3 multi	5.00	5.00
b.	A215	$3 multi	5.00	5.00
	Nos. 1418-1420 (3)		15.80	15.80

Miniature Sheet
Stamps Without White Frame

1421		Sheet of 6	16.00	16.00
a.	A210	80c multi	1.40	1.40
b.	A211	80c multi	1.40	1.40
c.	A212	90c multi	1.50	1.50
d.	A213	90c multi	1.50	1.50
e.	A214	$3 multi	5.00	5.00
f.	A215	$3 multi	5.00	5.00

Christmas.

Miniature Sheets

A215a

43rd Pacific Islands Forum, Rarotonga — A215b

No. 1422G: i, Woman with Cook Islands sash with Minister of Education Teina Bishop, New Zealand Prime Minister John Key and John Carter, New Zealand High Commissioner to the Cook Islands. j, Canoe with sails. k, Women from Aitutaki holding a quilted bedspread. l, Leaders of Pacific islands seated in row. m, President of French Polynesia Oscar Temaru and Cook Islands Prime Minister Henry Puna in front of airplane. n, Australian Prime Minister Julia Gillard. o, Canoe on shore.

No. 1422H: p, Pres. Temaru, Prime Minister Puna, Cook Islands Deputy Prime Minister Tom Marsters and entourage walking away from airplane. q, Prime Minister Puna departing airplane, two women. r, U.S. airplane. s, People leaving Royal New Zealand Air Force airplane. t, Crowds near entrance to Aitutaki Airport. u, U.S. Secretary of State Hillary Clinton with Cook Island Minister of Finance Mark Brown. v, Aitutaki dancers performing for leaders.

2012, Nov. 30   Litho.   Perf. 14

1421G	A215a	80c Sheet of 7, #i-o, + label	9.50	9.50
1421H	A215b	90c Sheet of 7, #p-v, + label	10.50	10.50

Personalizable Stamps — A217

2012, Dec. 21   Litho.   Perf. 14x14¾

1422	A216	$4 multi	6.75	6.75
1423	A217	$4 multi	6.75	6.75

Items Commemorating British Coronations — A218

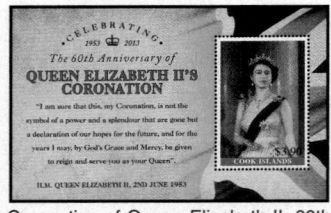

Coronation of Queen Elizabeth II, 60th Anniv. — A219

Various items commemorating the coronation of: 80c, Queen Victoria. 90c, King Edward VII. $1.10, King George V. $1.20, Seed packet for Coronation mixture of sweet pea seeds. $3.60, Illustration from *The Coronation Cut-Out Story Book*. $3.90, Queen Elizabeth II.

2013, Feb. 6   Litho.   Perf. 14

1424-1428	A218	Set of 5	12.50	12.50

Souvenir Sheet
Perf. 15x14

1429	A219	$3.90 multi	6.50	6.50

Nos. 1424-1428 each were printed isn sheets of 8 + central label.

A220

A221

Cook Islands 80c COOK ISLANDS MARINE PARK
A222

A223
90c COOK ISLANDS MARINE PARK

90c COOK ISLANDS MARINE PARK
A224

Cook Islands Marine Park
A225
90c COOK ISLANDS MARINE PARK

2013, Feb. 20   Litho.   Perf. 14
1430	A220	80c multi	1.40	1.40
1431	A221	80c multi	1.40	1.40
1432	A222	80c multi	1.40	1.40
1433	A223	90c multi	1.50	1.50
1434	A224	90c multi	1.50	1.50
1435	A225	90c multi	1.50	1.50
	Nos. 1430-1435 (6)		8.70	8.70

New Year 2013 (Year of the Snake) A226

No. 1436 — Snake with background color of: a, Green. b, Red.

Perf. 14¾x14¼
2013, Feb. 21   Litho.
1436	A226	$1.20 pair, #a-b	4.00	4.00

Printed in sheets containing 2 each of Nos. 1436a-1436b.

Nos. 1328, 1330-1337 Surcharged in Gold

COOK ISLANDS 20c CATHARANTHUS ROSEUS

Methods and Perfs. As Before
2013, Apr. 9
1437	A191	20c on 10c #1328	.35	.35
1438	A191	20c on 30c #1330	.35	.35
1439	A191	20c on 50c #1331	.35	.35
1440	A191	20c on 80c #1332	.35	.35
1441	A191	20c on 90c #1333	.35	.35
1442	A191	20c on $1 #1334	.35	.35
1443	A191	20c on $1.10 #1335	.35	.35
1444	A191	20c on $1.20 #1336	.35	.35
1445	A191	20c on $2 #1337	.35	.35
	Nos. 1437-1445 (9)		3.15	3.15

Ships — A227

No. 1446, 20c: a, Ndrua. b, Hamatafua.
No. 1447, 50c: a, Single-masted Vaa Kalua. b, Double-masted Vaa Kalua.
No. 1448, 60c: a, Vaka Motu. b, Toniaki.
No. 1449, 80c: a, Vaka. b, Pahi.
No. 1450, 90c: a, Vaka, diff. b, Pahi, diff.
No. 1451, $2.30: a, Vaka Motu, diff. b, Tipaerua.
No. 1452, $4.50: a, Pahi, diff. b, Waka Tou. c, Tipaerua, diff.

2013, May 24 Litho.   Perf. 14¾x14¼
Horiz. Pairs, #a-b
1446-1451	A227	Set of 6	17.00	17.00

Souvenir Sheet
1452	A227	$4.50 Sheet of 3, #a-c	22.00	22.00

Animals — A228

Designs: No. 1453, $1.50, American bison. No. 1454, $1.50, Gazella dama. No. 1455, $1.50, Phascolarctos cinereus. No. 1456, $1.50, Eurasian lynx. No. 1457, $1.50, Loxodonta africana. No. 1458, $1.50, Grus americana.

2013, May 31   Litho.   Perf. 14x14¾
1453-1458	A228	Set of 6	14.50	14.50

Miniature Sheet

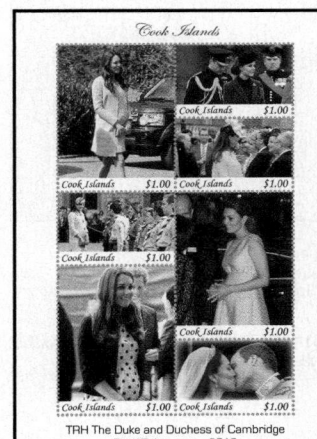

TRH The Duke and Duchess of Cambridge
Royal Baby • 2013

Duchess of Cambridge — A229

No. 1459 — Duchess of Cambridge: a, Wearing pink dress (40x52mm). b, Wearing dark blue jacket and black hat (40x26mm). c, Wearing yellow jacket and hat, meeting with group of dignitaries (40x26mm). d, Wearing white dress and hat, reviewing Scout troop (40x26mm). e, Wearing light blue dress (40x52mm). f, Wearing polka dot dress (40x52mm). g, Wearing wedding gown, kissing Duke of Cambridge (40x26mm).

2013, Aug. 1   Litho.   Perf. 13¼
1459	A229	$1 Sheet of 7, #a-g	11.50	11.50

Alphitobius diaperinus 30¢

Insects and Spiders A230

Designs: 30c, Alphitobius diaperinus. 50c, Leptocoris rufomarginatus. 70c, Nabis capsiformis. $1, Polistes jokahamae. $1.30,

Agrius convulvi. $1.50, Harmonia octomaculata. $1.70, Cosmopolites sordidus. $3.80, Graeffea crouanii. $4.10, Leptoglossus australis. $5.30, Nezara viridula. $6.50, Neoscona theisi. $8.50, Tholumis tillarga.

2013, Sept. 2   Litho.   Perf. 14
Stamps With White Frames
1460	A230	30c multi	.50	.50
1461	A230	50c multi	.85	.85
1462	A230	70c multi	1.25	1.25
1463	A230	$1 multi	1.60	1.60
1464	A230	$1.30 multi	2.10	2.10
1465	A230	$1.50 multi	2.50	2.50
1466	A230	$1.70 multi	2.75	2.75
1467	A230	$3.80 multi	6.25	6.25
1468	A230	$4.10 multi	6.75	6.75
1469	A230	$5.30 multi	8.75	8.75
1470	A230	$6.50 multi	10.50	10.50
1471	A230	$8.50 multi	14.00	14.00
	Nos. 1460-1471 (12)		57.80	57.80

Miniature Sheet
Stamp Without White Frame
1472		Sheet of 12	58.00	58.00
a.	A230	30c multi	.50	.50
b.	A230	50c multi	.85	.85
c.	A230	70c multi	1.25	1.25
d.	A230	$1 multi	1.60	1.60
e.	A230	$1.30 multi	2.10	2.10
f.	A230	$1.50 multi	2.50	2.50
g.	A230	$1.70 multi	2.75	2.75
h.	A230	$3.80 multi	6.25	6.25
i.	A230	$4.10 multi	6.75	6.75
j.	A230	$5.30 multi	8.75	8.75
k.	A230	$6.50 multi	10.50	10.50
l.	A230	$8.50 multi	14.00	14.00

See Nos. 1491-1503.

COOK ISLANDS 2013
Worlds First Postage Stamp $8.00
Great Britain No. 1 — A231

Litho. & Embossed With Foil Application
2013, Sept. 18   Perf. 13x13¼
1473	A231	$8 blk & gold	13.50	13.50

Souvenir Sheets

China International Collection Expo 2013
Cultures Reflected In Appreciation,
Pleasures Relished Through Collecting.
Cook Islands

2013 China International Collection Exposition, Beijing — A232

No. 1474 — Stamps inscribed "Cook Islands": a, $1, Painting by Paul Gauguin. b, $3, Beijing Exhibition Center.
No. 1475 — Stamps inscribed "Rarotonga / Cook Islands": a, $1, Painting by Paul Gauguin, diff. b, $3, Beijing Exhibition Center.

2013, Sept. 26   Litho.   Perf. 12
1474	A232	Sheet of 2, #a-b	6.75	6.75
1475	A232	Sheet of 2, #a-b	6.75	6.75

$2.40 50 Year Commemorative John F. Kennedy
Cook Islands 2013

Pres. John F. Kennedy (1917-63) A233

Designs: $2.40, Pres. Kennedy. $3.10, Pres. Kennedy and quote,

2013, Nov. 8   Litho.   Perf. 14¼
1476-1477	A233	Set of 2	9.00	9.00

Christmas — A234

Paintings by: $1, Gerard van Honthorst. $1.30, Michelangelo Merisi da Caravaggio. No. 1480, $1.50, Rembrandt.
No. 1481: a, $1.50, Bernardo Daddi. b, $1.70, Pieter Aertsen. c, $4.50, Lorenzo Lotto.

2013, Nov. 18   Litho.   Perf. 13¼
1478-1480	A234	Set of 3	6.25	6.25

Souvenir Sheet
1481	A234	Sheet of 3, #a-c	13.00	13.00

Highland Paradise Scenes — A235

Various scenes from Highland Paradise tourist educational show.

2014, Jan. 3   Litho.   Perf. 13¼
1482	A235	10c multi	.25	.25
1483	A235	20c multi	.35	.35
1484	A235	30c multi	.50	.50
1485	A235	50c multi	.85	.85
1486	A235	60c multi	1.00	1.00
1487	A235	$1 multi	1.60	1.60
1488	A235	$1.30 multi	2.10	2.10
1489	A235	$1.50 multi	2.50	2.50
1490	A235	$1.70 multi	2.75	2.75
	Nos. 1482-1490 (9)		11.90	11.90

Dated "2013."

Insects and Spiders Type of 2013

Designs: 10c, Teleogryllus oceanicus. 40c, Euconocephalus roberti. $1, Apis mellifera. $2.10, Crocidolomia pavonana. $2.50, Junonia villida. $3, Aedes polynesiensis. $3.50, Homalodisca coagulata. $4.50, Lygus flavoscutellatus. $5.50, Euploea lewinii perryi. $6.70, Hypolimnas bolina. $7, Porcellio laevis. $10.10, Vagrans egista bodenia.

2014, Jan. 6   Litho.   Perf. 14
Stamps With White Frames
1491	A230	10c multi	.25	.25
1492	A230	40c multi	.65	.65
1493	A230	$1 multi	1.60	1.60
1494	A230	$2.10 multi	3.50	3.50
1495	A230	$2.50 multi	4.00	4.00
1496	A230	$3 multi	5.00	5.00
1497	A230	$3.50 multi	5.75	5.75
1498	A230	$4.50 multi	7.25	7.25
1499	A230	$5.50 multi	9.00	9.00
1500	A230	$6.70 multi	11.00	11.00
1501	A230	$7 multi	11.50	11.50
1502	A230	$10.10 multi	16.50	16.50
	Nos. 1491-1502 (12)		76.00	76.00

Miniature Sheet
Stamp Without White Frame
1503		Sheet of 12	76.00	76.00
a.	A230	10c multi	.25	.25
b.	A230	40c multi	.65	.65
c.	A230	$1 multi	1.60	1.60
d.	A230	$2.10 multi	3.50	3.50
e.	A230	$2.50 multi	4.00	4.00
f.	A230	$3 multi	5.00	5.00
g.	A230	$3.50 multi	5.75	5.75
h.	A230	$4.50 multi	7.25	7.25
i.	A230	$5.50 multi	9.00	9.00
j.	A230	$6.70 multi	11.00	11.00
k.	A230	$7 multi	11.50	11.50
l.	A230	$10.10 multi	16.50	16.50

Souvenir Sheet

New Year 2014 (Year of the Horse) — A236

No. 1504 — Horse, with denomination color of: a, Red. b, White.

2014, Jan. 8   Litho.   Perf. 13¼
1504 A236 $3 Sheet of 2, #a-b   9.75 9.75

Souvenir Sheet

Christening of Prince George of Cambridge — A237

No. 1505 — Prince George being held by: a, $4, Duchess of Cambridge. b, $5, Duke of Cambridge.

2014, Jan. 14   Litho.   Perf. 14
1505 A237   Sheet of 2, #a-b   14.50 14.50

Easter — A238

No. 1506 — Religious painting by: a, 50c, Il Moro. b, $1, Tintoretto. c, $1.30, Giovanni Bellini. d, $1.50, Raphael (Sanzio). e, $1.70, William Blake.
$9.50, Painting by Hans Memling.

2014, Apr. 9   Litho.   Perf. 13¼
1506 A238   Sheet of 5, #a-e,
+ label   10.50 10.50
Souvenir Sheet
1507 A238 $9.50 multi   16.50 16.50

Small Island Developing States — A239

No. 1508: a, Tropical cyclone. b. Rising sea levels at Rarotonga. c, Pacific Small Island Developing States emblem. d, Map of Cook Islands. e, "Island Voices Global Choices" emblem. f, Fishing boats. g, Sailboat. h, Cruise liner. i, Kayak. j, Wind surfing. k, Nurse shark. l, Barracuda. m, Triggerfish. n, Pilot whale. o, Manta ray. p, Flag of Cook Islands.
No. 1509: a, Like #1508a. b, Like #1508p. c, Like #1508b. d, Like #1508c. e, Like #1508d. f, Like #1508e.
No. 1510: a, Like #1508f. b, Like #1508p. c, Like #1508g. d, Like #1508h. e, Like #1508i. f, Like #1508j.
No. 1511: a, Like #1508k. b, Like #1508p. c, Like #1508l. d, Like #1508m. e, Like #1508n. f, Like #1508o.

2014, May 9   Litho.   Perf. 13¼
1508   Block of 18, #1508a-
1508o, 3 #1508p   15.50 15.50
  a.-p. A239 50c Any single   .85   .85
Miniature Sheets
1509   Sheet of 6   21.00 21.00
  a.-f. A239 $2 Any single   3.50 3.50
1510   Sheet of 6   25.50 25.50
  a.-f. A239 $2.40 Any single   4.25 4.25
1511   Sheet of 6   27.00 27.00
  a.-f. A239 $2.60 Any single   4.50 4.50
    Nos. 1509-1511 (3)   73.50 73.50

No. 1508 was printed in sheets containing 3 blocks of 18. The frame on each stramp in the sheet, depicting a map of the Pacific Ocean, differs.

Souvenir Sheet

Nelson Mandela (1918-2013), President of South Africa — A240

No. 1512 — Mandela with: a, $2.50, Child. b, $4.50, U. S. Pres. Bill Clinton.

2014, May 13   Litho.   Perf. 14
1512 A240   Sheet of 2, #a-b   12.00 12.00

Tourism — A241

No. 1513, 30c: a, Relaxing. b, Shopping. c, Dancing. d, Dining.
No. 1514, 50c: a, Church service. b, Scootering. c, Hiking. d, Snorkeling.
No. 1515, $1: a, Kayaking. b, Swimming. c, Scuba diving. d, Fishing.
No. 1516, $1.70: a, Vaka sailing. b, Windsurfing. c, Kitesurfing. d, Paddleboarding.
No. 1517, $3.80: a, Whale watching, b, Sightseeing. c, Glass bottom boat. d, Birdwatching.
No. 1518, $4.10: a, Rugby. b, Beach volleyball. c, Golfing. d, Bike riding.

2014, June 23   Litho.   Perf. 14¼x14
Blocks of 4, #a-d
1513-1518 A241   Set of 6   80.00 80.00

Insects — A242

No. 1519: a, $4, Western honey bee. b, $11.50, Castor semi-looper moth. c, $13.60, Spotted ladybird.

2014, Sept. 12   Litho.   Perf. 13¼
1519 A242   Horiz. strip of 3,
#a-c, + 3 labels   46.00 46.00

Worldwide Fund for Nature (WWF) — A243

Various depictions of spotless crake: Nos. 1520, 1524a, $1. Nos. 1521, 1524b, $1.30. Nos. 1522, 1524c, $1.50. Nos. 1523, 1524d, $1.70.
$7.50, Spotless crake, diff.

Perf. 14¾x14¼
2014, Nov. 28   Litho.
Stamps With White Frame
1520-1523 A243   Set of 4   8.75 8.75
Stamps Without White Frame
1524 A243   Strip of 4, #a-d   8.75 8.75
Souvenir Sheet
1525 A243 $7.50 multi   12.00 12.00

Souvenir Sheet

Christmas — A244

No. 1526 — Religious paintings by: a, Giotto di Bondone. b, Jan Gossaert. c, Caravaggio.

2014, Dec. 12   Litho.   Perf. 14¾x14¼
1526 A244 $1.50 Sheet of 3, #a-
c   7.00 7.00

Souvenir Sheet

New Year 2015 (Year of the Sheep) — A245

No. 1527: a, $3.80, Red ram. b, $4.10, Blue ram.

2015, Jan. 5   Litho.   Perf. 13¼
1527 A245   Sheet of 2, #a-b   11.50 11.50

Miniature Sheet

Easter — A246

No. 1528 — Religious paintings by: a, Matthias Grünewald. b, Peter Paul Rubens. c, Jean Jouvenet. d, Giampietrino.

2015, Mar. 31   Litho.   Perf. 14
1528 A246 $2 Sheet of 4, #a-d 12.50 12.50

Souvenir Sheet

Birth of Princess Charlotte of Cambridge — A247

No. 1529: a, Duchess of Cambridge holding Princess Charlotte. b, Duke of Cambridge holding Prince George.

Perf. 14¾x14¼
2015, June 23   Litho.
1529 A247 $4.50 Sheet of 2,
#a-b   12.00 12.00

Magna Carta, 800th Anniv. A248

Quotations starting with: $1, "To no one will we deny or delay. . ." $1.30, "No free man shall be seized. . ." $1.50, "Given by our hand in the meadow. . ." $1.70, "To no one will we deny or delay. . .," diff.

2015, July 15   Litho.   Perf. 14¼x14¾
1530-1533 A248   Set of 4   7.25 7.25

A249

Self-Government, 50th Anniv. — A250

No. 1535 — Cook Islands stamps: a, #162. b, #164. c, #195. d, #233. e, #253. f, #288. g, #301. h, #322. i, #357. j, #409.

No. 1536 — Cook Islands stamps: a, #435. b, #464. c, #479. d, #502. e, #531. f, #549. g, #660. h, #685. i, #696a. j, #760. k, #877. l, #919. m, #B113. n, #998a. o, #1010b.

No. 1537 — Cook Islands stamps: a, #1029. b, #1048. c, #1111. d, #1140. e, #1191b. f, #1198b. g, #1204. h, #1214a. i, #O68. j, #1234. k, #1238. l, #1241. m, #1258. n, #1265. o, #1269.

No. 1538 — Cook Islands stamps: a, #1271. b, #1291a. c, #1296c. d, #1299. e, #1343a.f, #1383. g, #1422Hq. h, #1434. i, #1482. j, #1534.

2015, Aug. 5   Litho.   Perf. 14
1534	A249	$1 multi	1.25	1.25

Miniature Sheets
Perf. 13¾
1535		Sheet of 10	1.25	1.25
a.-j.	A250	10c Any single	.25	.25
1536		Sheet of 15	6.00	6.00
a.-o.	A250	30c Any single	.40	.40
1537		Sheet of 15	7.50	7.50
a.-o.	A250	40c Any single	.50	.50
1538		Sheet of 10	6.50	6.50
a.-j.	A250	50c Any single	.65	.65
		Nos. 1535-1538 (4)	21.25	21.25

New Year 2016 (Year of the Monkey) A251

Designs: $2.60: Adult and juvenile monkeys, leaves. $3, Juvenile monkey on back of adult. No. 1541: a, $3.80, Like $2.60. b, $4.10, Like $3.

2015, Sept. 25   Litho.   Perf. 13¼
1539-1540	A251	Set of 2	7.25	7.25

Self-Adhesive
1541	A251	Sheet of 2, #a-b	10.50	10.50

No. 1541 contains two 51x51mm diamond-shaped stamps.

Miniature Sheet

Queen Elizabeth II, Longest-Reigning British Monarch — A252

No. 1542 — Various photographs of Queen Elizabeth II: a, $1.30. b, $1.50. c, $1.70. d, $2.

2015, Nov. 20   Litho.   Perf. 14
1542	A252	Sheet of 4, #a-d	8.75	8.75

Souvenir Sheet

Christmas — A253

No. 1543 — Details from Nativity, by Antoniazzo Romano: a, Joseph and saint. b, Infant Jesus and animals. c, Virgin Mary and saint.

2015, Dec. 9   Litho.   Perf. 13¼
1543	A253	$1 Sheet of 3, #a-c	4.00	4.00

A254

A255

Night Skies — A256

Various depictions of night sky, as shown.

Perf. 14¾x14¼
2015, Dec. 29   Litho.
1544	A254	30c Block of 4, #a-d	1.60	1.60
1545	A255	$1 Block of 4, #a-d	5.50	5.50
1546	A256	$1.30 Block of 4, #a-d	7.00	7.00
		Nos. 1544-1546 (3)	14.10	14.10

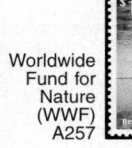

Worldwide Fund for Nature (WWF) A257

Various depictions of Reef manta ray: Nos. 1547, 1551a, $1. Nos. 1548, 1551b, $1.50. Nos. 1549, 1551c, $1.70. Nos. 1550, 1551d, $2.

2016, Feb. 15   Litho.   Perf. 14¾x14
Stamps With White Frames
1547-1550	A257	Set of 4	8.25	8.25

Stamps Without White Frames
1551	A257	Horiz. strip of 4, #a-d	8.25	8.25

No. 1551 printed in sheets containing two strips.

Souvenir Sheet

Queen Elizabeth II, 90th Birthday — A258

No. 1552 — Queen Elizabeth II: a, Holding parasol. b, Wearing coat.

2016, May 10   Litho.   Perf. 13¼
1552	A258	$3 Sheet of 2, #a-b	8.25	8.25

Marae Moana Marine Park — A259

Designs: 30c, Sperm whales. 80c, Melon-headed whales. $1, Emblem of Marae Moana Marine Park. $1.10, Spinner dolphin. $1.30, Spotted dolphins. $1.50, Whale shark. $1.70, Tiger shark. $2, Staghorn coral. $2.40, Yellow scroll coral. $2.50, Black saddled coral groupers. $2.60, Green turtles. $3, Bristle-thighed curlews.

2016, May 27   Litho.   Perf. 14¼x14¾
1553	A259	30c multi	.40	.40
1554	A259	80c multi	1.10	1.10
1555	A259	$1 multi	1.40	1.40
1556	A259	$1.10 multi	1.50	1.50
1557	A259	$1.30 multi	1.75	1.75
1558	A259	$1.50 multi	2.10	2.10
1559	A259	$1.70 multi	2.40	2.40
1560	A259	$2 multi	2.75	2.75
1561	A259	$2.40 multi	3.25	3.25
1562	A259	$2.50 multi	3.50	3.50
1563	A259	$2.60 multi	3.50	3.50
1564	A259	$3 multi	4.25	4.25
		Nos. 1553-1564 (12)	27.90	27.90

New Year 2017 (Year of the Rooster) A260

Designs: $2.30, Red rooster. $4.50, Turquoise blue rooster.

2016, Aug. 10   Litho.   Perf. 13¼
1565-1566	A260	Set of 2	10.00	10.00
1566a		Souvenir sheet of 2, #1565-1566	10.00	10.00

2016 Summer Olympics, Rio de Janeiro A261

No. 1567: a, Sailing. b, Canoeing slalom. c, Weight lifting. d, Swimming. e, Track and field.

2016, Sept. 6   Litho.   Perf. 13¾
1567		Horiz. strip of 5	15.00	15.00
a.-e.	A261	$2 Any single	3.00	3.00

A262

Christmas A263

No. 1568: a, Stained-glass window depicting Holy Family. b, Five-sectioned stained-glass window.

No. 1569: a, Stained-glass window depicting Holy Family, diff. b, Two-sectioned stained-glass window.

2016, Dec. 19   Litho.   Perf. 13¼
1568	A262	50c Vert. pair, #a-b	1.40	1.40
1569	A263	$1 Vert. pair, #a-b	2.75	2.75

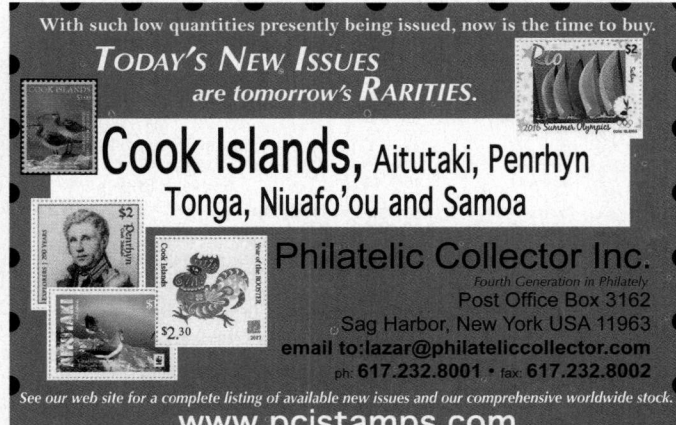

SEMI-POSTAL STAMPS

Catalogue values for unused stamps in this section are for Never Hinged items.

Nos. 203-204, 223, 210, 213, 215-216
Surcharged

No. B1

No. B3

No. B7

Perf. 14x13½, 13½

1968, Feb. 12			**Photo.**	
B1	A34	3c + 1c multi	.25	.25
B2	A34	4c + 1c multi	.25	.25
B3	A37	5c + 2c multi	.25	.25
B4	A34	10c + 2c multi	.25	.25
B5	A34	25c + 5c multi	.30	.30
B6	A34	50c + 10c multi	.60	.60
B7	A35	$1 + 10c multi	1.00	1.00
		Nos. B1-B7 (7)	2.90	2.90

Surtax for the victims of hurricane of Dec. 15-18, 1967. The surcharge on No. B3 is printed on a silver rectangle. The surcharge on No. B7 is in smaller type with serifs, measuring 7½mm in depth.

Nos. 210, 213-214 Surcharged in Ultramarine

1971, Sept. 8		**Photo.**	**Perf. 14x13½**	
B8	A34	10c + 1c multi	.25	.25
B9	A34	10c + 3c multi	.25	.25
B10	A34	25c + 1c multi	.40	.40
B11	A34	25c + 5c multi	.40	.40
B12	A34	30c + 1c multi	.50	.50
B13	A34	30c + 3c multi	.50	.50
		Nos. B8-B13 (6)	2.30	2.30

4th South Pacific Games, Papeete, French Polynesia, Sept. 8-19.

Christmas Type of Regular Issue
Souvenir Sheet

50c+5c, Holy Family in a Garland of Flowers, by Jan Brueghel and Pieter van Avont.

1971, Nov. 30			**Perf. 13½**	
B14	A50	50c + 5c gold & multi	1.10	1.10

No. B14 contains one stamp 45x40mm.

Nos. 316-318, 211, 213 and 215
Surcharged in Red or Black

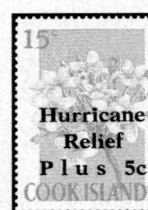

a   b

1972, Mar. 30		**Photo.**	**Perf. 13½**	
B15	A46(a)	5c + 2c multi (R)	.25	.25
B16	A46(a)	10c + 2c multi (R)	.25	.25
B17	A34(b)	15c + 5c multi	.25	.25
B18	A34(b)	25c + 5c multi	.40	.40
B19	A46(a)	30c + 5c multi (R)	.50	.50
B20	A34(b)	50c + 10c multi	.60	.60
		Nos. B15-B20 (6)	2.25	2.25

Surtax for victims of hurricane of Mar. 22-26.

Nos. 319-322c with Surcharge Similar to Type "a"

1972, May 24		**Photo.**	**Perf. 13½**	
B21	A51	5c + 2c, pair, #a.-b.	.35	.35
B22	A51	10c + 2c, pair, #a.-b.	.45	.45
B23	A51	25c + 2c, pair, #a.-b.	.55	.55
B24	A51	30c + 2c, pair, #a.-b.	.65	.65
c.		Souvenir sheet of 8	3.50	3.50
		Nos. B21-B24 (4)	2.00	2.00

Surtax for victims of hurricane of Mar. 22-26. Stamps of No. B24c each surcharged 3c.

Olympic Type of Regular Issue
Souvenir Sheet

50c+5c, Pierre de Coubertin, Olympic rings.

1972, June 26			
B29	A52	50c + 5c multi	2.00	2.00

Christmas Type of Regular Issue
Souvenir Sheet

Design: 50c+5c, Nativity, by Correggio.

1972, Oct. 11		**Photo.**	**Perf. 13½**	
B30	A53	50c + 5c multi	1.50	1.25

No. B30 contains one stamp 30x40mm.

Easter Type of Regular Issue
Souvenir Sheets

1973, Apr. 30		**Photo.**	**Perf. 13½x14**	
B31	A56	50c + 5c like #346	.50	.50
B32	A56	50c + 5c like #347	.50	.50
B33	A56	50c + 5c like #348	.50	.50
		Nos. B31-B33 (3)	1.50	1.50

Surtax was for school children.

Christmas Type of Regular Issue
Souvenir Sheets

1973, Dec. 3		**Photo.**	**Perf. 13x13½**	
B34	A59	50c + 5c like #364	.35	.35
B35	A59	50c + 5c like #365	.35	.35
B36	A59	50c + 5c like #366	.35	.35
B37	A59	50c + 5c like #367	.35	.35
B38	A59	50c + 5c like #368	.35	.35
		Nos. B34-B38 (5)	1.75	1.75

Surtax was for school children.

Easter Type of 1973
Dated "1974"
Souvenir Sheets

1974, Apr. 22			**Perf. 13½x14**	
B39	A56	50c + 5c like #378	.50	.50
B40	A56	50c + 5c like #379	.50	.50
B41	A56	50c + 5c like #380	.50	.50
		Nos. B39-B41 (3)	1.50	1.50

Christmas Type of 1974
Souvenir Sheets

1974		**Photo.**	**Perf. 13½x13**	
B42	A68	50c + 5c like #412	.35	.35
B43	A68	50c + 5c like #413	.35	.35
B44	A68	50c + 5c like #414	.35	.35
B45	A68	50c + 5c like #415	.35	.35
B46	A68	50c + 5c like #416	.35	.35
		Nos. B42-B46 (5)	1.75	1.75

Christmas Type of 1975
Souvenir Sheets

1975, Dec. 1			**Perf. 13½**	
B47	A75	75c + 5c like #437	.50	.50
B48	A75	75c + 5c like #438	.50	.50
B49	A75	75c + 5c like #439	.50	.50
B50	A75	75c + 5c like #440	.50	.50
B51	A75	75c + 5c like #441	.50	.50
		Nos. B47-B51 (5)	2.50	2.50

Size of stamps: 23x40mm.

Easter Type of 1976
Souvenir Sheets

1976, May 3		**Photo.**	**Perf. 13½**	
B52	A76	60c + 5c like #442	.55	.55
B53	A76	60c + 5c like #443	.55	.55
B54	A76	60c + 5c like #444	.55	.55
		Nos. B52-B54 (3)	1.65	1.65

Size of stamps: 36x36mm.

Christmas Type of 1976
Souvenir Sheets

1976, Nov. 2		**Photo.**	**Perf. 14x13½**	
B55	A80	75c + 5c like #459	.50	.50
B56	A80	75c + 5c like #460	.50	.50
B57	A80	75c + 5c like #461	.50	.50
B58	A80	75c + 5c like #462	.50	.50
B59	A80	75c + 5c like #463	.50	.50
		Nos. B55-B59 (5)	2.50	2.50

Easter Type of 1977
Souvenir Sheets

1977, Apr. 18		**Photo.**	**Perf. 13½x14**	
B60	A83	60c + 5c like #471	.60	.60
B61	A83	60c + 5c like #472	.60	.60
B62	A83	60c + 5c like #473	.60	.60
		Nos. B60-B62 (3)	1.80	1.80

Size of stamps: 30x42mm.

Christmas Type of 1977
Souvenir Sheets

1977, Oct. 31		**Photo.**	**Perf. 14x13½**	
B63	A84	75c + 5c like #474	.45	.45
B64	A84	75c + 5c like #475	.45	.45
B65	A84	75c + 5c like #476	.45	.45
B66	A84	75c + 5c like #477	.45	.45
B67	A84	75c + 5c like #478	.45	.45
		Nos. B63-B67 (5)	2.25	2.25

Easter Type of 1978
Souvenir Sheets

1978, Apr. 10		**Photo.**	**Perf. 14x13½**	
B68	A87	60c + 5c like #483	.45	.45
B69	A87	60c + 5c like #484	.45	.45
B70	A87	60c + 5c like #485	.45	.45
		Nos. B68-B70 (3)	1.35	1.35

Christmas Type of 1978
Souvenir Sheets

1979, Jan. 12		**Photo.**	**Perf. 13**	
B71	A89	75c + 5c like #503	.45	.45
B72	A89	75c + 5c like #504	.45	.45
B73	A89	75c + 5c like #505	.45	.45
		Nos. B71-B73 (3)	1.35	1.35

Easter Type of 1979
Souvenir Sheet

1979, Apr. 5		**Photo.**	**Perf. 13**	
B74		Sheet of 4	1.00	1.00
a.	A90	10c + 2c like #506	.25	.25
b.	A90	12c + 2c like #507	.25	.25
c.	A90	15c + 2c like #508	.25	.25
d.	A90	20c + 2c like #509	.25	.25

IYC Type of 1979
Souvenir Sheet

1979, Oct. 10				
B75		Sheet of 3	1.40	1.40
a.	A93	30c + 5c like #529	.30	.30
b.	A93	50c + 5c like #530	.40	.40
c.	A93	65c + 5c like #531	.50	.50

Christmas Type of 1979

1980, Jan. 15		**Photo.**	**Perf. 14**	
B76	A95	6c + 2c like #537	.25	.25
B77	A95	10c + 2c like #538	.25	.25
B78	A95	12c + 2c like #539	.25	.25
B79	A95	15c + 2c like #540	.25	.25
		Nos. B76-B79 (5)	1.00	1.00

Easter Type of 1980
Souvenir Sheets

1980, Mar. 31		**Photo.**	**Perf. 13**	
B80	A96	Sheet of 6, #a.-f.	1.40	1.40

No. B80 contains Nos. 541-543, each stamp with 2c surcharge.

1980, Apr. 23   Souvenir Sheets

B81	A96	75c + 5c like #541a	.50	.50
B82	A96	75c + 5c like #541b	.50	.50
B83	A96	75c + 5c like #542a	.50	.50
B84	A96	75c + 5c like #542b	.50	.50
B85	A96	75c + 5c like #543a	.50	.50
B86	A96	75c + 5c like #543b	.50	.50
		Nos. B81-B86 (6)	3.00	3.00

Surtax was for school children.

Rotary Type of 1980
Souvenir Sheet

1980, May 27		**Photo.**	**Perf. 14**	
B87		Sheet of 3	1.50	1.50
a.	A97	30c + 3c like #547	.35	.35
b.	A97	35c + 3c like #548	.45	.45
c.	A97	50c + 3c like #549	.60	.60

Christmas Type of 1980
Souvenir Sheets

1981, Jan. 9		**Photo.**	**Imperf.**	
B88	A102a	75c + 5c like #652	.50	.50
B89	A102a	75c + 5c like #653	.50	.50
B90	A102a	75c + 5c like #654	.50	.50
B91	A102a	75c + 5c like #655	.50	.50
		Nos. B88-B91 (4)	2.00	2.00

Easter Type of 1981
Souvenir Sheets

1981, Apr. 10		**Photo.**	**Perf. 13½**	
B92		Sheet of 3	1.20	1.20
a.	A103	15c + 2c like #656	.25	.25
b.	A103	25c + 2c like #657	.30	.30
c.	A103	40c + 2c like #658	.50	.50

1981, Apr. 28			**Imperf.**	
B93	A103	75c + 5c like #656	.65	.65
B94	A103	75c + 5c like #657	.65	.65
B95	A103	75c + 5c like #658	.65	.65
		Nos. B93-B95 (3)	1.95	1.95

Surtax was for school children.

Espana '82 Soccer Type
Souvenir Sheet

1981		**Photo.**	**Perf. 13½**	
B96	A105	Sheet of 8, #a.-h.	6.50	6.50

No. B96 contains Nos. 661-664, each stamp with 3c surcharge.

Royal Wedding Type of 1981
Nos. 659-660a Surcharged in Black

1981, Nov. 10		**Photo.**	**Perf. 14**	
B97	A104	$1 + 5c multi	.75	1.50
B98	A104	$2 + 5c multi	1.50	2.50
a.		Souvenir sheet of 2	3.50	4.00

Intl. Year of the Disabled. No. B98a contains Nos. B97-B98 each with 10c surtax, which was for benefit of the disabled; black overprint in margin.

Christmas Type of 1981
Souvenir Sheet

1981, Dec. 14		**Photo.**	**Perf. 13½**	
B99		Sheet of 4	2.75	2.75
a.	A107	8c + 3c like #669	.25	.25
b.	A107	15c + 3c like #670	.35	.35
c.	A107	40c + 3c like #671	.75	.75
d.	A107	50c + 3c like #672	1.00	1.00

Surtax was for school children.

Nos. 919-923 Surcharged in Silver

No. B100

No. B104

1986, Nov. 21   Litho.   Perf. 13½

B100	A138	55c + 10c multi	2.50	2.50
B101	A138	$1.30 + 10c multi	5.25	5.25
B102	A138	$2.75 + 10c multi	10.00	10.00
		Nos. B100-B102 (3)	17.75	17.75

Souvenir Sheets

B103		Sheet of 3	16.00	16.00
a.-c.		A138 $2.40 + 10c on Nos. 922a-922c, any single	5.25	5.25
B104		A138 $6.40 + 50c multi	16.00	16.00

No. B103 ovptd. in margin "VISIT TO SOUTH PACIFIC / OF POPE JOHN PAUL II" and "FIRST PAPAL VISIT / NOVEMBER 21-24 1986."
For surcharge see No. B112.

Stamps of 1982 and 1987 Surcharged in Sans-serif Capitals

No. B109

Perfs. as before

1987, June 30   Photo.

Surcharged +25c

B105	A121	55c on #958	1.10	1.10
B106	A121	65c on #960	1.25	1.25
B107	A121	75c on #963	1.40	1.40
B108	A121	95c on #965	1.60	1.60

Surcharged +50c

B109	A101	$2.80 on #582	4.50	4.50
B110	A101	$5 on #583	7.75	7.75
B111	A102	$6.40 on #978	9.50	9.50
		Nos. B105-B111 (7)	27.10	27.10

Stamps of 1985-86 Surcharged in Silver or Black

1987   Perfs. as before

Surcharged +50c

B112	A138	55c on #B100	1.40	1.40
B113	A133	55c on #897 (B)	1.40	1.40
B114	A128	65c on #871	1.50	1.50
B115	A133	65c on #898	1.50	1.50
B116	A128	75c on #872	1.60	1.60
B117	A133	75c on #899	1.60	1.60
B118	A134	95c on #908 (B)	1.90	1.90
B119	A135	$1 on #910	2.10	2.10
B120	A136	$1 on #913	2.10	2.10
B121	A137	$1 on #916	2.10	2.10
B122	A134	$1.15 on #873	2.25	2.25
B123	A133	$1.25 on #900	2.25	2.25
B124	A134	$1.25 on #905	2.25	2.25
B125	A136	$1.25 on #914 (B)	2.25	2.25
B126	A138	$1.30 on #920	2.50	2.50
B127	A134	$1.50 on #906 (B)	2.50	2.50
B128	A135	$1.50 on #911 (B)	2.50	2.50
B129	A133	$2 on #901 (B)	3.25	3.25
B130	A135	$2 on #912 (B)	3.25	3.25
B131	A137	$2 on #917	3.25	3.25
B132	A136	$2.75 on #915	4.50	4.50
B133	A138	$2.75 on #921	4.50	4.50
B134	A128	$2.80 on #874	4.50	4.50
B135	A137	$3 on #918	4.75	4.75
		Nos. B112-B135 (24)	61.70	61.70

Souvenir Sheets

B136	A134	$1.10 on #907 (B)	2.00	2.00
B137	A134	$1.95 on #908	3.00	3.00
B138	A138	$2.40 on #922	11.00	11.00
B139	A134	$2.45 on #909 (B)	3.75	3.75
B140	A128	$5.30 on #875	7.25	7.25
B141	A138	$6.40 on #B104	8.50	8.50
		Nos. B136-B141 (6)	35.50	35.50

Issued: Nos. B118, B121, B124, B127, B131, B135-B137, B139-B140, 7/31; others 6/30.

No. 1230 Surcharged in Silver
Souvenir Sheet

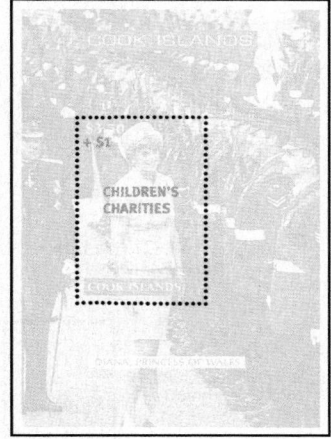

1998, Nov. 20   Litho.   Perf. 14

B142	A179	$3.50 +$1 multi	4.75	4.75

AIR POST STAMPS

Catalogue values for unused stamps in this section are for Never Hinged items.

Stamps of 1936-63 Overprinted and Surcharged

Perf. 13x13½, 13½x13
Litho., Engr.

1966, Apr. 22   Wmk. 253

C1	A25	6p on #152	.70	.25
C2	A26	7p on 8p #153	1.00	.25
C3	A25	10p on 3p #150	.65	.35
C4	A25	1sh on #154	.70	.45
C5	A27	1sh6p on #155	1.25	1.25
C6	A28	2sh3p on 3sh #157	1.00	1.00
C7	A28	5sh on #158	1.60	1.75
C8	A28	10sh on 2sh #156	2.00	8.00

No. 106 Overprinted

Perf. 14
Typo.

C9	PF5	£1 pink	12.00	16.00
a.		Airplane missing	37.50	50.00
		Nos. C1-C9 (9)	20.90	29.30

No. C9a occurs on all stamps from the right vertical column of the sheet due to a lack of airplane symbols. The size and position of the airplane symbol varies in relation to "Airmail" on the other stamps. The surcharges are printed on silver ovals.

2nd So. Pacific Games' Type
Sport: 10p, Women runners and Games' emblem. 2sh3p, Runner and team emblem.

Perf. 13½

1967, Jan. 12   Unwmk.   Photo.

C10	A32	10p org & multi	.25	.25
C11	A32	2sh3p multi	.25	.25

Capt. Cook Type of Regular Issue
6c, The "Resolution" and "Discovery" Beating Through the Ice, by Webber. 10c, The Island of Otaheite, by Hodges, and Queen Elizabeth II. 15c, View of Karakakooa (Kealakekua), Hawaii, by Webber. 25c, The Landing at Middleburg, Tonga, by Hodges, & Captain Cook. (All horiz.)

1968, Sept. 12   Photo.   Perf. 13

C12	A39	6c gold & multi	.35	.35
C13	A39	10c gold & multi	.40	.40
C14	A39	15c gold & multi	.45	.45
C15	A39	25c gold & multi	1.00	1.00
		Nos. C12-C15 (4)	2.20	2.20

See note after No. 236.

Christmas Type of 1979

1979, Dec. 14   Photo.   Perf. 14

C16	A95	20c like #537	.25	.25
C17	A95	25c like #538	.25	.25
C18	A95	30c like #539	.30	.30
C19	A95	35c like #540	.40	.40
		Nos. C16-C19 (4)	1.20	1.20

Franklin D. Roosevelt — AP1

80c, Benjamin Franklin. $1.40, George Washington, by Gilbert Stuart.

1982, Sept. 30   Photo.   Perf. 14

C20	AP1	60c multicolored	.80	.80
C21	AP1	80c multicolored	1.00	1.00
C22	AP1	$1.40 multicolored	1.75	1.75
a.		Souvenir sheet of 3	4.00	4.00
		Nos. C20-C22 (3)	3.55	3.55

No. C22a contains Nos. C20-C22, perf. 13½ with portraits in square frames.

No. C22 Overprinted in Gold and Black

1983, Aug. 12   Photo.   Perf. 14

C23	AP1	96c on $1.40 multi	1.60	1.60

Endangered Bird Species Type
Souvenir Sheets

Nos. 1020-1023 Overprinted

1990, Dec. 5   Litho.   Perf. 13½

C24	A145	$1 Flycatcher	3.50	3.50
C25	A145	$1.25 Flycatchers	4.25	4.25
C26	A145	$1.50 Fruit dove	5.50	5.50
C27	A145	$1.75 Fruit doves	6.25	6.25
		Nos. C24-C27 (4)	19.50	19.50

Birdpex '90, 20th Intl. Ornithological Cong., New Zealand.

AIR POST SEMI-POSTAL STAMPS

Catalogue values for unused stamps in this section are for Never Hinged items.

Christmas Type of 1979

1980, Jan. 15   Photo.   Perf. 14

CB1	A95	20c + 4c like #C16	.25	.25
CB2	A95	25c + 4c like #C17	.30	.30
CB3	A95	30c + 4c like #C18	.35	.35
CB4	A95	35c + 4c like #C19	.40	.40
		Nos. CB1-CB4 (4)	1.30	1.30

OFFICIAL STAMPS

Flower Issue of 1967-69 Overprinted or Surcharged in Black on Silver

1975   Photo.   Unwmk.   Perf. 14x13½

O1	A34	1c multi (#200)	.25
O2	A34	2c multi (#201)	.25
O3	A34	3c multi (#203)	.25
O4	A34	4c multi (#205)	.25
O5	A34	5c on 2½c multi (#202)	.25
O6	A34	8c multi (#208)	.30
O7	A34	10c on 6c multi (#207)	.30
O8	A34	18c on 20c multi (#212)	.35
O9	A34	25c on 9c multi (#209)	.55
O10	A34	30c on 15c multi (#211)	.65
O11	A34	50c multi (#215)	.70
O12	A35	$1 multi (#216)	1.30
O13	A35	$2 multi (#217)	2.00
O14	A36	$4 multi (#218)	3.75
O15	A36	$6 multi (#219)	4.50
		Nos. O1-O15 (15)	15.65

No. O1-O15 were not sold to the public unused. Arrangement of surcharge varies on different denominations.
Silver panel on Nos. O14-O15 measures 26½x6mm and is rounded at both ends.
Issue dates: 1c-$2, Mar. 17, $4-$6, May 19.

Catalogue values for unused stamps in this section, from this point to the end of the section, are for Never Hinged items.

Nos. 381-382, 389, 393-396, 467, 446 Ovptd. or Srchd. in Silver or Black

No. O16

No. O18

Photo., Litho.

1978, Oct. 19   Perf. 13½

O16	A62	1c multi (S)	.85	.25
O17	A62	2c on ½c multi	.85	.25
O18	A62	5c on ½c multi	.95	.25
O19	A62	10c on 8c multi (S)	1.10	.25
O20	A62	15c on 50c multi (S)	1.25	.25
O21	A62	18c on 60c multi (S)	1.25	.25
O22	A62	25c multicolored	1.60	.25
O23	A62	30c multi (S)	1.60	.30
O24	A62	35c on 60c multi (S)	1.60	.35
O25	A62	50c multi (S)	2.10	.50
O26	A62	60c multi (S)	2.40	.60
O27	A82	$1 Pair, #a.-b. (S)	10.00	2.00
O29	A77	$2 multicolored	7.25	.75
O30	A64	$4 multi ('79)	13.50	3.50
O31	A64	$6 multi ('79)	13.50	5.50
		Nos. O16-O31 (15)	59.80	16.75

Diagonal overprints on No. O27. Overprint on No. O29-O31: 19x4mm.

Nos. 790-791,
795, 797, 799,
805, 807, 809-
810 Ovptd. or
Srchd. in Silver

1985, July 10 Photo. Perf. 13½x13

O32	A121	5c multi	.55	.55
O33	A121	10c multi	.55	.55
O34	A121	20c multi	.65	.65
O35	A121	30c multi	.65	.65
O36	A121	40c multi	.65	.65
O37	A121	55c on 85c multi	.80	.80
O38	A121	60c multi	.80	.80
O39	A121	$1.10 multi	1.60	1.25
O40	A121	$2 on $1.20 multi	3.25	2.50
		Nos. O32-O40 (9)	9.50	8.40

Nos. 792-794, 802, 806, 696 and 583-
586 Ovptd. or Srchd. in Silver, Gold
(75c) or Black and Silver ($5, $18)

No. O41

No. O53

1986-90 Photo. Perfs. as Before

O41	A121	12c multi	5.00	5.00
O42	A121	14c multi	5.00	5.00
O43	A121	18c multi	5.00	5.00
O44	A121	50c multi	6.25	6.25
O45	A121	70c multi	6.75	6.75
O46	A111	75c on 60c, #a.- d.	13.50	13.50
O50	A102	$5 on $3 multi	17.00	17.00
O51	A102	$9 on $4 multi	9.00	9.00
O52	A102	$14 on $6 multi	14.00	14.00
O53	A102	$18 on $10 multi	20.00	20.00
		Nos. O41-O53 (10)	101.50	101.50

Issued: $9, 5/30/89; $14, 7/12/89; $18,
6/4/90; others 5/5/86.

Nos. 1058-
1059, 1062,
1064-1066,
1071, 1076-
1078, 1080-
1083, 1085,
1087 Ovptd.
in Silver

1995-98 Litho. Perf. 14½x13½

O54	A155	5c multicolored	.40	.40
O55	A155	10c multicolored	.40	.40
O56	A155	15c multicolored	.50	.50
O57	A155	20c multicolored	.55	.55
O58	A155	25c multicolored	.60	.60
O59	A155	30c multicolored	.65	.65
O60	A155	50c multicolored	.80	.80
O61	A155	80c multicolored	1.30	1.30
O62	A155	85c multicolored	1.30	1.30
O63	A155	90c multicolored	1.30	1.30
O64	A155	$1 multicolored	1.50	1.50
O65	A155	$2 multicolored	2.40	2.40
O66	A155a	$3 multicolored	3.75	3.75
O67	A155a	$5 multicolored	4.75	4.75
O68	A155a	$7 multicolored	6.75	6.75
O69	A155a	$10 multi	8.50	8.50
		Nos. O54-O69 (16)	35.45	35.45

Overprint on Nos. O66-O69 has larger, sans
serif letters.
Nos. O66-O69 were not sold unused to local
customers.
Issued: 5c-90c, 2/24/95; $1-$2, 5/15/95; $3-
$7, 7/17/98; $10, 11/12/98.

Nos. 1305-1322 Overprinted in Gold

2010, Oct. 12 Litho. Perf. 13¾
Sizes: 60x37mm, 37x60mm

O70	A191	10c multi	.25	.25
O71	A191	20c multi	.30	.30
O72	A191	30c multi	.50	.50
O73	A191	40c multi	.65	.65
O74	A191	50c multi	.80	.80
O75	A191	70c multi	1.10	1.10
O76	A191	80c multi	1.25	1.25
O77	A191	90c multi	1.50	1.50
O78	A191	$1 multi	1.60	1.60
O79	A191	$1.10 multi	1.75	1.75
O80	A191	$1.20 multi	1.90	1.90
O81	A191	$2 multi	3.25	3.25
O82	A191	$3 multi	4.75	4.75
O83	A191	$4 multi	6.50	6.50
O84	A191	$5 multi	8.00	8.00

Size: 60x37mm

O85	A191	$7.50 multi	12.00	12.00
O86	A191	$10 multi	16.00	16.00
O87	A191	$20 multi	32.00	32.00
		Nos. O70-O87 (18)	94.10	94.10

Overprint reads up on vertical stamps.

**Nos. 1305-1309 Overprinted in
Metallic Green Like No. O70**

2010, Oct. 12 Litho. Perf. 13¾
Sizes: 60x37mm, 37x60mm

O88	A191	10c multi	.25	.25
O89	A191	20c multi	.30	.30
O90	A191	30c multi	.50	.50
O91	A191	40c multi	.65	.65
O92	A191	50c multi	.80	.80
O93	A191	70c multi	1.10	1.10
O94	A191	80c multi	1.25	1.25
O95	A191	90c multi	1.50	1.50
O96	A191	$1 multi	1.60	1.60
O97	A191	$1.10 multi	1.75	1.75
O98	A191	$1.20 multi	1.90	1.90
O99	A191	$2 multi	3.25	3.25
O100	A191	$3 multi	4.75	4.75
O101	A191	$4 multi	6.50	6.50
O102	A191	$5 multi	8.00	8.00
		Nos. O88-O102 (15)	34.10	34.10

Overprint reads up on vertical stamps.

**Nos. 1305-1309 Overprinted in
Metallic Red Like No. O70**

2010, Oct. 12 Litho. Perf. 13¾
Sizes: 60x37mm, 37x60mm

O103	A191	10c multi	.25	.25
O104	A191	20c multi	.30	.30
O105	A191	30c multi	.50	.50
O106	A191	40c multi	.65	.65
O107	A191	50c multi	.80	.80
O108	A191	70c multi	1.10	1.10
O109	A191	80c multi	1.25	1.25
O110	A191	90c multi	1.50	1.50
O111	A191	$1 multi	1.60	1.60
O112	A191	$1.10 multi	1.75	1.75
O113	A191	$1.20 multi	1.90	1.90
O114	A191	$2 multi	3.25	3.25
O115	A191	$3 multi	4.75	4.75
O116	A191	$4 multi	6.50	6.50
O117	A191	$5 multi	8.00	8.00
		Nos. O103-O117 (15)	34.10	34.10

Overprint reads up on vertical stamps.

CORFU

kor-'fü

LOCATION — An island in the Ionian
Sea opposite the Greek-Albanian
border
GOVT. — A department of Greece
AREA — 245 sq. mi.
POP. — 114,620 (1938)
CAPITAL — Corfu

In 1922 Italy occupied Corfu (Ker-
kyra) during a controversy with Greece
over the assassination of an Italian official in Epirus. Italy again occupied
Corfu in 1941-43.

100 Centesimi = 1 Lira
100 Lepta = 1 Drachma

Watermark

Wmk. 140 —
Crown

Wmk. 252 —
Crowns

ISSUED UNDER ITALIAN
OCCUPATION

Italian Stamps of 1901-
23 Overprinted

1923, Sept. 20 Wmk. 140 Perf. 14

N1	A48	5c green	6.00	11.00
N2	A48	10c claret	6.00	11.00
N3	A48	15c slate	6.00	11.00
N4	A50	20c brown or- ange	6.00	11.00
N5	A49	30c orange brown	6.00	11.00
N6	A49	50c violet	6.00	11.00
N7	A49	60c blue	6.00	11.00
a.		Vert. pair, one without overprint	1,500.	
N8	A46	1 l brown & green	6.00	11.00
		Nos. N1-N8 (8)	48.00	88.00
		Set, never hinged	115.00	

Italian Stamps of 1901-
23 Surcharged

1923, Sept. 24

N9	A48	25 l on 10c claret	60.00	45.00
N10	A49	60 l on 25c blue	10.00	
N11	A49	70 l on 30c org brn	10.00	
N12	A49	1.20d on 50c violet	25.00	45.00
N13	A46	2.40d on 1 l brn & grn	25.00	45.00
N14	A46	4.75d on 2 l grn & org	15.00	
		Nos. N9-N14 (6)	145.00	
		Set, never hinged	265.00	

Nos. N10, N11, N14 were not placed in use.

Issue for Corfu and Paxos

Nos. N15-N34, NC1-NC12, NJ1-
NJ11 and NRA1-NRA3 have been
extensively counterfeited, some with
forged cancellations.

Stamps of
Greece,
1937-38,
Overprinted
in Black

Perf. 12x13½, 12½x12, 13½x12
1941, June 5 Wmk. 252

N15	A69	5 l brn red & blue	5.75	3.75
a.		Inverted overprint	60.00	47.50
b.		Double overprint	80.00	110.00
N16	A70	10 l bl & brn red (On 397)	1.90	2.75
N17	A70	10 l bl & brn red (On 413)	1,550.	1,350.
N18	A71	20 l black & grn	2.75	3.75
a.		Inverted overprint	80.00	47.50
N19	A72	40 l green & blk	3.25	4.25
a.		Inverted overprint	80.00	47.50
b.		Double overprint	80.00	110.00
N20	A73	50 l brown & blk	1.90	2.75
a.		Inverted overprint	55.00	47.50
N21	A74	80 l ind & yel brn	3.75	5.00
N22	A67	1d green	14.50	14.50
N23	A84	1.50d green	14.50	14.50
N24	A75	2d ultra	7.75	11.00
N25	A67	3d red brown	7.75	11.00
N26	A76	5d red	7.75	11.00
N27	A77	6d olive brown	7.75	11.00
N28	A78	7d dark brown	12.00	12.00
N29	A67	8d deep blue	24.50	24.50
N30	A79	10d red brown	700.00	375.00
N31	A80	15d green	28.00	28.00
N32	A81	25d dark blue	28.00	28.00
N33	A84	30d org brn	115.00	100.00
N34	A67	100d carmine lake	375.00	350.00
		Nos. N15-N34 (20)	2,912.	2,363.
		Set, never hinged	3,900.	

AIR POST STAMPS

Greece Nos. C37 and C26-C35,
Overprinted Like Nos. N15-N34
Perf. 12½x13, 13x12½, 13½x12½
1941, June 5 Unwmk.

NC1	D3	50 l dk brown	11.00	7.75
NC2	AP16	1d red	750.00	275.00
NC3	AP17	2d gray blue	11.00	7.75
NC4	AP18	5d violet	13.50	13.00
NC5	AP19	7d deep ultra	17.50	13.00
NC6	AP20	10d bister brn (On C26)	950.00	400.00
NC7	AP20	10d brown org (On C35)	62.50	50.00
NC8	AP21	25d rose	135.00	60.00
NC9	AP22	30d dk grn	145.00	90.00
NC10	AP23	50d violet	145.00	90.00
a.		Double overprint		550.00
NC11	AP24	10d brown	1,300.	650.00

On No. C36
Serrate Roulette 13½

NC12	D3	50 l vio brn	90.00	23.00
a.		On No. C36a	350.00	
		Nos. NC1-NC12 (12)	3,631.	1,680.
		Set, never hinged	5,500.	

POSTAGE DUE STAMPS

Postage Due Stamps of Greece,
1913-35 Overprinted Like #N15-N34
1941, June 5 Unwmk.
Serrate Roulette 13½

NJ1	D3	10 l carmine	4.50	5.00
NJ2	D3	25 l ultra	4.50	5.00
NJ3	D3	80 l lilac brown	1,150.	450.00

Perf. 12½x13, 13½x12½

NJ4	D3	1d lt bl (On J80)	1,600.	800.00
NJ5	D3	2d light red	8.50	14.00
NJ6	D3	5d gray	22.50	24.00
NJ7	D3	10d gray green	22.50	24.00
NJ8	D3	15d red brown	22.50	24.00
NJ9	D3	25d light red	22.50	24.00
NJ10	D3	50d orange	22.50	24.00
NJ11	D3	100d slate green	600.00	450.00
		Nos. NJ1-NJ11 (11)	3,480.	1,844.
		Set, never hinged	5,000.	

POSTAL TAX STAMPS

**Greece Nos. RA61-RA63
Overprinted Like Nos. N15-N34
Wmk., Unwmk.**

1941, June 5   **Perf. 13½**

NRA1	PT7	10 l brt rose, *pale rose*	3.25	4.50
NRA2	PT7	50 l gray grn, *pale green*	5.50	7.00
NRA3	PT7	1d dull blue, *lt blue*	37.50	45.00
		Nos. NRA1-NRA3 (3)	46.25	56.50
		Set, never hinged	67.50	

Stamps overprinted "CORFU" were replaced by Italian stamps overprinted "Isole Jonie." See Ionian Islands.

COSTA RICA

ˌkōs-tə-'rē-kə

LOCATION — Central America between Nicaragua and Panama
GOVT. — Republic
AREA — 19,730 sq. mi.
POP. — 3,674,490 (1999 est.)
CAPITAL — San Jose

8 Reales = 100 Centavos = 1 Peso
100 Centimos = 1 Colon (1900)

Catalogue values for unused stamps in this country are for Never Hinged items, beginning with Scott 238 in the regular postage section, Scott C117 in the air post section, Scott CE1 in the air post special delivery section, Scott E1 in the special delivery section, and Scott RA1 in the postal tax section.

Watermarks

Wmk. 215 — Small Star in Shield, Multiple

Wmk. 229 — Wavy Lines

Wmk. 334 — Rectangles

Values for unused stamps are for examples with original gum as defined in the catalogue introduction. Very fine examples of Nos. 1-22 will have perforations just clear of the design on one or more sides due to the placement of the stamps on the plates and to imperfect perforating methods.

Coat of Arms — A1

1863   **Unwmk.**   **Engr.**   **Perf. 12**

1	A1	½r blue	.40	1.10
a.		½r light blue	.40	1.10
b.		Pair, imperf. horiz.	6,000.	
2	A1	2r scarlet	1.75	2.25
3	A1	4r green	16.00	16.00
4	A1	1p orange	42.50	42.50
		Nos. 1-4 (4)	60.65	61.85

The ½r was printed from two plates. The second is in light blue with little or no sky over the mountains.
Imperforate stamps of Nos. 1-2 are corner stamps from poorly perforated sheets.

Nos. 1-3 Surcharged in Red or Black

a   b

c   d

e

1881-82   **Red or Black Surcharge**

7	A1(a)	1c on ½r ('82)	3.00	6.00
a.		On No. 1a	15.00	
8	A1(b)	1c on ½r ('82)	18.00	30.00
9	A1(c)	2c on ½r, #1a	3.00	2.75
a.		On No. 1	8.00	
12	A1(c)	5c on ½r	15.00	
13	A1(d)	5c on ½r ('82)	3.00	
14	A1(d)	10c on 2r (Bk) ('82)	72.50	
15	A1(e)	20c on 4r ('82)	300.00	—

Overprints with different fonts and "OFICIAL" were never placed in use, and are said to have been surcharged to a dealer's order. The ½r surcharged "DOS CTS" is not a postage stamp. It probably is an essay.
Postally used examples of Nos. 7-15 are rare. Nos. 13-15 exist with a favor cancel having a hyphen between "San" and "Jose." Values same as unused. Fake cancellations exist.
Counterfeits exist of surcharges on Nos. 7-15.

Gen. Prospero Fernández — A6

1883, Jan. 1

16	A6	1c green	3.00	1.50
17	A6	2c carmine	3.25	1.50
18	A6	5c blue violet	32.50	2.00
19	A6	10c orange	150.00	12.00
20	A6	40c blue	3.00	3.00
		Nos. 16-20 (5)	191.75	20.00

Unused examples of 40c usually lack gum.
For overprints see Nos. O1-O20, O24, Guanacaste 1-38, 44.

President Bernardo Soto Alfaro — A7

1887

21	A7	5c blue violet	7.00	.50
22	A7	10c orange	4.00	3.00

Unused examples of 5c usually lack gum.
For overprints see Nos. O22-O23, Guanacaste 42-43, 45.

CORREOS   CORREOS

A8   A9

1889   **Black Overprint**

23	A8	1c rose	5.00	3.00
24	A9	5c brown	7.00	3.00

Vertical and inverted overprints are fakes.
For overprints see Guanacaste Nos. 47-54.

President Soto Alfaro
A10   A11

A12   A13

A14   A15

A16   A17

A18   A19

1889   **Perf. 14-16 & Compound**

25	A10	1c brown	.35	.45
a.		Horiz. pair, imperf. vert	150.00	
b.		Imperf. pair	150.00	
c.		Horiz. or vert. pair, imperf. btwn.	150.00	
26	A11	2c dark green	.35	.45
a.		Imperf., pair	50.00	
b.		Vert. pair, imperf. horiz.	125.00	
c.		Horiz. pair, imperf. btwn.	125.00	
27	A12	5c orange	.45	.35
a.		Imperf., pair		750.00
b.		Horiz. pair, imperf. btwn.	350.00	
28	A13	10c red brown	.40	.35
a.		Vert. or horiz. pair, imperf. btwn.	150.00	500.00
29	A14	20c yellow green	.30	.35
a.		Vert. pair, imperf. horiz.	200.00	
b.		Horizontal pair, imperf. btwn.	150.00	
30	A15	50c rose red	1.00	
		Telegram cancel		.75
31	A16	1p blue	1.25	
		Telegram cancel		.75
32	A17	2p dull violet	6.00	
a.		2p slate	6.00	
		Telegram cancel		4.00
33	A18	5p olive green	25.00	
		Telegram cancel		10.00
34	A19	10p black	100.00	
		Telegram cancel		45.00
		Nos. 25-34 (10)	135.10	1.95

Nos. 30-34 normally were used on telegrams and most examples were removed from the forms and sold by the government.
Most unused examples of No. 34 have no gum or only part gum. These sell for somewhat less.

For overprints see Nos. O25-O30, Guanacaste 55-67.

Arms of Costa Rica
A20   A21

A22   A23

A24   A25

A26   A27

A28   A29

1892   **Perf. 12-15 & Compound**

35	A20	1c grnsh blue	.30	.40
36	A21	2c yellow	.30	.40
37	A22	5c red lilac	.30	.25
a.		5c violet	60.00	.30
38	A23	10c lt green	.80	.35
a.		Horiz. pair, imperf. btwn.		100.00
39	A24	20c scarlet	12.00	.25
a.		Horiz. pair, imperf. btwn.		100.00
40	A25	50c gray blue	4.00	4.25
41	A26	1p green, *yel*	1.25	1.00
42	A27	2p brown red, *lilac*	3.00	1.00
a.		2p rose red, *pale lil*	12.00	1.00
43	A28	5p dk blue, *blue*	2.00	1.00
44	A29	10p brown, *pale buff*	35.00	5.00
a.		10p brown, *yellow*	8.00	
		Nos. 35-44 (10)	58.95	13.90

Imperfs. of Nos. 35-44 are proofs.
For overprints see Nos. O31-O36.

Statue of Juan Santamaría
A30

Juan Mora Fernández
A31

View of Port Limón — A32

Braulio Carrillo ("Branlio" on stamp) — A33

National Theater — A34

José M. Castro — A35

Birris Bridge — A36

Juan Rafael Mora — A37

Jesús Jiménez — A38

Coat of Arms — A39

1901, Jan.   *Perf. 12-15½*

45	A30	1c green & blk	3.25	.30
a.		Horiz. pair, imperf. btwn.	150.00	
46	A31	2c ver & blk	1.25	.30
47	A32	5c gray blue & blk	3.25	.30
a.		Vert. pair, imperf. btwn.		300.00
48	A33	10c ocher & blk	3.25	.35
49	A34	20c lake & blk	22.50	.25
a.		Vert. pair, imperf. btwn.	1,000.	
50	A35	50c dull lil & dk bl	5.50	1.00
51	A36	1col ol bis & blk	110.00	3.50
52	A37	2col car rose & dk grn	16.00	3.00
53	A38	5col brown & blk	75.00	3.50
54	A39	10col yel grn & brn red	29.00	3.00
		Nos. 45-54 (10)	269.00	15.50

The 2c exists with center inverted. Value $77,500.

Nos. 45-57 in other colors are private reprints made in 1948. They have little value.

For surcharge and overprints see Nos. 58, 78, O37-O44.

Remainders

In 1914 the government sold a large quantity of stamps at very much less than face value. The lot included most regular issues from 1901 to 1911 inclusive, postage due stamps of 1903 and Official stamps of 1901-03. These stamps were canceled with groups of thin parallel bars. The higher valued used stamps, such as Nos. 64, 65-68a, sell for much less than the values quoted, which are for stamps with regular postal cancellations. A few sell for much higher prices.

José M. Cañas — A40

Julián Volio — A41

Eusebio Figueroa Oreamuno — A42

1903   *Perf. 13½, 14, 15*

55	A40	4c red vio & blk	2.00	.70
56	A41	6c olive grn & blk	7.25	4.00
57	A42	25c gray lil & brn	16.00	.30
		Nos. 55-57 (3)	25.25	5.00

See note on private reprints following No. 54.
For overprints see Nos. 81, O45-O47.

No. 49
Surcharged in Black:

1905

58	A34	1c on 20c lake & blk	.60	.60
a.		Inverted surcharge	10.00	10.00
b.		Diagonal surcharge	.60	.60

Examples surcharged in other colors are proofs.

Statue of Juan Santamaria A43

Juan Mora Fernández A44

José M. Cañas A45

Mauro Fernández A46

Braulio Carrillo — A47

Julián Volio — A48

Eusebio Figueroa Oreamuno A49

José M. Castro A50

Jesús Jiménez — A51

Juan Rafael Mora — A52

Perf. 11x14, 14 (1c, 5c, 10c, 25c)

1907   **Unwmk.**

59	A43	1c red brn & ind	8.00	.40
a.		Perf. 11x14	60.00	10.00
b.		Imperf pair	15.00	—
60	A44	2c yel grn & blk	3.00	.30
a.		Perf. 14	3.00	.30
b.		Imperf pair	15.00	—
61	A45	4c car & indigo	12.00	2.50
a.		Perf. 14	500.00	45.00
b.		Imperf pair	15.00	—
62	A46	5c yel & dull bl	3.00	.30
a.		Perf. 11x14	60.00	10.00
b.		Imperf pair	15.00	—
63	A47	10c blue & blk	10.00	1.00
a.		Perf. 11x14	20.00	1.00
b.		Imperf pair	30.00	—
64	A48	20c olive grn & blk	25.00	6.00
a.		Perf. 14	25.00	6.00
		Remainder cancel		2.00
65	A49	25c gray lil & blk	3.00	3.00
		Remainder cancel		1.00
a.		Perf. 11x14	150.00	50.00
66	A50	50c red lil & blue	75.00	25.00
		Remainder cancel		2.00
a.		Perf. 14	175.00	50.00
b.		Imperf pair	100.00	

67	A51	1col brown & blk	25.00	20.00
a.		Perf. 14	25.00	20.00
		Remainder cancel		2.00
b.		Imperf pair		
68	A52	2col claret & grn	160.00	100.00
		Remainder cancel		3.00
a.		Perf. 14	300.00	150.00
b.		Imperf pair	200.00	
		Nos. 59-68 (10)	324.00	158.00

The remainder cancel value applies to both perforations.

The imperforate varieties of the above set are valued without gum. Ungummed stamps were probably placed on the market in London, while gummed stamps appear to have been sent to Costa Rica and accepted for postal use. There is a small premium for gummed stamps.

The 1c, 2c, 5c, 20c, 50c, 1 col and 2 col exist with center inverted. Value, set $62,500. Nos. 59-68 exist with papermaker's watermark.

No. 65b with brown vignette is a proof. Value, pair $40. The actual No. 65b (black vignette) is worth much more.

For overprints see Nos. 77, 79-80, 82-84, O48-O55, O60-O64.

Statue of Juan Santamaria A53

Juan Mora Fernández A54

José M. Cañas A55

Mauro Fernández A56

Braulio Carrillo — A57

Julián Volio — A58

Eusebio Figueroa Oreamuno A59

Jesús Jiménez A60

1910   *Perf. 12*

69	A53	1c brown	.25	.25
70	A54	2c dp green	.30	.25
71	A55	4c scarlet	.35	.35
72	A56	5c orange	1.00	.25
73	A57	10c deep blue	.40	.25
74	A58	20c olive grn	.50	.35
75	A59	25c dp violet	17.00	1.50
76	A60	1col dk brown	.50	.50
		Nos. 69-76 (8)	20.30	3.70

For overprints and surcharge see Nos. 111C-111J, B1, C2, O56-O59.

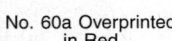

No. 60a Overprinted in Red

1911   *Perf. 14*

77	A44	2c yel grn & blk	3.00	1.10
a.		Inverted overprint	6.00	5.00
b.		Double overprint, both inverted	45.00	

Stamps of 1901-07 Overprinted in Red or Black

78	A30	1c grn & blk (R)	3.00	1.00
a.		Black overprint	32.50	18.00
b.		Inverted overprint		
79	A43	1c red brn & ind (Bk)	1.25	.40
a.		Inverted overprint	4.50	3.50
b.		Double overprint	5.50	5.00
80	A44	2c yel grn & blk (Bk)	1.00	.40
a.		Inverted overprint	3.75	3.50
b.		Dbl. ovpt., one as on No. 77	40.00	27.50
c.		Double overprint, one inverted	15.00	15.00
d.		Pair, one stamp No. 77	25.00	18.00
e.		Perf. 11x14	30.00	1.00

No. 55 Overprinted in Black

81	A40	4c red vio & blk	1.50	.65

Stamps of 1907 Overprinted in Blue, Black or Rose

Perf. 14, 11x14 (#83, 84)

82	A46	5c yel & bl (Bl)	2.00	.25
a.		"Habilitada"	3.25	2.50
b.		"2911"	5.50	3.25
c.		Roman "I" in "1911"	4.00	2.50
d.		Double overprint	5.50	5.00
e.		Inverted overprint	6.00	3.75
f.		Black overprint	250.00	2.00
g.		Triple overprint	6.00	
h.		Vert. pair, imperf. horiz.	100.00	
83	A47	10c blue & blk (Bk)	5.00	1.40
a.		As #83, Roman "I" in "1911"	7.00	5.00
c.		As #83, double overprint	20.00	11.50
d.		Perf. 14	45.00	5.25
84	A47	10c blue & blk (R)	15.00	13.50
a.		Roman "I" in "1911"	100.00	100.00
c.		Perf. 14	100.00	100.00
		Nos. 77-84 (8)	31.75	18.70

Many counterfeits of overprint exist.

Telegraph Stamps Surcharged in Rose, Blue or Black

A61

Correos Dos centimos 2

A62

Correos 5 5 centimos

A63

1911   *Perf. 12*

86	A61	1c on 10c bl (R)	.50	.25
a.		"Coereos"	7.75	6.00
b.		Inverted surcharge		
87	A61	1c on 10c bl (Bk)	210.00	87.50
88	A61	1c on 25c vio (Bk)	.50	.25
a.		"Coereos"	8.75	6.00
b.		Pair, one without surcharge	20.00	
c.		Double surcharge	9.00	
d.		Double surch., one inverted	12.50	
89	A61	1c on 50c red brn (Bl)	.55	.40
a.		Inverted surcharge	5.50	5.00
b.		Double surcharge	4.50	
90	A61	1c on 1col brn (R)	.55	.40
91	A61	1c on 5col red (Bl)	1.00	.55
92	A61	1c on 10col dk brn (R)	1.50	.70

Perf. 14

93	A62	2c on 5c brn org (Bk)	3.50	1.90
a.		Inverted surcharge	9.00	3.75
b.		"Correos" inverted	17.50	
c.		Double surcharge	9.00	

Perf. 14x11

94	A62	2c on 10c bl (R)	100.00	100.00
a.		Perf. 14	350.00	350.00
b.		"Correos" inverted	2,000.	
c.		As "b," perf. 14		

95	A62 2c on 50c cl (Bk)		1.00	.55
a.	Inverted surcharge		4.50	3.25
b.	Double surcharge		12.50	
c.	Perf. 14		45.00	20.00
96	A62 2c on 1col brn (Bk)		1.25	.70
a.	Inverted surcharge		12.50	
b.	Double surcharge		16.00	
c.	Perf. 14		2.00	.80
97	A62 2c on 2col car (Bk)		1.25	.60
a.	Inverted surcharge		8.00	5.00
b.	"Correos" inverted		10.00	5.50
c.	Double surcharge			
d.	Perf. 14		27.50	16.00
98	A62 2c on 5col grn (Bk)		1.00	.70
a.	Inverted surcharge		10.00	7.00
b.	"Correos" inverted		16.00	4.25
c.	Perf. 14		6.00	3.00
99	A62 2c on 10col mar (Bk)		1.50	.70
a.	"Correos" inverted		400.00	
b.	Perf. 14		6.00	3.00

Perf. 12

100	A63 5c on 5c org (Bl)		.40	.25
a.	Double surcharge		27.50	16.00
b.	Inverted surcharge		27.50	9.50
c.	Pair, one without surcharge		16.00	

Counterfeits exist of Nos. 87, 94 and all minor varieties. Genuine used examples of No. 94 are rare and have a cancel only used on registered mail. Genuine "Coereos" errors do not exist on No. 87. Used examples of No. 94 with target cancels are counterfeits. No. 94c is unique. All examples of Nos. 94b and 94c have stains and are valued thus.

Nos. 93-99 exist with papermaker's watermark.

Coffee Plantation — A64

1921, June 17   Litho.   Perf. 11½

103	A64 5c bl & blk		3.00	3.00
a.	Tête bêche pair		15.00	6.50
b.	Imperf., pair		40.00	
c.	As "a," imperf.		150.00	

Centenary of coffee raising in Costa Rica.

Liberty with Torch of Freedom — A65

1921   Typo.   Perf. 11

104	A65 5c violet		1.00	.40
a.	Imperf, pair		10.00	

Cent. of Central American independence. Beware of trimmed singles that look like No. 104a.

For overprint see No. 111.

Juan Mora and Julio Acosta — A66

1921, Sept. 15   Perf. 11½

105	A66 2c orange & blk		2.00	2.00
106	A66 3c green & blk		2.00	2.00
107	A66 6c scarlet & blk		3.75	3.75
108	A66 15c dk blue & blk		8.00	8.00
109	A66 30c orange brn & blk		10.00	10.00
	Nos. 105-109 (5)		25.75	25.75

Centenary of Central American independence. Issue requested by Costa Rican Philatelic Society. Authorized by decree calling for 2,000 of 30c and 5,000 each of other values. Nos. 105-109 imperf were not regularly issued. Inverted centers exist of both perf and imperf. They are rare. Used values are for Independence commemorative cancel.

Each sheet of 20 (4x5) contains 5 tête-bêche pairs. Value, set of 5 pairs $40.

Simón Bolívar — A67

1921   Engr.   Perf. 12

110 A67 15c deep violet   .75 .25

For overprint see No. 111H. For surcharge see No. 148.

No. 104 Overprinted

1922   Perf. 11

111	A65 5c violet	.75	.40
a.	Inverted overprint	10.00	
b.	Double overprint	15.00	

Stamps of 1910-1921 Overprinted in Blue, Red, Black or Gold

1922   Perf. 12

111C	A53 1c brown (Bl)	.30	.25
111D	A54 2c deep green (R)	.40	.25
111E	A55 4c scarlet	.30	.25
111F	A56 5c orange	3.00	.40
111G	A57 10c deep blue (R)	.75	.40
111H	A67 15c deep violet (G)	5.50	2.00
	Nos. 111C-111H (6)	10.25	3.55

Inverted overprints occur on all values. Value, set $20. Counterfeits predominate.

No. 72 Overprinted

1923

111J	A56 5c orange	3.00	.75
k.	"VD." for "UD."	75.00	75.00

Jesús Jiménez — A68

1923, June 18   Litho.   Perf. 11½

112	A68 2c brown	.40	.40
113	A68 4c green	.40	.40
114	A68 5c blue	.60	.40
115	A68 20c carmine	.85	.50
116	A68 1col violet	1.10	1.25
	Nos. 112-116 (5)	3.35	2.95

Pres. Jesús Jiménez (1823-98). Nos. 112-116, imperf, were not regularly issued. Value, set $5.

For overprints see Nos. O65-O69.

National Monument A70

Harvesting Coffee — A71

Banana Growing — A73

General Post Office A74

Columbus Soliciting Aid of Isabella A75

Christopher Columbus A76

Columbus at Cariari A77

Map of Costa Rica — A78

Manuel M. Gutiérrez — A79

1923-26   Engr.   Perf. 12

117	A70 1c violet	.25	.25
118	A71 2c yellow	.50	.25
119	A73 4c deep green	.75	.30
120	A74 5c light blue	1.50	.25
121	A74 5c yellow grn ('26)	.50	.25
122	A75 10c red brown	3.00	.25
123	A75 10c car rose ('26)	.50	.25
124	A76 12c carmine rose	10.00	3.00
125	A77 20c deep blue	10.00	.65
126	A78 40c orange	11.00	3.00
127	A79 1col olive green	2.40	.80
	Nos. 117-127 (11)	40.40	9.25

See Nos. 151-156. For surcharges & overprints see Nos. 136-140, 147, 189, 218, C2.

Rodrigo Arias Maldonado — A80

1924   Perf. 12½

128	A80 2c dark green	.25	.25
a.	Perf. 14	.50	.25

See No. 162.

Map of Guanacaste A81

Mission at Nicoya A82

1924   Litho.   Perf. 12

129	A81 1c carmine rose	.30	.25
130	A81 2c violet	.40	.25
131	A81 5c green	.40	.25
132	A81 10c orange	2.25	.50
133	A82 15c light blue	1.00	.50
134	A82 20c gray black	2.00	1.00
135	A82 25c light brown	3.00	1.50
	Nos. 129-135 (7)	9.35	4.25

Centenary of annexation of Province of Guanacaste to Costa Rica.
Exist imperf. Value, set, $50.

Stamps of 1923 Surcharged

a

b

1925

136	A74(a) 3c on 5c lt blue	.30	.25
137	A75(a) 6c on 10c red brn	.40	.25
138	A78(a) 30c on 40c orange	1.50	.40
139	A79(b) 45c on 1col ol grn	1.50	.50
a.	Double surcharge	250.00	
	Nos. 136-139 (4)	3.95	1.40

No. 124 Surcharged

1926

140 A76 10c on 12c car rose   1.50 .30

College of San Luis, Cartago A83

Chapui Asylum, San José — A84

Normal School, Heredia A85

Ruins of Ujarrás A86

1926 Unwmk. Engr. Perf. 12½
143	A83	3c ultra	.55	.25
144	A84	6c dark brown	.55	.25
145	A85	30c deep orange	3.00	.40
146	A86	45c black violet	5.00	1.60
		Nos. 143-146 (4)	9.10	2.50

For surcharges see Nos. 190-190D, 217.

No. 124 Surcharged in Black

1928, Jan. 7 Perf. 12
147	A76	10c on 12c car rose	4.75	4.75

Issued in honor of Col. Charles A. Lindbergh during his Good Will Tour of Central America.
The surcharge was privately reprinted using an original die. Reprints can be distinguished by distinct dots under the "10s." All errors and inverted surcharges are reprints.

No. 110 Surcharged

1928
148	A67	5(c) on 15c dp violet	.25	.25
a.		Inverted surcharge		35.00

Type I — A88

Type II

Type III

Type IV

Type V

Surcharge Typo. (I-V) & Litho. (V)
1929 Perf. 12½
149	A88	5c on 2col car (I)	.50	.25
a.-d.		Types II-V	.60	.25
e.		Type V (litho.)	3.00	3.00

Telegraph Stamp Surcharged for Postage as in 1929, Surcharge Lithographed
1929
150	A88	13c on 40c deep grn	.35	.25
a.		Inverted surcharge	1.00	1.00

Excellent counterfeits exist of No. 150a.

Types of 1923-26 Issues Dated "1929"
Imprint of Waterlow & Sons
1930 Size: 26x21½mm Perf. 12½
151	A70	1c dark violet	.70	.25
155	A74	5c green	.70	.25
156	A75	10c carmine rose	.70	.25
		Nos. 151-156 (3)	2.10	.75

Juan Rafael Mora — A89

1931, Jan. 29
157	A89	13c carmine rose	.60	.25

For surcharge see No. 209.

Seal of Costa Rica Philatelic Society ("Octubre 12 de 1932") — A90

1932, Oct. 12 Perf. 12
158	A90	3c orange	.25	.25
159	A90	5c dark green	.40	.25
160	A90	10c carmine rose	.50	.25
161	A90	20c dark blue	.85	.40
		Nos. 158-161 (4)	2.00	1.15

Phil. Exhib., Oct. 12, 1932. See Nos. 179-183.

Maldonado Type of 1924
1934, Aug. 11 Perf. 12½
162	A80	3c dark green	.25	.25

Red Cross Nurse — A91

1935, May 31 Perf. 12
163	A91	10c rose carmine	7.50	.25

50th anniv. of the founding of the Costa Rican Red Cross Society.

Air View of Cartago A92

Miraculous Statuette and View of Cathedral A93

Vision of 1635 — A94

1935, Aug. 1 Perf. 12½
164	A92	5c green	.25	.25
165	A93	10c carmine	.25	.25
166	A92	30c orange	.25	.25
167	A94	45c dark violet	1.00	.55
168	A93	50c blue black	1.00	1.00
		Nos. 164-168 (5)	2.75	2.30

Tercentenary of the Patron Saint, Our Lady of the Angels, of Costa Rica.

Map of Cocos Island A95

1936, Jan. 29 Perf. 14, 11½ (25c)
169	A95	4c ocher	.50	.25
170	A95	8c dark violet	.65	.25
171	A95	25c orange	.80	.25
172	A95	35c brown vio	.95	.25
173	A95	40c brown	1.25	.40
174	A95	50c yellow	1.50	.60
175	A95	2col yellow grn	11.00	10.00
176	A95	5col green	30.00	25.00
		Nos. 169-176 (8)	46.65	37.00

Exist imperf. Value, set, $50.
For surcharges see Nos. 196-200, C55-C56.

Map of Cocos Island and Ships of Columbus A96

1936, Dec. 5 Perf. 12
177	A96	5c green	.40	.25
178	A96	10c carmine rose	.55	.25

For overprints see Nos. 247, O80-O81.

Seal of Costa Rica Philatelic Society ("Diciembre 1937") — A97

1937, Dec. 15
179	A97	2c dark brown	.45	.25
180	A97	3c black	.45	.25
181	A97	5c green	.45	.25
182	A97	10c orange red	.45	.25
		Nos. 179-182 (4)	1.80	1.00

Souvenir Sheet
Imperf
183		Sheet of 4	6.50	4.00
a.	A97	2c dark brown	.25	.25
b.	A97	3c black	.25	.25
c.	A97	5c green	.25	.25
d.	A97	10c orange red	.25	.25

Phil. Exhib., Dec. 1937.

Purple Guaria Orchid, National Flower — A98

Tuna — A99

Native with Donkey Carrying Bananas A101

3c, Cacao pod. 10c, Coffee harvesting.

1937-38 Wmk. 229 Perf. 12½
184	A98	1c green & vio ('38)	.55	.25
185	A98	3c chocolate ('38)	.55	.25

Unwmk. Perf. 12
186	A99	2c olive gray	.40	.25
187	A101	5c dark green	.55	.25
188	A101	10c carmine rose	.90	.25
		Nos. 184-188 (5)	2.95	1.25

National Exposition.

No. 125 Overprinted in Black

1938, Sept. 23 Unwmk. Perf. 12
189	A77	20c deep blue	1.50	.30

No. 146 Surcharged in Red

a

b

c

d

e

1940 Perf. 12½
190	A86(a)	15c on 45c blk vio	.60	.30
190A	A86(b)	15c on 45c blk vio	.60	.30
190B	A86(c)	15c on 45c blk vio	.60	.30
190C	A86(d)	15c on 45c blk vio	.60	.30
190D	A86(e)	15c on 45c blk vio	.60	.30
		Nos. 190-190D (5)	3.00	1.50

No. 190D exists with inverted surcharge. Value, $5.

Allegory A103

Black Overprint
1940, Dec. 2 Engr. Perf. 12
191	A103	5c green	.35	.25
192	A103	10c rose carmine	.75	.25
193	A103	20c deep blue	2.00	1.00
194	A103	40c brown	6.00	2.75
195	A103	55c orange yellow	15.00	10.00
		Nos. 191-195 (5)	24.10	14.25

Pan-American Health Day. See Nos. C46-C54.
Exist without overprint.

Stamps of 1936 Srchd. in Black

1941 *Perf. 14, 11½*
196 A95 15c on 25c orange .50 .50
197 A95 15c on 35c brn vio .50 .50
198 A95 15c on 40c brown .50 .50
199 A95 15c on 2col yel grn .50 .50
200 A95 15c on 5col green 1.00 1.00
Nos. 196-200 (5) 3.00 3.00

Nos. 196-200 exist with surcharge inverted. Value, set of 5, $20.

National Stadium A104

Engr.; Flags Typo. in Natl. Colors
1941, May 8 *Perf. 12½*
201 A104 5c green .70 .25
 a. Flags omitted 250.00
202 A104 10c orange .55 .30
203 A104 15c car rose .80 .40
204 A104 25c dk blue .85 .55
205 A104 40c chestnut 3.25 1.40
206 A104 50c purple 4.25 2.00
207 A104 75c red orange 6.75 5.75
208 A104 1col dk carmine 13.00 10.50
Nos. 201-208 (8) 30.15 21.15

Caribbean and Central American Soccer Championship. See Nos. C57-C66, C121-C123.

No. 157 Surcharged in Black

1941, July 26 *Perf. 12*
209 A89 5c on 13c car rose .25 .25

Cleto González Viquez — A105

Design: 5c, José Rodriguez.

1941-45 **Engr.** *Perf. 12½*
210 A105 3c dp orange .25 .25
210A A105 3c dp plum ('43) .25 .25
210B A105 3c carmine ('45) .25 .25
211 A105 5c dp violet .25 .25
211A A105 5c brown blk ('43) .25 .25
Nos. 210-211A (5) 1.25 1.25

See No. 256.

Old University of Costa Rica A106

New National University A107

1941, Aug. 26 *Perf. 12*
212 A106 5c green .40 .25
213 A107 10c yellow org .40 .25
214 A106 15c lilac rose .75 .25
215 A107 25c dull blue 1.00 .35
216 A106 50c fawn 7.50 2.25
Nos. 212-216 (5) 10.05 3.35

National University, founded in 1940. See Nos. C74-C80.

Nos. 144, 189 Srchd. in Black or Red

1942, April *Perf. 12½, 12*
217 A84 5c on 6c dk brn .35 .25
218 A77 15c on 20c dp bl (R) 1.50 .25

Nos. 217-218 exist with inverted surcharge. Value, each $10.

Torch of Freedom, "Victory" and Flags of American Nations — A108

1942, Sept. 25 *Perf. 12*
219 A108 5c rose .30 .25
220 A108 5c yellow grn .30 .25
221 A108 5c purple .30 .25
222 A108 5c dp blue .30 .25
223 A108 5c red orange .30 .25
Nos. 219-223 (5) 1.50 1.25

For overprints see Nos. 238-241.

Juan Mora Fernández — A109

Designs: 2c, Bruno Carranza. 3c, Tomas Guardia. 5c, Manuel Aguilar. 15c, Francisco Morazan. 25c, Jose M. Alfaro. 50c, Francisco M. Oreamuno. 1col, Jose M. Castro. 2col, Juan Rafael Mora.

1943-47 **Engr.**
224 A109 1c red lilac .25 .25
225 A109 2c black .25 .25
226 A109 3c deep blue .25 .25
227 A109 5c brt blue grn .25 .25
 a. 5c bright green ('47) .25 .25
228 A109 15c scarlet .25 .25
229 A109 25c brt ultra 1.00 .25
230 A109 50c dp violet 3.00 .45
231 A109 1col black brown 4.00 2.00
232 A109 2col deep orange 5.00 3.00
Nos. 224-232 (9) 14.25 6.95

See Nos. 344-368, C81-C91A, C124-C127, C154-C158, C179-C181, C768-C772, C790-C794, C854-C858. For surcharges see Nos. C154-C158, C182, C184-C185.

View of San Ramón A118

1944, Jan. 19
233 A118 5c dark green .25 .25
234 A118 10c orange .25 .25
235 A118 15c rose pink .30 .25
236 A118 40c gray black 1.25 .80
237 A118 50c deep blue 2.40 1.60
Nos. 233-237 (5) 4.45 3.15

100th anniv. of the founding of the City of San Ramón. See Nos. C94-C102.

Catalogue values for unused stamps in this section, from this point to the end of the section, are for Never Hinged items.

Nos. 220-223 Overprinted in Red or Black

1944, Sept. 18
238 A108 5c yel green .30 .25
239 A108 5c purple (R) .30 .25
240 A108 5c dp blue (R) .30 .25
241 A108 5c red orange .30 .25
Nos. 238-241 (4) 1.20 1.00

Amicable settlement of a boundary dispute with Panama. This overprint also exists on No. 219.

Mauro Fernández (1844-1905), Statesman — A119

Unwmk.
1945, July 21 **Engr.** *Perf. 14*
242 A119 20c deep green .30 .25

For surcharge see No. 246.

Coffee Harvesting — A120

1945, Oct. 9 *Perf. 12*
243 A120 5c dk green & blk .30 .25
244 A120 10c orange & blk .30 .25
245 A120 20c car rose & blk .50 .25
Nos. 243-245 (3) 1.10 .75

No. 242 Surcharged in Red Brown
1946 **Unwmk.** *Perf. 14*
246 A119 15c on 20c dp green .30 .25

Exists with inverted surcharge. Value, $6.

No. O80 Overprinted in Red

1947, Mar. 19 *Perf. 12*
247 A96 5c green .30 .25

Exist with inverted overprint. Value, $10.

Cervantes — A121

Wmk. 215
1947, Nov. 10 **Engr.** *Perf. 14*
249 A121 30c deep blue .45 .25
250 A121 55c deep carmine .80 .40

Miguel de Cervantes Saavedra, novelist, playwright & poet, 400th birth anniv.

A122

1947, Aug. 26 **Unwmk.** *Perf. 12*
251 A122 5c brt green .25 .25
252 A122 10c car rose .25 .25
253 A122 15c ultra .25 .25
254 A122 25c orange red .35 .25
255 A122 50c lilac .55 .30
Nos. 251-255,C160-C167 (13) 7.35 6.30

Franklin D. Roosevelt. For surcharges see Nos. C224-C226.

Small Portrait Type of 1941

Design: 3c, Bishop Bernardo A. Thiel.

1948 *Perf. 12½*
256 A105 3c deep ultra .25 .25

Old University of Costa Rica A123

Black Surcharge
1953, June 25 **Litho.** *Perf. 12*
257 A123 5c on 10c green .35 .25

Revenue Stamp Surcharged in Red or Blue — A124

1955-56 **Unwmk.** **Engr.** *Perf. 12*
258 A124 5c on 2c emerald .25 .25
259 A124 15c on 2c emer (Bl) .25 .25
260 A124 15c on 2c emer ('56) .25 .25
Nos. 258-260,C341-C344 (7) 2.35 2.10

For surcharges see Nos. C341-C344, C431-C433.

Justo A. Facio — A125

1960, Apr. 20 **Photo.** *Perf. 13½*
261 A125 10c brown red .40 .25

Centenary of the birth (in 1859) of Prof. Justo A. Facio. Exists imperf. Value, $35.

Nos. RA12-RA15 Surcharged in Red

1963, Mar.
262 PT3 10c on 5c dk car .40 .25
263 PT3 10c on 5c sepia .40 .25
264 PT3 10c on 5c dull grn .40 .25
265 PT3 10c on 5c blue .40 .25
Nos. 262-265 (4) 1.60 1.00

Anglo-Costa Rican Bank — A126

1963 **Unwmk.** *Perf. 13½*
266 A126 10c gray .35 .25

Centenary of the Anglo-Costa Rican Bank.

Arms of San
José — A127

Coats of Arms: 35c, Cartago. 50c, Heredia.
55c, Alajuela. 65c, Guanacaste. 1col,
Puntarenas. 2col, Limon.

1969, Sept. 14   Litho.   Perf. 14x13½
267 A127 15c multicolored   .30 .25
268 A127 35c multicolored   .30 .25
269 A127 50c gray & multi   .30 .25
270 A127 55c buff & multi   .30 .25
271 A127 65c multicolored   .75 .25
272 A127 1col pink & multi   2.75 .40
273 A127 2col multicolored   3.75 .60
   Nos. 267-273 (7)   8.45 2.25

Alberto M.
Brenes
Mora — A128

1976, Mar. 1   Litho.   Perf. 10½
274 A128 1col violet blue   .65 .25
   Nos. 274,C653-C657 (6)   9.15 4.40

Prof. Alberto Manuel Brenes Mora, botanist,
birth centenary.

Map of Costa
Rica, Reader
with
Book — A129

1978, July 17   Litho.   Perf. 13½
275 A129 50c multicolored   .40 .25

National five-year literacy plan.

World
Communications
Year — A130

1983, May 17   Litho.   Perf. 13x13½
276 A130 10c multicolored   .40 .25
277 A130 50c multicolored   .35 .25
278 A130 10col multicolored   1.40 .30
   Nos. 276-278 (3)   2.15 .80

A131

1983, May 30   Litho.   Perf. 10½
279 A131 20col black   2.40 .55

1st World Cong. of Human Rights, 1982.

UPU Membership Centenary — A132

3col, #17, UPU monument. 10col, #20, San
Jose post office.

1983, June 30   Litho.   Perf. 16
280 A132 3col multi   1.25 .25
281 A132 10col multi   2.40 .50

French Alliance
Centenary — A133

Scene in San Jose, by Christina Fournier.

1983, July 21   Litho.   Perf. 11
282 A133 12col multicolored   2.00 .55

Christmas 1983 — A134

Nativity tableau in continuous design.

1983, Dec. 5   Litho.   Perf. 13½
283   1.50col multi   .25 .25
284   1.50col multi   .25 .25
285   1.50col multi   .25 .25
  a. A134 Strip of 3, #283-285 1.60 1.60

Costa Rican Gardens Association.

Fishery Development
Administration
A135

1983, Dec. 19   Litho.   Perf. 13½
286 A135 8.50col multi   .80 .30

Local
Birds — A136

10c, Quetzal. 50c, Cyanerpes cyaneus.
1col, Turdus grayi. 1.50col, Momotus momota.
3col, Colibri thalassinus. 10col, Notioche-
lindon cyanoleuca.

1984, Jan. 9   Litho.   Perf. 13½
287 A136   10c multicolored   .55 .25
288 A136   50c multicolored   .65 .25
289 A136   1col multicolored   .65 .25
290 A136 1.50col multicolored .65 .25
291 A136   3col multicolored 1.50 .25
292 A136 10col multicolored 4.75 .30
   Nos. 287-292 (6)   8.75 1.55

Dated 1983. 10c, 1.50col, 3col vert.

José Joaquin Mora, Hero of 1856
Independence Campaign — A137

Paintings, Juan Santamaria Museum, San
José: 1.50col, Pancha Carrasco. 3 col, Death
of Juan Santamaria, horiz. 8.50col, Juan Rafael Mora Porras.

1984, Apr. 10   Litho.   Perf. 10½
293 A137   50c multi   .25 .25
294 A137 1.50col multi   .25 .25
295 A137   3col multi   .25 .25
296 A137 8.50col multi   .80 .55
   Nos. 293-296 (4)   1.55 1.30

For surcharge see No. 440.

Jesus Bonilla
Chavarria,
Composer
A138

Musicians and Composers: 5col, Benjamin
Gutierrez (b. 1937). 12col, Pilar Jimenez
(1835-1922). 13col, Jose Daniel Zuniga
Zeledon (1889-1981).

1984, May 30   Litho.   Perf. 13½
297 A138 3.50col black & lil   .30 .25
298 A138   5col black & pink   .40 .25
299 A138 12col black & grn   1.00 .80
300 A138 13col black & yel   1.25 .90
   Nos. 297-300 (4)   2.95 2.20

Figurines, Jade
Museum — A139

1984, June 27   Litho.   Perf. 13½
301 A139 4col Man (pendant)   .80 .25
302 A139 7col Seated man   1.60 .40
303 A139 10col Dish, horiz.   2.10 .50
   Nos. 301-303 (3)   4.50 1.15

1984 Summer
Olympics
A140

1984, July 27
304 A140 1col Basketball   .25 .25
305 A140 8col Swimming   .65 .25
306 A140 11col Bicycling   .90 .40
307 A140 14col Running   1.25 .65
308 A140 20col Boxing   1.60 1.25
309 A140 30col Soccer   2.50 1.40
   Nos. 304-309 (6)   7.15 4.20

Public Street
Lighting
Centenary
A141

6col, Street scene by Luis Chacon.

1984, Aug. 9   Litho.   Perf. 10½
310 A141 6col multi   .55 .40

10th Natl. Stamp Exhibition, Sept. 10-
16 — A142

No. 311, Natl. monument. No. 312, Juan
Mora Fernandez monument.

1984, Sept. 10   Litho.   Perf. 10½
311 A142 10col multicolored   .90 .55
312 A142 10col multicolored   .90 .55
  a. Min. sheet, 2 each #311-312 15.00 10.00

Natl.
Arms — A143

1984, Oct. 29   Engr.   Perf. 14x13½
313 A143 100col dk green   8.00 3.75
314 A143 100col yel org   8.00 3.75

Detail from Sistine Virgin by
Raphael — A144

1984, Dec. 7   Litho.   Perf. 10½
315   3col multicolored   .25 .25
316   3col multicolored   .25 .25
  a. A144 Pair, #315-316   2.00 2.00

20th Intl. Bicycle
Race, Costa
Rica — A146

1984, Dec. 19   Litho.   Perf. 13½
317 A146 6col multi   .65 .30

Intl.
Youth
Year
A147

11col, IYY emblem, #C476.

1985, Jan. 31   **Perf. 10½**
322 A147 11col multi   1.60 .55
Scouting Movement, 75th anniv.

Labor Monument,
San Jose — A148

Natl. values: 11col, Freedom of speech-wooden hand printing press. 13col, Neutrality-dove, natl. flag, outline map.

1985, Feb. 28
323 A148 6col shown   .80 .30
324 A148 11col bl, blk & yel   1.25 .50
325 A148 13col multi   1.40 .55
    Size: 68x38mm
326 A148 30col Nos. 323-325   4.00 1.10
    Nos. 323-326 (4)   7.45 2.45

Natl. Red Cross Cent., UN 40th Anniv. A149

1985, May 3   **Perf. 10½**
327 A149 3col No. 163, horiz.   2.00 .25
328 A149 5col No. C120   3.00 .25

Club Emblem A150

1st Club Pres., Ricardo Saprissa Ayma A151

Design: No. 330, Hands holding soccer ball.

1985, July 16   **Perf. 10½**
329 A150 3col multi   .50 .25
330 A150 3col multi   .50 .25
a.   Pair, #329-330   1.50 1.00
331 A151 6col multi   1.00 .30
   Nos. 329-331 (3)   2.00 .80
Saprissa Soccer Club, 50th Anniv.

Orchids — A152

No. 332, Brassia arcuigera. No. 333, Encyclia peraltensis. No. 334, Maxillaria especie. No. 335, Oncidium turialbae. No. 336, Trichopilia marginata. No. 337, Stanhopea ecornuta.

1985, Dec. 3
332 A152 6col multicolored   4.00 .80
333 A152 6col multicolored   4.00 .80
334 A152 6col multicolored   4.00 .80
a.   Strip of 3, #332-334   16.50 5.00
335 A152 13col multicolored   3.50 1.40
336 A152 13col multicolored   3.50 1.40

337 A152 13col multicolored   3.50 1.40
a.   Strip of 3, #335-337   14.50 5.50
   Nos. 332-337 (6)   22.50 6.60

11th Natl. Philatelic Exposition A153

1985, Dec. 3   **Litho.**   **Perf. 13½**
338 A153 20col No. C41   1.25 .55

Christmas 1985 — A153a

1985, Dec. 12   **Litho.**   **Perf. 10½**
338A A153a 3col multi   .40 .25

Compulsory Education, Cent. A154

Designs: 3col, Primary school, horiz. 30col, Mauro Fernandez Acuna, founder.

1986, Feb. 28   **Perf. 13½**
339 A154 3col pale yel & brn   .25 .25
340 A154 30col pale pink & brn   1.60 .80

Agriculture Students — A155

No. 341, Students on farm. No. 342, IDB emblem. No. 343, Capo Bianco fisherman.

1986, Mar. 21   **Perf. 10½**
341 10col multi   .50 .25
342 10col multi   .50 .25
343 10col multi   .50 .25
a.   A155 Strip of 3, #341-343   3.00 3.00
   Nos. 341-343 (3)   1.50 .75
Inter-American Development Bank Annual Governors' Assembly, San Jose.

Presidents Type of 1943
Designs: Nos. 344, 349, 354, 359, 364, Francisco J. Orlich Bolmarcich, 1962-66.
Nos. 345, 350, 355, 360, 365, Jose Joaquin Trejos Fernandez, 1966-70.
Nos. 346, 351, 356, 361, 366, Daniel Oduber Quiros, 1974-78.
Nos. 347, 352, 357, 362, 367, Rodrigo Carazo Odio, 1978-82.
Nos. 348, 353, 358, 363, 368, Luis Alberto Monge Alvarez, 1982-86.

1986, May 12   **Litho.**   **Perf. 10½**
344 A109 3col turq blue   .40 .25
345 A109 3col turq blue   .40 .25
346 A109 3col turq blue   .40 .25
347 A109 3col turq blue   .40 .25
348 A109 3col turq blue   .40 .25
a.   Strip of 5, #344-348   2.25 1.90
349 A109 6col yel brn   .65 .25
350 A109 6col yel brn   .65 .25
351 A109 6col yel brn   .65 .25
352 A109 6col yel brn   .65 .25
353 A109 6col yel brn   .65 .25
a.   Strip of 5, #349-353   5.00 4.50
354 A109 10col brn org   .95 .30
355 A109 10col brn org   .95 .30
356 A109 10col brn org   .95 .30
357 A109 10col brn org   .95 .30
358 A109 10col brn org   .95 .30
a.   Strip of 5, #354-358   8.25 8.00
359 A109 11col slate gray   1.25 .40
360 A109 11col slate gray   1.25 .40
361 A109 11col slate gray   1.25 .40
362 A109 11col slate gray   1.25 .40
363 A109 11col slate gray   1.25 .40
a.   Strip of 5, #359-363   10.00 9.00

364 A109 13col olive   1.60 .45
365 A109 13col olive   1.60 .45
366 A109 13col olive   1.60 .45
367 A109 13col olive   1.60 .45
368 A109 13col olive   1.60 .45
a.   Strip of 5, #364-368   13.50 10.50
   Nos. 344-368 (25)   24.25 8.25
   Nos. 348a-368a (5)   39.00

1986 World Cup Soccer Championships, Mexico — A156

No. 369, Players. No. 370, Character trademark, vert. No. 373, Players, diff.

1986, May 30   **Litho.**   **Perf. 13½**
369 A156 1col multi   .30 .25
370 A156 1col multi   .30 .25
371 A156 4col as No. 370   1.40 .25
372 A156 6col as No. 369   2.00 .25
373 A156 11col multi   4.00 .40
   Nos. 369-373 (5)   8.00 1.40

A second printing of No. 370 differs in paper and shade from the first printing, but the most obvious difference is in the absence of the initials "LIL" by the left foot of the soccer player. Unused stamps are rare. Value for used, $3.

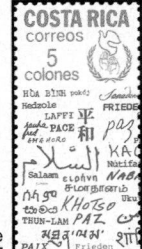

Intl. Peace Year — A157

Peace in many languages: a, "Hoa binh," etc. b, "Vrede," etc. c, "Pace," etc.

1986, July 31   **Litho.**   **Perf. 10½**
374   Strip of 3   4.50 1.25
a.-c. A157 5col, any single   .55 .25

A158

Gold Museum, Central Bank of Costa Rica — A158a

Designs: Various undescribed works of Pre-Columbian art.

1986, Sept. 19   **Perf. 10½**
375 A158 Strip of 5   10.00 2.50
a.-e. 6col any single   .80 .25
376 A158a Strip of 5   6.00 2.00
a.-e. 13col any single   .40 .40

Exist perf 13½, value $17.50 for the two strips of 5 unused

A159

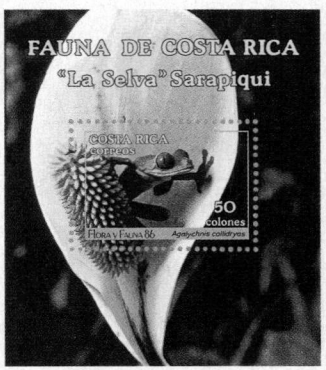

Fauna and Flora — A160

2col, Centurio senex. 3col, Glossophaga soricina. 4col, Ectophylla alba. 5col, Ectophylla alba, diff. 6col, Agalychnis callidryas. 10col, Dendrobates pumilio. 11col, Hyla ebraccata. 20col, Phyllobates lugubris. 50col, Agalychnis callidryas, diff.

1986, Dec. 16   **Litho.**   **Perf. 13x13½**
377 A159 2col multicolored   .25 .25
378 A159 3col multicolored   .45 .25
379 A159 4col multicolored   .60 .25
380 A159 5col multicolored   .85 .25
381 A159 6col multicolored   1.00 .25
382 A159 10col multicolored   1.40 .25
383 A159 11col multicolored   1.60 .40
384 A159 20col multicolored   2.40 .65
   Nos. 377-384 (8)   8.55 2.55

   Souvenir Sheet
    Perf. 12½x12
385 A160 50col multicolored   60.00 40.00

Natl. Science and Technology Day — A161

Mural (detail), by Francisco Amighetti, Clorito Picado Social Security Clinic.

1987, July 31   **Litho.**   **Perf. 10½**
386 A161 8col multi   4.00 .25

Natl. Museum, Cent. A162

Artifacts: No. 387a, Dowel-shaped figure of a man. No. 387b, Ape-like carved stone figurine. No. 387c, Polished stone ritual figure. No. 387d, Carved granite capital. No. 387e, Two-legged pot. No. 388a, Bowl. No. 388b, Sculpture. No. 388c, Water jar.

1987, Aug. 7
387   Strip of 5   5.00 2.40
a.-e. A162 8col any single, vert.   .40 .25
388   Strip of 3   5.00 2.75
a.-c. A162 15col any single   .65 .25
   Nos. 387-388 (2)   10.00 5.15

Horse-drawn Wagon — A163

No. 390, Street in old San Jose. No. 391, Provincial coat of arms.

1987, Oct. 26

389	A163	20col shown	.95	.50
390	A163	20col multicolored	.95	.50
a.		Pair, #389-390	2.00	2.00
391	A163	20col multicolored	.95	.50
		Nos. 389-391 (3)	2.85	1.50

City of San Jose, 250th anniv. Rotary Club, 60th anniv.

Columbus Day A164

1987, Oct. 26   **Perf. 10½**

392	A164	30col Map, 16th cent.	2.25	.65

Day of the Race; 495th anniv. of Columbus's departure from Palos, Spain, on first journey to the New World.

Discovery of America, 500th Anniv. (in 1992) — A165

Maps of Honduras, Nicaragua, Costa Rica and Panama, believed to be Asia by Columbus: No. 393, Costa Rica, 16th cent. No. 394, Map of "Asia" by Bartholomeu Columbus (1461-1514).

1987, Nov. 20   **Litho.**   **Perf. 13½**

393	A165	4col yel & dk red brn	.25	.25
394	A165	4col yel & dk red brn	.25	.25
a.		Pair, #393-394	2.00	2.00

Pres. Oscar Arias, 1987 Nobel Peace Prize Winner — A166

1987, Dec. 2   **Perf. 10½**

395	A166	10col multi	2.50	.30

Two Houses, a Watercolor by Fausto Pacheco (1899-1966) A167

1987, Dec. 22   **Litho.**   **Perf. 10½**

396	A167	1col multi	.55	.30

Intl. Year of Shelter for the Homeless.

17th General Conference for the Preservation of Natural Resources A168

No. 397, Green turtle. No. 398, Emblem, golden toad. No. 399, Blue butterfly.

1988, Feb. 1   **Litho.**   **Perf. 13½**

397	A168	5col multi	.80	.25
398	A168	5col multi	.80	.25
399	A168	5col multi	.80	.25
a.		A168 Strip of 3, #397-399	2.50	2.50

Intl. Red Cross and Red Crescent Organizations, 125th Annivs. — A169

1988, Apr. 18   **Litho.**   **Perf. 10½**

400	A169	30col lt blue & dark red	1.40	.65

North and South Campaign A170

18col, Adult education. 20col, Cultural radio programs.

1988, June 6   **Photo.**   **Perf. 11½**
Granite Paper

401	A170	18col multi	2.40	.25
402	A170	20col multi	2.40	.25

Cultural cooperation with Liechtenstein. See Liechtenstein Nos. 886-887. For overprint see No. C921.

A171

1988, June 27   **Litho.**   **Perf. 10½**

403	A171	3col dk blue, dark red & yel	.40	.25

Anglo-Costa Rican Bank, 125th anniv.

A172

No. 404, Character trademark. No. 405, Games emblem.

1988, Sept. 16   **Litho.**   **Perf. 13½**

404	A172	25col multicolored	.95	.50
405	A172	25col multicolored	.95	.50
a.		Pair, #404-405	5.00	5.00

1988 Summer Olympics, Seoul.

Girls' High School, Cent. A173

10col, Student, courtyard.

1988, Oct. 17   **Litho.**   **Perf. 10½**

406	A173	10col cream, brown	.50	.25

A174

1988, Nov. 18

407	A174	10col gray, greenish bl & red brn	.40	.25

Educator Omar Dengo (1888-1928) and the Teachers' College, Heredia.

A175

Indian glass-bead and lion-tooth necklace.

1988, Nov. 28   **Perf. 13½**

408	A175	4col multi	.25	.25

Discovery of America, 500th anniv. (in 1992).

A176

1988, Dec. 26   **Litho.**   **Perf. 10½**

409	A176	2col Observation tower	.65	.30

Natl. Meteorological Institute, cent. For surcharge see No. 439.

A177

Indigenous flora: 5col, Eschweilera costarricensis. 10col, Heliconia wagneriana. 15col, Heliconia lophocarpa. 20col, Aechmea magdalenae. 25col, Psammisia ramiflora. 30col, Passiflora vitifolia.

1989, Feb. 28

410	A177	5col multicolored	.50	.25
411	A177	10col multicolored	.95	.25
412	A177	15col multicolored	1.25	.25
413	A177	20col multicolored	1.50	.25
414	A177	25col multicolored	1.75	.25
415	A177	30col multicolored	2.25	.25
		Nos. 410-415 (6)	8.20	1.50

Nation at Arms — A178

1989, July 1   **Litho.**   **Perf. 10½**

416	A178	30col multi	1.40	.50

French Revolution, bicent.

Sugar Mill — A179

1989, Aug. 28   **Litho.**   **Perf. 13½**

417	A179	10col multi	.65	.25

Grecia County, 151st anniv. For overprints see Nos. RA106-RA109.

America Issue — A180

UPAE emblem and pre-Columbian stone carvings: 50col, Three-footed bench for grinding corn. 100col, Sphere.

Litho. & Engr.
Perf. 12½x12

1989, Oct. 12   **Wmk. 334**

418	A180	50col multi	2.50	1.10
419	A180	100col multi	5.50	1.75

For overprint see No. C916.

Orchid — A181

Perf. 10½

1989, Oct. 23   **Litho.**   **Unwmk.**

420	A181	10col multi	2.00	.25

"100 Years of Democracy" summit of Presidents.

Map, H.F. Pittier, Emblem — A182

Perf. 13½

1989, Nov. 27   **Litho.**   **Unwmk.**

421	A182	18col multi	.80	.25

Natl. Geographic Institute, cent. For surcharge see No. 452.

America Issue — A183

Pre-Columbian gold frog figurine and facing portraits of Ferdinand V and Isabella I on gold coin struck by Spain from 1476 to 1516.

1989, Dec. 4   **Perf. 10½**

422	A183	4col multicolored	1.00	.25

Discovery of America, 500th anniv. (in 1992).

Natl. Theater, Cent. A184

Perf. 10½

1990, Feb. 27 **Litho.** **Unwmk.**
423 A184 5col Coffee Allegory .65 .30

World Cup Soccer Championships, Italy — A185

1990, June 1 **Litho.** **Perf. 10½**
424 A185 5col multicolored .25 .25

Univ. of Costa Rica, 50th Anniv. A187

1990, Aug. 24 **Litho.** **Perf. 10½**
426 A187 18col multicolored .75 .25

Education, Democracy, Peace — A188

Litho. & Engr.
1990, Oct. 31 **Perf. 12½**
427 A188 100col shown 2.25 1.10
428 A188 200col Flag as map 4.50 1.75
429 A188 500col National arms 12.00 4.50
Nos. 427-429 (3) 18.75 7.35

"Invisible" security printing is sometimes visible.

For overprints see Nos. 448, C920. For surcharges see Nos. 546-548, 553.

Hospitals — A190

No. 431, St. Vincent de Paul Hospital, Heredia. No. 432, Natl. Psychiatric hospital.

1990, Dec. 18 **Engr.** **Perf. 13x12½**
431 A190 50col multicolored 1.90 .60
432 A190 100col multicolored 3.25 .80

America Issue — A191

No. 433, Ara macao. No. 434, Ara ambigua. No. 435, Cassia grandis. No. 436, Tabebuia ochracea.

1990, Dec. 21 **Litho.** **Perf. 10½**
433 A191 18col multi 1.00 .40
434 A191 18col multi 1.00 .40
a. Pair, #433-434 8.00 8.00

435 A191 24col multi 1.90 1.90
436 A191 24col multi 1.90 1.90
a. Pair, #435-436 8.00 8.00
Nos. 433-436 (4) 5.80 4.60

Costa Rica-Panama Border Treaty, 50th Anniv. — A192

Designs: a, Flags, national arms. b, Presidents. c, Map.

1991, May 24 **Litho.** **Perf. 10½**
437 Strip of 3 4.00 2.50
a.-c. A192 10col Any single 1.00 .60

Discovery of America, 500th Anniv. (in 1992) — A193

1991, Oct. 11 **Litho.** **Perf. 13½**
438 A193 4col multicolored .70 .25

No. 409 Surcharged

No. 296 Surcharged

1991, Oct. 21 **Litho.** **Perf. 10½**
439 A176 1col on 2col #409 .30 .25
440 A137 3col on 8.50col #296 .30 .25

Former Presidents, Supreme Court of Justice — A194

Designs: a, Benito Serrano Jimenez. b, Luis Davila Solera. c, Fernando Baudrit Solera. d, Alejandro Alvarado Garcia.

Perf. 14½x13½
1992, Feb. 28 **Litho.**
441 A194 5col Strip of 4, #a.-d. 3.50 2.00
A sheet exists containing an unissued 5th stamp. Value, sheet $500.

America Issue — A191

No. 433, Ara macao. No. 434, Ara ambigua. No. 435, Cassia grandis. No. 436, Tabebuia ochracea.

DINADECO, Natl. Directorate of Community Development, 25th Anniv. A195

1992, Apr. 28 **Litho.** **Perf. 10½**
442 A195 15col multicolored 3.00 .60
Compare with No. C505.

A196

1992, May 26 **Litho.** **Perf. 13½**
443 A196 15col lake & black 1.25 .35
Dr. Solon Nunez Frutos, public health pioneer.

Solar Eclipse — A197

a, Total eclipse. b, Post Office Bldg. during eclipse. c, Partial eclipse.

1992, July 17 **Litho.** **Perf. 13**
444 A197 45col Strip of 3, #a.-c. 10.00 6.00

A198

1992, Aug. 14 **Litho.** **Perf. 13½**
445 A198 35col multicolored 2.00 .60
Interamerican Institute for Agricultural Cooperation, 50th anniv.

A199

1992, Nov. 5 **Litho.** **Perf. 10½**
446 A199 2col Waterfall .70 .30
447 A199 15col Coastline 1.00 .40
Cocos Island, 450th anniv. of discovery.

No. 427 Overprinted

Litho. & Engr.
1992, Nov. 27 **Perf. 12½**
448 A188 100col black & blue 5.00 2.50

America Issue A200

15col, Anolis townsendi. 35col, Pinaroloxias inornata.

1992, Dec. 15 **Litho.** **Perf. 10½**
449 A200 15col multi 3.50 .30
450 A200 35col multi 5.50 .50

Natl. Theater A201

Detail from painting "Allegory of Fine Arts," by Roberto Fontana.

1993, Jan. 29 **Litho.** **Perf. 10½**
451 A201 20col multicolored .80 .25

No. 421 Surcharged

1993, Mar. 26 **Litho.** **Perf. 13½**
452 A182 5col on 18col multi .50 .25

50,000 stamps originally were overprinted with a tiny block and four thin bars over the value, but this was considered unacceptable. So these stamps plus 1,550,000 unoverprinted stamps were overprinted with the large black square and surcharge, as shown.

Protection of the Dolphin A202

10col, Delphinus delphis. 20col, Stenella coeruleoalbus.

1993, May 17 **Litho.** **Perf. 10½**
453 A202 10col multicolored 2.50 .50
454 A202 20col multicolored 4.50 .50

Costa Rican Civil Service, 40th Anniv. — A203

1993, May 28 **Litho.** **Perf. 13½**
455 A203 5col multicolored .45 .25

Costa Rican Chamber of Industries, 50th Anniv. A204

1993, July 15   **Perf. 10½**
456 A204 45col multicolored   1.40   .90

School of Communication Sciences, University of Costa Rica, 25th Anniv. — A205

1993, Aug. 19   **Litho.**   **Perf. 13½**
457 A205 20col black, blue & red   1.00   .50

Protection of the Tropical Rain Forest — A206

2col, Passiflora vitifolia. 35col, Gurania megistantha.

1993, Aug. 27   **Perf. 10½**
458 A206 2col multi   1.40   .40
459 A206 35col multi   2.50   .80

Social Guarantees and Labor Code, 50th Anniv. A207

1993, Sept. 14   **Litho.**   **Perf. 10½**
460 A207 20col multicolored   .50   .30

A208

1993, Oct. 25   **Litho.**   **Perf. 13½**
461 A208 45col multicolored   1.00   .70

Intl. Assoc. of Professional Custom-House Agents, 15th Congress.

A209

1993, Nov. 26   **Perf. 10½**
462 A209 20col multicolored   .65   .30

Miguel Angel Castro Carazo (1893-1960), educator and humanitarian.
For surcharge see No. 481.

Law School of Costa Rica, 150th Anniv. — A211

1993, Dec. 23   **Litho.**   **Perf. 10½**
464 A211 20col multicolored   .55   .30

Natl. Theater — A212

1994, Mar. 18   **Litho.**   **Perf. 13**
465 A212 20col multi   .55   .30

Marine Life — A213

5col, Cyphoma gibbosum. 10col, Ophioderma rubicundum. 15col, Myripristis jacobus. 20col, Holocanthus passer. 35col, Paranthias furcifer. 45col, Tubastraea coccinea. 50col, Acanthaster planci. 55col, Ocypode. 70col, Arothron meleagris. 100col, Thalassoma lucasanum.

Litho. & Embossed
1994, Apr. 29   **Perf. 12½x12**
466 A213 5col multicolored   .40   .25
467 A213 10col multicolored   .80   .25
468 A213 15col multicolored   1.25   .30
469 A213 20col multicolored   1.60   .35
470 A213 35col multicolored   2.75   .55
471 A213 45col multicolored   3.50   .75
472 A213 50col multicolored   4.00   .85
473 A213 55col multicolored   4.50   .95
474 A213 70col multicolored   5.50   1.25
    Nos. 466-474 (9)   24.30   5.50

Souvenir Sheet
Perf. 13
475 A213 100col multicolored   11.00   8.00

America Issue A214

Illustrations from 19th century Book of Figueroa: a, Man on horseback. b, Back of ox carrying bundles.

1994, Dec. 19   **Litho.**   **Perf. 10½**
476 A214 20col Pair, #a.-b. + label   1.75   1.40

No. 476 is a continuous design.

Rotary Intl., 90th Anniv. — A215

1995, Mar.   **Litho.**   **Perf. 13½**
477 A215 20col multicolored   .90   .40

Antonio Jose de Sucre (1795-1830) — A216

Design: 30col, Jose Marti (1853-95).

1995, June   **Litho.**   **Perf. 10½**
478 A216 10col multicolored   .25   .25
479 A216 30col multicolored   .65   .65

Guanacaste Institute, 50th Anniv. — A217

1995, July 24   **Perf. 13½**
480 A217 50col ol grn, blk & cream   1.00   1.00

No. 462 Surcharged in Blue or Black

1995, Sept. 11   **Litho.**   **Perf. 10½**
481 A209 5col on 20col multi   .30   .25

UN, 50th Anniv. — A218

1995, Oct. 24   **Litho.**   **Perf. 10½**
482 A218 5col multicolored   .40   .25

13th Natl. Philatelic Expo — A219

Paintings by Lola Fernández: No. 483, Noviembre. No. 484, Enero.

1995, Dec. 1
483 A219 50col multicolored   1.00   1.00
484 A219 50col multicolored   1.00   1.00
  a.   Pair, Nos. 483-484   3.00   3.00

America Issue A220

30col, Jabiru mycteria. No. 486, View of coast. No. 487, River, trees. 50col, Atta cephalotes.

1995, Dec. 25   **Litho.**   **Rouletted 13½**
485 A220 30col multicolored   1.50   .80
486 A220 40col multicolored   1.50   1.25
487 A220 40col multicolored   1.50   1.25
  a.   Pair, #486-487   3.50   3.00
488 A220 50col multicolored   2.00   1.50
  a.   Souvenir sheet, #485-488   12.00   8.00
    Nos. 485-488 (4)   6.50   4.80

Seaport City of Limón A221

Designs: a, Early picture of steam train. b, Photo of ship in port, 1922. c, Aerial view of seaport, 1995. d, Painting of fruit seller, by Diego Villalobos. e, Drawing of Calipso singers, by Jorge Esquivel.

1996, Jan. 31   **Litho.**   **Perf. 10½**
489   Strip of 5   6.00   5.00
  a.-e.   A221 30col Any single   1.00   .60

Jerusalem, 3000th Anniv. — A222

1996, May 17   **Litho.**   **Perf. 13½**
490 A222 30col multicolored   .80   .65

1996 Summer Olympic Games, Atlanta A223

Olympic swimmers, coaches from Costa Rica: a, F. Rivas, M.M. Paris. b, S. Poll, R. Yglesias. c, C. Poll, A. Cruz.

1996, July 18   **Litho.**   **Perf. 10½**
491   Strip of 3   3.00   3.00
  a.-c.   A223 5col Any single   1.00   .50

No. 491 is a continuous design.

A224

First lady, presidents: a, Juana del Castillo. b, Juan Mora Fernández. c, J.M. Castro Madriz. d, Pacífica Fernández.

1996, Sept. 13   **Litho.**   **Perf. 10½**
492   Block of 4, #a.-d.   3.00   3.00
  a.-d.   A224 30col Any single   1.00   .60

Independence, 175th anniv. No. 492 was issued in sheets of 16 stamps.

A225

1996, Oct. 4   **Litho.**   **Perf. 13½**
493 A225 15col multicolored   .40   .25

Aqueducts and sewage systems, 35th anniv. Exists imperf.

A226

America issue (Paintings): No. 494, Black from Lemon, by Manuel da la Cruz González. No. 495, Peasant Women, by Gonzalo Morales Alvarado, vert.

1996, Dec. 16   *Perf. 10½*
494 A226 45col multicolored   2.50 1.00
495 A226 45col multicolored   2.50 1.00

A227

Entrance of the Saints at San Ramón, parade of people: a, Building with palm trees on top. b, Church on hill. c, Tree, holy family.

1997, Aug. 14   **Litho.**   *Perf. 13½*
496 A227 30col Strip of 3, #a.-c.   4.00 2.50
Costa Rican traditions.

School of Fine Arts, Cent. A228

1997, Sept. 24   *Perf. 10½*
497 A228 50col multicolored   1.40 .70

Radio Netherlands, 50th Anniv. — A229

1997, Sept. 26   *Perf. 13½*
498 A229 45col multicolored   1.10 .65
Exists imperf.

14th Natl. Philatelic Exhibition A230

1997, Oct. 9   *Perf. 10½*
499 A230 30col Postmen   1.00 .50
America Issue.

Church of the Immaculate Conception, Heredia, Bicent. — A231

1997, Nov. 10   **Litho.**   *Perf. 10½*
502 A231 50col multicolored   1.25 1.00

Second Republic, 50th Anniv. — A232

Former Pres. José Figueres demolishing wall of Fort Bellavista: 10col, 45col, Complete photo. 30col, Detail of Figueres' head. 50col, Hammer head hitting wall.

Litho. & Engr.
1998, Mar. 30   *Perf. 12½*
503 A232 10col multicolored   .60 .30
504 A232 30col multicolored   .90 .30
505 A232 45col multicolored   1.40 .30
506 A232 50col multicolored   1.50 .40
   a.   Souvenir sheet of 2, #504, 506   4.50 3.25

Natl. University, 25th Anniv. — A233

1998, July 27   **Litho.**   *Perf. 10½*
507 A233 50col multicolored   2.50 1.25

Butterflies A234

10col, Caligo memnon. 15col, Morpho peleides. 20col, Papilio thoas. 30col, Siproeta stelenes. 35col, Ascia monuste. 40col, Parides iphidamas. 45col, Smyrna blonfildia. 50col, Callicore pitheas. 55col, Historis odius. 60col, Danaus plexippus.

1998, July 16
508 A234 10col multicolored   .80 .30
509 A234 15col multicolored   1.25 .40
510 A234 20col multicolored   1.75 .60
511 A234 30col multicolored   2.50 .90
512 A234 35col multicolored   3.00 1.10
513 A234 40col multicolored   3.25 1.25
514 A234 45col multicolored   3.50 1.40
515 A234 50col multicolored   4.00 1.50
516 A234 55col multicolored   4.50 1.75
517 A234 60col multicolored   5.50 1.90
   Nos. 508-517 (10)   30.05 11.10

1998 World Cup Soccer Championships, France — A235

1998, Feb. 27   **Litho.**   *Perf. 10½*
518 A235 50col multicolored   1.25 1.00

A236

1998, Nov. 30   **Litho.**   *Perf. 13½*
519 A236 50col brn, yel brn & lt yel   2.00 .80
Carmen Lyra (1888-1949), author.

Gandhi (1869-1948) — A237

1998, Dec. 11   **Litho.**   *Perf. 13½*
520 A237 50col multicolored   2.50 1.40

Intl. Union for the Conservation of Nature, 50th Anniv. A238

Turtles: a, Rhinociemmys pulcherrima. b, Trachemys scripta. c, Chelydra serpentina.

1998, Dec. 1
521 A238 Strip of 3   10.00 10.00
   a.   A238 70col multi   3.50 3.50
   b.   A238 60col multi   3.00 3.00
   c.   A238 70col multi   3.50 3.50

Mushrooms A239

No. 522: a, Morchella esculenta. b, Boletus edulis.

1999, July 2   **Litho.**   *Perf. 10½*
522   Pair   4.50 4.50
   a.-b.   A239 50col Either single   2.25 2.25

SOS Children's Villages, 50th Anniv. — A240

1999, June   **Litho.**   *Perf. 10½*
523 A240 50col multicolored   2.50 .90

Costa Rican Institute of Electricity, 50th Anniv. A241

1999, Sept. 21   **Litho.**   *Perf. 13¼*
524 A241 75col multi   .80 .60

A242

1999, Oct. 7   **Engr.**   *Perf. 13¾x14*
525 A242 300col violet   3.00 3.00
Archbishop Víctor M. Sanabria (1899-1952). See No. 538.

Intl. Year of Older Persons — A243

1999, Oct. 29   **Litho.**   *Perf. 13¼*
526 A243 50col multi   .80 .50

Supreme Election Tribunal, 50th Anniv. A244

1999, Nov. 5   *Perf. 10½*
527 A244 70col multi   1.80 .80

UPU, 125th Anniv. — A245

1999, Dec. 1   *Perf. 13¼*
528 A245 75col multi   .90 .70

Carmen Granados (1915-99), Humorist — A246

1999, Dec. 1
529 A246 50col multi   .90 .60

America Issue, A New Millennium Without Arms — A247

70col, Male face, both hands.

1999, Dec. 1
530 A247 50col shown   .75 .50
531 A247 70col multicolored   1.00 .70

PhilexFrance '99 — A248

No. 533, Flower, Eiffel Tower.

1999, Dec. 1
532 A248 300col shown   5.00 3.50
533 A248 300col multi   5.00 3.50

Natl. Bank, 50th Anniv. — A249

No. 534 — Pre-Columbian artifacts: a, Jaguar. b, Scorpion. c, Bat. d, Crab. e, Beast with horns.
No. 535 — Obverse and reverse of coins: a, Gold, from 1825. b, Gold, from 1850. c, Silver one-eighth peso. d, Gold 20-peso. e, 1935 1-colon.

2000, Jan. 28	**Litho.**		**Perf. 13¼**	
534	Vert. strip of 5		9.50	7.00
a.-e.	A249 60col Any single		1.25	1.00
535	Vert. strip of 5		22.50	12.50
a.-e.	A249 90col Any single		3.00	1.50

2000 Summer Olympics, Sydney — A250

No. 536, 60col: a, Taekwando. b, Cycling. c, Swimming. d, Soccer.
No. 537, 70col: a, Running. b, Boxing. c, Men's rings. d, Tennis.

2000, Aug. 31	**Blocks of 4, #a-d**		
536-537	A250	Set of 2	10.00 10.00

There were two printings of Nos. 536-537. In the first printing, colors are paler, and the green Olympic ring is misregistered on Nos. 536a-536d. In the second, colors are more intense, and the green ring is properly registered. Values same.

Famous Person Type of 1999

Pres. Rafael A. Calderón Guardia (1900-70).

2000, Sept. 14	**Engr.**		**Perf. 12½**	
538	A242 100col deep blue		1.10	.50
a.	Perf 13¾x14		3.25	1.50

Paintings by Max Jiménez — A251

No. 539: a, Fishermen in Cojimar. b, Adamant.

2000, Nov.	**Litho.**		**Perf. 10½**	
539	Horiz. pair		4.00	2.50
a.-b.	A251 50col Either single		1.00	.50

America Issue, Fight Against AIDS — A252

Designs: 60col, Stylized people. 90col, Stylized person.

2000, Dec.			**Perf. 13¼**	
540-541	A252	Set of 2	2.50	2.00

Christmas — A253

2000, Dec.			
542	A253 100col multi	1.60	1.25

America Issue — UNESCO World Heritage A254

Birds form Cocos Island Natl. Park: 95col, Coccyzus ferrugineus. 115col, Pinaroloxias inornata.

2001, Apr. 5	**Litho.**	**Perf. 10½**	
543-544	A254 Set of 2	6.00	4.00

Costa Rica — Netherlands Diplomatic Relations, 150th Anniv. — A255

2001, July 20			
545	A255 65col multi	1.00	.75

No. 429 Surcharged

2001	**Method and Perf. As Before**		
546	A188 65col on 500col multi	1.00	.75
547	A188 80col on 500col multi	1.25	1.00
548	A188 95col on 500col multi	1.50	1.10
	Nos. 546-548 (3)	3.75	2.85

Issued: No. 846, 8/24. Nos. 547-548, 9/7.

Third Hispanic-Costa Rican Exposition — A256

Orchids: a, Guaria turrialba. b, Tricopilia.

2001, Oct. 5	**Litho.**	**Perf. 13¼**	
549	A256 65col Horiz. pair, #a-b	2.50	2.50

Campaign Against Child Labor — A257

2001, Nov. 15		**Perf. 13¼**	
550	A257 100col multi	1.60	1.25

Pres. Tomás Guardia (1832-82) and Locomotive — A258

2001, Nov. 21			
551	A258 65col multi	2.00	.80

A second printing of No. 551 was issued in 2002. It features a lighter beige and has yellow gum. This printing of 500 sheets of 15 stamps was made to complete the contract. Value, unused $25.

Costa Rican Team for 2002 World Cup Soccer Championships, Japan and Korea — A259

2002, Mar. 15		**Perf. 10½**	
552	A259 65col multi	2.00	.80

No. 428 Surcharged in Red

Litho. & Engr.

2002, Jan. 24		**Perf. 12½**	
553	A188 65col on 200col multi	1.00	.75

America Issue — Youth, Education and Literacy — A260

Designs: 65col, Children and globe. 100col, Blind person reading Braille.

Litho. & Embossed

2002, Mar.		**Perf. 10½**	
554-555	A260 Set of 2	2.50	2.00

Taiwan Friendship Bridge A261

2002, Apr. 3		**Litho.**	
556	A261 95col multi	1.25	1.00

16th Rio Group Congress A262

2002, Apr. 10			
557	A262 65col blue & green	1.00	.75

Pan-American Health Organization, Cent. — A263

No. 558: a, People (red denomination at UR). b, Emblem. c, Mother and child (black denomination at LR). d, Child and man (red denomination at LR).
50col, Emblem.

2002, July 5				
558	A263 10col Block of 4, #a-d		.65	.65
559	A263 50col multi		.70	.70

In Remembrance of Sept. 11, 2001 Terrorist Attacks — A264

Litho. & Embossed

2002, Sept. 11			
560	A264 110col multi	4.00	2.00

Marine Life of Uvita Island A265

Designs: No. 561, 75col, Gorgona flabellum. No. 562, 75col, Ulva lactuca. No. 563, 75col, Cittarium pica. No. 564, 75col, Liriope tetraphyla.

Litho & Embossed

2002, Sept. 25			
561-564	A265 Set of 4	6.00	6.00

Space Exploration — A266

No. 565: a, Dr. Franklin Chang-Diaz, astronaut, and space shuttle. b, Phanaeus changdiazi and satellite.

Litho. & Embossed

2003, June 15		**Perf. 10½**	
565	A266 115col Horiz. pair, #a-b	4.00	4.00

Coco Island National Park — A267

No. 566: a, Denomination at UR. b, Denomination at UL.

2003, Aug. 1			
566	A267 75col Horiz. pair, #a-b	3.00	3.00

America Issue - Fish — A268

No. 567: a, Archocentrus sajica. b, Astatheros diquis.

2003			
567	A268 110col Horiz. pair, #a-b	5.00	5.00

Scenes from Cocorí, by Joaquín Gutiérrez — A269

No. 568: a, Boy, turtle, monkey and bird. b, Boy looking at reflection in water. c, Toucan in tree, boy and monkey on ground. d, Sailor, girl and boy. e, Boy, bird on branch. f, Jaguar, turtle armadillo, monkey, boy and father. g, Boy and monkey pushing turtle. h, Monkey with open arms, turtle, boy. i, Mother and boy. j, Mother, boy, rose bush. k, Boy, father playing musical instrument (80x150mm).

Litho. & Embossed

2003, Sept. 3   **Perf. 10½**
568   A269   Sheet of 11   15.00 15.00
   a.-j.   25col Any single   .80   .60
   k.   225col multi   5.00 5.00

National Anthem, Cent. — A270

No. 569: a, Lyricist José María Zeledón (24x35mm). b, Flag, text of anthem (49x35mm).

2003, Sept. 10   **Litho.**
569   A270   75col Horiz. pair, #a-b   4.00 4.00

Election of Pope John Paul II, 25th Anniv. — A271

2003, Oct. 16 Litho.   **Perf. 13¼x13½**
570   A271   130col multi   3.00 3.00

Charles Lindbergh's Flight to Costa Rica, 75th Anniv. — A272

Litho. & Embossed

2003, Dec. 16   **Perf. 13½x13¼**
571   A272   110col multi   2.00 2.00

Guayabo de Turrialba Archaeological Monument — A273

2003, Dec. 18
572   A273   110col multi   2.00 2.00

America Issue A274

Flora: No. 573, 75col, Ceiba pentandra. No. 574, 75col, Tetranema floribundum. 90col, Ceiba pentandra, diff. 110col, Tetranema gamboanum.

2004, Mar. 23   **Litho.**   **Perf. 10½**
573-576   A274   Set of 4   6.00 6.00

Volcanoes A275

Designs: 85col, Arenal. 120col, Irazú. 140col, Poás.

2004-05   **Perf. 10½**
577-579   A275   Set of 3   6.00 6.00
577a   Perf. 13¼ ('05)   1.50 1.50
578a   Perf. 13¼ ('05)   2.00 2.00
579a   Perf. 13¼ ('05)   2.50 2.50

Issued: Nos. 577-579, 6/24/04; 577a, 578a, 579a, 2005.
Nos. 577a, 578a and 579a have printer's inscription "LIL S.A."

2004 Summer Olympics, Athens A276

No. 580 — Various athletes in: a, Blue. b, Yellow orange. c, Green. d, Red.

2004, July 15
580   Horiz. strip of 4   8.00 8.00
   a.-d.   A276 120col Any single   2.00 2.00

Dr. Miguel Angel Rodríguez, Organization of American States President A277

2004, Sept. 15
581   A277   120col multi   2.00 2.00

FIFA (Fédération Internationale de Football Association), Cent. — A278

No. 582: a, Emblem (34x34mm). b, Soccer player and field (39x34mm).

2004, Feb. 15   **Litho.**   **Perf. 10½**
582   A278   140col Horiz. pair, #a-b   5.00 5.00

Rotary International, Cent. — A279

No. 583: a, Emblem and frog. b, Centenary emblem. c, Emblem and butterfly.

2005, Feb. 23
583   Horiz. strip of 3   7.50 7.50
   a.-c.   A279 140col Any single   2.50 2.50

Souvenir Sheet

Popes — A280

No. 584: a, Pope John Paul II (1920-2005). b, Pope Benedict XVI.

2005, Aug. 22
584   A280   140col Sheet of 4, 2 each #a-b   10.00 10.00
   a.-   A281 95col Either single
   b.   5.00 5.00

An imperf. sheet lacking postal validity exists. Value, $150.

Intl. Year of Physics — A281

No. 585: a, Albert Einstein (1879-1955). b, Max Planck (1858-1947).

2005, June 7
585   Horiz. pair   3.50 3.50
   a.-b.   A281 95col Either single   1.75 1.75

Flora and Fauna in National Parks — A282

No. 586: a, Passiflora vitifolia. b, Dryas iulia moderata. c, Potos flavus.

2005, Oct. 11   **Litho.**   **Perf. 10½**
586   Strip of 3   4.50 4.50
   a.-c.   A282 85col Any single   1.40 1.40

America Issue, Fight Against Poverty — A283

No. 587: a, Child at computer. b, Man sawing wood. c, Medical worker.

2005, Oct. 19
587   Strip of 3   6.50 6.50
   a.-c.   A283 120col Any single   2.10 2.10

Intl. Year of Sports and Physical Education A284

2005, Dec. 6
588   A284   85col multi   1.50 1.50

Cartago Sport Club, Cent. — A285

2006, Mar. 20
589   A285   85col multi   1.75 1.75

Miniature Sheet

National Campaign Against Nicaraguan Pres. William Walker, 150th Anniv. — A286

No. 590: a, Juan Rafael Mora, National Monument. b, Juan Santamaría Monument, barracks. c, Map (50x40mm). d, Gen. José María Cañas, Santa Rosa House. e, Luis Molina, Joaquín Bernardo Calvo.

2006, Apr. 7
590   A286   85col Sheet of 5, #a-e   8.50 8.50

2006 World Cup Soccer Championships, Germany — A287

2006, May 15
591   A287   120col multi   2.40 2.40

America Issue, Energy Conservation — A288

2006, July 31   **Litho.**   **Perf. 10½**
592   A288   155col multi + label   3.00 3.00

Miniature Sheet

Birds and Marine Life of Cocos
Island — A289

No. 593: a, Sula sula. b, Mycteroperca olfax.
c, Zanclus cornutis. d, Eretmochely imbricaas.
e, Tursiops truncatus. f, Myripristis berndti. g,
Dendroica petechia aureola. h, Carcharhinus
limbatus. i, Anous stolidus. j, Acarus
rubroviolaceus.

2006, Aug. 25　Litho.　Perf. 10½
593　A289　180col Sheet of 10,
　　　#a-j　　　　　35.00　35.00

Pres. José Figueres Ferrer (1906-
90) — A290

2006, Sept. 25　　　　Perf. 10½
594　A290　115col gray & multi　3.00　3.00
Souvenir Sheet
Imperf
595　A290　1000col tan & multi　30.00　30.00
No. 594 was printed in sheets of 6 + 3
labels. Value, $20.

Fruits —
A291

No. 596: a, Hymenaea courbaril. b, Bixa
orellana. c, Garcinia intermedia.

2006, Oct. 12　　　　Perf. 10½
596　　　Strip of 3　　　9.00　9.00
a.-c.　A291 155col Any single　3.00　3.00

National Symbols — A292

No. 597: a, Flag. b, Coat of arms.

2006, Nov. 27
597　A292 155col Pair, #a-b　6.00　6.00
Printed in sheets containing two pairs.
Value, $12.50.

Pres. Francisco J. Orlich (1907-
69) — A293

2007, Mar. 7
598　A293 115col multi　　　2.25　2.25

Orchids — A294

No. 599: a, Guarianthe skinneri (pink flowers). b, Galeandra arundinis. c, Encyclia
ossenbachiana. d, Dracula inexperata. e,
Guarianthe skinneri (white flowers). f, Kefer-
steinia retanae. g, Coryanthes kaiseriana. h,
Psychopsis krameriana. i, Chondroscaphe
yamilethae. j, Cattleya dowiana.
　1000col, Brassia suavissima.

2007, Mar. 19　Litho.　Perf. 10½
599　A294　180col Sheet of 10,
　　　#a-j　　　　　18.00　18.00
Souvenir Sheet
Imperf
600　A294 1000col multi　　40.00　40.00
No. 599 contains ten 45x37mm stamps. No.
600 has simulated perforations.

Salesian Order
in Costa Rica,
Cent. — A295

2007, Apr. 30　　　　Perf. 10½
601　A295　110col multi　　2.25　2.25

Miniature Sheet

Pre-Columbian Art — A296

No. 602: a, Frog-shaped gold pendant
(25x45mm). b, Bird-shaped jadeite pendant
(25x45mm). c, Stone metate, horiz.
(50x30mm). d, Ceramic censer with alligator
(25x45mm). e, Stone figure of warrior
(25x45mm).

2007, May 4
602　A296 155col Sheet of 5,
　　　#a-e　　　　15.00　15.00

America Issue, Education For
All — A297

No. 603: a, 115col, Teacher and students. b,
155col, Family around fire.

2007, June 8
603　A297　Horiz. pair, #a-b　6.00　6.00

Plasma Technology — A298

No. 604: a, Astronaut and spacecraft's robot
arm. b, Plasma containment vessel.

2007, July 6
604　A298 240col Horiz. pair, #a-b 9.50　9.50
Nos. 604a and 604b were printed in sheets
of containing two of each stamp. Value, $19.

Guanacaste Musical
Instruments — A299

Designs: No. 605, 115col, Marimba. No.
606, 115col, Quijongo, vert. (30x50mm).

2007, July 25
605-606 A299　Set of 2　4.50　4.50
Nos. 605-606 were printed in sheets containing two of each stamp + label. Value, $9.

Virgin of the Angels Icon, 225th Anniv.
as Patron of Cartago — A300

No. 607 — Icon with denomination at: a, LR.
b, LL.
　1000col, Interior of Cartago Basilica, vert.

2007, July 27
607　A300　115col Horiz. pair,
　　　#a-b　　　　4.50　4.50
Souvenir Sheet
608　A300 1000col multi　　30.00　30.00
No. 608 contains one 75x115mm stamp.

Fauna of
National
Parks — A301

No. 609: a, Oxybelis fulgidus. b, Stagmo-
mantis sp. c, Heliodoxa jacula. d, Pulsatrix
perspicillata.

2007, Aug. 17　Litho.　Perf. 10½
609　　　Horiz. strip of 4　18.00　18.00
a.-d.　A301 235col Any single　4.50　4.50

2007 Special Olympics,
Shanghai — A302

No. 610: a, Cycling. b, Swimming. c,
Running.

2007, Sept. 10
610　　　Horiz. strip of 3　14.00　14.00
a.-c.　A302 240col Any single　3.50　3.50

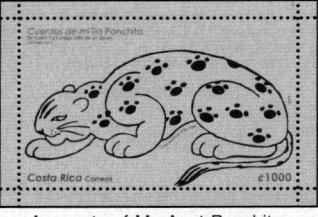

Accounts of My Aunt Panchita,
Children's Book by Carmen
Lyra — A303

No. 611, vert. — Text: a, Por qué Tío Conejo
tiene las orejas tan largas. b, La Mica. c,
Uvieta. d, Tío Conejo y los caites de su
abuela.
　1000col, De como Tío Conejo salió de un
apuro.

2007, Oct. 18
611　A303　100col Sheet of 4,
　　　#a-d　　　　8.00　8.00
Souvenir Sheet
612　A303 1000col multi　　30.00　30.00
No. 611 contains four 37x50mm stamps.

Ox Cart Heritage — A304

No. 613: a, Man with oxen. b, Decorated
wheel.

2007, Nov. 23
613　A304 180col Vert. pair, #a-b,
　　　　　+ central label 7.00　7.00
Nos. 613a and 613b were printed in sheets
of containing two of each stamp. Value, $14.

Esquipulas II Central American Peace Accords, 20th Anniv. — A305

No. 614 — Nobel Peace medal of Pres. Oscar Arias Sánchez: a, Reverse (three men). b, Obverse (Alfred Nobel).

2007, Dec. 10
614 A305 135col Horiz. pair, #a-b 5.25 5.25

Dr. Fernando Centeno Güell (1907-93), Poet and Educator — A306

2008, Feb. 14
615 A306 115col multi 2.25 2.25

Churches — A307

No. 616: a, Our Lord of Agony Chapel, Guanacaste. b, San Francisco Church, San José. c, Our Lady of Sorrow Church, San José. d, Santa Ana Church, San José. e, Our Lady of Carmel Cathedral, Puntarenas. f, San Bartolomé Apóstol Church, Heredia.
1000col, Our Lady of Mercy Parish Church, San José.

2008, Mar. 17
616 A307 230col Sheet of 6,
#a-f 27.50 27.50
Souvenir Sheet
617 A307 1000col multi 50.00 30.00
No. 616 contains six 40x40mm stamps.

Souvenir Sheet

Women's Superior College, 120th Anniv. — A308

2008, Mar. 31
618 A308 1000col multi 30.00 30.00

Miniature Sheet

Marine Mammals — A309

No. 619: a, Megaptera novaengliae, side view. b, Sotalia guianensis. c, Stenella attenuata. d, Megaptera novaengliae flukes.

2008, June 16 Litho. Perf. 10½
619 A309 240col Sheet of 4,
#a-d 19.00 19.00

Intl. Year of Planet Earth — A310

No. 620: a, San Vicente Cataracts. b, Santa Elena Peninsula.

2008, July 1
620 Pair 7.00 7.00
a.-b. A310 175col Either single 3.50 3.50
Nos. 620a and 620b were printed in sheets of containing two of each stamp. Value, $14.

Miniature Sheet

Art — A311

No. 621: a, La Ultima Escena, by Rudy Espinoza. b, Mujer que Avanza, sculpture by Crisanto Badilla. c, Transitoriedad del Hombre, by Miguel Hernández. d, Arquetipo, by Lola Fernández.

2008, July 3
621 A311 240col Sheet of 4,
#a-d 19.00 19.00

Miniature Sheet

Ministry of Labor and Social Security, 80th Anniv. — A312

No. 622 — Details from mural "The Second Republic," by Luccio Ranucci: a, Man with hat, striped pole. b, Woman with basket of fruit. c, Man and woman embracing. d, Man carrying sack on head.

2008, Aug. 28 Litho. Perf. 10½
622 A312 240col Sheet of 4,
#a-d 19.00 19.00

Masks — A313

No. 623 — Masks with background colors of: a, 115col, Brown orange. b, 155col, Green.

2008, Oct. 31
623 A313 Horiz. pair, #a-b 5.50 5.50
Nos. 623a and 623b were printed in sheets of containing two of each stamp. Value, $11.

Hogar Crea Drug Rehabilitation Centers in Costa Rica, 25th Anniv. — A314

2009, Feb. 25 Litho. Perf. 10½
624 A314 160col multi 3.20 3.20

Carlos Luis Fallas (1906-66), Author — A315

2009, Apr. 30 Litho. Perf. 10½
625 A315 150col multi 2.00 2.00

Miniature Sheet

Children's Literature — A316

No. 626: a, Tolo, the Giant North Wind (kite), by Adela Ferreto de Saénz. b, The Ship of the Stars (ship and boy), by Alfredo Cardona Peña. c, Old Stories (rabbit and gourds), by María Leal de Noguera. d, Paul's Music (boy holding box), by Lara Ríos.

2009, May 27
626 A316 65col Sheet of 4, #a-d 5.00 5.00

Alberto Martén, Economist, Solidarity Movement Founder — A317

2009, June 19
627 A317 135col multi 2.50 2.50

Miniature Sheet

Costa Rican Electrical Institute (ICE), 60th Anniv. — A318

No. 628: a, People and ICE building. b, Construction workers in tunnel. c, Lineman on ladder. d, Computers and satellite dishes. e, Houses and windmills. f, Hand planting seedling, girl.

2009, June 30
628 A318 340col Sheet of 6,
#a-f 15.00 15.00

Diplomatic Relations Between Costa Rica and Switzerland — A319

2009, July 8
629 A319 225col multi 4.00 4.00

Miniature Sheet

National Parks — A320

No. 630: a, Arenal Volcano. b, Celeste River. c, Cerro Chirripó. d, Cocos Island. e, Monteverde. f, Poás Volcano. g, Tortuguero.

2009, Aug. 24
630 A320 240col Sheet of 7, #a-g 8.25 8.25

America Issue, Traditional Games — A321

No. 631: a, Marbles. b, Kite flying.

2009, Sept. 9 **Litho.** **Perf. 10½**
631   Horiz. pair   2.00 2.00
a.-b.   A321 135col Either single   .75 .75

Intl. Holocaust Remembrance Day — A322

2010, Jan. 27 **Perf. 13¼**
632 A322 500col gray & black 4.00 4.00
No. 632 was printed in sheets of four with labels at left, bottom and right. Value, $27.50.

Miniature Sheet

Locomotives — A323

No. 633: a, Steam locomotive, 1889. b, Electric Series AEG locomotive, 1926. c, Yellow and white Apolo Series Diesel-electric locomotive, 1990. d, Blue, white and red Diesel-electric locomotive, 1979-80.

2010, May 4 **Litho.** **Perf. 10½**
633 A323 200col Sheet of 4, #a-d 3.25 3.25

America Issue, National Symbols — A324

2010, June 24
634   Horiz. pair   6.00 6.00
a.   A324 280col Turdus grayi   1.25 1.25
b.   A324 340col Odocoileus virginianus   1.50 1.50
No. 634 was printed in sheets containing two pairs. Value, $15.

Miniature Sheet

Endangered Birds — A325

No. 635: a, 400col, Platalea ajaja. b, 400col, Icterus mesomelas. c, 1000col, Morphnus guianensis. d, 1000col, Harpia harpyja.

2010, June 24 **Litho.** **Perf. 10½**
635 A325 Sheet of 4, #a-d 15.00 15.00

University Anniversaries — A326

No. 636: a, Mural by Eduardo Torijano at University of Costa Rica. b, Monument to Disarmament, Work and Peace by Thelvia Marin at Univeristy for Peace.

2010, Aug. 26
636 A326 500col Pair, #a-b 4.00 4.00
University of Costa Rica, 70th anniv., University for Peace, 30th anniv.

Miniature Sheet

Details of Sculptures by Jiménez Deredia — A327

No. 637: a, 225col, Pareja. b, 225col, Ricordo Profondo. c, 395col, Continuación. d, 395col, Génesi Ricordo Profondo. Names of sculptures are in sheet margin above stamps.

Perf. 10½ on 2 or 3 Sides
2011, Feb. 23
637 A327 Sheet of 4, #a-d, + label 5.00 5.00

Souvenir Sheet

Opening of New National Stadium — A328

No. 638 — National Stadium built in: a, 1924. b, 2011.

2011, Mar. 26 **Perf. 10½**
638 A328 1000col Sheet of 2, #a-b 8.00 8.00

Pres. Laura Chinchilla A329

2011, May 9 **Perf. 10½ Vert.**
639 A329 340col multi 2.00 2.00

Souvenir Sheet

Cartoons by Costa Rican Artists — A330

No. 640 — Cartoons by: a, 500col, Francisco "Paco" Hernández (1885-1961) and Noé Solano (1889-1971). b, 1000col, Hugo Diaz

"Lalo" (1930-2001) and Jorge Chavarria "Kokin" (1932-94).

2011, June 15 **Perf. 10½**
640 A330 Sheet of 2, #a-b 6.00 6.00

Miniature Sheet

Athletes — A331

No. 641: a, 200col, Hanna Gabriel, boxer. b, 200col, Nery Brenes, sprinter. c, 330col, Bryan Ruiz, soccer player. d, 330col, Andrey Amador, cyclist.

2011, July 14
641 A331 Sheet of 4, #a-d 4.25 4.25

Rights of the Child — A332

No. 642 — Banner inscribed: a, Participación. b, No Discriminación. c, Educación.

2011, Aug. 12
642   Horiz. strip of 3   4.75 4.75
a.   A332 225col multi   .90 .90
b.   A332 340col multi   1.40 1.40
c.   A332 600col multi   2.40 2.40

Miniature Sheet

Flora and Fauna of Monteverde Children's Forest — A333

No. 643: a, 500col, Forest and lake. b, 500col, Lithobates vibicarius. c, 1000col, Lepanthes ciliisepala. d, 1000col, Leopardus wiedii.

2011, Aug. 24 **Perf. 10½ on 3 Sides**
643 A333 Sheet of 4, #a-d, + 2 labels 15.00 15.00

Tricolín, Comic Strip by Carlos Figueroa — A334

No. 644: a, Tricolín, Tricolína and Costa Rican flag. b, Tricolín and Tricolína donating money for Red Cross. c, Tricolín and Pepín planting flower. d, Tricolín, Tricolína, and Pepín.

2011, Sept. 9 **Die Cut Perf. 12x11½ Self-Adhesive**
644   Block or horiz. strip of 4 5.50
a.   A334 300col multi   1.25 1.25
b.   A334 320col multi   1.25 1.25
c.   A334 350col multi   1.40 1.40
d.   A334 395col multi   1.60 1.60

Mailboxes — A335

No. 645: a, Black mailbox. b, Blue mailbox.

2011, Oct. 10   *Perf. 10½*
645 A335 400col Pair, #a-b   5.00 5.00
   America issue. No. 645 was printed in sheets containing two pairs. Value, $12.50.

Souvenir Sheet

Scouting in Costa Rica, Cent. — A336

No. 646 — Boy Scouts and Girl Guides: a, Near tents. b, Around campfire.

2011, Oct. 28
646 A336 340col Sheet of 2, #a-b 2.75 2.75

Souvenir Sheet

National Museum, 125th Anniv. — A337

No. 647: a, Grinding stone, butterfly at right. b, Butterfly at left, Pre-Columbian stone sphere.

2012, May 4
647 A337 395col Sheet of 2, #a-b 3.25 3.25

Bank of Costa Rica, 135th Anniv. A338

2012, June 7
648 A338 275col multi   1.50 1.50
   No. 648 was printed in sheets of 2. Value, $3.50.

Souvenir Sheet

2012 Summer Olympics, London — A339

No. 649: a, 365col, Runner. b, 435col, Taekwondo.

2012, June 25
649 A339   Sheet of 2, #a-b   3.25 3.25

Souvenir Sheet

Intl. Year of Cooperatives — A340

No. 650: a, 275col, People holding rainbow and trees. b, 395col, People wrapping ribbons around sphere.

2012, July 6
650 A340   Sheet of 2, #a-b   2.75 2.75

Manuel Antonio National Park — A341

2012, Aug. 24   *Perf. 10½ Horiz.*
Booklet Stamp
651 A341 545col multi   3.00 3.00
  a.   Booklet pane of 3   15.00 —
     Complete booklet, #651a   15.00

Souvenir Sheet

America Issue — A342

No. 652: a, 385col, Legend of La Segua. b, 485col, Legend of the Cart Without Oxen.

2012, Oct. 9   *Perf. 10½*
652 A342   Sheet of 2, #a-b   3.50 3.50

Souvenir Sheet

First Costa Rican Postage Stamps, 150th Anniv. — A343

No. 653: a, Costa Rica #1. b, Costa Rica #2.

Litho. & Embossed With Foil Application
2013, Apr. 17
653 A343 1000col Sheet of 2, #a-
     b   8.00 8.00

Souvenir Sheet

Bancrédito Commercial Bank, 95th Anniv. — A344

2013, May 15   *Litho.*
654 A344 400col multi   1.60 1.60

"Costa Rica, Land of Immigrants" A345

2013, June 20
655 A345 500col multi   2.00 2.00
   No. 655 was printed in sheets of 2. Value, $4.50.

Souvenir Sheet

Braulio Carrillo National Park — A346

2013, Aug. 23   *Litho.*   *Perf.*
656 A346 1500col multi   6.00 6.00

Jorge Manuel Dengo (1918-2012), Vice-President — A347

2013, Sept. 18   *Litho.*   *Perf. 10½*
657 A347 500col multi   2.00 2.00
   No. 657 was printed in sheets of 2. Value, $4.50.

Campaign Against Discrimination — A348

2013, Oct. 9   *Litho.*   *Perf. 10½*
658 A348 300col multi   1.50 1.50
   America issue. No. 658 was printed in sheets of 2 + central label. Value, $3.50.

Souvenir Sheet

Pres. Juan Rafael Mora Porras (1814-60) — A349

2014, Feb. 7   *Litho.*   *Perf. 10½*
659 A349 360col multi   1.40 1.40
   America issue.

Souvenir Sheet

Election of Pope Francis, 1st Anniv. — A350

2014, Mar. 19   *Litho.*   *Perf. 10½*
660 A350 300col multi   2.00 2.00

Souvenir Sheet

2014 World Cup Soccer Championships, Brazil — A351

No. 661: a, 500col, 2014 World Cup mascot. b, 710col, World Cup.

2014, Apr. 24　Litho.　Perf. 10½
661 A351　Sheet of 2, #a-b　　6.00 6.00

Souvenir Sheet

Endangered Cats in Corcovado National Park — A352

No. 662: a, 690col, Puma yagouaroundi. 1220col, Panthera onca.

2014, Aug. 22　Litho.　Perf. 13
662 A352　Sheet of 2, #a-b　　9.00 9.00

Souvenir Sheet

National Bank, Cent. — A353

2014, Nov. 3　Litho.　Perf. 10½
663 A353　500col multi　　1.90 1.90

Vuelta de Costa Rica Bicycle Race, 50th Anniv. A354

2014, Dec. 11　Litho.　Perf. 13¼
664 A354　500col multi　　2.25 2.25
　No. 664 was printed in sheets of 2. Value, $5.

Souvenir Sheet

Forensic Medicine in Costa Rica, 50th Anniv. — A355

2015, Jan. 30　Litho.　Perf. 10½
665 A355　360col multi　　1.40 1.40

Costa Rica Chamber of Commerce, Cent. — A356

2015, Mar. 4　Litho.　Perf. 10½
666 A356　500col multi　　1.90 1.90
　No. 666 was printed in sheets of 2. Value, $4.

Souvenir Sheet

El Buen Pastor Episcopal Church, San José, 150th Anniv. — A357

2015, Apr. 23　Litho.　Imperf.
667 A357　1000col multi　　5.00 5.00
　No. 667 has simulated perforations.

Souvenir Sheet

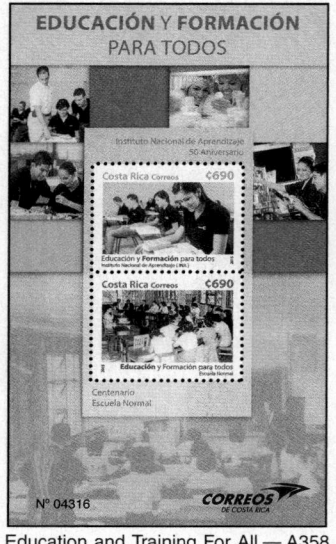

Education and Training For All — A358

　No. 668 — Adult students with denomination in: a, Orange yellow. b, Blue.

2015, May 7　Litho.　Perf. 10½
668 A358　690col Sheet of 2, #a-b 5.25 5.25
　National Apprentice Institute, 50th anniv.; Normal School, cent.

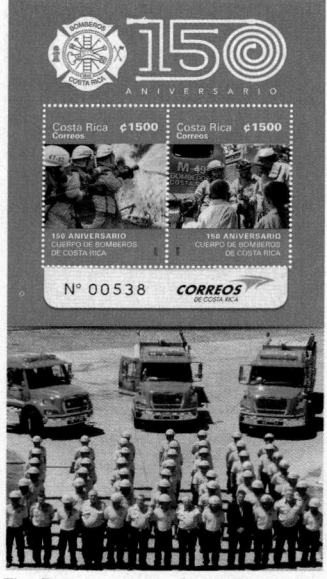

Fire Departments in Costa Rica, 150th Anniv. — A359

　No. 669: a, Fire fighters spraying water on fire. b, Fire fighters, truck and children.

2015, July 16　Litho.　Perf. 14
669 A359　1500col Sheet of 2,
　　　　　#a-b　　11.50 11.50

Nelson Mandela (1918-2013), President of South Africa — A360

2015, July 18　Litho.　Perf. 10½
　　　　Booklet Stamp
670 A360　1220col multi　　4.75 4.75
　a.　Booklet pane of 3　　14.50 —
　　　Complete booklet, #670a　14.50

Coral Reefs of Cahuita National Park — A361

No. 671: a, Coral and sea urchin. b, Coral. 1000col, Coral, diff.

2015, Aug. 24　Litho.　Perf. 13x13¼
671 A361　500col Sheet of 2,
　　　　　#a-b　　3.75 3.75
　　　Souvenir Sheet
672 A361　1000col multi　　5.00 5.00

Campaign Against Human Trafficking A362

2015, Oct. 9　Litho.　Perf. 10½
673 A362　500col black & blue　1.25 1.90
　America Issue. No. 673 was printed in sheets of 2. Value, $3.

Coope Ande Credit Union, 50th Anniv. — A363

2015, Nov. 4　Litho.　Perf. 10½
674 A363　600col multi　　2.25 2.25
　No. 674 was printed in sheets of 2.

Souvenir Sheet

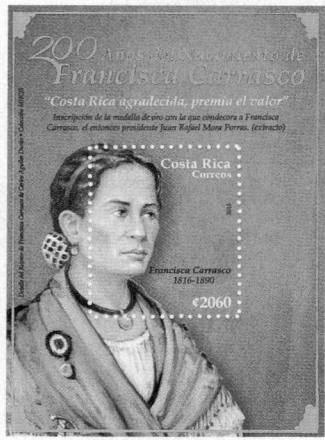

Francisca Carrasco (1816-90), First Woman in Costa Rican Military — A364

Litho., Sheet Margin Litho. With Foil Application

2016, Apr. 4   **Perf. 10½**
675 A364 2060col multi   7.75 7.75

Souvenir Sheet

Pres. José Joaquín Trejos Fernández (1916-2010) — A365

2016, Apr. 18   **Litho.**   **Perf. 10½**
676 A365 1950col multi   7.50 7.50

Souvenir Sheet

Archaeological Sites — A366

Diquís Culture Stone Spheres: No. 677: a, Stone sphere. b, Stone sphere and triangular ramp of stones at archaeological dig site.

Litho. & Thermography

2016, June 23   **Perf. 13¼x13½**
677 A366 650col Sheet of 2, #a-b 4.75 4.75

Souvenir Sheet

2016 Summer Olympics, Rio de Janeiro — A367

No. 678: a, 600col, Fencing. b, 1400col, Mountain biking.

2016, July 15   **Litho.**   **Perf. 10½**
678 A367 Sheet of 2, #a-b   7.50 7.50

Dermochelys Coriacea — A368

No. 679 —Turtle facing: a, 1370col, Right. b, 2100col, Left.
1100col, Turtle facing forward.

Litho. & Embossed

2016, Aug. 24   **Perf. 13½x13¼**
679 A368 Sheet of 2, #a-b   12.50 12.50

Souvenir Sheet

680 A368 1100col multi   4.00 4.00

Fauna of Marino Las Baulas National Park.

Souvenir Sheet

Writers — A369

No. 681: a, 420col, Aquileo J. Echeverría (1866-1909). b, 650col, Yolanda Oreamuno (1916-56).

2016, Oct. 10   **Litho.**   **Perf. 10½**
681 A369   Sheet of 2, #a-b   4.00 4.00

POSTAL-FISCAL STAMPS

From April 1884 through September 1889 revenue stamps were permitted for postal use, when post offices exhausted supplies of regular postage stamps.

Used values are for stamps with postal cancels.

PF1

1884   **Engr.**   **Perf. 12**
AR1 PF1 1c rose   .50 5.00
AR2 PF1 2c light blue   20.00 5.00

PF2

1888
AR3 PF2 5c brown   .50 3.00
AR4 PF2 10c blue   .25 3.00

Nos. AR2-AR4 are normally found without gum.

SEMI-POSTAL STAMPS

No. 72 Surcharged in Red

1922   **Unwmk.**   **Perf. 12**
B1 A56 5c + 5c orange   1.00 .40

Issued for the benefit of the Costa Rican Red Cross Society. In 1928, owing to a temporary shortage of the ordinary 5c stamp, No. B1 was placed on sale as a regular 5c stamp, the surtax being disregarded.

Discus Thrower SP1

Trophy SP2

Parthenon SP3

1924   **Litho.**   **Imperf.**
B2 SP1 5c dark green   1.60 2.00
B3 SP2 10c carmine   1.60 2.00
B4 SP3 20c dark blue   20.00 20.00
a.   Tête bêche pair   60.00 60.00

Perf. 12
B5 SP1 5c dark green   1.60 2.25
B6 SP2 10c carmine   1.60 2.25
B7 SP3 20c dark blue   3.50 4.00
a.   Tête bêche pair   16.00 20.00
Nos. B2-B7 (6)   29.90 32.50

These stamps were sold at a premium of 10c each, to help defray the expenses of athletic games held at San José in Dec. 1924.

AIR POST STAMPS

Airplane AP1

Perf. 12½
1926, June 4   **Unwmk.**   **Engr.**
C1 AP1 20c ultramarine   3.00 .65

No. 123 Overprinted

1930, Mar. 14   **Perf. 12**
C2 A75 10c carmine rose   2.00 .25

Inverted or double overprints are fakes.

AP3

1930-32   **Perf. 12½**
C3 AP3 5c on 10c dk brn ('32)   .40 .25
C4 AP3 20c on 50c ultra   .50 .25
C5 AP3 40c on 50c ultra   .60 .25
Nos. C3-C5 (3)   1.50 .75

The existence of genuine inverted or double surcharges of Nos. C3-C5 is in doubt.

Telegraph Stamp Overprinted

1930, Mar. 19
C6 AP3 1col orange   2.00 .50

No. O79 Surcharged in Red

1930, Mar. 11
C7 O7 8c on 1col lilac & blk   .80 .65
C8 O7 20c on 1col lilac & blk   1.25 .70
C9 O7 40c on 1col lilac & blk   2.40 1.50
C10 O7 1col on 1col lilac & blk   3.50 2.00
Nos. C7-C10 (4)   7.95 4.85

AP6

Red Surcharge on Revenue Stamps

1931-32   **Perf. 12**
C11 AP6 2col on 2col gray   grn   35.00 35.00
C12 AP6 3col on 5col lil brn   35.00 35.00
C13 AP6 5col on 10col gray   blk   35.00 35.00
Nos. C11-C13 (3)   105.00 105.00

There were two printings of this issue which were practically identical in the colors of the stamps and the surcharges.

Nos. C11 and C13 have the date "1929" on the stamp, No. C12 has "1930."

AP7

Black Overprint on Telegraph Stamp

1932, Mar. 8   **Perf. 12½**
C14 AP7 40c green   3.00 .30
a.   Inverted overprint   32.50 27.50

Unofficial "proofs," inverts and double overprints were made from a defaced plate.

Mail Plane about to Land AP8

Allegory of Flight AP9

1934, Mar. 14   **Perf. 12**
C15 AP8 5c green   .25 .25
C16 AP8 10c carmine rose   .25 .25
C17 AP8 15c chocolate   .40 .25
C18 AP8 20c deep blue   .40 .25
C19 AP8 25c deep orange   .55 .25
C20 AP8 40c olive blk   1.75 .25
C21 AP8 50c gray blk   .85 .25
C22 AP8 60c orange yel   1.50 .25
C23 AP9 75c dull violet   2.75 .50
C24 AP9 1col deep rose   1.50 .25
C25 AP9 2col lt blue   7.50 .95
C26 AP9 5col black   7.50 4.75
C27 AP9 10col red brown   10.00 8.00
Nos. C15-C27 (13)   35.20 16.45

Nos. C15-C27 with holes punched through were for use of government officials.
See Nos. C216-C219. For overprints see Nos. C67-C73, C92-C93, C103-C116, CO1-CO13.

Airplane over Poás Volcano — AP10

1937, Feb. 10
C28 AP10 1c black   .45 .35
C29 AP10 2c brown   .45 .35
C30 AP10 3c dk violet   .45 .35
Nos. C28-C30 (3)   1.35 1.05

First Fair of Costa Rica.

Puntarenas — AP11

Perf. 12, 12½

1937, Dec. 15   **Unwmk.**
C31	AP11	2c black gray	.25	.25
C32	AP11	5c green	.30	.25
C33	AP11	20c deep blue	.25	.25
C34	AP11	1.40col olive brn	2.50	2.50
		Nos. C31-C34 (4)	3.35	3.25

National Bank AP12

1938, Jan. 11   **Wmk. 229**   **Perf. 12½**
C35	AP12	1c purple	.25	.25
C36	AP12	3c red orange	.25	.25
C37	AP12	10c carmine rose	.30	.25
C38	AP12	75c brown	2.50	2.00
		Nos. C35-C38 (4)	3.30	2.75

Nos. C31-C38 for the Natl. Products Exposition held at San José, Dec. 1937.

Airport Administration Building, La Sabana — AP13

1940, May 2   **Engr.**   **Unwmk.**
C39	AP13	5c green	.30	.25
C40	AP13	10c rose pink	.30	.25
C41	AP13	25c lt blue	.40	.25
C42	AP13	35c red brown	.40	.25
C43	AP13	60c red org	.55	.40
C44	AP13	85c violet	1.40	1.00
C45	AP13	2.35col turq grn	6.50	5.50
		Nos. C39-C45 (7)	9.85	7.90

Opening of the Intl. Airport at La Sabana.

Duran Sanatorium AP14

Overprinted in Black

1940, Dec. 2   **Perf. 12**
C46	AP14	10c scarlet	.25	.25
C47	AP14	15c purple	.25	.25
C48	AP14	25c lt blue	.50	.40
C49	AP14	35c bister brn	.70	.65
C50	AP14	60c pck green	1.00	.95
C51	AP14	75c olive	2.75	2.50
C52	AP14	1.35col red org	8.75	8.00
C53	AP14	5col sepia	45.00	40.00
C54	AP14	10col red lilac	140.00	100.00
		Nos. C46-C54 (9)	199.20	153.00

Pan-American Health Day. Nos. C46-C54 exist without overprint. Value, set $5,000.

No. 174 Surcharged in Black or Blue

1940, Dec. 17   **Perf. 14**
C55	A95	15c on 50c yel (Bk)	1.00	1.00
C56	A95	30c on 50c yel (Bl)	1.00	1.00

Pan-American Aviation Day, proclaimed by President F. D. Roosevelt.
The 15c surcharge exists normal and inverted on No. 171, Value, normal $30. Inverted surcharge is worth more.

International Soccer Game at National Stadium — AP15

1941, May 8   **Perf. 12**
C57	AP15	15c red	.80	.25
C58	AP15	30c dp ultra	.90	.25
C59	AP15	40c red brn	.95	.35
C60	AP15	50c purple	1.40	.80
C61	AP15	60c brt green	1.60	.90
C62	AP15	75c yel org	2.75	1.40
C63	AP15	1col dull vio	4.75	4.50
C64	AP15	1.40col rose	9.50	8.75
C65	AP15	2col blue grn	20.00	17.50
C66	AP15	5col black	52.50	37.50
		Nos. C57-C66 (10)	95.15	72.20

Caribbean and Central American Soccer Championship. See Nos. C121-C123. For surcharges see Nos. C145-C147.

Air Post Stamps of 1934 Overprinted or Surcharged in Black

1941, June 2
C67	AP8	5c on 20c dp bl	.25	.25
C68	AP8	15c on 20c dp bl	.25	.25
C69	AP8	40c on 75c dl vio	.35	.25
C70	AP9	65c on 1col dp rose	.65	.50
C71	AP9	1.40col on 2col lt bl	3.25	3.25
C72	AP9	5col black	12.00	12.00
C73	AP9	10col red brn	14.50	12.50
		Nos. C67-C73 (7)	31.25	29.00

Issued in commemoration of the settlement of the Costa Rica-Panama border dispute.
Nos. C67-C73 are found with hyphen omitted in overprint.
Nos. C67-C69 exist with inverted overprint. Value, each, $35.

University Types of 1941

1941, Aug. 26   **Perf. 12**
C74	A107	15c salmon	.25	.25
C75	A106	30c lt blue	.30	.25
C76	A107	40c orange	.40	.30
C77	A106	60c turq green	.50	.40
C78	A107	1col violet	1.90	1.90
C79	A106	2col black	4.75	4.75
C80	A107	5col sepia	16.00	16.00
		Nos. C74-C80 (7)	24.10	23.85

Portrait Type of 1943-47

Designs: 40c, Manuel Aguilar. No. C83, Francisco Morazan. No. C83A, Jose R. De Gallegos. 50c, Jose M. Alfaro. 60c, Francisco M. Oreamuno. 65c, Jose M. Castro. 85c, Juan Rafael Mora. 1col, Jose M. Montealegre. 1.05col, Braulio Carrillo. 1.15col, Jesus Jimenez. 1.40col, Bruno Carranza. 2col, Tomas Guardia.

1943-45   **Engr.**
C81	A109	10c rose pink	.25	.25
C82	A109	40c blue	.30	.25
C82A	A109	40c car rose	.30	.25
C83	A109	45c magenta	.50	.30
C83A	A109	45c black	.25	.25
C84	A109	50c turq grn	1.75	.25
C84A	A109	50c red org	.40	.25
C85	A109	60c brt ultra	.65	.25
C85A	A109	60c brt green	.25	.25
C86	A109	65c scarlet	.95	.30
C86A	A109	65c brt ultra	.30	.25
C87	A109	85c dp org	1.25	.50
C87A	A109	85c dull pur	1.60	.65
C88	A109	1col black	1.60	.50
C88A	A109	1col scarlet	.65	.40
C88B	A109	1.05col bis brn	.90	.55
C89	A109	1.15col red brn	2.10	1.75
C89A	A109	1.15col green	3.00	1.25
C90	A109	1.40col dp vio	3.25	2.40
C90A	A109	1.40col org vel	1.75	1.60
C91	A109	2col black	5.25	1.25
C91A	A109	2col olive grn	1.60	.50
		Nos. C81-C91A (22)	28.85	14.20

Issued: Nos. C82A, C83A, C84A, C85A, C86A, C87A, C88A, C88B, C89A, C90A, C91A, 1945.

See Nos. C124-C127, C179-C181. For surcharges see Nos. C154-C158, C182, C184-C185.

Nos. C26-C27 Ovptd. in Red or Blue

1943, Sept. 16
C92	AP9	5col black (R)	4.50	3.00
C93	AP9	10col red brown (Bl)	5.25	3.25

Mercury and Plane AP31

1944, Jan. 19
C94	AP31	10c red org	.25	.25
C95	AP31	15c dk car	.25	.25
C96	AP31	40c brt ultra	.40	.25
C97	AP31	45c dp red lil	.40	.30
C98	AP31	60c turq org	.55	.40
C99	AP31	1col dk red brn	1.60	.80
C100	AP31	1.40col gray blk	8.75	5.25
C101	AP31	5col violet	24.00	16.00
C102	AP31	10col black	70.00	62.50
		Nos. C94-C102 (9)	106.20	86.00

City of San Ramón founding, 100th anniv.

No. CO10 With Additional Overprint in Black

1944, Nov. 22
C103	AP9	1col deep rose	2.00	.95
a.		Blue overprint	100.00	100.00

Nos. CO1-CO13 Overprinted in Carmine or Black

1945, Jan. 12   **Unwmk.**   **Perf. 12**
C104	AP8	5c green	.60	.50
C105	AP8	10c car rose (Bk)	.60	.55
C106	AP8	15c chocolate	.60	.55
C107	AP8	20c deep blue	.50	.40
C108	AP8	25c dp org (Bk)	.60	.60
C109	AP8	40c olive blk	.35	.35
C110	AP8	50c gray blk	.60	.60
C111	AP8	60c org yel (Bk)	.90	.35
C112	AP8	75c dull violet	.75	.50
C113	AP9	1col dp rose (Bk)	.75	.35
C114	AP9	2col light blue	8.00	4.50
C115	AP9	5col black	8.00	5.50
C116	AP9	10col red brn (Bk)	11.00	8.25
		Nos. C104-C116 (13)	33.25	23.00

No. C104 exists inverted & overprinted in black. This is probably a trial color. Value, $50.

> **Catalogue values for unused stamps in this section, from this point to the end of the section, are for Never Hinged items.**

AP32

Telegraph Stamps Overprinted in Black or Carmine

1945, Feb. 28   **Unwmk.**   **Perf. 12½**
C117	AP32	40c green (C)	.30	.25
C118	AP32	50c ultra (C)	.30	.25
C119	AP32	1col orange (Bk)	1.00	.40
		Nos. C117-C119 (3)	1.60	.90

No. C117 exists with inverted overprint. Value, $10.

Florence Nightingale and Edith Cavell AP33

1945   **Engr.**
C120	AP33	1col black & car	1.00	.50

Costa Rican Red Cross Soc., 60th anniv For surcharge see No. C183.

Soccer Type of 1941 Inscribed: "Febrero 1946"

1946, May 13   **Perf. 12**
C121	AP15	25c green	1.60	.65
C122	AP15	30c dull yellow	2.00	.65
C123	AP15	55c deep blue	2.40	.65
		Nos. C121-C123 (3)	6.00	1.95

Portrait Type of 1943-47

Designs: 25c, Aniceto Esquivel. 30c, Vicente Herrera. 55c, Prospero Fernandez. 75c, Bernardo Soto.

1946, May 12
C124	A109	25c blue	.25	.25
C125	A109	30c red brown	.25	.25
C126	A109	55c plum	.40	.30
C127	A109	75c blue green	.60	.40
		Nos. C124-C127 (4)	1.50	1.20

Hospital of St. John of God AP38

1946, June 24   **Unwmk.**   **Perf. 12½**
Center in Black
C128	AP38	5c yellow grn	.40	.25
C129	AP38	10c dk brown	.50	.25
C130	AP38	15c carmine	.50	.25
C131	AP38	25c dk blue	.50	.25
C132	AP38	30c dp orange	.95	.25
C133	AP38	40c olive grn	.50	.25
C134	AP38	50c violet	.95	.25
C135	AP38	60c dk sl grn	1.90	.55
C136	AP38	75c brown	1.40	.40
a.		Horiz. pair, imperf. btwn.	100.00	
C137	AP38	1col blue	1.90	.35
C138	AP38	2col brn org	2.40	.80
C139	AP38	3col dk vio brn	4.75	2.00
C140	AP38	5col yellow	6.50	2.40
		Nos. C128-C140 (13)	23.15	8.25

Nos. C128, C129, C132 and C135 exist imperf.

Rafael Iglesias — AP39

3col, Ascensión Esquivel. 5col, Cleto González Viquez. 10col, Ricardo Jiménez Oreamuno.

1947, Jan. 15   **Wmk. 215**   **Perf. 14**
Center in Black
C141	AP39	2col blue	2.00	1.25
C142	AP39	3col dp car	2.75	1.60
C143	AP39	5col dk green	4.75	2.00
C144	AP39	10col orange	7.25	5.25
		Nos. C141-C144 (4)	16.75	10.10

Nos. C141-C144 also exist in a souvenir sheet of 4. Value, $600. The sheet in sepia is a proof and worth less.

Nos. C121-C123 Surcharged in Black

1947, May 5   **Unwmk.**   *Perf. 12*
C145 AP15 15c on 25c green .95 .80
C146 AP15 15c on 30c dull yel .95 .80
C147 AP15 15c on 55c dp blue .95 .80
    Nos. C145-C147 (3)   2.85 2.40
   Nos. C145-C147 exist with inverted surcharge.

Columbus in Cariari AP43

1947, May 18   **Engr.**   *Perf. 12½*
Center in Black
C148 AP43 25c green .30 .25
C149 AP43 30c dp ultra .40 .25
C150 AP43 40c red orange .50 .25
C151 AP43 45c violet .65 .30
C152 AP43 50c brt carmine .70 .25
C153 AP43 65c brown org 2.00 .95
    Nos. C148-C153 (6)   4.55 2.25
   For surcharges see Nos. C178, C220-C223.

Nos. C84A, C85A, C127, C88A, and C88B Surcharged with New Value in Black or Red

1947, June 3   *Perf. 12*
C154 A109 15c on 50c red org .40 .30
C155 A109 15c on 60c brt grn (R) .40 .30
C156 A109 15c on 75c bl grn (R) .40 .30
C157 A109 15c on 1col scar .55 .50
C158 A109 15c on 1.05col bis brn .40 .30
    Nos. C154-C158 (5)   2.15 1.70
   No. C155 is known with black surcharge. Value, $10. No. C156 with inverted surcharge. Value, $10.

Early Steam Locomotive — AP44

1947, Nov. 10   *Perf. 12½*
C159 AP44 35c bl grn & blk 2.40 .55
   Electric railroad to the Pacific coast, 50th anniv.

Roosevelt Type of Regular Issue
1947, Aug. 26   *Perf. 12*
C160 A122 15c green .25 .25
C161 A122 30c car rose .25 .25
C162 A122 45c red brown .25 .25
C163 A122 65c orange yel .25 .25
C164 A122 75c blue .30 .25
C165 A122 1col olive grn .50 .35
C166 A122 2col black 1.40 1.00
C167 A122 5col scarlet 2.50 2.40
    Nos. C160-C167 (8)   5.55 4.60
   For surcharges see Nos. C224-C226.

National Theater AP46   Rafael Iglesias AP47

1948, Jan. 26   *Perf. 12½*
Center in Black
C168 AP46 15c brt ultra .25 .25
C169 AP46 20c red .25 .25
C170 AP47 35c dk green .40 .25
C171 AP46 45c purple .50 .25
C172 AP46 50c carmine .50 .25
C173 AP46 75c red violet 1.10 .80
C174 AP46 1col olive 2.00 1.10
C175 AP46 2col red brn 3.25 1.60
C176 AP47 5col org yel 5.25 4.00
C177 AP47 10col brt blue 12.00 8.00
    Nos. C168-C177 (10)   25.50 16.75
   50th anniversary of National Theater.

No. C150 Surcharged in Carmine

1948, Apr. 21
C178 AP43 35c on 40c 1.10 .50
   Exists with surcharge inverted.

Portrait Type of 1943-47
5c, Salvador Lara. 15c, Carlos Duran.

1948   **Engr.**   *Perf. 12*
C179 A109 5c sepia .25 .25
C180 A109 10c olive brown .25 .25
C181 A109 15c violet .25 .25
    Nos. C179-C181 (3)   .75 .75

Nos. C88B, C120, C89A and C90A Surcharged in Carmine or Black

Perf. 12½, 12
1949, Aug. 28   **Unwmk.**
C182 A109 35c on 1.05col bis brn .35 .25
C183 AP33 50c on 1col blk & car .60 .45
   a. 2nd & 3rd lines both read "125 Aniversario" 5.00 3.00
C184 A109 50c on 1.15col grn .85 .70
C185 A109 55c on 1.40col org yel (Bk) .90 .60
    Nos. C182-C185 (4)   2.70 2.00
   125th anniv. of the annexation of the province of Guanacaste.
   Overprint differs on No. C183, with "Guanacaste" in capitals, and lower case "a" in "Anexión."
   The variety "I" for "i" in "Anexion" is found on Nos. C182, C184 and C185.

Symbols of UPU AP48

1950, Jan. 11   **Photo.**   *Perf. 11½*
C186 AP48 15c lilac rose .25 .25
C187 AP48 25c chalky blue .40 .40
C188 AP48 1col gray green .55 .55
    Nos. C186-C188 (3)   1.20 1.20
   75th anniv. of the UPU.

Battle of El Tejar, Cartago AP49

Occupation of Limón — AP50

   25c, Lucha ranch. 35c, Trenches of San Isidro Battalion. 55c, 75c, Observation post. 80c, 1col, Dr. Carlos Luis Valverde.

Inscribed: "Guerra de Liberacion Nacional 1948"
Engraved; Center Photogravure
1950, July 20   *Perf. 12½*
Center in Black
C189 AP49 15c brt car .25 .25
C190 AP50 20c dull green .25 .25
C191 AP49 25c dull blue .30 .25
C192 AP49 35c chestnut .40 .25
C193 AP49 55c lilac .70 .25
C194 AP49 75c red org 1.10 .30
C195 AP50 80c gray 1.10 .50
C196 AP50 1col org yel 1.50 .55
    Nos. C189-C196 (8)   5.60 2.60
   2nd anniv. of the War for Natl. Liberation.

Bull (Cattle Raising) — AP51

   1c, 10c, 2col, Bull. 2c, 30c, 3col, Tuna fishing. 3c, 65c, Pineapple. 5c, 50c, 5col, Bananas. 45c, 80c, 10col, Coffee picker.

Inscribed: "Feria Nacional Agricola Ganadera e Industrial Cartago 1950"
1950, July 27   **Center in Black**
C197 AP51 1c brt green .55 .25
C198 AP51 2c brt blue .55 .25
C199 AP51 3c chocolate .65 .25
C200 AP51 5c dp ultra .65 .25
C201 AP51 10c green .65 .25
C202 AP51 30c purple .65 .25
C203 AP51 45c vermilion .70 .25
C204 AP51 50c blue gray .80 .25
C205 AP51 65c dk blue .80 .25
C206 AP51 80c dp rose 2.00 .65
C207 AP51 2col org yel 4.00 1.60
C208 AP51 3col blue 7.25 4.00
C209 AP51 5col carmine 10.50 6.50
C210 AP51 10col dp claret 10.50 6.50
    Nos. C197-C210 (14)   40.25 21.50
   National Agricultural, Livestock and Industrial Fair, Cartago, 1950.
   For surcharge see No. RA1.

Queen Isabella I and Caravels of Columbus AP52

Unwmk.
1952, Mar. 4   **Engr.**   *Perf. 13*
C211 AP52 15c carmine .30 .25
C212 AP52 20c orange .55 .25
C213 AP52 25c ultra .80 .25
C214 AP52 55c dp green 2.75 .25
C215 AP52 2col violet 5.25 .50
    Nos. C211-C215 (5)   9.65 1.50
   Birth of Queen Isabella I of Spain, 500th anniv.

Mail Plane Type of 1934
1952-53   *Perf. 12*
C216 AP8 5c blue .40 .25
C217 AP8 10c green .55 .25
C218 AP8 15c car rose ('53) .55 .25
C219 AP8 35c purple 1.40 .25
    Nos. C216-C219 (4)   2.75 1.00
   Nos. C216-C217 were reprinted in 1953 in different shades. Values the same.

Nos. C149-C151, C153 Surcharged in Red: "HABILITADO PARA CINCO CENTIMOS 1953"
1953, Apr. 24   *Perf. 12½*
Center in Black
C220 AP43 5c on 30c dp ultra 2.00 1.50
C221 AP43 5c on 40c red org .40 .30
C222 AP43 5c on 45c vio .40 .30
C223 AP43 5c on 65c brn org .40 .30
    Nos. C220-C223 (4)   3.20 2.40

Nos. C161-C163 Surcharged in Black

1953, Apr. 11   *Perf. 12*
C224 A122 15c on 30c car rose .30 .25
C225 A122 15c on 40c red brn .30 .25
C226 A122 15c on 65c org yel .30 .25
    Nos. C224-C226 (3)   .90 .75

Refinery of Vegetable Oils and Fats — AP53

   Industries: 10c, Pottery. 15c, Sugar. 20c, Soap. 25c, Lumber. 30c, Matches. 35c, Textiles. 40c, Leather. 45c, Tobacco. 50c, Preserving. 55c, Canning. 60c, General. 65c, Metals. 75c, Pharmaceuticals. 80c, Pharmaceuticals. 1col, Paper. 2col, Rubber. 3col, Airplane maintenance. 5col, Marble. 10col, Beer.

Engraved; Center Photogravure
1954-59   **Unwmk.**   *Perf. 13x12½*
Center in Black
C227 AP53 5c red .25 .25
C228 AP53 10c dk blue .25 .25
C229 AP53 15c green .25 .25
C230 AP53 20c violet .25 .25
C231 AP53 25c magenta .30 .25
C232 AP53 30c purple .65 .40
C233 AP53 35c red vio .40 .25
C234 AP53 40c black .65 .30
C235 AP53 45c dk green 1.25 .40
C236 AP53 50c vio brown .80 .25
C237 AP53 55c yellow .65 .25
C238 AP53 60c brown 1.50 .65
C239 AP53 65c carmine 1.75 .95
C240 AP53 75c violet 2.40 .80
C240A AP53 80c pur & gray 1.25 .80
C241 AP53 1col blue .80 .40
   a. Imperf., pair 200.00
C242 AP53 2col rose pink 2.40 1.25
C243 AP53 3col ol grn 3.25 2.00
C244 AP53 5col black 5.25 1.60
C245 AP53 10col yellow 14.50 9.50
    Nos. C227-C245 (20)   38.80 21.05
   Issued: 30c, 35c, 60c, 65c, 75c, 2col, 3col, Oct. 20; 80c, Oct. 2, 1959; others, Sept. 1.
   See Nos. C252-C255. For surcharges and overprint, see Nos. C314-C315, C334-C336, RA2, RA11.

Globe, Rotary Emblem — AP54

   25c, Hand protecting boy. 40c, 2col, Hospital. 45c, Globe & palm leaves. 60c, Lighthouse.

1956, Feb. 7   **Engr.**   *Perf. 12*
C246 AP54 10c green .25 .25
C247 AP54 25c dk blue .25 .25
C248 AP54 40c dk brown .50 .40
C249 AP54 45c brt red .30 .25
C250 AP54 60c dk red vio .50 .30
C251 AP54 2col yel org 1.25 .65
    Nos. C246-C251 (6)   3.05 2.10
   50th anniv. of Rotary Intl. (in 1955).

Industries Type of 1954

Designs as in 1954.

Engraved; Center Photogravure
1956, Feb. 17   **Perf. 12**
Center in Black
C252	AP53	5c ultra	.30	.25
C253	AP53	10c violet blue	.40	.25
C254	AP53	15c orange yel	.50	.25
C255	AP53	75c red orange	.80	.30
		Nos. C252-C255 (4)	2.00	1.05

Map of Costa Rica — AP55

10c, Map of Guanacaste. 15c, Inn. 20c, House of Santa Rosa. 25c, Gen. Jose Manuel Quiros. 30c, Old Presidential Palace. 35c, Joaquin Bernardo Calvo. 40c, Luis Molina. 45c, Gen. Jose Joaquin Mora. 50c, Gen. Jose Maria Canas. 55c, Juan Santamaria monument. 60c, National monument. 65c, Antonio Vallerriestra. 70c, Ramon Castilla y Marquesado. 75c, San Carlos fortress. 80c, Francisco Maria Oreamuno. 1col, Pres. Juan Rafael Mora.

1957, June 21   **Engr.**   **Perf. 13½x13**
C256	AP55	5c lt blue	.25	.25
C257	AP55	10c green	.30	.25
C258	AP55	15c dp orange	.30	.25
C259	AP55	20c lt brown	.30	.25
C260	AP55	25c vio blue	.40	.25
C261	AP55	30c violet	.50	.25
C262	AP55	35c car rose	.55	.25
C263	AP55	40c slate	.55	.25
C264	AP55	45c rose red	.65	.25
C265	AP55	50c ultra	.70	.25
C266	AP55	55c ocher	1.10	.25
C267	AP55	60c brt car	.95	.30
C268	AP55	65c carmine	1.10	.30
C269	AP55	70c orange yel	1.25	.30
C270	AP55	75c emerald	1.25	.30
C271	AP55	80c dk brown	1.60	.40
C272	AP55	1col black	1.75	.40
		Nos. C256-C272 (17)	13.50	4.75

Centenary of War of 1856-57.

Cleto Gonzalez Viquez — AP56

Highway and Gonzalez Viquez AP57

Designs: 10c, Ricardo Jimenez Oreamuno. 20c, Puntarenas wharf and Jimenez. 35c, Post and Telegraph Bldg. and Jimenez. 55c, Pipeline and Gonzalez Viquez. 80c, National Library and Gonzalez Viquez. 1col, Electric train and Jimenez. 2col, Gonzales and Jimenez.

1959, Nov. 23   **Engr.**   **Perf. 13½**
C274	AP56	5c car & ultra	.25	.25
C275	AP56	10c red & gray	.25	.25

Perf. 13½x13
C276	AP57	15c dk bl grn & blk	.25	.25
C277	AP57	20c car & brn	.50	.25
C278	AP57	35c rose lil & bl	.25	.25
C279	AP57	55c olive & vio	.50	.25
C280	AP57	80c ultra	.60	.35
C281	AP57	1col orange & mar	.85	.50
C282	AP57	2col gray & mar	2.00	1.60
		Nos. C274-C282 (9)	5.45	3.95

For surcharge and overprint see Nos. C337, C339.

Soccer AP58

Designs: Various soccer scenes.

Perf. 13½
1960, Mar. 7   **Unwmk.**   **Photo.**
C283	AP58	10c black	.30	.30
C284	AP58	25c ultra	.30	.30
C285	AP58	35c red orange	.30	.30
C286	AP58	50c red brown	.40	.30
C287	AP58	85c Prus green	1.10	.90
C288	AP58	5col dp claret	2.50	2.50
		Nos. C283-C288 (6)	4.90	4.60

Souvenir Sheet
Imperf
C289	AP58	2col blue		6.50 6.50

3rd Pan-American Soccer Games, San José, Mar. 1960.
Nos. C283-C288 exist imperf. Value, pair $150.

WRY Uprooted Oak Emblem — AP59

1960, Apr. 7   **Unwmk.**   **Perf. 11½**
Granite Paper
C290	AP59	35c vio bl, blk & yel	.30	.25
C291	AP59	85c black & brt pink	.65	.55

Refugee Year, July 1, 1959-June 30, 1960.

Banner and "OEA" — AP60

35c, "OEA" in oval. 55c, Clasped hands. 2col, "OEA" & map of Americas. 5col, Flags forming bird. 10col, Map of Costa Rica, flags & "OEA."

1960, Aug. 15   **Litho.**   **Perf. 10**
C292	AP60	25c black & multi	.25	.25
a.		Multi, impression sideways	60.00	
C293	AP60	35c multicolored	.30	.30
a.		Pair, imperf. between	60.00	
C294	AP60	55c multicolored	.50	.40
C295	AP60	5col multicolored	3.00	2.75
C296	AP60	10col black & multi	5.00	4.50
		Nos. C292-C296 (5)	9.05	8.20

Souvenir Sheet
Imperf
C297	AP60	2col multicolored	2.75	2.75

Pan-American Conf., San Jose, Aug. 15.

St. Louisa de Marillac and Orphanage — AP61

St. Vincent de Paul — AP62

25c, St. Vincent & old seminary. 50c, St. Louisa & sickroom. 1col, St. Vincent & new seminary.

1960, Oct. 26   **Engr.**   **Perf. 14x13½**
C298	AP61	10c green	.25	.25
C299	AP61	25c carmine	.25	.25
C300	AP61	50c dk blue	.25	.25
C301	AP61	1col brown org	.40	.30
C302	AP62	5col brown	2.10	1.75
		Nos. C298-C302 (5)	3.25	2.80

St. Vincent (1581?-1660) and St. Louisa (1591-1660). Nos. C298-C302 exist imperf.

Runner AP63

Sports: 2c, Woman swimmer. 3c, Bicyclist. 4c, Weight lifter. 5c, Woman tennis player. 10c, Boxers. 25c, Soccer player. 85c, Basketball player. 1col, Baseball batter. 5col, Romulus and Remus statue. 10col, Pistol marksman.

Perf. 13½x14
1960, Dec. 14   **Photo.**   **Unwmk.**
Designs in Black
C303	AP63	1c brt yellow	.25	.25
C304	AP63	2c lt ultra	.25	.25
C305	AP63	3c dp rose	.25	.25
C306	AP63	4c yellow	.25	.25
C307	AP63	5c brt yel grn	.25	.25
C308	AP63	10c pink	.25	.25
C309	AP63	25c lt bl grn	.25	.25
C310	AP63	85c lilac	1.25	.80
C311	AP63	1col gray	1.40	1.00
C312	AP63	10col lt violet	10.50	8.00
		Nos. C303-C312 (10)	14.90	11.55

Souvenir Sheets
Perf. 14x13½
C313	AP63	5col multi	6.00	6.00

17th Olympic Games, Rome, 8/25-9/11. Nos. C303-C313 exist imperf.

No. C255 Srchd. and Ovptd. in Blue or Ultramarine

Engraved and Photogravure
1961, Apr. 21   **Perf. 12**
Center in Black
C314	AP53	25c on 75c red org (Bl)	.25	.25
C315	AP53	75c red orange (U)	.55	.25

15th Amateur Baseball Championships.

Alberto Brenes C. — AP64

No. C317, Manuel Aguilar. No. C318, Agustin Gutierrez L. No. C319, Vicente Herrera.

1961, June 12   **Photo.**   **Perf. 12**
C316	AP64	10c deep claret	.25	.25
C317	AP64	10c blue	.25	.25
C318	AP64	25c bright violet	.25	.25
C319	AP64	25c gray	.25	.25
		Nos. C316-C319 (4)	1.00	1.00

First Continental Congress of Lawyers, San José, June 11-15. Exist imperf. See Nos. C330-C333.

Miguel Obregon — AP65

1961, July 19   **Litho.**   **Perf. 13½**
C320	AP65	10c Prussian green	.40	.25

Birth centenary of Prof. Miguel Obregon L. Exists imperf. Value $50.

UN Food and Agriculture Organization AP66

UN day (UN Organizations): 20c, WHO. 25c, ILO. 30, ITU. 35c, World Meteorological Organization. 45c, UNESCO. 85c, ICAO. 5col, "United Nations" holding the world. 10col, Int. Bank for Reconstruction and Development.

Perf. 11½
1961, Oct. 24   **Unwmk.**   **Engr.**
C321	AP66	10c lt green	.25	.25
C322	AP66	20c orange	.25	.25
C323	AP66	25c Prus grn	.25	.25
C324	AP66	30c dk blue	.25	.25
C325	AP66	35c carmine rose	.90	.25
C326	AP66	45c violet	.30	.25
C327	AP66	85c blue	.65	.55
C328	AP66	10col dk sl grn	5.25	4.50
		Nos. C321-C328 (8)	8.10	6.55

Souvenir Sheet
Imperf
C329	AP66	5col ultra	4.50	4.50

For overprint see No. C338.

Portrait Type of 1961

No. C330, Dr. José Maria Soto Alfaro. No. C331, Dr. Elias Rojas Roman. No. C332, Dr. Andres Saenz Llorente. No. C333, Dr. Juan José Ulloa Giralt.

1961   **Photo.**   **Perf. 13½**
C330	AP64	10c blue green	.25	.25
C331	AP64	10c violet	.25	.25
C332	AP64	25c dark gray	.30	.25
C333	AP64	25c deep claret	.30	.25
		Nos. C330-C333 (4)	1.10	1.00

9th Congress of Physicians of Central America and Panama.

Nos. C229, C236 and C280 Surcharged in Black, Orange or Red

No. C334

No. C334A

Engraved; Center Photogravure
1962   **Perf. 13x12½, 13½x13**
C334	AP53	10c ("10") on 15c	.25	.25
C334A	AP53	10c ("c0.10") on 15c (R)	.25	.25
C335	AP53	25c on 15c	.25	.25
C336	AP53	35c on 50c (O)	.30	.25

Engr.
C337	AP57	85c on 80c (R)	.95	.80
		Nos. C334-C337 (5)	2.00	1.80

No. C336 exists with double surcharge. Value, $35.

Nos. C324 and C282 Overprinted in Red

1962, Sept. 12   *Perf. 11½, 13½x13*
C338 AP66 30c dark blue   .55 .40
C339 AP57 2col gray & mar   1.60 1.25
2nd Central American Phil. Convention.

Revenue Stamp Surcharged in Red

1962   **Engr.**   *Perf. 12*
C341 A124 25c on 2c emer   .25 .25
C342 A124 35c on 2c emer   .25 .25
C343 A124 45c on 2c emer   .40 .30
C344 A124 85c on 2c emer   .70 .55
   Nos. C341-C344 (4)   1.40 1.20

Arms and Malaria Eradication Emblem AP67

1963, Feb. 14   **Photo.**   *Perf. 11½*
C345 AP67 25c brt rose   .25 .25
C346 AP67 35c brown org   .25 .25
C347 AP67 45c ultra   .30 .25
C348 AP67 85c blue grn   .65 .50
C349 AP67 1col dk blue   1.10 .65
   Nos. C345-C349 (5)   2.55 1.90
WHO drive to eradicate malaria.

Central American Tapir — AP68

Designs: 5c, Paca. 25c, Jaguar. 30c, Ocelot. 35c, Whitetail deer. 40c, Manatee. 85c, White-throated capuchin monkey. 5col, White-lipped peccary.

     Perf. 13½
1963, May   **Unwmk.**   **Photo.**
C354 AP68 5c yel ol & brn   .25 .25
C355 AP68 10c orange & sl   .30 .25
C356 AP68 25c blue & yel   .50 .35
C357 AP68 30c lt yel grn & brn   .70 .40
C358 AP68 35c bis & red brn   1.00 .40
C359 AP68 40c emer & sl bl   1.25 .55
C360 AP68 85c green & blk   4.00 .55
C361 AP68 5col gray grn & choc   12.00 4.00
   Nos. C354-C361 (8)   20.00 6.75
   See Nos. C367-C370.

Stamp of 1863 and Packet "Monarch" — AP69

Issue of 1863 and: 2col, Recaredo Bonilla Carrillo, Postmaster, 1862-63. 3col, Burros, overland mail transport, 1839. 10col, Burro railway car.

1963, June 26   **Litho.**
C362 AP69 25c dl rose & chlky bl   .25 .25
C363 AP69 2col gray bl & org   1.75 1.25
C364 AP69 3col bister & emer   3.00 2.00
C365 AP69 10col dl grn & ocher   10.50 6.00
   Nos. C362-C365 (4)   15.50 9.50
Centenary of Costa Rica's stamps. No. C362 is inscribed "William Le Lacheur," the builder and captain of the "Monarch."

Souvenir Sheets

Stamps of 1863 and San José Postmark — AP70

Perf. 13½, Imperf.
1963, June 26   **Unwmk.**
C366 AP70 5col bl, red, grn & org   5.50 5.50
   Cent. of Costa Rica's stamps.
In 1968 examples of No. C366 were overprinted "2-4 Agosto 1968" and "III Exposicion Filatelica Nacional / 'Costa Rica 68'". Value, $10.50.

Animal Type of 1963 Surcharged in Red

No. C367, Little anteater. No. C368, Gray fox. No. C369, Armadillo. No. C370, Great anteater.

1963, Sept. 14   **Photo.**   *Perf. 13½*
C367 AP68 10c on 1c brt grn & org brn   1.10 .30
C368 AP68 25c on 2c org yel & ol grn   1.10 .30
C369 AP68 35c on 3c bluish grn & brn   1.50 .30
C370 AP68 85c on 4c dp rose & dk brn   2.75 .65
   Nos. C367-C370 (4)   6.45 1.55
Examples of No. C370 exist without surcharge. Value, $1,000, less than 10 exist.

Pres. Kennedy — AP71

Portraits — Presidents: 25c, Francisco J. Orlich, Costa Rica. 30c, Julio A. Rivera, El Salvador. 35c, Miguel Ydigoras F., Guatemala. 85c, Dr. Ramon Villeda M., Honduras. 1col, Luis A. Somoza, Nicaragua. 3col, Roberto F. Chiari, Panama.

1963, Dec. 7   **Unwmk.**   *Perf. 14*
Portraits in Black Brown
C371 AP71 25c violet brn   .30 .25
C372 AP71 30c brt lil rose   .30 .25
C373 AP71 35c ocher   .30 .25
C374 AP71 85c gray blue   .50 .25
C375 AP71 1col orange brn   .55 .30
C376 AP71 3col lt ol grn   2.50 1.60
C377 AP71 5col gray   3.25 2.25
   Nos. C371-C377 (7)   7.70 5.15
Meeting of Central American Presidents with Pres. John F. Kennedy, San José, Mar. 18-20, 1963.

Ancestral Figure — AP72

Ancient Art: 5c, Dog, horiz. 10c, Ornamental stool, horiz. 25c, Male figure. 30c, Ceremonial dancer. 35c, Ceramic vase. 50c, Frog. 55c, Bell. 75c, Six-limbed figure. 85c, Seated man. 90c, Bird-shaped jug. 1col, Twin human beaker, horiz. 2col, Alligator, horiz. 3col, Twin-tailed lizard. 5col, Figure under arch. 10col, Polished stone figure.

1963-64   **Photo.**   *Perf. 12*
C378 AP72 5c lt yel grn & Prus grn   .25 .25
C379 AP72 10c buff & dk grn   .25 .25
C380 AP72 25c rose & dk brn   .25 .25
C381 AP72 30c ocher & Prus grn ('64)   .25 .25
C382 AP72 35c sal & sl grn   .25 .25
C383 AP72 45c lt bl & dk brn   .25 .25
C384 AP72 50c dl bl & dk brn   .40 .25
C385 AP72 55c yel grn & dk brn   .55 .25
C386 AP72 75c ocher & dk red brn   .55 .25
C387 AP72 85c yel & red brn   1.40 1.40
C388 AP72 90c cit & red brn   1.75 1.75
C389 AP72 1col lt bl & dk brn ('64)   1.00 .30
C390 AP72 2col buff & dk grn ('64)   1.60 .65
C391 AP72 3col yel grn & dk brn ('64)   5.25 .95
C392 AP72 5col cit & sep ('64)   5.25 5.25
C393 AP72 10col rose lil & sl grn   8.75 8.75
   Nos. C378-C393 (16)   28.00 21.30
For surcharges and overprint see Nos. C395, C397-C398, C400, C426-C428.

Flags of Central American States — AP73

1964, Mar. 11   *Perf. 14*
C394 AP73 30c bl, gray, red & blk   1.00 .35
Central American Independence issue. For surcharge see No. C396.

Nos. C381, C394 and C387 Surcharged

1964, Oct.   *Perf. 12, 14*
C395 AP72 5c on 30c   .55 .25
C396 AP73 15c on 30c   .55 .25
C397 AP72 15c on 85c   .55 .25
   Nos. C395-C397 (3)   1.65 .75

No. C388 Surcharged in Black

1964, Nov. 22   *Perf. 12*
C398 AP72 15c on 90c cit & red brn   .50 .25
Paris Postal Conference.

Alfredo Gonzalez F. — AP74

1965, June   **Photo.**   *Perf. 12*
C399 AP74 35c dk blue green   3.25 .25
50th anniv. of the National Bank and honoring Alfredo Gonzalez Flores (1877-1962), 1st governor of the bank.

No. C390 Overprinted in Black

1965, Aug. 14   **Unwmk.**   *Perf. 12*
C400 AP72 2col buff & dk grn   1.40 .80
75th anniv. of Chapui Asylum, San José.

Girl, FAO Emblem and Hands Holding Grain — AP75

FAO Emblem and: 15c, Map of Costa Rica and silos, horiz. 50c, World population chart and children. 1col, Plane over map of Costa Rica, horiz.

1965, Oct. 25   **Litho.**   *Perf. 14*
C401 AP75 15c lt brn & blk   .25 .25
C402 AP75 35c black & red   .25 .25
C403 AP75 50c ultra & dk grn   .25 .25
C404 AP75 1col grn, blk & sil   .40 .25
   Nos. C401-C404 (4)   1.15 1.00
FAO "Freedom from Hunger" campaign.

Church of Nicoya — AP76

5c, Leonidas Briceno B. 15c, Scroll dated "25 de Julio de 1964." 35c, Map of Guanacaste and Nicoya peninsula. 50c, Dancing couple. 1col, Map showing local products.

1965, Dec. 20   *Perf. 13½x14*
C405 AP76 5c red brn & blk   .40 .25
C406 AP76 10c blue & gray   .40 .25
C407 AP76 15c bis & slate   .40 .25
C408 AP76 35c blue & slate   .40 .25

C409	AP76	50c gray & vio bl	.55 .25
C410	AP76	1col buff & slate	1.10 .40
	Nos. C405-C410 (6)		3.25 1.65

Acquisition of the Nicoya territory.

Runner and Olympic Rings — AP77

Olympic Rings and Emblem: 10c, Bicyclists. 40c, Judo. 65c, Basketball. 80c, Soccer. 1col, Hands holding torches, and Mt. Fuji.

1965, Dec. 23   **Perf. 13x13½**

C411	AP77	5c bister & multi	.25 .25
C412	AP77	10c lt lil & multi	.25 .25
C413	AP77	40c multicolored	.25 .25
C414	AP77	65c lemon & multi	.25 .25
C415	AP77	80c tan & multi	.40 .25
C416	AP77	1col multicolored	.50 .30
a.		Souvenir sheet of 2	6.00 3.00
	Nos. C411-C416 (6)		1.90 1.55

18th Olympic Games, Tokyo, Oct. 10-25, 1964. No. C416a contains two 1col stamps, one like No. C416, the other with gray background replacing yellow orange.

No. C416a was issued both perf and imperf. Same values.

Nos. C411-C416 exist imperf.

Pres. Kennedy Speaking in San José Cathedral — AP78

Designs: 45c, Friendship 7 capsule circling globe, and Kennedy, horiz. 85c, Kennedy and John, Jr. 1col, Curtis-Lee Mansion and flame from Kennedy grave, Arlington, Va.

Perf. 13½x13, 13x13½

1965, Dec. 23   **Litho.**   **Unwmk.**

C417	AP78	45c brt bl & lil	.25 .25
C418	AP78	55c org & brt bl	.30 .25
C419	AP78	85c gray, dk brn & red brn	.55 .40
C420	AP78	1col multicolored	.65 .50
a.		Souvenir sheet of 2	1.25 1.25
	Nos. C417-C420 (4)		1.75 1.40

President John F. Kennedy (1917-63). No. C420a contains two 1col stamps, one like No. C420, the other with green background replacing dark blue. Exists with light blue background instead of green; value $150.

No. C420a was issued both perf and imperf. Same values.

Nos. C417-C420 exist imperf.

For surcharges see Nos. C429-C430.

Firemen with Hoses — AP79

Designs: 5c, Fire engine "Knox," horiz. 10c, 1866 fire pump. 35c, Fireman's badge. 50c, Emblem and flags of Confederation of Central American Fire Brigades.

1966, Mar. 12   **Litho.**   **Perf. 11**

C421	AP79	5c black & red	.50 .25
C422	AP79	10c bister & red	.75 .25
C423	AP79	15c blk, red brn & red	1.00 .25
C424	AP79	35c black & yel	2.00 .25
C425	AP79	50c dk blue & red	4.00 .50
	Nos. C421-C425 (5)		8.25 1.50

Centenary of San José Fire Brigade.

Nos. C381, C383, C386 and C418-C419 Surcharged

a

b

1966, Dec.   **Photo.**   **Perf. 12**

C426	AP72(a)	15c on 30c	.25 .25
C427	AP72(a)	15c on 45c	.25 .25
C428	AP72(a)	35c on 75c	.25 .25

     Litho.   **Perf. 13x13½**

C429	AP78(a)	35c on 55c	.25 .25
C430	AP78(b)	50c on 85c	.45 .45
	Nos. C426-C430 (5)		1.45 1.25

Revenue Stamps (Basic Type of A124) Surcharged

1967, Jan.   **Engr.**   **Perf. 12**

C431	A124	15c on 5c blue	.25 .25
C432	A124	35c on 10c claret	.30 .25
C433	A124	50c on 20c rose red	.50 .25
	Nos. C431-C433 (3)		1.05 .75

Central Bank of Costa Rica — AP80

1967, Mar. 1   **Litho.**   **Perf. 11**

C434	AP80	5c brt green	.35 .25
C435	AP80	15c brown	.35 .25
C436	AP80	35c scarlet	.35 .25
	Nos. C434-C436 (3)		1.05 .75

Power Lines — AP81

Telecommunications Building, San Pedro — AP82

Electrification Program: 15c, Telephone Central. 25c, La Garita Dam. 35c, Rio Mache Reservoir. 50c, Cachi Dam.

1967, Apr. 24   **Litho.**   **Perf. 11**

C437	AP81	5c dark gray	.25 .25
C438	AP82	10c brt rose	.25 .25
C439	AP81	15c brown org	.25 .25
C440	AP82	25c brt ultra	.25 .25
C441	AP82	35c brt green	.30 .25
C442	AP82	50c red brown	.40 .30
	Nos. C437-C442 (6)		1.70 1.55

Chondrorhyncha Aromatica — AP83

Orchids: 10c, Miltonia endresii. 15c, Stanhopea cirrhata. 25c, Trichopilia suavis. 35c, Odontoglossum schlieperianum. 50c, Cattleya skinneri. 1col, Cattleya dowiana. 2col, Odontoglossum chiriquense.

1967, June 15   **Engr.**   **Perf. 13x13½**
Orchids in Natural Colors

C443	AP83	5c multicolored	.25 .25
C444	AP83	10c olive & multi	.40 .25
C445	AP83	15c multicolored	.55 .30
C446	AP83	25c multicolored	.95 .30
C447	AP83	35c dull vio & multi	1.25 .30
C448	AP83	50c brown & multi	1.60 .30
C449	AP83	1col vio & multi	3.50 .80
C450	AP83	2col dk ol bis & multi	6.00 1.50
	Nos. C443-C450 (8)		14.50 4.05

Issued for the University Library.

Institute Emblem — AP84

1967, Oct. 6   **Litho.**   **Perf. 13x13½**

C451	AP84	50c vio bl, lt bl & bl	.40 .25

Inter-American Agriculture Institute, 25th anniv.

Church of Solitude — AP85

Costa Rican Churches: 10c, Basilica of Santo Domingo, Heredia. 15c, Cathedral of Tilaran. 25c, Cathedral of Alajuela. 30c, Mercy Church. 35c, Basilica of Our Lady of Angels. 40c, Church of St. Raphael, Heredia. 45c, Ujarras ruins. 50c, Ruins of parish church, Cartago. 55c, Cathedral of San José. 65c, Parish church, Puntarenas. 75c, Church of Orosi. 80c, Cathedral of St. Isidro, the General. 85c, St. Ramon Church. 90c, Church of the Abandoned. 1col, Coronado Church. 2col, Church of St. Teresita. 3col, Parish Church, Heredia. 5col, Carmelite Church. 10col, Limon Cathedral.

1967, Dec. 15   **Engr.**   **Perf. 12½**

C452	AP85	5c green	.25 .25
C453	AP85	10c blue	.25 .25
C454	AP85	15c lilac	.25 .25
C455	AP85	25c dull yel	.25 .25
C456	AP85	30c orange brn	.25 .25
C457	AP85	35c lt blue	.25 .25
C458	AP85	40c dp orange	.30 .25
C459	AP85	45c dl bl grn	.30 .25
C460	AP85	50c olive	.40 .25
C461	AP85	55c brown	.40 .25
C462	AP85	65c car rose	.65 .25
C463	AP85	75c sepia	.70 .30
C464	AP85	80c yellow	1.40 .45
C465	AP85	85c violet blk	1.60 .45
C466	AP85	90c emerald	1.60 .65
C467	AP85	1col slate	1.25 .35
C468	AP85	2col brt green	5.00 1.75
C469	AP85	3col orange	7.25 3.00
C470	AP85	5col vio blue	8.00 3.00
C471	AP85	10col carmine	9.75 4.50
	Nos. C452-C471 (20)		40.60 17.20

Nos. C452 and C454 exist imperf; Nos. C455 and C470 exist imperf horiz.

See Nos. C561-C576.

LACSA Emblem — AP86

45c, LACSA emblem, jet, horiz. 50c, Decorated wheel, anniversary emblem.

Perf. 13x13½, 13½x13

1967, Dec. 12   **Litho. & Engr.**

C472	AP86	40c ultra, grnsh bl & gold	.25 .25
C473	AP86	45c blk, pale grn, ultra & gold	.30 .25
C474	AP86	50c blue & multi	.40 .25
	Nos. C472-C474 (3)		.95 .75

20th anniv. (in 1966) of Lineas Aereas Costaricenses, LACSA, Costa Rican Airlines.

Scout Directing Traffic — AP87

Designs: 25c, Campfire under tree. 35c, Flag of Costa Rica, Scout flag and emblem. 50c, Encampment, horiz. 65c, Photograph of first Scout troop, horiz.

1968, Mar. 15   **Perf. 13**

C475	AP87	15c lt bl, blk & lt brn	.25 .25
C476	AP87	25c lt ultra, vio bl & org	.25 .25
C477	AP87	35c blue & multi	.40 .25
C478	AP87	50c multicolored	.65 .30
C479	AP87	65c sal, dk bl & brn	.80 .40
	Nos. C475-C479 (5)		2.35 1.45

Costa Rican Boy Scouts, 50th anniversary.

Runner — AP88

Sports: 40c, Women's running. 55c, Boxing. 65c, Bicycling. 75c, Weight lifting. 1col, High diving. 3col, Rifle shooting.

1969, Jan. 17   **Litho.**   **Perf. 10x11**

C481	AP88	30c multi	.25 .25
C482	AP88	40c multi	.25 .25
C483	AP88	55c multi	.25 .25
C484	AP88	65c lil & multi	.30 .25
C485	AP88	75c multi	.30 .25
C486	AP88	1col multi	.40 .25
C487	AP88	3col multi	1.60 .95
	Nos. C481-C487 (7)		3.35 2.45

19th Olympic Games, Mexico City, 10/12-27.

Philatelic Exhibition Emblem — AP89

1969, June 5   **Litho.**   **Perf. 11x10**

C488	AP89	35c multicolored	.25 .25
C489	AP89	40c pink & multi	.25 .25
C490	AP89	50c lt blue & multi	.25 .25
C491	AP89	2col multicolored	.95 .55
	Nos. C488-C491 (4)		1.70 1.30

4th Natl. Philatelic Exhib., San José, 6/5-8.

ILO Emblem
AP90

1969, Oct. 29   Litho.   Perf. 10
C492 AP90 35c bl grn & blk   .25 .25
C493 AP90 50c scarlet & blk   .25 .25

50th anniv. of the ILO.

Soccer — AP91

Designs: 65c, Soccer ball, map of North and Central America. 85c, Soccer player. 1col, Two players in action.

1969, Nov. 23   Litho.   Perf. 11x10
C494 AP91 65c gray & multi   .30 .25
C495 AP91 75c multicolored   .30 .25
C496 AP91 85c multicolored   .40 .30
C497 AP91 1col pink & multi   .55 .40
     Nos. C494-C497 (4)   1.55 1.20

Issued to publicize the 4th Soccer Championships (CONCACAF), Nov. 23-Dec. 7.

Stylized
Crab — AP92

1970, May 14   Litho.   Perf. 12½
C498 AP92 10c blk & lil rose   .25 .25
C499 AP92 15c blk & yel   .25 .25
C500 AP92 25c blk & brn org   .25 .25
C501 AP92 1.10col blk & emer   .55 .25
     Nos. C498-C501 (4)   1.30 1.00

10th Inter-American Cancer Cong., 5/22-29.

Costa Rica No. 124, Magnifying Glass and Stamps — AP93

2col, Father, son with stamps, album.

1970, Sept. 14   Litho.   Perf. 11
C502 AP93 1col ultra, brn & car
          rose   1.00 .25
C503 AP93 2col blk, pink & ultra   1.25 .55

The 5th National Philatelic Exhibition.

EXPO Emblem and Costa Rican Cart — AP94

EXPO Emblem and: 10c, Japanese floral arrangement, vert. 35c, Pavilion and Tower of the Sun. 40c, Japanese tea ceremony. 45c, Woman picking coffee, vert. 55c, Earth seen from moon, vert.

1970, Oct. 22   Litho.   Perf. 13x13½
C504 AP94 10c multicolored   .25 .25
C505 AP94 15c green & multi   .25 .25
C506 AP94 35c blue & multi   .55 .25
C507 AP94 40c gray & multi   .65 .25
C508 AP94 45c multicolored   .70 .25
C509 AP94 55c black & multi   1.90 .30
     Nos. C504-C509 (6)   4.30 1.55

EXPO '70 International Exhibition, Osaka, Japan, Mar. 15-Sept. 13.

Escazu Valley, by Margarita Bertheau — AP95

Paintings: 25c, "Irazu," by Rafael A. Garcia, vert. 80c, Shore landscape, by Teodorico Quiros. 1col, "The Other Face," by Cesar Valverde. 2.50col, Mother and Child, by Luis Daell, vert.

1970, Nov. 4   Litho.   Perf. 12½
C510 AP95 25c multi   .80 .30
C511 AP95 45c multi   .80 .30
C512 AP95 80c multi   1.25 .55
C513 AP95 1col multi   1.25 .65
C514 AP95 2.50col multi   2.50 2.00
     Nos. C510-C514 (5)   6.60 3.80

Arms of Costa Rica, 1964 — AP96

Various Coats of Arms, dated: 10c, Nov. 27, 1906. 15c, Sept. 29, 1848. 25c, Apr. 21, 1840. 35c, Nov. 22, 1824. 50c, Nov. 2, 1824. 1col, Mar. 6, 1824. 2col, May 10, 1823.

1971, Feb. 10   Litho.   Perf. 14x13½
C515 AP96 5c buff & multi   .40 .25
C516 AP96 10c multi   .40 .25
C517 AP96 15c yel & multi   .50 .25
C518 AP96 25c pink & multi   .50 .25
C519 AP96 35c multi   .65 .25
C520 AP96 50c rose & multi   .70 .25
C521 AP96 1col beige & multi   .80 .40
C522 AP96 2col multi   1.60 .80
     Nos. C515-C522 (8)   5.55 2.70

National Theater AP97

1971, Apr. 14   Litho.   Perf. 11
C523 AP97 2col plum   .40 .30

Organization of American States meeting.

José Matias Delgado, Manuel José Arce AP98

Flag of Costa Rica — AP99

Independence Leaders: 10c, Miguel Larreinaga and Manuel Antonio de la Cerda, Nicaragua. 15c, José Cecilio del Valle, Dionisio de Herrera, Honduras. 35c, Pablo Alvarado and Florencio del Castillo, Costa Rica. 50c, Antonio Larrazabal and Pedro Molina, Guatemala. 2col, Costa Rica coat of arms.

1971, Sept. 14   Perf. 13
C524 AP98 5c multi   .25 .25
C525 AP98 10c multi   .25 .25
C526 AP98 15c gray, brn & blk   .25 .25
C527 AP98 35c multi   .25 .25
C528 AP98 50c multi   .25 .25
C529 AP99 1col multi   .25 .25
C530 AP99 2col multi   .40 .40
     Nos. C524-C530 (7)   1.90 1.90

Central American independence, sesqui.

Soccer Federation Emblem — AP100

1971, Dec. 6
C531 AP100 50c multi   .30 .25
C532 AP100 60c multi   .30 .25

50th anniv. of Soccer Federation of Costa Rica.

Children of the World — AP101

1972, Jan. 11   Perf. 12½
C533 AP101 50c multi   .25 .25
C534 AP101 1.10col red & multi   .40 .25

25th anniv. (in 1971) of UNICEF.

Tree of Guanacaste AP102

Designs: 40c, Hermitage, Liberia. 55c, Petroglyphs, Rincón Brujo. 60c, Painted head, sculpture from Curubandé, vert.

1972, Feb. 28   Perf. 11
C535 AP102 20c brn, ol & brt grn   .40 .25
C536 AP102 40c brn & ol   .40 .25
C537 AP102 55c blk & brn   .40 .25
C538 AP102 60c blk, buff & ver   .40 .25
     Nos. C535-C538 (4)   1.60 1.00

Bicentenary of the founding of the city of Liberia, Guanacaste.

Farm and Family — AP103

Designs: 45c, Cattle, dairy products and meat, horiz. 50c, Kneeling figure with plant. 10col, Farmer and map of Americas.

1972, June 30   Litho.   Perf. 12½
C539 AP103 20c multi   .30 .25
C540 AP103 45c multi   .30 .25
C541 AP103 50c dp yel, grn &
           blk   .30 .25
C542 AP103 10col brn, org & blk   2.50 1.75
     Nos. C539-C542 (4)   3.40 2.50

30th anniversary of the Inter-American Institute of Agricultural Sciences.

Inter-American Exhibitions AP104

1972, Aug. 26   Litho.   Perf. 13
C543 AP104 50c orange & brn   .25 .25
C544 AP104 2col blue & vio   .40 .30

4th Interamerican Philatelic Exhibition, EXFILBRA, Rio de Janeiro, Aug. 26-Sept. 2.

First Book Printed in Costa Rica — AP105

Intl. Book Year: 50c, 5col, Natl. Library, horiz.

1972, Dec. 7   Litho.   Perf. 12½
C545 AP105 20c brt blue   .40 .25
C546 AP105 50c gold & multi   .40 .25
C547 AP105 75c multicolored   .40 .25
C548 AP105 5col multicolored   1.90 .95
     Nos. C545-C548 (4)   3.10 1.70

No. C545 exists on thin dull paper with shiny gum. Values: unused $20, used $10.

Road to Irazú Volcano AP106

15c, Coco-Culebra Bay. 40c, Manuel Antonio Beach. 45c, Tourist Office emblem. 50c, Lindora Lake. 60c, San Jose P.O., vert.

1972-73   Perf. 11x11½, 11½x11
C549 AP106 5c like 20c   .30 .25
C550 AP106 15c like 20c   .30 .25
C551 AP106 20c shown   .30 .25
C552 AP106 25c like 15c   .30 .25
C553 AP106 40c multi   .30 .25
C554 AP106 45c multi   .30 .25
C555 AP106 50c multi   .30 .25
C556 AP106 60c multi   .30 .25
C557 AP106 80c like 40c   .40 .25
C558 AP106 90c like 45c   .40 .25
C559 AP106 1col like 50c   .40 .25
C560 AP106 2col like 60c   .70 .50
     Nos. C549-C560 (12)   4.30 3.25

Tourism year of the Americas.
Issued: 20c, 25c, 80c, 90c, 1col, 2col, 12/26; others, 3/21/73.
No. C555 exists with inverted center, used only. Value $10,000.

Church Type of 1967

Designs as before.

1973, July 16   Engr.   Perf. 12½
C561 AP85 5c slate grn   .25 .25
C562 AP85 10c olive   .25 .25
C563 AP85 15c orange   .25 .25
C564 AP85 25c brown   .25 .25
C565 AP85 30c rose claret   .25 .25
C566 AP85 35c violet   .25 .25
C567 AP85 40c brt green   .25 .25
C568 AP85 45c dull yellow   .25 .25
C569 AP85 50c rose magenta   .25 .25
C570 AP85 55c blue   .25 .25
C571 AP85 65c black   .30 .25
C572 AP85 75c rose red   .40 .25
C573 AP85 80c yellow grn   .45 .25
C574 AP85 85c lilac   .50 .25
C575 AP85 90c brt pink   .55 .25
C576 AP85 1col dark blue   .65 .25
     Nos. C561-C576 (16)   5.35 4.00

Human Rights
Flame — AP107

1973, Dec. 10   Photo.   Perf. 10½
C577 AP107 50c black & red   .40   .25
25th anniversary of the Universal Declaration of Human Rights.

OAS
Emblem — AP108

1973, Dec. 17   Litho.   Perf. 10½
C578 AP108 20c dk bl & dp car   .40   .25
25th anniv. of the OAS.

Joaquin Vargas
Calvo — AP109

No. C580, Alejandro Monestel. No. C581, Julio Mata. No. C582, Julio Fonseca. No. C583, Rafael A. Chaves. No. C584, Manuel M. Gutierrez.

1974, Jan. 14
C579 AP109 20c shown   .40   .25
C580 AP109 20c multicolored   .40   .25
C581 AP109 20c multicolored   .40   .25
C582 AP109 60c multicolored   .40   .25
C583 AP109 2col multicolored   .90   .30
C584 AP109 5col multicolored   2.10   1.25
  Nos. C579-C584 (6)   4.60   2.55
Costa Rican composers honored by the National Symphony Orchestra.

Revenue Stamps
Overprinted in
Black — AP110

1974, Apr. 5   Engr.   Perf. 12
C585 AP110 50c brown   .25   .25
C586 AP110 1col violet   .30   .25
C587 AP110 2col orange   .70   .40
C588 AP110 5col olive   1.75   1.75
  Nos. C585-C588 (4)   3.00   2.65

Telephone
Building, San
Pedro — AP111

Designs: 65c, Rio Macho Control, horiz. 85c, Turbines, Rio Macho Center. 1.25col, Cachi Dam and reservoir, horiz. 2col, I.C.E. Headquarters.

1974, July 30   Litho.   Perf. 10½
C589 AP111 50c gold & multi   .25   .25
C590 AP111 65c gold & multi   .25   .25
C591 AP111 85c gold & multi   .30   .25
C592 AP111 1.25col gold & multi   .40   .25
C593 AP111 2col gold & multi   .80   .40
  Nos. C589-C593 (5)   2.00   1.40
25th anniversary of Costa Rican Electrical Institute (I.C.E.).

EXFILMEX 74
Emblem
AP112

1974, Aug. 22   Perf. 13
C594 AP112 65c green   .25   .25
C595 AP112 3col lilac rose   .65   .40
5th Inter-American Philatelic Exhibition, EXFILMEX-74 UPU, Mexico City, Oct. 26-Nov. 3.

Map of
Costa Rica,
4-S Emblem
AP113

50c, Young harvesters and 4-S emblem.

1974, Oct. 7   Litho.   Perf. 12x11
C596 AP113 20c brt green   .40   .25
C597 AP113 50c multicolored   .40   .25
25th anniversary of 4-S Clubs of Costa Rica (similar to US 4-H Clubs).

Roberto Brenes
Mesen — AP114

Designs: 85c, "Love and Death," manuscript. 5col, Hands of writer, horiz.

1974, Oct. 14   Litho.   Perf. 10½
C598 AP114 20c black & brn   .25   .25
C599 AP114 85c black & red   .25   .25
C600 AP114 5col black & red brn   1.60   .90
  Nos. C598-C600 (3)   2.10   1.40
Mesen, educator & writer, birth centenary.

"Life Insurance"
AP115

Designs: 20c, Ricardo Jiménez Oreamuno and Tomás Soley Güell, horiz. 50c, Harvest Insurance (hand holding shovel), horiz. 85c, Maritime insurance (hand holding paper boat). 1.25col, INS emblem. 2col, Workers rehabilitation (arm with crutch). 2.50col, Workers' Compensation (hand holding wrench). 20col, Fire insurance (hands protecting house).

1974, Oct. 30   Perf. 14
C601 AP115 20c multi   .25   .25
C602 AP115 50c multi   .25   .25
C603 AP115 65c multi   .25   .25
C604 AP115 85c multi   .25   .25
C605 AP115 1.25col multi   .30   .25
C606 AP115 2col multi   .55   .25
C607 AP115 2.50col multi   .65   .40
C608 AP115 20col multi   4.50   4.50
  Nos. C601-C608 (8)   7.00   6.40
Costa Rican Insurance Institute (Instituto Nacional de Seguros, INS), 50th anniversary.
For surcharges see Nos. C721-C722.

WPY
Emblem — AP116

1974, Nov. 13   Litho.   Perf. 11x11½
C609 AP116 2col vio bl & red   .50   .25
World Population Year.

Oscar J. Pinto
F. — AP117

Designs: 50c, Alberto Montes de Oca D., champion sharpshooter. 1col, Eduardo Garnier, sports promoter. O. J. Pinto, introducer of soccer.

1974, Dec. 2   Perf. 13
C610 AP117 20c gray & dk bl   .25   .25
C611 AP117 50c gray & dk bl   .25   .25
C612 AP117 1col gray & dk bl   .50   .25
  Nos. C610-C612 (3)   1.00   .75
First Central American Olympic Games, held in Guatemala, 1973.

Mormodes
Buccinator
AP118

Masdevallia
Ephippium
AP119

Orchids: No. C614, Gongora claviodora. No. C616, Encyclia spondiadum. No. C617, Lycaste skinneri alba. No. C618, Peristeria elata. No. C619, Miltonia roezelii. No. C620, Brassavola digbyana. No. C621, Epidendrum mirabile. No. C622, Barkeria lindleyana. No. C623, Cattleya skinneri. No. C624, Sobralia macrantha. No. C625, Lycaste cruenta. No. C626, Oncidium obryzatum. No. C627, Gongora armeniaca. No. C628, Sievekingia suavis. No. C629, Hexisea imbricata. No. C630, Warcewiczella discolor. No. C631, Oncidium kramerianum. No. C632, Cattleya dowiana.

1975, Mar. 7   Litho.   Perf. 10½, 13½
C613 AP118 25c shown   .65   .25
C614 AP118 25c multi   .65   .25
C615 AP119 25c shown   .65   .25
C616 AP119 25c multi   .65   .25
  a.   Block of 4, #C613-C616   2.60   1.25
  b.   As "a," perf. 10½   1.60   1.25
C617 AP118 65c multi   1.60   .25
C618 AP118 65c multi   1.60   .25
C619 AP119 65c multi   1.60   .25
C620 AP119 65c multi   1.60   .25
  a.   Block of 4, #C617-C620, perf. 13½   6.50   2.25
  b.   As "a," perf. 10½   16.00   2.25
C621 AP118 80c multi   2.25   .30
C622 AP118 80c multi   2.25   .30
C623 AP119 80c multi   2.25   .30
C624 AP119 80c multi   2.25   .30
  a.   Block of 4, #C621-C624   9.00   2.50
  b.   As "a," perf. 10½   16.00   2.50
C625 AP118 1.40col multi   2.75   .40
C626 AP118 1.40col multi   2.75   .40
C627 AP119 1.40col multi   2.75   .40
C628 AP119 1.40col multi   2.75   .40
  a.   Block of 4, #C625-C628   11.00   4.50

---

  b.   As "a," perf. 10½   9.75   4.50
Perf. 13½
C629 AP118 1.75col multi   1.60   .40
C630 AP118 2.15col multi   1.60   .55
C631 AP119 2.50col multi   2.75   1.10
C632 AP119 3.25col multi   3.25   1.40
  Nos. C613-C632 (20)   38.20   8.25
5th National Orchid Exhibition.
Nos. C613-C628 were printed in both perforations on two different papers: dull finish and shiny. Nos. C629-C632 were printed on shiny paper.
Most examples of Nos. C617-C620, perf 10½, were surcharged.
For overprints and surcharges see Nos. C715-C720, C723-C728.

Radio Club
Emblem
AP120

Members' Flags and
Emblem — AP121

Design: 2col, Federation emblem.

1975, Apr. 16   Litho.   Perf. 13½
C633 AP120 1col blk & red lil   .50   .25
C634 AP121 1.10col multi   .55   .25
C635 AP120 2col black & bl   .95   .25
  Nos. C633-C635 (3)   2.00   .75
16th Central American Radio Amateurs' Convention, San José, May 2-4.

Nicoya Beach
AP122

Designs: 75c, Driving cattle. 1col, Colonial Church, Nicoya. 3col, Savannah riders, vert.

1975, Aug. 1   Litho.   Perf. 13½
C636 AP122 25c gray & multi   .25   .25
C637 AP122 75c gray & multi   .25   .25
C638 AP122 1col gray & multi   .30   .25
C639 AP122 3col gray & multi   1.00   .85
  Nos. C636-C639 (4)   1.80   1.60
Sesqui. of annexation of Nicoya District.

Costa
Rica #158
AP123

Designs (Type A90 of 1932): No. C641, #159. No. C642, #160. No. C643, #161.

1975, Aug. 14   Litho.   Perf. 12
C640 AP123 2.20col blk & org   .40   .35
C641 AP123 2.20col blk & dk grn   .40   .35
C642 AP123 2.20col blk & car rose   .40   .35
C643 AP123 2.20col blk & dk bl   .40   .35
  a.   Block of 4, #C640-C643   4.00   4.00
6th Natl. Phil. Exhib., San José, Aug. 14-17.
For surcharges see Nos. C885-C892.

IWY Emblem
AP124

1975, Oct. 9　**Litho.**　**Perf. 10½**
C644	AP124	40c vio bl & red	.25	.25
C645	AP124	1.25col blk & ultra	.40	.25

International Women's Year 1975.

UN Emblem
AP125

UN, 30th Anniv.: 60c, UN General Assembly, horiz. 1.20col, UN Headquarters, NY.

1975, Oct. 24　　　　　**Perf. 12**
C646	AP125	10c bl & blk	.25	.25
C647	AP125	60c multi	.25	.25
C648	AP125	1.20col multi	.40	.25
	Nos. C646-C648 (3)		.90	.75

The Visitation,
by Jorge
Gallardo
AP126

Paintings by Jorge Gallardo: 1col, Nativity and Star. 5col, St. Joseph in his Workshop, Virgin and Child.

1975, Nov. 3　　　　　**Perf. 10½**
C649	AP126	50c multi	.30	.25
C650	AP126	1col multi	.50	.25
C651	AP126	5col multi	1.75	.70
	Nos. C649-C651 (3)		2.55	1.20

Christmas 1975.

"20-30" Club
Emblem — AP127

1976, Jan. 16　**Litho.**　**Perf. 12**
C652	AP127	1col multi	.40	.25

"20-30" Club of Costa Rica, 20th anniv.

Quercus Brenessi
Trel — AP128

Plants: 30c, Maxillaria albertii schecht. 55c, Calathea brenesii standl. 2col, Brenesia costaricensis schlecht. 10col, Philodendron brenesii standl.

1976, Mar. 1　　　　　**Perf. 10½**
C653	AP128	5c multi	.50	.25
C654	AP128	30c multi	.50	.25
C655	AP128	55c multi	.75	.25
C656	AP128	2col tan & multi	1.25	.40
C657	AP128	10col multi	5.50	3.00
	Nos. C653-C657 (5)		8.50	4.15

Prof. Alberto Manuel Brenes Mora, botanist, birth centenary.

"Literary
Development"
AP129

Designs: 1.10col, Man holding book, stylized. 5col, Costa Rican flag emanating from book, horiz.

1976, Apr. 9　**Litho.**　**Perf. 16**
C658	AP129	15c multi	.25	.25
C659	AP129	1.10col multi	.25	.25
C660	AP129	5col multi	.95	.80
	Nos. C658-C660 (3)		1.45	1.30

Publishing in Costa Rica.
Nos. C658-C660 exist imperf.

Postrider, 1839 — AP130

Costa
Rica No.
13, Post
Office
AP131

Designs: 65c, Costa Rica No. 14 and Post Office. 85c, Costa Rica No. 15 and Post Office. 2col, UPU Monument, Bern, vert.

1976, May 24　　　　　**Perf. 10½**
C661	AP130	20c apple grn & blk	.30	.25
C662	AP131	50c bister & multi	.30	.25
C663	AP131	65c multi	.30	.25
C664	AP131	85c multi	.30	.25
C665	AP130	2col blk & lt bl	.80	.50
	Nos. C661-C665 (5)		2.00	1.50

Cent. of UPU (in 1974).
Nos. C662-C664 exist without the surcharges on reproductions of Nos. 13-15.

Telephones, 1876
and 1976 — AP132

Designs: 2col, Wall telephone. 5col, Alexander Graham Bell.

1976, June 28
C666	AP132	1.60col lt bl & blk	.40	.25
C667	AP132	2col multicolored	.50	.25
C668	AP132	5col yellow & blk	1.25	.95
	Nos. C666-C668 (3)		2.15	1.45

Centenary of first telephone call by Alexander Graham Bell, Mar. 10, 1876.

Inverted Center Stamp of 1901 and
Association Emblems — AP133

Design: 5col, 1901 stamp between Costa Rican Philatelic Society and Interamerican Philatelic Federation emblems.

1976, Nov. 11　**Litho.**　**Perf. 10½**
C669	AP133	50c multi	.25	.25
C670	AP133	1col multi	.25	.25
C671	AP133	2col multi	.40	.25
	Nos. C669-C671 (3)		.90	.75

Souvenir Sheet
Perf. 12
C672	AP133	5col multi	5.25	2.50

7th Natl. Phil. Exhib. and 9th Plenary Assembly of the Interamerican Phil. Fed. (FIAF), San José, Nov. 1976.
No. C670 exists in colors of No. C671.
No. C671 exists on thin dull paper, with bright gum. Value, mint, $25.
No. C672 was issued both perf and imperf. Same values.

"Seeing Eye"
and Map of
Costa Rica
AP134

Amadeo Quiros
Blanco — AP135

1976, Nov. 22　　　　　**Perf. 16**
C673	AP134	35c black & blue	.25	.25
C674	AP135	2col multicolored	.55	.40

General Audit Office, 25th anniversary.

Nurse Attending
Child — AP136

1.10col, National Children's Hospital, horiz.

1976, Nov. 29
C675	AP136	90c multi	.25	.25
C676	AP136	1.10col multi	.25	.25

5th Panamerican Congress of Pediatric Surgery and 12th Congress of Pediatrics.

LACSA Circling
Globe — AP137

Designs: 1.20col, Route map. 3col, LACSA emblem and Costa Rican flag.

1976, Dec. 1　　　　　**Perf. 10½**
C677	AP137	1col multi	.25	.25
C678	AP137	1.20col multi	.40	.25
C679	AP137	3col multi	1.10	.70
	Nos. C677-C679 (3)		1.75	1.20

Costa Rican Air Lines (LACSA), 30th anniversary.

Boston Tea
Party
AP138

US Bicent.: 5col, Declaration of Independence. 10col, Ringing Liberty Bell to announce Independence, vert.

1976, Dec. 24
C680	AP138	2.20col multi	.40	.30
C681	AP138	5col multi	1.00	.70
C682	AP138	10col multi	1.75	1.40
	Nos. C680-C682 (3)		3.15	2.40

Tree of
Guanacaste
AP139

Felipe J.
Alvarado
AP140

Designs (Rotary Emblem and): 60c, Dr. Paul Blanco Cervantes Hospital, horiz. 3col, Map of Costa Rica, horiz. 10col, Paul Harris.

1977, Mar. 31　**Litho.**　**Perf. 16**
C683	AP139	40c multi	.25	.25
C684	AP140	50c multi	.25	.25
C685	AP139	60c multi	.25	.25
C686	AP139	3col multi	.95	.65
C687	AP140	10col multi	3.25	2.50
	Nos. C683-C687 (5)		4.95	3.90

Rotary Club of San José, 50th anniversary.

Boruca Cloth
AP141

Design: 1.50col, Painted wood ornament.

1977, Feb. 22
C688	AP141	75c multi	.25	.25
C689	AP141	1.50col multi	.30	.25

Natl. Artisan & Small Industry Program.

Juana
Pereira — AP142

Designs: 1col, First Church of Our Lady of the Angels, horiz. 1.10col, Our Lady of the Angels (gold sculpture). 1.25col, Crown of Our Lady of the Angels.

1977, June 6　**Litho.**　**Perf. 10½**
C690	AP142	50c multi	.25	.25
C691	AP142	1col multi	.25	.25
C692	AP142	1.10col multi	.25	.25
C693	AP142	1.25col multi	.40	.25
	Nos. C690-C693 (4)		1.15	1.00

50th anniv. of the coronation of Our Lady of the Angels, patron saint of Costa Rica.

Alonso de
Anguiciana de
Gamboa — AP143

Designs: 75c, Church of Esparza. 1col, Statue of Our Lady of Candlemas. 2col, Statue of Diego de Artieda y Chirino.

1977, July 4　**Litho.**　**Perf. 10½**
C694	AP143	35c multi	.25	.25
C695	AP143	75c multi	.25	.25
C696	AP143	1col multi	.30	.25
C697	AP143	2col multi	.65	.40
	Nos. C694-C697 (4)		1.45	1.15

400th anniv. of the founding of Esparza.
For surcharge see No. C883.

CARE Emblem and Child — AP144

1col, CARE emblem and soybeans, horiz.

1977, Sept. 14   Litho.   Perf. 16
C698 AP144 80c multi   .25   .25
C699 AP144 1col multi   .40   .25
    20th anniversary of CARE (relief organization) in Costa Rica.

Institute's Emblem — AP145

First Map of Americas, 1540 — AP146

1977, Oct. 21   Litho.   Perf. 16
C700 AP145   50c blk & multi   .50   .25
C701 AP146 1.40col blk & multi   .95   .40
    Hispanic Cultural Institute of Costa Rica, 25th anniversary.

Mercy Church, by Ricardo Ulloa B. — AP147

Paintings: 1col, Christ, by Floria Pinto de Herrero. 5col, St. Francis and the Birds, by Louisa Gonzalez Y Saenz.

1977, Nov. 9   Litho.   Perf. 10½
C702 AP147 50c multi   .40   .25
C703 AP147 1col multi   .40   .25
C704 AP147 5col multi   1.75   .70
    Nos. C702-C704 (3)   2.55   1.20

Health Ministry Emblem — AP148

1977, Nov. 16   Perf. 16
C705 AP148 1.40col multi   .40   .25
    Creation of Ministry of Health.

Picnic — AP149

Designs: 50c, Weaver. 2col, Beach scene. 5col, Fruit and vegetable market. 10col, Swans on lake.

1978, Mar. 21   Litho.   Perf. 10½
C706 AP149 50c blk & multi   .25   .25
C707 AP149 1col blk & multi   .40   .25
C708 AP149 2col blk & multi   1.00   .25
C709 AP149 5col blk & multi   1.90   .85
C710 AP149 10col blk & multi   2.50   1.90
    Nos. C706-C710 (5)   6.05   3.50
    Conf. of Latin American Tourist Organizations.

San Martin — AP150

1978, Aug. 7   Litho.   Perf. 10½
C711 AP150 5col multi   1.25   .80
    Gen. José de San Martin (1778-1850), soldier and statesman, fought for South American independence.

Geographical Institute Emblem — AP151

1978, Aug. 28   Litho.   Perf. 12½
C712 AP151 5col multi   1.25   .65
    Pan-American Geography and History Institute, 50th anniversary. Exists imperf.

University Federation Emblem — AP152

1978, Sept. 18   Perf. 11
C713 AP152 80c ultra   .40   .25
    Central American University Federation, 30th anniversary.

Emblems — AP153

1978, Oct. 24   Perf. 16
C714 AP153 2col aqua, blk & gold   .55   .40
    6th Interamerican Philatelic Exhibition, Argentina 78, Buenos Aires, Oct. 1978.

Nos. C629-C631 Overprinted

1978, Nov. 1   Litho.   Perf. 13½
C715 AP118 1.75col multi   .55   .30
C716 AP118 2.15col multi   .70   .40
C717 AP119 2.50col multi   .95   .55
    Nos. C715-C717 (3)   2.20   1.25
1st Pan Am flight in Costa Rica, 50th anniv.

Nos. C629-C631 Overprinted: "50 Aniversario de la / visita de Lindbergh a / Costa Rica 1928-1978"

1978, Nov. 1
C718 AP118 1.75col multi   1.40   .30
C719 AP118 2.15col multi   1.60   .40
C720 AP119 2.50col multi   2.10   .50
    Nos. C718-C720 (3)   5.10   1.20
    50th anniversary of Lindbergh's visit.

Nos. C603 and C607 Surcharged

1978, Nov. 8   Perf. 14
C721 AP115 50c on 65c multi   .25   .25
C722 AP115 2col on 2.50col multi   .55   .25
    Asilo Carlos Maria Ulloa, birth centenary.

No. C617-C620, C630-C631 Surcharged

Perf. 10½, 13½
1978, Nov. 13   Litho.
C723 AP118   50c on 65c   .65   .60
C724 AP118   50c on 65c   .65   .60
C725 AP119   50c on 65c   .65   .60
C726 AP119   50c on 65c   .65   .60
    a.   Block of 4, #C723-C726   2.75   2.75
C727 AP118 1.20col on 2.15col   1.25   .55
C728 AP119   2col on 2.50col   1.25   .55
    Nos. C723-C728 (6)   5.10   3.50

    Nos. C723-C726, perf. 13½, value $20, unused, $10, used, each. No. C726a, unused, $400.

Star over Map of Costa Rica — AP154

1978, Nov. 13   Perf. 10½
C729 AP154 50c blue & blk   .25   .25
C730 AP154 1col rose lil & blk   .25   .25
C731 AP154 5col orange & blk   1.40   .65
    a.   Strip of 3, #C729-C731   2.00   2.00
    Christmas 1978. Nos. C729-C731 printed in sheets of 100 and se-tenant in sheet of 15 (3x5). Value, se-tenant sheet, $20.

"Flying Men," Chorotega AP155

Designs: 1.20col, Oviedo giving his History of Indies to Duke of Calabria, horiz. 10col, Lord of Oviedo's coat of arms.

1978, Nov. 20   Perf. 11½
C732 AP155   85c multi   .25   .25
C733 AP155 1.20col blk & lt bl   .25   .25
C734 AP155   10col multi   2.00   2.00
    Nos. C732-C734 (3)   2.50   2.50
    500th birth anniv. of Gonzalo Fernandez de Oviedo, 1st chronicler of Spanish Indies.

Msgr. Domingo Rivas AP156

San José Cathedral AP157

1978, Dec. 6   Perf. 16, 13½ (20col)
C735 AP156 1col black & indigo   .25   .25
C736 AP157 20col multicolored   3.75   3.50
    Centenary of the Cathedral of San José.

View of Coco Island AP158

Designs: 2.10, 3, 5 col, various views of Coco Island. 10col, Installation of memorial plaque, people and flag. 5, 10col vert.

1979, Apr. 30   Perf. 10½
C737 AP158 90c multi   .40   .25
C738 AP158 2.10col multi   .80   .40
C739 AP158 3col multi   1.25   .55
C740 AP158 5col multi   1.90   1.00
C741 AP158 10col multi   3.75   2.25
    a.   Souv. sheet, #C737-C741   12.00   12.00
    Nos. C737-C741 (5)   8.10   4.45
    Visit of Pres. Rodrigo Carazo Odio to Coco Island, June 24, 1978, in the interest of national defense.
    No. C741a exists imperf. Value $750.

Shrimp AP159

Designs: 85c, Mahogany snapper. 1.80col, Corvina. 3col, Crayfish. 10col, Tuna.

1979, May 14   Litho.   Perf. 13½
C742 AP159 60c multi   .50   .25
C743 AP159 85c multi   .50   .25
C744 AP159 1.80col multi   .95   .25
C745 AP159 3col multi   1.40   .55
C746 AP159 10col multi   5.00   3.50
    Nos. C742-C746 (5)   8.35   4.80
    Marine life protection.

Hungry Nestlings, IYC Emblem — AP160

1979, May 24   **Perf. 11**
C747	AP160	1col multi	.80 .25
C748	AP160	2col multi	1.60 .50
C749	AP160	20col multi	10.50 5.50
	Nos. C747-C749 (3)		12.90 6.25

International Year of the Child.

Microwave Transmitters, Mt. Irazu — AP161

Design: 1col, Arenal Dam, horiz.

1979, June 28   **Litho.**   **Perf. 14**
C750	AP161	1col multi	.25 .25
C751	AP161	5col multi	1.10 .70

Costa Rican Electricity Institute, 30th anniversary.

Costa Rica No. 1 and Rowland Hill AP162

Design: 10col, Penny Black and Hill.

1979, July 16   **Perf. 13**
C752	AP162	5col lil rose & bl gray	1.25 .55
C753	AP162	10col dl bl & blk	2.40 1.25

Sir Rowland Hill (1795-1879), originator of penny postage.

Poverty, by Juan Ramon Bonilla AP163

National Sculpture Contest: 60c, Hope, by Hernan Gonzalez. 2.10col, Cattle, by Victor M. Bermudez, horiz. 5col, Bust of Clorito Picado, by Juan Rafael Chacon. 20col, Mother and Child, by Francisco Zuniga.

1979, July 16   **Litho.**   **Perf. 12**
C754	AP163	60c multi	.25 .25
C755	AP163	1col multi	.30 .25
C756	AP163	2.10col multi	.65 .25
C757	AP163	5col multi	1.60 1.10
C758	AP163	20col multi	5.25 2.50
	Nos. C754-C758 (5)		8.05 4.35

Danaus Plexippus — AP164

Butterflies: 1col, Phoebis philea. 1.80col, Rothschildia. 2.10col, Prepona omphale. 2.60col, Marpesia marcella. 4.05col, Morpho cypris.

1979, Aug. 31   **Litho.**   **Perf. 13½**
C759	AP164	60c multi	3.00	.40
C760	AP164	1col multi	5.00	.40
C761	AP164	1.80col multi	7.00	.65
C762	AP164	2.10col multi	10.00	1.25
C763	AP164	2.60col multi	10.00	2.50
C764	AP164	4.05col multi	18.00	3.50
	Nos. C759-C764 (6)		53.00	8.70

SOS Emblem, Houses AP165

Children's Drawings: 5col, 5.50col, Landscapes, diff.

1979, Sept. 18
C765	AP165	2.50col multi	.95 .40
C766	AP165	5col multi	2.00 .60
C767	AP165	5.50col multi	2.40 .90
	Nos. C765-C767 (3)		5.35 1.90

SOS Children's Villages, 30th anniversary.

President Type of 1943

Presidents of Costa Rica: 60c, Rafael Yglesias C. 85c, Ascension Esquivel Ibarra. 1col, Cleto Gonzalez Viquez. 2col, Ricardo Jimenez Oreamuno.

1979, Oct. 8   **Litho.**   **Perf. 13½**
C768	A109	10c dk blue	.25 .25
C769	A109	60c dull purple	.25 .25
C770	A109	85c red orange	.25 .25
C771	A109	1col red orange	.30 .25
C772	A109	2col brown	.65 .40
a.		Strip of 5, #C768-C772	1.75 1.40
	Nos. C768-C772 (5)		1.70 1.40

Printed in sheets of 100 and se-tenant in sheets of 25 (5x5).
See Nos. C790-C794.

Holy Family, Creche — AP167

1979, Nov. 16   **Litho.**   **Perf. 12½**
C773	AP167	1col multi	.25 .25
C774	AP167	1.60col multi	.65 .25

Christmas 1979.

Reforestation AP168

1980, Jan. 14   **Litho.**   **Perf. 11**
C775	AP168	1col multi	.25 .25
C776	AP168	3.40col multi	.65 .50

Anatomy Lesson, by Rembrandt AP169

1980, Feb. 7   **Litho.**   **Perf. 10½**
C777	AP169	10col multi	4.00 1.75

Legal medicine teaching in Costa Rica, 50th anniversary.

Rotary Intl., 75th Anniv. — AP170

1980, Feb. 26   **Perf. 16**
C778	AP170	2.10col multi	.35 .25
C779	AP170	5col multi	1.00 .65

14th Intl. Symposium on Remote Sensing of the Environment, San José, Apr. 23-30 — AP171

Designs: 2.10col, Puerto Limon. 5col, Gulf of Nicoya, satellite photo.

1980, Mar. 10   **Litho.**   **Perf. 12½**
C780	AP171	2.10col multi	.35 .25
C781	AP171	5col multi	1.00 .65

Exist imperf.

Soccer, Moscow '80 Emblem — AP172

3col, Bicycling. 4.05col, Baseball. 20col, Swimming.

1980, Apr. 16   **Litho.**   **Perf. 10½**
C782	AP172	1col shown	.50 .25
C783	AP172	3col multi	8.00 .75
C784	AP172	4.05col multi	8.00 1.00
C785	AP172	20col multi	8.00 5.00
	Nos. C782-C785 (4)		24.50 7.00

22nd Summer Olympic Games, Moscow, July 19-Aug. 3.

Poas Volcano AP173

2.50col, Cahuita Beach.

1980, May 14   **Litho.**   **Perf. 10½**
C786	AP173	1col shown	.25 .25
C787	AP173	2.50col multi	.55 .40

National Parks Service, 10th anniversary.

José Maria Zeledon Brenes, Score — AP174

Design: 10col, Manuel Maria Gutierrez.

1980, June 25   **Litho.**   **Perf. 12½**
C788	AP174	1col multi	.25 .25
C789	AP174	10col multi	1.60 1.40

National anthem composed by Brenes (words) and Gutierrez (music). Nos. C788-C789 exist imperf.

President Type of 1943

1col, Alfredo Gonzalez F. 1.60col, Federico Tinoco G. 1.80col, Francisco Aguilar B. 2.10col, Julio Acosta G. 3col, Leon Cortes C.

1980, Aug. 14   **Litho.**   **Perf. 11**
C790	A109	1col dk red	.25 .25
C791	A109	1.60col slate bl	.40 .25
C792	A109	1.80col brown	.40 .25
C793	A109	2.10col dull green	.50 .25
C794	A109	3col dark purple	.80 .50
	Nos. C790-C794 (5)		2.35 1.50

8th Natl. Phil. Exhib. — AP175

1980, Sept. 11   **Perf. 13½**
C795	AP175	5col multi	.80 .60
C796	AP175	20col multi	3.25 2.75

Fruits — AP176

60c, Cacao. 1col, Coffee. 2.10col, Bananas. 3.40col, Flowers. 5col, Sugar cane.

1980, Sept. 24   **Perf. 10½**
C797	AP176	10c shown	.25 .25
C798	AP176	60c multi	.50 .25
C799	AP176	1col multi	.80 .25
C800	AP176	2.10col multi	1.60 .25
C801	AP176	3.40col multi	2.00 .50
C802	AP176	5col multi	2.40 .95
	Nos. C797-C802 (6)		7.55 2.45

Giant Tree, by Jorge Carvajal — AP177

Paintings: 2.10col, Secret Look, by Rolando Cubero. 2.45col, Consuelo, by Fernando Carballo. 3col, Volcano, by Lola Fernandez. 4.05col, attending Mass, by Francisco Amighetti.

1980, Oct. 22   **Litho.**   **Perf. 10½**
C803	AP177	1col multi	.40 .25
C804	AP177	2.10col multi	.55 .25

Size: 28x30mm
C805	AP177	2.45col multi	.70 .30

Size: 22x36mm
C806	AP177	3col multi	.80 .40
C807	AP177	4.05col multi	1.25 .50
	Nos. C803-C807 (5)		3.70 1.70

Virgin and Child, by Raphael AP178

Christmas 1980: 10col, Virgin and Child and St. John, by Raphael.

1980, Nov. 11   **Perf. 13½**
C808	AP178	1col multi	.40 .30
C809	AP178	10col multi	2.40 1.75

Juan Santamaria International Airport AP179

1col, Caldera Harbor. 2.10col, Rio Frio Railroad Bridge. 2.60col, Highway to Colon. 5col, Huetar post office.

1980, Dec. 11   Litho.   Perf. 10½
Sizes: 30x30mm, 31x25mm (1.30col), 25x32mm (2.60col)

C810	AP179	1col multi	.25	.25
C811	AP179	1.30col shown	.40	.25
C812	AP179	2.10col multi	.80	.40
C813	AP179	2.60col multi	.80	.40
C814	AP179	5col multi	1.25	.80
	Nos. C810-C814 (5)		3.50	2.10

Paying your taxes means progress. For surcharge see No. C884.

Repertorio Americano Cover, J. Garcia Monge and Signature — AP180

1981, Jan. 2   Litho.   Perf. 10½

C815	AP180	1.60col multi	.30	.25
C816	AP180	3col multi	.60	.40

Birth centenary of J. Garcia Monge, founder of Repertorio Americano journal.

Arms of Aserri (Site of Cornea Bank) — AP181

1981, Jan. 28   Litho.   Perf. 13½

C817	AP181	1col shown	.30	.25
C818	AP181	1.80col Eye	.85	.25
C819	AP181	5col Rojas	2.50	.80
	Nos. C817-C819 (3)		3.65	1.30

Establishment of human cornea bank, founded by Abelardo Rojas.

Harpia Harpyja — AP182

2.50col, Ara macao. 3col, Felis concolor. 5.50col, Ateles geoffrovi.

1980, Dec. 23   Perf. 11

C820	AP182	2.10col shown	1.60	.40
C821	AP182	2.50col multi	2.10	.55
C822	AP182	3col multi	2.75	.65
C823	AP182	5.50col multi	5.50	1.10
	Nos. C820-C823 (4)		11.95	2.70

Medical and Surgical Clinic AP183

1981, Apr. 8   Litho.   Perf. 10½

C824	AP183	5c multi	.25	.25
C825	AP183	10c multi	.25	.25
C826	AP183	50c multi	.25	.25
C827	AP183	1.30col multi	.40	.25

C828	AP183	3.40col multi	.55	.50
C829	AP183	4.05col multi, vert.	.80	.55
	Nos. C824-C829 (6)		2.50	2.05

University of Costa Rica, 40th anniversary.

Mail Transport by Horse — AP184

2.10col, Train, 1857. 10col, Mail carriers, 1858.

1981, May 6   Litho.   Perf. 10½

C830	AP184	1col shown	.25	.25
C831	AP184	2.10col multi	.55	.25
C832	AP184	10col multi	2.40	1.60
	Nos. C830-C832 (3)		3.20	2.10

Heinrich von Stephan (1831-97), UPU founder.

13th World Telecommunications Day — AP185

1981, May 18   Perf. 11

C833	AP185	5col multi	3.00	.60
C834	AP185	25col multi	7.50	4.00

Bishop Bernardo Thiel — AP186

1981, June 8   Litho.   Perf. 10½

C835		Strip of 5, stained glass windows	3.50	3.50
a.	AP186	1col Sts. Peter & Paul	.30	.30
b.	AP186	1col St. Vincent de Paul	.30	.30
c.	AP186	1col Death of St. Joseph	.30	.30
d.	AP186	1col Archangel Michael	.30	.30
e.	AP186	1col Holy Family	.30	.30
C836	AP186	2col shown	.85	.40

Consecration of Bernardo Augusto Thiel as Bishop of San Jose.

Juan Santamaria AP187

2.40col, Alajuela Cathedral, horiz.

1981, June 26   Perf. 13½

C837	AP187	1col shown	.25	.25
C838	AP187	2.45col multi	.50	.40

Alajuela province.

Potters — AP188

1.60col, Bricklayers. 1.80col, Farmers. 2.50col, Fishermen. 3col, Nurse, patient. 5col, Children, traffic policeman.

1981, July 10   Litho.   Perf. 10½

C839	AP188	15c shown	.25	.25
C840	AP188	1.60col multi	.25	.25
C841	AP188	1.80col multi	.25	.25
C842	AP188	2.50col multi	.25	.25
C843	AP188	3col multi	.40	.25
C844	AP188	5col multi	.70	.25
	Nos. C839-C844 (6)		2.10	1.50

Model of New Natl. Archives AP189

Natl. Archives Centenary: 1.40col, Leon Fernandez Bonilla, founder, vert. 2col, Arms, vert. 3col, St. Thomas University, former headquarters.

1981, Aug. 24   Litho.   Perf. 13½

C845	AP189	1.40col multi	.30	.25
C846	AP189	2col multi	.50	.25
C847	AP189	3col multi	.65	.50
C848	AP189	3.50col multi	.70	.60
	Nos. C845-C848 (4)		2.15	1.60

Men Reaching for Sun, Map AP190

1col, Man in wheelchair, stairs, vert. 2.60col, Man reaching for scale, vert.

1981, Sept. 9   Litho.   Perf. 11

C849	AP190	1col multi	.30	.25
C850	AP190	2.60col multi	.80	.25
C851	AP190	10col shown	3.50	.80
	Nos. C849-C851 (3)		4.60	1.30

Intl. Year of the Disabled.

World Food Day — AP191

1981, Oct. 16   Litho.   Perf. 10½

C852	AP191	5col multi	.40	.25
C853	AP191	10col multi	.80	.55

President Type of 1943

1col, Rafael A. Calderon Guardia, 1940. 2col, Teodoro Picado Michalski, 1944. 3col, José Figueres Ferrer, 1953. 5col, Otilio Ulate Blanco, 1949. 10col, Mario Echandi Jimenez, 1958.

1981, Dec. 7   Litho.   Perf. 13½

C854	A109	1col pink	.55	.55
C855	A109	2col orange	.55	.55
C856	A109	3col green	.70	.55
C857	A109	5col dk bl	1.25	.90
C858	A109	10col blue	2.50	2.00
	Nos. C854-C858 (5)		5.55	4.55

Bar Assoc. of Costa Rica Centenary (1981) AP192

1col, Emblem, horiz. 2col, E. Figueroa, 1st president. 20col, Bar building, horiz.

1982, Mar. 22   Litho.   Perf. 13½

C859	AP192	1col multi	.25	.25
C860	AP192	2col multi	.25	.25
C861	AP192	20col multi	2.50	1.40
	Nos. C859-C861 (3)		3.00	1.90

National Progress AP193

95c, Housing. 1.15col, Agricultural fair. 1.45col, Education. 1.65col, Drinkable water. 1.80col, Rural medical care. 2.10col, Recreational areas. 2.35col, Natl. Theater Square. 2.60col, Communications. 3col, Electric railroad. 4.05col, Irrigation.

1982   Perf. 10½

C862	AP193	95c multi	.35	.35
C863	AP193	1.15col multi	.35	.35
C864	AP193	1.45col multi	.35	.35
C865	AP193	1.65col multi	.35	.35
C866	AP193	1.80col multi	.35	.35
C867	AP193	2.10col multi	.35	.35
C868	AP193	2.35col multi	.55	.55
C869	AP193	2.60col multi	.75	.75
C870	AP193	3col multi	1.00	1.00
C871	AP193	4.05col multi	1.25	1.25
	Nos. C862-C871 (10)		5.65	5.65

Issue dates: 1.80col, 2.10col, 2.60col, 3col, 4.05col, May 5; others, June 16.

City of Alajuela Bicentenary AP194

Designs: 5col, Central Park Fountain. 10col, Juan Santamaria Historical and Cultural Museum, horiz. 15col, Church of Christ of Esquipulas. 20col, Monsignor Esteban Lorenzo de Tristan. 25col, Father Juan Manuel Lopez del Corral.

1982, Aug. 9

C872	AP194	5col multi	.55	.30
C873	AP194	10col multi	1.25	.55
C874	AP194	15col multi	1.75	1.25
C875	AP194	20col multi	2.40	1.25
C876	AP194	25col multi	3.00	1.60
	Nos. C872-C876 (5)		8.95	4.95

Perez Zeledon County, 50th Anniv. (1981) — AP195

Designs: 10c, Saint's Stone. 50c, Monument to Mothers. 1col, Pedro Perez Zeledon. 1.25col, St. Isidore Labrador Church. 3.50col, Municipal Building, horiz. 4.25col, Arms.

1982, Aug. 30

C877	AP195	10c multi	.30	.30
C878	AP195	50c multi	.30	.30
C879	AP195	1col multi	.30	.30
C880	AP195	1.25col multi	.30	.30
C881	AP195	3.50col multi	.45	.30
C882	AP195	4.25col multi	.60	.30
	Nos. C877-C882 (6)		2.25	1.80

Nos. C695 and C813 Surcharged

No. C883

No. C884

1982, Oct. 28   Litho.   Perf. 10½
C883 AP143 3col on 75c multi   .40   .25
C884 AP179 5col on 2.60col mul-
             ti   .55   .25

**Nos. C640-C643 Surcharged and
Overprinted**

1982, Oct. 28   Perf. 12
C885 AP123 8.40col on #C640   .55   .40
C886 AP123 8.40col on #C641   .55   .40
C887 AP123 8.40col on #C642   .55   .40
C888 AP123 8.40col on #C643   .55   .40
C889 AP123 9.70col on #C640   .65   .55
C890 AP123 9.70col on #C641   .65   .55
C891 AP123 9.70col on #C642   .65   .55
C892 AP123 9.70col on #C643   .65   .55
      Nos. C885-C892 (8)   4.80 3.80
9th Natl. Stamp Exhibition.

TB Bacillus
Centenary
AP196

1.50col, Koch. 3col, Koch, slide. 3.30col,
Health Ministry.

1982, Nov. 19   Perf. 13½
C893 AP196 1.50col multi   .25   .25
C894 AP196 3col multi   .40   .25
C895 AP196 3.30col multi   .40   .25
      Nos. C893-C895 (3)   1.05   .75

Pan-American
Blood Donors'
Society, 7th
Cong. — AP197

30col, Natl. Blood Assoc. emblem. 50col,
Cong. emblem.

1982, Nov. 25   Perf. 11
C896 AP197 30col multi   2.00 1.40
C897 AP197 50col multi   3.25 2.00

AP198

8.40col, Emblem, horiz. 9.70col, Emblem,
diff. 11.70col, Handshake, horiz. 13.05col,
Emblem, diff., horiz.

1982, Dec. 13   Litho.   Perf. 10½
C898 AP198 8.40col multi   .55   .25
C899 AP198 9.70col multi   .80   .40
C900 AP198 11.70col multi   .80   .40
C901 AP198 13.05col multi   .95   .50
      Nos. C898-C901 (4)   3.10 1.55
Inter-Governmental Migration Committee,
30th anniv.

AP199

4.80col, St. Francis of Assisi, by El Greco.
7.40col, Portrait, diff.

1983, Jan. 3   Perf. 16
C902 AP199 4.80col multi   .55   .25
C903 AP199 7.40col multi   .80   .25
For surcharges see Nos. C908-C911.

Visit of Pope John
Paul II — AP200

1983, Mar. 1   Litho.   Perf. 10½
C904 AP200 5col multi   2.75   .25
C905 AP200 10col multi   2.75   .50
C906 AP200 15col multi   6.00   .75
      Nos. C904-C906 (3)   11.50 1.50

Bolivar, by Francisco
Zuniga
Chavarria — AP201

1983, July 22   Litho.   Perf. 16
C907 AP201 10col multi   1.10   .25

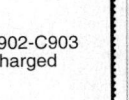

Nos. C902-C903
Surcharged

1983, Sept. 23   Litho.   Perf. 16
C908 AP199 10c on 4.80col   .25   .25
C909 AP199 50c on 4.80col   .25   .25
C910 AP199 1.50col on 7.40col .25 .25
C911 AP199 3col on 7.40col   .25   .25
      Nos. C908-C911 (4)   1.00 1.00

LACSA Costa
Rica Airlines,
40th
Anniv. — AP202

Various childrens' drawings: 1col, Adriana
E. Hidalgo. 7col, Osvaldo A.G. Vega. 16col,
David V. Rodriguez.

1986, Dec. 12   Litho.   Perf. 13½
C912 AP202 1col multi   .55   .25
C913 AP202 7col multi   3.50   .30
C914 AP202 16col multi   8.00   .75
      Nos. C912-C914 (3)   12.05 1.30
Nos. C912-C913 exist perf 11. Unused
examples are rare. Value used, $5 each.

Roman
Macaya
Lahmann,
Aviation
Pioneer
AP203

1988, Sept. 26   Litho.   Perf. 10½
C915 AP203 10col multi   .50   .25

No. 418
Overprinted

1990, Nov. 5
C916 A180 50col multicolored 4.00 1.50

Bagging Coffee
Beans — AP204

Perf. 10½
1990, Nov. 16   Litho.   Unwmk.
C917 AP204 50col multicolored 3.00   .80

AP205

1990, Dec. 6
C918 AP205 50col blue & black 3.50   .80
First postage stamps, 150th anniv.

National
Theater — AP206

Banana Picker, 1897, by Alleardo Villa.

1991, Mar. 25   Litho.   Perf. 10½
C919 AP206 30col multicolored 2.00   .40

No. 428
Overprinted

Litho. & Engr.
1991, Sept. 13   Perf. 12½
C920 A188 200col   8.00 2.00
12th Natl. Philatelic Exposition.

No. 402
Overprinted

1991, Oct. 11   Litho.   Perf. 11½
Granite Paper
C921 A170 20col multicolored 4.00 1.50
Basketball, cent.

Social Security
Administration,
50th Anniv.
AP207

1991, Nov. 1   Litho.   Perf. 13½
C922 AP207 15col multicolored 3.00   .50

La Poesia by
Vespasiano
Bignami — AP208

1992, Jan. 24   Litho.   Perf. 10½
C923 AP208 35col multicolored 5.00 1.50
National Theater.

Discovery of
America, 500th
Anniv.
AP209

No. C924 — Columbus' ships: a, Nina. b,
Santa Maria. c, Pinta.

1992, Oct. 8   Litho.   Perf. 13½
C924   Strip of 3   5.00 3.00
a.-c. A209 45col Any single   1.50   .90

Intl. Arts
Festival — AP210

1993, Mar. 15   Litho.   Perf. 13½
C925 AP210 45col multicolored 1.40   .50

Telecommunications Institute, 30th
Anniv. — AP211

1993, Nov. 25   Litho.   Perf. 13½
C926 AP211 45col multicolored 1.00   .70

Ministry of
the Interior,
150th
Anniv.
AP212

1994, Mar. 8   Litho.   Perf. 10½
C927 AP212 45col multicolored   1.00 .70

Intl. Year of the
Family — AP213

1994, May 5   Litho.   Perf. 10½
C928 AP213 45col multicolored   2.50 1.30

LACSA, 50th
Anniv.
AP214

5col, Douglas DC-3. 10col, Curtiss C-46.
20col, Beechcraft. 30col, DC-6B. 35col, BAC
1-11. 40col, Convair CV 440. 45col, Electra L-
188. 50col, Boeing 727-200. 55col, Douglas
DC-8. 60col, Airbus A320.

1996, Mar. 29   Litho.   Perf. 10½
C929 AP214 5col multi   .25 .25
C930 AP214 10col multi   .25 .25
C931 AP214 20col multi   .40 .40
C932 AP214 30col multi   .65 .65
C933 AP214 35col multi   .70 .70
C934 AP214 40col multi   .90 .90
C935 AP214 45col multi   .95 .95
C936 AP214 50col multi   1.00 1.00
C937 AP214 55col multi   1.25 1.25
C938 AP214 60col multi   1.40 1.40
  Nos. C929-C938 (10)   7.75 7.75

No. C932
Surcharged

2001, Oct. 5   Litho.   Perf. 10½
C939 AP214 5col on 30col multi   .40 .25

10th Intl. Art
Festival — AP215

2006, Mar. 17   Litho.   Perf. 10½
C940 AP215 120col multi   2.00 2.00

AIR POST SPECIAL DELIVERY STAMPS

Catalogue values for unused
stamps in this section are for
Never Hinged items.

UPU Headquarters and Monument,
Bern — APSD1

Perf. 10x11
1970, May 20   Litho.   Unwmk.
CE1 APSD1 35c multi   .75 .25
CE2 APSD1 60c multi   .75 .25
  Opening of the UPU Headquarters in Bern.
The red and black label attached to the 60c is
inscribed "EXPRES." Values are for stamps
with label attached.
  Stamps with labels removed were used for
regular airmail.

AIR POST OFFICIAL STAMPS

Air Post
Stamps of
1934
Ovptd. in
Red

1934   Unwmk.   Perf. 12
CO1 AP8 5c green   .25 .25
CO2 AP8 10c car rose   .25 .25
CO3 AP8 15c chocolate   .50 .50
CO4 AP8 20c deep blue   .80 .80
CO5 AP8 25c deep org   .80 .80
CO6 AP8 40c olive blk   .80 .80
CO7 AP8 50c gray blk   .80 .80
CO8 AP8 60c org yel   .95 .95
CO9 AP8 75c dull vio   .95 .95
CO10 AP9 1col deep rose   1.60 1.60
CO11 AP9 2col light blue   4.75 4.75
CO12 AP9 5col black   8.00 8.00
CO13 AP9 10col red brown   12.00 12.00
  Nos. CO1-CO13 (13)   32.45 32.45
  For overprints see Nos. C103-C116.

SPECIAL DELIVERY STAMPS

Catalogue values for unused
stamps in this section are for
Never Hinged items.

Winged
Letter
SD1

Unwmk.
1972, Mar. 20   Litho.   Perf. 11
E1 SD1 75c brown & red   .30 .30
E2 SD1 1.50col blue & red   .50 .40

1973   Perf. 11x12
E3 SD1 75c green & red   .30 .30

1973, Nov. 5   Litho.   Perf. 12
E4 SD1 75c lilac & orange   1.50 .75
  Exists perf 11x11 ½.

Concorde
SD2

1976, May 17   Litho.   Perf. 16
E5 SD2 1col vermilion & multi   .75 .75

SD3

1979, June 15   Litho.   Perf. 12½
E6 SD3 2col multi   .90 .50

SD4

1980, Dec. 18   Litho.   Perf. 12½
E7 SD4 2col multi   .80 .50

1982, Dec. 20   Litho.   Perf. 11
E8 SD4 4col multi   .65 .40

POSTAGE DUE STAMPS

D1

1903   Unwmk.   Engr.   Perf. 14
Numerals in Black
J1 D1 5c slate blue   6.75 1.25
J2 D1 10c brown orange   6.75 1.25
J3 D1 15c yellow green   3.50 1.75
J4 D1 20c carmine   4.75 1.75
J5 D1 25c slate gray   4.75 2.40
J6 D1 30c brown   6.00 2.50
J7 D1 40c olive bister   6.75 2.50
J8 D1 50c red violet   6.75 2.50
  Nos. J1-J8 (8)   46.00 15.90

D2

1915   Litho.   Perf. 12
J9 D2 2c orange   1.25 .55
J10 D2 4c dark blue   1.25 .55
J11 D2 8c gray green   1.25 .55
J12 D2 10c violet   1.25 .55
J13 D2 20c brown   1.25 .55
  Nos. J9-J13 (5)   6.25 2.75

OFFICIAL STAMPS

Values for unused stamps are for
examples with original gum as defined
in the catalogue introduction. Examples
without gum have probably been used
and are so regarded.

Very fine examples of Nos. O1-O24
will have perforations just clear of the
design on one or more sides.
  Nos. O1-O55, to about 1915, normally were not canceled when affixed to
official mail. Occasionally they were
canceled in a foreign country of destination. Used values are for favor-canceled
stamps or for stamps without gum.

Regular Issues Overprinted

Overprinted in Red,
Black, Blue or Green

1883-85   Unwmk.   Perf. 12
O1 A6 1c green (R)   2.00 1.10
O2 A6 1c green (Bk)   4.00 1.10
O3 A6 2c carmine (Bk)   4.00 1.40
O4 A6 2c carmine (Bl)   2.40 1.60
O5 A6 5c blue vio (R)   7.00 3.00
O6 A6 10c orange (G)   10.00 4.00
O7 A6 40c blue (R)   10.00 4.00
  Nos. O1-O7 (7)   39.40 16.20

Overprinted

1886
O8 A6 1c green (Bk)   3.50 1.10
O9 A6 2c carmine (Bk)   3.50 1.60
O10 A6 5c blue vio (R)   24.00 11.00
O11 A6 10c orange (Bk)   24.00 11.00
  Nos. O8-O11 (4)   55.00 24.70

Overprinted

O12 A6 1c green (Bk)   3.50 1.00
O13 A6 2c carmine (Bk)   3.50 1.40
O14 A6 5c blue vio (R)   24.00 11.00
O15 A6 10c orange (Bk)   24.00 11.00
  Nos. O12-O15 (4)   55.00 24.40
  Nos. O8-O11 and O12-O15 exist se-tenant
in vertical pairs.

Overprinted in Black

O16 A6 5c blue vio   60.00 35.00
O17 A6 10c orange   — 275.00

Overprinted

1887
O18 A6 1c green   1.25 .55
O19 A6 2c carmine   1.25 .50
O21 A6 10c orange   37.50 24.00
  c. Double overprint   42.50
O22 A7 5c blue vio   12.00 3.50
O23 A7 10c orange   .90 .50
  c. Double overprint   27.50
O24 A6 40c blue   1.25 .50
  Nos. O18-O24 (6)   54.15 29.55

Overprinted "OFICAL"

O18a A6 1c green
O19a A6 2c carmine   14.50 14.50
O22a A7 5c blue violet   14.50

O23a	A7	10c orange	14.50	3.50
O24a	A6	40c blue	17.00	17.00
		Nos. O18a-O24a (5)	60.50	

Dangerous counterfeits exist of Nos. O18a-O24a.

Without Period

O18b	A6	1c green	14.50	10.00
O19b	A6	2c carmine	14.50	10.00
O22b	A7	5c blue violet	14.50	10.00
O23b	A7	10c orange	14.50	10.00
		Nos. O18b-O23b (4)	58.00	40.00

Nos. O18b-O23b are from a separate plate without periods. No. O23 exists without period (position 32). These must be collected in pairs.

Issues of 1889-1901 Overprinted

1889			*Perf. 14, 15*	
O25	A10	1c brown	.25	.25
O26	A11	2c dk green	.25	.25
O27	A12	5c orange	.25	.25
O28	A13	10c red brown	.25	.25
O29	A14	20c yellow grn	.40	.25
O30	A15	50c rose red	1.40	1.40
		Nos. O25-O30 (6)	2.80	2.65

1892				
O31	A20	1c grnsh blue	.25	.25
O32	A21	2c yellow	.25	.25
O33	A22	5c violet	.25	.25
O34	A23	10c lt green	3.50	1.60
O35	A24	20c scarlet	.25	.25
O36	A25	50c gray blue	.65	.55
		Nos. O31-O36 (6)	5.15	3.15

1901-02				
O37	A30	1c green & blk	.40	.40
O38	A31	2c ver & blk	.40	.40
O39	A32	5c gray bl & blk	.40	.40
O40	A33	10c ocher & blk	.80	.80
O41	A34	20c lake & blk	1.25	1.25
O42	A35	50c lilac & dk bl	10.00	4.00
O43	A36	1col ol bis & blk	17.50	10.00
		Nos. O37-O43 (7)	30.75	17.25

No. 46 Overprinted in Green

1903				
O44	A31	2c ver & blk	3.00	3.00
b.		"PROVISIORO"	10.00	10.00
d.		Inverted overprint	10.00	10.00
f.		As "b," inverted	13.00	10.00

Counterfeit overprints exist.

Regular Issue of 1903 Overprinted Like Nos. O25-O43

1903			*Perf. 14, 12½x14*	
O45	A40	4c red vio & blk	1.40	1.40
O46	A41	6c ol grn & blk	1.75	1.75
O47	A42	25c gray lil & brn	9.50	6.00
		Nos. O45-O47 (3)	12.65	9.15

Counterfeit overprints exist.

Regular Issue of 1907 Overprinted

1908			*Perf. 14*	
O48	A43	1c red brn & ind	.25	.25
O49	A44	2c yel grn & blk	.25	.25
O50	A45	4c car & ind	.25	.25
O51	A46	5c yel & dull bl	.25	.25
O52	A47	10c blue & blk	.80	.80
O53	A49	25c gray lil & blk	.30	.30
O54	A50	50c red lil & bl	.55	.55
O55	A51	1col brown & blk	1.25	1.25
		Nos. O48-O55 (8)	3.90	3.85

Various varieties of the overprint and basic stamps exist.
Imperf examples of Nos. O48, O49, O53 were found in 1970.

Regular Issue of 1910 Overprinted in Black

1917				
O56	A56	5c orange	.40	.40
a.		Inverted overprint	6.00	3.50
O57	A57	10c deep blue	.25	.25
a.		Inverted overprint	3.50	3.50

No. 74 Surcharged

1920		**Red Surcharge**	*Perf. 12*	
O58	A58	15c on 20c olive grn	.55	.55

Nos. 72, 61, 59, 65-67 Surcharged or Overprinted

1921		**Black Surcharge**	*Perf. 12*	
O59	A56	10c on 5c orange	.50	.50
a.		"10 CTS." inverted	17.50	
			Perf. 14	
O60	A45	4c car & indigo	.40	.40
a.		"1291" for "1921"	12.00	
O61	A43	6c on 1c red brn & ind	.55	.55
O62	A49	20c on 25c gray lil & blk	.55	.55

Overprinted like No. O60

O63	A50	50c red lil & bl	2.50	1.75
O64	A51	1col brown & blk	5.00	3.00
		Nos. O59-O64 (6)	9.50	6.75

Nos. O60 to O64 exist with date and new values inverted. These may be printer's waste but probably were deliberately made.

Regular Issue of 1923 Overprinted

1923			*Perf. 11½*	
O65	A68	2c brown	.25	.25
O66	A68	4c green	.25	.25
O67	A68	5c blue	.40	.40
O68	A68	20c carmine	.25	.25
O69	A68	1col violet	.50	.50
		Nos. O65-O69 (5)	1.65	1.65

Nos. O65 to O69 exist imperforate but were not regularly issued in that condition.

O7

1926		**Unwmk. Engr.**	*Perf. 12½*	
O70	O7	2c ultra & blk	.25	.25
O71	O7	3c mag & blk	.25	.25
O72	O7	4c lt bl & blk	.25	.25
O73	O7	5c grn & blk	.25	.25
O74	O7	6c ocher & blk	.25	.25
O75	O7	10c rose red & blk	.25	.25
O76	O7	20c ol grn & blk	.25	.25
O77	O7	30c red org & blk	.25	.25
O78	O7	45c brown & blk	.25	.25
O79	O7	1col lilac & blk	.50	.50
		Nos. O70-O79 (10)	2.75	2.75

See Nos. O82-O94. For surcharges see Nos. C7-C10.

Regular Issue of 1936 Overprinted in Black

1936		**Unwmk.**	*Perf. 12*	
O80	A96	5c green	.25	.25
O81	A96	10c carmine rose	.25	.25

Type of 1926

1937	O7		*Perf. 12½*	
O82	O7	2c vio & blk	.25	.25
O83	O7	3c bis brn & blk	.25	.25
O84	O7	4c rose car & blk	.25	.25
O85	O7	5c ol grn & blk	.25	
O86	O7	8c blk brn & blk	.25	
O87	O7	10c rose lake & blk	.25	
O88	O7	20c ind & blk	.25	.25
O89	O7	40c red org & blk	.25	
O90	O7	55c dk vio & blk	.25	
O91	O7	1col brn vio & blk	.30	.30
O92	O7	2col gray bl & blk	.70	.70
O93	O7	5col dl yel & blk	3.00	3.00
O94	O7	10col blue & blk	45.00	20.00
		Nos. O82-O94 (13)	51.25	

Nine stamps of this series exist with perforated star (2c, 3c, 4c, 20c, 40c, 1col, 2col, 5col, 10col). These were issued to officials for postal purposes. Unpunched stamps were sold to collectors but had no franking power. Values for unused are for unpunched.

POSTAL TAX STAMPS

The 1927 postal tax stamps covered the 10c per book charge for books sent by mail. The stamps were sold at the post office and applied to any package containing books.

Regular Stamps and Revenue Stamps Overprinted in Black

Nos. RA1B-RA1D Overprinted

1927, Mar. 17				
RA1A	A75	10c red brown	25.00	5.00
RA1B		50c brown (overprinted on revenue stamp)	35.00	10.00
RA1C	A79	1col olive green	35.00	10.00
RA1D		2col blue green (overprinted on revenue stamp)	750.00	400.00
		Nos. RA1A-RA1D (4)	845.00	425.00

No. 124 Surcharged in Black

1927, Dec. 23				
RA1E	A76	10c on 12c carmine rose	25.00	5.00

> **Catalogue values for unused stamps in this section are for Never Hinged items.**

Most postal tax issues were to benefit the Children's Village and were obligatory on all mail during Dec.

No. C198 Surcharged in Red

Engraved; Center Photogravure

1958		**Unwmk.**	*Perf. 12½*	
RA1	AP51	5c on 2c brt bl & blk	.30	.25

Type of 1954 Surcharged in Green

RA2	AP53	5c on 10c dk bl & blk	.50	.25
a.		Inverted surcharge	8.50	

Design: Like No. C228, pottery.

Father Edward J. Flanagan — PT1

Paintings: No. RA4, Boy by El Greco. No. RA5, Boy by Jose Ribera. No. RA6, Girl by Amadeo Modigliani.

			Perf. 13½	
1959, Nov. 25		**Unwmk.**	**Photo.**	
RA3	PT1	5c green	.65	.25
RA4	PT1	5c dl gray vio	.65	.25
RA5	PT1	5c olive	.65	.25
RA6	PT1	5c lilac rose	.65	.25
		Nos. RA3-RA6 (4)	2.60	1.00

Nos. RA3-RA6 exist imperf.

Father Peralta — PT2

Designs: No. RA8, Girl by Renoir. No. RA9, Boys with cups by Velazquez. No. RA10, Singing children, sculpture by F. Zuñiga.

1960		**Litho.**	*Perf. 14*	
RA7	PT2	5c chocolate	.65	.25
RA8	PT2	5c dp org	.65	.25
RA9	PT2	5c plum	.65	.25
RA10	PT2	5c grysh bl	.65	.25
		Nos. RA7-RA10 (4)	2.60	1.00

Nos. RA7-RA10 exist imperf.

No. C229 Surcharged in Black

Engraved; Center Photogravure

1961			*Perf. 13x12½*	
RA11	AP53	5c on 15c grn & blk	.40	.25

Nicolas, Son of Rubens — PT3

Designs: No. RA13, Madonna by Bellini. RA14, Angel playing stringed instrument by Melozzo. RA15, Msgr. Rubén Odio H.

1962		Photo.	Perf. 13½	
RA12	PT3	5c dark carmine	.70	.25
RA13	PT3	5c sepia	.70	.25
RA14	PT3	5c dull green	.70	.25
RA15	PT3	5c blue	.70	.25
		Nos. RA12-RA15 (4)	2.80	1.00

For surcharges see Nos. 262-265.

Type of 1962, Inscribed "1963"

Designs as before.

1963		Photo.	Perf. 13½	
RA16	PT3	5c sepia (RA12)	.45	.25
RA17	PT3	5c ultra (RA13)	.45	.25
RA18	PT3	5c dk car (RA14)	.45	.25
RA19	PT3	5c black (RA15)	.45	.25
		Nos. RA16-RA19 (4)	1.80	1.00

Boys in Workshop — PT4

Designs: No. RA21, Two playing boys. No. RA22, Teacher and children. No. RA23, Priest with boys.

1964		Litho.	Perf. 12½	
RA20	PT4	5c bright green	.40	.25
RA21	PT4	5c rose lilac	.40	.25
RA22	PT4	5c blue	.40	.25
RA23	PT4	5c brown	.40	.25
		Nos. RA20-RA23 (4)	1.60	1.00

Brother Casiano de Madrid — PT5

Designs: No. RA25, National Children's Hospital. No. RA26, Poinsettia. No. RA27, Santa Claus with children (diamond).

1965, Dec. 10		Litho.	Perf. 10	
RA24	PT5	5c red brown	.25	.25
RA25	PT5	5c green	.25	.25
RA26	PT5	5c red	.25	.25
RA27	PT5	5c ultra	.25	.25
		Nos. RA24-RA27 (4)	1.00	1.00

Christmas Ornaments — PT6

1966		Litho.	Perf. 11	
RA28	PT6	5c shown	.25	.25
RA29	PT6	5c Angel	.25	.25
RA30	PT6	5c Church	.25	.25
RA31	PT6	5c Reindeer	.25	.25
		Nos. RA28-RA31 (4)	1.00	1.00

General Post Office, San José — PT7

1967, Mar.		Litho.	Perf. 11	
RA32	PT7	10c blue	.40	.25

No. RA32 was issued as a postal tax stamp to be used by organizations normally allowed free postage. On Dec. 15, 1972, it was authorized for use as an ordinary postage stamp.

Madonna and Child — PT8

1967		Litho.	Perf. 11	
RA33	PT8	5c olive green	.25	.25
RA34	PT8	5c dp lil rose	.25	.25
RA35	PT8	5c brt blue	.25	.25
RA36	PT8	5c grnsh blue	.25	.25
		Nos. RA33-RA36 (4)	1.00	1.00

Star of Bethlehem, Mother and Child — PT9

1968, Dec.		Litho.	Perf. 12½	
RA37	PT9	5c gray	.25	.25
RA38	PT9	5c rose red	.25	.25
RA39	PT9	5c dk rose brn	.25	.25
RA40	PT9	5c bister brn	.25	.25
		Nos. RA37-RA40 (4)	1.00	1.00

Madonna and Child — PT10

1969, Dec.		Litho.	Perf. 12½	
RA41	PT10	5c dk blue	.25	.25
RA42	PT10	5c orange	.25	.25
RA43	PT10	5c brown red	.25	.25
RA44	PT10	5c blue green	.25	.25
		Nos. RA41-RA44 (4)	1.00	1.00

Christ Child, Star — PT11

1970, Dec.		Litho.	Perf. 12½	
RA45	PT11	5c brt purple	.35	.25
RA46	PT11	5c lilac rose	.35	.25
RA47	PT11	5c olive	.35	.25
RA48	PT11	5c ocher	.35	.25
		Nos. RA45-RA48 (4)	1.40	1.00

Christ Child and "PAX" — PT12

1971, Nov. 29				
RA49	PT12	10c dk blue	.25	.25
RA50	PT12	10c orange	.25	.25
RA51	PT12	10c brown	.25	.25
RA52	PT12	10c green	.25	.25
		Nos. RA49-RA52 (4)	1.00	1.00

Madonna and Child — PT13

1972, Nov. 30			Perf. 11x11½	
RA53	PT13	10c dk blue	.25	.25
RA54	PT13	10c brt red	.25	.25
RA55	PT13	10c lilac	.25	.25
RA56	PT13	10c green	.25	.25
		Nos. RA53-RA56 (4)	1.00	1.00

Madonna and Child — PT14

1973, Nov. 30		Litho.	Perf. 12½	
RA57	PT14	10c purple	.25	.25
RA58	PT14	10c car rose	.25	.25
RA59	PT14	10c gray	.25	.25
RA60	PT14	10c orange brn	.25	.25
		Nos. RA57-RA60 (4)	1.00	1.00

Boys Eating Cake, by Murillo — PT15

Paintings: No. RA62, Virgin and Child, with St. John, by Raphael. No. RA63, Maternity, by Juan R. Bonilla. No. RA64, Praying Child, by Reynolds.

1974, Nov. 25			Perf. 13	
RA61	PT15	10c brt pink	.30	.25
RA62	PT15	10c rose lilac	.30	.25
RA63	PT15	10c dk gray	.30	.25
RA64	PT15	10c violet bl	.30	.25
		Nos. RA61-RA64 (4)	1.20	1.00

See No. RA110.

"Happy Dreams," by Sonia Romero — PT16

Paintings: No. RA66, Virgin with Carnation, by Leonardo da Vinci. No. RA67, Children with Tortoise, by Francisco Amighetti. No. RA68, Boy with Pigeon, by Picasso.

1975, Nov. 25		Litho.	Perf. 10½	
RA65	PT16	10c gray	.45	.30
RA66	PT16	10c red lilac	.45	.30
RA67	PT16	10c orange brown	.45	.30
RA68	PT16	10c brt blue	.45	.30
		Nos. RA65-RA68 (4)	1.80	1.20

Virgin and Child, by Hans Memling — PT17

Paintings: No. RA70, Girl with Sombrero, by Auguste Renoir. No. RA71, Meditation (boy), by Floria Pinto de Herrero. No. RA72, Gaston de Mezerville (boy), by Lolita Zeller de Peralta.

1976, Nov. 24		Litho.	Perf. 10½	
RA69	PT17	10c rose lilac	.30	.25
RA70	PT17	10c rose carmine	.30	.25
RA71	PT17	10c gray	.30	.25
RA72	PT17	10c violet blue	.30	.25
		Nos. RA69-RA72 (4)	1.20	1.00

Boy's Head, by Amparo Cruz — PT18

Paintings: No. RA74, Girl's head, by Rubens. No. RA75, Girl and infant, by Cristina Fournier. No. RA76, Mariano Goya, by Goya.

1977, Nov.			Perf. 10½	
RA73	PT18	10c gray olive	.30	.25
RA74	PT18	10c rose red	.30	.25
RA75	PT18	10c brt ultra	.30	.25
RA76	PT18	10c brt rose lil	.30	.25
		Nos. RA73-RA76 (4)	1.20	1.00

Boy with Kite — PT19

Designs: Nos. RA78-RA79, Girl flying kite.

1978, Nov. 20		Litho.	Perf. 12½	
RA77	PT19	10c magenta	.30	.25
RA78	PT19	10c slate	.30	.25
RA79	PT19	10c lilac	.30	.25
RA80	PT19	10c violet blue	.30	.25
		Nos. RA77-RA80 (4)	1.20	1.00

Boy Leaning on Tree — PT20

1979, Nov. 19		Litho.	Perf. 12½	
RA81	PT20	10c blue	.25	.25
RA82	PT20	10c orange	.25	.25
RA83	PT20	10c magenta	.25	.25
RA84	PT20	10c green	.25	.25
		Nos. RA81-RA84 (4)	1.00	1.00

Boy on Swing — PT21

1980, Nov. 18		Litho.	Perf. 12½	
RA85	PT21	10c brt blue	.25	.25
RA86	PT21	10c brt yellow	.25	.25
RA87	PT21	10c crimson rose	.25	.25
RA88	PT21	10c brt green	.25	.25
		Nos. RA85-RA88 (4)	1.00	1.00

Boy Riding Toy Car — PT22

1981, Nov. 19		Litho.	Perf. 11	
RA89	PT22	10c blue	.25	.25
RA90	PT22	10c green	.25	.25
RA91	PT22	10c red	.25	.25
RA92	PT22	10c orange	.25	.25
		Nos. RA89-RA92 (4)	1.00	1.00

Youth Running Machine — PT23

1982, Nov. 19		Litho.	Perf. 10½	
RA93	PT23	10c red	.25	.25
RA94	PT23	10c gray	.25	.25
RA95	PT23	10c purple	.25	.25
RA96	PT23	10c grnsh blue	.25	.25
		Nos. RA93-RA96 (4)	1.00	1.00

Youths Working on Wheelchair — PT24

1983, Nov. 24   **Litho.**   *Perf. 16*
RA97 PT24 10c red   .25 .25
RA98 PT24 10c orange   .25 .25
RA99 PT24 10c ultra   .25 .25
RA100 PT24 10c green   .25 .25
    Nos. RA97-RA100 (4)   1.00 1.00
     Christmas 1983.

Girl on Bicycle — PT25

1984, Nov. 20   **Litho.**   *Perf. 10½*
RA101 PT25 10c violet   .70 .30
     Christmas 1984.

Taking a Child in Out of the Cold — PT26

1985, Dec. 1   **Litho.**   *Perf. 13*
RA102 PT26 10c dull brown   .70 .30
     Christmas 1985.

Depressed Child — PT27

1986, Dec. 1   **Litho.**   *Perf. 10½*
RA103 PT27 10c lemon   .70 .30
    Christmas stamps, 25th anniv.; Christmas 1986.

Christmas — PT28

1987, Dec. 1   **Litho.**   *Perf. 10½*
RA104 PT28 10c dk ol bis & brt bl   .60 .30
   No postal tax stamp was issued for 1988.

Teaching Children — PT29

1989, Dec. 1   **Litho.**   *Perf. 13½*
RA105 PT29 1col blue, blk & brt apple grn   .60 .30
     Christmas 1989.

No. 417 Ovptd. in Red, Blue, Green, or Orange

1990, Nov. 16   **Litho.**   *Perf. 13½*
RA106 A179 10col multi (R)   .90 .25
RA107 A179 10col multi (Bl)   .90 .25
RA108 A179 10col multi (G)   .90 .25
RA109 A179 10col multi (O)   .90 .25
    Nos. RA106-RA109 (4)   3.60 1.00
   No. RA109 exists with a silver overprint.

Art Type of 1974

Design: 10col, Praying Child, by Reynolds.

1991, Nov. 18   **Litho.**   *Perf. 10½*
RA110 PT15 10col dark ultra   1.20 .35

Christmas — PT30

Boy in workshop.

1992, Dec. 1   **Litho.**   *Perf. 10½*
RA111 PT30 10col red   .60 .30

Christmas PT31

1993, Nov. 17
RA112 PT31 10col multicolored   .50 .30

Christmas PT32

1994, Nov. 23   **Litho.**   *Perf. 10½*
RA113 PT32 11col lilac & slate   .70 .30
   No. RA113 exists imperf.

Christmas — PT33

Painting of mother and child, by Claudio Carazo.

1995, Dec. 1   *Perf. 13½*
RA114 PT33 12col multicolored   .70 .30
   a.   Miniature sheet, #RA114 + 5 labels   3.25 3.25
   No. RA114a contains 4 progressive proofs of No. RA114 + one label of text and sold for 112col.

Sculpture — PT34

1996, Dec. 1   **Litho.**   *Perf. 10½*
RA115 PT34 14col multi   .60 .30

Christmas — PT35

Bust of Antonio Obando Chan, by Olger Villegas Cruz.

1997, Dec. 1
RA116 PT35 15col multicolored   .50 .30

Christmas PT36

No. RA117: a, Flower. b, Flower up close, one in background. c, Berries on branch.

1998   **Litho.**   *Perf. 13½*
RA117   Strip of 3   1.75 1.30
   a.-c.   PT36 16col Any single   .50 .30

Children's Village PT37

1999, Dec. 1   **Litho.**   *Perf. 13¼*
RA118 PT37 17col multi   .50 .30

Child — PT38

Color: a, Green. b, Red. c, Blue. d, Brown.

2000, Dec. 1   **Litho.**   *Perf. 10½*
RA119   Horiz. strip of 4   4.50 2.50
   a.-d.   PT38 20col Any single   .80 .40

Child Examining Stamp — PT39

Panel color: a, Purple. b, Green. c, Red. d, Orange.

2001, Dec. 1   **Litho.**   *Perf. 10½*
RA120   Horiz. strip of 4   2.00 1.40
   a.-d.   PT39 21col Any single   .40 .30

Child — PT40

Panel color: a, Purple. b, Blue. c, Orange. d, Green.

2002   **Litho.**   *Perf. 10½*
RA121   Horiz strip of 4   1.85 1.50
   a.-d.   PT40 22col Any single   .40 .30

Child Pointing at Star — PT41

No. RA122 — Background color: a, Purple. b, Green. c, Red. d, Yellow orange.

2003, Dec. 1   **Litho.**   *Perf. 13½x13¼*
RA122   Horiz. strip of 4   1.80 1.50
   a.-d.   PT41 23col Any single   .40 .30

Three Magi — PT42

No. RA123 — Magi in: a, Lemon. b, Green. c, Purple. d, Red violet.

2004   **Litho.**   *Perf. 13¼*
RA123   Horiz. strip of 4   2.50 2.00
   a.-d.   PT42 25col Any single   .50 .40

Children — PT43

No. RA124 — Denomination color: a, White. b, Buff. c, Dull orange. d, Red.

2005, Dec. 1   **Litho.**   *Perf. 10½*
RA124   Horiz. strip of 4   2.50 2.00
   a.-d.   PT43 28col Any single   .50 .40
    Surtax for Children's Village.

Child Reading PT44

No. RA125 — Frame color: a, Yellow bister. b, Dull brown. c, Olive green. d, Orange brown.

2006, Dec. 1   **Litho.**   *Perf. 10½*
RA125   Horiz. strip of 4   2.60 2.25
   a.-d.   PT44 32col Any single   .60 .55

Children's Art — PT45

No. RA126: a, Family and hearts. b, Children at school. c, Children on playground equipment. d, Boy on skateboard.

2007, Dec. 1   **Litho.**   *Perf. 10½*
RA126   Horiz. strip of 4   2.60 2.60
   a.-d.   PT45 35col Any single   .60 .60

    Surtax for Children's Village.

Children's Art — PT46

No. RA127: a, Child flying kite, by Luis Paulino Murillo Méndez. b, Boy and jaguar, by David Malavassi Zúñiga. c, Bird and sailboat, by Valeria Vargas Arias. d, Child in water, by Dannia María Berrocal Fonseca.

2008, Dec. 1 Litho. Perf. 13½
RA127   Horiz. strip of 4   4.25   4.25
a.-d.   PT46 40col Any single   .75   .75
Surtax for Children's Village.

Miniature Sheet

Masquerade Costumes — PT47

No. RA128: a, Devil and man in purple hat. b, Bull and clown. c, Grim reaper. d, Stilt walker and tall woman.

2009, Dec. 1 Litho. Perf. 10½
RA128 PT47 45col Sheet of 4,
     #a-d   2.50   2.50
Surtax for Children's Village.

Children's Art — PT48

No. RA129: a, School, tree and sun (gray panels). b, Child in workshop (blue panels). c, Sun, hills, flora and fauna (pink panels). d, Sun, house on hill (yellow panels).

2010, Dec. 1
RA129   Horiz. strip of 4   2.00   2.00
a.-d.   PT48 45col Any single   .40   .30
Surtax for Children's Village.

Children's Art — PT49

No. RA130: a, Head (orange yellow panel). b, Children with banner (blue panel). c, Children in playground (yellow green panel). d, Various children (bright rose panel).

2011, Dec. 1
RA130 PT49 55col Block of 4,
     #a-d   3.00   3.00
Surtax for Children's Village.

Boy Holding Sun — PT50

No. RA131 — Background color: a, Light blue. b, Blue. c, Brown orange. d, Yellow bister.

2012, Dec. 1 Litho. Perf. 10½
RA131   Horiz. strip of 4   1.50   1.50
a.-d.   PT50 60col Any single   .30   .30
Surtax for Children's Village.

PT51

No. RA132: a, Forest (denomination in olive green). b, Arches in wall (denomination in orange). c, Rock formation (denomination in lilac). d, Toucan (denomination in blue).

2013, Dec. 2 Litho. Perf. 10½
RA132 PT51 60col Block of 4,
     #a-d   2.00   2.00

No. RA132 was printed in sheets of 20 (5 of each stamp) + 4 labels. Surtax for Children's Village.

Traditional Dishes — PT52

No. RA133: a, Gallo pinto. b, Olla de carne. c, Casado con pollo. d, Picadillo de Vainica.

2014, Dec. 1 Perf. 13½x13
RA133   Strip of 4   1.00   1.00
a.-d.   PT52 65col Any single   .25   .25
Surtax for Children's Village.

PT53

No. RA134: a, Our Lady of Consolation Church (pink panels). b, Welder (blue panels). c, Fountain and building, San Agustín Technical College (orange panels). d, Sculpure and building, San Agustín Technical College (green panels).

2015, Dec. 1 Litho. Perf. 14
RA134 PT53 65col Block or vert.
     strip of 4,
     #a-d   1.00   1.00
Surtax for Children's Village.

GUANACASTE

ˌgwä-nə-ˈkästä

(A province of Costa Rica)

LOCATION — Northwestern coast of Central America
AREA — 4,000 sq. mi. (approx.)
POP. — 69,531 (estimated)
CAPITAL — Liberia

Residents of Guanacaste were allowed to buy Costa Rican stamps, overprinted "Guanacaste," at a discount from face value because of the province's isolation and climate, which make it difficult to keep mint stamps. Use was restricted to the province.

Counterfeits of most Guanacaste overprints are plentiful.

For 5c stamps between Nos. 5-43, unused examples without gum sell for slightly more than the used value.

Very fine examples of Nos. 1-54 will have perforations just clear of the design on one or more sides.

Dangerous counterfeits exist of Nos. 1-63.

On Issue of 1883

16mm

1885 Unwmk. Perf. 12
Overprinted Horizontally in Black
1   A6   1c green   4.00   3.25
2   A6   2c carmine   4.00   3.25
   a.   "Gnanacaste"   250.00
3   A6   10c orange   35.00   21.00
   a.   "Gnanacaste"   500.00
Same Overprint in Red
4   A6   1c green   4.00   3.25
   a.   200.00
   b.   Overprinted in black & red   300.00
5   A6   5c blue violet   30.00   4.00
   a.   "Gnanacaste"   350.00
6   A6   40c blue   25.00   21.00

17½mm

Overprinted Horizontally in Black
7   A6   1c green   10.00   7.00
8   A6   2c carmine   10.00   7.00
9   A6   5c blue violet   60.00   15.00
10   A6   10c orange   75.00   35.00
11   A6   40c blue   75.00   60.00
Same Overprint in Red
12   A6   5c blue violet   2,000.   250.00
13   A6   40c blue   2,000.

18½mm — c

Overprinted Horizontally in Black
14   A6   2c carmine   10.00   7.00
15   A6   10c orange   100.00   75.00
Same Overprint in Red
16   A6   1c green   7.00   7.00
   a.   Double ovpt., one in blk   250.00
17   A6   5c blue violet   45.00   15.00
18   A6   40c blue   75.00   75.00
Same Overprint, Vertically in Black
19   A6   1c green   5,000.
20   A6   2c carmine   4,250.
21   A6   5c blue violet   800.00   200.00
22   A6   10c orange   200.00   200.00

e   f

---

g

h

i

Overprinted Type e, Vertically
23   A6   1c green   3,000.   2,000.
24   A6   2c carmine   1,500.   300.00
25   A6   5c blue violet   400.00   75.00
26   A6   10c orange   75.00   75.00

Overprinted Type f, Vertically
27   A6   1c green   2,000.   2,000.
28   A6   2c carmine   1,000.   400.00
29   A6   5c blue violet   400.00   125.00
30   A6   10c orange   100.00   100.00

Overprinted Type g, Vertically
31   A6   1c green   3,000.   2,500.
32   A6   2c carmine   1,500.   1,000.
33   A6   5c blue violet   800.00   250.00
34   A6   10c orange   200.00   150.00

Overprinted Type h, Vertically
35   A6   1c green   3,000.   1,500.
36   A6   2c carmine   1,000.   300.00
37   A6   5c blue violet   600.00   75.00
38   A6   10c orange   100.00   60.00

Overprinted Type i, Vertically
39   A6   1c green   500.00
39A   A6   2c carmine   300.00
40   A6   5c blue violet   20.00
41   A6   10c orange   250.00

On Issues of 1883-87

Overprinted Horizontally in Black

1888-89
42   A7   5c blue violet   15.00   3.00

Overprinted Horizontally in Black

43   A7   5c blue violet   15.00   3.00

Overprinted Horizontally in Black

44   A6   2c carmine   4.00
45   A7   10c orange   4.00
Inverted overprints are fakes.

On Issue of 1889
Overprinted Like Nos. 7-13

1889   Horizontally
47   A8   2c blue   25.00
Vertically
48   A8   2c blue (c)   250.00
49   A8   2c blue (e)   100.00
51   A8   2c blue (f)   100.00
52   A8   2c blue (g)   350.00
54   A8   2c blue (h)   100.00

Nos. 47-54 are overprinted "Correos." Stamps without "Correos" are known postally used. Unused examples are valued the same as Nos. 47-54, unused. The 1c without "Correos" is known postally used. The 1c with "Correos" is counterfeit.

On Nos. 25-33
Overprinted
Horizontally in Black

1889 *Perf. 14 and 15*

55	A10	1c brown	10.00	3.50
56	A11	2c dark green	4.50	1.50
57	A12	5c orange	6.75	2.10
58	A13	10c red brown	6.75	2.10
59	A14	20c yellow green	1.00	.70
60	A15	50c rose red	1.75	1.50
61	A16	1p blue	4.50	4.50
62	A17	2p violet	13.00	6.75
63	A18	5p olive green	60.00	37.50
		Nos. 55-63 (9)	108.25	60.15

Overprinted "GUAGACASTE"

60a	A15	50c rose red	325.00	325.00
61a	A16	1p blue	325.00	325.00
62a	A17	2p violet	400.00	400.00
63a	A18	5p olive green	600.00	600.00

Values for Nos. 60a-63a used are for examples with remainder cancels.

Overprinted
Horizontally in Black

64	A10	1c brown	2.25	1.50
a.	Vert. pair, imperf. between			
65	A11	2c dark green	2.25	1.50
66	A12	5c orange	2.25	1.50
67	A13	10c red brown	2.25	1.50
		Nos. 64-67 (4)	9.00	6.00

CRETE

'krēt

LOCATION — An island in the Mediterranean Sea south of Greece
GOVT. — A department of Greece
AREA — 3,235 sq. mi.
POP. — 336,150 (1913)
CAPITAL — Canea

Formerly Crete was a province of Turkey. After an extended period of civil wars, France, Great Britain, Italy and Russia intervened and declaring Crete an autonomy, placed it under the administration of Prince George of Greece as High Commissioner. In October, 1908, the Cretan Assembly voted for union with Greece and in 1913 the union was formally effected.

40 Paras = 1 Piaster
4 Metallik = 1 Grosion (1899)
100 Lepta = 1 Drachma (1900)

Issued Under Joint Administration of France, Great Britain, Italy and Russia
British Sphere of Administration District of Heraklion (Candia)

A1

Handstamped
1898 Unwmk. *Imperf.*

1	A1	20pa violet	400.00	225.00

A2

1898 **Litho.** *Perf. 11½*

2	A2	10pa blue	6.50	2.00
a.	Horiz. pair, imperf. btwn.		200.00	
b.	Imperf., pair		225.00	
c.	Horiz. pair, imperf. vert.		225.00	
3	A2	20pa green		6.50	2.00
a.	Imperf., pair		225.00	

1899

4	A2	10pa brown	6.50	2.00
a.	Horiz. pair, imperf. btwn.		200.00	
b.	Imperf., pair		225.00	
5	A2	20pa rose		8.00	2.00
a.	Imperf., pair		225.00	

Used values for Nos. 2-5 are for stamps canceled by the straight-line "Heraklion" town postmark. Stamps canceled with any other postmark used for postal duty are scarce and worth much more. Other cancellations, values from: Ag. Thomas, $65; Ag. Myron, $70; Arkanais, $90; Episkopi, $170; Kastelli, $175; Moirais, $175; Xarakas, $190; Chersonissos, $235; and Moxos.
Counterfeits exist of Nos. 1-5.

Russian Sphere of Administration District of Rethymnon

Coat of Arms
A3   A4

1899 **Handstamped** *Imperf.*
Laid paper
No Gum

10	A3	1m green	13.50	5.50
11	A3	2m black	11.00	4.00
12	A3	2m rose	325.00	225.00
13	A4	1m blue	100.00	75.00

Wove paper

10E	A3	1m green	13.00	5.00
11E	A3	2m black	13.00	5.00
12E	A3	2m rose	225.00	165.00
13E	A4	1m blue	100.00	60.00

Quadrille paper

10J	A3	1m green	350.00	
11J	A3	2m black	350.00	80.00
12J	A3	2m rose	500.00	
13J	A4	1m violet		650.00

Nos. 10-13 normally have a circular control mark applied in violet or blue on blocks of four stamps. They also are known without this control mark (errors) and occasionally with the small round control marks of the next issue, in blue or violet (probably proofs). They are sometimes found with pin-perforations. Other varieties exist.
Counterfeits exist.

Poseidon's Trident — A5a
A5

1899 **Litho.** *Perf. 11½*
With Control Mark Overprinted in Violet
Without Stars at Sides

14	A5	1m orange	175.00	115.00
15	A5	2m orange	175.00	115.00
16	A5	1gr orange	175.00	115.00
17	A5	1m green	175.00	115.00
18	A5	2m green	175.00	115.00
19	A5	1gr green	175.00	115.00
20	A5	1m yellow	175.00	115.00
21	A5	2m yellow	175.00	115.00
22	A5	1gr yellow	175.00	115.00
23	A5	1m rose	175.00	115.00
24	A5	2m rose	175.00	115.00
25	A5	1gr rose	175.00	115.00
26	A5	1m violet	175.00	115.00
27	A5	2m violet	175.00	115.00
28	A5	1gr violet	175.00	115.00
29	A5	1m blue	175.00	115.00
30	A5	2m blue	175.00	115.00
31	A5	1gr blue	175.00	115.00
32	A5	1m black	1,250.	1,150.
33	A5	2m black	1,250.	1,150.
34	A5	1gr black	1,250.	1,150.

With Stars at Sides

35	A5a	1m blue	37.50	30.00
36	A5a	2m blue	15.00	12.50
37	A5a	1gr blue	13.00	8.50
38	A5a	1m rose	160.00	70.00
39	A5a	2m rose	15.00	12.00
40	A5a	1gr rose	12.50	8.50
41	A5a	1m green	37.50	30.00
42	A5a	2m green	15.00	12.00
43	A5a	1gr green	12.50	8.50
44	A5a	1m violet	37.50	30.00
45	A5a	2m violet	15.00	12.00
46	A5a	1gr violet	12.50	8.50
a.	Horiz. pair, imperf. btwn.		250.00	
b.	Vert. pair, imperf. horiz.		190.00	
		Nos. 35-46 (12)	383.00	242.50

Almost all of Nos. 14 to 46 may be found without control mark, with double control marks and in various colors.
Used values for Nos. 35-46 are for stamps with postmarks of Rethymnon. Thirteen other post offices existed, and stamps with postmarks other than Rethymnon are scarce and command significant premiums: Ag. Galini, $125; Amari, $90; Anogeia, $525; Garazo, $160; Damasta, $550; Kastelli, $125; Margaritais, $550; Melampes, $375; Pigi, $125; Roystika, $70; Xenia, $105; Spili, $105; Fodede, $550.
Counterfeits exist of Nos. 14-46.
Nos. 14-31 exist imperf. Value, unused pair each $1,150.

Issued by the Cretan Government

Hermes — A6   Hera — A7

Prince George of
Greece — A8

1900, Mar. 1 **Engr.** *Perf. 14*

50	A6	1 l violet brown	.40	.45
51	A7	5 l green	1.80	.45
52	A8	10 l red	1.35	.45
53	A7	20 l carmine rose	5.00	2.00
		Nos. 50-53 (4)	8.55	3.35

See #64-71. For overprints and surcharges see #54-63, 72-73, 85, 88, 93, 97-99, 108, 111.

Overprinted

Red Overprint

54	A8	25 l blue	.80	1.00
55	A6	50 l lilac	2.00	1.35
56	A9	1d gray violet	11.00	13.50
57	A10	2d brown	55.00	32.50
58	A11	5d green & blk	185.00	200.00
		Nos. 54-58 (5)	253.80	248.35

Black Overprint

59	A8	25 l blue	1.60	.75
60	A6	50 l lilac	1.60	1.50
61	A9	1d gray violet	8.75	5.75
a.	Inverted overprint		350.00	350.00
62	A10	2d brown	23.00	17.00
63	A11	5d green & blk	100.00	110.00
		Nos. 59-63 (5)	134.95	135.00

Talos — A9   Minos — A10

St. George and the
Dragon — A11

1901 **Without Overprint**

64	A6	1 l bister	1.00	1.15
65	A7	20 l orange	3.00	1.15
66	A8	25 l blue	8.75	.85
67	A6	50 l lilac	37.50	27.50
68	A6	50 l ultra	13.00	13.00
69	A9	1d gray violet	40.00	27.50
70	A10	2d brown	13.00	11.50
71	A11	5d green & blk	16.50	13.00
		Nos. 64-71 (8)	132.75	95.65

No. 64 is a revenue stamp that was used for postage for short periods in 1901 and 1904.
Types A6 to A8 in olive yellow, and types A9 to A11 in olive yellow and black are revenue stamps.
See note following No. 53.

Surcharges with the year "1922" on designs A6, A8, A9, A11, A13, A15-A23 and D1 are listed under Greece.

No. 66 Overprinted in
Black

ΠΡΟΣΩΡΙΝΟΝ

1901

72	A8	25 l blue	22.50	.75
a.	First letter of ovpt. invtd.		475.00	300.00
b.	Inverted overprint		700.00	350.00
c.	"S" of "PROSORINON" omitted		200.00	80.00

No. 65 Surcharged in
Black

1904, Dec.

73	A7	5 l on 20 l orange	2.25	.75
a.	Without "5" at right		150.00	150.00

Mycenaean
Seal — A12

Britomartis
(Cortyna
Coin) — A13

Prince
George — A14

Kydon and Dog
(Cydonia
Coin) — A15

Triton (Itanos
Coin) — A16

Ariadne
(Knossos
Coin) — A17

Zeus as Bull Abducting Europa (Cortyna Coin) A18

Palace of Minos Ruins, Knossos A19

Arkadi Monastery and Mt. Ida — A20

1905, Feb. 15

74	A12	2 l dull violet	1.25	.35
75	A13	5 l yellow grn	1.50	.35
76	A14	10 l red	1.50	.75
77	A15	20 l blue grn	5.50	1.00
78	A16	25 l ultra	7.00	1.00
79	A17	50 l yellow brn	7.50	3.25
80	A18	1 d rose car & dp brn	72.50	62.50
81	A19	3 d orange & blk	50.00	40.00
82	A20	5 d ol grn & blk	25.00	25.00
		Nos. 74-82 (9)	171.75	134.20

For overprints see Nos. 86-87, 89, 91-92, 94-95, 104, 106, 109-110, 112-113, 115-120.

The so-called revolutionary stamps of 1905 were issued for sale to collectors and, so far as can be ascertained, were of no postal value.

A. T. A. Zaimis A21

Prince George Landing at Suda A22

1907, Aug. 28

83	A21	25 l blue & blk	36.00	.85
84	A22	1 d green & blk	9.00	7.00

Administration under a High Commissioner. For overprints see Nos. 90, 105, 107.

Stamps of 1900-1907 Overprinted in Black

1908, Sept. 21

85	A6	1 l violet brn	.55	.40
a.		Inverted overprint	—	
86	A12	2 l dull violet	.55	.40
a.		Pair, one without ovpt.	—	
87	A13	5 l yellow grn	.55	.40
88	A8	10 l red	1.15	.80
a.		Pair, one without ovpt.	—	
89	A15	20 l blue grn	3.00	1.00
90	A21	25 l blue & blk	8.50	2.50
91	A17	50 l yellow brn	11.50	4.25
a.		Inverted overprint	—	
92	A18	1 d rose car & dp brn	95.00	67.50
93	A10	2 d brown	10.00	8.00
94	A19	3 d orange & blk	45.00	37.50
95	A20	5 d ol grn & blk	35.00	30.00
		Nos. 85-95 (11)	210.80	152.75
		Set, never hinged	400.00	

This overprint exists inverted and double, as well as with incorrect, reversed, misplaced and omitted letters. Similar errors are found on the

Postage Due and Official stamps with this overprint.

Hermes by Praxiteles — A23

1908

96	A23	10 l brown red	2.75	.80
a.		Pair, one without overprint	150.00	150.00
b.		Inverted overprint	—	
c.		Double overprint	—	

Nos. 96 and 114 were not regularly issued without overprint.

For overprints see Nos. 103, 114.

No. 53 Surcharged

1909

97	A7	5 l on 20 l car rose	220.00	245.00

Forgeries exist of No. 97.

On No. 65

98	A7	5 l on 20 l orange	1.25	1.10
a.		Inverted surcharge	150.00	150.00
b.		Double surcharge	120.00	120.00

Overprinted on Nos. 64, J1

99	A6	1 l bister	3.50	3.50
100	D1	1 l red	1.25	1.25

No. J4 Surcharged

101	D1	2 l on 20 l red	1.25	1.25
b.		Inverted surcharge	75.00	
c.		Second letter of surcharge "D" instead of "P"	50.00	50.00

No. J4 Surcharged

102	D1	2 l on 20 l red	1.25	1.25
a.		Double overprint	125.00	125.00

Overprinted in Black

a

b

c

103	A23(a)	10 l brown red	3.00	1.00
a.		Inverted overprint	110.00	
104	A15(a)	20 l blue grn	4.00	1.00
105	A21(c)	25 l blue & blk	5.00	2.00
106	A17(a)	50 l yellow brn	7.00	4.00
107	A22(b)	1 d green & blk	12.50	7.00
108	A10(a)	2 d brown	12.50	10.00
109	A19(b)	3 d org & blk	125.00	115.00
110	A20(b)	5 d ol grn & blk	52.50	52.50
		Nos. 103-110 (8)	221.50	192.50

Stamps of 1900-08 Overprinted in Red or Black

1909-10

111	A6	1 l violet brown	.35	.25
112	A12	2 l dull violet	.35	.25
113	A13	5 l yellow green	.35	.25
114	A23	10 l brown red (Bk)	.60	.60
115	A15	20 l blue green	2.00	.70
116	A16	25 l ultra	2.50	.75
117	A17	50 l yellow brn	7.00	2.00
118	A18	1 d rose car & dp brn (Bk)	100.00	100.00
119	A19	3 d orange & blk	85.00	85.00
120	A20	5 d ol grn & blk	55.00	55.00
		Nos. 111-120 (10)	253.15	244.80

POSTAGE DUE STAMPS

D1

1901 Unwmk. Litho. Perf. 14

J1	D1	1 l red	.30	.30
J2	D1	5 l red	.50	.30
J3	D1	10 l red	.75	.40
J4	D1	20 l red	1.00	.50
J5	D1	40 l red	11.50	11.50
J6	D1	50 l red	11.50	11.50
J7	D1	1 d red	22.50	22.50
J8	D1	2 d red	14.00	12.50
		Nos. J1-J8 (8)	62.05	59.50
		Set, never hinged	115.00	

For overprints and surcharges see Nos. 100-102, J9-J26.

Surcharged in Black

1901

J9	D1	1 d on 1 d red	11.00	10.00

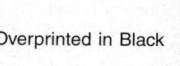

Overprinted in Black

1908

J10	D1	1 l red	.35	.35
J11	D1	5 l red	.60	.60
J12	D1	10 l red	.60	.60
J13	D1	20 l red	2.00	2.00
J14	D1	40 l red	8.25	7.50
J15	D1	50 l red	10.50	9.00
J16	D1	1 d red	475.00	475.00
a.		Pair, one without ovpt.	—	

J17	D1	1 d on 1 d red	11.50	10.00
J18	D1	2 d red	19.00	10.00
		Nos. J10-J18 (9)	527.80	515.05

Nos. J10-J18 exist with inverted overprint. See note after No. 95.
Counterfeits of No. J16 exist.

Overprinted in Black

O1 O2

1910

J19	D1	1 l red	.45	.30
J20	D1	5 l red	1.00	.35
J21	D1	10 l red	1.00	.35
J22	D1	20 l red	3.25	1.75
J23	D1	40 l red	11.00	6.00
J24	D1	50 l red	16.50	12.00
J25	D1	1 d red	27.50	27.50
J26	D1	2 d red	27.50	27.50
		Nos. J19-J26 (8)	88.20	75.75

OFFICIAL STAMPS

1908, Jan. 14   Unwmk.   Litho.   Perf. 14

O1	O1	10 l dull claret	18.00	1.50
O2	O2	30 l blue	37.50	1.50

Nos. O1-O2 exist imperf.

Nos. O1-O2 Overprinted

O3	O1	10 l dull claret	13.00	1.20
a.		Inverted overprint	100.00	100.00
O4	O2	30 l blue	27.50	1.20
a.		Inverted overprint	200.00	200.00

See note after No. 95.

Nos. O1-O2 Overprinted

1910

O5	O1	10 l dull claret	2.25	1.40
O6	O2	30 l blue	2.25	1.40

Nos. O5-O6 remained in use until 1922, nine years after union with Greece.

CROATIA

krō-'ā-shē̠-ə

LOCATION — Southeastern Europe
GOVT. — Independent state
AREA — 44,453 sq. mi.
POP. — 7,000,000 (approx.)
CAPITAL — Zagreb

The Independent Croatian State of 1941-45 became part of the Yugoslav Federation in 1945.
Croatia declared its independence in 1991.

100 Paras = 1 Dinar
100 Banica = 1 Kuna

Catalogue values for unused stamps in this country are for Never Hinged items, beginning with Scott 1 in the regular postage section, Scott B1 in the semi-postal section, Scott C1 in the airmail section and Scott RA1 in the postal tax section.

Watermark

Wmk. 278 — Network Connecting Circles

Yugoslavia Nos. 143 to 148B Overprinted in Black

Perf. 12½

1941, Apr. 12   Unwmk.   Typo.

1	A16	50p orange	4.50	3.75
a.		Inverted overprint	225.00	
2	A16	1d yellow grn	5.25	3.75
a.		Double overprint	110.00	
3	A16	1.50d red	6.00	2.25
a.		Double overprint	110.00	
4	A16	2d deep magenta	6.75	3.75
5	A16	3d dull red brn	11.00	6.75
a.		Double overprint	110.00	
6	A16	4d ultra	15.00	7.50
7	A16	5d dark blue	18.50	8.25
8	A16	5.50d dk violet brn	22.50	9.00
a.		Double overprint	110.00	
		Nos. 1-8 (8)	89.50	45.00

Counterfeit overprints exist of Nos. 1-8, especially the inverted and double overprint varieties.

Yugoslavia Nos. 142 to 154 Overprinted in Black

1941, Apr. 21

9	A16	25p black	.75	.50
a.		Inverted overprint	75.00	
b.		Double overprint	75.00	
10	A16	50p orange	.75	.50
a.		Inverted overprint	75.00	
11	A16	1d yellow grn	.75	.50
a.		Inverted overprint	—	
12	A16	1.50d red	.80	.50
a.		Double overprint	150.00	
13	A16	2d deep magenta	.80	.50
14	A16	3d dull red brn	1.10	.95
15	A16	4d ultra	1.50	1.40
16	A16	5d dark blue	1.90	1.40
a.		Double overprint	200.00	
17	A16	5.50d dk violet brn	2.25	1.40
a.		Inverted overprint	375.00	
b.		Double overprint	200.00	
18	A16	6d slate blue	3.00	2.25
19	A16	8d sepia	3.75	2.25
20	A16	12d brt violet	4.50	3.00
a.		Inverted overprint	375.00	

21	A16	16d dull violet	5.25	4.50
a.		Double overprint	200.00	
22	A16	20d blue	6.75	5.25
23	A16	30d bright pink	12.00	10.00
		Nos. 9-23 (15)	45.85	34.90

The overprint exists double, both inverted, on Nos. 16, 18 and 19.

Yugoslavia Nos. 147, 148 Surcharged in Black

1941, May 16

24	A16	1d on 3d dull red brn	.40	.40
a.		Inverted overprint	75.00	
b.		Double overprint	75.00	
25	A16	2d on 4d ultra	.40	.40
a.		Inverted overprint	75.00	
b.		Double overprint	75.00	

Postage Due Stamps of Yugoslavia, Nos. J28, J30 to J32, Overprinted in Black

1941, May 17

26	D4	50p violet	.50	.45
27	D4	2d deep blue	1.35	1.25
28	D4	5d orange	1.90	1.40
29	D4	10d chocolate	2.25	1.60
		Nos. 26-29 (4)	6.00	4.70

Counterfeit cancellations exist for Nos. 1-29 on cover.

Imperforates

Nearly all Croatian stamps, from No. 30 through 80, B3 through B76, J6 through J25, O1 through O24 and RA1 through RA7 exist imperforate, imperforate vertically, and imperforate horizontally. These are primarily from the special Ministerial Albums issued by the State Printing Office.

Ozalj Castle — A1

Designs: 50b, City of Jajce. 75b, Old Warasdin. 1k, Velebit Mountains. 1.50k, Zelanjak. 2k, Zagreb Cathedral. 3k, Osjek Cathedral. 4k, Drina River. No. 38, Konjic. No. 39, Zemun. 6k, Dubrovnik. 7k, Save River. 8k, Sarajevo. 10k, Plitvice. 12k, Klis Fortress, Split. 20k, Hvar. 30k, Syrmia. 50k, Senj. 100k, Banjaluka (without "F.I.").

Perf. 11¼.

1941-43   Unwmk.   Photo.
Ordinary Paper

30	A1	25b henna	.25	.25
31	A1	50b slate blue	.25	.25
32	A1	75b dk olive grn	.25	.25
33	A1	1k Pruss grn	.25	.25
34	A1	1.50k deep green	.25	.25
35	A1	2k carmine lake	.25	.25
36	A1	3k brown red	.25	.25
37	A1	4k deep ultra	.25	.25
38	A1	5k black	2.00	1.15
39	A1	5k blue	.25	.25
40	A1	6k lt olive brn	.25	.25
41	A1	7k orange red	.30	.25
42	A1	8k chestnut	.40	.30
43	A1	10k dark plum	.90	.45
44	A1	12k olive brown	1.50	.50
45	A1	20k golden brown	1.10	.40
46	A1	30k black brown	1.50	.50
47	A1	50k dk slate green	3.75	1.50
48	A1	100k violet	5.25	3.00
		Nos. 30-48 (19)	19.20	11.05

Nos. 30-48 exist with a variety of perforations, including 11¼x10¾ and 12. Examples of Nos. 30, 36 and 48 exist with a special printer's mark in the design. Two varieties of printer's mark are known for No. 30, one for the first printing, and one for the second. Usually one stamp per pane has the printer's mark.

Nos. 31, 35 and 43 exist on thin to pelure paper, as does No. 32, though the latter was not issued to the public. Shades of all values exist.
For overprints and surcharge see Nos. 49-51, 53.

Tête bêche Pairs

30a	A1	25b	1.75	2.75
31a	A1	50b	2.00	3.50
33a	A1	1k	2.50	4.00
34a	A1	1.50k	2.75	5.00
35a	A1	2k	3.00	6.00
37a	A1	4k	3.95	6.50
38a	A1	5k	7.00	7.50
40a	A1	6k	4.00	7.00
41a	A1	7k	4.50	7.25
42a	A1	8k	5.00	8.00
43a	A1	10k	5.50	9.50
45a	A1	20k	6.50	10.00
46a	A1	30k	7.25	11.00
47a	A1	50k	13.00	13.00
		Nos. 30a-47a (14)	68.70	101.00

Types of 1941 Overprinted in Brown or Green

1942, Apr. 9

49	A1	2k dark brown	.60	.40
50	A1	5k dark carmine	.90	.85
51	A1	10k dark blue green (G)	1.50	1.25
		Nos. 49-51 (3)	3.00	2.50

First anniversary of Croatian independence. The overprint exists double on No. 50.
Tête bêche pairs of Nos. 49-51 are from Ministerial Albums.

Banjaluka ("F.I." at upper right) — A20

1942, June 13

| 52 | A20 | 100k violet | 4.25 | 4.25 |

Banjaluka Philatelic Exhibition.
No. 52 exists in se-tenant pair with No. 48. Value unused, $300.
No. 52 exists with a special printer's mark in the design. The mark typically appears on one stamp in a given pane.

No. 35 Surcharged in Red Brown with New Value and Bar

1942, June 23

| 53 | A1 | 25b on 2k carmine lake | .55 | .55 |
| a. | | Tête bêche pair | 3.25 | 3.25 |

No. 53 exists with double surcharge. It is not scarce.

Trakoscan Castle — A21

Design: 12.50k, Citadel of Veliki Tabor.

1943, Mar. 28   Pelure Paper

| 54 | A21 | 3.50k brown carmine | .75 | .55 |
| 55 | A21 | 12.50k violet black | 1.00 | .85 |

Nos. 54 was reissued in 1944 on ordinary paper, perf 12. Value the same for both varieties. No. 55 also exists on ordinary paper. It is scarce.

Catherine Zrinski — A23

2k, Fran Krsto Frankopan. 3.50k, Peter Zrinski.

Various Frames

1943, June 7   Engr.   Perf. 12¼x12½

56	A23	1k dark blue	.40	.40
57	A23	2k dark olive green	.40	.40
58	A23	3.50k dark red	.50	.55
		Nos. 56-58 (3)	1.30	1.35

Many perforation varieties of this issue exist, including 12x12½, 12½x13, 12½, 13, 12½x14, 13x12½, and 14x12½.

Rudjer Boscovich — A26

1943, Dec. 13   Perf. 11

| 59 | A26 | 3.50k copper red | .50 | .40 |
| 60 | A26 | 12.50k dk violet brn | .65 | .50 |

Rugjer Boscovich (1711-1787). Mathematician and physicist.
No. 60 exists with a special printer's mark in the design. The mark typically appears on one stamp in a given pane.

Ante Pavelich — A27

1943-44   Litho.   Perf. 12½, 14

61	A27	25b orange ver	.30	.25
62	A27	50b Prus blue	.30	.25
63	A27	75b olive green	.30	.25
64	A27	1k lt green	.30	.25
65	A27	1.50k dull gray vio	.30	.25
66	A27	2k rose lake	.30	.25
67	A27	3k rose brown	.30	.25
68	A27	3.50k bright blue	.30	.25
a.		3.50k dark blue, perf. 11½	4.00	4.75
69	A27	4k brt red violet	.30	.25
70	A27	5k ultra	.30	.25
71	A27	8k orange brn	.35	.25
72	A27	9k rose pink	.35	.25
73	A27	10k violet brn	.40	.25
74	A27	12k dk olive bis	.45	.25
75	A27	12.50k gray black	.55	.25
76	A27	18k dull brown	.70	.30
77	A27	32k dark brown	.75	.30
78	A27	50k grnsh blue	1.50	.50
79	A27	70k orange	1.90	.90
80	A27	100k violet	3.00	1.50
		Nos. 61-80 (20)	12.95	7.25

Nos. 61 and 63 measure 20½x26mm. Nos. 62 and 64-80 measure 22x27½mm.
Nos. 61, 63, 67, 70, 71 and 72 are perf 12½. Nos. 62, 64-66, 68, 69, 73 and 75-80 are perf 14. No. 74 exists either perf 12½ or 14.
No. 80 exists with a special printer's mark in the design. The mark typically appears on one stamp in a given pane.
Issue dates: 2k, 1943; No. 68a, June 13, 1943, Pavelich's Saint's Day; others, 1944.

"Labor Day 1945" — A28

1945   Photo.   Perf. 11½

| 81 | A28 | 3.50k red brown | .85 | 1.60 |

No. 81 exists imperforate. Value, never hinged $900.

From 1951 to 1972 44 labels were circulated by a Croatian Government in Exile. These had no postal value.

GOVT. — Independent state
AREA — 21,823 sq. mi.
POP. — 4,676,865 (1999 est.)
CAPITAL — Zagreb

Croatia declared its independence from Yugoslavia in 1991.

100 Paras = 1 Dinar (1991)
100 Lipa = 1 Kuna (1994)

Nos. RA20, RA20a Srchd. in Black and Gold

1991, Nov. 21   Litho.   Perf. 14
100 PT10 4d on 1.20d #RA20   .70 .70
a.   Perf. 11x10½   .50 .50
b.   Perf. 11   7.50 7.50

A35

1991, Dec. 10   Perf. 12
101 A35 30d multicolored   2.00 2.00
Declaration of independence, 10/8/91.

Christmas — A36

Creche figures of the Holy Family from Kosljun Monastery.

1991, Dec. 11   Perf. 12
102 A36 4d multicolored   .80 .80

No. RA21 Surcharged in Black and Gold

1992, Jan. 3   Perf. 10½x11
103 PT11 20d on 1.70d #RA21   5.75 5.75

Croatian Arms — A37

1992, Jan. 15   Perf. 11x10½
104 A37 10d multicolored   .60 .60
a.   Perf. 14   .40 .40
See No. RA22.

1992 Winter Olympics, Albertville A38

1992, Feb. 4   Perf. 11x10½
105 A38 30d multicolored   1.50 1.50

Croatian Cities and Landmarks A39

A39a

Designs: 6d, Knin. 7d, Eltz Castle, Vukovar. 20d, Church, Ilok. 30d, Starcevic Street, Gospic. 45d, Rector's Palace, Dubrovnik. 50d, St. Jakov's Cathedral, Sibenik. 100d, Vinkovci. 200d, Pazin, vert. No. 115, Beli Manastir. 500d, Slavonski Brod. 1000d, Varazdin. 2000d, Karlovac. 5000d, Zadar, vert. 10,000d, Vis.

1992-94   Perf. 14
107 A39   6d multi   .25 .25
108 A39   7d multi   .25 .25
109 A39   20d multi   .35 .35
a.   Perf. 11x10½   1.00 1.00
110 A39   30d multi   .90 .90
111 A39   45d multi   .90 .90
112 A39   50d multi   .90 .90
113 A39a   100d multi   .65 .65
114 A39a   200d multi   .35 .35
115 A39   300d multi   2.00 2.00
117 A39a   500d multi   1.90 1.90
118 A39a   1000d multi   1.00 .70
119 A39a   2000d multi   2.00 1.50
120 A39a   5000d multi   3.00 2.50
121 A39a   10,000d multi   5.50 5.00
Nos. 107-121 (14)   19.95 18.15

Issued: 6d, 4/18; 7d, 4/8; No. 109, 2/28; No. 109a, 9/9; 30d, 5/21; 45d, 4/14; 50d, 4/28; 115, 6/26; 100d, 12/14; 500d, 2/9/93; 1000d, 3/16/93; 200d, 4/9/93; 2000d, 5/20/93; 5000d, 9/24/93; 10,000d, 2/22/94.
See Nos. 355-356, 437A, 456.

Statue of King Tomislav — A40

**1992, May 5   Engr.   Perf. 12½ Horiz.
Coil Stamp**
124 A40 10d dark green   .40 .40

Railroad Station, Zagreb, Cent. — A41

1992, June 30   Litho.   Perf. 14
125 A41 30d multicolored   .40 .30

Matica, Society of Knowledge and Literacy, 150th Anniv. — A42

1992, July 8
126 A42 20d red, gold & black   .35 .30

Bishop Josip Juraj Strossmayer, Founder — A43

1992, July 9
127 A43 30d multicolored   .40 .40
Croatian Academy of Arts and Sciences, 125th anniv., in 1991.

1992 Summer Olympics, Barcelona A44

Design: 105d, Abstract design.

1992, July 25
128 A44 40d shown   .30 .30
129 A44 105d multicolored   1.25 1.25

Flowers A45

Designs: 30d, Edraianthus pumilio. 85d, Degenia velebitica, vert.

1992, July 28
130 A45 30d multicolored   .35 .35
131 A45 85d multicolored   .90 .90

Wildlife — A46

40d, Monticola solitarius. 75d, Elaphe situla.

1992, July 31
132 A46 40d multicolored   .45 .45
133 A46 75d multicolored   .85 .85

Discovery of America, 500th Anniv. — A47

Europa: 30d, 60d, Sailing ship. 75d, 130d, Indian in Chicago, by Ivan Mestrovic (1883-1962).

1992, Sep. 4   Litho.   Perf. 14
134 A47 30d multicolored   .55 .55
135 A47 60d multicolored   1.15 1.15
136 A47 75d red & black   1.30 1.30
137 A47 130d red, blk & gold   2.00 2.00
Nos. 134-137 (4)   5.00 5.00
Issued: 30d, 75d, July 31; others, Sept. 4.

A48

1992, Oct. 2
138 A48 40d reddish org & blue   .35 .35
139 A48 130d pale blue & pur   1.00 1.00
Declaration of Croatian Literary Language, 25th Anniv. (No. 138). Spelling reform by Dr. Ivan Broz, cent. (No. 139).

A49

1992, Oct. 16
140 A49 90d multicolored   .65 .40
City of Samobor, 750th Anniv.

Gift of the St. Juraj Church by Archbishop Mucimir, 1100th Anniv. — A50

1992, Oct. 30
141 A50 60d multicolored   .40 .30

Reign of King Bela IV, 750th Anniv. — A51

1992, Nov. 16   Litho.   Perf. 14
142 A51 180d multicolored   .85 .85

Christmas A52

1992, Dec. 7
143 A52 80d multicolored   .40 .35

Blaz Lorkovic (1839-1892), Scientist — A53

1992, Dec. 21
144 A53 250d multicolored   .90 .90

Kolo Literature Review, 150th Anniv. — A54

1992, Dec. 22
145 A54 300d multicolored 1.10 1.10

Ivan Bunic-Vucic (1592-1658) A55

1992, Dec. 29
146 A55 350d multicolored 1.10 1.10

800th Anniv. of Krapina — A55a

1993, Jan. 15
146A A55a 300d multicolored .70 .70

Nikola Tesla (1856-1943), Physicist A56

1993, Jan. 30
147 A56 250d multicolored .70 .70

Self-Portrait, by Ferdo Quiquerez (1845-1893) A57

1993, Feb. 10
148 A57 100d multicolored .40 .40

Wildlife — A58

500d, Cervus elaphus. 550d, Haliaeetus albicilla.

1993, Feb. 23 **Litho.** **Perf. 14**
149 A58 500d multi 1.00 1.00
150 A58 550d multi 1.00 1.00

Self-Portrait, by Zlatko Sulentic (1893-1971) A59

1993, Mar. 17
151 A59 350d multicolored .55 .55

Lipik Health and Convalescent Home, Cent. — A60

1993, Apr. 22 **Litho.** **Perf. 14**
152 A60 400d multicolored .55 .55

Ivan Goran Kovacic (1913-1943), Author — A61

1993, Apr. 24
153 A61 200d multicolored .35 .35

59th PEN Congress, Dubrovnik A62

1993, Apr. 24
154 A62 800d multicolored 1.25 1.25

Ivan Kukuljevic (1816-89), Politician, Historian, Writer — A63

1993, May 2 **Litho.** **Perf. 14**
155 A63 500d multicolored .65 .65

Croatian Natl. Theatre, Split, Cent. — A64

1993, May 6 **Litho.** **Perf. 14**
156 A64 600d multicolored .75 .75

Pag, 500th Anniv. — A65

1993, May 18
157 A65 800d multicolored .75 .75

Croatian Membership in United Nations, 1st Anniv. — A66

1993, May 22
158 A66 500d multicolored .60 .60

Europa A67

Contemporary paintings by: 700d, Ivo Dulcic (1916-75). 1000d, Miljenko Stancic (1926-77). 1100d, Ljubo Ivancic (b. 1925).

1993, June 5
159 A67 700d multicolored .75 .75
160 A67 1000d multicolored 1.50 1.50
161 A67 1100d multicolored 2.25 2.25
a. Min. sheet, 2 each #159-161 9.00 9.00
Nos. 159-161 (3) 4.50 4.50

Intl. Art Biennial, Venice — A68

Works of art by: 250d, Milivoj Bijelic. 600d, Ivo Dekovic. 1000d, Zeljko Kipke.

1993, June 10 **Litho.** **Perf. 14**
162 A68 250d multicolored .30 .30
a. Souvenir sheet of 4 1.00 1.00
163 A68 600d multicolored .85 .85
a. Souvenir sheet of 4 3.00 3.00
164 A68 1000d multicolored 1.20 1.20
a. Souvenir sheet of 4 4.00 4.00
Nos. 162-164 (3) 2.35 2.35

1993 Mediterranean Games — A69

1993, June 15 **Litho.** **Perf. 14**
165 A69 700d multicolored .65 .65

Adolf Waldinger (1843-1904), Painter — A70

1993, June 16
166 A70 300d multicolored .35 .35

Famous Croatian Battles A71

800d, Krbavskom, 1493. 1300d, Sisak, 1593.

1993, July 6 **Litho.** **Perf. 14**
167 A71 800d multi .65 .65
168 A71 1300d multi 1.10 1.10

Miroslav Krleza (1893-1981), Writer — A72

1993, July 7
169 A72 400d multicolored .40 .40

Croatian Membership in UPU, 1st Anniv. — A73

1993, July 20 **Litho.** **Perf. 14**
170 A73 1800d multicolored 1.25 .80

Vlaho Paljetak (1893-1944), Composer A74

1993, Aug. 7
171 A74 500d multicolored .45 .45

Stamp Day — A75

1993, Sept. 9 **Litho.** **Perf. 14**
172 A75 600d multicolored .50 .50

Map of Istria, 1620 — A76

1993, Sept. 20
173 A76 2200d multicolored   1.20 1.20
Incorporation of Istria, Rijeka and Zadar into Croatia, 50th anniv.

Tadija Smiciklas (1843-1914), Historian — A77

1993, Oct. 1
174 A77 800d black, gold & red   .60 .60

Archaelogical Museum, Split, Cent. — A78

1993, Oct. 27
175 A78 1000d multicolored   .60 .60

A79

1993, Nov. 17   Litho.   Perf. 14
176 A79 3000d multicolored   1.50 1.50
Uprising of 13th Pioneer Battalion, Villefranche-de-Rouergue, France, 50th anniv.

A80

Josip Eugen Tomic (1843-1906), writer.

1993, Nov. 18
177 A80 900d multicolored   .50 .50

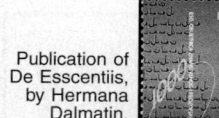

Publication of De Esscentiis, by Hermana Dalmatin, 850th Anniv. — A81

1993, Nov. 30
178 A81 1000d multicolored   .50 .50

Christmas A82

Paintings: 1000d, Christmas at the Front, by Miroslav Sutej. 4000d, Birth of Christ, 15th cent. fresco, Marienkirch of Dvigrad.

1993, Dec. 3
179 A82 1000d multicolored   1.00 1.00
180 A82 4000d multicolored   2.00 2.00
Nos. 179-180 are known with gold omitted. Values: No. 179, $90 mint; No. 180, $175 mint.

Organized Skiing in Croatia, Cent. — A83

1993, Dec. 15
181 A83 1000d multicolored   .80 .80

Croatian Natl. Guard, 125th Anniv. A84

1993, Dec. 22
182 A84 1100d multicolored   .80 .80

Printers of Senj, 500th Anniv. — A85

1994, Jan. 29
183 A85 2200d multicolored   1.10 .80

1994 Winter Olympics, Lillehammer A86

1994, Feb. 12
184 A86 4000d multicolored   1.90 1.60

Dinosaurs from Western Istria — A87

a, 2400d, Iguanodons. b, 4000d, Map, skeleton.

1994, Mar. 7
185 A87 Pair, #a.-b.   3.25 3.25
Nos. 185a-185b are a continuous design.

Zora Dalmatinska Magazine, 150th Anniv. — A88

1994, Mar. 15
186 A88 800d multicolored   .50 .35

Croatian University, Zagreb, 325th Anniv. — A89

Design: 2200d, University building, Emperor Leopold I's seal, vice-chancellor's chain.

1994, Apr. 19   Litho.   Perf. 14
187 A89 2200d multicolored   1.10 .75

Protect the Environment A90

1994, Apr. 22   Litho.   Perf. 14
188 A90 3800d Canis lupus   2.00 1.75

ILO, 75th Anniv. — A91

1994, May 2
189 A91 1000d multicolored   .60 .40

Europa — A93

European inventions, discoveries: 3800d, Faust Vrancic (1551-1617), parachute. 4000d, Slavoljub Penkala (1871-1922), fountain pen.

1994, May 16
190 A92 3800d multicolored   *2.25 2.00*
191 A93 4000d multicolored   *2.75 2.00*

Flowers — A94

2.40k, Iris croatica. 4k, Colchicum visianii.

1994, June 3
192 A94 2.40k multicolored   1.00 .60
193 A94 4k multicolored   1.60 1.25

A95

Drazen Petrovic (1964-93), basketball player.

1994, June 7
194 A95 1k multicolored   .75 .75

Tourism in Croatia, 150th Anniv. — A96

Designs: 80 l, Plitvice Lakes Natl. Park. 1k, Waterfalls, Krka River. 1.10k, Kornati Islands Natl. Park. 2.20k, Kopacki Trscak nature reserve. 2.40k Sailboats, Opatijska Riviera resort. 3.80k, Brijuni islands. 4k, Trakoscan castle, Zagorje.

1994, June 15   Litho.   Perf. 14
196 A96 80 l multicolored   .45 .25
197 A96   1k multicolored   .50 .30
198 A96 1.10k multicolored   .55 .35
199 A96 2.20k multicolored   1.25 .40
200 A96 2.40k multicolored   1.40 .60
201 A96 3.80k multicolored   2.10 .75
202 A96   4k multicolored   2.40 1.00
a.   Min. sheet of 7, #196-202 + 2 labels   8.50 8.00
  Nos. 196-202 (7)   8.65 3.65

Croatian Musicians A97

Designs: 1k, Kresimir Baranovic (1894-1975), composer, vert. 2.20k, Vatroslav Lisinski (1819-54), composer, vert. 2.40k, Pauline song-book (1644), harpist.

1994, June 20
211 A97   1k multicolored   .50 .35
212 A97 2.20k multicolored   1.10 .75
213 A97 2.40k multicolored   1.25 .85
  Nos. 211-213 (3)   2.85 1.95

Croatian Fraternal Union, Cent. — A98

1994, Aug. 15   Litho.   Perf. 14
214 A98 2.20k multicolored   1.25 1.25

Intl. Year of the Family — A99

1994, Aug. 31
215 A99 80 l multicolored .50 .50

A100

1994, Sept. 10
216 A100 1k multicolored .60 .60
Intl. Olympic Committee, cent.

Visit of Pope John Paul II — A101

1994, Sept. 10
217 A101 1k multicolored .75 .75
No. 217 printed with se-tenant label.

Antoine de Saint-Exupery (1900-44), Aviator, Author A102

1994, Sept. 20
218 A102 3.80k multicolored 1.90 1.40

13th Intl. Congress on Early Christian Archeology A103

1994, Sept. 23
219 A103 4k multicolored 2.00 1.40
No. 219 printed with se-tenant label.

Modern Croatian Paintings A104

Designs: 2.40k, Still Life with Fruits and Basket, by Marino Tartaglia, 1926. 3.80k, In the Park, by Milan Steiner, c. 1918. 4k, Self-portrait, by Vilko Gecan, 1929.

1994, Oct. 12
220 A104 2.40k multicolored 1.00 .75
221 A104 3.80k multicolored 1.60 1.25
222 A104 4k multicolored 1.75 1.25
  Nos. 220-222 (3) 4.35 3.25

Ivan Belostenec (1594-1675), Writer & Lexicographer A105

1994, Nov. 9
223 A105 2.20k multicolored 1.10 .90

City of Zagreb, Zagreb Bishopric, 900th Anniv. — A106

Designs: No. 224a, 1k, Zagreb exchange building, designed by V. Kovacic, S. Penkala's airplane, Cibona office tower, designed by Hrzic, Pitesa and Serbetic. b, 1k, Maxi Cat, by Zlatko Grgic, Zagreb School of Animated Film. c, 1k, St. Mark's Church, Gradec; photo of gas lantern, by Toso Dabac. d, 4k, Late Gothic bishop's staff, Valvasor's view of Zagreb. 13.50k, Zagreb street scene, Penkala's airplane, vert.

1994, Nov. 16
224 A106 Strip of 4, #a.-d. 3.00 3.00
Souvenir Sheet
225 A106 13.50k multicolored 5.00 5.00
No. 224 is a continuous design. No. 225 contains one 24x48mm stamp.

Christmas A107

Design: 1k, Epiphany, by unknown sculptor.

1994, Dec. 1 Litho. Perf. 14
226 A107 1k multicolored .60 .50

Virgin Mary's Sanctuary, Loreto, 700th Anniv. — A108

Design: 4k, The Moving of the Holy House, by Giovanni Battista Tiepolo.

1994, Dec. 10
227 A108 4k multicolored 2.00 1.50

Necktie in Croatia — A109

Tie designs: 1.10k, Businessman's, 1995. 3.80k, English Dandy, 1810. 4k, Croatian soldier, 1630.

1995, Jan. 19 Litho. Perf. 14
228 A109 1.10k multicolored .60 .45
229 A109 3.80k multicolored 1.90 1.50
230 A109 4k multicolored 2.00 1.90
  a. Souvenir sheet of 3, #228-230 4.75 4.75
  Nos. 228-230 (3) 4.50 3.85

Croatian Monasteries — A110

1k, Jesuit Monastery, Zagreb, 350th anniv. 2.40k, Franciscan Monastery, Visovac, 550th anniv.

1995, Feb. 16
231 A110 1k multicolored .50 .30
232 A110 2.40k multicolored 1.25 .95

Hunting Dogs — A111

Designs: 2.20k, Istrian short-haired. 2.40k, Posavinian. 3.80k, Istrian wire-haired.

1995, Mar. 9 Litho. Perf. 14
233 A111 2.20k multicolored 1.00 .75
234 A111 2.40k multicolored 1.25 .80
235 A111 3.80k multicolored 1.75 1.40
  Nos. 233-235 (3) 4.00 2.95

Town of Split, 1700th Anniv. — A112

No. 236: a, 1k, Drawing of reconstruction of Diocletian's Palace. b, 2.20k, "Split Harbour," by Emanuel Vidovic, 1937. c, 4k, Modern view of town, bust of Marko Marulic by Ivan Mestrovic. 13.40k, Buildings, vert.

1995, Apr. 20 Litho. Perf. 14
236 A112 Strip of 3, #a.-c. 4.00 4.00
Souvenir Sheet
237 A112 13.40k multicolored 6.25 6.25
No. 237 contains one 24x48mm stamp.

World Team Handball Championships, Iceland — A113

1995, May 4
238 A113 4k multicolored 2.00 1.25

Peace & Freedom A114

Europa: 2.40k, Clearing storm clouds. 4k, Hands of angel, by Francisco Robba.

1995, May 9
239 A114 2.40k multicolored 1.75 1.25
240 A114 4k multicolored 2.25 1.60

Anti-Austria Demonstrations, 150th Anniv. — A115

1995, May 15
241 A115 1.10k multicolored .65 .45
242 A115 3.80k multicolored 1.25 1.10
Croatian surrender to British forces at Bleiburg, 50th anniv. (No. 242).

Independence Day — A116

1995, May 30 Litho. Perf. 14
243 A116 1.10k multicolored .75 .40

Croatian Sculptures at Venice Biennial, 1995 — A117

2.20k, Installation (a part), by Martina Kramer. 2.40k, Paracelsus Paraduchamps, by Mirko Zrinscak, vert. 4k, Shadows, by Goran Petercol.

1995, June 8 Litho. Perf. 14
244 A117 2.20k multicolored 1.00 .65
245 A117 2.40k multicolored 1.10 .75
246 A117 4k multicolored 1.90 1.75
  Nos. 244-246 (3) 4.00 3.15

St. Anthony of Padua (1195-1231) — A118

1995, June 13
247 A118 1k multicolored .45 .30

Marine Life — A119

2.40k, Caretta caretta. 4k, Tursiops truncatus.

1995, June 29 Litho. Perf. 14
248 A119 2.40k multi 1.00 .90
249 A119 4k multi 1.75 1.50

Liberation of the City of Knin — A120

1995, Aug. 5 Litho. Perf. 14
250 A120 1.30k multicolored .75 .60

Krka River Hydroelectric Power Plant, Cent. — A121

1995, Aug. 28
251 A121 3.60k multicolored 1.45 1.00

Stamp Day — A122

1995, Sept. 9 Litho. *Perf. 14*
252 A122 1.30k multicolored .70 .70

Franz von Suppe (1819-95), Composer A123

1995, Sept. 15
253 A123 6.50k multicolored 3.00 2.00
See Austria Nos. 1686-1687.

Liberation of Petrinja from Turkish Rule, 400th Anniv. — A124

1995, Sept. 21
254 A124 2.20k multicolored 1.10 .90

Croatian Music — A125

Composers, conductors: 1.20k, Ivo Tijardovic (1895-1976). 1.40k, Lovro Von Matacic (1899-1985). 6.50k, Jakov Gotovac (1895-1982).

1995, Sept. 23
255 A125 1.20k multicolored .55 .55
256 A125 1.40k multicolored .65 .60
257 A125 6.50k multicolored 3.25 2.50
Nos. 255-257 (3) 4.45 3.65

Herman Bollé (1845-1926), Architect — A126

2.40k, Izidor Krsnjavi (1845-1927), painter. 3.60k, Croatian National Theatre, cent.

1995, Oct. 14 Litho. *Perf. 14*
258 A126 1.80k multicolored .80 .50
259 A126 2.40k multicolored 1.00 .70
260 A126 3.60k multicolored 1.75 1.25
Nos. 258-260 (3) 3.55 2.45

Croatian Towns — A127

1995, Oct. 20
261 A127 1k Bjelovar .45 .45
262 A127 1.30k Osijek, vert. .55 .55
263 A127 1.40k Cakovec, vert. .60 .60
264 A127 2.20k Rovinj 1.10 1.10
265 A127 2.40k Korcula 1.25 1.25
266 A127 3.60k Zupanja 1.60 1.60
Nos. 261-266 (6) 5.55 5.55
See No. 448.

UN, FAO, 50th Anniv. — A128

No. 268, "5, 0" in form of cracker, FAO.

1995, Oct. 24
267 A128 3.60k multicolored 1.40 1.00
268 A128 3.60k multicolored 1.60 1.00
a. Pair, #267-268 3.25 3.25

Croatian Scientists — A129

1k, Spiro Brusina (1845-1908). 2.20k, Bogoslav Sulek (1816-95). 6.50k, Front of European language dictionary, published by Faust Vrancic (1551-1617).

1995, Oct. 30
269 A129 1k multicolored .65 .30
270 A129 2.20k multicolored 1.00 .65
271 A129 6.50k multicolored 3.00 2.25
Nos. 269-271 (3) 4.65 3.20

Institute for Blind Children, Cent. — A130

1995, Nov. 23 Litho. *Perf. 14*
272 A130 1.20k multicolored 1.00 1.00

Christmas A131

1995, Dec. 1
273 A131 1.30k multicolored .65 .45

Maroc Polo's Return from China, 700th Anniv. A132

1995, Dec. 7
274 A132 3.60k multicolored 1.75 1.50

Liberated Towns A133

20 l, Hrvatska Kostajnica. 30 l, Slunj. 50 l, Gracac. 1.20k, Drnis, vert. 6.50k, Glina. 10k, Obrovac, vert.

1995, Dec. 16
275 A133 20 l multi .25 .25
276 A133 30 l multi .25 .25
277 A133 50 l multi .35 .35
278 A133 1.20k multi .70 .70
279 A133 6.50k multi 3.25 3.25
280 A133 10k multi 4.50 4.50
Nos. 275-280 (6) 9.30 9.30

Incunabula A134

Designs: 1.40k, Lectionary of Bernardin of Split. 3.60k, Spovid Opcena (General Confession).

1995, Dec. 28
281 A134 1.40k multicolored .75 .40
282 A134 3.60k multicolored 1.75 1.25

Spirituality of the Croats — A135

Designs: No. 283, Mosaic of St. Marko Krizevcanin (1589-1619), Catholic martyr. No. 284, Veneration of Miraculous Crucifix, St. Guido's Church, Rijeka, 700th anniv. No. 285, Ivan Merz (1896-1928), Catholic educator.

1996, Jan. 18 Litho. *Perf. 14*
283 A135 1.30k multicolored .60 .50
284 A135 1.30k multicolored .60 .50
285 A135 1.30k multicolored .60 .50
a. Strip of 3, Nos. 283-285 2.00 2.00

Political Anniversaries A136

1.20k, Rakovica Uprising by Eugen Kvaternik, 125th anniv., horiz. 1.40k, Ante Starcevic (1823-96). 2.20k, Constitution of Neutral Peasant Republic of Croatia, 75th anniv., Stjepan Radic (1871-1928). 3.60k, Labin Republic, 75th anniv.

1996, Feb. 28
286 A136 1.20k multicolored .60 .50
287 A136 1.40k multicolored .70 .60
288 A136 2.20k multicolored .95 .80
289 A136 3.60k multicolored 1.75 1.40
Nos. 286-289 (4) 4.00 3.30

Institute for Pharmacognosy, University of Zagreb, Cent. — A137

1996, Mar. 23 Litho. *Perf. 14*
290 A137 6.50k multicolored 3.00 2.00

Croatian Music — A138

a, Vinko Jelić (1596-1636), composer. b, First performance of opera "Love and Music." c, Josip Stolcer Slavenski (1896-1955), composer. d, "Lijepa Nasa," Croatian national anthem, 150th anniv.

1996, Mar. 28
291 A138 2.20k Strip of 4, #a.-d. 3.75 3.75

A139

Famous Women Writers (Europa): 2.20k, Cvijeta Zuzoric (b. 1551 or 1552). 3.60k, Ivana Brlic Mazuranic (1874-1938).

1996, Apr. 11 Litho. *Perf. 14*
292 A139 2.20k multicolored 1.60 1.60
293 A139 3.60k multicolored 2.25 2.25

A140

The Zrinskis and The Frankopans: 1.30k, Nikola Subic Zrinski of Sziget (1508-56). 1.40k, Nikola Zrinski (1620-64). 2.20k, Petar Zrinski (1621-71). 2.40k, Katarina Zrinski (1625-73). 3.60k, Fran Krsto Frankopan (1643-71).

1996, Apr. 30
294 A140 1.30k multicolored .55 .55
295 A140 1.40k multicolored .60 .60
296 A140 2.20k multicolored 1.00 1.00
297 A140 2.40k multicolored 1.10 1.10
298 A140 3.60k multicolored 1.40 1.40
a. Sheet of 5, #294-298 5.00 5.00
Nos. 294-298 (5) 4.65 4.65

Natl. Guard, 5th Anniv. — A141

1996, May 28 Litho. *Perf. 14*
299 A141 1.30k multicolored .65 .65

Flowers — A142

Designs: 2.40k, Campanula istriaca. 3.60k, Centaurea ragusina.

1996, June 5
300 A142 2.40k multicolored 1.00 1.00
301 A142 3.60k multicolored 1.60 1.60

England '96,
European
Soccer
Championship
A143

1996, June 8
302 A143 2.20k red & black 1.10 .90

Father Ferdinand
Konscak's
Expedition to
Lower California,
250th
Anniv. — A144

1996, June 10
303 A144 2.40k multicolored 1.10 1.00

1996 Summer
Olympics,
Atlanta
A145

1996, July 4
304 A145 3.60k multicolored 1.75 1.25

A146

1996, July 4
305 A146 1.40k multicolored .65 .60

Josip Fon, founder of Croatian Sokol Gymnastics Society, 150th birth anniv.

A147

1996, Sept. 9   Litho.   Perf. 14
306 A147 1.30k multicolored .65 .40

Croatian postage stamps, 5th anniv.

1st Written
Reference,
Zumberak
Region, 700th
Anniv. — A148

1996, Sept. 14
307 A148 2.20k multicolored 1.00 1.00

A149

1996, Sept. 19
308 A149 1.30k multicolored .60 .60

First written record of fishing in Croatia, 1000th anniv.

A150

Events of the early Middle Ages: 1.20k, Vekenega's Book of Gospels, 900th anniv. 1.40k, Visit by Saxon Benedictine abbot Gottschalk (805-870), to Duke Trpimir's court, 1150th anniv.

1996, Sept. 19
309 A150 1.20k multicolored .55 .50
310 A150 1.40k multicolored .65 .55

Scientists
A151

Designs: a, Gjuro Pilar (1846-93), geologist. b, Frane Bulic (1846-1934), archeologist. c, Ante Sercer (1896-1968), otolaryngologist.

1996, Oct. 4   Litho.   Perf. 14
311 A151 2.40k Strip of 3, #a.-c. 3.25 3.25

Beginning of Higher Education in
Croatia, 600th Anniv. — A152

Oldest preserved Croatian text written in Latin script, "Order and Law" of Dominican nuns, Zadar.

1996, Oct. 16   Perf. 13½
312 A152 1.40k multicolored .70 .50

Paintings — A153

Designs: 1.30k, Rain, by Menci Clement Crncic (1865-1930). 1.40k, The Peljesac-Korcula Channel, by Mato Celestin Medovic (1857-1919). 3.60k, Pink Dream, by Vlaho Bukovac (1855-1922).

1996, Nov. 7   Litho.   Perf. 14
313 A153 1.30k multicolored .60 .60
314 A153 1.40k multicolored .70 .70
315 A153 3.60k multicolored 1.75 1.75
 Nos. 313-315 (3) 3.05 3.05

UNICEF, 50th
Anniv. — A154

1996, Nov. 15
316 A154 3.60k multicolored 1.60 1.25

City of Osijek,
800th
Anniv. — A155

Views of city: No. 317, River bank, church, coat of arms. No. 318, Boats in water, view looking down covered walkway through building.

1996, Dec. 2   Litho.   Perf. 14
317 A155 2.20k multicolored 1.00 .75
318 A155 2.20k multicolored 1.00 .75
 a.   Pair, #317-318 2.25 2.25

Christmas — A156

1996, Dec. 3
319 A156 1.30k multicolored .70 .50

First Croatian
Savings Bank,
Zagreb, 150th
Anniv. — A157

Design: 3.60k, Publishing of "The Bases of Corn Trade," by Josip Sipus, bicent.

1996, Dec. 14
320 A157 2.40k multicolored 1.00 .80
321 A157 3.60k multicolored 1.75 1.25

Motion
Pictures,
Cent. — A158

Designs: a, Shooting of film, "Vatroslav Lisinski," Oktavijan Miletic, cameraman, director. b, Characters from animated series, "Professor Baltazar." c, Mirjana Bohanec, Relja Basic in "Who Sings Means No Harm."

1997, Jan. 16   Litho.   Perf. 14
322 A158 1.40k Strip of 3, #a.-c. 2.00 2.00

Great Europeans
A159

Designs: 2.20k, Miguel de Cervantes (1547-1676), author. 3.60k, Johannes Gutenberg (1397-1468), printer, horiz.

1997, Feb. 7
323 A159 2.20k multicolored .90 .65
324 A159 3.60k multicolored 1.50 1.10

Legends
A160

Europa: 1.30k, Home Genies, from story, "Stribor's Forest." 3.60k, "Vili Joze," by Vladimir Nazor, vert.

1997, Mar. 6   Litho.   Perf. 14
325 A160 1.30k multicolored *1.10 1.10*
326 A160 3.60k multicolored *2.75 2.75*

Fauna of
Croatia — A161

1997, Apr. 22   Litho.   Perf. 14
327 A161 1.40k Pinna nobilis .60 .60
328 A161 2.40k Radziella styx 1.00 1.00
329 A161 3.60k Tonna galea 1.60 1.60
 Nos. 327-329 (3) 3.20 3.20

Admission
of Croatia
to UN, 5th
Anniv.
A162

6.50k, Pres. Franjo Tudjman.

1997, May 22   Litho.   Perf. 14
330 A162 6.50k multi 3.00 3.00

First
Croatian
Esperantist
Conference,
90th Anniv.
A163

Ludwig Lazarus Zamenhof, conf. logo.

1997, May 31
331 A163 1.20k multicolored .70 .70

Congress of
Intl. Amateur
Rugby
Federation,
Dubrovnik
A164

1997, June 6
332 A164 2.20k multicolored 1.10 .80

Siege of Vukovar, Serbo-Croatian War, 1991 — A165

Painting by Zlatko Kauzlaric Atac.

1997, June 8		Litho.		**Perf. 14**
333	A165	6.50k multicolored	3.00	3.00

Croatian Kings — A166

1.30k, King Peter Svacic, 900th death anniv. 2.40k, King Stephen Drzislav, 1000th death anniv.

1997, July 3				
334	A166	1.30k multicolored	.60	.60
335	A166	2.40k multicolored	1.25	1.25

16th Century Courier from Dubrovnik A167

1997, Sept. 9		Litho.		**Perf. 14**
336	A167	2.30k multicolored	1.10	.90

Stamp Day.

Croatian Olympic Medals — A168

Designs: 1k, Tennis, bronze, Barcelona, 1992. 1.20k, Basketball, silver, Barcelona 1992. 1.40k, Water polo, silver, Atlanta, 1996. 2.20k, Handball, gold, Atlanta, 1996.

1997, Sept. 10				
337	A168	1k multicolored	.40	.40
338	A168	1.20k multicolored	.50	.50
		Size: 27x31mm		
339	A168	1.40k multicolored	.75	.75
340	A168	2.20k multicolored	1.00	1.00
		Nos. 337-340 (4)	2.65	2.65

Defense of Sibenik — A169

Designs: No. 341, Fort, airplanes. No. 342, Turkish cavalry, fort.

1997, Sept. 18				
341	A169	1.30k multicolored	.50	.50
342	A169	1.30k multicolored	.50	.50
a.		Pair, #341-342	1.25	1.25

Serbo-Croatian War, 1991 (No. 341). War with the Turks, 350th anniv. (No. 342).

Anniversaries A170

No. 343: a, Frane Petrić (1529-97), philosopher. b, Vicko Lovrin, 16th century painter. c, Frano Krsiníc (1897-1982), sculptor. d, Dubravko Dujsin (1894-1947), actor.

1997, Oct. 17		Litho.		**Perf. 14**
343	A170	1.40k Strip of 4, #a.-d.	2.75	2.75

A171

A172

1997, Oct. 23				
344	A171	2.20k multicolored	1.00	.70
345	A172	3.60k multicolored	1.50	1.00

Use of Croatian language in parliament, 150th anniv. (No. 344). Croatian Grammar School, Zadar, cent. (No. 345).

Palaeontological Finds in Croatia — A173

Designs: 1.40k, Gomphotherium angustidens. 2.40k, Viviparus novskaensis.

1997, Nov. 6				
346	A173	1.40k multicolored	.60	.60
347	A173	2.40k multicolored	1.10	1.10

Modern Art A174

Paintings: 1.30k, Painter in the Pond, by Nikola Masic (1852-1902). 2.20k, Angelus, by Emanuel Vidovic (1870-1953). 3.60k, Tree in the Snow, by Slava Raskaj (1877-1906).

1997, Nov. 14				
348	A174	1.30k multicolored	.60	.45
349	A174	2.20k multicolored	.90	.55
350	A174	3.60k multicolored	1.75	1.25
		Nos. 348-350 (3)	3.25	2.25

Contemporary Christmas Painting, by Ivan Antolcic — A175

"Birth of Jesus," by Isidor Krsnjavi A176

1997, Nov. 28		Litho.		**Perf. 13½**
351	A175	1.30k multicolored	.50	.40
				Perf. 14
352	A176	3.60k multicolored	1.60	1.10

Croatian Literature — A177

1997, Dec. 18				**Perf. 14**
353	A177	1k shown	.55	.40
354	A177	1.20k Book, words	.60	.40

Printing of the translation of "Electra," by Dominko Zlataric, 400th anniv. (No. 353). Publication of "The Best of Folk Speech and the Illyric or Croatian Language," by Filip Grabovac, 250th anniv. (No. 354).

Cities and Landmarks Type of 1992

1997		Litho.		**Perf. 14**
355	A39	5 l Ilok	.25	.25
356	A39	10 l Dubrovnik	.25	.25

Events and Festivals — A178

Europa: 1.45k, Varazdin Baroque Evenings, musical notes. 4k, Dubrovnik Summer Festival.

1998, Jan. 23				**Perf. 13½**
357	A178	1.45k multicolored	1.00	1.00
358	A178	4k multicolored	2.50	2.50

1998 Winter Olympic Games, Nagano — A179

1998, Feb. 7				**Perf. 14**
359	A179	2.45k multicolored	1.10	.75

Croatian Events of 1848 — A180

a, 1.60k, Flag, battle near Moor. b, 4k, Portrait of Ban Josip Jelacic. c, 1.60k, Croatian Assembly.

1998, Mar. 25		Litho.		**Perf. 14**
360	A180	Strip of 3, #a.-c.	3.25	3.25

No. 360b is 21x32mm.

Ante Topic Mimara (1898-1987), Art Collector, Painter A181

1998, Apr. 7		Litho.		**Perf. 14**
361	A181	2.65k multicolored	1.25	.90

A182

Mushrooms: a, 1.30k, Amanita caesarea. b, 7.20k, Morchella conica. c, 1.30k, Lactarius deliciosus.

1998, Apr. 22				
362	A182	Strip of 3, #a.-c.	4.50	4.50

A183

1998, May 8				
363	A183	1.50k multicolored	.65	.65

Archbishop Alojzije Stepinac (1898-1960).

27th European Regional Conference of Interpol, Dubrovnik A184

1998, May 13				
364	A184	2.45k multicolored	1.10	.90

Souvenir Sheet

Expo '98, Lisbon — A185

14.85k, Fishing boat, Falkusa.

1998, June 3   Litho.   Perf. 14
365 A185 14.85k multi   6.25 6.25

1998 World Cup Soccer
Championships, France — A186

1998, June 10
366 A186 4k multicolored   2.00 1.50

Writers
A187

1.20k, Juraj Barakovic (1548-1628). 1.50k,
Milan Begovic (1876-1948). 1.60k, Mate
Balota (Mijo Mirkovic, 1898-1963). 2.45k,
Antun Gustav Matos (1873-1914). 2.65k,
Matija Antun Relkovic (1732-98). 4.00k, Antun
Branko Simic (1898-1925).

1998, June 13   Litho.   Perf. 14
367 A187 1.20k multicolored   .60   .50
368 A187 1.50k multicolored   .70   .60
369 A187 1.60k multicolored   .75   .70
370 A187 2.45k multicolored   1.00   .90
371 A187 2.65k multicolored   1.10 1.00
372 A187 4k multicolored   1.75 1.60
      Nos. 367-372 (6)   5.90 5.30

19th
Conference of
the Countries
of the Danube
Region,
Osijek — A188

1998, June 15
373 A188 1.80k multicolored   .75   .65

Stjepan
Betlheim
(1898-1970),
Psychiatrist
A189

1998, July 22
374 A189 1.50k multicolored   .65   .50

Souvenir Sheet

Croatian Soccer Team, Bronze
Medalists at 1998 World Cup Soccer
Championships, France — A190

Portions of team picture, denomination: a,
red, LL. b, yellow, CR (player in yellow & blue
shirt). c, yellow, CL. d, yellow, LR.

1998, July 24
375 A190 4k Sheet of 4, #a.-d.   7.25 7.25

Croatian
Ships — A191

1.20k, Serilia Liburnica. 1.50k, Condura
Croatica. 1.60k, Dubrovnik carrack. 1.80k,
Bracera. 2.45k, Ship from the Neretva. 2.65k,
Bark. 4k, Training ship, "Villa Velebita." 7.20k,
Passenger ship, "Amorella." 20k, Missile gun
boat, "Kralj Petar Kresimir IV."

1998, Aug. 27   Litho.   Perf. 14
376   A191 1.20k multi   .70   .70
376A A191 1.50k multi   .80   .80
376B A191 1.60k multi   .85   .85
376C A191 1.80k multi   .90   .90
376D A191 2.45k multi   1.30 1.30
376E A191 2.65k multi   1.50 1.50
376F A191 4k multi   2.00 2.00
376G A191 7.20k multi   3.50 3.50
376H A191 20k multi   9.25 9.25
      i. Sheet of 9, #376-376H +
          3 labels   20.00 20.00
      Nos. 376-376H (9)   20.80 20.80

Stamp
Day — A192

1998, Sept. 9
377 A192 1.50k multicolored   .65   .50

Bishopric of Sibenik, 700th
Anniv. — A193

1998, Sept. 29   Litho.   Perf. 14
378 A193 4k multicolored   1.60 1.60

Pope
John Paul
II, Second
Visit to
Croatia
A194

1998, Oct. 2
379 A194 1.50k multicolored   .90   .90

History of
Public
Transportation
A195

Designs: a, 1.50k, Horse tram. b, 1.50k,
First automobile in Zagreb, 1901. c, 7.20k,
Zagreb funicular. d, 1.50k, Karlovac-Rijeka
Railway Line, 1873. e, 1.50k, New Highway,
Zagreb-Rijeka.

1998, Oct. 23   Litho.   Perf. 14
380 A195 Strip of 5, #a.-e.   6.00 6.00
      No. 380c is 20x24mm.

Christmas — A196

Adoration of the Shepherds, by Juraj Julije
Klovic (1498-1578).

1998, Nov. 21   Perf. 14x13
381 A196 1.50k multicolored   .80   .75
      See Vatican City No. 1088.

Father Luka
Ibrisimovic
(1620-98)
A197

1998, Nov. 30   Litho.   Perf. 14
382 A197 1.90k multicolored   .90   .75

Universal
Declaration
of Human
Rights,
50th
Anniv. — A198

1998, Dec. 10
383 A198 5k multicolored   2.00 2.00

Modern
Art
A199

Paintings: 1.90k, Paromlin Road, by Josip
Vanista. 2.20k, Cypresses, by Frano Simu-
novic, vert. 5k, Koma, by Dalibor Martinis, vert.

1998, Dec. 15
384 A199 1.90k multicolored   .90   .90
385 A199 2.20k multicolored   1.00 1.00
386 A199 5k multicolored   2.10 2.10
      Nos. 384-386 (3)   4.00 4.00

Zagreb Intl. Trade
Fair — A200

1999, Jan. 21   Litho.   Perf. 14
387 A200 1.80k multicolored   .90   .80

Cardinal Juraj
Haulik (1788-
1869),
Archbishop of
Zagreb — A201

Photo. & Engr.
1999, Jan. 28   Perf. 11½
388 A201 5k multicolored   2.10 2.10
      See Slovakia 321.

National
Parks — A202

Europa: 1.80k, Mljet Island. 5k, Lonja Field.

1999, Mar. 12   Litho.   Perf. 14
389 A202 1.80k multicolored   *2.00 2.00*
390 A202 5k multicolored   *3.50 3.50*

Vipera
Ursinii — A203

World Wildlife Fund: a, One coiled in grass
and rock. b, Two. c, Head. d, One coiled on
rock.

1999, Apr. 27   Litho.   Perf. 14
391 A203 2.20k Strip of 4, #a.-d. 4.25 4.25

Council of
Europe, 50th
Anniv. — A204

1999, May 5
392 A204 2.80k multicolored   1.25 1.25

19th Convention of
the Foundation of
European Carnival
Cities,
Dubrovnik — A205

1999, May 8
393 A205 2.30k multicolored   1.10 1.10

Croatian
Coins — A206

Designs: a, 2.30k, Obv., rev. of 1849 kreut-
zer. b, 5k, One kuna.

1999, May 30   Litho.   Perf. 14
394 A206 Pair, #a.-b.   3.25 3.25
      Minting of Jelacic kreutzer, 150th anniv.
(No. 394a). Croatian kuna, 5th anniv. (No.
394b).

Famous
Croats — A207

1.80k, Vladimir Nazor (1876-1949), poet.
2.30k, Ferdo Livadic (1799-1879), composer.
2.50k, Ivan Rendic (1849-1932), sculptor.
2.80k, Milan Lenuci (1849-1924), architect.
3.50k, Vjekoslav Klaic (1849-1929), historian.
musician. 4k, Emilij Laszowski (1868-1949),
historian. 5k, Antun Kanizlic (1699-1777),
poet, missionary.

1999, June 18
395 A207 1.80k multicolored   .65   .65
396 A207 2.30k multicolored   .95   .90
397 A207 2.50k multicolored   1.25 1.10
398 A207 2.80k multicolored   1.30 1.30
399 A207 3.50k multicolored   1.40 1.40
400 A207 4k multicolored   1.60 1.60
401 A207 5k multicolored   2.10 2.10
      Nos. 395-401 (7)   9.25 9.05

Euphrasian Basilica, Porec — A208

1999, June 25
402 A208 4k multicolored   1.75 1.75

2nd World Military Games, Zagreb A209

1999, Aug. 7   **Litho.**   **Perf. 14**
403 A209 2.30k multicolored   1.10 .90

Discovery of Early Krapina Man, Cent. — A210

Designs: a, 1.80k, Bones, rendition of Krapina man. b, 4k, Ancient bones, paleontologist Dragutin Gorjanovic-Kramberger.

1999, Aug. 23
404 A210 Pair, #a.-b.   3.00 3.00

Stamp Day and UPU, 125th Anniv. — A211

1999, Sept. 9   **Litho.**   **Perf. 14**
405 A211 2.30k multicolored   1.10 1.00

Paulist Order in Lepoglava, 600th Anniv. — A212

a, Lace, Jesus Expelling the Money Changers from Temple, by Ivan Ranger, altar angel from St. Mary's Church, Lepoglava. b, St. Mary's Church facade, altar angel. c, St. Elizabeth, lace.

1999, Sept. 11   **Litho.**
406 A212 5k Strip of 3, #a.-c.   6.50 6.50

150th Anniv. of "Jelacic March" by Johann Strauss the Elder — A213

1999, Sept. 16   **Litho.**
407 A213 3.50k multicolored   1.75 1.75

World Ozone Layer Protection Day A214

1999, Sept. 16   **Litho.**
408 A214 5k multicolored   2.10 2.10

Grammar School Anniversaries A215

2.30k, Pazin, cent. 3.50k, Pozega, 300th anniv.

1999, Oct. 15   **Litho.**   **Perf. 14**
409 A215 2.30k multi   1.00 .90
410 A215 3.50k multi   1.50 1.25

Andrija Hebrang (1899-1949), Politician — A216

1999, Oct. 21
411 A216 1.80k multicolored   .80 .80

Our Lady of the Rose Garden, by Blaz Jurjev Trogiranin A217

1999, Oct. 28
412 A217 5k multicolored   2.00 2.00
Christmas, opening of exhibition of Croatian religious art and artifacts, Vatican City.

Christmas — A218

1999, Nov. 24   **Litho.**   **Perf. 14**
413 A218 2.30k multicolored   1.10 1.10

Modern Art A219

Designs: 2.30k, Winter Landscape, by Gabrijel Jurkic (1886-1974). 3.50k, Klek, by Oton Postruznik (1900-78). 5k, Stone Table, by Ignjat Job (1895-1936), vert.

1999, Dec. 15
414 A219 2.30k multicolored   1.10 1.10
415 A219 3.50k multicolored   1.40 1.40
416 A219 5k multicolored   2.00 2.00
    Nos. 414-416 (3)   4.50 4.50

Pres. Franjo Tudjman (1922-99) — A220

               Vignette Color
1999, Dec. 16
417 A220 2.30k black   1.10 1.00
418 A220 5k blue   2.50 2.00

Millennium A221

2000, Jan. 1   **Litho.**   **Perf. 14**
419 A221 2.30k multi   2.75 2.25

Valentine's Day — A222

2000, Feb. 1
420 A222 2.30k multi   2.00 1.60

Split Grammar School, 300th Anniv. — A223

2000, Mar. 25   **Litho.**   **Perf. 14**
421 A223 2.80k multi   1.25 1.10

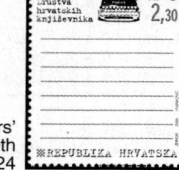

Croatian Writers' Assoc., 100th Anniv. — A224

2000, Apr. 22   **Litho.**   **Perf. 14**
422 A224 2.30k black & red   2.75 2.75

A225

A226

A227

A228

A229

(1.80k) Lo Schiavone (Andrija Medulic, c. 1500-63), painter; (2.30k) Matija Petar Katancic (1750-1825), writer; (2.80k) Marija Ruzicka-Strozzi (1850-1937), actress; (3.50k) Marko Marulic (1450-1524), writer; (5k) Blaz Jurjev Trogiranin (c. 1390-1450), painter.

2000, Apr. 22
423 A225 1.80k multi   .65 .65
424 A226 2.30k multi   .95 .95
425 A227 2.80k multi   1.10 1.10
426 A228 3.50k multi   1.40 1.40
427 A229 5k multi   1.90 1.90
    Nos. 423-427 (5)   6.00 6.00

Europa, 2000
Common Design Type and

A230

2000, May 9
428 A230 2.30k multi   2.00 2.00
429 CD17 5k multi   4.25 4.25

Independence Day — A231

2000, May 30   **Litho.**   **Perf. 14**
430 A231 2.30k multi   1.50 1.50

Souvenir Sheet

Expo 2000, Hanover — A232

2000, June 1
431 A232 14.40k multi   6.25 6.25

Flora — A233

No. 432: a, 3.50k, Micromeria croatica. b, 5k, Geranium dalmaticum.

2000, June 5
432 A233 Pair, #a-b   4.00 4.00
    c.   Booklet pane of 10 #432a   15.00
        Booklet, #432c   16.00
    d.   Booklet pane of 10 #432b   20.00
        Booklet, #432d   21.00

Kastav Statute, 600th Anniv. — A234

2000, June 6
433 A234 1.80k multi .85 .85

World Mathematics Year — A235

2000, June 15
434 A235 3.50k multi 1.60 1.60

Ivan Ranger (1700-53), Artist — A236

2000, June 19
435 A236 1.80k multi .85 .85

Souvenir Sheet

Baska Stone Tablet, 900th Anniv. — A237

2000, June 24
436 A237 16.70k multi 7.25 7.25

Archdeacon Toma of Split (1200-68) A238

2000, July 10
437 A238 3.50k multi 1.60 1.60

Type of 1992-94 Redrawn
2000, Aug. 1 **Litho.** **Perf. 14**
437A A39a 3.50k Vis 1.60 1.60
No. 437A has "HP" and post horn in LR corner.

Stamp Day — A239

No. 438: a, 2.30k, Austria #5. b, 2.30k, Automatic mail sorting equipment.
2000, Sept. 9 **Litho.** **Perf. 14**
438 A239 Pair, #a-b 2.25 2.25
First stamps used in Croatia, 150th anniv. (No. 438a).

2000 Summer Olympics, Sydney A240

2000, Sept. 15
439 A240 5k multicolored 3.00 3.00

Altarpiece, Church of the Blessed Virgin Mary, Ostarije A241

2000, Nov. 23
440 A241 2.30k multi 1.10 1.10
a. Booklet pane of 10 11.00
Booklet, #440a 11.50

Modern Art A242

Designs: 1.80k, Korcula, by Vladimir Varlaj. 2.30k, Brusnik, by Duro Tiljak. 5k, Boats, by Ante Kastelacic.
2000, Dec. 1
441-443 A242 Set of 3 4.00 4.00
See Nos. 471-473, 505-507.

Start of New Millennium A243

2001, Jan. 1 **Litho.** **Perf. 14**
444 A243 2.30k multi 1.75 1.75

Souvenir Sheet

Equestrian Statue of Charlemagne — A244

2001, Jan. 19
445 A244 14.40k multi 6.25 6.25
Crowning of Charlemagne as Emperor of the Romans, 1200th anniv. (in 2000).

Dzore Drzic (1461-1501), Writer — A245

2001, Mar. 15 **Litho.** **Perf. 14**
446 A245 2.80k multi 1.40 1.40

Comic Strip "Black Rider," by Andrija Maurovic (1901-81) A246

2001, Mar. 29
447 A246 5k multi 2.25 2.25

Makarska A247

2001, Mar. 30
448 A247 2.30k multi 1.00 1.00
a. Perf. 14 syncopated 1.00 1.00
Issued: No. 448a, 6/2/06.

Janica Kostelic, Skier — A248

2001, Apr. 19 **Litho.** **Perf. 14**
449 A248 2.80k multi 2.40 2.00

Kastel Stafilic Olive Trees, 1500th Anniv. — A249

2001, Apr. 20
450 A249 1.80k multi .85 .85

Europa — A250

No. 451: a, 3.50k, Denomination at R. b, 5k, Denomination at L.
2001, May 9
451 A250 Horiz. pair, #a-b 3.50 3.50

World No Smoking Day — A251

2001, May 31
452 A251 2.50k multi 1.10 1.10

Butterflies A252

Designs: 2.50k, Parnassius apollo. 2.80k, Maculinea teleius. 5k, Coenonympha oedippus.
2001, June 5
453-455 A252 Set of 3 4.75 4.75

Type of 1992 Redrawn
2.80k, Eltz Castle, Vukovar.
2001, June 21 **Litho.** **Perf. 14**
456 A252 1.25 1.25
a. Perf. 14 syncopated 1.10 1.10
No. 456 has "1991-2001" inscription, and "HP" and post horn at LL. Issued: No. 456a, 6/19/06.

Souvenir Sheet

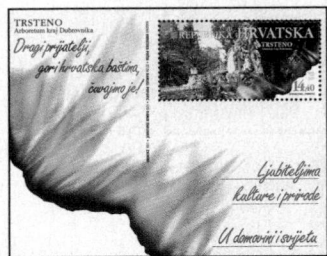

Trsteno Arboretum — A253

2001, July 12 **Litho.** **Perf. 14**
457 A253 14.40k multi 6.50 6.50

World Esperanto Congress, Zagreb — A254

2001, July 21
458 A254 5k multi 2.40 2.40

Refugee Organizations, 50th Annivs. A255

Designs: 1.80k, UN High Commissioner for Refugees. 5k, Intl. Organization for Migration.
2001, July 28
459-460 A255 Set of 2 3.25 3.25

Victory of Goran Ivanisevic at Wimbledon A256

2001, Aug. 31
461 A256 2.50k multi 2.50 2.25
Printed in sheets of 9 + label.

Stamp Day — A257

2001, Sept. 9
462 A257 2.50k multi .90 .90
Printed in sheets of 16 + 4 labels.

Native Dog Breeds A258

Designs: 1.80k, Croatian sheepdog. 5k, Dalmatian.

2001, Oct. 4
463-464 A258 Set of 2 3.25 3.25

Independence, 10th Anniv. — A259

2001, Oct. 8
465 A259 2.30k multi 1.10 1.10

Printed in sheets of 25 + 5 labels.

Year of Dialogue Among Civilizations — A260

2001, Oct. 9
466 A260 5k multi 4.00 4.00

Fortresses — A261

Designs: 1.80k, Klis, 16th cent. 2.50k, Ston, 14th-15th cents. 3.50k, Sisak, 16th cent.

2001, Oct. 26 Litho. Perf. 14
467-469 A261 Set of 3 3.50 3.50

See Nos. 499-501, 525-527, 565-567, 594-596, 630-632.

Adoration of the Magi Altarpeice, Church of the Visitation of Mary, Cucerje — A262

2001, Nov. 22 Litho. Perf. 14
470 A262 2.30k multi 1.10 1.00
a. Booklet pane of 10 11.00 11.00
Complete booklet, #470a 11.00

Modern Art Type of 2000

Designs: No. 471, 2.50k, Maternité du Port-Royal, by Leo Junek. No. 472, 2.50k, Amphitheater Ruins, by Vjekoslav Parac. 5k, Nude with a Baroque Figure, by Slavko Sohaj, vert.

2001, Dec. 1
471-473 A242 Set of 3 4.75 4.75

Croatian Nobel Laureates — A263

Laureates: 2.80k, Lavoslav (Leopold) Ruzicka, Chemistry, 1939. 3.50k, Vladimir Prelog, Chemistry, 1975. 5k, Ivo Andric, Literature, 1961.

2001, Dec. 5
474-476 A263 Set of 3 5.50 5.50

Famous Croats and Events A264

Designs: 1.80k, Ivan Gucetic (1451-1502), writer. 2.30k, Dobrisa Cesaric (1902-80), writer. 2.50k, Publishing of Juraj Rattkay's *History of Croatian Rulers*, 350th anniv. 2.80k, Franjo Vranjanin Laurana (c. 1420-1502), sculptor. 3.50k, Beatification of Bishop Augustin Kazotic (c. 1260-1323), 300th anniv. 5k, Matko Laginja (1852-1930), politician and writer.

2002, Jan. 24 Litho. Perf. 14
477-482 A264 Set of 6 8.00 8.00

2002 Winter Olympics, Salt Lake City — A265

2002, Feb. 8
483 A265 5k multi 2.40 2.40

Croatian Chamber of Economy, 150th Anniv. — A266

2002, Feb. 16
484 A266 2.50k multi 1.25 1.25

Souvenir Sheet

Trpimir's Deed of Gift, 1150th Anniv. — A267

2002, Mar. 4
485 A267 14.40k multi 6.50 6.50

Franjo Cardinal Kuharic (1919-2002) A268

2002, Mar. 25
486 A268 2.30k multi .90 .90

Divan, by Vlaho Bukovac — A269

Litho. & Engr.
2002, Apr. 23 Perf. 11¾
487 A269 5k multi 2.40 2.40

See Czech Republic No. 3169.

Royal Borough of Krizevci, 750th Anniv. — A270

2002, Apr. 24 Litho. Perf. 14
488 A270 1.80k multi .85 .85

Varazdin Post Office, Cent. — A271

2002, Apr. 26
489 A271 2.30k multi 1.10 1.10

Europa — A272

Clown color: a, 3.50k, Orange. b, 5k, Blue.

2002, May 9 Litho. Perf. 14
490 A272 Horiz. pair, #a-b 4.25 4.25

2002 World Cup Soccer Championships, Japan and Korea — A273

Stylized players facing: a, 3.50k, Left. b, 5k, Right.

2002, May 15
491 A273 Horiz. pair, #a-b 4.00 4.00

World Bowling Championships, Osijek — A274

2002, May 18
492 A274 3.50k multi 1.60 1.60

Oak Trees — A275

Designs: 1.80k, Quercus rober. 2.50k, Quercus petraea. 2.80k, Quercus ilex.

2002, June 5
493-495 A275 Set of 3 3.25 3.25
493a Booklet pane of 10 6.00
Complete booklet, #493a 6.25
494a Booklet pane of 10 12.00 —
Complete booklet, #494a 12.50
495a Booklet pane of 10 14.75 —
Complete booklet, #495a 15.25

15th World Animated Films Festival, Zagreb — A276

2002, June 18
496 A276 5k multi 2.40 2.40

Lace — A277

Lace from: 3.50k, Pag Island, Croatia. 5k, Liedekerke, Belgium.

2002, July 13 Photo. Perf. 11½
497-498 A277 Set of 2 4.00 4.00

See Belgium Nos. 1927-1928.

Fortresses Type of 2001

Designs: No. 499, 2.50k, Nehaj, 16th cent. No. 500, 2.50k, Skocibuha, 16th cent. 5k, Veliki Tabor, 16th cent.

2002, Sept. 20 Litho. Perf. 14
499-501 A261 Set of 3 4.50 4.50

Old Slavonic Academy, Krk, Cent. — A278

2002, Oct. 3 Litho. & Embossed
502 A278 4k red & black 1.75 1.75

Children's Help Line 48 26 051, 5th Anniv. — A279

2002, Oct. 15 Litho.
503 A279 2.30k multi 1.10 1.10

Christmas A280

2002, Nov. 21
504 A280 2.30k multi 1.25 1.25
a. Booklet pane of 10 12.50 —
Complete booklet, #504a 13.00

Modern Art Type of 2002

Designs: No. 505, 2.50k, Flowers on the Window, by Antun Motika (1902-92), vert. No. 506, 2.50k, The Girl in the Boat, by Milivoj Uzelac (1897-1977), vert. 5k, On the Drava River, by Krsto Hegedusic (1901-75).

2002, Dec. 2 Litho. Perf. 14
505-507 A242 Set of 3 4.75 4.75

Zagreb Bishopric, 150th Anniv. — A281

2002, Dec. 11
508 A281 2.80k multi   1.40 1.40
Printed in sheets of 19 + label.

Pavao Ritter Vitezovic (1652-1713), Writer — A282

2002, Dec. 13
509 A282 2.30k multi   1.10 1.10

Pacta Conventa, 900th Anniv. — A283

2002, Dec. 14
510 A283 3.50k multi   1.60 1.60

Fairies From Stories by Ivana Brlic Mazuranic — A284

No. 511: a, 2.30k, Kosjenka, fairy character from *Regoc*. b, 2.80k, Tintilinic, fairy character from *Suma Striborova*.

2003, Jan. 15
511 A284 Horiz. pair, #a-b   2.40 2.40

St. Valentine's Day — A285

Litho. With Foil Application
2003, Feb. 1
512 A285 2.30k multi   1.10 1.10

Astronomy and Meteorology A286

No. 513: a, 1.80k, Zagreb Astronomical Observatory, cent. b, 3.50k, Meteorological

measurements in Zagreb, 150th anniv.; Meteorological station on Zavizan, 50th anniv.

2003, Feb. 17   **Litho.**
513 A286 Pair, #a-b   2.25 2.25

Souvenir Sheet

Croatia, 2003 World Handball Champions — A287

No. 514: a, Five team members, one wearing red shirt. b, Eight team members, one with arm extended. c, Six team members. d, Four team members, one wearing blue shirt.

2003, Feb. 20
514 A287 4k Sheet of 4, #a-d   7.00 7.00

Paulist High School, Lepoglava, 500th Anniv. — A288

2003, Mar. 1
515 A288 5k multi   2.40 2.40

Missal of Hrvoje Vukcic Hrvatinic, 600th Anniv. — A289

2003, Mar. 25
516 A289 5k multi   2.40 2.40

Land Mine Danger A290

2003, Apr. 8
517 A290 2.30k multi   1.10 1.10

Alpine Skiing World Cup Victories of Janica and Ivica Kostelic A291

No. 518: a, Janica. b, Ivica.

2003, Apr. 16
518 A291 3.50k Pair, #a-b   5.00 5.00
Printed in sheets containing 4 vertical pairs and 2 labels.

Christian Institutions in Rome Founded by Croatian Roman Brotherhood of St. Jerome, 550th Anniv. — A292

2003, Apr. 22
519 A292 2.80k multi   1.25 1.25

Famous Croatians A293

Designs: 1.80k, Antun Soljan (1932-93), writer. 2.30k, Hanibal Lucic (1485-1553), writer. 5k, Federiko Benkovic (1667-1753), painter.

2003, Apr. 22
520-522 A293 Set of 3   4.25 4.25

Poster for Performance of Marya Delvard, by Tomislav Krizman, 1907 — A294

Poster for Performance of "The Firebird," by Boris Bucan, 1983 — A295

2003, May 9   **Litho.**   **Perf. 14**
523 A294 3.50k multi   1.50 1.50
524 A295 5k multi   2.25 2.25
Europa.

Fortresses Type of 2001

Designs: 1.80k, Kostajnica, 15th-18th cent. 2.80k, Slavonski Brod, 18th cent. 5k, Minceta Tower, 15th cent., vert.

2003, May 13
525-527 A261 Set of 3   4.25 4.25

Visit of Pope John Paul II — A296

2003, June 2
528 A296 2.30k multi   1.75 1.75

Rodents A297

Designs: 2.30k, Sciurus vulgaris. 2.80k, Glis glis. 3.50k, Castor fiber.

2003, June 5
529-531 A297 Set of 3   4.00 4.00
531a Booklet pane, 6 #529, 2
      each #530-531   13.00 —
      Complete booklet, #531a 13.00

Souvenir Sheet

Robe of King Ladislaus, 11th Cent. — A298

2003, June 13
532 A298 10k multi   4.25 4.25

Stamp Day — A299

2003, Sept. 9   **Litho.**   **Perf. 14**
533 A299 2.30k multi   1.10 1.10

Souvenir Sheet

Primosten Vineyards — A300

Litho. with Foil Application
2003, Sept. 19
534 A300 10k multi   4.75 4.75

Ursuline Sisters in Croatia, 300th Anniv. — A301

2003, Oct. 20   **Litho.**
535 A301 2.50k multi   1.10 1.10

Christmas A302

2003, Nov. 20   **Litho.**   **Perf. 14**
536 A302 2.30k multi   1.00 1.00

Self-Adhesive
Serpentine Die Cut 5¼
537 A302 2.30k multi   1.00 1.00

Modern Art A304

Designs: 1.80k, Flower Girl II, by Slavko Kopac, vert. No. 539, 3.50k, Dry Stone Wall 5-71, by Oton Gliha. No. 540, 3.50k, Pont des Arts, by Josip Racic.

2003, Nov. 21   **Perf. 14**
538-540 A304   Set of 3   4.00 4.00

    See Nos. 568-570, 604-606, 636-638, 668-670, 712-714, 749-751.

18th World Women's Handball Championships — A305

2003, Dec. 1
541 A305 5k multi   2.25 2.25

Musicians — A306

    No. 542: a, Josip Hatze (1879-1959), composer. b, Zagreb Soloists, 50th anniv.

2004, Jan. 5   **Litho.**   **Perf. 14**
542 A306 5k Horiz. pair, #a-b   4.50 4.50

Hval's Manuscript, 600th Anniv. — A307

2004, Jan. 22
543 A307 2.30k multi   1.40 1.40

European Boxing Championships, Pula — A308

2004, Feb. 19   **Litho.**   **Perf. 14**
544 A308 2.80k multi   1.25 1.25

Worldwide Fund for Nature (WWF) — A309

    Ardea purpurea: a, In grass. b, Standing with head extended. c, With young. d, In flight.

2004, Mar. 22
545   Strip or block of 4   8.50 8.50
   a.-d.   A309 5k Any single   1.75 1.75

Famous Croats — A310

    Designs: 2.30k, Ivan Lucic (1604-79), historian. No. 547, 3.50k, Antun Vrancic (1504-75), archbishop, writer. No. 548, 3.50k, St. Jerome, sculpture by Andrija Alesi (c. 1425-1504). 10k, Printing of Croatian grammar book, by Bartol Kasic (1575-1650), 400th anniv.

2004, Apr. 22
546-549 A310   Set of 4   8.25 8.25

Souvenir Sheet

Risnjak National Park — A311

2004, Apr. 22
550 A311 10k multi   5.25 5.25

Martyrdom of St. Domnio, 1700th Anniv. — A312

2004, May 7
551 A312 3.50k multi   1.75 1.75

Europa A313

    Designs: No. 552, 3.50k, Summer vacation items. No. 553, 3.50k, Winter vacation items.

2004, May 9
552-553 A313   Set of 2   3.00 3.00

FIFA (Fédération Internationale de Football Association), Cent. A314

2004, May 21   **Litho.**   **Perf. 14**
554 A314 2.50k multi   1.25 1.25

Medicinal Herbs — A315

    Designs: 2.30k, Rosa canina. 2.80k, Viola odorata. 3.50k, Mentha piperita.

2004, June 5
555-557 A315   Set of 3   4.00 4.00
555a   Booklet pane of 10   10.00 —
    Complete booklet, #555a   10.50
556a   Booklet pane of 10   12.50 —
    Complete booklet, #556a   13.00
557a   Booklet pane of 10   16.50 —
    Complete booklet, #557a   17.50

    Nos. 555-557 are impregnated with a floral scent.

Intl. Marionette Union Congress, Intl. Puppetry Art Festival, Rijeka A316

2004, June 6
558 A316 3.50k multi   1.75 1.75

European Soccer Championships, Portugal — A317

2004, June 12
559 A317 3.50k multi   1.75 1.75
    Values are for stamps with surrounding selvage.

Restoration of Old Bridge, Mostar, Bosnia & Herzegovina A318

2004, July 23   **Litho.**   **Perf. 14**
560 A318 3.50k multi   1.75 1.75

2004 Summer Olympics, Athens — A319

2004, Aug. 13
561 A319 3.50k multi   1.75 1.75

Virovitica A320

2004, Aug. 16
562 A320 5k multi   2.40 2.40
   a.   Perf. 14 syncopated

    Issued: No. 562a, 12/7/07. For surcharge see No. 779.

Zagreb Post Office, Cent. A321

2004, Sept. 9
563 A321 2.30k multi   1.00 1.00
    Printed in sheets of 16 + 4 labels.

Father Andrija Kacic Miosic (1704-60), Poet — A322

2004, Sept. 15
564 A322 2.80k multi   1.25 1.25

Fortresses Type of 2001

    Designs: No. 565, 3.50k, Dubovac, 15th-19th cent. No. 566, 3.50k, Gripe, 17th cent. No. 567, 3.50k, Valpovo, 15th-18th cent.

2004, Sept. 29
565-567 A261   Set of 3   4.75 4.75

Modern Art Type of 2003

    Designs: No. 568, 2.30k, Self-portrait, by Miroslav Kraljevic, vert. No. 569, 2.30k, Noon in Supetar, by Jerolim Mise, vert. No. 570, 2.30k, Stari Grad, by Juraj Plancic, vert.

2004, Nov. 15   **Litho.**   **Perf. 14**
568-570 A304   Set of 3   3.25 3.25

Christmas A323

2004, Nov. 25
571 A323 2.30k multi   1.10 1.10

Antun and Stjepan Radic and Plowman — A324

2004, Dec. 22   **Litho.**   **Perf. 14**
572 A324 7.20k multi   3.25 3.25
    Croatian People's Peasant Party, Cent.

Fairy Tale Characters — A325

    No. 573: a, Mermaid Halugica. b, Dwarf Pedalj Muza Lakat Brade.

2005, Jan. 14
573 A325 5k Horiz. pair, #a-b   4.50 4.50

World Conference on the Information Society, Tunis — A326

2005, Feb. 10
574 A326 2.80k multi 1.40 1.40
Values are for stamps with surrounding selvage.

Souvenir Sheet

Bust of Livia Drusilla — A327

2005, Feb. 24
575 A327 10k multi 5.00 5.00

Souvenir Sheet

Expo 2005, Aichi, Japan — A328

2005, Mar. 25 *Perf.*
576 A328 10k multi 5.00 5.00

Pope John Paul II (1920-2005) A329

2005, Apr. 8 *Perf. 14*
577 A329 2.30k multi 1.25 1.25

World Music Days, Zagreb A330

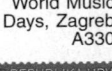

Stjepan Sulek (1914-86), Composer A331

2005, Apr. 15
578 A330 2.30k multi 1.10 1.10
579 A331 2.30k multi 1.10 1.10

Insects — A332

Designs: 1.80k, Coccinella septempunctata. 2.30k, Rosalia alpina. 3.50k, Lucanus cervus.

2005, Apr. 22
580-582 A332 Set of 3 3.75 3.75

Liberation of Western Slavonia, 10th Anniv. A333

2005, May 1
583 A333 1.80k multi .95 .95

Dr. Josip Buturac (1905-93), Historian — A334

2005, May 6
584 A334 2.80k multi 1.25 1.25

Europa — A335

No. 585: a, Loaf of bread. b, Glass of wine.

2005, May 9
585 A335 3.50k Horiz. pair, #a-b 3.50 3.50

Coast of Hvar Island — A336

No. 586: a, Rock at L, tree tops at bottom. b, Tree tops at LL. c, Rock at R. d, Canoe, rock at R. e, Small rock in center. f, Rocks at UL, trees. g, Rocks at R, trees. h, Tree tops at LL corner, rock at UR corner. i, Rocks at UL and LL corners. j, Rocks at LL.

2005, May 24 **Litho.** *Perf. 14*
586 A336 Booklet pane of
10 13.00 —
a.-e. 1.80k Any single .90 .90
f.-j. 3.50k Any single 1.40 1.40
Complete booklet, #586 14.00

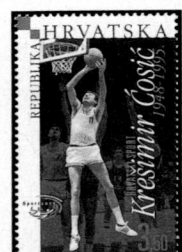

Kresimir Cosic (1948-95), Basketball Player — A337

2005, May 25
587 A337 3.50k multi 1.50 1.50
Printed in sheets of 9 + 1 label.

Krapanj Island Sponge and Coral Diving — A338

2005, June 2 **Litho.**
588 A338 3.50k multi 1.75 1.75
Portions of the design were applied by a thermographic process producing a shiny, raised effect.

Emperor Constantine's Bath, Varazdinske Toplice A339

2005, June 20 *Perf. 14*
589 A339 1.80k multi 1.00 1.00

Intl. Fire Brigade Olympics, Varazdin — A340

2005, July 15
590 A340 2.30k multi 1.25 1.25
Printed in sheets of 8 + 2 labels.

European Philatelic Cooperation, 50th Anniv. (in 2006) A341

Designs: 7.20k, Vignette of #134. 8k, Stylized gull.

2005, Sept. 8
591-592 A341 Set of 2 7.00 7.00
592a Souvenir sheet, #591-592 60.00 60.00
Europa stamps, 50th anniv. (in 2006).

Telegraph A342

2005, Sept. 9
593 A342 2.30k multi 1.25 1.25
First overhead telegraph lines in Croatia, 155th anniv., Stamp Day.

Fortresses Type of 2001

Designs: 1k, Ilok, 14th-15th cents. 2.30k, Motovun, 13th-15th cents., vert. 3.50k, St. Nicholas, 16th cent.

2005, Sept. 15
594-596 A261 Set of 3 3.50 3.50

Famous People — A343

Designs: 1k, Adam Baltazar Krcelic (1715-78), historian. No. 598, 2.30k, Dragutin Tadijanovic (b. 1905), poet. No. 599, 2.30k, Tin Ujevic (1891-1955), poet. 2.80k, Madonna and Child, by Juraj Culinovic (c.1433-1504).

2005, Nov. 4
597-600 A343 Set of 4 4.00 4.00

Clock Tower, Rijeka — A344

2005, Nov. 10 **Litho.** *Perf. 14*
601 A344 3.50k multi 1.75 1.75
a. Perf. 14 syncopated 1.75 1.75
Issued: No. 601a, 6/12/06. For surcharge see No. 778.

Christmas A345

2005, Nov. 22 *Perf. 14*
602 A345 2.30k multi 1.25 1.25

Booklet Stamp
Self-Adhesive
Serpentine Die Cut 5¼
603 A345 2.30k multi 1.25 1.25
a. Booklet pane of 10 12.50 12.50
Complete booklet, #603a 12.50 12.50

Modern Art Type of 2003

Designs: 1.80k, Zadar, by Edo Murtic. 5k, Meander, by Julije Knifer. 10k, Drawing, by Miroslav Sutej, vert.

2005, Dec. 1 *Perf. 14*
604-606 A304 Set of 3 8.75 8.75

Davis Cup and Members of Croatian Tennis Team — A346

2005, Dec. 22 **Litho.** *Perf. 14*
607 A346 5k multi 2.75 2.75
Croatia, winners of 2005 Davis Cup. Printed in sheets of 9 + label.

Composers A347

Designs: 1.80k, Boris Papandopulo (1906-91). 2.30k, Milo Cipra (1906-85). 2.80k, Ivan Brkanovic (1906-87).

2006, Jan. 17
608-610 A347 Set of 3 3.50 3.50

2006 Winter Olympics, Turin — A348

2006, Feb. 10
611 A348 3.50k multi 1.90 1.90

Rembrandt (1606-69), Painter A349

2006, Mar. 7
612 A349 5k multi 2.75 2.75

Famous Men — A350

Designs: No. 613, 1k, Andrija Ljudevit Adamic (1766-1828), merchant. No. 614, 1k, Josip Kozarac (1858-1906), writer. 5k, Vanja Radaus (1906-75), sculptor. 7.20k, Ljubo Karaman (1886-1971), art historian.

2006, Mar. 21   Perf. 14 Syncopated
613-616 A350 Set of 4 7.25 7.25

European Track and Field Championships, Göteborg, Sweden — A351

2006, Apr. 4
617 A351 2.30k multi 1.25 1.25

2006 World Cup Soccer Championships, Germany A352

2006, Apr. 4
618 A352 2.80k multi 1.25 1.25

Flag and Crowd — A353

No. 619 — Location and placement of denomination: a, At left, with denomination above crowd. b, At right, with top of numerals over red in flag. c, At left, with top of "8" and "0" above white in flag. d, At left, with serif of "1" above red in flag. e, At left, with entire denomination above red in flag. f, At right, with parts of "5" and "0" above red in flag. g, At right, with entire denomination above red in flag. h, At right, with entire denomination above white in flag. i, At left, with entire denomination above red in flag. j, At right, with denomination above crowd.

2006, Apr. 25
619   A353   Booklet pane of
        10   16.00   —
a.-e.   1.80k Any single   1.00   1.00
f.-j.   3.50k Any single   2.10   2.10
        Complete booklet, #619   17.00

Europa — A354

No. 620: a, Denomination at left. b, Denomination at right.

2006, May 9
620 A354 3.50k Horiz. pair, #a-b 3.50 3.50

Worldwide Fund for Nature (WWF) A355

No. 621 — Various views of Sterna albifrons with denomination in: a, Gray. b, Dull green. c, Yellow orange. d, Red.

2006, May 23
621   Strip of 4   10.00 10.00
a.-d.   A355 5k Any single   2.40   2.40

Croatian Automobile Club, Cent. — A356

Perf. 13¾x14 Syncopated
2006, June 4
622 A356 5k multi 2.75 2.75

Aquatic Flowers A357

Designs: 2.30k, Nymphaea alba. 2.80k, Nuphar lutea. 3.50k, Menyanthes trifoliata.

2006, June 5   Perf. 14 Syncopated
623-625 A357   Set of 3   4.50   4.50
623a   Booklet pane of 10   12.50 12.50
         Complete booklet, #623a 12.50
624a   Booklet pane of 10   14.00 14.00
         Complete booklet, #624a 14.00
625a   Booklet pane of 10   18.00 18.00
         Complete booklet, #625a 18.00

Nikola Tesla (1856-1943), Inventor — A358

Perf. 14x13½ Syncopated
2006, July 10   Litho.
626 A358 3.50k multi 1.75 1.75

Bjelovar, 250th Anniv. A359

Perf. 14 Syncopated
2006, Aug. 22   Litho.
627 A359 2.80k multi 1.50 1.50

Stamp Day — A360

2006, Sept. 9   Litho. & Embossed
628 A360 2.30k multi 1.25 1.25

Jewish Community of Zagreb, 200th Anniv. — A361

Perf. 14¼x13¾ Syncopated
2006, Sept. 15   Litho.
629 A361 5k multi 2.75 2.75

Fortresses Type of 2001

Designs: No. 630, 1k, St. Mary of Mercy Church, Vrboska, 16th cent. No. 631, 1k, Church of the Holy Spirit, Sudurad, 16th cent. 7.20k, Frankapan Citadel, Ogulin, 16th cent.

Perf. 13¾x14¼ Syncopated
2006, Sept. 21
630-632 A261 Set of 3 4.75 4.75

White Cane Safety Day — A362

Perf. 14 Syncopated
2006, Oct. 15   Litho. & Embossed
633 A362 1.80k black & red 1.00 1.00

Christmas A363

Perf. 14¼ Syncopated
2006, Nov. 27   Litho.
634 A363 2.30k multi 1.25 1.25

Booklet Stamp
Self-Adhesive
Serpentine Die Cut 5¼

635   A363 2.30k multi   1.25   1.25
a.   Booklet pane of 10   12.50
         Complete booklet, #635a 12.50

Modern Art Type of 2003

Designs: 1k, Still Life, by Vladimir Becic. 1.80k, Composition Tyma 3, by Ivan Picelj.

10k, Self-portrait as Hunter, by Nasta Rojc, vert.

2006, Dec. 1   Perf. 14 Syncopated
636-638 A304 Set of 3 6.00 6.00

Classical Gymnasium, Zagreb, 400th Anniv. — A364

Perf. 14 Syncopated
2007, Jan. 9   Litho.
639 A364 5k multi 2.40 2.40

Fairy Tale Characters — A365

No. 640: a, Monster Orko. b, Devil Macic.

2007, Jan. 18
640 A365 2.30k Horiz. pair, #a-b 2.50 2.50

National and University Library, Zagreb, 400th Anniv. A366

2007, Feb. 22
641 A366 5k multi 2.50 2.50

Crustaceans A367

Designs: 1.80k, Palinurus elephas. 2.30k, Nephrops norvegicus. 2.80k, Astacus astacus.

2007, Mar. 15
642   A367 1.80k multi   .85   .85
a.   Booklet pane of 10   8.50
         Complete booklet, #642a 8.50
643   A367 2.30k multi   1.05   1.05
a.   Booklet pane of 10   10.50
         Complete booklet, #643a 10.50
644   A367 2.80k multi   1.35   1.35
a.   Booklet pane of 10   13.50
         Complete booklet, #644a 13.50
         Nos. 642-644 (3)   3.25   3.25

Native Breeds of Farm Animals A368

Designs: 2.80k, Istrian ox. 3.50k, Posavina horse. 5k, Dalmatian donkey.

2007, Mar. 20
645-647 A368 Set of 3 5.75 5.75

Europa — A369

No. 648: a, Scouting emblem and dove. b, Scout neckerchief.

2007, Apr. 16
648 A369 3.50k Horiz. pair, #a-b   3.25 3.25
Scouting, cent.

Scientists — A370

Designs: 5k, Andrija Mohorovicic (1857-1936), seismologist. 7.20k, Duro Baglivi (1668-1707), physician.

Perf. 14x13½ Syncopated
2007, Apr. 23
649-650 A370   Set of 2   6.00 6.00

Souvenir Sheet

World Championship Victory of Croatian Water Polo Team — A371

No. 651: a, Man with red shirt at right, denomination at UL. b, Man with red shirt at LR, denomination at UR. c, Man with red shirt at left, denomination at UR.

Litho. With Foil Application
2007, May 3   *Perf. 14¼ Syncopated*
651 A371 5k Sheet of 3, #a-c   7.75 7.75

World Table Tennis Championships, Zagreb — A372

Perf. 14 Syncopated
2007, May 21   Litho. & Embossed
652 A372 3.50k multi   1.75 1.75

Starting with No. 652 some stamps have an imprinted wing-shaped tagging design that looks like a watermark.

Diplomatic Relations Between Croatia and People's Republic of China, 15th Anniv. — A373

No. 653: a, "China" in Glagolitic letters. b, "Croatia" in Chinese characters.

2007, May 30   Litho.   Perf. 12
653 A373 5k Horiz. pair, #a-b   5.00 5.00

Zagreb City Museum, Cent. — A374

2007, May 31   *Perf. 14 Syncopated*
654 A374 2.30k multi   1.10 1.10

Souvenir Sheet

Red Lake — A375

2007, June 8
655 A375 10k multi   4.50 4.50

First Croatian Philatelic Exhibition, Cent. — A376

Perf. 14 Syncopated
2007, Sept. 9   Litho. & Embossed
656 A376 2.80k multi   1.25 1.25
Stamp Day.

Lighthouses — A377

Designs: No. 657, 5k, St. John on the Sea Lighthouse. No. 658, 5k, Porer Lighthouse. No. 659, 5k, Savudrija Lighthouse.

Perf. 13¾x14¼ Syncopated
2007, Sept. 14   Litho.
657-659 A377   Set of 3   7.00 7.00

Veprinac Statute, 500th Anniv. — A378

Perf. 14¼x13¾ Syncopated
2007, Oct. 2
660 A378 2.70k multi   1.25 1.25

City Views — A379

Designs: 1.80k, Omis. 2.30k, Koprivnica, horiz. 2.80k, Krk.

2007, Oct. 30   *Perf. 14 Syncopated*
661 A379 1.80k multi   .85 .85
a.   Perf. 14 ('10)   .70 .70
662 A379 2.30k multi   1.00 1.00
663 A379 2.80k multi   1.30 1.30
Nos. 661-663 (3)   3.15 3.15

For surcharge see No. 777.

Blanka Vlasic, 2007 World Women's High Jump Champion A380

2007, Nov. 8
664 A380 2.30k multi   1.25 1.25

Christmas A381

Perf. 14¼ Syncopated
2007, Nov. 15   Litho.
665 A381 2.30k multi   1.25 1.25

Booklet Stamp
Self-Adhesive
Serpentine Die Cut 5¼
666 A381 2.30k multi   1.25 1.25
a.   Booklet pane of 10   12.50
Complete booklet, #666a   12.50

Marija Juric Zagorka (1873-1957), Writer — A382

Perf. 14¼x13¾ Syncopated
2007, Nov. 16
667 A382 7.20k multi   3.25 3.25

Modern Art Type of 2003
Designs: 2.80k, Area by the Sava River, by Branko Senoa. No. 669, 5k, Pegasus's Garden, by Ferdinand Kulmer. No. 670, 5k, Bridgeport, by Ivan Benkovic.

Perf. 14 Syncopated
2007, Dec. 1   Litho.
668-670 A304   Set of 3   5.75 5.75

New Year 2008 — A383

2007, Dec. 5
671 A383 1.80k multi   .80 .80

Composers A384

Designs: No. 672, 2.30k, Igor Kuljeric (1938-2006). No. 673, 2.30k, Krsto Odak (1888-1965).

2008, Jan. 22
672-673 A384   Set of 2   2.25 2.25

Publication of *Arithmetika Horvatszka*, by Mijo Silobod Bolsic, 250th Anniv. — A385

Perf. 13¾x14 Syncopated
2008, Jan. 25
674 A385 3.50k multi   1.75 1.75

Steam Locomotives — A386

Designs: No. 675, 5k, MAV 601/JZ 32. No. 676, 5k, MAV 651/JZ 31.

2008, Feb. 15   Set of 2   4.50 4.50
675-676 A386
Nos. 675-676 were printed in sheets of 6 containing three of each stamp.

St. Nicholas Church, Cavtat A387

Perf. 14 Syncopated
2008, Mar. 8   Litho.
677 A387 7.20k multi   3.25 3.25

For surcharge see No. 780.

2008 Summer Olympics, Beijing A388

2008, Mar. 11
678 A388 5k multi   2.00 2.00

Printed in sheets of 9 + label.

Flowers — A389

Designs: 1.80k, Helleborus niger. 2.80k, Onosma stellulata. 3.50k, Lonicera glutinosa.

2008, Mar. 20
679 A389 1.80k multi   .95 .95
a.   Booklet pane of 10   9.50
Complete booklet, #679a   9.50
680 A389 2.80k multi   1.50 1.50
a.   Booklet pane of 10   15.00
Complete booklet, #680a   15.00
681 A389 3.50k multi   1.75 1.75
a.   Booklet pane of 10   17.50
Complete booklet, #681a   17.50
Nos. 679-681 (3)   4.20 4.20

Famous Writers — A390

Designs: 2.30k, Petar Zoranic (1508-c. 1569), novelist. 2.80k, Silvije Strahimir Kranjcevic (1865-1908), poet. 7.20k, Marin Drzic (1508-67), dramatist.

Perf. 14 Syncopated

2008, Apr. 22			**Litho.**
682-684	A390	Set of 3	5.75 5.75

Waterfall, Plitvice Lakes National Park — A391

No. 685 — Part of waterfall with: a, Country name in white, denomination at UL, "HP" symbol in white at LL. b, Country name in white, denomination at UR, "HP" symbol in white at LL, green foliage at UL. c, Country name in black, denomination at UR. d, Country name in white, denomination at UR, "HP" symbol in black at LL. e, Country name in white, denomination at UR, "HP" symbol in white at LL, green foliage at UR. f, Country name in white, denomination in black at LR, "HP" symbol in black at LL, rock with foliage in center. g, Country name in white, denomination in black at LR, "HP" symbol in black at LL, all rocks covered by spray. h, Country name in black, denomination at LR. i, Country name in white, denomination in white at LR. j, Country name in white, denomination in black at LR, "HP" symbol in white at LL.

Perf. 14 Syncopated

2008, Apr. 25			**Litho.**
685		Booklet pane of 10	17.50 —
a.-j.	A391	3.50k Any single	1.75 1.75
		Complete booklet, #685	17.50

2008 Volkswagen Beetle — A392

2008, May 8			
686	A392	2.30k multi + label	1.10 1.10

Europa A393

Designs: 3.50k, Insured envelope with wax seal. 5k, Airmail envelope.

2008, May 9			**Litho.**
687	A393	3.50k multi	1.60 1.60

Litho. & Embossed

688	A393	5k multi	2.40 2.40

Portions of the design of No. 687 were applied using a thermographic process producing a shiny raised effect.

UEFA Euro 2008 Soccer Championships, Austria and Switzerland — A394

2008, May 14	**Litho.**	**Perf. 14x13½**	
689	A394	3.50k multi	1.50 1.50

Values are for stamps with surrounding selvage. Printed in sheets of 9 + label.

Adris Group — A395

2008, May 16		**Perf. 14 Syncopated**	
690	A395	2.30k multi + label	1.10 1.10

Souvenir Sheet

Ivan Vucetic (1858-1925), Fingerprint Classifier — A396

2008, Apr. 20			
691	A396	10k multi	5.00 5.00

Souvenir Sheet

Expo Zaragoza 2008 — A397

Litho. With Foil Application

2008, June 16			
692	A397	10k multi	4.50 4.50

Souvenir Sheet

Lujzinske Road, 200th Anniv. — A398

No. 693 — Parts of map of Lujzinske Road with denomination in: a, Red. b, Green. c, White.

Perf. 14x13½ Syncopated

2008, June 17			**Litho.**
693	A398	5k Sheet of 3, #a-c	7.00 7.00

Western Union — A399

2008, July 11		**Perf. 14 Syncopated**	
694	A399	3.50k multi + label	1.50 1.50

Postal Workers' Games — A400

Litho. With Foil Application

2008, Sept. 9		**Perf. 14 Syncopated**	
695	A400	2.80k multi	1.30 1.30

Stamp Day.

Lighthouses A401

Designs: No. 696, 5k, Pinida Lighthouse. No. 697, 5k, Vnetak Lighthouse. No. 698, 5k, Zaglav Lighthouse.

Perf. 14¼x13¾ Syncopated

2008, Sept. 12			**Litho.**
696-698	A401	Set of 3	7.00 7.00

Order of St. Clare, Split, 700th Anniv. — A402

2008, Sept. 16			
699	A402	2.80k multi	1.25 1.25

Details From Native Costumes A403

Costume from: 10 l, Sunja. 20 l, Bistra. 50 l, Bizovac. 1k, Ravni Kotari. 10k, Pag.

2008, Sept. 30		**Perf. 14 Syncopated**	
700-704	A403	Set of 5	6.00 6.00
701a		Perf. 14 ('10)	.25 .25
703a		Perf. 14 ('10)	.35 .35
704a		Sheet of 5, #700-704 + label	6.00 6.00

European Healthy Cities Movement, 20th Anniv. — A404

2008, Oct. 17		**Perf. 14¼ Syncopated**	
705	A404	2.80k multi + label	1.25 1.25

Collegium Ragusinum, Dubrovnik, 350th Anniv. — A405

Perf. 14¼x13¾ Syncopated

2008, Nov. 7		**Litho. & Embossed**	
706	A405	7.20k multi	3.00 3.00

Intl. Amateur Radio Union Region 1 Conference, Cavtat — A406

Perf. 13¾x14¼ Syncopated

2008, Nov. 14			**Litho.**
707	A406	3.50k multi	1.50 1.50

The Book on the Art of Trading, by Benedikt Kotruljevic, 550th Anniv. of Publication A407

Perf. 14¼x13¾ Syncopated

2008, Oct. 22			**Litho.**
708	A407	2.80k multi	1.25 1.25

New Year's Day — A408

Perf. 14 Syncopated

2008, Nov. 21			**Litho.**
709	A408	1.80k multi	.75 .75

Christmas A409

2008, Nov. 27		**Perf. 14 Syncopated**	
710	A409	2.80k multi	1.50 1.50

Booklet Stamp
Self-Adhesive

711 A409 2.80k multi   1.00 1.00
a.   Booklet pane of 10   10.00
   Complete booklet, #711a   10.00

Modern Art Type of 2003

Designs: 1.65k, Two Trees at the Foot of a Hill, by Oskar Herman. 1.80k, Carousel, by Nevenka Djordjevic. 6.50k, Still Life, by Ivo Rezek.

Perf. 14 Syncopated
2008, Dec. 1   Litho.
712-714 A304   Set of 3   4.50 4.50

Zora Choral Society, 150th Anniv. — A410

Perf. 14x13¾ Syncopated
2008, Dec. 5
715 A410 1.65k multi   .75 .75

Ivan Mestrovic (1883-1962), Sculptor — A411

Perf. 14 Syncopated
2008, Dec. 15   Litho.
716 A411 5k multi   2.10 2.10

21st Men's World Handball Championships — A412

Perf. 13¾x14¼ Syncopated
2009, Jan. 16   Litho. & Embossed
717 A412 3.50k multi   1.50 1.50

Printed in sheets of 9 + label

Bruno Bjelinski (1909-92), Composer A413

Josip Andreis (1909-82), Musicologist A414

Perf. 14¼x13¾ Syncopated
2009, Jan. 21   Litho.
718 A413 1.80k multi   .75 .75
719 A414 3.50k multi   1.50 1.50

Street and Bridge, Sisak — A415

2009, Jan. 22   *Perf. 14 Syncopated*
720 A415 8k multi   3.50 3.50

Remains of St. Tryphon in Kotor, 1200th Anniv. — A416

No. 721 — St. Tryphon: a, Drawing. b, Sculpture from altarpiece, Kotor Cathedral.

2009, Feb. 3   *Perf. 14¼ Syncopated*
721 A416 3.50k Horiz. pair, #a-b   2.75 2.75

Fairy Tale Characters — A417

No. 722: a, Svarozic. b, Bjesomar.

2009, Feb. 27
722 A417 1.65k Horiz. pair, #a-b   1.50 1.50

Souvenir Sheet

Protection of Polar Regions and Glaciers — A418

No. 723: a, Sun over glacier. b, Intl. Polar Year emblem and glacier.

2009, Mar. 27   Litho. & Embossed
723 A418 5k Sheet of 2, #a-b   3.75 3.75

Easter A419

Perf. 14 Syncopated
2009, Mar. 30   Litho.
724 A419 3.50k multi   1.60 1.60

Entry Into NATO A420

2009, Apr. 4
725 A420 8k multi   3.00 3.00

Juraj Sizgoric (1445-c. 1509), Poet — A421

Juraj Habdelic (1609-78), Writer — A422

Ljudevit Gaj (1809-72), Writer, Illyrian Movement Leader — A423

Petar Segedin (1909-98), Writer — A424

Perf. 14¼x13¾ Syncopated
2009, Apr. 22
726 A421 3.50k multi   1.25 1.25
727 A422 3.50k multi   1.25 1.25
728 A423 5k multi   1.90 1.90
729 A424 5k multi   1.90 1.90
   Nos. 726-729 (4)   6.30 6.30

Europa — A425

No. 730 — Image of space from Hubble Space Telescope with red diamond at: a, Left. b, Right.

Perf. 14x13½ Syncopated
2009, May 9   Litho.
730 A425 8k Horiz. pair, #a-b   6.00 6.00

Intl. Year of Astronomy. Values are for stamps with surrounding selvage.

Franciscans in Cakovec, 350th Anniv. — A426

2009, May 20   *Perf. 14 Syncopated*
731 A426 3.50k multi   1.40 1.40

Souvenir Sheet

King Andrew's Charter Proclaiming Varazdin as Free Royal Borough, 800th Anniv. — A427

Perf. 14 Syncopated
2009, June 9   Litho.
732 A427 15k multi   6.00 6.00

Souvenir Sheet

St. John, Sculpture by Ivan Duknovic (c. 1440-1509) — A428

2009, June 23   *Perf. 14*
733 A428 10k multi   4.75 4.75

Zagreb Jazz Quartet, 50th Anniv. A429

2009, June 29
734 A429 10.70k multi   5.00 5.00

Fish — A430

Designs: 3.50k, Acipenser naccarii. No. 736, 5k, Knipowitschia mrakovcici. No. 737, 5k, Ballerus sapa.

2009, Sept. 1   Litho.   Perf. 14

735	A430	3.50k multi	1.75	1.75
a.		Booklet pane of 10	17.50	—
		Complete booklet, #735a	17.50	
736	A430	5k multi	2.50	2.50
a.		Booklet pane of 10	25.00	
		Complete booklet, #736a	25.00	
737	A430	5k multi	2.50	2.50
a.		Booklet pane of 10	25.00	
		Complete booklet, #737a	25.00	
		Nos. 735-737 (3)	6.75	6.75

Stamp Day — A431

2009, Sept. 9

738	A431	3.50k multi	1.50	1.50

Croatian Post Inc., 10th Anniv.

Lighthouses A432

Designs: No. 739, 3.50k, Gruica Lighthouse. No. 740, 3.50k, Strazica Lighthouse. 8k, Voscica Lighthouse.

2009, Sept. 11

739-741	A432	Set of 3	5.75	5.75

Franciscan Order, 800th Anniv. — A433

2009, Sept. 17   Litho.   Perf. 14

742	A433	3.50k multi	1.60	1.60

Souvenir Sheet

Stone Buildings — A434

No. 743 — Stone building in: a, Pazin, Croatia. b, Kopriva na Krasu, Slovenia.

2009, Sept. 25

743	A434	8k Sheet of 2, #a-b	7.50	7.50

See Slovenia No. 812.

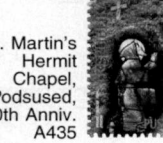

St. Martin's Hermit Chapel, Podsused, 800th Anniv. A435

2009, Oct. 29

744	A435	3.50k multi	1.60	1.60

National Folk Dance Ensemble, 60th Anniv. A436

2009, Nov. 11

745	A436	3.50k multi	1.60	1.60

Rights of the Child A437

2009, Nov. 20

746	A437	3.50k multi	1.30	1.30

Declaration of the Rights of the Child, 50th anniv.; UN Convention on the Rights of the Child, 20th anniv.

New Year's Day — A438

2009, Nov. 24   Litho.   Perf. 14

747	A438	3.50k multi	1.50	1.50

Serpentine Die Cut 5¼
Booklet Stamp
Self-Adhesive

748	A438	3.50k multi	1.50	1.50
a.		Booklet pane of 10	15.00	
		Complete booklet, #748a	15.00	

Modern Art Type of 2003

Designs: No. 749, 1.80k, Gray Sail, by Zlatko Prica. No. 750, 1.80k, A Bosom Full of Wind, by Nives Kavuric Kurtovic, vert. No. 751, 1.80k, Flora, by Ordan Petlevski.

2009, Dec. 1   Litho.   Perf. 14

749-751	A304	Set of 3	2.00	2.00

A439

Christmas A440

2009, Dec. 4   Litho.   Perf. 14

752	A439	3.50k multi	1.50	1.50
753	A440	8k multi	3.25	3.25

Serpentine Die Cut 5¼
Booklet Stamp
Self-Adhesive

754	A439	3.50k multi	1.50	1.50
a.		Booklet pane of 10	15.00	
		Complete booklet, #754a	15.00	

Statute of Lastovo, 700th Anniv. — A441

2010, Jan. 8   Litho.   Perf. 14

755	A441	3.50k multi	1.60	1.60

2010 Winter Olympics, Vancouver A442

2010, Feb. 12   Perf. 14¼x14

756	A442	3.50k multi	1.60	1.60

Souvenir Sheet

Peonies — A443

No. 757: a, Paeonia mascula. b, Paeonia officinalis.

2010, Mar. 8   Litho.   Perf. 14

757	A443	3k Sheet of 2, #a-b	3.00	3.00

Embroidery A444

Embroidery from: 1.60k, Primorje. 3.10k, Medimurje. 4.60k, Posavina. 7.10k, Draganic.

2010, Mar. 15

758-761	A444	Set of 4	7.75	7.75
761a		Sheet of 4, #758-761	7.75	7.75

Fruit A445

Designs: 1k, Fragaria vesca. No. 763, Vitis vinifera. No. 764, Ribes uva-crispa.

2010, Mar. 16   Litho. & Embossed

762	A445	1k multi	.45	.45
a.		Booklet pane of 10	4.50	
		Complete booklet, #762a	4.50	
763	A445	4k multi	1.75	1.75
a.		Booklet pane of 10	17.50	
		Complete booklet, #763a	17.50	
764	A445	4k multi	1.75	1.75
a.		Booklet pane of 10	17.50	
		Complete booklet, #764a	17.50	
		Nos. 762-764 (3)	3.95	3.95

Easter A446

2010, Mar. 19   Litho.   Perf. 14

765	A446	3.10k multi	1.40	1.40

Establishment of Bjelovar-Krizevci Diocese — A447

2010, Mar. 19

766	A447	6.50k multi	2.75	2.75

Printed in sheets of 8 + 2 labels.

Steam Locomotives — A448

No. 767: a, Series MAV 326/JZ 125. b, Series SüdB 18.

2010, Mar. 29

767		Vert. pair + central label	6.75	6.75
a.-b.		A448 7.10k Either single	3.25	3.25

Capuchin Order in Croatia, 400th Anniv. — A449

2010, Apr. 15

768	A449	6.10k multi	2.75	2.75

Famous
Men — A450

Designs: 1.60k, Grgo Gamulin (1910-97), art historian. 3.10k, Janko Polic Kamov (1886-1910), writer. 4.50k, Ivan Matetic Ronjgov (1880-1960), composer. 6.10k, Marko Antun de Dominis (1560-1624), archbishop and physicist.

2010, Apr. 22
769-772 A450 Set of 4   7.00 7.00

Souvenir Sheet

Expo 2010, Shanghai — A451

2010, Apr. 29
773 A451 10k multi   4.50 4.50

Europa — A452

No. 774 — Children's book and: a, Fairy on branch, fairy with horn. b, Fairy looking at butterfly, fairy on flower.

Litho. With Foil Application
2010, May 7   Perf. 14
774 A452 7.10k Horiz. pair, #a-b   6.25 6.25

Souvenir Sheet

Lubenice — A453

2010, May 21   Litho.
775 A453 10k multi   4.75 4.75

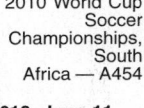

2010 World Cup
Soccer
Championships,
South
Africa — A454

2010, June 11
776 A454 4.50k multi   2.25 2.25
Printed in sheets of 9 + label.

Nos. 562a, 601,
661a and 677
Surcharged

Methods and Perfs. As Before
2010
777 A379 1.60k on 1.80k #661a   .65 .65
778 A344 3.10k on 3.50k #601   1.25 1.25
779 A320 4.50k on 5k #562a   2.10 2.10
780 A367 7.10k on 7.20k #677   3.25 3.25
      Nos. 777-780 (4)   7.25 7.25
    Issued: Nos. 777-778, 5/17; Nos. 779-780, 7/19.

Lighthouses
A455

Designs: No. 781, 3.10k, Vir Lighthouse. No. 782, 3.10k, Veli Rat Lighthouse. No. 783, 3.10k, Tajer Lighthouse.

2010, Sept. 7   Litho.   Perf. 14
781-783 A455 Set of 3   4.50 4.50

Souvenir Sheet

Minerals — A456

No. 784: a, Calcite from Brac. b, Agate from Lepoglava.

Litho. & Embossed (#784a), Litho.
2010, Oct. 15
784 A456 3.10k Sheet of 2, #a-b   3.00 3.00

Souvenir Sheet

Dubrovnik Tramway, Cent. — A457

2010, Nov. 22   Litho.   Perf. 14
785 A457 15k multi   7.00 7.00

Adoration of
the
Shepherds, by Josip
Biffel — A458

2010, Nov. 25
786 A458 3.10k multi   1.50 1.50

Booklet Stamp
Self-Adhesive
Serpentine Die Cut 5¼
787 A458 3.10k multi   1.50 1.50
  a.   Booklet pane of 10   15.00
       Complete booklet, #787a   15.00
    Christmas.

A459

2010, Dec. 1   Litho.   Perf. 14
788 A459 3.10k multi   1.40 1.40
    Croatian Journalist Society, cent.

New Year
2011 — A460

2010, Dec. 6
789 A460 1.60k multi   .75 .75

Intl. Children's
Festival,
Sibenik — A461

2011, Feb. 14   Litho.   Perf. 14
790 A461 1.60k multi   .85 .85

Fauna — A462

Designs: 1.60k, Ursus arctos. 3.10k, Falco eleonorae. 4.60k, Monachus monachus.

2011, Mar. 15
791 A462 1.60k multi   .80 .80
  a.   Booklet pane of 10   8.00
       Complete booklet, #791a   8.00
792 A462 3.10k multi   1.60 1.60
  a.   Booklet pane of 10   16.00
       Complete booklet, #792a   16.00
793 A462 4.60k multi   2.40 2.40
  a.   Booklet pane of 10   24.00
       Complete booklet, #793a   24.00
       Nos. 791-793 (3)   4.80 4.80

Stations of the
Cross — A463

No. 794 — Station: a, 1. b, 2. c, 3. d, 4. e, 5. f, 6. g, 7. h, 8. i, 9. j, 10. k, 11. l, 12. m, 13. n, 14.

2011, Mar. 23
794   Booklet pane of 14   24.50 —
  a.-n. A463 3.10k Any single   1.75 1.75
         Complete booklet, #794   24.50

Visit to Croatia of Pope Benedict
XVI — A464

2011, Apr. 4   Litho.
795 A464 3.10k multi   1.75 1.75

Souvenir Sheet

Wreck of the Elhawi Star, Rijeka
Harbor — A465

2011, Apr. 14   Perf. 14
796 A465 10k multi   5.00 5.00

Souvenir Sheet

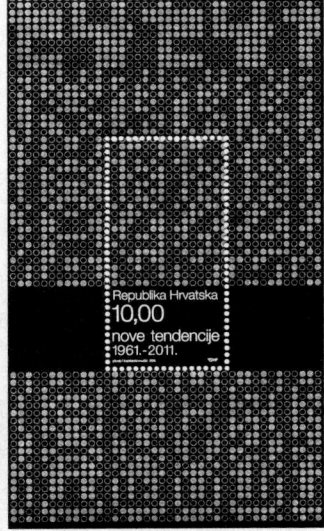

New Tendencies Art Exhibit, 50th
Anniv. — A466

2011, Apr. 15
797 A466 10k black & silver   5.00 5.00

Famous
People — A467

Designs: No. 798, 1.60k, Jagoda Truhelka (1864-1957), writer. No. 799, 1.60k, August Harambasic (1861-1911), poet and politician. No. 800, 1.60k, Grigor Vitez (1911-66), writer.

2011, Apr. 22
798-800 A467 Set of 3   2.25 2.25

Croatian Academy of Sciences and Arts, 150th Anniv. — A468

2011, Apr. 29
801 A468 9.50k multi 4.50 4.50

Europa — A469

No. 802 — Paintings: a, Beech, by Josip Zanki. b, Forest Scene with Spider's Web, by Lovro Artukovic.

2011, May 5
802 A469 7.10k Horiz. pair, #a-b 6.25 6.25
Intl. Year of Forests.

Castles and Palaces A470

Arms and: No. 803, 3.10k, Pejacevic Castle, Nasice. No. 804, 3.10k, Hilleprand-Mailáth Castle, Donji Miholjac. No. 805, 4.60k, Hilleprand-Prandau Normann-Ehrenfels Castle, Valpovo. No. 806, 4.60k, Palace of Prince Eugene of Savoy, Bilje.

2011, June 16   Litho.   Perf. 14
803-806 A470   Set of 4   7.00 7.00
806a   Sheet of 8, 2 each #803-806, + 8 labels   15.00 15.00

Nos. 803-806 each were printed in sheets of 9 + label. See Nos. 876-879, 956-959.

Independence, 20th Anniv. — A471

2011, June 24
807 A471 3.10k multi 1.50 1.50
Printed in sheets of 25 + 5 labels.

Eucharistic Miracle of Ludbreg, 600th Anniv. — A472

2011, Sept. 1
808 A472 5k multi 2.50 2.50

Quick Response Code — A473

2011, Sept. 9
809 A473 3.10k brown & black 1.60 1.60
Stamp Day.

Rudjer Boskovich (1711-87), Astronomer, and Dome of St. Peter's Basilica — A474

2011, Sept. 13
810 A474 7.10k multi 3.75 3.75
See Vatican City No. 1482.

Lighthouses — A475

Designs: No. 811, 3.10k, Prisnjak Lighthouse. No. 812, 3.10k, Mulo Lighthouse. 7.10k, Blitvenica Lighthouse.

2011, Oct. 18
811-813 A475   Set of 3   6.50 6.50

Institute of Art History, Zagreb, 50th Anniv. — A476

2011, Oct. 28
814 A476 4.60k multi 2.50 2.50

The Birth of Jesus, Fresco by Zeljko Hegedusic and Eugen Kokot — A477

2011, Nov. 3
815 A477 3.10k multi 1.75 1.75
Serpentine Die Cut 5¼
Booklet Stamp
Self-Adhesive
816 A477 3.10k multi 1.75 1.75
a.   Booklet pane of 10 17.50
      Complete booklet, #816a 17.50
Christmas.

Siege of Vukovar, 20th Anniv. A478

2011, Nov. 18   Perf. 14
817 A478 3.10k multi 1.75 1.75

Ivica Kostelic, 2011 World Cup Skiing Overall Champion A479

2011, Nov. 23
818 A479 7.10k multi 3.50 3.50
Printed in sheets of 9 + label.

New Year 2012 A480

Litho. With Foil Application
2011, Nov. 24
819 A480 3.10k multi 1.60 1.60

Art A481

Designs: 3.10k, Space-B, by Ante Kuduz. 4.50k, Woman with Cat, by Marijan Trepse, vert. 9.50k, Lovers, by Anka Krizmanic.

2011, Dec. 1   Litho.   Perf. 14
820-822 A481   Set of 3   8.00 8.00

Vasa Posta Foundation A482

2011, Dec. 5
823 A482 3.10k multi 1.60 1.60
Printed in sheets of 8 + label.

New Year 2012 (Year of the Dragon) A483

2012, Jan. 4
824 A483 1.60k ol brn & blk .90 .90

St. Valentine's Day — A484

2012, Feb. 1   Perf. 14x13¾
825 A484 3.10k multi + 2 labels 2.25 2.25
a.   Booklet pane of 4 + 8 labels 9.00 —
      Complete booklet, #825a 9.00

No. 825 was printed in sheets of 4 stamps + 8 labels. These sheets were affixed inside booklet covers, and booklet panes have folds along the left margin and throuch the center row of perforations.

Cats — A485

No. 826: a, 1.60k, Ragdoll cat and bird. b, 1.60k, Domestic cat and ball. c, 3.10k, Siamese cat and sock. d, 3.10k, Persian cat and mouse.

2012, Feb. 21   Perf. 14
826 A485   Block of 4, #a-d   4.50 4.50

Flowers A486

Designs: 1.60k, Galanthus nivalis. 3.10k, Primula vulgaris. 4.60k, Crocus vernus.

2012, Mar. 15
827 A486 1.60k multi .80 .80
a.   Booklet pane of 10 8.00
      Complete booklet, #827a 8.00
828 A486 3.10k multi 1.50 1.50
a.   Booklet pane of 10 15.00
      Complete booklet, #828a 15.00
829 A486 4.60k multi 2.25 2.25
a.   Booklet pane of 10 22.50
      Complete booklet, #829a 22.50
Nos. 827-829 (3) 4.55 4.55

Easter A487

2012, Mar. 16
830 A487 3.10k multi 1.50 1.50
a.   Booklet pane of 4 6.00
      Complete booklet, #830a 6.00

Famous People A488

Designs: No. 831, 1.60k, Bishop Juraj Dobrila (1812-82). No. 832, 1.60k, Vesna Parun (1922-2010), poet. No. 833, 1.60k, Dragojla Jarnevic (1812-75), poet.

2012, Apr. 19
831-833 A488   Set of 3   2.25 2.25

Statute of Split, 700th Anniv. A489

2012, Apr. 25
834 A489 3.10k multi 1.50 1.50
No. 834 was printed in sheets of 10 + 2 labels.

Paklenica National Park — A490

Apoxyomenos Statue Found in the Adriatic Sea — A491

2012, May 9
835 A490 7.10k multi 3.50 3.50
836 A491 7.10k multi 3.50 3.50
Europa.

Croatian Chess Federation, Cent. A492

2012, May 12
837 A492 4.60k multi 2.25 2.25
No. 837 was printed in sheets of 9 + label.

Lighthouses — A493

Designs: 3.10k, St. Peter's Lighthouse. No. 839, 7.10k, St. Nicholas's Lighthouse. No. 840, 7.10k, Pokonji Dol Lighthouse.

2012, May 31
838-840 A493 Set of 3 8.25 8.25

Croatian Soccer Team's Participation in 2012 European Soccer Championships A494

2012, June 8
841 A494 4.60k multi 2.00 2.00
Printed in sheets of 9 + label.

UNESCO Intangible Cultural Heritage of Croatia A495

Designs: 1.60k, Festival of St. Blaise (Festa Sv. Vlaha). 3.10k, Lacemaking, Hvar. 4.60k, Gingerbread heart, butterfly and cross. 7.10k, Carved wooden bird toy.

2012, June 12
842-845 A495 Set of 4 6.50 6.50
845a Souvenir sheet of 4, #842-
845 + 5 labels 6.50 6.50

Miniature Sheet

Seafood Dishes — A496

No. 846: a, Rakovica (spider crab). b, Kamenice (oysters). c, Hobotnica (octopi). d, Orada (gilthead sea bream).

2012, July 2 Serpentine Die Cut 5¼
Self-Adhesive
846 A496 4.60k Sheet of 4, #a-d, + 4 etiquettes 7.50 7.50

2012 Summer Olympics, London — A497

2012, July 23 Perf. 14
847 A497 3.10k multi 1.25 1.25
Printed in sheets of 9 + label.

A498

A499

A500

Hemaris Croatica — A501

2012, Sept. 18
848 Strip of 4 7.00 7.00
a. A498 4.60k multi 1.75 1.75
b. A499 4.60k multi 1.75 1.75
c. A500 4.60k multi 1.75 1.75
d. A501 4.60k multi 1.75 1.75
Worldwide Fund for Nature (WWF).

Theater in Hvar, 400th Anniv. — A502

2012, Sept. 25
849 A502 1.60k multi .65 .65

Locomotives — A503

No. 850: a, MAV 424/JDZ/JZ 11. b, SüdB 29/JDZ 124.

2012, Oct. 1
850 Vert. pair + 2 central labels 5.50 5.50
a.-b. A503 7.10k Either single 2.75 2.75
First locomotives on Zidani Most-Sisak line, 150th anniv.

Souvenir Sheet

Diplomatic Relations Between Croatia and San Marino, 20th Anniv. — A504

No. 851 —Traditional costumes with denom-ination at: a, LR. b, LL.

2012, Oct. 16
851 A504 7.10k Sheet of 2, #a-b 5.50 5.50
See San Marino No. 1874.

Euroherc Insurance Company, 20th Anniv. — A505

2012, Oct. 19
852 A505 3.10k multi + label 1.25 1.25

Souvenir Sheet

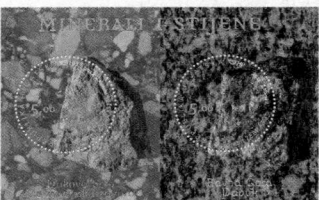

Rocks and Minerals — A506

No. 853: a, Roselite. b, Zebrato granite.

Litho. & Embossed With Foil Application
2012, Oct. 24 Perf.
853 A506 5k Sheet of 2, #a-b 4.00 4.00

Intl. Day of the Romani Language — A507

2012, Nov. 5 Litho. Perf. 14
854 A507 3.10k multi 1.25 1.25

Krapina Neanderthal Man Museum A508

Designs: 1.60k. Timeline and statues of hominids. 3.10k, Diorama of Neanderthals in cave.

2012, Nov. 7
855-856 A508 Set of 2 1.90 1.90

Christmas A509

Litho. With Foil Application
2012, Nov. 15 Perf. 14
857 A509 3.10k multi 1.25 1.25

Booklet Stamp
Self-Adhesive
Serpentine Die Cut 5¼
858 A509 3.10k multi 1.25 1.25
a. Booklet pane of 10 12.50
Complete booklet, #858a 12.50

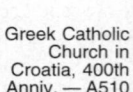

Greek Catholic
Church in
Croatia, 400th
Anniv. — A510

2012, Nov. 27 **Litho.** **Perf. 14**
859 A510 3.10k multi 1.25 1.25

New Year
2013 — A511

Litho. With Foil Application
2012, Dec. 4
860 A511 3.10k multi 1.25 1.25

Dogs — A512

No. 861: a, German shepherd with bone. b,
Yorkshire terrier with sausages. c, Golden
retriever with newspaper. d, Bichon frisé in
basket.

2013, Feb. 21 **Litho.**
861 A512 3.10k Block or vert.
strip of 4, #a-d 4.25 4.25

Easter
A513

2013, Mar. 11
862 A513 3.10k multi 1.10 1.10

Amphibians
A514

Designs: 1.60k, Bombina bombina. 3.10k,
Salamandra salamandra. 4.60k, Proteus
anguinus.

2013, Apr. 8
863 A514 1.60k multi .55 .55
a. Booklet pane of 10 5.50
Complete booklet, #863a 5.50
864 A514 3.10k multi 1.10 1.10
a. Booklet pane of 10 11.00
Complete booklet, #864a 11.00
865 A514 4.60k multi 1.60 1.60
a. Booklet pane of 10 16.00
Complete booklet, #865a 16.00
Nos. 863-865 (3) 3.25 3.25

Famous
People
A515

Designs: No. 866, 1.20k, Stjepan Gradic
(1613-83), diplomat. No. 867, 1.20k, Antonija
Krasnik (1874-1956), decorative artist. No.
868, 5.80k, Ranko Marinkovic (1913-2001),
writer. No. 869, 5.80k, Milka Trnina (1863-
1941), opera singer.

2013, Apr. 16
866-869 A515 Set of 4 5.00 5.00

Souvenir Sheet

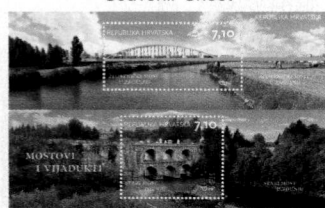

Bridges — A516

No. 870: a, Railway Bridge, Zagreb
(49x24mm). b, Old Bridge, Tounj (36x30mm).

2013, Apr. 29
870 A516 7.10k Sheet of 2, #a-b 5.00 5.00

Europa — A517

Postal vehicles: No. 871, 7.10k, Moped. No.
872, 7.10k, Van.

2013, May 9
871-872 A517 Set of 2 5.25 5.25

A518

Admission of Croatia to European
Union — A519

2013, July 1
873 A518 3.10k multi 1.10 1.10
Souvenir Sheet
874 A519 20k multi 7.00 7.00
No. 873 was printed in sheets of 25 stamps
+ 5 labels.

Pula Film
Festival,
60th
Anniv.
A520

2013, July 2
875 A520 3.10k multi 1.10 1.10

Castles and Palaces Type of 2011

Arms and: No. 876, 1.60k, Odescalchi Cas-
tle, Ilok. No. 877, 1.60k, Eltz Castle, Vukovar.
No. 878, 1.60k, Pejacevic Castle, Virovitica.
No. 879, 1.60k, Turkovic Castle, Kutjevo.

2013, July 18
876-879 A470 Set of 4 2.25 2.25
879a Souvenir sheet of 8, 2 each
#876-879, + 8 labels 4.50 4.50

Mushrooms
A521

No. 880: a, Macrolepiota procera. b, Boletus
regius. c, Tuber magnatum, Tuber
melanosporum.

2013, Sept. 3 **Perf. 14**
880 Horiz. strip of 3 5.25 5.25
a.-c. A521 4.60k Any single 1.75 1.75

Lapitch, the
Little
Shoemaker
A522

2013, Sept. 4
881 A522 3.10k multi 1.10 1.10
Publishing of Lapitch, the Little Shoemaker,
children's book by Ivana Brlic Mazuranic, cent.

Souvenir Sheet

Portrait of Count Teodor Pejacevic
(1855-1928), by Vlaho
Bukovac — A523

2013, Sept. 18
882 A523 11k multi 4.00 4.00
Diplomatic relations between Croatia and
the Sovereign Military Order of Malta, 20th
anniv.

Lighthouses — A524

Designs: 4.60k, Plocica Lighthouse. 5.80k,
Stoncica Lighthouse. 7.60k, Sucuraj
Lighthouse.

2013, Sept. 26 **Perf. 14**
883-885 A524 Set of 3 6.50 6.50

Salesians in
Croatia,
Cent. — A525

2013, Oct. 1 **Litho.** **Perf. 14**
886 A525 1.20k multi .45 .45

Gas Lighting
System in
Zagreb, 150th
Anniv. — A526

2013, Oct. 3 **Litho.** **Perf. 14**
887 A526 7.60k multi 2.75 2.75
No. 887 was printed in sheets of 8 + label.

Souvenir Sheet

Peasant's Revolt, 440th Anniv. — A527

2013, Oct. 11 **Litho.** **Perf. 14**
888 A527 11k multi 4.00 4.00

Mirko (1871-1913) and Stevo (1875-
1936) Seljan, Explorers, Map of
Guayra Falls, South America — A528

2013, Oct. 15 **Litho.** **Perf. 14**
889 A528 7.60k multi 2.75 2.75

Faros Swimming Marathon — A529

2013, Nov. 5 **Litho.** **Perf. 14**
890 A529 7.60k multi 2.75 2.75
No. 890 was printed in sheets of 9 + label.

Christmas
A530

Litho. With Foil Application

2013, Nov. 27 *Perf. 14*
891 A530 3.10k multi 1.10 1.10

Litho.
Booklet Stamp
Self-Adhesive

Serpentine Die Cut 5¼

892 A530 3.10k multi 1.10 1.10
 a. Booklet pane of 10 11.00
 Complete booklet, #892a 11.00

Art — A531

Designs: 1.20k, Black Flag, by Ljubo Babic. 3.10k, Sappho, by Bela Cikos Sesija. 5.80k, PAFAMA, by Josip Seissel.

2013, Dec. 3 *Litho.* *Perf. 14*
893-895 A531 Set of 3 3.75 3.75

New
Year
2014
A532

Litho. With Foil Application

2013, Dec. 5 *Perf. 14*
896 A532 3.10k multi 1.10 1.10

2014 Winter
Olympics,
Sochi, Russia
A533

2014, Feb. 7 *Litho.* *Perf. 14*
897 A533 3.10k multi 1.10 1.10

No. 897 was printed in sheets of 9 + label.

Pets — A534

No. 898: a, Chinchilla eating apple slice. b, Guinea pig eating biscuit. c, Rabbit in top hat. d, Hamster with carrot.

2014, Feb. 21 *Litho.* *Perf. 14*
898 A534 3.10k Block of 4, #a.-d. 4.50 4.50

Temple of Augustus,
Pula — A535

2014, Mar. 3 *Litho.* *Perf. 14*
899 A535 2.80k multi 1.00 1.00

Souvenir Sheet

University of Zagreb Faculty of
Science Botanical Garden, 125th
Anniv. — A536

2014, Apr. 1 *Litho.* *Perf. 14*
900 A536 11k multi 4.00 4.00

Dalmatian
Braided
Bread — A537

2014, Apr. 2 *Litho.* *Perf. 14*
901 A537 3.10k multi 1.10 1.10

Easter.

Miniature Sheet

Marine Life — A538

No. 902: a, Ornate wrasse (Vladika arbanaska). b, Golden sponge (Promjenjiva sumporaca). c, European fan worm (Kozasti perjanicar). d, mediterranean violet aeolid (Ljubicasta flabelina).

Serpentine Die Cut 5¼

Self-Adhesive

2014, Apr. 9 *Litho.*
902 A538 Sheet of 4 + 4 etiquettes 8.50
 a.-d. 5.80k Any single 2.10 2.10

Orchids
A539

Designs: No. 903, Ophrys dinarica. No. 904, Serapias istriaca. 3.10k, Ophrys libunica.

2014, Apr. 11 *Litho.* *Perf. 14*
903 A539 2.80k multi 1.00 1.00
 a. Booklet pane of 10 10.00
 Complete booklet, #903a 10.00
904 A539 2.80k multi 1.00 1.00
 a. Booklet pane of 10 10.00
 Complete booklet, #904a 10.00
905 A539 3.10 multi 1.10 1.10
 a. Booklet pane of 10 11.00
 Complete booklet, #905a 11.00

Famous
People
A540

Designs: 1.20k, Ivan Bjelovucic (1889-1949), first man to fly over Alps. 2.80k, Ivan Gundulic (1589-1638), writer. 3.10k, Ivan Mazuranic (1814-90), poet. 7.60k, Dora Pejacevic (1885-1923), composer.

2014, Apr. 18 *Litho.* *Perf. 14*
906-909 A540 Set of 4 5.50 5.50

Canonization of
Popes John Paul
II and John
XXIII — A541

No. 910—Arms and portrait of: a, Pope John Paul II. b, Pope John XXIII.

2014, Apr. 25 *Litho.* *Perf. 14*
910 A541 7.60k Pair, #a.-b. 5.75 5.75

Europa
A542

Musical instruments: 3.10k, Lijerica. 7.60k, Sopile.

2014, May 9 *Litho.* *Perf. 14*
911-912 A542 Set of 2 4.00 4.00

Lighthouses — A543

Designs: 2.80k, Palagruza Lighthouse. No. 914, 5.80k, Struga Lighthouse. No. 915, 5.80k, Susac Lighthouse.

2014, May 30 *Litho.* *Perf. 14*
913-915 A543 Set of 3 5.25 5.25

Villa
Angiolina,
Opatija, 170th
Anniv.
A544

2014, June 11 *Litho.* *Perf. 14*
916 A544 2.80k multi 1.00 1.00

No. 916 was printed in sheets of 8 + central label.

2014 World Cup
Soccer
Championships,
Brazil — A545

2014, June 12 *Litho.* *Perf. 14*
917 A545 7.60k multi 2.75 2.75

No. 917 was printed in sheets of 9 + label.

Volunteer Fire
Departments in
Croatia, 150th
Anniv. — A546

2014, June 17 *Litho.* *Perf. 14*
918 A546 5k multi 1.90 1.90

No. 918 was printed in sheets of 8 + 2 labels.

Prelog, 750th
Anniv. — A547

2014, Sept. 23 *Litho.* *Perf. 14*
919 A547 3.10k multi 1.10 1.10

Souvenir Sheet

Carved Wooden Doorway of Split
Cathedral, 800th Anniv. — A548

2014, Sept. 23 *Litho.* *Perf. 14*
920 A548 11k multi 3.75 3.75

Statute of the
Town and
Island of
Korcula, 800th
Anniv. — A549

2014, Sept. 26 *Litho.* *Perf. 14*
921 A549 2.80k multi .95 .95

St. Nicholas Benedictine Monastery, Trogir, 950th Anniv. — A550

2014, Sept. 30   Litho.   Perf. 14
922   A550   2.80k multi   .95   .95

Locomotives — A551

No. 923: a, KkStB 229/JDZ/JZ 116. b, MAV 375/JDZ/HDZ/JZ 51.

2014, Oct. 1   Litho.   Perf. 14
923   Vert. pair + 2 central labels   3.50   3.50
a.-b.   A551 5k Either single   1.75   1.75

Monument in Mirogoj Cemetery, Zagreb A552

2014, Oct. 14   Litho.   Perf. 14
924   A552   7.60k multi   2.50   2.50
World War I, cent.

Details from Traditional Costumes — A553

Detail from costume from: 3.10k, Slavonia. 5.80k, Vrlika. 7.60k, Gorski Kotar. 11k, Lovas.

2014, Oct. 20   Litho.   Perf. 14
925   A553   3.10k multi   1.00   1.00
926   A553   5.80k multi   1.90   1.90
927   A553   7.60k multi   2.50   2.50
928   A553   11k multi   3.75   3.75
a.   Souvenir sheet of 4, #925-928   9.25   9.25
Nos. 925-928 (4)   9.15   9.15

Souvenir Sheet

Rocks and Minerals — A554

No. 929: a, Green schist (green background). b, Prehnite (blue background).

Litho. & Embossed
2014, Oct. 24   Perf.
929   A554   5k Sheet of 2, #a-b   3.25   3.25

Souvenir Sheet

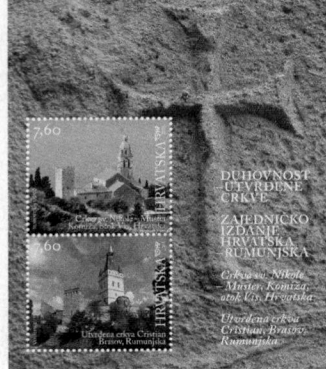

Fortified Churches — A555

No. 930: a, St. Nicholas Church, Komiza. b, Evangelical Church, Cristian, Romania.

2014, Nov. 14   Litho.   Perf. 14
930   A555   7.60k Sheet of 2, #a-b   5.00   5.00
See Romania Nos. 5625-5626.

Requisition, by Ivan Generalic (1914-92) — A556

2014, Nov. 17   Litho.   Perf. 14
931   A556   3.10k multi   1.00   1.00

Christmas — A557

Litho. With Foil Application
2014, Nov. 27   Perf. 14
932   A557   3.10k multi   1.00   1.00

Booklet Stamp
Self-Adhesive
Serpentine Die Cut 5¼
933   A557   3.10k multi   1.00   1.00
a.   Booklet pane of 10   10.00
Complete booklet, #933a   10.00

Royal University Library and Land Archives A558

Designs: No. 934, 4.60k, Building exterior. No. 935, 4.60k, Reading room. No. 936, 4.60k, Table lamps, vert.

2014, Dec. 1   Litho.   Perf. 14
934-936   A558   Set of 3   4.50   4.50

New Year 2015 — A559

2014, Dec. 4   Litho.   Perf. 14
937   A559   3.10k multi   1.00   1.00

St. Valentine's Day — A560

2015, Feb. 4   Litho.   Perf. 14
938   A560   6.50k multi   1.90   1.90
Values are for stamps with surrounding selvage.

112 Emergency Services Day — A561

2015, Feb. 11   Litho.   Perf. 14
939   A561   6.50k brt orange & blk   1.90   1.90

Pet Birds — A562

No. 940: a, Canary wearing horned helmet. b, Budgerigar wearing captain's hat. c, Zebra finch with didgeridoo. d, Sulphur-crested cockatoo wearing leather jacket.

2015, Feb. 19   Litho.   Perf. 14
940   A562   3.10k Block of 4, #a-d   3.75   3.75

Rotary International District 1913, 110th Anniv. — A563

2015, Feb. 23   Litho.   Perf. 14
941   A563   3.10k multi   .90   .90

Easter — A564

Litho. With Foil Application
2015, Mar. 16   Perf. 14
942   A564   3.10k multi   .90   .90

Croatian Paralympic Committee, 50th Anniv. — A565

2015, Mar. 23   Litho.   Perf. 14
943   A565   5k multi   1.50   1.50
No. 943 was printed in sheets of 9 + label.

Lace — A566

No. 944: a, Colors of Croatian flag, lace from Lepoglav. b, Colors of Spanish flag, lace from Seville.

2015, Mar. 31   Litho.   Perf. 14
944   A566   7.60k Pair, #a-b   4.50   4.50
See Spain No. 4037.

Wildlife — A567

Designs: 2.80k, Capreolus capreolus. 4.60k, Vulpes vulpes. 6.50k, Sus scrofa.

2015, Apr. 15   Litho.   Perf. 14
945   A567   2.80k multi   .85   .85
a.   Booklet pane of 10   8.50
Complete booklet, #945a   8.50
946   A567   4.60k multi   1.40   1.40
a.   Booklet pane of 10   14.00
Complete booklet, #946a   14.00
947   A567   6.50k multi   2.00   2.00
a.   Booklet pane of 10   20.00
Complete booklet, #947a   20.00
Nos. 945-947 (3)   4.25   4.25

Famous People — A568

Designs: No. 948, 3.10k, Ivan Supek (1915-2007), scientist and writer. No. 949, 3.10k, Luka Sorkocevic (1734-89), composer. No. 950, 3.10k, Josip Juraj Strossmayer (1815-1905), bishop and politician.

2015, Apr. 21   Litho.   Perf. 14
948-950   A568   Set of 3   2.75   2.75

1000th Stamp Design of Croatia Post — A569

2015, Apr. 27   Litho.   Perf. 14
951   A569   3.10k multi   .95   .95

Souvenir Sheet

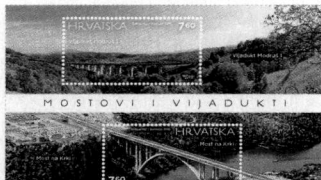

Bridges — A570

No. 952: a, Modrus 1 Bridge. b, Krka River Bridge.

2015, Apr. 29 Litho. *Perf. 14*
952 A570 7.60k Sheet of 2, #a-b 4.50 4.50

Europa A571

Toys: 4.60k, To Tak wood pieces and connectors. 7.60k, Porcelain doll.

2015, May 7 Litho. *Perf. 14*
953-954 A571 Set of 2 3.75 3.75

International Telecommunications Union, 150th Anniv. — A572

2015, May 15 Litho. *Perf. 14*
955 A572 10k multi 3.00 3.00

Castles and Palaces Type of 2011

Designs: No. 956, 4.60k, Jankovic Castle, Daruvar. No. 957, 4.60k, Markovic-Kulmer Castle, Cernik. No. 958, 4.60k, Erdödy-Rubido Castle, Gornja Rijeka. No. 959, 4.60k, Old Town, Durdevac.

2015, May 20 Litho. *Perf. 14*
956-959 A470 Set of 4 5.50 5.50
959a Souvenir sheet of 8, 2
each #956-959, + 8 labels 11.00 11.00

Lighthouses — A573

Designs: 2.80k, Daksa Lighthouse. 3.10k, Glavat Lighthouse. 4.60k, Grebeni Lighthouse. 6.50k, Sveti Andrija Lighthouse.

2015, June 10 Litho. *Perf. 14*
960-963 A573 Set of 4 5.00 5.00

Bracera — A574

2015, July 9 Litho. *Perf. 14*
964 A574 5.80k multi 1.75 1.75

A575

UNESCO Intangible Cultural Heritage — A576

Designs: No. 965, 3.10k, Zvoncari (carnival procession of bell ringers from Kastav). No. 966, 3.10k, Becarac (musician with stringed instrument). No. 967, 3.10k, Klapsko Pjevanje (a capella singers). No. 968, 3.10k, Sinjska Alka (horseman at Alka Chivalric Tournament, Sinj).

11k, Alka Chivalric Tournament, 300th anniv.

2015, July 27 Litho. *Perf. 14*
965-968 A575 Set of 4 3.75 3.75
968a Souvenir sheet of 4, #965-968, + 5 labels 3.75 3.75

Souvenir Sheet
Litho., Sheet Margin Litho. With Foil Application

969 A576 11k multi 3.25 3.25

Victory and Homeland Thanksgiving Day — A577

2015, Aug. 3 Litho. *Perf. 14*
970 A577 3.10k multi .90 .90

2015 Men's European Basketball Cahmpionships, Zagreb — A578

2015, Sept. 4 Litho. *Perf. 14*
971 A578 5k multi 1.50 1.50

No. 971 was printed in sheets of 8 + label.

Traffic Safety — A579

2015, Sept. 7 Litho. *Perf. 14*
972 A579 3.10k multi .95 .95

Christmas A580

2015, Nov. 25 Litho. *Perf. 14*
973 A580 3.10k multi .90 .90

Booklet Stamp
Self-Adhesive
Serpentine Die Cut 5¼

974 A580 3.10k multi .90 .90
a. Booklet pane of 10 9.00
Complete booklet, #974a 9.00

Sculpture A581

Designs: 1.20k, Metal Sculpture XX, by Dusan Dzamonja. 3.10k, Dunja I, by Kosta Angeli Radovani. 4.60k, The Bull, by Vojin Bakic.

2015, Dec. 1 Litho. *Perf. 14*
975-977 A581 Set of 3 2.50 2.50

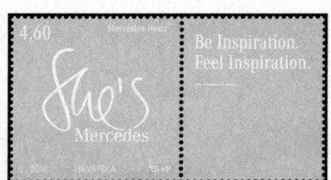

Advertising Slogan for Mercedes-Benz Automobiles — A582

2016, Feb. 2 Litho. *Perf. 14*
978 A582 4.60k lt bl + label 1.40 1.40

St. Blaise, by Carmelo Reggio — A583

2016, Feb. 3 Litho. *Perf. 14*
979 A583 3.10k multi .90 .90

St. Blaise (d. 316), patron saint of Dubrovnik.

Pet Fish — A584

No. 980: a, Angelfish and baby carriage. b, Goldfish, hat, gold and miner's pan. c, Guppy, rainbow, airplane. d, Siamese fighting fish, castle, shield and lance.

2016, Feb. 22 Litho. *Perf. 14*
980 A584 3.10k Block of 4, #a-d 3.50 3.50

Easter A585

2016, Mar. 8 Litho. *Perf. 14*
981 A585 3.10k multi .95 .95

Herbs — A586

Designs: 2.80k, Rosmarinus officinalis. 3.10k, Lavandula angustifolia. 4.60k, Helichrysum italicum.

2016, Mar. 21 Litho. *Perf. 14*
982 A586 2.80k multi .85 .85
a. Booklet pane of 10 8.50
Complete booklet, #982a 8.50
983 A586 3.10k multi .95 .95
a. Booklet pane of 10 9.50
Complete booklet, #983a 9.50
984 A586 4.60k multi 1.40 1.40
a. Booklet pane of 10 14.00 —
Complete booklet, #984a 14.00
Nos. 982-984 (3) 3.20 3.20

Nos. 982-984 are impregnated with the scent of the depicted plant.

Famous People — A587

Designs: No. 985, 3.10k, Sidonija Erdödy Rubido (1819-84), opera singer. No. 986, 3.10k, Slavko Kolar (1891-1963), writer. No. 987, 3.10k, Mia Corak Slavenska (1916-2002), ballerina. No. 988, 3.10k, Mirko Bogovic (1816-93), poet.

2016, Apr. 20 Litho. *Perf. 14*
985-988 A587 Set of 4 3.75 3.75

Radio Announcer and Cameraman — A588

2016, Apr. 26 Litho. *Perf. 14*
989 A588 3.10k multi + label .95 .95

Croatian radio broadcasting 90th anniv.; Croatian television broadcasting, 60th anniv.

Islamic Center, Zagreb — A589

2016, Apr. 27 Litho. *Perf. 14*
990 A589 3.10k multi .95 .95

Islam in Croatia, cent.

Croatian Inventors and Their Inventions A590

Designs: 5k, Giovanni Biagio Luppis (1813-75) and torpedo. 6.50k, Eduard Slavoljub Penkala (1871-1922) and mechanical pencil, vert.

2016, Apr. 27	Litho.	Perf. 14	
991-992 A590 Set of 2		3.50	3.50

A591

Europa A592

2016, May 9	Litho.	Perf. 14	
993 A591 4.60k multi		1.40	1.40
994 A592 7.60k multi		2.25	2.25

Think Green Issue.

Dominican Order, 800th Anniv. — A593

2016, May 24	Litho.	Perf. 14	
995 A593 3.10k multi		.95	.95

Greetings to the Sun, by Nikola Basic — A594

Sea Organ, by Basic A595

2016, June 1	Litho.	Perf. 14	
996 A594 2.80k multi		.85	.85
997 A595 4.60k multi		1.40	1.40

Monuments in Zadar.

Declaration of Statehood, 25th Anniv. — A596

2016, June 23	Litho.	Perf. 14	
998 A596 3.10k multi		.95	.95

No. 998 was printed in sheets of 26 + 4 labels.

2016 European University Games, Zagreb and Rijeka — A597

2016 European Junior Synchronized Swimming and Diving Championships, Rijeka — A598

2016, June 28	Litho.	Perf. 14	
999 A597 3.10k multi		.95	.95
1000 A598 3.10k multi		.95	.95

Nos. 999-1000 were each printed in sheets of 9 + label.

Ocellated Wrasse — A599

2016, July 7	Litho.	Perf. 14	
1001 A599 5.80k multi		1.75	1.75

Souvenir Sheet

Battle of Lissa (Vis), 150th Anniv. — A600

2016, July 18	Litho.	Perf. 14	
1002 A600 7.60k multi		2.25	2.25

See Slovenia No. 1188.

2016 Summer Olympics, Rio de Janeiro — A601

2016, Aug. 3	Litho.	Perf. 14	
1003 A601 4.60k multi		1.40	1.40

No. 1003 was printed in sheets of 8 + label.

Souvenir Sheet

Battle of Szigetvár, 450th Anniv. — A602

No. 1004: a, 4.70k, Szigetvár coat of arms. b, 6.50k, Zrinski's Charge from the Szigetvár Fortress, by Bertalan Székely.

2016, Sept. 5	Litho.	Perf. 14	
1004 A602 Sheet of 2, #a-b		3.25	3.25

See Hungary No. 4402.

Resumption of Croatian Postage Stamps, 25th Anniv. — A603

Litho. & Embossed With Hologram Affixed

2016, Sept. 9		Perf. 14	
1005 A603 11k multi		3.25	3.25

St. James Cathedral, Sibenik A604

2016, Sept. 15	Litho.	Perf. 14	
1006 A604 3.10k multi		.95	.95

Sibenik, 950th anniv.

Campaign Against Hate Speech A605

2016, Sept. 21	Litho.	Perf. 14	
1007 A605 3.10k multi		.95	.95

Locomotives — A606

No. 1008: a, Steam locomotive model 207. b, Steam locomotive JDZ/HDZ/JZ 83-106.

2016, Oct. 1	Litho.	Perf. 14	
1008 Vert. pair + 2 central labels		6.00	6.00
a.-b. A606 9.50k Either single		3.00	3.00

Depictions of Fossilized Animals — A607

No. 1009: a, Panthera leo fossils (Lion of Dramalj). b, Mesocetus agrami (Whale of Zagreb).

2016, Oct. 12	Litho.	Perf. 14	
1009 A607 5k Pair, #a-b		3.00	3.00

Souvenir Sheet

Minerals — A608

No. 1010: a, 4.50k, Sea salt crystals (35mm diameter). b, 6.50k, Rhyolite (30x36mm).

Perf. (4.50k), Perf. 14 (6.50k)

2016, Oct. 24	Litho. & Embossed		
1010 A608 Sheet of 2, #a-b		3.25	3.25

Canonization of St. Teresa of Calcutta (Mother Teresa) — A609

2016, Nov. 15	Litho.	Perf. 14	
1011 A609 7.60k multi		2.25	2.25

Adoration of the Magi, by an Italo-Cretan Master — A610

2016, Nov. 24	Litho.	Perf. 14	
1012 A610 3.10k multi		.90	.90

Booklet Stamp
Self-Adhesive
Serpentine Die Cut 5¼

1013 A610 3.10k multi		.90	.90
a. Booklet pane of 10		9.00	
Complete booklet, #1013a		9.00	

Christmas.

Adris Foundation — A611

2016, Nov. 28	Litho.	Perf. 14	
1014 A611 3.10k multi + label		.90	.90

No. 1014 was printed in sheets of 10 + 10 labels.

Viktor Kovacic (1874-1924), Architect — A612

Designs: 2.80k, Furniture in room of Kovacic's apartment. 4.60k, Decorative detail by Kovacic, vert. 7.60k, Stock Exchange Palace (Croatian National Bank), Zagreb, vert.

2016, Dec. 1	Litho.	Perf. 14	
1015-1017 A612 Set of 3		4.25	4.25

Souvenir Sheet

Statue of Ban Josip Jelacic, Zagreb, 150th Anniv. — A613

2016, Dec. 5   **Litho.**   ***Perf. 14***
1018 A613 15k multi   4.25 4.25

Black Luca, Hrvatko and Emblem of Croatian National Bank — A614

2016, Dec. 9   **Litho.**   ***Perf. 14***
1019 A614 3.10k multi + label   .85 .85

No. 1019 was printed in sheets of 10 + 10 labels.

SEMI-POSTAL STAMPS

> Catalogue values for unused stamps in this section are for Never Hinged items.

Types of Yugoslavia, 1941, Overprinted in Gold "NEZAVISNA / DRZAVA / HRVATSKA"
Perf. 11½

1941, May 10   **Unwmk.**   **Engr.**
B1 SP80 1.50d + 1.50d bl blk   22.50 22.50
B2 SP81   4d + 3d choc   22.50 22.50

Panes of 16 stamps and 9 labels.
This overprint exists on Yugoslavia No. B124. Value $2,500.

In 1941, 5,000 sets of Yugoslavia Nos. 142-154 were overprinted "NEZAVISNA DRZAVA HRVATSKA 10. IV. 1941" and with a small shield in red or blue. Sold for double face value. Value: set, $550.

Costume of Sinj, Dalmatia — SP1

Designs (Costumes): 2k+2k, Travnik, Bosnia. 4k+4k, Turopolje, Croatia.

1941, Oct. 12   **Photo.**   ***Perf. 10½x10***
B3 SP1   1.50k + 1.50k Prus
     bl & red   1.00 1.00
B4 SP1   2k + 2k ol brn &
     red   1.25 1.25
B5 SP1   4k + 4k brn lake
     & red   2.25 2.25
   Nos. B3-B5 (3)   4.50 4.50

The surtax aided the Croatian Red Cross.
Nos. B3-B5 were issued in panes of 20 stamps and 5 labels.
Nos. B3-B5 exist with a special printer's mark in the design. The printer's mark appears on one stamp in one pane of the four in the printed sheet. Value, $35 each.

Soldiers with Arms of the Axis States — SP4

1941, Dec. 3   ***Perf. 11***
B6 SP4 4k + 2k blue   3.75 4.00

The surtax was used for Croatian Volunteers in the East.
Issued in panes of 100 stamps.

Model Plane — SP5

Model Plane — SP6

Designs: 3k+3k, Boy with model plane. 4k+4k, Model seaplane in flight.

1942, Mar. 25
B7 SP5   2k + 2k sepia   1.90 1.90
B8 SP6   2.50k + 2.50k dl grn   1.90 1.90
B9 SP5   3k + 3k brn car   1.90 1.90
B10 SP6   4k + 4k dp bl   1.90 1.90
   Nos. B7-B10 (4)   7.60 7.60

Nos. B7-B10 were issued both in panes of 25 and in panes of 24 plus label.
Nos. B7-B10 exist with a special printer's mark in the design. The mark appears on one stamp in every pane. Value, $10

> Values for used souvenir sheets are for those with special philatelic cancels. Faked postal cancellations on souvenir sheets are common, especially using cancellers stolen after WWII. Genuine postal cancellations are the exception and sell for much more. Expertization is recommended.

Souvenir Sheets
Perf. 11
B11   Sheet of 2   45.00 45.00
  a.   SP5 2k+8k brown carmine   15.00 15.00
  b.   SP5 3k+12k deep blue   15.00 15.00
Imperf
B12   Sheet of 2   45.00 45.00
  a.   SP5 2k+8k deep blue   15.00 15.00
  b.   SP5 3k+12k brown carmine   15.00 15.00

The sheets measure 125x110mm.
Aviation Exposition of Zagreb. The surtax aided society of Croatian Wings (Hrvatska Krila).
Nos. B11-B12 exist with colors of stamps and inscriptions transposed, with missing colors and with one stamp missing.
Nos. B11-B12 exist with a special printer's mark in the design. The mark typically appears on one stamp in a given pane.

Boy Trumpeters SP10

Triumphal Arch — SP11

Mother and Child — SP12

1942, July 5   ***Perf. 11½***
B13 SP10 3k + 1k lake   1.50 1.50
B14 SP11 4k + 2k dk brn   1.60 1.60
B15 SP12 5k + 5k dp bl grn   2.40 2.40
   Nos. B13-B15 (3)   5.50 5.50

The surtax was for national welfare.
Issued in panes of 25.
Nos. B13-B15 exist with a special printer's mark in the design. The printer's mark appears on one stamp in one pane of the four in the printed sheet. Value, $40 each.

Matthew Gubec SP13

Ante Starcevich SP14

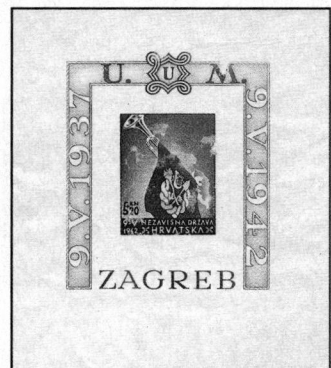

SP15

1942, Nov. 22   ***Perf. 14½***
B16 SP13 3k + 6k dark red   1.00 1.00
B17 SP14 4k + 7k sepia   1.00 1.00
Souvenir Sheets
Perf. 12, Imperf.
B18 SP15 5k + 20k dull blue   24.00 24.00

Heroes of Senj, May 9, 1937. Nos. B16-B17 were printed in panes of 16 + 9 labels, each bearing a hero's name. The surtax aided the Natl. Youth Soc.

Sestine Peasant — SP16

Designs: 3k+1k, Slavonian peasant. 4k+2k, Bosnian peasant. 10k+5k, Dalmatian peasant. 13k+6k, Sestine peasant.

1942, Oct. 4   ***Perf. 11½***
B20 SP16 1.50k + 50b org brn
     & red   1.40 1.40
B21 SP16 3k + 1k dl pur &
     red   1.40 1.40
B22 SP16 4k + 2k dp bl &
     red   2.10 2.10

B23 SP16 10k + 5k dk ol bis
     & red   3.00 3.00
B24 SP16 13k + 6k rose lake
     & red   5.50 5.50
   Nos. B20-B24 (5)   13.40 13.40

The surtax aided the Croatian Red Cross. Issued in panes of 24 stamps plus label.

Croatian Labor Corpsman — SP20

Designs: 3k+3k, Corpsman with wheelbarrow. 7k+4k, Corpsman plowing.

1943, Jan. 17   **Wmk. 278**   ***Perf. 11***
B25 SP20 2k + 1k ol gray &
     sepia   4.75 5.00
B26 SP20 3k + 3k brn & sepia   4.75 5.00
B27 SP20 7k + 4k gray bl &
     sepia   4.75 5.00
   Nos. B25-B27 (3)   14.25 15.00

The surtax aided the State Labor Service (Drzavna Radna Sluzba). Issued in panes of 9.

Arms of Zagreb and "Golden Bull" — SP23

1943, Mar. 21   **Unwmk.**
B28 SP23 3.50k (+ 6.50k) ultra   4.50 4.75

700th anniversary of Zagreb's "Golden Bull," a Magna Carta of civic rights and privileges granted to the city in 1242 by King Bela because the Croats annihilated Tartar hordes at Grobnik.
Issued in panes of 8 with marginal inscriptions.

Ante Pavelich — SP24

1943, Apr. 10   ***Perf. 13¾x14***
B29 SP24 5k + 3k copper red   .60 .60
  a.   Sheetlet of 16 #B29 + 9 labels   12.00 12.00
B30 SP24 7k + 5k dark green   .60 .60
  a.   Sheetlet of 16 #B30 + 9 labels   12.00 12.00

Surtax aided the National Youth Society.
Nos. B29-B30 were issued in panes of 100 stamps. Nos. B29a and B30a were issued Apr. 12 and are perf 14½.

Souvenir Sheets
1943, May 17   ***Perf. 12, Imperf.***
B31 SP24 12k + 8k dp ultra   30.00 30.00

Sailor at Sea of Azov — SP26

Designs: 2k+1k, Flier at Sevastopol and Rzhev. 3.50k+1.50k, Infantrymen at Stalingrad. 9k+4.50k, Panzer Division at Don River.

1943, July 1   ***Perf. 11***
B33 SP26 1k + 50b grn   .40 .25
B34 SP26 2k + 1k dk red   .40 .25
B35 SP26 3.50k + 1.50k dk bl   .40 .25
B36 SP26 9k + 4.50k chestnut   .40 .25
   Nos. B33-B36 (4)   1.60 1.00

Souvenir Sheets
Perf. 11, Imperf.

B37 Sheet of 4   7.50   7.50
   a. SP26 1k+50b dark blue   1.40   1.40
   b. SP26 2k+1k green   1.40   1.40
   c. SP26 3.50k+1.50k dk red brown   1.40   1.40
   d. SP26 9k+4.50k bluish black   1.40   1.40

Surtax aided the National Youth Society. Issued to honor the Croatian Legion which fought with the Germans in Russia. The surtax aided the Legion.
Issued in panes of 100.

St. Mary's Church and Cistercian Cloister, Zagreb, in 1650 — SP31

1943, Sept. 12   **Engr.**   **Perf. 14½**
B39 SP31 18k + 9k dl gray vio   5.25   5.25

Souvenir Sheet
Perf. 12½
B40 SP31 18k + 9k blk brn   13.00   13.00

Croatian Phil. Soc. Exhibition at Zagreb. No. B39 issued in pane of 40.
Nos. B39-B40 exist with a special printer's mark in the design. The printer's mark appears on one stamp in the pane for No. B39, value $30; the mark appears on one souvenir sheet of the six in the printed sheet for No. B40, value $52.50.

No. B39 Ovptd. in Red

1943, Sept. 12
B41 SP31 18k + 9k dl gray vio   12.00   14.00

Return to Croatia of the Dalmatian and Croatian coasts.
The overprint exists inverted, double, and double, one inverted.
No. B41 exists with a special printer's mark in the design. The mark typically appears on one stamp in a given pane.

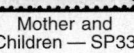

Mother and Children — SP33   Nurse and Patient — SP34

1943, Oct. 3   **Litho.**   **Perf. 11**
Cross in Red
B42 SP33   1k + 50b bl grn   .75   .75
B43 SP33   2k + 1k bril car   .75   .75
B44 SP33   3.50k + 1.50k brt bl   .75   .75
B45 SP34   8k + 3k red brn   .90   .90
B46 SP34   9k + 4k yel grn   1.00   1.00
B47 SP33   10k + 5k dp vio   1.00   1.00
B48 SP34   12k + 6k brt ultra   1.25   1.25
B49 SP33   12.50k + 6k dk brn   1.75   1.75
B50 SP34   18k + 8k brn org   2.00   2.00

B51 SP34   32k + 12k dk gray   3.25   3.25
   Nos. B42-B51 (10)   13.40   13.40

The surtax aided the Croatian Red Cross. Issued in panes of 100.

Post Horn and Arms — SP35

Carrier Pigeon and Plane — SP36   Mercury — SP37

Winged Wheel — SP38

1944, Feb. 3
B52 SP35 7k + 3.50k ol bis & red   .90   .90
   a. Double impression of red
B53 SP36 16k + 8k bl & dk bl   .90   .90
B54 SP37 24k + 12k red & rose red   .90   .90
B55 SP38 32k + 16k gray & red   .90   .90
   Nos. B52-B55 (4)   3.60   3.60

The surtax benefited communications and railway employees. Panes of 9.

St. Sebastian — SP39

War Invalids SP40

Statue of Ancient Croatian King — SP41

Death of King Peter Svacic, 1097 — SP42

1944, Feb. 15
B56 SP39 7k + 3.50k org red & rose car   1.00   1.00
B57 SP40 16k + 8k yel grn & dk grn   1.00   1.00
B58 SP41 24k + 12k yel brn & red   1.00   1.00
B59 SP42 32k + 16k bl & dk brn   1.00   1.00
   Nos. B56-B59 (4)   4.00   4.00

The surtax aided wounded war victims.

Issued in panes of eight stamps, with marginal inscriptions and a central label picturing St. Sebastian.

Black Legion in Combat — SP43

Guarding the Drina — SP44

Jure Francetic — SP45

1944, May 22   **Photo.**   **Imperf.**
B60 SP43 3.50k + 1.50k brn red   .25   .25
B61 SP44 12.50k + 6.50k slate bl   .25   .25
B62 SP45 18k + 9k olive brn   .25   .25
   Nos. B60-B62 (3)   .75   .75

Third anniversary of Croatian independence. The surtax aided the National Youth Society. Panes of 20.

Perf. 14½
B63 SP45 12.50k + 287.50k int blk   12.00   14.50

Issued to commemorate Jure Francetic. Issued in pane of 30.

Labor Corpsmen Marching SP46   Corpsman Digging SP47

Designs: 18k+9k, Officer instructing corpsman. 32k+16k, Pavelich reviewing Labor Corps. Panes of 8 plus label.

Perf. 11½, 12½, 14½

1944, Aug. 20   **Engr.**
B65 SP46 3.50k + 1k dk red   .50   .50
B66 SP47 12.50k + 6k sepia   .50   .50
B67 SP47 18k + 9k dk bl   .50   .50
B68 SP47 32k + 16k gray grn   .50   .50
   Nos. B65-B68 (4)   2.00   2.00

Nos. B68 exists only perf 12½, while B65-B67 exist perf 11½, 12½ or 14½. Values are for copies perf 11½ or 12½. Values Nos. B65-B67 perf 14½, $5 each unused or used.

Souvenir Sheet
Perf. 12½
B69 SP47 32k + 16k dk brn, *cr*   4.50   5.00

The surtax aided the State Labor Service (Drzavna Radna Sluzba).

Palm Leaf — SP51

1944, Nov. 12   **Litho.**   **Perf. 11**
B70 SP51 2k + 1k dl grn & red   .45   .45
B71 SP51 3.50k + 1.50k car lake & red   .45   .45
B72 SP51 12.50k + 6k ind & red   .45   .45
   Nos. B70-B72 (3)   1.35   1.35

The surtax aided the Croatian Red Cross. Panes of 16.

Men of Storm Division — SP52

70k+70k, Soldiers of Storm Division in action. 100k+100k, Storm Division emblem.

1944   **Unwmk.**   **Litho.**   **Perf. 11**
B73 SP52 50k + 50k brick red   175.00   190.00
B74 SP52 70k + 70k sepia   175.00   190.00
B75 SP52 100k + 100k chlky, pale & dp bl   175.00   190.00
   Nos. B73-B75 (3)   525.00   570.00

Nos. B73-B75 issued in panes of 20.

Souvenir Sheet
B76 Sheet of 3   1,650.   1,650.
   a. SP52 50k + 50k brick red   400.   400.
   b. SP52 70k + 70k sepia   400.   400.
   c. SP52 100k + 100k chalky, pale & deep blue   400.   400.

Nos. B76a to B76c are inscribed "O. A." in brick red at right below design. The sheet measures 216x132mm. The surtax aided the First Croatian Storm Division. Counterfeits are plentiful.

Postman SP55   Telephone Line Repairman SP56

24k+12k, Switchboard operator. 50k+25k, 100k+50k, Postman delivering parcel.

1945   **Photo.**
B77 SP55 3.50k + 1.50k sl gray   .40   .40
B78 SP56 12.50k + 6k brn car   .40   .40
B79 SP56 24k + 12k dk grn   .40   .40
B80 SP56 50k + 25k brn vio   .40   .40
   Nos. B77-B80 (4)   1.60   1.60

Souvenir Sheet
B81 SP56 100k + 50k dp brn   11.00   11.00

The surtax on #B77-B81 aided employees of the P.T.T. Panes of 8.

Famous Croatians SP60

No. B100, Ban Josip Jelacic (1801-59). No. B101, Dr. Ante Starcevic (1823-96). 7d + 3d, Stjepan Radic (1871-1928).

1992 **Litho.** **Perf. 11x10½**
B100	SP60	4d +2d multi	.65	.65
B101	SP60	4d +2d multi	.65	.65

Perf. 14
B102	SP60	7d +3d multi	.65	.65
		Nos. B100-B102 (3)	1.95	1.95

Issued: No. B100, 2/1; No. B101, 3/4; No. B102, 4/2.

The surcharge on Nos. B100-B102 was initially an obligatory tax on all internal and overseas mail. From May 15, 1992, these stamps were valid for postage at their 6d or 10d face values.

AIR POST STAMPS

> Catalogue values for unused stamps in this section are for Never Hinged items.

Airplane, Zagreb Cathedral and Port of Dubrovnik AP1

Airplane Over Ruins of Diocletian's Palace, Split — AP2

Coat of Arms, Airplane, Zagreb Cathedral and Pula Amphitheatre AP3

Paper Airplane Made From Picture of Osijek Cathedral AP4

1991-92 **Litho.** **Perf. 11x10½**
C1	AP1	1d multicolored	.50	.50
		Perf. 14	.50	.50
C2	AP2	2d multicolored	1.50	.50
		Perf. 14	.50	.50
C3	AP3	3d multicolored	.50	.50
C4	AP4	4d multicolored	.50	.50
		Nos. C1-C4 (4)	3.00	2.00

Issued: No. C1, 9/9/91; No. C1a, 6/24/92; No. C2, 10/9/91; No. C2a, 1992; No. C3, 11/20/91; No. C4, 2/14/92.

Miniature Sheet

Marine Life — AP5

No. C5: a, Long-snouted seahorse (konjic dugokljunic). b, Violescent sea-whip (velika roznjaca). c, Cylinder anemone (opnena voskovica). d, Neptune's lace (neptunova cipka).

Serpentine Die Cut 5½x5¼
2015, June 15 **Litho.**
Self-Adhesive
C5	AP5	Sheet of 4	7.00	
a.-d.		5.80k Any single	1.75	1.75

POSTAGE DUE STAMPS

Yugoslavia Nos. J28-J32 Overprinted in Black

1941, Apr. 26 **Unwmk.** **Perf. 12½**
J1	D4	50p violet	.40	.65
a.		Double overprint	150.00	
b.		50p rose violet	9.00	18.00
c.		As "b," double overprint		200.00
J2	D4	1d deep magenta	.40	.65
a.		Inverted overprint	200.00	
b.		Double overprint		300.00
J3	D4	2d deep blue	10.00	20.00
a.		Double overprint	300.00	
J4	D4	5d orange	1.25	2.00
a.		Double overprint	300.00	
J5	D4	10d chocolate	6.00	12.00
		Nos. J1-J5 (5)	18.05	35.30
		Set, never hinged	40.00	

Counterfeit overprints exist, particularly of Nos. J3 and J5.

D1

1941, Sept. 12 **Litho.** **Perf. 11**
J6	D1	50b carmine lake	.25	.50
J7	D1	1k carmine lake	.25	.50
J8	D1	2k carmine lake	.30	.70
J9	D1	5k carmine lake	.50	1.00
J10	D1	10k carmine lake	.75	1.40
		Nos. J6-J10 (5)	2.05	4.10
		Set, never hinged	5.00	

D2

1943 **Perf. 11½, 12x12½, 12½**
Size: 24x24mm
J11	D2	50b lt blue & gray	.25	.25
J12	D2	1k lt blue & gray	.25	.25
J13	D2	2k lt blue & gray	.25	.25
J14	D2	4k lt blue & gray	.25	.35
J15	D2	5k lt blue & gray	.25	.40
J16	D2	6k lt blue & gray	.25	.45
J17	D2	10k lt blue & indigo	.25	.40
J18	D2	15k blue & indigo	.25	1.10
J19	D2	20k blue & indigo	.65	1.60
		Nos. J11-J19 (9)	2.65	5.05
		Set, never hinged	5.00	

1942, July 30 **Perf. 10½, 11½**
Size: 25x24¼mm
J20	D2	50b lt blue & gray	.25	.40
J21	D2	1k lt blue & gray	.25	.50
J22	D2	2k lt blue & gray	.25	.50
J23	D2	5k lt blue & gray	.25	.50
J24	D2	10k lt blue & blue	.65	1.10
J25	D2	20k lt blue & blue	.90	1.60
		Nos. J20-J25 (6)	2.55	4.60
		Set, never hinged	6.00	

Nos. J21-J25 exist both perf 10½ and 11½. No. J20 exists only perf 11½.

OFFICIAL STAMPS

Croatian Coat of Arms
O1   O2

1942-43 **Unwmk.** **Litho.**
Ordinary Paper
Perf. 11½
O1	O1	25b rose lake	.25	.25
O2	O1	50b slate blk	.25	.25
O3	O1	75b gray grn	.25	.25
O4	O1	1k orange brn	.25	.25
O5	O1	2k turq blue	1.10	1.10
O6	O1	3k vermilion	.25	.25
O7	O1	4k brown vio	.25	.25
O8	O1	5k ultra, *thin paper*	.25	.40
O9	O1	6k brt violet	.25	.25
O10	O1	10k lt green	.25	.30
O11	O1	12k brown rose	.25	.35
O12	O1	20k dark blue	.25	.40
O13	O2	30k brn vio & gray	.25	.40
O14	O2	40k vio blk & gray	.30	.50
O15	O2	50k brn lake & gray	.65	1.00
O16	O2	100k black & pink	.65	1.00
		Nos. O1-O16 (16)	5.70	7.20
		Set, never hinged	8.00	

Perf. 10½
O1a	O1	25b rose lake	.25	.25
O2a	O1	50b slate blk	.25	.25
O3a	O1	75b gray grn	.25	.25
O4a	O1	1k orange brn	.25	.25
O5a	O1	2k turq blue	1.10	2.00
O6a	O1	3k vermilion	.25	.25
O7a	O1	4k brown vio	.25	.25
O8a	O1	5k ultra	.95	1.75
O9a	O1	6k brt violet	1.40	2.50
O10a	O1	10k lt green	.25	.25
O11a	O1	12k brown rose	1.25	2.25
O12a	O1	20k dark blue	1.25	2.25
O13a	O2	30k brn vio & gray	.25	.40
O14a	O2	40k vio blk & gray	.30	.50
O15a	O2	50k brn lake & gray	.65	1.00
O16a	O2	100k black & pink	.65	1.00
		Nos. O1a-O16a (16)	9.55	15.40
		Set, never hinged	15.00	

1943-44 **Thin Paper** **Perf. 11½**
O17	O1	25b claret	.25	.25
O18	O1	50b gray	.25	.25
O19	O1	75b dull green	.25	.25
O20	O1	1k orange brn	.25	.25
O21	O1	2k slate blue	.25	.25
O22	O1	3.50k car rose	.25	.25
a.		Ordinary paper	3.00	3.00
O23	O1	6k brt red vio	.25	.25
O24	O1	12.50k deep orange	.25	.25
a.		Ordinary paper	2.00	2.00
		Set, never hinged	1.50	

POSTAL TAX STAMPS

> Catalogue values for unused stamps in this section are for Never Hinged items.

Nurse and Soldier — PT1

Unwmk.
1942, Oct. 4 **Litho.** **Perf. 11**
RA1	PT1	1k olive grn & red	.85	.80

The tax aided the Croatian Red Cross. Issued in sheets of 24 plus label.

No. RA1 can be found with a red cross printed on the nurse's hat. The original design included this element, but it was removed from the final approved design. Early printings of No. RA1, probably trial printings, included the red cross.

Wounded Soldier — PT2

1943, Oct. 3
RA2	PT2	2k blue & red	.70	.70

The tax aided the Croatian Red Cross.

Ruins — PT3

Wounded Soldier — PT4

1944, Jan. 1 **Photo.** **Perf. 12**
RA3	PT3	1k dk slate green	.25	.25
RA4	PT4	2k carmine lake	.30	.30
RA5	PT4	5k black	.35	.35
RA6	PT4	10k deep blue	.55	.40
RA7	PT4	20k brown	1.10	.90
		Nos. RA3-RA7 (5)	2.55	2.20

Interior of Zagreb Cathedral PT10

1991, Apr. 1 **Litho.** **Perf. 14**
RA20	PT10	1.20d black & gold	.65	.55
a.		Perf. 11x10½	.85	.80
b.		Perf. 11	15.00	12.00
c.		Imperf	.90	.90

Worker's Fund. Required on mail during April 1991.

For surcharges see Nos. 100, 100a.

Shrine of the Virgin, 700th Anniv. PT11

1991, May 16 **Perf. 10½x11**
RA21	PT11	1.70d multicolored	.80	.65
a.		Imperf	1.25	1.10

Workers' Fund. Required on mail May 16-31.

Croatian Arms Type of 1992
1991, July 1 **Perf. 11x10½**
RA22	A37	2.20d multicolored	.80	.70
a.		Imperf	1.25	1.00

Required on mail during July.

Members of
Parliament
PT12

1991, Aug. 1   *Perf. 11x10½*
RA23 PT12 2.20d multicolored .80 .70
a. Imperf. 1.25 1.00

Worker's Fund. Required on mail during Aug.

Red Cross and
Tuberculosis
PT13

1991, Sept 14   *Perf. 11*
RA24 PT13 2.20d blue & red .50 .45
Required on mail Sept. 14-21.

Re-erection of
Ban Josip
Jelacic
Equestrian
Statue, Zagreb
PT14

1991, Nov. 1   *Perf. 11x10½*
RA25 PT14 2.20d multicolored .80 .70
a. Imperf. 1.25 1.00

Worker's Fund. Required on mail during Nov.

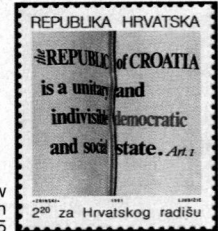

New
Constitution
PT15

1991, Dec. 2   Litho.   *Perf. 10¾x10½*
Language of Inscription
RA26 PT15 2.20d English 3.25 3.00
RA27 PT15 2.20d Croatian 1.15 1.00
RA28 PT15 2.20d French 3.25 3.00
RA29 PT15 2.20d German 3.25 3.00
RA30 PT15 2.20d Russian 3.25 3.00
RA31 PT15 2.20d Spanish 3.25 3.00
a. Vert. strip, #RA26-RA31 35.00 35.00
Nos. RA26-RA31 (6) 17.40 16.00

Nos RA26-RA31 were printed in sheet containing 15 of No. RA27, 2 each of the other stamps and five labels. Obligatory on mail Dec. 2-31.
Sheet exists imperf. Value $225.

"VUKOVAR"
with Barbed
Wire — PT16

1992, Jan. 1   Litho.   *Perf. 11x10½*
RA32 PT16 2.20d black & brown 1.15 .90
a. Imperf. 1.60 1.40

Vukovar Refugee's Fund. Required on mail during Jan.

Red Cross
PT17

Red Cross
and Solidarity
PT18

1992   *Perf. 11*
RA33 PT17 3d red & black .50 .50
RA34 PT18 3d red & black .30 .30

Issued: No. RA33, May 8. No. RA34, June 1. No. RA33 was required on mail May 8-15; No. RA34, June 1-7.

Madonna of
Bistrica — PT19

1992, Aug. 1   Litho.   *Perf. 14*
RA35 PT19 5d blue & gold .45 .40
Required on mail, Aug. 1-8.

Red
Cross — PT20

1992, Sept. 21   Litho.   *Perf. 11*
RA36 PT20 5d black & red .50 .30
Required on mail Sept. 14-21.

St. George
Slaying
Dragon
PT21

1992, Nov. 4   *Perf. 14*
RA37 PT21 15d multicolored .50 .30
Cancer Research League. Required on mail Nov. 4-11.
See No. RA43.

Red
Cross — PT22

1993, May 8   Litho.   *Rough Perf. 11*
RA38 PT22 80d black & red .50 .30
Required on mail May 8-15.

Red Cross
and Solidarity
PT23

1993, June 1
RA39 PT23 100d black & red .50 .30
Required on mail June 1-7.

Cardinal Stepinac
(1898-1960)
PT24

1993, July 15   Litho.   *Perf. 14*
RA40 PT24 150d multicolored .50 .30
Required on mail July 15-22.

Zrinski-Frankopan Foundation — PT25

Design: 200d, Gen. Peter Zrinski (1621-1671), Politician and Fran Krsto Frankopan, Count of Tersat (1643-1671), Poet.

1993, Aug. 12   Litho.   *Perf. 14*
RA41 PT25 200d gray & blue .50 .30
Required on mail Aug. 12-19.

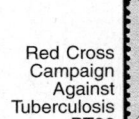

Red Cross
Campaign
Against
Tuberculosis
PT26

1993, Sept. 14   Litho.   *Perf. 11*
RA42 PT26 300d gray, red & black .50 .45
Required on mail Sept. 14-21.

St. George Slaying Dragon Type of 1992
1993, Oct. 11   Litho.   *Perf. 14*
RA43 PT21 400d multicolored .45 .40
Cancer Research League. Required on mail Oct. 11-31.

Save the
Children of
Croatia
PT27

1993, Nov. 1   *Perf. 13½x14*
RA44 PT27 400d multicolored .50 .45
Required on mail Nov. 1-30.

Croatian Red
Cross — PT28

1994, May 5   Litho.   *Perf. 11*
RA45 PT28 500d multicolored .50 .45
Required on mail May 8-15.

Red Cross
Solidarity — PT29

1994, May 5   Litho.   *Perf. 11*
RA46 PT29 50 l multicolored .50 .45
Required on mail June 1-7.

Ludberg
Church — PT30

1994, July 15   *Perf. 14*
RA47 PT30 50 l multicolored .50 .30
Required on mail July 15-22.

Save the Children
of
Croatia — PT31

1994, Aug. 16   Litho.   *Perf. 14*
RA48 PT31 50 l multicolored .50 .30
Required on mail Aug. 16-29.

St. George
Slaying
Dragon — PT32

1994, Sept. 1
RA49 PT32 50 l multicolored .50 .30
Cancer Research League. Required on mail Sept. 1-8.

PT33

1994, Sept. 14   *Perf. 11*
RA50 PT33 50 l blk, grn & red .50 .30
Red Cross Campaign against Tuberculosis. Required on mail Sept. 14-21.

PT34

1994, Oct. 15   Litho.   *Perf. 14*
RA51 PT34 50 l multicolored .50 .35
Town of Slavonski Brod, 750th anniv.

Homage to Olympia, by Ivan Lackovic PT35

Intl. Olympic Committee, Cent. — PT36

Designs: a, Tennis. b, Soccer. c, Basketball. d, Team handball. e, Canoeing, kayaking. f, Water polo. g, Track and field. h, Gymnastics.

1994, Nov. 2 **Litho.** *Perf. 14*
RA52 PT35 50 l Pair, #a.-b. 1.40 1.25
RA53 PT36 50 l Sheet of 8, #a.-h. 5.75 5.75
RA54 PT36 50 l Sheet of 8, #a.-h. 5.75 5.75

Nos. RA52b, RA53a, RA53d-RA53e, RA53h, RA54b-RA54c, RA54f-RA54g have IOC centennial emblem. Others have emblem of Croatian Olympic Committee. Required on mail Nov. 2-15.

Natl. Olympic Committee PT37

Designs: a, Rowing. b, Pétanque. c, Monument to Drazen Petrovic, Olympic Park, Lausanne. d, Tennis. e, Basketball.

1995, Apr. 17 **Litho.** *Perf. 14*
RA55 PT37 50 l Strip of 5, #a.-e. 2.00 2.00
Required on mail Apr. 17-30.

Red Cross Stamps — PT38

1995, May 8 *Perf. 11*
RA56 PT38 50 l multicolored .50 .30
Required on mail May 8-15.

Red Cross Stamps — PT39

1995, June 1
RA57 PT39 50 l multicolored .50 .30
Required on mail June 1-7.

Sts. Peter and Paul Cathedral, Osijek — PT40

1995, July 17 *Perf. 14*
RA58 PT40 65 l multicolored .50 .40
Required on mail July 17-30.

Holy Mother of Freedom PT41

Design: No. RA59, Like No. RA60, but with black surcharge on white panel. #RA60, Croatian Pieta, by Ivan Lackovic. #RA61, Gedenkstatte Church Project.

1995, Aug. 14 **Litho.** *Perf. 14*
RA59 PT41 65 l on 50 l multi 2.50 2.50
RA60 PT41 65 l multicolored .55 .50
RA61 PT41 65 l multicolored .55 .50
Nos. RA59-RA61 (3) 3.60 3.50

No. RA59 not issued without surcharge. Examples without surcharge are printer's waste. Required on mail Aug. 14-27.

Red Cross and Tuberculosis — PT42

1995, Sept. 14 *Perf. 11*
RA62 PT42 65 l multicolored .50 .40
Required on mail Sept. 14-21.

Save the Croatian Children — PT43

1995, Oct. 16 *Perf. 14*
RA63 PT43 65 l multicolored .50 .40
Required on mail Oct. 16-29.

PT44

Performance scene: a, Woman seated at top of steps. b, Gathering of people. c, People, large statue in background.

1995, Oct. 16
RA64 PT44 65 l Strip of 3, #a.-c. 1.50 1.50
Croatian Natl. Theater, Zagreb, cent. No. RA64 has continuous design. Required on mail 10/16-29.

Fight Against Drugs — PT45

1995, Nov. 6 **Litho.** *Perf. 14*
RA65 PT45 65 l multicolored .50 .35
Required on mail Nov. 20-30.

PT46

1995, Nov. 20 **Litho.** *Perf. 14x13¾*
RA66 PT46 65 l multicolored .50 .35
Croatian Anti-Cancer League. Required on mail Nov. 20-30.

PT47

1996, Feb. 15 **Litho.** *Perf. 14x13½*
RA67 PT47 65 l multicolored .50 .35
Croatian Anti-Cancer League. Required on mail Feb. 15-28.

PT48

1996, Mar. 18 **Litho.** *Perf. 14*
RA68 PT48 65 l multicolored .50 .35
Sanctuary of the Virgin Mary of Bistrica. Required on mail Mar. 18-31.

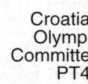

Croatian Olympic Committee PT49

1996, Apr. 17 **Litho.** *Perf. 14*
RA69 PT49 65 l multi .60 .35
No. RA69 exists imperf. and in booklets, which were not placed on sale. Required on mail Apr. 17-30.

Red Cross — PT50

1996, May 8 **Litho.** *Perf. 11*
RA70 PT50 65 l multicolored .50 .35
Required on mail May 8-15.

Red Cross Solidarity Week — PT51

1996, June 6 **Litho.** *Perf. 11*
RA71 PT51 65 l multicolored .50 .35
Required on mail June 1-7.

Croatian Children — PT52

1996, June 14 **Litho.** *Perf. 14x13½*
RA72 PT52 65 l multicolored .50 .35
Required on mail 6/14-27.

PT53

1996, July 3 **Litho.** *Perf. 14*
RA73 PT53 65 l multicolored .50 .35
Osijek, 800th anniv. Required on mail July 3-16.

PT54

1996, July 17 **Litho.** *Perf. 14*
RA74 PT54 65 l multicolored .50 .35
Renovation of Dakovo Cathedral. Required on mail July 17-30.

Split, 1700th Anniv. — PT55

1996, Aug. 1 **Litho.** *Perf. 14*
RA75 PT55 65 l multicolored .50 .35
Required on mail Aug. 1-14.

Aid to Vukovar — PT56

1996, Aug. 16 **Litho.** *Perf. 14x13½*
RA76 PT56 65 l multicolored .50 .35
Required on mail 8/16-29.

Fight Against Drugs — PT57

1996, Sept. 1   Litho.   Perf. 14
RA77 PT57 65 l multicolored   .55   .35
   Required on mail Sept. 1-12.

PT58

1996, Sept. 14   Litho.   Perf. 11
RA78 PT58 65 l multicolored   .50   .35
   Red Cross Tuberculosis Week. Required on mail Sept. 14-21.

PT59

1996, Oct. 10   Litho.   Perf. 14
RA79 PT59 65 l multicolored   .55   .35
   Isolation of insulin, 75th anniv. Required on mail Oct. 10-17.

PT60

1996, Nov. 11   Litho.   Perf. 14
RA80 PT60 65 l multicolored   .50   .35
   Remete pilgrimage. Required on mail Nov. 11-24.

PT61

1997, Jan. 6   Litho.   Perf. 14
RA81 PT61 65 l multicolored   .50   .35
   Antun Mihanovic (1796-1861), natl. anthem lyricist. Required on mail Jan. 6-26.

House of Dr. Ante Starcevic PT62

1997, Jan. 27   Litho.   Perf. 14
RA82 PT62 65 l multicolored   .50   .35
   Required on mail Jan. 27-Feb. 14.

PT63

1997, Feb. 15   Litho.   Perf. 14
RA83 PT63 65 l multicolored   .50   .35
   Croatian Anti-Cancer League. Required on mail Feb. 15-28.

Red Cross — PT64

1997, May 8   Litho.   Perf. 10½x11
RA84 PT64 65 l multicolored   .50   .35
   a.   Perf 10½   .50   .35
   b.   Perf 11   35.00
   Required on mail May 8-15.

Numerous charity stamps were issued between 1997 and 2001, but their use on mail was not obligatory.

Red Cross Solidarity Week — PT65

2001, Dec. 8   Litho.   Perf. 14
RA85 PT65 1.15k red & black   1.25   1.00
   Obligatory on mail Dec. 8-15.

Red Cross Week — PT66

2002, May 8
RA86 PT66 1.15k multi   1.25   1.10
   Obligatory on mail May 8-15.

Red Cross Anti-Tuberculosis Week — PT67

2002, Sept. 14
RA87 PT67 1.15k multi   1.25   1.00
   Obligatory on mail Sept. 14-21.

Red Cross Solidarity Week — PT68

2002, Dec. 8
RA88 PT68 1.15k multi   1.25   1.00
   Obligatory on mail Dec. 8-15.

Red Cross Week — PT69

2003, May 8
RA89 PT69 1.15k multi   1.25   1.10
   Obligatory on mail May 8-15.

Red Cross Anti-Tuberculosis Week — PT70

2003, Sept. 14
RA90 PT70 1.15k multi   1.25   1.10
   Obligatory on mail Sept. 14-21.

Red Cross Solidarity Week — PT71

2003, Dec. 8
RA91 PT71 1.15k multi   1.25   1.10
   Obligatory on mail Dec. 8-15.

Red Cross Week — PT72

2004, May 8
RA92 PT72 1.15k multi   1.25   1.10
   Obligatory on mail May 8-15.

Red Cross Anti-Tuberculosis Week — PT73

2004, Sept. 14
RA93 PT73 1.15k multi   .50   .50
   Obligatory on mail Sept. 14-21.

Red Cross Solidarity Week — PT74

2004, Dec. 8
RA94 PT74 1.15k multi   .50   .50
   Obligatory on mail Dec. 8-15.

Red Cross Week — PT75

2005, May 8   Litho.   Perf. 14
RA95 PT75 1.15k multi   .60   .60
   Obligatory on mail May 8-15.

Red Cross Anti-Tuberculosis Week — PT76

2005, Sept. 14
RA96 PT76 1.15k multi   .50   .50
   Obligatory on mail Sept. 14-21.

Red Cross Solidarity Week — PT77

2005, Dec. 8
RA97 PT77 1.15k multi   .50   .50
   Obligatory on mail Dec. 8-15.

Red Cross Week — PT78

2006, May 8   Litho.   Perf. 14
RA98 PT78 1.15k multi   1.25   1.25
   Obligatory on mail May 8-15.

Red Cross Anti-Tuberculosis Week — PT79

2006, Sept. 14
RA99 PT79 1.15k multi   1.25   1.25
   Obligatory on mail Sept. 14-21.

Red Cross Solidarity
Week — PT80

2006, Dec. 8
RA100 PT80 1.15k multi   1.25 1.25
Obligatory on mail Dec. 8-15.

Red Cross
Week — PT81

2007, May 8   **Litho.**   **Perf. 14¼**
RA101 PT81 1.15k multi   — —
Obligatory on mail May 8-15.

Red Cross Anti-
Tuberculosis
Week — PT82

2007, Sept. 14   **Litho.**   **Perf. 14¼**
RA102 PT82 1.15k multi   — —
Obligatory on mail Sept. 14-21.

Red Cross Solidarity
Week — PT83

2007, Dec. 8   **Litho.**   **Perf. 14¼**
RA103 PT83 1.15k multi   — —
Obligatory on mail Dec. 8-15.

Red Cross
Week — PT84

2008, May 8   **Litho.**   **Perf. 14¼**
RA104 PT84 1.15k multi   — —
Obligatory on mail May 8-15.

Red Cross Anti-
Tuberculosis
Week — PT85

2008, Sept. 14   **Litho.**   **Perf. 14¼**
RA105 PT85 1.15k multi   .45 .45
Obligatory on mail Sept. 14-21.

Red Cross Solidarity
Week — PT86

2008, Dec. 8   **Litho.**   **Perf. 14¼**
RA106 PT86 1.15k multi   — —
Obligatory on mail Dec. 8-15.

Red Cross
Week — PT87

2009, May 8   **Litho.**   **Perf. 14¼**
RA107 PT87 1.75k multi   — —
Obligatory on mail May 8-15.

Red Cross Anti-
Tuberculosis
Week — PT88

2009, Sept. 14   **Litho.**   **Perf. 14¼**
RA108 PT88 1.75k multi   — —
Obligatory on mail Sept. 14-21.

Red Cross Solidarity
Week — PT89

2009, Dec. 8   **Litho.**   **Perf. 14¼**
RA109 PT89 1.75k multi   — —
Obligatory on mail Dec. 8-15.

Red Cross
Week — PT90

2010, May 8   **Litho.**   **Perf. 14¼**
RA110 PT90 1.55k on 1.75k multi   — —
Obligatory on mail May 8-15. No. RA110
was not issued without surcharge.

Red Cross Anti-
Tuberculosis
Week — PT91

2010, Sept. 14   **Litho.**   **Perf. 14¼**
RA111 PT91 1.55k multi   — —
Obligatory on mail Sept. 14-21.

Red Cross Solidarity
Week — PT92

2010, Dec. 8   **Litho.**   **Perf. 14¼**
RA112 PT92 1.55k multi   — —
Obligatory on mail Dec. 8-15.

Red Cross
Week — PT93

2011, May 8   **Litho.**   **Perf. 14¼**
RA113 PT93 1.55k multi   — —
Obligatory on mail May 8-15.

Red Cross Anti-
Tuberculosis
Week — PT94

2011, Sept. 14   **Litho.**   **Perf. 14¼**
RA114 PT94 1.55k multi   — —
Obligatory on mail Sept. 14-21.

Red Cross Solidarity
Week — PT95

2011, Dec. 8   **Litho.**   **Perf. 14¼**
RA115 PT95 1.55k multi   — —
Obligatory on mail Dec. 8-15.

Red Cross
Week — PT96

2012, May 8   **Litho.**   **Perf. 14¼**
RA116 PT96 1.55k multi   — —
Obligatory on mail May 8-15.

Red Cross Anti-
Tuberculosis
Week — PT97

2012, Sept. 14   **Litho.**   **Perf. 14¼**
RA117 PT97 1.55k multi   — —
Obligatory on mail Sept. 14-21.

Red Cross Solidarity
Week — PT98

2012, Dec. 8   **Litho.**   **Perf. 14¼**
RA118 PT98 1.55k multi   — —
Obligatory on mail Dec. 8-15.

Red Cross
Week — PT99

2013, May 8   **Litho.**   **Perf. 14¼**
RA119 PT99 1.55k multi   — —
Obligatory on mail May 8-15.

Red Cross Anti-Tuberculosis
Week — PT100

2013, Sept. 14   **Litho.**   **Perf. 14¼**
RA120 PT100 1.55k multi   — —
Obligatory on mail Sept. 14-21.

Red Cross
Solidarity
Week
PT101

2013, Dec. 8   **Litho.**   **Perf. 14¼**
RA121 PT101 1.55k multi   — —
Obligatory on mail Dec. 8-15.

CUBA

'kyü-bə

LOCATION — The largest island of the West Indies; south of Florida
GOVT. — Former Spanish possession
AREA — 44,206 sq. mi.
POP. — 11,096,395 (1999 est.)
CAPITAL — Havana

Formerly a Spanish possession, Cuba made several unsuccessful attempts to gain her freedom, which finally led to the intervention of the US in 1898. In that year under the Treaty of Paris, Spain relinquished the island to the US in trust for its inhabitants.

In 1902 a republic was established and the Cuban Congress took over the government from the military authorities.

8 Reales Plata = 1 Peso
100 Centesimos = 1 Escudo or Peseta (1867)
1000 Milesimas =
100 Centavos = 1 Peso

Catalogue values for unused stamps in this country are for Never Hinged items, beginning with Scott 402 in the regular postage section, Scott B3 in the semipostal section, Scott C38 in the airpost section, Scott CB1 in the airpost semi-postal section, Scott E13 in the special delivery section, and Scott RA1 in the postal tax section.

Pen cancellations are common on the earlier stamps of Cuba. Stamps so canceled sell for very much less than those with postmark cancellations.

Watermarks

Wmk. 104 — Loops

Loops from different rows may or may not be directly opposite each other.

Wmk. 105 — Crossed Lines

Wmk. 106 — Star

Wmk. 229 — Wavy Lines

Wmk. 320

Wmk. 321 — "R de C"

Wmk. 376 — "R de C"

Issued under Spanish Dominion

Used also in Puerto Rico: Nos. 1-3, 9-14, 17-21, 32-34, 35A-37, 39-41, 43-45, 47-49, 51-53, 55-57.
Used also in the Philippines: Nos. 2-3.
Identifiable cancellations of those countries will increase the value of the stamps.

Queen Isabella II — A1

Blue Paper

		1855 Typo. Wmk. 104 Imperf.		
1	A1	½ r p blue green	100.00	7.50
a.		½ r p blackish green	250.00	30.00
2	A1	1 r p gray green	100.00	6.50
3	A1	2 r p carmine	1,000.	15.00
4	A1	2 r p orange red	1,500.	20.00
a.		2 r p vermilion	1,600.	22.00
		Nos. 1-4 (4)	2,700.	49.00

See Nos. 9-14. For surcharges see Nos. 5-8, 15.

Counterfeit surcharges are plentiful.

Nos. 3-4 Surcharged

		1855-56		
5	A1	¼ r p on 2 r p car	1,500.	400.00
a.		Without fraction bar	3,000.	2,000.
6	A1	¼ r p on 2 r p org red	4,000.	800.00
a.		Without fraction bar	—	3,000.

Surcharged

7	A1	¼ r p on 2 r p car	1,250.	300.00
a.		Without fraction bar	2,500.	1,500
8	A1	¼ r p on 2 r p org red	1,800.	600.00
a.		Without fraction bar		

The "Y ¼" surcharge met the "Ynterior" rate for delivery within the city of Havana.

Rough Yellowish Paper

		1856 Wmk. 105		
9	A1	½ r p yellow grn	10.00	2.00
10	A1	1 r p green	1,250.	30.00
a.		1 r p emerald	1,750.	100.00
11	A1	2 r p orange red	700.00	40.00

White Smooth Paper

		1857 Unwmk.		
12	A1	½ r p blue	5.00	1.00
13	A1	1 r p gray green	5.00	1.00
a.		1 r p pale yellow green	5.00	3.25
14	A1	2 r p dull rose	25.00	5.00
		Nos. 12-14 (3)	35.00	7.00

Surcharged

		1860		
15	A1	¼ r p on 2 r p dl rose	300.00	100.00
a.		1 of ¼ inverted	500.00	200.00
		On cover		1,500.
b.		"Y ¼" instead of "1 ¼"		

Queen Isabella II
A2   A3

		1862-64 Imperf.		
16	A2	¼ r p black	30.00	60.00
17	A3	¼ r p blk, buff ('64)	30.00	60.00
18	A3	½ r p green ('64)	5.00	1.00
19	A3	½ r p grn, pale rose ('64)	15.00	3.00
20	A3	1 r p bl, sal ('64)	6.00	2.00
a.		Diagonal half used as ½ r p on cover		300.00
21	A3	2 r p ver, buff ('64)	30.00	8.00
a.		2 r p red, buff	35.00	15.00
		Nos. 16-21 (6)	116.00	134.00

No. 17 Overprinted in Black

		1866		
22	A3	¼ r p black, buff	85.00	120.00

Exists with handstamped "1866."

A5

		1866		
23	A5	5c dull violet	50.00	60.00
24	A5	10c blue	6.00	1.10
25	A5	20c green	4.00	1.10
a.		Diag. half used as 10c on cover		
26	A5	40c rose	50.00	60.00
		Nos. 23-26 (4)	110.00	122.20

For the Type A5 20c in dull lilac, see Spain No. 87.

Stamps Dated "1867"

		1867 Perf. 14		
27	A5	5c dull violet	40.00	35.00
28	A5	10c blue	35.00	4.00
a.		Imperf., pair	110.00	6.50
b.		Diagonal half used as 5c on cover		300.00
29	A5	20c green	30.00	5.00
a.		Imperf., pair	110.00	75.00
b.		Diag. half used as 10c on cover		325.00
30	A5	40c rose	20.00	30.00
		Nos. 27-30 (4)	125.00	74.00

A6

Stamps Dated "1868"

		1868		
31	A6	5c dull violet	30.00	20.00
32	A6	10c blue	5.00	2.00
a.		Diagonal half used as 5c on cover		250.00
33	A6	20c green	10.00	4.00
a.		Diag. half used as 10c on cover		275.00
34	A6	40c rose	25.00	15.00
a.		Diag. half used as 20c on cover		175.00
		Nos. 31-34 (4)	70.00	41.00

Nos. 31-34 Overprinted in Black

		1868		
35	A6	5c dull violet	75.00	32.50
35A	A6	10c blue	75.00	32.50
36	A6	20c green	75.00	32.50
37	A6	40c rose	75.00	32.50
		Nos. 35-37 (4)	300.00	130.00

		1869 Stamps Dated "1869"		
38	A6	5c rose	50.00	40.00
39	A6	10c red brown	5.00	2.00
a.		Diagonal half used as 5c on cover		140.00
40	A6	20c orange	10.00	3.00
41	A6	40c dull violet	40.00	30.00
		Nos. 38-41 (4)	105.00	75.00

Nos. 38-41 Ovptd. Like Nos. 35-37

42	A6	5c rose	100.00	40.00
43	A6	10c red brown	100.00	40.00
44	A6	20c orange	100.00	40.00
45	A6	40c dull violet	100.00	40.00
		Nos. 42-45 (4)	400.00	160.00

"Espana" — A8

1870   *Perf. 14*

46	A8	5c blue	250.00	125.00
47	A8	10c green	5.00	2.00
a.		Diagonal half used as 5c on cover		250.00
48	A8	20c red brown	4.00	3.00
a.		Diag. half used as 10c on cover		300.00
49	A8	40c rose	300.00	100.00

"Espana" — A9

1871

50	A9	12c red lilac	25.00	12.00
a.		Imperf., pair	100.00	
51	A9	25c ultra	3.00	1.00
a.		Imperf., pair	50.00	
b.		Diagonal half used as 12c on cover		125.00
52	A9	50c gray green	4.00	2.00
a.		Imperf., pair	75.00	
b.		Diagonal half used as 25c on cover		250.00
53	A9	1p yel brown	40.00	15.00
a.		Imperf., pair	125.00	
		Nos. 50-53 (4)	72.00	30.00

King Amadeo — A10

1873   *Perf. 14*

54	A10	12½c dark green	40.00	30.00
a.		Diagonal half used as 12½c on cover		120.00
b.		25c lilac	10.00	4.00
c.		As "b," half used as 12½c on cover		150.00
d.		As "b," imperf., pair	50.00	
56	A10	50c brown	3.00	1.00
a.		Imperf., pair	75.00	
b.		Half used as 25c on cover		200.00
57	A10	1p red brown	450.00	75.00
a.		Diagonal half used as 50c on cover		750.00

"España" — A11

1874

58	A11	12½c brown	30.00	25.00
a.		Half used as 5c on cover		500.00
59	A11	25c ultra	1.00	.60
a.		Diagonal half used as 12½c on cover		100.00
60	A11	50c dp violet	2.00	5.00
a.		Diagonal half used as 25c on cover		200.00
b.		"1374" instead of "1874"	—	—
61	A11	50c gray	5.00	2.00
a.		Diagonal half used as 25c		175.00
62	A11	1p carmine	350.00	400.00
a.		Imperf., pair	700.00	250.00
		Nos. 58-62 (5)	388.00	432.60

Examples of Nos. 61, 63-65, 67-87 with fine impressions in slightly different colors are proofs.

Coat of Arms — A12

1875

63	A12	12½c lt violet	1.50	2.00
a.		Imperf., pair	100.00	
64	A12	25c ultra	1.25	1.60
a.		Imperf., pair	100.00	
b.		Diagonal half used as 12½c on cover		100.00
65	A12	50c blue green	1.00	2.00
a.		Imperf., pair	100.00	
b.		Diag. half used as 25c on cover		80.00
66	A12	1p brown	15.00	10.00
a.		Diag. half used as 50c on cover		135.00
		Nos. 63-66 (4)	18.75	15.60

King Alfonso XII — A13

1876

67	A13	12½c green	3.00	6.00
a.		12½c emerald green	3.75	6.00
68	A13	25c gray	4.00	3.00
a.		Diagonal half used as 12½c on cover		100.00
b.		25c pale violet	4.50	3.25
d.		25c bluish gray	4.50	3.25
69	A13	50c ultra	3.00	6.00
a.		Imperf., pair	75.00	16.00
b.		Diag. half used as 25c on cover		100.00
70	A13	1p black	15.00	25.00
a.		Imperf., pair	40.00	40.00
b.		Diag. half used as 50c on cover		125.00
		Nos. 67-70 (4)	25.00	40.00

King Alfonso XII — A14

1877

71	A14	10c lt green	40.00	—
72	A14	12½c gray	6.00	12.50
a.		Imperf., pair	100.00	
b.		Diagonal half used on cover		300.00
73	A14	25c dk green	1.00	.50
a.		Imperf., pair	100.00	
b.		Diagonal half used as 12½c on cover		75.00
74	A14	50c black	1.00	1.50
a.		Imperf., pair	100.00	
b.		Half used as 25c on cover		100.00
75	A14	1p brown	30.00	25.00
		Nos. 71-75 (5)	78.00	

No. 71 was not placed in use.

1878   **Stamps Dated "1878"**

76	A14	5c blue	1.00	2.00
77	A14	10c black	100.00	
78	A14	12½c brown bis	6.00	10.00
b.		12½c olive brown	6.00	10.00
c.		Diagonal half used on cover		200.00
d.		As "a," diagonal half used on cover		200.00
79	A14	25c yel green	1.00	2.00
b.		No. 79, diagonal half used as 12½c on cover		100.00
c.		25c deep green	1.00	2.00
80	A14	50c dk blue grn	1.00	2.00
b.		Diagonal half used as 25c on cover		100.00
81	A14	1p carmine	25.00	15.00
b.		1p rose	16.00	500.00
c.		Diagonal half used as 50c on cover		900.00
		Nos. 76-81 (6)	134.00	31.00

No. 77 was not placed in use.

Imperf., Pairs

76a	A14	5c blue	100.00	
77a	A14	10c black	400.00	
78b	A14	12½c brown bister	100.00	
79a	A14	25c deep green	100.00	
80a	A14	50c dk blue green	200.00	
81a	A14	1p carmine	150.00	

1879   **Stamps Dated "1879"**

82	A14	5c slate black	1.00	3.00
83	A14	10c orange	200.00	75.00
84	A14	12½c rose	1.00	3.00
85	A14	25c ultra	1.00	2.00
a.		Diagonal half used as 12½c on cover		100.00
b.		Imperf., pair	75.00	
86	A14	50c gray	1.00	1.00
a.		Diag. half used as 25c on cover		100.00
87	A14	1p olive bister	25.00	30.00
		Nos. 82-87 (6)	229.00	114.00

Forgeries exist of No. 83.

A15

1880

88	A15	5c green	1.00	2.00
89	A15	10c lake	125.00	
a.		Double impression of frame and lettering	200.00	
90	A15	12½c gray	1.00	.50
91	A15	25c gray blue	1.00	.50
a.		Diagonal half used as 12½c on cover		100.00
92	A15	50c brown	1.00	.50
a.		Diagonal half used as 25c on cover		100.00
93	A15	1p yellow brn	8.00	5.00
a.		Diagonal half used as 50c on cover		400.00
		Nos. 88-93 (6)	137.00	8.50

No. 89 was not placed in use.

A16

1881

94	A16	1c green	1.00	.50
95	A16	2c lake	50.00	
96	A16	2½c olive bister	1.00	.50
97	A16	5c gray blue	.50	.25
98	A16	10c yellow brown	.50	.25
a.		Diagonal half used as 5c on cover		100.00
99	A16	20c dark brown	6.00	10.00
		Nos. 94-99 (6)	59.00	11.50

No. 95 was not placed in use.

A17

1882

100	A17	1c green	.75	.50
a.		Diag. half used as ½c on cover		150.00
101	A17	2c lake	5.00	3.00
a.		Diag. half used as 1c on cover		100.00
102	A17	2½c dk brown	10.00	5.00
103	A17	5c gray blue	8.00	.50
a.		Diag. half used as 2½c on cover		100.00
104	A17	10c olive bister	.75	.50
a.		Diag. half used as 5c on cover		100.00
105	A17	20c red brown	130.00	50.00
a.		Diag. half used as 10c on cover		500.00
		Nos. 100-105 (6)	154.50	59.50

See Nos. 121-131. For surcharges see Nos. 106-120.

Issue of 1882 Surcharged or Overprinted in Black, Blue or Red

a

b

c

d

e

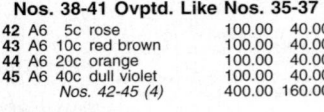

1883   **Type "a"**

106	A17	5 on 5c (R)	3.00	2.00
a.		Triple surcharge	25.00	25.00
b.		Double surcharge	25.00	25.00
c.		Inverted surcharge	30.00	30.00
d.		Without "5" in surcharge	20.00	20.00
e.		Dbl. surch., types "a" & "d"	75.00	—
107	A17	10 on 10c (Bl)	3.50	2.50
a.		Inverted surcharge	75.00	
b.		Double surcharge	30.00	
108	A17	20 on 20c	45.00	75.00
a.		"10" instead of "20"	75.00	75.00
b.		Double surcharge	75.00	
c.		As "a," inverted surcharge	90.00	90.00

Type "b"

109	A17	5 on 5c (R)	3.00	2.00
a.		Inverted surcharge	30.00	30.00
b.		Double surcharge	25.00	25.00
110	A17	10 on 10c (Bl)	10.00	12.00
a.		Inverted surcharge	35.00	35.00
b.		Double surcharge	35.00	35.00
111	A17	20 on 20c	120.00	150.00
a.		Double surcharge		
b.		Dbl. surch., types "b" & "c"		

Type "c"

112	A17	5 on 5c (R)	2.50	2.00
a.		Inverted surcharge	35.00	35.00
b.		Dbl. surch., types "c" & "d"		
c.		Dbl. surch., types "c" & "a"		
113	A17	10 on 10c (Bl)	10.00	12.00
a.		Inverted surcharge	40.00	40.00
b.		Double surcharge	40.00	40.00
114	A17	20 on 20c	60.00	100.00
a.		"10" instead of "20"	100.00	120.00
b.		Double surcharge	100.00	120.00
c.		Dbl. surch., types "a" & "c"	100.00	120.00

Type "d"

115	A17	5 on 5c (R)	3.00	2.00
a.		Inverted surcharge	35.00	35.00
b.		Double surcharge	30.00	30.00
116	A17	10 on 10c (Bl)	4.00	3.00
a.		Inverted surcharge	40.00	40.00
c.		Dbl. surch., types "d" & "c"		
117	A17	20 on 20c	85.00	100.00
a.		Dbl. surch., types "a" & "d"		

Type "e"

118	A17	5c gray blue (R)	4.00	3.00
a.		Double overprint	40.00	40.00
119	A17	10c olive bis (Bl)	12.00	15.00
a.		Double overprint	40.00	40.00
120	A17	20c red brown	250.00	300.00
a.		Double overprint	300.00	300.00
		Nos. 106-120 (15)	615.00	780.50

Handstamped overprints and surcharges are counterfeits.
Numerous other varieties exist.

Type of 1882

Original   1st retouch 2nd retouch

The differences between the stamps of 1882 and the various retouches are as follows:

Original state: The medallion is surrounded by a heavy line of color of nearly even thickness, touching the horizontal line below the word "Cuba" (or "Filipinas," "Puerto Rico," as the case may be); the opening in the hair above the temple is narrow and pointed.

1st retouch: The line around the medallion is thin, except at the upper right, and does not touch the horizontal line above it; the opening in the hair is slightly wider and a trifle rounded; the lock of hair above the forehead is shaped like a broad "V" and ends in a point; there is a faint white line below it, which is not found on the stamps in the original state. Owing to wear of the plate the shape of the lock of hair and the width of the white line below it vary.

2nd retouch: The opening in the hair forms a semi-circle; the lock above the forehead is nearly straight, having only a slight wave, and the white line is much broader than before.

1883-86

121	A17	1c grn, 2nd retouch	150.00	40.00
122	A17	2½c olive bister	.50	.30
124	A17	2½c violet	1.00	.40
a.		2½c red lilac ('85)	1.00	.40
b.		2½c ultramarine	125.00	150.00
125	A17	5c gray bl, 1st retouch	100.00	.50
a.		Diag. half used as 2½c on cover		75.00
126	A17	5c gray bl, 2nd retouch	120.00	2.00
a.		Diag. half used as 2½c on cover		125.00
127	A17	10c brn, 1st retouch	3.00	1.00
a.		Diagonal half used as 5c on cover		75.00
c.		Imperf, pair	300.00	—
		Nos. 121-128 (7)	389.50	54.20

1888

129	A17	2½c red brown	1.75	.85
130	A17	10c blue	1.50	1.00
a.		Diagonal half used as 5c on cover		175.00
131	A17	20c brnsh gray	15.00	10.00
		Nos. 129-131 (3)	18.25	11.85

King Alfonso
XIII — A18

1890-97

132	A18	1c gray brown	20.00	6.50
133	A18	1c ol gray ('91)	10.00	4.00
134	A18	1c ultra ('94)	5.00	.50
135	A18	1c dk vio ('96)	1.50	.50
136	A18	2c slate blue	10.00	3.00
137	A18	2c lilac brn ('91)	2.00	.75
138	A18	2c rose ('94)	35.00	5.00
139	A18	2c claret ('96)	9.00	5.00
140	A18	2½c emerald	12.50	5.00
141	A18	2½c salmon ('91)	60.00	5.00
142	A18	2½c lilac ('94)	4.00	3.00
143	A18	2½c rose ('96)	4.00	6.00
144	A18	5c olive gray	1.00	.75
b.		Diagonal half used as 2½c on cover		500.00
145	A18	5c emerald ('96)	1.00	.50
b.		Diagonal half used as 2½c on cover		500.00
146	A18	5c sl blue ('96)	.75	1.00
b.		Diagonal half used as 2½c on cover		600.00
147	A18	10c brown violet	6.00	1.00
b.		Diagonal half used as 5c on cover		500.00
148	A18	10c claret ('91)	2.50	.50
b.		Diagonal half used as 5c on cover		400.00
149	A18	10c emerald ('96)	1.00	1.50
150	A18	20c dk violet	2.00	1.00
151	A18	20c ultra ('91)	25.00	8.00
152	A18	20c red brn ('94)	20.00	30.00
153	A18	20c violet ('96)	15.00	10.00
b.		Diagonal half used as 10c on cover		600.00
154	A18	40c orange brn ('97)	40.00	35.00
155	A18	80c lilac brn ('97)	80.00	70.00
		Nos. 132-155 (24)	367.25	203.50

Imperf., Pairs

134a	A18	1c ultramarine	100.00
135a	A18	1c dark violet	100.00
138a	A18	2c rose	100.00
139a	A18	2c claret	100.00
142a	A18	2½c lilac	100.00
143a	A18	2½c rose	100.00
145a	A18	5c emerald	100.00
146a	A18	5c slate blue	100.00
148a	A18	10c claret	100.00
149a	A18	10c emerald	100.00
152a	A18	20c red brown	135.00
153a	A18	20c violet	125.00
154a	A18	40c orange brown	115.00
155a	A18	80c red brown	175.00

King Alfonso
XIII — A19

1898

156	A19	1m orange brn	.75	1.00
157	A19	2m orange brn	.30	1.00
158	A19	3m orange brn	.30	1.00
159	A19	4m orange brn	6.00	12.00
160	A19	5m orange brn	.30	1.00
161	A19	1c black vio	.30	1.00
162	A19	2c dk blue grn	.30	1.00
163	A19	3c dk brown	.30	1.00
164	A19	4c orange	16.00	12.00
165	A19	5c car rose	1.25	.50
166	A19	6c dk blue	.50	1.50
167	A19	8c gray brown	2.00	4.00
168	A19	10c vermilion	1.30	.75
169	A19	15c slate green	6.00	10.00
170	A19	20c maroon	4.00	1.00
171	A19	40c dark lilac	5.00	8.00
172	A19	60c black	10.00	20.00
173	A19	80c red brown	20.00	25.00
174	A19	1p yel green	20.00	25.00
175	A19	2p slate blue	35.00	40.00
		Nos. 156-175 (20)	129.60	166.75

Nos. 156-160 were issued for use on newspapers.

Nos. 156-175 exist imperf. Value, unused pairs, $7,500. Only one set of pairs is currently known.

For surcharges see Nos. 176-189C, 196-200.

Issued under Administration of the United States
Puerto Principe Issue
Issues of Cuba of 1898 and 1896
Surcharged

Black Surcharge on Nos. 156-158, 160

1898-99

Types a, c, d, e, f, g and h are 17½mm high, the others are 19½mm high.

176	A19 (a)	1c on 1m		
		org brn	50.00	30.00
177	A19 (b)	1c on 1m		
		org brn	45.00	40.00
a.		Broken figure "1"	75.00	65.00
b.		Inverted surcharge		200.00
d.		As "a," inverted		250.00

178	A19 (c)	2c on 2m		
		org brn	28.00	21.50
a.		Inverted surcharge	250.00	50.00
179	A19 (d)	2c on 2m		
		org brn	40.00	35.00
a.		Inverted surcharge	350.00	100.00

179B	A19 (k)	3c on 1m		
		org brn	300.	175.
c.		Double surcharge	1,500.	750.

An unused example is known with "cents" omitted.

179D	A19 (l)	3c on 1m		
		org brn	1,500.	750.
e.		Double surcharge		

179F	A19 (e)	3c on 2m		
		org brn		1,500.

Value is for examples with minor faults.

179G	A19 (f)	3c on 2m		
		org brn	—	2,000.

Value is for examples with minor faults.

180	A19 (e)	3c on 3m		
		org brn	30.	30.
a.		Inverted surcharge		110.
181	A19 (f)	3c on 3m		
		org brn	75.	75.
a.		Inverted surcharge		200.

182	A19 (g)	5c on 1m		
		org brn	700.	250.
a.		Inverted surcharge		500.
183	A19 (h)	5c on 1m		
		org brn	1,300.	500.
a.		Inverted surcharge		700.
184	A19 (g)	5c on 2m		
		org brn	750.	275.
185	A19 (h)	5c on 2m		
		org brn	1,500.	500.
186	A19 (g)	5c on 3m		
		org brn	650.	175.
a.		Inverted surcharge	1,200.	700.
187	A19 (h)	5c on 3m		
		org brn		400.
a.		Inverted surcharge		1,000.
188	A19 (g)	5c on 5m		
		org brn	100.	80.
a.		Inverted surcharge	400.	200.
b.		Double surcharge		
189	A19 (h)	5c on 5m		
		org brn	350.	250.
a.		Inverted surcharge		425.
b.		Double surcharge	—	

The 2nd printing of Nos. 188-189 has shiny ink. Values are for the 1st printing.

189C	A19 (i)	5c on 5m		
		org brn		8,000.

No. 191

Black Surcharge on No. P25

190	N2 (g)	5c on ½m bl		
		grn	250.	75.
a.		Inverted surcharge	500.	150.
b.		Pair, one without surcharge		500.

Value for 190b is for pair with unsurcharged stamp at right. Also exists with unsurcharged stamp at left.

191	N2 (h)	5c on ½m bl		
		grn	300.	90.
a.		Inverted surcharge		200.
192	N2 (i)	5c on ½m bl		
		grn	550.	200.
a.		Dbl. surch., one diagonal		11,500.
193	N2 (j)	5c on ½m bl		
		grn	800.	300.

Red Surcharge on No. 161

196	A19 (k)	3c on 1c blk		
		vio	65.	35.
a.		Inverted surcharge		325.
197	A19 (l)	3c on 1c blk		
		vio	125.	55.
a.		Inverted surcharge		400.
198	A19 (i)	5c on 1c blk		
		vio	25.	30.
a.		Inverted surcharge		125.
b.		Surcharge vert. reading up		3,500.
c.		Double surcharge	400.	600.
d.		Double invtd. surch.		

Value for No. 198b is for surcharge reading up. One example is known with surcharge reading down.

199	A19 (j)	5c on 1c blk		
		vio	55.	55.
a.		Inverted surcharge		250.
b.		Vertical surcharge		2,000.
c.		Double surcharge	1,000.	700.

m

200	A19 (m)	10c on 1c blk	20.	50.
a.		Broken figure "1"	40.	100.

Black Surcharge on Nos. P26-P30

201	N2 (k)	3c on 1m bl		
		grn	350.	350.
a.		Inverted surcharge		450.
b.		"EENTS"	550.	450.
c.		As "b," inverted		850.
202	N2 (l)	3c on 1m bl		
		grn	550.	400.
a.		Inverted surcharge		850.
203	N2 (k)	3c on 2m bl		
		grn	900.	400.
a.		"EENTS"	1,250.	500.
b.		Inverted surcharge		1,150.
c.		As "a," inverted		950.
204	N2 (l)	3c on 2m bl		
		grn	1,250.	875.
a.		Inverted surcharge		950.
205	N2 (k)	3c on 3m bl		
		grn	900.	400.
a.		Inverted surcharge		750.
b.		"EENTS"	1,250.	450.
c.		As "b," inverted		700.
206	N2 (l)	3c on 3m bl		
		grn	1,200.	550.
a.		Inverted surcharge		700.
211	N2 (i)	5c on 1m bl		
		grn		1,800.
a.		"EENTS"	—	2,500.
212	N2 (j)	5c on 1m bl		
		grn		2,250.
213	N2 (i)	5c on 2m bl		
		grn		1,800.
a.		"EENTS"		1,900.
214	N2 (j)	5c on 2m bl		
		grn		2,300.
215	N2 (i)	5c on 3m bl		
		grn		550.
a.		"EENTS"		1,000.
216	N2 (j)	5c on 3m bl		
		grn		1,000.
217	N2 (i)	5c on 4m bl		
		grn	2,500.	900.
a.		"EENTS"	3,000.	1,500.
b.		Inverted surcharge		2,500.
c.		As "a," inverted		2,000.
218	N2 (j)	5c on 4m bl		
		grn		1,500.
a.		Inverted surcharge		2,000.
219	N2 (i)	5c on 8m bl		
		grn	2,500.	1,250.
a.		Inverted surcharge		1,500.
b.		"EENTS"		1,800.
c.		As "b," inverted		2,500.
220	N2 (j)	5c on 8m bl		
		grn	2,000.	1,250.
a.		Inverted surcharge		2,500.

Beware of forgeries of the Puerto Principe issue. Obtaining expert opinions is recommended.

United States Stamps Nos. 279, 267, 267b, 279Bf, 279Bh, 268, 281, 282C and 283 Surcharged in Black

CUBA
1 c.
de PESO

1899		**Wmk. 191**		**Perf. 12**
221	A87	1c on 1c yel		
		grn	4.50	.40
		Never hinged	11.50	

222	A88	2c on 2c reddish car, III	10.00	.75	
		Never hinged	25.00		
b.		2c on 2c vermilion, type III	10.00	.75	
222A	A88	2c on 2c reddish car, IV	6.00	.40	
		Never hinged	15.00		
c.		2c on 2c vermilion, IV	6.00	.40	
d.		As No. 222A, inverted surcharge	5,500.	4,000.	
223	A88	2½c on 2c reddish car, III	6.00	.80	
		Never hinged	15.00		
b.		2½c on 2c vermilion, III	6.00	.80	
223A	A88	2½c on 2c reddish car, IV	3.50	.50	
		Never hinged	8.75		
c.		2½c on 2c vermilion, IV	3.50	.50	
224	A89	3c on 3c purple	12.00	1.75	
		Never hinged	30.00		
a.		Period between "B" and "A"	40.00	35.00	
225	A91	5c on 5c blue	12.50	2.00	
		Never hinged	30.00		
226	A94	10c on 10c brn, I	25.00	6.00	
		Never hinged	70.00		
b.		"CUBA" omitted	7,000.	4,000.	
226A	A94	10c on 10c brn, II	6,000.		
		Nos. 221-226 (8)	79.50	12.60	

The 2½c was sold and used as a 2c stamp. Excellent counterfeits of this and the preceding issue exist, especially inverted and double surcharges.

Issues of the Republic under US Military Rule

Statue of Columbus
A20

Royal Palms
A21

"Cuba" — A22

Ocean Liner — A23

Cane Field — A24

1899	**Wmk. US-C (191C)**	**Perf. 12**		
227	A20	1c yellow green	3.50	.25
		Never hinged	8.75	
228	A21	2c carmine	3.50	.25
		Never hinged	8.75	
a.		scarlet	3.50	.25
b.		Booklet pane of 6	5,500.	
229	A22	3c purple	3.50	.30
		Never hinged	8.75	
230	A23	5c blue	4.50	.30
		Never hinged	11.00	
231	A24	10c brown	11.00	.80
		Never hinged	27.50	
		Nos. 227-231 (5)	26.00	1.90

No. 228b was issued by the Republic.
See Nos. 233-237 in Scott Standard Catalogue Vol 2. For surcharge see No. 232.

Issues of the Republic

No. 229 Surcharged in Carmine

1902, Sept. 30

232	A22	1c on 3c purple	2.75	.50
a.		Inverted surcharge	150.00	150.00
b.		Surcharge sideways (numeral horizontal)	200.00	200.00
c.		Double surcharge	200.00	200.00

Counterfeits of the errors are plentiful.

Re-engraved

The re-engraved stamps of 1905-07 may be distinguished from the issue of 1899 as follows:

ORIGINAL   RE-ENGRAVED

1c — The ends of the label inscribed "Centavo" are rounded instead of square.
2c — The foliate ornaments, inside the oval disks bearing the numerals of value, have been removed.
5c — Two lines forming a right angle have been added in the upper corners of the label bearing the word "Cuba."
10c — A small ball has been added to each of the square ends of the label bearing the word "Cuba."

1905		**Unwmk.**	**Perf. 12**	
233	A20	1c green	1.75	.25
234	A21	2c rose	1.20	.25
a.		Booklet pane of 6	150.00	
236	A23	5c blue	42.50	1.00
237	A24	10c brown	3.50	.50
		Nos. 233-237 (4)	48.95	2.00

Maj. Gen. Antonio Maceo — A26

1907

238	A26	50c gray bl & blk	1.75	.80

Bartolomé Masó
A27

Máximo Gómez
A28

Julio Sanguily
A29

Ignacio Agramonte
A30

Calixto García
A31

José M. Rodriguez y Rodriquez (Mayia)
A32

Carlos Roloff — A33

1910, Feb. 1

239	A27	1c grn & vio	1.00	.30
a.		Center inverted	260.00	260.00
240	A28	2c car & grn	1.90	.30
a.		Center inverted	575.00	575.00
241	A29	3c vio & bl	1.35	.30
242	A30	5c bl & grn	20.00	.80
243	A31	8c ol & vio	1.35	.30
244	A32	10c brn & bl	8.00	.65
a.		Center inverted	850.00	
245	A26	50c vio & blk	1.90	.50
246	A33	1p slate & blk	9.25	4.00
		Nos. 239-246 (8)	44.75	7.15
		Set, never hinged	72.50	

1911-13

247	A27	1c green	1.00	.25
248	A28	2c car rose	1.35	.25
a.		Booklet pane of 6 ('13)	82.50	
250	A30	5c ultra	3.75	.25
251	A31	8c ol grn & blk	2.00	.60
252	A33	1p black	9.50	2.00
		Nos. 247-252 (5)	17.60	3.35
		Set, never hinged	25.00	

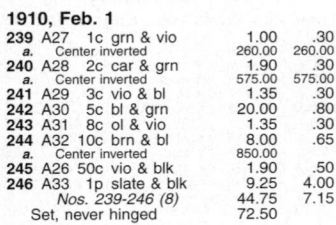

Map of Cuba — A34

1914-15

253	A34	1c green	.80	.25
a.		Booklet pane of 6	100.00	
254	A34	2c car rose	.95	.25
a.		Booklet pane of 6	100.00	
255	A34	2c red ('15)	1.50	.25
a.		Booklet pane of 6	100.00	
256	A34	3c violet	4.75	.35
257	A34	5c blue	6.50	.25
258	A34	8c ol grn	5.25	.70
259	A34	10c brown	9.50	.35
260	A34	10c ol grn ('15)	11.50	.55
261	A34	50c orange	75.00	10.00
262	A34	1p gray	110.00	24.00
		Nos. 253-262 (10)	225.75	36.95
		Set, never hinged	400.00	

Complete set of eight 1914 stamps, imperf. pairs, value $1,500.
Nos. 253, 254, 256 and E5 exist with "1917 GOB./CONSTITUCIONAL/CAMAGUEY" overprint. These were not authorized.

Gertrudis Gómez de Avellaneda, Cuban Poetess (1814-73)
A34a

1914

263	A34a	5c blue	18.00	5.00
		Never hinged	30.00	

José Martí
A35

Máximo Gómez
A36

José de la Luz Caballero
A37

Ignacio Agramonte
A39

Tomás Estrada Palma
A40

José A. Saco — A41

Antonio Maceo — A42

Calixto García
A38

Carlos Manuel de Céspedes — A43

1917-18		**Unwmk.**	**Perf. 12**	
264	A35	1c bl grn	1.00	.25
a.		Booklet pane of 6	40.00	
b.		Booklet pane of 30	250.00	
265	A36	2c rose	1.05	.25
a.		Booklet pane of 6	50.00	
b.		Booklet pane of 30	210.00	

266	A36	2c lt red ('18)	.85	.25
a.		Booklet pane of 6	50.00	
267	A37	3c violet	1.10	.25
a.		Imperf. pair	275.00	
b.		Booklet pane of 6	50.00	
268	A38	5c dp bl	1.05	.25
269	A39	8c red brn	5.50	.25
270	A40	10c yel brn	3.25	.25
271	A41	20c gray grn	18.50	1.60
272	A42	50c dl rose	18.50	.70
273	A43	1p black	19.00	.70
		Nos. 264-273 (10)	69.80	4.75
		Set, never hinged	110.00	

1925-28 Wmk. 106 Perf. 12

274	A35	1c bl grn	1.10	.25
a.		Booklet pane of 6	350.00	
275	A36	2c brt rose	1.20	.25
a.		Booklet pane of 6	75.00	
b.		Booklet pane of 30	350.00	
276	A38	5c dp bl	2.50	.25
277	A39	8c red brn ('28)	5.75	.65
278	A40	10c yel brn ('27)	7.00	.70
279	A41	20c olive grn	11.00	1.10
		Nos. 274-279 (6)	28.55	3.20
		Set, never hinged	50.00	

1926 Imperf.

280	A35	1c blue green	2.75	2.00
281	A36	2c brt rose	2.75	2.00
282	A38	5c deep blue	3.50	2.75
		Nos. 280-282 (3)	9.00	6.75
		Set, never hinged	10.00	

See Nos. 304-310. For overprint and surcharge see Nos. 317-318, 644.

Arms of Republic A44

1927, May 20 Unwmk. Perf. 12

283	A44	25c violet	18.00	3.50
		Never hinged	27.50	

25th anniversary of the Republic.
For surcharges see Nos. 355, C3.

Tomás Estrada Palma A45

Designs: 2c, Gen. Gerardo Machado. 5c, Morro Castle. 8c, Havana Railway Station. 10c, Presidential Palace. 13c, Tobacco Plantation. 20c, Treasury Building. 30c, Sugar Mill. 50c, Havana Cathedral. 1p, Galician Clubhouse, Havana.

1928, Jan. 2 Wmk. 106

284	A45	1c deep green	.60	.30
285	A45	2c brt rose	.60	.30
286	A45	5c deep blue	1.75	.50
287	A45	8c lt red brn	3.75	1.10
288	A45	10c bister brn	1.50	.80
289	A45	13c orange	2.10	.80
290	A45	20c olive grn	2.50	.95
291	A45	30c dk violet	5.25	.75
292	A45	50c carmine rose	8.00	2.75
293	A45	1p gray black	16.00	6.25
		Nos. 284-293 (10)	42.05	14.50
		Set, never hinged	67.50	

Sixth Pan-American Conference.

Capitol, Havana A55

1929, May 18

294	A55	1c green	.50	.35
295	A55	2c carmine rose	.50	.30
296	A55	5c blue	.65	.40
297	A55	10c bister brn	1.35	.50
298	A55	20c violet	4.50	2.75
		Nos. 294-298 (5)	7.50	4.30
		Set, never hinged	12.00	

Opening of the Capitol, Havana.

Hurdler — A56

1930, Mar. 15 Engr.

299	A56	1c green	.95	.45
300	A56	2c carmine	.95	.50
301	A56	5c deep blue	1.25	.50
302	A56	10c bister brn	2.50	.95
303	A56	20c violet	15.00	3.25
		Nos. 299-303 (5)	20.65	5.65
		Set, never hinged	32.50	

2nd Central American Athletic Games.

Types of 1917 Portrait Issue
Flat Plate Printing

1930-45 Wmk. 106 Engr. Perf. 10

304	A35	1c blue green	.80	.25
a.		Booklet pane of 6	50.00	
b.		Booklet pane of 30		
305	A36	2c brt rose	75.00	—
a.		Booklet pane of 6	1,200.	
305B	A37	3c dk rose vio ('42)	4.00	.75
c.		Booklet pane of 6	42.50	
306	A38	5c dk blue	2.75	.25
306A	A39	8c red brn ('45)	2.75	.25
307	A40	10c brown	2.75	.25
a.		10c yellow brown ('35)	3.50	.75
307B	A41	20c olive grn ('41)	4.75	.75
		Nos. 304-307B (7)	92.80	2.50

Nos. 305 and 305B were printed for booklet panes and all examples have straight edges. For surcharge see No. 644.

Rotary Press Printing

308	A35	1c blue grn	1.10	.25
309	A36	2c brt rose	1.10	.25
a.		Booklet pane of 50		
310	A37	3c violet	1.50	.25
a.		3c dull violet ('38)	1.10	.25
b.		3c rose violet ('41)	1.10	.25
c.		Booklet pane of 50		
		Nos. 308-310 (3)	3.70	.75

Flat plate stamps measure 18½x21½mm; rotary press, 19x22mm.

The Mangos of Baragua — A57

War Memorial — A61

Battle of Mal Tiempo A58

Battle of Coliseo A59

Maceo, Gómez and Zayas A60

Wmk. 229

1933, Apr. 23 Photo. Perf. 12½

312	A57	3c dk brown	2.00	.30
313	A58	3c dk blue	1.75	.40
314	A59	10c emerald	3.50	.40

315	A60	13c red	4.00	1.10
316	A61	20c black	7.75	3.00
		Nos. 312-316 (5)	19.00	5.20
		Set, never hinged	29.00	

War of Independence and dedication of the "Soldado Invasor" (the American Army that came to the aid of the revolution against Spain) monument.

Types of 1917 Issues with Carmine or Black Overprint Reading Up or Down

Rotary Press Printing
Wmk. 106

1933, Dec. 23 Engr. Perf. 10

317	A35	1c blue green (C)	1.50	.25

With Additional Surcharge of New Value and Bars

318	A37	2c on 3c vio (Bk)	1.50	.25

Establishment of a revolutionary junta.
Catalogue values for Nos. 317-318 unused are for examples with overprint reading up. Values for overprint reading down, $4.

Dr. Carlos J. Finlay — A62

1934, Dec. 3 Engr. Perf. 10

319	A62	2c dark carmine	1.35	.50
320	A62	5c dark blue	3.75	1.50
		Set, never hinged	8.00	

Cent. of the birth of Dr. Carlos J. Finlay (1833-1915), physician-biologist who found that a mosquito transmitted yellow fever.

Pres. José Miguel Gómez — A63

Gómez Monument A64

1936, May Perf. 10

322	A63	1c green	2.25	.40
323	A64	2c carmine	3.25	.50
		Set, never hinged	8.00	

Unveiling of a monument to Gen. José Miguel Gómez, ex-president.

Matanzas Issue

Map of Cuba A65

2c, Map of Free Zone. 4c, S. S. "Rex" in Matanzas Bay. 5c, Ships in Matanzas Bay. 8c, Caves of Bellamar. 10c, Valley of Yumuri. 20c, Yumuri River. 50c, Ships Leaving Port.

Wmk. 229

1936, May 5 Photo. Perf. 12½

324	A65	1c blue green	.45	.25
325	A65	2c red	.70	.25
326	A65	4c claret	1.20	.25
327	A65	5c ultra	1.75	.25
328	A65	8c orange brn	3.00	.70
329	A65	10c emerald	3.25	.70

330	A65	20c brown	6.25	2.50
331	A65	50c slate	11.50	3.50
		Nos. 324-331,C18-C21,CE1,E8 (14)	55.70	21.85
		Set, never hinged	92.50	

Exist imperf. Value 20% more.

"Peace and Work" A73

Máximo Gómez Monument — A74

Torch — A75

"Independence" — A76

"Messenger of Peace" — A77

1936, Nov. 18 Perf. 12½

332	A73	1c emerald	.75	.25
333	A74	2c crimson	.90	.30
334	A75	4c maroon	1.05	.30
335	A76	5c ultra	4.00	.55
336	A77	8c dk green	6.00	1.20
		Nos. 332-336,C22-C23,E9 (8)	26.55	7.20
		Set, never hinged	48.00	

Maj. Gen. Máximo Gómez, birth centenary. Issued both perf and imperf. Values for imperfs are approx. 400% higher.

Sugar Cane — A78

Primitive Sugar Mill — A79

Modern
Sugar
Mill — A80

Wmk. 106

1937, Oct. 2	**Engr.**	**Perf. 10**	
337 A78	1c yellow green	1.75	.40
338 A79	2c red	1.00	.25
339 A80	5c bright blue	2.25	.40
	Nos. 337-339 (3)	5.00	1.05
	Set, never hinged	8.50	

Cuban sugar cane industry, 400th anniv.

Argentine
Emblem — A81

Mountain Scene
(Bolivia) — A82

Arms of
Brazil — A83

Canadian
Scene — A84

Camilo
Henriquez
(Chile)
A85

Gen, Francisco
de Paula
Santander
(Colombia)
A86

Natl. Monument
(Costa
Rica) — A87

Autograph of
José Marti
(Cuba) — A88

Columbus
Lighthouse
(Dominican
Rep.) — A89

Juan Montalvo
(Ecuador) — A90

Abraham Lincoln
(US)
A91

Quetzal and
Scroll
(Guatemala)
A92

Arms of Haiti
A93

Francisco
Morazán
(Honduras)
A94

Fleet of
Columbus — A95

Wmk. 106

1937, Oct. 13	**Engr.**	**Perf. 10**	
340 A81	1c deep green	.75	.75
341 A82	1c green	.75	.75
342 A83	2c carmine	.75	.75
343 A84	2c carmine	.75	.75
344 A85	3c violet	1.75	1.75
345 A86	3c violet	1.75	1.75
346 A87	4c bister brown	2.10	2.10
347 A88	4c bister brown	3.75	3.75
348 A89	5c blue	1.90	1.90
349 A90	5c blue	1.90	1.90
350 A91	8c citron	7.00	7.00
351 A92	8c citron	3.25	3.25
352 A93	10c maroon	3.25	3.25
353 A94	10c maroon	3.25	3.25
354 A95	25c rose lilac	35.00	35.00
	Nos. 340-354,C24-C29,E10-		
	E11 (23)	132.90	132.90
	Set, never hinged	170.00	

Nos. 340-354 were sold by the Cuban PO
for 3 days, Oct. 13-15, during which no other
stamps were sold. They were postally valid for
the full face value. Proceeds from their three-
day sale above 30,000 pesos were paid by the
Cuban POD to the Assoc. of American Writers
and Artists. Remainders were overprinted
"SVP" (Without Postal Value).

No. 283
Surcharged
in Green

1937, Nov. 19	**Unwmk.**	**Perf. 12**	
355 A44	10c on 25c violet	16.00	4.00
	Never hinged	22.50	

Centenary of Cuban railroads.

Ciboney Indian
and
Cigar — A96

Cigar and
Globe — A97

Tobacco Plant and
Cigars — A98

1939, Aug. 28	**Wmk. 106**	**Perf. 10**	
356 A96	1c yellow green	.75	.25
357 A97	2c red	1.00	.25
358 A98	5c brt ultra	1.75	.30
	Nos. 356-358 (3)	3.50	.80
	Set, never hinged	5.25	

General Calixto García

A99 A100

1939, Nov. 6		**Perf. 10, Imperf.**	
359 A99	2c dark red	.95	.25
360 A100	5c deep blue	1.25	.40
	Set, never hinged	3.50	

Birth centenary of General Garcia.
Values are for perf examples. Value of
imperfs approx. 20% higher.

Gonzalo de
Quesada — A101

1940, Apr. 30	**Engr.**	**Perf. 10**	
361 A101	2c rose red	1.75	.50
	Never hinged	2.75	

Pan American Union, 50th anniversary.

Rotary Club
Emblem, Cuban
Flag and Tobacco
Plant — A102

1940, May 18	**Wmk. 106**	**Perf. 10**	
362 A102	2c rose red	2.75	.75
	Never hinged	4.00	

Rotary Intl. Convention held at Havana.

Lions Emblem,
Cuban Flag and
Royal
Palms — A103

1940, July 23			
363 A103	2c orange vermilion	2.75	.75
	Never hinged	4.00	

Lions International Convention, Havana.

Dr.
Nicolás J.
Gutiérrez
A104

1940, Oct. 28

364 A104	2c orange ver	1.90	.30
365 A104	5c blue	2.50	.30
a.	Sheet of four, imperf., unwmkd.	8.50	3.00
	Never hinged	12.00	
b.	As "a," black overprint ('51)	11.00	4.75
	Never hinged	17.00	
	Set, never hinged	5.50	

100th anniv. of the publication of the 1st
Cuban Medical Review, "El Repertorio Medico
Habanero."

No. 365a contains 2 each of Nos. 364-365
imperf. and sold for 25c.

For overprint see No. C43A.

In 1951 No. 365a was overprinted in black:
"50 Aniversario Descubrimiento Agente Trans-
misor de la Flebre Amarilla por el Dr. Carlos J.
Finlay Honor a los Martires de la Ciencia 1901
1951." The overprint is illustrated over No.
C43A, but does not include the plane and
"Correo Aereo."

Major General
Guillermo
Moncada — A105

Moncada
Riding into
Battle
A106

1941, June 25

366 A105	3c dk brown, *buff*	1.75	.50
367 A106	5c bright blue	1.75	.50
	Set, never hinged	5.50	

Maj. Gen. Guillermo Moncada (1841-96).

Globe Showing
Western
Hemisphere
A107

Maceo,
Bolívar,
Juárez,
Lincoln
and Arms
of Cuba
A108

"Labor: Wealth of
America" — A109

Tree of
Fraternity,
Havana
A110

Statue of
Liberty — A111

Perf. 10, Imperf.

1942, Feb. 23		**Wmk. 106**	
368 A107	1c emerald	.45	.25
369 A108	3c orange brown	.70	.25
370 A109	5c blue	1.20	.25
371 A110	10c red violet	3.00	1.00
372 A111	13c red	2.10	.65
	Nos. 368-372 (5)	7.45	2.40
	Set, never hinged	11.00	

Spirit of Democracy in the Americas.

The imperforate varieties are without gum. Value, set mint $10, used $5.

Ignacio Agramonte Loynaz — A112

Rescue of Sanguily by Agramonte A113

1942, Apr. 10   **Perf. 10**
373 A112 3c bister brn   1.35 .50
374 A113 5c brt blue, *bluish*   2.75 1.00
    Set, never hinged   6.25
    100th anniv. of the birth of Ignacio Agramonte Loynaz, patriot.

"Unmask the Fifth Columnists" — A114

"Be Careful, The Fifth Column is Spying on You" — A115

"Destroy it. The Fifth Column is like a Serpent" — A116

"Fulfill your Patriotic Duty by Destroying the Fifth Column" — A117

"Don't be Afraid of the Fifth Column. Attack it" — A118

1943, July 5
375 A114 1c dk blue grn   .50 .30
376 A115 3c red   .85 .30
377 A116 5c brt blue   .85 .30
378 A117 10c dull brown   3.00 .70
379 A118 13c dull rose vio   4.25 1.50
    Nos. 375-379 (5)   9.45 3.10
    Set, never hinged   13.50

General Eloy Alfaro and Flags of Cuba and Ecuador A119

1943, Sept. 20
380 A119 3c green   2.50 .30
    Never hinged   3.00
    General Eloy Alfaro of Ecuador, 100th birth anniv.

Retirement Security A120

1943, Nov. 8   **Wmk. 106**   **Perf. 10**
381 A120 1c yellow green   .65 .30
382 A120 3c vermilion   .65 .30
383 A120 5c bright blue   1.00 .40

1944, Mar. 18
384 A120 1c bright yel grn   1.40 .40
385 A120 3c salmon   1.40 .40
386 A120 5c light blue   3.00 1.10
    Nos. 381-386 (6)   8.10 2.90
    Set, never hinged   12.00
    Half the proceeds from the sale of Nos. 381-386 were used for the Communications Ministry Employees' Retirement Fund.

Portrait of Columbus — A121

Bartolomé de Las Casas — A122

First Statue of Columbus at Cárdenas — A123

Discovery of Tobacco A124

Columbus Sights Land A125

1944, May 19
387 A121 1c dk yellow grn   .35 .25
   a.   Pair, imperf horiz.   150.00
388 A122 3c brown   .55 .25
389 A123 5c brt blue   1.00 .25
390 A124 10c dark violet   3.00 .75
391 A125 13c dark red   5.00 1.75
    Nos. 387-391,C36-C37 (7)   13.50 4.40
    Set, never hinged   27.50
    450th anniv. of the discovery of America.

Major General Carlos Roloff — A126

1944, Aug. 21
392 A126 3c violet   1.35 .30
    Never hinged   2.50
    Maj. Gen. Carlos Roloff, 100th birth anniv.

Americas Map and 1st Brazilian Postage Stamps — A127

1944, Dec. 20   **Engr.**
393 A127 3c brown orange   3.00 .75
    Never hinged   4.50
    Cent. of the 1st postage stamps of the Americas, issued by Brazil in 1843.

Seal of the Society — A128

Luis de las Casas and Luis Maria Penalyer A129

1945, Oct. 5   **Wmk. 106**   **Perf. 10**
394 A128 1c yellow green   .50 .25
395 A129 2c scarlet   1.25 .25
    Set, never hinged   2.75
    Sesquicentenary of the founding of the Economic Society of Friends of the Country.

Aged Couple A130

1945, Dec. 27
396 A130 1c dk yellow grn   .25 .25
397 A130 2c scarlet   .40 .25
398 A130 5c cobalt blue   .90 .25

1946, Mar. 26
399 A130 1c brt yellow grn   .75 .25
400 A130 2c salmon pink   .45 .25
401 A130 5c light blue   .75 .25
    Nos. 396-401 (6)   3.50 1.50
    Set, never hinged   5.00
    See note after No. 386.

> Catalogue values for unused stamps in this section, from this point to the end of the section, are for Never Hinged items.

Gabriel de la Concepcion Valdés Plácido A131

1946, Feb. 5
402 A131 2c scarlet   1.25 .30
    Cent. of the death of the poet Gabriel de la Concepcion Valdés.

Manuel Marquez Sterling — A132

1946, Apr. 30
403 A132 2c scarlet   3.50 .30
    Founding of the Manuel Marquez Sterling Professional School of Journalism, 3th anniv.

Globe and Cross — A133

1946, July 4   **Engr.**
404 A133 2c scarlet, *pink*   1.25 .25
    80th anniv. of the Intl. Red Cross.

Cow and Milkmaid — A134

1947, Feb. 20   **Wmk. 106**   **Perf. 10**
405 A134 2c scarlet   3.50 .40
    1947 National Livestock Exposition.

Franklin D. Roosevelt — A135

1947, Apr. 12
406 A135 2c vermilion   3.50 .40
2nd anniv. of the death of Franklin D. Roosevelt.

Antonio Oms Sarret and Aged Couple A136

1947, Oct. 20
407 A136 1c dp yellow grn   .50 .30
408 A136 2c scarlet   .50 .30
409 A136 5c lt blue   1.00 .55
   Nos. 407-409 (3)   2.00 1.15
See note after No. 386.

Marta Abreu Arenabio de Estevez — A137   "Charity" — A138

Marta Abreu Monument, Santa Clara A139   "Patriotism" A140

1947, Nov. 29
410 A137 1c dp yellow grn   .70 .30
411 A138 2c scarlet   1.25 .30
412 A139 5c brt blue   2.50 .40
413 A140 10c dk violet   4.50 1.00
   Nos. 410-413 (4)   8.95 2.00
Birth cent. of Marta Abreu Arenabio de Estevez, philanthropist and humanitarian.

Armauer Hansen A141

1948, Apr. 9
414 A141 2c rose carmine   2.50 .40
International Leprosy Congress, Havana.

Mother and Child A142

1948, Oct. 15   **Engr.**
415 A142 1c yellow grn   .40 .25
416 A142 2c scarlet   .50 .25
417 A142 5c brt blue   1.20 .40
   Nos. 415-417 (3)   2.10 .90
See note after No. 386.

Death of José Martí — A143

Martí Rowing to Shore — A144

1948, Nov. 10   **Wmk. 106**   **Perf. 10**
418 A143 2c scarlet   .85 .25
419 A144 5c brt blue   2.50 .45
50th anniversary of the death of José Martí, patriot (in 1945).

Tobacco Picking — A145   Liberty Carrying Flag and Cigars — A146

Cigar and Arms of Cuba — A147

1948, Dec. 6   **Size: 22½x26mm**
420 A145 1c green   .35 .25
421 A146 2c rose car   .50 .30
422 A147 5c brt blue   1.00 .30
   Nos. 420-422 (3)   1.85 .85
Cuba's tobacco industry. See Nos. 445-447. For overprints and surcharge see Nos. 448-451, 512.

Equestrian Statue of Gen. Antonio Maceo — A148

Sword Salute to Maceo A149

Designs: 2c, Portrait of Maceo. 5c, Mausoleum, El Cacahual. 10c, East to West invasion. 20c, Battle of Peralejo. 50c, Declaration of Baragua. 1p, Death of Maceo at San Pedro.

1948, Dec. 15   **Wmk. 229**   **Perf. 12½**
423 A148 1c blue green   .40 .25
424 A148 2c red   .45 .25
425 A148 5c blue   .60 .25
426 A149 8c black & brown   1.10 .40
427 A149 10c brown & bl grn   1.10 .25

428 A149 20c blue & car   4.50 1.10
429 A149 50c car & ultra   7.25 2.75
430 A149 1p black & violet   16.00 4.25
   Nos. 423-430 (8)   31.40 9.50
Birth cent. (in 1945) of Maceo.

Symbol of Pharmacy A150

1948, Dec. 28   **Perf. 10**
431 A150 2c rose carmine   1.75 .40
1st Pan-American Congress of Pharmacy, Havana, Dec. 1948.

Morro Lighthouse — A151

1949, Jan. 17   **Wmk. 229**   **Perf. 12½**
432 A151 2c carmine   2.50 .40
Centenary (in 1944) of the erection of the Morro Lighthouse.

Jagua Castle, Cienfuegos A152

1949, Jan. 27   **Wmk. 106**   **Perf. 10**
433 A152 1c yellow green   1.00 .30
434 A152 2c rose red   2.00 .30
200th anniv. of the construction of Jagua Castle and the cent. of the publication of the 1st newspaper in Cienfuegos.

Manuel Sanguily y Garritt — A153

1949, Mar. 31
435 A153 2c rose red   1.00 .30
436 A153 5c blue   2.50 .30
Manuel Sanguily y Garritt (1848-1925), cabinet member, editor, author.

Map of Isle of Pines — A154

1949, Apr. 26
437 A154 5c blue   3.00 .75
20th anniv. of the recognition of Cuban ownership of the Isle of Pines.

Ismael Cespedes — A155

1949, Sept. 28
438 A155 1c yellow green   .60 .30
439 A155 2c scarlet   .60 .30
440 A155 5c brt blue   1.25 .30
   Nos. 438-440 (3)   2.45 .90
See note after No. 386.

Gen. Enrique Collazo — A156

1950, Feb. 28   **Engr.**   **Perf. 10**
441 A156 2c scarlet   .90 .25
442 A156 5c brt blue   2.50 .45
Centenary (in 1948) of the birth of General Enrique Collazo.

Enrique José Varona — A157

1950, Feb. 28
443 A157 2c scarlet   .90 .25
444 A157 5c brt blue   2.50 .25
Centenary of the birth of Enrique José Varona, writer and patriot.

Tobacco Types of 1948
1950, June 20   **Re-engraved**
   Size: 21x25mm
445 A145 1c green   1.25 .30
446 A146 2c rose red   1.25 .30
447 A147 5c blue   2.00 .30
   Nos. 445-447 (3)   4.50 .90
The re-engraved stamps show slight differences in many minor details.
For overprints and surcharge see Nos. 448-451, 512.

No. 446 Overprinted in Black

1950, Apr. 27
448 A146 2c rose red   2.25 .30
Natl. Bank of Cuba opening, Apr. 27, 1950.

Re-engraved Tobacco Types of 1950 Overprinted in Carmine

1950, May 18

449	A145	1c yellow green	.50 .30
450	A146	2c lilac rose	.75 .30
451	A147	5c light blue	2.25 .30
		Nos. 449-451 (3)	3.50 .90

75th anniv. (in 1949) of the UPU.
No. 451 exists with surcharge inverted.

Manuel Balanzategui, Antonio L. Pausa and Train Wreck A158

1950, Sept. 21   **Engr.**

452	A158	1c yellow grn	1.50 .75
453	A158	2c scarlet	1.50 .75
454	A158	5c brt blue	4.25 1.25
		Nos. 452-454 (3)	7.25 2.75

Fernando Figueredo — A159

1951, Mar. 17   **Wmk. 106**   *Perf. 10*

455	A159	1c green	1.40 .25
456	A159	2c scarlet	1.40 .25
457	A159	5c brt blue	2.25 .25
		Nos. 455-457 (3)	5.05 .75

Three-fourths of the proceeds from the sale of these stamps were used for the Communication Ministry Employees' Retirement Fund. See Nos. 474, C51-C56, E15. For surcharges see Nos. 474, C51-C56, E15.

Miguel Teurbe Tolón and Flag — A160

Narciso Lopez — A161

Emilia Teurbe Tolón Sewing Flag — A162

Cuban Flag — A163

Engraved and Lithographed

1951, July 3   **Wmk. 229**   *Perf. 13*

458	A160	1c Prus grn, ultra & red	.75 .30
459	A161	2c red & gray blk	1.00 .30
460	A162	5c ultra & red	3.00 .45
461	A163	10c rose vio, bl & red	5.00 .60
		Nos. 458-461,C41-C43,E13 (8)	31.25 5.40

Centenary of adoption of Cuba's flag.

Clara Louise Maass and Hospitals A164

Hospitals: Lutheran Memorial, Newark, N.J. and Las Animas, Havana.

Wmk. 106

1951, Aug. 24   **Engr.**   *Perf. 10*

462	A164	2c scarlet	3.00 .50

75th anniv. of the birth of Clara Louise Maass, (1876-1901), American nurse and martyr in yellow fever fight.

Airmail Type and

José Raul Capablanca — A165

Capablanca Club, Havana A166

Wmk. 229

1951, Nov. 1   **Photo.**   *Perf. 13*

463	A165	1c blue grn & org	6.25 .65
464	AP27	2c rose car & dk brn	8.00 1.25
465	A166	5c black & dp ultra	16.00 1.90
		Nos. 463-465,C44-C46,E14 (7)	95.25 13.60

Jose Raul Capablanca, World Chess titlist (1921). Value imperf., set of 7 pairs, $1,500.

Antonio Guiteras Holmes — A167

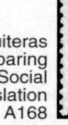

Guiteras Preparing Social Legislation A168

Fort of the Morrillo A169

Wmk. 106

1951, Oct. 22   **Engr.**   *Perf. 10*

466	A167	1c yellow green	.45 .25
467	A168	2c rose carmine	.75 .25
468	A169	5c deep blue	1.50 .40
		Nos. 466-468,C47-C49 (6)	19.20 4.60

16th anniv. of the Action of the Morrillo and to honor Antonio Guiteras Holmes, who was killed there.
Souvenir sheets containing stamps similar to Nos. 466-468, but in different colors, are listed as Nos. C49a-C49b.

Poinsettia — A170

1951, Dec. 1   **Engr. and Typo.**

469	A170	1c green & car	5.00 .25
470	A170	2c rose car & grn	5.50 .50
		See Nos. 498-499.	

Maj. Gen. José Maceo — A171

1952, Feb. 6   **Engr.**

471	A171	2c yellow brown	.75 .25
472	A171	5c indigo	1.50 .25

Birth centenary of Maceo.

Isabella I — A172

1952, Feb. 22

473	A172	2c bright red	2.25 .50

500th anniv. of the birth of Queen Isabella I of Spain.
Souvenir sheets containing 2c stamps of type A172 are listed as Nos. C50a-C50b.

Type of 1951 Surcharged in Green

1952, Mar. 18

474	A159	10c on 2c yel brn	2.75 .40

Receipt of Autonomy A173

Designs: 2c, Tomas Estrada Palma and Luis Estevez Romero. 5c, Barnet, Finlay, Guiteras and Nuñez. 8c, Capitol. 20c, Map, Central Highway. 50c, Sugar Mill.

Centers in Black

Wmk. 106

1952, May 27   **Engr.**   *Perf. 12½*

475	A173	1c dk green	.35 .25
476	A173	2c dk carmine	.40 .25
477	A173	5c dk blue	.60 .25
478	A173	8c dk brown car	.95 .25
479	A173	20c dk olive grn	2.40 .40
480	A173	50c dp orange	4.75 .80
		Nos. 475-480,C57-C60,E16 (11)	21.65 4.75

50th anniv. of the Republic of Cuba.

Hands Holding Coffee Beans A174

Designs: 2c, Map and man picking coffee beans. 5c, Farmer with pan of beans.

1952, Aug. 22   **Wmk. 229**   *Perf. 13½*

481	A174	1c green	.70 .25
482	A174	2c rose red	1.70 .30
483	A174	5c dk vio bl & aqua	2.50 .40
		Nos. 481-483 (3)	4.90 .95

Bicentenary of coffee cultivation.

Col. Charles Hernandez y Sandrino — A175

1952, Oct. 7   **Wmk. 106**   *Perf. 10*

484	A175	1c yellow grn	.30 .30
485	A175	2c scarlet	.55 .30
486	A175	5c blue	.65 .30
487	A175	8c black	1.90 .45

488	A175	10c brown red	1.90 .45
489	A175	20c brown	9.00 3.75
		Nos. 484-489,C63-C72,E17 (17)	63.95 25.15

See note after No. 457.

Alonso Alvarez de la Campa — A176

Portraits: 2c, Carlos A. Latorre. 3c, Anacleto Bermudez. 5c, Eladio G. Toledo. 8c, Angel Laborde. 10c, Jose M. Medina. 13c, Pascual Rodriguez. 20c, Carlos Verdugo.

Frame Engraved; Center in Black

1952, Nov. 27

490	A176	1c green	.50 .25
491	A176	2c carmine	.75 .25
492	A176	3c purple	.90 .25
493	A176	5c blue	.90 .60
494	A176	8c bister brn	2.00 .50
495	A176	10c orange brn	1.50 .50
496	A176	13c lilac rose	3.00 .75
497	A176	20c olive grn	4.50 1.25
		Nos. 490-497,C73-C74 (10)	23.30 6.15

Execution of 8 medical students, 81st anniv.

Christmas Type of 1951

Centers: Tree.

Frame Engr.; Center Typo.

1952, Dec. 1   Dated "1952-1953"

498	A170	1c yel grn & car	7.25 1.75
499	A170	3c vio & dk grn	7.25 1.75

Birthplace of José Martí — A177

Marti at St. Lazarus Quarry — A178

No. 501, Court martial. No. 502, Martiano house, Havana. No. 504, El Abra ranch, Isle of Pines. No. 505, Symbols, "Marti the Poet." No. 506, Marti and Bolivar statue, Caracas. No. 507, At desk in New York. No. 508, House where revolutionary party was formed. No. 509, 1st issue of "Patria."

1953   *Perf. 10*

500	A177	1c dk grn & red brn	.50 .25
501	A177	1c dk grn & red brn	.50 .25
502	A177	3c purple & brn	.55 .25
503	A178	3c purple & brn	.55 .25
504	A177	5c dp bl & dk brn	1.00 .25
505	A178	5c ultra & brn	1.00 .25
506	A178	10c red brn & blk	2.00 .40
507	A178	10c dk brn & blk	2.00 .40
508	A178	13c dk ol grn & dk brn	3.25 .80
509	A177	13c dk ol grn & brn	3.25 1.00
		Nos. 500-509,C79-C89 (21)	38.75 13.40

Centenary of birth of José Marti.

Rafael Montoro Valdez — A179

1953, Mar. 5

510	A179	3c dark violet	2.10 .30

Rafael Montoro Valdez, statesman, birth cent.

Francisco Carrera Justiz — A180

1953, Mar. 9
511 A180 3c rose red   2.10 .30
Francisco Carrera Justiz, educator, statesman.

No. 446 Surcharged with New Value
1953, June 16
512 A146 3c on 2c rose red   1.50 .25

Board of Accounts Bldg., Havana — A181

1953, Nov. 3   **Engr.**
513 A181 3c blue   1.35 .45
     Nos. 513,C90-C91 (3)   7.60 2.25
1st Intl. Cong. of Boards of Accounts, Havana, Nov. 2-9.

Miguel Coyula Llaguno — A182

Communications Assoc. Flag — A183

Designs: 3c, 8c, Enrique Calleja Hensell. 10c, Antonio Ginard Rojas.

1954   **Dated 1953**
514 A182 1c green   .30 .25
515 A182 3c rose red   .30 .25
516 A183 5c blue   1.40 .25
517 A182 8c brn car   2.25 .40
518 A182 10c brown   3.50 .65
     Nos. 514-518,C92-C95,E19 (10) 25.35 8.25
Nos. 515 and 517 show the same portrait, but inscriptions are arranged differently. See note after No. 457.

Carlos J. Finlay — A184   Maximo Gomez — A184a

Portraits: 1c, José Marti. 3c, José de la Luz Caballero. 4c, Miguel Aldama. 5c, Calixto Garcia. 8c, Ignacio Agramonte. 10c, Tomas Estrada Palma. 14, Serafin Sanchez. 20c, José Antonio Saco. 50c, Antonio Maceo. 1p, Carlos Manuel de Cespedes.

1954-56   **Wmk. 106**   **Perf. 10**
519 A184 1c green   .45 .25
520 A184a 2c rose car   .45 .25
521 A184 3c violet   .45 .25
521A A184 4c red lil ('56)   .50 .25
522 A184a 5c slate bl   .60 .25
523 A184a 8c car lake   .90 .25
524 A184 10c sepia   .90 .25
525 A184a 13c org red   .75 .25
525A A184a 14c gray ('56)   1.25 .25
526 A184 20c olive   2.50 .25
527 A184a 50c org yel   3.50 .45
528 A184a 1p orange   7.00 .45
     Nos. 519-528 (12)   19.25 3.40
See Nos. 674-680. For surcharges see Nos. 636, 641-643.

Maj. Gen. José M. Rodriguez — A185

Design: 5c, Gen. Rodriguez on horseback.

1954, June 8   **Engr.**   **Perf. 12½**
     Center in Dark Brown
529 A185 2c dark carmine   .90 .25
530 A185 5c deep blue   2.40 .40
Cent. of the birth of Maj. Gen. José Maria Rodriguez (in 1851).

Gen. Batísta Sanatorium — A186

1954, Sept. 21   **Wmk. 106**   **Perf. 10**
531 A186 3c deep blue   1.50 .25
See No. C107.

Santa Claus — A187

1954, Dec. 15
532 A187 2c dk grn & car   7.25 1.25
533 A187 4c car & dk grn   7.25 1.25
Christmas 1954.

Maria Luisa Dolz — A188

1954, Dec. 23
534 A188 4c deep blue   1.75 .30
Cent. of the birth of Maria Luisa Dolz, educator and defender of women's rights. See No. C108.

Cuban Flag and Scouts Saluting A189

1954, Dec. 27   **Perf. 12½**
535 A189 4c dark green   2.25 .30
Issued to publicize the national patrol encampment of the Boy Scouts of Cuba.

Rotary Emblem and Paul P. Harris — A190

1955, Feb. 23   **Engr.**   **Wmk. 106**
536 A190 4c blue   2.75 .25
Rotary International, 50th anniversary. See No. C109.

Maj. Gen. Francisco Carrillo — A191

Portrait: 5c, Gen. Carrillo standing.

1955, Mar. 8   **Perf. 10**
537 A191 2c brt red & dk bl   .75 .25
538 A191 5c dk bl & dk brn   1.50 .30
Cent. of the birth of Maj. Gen. Francisco Carrillo (1851-1926).

Stamp of 1885 and Convent of San Francisco — A192

Designs (including 1855 stamp): 4c, Volanta carriage. 10c, Havana, 19th century. 14c, Captain general's residence.

1955, Apr.   **Perf. 12½**
539 A192 2c lil rose & dk grnsh bl   .95 .25
540 A192 4c ocher & dk grn   1.25 .30
541 A192 10c ultra & dk red   3.00 .85
542 A192 14c grn & dp org   7.00 2.00
     Nos. 539-542,C110-C113 (8) 20.55 6.65
Cent. of Cuba's 1st postage stamps.

Maj. Gen. Mario G. Menocal A193   Gen. Emilio Nuñez A194

Portraits: 10c, J. G. Gomez. 14c, A. Sanchez de Bustamante.

1955, June 22
543 A193 2c dark green   .65 .25
544 A194 4c lilac rose   .80 .25
545 A193 10c deep blue   1.50 .40
546 A194 14c gray violet   3.00 .90
     Nos. 543-546,C114-C116,E20 (8) 18.95 6.05
See note after No. 457.

Turkey — A195

1955, Dec. 15   **Engr.**
547 A195 2c slate grn & dk car   6.75 1.50
548 A195 4c rose lake & brt grn   6.75 1.50
Christmas 1955.

Gen. Emilio Nuñez — A196

1955, Dec. 27
549 A196 4c claret   1.75 .45
     Nos. 549,C127-C128 (3)   7.00 1.90
Cent. of the birth of Gen. Emilio Nunez, Cuban revolutionary hero.

Francisco Cajigal de la Vega (1695-1777) A197

1956, Mar. 27   **Perf. 12½**
552 A197 4c rose brn & slate bl 2.00 .55
Cuban post bicent. See No. C129.

Julian del Casal — A198

Portraits: 4c, Luisa Perez de Zambrana. 10c, Juan Clemente Zenea. 14c, José Joaquin Palma.

1956, May 2   **Portraits in Black**
553 A198 2c green   .50 .25
554 A198 4c rose lilac   .50 .25
555 A198 10c blue   1.75 .25
556 A198 14c violet   3.25 .25
     Nos. 553-556,C131-C133,E21 (8) 16.75 3.75
See note after No. 457.

Victor Muñoz — A199

1956, May 13
557 A199 4c brown & green   1.50 .55
Victor Munoz (1873-1922), founder of Mother's Day in Cuba. See No. C134.

Masonic Temple, Havana — A200

1956, June 5
558 A200 4c blue   1.50 .55
See No. C135.

Virgin of Charity, El Cobre — A201

1956, Sept. 8   **Perf. 12½**
559 A201 4c brt blue & yel   1.25 .30
Issued in honor of Our Lady of Charity of Cobre, patroness of Cuba. See No. C149.

"The Cry of Yara" — A202

1956, Oct. 10
560 A202 4c dk grn & brn 1.40 .30
Cuba's independence from Spain.

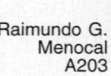

Raimundo G. Menocal A203

1956, Dec. 3 Wmk. 106 Perf. 12½
561 A203 4c dark brown 1.25 .30
Cent. of the birth of Prof. Raimundo G. Menocal, physician.

The Three Wise Men — A204

1956, Dec. 1
562 A204 2c red & slate grn 6.50 1.25
563 A204 4c slate grn & red 6.50 1.25
Christmas 1956.

Martin Morua Delgado — A205

1957, Jan. 30
564 A205 4c dark green 1.00 .30
Delgado, patriot, birth cent.

Boy Scouts at Campfire — A206

1957, Feb. 22 Wmk. 106 Perf. 12½
565 A206 4c slate grn & red 1.50 .40
Cent. of the birth of Lord Baden-Powell, founder of the Boy Scouts. See No. C152.

"The Blind," by M. Vega A207

Paintings: 4c, "The Art Critics" by M. Melero. 10c, "Volanta in Storm" by A. Menocal. 14c, "The Convalescent" by L. Romañach.

1957, Mar. Engr. Perf. 12½
Side and Lower Inscriptions in Dark Brown
566 A207 2c olive green .50 .25
567 A207 4c orange red .90 .30
568 A207 10c olive green 1.25 .50
569 A207 14c ultra 1.50 .55
Nos. 566-569,C153-C155,E22 (8) 14.40 4.30
See note after No. 457.

Emblem of Philatelic Club of Cuba — A208

1957, Apr. 24
570 A208 4c ocher, blue & red 2.00 .30
Issued for Stamp Day, Apr. 24, and the National Philatelic Exhibition. See No. C156.

Juan F. Steegers — A209

1957, Apr. 30
571 A209 4c blue 1.40 .30
Juan Francisco Steegers y Perera (1856-1921), dactyloscopy pioneer. See No. C157.

Victoria Bru Sanchez — A210

1957, June 3 Wmk. 106 Perf. 12½
572 A210 4c indigo 1.75 .30

Joaquin de Aguero in Battle of Jucaral — A211

1957, July 4
573 A211 4c dark green 1.60 .30
Issued to honor Joaquin de Aguero, Cuban freedom fighter and patriot. See No. C162.

Boy, Dogs and Cat — A212

1957, July 17
574 A212 4c Prus green 2.00 .55
Mrs. Jeanette Ryder, founder of the Humane Society of Cuba. See Nos. C163-C163a.

Col. Rafael Manduley del Rio — A213

1957, July 31
575 A213 4c Prus green 2.75 1.50
Issued to honor Col. Manduley del Rio, patriot, on the cent. of his birth (in 1856).

Palace of Justice A214

1957, Sept. 2 Engr. Perf. 12½
576 A214 4c blue gray 1.25 .40
Opening of the new Palace of Justice in Havana. See No. C165.

Generals of the Liberation — A215

1957, Sept. 26
577 A215 4c dl grn & red brn 1.00 .30
578 A215 4c dl bl & red brn 1.00 .30
579 A215 4c rose & brown 1.00 .30
580 A215 4c org yel & brn 1.00 .30
581 A215 4c lt violet & brn 1.00 .30
Nos. 577-581 (5) 5.00 1.50
Generals of the army of liberation.

1st Publication Printed in Cuba — A216

1957, Oct. 18 Wmk. 106 Perf. 12½
582 A216 4c slate blue 1.00 .40
Nos. 582,C167-C168 (3) 3.75 1.15
José Marti National Library.

Patio — A217

1957, Nov. 19
583 A217 4c red brn & grn 1.00 .40
Nos. 583,C173-C174 (3) 6.00 1.40
Cent. of the 1st Cuban Normal School.

Trinidad, Founded 1514 — A218

Fortifications, Havana, 1611 — A219

Views: 10c, Padre Pico street, Santiago de Cuba. 14c, Church of Our Lady, Camaguey.

1957, Dec. 17 Engr. Perf. 12½
584 A218 2c brown & indigo .30 .25
585 A219 4c slate grn & brn .70 .25
586 A219 10c sepia & red 1.60 .30
587 A219 14c green & dk red 2.40 .25
Nos. 584-587,C175-C177,E23 (8) 13.80 3.50
See note after No. 457.

Nativity — A220

1957, Dec. 20
588 A220 2c multicolored 4.50 .90
589 A220 4c multicolored 4.50 .90
Christmas 1957.

Dayton Hedges and Ariguanabo Textile Factory A221

1958, Jan. 30 Wmk. 106 Perf. 12½
590 A221 4c blue .65 .75
Issued to honor Dayton Hedges, founder of Cuba's textile industry. See No. C178.

Dr. Francisco Dominguez Roldan — A222

1958, Feb. 21
591 A222 4c green 1.25 .30
Roldan (1864-1942), who introduced radiotherapy and physiotherapy to Cuba.

José Ignacio Rivero y Alonso — A223

1958, Apr. 1
592 A223 4c lt olive green 1.25 .70
José Ignacio Rivero y Alonso, editor of Diario de la Marina, 1919-44. See No. C179.

Map of Cuba and Mail Route, 1756 A224

1958, Apr. 24 Perf. 12½
593 A224 4c dk grn, aqua & buff 1.00 .30
Issued for Stamp Day, Apr. 24 and the National Philatelic Exhibition. See No. C180.

Maj. Gen. José Miguel Gomez — A225

1958, June 6   Wmk. 106   Perf. 12½
594 A225 4c slate   1.00   .40
Maj. Gen. José Miguel Gomez, President of Cuba, 1909-13. See No. C181.

Nicolas Ruiz Espadero — A226

Musicians: 4c, Ignacio Cervantes. 10c, José White. 14c, Brindis de Salas.

1958, June 27   Perf. 12½
Indigo Emblem
595 A226 2c brown   .60   .25
596 A226 4c dark gray   .60   .25
597 A226 10c olive green   .80   .25
598 A226 14c red   1.10   .25
Green Emblem
Physicians: 2c, Tomas Romay Chacon. 4c, Angel Arturo Aballi. 10c, Fernando Gonzalez del Valle. 14c, Vicente Antonio de Castro.
599 A226 2c brown   .70   .25
600 A226 4c gray   1.10   .25
601 A226 10c dark carmine   .80   .25
602 A226 14c dark blue   1.10   .25
Red Emblem
Lawyers: 2c, Jose Maria Garcia Montes. 4c, Jose A. Gonzalez Lanuza. 10c, Juan B. Hernandez Barreiro. 14c, Pedro Gonzalez Llorente.
603 A226 2c sepia   .50   .25
604 A226 4c gray   .80   .25
605 A226 10c olive grn   1.00   .25
606 A226 14c slate blue   1.10   .25
Nos. 595-606 (12)   10.20 3.00
For surcharges see Nos. 629-631.

Carlos de la Torre — A227

1958, Aug. 29   Engr.   Wmk. 321
607 A227 4c violet blue   1.50   .40
Nos. 607,C182-C184 (4)   26.00 5.50
Dr. Carlos de la Torre y Huerta (1858-1950), naturalist. For surcharge see No. 632.

Poey's "Memorias" Title Page — A228

Felipe Poey — A229

1958, Sept. 26   Wmk. 106
608 A228 2c black & lt violet   .80   .25
609 A229 4c brown black   .95   .25
Nos. 608-609,C185-C191,E26-E27 (11)   91.00 22.60
Felipe Poey (1799-1891), naturalist.

Theodore Roosevelt — A230

1958, Oct. 27   Perf. 12½
610 A230 4c gray green   1.25   .40
Theodore Roosevelt, birth cent. See No. C192.

Cattleyopsis Lindenii Orchid — A231

4c, Oncidium Guibertianum Orchid.

Engraved and Photogravure
1958, Dec. 16   Wmk. 321   Perf. 12½
611 A231 2c multicolored   5.50 1.25
612 A231 4c multicolored   5.50 1.25
Christmas. For surcharge see No. 633.

Flag and Revolutionary A232

Engr. & Typo.
1959, Jan. 28   Wmk. 321
613 A232 2c car rose & gray   .75   .30
Day of Liberation, Jan. 1, 1959.

Gen. Adolfo Flor Crombet (1848-95) — A233

1959, Mar. 18   Engr.   Wmk. 106
614 A233 4c slate green   1.10   .40
For surcharge see No. 634.

Maria Teresa Garcia Montes — A234

1959, Nov. 11   Perf. 12½
615 A234 4c brown   1.10   .40
Maria Teresa Garcia Montes (1880-1930), founder of the Musical Arts Society. See No. C198. For surcharge see No. 635.

Carlos Manuel de Cespedes — A235

Presidents: No. 617, Salvador Cisneros Betancourt. No. 618, Manuel de Jesus Calvar. No. 619, Bartolomé Maso. No. 620, Juan B. Spotorno. No. 621, Tomas Estrada Palma. No. 622, Francisco Javier de Céspedes. No. 623, Vicente Garcia.

1959, Oct. 10   Wmk. 106   Perf. 12½
616 A235 2c slate blue   .55   .25
617 A235 2c green   .55   .25
618 A235 2c deep violet   .55   .25
619 A235 2c orange brown   .55   .25
620 A235 4c dark carmine   .70   .25
621 A235 4c deep brown   .70   .25
622 A235 4c dark gray   .70   .25
623 A235 4c dark violet   .70   .25
Nos. 616-623 (8)   5.00 2.00
Issued to honor former Cuban presidents.

No. B3 Surcharged in Red

1960
624 SP2 2c on 2c + 1c car & ultra   1.00   .25
See No. C199.

Rebel Attack on Moncada Barracks A236

Designs: 2c, Rebels disembarking from "Granma." 10c, Battle of the Uvero. 12c, Map of Cuba and rebel ("The Invasion").

1960, Jan. 28   Wmk. 320
625 A236 1c gray ol, bl & ver   .25   .25
626 A236 2c bl, gray ol & brn   .70   .25
627 A236 10c bl, gray ol & red   1.75   .65
628 A236 12c brt bl, brn & grn   2.40   .30
Nos. 625-628,C200-C202 (7)   17.10 3.85
First anniversary of revolution.

Stamps of 1956-59 Surcharged with New Value in Carmine or Silver
1960, Feb. 3
629 A226 1c on 4c dk gray & ind   .50   .25
630 A226 1c on 4c gray & grn   .50   .25
631 A226 1c on 4c gray & red   .50   .25
632 A227 1c on 4c violet bl   .50   .25
633 A231 1c on 4c multi (S)   .60   .50
634 A233 1c on 4c slate grn   .50   .25
635 A234 1c on 4c brown   .50   .25
636 A184a 2c on 14c gray   .90   .25
Nos. 629-636,C203-C204 (10)   8.00 3.55

Tomas Estrada Palma Statue, Havana — A237

Statues: 2c, Mambi Victorioso (Battle of San Juan Hill), Santiago de Cuba. 10c, Marta Abreo de Estevez. 12c, Ignacio Agramonte, Camaguey.

Wmk. 321
1960, Mar. 28   Engr.   Perf. 12½
637 A237 1c brn & dk bl   .25   .25
638 A237 2c green & red   .30   .25
639 A237 10c choc & red   .90   .25
640 A237 12c gray ol & vio   1.25   .45
Nos. 637-640,C206-C208 (7)   7.40 2.95
See note after No. 386.

Nos. 521A, 522 and 525 Surcharged in Violet Blue, Red or Black

1960   Wmk. 106   Perf. 10
641 A184 2c on 4c red lil (VB)   .80   .40
642 A184a 2c on 5c sl bl (R)   1.25   .40
643 A184 2c on 13c org red   1.25   .40

No. 307B Surcharged in Black

644 A41 10c on 20c ol grn   1.25   .50
Nos. 641-644 (4)   4.55 1.70

17th Olympic Games, Rome, Aug. 25-Sept. 11 — A238

Wmk. 321
1960, Sept. 22   Engr.   Perf. 12½
645 A238 1c Sailboats   .45   .25
646 A238 2c Marksman   .55   .25
Nos. 645-646,C212-C213 (4)   3.30 1.25
For souvenir sheet see No. C213a.

Camilo Cienfuegos and View of Escolar A239

1960, Oct. 27   Litho.   Unwmk.
647 A239 2c brn, bl, grn & red   1.25   .25
1st anniv. of the death of Camilo Cienfuegos, revolutionary hero.

Morning Glory A240

Tobacco and Christmas Hymn A241

1960   Litho.   Perf. 12½
648 A240 1c red   .75   .75
649 A241 1c Tobacco   1.50 1.50
650 A241 1c Mariposa   1.50 1.50
651 A241 1c Guaiacum   1.50 1.50
652 A241 1c Coffee   1.50 1.50
 a.   Block of 4, #649-652   7.00
653 A240 2c ultra   1.00 1.00
654 A241 2c Tobacco   3.00 3.00
655 A241 2c Mariposa   3.00 3.00
656 A241 2c Guaiacum   3.00 3.00
657 A241 2c Coffee   3.00 3.00
 a.   Block of 4, #654-657   14.00
658 A240 10c ocher   3.00 2.50
659 A241 10c Tobacco   10.00 6.00
660 A241 10c Mariposa   10.00 6.00
661 A241 10c Guaiacum   10.00 6.00
662 A241 10c Coffee   10.00 6.00
 a.   Block of 4, #659-662   47.50
Nos. 648-662 (15)   62.75 46.25
Issued for Christmas 1960.
Nos. 648-662 were printed in three sheets of 25. Nine stamps of type A240 form a center cross, stamps of type A241 form a block of four in each corner with the musical bars joined in an oval around the floral designs.

"Public Capital for Economic Benefit" — A242

Designs: 2c, Chart and symbols of agriculture and industry. 6c, Cogwheels.

			Perf. 11½	
1961, Jan. 10		Unwmk.	Photo.	
663	A242	1c yel, blk & org	.40	.25
664	A242	2c bl, blk & red	.40	.25
665	A242	6c yel, red org & blk	1.00	.25
		Nos. 663-665,C215-C218 (7)	9.90	2.90

Issued to publicize the conference of underdeveloped countries, Havana.

Jesus Menéndez and Sugar Cane — A243

1961, Jan. 22		Litho.	Perf. 12½	
666	A243	2c dk grn & brn	.60	.25

Jesus Menéndez, leader in sugar industry.

Overprinted in Red

1961, May 2			
667	A243	2c dk grn & brn	1.50	.25

Issued for May Day, 1961.

Dove and UN Emblem — A244

			Perf. 12½	
1961, Apr. 12		Litho.		
668	A244	2c red brn & yel grn	.60	.25
669	A244	10c emer & rose lil	1.25	.45
a.		Souv. sheet, #668-669, imperf.	5.00	
		Nos. 668-669,C222-C223 (4)	3.95	1.45

15th anniv. (in 1960) of the UN.

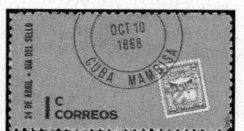

Stamp Day A245

Stamp Day: 1c, Revolutionary 10c stamp of 1874, 1868 "cancel." 2c, #238, 1902 "cancel." 10c, #613, 1959 "cancel."

1961, Apr. 24		Unwmk.	
670	A245	1c dull rose & dk grn	.35	.25
671	A245	2c salmon & dk grn	.40	.25
672	A245	10c pale grn, car rose & blk	2.00	.40
		Nos. 670-672 (3)	2.75	.90

For overprint see No. 681.

Hand Releasing Dove — A246

			Perf. 12½	
1961, July 26				
673	A246	2c blk, red, yel & gray	1.50	.25

26th of July (1953) movement, Castro's revolt against Fulgencio Batista.

Burelage on back consisting of wavy lines and diagonal rows of "CUBA CORREOS" in pale salmon.

Portrait Type of 1954

Designs: Same as before. On the 2c, "1833" is replaced by "?."

Wmk. 321 (Nos. 674, 676); Unwmkd.
Perf. 12½ (Nos. 674, 676); Rouletted

			1961-69	Engr.	
674	A184	1c brown red		.50	.25
675	A184	1c lt blue ('69)		.30	.25
676	A184a	2c slate green		.50	.25
677	A184a	2c yel grn ('69)		.30	.25
678	A184	3c org ('64)		1.50	.25
679	A184	13c brn ('64)		1.50	.30
680	A184	20c lilac ('69)		1.75	.25
		Nos. 674-680 (7)		6.35	1.80

Issued: Nos. 674, 676, 8/1; Nos. 678-679, 12/764; others, 9/69.
For Nos. 675, 677-680, see embargo note following No. 702.

No. 672 Ovptd. in Red

		Perf. 12½	
1961, Oct. 7		Litho.	Unwmk.
681	A245	10c pale grn, car rose & blk	2.00	.45

1st Official Phil. Exhib., Havana, Oct. 7-17.

Education Year — A247

Designs: One letter (per stamp) of "CUBA," book and various quotations by Jose Marti about the virtues of literacy.

1961, Nov. 22			
682	A247	1c pale grn, red & blk	.25	.25
683	A247	2c blue, red & blk	.25	.25
684	A247	10c vio, red & blk	.90	.25
685	A247	12c org, red & blk	1.75	.60
		Nos. 682-685 (4)	3.15	1.35

A248

Christmas A249

No. 686, Polymita flammulata. No. 687, Polymita fulminata. No. 688, Polymita nigrofasciata. No. 689, Polymita fuscolimbata. No. 690, Polymita roseolimbata. No. 691, Tiaris canorus. No. 692, Ara tricolor. No. 693, Priotelus temnurus. No. 694, Mellisuga helenae. No. 695, Campephilus principalis. No. 696, Othreis toddi. No. 697, Uranidia boisduvalii. No. 698, Phoebis avellaneda. No. 699,

Phaloe cubana. No. 700, Papilio gundlachianus.
1c, Snails. 2c, Birds, vert. 10c, Butterflies.

1961, Dec. 1			
686	A248	1c multicolored	.50	.25
687	A249	1c multicolored	.50	.25
688	A249	1c multicolored	.50	.25
689	A249	1c multicolored	.50	.25
690	A249	1c multicolored	.50	.25
a.		Block of 5 + label, Nos. 686-690	2.50	1.50
691	A248	2c multicolored	2.00	.50
692	A249	2c multicolored	2.00	.50
693	A249	2c multicolored	2.00	.50
694	A249	2c multicolored	2.00	.50
695	A249	2c multicolored	2.00	.50
a.		Block of 5 + label, Nos. 691-695	12.50	4.00
696	A248	10c multicolored	3.00	1.00
697	A249	10c multicolored	3.00	1.00
698	A249	10c multicolored	3.00	1.00
699	A249	10c multicolored	3.00	1.00
700	A249	10c multicolored	3.00	1.00
a.		Block of 5 + label, Nos. 696-700	15.00	7.50
		Nos. 686-700 (15)	27.50	8.75

Stamps of the same denomination printed se-tenant in sheets of 20 stamps plus 5 labels picturing bells and star. Stamps of Type A249 are arranged in blocks of 4; Type A248 stamps and labels form a cross in sheet.
See Nos. 760-774, 912-926, 1025-1039, 1179-1193, 1303-1317, 1464-1478, 1572-1586.

3rd Anniv. of the Revolution A250

1962, Jan. 3			
701	A250	1c multi	.85	.35
702	A250	2c multi	1.75	.45

See Nos. C226-C228.

Cuban goods have been embargoed by the United States since a Feb. 7, 1962 proclamation by President Kennedy, but according to the Office of Foreign Assets Control of the Treasury Department, used Cuban stamps can be imported and sold without limitation, and unused stamps may be imported for personal use, but not resold.

Natl. Militia A251

Silhouettes of militiamen and women and their peace-time occupations: 1c, Farmer. 2c, Welder. 3c, Seamstress.

1962, Feb. 26			
703	A251	1c blue grn & blk	.30	.25
704	A251	2c deep blue & blk	.60	.25
705	A251	10c brt org & blk	2.10	.55
		Nos. 703-705 (3)	3.00	1.05

Bay of Pigs Invasion, 1st Anniv. — A252

1962, Apr. 17			
706	A252	2c multi	.45	.25
707	A252	3c multi	.45	.25
708	A252	10c multi	3.00	.65
		Nos. 706-708 (3)	3.90	1.15

1st West Indies Packet A253

1962, Apr. 24			
709	A253	10c red & gray	3.25	.90

Stamp Day. See No. E32.

Intl. Labor Day — A254

1962, May 1			
710	A254	2c ocher & blk	.35	.25
711	A254	3c ver & blk	.75	.25
712	A254	10c greenish blue & blk	2.50	.70
		Nos. 710-712 (3)	3.60	1.20

Natl. Sports Institute (INDER) Emblem and Athletes — A255

No. 713, Judo. No. 714, Discus. No. 715, Gymnastics. No. 716, Wrestling. No. 717, Weight lifting. No. 718, Roller skating. No. 719, Equestrian. No. 720, Archery. No. 721, Bicycling. No. 722, Bowling. No. 723, Power boating. No. 724, One-man kayak. No. 725, Swimming. No. 726, Sculling. No. 727, Yachting. No. 728, Soccer. No. 729, Volleyball. No. 730, Baseball. No. 731, Basketball. No. 732, Tennis. No. 733, Boxing. No. 734, Underwater fishing. No. 735, Model-plane flying. No. 736, Pistol shooting. No. 737, Water polo. No. 738, Paddleball. No. 739, Fencing. No. 740, Sports Palace. No. 741, Chess. No. 742, Jai alai.

			Wmk. 321	
1962, July 25				
713	A255	1c multi	.35	.25
714	A255	1c multi	.35	.25
715	A255	1c multi	.35	.25
716	A255	1c multi	.35	.25
717	A255	1c multi	.35	.25
718	A255	2c multi	.35	.25
719	A255	2c multi	.35	.25
720	A255	2c multi	.35	.25
721	A255	2c multi	.35	.25
722	A255	2c multi	.35	.25
723	A255	3c multi	1.00	.25
724	A255	3c multi	1.00	.25
725	A255	3c multi	1.00	.25
726	A255	3c multi	1.00	.25
727	A255	3c multi	1.00	.25
728	A255	9c multi	.90	.35
729	A255	9c multi	.90	.35
730	A255	9c multi	.90	.35
731	A255	9c multi	.90	.35
732	A255	9c multi	.90	.35
733	A255	10c multi	.90	.35
734	A255	10c multi	.90	.35
735	A255	10c multi	.90	.35
736	A255	10c multi	.90	.35
737	A255	10c multi	.90	.35
738	A255	13c multi	1.00	.50
739	A255	13c multi	1.00	.50
740	A255	13c multi	1.00	.50
741	A255	13c multi	1.00	.50
742	A255	13c multi	1.00	.50
		Nos. 713-742 (30)	22.50	9.75

Stamps of the same denomination printed se-tenant in sheets of 25. Various combinations possible.

9th Anniv. of the Revolution A256

Attack on Moncada Barracks: Abel Santamaria and: 2c, Barracks under siege. 3c, Children at Moncada School.

1962, July 26
743	A256	2c brn car & dark ultra	.65	.35
744	A256	3c dark ultra & brn car	1.10	.55

8th World Youth Festival for Peace and Friendship, Helsinki, July 28-Aug. 6 — A257

1962, July 28
745	A257	2c Dove, emblem	1.00	.25
746	A257	3c Hand grip, emblem	1.75	.55
a.		Min. sheet of 2, Nos. 745-746, imperf.	6.50	6.50

9th Central American and Caribbean Games, Kingston, Jamaica, Aug. 11-25
A258

1962, Aug. 27
747	A258	1c Boxing	.25	.25
748	A258	2c Tennis	.25	.25
749	A258	3c Baseball	.25	.25
750	A258	13c Fencing	2.40	.80
		Nos. 747-750 (4)	3.15	1.55

A259

First Natl. Congress of the Federation of Cuban Women — A260

1962, Oct. 1
751	A259	9c rose, blk & grn	1.10	.25
752	A260	13c blk, grn & lt blue	2.40	.65

Latin American University Games — A261

1962, Oct. 13   **Wmk. 106**
753	A261	1c Running	.40	.25
754	A261	2c Baseball	.85	.25
755	A261	3c Basketball	1.25	.25
756	A261	13c World map	2.50	.55
		Nos. 753-756 (4)	5.00	1.30

World Health Organization Campaign to Eradicate Malaria — A262

Designs: 1c, Magnified specimen of the parasitic protozoa, microscope. 2c, Swamp and mosquito. 3c, Chemist's structural formulas for quinine, cinchona plant.

1962, Dec. 14
757	A262	1c multi	.50	.25
758	A262	2c multi	.50	.25
759	A262	3c multi	1.75	.45
		Nos. 757-759 (3)	2.75	.95

Christmas Type of 1961

No. 760, Epicrates anqulifer. No. 761, Cricosaurus typica. No. 762, Anolis equestris. No. 763, Tropidophis wrighti. No. 764, Cyclura macleayi. No. 765, Cubispa turquino. No. 766, Chrysis superba. No. 767, Essostruta roberto. No. 768, Hortensia conciliata. No. 769, Lachnopus argus. No. 770, Monophyllus cubanus. No. 771, Capromys pilorides. No. 772, Capromys pre-hensilis. No. 773, Solenodon cubensis. No. 774, Capromys pilorides (Blanca).

2c, Reptiles. 3c, Insects, vert. 10c, Rodents.

1962, Dec. 21   **Unwmk.**
760	A248	2c multi	.65	.25
761	A249	2c multi	.65	.25
762	A249	2c multi	.65	.25
763	A249	2c multi	.65	.25
764	A249	2c multi	.65	.25
a.		Block of 5 + label, Nos. 760-764	3.50	1.50
765	A248	3c multi	1.00	.60
766	A249	3c multi	1.00	.60
767	A249	3c multi	1.00	.60
768	A249	3c multi	1.00	.60
769	A249	3c multi	1.00	.60
a.		Block of 5 + label, Nos. 765-769	5.50	4.50
770	A248	10c multi	4.00	1.25
771	A249	10c multi	4.00	1.25
772	A249	10c multi	4.00	1.25
773	A249	10c multi	4.00	1.25
774	A249	10c multi	4.00	1.25
a.		Block of 5 + label, Nos. 770-774	21.00	9.00
		Nos. 760-774 (15)	28.25	10.50

Christmas 1962. See note after No. 700.

Around 1962 a 1ctv. label picturing Fidel Castro was used as a voluntary contribution stamp. It is not inscribed "Correos" and was not valid for postage.

Soviet Space Flights — A263

Spacecraft and cosmonauts: 1c, Vostok 1, Yuri A. Gagarin, Apr. 12, 1961. 2c, Vostok 2, Gherman S. Titov, Aug. 6-7, 1961. 3c, Vostok 3, Andrian G. Nikolaev, Aug. 11-15, 1962, and Vostok 4, Pavel R. Popovich, Aug. 12-15, 1962. 9c, Vostok 5, Valery F. Bykovsky, June 14-19, 1963. 13c, Vostok 6, Valentina V. Tereshkova, June 16-19, 1963.

1963-64   **Wmk. 321**
775	A263	1c ultra, red & yel	.35	.25
776	A263	2c grn, yel & rose lake	.65	.25
777	A263	3c yel, vio & ver	.65	.25
778	A263	9c red, dark vio & yel	1.25	.45
779	A263	13c dark blue green, dull red brown & yel	3.25	.70
		Nos. 775-779 (5)	6.15	1.90

Issued: 1c, 2c, 3c, 2/26/63; others, 8/15/64.

Attack of the Presidential Palace, 6th Anniv. — A264

9c, Guerillas attacking palace. 13c, Four student leaders. 30c, Jose A. Echeverria, Menelao Mora.

1963, Mar. 13
780	A264	9c dark red & blk	1.10	.25
781	A264	13c chalky blue & sep	1.40	.45
782	A264	30c org & grn	3.50	1.00
		Nos. 780-782 (3)	6.00	1.70

4th Pan American Games, Sao Paulo, Brazil, Apr. 20-May 5 — A265

1963, Apr. 20
783	A265	1c Baseball	1.25	.35
784	A265	13c Boxing	3.25	.65

Stamp Day A266

3c, Mask mailbox, 19th cent. 10c, Mask mailbox at the Plaza de la Catedral, Havana.

1963, Apr. 25
785	A266	3c black & dark org	1.00	.25
786	A266	10c black & pur	2.50	.50

See Nos. 828-829, 956-957 and 1102-1103.

Labor Day — A267

1963, May 1
787	A267	3c shown	.50	.25
788	A267	13c Four workers	1.75	.60

Intl. Children's Week, June 1-7 — A268

1963, June 1
789	A268	3c blue blk & bister brn	.50	.25
790	A268	30c blue blk & red	2.75	.80

Ritual Effigy — A269

Taino Civilization artifacts: 3c, Wood-carved throne, horiz. 9c, Stone-carved figurine.

1963, June 29
791	A269	2c org & red brn	.75	.25
792	A269	3c ultra & red brn	.90	.25
793	A269	9c rose & gray	1.60	.45
		Nos. 791-793 (3)	3.25	.95

Montane Anthropology Museum, 60th anniv.

Broken Chains at Moncada A270

2c, Attack on the Presidential Palace. 3c, The insurrection. 7c, Strike of April 9. 9c, Triumph of the revolution. 10c, Agricultural reform and nationalization of industry. 13c, Bay of Pigs victory.

1963, July 26
794	A270	1c pink & blk	.25	.25
795	A270	2c lt blue & vio brn	.25	.25
796	A270	3c lt vio & brn	.25	.25
797	A270	7c apple green & rose	.25	.25
798	A270	9c olive bister & rose vio	.50	.30
799	A270	10c beige & sage grn	1.50	.50
800	A270	13c pale org & slate blue	2.25	.90
		Nos. 794-800 (7)	5.25	2.70

Indigenous Fruit — A271

1963, Aug. 19
801	A271	1c Star apple	.25	.25
802	A271	2c Cherimoya	.25	.25
803	A271	3c Cashew nut	.35	.25
804	A271	10c Custard apple	2.00	.45
805	A271	13c Mangoes	2.50	1.40
		Nos. 801-805 (5)	5.35	2.60

Geometric Shapes A272

View of a Town — A273

Designs: No. 806, Circle, triangle, square, vert. No. 807, Roof, window, vert. No. 808, View of a town. No. 809, View of a town in blue. No. 810, View of a town in olive bister and red. No. 811, Circle, triangle, vert. No. 812, House, roof and doorway, vert. No. 813, House, girders.

1963, Sept. 29   **Unwmk.**
806	A272	3c multi	.50	.25
807	A272	3c multi	.50	.25
808	A273	3c multi	.50	.25
809	A273	3c multi	.50	.25
810	A273	13c multi	1.50	.55
811	A272	13c multi	1.50	.55
812	A272	13c multi	1.50	.55
813	A272	13c multi	1.50	.55
		Nos. 806-813 (8)	8.00	3.20

7th Intl. Congress of the Intl. Union of Architects.

Ernest Hemingway (1899-1961), American Author — A274

Hemingway and: 3c, The Old Man and the Sea. 9c, For Whom the Bell Tolls. 13c, Hemingway Museum (former residence), San Francisco de Paula, near Havana.

1963, Dec. 5   **Wmk. 321**
814	A274	3c brn & lt blue	.75	.25
815	A274	9c sage grn & pink	1.75	.25
816	A274	13c blk & yel grn	3.00	.60
		Nos. 814-816 (3)	5.50	1.10

Natl. Museum, 50th Anniv. — A275

Works of art: 2c, El Zapateo (Dance), by Victor P. Landaluze. 3c, Abduction of the Mulatto Women, by Carlos Enriquez, vert. 9c, Greek Panathean amphora, vert. 13c, My Beloved (bust of a young woman), by Jean Antoine Houdon, vert.

1964, Mar. 19			Unwmk.	
817	A275	2c multi	.25	.25
818	A275	3c multi	.80	.25
819	A275	9c multi	1.10	.40
820	A275	13c multi	2.40	.65
	Nos. 817-820 (4)		4.55	1.55

General Strike on Apr. 9, 6th Anniv. — A276

Rebel leaders: 2c, Bernardo Juan Borrell. 3c, Marcelo Salado. 10c, Oscar Lucero. 13c, Sergio Gonzalez.

1964, Apr. 9				
821	A276	2c blk, yel grn & dull org	.40	.25
822	A276	3c blk, red & dull org	.70	.25
823	A276	10c blk, pur & beige	1.25	.30
824	A276	13c blk, brt blue & beige	2.50	.60
	Nos. 821-824 (4)		4.85	1.40

Bay of Pigs Invasion, 3rd Anniv. A277

Designs: 3c, Fish in net. 10c, Victory Monument. 13c, Fallen eagle, vert.

1964, Apr. 17				
825	A277	3c multi	.30	.25
826	A277	10c multi	.70	.35
827	A277	13c multi	2.00	.70
	Nos. 825-827 (3)		3.00	1.30

Stamp Day Type of 1963

3c, Vicente Mora Pera, 1st postal director. 13c, Unissued provisional stamp, 1871.

1964, Apr. 24				
828	A266	3c ocher & dull lil	.50	.25
829	A266	13c dull vio & lt olive grn	2.50	.50

Labor Day — A278

1964, May 1				
830	A278	3c Industry	.40	.25
831	A278	13c Agriculture	1.60	.55

Diplomatic Relations with China — A279

Designs: 1c, China Monument, Havana. 2c, Cuban and Chinese farmers. 3c, Natl. flags.

1964, May 15				
832	A279	1c multi	.35	.25
833	A279	2c org brn, blk & apple grn	.70	.25
834	A279	3c multi	1.40	.25
	Nos. 832-834 (3)		2.45	.75

15th UPU Congress, Vienna, May-June A280

13c, Hemispheres on world map. 30c, Heinrich von Stephan. 50c, UPU Monument, Bern.

1964, May 29				
835	A280	13c multicolored	.85	.30
836	A280	30c multicolored	1.90	.80
837	A280	50c multicolored	4.00	1.40
	Nos. 835-837 (3)		6.75	2.50

Development of Natl. Industry A281

1964, June 16				
838	A281	1c Fish	.40	.25
839	A281	2c Cow	.60	.25
840	A281	13c Chickens	2.50	.60
	Nos. 838-840 (3)		3.50	1.10

Merchant Fleet — A282

1964, June 30				
841	A282	1c Rio Jibacoa	.25	.25
842	A282	2c Camilo Cienfuegos	.40	.25
843	A282	3c Sierra Maestra	.60	.25
844	A282	9c Bahia de Siguanea	1.25	.50
845	A282	10c Oriente	3.50	.90
	Nos. 841-845 (5)		6.00	2.15

Unification of Viet Nam — A283

Designs: 2c, Vietnamese guerrilla, American soldier. 3c, Northerner and southerner shaking hands over map of united Viet Nam. 10c, Ox-drawn plow, machinised harvester. 13c, Natl. flags and profiles of Cuban and Vietnamese farmers.

1964, July 20				
846	A283	2c multi	.30	.25
847	A283	3c multi	.45	.25
848	A283	10c multi	1.00	.25
849	A283	13c multi	2.75	.60
	Nos. 846-849 (4)		4.50	1.35

11th Anniv. of the Revolution — A284

Designs: 3c, Raul Gomez Garcia and poem. 13c, Cover of La Historia Me Absolvera, by Fidel Castro.

1964, July 25				
850	A284	3c red, tan & blk	.50	.25
851	A284	13c multi	3.00	.40

1964 Summer Olympics, Tokyo, Oct. 10-25 — A285

1c, Gymnastics. 2c, Rowing. 3c, Boxing. 7c, Running, horiz. 10c, Fencing, horiz. 13c, Foil, cleats, oar, boxing glove, sun, horiz.

1964, Oct. 10			Wmk. 376	*Perf. 10*	
852	A285	1c multi		.30	.25
853	A285	2c multi		.30	.25
854	A285	3c multi		.30	.25
855	A285	7c multi		.70	.25
856	A285	10c multi		1.50	.55
857	A285	13c multi		2.50	.85
	Nos. 852-857 (6)			5.60	2.40

Satellite and Globe A286

Satellite and Partial Globe A287

No. C31 and Partial Globe A288

Various satellites and rockets.

1964, Oct. 15				
858	A286	1c shown	.25	.25
859	A287	1c shown	.25	.25
860	A287	1c Globe LL	.25	.25
861	A287	1c Globe UR	.25	.25
862	A287	1c Globe UL	.25	.25
a.	Block of 5 + label, Nos. 858-862		1.00	1.00
863	A286	2c Spacecraft and globe	.55	.25
864	A287	2c Globe LR	.55	.25
865	A287	2c Globe LL	.55	.25
866	A287	2c Globe UR	.55	.25
867	A287	2c Globe UL	.55	.25
a.	Block of 5 + label, Nos. 863-867		3.00	1.50
868	A286	3c Satellite and globe	.75	.35
869	A287	3c Globe LR	.75	.35
870	A287	3c Globe LL	.75	.35
871	A287	3c Globe UR	.75	.35
872	A287	3c Globe UL	.75	.35
a.	Block of 5 + label, Nos. 868-872		4.00	2.50

873	A286	9c Satellite and globe, diff	1.75	.70
874	A287	9c Globe LR	1.75	.70
875	A287	9c Globe LL	1.75	.70
876	A287	9c Globe UR	1.75	.70
877	A287	9c Globe UL	1.75	.70
a.	Block of 5 + label, Nos. 873-877		11.00	5.00
878	A286	13c Satellite and globe, diff	2.40	1.75
879	A287	13c Globe LR	2.40	1.75
880	A287	13c Globe LL	2.40	1.75
881	A287	13c Globe UR	2.40	1.75
882	A287	13c Globe UL	2.40	1.75
a.	Block of 5 + label, Nos. 878-882		16.00	10.00
883	A288	50c blk & lt grn	4.00	2.50
a.	Souvenir sheet of one, Wmk. 321		15.00	12.50
	Nos. 858-883 (26)		32.50	19.00

Experimental Cuban postal rocket flight, 25th anniv. Stamps of the same denomination printed se-tenant in sheets of 20 stamps and 5 inscribed labels. Stamps of Type A287 arranged in blocks of 4 with a complete globe in center of block; Type A286 stamps and labels form a cross in center of sheet. Inscribed "1939-Cohete Postal Cubano-1964." No. 883a contains one 46x28mm stamp.

Type of A288 Ovptd. in Silver

1964, Oct. 17			Unwmk.	
884	A288	50c dk red brn & lt grn	5.00	1.50

No. 884 not issued without overprint.

40th Death Anniv. of Lenin — A289

Designs: 13c, Lenin Mausoleum, horiz. 30c, Lenin, star, hammer and sickle.

1964, Nov. 7			Wmk. 376	
885	A289	3c org & blk	.40	.25
886	A289	13c pur, pink & blk	1.10	.35
887	A289	30c blue & blk	2.25	.80
	Nos. 885-887 (3)		3.75	1.40

Havana Zoo — A290

1c, Leopard, horiz. 2c, Elephant. 3c, Fallow deer. 4c, Kangaroo, horiz. 5c, Lions, horiz. 6c, Eland, horiz. 7c, Zebra, horiz. 8c, Hyena, horiz. 9c, Tiger, horiz. 10c, Guanaco, horiz. 13c, Chimpanzees, horiz. 20c, Peccary, horiz. 30c, Raccoon. 40c, Hippopotamus, horiz. 50c, Tapir, horiz. 60c, Dromedary. 70c, Bison, horiz. 80c, Black bear. 90c, Water buffalo, horiz. 1p, Deer in nature park, horiz.

1964, Nov. 25				
888	A290	1c multi	.30	.25
889	A290	2c multi	.30	.25
890	A290	3c multi	.30	.25
891	A290	4c multi	.30	.25
892	A290	5c multi	.40	.25
893	A290	6c multi	.50	.25
894	A290	7c multi	.50	.25
895	A290	8c multi	.75	.25
896	A290	9c multi	.75	.25
897	A290	10c multi	.80	.25
898	A290	13c multi	.90	.25
899	A290	20c multi	1.10	.25
900	A290	30c multi	1.60	.60
901	A290	40c multi	2.75	1.00

902	A290	50c multi	3.00	1.40
903	A290	60c multi	4.50	1.90
904	A290	70c multi	4.75	1.90
905	A290	80c multi	5.00	2.40
906	A290	90c multi	5.50	3.00

Size: 47x32mm

907	A290	1p multi	9.25	3.00
	Nos. 888-907 (20)		43.25	18.20

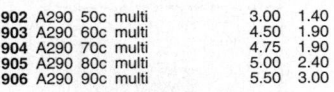

Heroes of the 1895 War of Independence — A291

1964, Dec. 7

908	A291	1c Jose Marti	.25	.25
909	A291	2c Antonio Maceo	.40	.25
910	A291	3c Maximo Gomez	.75	.35
911	A291	13c Calixto Garcia	1.90	.70
	Nos. 908-911 (4)		3.30	1.55

Christmas Type of 1961

No. 912, Dwarf cup coral. No. 913, Eusmilia fastigiata. No. 914, Acropora palmata. No. 915, Acropora profilera. No. 916, Diploria labyrinthiformis. No. 917, Condylactis gigantea. No. 918, Physalia physalis. No. 919, Aurelia aurita. No. 920, Linuche unguiculata. No. 921, Cassiopea frondosa. No. 922, Neocrinus blakei. No. 923, Eucidaris tribuloidas. No. 924, Tripneutes. No. 925, Ophiocoma echinata. No. 926, Oreaster celiculatus.

2c, Coral. 3c, Jellyfish. 10c, Starfish, sea-urchins.

1964, Dec. 18

912	A248	2c multi	.80	.30
913	A249	2c multi	.80	.30
914	A249	2c multi	.80	.30
915	A249	2c multi	.80	.30
916	A249	2c multi	.80	.30
a.	Block of 5 + label, Nos. 912-916		4.50	2.00
917	A248	3c multi	1.25	.50
918	A249	3c multi	1.25	.50
919	A249	3c multi	1.25	.50
920	A249	3c multi	1.25	.50
921	A249	3c multi	1.25	.50
a.	Block of 5 + label, Nos. 917-921		7.50	3.00
922	A248	10c multi	2.25	1.00
923	A249	10c multi	2.25	1.00
924	A249	10c multi	2.25	1.00
925	A249	10c multi	2.25	1.00
926	A249	10c multi	2.25	1.00
a.	Block of 5 + label, Nos. 922-926		12.50	7.00
	Nos. 912-926 (15)		21.50	9.00

Christmas 1964. See note after No. 700.

Dr. Tomas Romay (1764-1849), Physician and Scientist — A292

Romay Monument — A293

Designs: 2c, First vaccination against small-pox. 3c, Portrait and treatise on vaccination.

1964, Dec. 21

927	A292	1c blk & olive brn	.50	.25
928	A292	2c blk & tan	.50	.25
929	A293	3c olive & dk red brn	.60	.25
930	A293	10c bister & blk	2.40	.40
	Nos. 927-930 (4)		4.00	1.15

Second Declaration of Havana A294

Map of Latin America and ripples or map of Cuba and peasant breaking shackles under text from the Declaration of Havana: No. 931a, 932a "Visperas de su muerte..." No. 931b, 932b, "Un continente, que juntos suponen representos..." No. 931c, 932c, "Y no se ocultaran ni el gobierna..." No. 931d, 932d, "Millones de mulatos latinamericanos que saben..." No. 931e, "A labran la tierra en condiciones..."

1964, Dec. 23

931		Strip of 5	5.00	3.50
a.-e.	A294 3c any single		.75	.40
932		Strip of 5	15.00	12.50
a.-e.	A294 13c any single		1.75	1.50

Nos. 931-932 printed in sheets of 25 (5x5).

Dioramas in New Cuban Postal Museum — A295

1965, Jan. 4
Yellow & Black Border

933	A295	13c Maritime Post	3.25	.85
934	A295	30c Insurrection Post	2.50	1.25

Souvenir Sheet
Imperf

935		Sheet of 2	8.50	7.50
a.	A295 13c like #933, blue & blk border		1.00	1.00
b.	A295 30c like #934, blue & blk border		3.00	3.00
	Nos. 933-935 (3)		14.25	9.60

Stamps in No. 935 have simulated perforations; buff margin is inscribed "PRECIO 50c" LR.

Fishing Fleet — A296

1965, May 1

936	A296	1c Schooner	.25	.25
937	A296	2c Omicron	.30	.25
938	A296	3c Victoria	.45	.25
939	A296	9c Cardenas	.70	.30
940	A296	10c Sigma	2.75	.60
941	A296	13c Lambda	4.25	1.00
	Nos. 936-941 (6)		8.70	2.65

Intl. Women's Day — A297

1965, Mar. 8

942	A297	3c Lidia Doce	1.10	.30
943	A297	13c Clara Zetkin	1.60	.60

Technical Revolution — A298

Designs: 3c, Jose Antonio Echeverria University School. 13c, Stylized symbols of science and research, molecular structure and satellite dish.

1965, Mar. 31

944	A298	3c tan, blk & dark red brn	.50	.25
945	A298	13c multi	2.50	.70

Cosmonauts, Rocket — A299

30c, Cosmonauts Pavel I. Balyayev, Aleksei A. Leonov taking first space walk.

1965, Apr. 2

946	A299	30c dark blue, blk & brn	2.50	.70
947	A299	50c brt pink & blue blk	4.50	1.40

Flight of Voskhod 2, the first man to walk in space, Mar. 17.

Abstract Wood Carving by Eugenio Rodriguez A300

Paintings in the Natl. Museum, Havana: 3c, Garden with Sunflowers, by Victor Manuel. 10c, Abstract, by Wilfredo Lam, horiz. 13c, Children, by Enrique Ponce, horiz.

1965, Apr. 12

948	A300	2c multi	.35	.25

Size: 35x46mm

949	A300	3c multi	.55	.25

Size: 46x35mm

950	A300	10c multi	1.50	.45

Size: 43x37mm

951	A300	13c multi	2.50	.80
	Nos. 948-951 (4)		4.90	1.75

Abraham Lincoln — A301

Designs: 1c, Log cabin, birth site, horiz. 2c, Memorial, Washington, DC, horiz. 3c, Monument, Washington, DC. 13c, Portrait, quote.

1965, Apr. 15

952	A301	1c yel bister, red brn & gray	.25	.25
953	A301	2c lt blue & dark blue	.45	.25
954	A301	3c red org, blk & blue blk	1.25	.35
955	A301	13c org, blk & blue blk	2.50	.60
	Nos. 952-955 (4)		4.45	1.45

Stamp Day Type of 1963

Stamp Day 1965: 3c, 18th Cent. postmarks and packet. 13c, No. C16 and airplanes over capital.

1965, Apr. 24

956	A266	3c sep & dark org	3.00	.25
957	A266	13c brt blue, sal rose & blk	2.75	.60

Intl. Quiet Sun Year — A302

1c, Sun, Earth's magnetic pole, horiz. 2c, Sun Year emblem. 3c, Earth's magnetic field, horiz. 6c, Atmospheric currents, horiz. 30c, Solar rays on planet surface. 50c, Effect on satellite orbits, horiz.

1965, May 10

958	A302	1c multicolored	.25	.25
959	A302	2c multicolored	.25	.25
960	A302	3c multicolored	.55	.25
961	A302	6c multicolored	.60	.25
962	A302	30c multicolored	2.10	.55
963	A302	50c multicolored	2.75	1.40
a.	Souv. sheet of one, imperf.		8.00	8.00
b.	As "a," changed colors		14.00	14.00
	Nos. 958-963 (6)		6.50	2.95

Stamps in Nos. 963a-963b have simulated perforations.

Stamp in No. 963b is blue blk, Prus blue, org yel & red. Issued Oct. 10 for the Philatelic Space Exhibition, Havana, Oct. 10-17.

Intl. Telecommunications Union, Cent. — A303

1c, Station, horiz. 2c, Satellite. 3c, Telstar, horiz. 10c, Telstar, receiving station. 30c, ITU emblem, horiz.

1965, May 17

964	A303	1c gold & multi	.25	.25
965	A303	2c multi	.25	.25
966	A303	3c multi	.30	.25
967	A303	10c multi	1.10	.25
968	A303	30c multi	3.00	.90
	Nos. 964-968 (5)		4.90	1.90

9th Communist World Youth and Students Congress — A304

13c, Flags of Cuba and Algeria, emblem. 30c, Flags, guerrillas.

1965, June 10

969	A304	13c multi	1.50	.30
970	A304	30c multi	2.50	.50

Matias Perez, Cuban Aeronautics Pioneer — A305

1965, June 23

971	A305	3c pink & blk	1.75	.95
972	A305	13c dull vio & blk, diff.	2.75	.95

Flowers and Maps of Their Locations A306

1c, Rosa canina, Europe. 2c, Chrysanthemum hortorum, Asia. 3c, Strelitzia reginae, Africa. 4c, Dahlia pinnata, No. America. 5c, Cattleya labiata, So. America. 13c, Grevillea banksii, Oceania. 30c, Brunfelsia nitida, Cuba.

1965, July 20

973	A306	1c multicolored	.25	.25
974	A306	2c multicolored	.30	.25
975	A306	3c multicolored	.30	.30
976	A306	4c multicolored	.30	.25
977	A306	5c multicolored	1.60	.25
978	A306	13c multicolored	3.25	.95
979	A306	30c multicolored	4.75	1.60
		Nos. 973-979 (7)	10.75	3.85

1st Natl. Games — A307

1965, July 25

980	A307	1c Swimming	.25	.25
981	A307	2c Basketball	.35	.25
982	A307	3c Gymnastics	.70	.25
983	A307	30c Hurdling	2.75	.70
		Nos. 980-983 (4)	4.05	1.45

Revolution Museum Opening A308

1c, Anti-tank guns. 2c, Tanks. 3c, Bazookas. 10c, Uniform, guerillas. 13c, Compass, yacht Granma.

1965, July 26

984	A308	1c multi	.25	.25
985	A308	2c multi	.25	.25
986	A308	3c multi	.25	.25
987	A308	10c multi	.75	.25
988	A308	13c multi	2.10	.45
		Nos. 984-988 (5)	3.60	1.45

A309

1c, Finlay's signature. 2c, Anopheles mosquito. 3c, Portrait. 7c, Microscope. 9c, Dr. Claudio Delgado. 10c, Monument. 13c, Discussing theory with doctors.

1965, Aug. 20

989	A309	1c multicolored	.25	.25
990	A309	2c multicolored	.25	.25
991	A309	3c multicolored	.35	.25
992	A309	7c multicolored	.45	.25
993	A309	9c multicolored	.75	.25
994	A309	10c multicolored	1.90	.30
995	A309	13c multicolored	3.00	.65
		Nos. 989-995 (7)	6.95	2.20

Carlos J. Finlay (1833-1915), discovered transmission of yellow fever via aedes aegypti (not anopheles) mosquito. Nos. 990-995 vert.

Butterflies A310

No. 996, Dismorphia cubana. No. 997, Anetia numidia briarea. No. 998, Carathis gortynoides. No. 999, Hymenitis cubana. No. 1000, Eubaphe heros. No. 1001, Lycorea ceres demeter. No. 1002, Eubaphe disparitis. No. 1003, Siderone nemesis. No. 1004, Syntomidopsis variegata. No. 1005, Ctenuchidia virgo. No. 1006, Prepona antimache crossina. No. 1007, Sylepta reginalis. No. 1008, Chlosyne perezi perezi. No. 1009, Anaea clytemnestra iphigenia. No. 1010, Anetia cubana.

1965, Sept. 22   **Unwmk.**

996	A310	2c multicolored	.50	.25
997	A310	2c multicolored	.50	.25
998	A310	2c multicolored	.50	.25
999	A310	2c multicolored	.50	.25
1000	A310	2c multicolored	.50	.25
a.		Strip of 5, Nos. 996-1000	3.75	2.50
1001	A310	3c multicolored	.75	.25
1002	A310	3c multicolored	.75	.25
1003	A310	3c multicolored	.75	.25
1004	A310	3c multicolored	.75	.25
1005	A310	3c multicolored	.75	.25
a.		Strip of 5, Nos. 1001-1005	5.00	3.25
1006	A310	13c multicolored	3.00	.80
1007	A310	13c multicolored	3.00	.80
1008	A310	13c multicolored	3.00	.80
1009	A310	13c multicolored	3.00	.80
1010	A310	13c multicolored	3.00	.80
a.		Strip of 5, Nos. 1006-1010	17.00	8.25
		Nos. 996-1010 (15)	21.25	6.50

Cuban Mint, 50th Anniv. A311

Coins (obverse and reverse): No. 1011, 20 centavos, 1962. No. 1012, 1 peso, 1934. No. 1013, 40 centavos, 1962. No. 1014, 1 peso, 1915. No. 1015, Marti peso, 1953. No. 1016, 20 pesos, 1915.

1965, Oct. 13

1011	A311	1c multicolored	.30	.25
1012	A311	2c multi	.30	.25
1013	A311	3c multi	.30	.25
1014	A311	8c multi	.80	.25
1015	A311	10c multi	1.90	.40
1016	A311	13c multi	2.75	.50
		Nos. 1011-1016 (6)	6.35	1.90

Tropical Fruit — A312

1965, Nov. 15   **Perf. 12½**

1017	A312	1c Oranges	.25	.25
1018	A312	2c Custard apples	.25	.25
1019	A312	3c Papayas	.25	.25
1020	A312	4c Bananas	.35	.25
1021	A312	10c Avocado	.60	.25
1022	A312	13c Pineapple	.95	.70
1023	A312	20c Guavas	2.50	.70
1024	A312	50c Marmalade plums	5.50	1.25
		Nos. 1017-1024 (8)	10.65	3.90

Christmas Type of 1961

Birds: No. 1025, Icterus galbula. No. 1026, Passerina ciris. No. 1027, Setophaga ruticillar. No. 1028, Dendroica tusca. No. 1029, Pheucticus ludovicianus. No. 1030, Pyranga olivacea. No. 1031, Dendroica dominica. No. 1032, Vermivora pinus. No. 1033, Protonotaria citrea. No. 1034, Wilsonia citrina. No. 1035, Passerina cyanea. No. 1036, Anas discors. No. 1037, Aix sponsa. No. 1038, Spatula clypeata. No. 1039, Nycticorax hoactli.

1965, Dec. 1

1025	A248	3c multicolored	1.60	1.25
1026	A249	3c multicolored	1.60	1.25
1027	A249	3c multicolored	1.60	1.25
1028	A249	3c multicolored	1.60	1.25
1029	A249	3c multicolored	1.60	1.25
a.		Block of 5 + label, Nos. 1025-1029	9.00	7.25
1030	A248	5c multicolored	1.75	1.75
1031	A249	5c multicolored	1.75	1.75
1032	A249	5c multicolored	1.75	1.75
1033	A249	5c multicolored	1.75	1.75
1034	A249	5c multicolored	1.75	1.75
a.		Block of 5 + label, Nos. 1030-1034	10.00	10.00
1035	A248	13c multicolored	4.00	3.00
1036	A249	13c multicolored	4.00	3.00
1037	A249	13c multicolored	4.00	3.00
1038	A249	13c multicolored	4.00	3.00
1039	A249	13c multicolored	4.00	3.00
a.		Block of 5 + label, Nos. 1035-1039	21.00	20.00
		Nos. 1025-1039 (15)	36.75	30.00

Christmas 1965. See note after No. 700.

Intl. Athletic Competition, Havana, 7th Anniv. — A313

1965, Dec. 11   **Wmk. 376**   **Perf. 10**

1040	A313	1c Hurdling	.25	.25
1041	A313	2c Discus	.25	.25
1042	A313	3c Shot put	.55	.25
1043	A313	7c Javelin	.55	.25
1044	A313	9c High jump	.70	.35
1045	A313	10c Hammer throw	1.40	.60
1046	A313	13c Running	2.00	.90
		Nos. 1040-1046 (7)	5.70	2.85

Fish in the Natl. Aquarium — A314

1c, Echeneis naucrates. 2c, Katsuwonus pelamis. 3c, Abudefduf saxatilis. 4c, Istiophorus. 5c, Epinephelus striatus. 10c, Lutianus analis. 13c, Ocyurus chrysurus. 30c, Holocentrus ascensionis.

1965, Dec. 5   **Unwmk.**   **Perf. 12½**

1047	A314	1c multicolored	.25	.25
1048	A314	2c multicolored	.25	.25
1049	A314	3c multicolored	.55	.25
1050	A314	4c multicolored	.65	.25
1051	A314	5c multicolored	.65	.25
1052	A314	10c multicolored	.80	.30
1053	A314	13c multicolored	2.75	.80
1054	A314	30c multicolored	4.50	1.25
		Nos. 1047-1054 (8)	10.40	3.60

Andre Voisin (d. 1964), French Naturalist — A315

13c, Portrait, flags, microscope, plant.

1965, Dec. 21   **Wmk. 376**

1055	A315	3c shown	1.00	.25
1056	A315	13c multicolored	2.50	.55

Transportation — A316

1c, Skoda bus, Czechoslovakia. 2c, Ikarus bus, Hungary. 3c, Leyland bus, G.B. 4c, TEM-4 locomotive, USSR. 7c, BB-69.000 locomotive, France. 10c, Remolcador tugboat, DDR. 13c, 15 de Marzo freighter, Spain. 20c, Ilyushin 18 jet, USSR.

1965, Dec. 30

1057	A316	1c multicolored	.25	.25
1058	A316	2c multicolored	.25	.25
1059	A316	3c multicolored	.25	.25
1060	A316	4c multicolored	3.00	.70
1061	A316	7c multicolored	3.00	.70
1062	A316	10c multicolored	1.25	.35
1063	A316	13c multicolored	2.00	.60
1064	A316	20c multicolored	2.50	1.00
		Nos. 1057-1064 (8)	12.50	4.10

A317

7th Anniv. of the Revolution A318

1c, Guerrillas. 2c, Commander and tank. 3c, Sailor, patrol boat. 10c, Jet aircraft. 13c, Rocket.

1966, Jan. 2

1065	A317	1c multi	.25	.25
1066	A317	2c multi	.25	.25
1067	A317	3c multi	.90	.25
1068	A318	10c multi	1.90	.45
1069	A318	13c multi	2.25	.70
		Nos. 1065-1069 (5)	5.55	1.90

Conference of Asian, African and South American Countries, Havana — A319

1966, Jan. 3

1070	A319	2c Emblem at R	.25	.25
1071	A319	3c Emblem at L	.40	.25
1072	A319	13c Emblem at center	2.10	.55
		Nos. 1070-1072 (3)	2.75	1.05

Guardalabarca Beach — A320

2c, Gran Piedra mountain. 3c, Guama Village. 13c, Soroa waterfall, vert.

1966, Feb. 10

1073	A320	1c shown	.30	.25
1074	A320	2c multi	.30	.25
1075	A320	3c multi	.90	.25
1076	A320	13c multi	2.50	.60
		Nos. 1073-1076 (4)	4.00	1.35

11th Medical and 7th Natl. Dental Congresses — A321

1966, Feb. 28   **Wmk. 376**
1077 A321 3c multi   .30   .25
1078 A321 13c multi, diff.   1.50   .55

Folk Art A322

1c, Afro-cuban ritual puppet. 2c, Sombreros. 3c, Ceramic vase. 7c, Lanterns, lamp. 9c, Table lamp. 10c, Shark, wood sculpture. 13c, Snail-shell necklace, earrings.

1966, Feb. 28   **Unwmk.**
1079 A322 1c multicolored   .25   .25
1080 A322 2c multicolored   .25   .25
1081 A322 3c multicolored   .25   .25
1082 A322 7c multicolored   .25   .25
1083 A322 9c multicolored   .80   .25
1084 A322 10c multicolored   1.25   .30
1085 A322 13c multicolored   2.50   .60
        Nos. 1079-1085 (7)   5.55   2.15

Nos. 1079-1083 vert.

Chelsea College, by Canaletto — A323

Ceramics and paintings in the National Museum: 1c, Ming vase. 3c, Portrait of a Lady, by Goya. 13c, Portrait of Fayum, encaustic painting. Nos. 1086, 1088-1089 vert.

1966, Mar. 31   **Wmk. 376**
1086 A323 1c multi   .25   .25
1087 A323 2c multi   .85   .25
1088 A323 3c multi   .75   .25
1089 A323 13c multi   3.00   .70
        Nos. 1086-1089 (4)   4.85   1.45

First Man in Space, 5th Anniv. A324

Designs: 1c, Konstantin Eduardovich Tsiolkovsky (1857-1935), Soviet rocket and space sciences pioneer. 2c, Cosmonauts in training, vert. 3c, Yuri Gagarin, rocket, Earth. 7c, Cosmonauts Nikolaev and Popovich, vert. 9c, Tereshkova and Bykovsky. 10c, Komarov, Feoktistov and Yegorov. 13c, Leonov taking first space walk.

1966, Apr. 12
1090 A324 1c multi   .25   .25
1091 A324 2c multi   .25   .25
1092 A324 3c multi   .35   .25
1093 A324 7c multi   .60   .25
1094 A324 9c multi   .85   .25
1095 A324 10c multi   1.10   .30
1096 A324 13c multi   2.25   .55
        Nos. 1090-1096 (7)   5.65   2.10

Bay of Pigs Invasion, 5th Anniv. A325

2c, Tank. 3c, Burning ship, plane crash. 9c, Tank in ditch. 10c, Soldier, gunners. 13c, Operations map.

1966, Apr. 17
1097 A325 2c multi   .25   .25
1098 A325 3c multi   .95   .25
1099 A325 9c multi   .40   .25
1100 A325 10c multi   1.75   .25
1101 A325 13c multi   3.00   .70
        Nos. 1097-1101 (5)   6.35   1.70

Stamp Day Type of 1963

Designs: 3c, Cuban Postal Museum interior. 13c, No. 613 and stamp collector.

1966, Apr. 24
1102 A266 3c sage grn & sal
             rose   1.25   .25
1103 A266 13c brn, sal rose &
             blk   3.50   .80

Stamp Day 1966. 1st Anniv. of the Cuban Postal Museum (No. 1102); 1st anniv. of the Cuban Philatelic Federation (No. 1103).

Flowers and Symbols of Industry — A326

2c, Anvil. 3c, Machete. 10c, Hammer. 13c, Hemisphere, gearwheel.

1966, May 1
1104 A326 2c multi   .25   .25
1105 A326 3c multi   .30   .25
1106 A326 10c multi   .70   .25
1107 A326 13c multi   1.75   .90
        Nos. 1104-1107 (4)   3.00   1.65

Labor Day.

Opening of the World Health Organization Headquarters, Geneva — A327

Views of WHO headquarters and emblem or emblem on flag.

1966, May 3
1108 A327 2c blk & yel org   .25   .25
1109 A327 3c blk, lt blue & yel
             org   .70   .25
1110 A327 13c blk, lt blue & yel
             org   2.10   .55
        Nos. 1108-1110 (3)   3.05   1.05

10th Central American and Caribbean Games, Puerto Rico, June 11-25 A328

1966, June 11
1111 A328 1c Running, vert.   .25   .25
1112 A328 2c Rifle shooting   .30   .25
1113 A328 3c Baseball, vert.   .45   .25
1114 A328 7c Volleyball, vert.   .45   .25
1115 A328 9c Soccer, vert.   .80   .25

1116 A328 10c Boxing, vert.   1.40   .25
1117 A328 13c Basketball, vert.   3.50   .55
        Nos. 1111-1117 (7)   7.15   2.05

Progress in Education A329

Designs: 1c, Makarenko School, Playa de Tarara. 2c, Natl. Literacy Campaign Museum. 3c, Lantern, literacy campaign emblem for 1961. 10c, Frank Pais education team in the mountains. 13c, Farmer, factory worker.

1966, June 15
1118 A329 1c grn & blk   .25   .25
1119 A329 2c yel, olive bister &
             blk   .25   .25
1120 A329 3c brt blue, lt blue &
             blk   .30   .25
1121 A329 10c golden brn, brn &
             blk   .90   .25
1122 A329 13c multi   2.40   .45
        Nos. 1118-1122 (5)   4.10   1.45

1st Graduating class of Makarenko School (1c), 5th anniv. of the Natl. Literacy Campaign (3c), 4th anniv. of agricultural and industrial trade education (13c).

12th Congress of the Cuban Labor Organization — A330

1966, Aug. 12
1123 A330 3c multi   .75   .25

Sea Shells — A331

1c, Liguus flammellus. 2c, Cypraea zebra. 3c, Strombus pugilis. 7c, Aequipecten muscosu. 9c, Liguus fasciatus crenatus. 10c, Charonia variegata. 13c, Liguus fasciatus archeri.

1966, Aug. 25   **Unwmk.**
1124 A331 1c multicolored   .35   .25
1125 A331 2c multicolored   .45   .25
1126 A331 3c multicolored   .70   .25
1127 A331 7c multicolored   .80   .25
1128 A331 9c multicolored   .90   .25
1129 A331 10c multicolored   1.75   .40
1130 A331 13c multicolored   3.50   .80
        Nos. 1124-1130 (7)   8.45   2.45

Breeding Messenger Pigeons — A332

2c, Timer. 3c, Coops. 7c, Breeder tending coops. 9c, Pigeons in yard. 10c, Two men, message. 13c, Baracoa to Havana championship flight, July 26, 1959.

1966, Sept. 18   **Wmk. 376**
1131 A332 1c shown   .40   .25
1132 A332 2c multicolored   .40   .25
1133 A332 3c multicolored   .40   .25
1134 A332 7c multicolored   .80   .25
1135 A332 9c multicolored   .80   .35
1136 A332 10c multicolored   2.50   .50

Size: 47x32mm
1137 A332 13c multicolored   3.75   .90
        Nos. 1131-1137 (7)   9.05   2.75

Provincial and Natl. Coats of Arms, Map of Cuba A333

1966, Oct. 10
1138 A333 1c Pinar del Rio   .25   .25
1139 A333 2c Havana   .30   .25
1140 A333 3c Matanzas   .30   .25
1141 A333 4c Las Villas   .40   .25
1142 A333 5c Camaguey   .60   .25
1143 A333 9c Oriente   1.00   .45

Size: 30x48mm
1144 A333 13c National arms   2.25   .55
        Nos. 1138-1144 (7)   5.10   2.25

17th World Chess Olympiad, Havana — A334

1c, Pawn. 2c, Rook. 3c, Knight. 9c, Bishop. 10c, Queen, games, horiz. 13c, King and emblem, horiz.
30c, Capablanca Vs. Lasker, 1914, horiz.

1966, Oct. 18
1145 A334 1c multicolored   .30   .25
1146 A334 2c multicolored   .30   .25
1147 A334 3c multicolored   .50   .25
1148 A334 9c multicolored   1.00   .25
1149 A334 10c multicolored   2.40   .25
1150 A334 13c multicolored   3.25   .60
        Nos. 1145-1150 (6)   7.75   1.85

Souvenir Sheet
Imperf
1151 A334 30c multicolored   12.00 12.00

No. 1151 contains one 49½x31mm stamp.

Cuban-Soviet Diplomatic Relations — A335

2c, Lenin Hospital. 3c, Oil tanker, world map. 10c, Workers, gearwheels. 13c, Agriculture.

1966, Nov. 7
1152 A335 2c multicolored   .25   .25
1153 A335 3c multicolored   .35   .25
1154 A335 10c multicolored   1.10   .25
1155 A335 13c multicolored   2.25   .70
        Nos. 1152-1155 (4)   3.95   1.45

2nd Song Festival A336

Cuban composers and their compositions: 1c, Amadeo Roldan. 2c, Eduardo Sanchez de Fuentes. 3c, Moises Simons. 7c, Jorge Anckermann. 9c, Alejandro G. Caturla. 10c, Eliseo Grenet. 13c, Ernesto Lecuona.

1966, Nov. 18
1156 A336 1c multicolored   .25   .25
1157 A336 2c multicolored   .30   .25
1158 A336 3c multicolored   .30   .25

1159	A336	7c multicolored	.80	.25
1160	A336	9c multi	.80	.25
1161	A336	10c multicolored	3.00	.45
1162	A336	13c multicolored	4.00	.90
		Nos. 1156-1162 (7)	9.45	2.60

Viet Nam War — A337

Flag of Viet Nam and: 2c, US aircraft discharging bombs, dead cattle. 3c, Gas mask and victims. 13c, US bombs, women and children.

1966, Nov. 23

1163	A337	2c multi	.40	.25
1164	A337	3c multi	.60	.25
1165	A337	13c multi	2.00	.60
		Nos. 1163-1165 (3)	3.00	1.10

10th Anniv. of Successful Revolution Campaigns — A338

Revolution leaders, scenes of the insurrection: 1c, Antonio Fernandez. 2c, Candido Gonzalez. 3c, Jose Tey. 7c, Tony Aloma. 9c, Otto Parellada. 10c, Juan Manuel Marquez. 13c, Frank Pais.

1966, Nov. 30

1166	A338	1c multicolored	.25	.25
1167	A338	2c multicolored	.25	.25
1168	A338	3c multicolored	.25	.25
1169	A338	7c multicolored	.30	.25
1170	A338	9c multicolored	.60	.25
1171	A338	10c multicolored	2.00	.50
1172	A338	13c multicolored	1.90	.80
		Nos. 1166-1172 (7)	5.55	2.55

Intl. Leisure Time and Recreation Seminar — A339

9c, World map, stopwatch, eye. 13c, Earth, clock, emblem.

1966, Dec. 2

1173	A339	3c shown	.25	.25
1174	A339	9c multicolored	1.40	.25
1175	A339	13c multicolored	1.75	.60
		Nos. 1173-1175 (3)	3.40	1.10

1st Natl. Telecommunications Forum — A340

1966, Dec. 12

1176	A340	3c shown	.75	.25
1177	A340	10c Satellite in orbit	3.75	.25
1178	A340	13c Shell, satellite	5.50	.70
a.		Souv. sheet of 3, #1176-1178, imperf	15.00	15.00
		Nos. 1176-1178 (3)	10.00	1.20

No. 1178a sold for 30c.

Christmas Type of 1961

No. 1179, Cypripedium eurylochus. No. 1180, Cattleya speciosissima. No. 1181, Cattleya mendelii majestica. No. 1182, Cattleya trianae amesiana. No. 1183, Cattleya labiata macfarlanei. No. 1184, Cypripedium morganiae burfordense. No. 1185, Cattleya Countess of Derby. No. 1186, Cypripedium hookerae volunteanum. No. 1187, Cattleya warscewiczii reginae burfordense. No. 1188, Cypripedium stonei cannartae. No. 1189, Cattleya mendelii Duchess of Montrose. No. 1190, Oncidium macranthum. No. 1191, Cypripedium stonei platytoenium. No. 1192, Cattleya dowiana aurea. No. 1193, Laelia anceps.

1966, Dec. 20 — Unwmk.

1179	A248	1c multicolored	.90	.25
1180	A249	1c multicolored	.90	.25
1181	A249	1c multicolored	.90	.25
1182	A249	1c multicolored	.90	.25
1183	A249	1c multicolored	.90	.25
a.		Block of 5 + label, #1179-1183	5.00	1.00
1184	A248	3c multicolored	1.40	.25
1185	A249	3c multicolored	1.40	.25
1186	A249	3c multicolored	1.40	.25
1187	A249	3c multicolored	1.40	.25
1188	A249	3c multicolored	1.40	.25
a.		Block of 5 + label, #1184-1188	8.00	1.00
1189	A248	13c multicolored	5.00	.50
1190	A249	13c multicolored	5.00	.50
1191	A249	13c multicolored	5.00	.50
1192	A249	13c multicolored	5.00	.50
1193	A249	13c multicolored	5.00	.50
a.		Block of 5 + label, #1189-1193	27.50	2.75
		Nos. 1179-1193 (15)	36.50	5.00

Christmas 1966. See note after No. 700.

8th Anniv. of the Revolution — A341

No. 1194, Liberation, 1959. No. 1195, Agrarian Reform, 1960. No. 1196, Education, 1961. No. 1197, Agriculture, 1965. No. 1198, Rodin's Thinker, Planning, 1962. No. 1199, Organization, 1963. No. 1200, Economy, 1964. No. 1201, Solidarity, 1966.

1967, Jan. 2

1194	A341	3c multicolored	.30	.25
1195	A341	3c multicolored	.30	.25
1196	A341	3c multicolored	.30	.25
1197	A341	3c multicolored	.30	.25
a.		Strip of 4, Nos. 1194-1197	1.25	.90
1198	A341	13c multicolored	1.90	.45
1199	A341	13c multicolored	1.90	.45
1200	A341	13c multicolored	1.90	.45
1201	A341	13c multicolored	1.90	.45
a.		Strip of 4, Nos. 1198-1201	7.75	4.25
		Nos. 1194-1201 (8)	8.80	2.80

Nos. 1198-1201 vert.

Spring, by Jorge Arche — A342

Paintings in the Natl. Museum: 1c, Coffee Machine, by Angel Acosta Leon, vert. 2c, Country People, by Eduardo Abela, vert. 13c, Still-life, by Amelia Pelaez, vert. 30c, Landscape, by Gonzalo Escalante.

1967, Feb. 27

1202	A342	1c multi	.30	.25
1203	A342	2c multi	.50	.25
1204	A342	3c multi	.70	.25
1205	A342	13c multi	2.00	.80
1206	A342	30c multi	5.50	1.50
		Nos. 1202-1206 (5)	9.00	3.05

Natl. Events, Mar. 13, 1957 A343

3c, Attack on Presidential Palace. 13c, Landing of Corynthia. 30c, Cienfuegos revolt.

1967, Mar. 13 — Wmk. 376

1207	A343	3c multicolored	.25	.25

Size: 41x28mm

1208	A343	13c multicolored	2.50	.70
1209	A343	30c multicolored	2.40	.80
		Nos. 1207-1209 (3)	5.15	1.75

Evolution of Man — A344

Prehistoric men: 2c, Australopithecus. 3c, Pithecanthropus erectus. 4c, Sinanthropus pekinensis. 5c, Neanderthal man. 13c, Cro-magnon man carving tusk. 20c, Cro-magnon man painting petroglyph.

1967, Mar. 31 — Unwmk.

1210	A344	1c multi	.30	.25
1211	A344	2c multi	.50	.25
1212	A344	3c multi	.50	.25
1213	A344	4c multi	.75	.25
1214	A344	5c multi	1.10	.25
1215	A344	13c multi	3.75	.50
1216	A344	20c multi	7.50	.90
		Nos. 1210-1216 (7)	14.40	2.65

Stamp Day A345

Carriages.

1967, Apr. 24

1217	A345	3c Victoria	.35	.25
1218	A345	9c Volante	2.00	.45
1219	A345	13c Quitrin	3.00	.80
		Nos. 1217-1219 (3)	5.35	1.50

EXPO '67, Montreal, Apr. 28-Oct. 27 — A346

1c, Cuban pavilion. 2c, Space exploration. 3c, Petroglyph, hieroglyph. 13c, Agriculture, computer technology. 20c, Athletes.

1967, Apr. 28

1220	A346	1c multicolored	.40	.25
1221	A346	2c multicolored	.40	.25
1222	A346	3c multicolored	.55	.25
1223	A346	13c multicolored	3.00	.70
1224	A346	20c multicolored	3.50	.80
		Nos. 1220-1224 (5)	7.85	2.25

Botanical Gardens, Sequicentennial A347

Flowering plants: 1c, Eugenia malaccensis. 2c, Jacaranda filicifolia. 3c, Coroupita guianensis. 4c, Spathodea campanulata. 5c, Cassia fistula. 13c, Plumieria alba. 20c, Erythrina poeppigiana.

1967, May 30

1225	A347	1c multicolored	.25	.25
1226	A347	2c multicolored	.25	.25
1227	A347	3c multicolored	.45	.25
1228	A347	4c multicolored	.45	.25
1229	A347	5c multicolored	.90	.25
1230	A347	13c multicolored	2.75	.55
1231	A347	20c multicolored	4.75	.65
		Nos. 1225-1231 (7)	9.80	2.45

Natl. Ballet — A348

1967, June 15

1232	A348	1c Giselle	.35	.25
1233	A348	2c Swan Lake	.35	.25
1234	A348	3c Don Quixote	.50	.25
1235	A348	4c Calaucan	1.00	.25
1236	A348	13c Swan Lake	2.75	.70
1237	A348	20c Nutcracker	4.00	1.25
		Nos. 1232-1237 (6)	8.95	2.95

Intl. Ballet Festival, Havana.

5th Pan American Games, Winnipeg, Canada, July 22-Aug. 7 — A349

1c, Baseball, horiz. 2c, Swimming, horiz. 3c, Basketball. 4c, Gymnastic rings. 5c, Water polo. 13c, Weight lifting, horiz. 20c, Javelin.

1967, July 22

1238	A349	1c multi	.25	.25
1239	A349	2c multi	.35	.25
1240	A349	3c multi	.50	.25
1241	A349	4c multi	.85	.25
1242	A349	5c multi	1.00	.25
1243	A349	13c multi	3.00	.45
1244	A349	20c multi	4.75	.80
		Nos. 1238-1244 (7)	10.70	2.50

1st Conference of Latin American Solidarity Organization (OLAS) — A350

Portrait of representative, map of South American homeland: No. 1245, Camilo Torres, Colombia. No. 1246, Luis de la Puente Uceda,

Peru. No. 1247, Luis A. Turcios Lima, Guatemala. No. 1248, Fabricio Ojeda, Venezuela.

1967, July 28 **Wmk. 376**

1245	A350	13c pale grn, blk & red	2.00	.50
1246	A350	13c lil, blk & red	2.00	.50
1247	A350	13c dark chalky blue, blk & red	2.00	.50
1248	A350	13c golden brn, blk & red	2.00	.50
	Nos. 1245-1248 (4)		8.00	2.00

Portrait of Sonny Rollins, by Alan Davie — A351

Bathers, by Gustave Singier A352

Modern Art: No. 1250, Twelve Selenites, by Felix Labisse. No. 1251, Night of the Drinker, by Friedensreich Hundertwasser. No. 1252, Figure, by Mariano. No. 1253, All-Souls, by Wilfredo Lam. No. 1254, Darkness and Cracks, by Antonio Tapies. No. 1256, Torso of a Muse, by Jean Arp. No. 1257, Figure, by M.W. Svanberg. No. 1258, Oppenheimer's Information, by Erro. No. 1259, Where Cardinals Are Born, by Max Ernst. No. 1260, Havana Landscape, by Portocarrero. No. 1261, EG 12, by Victor Vasarely. No. 1262, Frisco, by Alexander Calder. No. 1263, The Man with the Pipe, by Picasso. No. 1264, Abstract Composition, by Sergei Poliakoff. No. 1265, Painting, by Bram van Velde. No. 1266, Sower of Fires, by R. Matta. No. 1267, The Art of Living, by Rene Magritte. No. 1268, Poem, by Joan Miro. No. 1269, Young Tigers, by Jean Messagier. No. 1270, Painting, by M. Vieira da Silva. No. 1271, Live Cobra, by Pierre Alechinsky. No. 1272, Stalingrad, by Asger Jorn. 30c, Warriors, by Edouard Pignon. 50c, Cloister, a mural at the exhibition representing the Salon de Mayo pictures.

1967, July 29 **Unwmk.**

1249	A351	1c shown	.80	.25
1250	A351	1c multi	.80	.25
1251	A351	1c multi	.80	.25
1252	A351	1c multi	.80	.25
1253	A351	1c multi	.80	.25
a.		Strip of 5, Nos. 1249-1253	4.50	1.50

Sizes: 36½x54mm, 36½x53mm, 36½x45mm, 36½x41mm

1254	A352	2c multi	.80	.25
1255	A352	2c shown	.80	.25
1256	A352	2c multi	.80	.25
1257	A352	2c multi	.80	.25
1258	A352	2c multi	.80	.25
a.		Strip of 5, Nos. 1254-1258	4.50	2.50

Sizes: 36½x54mm, 36½x40mm, 36½x42mm, 36½x49mm

1259	A352	3c multi	1.50	.25
1260	A352	3c multi	1.50	.25
1261	A352	3c multi	1.50	.25
1262	A352	3c multi	1.50	.25
1263	A352	3c multi	1.50	.25
a.		Strip of 5, Nos. 1259-1263	7.50	3.50

Sizes: 35x15mm, 35x67mm, 35x46½mm, 35x55mm

1264	A352	4c multi	1.75	.80
1265	A352	4c multi	1.75	.80
1266	A352	4c multi	1.75	.80
1267	A352	4c multi	1.75	.80
1268	A352	4c multi	1.75	.80
a.		Strip of 5, Nos. 1264-1268	9.00	4.00

Sizes: 49x32mm, 49x35mm, 49x46mm

1269	A351	13c multi	4.50	2.75
1270	A351	13c multi	4.50	2.75
1271	A351	13c multi	4.50	2.75
1272	A351	13c multi	4.50	2.75
a.		Strip of 4, Nos. 1269-1272	19.00	11.00

Size: 54x32mm

1273	A351	30c multi	17.50	11.00
	Nos. 1249-1273 (25)		59.75	29.75

Souvenir Sheet
Imperf

1274	A351	50c multi	25.00	12.50

Salon de Mayo Art Exhibition, Havana. No. 1274 contains one 88x45mm stamp with simulated perforations. Issued Oct. 7.

World Underwater Fishing Championships — A353

1967, Sept. 5

1275	A353	1c Green moray	.25	.25
1276	A353	2c Octopus	.25	.25
1277	A353	3c Great barracuda	.25	.25
1278	A353	4c Blue shark	.75	.25
1279	A353	5c Spotted jewfish	1.60	.25
1280	A353	13c Sting ray	3.25	.70
1281	A353	20c Green turtle	6.50	.85
	Nos. 1275-1281 (7)		12.85	2.80

Soviet Space Program A354

1967, Oct. 4 **Wmk. 376**

1282	A354	1c Sputnik 1	.25	.25
1283	A354	2c Lunik 3	.25	.25
1284	A354	3c Venusik	.25	.25
1285	A354	4c Cosmos	.40	.25
1286	A354	5c Mars 1	.65	.25
1287	A354	9c Electron 1 & 2	.75	.25
1288	A354	10c Luna 9	1.10	.45
1289	A354	13c Luna 10	2.50	.60
a.		Souv. sheet of 8, #1282-1289, imperf.	15.00	15.00
	Nos. 1282-1289 (8)		6.15	2.55

Stamps in No. 1289a have simulated perfs.

50th Anniv. of the October Revolution, Russia A355

Paintings: 1c, Storming the Winter Palace, by Sokolov-Skalia and Miasnikov. 2c, Lenin Addressing Congress, by W.A. Serov. 3c, Lenin, by H.D. Nalbandian. 4c, Lenin Explaining Electrification Map, by L.A. Schmatko. 5c, Dawn of the Five-Year Plan, by J.D. Romas. 13c, Kusnetzkroi Steel Furnace No. 1, by P. Kotov. 30c, Victory, by A. Krivonogov.

1967, Nov. 7 **Unwmk.**

1290	A355	1c 64x36mm	.25	.25
1291	A355	2c 48x36mm	.25	.25
1292	A355	3c 35x37mm	.45	.25
1293	A355	4c 48x36mm	.45	.25
1294	A355	5c 50x36mm	3.75	.50
1295	A355	13c 36x50mm	3.00	.50
1296	A355	30c 50x36mm	4.00	.85
	Nos. 1290-1296 (7)		12.15	2.85

Castle of the Royal Forces, Havana — A356

Historic architecture: 2c, Iznaga Tower, Trinidad, vert. 3c, Castle of Our Lady of the Angels, Cienfuegos. 4c, St. Francis de Paula Church, Havana. 13c, St. Francis Convent, Havana. 30c, Castle del Morro, Santiago de Cuba.

1967, Nov. 7 **Wmk. 376**
Sizes: 26x47mm (1c), 41x29mm (3c, 4c), 38½x31mm (13c)

1297	A356	1c multi	.25	.25
1298	A356	2c multi	.25	.25
1299	A356	3c multi	.65	.25
1300	A356	4c multi	.65	.25
1301	A356	13c multi	3.25	.50
1302	A356	30c multi	5.00	1.00
	Nos. 1297-1302 (6)		10.05	2.50

Christmas Type of 1961

Birds: No. 1303, Struthia camelus australis. No. 1304, Chysolophus pictus. No. 1305, Ciconia ciconia ciconia. No. 1306, Balearica pavonina. No. 1307, Dromiceius novaehollandiae. No. 1308, Anodorhynchus hyacinthus. No. 1309, Psittacus erithacus. No. 1310, Domicella garrula. No. 1311, Ramphastos sulfuratus. No. 1312, Kakatoe galerita galerita. No. 1313, Phoenicopterus ruber. No. 1314, Pelecanus erythrorhynchos. No. 1315, Alopochen aegyptiacus. No. 1316, Dendronessa galericulata. No. 1317, Chenopsis atrata.

1967, Dec. 20

1303	A248	1c multicolored	1.75	.60
1304	A249	1c multicolored	1.75	.60
1305	A249	1c multicolored	1.75	.60
1306	A249	1c multicolored	1.75	.60
1307	A249	1c multicolored	1.75	.60
a.		Block of 5 + label, Nos. 1303-1307	10.00	3.25
1308	A248	3c multicolored	2.40	1.00
1309	A249	3c multicolored	2.40	1.00
1310	A249	3c multicolored	2.40	1.00
1311	A249	3c multicolored	2.40	1.00
1312	A249	3c multicolored	2.40	1.00
a.		Block of 5 + label, Nos. 1308-1312	14.00	5.50
1313	A248	13c multicolored	4.50	1.75
1314	A249	13c multicolored	4.50	1.75
1315	A249	13c multicolored	4.50	1.75
1316	A249	13c multicolored	4.50	1.75
1317	A249	13c multicolored	4.50	1.75
a.		Block of 5 + label, Nos. 1313-1317	25.00	9.00
	Nos. 1303-1317 (15)		43.25	16.75

Christmas 1967. See note after No. 700.

Ernesto "Che" Guevara (1928-1967), Revolution Leader — A356a

1968, Jan. 3

1318	A356a	13c blk, dark red & buff	2.50	.55

Cultural Congress, Havana — A357

Abstract designs: No. 1319, Independence fostering culture. No. 1320, Integral formation

of man. No. 1321, Responsibility of intellectuals. No. 1322, Relationship between culture and the mass media. No. 1323, The arts versus science and technology.

1968, Jan. 4

1319	A357	3c multi, vert.	.25	.25
1320	A357	3c multi, vert.	.25	.25
1321	A357	13c multi, vert.	1.50	.40
1322	A357	13c multi, vert.	1.75	.45
1323	A357	30c multi	2.40	.85
	Nos. 1319-1323 (5)		6.15	2.25

Canaries and Breeding Cycles A358

1968, Apr. 13

1324	A358	1c F.C.C. 4016	.25	.25
1325	A358	2c A.C.C. 774	.25	.25
1326	A358	3c A.C.C. 122	.40	.25
1327	A358	4c F.C.C. 4477	.40	.25
1328	A358	5c A.C.C. 117	.75	.25
1329	A358	13c A.N.R. 1175	4.00	.55
1330	A358	20c A.C.C. 777	5.50	.70
	Nos. 1324-1330 (7)		11.55	2.50

Stamp Day A359

Paintings: 13c, The Village Postman, by J. Harris. 30c, The Philatelist, by G. Sciltian.

1968, Apr. 24 **Unwmk.**

1331	A359	13c multi	2.00	.50
1332	A359	30c multi	3.00	.70

World Health Organization, 20th Anniv. — A360

13c, Nurse, mother, child. 30c, Surgeons.

1968, May 10 **Wmk. 376**

1333	A360	13c multi	1.60	.55
1334	A360	30c multi	2.10	.80

Intl. Children's Day — A361

1968, June 1

1335	A361	3c multi	1.25	.25

Seville Camaguey Flight, 35th
Anniv. — A362

13c, Plane Four Winds. 30c, Capt.
Barberan, Lt. Collar, pilots.

1968, June 20
1336	A362	13c multi	2.25	.45
1337	A362	30c multi	2.75	.60

Natl. Food Production — A363

1c, Yellow tuna, can. 2c, Cow, dairy products. 3c, Rooster, eggs. 13c, Rum, sugar cane. 20c, Crayfish, box.

1968, June 29
1338	A363	1c multi	.25	.25
1339	A363	2c multi	.25	.25
1340	A363	3c multi	.50	.25
1341	A363	13c multi	3.00	.50
1342	A363	20c multi	3.50	.70
		Nos. 1338-1342 (5)	7.50	1.95

Attack of
Moncada
Barracks,
15th
Anniv.
A364

3c, Siboney farmhouse. 13c, Assault route, Santiago de Cuba. 30c, Students, school.

1968, July 26
Size: 43x29mm (13c)
1343	A364	3c multi	.25	.25
1344	A364	13c multi	1.75	.55
1345	A364	30c multi	3.00	.80
		Nos. 1343-1345 (3)	5.00	1.60

Committee for
the Defense
of the
Revolution,
8th
Anniv. — A365

1968, Sept. 28
1346	A365	3c multi	2.00	.25

Guerilla
Day
A366

Che Guevara and: 1c, Rifleman and "En Cualquier Lugar..." 3c, Machine gunners and "Crear tres muchos Viet Nam." 9c, Silhouette of battalion and "Este Tipo De Lucha..." 10c, Guerillas cheering and "Hoy aquilatamos..." 13c, Map of Caribbean, So. America and "Hasta La Victoria Siempre."

1968, Oct. 8
1347	A366	1c gold, brt blue grn & blk	.25	.25
1348	A366	3c gold, org brn blk	.25	.25
1349	A366	9c multi	.60	.25
1350	A366	10c gold, lt olive grn & blk	1.40	.25
1351	A366	13c gold, red org & blk	2.50	.70
		Nos. 1347-1351 (5)	5.00	1.70

Cuban War of Independence,
Cent. — A367

Independence fighters and scenes: No. 1352, C.M. de Cespedes, broken wheel. No. 1353, E. Betances, horsemen, flag. No. 1354, I. Agramonte, Clavellinas Monument. No. 1355, A. Maceo, Baragua Protest. No. 1356, J. Marti, horsemen. No. 1357, M. Gomez, The Invasion. No. 1358, J.A. Mella, declaration. No. 1359, A. Guiteras, El Morrillo monument. No. 1360, A. Santamaria, attack on Moncada Barracks. No. 1361, F. Pais memorial. No. 1362, J. Echeverria, student protest. No. 1363, C. Cienfuegos, insurrection. No. 1364, Che Guevara, 1st Declaration of Havana.

1968, Oct. 10   **Unwmk.**
1352	A367	1c multicolored	.25	.25
1353	A367	1c multicolored	.25	.25
1354	A367	1c multicolored	.25	.25
1355	A367	1c multicolored	.25	.25
1356	A367	1c multicolored	.25	.25
a.		Strip of 5, Nos. 1352-1356	1.00	1.00
1357	A367	3c multicolored	.25	.25
1358	A367	3c multicolored	.25	.25
1359	A367	3c multicolored	.25	.25
1360	A367	3c multicolored	.25	.25
1361	A367	3c multicolored	.25	.25
a.		Strip of 5, Nos. 1357-1361	1.75	1.00
1362	A367	9c multicolored	1.25	.25
1363	A367	13c multicolored	3.00	.70
1364	A367	30c multicolored	3.50	1.10
		Nos. 1352-1364 (13)	10.25	4.55

Souvenir Sheet

The Burning of Bayamo, by J.E.
Hernandez Giro — A368

1968, Oct. 18   *Imperf.*
1365	A368	50c multi	9.00	9.00

Natl. Philatelic Exhibition, independence cent. Stamp in No. 1365 has simulated perforations.

19th Summer Olympics, Mexico City,
Oct. 12-27 — A369

1c, Parade of athletes. 2c, Women's basketball, vert. 3c, Hammer throw, vert. 4c, Boxing. 5c, Water polo. 13c, Pistol shooting. 30c, Mexican flag, calendar stone. 50c, Running.

1968, Oct. 21   *Perf. 12½*
1366	A369	1c multicolored	.25	.25
1367	A369	2c multicolored	.25	.25
1368	A369	3c multicolored	.25	.25
1369	A369	4c multicolored	.25	.25
1370	A369	5c multicolored	.45	.25
1371	A369	13c multicolored	3.00	.55
		Size: 32x50mm		
1372	A369	30c multicolored	4.50	.80
		Nos. 1366-1372 (7)	8.95	2.60

Souvenir Sheet
Imperf
1373	A369	50c multicolored	15.00	4.00

Stamp in No. 1373 has simulated perforations.

Civilian
Activities
of the
Armed
Forces
A370

3c, Crop dusting. 9c, Che Guevara's Brigade. 10c, Road building. 13c, Plowing, harvesting.

1968, Dec. 2   **Wmk. 376**   **Perf. 12½**
1374	A370	3c multicolored	.25	.25
1375	A370	9c multicolored	.60	.25
1376	A370	10c multicolored	1.00	.25
1377	A370	13c multicolored	2.10	.70
		Nos. 1374-1377 (4)	3.95	1.45

San Alejandro School of Painting,
Sesquicentennial — A371

Paintings: 1c, Manrique de Lara's Family, by Jean Baptiste Vermay, vert. 2c, Seascape, by Leopoldo Romanach. 3c, Wild Cane, by Antonio Rodriguez, vert. 4c, Self-portrait, by Miguel Melero, vert. 5c, The Lottery List, by Jose Joaquin Tejada. 13c, Portrait of Nina, by Armando B. Menocal, vert. 30c, Landscape, by Esteban B. Chartrand. 50c, Siesta, by Guillermo Collazo.

1968, Dec. 30   **Unwmk.**
Sizes: 38x48mm (1c, 3c), 39x50mm (4c, 13c), 53x36mm (30c)
1378	A371	1c multi	.25	.25
1379	A371	2c multi	.25	.25
1380	A371	3c multi	.30	.25
1381	A371	4c multi	.30	.25
1382	A371	5c multi	1.40	.40
1383	A371	13c multi	4.00	.70
1384	A371	30c multi	6.25	1.10
		Nos. 1378-1384 (7)	12.75	3.20

Souvenir Sheet
Imperf
1385	A371	50c multi	9.00	3.50

No. 1385 contains one 52x41½mm stamp that has simulated perforations.

10th Anniv.
of the
Revolution
A372

1969, Jan. 3   **Wmk. 376**   **Perf. 12½**
1386	A372	13c multi	2.00	.60

Villaclarenos Rebellion, Cent. — A373

3c, Gutierrez and Sanchez.

1969, Feb. 6
1387	A373	3c multi	1.00	.25

Women's
Day — A374

Design: Mariana Grajales, rose and statue.

1969, Mar. 8
1388	A374	3c multi	1.25	.25

Cuban Pioneers and Young
Communists Unions — A375

3c, Pioneers. 13c, Young Communists.

1969, Apr. 4
1389	A375	3c multi	.40	.25
1390	A375	13c multi	2.25	.80

Guaimaro Assembly, Cent. — A376

1969, Apr. 10
1391	A376	3c dark brn	1.00	.25

The
Postman,
by Jean
C. Cazin
A377

Paintings: 30c, Portrait of a Young Man, by George Romney.

1969, Apr. 24   **Unwmk.**
1392	A377	13c multi	2.50	.60
		Size: 35½x43½mm		
1393	A377	30c multi	4.00	.90

Stamp Day.

Agrarian
Reform,
10th
Anniv.
A378

1969, May 17   **Wmk. 376**
1394	A378	13c multi	2.25	.70

Marine Life
A379

1c, Petrochirus bahamensis. 2c, Stenopus hispidus. 3c, Panulirus argus. 4c, Callinectes sapidus. 5c, Gecarcinus ruricola. 13c, Macrobrachium carcinus. 30c, Carpilius coralinus.

			Unwmk.	
1969, May 20				
1395	A379	1c multicolored	.25	.25
1396	A379	2c multicolored	.40	.25
1397	A379	3c multicolored	.40	.25
1398	A379	4c multicolored	.50	.25
1399	A379	5c multicolored	.50	.25
1400	A379	13c multicolored	3.50	.45
1401	A379	30c multicolored	5.25	.80
	Nos. 1395-1401 (7)		10.80	2.50

Intl. Labor Organization, 50th Anniv. — A380

13c, Blacksmith breaking chains.

			Wmk. 376	
1969, June 6				
1402	A380	3c shown	.45	.25
1403	A380	13c multi	2.25	.70

Paintings in the Natl. Museum — A381

Designs: 1c, Flowers, by Raul Milian, vert. 2c, Annunciation, by Antonia Eiriz. 3c, Factory, by Marcelo Pogolotti, vert. 4c, Territorial Waters, by Luis Martinez Pedro, vert. 5c, Miss Sarah Gale, by John Hoppner, vert. 13c, Two Women Wearing Mantilla, by Ignacio Zuloaga. 30c, Virgin and Child, by Francisco de Zurbaran.

			Unwmk.	
1969, June 15				
1404	A381	1c 39x59mm	.25	.25
1405	A381	2c 49x40mm	.25	.25
1406	A381	3c 39½x49mm	1.10	.25
1407	A381	4c 39½x43mm	.30	.25
1408	A381	5c 39½x45½mm	.30	.25
1409	A381	13c 38x41½mm	2.10	.70
1410	A381	30c 39x45mm	3.25	.90
	Nos. 1404-1410 (7)		7.55	2.85

Broadcasting Institute — A382

13c, Hemispheres, tower. 1p, Waves on graph.

			Wmk. 376	
1969, July 5				
1411	A382	3c shown	.40	.25
1412	A382	13c multicolored	2.10	.80
1413	A382	1p multicolored	5.00	1.75
	Nos. 1411-1413 (3)		7.50	2.80

Fish
A383

1c, Apogon maculatus. 2c, Bodianus rufus. 3c, Microspathodon chrysurus. 4c, Gramma loreto. 5c, Chromis marginatus. 13c, Myripristis jacobus. 30c, Nomeus gronovii, vert.

			Unwmk.	
1969, July 20				
1414	A383	1c multicolored	.25	.25
1415	A383	2c multicolored	.25	.25
1416	A383	3c multicolored	.40	.25
1417	A383	4c multicolored	.40	.25
1418	A383	5c multicolored	.60	.25
1419	A383	13c multicolored	3.75	.55
1420	A383	30c multicolored	5.25	.90
	Nos. 1414-1420 (7)		10.90	2.70

Natl. Film Industry, 10th Anniv. — A384

			Wmk. 376	
1969, Aug. 5				
1421	A384	1c Poster	.25	.25
1422	A384	3c Documentaries	.25	.25
1423	A384	13c Cartoons	3.00	.60
1424	A384	30c Entertainers	3.50	.70
	Nos. 1421-1424 (4)		7.00	1.80

Napoleon in Milan, by Andrea Appiani — A385

Paintings in the Napoleon Museum, Havana: 2c, Hortensia de Beauharnais, by Francois Gerard. 3c, Napoleon as First Consul, by J.B. Regnault. 4c, Elisa Bonaparte, by Robert Lefevre. 5c, Napoleon Planning Coronation Ceremony, by J.G. Vibert, horiz. 13c, Napoleon as Cuirassier Corporal, by Jean Meissonier. 30c, Napoleon Bonaparte, by LeFevre.

			Unwmk.	
1969, Aug. 20				
1425	A385	1c 46x56mm	.25	.25
1426	A385	2c 41½x55mm	.25	.25
1427	A385	3c 45½x56mm	.25	.25
1428	A385	4c 43x62½mm	.45	.25
1429	A385	5c 63x47½mm	.70	.30
1430	A385	13c 43x62½mm	3.25	.70
1431	A385	30c 45x59½mm	4.25	.90
	Nos. 1425-1431 (7)		9.40	2.90

See Nos. 2448-2453.

Cuba's Victory at the 17th World Amateur Baseball Championships, Santo Domingo — A386

1969, Sept. 11
1432 A386 13c multi   2.75 .60

No. 1432 printed se-tenant with inscribed label listing finalists.

Alexander von Humboldt (1769-1859), German Naturalist — A387

1969, Sept. 14				
1433	A387	3c Surinam eel	.25	.25
1434	A387	13c Night ape	2.50	1.00
1435	A387	30c Condors	4.00	.85
	Nos. 1433-1435 (3)		6.75	2.10

World Fencing Championships, Havana — A388

Designs: 1c, Ancient Egyptians in combat. 2c, Roman gladiators. 2c, Viking and Norman. 4c, Medieval tournament. 5c, French musketeers. 13c, Japanese samurai. 30c, Mounted Cubans, War of Independence. 50c, Modern fencers.

1969, Oct. 2				
1436	A388	1c multi	.25	.25
1437	A388	2c multi	.25	.25
1438	A388	3c multi	.25	.25
1439	A388	4c multi	.40	.25
1440	A388	5c multi	.65	.25
1441	A388	13c multi	3.00	.45
1442	A388	30c multi	4.75	.80
	Nos. 1436-1442 (7)		9.55	2.50

Souvenir Sheet
Imperf

1443 A388 50c multi   12.00 5.00

Stamp in No. 1443 has simulated perforations.

Natl. Revolutionary Militia, 10th Anniv. — A389

			Wmk. 376	
1969, Oct. 26				
1444	A389	3c multi	1.25	.25

Disappearance of Maj. Camilo Cienfuegos, 10th Anniv. — A390

1969, Oct. 28
1445 A390 13c multi   2.50 .60

Agriculture — A391

No. 1446, Strawberries, grapes. No. 1447, Onions, asparagus. No. 1448, Rice. No. 1449, Banana. No. 1450, Pineapple, vert. No. 1451, Tobacco, vert. No. 1452, Citrus fruits, vert. No. 1453, Coffee, vert. No. 1454, Rabbits, vert. No. 1455, Pigs, vert. No. 1456, Sugar cane. No. 1457, Bull.

			Unwmk.	
1969, Nov. 2				
1446	A391	1c multicolored	.25	.25
1447	A391	1c multicolored	.25	.25
1448	A391	1c multicolored	.25	.25
1449	A391	1c multicolored	.25	.25
a.	Strip of 4, #1446-1449		1.00	.80
1450	A391	3c multicolored	.50	.50
1451	A391	3c multicolored	.50	.50
1452	A391	3c multicolored	.50	.50
1453	A391	3c multicolored	.50	.50
1454	A391	3c multicolored	.50	.50
a.	Strip of 5, #1450-1454		2.75	2.50
1455	A391	10c multicolored	.50	.50
1456	A391	13c multicolored	2.75	.60
1457	A391	30c multicolored	4.00	.85
	Nos. 1446-1457 (12)		10.75	5.20

Sporting Events — A392

1c, 2nd Natl. Games. 2c, 11th Anniv. Games. 3c, Barrientos Commemorative, vert. 10c, 2nd Olympic Trials, vert. 13c, 6th Socialist Bicycle Race, vert. 30c, 6th Capablanca Memorial Chess Championships, vert.

1969, Nov. 15				
1458	A392	1c multicolored	.25	.25
1459	A392	2c multicolored	.25	.25
1460	A392	3c multicolored	.25	.25
1461	A392	10c multicolored	.40	.25
1462	A392	13c multicolored	2.75	.80
1463	A392	30c multicolored	4.00	1.25
	Nos. 1458-1463 (6)		7.90	3.05

Christmas Type of 1961

Flowering plants: No. 1464, Plumbago capensis. No. 1465, Petrea volubilis. No. 1466, Clitoria ternatea. No. 1467, Duranta repens. No. 1468, Ruellia tuberosa. No. 1469, Turnera ulmifolia. No. 1470, Thevetia peruviana. No. 1471, Hibiscus elatus. No. 1472, Allamanda cathartica. No. 1473, Cosmos sulphureus. No. 1474, Delonix regia. No. 1475, Neriun oleander. No. 1476, Cordia sebestena. No. 1477, Lochnera rosea. No. 1478, Jatropha integerrima.

1969, Dec. 1				
1464	A248	1c multicolored	.40	.25
1465	A249	1c multicolored	.40	.25
1466	A249	1c multicolored	.40	.25
1467	A249	1c multicolored	.40	.25
1468	A249	1c multicolored	.40	.25
a.	Block of 5 + label, Nos. 1464-1468		3.00	1.00
1469	A248	3c multicolored	1.00	.25
1470	A249	3c multicolored	1.00	.25
1471	A249	3c multicolored	1.00	.25
1472	A249	3c multicolored	1.00	.25
1473	A249	3c multicolored	1.00	.25
a.	Block of 5 + label, Nos. 1469-1473		6.00	1.25
1474	A248	13c multicolored	2.25	1.00
1475	A249	13c multicolored	2.25	1.00

1476	A249	13c multicolored	2.25	1.00
1477	A249	13c multicolored	2.25	1.00
1478	A249	13c multicolored	2.25	1.00
a.		Block of 5 + label, Nos. 1474-1478	11.00	5.00
		Nos. 1464-1478 (15)	18.25	7.50

Christmas 1969. See note after No. 700.

Zapata Swamp Fauna — A393

1c, Trelanorhynus variabilis. 2c, Hyla insulsa. 3c, Atractosteus tristoechus. 4c, Capromys nana. 5c, Crocodylus rhombifer. 13c, Amazona leucocephala. 30c, Agelaius phoeniceus assimilis.

1969, Dec. 15

1479	A393	1c multicolored	.25	.25
1480	A393	2c multicolored	.25	.25
1481	A393	3c multicolored	.25	.25
1482	A393	4c multicolored	.25	.25
1483	A393	5c multicolored	.25	.25
1484	A393	13c multicolored	4.50	.55
1485	A393	30c multicolored	5.00	1.00
		Nos. 1479-1485 (7)	10.75	2.80

Nos. 1482, 1484-1485 vert.

Tourism
A394

1c, Jibacoa Beach. 3c, Trinidad City. 13c, Santiago de Cuba. 30c, Vinales Valley.

1970, Jan. 25   **Wmk. 376**

1486	A394	1c multi	.25	.25
1487	A394	3c multi	.25	.25
1488	A394	13c multi	1.90	.80
1489	A394	30c multi	2.75	1.00
		Nos. 1486-1489 (4)	5.15	2.30

Medicinal
Plants — A395

1c, Guarea guara. 3c, Ocimum sanctum. 10c, Canella winterana. 13c, Bidens pilosa. 30c, Turnera ulmifolia. 50c, Picramnia pentandra.

1970, Feb. 10   **Unwmk.**

1490	A395	1c multi	.25	.25
1491	A395	3c multi	.25	.25
1492	A395	10c multi	.45	.25
1493	A395	13c multi	2.25	.70
1494	A395	30c multi	2.75	.85
1495	A395	50c multi	4.00	1.00
		Nos. 1490-1495 (6)	9.95	3.30

11th Central American and Caribbean Games, Panama, Feb. 28-Mar. 14 — A396

1970, Feb. 28   **Wmk. 376**

1496	A396	1c Weight lifting	.25	.25
1497	A396	3c Boxing	.25	.25
1498	A396	10c Gymnastics	.25	.25
1499	A396	13c Running	2.40	.65
1500	A396	30c Fencing	3.50	.90
		Nos. 1496-1500 (5)	6.65	2.30

Souvenir Sheet

Imperf

1501	A396	50c Baseball	12.00	6.00

No. 1501 contains one 50x37mm stamp that has simulated perforations.

EXPO '70, Osaka, Japan, Mar. 15-Sept. 13 — A397

1c, Enjoying life. 2c, Improving on nature, vert. 3c, Better living standard. 13c, Intl. cooperation, vert. 30c, Cuban pavilion.

1970, Mar. 15

1502	A397	1c multicolored	.25	.25
1503	A397	2c multicolored	.40	.25
1504	A397	3c multicolored	.40	.25
1505	A397	13c multicolored	2.75	.55
1506	A397	30c multicolored	4.00	.80
		Nos. 1502-1506 (5)	7.80	2.10

Speleological Soc., 30th Anniv. — A398

Petroglyphs in Cuban caves: 1c, Ambrosio Cave, Varadero Matanzas. 2c, Cave No. 1, Punta del Este, Isle of Pines. 3c, Pichardo Cave, Cubitas Camaguey Mountains. 4c, Ambrosio Cave, diff. 5c, Cave No. 1, diff. 13c, Garcia Ribiou Cave, Havana. 30c, Cave No. 2, Punta del Este.

1970, Mar. 28   **Unwmk.**
Sizes: 29x45mm (1c, 3c, 4c, 13c)

1507	A398	1c multi	.25	.25
1508	A398	2c shown	.25	.25
1509	A398	3c multi	.25	.25
1510	A398	4c multi	.25	.25
1511	A398	5c multi	.25	.25
1512	A398	13c multi	2.25	.70
1513	A398	30c multi	4.75	.80
		Nos. 1507-1513 (7)	8.25	2.75

Aviation Pioneers — A399

1970, Apr. 10

1514	A399	3c Jose D. Blino	1.00	.25
1515	A399	13c Adolfo Teodore	3.50	.70

Lenin Birth Centenary — A400

Paintings and quotes: 1c, Lenin in Kazan, by O. Vishniakov. 2c, Young Lenin, by V. Prager. 3c, Second Socialist Party Congress, by Y. Vinogradov. 4c, First Manifesto, by F. Golubkov. 5c, First Day of Soviet Power, by N. Babasiuk. 13c, Lenin in Smolny, by M. Sokolov. 30c, Autumn in Gorky, by A. Varlamov. 50c, Lenin at Gorky, by N. Baskakov.

1970, Apr. 22
Sizes: 67½x46mm (1c, 4c, 5c)

1516	A400	1c multi	.25	.25
1517	A400	2c shown	.25	.25
1518	A400	3c multi	.25	.25
1519	A400	4c multi	.25	.25
1520	A400	5c multi	.25	.25
1521	A400	13c multi	2.75	.55
1522	A400	30c multi	3.25	.70
		Nos. 1516-1522 (7)	7.25	2.50

Souvenir Sheet

Imperf

1523	A400	50c multi	13.00	6.50

No. 1523 contains one 48x46mm stamp that has simulated perforations.

Stamp Day — A401

13c, The Letter, by J. Arche. 30c, Portrait of A Cadet, Anonymous.

1970, Apr. 24

1524	A401	13c multicolored	3.00	.60

Size: 30x44mm

1525	A401	30c multicolored	3.75	.80

Da Vinci's Anatomical Drawing, Earth, Moon — A402

1970, May 17   **Wmk. 376**

1526	A402	30c multi	3.50	.60

World Telecommunications Day.

Ho Chi Minh (1890-1969), President of North Viet Nam — A403

No. 1527, Vietnamese fisherman. No. 1528, Two women. No. 1529, Plowing field. No. 1530, Teacher, students in air-raid shelter. No. 1531, Nine women in paddy. No. 1532, Camouflaged machine shop.

1970, May 19   **Unwmk.**

1527	A403	1c multicolored	.25	.25

Size: 32x44mm

1528	A403	3c multicolored	.50	.25
1529	A403	3c multicolored	.50	.25

Size: 33x45mm

1530	A403	3c multicolored	.50	.25
1531	A403	3c multicolored	.70	.25

Size: 34x41½mm

1532	A403	3c multicolored	.70	.25

Size: 34x39mm

1533	A403	13c shown	3.25	.70
		Nos. 1527-1533 (7)	6.40	2.20

Cuban Cigar Industry A404

3c, Plantation, Eden cigar band. 13c, Factory, El Mambi band. 30c, Packing cigars, Lopez Hermanos band.

1970, July 5

1534	A404	3c multicolored	.25	.25
1535	A404	13c multicolored	2.25	.70
1536	A404	30c multicolored	3.25	1.00
		Nos. 1534-1536 (3)	5.75	1.95

Projected Sugar Production: Over 10 Million Tons — A405

1c, Cane-crushing. 2c, Sowing and crop dusting. 3c, Cutting sugar cane. 10c, Transporting cane. 13c, Modern cutting machine. 30c, Intl. Brigade, cane cutters, vert. 1p, Sugar warehouse.

1970, July 26

1537	A405	1c multicolored	.25	.25
1538	A405	2c multicolored	.25	.25
1539	A405	3c multicolored	.25	.25
1540	A405	10c multicolored	5.00	.45
1541	A405	13c multicolored	1.50	.25
1542	A405	30c multicolored	2.25	.70
1543	A405	1p multicolored	4.00	2.00
		Nos. 1537-1543 (7)	13.50	4.15

Pedro Figueredo (d. 1870), Composer — A406

Versions of the Natl. Anthem.

1970, Aug. 17

1544	A406	3c 1868 Version	.30	.25
1545	A406	20c 1898 Version	2.75	.60

Women's Federation, 10th Anniv. — A407

1970, Aug. 23

1546	A407	3c multi	1.00	.50

Militia, by Servando C. Moreno — A408

Paintings in the Natl. Museum: 2c, Washerwomen, by Aristides Fernandez. 3c, Puerta del Sol, Madrid, by L. Paret Y Alcazar. 4c, Fishermen's Wives, by Joaquin Sorolla. 5c, Portrait of a Woman, by Thomas de Keyser. 13c, Mrs. Edward Foster, by Sir Thomas Lawrence. 30c, Tropical Gypsy, by Victor M. Garcia.

1970, Aug. 31

1547	A408	1c shown	.25	.25

Size: 45x41mm

1548	A408	2c multi	.25	.25
1549	A408	3c multi	.25	.25

Size: 40x41mm

1550	A408	4c multi	.25	.25

Size: 38x45½mm

1551	A408	5c multi	.25	.25
1552	A408	13c multi	2.50	.50
1553	A408	30c multi	4.00	.80
		Nos. 1547-1553 (7)	7.75	2.55

See Nos. 1640-1646, 1669-1675, 1773-1779.

Havana Declaration, 10th Anniv. — A409

1970, Sept. 2

1554	A409	3c Jose Marti Square	.75	.25

Committee for the Defense of the Revolution, 10th Anniv. A410

1970, Sept. 28

1555	A410	3c multi	.55	.25

39th Sugar Technician's Assoc. (ATAC) Conference — A411

1970, Oct. 11

1556	A411	30c multi	3.25	.70

Wildlife — A412

1c, Numida meleagris galeata. 2c, Dendrocygna arborea. 3c, Phasianus colchicus torquatus. 4c, Zenaida macroura macroura. 5c, Colinus virginianus cubanensis. 13c, Sus scrofa. 30c, Odocoileus virginianus.

1970, Oct. 20

1557	A412	1c multicolored	.70	.25
1558	A412	2c multicolored	.80	.25
1559	A412	3c multicolored	.95	.25
1560	A412	4c multicolored	1.10	.25
1561	A412	5c multicolored	1.25	.25
1562	A412	13c multicolored	2.00	1.00
1563	A412	30c multicolored	3.25	1.50
		Nos. 1557-1563 (7)	10.05	3.75

Black-magic Feast, by M. Puente — A413

Afro-Cuban folk paintings: 3c, Hat Dance, by V.P. Landaluze. 10c, Los Hoyos Conga Dance, by Domingo Ravenet. 13c, Climax of the Rumba, by Eduardo Abela.

1970, Nov. 5

Sizes: 36x48½mm (3c, 13c), 44½x44mm (10c)

1564	A413	1c shown	.25	.25
1565	A413	3c multi	.35	.25
1566	A413	10c multi	.90	.45
1567	A413	13c multi	2.50	.70
		Nos. 1564-1567 (4)	4.00	1.65

Road Safety Week A414

1970, Nov. 15

1568	A414	3c Zebra, road signs	1.10	.25
1569	A414	9c Prudence the Bear	1.60	.25

Intl. Education Year — A415

1970, Nov. 20

1570	A415	13c Abacus, "a"	2.50	.25
1571	A415	30c Cow, microscope	3.25	.70

Christmas Type of 1961

Birds: No. 1572, Dives atroviolaceus. No. 1573, Glaucidium siju siju. No. 1574, Todus multicolor. No. 1575, Xiphidiopicus percussus percussus. No. 1576, Ferminia cerverai. No. 1577, Teretistris fornsi. No. 1578, Myadestes elisabeth elisabeth. No. 1579, Polioptila lembeyei. No. 1580, Vireo gundlachii gundlachii. No. 1581, Teretistris fernandinae. No. 1582, Torreornis inexpectata inexpectata. No. 1583, Chondrohierax wilsonii. No. 1584, Accipiter gundlachi. No. 1585, Starnoenas cyanocephala. No. 1586, Aratinga euops.

1970, Dec. 1

1572	A248	1c multicolored	.80	.25
1573	A249	1c multicolored	.80	.25
1574	A249	1c multicolored	.80	.25
1575	A249	1c multicolored	.80	.25
1576	A249	1c multicolored	.80	.25
a.		Block of 5 + label, Nos. 1572-1576	5.00	1.00
1577	A248	3c multicolored	1.75	.35
1578	A249	3c multicolored	1.75	.35
1579	A249	3c multicolored	1.75	.35
1580	A249	3c multicolored	1.75	.35
1581	A249	3c multicolored	1.75	.35
a.		Block of 5 + label, Nos. 1577-1581	10.00	2.00
1582	A249	13c multicolored	2.50	.90
1583	A249	13c multicolored	2.50	.90
1584	A249	13c multicolored	2.50	.90
1585	A249	13c multicolored	2.50	.90
1586	A249	13c multicolored	2.50	.90
a.		Block of 5 + label, Nos. 1582-1586	15.00	5.00
		Nos. 1572-1586 (15)	25.25	7.50

Christmas 1970. See note after No. 700.

Camilo Cienfuegos Military Academy — A416

1970, Dec. 2

1587	A416	3c multi	1.25	.25

7th Congress of the Intl. Organization of Journalists — A417

1971, Jan. 4

1588	A417	13c multi	2.25	.50

World Meteorology Day — A418

1c, Class, weather chart, computer, vert. 3c, Weather map. 8c, Equipment, vert.

Size: 39½x35½mm (3c)

1971, Feb. 16

1589	A418	1c multi	.25	.25
1590	A418	3c multi	.25	.25
1591	A418	8c multi	1.00	.25
1592	A418	30c shown	4.75	1.25
		Nos. 1589-1592 (4)	6.25	2.00

6th Pan American Games, Cali, Colombia — A419

1c, Emblem, vert. 2c, Women's running, vert. 3c, Rifle shooting. 4c, Gymnastics, vert. 5c, Boxing, vert. 13c, Water polo. 30c, Baseball.

1971, Feb. 20

1593	A419	1c multicolored	.25	.25
1594	A419	2c multicolored	.25	.25
1595	A419	3c multicolored	.25	.25
1596	A419	4c multicolored	.25	.25
1597	A419	5c multicolored	.25	.25
1598	A419	13c multicolored	2.40	.30
1599	A419	30c multicolored	3.00	.55
		Nos. 1593-1599 (7)	6.65	2.10

Porcelain and Mosaics in the Metropolitan Museum, Havana — A420

Designs: 1c, Parisian vase, 19th cent. 3c, Mexican bowl, 17th cent. 10c, Parisian vase, diff. 13c, Colosseum, Italian mosaic, 19th cent. 20c, Mexican bowl, 17th cent. 30c, St. Peter's Square, Italian mosaic, 19th cent.

1971, Mar. 11

Sizes: 34½x53mm (1c, 10c), 46x53mm (3c), 42x48mm (20c)

1600	A420	1c multi	.25	.25
1601	A420	3c multi	.25	.25
1602	A420	10c multi	.40	.25
1603	A420	13c shown	2.25	.25
1604	A420	20c multi	2.25	.55
1605	A420	30c multi	2.75	.65
		Nos. 1600-1605 (6)	8.15	2.20

See Nos. 1699-1705.

Natl. Child Centers, 10th Anniv. — A421

1971, Apr. 10

1606	A421	3c multicolored	.75	.25

Manned Space Flight 10th Anniv. — A422

Cosmonauts in training.

1971, Apr. 12

1607	A422	1c multi	.25	.25
1608	A422	2c multi, diff.	.25	.25
1609	A422	3c multi, diff.	.25	.25
1610	A422	4c multi, diff.	.25	.25
1611	A422	5c multi, diff.	.25	.25
1612	A422	13c multi, diff.	2.25	.30
1613	A422	30c multi, diff.	3.25	.65
		Nos. 1607-1613 (7)	6.75	2.20

Souvenir Sheet

Imperf

1614	A422	50c multi	10.00	10.00

Stamp in No. 1614 has simulated perf.

Bay of Pigs Invasion, 10th Anniv. A423

1971, Apr. 17

1615	A423	13c multi	2.00	.60

Stamp Day — A424

Packets: 13c, Jeune Richard attacking the Windsor Castle, 1807. 30c, Orinoco.

1971, Apr. 24

1616	A424	13c multi	2.40	.80
1617	A424	30c multi	3.50	1.00

Cuban Intl. Broadcast Service, 10th Anniv. — A425

1971, May 1   **Wmk. 376**
1618	A425	3c multi	.40	.25
1619	A425	50c multi	4.50	.90

Orchids A426

1c, Cattleya skinnerii. 2c, Vanda hibrida. 3c, Cypripedium collossum. 4c, Cypripedium gloucophyllum. 5c, Vanda tricolor. 13c, Cypripedium mowgh. 30c, Cypripedium solum.

1971, May 15
1620	A426	1c multicolored	.25	.25
1621	A426	2c multicolored	.25	.25
1622	A426	3c multicolored	.25	.25
1623	A426	4c multicolored	.25	.25
1624	A426	5c multicolored	.25	.25
1625	A426	13c multicolored	2.40	.45
1626	A426	30c multicolored	4.75	.85
		Nos. 1620-1626 (7)	8.40	2.55

See Nos. 1677-1683 and 1780-1786.

Enrique Loynaz del Castillo (b. 1861), Composer — A427

3c, Portrait, Invasion Hymn.

1971, June 5   **Wmk. 376**
1627	A427	3c multicolored	.90	.25

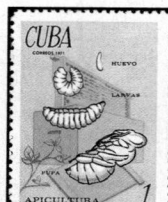

Bee Keeping — A428

1971, June 20   **Unwmk.**
1628	A428	1c Egg, larvae, pupa	.25	.25
1629	A428	3c Worker	.25	.25
1630	A428	9c Drone	.45	.25
1631	A428	13c Defense of hive	2.25	.80
1632	A428	30c Queen	3.50	.80
		Nos. 1628-1632 (5)	6.70	1.85

Children's Drawings — A429

1c, Sailboat. 3c, The Little Train. 9c, Sugar Cane Cutter. 10c, Return of the Fishermen. 13c, The Zoo. 20c, House and Garden. 30c, Landscape.

1971, Aug. 30   **Size: 45x39mm**
1633	A429	1c multi	.25	.25
1634	A429	3c multi	.85	.25

Sizes: 45½x35½mm (9c, 13c), 47x37½mm (10c)
1635	A429	9c multi	.25	.25
1636	A429	10c multi	.40	.25
1637	A429	13c multi	1.60	.30

Size: 47x42mm
1638	A429	20c multi	2.50	.55

Size: 31½x50mm
1639	A429	30c multi	2.75	.85
		Nos. 1633-1639 (7)	8.60	2.70

Art Type of 1970

Paintings in the Natl. Museum: 1c, St. Catherine of Alexandria, by F. Zurburan. 2c, The Cart, by Federico Americo. 3c, St. Christopher and Child, by J. Bassano. 4c, Little Devil, by Rene Portocarrero. 5c, Portrait of a Woman, by Nicolas Maes. 13c, Phoenix, by Raul Martinez. 30c, Sir William Pitt, by Thomas Gainsborough.

1971, Sept. 20
1640	A408	1c 31x55mm	.25	.25
1641	A408	2c 48x37mm	.25	.25
1642	A408	3c 31x55mm	.25	.25
1643	A408	4c 37x48mm	.25	.25
1644	A408	5c 37x48mm	.40	.25
1645	A408	13c 39x48½mm	2.25	.45
1646	A408	30c 39x48½mm	3.25	.75
		Nos. 1640-1646 (7)	6.90	2.45

Sport Fishing — A431

1c, Albula vulpes. 2c, Seriola species. 3c, Micropterus salmoides. 4c, Coryphaena hippurus. 5c, Megalops atlantica. 13c, Acanthocybium solandri. 30c, Makaira ampla.

1971, Oct. 30
1647	A431	1c multicolored	.25	.25
1648	A431	2c multicolored	.25	.25
1649	A431	3c multicolored	.25	.25
1650	A431	4c multicolored	.25	.25
1651	A431	5c multicolored	.30	.25
1652	A431	13c multicolored	2.00	.55
1653	A431	30c multicolored	3.25	.95
		Nos. 1647-1653 (7)	6.55	2.75

19th World Amateur Baseball Championships — A432

1971, Nov. 22   **Wmk. 376**
1654	A432	3c shown	.25	.25
1655	A432	1p Globe as baseball	6.25	1.40

Execution of Medical Students, Cent. A433

Paintings: 3c, Dr. Fermin Valdez Dominguez, anonymous. 13c, Execution of the Medical Students, by M. Mesa. 30c, Capt. Federico Capdevila, anonymous.

1971, Nov. 27   **Unwmk.**
Size: 61½x46mm (13c)
1656	A433	3c multi	.35	.25
1657	A433	13c multi	1.90	.40
1658	A433	30c multi	3.00	.55
		Nos. 1656-1658 (3)	5.25	1.20

Spindalis Zena Pretrei — A434

Birds: 1c, Falco sparverius sparverioides vigors. 2c, Glaucidium siju siju. 3c, Priotelus temnurus temnurus. 4c, Saurothera merlini merlini. 5c, Nesoceleus fernandinae. 30c, Mimocichla plumbea rubripes. 50c, Chlorostilbon ricordii ricordii and Archilochus colubris. Nos. 1659-1663 vert.

1971, Dec. 10
1659	A434	1c multi	.40	.25
1660	A434	2c multi	.40	.25
1661	A434	3c multi	.65	.25
1662	A434	4c multi	.70	.25
1663	A434	5c multi	.90	.25
1664	A434	13c shown	1.60	.55
1665	A434	30c multi	3.25	1.75
		Nos. 1659-1665 (7)	7.90	3.55

Size: 55½x29mm
1666	A434	50c multi	6.00	1.75

Death centenary of Ramon de la Sagra, naturalist.

Cuba's Victory at the World Amateur Baseball Championships — A435

1971, Dec. 8   **Wmk. 376**
1667	A435	13c multi	2.00	.60

UNICEF, 25th Anniv. A436

1971, Dec. 11
1668	A436	13c multi	2.50	.70

Art Type of 1970

Paintings in the Natl. Museum: 1c, Arrival of an Ambassador, by Vittore Carpaccio. 2c, Senora Malpica, by G. Collazo. 3c, La Chorrera Tower, by Esteban Chartrand. 4c, Creole Landscape, by Carlos Enriquez. 5c, Sir William Lemon, by George Romney. 13c, Landscape, by Henry Cleenewerk. 30c, Valencia Beach, by Joaquin Sorolla y Bastida.

1972, Jan. 25   **Unwmk.**
1669	A408	1c 50x33mm	.25	.25
1670	A408	2c 27½x52mm	.25	.25
1671	A408	3c 50x33mm	.25	.25
1672	A408	4c 35x43mm	.25	.25
1673	A408	5c 35x43mm	.25	.25
1674	A408	13c 43x33mm	2.00	.40
1675	A408	30c 43x33mm	3.50	.95
		Nos. 1669-1675 (7)	6.75	2.60

Academy of Sciences, 10th Anniv. — A437

13c, Capitol Type of 1929.

1972, Feb. 20   **Wmk. 376**
1676	A437	13c multi	2.00	.50

Orchid Type of 1971

1c, Brasso cattleya sindorossiana. 2c, Cypripedium doraeus. 3c, Cypripedium exul. 4c, Cypripedium rosy dawn. 5c, Cypripedium champolliom. 13c, Cypripedium bucolique. 30c, Cypripedium sullanum.

1972, Feb. 25   **Unwmk.**
1677	A426	1c multicolored	.25	.25
1678	A426	2c multicolored	.25	.25
1679	A426	3c multicolored	.25	.25
1680	A426	4c multicolored	.25	.25
1681	A426	5c multicolored	.25	.25
1682	A426	13c multicolored	2.75	.65
1683	A426	30c multicolored	3.50	.80
		Nos. 1677-1683 (7)	7.50	2.70

Eduardo Agramonte (1849-1872), Revolutionary, Physician — A438

3c, Portrait by F. Martinez.

1972, Mar. 8
1684	A438	3c multi	.60	.25

World Health Day — A439

1972, Apr. 7   **Wmk. 376**
1685	A439	13c multicolored	2.00	.50

Soviet Space Program — A440

1c, Sputnik 1. 2c, Vostok 1. 3c, Valentina Tereshkova. 4c, Alexei Leonov. 5c, Lunokhod 1, moon vehicle. 13c, Linking Soyuz capsules. 30c, Victims of Soyuz 11 accident.

1972, Apr. 12   **Unwmk.**
1686	A440	1c multicolored	.25	.25
1687	A440	2c multicolored	.25	.25
1688	A440	3c multicolored	.25	.25
1689	A440	4c multicolored	.25	.25
1690	A440	5c multicolored	.25	.25
1691	A440	13c multicolored	2.10	.40
1692	A440	30c multicolored	2.50	.70
		Nos. 1686-1692 (7)	5.85	2.35

Stamp
Day — A441

Designs: 13c, Postmaster-Gen. Vicente
Mora Pera, by Ramon Loy. 30c, Soldier's Letter, Cuba to Venezuela, 1897.

1972, Apr. 24
1693 A441 13c shown   1.75   .50
Size: 48x39mm
1694 A441 30c multicolored   2.75   .55

Labor
Day — A442

1972, May 1   **Wmk. 376**
1695 A442 3c multicolored   .90   .25

Jose Marti, Ho
Chi Minh — A443

3rd Conference Against War in Indo-
China, May 19 — A444

30c, Roses, conference emblem.

1972, May 19
1696 A443 3c shown   .40   .25
1697 A443 13c shown   1.60   .40
1698 A443 30c multicolored   2.00   .55
   Nos. 1696-1698 (3)   4.00 1.20

Metropolitan Museum Type of 1971

Portraits: 1c, Salvador del Muro, by J. Del
Rio. 2c, Luis de las Casas, by Del Rio. 3c,
Cristopher Columbus, anonymous. 4c, Tomas
Gamba, by V. Escobar. 5c, Maria Galarraga,
by Escobar. 13c, Isabel II, by Federico
Madrazo. 30c, Carlos III, by Miguel Melero.

1972, May 25   **Unwmk.**
Size: 34x43½mm
1699 A420 1c multi   .25   .25
1700 A420 2c multi   .25   .25
1701 A420 3c multi   .25   .25
1702 A420 4c multi   .40   .25
1703 A420 5c multi   .40   .25
Size: 34x51½mm
1704 A420 13c multi   2.00   .40
1705 A420 30c multi   2.50   .70
   Nos. 1699-1705 (7)   6.05 2.35

Children's
Songs
Competition,
Natl. Library
A445

1972, June 5   **Wmk. 376**
1706 A445 3c multi   .80   .25

Thoroughbred Horses — A446

1972, June 30   **Unwmk.**
1707 A446 1c Tarpan   .25   .25
1708 A446 2c Kertag   .25   .25
1709 A446 3c Creole   .25   .25
1710 A446 4c Andalusian   .25   .25
1711 A446 5c Arabian   .25   .25
1712 A446 13c Quarter horse   3.00   .55
1713 A446 30c Pursang   3.50   .80
   Nos. 1707-1713 (7)   7.75 2.60

Frank Pais (d. 1957), Educator,
Revolutionary — A447

1972, July 26   **Wmk. 376**
1714 A447 13c blk & red   1.75   .50

1972 Summer Olympics, Munich, Aug.
26-Sept. 10 — A448

1c, Athlete, emblems, vert. 2c, "M," boxing.
3c, "U," weight lifting. 4c, "N," fencing. 5c, "I,"
rifle shooting. 13c, "C," running. 30c, "H,"
basketball.
50c, Gymnastics.

1972, Aug. 26   **Unwmk.**
1715 A448 1c multicolored   .25   .25
1716 A448 2c multicolored   .25   .25
1717 A448 3c multicolored   .25   .25
1718 A448 4c multicolored   .25   .25
1719 A448 5c multicolored   .25   .25
1720 A448 13c multicolored   2.00   .35
1721 A448 30c multicolored   2.50   .65
   Nos. 1715-1721 (7)   5.75 2.25
Souvenir Sheet
Imperf
1722 A448 50c multicolored   6.00 1.90
Stamp in No. 1722 has simulated
perforations.

Intl. Hydrological Decade — A449

Landscapes: 1c, Tree Trunks, by Domingo
Ramos. 3c, Cyclone, by Tiburcio Lorenzo. 8c,
Vinales, by Ramos. 30c, Forest and Brook, by
Antonio R. Morey, vert.

1972, Sept. 20
1723 A449 1c multi   .25   .25
1724 A449 3c multi   .25   .25
1725 A449 8c multi   .80   .25
1726 A449 30c multi   2.50   .55
   Nos. 1723-1726 (4)   3.80 1.30

Butterflies from the Gundlach
Collection — A450

1c, Papilio thoas oviedo. 2c, Papilio devil-
liers. 3c, Papilio polixenes polixenes. 4c,
Papilio androgeus epidaurus. 5c, Papilio
cayguanabus. 13c, Papilio andraemon her-
nandezi. 30c, Papilio celadon.

1972, Sept. 25
1727 A450 1c multicolored   .25   .25
1728 A450 2c multicolored   .25   .25
1729 A450 3c multicolored   .25   .25
1730 A450 4c multicolored   .25   .25
1731 A450 5c multicolored   .30   .25
1732 A450 13c multicolored   3.50   .85
1733 A450 30c multicolored   4.75 1.10
   Nos. 1727-1733 (7)   9.55 3.20

A451

Miguel de Cervantes Saavedra (1547-
1616), Spanish Author — A452

Paintings by A. Fernandez: 3c, In La
Mancha, vert. 13c, Battle with Wine Skins.
30c, Don Quixote de La Mancha, vert. 50c,
Scene from Don Quixote, by Jose Moreno
Carbonero.

1972, Sept. 29
Size: 34½x46mm (3c, 30c)
1734 A451 3c multi   .25   .25
1735 A451 13c shown   2.10   .50
1736 A451 30c multi   2.25   .55
   Nos. 1734-1736 (3)   4.60 1.30
Souvenir Sheet
Perf. 12½ on 3 Sides
1737 A452 50c shown   5.00 2.25

Guerrilla Day, 5th Anniv. — A453

3c, Ernesto "Che" Guevara. 13c, Tamara
"Tania" Bunke. 30c, Guido "Inti" Peredo.

1972, Oct. 8
1738 A453 3c multicolored   .25   .25
1739 A453 13c multicolored   2.25   .45
1740 A453 30c multicolored   2.50   .60
   Nos. 1738-1740 (3)   5.00 1.35

Traditional
Musical
Instruments
A454

3c, Abwe (rattles). 13c, Bonko enchemiya
(drum). 30c, Iya (drum).

1972, Oct. 25
1741 A454 3c multi   .25   .25
1742 A454 13c multi   2.25   .45
1743 A454 30c multi   2.50   .55
   Nos. 1741-1743 (3)   5.00 1.25

MATEX '72, 3rd Natl. Philatelic
Exhibition, Matanzas — A455

1972, Nov. 18   **Wmk. 376**
1744 A455 13c No. 467   2.50   .45
1745 A455 30c No. C49   3.00   .55
Nos. 1744-1745 printed se-tenant with
insribed labels picturing Type A232, emblem
of the Cuban Philatelic Federation.

Historic
Ships
A456

1c, Viking long boat, 6th-9th cent. 2c, Caravel, 15th cent., vert. 3c, Galleass, 16th cent.
4c, Galleon, 17th cent., vert. 5c, Clipper, 19th
cent. 13c, Steam packet, 19th cent. 30c,
Atomic icebreaker Lenin.

1972, Nov. 30   **Unwmk.**
1746 A456 1c multicolored   .25   .25
1747 A456 2c multicolored   .25   .25
1748 A456 3c multicolored   .25   .25
1749 A456 4c multicolored   .30   .25
1750 A456 5c multicolored   .35   .25
1751 A456 13c multicolored   2.10   .75
Size: 52½x29mm.
1752 A456 30c multicolored   6.00 1.25
   Nos. 1746-1752 (7)   9.50 3.25

UNESCO Save Venice
Campaign — A457

3c, Lion of St. Mark. 13c, Bridge of Sighs, vert. 30c, St. Mark's Cathedral.

1972, Dec. 8

1753	A457	3c multicolored	.25	.25
1754	A457	13c multicolored	1.75	.45
1755	A457	30c multicolored	2.25	.85
		Nos. 1753-1755 (3)	4.25	1.55

Cuba, World Amateur Baseball Champion in 1972 — A458

1972, Dec. 15

1756	A458	3c Umpire	1.25	.30

Sport Events, 1972 — A459

1972, Dec. 22

1757	A459	1c shown	.25	.25
1758	A458	2c Pole vault	.25	.25
1759	A458	3c like No. 1756	.25	.25
1760	A458	4c Wrestling	.25	.25
1761	A458	5c Fencing	.25	.25
1762	A458	13c Boxing	1.75	.55
1763	A458	30c Marlin	2.50	.80
		Nos. 1757-1763 (7)	5.50	2.60

Barrientos Memorial Athletics Championships, 11th Amateur Baseball Championships, Cerro Pelado Intl. Tournament, Central American and Caribbean Fencing Tournament, Giraldo Cordova Tournament, Ernest Hemingway Natl. Fishing Contest.

No. 1759 inscribed "XI serie nacional de beisbol aficionado."

Medals Won by Cubans at the 1972 Summer Olympics, Munich A460

1c, Bronze, Women's 100-meter. 2c, Bronze, women's relay. 3c, Gold, 54kg boxing. 4c, Silver, 81kg boxing. 5c, Bronze, 51kg boxing. 13c, Gold, 87kg boxing. 30c, Gold, silver cup, heavyweight boxing. 50c, Bronze, basketball.

1973, Jan. 28

1764	A460	1c multi	.25	.25
1765	A460	2c multi	.25	.25
1766	A460	3c multi	.25	.25
1767	A460	4c multi	.25	.25
1768	A460	5c multi	.25	.25
1769	A460	13c multi	1.75	.60
1770	A460	30c multi	2.25	.90
		Nos. 1764-1770 (7)	5.25	2.75

Souvenir Sheet

Imperf

1771	A460	50c multi	6.00	2.25

Stamp in No. 1771 has simulated perforations.

Portrait by A.M. Esquivel — A461

1973, Feb. 10

1772	A461	13c multi	2.25	.45

Gertrudis Gomez de Avellaneda (1814-1873), poet.

Art Type of 1970

Paintings in the Natl. Museum: 1c, Bathers in the Lagoon, by C. Enriquez. 2c, Still-life, by W.C. Heda. 3c, Gallantry, by P. Landaluze. 4c, Return in the Late Afternoon, by C. Troyon. 5c, Elizabetta Mascagni, by F.X. Fabre. 13c, The Picador, by De Lucas Padilla, horiz. 30c, In the Garden, by Arburu Morell.

1973, Feb. 28

Sizes: 36x46mm, 46x36mm

1773	A408	1c multi	.25	.25
1774	A408	2c multi	.25	.25
1775	A408	3c multi	.25	.25
1776	A408	4c multi	.25	.25
1777	A408	5c multi	.25	.25
1778	A408	13c multi	1.60	.55
1779	A408	30c multi	2.25	.80
		Nos. 1773-1779 (7)	5.10	2.60

Orchid Type of 1971

1c, Dendrobium hybrid. 2c, Cypripedium exul. 3c, Vanda miss. joaquin rose marie. 4c, Phalaenopsis schilleriana. 5c, Vanda gilbert tribulet. 13c, Dendrobium hybrid, diff. 30c, Arachnis catherine.

1973, Mar. 26

1780	A426	1c multicolored	.25	.25
1781	A426	2c multicolored	.25	.25
1782	A426	3c multicolored	.25	.25
1783	A426	4c multicolored	.25	.25
1784	A426	5c multicolored	.40	.25
1785	A426	13c multicolored	3.00	.55
1786	A426	30c multicolored	3.50	.80
		Nos. 1780-1786 (7)	7.90	2.60

A462

1973, Apr. 7   **Wmk. 376**

1787	A462	10c multi, *buff*	1.25	.30

World Health Day. World Health Organization, 25th anniv.

Anti-Polio Campaign — A463

1973, Apr. 9   **Unwmk.**

1788	A463	3c multi	.70	.25

Soviet Space Program — A464

1c, Soyuz rocket launch, vert. 2c, Luna 1, Moon. 3c, Luna 16 taking-off from Moon, vert.

4c, Venera 7. 5c, Molniya 1, vert. 13c, Mars 3. 30c, Radar observation ship, Yuri Gagarin.

1973, Apr. 12

1789	A464	1c multicolored	.25	.25
1790	A464	2c multicolored	.25	.25
1791	A464	3c multicolored	.25	.25
1792	A464	4c multicolored	.25	.25
1793	A464	5c multicolored	.25	.25
1794	A464	13c multicolored	1.25	.70
1795	A464	30c multicolored	3.50	.85
		Nos. 1789-1795 (7)	6.00	2.80

Stamp Day A465

Postmarks: 13c, Santiago de Cuba, 1760. 30c, Havana, 1760.

1973, Apr. 24

1796	A465	13c multi	1.90	.50
1797	A465	30c multi	2.10	.60

See Nos. 1888-1891.

Portrait by A. Espinosa A466

1973, May 11

1798	A466	13c multi	1.50	.45

Maj.-Gen. Ignacio Agramonte (1841-1873).

Birthplace, Torun, and Inventions — A467

Copernicus Monument, Warsaw — A468

13c, Copernicus, spacecraft. 30c, Manuscript, Frombork Tower.

1973, May 25

1799	A467	3c shown	.25	.25
1800	A467	13c multicolored	1.60	.45
1801	A467	30c multicolored	3.00	.60
		Nos. 1799-1801 (3)	4.85	1.30

Souvenir Sheet

Perf. 12½ on 3 Sides

1802	A468	50c shown	6.50	2.25

500th anniversary of the birth of Nicolaus Copernicus (1473-1543), Polish astronomer.

Improvement of School Education — A469

1973, June 12   **Wmk. 376**

1803	A469	13c multi	1.50	.25

Cattle — A470

1973, June 28   **Unwmk.**

1804	A470	1c Jersey	.25	.25
1805	A470	2c Charolaise	.25	.25
1806	A470	3c Creole	.25	.25
1807	A470	4c Swiss	.25	.25
1808	A470	5c Holstein	.25	.25
1809	A470	13c Santa Gertrudis	1.60	.40
1810	A470	30c Brahman	3.25	.75
		Nos. 1804-1810 (7)	6.10	2.40

A471

1973, July 10   **Wmk. 376**

1811	A471	13c multi	1.50	.30

10th Communist Festival of Youths and Students, East Berlin.

A472

3c, Siboney Farm, Santiago de Cuba. 13c, Moncada Barracks. 30c, Revolution Plaza, Havana.

1973, July 26   **Unwmk.**

1812	A472	3c multicolored	.35	.25
1813	A472	13c multicolored	1.50	.30
1814	A472	30c multicolored	2.25	.45
		Nos. 1812-1814 (3)	4.10	1.00

20th anniv. of the Revolution.

10th Anniv. of the Revolutionary Navy — A473

3c, Midshipman, missile frigate.

1973, Aug. 3   **Wmk. 376**

1815	A473	3c multicolored	.85	.30

Interior, by Manuel Vicens
A474

Paintings in the Natl. Museum: 1c, Amalia of Saxony, by J.K. Rossler. 3c, Margarita of Austria, by J. Pantoja de la Cruz. 4c, City Hall Official, anonymous. 5c, View of Santiago de Cuba, by Hernandez Giro. 13c, The Catalan, by J.J. Tejada. 30c, Alley in Guayo, by Tejada.

1973, Aug. 30   **Unwmk.**
Sizes: 26½x41mm (1c, 3c),
28½x39mm (4c, 13c, 30c)
1816	A474	1c multi	.25	.25
1817	A474	2c multi	.25	.25
1818	A474	3c multi	.25	.25
1819	A474	4c multi	.25	.25
1820	A474	5c multi	.25	.25
1821	A474	13c multi	1.90	.60
1822	A474	30c multi	2.50	.70
	Nos. 1816-1822 (7)		5.65	2.55

WMO Emblem, Paintings by J. Madrazo
A475

1973, Sept. 4
1823	A475	8c Spring	.75	.25
1824	A475	8c Summer	.75	.25
1825	A475	8c Fall	.75	.25
1826	A475	8c Winter	.75	.25
	Nos. 1823-1826 (4)		3.00	1.00

World Meteorogological Organization, cent. Nos. 1823-1826 printed se-tenant in strips of 4; frame reversed on 2nd and 4th stamp in strip.

A476

27th World and 1st Pan American Weight Lifting Championships: Various weightlifting positions.

1973, Sept. 12
1827	A476	1c multi, diff.	.25	.25
1828	A476	2c shown	.25	.25
1829	A476	3c multi, diff.	.25	.25
1830	A476	4c multi, diff.	.25	.25
1831	A476	5c multi, diff.	.25	.25
1832	A476	13c multi, diff.	1.60	.45
1833	A476	30c multi, diff.	2.75	.90
	Nos. 1827-1833 (7)		5.60	2.60

A477

Flowering plants: 1c, Erythrina standleyana. 2c, Lantana camara. 3c, Canavalia maritima. 4c, Dichromena colorata. 5c, Borrichia arborescens. 13c, Anguria pedata. 30c, Cordia sebestena.

1973, Sept. 28
1834	A477	1c multicolored	.25	.25
1835	A477	2c multicolored	.25	.25
1836	A477	3c multicolored	.25	.25
1837	A477	4c multicolored	.25	.25
1838	A477	5c multicolored	.25	.25

1839	A477	13c multicolored	2.10	.65
1840	A477	30c multicolored	3.25	.90
	Nos. 1835-1840 (6)		6.35	2.55

8th World Trade Union Congress, Varna, Bulgaria — A478

1973, Oct. 5   **Wmk. 376**
1841	A478	13c multi	1.50	.35

Cuban Natl. Ballet, 25th Anniv. — A479

1973, Oct. 28   **Unwmk.**
1842	A479	13c gold & brt ultra	2.00	.40

Sea Shells — A480

1c, Liguus fasciatus fasciatus. 2c, Liguus fasciatus guitarti. 3c, Liguus fasciatus whartoni. 4c, Liguus fasciatus angelae. 5c, Liguus fasciatus trinidadense. 13c, Liguus blainianus. 30c, Liguus vittatus.

1973, Oct. 29
1843	A480	1c multicolored	.25	.25
1844	A480	2c multicolored	.25	.25
1845	A480	3c multicolored	.25	.25
1846	A480	4c multicolored	.25	.25
1847	A480	5c multicolored	.25	.25
1848	A480	13c multicolored	2.75	.70
1849	A480	30c multicolored	3.75	.85
	Nos. 1843-1849 (7)		7.75	2.80

Maps of Cuba
A481

1c, Juan de la Cosa, 1502. 3c, Ortelius, 1572. 13c, Bellini, 1762. 40c, 1973.

1973, Oct. 29
1850	A481	1c multi	.25	.25
1851	A481	3c multi	.25	.25
1852	A481	13c multi	1.75	.25
1853	A481	40c multi	2.10	.80
	Nos. 1850-1853 (4)		4.35	1.55

15th Anniversary of the Revolution — A482

1974, Jan. 2
1854	A482	1c No. 625	.25	.25
1855	A482	3c No. 626	.25	.25
1856	A482	13c No. C200	4.00	.55
1857	A482	40c No. C201	1.60	.80
	Nos. 1854-1857 (4)		6.10	1.85

Woman, by F. Ponce de Leon — A483

Portraits in the Camaguey Museum: 3c, Mexican Girls, by J. Arche. 8c, Young Woman, by A. Menocal. 10c, Mulatto Woman Drinking from Coconut, by L. Romanach. 13c, Head of an Old Man, by J. Arburu.

1974, Jan. 10
1858	A483	1c multi	.25	.25
1859	A483	3c multi	.25	.25
1860	A483	8c multi	.35	.25
1861	A483	10c multi	1.10	.25
1862	A483	13c multi	1.60	.40
	Nos. 1858-1862 (5)		3.55	1.40

Amilcar Cabral — A484

1974, Jan. 20
1863	A484	13c multi	1.40	.25

Amilcar Cabral, Guinea-Bissau freedom fighter, 1st death anniv.

Lenin, by I.V. Kosmin — A485

1974, Jan. 21
1864	A485	30c multi	3.00	.55

50th death anniv. of Lenin.

12th Central American and Caribbean Games, Santo Domingo — A486

1974, Feb. 8
1865	A486	1c Emblem	.25	.25
1866	A486	2c Javelin	.25	.25
1867	A486	3c Boxing	.25	.25
1868	A486	4c Baseball, horiz.	.25	.25
1869	A486	13c Basketball, horiz.	1.60	.25
1870	A486	30c Volleyball, horiz.	2.40	.70
	Nos. 1865-1870 (6)		5.00	1.95

Portrait by F. Martinez — A487

1974, Feb. 27
1871	A487	13c multi	1.40	.25

Carlos M. de Cespedes (d. 1874), patriot.

Portrait of a Man, by J.B. Vermay — A488

Paintings in the Natl. Museum: 2c, The Wet Nurse, by C.A. Van Loo. 3c, Cattle in River, by R. Morey. 4c, Village, by Morey. 13c, Faun and Bacchus, by Rubens. 30c, Young Woman Playing Cards, by R. Madrazo.

1974, Mar. 7
1872	A488	1c shown	.25	.25
1873	A488	2c multi	.25	.25
1874	A488	3c multi	.25	.25
1875	A488	4c multi	.25	.25
1876	A488	13c multi	1.40	.25
1877	A488	30c multi	2.50	.55
	Nos. 1872-1877 (6)		4.90	1.80

Council for Mutual Economic Assistance (COMECON), 25th Anniv. — A489

30c, Comecon building, Moscow.

1974, Mar. 15
1878	A489	30c multicolored	2.00	.70

Visit of Leonid I. Brezhnev to Cuba, Jan. 28-Feb. 3 — A490

13c, Jose Marti, Lenin, flags. 30c, Brezhnev, Fidel Castro.

1974, Mar. 28
1879	A490	13c multicolored	2.00	.30
1880	A490	30c multicolored	2.10	.55
	Nos. 1879-1880 (2)		4.10	.85

Science Fiction A491

Paintings by A. Sokolov: 1c, Martian Crater. 2c, Fiery Labyrinth. 3c, Amber Wave. 4c, Flight Through Space. 13c, Planet in Nebula. 30c, World of Two Suns.

1974, Apr. 12

1881	A491	1c multi	.25	.25
1882	A491	2c multi	.25	.25
1883	A491	3c multi	.25	.25
1884	A491	4c multi	.25	.25
1885	A491	13c multi	2.00	.25
1886	A491	30c multi	3.25	.60
	Nos. 1881-1886 (6)		6.25	1.85

Cosmonauts Day.

UPU,
Cent.
A492

1974, Apr. 15

1887	A492	30c Letter, 1874	2.50	.60

Stamp Day Type of 1973

Postmarks.

1974, Apr. 24

1888	A465	1c Havana	.25	.25
1889	A465	3c Matanzas	.40	.25
1890	A465	13c Trinidad	1.50	.25
1891	A465	20c Guana Vacoa	2.25	.35
	Nos. 1888-1891 (4)		4.40	1.10

18th Sports
Congress of
Friendly
Armies — A493

1974, May 5   **Wmk. 376**

1892	A493	3c multi	.80	.25

Felipe Poey (1799-1891),
Naturalist — A494

1c, Eumaeus atala atala. 2c, Pineria terebra. 3c, Chaetodon sedentarius. 4c, Eurema dina dina. 13c, Hemitrochus fuscolabiata. 30c, Eupomacentrus partitus. 50c, Apogon binotatus.

1c, 4c, Butterflies. 2c, 13c, Sea shells. 3c, 30c, 50c, Fish.

1974, May 26   **Perf. 12½x12**

1893	A494	1c multicolored	.25	.25
1894	A494	2c multicolored	.25	.25
1895	A494	3c multicolored	.25	.25
1896	A494	4c multicolored	.80	.25
1897	A494	13c multicolored	2.75	.45
1898	A494	30c multicolored	3.50	.55
	Nos. 1893-1898 (6)		7.80	2.00

Souvenir Sheet

Imperf

1899	A494	50c multicolored	7.00	2.50

Stamp in No. 1899 has simulated perforations.

Havana Philharmonic Orchestra, 50th
Anniv. — A495

1c, Antonio Mompo, cello. 3c, Cesar Perez Sentenat, piano. 5c, Pedro Mercado, trumpet. 10c, Pedro Sanjuan, Havana Philharmonic emblem. 13c, Roberto Ondina, flute.

1974, June 8   **Perf. 12½**

1900	A495	1c multi	.25	.25
1901	A495	3c multi	.25	.25
1902	A495	5c multi	.25	.25
1903	A495	10c multi	1.40	.25
1904	A495	13c multi	1.75	.25
	Nos. 1900-1904 (5)		3.90	1.25

Garden
Flowers — A496

1c, Heliconia humilis. 2c, Anthurium andraeanum. 3c, Canna generalis. 4c, Alpinia purpurata. 13c, Gladiolus grandiflorus. 30c, Amomum capitatum.

1974, June 12

1905	A496	1c multicolored	.25	.25
1906	A496	2c multicolored	.25	.25
1907	A496	3c multicolored	.25	.25
1908	A496	4c multicolored	.25	.25
1909	A496	13c multicolored	1.75	.25
1910	A496	30c multicolored	4.50	.60
	Nos. 1905-1910 (6)		7.25	1.85

A497

World Amateur Boxing Championships: Emblem and various boxers.

     Perf. 12x12½

1974, Aug. 24   **Litho.**   **Unwmk.**

1911	A497	1c multi	.25	.25
1912	A497	3c multi	.35	.25
1913	A497	13c multi	1.60	.25
	Nos. 1911-1913 (3)		2.20	.75

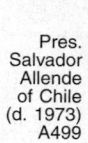

Extinct
Birds — A498

1c, Dodo. 3c, Ara de Cuba (parrot). 8c, Passenger pigeon. 10c, Moa. 13c, Great auk.

1974, Aug. 28   **Perf. 13**

1914	A498	1c multi	.40	.25
1915	A498	3c multi	.40	.25
1916	A498	8c multi	.85	.25
1917	A498	10c multi	2.75	.55
1918	A498	13c multi	3.50	.80
	Nos. 1914-1918 (5)		7.90	2.10

Pres.
Salvador
Allende
of Chile
(d. 1973)
A499

1974, Sept. 11

1919	A499	13c multi	1.25	.45

Wildflowers
A500

1c, Suriana maritima. 3c, Cassia ligustrina. 8c, Flaveria linearis. 10c, Stachytarpheta jamaicensis. 13c, Bacopa monnieri.

1974, Sept. 14   **Perf. 13x12½**

1920	A500	1c multi	.25	.25
1921	A500	3c multi	.25	.25
1922	A500	8c multi	.30	.25
1923	A500	10c multi	2.10	.25
1924	A500	13c multi	3.50	.85
	Nos. 1920-1924 (5)		6.40	1.85

Model
Aircraft — A501

3c, Sky diving. 8c, Glider. 10c, Crop dusting. 13c, Commercial aviation.

1974, Sept. 22   **Perf. 12½**

1925	A501	1c shown	.25	.25
1926	A501	3c multi	.25	.25
1927	A501	8c multi	.45	.25
1928	A501	10c multi	1.25	.25
1929	A501	13c multi	2.00	.25
	Nos. 1925-1929 (5)		4.20	1.25

Civil Aeronautic Institute, 10th anniv. Nos. 1927-1929 horiz.

History of Cuban Baseball — A502

1c, Indians playing ball. 3c, 1st Official game, 1874. 8c, Emilio Sabourin. 10c, Umpire, players, 1974. 13c, Latin-American Stadium, Havana.

1974, Oct. 3   **Perf. 13**

1930	A502	1c multicolored	.25	.25
1931	A502	3c multicolored	.25	.25
1932	A502	8c multicolored	.40	.25
1933	A502	10c multicolored	1.25	.25
1934	A502	13c multicolored	2.10	.25
	Nos. 1930-1934 (5)		4.25	1.25

Nos. 1930-1932 vert.

Mambi 10c Stamp (Revolutionary
Junta Issue), Cent. — A503

1974, Oct. 10

1935	A503	13c multi	1.50	.25

16th Conference of Customs
Organizations of Socialist
Countries — A504

30c, Comecon Building, Moscow.

1974, Oct. 15

1936	A504	30c multicolored	2.00	.55

Disappearance
of Major Camilo
Cienfuegos,
15th
Anniv. — A505

     Wmk. 376

1974, Oct. 28   **Litho.**   **Perf. 13**

1937	A505	3c multi	.75	.25

8th World Mining Conference — A506

1974, Nov. 3

1938	A506	13c multi	1.50	.25

Petroleum Institute, 15th
Anniv. — A507

1974, Nov. 20

1939	A507	3c multi	.70	.25

Intersputnik Earth Station
Opening — A508

13c, Satellite, satellite dish. 1p, Satellite, flags.

1974, Nov. 30   **Unwmk.**

1940	A508	3c shown	.25	.25
1941	A508	13c multicolored	1.25	.25
1942	A508	1p multicolored	3.25	1.10
	Nos. 1940-1942 (3)		4.75	1.60

Philatelic Federation, 10th
Anniv. — A509

1974, Nov. 30   **Perf. 12½x13**
1943 A509 30c multi   2.40 .45

Souvenir Sheet

Mercury — A510

1974, Dec. 6   *Imperf.*
1944 A510 50c multi   6.00 1.25
4th Natl. Phil. Exhib., Havana.

1st World
Peace
Congress, 25th
Anniv. — A511

30c, F. Joliot-Curie, by Picasso.

1974, Dec. 16   **Wmk. 376**   **Perf. 13**
1945 A511 30c red, blk & buff   3.00 .45

Ruben Martinez Villena (b. 1899),
Revolutionary — A512

1974, Dec. 20   **Unwmk.**
1946 A512 3c red org & yel   .75 .25

Souvenir Sheet

Cuban Victories, 1st Amateur Boxing
Championships — A513

1975, Jan. 6   **Litho.**   *Imperf.*
1947 A513 50c Trophy   6.00 1.25

*The
Word,* by
Marcelo
Pogolotti
A514

Paintings in the Natl. Museum: 2c, *The Silk-Cotton Tree,* by Henry Cleenewerk. 3c, *Landscape,* by Guillermo Collazo. 5c, *Still-life,* by Francisco Peralta. 13c, *Maria Wilson,* by Federico Martinez, vert. 30c, *The Couple,* by Mariano Fortuny.

1975, Jan. 20   **Perf. 13**
1948 A514 1c multi   .25 .25
1949 A514 2c multi   .25 .25
1950 A514 3c multi   .25 .25
1951 A514 5c multi   .25 .25
1952 A514 13c multi   1.50 .25
1953 A514 30c multi   2.75 .45
    Nos. 1948-1953 (6)   5.25 1.70

Intl.
Women's
Year
A515

1975, Feb. 6
1954 A515 13c multi   1.25 .25

Fishing Industry
A516

Various fish and fishing vessels: 1c, Long-finned tuna. 2c, Tuna. 3c, Mediterranean grouper. 8c, Hake. 13c, Prawn. 30c, Lobster.

1975, Feb. 22
1955 A516 1c multicolored   .25 .25
1956 A516 2c multicolored   .25 .25
1957 A516 3c multicolored   .25 .25
1958 A516 8c multicolored   .25 .25
1959 A516 13c multicolored   1.10 .70
1960 A516 30c multicolored   3.25 .70
    Nos. 1955-1960 (6)   5.35 2.40

Minerals — A517

1975, Mar. 15   **Litho.**   **Perf. 13x12½**
1961 A517 3c Nickel   .40 .25
1962 A517 13c Copper   1.60 .25
1963 A517 30c Chromium   2.75 .45
    Nos. 1961-1963 (3)   4.75 .95

Cosmonaut's Day — A518

1c, Cosmodrome. 2c, Probe, vert. 3c, Eclipse. 5c, Threshold to Space. 13c, Midday on Mars. 30c, Cosmonaut's view of Earth.

1975, Apr. 12   **Perf. 13x12½, 12½x13**
1964 A518 1c multicolored   .25 .25
1965 A518 2c multicolored   .25 .25
1966 A518 3c multicolored   .25 .25
1967 A518 5c multicolored   .40 .25
1968 A518 13c multicolored   1.50 .25
1969 A518 30c multicolored   2.50 .45
    Nos. 1964-1969 (6)   5.15 1.70
    The future of space.

Stamp
Day
A519

Various covers.

1975, Apr. 24   **Perf. 13**
1970 A519 3c multi   .25 .25
1971 A519 13c multi   1.40 .25
1972 A519 30c multi   2.10 .40
    Nos. 1970-1972 (3)   3.75 .90

Victory Over Fascism, 30th
Anniv. — A520

Design: Raising red flag over Reichstag, Berlin.

1975, May 9   **Perf. 13x12½**
1973 A520 30c multi   2.00 .40

A521

Works in the Decorative Art
Museum — A522

1c, Sevres porcelain vase, vert. 2c, Meissen porcelain statue *Shepherdess and Dancers,* vert. 3c, Chinese porcelain dish *Lady with Parasol.* 5c, Chinese screen detail *The Phoenix,* vert. 13c, *Allegory of Music,* by Francois Boucher (1703-70), vert. 30c, *Portrait of a Lady,* by L. Tocque, vert. 50c, *The Swing,* by Hubert Robert (1733-1808).

1975, May 10   **Perf. 12½x13, 13x12½**
1974 A521 1c multi   .25 .25
1975 A521 2c multi   .25 .25
1976 A521 3c shown   .25 .25
1977 A521 5c multi   .40 .25
1978 A521 13c multi   1.50 .25
1979 A521 30c multi   2.00 .40
    Nos. 1974-1979 (6)   4.65 1.65

Souvenir Sheet
Perf. 13x12½ on 3 Sides
1980 A522 50c shown   5.50 1.25
No. 1980 contains one 25x39mm stamp.

Intl. Children's Day — A523

Wmk. 376
1975, May 31   **Litho.**   **Perf. 13**
1981 A523 3c multi   .50 .25

Indigenous
Birds — A524

Designs: 1c, Vireo gundlachi. 2c, Gymnoglaux lawrenci. 3c, Aratingo eoups. 5c, Staroenas cyanocephala. 13c, Chondrohierax wilsoni. 30c, Cyanolimnas cerverai.

1975, June 18   **Unwmk.**
1982 A524 1c multicolored   .25 .25
1983 A524 2c multicolored   .25 .25
1984 A524 3c multicolored   .25 .25
1985 A524 5c multicolored   .40 .25
1986 A524 13c multicolored   1.75 .40
1987 A524 30c multicolored   2.50 .70
    Nos. 1982-1987 (6)   5.40 2.10

See Nos. 2121-2125, 2180-2182, C276-C276.

Scientific Investigation Center, 10th
Anniv. — A525

1975, July 1   **Perf. 12½**
1988 A525 13c multi   1.40 .25

Irrigation and Drainage Commission,
25th Anniv. — A526

1975, Aug. 2   **Perf. 13**
1989 A526 13c multi   1.40 .25

Afforestation
A527

Designs: 1c, Cedrela mexicana. 3c, Swietenia mahagoni. 5c, Calophyllum brasiliense. 13c, Hibiscus tiliaceus. 30c, Pinus caribaea.

1975, Aug. 20

1990	A527	1c multicolored	.25	.25
1991	A527	3c multicolored	.40	.25
1992	A527	5c multicolored	.40	.25
1993	A527	13c multicolored	1.10	.25
1994	A527	30c multicolored	1.75	.40
		Nos. 1990-1994 (5)	3.90	1.40

Cuban Women's Federation, 15th Anniv. — A528

1975, Aug. 23

1995	A528	3c multi	.50	.25

Intl. Conference on the Independence of Puerto Rico — A529

1975, Sept. 5   Litho.

1996	A529	13c multi	1.00	.25

A530

7th Pan American Games, Mexico: Aztec calendar stone and various athletes.

1975, Sept. 20   Perf. 12½x13

1997	A530	1c Baseball	.25	.25
1998	A530	3c Boxing	.25	.25
1999	A530	5c Basketball	.25	.25
2000	A530	13c High jump	1.50	.30
2001	A530	30c Weight lifting	2.10	.30
		Nos. 1997-2001 (5)	4.35	1.35

Souvenir Sheet
Imperf

2002	A530	50c Stone, emblem	4.00	1.25

A531

1975, Sept. 28   Perf. 12½x13

2003	A531	3c multi	.50	.25

Revolutionary Defense Committees (CDR), 15th anniv.

Friendship Among the Peoples Institute, 15th Anniv. A532

1975, Oct. 8   Perf. 12½x13

2004	A532	3c multi	.30	.25

Natl. Bank, 25th Anniv. A533

Designs: 1-peso coins and banknotes identified by serial numbers.

1975, Oct. 13   Perf. 13x12½

2005	A533	13c	Coin, 1915	1.10	.25
2006	A533	13c	C882736A, 1934	1.10	.25
2007	A533	13c	A000387A, 1946	1.10	.25
2008	A533	13c	933906, 1964	1.10	.25
2009	A533	13c	K000000, 1976	1.10	.25
a.			Strip of 5, Nos. 2005-2009	6.00	1.50
			Nos. 2005-2009 (5)	5.50	1.25

Locomotives — A534

1c, La Junta, 1837. 3c, Steam engine 2-8-0 No. 12. 5c, Diesel TEM 4 No. 51010. 13c, Diesel DVM 9I-7 55. 30c, Diesel M 62K No. 61601.

1975, Oct. 28   Unwmk.   Perf. 12½

2010	A534	1c multicolored	.25	.25
2011	A534	3c multicolored	.30	.25
2012	A534	5c multicolored	.30	.25
2013	A534	13c multicolored	2.50	.25
2014	A534	30c multicolored	3.00	.45
		Nos. 2010-2014 (5)	6.35	1.45

Railway history.

Development of the Textile Industry — A535

13c, Bobbins, flag, loom operator.

1975, Nov. 10   Perf. 13x12½

2015	A535	13c multi	1.25	.25

Veterinary Medicine — A536

Parasites and host species: 1c, Haemonchus, lamb. 2c, Ancylostoma caninum, dog. 3c, Dispharynx nasuta, rooster. 5c, Gasterophilus intestinalis, horse. 13c, Ascaris lumbricoides, pig. 30c, Boophilus microplus, bull.

1975, Nov. 25   Litho.   Perf. 13

2016	A536	1c multicolored	.25	.25
2017	A536	2c multicolored	.25	.25
2018	A536	3c multicolored	.25	.25
2019	A536	5c multicolored	.25	.25

2020	A536	13c multicolored	1.40	.25
2021	A536	30c multicolored	2.50	.40
		Nos. 2016-2021 (6)	4.90	1.65

Manuel Ascunce Domenech Educational Detachment A537

1975, Nov. 27   Litho.

2022	A537	3c multi	.40	.25

Development of Agriculture and Irrigation — A538

1975, Dec. 15   Litho.   Perf. 13x12½

2023	A538	13c Irrigation	1.25	.25

1st Communist Party Congress — A539

3c, "1," revolutionaries, vert. 30c, Party leaders.

1975, Dec. 17   Perf. 12½x13, 13x12½

2024	A539	3c multi	.25	.25
2025	A539	13c shown	1.10	.25
2026	A539	30c multi	1.50	.30
		Nos. 2024-2026 (3)	2.85	.80

8th Latin-American Obstetrics and Gynecology Congress — A540

1976, Jan. 24   Perf. 13

2027	A540	3c multi	.60	.25

Paintings in Natl. Museums — A541

Designs: 1c, *Seated Woman*, by Victor Manuel, vert. 2c, *Garden*, by Santiago Rusinol. 3c, *Guadalquivir River*, by Manuel Barron y Carrillo. 5c, *Self-portrait*, by Jan Havicksz Steen, vert. 13c, *Portrait of a Woman*, by Louis Michel Van Loo, vert. 30c, *La Chula*, by Jose Arburu Morell, vert.

**Sizes: 29x40mm (1c, 5c, 13c),
40x29mm (2c), 44x27mm (3c),
27x44mm (30c)**

Perf. 13, 12½ (3c, 30c)

1976, Jan. 30

2028	A541	1c multi	.25	.25
2029	A541	2c multi	.25	.25
2030	A541	3c multi	.25	.25

2031	A541	5c multi	.25	.25
2032	A541	13c multi	1.40	.25
2033	A541	30c multi	2.25	.50
		Nos. 2028-2033 (6)	4.65	1.75

10th Cong. of Ministers from Socialist Communications Organizations, Feb. 12, Havana — A542

1976, Feb. 12   Litho.   Perf. 13

2034	A542	13c multi	1.40	.25

Hunting Dogs A543

1c, American foxhound. 2c, Labrador retriever. 3c, Borzoi. 5c, Irish setter. 13c, Pointer. 30c, Cocker spaniel.

1976, Feb. 20

2035	A543	1c multi	.25	.25
2036	A543	2c multi	.25	.25
2037	A543	3c multi	.25	.25
2038	A543	5c multi	.25	.25
2039	A543	13c multi	2.40	.30
2040	A543	30c multi	3.25	.40
		Nos. 2035-2040 (6)	6.65	1.70

Socialist Constitution — A544

13c, Natl. flag, arms, anthem.

1976, Feb. 24   Perf. 12½

2041	A544	13c multi	1.40	.25

Chess Champions — A545

Designs: 1c, Ruy Lopez Segura and chessboard. 2c, Francois Philidor and frontispiece of his book, *Analysis of the Game of Chess*. 3c, Wilhelm Steinitz and knight. 13c, Emanuel Lasker and king. 30c, Jose Raul Capablanca learning to play chess as a small boy.

1976, Mar. 15   Perf. 13x12½

2042	A545	1c multi	.25	.25
2043	A545	2c multi	.25	.25
2044	A545	3c multi	.25	.25
2045	A545	13c multi	1.75	.25
2046	A545	30c multi	1.90	.55
		Nos. 2042-2046 (5)	4.40	1.55

Havana Radio Intl. Broadcasts, 15th Anniv. — A546

1976, Mar. 26
2047 A546 50c multi   2.00 .70

World Health Day — A547

1976, Apr. 7
2048 A547 30c multi   1.50 .45

Child Care Centers, 15th Anniv. — A548

1976, Apr. 10   *Perf. 12½x13*
2049 A548 3c multi   .60 .25

1st Manned Space Flight, 15th Anniv. A549

1c, Gagarin, lift-off. 2c, V. Tesreshkova, rockets. 3c, A. Leonov's space walk, vert. 5c, Spacecraft, vert. 13c, Spacecraft, diff., vert. 30c, Space link-up.

1976, Apr. 12   *Perf. 13*
2050	A549	1c multicolored	.25	.25
2051	A549	2c multicolored	.25	.25
2052	A549	3c multicolored	.25	.25
2053	A549	5c multicolored	.40	.25
2054	A549	13c multicolored	1.10	.25
2055	A549	30c multicolored	1.75	.35
		Nos. 2050-2055 (6)	4.00	1.60

Bay of Pigs Invasion, 15th Anniv. — A550

13c, Bomber, pilot. 30c, Soldiers exulting, vert.

1976, Apr. 17   *Perf. 13x12½, 12½x13*
2056	A550	3c shown	.25	.25
2057	A550	13c multi	.95	.25
2058	A550	30c multi	1.75	.45
		Nos. 2056-2058 (3)	2.95	.95

Natl. Militia, 17th anniv. (3c); Air Force, 15th anniv. (13c); proclamation of the socialist revolution, 15th anniv. (30c).

Nat. Assoc. of Small Farmers (ANAP), 15th Anniv. — A551

1976, May 17   *Perf. 13x12½*
2059 A551 3c multi   .60 .25

1976 Summer Olympics, Montreal — A552

1c, Volleyball. 2c, Basketball. 3c, Long jump. 4c, Boxing. 5c, Weight lifting. 13c, Judo. 30c, Swimming.

50c, Character trademark (beaver).

1976, May 25   *Perf. 12½x13*
2060	A552	1c multi	.25	.25
2061	A552	2c multi	.25	.25
2062	A552	3c multi	.25	.25
2063	A552	4c multi	.25	.25
2064	A552	5c multi	.25	.25
2065	A552	13c multi	1.10	.25
2066	A552	30c multi	1.75	.45
		Nos. 2060-2066 (7)	4.10	1.95

Souvenir Sheet
Imperf
2067 A552 50c multi   4.00 1.25
See Nos. 2106, 2112.

Modern Secondary Schools — A553

1976, June 12   Litho.   *Perf. 13*
2068 A553 3c red, pale grn & blk   .60 .25

Indigenous Birds — A554

Designs: 1c, Teretistris fornsi. 2c, Glaucidium siju. 3c, Nesoceleus fernandinae. 5c, Todus mutlicolor. 13c, Accipiter gundlachi. 30c, Priotelus temnurus.

1976, June 15   *Perf. 13x12½*
2069	A554	1c multicolored	.30	.25
2070	A554	2c multicolored	.30	.25
2071	A554	3c multicolored	.40	.25
2072	A554	5c multicolored	.70	.25
2073	A554	13c multicolored	1.40	.25
2074	A554	30c multicolored	3.25	.80
		Nos. 2069-2074 (6)	6.35	2.05

EXPO '76, USSR A555

Designs: 1c, Anatomical scanning device. 3c, Child, doe. 10c, Cosmonauts. 30c, Tupolev supersonic jet.

1976, July 5   *Perf. 12½x13, 13x12½*
2075	A555	1c multicolored	.25	.25
2076	A555	3c multicolored	.25	.25
2077	A555	10c multicolored	.50	.25
2078	A555	30c multicolored	2.50	.55
		Nos. 2075-2078 (4)	3.50	1.30

Public health and industrial safety (1c), environmental protection (3c), space exploration (10c) and modern transportation (30c). Nos. 2075-2077 vert.

Death Cent. of "El Inglesito" A556

1976, Aug. 4   *Perf. 13*
2079 A556 13c Henry M. Reeve   .70 .25

Portrait of G. Collazo, by Jean Dabour — A557

Paintings by Collazo: 2c, The Art Lovers, horiz. 3c, The Patio. 5c, Coconut Tree. 13c, New York Studio, horiz. 30c, R. Emelina Collazo.

Sizes: 33x44mm, 44x33mm (2c), 31x46mm (5c, 30c), 46x31mm (13c)

Perf. 13, 12½x13 (5c, 30c), 13x12½ (13c)

1976, Sept. 2
2080	A557	1c multi	.25	.25
2081	A557	2c multi	.25	.25
2082	A557	3c multi	.25	.25
2083	A557	5c multi	.25	.25
2084	A557	13c multi	.65	.25
2085	A557	30c multi	2.10	.50
		Nos. 2080-2085 (6)	3.75	1.75

Camilo Cienfuegos Military Schools, 10th Anniv. — A558

1976, Sept. 23   *Perf. 13*
2086 A558 3c multi   .40 .25

Development of the Merchant Marine — A559

Various cargo and passenger ships.

1976, Oct. 2   *Perf. 12½*
2087	A559	1c multi	.30	.25
2088	A559	2c multi	.30	.25
2089	A559	3c multi	.30	.25
2090	A559	5c multi	.45	.25
2091	A559	13c multi	1.40	.25
2092	A559	30c multi	2.75	.80
		Nos. 2087-2092 (6)	5.50	2.25

8th Intl. Health Film Festival of Socialist Countries, Havana — A560

1976, Oct. 4   *Perf. 13x12½*
2093 A560 3c multi   .40 .25

5th Intl. Ballet Festival, Havana A561

Scenes from ballets: 1c, Apollo. 2c, The River and the Forest, vert. 3c, Giselle. 5c, Oedipus Rex, vert. 13c, Carmen, vert. 30c, Vital Song, vert.

1976, Nov. 6   *Perf. 13*
2094	A561	1c multicolored	.25	.25
2095	A561	2c multicolored	.25	.25
2096	A561	3c multicolored	.25	.25
2097	A561	5c multicolored	.25	.25
2098	A561	13c multicolored	1.10	.25
2099	A561	30c multicolored	2.10	.35
		Nos. 2094-2099 (6)	4.20	1.60

3rd Military Games A562

1976, Nov. 25   *Perf. 13*
2100 A562 3c multi   .50 .25

Granma Landings, 20th Anniv. — A563

1976, Dec. 2   *Perf. 13x12½*
2101	A563	1c Landing craft	.25	.25
2102	A563	3c Landing force	.25	.25
2103	A563	13c Castro, soldiers	1.00	.25
2104	A563	30c Globe, rifles	1.60	.55
		Nos. 2101-2104 (4)	3.10	1.30

Souvenir Sheet

Cuban Landscape, by F. Cadava — A564

1976, Dec. 8   *Perf. 13x13½*
2105 A564 50c multi   5.25 2.00
CIENFUEGOS '76, 5th natl. phil. exhib.

Summer Olympics Type of 1976 and

Victory of Cuban Athletes at the Montreal Games — A565

1c, Volleyball. 2c, Hurdles. 3c, Running (starting blocks). 8c, Boxing. 13c, Running (finish line). 30c, Judo.

1976, Dec. 10   **Perf. 12½x13**
2106	A565	1c multicolored	.25	.25
2107	A565	2c multicolored	.25	.25
2108	A565	3c multicolored	.25	.25
2109	A565	8c multicolored	.25	.25
2110	A565	13c multicolored	.85	.25
2111	A565	30c multicolored	1.75	.45
		Nos. 2106-2111 (6)	3.60	1.70

Souvenir Sheet
Imperf
2112	A552	50c like No. 2063	5.00	1.25

Paintings in the Natl. Museum A566

1c, *Golden Cross Inn*, by S. Scott. 3c, *Portrait of a Man*, by J.C. Verspronck, vert. 5c, *Venetian Landscape*, by Francesco Guardi. 10c, *Valley Corner*, by H. Cleenewerck, vert. 13c, *F. Xaviera Paula*, anonymous, vert. 30c, *F. de Medici*, by C. Allori, vert.

Perf. 13, 12½x13 (3c, 10c, 30c) 12½ (13c)

1977, Jan. 18
Sizes: 40x29mm, 27x42mm (3c, 10c, 30c), 27x43½mm (13c)
2113	A566	1c multi	.25	.25
2114	A566	3c multi	.25	.25
2115	A566	5c multi	.25	.25
2116	A566	10c multi	.55	.25
2117	A566	13c multi	.85	.25
2118	A566	30c multi	2.10	.40
		Nos. 2113-2118 (6)	4.25	1.65

Rural Transport A567

1977, Feb. 15   **Perf. 13**
2119	A567	3c multi	.80	.25

Constitution of Popular Government — A568

1976, Dec. 1   **Perf. 13x12½**
2120	A568	13c multi	.70	.25

Bird Type of 1975

Designs: 1c, Xiphidiopicus percussus. 4c, Tiaris canora. 10c, Dives atroviolaceus. 13c, Ferminia cerverai. 30c, Mellisuga helenae.

1977, Feb. 25   **Perf. 13**
2121	A524	1c multicolored	.40	.25
2122	A524	4c multicolored	.45	.25
2123	A524	10c multicolored	.95	.25
2124	A524	13c multicolored	1.40	.25
2125	A524	30c multicolored	2.75	.65
		Nos. 2121-2125 (5)	5.95	1.65

Lenin Park Aquarium, Havana — A569

Designs: 1c, Chichlasoma meeki. 3c, Barbus tetrazona tetrazona. 5c, Cyprinus carpio. 10c, Betta splendens. 13c, Pterophyllum scalare, vert. 30c, Hemigrammus caudovittatus.

1977, Mar. 15
2126	A569	1c multicolored	.25	.25
2127	A569	3c multicolored	.25	.25
2128	A569	5c multicolored	.25	.25
2129	A569	10c multicolored	.30	.25
2130	A569	13c multicolored	1.25	.25
2131	A569	30c multicolored	2.50	.50
		Nos. 2126-2131 (6)	4.80	1.75

Sputnik (1st Artificial Satellite), 20th Anniv. — A570

1c, DDR #370, *Sputnik*. 3c, Hungary #1216, *Luna 16*. 5c, North Korea #134, *Cosmos*. 10c, Poland #822, *Sputnik 3*. 13c, Yugoslavia #870, Earth, Moon. 30c, Cuba #866, Earth, Moon. 50c, Russia #2021, *Sputnik*.

1977, Apr. 12   **Perf. 13x12½**
2132	A570	1c multi	.25	.25
2133	A570	3c multi	.25	.25
2134	A570	5c multi	.25	.25
2135	A570	10c multi	.35	.25
2136	A570	13c multi	1.10	.25
2137	A570	30c multi	1.90	.40
		Nos. 2132-2137 (6)	4.10	1.65

Souvenir Sheet
Imperf
2138	A570	50c multi	4.25	1.25

No. 2138 has simulated perfs.

Antonio Maria Romeu (1876-1955), Composer — A571

1977, May 10   **Litho.**   **Perf. 13**
2139	A571	3c multi	.35	.25

See No. C251.

Flowering Plants — A572

Designs: 1c, Hibiscus rosa sinensis. 2c, Nerium oleander. 5c, Allamanda cathartica. 10c, Pelargonium zonale.

1977, May 31
2140	A572	1c multicolored	.25	.25
2141	A572	2c multicolored	.25	.25
2142	A572	5c multicolored	.25	.25
2143	A572	10c multicolored	.40	.25
		Nos. 2140-2143 (4)	1.15	1.00

Dr. Juan Tomas Roig (b. 1877), botanist. See Nos. C252-C254.

Fire Prevention Week — A573

2c, Horse-drawn fire pump, diff. 6c, Early motorized vehicle. 10c, Modern truck. 13c, Turntable-ladder truck. 30c, Crane vehicle.

1977, June 20
2144	A573	1c shown	.25	.25
2145	A573	2c multicolored	.25	.25
2146	A573	6c multicolored	.25	.25
2147	A573	10c multicolored	.50	.25
2148	A573	13c multicolored	.90	.25
2149	A573	30c multicolored	1.90	.40
		Nos. 2144-2149 (6)	4.05	1.65

Natl. Decorations (Ribbons and Medals of Honor) — A574

1977, July 26   **Perf. 12x12½**
2150	A574	1c shown	.25	.25
2151	A574	3c multi, diff.	.25	.25

See Nos. C255-C256.

Paintings by Jorge Arche — A575

1c, *Portrait of Mary*. 3c, *Jose Marti*. 5c, *Portrait of Aristides*. 10c, *Bathers*.

Perf. 13x12½, 12½x13 (10c), 13 (5c)
1977, Aug. 25
Sizes: 26x38mm, 29x40mm (5c), 38x26mm (10c)
2152	A575	1c multicolored	.25	.25
2153	A575	3c multicolored	.25	.25
2154	A575	5c multicolored	.25	.25
2155	A575	10c multicolored	.50	.25
		Nos. 2152-2155 (4)	1.25	1.00

Nos. 2152-2154 vert. See Nos. C257-C259.

4th Military Spartakiad (Summer Sports) — A576

1977, Sept. 10   **Perf. 13**
2156	A576	1c Boxing	.25	.25
2157	A576	3c Volleyball	.25	.25
2158	A576	5c Parachuting	.25	.25
2159	A576	10c Running	.35	.25
		Nos. 2156-2159 (4)	1.10	1.00

See Nos. C260-C261.

Intl. Airmail Service, 50th Anniv. A577

Designs: 1c, Biplane and No. C62. 2c, Three-engine plane and Cuba-Key West 1st flight cancel, Oct. 28, 1927. 5c, Flying boat and intl. airmail service 1st flight cachet. 10c, Jet aircraft and Havana-Madrid cachet, Apr. 26, 1948.

1977, Oct. 27   **Litho.**   **Perf. 12x12½**
2160	A577	1c multi	.25	.25
2161	A577	2c multi	.25	.25
2162	A577	5c multi	.25	.25
2163	A577	10c multi	.50	.25
		Nos. 2160-2163 (4)	1.25	1.00

See Nos. C263-C264.

October Revolution, Russia, 60th Anniv. — A578

3c, Cruiser *Aurora*. 13c, Lenin, Flags. 30c, Hammer, sickle, symbols of agriculture, technology.

1977, Nov. 7   **Perf. 13x12½**
2164	A578	3c multicolored	.25	.25
2165	A578	13c multicolored	.40	.25
2166	A578	30c multicolored	1.40	.40
		Nos. 2164-2166 (3)	2.05	.90

Felines, Havana Zoo — A579

1977, Nov. 24   **Litho.**   **Perf. 13**
2167	A579	1c Cat	.25	.25
2168	A579	2c Black panther	.25	.25
2169	A579	8c Puma	.25	.25
2170	A579	10c Leopard	1.10	.25
		Nos. 2167-2170 (4)	1.85	1.00

See Nos. C266-C267.

Martyrs of the Revolution, 20th Death Annivs. — A580

3c, Cienfuegos Uprising. 20c, Siege on the Presidential Palace.

1977, Dec. 2   **Perf. 12½x12**
2171	A580	3c multicolored	.25	.25
2172	A580	20c multicolored	1.00	.25

See No. C268.

Intl. Measurement System — A581

1977, Dec. 9
2173 A581 3c multicolored .40 .25

Havana University, 250th Anniv. — A582

1978, Jan. 5 *Perf. 13x12½*
2174 A582 3c multicolored .25 .25
See Nos. C270-C271.

Landscape with Figures, by J. Pilliment — A583

Paintings in the Natl. Museum of Art: 1c, *Seated Woman*, by R. Madrazo, vert. 4c, *Girl*, by J. Sorolla, vert. 10c, *The Cow*, by E. Abela.

Perf. 12x12½, 13 (4c, 6c, 10c)
1978, Feb. 20
Sizes: 27x42mm, 29x40mm (4c),
40x29mm (6c, 10c)
2175 A583 1c multi .25 .25
2176 A583 4c multi .25 .25
2177 A583 6c shown .25 .25
2178 A583 10c multi .60 .25
    Nos. 2175-2178 (4) 1.35 1.00
See Nos. C273-C274.

Frontier Troops, 15th Anniv. — A584

1978, Mar. 5 *Perf. 13*
2179 A584 13c multi 1.50 .25

Bird Type of 1975

Birds: 1c, Myadestes elisabeth. 4c, Palioptila lembeyei. 10c, Teretistris fernandinae.

Perf. 13, 12½x12 (4c)
1978, Mar. 10 **Size: 42x27mm**
2180 A524 1c multicolored .45 .25
2181 A524 4c multicolored .55 .25
2182 A524 10c multicolored 1.40 .25
    Nos. 2180-2182 (3) 2.40 .75

Name of bird inscribed below vignette. See Nos. C275-C276.

Cosmonaut's Day — A585

1978, Apr. 12 *Perf. 13*
2183 A585 1c Intercosmos, vert. .25 .25
2184 A585 2c Luna 24 .25 .25
2185 A585 5c Venera 9, vert. .35 .25
2186 A585 10c Cosmos .35 .25
    Nos. 2183-2186 (4) 1.20 1.00
See Nos. C278-C279.

9th World Trade Unions Congress, Prague — A586

1978, Apr. 16
2187 A586 30c ver, deep brn & blk 1.00 .45

Cactus Flowers — A587

Designs: 1c, Melocactus guitarti. 4c, Leptocereus wrightii. 6c, Opuntia militaris. 10c, Cylindropuntia hystrix.

1978, May 15 *Perf. 12½x13 (1c), 13*
2188 A587 1c multicolored .25 .25
2189 A587 4c multicolored .25 .25
2190 A587 6c multicolored .25 .25
2191 A587 10c multicolored .65 .25
    Nos. 2188-2191 (4) 1.40 1.00
Natl. Botanical Gardens. See Nos. C281-C282.

Lenin Park Aquarium, Havana — A588

Designs: 1c, Barbus arulios. 4c, Hiphessobrycon flammeus. 6c, Poecilia reticulata. 10c, Colis lalia.

1978, June 15 *Perf. 13*
2192 A588 1c multicolored .25 .25
2193 A588 4c multicolored .25 .25
2194 A588 6c multicolored .30 .25
2195 A588 10c multicolored .65 .25
    Nos. 2192-2195 (4) 1.45 1.00
See Nos. C286-C287.

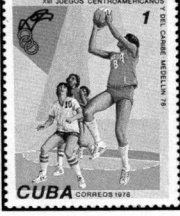

MEDELLIN '78, 13th Central American and Caribbean Games — A589

1978, July 1
2196 A589 1c Basketball .25 .25
2197 A589 3c Boxing .25 .25
2198 A589 5c Weight lifting .25 .25
2199 A589 10c Fencing, horiz. .45 .25
    Nos. 2196-2199 (4) 1.20 1.00
See Nos. C288-C289.

Attack on Moncada Barracks, 25th Anniv. — A590

1978, July 26
2200 A590 3c multi .25 .25
See Nos. C290-C291.

World Youth and Students Festival, Havana A591

Natl. flags and views of host cities.

1978, July 28
2201 A591 3c Prague, 1947 .25 .25
2202 A591 3c Budapest, 1949 .25 .25
2203 A591 3c Berlin, 1951 .25 .25
2204 A591 3c Bucharest, 1953 .25 .25
2205 A591 3c Warsaw, 1955 .25 .25
  a. Strip of 5, Nos. 2201-2205 1.40 1.40
    Nos. 2201-2205 (5) 1.25 1.25
See Nos. C292-C297.

Young Workers' Army, 5th Anniv. — A592

1978, Aug. 3
2206 A592 3c multi .30 .25

Tuna Industry A593

1c, Tuna boat. 2c, Processing ship. 5c, Shrimp boat. 10c, Inshore stern trawler.

1978, Aug. 30 *Perf. 12½x12*
2207 A593 1c multicolored .25 .25
2208 A593 2c multicolored .25 .25
2209 A593 5c multicolored .25 .25
2210 A593 10c multicolored .40 .25
    Nos. 2207-2210 (4) 1.15 1.00
See Nos. C298-C299.

Paintings by Amelia Pelaez del Casal (1896-1968) — A594

1c, *The White Mantle*. 3c, *Still-life with Flowers*, vert. 6c, *Women*, vert. 10c, *Fish*, vert.

Perf. 13x12½, 13 (3c, 6c), 12½x13
1978, Sept. 15
2211 A594 1c multicolored .25 .25
2212 A594 3c multicolored .25 .25
2213 A594 6c multicolored .25 .25
2214 A594 10c multicolored .45 .25
    Nos. 2211-2214 (4) 1.20 1.00
See Nos. C301-C303.

African Fauna, Havana Zoo A595

1978, Oct. 20 *Perf. 13*
2215 A595 1c Rhinoceros .25 .25
2216 A595 4c Okapi, vert. .25 .25
2217 A595 6c Mandrill .25 .25
2218 A595 10c Giraffe, vert. .65 .25
    Nos. 2215-2218 (4) 1.40 1.00
See Nos. C307-C308.

Natl. Ballet, 30th Anniv. — A596

3c, *Grande Pas de Quatre*.

1978, Oct. 28 *Perf. 13x12½*
2219 A596 3c multicolored .25 .25
See Nos. C309-C310.

A597

Flowers of the Pacific: Various species.

1978, Nov. 30 *Litho.* *Perf. 13*
2220 A597 1c multi .25 .25
2221 A597 4c multi .25 .25
2222 A597 6c multi .25 .25
2223 A597 10c multi .50 .25
    Nos. 2220-2223 (4) 1.25 1.00
See Nos. C311-C312.

A598

3c, Castro, soldier. 13c, Industry. 1p, Flag, globe, flame.

1979, Jan. 1 *Perf. 12½x13 (3c), 13*
2224 A598 3c multicolored .25 .25
2225 A598 13c multicolored .50 .25
2226 A598 1p multicolored 3.25 1.25
    Nos. 2224-2226 (3) 4.00 1.75
Triumph of the Revolution, 20th anniv.

Doves and Pigeons
A599

Designs: 1c, Starnoenas cyanocephala. 3c, Geotrygon chysia. 7c, Geotrygon caniceps. 8c, Geotrygon montana. 13c, Columba leucocephala. 30c, Columba inornata.

1979, Jan. 30   *Perf. 13*

2227	A599	1c multicolored	.35	.25
2228	A599	3c multicolored	.40	.25
2229	A599	7c multicolored	.40	.25
2230	A599	8c multicolored	.50	.25
2231	A599	13c multicolored	.90	.25
2232	A599	30c multicolored	1.90	.80
		Nos. 2227-2232 (6)	4.45	2.05

Paintings in the Natl. Museum of Art
A600

Designs: 1c, *Genre Scene,* by David Teniers. 3c, *Arrival of Spanish Troops,* by J. Louis Meissonier. 6c, *A Joyful Gathering,* by Sir David Wilkie. 10c, *A Robbery,* by E. De Lucas Padilla. 13c, *Tea Time,* by R. Madrazo, vert. 30c, *Peasants in Front of a Tavern,* by Adriaen van Ostade.

1979, Feb. 20

2233	A600	1c multi	.25	.25
2234	A600	3c multi	.25	.25
2235	A600	6c multi	.30	.25
2236	A600	10c multi	.45	.25
2237	A600	13c multi	.80	.25
2238	A600	30c multi	1.75	.30
		Nos. 2233-2238 (6)	3.80	1.55

See Nos. 2262-2267, C317.

Marine Flora — A601

Designs: 3c, Nymphaea capensis. 10c, Nymphaea ampla. 13c, Nymphaea coerulea. 30c, Nymphaea rubra.

1979, Mar. 20

2239	A601	3c multicolored	.25	.25
2240	A601	10c multicolored	.40	.25
2241	A601	13c multicolored	.65	.25
2242	A601	30c multicolored	1.50	.40
		Nos. 2239-2242 (4)	2.80	1.15

All are incorrectly inscribed "Nymphaca."

Cuban Film Industry, 20th Anniv. — A602

1979, Mar. 24
2243   A602   3c multicolored   .25   .25

Cosmonaut's Day — A603

1979, Apr. 12

2244	A603	1c Rocket launch	.25	.25
2245	A603	4c Soyuz	.25	.25
2246	A603	6c Salyut	.35	.25
2247	A603	10c Link-up	.50	.25
2248	A603	13c Soyuz, Salyut	.85	.25
2249	A603	30c Parachute landing	1.90	.25
		Nos. 2244-2249 (6)	4.10	1.50

See No. C315.

6th Summit Meeting of Non-Aligned Countries — A604

3c, Understanding, cooperation. 13c, Fight colonialism. 30c, New world economic order.

1979, Apr. 17

2250	A604	3c multicolored	.25	.25
2251	A604	13c multicolored	.50	.25
2252	A604	30c multicolored	1.40	.40
		Nos. 2250-2252 (3)	2.15	.90

House of the Americas Museum, 20th Anniv. — A605

13c, Cuna Indian tapestry.

1979, Apr. 28   *Perf. 13x12½*
2253   A605   13c multicolored   .40   .25

Agrarian Reform, 20th Anniv. — A606

1979, May 17   *Perf. 12½x12*
2254   A606   3c multicolored   .40   .25

Souvenir Sheet

The Party, by Jules Pascin — A607

1979, May 18   *Perf. 13*
2255   A607   50c multi   3.50   1.25
PHILASERDICA '79 phil. exhib., Sofia.

Nocturnal Butterflies — A608

Designs: 1c, Eulepidotis rectimargo. 4c, Othreis materna. 6c, Noropsis hieroglyphica. 10c, Heterochroma. 13c, Melanchroia regnatrix. 30c, Attera gemmata.

1979, May 25

2256	A608	1c multicolored	.25	.25
2257	A608	4c multicolored	.25	.25
2258	A608	6c multicolored	.40	.25
2259	A608	10c multicolored	.40	.25
2260	A608	13c multicolored	.80	.25
2261	A608	30c multicolored	2.00	.45
		Nos. 2256-2261 (6)	4.10	1.70

Art Type of 1979

Paintings by Victor Manuel Garcia (d. 1969): 1c, *Main Avenue, Paris.* 3c, *Portrait of Enmita.* 6c, *San Juan River, Matanzas.* 10c, *Woman Carrying Hay.* 13c, *Still-life with Vase.* 30c, *Street at Night.* Nos. 2262-2267 vert.

1979, June 15

2262	A600	1c multi	.25	.25
2263	A600	3c multi	.25	.25
2264	A600	6c multi	.25	.25
2265	A600	10c multi	.30	.25
2266	A600	13c multi	.45	.25
2267	A600	30c multi	1.60	.45
		Nos. 2262-2267 (6)	3.10	1.70

See No. C317.

World Peace Council, 30th Anniv. A609

1979, June 29   *Perf. 12½x13*
2268   A609   30c multi   1.00   .35

1980 Summer Olympics, Moscow — A610

1c, Wrestling. 4c, Boxing. 6c, Women's volleyball. 10c, Shooting. 13c, Weight lifting. 30c, High jump.

1979, July 30   *Perf. 13x12½*

2269	A610	1c multicolored	.30	.25
2270	A610	4c multicolored	.30	.25
2271	A610	6c multicolored	.30	.25
2272	A610	10c multicolored	.40	.25
2273	A610	13c multicolored	.65	.25
2274	A610	30c multicolored	2.10	.30
		Nos. 2269-2274 (6)	4.05	1.55

Roses — A611

Designs: 1c, Rosa eglanteria. 2c, Rosa centifolia anemonoides. 3c, Rosa indica vulgaris. 5c, Rosa eglanteria punicea. 10c, Rosa sulfurea. 13c, Rosa muscosa alba. 20c, Rosa gallica purpurea velutina.

1979, Aug. 20   *Perf. 13*

2275	A611	1c multicolored	.25	.25
2276	A611	2c multicolored	.25	.25
2277	A611	3c multicolored	.25	.25
2278	A611	5c multicolored	.25	.25
2279	A611	10c multicolored	.30	.25
2280	A611	13c multicolored	.50	.25
2281	A611	20c multicolored	1.00	.25
		Nos. 2275-2281 (7)	2.80	1.75

A612

1979, Aug. 30
2282   A612   13c multicolored   .50   .25

Council for Mutual Economic Assistance, 30th anniv.

Cubana Airlines, 50th Anniv. A613

Various aircraft.

1979, Oct. 8

2283	A613	1c Ford trimotor	.25	.25
2284	A613	2c Sikorsky S-38	.25	.25
2285	A613	3c Douglas DC-3	.35	.25
2286	A613	4c Brittania	.35	.25
2287	A613	13c Ilyushin IL-14	.90	.25
2288	A613	40c Tupolev TU-104	2.50	.40
		Nos. 2283-2288 (6)	4.60	1.65

Disappearance of Camilo Cienfuegos, 20th Anniv. — A614

1979, Oct. 28
2289   A614   3c multi   .30   .25

Reinoso, Sugar Cane and Blossom A615

1979, Nov. 12
2290   A615   13c multi   .75   .25

Sugar Cane Research Institute, 15th anniv., and sesquicentennial of the birth of Alvaro Reinoso.

Zoo Animals
A616

1979, Nov. 15

2291	A616	1c	Chimpanzees	.25	.25
2292	A616	2c	Leopards	.25	.25
2293	A616	3c	Deer	.25	.25
2294	A616	4c	Lion cubs	.25	.25
2295	A616	5c	Bear cubs	.25	.25
2296	A616	13c	Squirrels	.30	.25
2297	A616	30c	Pandas	.70	.30
2298	A616	50c	Tiger cubs	1.40	.60
		Nos. 2291-2298 (8)		3.65	2.40

Insects
A617

Designs: 1c, *Rhina oblita.* 5c, *Odontocera josemartii,* vert. 6c, *Pinthocoelium columbinum.* 10c, *Calasoma splendida,* vert. 13c, *Homophileurus cubanus,* vert. 30c, *Heterops dimidiata,* vert.

1980, Jan. 25

2299	A617	1c	multicolored	.25	.25
2300	A617	5c	multicolored	.25	.25
2301	A617	6c	multicolored	.25	.25
2302	A617	10c	multicolored	.50	.25
2303	A617	13c	multicolored	.95	.25
2304	A617	30c	multicolored	2.10	.70
		Nos. 2299-2304 (6)		4.30	1.95

1980 Summer Olympics,
Moscow — A618

1980, Feb. 20   Perf. 12½

2305	A618	1c	Weight lifting	.25	.25
2306	A618	2c	Shooting	.25	.25
2307	A618	5c	Javelin	.30	.25
2308	A618	6c	Wrestling	.30	.25
2309	A618	8c	Judo	.30	.25
2310	A618	10c	Running	.30	.25
2311	A618	13c	Boxing	.65	.25
2312	A618	30c	Women's volley-ball	1.60	.60
		Nos. 2305-2312 (8)		3.95	2.35

Souvenir Sheet
Imperf

2313	A618	50c	Mischa character	3.00	1.60

No. 2313 contains one 32x40mm stamp.

Paintings
in the
Natl.
Museum
A619

Designs: 1c, *The Oak Trees,* by Henry Joseph Harpignies, vert. 4c, *Family Reunion,* by Willem van Mieris. 6c, *Domestic Fowl,* by Melchior De Hondecoeter, vert. 9c, *Innocence,* by William A. Bougereau, vert. 13c, *Venetian Scene II,* by Michele Marieschi. 30c, *Spanish Peasant Woman,* by Joaquin Dominguez Bequer, vert.

Sizes: 29x40mm, 40x29mm (4c), 28x42mm (9c, 30c), 38x26mm (13c)

Perf. 12½, 13 (9c, 30c), 12½x13 (13c)

1980, Mar. 11

2314	A619	1c	multi	.25	.25
2315	A619	4c	multi	.25	.25
2316	A619	6c	multi	.25	.25
2317	A619	9c	multi	.65	.25
2318	A619	13c	multi	.85	.25
2319	A619	30c	multi	1.90	.65
		Nos. 2314-2319 (6)		4.15	1.90

Souvenir Sheet

LONDON '80 — A620

50c, *Malvern Hall,* by John Constable.

1980, Apr. 1   Perf. 13

2320	A620	50c multi	3.50	1.60

Intercosmos Program — A621

1c, Emblem, flags. 4c, Astrophysics. 6c, Satellite communications. 10c, Meteorology. 13c, Biology and medicine. 30c, Surveying satellite.

1980, Apr. 12

2321	A621	1c	multicolored	.25	.25
2322	A621	4c	multicolored	.25	.25
2323	A621	6c	multicolored	.25	.25
2324	A621	10c	multicolored	.45	.25
2325	A621	13c	multicolored	.60	.25
2326	A621	30c	multicolored	1.90	.65
		Nos. 2321-2326 (6)		3.70	1.90

Cuban Postage Stamps, 125th
Anniv. — A622

30c, Nos. 1, 7 and 613.

1980, Apr. 24   Perf. 12½

2327	A622	30c multi	1.25	.45

Orchids — A623

Designs: 1c, *Bletia purpurea.* 4c, *Oncidium leiboldii.* 6c, *Epidendrum cochieatum.* 10c, *Cattleyopsis lindenii.* 13c, *Encyclia fucata.* 30c, *Encyclia phoenicea.*

1980, May 20   Perf. 13

2328	A623	1c	multicolored	.25	.25
2329	A623	4c	multicolored	.25	.25
2330	A623	6c	multicolored	.25	.25
2331	A623	10c	multicolored	.50	.25
2332	A623	13c	multicolored	.90	.25
2333	A623	30c	multicolored	1.90	.60
		Nos. 2328-2333 (6)		4.05	1.85

Marine Mammals — A624

Designs: 1c, *Tursiops truncatus.* 3c, *Megaptera novaeangliae,* vert. 13c, *Ziphius cavirostris.* 30c, *Monachus tropicalis.*

1980, June 20

2334	A624	1c	multicolored	.50	.25
2335	A624	3c	multicolored	.50	.25
2336	A624	13c	multicolored	1.50	.25
2337	A624	30c	multicolored	3.50	.50
		Nos. 2334-2337 (4)		6.00	1.25

Urban Reform
Campaign, 20th
Anniv. — A625

Nationalization of Foreign Industry,
20th Anniv. — A626

1980, July 26   Perf. 13x12½, 12½x13

2338	A625	3c multi	.25	.25
2339	A626	13c multi	.35	.25

Moncada Program.

Colonial
Copperware
A627

3c, Wine pitcher, 19th cent. 13c, Oil jar, 18th cent. 30c, Lidded pitcher, 19th cent.

Perf. 12½, 12½x13 (13c)
1980, July 29
Sizes: 27x43½mm, 38x26mm (13c)

2340	A627	3c	multicolored	.25	.25
2341	A627	13c	multicolored	.70	.25
2342	A627	30c	multicolored	1.40	.30
		Nos. 2340-2342 (3)		2.35	.80

Cuban Women's
Federation, 20th
Anniv. — A628

1980, Aug. 23   Perf. 13

2343	A628	3c multi	.40	.25

Souvenir Sheet

ESPAMER '80, Madrid — A629

Design: *Clotilde Passing Through the Country Garden,* by Joaquin Sorolla y Bastida.

1980, Aug. 29

2344	A629	50c multi	3.50	1.60

Postage stamps of Spain, 130th anniv.

1st Havana
Declaration,
20th
Anniv. — A630

1980, Sept. 2

2345	A630	13c multi	.50	.25

Construction of Naval Vessels in
Cuba, 360th Anniv. — A631

Ships under construction: 1c, *Our Lady of Atocha,* galleon, 1620. 3c, *El Rayo,* warship, 1749. 7c, *Santisima Trinidad,* 1769. 10c, *Santisima Trinidad,* diff., 1805, vert. 13c, Steamships *Congreso* and *Colon,* 1851. 30c, Cardenas and Chullima shipyards.

1980, Sept. 15

2346	A631	1c	multi	.25	.25
2347	A631	3c	multi	.25	.25
2348	A631	7c	multi	.25	.25
2349	A631	10c	multi	.50	.25
2350	A631	13c	multi	.95	.25
2351	A631	30c	multi	1.60	.60
		Nos. 2346-2351 (6)		3.80	1.85

A633

1980, Sept. 26   Perf. 13

2354	A633	13c multi	.60	.25

Fidel Castro's 1st speech before the UN General Assembly, 20th anniv.

A634

1980, Sept. 28   Perf. 13x12½

2355	A634	3c multi	.30	.25

Revolutionary defense committees, 20th anniv.

Souvenir Sheet

ESSEN '80, 49th Intl. Philatelic
Federation Congress — A635

Painting: *Portrait of a Lady,* by Ludger Tom Ring The Younger.

1980, Oct. 2 **Litho.** *Perf. 13*
2356 A635 50c multi 3.75 1.25

Early Locomotives — A636

1c, Josefa. 2c, Chaparra Sugar Co. No. 22. 7c, Steam storage locomotive. 10c, 2-4-2 locomotive. 13c, 2-4-0 locomotive. 30c, Oil combustion engine, 1909.

1980, Oct. 15
2357 A636 1c multicolored .25 .25
2358 A636 2c multicolored .25 .25
2359 A636 7c multicolored .25 .25
2360 A636 10c multicolored .40 .25
2361 A636 13c multicolored .65 .25
2362 A636 30c multicolored 1.60 .60
    Nos. 2357-2362 (6) 3.40 1.85

Lighthouses A637

3c, Roncali, San Antonio. 13c, Jagua, Cienfuegos. 30c, Maisi Point, Guantanamo.

1980, Oct. 30
2363 A637 3c multicolored .25 .25
2364 A637 13c multicolored .70 .25
2365 A637 30c multicolored 1.60 .25
    Nos. 2363-2365 (3) 2.55 .75

See Nos. 2440-2442, 2553-2555, 2614-2616.

Victory of Cuban Athletes at the 1980 Summer Olympics, Moscow — A638

1980, Nov. 10 **Litho.** *Perf. 12½x12*
2366 A638 13c Bronze medals .50 .25
2367 A638 30c Silver medals 1.10 .25
2368 A638 50c Gold medals 2.25 .55
    Nos. 2366-2368 (3) 3.85 1.05

Nos. 2366-2368 each printed se-tenant with label containing statistical data.

Wildflowers A639

Designs: 1c, Pancratium arenicolum. 4c, Urechites lutea. 6c, Solanum elaegnifolium. 10c, Hamelia patens. 13c, Morinda royoc. 30c, Centrosema virginianum.

1980, Nov. 20 *Perf. 13*
2369 A639 1c multicolored .25 .25
2370 A639 4c multicolored .25 .25
2371 A639 6c multicolored .30 .25
2372 A639 10c multicolored .50 .25
2373 A639 13c multicolored .95 .25
2374 A639 30c multicolored 2.25 .40
    Nos. 2369-2374 (6) 4.50 1.65

Souvenir Sheet

7th Natl. Stamp Exhibition — A640

1980, Nov. 22
2375 A640 50c Mail train 3.00 1.25

2nd Communist Party Congress A641

13c, Industry, communication. 30c, Athletics, elderly, education.

1980, Dec. 17
2376 A641 3c shown .25 .25
2377 A641 13c multicolored .40 .25
2378 A641 30c multicolored 1.10 .25
    Nos. 2376-2378 (3) 1.75 .75

Paintings in the Natl. Museum of Art A642

Designs: 1c, *Lady Mayo,* by Anton Van Dyck, vert. 6c, *The Spinner,* by Giovanni Battista Piazzetta, vert. 10c, *Daniel Collyer,* by Francis Cotes, vert. 13c, *Gardens, Palma de Mallorca,* by Santiago Rusinol Prats. 20c, *Landscape with Roadway and Houses,* by Frederick Waters Watts. 50c, *Landscape with Sheep,* by Jean-Francois Millet.

1981, Jan. 20
2379 A642 1c multi .25 .25
2380 A642 6c multi .25 .25
2381 A642 10c multi .50 .25
2382 A642 13c multi .60 .25
2383 A642 20c multi 1.00 .30
2384 A642 50c multi 2.10 .60
    Nos. 2379-2384 (6) 4.70 1.90

See Nos. 2510-2515.

Pelagic Fish A643

Designs: 1c, Isurus oxyrhynchus. 3c, Lampris regius. 10c, Istiophorus platypterus. 13c, Mola mola, vert. 30c, Coruphaena hippurus. 50c, Tetrapturus albidus.

1981, Feb. 25
2385 A643 1c multicolored .25 .25
2386 A643 3c multicolored .25 .25
2387 A643 10c multicolored .45 .25
2388 A643 13c multicolored 1.75 .25
2389 A643 30c multicolored 1.10 .40
2390 A643 50c multicolored 2.00 .95
    Nos. 2385-2390 (6) 5.80 2.35

1982 World Cup Soccer Championships, Spain — A644

Globe and various soccer players.

1981, Mar. 20 *Perf. 12½*
2391 A644 1c multi .25 .25
2392 A644 2c multi .25 .25
2393 A644 3c multi .25 .25
2394 A644 10c multi, vert. .45 .25
2395 A644 13c multi, vert. .45 .25
2396 A644 50c multi 1.75 .65
    Nos. 2391-2396 (6) 3.40 1.90

Souvenir Sheet
Perf. 13
2397 A644 1p Soccer ball, flag 4.75 2.00

No. 2397 contains one 40x32mm stamp.

Opening of the 1st Kindergarten, 20th Anniv. — A645

1981, Apr. 10 *Perf. 13*
2398 A645 3c multi .65 .25

1st Man in Space, 20th Anniv. — A646

Designs: 1c, Jules Verne, Russian scientist Konstantin E. Tsiolkovski, and Sergei P. Korolev, designer of the 1st Soviet spacecraft, vert. 2c, Yuri Gagarin, 1st man in space. 3c, Valentina Tereshkova, 1st woman in space, and *Vostok 6.* 5c, Aleksei A. Leonov, 1st man to walk in space. 13c, Konstantin Feoktistov, Boris Yegorov and Vladimir Komarov, *Voskhod 1* crew, 1st 3-man orbital flight. 30c, Valeri Ryumin and Leonid Popov, set a space endurance record. 50c, Arnaldo Tamayo Mendez, 1st Cuban cosmonaut, and Soviet cosmonaut Yuri Romanenko on joint space flight, vert.

1981, Apr. 12 *Perf. 12½*
2399 A646 1c multi .25 .25
2400 A646 2c multi .25 .25
2401 A646 3c multi .25 .25
2402 A646 5c multi .25 .25
2403 A646 13c multi .45 .25
2404 A646 30c multi 1.00 .35
2405 A646 50c multi 2.25 .60
    Nos. 2399-2405 (7) 4.70 2.20

A647

Designs: 3c, Rocket, aircraft. 13c, Hand raising gun.

1981, Apr. 19 **Litho.** *Perf. 13*
2406 A647 3c multi, vert. .25 .25
2407 A647 13c multi, vert. .40 .25
2408 A647 30c multi .95 .60
    Nos. 2406-2408 (3) 1.60 1.10

Creation of armed forces (DAAFAR) (3c), Bay of Pigs Invasion, 20th Anniv. (13c), Proclamation of the socialist revolution (30c).

Attack on Goicuria Barracks, 25th Anniv. — A648

1981, Apr. 29
2409 A648 3c multi .30 .25

Natl. Assoc. of Small Farmers (ANAP), 20th Anniv. A649

1981, May 17
2410 A649 3c multi .50 .25

Souvenir Sheet

WIPA '81 — A650

1981, May 22 **Litho.**
2411 A650 50c Austria No. 643 4.00 1.50

Fighting Cocks A651

1981, May 25 *Perf. 12½x13, 13x12½*
2412 A651 1c Canelo, vert. .25 .25
2413 A651 3c Cenizo .25 .25
2414 A651 7c Blanco, vert. .25 .25
2415 A651 13c Pinto, vert. .50 .25
2416 A651 30c Giro 1.60 .35
2417 A651 50c Jabao, vert. 2.40 .60
    Nos. 2412-2417 (6) 5.25 1.95

Ministry of the Interior, 20th Anniv. — A652

1981, June 6 *Perf. 13*
2418 A652 13c multi .40 .25

Souvenir Sheet

Mother and Child, by Zlatka Dabova — A653

1981, June 14
2419 A653 50c gold, sil & blk 2.25 1.10
Bulgaria, 1300th anniv. BULGARIA '81 phil. exhib.

Horse-drawn Carriages — A654

1981, June 25
2420	A654	1c Streetcar	.25	.25
2421	A654	4c Bus	.25	.25
2422	A654	9c Breake	.25	.25
2423	A654	13c Landau	.40	.25
2424	A654	30c Phaeton	1.40	.45
2425	A654	50c Funeral coach	2.50	.75
	Nos. 2420-2425 (6)		5.05	2.20

House in the Country, by Mario Caridad — A655

1981, July 15 *Perf. 12½*
2426 A655 30c multi 1.25 .30
Intl. Year of the Disabled.

Sandinistas, 25th Anniv. — A656

1981, July 23 *Perf. 13*
2427 A656 13c multi .50 .25

State Institutions, 20th Annivs. — A657

1981, July 26 *Perf. 12½*
2428	A657	3c multi	.25	.25
2429	A657	13c multi, diff.	.45	.25
2430	A657	30c multi, diff.	1.25	.25
	Nos. 2428-2430 (3)		1.95	.75

Institute for Sports, Physical Education and Recreation (3c); Radio Havana (13c); and Ministry of Foreign Trade (MINCEX) (30c).

Carlos J. Finlay and Cent. of His Theory of Biological Vectors — A658

1981, Aug. 14 *Perf. 13*
2431 A658 13c multi 1.00 .25

Nonaligned Countries Movement, 20th Anniv. — A659

1981, Sept. 1
2432 A659 50c multi 1.50 .80

Horses — A660

Nos. 2433-2437 vert.

1981, Sept. 15 *Perf. 13*
Size: 29x40mm
2433	A660	1c multi	.25	.25
2434	A660	3c multi, diff.	.25	.25
2435	A660	8c multi, diff.	.25	.25
2436	A660	13c multi, diff.	.35	.25
2437	A660	30c multi, diff.	1.10	.45

Size: 68x27mm
Perf. 12½
2438	A660	50c Herd	1.75	.75
	Nos. 2433-2438 (6)		3.95	2.20

Souvenir Sheet

Idyll in a Tea House, by Kitagawa Utamaro — A661

1981, Oct. 9 *Perf. 13*
2439 A661 50c multi 2.75 1.25
PHILATOKYO '81.

Lighthouse Type of 1980
1981, Oct. 15 **Litho.**
2440	A637	3c North Rock	.25	.25
2441	A637	13c Lucrecia Point	.50	.25
2442	A637	40c East Guano	2.10	.50
	Nos. 2440-2442 (3)		2.85	1.00

Jose Marti Natl. Library, 80th Anniv. — A662

Sugar mills, lithographs from *Los Ingenios,* by Eduardo Laplante (b. 1818): 3c, Flor de Cuba, 1838. 13c, El Progreso, 1845. 30c, Santa Teresa, 1847.

1981, Oct. 18 *Perf. 12½x12*
2443	A662	3c multi	.25	.25
2444	A662	13c multi	.35	.25
2445	A662	30c multi	1.25	.55
	Nos. 2443-2445 (3)		1.85	1.05

Pablo Picasso (b. 1881) and No. 1263 A663

1981, Oct. 25 *Perf. 12½x13*
2446 A663 30c multi 1.25 .40

Souvenir Sheet

ESPAMER '81, Buenos Aires — A664

1981, Nov. 13 *Perf. 13*
2447 A664 1p Packet 4.00 2.00

Art Type of 1969
Paintings in the Napoleon Museum: 1c, *Napoleon in Coronation Costume,* anonymous. 3c, *Napoleon with Landscape in the Background,* by Jean Horace Vernet. 10c, *Bonaparte in Egypt,* by Edouard Detaille. 13c, *Napoleon on Horseback,* by Hippolyte Bellange. 30c, *Napoleon in Normandy,* by Bellange. 50c, *Death of Napoleon,* anonymous.

1981, Dec. 1 *Perf. 12½*
Sizes: 42x58mm, 58x42mm (3c, 13c, 30c, 50c)
2448	A385	1c multi	.25	.25
2449	A385	3c multi, horiz.	.25	.25
2450	A385	10c multi	.40	.25
2451	A385	13c multi, horiz.	.40	.25
2452	A385	30c multi, horiz.	1.25	.40
2453	A385	50c multi, horiz.	2.10	.70
	Nos. 2448-2453 (6)		4.65	2.10

Napoleon Museum, 20th anniv.

25th Anniv. A665

3c, Revolutionaries, vert. 20c, Marksman. 1p, Yacht *Granma.*

1981, Dec. 2 *Perf. 13*
2454	A665	3c multi	.25	.25
2455	A665	20c multi	.45	.25
2456	A665	1p multi	5.25	1.40
	Nos. 2454-2456 (3)		5.95	1.90

November 30th insurrection (3c); creation of the revolutionary armed forces (20c); and disembarking of revolutionary forces (1p).

Fauna — A666

1981, Dec. 14 **Litho.** *Perf. 12½x12*
2457	A666	1c Hummingbird	.60	.25
2458	A666	2c Parakeet	.95	.25
2459	A666	5c Hutia	.25	.25
2460	A666	20c Almiqui	.65	.25
2461	A666	35c Manatee	1.25	.25
2462	A666	40c Crocodile	1.00	.55
	Nos. 2457-2462 (6)		4.70	1.80

Fernando Ortiz, Folklorist, Birth Cent. A667

3c, Portrait by Jorge Arche y Silva. 10c, Hanging idol. 30c, Arara drum. 50c, Chango statue.

1981, Dec. 20 *Perf. 12½x13*
2463	A667	3c multi	.25	.25
2464	A667	10c multi	.40	.25
2465	A667	30c multi	1.50	.45
2466	A667	50c multi	2.25	.70
	Nos. 2463-2466 (4)		4.40	1.65

Literacy Campaign, 20th Anniv. — A668

No. 2467, Conrado Benitez. No. 2468, Manuel Asunce.

1981, Dec. 25 *Perf. 12½x12*
2467	A668	5c multi	.30	.25
2468	A668	5c multi	.30	.25
a.	Pair, #2467-2468		.75	.25
	Nos. 2467-2468 (2)		.60	.50

A669

1982 World Cup Soccer
Championships, Spain — A670

Various athletes.

1982, Jan. 15			Perf. 13	
2469	A669	1c multi, vert.	.25	.25
2470	A669	2c multi, vert.	.25	.25
2471	A669	5c multi, vert.	.25	.25
2472	A669	10c multi, vert.	.30	.25
2473	A669	20c shown	.70	.25
2474	A669	40c multi	1.25	.50
2475	A669	50c multi, vert.	1.60	.70
	Nos. 2469-2475 (7)		4.60	2.45

Souvenir Sheet

2476	A670	1p shown	5.00	2.50

No. 2476 contains one 32x40mm stamp.

10th World
Trade Unions
Congress,
Havana — A671

30c, Lazaro Pena, delegate.

1982, Feb. 10			Litho.	
2477	A671	30c multi	1.00	.40

Butterflies — A672

Designs: 1c, Euptoieta hegesia. 4c,
Metamorpha stelenes insularis. 5c, Heliconius
charithonius ramsdeni. 20c, Phoebis avellaneda. 30c, Hamadryas ferox diasia. 60c,
Marpesia eleuchea.

1982, Feb. 25			Perf. 12½	
2478	A672	1c multicolored	.25	.25
2479	A672	4c multicolored	.25	.25
2480	A672	5c multicolored	.25	.25
2481	A672	20c multicolored	1.40	.30
2482	A672	30c multicolored	2.25	.55
2483	A672	50c multicolored	4.00	.95
	Nos. 2478-2483 (6)		8.40	2.55

Exports — A673

3c, Sugar (processing plant). 4c, Lobster
(fishing boat). 6c, Canned fruits. 7c, Agricultural machinery. 8c, Nickel (passenger jet,
industrial complex, car). 9c, Rum. 10c, Coffee.
30c, Fresh fruit. 50c, Tobacco. 1p, Cement.
Nos. 2489-2493 vert.

1982, Feb. 26			Perf. 12x12½, 12½x12	
2484	A673	3c lt grn	.25	.25
2485	A673	4c car rose	.25	.25
2486	A673	6c dull blue	.25	.25
2487	A673	7c brt org	.40	.25
2488	A673	8c brt vio	.40	.25
2489	A673	9c slate	.40	.25
2490	A673	10c dull red brn	.50	.25
2491	A673	30c bister	.75	.25
2492	A673	50c orange	2.10	.40
2493	A673	1p olive bister	4.00	1.25
	Nos. 2484-2493 (10)		9.30	3.65

Tulips
A674

1982, Mar. 30			Perf. 12½x13	
2494	A674	1c Greenland	.25	.25
2495	A674	3c Mariette	.25	.25
2496	A674	8c Ringo	.25	.25
2497	A674	20c La Tulipe Noire	.80	.25
2498	A674	30c Jewel of Spring	1.40	.25
2499	A674	50c Orange Parrot	1.90	.60
	Nos. 2494-2499 (6)		4.85	1.85

Communist Youth Organization, 20th
Anniv. — A675

1982, Apr. 4			Perf. 13	
2500	A675	5c multi	.30	.25

2nd UN Congress on the Peaceful
Use of Outer Space — A676

1c, Gorizont. 3c, Meteor. 6c, Salyut-Soyuz
link-up. 20c, Lunokhod moon vehicle. 30c,
Venera with heat shield. 50c, Intelsat-4a.

1982, Apr. 12				
2501	A676	1c multicolored	.25	.25
2502	A676	3c multicolored	.25	.25
2503	A676	6c multicolored	.25	.25
2504	A676	20c multicolored	.50	.25
2505	A676	30c multicolored	1.40	.30
2506	A676	50c multicolored	2.00	.60
	Nos. 2501-2506 (6)		4.65	1.90

Cover
A677

1982, Apr. 24			Perf. 12½x12	
2507	A677	20c Havana-Veracruz	.75	.25
2508	A677	30c Havana-Tampico	1.25	.25

Stamp Day. English post office, 1842-1877
(20c); and French post office, 1862-1877
(30c).

Broadcasting and
Television
Institute (ICRT),
20th
Anniv. — A678

1982, May 24			Perf. 12x12½	
2509	A678	30c multi	1.00	.25

Art Type of 1981 With Larger Type

Paintings in the Natl. Museum of Art: 1c,
Portrait of a Youth (girl), by Jean B. Greuze,
vert. 3c, *Procession in Brittany,* by Jules
Breton. 9c, *Landscape,* by Jean Piliment. 20c,
Late Afternoon, by William A. Bouguereau,
vert. 30c, *Tiger,* by Ferdinand V.E. Delacroix.
40c, *The Chair,* by Wilfredo Lam, vert.

1982, May 31		Perf. 13, 13x12½ (3c), 12x12½ (20c, 40c), 12½x12 (30c)	Litho.	
2510	A642	1c 29x40mm	.25	.25
2511	A642	3c 46x36mm	.25	.25
2512	A642	9c 40x29mm	.25	.25
2513	A642	20c 27x42mm	.65	.25
2514	A642	30c 42x27mm	1.25	.40
2515	A642	40c 27x42mm	2.00	.40
	Nos. 2510-2515 (6)		4.65	1.80

Souvenir Sheet

PHILEXFRANCE '82 — A679

1p, Steamship Louisiana at St. Nazaire.

1982, June 7			Perf. 13	
2516	A679	1p multicolored	5.00	2.50

DEPORFILEX '82 — A680

1982, June 10			Perf. 13x12½	
2517	A680	20c Hurdler, No. 300	1.50	.25

Reptiles
A681

Designs: 1c, Pseudemys decussata. 2c,
Tropidophis pardalis. 3c, Crocodylus
rhombifer. 20c, Cyclura nubila. 30c, Anolis
allisonis. 50c, Alsophis cantherigerus.

1982, June 15			Perf. 13	
2518	A681	1c multicolored	.25	.25
2519	A681	2c multicolored	.25	.25
2520	A681	3c multicolored	.25	.25
2521	A681	20c multicolored	.85	.25
2522	A681	30c multicolored	1.25	.30
2523	A681	50c multicolored	2.40	.50
	Nos. 2518-2523 (6)		5.25	1.80

George Dimitrov
(1882-1949),
Bulgarian Prime
Minister — A682

1982, June 18				
2524	A682	30c multi	1.00	.25

Koch,
Bacillus
A683

1982, July 18				
2525	A683	20c multi	1.25	.25

Discovery of the tubercle bacillus by Dr.
Robert Koch, cent.

14th Central
American and
Caribbean
Games — A684

1982, Aug. 1				
2526	A684	1c Baseball	.25	.25
2527	A684	2c Boxing	.25	.25
2528	A684	10c Water polo	.35	.25
2529	A684	20c Javelin	.80	.30
2530	A684	35c Weight lifting	1.25	.25
2531	A684	50c Volleyball	2.00	.55
	Nos. 2526-2531 (6)		4.90	2.10

Hydraulic Development Plan, 20th
Anniv. — A685

5c, Fruit, *Eichornia crassipes,* ship. 20c,
Arid soil, *Nymphaea alba,* irrigation & reservoir
systems.

1982, Aug. 9				
2532	A685	5c multi	.40	.25
2533	A685	20c multi	1.25	.25

Souvenir Sheet

DEPORFILEX '82, Intl. Stamp and
Coin Exhibition — A686

1p, Cuco, character trademark.

1982, Aug. 10			Litho.	
2534	A686	1p multi	4.75	2.25

14th Central American and Caribbean
Games.

Namibia Day — A687

1982, Aug. 26
2535 A687 50c multi   1.75 .75

1982 World Cup Soccer Championships, Spain — A688

Various athletes.

1982, Aug. 30
2536 A688 5c multi   .25 .25
2537 A688 20c multi   .75 .30
2538 A688 30c multi   1.10 .40
2539 A688 50c multi   1.90 .80
    Nos. 2536-2539 (4)   4.00 1.75

Also exist in miniature sheets of 16 + 9 labels containing 4 each Nos. 2536-2539 in blocks of 4.

Natl. Folklore Ensemble, 20th Anniv. — A689

Paintings by V.P. Landaluze.

1982, Sept. 10
2540 A689 20c Little Devil, vert.   .80 .25
2541 A689 30c Day of Kings   1.10 .45

Prehistoric Fauna — A690

Designs: 1c, Ornimegalonyx oteroi, vert. 5c, Crocodylus rhombifer. 7c, Aquila borrasi, vert. 20c, Geocapromys colombianus. 35c, Megalocnus rodens, vert. 50c, Nesophontes micrus.

1982, Sept. 15   **Litho.**
2542 A690 1c multicolored   .65 .25
2543 A690 5c multicolored   .25 .25
2544 A690 7c multicolored   2.75 .40
2545 A690 20c multicolored   .65 .25
2546 A690 35c multicolored   1.00 .50
2547 A690 50c multicolored   1.40 .65
    Nos. 2542-2547 (6)   6.70 2.30

15th Death Anniv. of Che Guevara — A691

1982, Oct. 8   **Perf. 13x12½**
2548 A691 20c multi   .70 .25

Discovery of America, 490th Anniv. — A692

1982, Oct. 12   **Perf. 13**
2549 A692 5c shown   1.10 .25
2550 A692 20c Santa Maria, vert. 1.25 .40
2551 A692 35c Pinta, vert.   1.90 .90
2552 A692 50c Nina, vert.   2.40 1.10
    Nos. 2549-2552 (4)   6.65 2.65

Lighthouse Type of 1980

5c, Jutias Caye. 20c, Paredon Grande Caye. 30c, Morro Santiago de Cuba.

1982, Oct. 25
2553 A637 5c multicolored   1.00 .25
2554 A637 20c multicolored   2.75 .25
2555 A637 30c multicolored   3.75 .45
    Nos. 2553-2555 (3)   7.50 .95

George Washington, 250th Birth Anniv. — A693

Designs: Quotations and anonymous oil paintings, 18th-19th cent.

1982, Oct. 29   **Perf. 12x12½**
2556 A693 5c multi   .25 .25
2557 A693 20c multi, diff.   .75 .25

Souvenir Sheet

8th Natl. Philatelic Exposition, Ciego de Avila — A694

1p, Paddle steamer Almendares.

1982, Nov. 13
2558 A694 1p multi   5.00 2.50

8th Congress of the Cuban Philatelic Federation, Nov. 13-22.

Lenin Park, 10th Anniv. A695

1982, Dec. 28
2559 A695 5c multi   .65 .25

Chess Champion Jose Raul Capablanca and King — A696

1982, Dec. 29
2560 A696 5c shown   .25 .25
2561 A696 20c Rook   1.10 .25
2562 A696 30c Knight   1.40 .50
2563 A696 50c Queen   2.25 .80
   a.   Bkt. pane of 4, Nos. 2560-
      2563   20.00 10.00
    Nos. 2560-2563 (4)   5.00 1.80

Exist in sheets of 4+2 labels picturing chessmen.

USSR, 60th Anniv. — A697

1982, Dec. 30   **Perf. 13x12½**
2564 A697 30c multi   1.25 .25

World Communications Year — A698

1983, Jan. 24   **Litho.**   **Perf. 13**
2565 A698 20c multi   .75 .25

No. 507 and Birthplace — A699

1983, Jan. 28   **Perf. 13x12½**
2566 A699 5c multi   .30 .25

Jose Marti (b. 1853), writer, revolution leader.

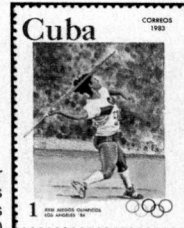

1984 Summer Olympics, Los Angeles A700

1983, Jan. 31   **Perf. 13**
2567 A700 1c Javelin   .25 .25
2568 A700 5c Volleyball   .25 .25
2569 A700 6c Basketball   .25 .25
2570 A700 20c Weight lifting   .80 .25
2571 A700 30c Wrestling   1.10 .40
2572 A700 50c Boxing   1.75 .60
   a.   Block of 6, #2567-2572   4.50 2.00
    Nos. 2567-2572 (6)   4.40 2.00

Souvenir Sheet
Perf. 13½x13

2573 A700 1p Judo   5.00 2.50

No. 2573 contains one 32x40mm stamp.

Radio Rebelde, 25th Anniv. — A701

1983, Feb. 24   **Perf. 13**
2574 A701 20c multi   .70 .25

Karl Marx, Death Cent. A702

1983, Mar. 14
2575 A702 30c multi   1.00 .40

1st Manned Balloon Flight, Bicent. — A703

Various balloons.

1983, Mar. 30
2576 A703 1c multi   .25 .25
2577 A703 3c multi   .25 .25
2578 A703 5c multi   .25 .25
2579 A703 7c multi   .35 .25
2580 A703 30c multi   2.10 .70
2581 A703 50c multi   2.10 .70
    Nos. 2576-2581 (6)   5.30 2.40

Souvenir Sheet
2582 A703 1p Jose D. Blino   4.00 2.00

No. 2582 contains one 32x40mm stamp.

Cosmonauts' Day — A704

1c, *Vostok 1.* 4c, Satellite *Frances D1.* 5c, *Mars 2.* 20c, *Soyuz.* 30c, Meteorological satellite. 50c, Intercosmos satellite.

1983, Apr. 12			Litho.	
2583	A704	1c multicolored	.25	.25
2584	A704	4c multicolored	.25	.25
2585	A704	5c multicolored	.25	.25
2586	A704	20c multicolored	.75	.25
2587	A704	30c multicolored	1.10	.50
2588	A704	50c multicolored	1.75	.70
		Nos. 2583-2588 (6)	4.35	2.20

Stamp Day A705

20c, Havana-Key West cover. 30c, Spain-Havana cover.

1983, Apr. 24				
2589	A705	20c multicolored	.75	.30
2590	A705	30c multicolored	1.25	.30
		1st Intl. airmail services.		

Souvenir Sheet

TEMBAL '83, Basel — A706

1983, May 21		Perf. 13½x13	
2591	A706	1p Weasel	5.00	2.50

Simon Bolivar, Liberator of South America A707

5c, Jose Rafael de las Heras. 20c, Bolivar.

1983, July 24		Perf. 12½x13	
2592	A707	5c multicolored	.25	.25
2593	A707	20c multicolored	.60	.25

Attack of Moncada Barracks, 30th Anniv. — A708

Designs: 5c, Jose Marti, Moncada barracks. 20c, Abel Santamaria, Jose Luis Tasende and Boris Luis Santa Coloma, martyrs, vert. 30c, *History Will Absolve Me,* declaration of Fidel Castro, vert.

1983, July 26			Perf. 13	
2594	A708	5c multi	.25	.25
2595	A708	20c multi	.70	.25
2596	A708	30c multi	.90	.50
		Nos. 2594-2596 (3)	1.85	1.00

Souvenir Sheet

Alberto Santos-Dumont (1873-1932) — A709

1983, July 29		Perf. 13x13½	
2597	A709	1p Dumont's aircraft	5.00	2.50

BRASILIANA '83, Rio; 140th anniv. of 1st stamp issued in the Americas.

9th Pan American Games, Caracas — A710

1983, Aug. 14			Perf. 13x12½	
2598	A710	1c Weight lifting	.25	.25
2599	A710	2c Volleyball	.25	.25
2600	A710	3c Baseball	.25	.25
2601	A710	20c High jump	.75	.25
2602	A710	30c Basketball	1.10	.25
2603	A710	50c Boxing	1.75	.70
		Nos. 2598-2603 (6)	4.35	2.20

Port, by Claude Joseph Vernet — A711

1983, Sept. 5			
2604	A711	30c multi	1.75	.55
		French alliance, cent.		

Pres. Salvador Allende of Chile (d. 1973) — A712

1983, Sept. 12			
2605	A712	20c multi	.70	.25

1st Congress of Farmers at Arms, 25th Anniv. — A713

1983, Sept. 21		Perf. 12½x12	
2606	A713	5c multi	.25	.25

Raphael, 500th Birth Anniv. — A714

1c, *Girl with Veil.* 2c, *The Cardinal.* 5c, *Francesco M. Della Rovere.* 20c, *Portrait of a Youth.* 30c, *Magdalena Doni.* 50c, *La Fornarina.*

1983, Sept. 30		Litho.	Perf. 13	
2607	A714	1c multi	.25	.25
2608	A714	2c multi	.25	.25
2609	A714	5c multi	.25	.25
2610	A714	20c multi	.75	.25
2611	A714	30c multi	1.10	.40
2612	A714	50c multi	1.75	.65
		Nos. 2607-2612 (6)	4.35	2.05

State Quality Seal A715

1983, Oct. 14			
2613	A715	5c multi	.40	.25

Lighthouse Type of 1980

1983, Oct. 20				
2614	A637	5c Carapachibey	.25	.25
2615	A637	20c Cadiz Bay	.80	.30
2616	A637	30c Gobernadora Point	2.00	.80
		Nos. 2614-2616 (3)	3.05	1.35

Turtles A716

Designs: 1c, Eretmochelys imbricata. 2c, Lepidochelys kempi. 5c, Chrysemys decussata. 20c, Caretta caretta. 30c, Chelonia mydas. 50c, Dermochelys coriacea.

1983, Nov. 15				
2617	A716	1c multicolored	.25	.25
2618	A716	2c multicolored	.25	.25
2619	A716	5c multicolored	.25	.25
2620	A716	20c multicolored	.80	.25
2621	A716	30c multicolored	1.40	.25
2622	A716	50c multicolored	2.75	.75
		Nos. 2617-2622 (6)	5.70	2.00

World Communications Year — A717

1c, Bell's Gallow Frame, telephone. 5c, Telegram, airmail. 10c, Satellite, satellite dish. 20c, Television, radio. 30c, 24th Communications conference.

1983, Nov. 23				
2623	A717	1c multicolored	.25	.25
2624	A717	5c multicolored	.25	.25
2625	A717	10c multicolored	.45	.25
2626	A717	20c multicolored	.75	.25
2627	A717	30c multicolored	1.10	.40
		Nos. 2623-2627 (5)	2.80	1.40

Nos. 319 and 990 A718

1983, Dec. 3		Perf. 13x12½	
2628	A718	20c multi	.70	.25
		See note after No. 320.		

Flowers, Birds — A719

Designs: No. 2629, Opuntia dillenii. No. 2630, Euphorbia podocarpifolia. No. 2631, Dinema cubincola. No. 2632, Guaiacum officinale. No. 2633, Magnolia cubensis. No. 2634, Jatropha angustifolia. No. 2635, Cochlospermum vitifolium. No. 2636, Tabebuia lepidota. No. 2637, Kalmiella ericoides. No. 2638, Jatropha integerrima. No. 2639, Melocactus actinacanthus. No. 2640, Cordia sebestana. No. 2641, Tabernae - montana apoda. No. 2642, Lantana camara. No. 2643, Cordia gerascanthus. No. 2644, Tiaris canora. No. 2645, Phaethon lepturus. No. 2646, Myadestes elisabeth. No. 2647, Saurothera merlini. No. 2648, Polioptila lembeyei. No. 2649, Mellisuga helenae. No. 2650, Mimus polyglottos. No. 2651, Todus multicolor. No. 2652, Amazona leucocephala. No. 2653, Ferminia cerverai. No. 2654, Pelecanus occidentalis. No. 2655, Melanerpes superciliaris. No. 2656, Mimocichla plumbea. No. 2657, Aratinga euops. No. 2658, Sturnella magna.

No. 2658B, Hedychium coronarium. No. 2658C, Priotelus temnurus.

1983, Dec. 20			Perf. 13	
2629	A719	5c multicolored	.55	.25
2630	A719	5c multicolored	.55	.25
2631	A719	5c multicolored	.55	.25
2632	A719	5c multicolored	.55	.25
2633	A719	5c multicolored	.55	.25
a.		Strip of 5, Nos. 2629-2633	4.00	2.00
2634	A719	5c multicolored	.55	.25
2635	A719	5c multicolored	.55	.25
2636	A719	5c multicolored	.55	.25
2637	A719	5c multicolored	.55	.25
2638	A719	5c multicolored	.55	.25
2639	A719	5c multicolored	.55	.25
2640	A719	5c multicolored	.55	.25
2641	A719	5c multicolored	.55	.25
2642	A719	5c multicolored	.55	.25
2643	A719	5c multicolored	.55	.25
a.		Block of 10, Nos. 2634-2643	6.50	4.00
2644	A719	5c multicolored	.55	.25
2645	A719	5c multicolored	.55	.25
2646	A719	5c multicolored	.55	.25
2647	A719	5c multicolored	.55	.25

2648	A719	5c multicolored	.55	.25
a.		Strip of 5, Nos. 2644-2648	4.00	2.00
2649	A719	5c multicolored	.55	.25
2650	A719	5c multicolored	.55	.25
2651	A719	5c multicolored	.55	.25
2652	A719	5c multicolored	.55	.25
2653	A719	5c multicolored	.55	.25
2654	A719	5c multicolored	.55	.25
2655	A719	5c multicolored	.55	.25
2656	A719	5c multicolored	.55	.25
2657	A719	5c multicolored	.55	.25
2658	A719	5c multicolored	.55	.25
a.		Block of 10, Nos. 2649-2658	6.50	4.00
		Nos. 2629-2658 (30)	16.50	7.50

Souvenir Sheets

2658B	A719	100c multicolored	5.00	4.50
2658C	A719	100c multicolored	5.00	4.50

Flowers — A720

1983, Dec. 30   **Perf. 12½**

2659	A720	60c Tobacco	1.75	.55
2660	A720	70c Lily	2.25	.60
2661	A720	80c Mariposa	2.50	.70
2662	A720	90c Orchid	3.50	1.00
		Nos. 2659-2662 (4)	10.00	2.85

25th Anniv. of the Revolution — A721

20c, Flags, Santa Clara Railway tracks.

1983, Dec. 31   **Litho.**   **Perf. 13**

2663	A721	5c shown	.25	.25
2664	A721	20c multicolored	3.50	1.00

25th Anniv. of the Revolution — A722

No. 2665, Guevara, Castro. No. 2666, Star. No. 2667, PCC emblem, workers.

1984, Jan. 8

2665	A722	20c multi	.70	.25
2666	A722	20c multi	.70	.25
2667	A722	20c multi	1.75	.80
a.		Strip of 3, #2665-2667	3.25	1.50
		Nos. 2665-2667 (3)	3.15	1.30

Lenin, 60th Death Anniv. A723

30p, Spasski Tower, Russia Nos. 295, 265.

1984, Jan. 21   **Perf. 12½x12**

2668	A723	30p multi	1.25	.25

Cuban Labor Union, 45th Anniv. A724

1984, Jan. 28   **Perf. 13**

2669	A724	5c multi	.25	.25

Butterflies — A725

Designs: 1c, Ixias balice. 2c, Phoebis avellaneda. 3c, Anthocaris sara. 5c, Victorina. 20c, Heliconius cydno cydnides. 30c, Parides gundlachianus calzadillae. 50c, Catagramma sorana.

1984, Jan. 31   **Perf. 13x12½**

2670	A725	1c multicolored	.25	.25
2671	A725	2c multicolored	.25	.25
2672	A725	3c multicolored	.25	.25
2673	A725	5c multicolored	.25	.25
2674	A725	20c multicolored	.80	.25
2675	A725	30c multicolored	1.40	.65
2676	A725	50c multicolored	2.40	.95
		Nos. 2670-2676 (7)	5.60	2.85

Marine Mammals — A726

Designs: 1c, Grampus griseus, vert. 2c, Delphinus delphis, vert. 5c, Physeter catodon. 6c, Stenella plagiodon, vert. 10c, Pseudorca crassidens. 30c, Tursiops truncatus, vert. 50, Megaptera novaeangliae.

1984, Feb. 15   **Perf. 12x12½, 12½x12**

2677	A726	1c multicolored	.25	.25
2678	A726	2c multicolored	.25	.25
2679	A726	5c multicolored	.25	.25
2680	A726	6c multicolored	.25	.25
2681	A726	10c multicolored	.70	.25
2682	A726	30c multicolored	1.60	.40
2683	A726	50c multicolored	2.75	.70
		Nos. 2677-2683 (7)	6.05	2.35

Augusto C. Sandino (1893-1934), Nicaraguan Revolutionary — A727

1984, Feb. 21   **Perf. 13**

2684	A727	20c multicolored	.70	.25

Red Cross in Cuba, 75th Anniv. — A728

1984, Mar. 10

2685	A728	30c Flag, No. 404	1.25	.35

Cuban Film Industry, 25th Anniv. A729

1984, Mar. 24

2686	A729	20c multi	.80	.30

Caribbean Flowers — A730

Designs: 1c, Brownea grandiceps. 2c, Couroupita guianensis. 5c, Triplaris surinamensis. 20c, Amherstia nobilis. 30c, Plumieria alba. 50c, Delonix regia.

1984, Mar. 29

2687	A730	1c multicolored	.25	.25
2688	A730	2c multicolored	.25	.25
2689	A730	5c multicolored	.25	.25
2690	A730	20c multicolored	.80	.30
2691	A730	30c multicolored	1.10	.50
2692	A730	50c multicolored	2.00	.90
		Nos. 2687-2692 (6)	4.65	2.45

Cosmonauts' Day — A731

2c, *Electron 1*, 1964. 3c, *Electron 2*, 1964. 5c, *Intercosmos 1*, 1969. 10c, *Mars 5*, 1974. 30c, *Soyuz*, 1969. 50c, USSR-Bulgaria space flight, 1979.
1p, *Luna 1*, 1959.

1984, Apr. 12

2693	A731	2c multi	.25	.25
2694	A731	3c multi	.25	.25
2695	A731	5c multi	.25	.25
2696	A731	10c multi	.40	.25
2697	A731	30c multi	1.10	.50
2698	A731	50c multi	2.00	.90
		Nos. 2693-2698 (6)	4.25	2.40

Souvenir Sheet
Perf. 12½

2699	A731	1p multi	4.00	2.00

No. 2699 contains one 32x40mm stamp.

Mothers' Day — A732

1984, Apr. 19   **Perf. 13**

2700	A732	20c Red roses	.80	.30
2701	A732	20c Pink roses	.80	.30

Stamp Day — A733

Designs: Mural, by R. Rodriguez Radillo (details): 20c, Mexican runner. 30c, Egyptian boatman.

1984, Apr. 24   **Perf. 13x12½**

2702	A733	20c multicolored	.80	.30
2703	A733	30c multicolored	1.10	.50

See Nos. 2787-2788, 2860-2861, 3025-3026, 3122-3123, 3213-3214.

Souvenir Sheet

ESPANA '84, Madrid — A734

1984, Apr. 27   **Perf. 13x13½**

2704	A734	1p Clipper ship	4.75	2.25

Women's Basketball, 1984 Summer Olympics A735

1984, May 5   **Perf. 13**

2705	A735	20c multi	1.25	.35

Agrarian Reform Act, 25th Anniv. — A736

1984, May 17   **Perf. 13½x13**

2706	A736	5c multi	.40	.25

Banco Popular de Ahorro, 1st Anniv. — A737

1984, May 18   **Perf. 13**

2707	A737	5c multi	.40	.25

Early Locomotives — A738

1984, June 11   **Perf. 12½x12**

2708	A738	1c multi	.25	.25
2709	A738	4c multi, diff.	.25	.25
2710	A738	5c multi, diff.	.25	.25
2711	A738	10c multi, diff.	.40	.25
2712	A738	30c multi, diff.	1.25	.40
2713	A738	50c multi, diff.	2.10	.80
		Nos. 2708-2713 (6)	4.50	2.20

Souvenir Sheet

19th UPU Congress, HAMBURG '84 — A739

1984, June 19   *Perf. 13x13½*
2714   A739   1p Nos. 73, 232   4.50   2.25

Intl. Olympic Committee, 90th Anniv. — A740

30c, Coubertin, torch-bearer.

1984, June 23   *Perf. 13*
2715   A740   30c multi   1.40   .50

Children's Day
A741

1984, July 15   *Perf. 12½x13*
2716   A741   5c multi   .25   .25

1984 Summer Olympics, Los Angeles
A742

1984, July 28   *Perf. 13*
2717   A742   1c Wrestling   .25   .25
2718   A742   3c Discus   .25   .25
2719   A742   5c Volleyball   .25   .25
2720   A742   20c Boxing   .80   .30
2721   A742   30c Basketball   1.10   .50
2722   A742   50c Weight lifting   2.00   .90
    Nos. 2717-2722 (6)   4.65   2.45

Souvenir Sheet
Perf. 12½
2723   A742   1p Baseball   4.50   2.25
No. 2723 contains one 32x40mm stamp.

Emilio Roig de Leuchsenring (1889-1964), Historian
A743

1984, Aug. 8   *Perf. 13*
2724   A743   5c multi   .25   .25

Friendship Games, Aug. 18-26, Havana — A744

3c, Volleyball. 5c, Women's volleyball. 8c, Water polo. 30c, Boxing.

1984, Aug. 18
2725   A744   3c multicolored   .25   .25
2726   A744   5c multicolored   .35   .25
2727   A744   20c multicolored   .35   .25
2728   A744   30c multicolored   1.25   .35
    Nos. 2725-2728 (4)   2.20   1.10

Cattle Breeding
A745

1984, Sept. 20
2729   A745   2c Artificial pastures   .25   .25
2730   A745   3c Cuban carib   .25   .25
2731   A745   5c Charolaise, vert.   .25   .25
2732   A745   30c Cuban cebu, vert.   1.25   .40
2733   A745   50c White-udder   2.25   .75
    Nos. 2729-2733 (5)   4.25   1.90

Souvenir Sheet

AUSIPEX '84, Sept. 21-30, Melbourne — A746

1984, Sept. 21   *Perf. 12½*
2734   A746   1p Emu   5.00   2.75

Fauna — A747

Designs: 1c, Polymita. 2c, Solenodon cubanus. 3c, Alsophis cantherigerus. 4c, Osteopilus septentrionalis. 5c, Mellisuga helenae. 10c, Capromys melanurus. 30c, Todus multicolor. 50c, Parrots (cotorra).

1984, Oct. 10   *Perf. 13*
2735   A747   1c multicolored   .25   .25
2736   A747   2c multicolored   .25   .25
2737   A747   3c multicolored   .25   .25
2738   A747   4c multicolored   .25   .25
2739   A747   5c multicolored   .55   .25
2740   A747   10c multicolored   .30   .25
2741   A747   30c multicolored   2.40   .95
2742   A747   50c multicolored   3.75   1.25
    Nos. 2735-2742 (8)   8.00   3.70

ESPAMER '85, Havana — A748

Columbus Day: a, Ferdinand, Isabella. b, Departure from Palos. c, *Nina, Pinta, Santa Maria.* d, Landing in America.

1984, Oct. 12
2743   Sheet of 4 + 2 labels   5.00   2.50
  a.   A748   5c multicolored   .25   .25
  b.   A748   20c multicolored   1.50   .70
  c.   A748   30c multicolored   2.25   1.10
  d.   A748   50c multicolored   1.00   .50

Souvenir Sheet

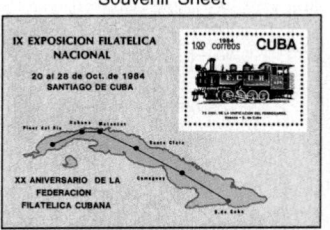

9th Natl. Phil. Exhibition, Oct. 20-28, Santiago de Cuba — A749

1984, Oct. 20   *Perf. 12½*
2744   A749   1p multicolored   4.50   2.25

Natl. Revolutionary Militia, 25th Anniv. — A750

1984, Oct. 26   *Perf. 12½x13*
2745   A750   5c multi   .30   .25

Disappearance of Camilo Cienfuegos, 25th Anniv. — A751

1984, Oct. 28   *Perf. 13x12½*
2746   A751   5c multi   .40   .25

UN Child Survival Campaign
A752

1984, Nov. 11   *Perf. 13*
2747   A752   5c Breast-feeding   .40   .25

Classic Automobiles — A753

1c, 1909 Morgan. 2c, 1922 Austin. 5c, 1903 De Dion-Bouton. 20c, 1908 Ford Model T. 30c, 1885 Benz. 50c, 1910 Benz.

1984, Nov. 25
2748   A753   1c multi   .25   .25
2749   A753   2c multi   .25   .25
2750   A753   5c multi   .25   .25
2751   A753   20c multi   .95   .25
2752   A753   30c multi   1.50   .35
2753   A753   50c multi   2.75   .70
    Nos. 2748-2753 (6)   5.95   2.05

Postal Museum, 20th Anniv. — A754

1985, Jan. 2   *Perf. 13x12½*
2754   A754   20c multi   .75   .25

Portrait of Celia Sanchez, by E. Escobedo
A755

1985, Jan. 11   *Perf. 13*
2755   A755   5c multi   .40   .25
Celia Sanchez (1920-1980), party leader.

PORTO '85, Intl. Pigeon Exhibition — A756

1985, Jan. 23
2756   A756   20c multi   1.25   .25

1986 World Cup Soccer Championships, Mexico — A757

Athletes and Flags of previous host nations: 1c, Chile, 1962. 2c, Great Britain, 1966. 3c, Mexico, 1970. 4c, Federal Republic of Germany, 1974. 5c, Argentina, 1978. 30c, Spain, 1982. 50c, Sweden, 1958. 1p, Mexico, 1986.

1985, Jan. 25
2757   A757   1c multi   .25   .25
2758   A757   2c multi   .25   .25
2759   A757   3c multi   .25   .25
2760   A757   4c multi   .25   .25
2761   A757   5c multi   .25   .25

2762	A757 30c multi	1.40	.50
2763	A757 50c multi	2.25	.65

Nos. 2757-2763 (7) 4.90 2.40

Souvenir Sheet
Perf. 12½

2764	A757 1p multi	4.00	2.00

No. 2764 contains one 40x32mm stamp.

Baconao Natl. Park — A758

Dinosaurs.

1985, Feb. 14 Perf. 13x12½

2765	A758 1c Pteranodon	.30	.25
2766	A758 2c Brontosaurus	.30	.25
2767	A758 4c Iguanodontus	.30	.25
2768	A758 5c Estegosaurus	.30	.25
2769	A758 8c Monoclonius	.50	.25
2770	A758 30c Corythosaurus	1.50	.50
2771	A758 50c Tyrannosaurus	2.75	.75

Nos. 2765-2771 (7) 5.95 2.45

13th Congress of the Postal Unions of
the Americas, Havana — A759

Design: Uruguay #196, congress emblem
and Argentina #287.

1985, Mar. 11 Perf. 12½x12

2772	A759 20c multi	2.50	.70

ESPAMER
'85 — A760

Indian activities: 1c, Playing ball. 2c,
Medicine man preparing calumet and other ritual items. 5c, Net and spear fishing. 20c, Potter. 30c, Hunting. 50c, Hollowing-out canoe,
decorating paddle. 1p, Cooking.

1985, Mar. 19 Perf. 12½x13

2773	A760 1c multi	.25	.25
2774	A760 2c multi	.25	.25
2775	A760 5c multi	.40	.25
2776	A760 20c multi	.40	.25
2777	A760 30c multi	.65	.40
2778	A760 50c multi	2.75	.80

Nos. 2773-2778 (6) 4.70 2.20

Souvenir Sheet
Perf. 12½

2779	A760 1p multi	5.00	2.50

No. 2779 contains one 32x40mm stamp.
An imperf. souvenir sheet exists containing
Nos. 2773-2779.

Cosmonauts' Day — A761

Designs: 2c, Spacecraft orbiting Moon. 3c,
Two spacecraft. 10c, Space walkers linked.
13c, Space walkers welding. 20c, Vostok 2.
50c, Lunokhod 1 moon vehicle.

1985, Apr. 12 Perf. 13x12½

2780	A761 2c multi	.25	.25
2781	A761 3c multi	.25	.25
2782	A761 10c multi	.45	.25
2783	A761 13c multi	.65	.25
2784	A761 20c multi	.75	.25
2785	A761 50c multi	2.50	.70

Nos. 2780-2785 (6) 4.85 1.95

12th Youth and
Students
Festival,
Moscow
A762

1985, Apr. 19 Perf. 13

2786	A762 30c Lenin Mausoleum	.65	.50

Stamp Day Type of 1984

Mural, by R. Rodriguez Radillo (1967),
details: 20c, Roman charioteer (courier of Cur-
sus Publicus). 35c, Medieval nobleman,
monks (monastic messenger mail).

1985, Apr. 24 Perf. 13x12½

2787	A733 20c multi	.80	.25
2788	A733 35c multi	1.10	.40

Mothers'
Day — A763

1985, May 2 Perf. 13

2789	A763 1c Peonies	.25	.25
2790	A763 4c Carnations	.25	.25
2791	A763 5c Dahlias	.25	.25
2792	A763 13c Roses	.45	.25
2793	A763 20c Roses, diff.	.75	.25
2794	A763 50c Tulips	2.00	.55

Nos. 2789-2794 (6) 3.95 1.80

50th Death Anniv. of Antonio Guiteras
and Carlos Aponte,
Revolutionaries — A764

1985, May 9 Perf. 12½x12

2795	A764 5c multi	.25	.25

End of
WWII,
40th
Anniv.
A765

20c, Soviet memorial, Berlin-Treptow. 30c,
Dove.

1985, May 10

2796	A765 5c shown	.25	.25
2797	A765 20c multicolored	.65	.30
2798	A765 30c multicolored	1.10	.55

Nos. 2796-2798 (3) 2.00 1.10

Souvenir Sheet

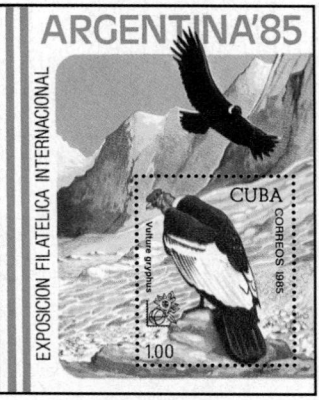

ARGENTINA '85, Buenos
Aires — A766

1985, June 5 Perf. 13½x13

2799	A766 1p Vulture gryphus	4.50	2.25

Motorcycle, Cent. — A767

2c, 1885 Daimler. 5c, 1910 Kaiser Tricycle.
10c, 1925 Fanomobile. 30c, 1926 Mars A20.
50c, 1936 Simson BSW.

1985, June 28 Perf. 13

2800	A767 2c multi	.25	.25
2801	A767 5c multi	.25	.25
2802	A767 10c multi	.55	.25
2803	A767 30c multi	1.50	.30
2804	A767 50c multi	2.75	.70

Nos. 2800-2804 (5) 5.30 1.75

Development of Health Care Since the
Revolution — A768

1985, July 18 Perf. 12½x12

2805	A768 5c Hospitals	.25	.25

Federation of Cuban Women (FMC),
25th Anniv. — A769

1985, Aug. 23

2806	A769 5c multi	.25	.25

No. 2806 printed se-tenant with label picturing federation emblem.

Universiade
Games,
Japan — A770

1985, Aug. 27 Perf. 13

2807	A770 50c multi	1.75	.55

1st Havana Declaration, 25th
Anniv. — A771

5c, Jose Marti statue, revolutionaries.

1985, Sept. 2

2808	A771 5c multicolored	.40	.25

Souvenir Sheet

ITALIA '85 — A772

1985, Sept. 25 Perf. 12½

2809	A772 1p Roman galley	5.00	2.50

Revolutionary Defense Committees
(CDR), 25th Anniv. — A773

1985, Sept. 28 Perf. 13

2810	A773 5c multicolored	.25	.25

Aquarium Fish — A774

Designs: 1c, Centropyge argi. 3c, Holacanthus tricolor. 5c, Chaetodon capistratus.
10c, Chaetodon sedentarius. 20c, Chaetodon
ocellatus. 50c, Holacanthus ciliaris.

1985, Sept. 30 Litho.

2811	A774 1c multicolored	.25	.25
2812	A774 3c multicolored	.25	.25
2813	A774 5c multicolored	.25	.25
2814	A774 10c multicolored	.40	.25
2815	A774 20c multicolored	.95	.50
2816	A774 50c multicolored	2.40	1.60

Nos. 2811-2816 (6) 4.50 3.10

Communist Party
Central
Committee, 20th
Anniv. — A775

1985, Oct. 1

2817	A775 5c multicolored	.40	.25

Souvenir Sheet

EXFILNA '85 — A776

1p, Spain No. C45, Cuba No. 387.

1985, Oct. 18
2818 A776 1p multicolored   5.00 2.50

UN, 40th Anniv. — A777

1985, Oct. 24
2819 A777 20c multicolored   .90 .25

Sites on the UNESCO World Heritage List — A778

Designs: 2c, Plaza Vieja, 16th cent. 5c, Royal Army Castle, c. 1558. 20c, Havana Cathedral, c. 1748. 30c, Captains-General Palace (Havana City Museum), 1776. 50c, The Temple, 1827.

1985, Nov. 25
2820	A778	2c multi	.25	.25
2821	A778	5c multi	.25	.25
2822	A778	20c multi	.95	.25
2823	A778	30c multi	1.50	.45
2824	A778	50c multi	2.40	.60
		Nos. 2820-2824 (5)	5.35	1.80

1986 World Cup Soccer Championships, Mexico — A779

Various athletes.

1986, Jan. 20
2825	A779	1c multi	.25	.25
2826	A779	4c multi	.25	.25
2827	A779	5c multi	.25	.25
2828	A779	10c multi	.30	.25
2829	A779	30c multi	1.10	.30
2830	A779	50c multi	1.60	.55
		Nos. 2825-2830 (6)	3.75	1.85

Souvenir Sheet
Perf. 13½x13
2831 A779 1p multi   4.50 2.25
No. 2831 contains one 32x40mm stamp.

3rd Communist Party Congress, Havana — A780

20c, Party and natl. flags, emblem.

1986, Feb. 4   *Perf. 13*
2832 A780 5c shown   .25 .25
2833 A780 20c multicolored   1.25 .25

Natl. Sports Institute (INDER), 25th Anniv. A781

1986, Feb. 23
2834 A781 5c multicolored   .30 .25

A782

1986, Feb. 23
2835 A782 5c multicolored   .30 .25
Ministry of Domestic Trade, 25th anniv.

A783

Exotic flowers in the Botanical Gardens: 1c, Tecomaria capensis. 3c, Michelia champaca. 5c, Thunbergia grandiflora. 8c, Dendrobium phalaenopsis. 30c, Allamanda violacea. 50c, Rhodactus bleo.

1986, Feb. 25   *Perf. 12½x12*
2836	A783	1c multicolored	.25	.25
2837	A783	3c multicolored	.25	.25
2838	A783	5c multicolored	.25	.25
2839	A783	8c multicolored	.30	.25
2840	A783	30c multicolored	1.25	.25
2841	A783	50c multicolored	1.90	.40
		Nos. 2836-2841 (6)	4.20	1.65

Gundlach and Birds — A784

Designs: 1c, Agelaius assimilis. 3c, Dendroica pityophila. 7c, Myiarchus sagrae. 9c, Dendroica petechia gundlachi. 30c, Geotrygon caniceps. 50c, Colaptes auratus chrysocaulosus.

1986, Mar. 14   Litho.   Perf. 13½x13
2842	A784	1c multicolored	.30	.25
2843	A784	3c multicolored	.30	.25
2844	A784	7c multicolored	.55	.40
2845	A784	9c multicolored	.70	.50
2846	A784	30c multicolored	3.00	2.00
2847	A784	50c multicolored	4.75	3.25
		Nos. 2842-2847 (6)	9.60	6.65

Juan Cristobal Gundlach (d. 1896), ornithologist.

Pioneers Youth Organization, 25th Anniv. — A785

1986, Apr. 3   *Perf. 13*
2848 A785 5c Induction   .30 .25

150th Birth Anniv. of Maximo Gomez — A786

1986, Apr. 4
2849 A786 20c multicolored   .90 .25

A787

1986, Apr. 10   *Perf. 12½*
2850 A787 5c multicolored   .40 .25
Kindergartens, 25th anniv.

A788

1st Man in Space, 25th Anniv.: 1c, *Vostok* and rocket designer Sergei Korolev. 2c, Yuri Gagarin, *Vostok 1.* 5c, Valentina Tereshkova, *Vostok 6.* 20c, *Salyut-Soyuz* space link. 30c, Capsule landing. 50c, *Soyuz* rocket launch. 1p, Konstantin Tsiolkovski (1857-1935), rocket scientist.

1986, Apr. 12   *Perf. 13x13½*
2851	A788	1c multi	.25	.25
2852	A788	2c multi	.25	.25
2853	A788	5c multi	.25	.25
2854	A788	20c multi	.60	.25
2855	A788	30c multi	.80	.25
2856	A788	50c multi	1.75	.55
		Nos. 2851-2856 (6)	3.90	1.80

Souvenir Sheet
Perf. 12½
2857 A788 1p multi   4.50 2.25
No. 2857 contains one 32x40mm stamp.

Natl. Flag and No. 2407 A789

20c, Banners, natl. crest.

1986, Apr. 19   *Perf. 13*
2858 A789 5c shown   .25 .25
2859 A789 20c multicolored   1.10 .25
Bay of Pigs invasion, 25th anniv. (5c); Proclamation of Socialist Revolution, 25th anniv. (20c).

Stamp Day Type of 1984

Mural, by R. Rodriguez Radillo (1967), details: 20c, Mail coach, 18th-19th cent. 30c, Pony Express.

1986, Apr. 24   *Perf. 13x12½*
2860 A733 20c multi   .75 .25
2861 A733 30c multi   1.00 .25

Radio Havana, 25th Anniv. — A790

1986, May 1
2862 A790 5c multicolored   .40 .25

EXPO '86, Vancouver — A791

Locomotives: 1c, *Stourbridge Lion*, 1829, US. 4c, Stephenson's *Rocket*, 1829, GB. 5c, 1st Russian locomotive, 1845. 8c, Seguin's locomotive, 1830, France. 30c, 1st Canadian locomotive, 1836. 50c, Urban locomotive, Belgian Grand Central Rlwy., 1872. 1p, US locomotive pulling Cuban sugar train, 1837.

1986, May 2   Litho.   Perf. 12½x12
2863	A791	1c multi	.25	.25
2864	A791	4c multi	.25	.25
2865	A791	5c multi	.25	.25
2866	A791	8c multi	.25	.25
2867	A791	30c multi	.80	.30
2868	A791	50c multi	2.10	.55
		Nos. 2863-2868 (6)	3.90	1.85

Souvenir Sheet
Perf. 13x13½
2869 A791 1p multi   5.00 2.50
No. 2869 contains one 40x32mm stamp.

Assoc. of Small Farmers, (ANAP), 25th Anniv. — A792

1986, May 17   *Perf. 13*
2870 A792 5c multicolored   .40 .25

Intl. Peace Year A793

1986, June 2
2871 A793 30c multicolored   1.00 .25

Ministry of the Interior (MININT), 25th Anniv. — A794

1986, June 6
2872 A794 5c multicolored .40 .25

Martin Luther King, Jr. A795

1986, June 27 *Perf. 13½x13*
2873 A795 20c multicolored 1.00 .25

Bonifacio Byrne (d. 1936), Poet A796

1986, July 5 *Perf. 13*
2874 A796 5c multicolored .30 .25

Cuban Union of Writers and Artists (UNEAC), 25th Anniv. — A797

1986, July 10 *Perf. 13x12½*
2875 A797 5c multi .30 .25

Sandinista Movement in Nicaragua (FSLN), 25th Anniv. — A798

Augusto Cesar Sandino and Carlos Fonseca.

1986, July 23 *Perf. 13x12*
2876 A798 20c multi .75 .25

Ministry of Transportation, 25th Anniv. — A799

1986, Aug. 1 *Perf. 13*
2877 A799 5c multicolored .50 .25

7th University Games of Central America and the Caribbean A800

1986, Aug. 9
2878 A800 20c multicolored 1.00 .25

Souvenir Sheet

STOCKHOLMIA '86 — A801

Designs: a, 2c Mambi Revolutionary stamp of 1897. b, Sweden Type A7, cancellation.

1986, Aug. 28 *Perf. 12½*
2879 A801 Sheet of 2 4.50 2.25
 a.-b. 50c multi

Nonaligned Countries Movement, 25th Anniv. — A802

1986, Sept. 1 *Perf. 13½x13*
2880 A802 50c multi 2.00 .45

Orchids — A803

Designs: 1c, Cattleya hardyana. 4c, Brasso-laelio cattleya. 5c, Phalaenopsis marget moses. 10c, Laelio cattleya prism palette. 30c, Phalaenopsis violacea. 50c, Disa uniflora.

1986, Sept. 15 *Perf. 12½*
2881 A803 1c multicolored .25 .25
2882 A803 4c multicolored .25 .25
2883 A803 5c multicolored .25 .25
2884 A803 10c multicolored .30 .25
2885 A803 30c multicolored 1.25 .30
2886 A803 50c multicolored 1.90 .50
 Nos. 2881-2886 (6) 4.20 1.80

Latin American History — A804

Pre-Columbian artifacts: No. 2887, Mayan dwelling and votive jade sculpture. No. 2888, Inca vase and Tiahuanaco sun gate (Bolivia). No. 2889, Spain No. C47, discovery of America 500th anniv. emblem, scroll. No. 2890, Diaguitan duck-shaped pitcher and Pucara de Quitor ruins (Chile). No. 2891, San Agustin Archaeological Park megaliths and Quimbayan sculpture (Colombia). No. 2892, Moler grinding stone and Chorotega ceramic figurine. No. 2893, Tabaco idol and Indian

dwelling (Cuba). No. 2894, Spain No. C38. No. 2895, Taino dwelling and chair (Dominica). No. 2896, Tolita statue and Ingapirca Castle ruins. No. 2897, Maya vase and Tikal Temple (Guatemala). No. 2898, Copan ruins and Maya idol. No. 2899, Spain No. C37. No. 2900, Chichen Itza Temple and Zapotecan urn (Mexico). No. 2901, Punta de Zapote megaliths and Ometepe ceramic figurine. No. 2902, Tonosi lidded ceramic bowl and Barriles monoliths. No. 2903, Ruins at Machu-Picchu and Inca statue (Peru). No. 2904, Spain No. C49. No. 2905, Teepees and triangular sculpture (Puerto Rico). No. 2906, Fertility statue from Santa Ana and Santo Domingo Cave.

1986, Oct. 12 *Perf. 13*
2887 A804 1c multi .25 .25
2888 A804 1c multi .25 .25
2889 A804 1c multi .25 .25
2890 A804 1c multi .25 .25
2891 A804 1c multi .25 .25
 a. Strip of 5, Nos. 2887-2891 1.00 1.00
2892 A804 5c multi .25 .25
2893 A804 5c multi .25 .25
2894 A804 5c multi .25 .25
2895 A804 5c multi .25 .25
2896 A804 5c multi .25 .25
 a. Strip of 5, Nos. 2892-2896 1.00 1.00
2897 A804 10c multi .30 .25
2898 A804 10c multi .30 .25
2899 A804 10c multi .30 .25
2900 A804 10c multi .30 .25
2901 A804 10c multi .30 .25
 a. Strip of 5, Nos. 2897-2901 1.50 1.00
2902 A804 20c multi .70 .30
2903 A804 20c multi .70 .30
2904 A804 20c multi .70 .30
2905 A804 20c multi .70 .30
2906 A804 20c multi .70 .30
 a. Strip of 5, Nos. 2902-2906 3.50 1.50
 Nos. 2887-2906 (20) 7.50 5.25

Discovery of America, 500th anniv. (in 1992). See Nos. 2966-2985, 3065-3084, 3253-3272, 3463-3466.

Intl. Brigades, Spain, 50th Anniv. — A805

1986, Oct. 14 *Perf. 12½x12*
2907 A805 30c multicolored .75 .35

Paintings in the Natl. Museum A806

Designs: 2c, *Two Children*, by Gutierrez de la Vega, vert. 4c, *Sed*, by Jean-Georges Vibert. 6c, *Virgin and Child*, by Niccolo Abbate, vert. 10c, *Bullfight*, by Eugenio de Lucas Velazquez. 30c, *The Five Senses*, anonymous. 50c, *Arrival at Thomops Castle*, by Jean Louis Ernest.

1986, Nov. 5 *Perf. 13*
2908 A806 2c multi .25 .25
2909 A806 4c multi .25 .25
2910 A806 6c multi .25 .25
2911 A806 10c multi .40 .25
2912 A806 30c multi 1.10 .30
2913 A806 50c multi 1.90 .55
 Nos. 2908-2913 (6) 4.15 1.85

Anniversaries — A807

1986, Dec. 2 *Litho.* *Perf. 12½*
2914 A807 5c *Granma* .45 .25

Size: 26x38mm
2915 A807 20c Soldier, rifle, flag 1.50 .25

Granma Landings, 30th anniv. (5c); Revolutionary Armed Forces, 30th anniv. (20c).

Scholarship Program, 25th Anniv. — A808

1986, Dec. 22 *Perf. 13*
2916 A808 5c Guevara, students .30 .25

Natl. Literacy Campaign, 25th Anniv. — A809

5c, Marti, man learning to write.

1986, Dec. 25 *Perf. 13x12½*
2917 A809 5c multicolored .30 .25

Siege of La Plata, 30th Anniv. A810

5c, Map, revolutionaries.

1987, Jan. 17 *Perf. 12½x12*
2918 A810 5c multicolored .30 .25

Paintings in the Natl. Museum A811

3c, *Gypsy*, by Joaquin Sorolla. 5c, *Sir Walter Scott*, by Sir John W. Gordon. 10c, *Farm Meadows*, by Alfred de Breanski. 20c, *Still-life*, by Isaac van Duynen. 30c, *Landscape with Figures*, by Francesco Zuccarelli. 40c, *The Failure* (defeated bullfighter), by Ignacio Zuloaga.

1987, Feb. 5 *Perf. 13*
2919 A811 3c multi, vert. .25 .25
2920 A811 5c multi, vert. .25 .25
2921 A811 10c multi .40 .25
2922 A811 20c multi 1.00 .25
2923 A811 30c multi 1.10 .30
2924 A811 40c multi, vert. 1.60 .50
 Nos. 2919-2924 (6) 4.60 1.80

Siege of the Presidential Palace, 30th Anniv. — A812

5c, Palace, van, Echeverra.

1987, Mar. 13 *Perf. 12½x12*
2925 A812 5c multicolored .30 .25

Lazarus Ludwig Zamenhof and Russia Type A77 — A813

1987, Mar. 16   *Perf. 13½x13*
2926 A813 30c multicolored   1.00 .30

Esperanto, cent.

Souvenir Sheet

EXFILNA '87, 10th Natl. Stamp Exposition, Holguin — A814

1987, Mar. 28   *Perf. 13x13½*
2927 A814 1p Nos. 552, C129   4.50 2.25

25th Anniv. and 5th Cong. of the Youth Communist League (U.J.C.) — A815

1987, Apr. 4   *Perf. 13*
2928 A815 5c multicolored   .30 .25

Intercosmos, 20th Anniv. — A816

3c, Intercosmos 1. 5c, Intercosmos 2. 10c, TD. 20c, Cosmos 93. 30c, Prognoz. 50c, Vostok 3.

1p, Rocket, Vostok 3.

1987, Apr. 12   **Litho.**   *Perf. 12½x12*
2929 A816 3c multicolored   .25 .25
2930 A816 5c multicolored   .25 .25
2931 A816 10c multicolored   .30 .25
2932 A816 20c multicolored   .75 .25
2933 A816 30c multicolored   1.00 .30
2934 A816 50c multicolored   1.60 .55
   Nos. 2929-2934 (6)   4.15 1.85

Souvenir Sheet
Perf. 13½x13
2935 A816 1p multi   4.50 2.25

No. 2935 contains one 32x40mm stamp.

Stamp Day A817

Stamped covers and canceled stamps: 30c, Havana, 1890. 50c, Santiago de Cuba, 1869.

1987, Apr. 24   *Perf. 13*
2936 A817 30c multi   1.25 .30
2937 A817 50c multi   2.10 .60

Mothers' Day — A818

Various dahlias and roses.

1987, May 2
2938 A818 3c multi   .25 .25
2939 A818 5c multi   .25 .25
2940 A818 10c multi   .25 .25
2941 A818 13c multi   .30 .25
2942 A818 30c multi   .70 .25
2943 A818 50c multi   1.25 .50
   Nos. 2938-2943 (6)   3.00 1.75

Bone-lengthening Procedure (Femur in Frame) — A819

1987, May 4
2944 A819 5c multi   .30 .25

ORTOPEDIA '87, medical congress for orthopedists from Spanish and Portuguese-speaking countries, Havana.

Cuban Broadcasting and Television Institute, 25th Anniv. — A820

1987, May 24   *Perf. 13*
2945 A820 5c multi   .30 .25

Battle of Uvero, 30th Anniv. A821

Views of monument, Sierra Maestra Mts.

1987, May 28   *Perf. 13½x13*
2946 A821 5c multicolored   .30 .25

CAPEX '87 — A822

Natl. flags, stamps and 19th cent. mail carriers pictured on cigarette cards: 3c, Messenger, llamas and Bolivia Type A9. 5c, Early p.o., automobile and France Type A17. 10c, Messengers riding elephants and Thailand Type A2. 20c, Messenger riding camel and stamp of Egypt, 1879. 30c, Mail troika and stamp of Russia. 50c, Post rider and stamp of Indo-China. 1p, Post rider and Mambi Revolutionary stamp.

1987, June 15   *Perf. 12½x13*
2947 A822 3c multi   .25 .25
2948 A822 5c multi   .25 .25
2949 A822 10c multi   .25 .25
2950 A822 20c multi   .50 .25
2951 A822 30c multi   .70 .25
2952 A822 1.25c multi   1.25 .50
   Nos. 2947-2952 (6)   3.20 1.75

Souvenir Sheet
Perf. 13½x13
2953 A822 1p multi   4.50 2.25

No. 2953 contains one 32x40mm stamp.

Dinosaur Exhibits, Bacanao Natl. Park A823

1987, June 25   *Perf. 13*
2954 A823 3c multi   .25 .25
2955 A823 5c multi   .25 .25
2956 A823 10c multi   .40 .25
2957 A823 20c multi   .90 .25
2958 A823 35c multi   1.40 .30
2959 A823 40c multi   1.60 .40
   Nos. 2954-2959 (6)   4.80 1.70

Frank Pais (d. 1957), Teacher and Student Leader — A824

5c, Pais, Rafael Maria Mendive University.

1987, July 30   *Perf. 12½x12*
2960 A824 5c multicolored   .30 .25

10th Pan American Games, Indianapolis — A825

1987, Aug. 8
2961 A825 50c multicolored   1.75 .45

Printed se-tenant with inscribed label picturing the 1991 Havana Games character trademark.

Siege of Cienfuegos, 30th Anniv. — A826

1987, Sept. 5   *Perf. 13*
2962 A826 5c Memorial   .30 .25

Souvenir Sheet

HAFNIA '87, Denmark — A827

1p, Danish mailman, 1887, Type A6.

1987, Sept. 16   *Perf. 13½x13*
2963 A827 1p multi   4.50 2.25

Souvenir Sheet

ESPAMER '87, La Coruna, Oct. 2-12 — A828

1p, La Coruna Port, 1525.

1987, Oct. 2
2964 A828 1p multi   4.50 2.25

20th Heroic Guerrillas Day — A829

1987, Oct. 8   *Perf. 12½x12*
2965 A829 50c Coins, #1364   1.25 .55

Latin American History Type of 1986

Indians and birds: No. 2966, Tehuelche Indian of Argentina, *Habia rubica.* No. 2967, *Ramphastos cuvieri,* Tibirica Indian of Brazil. No. 2968, Spain #C31 & discovery of America 500th anniv. emblem. No. 2969, *Vultur gryphus,* Lautaro Indian of Chile. No. 2970, Calarca Indian of Colombia, *Opisthocomus hoazin.* No. 2971, *Priotelus temnurus,* Hatuey Indian of Cuba. No. 2972, *Columbigallina passerina,* Enriquillo Indian of the Dominican Republic. No. 2973, Spain #427. #2974, *Semnornis ramphastinus,* Ruminahui Indian of Ecuador. No. 2975, *Pharomachrus mocinno,* Tecum Uman Indian of Guatemala. No. 2976, Anacaona Indian of Haiti, *Aramus guarauna.* No. 2977, Lempira Indian of Honduras, *Diglossa baritula.* #2978, Spain #C42. No. 2979, *Onychorhinchus mexicanus,* Cuauhtemoc Indian of Mexico. No. 2980, *Setofaga picta,* Nicarao Indian of Nicaragua. No. 2981, *Rupicola peruviana,* Atahualpa Indian of Peru. No. 2982, Atlacatl Indian of El Salvador, *Bluteo jamaicensis.* #2983, Spain #432. No. 2984, Abayuba Indian of Uruguay, *Phytotoma rutila.* No. 2985, Guaycaypuro Indian of Venezuela, *Ara arauna.*

1987, Oct. 12   *Perf. 13*
2966 A804 1c multi   .25 .25
2967 A804 1c multi   .25 .25
2968 A804 1c multi   .25 .25
2969 A804 1c multi   .25 .25
2970 A804 1c multi   .25 .25
   a.   Strip of 5, Nos. 2966-2970   1.00 1.00
2971 A804 5c multi   .40 .25
2972 A804 5c multi   .40 .25
2973 A804 5c multi   .40 .25
2974 A804 5c multi   .40 .25
2975 A804 5c multi   .40 .25
   a.   Strip of 5, Nos. 2971-2975   2.00 1.00
2976 A804 10c multi   .65 .25
2977 A804 10c multi   .65 .25
2978 A804 10c multi   .65 .25
2979 A804 10c multi   .65 .25
2980 A804 10c multi   .65 .25
   a.   Strip of 5, Nos. 2976-2980   3.25 1.00
2981 A804 20c multi   1.00 .40
2982 A804 20c multi   1.00 .40
2983 A804 20c multi   1.00 .40
2984 A804 20c multi   1.00 .40

2985	A804	20c multi	1.00	.40
a.		Strip of 5, Nos. 2981-2985	5.00	2.00
		Nos. 2966-2985 (20)	11.50	5.75

Discovery of America, 500th anniv. (in 1992). *Vultur* is spelled incorrectly on No. 2969.

October Revolution, Russia, 70th Anniv. — A830

30c, Soviet spacecraft, Russia No. 379.

1987, Nov. 7   *Perf. 12½x12*
2986	A830	30c multi	1.00	.25

Cuban Railway, 150th Anniv. — A831

Stamps on stamps.

1987, Nov. 19   *Perf. 13x12½*
2987	A831	3c No. 453	.25	.25
2988	A831	5c No. 1061	.25	.25
2989	A831	10c No. 2010	.25	.25
2990	A831	20c No. 2011	.55	.25
2991	A831	35c No. 2360	1.00	.30
2992	A831	40c No. 2361	1.25	.40
		Nos. 2987-2992 (6)	3.55	1.70

Souvenir Sheet
Perf. 13x13½
2993	A831	1p No. 355	4.75	2.25

No. 2993 contains 40x32mm one stamp. An imperf. sheet containing Nos. 2987-2992 exists, inscribed to promote the 17th Pan American Railway Congress. Value, $7.

San Alejandro Art School, 170th Anniv. — A832

Paintings: 1c, *Landscape*, by Domingo Ramos. 2c, *Portrait of Rodriguez Morey*, by Eugenio Gonzalez Olivera. 3c, *Landscape with Malangas and Palm Trees*, by Valentin Sanz Carta. 5c, *Wagons*, by Eduardo Morales. 10c, *Portrait of Elena Herrera*, by Armando Menocal, vert. 30c, *Rape of Dejanira*, by Miguel Melero, vert. 50c, *The Card Player*, by Leopoldo Romanach.

1988, Jan. 12   *Perf. 13x12½, 12½x13*
2994	A832	1c multi	.25	.25
2995	A832	2c multi	.25	.25
2995A	A832	3c multi	.25	.25
2996	A832	5c multi	.25	.25
2997	A832	10c multi	.30	.25
2998	A832	30c multi	.85	.25
2999	A832	50c multi	1.50	.50
		Nos. 2994-2999 (7)	3.65	2.00

Poisonous Mushrooms A833

Designs: 1c, Boletus satanas. 2c, Amanita citrina. 3c, Tylopilus felleus. 5c, Paxillus involutus. 10c, Inocybe patouillardii. 30c, Amanita muscaria. 50c, Hypholoma fasciculare.

1988, Feb. 15   *Perf. 13*
3000	A833	1c multicolored	.25	.25
3001	A833	2c multicolored	.25	.25
3002	A833	3c multicolored	.25	.25
3003	A833	5c multicolored	.25	.25
3004	A833	10c multicolored	.55	.25
3005	A833	30c multicolored	1.50	.55
3006	A833	50c multicolored	2.40	1.00
		Nos. 3000-3006 (7)	5.45	2.80

Radio Rebelde, 30th Anniv. — A834

1988, Feb. 24   *Perf. 12½x12*
3007	A834	5c multi	.30	.25

Monuments A835

No. 3008, Mario Munoz, Santiago de Cuba. No. 3009, Frank Pais Memorial, eternal flame.

1988   **Litho.**   *Perf. 13*
3008	A835	5c multi	.45	.25
3009	A835	5c multi	.45	.25

Battle fronts, 30th annivs. Issue dates: No. 3008, Mar. 5. No. 3009, Mar. 11.

Mothers' Day — A836

1988, Mar. 30
3010	A836	1c Red roses	.25	.25
3011	A836	2c Pale pink peonies	.25	.25
3012	A836	3c Daisies	.25	.25
3013	A836	5c Dahlias	.25	.25
3014	A836	13c White roses	.30	.25
3015	A836	35c Carnations	.90	.25
3016	A836	40c Pink roses	1.10	.30
		Nos. 3010-3016 (7)	3.30	1.80

Cosmonauts' Day — A837

2c, Gorizont. 3c, Mir-Kvant space link. 4c, Signo 3. 5c, Mars, space probe. 10c, Phobos. 30c, Vega. 50c, Spacecraft. 1p, Spacecraft, diff.

1988, Apr. 12
3017	A837	2c multicolored	.25	.25
3018	A837	3c multicolored	.25	.25
3019	A837	4c multicolored	.25	.25
3020	A837	5c multicolored	.25	.25
3021	A837	10c multicolored	.30	.25
3022	A837	30c multicolored	.85	.25
3023	A837	50c multicolored	1.50	.50
		Nos. 3017-3023 (7)	3.65	2.00

Souvenir Sheet
Perf. 13½x13
3024	A837	1p multicolored	4.25	2.00

No. 3024 contains one 32x40mm stamp.

Stamp Day Type of 1984

Mural, by R. Rodriguez Radillo (1967) details: 30c, Mail coach, telegraph operator. 50c, Passenger pigeon.

1988, Apr. 24   *Perf. 13x12½*
3025	A733	30c multi	1.10	.40
3026	A733	50c multi	1.90	.50

Institute for Research on Sugar Cane and Byproducts (ICIDCA), 25th Anniv. — A838

1988, May 23   *Perf. 12½x12*
3027	A838	5c multi	.40	.25

Cubana Airlines Transatlantic Flights — A839

1988, May 25
3028	A839	2c Madrid, 1948	.25	.25
3029	A839	4c Prague, 1961	.25	.25
3030	A839	5c Berlin, 1972	.25	.25
3031	A839	10c Luanda, 1975	.30	.25
3032	A839	30c Paris, 1983	1.00	.25
3033	A839	50c Moscow, 1987	1.60	.50
		Nos. 3028-3033 (6)	3.65	1.75

Souvenir Sheet

FINLANDIA '88 — A840

1p, Steam packet Furst Menschikoff.

1988, June 1   *Perf. 12½*
3034	A840	1p multicolored	4.00	2.00

Postal Union of the Americas and Spain (UPAE) Conference on Stamps of the Americas, Havana — A841

1988, June 20   *Perf. 12½x12*
3035	A841	20c multi	1.25	.35

Beetles A842

Designs: 1c, Megasoma elephas fabricus. 3c, Platycoelia flavoscutellata ohaus, vert. 4c, Plusiotis argenteola bates. 5c, Heterosternus oberthuri ohaus. 10c, Odontotaenius zodiacus truqui. 35c, Chrysophora chrysochlora

latreille, vert. 40c, Phanaeus leander waterhouse.

1988, June 30   *Perf. 13*
3036	A842	1c multicolored	.25	.25
3037	A842	3c multicolored	.25	.25
3038	A842	4c multicolored	.25	.25
3039	A842	5c multicolored	.25	.25
3040	A842	10c multicolored	.40	.25
3041	A842	35c multicolored	1.25	.30
3042	A842	40c multicolored	1.60	.50
		Nos. 3036-3042 (7)	4.25	2.05

Jose Raul Capablanca (1888-1942), Chess Champion — A843

30c, Chessmen, vert. 40c, J. Corzo, Capablanca. 50c, Lasker, Capablanca. 1p, Winning configuration, 1921, vert. 3p, Portrait by E. Valderrama, vert. 5p, Chessmen, Capablanca.

1988, July 15   *Perf. 12½x13, 13x12½*
3043	A843	30c multicolored	.65	.30
3044	A843	40c multicolored	.90	.30
3045	A843	50c multicolored	.95	.40
3046	A843	1p multicolored	2.40	.90
3047	A843	3p multicolored	7.25	2.40
3048	A843	5p multicolored	13.00	4.50
		Nos. 3043-3048 (6)	25.15	8.80

Souvenir Sheets
3049	Sheet of 2	1.60	.80
a.	A843 30c No. 464, vert.	.60	.40
b.	like No. 3043, size: 32x40mm	.60	.40
3050	Sheet of 2	2.10	1.05
a.	A843 40c No. 465	.70	.40
b.	like No. 3044, size: 40x32mm	.70	.40
3051	Sheet of 2	3.00	1.50
a.	A843 50c No. C44	.75	.50
b.	like No. 3045, size: 40x32mm	.75	.50
3052	Sheet of 2	5.50	2.75
a.	A843 1p No. 464, vert.	2.10	1.00
b.	like No. 3046, size: 32x40mm	2.10	1.00
3053	Sheet of 2	16.00	8.00
a.	A843 3p No. C46, vert.	6.25	3.00
b.	like No. 3047, size: 32x40mm	6.25	3.00
3054	Sheet of 2	27.50	13.50
a.	A843 5p No. C45, vert.	10.50	5.00
b.	like No. 3048, size: 32x40mm	10.50	5.00
	Nos. 3049-3054 (6)	55.70	27.60

Attack on Moncada Barracks, 35th Anniv. A844

1988, July 26   *Perf. 13*
3055	A844	5c blk, yel ocher & red	.30	.25

Souvenir Sheet

PRAGA '88 — A845

1p, Czechoslovakia #45.

1988, Aug. 26   *Perf. 12½*
3056	A845	1p multicolored	4.00	2.00

Czechoslovakian postage stamps, 70th anniv.

Revolutionary Invasion Force, 30th Anniv. — A846

1988, Aug. 31   *Perf. 12½x12*
3057 A846 5c multicolored   .30 .25

World Marxist Review, 30th Anniv. A847

1988, Sept. 1   *Perf. 13*
3058 A847 30c multi   1.25 .35

Locomotives — A848

20c, Stephenson's Rocket, 1837. 30c, Miller, US, 1839. 50c, La Junta. 1p, J.G. Brill trolley, US, 1922. 2p, TEM 4K, USSR, c. 1960. 5p, CAP 9 electric, c. 1988.

1988, Sept. 19   *Perf. 12½x13*
3059 A848 20c multicolored   .50 .25
3060 A848 30c multicolored   .95 .45
3061 A848 50c multicolored   2.00 .90
3062 A848 1p multicolored   3.50 1.25
3063 A848 2p multicolored   6.75 3.00
3064 A848 5p multicolored   15.00 8.00
    Nos. 3059-3064 (6)   28.70 13.85

Latin American History Type of 1986

Natl. arms & patriots: No. 3065, San Martin, Argentina. No. 3066, M.A. Padilla, Bolivia. No. 3067, #390 & discovery of America 500th anniv. emblem. No. 3068, Tiradentes, Brazil. No. 3069, O'Higgins, Chile. No. 3070, A. Narino, Colombia. No. 3071, Marti, Cuba. No. 3072, #391 & emblem. No. 3073, Duarte, Dominican Republic. No. 3074, Sucre, Ecuador. No. 3075, M.J. Arce, El Salvador. No. 3076, Dessalines, Haiti. No. 3077, #C36 & emblem. No. 3078, Hidalgo, Mexico. No. 3079, J.D. Estrada, Nicaragua. No. 3080, Diaz, Paraguay. No. 3081, F. Bolognesi, Peru. No. 3082, #C37 & emblem. No. 3083, Artigas, Uruguay. No. 3084, Bolivar, Venezuela.

1988, Oct. 12   *Perf. 13*
3065 A804 1c multi   .25 .25
3066 A804 1c multi   .25 .25
3067 A804 1c multi   .25 .25
3068 A804 1c multi   .25 .25
3069 A804 1c multi   .25 .25
   a.   Strip of 5, Nos. 3065-3069   1.00 .50
3070 A804 5c multi   .25 .25
3071 A804 5c multi   .25 .25
3072 A804 5c multi   .25 .25
3073 A804 5c multi   .25 .25
3074 A804 5c multi   .25 .25
   a.   Strip of 5, Nos. 3070-3074   1.00 .50
3075 A804 10c multi   .25 .25
3076 A804 10c multi   .25 .25
3077 A804 10c multi   .25 .25
3078 A804 10c multi   .25 .25
3079 A804 10c multi   .25 .25
   a.   Strip of 5, Nos. 3075-3079   1.50 .75
3080 A804 20c multi   .45 .25
3081 A804 20c multi   .45 .25
3082 A804 20c multi   .45 .25
3083 A804 20c multi   .45 .25
3084 A804 20c multi   .45 .25
   a.   Strip of 5, Nos. 3080-3084   2.50 1.25
   b.   Sheet of 20, Nos. 3065-3084   7.50 7.50
    Nos. 3065-3084 (20)   6.00 5.00

Discovery of America, 500th anniv. (in 1992).

Havana Museum, 20th Anniv. — A849

Design: Captain-General's Palace and Maces of Municipal Havana.

1988, Oct. 16   Litho.   *Perf. 12½x12*
3085 A849 5c multi + label   .40 .25

Anniversaries — A850

No. 3086, Swan Lake. No. 3087, Theater in 1838 and 1988.

1988, Oct. 28   *Perf. 13*
3086 A850 5c multicolored   .60 .25
3087 A850 5c multicolored   .60 .25
   a.   Pair, Nos. 3086-3087   1.25 .40

Natl. Ballet, 40th anniv. (No. 3086); Grand Theater of Havana, 150th anniv. (No. 3087).

Intl. Literacy Year A851

1988, Dec. 5
3088 A851 5c multicolored   .30 .25

UN Declaration of Human Rights, 40th Anniv. — A851a

1988, Dec. 10
3088A A851a 30c multi   1.25 .35

Battle of Santa Clara, 30th Anniv. — A852

30c, Monument, Che Guevara Plaza.

1988, Dec. 28   *Perf. 13x12½*
3089 A852 30c multicolored   1.25 .35

30th Anniv. of the Revolution — A853

1989, Jan. 1   *Perf. 13*
3090 A853 5c multi   .25 .25
3091 A853 20c multi   .65 .25
3092 A853 30c multi   .85 .25
3093 A853 50c multi   1.75 .50
    Nos. 3090-3093 (4)   3.50 1.25

Edible Mushrooms — A854

Designs: 2c, Pleurotus levis. 3c, Pleurotus floridanus. 5c, Amanita caesarea. 10c, Lentinus cubensis. 40c, Pleurotus ostreatus (brown). 50c, Pleurotus ostreatus (yellow)

1989, Jan. 10
3094 A854 2c multicolored   .25 .25
3095 A854 3c multicolored   .25 .25
3096 A854 5c multicolored   .25 .25
3097 A854 10c multicolored   .45 .25
3098 A854 40c multicolored   1.60 .40
3099 A854 50c multicolored   1.75 .50
    Nos. 3094-3099 (6)   4.55 1.90

2c, 3c, 5c, 40c, 50c, vert.

Souvenir Sheet

INDIA '89 — A855

1p, Indian River Post, 1858.

1989, Jan. 20
3100 A855 1p multicolored   4.00 2.00

Central Organization of Cuban Trade Unions (CTC), 50th Anniv. — A856

5c, No. 2477, CTC emblem.

1989, Jan. 28   *Perf. 12½*
3101 A856 5c multicolored   .30 .25

Butterflies A857

Designs: 1c, Metamorpho dido. 3c, Callithea saphhira. 5c, Papilio zagreus. 10c, Mynes sestia. 30c, Papilio dardanus. 50c, Catagranma sorana.

1989, Feb. 15
3102 A857 1c multicolored   .25 .25
3103 A857 3c multicolored   .25 .25
3104 A857 5c multicolored   .25 .25
3105 A857 10c multicolored   .30 .25
3106 A857 30c multicolored   1.40 .30
3107 A857 50c multicolored   2.50 .65
    Nos. 3102-3107 (6)   4.95 1.95

1990 World Cup Soccer Championships, Italy — A858

Various athletes.

1989, Mar. 15   *Perf. 13*
3108 A858 1c multi   .25 .25
3109 A858 3c multi, diff.   .25 .25
3110 A858 5c multi, diff.   .25 .25
3111 A858 10c multi, diff.   .25 .25
3112 A858 30c multi, diff.   1.25 .25
3113 A858 50c multi, diff.   2.10 .40
    Nos. 3108-3113 (6)   4.35 1.65

Souvenir Sheet
Perf. 12½

3114 A858 1p multi, diff., horiz.   4.00 2.00

No. 3114 contains one 40x32mm stamp.

Natl. Revolutionary Police (PNR), 30th Anniv. — A859

1989, Mar. 23   *Perf. 13*
3115 A859 5c multicolored   .30 .25

Cosmonauts' Day — A860

Spacecraft and rocket mail covers: 1c, Zodiac and cover, Australia 1934. 3c, Lighthouse and cover, India, 1934. 5c, Cover, England, 1934. 10c, Icarus and cover, The Netherlands, 1935. 40c, La Douce France and cover, France, 1935. 50c, Rocket mail cover, Cuba, 1939.

1989, Apr. 12
3116 A860 1c multi   .25 .25
3117 A860 3c multi   .25 .25
3118 A860 5c multi   .25 .25
3119 A860 10c multi   .25 .25
3120 A860 40c multi   1.10 .40
3121 A860 50c multi   1.40 .55
    Nos. 3116-3121 (6)   3.50 1.95

Stamp Day Type of 1984

Details of mural by R. Rodriguez Radillo (1967): 30c, Mail coach, Satellite dish. 50c, Galleon, longboats, train, passenger pigeon, horses.

1989, Apr. 24   Litho.   *Perf. 13x12½*
3122 A733 30c multi   .65 .30
3123 A733 50c multi   4.75 2.00

Casa de Las Americas, 30th Anniv. A861

1989, Apr. 28   *Perf. 12½x13*
3124 A861 5c multi   .30 .25

Souvenir Sheet

BULGARIA '89 — A862

1989, May 1   **Perf. 12½**
3125 A862 1p Bulgaria No. 346   4.50 2.25

58th FIP Congress and 101st anniv. of Bulgarian Railways.

Cuban
Postal
Code
A863

1989, May 5   **Perf. 13**
3126 A863 5c multi   .30 .25

Mothers'
Day — A864

Perfume bottles and flowers: 1c, Habano, tobacco. 3c, Violeta, violets. 5c, Mariposa, mariposa. 13c, Coral Negro, roses. 30c, Ala Alonso, jasmine. 50c, D'Man, lemon blossoms.

1989, May 10
3127 A864 1c multi   .25 .25
3128 A864 3c multi   .25 .25
3129 A864 5c multi   .25 .25
3130 A864 13c multi   .35 .25
3131 A864 30c multi   1.00 .30
3132 A864 50c multi   1.75 .70
    Nos. 3127-3132 (6)   3.85 2.00

Agrarian Reform
Law, 30th
Anniv. — A865

1989, May 17   **Perf. 12x12½**
3133 A865 5c multi   .30 .25

Council for
Mutual
Economic
Assistance
(CAME),
40th Anniv.
A866

1989, June 1   **Litho.**   **Perf. 12½x13**
3134 A866 30c multi   1.25 .25

13th World Communist Youth and
Student Festival, Pyongyang — A867

1989, July 1   **Litho.**   **Perf. 12½**
3135 A867 30c multi   1.25 .25

Souvenir Sheet

Rouget de Lisle Singing La
Marseillaise, by Pils — A868

1989, July 7   **Perf. 13**
3136 A868 1p multi   4.00 2.00

PHILEXFRANCE '89, French revolution bicent. and Cuban revolution 30th anniv.

BRASILIANA '89 — A869

Exotic birds: 1c, Ramphastos toco. 3c, Agamia agami. 5c, Eudocimus ruber. 10c, Psophia leucoptera. 35c, Harpia harpyja. 50c, Cephalopterus ornatus.

1989, July 28   **Litho.**   **Perf. 12½**
3137 A869 1c multicolored   .25 .25
3138 A869 3c multicolored   .25 .25
3139 A869 5c multicolored   .25 .25
3140 A869 10c multicolored   .40 .25
3141 A869 35c multicolored   1.50 .50
3142 A869 50c multicolored   2.00 .70
    Nos. 3137-3142 (6)   4.65 2.20

Warships
A870

1989, Sept. 29   **Litho.**   **Perf. 12½**
3143 A870 1c El Fenix   .25 .25
3144 A870 3c Triunfo   .25 .25
3145 A870 5c El Rayo   .25 .25
3146 A870 10c San Carlos   .30 .25
3147 A870 30c San Jose   1.25 .40
3148 A870 50c San Genaro   1.90 .70
    Nos. 3143-3148 (6)   4.20 2.10

America Issue — A871

UPAE emblem and pre-Columbian art: 5p, Stone carving, Indians in dugout canoe. 20p, Petroglyph, Indian drawing on stone wall.

1989, Oct. 12   **Perf. 12½x12**
3149 A871 5c multi   .25 .25
3150 A871 20c multi   .80 .40

Latin American History — A872

Writers and orchids: No. 3151, Domingo Sarmiento (1811-1888), Argentine educator, and *Govenia utriculata.* No. 3152, Joaquim Maria Machado de Assis (1839-1908), Brazilian novelist, and *Laelia grandis.* No. 3153, Salvador No. 69 and discovery of America anniv. emblem. No. 3154, Jorge Isaacs (1837-1895), Colombian novelist, and *Cattleya trianae.* No. 3155, Alejo Carpentier, Cuban writer, and *Cochleanthes discolor.* No. 3156, Pablo Neruda (1904-1973), Chilean poet, and *Oxalis adenophylla.* No. 3157, Pedro Urena, Dominican writer, and *Epidendrum fragrans.* No. 3158, Salvador No. 86 and anniv. emblem. No. 3159, Juan Montalvo (1832-1889), Ecuadorian satirist, and *Miltonia vexillaria.* No. 3160, Miguel Asturias (1899-1974), Guatemalan writer awarded the 1966 Lenin Peace Prize and 1967 Nobel Prize for literature, and *Odontoglossum rossii.* No. 3161, Jose C. del Valle, Honduran writer, and *Laelia anceps.* No. 3162, Alfonso Reyes (1889-1959), Mexican poet, and *Laelia anceps alba.* No. 3163, Salvador No. 87 and anniv. emblem. No. 3164, Ruben Dario (1867-1917), Nicaraguan poet, and *Brassavola acaulis.* No. 3165, Belisario Porras (1856-1942), president of Panama, and *Pescatorea celina.* No. 3166, Ricardo Palma (1833-1919), Peruvian writer, and *Coryanthes leucocorys.* No. 3167, Eugenio Maria de Hostos (1839-1903), Puerto Rican writer, and *Guzmania berteroniana.* No. 3168, Salvador No. 88 and anniv. emblem. No. 3169, Jose E. Rodo (1872-1917), Uruguayan philosopher, essayist, and *Cypella hebertii.* No. 3170, Romulo Gallegos, Venezuelan writer, and *Cattleya mossiae.*

1989, Oct. 27   **Litho.**   **Perf. 13**
3151 A872 1c multicolored   .25 .25
3152 A872 1c multicolored   .25 .25
3153 A872 1c multicolored   .25 .25
3154 A872 1c multicolored   .25 .25
3155 A872 1c multicolored   .25 .25
  a.   Strip of 5, Nos. 3151-3155 1.00 .50
3156 A872 5c multicolored   .25 .25
3157 A872 5c multicolored   .25 .25
3158 A872 5c multicolored   .25 .25
3159 A872 5c multicolored   .25 .25
3160 A872 5c multicolored   .25 .25
  a.   Strip of 5, Nos. 3156-3160 1.00 .50
3161 A872 10c multicolored   .35 .25
3162 A872 10c multicolored   .35 .25
3163 A872 10c multicolored   .35 .25
3164 A872 10c multicolored   .35 .25
3165 A872 10c multicolored   .35 .25
  a.   Strip of 5, Nos. 3161-3165 2.00 1.00
3166 A872 20c multicolored   .55 .25
3167 A872 20c multicolored   .55 .25
3168 A872 20c multicolored   .55 .25
3169 A872 20c multicolored   .55 .25
3170 A872 20c multicolored   .55 .25
  a.   Strip of 5, Nos. 3166-3170 3.00 1.50
  b.   Sheet of 20, #3151-3170   8.00 8.00
    Nos. 3151-3170 (20)   7.00 5.00

Discovery of America 500th anniv. (in 1992).

Disappearance
of Camilo
Cienfuegos,
30th
Anniv. — A873

1989, Oct. 28
3171 A873 5c multicolored   .30 .25

Founding of
the City of
Trinidad,
475th
Anniv.
A874

1989, Nov. 6   **Perf. 12½x13**
3172 A874 5c multicolored   .30 .25

Paintings in the Natl. Museum — A875

Designs: 1c, *Familiar Scene,* by Antoine Faivre. 2c, *Flowers,* by Emile Jean Horace Vernet (1789-1863). 5c, *The Judgement of Paris,* by Charles Le Brun (1619-1690). 20c, *Outskirts of Nice,* by Eugene Louis Boudin (1824-1898). 30c, *Portrait of Sarah Bernhardt,* by G.J.V. Clairin. 50c, *Fishermen in Port,* by C.J. Vernet.

Perf. 12½, 12½x13 (30p)
1989, Nov. 20   **Litho.**
Size of 30p: 36x46mm
3173 A875 1c multicolored   .25 .25
3174 A875 2c multicolored   .25 .25
3175 A875 5c multicolored   .25 .25
3176 A875 20c multicolored   .85 .25
3177 A875 30c multicolored   1.10 .25
3178 A875 50c multicolored   2.25 .55
    Nos. 3173-3178 (6)   4.95 1.80

11th Pan-American Games, Havana,
1991 — A876

1989, Dec. 15   **Litho.**   **Perf. 12½**
3179 A876 5c Cycling   .25 .25
3180 A876 5c Fencing   .25 .25
3181 A876 5c Water polo   .25 .25
3182 A876 5c Shooting   .25 .25
3183 A876 5c Archery   .25 .25
3184 A876 20c Tennis, vert.   .65 .25
3185 A876 30c Swimming, vert.   1.10 .25
3186 A876 35c Diving, vert.   1.40 .30
3187 A876 40c Field hockey   1.50 .30
3188 A876 50c Basketball, vert. 2.25 .65
    Nos. 3179-3188 (10)   8.15 3.00

Jose Marti's
Golden Age,
Cent. — A877

1989, Dec. 20   **Perf. 13**
3189 A877 5c scar, lt blue & blk   .40 .25

Cuban Postal Museum, 25th
Anniv. — A878

1990, Jan. 2   *Perf. 13x12½*
3190 A878 5c *Almendares* .25 .25
3191 A878 30c Mail train 2.50 .80

Speleological Soc., 50th
Anniv. — A879

1990, Jan. 15   *Perf. 12½*
3192 A879 30c multicolored 2.00 .35

1990 World Cup
Soccer
Championships,
Italy — A880

Various Italian architecture and athletes: No.
3193a, Dribbling (in red and blue). No. 3193b,
Heading (in red and green). No. 3193c, Kicking (in green). 10c, Goalie catching ball. 30c,
Dribbling, diff. 50c, Kicking, diff. 1p, Goalie
catching ball, diff.

1990, Jan. 30   *Litho.*   *Perf. 12½*
3193   Strip of 3 .50 .25
a.-c.   A880 5c any single .25 .25
3194 A880 10c multicolored .25 .25
3195 A880 30c multicolored 1.25 .30
3196 A880 50c multicolored 2.10 .55
a.   Sheet of 6, #3193a-3193c,
    3194-3196 + 3 labels 4.25 2.10
    Nos. 3193-3196 (4) 4.10 1.35
Souvenir Sheet
3197 A880 1p multicolored 3.50 1.75
No. 3193 has a continuous design picturing
The Colosseum.

1992 Summer Olympics,
Barcelona — A881

1c, Baseball. 4c, Running. 5c, Basketball.
10c, Women's volleyball. 30c, Wrestling. 50c,
Boxing.
1p, High jump.

1990, Feb. 20   *Litho.*   *Perf. 12½*
3198 A881 1c multicolored .25 .25
3199 A881 4c multicolored .25 .25
3200 A881 5c multicolored .25 .25
3201 A881 10c multicolored .45 .25
3202 A881 30c multicolored 1.10 .30
3203 A881 50c multicolored 2.00 .65
    Nos. 3198-3203 (6) 4.30 1.95
Souvenir Sheet
3204 A881 1p multicolored 4.00 2.00
Nos. 3198-3201 and 3203 are vert.
No. 3204 contains one 40x32mm stamp.

75th Universal Esperanto
Congress — A882

1990, Mar. 7
3205 A882 30c Tower of Babel 1.25 .35
No. 3205 printed se-tenant with inscribed
label publicizing the congress.

Souvenir Sheet

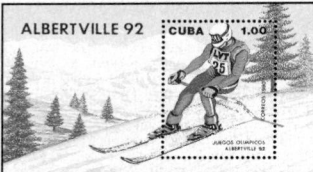

1992 Winter Olympics,
Albertville — A883

1990, Mar. 30   *Litho.*   *Perf. 13*
3206 A883 1p multicolored 4.50 2.25

Cosmonauts' Day — A884

Spacecraft and rocket mail covers: 1c, Austria, 1932. 2c, Germany, 1933. 3c, Netherlands, 1934. 10c, Belgium, 1935. 30c, Yugoslavia, 1935. 50c, United States, 1936.

1990, Apr. 12   *Perf. 12½*
3207 A884 1c multicolored .25 .25
3208 A884 2c multicolored .25 .25
3209 A884 3c multicolored .25 .25
3210 A884 10c multicolored .25 .25
3211 A884 30c multicolored 1.10 .25
3212 A884 50c multicolored 2.00 .55
    Nos. 3207-3212 (6) 4.10 1.80

Stamp Day Type of 1984
Details of mural by R. Rodriguez Radillo
(1967): 30c, Train station. 50c, Jet aircraft in
flight.

1990, Apr. 24   *Perf. 13x12½*
3213 A733 30c multicolored 2.40 .75
3214 A733 50c multicolored 1.40 .45

Labor
Day,
Cent.
A885

1990, Apr. 30   *Perf. 13*
3215 A885 5c multicolored .40 .25

Souvenir Sheet

Great Britain No. 1 on Cover — A886

1990, May 3
3216 A886 1p multicolored 4.00 2.00
Stamp World London '90, Penny Black
150th anniv.

Penny
Black,
150th
Anniv.
A887

Portraits of Sir Rowland Hill and stamps of
Great Britain: 2c, No. 1. 3c, No. 2. 5c, Type
A5. 10c, No. 5. 30c, First day postmark. 50c, 5
#1 on Mulready envelope.

1990, May 6   *Litho.*   *Perf. 12½x12*
3217 A887 2c multicolored .25 .25
3218 A887 3c multicolored .25 .25
3219 A887 5c multicolored .25 .25
3220 A887 10c multicolored .25 .25
3221 A887 30c multicolored 1.25 .25
3222 A887 50c multicolored 2.25 .60
    Nos. 3217-3222 (6) 4.50 1.85

Celia Sanchez Manduley (1920-
1980) — A888

1990, May 9   *Perf. 12½x13*
3223 A888 5c multicolored .50 .25

Ho Chi Minh
(1890-1969),
Vietnamese
Communist
Party
Leader — A889

1990, May 19   *Perf. 12½*
3224 A889 50c multicolored 1.40 .45

Oceanography Institute, 25th
Anniv. — A890

Designs: 5c, Specimen analysis and
Lachnolaimus maximus. 30c, Research ship,
fish, coral reef. 50c, Specimen collection and
Panulirus argus.

1990, June 18   *Litho.*   *Perf. 12½*
3225 A890 5c multicolored .25 .25
3226 A890 30c multicolored 1.00 .25
3227 A890 50c multicolored 1.60 .40
    Nos. 3225-3227 (3) 2.85 .90

5th Latin
American
Botanical
Conference
A891

Designs: 3c, Banara minutiflora. 5c, Oplonia
nannophylla. 10c, Jacquinia brunnescens.
30c, Rondeletia brachycarpa. 50c, Rondeletia
odorata.

1990, June 25   *Litho.*   *Perf. 12½*
3228 A891 3c multicolored .25 .25
3229 A891 5c multicolored .25 .25
3230 A891 10c multicolored .50 .25
3231 A891 30c multicolored 1.60 .25
3232 A891 50c multicolored 2.40 .60
    Nos. 3228-3232 (5) 5.00 1.60

Tourism
A892

1990, June 30
3233 A892 5c Wind surfing .25 .25
3234 A892 10c Spear fishing .35 .25
3235 A892 30c Deep sea fishing 1.00 .25
3236 A892 40c Hunting 1.60 .55
    Nos. 3233-3236 (4) 3.20 1.30
Nos. 3233, 3236 vert.

Art
Treasures
A893

5c, "La Flauta Del Dios Pan." 20c, "Un Pastor." 50c, "Ganimedes." 1p, "Venus
Anadiomena."

1990, July 20
3237 A893 5c multicolored .25 .25
3238 A893 20c multicolored .60 .25
3239 A893 50c multicolored 1.60 .40
3240 A893 1p multicolored 2.50 .85
a.   Sheet of 4, #3237-3240 5.00 5.00
    Nos. 3237-3240 (4) 4.95 1.75

Birds
A894

Designs: 2c, Podiceps cristatus. 3c, Galliral-
lus australis. 5c, Nestor notabilis. 10c, Xenicus
longipes. 30c, Cracticus torquatus. 50c, Pros-
themadera novaeseelandiae.
1p, Kiwi.

1990, Aug. 24   *Litho.*   *Perf. 13*
3241 A894 2c multicolored .25 .25
3242 A894 3c multicolored .25 .25
3243 A894 5c multicolored .25 .25
3244 A894 10c multicolored .50 .25
3245 A894 30c multicolored 1.50 .35
3246 A894 50c multicolored 2.40 .65
    Nos. 3241-3246 (6) 5.15 2.00
Souvenir Sheet
3247 A894 1p multicolored 4.50 2.25
New Zealand '90. No. 3247 contains one
39x31mm stamp.

8th UN
Congress on
Crime
Prevention
A895

1990, Aug. 27   *Litho.*   *Perf. 12½*
3248 A895 50c blue, silver & red 1.75 .45

Discovery of America, 500th Anniv. (in 1992) — A896

1990, Oct. 12   Litho.   Perf. 12½
3249	A896	5c Ship, shore	.25	.25
3250	A896	20c Columbus, village	1.00	.35

Cuban Television, 40th Anniv. — A897

1990, Oct. 12   Litho.   Perf. 13
3251	A897	5c multicolored	.35	.25

Nationalization of Railroads, 30th Anniv. — A898

1990, Oct. 13   Perf. 13x12½
3252	A898	50c multicolored	2.40	.75

Latin American History Type of 1986

Latin American stamps or flags and costumes: No. 3253, Argentina. No. 3254, Bolivia. No. 3255, Argentina No. 91. No. 3256, Colombia. No. 3257, Costa Rica. No. 3258, Cuba. No. 3259, Chile. No. 3260, Dominican Republic No. 110. No. 3261, Ecuador. No. 3262, El Salvador. No. 3263, Guatemala. No. 3264, Mexico. No. 3265, Puerto Rico No. 133. No. 3266, Nicaragua. No. 3267, Panama. No. 3268, Paraguay. No. 3269, Peru. No. 3270, El Salvador No. 103. No. 3271, Puerto Rico. No. 3272, Venezuela.

1990, Oct. 27   Perf. 12½
3253	A804	1c multicolored	.25	.25
3254	A804	1c multicolored	.25	.25
3255	A804	1c multicolored	.25	.25
3256	A804	1c multicolored	.25	.25
3257	A804	1c multicolored	.25	.25
a.		Strip of 5, Nos. 3253-3257	1.00	.50
3258	A804	5c multicolored	.25	.25
3259	A804	5c multicolored	.25	.25
3260	A804	5c multicolored	.25	.25
3261	A804	5c multicolored	.25	.25
3262	A804	5c multicolored	.25	.25
a.		Strip of 5, Nos. 3258-3262	1.00	.50
3263	A804	10c multicolored	.30	.25
3264	A804	10c multicolored	.30	.25
3265	A804	10c multicolored	.30	.25
3266	A804	10c multicolored	.30	.25
3267	A804	10c multicolored	.30	.25
a.		Strip of 5, Nos. 3263-3267	1.50	.75
3268	A804	20c multicolored	.85	.25
3269	A804	20c multicolored	.85	.25
3270	A804	20c multicolored	.85	.25
3271	A804	20c multicolored	.85	.25
3272	A804	20c multicolored	.85	.25
a.		Strip of 5, Nos. 3268-3272	4.50	2.25
b.		Sheet of 20, #3253-3272	5.00	5.00
		Nos. 3253-3272 (20)	8.25	5.00

Discovery of America, 500th anniv. (in 1992).

11th Jai Alai World Championships A899

1990, Nov. 14   Litho.   Perf. 12½
3273	A899	30c multicolored	1.25	.40

No. 3273 printed with se-tenant label.

11th Pan American Games, Havana — A900

No. 3274, Judo. No. 3275, Sailing. No. 3276, Kayak. No. 3277, Rowing. No. 3278, Equestrian. No. 3279, Table tennis. No. 3280, Men's gymnastics, vert. No. 3281, Baseball, vert. No. 3282, Team handball, vert. No. 3283, Soccer, vert.

1990, Nov. 15   Litho.   Perf. 12½
3274	A900	5c multicolored	.25	.25
3275	A900	5c multicolored	.25	.25
3276	A900	5c multicolored	.25	.25
3277	A900	5c multicolored	.25	.25
3278	A900	5c multicolored	.25	.25
3279	A900	10c multicolored	.30	.25
3280	A900	20c multicolored	.60	.25
3281	A900	30c multicolored	.90	.25
3282	A900	35c multicolored	1.10	.35
3283	A900	50c multicolored	1.60	.70
		Nos. 3274-3283 (10)	5.75	3.05

See Nos. 3311-3320.

A901

1990, Nov. 20   Litho.   Perf. 13
3284	A901	5c Boxing	.25	.25
3285	A901	30c Baseball	1.10	.25
3286	A901	50c Volleyball	1.90	.50
		Nos. 3284-3286 (3)	3.25	1.00

16th Central American and Caribbean Games, Mexico.

Butterflies A902

Designs: 2c, Chioides marmorosa. 3c, Composia fidelissima. 5c, Danaus plexippus. 10c, Hypolimnas misippus. 30c, Hypna iphigenia. 50c, Hemiargus ammon

1991, Jan. 25   Litho.   Perf. 12½
3287	A902	2c multicolored	.25	.25
3288	A902	3c multicolored	.25	.25
3289	A902	5c multicolored	.35	.25
3290	A902	10c multicolored	.50	.25
3291	A902	30c multicolored	1.40	.25
3292	A902	50c multicolored	2.25	.50
		Nos. 3287-3292 (6)	5.00	1.75

Jose Luis Guerra Aguiar (1914-1990), Director of Postal Museum — A903

1991, Feb. 17   Litho.   Perf. 12½
3293	A903	5c multicolored	.45	.25

A904

1991, Feb. 20
3294	A904	1c Long jump	.25	.25
3295	A904	2c Javelin	.25	.25
3296	A904	3c Field hockey	.25	.25
3297	A904	5c Weight lifting	.25	.25
3298	A904	40c Cycling	1.25	.35
3299	A904	50c Gymnastics	1.75	.50
		Nos. 3294-3299 (6)	4.00	1.85

Souvenir Sheet
3300	A904	1p Torchbearer	3.50	1.75

1992 Summer Olympics, Barcelona.

A905

1st Man in Space, 30th anniv.: 5c, Yuri Gagarin. No. 3302, Cosmonaut Y. Romanenko. No. 3303, Cosmonaut A. Tamayo Mendez. No. 3304, Mir space station. No. 3305, Mir space station, docked Soyuz, earth. 50c, Soviet space shuttle Buran.

1991, Apr. 12   Litho.   Perf. 13
3301	A905	5c multicolored	.25	.25
3302	A905	10c multicolored	.25	.25
3303	A905	10c multicolored	.25	.25
a.		Pair, #3302-3303	.40	.25
3304	A905	30c multicolored	1.00	.25
3305	A905	30c multicolored	1.00	.25
a.		Pair, #3304-3305	2.00	1.00
3306	A905	50c multicolored	1.60	.50
a.		Sheet of 6, #3301-3306	4.50	
		Nos. 3301-3306 (6)	4.35	1.75

Proclamation of the Socialist Revolution, 30th Anniv. — A906

Design: 50c, Ship, jet on fire.

1991, Apr. 19   Perf. 12½
3307	A906	5c multicolored	.25	.25
3308	A906	50c multicolored	1.60	.80

Bay of Pigs invasion, 30th anniv., No. 3308.

Stamp Day A907

Details from mural by R. Rodriguez Radillo: 30c, Rocket lift-off. 50c, Dish antenna, horiz.

1991, Apr. 24   Perf. 12½x13, 13x12½
3309	A907	30c multicolored	1.00	.30
3310	A907	50c multicolored	1.75	.40

11th Pan American Games Type of 1990

1991, May 15   Litho.   Perf. 12½
3311	A900	5c Volleyball	.25	.25
3312	A900	5c Rhythmic gymnastics	.25	.25
3313	A900	5c Synchronized swimming	.25	.25
3314	A900	5c Weight lifting	.25	.25
3315	A900	5c Baseball	.25	.25
3316	A900	10c Bowling	.25	.25
3317	A900	20c Boxing	.55	.25
3318	A900	30c Running	.85	.25
3319	A900	35c Wrestling	1.10	.30
3320	A900	50c Karate	1.50	.50
		Nos. 3311-3320 (10)	5.50	2.80

Nos. 3311-3315 & 3317 are vert.

Airships A908

Designs: 5c, First ellipsoidal, 1784, J.B.M. Meusnier. 10c, First with steam engine, 1852, H. Giffard. 20c, First with gas engine, 1872, P. Haenlein. 30c, First with gasoline engine, 1896, H. Wolfert. 50c, First rigid aluminum, 1897, D. Schwarz. 1p, LZ-129 Hindenburg, 1936, F. von Zeppelin.

1991, July 1   Litho.   Perf. 13
3321	A908	5c multicolored	.25	.25
3322	A908	10c multicolored	.35	.25
3323	A908	20c multicolored	.70	.30
3324	A908	30c multicolored	.90	.50
3325	A908	50c multicolored	1.60	.95
3326	A908	1p multicolored	3.25	1.60
		Nos. 3321-3326 (6)	7.05	3.85

Espamer '91, Buenos Aires, Argentina.

Simon Bolivar A909

1991, June 22   Litho.   Perf. 12½x13
3327	A909	50c multicolored	2.00	.60

Amphictyonic Cong. of Panama, 165th anniv.

Birds
A910

Designs: 45c, Melanerpes superciliaris. 50c, Myadestes elisabeth. 2p, Priotelus temnurus. 4p, Tiaris canora. 5p, Campephilus principalis. 10p, Amazona leucocephala, horiz. 16.45p, Mellisuga helenae, horiz.

1991, July 15   Perf. 12½x13, 13x12½

3328	A910	45c multicolored	1.25	.40
3329	A910	50c multicolored	1.50	.50
3330	A910	2p multicolored	5.25	2.00
3331	A910	4p multicolored	10.00	3.50
3332	A910	5p multicolored	12.50	4.25
3333	A910	10p multicolored	25.00	6.50
3334	A910	16.45p multicolored	40.00	13.00
		Nos. 3328-3334 (7)	95.50	30.15

Tourism — A911

Designs: No. 3335, Varadero Beach, vert. No. 3336, Cayo Largo, vert. No. 3337, Artillerymen at fortress San Carlos de la Cabana. No. 3338, Tres Reyes del Morro Castle.

1991, July 30

3335	A911	20c multicolored	.60	.25
3336	A911	20c multicolored	.60	.25
3337	A911	30c multicolored	1.00	.30
3338	A911	30c multicolored	1.00	.30
		Nos. 3335-3338 (4)	3.20	1.10

Panamfilex '91 — A912

11th Pan American Games venues: 5c, Pan American Stadium. 20c, Swimming venue. 30c, Multisports center. 50c, Velodrome. 1p, Havana City Coliseum and Sports Center.

1991, Aug. 4   Litho.   Perf. 12½

3339	A912	5c multicolored	.25	.25
3340	A912	20c multicolored	.60	.30
3341	A912	30c multicolored	.80	.30
3342	A912	50c multicolored	1.50	.90
		Nos. 3339-3342 (4)	3.15	1.95

Souvenir Sheet

3343	A912	1p multicolored	3.50	1.75

No. 3343 contains one 40x32mm stamp.

Paintings
A913

5c, Kataoka Dengoemon Takafusa, by Utagawa Kuniyoshi. 10c, Evening Walk, by Hosoda Eishi. 20c, Courtesans, by Torii Kiyonaga. 30c, Conversation, by Utamaro.

50c, Bridge at Inari-bashi, by Hiroshige. 1p, On the Terrace, by Kiyonaga.

1991, Sept. 9   Litho.   Perf. 12½x13

3344	A913	5c multicolored	.25	.25
3345	A913	10c multicolored	.35	.25
3346	A913	20c multicolored	.70	.30
3347	A913	30c multicolored	.90	.40
3348	A913	50c multicolored	1.60	.75
3349	A913	1p multicolored	3.25	1.75
		Nos. 3344-3349 (6)	7.05	3.70

Phila Nippon '91, Tokyo.

Souvenir Sheet

1992 Winter Olympics,
Albertville — A914

1991, Sept. 25   Litho.   Perf. 12½

3350	A914	1p multicolored	3.50	1.75

Cuban
Communist
Party, 4th
Congress
A915

1991, Oct. 10

3351	A915	5c shown	.25	.25
3352	A915	50c Congress symbol	1.75	.50

Discovery of America, 500th Anniv. (in 1992) — A916

Designs: 5c, Columbus, Vicente and Martin Pinzon. 20c, Santa Maria, Nina and Pinta.

1991, Oct. 12

3353	A916	5c multicolored	.25	.25
3354	A916	20c multicolored	1.25	.25

Jose
Marti
A917

1991, Oct. 15   Perf. 13x12½

3355	A917	50c multicolored	2.00	.40

Publication of "Simple Verses," cent.

Latin
American
History
A918

Stamps or musicians and instruments: No. 3356, Julian Aguirre, Argentina, charango. No. 3357, Eduardo Caba, Bolivia, antara. No. 3358, Chile #2. No. 3359, Heitor Villalobos, Brazil, resonator trumpet. No. 3360, Guillermo Uribe-Holguin, Colombia, drum. No. 3361, Miguel Failde, Cuba, claves. No. 3362, Enrique Soro, Chile, drum. No. 3363, Chile #57. No. 3364, Segundo L. Moreno, Ecuador, xylophone. No. 3365, Ricardo Castillo, Guatemala, marimba. No. 3366, Carlos Chavez, Mexico, guitar. No. 3367, Luis A. Delgadillo, Nicaragua, maracas. No. 3368, Chile #69. No. 3369, Alfredo De Saint-Malo, Panama, mejorana. No. 3370, Jose Asuncion Flores, Paraguay, harp. No. 3371, Daniel Alomia, Peru, flute. No. 3372, Juan Morell y Campos, Puerto Rico, cuatro. No. 3373, Chile #72. No. 3374, Eduardo Farini, Uruguay, drums. No. 3375, Juan V. Lecuna, Venezuela, cuatro, diff.

1991, Oct. 27   Perf. 13

3356	A918	1c multicolored	.25	.25
3357	A918	1c multicolored	.25	.25
3358	A918	1c multicolored	.25	.25
3359	A918	1c multicolored	.25	.25
3360	A918	1c multicolored	.25	.25
a.		Strip of 5, #3356-3360	1.00	.50
3361	A918	5c multicolored	.25	.25
3362	A918	5c multicolored	.25	.25
3363	A918	5c multicolored	.25	.25
3364	A918	5c multicolored	.25	.25
3365	A918	5c multicolored	.25	.25
a.		Strip of 5, #3361-3365	1.00	.50
3366	A918	10c multicolored	.40	.25
3367	A918	10c multicolored	.40	.25
3368	A918	10c multicolored	.40	.25
3369	A918	10c multicolored	.40	.25
3370	A918	10c multicolored	.40	.25
a.		Strip of 5, #3366-3370	2.00	1.00
3371	A918	20c multicolored	.80	.25
3372	A918	20c multicolored	.80	.25
3373	A918	20c multicolored	.80	.25
3374	A918	20c multicolored	.80	.25
3375	A918	20c multicolored	.80	.25
a.		Strip of 5, #3371-3375	4.00	2.00
b.		Sheet of 20, #3356-3375	8.00	
		Nos. 3356-3375 (20)	8.50	5.00

Discovery of America, 500th anniv. in 1992 (Nos. 3358, 3363, 3368, 3373).

Jose Marti
Pioneers
Organization,
1st Congress
A919

1991, Oct. 29

3376	A919	5c multicolored	.35	.25

Toussaint L'Ouverture (1743-1803) — A920

1991, Nov. 20   Perf. 12½x13

3377	A920	50c multicolored	2.00	.40

Haitian Revolution, Bicent.

Cuban Revolutionary Armed Forces,
35th Anniv. — A921

Design: 50c, Landing of the Granma expedition, 35th anniv., vert.

Perf. 12½x12, 12x12½

1991, Dec. 2   Litho.

3378	A921	5c multicolored	.25	.25
3379	A921	50c multicolored	1.75	.40

Gen. Ignacio Agramonte (1841-1873),
Revolutionary Hero — A922

1991, Dec. 23   Litho.   Perf. 12½x13

3380	A922	5c multicolored	.30	.25

Souvenir Sheet

1992 Winter Olympics,
Albertville — A923

1992, Jan. 15   Perf. 13

3381	A923	1p multicolored	3.50	1.75

1992 Summer Olympics,
Barcelona — A924

1992, Jan. 20   Litho.   Perf. 13x12½

3382	A924	3c Table tennis	.25	.25
3383	A924	5c Handball	.25	.25
3384	A924	10c Shooting	.30	.25
3385	A924	20c Long jump, vert.	.60	.25
3386	A924	35c Judo	1.25	.40
3387	A924	50c Fencing	1.60	.40
		Nos. 3382-3387 (6)	4.25	1.80

Souvenir Sheet

Perf. 12½

3388	A924	100c Rhythmic gymnastics, vert.	3.50	1.75

No. 3388 contains one 32x40mm stamp.

Environmental
Protection
A925

5c, Terraced hillsides. 20c, Save the whales. 35c, Ozone hole over Antarctica. 40c, Nuclear disarmament.

1992, Feb. 10   **Perf. 13**
3389	A925	5c multicolored	.25	.25
3390	A925	20c multicolored	.60	.25
3391	A925	35c multicolored	1.25	.40
3392	A925	40c multicolored	1.40	.40
		Nos. 3389-3392 (4)	3.50	1.30

Dogs
A926

5c, Boxer. 10c, Great dane. 20c, German shepherd. 30c, Various breeds. 35c, Doberman pinscher. 40c, Fox terrier. 50c, Poodle.
1p, Bichon frise, vert.

1992, Mar. 10 Litho.   **Perf. 13x12½**
3393	A926	5c multi	.25	.25
3394	A926	10c multi	.25	.25
3395	A926	20c multi	.65	.25
3396	A926	30c multi	1.10	.25
3397	A926	35c multi	1.10	.30
3398	A926	40c multi	1.40	.40
3399	A926	50c multi	1.75	.50
		Nos. 3393-3399 (7)	6.50	2.20

Souvenir Sheet
Perf. 12½
3400	A926	1p multi	4.00	2.00

No. 3400 contains one 32x40mm stamp. Nos. 3401-3404 will not be assigned.

Union of Young
Communists,
30th
Anniv. — A928

1992, Apr. 4 Litho.   **Perf. 13**
3405	A928	5c multicolored	.35	.25

Cuban Revolutionary Party,
Cent. — A929

1992, Apr. 10   **Perf. 13x12½**
3406	A929	5c multicolored	.25	.25
3407	A929	50c multicolored	1.75	.50

Discovery of America, 500th
Anniv. — A930

5c, Landing at Bariay. 20c, Landing at San Salvador.

1992, Apr. 14   **Perf. 12½**
3408	A930	5c multi	.25	.25
3409	A930	20c multi	.70	.25

Granada '92 Philatelic
Exhibition — A931

Views of the Alhambra, Granada: 5c, With Sierra Nevada mountains beyond. 10c, Arches at sunset. 20c, Interior architecture. 30c, Patio, fountain of lions. 35c, Bedroom. 50c, View of Albaicin.

1992, Apr. 17   **Perf. 13**
3410	A931	5c multicolored	.25	.25
3411	A931	10c multicolored	.25	.25
3412	A931	20c multicolored	.75	.25
3413	A931	30c multicolored	1.25	.25
3414	A931	35c multicolored	1.50	.40
3415	A931	50c multicolored	2.10	.50
		Nos. 3410-3415 (6)	6.10	1.90

La Bodeguita Del Medio Restaurant,
50th Anniv. — A932

1992, Apr. 26
3416	A932	50c multicolored	1.75	.50

Fish
A933

Designs: 5c, Holacanthus isabelita. 10c, Equetus lanceolatus. 20c, Acanthurus coeruleus. 30c, Abudefduf saxatilis. 50c, Microspathodon chrysurus.

1992, May 15 Litho.   **Perf. 12½**
3417	A933	5c multicolored	.25	.25
3418	A933	10c multicolored	.25	.25
3419	A933	20c multicolored	.65	.25
3420	A933	30c multicolored	1.10	.25
3421	A933	50c multicolored	1.90	.50
		Nos. 3417-3421 (5)	4.15	1.50

Orchids — A934

1992, June 20 Litho.   **Perf. 12½**
3422	A934	3c Cattleya hibrida	.25	.25
3423	A934	5c Phalaenopsis	.25	.25
3424	A934	10c Cattleyopsis lindenii	.25	.25
3425	A934	30c Bletia purpurea	1.00	.25
3426	A934	35c Oncidium luridum	1.10	.30
3427	A934	40c Vanda hibrida	1.40	.40
		Nos. 3422-3427 (6)	4.25	1.70

Soroa Orchid Garden, 40th anniv.

Mellisuga Helenae — A935

1992, July 7   **Perf. 13**
3428	A935	5c Sitting on nest	.40	.25
3429	A935	10c Wings extended	.60	.30
3430	A935	20c Sitting on branch	1.25	.40
3431	A935	30c In flight	2.00	1.00
		Nos. 3428-3431 (4)	4.25	1.95

World Wildlife Fund.

Tourism
A936

10c, Guardalavaca Beach. 20c, Bucanero Hotel. 30c, Sailing ship, Havana. 50c, Varadero Beach.

1992, July 15 Litho.   **Perf. 12½**
3432	A936	10c multicolored	.35	.25
3433	A936	20c multicolored	.60	.25
3434	A936	30c multicolored	1.10	.40
3435	A936	50c multicolored	1.50	.50
		Nos. 3432-3435 (4)	3.55	1.40

Souvenir Sheet

Expo '92, Seville — A937

1992, July 27 Litho.   **Perf. 13**
3436	A937	1.50p multicolored	4.50	2.25

1992
Summer
Olympics,
Barcelona
A938

Athlete, sport: 5c, Eligio (Kid Chocolate) Sardinas, boxing. 35c, Ramon Fonst, fencing. 40c, Sergio Martinez, cycling. 50c, Martin Dihigo, baseball.

1992, July 20 Litho.   **Perf. 12½x13**
3437	A938	5c multicolored	.25	.25
3438	A938	35c multicolored	1.10	.30
3439	A938	40c multicolored	1.25	.40
3440	A938	50c multicolored	1.75	.60
		Nos. 3437-3440 (4)	4.35	1.55

Olymphilex '92.

Discovery of America, 500th
Anniv. — A939

5c, Alvarez Cabral. 10c, Alonso Pinzon. 20c, Alonso de Ojeda. 30c, Amerigo Vespucci. 35c, Prince Henry the Navigator. 40c, Bartolomeu Dias. 1p, Columbus' fleet.

1992, Sept. 18 Litho.   **Perf. 12½**
3441	A939	5c multicolored	.25	.25
3442	A939	10c multicolored	.30	.25
3443	A939	20c multicolored	.70	.25
3444	A939	30c multicolored	1.10	.30
3445	A939	35c multicolored	1.25	.30
3446	A939	40c multicolored	1.50	.40
		Nos. 3441-3446 (6)	5.10	1.75

Souvenir Sheet
Perf. 13
3447	A939	1p multi, vert.	3.25	1.60

Genoa '92. No. 3447 contains one 32x40mm stamp.

1992 Summer Olympics Medal
Winners, Barcelona — A940

Medals and participants in events: No. 3448, Bronze, 4x100-meter relay, women's high jump, and women's 800-meter. No. 3449, Gold, high jump, women's discus. No. 3450, Silver, 4x400-meter relay, bronze, discus. No. 3451, Gold and silver, boxing. No. 3452, Gold, baseball. No. 3453, Gold, women's volleyball. No. 3454, Gold, silver, and bronze, judo. No. 3455, Gold and bronze, Greco-Roman and freestyle wrestling. No. 3456, Silver and bronze, fencing, silver, weight lifting.

1992, Sept. 24 Litho.   **Perf. 13**
3448	A940	5c multicolored	.25	.25
3449	A940	5c multicolored	.25	.25
3450	A940	5c multicolored	.25	.25
3451	A940	20c multicolored	.65	.25
3452	A940	20c multicolored	.65	.25
3453	A940	20c multicolored	.65	.25
3454	A940	50c multicolored	1.75	.50
3455	A940	50c multicolored	1.75	.50
3456	A940	50c multicolored	1.75	.50
		Nos. 3448-3456 (9)	7.95	3.00

6th
World
Track
and
Field
Cup,
Havana
A941

1992, Sept. 24 Litho.   **Perf. 13**
3457	A941	5c High jump	.25	.25
3458	A941	20c Javelin	.65	.25
3459	A941	30c Hammer throw	1.00	.25
3460	A941	40c Long jump, vert.	1.40	.40
3461	A941	50c Hurdles, vert.	1.75	.50
		Nos. 3457-3461 (5)	5.05	1.65

Souvenir Sheet
3462	A941	1p Women's relay	3.50	1.75

No. 3462 contains one 40x32mm stamp.

**Latin American History Type of
1986**

Discovery of America: No. 3463a, Columbus, Queen Isabella. b, Columbus at Rabida Monastery. c, Columbus, pointing up, outlining his plan. d, Columbus, with scroll, before Salamanca Council. e, Departure of Columbus' fleet from Palos.
No. 3464a, Three ships stopping at Canary Islands. b, Columbus speaking to crew. c, Land sighted, Oct. 12, 1492. d, Columbus landing in New World. e, Meeting natives.
No. 3465a, Grounding of Santa Maria at Hispanola. b, Arrival of Nina at Palos. c,

Columbus welcomed in Barcelona. d, Columbus describes his voyage to Ferdinand and Isabella. e, Departure of fleet from Cadiz on second voyage.

No. 3466a, King and Queen welcome Columbus. b, Fleet on Columbus' third voyage. c, Columbus deported from Hispanola to Spain as prisoner. d, Columbus on ship, fourth voyage. e, Death of Columbus, May 20, 1506 in Valladolid.

1992, Oct. 3   *Perf. 13*

3463	A804	1c Strip of 5, #a.-e.	.65	.30
3464	A804	5c Strip of 5, #a.-e.	.65	.30
3465	A804	10c Strip of 5, #a.-e.	1.25	.75
3466	A804	20c Strip of 5, #a.-e.	4.00	1.50
		Nos. 3463-3466 (4)	6.55	2.85

Jose Maria Chacon y Calvo (1892-1969), Historian A942

1992, Oct. 29   *Perf. 13*

3467	A942	30c multicolored	1.00	.40

Churches A943

Designs: 5c, Basilica of Nuestra Senora de la Caridad del Cobre. 20c, Santa Maria del Rosario Church. 30c, Espiritu Santo Church. 50c, Santo Angel Custodio Church.

1992, Nov. 10   *Litho.*   *Perf. 12½*

3468	A943	5c multicolored	.25	.25
3469	A943	20c multicolored	.75	.25
3470	A943	30c multicolored	1.00	.30
3471	A943	50c multicolored	2.00	.30
		Nos. 3468-3471 (4)	4.00	1.05

Development of the Diesel Engine — A944

1993, Jan. 20   *Litho.*   *Perf. 12½*

3472	A944	5c Truck	.25	.25
3473	A944	10c Automobile	.25	.25
3474	A944	30c Tugboat	.55	.40
3475	A944	40c Locomotive	2.50	1.25
3476	A944	50c Tractor	1.00	.65
		Nos. 3472-3476 (5)	4.55	2.80

Souvenir Sheet

3477	A944	1p Rudolf Diesel	3.50	1.75

No. 3477 contains one 40x32mm stamp. Rudolf Diesel, 80th anniv. of death (No. 3477).

Davis Cup Tennis Competition — A945

Various tennis players in action.

Perf. 12x12½, 12½x12

1993, Feb. 10   *Litho.*

3478	A945	5c multi, vert.	.25	.25
3479	A945	20c multi, vert.	.60	.25
3480	A945	30c multi, vert.	.90	.40

3481	A945	35c multicolored	1.00	.50
3482	A945	40c multicolored	1.25	.60
		Nos. 3478-3482 (5)	4.00	2.00

Souvenir Sheet
Perf. 12½

3483	A945	1p multicolored	2.50	1.25

No. 3483 contains one 40x32mm stamp.

Scientists A946

Designs: 3c, Pierre-Paul-Emile Roux (1853-1933), bacteriologist. 5c, Carlos J. Finlay (1833-1915), suggested mosquito as carrier of yellow fever. 10c, Ivan Petrovich Pavlov (1849-1936), physiologist, investigated conditioned reflexes. 20c, Louis Pasteur, chemist, developer of pasteurization. 30c, Santiago Ramon y Cajal (1852-1934), histologist, isolated the neuron. 35c, Sigmund Freud, psychoanalyst. 40c, Wilhelm Conrad Roentgen, physicist, discoverer of x-ray. 50c, Joseph Lister, surgeon, introduced principle of antisepsis. 1p, Robert Koch, bacteriologist, developer of tuberculin, vert.

1993, Mar. 3   *Litho.*   *Perf. 12½*

3484	A946	3c multicolored	.25	.25
3485	A946	5c multicolored	.25	.25
3486	A946	10c multicolored	.25	.25
3487	A946	20c multicolored	.55	.25
3488	A946	30c multicolored	.80	.40
3489	A946	35c multicolored	.90	.50
3490	A946	40c multicolored	1.10	.60
3491	A946	50c multicolored	1.25	.65
		Nos. 3484-3491 (8)	5.35	3.15

Souvenir Sheet

3492	A946	1p multicolored	2.75	1.40

Bicycles — A947

Bicycles designed by: 3c, Leonardo da Vinci, 15th cent. 5c, Karl Von Drais de Sauerbrun, 1813. 10c, Ernest Michaux, 1856. 20c, James Starley, 1869. 30c, Harry Lawson, 1879. 35c, Guaso (Cuba), 1992.

1993, Apr. 14   *Perf. 13*

3493	A947	3c multicolored	.25	.25
3494	A947	5c multicolored	.25	.25
3495	A947	10c multicolored	.45	.25
3496	A947	20c multicolored	.90	.25
3497	A947	30c multicolored	1.40	.40
3498	A947	35c multicolored	1.50	.50
		Nos. 3493-3498 (6)	4.75	1.90

Cuban Natl. Museum, 80th Anniv. A948

Paintings by Joaquin Sorolla y Bastida (1863-1923): 3c, Child Eating Watermelon, 1920, vert. 5c, Valencian Fisherwomen, 1909. 10c, Regattas. 20c, Contadina, 1889. 40c, Summer, 1904. 50c, Boats on the Ocean, 1908.

1993, May 29   *Litho.*   *Perf. 13x12½*

3499	A948	3c multicolored	.25	.25

Perf. 12½x13

3500	A948	5c multicolored	.30	.25
3501	A948	10c multicolored	.35	.25
3502	A948	20c multicolored	.65	.25
3503	A948	40c multicolored	1.25	.60
3504	A948	50c multicolored	1.75	.65
		Nos. 3499-3504 (6)	4.55	2.25

Water Birds A949

Designs: 3c, Jacana spinosa. 5c, Ardea herodias, vert. 10c, Himantopus mexicanus. 20c, Nycticorax nycticorax. 30c, Grus canadensis, vert. 50c, Aramus guarauna.

Perf. 12½, 13x12½ (5, 30c)

1993, June 15

3505	A949	3c multicolored	.25	.25
3506	A949	5c multicolored	.25	.25
3507	A949	10c multicolored	.40	.25
3508	A949	20c multicolored	.80	.25
3509	A949	30c multicolored	1.10	.40
3510	A949	50c multicolored	2.25	.65
		Nos. 3505-3510 (6)	5.05	2.05

Brasiliana '93. Nos. 3506, 3510 are 27x44mm.

Anniversaries — A950

No. 3511, Jose Marti, Moncada Barracks. No. 3512, "History Will Absolve Me," declaration of Fidel Castro, Marti. No. 3513, Jose Marti, Rafael M. Mendive, vert. No. 3514, Carlos Manuel de Cespedes, gear wheels.

1993, July 26   *Litho.*   *Perf. 13*

3511	A950	5c multicolored	.25	.25
3512	A950	5c multicolored	.25	.25
3513	A950	5c multicolored	.25	.25
3514	A950	5c multicolored	.25	.25
		Nos. 3511-3514 (4)	1.00	1.00

Attack on Moncada Barracks, 40th anniv. (No. 3511). Declaration of Fidel Castro, 40th anniv. (No. 3512). Birth of Jose Marti, 140th anniv. (No. 3513). Declaration of the Ten Years' War, 125th anniv. (No. 3514).

Flowers from Cienfuegos Botanical Gardens A951

Designs: 3c, Sedum allantoides. 5c, Heliconia caribaea. 10c, Anthurium andraeanum. 20c, Pseudobombax ellipticum. 35c, Ixora coccinea. 50c, Callistemon specious.

1993, Aug. 20

3515	A951	3c multicolored	.25	.25
3516	A951	5c multicolored	.25	.25
3517	A951	10c multicolored	.35	.25
3518	A951	20c multicolored	.70	.25
3519	A951	35c multicolored	1.10	.50
3520	A951	50c multicolored	1.90	.65
		Nos. 3515-3520 (6)	4.55	2.15

Bangkok '93, Intl. Philatelic Exhibition A952

Butterflies: 3c, Battus devillievs. 5c, Anteos maerula. 20c, Ascia monuste evonima. 30c, Junonia coenia. 35c, Anartia jatrophae guantanamo. 50c, Hypolimnas misippus.

1993, Sept. 10   *Litho.*   *Perf. 13*

3521	A952	3c multicolored	.25	.25
3522	A952	5c multicolored	.25	.25
3523	A952	20c multicolored	.70	.25
3524	A952	30c multicolored	1.00	.40
3525	A952	35c multicolored	1.10	.40
3526	A952	50c multicolored	1.60	.65
		Nos. 3521-3526 (6)	4.90	2.20

Endangered Species A953

5c, Phoenicopterus ruber. 50c, Ajaia ajaja.

1993, Oct. 12   *Litho.*   *Perf. 13*

3527	A953	5c multicolored	.25	.25
3528	A953	50c multicolored	1.75	.65

Latin American Revolutionaries A954

Flags, map and: No. 3529, Simon Bolivar. No. 3530, Jose Marti. No. 3531, Benito Juarez, Mexican President. No. 3532, Ernesto "Che" Guevara.

1993, Oct. 27   *Litho.*   *Perf. 13*

3529	A954	50c multicolored	1.40	.65
3530	A954	50c multicolored	1.40	.65
3531	A954	50c multicolored	1.40	.65
3532	A954	50c multicolored	1.40	.65
a.		Block of 4, #3529-3532	7.25	3.50
		Nos. 3529-3532 (4)	5.60	2.60

17th Central American and Caribbean Games, Ponce, Puerto Rico — A955

1993, Nov. 10   *Litho.*   *Perf. 12½*

3533	A955	5c Swimming	.25	.25
3534	A955	10c Pole vault	.25	.25
3535	A955	20c Boxing	.70	.25
3536	A955	35c Gymnastics, vert.	1.10	.40
3537	A955	50c Baseball, vert.	1.60	.65
		Nos. 3533-3537 (5)	3.90	1.80

Souvenir Sheet

3538	A955	1p Basketball	3.75	1.75

No. 3538 contains one 40x32mm stamp.

Mariana Grajales (1808-93), Patriot — A956

1993, Nov. 27   *Perf. 13*

3539	A956	5p multicolored	.30	.25

Peter I.
Tchaikovsky
(1840-93),
Composer
A957

1993, Nov. 30
3540	A957	5c Portrait	.25	.25
3541	A957	20c Swan Lake Ballet	.65	.25
3542	A957	30c Statue	.90	.40
3543	A957	50c Museum, horiz.	1.25	.65
		Nos. 3540-3543 (4)	3.05	1.55

A958

1994, Jan. 1   Litho.   Perf. 13
3544	A958	5c multicolored	.30	.25

35th anniv. of the Revolution.

A959

Various soccer players.

1994, Jan. 1
3545	A959	5c multicolored	.25	.25
3546	A959	20c multicolored	.60	.25
3547	A959	30c multicolored	.85	.40
3548	A959	35c multicolored	.95	.40
3549	A959	40c multicolored	1.25	.50
3550	A959	50c multicolored	1.40	.65
		Nos. 3545-3550 (6)	5.30	2.45

Souvenir Sheet
3551	A959	1p multicolored	3.00	1.50

1994 World Cup Soccer Championships,
US. No. 3551 contains one 40x31mm stamp.

Cats
A960

1994, Feb. 15   Litho.   Perf. 12½
3552	A960	5c Blue Persian	.25	.25
3553	A960	10c Havana	.25	.25
3554	A960	20c Maine coon	.70	.25
3555	A960	30c Blue British shorthair	1.00	.40
3556	A960	35c Bicolor Persian	1.10	.40
3557	A960	50c Gold chinchilla	1.60	.65
		Nos. 3552-3557 (6)	4.90	2.20

Souvenir Sheet
Perf. 13
3558	A960	1p Abyssinian, vert.	4.00	2.00

No. 3558 contains one 30x38mm stamp.

Medicinal
Plants — A961

Designs: 5c, Salvia officinalis. 10c, Aloe
barbadensis. 20c, Helianthus annuus. 30c,
Matricaria chamomilla. 40c, Calendula
officinalis. 50c, Tilia platyphyllos.

1994, Mar. 30   Litho.   Perf. 12½
3559	A961	5c multicolored	.25	.25
3560	A961	10c multicolored	.25	.25
3561	A961	20c multicolored	.65	.25
3562	A961	30c multicolored	.90	.40
3563	A961	40c multicolored	1.25	.50
3564	A961	50c multicolored	1.50	.65
		Nos. 3559-3564 (6)	4.80	2.30

Carriages — A962

Designs: 5c, Public coach, 1860. 10c,
Coach of Ferdinand VII, Maria Louisa. 30c,
Louis XV-style coach. 35c, Elizabeth II gala
day's coach. 40c, Catalina II's summer coach.
50c, Volanta habanera.

1994, Apr. 20   Perf. 12½x12
3565	A962	5c multicolored	.25	.25
3566	A962	10c multicolored	.25	.25
3567	A962	30c multicolored	1.00	.40
3568	A962	35c multicolored	1.10	.40
3569	A962	40c multicolored	1.40	.50
3570	A962	50c multicolored	1.60	.65
		Nos. 3565-3570 (6)	5.60	2.45

No. 3570 is 68x37mm.

Aquaculture — A963

Designs: 5c, Crassostrea rhizophorae. 20c,
Cardisoma guanhumi. 30c, Tilapia mela-
nopleura. 35c, Hippospongia lachne. 40c,
Panulirus argus. 50c, Cyprinus carpio.

1994, May 10   Litho.   Perf. 12½
3571	A963	5c multicolored	.35	.25
3572	A963	20c multicolored	.60	.25
3573	A963	30c multicolored	.85	.40
3574	A963	35c multicolored	1.00	.40
3575	A963	40c multicolored	1.25	.50
3576	A963	50c multicolored	1.50	.65
		Nos. 3571-3576 (6)	5.55	2.45

Intl. Olympic
Committee,
Cent. — A964

1994, June 23   Litho.   Perf. 12½
3577	A964	5c Flag, runners	.25	.25
3578	A964	30c Flag, world map	.85	.40
3579	A964	50c Flag, Olympic flame	1.50	.65
		Nos. 3577-3579 (3)	2.60	1.30

Scientists
A965

Designs: 5c, Michael Faraday (1791-1867),
physicist. 10c, Marie Curie (1867-1934), physical chemist. 20c, Pierre Curie (1859-1906),
chemist. 30c, Albert Einstein (1879-1955),
physicist, mathematician. 40c, Max Planck
(1858-1947), theoretical physicist. 50c, Otto
Hahn (1879-1968), physical chemist.

1994, July 20   Litho.   Perf. 12½
3580	A965	5c multicolored	.25	.25
3581	A965	10c multicolored	.25	.25
3582	A965	20c multicolored	.70	.25
3583	A965	30c multicolored	1.00	.40
3584	A965	40c multicolored	1.40	.50
3585	A965	50c multicolored	1.75	.65
		Nos. 3580-3585 (6)	5.35	2.30

Cactus
Flowers
A966

Designs: 5c, Opuntia dillenii. 10c, Opuntia
millspaughii, vert. 30c, Leptocereus
santamarinae. 35c, Pereskia marcanoi. 40c,
Dendrocereus nudiflorus, vert. 50c, Pilocereus
robinii.

1994, Aug. 15   Litho.   Perf. 12½
3586	A966	5c multicolored	.25	.25
3587	A966	10c multicolored	.30	.25
3588	A966	30c multicolored	1.00	.40
3589	A966	35c multicolored	1.10	.40
3590	A966	40c multicolored	1.50	.50
3591	A966	50c multicolored	1.75	.65
		Nos. 3586-3591 (6)	5.90	2.45

Souvenir Sheet

2nd Spanish-Cuban Philatelic
Exhibition, Havana — A967

Design: 1p, Cuban postal rocket, #C31.

1994, Sept. 18
3592	A967	1p multicolored	3.00	1.50

Experimental postal rocket flight, 55th anniv.

Dogs
A968

5c, Rough collie. 20c, American cocker
spaniel. 30c, Dalmatian. 40c, Afghan hound.
50c, English cocker spaniel.

1994, Sept. 20
3593	A968	5c multicolored	.25	.25
3594	A968	20c multicolored	.70	.25
3595	A968	30c multicolored	.95	.40
3596	A968	40c multicolored	1.40	.50
3597	A968	50c multicolored	1.60	.65
		Nos. 3593-3597 (5)	4.90	2.05

Cayo
Largo
Island
A969

Fauna: 15c, Carpilius corallinus. 65c,
Cyclura nubila, vert. 75c, Pelecanus
occidentalis. 1p, Chelonia mydas.

1994, Sept. 30   Litho.   Perf. 12½
3598	A969	15c multicolored	.30	.25
3599	A969	65c multicolored	1.50	.90
3600	A969	75c multicolored	1.75	1.00
3601	A969	1p multicolored	2.50	1.25
		Nos. 3598-3601 (4)	6.05	3.40

A970

1994, Oct. 28
3602	A970	15c multicolored	.50	.25

Camilo Cienfuegos Gorriaran, revolutionary,
35th anniv. of disappearance.

A971

Fauna of the Caribbean: 10c, Epinephelus
flavolimbatus, horiz. No. 3604, Phoenicopterus ruber. No. 3605, Aetobatus narinari.
No. 3606, Istiophorus platypterus, horiz. No.
3607, Tursiops truncatus, horiz. No. 3608,
Pelecanus occidentalis.

1994, Oct. 30
3603	A971	10c multicolored	.30	.25
3604	A971	15c multicolored	.30	.25
3605	A971	15c multicolored	.30	.25
3606	A971	15c multicolored	.30	.25
3607	A971	65c multicolored	1.75	.90
3608	A971	65c multicolored	1.75	.90
		Nos. 3603-3608 (6)	4.70	2.80

ICAO,
50th
Anniv.
A972

1994, Nov. 9
3609	A972	65c multicolored	1.75	.90

Zoological Garden, Havana, 55th Anniv. — A973

15c, Bronze monument. 65c, Ara chloroptera. 75c, Carduelis carduelis.

1994, Nov. 14   Litho.   Perf. 13
3610 A973 15c multicolored .25 .25
3611 A973 65c multicolored 1.40 .90
3612 A973 75c multicolored 1.60 1.00
Nos. 3610-3612 (3) 3.25 2.15

Cuban Philatelic Federation, 30th Anniv. — A974

1994, Nov. 20
3613 A974 15c multicolored .50 .25

America Issue — A975

Postal transportation: 15c, 18th Cent. Spanish galleon, maritime postal service, vert. 65c, 19th Cent. postal rider, insurgent postal service.

1994, Dec. 12
3614 A975 15c multicolored .25 .25
3615 A975 65c multicolored 1.75 .90

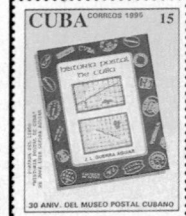

Postal Museum, 30th Anniv. — A976

1995, Jan. 2
3616 A976 15c multicolored .50 .25

Lizards — A977

Designs: 15c, Anolis baracoae. 65c, Sphaerodactylus ramsdeni. 75c, Leiocephalus raviceps. 85c, Sphaerodactylus ruibali. 90c, Anolis ophiolepis. 1p, Sphaerodactylus armasi.

1994, Nov. 30   Litho.   Perf. 12½
3617 A977 15c multicolored .30 .25
3618 A977 65c multicolored 1.60 .90
3619 A977 75c multicolored 1.75 1.00
3620 A977 85c multicolored 2.00 1.25
3621 A977 90c multicolored 2.25 1.25
3622 A977 1p multicolored 2.50 1.40
Nos. 3617-3622 (6) 10.40 6.05

Cuban War of Independence, Cent. — A978

1995, Feb. 24   Litho.   Perf. 12½
3623 A978 15c Jose Marti, flag .50 .25

Pan American Games, Mar del Plata, Argentina — A979

1995, Mar. 11   Litho.   Perf. 13
3624 A979 10c Boxing, vert. .25 .25
3625 A979 15c Weight lifting, vert. .25 .25
3626 A979 65c Volleyball, vert. 1.10 .80
3627 A979 75c Wrestling 1.25 1.00
3628 A979 85c Baseball 1.50 1.00
3629 A979 90c High jump 1.60 1.10
Nos. 3624-3629 (6) 5.95 4.40

National Aquarium, 35th Anniv. — A980

Fish: 10c, Holacanthus cillaris. 15c, Hypoplectrus guttavarius. 65c, Anisotremus virginicus. 75c, Amblycirrhitus pinos. 85c, Pomaacanthus paru. 90c, Acanthurus coeruleus.

1995, Apr. 28   Litho.   Perf. 13
3630 A980 10c multicolored .25 .25
3631 A980 15c multicolored .30 .25
3632 A980 65c multicolored 1.40 .70
3633 A980 75c multicolored 1.50 .80
3634 A980 85c multicolored 2.00 1.10
3635 A980 90c multicolored 2.00 1.10
Nos. 3630-3635 (6) 7.45 4.20

FAO, 50th Anniv. — A981

1995, Apr. 7   Litho.   Perf. 13
3636 A981 75c multicolored 1.40 1.00

First Cuban Postage Stamp, 140th Anniv. — A982

65c, Ornamental letter drop, envelope.

1995, Apr. 24   Litho.   Perf. 12½
3637 A982 15c blk & blue grn .30 .25
3638 A982 65c multicolored 1.40 .75

Jose Marti, Death Cent. — A983

Designs: 15c, Marti killed in combat, signature, portrait. 65c, Landing of Marti, Cuban patriots on Playitas beach. 75c, Montecristi Manifesto signed in Dominican Republic, Marti. 85c, Meeting of Marti, Maceo, Gomez at La Mejorana Farm. 90c, Marti's mausoleum, Santiago, Cuba, vert.

1995, May 19   Perf. 12½x13, 13x12½
3639 A983 15c multicolored .25 .25
3640 A983 65c multicolored 1.25 .80
3641 A983 75c multicolored 1.40 1.00
3642 A983 85c multicolored 1.75 1.00
3643 A983 90c multicolored 1.75 1.10
Nos. 3639-3643 (5) 6.40 4.15

Antonio Maceo (1845-96), Revolutionary — A984

1995, June 14   Litho.   Perf. 12½
3644 A984 15c multicolored .60 .25

Butterflies — A985

Designs: 10c, Dione vanillae. 15c, Eunica tatila. 65c, Melete salacia. 75c, Greta cubana. 85c, Eurema daira. 90c, Phoebis sennae.

1995, June 20   Perf. 12½x13
3645 A985 10c multicolored .25 .25
3646 A985 15c multicolored .25 .25
3647 A985 65c multicolored 1.25 .80
3648 A985 75c multicolored 1.40 1.00
3649 A985 85c multicolored 1.75 1.00
3650 A985 90c multicolored 1.75 1.10
Nos. 3645-3650 (6) 6.65 4.40

World War II Combat Planes — A986

Designs: 10c, Supermarine "Spitfire," Great Britain. 15c, IL-2, Russia. 65c, Curtiss P-40, US. 75c, Messerschmitt Bf-109, Germany. 85c, Morane-Saunier 406, France.

1995, July 30   Litho.   Perf. 12½
3651 A986 10c multicolored .30 .25
3652 A986 15c multicolored .30 .25
3653 A986 65c multicolored 1.40 .80
3654 A986 75c multicolored 1.60 1.00
3655 A986 85c multicolored 1.90 1.00
Nos. 3651-3655 (5) 5.50 3.30

A987

1995, Aug. 6   Litho.   Perf. 12½
3656 A987 15c multicolored .50 .25

Ernesto Lecuona, composer, pianist, birth cent.

A988

Color of Horse or Horses

1995, Aug. 10
3657 A988 10c golden brn, white .40 .25
3658 A988 15c white, horiz. .40 .25
3659 A988 65c dk brn, white 1.75 .80
3660 A988 75c red brown 2.10 1.00
3661 A988 85c tan 2.50 1.00
3662 A988 90c white 2.50 1.10
Nos. 3657-3662 (6) 9.65 4.40

Singapore '95.

Souvenir Sheet

Beijing Intl. Stamp & Coin Expo '95 — A989

1995, Aug. 28   Perf. 13
3663 A989 50c multicolored 1.25 .75

1996 Summer Olympics, Atlanta — A990

10c, Wrestling. 15c, Weight lifting. 65c, Women's volleyball. 75c, Women's athletics. 85c, Baseball. 90c, Women's judo. 1p, Boxing.

1995, Sept. 25   Litho.   Perf. 13
3664 A990 10c multicolored .25 .25
3665 A990 15c multicolored .25 .25
3666 A990 65c multicolored 1.10 .80
3667 A990 75c multicolored 1.25 1.00
3668 A990 85c multicolored 1.50 1.00
3669 A990 90c multicolored 1.60 1.10
Nos. 3664-3669 (6) 5.95 4.40

Souvenir Sheet
3670 A990 1p multicolored 3.00 1.50
No. 3670 contains one 30x36mm stamp.

Cuban Sugar Industry, 400th Anniv. A991

Paintings from "Los Ingenios," by Edouard Laplante, 1852: 15c, Steam train, sugar factory. 65c, Sugar factory, tower, bridge.

1995, Oct. 3
3671	A991	15c multicolored	1.75	.35
3672	A991	65c multicolored	1.00	.70

UN, 50th Anniv. A992

1995, Oct. 24 Litho. *Perf. 13*
3673	A992	65c multicolored	1.10	.80

Zoological Gardens, Havana — A993

Designs: 10c, Panthera leo, vert. 15c, Equus grevyi. 65c, Pongo pygmaeus, vert. 75c, Elephas maximus. 85c, Sciurus vulgaris. 90c, Procyon lotor.

1995, Oct. 30 Litho. *Perf. 13*
3674	A993	10c multicolored	.25	.25
3675	A993	15c multicolored	.30	.25
3676	A993	65c multicolored	1.25	.80
3677	A993	75c multicolored	1.50	1.00
3678	A993	85c multicolored	1.90	1.00
3679	A993	90c multicolored	2.10	1.10
		Nos. 3674-3679 (6)	7.30	4.40

UNESCO, 50th Anniv. — A994

UNESCO World Culture and National Heritage sites: 65c, Santa Clara de Asis Convent. 75c, San Francisco de Asis Minor Basilica.

1995, Nov. 4
3680	A994	65c multicolored	1.10	.80
3681	A994	75c multicolored	1.25	1.00

Orchids — A995

Designs: 5c, Epidendrum porpax. 10c, Cyrtopodium punctatum. 15c, Polyrrhiza lindeni. 40c, Bletia patula. 45c, Galeandra beyrichii. 50c, Vanilla dilloniana. 65c, Macradenia lutescens. 75c, Oncidium luridum. 85c, Ionopsis utricularioides.

1995, Nov. 10 *Perf. 12½*
3681A	A995	5c multicolored	.30	.25
3681B	A995	10c multicolored	.50	.25
3681C	A995	15c multicolored	.65	.25
3682	A995	40c multicolored	.80	.55
3683	A995	45c multicolored	.90	.55
3684	A995	50c multicolored	1.00	.65
3685	A995	65c multicolored	1.25	.80
3686	A995	75c multicolored	1.40	1.00
3687	A995	85c multicolored	1.75	1.00
		Nos. 3681A-3687 (9)	8.55	5.30

Issued: 40c-85c, 11/10/95; 5c-15c, 6/28/96.

Motion Pictures, Cent. — A996

1995, Dec. 7 *Perf. 13*
3688	A996	15c Lumiere Brothers	.30	.25
3689	A996	15c Marilyn Monroe	.30	.25
3690	A996	15c Marlene Dietrich	.30	.25
3691	A996	15c Vittorio DeSica	.30	.25
3692	A996	15c Charlie Chaplin	.30	.25
3693	A996	15c Greta Garbo	.30	.25
3694	A996	65c Humphrey Bogart	1.40	.80
3695	A996	75c Montaner	1.60	1.00
3696	A996	85c Cantinflas	1.90	1.00
		Nos. 3688-3696 (9)	6.70	4.30

Souvenir Sheet

4th Cuban-Spanish Philatelic Exhibition, Havana — A997

1995, Dec. 11 Litho. *Perf. 13*
3697	A997	1p multicolored	3.00	1.50

America Issue — A998

15c, Centurus superciliaris. 65c, Todus multicolor.

1995, Dec. 12
3698	A998	15c multicolored	.35	.25
3699	A998	65c multicolored	1.60	.80

Generals Who Died in 1895 War — A999

Designs: No. 3700, Alfonso Goulet Goulet, Francisco Adolfo Crombet Ballon. No. 3701, Jesus Calvar O, Jose Guillermo Moncada, Tomas Jordan. No. 3702, Francisco Borrero Lavadi, Francisco Inchaustegui Cabrera.

1995, Dec. 20 *Perf. 12½*
3700	A999	15c multicolored	.35	.25
3701	A999	15c multicolored	.35	.25
3702	A999	15c multicolored	.35	.25
a.		Strip of 3, #3700-3702	1.10	.90
		Nos. 3700-3702 (3)	1.05	.75

See Nos. 3758-3760.

Island of Coco Cay, Jardines del Rey A1000

Bird, scenic view: 10c, Sterna antillarum, aerial view of island. 15c, Eudocimus albus, people on beach. 45c, Spindalis zena, couple on steps of resort complex. 50c, Turdus plumbeus, resort. 65c, Mimus polyglottos, resort. 75c, Phoenicopterus ruber, couple in pool at resort.

1995, Dec. 23
3703	A1000	10c multicolored	.25	.25
3704	A1000	15c multicolored	.30	.25
3705	A1000	45c multicolored	1.00	.55
3706	A1000	50c multicolored	1.10	.60
3707	A1000	65c multicolored	1.40	.80
3708	A1000	75c multicolored	1.60	1.00
		Nos. 3703-3708 (6)	5.65	3.45

Patriots — A1001

Designs: 15c, Carlos M. de Céspedes (1819-74). 65c, José Marti (1853-95). 75c, Antonio Maceo (1845-96). 1.05p, Ignacio Agramonte (1841-73). 2.05p, Máximo Gómez (1836-1905). 3p, Calixto Garcia (1839-98).

1996, Jan. 10
3709	A1001	15c green	.25	.25
3710	A1001	65c blue	1.10	.80
3711	A1001	75c carmine	1.25	1.00
3712	A1001	1.05p lilac	1.90	1.40
3713	A1001	2.05p brown	3.75	2.50
3714	A1001	3p light brown	5.25	3.75
		Nos. 3709-3714 (6)	13.50	9.70

See Nos. 3755-3757.

Organization of Solidarity of the Peoples of Africa, Asia and Latin America (OSPAAAL), 30th Anniv. — A1002

1996, Jan. 14
3715	A1002	65c multicolored	1.50	.75

Scientists — A1003

10c, Leonardo da Vinci (1452-1519). 15c, Mikhail V. Lomonosov (1711-65), atmospheric scientist. 65c, James Watt (1736-1819), engineer, inventor. 75c, Guglielmo Marconi (1874-1937), physicist. 85c, Charles R. Darwin (1809-82), naturalist.

1996, Jan. 30 Litho. *Perf. 12½*
3716	A1003	10c multicolored	.35	.25
3717	A1003	15c multicolored	.35	.25
3718	A1003	65c multicolored	1.75	.80
3719	A1003	75c multicolored	2.00	1.00
3720	A1003	85c multicolored	2.25	1.00
		Nos. 3716-3720 (5)	6.70	3.30

1996 Summer Olympics, Atlanta — A1004

1996, Feb. 15 Litho. *Perf. 12½*
3721	A1004	10c Athletics, vert.	.30	.25
3722	A1004	15c Weight lifting, vert.	.30	.25
3723	A1004	15c Judo, vert.	1.40	.80
3724	A1004	75c Wrestling	1.60	1.00
3725	A1004	85c Boxing	1.90	1.00
		Nos. 3721-3725 (5)	5.50	3.30

Souvenir Sheet
3726	A1004	1p Baseball, vert.	3.00	1.50

No. 3726 contains one 40x32mm stamp.

Espamer '96, Aviation and Space, Philatelic Exhibition, Seville — A1005

1996, Mar. 4
3727	A1005	15c C-4 Autogiro	.25	.25
3728	A1005	65c CASA C-352	1.25	.80
3729	A1005	75c Alcotan C-201	1.60	1.00
3730	A1005	85c CASA C-212	1.75	1.00
		Nos. 3727-3730 (4)	4.85	3.05

Juan C. Gundlach (1810-1896), Ornithologist — A1006

Birds: 10c, Ceryle alcyon. 15c, Setophaga ruticilla. 65c, Geothlypis trichas. 75c, Passerina ciris. 85c, Bombycilla cedrorum. 1p, Vireo gundlachi.

1996, Mar. 15 *Perf. 12½*
3731	A1006	10c multicolored	.30	.25
3732	A1006	15c multicolored	.30	.25
3733	A1006	65c multicolored	1.40	.80
3734	A1006	75c multicolored	1.60	1.00
3735	A1006	85c multicolored	1.90	1.00
		Nos. 3731-3735 (5)	5.50	3.30

Souvenir Sheet
3736	A1006	1p multicolored	3.75	1.90

No. 3736 contains one 40x32mm stamp.

Souvenir Sheet

ESPAMER '96, Stamp Exhibition of America and Europe, Seville — A1007

1996, Mar. 14 Litho. *Perf. 12½*
3737	A1007	1p multicolored	3.00	1.50

First Man in Space, 35th Anniv. — A1008

Designs: 15c, Yuri A. Gagarin (1934-68). 65c, Spaceship, map showing orbital route.

1996, Apr. 12　Litho.　Perf. 12½
3738　A1008　15c multi　.25　.25
3739　A1008　65c multi, horiz.　1.10　.80

Bay of Pigs Invasion, 35th Anniv. — A1009

1996, Apr. 19
3740　A1009　15c shown　.35　.25
3741　A1009　65c Natl. flags　1.60　.80

Cuban Sailing Ships A1010

Designs: 10c, Bahama. 15c, Santísima Trinidad. 65c, Príncipe de Asturias. 75c, San Pedro de Alcántara. 85c, Santa Ana. 1p, San Genaro.

1996, May 8　Litho.　Perf. 12½
3742　A1010　10c multicolored　.25　.25
3743　A1010　15c multicolored　.30　.25
3744　A1010　65c multicolored　1.40　.80
3745　A1010　75c multicolored　1.60　1.00
3746　A1010　85c multicolored　1.75　1.00
　　Nos. 3742-3746 (5)　5.30　3.30

Souvenir Sheet

3747　A1010　1p multicolored　2.00　1.00

CAPEX '96. No. 3747 contains one 40x32mm stamp.

Fauna of the Caribbean A1011

Designs: 10c, Todus multicolor. No. 3749, Eulampis jugularis. No. 3750, Aix sponsa. No. 3751, Chaetodon ocellatus. No. 3752, Papilio cresphontes. No. 3753, Hypoplectrus indigo.

1996, June 18　Litho.　Perf. 12½
3748　A1011　10c multicolored　.30　.25
3749　A1011　10c multicolored　.30　.25
3750　A1011　15c multicolored　.30　.25
3751　A1011　15c multicolored　.30　.25
3752　A1011　65c multicolored　1.40　.80
3753　A1011　65c multicolored　1.40　.80
　　Nos. 3748-3753 (6)　4.00　2.60

Jose M. Maceo Grajales (1849-96), Revolutionary War Leader — A1012

1996, July 5
3754　A1012　15c multicolored　.50　.25

Patriot Type of 1996

Designs: 10c, Serafin Sánchez. 85c, Juan Gualberto Gomez. 90c, Quintin Bandera.

1996, July 10
3755　A1001　10c orange　.25　.25
3756　A1001　85c olive　1.75　1.00
3757　A1001　90c olive brown　2.00　1.10
　　Nos. 3755-3757 (3)　4.00　2.35

Generals Who Died in 1895 War Type of 1995

No. 3758, Esteban Tamayo (1843-96), Angel Guerra (1842-96). No. 3759, Juan Fernández Ruz (1821-96), José Maria Aguirre (1843-96), Serafin Sánchez (1846-96). No. 3760, Juan Bruno Zayas (1867-96), Pedro Vargas Sotomayor (1868-96).

1996, July 30
3758　A999　15c multicolored　.35　.25
3759　A999　15c multicolored　.35　.25
3760　A999　15c multicolored　.35　.25
　a.　　Strip of 3, #3758-3760　1.70　.90
　　Nos. 3758-3760 (3)　1.05　.75

Santiago de Cuba — A1013

Flower, scenic view: 15c, Jacaranda arborea, beach. 65c, Begonia bissei, Fort San Pedro de la Roca. 75c, Byrsonima crassifolia, palm trees, mountains, vert. 85c, Pereskia zinniiflora, church, vert.

Perf. 13x12½, 12½x13
1996, Sept. 27　Litho.
3761　A1013　15c multicolored　.30　.25
3762　A1013　65c multicolored　1.40　.80
3763　A1013　75c multicolored　1.60　1.00
3764　A1013　85c multicolored　1.75　1.00
　　Nos. 3761-3764 (4)　5.05　3.05

Steam Locomotives — A1014

Designs: 10c, Baldwin 0-4-2, 1878. 15c, American 2-6-0, 1904. 65c, Baldwin 4-6-0, 1906. 75c, Rogers 2-4-4, 1914. 90c, Baldwin 2-8-0, 1920.

1996, Sept. 30　Perf. 12½
3765　A1014　10c multicolored　.30　.25
3766　A1014　15c multicolored　.30　.25
3767　A1014　65c multicolored　1.40　.80
3768　A1014　75c multicolored　1.60　.90
3769　A1014　90c multicolored　1.75　1.00
　　Nos. 3765-3769 (5)　5.35　3.20

Traditional Costumes A1015

America Issue: 15c, Free black couple, 19th cent. 65c, Guayabera couple, 20th cent.

1996, Oct. 12　Litho.　Perf. 12½
3770　A1015　15c multicolored　.35　.25
3771　A1015　65c multicolored　1.60　.80

UNICEF, 50th Anniv. — A1016

1996, Nov. 8　Litho.　Perf. 12½
3772　A1016　15c multicolored　.50　.25

World Chess Championship Won by José Raúl Capablanca, 75th Anniv. — A1017

Designs: 15c, Portrait, chess board. 65c, Portrait, seated at chess board. 75c, Rook with top shaped as world, portrait. 85c, Playing chess as a child. 90c, In championship match, 1921.

1996, Nov. 30　Litho.　Perf. 12½
3773　A1017　15c multicolored　.25　.25
3774　A1017　65c multicolored　1.25　.80
3775　A1017　75c multicolored　1.40　1.00
3776　A1017　85c multicolored　1.60　1.00
3777　A1017　90c multicolored　1.75　1.10
　　Nos. 3773-3777 (5)　6.25　4.15

Revolutionary Armed Forces and Return of Castro from Mexico, 40th Anniv. — A1018

1996, Dec. 2
3778　A1018　15c Yacht Granma　.25　.25
3779　A1018　65c Armed forces　1.60　1.00

Maj. Gen. Antonio Maceo (1845-96) — A1019

Designs: 10c, Monument, Santiago, vert. No. 3781, Portrait, vert. No. 3782, Monument, Duaba. 65c, Detail of painting showing Maceo dying from combat wounds. 75c, Maceo, young man and monument, San Pedro.

1996, Dec. 7
3780　A1019　10c multicolored　.25　.25
3781　A1019　15c multicolored　.30　.25
3782　A1019　15c multicolored　.30　.25
3783　A1019　65c multicolored　1.60　1.10
3784　A1019　75c multicolored　1.90　1.40
　　Nos. 3780-3784 (5)　4.35　3.25

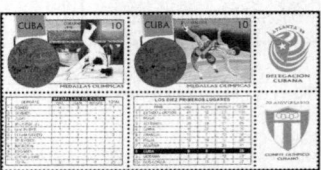

Medals Won at 1996 Summer Olympic Games, Atlanta — A1020

Medal, sport: No. 3785a, Gold, judo. b, Bronze, wrestling.
No. 3786: a, Gold, weight lifting. b, Gold, wrestling. c, Silver, fencing. d, Silver, swimming.
No. 3787: a, Gold, women's volleyball. b, Gold, boxing. c, Silver, women's running. d, Gold, baseball.

1996, Dec. 10
3785　A1020　10c Pair, #a-b + 4
　　　　labels　.50　.25
3786　A1020　15c Block, #a-d + 2
　　　　labels　1.25　.65
3787　A1020　65c Block, #a-d + 2
　　　　labels　5.00　2.50
　　Nos. 3785-3787 (3)　6.75　3.40

New Year 1996 (Year of the Rat) — A1021

1996, Dec. 28　Litho.　Perf. 12½
3788　A1021　15c multicolored　.50　.25

Espamer '98 — A1022

Locomotives: 15c, Minho Douro 0-6-0, Portugal. No. 3790, Vulcan Iron Works 0-4-0, Brazil. No. 3791, Baldwin 2-6-0, Dominican Republic. No. 3792, American Locomotive Co. 2-6-4, Panama. No. 3793, Baldwin 0-4-0, Puerto Rico. No. 3794, Slaughter, Gruning Co. 0-4-0, Spain. No. 3795, Yorkshire Engine Co. 4-4-0, Argentina. No. 3796, 2-6-0 Paraguay. No. 3797, H.K. Porter Co. 2-8-2, Chile. No. 3798, 2-6-0, Mexico.
1p, Baldwin 0-4-2 (1884), Cuba.

1996, Dec. 30
3789　A1022　15c multicolored　.30　.25
3790　A1022　65c multicolored　1.50　.85
3791　A1022　65c multicolored　1.50　.85
3792　A1022　65c multicolored　1.50　.85
3793　A1022　65c multicolored　1.50　.85
3794　A1022　65c multicolored　1.50　.85
3795　A1022　75c multicolored　1.75　1.00
3796　A1022　75c multicolored　1.75　1.00
3797　A1022　75c multicolored　1.75　1.00
3798　A1022　75c multicolored　1.75　1.00
　　Nos. 3789-3798 (10)　14.80　8.50

Souvenir Sheet

3799　A1022　1p multicolored　3.50　1.75

No. 3799 contains one 36x28mm.

Hong Kong '97, Intl. Philatelic Exhibition — A1023

Victory at Cuito Cuanavale, Angola, 10th Anniv. — A1060

1998, Mar. 23   Litho.   Perf. 12½
3911 A1060 15c multicolored   .65   .25

New Year 1998 (Year of the Tiger) — A1061

1998, Mar. 30
3912 A1061 15c multicolored   .65   .25

Dogs — A1062

1998, Apr. 15   Litho.   Perf. 12½
3913 A1062 10c Chihuahua   .40   .25
3914 A1062 15c Beagle   .45   .25
3915 A1062 15c Xoloitzcuintle   .45   .25
3916 A1062 65c German pointer   1.60 1.00
3917 A1062 75c Chow chow   1.90 1.25
Nos. 3913-3917 (5)   4.80 3.00

Evolution of the Chimpanzee A1063

Pan troglodytes and: 10c, Proconsul. No. 3919, Cranium. No. 3920, Right hand and foot. 65c, New-born chimpanzee. 75c, Map of Africa showing chimpanzee's range.

1998, May 15   Litho.   Perf. 12½
3918 A1063 10c multicolored   .40   .25
3919 A1063 10c multicolored   .40   .25
3920 A1063 15c multicolored   .40   .25
3921 A1063 65c multicolored   1.60 1.25
3922 A1063 75c multicolored   1.75 1.25
Nos. 3918-3922 (5)   4.55 3.25

Lisbon '98, World Stamp Exhibition — A1064

Deep sea fish: No. 3923, Raja batis. No. 3924, Eurypharynx pelecanoides. 65c, Caulophryne. 75c, Chauliodus sloani.

1998, May 22   Litho.   Perf. 12½
3923 A1064 15c multicolored   .40   .25
3924 A1064 15c multicolored   .40   .25
3925 A1064 65c multicolored   1.60 1.10
3926 A1064 75c multicolored   1.80 1.25
Nos. 3923-3926 (4)   4.20 2.85

Souvenir Sheet

Juvalux '98, World Stamp Exhibition for Youth Philately and Postal History, Luxembourg — A1065

1p, Postman on bicycle.

1998, May 20   Litho.   Perf. 12½
3927 A1065 1p multi   3.00 1.50

Federico Garcia Lorca (1898-1936), Poet — A1066

1998, June 2
3928 A1066 75c multicolored   2.25 1.25

Intl. Year of the Oceans A1067

No. 3929, Canarreos flower coral, coral crab, small fish. No. 3030, French angel fish, brain coral, gorgonia.

1998, June 5
3929 A1067 65c multicolored   1.50 1.00
3930 A1067 65c multicolored   1.50 1.00
a.   Pair, #3929-3930   3.50 1.75

Diana, Princess of Wales (1961-97) A1068

Various portraits, color of clothes: No. 3931, Pale yellow and pink. No. 3932, Black and white. No. 3933, Multicolored print. No. 3934, Red. No. 3935, Pink and black plaid. 65c, White. 75c, Blue.

1998, June 30   Litho.   Perf. 13
3931 A1068 10c multicolored   .30   .25
3932 A1068 10c multicolored   .30   .25
3933 A1068 10c multicolored   .30   .25
3934 A1068 15c multicolored   .40   .25
3935 A1068 15c multicolored   .40   .25
3936 A1068 65c multicolored   1.90 1.10
3937 A1068 75c multicolored   2.10 1.25
Nos. 3931-3937 (7)   5.70 3.60

Expo 2000, Hanover A1069

No. 3938, Mascot, "Twipsy." No. 3939, Mascot in London, 1851. No. 3940, Mascot in Brussels, 1958. No. 3941, German flag, map of Germany. 65c, Mascot in Paris, 1889. 75c, Mascot on top of world, fireworks.

1998, July 31   Perf. 12½
3938 A1069 15c multi, vert.   .40   .25
3939 A1069 15c multi   .40   .25
3940 A1069 15c multi   .40   .25
3941 A1069 15c multi   .40   .25
3942 A1069 65c multi, vert.   1.90 1.00
3943 A1069 75c multi   2.10 1.25
Nos. 3938-3943 (6)   5.60 3.25

Maracaibo '98, 18th Central America and Caribbean Games — A1070

1998, Aug. 8
3944 A1070 15c multicolored   .50   .25

Attack on Moncada Barracks, 45th Anniv. — A1071

Designs: 15c, Siboney farmhouse, Abel Santamaría. 65c, Barracks, José Marti.

1998, July 26   Litho.   Perf. 13
3945 A1071 15c multicolored   .40   .25
3946 A1071 65c multicolored   1.90   .95

Democratic Republic of Korea, 50th Anniv. — A1072

75c, Kim Il Sung (1912-94).

1998, Sept. 8   Litho.   Perf. 13
3947 A1072 75c multi   2.25 1.10

Japanese Immigration to Cuba, Cent. — A1073

1998, Sept. 9   Litho.   Perf. 13
3948 A1073 75c multicolored   2.25 1.10

Orchids A1074

10c, Coelogyne flaccida. No. 3950, Dendrobium fimbriatum. No. 3951, Arunding graminifolia. No. 3952, Bletia patula. No. 3953, Phaius tankervilliaea.

1998, Sept. 10
3949 A1074 10c multicolored   .30   .25
3950 A1074 15c multicolored   .50   .25
3951 A1074 15c multicolored   .50   .25
3952 A1074 65c multicolored   1.90 1.00
3953 A1074 65c multicolored   1.90 1.00
Nos. 3949-3953 (5)   5.10 2.75

5th Congress of the Revolution Defense Committees A1075

1998, Sept. 25   Litho.   Perf. 13
3954 A1075 15c multicolored   .45   .25

World Tourism Day — A1076

Holguin Province, reptiles: 10c, Looking through gateway, city of Gibara, anolis equestris, vert. 15c, Mayabe Valley, anolis vermiculatus, vert. 65c, Guardalavaca Beach, anolis allisoni. 75c, Mayari pine forest, anolis mestrei.

1998, Sept. 27
3955 A1076 10c multicolored   .30   .25
3956 A1076 15c multicolored   .50   .25
3957 A1076 65c multicolored   1.90   .95
3958 A1076 75c multicolored   2.10 1.25
Nos. 3955-3958 (4)   4.80 2.70

Women Who Aided Cuban Revolutionary Movements A1077

America Issue: 65c, Bernarda Toro Pelegrin (1852-1911). 75c, Maria Magdalena Cabrales Isaac (1842-1905).

1998, Oct. 12
3959 A1077 65c multicolored   1.90   .95
3960 A1077 75c multicolored   2.10 1.25

World Wildlife
Fund Protected
Fauna — A1078

Arantinga Euops: 10c, Two on tree branch.
15c, One looking out of nest. 65c, One on tree
branch. 75c, One up close.

1998, Oct. 21
3961	A1078	10c multicolored	.45	.30
3962	A1078	15c multicolored	.65	.50
3963	A1078	65c multicolored	2.75	.95
3964	A1078	75c multicolored	3.25	1.25
	Nos. 3961-3964 (4)		7.10	3.00

Cuban Natl.
Ballet, 50th
Anniv. — A1079

1998, Oct. 28
| 3965 | A1079 | 15c Swan Lake | .50 | .25 |
| 3966 | A1079 | 65c Giselle | 1.90 | .95 |

Massacre of O'Farrill and Goicuria,
40th Anniv. — A1080

Rogelio Perea, Angel Ameijeiras, Pedro
Gutiérrez.

1998, Nov. 8
| 3967 | A1080 | 15c multicolored | .45 | .25 |

Battle of
Guisa,
40th
Anniv.
A1081

Design: Capt. Braulio Coroneaux, tank.

1998, Nov. 30   Litho.   Perf. 12½
| 3968 | A1081 | 15c multicolored | .45 | .25 |

A1082

1998, Dec. 10   Litho.   Perf. 12½
| 3969 | A1082 | 65c multicolored | 1.90 | .95 |

Universal Declaration of Human Rights,
50th anniv.

A1083

Calixto Garcia Iñiguez (1839-98), revolutionary Major General.

1998, Dec. 11   Perf. 13
| 3970 | A1083 | 65c multicolored | 1.90 | .95 |

Padre Félix Varela (1788-
1853) — A1084

1998, Dec. 16
| 3971 | A1084 | 15c multicolored | 2.25 | 1.10 |

War for Independence, Cent. — A1085

War heroes, historical scene: No. 3972,
Carlos Manuel de Céspedes. No. 3973, Igna-
cio Agramonte. No. 3974, Máximo Gómez.
No. 3975, José Maceo. No. 3976, Salvador
Cisneros. No. 3977, Calixto Garcia. No. 3978,
Adolfo Flor. No. 3979, Serafin Sánchez. 65c,
José Marti. 75c, Antonio Maceo.

1998, Dec. 25   Litho.   Perf. 12½
3972	A1085	15c multicolored	.45	.25
3973	A1085	15c multicolored	.45	.25
3974	A1085	15c multicolored	.45	.25
3975	A1085	15c multicolored	.45	.25
3976	A1085	15c multicolored	.45	.25
3977	A1085	15c multicolored	.45	.25
3978	A1085	15c multicolored	.45	.25
3979	A1085	15c multicolored	.45	.25
3980	A1085	65c multicolored	1.90	.95
3981	A1085	75c multicolored	2.10	1.10
a.	Sheet of 10, #3972-3981 + 3 labels		8.00	8.00
	Nos. 3972-3981 (10)		7.60	4.05

Battle for
Palma
Soriano,
40th
Anniv.
A1086

1998, Dec. 27   Litho.   Perf. 13
| 3982 | A1086 | 15c multicolored | .45 | .25 |

Cuban Revolution, 40th
Anniv. — A1087

a, Boat, soldiers in water. b, Fidel Castro
with soldier. c, Castro giving speech, pigeons.

1999, Jan. 1
| 3983 | A1087 | 65c Strip of 3, #a.-c. | 4.75 | 2.40 |

Natl. Revolutionary Police, 40th
Anniv. — A1088

1999, Jan. 5
| 3984 | A1088 | 15c multicolored | .50 | .25 |

Cuban Workers'
Trade Union
Organization,
60th
Anniv. — A1089

1999, Jan. 28   Litho.   Perf. 12½
| 3985 | A1089 | 15c multicolored | .45 | .25 |

New Year 1999
(Year of the
Rabbit) — A1090

1999, Feb. 5   Perf. 13
| 3986 | A1090 | 75c multicolored | 1.60 | 1.10 |

Lenin (1870-1924) — A1091

1999, Feb. 21   Litho.   Perf. 12½
| 3987 | A1091 | 75c multicolored | 1.60 | 1.10 |

Dinosaurs — A1092

1999, Mar. 10
3988	A1092	10c Ornithosuchus	.30	.25
3989	A1092	15c Saltopus	.50	.25
3990	A1092	15c Bactrosaurus	.50	.25
3991	A1092	65c Protosuchus	1.90	.95
3992	A1092	75c Mussaurus	2.10	1.10
	Nos. 3988-3992 (5)		5.30	2.80

Cuban Musicians — A1093

No. 3993, Dámaso Pérez Prado. No. 3994,
Benny Moré. No. 3995, Chano Pozo. No.
3996, Miguelito Valdés. No. 3997, Bola de
Nieve. No. 3998, Rita Montaner.

1999, Mar. 22   Perf. 13
3993	A1093	5c multi	.25	.25
3994	A1093	15c multi	.50	.25
3995	A1093	15c multi	.50	.25
3996	A1093	35c multi	1.25	.25
3997	A1093	65c multi	1.90	.95
3998	A1093	75c multi	2.10	1.10
	Nos. 3993-3998 (6)		6.50	3.30

Simón Bolivar's
Visit to Cuba,
Bicent.
A1094

1999, Mar. 25
3999	A1094	65c Portrait	1.90	.95
4000	A1094	65c Monument	1.90	.95
a.	Pair, #3999-4000		4.25	2.00

State Security
Organization,
40th
Anniv. — A1095

1999, Mar. 26   Litho.   Perf. 12½
| 4001 | A1095 | 65c multicolored | 1.90 | .95 |

Souvenir Sheet

China '99 World Philatelic
Exhibition — A1096

1999, Apr. 10   Litho.   Perf. 12½
| 4002 | A1096 | 1p Giant panda | 3.00 | 1.50 |

Stamp
Day
A1097

1999, Apr. 24
| 4003 | A1097 | 15c Postal rocket | .50 | .25 |
| 4004 | A1097 | 65c Post rider | 1.90 | .80 |

Test of Cuban Postal Rocket, 60th anniv.
Insurgent Postal Service, 130th anniv.

Casa de las Américas, 40th
Anniv. — A1098

1999, Apr. 24
| 4005 | A1098 | 65c multicolored | 1.90 | .80 |

Souvenir Sheet

IBRA '99, World Philatelic Exhibition, Nuremberg — A1099

1999, Apr. 27
4006 A1099 1p Train   3.00 1.50

Agrarian Reform Law, 40th Anniv. A1100

1999, May 17
4007 A1100 65c multicolored   1.60 .80

Felipe Poey, Scientist, Birth Bicent. A1101

Fish: 5c, Gramma loreto Poey. 15c, Liopropoma rubre Poey. No. 4010, Hypoplectrus gummigutta. No. 4011, Stegastes dorsopunicans.
1p, Portrait of Poey, hypoplectrus guttavarius.

1999, May 26   Litho.   Perf. 12½
4008 A1101 5c multicolored   .25 .25
4009 A1101 15c multicolored   .40 .25
4010 A1101 65c multicolored   1.90 .80
4011 A1101 65c multicolored   1.90 .80
       Nos. 4008-4011 (4)   4.45 2.10

Souvenir Sheet
Perf. 13¼x13
4012 A1101 1p multicolored   3.00 1.00

No. 4012 contains one 32x40mm stamp.

Souvenir Sheet

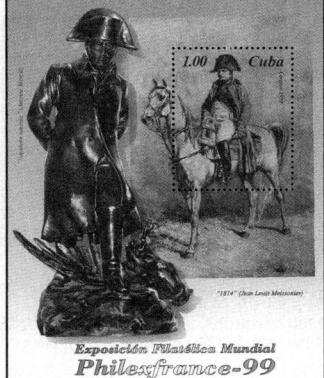

Philexfrance '99, World Philatelic Exhibition — A1102

Sculpture in sheet margin: "1814," by Jean Louis Meissonier (1815-1891).

1999, June 2   Perf. 13
4013 A1102 1p multicolored   3.00 1.50

1999 Pan-American Games, Winnipeg — A1103

1999, June 25   Litho.   Perf. 13
4014 A1103 15c Baseball   .40   .25
4015 A1103 65c Volleyball, vert 1.90 .80
4016 A1103 75c Boxing   2.10 .90
       Nos. 4014-4016 (3)   4.40 1.95

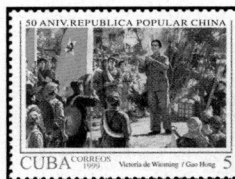

People's Republic of China, 50th Anniv. A1104

5c, Victory at Wioming, by Gao Hong. 15c, Nanchang Insurrection, by Cai Lang. 40c, Red Army Crossing a Swamp, by Gao Quan. 65c, Occupation of the Presidential Palace, by Cheng Yifei and Wei Jingshan. 75c, Proclamation of the People's Republic of China, by Dong Xiwen.

1999, Aug. 21   Litho.   Perf. 12¾
4017 A1104 5c multicolored   .25   .25
4018 A1104 15c multicolored   .40   .25
4019 A1104 40c multicolored   1.10   .70
4020 A1104 65c multicolored   1.75 1.10
4021 A1104 75c multicolored   2.00 1.40
       Nos. 4017-4021 (5)   5.50 3.70

China 1999 World Philatelic Exhibition, Beijing — A1105

No. 4022, Morning Glories, by Qi Baishi. No. 4023, Three Galloping Horses, by Xu Beihong. No. 4024, Hunan Woman, by Fu Baoshi. No. 4025, Birthplace of Luxun, by Wu Guanzhong. No. 4026, Horse Riders, by Huangzhou. 40c, Pine Tree, by He Xiangning. 65c, Sleep, by Jin Shangyi. 75c, Poetic Scene in Xun Yang, by Chen Yifei.

1999, Aug. 22   Litho.   Perf. 13
4022 A1105 5c multicolored   .25   .25
4023 A1105 5c multicolored   .25   .25
4024 A1105 15c multicolored   .40   .25
4025 A1105 15c multicolored   .40   .25
4026 A1105 15c multicolored   .40   .25
4027 A1105 40c multicolored   1.10   .70
4028 A1105 65c multicolored   1.75 1.10
4029 A1105 75c multicolored   2.00 1.25
 a.   Sheet of 8, #4022-4029 + label 8.00 8.00
       Nos. 4022-4029 (8)   6.55 4.30

UPU, 125th Anniv. A1106

1999, Sept. 16   Litho.   Perf. 12¾
4030 A1106 75c multicolored   1.50 1.00

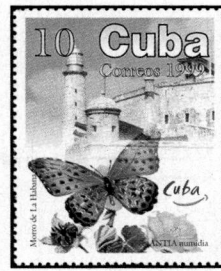

World Tourism Day A1107

Butterflies and Havana tourist sites: 10c, Antia numidia, Morro Castle. 15c, Papilio polyxenes, Havana Cathedral. 65c, Dryas julia, Convent of San Francisco. 75c, Eueides cleobaea, Capitol.

1999, Sept. 27   Perf. 12½x12¾
4031 A1107 10c multicolored   .25   .25
4032 A1107 15c multicolored   .40   .25
4033 A1107 65c multicolored   1.75 1.00
4034 A1107 75c multicolored   2.00 1.10
       Nos. 4031-4034 (4)   4.40 2.60

Expo 2000, Hanover, Germany A1108

5c, World map, Expo 2000 emblem. No. 4036, "Twipsy" mascot, vert. No. 4037, "Twipsy" and 1876 Philadelphia Exposition. No. 4038, "Twipsy" and 1970 Osaka Exposition. 65c, "Twipsy" and 2000 Exposition. 75c, "Twipsy" and 1967 Montreal Exposition.

1999, Oct. 1   Perf. 12¾
4035 A1108 5c multicolored   .25   .25
4036 A1108 15c multicolored   .35   .25
4037 A1108 15c multicolored   .35   .25
4038 A1108 15c multicolored   .35   .25
4039 A1108 65c multicolored   1.60 1.00
4040 A1108 75c multicolored   2.00 1.10
       Nos. 4035-4040 (6)   4.90 3.10

Cubana Airlines, 70th Anniv. — A1109

1999, Oct. 8   Perf. 12½x12¼
4041 A1109 15c Fokker   .35   .25
4042 A1109 15c DC-10   .35   .25
4043 A1109 65c A-320   1.60 1.00
4044 A1109 75c DC-3   2.00 1.10
       Nos. 4041-4044 (4)   4.30 2.60

America Issue, A New Millennium Without Arms — A1110

15c, Pigeon, mushroom cloud. 65c, Dove, globe.

1999, Oct. 12   Perf. 12¾
4045 A1110 15c multi   .40   .25
4046 A1110 65c multi   1.60 1.10

National Instiutions, 40th Anniv. — A1111

15c, MINFAR. 65c, Natl. Revolutionary Militia.

1999, Oct. 16   Perf. 12¾
4047 A1111 15c multi   .35   .25
4048 A1111 65c multi   1.50 1.00

Disappearance of Camilo Cienfuegos, 40th Anniv. — A1112

1999, Oct. 28   Litho.   Perf. 12¾
4049 A1112 15c multicolored   1.40 .25

Souvenir Sheet

12th Congress of Cuban Philatelic Federation — A1113

1999, Dec. 11   Perf. 13
4050 A1113 1p multicolored   2.50 1.25

Ernest Hemingway (1899-1961), Writer — A1114

1999, Dec. 15   Perf. 12½x12¼
4051 A1114 65c multicolored   1.50 1.00

9th Summit of Ibero-American Heads of State and Government, Havana — A1115

Designs: 65c, Plaza Vieja. 75c, Plaza of St. Francis of Assisi.
1p, Plaza de Armas.

1999, Nov. 5   Litho.   Perf. 12¾x12½
4052 A1115 65c multi   1.50 1.00
4053 A1115 75c multi   1.60 1.10

Souvenir Sheet
Perf. 13
4054 A1115 1p multi   2.50 1.25

No. 4054 contains one 40x31mm stamp.

Rubén Martínez Villena (1899-1934),
Revolutionary — A1116

1999, Dec. 20 **Perf. 12½x12¾**
4055 A1116 15c multi .40 .25

Dr. Tomás
Romay Chacón
(1764-1849)
A1117

1999, Dec. 21 **Perf. 13**
4056 A1117 65c multi 1.40 .90

New Year 2000 (Year of the
Dragon) — A1118

2000, Jan. 10 **Perf. 12½**
4057 A1118 15c multi .40 .25

Folklore
A1119

Paintings depicting Cuban folklore by Concepción Ferrant (1882-1968): 10c, Rumba Caliente. 15c, Cachumba. 65c, En Casa de un Babalao. 75c, Tata Cuñengue.

2000, Jan. 26 **Perf. 12½x12¾**
4058 A1119 10c multi .25 .25
4059 A1119 15c multi .35 .30
4060 A1119 65c multi 1.40 1.10
4061 A1119 75c multi 1.60 1.10
  Nos. 4058-4061 (4) 3.60 2.65

Butterflies — A1120

10c, Helcyra superba. No. 4063, Pantaporia punctata. No. 4064, Neptis themis. 65c, Curetis acuta. 75c, Chrysozephyrus ataxus.

2000, Feb. 25 **Perf. 12¾**
4062 A1120 10c multi .30 .25
4063 A1120 15c multi .40 .30
4064 A1120 15c multi .40 .30
4065 A1120 65c multi 1.60 1.25
4066 A1120 75c multi 1.90 1.40
  Nos. 4062-4066 (5) 4.60 3.50
  Bangkok 2000 Stamp Exhibition.

Group of 77 South Summit,
Havana — A1121

2000, Apr. 7 **Litho.** **Perf. 13x12½**
4067 A1121 75c multi 2.00 1.25

Lenin, 130th
Anniv. of
Birth — A1122

2000, Apr. 22 **Perf. 12¾**
4068 A1122 75c multi 2.00 1.25

Che
Guevara
in
Congo,
35th
Anniv.
A1123

2000, Apr. 24
4069 A1123 65c multi 1.75 1.10

Stamp
Day — A1124

Designs: 65c, Cuba #2, building. 90c, Airplane, cover, Jaime González, pilot of first experimental airmail flight in Cuba.

2000, Apr. 24
4070 A1124 65c multi 1.75 1.10
4071 A1124 90c multi 2.25 1.50

Capt. San Luis
(Eliseo Reyes),
Military Hero
(1940-67)
A1125

2000, Apr. 27
4072 A1125 65c multi 1.75 1.10

The
Stamp
Show
2000,
London
A1126

Locomotives: 5c, 1882 Baldwin 0-6-0. 10c, 1895 Baldwin 2-8-0. 15c, 1912 Baldwin 2-8-0. 65c, 1919 Alco 2-8-0. 75c, 1925 Alco 2-8-2. 1p, 1920 Henschel 2-6-0.

2000, May 5 **Perf. 12¾**
4073 A1126 5c multi .25 .25
4074 A1126 10c multi .30 .25
4075 A1126 15c multi .40 .30
4076 A1126 65c multi 1.60 1.10
4077 A1126 75c multi 1.90 1.25
  Nos. 4073-4077 (5) 4.45 3.15
Souvenir Sheet
Perf. 13
4078 A1126 1p multi 3.00 1.50
  No. 4078 contains one 40x32mm stamp.

WIPA 2000 Philatelic Exhibition,
Vienna — A1127

Airships of: 10c, Henri Giffard, 1852. 15c, Albert and Gaston Tissandier, 1883, vert. 50c, Charles Renard and Arthur Krebs, 1884. 65c, Pierre and Paul Lebaudy, 1903. 75c, August von Perseval, 1906. 1p, Ferdinand von Zeppelin.

Perf. 12½x12¼, 12¼x12½
2000, May 18
4079 A1127 10c multi .35 .25
4080 A1127 15c multi .50 .30
4081 A1127 50c multi 1.40 .90
4082 A1127 65c multi 1.90 1.10
4083 A1127 75c multi 2.10 1.25
  Nos. 4079-4083 (5) 6.25 3.80
Souvenir Sheet
Perf. 12½
4084 A1127 1p multi 3.00 1.50
  No. 4084 contains one 40x32mm stamp.

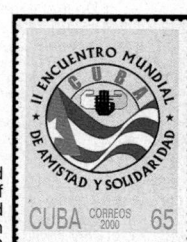

Second World
Meeting of
Friendship and
Solidarity With
Cuba — A1128

2000, June 23 **Litho.** **Perf. 12¾**
4085 A1128 65c multi 1.50 1.10

José de la Luz y Caballero (1800-62),
Educator — A1129

2000, July 11 **Perf. 12½x12¼**
4086 A1129 65c multi 1.50 1.10

Amadeo Roldan (1900-39),
Violinist — A1130

2000, July 12 **Perf. 12¾**
4087 A1130 65c multi 1.50 1.10

La Edad de
Oro, by José
Marti — A1131

5c, Bebé y El Señor Don Pomposo. 10c, La Muñeca Negra. 15c, Nene Traviesa. 50c, Los Dos Ruiseñores. 65c, Frontispiece of La Edad de Oro. 75c, El Camarón Encantado.

2000, July 20
4088-4093 A1131 Set of 6 6.00 4.25
4093a Sheet of 6, #4088-4093 6.00 6.00

Latin American Association for
Integration — A1132

2000, Aug. 12
4094 A1132 65c multi 1.75 1.25

Souvenir Sheet

Olymphilex 2000, Sydney — A1133

2000, Aug. 17 **Perf. 13**
4095 A1133 1p multi 2.25 1.10

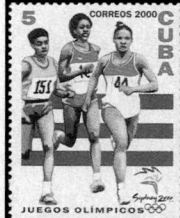

2000 Summer
Olympics,
Sydney
A1134

Designs: 5c, Runners. 15c, Soccer. 65c, Baseball. 75c, Cycling.

2000, Aug. 20 **Perf. 12¾**
4096-4099 A1134 Set of 4 4.50 4.00

Dr. Pedro Kouri Esmeja (1900-64) A1135

2000, Aug. 21   **Litho.**
4100 A1135 65c multi   1.75 1.25

Federation of Cuban Women, 40th Anniv. — A1136

2000, Aug. 23
4101 A1136 15c multi   .40 .30

España 2000 Intl. Philatelic Exhibition — A1137

Designs: 10c, 1851 Havana-Bilbao stampless cover, ship. No. 4103, 15c, Spain #1, Cibeles Fountain, Madrid. No. 4104, 15c, 1850 Zaragoza-Cadiz cover, Palacio de Cristal, Madrid. 65c, Spain #1-5, Palacio de Comunicaciones, Madrid. 75c, Cuba #1, Centro Gallego, Havana.

2000, Sept. 7   **Perf. 12¾x12½**
4102-4106 A1137   Set of 5   4.75 3.00
4106a   Sheet of 5, #4102-4106 + label   4.75 4.75

Souvenir Sheet
Perf. 12½
4107 A1137 100c Queen Isabella II, vert.   3.00 2.25

No. 4107 contains one 32x40mm stamp.

Beaches — A1138

No. 4108, Coconuts Bay, PRC. No. 4109, Varadero Beach, Cuba.

2000, Sept. 26   **Perf. 12½x12¼**
4108-4109 A1138 15c Set of 2   .80 .80
4109a   Pair, #4108-4109   .80 .80

See People's Republic of China No. 3052.

World Tourism Day A1139

Marine Life: 10c, Eretmochelys imbricata, vert. 15c, Epinephelus striatus, vert. 65c, Pomacanthus paru. 75c, Anisotremus surinamensis.

Perf. 12½x12¾, 12¾x12½
2000, Sept. 27
4110-4113 A1139 Set of 4   4.00 2.00

Committees of Defense of the Revolution, 40th Anniv. — A1140

2000, Sept. 28   **Perf. 12¾**
4114 A1140 15c multi   .40 .30

America Issue — AIDS Prevention A1141

Ribbon, heart-shaped map and: 15c, Family. 65c, Couple.

2000, Oct. 12
4115-4116 A1141 Set of 2   2.75 1.25

Cuban Military in Angola, 25th Anniv. — A1142

2000, Nov. 7
4117 A1142 75c multi   2.00 1.40

Visit by Alexander von Humboldt, Bicent. — A1143

Humboldt and: 15c, House in Trinidad. 65c, House in Havana, Political Essay on the Island of Cuba.

2000, Dec. 19   **Litho.**   **Perf. 12¾**
4118-4119 A1143 Set of 2   2.50 1.25

20th Pan-American Railway Congress A1144

2000, Sept. 18   **Litho.**   **Perf. 12¾**
4120 A1144 65c multi   1.75 1.25

Millennium — A1145

Snails: a, Polymita versicolor. b, Polymita picta iolimbata. c, Polymita picta roseolimbata. d, Polymita picta picta. e, Polymita picta nigrolimbata.

2000, Dec. 20
4121 A1145 65c Block of 5, #a-e, + label   8.00 4.00

New Year 2001 (Year of the Snake) — A1146

2001, Jan. 10
4122 A1146 15c multi   .50 .25

Hong Kong 2001 Stamp Exhibition — A1147

Birds: 5c, Aix galericulata. 10c, Chrysolophus pictus. 15c, Ardea cinerea. 65c, Gallus gallus. 75c, Streptotelia decaocto. 1p, Grus grus.

2001, Jan. 25   **Perf. 12¾**
4123-4127 A1147   Set of 5   4.50 3.25

Souvenir Sheet
Perf. 12½
4128 A1147 1p multi   3.00 1.25

No. 4128 contains one 32x40mm stamp.

National Institute for Sport Physical Education and Recreation, 40th Anniv. — A1148

2001, Feb. 23   **Perf. 12½x12¼**
4129 A1148 65c multi   1.60 .80

UN High Commissioner for Refugees, 50th Anniv. — A1149

2001, Mar. 15   **Perf. 12¾x12½**
4130 A1149 65c multi   1.50 .75

Antique Locomotives — A1150

Locomotives from, 10c, 1863. 15c, 1876. 40c, 1885. 65c, 1914. 75c, 1932.

2001, Mar. 20   **Perf. 12½x12¼**
4131-4135 A1150   Set of 5   4.75 2.40

105th Interparliamentary Union Congress, Havana — A1151

2001, Mar. 30   **Perf. 12¾**
4136 A1151 65c multi   1.75 .80

Bay of Pigs Invasion, 40th Anniv. — A1152

2001, Apr. 19   **Perf. 12¾x12½**
4137 A1152 65c multi   1.50 .75

Cats and Dogs A1153

Designs: 10c, Cats, emblem of Cat Aficionados Association. No. 4139, 15c, Dogs, Cats, emblem of Aniplant. No. 4140, 15c, Dogs, emblem of Cynological Federation of Cuba. 65c, Dogs, emblem of Sporting Dog Federation of Cuba. 75c, Dogs, cats.

2001, Apr. 25   **Perf. 12½x12¾**
4138-4142 A1153   Set of 5   4.00 2.00

Radio Havana, 40th Anniv. — A1154

2001, May 1 **Perf. 12½x12¼**
4143 A1154 65c multi 1.50 .75

Tourism Convention — A1155

2001, May 7 **Perf. 12¾x12½**
4144 A1155 65c multi 1.50 .75

Belgica 2001 Intl. Stamp Exhibition, Brussels A1156

Designs: 5c, St. Michel Cathedral. 10c, Sablon Church, horiz. 15c, Royal Residence, horiz. 65c, Sacred Heart Basilica, horiz. 75c, Atomium.
1p, Royal Palace.

2001, May 10 **Perf. 12¾**
4145-4149 A1156 Set of 5 4.00 2.00
Souvenir Sheet
Perf. 12½
4150 A1156 100c multi 2.40 1.25
No. 4150 contains one 32x40mm stamp.

Interior Ministry, 40th Anniv. A1157

2001, June 6 **Perf. 12¾**
4151 A1157 65c multi 1.75 .80

Phila Nippon '01, Japan A1158

Japanese trains: 5c., JR 500. 10c, JR 700. 15c, MAX 1. 65c, MAX 2. 75c, 300.

2001, June 20 **Litho.** **Perf. 12¾**
4152-4156 A1158 Set of 5 3.75 1.50
Souvenir Sheet
Perf. 12½
4157 A1158 100c Zero 2.40 1.25
No. 4157 contains one 40x32mm stamp.

Republic of San Marino, 1700th Anniv. — A1159

2001, July 20 Litho. **Perf. 12½x12¼**
4158 A1159 75c multi 1.75 .75

Aquaculture — A1160

Designs: 5c, Tinca tinca. 10c, Rana temporaria. 15c, Cardisoma guanhumi. 65c, Mytilus edulis. 75c, Tilapia mariae.
1p, Potamobius pallipes.

2001, Sept. 17 **Perf. 12¾**
4159-4163 A1160 Set of 5 3.75 1.50
Souvenir Sheet
Perf. 12½
4164 A1160 1p multi 2.40 1.25
No. 4164 contains one 40x32mm stamp.

Recovery of Raw Materials, 40th Anniv. — A1161

2001, Sept. 21 **Perf. 12¾x12½**
4165 A1161 65c multi 1.60 .75

Tourism — A1162

Designs: 10c, Valle de Viñales. 15c, Trinidad. 65c, Sirena Beach, Cayo Largo del Sur. 75c, Morro Castle, Havana.

2001, Sept. 27
4166-4169 A1162 Set of 4 3.75 1.75

Year of Dialogue Among Civilizations A1163

2001, Oct. 9 **Perf. 12¾**
4170 A1163 65c multi 1.50 .75

America Issue — UNESCO World Heritage A1164

Flora and fauna from Desembarco del Granma Natl. Park: 15c, Tetramicra malpighiarum. 65c, Liggus vittatus.

2001, Oct. 12 **Perf. 12½x12¾**
4171-4172 A1164 Set of 2 1.75 .85

José Marti National Library, Cent. A1165

2001, Oct. 18 **Perf. 12¾**
4173 A1165 15c multi .35 .25

Cuban Airliner Explosion Near Barbados, 25th Anniv. — A1166

Various details of painting.

2001, Oct. 22
4174 Horiz. strip of 5 3.25 1.60
a. A1166 5c shown .25 .25
b. A1166 10c multi .25 .25
c. A1166 15c multi .35 .25
d. A1166 50c multi 1.10 .55
e. A1166 65c multi 1.40 .90

Eduardo R. Chibas, Communist Leader, Cent. of Birth — A1167

2001, Nov. 27 **Litho.** **Perf. 13**
4175 A1167 65c multi 1.60 .80

Napoleonic Museum, 40th Anniv. — A1168

Equestrian statues of Napoleon and map of battle of: No. 4176, 10c, Eylau. No. 4177, 10c, Marengo. 65c, Waterloo. 75c, Aboukir.

2001, Dec. 1 **Perf. 12¾x12½**
4176-4179 A1168 Set of 4 3.75 1.75

Pablo de la Torriente Brau (1901-36), Writer — A1169

2001, Dec. 12 **Perf. 12¾**
4180 A1169 75c multi 1.75 .80

Cuban Federation of Pigeon Fanciers, 4th Congress A1170

Pigeons: No. 4181, 65c, Empedrado oscura 2021-61-ME. No. 4182, 65c, Empedrado claro 2241-55-ME. No. 4183, 65c, Mosaico 1561-66-HM. No. 4184, 65c, Mosaico, 3013-67-HM. No. 4185, 65c Bronceado, 338-59-HE.

2001, Dec. 14 **Perf. 12½**
4181-4185 A1170 Set of 5 7.00 3.50

Film Stars Who Never Won Academy Awards A1171

Designs: 5c, Tyrone Power. No. 4187, 10c, Ava Gardner. No. 4188, 10c, Steve McQueen. No. 4189, 15c, Rita Hayworth. No. 4190, 15c, Marilyn Monroe. No. 4191, 15c, James Dean. No. 4192, 65c, Rock Hudson. No. 4193, 65c, Natalie Wood. 75c, Richard Burton.

2001, Dec. 20
4186-4194 A1171 Set of 9 8.00 3.50
a. Sheet of 9, #4186-4194 8.00 3.50

New Year 2002 (Year of the Horse) — A1172

2002, Jan. 21 Litho. **Perf. 12½x12¾**
4195 A1172 15c multi .45 .30

Cigar Production — A1173

Cigars and: 5c, Hat, Cuba No. 358, tobacco leaf. 10c, Clock, cigar cylinder. 15c, Map of Cuba, Simon Bolivar. 65c, Cuba Nos. 356, 357, map, cigar smoker. 75c, Flag, tobacco field, man.

1p, Fidel Castro, map, star.

2002, Feb. 15   **Perf. 12¾**
4196-4200   A1173   Set of 5   4.00   2.00

Souvenir Sheet
Perf. 1313¼

4201   A1173   1p multi   2.50   1.25

Fourth Havana Festival, Cohiba brand, 36th anniv. No. 4201 contains one 40x32mm stamp.

Second UPAEP Information Workshop — A1174

2002, Feb. 21   **Perf. 12½x12¼**
4202   A1174   65c multi   1.50   .75

Explorers A1175

Explorers: 5c, Reading map. 15c, Tying knots. 50c, Starting campfire for cooking. 65c, Starting fire. 75c, Using orientation techniques.

2002, Mar. 20   **Perf. 12½**
4203-4207   A1175   Set of 5   5.00   2.50
   a.   Sheet of 5, #4203-4207, + label   7.00   3.50

Union of Young Communists, 40th Anniv. — A1176

2002, Apr. 4   **Perf. 12½x12¼**
4208   A1176   15c multi   .30   .25

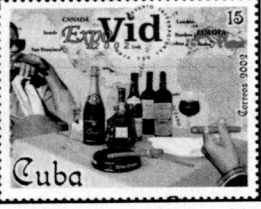

ExpoVid 2002 Wine Event — A1177

Designs: 15c, Cigar smokers, wine bottles and glasses, map of wine producing areas. 65c, Wine glass and barrels. 75c, Wine glass and vineyard.

2002, June 5   **Perf. 12¾x12½**
4209-4211   A1177   Set of 3   3.50   1.75

2002 World Cup Soccer Championships, Japan and Korea — A1178

Player and flag from: No. 4212, 15c, South Korea. No. 4213, 15c, France. No. 4214, 15c, Germany. No. 4215, 15c, Brazil. No. 4216, 15c, Spain. 65c, Argentina. 75c, Italy. 85c, Japan.

2002, Apr. 21   **Litho.**   **Perf. 12½**
4212-4219   A1178   Set of 8   6.50   3.25
  4219a   Sheet, #4212-4219   8.50   4.25

Souvenir Sheet

Hispano-Cubano Philatelic Exposition — A1179

2002, Apr. 27   **Perf. 13**
4220   A1179   1p multi   2.25   1.10

Juan Tomas Roig, Botanist, 125th Anniv. of Birth A1180

Designs: 5c, Bust of Roig, experimental agronomic station, Santiago de las Vegas. 10c, Bust and house of Roig. 15c, Roig, laboratory glassware and Nicotiana tabacum. 50c, Building, Allophyllum roiggi, and sculpture of Roig. 65c, Roig, laboratory glassware and botanical dictionary.

2002, May 10   **Perf. 12½x12¾**
4221-4225   A1180   Set of 5   3.25   1.50
  4225a   Sheet, #4221-4225, + label   5.00   2.40

Medi Cuba Suiza — A1181

2002, June 18   **Perf. 12¾x12½**
4226   A1181   75c multi   1.60   .80

Mushrooms A1182

Designs: 5c, Amanita junquillea. 15c, Lepiota puellaris. 45c, Cortinarius cumatilis. 65c, Pholliota adiposa. 75c, Coprinus comatus.

2002, June 20   **Perf. 12¾**
4227-4231   A1182   Set of 5   4.50   2.25
  4231a   Sheet, #4227-4231, + label   8.00   4.00

Nicolás Guillén (1902-89), Poet — A1183

2002, July 10   **Perf. 12¾x12½**
4232   A1183   65c multi   1.75   .90

Dockers, By Marcelo Pogolotti (1902-88) A1184

2002, July 12   **Perf. 12¾**
4233   A1184   15c multi   .50   .30

Agostinho Neto (1922-79), Pres. of Angola — A1185

2002, Sept. 17   **Perf. 12¾x12½**
4234   A1185   65c multi   1.75   .90

España 2002 Youth Philatelic Exposition, Salamanca — A1186

Birds: 5c, Calidris minutilla. 10c, Tringa melanoleucas. 15c, Charadius semipalmatus. 65c, Pluvialis squatarola. 75c, Arenaria interpres.

1p, Porzana carolina.

2002, Sept. 20   **Perf. 12½x12¼**
4235-4239   A1186   Set of 5   4.75   2.25
  4239a   Sheet, #4235-4239, + label   8.00   4.00

Souvenir Sheet
Perf. 13

4240   A1186   1p multi   2.50   1.25

No. 4240 contains one 40x31mm stamp.

Third Intl. Meeting of War Correspondents — A1187

2002, Oct. 7   **Perf. 12¾**
4241   A1187   65c multi   1.75   .90

Ernesto "Che" Guevara (1928-67), Revolutionary Leader — A1188

Various depictions of Guevara: 5c, 10c, 15c, 50c, 65c, 75c.

2002, Oct. 8   **Litho.**
4242-4247   A1188   Set of 6   5.25   2.75
  4247a   Sheet, #4242-4247   30.00   6.00

America Issue — Youth, Education and Literacy — A1189

Designs: 15c, Emblem of Literacy Army, man with book, teacher with student. 65c, Building, flag, children at computer.

2002, Oct. 12   **Perf. 12½x12¼**
4248-4249   A1189   Set of 2   2.00   1.00

Old Automobiles — A1190

Designs: No. 4250, 5c, 1956 Pontiac Catalina. No. 4251, 5c, 1957 Mercury Monterrey. 15c, 1959 Cadillac Fleetwood. 65c, Hudson Hornet. 75c, 1957 Chevrolet Bel Air. 85c, 1957 Mercedes-Benz 190SL.

2002, Oct. 19   **Perf. 12¾**
4250-4255   A1190   Set of 6   6.00   3.50
  a.   Sheet, #4250-4255, + 6 labels   16.00   4.00

15th Intercontinental Baseball Cup — A1191

Baseball players: 5c, G. Mesa. 15c, A. Pacheco. 50c, O. Linares. 65c, O. Kindelan. 75c, L. Ulacia.

2002, Nov. 1
4256-4260   A1191   Set of 5   5.00   3.00
  4260a   Sheet of 5, #4256-4260 + 4 labels   15.00   4.75

20th Havana Intl. Fair — A1192

2002, Nov. 3
4261   A1192   65c multi   1.75   .90

Railroads, 165th Anniv. — A1193

Designs: 5c, Rocket. 15c, Miller. 50c, Vulcan. 65c, Consolidation. 75c, Mikado.

2002, Nov. 12   **Perf. 12½x12¼**
4262-4266 A1193   Set of 5   5.00 3.00
4266a   Sheet, #4262-4266, + label   15.00 3.75

Camagüey Ballet, 35th Anniv. — A1194

Designs: 65c, Twelve dancers. 75c, Two dancers.

2002, Dec. 1   **Perf. 12¾**
4267-4268 A1194   Set of 2   3.50 2.00

Pan-American Health Organization, Cent. — A1195

2002, Dec. 2
4269 A1195 65c multi   1.50 .90

Paintings of Wilfredo Lam (1902-82) A1196

Designs: 15c, Emi Cosinca, 1950. 45c, Yo Soy, 1949. 65c, Retrado de H.H., 1941-42. 75c, Mujer Sentada, 1951.

2002, Dec. 8   **Perf. 12¾**
4270-4273 A1196   Set of 4   5.00 3.00
4273a   Sheet, #4270-4273, + 4 labels   14.00 3.00

Dulce M. Loynaz (1902-97), Writer A1197

      Perf. 12½x12¾
2002, Dec. 19   **Litho.**
4274 A1197 65c multi   1.50 .90

Souvenir Sheet

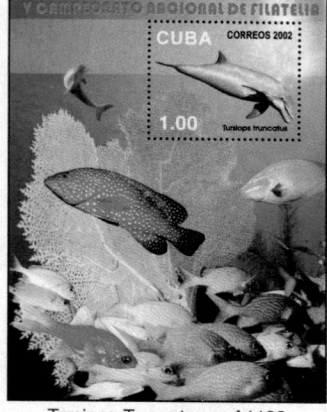

Tursiops Truncatus — A1198

2002, Dec. 20   **Perf. 12½**
4275 A1198 1p multi   3.00 1.50
Fifth National Philatelic Competition.

Prehistoric and Modern-Day Animals — A1199

Designs: 5c, Megaloceros, Cervus elaphus. 10c, Theropithecus, Papio anubis. 15c, Coelodonta, Diceros bicornis. 45c, Canis dirus, Canis lupus. 65c, Ursus spelaeus, Ursus arctos. 75c, Smilodon, Panthera leo. 1p, Mammuthus primigenius.

2002, Dec. 27   **Perf. 12½x12¼**
4276-4281 A1199   Set of 6   5.00 2.00
     Souvenir Sheet
      Perf. 13
4282 A1199 1p multi   2.75 1.10
No. 4282 contains one 40x32mm stamp.

New Year 2003 (Year of the Ram) A1200

Ram with background in: No. 4283, 15c, Green. No. 4284, 15c, Red.

2003, Jan. 6   **Perf. 12½**
4283-4284 A1200   Set of 2   .80 .40

San Alejandro Academy for Arts, 185th Anniv. — A1201

Paintings by: 5c, Amelia Pelaez. 15c, René Portocarrero. 65c, Mario Carreña, horiz. 75c, Servando Cabrera.

2003, Jan. 12   **Perf. 12¾**
4285-4288 A1201   Set of 4   4.00 2.00

José Martí (1853-95), Patriot — A1202

Designs: 15c, Birthplace. No. 4290, 65c, Martí and text. No. 4291, 65c, Martí, sky and text, horiz. 75c, Portrait. 1p, Martí, horiz.

2003, Jan. 28   **Perf. 12¾**
4289-4292 A1202   Set of 4   5.00 2.50
     Souvenir Sheet
      Perf. 12½
4293 A1202 1p multi   2.75 1.40
No. 4293 contains one 40x32mm stamp.

Arrival of Europeans at Havana, 510th Anniv. — A1203

Various Cuban stamps and: No. 4294, 15c, Woman with Cigar boxes, map of Cuba (diamond-shaped). No. 4295, 15c, Men at table holding cigars and drinks (diamond-shaped). 50c, Tobacco farmer, field, hands rolling cigar. 65c, Building, Trinidad. 75c, Cigar, building, palm tree, people in room. 1p, Indian lighting cigar, vert.

2003, Feb. 6   **Perf. 12½**
4294-4298 A1203   Set of 5   5.00 2.50
     Souvenir Sheet
4299 A1203 1p multi   2.75 1.40
No. 4299 contains one 32x40mm stamp.

Radio Rebelde, 45th Anniv. A1204

2003, Feb. 13   **Perf. 12¾**
4300 A1204 65c multi   1.50 .85

Félix Varela (1788-1853), Priest — A1205

2003, Feb. 25   **Perf. 12½**
4301 A1205 65c multi   1.50 .85

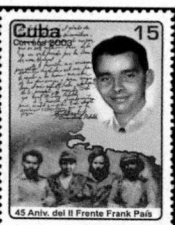

Military Units, 45th Anniv. — A1206

Designs: No. 4302, 15c, 2nd Frank Pais Front. No. 4303, 15c, 3rd Mario Muñoz Front.

2003   **Perf. 12¾**
4302-4303 A1206   Set of 2   1.10 .55
   Issued: No. 4302, 3/5; No. 4303, 3/11.

16th World Sexology Congress A1207

2003, Mar. 11
4304 A1207 65c multi   1.50 .85

Transportation and Shipping — A1208

Designs: 5c, Container ship. 10c, Truck. 15c, Train. 65c, Airplane and delivery van. 75c, Airplane and delivery van, diff.

2003, Apr. 10   **Perf. 12½**
4305-4309 A1208   Set of 5   4.00 2.00

Flora & Fauna — A1209

Designs: 5c, Nymphaea ampla, Lepisosteus tristoechus. 10c, Magnolia grandiflora, Spindalis zena pretrei. 15c, Lilium candidum, Polymita picta. 65c, Strelitzia regiae, Solenodon cubanus. 75c, Hibiscus rosasinensis, Mellisuga helenae.

2003, May 15
4310-4314 A1209   Set of 5   4.00 2.00

Pan American Games, Santo Domingo, Dominican Republic A1210

Designs: 5c, Kayaking. 15c, Judo. 50c, Track. 65c, Volleyball.

2003, June 27   **Perf. 12½x12¾**
4315-4318 A1210   Set of 4   3.00 1.50

Attack on Moncada Barracks, 50th Anniv. — A1211

Designs: 15c, Men and barracks. 65c, Fidel Castro, text.

2003, July 26   **Perf. 12¾**
4319-4320   A1211   Set of 2   1.75   .75

Railroads
A1212

Designs: 5c, Three-wheeled handcar, 1930-35. 10c, Crane, 1920. 15c, B-B 120/120 E locomotive, 1925. 65c, DVM-9 Ganz Mavag locomotive, 1969. 75c, 2-6-0 locomotive, 1905.

2003, Aug. 7
4321-4325   A1212   Set of 5   4.00 2.00

UN Conference to Combat
Desertification — A1213

2003, Aug. 25   **Perf. 12½x12¼**
4326   A1213   65c multi   1.50   .85

Expo Bangkok
A1214

Wildlife: 5c, Nyctea scandiaca. 10c, Fratercula arctica. 15c, Sula bassana. 65c, Ursus maritimus. 75c, Alopex lagopus. 1p, Pagophilus groenlandicus.

2003, Aug. 28   **Perf. 12¾**
4327-4331   A1214   Set of 5   4.00 2.00
     Souvenir Sheet
     Perf. 12½
4332   A1214   1p multi   2.75 1.40
No. 4332 contains one 32x40mm stamp.

Butterflies and Flowers — A1215

Designs: 5c, Dione juno, Gardenia jasminoides. 15c, Apatura ilia, Chrysanthemum sinence. 65c, Inachis io, Hibiscus rosasinensis. 75c, Marpesia iole, Althaea rosea. 1p, Danaus plexippus, Zantedeschia aethiopica, vert.

2003, Sept. 11   **Litho.**   **Perf. 12½**
4333-4336   A1215   Set of 4   4.00 2.00
     Souvenir Sheet
4337   A1215   1p multi   2.75 1.40
No. 4337 contains one 32x40mm stamp.

Ecotourism — A1216

Bird and location: 10c, Aratinga eops, Baracoa. 15c, Xiphidiopicus percussus, Valle de los Ingenios. 65c, Tiaris canora, Sierra Maestra. 75c, Priotelus temnurus, Granma.

2003, Sept. 27   **Perf. 12¾x12½**
4338-4341   A1216   Set of 4   4.00 2.00

Worldwide Fund for Nature
(WWF) — A1217

Crocodylus rhombifer: No. 4342, 15c, Eggs and hatchling. No. 4343, 15c, Adult at water's edge. 65c, Capturing prey. 75c, With open mouth.

2003, Sept. 30   **Litho.**   **Perf. 12¾**
4342-4345   A1217   Set of 4   5.00 2.50
4345a   Sheet, 4 each #4342-4345   20.00 12.50

America Issue
— Flora and
Fauna — A1218

Designs: 15c, Xiphidiopicus percussus. 65c, Encyclia phoenicea.

2003, Oct. 12
4346-4347   A1218   Set of 2   1.75   .85

35th Baseball World Cup — A1219

Cuban players: 5c, Antonio Muñoz. 10c, Lourdes Gourriel. No. 4350, 15c, Jorge L. Valdes. No. 4351, 15c, Lazaro Vargas. 65c, Lazaro Valle. 75c, Javier Mendez. 1p, Players celebrating, vert.

2003, Oct. 17   **Perf. 12½x12¼**
4348-4353   A1219   Set of 6   4.50 2.25
     Souvenir Sheet
     Perf. 12½
4354   A1219   1p multi   2.75 1.40
No. 4354 contains one 32x40mm stamp.

Ballet — A1220

Designs: No. 4355, 65c, National Ballet of Cuba, 55th anniv. No. 4356, 65c, Alicia Alonso as Giselle, 60th anniv., vert.

     Perf. 12¾x12½, 12½x12¾
2003, Oct. 28
4355-4356   A1220   Set of 2   3.00 1.50

Powered Flight, Cent. — A1221

Emblem and: 5c, Wright Brothers. 15c, Pitcairn PA-5. 65c, Stearman C-3MB. 75c, Douglas M-2.

2003, Dec. 17   **Perf. 12½x12¼**
4357-4360   A1221   Set of 4   4.00 2.00

Cuban
Revolution, 45th
Anniv. — A1222

2004, Jan. 1   **Perf. 12¾**
4361   A1222   65c multi   1.50   .85

Expocuba, 15th Anniv. — A1223

2004, Jan. 4   **Perf. 12½x12¼**
4362   A1223   65c multi   1.50   .85

2004 Summer Olympics,
Athens — A1224

Sports: 10c, Baseball. 15c, (No. 4363A), Track. 65c, Boxing. 75c, Equestrian.

2004, Jan. 6   **Litho.**
4363-4365   A1224   Set of 4   3.75 1.90

New Year 2004
(Year of the
Monkey)
A1225

Monkey with denomination in: No. 4366, 15c, Blue. No. 4367, 15c, Orange.

2004, Jan. 9   **Perf. 12¾**
4366-4367   A1225   Set of 2   1.00   .50

Julio A. Mella
(1903-29),
Communist
Leader
A1226

2004, Jan. 10
4368   A1226   65c multi   1.50 1.10

José Martí (1853-95) — A1227

Designs: No. 4369, 5c, Martí in 1862, Colegio San Pablo, Prado No. 88. No. 4370, 5c, Martí's father, Mariano, Tapineria No. 16, Valencia. No. 4371, 5c, Martí's mother, Leonor Pérez, birthplace, Paula No. 41. No. 4372, 10c, Martí's high school, 1862, Martí, Fermín Valdés Domínguez, 1869. No. 4373, 10c, Martí in 1869, Havana Royal Jail. No. 4374, 15c, Martí in 1870, El Abra farm, Isle of Pines. No. 4375, 15c, Martí in 1870, Martí Forge. No. 4376, 15c, Martí and son, José Francisco, 1879, Guanabacoa Lyceum. 65c, Martí and son, 1879, Mercaderes Law Offices. 75c, Martí in 1895, La Jatía farm, Oriente.

2004, Jan. 28   **Perf. 12½x12¼**
4369-4378   A1227   Set of 10   4.75 2.75
See Nos. 4525-4535, 4570-4578, 4691-4700, 4800-4807.

Town of Santa María de Puerto del
Principe, 490th Anniv. — A1228

2004, Feb. 2   **Perf. 12¾x12½**
4379   A1228   15c multi   .50   .25

Trolleys
A1229

Designs: 5c, Santiago. 10c, Havana. 15c, Camagüey. 65c, Matanzas. 75c, Camagüey, diff. 1p, Havana, diff.

2004, Feb. 20   **Perf. 12¾**
4380-4384   A1229   Set of 5   3.75 1.90
     Souvenir Sheet
     Perf. 12½
4385   A1229   1p multi   2.50 1.25
No. 4385 contains one 40x32mm stamp.

Souvenir Sheet

Cuba — Mexico Binational Philatelic Exhibition — A1230

| 2004, Feb. 25 | | **Perf. 12½** |
| 4386 | A1230 1p multi | 2.50 1.25 |

EGREM Recording Co., 40th Anniv. — A1231

Recording artists: 10c, Cascarita, Julio Cuevas. 15c, Carlos Puebla. 65c, Benny Moré. 75c, Compay Segundo.

| 2004, Mar. 24 | | **Perf. 12¾** |
| 4387-4390 | A1231 Set of 4 | 3.50 1.75 |

España 2004 Intl. Philatelic Exhibition — A1232

Dogs: 5c, Spanish pointer. 10c, Spanish hound. 15c, Mallorquin bulldog. 65c, Catalan sheepdog. 75c, Pyrenean mastiff. 1p, Spanish mastiff.

2004, Mar. 24		**Perf. 12½x12¼**
4391-4395	A1232 Set of 5	3.75 1.90
Souvenir Sheet		
Perf. 12½		
4396	A1232 1p multi	2.50 1.25

No. 4396 contains one 40x32mm stamp.

National Police, 45th Anniv. — A1233

| 2004, Mar. 26 | | **Perf. 12½x12¼** |
| 4397 | A1233 15c multi + label | .35 .25 |

Souvenir Sheet

Second Cuban Sports Olympiad — A1234

| 2004, Apr. 18 | | **Perf. 12½** |
| 4398 | A1234 1p multi | 2.50 1.25 |

Nature and Man Foundation, 10th Anniv. — A1235

| 2004, May 16 | **Litho.** | **Perf. 12¼x12½** |
| 4399 | A1235 65c multi | 1.50 .75 |

FIFA (Fédération Internationale de Football Association), Cent. — A1236

FIFA emblem and various players: 10c, 15c, 65c, 75c.

| 2004, May 21 | | **Perf. 12¾** |
| 4400-4403 | A1236 Set of 4 | 3.50 1.75 |

Pets A1237

Designs: 5c, Parakeets. 10c, Fish. 15c, Dogs. 65c, Cats. 75c, Finches. 1p, Horse, horiz.

2004, June 25		**Perf. 12½x12¾**
4404-4408	A1237 Set of 5	3.75 1.90
Souvenir Sheet		
Perf. 12½		
4409	A1237 1p multi	2.50 1.25

No. 4409 contains one 40x32mm stamp.

Intl. Chess Federation, 80th Anniv. — A1238

Chess players: 15c, Maria Teresa Mora. 65c, José Raúl Capablanca, horiz. 75c, Ernesto "Che" Guevara.

| 2004, July 20 | | **Perf. 12¾** |
| 4410-4412 | A1238 Set of 3 | 3.50 1.75 |

Minerals — A1239

Designs: 5c, Corundum. 10c, Thenardite. 15c, Uraninite. 65c, Realgar. 75c, Fluorite. 1p, Copper.

2004, July 30		**Perf. 13**
4413-4417	A1239 Set of 5	3.50 1.75
Souvenir Sheet		
Perf. 12½		
4418	A1239 1p multi	2.50 1.25

No. 4418 contains one 40x32mm stamp.

Convention Hall, 25th Anniv. — A1240

| 2004, Sept. 3 | | **Perf. 12¾** |
| 4419 | A1240 65c multi | 1.50 1.25 |

Cuban Aviation, 75th Anniv. — A1241

Designs: 15c, Lockheed Constellation. 65c, IL-62M. 75c, Airbus 330.

| 2004, Oct. 8 | | **Perf. 12½x12¼** |
| 4420-4422 | A1241 Set of 3 | 3.50 1.75 |

America Issue — A1242

Map of Cuba and: 15c, Bird over islands. 65c, Fish and marine life.

| 2004, Oct. 12 | | |
| 4423-4424 | A1242 Set of 2 | 1.75 .90 |

Marine Mammals — A1243

Designs: 5c, Delphinus delphis. 10c, Lagenorhynchus obliquidens. 15c, Stenella attenuata. 65c, Grampus griseus. 75c, Tursiops truncatus. 1p, Orcinus orca.

| 2004, Oct. 20 | | **Perf. 12½x12¼** |
| 4425-4429 | A1243 Set of 5 | 3.50 1.75 |

Souvenir Sheet
Perf. 13

| 4430 | A1243 1p multi | 2.50 1.25 |

No. 4430 contains one 40x32mm stamp.

Disappearance of Camilo Cienfuegos, 45th Anniv. A1244

| 2004, Oct. 28 | | **Perf. 12¾** |
| 4431 | A1244 65c multi | 1.50 .75 |

Railroad Stations, Cent. — A1245

Designs: 15c, Agramonte Station, 1906 ALCO No. 48 4-6-0. 65c, Aguacate Station, 1907 BLW No. 57 4-6-0. 75c, Guira de Melina Station, 1903 ALCO No. 7 4-4-0.

| 2004, Nov. 10 | | **Perf. 13** |
| 4432-4434 | A1245 Set of 3 | 3.50 1.75 |

Souvenir Sheet

13th Philatelic Congress, Havana — A1245a

| 2004, Nov. 20 | **Litho.** | **Perf. 12½** |
| 4434A | A1245a 1p multi | 2.25 2.25 |

Founding of San Cristóbal de la Habana, 485th Anniv. A1246

Designs: 15c, Temple. 65c, Painting showing priest in red vestments at base of tree. 75c, Paintig showing group of men at base of tree.

Perf. 12½x12¾

| 2004, Nov. 30 | | **Litho.** |
| 4435-4437 | A1246 Set of 3 | 3.00 1.50 |

Latin American Parliament Foundation, 40th Anniv. — A1246a

2004, Nov. 30   Litho.   Perf. 12¾
4437A A1246a 65c multi   1.40 .70

Ministry of Foreign Affairs, 45th Anniv. — A1247

2004, Dec. 23   Perf. 12½x12¼
4438 A1247 65c multi   1.40 .70

Alejo Carpentier (1904-80), Writer — A1248

2004, Dec. 26   Perf. 12¾
4439 A1248 65c multi   1.40 .70

First Baseball Game in Cuba, 130th Anniv. — A1249

Baseball players: 5c, Rey Vicente Anglada. 10c, Braudilio Vinent. 15c, Rogelio Garcia. 65c, Luis G. Casanova. 75c, Victor Mesa. 1p, Martin Dihigo, vert.

2004, Dec. 27   Perf. 12½x12¼
4440-4444 A1249   Set of 5   5.25 2.50
Souvenir Sheet
Perf. 12½
4445 A1249 1p multi   2.25 1.10
No. 4445 contains one 32x40mm stamp.

Jose L. Guerra Aguiar Cuban Postal Museum, 40th Anniv. — A1250

Designs: 15c, Plaza Mayor, Trinidad and 1855 Trinidad to Barcelona cover. 65c, Charity Sanctuary, El Cobre and 1861 El Cobre to Santiago de Cuba cover. 85c, Matanzas Cathedral, Matanzas and 1848 Mantanzas to Havana cover.

2005, Jan. 2   Perf. 12¾x12½
4446-4448 A1250   Set of 3   3.50 1.75

New Year 2005 (Year of the Rooster) A1251

Designs: No. 4449, 15c, Rooster in air. No. 4450, 15c, Rooster on ground.

2005, Jan. 4   Perf. 12¼x12½
4449-4450 A1251   Set of 2   .60 .30

Ministry of Information Technology and Communications, 5th Anniv. — A1252

2005, Jan. 12   Perf. 12½x12¼
4451 A1252 65c multi   1.40 .70

Dinosaurs — A1253

Designs: 5c, Carnotaurus. 10c, Oviraptor. 30c, Parasaurolophus. 65c, Sauropelta. 90c, Iguanodon. 1p, Velociraptor.

2005, Jan. 20 Litho. Perf. 12½x12¼
4452-4456 A1253   Set of 5   4.25 2.10
Souvenir Sheet
Perf. 13
4457 A1253 1p multi   2.25 1.10
No. 4457 contains one 40x32mm stamp.

Miguel de Cervantes and Title Page of *Don Quixote* — A1254

2005, Jan. 24   Perf. 12¾x12½
4458 A1254 65c multi   1.40 .70
Publication of *Don Quixote*, 400th anniv.

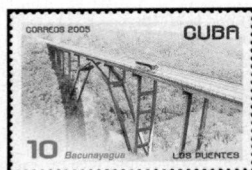

Bridges A1255

Designs: 10c, Bacunayagua Bridge. 15c, La Concordia Bridge. 50c, El Triunfo Bridge. 65c, Yayabo Bridge. 75c, Canimar Bridge. 1p, Plaza Bridge.

2005, Feb. 5   Perf. 13x12¾
4459-4463 A1255   Set of 5   4.75 2.40

Souvenir Sheet
Perf. 13
4464 A1255 1p multi   2.25 1.10
No. 4464 contains one 40x32mm stamp.

Cuban Telecommunications Enterprise, 10th Anniv. — A1256

2005, Feb. 24   Perf. 12½x12¾
4465 A1256 90c multi   1.90 .95

Parrots — A1257

Designs: 5c, Amazona ochrocephala, Amazona leucocephala. 10c, Agapornis personata, Agapornis fischeri. 15c, Cacatua galerita, Cacatua leadbeateri. 65c, Psittacula krameri, Psittacula himalayana, vert. 1.05p, Aratinga guarouba, Aratinga euops. 1p, Ara macao, Ara araruana, Anodorhynchus hyacythus.

Perf. 12½x12¼, 12¼x12½
2005, Feb. 23   Litho.
4466-4470 A1257   Set of 5   4.25 2.10
Souvenir Sheet
Perf. 13
4471 A1257 1p multi   2.25 1.10
No. 4471 contain one 32x40mm stamp.

Cats A1258

Various cats: 5c, 10c, 40c, 65c, 75c. 10c is vert.

2005, Mar. 15   Perf. 12¾
4472-4476 A1258   Set of 5   4.25 2.10
Perf. 13
4477 A1258 1p Two cats, vert.   2.25 1.10
No. 4477 contains one 32x40mm stamp.

Cuba — Canada Diplomatic Relations, 60th Anniv. — A1259

2005, Mar. 20   Perf. 12¾x12½
4478 A1259 65c multi   1.40 .70

Wildlife — A1260

2005, Mar. 21   Perf. 12½x12¼
4479 A1260 15c Manatee   .30 .25
4480 A1260 65c Parrot   1.40 .70
4481 A1260 75c Crocodile   1.50 .75
4482 A1260 90c Hummingbird   1.90 .95
Nos. 4479-4482 (4)   5.10 2.65

World Water Day — A1261

2005, Mar. 22   Perf. 13
4483 A1261 90c multi   1.90 .95

Boats — A1262

Designs: 10c, Fishing boat, fish. 20c, Schooner, fish. 30c, Bonito boat, bonito. 45c, Shrimp boat, shrimp. 90c, Lobster boat, lobster. 1p, Cargo ship, horiz.

2005, Apr. 15   Perf. 12½
4484-4488 A1262   Set of 5   4.25 2.10
Souvenir Sheet
4489 A1262 1p multi   2.25 1.10

First Cuban Postage Stamps, 150th Anniv. — A1263

Designs: 15c, St. Francis of Assisi Convent, Cuba #1. 65c, Morro Lighthouse, Cuba #2. 75c, Colonial Post Office, Cuba #3.

2005, Apr. 24   Perf. 12¾x12½
4490-4492 A1263   Set of 3   3.50 1.75

Social Security For All — A1264

2005, May 5   Litho.
4493 A1264 65c multi   1.40 .70

Major General Máximo Gómez (1836-1905) — A1265

2005, June 17   *Perf. 12½*
4494 A1265 1.05p multi   2.25 1.10

Souvenir Sheet

Santiago de Cuba, 490th
Anniv. — A1266

2005, July 4   *Perf. 13*
4495 A1266 1p multi   2.25 1.10

16th World Youth and Student Festival,
Venezuela — A1267

2005, July 29   *Perf. 12¾x12½*
4496 A1267 65c multi   1.40   .70

Dances
A1268

Parrot and: No. 4497, 65c, Samba dancers
and Brazilian flag. No. 4498, 65c, Son dancers, Cuban flag.

2005, Aug. 15   *Perf. 12¾*
4497-4498 A1268 Set of 2   2.75 1.50

See Brazil Nos. 2967-2968.

Cuban — Soviet Space Flight, 25th
Anniv. — A1269

No. 4499: a, Cosmonaut Arnaldo Tamayo
Mendez. b, Cosmonaut Yuri Romanenko.

2005, Sept. 18   *Perf. 12½*
4499 A1269 90c Horiz. pair, #a-b 4.00 2.00

Albert Einstein's
Visit to Cuba,
75th
Anniv. — A1270

Designs: 65c, Caricature of Einstein. 75c,
Equation for energy, Einstein writing.

2005, Sept. 21
4500-4501 A1270 Set of 2   4.00 2.00

Locomotives — A1271

Designs: 5c, DSB B40, 1869. 10c, Great
Northern, 1902. No. 4504, 15c, Minaret, 1929.
No. 4505, 15c, C. F. White, 1885. 2.05p,
Western Pacific FP7A 805D.
1p, 14th No. 4 Krauss & Co., 1884.

2005, May 10   *Litho.*   *Perf. 12¾*
4502-4506 A1271 Set of 5   5.50 2.75

Souvenir Sheet
Perf. 13

4507 A1271 1p multi   2.25 1.10
No. 4507 contains one 40x32mm stamp.

Zoo Animals
A1272

Designs: 10c, Loxodonta africana. 15c, Acu-
nonyx jubatus, horiz. 50c, Synceros caffer,
horiz. 65c, Giraffa camelopardalis. 75c,
Panthera leo.
1p, Equus burchelli, horiz.

2005, July 21   *Perf. 12¾*
4508-4512 A1272 Set of 5   4.75 2.40

Souvenir Sheet
Perf. 13

4513 A1272 1p multi   2.25 1.10
No. 4513 contains one 40x32mm stamp.

Santiago de Cuba, 490th
Anniv. — A1273

2005, Sept. 22   *Perf. 12¾x12½*
4514 A1273 75c multi   1.60   .80

Revolutionary Defense Committees,
45th Anniv. — A1274

2005, Sept. 28   *Perf. 12½x12¼*
4515 A1274 50c multi   1.10   .55

Diplomatic Relations Between Cuba
and People's Republic of China, 45th
Anniv. — A1275

No. 4516: a, Chinese General Secretary Hu
Jintao and Cuban Pres. Fidel Castro. b, Great
Wall of China and Morro Castle, Havana.

2005, Sept. 28   *Perf. 13x13½*
4516 A1275 15c Horiz. pair, #a-b 1.00   .50

America Issue,
Fight Against
Poverty
A1276

Designs: 50c, Starving children, map of
Africa. 75c, Woman and child, map of South
America.

2005, Oct. 12   *Perf. 12¾*
4517-4518 A1276 Set of 2   2.75 1.40

Horses
A1277

Breeds: 10c, Gelderlander. 20c, Arabian.
30c, Quarterhorse. 65c, Wild horses. 75c,
Lipizzaner.
100c, Holsteiner, vert.

2005, Oct. 21   *Perf. 12¾*
4519-4523 A1277 Set of 5   4.25 2.10

Souvenir Sheet
Perf. 12¾x12½

4524 A1277 100c multi   2.25 1.10
No. 4524 contains one 32x40mm stamp.

José Martí Type of 2004

Martí and: No. 4525, 5c, Central University,
Madrid, 1871. No. 4526, 5c, Zaragoza University, 1871. No. 4527, 5c, F. Valdés Dominguez, Teatro Principal, Zaragoza, 1872. No.
4528, 10c, Victor Hugo House, Paris, 1872.
No. 4529, 10c, Moneda No. 12, Mexico City,
1875. No. 4530, 15c, Normal School, Guatemala City, 1876. No. 4531, 15c, San Ildefonso
No. 40, Mexico City, 1894. No. 4532, 15c,
Plaza de Guardiola, Mexico City, 1894. 65c,
Plaza Bolívar, Caracas, 1885. 75c, Santa
María College, Caracas, 1893.
1p, Martínez Ibor Tobacco Factory, Tampa,
1892.

2005, Oct. 20   *Perf. 12½x12¼*
4525-4534 A1227 Set of 10   4.75 2.40

Souvenir Sheet
Perf. 13

4535 A1227 1p multi   2.25 1.10
No. 4535 contains one 40x32mm stamp.

World Summit on the Information
Society, Tunis — A1278

2005, Nov. 16   *Perf. 12½x12¼*
4536 A1278 75c multi   1.60   .80

Establishment of Local Delivery of Mail
in Havana, 150th Anniv. — A1279

Designs: 15c, Cuba #7, cover to Havana.
65c, Cuba #16, Colonial Havana mailbox.

2005, Nov. 19   *Perf. 12¾x12½*
4537-4538 A1279 Set of 2   1.60   .80

Cuban
Men
Convicted
of
Terrorism
Imprisoned
In the
United
States
A1280

2005, Nov. 25   *Perf. 12½x12¾*
4539 A1280 65c multi   2.00 1.00

Europa
Stamps,
50th Anniv.
(in 2006)
A1281

Designs: 1.30p, Spain #1126, Castilla de la
Fuerza, Havana. 2.05p, Spain #1010, Santisima Church, Trinidad, Cuba. 2.55p, Spain
#1526, Morro Castle, Santiago de Cuba.
3.90p, Spain #1263, San Cristóbal Cathedral,
Havana.

2005, Nov. 30   *Perf. 12½*
4540-4543 A1281 Set of 4   20.00 10.00
4543a   Souvenir sheet, #4540-
                   4543   20.00 10.00

Nos. 4540-4543, 4543a exist imperf. Values,
same.

Jewelry
A1282

Jewelry by: 5c, Antonio Barcala. 10c, Raúl
Valladares. 45c, Carlos de la Torre. 65c, J.
Carlo Rafart. 75c, Osvaldo Castilla.
1p, 19th cent. jewelry in Gold Museum.

2005, Dec. 1   *Perf. 12¾*
4544-4548 A1282 Set of 5   4.25 2.10

Souvenir Sheet
Perf. 12½
4549 A1282 1p multi 2.25 1.10
No. 4549 contains one 32x40mm stamp.

Friendship Among the Peoples Institute, 45th Anniv. — A1283

2005, Dec. 14 **Perf. 12¾x12½**
4550 A1283 1.05p multi 2.25 1.10

Snails and Mushrooms A1284

Designs: 10c, Clathrus cancellatus. 20c, Polymita genus picta. 30c, Lepiota puellaris. 65c, Polymita genus muscarum. 75c, Clitocybe infundibuliformis.
1p, Polymita genus versicolor, horiz.

2005, Dec. 15 **Perf. 12¾**
4551-4555 A1284 Set of 5 4.25 2.10
Souvenir Sheet
Perf. 13
4556 A1284 1p multi 2.25 1.10
No. 4556 contains one 40x32mm stamp.

Hotel Inglaterra, 130th Anniv. — A1285

2005, Dec. 23 **Perf. 12¾x12½**
4557 A1285 65c multi 1.40 .70

New Year 2006 (Year of the Dog) — A1286

Designs: No. 4558, 15c, Shih tzu. No. 4559, 15c, Pug.

2006, Jan. 4 **Perf. 12¼x12½**
4558-4559 A1286 Set of 2 .60 .30

Organization of Solidarity of the People of Asia, Africa and Latin America, 40th Anniv. A1287

2006, Jan. 16 **Perf. 12¾**
4560 A1287 65c multi 1.40 .70

Establishment of Cuban Postal Service, 250th Anniv. — A1288

Stampless cover and: 75c, Horse and rider. 2.05p, Ship.

2006, Mar. 1 **Perf. 12½x12¼**
4561-4562 A1288 Set of 2 6.00 3.00

OPEC Intl. Development Fund, 30th Anniv. — A1289

2006, Mar. 23 **Litho.**
4563 A1289 75c multi 1.60 .80

Souvenir Sheet

Havana '06 Intl. Philatelic Exhibition — A1290

2006, Mar. 25 **Perf. 12½**
4564 A1290 1p multi 2.25 1.10

Pope John Paul II (1920-2005) — A1291

Designs: 65c, Pope, Mass in Santa Clara. 75c, Mass in Camagüey (44x27mm). 90c, Mass in Santiago de Cuba (44x27mm). 1.05p, Pope, Mass in Havana.

2006, Apr. 2 **Perf. 12½x12¼**
4565-4568 A1291 Set of 4 7.25 3.75

Bay of Pigs Invasion, 45th Anniv. — A1292

2006, Apr. 17 **Perf. 12¼x12½**
4569 A1292 65c multi 1.40 .70

José Martí Type of 2004
Martí and: No. 4570, Madame Griffou's Hotel, New York, 1890. No. 4571, Gonzalo de Quesada, 116 West 64th Street, New York, 1893. No. 4572, Son, José Francisco, 324 Classon Ave., New York, 1885. No. 4573, Masonic Temple, New York, 1888.
No. 4574: a, Cajobabo beach, Gomez monument. b, Martí monument, monument at Dos Ríos.
Martí and: 75c, Hardman Hall, New York, 1891. 85c, Office, 120 Front Street, New York, 1891. 90c, María Mantilla, Bath Beach, Long Island.
1p, Home of Teodoro Pérez, Cayo Hueso, 1893.

2006, May 19 Litho. Perf. 12½x12¼
4570 A1227 5c multi .25 .25
4571 A1227 5c multi .25 .25
4572 A1227 10c multi .25 .25
4573 A1227 10c multi .25 .25
4574 A1227 15c Horiz. pair, #a-b .65 .65
4575 A1227 75c multi 1.60 1.60
4576 A1227 85c multi 1.90 1.90
4577 A1227 90c multi 1.90 1.90
Nos. 4570-4577 (8) 7.05 7.05
Souvenir Sheet
Perf. 13
4578 A1227 1p multi 2.25 2.25
No. 4578 contains one 40x32mm stamp.

Prehistoric Animals — A1293

Designs: 5c, Dsungaripetrus, Yangchuanosaurus. 10c, Pterodactylus, Sprinosaurus. 30c, Pteranodon, Pachycephalosaurus. 35c, Scaphognathus, Muttaburrasaurus. 65c, Quetzalcoatlus, Stegosaurus. 1.05p, Sordes, Saichania.
1p, Stenonychosaurus, vert.

2006, May 24 **Perf. 12½x12¼**
4579-4584 A1293 Set of 6 5.50 5.50
Souvenir Sheet
Perf. 12½
4585 A1293 1p multi 2.25 2.25
No. 4585 contains one 32x40mm stamp.

Ministry of the Interior, 45th Anniv. — A1294

2006, June 6 **Perf. 12½x12¼**
4586 A1294 75c multi 1.60 1.60

Fowl — A1295

Designs: 5c, Chickens. No. 4588, 15c, Turkeys. No. 4589, 15c, Guinea fowl. 45c, Geese. 50c, Pheasants. 75c, Peafowl.

2006, June 15 **Perf. 12½x12¼**
4587-4592 A1295 Set of 6 4.50 4.50
Souvenir Sheet
Perf. 13
4593 A1295 1p multi 2.25 2.25
No. 4593 contains one 40x32mm stamp.

Cerro Pelado Declaration, 40th Anniv. — A1296

Designs: 65c, Ship, man and crowd. 75c, People in cargo hoist. 85c, Men assisting woman down ship's stairs, flags of Cuba and Puerto Rico.

2006, June 25 **Perf. 12½x12¾**
4594-4596 A1296 Set of 3 4.75 4.75

2006 World Cup Soccer Championships, Germany — A1296a

Various Cuban soccer players: 15c, 45c, 65c, 75c.

2006, June Litho. Perf. 12¾
4596A-4596D A1296a Set of 4 4.00 4.00

Genetic Engineering and Biotechnology Center, 20th Anniv. — A1297

2006, July 1 **Perf. 12½x12¼**
4597 A1297 65c multi 1.40 1.40

Comic Strips by Virgilio Martínez — A1298

Designs: 15c, Pucho y Sus Perrerias. 65c, Cucho.

2006, July 16 **Perf. 12¾x12¼**
4598-4599 A1298 Set of 2 1.75 1.75

Airplanes — A1299

Designs: 10c, Granville GeeBee R2. No. 4601, 15c, Bücker Jungmann. No. 4602, 15c, Comte AC-4 Gentleman. 50c, Mustang TF-51. 75c, Supermarine Spitfire. 85c, Lavochkin La-9. 1p, Bücker Jungmeister.

2006, July 20   **Perf. 12¾**
4600-4605 A1299   Set of 6   5.50 5.50
Souvenir Sheet
Imperf
4606 A1299 1p multi   2.25 2.25
No. 4606 contains one 36x28mm stamp.

Dogs — A1300

Designs: 5c, Bulldog. 10c, American cocker spaniel. 15c, Shar-pei. 20c, Airedale terrier. 35c, Pomeranian. 2.05p, Dalmatian. 1p, Whippet, vert.

2006, Aug. 18   **Perf. 12½x12¼**
4607-4612 A1300   Set of 6   6.25 6.25
Souvenir Sheet
Perf. 13
4613 A1300 1p multi   2.25 2.25

Recovery of Raw Materials, 45th Anniv. — A1301

Designs: 15c, Ernesto "Che" Guevara. 65c, Cuban and recovery program flags.

2006, Aug. 24   **Perf. 12¾**
4614-4615 A1301   Set of 2   1.75 1.75

14th Congress of Non-Aligned Countries, Havana A1302

2006, Sept. 10
4616 A1302 65c multi   1.40 1.40

Pedro Santacilia, Benito Juárez and Mexico House, Havana — A1303

2006, Sept. 15   **Perf. 12½x12¼**
4617 A1303 65c multi   1.40 1.40
Benito Juárez (1806-72), President of Mexico.

Souvenir Sheet

7th Hispano-Cuban Philatelic Exposition — A1304

No. 4618: a, Statue, arms of Cuba, denomination at LR. b, Statue, arms of Spain, denomination at LL.

2006, Sept. 20   **Imperf**
4618 A1304 50c Sheet of 2, #a-b 2.25 2.25

España 06 World Philatelic Exposition, Malaga, Spain — A1305

Designs: 5c, Rio Hanabanilla. 10c, Laguna Bacanao. 15c, Sierra de la Gran Piedra. 20c, Valle de los Ingenios. 50c, Laguna del Tesoro. 75c, Sierra Maestra. 1p, Valle de Viñales.

2006, Sept. 20   **Perf. 12¾**
4619-4624 A1305   Set of 6   3.75 3.75
Souvenir Sheet
Perf. 13
4625 A1305 1p multi   2.25 2.25
No. 4625 contains one 40x32mm stamp.

America Issue, Energy Conservation — A1306

Equipment for harnessing energy source: No. 4626, 65c, Petroleum. No. 4627, 65c, Water. No. 4628, 65c, Solar. No. 4629, 65c, Wind.

2006, Oct. 12   **Perf. 12¾**
4626-4629 A1306   Set of 4   5.50 5.50

Saiz Brothers Association, 20th Anniv. A1307

2006, Oct. 18
4630 A1307 75c multi   1.60 1.60

20th Intl. Ballet Festival, Havana A1308

Dancers: 75c, Alicia Alonso and Igor Youskévitch. 85c, Alonso.

2006, Oct. 28   **Perf. 12¼x12½**
4631-4632 A1308   Set of 2   3.50 3.50

A1309

Belgica '06 Intl. Youth Philately Exposition, Belgium — A1310

Trains: 5c, Rocket and Intercity Diesel-electric. 10c, Turbine locomotive, Diesel-electric locomotive. 15c, Shinkasen and City of Los Angeles. 65c, Steam locomotive, Diesel locomotive. 75c, TEE Diesel-electric, TGV electric. 85c, Brisbane electric monorail, Wuppertal monorail.
No. 4639: a, Steam locomotive. b, Diesel locomotive.

2006, Nov. 2   **Perf. 12¾**
4633-4638 A1309   Set of 6   5.50 5.50
Souvenir Sheet
Perf. 12½
4639 A1310 50c Sheet of 2, #a-b 2.25 2.25

TeleFood Emblem — A1311

2006, Nov. 11   **Perf. 12¾**
4640 A1311 75c multi   1.60 1.60

Animals Serving Man — A1312

Designs: 5c, Equus caballus, Greek horse-drawn chariot. 15c, Camelus dromedarius, Ibn Battuta on camel. 30c, Capra aegagrus, Roman musician. 40c, Lama lama, Peruvian pre-Columbian ceramic llama. 50c, Felis catus, painting by Kuniyoshi Utagawa. 1.05p, Elephas maximus, elephant with Indian caparison.
1p, Canis familiaris, Grecian with dog.

2006, Oct. 1   **Litho.**   **Perf. 12½x12¼**
4641-4646 A1312   Set of 6   5.50 5.50
Souvenir Sheet
Perf. 12½
4647 A1312 1p multi   2.25 2.25
No. 4647 contains one 40x32mm stamp.

Fire Fighting and Rescue Equipment — A1313

Designs: 5c, 1899 Horse-drawn ambulance, Brazil, and megaphone. 10c, Fireman's hat, and 1898 Merryweather fire truck, England. 20c, 1910 Laurin & Klement fire truck, Bohemia, and fire hydrant. 30c, 1939 American La France ladder truck, US, and badge. 45c, 1925 Leyland Motors pumper motorcycle, United Kingdom, and portable hose and tank. 90c, Brussels fire badge and 1930 Magirus ladder truck, Germany.
1p, Fireman spraying water, vert.

2006, Nov. 13   **Perf. 12¾**
4648-4653 A1313   Set of 6   4.50 4.50
Souvenir Sheet
Perf. 12½
4654 A1313 1p multi   2.25 2.25
No. 4654 contains one 32x40mm stamp.

Santiago Rebellion, 50th Anniv. — A1314

2006, Nov. 30   **Perf. 12½x12¼**
4655 A1314 65c multi   1.40 1.40

Governmental Reorganization, 30th Anniv. — A1315

2006, Dec. 2
4656 A1315 75c multi   1.60 1.60

Granma Landings, 50th Anniv. — A1316

Revolutionary Armed Forces, 50th Anniv. — A1317

2006, Dec. 2   **Perf. 13**
4657 A1316 65c multi   1.40 1.40
4658 A1317 65c multi   1.40 1.40

General Antonio Maceo Grajales
(1845-96) — A1317a

2006, Dec. 7 Litho. Perf. 12½x12¼
4658A A1317a 1.05p multi 2.10 2.10

Intl. Film and Television School, 20th
Anniv. — A1318

2006, Dec. 15 Perf. 12¾
4659 A1318 75c multi 1.60 1.60

Martí Forge Museum, 55th
Anniv. — A1319

2006, Dec. 15 Perf. 12½x12¼
4660 A1319 90c multi 1.90 1.90

Literacy
Campaign,
45th Anniv.
A1320

2006, Dec. 19 Perf. 12¾
4661 A1320 65c multi 1.40 1.40

Major General Ignacio Agramonte y
Loinaz (1841-73) — A1321

2006, Dec. 23 Perf. 12½x12¼
4662 A1321 65c multi 1.40 1.40

Special Education, 45th
Anniv. — A1322

2007, Jan. 4 Perf. 12¾
4663 A1322 85c multi 1.75 1.75

Francesa
Pharmacy,
125th Anniv.
A1323

2007, Jan. 18 Litho.
4664 A1323 65c multi 1.40 1.40

Electric
Trains
A1324

Designs: 5c, First American electric locomotive, 1895. 10c, Locomotive, Netherlands. 15c, Interurban train, Australia. 65c, High-speed train, Italy. 85c, Helensburgh-Bridgeton train, Great Britain. 1.05p, Lyon-St. Etienne interurban train, France.
1p, High-speed train, Germany.

2007, Jan. 18 Perf. 12¾
4665-4670 A1324 Set of 6 6.00 6.00
Souvenir Sheet
Imperf
4671 A1324 1p multi 2.25 2.25

No. 4671 contains one 40x32mm stamp with simulated perforations.

12th Intl. Information Fair and
Convention — A1325

2007, Feb. 12 Perf. 12½x12¼
4672 A1325 75c multi 1.60 1.60

Cats
A1326

Designs: 10c, Two cats. No. 4674, 15c, Kitten with paw raised. No. 4675, 15c, Cat. 50c, Cat and telephone. 75c, Cat with ball. 90c, Cat, diff.
1p, Cat, diff.

2007, Feb. 14 Perf. 12¾
4673-4678 A1326 Set of 6 5.50 5.50
Souvenir Sheet
Imperf
4679 A1326 1p multi 2.25 2.25

No. 4679 contains one 40x32mm stamp with simulated perforations.

Fifth Congress of Cuban Pigeon
Fanciers Federation — A1327

2007, Feb. 24 Perf. 12¾
4680 A1327 75c multi 1.60 1.60

Souvenir Sheet

Patria Newspaper, 115th
Anniv. — A1328

Imperf. With Simulated Perforations
2007, Mar. 14
4681 A1328 1p multi 2.25 2.25

Animals in National Zoo — A1329

Designs: 5c, Ara ararauana. 10c, Tsetudo elephantopus. 15c, Balearica regulorum. 20c, Procyon lotor. 45c, Panthera pardus. 2.05p, Pongo pygmaeus.
1p, Giraffa camelopardalis, vert.

2007, Mar. 31 Perf. 12½x12¼
4682-4687 A1329 Set of 6 6.50 6.50
Souvenir Sheet
Imperf
4688 A1329 1p multi 2.25 2.25

No. 4688 contains one 32x40mm stamp with simulated perforations.

Raúl Roa
García (1907-
82), Foreign
Minister
A1330

2007, Apr. 18 Perf. 12¾
4689 A1330 65c multi 1.40 1.40

Union of Young Communists, 45th
Anniv. — A1331

2007, Apr. 4 Perf. 12½x12¼
4690 A1331 75c multi 1.60 1.60

José Martí Type of 2004

Martí and: No. 4691, 5c, Cuban High School, Tampa, 1892. No. 4692, 5c, Casa de los Pedrosa, Tampa, 1892. No. 4693, 10c, Hotel Duval, Cayo Hueso, 1891. No. 4694, 10c, Hotel Cherokee, Tampa, 1891. No. 4695, 15c, Cayo Hueso Committee, 1891 (68x28mm). No. 4696, 15c, F. Valdés Domínguez, Gato Brothers Cigar Factory, Cayo Hueso, 1894. 35c, Club San Carlos, Cayo Hueso, 1893. 40c, Hotel Myrtle Bank, Kingston, 1892. 50c, Gen. Francisco Gómez Toro, Friends of the Country Society Building, Santo Domingo, 1894. 65c, Máximo Gómez, Gómez's house, Montecristi.

2007, Apr. 10 Perf. 12½x12¼
4691-4700 A1227 Set of 10 5.50 5.50

World Food Program Children's Art
Exhibition, 10th Anniv. — A1332

2007, May 3 Litho. Perf. 12¾
4701 A1332 65c multi 1.40 1.40

Folklore
Union — A1333

2007, May 7 Perf. 12¼x12½
4702 A1333 75c multi 1.60 1.60

Islands and Wildlife — A1334

Designs: 5c, Cayo Guillermo, pelican. No. 4704, 15c, Cayo Las Brujas, sea gull. No. 4705, 15c, Cayo Levisa, conches. 20c, Cayo Santa Maria, iguana. 50c, Cayo Ensenachos, plover. 85c, Cayo Largo, Carey turtle.
1p, Cayo Coco, flamingos.

2007, May 8 Perf. 12½x12¼
4703-4708 A1334 Set of 6 4.25 4.25
Souvenir Sheet
Imperf
4709 A1334 1p multi 2.25 2.25

No. 4709 contains one 40x32mm stamp.

Singers and
Songwriters
A1335

Designs: 5c, Benny Moré. 10c, Ignacio Piñeiro. 30c, Arsenio Rodríguez. 35c, Miguelito Cuní. 65c, Pio Leyva. 75c, Ibrahim Ferrer.
1p, Miguel Matamoros.

2007, May 10 Perf. 12¾
4710-4715 A1335 Set of 6 4.75 4.75
Souvenir Sheet
Imperf
4716 A1335 1p multi 2.25 2.25

No. 4716 contains one 32x40mm stamp with simulated perforations.

Souvenir Sheet

Martí Studies Youth Seminary, 35th Anniv. — A1336

2007, May 19 *Imperf.*
4717 A1336 1p multi 2.25 2.25

Cuban Radio and Television Institute, 45th Anniv. — A1337

2007, May 24 *Perf. 12½x12¼*
4718 A1337 3p multi 6.50 6.50

Integral Development Group of the Capital, 20th Anniv. — A1338

2007, May 25 *Litho.*
4719 A1338 65c multi 1.40 1.40

Cuban Admission to the United Nations, 60th Anniv. A1339

2007, May 29 *Perf. 12¾*
4720 A1339 65c multi 1.40 1.40

2007 Pan American Games, Rio de Janeiro — A1340

Designs: No. 4721, 15c, Fencing. No. 4722, 15c, Boxing. 20c, Wrestling. 45c, Running. 65c, Gymnastics. 75c, Cycling.
1p, Games emblem, vert.

2007, June 20 *Perf. 12¾*
4721-4726 A1340 Set of 6 5.00 5.00
Souvenir Sheet
Imperf
4727 A1340 1p multi 2.25 2.25
No. 4727 contains one 32x40mm stamp.

Third Technological Transfer and Intl. Trade Workshop — A1341

2007, July 3 *Perf. 12½x12¼*
4728 A1341 65c multi 1.40 1.40

Frank País (1934-57), Revolutionary Hero — A1342

2007, July 30 *Perf. 12¾*
4729 A1342 65c multi 1.40 1.40

Radio Cubana, 85th Anniv. A1343

2007, Aug. 22 *Perf. 12¾*
4730 A1343 65c multi 1.40 1.40

Seven Wonders of the Modern World A1344

Designs: 10c, Great Wall of China. 15c, Petra, Jordan. 20c, Christ the Redeemer Statue, Brazil. 40c, Machu Picchu, Peru. 65c, Chichén Itzá Pyramids, Mexico. 75c, Roman Colosseum. 85c, Taj Mahal, India.

2007, Aug. 16 *Litho.* *Perf. 12¾*
4731-4737 A1344 Set of 7 6.25 6.25

Transportation — A1345

Designs: 10c, Cocotaxis (40x29mm). 15c, Lada 2105 taxi (40x29mm). 30c, Girón VI bus (40x29mm). 40c, Bus trailer on truck (44x27mm). 75c, DAF articulated bus (44x27mm). 85c, Yutong bus (44x27mm).
1p, La Gaviota train.

Perf. 12¾, 12½x12¼ (#4741-4743)
2007, Sept. 3
4738-4743 A1345 Set of 6 5.25 5.25
Souvenir Sheet
Imperf
4744 A1345 1p multi 2.00 2.00
No. 4744 contains one 40x32mm stamp with simulated perforations.

Central Youth Club, 20th Anniv. — A1346

2007, Sept. 8 *Perf. 12¼x12½*
4745 A1346 65c multi 1.40 1.40

Cubans Convicted of Espionage by United States A1347

Designs: No. 4746, 65c, Raised hand with "Cuban Five" emblem. No. 4747, 65c, Fernando González Liort. No. 4748, 65c, Gerardo Hernández Nordelo. No. 4749, 65c, Antonio Guerrero Rodríguez. No. 4750, 65c, Ramón Labañino Salazar. No. 4751, 65c, René González Schwerert.

2007, Sept. 12 *Perf. 12¾*
4746-4751 A1347 Set of 6 8.00 8.00

Tree Planting Campaign — A1348

2007, Oct. 24 *Perf. 12½x12¼*
4752 A1348 65c multi 1.40 1.40

Rose Varieties A1349

Designs: 5c, Pink Parfait. No. 4754, 15c, Alison Wheatcroft. No. 4755, 15c, Prima Ballerina. 45c, Fragrant Cloud. 50c, Blue Moon. 75c, Grandmère Jenny.
1p, Rosa highdownensis.

2007, Oct. 25 *Perf. 12¾*
4753-4758 A1349 Set of 6 4.25 4.25
Souvenir Sheet
Imperf
4759 A1349 1p multi 2.00 2.00
No. 4759 contains one 40x32mm stamp with simulated perforations.

International Design Conference — A1350

Designs: 75c, Electronic machine. 85c, Caricatures.

2007, Oct. 26 *Perf. 12½x12¼*
4760-4761 A1350 Set of 2 3.25 3.25

Souvenir Sheet

International Air Mail Service From Cuba, 80th Anniv. — A1351

2007, Oct. 27 *Imperf.*
4762 A1351 1p multi 2.00 2.00
Seventh Natl. Philatelic Championship. No. 4762 has simulated perforations.

Protected Animals — A1352

Designs: 5c, Eretmochelys imbricata. 10c, Trichechus manatus. 20c, Mesocapromys sanfelipensis. 30c, Mesocapromys nanus. 45c, Epinephelus itajara. 85c, Balistes vetula. 1p, Chelonia mydas.

2007, Nov. 15 *Perf. 12½x12¼*
4763-4768 A1352 Set of 6 4.00 4.00
Souvenir Sheet
Imperf
4769 A1352 1p multi 2.00 2.00
No. 4769 contains one 40x32mm stamp with simulated perforations.

Cuban UNESCO Commission, 60th Anniv. — A1353

2007, Nov. 17 *Perf. 12½x12¼*
4770 A1353 65c multi 1.40 1.40

Cuban Railroads, 170th Anniv. — A1354

2007, Nov. 19 *Perf. 12¾*
4771 A1354 3p multi 6.00 6.00

Camagüey Ballet, 40th Anniv. — A1355

2007, Dec. 1 *Litho.*
4772 A1355 75c multi 1.50 1.50

De la Torre y la Huerta and: 5c, Hand holding shells. 15c, Polymita picta nigrolimbata, light blue background. 50c, Polymita picta nigrolimbata, pink background. 65c, Polymita picta iolimbata. 75c, Polymita picta nigrolimbata, light green background. 90c, Polymita picta fuscolimbata.
1p, Liguus fasciatus.

2008 *Perf. 12½x12¼*
4893-4898 A1390 Set of 6 6.00 6.00
Souvenir Sheet
Imperf
4899 A1390 1p multi 2.00 2.00
No. 4899 contains one 40x32mm stamp with simulated perforations.

Paleolithic Man and Animals — A1391

Designs: 10c, Australopithecus afarensis and Megatherium. 15c, Australopithecus africanus and Toxodon. 50c, Australopithecus robustus and Bison. 65c, Homo habilis and Hippidion. 75c, Homo erectus and Megantereon. 90c, Neanderthal man and Mammoths.
1p, Coelodonts.

2008 *Perf. 12¾*
4900-4905 A1391 Set of 6 6.25 6.25
Souvenir Sheet
Imperf
4906 A1391 1p multi 2.00 2.00
No. 4906 contains one 45x34mm stamp with simulated perforations.

A1392

Transportation — A1392a

Designs: 15c, 1802 steam carriage of Richard Trevithick. 30c, 1829 steam carriage of Sir Goldsworthy Gurney. 40c, 1832 steam carriage of William Church. 65c, 1858 steam carriage of Thomas Rickett. 75c, 1890 Motorwagen of Karl Benz. 85c, 1836 steam omnibus of Walter Hancock.
1p, 1958 Panhard-Levassor automobile.

2008 *Perf. 12½x12¼*
4907-4912 A1392 Set of 6 6.25 6.25
Souvenir Sheet
Imperf
4913 A1392a 1p multi 2.00 2.00
No. 4913 has simulated perforations.

Matanzas, 315th Anniv. — A1393

Designs: 15c, Building arches, Plaza de la Vigía. 40c, Palacio Junco Provincial Museum.

50c, Fire house. 75c, Palace of Justice. 85c, Sauto Theater. 90c, Palace of Government.
1p, Unknown Soldier's Monument, vert.

2008 *Perf. 12½x12¼*
4914-4919 A1393 Set of 6 7.25 7.25
Souvenir Sheet
Imperf
4920 A1393 1p multi 2.00 2.00
No. 4920 has simulated perforations.

Triumph of the Cuban Revolution, 50th Anniv. — A1394

No. 4921, 15c: a, Liberation Day (man with wide-brimmed hat at left). b, Liberation Day (tank at left). c, Arrival of Fidel Castro in Havana. d, First march. e, Fidel Castro, Revolutionary Government Prime Minister, addressing crowd. f, Camilo Cienfuegos dissolves Bureau for the Repression of Communist Activities. g, Granting of Cuban citizenship to Ernesto "Che" Guevara. h, Fidel Castro's first visit to Venezuela. i, Creation of the P.N.R. (National Revolutionary Police). j, Creation of State Security organizations. k, Creation of T.G.F. (Border Guard). l, Agrarian Reform Law. m, Takeover of Cuban telephone system. n, Creation of the F.M.C. (Federation of Cuban Women). o, Creation of the C.D.R. (Committees for the Defense of the Revolution). p, Start of literacy campaign. q, Creation of I.N.D.E.R. (Institute of Sports, Physical Education and Recreation). r, Radio across Cuba. s, Designation of Guevara as Industry Minister. t, Creation of Union of Young Communists. u, Creation of the Civil Defense. v, Creation of the National Civil Defense Committee. w, First sugar harvest. x, Guevara speaks at the United Nations.
No. 4922, 15c: a, Constitution of the Central Committee of the Cuban Communist Party. b, Day of the Heroic Guerrilla. c, Free distribution of Guevara's diary. d, First National Education and Cultural Congress. e, First Congress of the P.C.C. (Cuban Communist Party). f, First Rural Education Congress. g, Establishment in Cuba of Intl. Children's Day. h, Vaccinations in Cuba, 205th anniv. i, Creation of M.I.N.A.Z. (Cuban Ministry of Sugar). j, Creation of I.N.P. (National Fishing Institute). k, Development of fishing industry. l, 11th World Youth and Student Festival. m, Cuban cosmonaut. n, Day of Cuban Science (building at right). o, Day of Cuban Science (building at left). p, Family doctors and nurses. q, Elimination of apartheid, 15th anniv. r, Beginning of Battle of Ideas. s, Social security. t, Creation of the E.I.E.D. u, National culture (ballet dancer at left). v, National culture (guitarists at right). w, Battle of Ideas program (classroom at right). x, Battle of Ideas program (people waving flags at right).
No. 4923, 1p, Cuban flags. No. 4924, 1p, Revolution Plaza, Havana.

2009, Jan. 1 *Litho.* *Perf. 12¾*
Sheets of 24, #a-x
4921-4922 A1394 Set of 2 14.50 14.50
Souvenir Sheets
Imperf
4923-4924 A1394 Set of 2 4.00 4.00
Nos. 4923-4924 have simulated perforations.

Ernesto "Che" Guevara and Cuban Flag — A1394a

2009 *Litho.* *Perf. 12¾*
4924A A1394a 75c multi 1.50 1.50
Cuban Revolution, 50th anniv. See Russia No. 7124.

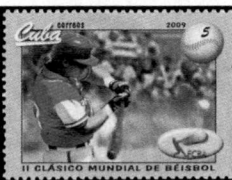
Second World Baseball Classic A1395

Designs: 5c, Batter swinging at ball. 10c, Play at home plate. 15c, Fielder stretching to catch ball. 45c, Pitcher in wind-up. 65c, Runner sliding into base. 75c, Runner and fielder watching ball.
1p, Cuban team.

2009, Jan. 27 *Perf. 12¾*
4925-4930 A1395 Set of 6 4.50 4.50
Souvenir Sheet
Imperf
4931 A1395 1p multi 2.00 2.00
No. 4931 has simulated perforations.

Souvenir Sheet

Cuban Workers' Union, 70th Anniv. — A1396

2009, Jan. 29 *Imperf.*
4932 A1396 1p multi 2.00 2.00
No. 4932 has simulated perforations.

Santa María del Puerto de Príncipe, 495th Anniv. A1397

2009, Feb. 2 *Perf. 12¾*
4933 A1397 90c multi 1.90 1.90

Souvenir Sheet

13th Intl. Information Fair and Convention, Havana — A1398

2009, Feb. 9 *Imperf.*
4934 A1398 1p multi 2.00 2.00
No. 4934 has simulated perforations.

Charles Darwin (1809-92), Naturalist A1398a

Designs: 10c, Darwin and his birthplace, Shrewsbury, England. 65c, HMS Beagle and map of its expedition. 75c, Publication of *On the Origin of Species*. 85c, Darwin and his notes.

Perf. 12½x12¼
2009, Feb. 12 *Litho.*
4934A-4934D A1398a Set of 4 4.75 4.75

Art — A1399

Designs: 15c, Coloritmo, by Alejandro Otero. 30c, Atmósfera Cromoplástica IV, by Luis Tomasello. 40c, Autopista del Sur, by León Ferrari. 65c, Tridim-L, by Victor Vasarely. 75c, Untitled work, by Jesús Soto. 85c, Untitled work, by Julio Le Parc.
1p, Physicromie 105, by Carlos Cruz Diez, horiz.

2009, Feb. 25 *Perf. 12¾*
4935-4940 A1399 Set of 6 6.25 6.25
Souvenir Sheet
Imperf
4941 A1399 1p multi 2.00 2.00
No. 4941 has simulated perforations.

High Speed Trains A1400

Designs: No. 4942, 15c, Acela Express, US. No. 4943, 15c, AVE, Spain. 30c, ATP Eurostar, Great Britain. 65c, ICE, Germany. 75c, ICN, Switzerland. 1.05p, TGV, France.
No. 4948: a, Shinkansen Model 500, Japan. b, Shinkansen Model 700, Japan.

2009, Feb. 27 *Perf. 12½x12¼*
4942-4947 A1400 Set of 6 6.25 6.25
Souvenir Sheet
Imperf
4948 A1400 50c Sheet of 2, #a-b 2.00 2.00
No. 4948 has simulated perforations.

Cuban Arts and Cinematographic Industry Institute, 50th Anniv. — A1401

Designs: No. 4949, 10c, Actress from *La Bella del Alhambra*. No. 4950, 10c, Actress from *Reina y Rey*. No. 4951, 15c, Character from animated film *Elpidio Valdés*. No. 4952, 15c, Actresses from *Lucía*. 45c, Actor from *Primera Carga al Machete*. 65c, Actor from *El Hombre de Maisinicú*. 75c, Actor and actress from *Clandestinos*. 90c, Actress from *Retrato de Teresa*. 1.05p, Santiago Alvarez, ICAIC reporter.
1p, Scene from *Fresa y Chocolate*.

2009, Mar. 24 *Perf. 12½x12¼*
4949-4957 A1401 Set of 9 8.75 8.75
Souvenir Sheet
Imperf
4958 A1401 1p multi 2.00 2.00
No. 4958 has simulated perforations.

State Security Organizations, 50th Anniv. — A1402

2009, Mar. 26   **Perf. 12¼x12½**
4959 A1402 65c multi   1.40 1.40

Motorcycles — A1403

Designs: 10c, Cagiva Mito N1. 15c, Honda CBR 900. 50c, Hyosung-GT 8. 65c, Kawasaki ZX-7R 750cc. 75c, Gussi MGS. 90c, Ducati Monster 900.
1p, Hyosung-GT 125-R-LD, vert.

2009, Apr. 8   **Perf. 12¾**
4960-4965 A1403 Set of 6   6.25 6.25
Souvenir Sheet
Imperf
4966 A1403 1p multi   2.00 2.00
China 2009 World Philatelic Exhibition, Luoyang. No. 4966 has simulated perforations.

Cats A1404

Designs: 10c, Cat and kittens. 15c, Kittens and baseball. 40c, Two cats clawing fabric. 65c, Two cats on tile floor. 75c, Cat. 1.05p, Cat eating food.
1p, Two cats on roof, vert.

2009, Apr. 12   **Perf. 12¾**
4967-4972 A1404 Set of 6   6.25 6.25
Souvenir Sheet
Imperf
4973 A1404 1p multi   2.00 2.00
No. 4973 has simulated perforations.

Tourism A1405

Art from hotels and restaurants: No. 4974, 10c, Stained-glass window, by René Portocarrero, Bodeguita del Medio Restaurant. No. 4975, Detail from mural, by Amelia Peláez, Hotel Habana Libre Tryp. 45c, Painting by Domingo Ramos, Hotel Nacional de Cuba, horiz. 65c, Detail from mural, by Mariano Rodríguez, Hotel Bello Caribe, horiz. 75c, Detail from mural, by Raúl Martínez, Hotel Bella Caribe, horiz. 85c, Mural, by Manuel A. Sosabravo, Hotel Habana Libre Tryp, horiz.
1p, Mural by various artists, Hotel Inglaterra, horiz.

2009, Apr. 21   **Perf. 12¾**
4974-4979 A1405 Set of 6   6.00 6.00

Souvenir Sheet
Imperf
4980 A1405 1p multi   2.00 2.00
No. 4980 has simulated perforations.

Haydee Santamaría Cuadrado (1922-80), Founder of Casa de las Americas — A1406

2009, Apr. 28   **Perf. 12¾**
4981 A1406 3p multi   6.00 6.00

World Heritage Sites A1407

Designs: 15c, Havana. 45c, Cienfuegos. 50c, Trinidad. 1.05p, Camagüey.

2009, May 8   **Litho.**
4982-4985 A1407 Set of 4   4.50 4.50
4985a   Souvenir sheet, #4982-4985   4.50 4.50

Parrots A1408

Designs: 5c, Guacamayo sereno. 10c, Guacamayo azul-dorado. 15c, Guacamayo de hombro rojo. No. 4989, 20c, Guacamayo cuellodorado. No. 4990, Guacamayo de Jacinto. 65c, Guacamayo escarlata. 75c, Guacamayo frente rojo. 90c, Guacamayo militar.

2009, May 16
4986-4993 A1408 Set of 8   6.00 6.00

Institute of Design, 25th Anniv. — A1409

2009, May 28   **Perf. 12½x12¼**
4994 A1409 65c multi   1.40 1.40

Souvenir Sheet

Ernesto Guevara Central Palace of Pioneers, 30th Anniv. — A1410

2009, June 1   **Imperf.**
4995 A1410 1p multi   2.00 2.00
No. 4995 has simulated perforations.

National Revolutionary Police, 50th Anniv. — A1411

2009, June 6   **Perf. 12½x12¼**
4996 A1411 1.05p multi   2.10 2.10

FORDES Gallery, 5th Anniv. — A1412

2009, June 14
4997 A1412 75c multi   1.50 1.50

Zoo Animals A1413

Designs: 5c, Ceratotherium simum. 10c, Syncerus caffer caffer. 15c, Acinonyx jubatus, vert. 30c, Papio hamadryas, vert. 40c, Struthio camelus, vert. 2.05p, Lycaon pictus, vert.
1p, Hippopotamus amphibius.

2009, June 20   **Perf. 12¾**
4998-5003 A1413 Set of 6   6.25 6.25
Souvenir Sheet
Imperf
5004 A1413 1p multi   2.00 2.00
No. 5004 contains one 47x30mm stamp with simulated perforations.

Cuban Cuisine — A1414

Designs: 40c, Arroz con pollo a la chorrera (chicken with rice). 45c, Plátano maduro frito (fried plantains). 50c, Frijoles negros dormidos (black beans with onion).

2009, June 29   **Perf. 12½x12¼**
5005-5007 A1414 Set of 3   2.75 2.75

Diplomatic Relations Between Cuba and Sri Lanka, 50th Anniv. — A1415

2009, July 29   **Perf. 12¼x12½**
5008 A1415 1.05p multi   2.10 2.10

Peace and National Sovereignty Movement, 60th Anniv. — A1416

2009, Aug. 4   **Perf. 12¾**
5009 A1416 65c multi   1.40 1.40

Los Malagones Peasant Militia, 50th Anniv. — A1417

2009, Aug. 31   **Perf. 12¼x12½**
5010 A1417 90c multi   1.90 1.90

Havana Convention Center, 30th Anniv. — A1418

2009, Sept. 3   **Perf. 12¾**
5011 A1418 50c multi   1.00 1.00

Tourism A1419

Birds: 15c, Coloptes fernandinae. 40c, Torreonis inexpectata. 50c, Ferminia cerverai. 65c, Agelaius assimilis. 75c, Mellisuga helenae. 90c, todus multicolor.
1p, Aratinga euops.

2009, Sept. 14   **Perf. 12¾**
5012-5017 A1419 Set of 6   6.75 6.75
Souvenir Sheet
Imperf
5018 A1419 1p multi   2.00 2.00
No. 5018 has simulated perforations.

People's Republic of China, 60th Anniv. A1420

2009, Sept. 28   **Litho.**   **Perf. 12¾**
5019 A1420 85c multi   1.75 1.75

Cubana Airlines, 80th Anniv. — A1421

Designs: 5c, Ford Trimotor. 15c, Sikorsky S-38B. 45c, DC-3. 50c, DC-4. 65c, IL-62M. 75c, IL-96 300.
1p, Tu-204.

2009, Oct. 8   *Perf. 12½x12¼*
5020-5025 A1421   Set of 6   5.25 5.25
Souvenir Sheet
Imperf
5026 A1421 1p multi   2.00 2.00
No. 5026 has simulated perforations.

America Issue, Traditional Games A1422

Designs: 15c, Kite. 65c, Top. 75c, Dominos. 2.05p, Jacks.

2009, Oct. 12   *Perf. 12¾*
5027-5030 A1422   Set of 4   7.25 7.25
5030a   Souvenir sheet, #5027-5030   7.25 7.25

Souvenir Sheet

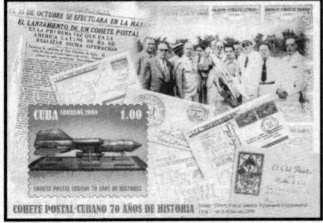

First Rocket Mail Flight in Cuba, 70th Anniv. — A1423

2009, Oct. 15   *Imperf.*
5031 A1423 1p multi   2.00 2.00

Ministry of the Revolutionary Armed Forces, 50th Anniv. — A1424

2009, Oct. 16   *Perf. 12¾*
5032 A1424 75c multi   1.50 1.50

Disappearance of Camilo Cienfuegos, 50th Anniv. — A1425

2009, Oct. 28   *Perf. 12½x12¼*
5033 A1425 65c multi   1.40 1.40

Rights of the Child Convention, 20th Anniv. A1426

2009, Nov. 20
5034 A1426 1.05p multi   2.10 2.10

Cuban Federation of Sport Fishing, 30th Anniv. — A1427

Designs: 15c, Fisherman pulling fish into boat. 30c, Fisherman in water holding rod and fish. 45c, Sailfish and boat. No. 5038, 65c, Fisherman in water holding rod and fish, horiz. 75c, Fish on line, two fishermen in boat, horiz. 85c, Fishermen on sea wall, horiz.
No,. 5041, 65c, Tilapia, horiz

Perf. 12¼x12½, 12½x12¼
2009, Nov. 21
5035-5040 A1427   Set of 6   6.50 6.50
Souvenir Sheet
Imperf
5041 A1427 65c multi   1.40 1.40
No. 5041 has simulated perforations.

Ministry of Foreign Relations, 50th Anniv. — A1428

2009, Dec. 23   *Perf. 12½x12¼*
5042 A1428 1.05p multi   2.10 2.10

Peony A1429

2009   *Perf. 13¼x13½*
5043 A1429 30c multi   .60 .60
Printed in sheets of 4.

José L. Guerra Aguiar Cuban Postal Museum, 45th Anniv. — A1430

2010, Jan. 2   *Perf. 12½x12¼*
5044 A1430 65c multi   1.40 1.40

A1431

A1432

A1433

New Year 2010 (Year of the Tiger) A1434

2010, Jan. 5   *Perf. 12¾*
5045 A1431 15c multi   .30 .30
5046 A1432 15c multi   .30 .30
5047 A1433 15c multi   .30 .30
5048 A1434 15c multi   .30 .30
a.   Souvenir sheet, #5045-5048   1.25 1.25
Nos. 5045-5048 (4)   1.20 1.20

January 1960 Speech of Fidel Castro, 50th Anniv. — A1435

2010, Jan. 15   *Perf. 12½x12¼*
5049 A1435 65c multi   1.40 1.40

Diplomatic Relations Between Cuba and Indonesia, 50th Anniv. — A1436

2010, Jan. 22
5050 A1436 85c multi   1.75 1.75

Trains A1438

Designs: 5c, Fidel Castro leaving train. 10c, DF7G-C locomotive. 15c, Tank car. 65c, Flat car carrying shipping containers. 75c, Box cars. 1.05p, DF7K-C locomotive.
1p, Locomotive at end of track, vert.

2010, Jan. 29   *Perf. 12¾*
5052-5057 A1438   Set of 6   5.50 5.50
Souvenir Sheet
Imperf
5058 A1438 1p multi   2.00 2.00

Diplomatic Relations Between Cuba and India, 50th Anniv. — A1439

2010, Feb. 10   *Perf. 12¾*
5059 A1439 85c multi   1.75 1.75

National Aquarium, 50th Anniv. — A1440

Designs: 10c, Bispira brunnea. No. 5061, 15c, Hypoplectrus gummigutta. No. 5062, 15c, Holocanthus ciliaris. 50c, Seal. 75c, Epinephelus guttatus. 85c, Tursiops truncatus.
1p, Acanthurus coeruleus.

2010, Feb. 12   *Perf. 12¾*
5060-5065 A1440   Set of 6   5.00 5.00
Souvenir Sheet
Imperf
5066 A1440 1p multi   2.00 2.00
No. 5066 has simulated perforations.

A1441

La Colmenita Youth Theater Company, 20th Anniv. — A1442

2010, Feb. 14   *Perf. 12¾*
5067 A1441 50c multi   1.00 1.00
5068 A1442 50c multi   1.00 1.00

Association of Rebel Youth, 50th Anniv. — A1437

2010, Jan. 28
5051 A1437 3p multi   6.00 6.00

Underwater Photography — A1443

Designs: 10c, Fish and coral. 15c, Coral and starfish. 45c, Crab and sea anemone. 50c, Sponges and feather duster worms. 75c, Sea cucumber and coral. 85c, Sea horse and diver photographing tube worm.
1p, Fish and diver.

2010, Feb. 20   Perf. 12½x12¼
5069-5074 A1443 Set of 6   5.75 5.75
Souvenir Sheet
Imperf
5075 A1443 1p multi   2.00 2.00

Central Planning, 50th Anniv. — A1444

2010, Mar. 11   Perf. 12½x12¼
5076 A1444 75c multi   1.50 1.50

Dogs and Art — A1445

Designs: 10c, Peruvian hairless dog, Mochica figurine of dog, Peru. 15c, Bichon Frise, pitcher depicting hunter and dogs. 40c, Neapolitan mastiff, Roman mosaic of hunter and dog. 65c, Chihuahua, figurine of dog, map of Colima, Mexico. 75c, Pug, Chinese painting of hunters and dog. 90c, King Charles spaniel, The Birth of Louis XIII, by Peter Paul Rubens.
1p, Pharaoh hound, Egyptian painting from tomb of Ipy.

2010, Mar. 12   Perf. 12¾
5077-5082 A1445 Set of 6   6.00 6.00
Souvenir Sheet
Imperf
5083 A1445 1p multi   2.00 2.00
No. 5083 has simulated perforations.

Diplomatic Relations Between Cuba and Canada, 65th Anniv. — A1446

2010, Mar. 16   Perf. 12¾
5084 A1446 65c multi   1.40 1.40

Bilateral Relations Between Cuba and Namibia, 20th Anniv. A1447

2010, Mar. 24   Litho.
5085 A1447 85c multi   1.75 1.75

2010 World Cup Soccer Championships, South Africa — A1448

Flags of competing nations, various soccer players and list of teams in: 15c, Groups A and B. 45c, Groups C and D. 65c, Groups E and F. 75c, Groups G and H.

2010, Mar. 24
5086-5089 A1448 Set of 4   4.00 4.00

Congress of the Young Communist's League — A1449

2010, Apr. 2
5090 A1449 65c multi   1.40 1.40

National Symphonic Orchestra, 50th Anniv. — A1450

Designs: 15c, Amadeo Roldán (1900-39), composer. 30c, Gonzalo Roig (1890-1970), composer. 40c, Enrique González Mántici (1912-74), composer. 75c, Manuel Duchesne Cuzán, General director of National Symphonic Orchestra.

2010, Apr. 11   Perf. 12½x12¼
5091-5094 A1450 Set of 4   3.25 3.25

Diplomatic Relations Between Cuba and Cambodia, 50th Anniv. — A1451

2010, Apr. 15
5095 A1451 85c multi   1.75 1.75

Cuban National Chorus, 50th Anniv. — A1452

2010, Apr. 17   Litho.
5096 A1452 90c multi   1.90 1.90

First Cuban Computer, 40th Anniv. — A1453

2010, Apr. 18   Perf. 12¾
5097 A1453 75c multi   1.50 1.50

First Cuban Stamps, 155th Anniv. — A1454

Designs: 75c, Matanzas mail box, 1859, bicyclist in front of building. 85c, Cuba #147, account book of first postal administrator, 1765.

2010, Apr. 24   Perf. 12½x12¼
5098-5099 A1454 Set of 2   3.25 3.25

Tourism A1455

Designs: 15c, Santiago de Cuba. 20c, Guantánamo. 35c, Holguín. 65c, Camagüey. 75c, Granma. 90c, Las Tunas.
1p, Santiago de Cuba, diff.

2010, May 4   Perf. 12¼x12½
5100-5105 A1455 Set of 6   6.00 6.00
Souvenir Sheet
Imperf
5106 A1455 1p multi   2.00 2.00

ICAIC Latin American Newsreels, 50th Anniv. — A1456

2010, June 1   Perf. 12¾
5107 A1456 75c multi   1.50 1.50

Flora and Fauna A1457

Designs: 15c, Dellia sp. 35c, Bietia purpurea. 40c, Anolis equestris. 65c, Broughtonia orgiesiana. 75c, Priotrochatella stellata. 85c, Todus multicolor, vert.
1p, Pinus caribaea.

Perf. 12½x12¼, 12¼x12½
2010, June 11
5108-5113 A1457 Set of 6   6.50 6.50
Souvenir Sheet
Imperf
5114 A1457 1p multi   2.00 2.00

Expo 2010, Shanghai — A1458

Map of China, aviation posters and aircraft: 5c, Savoia-Marchetti 55X. 10c, Farman 60 Goliath. 15c, Fokker VII. 45c, Koolhoven F.K. 50. 65c, Junkers 52/3M. 85c, Latécoère 28.
1p, Handley Page 42E.

2010, Apr. 26 Litho. Perf. 12½x12¼
5115-5120 A1458 Set of 6   4.50 4.50
Souvenir Sheet
Imperf
5121 A1458 1p multi   2.00 2.00
No. 5121 has simulated perforations.

Writings of José Martí — A1459

Designs: No. 5122, 15c, La Patria Libre, white warbler, flag similar to Chile's. No. 5123, 15c, La Nacion, great antshrike, flag of Argentina. No. 5124, 15c, Revista Universal, king vulture, flag of Mexico. No. 5125, 15c, Proclamation of President of Paraguay, plantcutter, flag of Paraguay. No. 5126, 15c, Patria, hummingbird, flag of Cuba. No. 5127, 15c, Montecristi Manifesto, woodpecker, flag similar to Dominican Republic's. No. 5128, 15c, La República Española y la Revolucion Cubana, house sparrow and flag similar to Spain's, vert. No. 5129, 15c, Mis Hijos (translation of Victor Hugo's Mes Fils), long-tailed tit, flag of France, vert. No. 5130, 15c, Guatemala, quetzal, flag of Guatemala, vert. 65c, Pamphlet for International Monetary Conference, crested gallito, flag of Uruguay, vert. 75c, Revista Venezolana, troupial, flag of Venezuela, vert. 90c, Books of poetry, quill pen and inkwell, vert.

Perf. 12½x12¼, 12¼x12½
2010, May 19
5122-5133 A1459 Set of 12   7.50 7.50

Birds Endemic to Various Countries — A1460

Designs: 5c, Eumomota superciliosa, Nicaragua. 10c, Priotelus temnurus, Cuba. 15c, Amazona imperialis, Dominica. No. 5137, 20c, Amazona guildingii, St. Vincent and the Grenadines. No. 5138, 20c, Fregata magnificens, Antigua and Barbuda. 65c, Vultur gryphus, Bolivia. 75c, Icterus icterus, Venezuela, vert. 90c, Turdus rufiventris, Brazil, vert.

2010, May 26   Perf. 12¾
5134-5141 A1460 Set of 8   6.00 6.00

Ernest Hemingway Intl. Fishing Tournament, 60th Anniv. — A1461

Emblem and: No. 5142, 65c, Fishing boat, rod and reel. No. 5143, 65c, Ernest Hemingway. No. 5144, 65c, Swordfish. No. 5145, 65c Trophy.

2010, May 29   *Perf. 12¼x12½*
5142-5145 A1461   Set of 4   5.25 5.25

Dr. Enrique Hart Ramírez (1900-89), Judge — A1462

2010, June 1   *Perf. 12¾*
5146 A1462 65c multi   1.40 1.40

Diplomatic Relations Between Cuba and North Korea, 50th Anniv. — A1463

2010, Aug. 29   Litho.
5147 A1463 85c multi   1.75 1.75

La Caridad Theater, Santa Clara, 125th Anniv. A1464

Designs: 15c, Theater in 1885. 30c, Theater in 2010. 75c, Theater interior. 90c, Marta Abreu de Estévez (1845-1909), philanthropist, vert.

2010, Sept. 8
5148-5151 A1464   Set of 4   4.25 4.25

Architectural Arches of Havana — A1465

Designs: 15c, Elliptical arch. 65c, Mixtilinear arch. 75c, Polylobular arch.

2010, Sept. 9   *Perf. 12½x12¼*
5152-5154 A1465   Set of 3   3.25 3.25

Lighthouses A1466

Maps and: No. 5155, 15c, Cayo Jutía Lighthouse, Pinar del Rio. No. 5156, 15c, Cayo Cruz del Padre Lighthouse, Matanzas. No. 5157, 15c, Cayo Lucrecia Lighthouse, Holguin. 2.05p, Morro Lighthouse, Santiago de Cuba.

2010, Sept. 15   *Perf. 12¼x12½*
5155-5158 A1466   Set of 4   5.00 5.00
5158a   Souvenir sheet, #5155-
     5158   5.00 5.00

Electric Automobiles — A1467

Designs: 5c, 1893 Jeantaud and Raffard. 10c, 1903 American Pope-Tribune. 15c, 1903 STAE. 20c, Matra Zoom. 45c, Zilent. 75c, Jeep Treo.
1p, Aptera, vert.

2010, Sept. 20   *Perf. 12¾*
5159-5164 A1467   Set of 6   3.50 3.50

Souvenir Sheet
Imperf
5165 A1467 1p multi   2.00 2.00
Portugal 2010 Intl. Philatelic Exhibition. No. 5165 has simulated perforations.

Tourism — A1468

Designs: 20c, Papilio androgeus epidaurus, Viñales National Park. 50c, Mesocapromys nanus, Ciénaga de Zapata National Park. 75c, Trichechus manatus manatus, Alejandro de Humboldt National Park. 90c, Amazona leucocephala, Desembarco del Granma National Park.

2010, Sept. 27   *Perf. 12½x12¼*
5166-5169 A1468   Set of 4   4.75 4.75

Diplomatic Relations Between Cuba and People's Republic of China, 50th Anniv. — A1469

Designs: No. 5170, 15c, Chinese Army, flag of People's Republic of China. No. 5171, 15c, Chinese landscape, arms of People's Republic of China. No. 5172, 85c, Cuban soldiers, horses and boat, flag of Cuba. No. 5173, 85c, Cuban landscape, arms of Cuba.

2010, Sept. 28
5170-5173 A1469   Set of 4   4.00 4.00

America Issue, National Symbols A1470

Designs: No. 5174, 65c, School children, Cuban flag and coat of arms, bust of José Marti. No. 5175, 65c, Cuban coat of arms. No. 5176, 65c, Cuban flag. No. 5177, 65c, Cuban national anthem.

2010, Oct. 12   Litho.   *Perf. 12¾*
5174-5177 A1470   Set of 4   5.25 5.25

World Statistics Day — A1471

2010   *Perf. 12½x12¼*
5178 A1471 65c multi   1.40 1.40

Cuban Television, 60th Anniv. A1472

2010, Oct. 24   *Perf. 12¾*
5179 A1472 1.05p multi   2.10 2.10

22nd Intl. Ballet Festival, Havana — A1473

2010, Oct. 28   *Perf. 12¼x12½*
5180 A1473 65c multi   1.40 1.40

Souvenir Sheet

14th Philatelic Congress, Havana — A1474

2010   *Imperf.*
5181 A1474 1p multi   2.00 2.00

Diplomatic Relations Between Cuba and Viet Nam, 50th Anniv. — A1475

2010, Dec. 2   *Perf. 12¼x12½*
5182 A1475 85c multi   1.75 1.75

Diplomatic Relations Between Cuba and Russia, 50th Anniv. — A1476

2010, Dec. 2   *Perf. 12¾*
5183 A1476 75c multi   1.50 1.50

Diplomatic Relations Between Cuba and Bulgaria, 50th Anniv. — A1477

No. 5184: a, Alexander Nevsky Cathedral, Sofia, Bulgaria, flag of Bulgaria. b, Flag of Cuba, Havana Cathedral.

2010, Dec. 10   *Perf. 12½x12¼*
5184 A1477 75c Horiz. pair, #a-b 3.00 3.00

Dora Alonso (1910-2001), Writer — A1478

2010, Dec. 22   *Perf. 12¾*
5185 A1478 75c multi   1.50 1.50

Diplomatic Relations Between Cuba and Mongolia, 50th Anniv. — A1479

2010   *Perf. 12¼x12½*
5186 A1479 85c multi   1.75 1.75

José Lezama Lima (1910-76), Writer — A1480

2010, Dec. 19   **Litho.**   **Perf. 12¾**
5187 A1480 65c multi   1.40 1.40

Souvenir Sheet

14th Intl. Information Convention and Fair, Havana — A1481

2011, Feb. 7   **Litho.**   **Imperf.**
5188 A1481 1p multi   2.00 2.00

Airplanes and Female Aviators — A1482

Designs: 10c, Bleriot, Matilde Moisant (1878-1964). 15c, Stinson "American Girl," Ruth Elder (1902-77). 20c, Lockheed Vega, Ruth Rowland (1901-60). 50c, Golden Eagle, Bobbi Trout (1906-2003). 65c, Seversky Executive, Jacqueline Cochran (1906-80). 90c, Lockheed Electra, Amelia Earhart (1897-1937).
1p, Curtiss Robin, Berta Moraleda, first Cuban aviatrix.

2011, Feb. 12   **Perf. 12½x12¼**
5189-5194 A1482   Set of 6   5.00 5.00
Souvenir Sheet
Imperf
5195 A1482 1p multi   2.00 2.00
Indipex 2011 Intl. Philatelic Exhibition, New Delhi.

New Year 2011 (Year of the Rabbit) A1483

Rabbit and background color of: No. 5196, 15c, Green. No. 5197, 15c, Red.

2011, Feb. 15   **Perf. 12¾**
5196-5197 A1483   Set of 2   .60 .60

Postal Union of the Americas, Spain and Portugal (UPAEP), Cent. — A1484

2011, Feb. 17
5198 A1484 65c multi   1.40 1.40

Central Army, 50th Anniv. — A1485

2011, Apr. 4   **Litho.**   **Perf. 12½x12¼**
5199 A1485 65c multi   1.40 1.40

Eastern Army, 50th Anniv. — A1486

2011, Apr. 21   **Litho.**   **Perf. 12½x12¼**
5200 A1486 65c multi   1.40 1.40

Earth Day A1487

Designs: 65c, Cart. 90c, Fountain.

2011, Apr. 22   **Perf. 12¾**
5201-5202 A1487   Set of 2   3.25 3.25

Radio Havana, 50th Anniv. — A1488

2011, May 1   **Perf. 12½x12¼**
5203 A1488 2.05p multi   4.25 4.25

Flora and Fauna A1489

Designs: 15c, Anolis vermiculata, Nymphaea. 35c, Apis mellifera, Bidens alba. 40c, Lycorea ceres demeter, Euphorbia helenae. 65c, Osteopilus septentrionalis, Plumeria obtusa. 75c, Ardea alba, Avicennia germinanas. 85c, Liguus fasciatus, Catopsis sp.
1p, Crocodylus rhombifer, Coccoloba uvifera, vert.

2011, June 6   **Perf. 12¾**
5204-5209 A1489   Set of 6   6.50 6.50
Souvenir Sheet
Imperf
5210 A1489 1p multi   2.00 2.00

Ministry of the Interior, 50th Anniv. — A1490

2011, June 8   **Perf. 12½x12¼**
5211 A1490 90c multi   1.90 1.90

Western Army, 50th Anniv. A1491

2011, June 14   **Perf. 12¾**
5212 A1491 75c multi   1.50 1.50

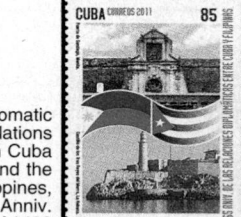

Dances A1492

Designs: No. 5213, 10c, Danzón. No. 5214, 10c, Mambo. 45c, Son. 65c, Rumba. 75c, Cha cha cha. 85c, Salsa.
No. 5219: a, Female Carnaval dancer. b, Male Carnaval dancer.

2011, June 29   **Perf. 12¼x12½**
5213-5218 A1492   Set of 6   6.00 6.00
Souvenir Sheet
Imperf
5219 A1492 50c Sheet of 2, #a-b   2.00 2.00

Diplomatic Relations Between Cuba and the Philippines, 65th Anniv. A1493

2011, July 1   **Perf. 12¾**
5220 A1493 85c multi   1.75 1.75

Locomotives — A1494

Designs: 5c, Best Friend of Charleston, 1830. 10c, Lafayette, 1837. 15c, Robert Stephenson Patentee, 1830. 65c, Thomas Ellis St. David, 1848. 75c, Stephenson long-boiler, 1848. 90c, 4-2-2 Stirling single-wheeler No. 1, 1870.
1p, Shinkansen, 1964.

2011, July 28   **Perf. 12½x12¼**
5221-5226 A1494   5.25 5.25
Souvenir Sheet
Imperf
5227 A1494 1p multi   2.00 2.00
Japan 2011 Intl. Philatelic Exhibition, Yokohama.

Baracoa, 500th Anniv. — A1495

2011, Aug. 15   **Perf. 12½x12¼**
5228 A1495 3p multi   6.00 6.00

Non-Aligned Countries Movement, 50th Anniv. — A1496

2011, Sept. 6   **Perf. 12¾**
5229 A1496 65c multi   1.40 1.40

Birds Endemic to Various Countries — A1497

Designs: 5c, Ramphastos sulfuratus, Belize. 10c, Melanerpes portoricensis, Puerto Rico. 15c, Icterus nigrogularis, Curaçao. 30c, Eumomota superciliosa, El Salvador. 50c, Vanellus chilensis lampronotus, Uruguay, vert. 65c, Pharomachrus mocinno, Guatemala, vert. 75c, Pelecanus occidentalis, St. Kitts and Nevis, vert. 85c, Orthorhycus cristatus, St. Eustatius, Caribbenan Netherlands, vert.

Perf. 12½x12¼, 12¼x12½
2011, Sept. 19
5230-5237 A1497   Set of 8   6.75 6.75

America Issue — A1498

Designs: No. 5238, 65c, Blue mailbox, denomination in pale orange. No. 5239, 65c, Blue green mailbox, denomination in pale rose. No. 5240, 65c, Three mailboxes, denomination in light blue. No. 5241, 65c, Blue green mailbox, denomination in lilac.

2011, Oct. 12   **Perf. 12¾**
5238-5241 A1498   Set of 4   5.25 5.25

Animals — A1499

Designs: 5c, Ursus maritimus, map of Arctic region. 10c, Cervus elaphus canadensis, map of North America. 15c, Lama glama, map of South America. 50c, Canis lupus, map of Europe. 65c, Pongo pygmaeus, map of East Asia. 85c, Phascolarctos cinereus, map of Australia.
1p, Panthera leo, map of Africa.

2011, Oct. 18   *Perf. 12½x12¼*
5242-5247 A1499   Set of 6   4.75 4.75
Souvenir Sheet
Imperf
5248 A1499 1p multi   2.00 2.00

Coral and Fish — A1500

Corals: 10c, Scolymia cubensis. 15c, Mussa angulosa. 20c, Manicina areolata. 30c, Mycetophyllia lamarckiana. 50c, Acropora prolifera. 65c, Tubastraea coccinea.
1p, Stylaster roseus.

2011, Oct. 18   *Perf. 12½x12¼*
5249-5254 A1500   Set of 6   4.00 4.00
Souvenir Sheet
Imperf
5255 A1500 1p multi   2.00 2.00

Revista Pionero, 50th Anniv. — A1501

2011, Nov. 25   *Perf. 12½x12¼*
5256 A1501 1.05p multi   2.10 2.10

Havana Tourist Attractions A1502

Designs: 5c, La Giraldilla, Castillo de la Fuerza. 10c, El Templete Monument. 15c, Plaza de la Catedra. 20c, Bacardi Building. 65c, Grand Theater of Havana. 75c, National Capitol (now Cuban Academy of Sciences).
1p, Morro Castle.

2011, Dec. 12   *Perf. 12¼x12½*
5257-5262 A1502   Set of 6   4.00 4.00
Souvenir Sheet
Imperf
5263 A1502 1p multi   2.00 2.00

Birds and Protected Habitats A1503

Designs: 5c, Contopus caribaeus, Hanabanilla Nature Preserve. 10c, Saurothera merlini, Caguanes National Park. 20c, Spindalis zena, Topes de Collantes Nature Preserve. 45c, Otus lawrencii, Jobo Rosado Protected Area. 65c, Teretistris fernandinae, Alturas de Banao Ecological Reserve. 85c, Priotelus temnurus, El Nicho Nature Preserve.
1p, Grus canadensis, Caguanes National Park.

2011, Dec. 13   *Perf. 12¼x12½*
5264-5269 A1503   Set of 6   4.75 4.75
Souvenir Sheet
Imperf
5270 A1503 1p multi   2.00 2.00

Stage Debut of Ballerina Alicia Alonso, 80th Anniv. — A1504

No. 5271 — Alonso with feet: a, Not visible. b, Visible.

2011, Dec. 29   *Perf. 12¼x12½*
5271 A1504 65c Horiz. pair, #a-b 2.60 2.60

African National Congress, Cent. — A1505

2012, Jan. 8   *Perf. 12¾*
5272 A1505 85c multi   1.75 1.75

Artemisa Province, 1st Anniv. A1506

2012, Jan. 9
5273 A1506 65c multi   1.40 1.40

Electrical Workers Day A1507

2012, Jan. 14
5274 A1507 75c multi   1.50 1.50

Communication Workers Day — A1508

2012, Feb. 24   *Perf. 12½x12¼*
5275 A1508 65c multi   1.40 1.40

Woman at a Window, by René Portocarrero (1912-85) A1509

2012, Feb. 24   *Perf. 12¾*
5276 A1509 1.05p multi   2.10 2.10

Diplomatic Relations Between Ukraine and Cuba, 20th Anniv. — A1510

2012, Mar. 12   *Perf. 12½x12¼*
5277 A1510 75c multi   1.50 1.50

Alejandro Robaina and His Automobile — A1511

No. 5278 — Tobacco field and: a, Robaina (1919-2010), farmer of cigar tobacco. b, Automobile.

2012, Mar. 20   *Perf. 12¾*
5278 A1511 65c Horiz. pair, #a-b 2.60 2.60

Diplomatic Relations Between Azerbaijan and Cuba, 20th Anniv. — A1512

2012, Apr. 16   *Litho.*
5279 A1512 75c multi   1.50 1.50

Diplomatic Relations Between Belarus and Cuba, 20th Anniv. — A1513

2012, Apr. 16   *Perf. 12½x12¼*
5280 A1513 75c multi   1.50 1.50

Capt. Orlando Pantoja Tamayo (1933-67), Capt. Eliseo Reyes Rodriguez (1940-67), First Lt. Antonio Briones Montoto (1939-67), Guerrillas in Intl. Conflicts — A1514

2012, Apr. 25   Litho.   *Perf. 12½x12¼*
5281 A1514 65c multi   1.40 1.40

Afro-Cuban Dances — A1515

Designs: 15c, Elegbá. 20c, Ogún. 30c, Shangó. 50c, Oyá. 65c, Yemayá. 75c, Obatalá.
1p, Oghún.

2012, May 7   Litho.   *Perf. 12¼x12½*
5282-5287 A1515   Set of 6   5.25 5.25
Souvenir Sheet
Imperf
5288 A1515 1p multi   2.00 2.00
No. 5288 has simulated perforations.

Butterflies — A1516

Designs: 5c, Phoebis avellaneda. 10c, Parides gundiachianus. 15c, Greta cubana. 35c, Eurytides celadon. 40c, Anartia chrysopelea. 65c, Dismorphia cubana. 75c, Calisto israel. 85c, Libytheana motya.

2012, May 22   Litho.   *Perf. 12¾*
5289-5296 A1516   Set of 8   6.75 6.75

Cuban Institute of Radio and Television, 50th Anniv. — A1517

2012, May 24   Litho.   *Perf. 12¾*
5297 A1517 90c multi   1.90 1.90

Visit of Pope Benedict XVI to Cuba — A1518

2012, June 6   Litho.   *Perf. 12¼x12½*
5298 A1518 75c multi   1.50 1.50

Shells
A1519

Designs: 10c, Cypraea auratum. 30c, Strombus pugilis. 45c, Voluta fulgetrum. 65c, Architectonica maximum. 75c, Murex beaui. 85c, Spondylus aurantium.
1p, Epitonium pretiosum, vert.

2012, June 6   Litho.   Perf. 12¾
5299-5304 A1519   Set of 6   6.25 6.25
Souvenir Sheet
Imperf
5305 A1519 1p multi   2.00 2.00
No. 5305 has simulated perforations.

Paulina Alvarez (1912-65), Singer — A1520

2012, June 13   Litho.   Perf. 12¾
5306 A1520 1.05p multi   2.10 2.10

2012 Summer Olympics, London A1521

Cuban Olympic gold medal winning athletes: 10c, Orlando Martinez. 15c, Téofilo Stevenson. 20c, Alberto Juantorena. 50c, María Caridad Colón. 65c, Driulys González. 90c, Mireya Luis.
1p, Javier Sotomayor, horiz.

2012, July 5   Litho.   Perf. 12¾
5307-5312 A1521   Set of 6   5.00 5.00
Souvenir Sheet
Imperf
5313 A1521 1p multi   2.00 2.00
No. 5313 has simulated perforations.

Diplomatic Relations Between Cuba and Timor, 10th Anniv. — A1522

2012, July 18   Litho.   Perf. 12½x12¼
5314 A1522 75c multi   1.50 1.50

Civil Defense, 50th Anniv. — A1523

2012, July 20   Litho.   Perf. 12½x12¼
5315 A1523 65c multi   1.40 1.40

Cienfuegos Military Insurrection, 55th Anniv. — A1524

2012, Sept. 5   Litho.   Perf. 12¼x12½
5316 A1524 65c multi   1.40 1.40

2012 National Census — A1525

2012, Sept. 6   Litho.   Perf. 12½x12¼
5317 A1525 65c multi   1.40 1.40

National Lyric Theater, 50th Anniv. — A1526

Perf. 12¼x12½
2012, Sept. 14   Litho.
5318 A1526 65c multi   1.40 1.40

Diplomatic Relations Between Cuba and Kiribati, Tonga, Cook Islands, Nauru, Solomon Islands and Fiji, 10th Anniv. — A1527

Perf. 12¼x12½
2012, Sept. 26   Litho.
5319 A1527 75c multi   1.50 1.50

Diplomatic Relations Between Cuba and France, 110th Anniv. — A1528

2012, Oct. 3   Litho.   Perf. 12¼x12½
5320 A1528 75c multi   1.50 1.50

Diplomatic Relations Between Cuba and Switzerland, 110th Anniv. — A1529

2012, Oct. 3   Litho.   Perf. 12¼x12½
5321 A1529 75c multi   1.50 1.50

Myths and Legends A1530

Designs: No. 5322, 65c, La Gaviota del Rio San Juan (The Gull of San Juan River). No. 5323, 65c, El Güije. No. 5324, 65c, La Giraldilla statue, La Macorina driving car. No. 5325, 65c, La Tatgua y las Matas de Guao.

2012, Oct. 12   Litho.   Perf. 12¾
5322-5325 A1530   Set of 4   5.25 5.25
America Issue.

Miner's Day — A1531

2012, Oct. 24   Litho.   Perf. 12½x12¼
5326 A1531 65c multi   1.40 1.40

Cirilo Villaverde (1812-94), Writer — A1532

2012, Oct. 27   Litho.   Perf. 12½x12¼
5327 A1532 75c multi   1.50 1.50

First Cuban Expedition to Antarctica, 30th Anniv. — A1533

2012, Nov. 7   Litho.   Perf. 12¾
5328 A1533 75c multi   1.50 1.50

Road Safety Campaign — A1534

Designs: 65c, Children's drawing of girl and traffic light. 90c, Children, car, traffic signs.

2012, Nov. 20   Litho.   Perf. 12¾
5329-5330 A1534   Set of 2   3.25 3.25

Ameijeiras Brothers Hospital, Havana, 30th Anniv. — A1535

2012, Nov. 26   Litho.   Perf. 12¾
5331 A1535 65c multi   1.40 1.40

Flora and Fauna A1536

Designs: 5c, Ardilla (squirrel). 10c, Bala de Cañón (cannonball tree flower). 15c, Flor de loto (lotus flower). 65c, Pavo real (peacock), vert. 75c, Polimita (snail), vert. 90c, Orquídea (orchid), vert.
1p, Zorzal real (red-legged thrush), vert.

Perf. 12½x12¼, 12¼x12½
2012, Nov. 29   Litho.
5332-5337 A1536   Set of 6   5.25 5.25
Souvenir Sheet
Imperf
5338 A1536 1p multi   2.00 2.00
Second Cuban Philatelic Cup.

Camagüey Ballet, 50th Anniv. — A1537

Designs: 75c, Fernando Alonso (1914-2013), ballet director, and dancers. 85c, Dancers in Don Quixote.

2012, Dec. 1   Litho.   Perf. 12¾
5339-5340 A1537   Set of 2   3.25 3.25

Diplomatic Relations Between Cuba and Jamaica, Trinidad & Tobago, Barbados and Guyana, 40th Anniv. — A1538

2012, Dec. 6   Litho.   Perf. 12¾
5341 A1538 65c multi   1.40 1.40

Program For Combatting Diabetic Foot Ulcers, 5th Anniv. — A1539

Designs: 65c, Person's feet. 75c, Boxes and vial of Heberprot-P.

2012, Dec. 14   Litho.   Perf. 12¾
5342-5343 A1539   Set of 2   3.00 3.00

Orchids
A1540

Various orchids: 5c, 10c, 15c, 65c, 75c, 90c. 1p, Orchid, diff.

2013, Jan. 15   Litho.   Perf. 12¾
5344-5349 A1540   Set of 6   5.25 5.25
Souvenir Sheet
Imperf
5350 A1540 1p multi   2.00 2.00
No. 5350 has simulated perforations.

Finland-Cuba Friendship Association,
50th Anniv. — A1541

2013, Jan. 17   Litho.   Perf. 12¾
5351 A1541 75c multi   1.50 1.50

Bust of José Martí, by Alberto Lescay Menencio A1542

2013, Jan. 19   Litho.   Perf. 12¾
5352 A1542 3p multi   6.00 6.00
Martí (1853-95), national hero.

National Museum, Cent. — A1543

Paintings: 5c, Torre de Babel (Tower of Babel), by School of Marten van Valckenborgh. 10c, Paisaje (Landscape), by Thomas Creswick. 50c, Saludos al Mar Caribe (Salute to the Caribbean Sea), by Mario Carreño. 65c, Jarrón con Flores (Vase with Flowers), by Amelia Peláez. 75c, Gallo Amarillo (Yellow Rooster), by Mariano Rodríguez. 85c, La Alicantina (Woman from Alicante), by Hermenegildo Anglada. 1p, Homenaje a la Soledad (Homage to Solitude), by Servando Cabrera Moreno.

2013, Jan. 25   Litho.   Perf. 12¾
5353-5358 A1543   Set of 6   6.00 6.00
Souvenir Sheet
Imperf
5359 A1543 1p multi   2.00 2.00
No. 5359 has simulated perforations.

Items Connected to José Martí (1853-95), National Hero — A1544

Designs: 10c, Braid of Martí's hair from childhood, drawing of woman sewing. 15c, Shackle, drawing of men trying to remove leg shackles. 20c, Rostrum from San Carlos Club, Tampa, Florida. 30c, Mambisa badge with flag design. 35c, Colt revolvers. 40c, Pen, drawing of Martí writing.

2013, Jan. 28   Litho.   Perf. 12¾
5360-5365 A1544   Set of 6   3.00 3.00

Chamber of Commerce, 50th Anniv. — A1545

2013, Feb. 1   Litho.   Perf. 12¾
5366 A1545 90c multi   1.90 1.90

Customs Department, 50th Anniv. — A1546

2013, Feb. 5   Litho.   Perf. 12¾
5367 A1546 1.05p multi   2.10 2.10

Third World Baseball Classic — A1547

No. 5368, 15c — Baseball and: a, Cuban uniform shirt., flags of Japan, People's Republic of China, Cuba and Brazil. b, Pitcher for Cuban team, trophy.
No. 5369, 65c — Baseball and: a, Player with glove, trophy. b, Flags of United States, Mexico, Italy and Canada, baseball glove.
No. 5370, 75c — Baseball and: a, Batter, trophy. b, Flags of Venezuela, Puerto Rico, Dominican Republic and Spain, batting helmet.
No. 5371, 85c — Baseball and: a, Catcher's mask, flags of South Korea, Netherlands, Australia and Republic of China. b, Catcher, trophy.

2013, Mar. 2   Litho.   Perf. 12½x12¼
Horiz. Pairs, #a-b
5368-5371 A1547   Set of 4   9.75 9.75

José Raúl Capablanca (1888-1942),
World Chess Champion — A1548

Capablanca and chess position in match between Capablanca and: 15c, Ossip Bernstein, 1911. 65c, Rudolf Spielmann, 1927.

75c, Mikhail Botvinnik, 1936. 85c, Jens Enevoldsen, 1939.

2013, Mar. 8   Litho.   Perf. 12½x12¼
5372-5375 A1548   Set of 4   5.00 5.00

Pets
A1549

Designs: 5c, Pigeon. 15c, Parrot, vert. 50c, Dog. 65c, Turtle. 75c, Cat. 85c, Rabbit. 1p, Horse.

Perf. 12½x12¼, 12¼x12½
2013, Mar. 12   Litho.
5376-5381 A1549   Set of 6   6.00 6.00
Souvenir Sheet
Imperf
5382 A1549 1p multi   2.00 2.00
No. 5382 has simulated perforations.

Souvenir Sheet

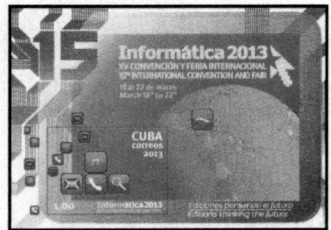

Informática 2013 International
Convention and Fair — A1550

2013, Mar. 18   Litho.   Imperf.
5383 A1550 1p multi   2.00 2.00

Prehistoric Animals — A1551

Designs: 5c, Cricosaurus. 15c, Pterosaurus, vert. 50c, Caribemys. 65c, Gallardosaurus. 75c, Camarasaurus. 85c, Ichthyosaurus. 1p, Vinialesaurus.

Perf. 12½x12¼, 12¼x12½
2013, Apr. 3   Litho.
5384-5389 A1551   Set of 6   6.00 6.00
Souvenir Sheet
Imperf
5390 A1551 1p multi   2.00 2.00
No. 5390 has simulated perforations.

Sauto Theater, 150th Anniv. A1552

2013, Apr. 6   Litho.   Perf. 12¾
5391 A1552 65c multi   1.40 1.40

Australia 2013 Intl. Philatelic
Exhibition, Melbourne — A1553

No. 5392, 15c: a, Parrot. b, Lyrebird.
No. 5393, 45c: a, Garfish. b, Platypus.
No. 5394, 85c: a, Hutia. b, Koala.
1p, Kangaroo and crocodile, horiz.

2013, Apr. 10   Litho.   Perf. 12¼x12½
Horiz. Pairs, #a-b
5392-5394 A1553   Set of 3   6.00 6.00
Souvenir Sheet
Imperf
5395 A1553 1p multi   2.00 2.00
No. 5392 has simulated perforations.

Labor Day — A1554

2013, May 1   Litho.   Perf. 12¾
5396 A1554 65c multi   1.40 1.40

Visit of Dr. Alexander Fleming to
Cuba, 60th Anniv. — A1555

2013, May 12 Litho. Perf. 12½x12¼
5397 A1555 65c multi   1.40 1.40

First Flight From Key West to Havana,
by Domingo Rosillo del Toro,
Cent. — A1556

2013, May 17 Litho. Perf. 12½x12¼
5398 A1556 2.05p multi   4.25 4.25

Souvenir Sheet

National Ballet of Cubaa, 65th
Anniv. — A1557

2013, May 20   Litho.   Imperf.
5399 A1557 1p multi   2.00 2.00
No. 5399 has simulated perforations.

Butterflies — A1558

Designs: 5c, Papilio caiguanabus. 10c, Proteides maysi. 15c, Allosmaitia coelebs. 40c, Anetia cubana. 65c, Kricogonia cabrerai. 75c, Papilio oxynius. 85c, Atlantea perezi. 90c, Eurema lucina.

2013, May 22   Litho.   Perf. 12¾
5400-5407 A1558   Set of 8   7.75 7.75
Compare with Type A1608.

Ministry of Construction, 50th Anniv. — A1559

2013, May 23   Litho.   Perf. 12¾
5408 A1559 90c multi   1.90 1.90

Debut of Alicia Alonso in Ballet *Giselle*, 70th Anniv. — A1560

Paintings of Alonso by: 5c, Servando Cabrera Moreno. 15c, Lorenzo Homar. 20c, Carlos Guzmán. 65c, Alicia Leal. 75c, Francisco Rodón (48x31mm). 90c, Agostino Brotto (48x31mm).
1p, Photograph of Alonso and other dancers, vert.

Perf. 12¾, 12½x12¾ (75p, 90p)
2013, June 5   Litho.
5409-5414 A1560   Set of 6   5.50 5.50
Souvenir Sheet
Imperf
5415 A1560 1p multi   2.00 2.00
No. 5415 contains one 31x48mm stamp with simulated perforations.

Eighth Federation of University Students Congress — A1561

2013, June 12   Litho.   Perf. 12¾
5416 A1561 65c multi   1.40 1.40

Souvenir Sheet

Seventh International Forum on Industrial Design, Havana — A1562

2013, June 18   Litho.   Imperf.
5417 A1562 1p multi   2.00 2.00
No. 5417 has simulated perforations.

Ernesto "Che" Guevara (1928-67), Guerrilla Leader A1563

2013, June 28   Litho.   Perf. 12¾
5418 A1563 65c multi   1.40 1.40

Birds A1564

Designs: 10c, Lophura diardi. 35c, Polyplectron bicalcaratum. 40c, Grus japonensis, vert. 50c, Pica sericea. 65c, Phasianus versicolor. 75c, Falco cherrug, vert. 1p, Pavo cristatus, vert.

Perf. 12½x12¼, 12¼x12½
2013, July 17   Litho.
5419-5424 A1564   Set of 6   5.50 5.50
Souvenir Sheet
Imperf
5425 A1564 1p multi   2.00 2.00
Thailand 2013 International Philatelic Exhibition, Bangkok. No. 5425 has simulated perforations.

Simón Bolívar (1783-1830), Liberator of South America — A1565

Designs: No. 5426, 65c, Paintings of Bolívar. No. 5427, 65c, Bolívar House, Havana, vert.

Perf. 12½x12¼, 12¼x12½
2013, July 24   Litho.
5426-5427 A1565   Set of 2   2.60 2.60
Bolívar House, 20th anniv. as museum.

Dr. Mario Muñoz Monroy (1912-53), Revolutionist A1566

2013, July 26   Litho.   Perf. 12¾
5428 A1566 75c multi   1.50 1.50

Assault on the Moncada and Carlos M. De Céspedes Barracks, 60th Anniv. — A1567

Designs: 45c, Moncada Barracks. 75c, Barracks, diff.

2013, July 26   Litho.   Perf. 12¾
5429-5430 A1567   Set of 2   2.40 2.40

Angerona Coffee Plantation, 200th Anniv. — A1568

2013, Aug. 12   Litho.   Perf. 12¾
5431 A1568 1.05p multi   2.10 2.10

El Brinco Cave A1569

2013, Sept. 6   Litho.   Perf. 12½x12¼
5432 A1569 75c multi   1.50 1.50

22nd Congress of the Postal Union of Spain, Portugal and the Americas, Havana — A1570

Designs: 65p, Quill pen writing on computer screen. 1p, UPAEP emblem.

2013, Sept. 9   Litho.   Perf. 12¾
5433 A1570 65c multi   1.40 1.40
Souvenir Sheet
Imperf
5434 A1570 1p multi   2.00 2.00
No. 5434 contains one 40x32mm stamp.

Armed Peasants Congress, 55th Anniv. — A1571

2013, Sept. 21   Litho.   Perf. 12¾
5435 A1571 85c multi   1.75 1.75

8th Congress of the Committee for the Defense of the Revolution — A1572

2013, Sept. 28   Litho.   Perf. 12¾
5436 A1572 65c multi   1.40 1.40

Mantanzas, 320th Anniv. — A1573

2013, Oct. 12   Litho.   Perf. 12¾
5437 A1573 65c multi   1.40 1.40

Campaign Against Discrimination — A1574

Campaign against: No. 5438, 65c, Child abuse. No. 5439, 65c, Homophobia. No. 5440, 65c, Racial discrimination. No. 5441, 65c, Disability discrimination.

2013, Oct. 12   Litho.   Perf. 12¾
5438-5441 A1574   Set of 4   5.25 5.25
America Issue.

North Korean National Holiday, 65th Anniv. — A1575

2013, Oct. 16   Litho.   Perf. 12¼x12½
5442 A1575 85c multi   1.75 1.75

Brasiliana 2013 International Philatelic
Exhibition, Rio de Janeiro — A1576

No. 5443, 15c: a, Cuica player. b, Tres
player.
No. 5444, 40c: a, Woman of Candomblé
religion. b, Woman of Cuban Santería religion.
No. 5445, 90c: a, Samba dancer. b, Rumba
dancer.
1p, Statue of Jesus Christ, Havana.

2013, Oct. 16 Litho. Perf. 12¼x12½
Horiz. Pairs, #a-b
5443-5445 A1576   Set of 3   6.00 6.00
Souvenir Sheet
Imperf
5446 A1576 1p multi   2.00 2.00
No. 5446 has simulated perforations.

Tenth National Championship of
Philately — A1577

Famous people: 15c, Mario Benedetti
(1920-2009), writer. 20c, Alexander von Humboldt (1769-1859), geographer and naturalist.
45c, Nat King Cole (1919-65), singer. 65c,
Juan Manuel Fangio (1911-95), race car
driver. 75c, Antonio Gades (1936-2004), flamenco dancer. 85c, María Félix (1914-2002),
actress.
1p, Ernest Hemingway (1899-1961), writer.

2013, Oct. 22 Litho. Perf. 12½x12¼
5447-5452 A1577   Set of 6   6.25 6.25
Souvenir Sheet
Imperf
5453 A1577 1p multi   2.00 2.00
No. 5453 has simulated perforations.

Bayamo, 500th
Anniv. — A1578

Designs: 50c, Church steeple. 65c, Carlos
M. Céspedes Barracks and flagpole, horiz.

2013, Nov. 5 Litho. Perf. 12¾
5454-5455 A1578   Set of 2   2.40 2.40

Arab House,
Havana, 30th
Anniv. — A1579

Designs: 75c, Bottle from Syria, 19th cent.
85c, Doorway.

2013, Nov. 13 Litho. Perf. 12¾
5456-5457 A1579   Set of 2   3.25 3.25

National Museum
of Dance,
Havana — A1580

Perf. 12¼x12½
2013, Nov. 25   Litho.
5458 A1580 75c multi   1.50 1.50

Cuban
Revolutionary
Fighters
Association,
20th
Anniv. — A1581

2013, Dec. 6 Litho. Perf. 12¾
5459 A1581 1.05p multi   2.10 2.10

General Prosecutor's Office, 40th
Anniv. — A1582

2013, Dec. 23 Litho. Perf. 12¾
5460 A1582 65c multi   1.40 1.40

Colonel Juan Delgado González
(1868-98) — A1583

Perf. 12½x12¼
2013, Dec. 27   Litho.
5461 A1583 90c multi   1.90 1.90

Triumph of
Cuban
Revolutionists,
55th
Anniv. — A1584

2013, Dec. 30 Litho. Perf. 12¾
5462 A1584 65c multi   1.40 1.40

Santísima
Trinidad, 500th
Anniv. — A1585

Designs: 40c, Trinidad Church. 85c,
Manaca-Iznaga Tower, locomotive.

2014, Jan. 12 Litho. Perf. 12¼x12½
5463-5464 A1585   Set of 2   2.50 2.50

Consecration of the Greek Orthodox
Cathedral of St. Nicholas, 10th
Anniv. — A1586

Designs: 90c, Cathedral, Archbishop Bartholomew of Constantinople, Fidel Castro. 1p,
St. Nicholas, vert.

2014, Jan. 25 Litho. Perf. 12½x12¼
5465 A1586 90c multi   1.90 1.90
Souvenir Sheet
Imperf
5466 A1586 1p multi   2.00 2.00
No. 5466 has simulated perforations.

2014 World Cup
Soccer
Championships,
Brazil — A1587

Designs: 35c, Soccer player. 65c, Maracana
Stadium, Rio de Janeiro. 75c, Mascot. 85c,
Player making bicycle kick.

2014, Feb. 1 Litho. Perf. 12¼x12½
5467-5470 A1587   Set of 4   5.25 5.25

Santa María del Puerto Príncipe
(Camagüey), 500th Anniv. — A1588

Famous people from Camagüey: 5c,
Enrique José Varona (1848-1933), writer. 10c,
Gertrudis Gómez de Avellaneda (1814-73),
writer. 15c, Vicentina de la Torre (1926-95),
dancer. 65c, Fidelio Ponce de León (1895-
1949), painter. 75c, Rafael Fortún (1919-82),
sprinter. 85c, Jorge González Allué (1910-
2001), composer.
1p, Plaza del Carmen, vert.

2014, Feb. 2 Litho. Perf. 12¾
5471-5476 A1588   Set of 6   5.25 5.25
Souvenir Sheet
Imperf
5477 A1588 1p multi   2.00 2.00
No. 5477 has simulated perforations.

Diplomatic Relations Between Cuba
and Haiti, 110th Anniv. — A1589

2014, Feb. 3 Litho. Perf. 12¾
5478 A1589 3p multi   6.00 6.00

Fans
A1590

Woman holding fan and fan from: 5c, 1860.
10c, 1860, diff. 15c, 1920. 45c, 1795-1800.
65c, 1850. 75c, 1717.

Perf. 12½x12¼
2014, Feb. 14 Set of 6   Litho.
5479-5484 A1590   Set of 6   4.50 4.50

20th Congress of Worker's Central
Union — A1591

Perf. 12½x12¼
2014, Feb. 21   Litho.
5485 A1591 75c multi   1.50 1.50

Community of
Latin American
States Summit,
Havana — A1592

Perf. 12¼x12½
2014, Feb. 24   Litho.
5486 A1592 75c multi   1.50 1.50

9th Congress of
Federation of
Cuban
Women — A1593

2014, Mar. 5 Litho. Perf. 12¼x12½
5487 A1593 65c multi   1.40 1.40

Hugo Chávez (1954-2013), President
of Venezuela — A1594

Chávez: 65c, Saluting. 75c, With hand over
heart. 85c, With arm raised.

2014, Mar. 5 Litho. Perf. 12½x12¼
5488-5490 A1594   Set of 3   4.50 4.50

Alejandro Robaina Pereda (1919-2010), Tobacco Grower — A1595

Cigar box and: 10c, Hand holding tobacco seedling, classification of tobacco leaves. 15c, Tobacco growers in field. 30c, Tobacco leaves and equipment for cigar making. 65c, Cigars with Robaina band. 75c, Cigar humidor, lit match. 85c, Cigar box art for Vegas Robaina cigars.

1p, Robaina, vert.

Perf. 12½x12¼
2014, Mar. 20 **Litho.**
5491-5496 A1595 Set of 6 5.75 5.75
Souvenir Sheet
Imperf
5497 A1595 1p multi 2.00 2.00
No. 5497 has simulated perforations.

Gertrudis Gomez de Avellaneda (1814-73), Writer — A1596

Perf. 12¼x12½
2014, Mar. 22 **Litho.**
5498 A1596 1.05p multi 2.10 2.10

Operation Transbordo, 50th Anniv. — A1597

Designs: 45c, Alberto Delgado Delgado (1932-64), undercover agent. 65c, Boat.

2014, Mar. 26 **Litho.** **Perf. 12¾**
5499-5500 A1597 Set of 2 2.25 2.25

Diplomatic Relations Between Antigua and Barbuda and Cuba, 20th Anniv. — A1598

2014, Apr. 4 **Litho.** **Perf. 12¾**
5501 A1598 65c multi 1.40 1.40

National Revolutionary Police, 55th Anniv. — A1599

2014, Apr. 19 **Litho.** **Perf. 12¾**
5502 A1599 90c multi 1.90 1.90

Ministry of Science, Technology and the Environment, 20th Anniv. — A1600

2014, Apr. 21 **Litho.** **Perf. 12½x12¼**
5503 A1600 90c multi 1.90 1.90

Flags of South Africa and Cuba, Nelson Mandela (1918-2013), President of South Africa — A1601

2014, Apr. 28 **Litho.** **Perf. 12¾**
5504 A1601 85c multi 1.75 1.75
Diplomatic relations between South Africa and Cuba, end of apartheid in South Africa, 20th anniv.

Labor Day — A1602

2014, May 1 **Litho.** **Perf. 12¼x12½**
5505 A1602 65c multi 1.40 1.40

Ernesto "Che" Guevara (1928-67), Minister of Industry, and Metallurgical Industries — A1603

Guevara, photographs of industry, plants or finished products and emblem of: 10c, Planta Mecanica. 45c, Profix. 75c, CIME. 85c, Inpud. 90c, Taino.

2014, May 2 **Litho.** **Perf. 12½x12¼**
5506-5510 A1603 Set of 5 6.25 6.25

State Council Historical Affairs Office, 50th Anniv. — A1604

2014, May 9 **Litho.** **Perf. 12½x12¼**
5511 A1604 75c multi 1.50 1.50

Bejucal, 300th Anniv. — A1605

2014, May 10 **Litho.** **Perf. 12¼x12½**
5512 A1605 65c multi 1.40 1.40

St. Francis of Assisi Basilica and Convent Museum, 20th Anniv. — A1606

2014, May 16 **Litho.** **Perf. 12½x12¼**
5513 A1606 90c multi 1.90 1.90

First Agrarian Reform Law, 55th Anniv. — A1607

2014, May 17 **Litho.** **Perf. 12½x12¼**
5514 A1607 65c multi 1.40 1.40

Butterflies — A1608

Designs: 5c, Eurema amelia. 10c, Astraptes cassander. 15c, Panoquina corrupta. 20c, Chioides marmorosa. 40c, Eunica heraclitus. 50c, Parachoranthus magdalia. 65c, Holguinia holguin. 75c, Eantis munroei. 90c, Oarisma nanus.

2014, May 22 **Litho.** **Perf. 12¾**
5515-5523 A1608 Set of 9 7.50 7.50
Compare with Type A1558.

Diplomatic Relations Between Cuba and Congo Republic, 50th Anniv. — A1609

2014, May 23 **Litho.** **Perf. 12¼x12½**
5524 A1609 85c multi 1.75 1.75

National Museum of Natural History, 50th Anniv. — A1610

2014, May 26 **Litho.** **Perf. 12½x12¼**
5525 A1610 75c multi 1.50 1.50

Souvenir Sheet

Hotel Cubanacan Comodoro — A1611

2014, May 31 **Litho.** **Imperf.**
5526 A1611 1p multi 2.00 2.00
Third Cuba Philately Cup.

Sancti Spiritus, 500th Anniv. — A1612

Designs: 65c, Rio Yayabo Bridge. 75c, Parroquial Mayor Church, vert.

Perf. 12½x12¼, 12¼x12½
2014, June 4 **Litho.**
5527-5528 A1612 Set of 2 3.00 3.00

Diplomatic Relations Between Nigeria and Cuba, 40th Anniv. — A1613

2014, July 1 **Litho.** **Perf. 12¼x12½**
5529 A1613 85c multi 1.75 1.75

Office of the Comptroller General, 5th Anniv. — A1614

2014, Aug. 1 **Litho.** **Perf. 12½x12¼**
5530 A1614 90c multi 1.90 1.90

Spanish Heritage Festival, 25th Anniv. — A1615

2014, Aug. 5 Litho. Perf. 12½x12¼
5531 A1615 65c multi 1.40 1.40

Show Jumping Horses — A1616

Designs: 15c, Golden Horse. 20c, Captain VZ. 30c, Fairmont R.E. 65c, Gigaa VDP. 75c, Google. 85c, Goldmann Jr.
1p, Fumuto and rider.

Perf. 12½x12¼
2014, Aug. 16 Litho.
5532-5537 A1616 Set of 6 6.00 6.00
Size: 83x83mm
Imperf
5538 A1616 1p multi 2.00 2.00
No. 5538 has simulated perforations.

African Animals and Map of Africa — A1617

2014, Sept. 2 Litho. Perf. 12½x12¼
5539 A1617 85c multi 1.75 1.75
Diplomatic relations between Cuba and Burundi, Cameroun, Gabon, Senegal, Uganda, Liberia and Madagascar, 40th anniv.

Latin American Parliament, 50th Anniv. — A1618

2014, Sept. 5 Litho. Perf. 12½x12¼
5540 A1618 65c multi 1.40 1.40

Diplomatic Relations Between Benin and Cuba, 40th Anniv. — A1619

2014, Sept. 12 Litho. Perf. 12¾
5541 A1619 85c multi 1.75 1.75

Guitars — A1620

Perf. 12¼x12½
2014, Sept. 25 Litho.
5542 A1620 65c multi 1.40 1.40
75th birthday of Leo Brouwer, guitarist and composer.

People's Republic of China, 65th Anniv. — A1621

Perf. 12½x12¼
2014, Sept. 29 Litho.
5543 A1621 85c multi 1.75 1.75

Lighthouses A1622

Designs: 15c, Morro Castle Lighthouse, Havana. 35c, Cayo Jutías Lighthouse, Pinar del Rio. 75c, Cayo Cruz del Padre Lighthouse, Matanzas. 85c, Morro Lighthouse, Santiago.

2014, Oct. 5 Litho. Perf. 12¼x12½
5544-5547 A1622 Set of 4 4.25 4.25

Philakorea 2014 Intl. Stamp Exhibition, Seoul — A1623

Dogs: 10c, Poodle (caniche). 20c, Yorkshire terrier. 30c, Schnauzer. 40c, Beagle. 65c, German shepherd (pastor aleman). 75c, Golden retriever.
1p, Collie (pastor escocés de pelo largo).

Perf. 12½x12¼
2014, June 15 Litho.
5548-5553 A1623 Set of 6 5.00 5.00
Souvenir Sheet
Imperf
5554 A1623 1p multi 2.00 2.00
No. 5554 contains one 43x33mm stamp with simulated perforations.

Malaysia 2014 Intl. Stamp Exhibition, Kuala Lumpur — A1624

Cats: 10c, Shorthaired cat (pelos cortos). 20c, Persian cat (Persas). 40c, Balinese cat (Balineses). 65c. Bengal cat (Bengalies). 75c, Siamese cat (Siameses), horiz. 85c, Semi-longhaired cat (pelos semi-largos).
1p, Cuban blue cat (azules cubanos).

Perf. 12¼x12½, 12½x12¼
2014, July 30 Litho.
5555-5560 A1624 Set of 6 6.00 6.00
Souvenir Sheet
Imperf
5561 A1624 1p multi 2.00 2.00
No. 5554 has simulated perforations.

Trains A1625

Designs: 5c, Talgo AVE series 100. 15c, Alstom FGC series 113. 50c, Siemens AVE series 103. 65c, Talgo AVE series 130. 75c, CRH380A. 85c, JR-Maglev MLX01.
1p, Cabina AVE series 102.

Perf. 12½x12¼
2014, Sept. 15 Litho.
5562-5567 A1625 Set of 6 6.00 6.00
Souvenir Sheet
Imperf
5568 A1625 1p multi 2.00 2.00
No. 5568 contains one 61x26mm trapezoidal stamp with simulated perforations.

Marine Life A1626

Designs: 5c, Volvarina moresi. 10c, Sepia officinalis. 30c, Amblyrhynchus cristatus. 65c, Physeter macrocephalus, vert. 75c, Aptenodytes patagonicus, vert. 85c, Eretmochelys imbricata, vert.
1p, Pomacanthus arcuatus, vert.

2014, Oct. 4 Litho. Perf. 12¾
5569-5574 A1626 Set of 6 5.50 5.50
Souvenir Sheet
Imperf
5575 A1626 1p multi 2.00 2.00
No. 5575 has simulated perforations.

Famous Men — A1626a

Designs: No. 5575A, 65c, José Martí (1853-95), writer. No. 5575B, 65c, Antonio Maceo Grajales (1845-96), military leader. No. 5575C, 65c, Ignacio Agramonte y Loynaz

(1841-73), revolutionist. No. 5575D, 65c, Carlos Manuel de Céspedes (1819-74), declarer of Cuban independence.

2014, Oct. 12 Litho. Perf. 12¾
5575A-5575D A1626a Set of 4 5.25 5.25
America Issue.

Airplanes of Cubana Arilines — A1627

Designs: 15c, Curtiss Robin. 20c, Bristol Britannia. 45c, Lockheed 10 Electra. 75c, Antonov 158.

2014, Oct. 22 Litho. Perf. 12½x12¼
5576-5579 A1627 Set of 4 3.25 3.25

Independence of Malawi, Tanzania and Zambia, 50th Anniv. — A1628

2014, Oct. 24 Litho. Perf. 12¼x12½
5580 A1628 85c multi 1.75 1.75

National Road Safety Day A1629

Children's drawings: 15c, Taxi and signs. 20c, Children in crosswalk. 40c, Tractor and cow on road. 50c, Car, sign and traffic light. 65c, Child chasing ball in street. 75c, Railroad crossing.
1p, Policeman, crosswalk, traffic light.

2014, Nov. 17 Litho. Perf. 12¾
5581-5586 A1629 Set of 6 5.50 5.50
Souvenir Sheet
Imperf
5587 A1629 1p multi 2.00 2.00
No. 5587 has simulated perforations.

Cuban Philatelic Treasures A1630

Designs: 10c, Stampless cover, ship. 20c, Cover with three stamps, mask. 30c, Havana local post cover with two stamps, watchtower, horiz. 65c, Cover with Mambí insurrection stamps, mounted soldier with Cuban flag. 75c, Cover with Puerto Principe surcharges, tower. 85c, Experimental rocket mail cover, rocket.
1p, Statue and birds, horiz.

Perf. 12¼x12½, 12½x12¼
2014, Nov. 20 **Litho.**
5588-5593 A1630 Set of 6 5.75 5.75
Souvenir Sheet
Imperf
5594 A1630 1p multi 2.00 2.00
No. 5554 contains one 44x31mm stamp with simulated perforations.

Diplomatic Relations Between Cuba and the Bahamas, 40th Anniv. — A1631

Perf. 12½x12¼
2014, Nov. 28 **Litho.**
5595 A1631 3p multi 6.00 6.00

José Antonio Echeverria City University, 50th Anniv. — A1632

2014, Dec. 2 Litho. Perf. 12½x12¼
5596 A1632 65c multi 1.40 1.40

2014 Diabetes Congress, Varadero Beach — A1633

Designs: 65c, Infected foot, bottle of medicine and surgeon's saw. 75c, People pulling on fabric covering over feet.

Perf. 12½x12¼
2014, Dec. 10 **Litho.**
5597-5598 A1633 Set of 2 3.00 3.00

Protected Flora and Fauna — A1634

Designs: 5c, Todus multicolor. 10c, Peireskia cubensis. 15c, Eretmochelys imbricata. 75c, Tetramicra eulophiae. 85c, Starnoenas cyanocephala. 90c, Bonnetia cubensis.
1p, Colaptes fernandinae, vert.

2014, Dec. 15 Litho. Perf. 12¾
5599-5604 A1634 Set of 6 5.75 5.75
Souvenir Sheet
Imperf
5605 A1634 1p multi 2.00 2.00
No. 5605 has simulated perforations.

Tomás Romay Chacón (1764-1849), Physician — A1635

Perf. 12½x12¼
2014, Dec. 21 **Litho.**
5606 A1635 65c multi 1.40 1.40

José Luis Guerra Aguiar Postal Museum, 50th Anniv. — A1636

Designs: 5c, 1826 stampless cover from Santiago de Cuba to Puerto Principe. 10c, 1883 cover with stamps depicting King Alfonso XII. 15c, Handstamp and free frank covers of General Máximo Gómez Báez. 20c, Cuba #238, printing stone for stamp similar to #238. 65c, Handstamp, cover with Cuba #C324-C325. 75c, Children looking at museum exhibit, magnifying glass and album pages.
1p, Cover with Cuba #935a-935b.

2015 Jan. 9 Litho. Perf. 12½x12¼
5607-5612 A1636 Set of 6 4.00 4.00
Souvenir Sheet
Imperf
5613 A1636 1p multi 2.00 2.00
No. 5613 contains one 44x33mm stamp with simulated perforations.

National Organization of Collective Law Offices, 50th Anniv. — A1637

2015, Jan. 22 Litho. Perf. 12½x12¼
5614 A1637 65c multi 1.40 1.40

Fish — A1638

Inscriptions: 5c, Siamese fighting fish (Luchador de Siam). 15c, Clown loach (Locha payaso), horiz. 45c, Pearl gourami (Gurami perla), horiz. 65c, Butterfly cichlid (Ciclido mariposa), horiz. 75c, Mollies (Pez molly), horiz. 90c, Goldfish, horiz.
1p, Angelfish (Escalar).

Perf. 12¼x12½, 12½x12¼
2015, Jan. 20 **Litho.**
5615-5620 A1638 Set of 6 6.00 6.00
Souvenir Sheet
Imperf
5621 A1638 1p multi 2.00 2.00
No. 5621 contains one 29x45mm stamp with simulated perforations.

Dogs A1639

Designs: 15c, Cocker spaniels. 30c, Golden retrievers. 40c, Border collies. 65c, Alaskan malamutes. 75c, Labrador retrievers. 85c, St. Bernards.
1p, German shepherds, vert.

2015, Jan. 20 Litho. Perf. 12½x12¼
5622-5627 A1639 Set of 6 6.25 6.25
Souvenir Sheet
Imperf
5628 A1639 1p multi 2.00 2.00
No. 5628 has simulated perforations.

Faustino Pérez Hernández (1920-92), Central Committee Member, Zaza Dam — A1640

Perf. 12½x12¼
2015, Feb. 15 **Litho.**
5629 A1640 1.05p multi 2.10 2.10

Ballet "Dioné," 75th Anniv. — A1641

Designs: 75c, Composer Eduardo Sánchez de Fuentes (1874-1944) and scene from ballet. 90c, Dancers Alicia and Fernando Alonso.

2015, Mar. 4 Litho. Perf. 12½x12¼
5630-5631 A1641 Set of 2 3.50 3.50

Ballet Performances of Anna Pavlova in Cuba, Cent. — A1642

Perf. 12¼x12½
2015, Mar. 18 **Litho.**
5632 A1642 65c multi 1.40 1.40

Manuel López Portilla (1940-60), State Security Agent — A1643

Perf. 12¼x12½
2015, Mar. 26 **Litho.**
5633 A1643 65c multi 1.40 1.40

Explosion of Ship "La Coubre" in Havana Harbor, 55th Anniv. — A1644

2015, Apr. 1 Litho. Perf. 12½x12¼
5634 A1644 3p multi 6.00 6.00

Railway Cars — A1645

Designs: 10c, Tanker cars. 20c, Flat cars. 50c, Lumber cars. 65c, Cars carrying intermodal containers. 75c, Coal cars. 85c, Automobile carrier.
1p, Poultry car.

2015, Mar. 4 Litho. Perf. 12½x12¼
5635-5640 A1645 Set of 6 6.25 6.25
Souvenir Sheet
Imperf
5641 A1645 1p multi 2.00 2.00
No. 5641 contains one 45x30mm stamp with simulated perforations.

Endangered Birds — A1646

Birds and maps of their range: 5c, Passerina ciris. 15c, Chiroxiphia caudata, vert. 20c, Amadina fasciata. 75c, Carduelis carduelis, vert. 85c, Chloebia gouldiae, vert. 90c, Leionthrix argentauris.
1p, Ferminia cerverai, vert.

Perf. 12½x12¼, 12¼x12½
2015, Apr. 10 **Litho.**
5642-5647 A1646 Set of 6 6.00 6.00
Souvenir Sheet
Imperf
5648 A1646 1p multi 2.00 2.00
No. 5648 has simulated perforations.

Landing of José Martí and General Máximo Gómez Báez at Playita, 120th Anniv. — A1647

No. 5649 — Playita and: a, 65c, Martí. b, 75c, Gómez.

2015, Apr. 11 Litho. Perf. 12¼x12½
5649 A1647 Horiz. pair, #a-b 3.00 3.00

Raúl Ferrer (1915-93), Poet and Educator — A1648

2015, Apr. 17 Litho. *Perf. 12¾*
5650 A1648 75c multi 1.50 1.50

Use of First Stamps in Cuba, 160th Anniv. — A1649

No. 5651: a, 10c, Havana postal badge, mailman and mailboxes. b, 30c, Padlock and key, horse-drawn postal wagons. c, 65c, Post office scale, postal workers sorting mail. d, 75c, Title of Postal Administration, post office.

2015, Apr. 24 Litho. *Perf. 12½x12¼*
5651 A1649 Block of 4, #a-d 3.75 3.75

Labor Day — A1650

2015, May 1 Litho. *Perf. 12¼x12½*
5652 A1650 75c multi 1.50 1.50

Diplomatic Relations Between Cuba and Russia, 55th Anniv. — A1651

2015, May 8 Litho. *Perf. 12¼x12½*
5653 A1651 85c multi 1.75 1.75

Havana Explosion and Fire of 1890, 125th Anniv. — A1652

Firefighter killed in explosion and horse-drawn: 5c, Cervantes pumper. 10c, Colón pumper. 15c, Fire wagon. 40c, Ambulance. 65c, Gámiz pumper. 75c, Cuba pumper.
1p, Megaphone and monument plaque listing the victims, vert.

2015, May 15 Litho. *Perf. 12¾*
5654-5659 A1652 Set of 6 4.25 4.25
Souvenir Sheet
Imperf
5660 A1652 1p multi 2.00 2.00
No. 5660 has simulated perforations.

Ferry "Pinero" — A1653

2015, May 16 Litho. *Perf. 12½x12¼*
5661 A1653 75c multi 1.50 1.50
Arrival of Fidel Castro and other Moncada Barracks attackers at Batabanó, 60th anniv.

International Telecommunication Union, 150th Anniv. — A1654

2015, May 17 Litho. *Perf. 12¼x12½*
5662 A1654 65c multi 1.40 1.40

Elisio Reyes (1940-67), Guerrilla Fighter — A1655

2015, May 23 Litho. *Perf. 12½x12¼*
5663 A1655 65c multi 1.40 1.40

Wild Cats A1656

Designs: 15c, Panthera onca, Olmec ceremonial hatchet. 35c, Puma concolor, gorget. 50c, Panthera tigris, carving of tiger. 65c, Panthera leo, Thracian grave decoration. 75c, Acinonyx jubatus, decorated Egyptian knife. 85c, Panthera pardus, Nigerian bronze plaque.
1p, Felis silvestris catus, Japanese drawing of cat.

2015, Apr. 15 Litho. *Perf. 12½x12¼*
5664-5669 A1656 Set of 6 6.50 6.50
Souvenir Sheet
Imperf
5670 A1656 1p multi 2.00 2.00
No. 5670 has simulated perforations.

Prehistoric Fauna — A1657

Designs: 10c, Carcharodon megalodon. 35c, Metaxytherium. 50c, Ptychodus. 65c, Aetomylaeus cubensis. 75c, Physetérid. 85c, Orycterocetus.
1p, Aspidorhynchus.

2015, May 6 Litho. *Perf. 12½x12¼*
5671-5676 A1657 Set of 6 6.50 6.50
Souvenir Sheet
Imperf
5677 A1657 1p multi 2.00 2.00
No. 5677 has simulated perforations.

Santiago de Cuba, 500th Anniv. — A1658

Designs: 5c, Lieutenant General Maceo Grajales, painting by Luis Desangles. 10c, Monument to Frank Pais. 15c, Fidel Castro at Mausoleum of José Martí. 30c, San Pedro de la Roca Castle. 75c, La Isabelica coffee plantation building, horiz. 85c, Tumba Francesa dancers and musicians, horiz.
1p, City Hall.

2015, May 20 Litho. *Perf. 12¾*
5678-5683 A1658 Set of 6 4.50 4.50
Souvenir Sheet
Imperf
5684 A1658 1p multi 2.00 2.00
No. 5684 has simulated perforations.

National Flowers of Central and South American Countries A1659

Flowers: 5c, Dahlia (Mexico). 15c, Golden trumpet (Brazil). 20c, Mayflower orchid (Venezuela). 30c, Ceibo (Argentina, Uruguay). 40c, Virgin orchid (Honduras). 65c, Rose (Ecuador). 75c, Copihue (Chile). 90c, White ginger (Cuba).

2015, May 26 Litho. *Perf. 12¼x12½*
5685-5692 A1659 Set of 8 7.00 7.00

Watercraft — A1660

Designs: 5c, SC CL Globe, China. 20c, Paraw, Philippines. 50c, Paddlewheeler Junco, Viet Nam. 65c, Kettuvallam, India. 75c, Dhoni, Maldive Islands, vert. 85c, Junk, China, vert.
1p, Turtle ship, Korea, vert.

Perf. 12½x12¼, 12¼x12½
2015, June 1 Litho.
5693-5698 A1660 Set of 6 6.00 6.00
Souvenir Sheet
Imperf
5699 A1660 1p multi 2.00 2.00
Singapore 2015 Intl. Philatelic Exhibition. No. 5699 contains one 32x48mm stamp with simulated perforations.

San Juan de los Remedios, 500th Anniv. — A1661

Designs: 65c, Buildings of San Juan de los Remedios. 75c, Alejandro García Caturla (1906-40), composer.

Perf. 12½x12¼
2015, June 24 Litho.
5700-5701 A1661 Set of 2 3.00 3.00

National Office of Tax Administration, 20th Anniv. — A1662

Perf. 12¼x12½
2015, June 28 Litho.
5702 A1662 65c multi 1.40 1.40

History of the Telephone A1663

Designs: 10c, 19th cent. desk telephone. 20c, 20th cent. wall telephone. 30c, 19th cent. desk telephone, diff. 50c, 20th cent. desk telephone. 65c, 20th cent. desk telephones, diff. 75c, 20th cent. two desk telphones.
1p, 20th cent. public pay telephone.

2015, July 14 Litho. *Perf. 12¾*
5703-5708 A1663 Set of 6 5.00 5.00
Souvenir Sheet
Imperf
5709 A1663 1p multi 2.00 2.00
No. 5709 has simulated perforations.

Mariana Grajales Coello (1808-93), Mother of Generals José and Antonio Maceo Grajales A1664

Designs: 65c, Mariana Grajales Coello and Cuban flag. 75c, Monument.

2015, July 24 Litho. *Perf. 12¼x12½*
5710-5711 A1664 Set of 2 3.00 3.00

Alicia Alonso National School of Ballet, 65th Anniv. — A1665

2015, Aug. 5 Litho. Perf. 12½x12¼
5712 A1665 65c multi   1.40 1.40

Cuban Court of International Commercial Arbitration, 50th Anniv. — A1666

Perf. 12¼x12½
2015, Sept. 16   Litho.
5713 A1666 3p multi   6.00 6.00

Committee for the Defense of the Revolution, 55th Anniv. — A1667

Perf. 12½x12¼
2015, Sept. 21   Litho.
5714 A1667 65c multi   1.40 1.40

Campaign Against Human Trafficking — A1668

Campaign against: No. 5715, 65c, Sexual exploitation (Explotación sexual). No. 5716, 65c, Forced labor (Trabajo forzado). No. 5717, 65c, Organ extraction (Extracción de órganos). No. 5718, 65c, Servitude (Servidumbre).

2015, Oct. 12 Litho. Perf. 12¼x12½
5715-5718 A1668 Set of 4   5.25 5.25
America Issue.

Paintings and Artifacts Connected to José Martí — A1669

Designs: 5c, Martí on horseback, spurs from Battle of Dos Ríos. 10c, House of General Máximo Gómez, Montecristi, and inkstand. 15c, Martí leading cavalrymen, Winchester rifle. 20c, Martí in rowboat, oarlocks. 30c, Martí reading *Patria* newpaper, plaque from Patria building. 40c, Martí addressing crowd, pulpit. 75c, María García Granados (1860-78), love interest of Martí and subject of Martí

poem, cushion. 85c, Martí writing, desk and chair.

2015, Oct. 15 Litho. Perf. 12¼x12½
5719-5726 A1669 Set of 8   5.75 5.75

Cuban Television, 65th Anniv. — A1670

2015, Oct. 24   Litho. Perf. 12¾
5727 A1670 75c multi   1.50 1.50
  a.   Dated "2015"
No. 5727 has "201" date at lower right.

Cuban Wushu and Qigong School, 20th Anniv. — A1671

2015, Oct. 26 Litho. Perf. 12½x12¼
5728 A1671 85c multi   1.75 1.75

Visit of Pope Francis — A1672

Perf. 12½x12¼
2015, Nov. 11   Litho.
5729 A1672 75c multi   1.50 1.50

11th National Stamp Championships — A1673

Designs: 10c, Marlon Brando (1924-2004), actor, Academy Award. 15c, Mother Teresa (St. Teresa of Calcutta) (1910-97), crucifix. 20c, Babe Ruth (1895-1948), baseball player, baseball. 65c, Charles A. Lindbergh (1902-74), aviator, Spirit of St. Louis. 75c, Gabriel García Márquez (1927-2014), writer, book, eyeglasses and butterflies. 85c, Diego Rivera (1886-1957), painter, detail of "The Uprising." 1p, Diego A. Maradona, soccer player, World Cup trophy.

Perf. 12½x12¼
2015, Nov. 20   Litho.
5730-5735 A1673 Set of 6   5.50 5.50
Souvenir Sheet
Imperf
5736 A1673 1p multi   2.00 2.00
No. 5736 has simulated perforations.

Nico López (1932-56), Revolutionary — A1674

2015, Dec. 2 Litho. Perf. 12½x12¼
5737 A1674 65c multi   1.40 1.40
Communist Party Schools, 55th anniv.

Souvenir Sheet

Alicia Alonso, Ballet Dancer — A1675

2016, Jan. 1 Litho. Imperf.
5738 A1675 1p multi   2.00 2.00
Reopening of Alicia Alonso Grand Theater, Havana.

Conrado Benítez (1942-61), Revolutionary Martyr — A1676

2016, Jan. 5 Litho. Perf. 12¾
5739 A1676 90c multi   1.90 1.90

Research Center for Animal Breeding of Tropical Livestock, 45th Anniv. — A1677

Designs: 65c, Research center, livestock. 75c, Researchers and livestock.

2016, Jan. 8 Litho. Perf. 12½x12¼
5740-5741 A1677 Set of 2   3.00 3.00

Mayabeque Province, 5th Anniv. — A1678

2016, Jan. 9 Litho. Perf. 12¼x12½
5742 A1678 90c multi   1.90 1.90

Francisco de Albear Fernández y de Lara (1816-87), Civil Engineer — A1679

2016, Jan. 11 Litho. Perf. 12½x12¼
5743 A1679 1.05p multi   2.10 2.10

Waterbirds — A1680

Designs: 10c, Alcedo atthis. 15c, Phaethon rubricauda. 45c, Branta canadensis. 75c, Threskiornis aethiopicus. 85c, Anas platyrhynchos. 90c, Branta canadensis, vert. 1p, Fratercula arctica, vert.

Perf. 12½x12¼, 12¼x12½
2016, Jan. 15   Litho.
5744-5749 A1680 Set of 6   6.50 6.50
Souvenir Sheet
Imperf
5750 A1680 1p multi   2.00 2.00
No. 5750 contains one 30x36mm stamp with simulated perforations. Bird name inscription on No. 5749 is incorrect.

General Calixto García University Hospital, Havana, 120th Anniv. — A1681

2016, Jan. 23 Litho. Perf. 12¼x12½
5751 A1681 65c multi   1.40 1.40

Second "Con Todos y Para el Bien de Todos" International Conference on Works of José Martí, Havana — A1682

2016, Jan. 25 Litho. Perf. 12¼x12½
5752 A1682 2.05p multi   4.25 4.25

Dinosaurs — A1683

Designs: 5c, Cryolophosaurus. 20c, Amargasaurus. 65c, Camarasaurus. 75c, Pachyrhinosaurus. 85c, Baryonyx. 90c, Allosaurus. 1p, Gorgosaurus.

2016, Jan. 31 Litho. Perf. 12½x12¼
5753-5758 A1683 Set of 6 7.00 7.00
Souvenir Sheet
Imperf
5759 A1683 1p multi 2.00 2.00
No. 5759 has simulated perforations.

Classic Automobiles — A1684

Designs: 5c, 1932 Duesenberg SJ Dual-cowl Phaeton. 15c, 1936 Bugatti Type 57SC Atlantic. 50c, 1931 Lincoln Model K. 65c, 1936 Mercedes-Benz 540 K. 75c, 1934 Chevrolet Master Sport Coupe. 85c, 1934 Ford Deluxe Roadster.
1p, 1938 Volkswagen Type 1.

Perf. 12½x12¼
2016, Feb. 20 Litho.
5760-5765 A1684 Set of 6 6.00 6.00
Souvenir Sheet
Imperf
5766 A1684 1p multi 2.00 2.00
No. 5766 has simulated perforations.

Ministry of Industry, 55th Anniv. — A1685

Perf. 12¼x12½
2016, Feb. 22 Litho.
5767 A1685 3p multi 6.00 6.00

Restoration of Teatro Martí, Havana — A1686

Designs: 45c, Building exterior. 50c, Stage. 65c, Seats and ceiling.

2016, Feb. 24 Litho. Perf. 12¾
5768-5770 A1686 Set of 3 3.25 3.25

Establishment of Cuban Postal Service, 260th Anniv. — A1687

Designs: 10c, Mail ship and captain, 1777. 40c, Postman, horse and carriage, 1902. 65c, Special delivery postman on motorcycle, 1950. 85c, Postman on bicycle, 2013.
1p, Postman on horse.

2016, Mar. 1 Litho. Perf. 12¾
5771-5774 A1687 Set of 4 4.00 4.00
Souvenir Sheet
Imperf
5775 A1687 1p multi 2.00 2.00
No. 5775 has simulated perforations.

Fe del Valle Ramos (1917-61), Department Store Worker Killed in Arson Fire — A1688

2016, Mar. 8 Litho. Perf. 12¾
5776 A1688 65c multi 1.40 1.40

Fauna — A1689

Designs: No. 5777, 90c, Buteo regalis, Bison bison. No. 5778, 90c, Ramphastos toco, Leopardus pardalis. No. 5779, 90c, Oncorhynchus mykiss. No. 5780, 90c, Trichechus manatus, Atractosteus tristoechus.

Perf. 12¼x12½
2016, Mar. 10 Litho.
5777-5780 A1689 Set of 4 7.25 7.25

Souvenir Sheet

16th Informática Intl. Convention and Fair — A1690

2016, Mar. 14 Litho. Imperf.
5781 A1690 1p multi 2.00 2.00

Central Army, 55th Anniv. — A1691

2016, Apr. 4 Litho. Perf. 12¼x12½
5782 A1691 65c multi 1.40 1.40

Sculptures by José Villa Soberón — A1692

Designs: 10c, Caballero de Paris. 35c, Tin Tan. 40c, Gabriel García Márquez. 75c, John Lennon. 85c, Benny Moré. 90c, Antonio Gades.
1p, Ernest Hemingway, vert.

2016, Apr. 5 Litho. Perf. 12½x12¼
5783-5788 A1692 Set of 6 6.75 6.75
Souvenir Sheet
Imperf
5789 A1692 1p multi 2.00 2.00
2016 Copa Cuba National Stamp Exhibition.
No. 5789 has simulated perforations.

Trains A1693

Designs: 10c, Liverpool & Manchester Railway train, 1830. 20c, American express train, 1885. 35c, Orient Express, 1883. 75c, Trans-Siberian train, 1883. 85c, Blue Train, 1903. 90c, Union Pacific train.
1p, Shinkansen Sereis 700 train.

2016, Apr. 5 Litho. Perf. 12½x12¼
5790-5795 A1693 Set of 6 6.50 6.50
Souvenir Sheet
Imperf
5796 A1693 1p multi 2.00 2.00
No. 5796 has simulated perforations.

Eastern Army, 55th Anniv. — A1694

2016, Apr. 21 Litho. Perf. 12½x12¼
5797 A1694 65c multi 1.40 1.40

National Association of Small Farmers, 55th Anniv. — A1696

2016, May 17 Litho. Perf. 12¼x12½
5799 A1696 85c multi 1.75 1.75

Musical Instruments — A1697

Designs: 5c, Laúd. 15c, Corneta China. 35c, Catá. 75c, Chequeré. 85c, Iyá.

2016, May 18 Litho. Perf. 12½x12¼
5800-5804 A1697 Set of 5 4.50 4.50

Enrique José Varona (1848-1933), Writer — A1698

2016, May 19 Litho. Perf. 12½x12¼
5805 A1698 75c multi 1.50 1.50
Cuban Academy of Language, 90th anniv.

Extinct and Endangered Hutias — A1699

Designs: 5c, Mesocapromys sanfelipensis. 15c, Mesocapromys nanus. 35c, Mesocapromys angelcabrerai. 45c, Mesocapromys auritus. 75c, Mysateles melanurus. 85c, Mysateles prehensilis.
1p, Capromys pilorides.

2016, May 23 Litho. Perf. 12¼x12½
5806-5811 A1699 Set of 6 5.25 5.25
Souvenir Sheet
Imperf
5812 A1699 1p multi 2.00 2.00
No. 5812 has simulated perforations.

National Flowers of North and South American Countries — A1700

Designs: 5c, Maga, Puerto Rico. 15c, Bougainvillea (bugambilia), Canada. 20c, Romerillo, St. Lucia. 30c, Plumeria (sacuanjoche), Nicaragua. 40c, Soufriere tree flower, St. Vincent and the Grenadines. 65c, Poinciana (framboyán), Haiti and St. Kitts and Nevis, vert. 75c, Dagger's log, Antigua and Barbuda, vert. 90c, Kantuta, Bolivia, vert.

2016, May 26 Litho. Perf. 12¾
5813-5820 A1700 Set of 8 7.00 7.00

Victims of Terrorism — A1701

Designs: 65c, Airplane, boat, people walking on street. 75c, Newspaper headline, people looking at wall of photographs.

2016, June 3 Litho. Perf. 12½x12¼
5821-5822 A1701 Set of 2 3.00 3.00

Ministry of the Interior, 55th Anniv. A1702

2016, June 5 Litho. Perf. 12¾
5823 A1702 90c multi 1.90 1.90

Western Army, 55th Anniv. — A1703

Perf. 12½x12¼
2016, June 14 Litho.
5824 A1703 65c multi 1.40 1.40

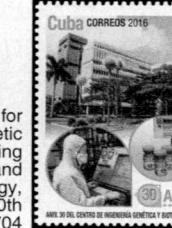

Center for Genetic Engineering and Biotechnology, 30th Anniv. — A1704

2016, July 1   Litho.   Perf. 12¾
5825 A1704 90c multi   1.90 1.90

Cuban Amateur Radio Federation, 50th Anniv. — A1705

2016, July 15   Litho.   Perf. 12¼x12½
5826 A1705 1.05p multi   2.10 2.10

SEMI-POSTAL STAMPS

Common Design Types pictured following the introduction.

Curie Issue
Common Design Type
Wmk. 106
1938, Nov. 23   Engr.   Perf. 10
B1 CD80 2c + 1c salmon   4.25 1.00
B2 CD80 5c + 1c deep ultra 4.25 1.40
Set, never hinged   12.00

40th anniv. of the discovery of radium by Pierre and Marie Curie. Surtax for the benefit of the Intl. Union for the Control of Cancer.

Catalogue values for unused stamps in this section, from this point to the end of the section, are for Never Hinged items.

"Agriculture" Supporting "Industry" SP2

Engr., Center Typo.
1959, May 7   Wmk. 321   Perf. 12½
B3 SP2 2c + 1c car & ultra   .70 .25

Agricultural reforms. See No. CB1. For surcharges see Nos. 624, C199.

Nurse — SP3

Wmk. 229
1959, Sept. 22   Photo.   Perf. 12½
B4 SP3 2c + 1c crimson rose .40 .25

Exists imperf, value about double.

AIR POST STAMPS

Seaplane over Havana Harbor AP1

Wmk. 106
1927, Nov. 1   Engr.   Perf. 12
C1 AP1 5c dark blue   8.00 1.00
  Never hinged   13.50

For overprint see No. C30.

Type of 1927 Issue Overprinted

1928, Feb. 8
C2 AP1 5c carmine rose   6.25 1.60
  Never hinged   10.00

No. 283 Surcharged in Red

1930, Oct. 27   Unwmk.
C3 A44 10c on 25c violet   5.75 1.60
  Never hinged   8.50

Airplane and Coast of Cuba — AP3

For Foreign Postage
1931, Feb. 26   Wmk. 106   Perf. 10
C4 AP3 5c green   .45 .25
C5 AP3 10c dk blue   .45 .25
C6 AP3 15c rose   .90 .30
C7 AP3 20c brown   .90 .25
C8 AP3 30c dk violet   1.25 .25
C9 AP3 40c dp orange   4.00 .35
C10 AP3 50c olive grn   6.75 .35
C11 AP3 1p black   10.00 .90
  Nos. C4-C11 (8)   24.70 2.90
  Set, never hinged   37.50

See No. C40. For surcharges see Nos. C16-C17, C203, C225.

Airplane AP4

For Domestic Postage
1931-46
C12 AP4 5c rose vio ('32) .40 .25
 a.   5c brown violet ('36) .40 .25
C13 AP4 10c gray blk   .40 .25
C14 AP4 20c car rose   3.25 .90
C14A AP4 20c rose pink ('46) 1.40 .25
C15 AP4 50c dark blue   5.25 .90
  Nos. C12-C15 (5)   10.70 2.55
  Set, never hinged   17.00

See #C130. For overprints see #C31, E29-E30.

Type of 1931 Surcharged in Black

1935, Apr. 24   Perf. 10
C16 AP3 10c + 10c red   15.00 9.50
  Never hinged   20.00

---

 a. Double surcharge   110.00
Imperf
C17 AP3 10c + 10c red   40.00 40.00
  Never hinged   55.00 55.00

Matanzas Issue

Air View of Matanzas AP5

10c, Airship "Macon." 20c, Airplane "The Four Winds." 50c, Air View of Fort San Severino.

Wmk. 229
1936, May 5   Photo.   Perf. 12½
C18 AP5 5c violet   .85 .30
C19 AP5 10c yellow orange 1.00 .50
C20 AP5 20c green   3.75 1.90
C21 AP5 50c greenish slate 9.00 3.75
  Nos. C18-C21 (4)   14.60 6.45
  Set, never hinged   22.50

Exist imperf. Value 20% more.

"Lightning" AP9

Allegory of Flight AP10

1936, Nov. 18
C22 AP9 5c violet   2.10 1.10
C23 AP10 10c orange brown 2.75 1.50
  Set, never hinged   6.00

Major Gen. Maximo Gomez, birth cent.

Flat Arch (Panama) — AP11

Carlos Antonio López (Paraguay) — AP12

Inca Gate, Cuzco (Peru) — AP13

Atlacatl (Salvador) AP14

José Enrique Rodó (Uruguay) AP15

Simón Bolívar (Venezuela) AP16

Wmk. 106
1937, Oct. 13   Engr.   Perf. 10
C24 AP11 5c red   7.75 7.75
C25 AP12 5c red   7.75 7.75
C26 AP13 10c blue   7.75 7.75
C27 AP14 10c blue   7.75 7.75
C28 AP15 20c green   10.00 10.00
C29 AP16 20c green   10.00 10.00
  Nos. C24-C29 (6)   51.00 51.00
  Set, never hinged   67.50

See note after No. 354.

Type of 1927 Ovptd. in Black

1938, May   Wmk. 106
C30 AP1 5c dark orange   7.25 1.60
  Never hinged   10.00

1st airplane flight from Key West to Havana, made by Domingo Rosillo, 1913.

Type of 1931-32 Overprinted

1939, Oct. 15
C31 AP4 10c emerald   32.50 6.50
  Never hinged   55.00

Issued in connection with an experimental postal rocket flight held at Havana.

Sir Rowland Hill, Map of Cuba and First Stamps of Britain, Spanish Cuba and Republic of Cuba — AP17

1940, Nov. 28   Engr.   Wmk. 106
C32 AP17 10c brown   6.75 2.00
  Never hinged   11.00

Souvenir Sheet
Unwmk.   Imperf.
C33   Sheet of 4   22.50 22.50
  Never hinged   35.00
 a.   AP17 10c light brown 5.50 3.50
  Never hinged   8.00

Cent. of the 1st postage stamp. Sheet sold for 60c.
No. C33 exists with each of the four stamps overprinted in black: "Exposicion de la ACNU/24 de Octubre de 1951/Dia de las Naciones" and "Historia de la Aviacion" in lower margin. Value, $80.
For overprints see Nos. C39, C211.

Poet José Heredia and Palms AP18

Heredia and Niagara Falls — AP19

1940, Dec. 30   Wmk. 106
C34 AP18 5c emerald   3.25 1.00
C35 AP19 10c greenish slate 4.00 1.60
  Set, never hinged   11.00

Death cent. of José Maria Heredia y Campuzano (1803-39), poet and patriot.

First Cuban Land Sighted by Columbus AP20

Columbus Lighthouse AP21

1944, May 19
C36 AP20 5c olive green 1.10 .40
C37 AP21 10c slate black 2.50 .75
450th anniv. of the discovery of America.

Catalogue values for unused stamps in this section, from this point to the end of the section, are for Never Hinged items.

Conference of La Mejorana (Maceo, Gomez and Marti) AP22

1948, May 21 Wmk. 229 Perf. 12½
C38 AP22 8c org yel & blk 4.50 .80
50th anniv. of the start of the War of 1895.

Souvenir Sheet
No. C33 Overprinted in Ultramarine

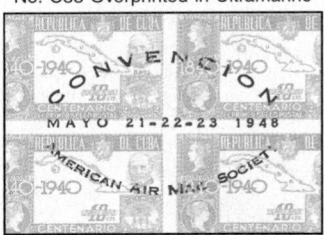

1948, May 21 Unwmk. Imperf.
C39 AP17 Sheet of 4 25.00 9.50
The overprint is applied in the center of the sheet, so that a part of the overprint falls on each stamp.
American Air Mail Soc. Convention, Havana, May 21 to 23, 1948. The sheets sold for 60c each.

Type of 1931
1948, June 15 Wmk. 106 Perf. 10
C40 AP3 8c orange brown 2.75 .80

Narciso Lopez Landing at Cárdenas AP23

Flag on Cuban Fort — AP24   Flag on Morro Castle, Havana — AP25

Engraved and Lithographed
1951, July 3 Wmk. 229 Perf. 13
C41 AP23 5c ol grn, ultra & red 2.75 .30
C42 AP24 8c red brn, bl & red 4.25 .30
C43 AP25 25c gray blk, bl & red 6.00 1.90
Nos. C41-C43 (3) 13.00 2.50
Centenary of adoption of Cuba's flag.

Souvenir Sheet
No. 365a Overprinted in Green

1951, Aug. 24 Unwmk. Imperf.
C43A Sheet of 4 19.00 9.00
50th anniv. of the discovery of the cause of yellow fever by Dr. Carlos J. Finlay, and to honor the martyrs of science.

Postage Type and

Resignation Play of Dr. Lasker AP26

Capablanca Making "The Exact Play" — AP27

Wmk. 229
1951, Nov. 1 Photo. Perf. 13
C44 AP26 5c shown 8.00 .80
C45 AP27 8c shown 12.00 1.25
C46 A165 25c Capablanca 22.50 3.25
Nos. C44-C46 (3) 42.50 5.30
30th anniv. of the winning of the World Chess title by José Raul Capablanca.

Morrillo Types of Regular Issue
Wmk. 106
1951, Nov. 22 Engr. Perf. 10
C47 A167 5c violet 3.25 .70
C48 A168 8c deep green 4.50 1.00
C49 A169 25c dark brown 8.75 2.00
a. Souv. sheet of 6, black brown, perf. 13 72.50 35.00
b. Souv. sheet of 6, green, imperf. 225.00 125.00
Nos. C47-C49 (3) 16.50 3.70
Nos. C49a and C49b contain one each of the 1c, 2c and 5c of types A167-A169 and of the 5c, 8c and 25c airmail stamps of types A167-A169. Sheets are unwatermarked and measure 124x133mm.

Isabella Type of Regular Issue, 1952
1952, Feb. 22
C50 A172 25c purple 5.75 1.25
a. Souv. sheet of 2, perf. 11 35.00 35.00
b. Souv. sheet of 2, imperf. 35.00 35.00
Nos. C50a and C50b contain one each of a 2c of type A172 and a 25c air-mail stamp of type A172. In No. C50a, the 2c and marginal inscriptions are brown carmine; the 25c, dark blue. In No. C50b, the 2c and marginal inscriptions are dark blue; the 25c, brown carmine. Sheets measure 108x18mm.

Type of Regular Issue of 1951 Surcharged in Various Colors

1952, Mar. 18
Color: Yellow Brown
C51 A159 5c on 2c .90 .30
C52 A159 8c on 2c (C) 1.75 .30
C53 A159 10c on 2c (Bl) 1.75 .30
C54 A159 25c on 2c (V) 3.25 1.50
C55 A159 50c on 2c (C) 13.50 3.00
C56 A159 1p on 2c (Bl) 20.00 12.00
Nos. C51-C56 (6) 41.15 17.40

Country School AP32

Entrance, University of Havana — AP33

10c, Presidential Mansion. 25c, Banknote.

Wmk. 106
1952, May 27 Engr. Perf. 12½
Centers Various Shades of Green
C57 AP32 5c dark purple .60 .25
C58 AP33 8c dark red .95 .25
C59 AP32 10c deep blue 1.90 .25
C60 AP32 25c dark violet brn 3.25 1.00
Nos. C57-C60 (4) 6.70 1.75
Foundation of the Republic of Cuba, 50th anniv.

Plane and Map — AP34   Agustín Parlá — AP35

1952, July 22 Engr. Perf. 10
C61 AP34 8c black 2.00 .55
a. Souv. sheet, 8c deep blue 18.00 10.00
b. Souv. sheet, 8c deep green 18.00 10.00
C62 AP35 25c ultra 5.50 1.60
a. Souv. sheet, 25c deep blue 18.00 10.00
b. Souv. sheet, 25c deep green 18.00 10.00
30th anniv. of the Key West-Mariel flight of Agustin Parla.
The four souvenir sheets are perf. 11.

Col. Charles Hernandez y Sandrino — AP36

1952, Oct. 7
C63 AP36 5c orange .80 .30
C64 AP36 8c brt yel grn .80 .30
C65 AP36 10c dk red 1.00 .30
C66 AP36 15c dk Prus grn 1.90 .80
C67 AP36 20c aqua 2.50 1.00
C68 AP36 25c crimson 1.90 1.00
C69 AP36 30c dk vio bl 5.25 2.50
C70 AP36 45c rose lilac 8.00 3.50
C71 AP36 50c indigo 6.50 2.50
C72 AP36 1p bister 16.00 5.00
Nos. C63-C72 (10) 44.65 17.20
Three-fourths of the proceeds from the sale were used for the Communications Ministry Employees' Retirement Fund.

Entrance, University of Havana — AP37

F. V. Dominguez, M. Estebanez and F. Capdevila — AP38

Engr.; Center Typo.
1952, Nov. 27
C73 AP37 5c indigo & dk blue 2.50 .40
C74 AP38 25c org & dk grn 6.75 1.40
Execution of 8 medical students, 81st anniv.

AP39

Lockheed Constellation Airliners — AP40

1953, May 22 Engr.
C75 AP39 8c orange brn 1.75 .25
C76 AP39 15c scarlet 3.25 .70
Typographed and Engraved
C77 AP40 2p dp green & dk brn 42.50 10.00
C78 AP40 5p blue & dk brn 82.50 17.50
Nos. C75-C78 (4) 130.00 28.45
See Nos. C120-C121. For surcharge, see No. C224.

Page of Manifesto of Montecristi — AP42

House of Maximo Gomez AP43

No. C79, Marti in Kingston, Jamaica. No. C80, With Workers in Tampa, Florida. No. C83, Marti addressing liberating army. No. C84, Portrait. No. C85, Dos Rios obelisk. No. C86, Marti's first tomb. No. C87, Present tomb. No. C88, Monument in Havana. No. C89, Martian forge.

1953 Engr. Perf. 10
C79 AP42 5c dk car & blk .30 .25
C80 AP42 5c dk car & blk .30 .25
C81 AP43 8c dk green & blk .65 .25
C82 AP43 8c dk green & blk .65 .25
C83 AP43 10c dk blue & dk car 1.75 .75
C84 AP43 10c dk blue & dk car 1.75 .75
C85 AP42 15c violet & gray 1.50 .90
C86 AP42 15c violet & gray 1.50 .90
C87 AP42 25c brown & car 4.75 1.25
C88 AP42 25c brown & car 4.75 1.25
C89 AP43 50c yellow & bl 6.25 2.50
Nos. C79-C89 (11) 24.15 9.30
Cent. of the birth of José Marti.

Board of Accounts
Building — AP44

25c, Plane above Board of Accounts Bldg.

1953, Nov. 3
| C90 | AP44 | 8c rose carmine | 2.25 | .70 |
| C91 | AP44 | 25c dk gray grn | 4.00 | 1.10 |

1st Intl. Cong. of Boards of Account,
Havana, Nov. 2-9, 1953.

Miguel Coyula   Antonio Ginard
Llaguno   Rojas
AP45   AP46

Designs: 10c, Gregorio Hernandez Saez.
1p, Communications Association Flag.

1954
C92	AP45	5c dark blue	.65	.25
C93	AP46	8c red violet	.80	.25
C94	AP46	10c orange	1.40	.35
C95	AP45	1p black	9.50	4.50
		Nos. C92-C95 (4)	12.35	5.35

See note after No. C72.

Alvaro
Reinoso — AP47

Plane and
Harvesters
Cutting Cane
AP48

Designs in Lower Triangle: 5c, Four-engine
Plane and Cane Field. 10c, Tractor pulling
loaded wagons. 15c, Train of sugar cane. 20c,
Modern mill. 25c, Evaporators. 30, Sacks of
sugar. 40c, Loading sugar on ship. 45c, Ox
cart. 50c, Primitive sugar mill.

1954, Apr. 27   **Engr.**
C96	AP47	5c yellow green	.55	.25
C97	AP48	8c brown	1.50	.50
C98	AP48	10c dark green	1.50	.50
C99	AP48	15c henna brn	3.75	.50
C100	AP48	20c blue	1.50	.25
C101	AP48	25c scarlet	1.15	.25
C102	AP48	30c lilac rose	3.00	.95
C103	AP48	40c deep blue	6.25	1.25
C104	AP48	45c violet	5.00	2.50
C105	AP48	50c brt blue	5.00	1.60
C106	AP47	1p dk gray blue	13.50	3.25
		Nos. C96-C106 (11)	42.70	11.80

For surcharges see Nos. C204.

Sanatorium Type of Regular Issue
1954, Sept. 21   Wmk. 106   Perf. 10
| C107 | A186 | 9c deep green | 2.50 | .65 |

Dolz Type of Regular Issue, 1954
1954, Dec. 23
| C108 | A188 | 12c carmine | 3.50 | .70 |

Rotary Type of Regular Issue, 1955
1955, Feb. 23
| C109 | A190 | 12c carmine | 2.50 | .65 |

Stamps
of 1855
and
1905,
Palace
of Fine
Arts
AP52

Designs (including 2 stamps): 12c, Plaza de
la Fraternidad. 24c, View of Havana. 30c,
Plaza de la Republica.

1955, Apr. 24   **Perf. 12½**
C110	AP52	8c dk grnsh bl & grn	1.00	.35
C111	AP52	12c dk ol grn & red	1.10	.35
C112	AP52	24c dk red & ultra	2.00	.95
C113	AP52	30c dp org & brn	4.25	1.60
		Nos. C110-C113 (4)	8.35	3.25

Cent. of Cuba's 1st postage stamps.

Mariel
Bay — AP53

Views: 12c, Varadero beach. 1p, Vinales
valley.

1955, June 22   **Wmk. 106**
C114	AP53	8c dk car & dk grn	.75	.25
C115	AP53	12c dk ocher & brt bl	1.75	.55
C116	AP53	1p dk grn & ocher	7.50	2.50
		Nos. C114-C116 (3)	10.00	3.30

See note after No. C72.

Map of
Crocier's 1914
Flight — AP54

Design: 30c, Crocier in plane.

1955, July 4   **Perf. 10**
| C117 | AP54 | 12c red & dk grn | 1.00 | .25 |
| C118 | AP54 | 30c dk grn & mag | 3.00 | .80 |

35th anniv. of the death of Jaime Gonzalez
Crocier, aviation pioneer.

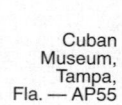

Cuban
Museum,
Tampa,
Fla. — AP55

1955, July 1   **Engr.**   **Perf. 12½**
| C119 | AP55 | 12c red & dk brn | 3.25 | .65 |

Cent. of Tampa's incorporation as a town.

Lockheed Type of 1953
Typographed and Engraved
1955, Sept. 21   **Wmk. 106**
| C120 | AP40 | 2p bl & ol grn | 29.00 | 6.50 |
| C121 | AP40 | 5p dp rose & ol grn | 62.50 | 15.00 |

Wright
Brothers'
Plane and
Stamps
AP56

Designs: 12c, Spirit of St. Louis. 24c, Graf
Zeppelin. 30c, Constellation passenger plane.
50c, Convair jet fighter.

Engraved and Photogravure
1955, Nov. 12   Wmk. 106   Perf. 12½
Inscription and Plane in Black
C122	AP56	8c car & bl	1.10	.35
C123	AP56	12c yel grn & car	2.50	.70
C124	AP56	24c vio & car	7.50	2.50
C125	AP56	30c bl & red org	6.50	3.25

C126	AP56	50c ol grn & red org	8.50	4.00
a.		Souvenir sheet of 5	57.50	26.00
		Nos. C122-C126 (5)	26.10	10.80

International Centenary Philatelic Exhibition
in Havana, Nov. 12-19, 1955.
No. C126a is printed on thick paper and
measures 140x178mm. It contains one each
of Nos. C122-C126 with the background of
each stamp printed in a different color from the
perforated stamps.

"Three
Friends"
and Gen.
Emilio
Nuñez
AP57

Design: 12c, Landing on the Cuban Coast.

1955, Dec. 27   **Engr.**   **Unwmk.**
| C127 | AP57 | 8c ultra & dk car | 2.00 | .55 |
| C128 | AP57 | 12c grn & dk red brn | 3.25 | .90 |

Gen. Emilio Nuñez, Cuban revolutionary
hero, birth cent.

Post Type of Regular Issue, 1956
Bishop P. A. Morell de Santa Cruz (1694-
1768).

1956, Mar. 27   **Wmk. 106**
| C129 | A197 | 12c dk brn & grn | 3.25 | .55 |

Plane Type of 1931-46
1956   **Engr.**   **Perf. 10**
| C130 | AP4 | 50c greenish blue | 5.00 | 1.00 |

Portrait Type of Regular Issue, 1956
Portraits: 8c, Gen. Julio Sanguily. 12c, Gen.
José Maria Aguirre. 30c, Col. Ernesto Fonts
Sterling.

1956, May 2   **Perf. 12½**
Portraits in Black
C131	A198	8c brown	1.25	.25
C132	A198	12c dull yellow	2.00	.25
C133	A198	30c indigo	3.00	1.50
		Nos. C131-C133 (3)	6.25	2.00

See note after No. C72.

Mother and
Child — AP60

1956, May 13   Wmk. 106   Perf. 12½
| C134 | AP60 | 12c ultra & red | 3.00 | .40 |

Issued in honor of Mother's Day 1956.

Masonic Temple
Havana — AP61

1956, June 5
| C135 | AP61 | 12c olive green | 3.25 | .55 |

Pigeon
AP62

Gundlach
Hawk — AP63

Birds: 8c, Wood duck. 19c, Herring gulls.
24c, White pelicans. 29c, Common mergan-
ser. 30c, Quail. 50c, Herons (great white,
great blue and Wurdemann's). 1p, Northern
caracara. 2p, Middle American jacana. 5p,
Ivory-billed woodpecker.

1956
C136	AP62	8c blue	.50	.25
C137	AP62	12c gray blue	10.00	.25
C138	AP63	14c green	2.25	.25
C139	AP63	19c redsh brn	1.50	.55
C140	AP63	24c lilac rose	1.60	.55
C141	AP62	29c green	2.50	.55
C142	AP62	30c dk olive bis	3.00	.80
C143	AP63	50c slate blk	5.75	1.10
C144	AP63	1p dk car rose	8.75	2.25
C145	AP62	2p rose violet	17.50	4.25
C146	AP63	5p brt red	47.50	8.75
		Nos. C136-C146 (11)	100.85	19.55

See Nos. C205, C235-C237. For
surcharges and overprints, see Nos. C147,
C151, C197, C209-C210.

Type of 1956
Surcharged

Design: 24c, White pelicans.

1956, July 13
| C147 | AP63 | 8c on 24c deep org | 2.50 | .75 |

Opening of the new building of the Cuba
Philatelic Club, Havana, July 14, 1956.

Hubert de
Blanck — AP64

1956, July 6
| C148 | AP64 | 12c ultra | 2.75 | .40 |

Hubert de Blanck (1856-1932), composer.

Church of Our
Lady of
Charity — AP65

1956, Sept. 8
| C149 | AP65 | 12c grn & car | 3.25 | .55 |
| a. | | Souvenir sheet of 2, imperf. | 18.00 | 9.50 |

Issued in honor of Our Lady of Charity of
Cobre, patroness of Cuba.
No. C149a contains one each of Nos. 559
and C149. No. C149a exists with yellow of No.
559 omitted.

Benjamin Franklin AP66

1956, Oct. 5   Engr.   Perf. 12½
C150 AP66 12c red brown   3.25   .55

Type of 1956 Surcharged in Blue

Design: 2p, Middle American jacana.

1956, Oct. 26   Wmk. 106
C151 AP62 12c on 2p dark gray   3.25   .95
Issued in honor of the 12th Inter-American Press Association Conference, Havana.

Lord Baden-Powell AP67

1957, Feb. 22
C152 AP67 12c slate   3.25   .70
Centenary of the birth of Lord Baden-Powell, founder of the Boy Scouts.

Hanabanilla Waterfall AP68

12c, Sierra de Cubitas. 30c, Puerto Boniato.

1957, Mar. 29
C153 AP68 8c blue & red   .75   .25
C154 AP68 12c green & red   2.75   .50
C155 AP68 30c ol grn & dk pur   3.25   .70
    Nos. C153-C155 (3)   6.75 1.45
See note after No. 457.

Philatelic Club, Havana — AP69

1957, Apr. 24   Wmk. 106   Perf. 12½
C156 AP69 12c yel, grn & brn   2.75   .40
Stamp Day, and the Natl. Phil. Exhib.

Fingerprint — AP70

1957, Apr. 30
C157 AP70 12c claret brown   2.40   .40
Birth cent. (in 1856) of Juan Francisco Steegers y Perera, dactyloscopy pioneer.

Baseball Player — AP71

1957, May 17   Wmk. 106   Perf. 12½
C158 AP71 8c shown   1.25   .40
C159 AP71 12c Ballerina   2.50   .50
C160 AP71 24c Girl diver   3.50 1.25
C161 AP71 30c Boxers   5.25 1.60
    Nos. C158-C161 (4)   12.50 3.75
Issued to honor young Cuban athletes.

Joaquin de Aguero — AP72

1957, July 4
C162 AP72 12c indigo   1.75   .40
Issued to honor Joaquin de Aguero, Cuban freedom fighter and patriot.

Jeanette Ryder — AP73

1957, July 17
C163 AP73 12c dk red brn   2.50   .55
    a.   Pair, #574, C163   7.00 3.50
Mrs. Jeanette Ryder, founder of the Humane Society of Cuba.

José M. de Heredia y Girard — AP74

1957, Aug. 16   Engr.   Wmk. 106
C164 AP74 8c dk blue vio   1.50   .30
José Maria de Heredia y Girard (1842-1905), Cuban born French poet.

Justice Type of Regular Issue, 1957
1957, Sept. 2   Perf. 12½
C165 A214 12c green   2.75   .50

John Robert Gregg — AP75

1957, Oct. 1
C166 AP75 12c dark green   2.50   .70
90th anniv. of the birth of John Robert Gregg, inventor of the Gregg shorthand system.

D. Figarola Caneda — AP76

José Marti National Library AP77

1957, Oct. 18   Wmk. 106   Perf. 12½
C167 AP76 8c ultra   .75   .25
C168 AP77 12c chocolate   2.00   .50
José Marti National Library.

Map of Cuba and UN Emblem AP78

1957, Oct. 24
C169 AP78 8c dk green & brn   1.15   .25
C170 AP78 12c car rose & grn   1.75   .55
C171 AP78 30c ind & brt pink   4.00 1.25
    Nos. C169-C171 (3)   6.90 2.05
Issued for United Nations Day, 1957.

Map of Cuba and Florida AP79

1957, Oct. 28
C172 AP79 12c dk red brn & bl   2.40   .80
30th anniv. of airmail service from Key West to Havana.

Type of Regular Issue, 1957 and

Stairway and Bell Tower AP80

Design: 12c, Facade of Normal School.

1957, Nov. 19   Engr.   Perf. 12½
C173 A217 12c indigo & ocher   1.75   .40
C174 AP80 30c dk car & gray   3.25   .60

View Types of Regular Issue, 1957
Views: 8c, El Viso Fort, El Caney. 12c, Sancti Spiritus Church. 30c, Concordia Bridge, Matanzas.

1957, Dec. 17   Perf. 12½
C175 A218 8c dk gray & red   .80   .30
C176 A219 12c brown & gray   1.50   .40
C177 A218 30c red brn & bl gray   3.50   .75
    Nos. C175-C177 (3)   5.80 1.45
See note after No. C72.

Hedges Types of Regular Issue, 1958
8c, Dayton Hedges & Matanzas rayon factory.

1958, Jan. 30   Wmk. 106   Perf. 12½
C178 A221 8c green   1.15   .80

Diario de la Marina Building — AP81

1958, Apr. 1
C179 AP81 29c black   4.25 1.10
Jose Ignacio Rivero y Alonso, editor of the newspaper, Diario de la Marina.

Map Showing Sea Mail Route, 1765 AP82

1958, Apr. 24   Wmk. 106   Perf. 12½
C180 AP82 29c dk bl aqua & buff   4.75 1.25
Issued for Stamp Day, Apr. 24, and the National Philatelic Exhibition.

Gen. Gomez in Battle — AP83

1958, June 6   Engr.
C181 AP83 12c slate green   2.00   .55
Issued in honor of Maj. Gen. José Miguel Gomez, President of Cuba, 1909-13.

Snail (Polymita Picta) — AP84

12c, Megalocnus Rodens. 30c, Ammonite.

1958, Aug. 29   Wmk. 321   Perf. 12½
C182 AP84 8c gray, red & yel   5.00 1.25
C183 AP84 12c brn, yel grn   7.50 1.75
C184 AP84 30c grn, pink   12.00 2.10
    Nos. C182-C184 (3)   24.50 5.10
Centenary of the birth of Dr. Carlos de la Torre, naturalist.

Papilio Caiguanabus AP85

Cuban Sea Bass — AP86

12c, Teria gundlachia. 14c, Teria ebriola. 19c, Nathalis felicia. 29c, Butter Hamlet. 30c, Tattler.

1958, Sept. 26   Wmk. 106   Perf. 12½
C185 AP85 8c multicolored   3.00   .65
C186 AP85 12c emer, blk & org   3.50   .65
C187 AP85 14c multicolored   5.25   .95
C188 AP85 19c bl, blk & yel   6.75 1.25
C189 AP86 24c multicolored   7.50 1.25
C190 AP86 29c blk, brn & ultra   11.00 1.60
C191 AP86 30c blk, yel grn & sep   16.00 2.25
    Nos. C185-C191 (7)   53.00 8.60
Felipe Poey (1799-1891), naturalist.

Battle of San Juan Hill, 1898 — AP87

Wmk. 106
1958, Oct. 27   Engr.   Perf. 12½
C192 AP87 12c black brown   2.75   .50
Birth centenary of Theodore Roosevelt.

UNESCO Building, Paris — AP88

Design: 30c, "UNESCO" and map of Cuba.

1958, Nov. 7
C193 AP88 12c dk slate grn 2.25 .50
C194 AP88 30c dp ultra 4.25 1.60
UNESCO Headquarters in Paris opening, Nov. 3.

Postal Notice of 1765 — AP89

Design: 30c, Administrative postal book of St. Cristobal, Havana, 1765.

1959, Apr. 24   Wmk. 321   Perf. 12½
C195 AP89 12c Prus blue & sep 1.50 .40
C196 AP89 30c sepia & Prus bl 2.50 1.40
Issued for Stamp Day, Apr. 24, and the National Philatelic Exhibition.

Type of 1956 Surcharged in Dark Blue

1959, Oct. 17   Wmk. 321   Perf. 12½
C197 AP63 12c on 1p emerald 2.40 1.40
Issued to publicize the meeting of the American Soc. of Travel Agents, Oct. 17-23.

Musical Arts Building — AP90

Wmk. 106
1959, Nov. 11   Engr.   Perf. 12½
C198 AP90 12c yellow green 3.00 .70
40th anniversary of the Musical Arts Society.

No. CB1 Surcharged in Red

Engr. & Typo.
1960   Wmk. 321   Perf. 12½
C199 SPAP1 12c on 12 + 3c car & grn 2.25 .75

Type of Regular Issue, 1960
8c, Battle of Santa Clara. 12c, Rebel forces entering Havana. 29c, Bank-note changing hands ("Clandestine activities in the cities").

Wmk. 320
1960, Jan. 28   Engr.   Perf. 12½
C200 A236 8c bl, gray ol & sal 2.25 .40
C201 A236 12c gray ol & ocher 3.25 .40
C202 A236 29c gray & car 6.50 1.50
Nos. C200-C202 (3) 12.00 2.40

Nos. C9 and C104 Srchd. in Red

1960, Feb. 3   Wmk. 106
C203 AP3 12c on 40c dp org 1.75 .65
C204 AP48 12c on 45c vio 1.75 .65

Pigeon Type of 1956
1960, Feb. 12   Wmk. 321
C205 AP62 12c brt blue grn 2.00 .55

Statue Type of Regular Issue, 1960.
Statues: 8c, José Marti, Matanzas. 12c, Heroes of the Cacarajicara, Pinar del Rio. 30c, Cosme de la Torriente, Isle of Pines, horiz.

1960, Mar. 28   Perf. 12½
C206 A237 8c gray & car .70 .25
C207 A237 12c blue & car 1.25 .25
C208 A237 30c violet & brn 2.75 1.25
Nos. C206-C208 (3) 4.70 1.75
See note after No. 386.

Type of 1956 and No. C33 Overprinted in Dark Blue

1960, Apr. 24   Wmk. 321   Perf. 12½
C209 AP62 8c orange yel .65 .40
C210 AP62 12c cerise 1.75 .65

Souvenir Sheet
C211 AP17 Sheet of 4 35.00 35.00
Stamp Day, 4/24/60, and Natl. Phil. Exhib. No. C211 has added marginal inscription in dark blue for cent. of the ¼r on 2r (No. 15).

Type of Olympic Games Issue, 1960
Wmk. 321
1960, Sept. 22   Engr.   Perf. 12½
C212 A238 8c Boxer .80 .25
C213 A238 12c Runner 1.50 .50
a. Souvenir sheet of 4 5.50 5.50
17th Olympic Games, Rome, Aug. 25-Sept. 11. No. C213a contains one each imperf. of types of Nos. 645-646 and Nos. C212-C213 in dark blue.

No. C3 and Flight Symbols of 1930, 1960 — AP91

1960, Oct. 30   Litho.   Unwmk.
C214 AP91 8c multicolored 3.50 2.00
30th anniv. of national air mail service.

Sword of Sheaf of Wheat — AP92

12c, Two workers, horiz. 30c, Three maps, horiz. 50c, Hand inscribed "Peace" in 5 languages.

1961, Jan. 10   Photo.   Perf. 11½
Granite Paper
C215 AP92 8c multicolored .60 .25
C216 AP92 8c multicolored 2.00 .25
C217 AP92 30c black & red 2.50 .65
C218 AP92 50c blk, bl & red 3.00 1.00
Nos. C215-C218 (4) 8.10 2.15
Conf. of Underdeveloped Countries, Havana.

José Marti and "Declaration of Havana" — AP93

Background in Spanish, English or French.

1961, Jan. 28   Litho.   Perf. 12½
C219 AP93 8c pale grn, blk & red 1.25 .85
C220 AP93 12c org yel, blk & pale vio 1.75 1.00
C221 AP93 30c pale bl, blk & pale brn 4.00 3.50
a. Souvenir sheet of 3 15.00 15.00
Nos. C219-C221 (3) 7.00 5.35
Declaration of Havana, Sept. 1, 1960. Sheets of 25 are imprinted in margin "E" for Spanish, "I" for English or "F" for French. No. C221a contains one each of Nos. C219-C221, imperf. The 8c has background in Spanish, the 12c in English and the 30e in French.

UN Type of 1961
1961, Apr. 12   Unwmk.   Perf. 12½
C222 A244 8c dp car & yel .60 .25
C223 A244 12c brt ultra & org 1.50 .50
a. Souv. sheet of 2, #C222-C223, imperf. 10.00 10.00

Nos. C76 and C7 Surcharged

Wmk. 106
1961, Oct. 1   Engr.   Perf. 10
C224 AP39 8c on 15c No. C76 1.00 .40
C225 AP3 8c on 20c No. C7 1.00 .40

Revolution Anniv. Type of 1962
Perf. 12½
1962, Jan. 3   Litho.   Unwmk.
C226 A250 8c multi .85 .30
C227 A250 12c multi 1.90 .55
C228 A250 30c multi 2.50 .90
Nos. C226-C228 (3) 5.25 1.75

1st Sugarcane Harvest in Socialist Cuba, 1st Anniv. — AP94

1962, Jan. 16
C229 AP94 8c salmon pink & dark brn 1.00 .25
C230 AP94 12c bluish lil & blk 2.50 .45

Cuban goods have been embargoed by the United States since a Feb. 7, 1962 proclamation by President Kennedy, but according to the Office of Foreign Assets Control of the Treasury Department, used Cuban stamps can be imported and sold without limitation, and unused stamps may be imported for personal use, but not resold.

Intl. Radio Service AP95

1962, Mar. 26   Wmk. 321
C231 AP95 8c multi 1.10 .25
C232 AP95 12c multi 2.25 .55
C233 AP95 30c multi 3.25 1.25
C234 AP95 1p multi 7.00 3.25
Nos. C231-C234 (4) 13.60 5.30

Bird Type of 1956
1962, July 20   Engr.   Wmk. 321
C235 AP63 1p like #C144, royal blue 5.75 5.75
C236 AP62 2p like #C145, dark red 17.00 15.00
C237 AP63 5p like #C146, rose lake 37.50 32.50
Nos. C235-C237 (3) 60.25 53.25

PRAGA '62 — AP96

No. C238, Czechoslovakia No. 1080.

1962, Aug. 18   Litho.
C238 AP96 31c multi 3.50 1.50

Souvenir Sheet
Imperf
C239 AP96 31c like No. C238 17.50 12.00
No. C239 contains one 60x35½mm stamp.

Achievements of the Revolution — AP97

1c, Agrarian reform. 2c, Industrialization. 3c, Urban reform. 7c, Eradication of unemployment. 9c, Education. 10c, Public health. 13c, Excerpt from La Historia Me Absolvera, by Castro.

1966, July 26   Wmk. 376   Perf. 12½
C240 AP97 1c multi .25 .25
C241 AP97 2c multi .25 .25
C242 AP97 3c multi .50 .25
C243 AP97 7c multi .50 .25
C244 AP97 9c multi .95 .25
C245 AP97 10c multi 2.10 .25
C246 AP97 13c multi 2.75 .45
Nos. C240-C246 (7) 7.30 1.95

Camaguey-Seville Flight, 35th Anniv. — AP98

13c, Aircraft. 30c, Map, Lieut. Menendez Palaez.

1971, Jan. 12   Unwmk.
C247 AP98 13c multi 2.75 .25
C248 AP98 30c multi 3.25 .70

Havana-Santiago de Chile Direct Air Service, 1st Anniv. — AP99

1972, June 26 **Wmk. 376**
C249 AP99 25c multi   3.00 .75

6th Congress of Latin American and Caribbean Exporters of Sugar, Havana — AP100

Perf. 12½x12
1977, Feb. 28 **Unwmk.**
C250 AP100 13c multi   .75 .25

Composer Type of 1977
13c, Jorge Ankerman and score.

1977, May 10 **Perf. 13**
C251 A571 13c multi   1.00 .25

Flower Type of 1977
Designs: 13c, Caesalpinia pulcherrima. 30c, Catharanthus roseus.

1977, May 31
C252 A572 13c multicolored   .85 .25
C253 A572 30c multicolored   1.75 .50

Souvenir Sheet
Perf. 13½x13
C254 A572 50c Juan Tomas Roig 4.00 .90

No. C254 contains one 32x40mm stamp.

Natl. Decorations Type of 1977
1977, July 26 **Perf. 12x12½**
C255 A574 13c multi, diff.   .80 .25
C256 A574 30c multi, diff.   1.50 .45

Art Type of 1977
Paintings by Jorge Arche: 13c, *My Wife and I*, vert. 30c, *Domino Players.* 50c, *Self-portrait,* vert.

1977, Aug. 25 **Perf. 13x12½**
Size: 26x38mm
C257 A575 13c multi   .65 .25
Size: 40x29mm
Perf. 13
C258 A575 30c multi   1.60 .40
Souvenir Sheet
Perf. 13½x13
C259 A575 50c multi   4.00 4.00

No. C259 contains one 32x40mm stamp.

Spartakiad Type of 1977
13c, Grenade-throwing. 30c, Rifle-shooting, horiz.

1977, Sept. 10 **Perf. 13**
C260 A576 13c multi   .60 .25
C261 A576 30c multi   1.50 .40

10th Heroic Guerrilla's Day AP101

13c, Guerrilla fighters.

1977, Oct. 8 **Perf. 12½x13**
C262 AP101 13c multi   1.00 .25

Airmail Service Type of 1977
13c, Havana-Mexico cachet. 30c, Havana-Prague cachet.

1977, Oct. 27 **Perf. 12x12½**
C263 A577 13c multi   .85 .25
C264 A577 30c multi   1.75 .55

Souvenir Sheet

Adoration of the Magi, by Rubens — AP102

1977, Nov. 18 **Perf. 13**
C265 AP102 50c multi   4.00 4.00

Rubens' 400th birth anniv.

Havana Zoo Type of 1977
1977, Nov. 24
C266 A579 13c Tiger   1.25 .25
C267 A579 30c Lion   1.90 .55

Revolution Martyrs Type of 1977
1977, Dec. 2 **Perf. 12½x12**
C268 A580 13c *Corynthia* landing .75 .25

Pan American Health Organization (OPS), 75th Anniv. — AP103

1977, Dec. 2
C269 AP103 13c multi   .75 .25

Havana University Type of 1978
13c, Crossed sabres, university. 30c, University, statue, crowd.

1978, Jan. 5 **Perf. 13x12½**
C270 A582 13c multi   .75 .25
C271 A582 30c multi   1.10 .50

Portrait of Jose Marti (b. 1853), by A. Menocal AP104

1978, Jan. 28
C272 AP104 13c multi   .80 .25

Art Type of 1978
Paintings in the Nat. Museum of Art: 13c, *El Guadalquivir,* by M. Barron. 30c, *Portrait of H.E. Ridley,* by J.J. Masqueries, vert.

13c, Guerrilla fighters.

1978, Feb. 20 **Perf. 12½x12, 13**
Sizes: 42x27mm, 29x40mm
C273 A583 13c multi   1.00 .25
C274 A583 30c multi   1.10 .40

Bird Type of 1975
Designs: 13c, Torreornis inexpectata, horiz. 30c, Ara tricolor.

1978, Mar. 10 **Perf. 12½x12, 13**
Size: 42x27mm, 27x42mm
C275 A524 13c multicolored   1.60 .50
C276 A524 30c multicolored   2.40 1.10

Baragua Protest, Cent. — AP105

13c, *Antonio Maceo,* by A. Melero.

1978, Mar. 15 **Perf. 13x13½**
C277 AP105 13c multi   .70 .25

Cosmonaut's Day Type of 1978
1978, Apr. 12 **Perf. 13**
C278 A585 13c Venera 10   .70 .25
Size: 36x46mm
Perf. 12½x13
C279 A585 30c Lunokhod 2, vert. 1.25 .50

SOCFILEX '78, Budapest — AP106

30c, Parliament, Hungary No. 217.

1978, May 7 **Perf. 13x12½**
C280 AP106 30c multi   1.75 .55

Cactus Type of 1978
Designs: 13c, Rhodocactus cubensis. 30c, Harrisia taetra.

1978, May 15 **Perf. 13**
C281 A587 13c multicolored   .90 .25
C282 A587 30c multicolored   1.90 .35

World Telecommunications Day — AP107

1978, May 17
C283 AP107 30c multi   1.25 .45

Organization of African Unity, 15th Anniv. — AP108

1978, May 25 **Perf. 13x12½**
C284 AP108 30c multi   1.00 .45

Souvenir Sheet

CAPEX '78, Toronto — AP109

50c, *Niven, Wales,* by G.H. Russell.

1978, June 9 **Perf. 13x13½**
C285 AP109 50c multi   3.50 2.25

Aquarium Type of 1978
Designs: 13c, Carassias auratus, vert. 30c, Symphysodon aequifasciata axelrodi.

1978, June 15 **Perf. 13**
C286 A588 13c multicolored   1.90 .25
C287 A588 30c multicolored   3.00 .50

MEDELLIN Games Type of 1978
1978, July 1
C288 A589 13c Volleyball   .60 .25
C289 A589 30c Running   1.25 .45

Attack on Moncada Type of 1978
13c, Soldiers bearing rifles. 30c, Stylized dove, banners.

1978, July 26
C290 A590 13c multi   .45 .25
C291 A590 30c multi   1.10 .35

Youth Festival Type of 1978
Natl. flags and views of host cities.

1978, July 28
C292 A591 13c Moscow, 1957   .70 .25
C293 A591 13c Vienna, 1959   .70 .25
C294 A591 13c Helsinki, 1962   .70 .25
C295 A591 13c Sofia, 1968   .70 .25
C296 A591 13c Berlin, 1973   .70 .25
a.   Strip of 5, Nos. C292-C296   3.75 1.75
Nos. C292-C296 (5)   3.50 1.25
Size: 46x36mm
Perf. 13x12½
C297 A591 30c Havana, 1978   1.50 .35

Tuna Industry Type of 1978
1978, Aug. 30 **Perf. 12½x12**
C298 A593 13c Stern trawler   .90 .25
C299 A593 30c Refrigerator ship 1.60 .60

Souvenir Sheet

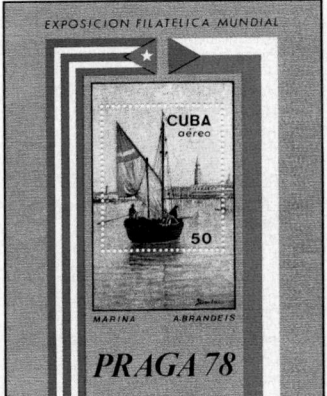

PRAGA '78 — AP110

50c, *Marina,* by A. Brandeis.

1978, Sept. 8 **Perf. 13**
C300 AP110 50c multi   3.75 2.00

Art Type of 1978

Paintings by Amelia Pelaez del Casal (1896-1968): 13c, *Yellow Flowers*, vert. 30c, *Still-life in Blue*, vert. 50c, *Portrait of Amelia*, by L. Romanach, vert.

1978, Sept. 15   **Perf. 12x12½, 13**
C301 A594 13c multi   .55 .25
C302 A594 30c multi   1.25 .45

Souvenir Sheet
Perf. 13½x13
C303 A594 50c multi   4.00 .90
No. C303 contains one 32x40mm stamp.

Socialist Communication Organizations Congress (OSS), 20th Anniv. — AP111

1978, Sept. 25   **Perf. 13**
C304 AP111 30c multi   1.25 .25

Souvenir Sheet

EXFILNA '78, 6th Natl. Philatelic Exposition — AP112

50c, 1st Postal Card, issued in 1878.

1978, Oct. 10   **Imperf.**
C305 AP112 50c multi   3.25 2.00
No. C305 has simulated perfs.

Intl. Anti-Apartheid Year — AP113

1978, Oct. 16   **Perf. 12½**
C306 AP113 13c multi   1.60 1.00

Zoo Type of 1978

Designs: 13c, Acinonyx jubatus. 30c, Loxodonta africana, vert.

1978, Oct. 20   **Perf. 13**
C307 A595 13c multicolored   1.00 .25
C308 A595 30c multicolored   2.40 .65

Natl. Ballet Type of 1978

1978, Oct. 28   **Perf. 12½x13**
C309 A596 13c *Giselle*, vert.   .85 .25
C310 A596 30c *Genesis*, vert.   1.60 .30

Pacific Flora Type of 1978

1978, Nov. 30   **Perf. 13**
C311 A597 13c multi, diff.   .80 .25
C312 A597 30c multi, diff.   1.60 .30

25th Death Anniv. of Julius and Ethel Rosenberg, American Communists Executed for Espionage — AP114

1978, Dec. 20
C313 AP114 13c multi   .60 .25

Julio A. Mella (d. 1929) AP115

1979, Jan. 10
C314 AP115 13c multi   .60 .25

Cosmonaut's Day Type of 1979

1979, Apr. 12   **Perf. 13½x13**
Souvenir Sheet
C315 A603 50c Orbital complex   3.75 2.00
No. C315 contains one 32x40mm stamp.

Intl. Year of the Child — AP116

1979, June 1   **Perf. 13x12½**
C316 AP116 13c multi   1.00 .25

Art Type of 1979

50c, Portrait of Victor Emmanuel Garcia, by J. Arche, vert.

1979, June 15   **Perf. 13½x13**
C317 A600 50c multicolored   3.50 1.75
No. C317 contains one 32x40mm stamp.

CARIFESTA '79, Festival of Caribbean Peoples, Havana AP117

1979, July 16   **Perf. 12½x13**
C318 AP117 13c multi   .75 .25

10th World Universiade Games, Mexico City — AP118

1979, Sept. 1   **Perf. 13x12½**
C319 AP118 13c grn, pale grn & gold   .75 .25

6th Conference of Nonaligned Countries — AP119

50c, Convention Palace.

1979, Sept. 3
C320 AP119 50c multi   1.75 .90

Sir Rowland Hill (d. 1879), Originator of Penny Postage — AP120

1979, Sept. 4   **Perf. 13½x13**
C321 AP120 30c Hill, casket   1.50 .25

SOCFILEX '79, Bucharest — AP121

30c, Romania No. 683, flags.

1979, Oct. 25   **Perf. 12½**
C322 AP121 30c multi   1.40 .40

Intl. Radio Consultative Committee (CCIR), 50th Anniv. — AP122

30c, Ground receiving station.

1979, Nov. 30   **Perf. 12½x12**
C323 AP122 30c multi   1.40 .40

1st Soviet-Cuban Joint Space Flight — AP123

1980, Sept. 23   **Perf. 12½**
C324 AP123 13c multi   .50 .25
C325 AP123 30c multi   1.50 .35

Capt. Mariano Barberan, Lt. Joaquin Collar, and Their Airplane Cuatro Vientos. — AP124

1993, June 11   **Litho.**   **Perf. 13**
C326 AP124 30c multicolored   1.00 .45
1st Flight Seville-Camaguey, 60th anniv.

AIR POST SEMI-POSTAL STAMP

> Catalogue values for unused stamps in this section are for Never Hinged items.

Farm Couple and Factory SPAP1

Engr. & Typo.
1959, May 7   **Wmk. 321**   **Perf. 12½**
CB1 SPAP1 12c + 3c car & grn   2.00 .80
Agricultural reforms. See No. C199.

AIR POST SPECIAL DELIVERY STAMPS

Matanzas Issue

Matanzas Harbor APSD1

Wmk. 229
1936, May 5   **Photo.**   **Perf. 12½**
CE1 ASPD1 15c light blue   5.00 3.50
   Never hinged   8.00
Exists imperf. Value $6.50 unused, $4.50 used.

SPECIAL DELIVERY STAMPS

Issued under Administration of the United States

US No. E5 Surcharged in Red

1899   **Wmk. 191**   **Perf. 12**
E1 SD3 10c blue   130. 100.
   Never hinged   300.
a.   No period after "CUBA"   575. 400.

Issue of the Republic under US Military Rule

Special Delivery Messenger SD2

Printed by the US Bureau of Engraving and Printing

1899   **Wmk. US-C (191C)**
Inscribed: "Immediata"

E2   SD2 10c orange   52.50   15.00
    Never hinged   120.00

Issues of the Republic
Inscribed: "Inmediata"

1902   *Perf. 12*
E3   SD2 10c orange   3.00   1.00

J. B. Zayas
SD3

1910   *Unwmk.*
E4   SD3 10c orange & blue   20.00   3.25
    Never hinged   30.00
    a.   Center inverted   1,250.

Airplane and
Morro
Castle
SD4

1914, Feb. 24   *Perf. 12*
E5   SD4 10c dark blue   15.00   1.25

    Exists imperf. Value, pair $500.

1927   **Wmk. Star (106)**
E6   SD4 10c deep blue   12.00   .50
    Never hinged   18.00

1935   *Perf. 10*
E7   SD4 10c blue   12.00   .40
    Never hinged   15.00

Matanzas Issue

Mercury
SD5

Wmk. Wavy Lines (229)
1936, May 5   *Perf. 12½*
E8   SD5 10c deep claret   8.00   3.50
    Never hinged   9.50

    Exists imperf. Value $7.50 unused, $5 used.

"Triumph of the Revolution" — SD6

1936, Nov. 18
E9   SD6 10c red orange   9.00   2.00
    Never hinged   11.00

    Maj. Gen. Máximo Gómez (1836-1905).

Temple of   Ruben Dario
Quetzalcoatl   (Nicaragua)
(Mexico)   SD8
SD7

Wmk. 106
1937, Oct. 13   **Engr.**   *Perf. 10*
E10   SD7 10c deep orange   7.00   7.00
E11   SD8 10c deep orange   7.00   7.00
    Set, never hinged   18.00

    Issued for the benefit of the Association of American Writers and Artists. See note after No. 354.

Letter and Symbols of
Transportation — SD9

1945, Oct. 30
E12   SD9 10c olive brown   2.75   .40
    Never hinged   4.00

> **Catalogue values for unused stamps in this section, from this point to the end of the section, are for Never Hinged items.**

Governor's
Building,
Cárdenas
SD10

Engraved and Lithographed
1951, July 3   **Wmk. 229**   *Perf. 13*
E13   SD10 10c henna brn, ultra
        & red   8.50   1.25

    Cent. of the adoption of Cuba's flag.

Chess Type of Regular Issue, 1951
1951, Nov. 1   **Photo.**
E14   A166 10c dk grn & rose
        brn   22.50   4.50

Type of Regular Issue
of 1951 Surcharged in
Red Violet

Wmk. 106
1952, Mar. 18   **Engr.**   *Perf. 10*
E15   A159 10c on 2c yel brn   5.50   1.40

Arms and Bars from
National
Hymn — SD12

1952, May 27   *Perf. 12½*
E16   SD12 10c dp org & bl   5.50   .80
    Republic of Cuba founding, 50th anniv.

Type of Air Post Stamps of 1952
Inscribed: "Entrega Especial"
1952, Oct. 7   *Perf. 10*
E17   AP36 10c pale olive grn   5.00   2.40

    Three-fourths of the proceeds from the sale of No. E17 were used for the Communications Ministry Employees' Retirement Fund.

Roseate
Tern — SD13

1953, July 28
E18   SD13 10c blue   5.75   1.60

Gregorio Hernandez
Saez — SD14

1954, Feb. 23
E19   SD14 10c olive green   5.25   1.10

Felix Varela — SD15

1955, June 22   *Perf. 12½*
E20   SD15 10c brown car   3.00   .95
    See note after No. E17.

Portrait Type of Regular Issue, 1956
Inscribed: "Entrega Especial"
    Portrait: 10c, Jose Jacinto Milanes.

1956, May 2   **Wmk. 106**
E21   A198 10c dk car rose & blk   4.50   .75
    See note after No. E17.

Painting Type of Regular Issue, 1957 Inscribed: "Entrega Especial"
    10c, "Yesterday" by E. Garcia Cabrera.

1957, Mar. 15   **Engr.**   *Perf. 12½*
E22   A207 10c dk brn & turq bl   3.50   1.25
    See note after No. E17.

View Type of Regular Issue, 1957 Inscribed: "Entrega Especial"
    10c, Independence square, Pino del Rio.

1957, Dec. 17
E23   A218 10c dk pur & brn   3.00   1.00
    See note after No. E17.

View in
Havana
and
Messenger
SD16

1958, Jan. 10   **Engr.**
E24   SD16 10c blue   2.75   .80
E25   SD16 20c green   3.50   .80
    See Nos. E28, E31.

Fish Type of Regular Issue, 1958 Inscribed: "Entrega Especial"
    Fish: 10c, Blackfish snapper. 20c, Mosquitofish.

1958, Sept. 26   **Wmk. 106**   *Perf. 12½*
E26   AP86 10c blk, bl, pink &
        yel   8.75   2.50
E27   AP86 20c blk, ultra & pink   27.50   11.00
    See note after No. C191.

Messenger Type of 1958
1960   **Wmk. 321**   *Perf. 12½*
E28   SD16 10c brt vio   3.50   .80

Plane Type
of Air Post
Issue, of
1931-46,
Srchd. in
Black or Red

1960   **Wmk. 106**   *Perf. 10*
E29   AP4 10c on 20c car rose   3.00   .50
E30   AP4 10c on 50c grnsh bl (R)   3.00   .50

Messenger Type of 1958
1961, June 28   **Wmk. 321**   *Perf. 12½*
E31   SD16 10c orange   3.50   .80

West Indies Packet Type of 1962
Perf. 12½
1962, Apr. 24   **Litho.**   *Unwmk.*
E32   A253 10c buff, dull ultra &
        brn   7.50   1.75

POSTAGE DUE STAMPS

Issued under Administration of the United States

Postage Due Stamps
of the United States
Nos. J38, J39, J41 and
J42 Srchd. in Black
Like Nos. 221-226A

1899   **Wmk. 191**   *Perf. 12*
J1   D2   1c dp claret   45.00   5.25
      Never hinged   110.00
J2   D2   2c dp claret   45.00   5.25
      Never hinged   110.00
    a.   Inverted surcharge   *3,500.*
J3   D2   5c dp claret   42.50   5.25
      Never hinged   105.00
J4   D2   10c dp claret   25.00   2.50
      Never hinged   60.00
    Nos. J1-J4 (4)   157.50   18.25

Issues of the Republic

D1

1914   **Unwmk.**   **Engr.**   *Perf. 12*
J5   D1   1c carmine rose   8.00   1.25
J6   D1   2c carmine rose   10.00   1.25
J7   D1   5c carmine rose   15.00   2.50
    Nos. J5-J7 (3)   33.00   5.00

1927-28
J8   D1   1c rose red   5.50   .90
J9   D1   2c rose red   8.50   .90
J10   D1   5c rose red   10.00   1.25
    Nos. J8-J10 (3)   24.00   3.05

NEWSPAPER STAMPS

Issued under Spanish Dominion

N1

1888   **Unwmk.**   **Typo.**   *Perf. 14*
P1   N1   ½m black   .25   .25
P2   N1   1m black   .25   .30
P3   N1   2m black   .25   .30
P4   N1   3m black   1.60   1.00
P5   N1   4m black   2.10   2.00
P6   N1   8m black   8.00   8.50
    Nos. P1-P6 (6)   12.45   12.35

N2

1890

P7	N2	½m red brown	.55	.65
P8	N2	1m red brown	.55	.65
P9	N2	2m red brown	.90	.95
P10	N2	3m red brown	1.10	1.10
P11	N2	4m red brown	8.25	5.50
P12	N2	8m red brown	8.25	5.50
		Nos. P7-P12 (6)	19.60	14.35

1892

P13	N2	½m violet	.25	.30
P14	N2	1m violet	.25	.30
P15	N2	2m violet	.25	.30
P16	N2	3m violet	1.10	.35
P17	N2	4m violet	4.25	1.90
P18	N2	8m violet	8.75	3.00
		Nos. P13-P18 (6)	14.85	6.15

1894

P19	N2	½m rose	.25	.30
a.		Imperf. pair	40.00	40.00
P20	N2	1m rose	.50	.35
P21	N2	2m rose	.55	.35
P22	N2	3m rose	2.10	1.40
P23	N2	4m rose	3.50	1.60
P24	N2	8m rose	6.00	4.00
		Nos. P19-P24 (6)	12.90	8.00

1896

P25	N2	½m blue green	.25	.30
P26	N2	1m blue green	.25	.30
P27	N2	2m blue green	.25	.30
P28	N2	3m blue green	2.75	1.50
P29	N2	4m blue green	5.75	7.00
P30	N2	8m blue green	10.50	10.00
		Nos. P25-P30 (6)	19.75	19.40

For surcharges see Nos. 190-193, 201-220.

POSTAL TAX STAMPS

Catalogue values for unused stamps in this section are for Never Hinged items.

Mother and Child — PT1

Wmk. Star. (106)

1938, Dec. 1   **Engr.**   **Perf. 10**
RA1 PT1 1c bright green   .90 .25

The tax benefited the National Council of Tuberculosis fund for children's hospitals. Obligatory on all mail during December and January. This note applies also to Nos. RA2-RA4, RA7-RA10, RA12-RA15, RA17-RA21.

Nurse with Child — PT2

1939, Dec. 1
RA2 PT2 1c orange vermilion   .90 .25

"Health" Protecting Children — PT3

1940, Dec. 1
RA3 PT3 1c deep blue   .90 .25

Mother and Child — PT4

1941, Dec. 1
RA4 PT4 1c olive bister   .95 .25

Victory — PT5

1942-44

RA5	PT5 ½c orange	.65	.25
RA6	PT5 ½c gray ('44)	.95	.25

Issued: No. RA5, 7/1/42; No. RA6, 10/3/44.

Type of 1941 Overprinted in Black

1942

1942, Dec. 1

RA7	PT4 1c salmon	.90	.30
a.	Inverted overprint	75.00	65.00

As PT3 — PT6

1943, Dec. 1
RA8 PT6 1c brown   .95 .25

As PT4 — PT7

1949, Dec. 9
RA9 PT7 1c blue   .75 .25

Type of 1949 Inscribed: "1950"

1950, Dec. 1   **Engr.**
RA10 PT7 1c rose red   .75 .25

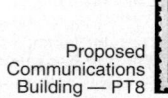

Proposed Communications Building — PT8

1951, June 5   **Wmk. 106**   **Perf. 10**
RA11 PT8 1c violet   .95 .25

The tax was to help build a new Communications Building. This note applies also to Nos. RA16, RA34, RA43.

Woman Holding Child Aloft — PT9

1951, Dec. 1

RA12	PT9 1c violet blue	.55	.25
RA13	PT9 1c brown carmine	.55	.25
RA14	PT9 1c olive bister	.55	.25
RA15	PT9 1c deep green	.55	.25
	Nos. RA12-RA15 (4)	2.20	1.00

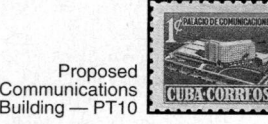

Proposed Communications Building — PT10

1952, Feb. 8
RA16 PT10 1c slate blue   .40 .25

See Nos. RA34, RA43.

Child — PT11

1952, Dec. 1

RA17	PT11 1c rose carmine	.75	.25
RA18	PT11 1c yellow green	.75	.25
RA19	PT11 1c blue	.75	.25
RA20	PT11 1c orange	.75	.25
	Nos. RA17-RA20 (4)	3.00	1.00

Hands Reaching for Lorraine Cross — PT12

1953, Dec. 1   **Perf. 9½**
RA21 PT12 1c rose carmine   .65 .30

Child's Head, Lorraine Cross — PT13

1954, Nov. 1   **Perf. 9½x10**

RA22	PT13 1c rose red	.75	.30
RA23	PT13 1c violet	.75	.30
RA24	PT13 1c bright blue	.75	.30
RA25	PT13 1c emerald	.75	.30
	Nos. RA22-RA25 (4)	3.00	1.20

The tax benefited the Natl. Council of Tuberculosis fund for children's hospitals. Obligatory on all mail during Nov., Dec., Jan. & Feb. This note also applies to Nos. RA26-RA33, RA35-RA42.

Rose and Watering Can — PT14

1955, Nov. 1

RA26	PT14 1c red orange	.75	.30
RA27	PT14 1c red lilac	.75	.30
RA28	PT14 1c bright blue	.75	.30
RA29	PT14 1c orange yellow	.75	.30
	Nos. RA26-RA29 (4)	3.00	1.20

Child and Protective Hands — PT15

1956, Nov. 1

RA30	PT15 1c rose red	.75	.30
RA31	PT15 1c yellow brown	.75	.30
RA32	PT15 1c bright blue	.75	.30
RA33	PT15 1c emerald	.75	.30
	Nos. RA30-RA33 (4)	3.00	1.20

Building Type of 1952

1957, Jan. 18   **Perf. 10**
RA34 PT10 1c rose red   .50 .30

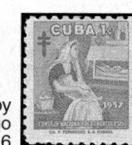

Mother and Child by Silvia Arrojo Fernandez — PT16

Wmk. 321

1957, Nov. 1   **Engr.**   **Perf. 10**

RA35	PT16 1c dull rose	.75	.30
RA36	PT16 1c bright blue	.75	.30
RA37	PT16 1c gray	.75	.30
RA38	PT16 1c emerald	.75	.30
	Nos. RA35-RA38 (4)	3.00	1.20

National Council of Tuberculosis — PT17

1958

RA39	PT17 1c rose red	.50	.30
RA40	PT17 1c red brown	.50	.30
RA41	PT17 1c gray	.50	.30
RA42	PT17 1c emerald	.50	.30
	Nos. RA39-RA42 (4)	2.00	1.20

Building Type of 1952

1958   **Wmk. 321**
RA43 PT10 1c rose red   .50 .30

CURACAO

ˈcər-ə-sau

LOCATION — North of Venezuela, east of Aruba in Caribbean Sea
AREA — 171 sq. mi.
POP. — 135,822 (2005)
CAPITAL — Willemstad

On Oct. 10, 2010, Curaçao, formerly part of Netherlands Antilles, became a constituent state within the Kingdom of the Netherlands. Stamps issued from 1873 to 1949 inscribed "Curaçao" were valid in all islands that comprised the Netherlands Antilles. These stamps are listed under "Netherlands Antilles."

100 Cents = 1 Gulden

> Catalogue values for all unused stamps in this country are for Never Hinged items.

Map of Curaçao and West Indies, Arms and Flag
A1

Perf. 13¾

2010, Oct. 10 Litho. Unwmk.
1 A1 111c multi 1.25 1.25

Souvenir Sheet

Touit Purpurata — A2

2010, Oct. 25 Litho. Perf. 13¾
2 A2 1500c multi 17.00 17.00

New Constitutional Status — A3

Designs: 1c, Sphere with colors of Curaçao flag, Diploria labyrinthiformis. 3c, Yellowtail snapper. 5c, Yellow goatfish. 30c, Blue hamlet. 63c, Rock beauty angelfish. 81c, Palometa jack. 112c, Spotfin butterflyfish. 166c, Cherubfish. 285c, Cocoa damselfish. 405c, Jewel damselfish. 630c, Schoolmaster snapper. Fish have colors of Curaçao flag.

2011, Jan. 11 Perf. 13¼x12¾
3 A3 1c multi .25 .25
4 A3 3c multi .25 .25
5 A3 5c multi .25 .25
6 A3 30c multi .35 .35
7 A3 63c multi .70 .70
8 A3 81c multi .90 .90
9 A3 112c multi 1.25 1.25
10 A3 166c multi 1.90 1.90
11 A3 285c multi 3.25 3.25
12 A3 405c multi 4.50 4.50
13 A3 630c multi 7.00 7.00
    Nos. 3-13 (11) 20.60 20.60
See Nos. 13A-13C, 215-216.

New Constitutional Status Type of 2011

Designs: 8c, Schoolmaster snapper. 115c, Spotfin butterflyfish. 171c, Cherubfish.

2012 Litho. Perf. 13¼x12¾
13A A3 8c multi — —
13B A3 115c multi — —
13C A3 171c multi — —

A4

Rabbit and: 112c, Big Wild Goose Pagoda, Xian, China. 145c, Great Wall of China, horiz. 166c, Temple of Heaven. 285c, Mountains near Li River, horiz. 405c, Paper lanterns.

Perf. 12¾x13¼, 13¼x12¾
2011, Feb. 11 Litho.
14-18 A4 Set of 5 12.50 12.50
New Year 2011 (Year of the Rabbit).

A5

Musical instruments: 49c, Double bass. 63c, Steel pan drums. 82c, Accordion. 145c, Saxophone. 166c, Djembe. 236c, Piano. 285c, Trombone. 405c, Pan flute. 700c, Cymbals.

2011, Mar. 11 Perf. 12¾x13¼
19-27 A5 Set of 9 24.00 24.00

Banknotes
A6

Designs: 63c, 1947 Curaçao 1-gulden note. 75c, 1970 Netherlands Antilles 2½-gulden note. 112c, 1958 Curaçao 5-gulden note. 175c, 1948 Curaçao 10-gulden note. 200c, 1970 Netherlands Antilles 1-gulden note. 250c, 1967 Netherlands Antilles 5-gulden note. 300c, 1979 Netherlands Antilles 25-gulden note. 350c, 1972 Netherlands Antilles 50-gulden note. 475c, 1967 Netherlands Antilles 250-gulden note. 500c, 1962 Netherlands Antilles 500-gulden note.

2011, Apr. 11 Perf. 14
28-37 A6 Set of 10 28.00 28.00
2011 Paper Money Fair, Maastricht, Netherlands.

Souvenir Sheet

Prehistoric Animals — A7

No. 38: a, 700c, Ankylosaurus. b, 800c, Spinosaurus. c, 1000c, Saurolophus.

2011, June 11 Perf. 13¼x12¾
38 A7 Sheet of 3, #a-c 28.00 28.00

New Technologies
A8

Designs: 275c, Social media. 375c, Fiber optics. 475c Blackberry PIN messaging. 625c, Cloud computing.

2011, July 11
39-42 A8 Set of 4 19.50 19.50

Souvenir Sheet

Preservation of Polar Regions and Glaciers — A9

No. 43 — Iceberg and: a, 112c, Emblem. b, 405c, Map of Antarctica.

2011, Aug. 11 Perf. 13½
43 A9 Sheet of 2, #a-b 5.75 5.75

Foods — A10

Designs: 63c, Almond cake. 81c, Apple pie. 112c, Blueberry pancakes. 145c, Broken glass cake. 166c, Lemon cake. 172c, Funchi (polenta cake). 195c, Chocolate cake. 285c, Fruit cake. 405c, Cherry cheesecake. 630c, Pumpkin cake

2011, Sept. 11 Perf. 13¼x12¾
44-53 A10 Set of 10 25.00 25.00

Christmas — A11

Evergreen branches, candle and: 63c, Christmas cake (Bolo di Pasku), candy cane and hard candies. 112c, Ayaka. 145c, New Year's cake (Pan dushi) and hard candies. 166c, Christmas ham (Ham di Pasku). 172c, Salmon (Salmou di bari). 250c, Nuts (Nechi). 405c, Pickled pork (Sult).

2011, Nov. 11 Perf. 12¾x13¼
54-60 A11 Set of 7 17.00 17.00

Miniature Sheet

Vegetables — A12

No. 61: a, 150c, Pumpkin and squashes. b, 200c, Okra. c, 225c, Onions. d, 325c, Bell peppers. c, 500c, Corn. f, 750c, Tomatoes.

2011, Dec. 11
61 A12 Sheet of 6, #a-f 22.00 22.00

Fish — A13

Designs: 25c, Myripristis botche. 150c, Neoniphon opercularis. 225c, Sargocentron spiniferum. 325c, Anyperodon leucogrammicus. 475c, Cephalopholis sonnerati. 500c, Epinephelus caeruleopunctatus. 700c, Abudefduf vaigiensis.

2012, Jan. 12 Perf. 14
62-68 A13 Set of 7 27.00 27.00
Nos. 62-68 were printed in sheets of 14 containing two of each stamp and a central label.

New Year 2012 (Year of the Dragon) A14

Designs: No. 69, 500c, Dragon. No. 70, 500c, Dragon facing left, horiz.
No. 71, 500c, Yin-yang, dragon, Chinese character.

Perf. 13½x14, 14x13½
2012, Feb. 13 Litho. & Embossed
69-70 A14 Set of 2 11.50 11.50
Souvenir Sheet
71 A14 500c multi 5.75 5.75

Miniature Sheet

Birds — A15

No. 72: a, 75c, Laughing gulls (24x27mm). b, 150c, Dunlins (36x27mm). c, 200c, Gannets (24x27mm). d, 225c, Frigatebirds (36x27mm). e, 300c, Snowy egret (24x27mm). f, 350c, Flamingos (36x27mm). g, 500c, Great blue heron (24x27mm). h, 700c, Pelican (36x27mm).

Perf. 13¼x13¾
2012, Mar. 12 Litho.
72 A15 Sheet of 8, #a-h 28.00 28.00

Miniature Sheet

Railways in Curacao — A16

No. 73: a, 200c, Dumping cars (40x21mm). b, 250c, Horse tram (30x39mm). c, 300c, Plymouth locomotive (30x42mm). d, 350c, Motor tram (40x18mm).

2012, Apr. 12   *Perf. 14x13½*
73 A16   Sheet of 4, #a-d, +   12.50 12.50
central label

Souvenir Sheet

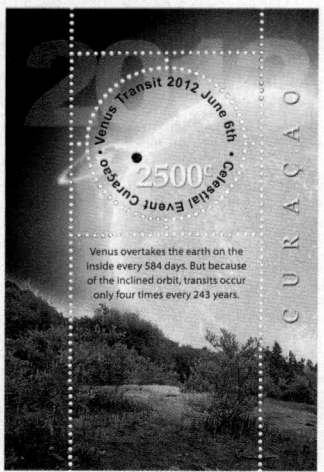

June 6, 2012 Transit of Venus — A17

2012, May 21   *Perf. 13¼*
74 A17 2500c multi   35.00 35.00

A18

Indonesia 2012 World Stamp
Exhibition, Jakarta — A19

2012, June 18   *Perf. 13½x13*
75 A18 10c multi   .25 .25

Souvenir Sheet
Perf.
76 A19 200c multi   2.25 2.25

Fruit — A20

Designs: 275c, Watermelons. 375c, Pineapples. 475c, Bananas. 625c, Mangos.

2012, June 12   *Perf. 13x13½*
77-80 A20   Set of 4   19.50 19.50

Miniature Sheet

Sports — A21

No. 81: a, 25c, Cycling. b, 50c, Swimming. c, 75c, Sailboarding. d, 100c, Soccer. e, 125c,

---

Handball. f, 150c, Judo. g, 175c, Track. h, 200c, Baseball.

2012, July 12   *Perf. 13¾*
81 A21   Sheet of 8, #a-h   10.00 10.00

Flora — A22

Designs: 75c, Datura metel. 100c, Opuntia wentiana. 150c, Caesalpina pulcherrima. 200c, Melocactus macracanthus. 250c, Crescentia cujete, horiz. 300c, Ritterocereus griseus, horiz. 350c, Calutropis procera, horiz. 450c, Zizyphus spina-cristi, horiz.

Perf. 13x13½, 13½x13
2012, Aug. 13
82-89 A22   Set of 8   21.00 21.00

Miniature Sheet

Tourist Attractions — A23

No. 90: a, Tafelberg. b, Penha. c, Brug di Ponton Koningin Emmabrug (Queen Emma Pontoon Bridge), Willemstad. d, Bark'i Fruta (fruit market). e, Kenepa Grandi Beach. f, Landhuis Zeelandia. g, Koningin Julianabrug (Queen Juliana Bridge). h, Houses along Berg Altena. i, Handelskade, Willemstad. j, Statuutmonument (Statute of Autonomy Monument).

2012, Sept. 27   *Perf. 13½x13*
90 A23 171c Sheet of 10, #a-j   19.50 19.50

Christmas — A24

Designs: 64c, Angel. 115c, Madonna and Child. 171c, Shepherd and donkey. 190c, Star of Bethlehem. 293c, Three Kings.

2012, Nov. 12   *Perf. 13x13¼*
91-95 A24   Set of 5   9.50 9.50

Souvenir Sheet

End of Mayan Calendar Cycle — A25

No. 96: a, 200c, Pyramid at Chichen Itza, Mexico. b, 400c, Mayan Calendar. c, 600c,

---

Date of end of Mayan Calendar cycle (Dec. 21, 2012).

2012, Dec. 21   *Perf.*
96 A25   Sheet of 3, #a-c   13.50 13.50

Faith — A26

Designs: 118c, Names of various deities. 175c, Words for "faith" in various languages. 200c, Candles. 250c, Statue of Buddha and prayer wheel. 300c, Cross and stained-glass window depicting saint. 350c, Star of David and Torah.

2013, Jan. 21   *Perf. 13¼x12¾*
97   A26 118c multi   1.40 1.40
   a.   Tete-beche pair   2.80 2.80
98   A26 175c multi   2.00 2.00
   a.   Tete-beche pair   4.00 4.00
99   A26 200c multi   2.25 2.25
   a.   Tete-beche pair   4.50 4.50
100 A26 250c multi   2.75 2.75
   a.   Tete-beche pair   5.50 5.50
101 A26 300c multi   3.50 3.50
   a.   Tete-beche pair   7.00 7.00
102 A26 350c multi   4.00 4.00
   a.   Tete-beche pair   8.00 8.00
   Nos. 97-102 (6)   15.90 15.90

New Year 2013 (Year of the Snake) A27

Various snakes and flowers: 175c, 301c, 428c.
500c, Snake in tree.

2013, Feb. 22   *Perf. 13¼x12¾*
103-105 A27   Set of 3   10.50 10.50

Souvenir Sheet
Perf. 14x13¼
106 A27 500c multi   5.75 5.75
No. 106 contains one 50x40mm stamp.

Abstract Art — A28

Various works of abstract art and silhouettes of people: 118c, 175c, 200c, 250c, 301c, 450c.
250c, 301c, 450c are vert.

Perf. 13¼x12¾, 12¾x13¼
2013, Mar. 13
107-112 A28   Set of 6   17.00 17.00

Suggestions for Environmentally
Friendly Living — A29

Inscriptions: 65c, Saving energy using LED lights. 118c, Drive Green. 175c, Solar energy. 181c, Recycle. 301c, Wind energy. 350c, Rainwater. 428c, Plant trees and protect wetlands.

2013, Apr. 15   *Perf. 13¼x12¾*
113-119 A29   Set of 7   18.00 18.00

Souvenir Sheet

Royal Transition in the
Netherlands — A30

No. 120 — Silhouette of: a, New King Willem-Alexander. b, Abdicating Queen Beatrix.

Litho. with Foil Application
2013, Apr. 30   *Perf. 13¾*
120 A30 1000c Sheet of 2, #a-b   22.50 22.50

Baseball A31

Designs: 65c, Batter hitting ball. 118c, Catcher. 175c, Pitcher. 181c, Team celebrating victory. 301c, Outfielder. 350c, Fielder tagging runner out at base. 428c, Baseball field.

2013, May 13 Litho.   *Perf. 13¼x12¾*
121-127 A31   Set of 7   18.00 18.00

Ocean Liner Freewinds A32

Freewinds and: 118c, Palm fronds. 175c, Birds.
250c, Bow of Freewinds, vert.

2013, June 1 Litho.   *Perf. 13½x13*
128-129 A32   Set of 2   3.25 3.25

Souvenir Sheet
Perf. 13x13½
130 A32 250c multi   3.00 3.00

Virtues — A33

Designs: 118c, Respect. 175c, Love. 250c, Hope. 301c, Forgiveness. 350c, Mercy. 428c, Peace.

2013, July 22 Litho.   *Perf. 12¾x13¼*
131-136 A33   Set of 6   18.00 18.00

Souvenir Sheet

Schottegat, Curaçao — A34

2013, Aug. 20 Litho.   *Perf. 13¾*
137 A34 1000c multi   11.50 11.50

Miniature Sheet

Tourist Attractions — A35

No. 138: a, Den Dunki Bridge. b, Spaanse (Spanish) Water. c, Blue Room. d, Veeris Hill. e, Boca Tabla Natural Bridge. f, Playa Kanoa. g, Noordkant. h, Blow hole near Watamula. i, Hato Caves. j, Natural Swimming Pool.

Perf. 13¼x12¾

2013, Sept. 27   Litho.
138 A35 175c Sheet of 10, #a-j 19.50 19.50

Fairy Tales — A36

Designs: 100c, The Wolf and the Seven Goats. 145c, The Frog Prince. 190c, Little Red Riding Hood. 293c, Pinocchio, vert. 301c, Puss in Boots, vert. 428c, Jack and the Beanstalk, vert.

Perf. 13¼x12¾, 12¾x13¼

2013, Oct. 21   Litho.
139-144 A36   Set of 6   16.50 16.50

Christmas A37

Fireworks and: 65c, Building with wreath and decorations in fence. 118c, Building with wreaths on gate. 175c, Shop, other buildings, street lights, Christmas tree. 190c, Church tower, vert. 301c, Clock tower with bells, street light, vert.

Perf. 13¼x12¾, 12¾x13¼

2013, Nov. 13   Litho.
145-149 A37   Set of 5   9.50 9.50

Beetles A38

Designs: 65c, Chlorocala africana oertzeni. 118c, Stephanorrhina julia. 175c, Amaurodes passerinii nyanzanus. 181c, Cetonischema speciosa jouselini protaetia. 250c, Goliathus orientalis. 301c, Eudicella aethiopica. 428c, Ranzania bertoloni. 500c, Dicronorrhina layardi.

Perf. 13¾x12¾

2013, Dec. 13   Litho.
150-157 A38   Set of 8   22.50 22.50

A39

A40

A41

Emancipation of Slaves in Kingdom of the Netherlands, 150th Anniv. — A42

2013   Litho.
158   Souvenir booklet   28.50
   a.   A39 500c multi, perf. 13¼   5.75   5.75
   b.   A40 500c multi, perf.   5.75   5.75
   c.   A41 750c multi, perf. 13¼   8.50   8.50
   d.   A42 750c multi, perf. 13¼x14   8.50   8.50

Nos. 158a-158d were each printed in booklet panes of 1.

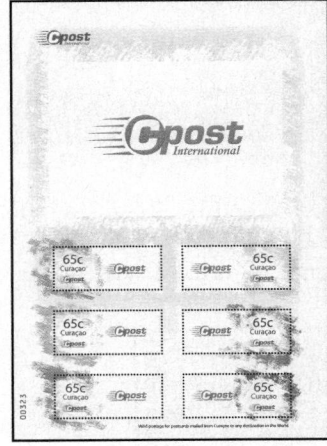

In 2014 Curacao began issuing personalizable stamps. Stamps were made available in sheets of 6 stamps. Numerous different frame designs, inscriptions, emblems and denominations have been reported.

Kingdom of the Netherlands, 200th Anniv. — A43

Designs: 150c, Crown and heraldic lion. 200c, Crown. 250c, Coat of arms. 300c, Post horn and motto, horiz. 350c, Heraldic lion and motto, horiz.

Perf. 12¾x13¼, 13¼x12¼

2014, Jan. 14   Litho.
159-163 A43   Set of 5   14.00 14.00

Miniature Sheet

New Year 2014 (Year of the Horse) — A44

No. 164 — Horse and: a, Men on boat (40x21mm). b, Building (30x42mm). c, Lanterns (30x39mm). d, Man carrying buckets (40x18mm).

2014, Jan. 31   Litho.   **Perf. 14x13¼**
164 A44 300c Sheet of 4, #a-d, + central label   13.50 13.50

Friendship — A45

Quote and heart with: 65c, Cake. 119c, Roses. 177c, Chocolate candies. 183c, Teddy bear. 305c, Gemstone. 434c, Drink with fruit garnishes.

Perf. 12¾x13¼

2014, Feb. 14   Litho.
165-170 A45   Set of 6   14.50 14.50

Birds of Prey — A46

Designs: 100c, Haliaeetus leucocephalus. 200c, Spizaetus ornatus. 250c, Aquila chrysaetos. 300c, Geranoaetus melanoleucus. 350c, Falconidae polyborinae. 400c, Pandion haliaetus.

2014, Mar. 14   Litho.   **Perf. 13¼**
171-176 A46   Set of 6   18.00 18.00

Miniature Sheet

William Shakespeare (1564-1616), Writer — A47

No. 177 — Shakespeare, with denomination at: a, Lower right. b, Upper right. c, Bottom center above name. d, Lower left, next to country name.

2014, Apr. 23 Litho.   Perf. 12¾x13¼
177 A47 400c Sheet of 4, #a-d 18.00 18.00

Automobiles A48

Designs: 65c, 1964 Ford Mustang. 119c, 1965 Ford Mustang Fastback. 177c, 2014 Ford Mustang. 183c, 1958 Porsche 356A Speedster. 430c, 1964 Porsche 356C. 676c, 2014 Porsche 911 Targa.

2014, May 14 Litho.   Perf. 13¼x12¾
178-183 A48   Set of 6   18.50 18.50

Miniature Sheet

Stadiums of the 2014 World Cup Soccer Championships, Brazil — A49

No. 184: a, 150c, Estadio Mineirao, Belo Horizonte. b, 200c, Arena Amazonia, Manaus. c, 250c, Arena de Sao Paulo, Sao Paulo. d, 300c, Estadio das Dunas, Natal. e, 350c, Estadio do Maracana, Rio de Janeiro. f, 400c, Arena Pernambuco, Recife.

2014, June 12   Litho.   Perf. 14x13¼
184 A49   Sheet of 6, #a-f   18.50 18.50

Peace — A50

Designs: 65c, Dove and "Peace." 119c, Hebrew, Dutch, French and Latin words for "peace." 177c, Hindi, German, Danish and Italian words for "peace." 183c, Family, Papiamento word for "peace," Papiamento, English, Spanish and French words for "family." 305c, Arabic, Farsi, Russian and Spanish words for "peace." 434c, Chinese, Icelandic, Greek and Finnish words for "peace."

2014, July 28 Litho.   Perf. 13¼x12¾
185-190 A50   Set of 6   14.50 14.50

Miniature Sheet

PhilaKorea 2014 World Stamp Exhibition, Seoul — A51

No. 191 — Pinwheel and: a, Girl facing left. b, Dove. c, Rainbow. d, Boy facing right.

2014, Aug. 7   Litho.   Perf. 12¾x13¼
191 A51 400c Sheet of 4, #a-d   18.00 18.00

Fight Against Cancer — A52

Ribbons and various silhouettes of people: 86c, 119c, 177c, 183c, 285c, 750c.

Perf. 12¾x13¼
2014, Aug. 22   Litho.
192-197 A52 Set of 6   18.00 18.00

World Orchid Conference, South Africa — A53

Orchids: 119c, Angraecum stella-africae. 177c, Disa longicornu. 183c, Stenoglottis fimbriata. 305c, Ansellia africana. 382c, Calanthe sylvatica. 434c, Disa uniflora.

Perf. 12¾x13¼
2014, Sept. 10   Litho.
198-203 A53 Set of 6   18.00 18.00

Miniature Sheet

XCOR Space Expeditions — A54

No. 204: a, Space plane at space port. b, Space plane control panel. c, Space port. d, Stars, wing of space plane. e, Nose of space plane. f, XCOR Space Expeditions emblem. g, Earth's horizon as seen from space. h, Burning exhaust of test engine. i, Burning exhaust of space plane in flight. j, Earth, wing of space plane.

2014, Sept. 26   Litho.   Perf. 14
204 A54 177c Sheet of 10, #a-j 20.00 20.00

Caricatures of Marine Life — A55

Designs: 100c, Turtle, starfish, shell. 119c, Fish, oyster with pearl. 177c, Octopus, snail.

305c, Dolphin. 500c, Crab, sea urchin, shells, starfish.

2014, Oct. 14   Litho.   Perf. 13x13½
205-209 A55 Set of 5   13.50 13.50

Christmas A56

Christmas gifts and various children: 65c, 119c, 117c, 183c, 305c.

2014, Nov. 14   Litho.   Perf. 13¼
210-214 A56 Set of 5   9.50   9.50

New Constitutional Status Type of 2011

Designs: 2c, Cocoa damselfish. 4c, Jewel damselfish.

2014   Litho.   Perf. 13¼x12¾
215 A3 2c multi   .25   .25
216 A3 4c multi   .25   .25

Miniature Sheet

Fish — A57

No. 217: a, Bladefin bass. b, Yellowbar basslet. c, Spanish flag. d, Spottail golden bass. e, Rough-tongue bass. f, Dragonette. g, Saber goby. h, Longfin-scorpionfish. i, Deep sea toad. j, Banded basslet.

2014, Nov. 30   Litho.   Perf. 14x13¾
217 A57 177c Sheet of 10, #a-j 20.00 20.00

Curaçao Carnaval, 45th Anniv. — A58

Various costumed participants: 65c, 119c, 177c, 183c, 305c, 434c.

2015, Jan. 19   Litho.   Perf. 13¼x13¾
218-223 A58 Set of 6   14.50 14.50

New Year 2015 (Year of the Goat) — A59

Various goats: 177c, 183c, 305c, 535c.

2015, Feb. 19   Litho.   Perf. 13½x14
224-227 A59 Set of 4   13.50 13.50

Miniature Sheet

Zeppelins — A60

No. 228 — Various zeppelins with color of: a, 343c, Purple. b, 350c, Red. c, 425c, Green. d, 500c, Yellow.

2015, Mar. 19   Litho.   Perf. 13x12¾
228 A60 Sheet of 4, #a-d   18.00 18.00

Miniature Sheet

Travels of Pope Francis — A61

No. 229: a, Pope Francis, two women. b, Dove, Pope Francis, hands and camera. c, Back of head of Pope Francis. d, Pope Francis kissing child.

2015, Apr. 20   Litho.   Perf. 13¼
229 A61 400c Sheet of 4, #a-d 18.00 18.00

Mammals A62

Designs: 65c, Solenodontidae. 119c, Hutias. 177c, Odocoileus virginianus curassavicus. 183c, Sylvilagus floridanus. 430c, Tursiops truncatus. 676c, Leptonycteris curasoae.

2015, May 19   Litho.   Perf. 13¾
230-235 A62 Set of 6   18.50 18.50

Miniature Sheet

Space — A63

No. 236: a, 200c, Pluto and Charon. b, 250c, First man on the Moon, 1969. c, 400c, Mars Lander. d, 750c, Mars Rover Curiosity.

2015, June 29   Litho.   Perf. 13¼
236 A63 Sheet of 4, #a-d   18.00 18.00

Miniature Sheet

World War I, Cent. — A64

No. 237 — Poppy and: a, 250c, Soldiers. b, 350c, Soldier's helmet and gas mask. c, 450c, Airplane, airship and tank. d, 550c, Medal and cemetery.

2015, July 15   Litho.   Perf. 13¾x13½
237 A64 Sheet of 4, #a-d   18.00 18.00

A65

A66

A67

A68

A69

Self-Portraits of Vincent van Gogh (1853-90) and Places in Curaçao — A70

Perf. 13¼x12¾, 12¾x13¼
2015, July 29   Litho.
238 A65 119c multi   1.40   1.40
239 A66 177c multi   2.00   2.00
240 A67 183c multi   2.10   2.10
241 A68 285c multi   3.25   3.25
242 A69 305c multi   3.50   3.50
243 A70 434c multi   5.00   5.00
    Nos. 238-243 (6)   17.25 17.25

Miniature Sheet

Singapore 2015 World Stamp Exhibition — A71

No. 244: a, 325c, Merlion statue. b, 400c, Orchid. c, 425c, Singapore coat of arms. d, 500c, Flag of Singapore.

2015, Aug. 14   Litho.   Perf. 12¾x13
244 A71 Sheet of 4, #a-d   18.50 18.50

Miniature Sheet

Elvis Presley (1935-77) — A72

No. 245: a, 300c, Presley and RCA Victor emblem. b, 400c, Presley. c, 400c, Presley holding microphone and guitar, horiz. d, 500c, Presley playing guitar, horiz.

Perf. 13½x14, 14x13½

2015, Aug. 28 **Litho.**
245 A72 Sheet of 4, #a-d 18.00 18.00

Dogs — A73

Dogs of various breeds: 86c, 119c, 177c, 183c, 305c, 434c.

2015, Sept. 24 **Litho.** **Perf. 13¾**
246-251 A73 Set of 6 14.50 14.50

Cactus
A79

Ship
A80

Klein Curaçao
Lighthouse
A81

Santa Claus,
Sleigh and
Reindeer
A82

Crane — A83

Queen Juliana Bridge — A84

2015, Nov. 26 **Litho.** **Perf. 14x13½**
261 A79 65c multi .75 .75
262 A80 86c multi 1.00 1.00
263 A81 119c multi 1.40 1.40
264 A82 177c multi 2.00 2.00
265 A83 183c multi 2.10 2.10
266 A84 305c multi 3.50 3.50
Nos. 261-266 (6) 10.75 10.75
Christmas.

Miniature Sheet

New Year 2016 (Year of the
Monkey) — A86

No. 273: a, 300c, Spider monkey. b, 400c, Orangutan. c, 500c, Emperor tamarin monkey. d, 600c, Red-faced spider monkey.

2016, Feb. 8 **Litho.** **Perf. 14x13½**
273 A86 Sheet of 4, #a-d 20.00 20.00

Bays — A89

Designs: 66c, Jan Kok Bay. 121c, Santa Martha Bay. 179c, Piscadera Bay. 308c, San Juan Bay. 440c, Spanish Water Bay, vert. 684c, Sint Joris Bay.

Perf. 14x13½, 13½x14

2016, Aug. 8 **Litho.**
286-291 A89 Set of 6 20.00 20.00
Parts of Nos. 286-291 are coated with a thick varnish containing grit.

SEMI-POSTAL STAMPS

Youth Care — SP1

Rabbit: 63c+26c, Writing molecular diagram on blackboard, molecular model. 112c+45c, With chemicals in test tubes and flasks. 166c+75c, Conducting experiment with plants and chemicals. 285c+125c, In rocket ship.

2011, Oct. 11 **Litho.** **Perf. 12¾x13¼**
B1-B4 SP1 Set of 4 10.00 10.00
Intl. Year of Chemistry.

Intl. Year of
Cooperatives
SP2

Stylized people and: 64c+26c, Construction tools, bird. 190c+75c, Rowboat, fish. 293c+125c, Rowboat, house, flower, bird, fish.

2012, Oct. 9 **Perf. 13¼x12¾**
B5-B7 SP2 Set of 3 8.75 8.75

SP3

SP4

SP5

Abolition of
Slavery, 150th
Anniv. — SP6

2013, July 1 **Litho.** **Perf. 13¼x12¾**
B8 SP3 65c +25c multi 1.00 1.00
B9 SP4 118c +45c multi 1.90 1.90
B10 SP5 175c +75c multi 2.75 2.75
B11 SP6 301c +125c multi 4.75 4.75
Nos. B8-B11 (4) 10.40 10.40

Wladimir "Coco"
Balantien, Holder of
New Record for
Home Runs in a
Japanese Baseball
Season — SP7

2013, Dec. 2 **Litho.** **Perf. 12¾x13¼**
B12 SP7 118c +100c multi 2.50 2.50

Pronunciation Symbols

ə .... banana, collide, abut

'ə, ˌə .... humdrum, abut

ə .... immediately preceding \l\, \n\, \m\, \ŋ\, as in battle, mitten, eaten, and sometimes open \'ō-pᵊm\, lock and key \-ᵊŋ-\; immediately following \l\, \m\, \r\, as often in French table, prisme, titre

ər .... further, merger, bird

'ər-
'ə-r } .... as in two different pronunciations of hurry \'hər-ē, 'hə-rē\

a .... mat, map, mad, gag, snap, patch

ā .... day, fade, date, aorta, drape, cape

ä .... bother, cot, and, with most American speakers, father, cart

à .... father as pronounced by speakers who do not rhyme it with bother; French patte

aů .... now, loud, out

b .... baby, rib

ch .... chin, nature \'nā-chər\

d .... did, adder

e .... bet, bed, peck

'ē, ˌē .... beat, nosebleed, evenly, easy

ē .... easy, mealy

f .... fifty, cuff

g .... go, big, gift

h .... hat, ahead

hw .... whale as pronounced by those who do not have the same pronunciation for both whale and wail

i .... tip, banish, active

ī .... site, side, buy, tripe

j .... job, gem, edge, join, judge

k .... kin, cook, ache

k̲ .... German ich, Buch; one pronunciation of loch

l .... lily, pool

m .... murmur, dim, nymph

n .... no, own

ⁿ .... indicates that a preceding vowel or diphthong is pronounced with the nasal passages open, as in French un bon vin blanc \œⁿ -bōⁿ -vaⁿ -bläⁿ\

ŋ .... sing \'siŋ\, singer \'siŋ-ər\, finger \'fiŋ-gər\, ink \'iŋk\

ō .... bone, know, beau

ȯ .... saw, all, gnaw, caught

œ .... French boeuf, German Hölle

œ̄ .... French feu, German Höhle

ȯi .... coin, destroy

p .... pepper, lip

r .... red, car, rarity

s .... source, less

sh .... as in shy, mission, machine, special (actually, this is a single sound, not two); with a hyphen between, two sounds as in grasshopper \'gras-ˌhä-pər\

t .... tie, attack, late, later, latter

th .... as in thin, ether (actually, this is a single sound, not two); with a hyphen between, two sounds as in knighthood \'nīt-ˌhud\

t̲h̲ .... then, either, this (actually, this is a single sound, not two)

ü .... rule, youth, union \'yün-yən\, few \'fyü\

ů .... pull, wood, book, curable \'kyůr-ə-bəl\, fury \'fyůr-ē\

ue .... German füllen, hübsch

ūe .... French rue, German fühlen

v .... vivid, give

w .... we, away

y .... yard, young, cue \'kyü\, mute \'myüt\, union \'yün-yən\

ʸ .... indicates that during the articulation of the sound represented by the preceding character the front of the tongue has substantially the position it has for the articulation of the first sound of yard, as in French digne \dēnʸ\

z .... zone, raise

zh .... as in vision, azure \'a-zhər\ (actually, this is a single sound, not two); with a hyphen between, two sounds as in hogshead \'hȯgz-ˌhed, 'hägz-\

\ .... slant line used in pairs to mark the beginning and end of a transcription: \'pen\

' .... mark preceding a syllable with primary (strongest) stress: \'pen-mən-ˌship\

ˌ .... mark preceding a syllable with secondary (medium) stress: \'pen-mən-ˌship\

- .... mark of syllable division

( ) .... indicate that what is symbolized between is present in some utterances but not in others: factory \'fak-t(ə-)rē\

÷ .... indicates that many regard as unacceptable the pronunciation variant immediately following: cupola \'kyü-pə-lə, ÷-ˌlō\

Illustrated Identifier

This section pictures stamps or parts of stamp designs that will help identify postage stamps that do not have English words on them.

Many of the symbols that identify stamps of countries are shown here as well as typical examples of their stamps.

See the Index and Identifier for stamps with inscriptions such as "sen," "posta," "Baja Porto," "Helvetia," "K.S.A.," etc.

Linn's Stamp Identifier is now available. The 144 pages include more than 2,000 inscriptions and more than 500 large stamp illustrations. Available from Linn's Stamp News, P.O. Box 4129, Sidney, OH 45365-4129.

1. HEADS, PICTURES AND NUMERALS

GREAT BRITAIN

Great Britain stamps never show the country name, but, except for postage dues, show a picture of the reigning monarch.

Victoria

Edward VII   George V   Edward VIII

George VI

George VI

Elizabeth II

Some George VI and Elizabeth II stamps are surcharged in annas, new paisa or rupees. These are listed under Oman.

Silhouette (sometimes facing right, generally at the top of stamp)

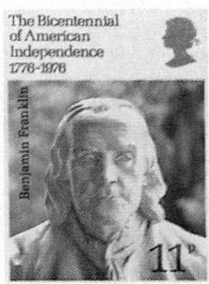

The silhouette indicates this is a British stamp. It is not a U.S. stamp.

VICTORIA

Queen Victoria

INDIA

Other stamps of India show this portrait of Queen Victoria and the words "Service" (or "Postage") and "Annas."

AUSTRIA

YUGOSLAVIA

(Also BOSNIA & HERZEGOVINA if imperf.)

BOSNIA & HERZEGOVINA

Denominations also appear in top corners instead of bottom corners.

HUNGARY

Another stamp has posthorn facing left

BRAZIL

AUSTRALIA

Kangaroo and Emu

GERMANY

Mecklenburg-Vorpommern

SWITZERLAND

PALAU

2. ORIENTAL INSCRIPTIONS

CHINA

Any stamp with this one character is from China (Imperial, Republic or People's Republic). This character appears in a four-character overprint on stamps of Manchukuo. These stamps are local provisionals, which are unlisted. Other overprinted Manchukuo stamps show this character, but have more than four characters in the overprints. These are listed in People's Republic of China.

Some Chinese stamps show the Sun.

Most stamps of Republic of China show this series of characters.

Stamps with the China character and this character are from People's Republic of China.

Calligraphic form of People's Republic of China

(一)	(二)	(三)	(四)	(五)	(六)
1	2	3	4	5	6
(七)	(八)	(九)	(十)	(一十)	(二十)
7	8	9	10	11	12

Chinese stamps without China character

REPUBLIC OF CHINA

PEOPLE'S REPUBLIC OF CHINA

Mao Tse-tung

MANCHUKUO

Temple   Emperor Pu-Yi

The first 3 characters are common to
many Manchukuo stamps.

The last 3 characters are common to
other Manchukuo stamps.

Orchid Crest

Manchukuo
stamp
without
these
elements

JAPAN

Chrysanthemum Crest   Country Name

Japanese stamps without these elements

The number of characters in the
center and the design of dragons on
the sides will vary.

RYUKYU ISLANDS

Country Name

PHILIPPINES
(Japanese Occupation)

Country Name

NETHERLANDS INDIES
(Japanese Occupation)

Indicates Japanese Occupation

Java   **Sumatra**

Country Name   Country Name

Moluccas, Celebes and
South Borneo

Country Name

NORTH BORNEO
(Japanese Occupation)

Indicates Japanese   Country
Occupation   Name

MALAYA
(Japanese Occupation)

Indicates Japanese   Country
Occupation   Name

BURMA
Union of Myanmar

Union of Myanmar

(Japanese Occupation)

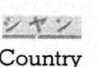

Indicates Japanese Occupation	Country Name

Other Burma Japanese Occupation stamps without these elements

Burmese Script

KOREA

These two characters, in any order, are common to stamps from the Republic of Korea (South Korea) or of the People's Democratic Republic of Korea (North Korea).

This series of four characters can be found on the stamps of both Koreas. Most stamps of the Democratic People's Republic of Korea (North Korea) have just this inscription.

Indicates Republic of Korea (South Korea)

South Korean postage stamps issed after 1952 do not show currency expressed in Latin letters. Stamps wiith " HW," "HWAN," "WON," "WN," "W" or "W" with two lines through it, if not illustrated in listings of stamps before this date, are revenues.
North Korean postage stamps do not have currency expressed in Latin letters.

Yin Yang appears on some stamps.

South Korean stamps show Yin Yang and starting in 1966, 'KOREA' in Latin letters

Example of South Korean stamps lacking Latin text, Yin Yang and standard Korean text of country name. North Korean stamps never show Yin Yang and starting in 1976 are inscribed "DPRK" or "DPR KOREA" in Latin letters.

THAILAND

Country Name

King Chulalongkorn

King Prajadhipok and Chao P'ya Chakri

3. CENTRAL AND EASTERN ASIAN INSCRIPTIONS

INDIA - FEUDATORY STATES

Alwar

Bhor

Bundi

Similar stamps come with
different designs in corners
and differently drawn daggers
(at center of circle).

Dhar   ### Duttia

Faridkot

Hyderabad

Similar stamps exist with
different central design which is
inscribed "Postage"
or "Post & Receipt."

Indore

Jammu & Kashmir

Text varies.

Jasdan

Jhalawar

Kotah

Size and text varies

Nandgaon

Nowanuggur

Poonch

Similar stamps exist
in various sizes with different text

Rajasthan

Rajpeepla

Soruth

Tonk

BANGLADESH

Country Name

NEPAL

Similar stamps are smaller, have squares in
upper corners and have five or nine
characters in central bottom panel.

TANNU TUVA　　ISRAEL

GEORGIA

This inscription
is found on other
pictorial stamps.

Country Name

ARMENIA

The four characters are found somewhere
on pictorial stamps. On some stamps only
the middle two are found.

4. AFRICAN INSCRIPTIONS

ETHIOPIA

5. ARABIC INSCRIPTIONS

١ ٢ ٣ ٤ ٥
1 2 3 4 5

٦ ٧ ٨ ٩ ٠
6 7 8 9 0

AFGHANISTAN

Many early Afghanistan stamps show Tiger's head, many of these have ornaments protruding from outer ring, others show inscriptions in black.

Arabic Script

Crest of King Amanullah

Mosque Gate & Crossed Cannons

The four characters are found somewhere on pictorial stamps. On some stamps only the middle two are found.

BAHRAIN

EGYPT

Postage

IRAN

Country Name

Royal Crown

Lion with Sword

Symbol

Emblem

IRAQ

JORDAN

LEBANON

Similar types have
denominations at top
and slightly different
design.

LIBYA

Country Name in various styles

Other Libya stamps show Eagle and
Shield (head facing either direction) or
Red, White and Black Shield (with or with-
out eagle in center).

Without Country Name

SAUDI ARABIA

Tughra (Central design)

← Palm Tree and Swords

SYRIA

Arab Government Issues

THRACE   **YEMEN**

PAKISTAN

PAKISTAN - BAHAWALPUR

Country Name in top panel, star and crescent

TURKEY

Star & Crescent is a device found on many Turkish stamps, but is also found on stamps from other Arabic areas (see Pakistan-Bahawalpur)

Tughra (similar tughras can be found on stamps of Turkey in Asia, Afghanistan and Saudi Arabia)

Mohammed V

Mustafa Kemal

Plane, Star and Crescent

TURKEY IN ASIA

Other Turkey in Asia pictorials show star & crescent. Other stamps show tughra shown under Turkey.

6. GREEK INSCRIPTIONS

GREECE

Country Name in various styles (Some Crete stamps overprinted with the Greece country name are listed in Crete.)

Lepta

ΔΡΑΧΜΗ **ΔΡΑΧΜΑΙ** **ΛΕΠΤΟΝ**

Drachma   Drachmas   Lepton

Abbreviated Country Name   **ΕΛΛ**

Other forms of Country Name

No country name

CRETE

Country Name

Crete stamps with a surcharge that have the year "1922" are listed under Greece.

EPIRUS

Similar stamps have text above the eagle.

IONIAN IS.

7. CYRILLIC INSCRIPTIONS

RUSSIA

Postage Stamp   Imperial Eagle

Postage in various styles

Abbreviation   Abbreviation   Russia
for Kopeck   for Ruble

Abbreviation for Russian Soviet
Federated Socialist Republic
RSFSR stamps were overprinted
(see below)

Abbreviation for Union of Soviet
Socialist Republics

This item is footnoted in Latvia

RUSSIA - Army of the North

"OKCA"

RUSSIA - Wenden

RUSSIAN OFFICES IN THE TURKISH EMPIRE

 These letters appear
on other stamps of the
Russian offices.

The unoverprinted ver-
sion of this stamp and a
similar stamp were over-
printed by various coun-
tries (see below).

ARMENIA

BELARUS

FAR EASTERN REPUBLIC

Country Name

FINLAND

Circles and Dots
on stamps similar
to Imperial
Russia issues

SOUTH RUSSIA

Country Name

BATUM

Forms of Country Name

TRANSCAUCASIAN FEDERATED REPUBLICS

 Abbreviation for
Country Name

KAZAKHSTAN

Country Name

KYRGYZSTAN

Country
Name

ROMANIA

TAJIKISTAN

Country Name & Abbreviation

UKRAINE

Country Name in various forms

The trident appears   Abbreviation for
on many stamps,   Ukrainian
usually as   Soviet
an overprint.   Socialist
                                          Republic

WESTERN UKRAINE

Abbreviation for
Country Name

AZERBAIJAN

AZƏRBAYCAN

Country Name

Abbreviation for Azerbaijan
Soviet Socialist Republic

MONTENEGRO

ЦРНА ГОРА

Country Name in various forms

Abbreviation
for country
name

No country name
(A similar Montenegro
stamp without coun-
try name has same
vignette.)

SERBIA

Country Name in various forms

Abbreviation for country name

No country name

No country name

MACEDONIA

МАКЕДОНИЈА

Country Name

Different form of Country Name

SERBIA & MONTENEGRO

YUGOSLAVIA

Showing country name

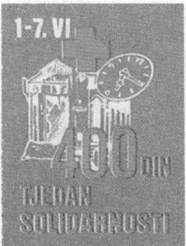

No Country Name

BOSNIA & HERZEGOVINA
(Serb Administration)

РЕПУБЛИКА СРПСКА

Country Name

Different form of Country Name

No Country Name

BULGARIA

Country Name   Postage

Stotinka

Stotinki (plural)   Abbreviation for
Stotinki

Country Name in various forms and styles

Н Р България

No country name

 Abbreviation
for Lev, leva

MONGOLIA

ШУУДАН   **төгрөг**

Country name in   Tugrik in Cyrillic
one word

МОНГОЛ ШУУДАН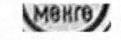

Country name in   Mung in Cyrillic
two words

 Mung
in Mongolian

Tugrik
in Mongolian

Arms

No Country Name

2016 Minkus Supplements

Whether you're updating your album or decided to start collecting a new country, Minkus supplements are the way to go. Heavy acid-free paper and the use of Scott numbers for easy identification makes collecting easy.

Country	Item No.	Retail	AA	Release Date
All-American				
All-American Part 1: US Reg Issues & Commems	MAA116	22.99	19.99	February
All-American Part 3: United Nations	MAA316	25.99	21.99	March
All-American Part 4: US Booklet Panes	MAA416	16.99	13.99	April
All-American Part 5: US Sheetlets	MAA516	22.99	19.99	April
All-American Part 6: US Plate Number Coils	MAA616	11.99	9.99	January
U.S. & U.N 3-Ring				
U.S. Booklet Panes	MUBK16	19.99	16.99	April
U.S. Commemoratives	MUSC16	16.99	13.99	February
U.S. Plate Blocks	MSPB16	22.99	19.99	April
U.S. Plate Number Coils	MPNC16	11.99	9.99	January
U.S. Regular Issues	MUSR16	16.99	13.99	February
U.S. Sheetlets	MSH16	22.99	19.99	April
U.N. Imprint Blocks	MUIB16	22.99	19.99	March
U.N. Postal Stationery	MNPS16	11.99	9.99	March
U.N. Singles	MUN16	25.99	21.99	March
Worldwide				
Andorra - French & Spanish	MAND16	11.99	9.99	July
Australia	MBO116	22.99	19.99	September
Austria	MAU16	19.99	16.99	May
Belgium	MBL16	22.99	19.99	August
Dependencies of Australia	MBO216	22.99	19.99	September
Brazil	MBR16	19.99	16.99	September
Canada	MCA16	34.99	29.99	May
Cyprus	MBE516	16.99	13.99	May
Czech Republic & Slovakia	MCZ16	22.99	19.99	August
Denmark/Faroe Islands/ Greenland/Iceland	MSC116	28.99	24.99	June
Finland	MSC216	22.99	19.99	June
France	MFR16	34.99	29.99	May
Germany	MGM16	16.99	13.99	May
Gibraltar	MBE416	16.99	13.99	May

Country	Item No.	Retail	AA	Release Date
Worldwide				
Great Britian, Ireland	MBE116	28.99	24.99	May
Greece	MGR16	22.99	19.99	June
Guernsey, Jersey, Isle of Man	MBE216	37.99	32.99	May
Hong Kong	MBA216	22.99	19.99	May
Hungary	MHU16	22.99	19.99	August
India	MIN116	22.99	19.99	July
Ireland	MIR16	16.99	13.99	May
Israel Singles	MIS16	16.99	13.99	August
Israel Tab Singles	MIST16	19.99	16.99	August
Italy	MIT16	22.99	19.99	July
Japan	MJA16	45.99	39.99	July
Latvia, Lithuania, Estonia	MSC516	19.99	16.99	August
Liechtenstein	MLT16	16.99	13.99	June
Luxembourg	MLX16	11.99	9.99	August
Malta	MBE316	16.99	13.99	May
Mexico	MMX16	19.99	16.99	September
Monaco	MMO16	16.99	13.99	May
Netherlands	MNE16	37.99	32.99	August
New Zealand	MBO316	22.99	19.99	September
Norway	MSC316	11.99	9.99	June
People's Republic of China	MPRC16	22.99	19.99	July
Poland	MPO16	19.99	16.99	August
Portugal	MPT16	22.99	19.99	July
Republic of China-Taiwan	MCT16	22.99	19.99	July
Russia	MRU16	34.99	29.99	September
San Marino	MSM16	11.99	9.99	July
Spain	MSP16	22.99	19.99	July
Sweden	MSC416	16.99	13.99	September
Switzerland	MSWZ16	16.99	13.99	June
Vatican City	MVA16	11.99	9.99	July
Global				
Global Part 1 (Countries U.S. & A-K)	MGL117	160.99	140.00	December
Global Part 2 (Countries L-Z)	MGL217	160.99	140.00	December

Visit AmosAdvantage.com

or Call 1-800-572-6885

Outside U.S. & Canada 937-498-0800
Mail to: P.O. Box 4129, Sidney OH 45365

INDEX AND IDENTIFIER

All page numbers shown are those in this Volume 2A.

Postage stamps that do not have English words on them are shown in the Illustrated Identifier.

SCOTT Specialty Series

Embark on a new collecting journey. There are Specialty pages available for more than 140 countries with some of them back in print after many years thanks to on-demand printing technology. Start a new collecting adventure with countries featured in Volume 2 of the new Scott Standard Postage Stamp Catalogue!

Specialty Series pages are sold as page units only. Binders, labels and slipcases are sold separately.

ALBUM SETS
These money-saving album sets include pages, binders and self-adhesive binder labels. Some set contents may vary, please call or visit or web site for specific information.

Item		# of Pgs.	Retail	AA
CANADA				
240CAN1	1851-1952	64	$44.99	$38.24
240CAN2	1953-1978	57	$44.99	$38.24
240CAN3	1979-1990	54	$44.99	$38.24
240CAN4	1991-1995	40	$32.99	$28.04
240CAN5	1996-2000	60	$44.99	$38.24
240CAN6	2001-2006	80	$57.99	$49.29
240S007	2007 #59	14	$19.99	$16.99
240S008	2008 #60	9	$13.99	$11.89
240S009	2009 #61	16	$19.99	$16.99
240S010	2010 #62	17	$19.99	$16.99
240S011	2011 #63	19	$19.99	$16.99
240S012	2012 #64	18	$19.99	$16.99
240S013	2013 #65	23	$21.99	$18.69
240S014	2014 #66	25	$21.99	$18.69
240S015	2015 #67	20	$21.99	$18.69
240S016	2016 #68		$25.99	$21.99
240BLANK	Blank Pages	20	$19.99	$16.99
LB012	Label: Canada		$2.29	$1.69
240SET	Album Set	430	$399.99	$299.99
Supplemented in May				
CAYMAN ISLANDS				
261CYI0	1900-1995	78	$52.99	$45.04
261CYI2	1996-2006	42	$32.99	$28.04
261CI07	2007 #11	4	$9.99	$8.49
261CI08	2008 #12	7	$9.99	$8.49
261CI09	2009 #13	4	$9.99	$8.49
261CI11	2011 #14	5	$9.99	$8.49
261CI12	2012 #15	4	$9.99	$8.49
261CI13	2013 #16	4	$9.99	$8.49
261CI14	2014 #17	3	$6.99	$5.94
CAYBLANK	Blank Pages	20	$19.99	$16.99
LB150	Label: Cayman Islands		$2.29	$1.69
261CISET	Album Set	140	$169.99	$124.99
Supplemented in June				
CHILE				
645CHL1	1853-1977	73	$49.99	$42.49
645CHL2	1978-1993	74	$49.99	$42.49
645CHL3	1994-1997	25	$21.99	$18.69
645CHL4	1998-2006	49	$49.99	$42.49
645S007	2007 #13	5	$9.99	$8.49
645S008	2008 #14	10	$13.99	$11.89
645S009	2009 #15	10	$13.99	$11.89
645S010	2010 #16	8	$13.99	$11.89
645S011	2011 #17	5	$9.99	$8.49
645S012	2012 #18	3	$6.99	$5.94
645S013	2013 #19	4	$9.99	$8.49
645S014	2014 #20	5	$9.99	$8.49
645S015	2015 #21	5	$9.99	$8.49
645SET	Album Set	260	$259.99	$189.99
Supplemented in September				
CHINA				
480CHN1	1878-1949	91	$59.99	$47.99
480CHN2	1865-1950	101	$69.99	$55.99
480SET	Album Set	192	$174.99	$134.99
CHINASET	Complete Parts	1115	$999.99	$699.99
COLOMBIA				
646COL1	1856-1976	151	$89.99	$76.49
646COL2	1977-1994	58	$44.99	$38.24
646COL3	1995-1997	15	$19.99	$16.99
646COL4	1998-2006	58	$44.99	$38.24
646S007	2007 #13	7	$9.99	$8.49
646S009	2008-2009 #14	11	$16.99	$14.44
646S010	2010 #15	14	$19.99	$16.99
646S011	2011 #16	8	$13.99	$11.89
646S012	2012 #17	9	$13.99	$11.89
646S013	2013 #18	4	$9.99	$8.49

Item		# of Pgs.	Retail	AA
646S015	2015 #19	4	$9.99	$8.49
646SET	Album Set	322	$329.99	$219.99
Supplemented in September				
CYPRUS				
203CYP0	1880-1997	85	$57.99	$49.29
203CYP2	1998-2006	33	$29.99	$25.49
203CY07	2007 #9	3	$6.99	$5.94
203CY08	2008 #10	5	$9.99	$8.49
203CY09	2009 #11	4	$9.99	$8.49
203CY10	2010 #12	4	$9.99	$8.49
203CY11	2011 #13	6	$9.99	$8.49
203CY12	2012 #14	4	$9.99	$8.49
203CY13	2013 #15	6	$9.99	$8.49
203CY14	2014 #16	3	$6.99	$5.94
203CY15	2015 #17	8	$13.99	$11.89
203CY16	2016 #18		$11.99	$9.99
CYPBLANK	Blank Pages	20	$19.99	$16.99
LB188	Label: Cyprus		$2.29	$1.69
203CYPSET	Album Set	139	$169.99	$119.99
Supplemented in May				
CZECHOSLOVAKIA				
307CZH1	1918-1959	121	$69.99	$59.49
307CZH2	1960-1972	89	$57.99	$49.29
307CZH3	1973-1986	82	$57.99	$49.29
307CZH4	1987-1994	46	$34.99	$29.74
307CZH5	1995-1999	37	$32.99	$28.04
307CZH6	2000-2006	58	$44.99	$38.24
307S007	2007 #58	10	$13.99	$11.89
307S008	2008 #59	10	$13.99	$11.89
307S009	2009 #60	13	$16.99	$14.44
307S010	2010 #61	10	$13.99	$11.89
307S011	2011 #62	18	$19.99	$16.99
307S012	2012 #63	15	$19.99	$16.99
307S013	2013 #64	11	$16.99	$14.44
307S014	2014 #65	11	$16.99	$14.44
307S015	2015 #66	13	$16.99	$14.44
307S016	2016 #67		$22.99	$19.99
CZEBLANK	Blank Pages	20	$19.99	$16.99
LB014	Label: Czechoslovakia		$2.29	$1.69
307SET	Album Set	494	$459.99	$319.99
Supplemented in August				
DENMARK				
345DEN1	1851-1995	81	$57.99	$49.29
345DEN2	1996-2009	96	$64.99	$55.24
345DM10	2010 #15	19	$19.99	$16.99
345DM11	2011 #16	17	$19.99	$16.99
345DM12	2012 #17	15	$19.99	$16.99
345DM13	2013 #18	9	$13.99	$11.89
345DM14	2014 #19	7	$9.99	$8.49
345DM15	2015 #20	7	$9.99	$8.49
345DM16	2016 #21		$16.99	$13.99
DENBLANK	Blank Pages	20	$19.99	$16.99
LB157	Label: Denmark		$2.29	$1.69
345DENSET	Album Set	261	$329.99	$229.99
Supplemented in June				
DOMINICAN REPUBLIC				
648DMR1	1865-1994	169	$99.99	$84.99
648DMR2	1995-2008	49	$44.99	$38.24
648S009	2009 #12	3	$6.99	$5.94
648S010	2010 #13	6	$9.99	$8.49
648S011	2011 #14	6	$9.99	$8.49
648S012	2012 #15	11	$16.99	$14.44
648S013	2013 #16	4	$9.99	$8.49
648S014	2014 #17	11	$16.99	$14.44
648S015	2015 #18	7	$9.99	$8.49
648S016	2016 #19		$16.99	$13.99

Item		# of Pgs.	Retail	AA
648BLANK	Blank Pages	20	$19.99	$16.99
LB205	Label: Dominican Rep.		$2.29	$1.69
Supplemented in September				
FALKLAND ISLANDS				
261FAI0	1878-1995	100	$69.99	$59.49
261FAI2	1996-2006	66	$44.99	$38.24
261FI07	2007 #12	9	$13.99	$11.89
261FI08	2008 #13	7	$9.99	$8.49
261FI09	2009 #14	8	$13.99	$11.89
261FI10	2010 #15	14	$19.99	$16.99
261FI11	2011 #16	7	$9.99	$8.49
261FI12	2012 #17	13	$16.99	$14.44
261FI13	2013 #18	11	$16.99	$14.44
261FI14	2014 #19	5	$9.99	$8.49
261FI15	2015 #20	8	$13.99	$11.89
LB170	Label: Falkland Islands		$2.29	$1.69
Supplemented in July				
FAROE ISLANDS				
345FIS0	1919-1995	30	$29.99	$25.49
345FIS2	1996-2009	46	$34.99	$29.74
345FI10	2010 #14	5	$9.99	$8.49
345FI11	2011 #15	4	$9.99	$8.49
345FI12	2012 #16	5	$9.99	$8.49
345FI13	2013 #17	4	$9.99	$8.49
345FI14	2014 #18	5	$9.99	$8.49
345FI15	2015 #19	5	$9.99	$8.49
345FI16	2016 #20		$11.99	$9.99
FAROBLANK	Blank Pages		$19.99	$16.99
LB158	Label: Faroe Islands		$2.29	$1.69
345FAISET	Album Set	85	$146.99	$114.99
Supplemented in June				
FIJI				
624FJI1	1870-1993	64	$44.99	$38.24
624FJI2	1994-1997	16	$19.99	$16.99
624FJI3	1998-2006	49	$39.99	$33.99
624S007	2007 #14	7	$9.99	$8.49
624S008	2008 #15	5	$9.99	$8.49
624S009	2009 #16	3	$6.99	$5.94
624S010	2010 #17	5	$9.99	$8.49
624S011	2011 #18	4	$9.99	$8.49
624S012	2012 #19	3	$6.99	$5.94
624S013	2013 #20	5	$9.99	$8.49
624S014	2014 #21	3	$6.99	$5.94
LB130	Label: Fiji		$2.29	$1.69
FIJISET	Album Set	153	$179.99	$124.99
Supplemented in August				
FINLAND				
345FIN1	1856-1995	108	$69.99	$59.49
345FIN2	1996-2003	45	$34.99	$29.74
345FN04	2004 #9	10	$13.99	$11.89
345FN05	2005 #10	9	$13.99	$11.89
345FN06	2006 #11	8	$13.99	$11.89
345FN07	2007 #12	9	$13.99	$11.89
345FN08	2008 #13	14	$19.99	$16.99
345FN09	2009 #14	7	$9.99	$8.49
345FN10	2010 #15	11	$16.99	$14.44
345FN11	2011 #16	15	$19.99	$16.99
345FN12	2012 #17	13	$16.99	$14.44
345FN13	2013 #18	11	$16.99	$14.44
345FN14	2014 #19	13	$16.99	$14.44
345FN15	2015 #20	13	$16.99	$14.44
345FN16	2016 #21		$22.99	$19.99
FINBLANK	Blank Pages	20	$19.99	$16.99
LB017	Label: Finland		$2.29	$1.69
345FINSET	Album Set	251	$229.99	$169.99
Supplemented in June				
FRANCE				
310FRN1	1849-1958	70	$49.99	$42.49
310FRN2	1959-1976	66	$44.99	$38.24

Item		# of Pgs.	Retail	AA
310FRN3	1977-1987	59	$44.99	$38.24
310FRN4	1988-1994	54	$44.99	$38.24
310FRN5	1995-2000	55	$44.99	$38.24
310FRN6	2001-2005	98	$64.99	$55.24
310FRN7	2006-2009	107	$69.99	$59.49
310S010	2010 #45	20	$19.99	$16.99
310S011	2011 #46	21	$21.99	$18.69
310S012	2012 #47	39	$32.99	$28.04
310S013	2013 #48	29	$24.99	$21.24
310S014	2014 #49	28	$24.99	$21.24
310S015	2015 #50	34	$29.99	$25.49
310S016	2016 #51		$34.99	$29.99
310BLANK	Blank Pages	20	$19.99	$16.99
LB018	Label: France		$2.29	$1.69
310SET	Album Set	552	$549.99	$369.99
Supplemented in May				
FRENCH AFRICA				
310FRA1	1886-1977	252	$129.99	$110.49
310FRAS1	2010 Supplement (Addendum)	8	$13.99	$11.89
310FRA2	1888-1974	235	$129.99	$110.49
310FRAS2	2010 Supplement (Addendum)	22	$19.99	$16.99
LB073	Label: French Africa		$2.29	$1.69
FRENCH COLONIES				
310FCP0	1859-1956	126	$72.99	$62.04
LB020	Label: French Colonies		$2.29	$1.69
FRENCH OFFICES ABROAD				
310FOA0	1885-1941	40	$32.99	$28.04
FRENCH POLYNESIA				
625FRP1	1892-1994	108	$69.99	$59.49
625FRP2	1995-2006	40	$32.99	$28.04
625S007	2007 #13	5	$9.99	$8.49
625S008	2008 #14	5	$9.99	$8.49
625S010	2010 #15	10	$13.99	$11.89
625S011	2011 #16	5	$9.99	$8.49
625S012	2012 #17	6	$9.99	$8.49
625S013	2013 #18	6	$9.99	$8.49
625S014	2014 #19	6	$9.99	$8.49
625S015	2015 #20	4	$9.99	$8.49
625S016	2016 #21		$11.99	$9.99
LB136	Label: French Polynesia		$2.29	$1.69
FRPOSET	Album Set	174	$189.99	$129.99
Supplemented in August				
FRENCH SOUTHERN & ANTARCTIC TERRITORIES				
626FSA1	1955-1994	38	$32.99	$28.04
626FSA2	1995-2006	37	$32.99	$28.04
626S007	2007 #10	6	$9.99	$8.49
626S008	2008 #11	6	$9.99	$8.49
626S010	2010 #12	6	$9.99	$8.49
626S011	2011 #13	4	$9.99	$8.49
626S012	2012 #14	7	$9.99	$8.49
626S013	2013 #15	7	$9.99	$8.49
626S014	2014 #16	9	$13.99	$11.89
626S015	2015 #17	3	$6.99	$5.94
626S016	2016 #18		$16.99	$13.99
LB141	Label: French & Antarctic Territories		$2.29	$1.69
FSASET	Album Set	97	$139.99	$99.99
Supplemented in August				

INDEX TO ADVERTISERS
2018 VOLUME 2A

SHOWGARD MOUNTS

Showgard mounts are manufactured with the highest archival qualities in mind. The foil used to produce the mounts is acid free and stronger than other mounts for maximum protection and durability. Selecting the right size mount for your stamp is easy. Simply use a millimeter ruler to measure the stamps' width then the height. Showgard incorporates these measurements into their product numbers to insure you get the right size. Mounts available with clear (c) or black (b) backgrounds. Please specify background preference when ordering.

Item	Description	Mounts	Retail	AA*
SGC50/31	50/31 U.S. Jumbo Singles - Horizontal	40	$3.95	$2.85
SGCV31/50	31/50 U.S. Jumbo Singles - Vertical	40	$3.95	$2.85
SGJ40/25	40/25 U.S. Commem. - Horizontal	40	$3.95	$2.85
SGJV25/40	25/40 U.S. Commem. - Vertical	40	$3.95	$2.85
SGE22/25	22/25 U.S. Regular Issues - Vertical	40	$3.95	$2.85
SGEH25/22	25/22 U.S. Regular Issues - Horizontal	40	$3.95	$2.85
SGT25/27	25/27 U.S. Famous Americans	40	$3.95	$2.85
SGU33/27	33/27 U.N., Germany	40	$3.95	$2.85
SGN40/27	40/27 United Nations	40	$3.95	$2.85
SGAH41/31	41/31 U.S. Semi Jumbo - Horizontal	40	$3.95	$2.85
SGAV31/41	31/41 U.S. Semi Jumbo - Vertical	40	$3.95	$2.85
SGDH52/36	52/36 U.S. Duck Stamps	30	$3.95	$2.85
SGS31/31	31/31 U.S. Celebrate the Century	30	$3.95	$2.85
SGUS2	Cut Style with Tray-8 Sizes	320	$32.95	$23.50
SGUS3	Strip Style w/Tray-No. 22 thru No. 52	75	$49.95	$35.75
SGUS1	U.S. Strip Sizes No. 22 thru No. 52	50	$24.50	$17.50
SG67/25	67/25 U.S. Coil Strips of 3	40	$8.35	$5.95
SG57/55	57/55 U.S. Regular Issue	25	$8.35	$5.95
SG106/55	106/55 U.S. 3¢, 4¢ Commemoratives	20	$8.35	$5.95
SG105/57	105/57 U.S. Giori Press Issues	20	$8.35	$5.95
SG127/70	127/70 U.S. Jumbo Issues	10	$8.35	$5.95
SG140/89	140/89 Postcards, Souvenir Sheets	10	$8.35	$5.95
SG165/94	165/94 First Day Covers	10	$8.35	$5.95
SG20	215/20 U.S. Mini Stamps, etc.	22	$9.75	$6.95
SG22	215/22 Narrow U.S. Airs	22	$9.75	$6.95
SG24	215/24 U.K. and Canada, early U.S.	22	$9.75	$6.95
SG25	215/25 U.S. Commem. & Regular Issues	22	$9.75	$6.95
SG27	215/27 U.S. Famous Americans, U.N.	22	$9.75	$6.95
SG28	215/28 Switzerland, Liechtenstein	22	$9.75	$6.95
SG30	215/30 U.S. Special Stamps, Jamestown	22	$9.75	$6.95
SG31	315/31 U.S. Squares & Semi Jumbo	22	$9.75	$6.95
SG33	215/33 U.K. Issues, Misc. Foreign	22	$9.75	$6.95
SG36	215/36 Duck Stamps, Misc. Foreign	15	$9.75	$6.95
SG39	215/39 U.S. Magsaysay, Misc. Foreign	15	$9.75	$6.95
SG41	215/41 U.S. Vertical Commem. Israel Tabs	15	$9.75	$6.95
SG44	215/44 Booklet Panes, Hatteras Quartet	15	$9.75	$6.95
SG48	215/48 Canada Reg. Issue & Comm Blocks	15	$9.75	$6.95
SG50	215/50 U.S. Plain Blocks of 4	15	$9.75	$6.95
SG52	215/52 France Paintings, Misc. Foreign	15	$9.75	$6.95
SG57	215/57 U.S. Commem. Plate Blocks	15	$9.75	$6.95
SG61	215/61 Souvenir Sheets, Tab Singles, etc.	15	$9.75	$6.95
SG63	240/63 U.S. Semi Jumbo Blocks	10	$11.95	$8.75
SG66	240/66 U.S. ATM Panes, SA Duck Panes	10	$11.95	$8.75
SG68	240/68 Canadian Plate Blocks, etc.	10	$11.95	$8.75
SG74	240/74 U.N. Inscription Blocks of 4	10	$11.95	$8.75
SG80	240/80 U.S. Commem. Blocks	10	$11.95	$8.75
SG82	240/82 U.N. Chagall SS, Canada Plate Blocks	10	$11.95	$8.75
SG84	240/84 Israel Plate Blocks, etc.	10	$11.95	$8.75
SG89	240/89 U.N. Inscription Blocks of 6	10	$11.95	$8.75
SG100	240/100 U.S. Squares Plate Blocks	7	$11.95	$8.75
SG120	240/120 Miniature Sheets	7	$11.95	$8.75
SG70	264/70 U.S. Jumbo Plate Blocks	10	$16.25	$11.50
SG91	264/91 U.K. Souvenir Sheets	10	$16.25	$11.50
SG105	264/105 U.K. Blocks, Covers, etc.	10	$16.25	$11.50
SG107	264/107 U.S. Plate No. Strip of 20	10	$16.25	$11.50
SG111	264/111 U.S. Floating Plate No. Strips of 20	5	$10.75	$7.75
SG127	264/127 Modern U.S. Definitive Sheets of 20	5	$11.95	$8.50
SG137	264/137 U.N. SS, U.K. Coronation	5	$12.95	$9.50
SG158	264/158 Miniature Sheets, Apollo Soyuz PB	5	$14.50	$10.50
SG175	264/175 U.S. Sheets-Pan American Reissues	5	$15.95	$11.75
SG188	264/188 U.S. Miniature Sheets-Hollywood, etc.	5	$16.95	$11.95
SG198	264/198 U.S. Miniature Sheets	5	$17.25	$12.50
SGMPK	Assortment No. 22 thru No. 41	12	$7.50	$5.50
SGMPK2	Assortment No. 76 thru No. 171	15	$32.75	$23.75
SGAB	U.S. SS to 1975-except White Plains	11	$8.75	$6.50
SGWSE	World Stamp Expo Souvenir Sheets	3	$2.75	$1.95
SGRP94	U.S. 1994 Souvenir Sheets	5	$10.25	$7.50
SGRPAC97	Pacific 97 Issues	7	$5.75	$4.25
SGDC2006	Washington 2006 Souvenir Sheets	4	$7.95	$5.75
SGTM	Trans-Mississippi Issues	11	$5.75	$4.25
SGSPC	Space Exploration Sheets	5	$7.25	$5.25
SGNY2016	New York 2016 WWS Releases		$12.50	$10.00
SG265/231	265/231 U.S. Full Sheets & Souvenir Cards	5	$21.25	$15.25
SG260/25	260/25 U.S. Coil Strips of up to 11 stamps	25	$12.75	$8.95
SG293/30	293/30 U.S. American Eagle Coil Strips of up to 11 stamps	5	$4.25	$3.25
SG260/40	260/40 U.S. Postal People Full Strip	10	$10.50	$7.50
SG260/46	260/46 U.S. Vending Booklets	10	$10.50	$7.50

Item	Description	Mounts	Retail	AA*
SG260/55	260/55 U.S. 13¢ Eagle Full Strip	10	$10.50	$7.50
SG260/59	260/59 U.S. Double Press Reg. Iss. Strips of 20	10	$10.50	$7.50
SG111/91	111/91 U.S. Columbian Souvenir Sheets	6	$5.50	$3.95
SG229/131	229/131 U.S. WWII Sheets, Looney Tunes	5	$10.75	$7.75
SG187/144	187/144 U.N. Flag Sheetlets	10	$18.50	$12.95
SG204/153	204/153 U.S. Commem. Sheets, Bicentennial	5	$11.25	$8.25
SG120/207	120/207 U.S. Ameripex Presidential Sheetlets	4	$7.75	$5.75
SG192/201	192/201 U.S. Classics Mini-Sheets	5	$13.50	$9.75
SG280/228	280/228 U.S. Greetings From America Sheets	5	$20.50	$14.75
SG191/229	191/229 U.S. Celebrate The Century Sheets	5	$15.25	$11.25
SG108/76	180/76 Bureau of Engraving and Printing Anniversary and other miniature panes	3	$2.50	$1.89
SG8983	89/83 Washington 2006 Souvenir sheet and other miniature panes	3	$2.50	$1.89
SG146/84	146/84 Distinguished Americans, Cycling Souvenir Sheet and other miniature panes	3	$3.75	$2.75
SG203/146	203/146 Hanukkah, Kwanzaa, Eid, Wedding Cake Series, Ronald Reagan, Dogs at Work, Jose Ferrer, Samuel de Champlain SS, etc.	3	$7.50	$5.50
SG178/181	178/181 Butterfly Series, Carmel Mission Express Mail, Celebrate Scouting, Cranes, etc.	3	$7.50	$5.50
SG151/192	151/192 29¢ Winter Olympics and other panes	3	$7.50	$5.50
SG148/196	148/196 $5.00 Waves of Color, Moon Landing 25th Anniversary, etc.	3	$7.50	$5.50
SG183/212	183/212 Wonders of the Sea, Arctic Animals, American Ballet, We the People. etc.	3	$7.50	$5.50
SG76	264/76 BEP SS, Booklets, Plate Blocks	5	$11.95	$8.75
SG96	264/96 Souvenir Sheets, Panes	5	$11.95	$8.75
SG109	264/109 Foreign Miniature Sheets	5	$11.95	$8.75
SG115	264/115 Foreign Miniature Sheets	5	$11.95	$8.75
SG117	264/117 Foreign Miniature Sheets	5	$11.95	$8.75
SG121	264/121 Foreign Miniature Sheets	5	$11.95	$8.75
SG131	264/131 Looney Toons, Misc. Sheetlets	5	$11.95	$8.75
SG135	264/135 Foreign Miniature Sheets	5	$11.95	$8.75
SG139	264/139 White House Pane, etc.	5	$11.95	$8.75
SG143	264/143 Victorian Love, Misc. Sheets	5	$11.95	$8.75
SG147	264/147 Cinco de Mayo, etc.	5	$14.95	$10.75
SG151	264/151 Antique Auto, Communication, etc.	5	$15.50	$11.08
SG163	264/163 Tropical Flowers, UN Human Rights	5	$14.95	$10.75
SG167	264/167 Misc. U.S. Sheetlets	5	$14.95	$10.75
SG171	264/171 Helping Children Learn, etc.	5	$14.95	$10.75
SG181	264/181 U.S. Sheets–Calder, All Aboard, etc.	5	$18.50	$13.25
SG201	264/201 Dinosaurs, etc.	5	$18.50	$13.25
SG215	264/215 U.S. Sheets–Arctic Animals, Ballet, etc.	5	$18.50	$13.25

7" LIGHTHOUSE STAMP MOUNT CUTTER

This affordable and versatile mount cutter features an attachable measuring scale up to 7" (180mm) with an adjustable stop for accurate and clean cuts every time.

Item	Retail	AA*
LH180MC	$23.99	$19.99

AMOS ADVANTAGE

Call **1-800-572-6885**

Outside U.S. & Canada: (937) 498-0800

Visit **AmosAdvantage.com**

Mail orders to: P.O. Box 4129, Sidney, OH 45365

2018
VOLUME 2A
DEALER DIRECTORY
YELLOW PAGE LISTINGS

This section of your Scott Catalogue contains advertisements to help you conveniently find what you need, when you need it...!

Accessories

BROOKLYN GALLERY COIN & STAMP, INC.
8725 4th Ave.
Brooklyn, NY 11209
PH: 718-745-5701
FAX: 718-745-2775
info@brooklyngallery.com
www.brooklyngallery.com

Aerophilately

HENRY GITNER PHILATELISTS, INC.
PO Box 3077-S
Middletown, NY 10940
PH: 845-343-5151
PH: 800-947-8267
FAX: 845-343-0068
hgitner@hgitner.com
www.hgitner.com

Appraisals

DR. ROBERT FRIEDMAN & SONS STAMP & COIN BUYING CENTER
2029 W. 75th St.
Woodridge, IL 60517
PH: 800-588-8100
FAX: 630-985-1588
drbobstamps@comcast.net
www.drbobfriedmanstamps.com

Argentina

GUILLERMO JALIL
Maipu 466,local 4
1006 Buenos Aires
Argentina
guillermo@jalilstamps.com
philatino@philatino.com
www.philatino.com
www.jalilstamps.com

Asia

KELLEHER & ROGERS LTD.
4 Finance Drive, Ste. 200
Danbury, CT 06810
PH: 203-297-6056
FAX: 203-297-6059
info@kelleherauctions.com
www.kelleherauctions.com

Auctions

DUTCH COUNTRY AUCTIONS
The Stamp Center
4115 Concord Pike
Wilmington, DE 19803
PH: 302-478-8740
FAX: 302-478-8779
auctions@dutchcountryauctions.com
www.dutchcountryauctions.com

KELLEHER & ROGERS LTD.
4 Finance Drive, Ste. 200
Danbury, CT 06810
PH: 203-297-6056
FAX: 203-297-6059
info@kelleherauctions.com
www.kelleherauctions.com

R. MARESCH & SON LTD.
5th Floor - 6075 Yonge St.
Toronto, ON M2M 3W2
CANADA
PH: 416-363-7777
FAX: 416-363-6511
www.maresch.com

British Commonwealth

ARON R. HALBERSTAM PHILATELISTS, LTD.
PO Box 150168
Van Brunt Station
Brooklyn, NY 11215-0168
PH: 718-788-3978
arh@arhstamps.com
www.arhstamps.com

COLLECTORS EXCHANGE ORLANDO STAMP SHOP
1814A Edgewater Drive
Orlando, FL 32804
PH: 407-620-0908
PH: 407-947-8603
FAX: 407-730-2131
jlatter@cfl.rr.com
www.BritishStampsAmerica.com
www.OrlandoStampShop.com

ROY'S STAMPS
PO Box 28001
600 Ontario Street
St. Catharines, ON
CANADA L2N 7P8
Phone: 905-934-8377
Email: roystamp@cogeco.ca

THE STAMP ACT
PO Box 1136
Belmont, CA 94002
PH: 650-703-2342
PH: 650-592-3315
FAX: 650-508-8104
thestampact@sbcglobal.net

British Commonwealth

WORLDSTAMPS/ FRANK GEIGER PHILATELISTS
PO Box 4743
Pinehurst, NC 28374
PH: 910-295-2048
info@WorldStamps.com
www.WorldStampsScott.com/British

Buying

DR. ROBERT FRIEDMAN & SONS STAMP & COIN BUYING CENTER
2029 W. 75th St.
Woodridge, IL 60517
PH: 800-588-8100
FAX: 630-985-1588
drbobstamps@comcast.net
www.drbobfriedmanstamps.com

Canada

CANADA STAMP FINDER
PO Box 92591
Brampton, ON L6W 4R1
PH: 514-238-5751
Toll Free in North America:
877-412-3106
FAX: 323-315-2635
canadastampfinder@gmail.com
www.canadastampfinder.com

ROY'S STAMPS
PO Box 28001
600 Ontario Street
St. Catharines, ON
CANADA L2N 7P8
Phone: 905-934-8377
Email: roystamp@cogeco.ca

Canada

WORLDSTAMPS/ FRANK GEIGER PHILATELISTS
PO Box 4743
Pinehurst, NC 28374
PH: 910-295-2048
info@WorldStamps.com
www.WorldStampsScott.com/Canada

China

KELLEHER & ROGERS LTD.
4 Finance Drive, Ste. 200
Danbury, CT 06810
PH: 203-297-6056
FAX: 203-297-6059
info@kelleherauctions.com
www.kelleherauctions.com

THE STAMP ACT
PO Box 1136
Belmont, CA 94002
PH: 650-703-2342
PH: 650-592-3315
FAX: 650-508-8104
thestampact@sbcglobal.net

Collections

DR. ROBERT FRIEDMAN & SONS STAMP & COIN BUYING CENTER
2029 W. 75th St.
Woodridge, IL 60517
PH: 800-588-8100
FAX: 630-985-1588
drbobstamps@comcast.net
www.drbobfriedmanstamps.com

Croatia

WORLDSTAMPS/
FRANK GEIGER PHILATELISTS
PO Box 4743
Pinehurst, NC 28374
PH: 910-295-2048
info@WorldStamps.com
www.WorldStampsScott.com/Croatia

Czechoslovakia

WORLDSTAMPS/
FRANK GEIGER PHILATELISTS
PO Box 4743
Pinehurst, NC 28374
PH: 910-295-2048
info@WorldStamps.com
www.WorldStampsScott.com/Czech

Denmark

WORLDSTAMPS/
FRANK GEIGER PHILATELISTS
PO Box 4743
Pinehurst, NC 28374
PH: 910-295-2048
info@WorldStamps.com
www.WorldStampsScott.com/Denmark

Ducks

MICHAEL JAFFE
PO Box 61484
Vancouver, WA 98666
PH: 360-695-6161
PH: 800-782-6770
FAX: 360-695-1616
mjaffe@brookmanstamps.com
www.brookmanstamps.com

Estonia

WORLDSTAMPS/
FRANK GEIGER PHILATELISTS
PO Box 4743
Pinehurst, NC 28374
PH: 910-295-2048
info@WorldStamps.com
www.WorldStampsScott.com/Estonia

Ethiopia

WORLDSTAMPS/
FRANK GEIGER PHILATELISTS
PO Box 4743
Pinehurst, NC 28374
PH: 910-295-2048
info@WorldStamps.com
www.WorldStampsScott.com/Ethiopia

Europe-Western

WORLDSTAMPS/
FRANK GEIGER PHILATELISTS
PO Box 4743
Pinehurst, NC 28374
PH: 910-295-2048
info@WorldStamps.com
www.WorldStampsScott.com/Europe

Falkland Islands

WORLDSTAMPS/
FRANK GEIGER PHILATELISTS
PO Box 4743
Pinehurst, NC 28374
PH: 910-295-2048
info@WorldStamps.com
www.WorldStampsScott.com/Falklands

France & Colonies

E. JOSEPH McCONNELL, INC.
PO Box 683
Monroe, NY 10949
PH: 845-783-9791
FAX: 845-782-0347
ejstamps@gmail.com
www.EJMcConnell.com

WORLDSTAMPS/
FRANK GEIGER PHILATELISTS
PO Box 4743
Pinehurst, NC 28374
PH: 910-295-2048
info@WorldStamps.com
www.WorldStampsScott.com/France

French S. Antarctic

E. JOSEPH McCONNELL, INC.
PO Box 683
Monroe, NY 10949
PH: 845-783-9791
FAX: 845-782-0347
ejstamps@gmail.com
www.EJMcConnell.com

WORLDSTAMPS/
FRANK GEIGER PHILATELISTS
PO Box 4743
Pinehurst, NC 28374
PH: 910-295-2048
info@WorldStamps.com
www.WorldStampsScott.com/FSAT

Japan

KELLEHER & ROGERS LTD.
4 Finance Drive, Ste. 200
Danbury, CT 06810
PH: 203-297-6056
FAX: 203-297-6059
info@kelleherauctions.com
www.kelleherauctions.com

Korea

KELLEHER & ROGERS LTD.
4 Finance Drive, Ste. 200
Danbury, CT 06810
PH: 203-297-6056
FAX: 203-297-6059
info@kelleherauctions.com
www.kelleherauctions.com

Latin America

GUY SHAW
PO Box 27138
San Diego, CA 92198
PH/FAX: 858-485-8269
guyshaw@guyshaw.com
www.guyshaw.com

Manchukuo

KELLEHER & ROGERS LTD.
4 Finance Drive, Ste. 200
Danbury, CT 06810
PH: 203-297-6056
FAX: 203-297-6059
info@kelleherauctions.com
www.kelleherauctions.com

Middle East-Arab

KELLEHER & ROGERS LTD.
4 Finance Drive, Ste. 200
Danbury, CT 06810
PH: 203-297-6056
FAX: 203-297-6059
info@kelleherauctions.com
www.kelleherauctions.com

New Issues

DAVIDSON'S STAMP SERVICE
Personalized Service since 1970
PO Box 36355
Indianapolis, IN 46236-0355
PH: 317-826-2620
ed-davidson@earthlink.net
www.newstampissues.com

WORLDSTAMPS/
FRANK GEIGER PHILATELISTS
PO Box 4743
Pinehurst, NC 28374
PH: 910-295-2048
info@WorldStamps.com
www.WorldStampsScott.com/NI

Proofs & Essays

HENRY GITNER
PHILATELISTS, INC.
PO Box 3077-S
Middletown, NY 10940
PH: 845-343-5151
PH: 800-947-8267
FAX: 845-343-0068
hgitner@hgitner.com
www.hgitner.com

Stamp Stores

California

BROSIUS STAMP, COIN &
SUPPLIES
2105 Main St.
Santa Monica, CA 90405
PH: 310-396-7480
FAX: 310-396-7455
brosius.stamp.coin@hotmail.com

Delaware

DUTCH COUNTRY AUCTIONS
The Stamp Center
4115 Concord Pike
Wilmington, DE 19803
PH: 302-478-8740
FAX: 302-478-8779
auctions@dutchcountryauctions.com
www.dutchcountryauctions.com

Florida

DR. ROBERT FRIEDMAN &
SONS STAMP & COIN
BUYING CENTER
PH: 800-588-8100
FAX: 630-985-1588
drbobstamps@comcast.net
www.drbobfriedmanstamps.com

Illinois

DR. ROBERT FRIEDMAN &
SONS STAMP & COIN
BUYING CENTER
2029 W. 75th St.
Woodridge, IL 60517
PH: 800-588-8100
FAX: 630-985-1588
drbobstamps@comcast.net
www.drbobfriedmanstamps.com

Indiana

KNIGHT STAMP & COIN CO.
237 Main St.
Hobart, IN 46342
PH: 219-942-4341
PH: 800-634-2646
knight@knightcoin.com
www.knightcoin.com

Stamp Stores

New Jersey

BERGEN STAMPS &
COLLECTIBLES
306 Queen Anne Rd.
Teaneck, NJ 07666
PH: 201-836-8987C

TRENTON STAMP & COIN CO
Thomas DeLuca
Store: Forest Glen Plaza
1804 Highway 33
Hamilton Square, NJ 08690
Mail: PO Box 8574
Trenton, NJ 08650
PH: 609-584-8100
FAX: 609-587-8664
TOMD4TSC@aol.com

New York

CHAMPION STAMP CO., INC.
432 W. 54th St.
New York, NY 10019
PH: 212-489-8130
FAX: 212-581-8130
championstamp@aol.com
www.championstamp.com

CK STAMPS
42-14 Union St. # 2A
Flushing, NY 11355
PH: 917-667-6641
ckstampsllc@yahoo.com

Ohio

HILLTOP STAMP SERVICE
Richard A. Peterson
PO Box 626
Wooster, OH 44691
PH: 330-262-8907 (O)
PH: 330-262-5378 (H)
hilltop@bright.net
www.hilltopstamps.com

Supplies

BROOKLYN GALLERY COIN &
STAMP, INC.
8725 4th Ave.
Brooklyn, NY 11209
PH: 718-745-5701
FAX: 718-745-2775
info@brooklyngallery.com
www.brooklyngallery.com

Topicals

E. JOSEPH McCONNELL, INC.
PO Box 683
Monroe, NY 10949
PH: 845-783-9791
FAX: 845-782-0347
ejstamps@gmail.com
www.EJMcConnell.com

WORLDSTAMPS/
FRANK GEIGER PHILATELISTS
PO Box 4743
Pinehurst, NC 28374
PH: 910-295-2048
info@WorldStamps.com
www.WorldStampsScott.com/Topic

Topicals-Columbus

MR. COLUMBUS
PO Box 1492
Fennville, MI 49408
PH: 269-543-4755
David@MrColumbus1492.com
www.MrColumbus1492.com

Topicals-Miscellaneous

HENRY GITNER
PHILATELISTS, INC.
PO Box 3077-S
Middletown, NY 10940
PH: 845-343-5151
PH: 800-947-8267
FAX: 845-343-0068
hgitner@hgitner.com
www.hgitner.com

United Nations

BRUCE M. MOYER
Box 99
East Texas, PA 18046
PH: 610-395-8410
FAX: 610-395-8537
moyer@unstamps.com
www.unstamps.com

United States

BROOKMAN STAMP CO.
PO Box 90
Vancouver, WA 98666
PH: 360-695-1391
PH: 800-545-4871
FAX: 360-695-1616
info@brookmanstamps.com
www.brookmanstamps.com

KEITH WAGNER
ACS Stamp Company
2914 W 135th Ave
Broomfield, Colorado 80020
303-841-8666
www.ACSStamp.com

U.S.-Classics/Moderns

BARDO STAMPS
PO Box 7437
Buffalo Grove, IL 60089
PH: 847-634-2676
jfb7437@aol.com
www.bardostamps.com

U.S.-Collections Wanted

DR. ROBERT FRIEDMAN &
SONS STAMP & COIN
BUYING CENTER
2029 W. 75th St.
Woodridge, IL 60517
PH: 800-588-8100
FAX: 630-985-1588
drbobstamps@comcast.net
www.drbobfriedmanstamps.com

DUTCH COUNTRY AUCTIONS
The Stamp Center
4115 Concord Pike
Wilmington, DE 19803
PH: 302-478-8740
FAX: 302-478-8779
auctions@dutchcountryauctions.com
www.dutchcountryauctions.com

Wanted-Worldwide Collections

DUTCH COUNTRY AUCTIONS
The Stamp Center
4115 Concord Pike
Wilmington, DE 19803
PH: 302-478-8740
FAX: 302-478-8779
auctions@dutchcountryauctions.com
www.dutchcountryauctions.com

Websites

KEITH WAGNER
ACS Stamp Company
2914 W 135th Ave
Broomfield, Colorado 80020
303-841-8666
www.ACSStamp.com

Wholesale

HENRY GITNER
PHILATELISTS, INC.
PO Box 3077-S
Middletown, NY 10940
PH: 845-343-5151
PH: 800-947-8267
FAX: 845-343-0068
hgitner@hgitner.com
www.hgitner.com

Worldwide

KELLEHER & ROGERS LTD.
4 Finance Drive, Ste. 200
Danbury, CT 06810
PH: 203-297-6056
FAX: 203-297-6059
info@kelleherauctions.com
www.kelleherauctions.com

Worldwide-Collections

DR. ROBERT FRIEDMAN &
SONS STAMP & COIN
BUYING CENTER
2029 W. 75th St.
Woodridge, IL 60517
PH: 800-588-8100
FAX: 630-985-1588
drbobstamps@comcast.net
www.drbobfriedmanstamps.com

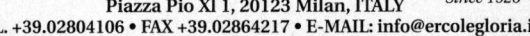

GET SOMEONE STARTED COLLECTING!

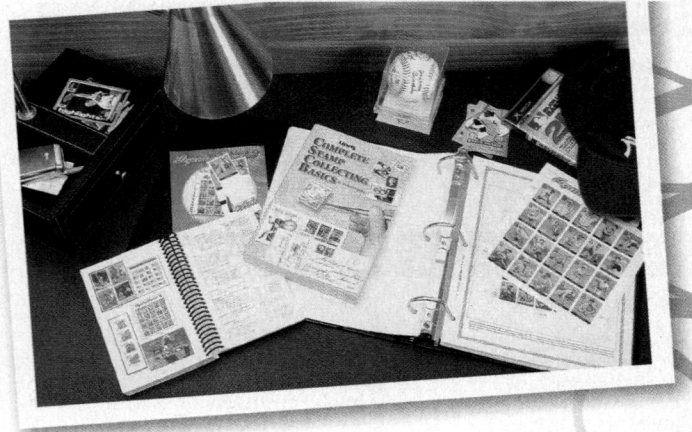

Thinking about starting a stamp collection? Here are the albums and the resources to get started.

MINUTEMAN ALBUM

America's number one stamp album makes collecting easy and fun. Album spaces are identified by Scott numbers and many of the spaces feature historic vignettes about the stamps. The three ring binder has been custom designed for the album pages. Now even the intermediate or beginner collector can have an album to fit their collecting interest without spending a small fortune. Save even more when you take advantage of money saving packages that are available!

ITEM	DESCRIPTION (PAGES ONLY)	PAGES	RETAIL	AA*
180PMM19	**19th Century 1840-1899**	15	$19.99	**$16.99**
180PMM20	**20th Century 1900-1999**	362	$69.99	**$59.49**
180PMM21	**21st Century 2000-2003**	78	$49.99	**$42.49**
180PMM21A	**Pages 2004-2009**	93	$69.99	**$59.49**

(Part and kit pages fit 3-ring binder only.)

MINUTEMAN ALBUM KIT

Includes all Minuteman album pages covering U.S. Stamps 1840-2015, as well as two Minuteman 3-ring binders.

ITEM	DESCRIPTION	RETAIL	AA*
180MMKIT	**Minuteman Kit**	$219.99	**$169.99**

MINUTEMAN 20th CENTURY ALBUM KIT

Includes Minuteman pages covering U.S. stamps from 1900 - 1999, as well as Minuteman 3-ring binder.

ITEM	DESCRIPTION	RETAIL	AA*
180AMM20	**20th Century Album Plus 3-Ring Binder**	$69.99	**$59.49**

MINUTEMAN SUPPLEMENTS & ACCESSORIES

ITEM	DESCRIPTION	PAGES	RETAIL	AA*
180S010	**2010 Supplement** (pages only)	14	$19.99	**$16.99**
180S011	**2011 Supplement** (pages only)	18	$19.99	**$16.99**
180S012	**2012 Supplement** (pages only)	20	$19.99	**$16.99**
180S013	**2013 Supplement** (pages only)	22	$19.99	**$16.99**
180S014	**2014 Supplement** (pages only)	20	$19.99	**$16.99**
180S015	**2015 Supplement** (pages only)	14	$19.99	**$16.99**
180S016	**2016 Supplement** (pages only)	18	$22.99	**$19.99**
180Z003	**Minuteman Blank Pages Pack** Fits both 2-post and 3-ring binders	20/pack	$19.99	**$16.99**

Starting with 2003, supplements fit both the 2-post Minuteman and 3-ring binders.

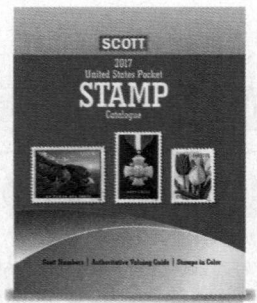

2017 U.S. STAMP POCKET CATALOGUE

With pages designed to be a convenient inventory checklist, the Scott U.S. Pocket Stamp Catalogue is a perfect compact companion at shows, club meetings, and your desk. Full-color stamp illustrations accompany listings and values for more than 4,000 U.S. stamps, all identified by Scott catalog numbers. Get your copy today!

ITEM	DESCRIPTION	RETAIL	AA*
P112017	**2017 U.S. Pocket Stamp Catalogue**	$32.50	**$26.99**

Get yours today by visiting **AmosAdvantage.com**

Or Call **1-800-572-6885** Outside U.S. & Canada Call: **1-937-498-0800**

P.O. Box 4129, Sidney, OH 45365

ScottMounts

PRE-CUT SINGLE MOUNTS

ITEM	W x H (mm)	DESCRIPTION	MOUNTS	RETAIL	AA*
901	40 x 25	U.S. Standard Comm. Hor. Water Activated	40	$3.50	$2.39
902	25 x 40	U.S. Standard Comm. Vert. Water Activated	40	$3.50	$2.39
903	25 x 22	U.S. Regular Issue – Hor. Water Activated	40	$3.50	$2.39
904	22 x 25	U.S. Regular Issue – Vert. Water Activated	40	$3.50	$2.39
905	41 x 31	U.S. Semi-Jumbo – Horizontal	40	$3.50	$2.39
906	31 x 41	U.S. Semi-Jumbo – Vertical	40	$3.50	$2.39
907	50 x 31	U.S. Jumbo – Horizontal	40	$3.50	$2.39
908	31 x 50	U.S. Jumbo – Vertical	40	$3.50	$2.39
909	25 x 27	U.S. Famous Americans/Champions Of Liberty	40	$3.50	$2.39
910	33 x 27	United Nations	40	$3.50	$2.39
911	40 x 27	United Nations	40	$3.50	$2.39
976	67 x 25	Plate Number Coils, Strips of Three	40	$6.25	$3.99
984	67 x 34	Pacific '97 Triangle	10	$3.50	$2.39
985	111 x 25	Plate Number Coils, Strips of Five	25	$6.25	$3.99
986	51 x 36	U.S. Hunting Permit/Express Mail	40	$6.25	$3.99
1045	40 x 26	U.S. Standard Comm. Hor. Self-Adhesive	40	$3.50	$2.39
1046	25 x 41	U.S. Standard Comm. Vert. Self-Adhesive	40	$3.50	$2.39
1047	22 x 26	U.S. Definitives Vert. Self Adhesive	40	$3.50	$2.39
966	Value Pack	(Assortment pre-cut sizes)	320	$23.25	$15.25
975	Best Pack	(Assortment pre-cut sizes - Black Only)	160	$14.75	$9.99

PRE-CUT PLATE BLOCK, FDC, POSTAL CARD MOUNTS

ITEM	W x H (mm)	DESCRIPTION	MOUNTS	RETAIL	AA*
912	57 x 55	Regular Issue Plate Block	25	$6.25	$3.99
913	73 x 63	Champions of Liberty	25	$6.25	$3.99
914	106 x 55	Rotary Press Standard Commemorative	20	$6.25	$3.99
915	105 x 57	Giori Press Standard Commemorative	20	$6.25	$3.99
916	127 x 70	Giori Press Jumbo Commemorative	10	$6.25	$3.99
917	165 x 94	First Day Cover	10	$6.25	$3.99
918	140 x 90	Postal Card Size/Submarine Booklet Pane	10	$6.25	$3.99
1048	152 x 107	Large Postal Cards	8	$10.25	$6.99

STRIPS 215MM LONG

ITEM	W x H (mm)	DESCRIPTION	MOUNTS	RETAIL	AA*
919	20	U.S. 19th Century, Horizontal Coil	22	$7.99	$5.25
920	22	U.S. Early Air Mail	22	$7.99	$5.25
921	24	U.S., Vertical Coils, Christmas (#2400, #2428 etc.)	22	$7.99	$5.25
922	25	U.S. Commemorative and Regular	22	$7.99	$5.25
1049	26	U.S. Commemorative and Regular	22	$7.99	$5.25
923	27	U.S. Famous Americans	22	$7.99	$5.25
924	28	U.S. 19th Century, Liechtenstein	22	$7.99	$5.25
1050	29	Virginia Dare, British Empire, etc.	22	$7.99	$5.25
925	30	U.S. 19th Century; Jamestown, etc; Foreign	22	$7.99	$5.25
926	31	U.S. Horizontal Jumbo and Semi-Jumbo	22	$7.99	$5.25
927	33	U.S. Stampin' Future, UN	22	$7.99	$5.25
928	36	U.S. Hunting Permit, Canada	15	$7.99	$5.25
1051	37	U.S., British Colonies	22	$7.99	$5.25
929	39	U.S. Early 20th Century	15	$7.99	$5.25
930	41	U.S. Vert. Semi-Jumbo ('77 Lafayette, Pottery, etc.)	15	$7.99	$5.25
931		Multiple Assortment: One strip of each size 22-41 above (SMKB) (2 x 25mm strips)	12	$7.99	$5.25
1052	42	U.S., British Colonies	22	$7.99	$5.25
1053	43	U.S., British Colonies	22	$7.99	$5.25
932	44	U.S. Vertical Coil Pair Garden Flowers Booklet Pane	15	$7.99	$5.25
933	48	U.S. Farley, Gutter Pair	15	$7.99	$5.25
934	50	U.S. Jumbo (Lyndon Johnson, '74 U.P.U., etc.)	15	$7.99	$5.25
935	52	U.S. Standard Commemorative Block (Butterflies)	15	$7.99	$5.25
936	55	U.S. Standard Plate Block - normal margins	15	$7.99	$5.25
937	57	U.S. Standard Plate Block - wider margins	15	$7.99	$5.25
938	61	U.S. Blocks, Israel Tabs, '99 Christmas Madonna Pane	15	$7.99	$5.25

STRIPS 240MM LONG

ITEM	W x H (mm)	DESCRIPTION	MOUNTS	RETAIL	AA*
939	63	U.S. Jumbo Commemorative Horizontal Block	10	$9.25	$5.99
940	66	U.S. CIPEX Souvenir Sheet, Self-Adhesive Booklet Pane (#2803a, 3012a)	10	$9.25	$5.99
941	68	U.S. ATM Booklet Pane, Farley Gutter Pair & Souvenir Sheet	10	$9.25	$5.99
942	74	U.S. TIPEX Souvenir Sheet	10	$9.25	$5.99
943	80	U.S. Standard Commemorative Vertical Block	10	$9.25	$5.99
944	82	U.S. Blocks of Four, U.N. Chagall	10	$9.25	$5.99
945	84	Israel Tab Block, Mars Pathfinder Sheetlet	10	$9.25	$5.99
946	89	Submarine Booklet, Souvenir Sheet World Cup, Rockwell	10	$9.25	$5.99
947	100	U.S. '74 U.P.U. Block, U.N. Margin Inscribed Block	7	$9.25	$5.99
948	120	Various Souvenir Sheets and Blocks	7	$9.25	$5.99

STRIPS 265MM LONG

ITEM	W x H (mm)	DESCRIPTION	MOUNTS	RETAIL	AA*
1035			12	$9.25	$5.99
949			10	$9.25	$5.99
981			10	$9.25	$5.99
1030			10	$9.25	$5.99
1036			10	$9.25	$5.99
950			10	$9.25	$5.99
951			10	$9.25	$5.99
952			10	$12.50	$8.50
1031			10	$12.50	$8.50
1032		, etc.	10	$12.50	$8.50
1060		t, etc.	10	$12.50	$8.50
953		anta	10	$12.50	$8.50
1033			10	$12.50	$8.50
1061			10	$12.50	$8.50
954		Number Strip	10	$12.50	$8.50
955			10	$12.50	$8.50
956			10	$14.75	$9.99
1062			10	$17.50	$11.99
957			10	$17.50	$11.99
1063		Plate Block	10	$17.50	$11.99
1064	133	U.S., Japan Gifts of Friendship sheet	10	$17.50	$11.99
958	137	Great Britain Coronation	10	$17.50	$11.99
1065	139	Sheets: Soda Fountain, Lady Bird Johnson, Earthscapes, etc.	10	$17.50	$11.99
1066	143	Sheets: Merchant Marine Ships, 2013 Hanukkah, etc.	10	$17.50	$11.99
1067	147	Sheets: Pickup Trucks, Animal Rescue, Washington D.C., etc.	10	$17.50	$11.99
1068	151	Sheets: Go Green, Bicycling, Happy New Year, Ben Franklin, etc.	10	$17.50	$11.99

STRIPS 265MM LONG, continued

ITEM	W x H (mm)	DESCRIPTION	MOUNTS	RETAIL	AA*
959	158	American Glass, U.S. Football Coaches Sheets	10	$17.99	$12.50
1069	163	Sheets: Modern Architecture, UN Human Rights, etc.	5	$12.50	$8.50
1070	167	Sheets: John F. Kennedy, Classics Forever, Made in America, etc.	5	$12.50	$8.50
1071	171	Film Directors, Foreign Souvenir Sheets	5	$12.50	$8.50
960	175	Large Block, Souvenir Sheet	5	$12.50	$8.50
1072	181	Sheets: Jimi Hendrix, Johnny Cash, American Photography, etc.	5	$17.50	$11.99
1073	185	Frank Sinatra, Ronald Reagan, Arthur Ashe, Creast Cancer, etc.	5	$17.50	$11.99
1074	188	Sheets: Yoda, 9/11 Heroes, Andy Warhol, Frida Kahlo, etc	5	$17.50	$11.99
1075	198	Sheets: Modern American Art, Super Heroes, Baseball Sluggers, etc.	5	$17.50	$11.99
1076	215	Celebrity Chefs sheets; Foreign sheets	5	$17.50	$11.99
961	231	U.S. Full Post Office Pane Regular and Commemorative	5	$17.99	$12.50

SOUVENIR SHEETS/SMALL PANES

ITEM	W x H (mm)	DESCRIPTION	MOUNTS	RETAIL	AA*
962	204 x 153	New Year 2000, U.S. Bicentennial S/S	4	$9.25	$5.99
963	187 x 144	55¢ Victorian Love Pane, U.N. Flag Sheet	9	$15.50	$10.25
964	160 x 200	U.N., Israel Sheet	10	$15.50	$10.25
965	120 x 207	U.S. AMERIPEX Presidential Sheet	4	$6.25	$3.99
968	229 x 131	World War II S/S Plate Block Only	5	$9.25	$5.99
970	111 x 91	Columbian Souvenir Sheet	6	$6.25	$4.75
972	148 x 196	Apollo Moon Landing/Carnivorous Plants	4	$7.99	$5.25
989	129 x 122	U.S. Definitive Sheet: Harte, Hopkins, etc.	8	$10.25	$6.99
990	189 x 151	Chinese New Year	5	$10.25	$6.99
991	150 x 185	Breast Cancer/Fermi/Soccer/'96 Folk Heroes	5	$10.25	$6.99
992	198 x 151	Cherokee Strip Sheet	5	$10.25	$6.99
993	185 x 151	Bernstein/NATO/Irish/Lunt/Gold Rush Sheets	5	$10.25	$6.99
994	198 x 187	Postal Museum	4	$10.25	$6.99
995	156 x 187	Sign Language/Statehood	5	$10.25	$6.99
996	188 x 197	Illustrators, '98 Music: Folk, Gospel; Country/Western	4	$10.25	$6.99
997	151 x 192	Olympic	5	$10.25	$6.99
998	174 x 185	Buffalo Soldiers	5	$10.25	$6.99
999	130 x 198	Silent Screen Stars	5	$10.25	$6.99
1000	190 x 199	Stars Stripes/Baseball/Insects & Spiders/Legends West/ Aircraft, Comics, '96 Olympics, Civil War	4	$10.25	$6.99
1001	178 x 181	Cranes	4	$10.25	$6.99
1002	183 x 212	Wonders of the Sea, We the People	3	$10.25	$6.99
1003	156 x 264	$14 Eagle	4	$10.25	$6.99
1004	159 x 270	$9.95 Moon Landing	4	$10.25	$6.99
1005	159 x 259	$2.90 Priority/$9.95 Express Mail	4	$10.25	$6.99
1006	223 x 187	Hubble, Hollywood Legends, O'Keefe Sheets	3	$10.25	$6.99
1007	185 x 181	Deep Sea Creatures, Olmsted Sheets	4	$10.25	$6.99
1008	152 x 228	Indian Dances/Antique Autos	5	$10.25	$6.99
1009	165 x 150	River Boat/Hanukkah	6	$10.25	$6.99
1010	275 x 200	Dinosaurs/Large Gutter Blocks	2	$10.25	$6.99
1011	161 x 160	Pacific '97 Triangle Mini Sheets	6	$10.25	$6.99
1012	174 x 130	Road Runner, Daffy, Bugs, Sylvester & Tweety	6	$10.25	$6.99
1013	196 x 158	Football Coaches	4	$10.25	$6.99
1014	184 x 184	American Dolls, Flowering Trees Sheets	4	$10.25	$6.99
1015	186 x 205	Classic Movie Monsters	3	$10.25	$6.99
1016	187 x 160	Trans-Mississippi Sheet	4	$10.25	$6.99
1017	192 x 230	Celebrate The Century	3	$10.25	$6.99
1018	156 x 204	Space Discovery	5	$10.25	$6.99
1019	182 x 209	American Ballet	5	$10.25	$6.99
1020	139 x 151	Christmas Wreaths	5	$10.25	$6.99
1021	129 x 126	Justin Morrill, Henry Luce	8	$10.25	$6.99
1022	184 x 165	Baseball Fields, Bright Eyes	4	$10.25	$6.99
1023	185 x 172	Shuttle Landing Pan Am Invert Sheets	4	$10.25	$6.99
1024	172 x 233	Sonoran Desert	3	$10.25	$6.99
1025	150 x 166	Prostate Cancer	5	$10.25	$6.99
1026	201 x 176	Famous Trains	4	$10.25	$6.99
1027	176 x 124	Canada - Historic Vehicles	5	$10.25	$6.99
1028	245 x 114	Canada - Provincial Leaders	5	$10.25	$6.99
1029	177 x 133	Canada - Year of the Family	5	$10.25	$6.99
1034	181 x 213	Arctic Animals	3	$10.25	$6.99
1037	179 x 242	Louise Nevelson	3	$10.25	$6.99
1038	179 x 217	Library Of Congress	3	$10.25	$6.99
1039	182 x 232	Youth Team Sports	3	$10.25	$6.99
1040	183 x 216	Lucille Ball Scott #3523	3	$10.25	$6.99
1041	182 x 244	American Photographers	3	$10.25	$6.99
1042	185 x 255	Andy Warhol	3	$10.25	$6.99
1043	165 x 190	American Film Making	4	$10.25	$6.99
1044	28 x 290	American Eagle PNC Strips of 11	12	$9.25	$5.99

Available in clear or black backgrounds. Please specify color choice when ordering.

2016 NATIONAL, MINUTEMAN OR ALL-AMERICAN SUPPLEMENT MOUNT PACKS

ITEM	DESCRIPTION	RETAIL	AA*
2016 B	2016 National, Minuteman or All-American Supplement Mount Pack - BLACK	$49.99	$39.99
2016 C	2016 National, Minuteman or All-American Supplement Mount Pack - CLEAR	$49.99	$39.99

Visit AmosAdvantage.com
Call 1-800-572-6885
Outside U.S. & Canada 937-498-0800
Mail to: P.O. Box 4129, Sidney OH 45365

ORDERING INFORMATION: *AA prices apply to paid subscribers of Amos Media titles, or orders placed online. Prices, terms and product availability subject to change. Taxes will apply in CA, OH, & IL. Shipping and handling rates will apply.
SHIPPING & HANDLING: United States: Order total $0-$10.00 charged $3.99 shipping; Order total $10.01-$79.99 charged $7.99 shipping; Order total $80.00 or more charged 10% of order total for shipping. Maximum Freight Charge $45.00. **Canada:** 20% of order total. Minimum charge $19.99; maximum charge $200.00. **Foreign:** Orders are shipped via FedEx Int'l. or USPS and billed actual freight.

AMOS ADVANTAGE

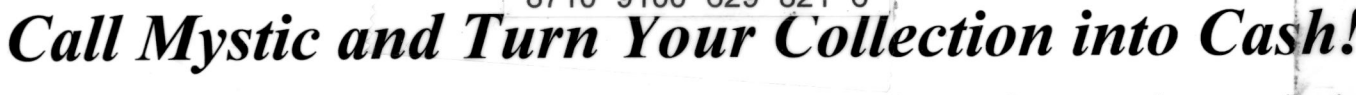

Want High Mar... ...r Your Stamps?
Call Mystic and Turn Your Collection into Cash!

Don Sundman
President
Mystic Stamp Company

When the time comes to sell your stamps, your biggest concern is getting top dollar for your collection. Lots of dealers claim to be the biggest and the best, so who should you trust?

The answer's simple – Mystic has a track record of treating stamp collectors with the honesty, respect and friendliness they deserve – for over 90 years.

Here are some of the many reasons you'll benefit from dealing with Mystic when you're ready to sell...

Mystic Buys and Sells More Stamps Than Anyone in America

Mystic has thousands of loyal customers with a variety of interests. Inside our 50,000-square-foot headquarters is the nation's largest dealer inventory of U.S. and worldwide stamps.

Each year we need millions of stamps to satisfy our collectors' needs. That means we must pay competitive prices to purchase stamps and coins – over $70 million in the past five years. That's great news if you're serious about selling your collection.

Our Expert Stamp Buyers Pay You Top Dollar

With Mystic, you get both high prices and fair treatment. We pay you what your stamps are really worth based on our many years of experience and our knowledge of current markets.

You Get Payment on the Spot

Mystic has the resources to pay you on the spot – whether you're selling a small collection, an estate or your entire dealer inventory. No middleman and no waiting.

Mystic Comes to You and Buys All Your Stamps

Mystic's expert stamp buyers will travel to your hometown for high-quality collections, accumulations and dealer inventories.

We need all types of stamps and stamp collections – U.S. and worldwide rare stamps, common stamps, and topical stamps (coins, too). And our buyers won't "cherry pick" your collection, leaving you to dispose of the rest.

You Benefit from Mystic's Small-Town Values

Mystic treats collectors fairly. We're located in a small village – Camden, New York – with a population of about 2,300. And most of Mystic's 150 colleagues live right here, too. Our small-town values of honesty, courtesy and plain talk come through each day.

Call Mystic Today – You'll Be Glad You Did!

Thousands of stamp collectors trust the folks at Mystic. We earn that trust daily – which means you can trust Mystic, too. So when it's time to sell your stamps, call Mystic and speak with an expert stamp buyer.

We're looking for:

* ✦ Worldwide new issues
* ✦ British and European colonies
* ✦ Rare/High-quality U.S. and foreign stamps
* ✦ U.S. collections of all qualities
* ✦ China stamps (all Asia stamps)
* ✦ Entire dealer stocks, store inventory, show dealer and mail order dealer stocks
* ✦ Accumulations and mixed collections (they don't need to be organized)
* ✦ Coin collections and accumulations of any size

ISBN 978-0-89487-518-2

Volume 2A of 2 Part Set
ISBN 978-0-89487-533-5

$134.99 Volume 2 Set (Part 2A, 2B)